THEON; in PARIS.

Bookman's Price Index

ISSN 0068-0141

Bookman's Price Index

VOLUME 27

A Guide to the Values of Rare and Other Out-of-Print Books

Edited by
Daniel F. McGrath

GALE RESEARCH COMPANY • BOOK TOWER • DETROIT, MICHIGAN 48226

Library of Congress Catalog Card Number 64-8723
ISBN 0-8103-0640-9
ISSN 0068-0141

Contents

How to Use This Book

All listings in this volume of *Bookman's Price Index* are based on descriptions of books offered for sale by leading dealers primarily in their 1983 catalogs.

Dealer's descriptions have been followed closely, although extensive details not essential to establishing condition or determining price have been condensed or omitted. In any case, however, there has been no addition to or revision of the content of the dealer's description, even in the few cases where a description might have been in error.

Every effort has been made to report prices and other details accurately; the user should keep in mind, however, that the possibility of typographical error—for which the publisher assumes no responsibility—does exist, and, furthermore, that an individual dealer's evaluation of a book may not represent a professional consensus.

Arrangement

Listings are alphabetical according to name of author, or, if no author is mentioned, according to the first word not an article in the title.

Names under which entries appear in *BPI* have been standardized as much as possible, and therefore are not always given in the exact form in which they appear on some title pages, or in the catalogs of some dealers. Familiar and common forms of names have been preferred.

In entering different editions of a single book, it has sometimes been necessary to depart from strict alphabetical order. Where this has been the case, the editor has elected to follow a chronological sequence. The second edition follows the first in such instances, even though this may disturb alphabetical regularity. In each such case, the editor has sought to consult the reader's convenience rather than any rigid consistency.

The reasons for the occasional uses of chronological order are two: First, as all bookmen know, a book often changed its title without changing its substance. The editor elected to hold all editions of such a book together under its most familiar title. The second reason is that book dealers, in preparing their catalogs, often transcribe only the second half of a lengthy Renaissance title page. Since the editor of *BPI* must work from such book dealers' descriptions, he felt well advised to arrange chronologically when there were several editions of one work.

The most obvious example of this particular editorial problem is, of course, the Bible. Title pages of Bibles can begin with such words as Complete, Holy, Authorized, Standard, New, Sacred, etc., etc.—it is still the same book. Therefore, all English Bibles appear in chronological order.

Most books, of course, are entered in alphabetical order, which suffices to gather all editions. The editor has then let first editions precede second, and first issues precede second issues. Collected works follow single works.

Order of Information

Within each entry, the following information is given in this order:

1. Author's name
2. Title
3. Place and date of publication
4. Description of the book, including its condition when offered by the dealer
5. Name of dealer publishing catalog
6. Number of catalog in which offered, and item number within catalog
7. Year date (or year of receipt) of catalog in which book is offered
8. Price at which offered

Dealers Represented in This Volume

RICHARD H. ADELSON
North Pomfret, Vermont 05053

ALEPH-BET BOOKS
670 Waters Edge
Valley Cottage, New York 10989

ARGOSY BOOK STORES, INC.
116 East 59th Street
New York, New York 10022

RICHARD B. ARKWAY, INC.
131 Fifth Avenue
New York, New York 10003

ARS LIBRI
711 Boylston Street
Boston, Massachusetts 02116

DAVID BICKERSTETH
38 Fulbrooke Road
Cambridge CB3 9EE, England

MEYER BOSWELL BOOKS
982 Hayes Street
San Francisco, California 94117

VAN ALLEN BRADLEY
Box 4130, Hopi Station
Scottsdale, Arizona 85258

BROMER BOOKSELLERS
607 Boylston Street
Boston, Massachusetts 02116

THE ARTHUR H. CLARKE COMPANY
P.O. Box 230
1264 South Central Avenue
Glendale, California 91204

DAWSON'S BOOK SHOP
535 North Larchmont Boulevard
Los Angeles, California 90004

DEIGHTON BELL & CO.
13 Trinity Street
Cambridge CB2 1TD, England

PHILIP C. DUSCHNES
699 Madison Avenue
New York, New York 10021

FRANCIS EDWARDS
83 Marylebone High Street
London W1M 4AL, England

JOSEPH J. FELCONE, INC.
P.O. Box 366
Princeton, New Jersey 08540

JAMES O'D. FENNING
12 Glenview Rochestown
Dun Laoghaire, County Dublin
Ireland

W. BRUCE FYE
1607 North Wood Avenue
Marshfield, Wisconsin 54449

JOHN GACH BOOKS
5620 Waterloo Road
Columbia, Maryland 21045

R.A. GEKOSKI
14 Portland Place West
Leamington Spa
Warwickshire CV32 5EU, England

MICHAEL GINSBERG BOOKS, INC.
P.O. Box 402
Sharon, Massachusetts 02067

ROBIN GREER
30 Sloan Court West
London SW3, England

RICK GRUNDER
915 Maxwell Terrace
Bloomington, Indiana 47401

R.D. GURNEY, LTD.
23 Campden Street
Kensington Church Station
London W8 7ED, England

T. & L. HANNAS
33 Farnaby Road
Bromley, Kent BR1 4BL, England

A.R. HEATH
179 Whiteladies Road, Clifton
Bristol 8, England

PETER MURRAY HILL
35 North Hill, Highgate
London N6, England

IAN HODGKINS & CO., LTD.
Mt. Vernon, Betterow, Rodborough
Stroud, Gloucestershire GL5 2LP, England

GEORGE J. HOULE
2277 Westwood Boulevard
Los Angeles, California 90066

IN OUR TIME
P.O. Box 386
Cambridge, Massachusetts 02139

JAMES F. JAFFE
P.O. Box 90
Bryn Mawr, Pennsylvania 19010

JARNDYCE BOOKS
68 Neal Street, Covent Garden
London WC2, England

JENKINS COMPANY
P.O. Box 2085
Austin, Texas 78768

PETER JOLIFFE
37 Bartlemas Road
Oxford OX4 1X11, England

K BOOKS
Waplington Hall
Allerthorpe
York Y04 4RS, England

KENNETH KARMIOLE, BOOKSELLER
P.O. Box 464
Santa Monica, California 90406

JOHN K. KING BOOKS
P.O. Box 363-A
Detroit, Michigan 48232

H.P. KRAUS
16 East 46th Street
New York, New York 10017

GEORGE MacMANUS COMPANY
1317 Irving Street
Philadelphia, Pennsylvania 19107

PATRICK McGAHERN BOOKS, INC.
783 Bank Street
Ottawa, Ontario K1S 3V5, Canada

EDWARD MORRILL & SON, INC.
25 Kingston Street
Boston, Massachusetts 02111

OAK KNOLL BOOKS
414 Delaware Street
New Castle, Delaware 19720

DAVID L. O'NEAL
263 Elm Hill Road
Peterborough, New Hampshire 03458

ROBERT PERATA
3170 Robinson Drive
Oakland, California 94602

PICKERING & CHATTO, LTD.
17 Pall Mall
London SW1Y 5NB, England

BERNARD QUARITCH, LTD.
5-8 Lower John Street, Golden Square
London W1R 4AU, England

QUILL & BRUSH
7649 Old Georgetown Road
Bethesda, Maryland 20014

THE RAVENSTREE COMPANY
Tor Haven, Route 1, Box 28
Wellton, Arizona 85356

WILLIAM REESE COMPANY
409 Temple Street
New Haven, Connecticut 06511

LEONA ROSTENBERG
Box 188, Gracie Station
New York, New York 10028

BERTRAM ROTA
30 & 31 Long Acre
London WC2E 9LT, England

WILLIAM SALLOCH
Pines Bridge Road
Ossining, New York 10562

CHARLES W. TRAYLEN
49-50 Quarry Street
Guildford, Surrey, England

TREBIZOND RARE BOOKS
667 Madison Avenue
New York, New York 10021

WHELDON & WESLEY
Lytton Lodge, Codicote
Hitchin, Herts SG4 8TE, England

XIMENES RARE BOOKS
120 East 85th Street
New York, New York 10028

ZEITLIN & VER BRUGGE
815 North La Cienega Boulevard
Los Angeles, California 90069

Bookman's
Price Index

A

A. E. PSEUD.
Please turn to
RUSSELL, GEORGE WILLIAM

A.L.O.E., PSEUD.
Please turn to
TUCKER, CHARLOTTE MARIA

ABBADIE, JACQUES   The History of the Late Conspiracy
against the King and the Nation. London: for Daniel Brown, 1696.
First edition. 8vo. Cont. calf, neatly rebacked, morocco label.
Traylen 94-1 1983 £32

ABBATE, FRANCESCO   Scultura napoletana del '400.
(Estratto dalla Storia di Napoli. Vol. IV.) Napoli, n.d. (48)
pp., 40 plates. 4to. Wraps. Ars Libri SB 26-1 1983 $30

ABBEY, EDWIN   Old Songs. N.Y.: Harp., 1889 (1888).
4to. Green decorated cloth. Light wear to spine extremities. Printed
on heavy stock. Line illus. in black & white by Abbey & Alfred Parsons.
Aleph-bet 8-1 1983 $30

ABBEY, EDWIN   Selections from the Poetry of Robert
Herrick. N.Y.: Harpers, 1882. First edition. 4to. Tan gilt and
pict. cloth. Some smudging, a.e.g. Many black & white illus. Very
good. Aleph-bet 8-2 1983 $30

ABBOT, JOSEPH   Philip Musgrave. J. Murray (Home and
Colonial Library), 1846. First edition thus, small 8vo, wrapper.
Fenning 61-2 1983 £24.50

ARBOT, RICHARD   The Wanderer. Darlington, Wm. Dresser,
1901. First edition, front. port. Orig. maroon cloth, bevelled
boards sl. marked. Jarndyce 31-854 1983 £10.50

ABBOT, WILLIS J.   Panama and the Canal in Picture and Prose.
NY, 1913. Photos, some color illus, folding map. 4to, pict. cloth,
blindstamp on title. Argosy 710-56 1983 $27.50

ABBOTT, ANTHONY   The Shudders. N.Y., Farrar & Rinehart,
(1943). First edition. Dust jacket (designed by Robert Graves),
small nicks, else very good. Houle 22-1 1983 $45

ABBOTT, EDWIN H.   A Review of the Report Upon the Physics
and Hydraulics of the Mississippi River Prepared by Capt. A. A.
Humphreys and Lt. H. L. Abbot... Boston, 1862. Orig. printed wraps.
Ginsberg 47-504 1983 $25

ABBOTT, J   Rollo's Museum. Boston, 1839. Small
12mo, 2 illus. Stamped cloth. Argosy 716-226 1983 $35

ABBOTT, J.   The T'Hakoorine, a Tale of Maandoo..
London, 1841. First edition. Sm.8vo. Half calf, slight wear.
From the Neilgherry Public Library with its stamp on the front board,
and labels inside. Good. Edwards 1044-2 1983 £95

ABBOTT, MAUDE   Appreciations and Reminiscences; Sir
William Osler Bart. Montreal, 1927. First edition. second printing.
8vo. Orig. binding. Limited edition of 1500 copies. Very fine
copy. Fye H-3-871 1983 $125

ABBOTT, MAUDE   Appreciations and Reminiscences; Sir
William Osler Bart. Montreal, 1927. 8vo. Orig. binding. Ex-
library. Water wrinkling of lower 2 inches of spine, else fine.
Fye H-3-872 1983 $100

ABBOTT, MAUDE   An Historical Sketch of the Medical
Faculty of McGill University. Reprinted from The Montreal Medical
Journal, Vol. 31, #8 (Aug. 1902). One half leather. Library book-
plate and spine label, top of spine taped. Inscribed to Adolf
Meyer and his wife. Gach 95-1 1983 $27.50

A'BECKET, THOMAS   The Life or the Ecclesiasticall Historie
of S. Thomas Archbishope of Canterbury. Paris: Widow of Jerome
Blagaert, 1639. First edition. 8vo. Cont. French brown morocco,
gilt, wide border enclosing a panel, gilt edges, spine repaired.
Traylen 94-62 1983 £550

A'BECKETT, GILBERT ABBOTT   The Comic History of England. (London):
Pub. at the Punch Office, 1847-8. 2 vols. 1st book ed. Contemp.
3/4 black morocco and marbled boards. With 10 color etchings and 120
woodcuts by John Leech. Very good set. Jenkins 153-815 1983 $1250

A'BECKETT, GILBERT ABBOTT   The Comic History of England. (London):
Published at the Punch Office, 1847-8. 2 vols. 1st book ed. Contemporary 3/4 black morocco and marbled boards. With ten color
etching and 120 woodcuts by John Leech. Very good set. Jenkins
155-1 1983 $150

A'BECKETT, GILBERT ABBOTT   The Comic History of England. London:
Published at The Punch Office, 1847-1853. Ten coloured etchings, and
120 woodcuts, by John Leech. 2 vols. Rebound in full cranberry calf,
gilt, with morocco labels on spines, original cloth covers bound in at
the backs. First edition. Very good copy. MacManus 277-2 1983
$150

A'BECKETT, GILBERT ABBOTT   The Comic History of England. The Comic
History of Rome. (London: Bradbury & Evans), 1848. 3 vols., illus.
by John Leech with hand-colored plates & many smaller woodcuts. 3/4
green morocco with cloth boards & marbled endpapers. First edition(s).
Some plates foxed. Spines trifle faded. Cloth box. Bookplate.
MacManus 277-3 1983 $350

A'BECKETT, GILBERT ABBOTT   The Comic History of England (and) The
Comic History of Rome. London, n.d. 3 vols. in 2. 8vo. Finely
bound in half olive green levant morocco, gilt, t.e.g., others uncut.
30 hand-coloured plates, and hundreds of woodcuts by John Leech.
Traylen 94-3 1983 £85

A'BECKETT, GILBERT ABBOTT   The Comic History of England. London,
Bradbury, Agnew, n.d. Illus. in color by John Leech. 2 vols. 4to.
Half calf, gilt tips. Tops of backstrips frayed. Morrill 287-542
1983 $60

A'BECKETT, GILBERT ABBOTT   King John, A Burlesque In One Act...
London: W. Strange, 1837. With a portrait of Mr. H. Hall. Orig.
wrappers. Very good copy. MacManus 277-1 1983 $25

A'BECKETT, GILBERT ABBOTT   King John Travestie. London: Thomas
Hailes Lacy, n.d. (c. mid-19th century). With an Illus. Orig. wrappers. MacManus 277-4 1983 $25

A'BECKETT, GILBERT ABBOTT   Man-Fred; A Burlesque Ballet Opera, In
One Act... London: G.H. Davidson, n.d. (c. mid-19th century). Orig.
wrappers. Embellished with a fine engraving, by Mr. Bonner. Very
good copy. MacManus 277-5 1983 $25

A'BECKETT, GILBERT ABBOTT   Pascal Bruno; A Burletta, In Two Acts,...
London: W. Strange, 1838. Orig. wrappers. Fine copy. MacManus
277-6 1983 $25

A'BECKETT, GILBERT ABBOTT   The Postilion: An Opera, In Three Acts...
London: G.H. Davidson, n.d. (c. mid-19th century). Orig. wrappers.
Good copy. MacManus 277-7 1983 $25

A'BECKETT, GILBERT ABBOTT   The Roof Scrambler. A Grand Burlesque
Ballet Opera, In Two Acts... London: John Cumberland, n.d. (c. mid-
19th century). Orig. wrappers. MacManus 277-8 1983 $25

A'BECKETT, GILBERT ABBOTT   Unfortunate Miss Bailey: An Interlude,
In One Act... London: Davidson, n.d. (c. mid-19th century). Orig.
wrappers. MacManus 277-9 1983 $25

ABEL, FREDERICK AUGUSTUS   Hand-Book of Chemistry... London:
Churchill, 1854. 8vo. Half red calf over boards with gilt. Spine
partially detached. Zeitlin 264-1 1983 $60

ABEL, MARY HINMAN   Practical Sanitary and Economic
Cooking. N.p.: American Public Health Association, 1890. Index.
Brown cloth. Karmiole 72-36 1983 $35

ABELL, IRVIN   A Retrospect of Surgery in Kentucky.
Louisville, 1923. First edition. 8vo. Very good. Fye H-3-1
1983 $25

ABER, ADOLF   Handbuch der Musikliteratur. Leipzig,
1922. 8vo, cloth (new binding). Salloch 387-260 1983 $40

ABER, SILVER DOLLAR   Star of Blood. (Denver, 1909). Orig.
printed wraps. First edition. Pages crinkled. Ginsberg 46-720
1983 $100

ABERCROMBIE, JOHN (1780-1844) Inquiries Concerning the Intellectual
Powers and the Investigation of Truth. Edinburgh: Waugh & Innes,
1830. Contemporary paneled calf, gilt. First edition, inscribed.
Gach 95-2 1983 $195

ABERCROMBIE, LASCELLES   Deborah. London: John Lane The Bodley
Head, 1913. Original cloth-backed boards with paper labels. First
edition. A review copy with a stamp on the title-page reading: "Review Copy With John Lane's Compliments." Binding a bit worn & soiled.
Good copy. MacManus 277-10 1983 $35

ABERCROMBIE, LASCELLES   Deborah. London, 1913. First edition.
Endpapers lightly foxed. Last eight leaves carelessly opened.
Inscription on flyleaf. Very good. Rota 230-1 1983 £15

ABERCROMBIE, LASCELLES   Emblems of Love. London, 1912. First
edition, second binding. Spine a little dull. S. Sassoon's initialled
autograph presentation inscription to R. Meiklejohn. Very good. Rota
230-528 1983 £25

ABERCROMBIE, LASCELLES   Emblems of Love designed in several
Discourses. London: John Lane, 1912. First edition. 8vo. Cloth
gilt. Traylen 94-4 1983 £20

ABERCROMBIE, LASCELLES   Emblems of Love. London: John Lane,
1912. Orig. pictorial cloth. First edition. Very good copy.
MacManus 277-11 1983 $20

ABERCROMBIE, LASCELLES   An Essay Towards a Theory of Art.
London: Martin Secker, 1922. Original cloth-backed boards. First
edition. Presentation copy from author inscribed: "Lionel Budde from
Lascelles Abercrombie." With two typescripts of poems by Abercrombie
laid in. Spine very lightly soiled. Edges a trifle worn. Very good
copy. MacManus 277-13 1983 $125

ABERCROMBIE, LASCELLES   An Essay Towards a Theory of Art. London:
Martin Secker, 1922. Original cloth-backed boards. Dust jacket (very
slightly worn). First edition. Endpapers slightly browned. Near-fine
copy. MacManus 277-12 1983 $35

ABERCROMBIE, LASCELLES   Interludes and Poems. London: John
Lane, 1908. Original cloth. T.e.g. First edition of author's first
book. Spine faded. Bookplate. Very good. MacManus 277-15 1983
$35

ABERCROMBIE, LASCELLES   Lyrics and Unfinished Poems. Newtown,
Wales, 1940. Sm folio, 1/2 morocco over marbled bds., morocco tips,
gilt extra. One of 175 copies printed on Barcham Green hand-made
paper. Inkspots to lower corners of 2 pages, former owner's name
in ink on front pastedown. Photograph of the author laid in.
Perata 28-70 1983 $400

ABERCROMBIE, LASCELLES   Phoenix. Tragicomedy in Three Acts.
London: Martin Secker, 1923. Original cloth-backed boards. First
edition, first binding. Presentation copy from author inscribed:
"H. Sydney Pickering from Lascelles Abercrombie. May 1929." Edges
a bit worn. Very good. MacManus 277-17 1983 $45

ABERCROMBIE, LASCELLES   Phoenix. Tragicomedy in Three Acts.
London: Martin Secker, 1923. Orig. cloth-backed boards. Dust
jacket. First edition. Fine. MacManus 277-16 1983 $20

ABERCROMBIE, LASCELLES   A Plea for the Liberty of Interpreting.
London: Humphrey Milford, (1930). Original wrappers. First edition.
Inscribed by author: "With the author's compliments. L.A." Wrappers
rather frayed and soiled at edges. Good. MacManus 277-18 1983 $40

ABERCROMBIE, LASCELLES   Progress in Literature. The Leslie
Stephen Lecture Delivered at Cambridge 10 May 1929. Cambridge:
University Press, 1929. Original wrappers. First edition. Presenta-
tion copy from author inscribed: "Catherine Abercrombie. L.A. May 10,
1929." Spine worn. All edges faded and a bit frayed. Good.
MacManus 277-19 1983 $65

ABERCROMBIE, LASCELLES   The Sale of Saint Thomas. In Six Acts.
London: Martin Secker, 1931. Original cloth. First edition. Presentation copy from author to his brother inscribed: "Ralph Abercrombie,
from L.A. Christmas, 1931." Edges rather worn. Covers a bit soiled.
Good. MacManus 277-20 1983 $50

ABERCROMBIE, LASCELLES   The Theory of Poetry. London, 1924.
First edition. 8vo, cloth backed boards. Argosy 714-1 1983 $25

ABERCROMBIE, LASCELLES   Twelve Idyls And Other Poems. London:
Martin Secker, 1928. Orig. cloth-backed boards. First edition. Presentation copy, inscribed on the front flyleaf "R(alph) A(bercrombie)
from L.A. October 1928." Spine darkened, boards rubbed. Good copy.
MacManus 277-22 1983 $40

ABERCROMBIE, LASCELLES   Twelve Idyls and Other Poems. London:
Martin Secker, 1928. Original cloth-backed boards. First edition.
Signed by author. Corners slightly bumped. Very good. MacManus
277-21 1983 $35

ABERCROMBIE, PATRICK   Greater London Plan 1944. H.M.S.O.,
1945. First edition, 2 folding coloured maps in an end pocket and
many other maps, plates and illus., some folding, 4to, orig. cloth;
a fine copy in a slightly frayed dust wrapper. Fenning 62-1 1983
£24.50

ABERCROMBIE, RALPH   Principles of Forecasting by means of
Weather Charts. London: Her Majesty's Stationery Office, 1885.
2nd revised ed., tall 8vo, cont. half calf gilt, marbled boards.
Frontis. map and many text illus. Hinges rubbed, but a good copy.
Trebizond 18-174 1983 $100

ABERDEEN, COUNTESSE OF   Through Canada with a Kodak. Edinburgh:
W.H. White & Co., 1893. 18 1/2cm. Ca. 118 illus. Orig. gilt
decorated cloth. Very good to fine. McGahern 53-1 1983 $45

ABERDEEN AND TEMAIR, JOHN CAMPBELL GORDON, 1ST MARQUIS OF   "We Twa;"
Reminiscences of Lord and Lady Aberdeen. London: W. Collins Sons,
(1925). Two vols., numberous illus. 23 cm. Orig. grey cloth, green
leather labels on spines. Nearly fine. First edition, second
impression. Each volume signed and stamped by Susa Young Gates.
Grunder 6-1 1983 $25

ABERIGH-MACKAY, G. R.   Twenty-One-Days in India. London, 1910.
10 plates, cr. 8vo., decorative cloth gilt. Good. Edwards 1044-1
1983 £14

ABERNETHY, JOHN   Surgical Observations on the
Constitutional Origin and Treatment of Local Diseases. London, 1826.
8vo, cloth. Argosy 713-1 1983 $100

ABERT, JAMES W.   Through the Country of the Comanche
Indians in the Fall of the Year 1845. San F., Kennedy, 1970. Illus.,
many colored plates, folded maps, etc. Orig. folio cloth, dust
jacket. Ginsberg 47-1 1983 $75

ABINGTON, FRANCES   The Life of...Celebrated Comic Actress.
Reader, 1888. First edition, half title, front. port. Orig. cream
boards, green leather label, v.g. Jarndyce 31-380 1983 £15

ABRAHAM, J. JOHNSTON   Lettsom his Life, Times, Friends and
Descendants. London, 1933. Large 8vo. Cloth. Numerous illus.
Gurney JJ-230 1983 £20

ABRAHAMS, ISAAC   The Powers of Chemistry in Relation to things Visible and Invisible... Philadelphia: R.T. Rawle, 1801. 8vo. Modern boards with title in ms. on spine. Ex-libris Denis L. Duveen. Some minor defects, but a very good copy. Zeitlin 264-2 1983 $90

AN ABRIDGMENT of the Prerogatives of St. Ann, Mother of the Mother of God. Printed for Ric. Chiswell, 1688. First edition of this translation (by Wm. Clagett?). 4to, old decorative floral paper wrapper (? original), uncut, little worn but sound. Very good. Fenning 60-1 1983 £24.50

ACCADEMIA DELLE SCIENZE DI TORINO.   Guarino Guarini e l'internazionalita del Barocco. Torino: Accademia delle Scienze, 1970. 2 vols. Prof. illus. 4to. Cloth. Ars Libri 33-185 1983 $150

AN ACCOUNT of a dream at Harwich. London: B. Bragg, 1708. 8vo. Disbound. First edition. Ximenes 63-582 1983 $45

AN ACCOUNT of Mrs. Elizabeth Johnson... Bristol: W. Pine, (ca. 1799). First edition. 12mo. Orig. half sheep. Slight wear. Heath 48-133 1983 £35

AN ACCOUNT of the Colony of Sierra Leone... London: James Phillips, 1795. 8vo. Folding map. Orig. sheep, red label, repair to blank area of title. Adelson Africa-128 1983 $135

ACCOUNT of the convalescent station of Malcolm Pait... London: reprinted, but not published, 1831. 8vo. Modern wrappers. Ximenes 63-197 1983 $80

ACCOUNT of the proceedings before His Majesty's most Hon. Privy Council, upon a petition for a third theatre in the metropolis. London: printed for W. H. Wyatt; by B. McMillan, 1810. 1st ed., 8vo, disbound. An uncut copy. Ximenes 64-3 1983 $125

ACCUM, FREDERICK   Culinary Chemistry, exhibiting the Scientific Principles of Cookery. Published by R. Ackermann, 1821. 12mo, coloured frontis., engraved title with hand-coloured vignette of a kitchen range. Orig. cloth, rebacked, preserving the orig. spine and end-papers, blocked in blind on the covers and in gilt on the spine. A fine copy. First edition. Bickersteth 75-208 1983 £145

ACCUM, FREDERICK   Elements of Crystallography... London, 1813. First edition. 8vo. Quarter-calf. 4 engraved plates and woodcut diagrams in text. Lacks half-title. Gurney 90-1 1983 £120

AN ACCURATE Description and History of the Cathedral and Metropolitan Church of St. Peter York... York: by A. Ward..., 1768. 8vo. Folding engraved plates. Cont. calf. Heath 48-578 1983 £45

ACHARIYAR, R. B. K. R.   A Handbook of Some Indian Grasses. Madras, 1921. Numerous illus., some slight wear. Good. Edwards 1044-3 1983 £15

ACKERKNECHT, ERWIN   Malaria in the Upper Mississippi Valley. Baltimore, 1945. 8vo. Wrappers. First edition. Very good. Fye H-3-6 1983 $40

ACKWORTH, JOHN   Doxie Dent. London: C.H. Kelly, 1899. First edition. Original cloth. Covers slightly soiled and worn at edges. Endpapers browned. Good copy. MacManus 277-23 1983 $30

ACLAND, C.   A Popular Account of the Manners and Customs of India... London, 1847 & 1845. Half calf, labels, gilt. Good. Edwards 1044-4 1983 £40

ACLAND, HENRY W.   The Oxford Museum. London: Smith, Elder and Co., 1859. First edition. Ads. Illus. with an engraved frontis., one full-page plate and a large folding plan. Orig. purple gilt-stamped cloth. Karmiole 73-1 1983 $75

ACOSTA, JORGE R.   El Palacio del Quetzalpapalotl. Mexico, 1964. 89 plates with 121 illus. (7 color). 13 plans. Large 4to. Cloth. Ars Libri 34-84 1983 $100

ACOSTA, JOSE DE (1539-1600)   De Natura Novi Orbis libri duo... Coloniae Agrippinae (Cologne) In Officina Birckmannica, Sumptibus Arnoldi Mylij, MDXCVI (1596). 8vo, vellum boards, paper covered spine. Title in MS. Lightly toned throughout. Endpapers foxed. Stamp on verso of t-p. "Bibl. pub. Basileensis." A.E. Lownes bookplate. Generally very good. Arkway 22-2 1983 $400

ACROSTICS: Original Acrostics. Bell and Daldy, 1864. First and apparently only edition, small 8vo, orig. green cloth, gilt. Fenning 60-2 1983 £18.50

ACTON, HAROLD   An Indian Ass. London, 1925. First edition. Bookplate. Endpapers browned. Spine faded. Very good. Jolliffe 26-1 1983 £17.50

ACTON, HAROLD   The Last Medici. London, 1932. First edition. Spine a little faded. Nice. Rota 230-4 1983 £20

ACTON, HENRY   Catching of the Whale and Seal. Salem: Ives & Jewett, 1838. First edition of a scarce juvenile. Plates, 12mo, orig. roan-backed boards with illus. on front cover. Slightly rubbed, occasional foxing. Morrill 286-582 1983 $85

ACWORTH, BERNARD   The Restoration of England's Sea Power. London, 1935. 8vo. Orig. cloth. Frontis. 12 plates. Spine faded. Good. Edwards 1042-1 1983 £15

ADAIR, BETHENIA ANGELINA   Dr. Owens-Adair. (Portland: Mann & Beach, n.d.) (1906?). 22 cm. 7 plates. (with a half-title but no full title page, and conforming to the Library of Congress copy). Orig. cloth. Ex-library copy with perforated stamp, etc. A solid working copy. Grunder 6-63 1983 $50

ADAIR, JAMES   The History of the American Indians. London, 1775. Large folding map. Quarto. Large uncut copy in new leatherette and cloth binding. Reese 18-108 1983 $1,250

ADAIR, JOHN   The Navajo and Pueblo Silversmiths. Norman: University of Oklahoma Press, 1946. 24 plates. Small 4to. Cloth. Ars Libri 34-85 1983 $40

ADAM, G. MERCER   The Canadian North-West: its History and its Troubles... Toronto: Rose Pub. Co., 1885. 19 1/2cm. Illus. Brown cloth. Gilt titles and decorations. Fine. McGahern 54-188 1983 $50

ADAM, H. L.   The Indian Criminal. London, 1909. Plates. Orig. cloth. 8vo. Good. Edwards 1044-5 1983 £25

ADAM, JAMES   The Vitality of Platonism. Cambridge, 1911. 8vo, cloth. Salloch 385-679 1983 $22

ADAM, LEONHARD   Nordwest-Amerikanische Indianerkunst. Berlin, (ca. 1910). Illus., plates, thin 8vo, boards, rebacked, paper label, edges slightly worn. Argosy 710-216 1983 $30

ADAMI, J. GEORGE   Charles White of Manchester (1728-1813)... First American edition. 8vo. Orig. binding. Scarce. Orig. binding. Fye H-3-998 1983 $50

ADAMI, MARIE   J. George Adami. Vice-Chancellor of the University of Liverpool 1919-26. London: Constable, 1930. 22cm. Frontis. portrait. Red cloth. Clipping laid down on the endpapers else fine, scarce. McGahern 54-1 1983 $45

ADAMS, ALICE D.   The Neglected Period of Anti-Slavery in America, (1808-1831). Boston & London, 1908. 8vo, mod. wrs. Argosy 716-14 1983 $25

ADAMS, ANDREW LEITH   Notes of a Naturalist in the Nile Valley and Malta. Edinburgh, 1870. Coloured geological map, 14 plates and other illus., a bit browned and some margins slightly frayed, a few library marks, modern quarter calf, bound. K Books 301-2 1983 £30

ADAMS, ANDY   The Log of a Cowboy. Boston, 1903. Illus. by E. Boyd Smith. Gilt pictorial cloth. About fine. Reese 19-2 1983 $175

ADAMS, ANDY   A Texas Matchmaker. Boston: Houghton,
Mifflin, 1904. First edition. Illus. by E. Boyd Smith. Orig.
olive pictorial gilt cloth. Fine. Jenkins 152-541 1983 $65

ADAMS, ANSEL   Camera & Lens. N.Y., Morgan, Lester,
1949. First edition. Profusely illus. with photos by Adams. Dust
jacket (small chips). Very good. Houle 22-3 1983 $60

ADAMS, ANSEL   My Camera in Yosemite Valley. Boston:
Houghton Mifflin, 1949. 24 photographs. Folio, orig. photographic
wrappers bound into black cloth. The fine Bancroft duplicate with a
few unobrusive markings. 1st ed. Jenkins 153-718 1983 $400

ADAMS, ANSEL   Yosemite and Range of Light. Boston,
1979. A fine copy in dust jacket. This copy signed by Adams.
In Our Time 156-3 1983 $150

ADAMS, C.   Great Campaigns. London, 1877. 8vo.
Orig. cloth. 5 folding maps. Very slightly worn. Ink ownership
inscription on title. Good. Edwards 1042-263 1983 £18

ADAMS, CHARLES FOLLEN   Leedle Yawcob Strauss, and Other Poems.
Boston & New York, 1878. (12)pp., frontis. 1st ed. Orig. pictorial
cloth, gilt. Supposedly illustrated by "Box". Fine copy. Jenkins
155-2 1983 $20

ADAMS, CHARLES FRANCIS (1835-1915)   The Sifted Grain and the
Grain Sifters. N.P., n.d. Printed gray wrappers. Bradley 64-1
1983 $20

ADAMS, DANIEL   The Scholar's Arithmetic. Leominister,
Mass., 1805. One internal leaf torn across with slight loss of text.
Old worn calf. Reese 18-271 1983 $25

ADAMS, EDWARD DEAN   Niagara Power. Niagara Falls, N.Y.:
Privately Printed, 1927. 4to. 28cm. 2 vols. Numerous portraits
and illus. (many folding) inc. diagrams and maps. Mapped endpapers.
Blue cloth. Very good to fine set. McGahern 54-187 1983 $45

ADAMS, FRANCIS   A Child of the Age. Boston: Roberts
Brothers, 1894. Original pictorial cloth. First American edition.
One of the Keynote Series. Covers a bit spotted. Good copy.
MacManus 277-24 1983 $30

ADAMS, FRANCIS WILLIAM L. LEICESTER   An Autogiography. George
Redway, 1885. First edition, 2 vols. Half title vol. 1, 2 pp ads
vol. 1; 16 pp ads vol. II. Orig. light blue cloth, blocked in dark
blue. Spine lettered in gilt. Very sl. marking. Very good. Jarndyce 30-262 1983 £85

ADAMS, FRANK   The Story of Little Jack Sprat. Methuen,
n.d. (ca.1905). Sm. 8vo. Colour pictorial title & 18 colour plates
printed by E. Evans. Buff boards. Onlaid colour plates. Greer 40-1
1983 £25

ADAMS, FRANKLIN P.   The Melancholy Lute. NY, 1936. First
edition. Limited to 400 copies signed by Adams. Near mint in limp
blue leather with rubbed gold slip-case. Bromer 25-1 1983 $60

ADAMS, FREDERICK B.   Radical Literature in America.
Stamford, 1939. Cloth, fine in slight chipped slipcase. Reese 19-50
1983 $185

ADAMS, FREDERICK B.   Radical Literature in America. Stamford, Conn.: Overbrook Press, 1939. 4to. Cloth. Slipcase. With
many fine full page plates. Limited to 650 copies. Some fading of
spine. Oak Knoll 49-3 1983 $90

ADAMS, GEORGE   Adam's New Directory of the City of
Boston... Boston, 1846. 1st number of this directory. 8vo. Orig.
boards, cloth back. Some rubbing. Morrill 289-412 1983 $37.50

ADAMS, GEORGE   Astronomical and Geographical Essays.
Printed by R. Hindmarsh...and sold by the author..., 1795. With engraved frontis. and 16 folding engr. plates. 8vo, cont. calf, gilt,
little rubbed but sound. A very good copy. Without the catalogue of
instruments bound in at end. Fenning 60-3 1983 £45

ADAMS, H. G.   Beautiful Butterflies. Groombridge,
1871. 8 coloured plates, cr. 8vo, original cloth, gilt. Wheldon
160-1014 1983 £18

ADAMS, HENRY   History of the United States of America
During the Administrations of Thomas Jefferson and Majes Madison.
New York, 1930. 9 vols. in 4. 8vo. Backstrips slightly faded.
Very fine. Morrill 289-257 1983 $60

ADAMS, HENRY K.   A Centennial History of St. Albans,
Vermont. St. Albans, 1889. First edition. 12mo, original wrappers.
Morrill 290-554 1983 $20

ADAMS, ISAAC   Darkness and Daybreak. Privately
printed, U.S.A., ca 1901. Illus., rather frayed cloth. K Books 301-
3 1983 £15

ADAMS, J. DONALD   The Poetry Society of America. New York:
Fine Editions Press, 1946. 8vo, cloth. Review of book pasted on inside endboard, tiny pinhole in front fly, else fine in rubbed dust
jacket. In Our Time 156-5 1983 $35

ADAMS, JAMES T.   Album of American History. N.Y., (1944)-
1948. Profusely illus. 4 vols. plus index. 5 vols. Argosy 716-
183 1983 $40

ADAMS, JAMES T.   Dictionary of American History. NY,
1940. First edition, 5 vols. + index. Large 8vo, blue cloth.
Argosy 716-184 1983 $175

ADAMS, JOHN   Anecdotes, Bons-Mots. London, 1789.
First edition. Recent full calf with gilt-stamped spine. New endpapers, orig. issued "Price Three Shillings, Sewed". King 45-144
1983 $85

ADAMS, JOHN QUINCY   An Address Delivered on the Occasion
of Reading the Declaration of Independence. Washington, 1821.
8vo, mod. wrappers. Argosy 710-1 1983 $30

ADAMS, JOHN QUINCY   Correspondence Between...Boston, 1829.
Sewed, uncut. Argosy 716-424 1983 $50

ADAMS, JOHN QUINCY   A Eulogy on the Life and Character of
James Monroe, fifth President of the United States. Boston: J. H.
Eastburn, 1831. 1st ed., 8vo, uncut copy, stitched as issued. A very
fine copy. Trebizond 18-175 1983 $50

ADAMS, JOHN QUINCY   A Letter to the Hon. Harrison Gray Otis.
Boston: Oliver and Munroe, 1808. Modern cloth. Second edition.
Felcone 22-1 1983 $50

ADAMS, JOHN QUINCY   Memoirs. Philadelphia, 1874-77. 1st
ed. 250 sets printed. 12 vols., 8vo. Bookplates, ends of spines
slightly frayed, small faded spots on backstrips from probably
removal of shelf labels, otherwise nice, clean set. Morrill 287-2
1983 $160

ADAMS, JOHN QUINCY   An Oration Addressed to the Citizens of
the Town of Quincy. Boston, 1831. Bound in half morocco, gilt. Orig.
front wrapper bound in. Inscribed and signed by President Adams to
Rev. W.W. Sprague. Fine. Jenkins 152-542 1983 $1,750

ADAMS, JOSEPH   An Illustration of Mr. Hunter's Doctrine.
London, Printed by W. Thorne, 1814. 1st ed., 8vo, titlepage, ads; a
little soiled, disbound. Pickering & Chatto 22-1 1983 $100

ADAMS, JOSIAH   The Genealogy of the Descendants of
Richard Haven of Lynn, Mass., and His Sons John, Nathaniel, and
Moses. Boston, 1843. Orig. pr. wraps. (backstrip taped). Signed
by Chas. E. Haven. Argosy 716-178 1983 $25

ADAMS, LEONIE   High Falcon and Other Poems. New York,
(1929). 8vo, cloth, boards. Very good-fine copy. In our Time 156-6
1983 $25

ADAMS, RAMON F.   Burs Under the Saddle. Norman, (1964).
First edition. Tan buckram. Very fine in dj. Bradley 65-26 1983
$85

ADAMS, RAMON F.   Charles M. Russell The Cowboy Artist.
Pasadena, 1948. 2 vols., half morocco, illus. Limited to 600 copies.
Fine copies. Includes separate sets of colored illustrations. Lacks
the box. Jenkins 151-299 1983 $225

ADAMS, RAMON F.   Charles M. Russell, the Cowboy Artist.
Pasadena, 1948. Cloth, very good in chipped dust jacket. Reese 19-
5 1983 $40

ADAMS, RAMON F.   Come An' Get it The Story of the Old Cowboy Cook. Norman, 1952. Illus. by Nick Eggenhofer. First edition.
Fine. Jenkins 152-1 1983 $30

ADAMS, RAMON F.   The Rampaging Herd. Norman: Univ. of
Oklahoma Press, (1959). First printing. 9 x 6 inches, cloth in dust
wrapper. Dawson 470-2 1983 $100

ADAMS, RAMON F.   Six-Guns and Saddle Leather. (Norman:
Univ. of Oklahoma Press, 1969). New edition, revised and enlarged.
Cloth in dust wrapper, two corners a little bumped. Dawson 470-4
1983 $75

ADAMS, RAMON F.   Western Words. Norman, 1944. First
edition in dust jacket. Long presentation copy from author. Jenkins
152-543 1983 $40

ADAMS, RANDOLPH   Three Americanists. Phila.: Univ. of
Pennsylvania Press, 1939. 8vo. Cloth. Oak Knoll 48-2 1983 $35

ADAMS, RANDOLPH   Three Americanists. Philadelphia:
University of Pennsylvania Press, 1939. Illus. Karmiole 71-1 1983
$25

ADAMS, RICHARD   Watership Down. London: Rex Collings,
1972. Orig. cloth. Dust jacket. First edition of author's now-
classic first book of which 2500 copies were printed. Very fine copy.
MacManus 277-26 1983 $650

ADAMS, RICHARD   Watership Down. New York: Macmillan,
(1972). Uncorrected Proof of the first American edition. 8vo.
Orig. wrappers. Mint. Jaffe 1-1 1983 $150

ADAMS, RICHARD   Watership Down. Paradine, 1976.
Royal 8vo. Orig. full green crushed morocco with gilt pictorial
front cover and gilt motifs on spine, marbled endpapers, a.e.g.,
by Sangorski & Sutcliffe, in marbled board slipcase. One of 250
copies specially bound, signed by Adams and John Lawrence, the
illustrator. Original watercolor by Lawrence on the front flyleaf.
Mint. Jaffe 1-2 1983 $575

ADAMS, ROBERT   The narrative of Robert Adams...
London: John Murray, 1816. 1 vol. 4to. Folding map. Modern
half brown calf. Marbled boards. Faint library blind stamp on
title. Repairs to map. Pages uncut. Adelson Africa-1 1983 $300

ADAMS, RUFUS   The Young Gentleman and Lady's
Explanatory Monitor. Zanesville, Ohio: Printed by David Chambers,
1815. Orig. calf-backed boards (front board wanting). A couple
of creases and marginal nicks, otherwise a very fine copy. Reese
18-484 1983 $175

ADAMS, SAMUEL   The Votes and Proceedings of the
Freeholders and Other Inhabitants of the Town of Boston, in Town
Meeting Assembled... Boston, (1770). Self-Wrappers, stitched. Good.
Reese 18-92 1983 $500

ADAMS, THOMAS F.   Typographia. New York: R. Hoe &
Co., 1856. 8vo. Orig. cloth with part of orig. spine laid down
on new cloth, new endpapers. Fine. Oak Knoll 48-3 1983 $125

ADAMS, THOMAS R.   The American Controversy... Providence,
1980. 2 vols. Boswell 7-11 1983 $80

ADAMS, WILLIAM   Observations on Contraction of the
Fingers. London, 1879. Full page plates & text illus. Thin 8vo,
first edition. Presentation copy, signed on half-title. Argosy
713-2 1983 $75

ADAMS, WILLIAM H. DAVENPORT   Memorable Battles in English History.
Lon., 1863. Boards in green leather with marbled paperwraps, edges
of spine worn and starting to separate, else very good. Inscription.
Quill & Brush 54-1648 1983 $35

ADAMS, WILLIAM L.   Centennial Address to the Oregon
State Fair, Oct. 13, 1876. Portland, Himes, 1876. Double columns.
Orig. printed wraps. First edition. Ginsberg 47-712 1983 $50

ADAM'S Tail: or, The First Metamorphosis... London: Printed for
John Bell...M.DCC.LXXIV. 4to, with half-title, clean tear in the
inner margin of the first two leaves. New marbled wraps. First
edition. Quaritch NS 7-1 1983 $250

ADANSON, MICHEL   A Voyage to Senegal, the Isle of
Goree, and the River Gambia. Printed for J. Nourse, 1759. First
edition in English, with a folding engraved map by Philip Buache.
8vo, errata, cont. calf, gilt, neatly rebacked. Fenning 61-5 1983
£225

ADCOCK, A   The Glory that was Grub Street. London,
(1928). First edition. 32 portraits by E.O. Hoppe. Covers a little
marked. Unopened. Nice. Rota 230-5 1983 £12

ADCOCK, A.   Gods of Modern Grub Street. London,
(1923). First edition. Covers a little marked and spine creased.
Reinforced dust wrapper. Bookplate. Nice. Rota 231-1 1983 £18.50

ADCOCK, A   More than Money. London: S.W. Partridge
& Co., n.d. (1903). With 12 illustrations. Original cloth. First
edition. Inscribed by author: "William and Eliza Adcock, from their
affectionate son, Arthur St. John Adcock. Oct. 1903." Binding worn
and soiled. Inner hinges cracking. Endpapers browning. MacManus
277-27 1983 $50

ADDINGTON, WILLIAM   An Abridgment of Penal Statutes.
W. Strahan & M. Woodfall for the author, 1790. Second edition, 4to,
calf, hinges cracked, label. Signed by author on title-page.
Jarndyce 31-42 1983 £42

ADDISON, ALBERT C.   The Romantic Story of the Puritan Fathers.
Boston: L.C. Page & Co., 1912. Frontis. and illus. Orig. pictorial
cloth, gilt. Very fine. Jenkins 152-2 1983 $45

ADDISON, GEORGE AUGUSTUS   Indian reminiscences or the Bengal
Moofussul miscellany. London: Edward Bull, 1837. First edition.
8vo. Orig. purple cloth. Trifle soiled, spine faded. Very good
copy. Ximenes 63-198 1983 $150

ADDISON, JOSEPH   The campaign, a poem. London: Tonson,
1705. Second edition. Folio. Quarter morocco. A couple of minor
marginal repairs; an uncut copy. Ximenes 63-354 1983 $150

ADDISON, JOSEPH   The Campaign: A Poem, to His Grace the
Duke of Marlborough. Printed for, and sold by H. Hills, 1710. 8vo,
new boards. Bickersteth 77-1 1983 £12

ADDISON, JOSEPH   The Drummer; or, the haunted house.
London: printed for Jacob Tonson, 1716. 1st edition, 4to, a little
browned at the beginning, want the half title. Disbound in wrappers.
Pickering & Chatto 19-1 1983 $350

ADDISON, JOSEPH   The Free-Holder. London: For D.
Midwinter and J. Tonson, 1729. Fourth edition. Half-title. 12mo.
Cont. panelled calf, gilt panelled spine and morocco label, gilt.
Traylen 94-7 1983 £12

ADDISON, JOSEPH   Interesting Anecdotes, Memoirs,
Allegories, Essays, and Protical Fragments Tending To Amuse the
Fancy and Inculcate Morality. London: Printed for the Author, 1794.
1st ed. Contemporary 3/4 calf and marbled boards. Fine copy of
this vol., one of a dozen published in the 1790's under this title
and authorship. Jenkins 155-4 1983 $75

ADDISON, JOSEPH   The Miscellaneous Works, In Verse and
Prose, Of the Right Honourable, Joseph Addison, Esq. London: Printed
for J. & R. Tonson, 1765. 4 vols. With some account of the life and
writtings of the author. Frontis. portrait. Full cont. tree calf with
red & green morocco labels on spines. Marbled endpapers. Bookplates.
Some foxing. Handsome set. MacManus 277-28 1983 $250

ADDISON, JOSEPH   Miscellaneous Works in Verse and Prose.
London: J. & R. Tonson, 1765. 4 vols. 8vo. Cont. calf, green
morocco labels, gilt. Portrait frontis. One joint slightly cracked.
Bookplate. Traylen 94-5 1983 £48

ADDISON, JOSEPH   Poems on Several Occasions. London:
Printed for E. Curll in Fleet-street, 1719-(1718). 8vo. Illus. with
frontis. portrait by M. Van der Gucht after Kneller. An engraving by
Kirkall, & engraved head- and tail-pieces. Full cont. panelled calf
with cont. lettering pieces on spine. First edition. Foxon 1, p.4.
Bookplate of Ross Winans. Very fine copy. MacManus 277-29 1983
$300

ADDISON, JOSEPH   Remarks on Several Parts of Italy, &c
In the Years 1701, 1702, 1703. London: Printed for J. Jonson, 1726.
Third edition, small 8vo, wood engraved head and tail pieces,
contemporary mottled calf, gilt back, morocco label gilt, backstrip
worn at head and tail, joints weak. Deighton 3-1 1983 £38

ADDISON, JOSEPH   Rosamond. An Opera. London: printed for
Jacob Tonson, 1707. 1st edition, 4to, wanting the half-title, some
foxing throughout, and scribbles in ink on several pages. Tear in
inner margin of last leaf slightly affecting the text, disbound,
in modern blue wrappers, detached. Pickering & Chatto 19-2 1983 $300

ADDISON, JOSEPH   The Works. Birmingham, John Baskerville
for J. & R. Tonson, 1761. 4to. 4 vols. Engraved portrait of Addison
by Miller after Kneller, 3 plates by Grignion after Hayman, & 13 plates
of cuts of coins. Cont. mottled calf with gilt role on sides, finely
rebacked with gilt spines & morocco labels. O'Neal 50-5 1983 $475

ADDISON, JOSEPH   The Works of the Late Right Honourable
Joseph Addison... Birmingham: John Baskerville for and J. and R.
Tonson, 1761. Baskerville edition. 4 vols. 4to. Cont. calf,
neatly rebacked with orig. backstrips laid down. Engraved frontis.
and the portrait by G. Kneller, vignette heading the Dedication,
3 plates by Hayman after Grignion, and 13 plates of medals. Traylen
94-6 1983 £120

ADDISON, THOMAS   A collection of the published writings
of the late Thomas Addison... London, 1868. 8vo. Colored illus.
Rebacked with orig. backstrip. Very good. Fye H-3-7 1983 $100

ADDRESSES on the Presentation of the Sword of Gen. Andrew Jackson to
the Congress of the United States. Washington: A.O.P. Nicholson,
1855. Orig. printed wrappers. Jenkins 153-277 1983 $30

ADE, GEORGE   Doc' Horne. Chicago: Herbert S. Stone,
1899. First edition, illus. 16mo, pict. buckram. Argosy 714-6
1983 $30

ADE, GEORGE   Fables in Slang. Chicago: Herbert S.
Stone & Company, 1900. First edition. Illus. Inscribed to Thomas
Perkins by Ade. With Perkins' engraved bookplate. Worn and soiled.
Bradley 66-1 1983 $27.50

ADE, GEORGE   In Pastures New. N.Y., 1906. First
edition. Illus., red cloth; rubbed. Argosy 714-7 1983 $20

ADE, GEORGE   More Fables. Chicago, 1900. First
edition. 16mo, dec. cloth. First edition. Argosy 714-9 1983 $20

ADE, GEORGE   Pink Marsh. Chicago: Herbert S. Stone,
1897. First edition. 16mo, pict. buckram. Illus. Argosy 714-8
1983 $40

ADE, GEORGE   Rollo Johnson or the Demon Bicycle
and Its Daring Rider. Arizona, (1903-4). 16mo. Total edition is
374 copies. Rear wrapper missing, front wrapper intact though
chipped. In Our Time 156-9 1983 $150

ADE, GEORGE   Samples: A Collection of Stories.
New York: Boni & Liveright, (1927). 8vo. Cloth. The colorful
dj for the book is chipped and worn, though mostly intact on the
front flap. A fine copy. In Our Time 156-683 1983 $85

ADELER, MAX, PSEUD.
Please turn to
CLARK, CHARLES HEBER

ADELMANN, HOWARD   Marcello Malpighi and the Evolution
of Embroyology. Ithaca, 1966. First edition. 8vo. 5 vols. Folio.
Boxed. New. Fye H-3-850 1983 $150

ADHEMAR, HELENE   Watteau. Sa vie, son oeuvre. Paris:
Pierre Tisne, 1950. 155 plates, text illus. Square 4to. Cloth.
Ars Libri 32-694 1983 $75

ADHEMAR, JEAN   Toulouse-Lautrec. His complete lithographs and drypoints. New York: Abrams, (1965). 368 illus. (54
color). Small folio. Cloth. Dust jacket. Ars Libri 32-664 1983
$175

ADIE, JOHN   On the Total Eclipse of the Sun.
Edinburgh: Printed by Neill and Company, 1851. Orig. offprint, 8vo,
disbound, nice lithographed plate. Pickering & Chatto 22-2 1983 $50

ADLER, ALFRED (1870-1937)   Beitraege Zur Lehre Von Der Organischen
Grundlage Der Psychoneuroses. (1912). With the author's presentation
stamp "vom autor". Gach 95-4 1983 $75

ADLER, ALFRED (1870-1937)   The Neurotic Constitution: Outlines
of a Comparative Individualistic Psychology and Psychotherapy. NY:
Moffat, Yard, 1916. First edition in English. Frontis. portrait.
Orig. red cloth. Good copy, slight dampstaining to upper outer
edges of first and last few leaves. Gach 95-5 1983 $75

ADLER, ALFRED (1870-1937)   Problems of Neurosis. NY: Cosmopolitan, 1930. First American edition. Gach 95-7 1983 $20

ADLER, ALFRED (1870-1937)   Study of Organ Inferiority and its
Physical Compensation. NY: N. M. D. Pub. Co., 1917. First edition
in English. Orig. boards. Fine copy. Gach 95-8 1983 $50

ADOLPHUS, JOHN   Memoirs of John Bannister, comedian.
London: Richard Bentley, n. d. (ca. 1846). 2 vols. in 1, 8vo,
original red cloth (spine worn and chipped). First ed., 2nd issue.
With two plates. Ximenes 64-6 1983 $40

ADONIA, a desultory story. London: printed for A. and J. Black,
etc., 1801. First edition. Four vols. 12mo. Cont. red half
morocco. Half-titles present. A little rubbed, slight wear to
tops of spines. Ximenes 63-114 1983 $350

ADVANTAGES of the use of gas in private houses in Calcutta...
Calcutta: Calcutta Gazette Office, etc., n.d. (1854). First
edition. Large slim 8vo. Orig. red cloth. Six folding plates.
Trifle rubbed. Very good copy. Ximenes 63-199 1983 $150

ADVENTURES of a Gold-Finder. Henry Colburn, 1850. First edition, 3
vols., half titles vol. I, 4 pp ads. vol. III. Inner hinges vol. I a
little weak. Orig. boards, cloth spines, paper labels a little rubbed.
Jarndyce 30-271 1983 £75

THE ADVENTURES of Baron Munchausen. Warne, nd (ca. 1890). 1st edn.
18 illus. printed in colours from orig. designs by A. Richard.
Frontis. Red cloth backed col'd pictorial bds. (edges & corners of
bds. some wear, bookpl. fr.ep., tear top margin p.v. & sml. tear
margin p.59), v.g. Hodgkins 27-353 1983 £35

THE ADVENTURES of Mr. Obadiah Oldbuck. Tilt and Bogue, circa, 1850.
Cartoon illus. on 84 numbered plates (including title), with text
beneath, oblong small 8vo, orig. (?) green cloth, gilt, v.g. copy.
Fenning 61-6 1983 £45

THE ADVERTISER. A Poem. London: Printed for J. Bew...MDCCLXXV. 4to,
inner margin of last leaf cut into, not affecting the text, new wraps.
First edition. A fresh, crisp copy. Quaritch NS 7-2 1983 $185

AELIANUS, CLAUDIUS   Claudii Aeliani...Opera, quae extant,
omnia, Graece Latineque e Regione... Tiguri apudGesneros Fratres,
(1556). Early vellum. First collected edition. Felcone 21-1 1983
$150

AESCHYLUS   Agamemnon. Chicago, 1903. 8vo, cloth-
backed boards, gilt-lettering. Title-page vignette, decorative border.
Translated by Fitzgerald. One of 160 (of 168) copies printed on
paper. Some cover wear. Very good. Perata 27-164 1983 $60

AECHYLUS Compositions from the Tragedies of
Aechylus. London, 1795. 32 engraved pl., oblong folio, 1/3 calf.
Designed by John Flaxman, engraved by Thomas Piroli. Salloch 385-282
1983 $165

AESCHYLUS Fabularum Aesopicarum Delectus. Oxoniae,
E Theatro Sheldoniano, 1698. 8vo, cont. panelled calf, rubbed, new
label, name on title, inscription on fly. Ravenstree 95-5 1983 $85

AESCHYLUS The Oresteia. Chiswick Press for Emery
Walker, Sydney Cockerell and A.W. Pollard, 1904. Sm. 4to, printed
throughout in red and black, uncut in original holland-backed paper
boards, paper label, a very fine entirely unopened copy. 225 copies
only on hand-made paper. The first use of the Proctor types.
Presentation copy inscribed in Dorothy Walker's hand: "To F G Salter
in memory of his friend Emery Walker (d. 1933)." Deighton 3-3
1983 £145

AESCHYLUS Tragoediae Quae Extant Septem.
Glasguae: In AEdibus Academicis. Excudebat Robertus Foulis, 1746.
2 vols., 12mo, orig. calf, little worn, one cover detached, minor
age-darkening. Apparently the variant pot 8vo. Ravenstree 95-3
1983 $175

AESCHYLUS Tragoediae. Lg, 1898. 1/2 calf, 8vo.
Salloch 385-414 1983 $20

AESCHYLUS Tragoediae. Oxford, OCT, 1902. 8vo,
cloth. Salloch 385-413a 1983 $20

THE AESOPIAD; a poem. Dublin, 1784-5. Disbound, 8vo, 1st edition.
Ximenes 64-7 1983 $400

AESOPUS Aesop's fables. Hull: printed for the
author, by Robert Peck, 1803. First edition. 8vo. 19th-century
green cloth, morocco label. Rare. Ximenes 63-60 1983 $150

AESOPUS The Fables... Newcastle, 1818. First
edition. Royal paper copy, roy. 8vo. Half polished calf. Gilt
spine with morocco labels, gilt, t.e.g. 188 wood-engraved headpieces to the fables and 136 other vignettes, tail-pieces, etc. by
Thomas Bewick. Traylen 94-8 1983 £180

AESOPUS Aesop's Fables. London: Printed for
J. Booker, et al. 1821. 16mo, illus. with wooducts by Bewick.
Old calf, rebacked, corners rubbed. Karmiole 71-2 1983 $100

AESOPUS Some of Aesop's Fables. N.Y.: Mac.,
1883. 4to. Brown pictorial cloth. Some shelfwear. Profusely illus.
by Randolph Caldecott. Very good. Aleph-bet 8-49 1983 $60

AESOPUS Aesop's Fables. N.Y., Doubleday, 1912.
First American edition thus. Color frontis. and 12 full page color
plates by Arthur Rackham, together with 50 b/w drawings. Orig. green
cloth stamped in black, large color pictorial paper label on front
cover (spine faded and some slight rubbing) else, very good. Houle
22-213 1983 $95

AESOPUS Aesop's Fables. Phila.: McKay, n.d.
(ca. 1930). Illus. by N. Fry. 8vo. Red cloth. Pictorial paste-On.
Full page color plates. Many black & whites in text on all pages.
Very good to fine. Aleph-bet 8-7 1983 $30

AESOPUS Fables of Aesop according to Sir Roger
L'Estrange. Paris: Harrison of Parris, n.d. 4to. Pictorial boards.
Slightly scuffed slipcase. Limited to 595 copies. "Not for Sale
Copy." Printed on Auvergne hand-made paper. Illus. with 50 drawings
by Calder. Uncut and unopened, with the orig. paper knife to use to
open the pages. Fine. Aleph-bet 8-50 1983 $300

AESOPUS The Fables of Aesop. Hodder & Stoughton,
n.d. 4to. Mounted colour frontis. & 22 mounted colour plates. Several text illus. Pictorial endpapers. Brown pictorial cloth, gilt.
Greer 40-88 1983 £65

AFLALO, FREDERICK G. A Sketch of the Natural History of
Australia. London: Macmillan and Co., 1896. With 31 illus. and 1
map. Green cloth. Karmiole 73-13 1983 $75

AFLALO, FREDERICK G The Sports of the World. London,
Cassell, n.d. (ca. early 1900s). Illus. from drawings and photos.
4to. Small piece torn from bottom of back cover at backstrip.
Morrill 287-3 1983 $37.50

AGASSIZ, L. Bibliographia Zoologiae et Geologiae.
Ray Society, 1848-54. 4 vols., 8vo, cloth. Good ex-library copy
with small stamps on endpapers and title-pages. A little light
foxing and bindings a trifle faded. Wheldon 160-205 1983 £90

AGASSIZ, L. Etudes sur les Glaciers. Neuchatel,
1840. Atlas of 18 lithograph plates by J. Bettannier and 14 key
plates, 2 vols., royal 8vo, and folio, contemporary calf and half
cloth. Contents of both volumes clean and unused. Wheldon 160-1354
1983 £1,650

AGATE, JAMES The Amazing Theatre. London, 1939.
First edition. Dust wrapper. Fine. Rota 230-10 1983 £12

AGATE, JAMES The Common Touch. London, 1926. First
edition. Fine. Rota 230-9 1983 £12.50

AGATE, JAMES Here's Richness. London, 1942. First
English edition. One of 100 numbered copies signed by the author and
Osbert Sitwell, who introduces the book. T.e.g. Half leather covers.
Inscription. Fore- and bottom edges faintly spotted. Spine slightly
faded. Very good indeed. Jolliffe 26-2 1983 £65

AGEE, JAMES Last Letter to Father Flye. Bos., 1969.
Limited to 500 copies, paperwraps, slight discoloration on cover, still
fine bright copy. Quill & Brush 54-6 1983 $75

AGEE, JAMES Notes for a Moving Picture. NY, 1937.
Very good or better in dust wrapper with faded spine color but lettering bright. Quill & Brush 54-8 1983 $35

AGEE, JAMES Permit Me Voyage. New Haven: 1934.
First edition. Very fine in slightly chipped and slightly stained
dust wrapper. Bromer 25-2 1983 $300

AGEE, JAMES Permit Me Voyage. NH, 1934. Very good
to fine. Quill & Brush 54-11 1983 $175

THE AGES of Female Beauty. Charles Tilt, 1838. Illus. with engravings from drawings. Blue vertical ribbed dec. cloth gilt, a.e.g.,
backstrip worn with some wear to rear joint, good copy. Hodgkins
27-239 1983 £15

AGGS, CHARLES M. A Letter Addressed to the Rev. R.
Burgess, Protestant Chaplain at Rome. Rome: Printed by Salvucci,
1836. First edition, 8vo, wrapper. Fenning 61-17.A 1983 £14.50

AGNELLO, GIUSEPPE I Vermexio. Firenze: "La Nuova
Italia'', 1959. 90 plates. Large 4to. Cloth. Dust jacket. Ars
Libri 33-380 1983 $125

AGNER, DWIGHT The Books of WAD, A Bibliography...
Baton Rouge: Press of the Nightowl, 1974. First edition. Small
4to. Half cloth over marbled paper covered boards. Limited to
206 numbered copies. With ornamentation printed in different
colored inks. Fine copy. Oak Knoll 49-437 1983 $95

AGUS, GIUSEPPE The Allemands. London, Welcker, n.d.
(1767). Engraved title and music. Oblong 8vo, marbled boards.
Salloch 387-1 1983 $135

AHLERS, FRANCISCO H. Instruccao sobre os Corpos Celestes...
Lisboa: Miguel Manscal da Costa, 1758. First edition. 8vo.
Cont. calf, gilt. Engraved frontis., folding engraved plates,
engraved vignette. Minor worming. Heath 48-481 1983 £75

AHRENS, FELIX B. Die Metallcarbide und Ihre Verwendung.
Stuttgart: Verlag von F. Enke, 1896. 8vo. Orig. printed orange
wrappers. Partially uncut. Ads. Internally a good copy. Zeitlin
264-3 1983 $60

AIKEN, CONRAD   Blue Voyage. New York: Scribners, 1927. 1st ed. orig. blue cloth, gilt. Good copy with four-line inscription from Aiken in 1930 to a woman with his notation "For Values Received". Jenkins 155-6 1983 $75

AIKEN, CONRAD   Blue Voyage. NY, 1927. One of 125 numbered and signed copies, edges slightly rubbed, otherwise good to very good in worn slipcase. Quill & Brush 54-12 1983 $65

AIKEN, CONRAD   Blue Voyage. New York, 1927. First edition. Covers a little marked. Nice. Rota 230-12 1983 £20

AIKEN, CONRAD   Blue Voyage. New York, 1927. First English edition. Spine a little creased. In a chipped and repaired dust wrapper. Nice. Rota 230-13 1983 £18

AIKEN, CONRAD   Blue Voyage. London: Gerald Howe, (1927). 1st English ed. Orig. blue cloth, gilt. Fine copy. Jenkins 155-7 1983 $30

AIKEN, CONRAD   Brownstone Eclogues. New York, 1942. First edition. Chipped dust wrapper. Inscription on flyleaf. Very nice. Rota 230-15 1983 £15

AIKEN, CONRAD   The Coming Forth by Day of Osiris Jones. New York, 1931. 1st issue. 8vo. Cloth. Date of publication penned on front flyleaf. Some fading to base of front endboard, else a fine copy in lightly chipped dj. In Our Time 156-12 1983 $85

AIKEN, CONRAD   Conversation, a Novel. New York, 1940. 8vo. Cloth. A fine copy in dj which has some light wear. In Our Time 156-13 1983 $75

AIKEN, CONRAD   Costumes by Eros. New York: Scribners, 1928. 1st ed. Orig. cloth, gilt. Some abrasions to front end paper, else nice copy with 1969 inscription from Aiken to a bookseller-friend. Jenkins 155-8 1983 $50

AIKEN, CONRAD   Gehenna. New York, 1930. 8vo. 1 of 875 copies. Light wear to paper label on spine, else vg-fine. In Our Time 156-11 1983 $20

AIKEN, CONRAD   The Kid. New York: Duell, Sloane and Pearce, (1947). Cloth. First edition. A fine copy in the very fragile dust jacket, which has only two minor nicks. Reese 20-14 1983 $45

AIKEN, CONRAD   The Kid. (Edinburgh), 1947. Some pages unopened, fine in dust wrapper. Quill & Brush 54-13 1983 $20

AIKEN, CONRAD   Landscape West Eden. London: Dent, (1934). 1st English ed. Orig. printed boards. Fine copy. Jenkins 155-9 1983 $20

AIKEN, CONRAD   Nocturne of Remembered Spring. Boston: Four Seas Company. 1917. 8vo. Cloth. Some light spotting to cloth, mainly a fine copy. This copy inscribed by Aiken to his publisher. In Our Time 156-10 1983 $250

AIKEN, CONRAD   Nocturne of Remembered Spring. London: Martin Secker (1921). 1st English ed. Orig. patterned boards, label uncut. Very good copy of an extremely fragile vol. Jenkins 155-10 1983 $25

AIKEN, CONRAD   Punch: The Immortal Liar. New York, 1921. 1st ed. Boards, with orange paper label wrapping around spine to show title front and back. Fine. Bradley 63-1 1983 $50

AIKEN, CONRAD   Punch: The Immortal Liar. New York, 1921. First edition. Orig. patterned boards. Spine darkened and a little rubbed. Very good. Rota 230-11 1983 £15

AIKEN, CONRAD   Punch: The Immortal Liar. London: Martin Secker (1921). 1st English ed. Orig. patterned boards, label, uncut. Very good copy of a fragile book. Jenkins 155-11 1983 $25

AIKEN, CONRAD   Scepticisms, Notes on Contemporary Poetry. New York: Knopf, 1919. First edition. Orig. red cloth, stamped in black. Back cover has a Fall 1919 booklist, front panel has a brief biography of Aiken. Fine copy in yellow dj with some tape repairs. Jenkins 155-12 1983 $65

AIKEN, CONRAD   The Soldier. Norfolk, (1944). Cover slightly sunned and endpapers very slightly offset, still very good in slightly darkened and soiled, very good dust wrapper with few short tears and some fraying. Quill & Brush 54-14 1983 $75

AIKEN, CONRAD   Thee. New York: Braziller, (1967). 1st ed., 1 of 100 numbered and signed copies, signed by both Aiken and Leonard Baskin whose drawings appear here. Orig. printed boards, box with label. Very fine copy. Jenkins 155-13 1983 $200

AIKEN, CONRAD   Thee. NY: George Braziller (1967). Tall 8vo, with 6 drawings. This is one of 100 special numbered copies signed by Leonard Baskin and Conrad Aiken. Green boards. Illus. Slipcase. Karmiole 73-5 1983 $150

AIKEN, CONRAD   Thee. NY: Braziller, (1967). Octavo. First edition. Illus. with 6 drawings by Leonard Baskin. Of an edition of 200 copies, 1/100 signed by Aiken and Baskin. Extremely fine in printed boards and slightly rubbed slip-case with large pictorial label. Bookplate. Bromer 25-139 1983 $150

AIKEN, CONRAD   Turns and Movies and Other Tales in Verse. London & Boston: Constable & Co., 1916. Quarto. Stiff boards. First edition. English issue from American sheets. Spine a trifle sunned, else a near fine copy. Reese 20-13 1983 $125

AIKEN, CONRAD   Twentieth Century American Poetry. New York, 1944. First American edition. With the ownership signature of Theodore Roethke. Corners bumped. Covers dull and very slightly soiled. Spine dull and rubbed. Very good. Jolliffe 26-435 1983 £18

AIKEN, HENRY   A Touch at the Fine Arts. London: Thomas M'lean, 1824. First edition. Small folio. Half title, ad. leaf. Cont. quarter green morocco. Orig. printed label pasted on front cover. 12 hand coloure Aquatint plates by Henry Alken. A good copy. Heath 48-26 1983 £275

AIKEN, JOHN   Labor and Wages, at Home and Abroad. Lowell, 1849. Disbound. Felcone 22-119 1983 $20

AIKEN, LUCY   The Life of Joseph Addison. Printed for Longman, Brown..., 1843. First edition, in two vols. With a portrait (lightly foxed), including half-titles. Large 12mo, orig. brown cloth, by Leighton Son & Hodge, with their ticket. Fenning 62-2 1983 £24.50

AIKEN, LUCY   Poetry for Children. London: Printed for R. Phillips and sold by B. Tabart, 1803. Second edition. 12mo. Ads. Tiny tears at bottom corner of few pages with very minor loss of letters; otherwise nice copy in orig. leather-backed marbled boards, rubbed at extremities. Contemporary owner's signature. Bromer 25-311 1983 $125

AIKIN, JOHN   The Arts of Life... Boston: Hosea Sprague for Samuel H. Parker, 1803. Full calf. Nice. Felcone 20-75 1983 $45

AIKIN, JOHN   The Arts of Life. London: J. Johnson, 1807. Second edition. 12mo. Ads. Fine in green vellum-backed marbled boards. Paper label on spine chipped and covers rubbed at extremities. Bromer 25-310 1983 $110

AIKIN, JOHN   Essays on Song-Writing. London: Printed for Joseph Johnson, St. Paul's Churchyard by William Eyres, Warrington, 1774. Second edition. Full morocco, title label and armorial of Thomas Hutton inset on red and green morocco. Nice. K Books 307-1 1983 £48

AIKIN, JOHN   Letters from a Father to his Son... London: for J. Johnson, 1796. Third edition. 2 vols. Cr. 8vo. Cont. calf, morocco labels, gilt, sides worn. Traylen 94-9 1983 £20

AIKMAN, DUNCAN   The Taming of the Frontier. New York:
Minton, Balch & Co., 1925. Frontis. and plates. First edition.
Scarce. Fine copy. Jenkins 153-2 1983 $45

AILLY, PIERRE D'   Tractatus super libros meteororum.
Cracow: Johann Haller, 1506. Second edition. Title with fine
large woodcut printer's mark. 4to. Modern boards with leather spine.
From the collection of Georg Tannstetter. Kraus 164-1 1983 $2,500.

AIMARD, GUSTAVE   The Trappers of Arkansas. (N.p.):
For the trade, 1867. Cloth, a waterstained and worn copy. Felcone
22-63 1983 $25

AINSA, J. Y.   History of the Crabb Expedition into N.
Sonora. Phoenix, 1951. Stapled into later manila covers. 52 pages.
Dawson 471-2 1983 $25

AINSLIE, KATHLEEN   Catharine Susan and Me's Coming Out.
London: Castell (ca. 1890's). 12mo. Full-page color illus. by
Ainslie throughout. Pictorial wrappers slightly soiled and rubbed
at extremities, otherwise fine. Owner's signature. Bromer 25-312
1983 $45

AINSLIE, KATHLEEN   Oh Poor Amelia Jane. Castell, n.d.
(ca. 1900). 14 colored illus. & printed written text, unpaginated.
Card pictorial covers in colour. Covers sl. marked & soiled, bruising
at edges, very good. Hodgkins 27-2 1983 $15

AINSWORTH, WILLIAM HARRISON   Boscobel: or, The Royal Oak. London:
Tinsley Brothers, 1872. Illus. by F.H. Rimbault. 3 vols. Orig.
decorated green cloth. First edition. Rubbed, especially on upper
cover of Vol. III. Outer hinge of Vol. I splitting at top. Scarce.
Good copy. MacManus 277-33 1983 $125

AINSWORTH, WILLIAM HARRISON   Cardinal Pole: or, The Days of Philip
and Mary. London: Chapman & Hall, 1863. 3 vols. Orig. cloth.
First edition. Fine. MacManus 277-34 1983 $600

AINSWORTH, WILLIAM HARRISON   Cardinal Pole. Chapman & Hall, 1863.
First edition. 3 vols., half titles. Library labels covered in
bookplates on inside front covers. Orig. green cloth, very sl.
rubbing of corners, v.g. Jarndyce 30-263 1983 £80

AINSWORTH, WILLIAM HARRISON   Crichton. Richard Bentley, 1837.
First edition, 3 vols. Orig. half calf, marbled boards. Gilt spines,
red and brown labels. Fine. Jarndyce 30-264 1983 £55

AINSWORTH, WILLIAM HARRISON   Crichton. Richard Bentley, 1837.
First edition. 3 vols. Large 12mo, lacks half-title in vol. II.
Orig. boards (new end-papers and spines, orig. labels re-mounted)
uncut. Contents leaf of vol. I misbound. Hannas 69-2 1983 £45

AINSWORTH, WILLIAM HARRISON   Guy Fawkes. R. Bentley, 1841. 3 vols.
Illus. by George Cruikshank. 22 etchings. Half maroon lea. backed
red marbled bds., with two dark green lea. title labels with each vol.,
t.e.g. others rough trimmed, marbled eps., early circulating lib.
stamp verso frontis. vol. 1., contents some thumbing with few repairs
to some pp., bookpl. both eps. each vol., scarce, vg. Hodgkins 27-240
1983 £65

AINSWORTH, WILLIAM HARRISON   Historical Novels. London, (1880).
16 vols. 8vo. Half red morocco, gilt panelled spines, t.e.g.
Full-page plates by George Cruikshank, etc. Orig. library edition.
Traylen 94-10 1983 £195

AINSWORTH, WILLIAM HARRISON   The Historical Romances. Phila.:
Printed for Subscribers Only by George Barrie & Sons, n.d. 19 (of 20)
vols. Illus. Orig. 3/4 red morocco & marbled boards. Marbled endpapers. Library edition, limited & numbered. Few spines slightly
rubbed. Very good set. MacManus 277-35 1983 $150

AINSWORTH, WILLIAM HARRISON   Jack Sheppard. London: Richard Bentley,
1839. Illus. by George Cruikshank. 3 vols. Orig. cloth. First edition. Covers slightly soiled and a little worn at the edges. Rear
inner hinge in Vol. I cracked. Some light foxing. Near-fine copy.
MacManus 277-36 1983 $150

AINSWORTH, WILLIAM HARRISON   Letters from Cockney Lands. London,
for W. Sams, 1727 (misprint for 1827). Third edition, sm. 8vo,
uncut in original pale mauve boards, surface of backstrip lacking
although original paper backing remains, as does the original paper
label. Firm and extremely clean copy. Errata slip pasted in. Neat
contemporary signature on boards of A M Grant. Deighton 3-4 1983
£55

AINSWORTH, WILLIAM HARRISON   The Lord Mayor of London: or, City Life
in the Last Century. London: Chapman & Hall, 1862. 3 vols. Orig.
decorated cloth. First edition. Spines faded. Rare in this condition. Bookplate. Near-fine, clean, and tight set. MacManus 277-37
1983 $650

AINSWORTH, WILLIAM HARRISON   Merry England: or, Nobles and Serfs.
London: Tinsley Brothers, 1874. 3 vols. Orig. green cloth. First
edition, in the remainder binding with the title spelled "Merry" rather
than "Merrie" on the spines. Near-fine copy. MacManus 277-39 1983
$350

AINSWORTH, WILLIAM HARRISON   Merry England; Or, Nobles And Serfs.
London: Tinsley Brothers, 1874. Orig. green decorated cloth (reading
"Merrie" on the spines). First edition, first binding. Spines and
covers slightly worn. Several pages coming loose in vol. III. Good
Set. MacManus 277-38 1983 $250

AINSWORTH, WILLIAM HARRISON   Merry England. Tinsley Brothers, 1874.
First edition, 3 vols. Half titles, orig. dark green cloth, spines
lettered in gilt ('Merry'). Very good copy. Jarndyce 30-267 1983
£110

AINSWORTH, WILLIAM HARRISON   Merry England. Tinsley, 1874. First
edition. 3 vols. Half titles, 16 pp ads. vols. II & III. Orig.
green cloth, rubbed, library labels on upper covers. A good copy.
This copy in first issue binding, with 'Merrie' on spines. Jarndyce
30-266 1983 £56

AINSWORTH, WILLIAM HARRISON   The Miser's Daughter: A Tale. London:
G. Routledge & Co., 1855. Illus. by George Cruikshank. Orig. blue
cloth. A re-issue of the first illustrated edition of 1848, part of
the Uniform Illustrated Editions of Ainsworth's Works. Bookplate.
Fine copy. MacManus 277-40 1983 $50

AINSWORTH, WILLIAM HARRISON   The Miser's Daughter. 1848. Illus.
by George Cruikshank, half red morocco, gilt decorated spine. K Books
307-2 1983 £20

AINSWORTH, WILLIAM HARRISON   Preston Fight. Tinsley Brothers, 1875.
First edition, 3 vols., orig. olive green dec. cloth. Fine.
Jarndyce 30-268 1983 £140

AINSWORTH, WILLIAM HARRISON   Preston fight or the insurrection of
1715. A tale. Tinsley Bros, 1875. First edition, 3 vols, 8vo,
no half-titles required, untrimmed in original dark green cloth,
spine gilt. Vols. I & II with small label removed from spine, Vol.
III faded and with library label removed from upper cover, new
endpapers. Scarce. Deighton 3-5 1983 £125

AINSWORTH, WILLIAM HARRISON   Saint James's. John Mortimer, 1844. 3
vols. Illus. by George Cruikshank. 9 etchings. Half tan lea. backed
marbled bds., black & brown title labels each vol., raised bands,
t.e.g., marbled eps., top corners of all vols. bumped, sl. foxing
prelims., vg. Hodgkins 27-241 1983 £65

AINSWORTH, WILLIAM HARRISON   The Spanish Match. Chapman & Hall,
1865. 2nd edition, 3 vols. Orig. blue cloth, v.g. Jarndyce 30-265
1983 £24

AINSWORTH, WILLIAM HARRISON   The Spendthrift. Leipzig, 1856. First
edition. Square 8vo, red half calf, gilt spine. Hannas 69-207 1983
£15

AINSWORTH, WILLIAM HARRISON   The Star-Chamber. G. Routledge, 1857.
Illus. by Phiz, 8vo, later qtr. roan, marbled sides. 8 plates.
Hill 165-1 1983 £15

AINSWORTH, WILLIAM HARRISON   Tower Hill. Leipzig, 1871. First
Tauchnitz edition. Square 8vo, quarter morocco, gilt spine. English
first edition. Hannas 69-208 1983 £10

AINSWORTH, WILLIAM HARRISON   The Tower of London. Richard Bentley, 1840. First edition. Front. & illus. by George Cruikshank. Crushed maroon morocco, gilt borders, dentelles and spine; repairs to hinges, t.e.g. Signed on the title: 'With affectionate remembrances from W. Harrison Ainsworth'. First issue. Jarndyce 31-403 1983 £85

AINSWORTH, WILLIAM HARRISON   The Tower of London. NY, 1903. Illus. by Cruikshank. New edition. Cloth covering top edge of rear corner slightly torn, still very good. Quill & Brush 54-15 1984 $35

AINSWORTH, WILLIAM HARRISON   Windsor Castle, An Historical Romance. London: Henry Colburn, 1844. 11 parts, illus. by George Cruikshank, Tony Johannot, and W.A. Delamotte. Orig. pictorial wrappers. First edition. Spines expertly rebacked. Several spine edges cracked slightly. Some plates slightly foxed. Very good set. Rare. MacManus 277-41 1983 $500

AINSWORTH, WILLIAM HARRISON   Windsor Castle. London: Henry Colburn, 1844. Illus. by George Cruikshank & Tony Johannot. With Designs on Wood, by W. Alfred Delamott. Rebound in 3/4 morocco & marbled boards. Marbled endpapers. New edition. Good copy, with original covers bound in. MacManus 277-42 1983 $75

AIRCRAFT Year Book. 1922. NY (1922). Photos, cloth, bookplate, slight stain on front cover else good. King 46-712 1983 $37.50

AIRD, THOMAS   The poetical works. Edinburgh: Blackwood, 1877. Fifth edition. 8vo. Orig. bright blue cloth. With mounted photographic portrait. Spine a trifle dull. Ximenes 63-430 1983 $40

AIRY, GEORGE BIDDELL   Instructions and Chart for Observations of Mars. London, Printed by G. Barclay, July, 1858. 1st ed., 8vo, folding engraved chart, uncut and unopened in the orig. printed wrappers, completely obscured by a later covering of brown paper pasted over. Pickering & Chatto 22-3 1983 $150

AKENSIDE, MARK   The Pleasures of the Imagination. London: Printed for R. Dodsley...M.DCC.XLIV. 4to, complete with half-title and leaf of ads. for Dodsley's Old Plays, vignette on titles, light foxing; cont. calf neatly rebacked. First edition, first of three 1744 issues, with five-line note on p. 9, and p. 20 misnumbered 22. Quaritch NS 7-4 1983 $375

AKENSIDE, MARK   The Pleasures of Imagination. Glasgow, printed by Robert and Andrew Foulis, 1775. 12mo, orig. sheep (quite worn, covers detached, spine chipped), other than a little foxing, internally nice. Ravenstree 94-104 1983 $37.50

AKENSIDE, MARK   The Poetical Works. London, 1857. Portrait, vignette title-page. Cr. 8vo. Dark blue calf, two line gilt borders with corner ornaments, gilt panelled spine, morocco label, gilt. Traylen 94-11 1983 £16

AKERMAN, JOHN YONGE   Wiltshire tales. London: John Russell Smith, 1853. First edition. 12mo. Orig. royal blue cloth. Trifle rubbed. Very good copy. Ximenes 63-141 1983 $85

AKERS, DWIGHT   Outposts of History in Orange County. Washingtonville, NY, (1937). Stiff pr. wraps. 2nd edition, one of 500 copies. Frontis., woodcuts by Fiske Boyd. Argosy 716-340 1983 $25

ALABAMA. LAWS.   General Assembly of Alabama, Acts of the 4th Biennial Session. Montgomery: Brittan & Blue, 1854. Disbound. Argosy 710-4 1983 $40

ALAZARD, JEAN   Ingres et l'Ingrisme. Paris: Albin Michel, 1950. 112 plates. 4to. Wrappers. Ars Libri 32-334 1983 $40

ALBANY FELT COMPANY.   Paper Machine Felts. Albany: Albany Felt Company, (1932). 8vo. Half leather over cloth, paper cover label. Covers rubbed. Oak Knoll 48-314 1983 $35

ALBEE, EDWARD   The American Dream. NY, (1961). Fine in very slightly soiled but still fine dustwrapper. Quill & Brush 54-17 1983 $75

ALBEE, EDWARD   The Zoo Story. New York: Coward-McCann, (1960). Cloth. First edition. A fine copy in very lightly soiled dust jacket, with a promotional photo of the author laid in. Reese 20-17 1983 $125

ALBEE, EDWARD   The Zoo Story, the Death of Bessie Smith, the Sandbox. NY, (1960). Cover lightly spotted, else near fine in slightly soiled, very good dustwrapper. Quill & Brush 54-18 1983 $125

ALBEE, FRED H.   Orphopedic and Reconstruction Surgery. Phila., 1919. 804 illus. Tall 8vo; ex-lib. Argosy 713-3 1983 $60

ALBINUS, BERNARD SIEGFRIED   Tables of the Skeleton and Muscles of the Human Body. H. Woodfall for John and Paul Knapton, London, 1749. Folio, engraving on title, 12 engraved plates of full length figures with backgrounds, each accompanied by an outline plate and 16 plates of bones; some foxing, mostly confined to the text and plate margins, last leaf of text (index) slightly smaller than the rest; nineteenth century half calf, rebacked. First edition in English. Quaritch NS 5-1 1983 $3,250

ALBUM de Cartagena de Indias. (Paris, 1927?). Illus. and ads. Oblong folio, orig. leatherette. Fine. Morrill 287-70 1983 $20

ALBUM Der Natuur. Een Werk Ter Verspreiding Van Natuurkennis Onder Beschaafde Lezers Van Allerlei Stand 1854. Te Haarlem 1854. Few illus., calf backed marbled boards, ink names, foxed, rubbed. King 46-499 1983 $20

ALBUM der Schweiz. Zurich, J. A. Preuss, n.d. (ca. 1890s). Plates from photographs and drawings; also fine advertising plates, some illustrated. 8vo, pictorial front cover. Morrill 288-475 1983 $35

ALCEDO, ANTONIO DE   Diccionario Geographico-historico de las Indias Occidentales o America. Madrid, 1786-89. First edition. 4to, 5 vols., cont. calf, spines gilt, cont. morocco labels. Half-titles, subscribers' list. Hole in margins of some leaves of final volume, not touching text. A fine copy of this scarce work. Trebizond 18-176 1983 $800

ALCOCK, FREDERICK   Trade & Travel in South America. London, Liverpool, 1903. First edition, 8vo, with 2 folding maps, 2 double-page charts, and numerous illustrations. Original brown cloth gilt, back faded and trifle marked. Deighton 3-6 1983 £18

ALCOTT, BRONSON   Pedlar's Progress. Boston, 1937. Thick 8vo, cloth backed boards. Ltd. first edition. One of 450 numbered copies, signed by the author. Argosy 714-12 1983 $50

ALCOTT, LOUISA MAY   Jo's Boys. Bos., 1886. Cover rubbed and spine slightly nicked, still good or better, tight copy. Quill & Brush 54-19 1983 $30

ALCOTT, LOUISA MAY   Little Men. Boston: Roberts, 1871. Frontis. 1st ed., 1st issue with signature mark and early ads. Orig. cloth, gilt, Very good copy. Jenkins 155-17 1983 $75

ALCOTT, LOUISA MAY   Little Women. Boston: Roberts, 1869. Frontis. 1st ed., later issue. Orig. green cloth, gilt. Slightly shaken, but a very good copy with almost no cover wear. Jenkins 155-18 1983 $50

ALCOTT, LOUISA MAY   Work: A Story of Experience. Bos., 1873. Hinges starting, cover worn, good. Quill & Brush 54-21 1983 $35

ALCOTT, WILLIAM A.   The Young Woman's Book of Health. Boston, 1850. Small 8vo. 1st ed. Morrill 289-1 1983 $27.50

ALDEN, EBENEZER   Early History of the Medical Profession in Norfolk Co., Mass. Boston, 1853. 1st separate ed. 8vo, later cloth, interleaved with lined up. Ex lib. Argosy 710-277 1983 $35

ALDEN, JOHN ELIOT   Rhode Island Imprints, 1727-1800. New York, 1949. First edition. 8vo, over 1700 items listed. Part of back cover water-stained, otherwise nice. Morrill 290-424 1983 $40

ALDEN, TIMOTHY   An Account of the Several Religious
Societies in Portsmouth, New-Hampshire... Boston, 1808. Disbound.
Reese 18-300 1983 $40

ALDERSON, E. A. H.   With the mounted infantry and the
Mashonaland Field Force 1896. London: Methuen & Co., 1898. 8vo.
Folding map, plan, 8 plates. Orig. cloth. Ex-lib. Adelson
Africa-153 1983 $50

ALDIN, CECIL   Old Inns. London: Heinemann (1921, ed.
of 1930). 4to. Black cloth spine, slightly faded. Full page color
illus. with tissue guards. Many full page & smaller black & white.
3 page handwritten letter from Aldin to poster artist John Hassall.
Very good. Aleph-bet 8-9 1983 $90

AL-DIN, NASIR   The Diary of H.M. The Shah of Persia.
John Murray, 1874. With a portrait and an additional coloured title-
page, 8vo, orig. cloth, gilt, the binding lightly marked, but otherwise
a fine copy. Fenning 60-293 1983 £24.50

ALDINGTON, RICHARD   Balls and Another Book for Suppression.
London: E. Lahr, 1931. Orig. wrappers. First edition. Fine copy.
MacManus 277-46 1983 $45

ALDINGTON, RICHARD   The Colonel's Daughter. London, Chatto
and Windus, 1931. First edition. One of 210 numbered copies signed
by the author. Green cloth, t.e.g., uncut, (spine a little faded),
else very good. Houle 22-10 1983 $65

ALDINGTON, RICHARD   The Colonel's Daughter. London: Chatto
& Windus, 1931. Original cloth. First edition. One of 210 copies
signed by Aldington. Almost fine. MacManus 277-47 1983 $50

ALDINGTON, RICHARD   The Colonel's Daughter. Chatto &
Windus, 1931. First edition, 8vo, orig. green buckram, top edges
gilt, a fine copy. Ltd. edition of 210 numbered copies signed by
the author. Fenning 62-3 1983 £24.50

ALDINGTON, RICHARD   The Colonel's Daughter. London, 1931.
First edition, first binding. Preliminaries a little foxed. Dust
wrapper. Very nice. Rota 230-18 1983 £12

ALDINGTON, RICHARD   The Complete Poems of Richard Aldington.
London, 1948. First edition. Dust wrapper. Fine. Rota 230-22 1983
£25

ALDINGTON, RICHARD   Death of a Hero. Paris, 1930. Authorised unexpurgated edition. 2 vols. 4to. Stiff paper wrappers,
uncut edges. Limited to 300 numbered copies. Spines a little worn.
Traylen 94-12 1983 £60

ALDINGTON, RICHARD   A Dream in the Luxembourg. Chatto &
Windux, 1930. First edition, 8vo, orig. cloth-backed decorated boards,
t.e.g., a fine copy. Ltd. edition of 308 numbered copies, signed by
the author. Fenning 62-4 1983 £32.50

ALDINGTON, RICHARD   Euripides and Alcestis. London,
Chatto & Windus, 1930. First edition. Half cloth over patterned
boards, t.e.g., uncut. One of 260 copies signed by the author.
Very good. Houle 22-11 1983 $45

ALDINGTON, RICHARD   Fifty Romance Lyric Poems. New York:
Crosby Gaige, 1928. First edition. One of 900 copies, printed under
the direction of Bruce Rogers. Autograph signatures of both Aldington
and Rogers. Fine. Rota 230-23 1983 £30

ALDINGTON, RICHARD   French Studies and Reviews. London,
1926. First edition. Spine a little darkened. Very nice. Rota
230-17 1983 £15

ALDINGTON, RICHARD   Images. London, the Egoist, (1919).
First edition. Half tan cloth over boards, paper labels, copy number
12, signed and numbered by the author. Printed by the Pelican Press.
Houle 22-12 1983 $100

ALDINGTON, RICHARD   Life Quest. Garden City, N.Y.: Doubleday, Doran & Co., Inc., 1935. Orig. cloth. First edition. Presentation copy from the author to Witter Bynner, inscribed on the front
flyleaf to "Witter Bynner, 'All the titles of good fellowship come to
you,' Richard Aldington, Aug. 1942." With Bynner's bookplate on the
front endsheet. Fine copy. MacManus 277-52 1983 $85

ALDINGTON, RICHARD   Life Quest. London: Chatto & Windus,
1935. First edition. 8vo. Orig. cloth, dust jacket. Slightly
dusty jacket. Fine. Jaffe 1-3 1983 $35

ALDINGTON, RICHARD   Literary Studies and Reviews. London,
1924. First edition, first binding. Spine a little darkened. Very
nice. Rota 230-16 1983 £15

ALDINGTON, RICHARD   Love and the Luxembourg. New York:
Covici, Friede, 1930. Orig. cloth. First edition. One of 475 signed
copies. Very good copy. MacManus 277-53 1983 $40

ALDINGTON, RICHARD   Roads to Glory. London, 1930. 8vo.
Cloth-backed boards, t.e.g., others uncut. Limited edition of 360
numbered copies signed by the author. Traylen 94-13 1983 £25

ALDINGTON, RICHARD   Soft Answers. London, 1932. 8vo,
cloth backed boards; inner hinges cracked. Ltd. first edition. One
of only 110 signed copies. Argosy 714-15 1983 $40

ALDINGTON, RICHARD   Stepping Heavenward. Florence: Orioli,
1931. First edition. One of 808 numbered copies on handmade paper,
signed by author. Dust wrapper. Fine. Rota 230-19 1983 £30

ALDINGTON, RICHARD   Two Stories. London: 1930. Orig.
cloth-backed boards (a little rubbed). First edition. One of 530
numbered copies, signed by author. About fine. MacManus 277-55
1983 $30

ALDINGTON, RICHARD   Women Must Work. London, 1934. First
edition, first binding. Frayed dust wrapper. Very nice. Rota 230-
20 1983 £12

ALDRICH, HENRY   The elements of civil architecture...
Oxford: printed by W. Baxter, for J. Parker, etc., 1824. Third
edition. 8vo. Orig. drab boards, printed paper label. With
engraved portrait and 55 plates. Spine dark and slightly worn at
the top. Some light spotting, but a fine copy. Ximenes 63-10
1983 $175

ALDRICH, JOHN   Lakeport's Ancient Homes. Lakeport, N.H.,
1917. First edition. Frontis. and plates. A.e.g. Orig. cloth.
Privately printed for author. Jenkins 152-716 1983 $40

ALDRICH, THOMAS BAILEY   Marjorie Daw. Boston: H.M., 1908.
First edition. Red gilt decorated cloth. 8vo. Full page color illus.
plus text illus. by J.C. Clay. Fine. Aleph-bet 8-10 1983 $25

ALDRIDGE, REGINALD   Life on a Ranch. London, 1884. Half
leather, some wear, old library stamp. Reese 19-14 1983 $375

ALDUS, DON   Coolie Traffic and Kidnapping. London,
McCorquodale & Co., 1876. 1st ed. Small 8vo. Slightly rubbed.
Morrill 289-587 1983 $47.50

ALEMAN, MATEO   The Rogue. Oxford, by William Turner,
for Robert Allot, 1630. Second English edition, first printed at
Oxford. Two parts. Folio. Lacks the two blank leaves. 19th
century calf (rebacked). Title laid down, first few leaves heavily
brown-stained. Hannas 69-3 1983 £100

ALEMBERT, JEAN LE ROND D'   Essai d'une Nouvelle Theorie de la
Resistance des Fluides. David l'aine, Paris, 1752. First edition.
4to, with 2 folding engraved plates; old library stamp on title
obliterated; a good copy in contemporary calf, gilt spine. Quaritch NS
5-2 1983 $950

ALEXANDER, MRS. A. H.
Please turn to
HECTOR, ANNIE FRENCH

ALEXANDER, ANN   Remarks on the Theatre, and on the late
fire at Richmond, in Virginia. York: printed by Thomas Wilson and
Son, for the author, and sold by William Alexander, etc., 1812. 8vo,
disbound, first ed. Ximenes 64-9 1983 $60

ALEXANDER, ARCHIBALD   Biographical Sketches of the Founder,
and Principal Alumni of the Log College. Princeton; J.T. Robinson,
1845. 12mo, lea. backed boards., (rubbed, foxed). Argosy 716-59
1983 $45

ALEXANDER, ARCHIBALD   A history of colonization on the
western coast of Africa. Phila: William S. Martien, 1846. 1 vol.
8vo. Folding map. Orig. cloth. Chipped at top. Rubbed. Light
foxing. Repairs to map. Adelson Africa-2 1983 $135

ALEXANDER, EDWARD PORTER   Iron Horses. New York, (1941). 1st ed.
Illus. 4to, dust wrapper. Morrill 286-2 1983 $22.50

ALEXANDER, EDWARD PORTER   Military Memoirs Of A Confederate.
NY, 1908. Portrait, maps, bookplate, inner hinges broken,
covers worn and soiled, spine slightly torn. King 46-38 1983 $40

ALEXANDER, FRANCES G.   Wayfarers in the Libyan Desert. N.Y.,
Putnam, 1912. First edition. Illustrated with sixty photographs;
maps, dust jacket (a few tears), else very good. Houle 21-7 1983
$25

ALEXANDER, HARTLEY BURR   North American Mythology. Boston, (1937).
Cloth. Illus. Blind-stamped names. Good. King 45-123 1983 $20

ALEXANDER, J. E.   Shigurf Namah I Velaet. London, 1827.
Hand-coloured lighograph portrait frontis. Half leather, worn.
8vo. Orig. cloth. Good. Edwards 1044-8 1983 £90

ALEXANDER, SAMUEL   Space, Time and Deity. London:
Macmillan, 1920. Two vols. Orig. gilt cloth. First edition. Reese
20-20 1983 $65

ALEXANDER, THOMAS
Please turn to
BROWNE, THOMAS ALEXANDER

ALEXANDER, WILLIAM   Picturesque Representations of the
Dress and Manners of the Russians. London: John Murray, 1814.
With 64 fine hand-colored plates of Russian 18th c. costume (including
Finland, Mongolia, etc.), each with facing page (or pages) of
description. Bound in full cont. red calf, gilt-stamped; inner
dentelles and raised bands. A.e.g. Spine rubbed and front cover sl.
soiled. Bookplate. Karmiole 75-43 1983 $450

ALEXANDRE, ARSENE   Maxime Maufra. Peintre marin et rustique
(1861-1918). Paris: Galeries Georges Petit, 1926. 100 illus. 4to.
Wrappers. Ars Libri 32-441 1983 $100

ALGONQUIN Prayer Book. Montaing: Fabre-Endatch, 1830. Small 16mo.
Sheep, newly rebacked. A fine copy. In Our Time 156-15 1983 $450

ALGREN, NELSON   Chicago: City on the Make. GC, 1951.
Signed by author. Very good or better in reinforced, still good dustwrapper that is rubbed on edges. Quill & Brush 54-22 1983 $75

ALGREN, NELSON   The Man With the Golden Arm. GC, 1949.
Short review tipped-in on front endpaper, else very good in chipped
and worn, soiled dustwrapper, owner's name. Quill & Brush 54-24 1983
$30

ALI, M. H.   Observations on the Mussulmauns of India.
London, 1932. 2 vols. Half calf, labels, slight wear. 8vo. Good.
Edwards 1044-9 1983 £85

ALI, S.   Handbook of the Birds of India and
Pakistan. 1968-74. Numerous coloured plates, maps and text-figures,
10 vols., royal 8vo, cloth. Scarce original edition. Wheldon
160-620 1983 £120

ALI, S   Indian Hill Birds. Oxford, 1949.
Maps on endpapers, 64 coloured plates, by G.M. Henry, 8 in black and
white. Sm.8vo. Orig. cloth. Good. Edwards 1044-10 1983 $36

ALI, S.   The Sikhs and Afghans. London, 1847.
Green calf, morocco labels, raised bands, spine gilt. 8vo. Good.
Edwards 1044-11 1983 £56

ALISON, ARCHIBALD   Essays on the Nature and Principles
of Taste. Edinburgh: for J.J.G. and G. Robinson, 1790. First
edition. 4to. Early nineteenth century polished calf, wide gilt
borders on sides, gully gilt panelled spine, marbled edges. From
the library of Lord Belper, with his bookplate. Traylen 94-14
1983 £250

ALISON, ARCHIBALD   Essays On The Nature And Principles Of
Taste. Edinburgh: Goerge Ramsay & Co., 1815. Fourth edition. 2 vols.
Fore-edge paintings on each vol. Full morocco. Spines worn and rubbed.
Very good. MacManus 278-1936 1983 $500

ALL About Amos 'N' Andy and Their Creators Correll and Gossden.
Chicago (1929). First edition. Photos, cloth, few pp missing
upper right corners, covers darkened and worn. King 46-403 1983
$25

ALLACK, WILLIAM   The California Overland Express. Los
Angeles, Historical Society of Southern California, 1935. First
edition. Illus.; folding maps. One of 150 copies printed by the
Ward Ritchie Press. Cloth over boards. Very good - fine. Houle
22-1184 1983 $125

ALLAIN, MARIE-FRANCOISE   The Other Man: Conversations with
Graham Greene. London, 1982. Wrappers. Uncorrected proof copy.
Very slightly creased proof dustwrapper. Fine. Jolliffe 26-232
1983 £35

ALLAN, JOHN R.   Farmer's Boy. London, 1935. First
English edition. Several full-page black and white drawings by
Douglas Percy Bliss. Chipped and slightly torn, price-clipped dustwrapper darkened at the spine. Very good. Jolliffe 26-59 1983
£15

ALLARDYCE, ALEXANDER   Balmoral. Edinburgh: Blackwood, 1893.
3 vols. Orig. cloth. First edition. Lacking the back free endpaper
in vol. two. Publisher's blind presentation stamp on the title page.
A fine, bright set. MacManus 277-58 1983 $85

ALLARDYCE, ALEXANDER   The City of Sunshine. Blackwood & Sons,
1877. First edition, 3 vols., half titles, orig. half calf, red and
black labels, v.g. Jarndyce 30-269 1983 £48

ALLBUT, ROBERT   Rambles in Dickens-Land. Chapman & Hall,
(1899). First edition, half title, front. & illus. by Helen M. James.
Orig. green cloth dec. in blind, spine lettered in gilt, v.g.
Jarndyce 31-577 1983 £10.50

ALLBUTT, T. CLIFFORD   Diseases of the Arteries Including
Angina Pectoris. London, 1915. 2 vols. Thick 8vo, mod. buckram;
ex-lib; uncut. First edition. Argosy 713-5 1983 $150

ALLEE, WARDER CLYDE   Animal Life and Social Growth. Baltimore: Williams & Wilkins, 1932. First Edition. Gach 94-1 1983 $20

ALLEN, ALBERT H.   Arkansas Imprints 1821-1876. New York:
Bowker, 1947. Some bumping. Dawson 470-8 1983 $25

ALLEN, ALBERT H.   Dakota Imprints 1858-1889. New York:
Bowker, 1947. Cloth. Dawson 470-9 1983 $35

ALLEN, BENJAMIN   The Natural History of the Chalybeat
and Purging Waters of England... London: by S. Smith..., 1699.
First edition. 8vo. Cont. calf, rebacked. Lightly browned.
Heath 48-482 1983 £175

ALLEN, BENJAMIN   The Natural History of the Chalybeat
and Purging Waters of England... London: S. Smith & B. Walford,
1699. First edition. 8vo. Cont. calf, with 2 woodcuts on last
page. Without ads. Binding rubbed, some light foxing, browning
and dampstains. Gurney 90-2 1983 £100

ALLEN, BRASSEYA   Pastorals, Elegies, Odes, Epistles, and
Other Poems. Abington, Md.: D.P. Ruff, 1806. 12mo, calf, (loose
boards, t.p. top torn, not affecting text). First edition. Argosy
716-414 1983 $85

ALLEN, CHARLES DEXTER   American Book-Plates, A Guide to their
Study with Examples. NY, 1894. Collectors ed., limited to 100
numbered copies printed on English hand-made paper, with 41 full page
plates printed from the original coppers. Cloth, Ex-Library,
covers worn. King 46-370 1983 $125

ALLEN, CHARLES DEXTER   American Book-plates. New York:
Macmillan and Co., 1894. First edition. 8vo. Orig. cloth, t.e.g.
Many illus. including 10 copper plates showing bookplates. Ink
inscription on free endpaper. Slightly shaken. Oak Knoll 48-62
1983 $35

ALLEN, D.   Frederic Remington and the Spanish-American War. New York: Crown, 1971. First edition, limited edition (No.80 of 150 copies in special binding and signed by author). Profusely illus. Orig. half calf over white linen. Mint in publisher's slipcase. Jenkins 152-345 1983 $175

ALLEN, ELIZA   The Female Volunteer. (Cincinnati, 1851). Orig. printed wraps., rebacked, rear wrapper repaired, but a sound copy. Reese 19-16 1983 $150

ALLEN, ETHAN   Allen's Captivity. Boston: Oliver L. Perkins, 1845. 18mo, straight-grained mor., gilt- & blind stamped, g.t. (lib. stamp on t.p. verso). Woodcut frontis. Argosy 716-454 1983 $50

ALLEN, ETHAN   Reason the Only Oracle of Man... Bennington: Haswell & Russell, 1784. Orig. calf, morocco label. Very slight chipping at head and toe of spine, otherwise a very fine copy, with the half-title and orig. blanks. Reese 18-147 1983 $2,850

ALLEN, FRANCIS W.   Bookplates, a Selection from the Works of Charles R. Capon, Together with a Foreward and Complete Check List. Portland: Anthoensen Press, (ca. 1950). Octavo. Limited to 300 copies. Near mint with glassine and rubbed slip-case, splitting at one edge. Bromer 25-158 1983 $65

ALLEN, GLOVER MORRILL   Birds and Their Attributes. Boston, (1925). First edition. Author's copy, with his signature. Illus., cloth, corners bumped, extremities worn. King 46-532 1983 $35

ALLEN, GRACIE   How to Become President. N.Y., Duell, Sloan & Pearce, (1940). First edition. Illus. by Charles Lofgren. Dust jacket (slight nicking). Signed by the author on the front free endpaper. Very good. Houle 22-13 1983 $60

ALLEN, GRANT   The British Barbarians. London: John Lane, 1895. Original pictorial cloth. First edition. Spine bruised. A volume of John Lane's "Keynotes" series (title-page designed by Aubrey Beardsley). Good copy. MacManus 277-60 1983 $25

ALLEN, GRANT   Evolution in Italian Art. London: Grant Richards, 1908. With 65 reproductions from photographs. Orig. cloth. First edition. Inner hinges starting, but a very good copy. MacManus 277-61 1983 $35

ALLEN, GRANT   Falling in Love. London: Smith, Elder & Co., 1889. Orig. cloth. First edition. Bookplate on front endsheet. Inner hanges weak. Extremities of spine rubbed. Good copy. MacManus 277-62 1983 $75

ALLEN, GRANT   Force and Energy. London, 1888. 1st ed. 8vo. Some pencil underlining, otherwise nice. Morrill 287-5 1983 $25

ALLEN, GRANT   In All Shades. London: Chatto & Windus, 1886. 3 vols. Orig. decorated cloth. First edition. Covers somewhat rubbed. Inner hinges weak, shaken. Very good copy. MacManus 277-64 1983 $350

ALLEN, HERVEY   Anthony Adverse. New York, 1933. 1st ed., 1st issue, with the Farrar & Rinehart emblem on copyright page and with the typographical errors. Pictorial title page and other decorations by Allen McNab. Blue cloth. Very fine in dj. Rare in this fine condition. Bradley 64-2 1983 $45

ALLEN, HERVEY   Anthony Adverse. NY, 1937. Limited Editions Club. Three vols., No. 1157 of 1500 copies signed by illus., E. A. Wilson. Vols. fine but box is coming apart. Quill & Brush 54-26 1983 $50

ALLEN, HERVEY   The Bride of Hiutzil. N.Y., Drake, 1922. Illus. with woodcuts by Bernhardt Wall. Red cloth over gilt patterned boards, paper spine label, uncut. One of 350 copies signed by the author. Printed by William E. Rudge. Typography by Bruce Rogers. Bookplate. Very good. Houle 22-14 1983 $60

ALLEN, HERVEY   The Bride of Huitzil, an Aztec Legend. New York: James F. Drake Inc., 1922. First edition. 8vo. Cloth-backed decorated boards, paper spine label. Limited to 350 copies. Numbered and signed by Allen. Designed and printed by William Edwin Rudge with typography by Bruce Rogers and illus. by Bernhardt Wall. Spine faded, covers rubbed. Oak Knoll 38-339 1983 $45

ALLEN, HERVEY   Carolina Chansons. N.Y., Macmillan, 1922. First edition. Half cloth, paper label on upper cover. Very good. One of a few copies for presentation, this being copy number 9, inscribed and signed by Allen, signed by Heyward. Houle 21-8 1983 $145

ALLEN, HERVEY   New Legends. NY, 1929. One of 175 numbered and signed copies, some pages uncut, edges slightly rubbed, still near fine in chipped, slightly frayed, aged dustwrapper that has been mended. Quill & Brush 54-27 1983 $50

ALLEN, HERVEY   Wampum and Old Gold. New Haven: Yale, 1921. Printed wraps. over boards. First edition. Small chip from head of spine, else a fine copy. One of 500 copies. Reese 20-22 1983 $35

ALLEN, HORATIO   Pacific Mail Steam Ship Company. N.Y., 1867. Orig. printed wraps. First edition. Ginsberg 46-714 1983 $30

ALLEN, J. GORDON   The Cheap Cottage and Small House. Letchworth: Garden City Press, 1912. Second edition. Profusely illus. Roy. 8vo, orig. cloth, gilt. A very good copy. Fenning 60-5 1983 £12.50

ALLEN, JAMES LANE   The Reign of Law, a Tale of the Kentucky Hemp Fields. New York: MacMillan, 1900. Frontis., plates. 1st ed. Orig. highly decorated cloth, gilt, t.e.g., untrimmed. Fine bright copy and a binding worth noting: the spine and front cover are plastered with vivid green decorations or cannabis. Jenkins 155-25 1983 $20

ALLEN, JOHN   Vindication of the Ancient Independence of Scotland. Charles Knight, 1833. First and apparently only edition, errata slip, 8vo, recent half calf. Fenning 62-5 1983 £12.50

ALLEN, JOHN HOUGHTON   San Juan. (San Antonio, 1945). Illus. by Harold Bugbee. Orig. stiff wraps. Ltd. to 420 copies. Ginsberg 47-6 1983 $50

ALLEN, LEWIS F.   American Cattle. New York, (1868). Cloth, very good. Reese 19-18 1983 $60

ALLEN, NATHAN   Population: Its Law of Increase. Lowell: Stone & Huse, 1870. Tall 8vo, orig. printed yellow wraps. Inscribed: "From N. Allen." Presentation copy. Rostenberg 88-110 1983 $85

ALLEN, P. S.   The Correspondence of an Early Printing-House, the Amorbachs of Basle. Glasgow: Jackson, Wylie & Co., 1932. First edition. Small 8vo. Stiff paper wrappers. Some foxing, corner of back cover is bent. Oak Knoll 49-4 1983 $20

ALLEN, PAUL   Original Poems, Serious and Entertaining. Salem: Joshua Cushing, 1801. Orig. calf, worn. First edition. Erasure of an ink name from the title, and scattered foxing and browning, but textually a good copy. Reese 18-241 1983 $65

ALLEN, W. E. D.   Caucasian Battlefields. Cambridge University Press, 1953. First edition. Thick roy. 8vo. Orig. blue buckram. Frontis. 7 plates, 8 folding and 17 full page maps, 14 text maps. Superb copy. Edwards 1042-265 1983 £40

ALLEN, WILLIAM A.   Adventures with Indians and Game. Chicago, 1903. First edition. Portrait frontispiece. Illustrated. Marbled boards with dark brown leather spine and corners, gilt top. Extremities worn, but very good soiled copy. Bradley 65-1 1983 $135

ALLEN, WILLIAM WALLACE   California Gold Book: First Nugget. San Francisco: 1893. First edition. Frontis., numerous other full-page plates. Orig. cloth. Fine. Bradley 66-476 1983 $85

ALLEN, ZACHARIAH   On the Dangerous Explosibility of Petroleum, Coal Oils, Camphene, Salt-Petre, Etc. Providence, 1862. 16mo, orig. pr. wraps., (front wr. & t.p. top trimmed, not affecting text). Argosy 716-140 1983 $25

ALLERTON, JAMES M.   Tom Quick, the Avenger. NY, 1888.
16mo, pink pr. wraps. Argosy 716-154 1983 $35

ALLESCH, JOHANNES VON   Michael Pacher. Leipzig: Insel-Verlag,
1931. 113 illus. 4to. Cloth. Dust jacket. Ars Libri 32-501 1983
$75

ALLESTREE, RICHARD   The Gentleman's Calling. Printed by
E. Jones, for E. Pawlet, 1696. With additional engraved title-page
and pages. Ads., including the orig. blank leaf L7, 8vo, cont.
panelled claf, gilt spine. Fenning 62-6 1983 £32.50

ALLGEYER, JULIUS   Anselm Feuerbach. Berlin/Stuttgart:
W. Spemann, 1904. 2 vols. 40 plates. Stout 4to. Cloth. Ars
Libri 32-219 1983 $125

ALLIBONE, SAMUEL AUSTIN   A Critical Dictionary of English
Literature and British and American Authors... (With): A
Supplement to Allibone... Philadelphia: J.B. Lippincott, 1891.
5 vols. in all. Thick 4to. Three-quarter leather over marbled
boards. Rebacked with hinges repaired. Complete set. Oak Knoll
48-391 1983 $150

ALLIBONE, SAMUEL AUSTIN   Critical Dictionary of English
Literature and British and American Authors. Detroit, 1965. 5 vols.
4to. Cloth. Traylen 94-15 1983 £65

ALLINGHAM, WILLIAM   The Music Master, A Love Story. London:
G. Routledge & Co., 1855. 9 woodcuts, 7 designed by Arthur Hughes.
8vo. Orig. blue embossed cloth. First edition, containing D.G.
Rossetti's first appearance as an illustrator of books. Bookplate.
Covers a little worn at edges. Inner hinges weak. Very good copy.
MacManus 277-67 1983 $550

ALLINSON, F. G.   Greek Lands and Letters. Boston & NY,
1909. 12 plates & maps. 8vo, cloth. Salloch 385-321 1983 $20

ALLISON, WILLIAM HENRY   A Guide to Historical Literature.
New York: The Macmillan Co., 1931. First edition. Thick 8vo.
Cloth. Library number on spine and library bookplate. Oak Knoll
48-392 1983 $25

ALLISON, YOUNG E.   The Old Kentucky Home. Bardstown, Ky.,
1923. 1 of 225 copies signed by author and publisher. Illus. Small
folio, orig. boards, cloth back. Morrill 286-561 1983 $20

ALLIX, PIERRE   An Historical Discourse Concerning the
Necessity of the Ministers Intention in Administrating the Sacraments.
Printed for Richard Chiswell, 1688. First edition, 4to, wrapper.
Fenning 61-8 1983 £12.50

ALLMAN, G. J.   A Monograph of the Gymnoblastic or
Tubularian Hydroids. Ray Society, 1871-72. 23 coloured plates, 2
vols. in 1, folio, half morocco (a little worming of covers, not
affecting contents). Occasional minor foxing and soiling, but a nice
copy. Wheldon 160-1241 1983 £85

ALLOM, T.   China, in a Series of Views... London,
c.1843. 4 engraved vignettes on titles, 124 plates, some occasional
foxing. 4 vols. 4to. Half morocco, gilt spines. Good. Edwards
1044-13 1983 $350

ALLPORT, ELLEN   The Desire of the Moth. London: Bentley,
1895. First edition. 2 vols. Orig. cloth. Covers a little soiled.
Endpapers partially torn. Very nice. MacManus 280-5333 1983 $85

ALLPORT, FLOYD HENRY   Institutional Behavior. Chapel Hill,
N.C.: Univ. of North Carolina Press, 1933. First edition. Good
copy, cloth rubbed, owner's name crossed out on flyleaf. Gach 95-11
1983 $20

ALLPORT, GORDON W.   The Use of Personal Documents in
Psychological Science. NY: SSRC, 1942. First printing. Wrappers.
Gach 95-12 1983 $25

ALLSOPP, FRED W.   Folklore of Romantic Arkansas. New
York: The Grolier Society, 1931. 2 volumes. First edition. Plates.
Uncut and unopened. Fine copies, scarce. Jenkins 153-17 1983 $125

ALLSTON, ROBERT F. W.   The South Carolina Rice Plantation
as Revealed in the Papers of... Chicago, (1946). Port., folding map.
Argosy 716-516 1983 $20

ALMACK, EDWARD   The History of the Second Dragoons.
London, 1908. Photogravure frontis., 3 coloured plates of uniform, 39
other plates. Small folio. Orig. white cloth backed grey buckram,
gilt. Very slightly soiled. T.e.g., others uncut. Some occasional
slight foxing. Fine. Edwards 1042-523 1983 £175

ALMON, JOHN   Anecdotes of the Life of the Right Hon.
William Chatham. Dublin, 1792. 2 vols. 2 folding tables, endpapers
foxed, cont. tree calf, a little worn. K Books 301-5 1983 £50

ALMON, JOHN   A letter concerning libels, warrants,
and the seizure of papers... London: printed for J. Almon, 1764.
Second edition. 8vo. Sewn, as issued. A fine uncut copy. Ximenes
63-172 1983 $125

ALPE, E. N.   Handy Book of Medicine... London,
ca. 1890. 8vo. Orig. cloth. Gurney JJ-3 1983 £15

ALPINI, PROSPERO   Historiae Aegypti Naturalis, pars prima
qua continentur Rerum Aegyptaryn...Pars secunda, sive de Plantis
Aegypti. Leyden, 1735. 102 engr. plates. 2 vols. 4to. Cont. calf,
gilt. Some worming in the lower inner blank margin at the beginning of
this volume but the text is not affected. Rare. Wheldon 160-342 1983
£500

ALPINI, PROSPERO   De Medicina Aegyptiorum, Libri Quatuor...
Venice: Franciscus de Franciscis, 1591. First edition. 4to. Old
vellum. 3 full-page woodcuts. Margins browned in the second half
of the book. Gurney 90-3 1983 £360

AL-QABISI   Libellus ysagogicus. Venice: Erhard
Ratdolt, 16 January 1482. 2 woodcut diagrams and several decorated
woodcut initials; heading on first page printed in red. Small 4to.
19th-century decorated flexible boards; in cloth drop-box. Early
ms. exlibris of an unidentified Franciscan library, bookplates of
Gilber R. Redgrave and Harrison D. Horblit. Kraus 164-3 1983
$4,500

ALSTON, C. H.   Wild Life in the West Highlands.
Glasgow, 1912. 8 plates (1 coloured), 8vo, cloth (trifled soiled).
Wheldon 160-343 1983 £12

ALSTON, CHARLES   Index Medicamentorum Simplicium Triplex.
(also): A Dissertation on Quick-Lime and Lime Water. Edinburgh,
1752. 8vo. 2 vols. in one. First editions. Orig. boards, rebacked,
uncut. Fine copy. Gurney 90-4 1983 £95

ALSTON, CHARLES   A Third Dissertation on Quick-Lime...
Edinburgh: Printed by Sands, Donaldson, Murray and Cochran, 1757.
1st ed., 8vo, title-page, uncut, modern wrappers. Pickering & Chatto
22-4 1983 $185

ALSTON, E. R.   Biologia Centrali-Americana: Mammalia.
1879-82. 22 plates, 4to, binder's cloth. Lower margin of one plate
slightly waterstained, and one or two small marginal tears in text,
but a good copy. Wheldon 160-540 1983 £200

ALTER, J. CECIL   James Bridger Trapper, Frontiersman,
Scout and Guide. Salt Lake City: Shepard Book Company, 1925.
Frontis and illus. 1st ed. Limited and signed by the author.
Jenkins 151-88 1983 $150

ALTHAM, MICHAEL   The Creed of Pope Pius the IV. Printed
for L. Meredith, 1687. First edition, 4to, wrapper, just a little
dusty and with a small hole in final leaf affecting two or three
letters only, a very good copy. Fenning 61-9 1983 £10.50

ALTHAM, MICHAEL   A Vindication of the Church of England
from the Foul Aspersians of Schism and Heresie unjustly Cast Upon Her
by the Church of Rome. Printed by J. H. for Luke Meredith, 1687.
First edition, 4to, wrapper. Fenning 61-10 1983 £21.50

ALTROCCHI, RUDOLPH   Sleuthing in the Stacks. Cambridge:
Harvard Univ. Press, 1944. First edition. 8vo. Cloth-backed
boards, paper cover label. 6 illus. Oak Knoll 48-9 1983 $30

ALTSHELER, JOSEPH A.   A Soldier of Manhattan, and His
Adventures at Ticonderoga and Quebec. Smith, Elder, 1898. Half
title, 2 pp ads. Orig. red cloth, v.g. First English edition.
Jarndyce 31-405 1983 £10.50

ALVAREZ, FRANCISCO   Narrative of the Portuguese Embassy to
Abyssinia during the years 1520-1527. London: Hakluyt Soc., 1881.
8vo. Folding maps. Modern cloth. Ex-lib. Adelson Africa-155 1983
$40

ALVERDES, F.   Social Life in the Animal World. 1927.
Some pencil underlining. Wheldon 160-457 1983 £12

AMADO, JORGE   The Miracle of the Birds. New York:
Targ Editions, 1983. 1st ed., limited to 250 copies, signed by
Amado. Orig. cloth-backed golden boards, gilt, tissue dj. Mint
copy. Jenkins 155-26 1983 $100

AMADO, JORGE   The Miracle of the Birds. New York:
Targ Edition No. 18, 1983. Oblong 12mo, decorated gilt boards and
cloth. Printed in red and black in an edition of 250 copies, each
signed by the author. First edition. Duschnes 240-2 1983 $90

AMBLER, ERIC   The Care of Time. NY, (1981). Limited
to 300 specially bound, numbered and signed copies, very fine in like
slipcase. Quill & Brush 54-32 1983 $75

AMBLER, ERIC   A Coffin for Dimitrios. N.Y., Knopf,
1939. First American edition. Dust jacket (some wear at edges,
traces of tape on verso and on endpapers), else a good-very good
copy. Houle 21-10 1983 $95

AMBLER, ERIC   Journey into Fear. N.Y., Knopf, 1940.
First American edition. Bookplate. Dust jacket (small nicks),
else very good. Houle 22-16 1983 $125

AMBLER, ERIC   Passage of Arms. N.Y., Knopf, 1960.
First American edition. With the two variant dust jackets. Very
good. Signed and inscribed by the author. Houle 21-14 1983 $125

AMBLER, ERIC   Passage of Arms. N.Y., Knopf, 1960.
First American edition. With the two variant dust jackets.
Presentation copy: "Robert Wehner, with best wishes, Eric Ambler,
get well soon." Houle 22-18 1983 $85

AMBLER, ERIC   The Schrimer Inheritance. NY, 1943.
Edges rubbed, else very good in very good dustwrapper with light wear
to edges. Quill & Brush 54-33 1983 $40

AMEER-ALI, TORICK   Memoirs of Sir Andres Nelvill.
London, 1918. First English translation. 8vo. Orig. cloth. Frontis.
folding map. 2 folding maps and 3 plates. Bookplate. Ink inscription
on endpapers. Good. Edwards 1042-412 1983 £18

AMERICAN Beer. NY: United States Brewers' Association, 1909. Orig.
brown cloth. Karmiole 73-97 1983 $30

THE AMERICAN Caravan. New York: Macaulay, (1927). 1st ed. Orig.
cloth, gilt. Very good copy of this anthology including works of
Hemingway, Robert Penn Warren, et al. Jenkins 155-549 1983 $20

AMERICAN COLLEGE OF SURGEONS.   A Catalogue of the H. Winnewet
Orr Historical Collection... Chicago: American College of Surgeons,
1960. First edition. 4to. Cloth. Some cover spotting. Oak Knoll
49-468 1983 $75

AMERICAN Common-Place Book of Poetry. Boston, 1832. 12mo, later 1/2
roan, foxed. Argosy 710-412 1983 $40

AMERICAN Common-Place Book of Poetry. Phila., 1841. Orig. cloth,
(mildly rubbed). Argosy 716-415 1983 $30

AMERICAN Criticism: 1926. New York, (1926). 8vo., cloth, price
clipped on jacket, else fine in almost perfect d.j. In Our Time
156-892 1983 $50

AMERICAN Decade: 68 Poems for the First Time in an Anthology.
Cummington, Mass.: Cummington Press, (1943). 1st ed., limited to
475 copies. Orig. blue cloth, dj. Contributions by Stevens,
Jeffers, et al. Fine copy in lightly used dj, and scarce thus.
Jenkins 155-1167 1983 $100

AMERICAN Decorations. Washington, GPO, 1927. First edition. 8vo.
Morrill 290-6 1983 $30

AMERICAN EXPRESS COMPANY   An Act To Incorporate the American
Express Company. New York: John H. Duyckinck, Printer to the Company,
1859. Orig. printed wrappers. Fine copy. Jenkins 153-729 1983
$450

AMERICAN Imprints Inventory... No. 2 Check List of Minnesota Imprints
1849-1865. Chicago: Historical Records Survey, 1938. 4to. Orig.
stiff paper wrappers. Some spotting of front cover. Oak Knoll 48-
463 1983 $45

AMERICAN Imprints Inventory... No. 7 A Check List of Nevada Imprints,
1859-1890. Chicago: Historical Records Survey, 1939. 4to. Cloth.
Leather spine label. Oak Knoll 48-466 1983 $55

AMERICAN Imprints Inventory... No. 15 A Check List of Iowa Imprints,
1838-1860. Chicago: WPA Historical Records Survey Project, 1940.
4to. Cloth. Leather spine label. Oak Knoll 48-446 1983 $55

AMERICAN INSTITUTE OF GRAPHIC ARTS.   Fifty Books Exhibited by the
Institute. New York: John Day Co., 1927. Tall 4to. Half cloth over
boards. Some cover wear along edges of boards. Oak Knoll 49-168
1983 $40

THE AMERICAN Journal of Pharmacy. Philadelphia, 1853-1855. 3 vols.
8vo, contemporary calf, leather labels. Morrill 289-2 1983 $30

AMERICAN LEGION. NATIONAL AMERICANISM COMMISSION.   ISMS, A
Review of Alien Isms, Revolutionary Communism and their Active
Sympathizers in the United States. Indianapolis: American Legion,
1937. Ex-library, cloth, cover discolor. 2nd edition. King 46-20
1983 $25

THE AMERICAN Medical Times. New York, July 7, 1860-Sept. 3, 1864.
9 vols. in 4. 4to, contemporary boards, calf backs and corners.
Morrill 289-3 1983 $100

THE AMERICAN Origin of the Augustana Synod from Contemporary
Lutheran Periodicals, 1851-1860. Rock Island, Ill., 1942. Orig.
printed wraps. First edition. Ginsberg 46-16 1983 $25

AMERICAN Plays Printed 1714-1830: A Bibliographical Record.
Stanford Univ. Press, (1934). Frontis. 1st ed. Orig. cloth, dj.
Fine copy in mildly creased dj. Jenkins 155-78 1983 $35

AMERICAN TEMPERANCE SOCIETY   Permanent Temperance Documents of...
Boston: Seth Bliss, and Perkins, Marvin and Co., 1835. Cloth
spine, boards (stained), some foxing to text. First nine reports.
Gach 95-14 1983 $25

AMERICAN Turf Register and Sporting Magazine. Baltimore and New York:
J.S. Skinner (et al). Vol. 1 number 1, September 1829, through
vol. XV, December 1844. Illus. Plates, folding charts. Calf-backed
boards (several bindings breaking). Some scattered foxing.
Felcone 21-3 1983 $8,000

AMERICAN TYPE FOUNDERS COMPANY.   Specimens of Printing Types.
London: American Type Founders Company, n.d. (1898). 8vo. Orig.
cloth. All edges stained red. Illuminated title page. Some cover
rubbing and cuts removed in two places. Oak Knoll 49-383 1983
$85

AMERICAN TYPE FOUNDRY.   Supplement No. 2, American Line Type
Book... N.P.: American Type Foundry, 1911. Small 4to. Stiff
paper wrappers. Many colors are used. A few pencil marks, edge
of front cover and a few pages are bumped. Oak Knoll 48-373 1983
$20

AMERICANA - Beginnings. Morristown: J. J., 1952. First edition.
One of 325 copies. Blue wrappers. Some fading and spotting on cover.
Bradley 66-471 1983 $200

AMES, AZEL   The May-Flower & Her Log, July 15, 1620-
May 6, 1621. Boston: Riverside Press, 1901. 1st ed. 11 maps &
illus., 4to, buckram, ex-library. Argosy 710-94 1983 $45

AMES, FISHER   Works. Boston, 1809. First edition,
port., orig. calf, leather label. Argosy 710-415 1983 $35

AMES, NATHANIEL   An Astronomical Diary or Almanack for
the Year of Our Lord Christ 1771. Boston: Printed and Sold by the
Printers and Booksellers, (1770). 1st ed., 1st known printing.
Orig. self-wrappers, uncut, stitched, as issued. Fine copy. Jenkins
155-440 1983 $300

AMES, O.   Schedulae Orchidianae. Boston, 1922-
30. Text-figures and 24 plates, 10 parts and index, 8vo. Scarce.
A complete set, although parts 5 and 6 are in xerox. Wheldon 160-
2035 1983 £30

AMES, OAKES   Defence of...Against the Charge of
Selling to Members of Congress Shares of the Capital Stock of the
Credit Mobilier of America. (Wash.), 1873. Sewn as issued.
First edition. Ginsberg 47-771 1983 $35

AMHURST, NICHOLAS   Terrae-Fillius. Printed for R. Francklin,
1726. 12mo, ad. leaf, bound in 2 vols., cont. panelled calf, with
the same engraved frontis. by William Hogarth in each volume. First
edition in book form. Bickersteth 75-2 1983 £40

AMIS, KINGSLEY   Dear Illusion. (London) Covent Garden
Press, 1972. First edition. Small 4to, stiff pictorial wraps. Fine.
Houle 21-17 1983 $75

AMIS, KINGSLEY   A Frame of Mind. Reading: University of
Reading, 1953. Limited to 150 copies, with signature of ownership on
free end-paper. Unevenly browned wrappers. A very good copy. Scarce.
Gekoski 2-2 1983 £100

AMIS, KINGSLEY   A Look Round the Estate. London:
Cape, (1967). 1st ed., uncorrected proofs. Orig. blue printed
wrappers, prepared for review. Fine copy. Jenkins 155-27 1983
$75

AMITY, JOHN   An Island Interlude. London: John Long,
1901. Orig. pictorial cloth. First edition. Edges and corners
slightly worn. Covers very slightly soiled. Endpapers browned. Good.
MacManus 277-70 1983 $35

AMMAN, J.   Stirpium Rariorum in Imperio Rutheno
Sponte Provenientium. St. Petersburg, 1739. 35 engraved plates on
34 leaves, 4to, boards. A very rare early flora of Russia. A light
waterstain in the lower part affecting the lower blank margins.
Wheldon 160-1643 1983 £220

AMMEN, DANIEL   The Old Navy and The New. Phila., 1891.
8vo. Orig. decorated cloth in silver and gilt. Portrait frontis.
Plate. 4 pp. facsimile letter. Very slightly worn. Good. Edwards
1042-193 1983 £75

AMMON, WOLFGANG   Neuw Gesangbuch Teutsch und Lateinisch.
Frankfurt, Egenolph's Erben, 1581. 240 leaves, title in red and black,
woodcut on verso. With 13 woodcuts, numerous woodcut decorations,
Thick 12mo, cont. vellum. Salloch 387-4 1983 $3,000

AMOREUX, D. M.   Memoire sur les Haies destinees a
la cloture des Pres... Paris: Chez Cuchet, 1787. First edition.
8vo. Half title, uncut in early boards. Heath 48-1 1983 £45

AMORY, MARTHA BABCOCK   The Domestic and Artistic Life of
John Singleton Copley, R.A. Boston: Houghton Mifflin, 1882.
Frontis. 4to. Cloth. Ars Libri 32-120 1983 $125

AMORY, THOMAS   The Life of John Buncle, Esq. Printed
for J. Noon (Vol.11) for J. Johnson and B. Davenport, 1756-66.
2 vols, 8vo, old tree calf (not uniform) rebacked: one hinge cracking
again; 1st ed. of both vols.; scarce. Hill 165-2 1983 £175

AMORY, THOMAS   The Life of John Buncle... London:
J. Noon, 1756. First edition. Thick 8vo. Cont. calf, neatly
rebacked with morocco label, gilt. Traylen 94-16 1983 £70

AMORY, THOMAS   The Life of John Buncle, Esq. A New
Edition. Septimus Prowett, 1825. 3 vols, 8vo, 19th cent. half calf,
gilt backs; half-titles; a nice set. Hill 165-3 1983 £55

AMOS, SHELDON   Fifty Years of the English Constitution,
1830-1880. Longmans, Green, 1880. Half title, 12 pp ads. Orig.
red cloth, spine faded, v.g. Jarndyce 31-85 1983 £10.50

AMPERE, ANDRE-MARIE   Correspondance et Souvenirs... Paris,
1875. Second edition. 8vo. 2 vols. Old quarter leather, rubbed.
Gurney JJ-4 1983 £30

AMPERE, ANDRE-MARIE   Expose Methodique des Phenomenes
Electrodynamiques, et des Lois de ces Phenomenes... Paris, Bachelier,
1823. 1st ed., 8vo; uncut stitched in the orig. plain pink paper
wrapper, almost detached. Pickering & Chatto 22-6 1983 $500

AMPERE, ANDRE-MARIE   Memoire Sur Quelques Nouvelles Proprietes
des Axes Permanens de Rotation Des Corps... Paris, de l'Imprimerie
royale. Chez Bachelier...1823. 1st separate ed. (corrected), 4to,
disbound. Pickering & Chatto 22-5 1983 $350

AMPERE, ANDRE-MARIE   Precis de la Theorie des Phenomones
Electro-Dynamiques... Paris, chez Crochard...et Bachelier...1824.
1st ed., 8vo, 1 folding engraved plate; uncut and stitched in the
orig. plain blue paper wrapper; presentation copy inscribed. Pickering
& Chatto 22-7 1983 $600

AMPERE, ANDRE-MARIE   Precis D'un Memoire sur L'Electro-
Dynamique... l'Academie royale des sciences dans sa seance du 21
novembre 1825. Offprint, 8vo, 1 folding engraved plate; uncut and
stitched in the orig. plain blue paper wrapper. Pickering & Chatto 22-
8 1983 $350

AMPERE, ANDRE MARIE   Sur les Experiences Electro-Magnetiques
de MM. Oersted (sic) et Ampere. Paris, 1820. First separate
edition. 4to. Orig. blue wrappers. Uncut. Kraus 164-5 1983
$1,250

AMSAYE, TERRY   A Million and One Nights. N.Y., S&S,
1926. First edition, 4to, illus. Blue cloth. 2 vols. Fine set.
One of 327 copies on large paper. Signed by Thomas Edison and the
author. Houle 21-745 1983 $650

AMSDEN, CHARLES AVERY   Navaho Weaving. Albuquerque: Univ.
of New Mexico Press, 1949. 123 plates. 4to. Cloth. Slightly
worn. Ars Libri 34-92 1983 $85

AMUCHASTEGUI, AXEL   Studies of Birds and Mammals of South
America. (1967). Small folio, 24 coloured plates and specially drawn
lithograph at beginning, orig. half morocco with ornamental boards.
Bickersteth 75-209 1983 £48

AMUNDSEN, ROALD   My Life as an Explorer. Heineman (U.S.A.
printed), 1927. First edition, with frontis., 2 maps and a few other
illus., roy. 8vo, orig. cloth, gilt, a very good copy. Fenning 60-7
1983 £18.50

AMYDENUS, THEODORUS   Pietas Romana et Parisiensis...
Oxford, 1687. First edition. 2 parts in one vol. Small 4to.
Cont. calf, neatly rebacked with morocco label, gilt. Traylen
94-17 1983 £30

ANACREON   Anacreontis odaria ad textus Barnesiani
fidem emendata. Accedunt variae lectiones cura Eduardi Forster.
Bulmer, 1802. 8vo, 20 large engraved head and tail pieces, 19th cent.
quarter roan gilt over patterned paper boards, binding slightly worn
at extremities, some spotting and staining and 5 leaves browned,
armorial bookplate and 2 signatures on front endpapers. A large paper
copy. Printed on heavy paper. Deighton 3-8 1983 £42

ANACREON   The odes of Anacreon. York: printed
by Wilson, Spence, and Mawman, etc., 1796. First edition of this
translation, done by Rev. Thomas Gilpin. Small 8vo. Orig. marbled
boards, drab paper spine, orange paper label (rubbed). Partly unopened.
A fine copy. Ximenes 63-61 1983 $125

ANACREON   The odes of Anacreon. Yarmouth:
printed by John Beart, for G.G. and J. Robinson (London), n.d.
(1803). First edition. 12mo. Cont. red straight-grained morocco,
gilt. Ximenes 63-62 1983 $100

ANANOFF, ALEXANDRE   Boucher. Peintures. Lausanne/Paris:
La Bibliotheque des Arts, 1976. 2 vols. 16 color plates. 1795
illus. Folio. Cloth. Dust jacket. Ars Libri 32-55 1983 $275

ANBUREY, THOMAS   Travels Through the Interior Parts of
America. Boston, 1923. 2 vols. Map. Boards, cover water-stained,
contents good. Clark 741-225 1983 $40.00, set

ANCIENT and Modern Scottish Songs, Heroic Ballads, etc. Edinburgh:
Printed by John Wotherspoon. For James Dickson and Charles Elliot,
1776. Two vols. 12mo, engraved vignettes on the titles, orig. calf,
spines chipped at head and foot, rubbed, upper joints cracked, but
bindings firm. First edition thus. Bickersteth 77-3 1983 £68

ANDERIDA; or, the Briton & the Saxon, A.D. London: Bickers, 1875.
3 vols. Original cloth. First edition. Covers a little darkened and
worn. Few inner hinges cracked. Very good copy. MacManus 277-76
1983 $125

ANDERS, FERDINAND   Codex Ixtlilxochitl. Graz: Akademische Druck- und Verlagsanstalt, 1976. 50 facsimile plates. 3
supplementary plates loose in rear pocket, as issued. Large 4to.
Cloth. Ars Libri 34-93 1983 $125

ANDERSEN, HANS CHRISTIAN   Danish Fairy Tales and Legends. Alexander Gardner, Paisley, n.d. (after 1901). Colour frontis. 15 plates.
Red cloth gilt. Greer 39-107 1983 £35

ANDERSEN, HANS CHRISTIAN   The Fairy Tales of... Newnes, 1899.
With upwards of 400 illus. by Helen Stratton. Cream cloth with gilt
& blue decor. fr. cvr. & bkstrip., bevelled boards, a.e.g. Occas.
foxing, eps. cracked at hinges, nice copy. Hodgkins 27-6 1983 £40

ANDERSEN, HANS CHRISTIAN   Fairy Tales. Archibald Constable, n.d.
(ca. 1900). Colour frontis. Colour pictorial title, 28 full-page and
153 text illus. Colour decorated cloth, rubbed. Greer 40-210 1983
£25

ANDERSEN, HANS CHRISTIAN   Hans Brinker or The Silver Skates.
Phila.: McKay, 1918. First edition. 4to. Pink cloth. Pictorial
paste-on. T.e.g. Color illus. by M. W. Enright. Very good to fine.
Aleph-bet 8-89 1983 $35

ANDERSEN, HANS CHRISTIAN   Hans Christian Andersen's Visits to
Charles Dickens, as Described in his Letters. 1937. Edition ltd. to
200 copies, signed by the editor. Orig. boards, label, v.g. 4to.
First edition. Jarndyce 30-141 1983 £16

ANDERSEN, HANS CHRISTIAN   H. C. Andersen's Historier. Copenhagen,
C.A. Reitzel, 1855. 1st illus. ed. 12mo, orig. quarter leather,
rubbed. Morrill 288-9 1983 $75

ANDERSEN, HANS CHRISTIAN   The Improvisatore. Richard Bentley,
1845. First edition, 2 vols., half titles, orig. boards, blue cloth
spines, paper labels, v.g. Jarndyce 30-270 1983 £52

ANDERSEN, HANS CHRISTIAN   The Improvisatore. Richard Bentley,
1845. First English edition. 2 vols. Large 12mo, orig. boards,
cloth spine (re-cased), paper labels, uncut. Hannas 69-98 1983 £45

ANDERSEN, HANS CHRISTIAN   The Improvisatore: or, Life in Italy.
London: Richard Bentley, 1845. 1st ed. of English translation,
tall 12mo, 2 vols., original half cloth, gray boards, paper labels,
uncut copy with half-titles. Advertisements in vol. I. Bindings
rubbed and shaken; internally a very good and generally clean copy.
Trebizond 18-105 1983 $75

ANDERSEN, HANS CHRISTIAN   The Improvisatore. London, Ward, Lock
& Co., n.d. Illus. 12mo. Full white vellum boards with gilt dec.
Former owner's inscription dated 1887. Very nice. Morrill 289-258
1983 $75

ANDERSEN, HANS CHRISTIAN   Life in Italy. New-York, published by
Harper & Brothers, 1845. First American edition. Large 8vo, double
column. Two advertisement leaves at end. Cont. half vellum. Some
traces of use. Hannas 69-99 1983 £25

ANDERSEN, HANS CHRISTIAN   The Old Man is Always Right. N.Y.:
Harp., (1940). Stated first edition. Sq. 4to. Slightly worn dust
wrapper. Cloth backed boards. Full-page color illus. plus black &
whites. Very good. Aleph-bet 8-226 1983 $30

ANDERSEN, HANS CHRISTIAN   Only a Fiddler! Richard Bentley, 1845.
First English edition. 3 vols. in one. Large 12mo, orig. cloth
head-band snagged, uncut. Fore margin of 1 leaf cut away. This
one-volume issue bears the spine title, "Only a Fiddler. By Mary
Howitt." Hannas 69-100 1983 £55

ANDERSEN, HANS CHRISTIAN   Only a Fiddler. H.G. Clarke & Co.,
1845. First edition of this translation. 2 vols. 12mo, orig. cloth
(recased), a.e.g., in slip-case. Hannas 69-5 1983 £20

ANDERSEN, HANS CHRISTIAN   Only a Fiddler! and O.T. or, Life in
Denmark. London: Bentley, 1847. 3 vols. Cont. 3/4 calf. Marbled
boards. Apparently the second English edition. Covers a bit worn.
A good, sound copy. MacManus 277-71 1983 $150

ANDERSEN, HANS CHRISTIAN   Pictures of Sweden. Richard Bentley,
1851. First edition, 8vo, orig. cloth, a little wear at head of
spine and light finger marks in a very few places, a very good copy.
Fenning 62-7 1983 £32.50

ANDERSEN, HANS CHRISTIAN   A Poet's Bazaar. London: Bentley,
1846. 3 vols. Cont. 3/4 calf. First edition in English. Somewhat
foxed. Spines a bit worn. Good sound set. MacManus 277-72 1983
$150

ANDERSEN, HANS CHRISTIAN   Stories. Hodder & Stoughton, n.d. First
edition. Large 4to. Mounted colour frontis. & 27 mounted colour
plates, back endpaper torn. Decorated endpaper, brown decorated cloth,
gilt. Greer 40-94 1983 £65

ANDERSEN, HANS CHRISTIAN   Stories and Tales. George Routledge,
n.d. (ca. 1879). 100 illus. by A.W. Bayes & 6 col. plates, engr'd &
printed by Bros. Dalziel. New edn. Brown fine diagonal ribbed cloth,
black decor. fr. cvr. & bkstrip., bevelled boards. Re-cased new eps.,
contemp. inscription verso frontis., occasional foxing, very good.
Hodgkins 27-5 1983 £15

ANDERSEN, HANS CHRISTIAN   Stories and Fairy Tales. George Allen,
1893. 2 vols. Frontis. Title vignettes. About 100 illus. Green
pictorial cloth, gilt. Greer 40-99 1983 £40

ANDERSEN, HANS CHRISTIAN   What the Moon Saw... Routledge, 1867.
Re-issue, 80 illus. by A.W. Bayes, engr'd by Bros. Dalziel, adverts.
Brown sand grain cloth, blind stamped design covrs., gilt titling.
Binding signed C.B. Presentation bookplate fr. ep - sl. foxing few
pp. Very nice copy. Hodgkins 27-4 1983 £20

ANDERSON, A.   A Narrative of the British Embassy to
China... London, 1796. Third edition. Calf, spine rubbed and chipped
at head. 8vo. Good. Edwards 1044-14 1983 £120

ANDERSON, ALEXANDER   The Looking-Glass for the Mind.
Philadelphia: Alexander Towar, 1832. 12mo. Numerous wood engravings by Anderson. Occasional light foxing. Slightly rubbed half-
leather and boards. Bromer 25-317 1983 $50

ANDERSON, ALEXANDER D.   The Silver Country of the Great Southwest.
New York: 1877. First edition. Folding map in color with minor
breaks at folds. Orig. green cloth. Fine copy. Bradley 66-447 1983
$85

ANDERSON, ALEXANDER D.   The Silver Country of the Great
Southwest. N.Y., 1877. Illus., folded map. Orig. cloth. Library
stamp on title page. First edition. Ginsberg 47-7 1983 $75

ANDERSON, ANNE   The Podgy-Puppy Book. T. Nelson, n.d.
Sm. 4to. Colour frontis. Title vignette. 11 colour plates with text
illus. around each plate. Cream pictorial boards, spine worn.
Greer 40-21 1983 £16

ANDERSON, C. L. G.   Old Panama and Castilla del Oro.
Washington, The Sudwarth Company, 1911. 1st ed., limited. Maps
and rare illus. 8vo. Fine. Morrill 286-4 1983 $40

ANDERSON, EDWARD   Camp Fire Stories. Chicago, (1900).
Orig. pictorial cloth, illus. Jenkins 152-779 1983 $75

ANDERSON, EDWARD   Camp Fire Stories. Chicago, 1900.
Cloth, very good. Reese 19-24 1983 $60

ANDERSON, GREGG   Recollections of the Grabhorn Press. Meriden, Conn.: Privately printed, 1935. Narrow 8vo, cloth-backed boards, vignette on upper cover. Frontis photo. by Will Connell. One of 70 copies. Occasional foxing. Quite scarce. Perata 28-1 1983 $125

ANDERSON, JAMES   Collections Relating to the History of Mary Queen of Scotland. Edinburgh: Printed by John Mosman and William Brown (by Thomas Ruddiman), 1727-1728. 4 vols., 4to, cont. calf with red morocco labels, final volume rebacked, preserving orig. labels. Inserted into the fourth volume at the beginning are 22 pages of manuscript copies of documents, and at page 149 are a further 7 pages in pen type-facs. Bickersteth 77-95 1983 £120

ANDERSON, JOHN   Box Office. N.Y., Jonathan Cape & Harrison Smith, (1929). First edition. Deco design endpapers and pictorial dust jacket (slight soiling and nicking). Endpapers and dust jacket designed by "Gene." Very good. Houle 22-671 1983 $27.50

ANDERSON, JOHN   The Unknown Turner. NY: Privately printed for the author. 1926. Folio. Color frontis. + 58 plates. Index. Edition ltd. to 1,000 copies (this copy not numbered). Dust jacket. Fine copy. Karmiole 75-11 1983 $100

ANDERSON, JOHN (1833-1900)   Anatomical and Zoological Researches: comprising an account of the Zoological Results of Two Expeditions to Western Yunnan in 1868 and 1875. 1878 (1879). 2 vols, 4to, original cloth (neatly repaired), plates. Rare, only 250 copies printed. Bindings neatly repaired, but a good clean copy. Wheldon 160-1 1983 £885

ANDERSON, JOHN REDWOOD   The Legend of Eros and Psyche. London, 1908. First edition. Dust wrappers. Inscription on flyleaf. Fine. Rota 230-26 1983 £25

ANDERSON, JOHN REDWOOD   The Music of Death. London, 1904. First edition. Dust wrappers. Inscription on flyleaf. Very nice. Rota 230-25 1983 £30

ANDERSON, MARGARET   My Thirty Years' War. London, 1930. First English edition. Free endpapers slightly browned. Very good. Jolliffe 26-10 1983 £25

ANDERSON, MAXWELL   High Tor. Washington, D.C.: Anderson House, 1937. First edition. 8vo. Orig. cloth. Dust jacket. Fine copy. Jaffe 1-4 1983 $45

ANDERSON, MAXWELL   You Who Have Dreams. NY, 1925. Limited to 1000 copies, spine and edges slightly darkened, edges rubbed and corners slightly worn, still good. Quill & Brush 54-36 1983 $35

ANDERSON, MAXWELL   You Who Have Dreams. New York: Simon & Schuster, 1925. 1st ed., 1 of 1,000 numbered copies. Orig. boards, labels. Near fine copy. Jenkins 155-29 1983 $30

ANDERSON, POUL   The Avatar. New York: Berkley, (1978). 1st ed. Printed light blue wrappers. Uncorrected proof for limited distribution. Advance copy for reviewers. Very fine. Bradley 64-3 1983 $75

ANDERSON, R. P.   Victories and Defeats. London, 1873. 8vo. Orig. cloth. Spine slightly soiled and faded. Ink stamp on title. Sole slight foxing. Good. Edwards 1042-268 1983 £12

ANDERSON, SHERWOOD   American County Fair. New York, 1930. 8vo. Wraps. 1 of 875 copies. Little wear to paper label on spine, else very good copy. In Our Time 156-21 1983 $25

ANDERSON, SHERWOOD   Dark Laughter. New York, 1925. 8vo. Cloth. A fine copy in dust jacket. Jacket has some chipping at the spinal extremities. In Our Time 156-19 1983 $125

ANDERSON, SHERWOOD   Hello Towns. New York, 1929. 8vo. Cloth. Little foxing to a few pages, else a fine copy in near perfect dj. In Our Time 156-20 1983 $125

ANDERSON, SHERWOOD   Hello Towns! New York: Liveright, 1929. 1st ed., 1st issue. Orig. tan cloth. Fine copy. Jenkins 155-30 1983 $20

ANDERSON, SHERWOOD   Home Town. N.Y., (1940). Photographic illus. by Farm Security Photographers. 4to, linen. First edition. Argosy 714-17 1983 $65

ANDERSON, SHERWOOD   Horses and Men. New York: Huebsch, 1923. Cloth, paper label. First edition, first state, with top edge stained orange. A fine copy in dust jacket (long closed tear in rear panel). Reese 20-28 1983 $75

ANDERSON, SHERWOOD   Mid-American Chants. New York, 1918. 1st ed. Decorated tan buckram, gilt. Association copy, inscribed in ink by Anderson to the critic Van Wyck Brooks, whose name he misspells "Van Wyke". Fine copy, protected by acetate wrapper. Bradley 63-5 1983 $250

ANDERSON, SHERWOOD   The Modern Writer. San Francisco, Latern Press, 1925. Title page drawing and initials in red by Donald McKay. Half orange cloth over blue boards (spine a little darkened). Slipcase. One of 50 numbered copies on Japan vellum signed by the author on colophon. Printed by Grabhorn Press. Fine. Houle 22-440 1983 $375

ANDERSON, SHERWOOD   No Swank. Philadelphia: The Centaur Press, 1934. 8vo. Cloth. A copy for review with slip from the publisher laid in. Endpaper browned, else a fine copy in the uncommon jacket. Jacket has some light wear but is intact. In Our Time 156-22 1983 $150

ANDERSON, SHERWOOD   No Swank. Philadelphia: Centaur Press, 1934. First edition. Black cloth. Fine in chipped dust jacket. Bradley 66-6 1983 $50

ANDERSON, SHERWOOD   Plays. Winesburg and Others. New York: Scribners, 1937. Brown cloth. First edition. This copy is in brown cloth. Fine in lightly used dust jacket, with one tiny inner mend. Reese 20-29 1983 $75

ANDERSON, SHERWOOD   A Story Teller's Story. New York, 1924. First edition. Inscription on flyleaf. Nice. Rota 230-28 1983 £15

ANDERSON, SHERWOOD   A Story Teller's Story. London, 1925. First English edition. Spine just a little darkened. Nice. Rota 231-11 1983 £15

ANDERSON, SHERWOOD   Winesburg, Ohio. New York, 1919. 8vo. Cloth, spine label. Laid in is a legal size mimeographed sheet of a review blurb by an unknown author. A very good copy in defective dj: about two inches missing at foot of spine and a panel of erasure on front cover. In Our Time 156-18 1983 $150

ANDERSON, SHERWOOD   Winesburg, Ohio. New York: Huebsch, 1919. 1st ed., later issue. Orig. yellow cloth, label. Label a little rubbed, else a very nice copy. Jenkins 155-32 1983 $60

ANDERSON, T. C.   Ubique: War Services... Calcutta, (1863). Title guarded, cloth. 8vo. Good. Edwards 1044-16 1983 £60

ANDERSON, THOMAS   On the Constitution of Anthracene or Paranaphthaline... Edinburgh, 1861. Offprint. 4to. Paper wrappers. Internally a good copy. Zeitlin 264-4 1983 $40

ANDERSSON, CHARLES JOHN
Please turn to
ANDERSSON, KARL JOHAN

ANDERSSON, KARL JOHAN   Lake Ngami. London: Hurst & Blackett, 1856. 8vo. Folding map. 16 plates. Numerous text engravings. Modern 1/4 black calf. Red label. Some light foxing and staining. Adelson Africa-3 1983 $250

ANDERSSON, KARL JOHAN   Lake Ngami. New York: Harper, 1856. 12mo. Text illus. Orig. blue cloth, rubbed. Adelson Africa-156 1983 $20

ANDERSSON, KARL JOHAN   The Okavango River: A narrative of travel, exploration, and adventure. London: Hurst & Blackett, 1861. 8vo. Engraved title. 16 plates. Orig. red cloth. Rubbed. Adelson Africa-4 1983 $275

ANDRADE, EDWARD NEVILLE DA COSTA   The New Chemistry. London:
G. Bell, 1936. 8vo. Orig. green cloth-backed boards. 8 photographic plates. First edition. Some minor flaws, but a very good
copy. Zeitlin 264-6 1983 $30

ANDRADE, EDWARD NEVILLE DA COSTA   The Structure of the Atom.
London: G. Bell, 1923. First edition. 8vo. 4 plates, 49 text
illus. Zeitlin 264-7 1983 $75

ANDRE, ALBERT   Renoir. Paris: G. Cres, 1928.
120 plates (4 color). Text illus. Boards, 1/4 cloth. From the
library of James Thrall Soby. Backstrip chipped at extremities.
Ars Libri 32-571 1983 $60

ANDRE, E.   Species des Hymenopteres d'Europe
et d'Algerie. Beaune, 1888. Vol. 4, 18 plates (13 coloured),
8vo, half morocco (trifle used). Wheldon 160-1015 1983 £45

ANDRE, E.   Species des Hymenopteres d'Europe et
d'Algerie. Paris, 1904. Vol. 9, 21 plates (7 coloured), 8vo,
new cloth. Wheldon 160-1016 1983 £30

ANDRE, JOHANN   Systematischer Theil. Offenbach, 1900.
Small folio, cloth-backed orig. printed boards. Salloch 387-357
1983 $60

ANDRE, R.   The Cruise of the Walnut Shell. Sampson
Low, n.d. 4to. Colour pictorial half-title & title. Colour frontis.
& 28pp with colour text illus. Brown colour glazed boards, rubbed.
Greer 40-24 1983 £25

ANDRE, R.   The Nightingale Dished up on China Plates.
George Allen, 1899. Sm. 4to. Frontis. Pictorial title. 19 plates
& 19 text illus. Green pictorial boards. Greer 40-25 1983 £12.50

ANDREAE, ANTONIUS   Quaestiones super XII libros Meta-
physicae Aristotelis. (London): Johannes Lettou for William
Wilcock, 1480. Folio. English 19th-century dark blue morocco,
blind-tooled, gilt back. Some damp marks throughout. From the
library of Sion College, with their engraved bookplate. 8-leaf
index bound in at the beginning. Scarce. Kraus 164-6 1983 $65,000

ANDREAS, A. T.   History of Chicago From the Earliest
Period to the Present Time. Chicago: A.T. Andreas, Publisher, 1884.
3 vols. Illus. with plates and maps. A.e.g. Full morocco, gilt.
Some wear and repairs to binding. Fairly nice. Jenkins 152-8 1983
$300

ANDREE, JOHN   An Account of the Tilbury Water. London:
Printed for W. Meadows, 1740. 2nd ed., 8vo in 4s (prelims misnumbered);
inscribed "Thomas Coffee House Janr.1 1739" on title, title soiled
and prelims torn in the inner margin affecting a few letters. Rare.
Pickering & Chatto 22-9 1983 $100

ANDREWS, ALEXANDER   The History of British Journalism.
Richard Bentley, 1859. First edition, 2 vols. Half titles, orig.
red cloth, v.g. Jarndyce 31-77 1983 £85

ANDREWS, CECILY   D. H. Lawrence. London: Martin Secker,
1930. First trade edition. Orig. cloth. Dust jacket (a bit dusty).
Fine. MacManus 279-3172 1983 $25

ANDREWS, CECILY   Elegy. N.Y.: Phoenix Book Shop, Inc.,
1930. First edition. Orig. cloth. Tissue dust jacket (torn). Limited to 250 copies signed by author. Bookplate. Fine. MacManus 280-
5510 1983 $80

ANDREWS, CECILY   Henry James. London, (1916). First
edition. 16mo, blue cloth. Argosy 714-793 1983 $45

ANDREWS, CECILY   The Return of the Soldier. London:
Nisbet & Co., Ltd., (1918). First edition. Orig. cloth. Inner hinges
repaired. Fine. MacManus 280-5513 1983 $50

ANDREWS, CECILY   The Strange Necessity. London, (1928).
First edition. 8vo, cloth; faded. Presentation to Edith Sitwell,
"with increasing admiration." Argosy 714-794 1983 $150

ANDREWS, CECILY   War Nurse. New York: Cosmopolitan,
1930. 1st ed. Orig. black cloth, gilt, dj. Very fine copy in fine
dj. Scarce. Jenkins 155-1295 1983 $60

ANDREWS, CHARLES M.   The Colonial Period of American History.
New Haven (1934-37). Thick 8vo, 4 vols. Argosy 710-95 1983 $100

ANDREWS, ISREAL WARD   Washington County and the Early
Settlement of Ohio. Cincinnati, 1877. Orig. printed wraps. First
edition. Ginsberg 46-570 1983 $50

ANDREWS, JANE   The Seven Little Sisters Prove their
Sisterhood. Boston, U.S.A.: Ginn & Co., 1893. Illus. half-title.
17-1/2 cm. Plates. Orig. decorated maroon cloth, spotted with
extremities somewhat rubbed. Grunder 7-85 1983 $25

ANDREWS, JOHN WILLIAM   Prelude to "Icaros". New York, (1936).
8vo, cloth. One of 1500 copies signed by the poet. Paper label which
covers the spine is rubbed, otherwise very good-fine. In Our Time
156-23 1983 $20

ANDREWS, MILES PETER   Fire and Water! A comic opera: in two
acts. London: printed for T. Cadell, 1780. 8vo, cont. half calf
(worn, front cover detached). 1st edition. The text has been
interleaved, but has not actually been marked up. Half-title present
(bit soiled). Ximenes 64-12 1983 $40

ANDREWS, PHILLIP   Air News Year Book. New York, (1942).
1st ed. Illus. Oblong 4to, torn dust wrapper. Morrill 286-34 1983
$30

ANDREWS, PHILLIP   Air News Yearbook. N.Y., (1942).
First edition. Cloth. Blind-stamped names and rubber stamp. Chipped
and torn dust wrapper. Very good. King 45-508 1983 $25

ANDREWS, ROBERT W.   The Life and Adventures, Extending Over
a Period of 97 Years. Boston: for the author, 1887. Orig. pr.
wraps. Frontis. Argosy 716-517 1983 $25

ANDREWS, ROY CHAMPAN   On The Trail Of Ancient Man. N.Y.:
G.P. Putnam's Sons, (1926). Fifth printing. Intro. by Henry Osborn.
Illus. Orig. green cloth. Presentation copy inscribed: "To Mr. & Mrs.
John Galsworthy, Whose 'Forsythe Saga' gave us all many happy hours in
this desert. Roy Chapman Andrews, by request of Peggy Fletcher."
Spine and covers slightly worn. Very good. MacManus 278-2136 1983
$45

ANDREWS, WILLIAM   Bygone Punishments. William Andrews,
1899. First edition, with full-page and other illus. 8vo, orig.
cloth, t.e.g. A very good copy. Fenning 60-8 1983 £18.50

ANDREWS, WILLIAM   North country poets. London, 1888.
8vo. Orig. dark blue cloth. Fine copy. Ximenes 63-431 1983 $20

ANDREWS, WILLIAM LORING   The Heavenly Jerusalem. NY: 1908.
Octavo. Limited to 120 copies printed at Gilliss Press. Several
facsimile illus., one with gold initials, 2 etchings by Sidney L.
Smith. Very fine in gilt-printed wrappers and slip-case. Bromer
25-133 1983 $85

ANDREWS, WILLIAM LORING   James Lyne's Survey... New York:
Dodd, Mead & Co., 1900. First edition. 8vo. Cloth. Limited
to 202 copies printed at the Gilliss Press. With three fold-out
facsimile reproductions of maps. Fine. Oak Knoll 49-10 1983
$150

ANDREWS, WILLIAM LORING   New York as Washington Knew It After
the Revolution. N.Y., Scribner, 1905. First edition. Illus. with
copperplate engravings by "Mr. Smith," and facs. of title pages,
etc. Full Japan vellum stamped in gilt, t.e.g., uncut. One of
32 copies on Japan vellum, printed at the Gillis Press. Very good -
fine. Houle 22-1007 1983 $225

ANDREWS, WILLIAM LORING   New York as Washington Knew It After
the Revolution. New York: Charles Scribners Sons, 1905. 8vo.
White parchment. T.e.g. Limited to 167 copies. With 15 plates
designed by Sidney L. Smith and three other illus. Bookplates
of Roderick Terry and Newport Historical Society, both stamped
withdrawn. Some foxing. Oak Knoll 49-11 1983 $150

ANDREWS WILLIAM LORING   A Trio of Eighteenth Century French
Engravers of Portraits in Miniature. NY: 1899. Octavo. Illus.
with 28 photogravures. Limited to 161 copies. Author's copy with
his bookplate. Very fine in faintly rubbed full brown morocco with
gilt-ornamented spine, covers and dentelles. Bromer 25-132 1983
$225

ANDREYEV, LEONID   Abyss. Waltham Saint Lawrence, 1929.
Translated by John Cournos. 12mo, cloth-backed bds., gilt, t.e.g.
One of 500 copies with engravings by Ivan Lebedeff. Perata 27-49
1983 $65

THE ANDRUS Bindery, A History of the Shop, 1831-1838. Hartford,
Conn.: Privately printed at The Sign of the Stone Book, 1940.
First edition. 8vo. Half-cloth over boards. Bookplate. Oak
Knoll 48-33 1983 £55

ANDRY, CHARLES FRANCOIS   Recherches sur la Rage. Paris, 1780.
12mo, cont. calf, (worn). At end, with separate pagination. Argosy
713-9 1983 $100

ANECDOTES of the life and character of John Howard, Esq. F.R.S.
London: printed for the author; sold by Hockham, etc., 1790. First
edition. 8vo. Disbound. With an etched frontis. portrait. Scarce.
Ximenes 63-82 1983 $150

ANET, CLAUDE   Ariange, Jeune Fille Russe. Paris,
Fayard, (1932). With 29 woodcuts by Angelina Beloff. Printed wraps.,
a bit worn, else good-very good. Houle 21-19 1983 $25

ANGEL NOVELTY CO.   Standardized Interior Woodwork, 1931.
Fitchburg, 1931. Illus. 4to, orig. wrappers. 3-in. tear on 4 leaves.
Good. Morrill 288-130 1983 $20

ANGELI, DIEGO   Mino da Fiesole. Firenze: Alinari,
1905. 11 plates. Numerous text illus. 4to. Cloth. Worn at
edges. Ars Libri 33-251 1983 $100

ANGELINI, LUIGI   Le opere in Venezia di Mauro Codussi.
Milano: Emilio Bestetti, 1945. 134 plates. 4to. Boards. Faint
waterstaining of upper edge towards rear. Ars Libri 33-113 1983
$75

ANGELO, VALENTI   Chinese Love Tales. N.Y.: Three Sirens
Press, 1935. First edition. 8vo, silk cloth, boxed. Illus. by
Valenti Angelo. Argosy 714-18 1983 $25

ANGELUS, JOHANNES   Astrolabium. Venice: Johannes Emericus
de Spira for Lucantononio Giunta, 9 June 1494. Full-page woodcut
of an astronomer (the author, acc. to an old inscription in this copy)
on verso of title, 439 text woodcuts, publisher's device on title,
printer's device at end, several ornamental woodcut initials. Small
4to. Cont. English calf over wooden boards, blind-tooled, 2 brass
catches, vellum endleaves, fly-leaf from an early printed book. Dampstaining, slightly soiled. Kraus 164-7 1983 $5,600

ANGLE, PAUL M.   A Shelf of Lincoln Books... New
Brunswick: Rutgers Univ. Press, 1946. First edition. 8vo.
Cloth. Limited to 1000 copies. Lee Edmonds Grove's copy. Oak
Knoll 49-268 1983 $35

ANGLICUS, BARTHOLOMAEUS
Please turn to
BARTHOLOMAEUS ANGLICUS

ANGOULEME, MARGUERITE D'
Please turn to
MARGUERITE D'ANGOULEME

ANIMAL Behaviour. 1958-81. Series complete from Jan. 1958 to Nov.
1981, vols. 6-29, royal 8vo, parts as issued. Wheldon 160-458 1983
£120

THE ANIMAL Museum. J. Harris, (1825). First edition, with 92 numbered
engravings on 25 plates, including half-title, large 12mo, cont. roan-
backed cloth. Very good. Fenning 60-9 1983 £32.50

ANNALES De Chimie. Paris, 1769-93. Several copperplates, 8vo, cont.
sprinkled bds, calf backs, leather labels. Vols. 2 and 4 somewhat
dampstained at lower edges. Argosy 713-10 1983 $850

THE ANNALS of the green room, and biography of the stage!...Memoirs
of Mrs. Honey. London: H. Smith, n.d. (ca. 1830). 12mo, cont.
wrappers (worn), first edition. Ximenes 64-13 1983 $100

ANNUAL of Advertising Art in the United States. N.Y., 1921-29.
Vols. 1 & 3 thru 8. Well illus. Cloth and boards. Blind-stamped
name, all vols. worn. Vol. 5 spine detached. Nice. King 45-307 $160

ANNUALS of Advertising Art. For the years: 1943, 1945, 1946 & 1947.
Illus., cloth, covers worn and soiled. King 46-381 1983 $100

ANNUNZIO, GABRIELE D'   The Flame of Life. London: William
Heinemann, 1900. First English edition. Orig. cloth. Covers
darkened. MacManus 278-1264 1983 $20

ANNUNZIO, GABRIELE D'   The Triumph of Death. London: William
Heinemann, 1898. First English edition. Orig. cloth. Very good.
MacManus 278-1265 1983 $25

ANNUNZIO, GABRIELE D'   The Victim. London: William Heinemann,
1899. First English edition. Orig. cloth. Covers darkened. Good.
MacManus 278-1266 1983 $20

ANSTEY, CHRISTOPHER   An Election Ball in Poetical Letters...
Dublin: by George Bonham, 1776. First Dublin edition. 8vo.
Wrappers. Heath 49-235 1983 £75

ANSTEY, CHRISTOPHER   Ad C W Bampfylde epistola poetica
familiaris...cui titulus. An Election Ball. Bathoniae, Hazard;
London, Dodsley & Wilkie; Cantab, Fletcher & Hodson; Oxon, Fletcher,
1776. 1st edition, sm. 4to, engraved title and 5 large engraved
scenes, contemporary quarter calf over marble boards, vellum-tipped
corners, excellent copy. Deighton 3-12 1983 £68

ANSTEY, CHRISTOPHER   A Familiar Epistle from C. Anstey Esq.
to C.W. Bampfylde, Esq. London: Printed by H. Reynell...for J. Almon.
MDCCLXXVII. First edition in English. 4to, new wraps. Quaritch
NS 7-5 1983 $150

ANSTEY, CHRISTOPHER   The new Bath guide. Cambridge, 1766.
Second edition, 8vo, original quarter calf, morocco label over
marbled paper boards, calf-tipped corners, slightly rubbed. Deighton
3-10 1983 £15

ANSTEY, CHRISTOPHER   The new Bath guide. London, Dodsley,
1766. Third edition. 8vo, original quarter calf over marbled paper
boards, slightly rubbed, one sig. foxed, extreme edges spotted, good.
Deighton 3-11 1983 £12

ANSTEY, CHRISTOPHER   The New Bath Guide. Hurst, Chance &
Co., 1830. Frontis. & title vignette by S. Williams & 5 etchings by
George Cruikshank. Plum cloth, paper title label on bkstrip, uncut,
cloth much faded & discol'd, plates sl. foxed, corners of cvrs. &
bkstrip worn, good copy. Hodgkins 27-243 1983 £40

ANSTEY, CHRISTOPHER   The patriot, a Pindaric address to
Lord Buckhorse. Cambridge: printed by Fletcher and Hodson, sold
by J. Dodsley, etc., 1767. 4to. Disbound. Ximenes 63-548 1983
$125

ANSTEY, CHRISTOPHER   The Priest Dissected, a Poem. Bath:
by S. Hazard, 1774. First edition. 4to. Wrappers. Engraved
vignette on title. Heath 49-236 1983 £75

ANSTIE, FRANCIS E.   Neuralgia & the Diseases that Resemble
it. Phila., 1871. First edition. Argosy 713-11 1983 $85

AN ANSWER to War in Disguise. New York: Hopkins and Seymour for
I. Riley & Co., February 1806. First edition. Orig. printed
wraps. Felcone 22-4 1983 $50

ANTHEIL, GEORGE   Bad Boy of Music. New York, 1945. First
edition. Nice. Rota 230-30 1983 £15

ANTHERTON, WILLIAM   Narrative of the Suffering & Defeat of
the North-Western Army, Under General Winchester. Frankfort, Ky.,:
A. G. Hodges, 1842. 1st ed., privately printed, original marbled
boards with printed label on front, morocco spine expertly repaired.
Library stamp on title-page, else a good crisp copy. Jenkins 151-
357 1983 $200

ANTHING, FREDERICK   History of the Campaigns of Count
Alexander Suworow Rymnikski. 1799. 2 vols., portrait, half calf.
K Books 307-5 1983 £48

ANTHOLOGIA Lyrica. Lg (T), 1913. 4th ed., 8vo, cloth. Salloch 385-
423 1983 $20

ANTHOLOGY of Magazine Verse for 1915. New York: Gomme & Marshall,
1915. 1st ed. Very good copy. Jenkins 155-119 1983 $35

ANTHONY, IRVIN   Paddle Wheels and Pistols. Phila.,
(1929). 1st ed. Illus., some in color. Clark 741-437 1983 $26.50

ANTI-SUFFRAGE Essays by Massachusetts Women. Boston, 1916. 1st ed.
Small 8vo. Morrill 286-5 1983 $25

THE ANTI-WEESILS. London: R. Taylor, 1691. First edition. Small
4to. Modern quarter morocco. A few headlines shaved. Ximenes 63-
355 1983 $140

ANTON, FERDINAND   Primitive Art. Pre-Columbian, North
American, Indian, African, Oceanic. New York: Abrams, 1979. 7
maps, 2 charts, 563 illus. (302 color). 4to. Cloth. Dust jacket.
Ars Libri 34-2 1983 $100

ANTONINUS, BROTHER   The Residual Years. (NY, 1948). Tiny
tear to paper covering front hinge, else very good in slightly chipped,
lightly stained, very good dustwrapper. Quill & Brush 54-427 1983
$50

ANTONINUS, BROTHER   Tendril in the Mesh. (N.p.): Cayucos
Books, 1973. Quarto. Half calf and boards. First edition. One of
250 numbered copies, printed by Clifford Burke at the Cranium Press,
and signed by the author. Very fine copy, with the prospectus laid
in. Reese 20-191 1983 $75

ANTONINUS, BROTHER   Triptych for the Living. (N.p.): The
Seraphim Press, 1951. Quarto. Full goat vellum, silk ties. Illus.
with woodcuts by Mary Fabilli. A very fine copy. This copy is
inscribed by Everson on the colophon to California printer Lawton
Kennedy. One of fewer than 100 copies, handprinted in Hammer Uncial
type on Tovil handmade paper. Reese 20-385 1983 $1,750

APIANUS, PETRUS   Isagoge in Typum Cosmographicum seu
Mappam Mundi. Landshut: Joannes Weyssenburger, ca. 1521-1522.
With a large woodcut on the title, displaying an Asia-Africa-Europe
map surround by wind-heads. 4to. Half vellum, in half morocco case.
First edition. Kraus 164-8 1983 $3,500

THE APOCALYPSE of St. John. London, 1909. 5 plates, map, 3rd edition.
8vo, cloth. Salloch 385-427 1983 $70

APOLLONIUS, RHODIUS   The Argonautics... Dublin: printed
by Graisberry and Campbell, for the author, 1803. First edition of
this translation by William Preston. 3 vols. 8vo. Cont. straight
grained purple morocco. Very slightly faded. A fine set. Ximenes
63-63 1983 $200

AN APOLOGY and a shield for protestant dissenters... London: C.
Dilly, 1784. First edition. 8vo. Early 19th-century half calf,
spine gilt. Rubbed. Ximenes 63-585 1983 $90

AN APOLOGY for the Protestants of France, in Reference to the
Persecutions they are Under at this Day; in Six Letters. Printed for
John Holford, 1683. 4to, wrapper, light browning, but a good to very
good copy. Fenning 61-13 1983 £14.50

AN APOLOGY for the United States of America. Liverpool, 1829.
First edition. Dbd. Ginsberg 46-14 1983 $50

APPERLEY, CHARLES JAMES   The Chace, the Turf, and the Road.
John Murray, 1843. Illus. by Alken and Gilbert. Second edition.
With additional engraved title, 11 plates and a few vignette
illus., 8vo, orig. pink cloth, gilt, a very good copy. Fenning 62-8
1983 £48.50

APPERLEY, CHARLES JAMES   The Horse and the Hound. Edinburgh:
Adam & Charles Black, 1842. First edition. Extra-illus. Cont. 3/4
red morocco and marbled boards. Foxing. Few annotations in ink in
the text. Very good. MacManus 278-1969 1983 $125

APPERLEY, CHARLES JAMES   The Life of a Sportsman. London: Kegan
Paul, Trench, Trubner, & Co., Ltd., 1914. 36 illus. by Henry Alken.
4to. Full cranberry morocco, gilt, with green & blue morocco labels
on spine, marbled endpapers. A.e.g., by Riviere & Son. MacManus 277-
101 1983 $450

APPERLEY, CHARLES JAMES   Memoirs of The Life of the late John
Maytton. London: Reprinted (with considerable Additions) from the
New Sporting Magazine, Kegan Paul, Trench, Trubner & Co. Ltd., n.d.
Illus. by H. Alken and T.J. Rawlins. 4to. Cont. 3/4 red morocco &
cloth. First extra-illustrated edition, with an introduction by
Joseph Grego. Fine copy. MacManus 277-102 1983 $200

APPERLEY, CHARLES JAMES   My Life and Times. Edinburgh & London,
1927. Illus. 8vo. Morrill 288-576 1983 $25

APPERLEY, CHARLES JAMES   Nimrod Abroad. London: Henry Colburn,
1842. 2 vols. Later full polished calf with morocco labels,
by Riviere. First edition. Some foxing. Very good copy. Each vol. in
a separate slipcase. MacManus 277-103 1983 $150

APPERLEY, CHARLES JAMES   Nimrod's Hunting Tours. London: M. A.
Pittman, 1835. Added are Nimrod's Letters on Riding to Hounds. Orig.
boards. First edition. Bookseller's label inside front cover and prelims edtached. A very good copy in a folding cloth slipcase. Very
scarce. MacManus 277-104 1983 $250

APPERLEY, CHARLES JAMES   Remarks on the Condition of Hunters, The
Choice of Horses, and Their Management. London: M. A. Pittman, 1831.
With Notes and a Copious Index. Orig. boards with paper label on spine.
First edition. Rare. Bookseller's label on the front cover. Hinges
cracked. In half-morocco slipcase. Very good copy. MacManus 277-105
1983 $295

APPLES of Gold in Pictures of Silver. Printed for William Cole n.d.
(ca. 1825). With numerous coloured engrs. Hand-col'd frontis. & 14
small hand-col'd wood cuts. Bound in maroon leather backed marbled
boards. Occasional fox mark, nice copy. Hodgkins 27-7 1983 £35

APPLETON, HONOR C.   The Bad Mrs. Ginger. Grant Richards,
1902. Royal 32mo. 24 colour plates (1 short tear). Green cloth.
No. 16 of the Dumpy Books. Greer 39-16 1983 £28

APPLETON, LE ROY H.   Indian Art of the Americas. New York:
Charles Scribner's Sons, 1950. 79 color plates. Large 4to. Cloth.
Ars Libri 34-105 1983 $40

APPLETON'S Cyclopaedia of American Biography. New York: D. Appleton,
1888-89. 6 vols., calf, quite worn, hinges cracked, one cover detached. Portraits and facs. signatures. Dawson 470-14 1983 $30

APPOLONIUS OF TYRE   Historia Apollonii Regis Tyri. London:
The Golden Cockerel Press, 1956. Cloth, gilt, orange morocco spine,
gilt, t.e.g. 6 line-engravings by Mark Severin. Limited edition of
300 numbered copies. Traylen 94-21 1983 £75

APRA, NIETTA   Ambrogio da Fossano detto il Bergognone.
Milano: G.G. Gorlich, 1945. 90 illus. Small folio. Wrappers.
Slightly worn. Foot of spine chipped. Edition limited to 750
numbered copies. Ars Libri 33-26 1983 $65

APULEIUS, LUCIUS   The Marriage of Cupid and Psyche. NY:
Limited Editions Club, 1951. Octavo. 6 full-page color illus. by
Edmund Dulac. Limited to 1500 copies signed by Dulac. Extremely
fine in gilt-stamped white boards. Slip-case slightly darkened.
Bromer 25-193 1983 $175

APULEIUS, LUCIUS   The Story of Cupid & Psyche. D. Nutt,
1903. 1st edn. Illus. by Jessie Mothersole. Large paper copy.
Decor. initial letters in red, printed on hand-made paper. Cream
cloth, red titling, yapped edges, uncut (cvrs. & eps. & half title sl.
discol'd), vg. Hodgkins 27-401 1983 £18.50

AQUILA, JOANNES   Opusculum Enchiridium Appellatum de
Omni Ludorum Genere. Oppenheim (Jacob Koebel), 1516. Full-page
woodcut on verso of title, woodcut initials printed white on black.
4to, antiphonal vellum. Salloch 387-5 1983 $950

ARABIAN NIGHTS   Aladdin, ou la Lampe Merveilleuse. Paris, 1896. Very slightly shaken, else fine in gilt stamped stiff wrappers. Bromer 25-408 1983 $65

ARABIAN NIGHTS   Arabian Nights Entertainment. London: Cass., Pett., Gal., n.d. (ca.1880). Thick 4to. Blue cloth. Extensive gilt & silver decoration. Foredge & title page slightly foxed. Thousands of black & whites, full page & smaller. Very good. Aleph-bet 8-15 1983 $40

ARABIAN NIGHTS   The Arabian Nights. London: Raphael Tuck & Sons (ca. 1890). Octavo. 12 full-page chromolithographs. Numerous monochrome vignettes. Very lightly rubbed at corners, else fine in cloth-backed, color pictorial boards. Bromer 25-322 1983 $55

ARABIAN NIGHTS   Arabian Nights. N.Y.: Dodd, 1917. 8vo. Blue pictorial cloth. Prelims. foxed. 8 tipped in color plates by Bull, black & whites in text. One page handwritten letter by Bull with sketch, dated 1900, signed. Very good. Aleph-bet 8-45 1983 $150

ARABIAN NIGHTS   Arabian Nights: Tales of Wonder & Magnificence. N.Y.: Mac., 1923. First edition. 8vo. Blue cloth. Spine faded. Color frontis. plus numerous black & whites (full page and in text) by E. Pape. Good to very good. Aleph-bet 8-16 1983 $25

ARABIAN NIGHTS   Sinbad the Sailor & Other Stories. London, Hodder & Stoughton, n.d. Illus. in color by Edmund Dulac. 4to. Slightly rubbed at corners. Morrill 288-93 1983 $50

ARABIAN NIGHTS   Stories from the Arabian Nights. London: Hodd. & Stought., (1911). 8vo. Green cloth. Pictorial inset. Light wear. Illus. with 27 color plates with tissue guards. Very good. Aleph-bet 8-96 1983 $37

ARABIAN NIGHTS   Stories from the Arabian Nights. Garden City, ca. 1920. Illus. with seven color plates by Culac and Frank Schoonover. Black cloth, large color label. Spine faded, good-very good. Houle 21-422 1983 $22.50

ARABIAN NIGHTS   The Thousand and One Nights: The Arabian Nights Entertainments. London, Knight, 1839-41. First edition thus. Thick 4to, illus. with engravings based on the designs of William Harvey. Full green 19th century morocco, spines decorated in gilt, covers stamped in gilt and blind, gilt inner dentelles, edges extra gilt. Bookplate of Elkin Matthews. Very good-fine. 3 vols. Houle 22-553 1983 $275

ARABIAN NIGHTS   The Thousand and One Nights. Charles Knight, 1841. 3 vols. Illus. engrs. on wood by William Harvey. Dark green fine bead grain cloth with central gilt vignettes cvrs., & bkstrips. Binder's ticket of Westleys & Clark. Corners sl. bruised & worn, eps. broken at hinges, rear joint of vol. 1 repr'd, some foxing fore-edges, nice copy. Hodgkins 27-244 1983 £65

ARABIAN NIGHTS   The Thousand and One Nights. John Murray, 1859. 3 vols., large 8vo, engr. half titles and many hundred woodcuts by Wm. Harvey. Orig. red riple-grained cloth, gilt. Fine. Jarndyce 31-775 1983 £42

ARABIAN NIGHTS   The Book of the Thousand Nights and A Night. N.Y.: Printed by Burton Club for Subscribers. Medina edition. Limited to 1000 numbered sets (this not num.). 17 vols. 4to. 3/4 leather. Marbled boards. Some volumes show wear to extremities. Illus. in black & white with tissue guards. Includes supp. nights, n.d. (ca.1885), no artist named. Very good. Aleph-bet 8-14 1983 $150

ARAGON, LOUIS   Henri Matisse. A novel. New York: Harcourt Brace Jovanovitch, 1972. 2 vols. 234 illus. (76 color). 307 illus. (79 color). Large 4to. Cloth. Dust jacket. Boxed. Ars Libri 32-438 1983 $175

ARBER, AGNES   Herbals their Origin and Evolution. Cambridge, 1938. 8vo. Cloth. Dust wrapper. Plates and illus. Gurney JJ-9 1983 £20

ARBER, EDWARD   Travels and Works of Captain John Smith... Edinburgh, 1910. Illus. 2 vols., 8vo. Morrill 286-6 1983 $40

ARBLAY, FRANCES BURNEY D'   Cecilia, Or, Memoirs of an Heiress. Dublin: Printed for Messrs. Price, Moncreiffe... 1783. 1st Dublin edition. 3 vols, 12mo, contemporary calf, red and green labels. Hill 165-16 1983 £45

ARBLAY, FRANCES BURNEY D'   Diary and Letters of Madame D'Arblay. London, 1842-46. 7 vols. Rebound in leather, cloth. A fine set. In Our Time 156-127 1983 $250

ARBLAY, FRANCES BURNEY D'   Diary and Letters of Madame D'Arblay... London, 1904-05. Edition-de-Luxe. 6 vols. 8vo. Red cloth, white buckram spines, gilt, uncut edges. Frontis. and other illus. Limited to 100 copies. Traylen 94-235 1983 £75

ARBLAY, FRANCES BURNEY D'   Diary and Letters of Madame D'Arblay... London, 1904-05. 6 vols. 8vo. Orig. red cloth, gilt. Frontis. and other illus. Traylen 94-236 1983 £45

ARBLAY, FRANCES BURNEY D'   Evelina. London: Geo. Newnes Ltd., 1898. First edition, later issue. Illus. by A. Rackham. Orig. decorated cloth. Bookplate on front endsheet. Covers somewhat rubbed and soiled. Very good. MacManus 280-4292 1983 $125

ARBLAY, FRANCES BURNEY D'   Evelina or The History of a Young Lady's Entrance into the World. London: Macmillan & Co., n.d. First of this illus. edition. Intro. by A. Dobson. Illus. by H. Thomson. Orig. gilt-decorated cloth. Dust jacket (torn, chipped). Very fine. MacManus 280-5225 1983 $150

ARBLAY, FRANCES BURNEY D'   The Wanderer; or female difficulties. London: for Longman, etc., 1814. First edition. 5 vols. 12mo. Cont. calf, morocco labels, gilt. Half-titles in vols. 2, 4, and 5, 4 pp. of ads. in vol. 5. One joint cracking. Traylen 94-132 1983 £120

ARBLAY, FRANCES BURNEY D'   The Wanderer. For Longman, Hurst, etc., 1814. First edition. 5 vols. 12mo, lacks half-titles, final blank leaves and advertisement leaves. Cont. half calf (joints weak). Faint water-stains in all vols., one leaf torn with no loss of text. Hannas 69-20 1983 £35

ARBUTHNOT, JOHN   An Essay concerning the Effects of Air on Human Bodies. London: for J. Tonson, 1733. First edition. 8vo. Cont. calf, gilt. Half title. Slight wear. Heath 48-483 1983 £150

ARBUTHNOT, JOHN   John Bull's Last Will and Testament... London: by S. Popping, 1713. Second edition, corrected by the author's own hand. Modern blue cloth. Neat repair at lower inner margin of title. Heath 49-237 1983 £75

ARBUTHNOT, JOHN   Law is a Bottomless Pit. Boston: J.W. Folsom, 1794. First American edition. 12mo, cont. calf, (foxed). Ex lib. Argosy 716-234 1983 $45

ARBUTHNOT, JOHN   Le Proces Sans Fin... Londres: chez J. Nours, 1753. First edition in French. 12mo. Cont. mottled calf, gilt. Slight wear. Heath 48-429 1983 £105

ARCANGELI, G.   Compendio della flora Italiana. Turin, 1894. Cr. 8vo, cloth, second edition. Two leaves stained where a specimen has been pressed between them. Wheldon 160-1646 1983 £25

ARCHER, LOU ELLA   Canyon Shadows. (Phoenix, AZ: The Author, 1931). Oblong 8vo, 7 color plates by Lillian Wilhelm Smith. Presentation copy, signed by the illustrator. Tan cloth, foxed, with mounted cover illus. Karmiole 75-6 1983 $60

ARCHER, THOMAS   Charles Dickens. Cassell, nd (ca. 1900). 28 full page sketches by Frederick Barnard & other illus. 18 mounted photogravures on heavy paper, plates (each plate having a printed guard). Half crimson morocco, fine ribbed crimson cloth boards, gilt tooled bkstrip, marbled eps., a.e.g. (bottom of bkstrip broken away & extremities rubbed, some foxing to margins of plates, occasional thumbing), v.g. Hodgkins 27-577 1983 £45

ARCHER, WILLIAM   About the Theatre. Essays and Studies. London: T. Fisher Unwin, 1886. First edition, 8vo, original dark green cloth. Presentation copy, inscribed on the half-title: "John Robertson from W. A. 6 July: 86." Some cracking of the inner hinges, but a very good copy. Ximenes 64-15 1983 $45

ARCHER, WILLIAM   Colour-Blind Neutrality. London: Hodder & Stoughton, 1916. Orig. wrappers. First edition. A bit dust-soiled. Very good copy. MacManus 277-106 1983 $35

ARCHER, WILLIAM   Shirking the Issue. London: Hodder & Stoughton, 1917. Orig. wrappers. First edition. Fine copy. MacManus 277-107 1983 $35

ARCHER, WILLIAM   Six of One and Half-a-Dozen of the Other. London: T. Fisher Unwin, 1917. Orig. wrappers. First edition. Fine copy. MacManus 277-108 1983 $45

THE ARCHER'S guide. London: T. Hurst, 1833. First edition. 12mo. Orig. green cloth. One hand-colored folding plate in three parts by Robert Cruikshank. Worn at one fold. Ximenes 63-549 1983 $150

ARCHIBALD, RAYMOND CLARE   Carlyle's First Love, Margaret Gordon, Lady Bannerman. John Lane, 1910. Front. & Illus. Half title, 16 pp ads. Orig. green cloth, t.e.g. Jarndyce 30-944 1983 £15

ARCTIC Bibliography. Washington, Montreal and London: Department of Defense and McGill-Queens Univ. Press, 1953-1969. 14 vols. Cloth, some corners bumped, a couple of hinges weak or repaired inside, but overall a fine bright set. Dawson 470-15 1983 $400

ARDITTI, J.   Orchid Biology. Cornell, 1982. Illus., royal 8vo, cloth. Wheldon 160-2036 1983 £39 .

ARDIZZONE, EDWARD   Game Pie: A Guinnes Indoor Sportfolio. (London: Arthur Guinnes), n.d. Octavo. Very fine copy in pictorial self-wrappers. Publisher's printed presentation card laid-in. Bromer 25-320 1983 $95

ARETINO, PIETRO   The Ragionamenti or Dialogues. Paris, Lisieux, 1889. 2 vols., portrait, red and black titles, binders cloth, deckle edges, with the booklabel on William Neely Ross. K Books 301-7 1983 £35

ARETZ, GERTRUDE   Napoleon and His Women Friends. London, 1927. 8vo. Orig. cloth. Portrait frontis. 15 portraits plates. Spine slightly faded. Good. Edwards 1042-423 1983 £15

ARGLES, MAGGIE
Please turn to
HUNGERFORD, MRS. MARGARET WOLFE HAMILTON

ARGLES, MRS. MARGARET HAMILTON
Please turn to
HUNGERFORD, MRS. MARGARET WOLFE HAMILTON

ARGYLE, ARCHIE   Cupid's Album. N.Y., 1866. Orig. cloth. First edition. Ginsberg 47-9 1983 $125

ARGYLE, HARVEY   As I Saw It. San F., (1902). Illus. Orig. cloth. First edition. Ginsberg 47-490 1983 $50

ARGYLL, JOHN   The Canadian North-West. Ottawa, 1883. Folded map. Dbd. Small rubber library stamp on title page. Ginsberg 46-132 1983 $50

ARIGO Minerbi. Pensieri, confessioni, ricordi. Milano: Ceschina, n.d. 102 collotype plates. Small folio. Cloth. Edition limited to 1500 copies. Ars Libri 33-529 1983 $85

ARISTOMENES: A Grecian Tale. London: Robert Tyas, 1838. Frontispieces. Orig. cloth. First edition. Light marginal dampstain to Vol. I, affecting margin of frontispiece. A very good copy. MacManus 277-77 1983 $125

ARISTOPHANES   The Birds. Printed for Taylor and Hessey, 1824. First edition of this translation, without the half-title, 8vo, cont. half calf, a little wear to the headband, but otherwise a nice copy. Fenning 60-11 1983 £24

ARISTOPHANES   Comoediae. Lg, 1921 & 1913. (Spine repaired). 2 vols. 8vo, cloth. Salloch 385-438 1983 $55

ARISTOPHANES   Comodiae Duae Plutus & Nubes; Cum Scholiis Graecis... Londoni, Rob. Clavel, 1695. 8vo, cont. calf rebacked, inner blank margin of title slightly defective and fixed to endpaper. Ravenstree 95-13 1983 $85

ARISTOPHANES   The Eleven Comedies of Aristophanes. New York, 1928. 8vo, full niger morocco, decorated spines and dentelles, cockerell endleaves, a.e.g. by Bayntun. With 32 illus. of which 16 are in colors and gold by Jean de Bosschere. One of a limited numbered edition published for subscribers only. Two vols. Duschnes 240-13 1983 $375

ARISTOPHANES   Plutus, or, the god of riches. London: printed for Wheatley and Adlard, etc., 1825. First edition. 8vo. Orig. grey boards, printed paper label. Spine a bit worn, label rubbed. Very good copy. Ximenes 63-64 1983 $35

ARISTOTELES   Aristotelian Papers. Ithaca, 1939. 8vo, cloth. Salloch 385-469 1983 $20

ARISTOTELES   The Basic Works. NY, 1941. 8vo, cloth. Salloch 385-446 1983 $25

ARISTOTELES   Constitution of Athens. London, 1893. Illus. 8vo, cloth. Salloch 385-447 1983 $45

ARISTOTELES   De Generatione et interitu duos... Venice: Bernardinus Vitales, April 1521. 2 vols. Uncut. Folio. Orig. boards covered with 14th-century manuscript vellum (vol. 1 with only the back so covered). From the library of Giulio Giovio with his manuscript exlibris. Kraus 164-9 1983 $1,500

ARISTOTELES   The Nicomachean Ethics. London, 1920. 8vo, cloth. Salloch 385-450 1983 $25

ARISTOTELES   On the part of Animals. 1882. 8vo, cloth. Wheldon 160-459 1983 £20

ARISTOTELES   The Poetics. London, 1917. A few pencil marks and underlinings. Salloch 385-454 1983 $35

ARISTOTELES   The Politics. Oxford, 1948. 8vo, cloth. Salloch 385-460 1983 $25

ARISTOTELES   Politics. Oxford, 1948. 8vo, cloth. Salloch 385-459 1983 $24

ARISTOTELES   The Rhetoric. Cambridge, 1877. Tall 8vo, three vols. Orig. green cloth. Salloch 385-461 1983 $125

ARIZONA and the West. Tucson, 1959-73. Vols. 1-15. Orig. printed wraps. First edition. Ginsberg 47-12 1983 $350

ARIZONA Highways for 1947 (XXIII: 1-12). Twelve issues bound together in blue buckram, gilt-lettered (very good). In very fine condition. Grunder 6-3 1983 $25

THE ARKANSAS Traveller's Songster... N.Y., (1864). 71, (1)pp. Original pictorial wrappers. Jenkins 151-7 1983 $45.

ARLEN, MICHAEL   May Fair. London, 1925. First edition. Covers and spine a little marked and worn. Author's signed autograph presentation inscription. Nice. Rota 231-19 1983 £20

ARLEN, MICHAEL   A Young Man Comes to London. London: Marshalsea Press, n.d. (ca.1920). 4to. Cloth. Classic Art Deco covers with matching endpapers. Light wear. Full page black & whites by Beaton. Fold-out color plates. Very good. Aleph-bet 8-19 1983 $35

ARLISS, GEORGE   My Ten Years in the Studios. Boston, Little, Brown, 1940. First edition. Illus. brown cloth, lightly soiled, else good-very good. Houle 21-22 1983 $20

ARMENGAUD, JACQUES E.   The Practical Draughtsman's Book of Industrial Design. Longman, Brown, 1853. First edition thus, with 55 double-page folding and other plates, 58 text illus., 4to, cont. half calf, a very good copy. Fenning 62-10 1983 £65

ARMER, LAURA A.   Southwest. New York, 1935. 1st ed. Illus. Clark 741-446 1983 $25

ARMER, LAURA A   Waterless Mountain. New York, 1931. 1st ed. Illus. Clark 741-290 1983 $21

ARMFIELD, CONSTANCE S.   The Flower Book. Chatto & Windus, 1910. 4to. Colour frontis. Colour decorated title & 18 colour plates, foxing. Grey backed green pictorial boards. Greer 40-34 1983 £17.50

ARMITAGE, MERLE   Dance Memoranda. N.Y., Dueel, Sloan & Pearce. (1946). First edition. 4to, profusely illus., title page woodblock and others by Gordon Craig. Dust jacket (slightly faded). Very good - fine. Houle 22-31 1983 $75

ARMITAGE, MERLE   "Fit for a King": The Merle Armitage Book of Food. N.Y., Duell, Sloan & Pearce, (1949). 4to, illus. by Elise, with 4 halftone photos by Edward Weston. Pictorial endpapers. Green cloth stamped in red. Very good. Houle 22-32 1983 $35

ARMITAGE, MERLE   Millard Sheets. Los Angeles, Hatfield, 1935. First edition. 4to, frontis. portrait by Edward Weston; 28 plates of reproductions. Blue decorated boards. Very good. With an orig. signed litho by sheets. One of 1,000 copies. Designed and written in part by Armitage. Houle 21-25 1983 $175

ARMITAGE, MERLE   Post-Caviar. N.Y., Longmans, 1939. First edition. Illus. Pictorial endpapers. Black cloth stamped in red (edges of upper cover bumped), else, very good. Houle 22-33 1983 $25

ARMOUR, G. D.   A Hunting Alphabet. Country Life, 1929. Large 4to. 26 mounted colour plates. Red boards, decorated dust wrapper. Very good. Greer 39-2 1983 $85

ARMOUR, G. D.   A Hunting Alphabet. Country Life, 1929. Large 4to. 26 mounted colour plates. Red boards, decorated dust wrappers. Very good. Greer 40-15 1983 £65

ARMSTRONG, E. A.   Bird Display and Behaviour. 1947. Revised and enlarged edition. Wheldon 160-624 1983 £12

ARMSTRONG, EDWARD FRANKLAND   Chemistry in the Twentieth Century. London: Ernst Benn, 1924. 8vo. Orig. black cloth with gilt. 9 plates and various diagrams. Zeitlin 264-11 1983 $40

ARMSTRONG, HENRY EDWARD   Essays on the Art and Principles of Chemistry... London: Benn, 1927. 8vo. Orig. red cloth. 2 plates, text illus. A very good copy. Zeitlin 264-12 1983 $40

ARMSTRONG, JOHN   The Art of Preserving Health. Printed for A. Millar, 1744. 4to, recent half calf antique with new end papers. Without the half title. First edition. Bickersteth 77-4 1983 £110

ARMSTRONG, JOHN   The Art of Preserving Health: A Poem. London: Printed for A. Millar, opposite to Katharine-Street in the Strand, 1744. 4to. Later boards. First edition. Very good copy. MacManus 277-109 1983 $100

ARMSTRONG, JOHN   Facts, Observations, & Practical Illustrations, Relative to Puerperal Fever, Scarlet Fever, Pulmonary Consumption & Measles. Phila., 1826. 3 parts in 1 vol., separate titles & paging. 8vo, cont. mottled calf, leather label. Argosy 713-12 1983 $75

ARMSTRONG, JOHN   The history of the island of Minorca. London: C. Davis, 1752. First edition. 8vo. Cont. calf. Folding map and two folding plates. Clean tear in one leaf. Ximenes 63-612 1983 $325

ARMSTRONG, JOHN   Miscellanies. London, 1770. 2 vols. 12 mo., contemporary calf, leather labels. Hinges cracked, some rubbing. 1st collected ed. Morrill 289-6 1983 $50

ARMSTRONG, JOHN S.   Court of Queen's Bench, Ireland. Dublin: Hodges and Smith, 1844. First edition. 8vo, orig. cloth, printed paper label, light foxing at beginning and end, but a very good copy. Fenning 61-322 1983 £28.50

ARMSTRONG, MARGARET   Murder in Stained Glass. NY (1939). First edition. Two-tone cloth. Very good in slightly worn dust wrapper. King 46-247 1983 $35

ARMSTRONG, MARTIN   Exodus and Other Poems. London: Lynwood & Co., Ltd., 1912. Orig. cloth-backed boards. First edition. Signed by Armstrong on the front free endpaper. Possibly Frederick Prokosch's copy, in a dust-jacket of aluminum foil and paper label with title-in manuscript by Prokosch on the spine. Spine stained. Good copy. MacManus 277-110 1093 $85

ARMSTRONG, MARTIN   Portrait of the Misses Harlowe, A Story. London: Elkin Mathews & Marrott, 1928. Orig. boards. Dust jacket (slightly soiled). First edition. One of 530 signed by the author. Very good copy. MacManus 277-111 1983 $12.50

ARMSTRONG, MARTIN   Saint Christopher's Day. London: Victor Gollancz Ltd., 1928. Orig. half-vellum. First edition. One of 50 copies signed. Fine copy. MacManus 277-112 1983 $40

ARMSTRONG, MARTIN   Saint Christopher's Day. London, 1928. First edition. One of 50 numbered copies, signed by author. Half parchment. Fine. Rota 231-21 1983 £15

ARMSTRONG, MARTIN   Saint Hercules and Other Stories. London: n.d. With drawings by Paul Nash. 4to, cloth-backed decorated bds. Scarce. One of 310 copies. A very good copy. Scarce. Perata 27-34 1983 $135

ARMSTRONG, MARTIN   The Sleeping Fury. London: Victor Gollancz Ltd., 1929. Orig. half-vellum. First edition. Limited to 125 copies signed. Spine a trifle darkened. Fine copy. MacManus 277-113 1983 $35

ARMSTRONG, MOSES K.   Early Empire Builders of Great West. St. Paul, 1901. Illus. Clark 741-241 1983 $31.50

ARMSTRONG, NELSON   Nuggets of Experience...The Sixties and Other Days... San Bernardino, Calif., 1906. 1st ed. Privately printed. Scarce. Jenkins 153-735 1983 $85

ARMSTRONG, NELSON   Nuggets of Experience. (L.A.), 1906. Illus., orig. cloth. First edition. Ginsberg 47-20 1983 $75

ARMSTRONG, WALTER   Sir Henry Raeburn. London: William Heinemann, 1901. 48 photogravure plates with tissue guards. 8 plates in text. Folio. Cloth. Somewhat worn. Ars Libri 32-544 1983 $125

ARMSTRONG, WALTER   Turner. London etc. (Thos. Agnew & Sons, 1902. 103 gravure illus. (79 hors texte). Titled tissue guards. Folio. Cloth. Uncut. Ars Libri 32-678 1983 $100

ARNAUD DE RONSIL, GEORGES   Anatomisch-chirurgische Abhandlung ueber die Hermaphroditen. Strassburg: Amand Koenig, 1777. 6 engraved folding plates. 4to. Cont. boards. Engraved bookplate of Joseph Rehmann (18th century). Kraus 164-10 1983 $850

ARNETT, ALEX M.   The Populist Movement in Georgia. NY: Columbia Univ., 1922. Pr. wraps., backstrip somewhat chipped. Argosy 716-202 1983 $25

ARNOLD, A. S.   Broughton, A Novel. London: Ward & Downey, 1890. 3 vols. Orig. decorated blue cloth. First edition. Spines darkened and slightly worn at the ends and edges. A good, tight set. MacManus 277-114 1983 $185

ARNOLD, ABRAM BLUMENTHAL (1820-1904)   Manual of Nervous Diseases.
San Francisco: The Bancroft Co., 1890 (1855). Second edition,
revised and enlarged. 12mo. Publisher's green cloth. Gach 95-17
1983 $25

ARNOLD, ARTHUR   Through Persia by Caravan. London, 1877.
2 vols., slight foxing, one section in vol. 2 loose, otherwise a
good set. K Books 307-7 1983 £70

ARNOLD, C. A.   An Introduction to Paleobotany. New
York, 1947. 187 illus., 8vo, cloth. Wheldon 160-1356 1983 £15

ARNOLD, E. L.   On the Indian Hills... London, 1893.
New edition. Frontis., illus., slightly soiled. 8vo. Orig. cloth.
Good. Edwards 1044-20 1983 £26

ARNOLD, EDWIN   The Poets of Greece. London: Cassell,
Petter, & Galpin, 1869. Orig. cloth. First edition. Bookplate.
Extremities a bit rubbed. Good copy. MacManus 277-115 1983 $35

ARNOLD, HUGH   Stained Glass of the Middle Ages in
England and France. 1925. Colour plates, slightly worn but good.
K Books 307-8 1983 £18

ARNOLD, MATTHEW   Culture and Anarchy. London: Smith,
Elder, & Co., 1894. Popular Edition. Orig. cloth. Presentation copy,
inscribed by Chesterton on the verso of the flyleaf: "Mrs. Blogg.--
Charity covereth a multitude of virtues. GKC. June 10th, 1897."
With an additional inscription, a quotation from "Our Mutual Friend",
on the verso of the half-title in Chesterton's hand. Very good.
MacManus 277-595 1983 $200

ARNOLD, MATTHEW   Discourses in America. London: Macmillan
and Co., 1885. Orig. cloth. First edition. Two corners bumped. Endpapers slightly foxed. Good copy. MacManus 277-117 1983 $65

ARNOLD, MATTHEW   Essays in criticism. London: Macmillan, 1865. First edition. 8vo. Orig. brown cloth. A bit
rubbed and soiled, inner hinges cracked. Ximenes 63-231 1983
$150

ARNOLD, MATTHEW   Higher Schools and Universities in Germany. Macmillan, 1892. Third edition. Half title, 2 pp. ads. Orig.
dark blue cloth. Very good. Jarndyce 31-41 1983 £12.50

ARNOLD, MATTHEW   Last essays on church and religion.
London: Smith, Elder, 1877. First edition. 8vo. Orig. dark
brown cloth. Very good copy. Ximenes 63-577 1983 $70

ARNOLD, MATTHEW   Last Essays on Church and Religion.
London: Smith, Elder & Co., 1877. Orig. cloth. First edition. Spine
and covers slightly worn. Very good copy. MacManus 277-118 1983 $65

ARNOLD, MATTHEW   Letters 1848-1888. Macmillan, 1895.
First edition, half titles, 2 pp ads. vol. I. Orig. dark blue cloth,
v.g. Jarndyce 30-881 1983 £24

ARNOLD, MATTHEW   Merope. A tragedy. London: Longman,
etc., 1857. First edition. 8vo. Orig. green cloth. In Carter's
"A" binding, with an inserted 32-page catalogue dated November 1857.
Ximenes 63-433 1983 $80

ARNOLD, MATTHEW   Mixed Essays. Smith, Elder, 1880. 2nd
edition. Half title, orig. blue cloth. Very good. Jarndyce 31-418
1983 £18

ARNOLD, MATTHEW   New Poems. London, 1867. First edition.
Covers a little marked. Initials on verso of flyleaf. Bookplate.
H. Walpole's copy, with his Brackenburn bookplate, his autograph
inscription, and a stanza copied out in his hand from Arnold's poem
"Obermann Once More." Nice. Rota 231-22 1983 £35

ARNOLD, MATTHEW   Poems, New and Complete Edition. Macmillan, 1877. 2 vols. Half titles. Orig. green cloth, slight ink
marking of spines, otherwise very good. Second collected edition.
Jarndyce 31-417 1983 £24

ARNOLD, MATTHEW   Poems. London: Macmillan & Co., 1885.
3 vols. Orig. cloth. First of this edition which Smart calls the
"Library Edition." Contains two new poems "Westminster Abbey" and
"Poor Matthias." Covers and spines very slightly worn, with some
foxing to the preliminary pages. Very good set. MacManus 277-119
1983 $85

ARNOLD, MATTHEW   Saint Brandan. London: E.W. & A. Skip-
with, 1867. Orig. brown paper wrappers. Probable forgery. John
Drinkwater's copy, with his signature and date of acquisition on the
half-title, with the pencil note: "The rare first edition, perfect,
in wrappers as issued." Tiny tear at base of spine. In a cloth case,
bearing Drinkwater's bookplate. Very fine copy. MacManus 277-120
1983 $250

ARNOLD, MATTHEW   The Scholar Gipsy. Thyrsis. London,
1910. Large quarto, full vellum over boards, gilt, g.t. With ten
illus. in color by W. Russel Flint. One of 100 copies printed on
Japanese vellum and signed by the artist. Duschnes 240-78 1983
$100

ARNOLD, MATTHEW   The Strayed Reveller, and Other Poems.
B. Fellowes, 1849. First edition. Orig. green cloth. Retford Book
Club on upper cover, and membership label inside back cover, both a
little torn. Otherwise very good. Jarndyce 31-416 1983 £110

ARNOLD, MATTHEW   Unpublished Letters of... New Haven:
Yale University Press, 1923. First edition, half title, orig. blue
cloth. Jarndyce 30-882 1983 £10.50

ARNOLD, MATTHEW   Works. London, 1903-04. 15 vols.
8vo. Orig. light blue satin cloth, gilt, gilt decorated spines.
Edition-de-Luxe, limited to 775 sets, portrait printed on Japon
vellum. Spine of vol. 1 damaged and neatly repaired, faded.
Traylen 94-22 1983 $100

ARNOLD, OREN   Wild Life in the Southwest. Dallas,
(1935). Illus. Clark 741-448 1983 $22

ARNOLD, SAMUEL BLAND   Defence and Prison Experiences of a
Lincoln Conspirator. Hattiesburg, 1943. Argosy 710-257 1983 $35

ARNOLD, THOMAS   History of Rome. 1848-50. Volume one,
fifth edition, volumes two and three, fourth editions. 3 vols. 8vo,
orig. cloth, a very good copy. Fenning 60-12 1983 £14.50

ARNOLD, THOMAS   Observations on the Nature, Kinds,
Causes, and Prevention of Insanity. London, 1806. Second edition.
8vo. 2 vols. Half-morocco. Portrait. Fine copy. Gurney 90-7
1983 £185

ARNOLD, WILLIAM HARRIS   First Editions of Bryant, Longfellow,
Emerson, Lowell... Jamaica, New York: The Marion Press, 1901. 2 vols.
in one. 8vo. Half leather with the orig. paper wrappers bound in.
Limited to 1200 and 1500 copies. The price list with the names of
buyers for the first sale is laid in. The second sales catalog is
priced by hand. Leather slightly rubbed. Oak Inoll 49-412 1983 $85

ARNOLDS, E.   Ecology and Coenology of Macrofungi
in Grasslands in the Netherlands. Bibl. Mycol., 1981-82. 8 coloured
plates and 295 text-figures, 3 vols. in 2, 8vo, cloth. Wheldon 160-
1784 1983 £83

ARNOW, HARRIETTE   Hunter's Horn. NY, (1949). Edges very
lightly worn, else very good in slightly soiled, lightly chipped and
frayed very good dustwrapper. Quill & Brush 54-47 1983 $50

ARNSTEIN, FLORIA J.   A Legacy of Hours. San Francisco:
privately printed at the Grabhorn Press, 1927. First edition.
Small 8vo. Cloth-backed decorated boards. Limited to 300 copies.
Presentation from the author. Covers rubbed. Ink spot on front
inside cover. Oak Knoll 48-176 1983 $20

ARP, W.   Avifauna Venezolana. Caracas, 1965.
130 coloured plates by the author, 4to, cloth, special edition
from the Central Bank of Venezuela. Wheldon 160-627 1983 £50

ARRHENIUS, SVANTE   Lehrbuch der Elektrochemie. Leipzig:
Von Quandt & Handel, 1901. 8vo. Modern brown buckram, orig.
paper covers preserved. Diagrams. A good copy. Zeitlin 264-13
1983 $75

ARRHENIUS, SVANTE   Text-book of Electrochemistry.
London: Longmans, 1902. 8vo. Orig. blue cloth with gilt. Ads.
Numerous text figures and tables. A very good copy. Zeitlin
264-14 1983 $45

ARRHENIUS, SVANTE   Theories of Chemistry... London:
Longmans, 1907. 8vo. Orig. red stamped cloth. Tables and charts.
Ownership inscription on title-page and front cover. Zeitlin 264-
15 1983 $40

ARRHENIUS, SVANTE   Theories of Solutions. New Haven:
Yale University Press, 1916. 8vo. Orig. blue cloth with gilt.
A good copy. Zeitlin 264-16 1983 $40

ARRIANUS, FLAVIUS   Ars Tactica. Apud Janssonie-Waesbergios,
1683. Sma. 8vo. Orig. cloth. Additional engraved title, 2 folding
maps and folding plate, text in Greek and Latin. Cont. calf, spine
gilt. Upper joint tender. Good. Edwards 1042-275 1983 £120

THE ART Work of Louis C. Tiffany. Garden City: Doubleday, Page &
Co., 1914. 62 plates with titled tissue-guards (tipped-in color
and photogravure). Small folio. Cloth. T.e.g. Uncut. One of
492 copies on japan paper, of a limited edition of 502 copies,
printed for private circulation. With the engraved armorial bookplate of Louis C. Tiffany tipped-in on a preliminary leaf. Ars
Libri 32-662 1983 $850

ART DIRECTORS CLUB OF CHICAGO   Record of Advertising Art. Chicago,
1944. Mostly illus. Cloth, tattered dust wrapper (blind-stamped names
on both endpapers). King 45-306 1983 $25

ART of Ancient Egypt. Vienna, Phaidon Press, (1936). 340 reproductions; rotogravure and colour plates. Tall 8vo. Illus. Morrill
286-29 1983 $25

ARTHUR, GEORGE   Life of Lord Kitchener. New York:
Macmillan, 1920. 3 vols. 8vo. Orig. red cloth. Adelson Africa-
157 1983 $40

ARTHUR, ROBERT   Treatment and Prevention of Decay of
the Teeth. Illus., 16mo; ex-lib. First edition. Argosy 713-13
1983 $35

ARTHUR, STANLEY C.   Audubon, an Intimate Life of the
American Woodsman. New Orleans, 1937. Illus. Inscription by
author on his stationery tipped in. Argosy 710-17 1983 $30

ARTHUR, STANLEY C.   The Story of the West Florida Rebellion.
St. Francisville, 1935. Orig. printed wrappers. Illus. Maps. Jenkins
152-209 1983 $75

ARTHUR, T. S.   The History of Kentucky, from its Earliest
Settlement to the Present Time. Phila., 1852. First edition.
Frontis. ("Daniel Boon"). Cloth. Spine ends chipped. Very good.
Felcone 20-83 1983 $35

ARTIOLI, NERIO   Bartolomeo Spani. Reggio Emilia:
Privately Printed, 1964. 67 plates (partly in color). Text
illus. Large 4to. Cloth. Dust jacket. Edition limited to 520
numbered copies. Ars Libri 33-347 1983 $135

ARTIST & Tradesman's Guide. NY, 1829. 12mo, calf, gilt spine,
last pp. dampstained. 3rd edition. Argosy 716-301 1983 $40

ARTISTIC Relief Ornamentation in Exterior Composition. Chicago (1916).
Photos, cloth, couple stamped names, some cover wear else good.
King 46-382 1983 $35

THE ART'S Anthology: Dartmouth Verse 1925. Mosher Press, 1925.
12mo. Boards. 1 of 500 copies. Name on fly, else fine. In Our
Time 156-237 1983 $75

ARTZYBASHEFF, BORIS   Seven Simeons. N.Y.: Viking, 1937.
First edition. Large 4to. Green cloth. Worn dust wrapper. Color
illus. Very good to fine. Aleph-bet 8-21 1983 $30

ARTZYBASHEFF, BORIS   Three and The Moon. N.Y.: Knopf, 1929.
Cloth-backed patterned boards, light wear. Limited edition of 250
copies, No. 61. Signed by Artzybasheff. Printed on Normandy vellum.
Full-page color illus., black & whites in text. Very good to fine.
Aleph-bet 8-20 1983 $275

ASCHAFFENBURG, GUSTAV   Ueber Die Stimmungsschwankungen Der
Epileptiker. Halle: Carl Marhold, 1906. First edition. Modern
cloth. M. J. Karpas' copy (unsigned) with his notes. Gach 95-18
1983 $37.50

ASCHAM, ROGER   The English Works of... London: for
R. and J. Dodsley and J. Newberry, 1761. First edition. 4to. Cont.
tree calf, fully gilt panelled spine, joints neatly repaired. Traylen
94-23 1983 £15

ASCHE, SIEGFRIED   Balthasar Permoser und die Barockskulptur des Dresdner Zwingers. Frankfurt: Weidlich, 1966. 322
illus. 4to. Cloth. Dust jacket. Ars Libri 32-507 1983 $75

ASCHE, SIEGFRIED   Balthasar Permoser. Leben und Werk.
Berlin: Deutscher Verein fur Kunstwissenschaft, 1978. 353 illus.
hors texte (4 color). Large 4to. Cloth. Dust jacket. Ars Libri
32-506 1983 $75

ASH, JOHN   The New and Complete Dictionary of the
English Language. Edward & Charles Dilly; and R. Baldwin, 1775.
Lacking front free end papers. Two vols. Calf rubbed; red labels,
defective vol. II. Jarndyce 31-21 1983 £75

ASHBEE, C. R.   American Sheaves & English Seed Corn:
Being a Series of Addresses Mainly Delivered in the United States,
1900-1901. N.p., 1901. 8vo, limp vellum, gilt. Printed in red and
black. Fine copy with large woodcut initials, tail-piece. Perata
27-42 1983 $175

ASHBEE, C. R.   Kingfisher out of Egypt. OUP, 1934.
7 illus. Blue decorated boards, white parchment backed. Edition
limited to 750 copies, No. 263. Presentation copy from Ashbee to
Rackham, dated, Xmas 1935. Greer 40-184 1983 $27.50

ASHBEE, C. R.   The Last Records of A Cotswold Community.
London: Essex House Press, 1904. Octavo. Almost completely unopened.
Illus. with drawings by Edmund H. New. Of 225 copies, 1/75 preferred
copies on Essex House paper. Covers slightly darkened, else very fine.
Bookplate. Bromer 25-200 1983 $400

ASHBERY, JOHN   Apparitions. Northridge, 1981. The
deluxe edition, ltd. to only 50 copies, each signed by all the poets.
Houle 21-33 1983 $85

ASHBERY, JOHN.   Fragment. Black Sparrow Press, 1969.
Illustrated by Alex Katz. 8vo. Leather, boards. 1 of 20 copies
lettered and signed by Ashbery and Katz. Each of the lettered
copies contain an original ink drawing by Katz, signed, tipped into
the book. A fine copy in acetate jacket and slipcase box. In Our
Time 156-28 1983 $750

ASHBERY, JOHN   The Tennis Court Oath. Middletown,
Connecticut, 1962. First edition. With the ownership signature of
the poet Peter Riley. Small stamp on front free endpaper. Nicked
dustwrapper darkened at the spine. Fine. Jolliffe 26-15 1983 £45

ASHBERY, JOHN   Three Plays. Calais, Vt.: Z Press, 1978.
First edition thus. One of 26 lettered copies, signed by the author.
Very good. Houle 21-42 1983 $75

ASHBURY, HERBERT   Carry Nation: the Woman with the
Hatchet. N.Y., Knopf, 1929. First edition. Black cloth decorated
with deco gilt design (spine faded). One of 150 copies on large
paper. Signed by the author. Good - very good. Houle 22-44 1983
$35

ASHBY, THOMAS   Turner's Vision of Rome. London, 1925.
12 tipped-in color plates, 16 monochrome plates. 4to. Cloth.
Salloch 385-323 1983 $40

ASHE, THOMAS   The Spirit of the Book. Allen & Co.,
1812. 3 vols., 12mo, final advertisement leaf. Cont. tree calf,
gilt. Hannas 69-4 1983 $35

ASHMEAD-BARTLETT, ELLIS   With the Turks in Thrace. Heinemann, 1913. First edition, with a folding map and 32 plates, errata slip, 8vo, orig. cloth, a very good copy. Fenning 61-15 1983 £18.50

ASHTON, JOHN   Humour, Wit and Satire of the Seventeenth Century. Chatto & Windus, 1883. First edition. Half title, frontis. & illus. 32 pp. ads. Orig. green dec. cloth. Very good. Signed presentation copy from the author, Oct. 1883, to Wm. Smith, FSA. Jarndyce 31-420 1983 £32

ASHTON, JOHN   Legendary History of the Cross. 1887. Sixty-four woodcuts. 8vo, pictorial decorated vellum, brass claps. K Books 307-10 1983 £48

ASHTON, JOHN   Real Sailor Songs... London: The Leadenhall Press, 1891. Folio. Orig. grey printed paper boards, vellum spine, uncut edges. Vignette title-page printed in red and black, 200 woodcuts, and 4 pp. of ads. Traylen 94-25 1983 £80

ASHWORTH, JOHN HENRY   Rathlynn. London: Hurst & Blackett, 1864. 3 vols. Orig. cloth. First edition. A few inner hinges cracked; slightly worn. Small portion of title page torn away in each vol. Scarce. MacManus 277-121 1983 £75

ASIMOV, ISAAC   3 by Asimov. New York: Targ Editions, 1981. First edition. One of 250 copies, signed by author. 4to. Full Belgian linen. Rice-paper wrapper. Fine. Rota 230-31 1983 £60

ASKINS, CHARLES   Modern Shotguns and Loads. Marshallton, Del., (1929). 1st ed. Illus. 8vo. Morrill 288-103 1983 $35

ASPINALL, JAMES   Roscoe's Library; or, Old Books and Old Times. Whittaker; Liverpool: Deighton & Laughton, 1853. First edition, Medallion half title, orig. blue cloth, v.g. Jarndyce 31-882 1983 £25

ASPLUND, KARL   Zorn's Engraved Work. Stockholm, 1920. 2 vols. Limited to 325 copies. Large 4to. Orig. wrappers. In the 2 orig. boxes; one box partly broken. Very nice. Morrill 289-260 1983 $550.

ASQUITH, CYNTHIA   This Mortal Coil. Sauk City, Wisconsin: Arkham House, 1947. Orig. cloth. Dust jacket. First edition. Fine copy. MacManus 277-123 1983 $25

ASQUITH, HERBERT   Poems, 1912-1933. London: Sidgwick & Jackson, Ltd., 1934. Orig. cloth. First edition. Presentation copy, inscribed on the flyleaf to "Vita Nicholson (Vita Sackville-West) from Herbert Asquith, 1934," with an ALS, 1 page. Covers partially faded. Nice copy. MacManus 277-124 1983 $100

ASSISI, FRANCIS OF
Please turn to
FRANCESCO D'ASSISI, SAINT

THE ASSOCIATION OF MAKERS OF ESPARTO PAPERS.   Esparto Paper. N.P.: Newman Neame, 1956. 4to. Blue cloth. Fine. Oak Knoll 48-318 1983 $85

ASTELL, MARY   An Essay in Defence of the Female Sex. London: for A. Roper and E. Wilkinson, and R. Clavel, 1696. First edition. 8vo. Cont. sheep. Engraved frontis. Small hole in corner of frontis., binding a little worn, early script on endpapers and front fly-leaf. Traylen 94-27 1983 £280

ASTON, FRANCIS WILLIAM   Mass-Spectra and Isotopes. London: Edward Arnold, 1933. First edition. 8vo. Orig. blue cloth with gilt. 8 plates, 7 tables. A little shook, ex-libris, otherwise a fine copy. Zeitlin 264-21 1983 $125

ASTON, FRANCIS WILLIAM   The Mass-Spectra of Chemical Elements. London, 1920. Offprint. 8vo. Paper wrappers. 1 plate. Ex-libris with a little wear, otherwise a very good copy. Zeitlin 264-22 1983 $60

AT SEA with Ahto. N.P., Privately Printed, 1937. Edition limited to 50 copies but not numbered. Illustrated; endpaper maps. Morrill 290-85 1983 $25

ATAL, C. K.   Cultivation and utilization of medicinal and aromatic plants. Jammu-Tawi, 1982. New edition, 2 vols., 8vo, cloth. Wheldon 160-2158 1983 £48

ATHERTON, GERTRUDE   The Conqueror. New York: MacMillan, 1902. 1st ed., 1st issue. Orig. maroon cloth, spangled in white and gilt, t.e.g. A very fine fresh copy. Jenkins 155-36 1983 $25

ATHERTON, GERTRUDE   The Splendid Idle Forties. New York: MacMillan, 1902. Frontis., plates. 1st ed. Orig. decorated red cloth, gilt. Fine bright copy. Jenkins 155-38 1983 $40

ATHERTON, GERTRUDE   The Splendid Idle Forties. N.Y., 1902. First edition. Illus. by H. Fisher. Decorated cloth. Ink inscription. Extremities worn, slightly soiled. King 45-145 1983 $25

ATHERTON, SARA   Brass-Eagles. Philadelphia, (1935). 8vo. Cloth. Very good-fine copy in rubbed dust jacket. Long blurb on front jacket by William Rose Benet. In Our Time 156-29 1983 $20

ATKINS, ARTHUR   Arthur Atkins. San Francisco, 1908. 1st ed. Illus. Small 8vo, orig. boards, vellum back. Morrill 288-577 1983 $25

ATKINS, WILLIAM   The Art and Practice of Printing... London: Sir Isaac Pitman & Sons, 1934. 8vo. Cloth. 5 vols. Library bookplate else very good condition. Oak Knoll 40-19 1983 $70

ATKINSON, BLANCHE   The Real Princess. A.D. Innes, 1894. Frontis. 4 full-page & 14 text illus. Silver decorated cloth. Greer 39-77 1983 £35

ATKINSON, C. T.   The Dorsetshire Regiment. Oxford, 1947. 2 vols. 7 folding maps at end, 48 maps in text, 3 plans (1 folding). Fine. Edwards 1042-542 1983 £35

ATKINSON, THOMAS WITLAM   Travels in the Regions of the Upper and Lower Amoor and the Russian Acquisitions on the Confines of India and China with Adventures Among the Mountain Kirghis. New York, 1860. Map, numerous illus., new cloth. K Books 301-10 1983 £30

ATKINSON, THOMAS   Hibernian eclogues, and miscellaneous poems. Dublin: W. Adams, 1802. First edition. 12mo, sewn fragments of original wrappers). Uncut. Ximenes 63-390 1983 $90

THE ATLANTIC and Gulf Coast Canal and Okeechobee Land Company. Jacksonville, (1881). Large folding map in color. Printed wrappers (detached). Wrappers and title page borders heavily dust-soiled. Rare prospectus. Bradley 65-70 1983 $55

ATLAS of the American Revolution. Chicago: Rand McNally: (1974). First edition. Numerous maps and illus. Folio. Full leather. Inscribed presentation note on title page. Bradley 66-446 1983 $75

ATLAS of the Boundaries of the City of Lowell... N.P., 1907. Maps. Large folio, orig. cloth, leather back, backstrip partly torn and top 5 inches lacking. Morrill 288-260 1983 $40

ATTERBURY, FRANCIS   An Answer to Some Considerations on the Spirit of Martin Luther and the Original of the Reformation. Oxford, Printed at the Theater, 1687. First edition, 4to, wrapper, little dusty, but a very good copy. Fenning 61-16 1983 £18.50

ATTERBURY, FRANCIS   Concio Ad Clerum Londinensem. Londini, typis J. B. impensis J. Bowyer, 1709. 1st edition, 4to, advertisements, stabsewn and unbound, but with the edges trimmed and gilt. Presentation copy from the author, inscribed on the half-title "Sr William Trumbull" in the author's hand. Pickering & Chatto 19-3 1983 $150

ATTERIDGE, A. H.   Napoleon's Brothers. London, 1909. First edition. 18 plates and 6 maps. 8vo. Bound in half red morocco, gilt, gilt panelled spine with Napoleonic emblems., edges gilt, by Bayntun. Traylen 94-626 1983 £28

ATTWELL, MABEL LUCIE   Fairy Tales. Valentine n.d. (inscr.1922). Pictorial title. 2 colour plates. 2 full-page & 6 text illus. Grey wrappers. Onlaid extra colour plate. Dusty & worn. Greer 39-21 1983 £12.50

ATTWELL, MABEL LUCIE   'Manty' A Fairy Tale. B. B., Ltd., n.d. 4to. 10 colour pictorial pages. Colour pictorial wrappers, rubbed. Greer 39-22 1983 £11

ATTWELL, MABEL LUCIE   Once Upon a Time. Tuck, n.d. 4to. Colour frontis. Title vignette & 15 tinted text illus. Beige wrappers pictorial. Extra onlaid colour plate, light wear. Greer 40-35 1983 £18.50

AUBLIGNAC, FRANCOIS HEDELIN, ABBE D'   The Whole Art of the Stage. London: printed for the author, and sold by William Cadman; Rich. Bentley; Sam. Smith; and T. Fox, 1684. 4to. cont. calf, spine gilt (neatly rebacked, original spine laid down, corners restored; a trifle worn). 1st edition in English. A fine copy. Ximenes 64-260 1983 $550

AUBRY, OCTAVE   Le Roi De Rome. Paris: Calmann Levy, (1936). 4to. Cloth backed pictorial boards. Frayed dust wrapper. Illus. by Carlegle. Fine. Aleph-bet 8-112 1983 $30

AUBRY, OCTAVE   St. Helena. London, 1937. 8vo. Half red morocco, gilt, t.e.g. Traylen 94-627 1983 £21

AUCASSIN & Nicolette. Hammersmith: Eragny Press, 1903. Octavo. From press of Lucien Pissaro with wood engr. by him as frontis. Last book printed in Vale type at Eragney. Limited to 230 copies. Lightly rubbed at extremities, else extremely fine in gilt-stamped and floral patterned boards. Bromer 25-199 1983 $175

AUCHINCLOSS, LOUIS   The Indifferent Children. NY, (1947). Cover lightly soiled, edges just starting to fray, else very good in frayed and wearing, still presentable dustwrapper. Quill & Brush 54-51 1983 $100

AUDAS, J. W.   Native trees of Australia. 1935. Numerous illus. (8 coloured), 8vo, cloth. Wheldon 160-2069 1983 £15

AUDEN, WYSTAN HUGH   The Age of Anxiety. N.Y., (1947). First edition. Small 12mo, d.w. Fine. Argosy 714-24 1983 $100

AUDEN, WYSTAN HUGH   The Age of Anxiety. New York, 1947. First edition. Frayed dust wrapper. Name of flyleaf. Very nice. Rota 230-33 1983 £25

AUDEN, WYSTAN HUGH   The Age of Anxiety. London, 1948. First English edition. Dust wrapper. Fine. Rota 231-29 1983 £20

AUDEN, WYSTAN HUGH   Another Time. London, 1940. First English edition. Torn dust wrapper. Name on flyleaf. Fine. Rota 231-27 1983 £30

AUDEN, WYSTAN HUGH   City Without Walls and Other Poems. New York, (1969). First edition, first printing. Tan cloth, red cloth spine. Very fine in dust jacket. Bradley 66-10 1983 $25

AUDEN, WYSTAN HUGH   The Dance of Death. (London): Faber & Faber, (1933). First edition. 8vo. Orig. boards. Dust jacket. Very fine copy. Jaffe 1-18 1983 $350

AUDEN, WYSTAN HUGH   The Dance of Death. London, 1933. First edition. Spine darkened and worn. Hinges cracked. Very good. Rota 231-25 1983 £30

AUDEN, WYSTAN HUGH   The Dog Beneath The Skin... London: Faber and Faber Limited, (1935). 8vo. Orig. cloth. Dust jacket. Slightly worn jacket, with the Group Theatre flyer laid in. First edition. Fine. Jaffe 1-21 1983 $185

AUDEN, WYSTAN HUGH   The Double Man. NY: (1941). First edition. Small stain to fore-edge, else fine with very slightly chipped dust wrapper. Bromer 25-3 1983 $125

AUDEN, WYSTAN HUGH   The Dyer's Hand and Other Essays. London, (1963). 1st English ed. 8vo. Cloth. Louis Untermeyer copy with a short ALS from Auden dated 1972 laid in. With envelope. Fine copy in dj which is lightly rubbed. In Our Time 156-31 1983 $125

AUDEN, WYSTAN HUGH   Epistle to a Godson. London, 1972. Inscribed on the title page to Elizabeth Jennings, and signed by Auden. Dustwrapper. Fine. Gekoski 2-205 1983 £125

AUDEN, WYSTAN HUGH   Journey to a War. London, 1939. First edition. Spine a little creased. Frayed dust wrapper. Very nice. Rota 230-36 1983 £30

AUDEN, WYSTAN HUGH   The Latest Ferrule. (Paris, Frederick Prokosch) Christmas, 1968 (1934). 32mo, printed on stiff blue-grey paper, stitched with dark red thread. Illus. with an orig. tipped in color erotic painting by Prokosch. Gold paper wraps., blue paper printed label on upper cover. Fine copy. This copy is marked: "Out of Series - Duplicate of Omega." Prokosch has altered the title page and inscribed the date 1968. One of two copies so issued. Houle 21-46 1983 $450

AUDEN, WYSTAN HUGH   Letters From Iceland. London: Faber and Faber, (1937). First edition. 8vo. Illus. Orig. cloth. Dust jacket. Slightly dust-soiled jacket, with the Book Society wrap-around band. Fine. Jaffe 1-22 1983 $125

AUDEN, WYSTAN HUGH   Letters from Iceland. London, 1937. First edition. Illus. Covers dust-marked. Name of flyleaf. Nice. Rota 230-37 1983 £21

AUDEN, WYSTAN HUGH   Look, Stranger! London: Faber & Faber Limited, (1936). First edition. 8vo. Orig. cloth. Dust jacket. Jacket a trifle nicked at head of spine, otherwise a very fine copy. Jaffe 1-19 1983 $225

AUDEN, WYSTAN HUGH   Look, Stranger! London, 1936. First edition. Edges of covers a little dust-marked. Nice. Rota 231-26 1983 £30

AUDEN, WYSTAN HUGH   New Year Letter. London, 1941. First English edition. Slightly torn dust wrapper. Very nice. Rota 231-28 1983 £30

AUDEN, WYSTAN HUGH   On This Island. New York, (1937). First American edition. Brown cloth. Fine in worn dust jacket. Bradley 66-13 1983 $55

AUDEN, WYSTAN HUGH   On This Island. New York, (1937). First American edition, first impression (with a flat spine). Brown cloth. Scarce. 2,000 issued. Fine in worn dj. Bradley 65-18 1983 $45

AUDEN, WYSTAN HUGH   The Orators. An English Study. London: Faber & Faber Limited, (1932). First edition. 8vo. Orig. cloth. Dust jacket. Unopened. Very fine. Jaffe 1-16 1983 $350

AUDEN, WYSTAN HUGH   The Orators, an English Study. London: (1932). First edition. Top of spine faintly rubbed and bottom corners lightly bumped, still fine. Signed on title-page by Auden. Bromer 25-4 1983 $200

AUDEN, WYSTAN HUGH   The Orators. London, 1932. First edition. One of 1000 copies. Spine slightly faded. Very nice. Rota 231-24 1983 £50

AUDEN, WYSTAN HUGH   Poems. London, 1930. First edition. Wrappers. Backstrip partially defective and margins of several leaves stained. Good reading copy. Rota 231-23 1983 £50

AUDEN, WYSTAN HUGH   Poems. London: Faber & Faber, (1933). Second edition. 8vo. Orig. cloth. Dust jacket. Jacket very slightly darkened and nicked, otherwise a fine unopened copy. Very scarce. Jaffe 1-17 1983 $425

AUDEN, WYSTAN HUGH   Poems. London, 1933. Second edition, revised. One of 1000 copies. Upper corners a little water-stained. Slightly frayed dust wrapper. Very good. Rota 230-32 1983 £20

AUDEN, WYSTAN HUGH   Poems. NY, (1934). First American edition. Very good in dustwrapper with some major losses and darkened spine. Quill & Brush 54-54 1983 $75

AUDEN, WYSTAN HUGH   Poems. NY, (1934). First American
edition. Very good. Quill & Brush 54-53 1983 $40

AUDEN, WYSTAN HUGH   The Poet's Tongue. London, 1935. First
One-Volume edition. Slightly frayed dust wrapper. Tipped in is a
slip bearing Auden's autograph signature. Very nice. Rota 230-35
1983 £30

AUDEN, WYSTAN HUGH   Sleep on Beside Me. (Paris, Frederick
Prokosch) Christmas, 1968 (1934). 32mo, illus. with an orig.
tipped erotic painting by Frederick Prokosch. Silver foil wraps.,
gold paper label, stitched with black thread; with an extra label
tipped in inside the back cover. Acetate jacket. Very good-fine.
Houle 21-47 1983 $450

AUDEN, WYSTAN HUGH   Spain. (London): Faber & Faber, (1937).
Printed wraps. First edition. Pub.'s review copy, with dated slip
laid in. Wraps. slightly darkened at edges, else fine. Reese 20-50
1983 $100

AUDEN, WYSTAN HUGH   Spain. (London): Faber and Faber,
(1937). First edition. 8vo. Orig. wrappers. Very fine copy.
Jaffe 1-20 1983 $100

AUDEN, WYSTAN HUGH   Three Songs for St. Cecilia's Day.
(N.Y.): Privately printed, 1941. Small 8vo, blue wraps. Stitched
with blue cord. One of 250 unnumbered copies, issued as a Christmas
greeting by Caroline Newton sent by A. E. Newton. Fine, in orig.
mailing envelope. Argosy 714-28 1983 $400

AUDSLEY, GEORGE ASHDOWN   The Art of Organ Building. NY, 1905.
Profusely illus. Tow vols. The orig. edition. Two vols. Frontis.
portrait etching. Titles in red and black. Thick folio, library
buckram. Ex-library, with bookplate and release. Fine set. Salloch
387-265 1983 $150

AUDUBON, JOHN JAMES   Audubon's America: The Narrative and
Experiences of... Boston, 1940. First edition. Quarto. Illus. with
17 double-page color plates, including self-portrait. Jenkins 151-10
1983 $65

AUDUBON, JOHN JAMES   The Birds of America. 1937. Portrait,
facsimile title-page and 500 coloured plates, royal 4to, original
buckram. Wheldon 160-630 1983 £50

AUDUBON, JOHN JAMES   The Birds of America. New York: 1937.
First printing of this edition. 500 color plates. Orig. green cloth,
gilt. Very good copy. Bradley 66-466 1983 $55

AUDUBON, JOHN JAMES   Delineations of American Scenery & Character. NY, 1926. Frontis. Argosy 710-16 1983 $30

AUDUBON, JOHN JAMES   Journal Made During His Trip to New
Orleans in 1820-1821. Cambridge, Business Historical Society, 1929.
8vo. Morrill 289-261 1983 $42.50

AUDUBON, JOHN JAMES   Journal of John James Audubon.
Cambridge: The Business Historical Society, 1929. 4to. Cloth.
Presentation copy from the publisher. Ars Libri 32-12 1983 $60

AUDUBON, JOHN JAMES   The Original Water-Color Paintings by
John James Audubon for the Birds of America. New York, 1966.
2 volumes. Small Folio. Profusely illustrated with lovely
colored bird plates. An extremely, fine and important edition.
Boxed. Jenkins 151-9 1983 $200

AUDUBON, JOHN JAMES   The Original Water-Color Paintings by...
for The Birds of America. New York: American Heritage, 1966. First
edition. 421 color plates. Quarto, 2 vols. Light brown cloth, marbled end papers. Very fine in slipcase, as issued. Bradley 66-467
1983 $125

AUDUBON, JOHN JAMES   The Original Water Color Paintings by
John James Audubon for the Birds of America. New York, 1966.
Frontispiece portrait in color, 431 color plates. 2 vols., brown
buckram. Original edition. Fine in slipcase. Bradley 65-20 1983
$145

AUDUBON, JOHN JAMES   Ornithological Biography. Edinburgh-
1831-39. 5 vols., royal 8vo, Vols. 3-5 original cloth (rebacked),
vols. 1-2 bound to match. Blind stamp on title-page of Vol. I.
Slight marginal stains in vol. I and a few leaves foxed in vol. 2.
An uncut copy. Wheldon 160-629 1983 £320

AUENBRUGGER, JOSEPH LEOPOLD Aphorismus Hippocratis, LII, Sect. II.
Vienna: Gregor Kurtzbock, 1752. Woodcut initial, head- and tail-
piece. Small 4to. Contemporary marbled wrappers. In a cloth box.
Very rare. Kraus 164-13 1983 $2,500

AUENBRUGGER, JOSEPH LEOPOLD Inventum nobum ex percussione thoracis
humani... Vienna: Johann Thomas Trattner, 1761. Woodcut headpieces and title-page vignette (tab on title). 8vo. Modern crimson
morocco. Front the library of Crawford M. Adams, with his bookplate.
First edition, first issue. Kraus 164-14 1983 $8,500

AUENBRUGGER, JOSEPH LEOPOLD Nouvelle methode pour reconnaitre
les maladies internes de la poitrine par la percussion de cette
cavite. Paris: Migneret, 1808. First edition of Corvisart's
translation. 8vo. Cont. half calf. Complete with the half-title
and final leaf of errata. A very fine copy. Ximenes 63-269 1983
$1,750

AUERBACH, G.   Anthracen Its Constitution, Properties,
Manufacture, and Derivatives... London: Longmans, 1877. 8vo.
Orig. red blind stamped cloth. Ads. Very good copy. Zeitlin 264-
23 1983 $50

AUERBACH, G.   Anthracen Its Constitution, Properties,
Manufacture, and Derivatives... London: Longmans, 1877. 8vo.
Modern cloth. Ads. Very good. Zeitlin 264-24 1983 $40

AUFRER, ANTHONY   The Cannibals' Progress. Newburyport,
(1798). Dsb. Reese 18-227 1983 $35

AUGUSTIN, JAMES M.   Official Souvenir Programme of the
Transfer of Louisiana from France to the United States. New Orleans,
1903. Illus. Orig. printed wraps. First edition. Ginsberg 46-415
1983 $25

AUGUSTUS, ARUELIUS   The Golden Book of Saint Augustine Commonly Called the Confessions. N.p.: 1935. Octavo. Printer's dummy.
Two proof engravings by Howard Simon included. Laid-in is binding
quote fron The Trade Bindery of San Francisco to the Windsor Press.
Very fine in cloth with leather spine. Bromer 25-245 1983 $1,000

AULUS GELLIUS   Noctes Atticae, Lvgdvni, Apvd
Haered. Seb. Gryphii, 1559. 16mo, old morocco, cover detached,
well-used copy with minor stains, blank edge of few pages nicked
as for index. Ravenstree 95-15 1983 $92

AUNGERVILLE, RICHARD   Philobiblon, a Treatise on the Love of
Books. London: Thomas Rodd, 1832. First English edition. 8vo.
Modern half leather over orig. boards, t.e.g. With the erratum slip.
Only minor cover wear, else very nice. Oak Knoll 49-321 1983 $400

AUNGERVILLE, RICHARD   The Philobiblon of Richard de Bury...
New York: The Grolier Club, 1889. 8vo. Full vellum, gilt
decorated, orig. slipcases. Limited to 300 copies. Worn slipcases.
Very good copy. Oak Knoll 48-322 1983 $225

AUNGERVILLE, RICHARD   The Philobiblon of Richard de Bury...
New York: Lockwood and Coombes, 1889. First U.S. edition of the
Thomas translation. 8vo. Red polished buckram, t.e.g., others
uncut. From the library of Lee Edmonds Grove. Spine faded, else
very good. Oak Knoll 49-322 1983 $50

AUNT Judy's Christmas Volume for 1873. Geo. Bell, 1873. Illus. by
Patterson, Griset, A.W. Bayes, A.W. Cooper, Petherick S. Hall, etc.
Pub's decor. cloth. Lower edges sl. worn, occasional fox mark, very
good. Hodgkins 27-8 1983 £18

AUNT Judy's Christmas Volume for 1875. Geo. Bell, 1875. Illus. by
Petherick, A.W. Bayes, Gordon Browne, A.S. Gatty, etc. Pub's decor.
cloth. Top fr. corner bumped, nice copy. Hodgkins 27-9 1983 £15

AUNT Louisa's National Album. F. Warne, n.d. (ca.1878). 4to.
24 plates colour printed by Kronheim. Brown pictorial cloth, gilt,
rubbed. Greer 40-78 1983 £32.50

AUNT Mavor's Alphabet. George Routledge, n.d. (ca.1858). 24 hand-coloured images on 8pp., edges repaired. Limp orange cloth. Greer 40-12 1983 £25

AURELIUS, MARCUS   Marci Antonini Imperatoris. Londini, Impensis Edv. Millingtoni, 1697. 4to, 19th century quarter calf, boards, much soiled and worn, front cover and fly leaf detached, small bookplate, spots of foxing. Ravenstree 95-17 1983 $37.50

AURELIUS, MARCUS   The Meditations. Glasgow, printed by Robert Foulis et al., 1742. 8vo, orig. calf (covers detached, cont. bookplate of "The Honble William Robertson" and with some age darkening throughout), decent copy. Ravenstree 95-18 1983 $95

AURELIUS ANTONINUS, MARCUS   The Meditations of...Newly Translated from the Greek. Glasgow: Printed by Robert Foulis, 1742. First edition of this translation, large 12mo, blank corner of one leaf torn off and name partially erased from upper blank margin of title, otherwise nice in cont. calf. Fenning 60-14 1983 £45

AUSTEN, JANE   Complete Novels. London, Heinemann, (1928). First edition thus. Thick 8vo, bound in full brown morocco, raised bands on gilt panelled spine, covers ruled in gilt, edges extra gilt, marbled endpapers, by Bayntun. A fine binding in fine condition. Houle 21-49 1983 $265

AUSTEN, JANE   Emma; a Novel. London: for John Murray, 1816. First edition. 12mo. 3 vols. Half brown morocco, gilt. Half-titles in vols. 1 and 2. Traylen 94-30 1983 £395

AUSTEN, JANE   Lady Susan. Oxford, Clarendon Press, 1925. 8vo, quarter buckram, paper boards, printed paper label, uncut, a fine copy. 250 copies printed by Humphrey Milford on hand-made paper. Deighton 3-14 1983 £35

AUSTEN, JANE   Mansfield Park: A Novel. London: for T. Egerton. First edition. 3 vols. 12mo. Half brown morocco, gilt, fore-margins trimmed. Traylen 94-31 1983 £330

AUSTEN, JANE   Northanger Abbey: and Persuasion. London: John Murray, 1818. First edition. 4 vols. 12mo. Half brown morocco, gilt. Traylen 94-32 1983 £375

AUSTEN, JANE   The Novels of Jane Austen. New York: Frank S. Holby, 1906. 10 vols. Illus. with color plates by C. E. & H. M. Brock. Orig. cloth with paper spine labels. Old Manor House Edition. One of 1000 copies. Spine labels slightly darkened and a trifle rubbed. Good, clean set. MacManus 277-126 1983 $165

AUSTEN, JANE   The Novels of Jane Austen. Edinburgh: John Grant, 1911-1912. Complete in 12 vols. Photogravure frontis. in volume 1. Fine set in blue cloth with gilt-stamped spines. T.e.g. Karmiole 75-15 1983 $350

AUSTEN, JANE   The Novels of Jane Austen. Oxford: the Clarendon Press, 1923. 5 vols. Roy. 8vo. Marbled boards, grey cloth spines, printed paper labels, uncut edges. Limited edition of 1000 sets on large paper. 45 illus., including 6 coloured costume plates. Traylen 94-28 1983 £275

AUSTEN, JANE   Plan of a Novel. Oxford, at the Clarendon Press, 1926. Printed from the originals. 4to, half title, facs. Marbled boards, cloth spine, label. Limited to 350 copies. Jarndyce 31-421 1983 £50

AUSTEN, JANE   Pride and Prejudice. Printed for T. Egerton, 1817. 3rd edition, 2 vols. Rebound in half calf, labels. Jarndyce 30-286 1983 £120

AUSTEN, JANE   Pride and Prejudice. NY: Bunce & Brother, Publishers, 1855. 10 pages of pub. ads. Orig. brown cloth, gilt spine. Karmiole 74-20 1983 $75

AUSTEN, JANE   Pride & Prejudice. Dent, 1907 (Eng. Idylls series). 1st edn. 24 colour plates by C.E. Brock. Pale green cloth gilt, t.e.g. others uncut, v. nice copy. Hodgkins 27-405 1983 £14

AUSTEN, JANE   Pride and Prejudice. London: for T. Egerton, 1913. Second edition. 3 vols. 12mo. Half brown morocco, gilt. Traylen 94-33 1983 £250

AUSTEN, JANE   Sense and Sensibility...The Second Edition. Printed for the Author, by C. Roworth...1813. 3 vols, 12mo, contemporary half red roan; with all half-titles; inkstain on pp. 186-7 of Vol. 111. Very fair copy. 2nd ed. Hill 165-4 1983 £285

AUSTEN, JANE   Sense and Sensibility. London: for the Author, 1813. Second edition. 3 vols. 12mo. Cont. half calf, gilt, some joints neatly repaired. Traylen 94-34 1983 £275

AUSTEN, JANE   Sense and Sensibility. London: for the Author, 1813. Second edition. 3 vols. 12mo. Cont. half brown morocco, gilt. Traylen 94-35 1983 £250

AUSTEN, JANE   Sense & Sensibility. Macmillan, 1897. Reprint, frontis. & 39 b&w illus. by Hugh Thomson. Dark red cl. with design in gilt by A.A. Turbayne, a.e.g. (bkstrip sl. faded, gilt sl. rubbed, name half title), v.g. Hodgkins 27-403 1983 £16

AUSTEN, JANE   Sense & Sensibility. Allen, 1899. 1st edn. Frontis. & 63 b&w illus. by Chris Hammond. Dk. green cloth gilt designed by A.A. Turbayne, a.e.g. (top of bkstrip rubbed, corners sl. bruised & sl. foxing prelims.), v.g. Hodgkins 27-404 1983 £16

AUSTEN, JANE   Three Evening Prayers. SF, 1940. 12mo, embroidered cloth. Set by hand in Centaur capitals and printed in red & black. A leaf of the manuscript in facsimile. One of 500 copies. Occasional foxing; a very nice copy. Perata 27-25 1983 $100

AUSTEN, JOHN   The ABC of Pen and Ink Rendering. London, 1937. First English edition. Numerous illus. by the author, Alan Odle, Eric Fraser, etc. Inscription. Torn and chipped dust-wrapper. Near fine. Jolliffe 26-21 1983 £35

AUSTEN, JOHN   "Rogues in Porcelain." London: Chapman & Hall Ltd., 1924. Compiled & decorated by John Austen. Large 8vo. Rebound in 3/4 calf and marbled boards. Marbled endpapers. T.e.g., with morocco labels on spine. First edition. Bookplate. Spine darkened. Edges somewhat rubbed. MacManus 277-132 1983 $45

AUSTEN, N. L.   Natural History Papers and Memoir. 1877. Portrait and 8 plates. Wheldon 160-118 1983 £12

AUSTEN, R. A. C.   On the Geology of the South-east of Devonshire. Trans. Geo. Soc., 1834-40. Coloured map and plate of sections, 4to, wrappers. Wheldon 160-1357 1983 £15

AUSTIN, ALFRED   Fortunatus the Pessimist. London, 1892. First edition. 8vo, green cloth. Fine. Argosy 714-31 1983 $35

AUSTIN, ALFRED   The Golden Age. Chapman & Hall, 1871. First edition, half title, erratum slip. Orig. brown cloth, v.g. Jarndyce 30-631 1983 £10.50

AUSTIN, ALFRED   Prince Lucifer. London: Macmillan & Co., 1887. Orig. two-tone cloth. First edition. Presentation copy, inscribed on the half-title "To Mrs. Edmund Yates from her old friend The Author, Oct. 1889." Spine darkened. Covers soiled. MacManus 277-136 1983 $35

AUSTIN, BENJAMIN   Constitutional Republicanism, in Opposition to Fallacious Federalism. Boston: Adams & Rhoades, 1803. Orig. paper-covered boards, uncut. Front cover detached, foxing. First collected edition. Felcone 22-9 1983 $45

AUSTIN, HERBERT H.   With MacDonald in Uganda. London, 1903. First edition. Map and illustrations. 8vo. Morrill 290-622 1983 $22.50

AUSTIN, HORACE   Minnesota. St. Paul, 1870. Large folded map. Orig. printed wraps. First edition. Inscribed by Austin to C.O. Lathrop. Ginsberg 46-471 1983 $65

AUSTIN, LEONARD   Around the World in San Francisco. Stanford: 1940. Pictures by Pauline Vinson. Oblong 4to, linen-backed decorated boards. Bookplate. Corners rubbed; a very nice copy. Perata 28-52 1983 $85

AUSTIN, MARY   Children Sing in the Far West. Boston, Houghton, 1928. First edition. Illus. by Gerald Cassidy. Pictorial red cloth (slight fading and fraying), else very good. Houle 21-53 1983 $45

AUSTIN, MARY   Everyman's Genius. Indianapolis, Bobbs-Merrill (1931). First edition. Purple cloth, paper labels (light fading), else very good. Houle 21-55 1983 $35

AUSTIN, MARY   Experiences Facing Death. Indianapolis, Bobbs-Merrill (1931). First edition. Purple cloth, paper labels (light fading), else very good. Houle 21-56 1983 $22.50

AUSTIN, MARY   The Land of Little Rain. Boston: Houghton, 1950. Quarto. Cloth. Illus. with plates by Ansel Adams. Dust jacket reproduces an Ansel Adams photograph. Reese 19-3 1983 $175

AUSTIN, MARY   The Land of Little Rain. Boston: Houghton, 1903. Quarto. Gilt pictorial cloth. First edition. Cont. ink sentiment, dated December, 1903. Reese 20-53 1983 $125

AUSTIN, MARY   The Land of Little Rain. Boston, 1903. 8vo, pict. cloth. First edition. Argosy 714-32 1983 $125

AUSTIN, MARY   Lost Borders. N.Y., Harper, 1909. First edition. Frontis. and six plates by Denman Fink. Pictorial green cloth (some light soiling), else good-very good copy. Houle 21-57 1983 $30

AUSTIN, MARY   The Mother of Felipe. (San Francisco), Book Club of California, 1950. Black cloth over decorated boards (spine a trifle faded). One of 400 copies printed by the Ward Ritchie Press. Decorations by Cas Duchow. Very good. Houle 22-1011 1983 $80

AUSTIN, MARY   The Trail Book. Boston, Houghton, 1918. First edition. Color frontis. and nineteen b/w text drawings by Milo Winter. Orange cloth (remnant of color pictorial label on upper cover), else good-very good. Houle 21-58 1983 $37.50

AUSTIN, MOSES   A Summary Description of the Lead Mines in Upper Louisiana. Wash., 1804. 1st ed. Jenkins 153-736 1983 $875

AUSTIN, MOSES   A Summary Description of the Lead Mines in Upper Louisiana. Washington, 1804. Cloth, leather label, very good. Reese 18-255 1983 $675

AUSTIN, STANLEY   The History of Engraving from its inception... London: T. Werner Laurie, n.d. (ca. 1910). First edition. 8vo. Orig. cloth. 18 illus. Oak Knoll 48-11 1983 $45

AUSTIN, WILLIAM   An Oration, Pronounced at Charlestown. Charlestown, Mass.: Samuel Etheridge, 1801. Stitched. Title chipped at edges. Very good. Felcone 20-4 1983 $20

AUSTRALIA and the South Seas.   London: Maggs Brothers, 1927. 28 full-page plates. Pictorial wrappers. Covers badly waterstained, few leaves at front lightly stained, but altogether a very good copy. Bradley 66-34 1983 $55

AUSTRALIAN Writers in England. 1899. Half title, frontis. 10 pp. ads. Orig. pale green cloth, photographic inset on front cover. Spine a little browned. Very good. Jarndyce 31-422 1983 £30

AUTENRIETH, H. F.   Discrimine Sexuali Jam in Seminibus Plantarum Dioicarum Apparente. Tubingen, 1821. 2 plates, 4to, boards (lower margin dampstained). Wheldon 160-1492 1983 £12

AN AUTHENTIC narrative of Mr. Kemble's retirement from the stage. London: printed for John Miller, 1817. 8vo, original drab boards, printed paper label (short split in upper hinge, minor wear to ends of spine). First edition. With a frontis. portrait (slightly foxed), and 3 plates (2 folding). A fine copy in original condition. Ximenes 64-335 1983 $150

AUTHENTICK memoirs of the life of, that justly celebrated actress, Mrs. Ann Oldfield. London printed, Dublin: reprinted, and sold by George Faulkner, 1731. 12mo, half morocco. First Irish edition. Excellent copy of a very rare pamphlet. Ximenes 64-398 1983 $450

AVERILL, JOHN   "Judge not a Book by its Cover." Chicago: Black Cat Press, 1938. 12mo. Illus. Limited to 100 copies. Extremely fine with very faintly chipped printed dust wrapper. Bromer 25-146 1983 $45

AVERMAETE, ROGER   Frans Masereel. Anvers: Fonds Mercator, 1975. Prof. illus. Small folio. Cloth. Dust jacket. Boxed. Ars Libri 32-430 1983 $100

AVIRETT, JAMES B.   The Old Plantation: How We Lived In Great House and Cabin Before the War. N.Y., (1901). 1st ed. Scarce. Jenkins 151-253 1983 $65

AVIS, R.   Bird-Preserving, Bird-Mounting and the Preservation of Birds' eggs. 1880. 12mo, text-figures, original limp boards (neatly rebacked). A little dustsoiling but a good copy. Scarce. Wheldon 160-633 1983 £20

AVRIL, PHILIPPE S. J.   Voyage en divers Etas d'Europe et d'Asie, entrepris pour decouvrir un nouveau Chemin a la Chine. Paris: Jean Boudot, 1693. 2nd ed., 12mo, modern half calf antique, marbled boards, engraved and printed title pages, engraved plates. Text lightly browned, but a very good copy. Trebizond 18-154 1983 $300

AYER, MARY F.   Boston Common in Colonial and Provincial Days. Boston, 1903. Illus. sw. 8vo, cloth-backed boards. One of 175 copies privately printed by D. B. Updike. Argosy 716-264 1983 $20

AYERS, JAMES J.   Gold and Sunshine, and San Francisco in 1849. Boston, (1922). Illus., index. Clark 741-77 1983 $45

AYERS, NATHANIEL M.   Building a New Empire. New York: Broadway Publishing, 1910. Illustrations. Original cloth. First edition. Jenkins 153-22 1983 $75

AYLESBURY, THOMAS   Paganisme and Papisme. Printed by George Eld, for Leonard Becket, 1624. First edition, 4to, wrapper, trifle dust soiled, but a good copy. Fenning 62-13 1983 £35

AYLIFFE, JOHN   The Ancient and Present State of the University of Oxford. Printed for W. Mears; and J. Hooke, 1723. 2 vols, 8vo, cont. calf, lacking the labels. Second issue with cancelled title pages. Bickersteth 75-4 1983 £65

AYLWARD, J. D.   The Small-Sword in England. London, n.d. (1945). Illus., cloth, rubbed. King 46-537 1983 $40

AYMAR, G. C.   Bird Flight. 1938. 200 photographs, royal 8vo, cloth. Wheldon 160-634 1983 £15

AYME, JEAN JACQUES   Deportation et Naufrage de J. J. Ayme. Paris: Maradan, n.d. (1800). 1st ed., 8vo, cont. qtr. calf gilt, morocco label, boards, half-title, advertisements. A very fine copy. Scarce. Trebizond 18-127 1983 $275

AYME, MARCEL   Le Mauvais Jars. Paris: Gallimard, 1935. 8vo. Cloth backed pictorial boards. Color illus. by N. Altman. Fine. Aleph-bet 8-115 1983 $30

AYROSA, PLINIO   Apontamentos para a Bibliografia da Lingua Tupi-Guarani. Sao Paulo, 1943. Frontispiece, plates, wrps., moderately soiled and chipped externally. One of 86 special numbered copies signed by author. Dawson 470-17 1983 $60

AYRTON, MICHAEL   British Drawings. London: Collins, 1946. 8 plates in colour and 25 illus. in black & white. 4to. Orig. boards. Dust jacket. First edition. Former owner's signature on flyleaf. Fine copy. MacManus 277-137 1983 $25

AYTOUN, WILLIAM EDMONSTOUNE   Lays of the Scottish Cavaliers and other Poems. Edinburgh: William Blackwood and Sons, 1870. Small 4to. Half morocco, gilt. 69 illus. engr. by Dalziel and others. Traylen 94-38 1983 £15

AYTOUN, WILLIAM EDMONSTOUNE   Lays of the Scottish Cavaliers and Other Poems. 1881. 4to, numerous fine woodengravings, white buckram gilt. Cover slightly soiled, but good copy. Bickersteth 77-186 1983 £12

AZURARA, GOMES EANNES DE   The chronicle of the discovery and conquest of Guinea. London: Hakluyt Soc., 1896. 2 vols. 8vo. Folding map. 7 plates. Orig. cloth. Ex-lib., spines darkened, chipped. Adelson Africa-158 1983 $30

B

BAARSLAG, KARL   Robbery by Mail. N.Y., Farrar & Rinehart, (1938). First edition. Illus. Pictorial dust jacket (slight rubbing and nicking) very good - fine. Houle 22-1151 1983 $27.50

BABAULT, G.   Mission Guy Babault dans les provinces centrales de l'Inde. Paris, 1920. 2 maps, 6 plates of view and 6 plates of birds, 4to, buckram. Wheldon 160-635 1983 £30

BABBAGE, CHARLES   Examples of the Solutions of Functional Equations, (1820). 8vo, 1 engraved plate; modern boards. Pickering & Chatto 22-10 1983 $250

BABBAGE, CHARLES   Reflections on the Decline of Science in England, and on Some of its Causes. For B. Fellowes, London, 1830. 8vo, very occasional minor spotting; uncut in orig. boards with printed label on spine, British and foreign library label on upper boards, worn, joints cracked. First edition. Quaritch NS 5-3 1983 $350

BARBITT, EDWIN D.   Principles of Light & Color. N.J., 1925. 4 color plates; over 200 text illus. Thick large 8vo, photo-engraved edition. Argosy 713-16 1983 $75

BABCOCK, ROBERT H.   Diseases of the Heart & Arterial System. N.Y., & London, 1903. First edition. Argosy 713-17 1983 $50

BABCOCK, WILLIAM WAYNE   Newer Surgical Methods of Treating Diseases of the Vascular System. N.Y., 1932. Illus. Tall 4to, buckram (ex-lib.) Argosy 713-18 1983 $85

BABELON, JEAN   Choix de bronzes de la collection Caylus donne au roi en 1762. (Les Tresors du Cabinet des Antiques.) Paris/Bruxelles, 1928. 56, (4)pp., 24 heliotype plates. Lrg. 4to. Wraps. Ars Libri SB 26-4 1983 $65

BABEUF, FRANCOIS NOEL   Du Systeme de Depopulation, Ou La Vie et Les Crimes de Carrier. Paris, Franklin, (1794). 1st ed., half-title and errata leaf, frontis. portrait, cont. calf-backed marbled boards, spine gilt, label. Pickering & Chatto 21-4 1983 $750

BABINGTON, C. C.   Memorials, Journal and Botanical Correspondence. Cambridge, 1897. 8vo, cloth, pedigree and 2 portraits. Wheldon 160-210 1983 £20

BABSON, JOHN J.   Notes and Additions to the History of Gloucester. Salem, 1891. 2nd series. 8vo, buckram, new endpapers. Morrill 288-637 1983 $20

BABY's Classics. London: Long., 1904. 4to. Pictorial cloth. Top of spine worn. Chosen by L. S. MacDonald, inscribed by MacDonald's sister. Very good. Aleph-bet 8-141 1983 $55

BACCHYLIDES   Carmina. Lg, 1904. 8vo, cloth. Salloch 385-486 1983 $45

BACCHYLIDES   The Poems and Fragments. Cambridge, 1905. 8vo, cloth. Salloch 385-485 1983 $125

BACCI, PELEO   La ricostruzione del pergami di Giovanni Pisano nel Duomo di Pisa. Milano/Roma: Bestetti & Tumminelli, ca. 1932. 110 illus. 4to. Cloth. Ars Libri 33-283 1983 $85

BACH, JOHANN SEBASTIAN   "Ich Will den Kreuzstab Gerne Tragen." Munich, 1921. Facs. edition from the autograph manuscript in Berlin. Folio, marbled boards with label. Salloch 387-12 1983 $100

BACHE, ALEXANDER D.   Report of the Superintendent of the Coast Survey, Showing the Progress of the Survey During the Year 1854. Washington, 1855. 58 plates (most folding). Cloth, endsheets foxed, fold wear to a few plates. Felcone 22-10 1983 $100

BACHE, FRANKLIN   Observations and Reflections on the Penitentiary System. Philadelphia, 1829. Dsb. Reese 18-639 1983 $100

BACHE, RICHARD MEADE   American Wonderland. Philadelphia, Claxton, Remsen and Haffelfinger, 1871. 1st ed. Frontispiece. Sm. 8vo. Morrill 288-21 1983 $25

BACHELLER, IRVING   The Light in the Clearing. Indianapolis: Bobbs-Merrill, (1917). 1st ed. Orig. cloth, dj. Mint copy in very nice dj. Jenkins 155-42 1983 $35

BACHELLER, IRVING   A Man for the Ages. Indianapolis, (1919). 8vo. Cloth, boards. In the scarce cloth dj for the book. Bookplate of a noted collector, a fine copy in dj. In Our Time 156-37 1983 $45

BACHELLER, IRVING   The Prodigal Village. Indianapolis: Bobbs-Merrill, (1920). 1st ed. Orig. pictorial boards, dj. Very fine. Jenkins 155-44 1983 $20

BACHMANN, HILDE   Gotische Plastik in den Sudetenlandern vor Peter Parler. (Beitrage zur Geschichte der Kunst im sudeten- und Karpathenraum. Vol. 7.) Brunn, 1943. 141, (3)pp., 68 plates. Sm. 4to. Boards (spine split). Ars Libri SB 26-5 1983 $50

BACILLY, BENIGNE DE   Remarques Curieuses sur l'Art de bien Chanter. Paris, 1668. 1 leaf, engraved title within frame of heraldry and olive branches. Small 8vo, new calf with red leather label, spine with four raised bands. First edition. Salloch 387-13 1983 $600

BACK, GEORGE   Narrative of the Arctic Land Expedition to the Mouth of the Great Fish River and Along the Shores of the Arctic Ocean in the Years 1833, 1834 and 1835. Phila., 1836. Illus., folded map. Orig. boards, cloth spine, paper label. First American edition. Ginsberg 47-22 1983 $175

BACK, GEORGE   Narrative of the Arctic Land Expedition to the Mouth of the Great Fish River and Along the Shores of the Arctic Ocean in the Years 1833, 1834 and 1835. Phila., 1836. Illus., folded map. Orig. boards, cloth spine, paper label. First American edition. Ginsberg 47-21 1983 $75

BACKHOUSE, JAMES   The Life and Correspondence of William and Alice Ellis, of Airton. London, 1849. 1st ed. Frontispiece. 8vo, slightly rubbed, inner hinges partly cracked. Morrill 288-22 1983 $25

BACKHOUSE, JAMES   A narrative of a visit to the Mauritius and South Africa. London: Hamilton, Adams, etc., 1844. First edition. Thick 8vo. Orig. grey-brown cloth. With a frontis. and 15 etched plates, two folding maps, and a number of wood-engraved illus. in the text. Ximenes 63-600 1983 $350

BACON, FRANCIS   A brief discourse of the happy union of the kingdoms of England and Scotland... London: for B. Griffin, sold by H. Newman, 1700. Third edition. Small 4to. Disbound. Light foxing. Ximenes 63-543 1983 $60

BACON, FRANCIS   Essays, Moral, Economical, and Political. Boston: Greenleaf, 1807. 1st ed. Contemporary 3/4 calf and marbled boards, raised bands, gilt label. Minor rubbing, else a very good attractive copy. Jenkins 155-45 1983 $125

BACON, FRANCIS   The Essayes or Counsels, civill and morall. London: John Haviland, 1632. Newly enlarged, 3rd. ed. containing the complete 58 essays. Cont. unlettered panelled calf, genuine first and final blanks present. Some minor worming and fraying to edges of initial leaves, but a very good copy. Trebizond 18-3 1983 $300

BACON, FRANCIS   Lord Bacon's Essays. Printed: And
sold by H. Parson, 1720. In two vols. Panelled calf, hinges sl.
weak, 19th C. labels. Jarndyce 31-12 1983 £45

BACON, FRANCIS   The Essayes or Counsels Civill & Morall
of... NY: Limited Editions Club, 1944. Quarto. Printed at Press
of William E. Rudge's Sons under direction of Bruce Rogers. Limited
to 1100 copies signed by BR. Near mint in cloth-backed decorated
boards with glassine. T.e.g. Folding box. Bromer 25-288 1983
$125

BACON, FRANCIS   Of the Advancement and Proficience of
Learning... Oxford: Printed by Leon: Lichfield, 1640. First
complete edition. Folio. Cont. calf, neatly rebacked. Engraved
decorated title and engraved portrait frontis., both by William
Marshall. Traylen 94-39 1983 £350

BACON, FRANCIS   A Speech Delivered by Sir Francis Bacon,
in the Lower House of Parliament Quinto Iacobi, Concerning the Article
of Naturalization of the Scottish Nation. Printed Anno, 1641.
First edition, 4to, wrapper. Complete with the first and final blank
leaves. Fenning 60-15 1983 £110

BACON, FRANCIS   Three Essays. Chelsea, 1926. 4to,
cloth-backed decorated bds., paper label. One of only 50 copies
printed in Caslon Old Black. Perata 28-165 1983 $85

BACON, FRANCIS   The Two Bookes of the Proficience and
Advancement of Learning, Diuine and Humane... At London, Printed
for Henrie Tomes...1605. 4to, t-p, 118 numbered 11 (with mistakes
should be 121). Bound in full morocco gilt by Riviere. Gold
dentelles, spine stamped and tooled in gilt between raised bands.
Triple gold fillet on board. A.E. Lownes bookplate. AEG. Small
hole in lower margin of 3D4 repaired with no text affected. This
copy is without the 2 errata leaves. Arkway 22-3 1983 $1,500

BACON, FRANCIS   The Twoo Bookes... London: for Henrie
Tomes, 1605. First edition. Small 4to. Newly bound in antique calf,
morocco label, gilt. Some light staining, mainly in the margins, and
edges of title-page frayed. Traylen 94-40 1983 £250

BACON, FRANCIS   De Verulam Angliae Cancelairii de
Augmentis Scientarum. Amsterdam, Ravesteiny, 1662. 16mo, engraved
title page. Full old calf (worn, front free endpaper loose). Good.
Houle 22-62 1983 $95

BACON, G. MACKENZIE   On the Writing of the Insane. London:
John Churchill & Sons, 1870. Five lithographed plates, 2 double-page
and 2 in color. Contemp. plum cloth, new backstrip, library stamp on
titlepage. First edition. Gach 95-21 1983 $75

BACON, LEE   Our Houseboat on the Nile. Boston,
1901. 1st ed. Illus. from water colors by Henry Bacon. 8vo.
Morrill 288-24 1983 $20

BACON, LEONARD   The Furioso. New York, 1932. 8vo.
Cloth. This copy inscribed by Bacon. Spine faded, else vg-fine
copy. In Our Time 156-43 1983 $20

BACON, MARTHA   Things Visible and Invisible. New
York, (1947). 8vo. Cloth. Fine in dj. In Our Time 156-45 1983
$20

BACON, NATHANIEL   A Relation of the Fearful Estate of
Francis Spira... London: for H.P., 1718. 16mo. Woodcut frontis.,
woodcuts in text, 19th century polished calf. First edition with
these illus. Heath 48-51 1983 £85

BACON, ROGER   Liber Alberti Magni de duabus sapientiis
et de recapitulatione omnium librorum Astronomie. (Nuremberg: Kaspar
Hochfeder, 1493-1496). Capital spaces with guide letters. 4to.
Boards, leather spine. From the collection of Georg Tannstetter.
First edition. Kraus 164-15 1983 $5,000

BACON, THOMAS   First Impressions and Studies from Nature
in Hindostan. London, 1837. 27 plates. 2 vols. Half calf, labels.
8vo. Good. Edwards 1044-24 1983 £120

BACULARD D'ARNAUD, FRANCOIS THOMAS   Warbeck: A Pathetic Tale.
Printed for William Lane, 1786. 1st ed., 2 vols., 12mo, contemporary
calf, red and green labels; half-titles; a fine copy. Hill 165-5
1983 £285

BADEN-POWELL, R. H.   Indian Memoires. London, 1915.
24 coloured illus. on 16 plates, numerous other plates by author.
8vo. Orig. cloth. Good. Edwards 1044-25 1983 £45

BADEN-POWELL, R. H.   The Indian Village. London, 1896.
Folding map. Orig. cloth. 8vo. Good. Edwards 1044-26 1983 £40

BADHAM, CHARLES DAVID   Prose haleutics or ancient and modern
fish tattle. London: Parker, 1854. First edition. 8vo. Orig.
dark blue cloth. Fine copy. Ximenes 63-550 1983 $75

BADISCHE Company Sole Importers of the Products Manufactured by
Badische Anilin- & Soda-Fabrik, Ludwigshafen o/ Rhine. N.P., n.d.
(ca. 1900). 12mo, orig. limp cloth. Very nice. Morrill 289-589
1983 $20

BAEDEKER, KARL   Egypt and the Sudan. Leipzig, 1914.
"7th remodelled edition". "22 maps, 85 plans, and 55 vignettes."
Red cloth. Index. First few pp slightly stained. Slightly chipped
and worn dust wrapper. Very good. King 45-540 1983 $25

BAEDEKER, KARL   Berlin and Its Environs. Leipzig:
Baedeker, 1903. With a slip cancel over this imprint: "Imported
by Charles Scribner's Sons, New York." 12mo, maps. Karmiole 72-
14 1983 $30

BAEDEKER, KARL   London and its Environs. Leipzig:
Karl Baedeker, 1905. Half title, 4 maps and 24 plans. Orig. flexible
red cloth covers, fine. Jarndyce 31-230 1983 £12.50

BAER, WARREN   The Duke of Sacramento. SF, 1934.
8vo, cloth-backed bds., paper label. Color illustrations by
Arvilla Parker. Perata 27-62 1983 $50

BAER, WARREN   The Duke of Sacramento. San Francisco:
The Grabhorn Press, 1934. Limited to 550 copies. Slight bumping to
corners. Also included is a sketch by Jane Bissell Grabhorn. Fine
copy overall. Jenkins 153-84 1983 $50

BAGEHOT, WALTER   Literary Studies. London: Longmans,
Green & Co., 1879. 2 vols. Illus. with Woodburytype frontis. port.
Orig. cloth. First edition. Hinges weak. Covers a little worn.
Good set. MacManus 277-139 1983 $25

BAGEHOT, WALTER   Lombard Street. New York: Charles
Scribner's Sons, 1883. Original brown cloth. First American edition?
Spine ends worn. A very good copy. MacManus 277-140 1983 $20

BAGGS, CHARLES M.   A Discourse on the Supremacy of the Roman
Pontiffs. Rome: Printed by Salviucci, 1836. First edition, 8vo,
wrapper. Fenning 61-17 1983 £12.50

BAGLEY, CLARANCE B.   The Acquisition and Pioneering of Old
Oregon. Seattle, Argus, 1924. Illus., some folded. Orig. small folio
printed wraps. First edition. Privately printed account. Ginsberg
46-594 1983 $125

BAGNALL, GIBBONS   A New Translation of Telemachus in English Verse. Dublin: Printed by William Porter, 1792. 2 vols. Calf,
leather labels on spines. Release stamp fron the AAS in both vols.
This set from library of Isaiah Thomas. It bears a presentation inscription by Thomas in both vols. to the American Antiquarian Society
and is dated 1820. Some light wear near the crown of spine on vol. 1,
otherwise a fine set. In Our Time 156-791 1983 $200

BAGNALL, J. E.   The Flora of Warwickshire. 1891.
Folding map in pocket, 8vo, cloth. Scarce. Edition limited to 500
numbered copies each signed by the author. Wheldon 160-1585 1983 £50

BAGNOLD, ENID   "National Velvet." London and Toronto:
William Heinemann Ltd., (1935). First edition. Drawings by Laurian
Jones. 8vo. Orig. cloth. Dust jacket. Inch-long chip out of front
panel of jacket, top of spine of jacket slightly chipped, otherwise
a very good copy. Jaffe 1-23 1983 $250

BAGROW, LEO   History of Cartography. London:
C.A. Watts, & Co., 1864. Revised edition. Thick small 4to. Cloth.
Dust jacket. 76 illus. in the text, 116 monochrome plates and 22
plates in full color. Jacket has a two-inch tear at head of spine,
else a fine copy. Oak Knoll 48-272 1983 $170

BAHR, HERMANN   Gustav Klimt. 50 Handzeichnungen.
Leipzig/Wien: Thyrsos-Verlag, 1922. 50 facsimile plates, loose in
portfolio, as issued. 4to. Boards, 1/2 calf. No. 235 of a limited
edition of 375 copies. Worn. Ars Libri 32-370 1983 $150

BAIF, LAZARE DE   De re Vestiaria Libellus, ex Baysio
Excerptus... Excudebat Rob. Stephanus Parisiis, Ann M.D. XXXVI. III.
Non. Maii., (1596). 8vo, late 17th century polished sheep with gilt
tooling on spine. Slightly scuffed. Ex-library copy. Arkway 22-4
1983 $275

BAIKIE, JAMES   The Charm of the Scott Country. Lon.,
1927. 25 pencil illus. by Gordon Home, flys offset from dustwrapper,
edges rubbed, else very good in internally mended, very good dustwrapper. Quill & Brush 54-1686 1983 $35

BAIKIE, R.   Observations on the Neilgherries. Calcutta, 1834. 3 folding coloured maps, 30 full page coloured route
maps and a full page map index. 10 hand-coloured plates, 1 black and
white plate, occasional slight browning. Panelled morocco by Mac-
Culloch of Calcutta, richly gilt and blindstamped, gilt inner dentelles.
Joints weakened by worming, front hinge cracked at head and tail.
Rubbed at corners. 8vo. Good. Edwards 1044-778 1983 £350

BAILEY, A. M.   Birds of Arctic Alaska. Denver, 1948.
Portrait, map and numerous illus. from photographs. Royal 8vo,
cloth. Wheldon 160-637 1983 £25

BAILEY, ALICE WARD   The Sage Brush Parson. Boston: Little,
Brown, 1906. Ads. Cloth. Dawson 471-163 1983 $40

BAILEY, EBENEZER   The Young Ladies' Class Book. Boston,
1832. Cont. lea. Argosy 710-155 1983 $25

BAILEY, F. M.   The Queensland Flora. Brisbane, 1899-
1902. 88 plates, 6 vols., 8vo, original cloth-backed boards. A
good copy of this scarce standard work. Wheldon 160-1648 1983 £170

BAILEY, ISAAC   American Naval Biography. Providence,
1815. Cont. calf, slight foxing, but very good. Reese 18-468 1983
$75

BAILEY, JAMES BLAKE   The Diary of a Resurrectionist 1811-
1812... London, 1896. 8vo. Orig. cloth. 10 plates. Gurney JJ-15
1983 £20

BAILEY, L. H.   The Cultivated Evergreens. 1923.
48 plates and 97 text-illustrations, royal 8vo, cloth. Wheldon 160-
2070 1983 £20

BAILEY, NATHANIEL   An Universal Etymological English
Dictionary. London: E. Bell, et al. 1724-1731. Second edition,
2 vols. Thick 8vo, unpaginated. Some woodcut illus. Old calf
rebacked. Bindings rubbed, but sound. Karmiole 73-39 1983 $100

BAILEY, NATHANIEL   An Universal Etymological English
Dictionary. J.J. & P. Knapton, D. Midwinter, 1735. Seventh edition,
panelled calf, worn but sound. Jarndyce 31-22 1983 £48

BAILEY, NATHANIEL   An Universal Etymological English
Dictionary. For T. Osborne, C. Hutch, L. Hawes, 1757. Rebound in
half calf, label. Jarndyce 31-23 1983 £58

BAILEY, NATHANIEL   An Universal Etymological English
Dictionary... London: for J. Buckland, etc., 1770. Thick 8vo.
Cont. calf, neatly rebacked with morocco label, gilt. Traylen 94-42
1983 £38

BAILEY, PETER   Sketches from St. George's Fields.
Stodart & Stewart, 1820. First edition, half title, vignette
woodcuts, erratum slip. Uncut. Later marbled boards, cloth spine,
paper label. Jarndyce 30-633 1983 £16.50

BAILEY, STEPHEN A.   A Memoir. Ithaca, New York, 1933. 1st
ed. Port., plates. Scarce. Clark 741-188 1983 $40

BAILEY, VERNON   The Prairie Ground Squirrels. Washington, 1893. 3 coloured plates and 4 maps, 8vo, half calf. Wheldon
160-538 1983 £12

BAILEY, VERNON   Wild Animals of Glacier National Park.
Washington, 1918. Profusely illus. Folding map. Orig. stiff printed
wrappers. Fine. Jenkins 152-18 1983 $50

BAILEY, WILLIAM   Records of Patriotism and Love of
Country. Wash., 1826. Later linen-backed boards, (title stained),
ex lib. Argosy 716-455 1983 $35

BAILLIE, A. F.   The Oriental Club and Hanover Square.
London, 1901. 14 plates, plan, roy.8vo., pictorial cloth. Good.
Edwards 1044-27 1983 £35

BAILLIE, MATTHEW   Morbid Anatomy of Some of the Most Important Parts of the Human Body. Phila., 1820. 8vo, sheep, modern calf
back. Argosy 713-21 1983 $150

BAILLIERE, H.   Catalogue des Livres de Medecine. Paris,
Janvier, 1852. 8vo, unbound & unopened. Argosy 713-22 1983 $40

BAILY, FRANCIS   Astronomical Collections. (Printed for
private circulation only.) London: March 1827. 1st ed., 8vo,
abrasion in centre of titlepage; contemp. wrappers with MS title.
Pickering & Chatto 22-12 1983 $180

BAILY, FRANCIS   The Catalogue of Stars of the British
Association for the Advancement of Science. Richard and John E.
Taylor, London, 1845. 4to, uncut and unopened in orig. grey boards,
rebacked. Only edition. Quaritch NS 5-4 1983 $325

BAIN, ALEXANDER   Mental and Moral Science. Longmans,
Green, 1872. 2 vols. bound as one. Third edition, 2 vols. Orig.
purple remainder cloth. Jarndyce 31-89 1983 £14.50

BAIN, ALEXANDER   Mind and Body. The Theories of Their
Relation. NY: D. Appleton, 1874. First American edition. 12mo.
Publisher's decorative red cloth. Gach 95-22 1983 $35

BAIN, ALEXANDER   The Senses and the Intellect. London:
Longmans, Green & Co., 1868. Third edition. Publisher's brown cloth.
Endpapers lacking, inner rear board and last few leaves of text damp-
stained. Good reading copy. Gach 94-517 1983 $50

BAIN, FRANCIS WILLIAM   The Substance of a Dream. Methuen & Co.,
(1919). First edition. 4to, frontis. Title in red and black.
Orig. paper boards, imitation vellum spine with printed label,
uncut and unopened. Hannas 69-6 1983 £15

BAIN, R. NISBET   Russian Fairy Tales. G.G. Harrap, 1915.
4to. Colour frontis. 3 colour plates & 12 other plates. Black cloth,
onlaid colour plate. Greer 40-152 1983 £25

BAINES, EDWARD   The History of the County Palatine and
Duchy of Lancaster. London and Manchester, 1868-1870. 2 vols., 4to,
recased and spines neatly relaid, orig. green cloth. K Books 301-11
1983 £50

BAINES, THOMAS   Explorations in South-West Africa.
London: Longman, Green, etc., 1864. 8vo. 3 folding maps.
colored frontis. 9 plates. Modern 1/2 brown calf. Black label.
Adelson Africa-5 1983 $400

BAINVILLE, JACQUES   Napoleon. London, 1932. 8vo. Bound
in half red morocco, gilt, t.e.g. Traylen 94-628 1983 £21

BAINVILLE, JACQUES   Petite Histoire de France. Maison Mame,
Tours, n.d. (1935). 4to. Colour front. 15 colour plates. 54 text
illus. Decorated endpapers. Colour pictorial boards. Greer 40-121
1983 £27.50

BAIRD, CHARLES W.   History of Rye. Westchester County, New York, 1660-1870. Illus. by Abram Hosier. NY: Anson D.F. Randolph and Co., 1871. Tall 8vo, with 18 plates (1 folding) and 3 maps (the folding plate at rear contains two of the maps.). With a 3-page orig. holograph letter, signed by Baird, laid in. Bound in orig. brown cloth. Bookplate. Karmiole 76-13 1983 $50

BAIRD, CHARLES W.   History of the Hugenot Emigration to America. N.Y., 1885. Two volumes. 15 maps and plates. Original cloth. First edition. Jenkins 153-24 1983 $100

BAIRD, FRANK   Fredericton's 100 Years. Then and Now. Fredericton: T. Amos Wilson, (1948). 23cm. Numerous illus. Stiff printed wrappers. Fine. McGahern 53-13 1983 $25

BAIRD, JOHN WALLACE   The Color Sensitivity of the Peripheral Retina. Washington, D.C.: Carnegie Inst. of Washington, 1905. Wrappers, piece torn from front cover. Gach 94-688 1983 $20

BAIRD, JOSEPH ARMSTRONG   California's Pictorial Letter Sheets, 1849-1869. San Francisco, Grabhorn & Hoyem, 1957. Edition limited to 475 copies. 60 reproductions of lettersheets, tinted. Folio, cloth-backed boards. Clark 741-279 1983 $147.50

BAIRD, JOSEPH ARMSTRONG   California's Pictorial Letter Sheets, 1849-1869. San Francisco: David Magee, 1967. Illus. Morocco and boards. Dawson 471-12 1983 $150

BAIRD, ROBERT   Impressions and Experiences of the West Indies and North America in 1849. Philadelphia: Lea & Blanchard, 1850. First American edition, sm. 8vo, original brown embossed cloth, lettered in gilt on spine, head and foot of spine and corners worn, one joint trifle split. Deighton 3-17 1983 £78

BAITAL-PACHIST   Vikram and the Vampire or tales of Hindu Devilry. London: Longmans, Green & Co., 1870. First edition, first issue. 8vo. 16 plates. orig. black cloth. Rebacked, part of orig. spine missing. Adelson Africa-41 1983 $75

BAITAL-PACHIST   Vikram and the Vampire or tales of Hindu Devilry. London: Tylston & Edwards, 1893. 8vo. 16 plates. Orig. black cloth. Rubbed, top of spine starting. Adelson Africa-172 1983 $50

BAKER, B. GRANVILLE   Old Cavalry Stations. London, 1934. First edition. Roy. 8vo. Orig. cloth. Coloured frontis and 46 illus. Good. Edwards 1042-278 1983 £15

BAKER, C. H. COLLINS   A Note on Gainsborough's Early Portraits. San Marino: The Huntington Library, 1946. 4to, wrappers, unsewn. Perata 28-58 1983 $15

BAKER, DANIEL B.   "A Soldier's Experience in the Civil War." Long Beach, Calif., 1914. 1st ed. Presentation copy to Daniel Comstock Baker. Orig. printed wrappers. Illus. Jenkins 153-737 1983 $75

BAKER, DAVID ERSKINE   Biographica Dramatica, or, a companion to the playhouse. Dublin: printed by T. Henshall, for W. and H. Whitestone, etc., 1782. 2 vols., 8vo, cont. calf, contrasting morocco labels. First Irish edition. Half-titles present. A fine copy. Ximenes 64-26 1983 $150

BAKER, DAVID ERSKINE   Biographica Dramatica, or, a companion to the playhouse. London: printed for Messrs. Rivingtons, etc., 1782. 2 vols, 2nd ed., 8vo, cont. calf, spines gilt (spines worn, hinges weak). Bound without half-titles. Ximenes 64-25 1983 $75

BAKER, DAVID ERSKINE   Biographica Dramatica; or, a companion to the playhouse. London: printed for Longman, etc., 1812. 3 vols. in 4 (as issued), 8vo, cont. half calf, spines gilt (slight wear). First edition thus; the last and most complete version. Very good copy. Ximenes 64-27 1983 $200

BAKER, DAVID ERSKINE   The Companion to the Play-House. London, 1764. First edition. 2 vols. 8vo. Newly bound in half antique calf, morocco labels, uncut edges. Errata and advertisement leaf in vol. 1. Traylen 94-43 1983 £160

BAKER, DAVID ERSKINE   The Companion to the Play-House: or, an historical account of all the dramatic writers that have appeared in Great Britain and Ireland. London: printed for T. Becket and P. A. Dehondt; C. Henderson; and T. Davies, 1764. 2 vols., 12mo, 1st ed. Cont. calf (spines worn, hinges tender; one title-label missing). Ximenes 64-24 1983 $150

BAKER, E. C. S.   The Game-Birds of India, Burma and Ceylon, Vol. III, Pheasants and Bustard-Quail. 1930. 20 plates (11 coloured), royal 8vo, original half cloth. Wheldon 160-640 1983 £80

BAKER, E. C. S.   The Indian Ducks and their Allies. 1908. 30 coloured plates by Gronvold, Lodge and Keulemans, royal 8vo, original half morocco. Binding somewhat rubbed, and slight foxing. Wheldon 160-639 1983

BAKER, ERNEST A.   The History of the English Novel. New York, 1967-69. 2 vols. 8vo. Cloth. Traylen 94-44 1983 £66

BAKER, EZEKIEL   Thirty-six years' practice and observations with rifle guns. London: L. Alexander, 1816. 8vo. Disbound. Nine plates (7 hand-colored). Sixth edition. Some soiling; headline of one plate shaved. Ximenes 63-170 1983 $125

BAKER, FRANK COLLINS   A Naturalist in Mexico. Chicago: David Oliphant, 1895. Errata. Maps and illus. Brown cloth. Karmiole 74-72 1983 $60

BAKER, HENRY   An Attempt towards a Natural History of the Polype... London, 1743. First edition. 8vo. Cont. calf, rebacked. One advertisement leaf, with frontis. and numerous illus. in text. Gurney 90-8 1983 £120

BAKER, HENRY   The Miroscope Made Easy or the Nature, Uses and Magnifying Powers of the Best Kinds of Microscopes... London: Printed for R. Dodsley...M.DCC.XLII (1742). 8vo, one folding table, fourteen engraved plates, some folding. Bound in full early calf. Double gold fillet on spine between raised bands. Hinges cracking, corners scuffed. Titlepage lightly toned and foxed. Title inscribed by early owner, Wm. Wavell. A.E. Lownes bookplate. First edition. Fine copy. Arkway 22-5 1983 $650

BAKER, HENRY   The Microscopy made Easy. London: R. Dodsley, 1742. First edition. 8vo. Calf. 14 folding plates. Gurney 90-9 1983 £185

BAKER, J. R.   Man and Animals in the New Hebrides. 1929. 43 illustrations, 8vo, cloth. Binding stained. Wheldon 160-344 1983 £20

BAKER, JAMES H.   History of Colorado. Denver, 1927. 5 vols. Contemp. 3/4 morocco, gilt. 1st ed. Jenkins 153-752 1983 $350

BAKER, JAMES H.   The Sources of the Mississippi. St. Paul, 1887. Orig. printed wraps. First edition. Ginsberg 47-505 1983 $25

BAKER, LAFAYETTE C.   History of the United States Secret Service. Philadelphia, 1868. Illus. 8vo. Binding partly faded. Morrill 287-22 1983 $22.50

BAKER, RACHEL   Devotional Somnium. New York, Printed for the Proprietor, 1815. First edition, small 8vo. Orig. printed boards, all edges untrimmed. Backstrip slightly cracked, occasional lettering on covers worn off. Nice. Morrill 289-61 1983 $65

BAKER, RAY STANNARD   Woodrow Wilson, Life and Letters. NY (1946). 7 vols. Potomac edition. Photos, cloth, spines a bit discolored. Minor wear and soil. King 46-241 1983 $75

BAKER, RICHARD   A Chronicle of the Kings of England... London: by J. Flesher and E. Cotes, 1653. Second edition. Folio. 18th century mottled calf, gilt. Engraved title-page by W. Marshall, title-page printed in red and black, frayed at the margins. Traylen 94-45 1983 £60

BAKER, RICHARD   Theatrum Redivivum, or the theatre
vindicated by Sir Richard Banker in answer to Mr. Pryn's Histriomastix.
London: printed by T. R. for Francis Eglesfield, 1662. 8vo, 18th-
cent. half calf, in a close case. 1st ed. Rare. Tear in one blank
margin, a couple of edges dusty, but a fine copy, entirely uncut.
Ximenes 64-28 1983 $1,250

BAKER, SAMUEL WHITE   The Albert N'Yanza, Great Basin of the
Nile... London: Macmillan & Co., 1866. 2 vols. 8vo. 2 maps.
15 plates. Orig. green cloth. Very good. Adelson Africa-6 1983
$325

BAKER, SAMUEL WHITE   The Albert N'yanza, Great Basin of the
Nile and Explorations of the Nile Sources. Philadelphia, 1866. Maps,
illus. and portraits, good ex-lib., orig. dec. cloth, map neatly repaired, recased and spine relaid, first American ed. K Books 301-12
1983 £70

BAKER, SAMUEL WHITE   Eight years' wanderings in Ceylon.
Chicago: Belford, Clarke, (1880). 12mo. Frontis. Orig. green
pictorial cloth. Adelson Africa-159 1983 $20

BAKER, SAMUEL WHITE   Ismailia. A narrative of the expedition
to central Africa... London: Macmillan & Co., 1874. 2 vols. 8vo.
2 maps. 52 plates. Orig. green cloth. Rubbed. Adelson Africa-8
1983 $300

BAKER, SAMUEL WHITE.   Ismailia. NY, 1875. Illus., folding
map, tipped-in magazine illus. on rear pastedown, edges very slightly
frayed. Quill & Brush 54-1691 1983 $125

BAKER, SAMUEL WHITE   Ismailia. London: Macmillan, 1875.
8vo. 2 maps, 51 plates. Orig. cloth. Spine faded, ex-lib.
Adelson Africa-161 1983 $50

BAKER, SAMUEL WHITE   Ismailia. London: Macmillan, 1879.
12mo. Map, 51 plates. Orig. green cloth. Rubbed, ex-lib.
Adelson Africa-160 1983 $80

BAKER, SAMUEL WHITE   The Nile tributaries of Abyssinia...
London: Macmillan & Co., 1867. 8vo. 2 maps. 23 plates. Orig.
blue cloth. Rubbed, spine ends starting, but a good copy. Adelson
Africa-7 1983 $225

BAKER, SAMUEL WHITE   The Nile Tributaries of Abyssinia, and
the Sword Hunters of the Hamran Arabs. 1867. 2 maps, portrait
frontis., 23 engraved plates. Orig. gilt cloth, spine inlaid but
slightly stained. K Books 307-11 1983 £75

BAKER, SAMUEL WHITE   Wild beasts and their ways. London:
Macmillan, 1890. 8vo. 28 plates. Orig. red cloth. Slightly
rubbed. Adelson Africa-162 1983 $75

BAKER, SARAH SCHOONMAKER   Keepsake for the Young. NY: Scribner,
n.d. 18-1/2 cm. Orig. green cloth decorated in black, red and gold.
Very good; a bit shaken. Grunder 6-39 1983 $65

BAKER, VALENTINE   The British cavalry. London: Longman,
etc.,1858. First edition. 8vo. Orig. blue cloth. Illus. with 2
hand-colored plates. A very good copy. Ximenes 63-309 1983 $95

BAKER, WILLIAM MUMFORD   Inside: A Chronicle Secession. New
York, 1866. Double columns. Illus. Stamped cloth, stained. Blank
leaves foxed. Good. Illus. by Thomas Nast. Reese 19-35 1983 $50

BAKST, LEON   Designs for the Sleeping Princess.
London, 1923. Folio, cloth with vellum back, t.e.g. Portrait
frontis. of Bakst by Picasso and 55 colored mounted plates, tissue
interleaved. One of 1000 copies. Corners worn, name on free endpaper. Duschnes 240-3 1983 $650

BALBOA by the Sea, Newport Bay, Orange County, California. Los Angeles:
Balboa Island Realty Co., (ca.1912). Illus. Blue wrappers. Dawson
471-14 1983 $100

BALDASS, LUDWIG VON   Hieronymous Bosch. New York: Abrams,
1960. 168 plates (48 color). Small square folio. Cloth. Ars
Libri 32-50 1983 $100

BALDINGER, ERNST GOTTFRIED   Catalogus dissertationum quae medicamentorum hisotiam... Altenburg: Officina Richteria, 1768. Woodcut
vignette, headpieces and tailpieces, 4to. Paper backstrip. Kraus
164-188 1983 $1,850

BALDINUCCI, FILIPPO   Vita di Gian Lorenzo Bernini. Milano:
Edizioni del Milione, 1948. 24 plates. Small 4to. Wrappers. Dust
jacket. Ars Libri 33-28 1983 $35

BALDWIN, CHARLES N.   A Universal Biographical Dictionary...
New York, 1825. Worn calf, good. Reese 18-584 1983 $20

BALDWIN, EBENEZER   Annals of Yale College, from Its
Foundation, to the Year 1831. New Haven, 1831. First edition, mod.
wraps., (foxed). Ex lib. Argosy 716-117 1983 $40

BALDWIN, JAMES   Go Tell it on the Mountain. NY, 1974.
Spine slighly sunned, else very good. Quill & Brush 54-56 1983 $75

BALDWIN, JAMES   If Beale Street Could Talk. NY, 1974.
Limited to 250 specially bound, numbered and signed copies. Mint in
slipcase. Quill & Brush 54-57 1983 $75

BALDWIN, JAMES   Nobody Knows My Name. London, 1964. Uncorrected proof copy, with the date of publication (24 Feb. 1964)
stamped on front cover. Fine. Gekoski 2-207 1983 £40

BALDWIN, JAMES MARK (1861-1934)   Fragments in Philosophy and
Science. London: John C. Nimmo, (1903). First British edition.
Gach 95-23 1983 $75

BALDWIN, JAMES MARK (1861-1934)   The Individual and Society.
London: Rebman, 1911. 12mo. Publisher's rose cloth, spine faded.
First British edition, with presentation stamp. Gach 95-24 1983
$35

BALDWIN, JAMES MARK (1861-1934)   The Story of the Mind. NY:
McClure, Phillips, 1904 (1899). Publisher's red cloth. Gach 95-
25 1983 $25

BALDWIN, JAMES MARK (1861-1934)   Thought and Things. London:
Swan Sonnenschein, NY: Macmillan, 1906. Publisher's maroon cloth.
Fine copy. First edition, American issue, with Macmillan imprint
on spine. Gach 95-26 1983 $50

BALDWIN, JAMES MARK (1861-1934)   Thought and Things. London:
Swan Sonnenschein, 1908. Vol. II Orig. crimson cloth. Second
issue binding with George Allen imprint. Good ex-library copy,
shelf-worn. Gach 95-27 1983 $35

BALDWIN, L. BLAKE   Syphilis in Dentistry. Chicago, 1903.
4 color plates, 12mo, buckram; uncut. First edition. Qrgosy 713-
24 1983 $40

BALDWIN, THOMAS   Narrative of the Massacre, by the
Savages, of the Wife and Children of...in the Extreme Western Part of
the State of Kentucky. N.Y., 1835. Illus., large foldout plate.
Orig. plain blue wraps. bound in half morocco. First edition.
Ginsberg 46-46 1983 $225

BALDWIN, THOMAS W.   Vital Records of Chelsea, Massachusetts,
to the Year 1850. Boston, 1916. 1st ed. 8vo. Small shelf label
removed from top of spine. Morrill 289-413 1983 $20

BALDWIN, WILLIAM CHARLES   African hunting and adventure from Natal
to the Zambesi. London: Richard Bentley, 1894. Third edition. 8vo.
Folding map. 17 plates. Orig. brown cloth. Lightly rubbed. Adelson
Africa-9 1983 $120

BALE, JOHN   The Actes of English Votaries...
London: John Tisdale, (1560). 12mo. 2 vols. in 1. Printed in
black letter. Later calf, one joint repaired. One single wormhole,
mainly in margin, else good copy. Heath 48-542 1983 £150

BALE, JOHN   Acta Romanorum Pontificum. Frankfurt/
Basel? 1560. Red and black title (neatly remargined), small 8vo,
lacks final blank, 19th century roan, gilt edges, a little rubbed.
K Books 301-13 1983 £150

BALFOUR, ALICE B.   Twelve Hundred Miles in a Waggon.
Edward Arnold, 1895. First edition, with a folding map and 38 full-
page and other illus., 32 ads., 8vo, orig. cloth, gilt, v.g. copy.
Fenning 61-18 1983 £45

BALFOUR, J. H.   Introduction to the study of Palaeon-
tological Botany. Edinburgh, 1872. 4 plates and 102 text-figures,
8vo, cloth. Wheldon 160-1359 1983 £15

BALFOUR, M. I.   The Work of Medical Women in India.
London, 1929. Large folding map, plates. 8vo. Orig. cloth. Good.
Edwards 10444-31 1983 £20

BALIANI, GIOVANNI BATISTA   De Motv Natvrali Gravivm Solidorvm
Ioannis Baptistae Baliani...Genvae (Genoa) Ex Typographia Io: Mariae
Favroni...MDCXXXVIII (1638). 4to, new vellum binding, new endpapers.
Margins trimmed, not affecting text. Modern MS on final page.
Occasional very light, very scattered foxing. Overall very good.
First edition. Arkway 22-6 1983 $1,800

BALIANI, GIOVANNI BATTISTA   De motu Naturali Gravium Solidorum et
Liquidorum... Genova, Gio. Maria Ferront, 1646. 4to, full vellum
binding. Lower board restored. Second edition. Very good.
Arkway 22-7 1983 $1,800

BALL, ELIZA CRAWFURD   The Christian Armour. NY: Charles Scribner & Co., 1866. 4to, ornate chromolithograph or gilt borders on each
page. Pub.'s deluxe gilt-stamped brown calf gilt binding. A.e.g.
Plates lithographed by Major & Knapp of New York City. Karmiole 73-29
1983 $200

BALL, JOHN   Autobiography of John Ball... Grand
Rapids, 1925. Plates. Original cloth. Dust jacket. Jenkins 153-
208 1983 $45

BALL, NICHOLAS   The Pioneers of '49. Boston: Lee and
Shepard, 1891. Ads. Engraved frontispiece portrait. 20 full-page
steel engravings. Original pictorial cloth. First edition. Nice.
Jenkins 153-26 1983 $100

BALL, NICHOLAS   Voyages of...from 1838 to 1853. Boston:
Privately Printed, 1895. Illustrations. Original cloth. First ed.
Jenkins 153-27 1983 $125

BALL, ROBERT S.   The Cause of an Ice Age. Kegan Paul...
1891. First edition, with a frontis. and 5 illus., 8vo, orig. cloth.
Fenning 60-16 1983 £14.50

BALLADS & Broadsides chiefly of the Elizabethan Period... Oxford:
the Roxburghe Club, 1912. Folio. Orig. half brown morocco, gilt,
t.e.g., others uncut. Limited edition, printed for Members only,
with 9 plates of facsimiles. Traylen 94-315 1983 £160

BALLADS and Songs of Southern Michigan. Ann Arbor, 1939. Cloth, minor
wear. Inscribed & signed by Emelyn Gardner. King 46-157 1983 $50

BALLANCE, CHARLES   Some Points in the Surgery of the Brain
and its Membranes. London: Macmillan, 1908. Text illus., 8vo, buckram. Argosy 713-25 1983 $125

BALLANCE, CHARLES   Some Points in the Surgery of the Brain
and its Membranes. London, 1908. 8vo. Orig. cloth. Illus. in text.
Initialled presentation inscription on half-title. Gurney JJ-18
1983 £25

BALLANTINE, JAMES   The Gaberlunzie's Wallet. Edinburgh,
1843. 13 steel-engraved plates, wood-engravings, rather foxed and
age-browned but good in half morocco, gilt spine. K Books 307-12
1983 £30

BALLANTYNE, ROBERT MICHAEL   The Battery and the Boiler or Adventures
in the Laying of Submarine Electric Cables. London: James Nisbet &
Co., 1883. Illus. by author. Orig. pictorial cloth. First edition.
Covers a bit rubbed. Fine copy. MacManus 277-146 1983 $225

BALLANTYNE, ROBERT MICHAEL   The Buffalo Runners. London, 1891.
First edition. Illus. by author. Pictorial cloth. Covers a little
marked. Bookplate. With author's autograph presentation inscription.
Very nice. Rota 230-42 1983 £50

BALLANTYNE, ROBERT MICHAEL   Charlie to the Rescue. London: James
Nisbet & Co., 1890. With illus. by author. Orig. pictorial cloth.
First edition. Contemporary owner's inscription on front flyleaf.
Inner hinges weak. A very good copy. MacManus 277-147 1983 $225

BALLANTYNE, ROBERT MICHAEL   The Gorilla Hunters. London: T. Nelson
& Sons, 1861. Illus. Orig. gilt-decorated cloth. First edition.
Spine faded. Contemporary owner's signature on front endsheet. Very
good copy. MacManus 277-148 1983 $175

BALLANTYNE, ROBERT MICHAEL   Hudson's Bay: or Every-Day Life In the
Wilds of North America. Boston, 1859. 1st ed. Plates, thick 16mo,
orig. cloth, pict. spine, minor foxing. Argosy 710-44 1983 $40

BALLANTYNE, ROBERT MICHAEL   In the Track of the Troops. James
Nisbet, 1878. First edition, with additional pictorial title and
5 plates, 8vo, orig. blue cloth, the preliminary leaves lightly foxed,
otherwise a very good copy. Fenning 60-17 1983 £24.50

BALLANTYNE, ROBERT MICHAEL   The Life of a Ship from the Launch to
the Wreck. London: Thomas Nelson, 1857. 4to. Green gilt cloth.
Stain on bottom blank margin of 3 pages. 8 full-page color illus.
printed one-side only engraved by F. Borders. Very good. Aleph-bet
8-25 1983 $65

BALLANTYNE, ROBERT MICHAEL   Red Rooney or The Last of the Crew.
London: James Nisbet & Co., 1886. Illus. Orig. pictorial cloth.
First edition. Contemporary owner's signature on verso of front free
endpaper. A fine copy. MacManus 277-149 1983 $250

BALLARD, G. A.   Rulers of the Indian Ocean. London, 1927.
Map and numerous plates. 8vo. Orig. cloth. Good. Edwards 1044-32
1983 £18

BALLARD, JOSEPH   England in 1815 as Seen by a Young
Boston Merchant. Boston: Houghton Mifflin Co., 1913. Edition ltd.
to 525 numbered copies. Blue cloth over boards; paper spine label.
Bookplate. Karmiole 72-16 1983 $25

BALLINGER, JOHN   The Cardiff Free Libraries. N.p., 1895.
First edition, n.p. Front. & illus. Orig. brown cloth, v.g.
Inscribed presentation copy from the author. Jarndyce 31-222 1983
£10.50

BALLO, FERDINANDO   Grosz. Milano: Rosa e Ballo, 1946.
63 plates (5 color). 1 tipped-in text illus. Small 4to. Wrappers.
Ars Libri 32-292 1983 $85

BALLOU, ADIN   Glimpses of the Supernatural. Liverpool:
Edward Howell, 1853. 17 cm. Orig. lavender printed boards, quite
worn, dated 1854. From the library of Sir Arthur Conan Doyle, signed
& dated by him on the title page in 1921. Grunder 6-16 1983 $185

BALLOU, ROBERT   Early Klickitat Valley Days. (Golden-
dale, Wash., 1938). 1st ed. Illus. Clark 741-405 1983 $27.50

BALLY, GUSTAV   Vom Ursprung Und Von Den Grenzen Der
Freiheit. Basel: Benno Schwabe & Co., (1945). First edition. Dust
jacket. Gach 95-29 1983 $20

BALSTON, THOMAS   The Cambridge University Press
Collection of Private Press Types... (Cambridge): University
Printer, 1951. First edition. Small 4to. Polished buckram.
Limited to 350 copies. Oak Knoll 48-92 1983 $150

BALTIMORE, F.   A Tour in the East. London, 1767.
Engraved title, folding map of Constantinople, 3 plates. Sm.8vo.
Full cont. red morocco, spine gilt, green label. Presentation copies
only were issued with plates. Previously belonged to Beckford, with
his manuscript marginal pencil note, J.H. Newman of Dorking, with his
bookplate, the neat Rosebery Library blindstamp at the head of the
title. Good. Edwards 1044-33 1983 £350

BALTIMORE MUSEUM OF ART   The Art of the Maya. Baltimore, 1937.
12 plates, 1 map. 4to. Wrappers. Ars Libri 34-112 1983 $20

BALTIMORE MUSEUM OF ART.   An Exhibition of African Art. Nov.
1946. Baltimore, 1946. 45 illus. 4to. Wrappers. Ars Libri
34-556 1983 $20

BALTIMORE Sun Almanac. Baltimore, 1876-1889. 1st 14 issues. 14 issues in 1. Thich 12mo. Orig. boards, orig. wrappers bound in. Binding worn and spine lacking. Morrill 289-409 1983 $25

BALWHIDDER, MICAH   Annals of the Parish. Edinburgh, 1821. 1st ed. 12mo, contemporary boards, calf back and corners. Morrill 289-590 1983 $20

BALZAC, HONORE DE   Eugenie Grandet, Nouvelle Edition, revue et corrigee. Paris: Charpentier, Librairie-Editeur, 1839. Cont. morocco with marbled endpapers. New edition, revised and corrected. Max Beerbohm's copy, inscribed on the half-title "ex dono Max Curtis, M.B. Rapallo 1931." Extremities of spine scuffed. MacManus 277-274 1983 $75

BALZAC, HONORE DE   Eugenie Grandet. Printed at the Curwen Press for the Limited Editions Club, 1960. 8vo, 20 hand coloured illustrations, straw buckram with two leather labels gilt, slip case with printed paper label. Edition limited to 1500 numbered copies signed by the illustrator. Deighton 3-18 1983 £38

BALZAC, HONORE DE   La Fille aux Yeux d'Or (The Girl with the Golden Eyes). London: Leonard Smithers, 1896. First edition. 6 illus. engraved on wood by Charles Conder. 4to. Orig. yellow cloth. Covers soiled. Good. MacManus 278-1621 1983 $125

BALZAC, HONORE DE   La Fille Aux Yeux D'Or. Leonard Smithers, 1896. 6 illus. engr'd on wood by Charles Conder. 1st edn. Variant binding. Yellow cloth with titling & decor. in purple on fr. cvr., gilt titling & decor. fr. cvr., uncut (fr. cvr. some mottling with sl. mark down centre of fr., some foxing contents), v.g. copy. Hodgkins 27-407 1983 £55

BALZAC, HONORE DE   La Fille Aux Yeux D'Or. Leonard Smithers, 1896. 6 illus. engr'd on wood by Charles Conder. Purple cloth, gilt titling & decor. fr. cvr., uncut (new fr. ep., corners sl. brused & bkstrip sl. soiled), v.g. Hodgkins 27-406 1983 £40

BALZAC, HONORE DE   Human Comedy. London: Printed only for Subscribers by Leonard Smithers, 1897. 16 etchings by Frederic-Emile Jeannin and Ricardo de Los Rios. Paintings by G. Bussiere. 11 vols. Illus. Orig. gilt-decorated parchment designed by Aubrey Beardsley. One of 50 sets printed on Japanese vellum. Covers dust-soiled. Good set. MacManus 277-234 1983 $350

BAMFORD, SAMUEL   Passages in the Life of a Radical. W. Strange; Edinburgh: W. Tait; Manchester: A. Heywood and J. Gadsby, (1840)-44. Half calf, green cloth boards, a little rubbed. Jarndyce 30-886 1983 £55

BANCE, WILLIAM   Ralph; a Legend of the Gipsies. Sold by the author at Charlton, 1845. First edition, orig. dark green cloth a little worn. Jarndyce 30-635 1983 £24

BANCKS, JOHN   A Compendious History of the House of Austria, and the German Empire. London: Printed By and For J. Mechell, n.d. 8vo, with a large folding engraved coloured map. Ex-library, contemporary polished calf, without the label, joints weak. Deighton 3-19 1983 £65

BANCROFT, ANNE   The Memorable Lives of Bummer & Lazarus (Citizens of San Francisco) 185? - 1865. Los Angeles, 1939. 8vo, cloth-backed bds., paper label, d/w. Illustrated with cartoons of the period by Edward Jump and others. One of 500 copies. A very nice copy. Perata 27-173 1983 $40

BANCROFT, FREDERIC   Slave-Trading in the Old South. Baltimore, (1932). Illus. 8vo, lacks front endleaf. Morrill 288-27 1983 $20

BANCROFT, GEORGE   History of the United States. Boston, 1862. 9 vols. 19th edition, 8vo, 1/2 leather, gilt-dec. spines, marbled boards. Argosy 716-185 1983 $200

BANCROFT, GEORGE   History of the United States of America, From the Discovery of the Continent. Boston, 1879. 6 vols. Cloth, sm. bookplate, bookseller's stamps. Spines a bit frayed, sm. paint spotting else a good used set. Centenary edition. King 46-9 1983 $35

BANCROFT, GEORGE   Literary and Historical Miscellanies. NY, 1855. First edition, 8vo, 1/2 crimson mor., g.t. Argoy 716-156 1983 $40

BANCROFT, HUBERT HOWE   California Inter Pocula. San Francisco, 1888. Blind-stamped cloth, ex lib. Argosy 716-29 1983 $35

BANCROFT, HUBERT HOWE   California Pastoral, 1769-1848. San Francisco, 1888. Blindstamped cloth, ex lib. Argosy 716-30 1983 $35

BANCROFT, HUBERT HOWE   History of British Columbia 1792-1887. San Francisco, 1887. Maps, blindstamped cloth, ex lib. Argosy 716-43 1983 $50

BANCROFT, HUBERT HOWE   History of Mexico. San Francisco: Bancroft, 1883. 6 vols., complete, maps. Maroon buckram, leather spine labels. Very fine set. Jenkins 153-28 1983 $250

BANCROFT, HUBERT HOWE   History of Oregon. San Francisco, 1886. 2 vols., maps, thick 8vo, blindstamped cloth. Ex lib. Argosy 716-393 1983 $60

BANCROFT, HUBERT HOWE   History of the Life of John Deane. San F., 1889. Orig. cloth. First edition. Ginsberg 47-42 1983 $25

BANCROFT, HUBERT HOWE   History of Washington, Idaho, Montana 1845-1889. San Francisco, 1890. Blindstamped cloth, ex lib. Argosy 716-601 1983 $35

BANCROFT, HUBERT HOWE   Literary Industries. San Francisco, 1890. Blindstamped cloth, ex lib. Argosy 716-186 1983 $25

BANCROFT, HUBERT HOWE   Works. San Francisco, 1882-1890. Orig. full tree calf. 39 vols., complete. Maps, illus. Orig. red and green leather labels. Spines extra gilt, a.e.g. A fine set in especially handsome bindings. Jenkins 152-19 1983 $3,750

BANCROFT, HUBERT HOWE   Works. San F., 1882-91. 39 vols. Orig. cloth. First edition. Ginsberg 47-23 1983 $1,250

BANCROFT, HUBERT HOWE   Works. San Francisco, 1883-90. 39 vols. 8vo, original 1/2 morocco, marbled boards & edges (some binding wear). Argosy 710-18 1983 $900

BANCROFT, S. B.   Mr. and Mrs. Bancroft, On and Off the Stage. London: Richard Bentley and Son, 1888. 2 vols. Half brown morocco, worn. Written by themselves. Dawson 471-316 1983 $50

BANDINEL, JAMES   The Star of Lovell; a Tale of the Poor Clergy. London: Saunders, Otley, and Co., 1862. 3 vols. Orig. cloth. First edition. Corners bumped. One hinge cracked. Covers a bit soiled. All edges a little worn. A good set. MacManus 277-151 1983 $225

BANGE, E. F.   Die deutschen Bronzestatuetten des 16. Berlin, 1949. Sm. folio, text illus., 203 plates. Boards, 1/4 cloth. Ars Libri SB 26-6 1983 $185

BANGEL, RUDOLF   Johann Georg Trautmann und seine Zeitgenossen. Strassburg: J.H. Ed. Heitz, 1914. 11 plates. 4to. Wrappers. Lacking back cover. Ars Libri 32-676 1983 $85

BANGS, JOHN KENDRICK   A House-Boat on the Styx. NY, 1896. Front hinge starting, one plate loose, good, owner's name. Quill & Brush 54-60 1983 $35

BANGS, JOHN KENDRICK   A House-Boat on the Styx. New York, Harper, 1896. Frontis., plates. First edition. Orig. pictorial green cloth, gilt. Few specks, but a fine copy. Jenkins 155-46 1983 $35

BANGS, JOHN KENDRICK   Mephistopheles: A Profanation. New York, 1889. 8vo. Stiff red wrappers. This copy inscribed by the author. Some light wear to edge of spine, mainly fine. In Our Time 156-48 1983 $50

BANGS, JOHN KENDRICK   Paste Jewels. New York & London, 1897.
1st ed. Orig. decorated pale green cloth, gilt. A few faint spots
on rear cover, else fine copy. Jenkins 155-48 1983 $20

BANGS, JOHN KENDRICK   The Pursuit of the House-Boat, Being
Some Further Account of the Divers Doings of the Associated Shades,
under the Leadership of Sherlock Holmes, Esq. New York: Harper,
1897. Frontis. 1st ed., state A. Orig. pictorial tan cloth, gilt.
Near fine copy of this vol. dedicated to A. Conan Doyle "with the
author's sincerest regards..." Jenkins 155-49 1983 $25

BANIM, JOHN   The Smuggler; a Tale. London: Bentley,
1831. 3 vols. Orig. boards. Paper labels. First edition, with the
correct pagination in volumes one and three. Spines and labels defective; a few covers and preliminaries loose. A good set. Containing
an inserted publisher's catalogue, dated, "August 1831," at the front
of volume one. MacManus 277-153 1983 $185

BANISTER, DOUGLAS   Life of Mr. John Reeve, with original
anecdotes. London: Richardson and Son, n.d. (1838). 1st ed., 8vo,
original grey printed wrappers (a bit dusty, some wear to spine).
With a frontis. portrait. Very good copy of a very uncommon piece
of theatrical biography. Ximenes 64-31 1983 $150

BANKS, CHARLES EDWARD   The History of Martha's Vineyard.
Edgartown: 1966. Orig. published in 1911. 3 vols. Illus.
Argosy 710-279 1983 $125

BANKS, HOMER   The Story of San Clemente. (San
Clemente: El Heralde de San Clemente, 1930). With 24 plates. This
is a pres. copy, signed by Ole Hanson, the founder of San Clemente.
Red cloth, a bit shelfworn. Karmiole 76-26 1983 $35

BANKS, JOHN   Vertue Betray'd; or. Anna Bullen.
London: R. Bentley and M. Magnes, 1682. First edition. Small
4to. Modern green morocco, title backed and imprint cropped. With
library stamp on verso of title-page. Very scarce. Traylen 94-46
1983 £135

BANNER, H. S.   Romantic Java as It Was and Is. London,
1927. Map, plates. 8vo. Orig. cloth. Good. Edwards 1044-35 £30

BANNERMAN, ANNE   Tales of superstition and chivalry.
London: Vernor and Hood, 1802. First edition. Small 8vo. Cont.
calf. 2 plates (some stains, slight marginal tear). Calf worn.
Some foxing. Ximenes 63-391 1983 $40

BANNERMAN, D. A.   Birds of Cyprus. 1958. 16 coloured and
15 half-tone plates, map, imp. 8vo, original cloth. Wheldon 160-
643 1983 £95

BANNERMAN, D. A.   The Birds of the British Isles. 1953-63.
12 vols., imp. 8vo, cloth, plain and coloured plates. Orig. dust
jackets. Scarce. A nice set. Wheldon 160-3 1983 £300

BANNERMAN, D. A.   The Birds of Tropical West Africa.
1930-51. 8 vols., imp. 8vo, original cloth, maps, plates. A complete
set of a very scarce work. Some worming in the outer margins of
vols. 2 and 3 at the beginning and end and slight foxing. Bindings of
vols. 5 to 8 a trifle stained. Wheldon 160-2 1983 £400

BANNERMAN, D. A.   The Birds of Tropical West Africa,
Vol. 7, Weaver birds. 1949. 14 coloured plates by G. Lodge, 4to,
cloth. Wheldon 160-641 1983 £75

BANNERMAN, D. A.   The Birds of Tropical West Africa,
Vol. 8, Supplement and General Index. 1951. 4to, cloth. Wheldon
160-642 1983 £45

BANNERMAN, HELEN   Little Degchie-Head. Nisbet, 1903.
Numerous col'd illus. Printed on one side of page only. Green mottled pictorial decor. pasted fr. cvr., red titling fr. cvr. & bkstrip.
Re-backed with portion of orig. bkstrip, extremities rubbed & some
thumbing of contents, good. Hodgkins 27-10 1983 £15

BANNERMAN, HELEN   The New Animated Little Black Sambo.
N.Y.: Garden City, (1933). Large 8vo. Yellow pictorial cloth. Illus.
with 27 full-page color illus. by K. Wiese. In a frayed dust wrapper
(slightly bowed). Near fine. Aleph-bet 8-27 1983 $85

BANNERMAN, HELEN   Sambo and the Twins. N.Y.: Stokes, 1936.
First edition. 12mo. Red cloth. Fine in frayed dust wrapper. Full-
page color illus. throughout. Aleph-bet 8-26 1983 $45

BANNING, HANCOCK   Santa Catalina Island, Winter & Summer.
Los Angeles: Wilmington Transportation Co., (1895). Illus. Wrappers.
Dawson 471-16 1983 $40

BANNING, WILLIAM   Six Horses. N.Y., Century, (1930).
First edition. Illus. with 49 halftones. Dust jacket (small chip).
Very good. Houle 22-1016 1983 $65

BANNING, WILLIAM   Six Horses. New York, (1930). 1st ed.
Port., plates, map, dj. Clark 741-474 1983 $50

BANNISTER, S.   William Peterson, the merchant statesman... Edinburgh, 1859. Second edition. 12mo. Orig. cloth.
Heath 48-32 1983 £20

BANQUET. MA, 1978. No. 28 of 225 copies signed by all contributors.
Mint in mint slipcase. Quill & Brush 54-1037 1983 $90

BANTA, WILLIAM   Twenty-Seven Years on the Texas Frontier.
Council Hill, Okla., (1933). Illus., wrps. Clark 741-465 1983
$23.50

BANVARD, JOHN   Description of Banvard's Panorama of the
Missippi River. Boston, 1847. Orig. printed wraps. First edition.
Ginsberg 46-51 1983 $250

BANVARD, JOHN   Description of Banvard's Panorama of the
Mississippi River, Painted on Three Miles of Canvas. Boston, 1847.
First edition. Orig. printed wrappers. Some foxing, particularly on
title. Includes a description of the scenes depicted in the painting
and an account of life on the Mississippi. Very good. Felcone 20-10
1983 $100

BARBANTINI, NINO   Medardo Rosso. Venezia: Neri Pozza,
1950. 38 plates. Large 8vo. Boards. Ars Libri 33-577 1983
$30

BARBARA, J. WESLEY   The Printers' Text Book... Boston:
Dodd's Newspaper Advertising Agency and Printers' Supply Depot, (1875).
Small 4to. Orig. cloth. The covers are rubbed with some discoloration
along edges. The cloth on the hinge has been partially worn off in two
places and the bottom of the spine is chipped off. Back cover is discolored. Oak Knoll 49-24 1983 $250

BARBE-MAUROIS, FRANCOIS   Our Revolutionary Forefathers. N.Y.,
1929. Illus. Argosy 716-456 1983 $30

BARBEAU, MARIUS   Cornelius Kreighoff. Pioneer Painter
of North America. Toronto: MacMillan, 1934. 24 1/2cm. 16 colour
plates. Catalogue raisonee. Orig. red cloth, gold stamped titles
on the spine and upper cover, spine slightly faded else very good
to fine copy. McGahern 54-8 1983 $300

BARBEAU, MARIUS   Cornelius Kreighoff. Toronto: Ryerson,
1948. 18cm. First edition. 16 illus. (4 being colour). Red cloth.
Fine. McGahern 54-9 1983 $35

BARBEAU, MARIUS   Haida Myths. Ottawa: National
Museum, 1953. 25cm. First edition. 328 illus. Colour illus'd
endpapers, decorated stiff wrappers. Fine. McGahern 54-10 1983
$85

BARBEAU, MARIUS   Totem Poles. Ottawa, 1950. 2 vols.
561 illus. 4to. Wrappers. Ars Libri 34-113 1983 $85

BARBER, DANIEL   History of My Own Times. Washington,
1827. Later calf and boards, rear board detached. Newberry
duplicate. Reese 18-610 1983 $20

BARBER, JAMES   Tom K----g's: or, the Paphian Grove.
London: printed for J. Robinson, 1738. 8vo, disbound, 1st ed.
Original printing; very rare. Engraved frontis. and two other
plates. A nice copy. Ximenes 64-32 1983 $550

BARBER, JOHN WARNER   City Guide to New Haven. New Haven 1860.
24mo, orig. cloth, front hinge broken, ex lib. Argosy 710-113
1983 $50

BARBER, JOHN WARNER   Connecticut Historical Collections.
New Haven, (1838). Illus. 7 plates, colored folding map. Later
cloth. Felcone 22-36 1983 $50

BARBER, JOHN WARNER   Historical Collections...of Every Town
in Massachusetts... Worcester, 1840. Folding map and 200 engravings.
8vo. Contemporary calf. Rubbed; some foxing; front hinge partly
broken. Morrill 289-414 1983 $50

BARBER, JOHN WARNER   Historical Collections of the State of
New Jersey... New York, 1844. 2 colored plates, 8 black and white
plates, text illus. 1st ed. 8vo, contemporary calf. Worn, some
foxing, hinges cracked. Morrill 289-457 1983 $40

BARBER, T.   Picturesque Illustrations of the Isle
of Wight. (ca. 1836). Engraved title-page, 40 engraved plates and a
map, 8vo, original decorated cloth (front joint loose). Wheldon
160-345 1983 £35

BARBOSA, DUARTE   A description of the coasts of east
Africa and Malabar... London: Hakluyt Soc., 1866. 8vo. 2
facsimiles. Modern cloth. Ex-library. Adelson Africa-163 1983
$40

BARBOUR, A. H. FREELAND   Spinal Deformity in Relation to
Obstetrics. N.Y., ca. 1885. 39 fine plates, the first 15 in tint.
Thin folio, orig. cloth (rebacked). First edition. Argosy 713-26
1983 $125

BARBOUR, GEORGE M.   Florida for Tourists, Invalids,
and Settlers... New York, 1883. Illus. Ads. Folding map. Cloth,
waterstain along extreme bottom edge of text, some cover soiling.
Felcone 22-65 1983 $20

BARBOUR, PHILIP   Journals of Late Brevet-Major, Captain
3rd Reg...London, 1936. Printed for the author in a limited edition
each numbered and signed. Portraits, facsimile, plate and chart.
8vo, original cloth, uncut, as new. Clark 741-450 1983 $27.50

BARBOUS, JACQUES   Essai D'Une Psychologie de L'Angleterre
Contemporaine. Paris: Felix Alcan, 1907. Grey polished calf, marbled
boards, preserving orig. wrappers. Very good ex-library copy, spine
bands rubbed. Gach 94-102 1983 $25

BARBOZA DU BOCAGE, J. V.   Ornithologie d'Angola. Lisbon, 1881.
Roy. 8vo, half-cloth, 10 hand-coloured plates by Keulemans. Rare.
Some foxing and a stamp on the title-page, else in good condition.
Wheldon 160-4 1983 £140

BARBUSSE, HENRI   Le Feu. Paris: Ernest Flammarion,
Editeur, (1916). Orig. printed wrappers. First trade edition. Inscribed at a later date on the half-title by the author: "A David...
hommage cordial et devoue Henri Barbusse, New York, Nov. 33." Preserved in a cloth slipcase with leather labels. A fine copy of this
important novel. MacManus 277-155 1983 $250

BARCLAY, FLORENCE LOUISA CHARLESWORTH   Guy Mervyn. London: Spencer
Blackett, 1891. First edition. 3 vols. Orig. cloth. Presentation
copy, inscribed on the verso of the flyleaf, with a quotation written
on the title-page. Lacking half-title in Vol. I. Front cover of
Vol. II soiled. Good. MacManus 280-4424 1983 $125

BARCLAY, JOHN   John Barclay His Argenis. By Felix
Kyngston, for Richard Meighen, 1629. Second edition of this
translation. 4to. Cont. calf, (joints cracked). Hannas 69-7 1983
£80

BARCLAY, JOHN   Euphormio's Satyricon. (London), 1954.
Quarto, full red morocco, gilt cockerel device on front cover,
t.e.g., others uncut. Ten wood-engravings by Derrick Harris. One of
60 copies on an edition of 260. Slipcase. Duschnes 240-92 1983
$250

BARCLAY, JOHN   Euphormio's Satyricon. (London), 1954.
Quarto, cloth-backed boards. One of 200 copies. Corners bumped.
Duschnes 240-93 1983 $125

BARCLAY, JOHN   An Inquiry into the Opinions, Ancient
and Modern, concerning Life and Organisation. Edinburgh, 1822.
8vo, cont. calf, rubbed, label defective. Bickersteth 77-256 1983
£68

BARCLAY, JOHN   A New Anatomical Nomenclature. Edinburgh, 1803. First edition. Thin 8vo, cont. bds., (back slightly
damaged); uncut. Argosy 713-27 1983 $85

BARCLAY, JOHN   A Selection from the Letters and Papers
of the Late John Barclay. Harvey and Darton, 1841. First edition,
8vo, orig. cloth. A little wear to spine. Fenning 60-18 1983
£10.50

BARCLAY, ROBERT   Apologie de la Veritable Theologie
Chretienne... A. Londres, T. Sowle, 1702. Cont. calf, label. 1st
ed. in French. O'Neal 50-3 1983 $60

BARD, SAMUEL   Two Discourses dealing with Medical
Education in early New York. New York, 1921. 8vo. Facs. of 1769
and 1819 works. Very good. Fye H-3-19 1983 $30

BARD, SAMUEL   Waikna: Or Adventures on the Mosquito
Shore. NY, 1855. Many illus., bottom edge of spine just starting to
wear, cover faded and rubbed, some interior foxing, very good, name
stamp on page 73. Quill & Brush 54-1693 1983 $65

BARD, SAMUEL   Waikna. NY, 1855. Map, many illus.
Orig. cloth, (worn, some pp. dampstained, t.p. blindstamped). Argosy
716-628 1983 $20

BARDSLEY, SAMUEL A.   Medical Reports of Cases and
Experiments...(with) an Enquiry into the Origin of Canine Madness.
London, 1807. First edition. Marbled boards, (crudely rebacked;
ex-lib.). Argosy 713-28 1983 $75

BAREFOOT, A. C.   Identification of Modern and Tertiary
Woods. Oxford, 1982. Numerous figures, 4to, boards. Wheldon 160-
2071 1983 £49

BARETTI, JOSEPH   An account of the manners and customs
of Italy. London: for T. Davies, etc., 1768. First edition. 8vo.
2 vols. Cont. calf. Spines gilt. Two leaves of engraved music in
vol. II. Some browning, binding a bit worn. Ximenes 63-613 1983
$125

BARGELLINI, PIERO   Il Concilio di Firenze e gli affreschi
di Benozzo. Firenze: Cassa di Risparmio di Firenze, 1961. 80
color plates. Large 4to. Cloth. Ars Libri 33-176 1983 $135

BARGELLINI, PIERO   La soave mestizia del Perugino.
Firenze: Del Turco, 1950. 4 color plates. 94 illus. Large 8vo.
Boards. Dust jacket. Ars Libri 33-266 1983 $20

BARHAM, R. H. DALTON   The Life and Letters of Rev. Richard
Harris Barham. Richard Bentley, 1880. Half title, frontis., 1 page
of ads. Orig. black cloth blocked in red and gilt. Jarndyce 30-
887 1983 £15

BARHAM, RICHARD HARRIS   The Ingoldsby Legends or Mirth and
Marvels. London: Richard Bentley, 1840. Original cloth. First
edition. Corners slightly bumped. A few small waterspots on the
front cover. A touch of foxing. A near-fine copy. MacManus 277-156
1983 $185

BARHAM, RICHARD HARRIS   The Ingoldsby Legends or Mirth and
Marvels. London: Richard Bentley, 1846-1847. 3 vols. Illus.
Rebound in full red morocco, gilt, by Morrell. Third edition. Some
foxing. A very good copy. MacManus 277-157 1983 $150

BARHAM, RICHARD HARRIS   The Ingoldsby Legends. Richard Bentley,
1852. Engr. titles, illus. by G. Cruikshank, Leech, etc. Plates
browned. Orig. blue cloth, spines gilt, v.g. Jarndyce 30-291 1983
£24

BARHAM, RICHARD HARRIS   Ingoldsby Legends. London, Bentley,
1876. Annotated edition, large 8vo, illus. by George Cruikshank,
John Leech and others. Full tan calf by Tout, with gilt spines,
red and blue leather labels. T.e.g., marbled endpapers. Very good.
2 vols. Houle 21-433 1983 $250

BARHAM, RICHARD HARRIS   The Ingoldsby Legends. London, 1898.
First edition with these illus. (by A. Rackham). Illus. in colour and
black and white. Reading copy only. Rota 230-501 1983 £30

BARHAM, RICHARD HARRIS   The Ingoldsby Legends, Mirth & Marvels.
London & N.T.: J.M. Dent & E.P. Dutton, 1907. First of this edition.
Folio. Illus. by A. Rackham. Orig. decorated vellum. One of 560
copies signed by Rackham. Contains many color plates and black & white
illustrations. Yellow silk ties torn. In a cloth slipcase. Fine.
MacManus 280-4325 1983 $500

BARHAM, RICHARD HARRIS   The Ingoldsby Legends. J.M. Dent, 1907.
4to. Mounted colour frontis. Decorated title. 23 mounted colour
plates, 12 tinted plates & 66 text illus. Pictorial endpapers. Full
white vellum pictorial, gilt. Lacks ties. Edition limited to 500
copies, No. 157, signed by Rackham. Greer 40-178 1983 £195

BARHAM, RICHARD HARRIS   The Ingoldsby Legends, or Mirth and
Marvels...Illustrated by Arthur Rackham. London: Dent, 1907.
Frontis., color plates tipped. 1st ed. Orig. pictorial green cloth,
t.e.g., others uncut. Light signs of rubbing, but fine copy.
Jenkins 155-1418 1983 $185

BARHAM, RICHARD HARRIS   The Jackdaw of Rheims. London: Richard
Bentley, 1870. Octavo. 12 color-printed illus. tipped in. Inner
hinges split, else fine in Victorian-style, pictorially gilt-stamped
cloth, lightly rubbed at extremities. A.e.g. Owner's signature.
Bromer 25-354 1983 $45

BARHAM, RICHARD HARRIS   The Windmill. London, 1923. First
edition. Illus. Sm. 4to. Lower corners a little bruised. Inscription on flyleaf. Nice. Rota 230-502 1983 £15

BARI, VALESKA   The Course of an Empire. New York,
1931. Illus. Clark 741-78 1983 $27.50

BARIGOZZI BRINI, AMALIA   Carlo Innocenzo Carloni. Milano:
Ceschina, 1967. 12 color plates. 88 illus. 4to. Cloth. Dust
jacket. Ars Libri 33-84 1983 $75

BARILI, ANTONIO   Castiglione Olona e Masolina da
Panicale. Milano: Unione Tipografico, 1938. Prof. illus. Small
4to. Wrappers. Ars Libri 33-228 1983 $27.50

BARING, ALEXANDER   An Inquiry into the Causes and Conse-
quences of the Orders in Council and an Examination of the Conduct of
Great-Britain Towards the Neutral Commerce of America. New York, 1808.
Second American edition. Stitched, uncut. Bradley 64-181 1983 $20

BARING, MAURICE   Algae. An Anthology of Phrases. London:
William Heinemann, Ltd., 1928. (With:) Algae. An Anthology of
Phrases. Second Series. Cambridge: The University Press, 1929.
Orig. wrappers. First editions; first ordinary edition of first
series, limited edition, of 50 copies of second series. Presentation copy, inscribed by Baring in 1931 in each volume. Wrappers a
little worn, but a very good pair. MacManus 277-158 1983 $150

BARING, MAURICE   Cecil Spencer. Lon., (1929). One of
525 numbered and signed copies, cover slightly soiled, else very good.
Quill & Brush 54-61 1983 $50

BARING, MAURICE   Cecil Spencer. London: William Heinemann Ltd., (1929). 4to. Orig. parchment. First edition. Limited to
525 copies signed by the author. Covers somewhat soiled and darkened.
A good copy. MacManus 277-159 1983 $35

BARING, MAURICE   Daphne Adeane. London: William Heinemann Ltd., (1926). Orig. cloth. First edition. With an autograph
note from Baring tipped to the title-page. Very good copy. MacManus
277-160 1983 $35

BARING, MAURICE   The Lonely Lady of Dulwich. London:
William Heinemann Ltd., (1934). Orig. cloth. First edition. Presen-
tation copy, inscribed on the front flyleaf to "E.V. (Knox) fr. Maurice,
July 25, 1934." Very good copy. MacManus 277-161 1983 $45

BARING, MAURICE   Poems: 1914-1919. London: Martin
Secker, (1920). Orig. blue boards with paper label on spine. First
edition. One of 100 copies printed on Japon vellum and signed by
author. Fine copy. MacManus 277-163 1983 $85

BARING, MAURICE   Robert Peckham. (London: The Fanfare
Press), Privately Printed for the Author, 1934. Orig. wrappers.
First edition. One of 100 copies signed by the author. Front cover
marked. Spine worn. MacManus 277-164 1983 $40

BARING, MAURICE   Sonnets and Short Poems. Oxford: B. H.
Blackwell, 1906. Orig. wrappers. First edition. Wrappers a bit faded
and frayed at edges. In cloth folding box. Good. MacManus 277-166
1983 $75

BARING, MAURICE   Tinker's Leave. London: William Heinemann Ltd., (1927). 8vo. Original green cloth. First edition.
MacManus 277-167 1983 $10

BARING-GOULD, SABINE   A Book of Brittany. London: Methuen &
Co., 1901. 69 illus. Original cloth. First edition. Spine very
slightly faded. Bookseller's stamp on endpaper. Corners a little
bumped. A very good copy. MacManus 277-168 1983 $45

BARING-GOULD, SABINE   A Book of the West. London: Methuen &
Co., 1899. 2 vols. Original cloth. First edition. Binding of vol.
2 very slightly waterstained. All edges a little worn. Bookseller's
tickets and previous owners' signatures on endpapers (bit of browning).
A very good set. MacManus 277-169 1983 $50

BARING-GOULD, SABINE   The Book of Were-Wolves. London, 1865.
First edition. 8vo, gilt pict. red cloth; extremes of backstrip
rubbed; front hinge starting. Argosy 714-33 1983 $100

BARING-GOULD, SABINE   Chris of All-Sorts. London: Methuen &
Co., 1903. Orig. cloth. First edition. Edges and corners very
slightly worn. Covers a trifle soiled. Rear inner hinges cracking.
Some light foxing. MacManus 277-170 1983 $45

BARING-GOULD, SABINE   Cliff Castles and Cave Dwellings of
Europe. London: Seeley and Co., 1911. With 51 illus. and diagrams.
Orig. pictorial cloth. First edition. Edges slightly worn. Covers
a little soiled. Endpapers a bit soiled. A very good copy. MacManus
277-171 1983 $35

BARING-GOULD, SABINE   Court Royal. London: Smith, Elder & Co.,
1886. 3 vols. Original decorated cloth. First edition. Corners and
edges very slightly worn. Covers a bit soiled and waterspotted.
Signature on each front pastedown endpaper. Hinges cracked in vol. 1.
A good set. MacManus 277-172 1983 $350

BARING-GOULD, SABINE   Family Names and Their Story. London:
Seeley & Co., 1910. Original cloth. First edition. Edges and corners
very slightly worn. A little light foxing. A very good to near-fine
copy. MacManus 277-173 1983 $35

BARING-GOULD, SABINE   In Exitu Israel. London: Macmillan and
Co., 1870. 2 vols. Original cloth. First edition of Baring-Gould's
second novel, which followed the anonymously published "Through Flood
and Fame." With the publisher's catalogue dated May, 1870. Spines
and covers quite soiled. Some light foxing. Edges a little worn.
A good set. MacManus 277-174 1983 $125

BARING-GOULD, SABINE   John Herring. London: Smith, Elder,
& Co., 1883. 3 vols. Orig. cloth. First edition. By the Author
of "Mehalah." Covers soiled (library labels removed from front
covers). All edges and corners a bit worn. Bookplates. A good set.
MacManus 277-181 1983 $275

BARING-GOULD, SABINE   Legends of Old Testament Characters, from
the Talmud and Other Sources. London: Macmillan, 1871. 2 vols.
Orig. cloth. First edition. Covers worn and soiled. A good sound
copy. MacManus 277-175 1983 $75

BARING-GOULD, SABINE   The Lost and Hostile Gospels: An Essay
on the Toledoth Jeschu, and the Petrine and Pauline Gospels of the
First Three Centuries of Which Fragments Remain. London: William
and Norgate, 1874. Original cloth. First edition. Edges and corners
a bit worn. Former owners' signatures. Very good. MacManus 277-176
1983 $45

BARING-GOULD, SABINE   Old Country Life. London: Methuen and
Co., 1890. Illus. Orig. pictorial cloth. First edition. An advance
copy, inscribed on the verso of the front free endpaper: "With the
publisher's compliments." Edges and corners a little worn. A very
good copy. MacManus 277-177 1983 $50

BARING-GOULD, SABINE   Old English Fairy Tales. Methuen, 1895. 13 plates and 6 text illus. Light green pictorial cloth gilt, rubbed. Greer 40-47 1983 £22.50

BARING-GOULD, SABINE   Richard Cable. The Lightshipman. London: Smith, Elder & Co., 1888. 3 vols. Orig. decorated cloth. First edition. Presentation copy from the author inscribed: "Rev' I. VS Hughes with the author's kindest regards. January 20/ '88." Spines slightly worn with a few small tears to the corners, inner hinges cracking although cords intact. A clean set. MacManus 277-179 1983 $450

BARING-GOULD, SABINE   Siegfried. Dean & Son, 1904. Frontis. in blue. Title vignette. 10 plates & 11 other illus. Red decorated cloth, gilt. Ex-Library. Greer 40-185 1983 £45

BARING-GOULD, SABINE   The Silver Store. London: Longmans, Green, & Co., 1868. Orig. cloth. First edition. Library labels removed from endpapers. Covers dull. A good copy. MacManus 277-180 1983 $85

BARING-GOULD, SABINE   Strange Survivals. London: Methuen & Co., 1892. Original cloth. First edition. Covers soiled, edges and corners a bit worn. Hinge cracked. Endpapers browned. Good. MacManus 277-178 1983 $35

BARING-GOULD, SABINE   The Tragedy of the Caesars. London, 1905. 4to, cloth. Salloch 385-209 1983 $25

BARING-GOULD, SABINE   The Tragedy of the Caesars. London, 1923. 117 plates and illus. Royal 8vo. Half levant morocco, gilt, t.e.g. Traylen 94-50 1983 £22

BARKER, ANSELM H.   Anselm Holcomb Barker 1822-1895 Pioneer Builder and Early Settler of Auraria. Denver, 1959. 83pp. Tipped in frontis. Folding map. First edition limited to 500 numbered and signed copies. Including nine keepsakes in rear pocket. Fine copy. Jenkins 151-11 1983 $75

BARKER, BERNARD   Eliot the Younger. Samuel Tinsley, 1878. 2nd edition, 3 vols. Orig. maroon cloth, spines lettered in gilt. Mint. Jarndyce 30-288 1983 £62

BARKER, CICELY M.   Children's Book of Hymns. N.Y.: Revell, n.d. (ca. 1938). 4to. Blue cloth. Tipped in plates by Barker. Black and whites, musical notation and words. Very good. Aleph-bet 8-28 1983 $30

BARKER, CICELY M.   The Children's Book of Hymns. Blackie, n.d. 4to. Mounted colour frontis. Title vignette. 11 mounted colour plates. 12 text illus. Pictorial endpapers. Blue cloth gilt. Greer 40-41 1983 £12.50

BARKER, GEORGE   Poems. London, 1935. First edition. Spine and covers faded and marked. Nice. Rota 231-37 1983 £25

BARKER, GRANVILLE   Anatol: A Sequence of Dialogues... N.Y.: Mitchell Kennerley, 1911. Orig. cloth. Dust jacket (defective). First American edition. Pencil inscription on front flyleaf. A good copy. MacManus 277-182 1983 $20

BARKER, JACOB   Jacob Barker's Letters, Developing the Conspiracy Formed in 1826 for His Ruin. (New York. 1827). Self-wraps., stitched, very good. Reese 18-611 1983 $125

BARKER, JACOB   The Speeches of Barker and His Counsel. NY, 1826. First edition. 8vo, sewed. Argosy 716-594 1983 $35

BARKER, JAMES N.   Sketches of the Primitive Settlements on the River Delaware. Philadelphia, 1827. Dsb., very good. Reese 18-612 1983 $60

BARKER, JAMES P.   The Log of a Limejuicer. Putman, 1934. First U.K. edition, with 12 plates, 8vo, orig. cloth, a very good copy in a slightly worn dust wrapper. Fenning 62-16 1983 £10.50

BARKER, LEWELLYS F   A Case of Circumscribed Unilateral, and Elective Sensory Paralysis. NY, 1896. First edition. Tall 8vo, new wrs. Argosy 713-29 1983 $75

BARKER, LEWELLYS F.   Introduction to Diseases of the Nervous System. Philadelphia: Lea & Febiger, (n.d.). Orig. printed wrappers, top of spine chipped. With Meyer's pencil-lining and pencil notes. Inscription to Professor Adolf Meyer. Gach 95-30 1983 $35

BARKER, SHIRLEY   The Dark Hills Under. Yale U.P., 1933. 8vo. Cloth. Remnants of a bookplate on front endboard, else a vg-fine copy. In Our Time 156-49 1983 $35

BARLOW, JANE   Maureen's Fairing and Other Stories. London: J.M. Dent & Co., 1895. Illus. by Bertha Newcombe. Orig. gilt-decorated cloth. First edition. Covers a bit spotted. Endpapers partially browned. A very good copy. MacManus 277-183 1983 $45

BARLOW, JOEL   Advice to the Priviledged Orders... Paris: English Press, 1793. 8vo, stitched. In box. Early imprint of the English Press of Paris. Rostenberg 88-25 1983 $185

BARLOW, JOEL   A Letter to the National Convention of France on the Defects in the Constitution of 1791...to which is added The Conspiracy of Kings. New York: Greenleaf for Fellows, (1793). 8vo, wraps. Extra-illus. with 2 port. of Barlow. First American edition. Rostenberg 88-111 1983 $125

BARLOW, THOMAS   Bishop of Lincoln. Printed by S. Roycroft for Robert Clavell, 1681. First edition, 4to, wrapper, title and final page evenly dusty, but otherwise a very good copy. Fenning 61-19 1983 £24.50

BARNARD, ANNE   South Africa a century ago. London: Smith, Elder, 1901. 8vo. Portrait. Orig. cloth. Rubbed. Adelson Africa-164 1983 $25

BARNARD, EDWARD   A Sermon Preached before his Excellency Francis Bernard...and the Honourable House of Representatives of the Province of the Massachusetts-Bay...1766. Boston, 1766. Dsb. Slight staining. Very good. Reese 18-83 1983 $65

BARNARD, EVAN G.   A Rider of the Cherokee Strip. Boston, 1936. Illus. Orig. cloth, slightly worn. Ginsberg 47-25 1983 $30

BARNARD, EVAN G.   A Rider of the Cherokee Strip. Boston, 1936. Frontis. and plates. First edition. Some wear and the usual faded spine. Jenkins 153-29 1983 $30

BARNARD, FREDERICK   Behind a Brass Knocker. Chatto & Windus, 1883. First edition. Orig. olive green cloth, upper cover blocked in black and gilt, as a panelled front door. Very good. Jarndyce 31-424 1983 £24

BARNARD, GEORGE   The Theory & Practice of Landscape Painting in Watercolours. Routledge, 1871. New edn. 26 col. plates printed by Leighton Bros. Red sand grain cloth gilt, a.e.g. (new eps., some plates sl. marks margins, corners sl. bruised & worn, re-cased & bkstrip repr'd at top but split down fr. joint, cvrs. some soiling. Hodgkins 27-354 1983 £35

BARNARD, HENRY   A Discourse (on) the Life, Character and Services of the Rev. Thomas H. Gallaudet. Hartford, 1852. Orig. pr. wrs. Argosy 710-136 1983 $30

BARNARD, HENRY   School Architecture. New York, A.S. Barnes & Co., 1848. Second edition. With a frontis. and very many full-page and other illus., 8vo, orig. cloth. Fenning 62-17 1983 £55

BARNARD, THOMAS   An Historical Character relating to the holy and exemplary Life of the Right Honourable the Lady Elizabeth Hastings... Leedes: by James Lister, 1742. First edition. 12mo. Ad. leaf. Cont. calf. Rebacked. Heath 48-53 1983 £80

BARNES, A. S.   A Popular History of the U.S. of America. NY, (1878). Thick 8vo, 3/4 red, straight-grained mor., gilt-dec. spine, (corners slightly scuffed). Engr. plates, many illus., maps. Argosy 716-187 1983 $30

BARNES, DJUNA   The Book of Repulsive Women. Yonkers,
N.Y., Alicat Bookshop Press, 1948. First edition thus. Illus. with
five drawings by the author. One of 1,000 copies. Black paper wraps
printed in pink and black (slightly faded). Very good. Houle 22-69
1983 $85

BARNES, DJUNA   Ryder. New York, 1928. First edition.
Illus. by author. One of 3000 copies. Spine faded and lower edges
of covers marked. Nice. Rota 231-41 1983 £35

BARNES, GRACE   So This is Langtry. Boerne, Texas, 1946.
Orig. pictorial wrappers. Illus. Signed by the authors. First edition. Jenkins 153-625 1983 $25

BARNES, JOHN   A Tour through the Whole of France.
London: William Darton, 1815. First (only) ed., 12mo, full morocco
gilt, spine gilt, a.e.g., inner dentelles gilt by Bayntun. Folding
colored map, colored copperplates. A very good copy. Trebizond
18-129 1983 $275

BARNES, JOSHUA   Gerania: a new discovery of a little
sort of people... London: printed by W.G. for Obadiah Blagrave,
1675. First edition. 8vo. 19th-century blue straight-grained
morocco, gilt. Frontis. Spine rubbed, some dust-soiling. Ximenes
63-645 1983 $850

BARNES, WILL C.   Western Grazing Grounds and Forest
Ranges. Chicago: The Breeder's Gazette, 1913. Profusely illus.
with photographs, diagrams, and 6 chromolithograph plates. Green
cloth. Ex-library copy, with spine marking removed and bookplate.
Errata tipped-in. Karmiole 74-22 1983 $25

BARNES, WILLIAM   Poems Of Rural Life In The Dorset Dialect.
London: John Russell Smith, 1848. Orig. cloth. Second edition.
Contains the signature of William Allingham on the title-page. Spine
backing missing. Inner hinges weak. Clean copy with several penciled
notes in the text possibly in Allingham's hand. MacManus 277-66 1983
$50

BARNES, WILLIAM   Poems, Partly of Rural Life. London:
J.R. Smith, 1846. Orig. cloth with paper label. First edition.
Spine faded and label slightly worn, endpapers very slightly foxed.
Scarce in this condition. A very good copy. MacManus 277-184 1983
$350

BARNES, WILLIAM   - A Selection from Poems of Rural Life in
the Dorset Dialect. London: Kegan Paul, Trench, Trubner & Co. Ltd.,
1909. Frontis. 12mo. Orig. cloth. First of this edition. Former
owner's signature on flyleaf. A very good copy. MacManus 277-185

BARNEY, JAMES M.   Tales of Apache Warfare. (Phoenix),
1933. First edition. Printed gray wrappers. Scarce. Lower right
corner clipped, otherwise very good. Bradley 65-5 1983 $65

BARNUM, PHINEAS TAYLOR   Life of P. T. Barnum. Buffalo, 1888.
Presentation copy from Barnum, 1888, to Robert Collyer, and a further
presentation from Collyer. Illus. 8vo. Few small stains on front
cover. Morrill 287-24 1983 $125

BARNUM, PHINEAS TAYLOR   Struggles and Triumphs. New York, 1871.
Author's Ed. Illus. Inserted is ALS, Feb. 18, 1882 from author.
8vo, lacks blank leaves at end. Morrill 288-29 1983 $50

BARR, ALFRED H.   Picasso: Fifty Years of His Art.
New York: Museum of Modern Art, 1946. 6 color plates. 330 illus.
4to. Cloth. Dust jacket. Ars Libri 32-513 1983 $60

BARR, ROBERT   In the Midst of Alarms. London: Methuen
& Co., 1894. First English edition. Orig. decorated cloth. Presentation copy to Arthur Conan Doyle inscribed: "To Conan Doyle from Robert
Barr," with a sketch by Barr on the front free endpaper. Covers worn
and spotted, inside hinges weak and cracking. Some offsetting to the
endpapers. Slight foxing throughout. MacManus 278-1632 1983 $250

BARRA, EZEKIEL I.   A Tale of Two Oceans. San Francisco:
Privately Printed, 1893. Plates, first edition. Original pictorial
wrappers. Minor chipping. Jenkins 153-30 1983 $200

BARRE, UTTERE   Avondale of Avondale. Remington, 1877.
First edition, 3 vols., orig. orange cloth, blocked in black and
lettered in gilt. Very good. Jarndyce 30-293 1983 £48

BARREME, BERTRAND-FRANCOIS   Le Livre Necessaire pour les Comptables,
Avocats, Notairs, Procureurs, Negotians, & generalement a toute forte
de Conditions... A Paris, Chez Denys Thierry...M.DC.XCIV. (1694).
12mo, bound in full cont. calf. Corners scuffed. Upper hinge
slightly cracked. Spine stamped in gold between raised bands.
Gauffered edges. Early leaves with light marginal waterstaining.
Arkway 22-8 1983 $275

BARRETT, C. R. B.   History of the XIII. Hussars. London,
1911. 2 coloured frontis. and 4 other coloured plates of uniform,
81 plates, 25 illus., 10 folding maps. 2 vols., imp. 8vo. Orig.
blue decorated cloth, slightly worn. Ink ownership signature on endpapers. Uncut. Edges foxed. Good. Edwards 1042-527 1983 £125

BARRETT, EATON STANNARD   The Miss-Led General; A Serio-Comic..
Romance... Printed for H. Oddy, 1808. 1st ed., 12mo, orig. printed
boards uncut; title with vignette on upper, advertisements on lower,
cover; half-title; trivial wear to spine; no frontispiece present
nor sign of its removal. Hill 165-6 1983 £38

BARRETT, EATON STANNARD   Woman, a Poem. Henry Colburn, 1818.
2nd edition, half title, front., 6 pp ads. Uncut, orig. boards,
spine chipped, otherwise very good. Jarndyce 30-637 1983 £16.50

BARRETT, EDNA DUERINGER   Mrs. Collett. Los Angeles, Suttonhouse,
1936. Illus. by Henry Shire. Tan cloth stamped in red and yellow.
One of 500 copies printed by the Plantin Press. Very good. Houle
22-1017 1983 $45

BARRETT, J. LEE   Speed Boat Kings. Detroit, 1936.
First edition, authographed by Gar Wood. Photos, cloth, covers a
bit soiled and worn. King 46-538 1983 $45

BARRETT, J. LEE   Speed Boat Kings. Detroit, 1939.
Photos. Cloth. Index. Covers moderately rubbed and soiled. King
45-471 1983 $35

BARRETT, J. O.   "Old Abe:" The Live War-Eagle of Wisconsin. Madison, Wisc., 1876. First edition. Orig. pictorial wrappers.
Frontis. Map. Jenkins 152-551 1983 $85

BARRETT, WILSON   The Daughters of Babylon. London: John
Macqueen, 1899. Orig. pictorial cloth. First edition. Endpapers
foxed. A very good copy. MacManus 277-187 1983 $35

BARRIE, JAMES MATTHEW   The Admirable Crichton. Hodder, nd
(ca. 1910). 1st edn. Mounted colour frontis. & 19 mounted col.
plates, illus. by Hugh Thomson. Red cloth gilt (designed by Thomson),
v.g. Hodgkins 27-409 1983 £40

BARRIE, JAMES MATTHEW   The Allahakbarrie Book of Broadway
Cricket for 1899. (N.p., 1899). Illus. Orig. Japan vellum wraps.
A fine copy. First edition, privately printed. On the verso of
the half-title and on the dedication page appear the signatures, in
pencil, of all thirty-one players, including Barrie and the
dedicatee. Accompanied by four autograph letters signed by Barrie
(1900) to E.T. Reed, one of the players. Also accompanied by a photo
of the team. Felcone 21-5 1983 $500

BARRIE, JAMES MATTHEW   Auld Licht Idylls. London: Hodder &
Stoughton, 1888. Orig. cloth. First edition. Front inner hinge
cracked. A fine copy. MacManus 277-189 1983 $25

BARRIE, JAMES MATTHEW   Better Dead. London: Swan Sonnenschein
& Co., 1891. Frontis. Orig. cloth. Early edition of the author's
scarce first book, using the wrapper from the first edition as a
frontispiece. Bookseller's catalogue entry removed from front endsheet,
bookplate on recto of frontispiece. A very good copy. MacManus 277-
190 1983 $35

BARRIE, JAMES MATTHEW   The Boy David. London: Davies, 1938.
12mo. Orig. cloth. Dust jacket. First edition. Fine. MacManus
277-191 1983 $20

BARRIE, JAMES MATTHEW   Courage. Lon., (1922). Signed inscription from author, very minor interior foxing, white cover slightly
soiled, still very good. Quill & Brush 54-62 1983 $40

BARRIE, JAMES MATTHEW   Courage. London: Hodder & Stoughton,
(1922). Orig. cream backram. First edition, large-paper issue. In
the trade binding rather than vellum. A fine copy. MacManus 277-194
1983 $25

BARRIE, JAMES MATTHEW   Echoes of the War. London: Hodder &
Stoughton, (1918). Orig. cloth with paper spine and cover labels.
Dust jacket (spine slightly faded and rubbed). First edition, advance
review copy. Front inner hinge cracking. Spine and covers slightly
faded. A very good copy. MacManus 277-196 1983 $50

BARRIE, JAMES MATTHEW   George Meredith, 1909. London, (1909).
First edition One illus. 24mo. Covers soiled. Bradley 66-15 1983
$20

BARRIE, JAMES MATTHEW   George Meredith, 1909. First edition,
half title, illus. borders in red. Booklet, printed at the Chiswick
Press. Orig. cream boards, v.g. Jarndyce 30-1075 1983 £10.50

BARRIE, JAMES MATTHEW   George Meredith, 1909. London: (1909).
First edition. One illus. 24mo. Covers soiled. Bradley 66-15
1983 $20

BARRIE, JAMES MATTHEW   Jane Annie; or, The Good Conduct Prize.
London: Chappell & Co., 1893. Music by Ernest Ford. (With explanatory
notes down the margin by Caddie.) Orig. printed wrappers. First edition. Front wrapper detached, darkening of wrapper and title-page
owing to offsetting from leather folding case (defective). MacManus
277-198 1983 $65

BARRIE, JAMES MATTHEW   The Ladies' Shakespeare. (London: Privately printed by Clement Shorter, July 19, 1925). The substance of
a speech by Sir James Matthew Barrie, O.M., delivered at Stationers'
Hall upon the occasion of his receiving the Freedom of the Stationers'
Company, 3rd July 1925. Original printed wrappers. First edition.
Covers slightly faded and a trifle worn. A very good copy. MacManus
277-193 1983 $150

BARRIE, JAMES MATTHEW   The Little Minister. London: Cassell,
1891. 3 vols. Orig. cloth (slightly soiled). First edition. Barrie's
only three-decker. A grubby copy in a handsome half morrocco case.
MacManus 277-200 1983 $225

BARRIE, JAMES MATTHEW   The Little Minister. London, 1892.
2nd ed. 8vo. Cloth. With Barries's presentation inscription on
front endpaper "to Clement Scott from J.M. Barrie, Mar. 14, '92".
Also included is a one page ALS from Barrie to Scott. Some light
wear to crown of spine, otherwise a fine copy, with bookplate. In
Our Time 156-52 1983 $150

BARRIE, JAMES MATTHEW   The Little Minister. NY: Caldwell,
(1898). 23 cm. "Illustrated by photographs..." Orig. gilt-
decorated grey cloth, t.e.g. Uncut. Inscribed by the future apostle
to his wife: "...Mrs. Leah D. Widtsoe from John A. Widtsoe..."
Grunder 6-52 1983 $37.50

BARRIE, JAMES MATTHEW   The Little White Bird. NY, 1902. Edges
rubbed, minor cover pitting, else very good bright copy in frayed and
lightly chipped, internally mended dustwrapper. Quill & Brush 54-63
1983 $100

BARRIE, JAMES MATTHEW   Margaret Ogilvy. London: Hodder &
Stoughton, 1896. Orig. cloth. First edition. With a fine and important presentation inscription from Barrie to Sidney Colvin, dated in
the month of publication. Formerly owned by Arthur Swann. In a cloth
slipcase. A very nice copy. MacManus 277-203 1983 $350

BARRIE, JAMES MATTHEW   Margaret Ogilvy. London: Hodder &
Stoughton, 1896. 8vo. Orig. buckram. T.e.g. First English edition.
Endpapers lightly foxed. In a half morocco folding box. A very fine
copy. MacManus 277-204 1983 $45

BARRIE, JAMES MATTHEW   Margaret Ogilvy by Her Son. London:
Hodder & Stoughton, 1896. 8vo. Orig. buckram. T.e.g. First edition.
Good copy. MacManus 277-205 1983 $20

BARRIE, JAMES MATTHEW   Neither Dorking Nor the Abbey. Chicago:
Browne's Bookstore, 1912. First American edition. Tan wrappers.
Lightly soiled. Bradley 66-16 1983 $20

BARRIE, JAMES MATTHEW   The Novels and Sketches. London,
1896. 8 vols. Small 4to. Boards with vellum spines, t.e.g.,
others uncut. Frontis. to each vol. Author's edition, printed on
Japanese vellum. Limited to 150 numbered sets, signed by the
author. Traylen 94-51 1983 £160

BARRIE, JAMES MATTHEW   Peter and Wendy. New York: Scribner's
Sons, (1911). Illus. by F.D. Bedford. Orig. decorated cloth. First
American edition. Presentation copy from the author inscribed on the
front free endpaper: "Florence (?), from her friend J.M. Barrie, December 1911." Loosely laid in is an ALS, 1-1/2 pages, 3 Adelphi Terrace House, Strand W.C., 23 April, n.y., to the same Florence (?).
Spine edges a trifle worn. In a half-morocco folding case. A near-
fine copy. MacManus 277-206 1983 $450

BARRIE, JAMES MATTHEW   Peter and Wendy. New York: Scribner,
(1911). 1st American ed. Orig. green cloth, gilt, dj. Dj is blue-
grey paper printed in gilt. Fine copy in fine and very scarce dj
which repeats the designs on the pictorial covers. Jenkins 155-53
1983 $75

BARRIE, JAMES MATTHEW   Peter and Wendy. N.Y.: Scrib., 1940.
4to. Tan pictorial cloth, light wear. Illus. by E. Blampied with 12
full-page color plates and full-page black & whites. First edition.
Very good. Aleph-bet 8-29 1983 $35

BARRIE, JAMES MATTHEW   Peter Pan In Kensington Gardens. London:
Hodder & Stoughton, 1906. First edition. Illus. by A. Rackham.
Orig. decorated vellum. One of 500 copies signed by A. Rackham.
Yellow silk ties torn off. In a cloth slipcase. Fine. MacManus 280-
4288 1983 $1,000

BARRIE, JAMES MATTHEW   Peter Pan in Kensington Gardens...
London, (1906). 50 mounted coloured plates and other illus. from
drawings by Arthur Rackham. 4to. Orig. green cloth, gilt. Traylen
94-53 1983 £75

BARRIE, JAMES MATTHEW   Peter Pan in Kensington Gardens.
London: 1907. Fourth edition. 4to. maroon cloth, lettering &
design in gilt. With 50 tipped-in color plates by Rackham.
Light cover wear; a very nice copy. Perata 27-155 1983 $145

BARRIE, JAMES MATTHEW   Peter Pan in Kensington Gardens. London,
Hodder & Stoughton, n.d. (ca. 1910). Early edition. Small 4to,
illus. with 24 full page color plates by Arthur Rackham. 3/4 dark
green morocco by Bantun of Bath, spine richly decorated in gilt,
t.e.g., orig. cloth and pictorial endpapers bound in at rear. Fine.
Houle 22-70 1983 $225

BARRIE, JAMES MATTHEW   Peter Pan or The Boy Who Would Not Grow
Up. London: Hodder & Stoughton, 1928. Orig. cloth. Dust jacket,
(a little faded and soiled). First edition. Very good. MacManus
277-207 1983 $45

BARRIE, JAMES MATTHEW   The Plays. London: Hodder & Stoughton,
1928. Frontis. port. Orig. cloth. Dust jacket (darkened). First
edition. Very good copy. MacManus 277-208 1983 $25

BARRIE, JAMES MATTHEW   The Plays. London, 1945. Thick roy.
8vo. Half green morocco, gilt. Traylen 94-54 1983 £22

BARRIE, JAMES MATThEW   Quality Street, a Comedy in Four Acts.
Ca. 1925. 22 tipped-in colour plates, blue decorated end papers, orig.
cloth gilt, 4to. Bright crisp copy. K Books 307-14 1983 £38

BARRIE, JAMES MATTHEW   Sentimental Tommy. N.Y.: Charles
Scribner's Sons, 1896. Illus. by William Hatherell. Orig. decorated
cloth. First American edition. Inscribed by the author on the front
flyleaf "To Mr Van Wagenen, with my sincere regards, from J.M. Barrie,
Nov. '96." Good copy. MacManus 277-210 1983 $85

BARRIE, JAMES MATTHEW   Sentimental Tommy. London: Cassell &
Co., 1896. Orig. cloth. First edition. Spine rubbed. A good copy.
MacManus 277-209 1983 $20

BARRIE, JAMES MATTHEW   Tommy and Grizel. London: Cassell and
Co., 1900. Orig. cloth. First Colonial edition, marked on the spine:
"Cassell's Colonial Library." Covers very slightly worn and soiled.
Endpapers a little foxed. A good copy. MacManus 277-212 1983 $25

BARRIE, JAMES MATTHEW   Tommy and Grizel. London: Cassell, 1900.
First edition. Orig. cloth. MacManus 277-213 1983 $20

BARRIE, JAMES MATTHEW   Walker London. London: Samuel French,
Ltd., 1907. Frontis. Orig. green wrappers. First edition. Very
good copy. MacManus 277-214 1983 $125

BARRIE, JAMES MATTHEW   A Window in Thrums. London, 1892.
4to. Dark blue buckram, gilt, uncut edges. Vignette and 17 etched
plates from drawings by William Hole. Limited edition of 550
numbered copies. Traylen 94-55 1983 £20

BARRIE, JAMES MATTHEW   A Window in Thrums. London, 1894. 12th
ed. Orig. cloth. Good copy from Housman's library with his pencil
signature on half-title, and with a 1-1/4pp. ALS from Barrie to
Housman (dated 1928) tipped in at front. Fine assoc. vol. Jenkins
155-54 1983 $150

BARRIE, JAMES MATTHEW   The Works. London, 1913. The
Kirrieumuir edition. 10 vols. Roy. 8vo. Kelmscott boards, cloth
spines, gilt, t.e.g. Limited edition of 1,000 sets, numbered and
signed by the publishers, finely printed in large type on hand-
made paper. Traylen 94-52 1983 £70

BARRIE, JAMES MATTHEW   Works of... N.Y., Scribner's, (1929-
1931). The Peter Pan edition. Beige cloth over brown boards, "Peter
Pan" medallion stamped in gilt on front covers, paper labels on
spine, uncut and partially unopened, slipcase (a bit worn), else very
good - fine. Illus. with frontis. photoengravings. One of 1030
sets, signed by the publisher. Complete in 14 vols. Houle 22-71
1983 $250

BARRIE, JAMES MATTHEW   Works. N.Y., Scribner (1929-1931).
Peter Pan edition. Half beige cloth, uncut and partially unopened.
Illus. Complete in 14 vols. One of 1030 sets, signed by the
publisher. Houle 21-66 1983 $250

BARRIE, JAMES MATTHEW   Works of... NY, 1929. 14 Vols. Limited
to 1000 copies signed by publisher; ALS laid-in, mint in slipcases (2
damaged, rest fine). Quill & Brush 54-64 1983 $225

BARRILI, ANTON GIULIO   A Noble Kinsman. London: T. Fisher
Unwin, 1885. 2 vols. Orig. cloth. First edition in English. Very
worn and stained. MacManus 277-220 1983 $25

BARRINGTON, EMILIE ISABEL WILSON   G. F. Watts. Reminiscences. New
York: Macmillan, 1905. 40 plates. 4to. Cloth. Inside front hinge
cracked. Ex-library. Ars Libri 32-699 1983 $75

BARROW, JOHN   An account of travels into the interior
of southern Africa... London: T. Cadell Jun. & Wm. Davies, 1801,
1804. 2 vols. 4to. Folding frontis. 9 maps and plates. Cont.
calf. Rebacked. Green labels. Adelson Africa-10 1983 $775

BARROW, JOHN   Travels in China. London, 1804. First
edition. Coroured frontis., 7 plates, 4 coloured, 2 folding. 4to.
Diced, russia, some wear to corners and hinges. Good. Edwards 1044-
37 1983 £300

BARROW, JOHN   Travels in China. Philadelphia.
Rather age-browned throughout, a few marginal patches of worm, cont.
sheep, neatly rebacked. K Books 307-15 1983 £60

BARROW, JOHN   A voyage to Cochinchina... London:
T. Cadell & W. Davies, 1806. 4to. Folding map. 20 hand-coloured
plates. Orig. mottled calf, rebacked, red labels. Repairs to
folding plates. Adelson Africa-11 1983 $775

BARRON, S. B.   The Lone Star Defenders: A Chronicle
of the Third Texas Cavalry, Ross' Brigade. N.Y.: Neale, 1908.
1st edition. Rebound. Jenkins 151-235 1983 $350

BARROWCLIFFE, A. J.   Trust for Trust. Smither, Elder, 1859.
First edition, 3 vols. Front. vol. I by Phiz. 3 vols. bound as one.
Orig. red remainder cloth, inner hinges cracked. Jarndyce 30-294 1983
£48

BARROWS, JOHN R.   Ubet. Caldwell, Idaho, 1934. Cloth,
a very good copy in a split but still present dust jacket. Reese
19-38 1983 $75

BARROWS, SAMUEL J.   The Isles and Shrines of Greece. Boston,
1899. 19 plates. 8vo, cloth. Salloch 385-326 1983 $25

BARROWS, WILLIAM   The General. Boston, (1869). First
edition. Orig. pict. cloth. Illus. by G.G. White. Argosy 716-609
1983 $45

BARRUEL, AUGUSTIN   The History of the Clergy During the
French Revolution. Burlington, 1794. Leather and boards, worn.
Paper foxed and browned. Good. Reese 18-192 1983 $100

BARRUEL, AUGUSTIN   The History of the Clergy During the
French Revolution. Burlington: I. Neale, & H. Kammerer, June, 1794.
Full calf (covers and spine very worn, broken). Very good. Felcone
19-2 1983 $50

BARRY, JOHN S.   The History of Massachusetts. Boston,
1855-57. Thick 8vo, orig. blind-stamped cloth. 3 vols. Argosy
716-265 1983 $75

BARRY, THEODORE AUGUSTUS   Men and Memories of San Francisco in
1850. Oakland: Johnek & Seeger Press, 1947. Reissue of the 1873
original. Limited to 650 copies. In d.j. Illus. Map. Jenkins 153-
85 1983 $35

BARRY, THEODORE AUGUSTUS   San Francisco California 1850. Oakland:
Biobooks, 1947. Limited to 650 copies. Unopened. Handsome. Jenkins
153-31 1983 $35

BARTEN, SIGRID   Rene Lalique: Schmuck und Objets
d'art, 1890-1910. Munchen: Prestel, 1977. 1644 illus. (104
color). Stout oblong 4to. Cloth. Ars Libri 32-384 1983 $115

BARTH, A.   The Religions of India. London, 1882.
8vo. Orig. cloth. Slightly worn. Good. Edwards 1044-38 £20

BARTH, HENRY   Travels and discoveries in north
and central Africa. New York: Harper & Bros., 1857. 3 vols.
8vo. Folding map. Numerous plates. New 1/4 green morocco.
Adelson Africa-12 1983 $275

BARTH, HENRY   Travels and Discoveries in North and
Central Africa... N.Y., Harper, 1857-59. 3 vols. Large thick 8vo.
3 Frontispieces, folded, folded colored map, woodcut illus., both as
plates in text. Orig. cloth. 1st American ed. Fine. O'Neal 50-4
1983 $225

BARTH, HENRY   Travels and Discoveries in North and
Central Africa. Philadelphia, 1859. First American edition. Illus.
and folding map. 8vo, some rubbing. Morrill 290-31 1983 $25

BARTH, J. B. P.   A Manual of Auscultation and Percussion.
Philadelphia, 1845. 12mo. Orig. cloth. Advert. leaf before title.
Several ownership inscriptions and stamps of Dr. E.B. Shapleigh, and
a notice of his obituary pasted in. First American edition. Back
slightly torn. Gurney 90-11 1983 £50

BARTH, JOHN   Chimera. NY, (1972). One of 300 specially bound numbered and signed copies, fine in fine slipcase. Quill
& Brush 54-65 1983 $125

BARTH, JOHN   Chimera. New York: Random House,
(1972). 1st ed., 1 of 300 numbered and signed copies. Orig. cloth,
gilt, glassine, boxed. Mint copy. Jenkins 155-55 1983 $85

BARTH, JOHN   The Floating Opera. NY, (1956). Some
edge wear, otherwise very good in slightly frayed and soiled still
good dustwrapper that is chipped at top spine edge. Quill & Brush 54-
69 1983 $150

BARTH, JOHN   Letters. New York: (1979). First
edition. Printed orange wrappers. Advance "uncorrected proof for
limited distribution." Publisher's dated announcement slip affixed
to front wrapper and a blurb to inside of front wrapper. Very fine
copy. Bradley 66-17 1983 $175

BARTH, JOHN   Letters. New York: Putnam, (1979).
1st ed., 1 of 500 numbered and signed copies. Orig. cloth-backed
boards, gilt, boxed. Mint. Jenkins 155-56 1983 $75

BARTH, JOHN   Letters. New York, (1979). First ed.
Advance "uncorrected proofs for limited distribution." Printed orange
wrappers. With dated announcement slip and a blurb for the book attached to front wrapper. Very scarce. Bradley 65-22 1983 $150

BARTH, JOHN   Letters. N.Y., (1979). First edition. Cloth backed boards. Slipcase. Limited to 500 numbered copies, signed by author. Very good. King 45-146 1983 $75

BARTH, JOHN   Letters. NY, (1979). One of 500 specially bound, numbered and signed copies, fine in fine slipcase. Quill & Brush 54-66 1983 $75

BARTH, JOHN   The Literature of Exhaustion and the Literature of Replenishment. Northridge: Lord John Press, 1982. Cream linen, gilt. Deluxe issue, limited to 100 signed copies. Mint. Jenkins 155-57-A 1983 $125

BARTH, JOHN   The Literature of Exhaustion and the Literature of Replenishment. Northridge: Lord John Press, 1982. Quarto. Cloth. First edition in book form. One of 300 numbered copies, signed by the author. Mint as issued. Reese 20-64 1983 $75

BARTH, JOHN   The Literature of Exhaustion and the Literature of Replenishment. Northridge: Lord John Press, 1982. 1st ed., 1 of 300 numbered and signed copies. Orig. red cloth, gilt. Mint copy. Jenkins 155-57 1983 $75

BARTH, JOHN   Sabbatical. NY, (1982). One of 750 numbered, specially bound signed copies, very fine in fine slipcase. Quill & Brush 54-68 1983 $75

BARTH, JOHN   Todd Andrews to the Author. Northridge, 1979. Limited to 50 numbered and signed deluxe edition copies, very fine in full brown leather. Quill & Brush 54-70 1983 $150

BARTHELME, DONALD   Come Back, Dr. Caligari. Boston: Little, Brown, 1964. 1st ed. Orig. cloth, dj. Fine copy. Jenkins 155-1355 1983 $100

BARTHELME, DONALD   Her in the Village. Northridge, 1978. One of 50 numbered and signed copies, fine. Quill & Brush 54-73 1983 $125

BARTHOLOMAEUS ANGLICUS   De proprietatibus reru(m). Cologne: Johann Veldener for William Caxton, 1472). Thick folio (400 x 190mm). Cont. pigskin over wooden boards. Cont. ms. ex-libris of Benedictine Monastery at Weingarten and duplicate stamp of Koenigliche Hand-bibliothek (Landes bibliothek) Stuttgart (1901) on first leaf. Some worm punctures at beginning and end, a few leaves with slight marginal stains. Initials supplied in red, rubricated. Clasp remnants. In excellent condition. Kraus 164-16 1983 $95,000

BARTHOLOMEW, CHARLES   The Turkish Bath. Bristol, ca. 1870. 8vo. Plate. Orig. pink printed wrapper. Bound into modern boards. Heath 48-487 1983 £40

BARTLET, JOHN   Pharmacopoeia Bartleiana: or, Bartlet's gentleman farrier's repository... Eton: T. Pote, 1773. Third edition. 8vo. Cont. sheep. 2 plates. Rubbed. Ximenes 63-184 1983 $90

BARTLET, JOHN   Suite du Gentilhomme Marechal. Paris, chez C.A. Jombert, 1757. First edition in French, including the half-title, large 12mo, cont. calf, labels supplied and with a light water stain but still a very good copy. Fenning 61-21 1983 £65

BARTLETT, EDWARD EVERETT   The Typographic Treasures in Europe. New York and London, 1925. Folio, boards, cloth back, g.t. One of 585 copies. Dated presentation by the author on half title. Duschnes 240-4 1983 $125

BARTLETT, ELISHA   A Brief Memoir of Dr. Elisha Bartlett with Selections from His Writings and a Bibliography of the Same. Providence, 1878. 1 of 300 privately printed copies. 8vo. Orig. wrappers. Morrill 289-11 1983 $30

BARTLETT, ELISHA   The History, Diagnosis and Treatment of Typhoid and of Typhus Fever; with an Essay on the Diagnosis of Bilious Remittent and of Yellow Fever. Philadelphia, 1842. 1st ed. 8vo. Corners rubbed; binding partly faded. Morrill 289-10 1983 $75

BARTLETT, F. C.   Remembering. A Study in Experimental and Social Psychology. Cambridge: At the Univ. Press, 1932. First edition. Rust stain from paper clip to upper edge of first several leaves, else very good to fine. Gach 94-519 1983 $40

BARTLETT, JOHN   A Collection of Familiar Quotations. Boston, 1879. 7th ed., greatly enlarged. Orig. cloth. Historian Justin Windsor's copy with his signature and a rare proof leaflet of unattributed quotations sent to him by Bartlett for identification, with Bartlett's inscription. Very good copy, and a fine assoc. Jenkins 155-59 1983 $175

BARTLETT, JOHN RUSSELL   Bibliography of Rhode Island...Providence: Printed by Order of the General Assembly, 1864. Later cloth and boards, edges worn. Dawson 470-21 1983 $40

BARTLETT, JOHN RUSSELL   Dictionary of Americanism. Boston: Little, Brown. London: Trubner & Co., 1859. 16 pp Trubner ads. Orig. brown cloth, recased. Jarndyce 31-657 1983 £85

BARTLETT, JOSEPH   Aphorisms on Man, Manners, Principles & Things. Portsmouth, 1810. Orig. quarter calf and boards. Edges just a trifle rubbed, otherwise a fine copy. Reese 18-333 1983 $185

BARTLETT, WILLIAM HENRY   Canadian Scenery, Illustrated. Toronto: Peter Martin, 1967. 4to. 2 vols. Facsimile edition, with 120 plates inc. half-titles and frontis., cloth backed boards, spines slightly faded else fine, boxed. McGahern 54-11 1983 $75

BARTLETT, WILLIAM HENRY   The Pilgrim Fathers. London, 1854. 2nd ed. Revised. Steel engraved plates; woodcuts in text. Tall 8vo. Half morocco, marbled board sides. Rubbed. Morrill 289-265 1983 $47.50

BARTLEY, S. HOWARD   Vision. A Study of Its Basis. NY: Van Nostrand, 1941. First edition. Gach 94-689 1983 $20

BARTOLI, DANIELO   La Tensione, e la Pressioni disputanti qual di loro sostenga l'argentovivo ne' cannelli doppo fattone il vuoto. Gioseffo Longhi, Bologna, 1677. 12mo, with 2 folding plates containing 16 woodcut figures of barometry experiments; a little browned; cont. vellum. First edition. Quaritch NS 5-5 1983 $400

BARTOLINI, SIGFRIDO   Ardegno Soffici. Reggio Emilia: Prandi, 1972. 525 illus. (numerous color). Large 4to. Cloth. Dust jacket. Slipcase. Edition limited to 850 numbered copies. Ars Libri 33-592 1983 $250

BARTOLOZZI, FRANCESCO   One Hundred Examples of Engravings by Francesco, Bartolozzi, R.A... London: The Autotype Company, n.d. 4 parts. 101 mounted autotype plates. Folio. Boards, 3/4 cloth. Limited edition of 150 copies for parts II-IV. Printed on laid paper. Moderate wear. Several plates loosened. Ars Libri 32-21 1983 $175

BARTON, B. M.   The British Flora Medica. 1877. New edition, 48 coloured plates of 192 figures, 8vo, binder's cloth, used. A sound ex-library copy, with bookplate but no stamps. Wheldon 160-2159 1983 £55

BARTON, BERNARD   Devotional verses. For Holdsworth, 1826. First edition. tall 12mo, engraved title on plate paper, uncut in original blue and brown paper boards, paper label, spine darkened. A fine copy as issued. Deighton 3-21 1983 £30

BARTON, BERNARD   Poems. London: Baldwin, Cradock and Joy, 1821. Second edition. 12mo. Orig. grey boards, printed paper label (chipped). Spine worn. Ximenes 63-392 1983 £90

BARTON, BERNARD   Poetic Vigils. Baldwin, Cradock & Joy, 1824. First edition. Rebound in moire-patterned green cloth, label. Jarndyce 30-638 1983 £16

BARTON, BERNARD   Selections from the Poems and Letters. Hall, Virtue & Co., 1849. First edition, front. port. and one other plates. Long subscribers' list, errata slip. Orig. light blue cloth, blocked in blind and gilt. Spine faded, otherwise v.g. Jarndyce 30-642 1983 £15

BARTON, BERNARD   A widow's tale and other poems.
For Holdsworth, 1827. First edition, tall 12mo, advts, engraved
vignette title, uncut in original boards, paper label chipped, joints
worn, but a good clean copy. Deighton 3-22 1983 £24

BARTON, BERNARD   A Widow's Tale, and Other Poems.
John Hatchard, 1828. First edition, rebound in maroon moire-
patterned cloth. Jarndyce 30-641 1983 £15

BARTON, CLARA   The Red Cross. Washington, 1898.
First edition. 8vo. Numerous photographs. Orig. binding. Very
good. Fye H-3-25 1983 $75

BARTON, F. T.   Pheasants in Covert and Aviary. 1912.
4 coloured plates and 36 other illustrations, 4to, cloth, inscription
on half-title. Wheldon 160-645 1983 £30

BARTON, RALPH   Plea for an Age Movement. Stamford:
Overbrook Press, 1943. 12mo. Limited to 600 copies. Title-page
and wood engraving by Rudolph Ruzicka. Fine with very faintly
chipped glassine. Printed presentation slip from printers laid-in.
Bromer 25-272 1983 $40

BARTON, ROY FRANKLIN   The Kalingas, Their institutions and
Custom Law. Chicago, 1949. 1st ed. Map, photos. Clark 741-413
1983 $35

BARTON, WILLIAM   Memoirs of the Life of David
Rittenhouse. Philadelphia: Edward Parker, 1813. Port., folding
facs. Orig. paper-covered boards, uncut. Front cover detached,
endsheets foxed. With early printed book labels of Richard M.
Wistar and John Savage. First edition. Felcone 22-13 1983 $125

BARTON, WILLIAM E.   A Beautiful Blunder. Ind., (1926).
Signed, dated presentation, spine shows wear, label darkened, otherwise
good to very good. Quill & Brush 54-76 1983 $25

BARTON, WILLIAM E.   A Beautiful Blunder. Indianapolis,
(1926). Edition limited to 500 signed copies. Illustrated. 8vo,
paper label, boxed. Morrill 290-32 1983 $20

BARTRAM, WILLIAM   Travels Through North & South Carolina,
Georgia, East & West Florida, the Cherokee Country, the Extensive
Territories of the Muscogulges or Creek Confederacy, and the Country
of the Chactaws. Dublin: For J. Moore, 1793. First Irish edition,
8vo, without the folding map, 7 copper engraved plates, contemporary
calf, gilt panelled back, red morocco label, one inner joint cracked,
frontispiece and last blank trifle loose, some dampstaining, folding
plate trifle frayed and torn. Deighton 3-23 1983 £125

BARZAZ-BREIZ. Chants Populaires de la Bretagne. Paris, 1846. 8vo,
cont. 1/2 morocco over marbled boards, spines gilt, with 4 raised bands.
Fine set. Salloch 387-34 1983 $95

BASHKIRTSEFF, MARIA C.   The Journal of Marie Bashkirtseff.
Cassell & Company, 1891. With 3 plates, 8vo, orig. cloth, gilt. A
very good copy. Fenning 61-22 1983 £10.50

BASILE, GIAMBATTISTA   The Pentamerone. Lon., 1848. Illus. by
Cruikshank. Rebound in leather, some interior foxing, else very good
or better. Quill & Brush 54-77 1983 $125

BASILE, GIAMBATTISTA   Il Pentamerone; or, The Tale of Tales.
London: Henry and Co., 1893. 2 vols. Royal 8vo. Orig. black cloth.
Uncut, rubbed. Edition limited to 165 copies. Adelson Africa-56
1983 $300

BASILE, GIAMBATTISTA   Stories from the Pentamerone. MacMillan,
1911. Large 4to. Mounted colour frontis. & 31 mounted colour plates.
Some foxing. Full white parchment gilt, some marks. Edition de Luxe.
Limited to 150 copies. Greer 39-70 1983 £160

BASILE, NINO   La Cattedrale di Palermo: l'opera
di Ferdinando Fuga... Firenze: R. Bemporad, 1926. 3 plates
(2 large folding). Small 4to. Boards. Spine defective). Ars
Libri 33-148 1983 $75

BASILY-CALLIMAKI, MME. DE   J.-B. Isabey. Sa vie--son oeuvre,
1767-1855. Paris: Frazier-Soye, 1909. 75 plates with tissue
guards (3 color hors texte). 105 illus. Numerous other illus.
in text. Folio. Full calf, gold tooled. Orig. wrappers bound
in. Slipcase. Edition limited to 550 copies. A fine copy. Ars
Libri 32-340 1983 $575

BASKERVILLE, JOHN   Horace. Birmingham: Johannis
Baskerville, 1770. Quarto, frontis., 4 plates. 1st ed. Contemporary
full crimson morocco, raised bands, spine fully gilt, inner dentilles
gilt, a.e.g., silk marker. Besides the frontispiece, this copy has
all 4 plates by Gravelot. Fine copy. Jenkins 155-60 1983 $650

BASKIN, LEONARD   Caprices & Grotesques. Northampton:
Gehenna Press, 1965. Quarto. Line drawings. Limited to 500 copies.
Extremely fine in wrappers and slip-case. Bookplate. Bromer 25-212
1983 $135

BASKIN, LEONARD   Fifteen Woodcuts. Boston: The
Friends of Art, Boston University, 1962. Title page, colophon
page, one orig. woodblock from the Gehenna Press and 15 woodcut
plates, some printed in red & black. Edition ltd. to 500 copies,
this being 1 of 100 special roman numeral copies, signed by Baskin,
that also include an original woodcut on Japan paper, signed by
him. Housed in a beige linen portfolio, with ties. Paper cover
label. Karmiole 71-18 1983 $300

BASKIN, R. N.   Reminiscences of Early Utah. (Salt Lake
City), 1914. 6 portraits. Orig. cloth. Some wear. Jenkins 152-478
1983 $50

BASON, FREDERICK T.   A Bibliography of the Writings of
William Somerset Maugham. London: Unicorn Press, 1931. Notes in
Bason's hand call this one of 'four special copies for presentation'
and 'the only copy of the 950 (sic) to be signed by us both'. Cloth,
foxed. One of 50 (of 1000) numbered copies on mould-made paper,
signed by Maugham. Dawson 470-22 1983 $95

BASS, SAM   Life and Adventures of...the Nororious
Union Pacific and Texas Train Robber. (Austin, Gammell), n.d.
Illus. Orig. printed tan wraps. Ginberg 46-53 1983 $25

BASSET, ROBERT   The Lives of All the Roman Emperors.
London: George Hutton, 1636. First edition, 16mo, with engraved
title-page + 156 woodcut portraits of the Roman Emperors. Bound in
ca. 1900 full green morocco by the "Eedy Bindery"; elaborately
gilt-stamped; inner dentelles. A.e.g. Bookplate. Karmiole 75-20
1983 $200

BASSETT, DAVID L.   The Central Nervous System. Portland,
(1952). 34 color reels, & numerous text illus., with descriptive
text. 4 vols. Small 8vo, stiff pr. wrs, spiral bound. Argosy 713-
30 1983 $85

BASSETT, JOHN Y.   The Medical Reports... Springfield,
1941. First edition. 8vo. Orig. binding. Very good. Fye H-3-27
1983 $60

BASSI-RATHGEB, ROBERTO   Vincenzo Bonomini. Bergamo: Edizioni
Orobiche, 1942. 63 plates. Small 4to. Wrappers. Spine and inner
hinges taped. Edition limited to 700 copies. Ars Libri 33-40 1983
$75

BASSO, HAMILTON   Beauregard, The Great Creole.
NY, 1933. Covers slightly soiled and discolored else good.
Soiled and frayed dust wrappers. First edition. King 46-40 1983
$30

BASSO, HAMILTON   Beauregard the Great Creole. New York,
1933. First edition. 8vo. Orig. cloth. Portrait frontis. 6 plates,
3 full page and 3 text illus. Very slightly faded. Bookplate. Good.
Edwards 1042-194 1983 £18

BASTELAERS, RENE VAN   Les estampes de Peter Bruegel L'Ancien.
Bruxelles: G. Van Oest, 1908. 278 plates. Large 4to. Cloth.
Orig. wrappers bound in. Rare catalogue raisonne. Ars Libri 32-
68 1983 $400

BASTIAN, H. CHARLTON   Paralyses. London, 1886. First
edition. Illus. Argosy 713-31 1983 $125

BASTIAT, FREDERIC   La Loi. Paris, Guillaumin, 1850.
1st ed., small 8vo, uncut in original printed wrappers. Pickering
& Chatto 21-5 1983 $50

BATAILLE, M.-L.   Berthe Morisot. Paris: Les Beaux-
Arts, 1961. 818 plates and reference illus. 4to. Cloth. Ars
Libri 32-478 1983 $650

BATCHELDER, ANN   East of Bridgewater and Other Poems.
N.Y., Dutton, 1943. First edition. Small 8vo, dust jackets (slight
soiling on front) else, very good. Signed and inscribed by the author.
Houle 22-74 1983 $75

BATE, GEORGE   Pharmacopoeia Bateana... London:
Sam. Smith, 1691. 12mo. Cont. calf, rebacked. Ads. Recipe for
simple in cont. hand back flyleaf, shelf numbered on titles page.
Zeitlin 264-26 1983 £175

BATE, GEORGE   Pharmacopoeia Bateana... London:
Sam. Smith & Benj. Walford, 1700. Third edition. 12mo. Cont.
panelled calf, expertly rebacked. Ads. Very good copy. Zeitlin
264-25 1983 £110

BATEMAN, FREDERICK   On Aphasia, or Loss of Speech...
London, (1890). 8vo. Orig. cloth. With 2 plates. Presentation
copy, inscribed on flyleaf. Gurney JJ-23 1983 £25

BATEMAN, G. C.   The Vivarium. 1897. 28 plates, cr.
8vo, cloth (trifle used). Wheldon 160-936 1983 £15

BATEMAN, JAMES   The Orchidaceae of Mexico and Guatemala.
NY: Johnson Reprint Corp. (n.d. ca. 1973). Tall folio, facs.
reprint of the orig. edition published in 1843. With 40 full-page
color botanical plates. Edition ltd. to 1,000 numbered copies.
Yellow gilt-stamped cloth. Fine. Karmiole 76-23 1983 $250

BATEMAN, JAMES   The Orchidaceae of Mexico and Guatemala.
(1837-1843), 1974. A slightly reduced reproduction. 40 coloured
plates, imp. folio, cloth. Wheldon 160-5 1983 £165

BATEMAN, JOHN   The clavi lyra, or an improved harp
with keys. Brighouse: J. Utley, printer, n.d. (1813). 8vo. 2
leaves, disbound. 2 folding plates. A little browned. Very rare.
Ximenes 63-323 1983 $125

BATEMAN, THOMAS   Delineations of Cutaneous Diseases.
1828. 4to, 72 coloured plates, each with leaf of explanatory text,
cont. half dark red morocco with marbled boards, rubbed, small light
stain at top of inner margin of preliminary pages only, and small
dark stain at upper outer corner of front fly. Bickersteth 75-210
1983 £85

BATES, CHARLES FRANCIS   Custer's Indian Battles. Bronxville,
N.Y., 1936. Illus. Orig. folio printed wraps. First edition.
Ginsberg 46-852 1983 $25

BATES, E. S.   Touring in 1600. Boston and New York:
Houghton Mifflin, 1911. Plates, frontispiece. Cloth, somewhat dull
but tight. Dawson 470-23 1983 $30

BATES, EDWARD   Edward Bates Against Thomas Hart Benton.
St. Louis, 1828. Dsb. Reese 18-617 1983 $275

BATES, HERBERT ERNEST   The Black Boxer. (London): Pharos
Editions, 1932. First edition. 8vo. Orig. cloth. Dust jacket.
Jacket lightly dust-soiled, otherwise a fine copy. Jaffe 1-33
1983 $75

BATES, HERBERT ERNEST   Catherine Foster. London: Jonathan
Cape, (1929). First edition. 8vo. Orig. cloth. Dust jacket.
Spine of jacket darkened, but a fine copy. Jaffe 1-28 1983 $85

BATES, HERBERT ERNEST   Charlotte's Row. London: Jonathan
Cape, (1931). First edition. 8vo. Orig. cloth. Dust jacket.
Jacket slightly worn at corners, but a very good copy. Jaffe 1-32
1983 $65

BATES, HERBERT ERNEST   Cut And Come Again. Fourteen Stories.
London: Jonathan Cape, (1935). First edition. 8vo. Orig. cloth.
Dust jacket. Fine copy. Jaffe 1-38 1983 $85

BATES, HERBERT ERNEST   Day's End and other Stories. London:
Jonathan Cape, (1928). First edition. 8vo. Orig. cloth. Dust
jacket. Jacket partially darkened, otherwise a fine copy. Jaffe
1-27 1983 $85

BATES, HERBERT ERNEST   The Duet. London: Grayson & Grayson,
1935. First edition. 8vo. Orig. cloth. Dust jacket. Limited to
285 copies signed by the author. Fine copy. Jaffe 1-39 1983 $100

BATES, HERBERT ERNEST   Edward Garnett. London, 1950. First
English edition. Free endpapers slightly browned. Nicked dustwrapper.
Fine. Jolliffe 26-37 1983 £27.50

BATES, HERBERT ERNEST   The Fallow Land. London: Jonathan
Cape, (1932). First edition. 8vo. Orig. cloth. Dust jacket.
Fine copy. Jaffe 1-34 1983 $75

BATES, HERBERT ERNEST   A House of Women. London: Jonathan
Cape, (1936). First edition. 8vo. Orig. cloth. Dust jacket.
Jacket slightly stained, with small spot on front cover. Book of
the Month wraparound band. A fine copy. Jaffe 1-40 1983 $85

BATES, HERBERT ERNEST   The House With The Apricot and Two
Other Tales. London: Golden Cockerel Press, 1933. First edition.
4to. Illus. with wood-engravings by Agnes Miller Parker. Orig.
half-morocco and decorated boards. Limited to 300 copies designed
by Robert Gibbings and signed by the author. Very fine copy.
Jaffe 1-36 1983 $200

BATES, HERBERT ERNEST   The Last Bread. London: Labor Publishing Co., (1926). Orig. printed wrappers. First edition of the
author's first book. MacManus 277-223 1983 $35

BATES, HERBERT ERNEST   The Last Bread. London, 1926. First
English edition. Wrappers. 5 A.L.S.s, 3 written in 1953, the other
2 in 1962, from the author loosely inserted. Very good. Jolliffe
26-34 1983 £45

BATES, HERBERT ERNEST   The Last Bread. London: The Labour
Publishing Company Limited, (1926). First edition. 8vo. Orig.
wrappers. Fine copy. Jaffe 1-24 1983 $85

BATES, HERBERT ERNEST   The Seekers. London: John and Edward
Bumpus, 1926. First edition. 8vo. Orig. boards. Inscribed by the
author to Ben Martin, with Martin's bookplate on the front endsheet.
Fine copy. Jaffe 1-26 1983 $125

BATES, HERBERT ERNEST   The Seekers. London, 1926. First
edition. Orig. glassine wrapper. Very fine. Gekoski 2-5 1983
£35

BATES, HERBERT ERNEST   Seven Tales and Alexander. London:
The Scholartis Press, 1929. First edition. 8vo. Orig. cloth-
backed boards, dust jacket. Jacket slightly soiled and chipped,
otherwise a fine copy. Jaffe 1-29 1983 $40

BATES, HERBERT ERNEST   Spella Ho. London: Jonathan Cape,
(1938). First edition. 8vo. Orig. cloth. Dust jacket. Small
chip out of jacket at base of spine, otherwise a fine copy. Jaffe
1-41 1983 $85

BATES, HERBERT ERNEST   The Story Without An End and The
Country Doctor. London: The White Owl Press, 1932. First edition.
8vo. Orig. cloth-backed boards. Dust jacket. The fragile jacket
is slightly foxed and torn, otherwise a fine copy. Jaffe 1-35
1983 $75

BATES, HERBERT ERNEST   A Threshing Day. London: W. and G.
Foyle, Ltd., (1931). First edition. Tall thin 8vo. Orig. cloth.
Limited to 300 copies signed by the author. Fine copy. Jaffe 1-31
1983 $100

BATES, HERBERT ERNEST   A threshing day. Foyle, 1931.
First edition, tall slim 8vo, uncut in blue cloth gilt, slightly
faded along spine, very good. 300 numbered copies only. Deighton
3-24 1983 £32

BATES, HERBERT ERNEST   Through the Woods. London, 1936. First edition. 73 wood-engravings by A. Miller Parker. 4to. Spine slightly darkened. Good. Rota 231-44 1983 £12

BATES, HERBERT ERNEST   The Tree. London: Blue Moon Booklets, (1930). First edition. One of 100 numbered copies, signed by author. Wrappers foxed. Nice. Rota 230-46 1983 £25

BATES, HERBERT ERNEST   The Tree. London: E. Lahr, n.d. (1930). First edition. 8vo. Orig. wrappers. Fine copy. Jaffe 1-30 1983 $45

BATES, HERBERT ERNEST   The Two Sister. London: Jonathan Cape Limited, (1926). First edition. 8vo. Orig. cloth. Dust jacket. Inscribed by the author to Ben Martin on the front free endpaper, with Martin's bookplate on the front endsheet. Spine of jacket darkened and slightly nicked, otherwise a fine copy. Jaffe 1-25 1983 $125

BATES, HERBERT ERNEST   The Two Sisters. Lon., (1926). Spine edges frayed, minor cover soiling, else good or better. Quill & Brush 54-78 1983 $40

BATES, HERBERT ERNEST   The Woman Who Had Imagination. London, 1934. Chipped and frayed, price-clipped dustwrapper darkened at the spine. Near fine. Jolliffe 26-36 1983 £45

BATES, HERBERT ERNEST   The Woman who had Imagination and other Stories. London: Jonathan Cape, (1934). First edition. 8vo. Orig. cloth. Dust jacket. Jacket a little torn at base of spine, otherwise a very good copy. Jaffe 1-37 1983 $65

BATES, ISAAC C.   An Oration, Pronounced Before the Washington Benevolent Society of the County of Hampshire... Northampton, 1812. Dsb., good. Reese 18-366 1983 $20

BATES, RALPH   The Fields of Paradise. New York: E.P. Dutton & Co., Inc., (1940). First edition. 8vo. Orig. cloth. Dust jacket. Fine copy. Jaffe 1-46 1983 $50

BATES, RALPH   Lean Men. An Episode in a Life. London: Peter Davies, 1934. First edition. 8vo. Orig. cloth. Dust jacket. Fine copy. Jaffe 1-43 1983 $75

BATES, RALPH   Rainbow Fish. New York: E.P. Dutton & Co., Inc., 1937. First American edition. 8vo. Orig. cloth. Dust jacket. Fine copy. Jaffe 1-44 1983 $40

BATES, RALPH   Schubert. (London): Peter Davies Limited, 1934. First edition. Frontis. 8vo. Orig. cloth. Dust jacket. Fine copy. Jaffe 1-42 1983 $45

BATES, RALPH   Sirocco and other stories. New York: Random House, (1939). First American edition. 8vo. Orig. cloth. Dust jacket. Fine copy. Jaffe 1-45 1983 $35

BATES, SAMUEL P.   History of Pennsylvania Volunteers 1861-5. Harrisburg, PA, 1869-71. 5 vols. 3 coverless, 2 with covers. A research set only, some pages lacking, disbound, etc. swaf. King 46-41 1983 $75

BATES, W. H.   The Cure of Imperfect Sight by Treatment without Glasses. New York, (1920). 8vo, text illus., orig. buckram. First edition. Bickersteth 75-211 1983 £12

BATES, WILLIAM   The Maclise Portrait-Gallery of Illustrious Literary Characters... New York: Scribner and Welford, 1883. Thick 8vo. Three-quarter leather over marbled boards. 85 portraits. Spine slightly rubbed. Oak Knoll 49-27 1983 $40

BATESON, W.   Mendel's Principles of Heredity. Cambridge: Cambridge University Press, 1913. Third impression. 8vo. Cloth, rebacked. With 3 portraits, 6 coloured plates, and numerous uncoloured plates. Gurney JJ-267 1983 £20

BATH, WILLIAM PULTENEY, EARL OF   Considerations on the Present State of Public Affairs, and the Means of Raising the Necessary Supplies. London, 1779. Disbound, very good. Reese 18-129 1983 $125

BATH, WILLIAM PULTENEY, EARL OF   A Short View of the State of Affairs, with Relations to Great Britain... London, 1730. Old half morocco and boards, very good. Reese 18-47 1983 $150

BATHER, F. A.   A Treatise on Zoology, Part III The Echinoderma. 1900. 8vo, cloth, text-illustrations. Wheldon 160-1312 1983 £12

BATKA, J. B.   Monographie der Cassien Gruppe Senna. Prague, 1866. Map and 5 lithographic plates, 4to, original boards, rebacked. Wheldon 160-2160 1983 £20

BATTARRA, A. J. A.   Fungorum Agri Ariminensis Historia. Faenza, 1755. 40 engraved plates, 4to, contemporary vellum. Rare. Covers very slightly wormed but a good copy. Wheldon 160-1786 1983 £330

BATTELL, ANDREW   The strange adventures of Andrew Battell of Leigh... London: Hakluyt Soc., 1901. 8vo. 2 folding maps. Orig. cloth. Spine darkened, ex-lib. Adelson Africa-165 1983 $30

THE BATTLE of the two philosophies. London: Longmans, etc., 1866. First edition. 8vo. Orig. brown cloth. Minor rubbing. Ximenes 63-350 1983 $125

BATTY, BEATRICE   Forty Two Years Amongst the Indians and Eskimo. London, 1893. Illus. Orig. cloth. x-l. First edition. Ginsberg 46-135 1983 $75

BATTYE, AUBYN B. R. TREVOR   Camping in Crete. Witherby & Co., 1913. First edition, with a folding map and 32 plates, 8vo, orig. cloth, a very good copy. Fenning 61-24 1983 £21.50

BAUDELAIRE, CHARLES   Les Fleurs de Mal. Grund, Paris, 1939. 4to. Colour frontis. & 5 colour plates. Colour pictorial wrappers with extra design. Greer 39-79 1983 £45

BAUDELAIRE, CHARLES   Flowers of Evil. (London); Fanfare Press for The Limited Editions Club, 1940. Med. 4to, 24 lithographed illustrations, t.e.g, others uncut, red cloth gilt, red boards slip case gilt, fine. Deighton 3-25 1983 £75

BAUDELAIRE, CHARLES   Intimate Journals. London: Methueun, 1949. Cloth. First English edition. Portraits and plates. This copy is inscribed by Isherwood (translator): "For Frank, with love from Christopher March 1950." One of 750 copies. Fine in dust jacket, which is chipped at the head of the spine. Reese 20-68 1983 $200

BAUDELAIRE, CHARLES   Intimate Journals. Hollywood, 1947. First edition of Christopher Isherwood translation. Cloth, illus., very good in worn and soiled dust wrapper. King 46-251 1983 $35

BAUDELAIRE, CHARLES   Intimate Journals. London, 1949. First English edition with this intro. by H. W. Auden. Illus. One of 750 copies. Dust wrapper. Fine. Rota 230-34 1983 £35

BAUDY, JERMONE KEATING (1842-1914)   Diseases of the Nervous System. Philadelphia: J. B. Lippincott Co., 1892 (1876). Second edition. Publisher's mauve cloth, ex-library, hinges broken, worn copy. Gach 95-32 1983 $25

BAUER, CARL HUGO   Der Heutige Stand der Synthese von Pflanzenalkaloiden. Braunschweig: Viewig & Sohn, 1913. 8vo. Orig. printed cloth. Ads. Near fine condition. Zeitlin 264-27 1983 $25

BAUERLE, AMELIA   The Child Lovers Calendar. Chatto & Windus, 1908. Sm. 8vo. Colour title vignette & 12 colour plates. Green cloth. Onlaid colour plate extra. Greer 40-45 1983 £20

BAUHINUS, CASPAR   De Lapidis Bezaaris Oriental. &
Occident... Basle, 1625. 8vo. Old vellum. With a few woodcuts in
text. Piece cut from bottom of title, and lower portion of errata
leaf, both repaired; heavily browned. Gurney JJ-24 1983 £95

BAUM, JULIUS   Deutsche Bildwerke des 10. bis 18.
Jahrhunderts. (Kataloge der Kgl. Altertumersammlung in Stuttgart.
Vol. III.) Stuttgart/Berlin, 1917. x, (2), 392pp., 20 plates.
476 illus. Lrg. 4to. Cloth (covers slightly soiled). Ars Libri
SB 26-8 1983 $250

BAUM, JULIUS   Gotische Bildwerke Schwabens.
Augsburg, 1921. xvi, 184pp., 128 plates. 4to. Boards, 1/4 cloth.
Ars Libri SB 26-9 1983 $85

BAUM, LYMAN FRANK   Glinda of Oz. Chicago (1920). First
ed. Illus. by John R. Neill, cloth with pict. color label, slight
cover wear, minor pencil scribbles on foredge. King 46-443 1983 $75

BAUM, LYMAN FRANK   John Dough and the Cherob. Chicago,
Reilly & Britton, (1906). First edition, later state, with misprint
corrected on page 275 etc. Illus. in color and b/w by John R. Neill.
Pictorial tan cloth stamped in red, black and yellow (a little
rubbed, some occasional light soiling in text), else, quite nice and
very good. Houle 22-75 1983 $225

BAUM, LYMAN FRANK   The Land of Oz. Chicago (1904). Second
edition, second state. Illus. by John R. Neill. Tan cloth, inner
hinges broken, covers soiled and rubbed, some pp. torn, pieces lacking,
etc. King 46-444 1983 $40

BAUM, LYMAN FRANK   Little Wizard Series of Oz. Chicago:
Reilly & Britton, (1914). First edition, first state. Sq. 8vo.
Yellow cloth. Pictorial paste-on, various pagination. Covers show some
wear. New cover design by Neill. Many full-page color illus. Very
good. Aleph-bet 8-31 1983 $280

BAUM, LYMAN FRANK   The New Wizard of Oz. Bobbs Merrill,
(1903). Colored illus. by W.W. Denslow. 8vo, green pictorial cloth.
Second edition. Intermediary state, with the first issue binding
and second issue textual points. Argosy 714-42 1983 $200

BAUM, LYMAN FRANK   Ozma of Oz. Chicago (1907). Color
illus. by John R. Neill, pict. cloth, spine ends worn, covers
darkened. 4th state. King 46-445 1985 $85

BAUM, LYMAN FRANK   Ozma of Oz. Chicago, Reilly & Britton,
(1918). First edition, later printing. Small 4to, color frontis. and
39 full page color plates, and one b/w plate by John Neill. Olive
cloth stamped in black, large color pictorial paper label on upper
cover. First issue with the color pictorial label on upper cover.
Houle 22-76 1983 $85

BAUM, LYMAN FRANK   The Wizard of Oz. Akron: Saalfield,
1944. 8vo. Pictorial boards, spiral bound. 6 moveable pages by Wehr.
Fine. Aleph-bet 8-32 1983 $40

BAUM, VICKI   Martin's Summer. New York, 1931. 8vo.
Cloth. A fine copy in dj which has a small nick. In Our Time
156-55 1983 $30

BAUM, VICKI   Nanking Road. London, Bles (1939).
First edition. Dust jacket (short tears, nicks). Very good. Houle
21-71 1983 $30

BAUM, VICKI   Weeping Wood. N.Y., Doubleday, 1943.
First edition. Dust jacket designed by Artzybasheff (a few short
tears), else very good. Houle 21-72 1983 $30

BAUME, ANTOINE   Elements de Pharmacie Theoretique et
Pratique. Paris: Samson, 1790. 8vo, cont. mottled calf (worn),
gilt back. With pub.'s signature on verso of title. Argosy 713-
32 1983 $125

BAUMGART, FRITZ   Geschichte der abendlandischen
Plastick von den Anfangen bis zur Gegenwart. Koln, 1957 387, (1)
pp. 181 plates (10 tipped-in color). 4to. Cloth. D.j.
Ars Libri SB 26-10 1983 $75

BAUMGARTEN, F.   Die Hellenische Kultur. 1905. 400
illus. 7 color pl., 4to. Salloch 387-64 1983 $35

BAUMGARTNER, LEONA   A Bibliography of the Poem Syphilis
Sive Morbus Gallicus... New Haven, 1935. First edition. 8vo.
Orig. binding. Fye H-3-1008 1983 $20

BAUQUIER, GEORGES   Fernand Leger. Sa vie, son oeuvre,
son reve. Milano: Edizioni Applinqire, 1971. 218 illus. (including
monochrome and color plates, facsimile and documentary photographs).
Small folio. Wrappers. Dust jacket. Slipcase. Edition limited
to 1150 numbered copies, on handmade paper. Ars Libri 32-395 1983
$200

BAX, ARNOLD E. T.   A Dublin Ballad, and Other Poems.
Dublin: The Candel Press, 1918. First edition, orig. printed
paper wrapper, v.g. copy. One of 425 copies printed. Fenning 62-18
1983 £24.50

BAX, CLIFFORD   Up Stream. Oxford: Basil Blackwell,
1922. Edition ltd. to only 50 numbered copies, signed by the
author, and printed on Kelmscott handmade paper at the Shakespeare
Head Press. Gilt-stamped vellum spine over illus. boards. Fine
copy. Karmiole 73-92 1983 $75

BAXTER, ALBERT   History of the City of Grand Rapids,
Michigan. New York, 1891. Illus., quarto, buckram. 1st ed.
Jenkins 151-209 1983 $85

BAXTER, JAMES K.   Blow, Wind of Fruitfulness. Caxton Press,
Christchurch, 1948. First edition. Dust wrapper. Inscribed to
Madame Rambert from J.K.B. Very nice. Rota 231-47 1983 £40

BAXTER, JAMES PHINNEY   A Memoir of Jacques Cartier...New York,
1906. Ed. limited to 335 copies. Fac. of manuscript. Maps and
illus. 8vo, paper label. Morrill 288-34 1983 $47.50

BAXTER, JOHN M.   Life of...Being a Brief Account of
His Experiences as a Pioneer, Missionary, Bishop and Stake
President. S.L.C., 1932. Illus. Orig. cloth. First edition.
47-589 1983 $35

BAXTER, RICHARD   A Call to the Unconverted, to Turn and
Live. New Brunswick: Abraham Blauvelt, 1797. Full calf (worn).
Signature "Jacob Van Norstrand / His Book / April 28th 1797." Very
good. Felcone 19-3 1983 $45

BAXTER, W. E.   A Winter in India. London, 1882.
Folding map, 6 plates, 1 colour, spine marked, frayed at head and tail.
8vo. Orig. cloth. Good. Edwards 1044-41 1983 £30

BAY, J. CHRISTIAN   A Handfull of Western Books. Chicago &
Cedar Rapids, 1935, 1936, 1937. 3 vols. Cloth and boards. Orig. set.
Dawson 471-17 1983 $125

BAY, WILLIAM   An Inaugural Dissertation on the
Operation of Pestilential Fluids upon the Large Intestines, Termed
by Nosologists Dysentery. New York: T. and J. Swords, 1797. Disbound. Early library stamp on title. Felcone 22-144 1983 $85

BAYARD, NICHOLAS   A Narrative of an Attempt Made by the
French of Canada... New York: Dodd, Mead & Co., 1903. Facsimile
reprint of 1693 edition. Folio. Facsimile illus., recently rebound
in limp fabrikoid. One of 525 copies. Fine. McGahern 54-23 1983
$45

BAYARD, RALPH   Lone Star Vanguard the Catholic Re-
Occupation of Texas. St. Louis, 1945. First edition. Dust jacket.
Jenkins 153-35 1983 $35

BAYER, HERBERT   Herbert Bayer. Painter, designer,
architect. New York/London: Reinhold/Studio Vista, 1967. More
than 200 illus. (20 color). Large 4to. Cloth. Dust jacket.
Ars Libri 32-23 1983 $100

BAYER, JOHANNES   Explicatio Characterum Aeneis Urano-
metrias Imaginum... Augsburg: J. Praetorius for J. Gerlin, 1654.
Engraved printer's mark on title. Small 4to. Boards with leather
back. From the library of F.X. von Zach, with his stamp on title.
Kraus 164-17 1983 $1,500

BAYER, JOHANNES   Uranometria Omnium Asterismorum
Continens Schemata... Augustae Vindelicorum excudit Christophorus
Mangus... MDCIII (1603). Folio, unnumbered leaves, engr. title
page, with lower right corner repaired. 51 engr. charts. Full
calf, gold tooled. Spine and corners rubbed. Library stamps on
verso of title page. A.E. Lownes bookplate. First edition.
Arkway 22-10 1983 $5,500

BAYERISCHES Nationalmuseum. Munchen, 1956 Die Bilkwerke in Bronze
und in anderen Metallen. Mit einem Anhang; Die Bronzebildwerke
des Residenzmuseums. Bearbeitet von Hans R. Weihrauch.
(Bayerisches Nationalmuseum, Munchen. Kataloge. Vol. XIII, 5.)
(12), 239, (1)pp. 293 illus. Lrg. 4to. Cloth (slightly shaken).
Ars Libri SB 26-148 1983 $100

BAYLE, PIERRE   An Historical and Critical Dictionary.
Printed for C. Harper, D. Brown, J. Tonson (and ten other booksellers).
1710. 4 vols., folio, fine large engraved vignette by Van der Gucht
on each title, panelled calf, all vols. rebacked. A fine set. First
edition in English. Bickersteth 77-5 1983 £200

BAYLES, RICHARD M.   Historical and Descriptive Sketches of
Suffolk County. Port Jefferson, Privately Published, 1874. Argosy
710-344 1983 $35

BAYLES, W. HARRISON   Old Taverns of New York. New York,
Frank Allaben Genealogical Co., (1915). First edition. Illustrated.
Small 8vo. Ex-library. Morrill 290-347 1983 $20

BAYLEY, DANIEL   The American Harmony: or, Royal Melody
Complete... Newburyport: Daniel Bayley, 1771. Seventh edition.
Full calf. Leaf 95/96 at end, and possibly one other leaf, lacking.
Neat holographic music on blank leaves. Several signatures of Adon-
ijah Bidwell, jun., one 1774. Felcone 20-114 1983 $300

BAYLIES, FRANCIS   A Narrative of Major General Wool's
Campaign in Mexico... Albany: Little & Company, 1851. First ed.
Portrait frontispiece. Printed wrappers. Library stamp at top edge
of upper cover. Library stamp at top edge of upper cover. A very
fine copy except for tiny breaks at front wrapper and minor spine
wear. Bradley 65-139 1983 $225

BAYLIES, FRANCIS   A Narrative of Major General Wool's
Campaign in Mexico, in the Years 1846, 1847 and 1848. Albany, 1851.
Illus., frontis. Orig. printed wraps. First edition. Ginsberg 47-
500 1983 $175

BAYLOR, FRANCES COURTENAY   Claudia. Osgood, McIlvaine, 1894. Half
titles, 8 pp ads. in both vols. Orig. dark green cloth, Mudie's
labels, v.g. Jarndyce 30-296 1983 £68

BAYLY, ADA ELLEN   The Autobiography of a Slander. London:
Longmans, Green & Co., 1892. First illustrated edition. 20 illus.
from drawings by L. Speed. Orig. pictorial cloth. Very good. Mac-
Manus 279-3385 1983 $55

BAYLY, ADA ELLEN   Hope the Hermit. London: Longmans,
Green & Co., 1898. First edition. Orig. cloth. Edges and corners
worn. Some foxing. Previous owner's signature on title-page and verso
of front free endpaper. Covers slightly soiled. Good. MacManus 279-
3386 1983 $35

BAYLY, ADA ELLEN   In Spite of All. N.Y.: Longmans,
Green and Co., 1901. First edition. Orig. cloth. Spine and covers
a bit waterspotted. Bookseller's stamp on front pastedown endpaper.
Very good. MacManus 279-3387 1983 $35

BAYLY, ADA ELLEN   In the Golden Days. London: Hurst &
Blackett, 1885. First edition. 3 vols. Orig. cloth. Signatures of
former owner on title-pages. Fine. MacManus 279-3388 1983 $350

BAYLY, ADA ELLEN   Knight-Errant. London: Hurst & Blackett,
1887. First edition. Orig. cloth. Spines and covers rather soiled.
Very good. MacManus 279-3389 1983 $175

BAYLY, ADA ELLEN   We Two, A Novel. London: Hurst &
Blackett, 1884. First edition. 3 vols. Orig. brown cloth. Spines
and covers soiled and worn. Former owner's inscription in pencil.
Good. MacManus 279-3391 1983 $225

BAYLY, THOMAS HAYNES   Musings and Prosings. Boulogne, printed
by F. Birle, 1833. First edition, tall 8vo, half title, 4 pp list of
subscribers. Rebound in half calf, hand-marbled boards, v.g. Jarndyce
30-644 1983 £30

BAYLY, THOMAS HAYNES   Rough Sketches of Bath; Imitations of
Horace; and Other Poems. Printed and sold by Meyler & Son, Bath,
1817. First edition. A little dusted. Orig. wraps., old spine
repair, Hookham's Library label on upper cover. Jarndyce 30-643 1983

BAYLY, THOMAS HAYNES   Weeds of Witchery. Ackermann & Co.,
1837. First edition, large 8vo, 12 full-page plates in the style of
Cruikshank, foxed. Orig. green cloth, sl. marked. Jarndyce 30-645
1983 £35

BAYMA, JOSEPH   The Elements of Molecular Mechanics.
Macmillan, 1866. First edition, with 3 folding plates, ads., 8vo,
orig. cloth. Fenning 60-20 1983 £65

BAYNE, PETER   Two great English women: Mrs. Browning
and Charlotte Bronte... London: James Clarke, 1881. First edition.
8vo. Orig. blue cloth. Rubbed, spine rather marked by damp and a
bit worn at the ends. Ximenes 63-232 1983 $45

BAYNES, ROBERT EDWARD   Lessons of Thermodynamics. Oxford:
Clarendon, 1878. 8vo. Orig. russet cloth with gilt. Errata
leaf and ads. 1 folding table. First edition. Spine faced, otherwise very good. Zeitlin 264-28 1983 $30

BEACALL, THOMAS   Dyestuffs and Coal-Tar Products...
London: Lockwood, 1916. Second edition. 8vo. Orig. cloth.
Folding table, numerous text diagrams and illus. Ads. A very
good copy. Zeitlin 264-29 1983 $25

BEACH, REX   The Miracle of Coral Gables. Coral
Cables, (Fla.), 1926. First edition. 4to, illus. in color by Edward
A. Wilson. Japan vellum backed boards, paper label on upper cover
stamped in gilt, uncut (soiling to spine and boards) else, very
good. With the bookplate of Adrian Goldstone. Houle 22-77 1983
$35

BEACH, REX   Oh Shoot! N.Y., Harper, 1921. Early
printing. Illus. with photographs by the author. Dust jacket,
a few nicks. Very good. Houle 21-74 1983 $20

BEACH, REX   The Silver Horde. New York, 1909.
8vo. Cloth. A fine copy. In Our Time 156-57 1983 $25

BEACH, WILLIAM H.   The First New York (Lincoln) Cavalry
From April 19, 1861 - July 6, 1865. NY: Lincoln Cavalry Asso, 1902.
1st ed. Illus, ex lib. Argosy 710-79 1983 $35

BEADLE, CHARLES   The City of Shadows. London: Everett &
Co., 1911. Orig. pictorial cloth. First edition. Spine very slightly
faded. Endpapers lightly browned. A very good copy. MacManus 277-
230 1983 $25

BEADLE, J. H.   Life in Utah or, The Mysteries and Crimes
of Mormonism. Phila.: National Publishing Co., 1870. Illus. Folding
map of Utah. Orig. green cloth, gilt. Fine. Jenkins 152-555 1983
$50

BEADLE, J. H.   Polygamy Or, The Mysteries and Crimes of
Mormonism. (N.p., 1904). Later printing, illus., spine edges and cor-
ners slightly frayed and some minor cover soiling, else very good.
Quill & Brush 54-1614 1983 $25

BEADLE, N. C. W.   Vegetation of Australia. 1981. 416
figures and 91 tables, 8vo, cloth. Wheldon 160-1649 1983 £51.50

BEAGLE, PETER S.   A Fine and Private Place. NY, 1960.
Very good in slightly soiled very good dustwrapper. Quill & Brush 54-
80 1983 $75

BEAGLE, PETER S.   The Last Unicorn. New York: (1968).
First edition, first issue. Boards and cloth. Very fine in dust
jacket. Bradley 66-106 1983 $85

BEALE, DOROTHEA   Dorothea Beale of Cheltenham. 1910.
New edition, front. port. Half title. Orig. olive cloth. Jarndyce
30-888 1983 £10.50

BEAMES, THOMAS   The Rookeries of London. Thomas
Bosworth, 1850. First edition. Half title. Orig. red cloth, sl.
dulled, v.g. Jarndyce 31-232 1983 £48

BEAMES, THOMAS   The Rookeries of London: Past, Present,
and Prospective. London: Thomas Bosworth, 1850. Full morocco with
marbled endpapers. First edition. All edges a bit rubbed. Attractive
copy with dentelles and marbled edges. Previous owner's name on one
blank leaf. MacManus 277-232 1983 $50

BEAN, FLORENCE O.   Bookbinding for Beginners. Boston:
School Arts Publishing Co., (1914). First edition. 8vo. Cloth.
Spine ends chipped; endpaper foxed. Oak Knoll 48-39 1983 $25

BEAN, ORESTES U.   Corianton, an Aztec Romance. (N.p.,
ca. 1902). 12mo, orig. pr. wraps. Argosy 716-548 1983 $20

BEAN, PERCY   The Chemistry and Practice of Finishing.
Manchester (Eng.), 1905. 1st ed. Pasted in are numerous fabric
samples of different colors and shades; also other illus. 8vo. Lacks
endleaves, inner hinges cracked. Morrill 286-45 1983 $37.50

BEAN, W. J.   Trees and Shrubs hardy in the British
Isles. 1970-80. 8th edition, numerous plates and text-figures,
4 vols., 8vo, cloth. Revised and enlarged edition. Wheldon 160-
2074 1983 £164

BEANLAND, WILLIAM   A Dickens Dinner Party. Chas. Damiens,
1909. First edition, orig. dark green cloth, a little marked.
Inscribed presentation copy from the author. Jarndyce 31-582 1983
£12.50

BEARD, DAN   The Black Wolf Pack. New York:
Scribners, (1922). Plates. Pictorial cloth. First edition. Inscribed
and signed by the author, and signed by the author's wife as well.
A very good copy. Reese 20-73 1983 $35

BEARD, GEORGE M. (1839-1883) A Practical Treatise on Nervous
Exhaustion (Neurasthenia). NY: William Wood, 1880. Publisher's
green cloth. First edition. Gach 95-34 1983 $125

BEARDSLEY, AUBREY   The Best of Beardsley. Spring Books,
nd (ca. 1948). Re-issue, frontis. portrait, plates. Yellow cloth
with design by A.B. fr. cvr. (worn d/w, erasure top fr. free ep., top
of bkstrip soiled), v.g. Hodgkins 27-411 1983 £18

BEARDSLEY, AUBREY   The Best of Beardsley. London, Bodley
Head, (1948). 1st ed. 4to. Plates. Bookplate removed. Morrill
289-266 1983 $20

BEARDSLEY, AUBREY   Fifty Drawings by Aubrey Beardsley.
N.Y., Nichols, 1920. Folio. With 50 full page plates. Black cloth
stamped with gilt Art Deco floral designs after Beardsley, t.e.g.,
(spine a bit faded). One of 150 signed and numbered copies. With
the bookplate of Adrian Goldstone. Very good. Houle 22-79 1983
$150

BEARDSLEY, AUBREY   The Morte Darthur Portfolio. London:
1927. Forward by Aymer Vallance & a Note on the Omitted Design by
Rainforth Armitage. Sq 4to, calf-backed vellum bds., upper cover
in gilt, t.e.g. One of 300 copies. An exceptional copy.
Perata 27-10 1983 $350

BEARDSLEY, AUBREY   A Portfolio of Aubrey Beardsley's Drawings Illustrating "Salome" by Oscar Wilde. N.p.: n.d. (London:1920).
17 plates loose in parchment-&-board portfolio. First edition. Portfolio worn. The plates in fine condition. MacManus 277-235 1983
$125

BEARDSLEY, AUBREY   A Second Book of Fifty Drawings. L.
Smithers, 1899. 1st edn., limited to 1000 copies. Frontis. portrait,
leaf adverts. rear. Scarlet cloth with gilt design fr. cvr. & rear
cvr. by Beardsley, t.e.g. (eps. sl. foxed & sl. foxing few plates,
top fr. corner bumped & others sl. bumped, bkstrip faded & fr. cvr.
faded & marked, 2 sections sl. sprung), v.g. Hodgkins 27-410 1983
£65

BEARDSLEY, AUBREY   The Story of Venus and Tannhauser.
London: Printed for Private Circulation, 1907. First edition. Of
300 numbered copies, this is one of 50 on Japon vellum. White
parchment covers are quite clean, but a small tear at head of spine
has been neatly repaired. Endpaper discoloured. One flyleaf frayed
where it has become brittle. Rota 230-48 1983 £250

BEARDSLEY, AUBREY   The Story of Venus and Tannhauser in
which is set forth an exact account of the manner of State held by
Madam Venus. N.Y.: Issued Privately for Subscribers Only, 1927.
Illus. by B.R. Elliott. 4to. Orig. silk-backed boards. One of 750
copies. Fine copy in original slipcase (damaged). MacManus 277-236
1983 $45

BEARDSLEY, AUBREY   The Uncollected Works of Aubrey
Beardsley. London, Bodley Head, (1925). First edition. Large 4to,
frontis. etching. Profusely illus. Dust jacket (2" x 2" chip on
front) else, very good - fine. Houle 22-80 1983 $225

BEATON, CECIL   Ashcombe. London, Batsford (1949).
First edition. Dust jacket with illus. by Rex Whistler (short tear).
Illus. with photos and drawings by Beaton, Whistler and others.
Houle 21-80 1983 $45

BEATON, CECIL   Ballet. N.Y., Doubleday, 1951. First
American edition. Color title page and 56 halftone plates and
drawings. Dust jacket. V.g. Signed and inscribed by Beaton.
Houle 21-81 1983 $85

BEATON, CECIL   Cecil Beaton's New York. Phila.,
Lippincott, (1938). First American edition. Color frontis. and 80
pages of photos; numerous line drawings, mostly by Beaton. Very good
copy. Signed and inscribed by Beaton. Houle 21-82 1983 $85

BEATON, CECIL   Time Exposure. New York: Charles
Scribner's Sons, 1941. Orig. cloth. Dust jacket (quite chipped,
torn). First edition. From the library of Anita Loos, with her
bookplate. Edges slightly worn. A good copy. MacManus 277-246
1983 $75

BEATTIE, JAMES   Poems on Several Occasions. Edinburgh:
Printed for W. Creech. M.DCC.LXXVI. Small 8vo, crimson straight
grain morocco, elaborately gilt, morocco lettering piece; lacking
the first, probably blank, leaf. First edition. Quaritch NS 7-7
1983 $375

BEATTIE, JAMES   Poetical Works. London, 1857. Portrait,
vignette title-page. Cr. 8vo, dark blue calf, two-line gilt borders
with corner ornaments, gilt panelled spine, morocco label. Traylen
94-57 1983 £16

BEATTIE, WILLIAM   The Danube. London, Virtue and Co.,
n.d. Illus. by W.H. Bartlett. Engraved and printed titles, portrait
frontis., 2 maps and 93 steel-engraved plates, wood-engravings in
the text, 4to, half hard-grain morocco gilt. K Books 307-16 1983
£290

BEATTIE, WILLIAM   The Ports, Harbours, Watering-Places, and
Coast Scenery of Great Britain. 1842. 2 vols., engr. and printed
titles, 123 finely engr. steel plates, full morocco, gilt tooling on
spines and boards. Handsome set with some slight foxing. K Books
307-17 1983 £270

BEAUCHAMP, WILLIAM M.   Aboriginal Use of Wood in New York.
Albany: New York State Museum, 1905. 30 plates. Small 4to.
Wrappers. Slightly worn. Ars Libri 34-116 1983 $30

BEAUCLERK, HELEN   The Green Lacquer Pavilion. New York,
1926. First American edition. Illus. by E. Dulac. Dust wrapper.
Very nice. Rota 230-173 1983 £12.50

BEAUCLERK, HELEN   The Love of the Foolish Angel. London,
1929. First edition. Decorations by E. Dulac. Slightly frayed dust
wrapper. Very good. Rota 230-174 1983 £12

BEAUCLERK, HELEN   The Mountain and the Tree. Collins,
1935. Blue cloth. Orig. dust wrapper designed by Dulac. Wear.
Greer 39-64 1983 £12.50

BEAUCLERK, HELEN   The Tale of Igor. London: C.W. Beaumont. 1918. With 6 full-page plates. One of 100 numbered copies on antique paper (total edition 125). Bound in 1/4 green cloth over boards; paper labels. Boards a bit rubbed. Karmiole 76-14 1983 $75

BEAUFOY, MARY   Nautical and Hydraulic Experiments, with Numerous Scientific Miscellanies. Vol. I. London, Henry Beaufoy, May 1834. 4to, engraved silhouette portrait, 2 vignettes by G. Cooke and 16 plates; plates foxed and waterstained; presentation copy to Thomas Love Peacock with signature of Henry Harding on title; orig. decorated cloth, rebacked, uncut. Only edition. This copy numbered 145. Quaritch NS 5-6 1983 $600

BEAUMONT, CYRIL W.   Mysterious Toyshop. London, Beaumont, 1924. First edition. Color frontis.; two full page color plates; numerous decorations by Wyndham Payne. Half cloth, paper label. Very good. Houle 21-83 1983 $45

BEAUMONT, CYRIL W.   The Wonderful Journey. C. W. Beaumont, 1927. First edition. Illus. in colour by W. Payne. Spine faded. Nice. Rota 231-48 1983 £12

BEAUMONT, FRANCIS   A King and No King as it is now acted at the Theatre Royal... London: by Andr. Clark..., 1676. Seventh edition. 4to. Wrappers. Some discolouring. Heath 48-241 1983 £30

BEAUMONT, FRANCIS   Philaster or, Love Lies a Bleeding... London: for William Leake..., 1652. Fifth impression. 4to. Half red morocco. Corner of title cut with slight loss, generally browned. Heath 48-242 1983 £75

BEAUMONT, FRANCIS   The Wild-Goose Chase. London: Humphrey Moseley, 1652. First edition. Thin folio, full brown levant morocco, gilt, inner gilt dentelles, edges gilt, by Riviere. Traylen 94-60 1983 £390

BEAUMONT, FRANCIS   Works. London: E. Moxon, 1840. 2 vols. Roy. 8vo. Cont. half calf, gilt, gilt panelled spines with red and green morocco labels, gilt. 2 portraits and engraved vignette title-pages. Traylen 94-58 1983 £25

BEAUMONT, FRANCIS   The Works. Cambridge, 1905-12. The Cambridge English Classics. 10 vols. 8vo. Orig. red cloth, gilt, spines slightly faded. Traylen 94-59 1983 £50

BEAUMONT, GUSTAVE DE   Systeme Penitentaire aux Etats-Unis et de son application en France. Paris, Gosselin, 1845. 3rd ed., 8vo, some slight foxing, cont. red quarter morocco, spine gilt, black morocco label, upper joint beginning to crack at the head, but a nice copy. Pickering & Chatto 21-7 1983 $100

BEAUMONT, WILLIAM   Experiments and Observations on the Gastric Juice, and the Physiology of Digestion. Plattsburgh: Printed by F.P. Allen, 1833. Orig. muslin backed paper boards, paper label. First edition. Enclosed in a folding cloth case. Reese 19-41 1983 $3,250

BEAUMONT, WILLIAM   Experiments and Observations on the Gastric Juice... Plattsburgh: F.P. Allen, 1833. 3 wood engravings. 8vo. Cloth with leather back and corners. Presented to the New York Academy of Medicine by Henry S. Norris, with his name stamped in gold on front cover. Duplicate stamp of N.Y. Academy of Medicine. Acquisition stamp of the Library of the N.Y. Post Graduate Medical School. First edition. Kraus 164-18 1983 $2,000

BEAUMONT, WILLIAM   Experiments and Observations on the Gastric Juice... Plattsburgh, (N.Y.), F.P. Allen, 1833. 8vo, orig. quarter linen, boards, spine nearly perished and front cover held by 2 cords, light foxing, faint watermarks, 2B1 and 2B2 reversed in binding as are the following 2 leaves; a respectable copy, preserved in slipcase. First edition. Ravenstree 97-95 1983 $1,350

BEAUMONT, WILLIAM   Experiments and Observations on the Gastric Juice. Boston: Lilly, Wait, and Company, 1834. Orig. muslin backed paper boards, remains of paper label. First edition, second issue. Spine cracking slightly, some occasional minor foxing and light staining, otherwise a near fine copy. Reese 19-42 1983 $1,200

BEAUMONT, WILLIAM   Experiments & Observations on the Gastric Juice & the Physiology of Digestion. Boston, 1929. 8vo, cloth-backed boards, paper label. Facs. of the 1833 edition. Argosy 713-33 1983 $45

BEAUMONT, WILLIAM   Experiments and Observations on the Gastric Juice... Boston, 1929. Facsimile of the 1833 edition. First edition. 8vo. 1/2 inch has been cut from the top of the first six leaves, else a very fine copy. Fye H-3-28 1983 $40

BEAUMONT, WILLIAM   Experiments and Observations on the Gastric Juice... Boston, 1929. 8vo. Orig. binding. Ex-library. Very good. Fye H-3-29 1983 $40

BEAUMONT, WILLIAM   The Physiology of Digestion, with Experiments on the Gastric Juice. Burlington: Chauncey Goodrich, 1847. Orig. cloth, stamped in blind. Bookplate, very slight browning, and a few light spots on the rear board, otherwise a fine, bright copy. Reese 19-43 1983 $650

BEAUMONT, A Guide to the City and Its Environs. Houston, ca. 1940. Illus., first edition, minor wear. Jenkins 153-609 1983 $30

THE BEAUTIES of Poetry, British and American: Containing Some of the Productions of... Philadelphia: From the Press of M. Carey. 1791. 12mo, cont. sheep, neatly rebacked with orig. label preserved. Some slight browning, and a few closed tears, with no losses, otherwise a very good copy. First edition. Reese 18-172 1983 $375

THE BEAUTIES of Spring. London: Printed for the Author...MDCCLXXXI. 4to, with list of errata pasted on verso of title, and an ad. leaf at end. First edition. New wraps. Quaritch NS 7-8 1983 $125

BEAUTY in Common Things. S.P.C.K., nd (ca. 1865). 12 mounted col. plates by Mrs. J. Whymper. Chromolithographed in colours by William Dickes. 1st edn. Blue fine ribbed decor. cloth, bevelled boards, a.e.g. (traces bookpl. fr. ep., sl. occasional foxing, corners sl. bruised), v.g. Hodgkins 27-355 1983 £35

BEAUVOIR, SIMONE DE   The Mandarins. Cleveland: World, (1956). Cloth, first edition in English. One of 500 copies (175 for sale), specially bound and signed by the author. A very fine copy in glassine wrapper and slipcase. Reese 20-77 1983 $85

BEAUX & Belles of England. London, Grolier Society, (190?). 14 vols., 8vo, half morocco, marbled sides, raised bands, gilt tops, nice. Ed. limited to 1000 sets. Morrill 286-572 1983 $50

BEAUX & Belles of England. Edinburgh Press, printed by the Grolier Society, London, n.d. 8vo, cloth, paper labels. 14 vols. Colored frontis. Fine set. In Our Time 156-342 1983 $150

BEAVER, PHILIP   African Memoranda: Relative to an Attempt to Establish a British Settlement on the Island of Bulama. London, 1805. Folding map, 2 engraved plates, 4to, a little dusty and some minor foxing but good in half calf. K Books 307-18 1983 £200

BEAZLEY, SAMUEL   The Oxonians. Colburn & Bentley, 1830. First edition. 3 vols. Sections springing in vol. II. Half red morocco. Jarndyce 31-425 1983 £35

BECCARIA, GIOVANNI BATTISTA   Experimenta, Atque Observationes, quibus Electricitas Vindex late Constituitur, Atque Explicatur. Augustae Taurinorum, (Turin) Ex Typographia Regia. (1769). 4to, 2 folding diagrams. In paper wraps. Toned and scattered light foxing throughout. Good. Arkway 22-11 1983 $395

BECCARI, O.   Asiatic Palms: Corypheae. Calcutta, 1931. Revised and edited by U. Martelli. Atlas of 102 plates, 4to and folio, original wrappers. Wheldon 160-2073 1983 £60

BECCARI, O.   Asiatic Palms: Lepidocaryae: Supplement. Calcutta, 1914. Atlas of 83 plates, 2 vols., folio, original portfolios. Wheldon 160-2072 1983 £40

BECHDOLT, FREDERICK R.   When the West Was Young. New York: The
Century Co., 1922. Frontis. Original cloth. Jenkins 153-37 1983
$30

BECHER, H. C. R.   A Trip to Mexico. Toronto: Willing &
Williamson, 1830. First edition. Map, plate of hieroglyphics. Port.
of Diaz, 13 mounted album photographs (some after plates). Orig.
pictorial gilt brown cloth. Minor cover wear and a few blindstamps.
Fine. Jenkins 152-329 1983 $250

BECHINIE DE LAZIAN, GEORGIUS Aristotelis Ex Euripo Emersus...
Prague, Typis Universitatis Carolo Ferdinandae, (1670). 12mo, orig.
vellum, name at foot of allegorical engraved frontis., names and
stamp on title, bit age-darkened, light spotting, but a good copy
with all 10 emblematic allegorical plates by the Austrian, Wolffgang.
Ravenstree 95-14 1983 $185

BECHSTEIN, J. R.   Naturgeschichte der Stubenthiere, Vogel.
Gotha, 1800. Second edition, coloured title vignette, 4 hand-
coloured plates and a folding table, 8vo, contemporary calf-backed
boards (neatly repaired). Wheldon 160-646 1983 £75

BECHTEL, EDWIN DE T.   Jacques Callot. New York: George
Braziller, 1955. 98 gravure plates (3 folding) with 237 illus.
Large 4to. Cloth. Dust jacket. Ars Libri 32-74 1983 $75

BECK, EARL CLIFTON   Songs of the Michigan Lumberjacks.
Ann Arbor, 1941. 1st ed. Illus. and log brands. 8vo, dust wrapper,
very nice. Morrill 286-650 1983 $25

BECK, GEORG LEONHARD   Dissertatio inauguralis diatetico-medica
sistens quaestiones quasdam de suctione fumi tabaci... Altdorf, 1745.
First edition. Small 4to. Modern boards. Kraus 164-229 1983 $180

BECK, HENRY CHARLTON   Fare to Midlands. N.Y., 1939. First
edition, many illus. Argosy 716-331 1983 $40

BECK, HENRY CHARLTON   Forgotten Towns of Southern New Jersey.
New Brunswick, 1937. 1st ed. Illus., in gravure. Ex library.
Argosy 710-334 1983 $30

BECK, HENRY CHARLTON   More Forgotten Towns of Southern New
Jersey. New York, 1937. First edition. Inscribed by author. 85
illustrations in gravure. 8vo. Morrill 290-344 1983 $20

BECK, LEWIS C.   A Gazetteer of the States of Illinois
and Missouri. Albany: Charles R. & George Webster, 1823. First
edition. Orig. paper boards, later cloth spine. Illus. with five
plans, but lacking map. Jenkins 152-556 1983 $850

BECK, WARREN   Final Score. N.Y., Knopf, 1944. First
edition. Dust jacket (slight rubbing), with a special "presentation
edition" leaf signed by the author. Very good. Houle 22-86 1983
$45

BECKE, LOUIS   The Naval Pioneers of Australia.
London, 1899. 1st ed. Illus. 8vo. Slightly rubbed and faded.
Morrill 287-26 1983 $20

BECKE, LOUIS   Under Tropic Skies. London: T. Fisher
Unwin, 1905. Orig. cloth. First edition. Edges and corners very
slightly worn. Covers a trifle soiled. Some foxing. A good copy.
MacManus 277-249 1983 $45

BECKER, BERIL   Paul Gauguin: The Calm Madman. NY,
(1931). Illus., fine in lightly worn, very good dustwrapper with a
chip out of top edge of rear panel, bookplate. Quill & Brush 54-1650
1983 $25

BECKER, ROBERT H.   The Plains and the Rockies. San Francisco: Printed at the Arion Press for John Howell--Books, 1982. Fourth
edition, revised and enlarged. Illus. Cloth. Dawson 471-18 1983
$150

BECKETT, RONALD B.   Lely. (English Master Painters.)
London: Routledge and Kegan Paul, 1951. 129 illus. 4to. Cloth.
Ars Libri 32-398 1983 $75

BECKETT, SAMUEL   All That Fall. New York, (1957). 8vo.
Cloth, boards. 1 of 25 specially bound copies, numbered and signed
by Beckett. A fine copy in protective acetate jacket. In Our Time
156-58 1983 $900

BECKETT, SAMUEL   All that Fall. N.Y., 1957. Ltd.
edition, one of 100 numbered copies. Argosy 714-45 1983 $175

BECKETT, SAMUEL   Bing. (Paris: 1966). First edition.
One of 112 of an edition of 762 reserved for library of printer, Les
Editions de Minuit. Signed by Beckett. Near mint in printed
wrappers and glassine. Bromer 25-5 1983 $185

BECKETT, SAMUEL   Come and Go. London, 1967. First
edition in English. One of (100) numbered copies, signed by author.
Publisher's buckram, gilt. In slipcase. Fine. Rota 230-51 1983
£64

BECKETT, SAMUEL   Echo's Bones. Paris, 1935. First
edition. Of 327 copies, this is one of 50 "hors commerce." Wrappers.
Two leaves just a little soiled. Very nice. Rota 231-50 1983 £250

BECKETT, SAMUEL   Ill Seen, Ill Said. Northridge: Lord
John Press, 1982. 1st ed., 1 of 26 lettered copies signed by Beckett.
Orig. half and fore-edge morocco and paste-paper boards, gilt, uncut.
Mint copy of the deluxe issue that was sold out at publication, in
special binding by David Bourbeau with spine and full fore-edge of
both covers edged in dark blue morocco, with vertically grained midnight blue paste-paper between. Jenkins 155-62 1983 $350

BECKETT, SAMUEL   Ill Seen Ill Said. Northridge: Lord
John Press, 1982. Small quarto. Calf backed marbled boards. First
edition thus. One of 299 numbered copies, printed by Henry Morris,
bound by Bela Blau, and signed by the author on the half-title.
Mint as issued. Reese 20-83 1983 $100

BECKETT, SAMUEL   Ill Seen, Ill Said. Northridge: Lord
John Press, 1982. 1st ed., 1 of 299 numbered and signed copies.
Orig. leather-backed marbled boards, uncut, gilt. Mint copy of this
book printed by Henry Morris at the Bird & Bull Press using Bembo
types on mould-made Burgrabutten paper, and bound by Bela Blau.
Jenkins 155-63 1983 $100

BECKETT, SAMUEL   Imagination Dead Image. London: (1965).
First edition. Limited to 100 copies signed by Beckett. Mint in
slip-case. Bromer 25-6 1983 $200

BECKETT, SAMUEL   The North. London: Enitharmon Press,
1972. With 3 original etchings by Avigdor Arikha. Folio. Loose
sheets in cloth portfolio, slipcase. First edition. One of 12
"ad personam" copies out of a total edition of 137. This one inscribed
by the author on the title-page "for George & Jean (Reavey) with love
from Sam, Paris, July 73." Reavey published a number of Beckett's
early works under his Europa Press imprint. Very fine copy.
MacManus 277-250 1983 $1,250

BECKETT, SAMUEL   No's Knife. London, (1967). 8vo,
full white calf, a.e.g. One of 100 copies, Series A, numbered and
signed by the author. Duschnes 240-9 1983 $200

BECKETT, SAMUEL   Not I. (London): Faber & Faber, (1973).
Orig. wrappers. Reprint, but inscribed by the author on the title-page:
"for George & Jane (Reavey) with love from Sam, Paris, July 1973."
Fine copy. MacManus 277-251 1983 $150

BECKETT, SAMUEL   Premier Amour. (Paris): Les Editions de
Minuit, (1970). Orig. wrappers. Later printing, but inscribed by the
author "for George & Jane (Reavey) with love from Sam, Paris, August,
1972." Reavey published a number of Beckett's early works under the
Europa Press imprint. Fine copy. MacManus 277-252 1983 $150

BECKETT, SAMUEL   Proust. London, 1931. First edition.
Bookplate, which has been inscribed by Beckett. Slight browning
on spine of dust wrapper. Fine copy. Gekoski 2-10 1983 £135

BECKETT, SAMUEL   Proust. London: Chatto & Windus, 1931.
12mo. Orig. boards. First edition. In dust jacket. Very fine copy.
MacManus 277-253 1983 $250

BECKETT, SAMUEL   Proust. London, 1931. First edition.
Covers just a little spotted. Slightly rubbed dust wrapper. Very nice.
Rota 231-49 1983 £60

BECKETT, SAMUEL   Tous Ceux Qui Tombent (All That Fall).
Paris: Les Editions de Minuit, (1957). 1st French ed., printed
wrappers. 1 of 70 numbered copies. This copy inscribed by author.
A fine copy. In Our Time 156-59 1983 $450

BECKETT, SAMUEL   Waiting for Godot. London: Samuel
French, (1957). Printed wraps., first acting edition, signed by the
author on the title-page. Fine. Reese 20-80 1983 $225

BECKETT, SAMUEL   Waiting For Godot. London: Faber &
Faber, (1956). Orig. yellow cloth with red lettering. Dust jacket
(slightly faded and worn). First English edition. Near fine copy.
MacManus 277-254 1983 $150

BECKETT, SAMUEL   Waiting for Godot. London, (1956).
First English edition. Cloth. Slightly rubbed dust wrapper. Very
good. King 45-148 1983 $150

BECKETT, SAMUEL   Waiting for Godot. London, 1956. First
English edition. Inscription. Fore-edge slightly spotted. Free endpapers slightly browned. Price-clipped dustwrapper. Fine. Jolliffe
26-48 1983 £45

BECKETT, SAMUEL   Watt. Paris: Olympia Press, 1953.
First edition. Of 1125 copies, this is one of 1100 for general cir-
culation. Wrappers a little frayed and creased. Bookplate. Nice.
Rota 231-51 1983 £45

BECKFORD, WILLIAM   An Arabian Tale. London: for J.
Johnson, 1786. First edition. 8vo. Cont. calf, neatly rebacked,
gilt, morocco label, gilt. Errata leaf. Traylen 94-63 1983
£275

BECKFORD, WILLIAM   The History of the Caliph Vathek.
Nimmo, 1883. Large thick 8vo, 5 etched plates, uncut in the original
green cloth, printed paper label slightly rubbed, endpapers darkened,
a fine and entirely unopened copy. 150 numbered copies printed
by Ballantyne on laid paper with proof etchings on Whatman paper.
Deighton 3-27 1983 £58

BECKFORD, WILLIAM   Vathek. New York: John Day, 1928.
Gilt cloth. First edition thus, with illus. by Mahlon Blaine.
Very fine in almost fine dust jacket, and slightly defective slipcase.
Reese 20-87 1983 $35

BECKFORD, WILLIAM   Vathek. Bloomsbury: The Nonesuch Press,
1929. Vellum and boards. Illus. by M.V. Dorn. One of 1050 numbered
copies. Corners a trifle shelf-rubbed, otherwise a fine copy.
Reese 20-729 1983 $65

BECKMANN, JOHANN   A History of Inventions and Discoveries.
London, 1797. First English edition. 8vo. 3 vols. Cont. calf,
rubbed. Top margin of a few leaves at beginning of vol. 3 wormed.
Gurney 90-12 1983 £135

BECKMANN, JOHANN   A History of Inventions and Discoveries.
London, 1814. Second edition. 8vo. 4 vols. Old half-calf, spines
slightly worn. Gurney 90-13 1983 £115

BECQUEREL, ALEXANDRE-EDMOND   Effets Lumineaux... Paris Imprimerie de
Ch. Lahure et Cie...), 19 Avril 1861. 1st ed., 8vo, colophon leaf,
a few wood engraved text illus.; uncut and unopened in the orig.
printed wrapper, wrapper slightly soiled, signed G. Quinche, 1863, a
good copy. Pickering & Chatto 22-14 1983 $165

BECQUEREL, ANTOINE-CESAR   Elements d'Electro-Chimie appliquee
aux Sciences Naturelles et aux Arts... Paris: Didot Freres, 1843.
8vo. Cont. quarter calf over pebbled boards. 3 folding tables.
Errata. Zeitlin 264-30 1983 $180

BECQUEREL, ANTOINE-CESAR   Traite de Physique consideree dans ses
Rapports avec la Chimie... Paris: Didot Freres, 1842, 1844. 2 vols.
8vo. Cont. green calf prize binding. 13 folding plates. Zeitlin
264-31 1983 $100

BEDA VENERABILIS   De natura rerum et Science temporum
ratione libri duo. Basel: Henricus Petri, 1529. Woodcut headpiece
and several figurated woodcut initials. Small folio. 18th-century
quarter calf, back gilt. Ms. exlibris of Neustift monastery (Nova
Cella) in Tirol, dated 1549, and of two other owners on title; bookplate of Harrison D. Horblit. Editio princeps. Kraus 164-24 1983
$1,250

BEDA VENERABILIS   Opera quotquot reperiri potuerunt omnia.
Cologne: Anton Hierat sen. and Johann Gymnich IV, 1612. 8 vols. in
3. Vol. 1 with fine engraved title incorporating a view of Cologne,
by Peter Isselburg after Augustin Braun. Titles of vols. 2-8 with
large publisher's device. Woodcut musical notation in vol. 1. Vol. 2
with 60 fine text woodcuts. Large folio. 17th-century English calf.
From the libraries of the Earls of Ellesmere, and of Harrison D.
Horblit. Rebacked. Few leaves browned. Kraus 164-25 1983 $4,500

BEDA VENERABILIS   De temporibus sive de sex aetatibus
huius seculi. Venice: Joannes Tacuinus da Trino, 28 May 1505.
One large figurated and two smaller ornamental woodcut initials.
Small 4to. 18th-century boards. From the library of Harrison D.
Horblit, with his bookplate. Rebacked. Kraus 164-21 1983 $2,850

BEDA VENERABILIS   De temporibus sive de sex aetatibus
huius seculi. Paris: (Jean Marchant) for Jean Petit, 5 April 1507.
Full-page woodcut on verso of title, large publisher's device on
title, three decorative woodcut initials. Small 4to. Modern calf-
backed boards. Kraus 164-22 1983 $657

BEDA, VENERABILIS   De temporibus sive de sex aetatibus
huius seculi Liber. Venice: Joannes Tacuinus da Trino, 8 May 1509.
One large figurated and two smaller ornamental woodcut initials.
Small 4to. 18th-century mottled calf, back gilt. From the library
of Harris D. Horblit, with his bookplate. 3 ms. lines on title
inked out. Kraus 164-23 1983 $800

BEDDOES, THOMAS   Hygeia: or Essays Moral and Medical
on the Causes Affecting the Personal State of Our Middling and
Affluent Classes. Bristol (Eng.), 1802-1803. 1st ed. 3 vols., 8vo.
Orig. boards, paper labels, all edges untrimmed. Spines chipped;
front hinge of Vol. 2 cracked. Morrill 289-14 1983 $150

BEDFORD, ARTHUR   The Evil and Danger of Stage-Plays:
shewing their natural tendency to destroy religion, and introduce
a general corruption of manners. (London), n.p.: printed and sold
by W. Bonny, and the booksellers of Bristol; 1706. 8vo, old calf
(rebacked), spine gilt (quite worn). 1st ed. Some browning, with a
leaf of errata and the leaf of ads at the end. Ximenes 64-34 1983
$600

BEDFORD, HERBRAND A. RUSSELL, DUKE OF   Science and Fruit
Growing. 1919. With 4 plates and 47 other illus., 8vo, orig. cloth.
Fenning 62-20 1983 £10.50

BEDFORD, PAUL   Recollections and Wanderings of Paul
Bedford. London: Routledge, Warne & Routledge, 1864. Orig. decorated
cloth. First edition. Spine and covers somewhat worn and spotted.
Former owner's signature; bookshop blindstamp. In a half-morocco
slipcase. Good condition. MacManus 277-258 1983 $125

BEDFORD, PAUL   Recollections and wanderings of Paul
Bedford. Facts, not fancies. London: Routledge, Warne, and Routledge, 1864. 1st ed., 8vo, original red cloth (slight wear at the
top of the spine). Bookplate. A very good copy. Ximenes 64-35 1983
$125

BEDFORD, PAUL   Recollections and wanderings of Paul
Bedford. Facts, not fancies. London: Strand Printing and Publishing
Co. Ltd., 1867. 12mo, cont. half calf (rather worn). 2nd edition.
A yellowback, with the remains of a pictorial front wrapper bound in.
Ximenes 64-36 1983 $25

BEDICHEK, ROY   Adventures with a Texas Naturalist.
Garden City: Doubleday, 1947. First edition. Illus. by Ward Lockwood.
Chipped dust jacket. Printed label stating this copy was distributed
by the Texas Folklore Society. Fine. Jenkins 152-558 1983 $45

BEDLAM: A Poem. London (i.e., Edinburgh): Printed for J. Huggonson.
1741. 8vo, new wraps. Edinburgh piracy of the folio edition printed
in London. Quaritch NS 7-9 1983 $350

BEEBE, G. M.   Governor's Annual Message. (Lawrence,
1861. First edition. Marbled boards and calf. Bookplate removed.
Bradley 66-574 1983 $275

BEEBE, GILBERT J.   A Review and Refutation of Helper's
"Impending Crisis." Middletown, N.Y., 1860. Stitched. Felcone 22-
14 1983 $20

BEEBE, LUCIUS   High Iron. N.Y., Appleton, 1938.
First edition. With over 200 fine gravures. Dust jacket. Front
free endpaper lacking, else very good. Houle 21-994 1983 $85

BEEBE, WILLIAM   Galapagos, World's End. New York,
1925. 9 coloured plates, 83 other illustrations, royal 8vo, original
cloth. Fourth impression of the first edition. Wheldon 160-346
1983 £36

BEEBE, WILLIAM   A Monograph of the Pheasants. 1918-22.
90 coloured plates by Thornburn, Lodge, Gronvold and others, 88 photogravure plates, distribution maps. 4 vols., folio, cloth. Scarce.
The edition consisted of 600 copies. Vol. 1 is rebound to match vols.
2-4 which are in original cloth. Small labels removed from inside
front covers. A few tissues creased and a few plate margins a trifle
foxed. Bookplates. Wheldon 160-6 1983 £1,350

BEEBE, WILLIAM   Pheasant Jungles. NY 1927.
Photos, cloth, mediocre copy. King 46-539 1983 $20

BEEBE, WILLIAM   Pheasants. Garden City, 1926. First
Trade edition. 2 vols. Color illus. Index. T.e.g. Badly chipped
dust wrapper. Very good. King 45-473 1983 $125

BEEBE, WILLIAM   Tropical Wild Life in British Guiana...
Vol. 1. NY 1917. First edition. Color plates, photos, gilt-pict.
cloth, extremities worn. King 46-505 1983 $45

BEECHER, EDWARD   Narrative of Riots at Alton... Alton,
1838. 12mo, paper label. 1st ed. Morrill 289-615 1983 $37.50

BEECHER, HARRIS H.   The 114th Regiment, N.Y.S.V.: Where
it Went, What it Saw, and What it Did. Norwich, N.Y., 1866.
582pp. First edition. Original three-quarter calf over marbled
boards, with morocco spine labels. A handsome copy. Illus.
One of the finest of personal memoirs by a Union Army surgeon.
Scarce in such fine finding. Jenkins 151-13 1983 $125

BEECHER, HENRY WARD   Eyes and Ears. Boston, 1862. First
edition. Orig. designed cloth, exlib. Argosy 716-372 1983 $40

BEECHER, HENRY WARD   A Looking-Glass for H. W. Beecher. New
York, 1875. First edition. 12mo, original wrappers. Morrill
290-626 1983 $25

BEECHER, LYMAN   A Sermon Delivered at the Funeral
of Henry Obookiah, a Native of Owhyhee, and a Member of the Foreign
Mission School. Elizabeth-town, N.J., 1819. First edition. Dbd.
Ginsberg 46-856 1983 $50

THE BEECHER-TILTON Scandal. New York, 1874. 8vo. Orig. wrappers.
Wrappers chipped, torn at front hinge, and with notes by a former
owner on front wrapper; some underlining in text. Morrill 289-268
1983 $20

THE BEECHER Trial, a Review of the Evidence from New York Times Editor.
New York, 1875. Fourth edition. Orig. printed, gray wraps, bit worn
and spotted. Nice. Boswell 7-147 1983 $75

BEECHING, HENRY CHARLES   Pages from a Private Diary. London:
Smith, Elder, & Co., 1898. 8vo, 20 cm. Orig. green vertical ribbed
cloth. Occasional foxing and light wear. Very good. Inscribed in
Latin and initialled by the author. First edition in book form.
Grunder 7-5 1983 $45

BEEDHAM, R. JOHN   Wood Engraving. Ditchling, 1929.
Introduction & Appendix by Eric Gill. Third edition. Sm 8vo,
cloth-backed pictorial bds., illustrated with wood-engravings by
David Jones, Desmond Chute, et al. A very nice copy. Perata 27-
163 1983 $85

BEEDHAM, R. JOHN   Wood Engraving. London: Faber and
Faber Ltd., (1946). 8vo. Cloth. Dust jacket (slightly chipped).
Oak Knoll 48-168 1983 $20

BEEDOME, THOMAS   Select Poems: Diving and Humane.
Bloomsbury, 1928. 12mo, limp vellum, gilt, slipcase. One of 1250
copies. Perata 28-116 1983 $35

BEEDOME, THOMAS   Select Poems Divine and Humane. Bloomsbury: Nonesuch Press, 1928. Limited to 1250 copies; vellum covers
slightly darkened at spine, otherwise very good in darkened slipcase.
Quill & Brush 54-87 1983 $30

BEEDOME, THOMAS   Select Poems Divine and Humane.
Bloomsbury, 1928. 12mo, limp vellum. One of 1250 copies on
Van Gelder paper. Slipcase. Duschnes 240-171 1983 $25

BEERBOHM, MAX   And Even Now. London: William Heinemann, 1920. Orig. cloth with paper label on spine. First edition.
Inscribed by the author on the half-title: "Miss Zina Naylor's copy
of And Even Now intruded on by Max Beerbohm, May 1921." Covers soiled
and slightly worn. MacManus 277-261 1983 $225

BEERBOHM, MAX   And Even Now. London: William Heinemann, 1920. Orig. cloth, with paper label on spine. First edition.
Spine faded. A very good copy. MacManus 277-259 1983 $45

BEERBOHM, MAX   And Even Now. London: William Heinemann, 1920. Orig. cloth with paper label. First edition. Covers
soiled and worn. MacManus 277-260 1983 $20

BEERBOHM, MAX   The Book of Elizabethan Verse. Boston:
Herbert B. Turner & Co., 1907. Orig. blue cloth. Second edition.
From the library of Max Beerbohm, with the presentation inscription
"Florence and Max with love from Morris, 1914." Spine ends worn.
A good copy. MacManus 277-262 1983 $85

BEERBOHM, MAX   Cartoons. "The Second Childhood of John
Bull." London: Stephen Swift & Co. Ltd., (1911). Elephant folio.
Orig. cloth-backed boards. First edition. Covers slightly rubbed &
soiled. A very good copy. Rare. MacManus 277-263 1983 $350

BEERBOHM, MAX   Catalogue of an Exhibition Entitled
"Ghosts." London: Ernest Brown & Phillips, The Leicester Galleries,
December 1928. Small 4to. Orig. wrappers. First edition. One of 55
copies signed by Beerbohm. Wrappers a bit soiled. A very good copy.
MacManus 277-264 1983 $185

BEERBOHM, MAX   Gavarni. Par Eugene Forgues. Paris:
Librairie de L'Art, n.d. Orig. cloth. Max Beerbohm's copy, with a
slight pencil sketch on page 68, by Max. Covers loose. Foxed.
MacManus 277-265 1983 $125

BEERBOHM, MAX   Lytton Strachey. Cambridge: The University Press, 1943. 12mo. Orig. wrappers. First edition. Fine.
MacManus 277-266 1983 $25

BEERBOHM, MAX   Observations. London: William Heine-
mann Ltd., (1925). 4to. Illus. with colored frontis. & 19 plates.
Orig. cloth. First edition. Covers a bit soiled. A good copy.
MacManus 277-267 1983 $75

BEERBOHM, MAX   A Peep into the Past. (N.Y.): Privately
Printed, 1923. 4to. Illus. with caricatures & a facsimile of the
manuscript. Orig. cloth-backed boards with pictorial paper label.
First edition. One of only 300 copies printed on Japan vellum. Very
good copy. MacManus 277-268 1983 $150

BEERBOHM, MAX   Seven Men. London: Heinemann, 1919.
Orig. cloth. Dust jacket (a bit worn). First edition. Scarce in
dust jacket. Nice copy. MacManus 277-269 1983 $65

BEERBOHM, MAX   Seven Men. London: Heinemann, 1919.
Orig. cloth. First edition. Fine copy. MacManus 277-270 1983 $50

BEERBOHM, MAX   A Survey. London: Heinemann, 1921.
4to. Illus. with 51 caricature plates, each mounted. First edition.
Limited to 275 copies signed by the author. Spine and covers faded.
Some staining. Very good. MacManus 277-271 1983 $175

BEERBOHM, MAX   A Survey. Heinemann, 1921. First
edition, with 52 caricature plates, 1 coloured, 4to, orig. cloth,
gilt. Defective dust wrapper loosely inserted. Fenning 62-21 1983
£32

BEERBOHM, MAX   A survey. London, Heinemann, 1921.
First edition, 4to, mounted colour frontispiece and 51 other mounted
plates, uncut in red cloth gilt, title and contents leaves foxed,
spine very faded. Deighton 3-28 1983 £32

BEERBOHM, MAX   Things New and Old. London: Heinemann,
1923. Large 4to, 49 leaves of tipped-in plates by Beerbohm. With
titled tissue guards. Tipped-in color frontis. and a special color
plate signed and dated, "Max 1923," laid inside rear pocket. Edition
ltd. to 380 numbered copies, signed by Beerbohm, and with
the additional signed print. In beige cloth, gilt-stamped. A.e.g.
Karmiole 73-14 1983 $250

BEERBOHM, MAX   Things New and Old. Heinemann, 1923.
1st ed., 4to, coloured frontispiece and 49 other black and white
plates, original cloth gilt, slight tear on spine but a very good
copy. Deighton 3-29 1983 £58

BEERBOHM, MAX   This New and Old. Lon., 1923. Frontis.
loose, top page edge margin stained affecting a few plates, else good
or better, bookplate. Quill & Brush 54-88 1983 $60

BEERBOHM, MAX   The Works... London: John Lane, The
Bodley Head, 1896. Orig. red cloth with paper label on spine, new
labels tipped-in at the back. First English edition. With a later
TLS, 1 page. 8vo, Villino Chiaro, Raphallo, 2 February, 1955, to the
publisher William Targ regarding the rights to reprint. With Targ's
bookplate on the front endsheet. Covers somewhat rubbed & dust-soiled.
Endpapers foxed. In folding cloth box. A good copy. MacManus 277-272
1983 $225

BEERBOHM, MAX   The Works of Max Beerbohm. New York:
Scribner's, 1896. 1st ed., preceding the English ed. Orig.
decorative brown cloth, gilt, t.e.g., uncut. Slight wear at spine
tips, else a fine copy with all of the gilt and the cream butterflies
intact. Jenkins 155-64 1983 $200

BEERBOHM, MAX   The Works. N.Y., 1896. Small 12mo,
dec. brown cloth; slightly rubbed. First edition. Argosy 714-47
1983 $200

BEERBOHM, MAX   The Works. London, 1922-1928. 10
vols. 8vo. Orig. multi-coloured buckram, with printed paper labels,
spines a little faded, uncut. edges. Limited to 780 numbered copies,
signed by the author. Traylen 94-64 1983 £350

BEERBOHM, MAX   Zuleika Dobson, or an Oxford Love Story.
London: Heinemann, 1911. Orig. cloth. First edition. Rough cloth
binding. A very good copy. MacManus 277-273 1983 $150

BEERBOHM, MAX   Zueleika Dobson, or an Oxford Love
Story. New York: John Lane, 1912. 1st American ed. Orig. pic-
torial cream cloth, gilt. Light wear, but a close to fine copy.
Jenkins 155-65 1983 $80

BEERS, CLIFFORD W.A.   A Mind that Found Itself. N.Y., 1913.
Presentation copy, signed on fly-leaf. With TLS inserted. Argosy
713-36 1983 $50

BEERS, ETHEL LYNN   All Quiet Along the Potomac.
Philadelphia: Porter & Coates, (1879). 1st ed. Orig. cloth, gilt.
Fine copy of this family copy inscribed by C. Eliot Beers. Jenkins
155-67 1983 $25

BEERS, HENRY A.   The Ways of Yale in the Consulship of
Plancus. New York, 1895. Frontis. Pictorial buckram. Very good.
Reese 19-607 1983 $20

BEERS, HENRY PUTNEY   Bibliographies in American History. NY,
1942. Tall 8vo, ex lib. Argosy 710-19 1983 $37.50

BEERS, HENRY PUTNEY   Bibliographies in American History.
New York: H.W. Wilson, 1942. Cloth; ex-library, somewhat used, but
tight. Revised ed. Dawson 470-24 1983 $20

BEESLEY'S Illustrated Guide to St. Michael's Church, Charleston, S.C.
(Charleston, 1908). Photos, oblong 16mo, pr. blue wrs., tied.
Argosy 710-515 1983 $25

BEETHOVEN, LUDWIG VON   Arien und Gesaenge aus Fidelio. Berlin,
n.d. (c. 1830). 12mo, decorative paper with a design in a gold and
purple pattern. Inside foxed. Replacement performers' names written
in by hand. Salloch 387-17 1983 $35

BEETHOVEN, LUDWIG VON   Fidelio. Paris, chez A. Farrenc,
Editeur, Md. de Musique, Boulevard Poissoniere No. 22. Plate #A.F. 72
(1826). Engraved title, engraved music. With a list of subscribers.
Thick folio, uncut. Crimson 1/2 morocco over marbled boards.
First edition. Salloch 387-14 1983 $3,000

BEETHOVEN, LUDWIG VON   Grand Septuor pour Deux Pianofortes a 8
Mains. Leipzig, au Bureau de Musique de C.F. Peters. Plate # 2781.
(1841-1844?). 2 vols. Engraved title for one of the vols. Oblong
folio, unbound. Some foxing and margins slightly frayed. Small
stamps of Peters, Leipzig and Schaffenberg, New York (faded) on title
page. Dated by a former owner in pencil. Salloch 387-15 1983 $125

BEETHOVEN, LUDWIG VON   Beethoven's letters... London: Longman's, etc., 1866. First edition in English. 2 vols., 8vo. Orig.
purple cloth. Portrait and a folding plate of facs. manuscript.
Spines slightly faded. Ximenes 63-324 1983 $100

BEETHOVEN, LUDWIG VON   Ouverture in C. Vienna, Tobias
Haslinger, (?1838). Full score, engraved title, engraved music.
Folio, new cloth. Slightly foxed, faded waterstain in margin. From
the library of Thomas Scherman; his name gilt-stamped on binding.
First edition. Salloch 387-18 1983 $300

BEETS, N.   Lucas de Leyde. Bruxelles/Paris:
G. Van Oest, 1913. 33 plates. Small 4to. Wrappers. Ars Libri
32-412 1983 $45

BEGBIE, HAROLD   The Vigil. London: Hodder and Stoughton,
1907. Orig. cloth. First edition. Edges a little worn. Covers
slightly scratched and soiled. First few leaves heavily foxed.
Frontispiece loose. MacManus 277-281 1983 $25

BEGG, ROBERT BURNS   The Lochleven angler. Kinross: George
Barnet, etc., 1874. First edition. Small 8vo. Orig. limp green
cloth. Tinted frontis. and a folding map. Top of spine slightly
rubbed. Very good copy. Ximenes 63-551 1983 $50

THE BEGGAR'S Bension; or, a Hero Without a Name. London, Cassell,
Petter & Gilpin, 1866. First ed., illus. with pen and ink sketches
by G. Cruikshank. 2 vols. Orig. cloth. Bookplates, good, in a
publisher's pres. binding with full printed pres. slips from author to
Alexander Cassels in each vol. MacManus 277-1207 1983 $135

THE BEGGAR'S Benison; or, A Hero Without a Name. London: Cassell,
Petter & Galpin, 1866. First ed., illus. with pen and ink sketches
by G. Cruikshank. 2 vols., orig. cloth, very good. MacManus 277-
1206 1983 $125

BEHAL, AUGUSTE   Traite de Chimie Organique d'apres
les theories modernes... Paris: Octave Doin, 1901. 2 vols. in 1.
8vo. Cont. morocco backed boards. Slightly rubbed. Zeitlin 264-32
1983 $80

BEHAN, BRENDAN   The Quare Fellow. NY, (1956). First
American edition. Limited to 100 numbered copies, very good, owner's
name. Quill & Brush 54-89 1983 $100

BEHMEN, JACOB   Concerning the Three Principles of the
Divine Essence of the Eternal, Dark, Light, and Temporary World.
Cornhill, M.S., 1648. Cont. calf, rebacked with orig. spine laid
down (title page lacking, replaced with two facs., last signature with
tears and foredge wear, crudely repaired, with some of the test of
the tables near the margin slightly affected). This copy belonged
to Frater Achad, and bears his signature, and date, 1937. Houle
22-89 1983 $150

BEHRING, I.   Die Praktischen Ziele Der Blutserum-
Therapie Und Die Immunisirungsmethoden Zum Zweck Der Gewinnung Von
Heil-Serum II. Das Tetanusheilserum Und Seine Anwendung Auf
Tetanuskranke Menschen. Leipzig 1892. 2 vols. First ed. Cloth,
ex-library, well rubbed. King 46-506 1983 $100

BEHRMAN, S. H.   Rain from Heaven. N.Y., Random House,
(1935). First edition. Orig. tan cloth stamped in brown (frayed at
spine tips), Signed and inscribed by the author, NYC, Sept., 1935.
Good - very good. Houle 22-91 1983 $45

BEILFIELD, JACOB FRIEDRICH, BARON   Institutions Politiques. The Hague, Chez Pierre Gasse Junior, 1760. First ed., 2 vols. in one, 4to, 4 folding tables, half-titles, engraved frontis. portrait, engraved vignette on title-pages and on dedication leaf, woodcut ornaments and initials, title-pages in red and black, cont. mottled calf, spine elaborately gilt, red and black morocco labels, head of spine a little worn, a very good copy. Pickering & Chatto 21-8 1983 $450

BEINECKE, E. J.   A Stevenson Library. New Haven, 1951-54. 6 vols. Roy. 8vo. Orig. blue buckram gilt, t.e.g., others uncut. Portrait and 45 illus. of facimiles of manuscripts, etc. From the library of Desmond Flower, with his signature. Traylen 94-785 1983 £150

BEKE, CHARLES T.   A lecture on the sources of the Nile... London: The London Institution, 1864. 8vo. 3 maps. Full modern calf. Adelson Africa-13 1983 $240

BELANEY, GEORGE   Tales of an Empty Cabin. London: Lovat Dickson Ltd., 1936. First edition. 23cm. Limited edition of 250 copies on rag paper, this being no. 68, and signed by the author, with extra plate reproduced in colours. T.e.g., uncut. Blue cloth. Boxed. A fine copy. Rare. McGahern 53-185 1983 $200

BELCHER, C. F.   The Birds of Nyasaland. 1930. Folding map, 8vo, cloth. Wheldon 160-647 1983 £30

BELDENE, W. W.   The Martyr-Spirit of the Age: A Tribute to Gen. George B. Boomer... (Attleboro, Mass., Aug., 1863). 1st ed. Presented (by the author?) to Gideon Welles, with the latter's name in pencil on front cover. 32mo, orig. wrappers, nice. Morrill 287-27 1983 $22.50

BELISLE, ORVILLA S.   The Prophets. Phila., 1855. Illus. Orig. blind-stamped cloth, gilt-pict. spine (some foxing). Argosy 716-549 1983 $175

BELKNAP, HENRY W.   Artists and Craftsmen of Essex County Mass. Salem: Essex Institute, 1927. Illus. Argosy 710-281 1983 $27.50

BELKNAP, JEREMY   American Biography... Boston: Isaiah Thomas and Ebenezer T. Andrews, 1794 and 1798. 2 vols. 8vo. 3/4 leather over marbled boards. First editions of both vols. Vol. 1 is on thick paper, vol. 2 on thin. Ex library copies with old library bookplates pasted to the inside of both covers and pockets removed from the back covers. A library number is written on the spine. Covers are rubbed, but tight with good hinges. The leather of spine of vol. 1 damaged. Oak Knoll 49-374 1983 $65

BELKNAP, JEREMY   A Discourse, Intended to Commemorate the Discovery of America by Christopher Columbus... Boston, 1792. Two leaves of ads. New cloth, very good. Reese 18-176 1983 $125

BELKNAP, JEREMY   The Foresters, an American Tale. Boston: Isaiah Thomas and E.T. Andrews, 1792. 12mo, full brown crushed levant, a.e.g., by Sangorski & Sutcliffe. Engraved frontis. A fine, crisp copy. First edition, with the frontis. in Blanck's state A, and the footnote on page 77 in state B (no priority). Reese 18-177 1983 $450

BELKNAP, JEREMY   Sacred Poetry. Boston: Thomas Wells, 1818. Small 12mo, preserved copy in orig. red calf; gilt borders on both covers and gilt tooled spine. Karmiole 75-22 1983 $75

BELKNAP, WILLIAM W.   United States Troops in Alabama. Wash., 1875. Dbd. First edition. Ginsberg 46-3 1983 $25

BELL, A. E.   Christian Huygens and the Development of Science in the Seventeenth Century. London, 1947. 8vo. Cloth. Dust wrapper. Plates. Gurney JJ-188 1983 £15

BELL, A. N.   Climatology and Mineral Waters of the United States. New York, 1885. 8vo. Orig. binding. First edition. Fye H-3-31 1983 $35

BELL, ADRIAN   Folly Field. London: Cobden-Sanderson, (1933). Orig. cloth. Dust jacket (top of spine a bit chipped). First edition. Fine copy. MacManus 277-282 1983 $25

BELL, ADRAIN   Men & the Fields. B.T. Batsford, 1939. Colour frontis. 5 colour plates & text illus. Brown cloth, colour pictorial dust wrapper. Greer 40-147 1983 £12.50

BELL, ADRIAN   Men and the Fields. London, 1939. First edition. Drawings and lithographs by J. Nash. Gilt lettering on spine faded. Nice. Rota 231-444 1983 £12

BELL, ALEXANDER D.   Immigration. (San Francisco), 1870. Ginsberg 46-79 1983 $25

BELL, ALEXANDER GRAHAM   Upon the Electrical Experiments To Determine the Location of the Bullet in the Body of the Late President Garfield, and Upon a Successful Form of Induction Balance...With an Appendix. Washington: Gibson Brother, 1882. 1st ed. For private circulation. Illustrated. 8vo., orig. wrappers. Morrill 289-15 1983 $65

BELL, BENJAMIN   System of Surgery. Edinburgh, 1796. 8vo, mod. calf. Argosy 713-37 1983 $175

BELL, BENJAMIN   Trattato della Gonorrea Virulente e della Lue Venerea. Venezia, 1795. 2 vols. in 1. 1/4 leather. Argosy 713-38 1983 $125

BELL, BENJAMIN   A Treatise on the Theory and Management of Ulcers. Edinburgh, 1787. 8vo, cont. calf (worn, inner hinges repaired). Argosy 713-39 1983 $125

BELL, CHARLES   Exposition of the Natural System of the Nerves of the Human Body. Phila., 1825. 3 folding copperplates, text wood-engravings. 8vo, later 3/4 calf. Phila., 1825. First American Edition. Title & few leaves waterstained; old signature on title. Argosy 713-40 1983 $250

BELL, CHARLES   The Hand, its Mechanism and Vital Endowments as Evincing Design. William Pickering (printed by Charles Whittingham), London, 1833. First edition. 8vo, occasional slight foxing, 4 ads. dated March 1832; an unrestored copy in the orig. blue glazed cloth, printed paper label on spine, spine worn and lower joint split, uncut. Quaritch NS 5-7 1983 $375

BELL, CHARLES   The Hand. London, 1833. First edition. 8vo, full tooled green calf. Fine copy. Argosy 713-42 1983 $150

BELL, CHARLES   Illustrations of the Great Operations of Surgery. For Longman, Hurst, Rees, Orme and Brown, London, 1821. Oblong folio, with 20 engraved plates, of which 17 are partly coloured by hand; ownership inscription on title, some spotting and soiling; uncut in orig. boards, a little worn. First edition. Quaritch NS 5-8 1983 $1,600

BELL, CHARLES D.   The Four Seasons at the Lakes. Marcus Ward, nd. 1st edn. Illuminated by Blanche de Montmorency Conyers Morrell. 15 illuminated leaves printed in colours on heavy card. Blue sand grain decor. cloth, bevelled bds, a.e.g. (top/bottom of bkstrip worn, corners sl. bruised, bkstrip some fading, sl. foxing title, etc.), v.g. Hodgkins 27-356 1983 £40

BELL, CHARLES D.   Poems Old and New. Edward Arnold, 1893. First edition, 2 pp ads. Orig. green cloth a little marked. Jarndyce 30-646 1983 £8.50

BELL, CLIVE   Art. London: Chatto & Windus, 1928. Illus. Orig. cloth with paper label on spine. Dust jacket. Later edition. Fine copy. MacManus 277-283 1983 $20

BELL, CLIVE   On British Freedom. London, 1923. First edition. Dust wrapper. Fine. Rota 231-59 1983 £20

BELL, CLIVE   Since Cezanne. London, 1922. First edition. Illus. Torn dust wrapper. Fine. Rota 231-58 1983 £15

BELL, CURRER, PSEUD.
Please turn to
BRONTE, CHARLOTTE

BELL, D.   Wellington's Officers. London, 1938.
First edition. 8vo. Orig. cloth. Portrait frontis. 5 portrait
plates, 1 full page map. Some very slight foxing. Good. Edwards
1042-280 1983 £15

BELL, E.   The Great Parliamentary Bore. London,
1869. 8vo. Orig. cloth. Some wear. Presentation copy "W.E. Baxter
Esq. M.P. with the Author's Compliments." Good. Edwards 1044-46
1983 £50

BELL, E.   Memoir of General John Briggs. London,
1885. Portrait frontis., roy.8vo., half morocco. Good. Edwards 1044-
47 1983 £50

BELL, E.   The Rajah and the Principality of Mysore.
London, 1865. Small tear on title, not affecting text. 8vo. Orig.
cloth. Inscribed on the front free endpaper from the author, also with
the Earl of Ellenborough's stamp. Good. Edwards 1044-48 1983 £45

BELL, GERTRUDE   The Letters of Gertrude Bell. London,
1927. 2 vols. Plates, 8vo, orig. cloth. Good. Edwards 1044-49
1983 £25

BELL, HORACE   Reminiscences of a Ranger. Santa Barbara: 1927. First illus. edition. Wood engravings. Pictorial cloth.
Bright and fine in dust jacket. Bradley 66-477 1983 $60

BELL, J. J.   Jack of All Trades. John Lane, 1900.
Sm. 4to. Colour frontis. Colour pictorial title & 30 two-colour
plates. Beige colour pictorial cloth. Greer 40-187 1983 £45

BELL, J. J.   The New Noah's Ark. John Lane, 1899.
Sm. 4to. Colour frontis. Colour pictorial title & 36 colour illus.
Little loose. Beige colour pictorial cloth. Greer 40-186 1983 £45

BELL, JACOB   Historical Sketch of the Progress of
Pharmacy in Great Britain. London, 1880. Small 8vo, cloth. First
edition. Argosy 713-44 1983 $100

BELL, JAMES   The influence of physical research
on mental philosophy. Edinburgh: Black, etc., 1839. First edition.
Small 8vo. Cont. purple calf, gilt, spine gilt, by Orrock and
Romanes, Edinburgh, with their ticket. Inscribed by the author to
John Hope. Rubbed, small paper label on upper cover. Ximenes 63-
297 1983 $100

BELL, JOHN   The Mineral and Thermal Springs of the
United States and Canada. Philadelphia, Parry and McMillan, 1855.
1st ed. 12mo. Binding partly faded, ends of spine worn. Morrill
286-47 1983 $37.50

BELL, JOHN   The Pilgrim and the Pioneer. Lincoln,
Neb., 1907. Illus. 1st ed. Orig. cloth. Scarce. Jenkins 153-741
1983 $75

BELL, MAC KENZIE   Christina Rossetti. Boston: Roberts
Brothers, 1898. Ads. Blue gilt-stamped cloth. Six portraits and six
facs. Karmiole 71-19 1983 $30

BELL, MACKENZIE   Spring's immortality: and other
poems. London: Ward, Lock, and Bowden, 1893. First edition.
Small 8vo. Orig. blue cloth. Presentation copy, inscribed by the
author on the front endpaper to Annie S. Swem. Fine copy.
Ximenes 63-434 1983 $45

BELL, MALCOM   Sir Edward Burne-Jones. London: G. Bell
& Sons, 1910. Later edition. Illus. Orig. decorated cloth. Spine
very slightly darkened and worn. Endpapers somewhat faded. Very good.
MacManus 277-808 1983 $25

BELL, ROBERT   The Ladder of Gold. Richard Bentley,
1850. First edition, 3 vols. Ads. printed on end papers. Orig.
green cloth, sl. rubbed, v.g. Jarndyce 30-298 1983 £54

BELL, SAMUEL   Governor's Message. Concord, June 7,
1819. Tall untrimmed copy. Jenkins 153-384 1983 $100

BELL, THOMAS EVANS   The Bengal Reversion. 1872. First
edition, 8vo, orig. cloth, gilt. Very good copy. Fenning 62-22
1983 £14.50

BELL, THOMAS W.   The Practice of the Chancery Division of
the High Court of Justice in Ireland in Minor Matters. Dublin:
E. Ponsonby, 1886. Second edition. 8vo, orig. cloth, a very good
copy. Fenning 62-23 1983 £18.50

BELLAMY, EDWARD   Equality. NY, 1897. Front hinge starting at introduction, spine darkened and edges slightly worn, else very
good, owner's name. Quill & Brush 54-90 1983 $35

BELLAMY, EDWARD   Equality. New York: Appleton, 1896.
1st ed. Orig. blue-gray cloth, stamped in black and silver. Fine
copy. Jenkins 155-68 1983 $30

BELLAMY, EDWARD   Looking Backward 2000-1887. Bos., 1888.
Cloth covers soiled with edges slightly worn, top edge of spine torn
and frayed, front hinge cracked and minor staining to endpapers, good.
Quill & Brush 54-91 1983 $75

BELLAMY, EDWARD   Looking Backward 2000-1887. Boston &
New York: Houghton, Mifflin, 1889. 8vo, ads. at end. Orig. printed
pictorial wraps. with ads. The present copy of No. 38 Extra of
Ticknor's Paper Series of Choice Reading, dated on the front cover June
16, 1888. Early edition. Fine copy. Rostenberg 88-71 1983 $75

BELLAMY, FRANCIS   Effective Magazine Advertising. New
York, Mitchell Kennerley, (1909). Illus. Tall 8vo. Morrill 287-28
1983 $20

BELLAMY, GEORGE ANNE   An apology for the life of George Anne
Bellamy. London: printed for the author, sold by J. Bell, 1785.
2nd edition, 5 vols., 12mo, cont. half calf (spines rather worn, two
covers loose); in a half morocco slipcase. Half-titles present.
Ximenes 64-38 1983 $125

BELLAMY, GEORGE ANNE   An apology for the life of George Anne
Bellamy. London: printed for the author, and sold by J. Bell, 1786.
5 vols., 12mo, cont. calf, spines gilt, contrasting morocco labels
(spines rubbed, several hinges weak). 4th edition, the first to be
illustrated. There is a frontis. in each volume, and one other portrait. Half-titles present. Ximenes 64-40 1983 $100

BELLAMY, JOSEPH   Works. NY, 1811-12. 3 vols., 8vo.
Later half linen, ex-library. Last vol. dampstained in part. First
edition with errata leaf. Argosy 710-64 1983 $50

BELLAMY, THOMAS   The Beggar Boy: A Novel. Alexandria:
Virginia, 1802. 3 vols. in 1. 8vo. 1st American edition. A fine
copy. In Our Time 156-65 1983 $125

BELLARDI, L.   Saggio di Ditterologia Messicana.
Turin, Mem. R. Accad. Sci., 1859-62. 5 plates, 2 parts and appendix,
4to, wrappers. Wheldon 160-1023 1983 £45

BELLE, FRANCIS P.   Life and Adventures of the Celebrated
Bandit Joaquin Murrieta, His Exploits in the State of California.
Chicago, 1925. Orig. cloth, first edition. ltd. to 975 copies.
Ginsberg 47-609 1983 $40

BELLENDEN, JOHN   The Works. Edinburgh: for W. and C.
Tait, 1822. First collected edition. 3 vols. 4to. Cont. russia,
gilt, neatly rebacked, gilt, edges gilt. Traylen 94-65 1983 £48

BELLINI, LORENZO   Discorsi di Anatomia. Firenze, 1741-44.
First edition. 3 parts in 2 vols. Thick 8vo, cont. vellum & bds.
First edition. Argosy 713-45 1983 $1,250

BELLINI, LORENZO   Opera Omnia. Venetiis: M. Hertz,
1708. First Collected edition. Thick 4to, cont. vellum; spine
defective. Some full-page copperplates. Double-col. Argosy 713-
46 1983 $200

BELLINI, VINCENZO   La Sonnambula. Paris, Launer, c. 1835. Engraved music. With lithograph portrait. Folio, cloth-backed boards. Rubberstamps of Ricordi and Launder on title. Light foxing. Salloch 387-20 1983 $75

BELLOC, HILAIRE   The Bad Child's Book of Beasts. London: Duckworth, (1924). 8vo. Cloth backed pictorial boards. Black & whites by B.T. Blackwood. Very good. Aleph-bet 8-34 1983 $20

BELLOC, HILAIRE   Belinda. N.Y., Harper, 1929. First American edition. Color frontis. and seven tipped-in tinted plates by Joe Pye. Dust jacket (a little fading, a few nicks), but very good. Houle 21-90 1983 $65

BELLOC, HILAIRE   Cautionary Tales for Children. London: Eveleigh Nash, n.d. (1907). First edition. Small sq. 4to, pictorial boards. Pictures by B.T.B. Fine, except for two small stains on front cover. Argosy 714-49 1983 $150

BELLOC, HILAIRE   Cautionary Tales For Children. London: Eveleigh Nash, (1908). Illus. Orig. decorated boards. First edition. Spine and covers slightly faded and worn. Scarce in this condition. A very good copy. MacManus 277-285 1983 $85

BELLOC, HILAIRE   Cautionary Tales for Children. London: Duckworth, n.d. (ca.1910). 8vo. Pictorial boards, spine worn at extremities. Black & whites throughout by B.T. Blackwood. Very good. Aleph-bet 8-33 1983 $22

BELLOC, HILAIRE   Cautionary Tales for Children. Lon., (n.d.). Stiff paper boards, bottom corner of page 39 torn where it was creased, else an attractive copy. Quill & Brush 54-92 1983 $90

BELLOC, HILLAIRE   The Chanty of the Nona. Lon., 1928. Limited to 500 numbered and signed copies, edges very slightly worn, else near fine. Quill & Brush 54-93 1983 $40

BELLOC, HILAIRE   A Conversation with an Angel. London, (1928). First edition. Argosy 714-50 1983 $25

BELLOC, HILAIRE   Economics for Helen. London, Arrowsmith, (1924). First trade edition. Black cloth, a little foxed at edges, else very good. Houle 21-91 1983 $45

BELLOC, HILAIRE   Elizabethan Commentary. London, Cassell (1942). First edition. Red cloth (spine faded), else very good. Houle 21-92 1983 $45

BELLOC, HILAIRE   Emmanuel Burden. N.Y., Scribner, 1904. First American edition (reset and printed in USA). 34 illus. by G.K. Chesterton. Gilt stamped green cloth (spine faded), else v.g. Houle 21-94 1983 $35

BELLOC, HILAIRE   An Essay on the Nature of Contemporary England. London, (1937). First edition. Tan boards, light foxing at edges, else very good. Houle 21-93 1983 $22.50

BELLOC, HILAIRE   Europe and the Faith. N.Y., Paulist, 1920. First American edition. Blue cloth, a few marks on binding, else v.g. Houle 21-95 1983 $32.50

BELLOC, HILAIRE   First and Last. London, 1911. First edition. Spine just a little faded and lower cover marked. Nice. Rota 231-60 1983 £12

BELLOC, HILAIRE   Have You Anything to Declare? N.Y., Knopf, 1937. First American edition (reset and printed in U.S.A.). Dust jacket (small chips) else, very good. Houle 22-95 1983 $30

BELLOC, HILAIRE   An Heroic Poem in Praise of Wine. London: Peter Davies, 1932. Second (First Published) edition. One of 100 copies, this unnumbered. 4to. Boards marked and somewhat worn. From the library of the Curwen Press, with their printer's work note tipped-in. Very good. Rota 230-62 1983 £30

BELLOC, HILAIRE   How the Reformation Happened. London, Cape (1928). First edition. Blue cloth. Dust jacket (a few nicks), else very good. Houle 21-96 1983 $65

BELLOC, HILAIRE   James the Second. London, Faber & Faber, (1928). First edition. Frontis. Dust jacket (a bit faded). Very good. Houle 22-92 1983 $60

BELLOC, HILAIRE   Joan of Arc. London, Cassell, (1929). Red cloth. First edition. Fine. Houle 21-97 1983 $22.50

BELLOC, HILAIRE   Lambkin's Remains. Oxford: Published by The Proprietors of the J.C.B. at J. Vincent's 96, High Street, Oxford, 1900. 12mo. Orig. gilt decorated cloth. First edition. Mint copy. MacManus 277-286 1983 $50

BELLOC, HILAIRE   Lambkin's Remains. London, 1900. First edition. Nice. Rota 230-57 1983 £15

BELLOC, HILLAIRE   The Man Who Made Gold. Lon., (1930). Illus. by G. K. Chesterton, endpapers slightly offset by dustwrapper, else bright, near fine copy in reinforced, slightly worn and foxed still presentable dustwrapper, owner's name. Quill & Brush 54-94 1983 $90

BELLOC, HILAIRE   Many Cities. London, Constable, 1928. First edition. Illus. with 64 b/w drawings by Edmond Warre. Blue cloth, t.e.g., uncut. Very good. Houle 21-98 1983 $22.50

BELLOC, HILAIRE   Mercy of Allah. London, Chatto, 1922. First edition. Grey-blue cloth, stamped in white, spine a bit faded). Very good. Houle 21-99 1983 $35

BELLOC, HILAIRE   The Old Road. London, 1904. First edition. Illus. by W. Hyde. 4to. Spine dull, covers stained and foxing throughout. Good. Rota 230-59 1983 £12

BELLOC, HILAIRE   The Party System. London: Stephen Swift, 1911. Orig. cloth. First edition. In a half-morocco slipcase. Very fine copy. MacManus 277-287 1983 $100

BELLOC, HILARIE   The Path to Rome. London, 1902. First edition. Cahill's 'B' binding, with the coloured picture on the upper cover. Lower corners a little rubbed. Bookplate. Nice. Rota 230-58 1983 £25

BELLOC, HILAIRE   Pongo and the Bull. London: Constable & Company Limited, 1910. Orig. decorated cloth. First edition. Spine faded. A fine copy. MacManus 277-288 1983 $75

BELLOC, HILAIRE   River of London. Boston, LeRoy Phillips, n.d. First American edition. With imprint of Phillips on Title page and spine and with seven pages of ads for other Phillips books. 16 tipped-in color plates by John Muirhead. Dust jacket with large color pictorial label. Very good. Houle 21-100 1983 $95

BELLOC, HILAIRE   Sonnets & Verse. N.Y., Robert McBride, 1924. First American edition. Blue cloth over boards, t.e.g., uncut. One of 250 de-luxe copies of the American issue on handmade paper. Dust jacket (slight sunning on edges). Houle 22-93 1983 $85

BELLOC, HILAIRE   Sonnets and Verse. N.Y., 1924. Ltd. edition. One of 525 numbered copies on handmade paper. Argosy 714-862 1983 $60

BELLOC, HILAIRE   The Stane Street. London, 1913. First edition. Cahill's 'B' binding. Spine a little creased. Illus. Very nice. Rota 230-61 1983 £12.50

BELLOC, HILAIRE   Verses. London, 1911. New edition, reset. Covers a little marked. Note on rear endpaper. Author's signed autograph presentation inscription to his son. Nice. Rota 231-61 1983 £50

BELLOW, SAUL   Dangling Man. N.Y., (1944). First edition, 8vo, cloth, d.w. A very good copy. Dust wrapper only slightly chipped. Argosy 714-52 1983 $300

BELLOW, SAUL   Dangling Man. NY, (1944). Cover lightly soiled, binder's glue staining on hinge, rear endpaper missing, otherwise good or better in slightly chipped and worn good or better dustwrapper. Quill & Brush 54-95 1983 $175

BELLOW, SAUL   Mr. Sammler's Planet. N.Y., Viking (1970). First edition. Dust jacket. Signed by the author. Fine. Houle 22-1208 1983 $75

BELLOW, SAUL   A Silver Dish. New York: Albondocani Press, 1979. Cloth and marbled boards. First edition in book form. One of 326 numbered copies, printed by the Fergusons and signed by the author. Very fine in acetate dust jacket. Reese 20-93 1983 $75

BELLOW, SAUL   The Victim. NY, (1947). Very good in price clipped, slightly soiled, good dustwrapper that is lightly chipped and mended at spine edges. Quill & Brush 54-100 1983 $125

BELLOW, SAUL   The Victim. NY, (1947). Edges slightly pitted and some minor cover spots, paste-downs slightly offset, still good in frayed and chipped dustwrapper, inscription. Quill & Brush 54-99 1983 $75

BELLOW, SAUL   The Victim. N.Y., (1947). 8vo, cloth. First edition. Argosy 714-53 1983 $60

BELLOW, SAUL   The Victim. London, 1948. First edition. Edward Bawden dustwrapper. Fine. Gekoski 2-11 1983 £110

BELLOWS, ALBERT J.   The Philosophy of Eating. 12mo, buckram, ex-lib. First edition. Argosy 713-47 1983 $25

BELLOWS, GEORGE   George Bellows: His Lithographs. New York/London: Alfred A. Knopf, 1928. Revised edition. 197 plates. Large 4to. Cloth. Ars Libri 32-28 1983 $185

BELOE, WILLIAM   The Sexagenarian. London: for F.C. and J. Rivington, 1818. Second edition. 2 vols. 8vo. Cont. half speckled calf, gilt spines with crimson morocco labels, gilt. Pasted to the front fly-leaf of vol. 1 is an A.L.S. from the author. Traylen 94-67 1983 £40

BELSON, MARY   My Brother. (London: William Darton, 1812). 12mo. First edition. Single engraved sheet folded to make six sections. Mounted and folded to match orig. format and tipped into stiff wrappers. Illus. Bromer 25-321 1983 $110

BELSON, MARY   Poetic Gift. New Haven: S. Babcock, (n.d.). Illus. Printed wrappers. Very good. Felcone 20-76 1983 $25

BELTRAMI, EUTENIO   Delle Variabili Complesse... 1868. Orig. offprint, 4to, 1 blank leaf; orig. printed paper wrappers, wrappers a little frayed and detached, inscription on upper wrapper. Pickering & Chatto 22-13 1983 $65

BELTRAMI, LUCA   Il cartone di Raffaello Sanzio per l'affresco della "Scuola d'Atene"... Milano/Roma: Alfieri & Lacroix, 1920. 32 plates. Text illus. Large 4to. Cloth. From the library of Vittorio Emanuele III, King of Italy. Ars Libri 33-296 1983 $100

BELTRAMI, LUCA   Leonardo Da Vinci e la Sala delle "Asse" nel Castello di Milano. Milano: Privately Printed, 1902. Profusely illus. Large 4to. Wrappers. Edition limited to 300 copies. Spine chipped. Ars Libri 33-191 1983 $75

BELVIDERE Illustrated: Historical, Descriptive and Biographical. Belvidere: The Daily Republican, 1896. First edition. Illustrated. Quarto, cloth. Cover edges lightly rubbed, otherwise very good. Bradley 64-79 1983 $25

BELZONI, G.   Narrative of the Operations and Recent Discoveries within the Pyramids... London, 1821. Large folding map. Portrait frontis., slightly spotted. 4to. Modern boards, cloth spine. Uncut. Good. Edwards 1044-51 1983 £80

BEMAN, DAVID   The Mysteries of Trade. Boston, Printed for the Author, 1825. 1st ed. Orig. and compiled. 8vo, contemporary leather, leaf of errata. Slightly rubbed. Morrill 287-547 1983 $65

BEMELMANS, LUDWIG   The Blue Danube. New York, 1945. 8vo. Cloth. A fine copy in lightly rubbed dj. In Our Time 156-66 1983 $20

BEMELMANS, LUDWIG   The Eye of God. N.Y., 1949. First edition, d.w. Argosy 714-54 1983 $20

BEMELMANS, LUDWIG   The Eye of God. New York, 1949. 8vo. Cloth. A fine copy in dj. In Our Time 156-67 1983 $20

BEMELMANS, LUDWIG   Life Class. N.Y., 1938. First edition. Illus. by the author. Argosy 714-56 1983 $25

BEMELMANS, LUDWIG   Noodle. N.Y.: Stokes, 1937. First ed. Oblong 4to. Brown cloth. In frayed dust wrapper. Illus. by Munro Leaf with full-page and in text illus. Very good to fine. Aleph-bet 8-35 1983 $40

BEMIS, GEORGE   Report of the Case of John W. Webster... Boston: Little & Brown, 1850. Frontis., plates. 1st ed. Contemp. binder's cloth, leather label. Illus. Inserted is a fine ALS by Webster. A fine book and rare autograph. Jenkins 153-680 1983 $300

BEMIS, SAMUEL F.   John Quincy Adams, and the Foundations of American Foreign Policy. Maps. Port. Argosy 716-426 1983 $25

BENAVIDES, FRAY ALONZO   The Memorial of... Chicago, 1916. Cloth, very good. Reese 19-46 1983 $300

BENCHLEY, ROBERT   After 1903-What? N.Y., 1938. First edition. Illus. Argosy 714-58 1983 $40

BENCHLEY, ROBERT   Benchley or Else. N.Y., Harper (1947). First edition. With drawings by Gluyas Williams. Dust jacket, a bit faded, else very good. Houle 21-106 1983 $35

BENCHLEY, ROBERT   The Tooth, the Whole Tooth, and Nothing but the Tooth. N.Y., The Home Sector, 1920. 4to, wraps. designed by John Held. Cloth bound together three other issues. Houle 21-107 1983 $65

BENDEL, MAX   Tobias Stimmer. Leben und Werke. Zurich/Berlin: Atlantis-Verlag, 1940. 116 plates. Small 4to. Cloth. Ars Libri 32-647 1983 $75

BENDER, ROBERT J.   Grapes from the Thorn. Warrenville, IL: Pony Barn Press, December, 1937. Printed on handmade paper. Black cloth. Karmiole 73-28 1983 $25

BENDURE, ZELMA   America's Fabrics, Origin and History Manufacture, Characteristics and Uses. New York: The Macmillan Co., 1947. Second printing. Thick 8vo. Cloth. Prof. illus. including a few full color plates. Oak Knoll 49-33 1983 $25

BENEDEK, LADISLAUS   Arbeiten Aus Der Psychiatrisch-Neurologischen Universitaetsklinik Und Deren Hirnhistologischen Abteilung zu Budapest. Budapest: (no publisher), 1940. Library bookplate. Bound vol. of 77 psychiatric, psychopathological, and neurological offprints. Gach 95-39 1983 $35

BENEDEN, E. VAN   Recherches sur la Morphologie des Tuniciers. Ghent, Arch. de Biol., 1886. 10 plates, royal 8vo, half cloth. Wheldon 160-1247 1983 £15

BENESCH, OTTO   Artistic and Intellectual Trends from Rubins to Daumier... Cambridge: Harvard College Library, 1943. First edition. Tall 8vo. Cloth-backed boards. 66 plates. Limited to 300 copies printed at the Anthoensen Press. Minor cover soiling. Oak Knoll 48-19 1983 $35

BENESCH, OTTO   The Drawings of Rembrandt. London: Phaidon, 1973. 6 vols. 1788 illus. Numerous text illus. Large 4to. Cloth. Ars Libri 32-548 1983 $375

BENESCH, OTTO   Rembrandt. Selected drawings. London/
New York: Phaidon/Oxford, 1947. 292 photogravure illus. Large 4to.
Cloth. Dust jacket. Ars Libri 32-549 1983 $75

BENET, LAURA   Is Morning Sure? Poems. New York,
1947. 8vo. Cloth. Review copy with slip laid in. Fine in dj. In
Our Time 156-68 1983 $20

BENET, STEPHEN VINCENT   Ballads and Poems: 1915-1930. N.Y.,
1931. Small 4to, boards; backstrip darkened. Ltd. edition. One of
only 201 signed and numbered copies. Argosy 714-59 1983 $50

BENET, STEPHEN VINCENT   The Devil and Daniel Webster. Weston,
Vermont: Countryman Press, (1937). 1st ed., 1 of 700 numbered
copies, signed by Benet and Harold Denison, the illustrator. Orig.
red cloth, gilt, box. Fine copy in very good box. Jenkins 155-70
1983 $65

BENET, STEPHEN VINCENT   Five Men and Pompey: A Series of
Dramatic Portraits. Boston: Four Seas, 1915. 1st ed., 1st issue.
8vo. Bound in lavender wrappers. Ink notations on front cover.
Enclosed in a rough silk fabric. From the library of the publisher
Edmund Brown. Enclosed in a worn brown envelope. Tiny split at
edge of spine near base, otherwise a fine copy. In Our Time 156-69
1983 $350

BENET, STEPHEN VINCENT   Five Men and Pompey. Bos., 1915. Second
issue in brown wraps over stiff cardboard covers, slight tear with no
loss on front edge, otherwise fine. Quill & Brush 54-101 1983 $50

BENET, STEPHEN VINCENT   John Brown's Body. N.Y., 1928. First
edition. Presentation copy. Argosy 714-61 1983 $50

BENET, STEPHEN VINCENT   The Litter of the Rose Leaves. New
York, 1930. 8vo. Wraps, paper label. 1 of 875 copies. Very good.
In Our Time 156-70 1983 $20

BENET, STEPHEN VINCENT   Nightmare at Noon. New York: Farrar,
(1940). 1st ed. Orig. white boards, the less common binding. Fine
copy, sent out for review with TLS from publisher sending the book.
Jenkins 155-71 1983 $25

BENET, WILLIAM ROSE   The Burglar of the Zodiac and Other
Poems. New Haven, 1918. First edition. 8vo, cloth backed
boards. Presentation copy, with an ink sketch of an old car.
Jarndyce 31-64 1983 $50

BENET, WILLIAM ROSE   Merchants from Cathay. N.Y., 1913.
First edition. 8vo, cloth. With a T.L.S., agreeing to sign some
books. Argosy 714-65 1983 $65

BENET, WILLIAM ROSE   Rip Tide. New York, 1932. 8vo.
Cloth. A fine copy in lightly rubbed but intact dj. In Our Time
156-71 1983 $25

BENEZET, ANTHONY   Some Historical Account of Guinea. Phila:
Printed by Joseph Cruikshank, 1771. First edition. 12mo, rather
heavily browned throughout, some slight age-marking, old style half
calf. Scarce. K Books 307-19 1983 £150

BENEZET, ANTHONY   Some historical account of Guinea...
London: J. Phillips, 1788. 8vo. 1 adv. Orig. calf. Rebacked,
rubbed. Duke of Bedford's bookplate. Adelson Africa-14 1983 $150

BENGAL Troops on the Line of March. Day & Haghe, n.d. (1835). Hand-
coloured lithograph panorama, some 28 ft. long, most unusually with a
presentation inscription from 'The Disigner.' Round hand-coloured
pictorial case. Very good. Greer 39-92 1983 £485

BENGER, ELIZABETH   Memoirs of Mr. John Tobin, author of
The Honeymoon. London: printed for Longman, etc., 1820. 8vo,
cont. half dark blue straight-grained morocco, spine gilt. First
edition. Fine copy. Ximenes 64-42 1983 $125

BENGER, ELIZABETH   Memoirs of the Life of Anne Boleyn,
Queen of Henry VIII. 1821. In two vols. First edition, with engraved
frontis., Two vols. in one. 8vo, cont. half calf, binding worn but
sound. Very good copy. Fenning 61-26 1983 £10.50

BENGER, ELIZABETH   Memoirs of the Life of Mary Queen of
Scots. 1823. 2 vols., 8vo, portrait in vol. 1, cont. half calf,
lacking part of one label. First edition. Bickersteth 77-97 1983
£35

BENHAM, ASAHEL   Federal Harmony. New Haven: Abel Morse,
1794. Third edition. Calf-backed boards. Paper covering boards
lacking, as is the rear endsheet. Signature "Adonijah Bidwell's Book
1795." This copy is paginated. Very good. Felcone 20-115 1983 $225

BENHAM, W. GURNEY   Playing Cards: History of the Pack
and Explanations of its many Secrets. London: 1931. First
edition. 4to, red cloth, d/w. With 242 illustrations (102 in
color). A very nice copy. Perata 27-154 1983 $85

BENHAM'S City Directory and Annual Advertiser: 1849-50. Number Ten.
New Haven, 1849. Map. Calf-backed printed boards. Covers
detached. Felcone 22-37 1983 $50

BENLOWES, EDWARD   Sphinx Theologica, sive Musica Templi,
ubi Discordia Concors: in Tres Decades totidemque Libros divisa.
Liber I. Canabrigiae: Ex Academiae celebrimae Typographeo, (1636).
2nd ed., 8vo, modern half calf gilt, marbled boards. Very rare.
Despite absence of initial and final blank leaves, a fine copy.
Trebizond 18-4 1983 $800

BENNET, BENJAMIN   Discourses on the Credibility of the
Scriptures. New Brunswick: Abraham Blauvelt, 1795. Full calf (hinges
cracking). One front endsheet, "Mrs. Mary S. Smith, / Given by her
Father / Moses Scott Febr. 17th 1796." Very good. Felcone 19-4
1983 $75

BENNET, E.   Shots and Snapshots in British East
Africa. London, 1914. 1st ed. Illus. from photographs & maps.
8vo, ex-library. Morrill 288-581 1983 $25

BENNETT, AGNES MARIA   The Beggar Girl and Her Benefactors.
London: William Lane at the Minerva Press, 1797. First edition.
7 vols. 12mo. Cont. half calf. Half-titles. Slightly worn and
vol. 7 lacks lettering piece. Traylen 94-68 1983 £280

BENNETT, AGNES MARIA   The Beggar Girl and Her Benefactors.
Dublin: Printed by P. Wogan, 1797-98. First Irish edition, 3 vols.,
large 12mo, recent boards, a very good copy. Fenning 62-24 1983
£65

BENNETT, AGNES MARIA   The Beggar Girl and her Benefactors.
Dublin: Printed by P. Wogan, 1797. 3 vols, 12mo, contemporary
calf, spines chipped, one hinge cracking; some leaves waterstained at
foot. Hill 165-7 1983 £30

BENNETT, ALEXANDER HUGHES   Case of Cerebral Tumour. London, 1885.
First edition. Illus. 8vo, cloth. Ex-lib. First edition. Argosy
713-48 1983 $200

BENNETT, ARNOLD   Accident. London: Cassell & Co., (1929).
Orig. cloth. Dust jacket (spine darkened). First edition. Very good.
MacManus 277-289 1983 $20

BENNETT, ARNOLD   The Author's Craft. London: Hodder &
Stoughton, (1914). Orig. cloth. First edition. Fine copy. MacManus
277-291 1983 $50

BENNETT, ARNOLD   The Author's Craft. N.Y.: George H.
Doran Co., (1914). Orig. cloth-backed boards. First American edition.
Very good copy. MacManus 277-290 1983 $20

BENNETT, ARNOLD   The Clayhanger Family. London: Methuen,
1925. Orig. cloth. First collected edition of the Clayhanger Trilogy.
One of 200 copies signed by the author. Dampstaining along the lower
margins throughout the text. In a cloth wrapper. A very nice copy.
MacManus 277-293 1983 $75

BENNETT, ARNOLD   Don Juan de Marana. Lon., 1923. Limited
to 1000 numbered and signed copies, additional spine label tipped-in
at rear, fine in very slightly chipped dustwrapper. Quill & Brush 54-
103 1983 $75

BENNETT, ARNOLD　　　　　Don Juan de Marana. London: T. Werner Laurie, Ltd., 1923. Frontis. port. Orig. parchment-backed boards with paper label. Dust jacket (spine darkened; slightly worn). First edition. Limited to 1,000 copies signed by the author. MacManus 277-294 1983 $50

BENNETT, ARNOLD　　　　　Don Juan de Marana. Lon., 1923. Limited to 1000 numbered and signed copies, spine darkened, cover lightly soiled, corners slightly worn, else very good. Quill & Brush 54-102 1983 $40

BENNETT, ARNOLD　　　　　Elsie and the Child. London: Cassell & Co., (1924). Orig. cloth. Dust jacket (slightly chipped at extremities of spine). First edition. Top of spine a trifle worn. A fine copy. MacManus 277-295 1983 $55

BENNETT, ARNOLD　　　　　Elsie and the Child. London: Cassell & Co., (1924). Orig. cloth. First edition. Very good copy. MacManus 277-296 1983 $35

BENNETT, ARNOLD　　　　　The Feast of St. Friend. N.Y.: George H. Doran Co., (1911). Orig. boards. Dust jacket. In publisher's box. First American edition. In scarce dust jacket and scarcer box. Very fine copy. MacManus 277-297 1983 $35

BENNETT, ARNOLD　　　　　The Ghost. Boston: Herbert B. Turner & Co., 1907. Orig. decorated cloth. Dust jacket (slightly worn & soiled). First American edition. In the rare dust jacket. A very fine copy. MacManus 277-298 1983 $125

BENNETT, ARNOLD　　　　　The Glimpse: An Adventure Of The Soul. London: Chapman & Hall, 1912. Orig. brown cloth. Presentation copy from the author to John Galsworthy inscribed: "To J.G. from A.B." Spine and covers slightly worn. A good copy. MacManus 277-299 1983 $150

BENNETT, ARNOLD　　　　　The Honeymoon. London: Methuen & Co. Ltd., (1911). Orig. cloth. First edition. Former owner's stamp on front endsheet. Covers partially faded. MacManus 277-300 1983 $50

BENNETT, ARNOLD　　　　　How to Live on 24 Hours a Day. New York: George H. Doran Co., (1910). Orig. decorated boards. First American edition. Spine and covers very slightly faded and worn. A very good copy. MacManus 277-301 1983 $20

BENNETT, ARNOLD　　　　　How to Make the Best of Life. New York, 1923. Presentation copy from the author, inscribed. Ownership name stamped on each pastedown. T.e.g. Spin slightly faded and rubbed. Very good. Jolliffe 26-50 1983 £75

BENNETT, ARNOLD　　　　　How to Make the Best of Life. London: Hodder & Stoughton, (1923). Orig. cloth-backed boards. Dust jacket (spine a trifle darkened and rubbed). First edition. Fine copy. MacManus 277-302 1983 $75

BENNETT, ARNOLD　　　　　The Human Machine. N.Y.: George H. Doran Co., n.d. Orig. cloth-backed decorated boards. First American edition, called "Author's Edition." Inscription on flyleaf. A fine copy. MacManus 277-303 1983 $25

BENNETT, ARNOLD　　　　　Imperial Palace. London: Cassell & Co., (1930). Orig. vellum. T.e.g. First edition. Limited to 100 sets printed on handmade paper and signed by the author. 2 vols. Very good set. MacManus 277-304 1983 $165

BENNETT, ARNOLD　　　　　Imperial Palace. Lon., (1930). First trade, bright copy in near fine dustwrapper that is lightly frayed at edges. Quill & Brush 54-104 1983 $50

BENNETT, ARNOLD　　　　　Imperial Palace. London: Cassell & Co., (1930). Orig. cloth. Dust jacket (slightly chipped). First edition. Fine. MacManus 277-305 1983 $20

BENNETT, ARNOLD　　　　　The Journals, 1896-1910. Cassell, 1932. First edition, half title, front. port. Orig. light brown cloth. Jarndyce 30-889 1983 £10.50

BENNETT, ARNOLD　　　　　The Journals, 1896-1928. London, 1932-33. 3 vols. Fine. Rota 231-65 1983 £30

BENNETT, ARNOLD　　　　　Lord Raingo. London: Cassell, (1926). Gilt cloth. First edition. Inscribed by the author: "To Leonora Ervine as usual A.B." The spine is slightly faded, else about fine in slightly used dust jacket, enclosed in a red half morocco case. Reese 20-95 1983 $75

BENNETT, ARNOLD　　　　　The Matador of the Five Towns. London, 1912. First edition. Name on half-title page. Nice. Rota 231-64 1983 £15

BENNETT, ARNOLD　　　　　Milestones. London: Methuen & Co. Ltd., (1912). Orig. cloth. First edition. Very good copy. MacManus 277-306 1983 $35

BENNETT, ARNOLD　　　　　The Night Visitor and Other Stories. London: Cassell & Co., (1931). Orig. cloth. Dust jacket (torn). First edition. MacManus 277-307 1983 $25

BENNETT, ARNOLD　　　　　The Old Wives' Tale. London: Chapman & Hall, 1908. Orig. cloth. First edition. Covers badly stained and worn. MacManus 277-308 1983 $65

BENNETT, ARNOLD　　　　　The Old Wives' Tale. N.Y.: George H. Doran Co., 1927. 2 vols. 4to. Orig. holland-backed boards with paper labels on spines. First edition, American issue. One of 500 copies signed by the author. Spines and labels slightly soiled. A very good copy. MacManus 277-309 1983 $75

BENNETT, ARNOLD　　　　　The Old Wives' Tale. Oxford: Limited Editions Club, 1941. Illus. by John Austin. One of 1500 numbered and signed (by the illus.) copies. Boards and cloth, two vols., each very fine in very good, slightly torn dustwrappers, worn slipcase. Quill & Brush 54-105 1983 $75

BENNETT, ARNOLD　　　　　Our Women. London: Cassell, 1920. Original cloth. Dust jacket (very slightly faded). First edition. Scarce in this condition. Fine copy. MacManus 277-310 1983 $100

BENNETT, ARNOLD　　　　　The Plain Man and His Wife. London: Hodder & Stoughton, n.d. Orig. holland-backed boards. First edition. Front inner hinge partially cracked. A good copy. MacManus 277-311 1983 $45

BENNETT, ARNOLD　　　　　The Price of Love. N.Y.: Harper & Brothers, 1914. Orig. red boards with paper label on upper cover. Advance Copy for Private Distribution, Not for Sale. Text of the magazine issued where the story first appeared, bound up as a book. Inscribed "Compliments of Harper Brothers." Boards a little rubbed. A very good copy. MacManus 277-312 1983 $125

BENNETT, ARNOLD　　　　　Sacred and Profane Love. London: Chatto & Windus, 1919. Orig. cloth with paper label on spine. Dust jacket. First edition, with publisher's slip giving instructions regarding performance of the play laid in. The dust jacket specifies three rather than four acts. Fine copy. MacManus 277-313 1983 $45

BENNETT, ARNOLD　　　　　The Strange Vanguard. London: Cassell & Co., (1928). Orig. cloth. Dust jacket (spine chipped). First edition. Very good copy. MacManus 277-314 1983 $20

BENNETT, ARNOLD　　　　　These Twain. London: Methuen & Co. Ltd., (1916). Orig. cloth. Dust jacket (chipped). First English edition. Very good copy. Scarce in jacket. MacManus 277-316 1983 $40

BENNETT, ARNOLD　　　　　These Twain. London: Methuen & Co., (1916). Orig. cloth. First edition. Bookplate. Very good copy. MacManus 277-315 1983 $20

BENNETT, ARNOLD　　　　　Things That Have Interested Me. N.Y.: George H. Doran Co., (1923). Orig. cloth. Dust jacket (a bit chipped). First American edition. Fine copy. MacManus 277-317 1983 $25

BENNETT, ARNOLD　　　　　The Truth About An Author. Westminster: Archibald Constable & Co., 1903. First edition. 8vo. Two-toned cloth. Spine is age yellowed. Oak Knoll 48-20 1983 $30

BENNETT, ARNOLD　　　　　What the Public Wants. London: Frank Palmer, (1910). Orig. cloth. First edition. Very good copy. MacManus 277-318 1983 $35

BENNETT, E. T.   The Gardens and Menagerie of the
Zoological Society of London delineated. 1835. Numerous engravings,
2 vols., 8vo, cont. half morocco (trifle rubbed), some slight foxing.
Wheldon 160-463 1983 £40

BENNETT, ESTELLINE   Old Deadwood Days. New York, 1928.
Frontis and illustrations. First edition. Good copy. Jenkins
151-15 1983 $45

BENNETT, H. S.   Quia Amore Langueo. (London): Faber &
Faber, 1937. First edition. Illus. with engravings by Eric Gill.
Orig. cloth. One of 400 copies. Spine faded. Covers a bit spotted.
Very good. Bookplates. MacManus 278-2182 1983 $135

BENNETT, JAMES   Overland Journey to California. N.Y.,
1932. Orig. wraps. Ltd. edition of 200 copies from New Harmony
Times of 1906. Ginsberg 47-28 1983 $25

BENNETT, JAMES   Overland Journey to California... New
York, 1932. Stiff printed wrappers. Limited to 200 copies. Jenkins
153-38 1983 $25

BENNETT, JOHN   Letters to a Young Lady. Dublin, by
Pat Wogan, 1796 (or W. Porter, 1793). First Irish edition (?). 8vo,
orig. cloth, a fine copy in the dust wrapper. Fenning 62-35 1983
£12.50

BENNETT, L. G.   History of the Thirty-Sixth Regiment
Illinois Volunteers, During the War of the Rebellion. Aurora, Ill.:
Knickerbocker & Hodder, 1876. 1st ed. Portrait frontispiece and 9
other portraits, each with tissue guard. Three quarters calf and
boards. Covers rubbed, otherwise fine. Scarce. Bradley 64-38 1983
$110

BENNETT, ROLF   Mr. Pyecroft Goes to Heaven. London,
1933. 8vo. Cloth. A fine copy in colorful dj. In Our Time 156-73
1983 $25

BENNETT, VIRGINIA   The Field-Mouse Tale. Nister, n.d. (ca.
1890). Illus. by E. Stuart Hardy. Col'd frontis. & 3 col'd plates
& decor. title, full b&w illus. & 16 text illus. Blue decor. cloth.
Prize label fr. ep. & name, edges of some pp. discol'd & occasional
thumb marks, vg. Hodgkins 27-11 1983 £12.50

BENNETT, WILLIAM   A Practical Guide to American Nineteenth
Century Color Plate Books. New York: Bennett Book Studios, 1949.
1st ed., with errata. Orig. red cloth, gilt. Fine copy. Jenkins
155-237 1983 $50

BENNETT, WILLIAM P.   The First Baby in Camp, a Full Account
of the Scenes & Adventures During the Pioneer Days of '49. Salt Lake,
1893. Very fine. Argosy 716-551 1983 $90

BENNETT, WILLIAM P.   The First Baby in Camp. Salt Lake City,
1893. 12mo, orig. printed wrps. Clark 741-79 1983 $30

BENNETT, WILLIAM P.   The SkySifter. (N.p.), 1892. 12mo,
orig. pr. wraps. Illus. Privately printed. Argosy 716-550 1983
$150

BENNETT, WILLIAM P.   The Sky-Sifter. (Privately pub., 1892).
Wrappers. Little soiling. Dawson 471-19 1983 $30

BENNION, HARDEN   The Bennion Family of Utah. N.p., (1931).
Illus., color plate of arms, d.w., embossed cloth, (Lacks front fly-
leaf). With typed presentation slip to Herbert Auerbach, signed by
Bennion, laid in. Argosy 716-552 1983 $50

BENSON, ARTHUR CHRISTOPHER   The Altar Fire. London, 1907. First
edition. Very nice. Rota 231-67 1983 £15

BENSON, ARTHUR CHRISTOPHER   Lyrics. London: John Lane, 1895.
12mo. Orig. cloth. First edition. One of 550 copies. Very fine.
MacManus 277-320 1983 $20

BENSON, ARTHUR CHRISTOPHER   Ode In Memory Of The Rt. Honble. Eton:
Privately Printed by R. Ingalton Drake, 1898. 4to. Grey printed
wrappers. First edition. Presentation copy from the author inscribed:
"Frederic Chapman with author's compliments, February 15, 1900."
Covers slightly discolored. Unopened copy. Scarce. Nice. MacManus
277-321 1983 $350

BENSON, ARTHUR CHRISTOPHER   The Professor. Eton: George New, 1895.
4to. Orig. wrappers. First edition. One of 100 copies. The author's
own copy, with his corrections in pencil throughout. Laid in are 12
sheets of paper containing more corrections and additions, partially
typed and partially in Benson's hand. Front wrapper detached and
soiled. Spine chipped. A good copy in a rather worn cloth folding
box (with bookplate). MacManus 277-322 1983 $750

BENSON, ARTHUR CHRISTOPHER   Thomas Gray. Eton: R. Ingalton Drake,
1895. 4to. Orig. wrappers. First edition. Wrappers slightly soiled,
first few leaves very slightly soiled at the lower edges. A very good
copy. Rare. MacManus 277-323 1983 $350

BENSON, E. F.   An Act in a Backwater. London: William
Heinemann, 1905. Orig. decorated cloth. First edition. Edges slightly
worn. Spine a bit soiled. A good copy. MacManus 277-325 1983 $25

BENSON, E. F.   The Babe B. A. London and New York:
G.P. Putnam's Sons, 1897. Orig. cloth. First edition. Edges and
corners slightly worn. A very good copy. MacManus 277-326 1983 $45

BENSON, E. F.   The Challoners. London: Heinemann, 1904.
Orig. cloth. First edition. Near-fine copy. MacManus 277-327 1983
$25

BENSON, E. F.   Dodo. A Detail of Today. London:
Methuen, 1893. Orig. cloth. 2 vols. First edition. Former owner's
bookplates partially removed from front pastedowns. A fine copy.
MacManus 277-328 1983 $350

BENSON, E. F.   The Freaks of Mayfair. London: T.N.
Foulis, (1916). Orig. cloth. Dust jacket (soiled and stained;
chipped). First edition. Corners bumped. Head and foot of spine a
bit rubbed. MacManus 277-329 1983 $35

BENSON, E. F.   The House of Defence. London: Heinemann, 1907. Orig. cloth. First English ediiton. Former owner's
signature on flyleaves. Covers a bit dusty. MacManus 277-330 1983
$20

BENSON, E. F.   The Male Impersonator. London, 1929.
First edition, thin sq. 12mo, boards, d.w. One of 530 numbered
copies signed by Benson. Argosy 714-66 1983 $20

BENSON, E. F.   Paul. London: William Heinemann, 1906.
Orig. pictorial cloth. First edition. Covers and spine a bit soiled.
Good copy. MacManus 277-332 1983 $20

BENSON, E. F.   The Princess Sophia. London: William
Heinemann, 1900. Orig. pictorial cloth. First edition. Spine and
covers soiled. Good copy. MacManus 277-333 1983 $20

BENSON, E. F.   The Relentless City. London: William
Heinemann, 1903. Orig. pictorial cloth. First edition. Covers
slightly soiled. A little light foxing. A very good copy. MacManus
277-334 1983 $25

BENSON, E. F.   Scarlet and Hyssop. London: William
Heinemann, 1902. Orig. pictorial cloth. First edition. Spine and
covers soiled. Endpapers a trifle foxed. A good copy. MacManus 277-
335 1983 $20

BENSON, JOHN HOWARD   The Elements of Lettering. Newport:
1940. First edition. Large octavo. Limited to 100 copies printed
at Merrymount Press. Near mint. Bromer 25-176 1983 $85

BENSON, MARY ELEANOR   Streets and Lanes of the City. Privately
printed, (1891). Half titles, orig. maroon cloth. Jarndyce 31-233
1983 £20

BENSON, ROBERT HUGH   By What Authority? London: Sir Isaac
Pitman and Sons, 1908. Orig. pictorial cloth. Edges and corners very
slightly worn. Endpapers lightly browned. A very good, attractive
copy. MacManus 277-336 1983 $20

BENSON, ROBERT HUGH   Come Rack! Come Rope! London: Hutchinson & Co., 1912. Orig. cloth. First edition. Edges and corners
a little worn. Covers and spine a bit soiled. Some foxing. Former
owner's signatures on front free endpaper. MacManus 277-337 1983 $35

BENSON, ROBERT HUGH   Loneliness. London: Hutchinson & Co.,
1915. Orig. cloth. First edition. Covers slightly soiled, a little
foxing. Endpapers browned. Former owner's inscription. A good copy.
MacManus 277-338 1983 $65

BENSON, ROBERT HUGH   Lord of the World. Sir I. Pitman, 1907.
First edition, 8vo, orig. pictorial cloth, the binding just a little
dull but thoroughly sound and otherwise a good copy. Fenning 60-21
1983 £28.50

BENSON, ROBERT HUGH   The Necromancers. London: Hutchinson
& Co., (1910). Orig. cloth. First edition. Binding faded and soiled,
worn at corners. Endpapers slightly browned. Library label removed
from front cover. MacManus 277-339 1983 $35

BENSON, ROBERT HUGH   None Other Gods. London: Hutchinson
& Co., (1910). Orig. cloth. First edition. Binding worn and soiled.
Endpapers browned. A little foxing. MacManus 277-340 1983 $35

BENSON, ROBERT HUGH   Oddsfish! London: Hutchinson & Co.,
(1914). First edition. Spine and covers slightly faded. Orig. cloth.
Edges and corners a little worn. Former owner's signatures. A good
copy. MacManus 277-341 1983 $45

BENSON, STELLA   Kwan-Yin. (San Francisco: Black satin
over boards; spine label. Corners rubbed. Karmiole 72-49 1983
$100

BENSON, STELLA   The Poor Man. London: Hutchinson & Co.,
(1914). Orig. cloth. First edition. Dust jacket. Fine copy.
MacManus 277-342 1983 $20

BENT, A. C.   Life Histories of North American Birds
of Prey. Washington, 1937-38. 194 plates, 2 vols., 8vo, cloth.
Rare original issues. Wheldon 160-649 1983 £40

BENT, ALLEN H.   A Bibliography of the White Mountains.
Boston, 1911. Illus., 8vo, cloth, paper label, light foxing.
Argosy 710-330 1983 $35

BENT, CHARLES   History of Whiteside County, Illinois.
Morrison, Ill., 1877. First edition. Frontispiece map in color. New
red cloth. Very good copy. Bradley 65-101 1983 $100

BENT, JAMES T.   The Ruined Cities of Mashonaland.
London: Longmans, Green and Co., 1892. 1 folding map. Numerous
text illus. Small 4to. Cloth. Slightly worn and shaken. Ars
Libri 34-563 1983 $45

BENT, JAMES T.   The Sacred Cities of the Ethiopians.
Longmans, Green, 1896. New edition, with a folding map, 9 plates, and
65 other illus. 8vo, orig. cloth, gilt. Unchanged reprint of the
first edition with a new preface. Fenning 60-22 1983 £38.50

BENT, THEODOR   The Cyclades. London, 1885. Folding map.
8vo, cloth. Salloch 385-329 1983 $50

BENTHAM, G.   Flora Australiensis. Amsterdam, 1966.
7 vols., 8vo, cloth, (1863-78) reprint. Wheldon 160-1652 1983 £108

BENTHAM, G.   Genera Plantarum. 1862-83. 3 vols. in
7, royal 8vo, cloth (trifle used). Rare original issue. Library
stamp on title-pages. Wheldon 160-1493 1983 £200

BENTHAM, G.   Handbook of the British Flora. 1912-44.
3 vols., 8vo, cloth. Wheldon 160-1586 1983 £15

BENTHAM, JEREMY   The Correspondence of Jeremy Bentham,
Vol. 5... London, 1981. Boswell 7-9 1983 $84

BENTIVOGLIO, GUIDO   The History of the Wars of Flanders.
London: Dorman Newman, 1678. First complete edition in English.
Folio. Cont. unlettered panelled calf, engraved frontis. portrait.
Large folding map; 23 engraved portraits. Small wormhole in margin of
some early leaves, else a very good copy. Trebizond 18-179 1983
$250

BENTLEY, ELIZABETH   Poems, being the genuine compositions
of Elizabeth Bentley... Norwich: sold by the author, etc., 1821.
12mo. First edition. Orig. grey boards, printed paper label. With
a list of subscribers. Spine rubbed. Very scarce. Fine copy.
Ximenes 63-393 1983 $125

BENTLEY, RENSSELAER   The Pictorial Spelling Book. NY, 1843.
Illus. Orig. leather-backed boards. Argosy 716-494 1983 $25

BENTLEY, PHYLLIS   A Modern Tragedy. N.Y., MacMillian,
1934. First edition. Dust jacket, designed by Artzybasheff,
(small chips, slight rubbing), signed by the author, "1934". Houle
22-100 1983 $45

BENTON, FRANK   Cowboy Life on the Sidetrack. Denver,
1903. First edition, pict. cloth. Illus. Slight outer wear. Jenkins
153-39 1983 $75

BENTON, JESSE JAMES   Cow by the Tail. Boston, 1943. 1st
ed. Clark 741-422 1983 $32.50

BENTON, JESSE JAMES   Cow by the Tail. Boston, 1943. Illus.
Orig. cloth, dust jacket. First edition. Ginsberg 46-59 1983
$30

BENTON, JOSEPH A.   Some of the Problems of Empire. San
F., 1868. Orig. printed wraps. First edition. Ginsberg 47-44 1983
$35

BENTON, JOSIAH HENRY   The Story of the Old Boston Town House.
Boston, Privately Printed, 1908. One of 350 copies printed by Updike.
Portraits and illustrations. 8vo, original boards, cloth back.
Morrill 290-282 1983 $25

BENTON, JOSIAH HENRY   Voting in the Field. Boston, Privately
Printed, 1915. 1st ed. Portraits. 8vo, orig. boards, cloth back.
Some rubbing. Morrill 287-30 1983 $25

BENTON, PAUL   Surgery Through The Ages. N.Y., (1943).
Numerous photos. recreating early medical techniques, etc. Cloth.
Blind-stamped names on both endpapers. Tattered dust wrapper. Very
good. King 45-463 1983 $25

BENTON, THOMAS HART   Abridgement of the Debates of Congress,
from 1789-1856. NY, 1857. 16 vols., 1/2 leather, gilt-spine,
marbled boards. Argosy 716-427 1983 $750

BENTON, THOMAS HART   Circular of Instructions to the School
Fund Commissioners of the State of Iowa. Iowa City, 1848. Sewn
as issued. First edition. Ginsberg 47-349 1983 $50

BENTON, THOMAS HART   Mr. Benton's Letter to Maj. Gen. Davis,
of the State of Mississippi. Wash., 1835. Dbd. First edition.
Ginsberg 46-60 1983 $35

BENTON, THOMAS HART   Thirty Years' View; or, a History of the
Workings of the American Government... 1820-50. NY, 1856. 2 frontis.
2 vols, thick 8vo, sheep, leather labels. With Ms. inscription.
Argosy 710-416 1983 $65

BENTON, THOMAS HART   Thirty Years' View. New York, 1854-56.
1st ed. Frontispieces. 2 vols., 8vo, partly faded and slightly
rubbed. Morrill 288-39 1983 $22.50

BENTON, THOMAS HART   To Mrs. Nancy Preston, of Montgomery
County, Virginia, Widow of the Late Governor Preston, and Aunt of
Mrs. Benton. N.p., ca. 1854. Dbd. Ginsberg 46-58 1983 $25

BERDMORE, SAMUEL   Specimens of literary resemblance...
London: G. Wilkie, 1801. First edition. 8vo. Disbound. Very
scarce. Ximenes 63-233 1983 $100

BERDOE, EDWARD   A Catechism of Vivisection. London,
1903. 8vo. Orig. binding. First edition. Fye H-3-34 1983 $45

BERENGER, CHARLES RANDOM DE, BARON DE BEAUFAIN   Helps and Hints How
to Protect Life and Property. London: printed for the proprietor, by
T. Hurst, 1835. First ed., 8vo., later 19th century half morocco,
spine gilt, a.e.g. With two folding lithographed views, eight engraved plates, wood engraved vignettes. Half title present. Bit rubbed.
Ximenes 63-546 1983 $200

BERENSON, BERNARD   Sassetta. Firenze: Electa, 1946
52 plates. Small folio. Boards, 1/4 calf. Edition limited to
1040 copies. Ars Libri 33-326 1983 $75

BERESFORD, GILBERT   Sorrow. London: James Nisbet & Co.,
1862. Orig. cloth. First edition. Presentation copy, inscribed on
the title-page "For dear Mary Anne with GB's best love." Very good
copy. MacManus 277-344 1983 $20

BERESFORD, J. D.   Nineteen Impressions. London: Sidgwick
& Jackson, 1918. First edition, Colonial issue. Orig. blue cloth,
gilt. Very good copy. Jenkins 155-73 1983 $20

BERESFORD, JAMES   The Miseries of Human Life. London:
W. Miller, 1806. Fourth edition. Small 8vo. Orig. grey boards
with printed paper label, uncut edges. Coloured folding frontis.
by Thomas Rowlandson. Traylen 94-69 1983 £25

BERETTA FESTI, CESARE   Francesco Melanzio da Montefalco.
Milano: Privately Printed, 1973. 68 plates (3 tipped-in color).
Large 4to. Cloth. Dust jacket. Edition limited to 460 numbered
copies. Ars Libri 33-232 1983 $100

BERG, ALBAN   Georg Buechner's Wozzeck. Vienna (Uni-
versal-Edition), n.d. With 12 pp. "Glassar I & II" in a back pocket,
4to, flexible cloth. Dedication to "Alma Mahler" on the flyleaf.
Salloch 387-22 1983 $125

BERG, BENGT   To Africa with the Migratory Birds.
New York, 1930. 1st ed. Illus. 8vo. Morrill 287-31 1983 $20

BERGER, KLAUS   Odilon Redon. Fantasy and colour.
New York: McGraw-Hill, (1965). 21 tipped-in color plates, 82
text illus. Large 4to. Cloth. Ars Libri 32-546 1983 $175

BERGER, THOMAS   Reinhart in Love. NY, (1962). Bright
fine copy in slightly rubbed very good, price clipped dustwrapper with
small snag that has been internally mended. Quill & Brush 54-108
1983 $75

BERGH, R.   Die Opisthobranchiata der Siboga-
Expedition. Leiden, 1905. 20 plates (5 coloured), 4to, wrappers,
rebacked). Wheldon 160-1198 1983 £28

BERGIN, THOMAS G.   The New Science of Giambattista Vico.
Cornell Univ. Press, 1948. First edition. Gach 95-475 1983 $25

BERGLING, J. M.   Art Alphabets and Lettering. Chicago:
J.M. Bergling, 1918. 4to. Cloth. Third edition. Some cover
soiling. Name in ink. Oak Knoll 48-77 1983 $25

BERGLUND, ERNEST   History of Marshall. Austin, 1948. 1st
ed. Scarce. Fine copy. Jenkins 153-604 1983 $50

BERGSON, HENRI (1859-1941)   Dreams. London: T. Fisher Unwin,
(1914). First edition in English. Cloth faded. Gach 95-40 1983
$35

BERHAUT, J.   Flore Illustree du Senegal, Vols. 1-6.
Dakar, 1971-69. 6 vols., 4to, wrappers, numerous line-drawings.
Wheldon 160-1953 1983 £125

BERIGARD, CLAUDE GUILLERMET DE   Dubitationes in Dialogorum
Galilaei Galilaei. Florence: Petrus Nestus, 1632. Last leaf blank.
Woodcut diagram. 2 large woodcut historiated initials. Small 4to.
Half-morocco. With the bookplate of Prince Piero Ginori Conti.
First edition. Kraus 164-83 1983 $3,000

BERINGTON, JOSEPH   The History of the Lives of Abeillard
and Heloisa. Birmingham: M. Swinney..., 1787. Full cont. calf
(hinges broken). Half-title wanting. Armorial bookplate of William
Wilkinson. First edition. Felcone 21-8 1983 $125

BERKELEY, GRANTLEY F.   The English Sportsman in the Western
Prairies. London: Hurst Blackett, Publishers, 1861. Illustrations.
Original pictorial cloth. Spine repaired. Presentation copy from
the author. Jenkins 153-40 1983 $150

BERKELEY, GRANTLEY F.   A month in the forests of France.
London: Longman, etc., 1857. First edition. 8vo. Orig. red
cloth. 2 plates by John Leech, one hand-colored. Spine a little
dull, short tears in joints neatly repaired. Ximenes 63-615
1983 $80

BERKELEY, M. J.   Handbook of British Mosses. 1863.
1 plain and 23 hand-coloured plates, 8vo, binder's cloth. First ed.
Some ink annotations, edges of a few leaves frayed and 1 leaf torn
without loss of text, but a good copy. Wheldon 160-1788 1983 £30

BERKELEY, M. J.   Outlines of British Fungology. 1860.
1 plain and 23 hand-coloured plates by W. Fitch, 8vo, original cloth.
Wheldon 160-1787 1983 £40

BERKELEY, R.   The History of the Rifle Brigade.
London, 1927-36. Orig. cloth. Frontis. 26 plates, 14 folding and
38 full page maps. 2 vols. Imp. 8vo. Good. Edwards 1042-548 1983
£60

BERKENHOUT, JOHN   Clavis Anglica Linguae Botanicae.
Printed for T. Cadell, 1789. 8vo, orig. calf, upper joint weak, chip
in top of spine. Bickersteth 75-213 1983 £28

BERLAND, L.   Hymenopteres Vespiformes. Paris,
1925-28. Parts 1 and 2 (of 3), half cloth. Wheldon 160-1026 1983
£15

BERLIOZ, HECKTOR   Traite d'Instrumentation et d'Orchestra-
tion. Paris, Henri Lemoine & Co., n.d. Folio, cloth, orig. wrs.
bound in. Salloch 387-24 1983 $75

BERLYN, MRS. ALFRED   Sunrise-Land. London: Jarrold & Sons,
1894. First edition. Illus. by A. Rackham. Orig. decorated cloth.
Spine ends a trifle rubbed. Near-fine. MacManus 280-4289 1983 $225

BERMAN, EUGENE   Imaginary Promenades in Italy. New
York: Pantheon Books (1956). 8vo, pictorial boards and cloth,
full page drawings in black and white, some on colored paper. One
of 850 copies signed by the artist. Duschnes 240-11 1983 $85

BERNANOS, GEORGES   The Diary of a Country Priest. London:
Boriswood, 1937. Cloth, first edition in English. Ink name, else a
very fine copy in lightly used dust jacket. Reese 20-97 1983 $35

BERNARD, CLAUDE   Introduction a l'Etude de la Medecine
Experimentale. Paris, 1865. 8vo, uncut in half morocco, t.e.g.,
orig. wraps. bound in. First edition, the issue with London and
Madrid imprint. Quaritch NS 5-9 1983 $1,300

BERNARD, CLAUDE   An Introduction to the Study of
Experimental Medicine. New York, 1927. 8vo. Orig. binding. First
English translation. Fye H-3-35 1983 $50

BERNARD, CLAUDE   L'oeurvre de. Paris, 1881. First
edition. 8vo, cloth-backed bds, ex-lib; waterstained. Argosy 713-
51 1983 $175

BERNARD, FRANCIS   Letters to the Right Honorable the Earl
of Hillsborough, from Governor Bernard, General Gage, the the
Honorable His Majesty's Council. London, 1769. English pub.'s ads.
Modern buckram. Very good. Reese 18-87 1983 $150

BERNARD, JOHN   Retrospections of the Stage. London:
Henry Colburn and Richard Bentley, 1830. 2 vols., 12mo, cont. half
rose calf, spines gilt. 1st ed. With a portrait. A very good copy.
Ximenes 64-43 1983 $125

BERNARD, L. L.   Instinct. A Study in Social Psychology.
NY: Holt, (1924). First edition. Gach 94-521 1983 $25

BERNARD, W. D.   Narrative of the Voyages and Services of
the "Nemesis." London, 1844. 6 plates, 3 maps, woodcuts in text.
2 vols. Roy.8vo, rebacked, part of the orig. spine of vol. I and all
of the spine of vol. 2 laid down. Good. Edwards 1044-53 1983 £265

BERNARDI, MARZIANO   Antonio Fontanesi 1818-1882. Torino:
Municipi di Torino & Reggio Emilia, 1932. 113 plates. Small folio.
New cloth. Orig. wrappers bound in. Edition limited to 1500
numbered copies. Ars Libri 33-469 1983 $125

BERNARDI, MARZIANO   Antonio Fontanesi. Milano: A.
Mondadori, 1933. 4 color plates. Frontis. 60 plates. 20
text illus. Large 8vo. Cloth. Ars Libri 33-467 1983 $40

BERNARDINI, GIORGIO   Sebastiano del Piombo. Bergamo:
Istituto Italiano d'Arti Grafiche, 1908. Prof. illus. 4to.
Marbled boards, 1/2 cloth. Ars Libri 33-329 1983 $40

BERNETZKE, CHARLES R.   The Good Old Pioneers. Los Angeles:
Sturdevant, 1920. Boards. Colored frontispiece. Fine copy. Jenkins
153-87 1983 $45

BERNHEIM, BERTRAM   The Story of the Johns Hopkins. Kingswood, Surrey, 1949. 8vo. Orig. binding. First British edition.
Fye H-3-36 1983 $35

BERNHEIM, H.   Die Suggestion Und Ihre Heilwirkung.
Leipzig: Franz Deuticke, 1888. Modern blue cloth, mild staining to
the first several leaves of the zweiter teil, some staining to title-
page, 2" vertical tear to top of titlepage repaired. 10 page postscript and breif postscript added by Sigmund Freud. Gach 95-150 1983
$850

BERRETT, HOWARD D.   Who's Who in Topeka. Topeka: Adams,
Publishers, 1905. Orig. cloth with minor wear. Jenkins 152-180
1983 $30

BERRI, D. G.   Monograms, Historical and Practical.
London: Privately printed, 1869. 8vo. Orig. red cloth, a.e.g.
20 full page plates each showing multiple examples of monograms.
Frontis. Covers worn. Frontis. and title page have water spot.
Oak Knoll 48-21 1983 $35

BERRY, C. W.   A Miscellany of Wine. London: Constable
& Co., 1932. First edition. Foreword by Andre Simon. Orig. red cloth.
Presentation copy to John Galsworthy inscribed on the title-page,
and dated 12 December 1932. Spine and covers slightly faded and worn.
Good. MacManus 278-2138 1983 $45

BERRY, ERICK   Sojo. Cleveland: Harter, (1934). 8vo.
Pictorial boards. Light soil. Paper browning. Color covers, each
page illus. in black & white. Very good. Aleph-bet 8-180 1983 $20

BERRY, JOHN J.   Life of David Belden. N.Y. & Toronto:
Belden Brothers, 1891. Several loose pages. Cloth. Dawson 471-20
1983 $60

BERRY, ROBERT POTTER   A History of the Formation and Development of the Volunteer Infantry. London, 1903. First edition. Thick
roy. 8vo. Orig. blue cloth gilt. Coloured portrait frontis. 7
coloured and 4 other plates, extra coloured illus. pasted onto last
blank. Very slightly worn. Edges and preliminaries slightly foxed.
Ink signature in upper margin of title. Good. Edwards 1042-281 1983
£100

BERRY, S. S.   Review of Cephalopods of Western
N. America. Washington, Bull. Bur. Fisheries, 1912. 25 plates,
royal 8vo, wrappers. Wheldon 160-1199 1983 £15

BERRY, WENDELL   November Twenty Six Nineteen Hundred Sixty
Three, Poem. NY: (1963). Oblong octavo. First edition, Limited
edition signed by both poet and illustrator, Ben Shahn. Spine
darkened, else very fine in slightly rubbed slip-case. Bromer 25-
300 1983 $85

BERRY, WENDELL   November Twenty-Six Nineteen
Hundred Sixty Three. New York, (1964). Oblong 8vo, cloth. One of
the ltd. edition signed by the author and artist. Slipcase. Duschnes
240-200 1983 $95

BERRY, WILLIAM   The History of the Island of Guernsey.
1815. Folding map, one folding and 28 full page aquantint pages,
4to, some staining of page margins, full calf. K Books 307-20 1983
£150

BERRYMAN, JOHN   The Dispossessed. New York: William
Sloan, (1948). Cloth. First edition. Except for the slightest
traces of shelf-rubbing at the extremities of the dust jacket, a very
fine copy. Reese 20-98 1983 $325

BERRYMAN, JOHN   Love & Fame. NY, 1970. First edition.
Very fine in dust wrapper. Bromer 25-7 1983 $50

BERRYMAN, JOHN   Poems. Norfold, (1942). Paperwraps edition with dustwrapper a little faded, otherwise very good. Quill &
Brush 54-110 1983 $100

BERRYMAN, JOHN   Poems. Norfolk: New Directions (1942).
First edition. Fine in lightly stained wrappers. Bromer 25-8 1983
$65

BERRYMAN, JOHN   Stephen Crane. NY, (1950). Front fly
slightly offset from dustwrapper, cover lightly soiled, else very good
in lightly soiled very good dustwrapper. Quill & Brush 54-111 1983
$150

BERTALOTTI, ANGELO MICHELE   Regole per il Canto Fermo. N.p.,
(Bologna), Gamberini e Parmeggiani, 1820. 4to, orig. boards, spine
repaired. A few pages foxed. Salloch 387-25 1983 $125

BERTHELOT, MARCELLIN   Introduction a l'Etude de la Chimie...
Paris: Steinheil, 1889. 8vo. Numerous text illus. Zeitlin
264-34 1983 $125

BERTHELOT, MARCELLIN   Introduction a l'Etude de la Chimie...
Paris: Librairie des Sciences et des Arts, 1938. 8vo. Orig.
wrappers. Frontis. portrait. Internally very good. Zeitlin 264-
35 1983 $70

BERTHELOT, MARCELLIN   Lecons sur les Methodes Generales
de Synthese en Chimie Organique. Paris: Gauthiers-Villars, 1864.
First edition. 8vo. Orig. gray printed wrappers (covers detached
and torn). Internally good. Zeitlin 264-36 1983 $160

BERTHELOT, MARCELLIN   Les Origines de l'Alchemie. Paris:
Georges Steinheil, 1885. 8vo. Modern buckram. Frontis. portrait,
2 plates. Ex-libris E.N. da C. Andrade. Binding slightly rubbed.
Very good copy. Zeitlin 264-37 1983 $100

BERTHELOT, MARCELLIN   La Revolution Chimique Lavoisier...
Paris: Felix Alcan, 1890. 8vo. First edition. Ads. Frontis.
Orig. pebbled cloth, rebacked. Very good copy. Zeitlin 264-38
1983 $80

BERTHELOT, MARCELLIN   Sur la Force de la Poudre et des
Matieres Explosives. Paris: Gauthier-Villars, 1872. 12mo in
4s. Orig. printed paper wrappers, rebacked, edges frayed. Ads.
Zeitlin 264-39 1983 $40

BERTHELOT, MARCELLIN   Sur la Force de la Poudre et des
Matieres Explosives. Paris, 1872. Second edition. 12mo. Orig.
printed wrappers, rebacked, frayed. Zeitlin 264-40 1983 $40

BERTHELOT, MARCELLIN   La Synthese Chimique. Paris: Germer
Bailliere, 1876. 8vo. Orig. maroon pebbled cloth. Spine faded
and chipped. Zeitlin 264-41 1983 $80

BERTHELOT, MARCELLIN   Traite Elementaire de Chimie Organique.
Paris: Dunot, 1872. First edition. Half green morocco. Inside
front hinge detached. Some minor staining, but a very good copy.
Zeitlin 264-42 1983 $80

BERTHIER, J.-J.   Le tombeau de Saint Dominique.
Paris, n.d. ix, (1), 174, (4)pp., 37 heliogravure plates. Text
illus. Folio. Full morocco. A.E.G. No. 15 of a limited edition
of 80 copies on velin a la forme. Magnificent copy, armorially
bound for the Duke of Parma. Ars Libri SB 26-20 1983 $850

BERTHOLD, VICTOR M.   The Pioneer Steamer California 1848-
1849. Boston and New York: Houghton Mifflin Company, 1932. Plates.
Maps. Original cloth in slipcase. Limited to 550 copies. Fine copy.
Jenkins 153-41 1983 $65

BERTHOLD, VICTOR M.   The Pioneer Steamer California, 1848-1849.
Boston, 1932. Illus. Orig. cloth. First edition. Ltd. to 550
copies. Ginsberg 47-45 1983 $65

BERTHOLLET, CLAUDE LOUIS   Elements of the Art of Dyeing and
Bleaching... London: T. Tegg, 1841. 8vo. Orig. cloth. Ads.
Cloth chipped, edges worn. Zeitlin 264-43 1983 $80

BERTHOLLET, CLAUDE LOUIS   Suite des recherches sur les lois de
l'affinite de l'influence dans les affinites complexes. (Paris,
ca. 1801). 4to. Cont. boards, worn, chipped, hinges split. Internally a good copy. Zeitlin 264-44 1983 $110

BERTHOUD, FERDINAND   Essai sur l'horlogerie. Paris, 1763.
First edition. 2 vols., 4to, with 38 folding engraved plates; cont.
French mottled calf, the Leroy copy with his bookplate. Quaritch NS
5-10 1983 $1,750

BERTHOUD, FERDINAND   Traite des Horloges Marines, Contenant
la Theorie, la Construction, la Main-d'Oeuvre de ces Machines...
Paris, 1773. 4to, with engraved vignette on title, engraved head-
piece, and 27 folding engraved plates; cont. French mottled calf,
presentation copy inscribed by Berthoud to M. Le Moyne, and with
another owner's inscription, M. Grandhomme. Quaritch NS 5-11 1983
$2,250

BERTIE, WILLOUGHBY, EARL   Thoughts On The Letter Of Edmund Burke,
Esq. Oxford, Printed for W. Jackson; Sold by J. Almon, n.d. 1777.
1st ed., 8vo, reddish cloth, morocco label. Pickering & Chatto 21-17
1983 $150

BERTIN, RENE-JOSEPH-H.   Traite des Maladies du Coeur et des
gros Vaisseaux. Paris: J.B. Bailliere, 1824. First edition. 8vo,
orig. pr. wrs.' uncut. Argosy 713-53 1983 $250

BERTINI, ALDO   Michelangelo fino alla Sistina.
Torino: Giulio Einaudi, 1942. 150 plates. Large 4to. Cloth.
Dust jacket. Edition limited to 1400 numbered copies. Ars Libri
33-236 1983 $125

BERTRAM, WILLIAM   Travels through North and South Carolina,
Georgia, East and west Florida, the Cherokee Country... London: J.
Johnson, 1794. 8 engraved plates, map, 3/4 morocco. Tiny early
library stamp on title, else a fine wide-margined and uncut copy.
Felcone 21-6 1983 $750

BERUETE, A. DE   Velazquez. Paris: Librairie Renouard,
1898. Prof. illus. Small folio. Marbled boards, 3/4 leather.
Edition limited to 800 numbered copies. Ars Libri 32-683 1983 $150

BERZE, JOSEF   Die Hereditaeren Beziehungen Der
Dementia Praecos. Leipzig/Wien: Franz Deuticke, 1910. First
edition. Gach 95-41 1983 $25

BERZELIUS, JONS JACOB   Essai sur la Theorie des Proportions
Chimiques et sur l'Influence Chimique de l'Electricite... Mequignon-
Marvais, Paris, 1819. First separate edition and first edition in
French. 8vo, leaves B1 and 4 of the table are cancels; old stamps
on title, dedication and last leaf, title and prelims foxed; cont.
roan backed boards. Quaritch NS 5-12 1983 $1,100

BERZELIUS, JONS JAKOB   The Use of the Blowpipe in Chemical
Analysis... London, 1822. 8vo. Modern half calf. 3 plates (lacks
folding table). Zeitlin 264-47 1983 $70

BESANT, ANNIE   An Autobiography. T. Fisher Unwin,
1893. First edition, 3 photogravure illus. & 10 plates, half title,
12 + 16 pp ads. Orig. olive cloth. Jarndyce 30-893 1983 £25

BESANT, WALTER   All in a Garden Fair. London: Chatto &
Windus, 1883. Orig. pictorial cloth with floral endpapers. 3 vols.
First edition. All edges a bit worn, covers slightly soiled. Corners
bumped, former owner's signature on one endpaper. Small tear in the
middle of one spine. A good set. MacManus 277-345 1983 $150

BESANT, WALTER   All in a Garden Fair. The simple Story
of Three Boys and a Girl. London: Chatto & Windus, 1883. First edition. 8vo, 3 vols. Orig. pictorial cloth, spine gilt. Half-title in
vol. I. A fine copy. Trebizond 18-5 1983 $275

BESANT, WALTER   Beyond the Dreams of Avarice. London:
Chatto & Windus, 1895. Orig. decorated cloth with floral endpapers.
First edition. Endpapers soiled, one almost detached. All edges a
bit worn. Covers slightly soiled. Former owner's signature on one
blank leaf. Hinges cracking. MacManus 277-346 1983 $35

BESANT, WALTER   Constantinople, A Sketch Of Its History
From Its Foundations To Its Conquest By The Turks In 1453. London:
Seeley, Jackson & Halliday, 1879. Frontispiece map. Original decorated cloth. First edition. Spine and covers slightly worn. Some
foxing to the preliminary pages. A very good copy. MacManus 277-359
1983 $60

BESANT, WALTER   Dorothy Forster. London: Chatto &
Windus, 1884. 3 vols. Orig. decorated cloth. First edition. Slightly soiled. Signature of former owner on front flyleaf. A very good
set. MacManus 277-348 1983 $350

BESANT, WALTER   The Eulogy of Richard Jefferies. Chatto
& Windus, 1888. First edition, front. 32 pp ads. (Oct. 1888). Orig.
blue cloth. Jarndyce 30-1031 1983 £14.50

BESANT, WALTER   The Eulogy of Richard Jefferies. London:
Chatto & Windus, 1889. Second edition, with a portrait. Frontis.
Orig. cloth. Spine and extremities a bit rubbed. MacManus 279-2970
1983 $35

BESANT, WALTER   Fifty Years Ago. London: Chatto &
Windus, 1892. With 144 plates and woodcuts. Orig. cloth. Tipped in
is a TLS, 1 page, 8vo. Spine faded. MacManus 277-349 1983 $35

BESANT, WALTER   For Faith and Freedom. London: Chatto
& Windus, 1889. Illus. by A. Forestier & F. Waddy. 3 vols. First
edition. Library labels removed from upper covers. One illus. replaced with tape in Vol. II. A nice copy. MacManus 277-350 1983
$250

BESANT, WALTER   The Fourth Generation. London: Chatto
& Windus, 1900. Orig. decorated cloth. First edition. Edges slightly
worn. Covers a little soiled. Endpapers a bit browned. A good copy.
MacManus 277-347 1983 $40

BESANT, WALTER   Herr Paulus. His Rise, His Greatness,
and His Fall. London: Chatto & Windus, 1888. 3 vols. Orig. decorated cloth. First edition. A very fine, tight set. MacManus 277-351
1983 $350

BESANT, WALTER   Herr Paulus, His Rise, His Greatness,
and His Fall. Chatto & Windus, 1888. First edition, 3 vols., 32 pp
ads. vol. II. Orig. brown cloth, blocked in blue, gilt lettered,
very good. Jarndyce 30-299 1983 £60

BESANT, WALTER   In Deacon's Orders. London: Chatto &
Windus, 1895. With a frontis. by A. Forestier. Orig. decorated cloth.
First edition. Spine faded, a bit rubbed. Endpapers foxed. A good
copy. MacManus 277-352 1983 $45

BESANT, WALTER   The Master Craftsman. London: Chatto
& Windus, 1896. 2 vols. Orig. cloth. First edition. Library labels
removed from front covers. Covers worn, contents shaken. MacManus
277-353 1983 $85

BESANT, WALTER   No Other Way. London: Chatto & Windus,
1902. 12 illus. by Charles D. Ward. Orig. decorated red cloth. First
edition. Covers dull, foxing. Scarce. A very good copy. MacManus
277-355 1983 $65

BESANT, WALTER   Over the Sea With the Sailor. London,
Christmas, 1880. Orig. cloth. First edition. One of a few copies
of the Christmas number of "All the Year Round" for 1880 bound in a
special presentation binding. Covers a bit foxed. Rare. MacManus
277-356 1983 $50

BESANT, WALTER   The Revolt of Man. Wm. Blackwood,
1882. First edition, half title, 4 pp ads. Orig. orange cloth,
blocked on front cover in black, spine gilt. Sl. rubbing, otherwise
v.g. Jarndyce 31-426 1983 £62

BESANT, WALTER   St. Katherine's By the Tower. London:
Chatto & Windus, 1891. Illus. by Charles Green. 3 vols. Orig. cloth.
First edition. Covers a bit rubbed. A very good copy. MacManus
277-357 1983 $250

BESANT, WALTER   Verbena Camellia Stephanotis. London:
Chatto & Windus, 1892. Frontispiece. Orig. decorated cloth. First
edition. Spine and covers slightly faded and worn. Inner hinges
weak. Free endpapers faded, with some foxing to the edges and
preliminary pages. A good copy. MacManus 277-358 1983 $150

BESANT, WALTER   With Harp And Crown. London: Tinsley
Brothers, 1875. 3 vols. Orig. green decorated cloth. First edition.
Presentation copy from the authors inscribed on the title-page: "The
Hon. George Brown Toronto, with the authors' compliments and regards,
October 1875." Spine ends and edges worn. A very good set. MacManus
277-360 1983 $400

BESKOW, ELSA   Aunt Green, Aunt Brown & Aunt Lavender.
N.Y.: Harp., 1932. Oblong folio. Cloth backed pictorial boards,
light wear. Each page of text faces large full color illus. Very good.
Aleph-bet 8-36 1983 $40

THE BEST Poems of 1925. B, (1925). Near fine, bright copy in faded,
frayed dustwrapper. Quill & Brush 54-1146 1983 $35

BESTE, RICHARD   Alcazar; Or, The Dark Ages. London:
Hurst & Blackett, 1857. 3 vols. Orig. dark-green cloth. First
edition. Spines and covers spotted and slightly worn. A good set.
Contemporary owner's signature. MacManus 277-361 1983 $225

BESTERMAN, THEODORE   A World Bibliography of Bibliographies...
New York: Scarecrow Press, (1955). Four vols. in two. Thick 8vo.
Cloth. Oak Knoll 48-400 1983 $150

BETHAM, MARY M.   The Lay of Marie: a Poem. Printed for
Rowland Hunter, 1816. First edition, errata leaf, 8vo, cont. half
calf, a very good copy. Fenning 61-31 1983 £48.50

BETHUNE-BAKER, G. T.   Revision of the Amblypodia group of
butterflies of the family Lycaenidae. Trans. Zoo. Soc., 1903.
5 plates (3 coloured), 4to, wrappers. Wheldon 160-1027 1983 £20

BETJEMAN, JOHN   Antiquarian Prejudice. London:
Hogarth, 1939. Orig. wraps., sewn. First edition. Front wrap
slightly soiled, else a fine copy. Reese 20-100 1983 $65

BETJEMAN, JOHN   Antiquarian Prejudice. Hogarth Press,
1939. First edition. Wrappers. Fine. Rota 231-70 1983 £12

BETJEMAN, JOHN   Church Poems. London, 1981. First
edition. Illus. by J. Piper. One of 100 numbered copies, signed by
author and artist. Fine. Rota 231-78 1983 £60

BETJEMAN, JOHN   Collected Poems. London, 1958. First
edition. One of 100 numbered copies on Oxford India paper, signed
by author. Full red calf. Slipcase. Fine. Rota 231-76 1983 £90

BETJEMAN, JOHN   Collected Poems. London: John Murray,
1958. Orig. printed wrappers. Proof copy of the first edition. Two
dates stamped on fly-title. Slightly dust-soiled. A very good copy.
MacManus 277-362 1983 $100

BETJEMAN, JOHN   Continual Dew. London, 1937. First
edition. Illus. by Osbert Lancaster and two others. A.e.g. Front
free endpaper very slightly spotted. In price-clipped dustwrapper
by E. McKnight Kauffer. Fine. Jolliffe 26-53 1983 £45

BETJEMAN, JOHN   Continual Dew. London, 1937. First
edition. Tipped onto the rear endpaper is a portion of the dust
wrapper designed by E.M. Kauffer. Nice. Rota 231-69 1983 £35

BETJEMAN, JOHN   English Cities & Small Towns. London,
1943. First edition. Illus. in colour and black and white. Dust
wrapper. Fine. Rota 231-72 1983 £12

BETJEMAN, JOHN   A Few Late Chrysanthemums. London: John
Murray, 1954. Orig. white buckram with tissue dust jacket. First
edition. One of only 50 copies signed by the author. Very fine.
MacManus 277-366 1983 $100

BETJEMAN, JOHN   Ghastly Good Taste or, A Depressing Story
of the Rise and Fall of English Architecture. London: Chapman & Hall
Ltd., (1933). Illus. with folding plate. 2 vols. Orig. cloth-backed
printed boards with paper label on spines. First editions, first and
second issues, with pp. 119-120 in uncancelled and cancelled states.
Very good set. MacManus 277-367 1983 $125

BETJEMAN, JOHN   Ghastly Good Taste. (Lon., 1970).
Limited to 200 signed and numbered copies in olive cloth and leather
spine. Cloth very slightly frayed where it meets spine, still fine in
matching slipcase. Quill & Brush 54-112 1983 $125

BETJEMAN, JOHN   High and Low. London: John Murray,
(1966). Orig. white backram with acetate dust jacket. First edition.
One of 100 copies signed by the author. Mint. MacManus 277-368 1983
$100

BETJEMAN, JOHN   High and Low. London, 1966. First
edition. One of 100 numbered copies on handmade paper, signed by
author. Orig. glassene wrapper. Fine. Rota 231-77 1983 £65

BETJEMAN, JOHN   John Piper. Harmondsworth: Penguin
Books, (1944). Orig. wrappers. First edition. A little dusty. A
very good copy. MacManus 277-369 1983 $20

BETJEMAN, JOHN   Mount Zion or In Touch With The
Infinite. London: James Press, 1931. Signed by the author on the
title page. First state of binding (blue and gold patterned paper).
Corners bumped, spine slightly damaged, but a very good copy. Scarce
as such. Gekoski 2-13 1983 £275

BETJEMAN, JOHN   Murray's Buckinghamshire Architectural
Guide. London, 1948. First edition. Illus. Sm. 4to. Torn dust
wrapper. With Betjeman's signed autograph presentation inscription.
Very nice. Rota 230-68 1983 £20

BETJEMAN, JOHN   New Bats in Old Belfries. London, 1945.
First edition. Slightly frayed dust wrapper. One of "a few autographed
copies...printed on special paper and with a coloured Title Page."
Fine. Rota 231-73 1983 £100

BETJEMAN, JOHN   Old Lights for New Chancels. London,
1940. First edition. Dust wrapper. Inscribed by author to S. O'Sullivan, dated May 1941. With a Christmas card from author bearing his
signed autograph inscription. Rota 231-71 1983 £75

BETJEMAN, JOHN   Selected Poems. London: John Murray,
1948. Cloth. First edition. Neat ink inscription, else a fine
copy in dust jacket, which is slightly chipped at the top edge.
Reese 20-101 1983 $75

BETJEMAN, JOHN   Selected poems. London, 1948. First
edition. Preface by J. Sparrow. Torn dust wrapper. Nice. Rota 230-
64 1983 £12

BETJEMAN, JOHN   Summoned by Bells. London: John Murray,
1960. Frontis. port. by Michael Tree. Illus. Orig. green calf, gilt,
acetate dust jacket. First edition. One of 125 copies signed by the
author. Mint. MacManus 277-370 1983 $100

BETJEMAN, JOHN   Summoned by Bells. London, Murray, 1960.
First edition. Illus. with drawings and an etching by Michael Tree.
Full green morocco, richly stamped in gilt with bell motif (small
chip at head of spine, rubbed at spine tips). One of 125 numbered
copies signed by the author. Very good. Houle 22-104 1983 $95

BETT, W. R.   A Short History of some common Diseases.
London, 1934. 8vo. Orig. binding. First edition. Fye H-3-38
1983 $50

BETT, W. R.   A Short History of some common Diseases. London, 1934. 8vo. Orig. binding. Ex-library. Fye H-3-39 1983 $40

BETTANY, G. T.   Eminent Doctors their Lives and their Work. London, n.d. (ca. 1890). Second edition. 8vo. 2 vols. Orig. cloth. Gurney JJ-31 1983 £15

BETTEN, H. L.   Upland Game Shooting. Phila. (1940). First ed. Color illus., cloth, covers worn, title and frontis foxed. King 46-542 1983 $25

BETTER Living for the Indian: An Exchange of Letters. Ethete, Wy., St. Michael's Mission, (1924). Illus. Stapled as issued. First edition. Ginsberg 47-981 1983 $25

BETTERTON, THOMAS   The History of the English Stage, from the Restauration to the present time. London: printed for E. Curll, 1741. First edition. 8vo, cont. calf (trifle rubbed). Frontis. portrait and 5 medallion portraits. Some faint marginal dampstains, but a fine copy. Ximenes 64-44 1983 $400

BETZENDAHL, WALTER   Die Ausdrucksformen Des Wahnsinns. Berlin: S. Karger, 1935. First edition. Library buckram, preserving orig. printed wrappers. Gach 94-298 1983 $25

BEUDANT, F. S.   Traite Elementaire de Physique. Paris, 1833. 8vo. Old cloth. Back gilt. With 14 plates. Slightly foxed. Gurney Jj-32 1983 £20

BEUTENMULLER, W.   Monograph of the Sesiidae of America north of Mexico. New York, Mem. Am. Mus. Nat. Hist., 1901. Text-figures and 8 coloured plates, royal 4to, wrappers, margins of 3 plates waterstained. Wheldon 160-1028 1983 £20

BEVAN, EDWARD   The honey bee. Its natural history, physiology and management. London: Van Voorst, 1838. Second edition, revised and enlarged. 8vo. Orig. purple-brown cloth. Engraved title and wood-engraved frontis. Lacks front endpaper, otherwise a good copy. Ximenes 63-25 1983 $90

BEVAN, EDWYN   Sybils and Seers. London, 1928. 8vo, cloth. Salloch 385-65 1983 $20

BEVAN, H.   Thirty Years in India. London, 1839. Folding map, coloured frontis. and 2 other costume plates. 2 vols. Modern half red morocco. 8vo. Good. Edwards 1044-56 1983 £95

BEVERIDGE, ALBERT J.   Abraham Lincoln, 1809-1858. Boston, 1928. Illus. 4 vols. Standard Library Ed. Morrill 289-271 1983 $30

BEVERIDGE, H.   A Comprehensive History of India. London, 1871. 17 maps, 4 folding, 2 plans, 3 frontis., engraved half-titles. Numerous engravings in text, including maps and plans. 3 vols. Half crimson morocco, raised bands. 8vo. Good. Edwards 1044-57 1983 £75

BEVERLAND, HADRIAN   De Stolatae Virginitatis. Lugd. Bat., Typis Joannis Lindani, 1680. First edition, woodcut title-device, small 8vo, a slight waterstain, modern half vellum. K Books 301-21 1983 £140

BEVERLEY, ROBERT   The History and Present State of Virginia, in Four Parts. London, 1705. Engraved title, folding table, 14 plates. Tooled leather, fine. Reese 18-35 1983 $1,200

BEVERLEY, ROBERT MACKENZIE   The Redan: a poem. London: Hamilton, Adams, 1856. First edition. 8vo. Orig. red cloth. Spine a bit dark. Very good copy. Ximenes 63-435 1983 $35

BEVINGTON, HELEN   Doctor Johnson's Waterfall and Other Poems. Boston, 1946. 8vo. Cloth. Review copy with slip from publisher laid in. Review of book pasted to front endboard, else fine copy in dj. In Our Time 156-75 1983 $30

BEWICK, THOMAS   A General History of Quadrupeds. Newcastle, 1791. Second edition, wood-engravings, a bit age-marked, a few library marks, gilt decorated brown morocco with centre panels of countersunk tree calf, gilt top. K Books 307-22 1983 £80

BEWICK, THOMAS   A History of British Birds. Newcastle upon Tyne, 1809. Wood engravings, 3rd ed., numerous engravings, 2 vols. in 1, 8vo, modern half calf (antique style). Wheldon 160-7 1983 £120

BEWICK, THOMAS   A History of British Birds. Newcastle, Printed for T. Bewick by Edw. Walker, 1826. 6th edn., numerous wood engrs. 2 vols. Bookpl. of Mary Laura Foster each vol. Half dark green calf with dark green cl. boards, 2 red lea. title labels each vol. raised bands & simple gilt design, a.e.g., marbled eps., occas. fox mark, lea. sl. rubbed, nice set. Hodgkins 27-245 1983 £165

BEWICK, THOMAS   A History of British Birds. Newcastle: Printed by J. Blackwell & Co., 1847. 2 vols., numerous fine wood-engravings, demy 8vo, half green morocco, new title labels inset on red morocco. K Books 307-21 1983 £150

BEY, KESNIN   The Evil of the East. Vizetelly & Co., 1888. First edition, half title, orig. dark blue boards, blocked and lettered in red; edges sl. rubbed. Jarndyce 31-394 1983 £14.50

BEYER, OSKAR   Rudolf Koch. Ein schopferisches Leben. Kassel/Basel: Barenreiter, 1953. 10 plates (3 color). Prof. illus. 4to. Boards, 1/4 cloth. Presentation copy, inscribed by the author. Ars Libri 32-374 1983 $75

BEZANCON, G. DE   Les Medecins a la Censure ou Entretiens sur la Medecine. Paris: L. Gonthier, 1677. 12mo. Cont. calf. First edition. Old ownership inscription on title. Gurney JJ-34 1983 £35

BHATIA, B. L.   Fauna of British India - Protozoa. 1936-38. 13 plates and text-figures, 2 vols., 8vo, cloth. Good ex-library copies. Wheldon 160-1271 1983 £25

BIANCALE, MICHELE   Plinio Nomellini. Roma: Fratelli Palombi, 1946. 46 plates. 4to. Boards. Ars Libri 33-554 1983 $30

BIANCHI, MARTHA DICKINSON   Gabrille and Other Poems. New York: Duffield, 1913. First edition. Orig. grey boards, gilt, t.e.g., others uncut. Inscribed by author in the year of publication: "A blessed Christmas to dearest Aunt Kate, from Martha." Fine copy. Jenkins 155-316 1983 $50

BIANCHINI, FRANCESCO   Camera ed Inscrizioni Sepulcrali De'Liberti... Rome, G.M. Salvioni, 1727. Folio. Title in red & black, engraved vignettes on title and preface, engraved ornamental initials, 7 finely engraved plates (5 folded), numerous letterpress inscriptions in double column text. With half-title, in full cont. vellum. 1st ed. Plates are very fine engravings by Girolamo Rossi after Antonio Buonamici. Fine copy. O'Neal 50-6 1983 $275

BIASUZ, GIUSEPPE   Andrea Brustolon. Padova: Istituto Veneto di Arti Grafiche, 1969. 199 illus. 4to. Wrappers. Dust jacket. Catalogue raisonne. Ars Libri 33-55 1983 $85

BIBB, GEORGE M.   Report of...Communicating Information in Relation to the Claim to Land in the State of Louisiana Called the "Houmas Claim." Wash., 1845. Illus., 3 folded maps of the claim. Dbd. First edition. Contains 77 transcripts and copies of letters from 1841 to 1845. Ginsberg 47-442 1983 $75

BIBB, GEORGE M.   Report of...Communicating Statistical Information in Relation to the Condition of the Agriculture, Manufactures, Domestic Trade, Currency, and Banks of the United States... Wash., 1845. Dbd. First edition. Ginsberg 46-61 1983 $50

BIBBS, ASA   Autobiography of...Including a Journal of a Trip from North Carolina to New York in 1832. Raleigh, 1915. Orig. printed wraps. First edition. Small embossed library stamp. Ginsberg 46-62 1983 $25

BIBBY, A.H.   Machine Gun Manual. Winnipeg, (ca. 1915). Illus. 16mo, orig. cloth wrappers. Morrill 289-583 1983 $27.50

BIBELOT. (Mosher, Portland, ME, 1895-1915. Complete set. 21 vols., 12mo. Clark 741-57 1983 $87.40, set

BIBLE - ALGONQUIN

BIBLE.   The New Testament of Our Lord and Saviour Jesus Christ; Translated into the Indian Language... Cambridge, (Massachusetts): Samuel Green and Marmaduke Johnson, 1661. Small 4to. Orig. calf, covers with triple gilt frame borders and floral ornaments, spine with raised bands and gilt line ornament. One of the 40 copies for presentation sent by the commissioners of the United Colonies. John Evelyn's copy. "Catalogo Evelyni inscriptus: Meliora Retinete, 1661" Traylen 94-72 1983 £30,000

BIBLE - DAKOTA

BIBLE   Dakota Wowapi Wakan Kin. The New Testament in the Dakota Language. New York, 1900. Pub.'s morocco, hinges cracked but sound. Felcone 22-15 1983 $25

BIBLE - DUTCH

BIBLE   Biblia: dat is, De Gantsche Heylige Schrift/Grondelijck end trouwelijck verduytschet. Leyden: Jan Jacobszoon and Jan Bouwensz, 1590. Folding map. Cont. blind-tooled calf (edge wear, front hinge cracked but solid), brass clasps (straps lacking). Felcone 21-9 1983 $150

BIBLE - ENGLISH

BIBLE.   New Testament... Rhemes: John Fogny, 1582. First edition. 4to. Later calf, with the arms of the Countess of Sutherland on upper cover. Roman letter, title-border and decorated initials. A very fine copy. Rare. Traylen 94-635 1983 £320

BIBLE   The Text of the New Testament of Iesvs Christ, translated ovt of the vulgar Latine by the Papists of the traiterous Seminarie at Rhemes. 1589. Lacking B1-B6, engraved title, folio, calf, rebacked, a good clean copy. K Books 307-134 1983 £150

BIBLE   The Bible Translated According to the Ebrew and Greeke. London: Robert Barker, 1608. Includes 2 concordances. Fancy engraved titles. Rebacked (cloth) panelled calf. About 600 double-col. pp in black letter. A.e.g. Some heads cropped, some birth & marriage records from the 18th century noted. New endpapers. Pages yellowed. Good. King 45-644 1983 $185.

BIBLE   The Holy Bible. London: by Robert Barker, 1631. 8vo. Woodcut titles. 18th Century calf. Slight usage. Heath 48-545 1983 £125

BIBLE   Solomons Song of Songs in English Metre. N.p., 1642. Inter-leafed, 4to, new calf. K Books 301-4 1983 £55

BIBLE.   The Holy Bible, containing the Old Testament and the New. Cambridge: by John Baskerville, 1763. First edition. Folio. Cont. dark blue morocco, gilt panelled sides with corner ornaments, fully gilt panelled spine with crimson morocco label, gilt, inner gilt dentelles, edges gilt. Engraved title-page, list of subscribers in third state. Traylen 94-444 1983 £450

BIBLE   The Holy Bible, Containing the Old and New Testaments. Trenton: Isaac Collins, 1791. Modern 3/4 morocco. Title page and first few pages darkened. Bound. Ownership stamp of Rev. James A. McFaul, nineteenth century Bishop of Trenton. The first Bible printed in New Jersey, and the second quarto Bible printed in America. Contains the Apocrypha and the concordance. Very nice. Felcone 19-5 1983 $250

BIBLE   The Holy Bible, Containing the Old and New Testaments. Trenton: Isaac Collins, 1793. Octavo. Full calf (very worn). Very good. Felcone 19-6 1983 $100

BIBLE   The Holy Bible, Containing the Old and New Testaments. Philadelphia, William Young, 1794. 2 vols. in 1, thick 12mo, contemporary calf, unpaged. Rubbed, lacks endleaves at end. Morrill 287-35 1983 $45

BIBLE   The Holy Bible Containing the Old and New Testaments. London, Chiswick Press for John Reeves, 1811. Small 8vo, full cont. red morocco wallet style binding, a.e.g., gilt stamped heraldic arms on cover, spine stamped in blind (a little rubbed at edges), else very good. Houle 22-105 1983 $150

BIBLE.   The Holy Bible: Containing the Old and New Testaments... Baltimore: Published and sold by John Hagerty, 1812. 2 vols. 16mo. Full crimson straight grain morocco, elaborately gilt, raised bands, gilt inner dentelles, a.e.g. Gushy ownership inscriptions, and a small chip neatly repaired, else a fine set. Bookseller's ticket of "A. Finley, Philad." Reese 18-365 1983 $85

BIBLE   Child's Bible. N.Y., Nurst, ca. 1860. 64mo. 23 woodcuts. Gilt stamped brown cloth (inner joints starting), else very good. Houle 21-641 1983 $60

BIBLE   The Holy Bible. N.Y., American Bible Society, 1874. Small 8vo, full brown morocco stamped in gilt and blind, edges gilt. Good-very good. Houle 21-112 1983 $150

BIBLE   The Illustrated Bible, also Verses entitled Railway to Heaven. London: Goode Bros., (ca. 1890). 28 illus. Fine copy in dark blue, glazed wrappers lettered in gold. A.e.g. (2 1/4 x 1 5/8; 58x41mm). Bromer 25-442 1983 $35

BIBLE   The New Testament of the Lord and Savior Jesus Christ. Glasgow: David Bryce and Son, 1895. About fine in blue leather with bookplate of Arthur A. Houghton. (11/16 x 5/8; 18x16mm). Bromer 25-456 1983 $285

BIBLE   The Holy Bible, Containing the Old and New Testaments. Glasgow: David Bryce, 1896. Fine in slightly rubbed gilt-stamped full red morocco and matching slip-case with magnifying glass inserted into front surface. With bookplate of Arthur A. Houghton. Contemporary owner's signature. (1 5/8 x 1 1/8; 42x29mm). Bromer 25-439 1983 $125

BIBLE   The Song of Songs Which Is Solomon's. London: 1897. Quarto. Illus. 1/100 copies on Japanese paper printed for Guild of Women Binders. Bound in full brown morocco with green morocco, gilt-lettered inlaid border. Inner dentelles green morocco, gilt-lettered inlaid border. Spine gilt extra in 6 compartments. Signed by (R) Watson of London. Bookplate of M. C. D. Borden. Very fine copy in red morocco-covered slip-case. Bromer 25-155 1983 $3200

BIBLE   The Holy Bible, Containing the Old and New Testaments. Glasgow: David Bryce, (ca. 1900). Elaborately embossed full brown leather with chain attaching book to miniature wooden lectern. Rubbed publisher's printed note glued to underside of lectern base. Book is fine with slight rubbing to extremities. Stand in excellent condition with shelf for storing Bible. From collection of Arthur A. Houghton with miniature bookplate. (1 3/4 x 1 1/8; 45x30mm). Bromer 25-440 1983 $565

BIBLE   The Ninety-First Psalm. Hingham: Village Press, 1904. 12mo. Limited to 200 copies. Very fine in faintly soiled printed boards. Bromer 25-308 1983 $200

BIBLE   The Book of Genesis. London: 1914. 4to, limp vellum, gilt, t.e.g., green silk ties, silk page marker. With 10 mounted color plates by Robinson. One of a very few copies bound in full vellum. A very fine copy in worn d/w. Perata 28-149 1983 $350

BIBLE   The Songs of Songs being Love Lyrics from Ancient Palestine. (San Francisco), 1922. 12mo., full vellum over boards, gilt. 23 initials printed in blue by Joseph Sinel and headpiece decoration by Harold von Schmidt. One of 310 copies hand-set and printed in black and red. Duschnes 240-99 1983 $135

BIBLE.   The Holy Bible, reprinted according to the Authorised Version. London: Nonesuch Press, 1924-25. 5 vols. Small folio. Orig. vellum, gilt. Limited edition of 75 copies printed on Arnold unbleached rag paper, with 5 finely engraved emblematical titles by Stephen Gooden, and other full-page decorations and headpieces. Traylen 94-71 1983 £750

BIBLE   The Gospel According to Saint Mark.
Washington: Judd & Detweiler, 1932. 4to, cloth, lettering & design in
gilt, t.e.g. Illus. with line drawings by Earl Winslow. One of 475
copies signed by artist and designer. A fine copy in rubbed slipcase.
Perata 28-192 1983 $50

BIBLE   The Sermon on the Mount... New York:
Golden Cross Press, 1935. First edition. 4to. Half leather over
boards, leather tips. Limited to 110 copies designed and hand-illuminated by Valenti Angelo and printed by Edmund B. Thompson at Hawthorn
House. With one color illus., two initials and a hand illuminated
title page. Some darkening of leather on spine. Oak Knoll 49-14
1983 $125

BIBLE   The Book of Job, from the King James
Bible. The Cummington Press, 1944. With wood engravings by Gustav
Wolf and a note by Alfred Young Fisher. 4to. Leather spine, decorated paper over boards. Little light rubbing to leather spine,
mainly a fine copy. In Our Time 156-184 1983 $350

BIBLE.   Book of Job. Leigh-on-Sea, 1948.
4to. Half vellum, gilt, t.e.g., others uncut, by Sangorski and
Sutcliffe, preserved in the orig. slip-case. 33 orig. etchings
by Frank Brangwyn, each one individually signed in pencil by the
artist. Traylen 94-92 1983 £330

BIBLE   The Book of Jonah. Cambridge: Rampant
Lions Press, 1979. 1/10 trial spreads on vellum. Wood engraving by
David Jones. Mint. Laid into hinged box with outside front hinge
starting. Bromer 25-283 1983 $225

BIBLE - GREEK

BIBLE   Novum Testamentum Graecum. London:
Pickering, 1828. Ads. Engraved frontis. Cloth-covered boards
slightly faded, else fine. Printed in small Greek type. (3 1/2 x
2 1/8; 90x53mm). Bromer 25-457 1983 $110

BIBLE - HAWAIIAN

BIBLE   New Testament. Oahu: Na Na Misionari i
Pai, 1835. First edition of the first appearance in print of the
entire New Testament in the Hawaiian language and the first printing
of any complete book on an island press. 12mo. Cont. full calf, spine
gilt stamped. Usual light foxing perforated library stamp on title.
Orig. binding. Fine. Jenkins 152-147 1983 $1,250

BIBLE - LATIN

BIBLE.   Biblia Sacra Vulgatae Editionis.
Regensburg, 1922. 4to, 1/2 leather. Salloch 385-488 1983 $50

BIBLE   The Gutenberg Bible in Facsimile. New
York: Brussell & Brussell, 1968. 3 vols., boxed, 8 color plates,
facsims. 1st ed. thus. Orig. cloth, gilt. Very fine set. Jenkins
155-1357 1983 $150

BIBLE - PERSIAN

BIBLE   The New Testament...Translated from
the Original Greek, into Persian, by the Revd Henry Martyn. 1837.
Fourth edition, persian characters, sheep, slightly rubbed. K Books
301-23 1983 £20

A BIBLIOGRAPHICAL Check List of North and Middle American Indian
Linguistics in the Edward E. Ayer Collection. Chicago, 1941. 2 vols.
Jenkins 153-742 1983 $65

THE BIBLIOGRAPHY of American Literature. New Haven: Yale Univ.
Press, (1955-1983). 7 vols. Mint set. Jenkins 155-76 1983 $400

THE BIBLIOGRAPHY of American Literature. New Haven: Yale Univ.
Press, (1955-1983). Vol. 7 only. Mint. Jenkins 155-77 1983 $85

BIBLIOGRAPHY of Hookworm Disease. New York, 1922. First edition.
8vo. Orig. binding. One leaf supplied in Xerox Facsimile. Ex-
library. Fye H-3-1012 1983 $30

A BIBLIOGRAPHY of the Writings of Harvey Cushing. Springfield, 1939.
First edition. 8vo. Orig. binding. Ex-library. Fye H-3-1013
1983 $50

BIBLIOTHECA Diabolica. (New York): Scribner, Welford & Armstrong,
September 1874. Tall 8vo. 19th century half leather. Frontis.
Bookplate of J. Timothy Kenrick. Head of spine has leather chipped
away. Scarce. Oak Knoll 48-422 1983 $75

BIBLIOTHEQUE NATIONALE.   Exposition d'oeuvres de Rembrandt.
Dessins et gravures. Paris, 1908. 25 plates. 4to. Wrappers.
Ars Libri 32-564 1983 $50

BICHAT, MARIE FRANCOIS XAVIER   Anatomie Generale. Paris, 1812.
2 parts in 4 vols. 8vo, modern calf, ex-lib. Argosy 713-55 1983
$450

BICHAT, MARIE FRANCOIS XAVIER   General Anatomy. Boston, 1822. 8vo.
3 vols. Old scuffed calf. Ex-lib. Argosy 713-56 1983 $300

BICHAT, MARIE FRANCOIS XAVIER   Physiological Researches on Life
and Death. London, n.d. (1815). First English edition. 8vo, mod.
1/2 buckram. Argosy 713-54 1983 $85

BICKERSTAFFE, ISAAC   Lionel and Clarissa or, a school for
fathers. London: printed for John Bell, 1781. 8vo, old half calf
(worn, cover detached.) Bell's edition. With a frontispiece.
Ximenes 64-48 1983 $20

BICKERSTETH, HENRY   Medical Hints, designed for the use of
Clergymen... London, 1824. Second edition. 8vo. Orig. boards,
backstrip torn. Gurney JJ-35 1983 £20

BICKHAM, WILLIAM D.   From Ohio to the Rocky Mountains. Dayton: 1879. First edition. Green cloth. Autograph presentation copy.
Very good. Bradley 66-516 1983 $85

BICKNELL, WALTER L.   Keep Troth. Hurst & Blackett, 1884.
First edition, 3 vols., half title. Library labels as pastedowns.
Orig. light purple cloth, dulled. Vol. I a little loose. Jarndyce
30-300 1983 £42

BIDDLE, CHARLES   Autobiography. Philadelphia, 1883.
First edition, privately printed. 8vo. Morrill 290-400 1983 $27.50

BIDDLE, MONCURE   A Christmas Letter. George Borrow:
The Early Years. Phila.: Moncure Biddle & Co., 1941. First edition.
Illus. Orig. red morocco, grained cloth. Fine. MacManus 277-591
1983 $20

BIDDLECOMBE, GEORGE   The Art of Rigging. Salem, Mass.:
Marine Research Society, 1925. 8vo. Orig. cloth. Frontis. 16 plates.
Good. Edwards 1042-7 1983 £55

BIDDULPH, J.   The Nineteenth and Their Times.
London, 1899. Photogravure frontis. portrait. 2 portrait plates, 4
coloured plates, 5 maps. 8vo. Orig. decorated cloth. Very slightly
worn. Bookplate. Good. Edwards 1042-530 1983 £50

BIDDULPH, J.   The Pirates of Malabar and an Englishwoman in India 200 years ago. London, 1907. Folding map and frontis.
Thick 8vo. Half blue niger. Authors own copy, interleaved, with his
own corrections in manuscript. Good. Edwards 1044-59 1983 £50

BIDEN, C. L.   Sea-Angling Fishes of the Cape.
Oxford, 1930. 48 plates and 2 maps, 8vo, cloth (head of spine torn).
Wheldon 160-938 1983 £15

BIDWELL, JOHN   Echoes of the Past About California.
Chico, Ca., ca. 1914. Illus., orig. wraps. Ginsberg 47-29 1983
$50

BIDWELL, JOHN   Echoes of the Past About California.
Chico, Calif., (ca. 1914). First edition. Illustrated with 3 photos.
Pictorial green wrappers. Wright Howes' copy, with his pencil note
on end paper. Fine. Bradley 65-24 1983 $55

BIDWELL, JOHN   A Journey to Califronia, 1841. San Francisco: John Henry Nash, 1937. Intro. by H.I. Priestly. Cloth & boards. Dawson 471-21 1983 $60

BIDWELL, JOHN   A Journey to California. SF, 1937. Introduction by Herbert Ingram Priestley. Folio, linen-backed bds., paper label, d/w. A fine copy. Perata 27-139 1983 $60

BIEBER, M.   History of the Greek & Roman Theatre. Princeton, 1939. Folio. 8vo, cloth. Salloch 385-66 1983 $45

BIELFELD, JACOB FRIEDERICH VON   Letters of Baron Bielfeld, Secretary of Legation to the King of Prussia. 1768-1770. 4 vols., 12mo, slight wear at top of vol. 4 and foot of vol. 1 spines, but a sound set. First edition in English. Bickersteth 75-6 1983 £24

BIER, AUGUST   Hyperaemie als Heilmittel. Leipzig, 1906. Illus. Orig. cloth. Argosy 713-57 1983 $100

BIERCE, AMBROSE   Black Beetles in Amber. San Francisco: Western Authors Publishing Company, 1892. First edition, first issue, with the Western Authors imprint. Portrait frontis. sketch by Partington. Gray cloth, gilt. Covers dull, top beveled edges bumped, otherwise very good. Bradley 64-19 1983 $115

BIERCE, AMBROSE   Black Beetles in Amber. San Francisco: Western Authors Pub. Co., 1892. Frontis. 1st ed. Orig. grey cloth, gilt. Front free end paper excised, else a fine copy. Jenkins 155-85 1983 $75

BIERCE, AMBROSE   Fantastic Fables. NY, 1899. First printing. About fine in slightly soiled and darkened pictorially stamped covers. Bromer 25-9 1983 $165

BIERCE, AMBROSE   A Horseman in the Sky. San Francisco: Book Club of Calif. 1920. Page decorations by Ray F. Coyle. Ltd. to 400 copies, printed by John Henry Nash. Cloth over boards, a little soiled. Paper spine label. Karmiole 72-17 1983 $50

BIERCE, AMBROSE   In the Midst of Life. New York: Putnam, 1898. 1st ed. thus. Orig. maroon cloth, gilt. Some light rubbing to lower edges, but a bright very good copy. Jenkins 155-86 1983 $65

BIERCE, AMBROSE   The Monk and the Hangman's Daughter. Chicago: F.J. Schulte and Co., 1892. Frontis. and plates. Yellow printed wraps. First edition, Starrett's first issue. Wraps. very lightly soiled, otherwise a fine copy. Very scarce in collector's condition. Preserved in a fine half morocco slipcase. Reese 19-75 1983 $300

BIERCE, AMBROSE   The Shadow on the Dial and Other Essays. San Francisco, 1909. First edition. Tall 8vo, dec. buckram. Fine copy, in dust wrapper. Argosy 714-68 1983 $85

BIERCE, AMBROSE   Tales of Soldiers and Civilians. San Francisco: E.L.G. Steele, 1891. 1st ed. Orig. brown cloth (rarer than grey). Fine copy. Jenkins 155-87 1983 $225

BIERCE, AMBROSE   Tales of Soldiers and Civilians. New York, 1943. Tall 8vo, bound by Bayntun in turquoise and orange morocco. Front cover has a soldier in full gear etched in black and a civilian in gilt, wide dentelles, cockerell endleaves, a.e.g. Wood-engravings by Paul Landacre printed directly from the blocks. One of 1500 copies signed by the artist. Duschnes 240-15 1983 $200

BIERCE, AMBROSE   Tales of Soldiers and Civilians. New York: LEC, 1943. 1 of 1500 numbered copies, signed by the artist Paul Landacre who did the wood engravings. Orig. pictorial calf and linen, slipcased. Inner folding liner broken, else a nice copy. Jenkins 155-807 1983 $55

BIERCE, AMBROSE   Ten Tales. London: First Editions Club, 1925. First edition. Presentation copy from A.J.A. Symons, the author of the introduction. T.e.g. Free endpapers browned. Fine. Jolliffe 26-499 1983 £44

BIERRING, WALTER   100 Years of Iowa Medicine - 1850-1950. Iowa City, 1950. 8vo. Orig. binding. First edition. Fye H-3-40 1983 $35

BIG Top Circus Book. N.p.: n.d. (ca.1940). Cloth backed pictorial boards. Ribbon ties. Few small rips, repaired. Very good. Book can be opened up to form a "big top" circus tent. Aleph-bet 8-179 1983 $70

BIGELOW, E. VICTOR   A Narrative History of the Town of Cohasset, Massachusetts. (Boston), 1898. First edition. Maps and illustrations. 8vo, close to fine. Morrill 290-283 1983 $35

BIGELOW, HENRY J.   Medical Education in America. Cambridge, 1871. 8vo. Orig. binding. First edition. Very fine. Fye H-3-41 1983 $75

BIGELOW, HENRY J.   A Memoir of Henry Jacob Bigelow. Boston, 1900. First edition. 8vo. Orig. binding. Fye H-3-682 1983 $40

BIGELOW, HENRY J.   Science and Success. A Valedictory Address... Boston, 1859. Second edition. Wrappers. 8vo. Fye H-3-42 1983 $35

BIGELOW, JACOB   Florula Bostoniensis. Boston, 1840. Third edition, enlarged, 8vo, binder's cloth, a trifle foxed. Wheldon 160-1654 1983 £30

BIGELOW, JACOB   Modern Inquiries: Classical Professional, and Miscellaneous. Boston, 1867. 8vo. First edition. Orig. binding. Water-stain affecting margins, not affecting text, else a near fine copy. Fye H-3-43 1983 $60

BIGELOW, JOHN   France and the Confederate Navy, 1862-1868. New York, 1888. 1st ed. 8vo. Morrill 289-273 1983 $20

BIGELOW, JOHN   Retrospections of An Active Life. N.Y., 1909-1913. First edition. 5 thick vols. Jenkins 152-785 1983 $125

BIGGAR, C. R. W.   Sir Oliver Mowat. Toronto: Warwick Bor's. & Rutter, Ltd., 1905. 22 1/2cm. 2 vols. 2 portraits. Rear folding map. Red cloth. T.e.g. Very good to fine set. Scarce. McGahern 54-190 1983 $100

BIGLAND, J.   Essays on Various Subjects. Doncaster: by and for W. Sheardown..., 1805. First edition. 2 vols. 8vo. Half calf, gilt. List of Subscribers. Slight wear. Heath 48-244 1983 £45

BIGSBY, JOHN J.   The Shoe and Canoe. London, 1850. 2 vols. Illus., 2 frontis. 18 plates, 5 maps, 2 of which are folded. Orig. gold stamped pictorial cloth. First edition. Ginsberg 46-136 1983 $275

BILBO, JACK   Jack Bilbo, an Autobiography. Lon., 1948. Fine in near fine dustwrapper and good to very good box. Quill & Brush 54-1644 1983 $35

BILL, A. H.   The Beleaguered City. New York, 1946. 8vo. Orig. cloth. Frontis. 15 plates, 2 folding maps. Good. Edwards 1042-196 1983 £15

BILL, MAX   Robert Maillart. Erlenbach-Zurich: Verlag fur Architektur, 1949. 247 illus. Oblong 4to. Cloth. Designed by Bill. Ars Libri 32-415 1983 $65

BILLBERG, EDDY E.   The War Cry of the Sioux a Historical Romance from the Sioux Outbreak of 1862. Boston, 1930. Orig. cloth. First edition. Ginsberg 46-691 1983 $45

BILLING, ARCHIBALD   Practical Observations on Diseases of the Lungs and Heart. London, 1852. First edition. Argosy 713-59 1983 $75

BILLINGTON, ELIZABETH   Memoirs of Mrs. Billington, from her birth. London: printed for James Ridgway, 1792. 8vo, sewn as issued. First edition. With a portrait (blank corner stained); half-title present. First and last pages dust-soiled; stitching a bit loose. Ximenes 64-49 1983 $225

BILLINGE, CHARLES   Poems on Christian Charity, Contentment, and Melancholy. Wolverhampton: Printed for the Author, by J. Smart. MDCCLXXXIV. 8vo, upper edge of title slightly shaved, not affecting text, otherwise a good copy in new wraps. First and only edition. Quaritch NS 7-10 1983 $175

BILLROTH, THEODOR   General Surgical Pathology & Therapeutics. N.Y., 1872. Illus. 1/2 calf (rubbed). Argosy 713-61 1983 $150

BILLY, ANDRE   La Grece. Grenoble, 1937. 210 illus. in gravure. 8vo, cloth. Salloch 385-330 1983 $20

BIMA, CARLO   Giorgio da Sebenico. Milano: Italpress, 1954. 80 plates. Small 4to. Cloth. Ars Libri 33-164 1983 $100

BINDER, EARL   Lords of Creation. Philadelphia: The Prime Press, (1949). 1st ed., limited issue. One of 112 on special paper; one of the special copies issued without limitation label. Dark blue cloth, all edges untrimmed, some pages unopened. Fine without dj, as issued, in publisher's orig. cardboard box, which is worn. Bradley 64-20 1983 $50

BINDLOSS, HAROLD   In the Niger Country. Edinburgh: Wm. Blackwood, 1898. 8vo. 2 maps. Orig. blue cloth, ex-lib. Adelson Africa-166 1983 $40

BINET, ALFRED   Animal Magnetism. NY: Appleton, 1898. Ads. Publisher's decorative r-d cloth. Fine copy. Gach 95-42 1983 $30

BINGAY, MALCOLM W.   "Detroit Is My Own Home Town". Indianapolis (1946). Tiger Town edition, limited to 199 numbered copies, signed by the author. Photos, bound in fine blue 1/2 lea., with a gilt-stamped Ford radiator. Top edge gilt. Slight wear. King 46-140 1983 $35

BINGHAM, CALEB   The Columbian Orator. Boston: Bingham, 1817. 12mo, orig. calf, worn, early writing on cover and flyleaves. Argosy 710-473 1983 $50

BINGHAM, CLIFTON   The Animals' Trip to Sea. London & N.Y., n.d. (1890's?). 11 (incl. one double-page) full page nice color lithographed plates and numerous pictures drawn by G.H. Thompson. Cloth spine. Color litho boards. 3 old photos. glued to inside front cover. One plate with repairable tear. Inner hinges loose. Covers worn and soiled. King 45-436 1983 $35

BINGHAM, HIRAM   Inca Land. Boston: Houghton Mifflin Company, 1922. Profusely illus., including map. Gilt-stamped blue cloth. Karmiole 71-64 1983 $35

BINGLEY, WILLIAM   Memoirs of British Quadrupeds. 1809. 71 engraved plates mostly by S. Howitt, 8vo, contemporary calf, gilt. Some light foxing. Plates 7, 8, and 22 were not published. Joints beginning to crack but a good copy. Wheldon 160-539 1983 £70

BINGLEY, WILLIAM   Musical biography; or, memoirs of the lives and writings of the most eminent musical composers and writers... London: Colburn, etc., 1814. Second edition. 2 vols. 8vo. Cont. half calf, spine gilt. A bit rubbed, later labels. Very good copy. Ximenes 63-326 1983 $150

BINNS, ARCHIE   You Rolling River. NY, 1947. Paperwraps, proof, cover offset and lightly soiled, else very good. Quill & Brush 54-113 1983 $30

BINSTEAD, ARTHUR M.   Houndsditch Day by Day. Sands & Co., 1903. 1 p ads., half title, 8 pp ads. Orig. pink dec. cloth. Jarndyce 31-234 1983 £10.50

BINSTEAD, ARTHUR M.   Mop Fair. Edinburgh: Sands, 1905. Orig. pictorial cloth. First edition. With a signed presentation inscription from the author on the flyleaf. Covers worn; front inner hinge cracked. MacManus 277-373 1983 $20

BINSWANGER, LUDWIG (1881-1966)   Ueber Phaenomenologie. Berlin: Verlag von Julius Springer, 1923. Self-wrappers. Inscribed "Ueberreicht von Verfasser". Gach 95-43 1983 $50

BINSWANGER, OTTO (1852-1929)   Die Hysterie. Vienna: Alfred Hoelder, 1904. 43 text illustrations, 2 plates. Contemporary 1/2 leather, (dry, joints and edges rubbed). First edition. Gach 95-44 1983 $75

BINSWANGER, OTTO (1852-1929)   Zur Kenntnis Der Trophischen Vorgaenge. Goettingen: Druck der Univ. Buchdruckerei von E. A. Huth, 1878. Self-wrappers. Gach 95-45 1983 $75

BINYON, LAURENCE   Attila. London: Murray, 1907. Orig. cloth-backed boards. First edition. Signed by the author. MacManus 277-374 1983 $20

BINYON, LAURENCE   Odes. London: The Unicorn Press, 1901. Woodcut title-page. Orig. cloth. First edition. Very fine. MacManus 277-378 1983 $20

BINYON, LAURENCE   Painting In The Far East. London: Edward Arnold, 1908. Illus. Orig. decorated cloth. First edition. Spine and covers faded and slightly worn. Spine cracked although webbing intact. A good copy. MacManus 277-379 1983 $35

BINYON, LAURENCE   Painting in the Far East. New York, 1913. Second edition, revised throughout. 40 plates, 4to, gilt top. K Books 307-24 1983 £35

BINYON, LAURENCE   Paris and Oenone. London: A. Constable & Co., 1906. Orig. wrappers. First edition. Front wrapper rather browned. A good copy. MacManus 277-380 1983 $35

BINYON, LAURENCE   The Shah-Namah of Firdausi. London, 1931. First edition. 4to. Edges of covers a little faded. In neatly repaired dust wrapper. Bookplate. Nice. Rota 230-71 1983 £65

BINYON, LAURENCE   The Sirens. London: Macmillan & Co., 1925. Orig. cloth-backed boards. Dust jacket (chipped). First edition. Very good copy. MacManus 277-381 1983 $20

BINYON, LAURENCE   The Wonder Night. N.Y.: William Edwin Rudge, 1927. Orig. wrappers. First American edition, copyright issue, limited to only 27 copies, of which twelve were for sale. Mint copy. MacManus 277-382 1983 $135

BINZ, C.   Lectures on Pharmacology. London: New Sydenham Society, 1895-7. 2 vols. 8vo, cloth. Argosy 713-62 1983 $85

BINZ, KARL B.   Lectures on Pharmacology for Practitioners and Students... London: New Sydenham Society, 1895. 2 vols. 8vo. Orig. binding. Numerous text illus. Binding chipped, spine of vol. II faded. Zeitlin 264-48 1983 $60

A BIOGRAPHICAL History with Portraits of Prominent Men of the Great West. Chicago: Manhattan Publishing Co., 1894. Steel engraved portraits. Full corocco. A.e.g. Folio. Jenkins 152-240 1983 $300

BIOGRAPHICAL Review Volume XVIII. Boston, 1897. Portraits. 4to, full orig. leather, rubbed & partly stained, hinges slightly cracked. Morrill 288-262 1983 $30

BIOGRAPHICAL Review Volume 28. Boston, 1898. Portraits. Large heavy 4to, full orig. leather, rubbed. Morrill 288-263 1983 $25

BIOGRAPHICAL Review...Boston, 1899. Portraits. Large 4to. Orig. leather. Rubbed. Morrill 289-416 1983 $27.50

THE BIOGRAPHY of the British Stage; being correct narratives of the lives of all the principal actors and actresses...To which is added, a comic poem, entitled "The Actress." London: printed for Sherwood, Jones and Co., 1824. 12mo, original grey printed boards (spine worn). First edition, with a frontis., and numerous small wood-engraved illus. in the text. Ximenes 64-50 1983 $150

BIONDI, GIOVANNI FRANCESCO   Eromena, or, Love and Revenge. By Richard Badger, for Robert Allot, 1632. First English edition. Folio, lacks initial blank leaf. Modern panelled calf, old style. Stains on some leaves, final leaf dust-soiled, frayed and laid down. Hannas 69-11 1983 £140

BIRCH, E. A.   The Management and Medical Treatment of Children in India. Calcutta, 1895. Third edition, revised and enlarged. 8vo. Orig. cloth. Good. Edwards 1044-62 1983 £40

BIRCH, JOHN   Examples of Labourers' Cottages, &c. Edinburgh: Blackwood, 1892. With 35 plates, roy. 8vo, orig. cloth, gilt. Inside joints neatly repaired. A very good copy. Third edition. Fenning 60-26 1983 £32.50

BIRCH, JOHN GRANT   Travels in North and Central China. London: Hurst and Blackett, ltd. 1902. Ads. With 57 illus. Illus. blue cloth. Karmiole 73-112 1983 $75

BIRCH, SAMUEL   History of Ancient Pottery. J. Murray, 1873. New & revised edn. with coloured frontis. & 10 col'd plates printed by Wm. Clowes & Sons, 2 b&w plates & numerous wood engrs. in text. Dark blue cloth, gilt vignette fr. cvr., gilt decor. bkstrip, bevelled bds. (sl. wear joints of bkstrip), v.g. copy. Hodgkins 27-357 1983 £35

BIRCH, THOMAS   An Inquiry into the Share. Printed for A. Miller, 1747. 8vo, cont. half calf, joints cracked, but binding firm. First edition. Bickersteth 75-5 1983 £28

BIRCH, VERA   The Green Faced Toad. N.Y.: Stokes, 1923. 4to. Green cloth. 8 color plates by Lenski. Very good. Aleph-bet 8-163 1983 $40

BIRD, GEORGE W.   Wanderings in Burma. Bournemouth, F.J. Bright, 1897. First and apparently only edition, with 88 folding and other maps, plans and plates, errata slip, roy. 8vo, orig. cloth, gilt, t.e.g., with a few marginal pencil notes, but still a very good copy. Fenning 61-32 1983 £65

BIRD, GEORGE W.   Wanderings in Burma. London, 1897. Large folding map in end pocket. Numerous plates, some slight spotting. Recased, roy. 8vo. Good. Edwards 1044-63 1983 £50

BIRD, J. MALCOLM   "Margery" the Medium. Boston, (1925). 1st ed. Illus. 8vo. Morrill 288-41 1983 $22.50

BIRD, JOSEPH   Protection Against Fire...New York, 1873. First edition. Small 8vo. Morrill 290-628 1983 $65

BIRD, ROBERT MONTGOMERY   The Infidel. Philadelphia, 1835. 1st ed. 2 vols., small 8vo, paper labels. Binding stained, some rubbing, few endleaves lacking. Vol. 1 lacks pp. 15-22. With the ads. Morrill 286-54 1983 $37.50

BIRD, WILLIAM   A Treatise of the Nobilitie of the Realme... London, 1642. 8vo. Light dampstaining throughout, title page a bit chipped & dusty, last blank torn away, bound in full, contemporary sheep, quite worn, covers & spine double blind-ruled, some repairs effected to the head & tail of spine and to joints, clean copy. Boswell 7-19 1983 $200

BIRDS. (London): Routledge, n.d. 9 color-printed wood engravings, some with additional hand-coloring. Few pages slightly creased, otherwise fine in pictorial self-wrappers. (2 3/4 x 2 3/16; 71x56mm). Bromer 25-411 1983 $35

BIRGE, JULIUS C.   The Awakening of the Desert. Boston, (1912). End map, illus. Clark 741-219 1983 $27.50

BIRGE, JULIUS C.   The Awakening of the Desert. London, n.d. End map, illus. Clark 741-220 1983 $25

BIRINGUCCIO, VANNOCCIO   Of Typecasting in the Sixteenth Century. N.P.: Columbiad Club, 1941. Small 8vo. Stiff paper wrappers. Limited to 200 numbered copies printed by Carl Purington Rollins. Oak Knoll 39-51 1983 $25

BIRKBECK, MORRIS   Letters from Illinois. Dublin, 1818. 8vo, 3/4 red mor., (inner hinges mended), g.t. Extra ad. slip with manuscript notations. Argosy 716-208 1983 $125

BIRKBECK, MORRIS   Notes on a Journey in America, from the Coast of Virginia to the Territory of Illinois. London, 1818. 3rd ed. Folding map. 8vo, orig. boards. Rebacked, part of bookplate, good copy. Morrill 287-37 1983 $50

BIRKINBINE, JOHN   Report of John Birkinbine, C.E. on Location of Iron and Steel Works, at Duluth, Minn. (N.p., 1887). Cover title. Wraps. (edges chipped, library stamp). Privately printed for the West Duluth Land Co. Felcone 22-151 1983 $20

BIRNEY, HARRY HOFFMAN   Zealots of Zion. Philadelphia, Penn, (1931). First edition. Illus. with halftone photos. Dust jacket (lightly creased, nicks at edges) else fine. Two page TLS from author. Houle 22-1024 1983 $150

BIRNBAUM, KARL   Psychosen Mit Wahnbildung... Halle: Carl Marhold, 1908. First edition. Original printed boards, ex-library. Gach 94-299 1983 $25

BIRNEY, HARRY HOFFMAN   Zealots of Zion. Phila., Penn (1931). First edition. Illus. with halftones. Dust jacket. Two-page typed letter signed from be author laid in. Houle 21-1113 1983 $150

BIRRELL, AUGUSTINE   Collected Essays. London: Elliot Stock, 1899. 2 vols. Orig. cloth. First edition. Spines faded. Endpapers foxed. A good set. MacManus 277-385 1983 $25

BIRRELL, AUGUSTINE   Frederick Locker-Lampson, a Character Sketch. London: Constable and Co., 1920. With a small selection from letters addressed to him and bibliographical notes on a few of the books formerly in the Rowfant Library. Orig. decorated cloth. First edition. One of 100 copies numbered and signed by the author. Covers slightly soiled, corners bumped. Endpapers lightly browned. Bookplate. MacManus 277-386 1983 $65

BIRRELL, AUGUSTINE   In the Name of the Bodleian, and Other Essays. Elliot Stock, 1906. 2nd edition, half title, 1 p ads. Orig. green cloth, v.g. Jarndyce 31-427 1983 £10.50

BIRRELL, AUGUSTINE   Life of Charlotte Bronte. London, 1887. First edition. Half-title. 8vo. Cloth. T.e.g. Traylen 94-113 1983 £12

BIRRELL, AUGUSTINE   Obiter Dicta. London: Elliot Stock, 1887. Orig. cloth. First edition. Fine copy. MacManus 277-388 1983 $25

BIRRELL, AUGUSTINE   Seven Lectures on the Law and History of Copyright in Books. London: Cassell, 1899. First edition thus. 8vo. Orig. cloth. Oak Knoll 49-62 1983 $32.50

BISCHOFF, HERMANN   Deadwood to the Big Horns, 1877. (Bismarck, 1931). Lithographed. Orig. printed wraps. First edition. One of 50 copies printed for the family. Ginsberg 47-268 1983 $150

BISCHOFF, L. W. T.   Nervi Accessorii Willissii Anatomia et Physiologia. Heidelbergae, 1832. 1/2 mor; ex-lib. Argosy 712-63 1983 $75

BISCOE, C. E. TYNDALE   Kashmir in Sunlight & Shade. London, 1922. Folding map, 28 photographs. 8vo. Orig. cloth. Good. Edwards 1044-66 1983 £30

BISHOP, ABRAHAM   Oration in Honor of the Election of President Jefferson, and the Peaceable Acquisition of Louisiana Delivered at the National Festival... (New Haven), 1804. Cloth with leather label. Ginsberg 47-444 1983 $50

BISHOP, ABRAHAM   Proofs of a Conspiracy, Against Christianity, and the Government of the United States. Hartford: John Babcock, 1802. Uncut. Disbound. Title waterstained and dust soiled. Felcone 22-16 1983 $20

BISHOP, GEORGE   New-England Judged, by the Spirit of the Lord... Second part, Being a Farther Relation of the Cruel and Bloody Suffering...from Anno 1660, to anno 1665. London: Printed and sold by T. Sowle, 1703-02 (sic). Three quarter polished calf, gilt. A fine, clean copy, bound with the leaf of advertisements. Reese 18-34 1983 $600

BISHOP, HENRY G.   The Practical Printer: A Book of Instructions for Beginners... Oneonta, NY: Henry G. Bishop, (1895). Third edition, revised. Small 8vo. Orig. cloth. Illus. Covers rubbed. Oak Knoll 49-66 1983 $45

BISHOP, ISABELLA LUCY BIRD   Unbeaten Tracks in Japan. London, 1880. Third edition. Folding map, frontis. Numerous illus. 2 vols. Pictorial cloth. 8vo. Good. Edwards 1044-64 1983 £55

BISHOP, JOHN B.   Theodore Roosevelt and His Time Shown in His Own Letters. New York, 1920. Two vols., portraits. Plates. Bound in fine three quarter polished calf, spines gilt extra, t.e.g. A very fine set. Bookplates. Reese 19-477 1983 $35

BISHOP, JOHN PEALE   Minute Particulars. New York, 1935. 8vo. Wraps. Total edition is 165 numbered copies signed by author. Original glassine wrapper is tanned, else a fine copy. In Our Time 156-78 1983 $350

BISHOP, JOHN PEALE   Selected Poems. New York, 1941. 8vo. Cloth. Fine copy in scuffed but intact dj. In Our Time 156-79 1983 $50

BISHOP, JOSEPH B.   The Panama Gateway. T. Fisher Unwin, 1913. First U.K. edition, with a folding map and 48 plates, 8vo, orig. cloth, gilt, t.e.g. A very good copy. Fenning 60-29 1983 £18.50

BISHOP, NATHANIEL H.   Voyage of the Paper Canoe. Boston (1878). Illus., gilt-pict. cloth, ink inscription, hinges loose, moderately rubbed. King 46-756 1983 $40

BISHOP, S. C.   Handbook of Salamanders. Ithaca, NY, (1943). Coloured frontispiece, 144 other illus. and 56 maps, 8vo, cloth. Wheldon 160-940 1983 £18

BISHOP, ZEALIA   The Curse of Yig. Sauk City: Arkham House, 1953. First edition. Black cloth. Laid in is signed postcard from August Derleth, publisher. Very fine in dust jacket. Bradley 66-107 1983 $85

BISSET, WILLIAM   The Modern Fanatick... London: by A. Baldwin..., 1710. First edition. 8vo. Modern quarter calf. Heath 48-162 1983 £60

BISSETT, CLARK PRESCOTT   Abraham Lincoln, a Universal Man. San Francisco, John Howell, 1923. 1st ed., 1125 copies printed (by E & R Grabhorn). Portrait. 8vo, orig. boards, cloth back. Morrill 287-38 1983 $22.50

BISSETT, ROBERT   Douglas, Or, The Highlander. Dublin: Printed by William Porter...for P. Wogan, H. Colbert (etc), 1800. 4 vols. in 2, 12mo, contemporary tree calf; lacks title-labels. 1st Dublin edition Hill 165-9 1983 £50

BITTER To Sweet End. London: Samuel Tinsley, 1877. Orig. embossed cloth. First edition. Prelims foxed. A fine copy. MacManus 277-78 300

BITTREMIEUX, LEO   Symbolisme in de Negerkunst. Bruxelles: Vromant, 1937. 20 plates with 150 illustrations. 4to, wrappers. Ars Libri 34-568 1983 $85

BIZZELL, WILLIAM B.   Rural Texas. New York, 1924. Frontis. and illustrations. Jenkins 153-49 1983 $45

BLAAUW, F. E.   A Monograph of the Cranes. Leyden and London, 1897. 22 coloured plates, roy. folio, original decorated cloth. Rare; edition limited to 170 copies, of which this is no. 6. Corners of the binding a little worn, else in very good condition. Wheldon 160-8 1983 £1,250

BLACAM, AODH DE   Gaelic Literature Surveyed. Dublin: Talbot, 1929. First edition, 5 plates, 8vo, orig. cloth, a nice copy in the dust wrapper. Fenning 61-33 1983 £12.50

BLACK, A. P. OTT   End of the Long Horn Trail. Selfridge, N.D., (1936). Illus. Clark 741-195 1983 $25

BLACK, HELEN C.   Pen, Pencil, Baton and Mask. London: Spottiswoode & Co., 1896. Biographical Sketches. Illus. Orig. cloth. First edition. Signed by the author on the frontispiece portrait. Spine and covers soiled and worn. Some foxing to the endpapers. A good copy. MacManus 277-393 1983 $35

BLACK, JEANNETTE D.   A Rhode Island Chaplain in the Revolution. Providence: Rhode Island Society of the Cincinnati, 1949. First edition. Tall 8vo. Cloth. Limited to 900 copies. Three illus. Oak Knoll 49-67 1983 $30

BLACK, JEREMIAH S.   Federal Jurisdiction in the Territories. Wash., 1883. Orig. printed wraps. First edition. Ginsberg 47-901 1983 $35

BLACK, JOHN   A Wind Is Rising: A Book of Verse. New York, (1948). 8vo. Cloth. Fine in dj. In Our Time 156-81 1983 $20

BLACK, READING W.   The Life and Diary of..., A History of Uvalde. Uvalde, Texas: The El Progreso Club, 1943. Orig. printed wrappers. Frontis. Plates. Privately printed. 1st ed. Very scarce. Jenkins 153-559 1983 $100

BLACK, W. S.   The Mole and the Bat. George Waterston, n.d. (ca.1880). 6 colour printed plates & 6pp of music with decorated borders. Red & yellow pictorial boards. Edges worn. Greer 39-33 1983 £15

BLACK, WILLIAM   The Beautiful Wretch. London: Macmillan & Co., 1881. Three stories in three volumes. Orig. cloth. First edition. The Four Macmicols. The Pupil of Aurelius. A fine set. MacManus 277-394 1983 $375

BLACK, WILLIAM   Green Pastures and Piccadilly. London: Macmillan & Co., 1877. 3 vols. Orig. cloth. First edition. A fine set. MacManus 277-395 1983 $375

BLACK, WILLIAM   Judith Shakespeare. London: Macmillan, 1884. 3 vols. Orig. cloth. First edition. An exceptionally tight set; a flawless example of a three-decker. With the Douglas C. Ewing bookplate. MacManus 277-396 1983 $350

BLACK, WILLIAM   Judith Shakespeare, a Romance. Macmillan, 1884. First edition, 3 vols. Half titles, 32 pp ads. vol. I, 2 pp ads vol. II. Orig. blue cloth, rubbed, remains of Potter's Subscription Library tickets on upper covers. Jarndyce 30-301 1983 £18

BLACK, WILLIAM   MacLeod of Dare. London: Macmillan and Co., 1878. 3 vols. With illus. Orig. cloth. First edition. Edges and corners a bit worn. Spines slightly faded. Covers a trifle soiled. A very good set. MacManus 277-397 1983 $250

BLACK, WILLIAM   Sabina Zembra. London: Macmillan, 1887. Orig. cloth. 3 vols. First edition. Covers stained & worn; shaken; library labels in front paste-downs. MacManus 277-399 1983 $125

BLACK, WILLIAM   Shandon Bells. London: Macmillan, 1883. 3 vols. Orig. cloth. First edition. Inner hinge repaired in vol. 1 (with tape). Bindings worn. Library labels inside front covers. MacManus 277-400 1983 $55

BLACK, WILLIAM   The Strange Adventures of a Phaeton. London: Macmillan & Co., 1872. 2 vols. Orig. gilt-decorated blue cloth. First edition. Covers worn at edges. Inner hinges cracked, shaken. A good copy. MacManus 277-401 1983 $225

BLACK, WILLIAM   Sunrise: A Story Of These Times. London: Sampson Low, Marston, Searle & Rivington, 1881. 3 vols. Orig. decorated cloth. First edition. Spine ends slightly worn. A near-fine, bright set. MacManus 277-402 1983 $300

BLACK, WILLIAM   White Heather, A Novel. London: Macmillan & Co., 1885. 3 vols. Orig. dark blue cloth. First edition. Presentation copy from the publisher with his rubber stamp on the title-page. Rear inner hinges to vols. 2 & 3 repaired. Spines worn. A good set. MacManus 277-403 1983 $225

BLACK, WILLIAM   White Wings. London: Macmillan & Co.,
1880. 3 vols. Orig. cloth. First edition. Bookseller's blindstamp
on front free endpapers. Spines and covers slightly worn, with a few
small tears to the spines. A clean, bright set. Former owner's
signature. Bookplate. MacManus 277-404 1983 $350

BLACK, WILLIAM   Wolfenberg. Sampson Low, Marston,
1892. First edition, 3 vols., half title vol. I; 32 pp ads. vol. III.
Orig. maroon cloth, a little marked. Jarndyce 30-302 1983 £42

BLACK, WILLIAM   Yolande. The Story of a Daughter.
London: Macmillan & Co., 1883. First edition. 3 vols. Orig. blue
cloth. Former owner's signature on flyleaf of Vol. one. Covers badly
dampstained, several inner hinges stained. MacManus 277-405 1983
$135

.THE BLACK Hills Trails. Rapid City, 1924. Illus. Orig. cloth.
First edition. Ginsberg 47-270 1983 $125

BLACKBURN, HENRY   The Art of Illustration. Allen, 1894.
1st edn. 95 illus. Red cloth backed dark olive green cloth (name
label fr. ep., bkstrip faded), v.g. copy. Hodgkins 27-558 1983 £25

BLACKBURN, HENRY   Randolph Caldecott; A Personal Memoir
of his Early Art Career. R. Clay for Sampson Low, 1886. 1st ed.,
4to, mounted photographic portrait, illus., green cloth gilt, t.e.g.,
others uncut, slight internal cracking but an excellent copy.
Large paper format. Deighton 3-63 1983 £48

BLACKBURN, HENRY   Randolph Caldecott: A Personal Memoir
of his Early Art Career. New York: George Routledge & Sons, 1886.
First U.S. edition. 8vo. Stamped cloth, a.e.g. Only minor cover
rubbing and soiling, else a very good copy. Oak Knoll 48-26 1983
$55

BLACKBURN, ISAAC WRIGHT   Illustrations of the Gross Morbid
Anatomy of the Brain in the Insane. A Selection of Seventy-Five
Plates... Washington: GPO, 1908. 1st ed. 4to. Morrill 289-18
1983 $37.50

BLACKBURN, PAUL   Proensa. (N.p.): The Divers Press,
(1953). Quarto. Printed wraps. First edition. The wraps. are
slightly soiled, else a fine copy. Reese 20-133 1983 $125

BLACKENBURY, GEORGE   The Campaign in the Crimea. P. & D.
Colnaghi, 1855. With 40 tinted litho plates, including additional
litho title-page, small folio, half calf, a very good copy. Fenning
61-41 1983 £48.50

BLACKER, C. P.   Human Values in Psychological Medicine.
Oxford: Oxford U. Press, 1933. First edition. Library bookplate.
Gach 94-300 1983 $20

BLACKER, V.   Memoir of the Operations of the British
Army in India... London, 1821. 46 maps, many folding and some partially coloured. Title a little browned. 4to. Half modern red
morocco. T.e.g. Good. Edwards 1044-67 1983 £185

BLACKIE, WILLIAM GARDEN   The Personal Life. John Murray, 1880.
First edition, front. port. (foxed). 32 pp ads. Orig. brown cloth.
Jarndyce 30-1054 1983 £28

BLACKMORE, RICHARD   A Critical Dissertation upon the Spleen,
so far as Concerns the Following Question; whether the Spleen is
necessary or useful to the Animal Possess'd of it? Printed for J.
Pemberton, 1725. 8vo, 2 ad. leaves, modern buckram. First edition.
Bickersteth 77-257 1983 £36

BLACKMORE, RICHARD DODDRIDGE Alice Lorraine. A Tale of the South
Downs. London: Sampson, Low, 1875. 3 vols. Mixed set (first ed. of
vol. one, fourth ed. of vol. two, third ed. of vol. three). Library
labels removed from front covers; a .trifle worn. Orig. cloth.
MacManus 277-408 1983 $35

BLACKMORE, RICHARD DODDRIDGE Christowell. A Dartmoor Tale. London"
Sampson, Low, Marston, Searle & Rivington, 1882. First edition.
3 vols. Orig. cloth. All edges and corners worn, covers a bit soiled,
spines faded. Some foxing. Good. MacManus 277-409 1983 $225

BLACKMORE, RICHARD DODDRIDGE Dariel. A Romance of Surrey. Edinburgh:
Blackwood, 1897. First edition. Orig. cloth. MacManus 277-410 1983
$35

BLACKMORE, RICHARD DODRIDGE Dariel. A Romance of Surrey. London:
William Blackwood & Sons, 1897. First edition. Illus. by Chris
Hammond. 8vo. Orig. cloth. A few pencil markings. MacManus 277-412
1983 $35

BLACKMORE, RICHARD DODDRIDGE Lorna Doone: A Romance of Exmoor.
London: Sampson Low, Sone, & Marston, 1869. First edition. 3 vols.
Handsomely rebound in full green morocco, t.e.g., by Riviere. Bookplates. Spines lightly faded to uniform brown. Fine set. MacManus
277-414 1983 $500

BLACKMORE, RICHARD DODDRIDGE Lorna Doone. A Romance of Exmoor. Phila.:
Winston, n.d. First of this edition. 2 vols. Orig. decorated cloth
dust jackets and publisher's slipcase. Very fine. MacManus 277-413
1983 $50

BLACKMORE, RICHARD DODDRIDGE The Maid of Sker. Edinburgh: William
Blackwood & Sons, 1872. First edition. 3 vols. Orig. cloth. Slightly
rubbed at edges. Covers a little stained. Very good. MacManus 277-
415 1983 $350

BLACKMORE, RICHARD DODDRIDGE Mary Anerley, A Yorkshire Tale. London:
Sampson Low, Marston, Searle & Rivington, 1880. First edition. 3 vols.
Orig. blue cloth. Spines and covers slightly worn and darkened. Good.
MacManus 277-416 1983 $350

BLACKMORE, RICHARD DODDRIDGE The Remarkable History of Sir Thomas
Upmore. London: Sampson Low, 1884. First edition. 2 vols. Orig.
cloth. Labels removed from front covers. Vol. two recased with new
endpapers. Spine worn. MacManus 277-418 1983 $50

BLACKMORE, RICHARD DODDRIDGE Slain by the Doones, and other Stories.
N.Y.: Dodd, Mead & Co., 1895. First edition. Illus. title-page.
Orig. decorated cloth. Inner hinges weak. Fine. MacManus 277-419
1983 $50

BLACKMORE, RICHARD DODDRIDGE Springhaven. A Tale of the Great War.
London: Sampson Low, 1887. Third edition. 3 vols. Orig. pictorial
cloth. Spines faded and worn. Small institutional stamp on a few
preliminaries. Good set. MacManus 277-421 1983 $50

BLACKMORE, RICHARD DODDRIDGE Springhaven. A Tale of the Great War.
London: Sampson Low, Marston, Searle, & Rivington, 1888. First illus.
edition. Illus. by Alfred Parsons & F. Barnard. Slight soiling of the
backstrip. Fine. MacManus 277-420 1983 $75

BLACKMUR, R. P.   The Double Agent. NY, (1935). Minor ink
underling, tiny tear to top spine edge, else very good, owner's name.
Quill & Brush 54-114 1983 $35

BLACKSTONE, WILLIAM   An Analysis of the Laws of England.
Oxford, 1762. 5th ed. Half-title. 1st and only ed. to have postscript concerning Blackstone's Vinerian professorship. Bit of occasional spotting, but quite clean, bound in full contemp. calf, little
worn, newly rebacked, orig. spine, elaborately gilt, expertly laid down,
orig. crimsom morocco label, double gilt-ruled & lettered, orig. marbled endpapers, preserved. Boswell 7-21 1983 $350

BLACKSTONE, WILLIAM   Commentaries on the Laws of England.
London, 1825. 4 vols., 16th ed., only ed. by John Taylor Coleridge.
Bit of spotting throughout. Newly and uniformly bound in quarter
calf over grey boards, spines with contrasting crimson and black
labels, double gilt ruled and lettered. Boswell 7-22 1983 $375

BLACKSTONE, WILLIAM   Commentaries on the Laws of England.
Chicago, 1979. 4 vols. 1st ed. in facsimile. Boswell 7-23 1983
$100

BLACKWELL, THOMAS   Forma Sacra. Boston, 1774. Leather,
chipped at backstrip edges. Very good. Reese 18-100 1983 $45

BLACKWOOD, ALGERNON   The Human Chord. London: Macmillan,
1910. First edition. Orig. cloth. Scarce. MacManus 277-424 1983
$45

BLACKWOOD, ALGERNON   Pan's Garden. London: Macmillan & Co.,
1912. First edition. Drawings by W. Graham Robertson. Orig. decorated cloth. Fine. MacManus 277-429 1983 $35

BLACKWOOD, ALGERNON   A Prisoner in FairyLand. London: Macmillan, 1913. First edition. Orig. cloth. Near-fine. MacManus
277-427 1983 $25

BLACKWOOD, ALGERNON   Stange Stories. London: William Heinemann Ltd., (1929). First edition. Orig. cloth. Dust jacket (top of
spine slightly chipped). Fine. MacManus 277-428 1983 $35

BLACKWOOD, ALGERNON   The Wave, an Egyptian Aftermath. London:
Macmillan and Co., 1916. First edition. Orig. cloth. Edges and corners slightly worn. Inscription on front free endpaper. Fore-edges
of all pages dampstained, very slightly affecting some margins. Mac-
Manus 277-429 1983 $45

BLACKWOOD, VERNON   The Fringe of an Art. London, (1898).
8vo. Cloth. This copy inscribed by author to the composer Arthur
Sullivan, November 25, 1898. Cloth faded on spine, name on half-
title page, else a very good copy. In Our Time 156-82 1983 $100

BLADES, WILLIAM   The Enemies of Books. London:
Trubner & Co., 1881. Third edition. 8vo. Orig. parchment wrapper
over paper covers. Seven plates. Covers soiled with part of the
covering of the spine missing. Oak Knoll 48-27 1983 £45

BLAGDEN, CHARLES   Experiments on the Cooling of Water Below
Its Freezing Point... (Read at the Royal Society, Jan. 31, 1788).
Orig. offprint, 4to, title page, entirely uncut, unopened and unsewn,
a remarkable copy. Pickering & Chatto 22-15 1983 $250

BLAGDEN, CHARLES   Experiments on the Effect of Various
Substances in Lowering the Point of Congelation in Water. (Read at
the Royal Society, April 24, 1788). Orig. offprint, 4to, 1 blank
leaf, stab sewn in the orig. plain paper wrapper, a fine copy. Pickering & Chatto 22-16 1983 $350

BLAGDEN, CYPRIAN   Fire More Than Water... London:
Longmans, Green and Co., (1949). First edition. 8vo. Stiff
paper wrappers. Illus. Light foxing throughout. Oak Knoll 48-
254 1983 $20

BLAGDON, F. W.   An Historical Momento. London, 1814.
4to. 6 finely hand-coloured aquatint plates (virtually no offsetting).
Orig. cloth. Half red morocco. Some slight wear. Fine. Edwards
1042 1983 £450

BLAIR, HENRY WILLIAM   The Temperance Movement. Boston, 1888.
Orig. pict. stamped cloth. Illus. Ex lib. Argosy 716-529 1983
$35

BLAIR, HUGH   Lectures on Rhetoric and Belles
Lettres. London: for A. Strahan; T. Cadell; and W. Creech, 1790.
Fourth edition. 3 vols. 8vo. Cont. calf, gilt spines with morocco
labels, gilt. Portrait. Traylen 94-75 1983 £35

BLAIR, ROBERT   The Grave... London: by T. Bensley,
1808. First edition. Folio. Cont. half blue morocco, gilt, gilt
panelled spine, edges gilt. Portrait of William Blake by Schiavonetti, etched title-page, and 11 plates by Schiavonetti after Blake.
Traylen 94-76 1983 £580

BLAISDELL, F. E.   Monographic Revision of Coleoptera.
U.S. Nat. Mus. Bull, 1909. 13 plates, 8vo, wrappers. Wheldon 160-
1030 1983 £15

BLAKE, CHARLES   An Historical Account of the Providence
Stage. Providence, RI: George H. Whitney, 1868. Cloth. Dawson 471-
317 1983 $25

BLAKE, E. R.   Manual of Neotropical Birds. Chicago,
1977. Vol. 1. 12 coloured and plain plates, 68 text-figures and 237
distribution maps, royal 8vo, cloth. Wheldon 160-652 1983 £40

BLAKE, ELI E.   Original Solutions of Several Problems
in Aerodynamics. New Haven, 1882. First edition. Cloth. Jenkins
152-779a 1983 $125

BLAKE, J. P.   The Money God. London: William Heinemann, 1904. First edition. Orig. pictorial cloth. Covers very slightly soiled. Endpapers browned. Some light foxing. Former owner's
signature. Good. MacManus 277-430 1983 $30

BLAKE, JOHN WILLIAM   Europeans in west Africa, 1450-1560.
London: Hakluyt Soc., 1942. 2 vols. 8vo. 3 maps. Orig. blue
cloth. Ex-lib. Adelson Africa-167 1983 $40

BLAKE, LUCIUS O'BRIEN   Rich and Rare, a Tale of Anglo-Italian
Life. T. Cautley Newby, 1870. First edition. 2 vols., 2 vols. bound
as one. Orig. green remainder cloth, rubbed and inner hinges repaired.
Jarndyce 30-304 1983 £18.50

BLAKE, WILLIAM   All Religions Are One. (Paris: Trianon
Press, 1970). Facs. repro. by William Blake Trust. Quarto, full green
morocco, matching leather tipped slipcase. With ten plates in color.
One of 36 copies (of an edition of 630) containing a set of proofs
showing the progressive stages of collotype printing of the plates.
Duschnes 240-23 1983 $375

BLAKE, WILLIAM   The Book of Ahania. London: Trianon
Press, 1973. Quarto, leather back with marbled sides, slipcase to
match. With six plates, three in color. One of 750 copies.
Duschnes 240-24 1983 $95

BLAKE, WILLIAM   The Book of Los. Paris: Trianon
Press, 1976. Quarto, half morocco with marbled boards, matching
slipcase. With five plates, four in color. One of 480 copies.
Duschnes 240-26 1983 $100

BLAKE, WILLIAM   The Book of Thel. Paris: The Trianon
Press, 1965. Quarto, half morocco, marbled boards, matching slipcase.
With eight plates in color. One of 426 copies. Duschnes 240-22
1983 $275

BLAKE, WILLIAM   The Complete Portraiture of William
and Catherine Blake. Paris, Trianon Press, 1977. Folio, 52 monochrome
collotype illustrations. 36 specials in full morocco and slip-case.
With an essay and iconography by Geoffrey Kenes, who also signed
copy. Deighton 3-41 1983 £125

BLAKE, WILLIAM   The Complete Writings of William Blake.
London: The Nonesuch Press, 1957. Two-tone cloth. Fine copy.
Karmiole 75-24 1983 $35

BLAKE, WILLIAM   Compositions from the Works, Days and
Theogony of Hesiod. London, et al., 1817. Designed by John Flaxman.
Engraved by William Blake. Oblong folio, 38 engraved plates (incl.
half-title & pictorial title). Half black pebbled morocco, gilt &
marbled boards. 1st ed. Very fine. O'Neal 50-7 1983 $650

BLAKE, WILLIAM   Eight Songs. N.Y.: (William Edwin
Rudge), 1926. 8vo. Orig. boards. Limited to 200 copies. Extremities of spine worn. MacManus 277-431 1983 $30

BLAKE, WILLIAM   Jerusalem. London: the Chiswick Press,
1904. First edition. 4to. Boards, gilt, uncut edges. Traylen 94-
78 1983 £18

BLAKE, WILLIAM   Jerusalem the emanation of the giant
Albion. Paris, Trianon Press (1951). Folio, 5 fascicles, hand-
coloured collotype plates, half-page plates; uncut in original paper
wrappers with printed paper labels, contained in original folding
box of quarter cloth over blue paper boards. Very slight wear to the
box, very slight marginal spotting of the introductory fascicle,
but a fine copy. 516 numbered copies only. One of 250 copies for
distribution in England. Deighton 3-31 1983 £1,500

BLAKE, WILLIAM   Jerusalem. London: The William
Blake Trust, 1951. Quarto, cloth, enclosed in board and cloth
folding box. 100 plates of which 10 are full-page, 45 half-page
water colors and 45 decorated with color designs. An average of
44 applications of color by hand required for each page. One of
500 copies. Accompanied by a commentary by Joseph Widksteed, 8vo,
bound in cloth with 28 illus. Duschnes 240-17 1983 $1,850

BLAKE, WILLIAM   Jerusalem. New York: The Beechhurst
Press, (1955). 8vo. Leather. 1st complete ed. A fine copy. In
Our Time 156-83 1983 $100

BLAKE, WILLIAM   Jerusalem. Trianon Press, 1974. 4to,
25 colour facsimiles and 4 others. 32 specials in full morocco and
slip case. 500 copies in quarter morocco over marbled boards,
contained in slip-case. Deighton 3-32 1983 £260

BLAKE, WILLIAM　　　　Land of Dreams. N.Y., Macmillan, 1928. First edition. Full page b/w plates and text designs by Bianco. Dust jacket (tear), else very good. Houle 21-111　1983　$20

BLAKE, WILLIAM　　　　Laocoon, a last testament. Paris, Trianon Press, 1976. Sm. folio, 12 colour facsimiles. 32 specials in full morocco and slip-case. Deighton 3-40　1983　£80

BLAKE, WILLIAM　　　　The Marriage of Heaven and Hell. Paris: The Trianon Press, 1960. Folio, half green higer morocco, marbled board sides with matching slipcase. With twenty-seven plates in color. One of 526 copies. Duschnes 240-21　1983　$400

BLAKE, WILLIAM　　　　The Marriage of Heaven & Hell. Paris, Trianon Press, 1960. Folio, 27 colour facsimiles, quarter green morocco gilt, marbled paper boards, t.e.g., very slight internal crack, fine in slip-case. 480 numbered copies. Deighton 3-33　1983　£230

BLAKE, WILLIAM　　　　Milton: A Poem. (London: The Trianon Press for the William Blake Trust 1967). Folio. The facs. edition. 50 leaves facs, all printed in color by collotype and stencil. Printed in brown, with 1 facs. plate. Edition ltd. to 426 numbered copies, printed on Arches pure rag paper. Half calf over marbled boards; with matching slipcase. Fine copy. Karmiole 75-25　1983　$300

BLAKE, WILLIAM　　　　The Note-Book of William Blake called the Rossetti Manuscript. London: the Nonesuch Press, 1935. Small 4to. Buckram, morocco label, gilt. Limited edition of 350 copies, with 120 pages in facsimile. Traylen 94-79　1983　£110

BLAKE, WILLIAM　　　　Pencil Drawings. London: the Nonesuch Press, 1927. Half buckram, uncut edges. Limited edition of 1500 numbered copies. 82 plates. Traylen 94-80　1983　£90

BLAKE, WILLIAM　　　　Pencil Drawings. Nonesuch Press, 1956. Second series. 4to, cloth, uncut, fine in black and gold dustwrapper. 1440 numbered copies. Deighton 3-42　1983　£45

BLAKE, WILLIAM　　　　The Poetical Works of William Blake. London, Oxford University, 1913. First edition. 16 illus. 3/4 green calf over green cloth; spine stamped in gilt and blind (slightly faded), edges marbled. Very good - fine. Houle 22-108　1983　$95

BLAKE, WILLIAM　　　　The Song of Los. (Paris: Trianon Press, 1975). Folio, half morocco, with marbled paper sides, matching slipcase. Eight plates in color. One of 400 copies. Duschnes 240-25　1983　$250

BLAKE, WILLIAM　　　　The Songs of Innocence. (Paris: The Trianon Press, 1954). 8vo, full orange morocco, t.e.g., slipcase. With 31 color plates. One of 800 copies. Duschnes 240-19　1983　$175

BLAKE, WILLIAM　　　　Songs of Innocence. London: Trianon Press for the Blake Trust, 1954. 1st ed. thus. Orig. full morocco, marbled box. Of 1,600 copies, this is 1 of 800 numbered copies for the U.S.A. Fine copy of this fine facsimile of the superior Rosenwald copy of the orig. 1789 ed. published by Blake himself. Jenkins 155-93　1983　$125

BLAKE, WILLIAM　　　　Songs of Innocence. (London: Trianon Press, 1954). Orig. calf-backed boards (rubbed). One of 1600 numbered copies. This facsimile was made from the Rosenwald copy. Bibliographical statement by Geoffrey Keynes. Slipcased. MacManus 277-434　1983　$75

BLAKE, WILLIAM　　　　Visions of the Daughters of Albion, 1793. London: Trianon Press, 1959. Folio, cockerell marbled paper sides, half niger morocco, g.t., matching slipcase. With 11 plates reproduced in facs. One of 400 copies. Duschnes 240-20　1983　$200

BLAKE, WILLIAM　　　　Water Colour Designs for the Poems of Thomas Gray. London, 1972. Folio. Handcolored facs. of 116 designs by Blake. Half tan morocco (sm stain on one spine). Enclosed in morocco edges slipcases (one cracked), else fine. 3 vols. One of 518 copies by the Trianon Press. Houle 21-115　1983　$600

BLAKE, WILLIAM　　　　The Works of William Blake. London: Bernard Quaritch, 1893. 3 vols. Rebound in quarter leather, top edges gilt, all others untrimmed. A large paper copy of the ed. Total ed. was 150 copies. As no formal colophon page exists indicating the large paper, the most conclusive is sheet size. Reg. issue is 10 x 6-1/4. This large issue is 11 x 7-3/8. Some light scuffing to leather, mainly a fine set. In Our Time 156-908　1983　$1200

BLAKE, WILLIAM P.　　　　The Discovery of Tin Ore in the Black Hills, Dakota. N.Y., 1883. Half morocco. Ginsberg 47-269　1983　$75

BLAKEBOROUGH, JOHN F. FAIRFAX　　　Sporting Days and Sporting Stories of Turf and Chase. Philip Allan, 1925. First edition, roy. 8vo, orig. cloth, gilt. A very good copy. Fenning 60-30　1983　£12.50

BLAKEWELL, ROBERT　　　　An Introduction to Geology... London, 1833. 8vo. Old half-calf. Frontis. 8 plates (2 coloured) and illus. in text. Presentation inscription to Dr. Park, with bookplate of J.R. Park, M.D. Gurney JJ-17　1983　£25

BLAKEY, DOROTHY　　　　The Minerva Press, 1790-1820. London: Bibliographical Society, 1939. First edition. Square 8vo. Cloth-backed boards. A fine unopened copy. Oak Knoll 48-462　1983　$150

BLAKEY, ROBERT　　　　Hints on angling... London: Robinson, 1846. First edition. 8vo. Orig. green cloth, spine decorated in gilt. Fine copy. Ximenes 63-552　1983　$150

BLAKEY, ROBERT　　　　The history of political literature... London: Richard Bentley, 1855. First edition. 2 vols. 8vo. Orig. red cloth. A fine copy. Ximenes 63-459　1983　$175

BLAKISTON, J.　　　　Twelve Years' Military Adventure... London, 1829. 2 vols. A little spotting of a few early pages. Half calf. 8vo. Good. Edwards 1044-71　1983　£100

BLAN VAN URK, J.　　　　The Story of American Foxhunting: From Challenge to Full Cry. The Derrydale Press, New York, 1940. 4to. Cloth, leather labels. 2 vols. 1 of 950 sets. A fine copy. In Our Time 156-198　1983　$500

BLANC, HENRY　　　　A Narrative of Captivity in Abyssinia. London, 1868. 8 engraved plates, half calf, spine worn. 8vo. Good. Edwards 1044-72　1983　£50

BLANCH, WILLIAM HARNETT　　　The Blue-Coat Boys. London, 1877. First edition. Frontispiece. 12mo, original boards with colored pictorial front cover, nice. Morrill 290-41　1983　$27.50

BLANCHAN, NELTJE　　　　Birds That Hunt And Are Hunted. Garden City, 1912. Color and b/w photos, cloth, spine lettering worn off, spine ends and corners well worn, 1 illus. loose. King 46-543　1983　$25

BLANCHARD, AMY　　　　When Mother was a Little Girl. London: Nister; N.Y.: Dutton, n.d. (ca.1900). Sq. 8vo. Cloth. Pictorial paste-on. Illus. by Waugh with chromolithographs, most full-page. Victorian colorplate. Near fine. Aleph-bet 8-259　1983　$80

BLANCHARD, JEAN PIERRE　　　The First Air Voyage in America... Philadelphia, Penn Mutual, 1943. First edition. Illus. Tan cloth printed in blue. TLS from the editor laid in loose. Very good. Houle 22-1013　1983　$27.50

BLANCHARD, STEPHEN　　　Lexikon Medicum Graeco-Latino-Germanicum. Francofurti ad Viachum: Henrici Georg. Muselii, 1705. Fourth edition. 12mo in 8's. Contemp. green marbled boards. Boards a trifle rubbed. Very good copy. Gach 94-109　1983　$75

BLANCHET, AUGUSTIN M. A.　　　Voyage de l'eveque de Walla-Walla. Quebec, 1851. Number 9. Original printed wrappers bound in. Folding map repaired. Jenkins 153-50　1983　$125

BLANCHET, FRANCOIS N.　　　Memoire Presente a la S. Congregation de la Propaganda sur le Territoire de l' Oregon... Quebec, 1847. Laid in slipcase. Jenkins 153-448　1983　$150

BLANCK, JACOB   Peter Parley to Penrod. N.Y.: 1938.
First edition. Sm. 8vo, cloth, gilt. One of 500 copies. A very good
copy. Perata 28-7 1983 $135

BLANCK, JACOB   Peter Parley to Penrod, a Bibliographical Description... New York: R.R. Bowker Co., 1938. First
edition. 8vo. Cloth. Limited to 500 copies. Some cover wear
at spine extremities. Oak Knoll 49-430 1983 $75

BLANCO, MARIO   Gli affreschi di Pietro Paolo Vasta
nelle antiche chiese di Acireale. N.p.: Cassa Centrale di Risparmio
V.E. per le Province Siciliane, n.d. 24 color plates. 13 text
illus. (2 color). Folio. Boards. Dusty. Ars Libri 33-379 1983
$75

BLAND, HENRY MEADE   Like Dawn Sierran. SF, 1937 A
Sonnet Sequence. 8vo, cloth-backed decorated bds., paper labels,
plain d/w. One of 250 copies with initials in red. A pristine
copy. Prospectus laid in. Perata 28-50 1983 $50

BLAND, HUBERT   Essays. Mac Groschen, 1914. Portrait.
Blue cloth, gilt. Presentation from E. Nesbit to F. Evans. Orig.
Beardsley bookplate for Evans. Fascinating associations. Greer 40-
151 1983 £45

BLAND, J.   An Essay in Praise of Women. Edinburgh:
Printed for, and sold by W. Darling, 1767. 12mo, modern marbled boards
with calf spine, new end papers. Bickersteth 75-7 1983 £110

BLAND, ROBERT   The Four Slaves of Cythera. Longman,
Hurst, 1809. First edition, half title, calf, leading hinge
weakening, red label. Jarndyce 30-649 1983 £24

BLANDFORD, G. FIELDING   Insanity and its Treatment. Philadelphia:
Henry C. Lea, 1871. Orig. mauve cloth, shelfworn. First edition.
With summary by Isaac Ray. Gach 95-415 1983 $50

BLANDING, DON   Today is Here. New York, 1946.
8vo. Cloth. Illustrated by the author. Reviews of the book pasted
on the front endboard. A fine copy in dj. In Our Time 156-86 1983
$25

BLANE, WILLIAM   Cynegetica: or Essays on Sporting:
consisting of Observations on Hare Hunting. London: Stockdale,
1788. 3rd (first complete) edition, 8vo, modern half morocco gilt,
a.e.g., marbled boards. Engraved title page and frontis., errata
leaf, advertisements. One corner lightly dampstained thoughout,
not touching text; a very good copy. Trebizond 18-196 1983 $125

BLANEY, HENRY R.   Old Boston: a Poem. Boston, 1896.
8vo, sewed, half tone, plates, small 4to, dec. cloth (somewhat
darkened). A.e.g. Argosy 710-29 1983 $25

BLANFORD, W. T.   Scientific Results of the Second
Yarkand Mission: Geology. Calcutta, 1878. 12 diagrams, 4to, wrappers. Wheldon 160-1360 1983 £15

BLATCHFORD, AMBROSE N.   Idylls of Old Greece. Bristol: J.W.
Arrowsmith, (c. 1890). First edition, half title, orig. brown
cloth, fine. Jarndyce 30-650 1983 £8.50

BLATCHFORD, SAMUEL   Elements of the Greek Language. NY 1807.
12mo, calf, scuffed. Argosy 710-474 1983 $25

BLATTY, WILLIAM P.   The Exorcist. New York: Harper &
Row, (n.d.). Small quarto. Spiral bound wraps., paper label.
Uncorrected proofs of the first edition. Fine. Reese 20-136 1983
$100

BLAU, ABRAM   The Master Hand. NY: 1946. Good to
very good ex-library copy. Gach 95-46 1983 $25

BLEACKLEY, HORACE   The Monster. London: William Heinemann,
1920. First edition. Orig. cloth. Dust jacket (somewhat rubbed at
edges). Inscribed "With kind regards from Horace Bleackley" on the
front flyleaf. Numerous holograph corrections in the margins, possibly
in the author's hand. Rear inner hinge cracked. Near-fine. MacManus
277-436 1983 $45

BLEACKLEY, HORACE   Some Distinguished Victims of the
Scaffold. London: 1905. First edition. Frontis., 20 other full-
page plates. Blue cloth, gilt top edges, others uncut. Extremities
worn but very good copy. Bradley 66-413 1983 $37.50

BLEEKER, P.   Memoire sur les Cyprinoides de Chine.
Amsterdam, 1871. 14 plates, 4to, wrappers (rebacked). Wheldon
160-941 1983 £18

BLESSINGTON, CHARLES JOHN GARDINER, 1ST EARL OF BLESSINGTON   De
Vavasour. Henry Colburn, 1826. First edition, 3 vols. Ex-library
copy, a little marked internally. Sturdy half brown morocco.
Jarndyce 30-395 1983 £68

BLESSINGTON, MARGUERITE POWER FARMER GARDINER, COUNTESS OF   The Con-
fessions of an Elderly Gentleman. London: Longman, Rees, Orme, Brown,
& Longman, 1836. First edition. Illus. by Six Female Portraits, from
Highly Finished drawings by E. T. Parris. Cont. 3/4 morocco & cloth.
Bookplates. Some foxing. Very good. MacManus 277-437 1983 $185

BLESSINGTON, MARGUERITE POWER FARMER GARDINER, COUNTESS OF   Conversations of Lord Byron with the Countess of Blessington. London: published for Henry Colburn, R. Bentley, 1834. First edition. 8vo. Orig.
drab boards and patterned brown cloth spine, printed paper label. Portrait. Some rubbing, label a bit soiled. Scarce. Ximenes 63-42 1983
$250

BLESSINGTON, MARGUERITE POWER FARMER GARDINER, COUNTESS OF   Heath's
Book of Beauty. 1834. Longman, Rees, (1833). First edition, with
19 engr. plates (including additional engr. title-pages). 8vo. A
little tired, but thoroughly sound. A very good copy in orig. pub's.
dark green morocco, gilt, edges gilt, by F. Westley, with his ticket.
Fenning 60-31 1983 £21.50

BLESSINGTON, MARGUERITE POWER FARMER GARDINER, COUNTESS OF   The
Literary Life and Correspondence of... 1855. First edition. 3 vols.
Frontis. Half dark blue morocco, spines gilt, t.e.g. Very good.
Jarndyce 30-895 1983 £52

BLESSINGTON, MARGUERITE POWER FARMER GARDINER, COUNTESS OF   The
Literary Life and Correspondence... T. C. Newby, 1855. First edition.
3 vols. Rebound in green moire-patterned cloth, labels. Jarndyce
30-896 1983 £32

BLEULER, MANFRED   Der Rorschachsihe Formdeutversuch Bei
Geschwistern. Berlin: Julius Springer, 1928. Gach 95-52 1983 $30

BLEULER, PAUL EUGEN (1857-1939)   Das Autisch-undisziplinierte
Denken in der Medizin und seine Ueberwindung. (1920). Inscribed
"mit freundl. gruesse vom vf." Gach 95-47 1983 $75

BLEULER, PAUL EUGEN (1857-1939)   Diagnostischen Assoziationstudien.
Leipzig: Johann A. Barth. Orig. printed orange wrappers. Inscribed
"(?) gruesse d. V." Gach 95-48 1983 $75

BLEULER, PAUL EUGEN (1857-1939)   The Theory of Schizophrenic Nega-
tivism. NY: N. M. D. Publishing Co., 1912. Orig. printed brown
wrappers. Very fine copy. Gach 95-49 1983 $150

BLIGH, NEVILLE MELTON   The Evolution and Development of the
Quantum Theory. London: Edward Arnold, 1926. 8vo. Orig. cloth
with gilt. Frontis. portrait of Planck, 6 text figures. First
edition. Slightly rubbed and shook. Very good copy. Zeitlin 264-
51 1983 $50

BLIND, MATHILDE   George Eliot. W.H. Allen, 1883. 2nd
edition, half title, ad slip. Orig. dark green cloth a little
rubbed. Jarndyce 30-983 1983 £10.50

THE BLIND Made Happy. New York, 1837. 2 engraved plates plus 2
raised-letter plates. Cloth. Waterstain through the interior
and cover wear, but a sound copy. First edition. Felcone 22-17
1983 $50

BLISS, ARTHUR AMES   Theodore Bliss, publisher and bookseller. N.p.: Northampton Historical society, 1941. 8vo. Cloth-
backed boards. Limited to 1000 copies. Oak Knoll 48-28 1983
$25

BLISS, CAREY   Catalogue of Books & Manuscripts in the
Estelle Doheny Collection. Los Angeles: The Ward Ritchie Press, 1955.
Plates, some in color. Cloth. One of 100 copies printed at the
Ritchie Press. Dawson 470-30 1983 $100

BLISS, CAREY   The First School Book Printed in California. Los Angeles: The Zamorano Club, 1976. Cloth. Facsimile reproduction. Printed on all-rag handmade paper. Dawson 471-24 1983 $75

BLISS, ELIOT   Luminous Isle. London, 1934. First
edition. Author's signed autograph presentation inscription to John
Hampson. Good. Rota 230-73 1983 £12

BLISS, FRANK C.   St. Paul, Its Past and Present.
St. Paul, 1888. Illus., covers rubbed and moderately stained.
King 46-207 1983 $20

BLISS, GEORGE N.   First R.I. Cavalry at Middleburg,
Va., June 17 and 18, 1863. Providence, 1889. Orig. printed wraps.
First edition. One of 250 copies. Ginsberg 46-768 1983 $25

BLISS, GEORGE N.   Prison Life of Lieut. James M. Fales.
Providence, 1882. Orig. printed wraps. First edition. One of 250
copies. Ginsberg 46-252 1983 $25

BLITH, WALTER   The English Improover, or a New Survey
of Husbandry. London: I. Wright, 1649. Small 4to. Boards. Cont.
ms. exlibris of Thomas Pury. First edition. Fine. Kraus 164-26
1983 $350

BLOCH, GEORGES   Pablo Picasso: Catalogue de l'oeuvre
grave et lithographie. Berne: Kornfeld et Klipstein, 1971-1979.
4 vols. More than 2500 illus. (numerous color). Large 4to. Cloth.
Dust jacket. Ars Libri 32-514 1983 $400

BLOCH, M. E.   Histoire Naturelle des Poissons. Paris,
An IX (1801). Plates, 10 vols., 12mo, cont. half calf (somewhat
rubbed). Lacks a plates in vol. 9. Some slight waterstaining.
Wheldon 160-942 1983 £140

BLOCHMAN, LAWRENCE   See You at the Morgue. N.Y., Duell,
Sloan, (1941). First edition. Dust jacket (small tears, rubbed),
else very good. Houle 22-114 1983 $45

BLOCK, ANDREW   The Book Collector's Vade Mecum. The
Mitre Press, 1938. With illus., 8vo, orig. cloth, a very good to
nice copy in the dust wrapper. Second edition. Fenning 61-34
1983 £28.50

BLOGG, MINNIE WRIGHT   Bibliography of the Writings of Sir
William Osler. Baltimore, 1921. First edition. 8vo. Orig. binding.
Fye H-3-1016 1983 $50

BLOIS, JOHN T.   Gazetteer of the State of Michigan.
Detroit, 1838. Errata slip. Cloth. A rather worn copy, with some
spotting and slightly pulled signatures, but a sound copy. First
edition. Felcone 21-74 1983 $150

BLOIS, JOHN T.   Gazetteer of the State of Michigan.
Detroit: Sydney L. Rood & Co., 1840. Original cloth, spine neatly
repaired. Jenkins 151-210 1983 $200

BLOME, RICHARD   Hawking, or Faulconry. (London): The
Cresset Press, 1929. Small 4to, folding frontis. Illus. Edition
ltd. to 650 copies. Parchment-backed boards. Fine copy in a
chipped dust jacket. Karmiole 71-21 1983 $100

BLOMFIELD, CHARLES J.   A Letter on the Present Neglect of the
Lord's Day Addressed to the Inhabitants of London and Westminster.
For B. Fellowes, 1830. Third edition. 8vo, wrapper. Fenning 61-35
1983 £18.50

BLONDUS, FLAVIUS (1388-1463) De Roma Instaurata...de Italia
Illustrata... 1527. Lacks final blank (?), woodcut initials, a
few patches of worm affecting some letters, a bit age-marked, a
bit shaken, old boards. K Books 22-24 1983 £140

BLOOMFIELD, PAUL   The Traveller's Companion. London,
1931. First English edition. 7 black and white decorations and
coloured frontis. by Rex Whistler. Inscription. Spine and cover
edges faded. Slightly worn and torn dustwrapper by Rex Whistler.
Very good. Jolliffe 26-590 1983 £16

BLOOMFIELD, ROBERT   The Banks of Wye. London: for the
Author, 1811. First edition. Small 8vo. Boards, uncut edges, new
cloth spine and paper label. 4 plates (a little spotted). Traylen
94-85 1983 £25

BLOOMFIELD, ROBERT   The Horkey. London: Macmillan, 1882.
Octavo. Full-page color illus. Cloth-backed pictorial boards rubbed
at extremities, front endpaper loose. Small chromolithographed
greeting card glued to front cover. Nice copy. Owner's signature.
Bromer 25-337 1983 $75

BLOOMFIELD, ROBERT   The Horkey. Macmillan, 1882. Illus.
by George Cruikshank, Jr. Each page inc. title illus. in colour.
Printed by Richard Clay Sons & Taylor. Colour pictorial bds., corners
of bds. sl. worn, sl. foxing eps & cvrs., half title & last page some
discolouration, vg copy. Hodgkins 27-12 1983 £25

BLOOMFIELD, ROBERT   Rural Tales, Ballads and Songs.
London: Printed for Vernor and Hood, Poultry; and Longman and Rees,
Paternoster-Row, 1802. 1st ed., 8vo, cont. marbled boards, frontis.
of the author, half-title. Eleven original woodcut engravings by
Thomas Bewick. Except for small tear in the margin of one leaf, a
very good copy. Trebizond 18-9 1983 $150

BLOOMFIELD, ROBERT   Views in Suffolk, Norfolk, and Northhamp-
tonshire... London, 1806. 8vo. Uncut in orig. boards. Tall copy.
Engr. plates. One joint repaired. Fine. Heath 48-245 1983 £45

BLOOMFIELD, ROBERT   Wild Flowers. London, 1806. First
edition. Small 8vo. Cont. tree calf, rebacked. Scarce. Traylen
94-87 1983 £25

BLOOMINGDALE HOSPITAL   A Phychiatric Milestone. MY: 1921.
Unopened copy. Gach 94-110 1983 $30

BLOOMSTER, EDGAR L.   Sailing and Small Craft Down the Ages.
Annapolis, 1940. 1st ed. Drawings by author. 4to, orig. buckram
leather back. Morrill 287-548 1983 $35

BLOOMSTER, EDGAR L.   Sailing and Small Craft. Annapolis:
USNI, 1941. Illus. by author, limited to 700 numbered and signed
copies bound for US Naval Institute, fine, bookplate. Quill & Brush
54-1653 1983 $50

BLOUET, PAUL   A Frenchman in America. New York,
(1891). Illus. by E.W. Kemble. Cloth (spine lettering a bit dull).
Felcone 22-18 1983 $30

BLOUET, PAUL   A Frenchman in America. New York,
(1891). 1st American ed. Illus. by E.W. Kemble. Clark 741-15
1983 $25

BLOUNT, BERTRAM   Practical Electro-Chemistry. London:
Constable, 1901. 8vo. Orig. maroon cloth with gilt. Text illus.
Ads. Very good internally. Zeitlin 264-52 1983 $40

BLOUNT, THOMAS   Glossographia. Printed by Tho. Newcomb,
1670. Third edition. Calf, well rebacked and corners repaired.
Inscriptions, uncluding that of Mary Bromfield, January. Jarndyce
31-1 1983 £150

BLOXAM, CHARLES LOUDON   Chemistry, Organic and Inorganic,
With Experiments. London: Churchill, 1875. Third edition.
8vo. Cont. half calf. Numerous text illus. Very good copy.
Zeitlin 264-53 1983 $45

BLOXAM, CHARLES LONDON   Laboratory Teaching, or Progressive
Exercises in Practical Chemistry. London: Churchill, 1886. Orig.
cloth. 8vo. Inside hinge detached, spine slightly chipped.
Zeitlin 264-54 1983 $20

BLUME, C. L. DE   Flora Javae nec non Insularum Adjacentium. Brussels, 1828-51, 1862-97. 3 vols, folio, half green morocco, 238 plates. A fine clean copy of this rare work. Wheldon 160-8a 1983 £2,800

BLUME, C. L. DE   Rumphia. Leyden, 1835-48. 4 vols. in 3, portrait, 2 frontis., 12 views, 36 plain and 162 hand-coloured plates, half green morocco. A fine complete copy of this rare work. Wheldon 160-9 1983 £3,500

BLUMENBACH, JOHANN FRIEDRICH De Nisu Formativo et Generationis negotio numperae Observationes. Gottingen: J.C. Dieterich, 1787. First edition. 4to. Boards. 2 plates. Gurney 90-14 1983 £50

BLUMENBACH, JOHANN FRIEDRICH De Oculus Leucaethiopum et Iridis Motu Commentatio. Gottingen, 1786. First edition. 4to. Boards. 1 hand-coloured plate. Margin of title lightly dust-soiled. Gurney 90-15 1983 £115

BLUMENBACH, JOHANN FRIEDRICH Prolusio Anatomica de Sinibus Frontalibus. Gottingen: J.C. Dieterich, 1779. First edition. 4to. Boards. One plate. Foxed. Gurney 90-16 1983 £40

BLUMENTHAL, JOSEPH   Art of the Printed Book: 1455-1955. New York: 1973. 125 full-page illus. Folio, cloth. First edition. Very fine in dust jacket. Bradley 66-37 $75

BLUMENTHAL, JOSEPH   The Printed Book in America. Boston (1977). Quarto, cloth, dust-jacket. 70 full-page illus., with 32 in color. Duschnes 240-28 1983 $30

BLUNDELL, JAMES   The Principles and Practice of Obstetricy. Washington, 1834. First American edition. Thick 8vo, cont. calf. Illus. by Thomas Castle. Back cover mended. Argosy 713-65 1983 $100

BLUNDELL, JAMES   Researches Physiological and Pathological. London, 1825. 8vo. Orig. boards, rebacked. 3 plates. Ownership inscription of Sir Charles Sherrington. Some foxing; a few old library stamps. Gurney 90-17 1983 £275

BLUNDEN, EDMUND   After The Bombing And Other Short Poems. London: Macmillan & Co., 1949. First edition, advance review copy with the publisher's slip loosely laid in. Orig. red cloth. Presentation copy inscribed: "To one who can annotate the stanzas on pp. 43-5 as a bowler and a Gloucester lad, from a Sussex lobster. Leonard (Clark) from Edmund, on a very notable evening. 6 August 1957. Near-fine. MacManus 277-441 1983 $100

BLUNDEN, EDMUND   After the Bombing. London: Macmillan & Co., 1949. First edition, publisher's advance copy. Orig. cloth. Dust jacket (spine and covers somewhat faded and slightly worn). With some offsetting to back free endpaper. Very good. MacManus 277-440 1983 $35

BLUNDEN, EDMUND   The Augustan Books of Modern Poetry. London: Ernest Benn, (1925). First edition. Orig. printed wrappers. Presentation copy inscribed: "Inscribed a little belatedly for Leonard (Clark) by his poetical companion Edmund: Summer evening, 6 viii '57." Covers a trifle soiled. Very Good. MacManus 277-549 1983 $85

BLUNDEN, EDMUND   "A Ballad Of Titles". (N.p.: Privately Printed), Christmas 1937. First separate edition. 4 pages. Presentation copy from the Blundens to the Sassoons inscribed: "With love from Edmund (scripsit) & Sylvia." Near-fine. MacManus 277-443 1983 $85

BLUNDEN, EDMUND   The Bonadventure: A Random Journal of an Atlantic Holiday. London: Richard Cobden-Sanderson, (1922). First edition. Orig. blue cloth. Presentation copy to Siegfried Sasson inscribed: "S. S. the true Ulysses, from E. B. The Suffolk traveller, November 20, 1922." Front cover of dust jacket pasted to the front paste-down endpaper. Spine and covers slightly worn & soiled. Good. MacManus 277-455 1983 $450

BLUNDEN, EDMUND   The Bonadventure. London, 1922. First English edition. Edges and prelims spotted. Nicked and chipped dust-wrapper. Very good. Jolliffe 26-622 1983 £32

BLUNDEN, EDMUND   The Bonadventure. London, 1922. First edition. Preliminaries foxed. Frayed dust wrapper. Name of flyleaf. Nice. Rota 230-74 1983 £12.50

BLUNDEN, EDMUND   Christ's Hospital: A Retrospect. London: Christophers, (1923). First edition. Illus. Orig. blue cloth. Presentation copy to Siegfried Sassoon inscribed: "Siegfried Sassoon, 'Observe these blue profundities,' from Edmund Blunder, 11 December 1923." Loosely laid in is an 8vo leaf of autograph noted by Blunden for the review of a book of Bridewell. Paint spot to the rear cover. Good. MacManus 277-448 1983 $450

BLUNDEN, EDMUND   Christ's Hospital. A Retrospect. London: Christophers, (1923). First edition. Illus. Orig. cloth. Presentation copy, inscribed. ALS. Spine a trifle worn, with some offsetting to the rear endpapers. Very good. MacManus 277-449 1983 $250

BLUNDEN, EDMUND   Christ's Hospital: The Dede of Pitie. London: Christ's Hospital, 1953. First edition. Orig. grey printed wrappers. Kenneth Hopkin's copy, signed by Blunden, with an ALS presenting the book, dated 20 vii '53. Edges slightly darkened. Very good. MacManus 277-447 1983 $225

BLUNDEN, EDMUND   "College Songs." Tokyo: Tokyo Women's Christian College, 1950. First edition. Self-wrappers. Presentation copy to his friend Kenneth Hopkins inscribed. Front page has a holograph facsimile in Blunden's hand of the song. Fine. MacManus 277-450 1983 $200

BLUNDEN, EDMUND   An Elegy and other Poems. London: Cobden-Sanderson, (1937). First edition. Orig. cloth with spine label, dust jacket (faded, worn and soiled, with a few small tears to the spine and covers). Presentation copy inscribed to Siegfried Sassoon. Contains a holograph remark in Sassoon's hand. Near-fine. MacManus 277-460 1983 $450

BLUNDEN, EDMUND   Eleven Poems. Cambridge: The Golden Head Press, 1965. First edition. Illus, 22 pages, with white stiff wrappers covered by pastel green thin wrappers. One of 200 copies printed on Glastonbury Antique paper. Presentation copy to Siegfried Sassoon inscribed: "Siegfried: A trifle indeed, from his affectionate and mindfull friend Edmund 29 iii 1966". Spine very slightly faded. Near-fine. MacManus 277-461 1983 $350

BLUNDEN, EDMUND   English Poems. (London): Cobden-Sanderson, (1925). First edition. Orig. red buckram with paper spine label (slightly rubbed). Signed by S. Sassoon in monogram and dated January 1926. MacManus 280-4509 1983 $350

BLUNDEN, EDMUND   English Poems. London, 1925. First edition. Name of flyleaf. Dust wrapper. Nice. Rota 230-75 1983 £12

BLUNDEN, EDMUND   English Poetry. Volume 1, 1948. Tokyo: 1948. First edition. Orig. wrappers, illus. with a photo. of Blunden. Contains three poems by Blunden. Kenneth Hopkins's copy with his signature of the front cover. MacManus 277-465 1983 $35

BLUNDEN, EDMUND   The Face Of England In A Series Of Occasional Sketches. London: Longmans, Green & Co., (1949). Clifford Library edition. Intro. by John Squire. Orig. cloth. Dust jacket (slightly worn & soiled). Presentation copy inscribed to Kenneth Hopkins. Sighed by Hopkins. Good. MacManus 277-469 1983 $135

BLUNDEN, EDMUND   Favourite Studies in English Literature. Tokyo: The Hokuseido Press, 1950. First edition. Illus. Orig. cloth. Dust jacket (a trifle worn). Presentation copy to Kenneth Hopkins inscribed: "K.H. who helps us all with such favorite studies, from E.B. 28 October 1950". Signed by Hopkins. Spine slightly faded. Very good. MacManus 277-472 1983 $185

BLUNDEN, EDMUND   Halfway House. Lon., 1932. Limited to 70 numbered and signed copies, many pages uncut, cover lightly sunned, endpapers offset, else very good. Quill & Brush 54-118 1983 $125

BLUNDEN, EDMUND   The Harbingers: Poems. (Privately Printed): G.A. Blunden, 1916. First edition, second impression. Orig. violet printed wrappers. Presentation copy to his close friend Emile Jacot inscribed. Spine ends worn, spine and covers faded and worn at the edges. Some foxing. Good. MacManus 277-480 1983 $250

BLUNDEN, EDMUND   A Hong Kong House: Poems 1951-1961. London: Collins, 1962. First edition. Orig. blue cloth. Dust jacket (a trifle worn and soiled). Presentation copy inscribed: "The last so far and I am happy to find Leonard Clark still in the audience, Edmund Blunden, 20 ix '64." Near-fine. MacManus 277-483 1983 $85

BLUNDEN, EDMUND   Influential Books. (Tokyo): The Hokuseido Press, (1950). First edition. Illus. Orig. cloth. Dust jacket
(slightly worn). Presentation copy inscribed: "Kenneth Hopkins with
the best wishes of Edmund Blunden, 12 September 1950." Signed by
Hopkins. Spine slightly faded. Very good. MacManus 277-488 1983
$185

BLUNDEN, EDMUND   Japanese Garland. (London): The Beau-
mont Press, (1928). First edition. Decorations & color illus. Orig.
cloth-backed decorated boards. One of 310 copies on Japanese paper.
Presentation copy to Siegfried Sassoon inscribed: "Siegfried from his
Kentish neighbour Edmund, July 3, 1928." Spine slightly faded. Fine.
MacManus 277-490 1983 $450

BLUNDEN, EDMUND   John Clare: Poems Chiefly From Manuscript.
London: Richard Cobden-Sanderson, (1920). First edition. Frontis.
Orig. blue cloth with paper spine label (chipped and worn). Contains
a prefatory note by Blunden and Alan Porter. Presentation copy to
Emile Jacot inscribed: "E.W. Jacot, 'Registered,' Clare's Ghost 'E.
Blunden'." Spine and covers worn and slightly soiled. Good. MacManus
277-491 1983 $300

BLUNDEN, EDMUND   Keats's Publisher: A Memoir of John
Taylor (1781-1864). London: Jonathan Cape, (1936). First edition.
Illus. Orig. cloth. Dust jacket (faded, worn & slightly spotted).
Presentation copy to Siegfried Sassoon inscribed: "Siegfried and
Hester, 16 October 1936, 'as a proof of the esteem and respect which
I entertain towards you both,' p. 62--Edmund." Near-fine. MacManus
277-495 1983 $450

BLUNDEN, EDMUND   Masks of Time. (Westminster: Cyril
William Beaumont Press, January 1925). First edition. Decorations by
R. Schwabe. Orig. cloth-backed decorated boards. Sassoon's copy with
his monogram on the front paste-down endpaper, dated, May 1925.
One of 390 copies printed on hand-made paper. Spine slightly darkened.
Very good, clean. MacManus 280-4510 1983 $400

BLUNDEN, EDMUND   Near and Far. London: Cobden-
Sanderson, 1929. Cloth. First edition. One of 160 numbered copies
printed on handmade paper, and signed by the author. Spine unevenly
sunned, else about fine. Reese 20-137 1983 $65

BLUNDEN, EDMUND   Near and Far. London: Cobden-
Sanderson, 1929. 1st trade ed. Orig. green cloth, label, dj, extra
label at end, ad slip laid in. Very fine copy from the library of
Crosby Gaige with his book label. Jenkins 155-95 1983 $65

BLUNDEN, EDMUND   Near and Far; new poems. London, 1929.
First edition. One of 160 numbered copies, signed by author. Spine
faded, some leaves a little creased at the corners. Dust wrapper.
Name on flyleaf. Very nice. Rota 230-81 1983 £35

BLUNDEN, EDMUND   Near and Far; poems. London, 1929.
First edition. Dust wrapper. Name of flyleaf. Very nice. Rota
230-80 1983 £12

BLUNDEN, EDMUND   Near and Far. New York, 1930. First
American edition. One of 105 numbered copies, signed by author. Hand-
coloured frontis. signed by artist. Dust wrapper and publisher's box.
An additional proof inscribed by the artist mounted on the flyleaf.
Fine. Rota 231-82 1983 £75

BLUNDEN, EDMUND   On Several Occasions. N.p.: (The Corvinus Press, 1938). First edition. Orig. decorated cloth. In publisher's slipcase. One of only 60 copies hand-set in 18-pt. Corvinus
light italic type and printed on Arnold and Foster hand-made paper.
Signed by author. White decorated cloth foxed. Rare. Fine. Mac-
Manus 277-512 1983 $275

BLUNDEN, EDMUND   Pastorals. A Book of Verses. London:
Erskine Macdonald, 1916. First edition. 12mo. Orig. wrappers. Near-
fine. MacManus 277-514 1983 $125

BLUNDEN, EDMUND   The Poems of Edmund Blunden. London:
Cobden-Sanderson, 1930. First limited edition. Orig. blue buckram.
One of 210 copies signed by author. Presentation copy to his friend
Kenneth Hopkins, inscribed with a verse which acknowledges the fact
that this copy belonged to J.C. Squire (his signature appears on the
front free endpaper). Signed by Hopkins on the half-title page.
Spine darkened. Good. MacManus 277-517 1983 $450

BLUNDEN, EDMUND   Poems. 1930-1940. London: Macmillan,
1940. First edition. Orig. cloth. Dust jacket. Presentation copy
inscribed to Siegfried Sassoon. Endpapers somewhat faded. Fine.
MacManus 277-516 1983 $475

BLUNDEN, EDMUND   Records of Friendship. Kyushu: Kyushu
University Press, 1950. First edition. Frontis. portrait of the
Blundens. Orig. boards with paper cover label. Presentation copy in-
scribed: "The name of Kenneth Hopkins comes very naturally into this
copy from Edmund Blunden, 'The Falcon,' 12 ix 1950." One of 200 copies.
Near-fine. MacManus 277-525 1983 $185

BLUNDEN, EDMUND   Retreat. (London): Richard Cobden-
Sanderson, Thavies Inn, (1928). First limited edition. Orig. buckram.
Presentation copy from the author to Siegfried Sassoon inscribed on a
small piece of paper neatly pasted to the front endpaper. Loosely laid
in is an autograph note in verse. One of 112 copies signed by author.
Fine. MacManus 277-529 1983 $450

BLUNDEN, EDMUND   Retreat; poems. London, 1928. First
edition. One of 112 numbered copies, signed by author. Dust wrapper.
Name of flyleaf. Fine. Rota 230-77 1983 £40

BLUNDEN, EDMUND   Retreat; poems. New York, 1928. First
American edition. Slightly frayed dust wrapper. Inscribed. Very nice.
Rota 230-78 1983 £20

BLUNDEN, EDMUND   Shelley, A Life Story. London: Collins,
St. James's Place, (1946). First edition. Frontis. Orig. cloth.
Dust jacket (faded, worn and slightly soiled, with a few small tears
to the covers). Presentation copy to Siegfried Sassoon inscribed.
Contains numerous holograph corrections in Blunden's hand. Two short
sentences written in pencil by Sassoon on the half-title page.
Near-fine. MacManus 277-535 1983 $450

BLUNDEN, EDMUND   Shelley. A Life Story. London: Collins,
(1946). First edition. Frontis. Orig. cloth. Dust jacket (a bit
worn & faded). Very good. MacManus 280-4719 1983 $30

BLUNDEN, EDMUND   Shells by a Stream. London: Macmillan
& Co., 1944. First edition. Orig. cloth. Dust jacket (spine and
covers slightly darkened and worn). Very good. MacManus 277-536
1983 $35

BLUNDEN, EDMUND   The Shepherd And Other Poems. Thavies
Inn: Richard Cobden-Sanderson, 1922. First edition. Orig. blue cloth
with paper spine label (defective; worn). Presentation copy to
his friend, Emile Jacot, inscribed. Spine and covers slightly worn at
the edges. Good. MacManus 277-537 1983 $250

BLUNDEN, EDMUND   The Shepherd And Other Poems. (London):
Richard Cobden-Sanderson, Thavies Inn, 1922. First edition. Orig.
blue cloth with paper spine label. Dust jacket (spine rather worn and
darkened). From the library of Siegfried Sassoon who pasted a small
bookseller's catalogue entry to the rear endpaper, with a note, in
pencil, "March 1928." Fine. MacManus 277-538 1983 $50

BLUNDEN, EDMUND   The Shepherd and Other Poems of Peace
and War. Richard Cobden-Sanderson, 1922. 8vo, uncut and unopened.
Orig. cloth with printed paper label on spine. Paper label partly
defective. First edition. Bickersteth 75-110 1983 £18

BLUNDEN, EDMUND   Sons Of Light: A Series of Lectures on
English Writers. The Hosei University Press, 1949. First edition.
Orig. boards. Publisher's glassine jacket (worn, with a few small
tears). Presentation copy from the author inscribed in pencil to
Kenneth Hopkins 3 January 1950. Contains Hopkins' signature on the
front paste-down endpaper. Bottom spine end slightly worn. Near-fine.
MacManus 277-545 1983 $225

BLUNDEN, EDMUND   A Summer's Fancy. Lon., 1930. One of
325 numbered copies, spine very slightly darkened, flys very slightly
offset, else near fine in lightly chipped glassine wrapper in fine
slipcase. Quill & Brush 54-117 1983 $60

BLUNDEN, EDMUND   A Summer's Fancy. London: Beaumont
Press, 1930. 1st ed., 1 of 325 copies. Orig. linen-backed
decorated boards, gilt, uncut. Fine copy. Jenkins 155-96 1983
$30

BLUNDEN, EDMUND   To Themis; poems. Beaumont Press, 1931.
First edition. One of 325 numbered copies on handmade paper. Patterned
boards. Fine. Rota 230-82 1983 £20

BLUNDEN, EDMUND   Votive Tablets. London: Cobden-Sanderson, (1931). First edition. Orig. cloth. One of 50 copies signed by
author. Spine slightly faded. Covers a bit rubbed. Good. MacManus
277-559   1983 $85

BLUNDEN, EDMUND   The Waggoner And Other Poems. London:
Sidgwick & Jackson, 1920. First edition, first issue. Orig. purple
cloth with paper spine label. Presentation copy to his friend E.W.
Jacot, inscribed. Underneath inscription Jacot has made a "reply".
Signed by Jacot on the title-page. Spine faded. Good. MacManus 277-
560   1983 $375

BLUNDEN, EDMUND   The Waggoner and Other Poems. London:
Sidgwick & Jackson, 1920. First edition, second issue. Orig. green
cloth with paper spine label (worn and slightly darkened). One of 150
copies. Presentation copy inscribed: "To C(yril) W. Beaumont, the
author's salutations, August 9, 1923." Very good. MacManus 277-561
1983 $135

BLUNDEN, EDMUND   The Waggoner and Other Poems. Sidgwick
and Jackson Ltd., 1920. 8vo, uncut, orig. cloth with paper label on
spine. Paper label partly defective. First edition. Bickersteth
75-109   1983   £18

BLUNDEN, EDMUND   Winter Nights; a poem. London: Ariel
Poems, 1928. First edition. One of 500 numbered copies on large paper,
signed by author. Nice. Rota 230-79   1983   £25

BLUNT, ANTHONY   Francois Mansart and the Origins of
French Classical Architecture. London: The Warburg Institute,
1941. 34 plates. 5 figs. Small 4to. Cloth. Ars Libri 32-423
1983 $60

BLUNT, ANTHONY   Nicolas Poussin. New York: Pantheon,
1967. 2 vols. 271 illus. 265 plates. 4to. Cloth. Ars Libri
32-532   1983 $175

BLUNT, ANTHONY   The Paintings of Nicolas Poussin.
London: Phaidon, 1966. 38 plates. 4to. Cloth. Dust jacket.
Ars Libri 32-533   1983 $100

BLUNT, ANTHONY   Philibert de l'Orme. London: A.
Zwemmer, 1958. 106 illus. hors texte. 4to. Cloth. Dust jacket.
Flyleaf clipped at one corner. Ars Libri 32-161   1983 $75

BLUNT, EDWARD   The Merchant and Seaman's Expeditious
Measurer. (New York) 1825. Cont. tree calf. Upper hinge
cracked. Corners, edges rubbed, leather peeling from boards. Title
gilt stamped on red morocco label. Scattered light foxing. Arkway
22-12   1983 $425

BLUNT, WILFRID SCAWEN   Francis Thompson. London: Burns &
Oates Ltd., (1907). First edition. Small 4to. Orig. grey printed
wrappers. A presentation copy with an inscription on upper cover,
"Evan Wyndham Quin from her affec. cous. Wilfrid Scawen Blunt,
Newbuilding, June 1, 1914." Traylen 94-825   1983   £40

BLUNT, WILFRID SCAWEN   The Future of Islam. Kegan Paul, Trench
& Co., 1882. First edition. Orig. cloth. Edges a bit worn. Bookplate. Binding slight soiled. Scarce. MacManus 277-568   1983 $85

BLUNT, WILFRID SCAWEN   Poems. London, 1923. First edition.
Torn dust wrapper. Presentation blind stamp on title-page. Nice.
Rota 231-83   1983   £25

BLUNT, WILFRID SCAWEN   Secret history of the English occupation
of Egypt. London: T. Fisher Unwin, 1907. 8vo. Frontis. Orig.
cloth-backed boards. Adelson Africa-168   1983 $55

BLUNT, WILFRID SCAWEN   Secret History. London, 1907. 8vo.
Portrait frontis. Some slight spotting. Orig. blue boards, canvas
spine. Slightly soiled. Good. Edwards 1042-285   1983 $25

BLUTHGEN, VICTOR   Kleine Sippschaft. Glogan: n.d.
Quarto. Printed on one side, ads. Color illus. Fine copy in pictorial boards, cloth spine. Orig. printed dust wrapper, chipped. Bromer
25-380   1983 $150

BLY, ROBERT   The Light Around the Body. New York,
(1967). 8vo. Boards. Signed in full. With reviews laid in. This
copy contains a TLS from Robert Bly to Louis Untermeyer, dated
22 June 68. From the library of Louis Untermeyer. Tiny nick at
edge of spine, else a fine copy in dj. In Our Time 156-87   1983
$200

BOADEN, JAMES   The Life of Mrs. Jordan. London: Edward
Bull, 1831. First edition. 2 vols. Illus. with numerous engravings.
Half-calf with marbled boards. Engraved plates neatly tipped in.
Spines and covers slightly rubbed. Some foxing to the endpapers.
In a half-morocco slipcase. Very good. MacManus 279-3007   1983 $135

BOADEN, JAMES   The Life of Mrs. Jordan. London:
Edward Bull, 1831. 2 vols., 8vo, original light blue boards, grey
paper backstrips, printed paper labels (slight neat restoration to
the ends of the spines). First edition, with a portrait, and a
folding facsimile plate of handwriting. A fine fresh copy in original
condition. Ximenes 64-52   1983 $125

BOADEN, JAMES   Memoirs of Mrs. Inchbald. London:
Richard Bentley, 1833. 2 vols., 8vo, original grey boards, printed
paper labels. First edition. A very fine copy in original condition.
Ximenes 64-53   1983 $200

BOADEN, JAMES   Memoirs of Mrs. Siddons. London:
Henry Colburn, 1827. 2 vols., 8vo, original light blue boards,
printed paper labels (slight wear, one lower hinge weak). First ed.,
with a portrait (offset). Upper corners of vol. II stained; old
lending library label on one front cover. Ximenes 64-54   1983 $75

BOADEN, JAMES   Memoirs of Mrs. Siddons. London:
Henry Colburn and Richard Bentley, 1831. 2 vols., 8vo, original
qtr. cloth and boards, printed paper labels. 2nd edition, with an
additional preface, and 18 pages of supplement.
With a portrait; some signatures browning, else a very good set.
Ximenes 64-55   1983 $75

BOADEN, JAMES   Memoirs of the Life of John Philip
Kemble, Esq. London: printed for Longman, etc., 1825. 2 vols.,
8vo, original blue boards, grey paper backstrips, printed paper
labels (tops of spines defective). First ed. With a portrait and
armorial bookplates on front covers and a few pastedowns. A few
light waterstains. Ximenes 64-56   1983 $50

BOAK, ARTHUR E.   A History of Rome to 565 AD. NY, 1943.
Maps, 3rd edition. Salloch 385-210   1983 $30

BOAM, HENRY J.   20th Century Impressions of Canada.
London, 1914. Illus., folding map, 4to, dec. buckram, ex-library.
Argosy 710-45   1983 $45

BOATE, GERARD   Histoire Naturelle D'Irlande, Contenant
Une Description Tres Exact De Sa Situation... Paris, 1666. First
French edition, small 8vo, without the last free endpaper, contemporary
mottled calf, slightly rubbed. Deighton 3-45   1983   £125

BOCCACCIO, GIOVANNI   The decameron, or ten days entertainment
of Boccace. London: R. Dodsley, 1741. First edition of this
translation by Charles Balguy. 8vo. Cont. calf. A very fine copy.
Ximenes 63-115   1983 $425

BOCCACIO, GIOVANNI   The Decameron... London: Privately
Printed for the Villon Society, 1886. 3 vols. Small 4to. Bound in
3/4 crimson levant morocco, t.e.g., others uncut, by Ramage. Limited
numbered edition. Traylen 94-88   1983   £25

BOCCACCIO, GIOVANNI   Delle Opere Di M. Giovanni Boccacci.
Firenze, 1723-1724. 6 vols. Rebound in leather, with new labels.
One blank flyleaf clipped at the corner, some rubbing to leathers,
a very good-fine set. In Our Time 156-88   1983 $125

BOCCACCIO, GIOVANNI   The Nymphs of Fiesole. Verona:
Editiones Officinae Bodoni. 1952. Folio. Illus. with 23 orig.
woodcuts, recut by Fritz Kredel, and with one facs. plate. Edition
ltd. to 225 copies, printed on the hand-press on hand-made Fabriano
paper. Bound in 1/4 vellum over dec. boards. Gilt-stamped spine.
T.e.g. A fine copy in a very slightly soiled slipcase. Karmiole
76-81   1983 $850

BOCCACCIO, GIOVANNI   Philocholo. (Impresso in Milano, 1520).
4to, in eights. Two final blank leaves. Printed in double columns.
Leter vellum (a little worn and soiled). A few small holes in some
margins, not affecting text. First two leaves a little dust-stained.
Hannas 69-12 1983 £280

BOCCADOR, JACQUELINE   Statuaire medievale en France de 1400 a
1053. Zug, 1974. Lg. square 4to, wraps, d.j. 792 illus. Ars Libri
SB 26-26 1983 $100

BOCCALINI, TRAIANO   The New-found Politicke... London:
for Francis Williams, 1626. First English translation. 4to.
Corner of title and first leaf repaired with loss of a few words,
else good copy in modern full old style calf. Heath 48-56 1983
£300

BOCCONE, P.   Icones et Descriptiones Rariorum
Plantarum Siciliae, Melitae, Galliae et Italiae. Oxford, 1674.
52 engravings, 4to, leather-backed boards, somewhat worn. Very
scarce. An ex-library copy with stamp on flyleaf and bookplates
but no stamps on the text. Inner joints neatly repaired. Wheldon
160-1655 1983 £270

BOCHER, EMMANUEL   Augustin de Saint Aubin. Paris:
Damascene Morgand et Charles Fatout, 1879. Large 4to. New
wrappers, mounted with portion of orig. front cover. No. 78 of
450 copies on uncut papier verge, from the limited edition of 475
copies. Ars Libri 32-610 1983 $175

BOCK, F. S.   Versuch Einer Wirthschaftlichen Naturgeschichte von dem Konigreich Ost- und Westpreussen. Dessau, 1782-85.
4 vols (1, 3, 4, 5), 6 plates (3 coloured), 8vo, boards. Wheldon
160-347 1983 £50

BODDAM-WHETHAM, J. W.   Western Wanderings. London: Richard
Bentley and Son, 1874. First edition. Illus. Blue cloth. Bit
shaken, extremities worn. Bradley 66-470 1983 $125

BODE, WILHELM   Boticelli. Des Meisters Gemalde.
Stuttgart: Deutsche Verlags-Anstalt, 1926. 155 plates. 4to.
Cloth. Ar Libri 33-45 1983 $45

BODE, WILHELM   Die italienischen Bronzestatuetten der
Renaissance. Kleine, neu bearbeitete Auflage. Berlin, 1922.
viii, 106pp. Prof. illus. Lrg. 4to. Boards, 1/4 cloth (slightly
shaken). Ars Libri SB 26-29 1983 $100

BODE, WILHELM   Florentiner Bildhauer der Renaissance.
Vierte vermehrte Auflage. Berlin, 1921 334pp. 198 illu. 4to.
Marbled boards, 3/4 cloth (slightly shaken). From the library of
Hann- Swarzenski. Ars Libri SB 26-28 1983 $50

BODELSEN, MERETE   Gauguin's Ceramics. London: Faber
and Faber, 1964. 162 illus. 4to. Cloth. Dust jacket. Ars Libri
32-246 1983 $85

BODENHAUSEN, EBERHARD, FREIHERR VON   Gerard David und seine Schule.
Munchen: F. Bruckmann, 1905. 29 hinged plates (9 photogravure).
Numerous text illus. Large 4to. Cloth. Ars Libri 32-145 1983
$600

BODENHEIMER, F. S.   Prodromus Faunae Palestinae. Cairo,
Mem. Instit. d'Egypte no. 33, 1937. 4to, wrappers. Wheldon 160-348
1983 £35

BODLEY, THOMAS   The Life of Sir Thomas Bodley Written
by Himself... Chicago: A.C. McClurg & Co., 1906. 12mo. Cloth-
backed boards. Limited to 250 copies printed by D.B. Updike at the
Merrymount Press. Leather spine label is worn. Oak Knoll 49-69
1983 $25

BOECKH, AUGUST   Encyclopaedie & Methodologie der
Philologischen Wissenschaften. 1886. A little shaky in binding.
8vo, cloth. Salloch 385-68 1983 $30

BOECK, WILHELM   Joseph Anton Feuchtmayer. Tubingen:
Ernst Wasmuth, 1948. 581 illus. 4to. Boards, 1/4 cloth. Ars
Libri 32-218 1983 $100

BOECK, WILHELM   Picasso. New York/Amsterdam: Abrams,
(1955). 606 illus. (44 color). Small folio. Cloth (designed by
Picasso). Ars Libri 32-515 1983 $75

BOECKLER, ALBERT   Die Bronzeturen des Bonanus von Pisa
und des Barisanus von Trani. (Die Fruhmittelalterlichen
Bronzeturen. Vol. 4.) Berlin, 1953. 74, (4)pp., 108 collotype
plates with 200 illus. Lrg. 4to. Cloth. Ars Libri SB 26-31
1983 $150

BOEHM, M. F.   Examen Acidi Pinguis... Strasburg,
1769. 4to. Dutch gilt wrappers. Presentation inscription to Engel-
berger on title. Title soiled. Gurney 90-18 1983 £45

BOEMUS, JOHANNES   The Fardle of Facions containing the
Aunciente Maners, Customs, and Lawes, of the Peoples Enhabiting the
Two partes of the earth, called Affrike and Asie. Jhon Kingstone &
Henry Sutton, 1555. First edition in English. Black letter, title
within woodcut boarder, some slight soiling. Small worm hole in margin
not affecting text, without Z4 blank. Sm.8vo. Cont. vellum, preserved in morocco backed box. Good. Edwards 1044-75 1983 £2500

BOER, L. E. M. DE   The Orang Utan, its biology and conserva-
tion. The Hague, 1982. 8vo, cloth. Wheldon 160-542 1983 £47

BOERHAAVE, HERMANN   Dr. Boerhaave's Elements of Chymistry,
Faithfully Abridg'd...to which are Added, Curious and Useful Notes.
For J. Wilford, London, 1732. First edition in English. 8vo, with
17 engraved plates; text and plates offset; cont. panelled calf,
rebacked, worn and upper joint split. Quaritch NS 5-13 1983 $950

BOERHAAVE, HERMANN   Praelectiones Academicae in propriae
Insitutiones Rei Medicae edidit, et Notas addidit, Albertus Haller.
Turin, 1743. 2 vols. 4to, vellum. K Books 22-25 1983 £70

BOESINGER, W.   Richard Neutra: Buildings and Projects.
Zurich/New York: Girsberg/Praeger, 1951-1966. 3 vols. Prof. illus.
Oblong 4to. Cloth. Light wear. Ars Libri 32-492 1983 $225

BOGAN, LOUISE   Body of This Death. NY, 1923. Cloth
spine slightly foxed, small stain on front board, else fine. Quill
& Brush 54-119 1983 $60

BOGAN, LOUISE   Dark Summer. NY, 1929. Blue cloth with
aqua buckram spine, cover edges lightly sunned, very good. Quill &
Brush 54-120 1983 $50

BOGAN, LOUISE   Dark Summer. New York: Scribners,
1929. Cloth, paper label. First edition. Slightly dusty, but a
very good copy. Reese 20-139 1983 $40

BOGARDUS, ADAM H.   Field, Cover, and Trap Shooting.
NY 1874. First ed. Portrait, cloth, ink name, covers spotted,
extremities frayed. King 46-544 1983 $35

BOGEN, F. W.   The German in America. Boston, 1851.
1st ed. 16mo. Ex-library with no external marks, spine faded, nice.
Morrill 286-61 1983 $32.50

BOGGS, MAE H.   My Play House was a Concord Coach.
Oakland, (1942). Illus., maps, plates. Orig. small folio cloth,
first edition. Ginsberg 46-82 1983 $300

BOGGS, TOM   Lyrics in Brief. New York: Powgen
Press, (1938). 8vo. Wraps. Though the copy is numbered, there is
no formal limitation notice. Very good-fine. In Our Time 156-89
1983 $25

BOHLER, LORENZ   Technik der Knockenbruchbehandlung.
Wien, 1933. 1059 illus. Argosy 713-66 1983 $75

BOHN, HENRY G.   A Dictionary of Quotations, from the
English Poets. 1867. Printed for private distribution. Presentation
leaf, signed by Bohn, to Robert Turner. Orig. brown cloth, bevelled
boards, v.g. Jarndyce 31-428 1983 £24

BOHR, NIELS   The Theory of Spectra and Atomic Constitution... Cambridge, 1922. First English edition. 8vo. Orig. maroon cloth with gilt. Spine faded. Very good copy. Zeitlin 264-55 1983 $90

BOHUN, W.   A Tithing Table... In the Savoy: by E. & R. Nutt..., 1732. First edition. 8vo. Uncut, stitched. Title and last leaf dusty. Heath 48-216 1983 £35

BOILEAU, ETHEL   Clansmen. London: Hutchinson & Co., (1936). First edition. Orig. cloth. Dust jacket (slightly worn at the cover and spine margins). Presentation copy to Dennis Wheatley inscribed: "From Ethel Boileau, April 1936." Loosely laid in is an ALS, 6 pages, June 18, 1939. Edges foxed. Bookplate of Dennis Wheatley. Near-fine. MacManus 277-571 1983 $65

BOISACQ, EMILE   Dictionnaire Etymologique de la Langue Grecque. Heidelberg, 1938. 3rd edition. 4to. Salloch 385-88 1983 $90

BOISSIER, GASTON   La Conjuration de Catilina. Paris, 1908. 8vo, cloth. Salloch 385-211 1983 $25

BOISSIER, GASTON   La Religion Romaine d'Auguste Aux Antonines. Paris, 1906. 2 vols., 6th edition. Salloch 385-70 1983 $30

BOKUM, HERMANN   The Testimony of A Refugee From East Tennessee. Phila., 1863-1864. Later cloth, morocco label. Orig. printed wrappers on both pamphlets bound in. Jenkins 152-567 1983 $75

BOLDINI, MME.   Boldini. Milano: Edizioni Il Torchietto, 1966. 30 color plates. Numerous reference illus. Folio. Cloth. Dust jacket. Ars Libri 33-414 1983 $100

BOLDINI, MME.   Vie de Jean Boldini. Paris: Eugene Figuiere, 1931. 20 plates. 4to. Wrappers. Ars Libri 33-413 1983 $45

BOLDREWOOD, ROLF   Babes in the Bush. London: Macmillan & Co., Limited, 1900. First edition. Orig. cloth. Inner hinges weak. Covers a little rubbed and marked. Good. MacManus 277-573 1983 $85

BOLDREWOOD, ROLF   The Ghost Camp or The Avengers. London: Macmillan & Co., 1902. First edition. Orig. embossed cloth. Rare. Very fine. MacManus 277-574 1983 $135

BOLDREWOOD, ROLF   Plain Living, a bush idyll. London: Macmillan, 1898. First edition. Orig. cloth. Very good. MacManus 277-575 1983 $75

BOLDREWOOD, ROLF   A Romance of Canvas town and other Stories London: Macmillan & Co., 1898. First edition. Orig. cloth. Spine a trifle rubbed. Front inner hinge strained. Very good. MacManus 277-576 1983 $100

BOLDREWOOD, ROLF   The Sealskin Cloak. London: Macmillan, 1896. First edition. Orig. red cloth. Fine. MacManus 277-577 1983 $50

BOLDREWOOD, ROLF   A Sydney-Side Saxton. London: Macmillan & Co., 1891. First edition. Orig. cloth. Signature of former owner in two places. Bookseller's blind-stamp on rear free endpaper. Fine. MacManus 277-579 1983 $90

BOLDREWOOD, ROLF   A Sydney-Side Saxon. London: Macmillan & Co., 1891. First edition, in a variant binding. Orig. decorated cloth. Half red cloth and half tan cloth with red wreaths, one of which contains the Macmillan logo. Edges and corners a bit worn. Bookseller's stamp on front pastedown endpaper. Covers slightly soiled. Good. MacManus 277-578 1983 $50

BOLINGBROKE, HENRY ST. JOHN (1678-1751)   Letters on the Spirit of Patriotism. London: A. Millar, 1749. First edition. 8vo. Cont. calf, gilt, joints worn. Traylen 94-91 1983 £30

BOLINGBROKE, HENRY ST. JOHN (1678-1751)   Remarks on the History of England. London: R. Francklin, 1747. Second edition. 8vo. Cont. calf, spine gilt, leather label, bookplate. A very good copy. Trebizond 18-180 1983 $50

BOLLER, HENRY A.   Among the Indians. Phila., 1868. First edition. Large folding map. Orig. cloth, (backstrip ends chipped, blindstamp on t.p.). Inscribed by F.J. Boller. Argosy 716-610 1983 $350

BOLOGNA, FERDINANDO   Roviale Spagnuolo e la pittura napoletana del Cinquecento. Napoli: Edizioni Scientifiche Italiane, 1959. 115 plates. Square 4to. Boards, 1/4 cloth. Dust jacket. Ars Libri 33-316 1983 $100

BOLT, BEN   The Green Arrow. London, Ward, Lock, (1933). First edition. Dust jacket (two small chips) else, very good. Houle 22-115 1983 $45

BOLT, JUDSON   The Prodigal Nephew. London: Duckworth & Co., 1907. First edition. 6 illus. by Fred Bennett. Orig. pictorial cloth. Covers very slightly soiled. Near-fine. MacManus 277-580 1983 $35

BOLTON, ALBERT D.   The Labourers (Ireland) Acts, 1883 to 1906. Dublin: J. Falconer, 1908. Second edition, 8vo, orig. cloth. Fenning 62-36 1983 £16.50

BOLTON, CHARLES KNOWLES   The Elizabeth Whitman Mystery at the Old Bell Tavern in Danvers. Peabody, Mass., 1912. Ed. limited to 300 copies. Illus. 8vo, orig. boards, cloth back. Inner hinges slightly cracked. Morrill 286-275 1983 $30

BOLTON, HERBERT E.   Coronado, Knight of Pueblos and Plains. New York, 1949. Cloth, very good. Reese 19-78 1983 $40

BOLTON, HERBERT E.   Coronado, Knight of Pueblos and Plains. New York, (1949). 2nd prntg. End map. Clark 741-452 1983 $27.50

BOLTON, HERBERT E.   Outpost of Empire. New York, 1931. Cloth, very good. Reese 19-79 1983 $40

BOLTON, HERBERT E.   Rim of Christendom. New York, 1936. Cloth, very good. Reese 19-80 1983 $100

BOLTON, HERBERT E.   Rim of Christendom. N.Y., MacMillian, 1936. First edition. Large 8vo, illus. with plates, facs. and 8 maps. Gilt stamped green cloth. Very good. Houle 22-1027 1983 $65

BOLTON, HERBERT E.   The Spanish Borderlands. New Haven, 1921. Plates. Gild cloth, fine. Reese 19-81 1983 $25

BOLTON, REGINALD P.   A Woman Misunderstood. N.Y., 1931. Orig. cloth. First edition. 1,000 copies printed. Ginsberg 46-319 1983 $20

BONAR, JAMES   Malthus and His Work. Macmillan, 1885. First edition. Half title. Orig. dark olive cloth, sl. marked, v.g. Jarndyce 30-1064 1983 £56

BONAVIA, E.   The Cultivated Oranges and Lemons. 1888. 8vo, cloth. Some slight marginal worming. Does not include atlas of 260 outline plates. Wheldon 160-2111 1983 £15

BOND, ALLEN   When the Hopkins came to Baltimore. Baltimore, 1927. 8vo. WRappers. First edition. Fye H-3-46 1983 $35

BOND, FRANCIS T.   The Home of the Agricultural Labourer. Gloucester: J. Headland, 1873. Disbound. Jarndyce 31-341 1983 £12.50

BOND, FRED G.   Flatboating on the Yellowstone 1877. New York, 1925. Frontis. Orig. printed wrappers. Jenkins 152-23 1983 $45

BOND, JOHN   Ortus Occidentalis: or a Dawning in the
West... London: J. D. for Fr. Eglesfield, 1645. Sole edition. 4to.
Modern boards, leather label. Heath 48-55 1983 £30

BOND, JOHN W.   The Empire State of the New North-West.
St. Paul, Minn.: H.M. Smyth & Co., 1878. Orig. printed wrappers.
Some soiling. Large folding map of Minnesota. Jenkins 152-255 1983
$125

BOND, NELSON   Mr. Mergenthwirker's Lobbies and
Other Fantastic Tales. N.Y., Coward - McCann, (1946). First edition.
Dust jacket (slight rubbing). Very good. Houle 22-116 1983 $37.50

BOND, NELSON   The Thirty-First of February. NY,
(1949). Signed inscription from Bond. Fine in fine dustwrapper.
Quill & Brush 54-121 1983 $50

BOND, WILLIAM   The Quicksilver Mining Company. N.Y.,
1867. Orig. printed wraps. First edition. Ginsberg 47-46 1983 $75

BONDEGAARDEN: Ny Opstillingsbilledbog. Kobenhavn: (ca. 1950).
Full color, six sections. Hinges between sections reinforced with
tape. Slightly soiled, otherwise fine in colored pictorial boards.
Bromer 25-374 1983 $65

BONE, GERTRUDE   Children's Children. Duckworth and Co.,
1908. Small 4to, 62 illus. by Muirhead Bone, 24 of them full-page,
orig. pictorial cloth gilt. Bickersteth 75-111 1983 £14

BONE, JAMES   The London Perambulator. London, 1925.
First edition. Sm. 4to. Spine faded. Autograph signatures of author
and artist. Very good. Rota 230-88 1983 £12

BONE, MUIRHEAD   The Western Front. Garden City, N.Y.:
Doubleday, Page & Co., 1917. First American edition. 200 drawings
by Muirhead Bone. Intro. by General Sir Douglas Haig. Folio. Orig.
10 parts (6 in the orig. pictorial dust jackets), enclosed in two
folding cloth cases, in publisher's boxes (defective). Minor marginal
worming, not affecting plates. Scarce. Very good. MacManus 277-581
1983 75

BONE, MUIRHEAD   The Western Front. London, 1917. 1st
ed. Illus. 2 vols., 4to, orig. boards, buckram backs, leather
labels. Morrill 287-530 1983 $22.50

BONEL, AUGUST   Histoire de la Telegraphie Description
des Principaux Appareilis aeriens et electriques. Paris, Ballay et
Conchon. Caen, Buhour, 1857. 12mo, numerous text figures, orig.
green printed wraps., defective on spine in places, and sewing loose.
Presentation copy inscribed by the author on the fly. Bickersteth
77-259 1983 £65

BONFILS, WINIFRED BLACK   The Life and Personality of Phoebe
Apperson Hearst. San Francisco: William Randolph Hearst, 1928.
Folio. First edition. Frontis. and decorations by William Wilke.
Orig. full vellum, t.e.g. 1/1000 copies. Vellum boards a little
warped at lower ends, front and back. Bradley 66-430 1983 $37.50

BONHOEFFER, K.   Klinische Beitraege zur Lehre von den
Degenerations-Psychosen. Halle: Carl Marhold, 1907. First edition.
Modern cloth. Though unsigned, M. J. Karpas' copy with notes to
several pages. Gach 95-53 1983 $30

BONHOTE, J.   Historical Records of the West Kent
Militia. London, 1909. Portrait frontis. 6 coloured plates, 75
other plates (1 folding), 7 illus. (1 coloured), 2 extra plates.
Thick roy. 8vo. Orig. half morocco, rebacked. Spine neatly laid down,
portion of orig. cloth cover with gilt crest laid down on upper cover.
New endpapers. A.e.g. Good. Edwards 1042-560 1983 £50

BONING, E. H.   British Marine Algae. (c. 1880).
4to, morocco, g.e. Wheldon 160-1792 1983 £60

BONINO, ATTILIO   Giovanni Antonio Molineri. Torino:
S. Lattes, 1930. 32 plates. Small 4to. Wrappers. Ars Libri 33-
253 1983 $45

BONNER, MARY   Magic Journeys. N.Y.: Macauley, (1928).
4to. Orange cloth, in frayed dust wrapper. Fine. Aleph-bet 8-41
1983 $20

BONNER, WILLIAM THOMPSON   New York, the World's Metropolis...
New York, R.L. Polk, 1924. Illus. 4to, former owner's rubber stamp
on title, endleaves, etc. Morrill 288-337 1983 $30

BONNET, CHARLES   Considerations sur les corps organises...
Amsterdam: Rey, 1762. First edition. 2 vols. 8vo. Cont. half
calf, spines gilt, contrasting morocco labels. Ximenes 63-270 1983
$750

BONNET, CHARLES   Traite d'insectologie; ou observations
sur les pucerons. Paris: Durand, 1745. First edition. 2 vols.
Small 8vo. Cont. mottled calf, spines gilt. 2 folding tables and
eight folding plates of insects. A very fine copy. Ximenes 63-271
1983 $675

BONNEY, H. K.   Historic Notices in Reference to
Fotheringhay. Printed by and for T. Bell; and for Messrs Longman,
Hurst, Rees, Orme and Brown, London; and Archibald Constable,
Edinburgh, 1821. 8vo, 9 plates, cont. half calf, rebacked,
preserving the orig. spine. Bickersteth 77-98 1983 £32

BONNYCASTLE, JOHN   An Introduction to Astronomy in a
Series of Letters from a Preceptor to his Pupil. 1811. 19 finely
engraved copper plates (serveral folding), half calf. Sixth edition.
K Books 307-26 1983 £28

BONOMI, JOSEPH   Nineveh and its Palaces. Ca. 1852.
Illus., uniformly age-browned throughout, hard-grained morocco, a
little rubbed. K Books 307-27 1983 £36

BONSAL, STEPHEN   Edward Fitzgerald Beale. N.Y., 1912.
Illus. Orig. cloth. First edition. Ginsberg 46-54 1983 $35

BONSAL, STEPHEN   Edward Fitzgerald Beale. N.Y. & London:
G. P. Putnam's Sons, 1912. Plates. Cloth. Back cover waterstained.
Signed by Beale's son Truxtun. Dawson 471-29 1983 $30

BONSELS, NILS   Wolfgang Katzheimer von Bamberg.
Strassburg: J.H. Ed. Heitz, 1936. 8 plates. 4to. Bound in new
cloth. Ars Libri 32-357 1983 $55

THE BON-TON Directory. Chicago, 1879-80. Brown cloth, gilt. Fine
copy. Bradley 66-498 1983 $35

THE BOOK of Adventure & Sport. Raphael Tuck, n.d. (ca. 1930). 4to.
2 colour plates & 3 text illus. by C. E. B. Other illus. Red colour
pictorial boards. Corners bumped. Greer 39-37 1983 £14

THE BOOK of American Negro Poetry. NY, (1922). Minor cover wear,
near fine in moderately chipped presentable dustwrapper, owner's name.
Quill & Brush 54-710 1983 $100

THE BOOK of Beasts. NY, (1954). Review copy with slip laid in,
illus., cover slightly stained, edges slightly bumped, else near fine
in frayed, very good dustwrapper. Quill & Brush 54-1521 1982 $75

A BOOK of Drawings. London: Privately printed, 1891. Bound in
morocco, teg. The publisher's copy with the David bookplate on
inside front endboard, two title pages, the insertion of a letter
from Selwyn Image and a bookplate designed by same with his autograph beneath it. Page drawings in book are signed by Joseph Pennell,
Walter Wilson, Charles Wilkerson, R.M. Moore, J. Partridge, Louis
Wain, Selwyn Image et al. Some bumping at top of spine. Fine. In
Our Time 156-90 1983 $375

THE BOOK of Elegant Extracts. Edinburgh, W.P. Nimmo, nd (ca. 1869).
Numerous text illus. by Lawson, A. Small, G. Hay, et al. Brown sand
grain cloth gilt, bevelled boards, a.e.g., some wear top/bottom bkstrip, bookpl. fr. ep., some foxing prelims., contemp. insc. verso
fr. ep., vg. Hodgkins 27-246 1983 £12.50

THE BOOK of Jasher. New York, (1840). First edition, second state.
8vo. Binding faded; some foxing. Morrill 290-379 1983 $25

THE BOOK of Kells. NY, 1974. 126 color plates, small folio, very fine in fine slipcase. Quill & Brush 54-1658 1983 $75

THE BOOK of knowledge. Manchester: Innes, 1836. 12mo. Old wrappers. Torn. Ximenes 63-85 1983 $25

BOOK OF MORMON   The Book of Mormon: An Account Written by the Hand of Morman...Part I. N.Y., Russell Bros. for the Deseret Univ., 1869. 8vo, orig. pictorial leather-backed boards. First edition in the Deseret alphabet. Only 3 books were printed in these hieroglyphics. Fine. O'Neal 50-37 1983 $125

THE BOOK of Oz Cooper. Chicago: The Society of Typographic Arts, 1949. First edition. 4to. Cloth. Prof. illus. Oak Knoll 48-112 1983 $45

THE BOOK of the Knight of La Tour Landry. London: the Verona Society, 1930. 4to. White buckram, gilt, t.e.g. Limited edition of 500 numbered copies, printed in red and black. Traylen 94-508 1983 £18

THE BOOK of Wonder Voyages. David Nutt, 1896. Illus. by John D. Batten. 17 text illus., adverts. Pink decor. cloth designed by Batten, uncut. Free eps. sl. foxed, name fr. ep., bkstrip v. sl. discoloured, nice copy. Hodgkins 27-13 1983 £25

THE BOOKMAN, Volume 1. October 1891-March 1892. London: Hodder and Stoughton, 1892. Orig. cloth-backed boards. Covers slightly soiled. Endpapers browned. Very good. MacManus 277-582 1983 $75

BOOKS and Manuscripts on Old Medicine, Alchemy, Witchcraft, Pharmacy, Cookery, Tobacco. London: Maggs Brothers, 1926. Profusely illus. Pictorial wrappers. Some very light staining, covers dusty, but nice copy. Bradley 66-39 1983 $25

BOOKS, Manuscripts and Drawings relating to Tobacco from the Collection of George Arents, Jr... Washington: Library of Congress, 1938. 12mo. Paper wrappers. Oak Knoll 49-505 1983 $25

BOOKWALTER, JOHN W.   Siveria and Central Asia. NY: Frederick A. Stokes Co., (1899). Tall 8vo, profusely illus. + a large folding color map in rear pocket. Gilt-stamped blue cloth. Karmiole 71-33 1983 $100

BOOLE, GEORGE   A Treatise on the Calculus of Finite Differences. Macmillan, London, (printed at the Cambridge University Press), 1860. First edition. 8vo, orig. cloth. Quaritch NS 5-14 1983 $550

BOOLE, MARY EVEREST   The Forging of Passion into Power. NY: Mitchell Kennerley, 1911. First American edition. Very good ex-library copy. Gach 95-54 1983 $20

BOOTH, GEORGE R.   The Cranbrook Press... Detroit: Cranbrook Press, 1902. 1st ed., limited. Orig. cloth-backed boards, label. Very good copy. Hand-colored initial letter, tipped in plates. Jenkins 155-99 1983 $45

BOOTH, J. B.   Seventy Years of Song. London: Hutchinson & So., n.d. (1940). Orig. pictorial wrappers. First edition. Foreword by Max Beerbohm. Wrappers slightly soiled and worn. A good copy. MacManus 277-276 1983 $50

BOOTH, STEPHEN   The Book Called Holinshed's Chronicles. Book Club of California, 1868. Edition limited to 500 copies with a leaf from the 1587 edition. Illus. Small folio, orig. boards, cloth back, label, mint. Morrill 287-549 1983 $150

BOOTH, WILLIAM   The Expansion of Paper as a Guide to Watermark Detection. London: The Chiswick Press, n.d. 4to. Cloth. Limited to 150 numbered copies, signed by the author. With 3 illus. done in red ink. Fine copy. Oak Knoll 49-89 1983 $65

BOOTHBY, GUY   Across the World for a Wife. London: Ward, Lock & Co., Limited, 1898. First edition. Illus. by J. Ambrose Walton. Orig. pictorial cloth. Inner hinges cracked. Very good. MacManus 277-583 1983 $35

BOOTHBY, GUY   The Fascination of the King. London: Ward Locke, 1897. First edition. Illus. Orig. cloth. Fine. Macmanus 277-584 1983 $35

BOOTHBY, GUY   In Strange Company. London: Ward, Lock & Bowden, 1894. First edition. Illus. by Stanley L. Wood. Orig. pictorial cloth. Pencil inscriptions on front and back endpapers. Very good. MacManus 277-585 1983 $45

BOOTHBY, GUY   Long Live the King. London: Ward, Lock & Co., 1900. First edition. Orig. pictorial cloth. Edges and coners a little worn. Endpapers browned. Very good. MacManus 277-586 1983 $40

BOOTHBY, GUY   Love Made Manifest. London, (1899). First edition. Very nice. Rota 231-84 1983 £15

BOOTHBY, GUY   The Lust of Hate. London: Ward, Lock & Co., 1898. First edition. Orig. pictorial cloth. Corners very slightly worn. A little browning to the endpapers. Very good. MacManus 277-587 1983 $50

BOOTHBY, GUY   A Maker of Nations. London: Ward, Lock, and Co., 1900. First edition. Illus. by Gordon Browne. Orig. decorated cloth. Edges very slightly worn. Endpapers browned. Former owner's signature. Good. MacManus 277-588 1983 $45

BOOTHBY, GUY   A Maker of Nations. London, 1900. First edition. Very nice. Rota 231-85 1983 £15

BOREIN, EDWARD   Drawings & Paintings of the Old West. Vol. I, The Indians. Flagstaff, 1968. Fine in cloth, with dust jacket. Ltd. to 2,000 numbered copies. Reese 19-84 1983 $100

BOREL, PIERRE   A summary or compendium, of the life of the most famous philosopher Renatus Descartes. London: E. Okes, for G. Palmer, 1670. First edition in English. 8vo. Cont. sheep. Worn. Some light waterstains, but a very good copy. Ximenes 63-342 1983 $600

BOREMAN, THOMAS   Moral Reflections on the Short Life of the Ephemeron. Boston: 1970 Published by David R. Godine. Octavo. Color etchings by Lance Hidy. Limited to 100 copies signed by Hidy. Near mint with slip-case. Bromer 25-217 1983 $200

BORGES, JORGE LUIS   Deathwatch on the Southside. Cambridge, Mass., (1968). Oblong wrappers. Total ed. is 150 copies signed by author and Robert Fitzgerald, the translator. Fine copy. In Our Time 156-91 1983 $75

BORGES, JORGE LUIS   Irish Strategies. Dublin: Dolmen Press, 1975. First edition. Coloured illus. by B. Childs. One of 350 numbered copies, signed by the translators and artist. Slipcase. Fine. Rota 231-86 1983 £50

BORGIOTTI, MARIO   La lezione pittorica di Fattori. Milano: Aldo Martello/Galleria d'Arte Sant'Ambrogio, 1968. 62 tipped-in color plates. 10 tipped-in color text illus. Folio. Cloth. Dust jacket. Ars Libri 33-458 1983 $150

BORGIOTTI, MARIO   Mario Puccini e Ulvi Liegi... Milano: Edizioni d'Arte Sant'Ambrogio, 1969. 85 tipped-in color plates with commentary opposite. Square folio. Cloth. Dust jacket. Ars Libri 33-567 1983 $125

BORING, EDWIN G.   Sensation and Perception in the History of Experimental Psychology. NY: Appleton, (1947 (1942)). Gach 95-55 1983 $40

BORLASE, WILLIAM COPELAND   Naenia Cornubiae, a Descriptive Essay. London & Truro, 1872. Illus., neatly recased in the orig. gilt-decorated cloth. K Books 397-28 1983 £39

BORN, ESTER   The New Architecture in Mexico. NY: Architectural Record, 1937. Numerous photos, cloth, numerous stamped names on both end papers. Covers heavily soiled. First ed. King 46-383 1983 $35

BORN, IGNAZ VON   New Process of Amalgamation of Gold
and Silver Ores... London, 1790. First English edition. 4to.
Orig. boards, worn, rebacked, uncut. 22 plates. Some margins
dust-soiled. Gurney 90-19 1983 £210

BORN, MAX   The Constitution of Matter, Modern
Atomic and Electron Theories... London: Methuen & Co., 1923.
First edition. 8vo. Orig. green cloth. Numerous text illus.
and diagrmas. A very good copy. Zeitlin 264-56 1983 $60

BORNE, F. P.   El Latrodectus Formidabilis de Chile.
Santiago, 1892-94. 3 plates (1 coloured), 4to, wrappers. The paper
is of poor quality and brittle. Wheldon 160-1250 1983 £15

BORRA, POMPEO   Piero Della Francesca. Milano:
Istituto Editoriale Italiano, 1950. 137 plates. Small folio.
Cloth. Ars Libri 33-271 1983 $75

BORRELLI, GENNARO   Il presepe napoletano. Roma, 1970
516pp. 218 plates (partly in color). Square 4to, Cloth. D.j.
Ars Libri SB 26-34 1983 $150

BORRHAUS, MARTINUS CELLARIUS Elementale Cosmographicum, quo totius
& Astronomiae & Geographiae Rudimenta, certifisimis breussimisque
docentur apodixibus. Parisiis, Apud Gulielmum Cauellet, in pinqui
Gallina, ex aduerso collegii Cameracensis. 1551. Com priuilegio
Revis. 8vo, numerous woodcut illus. within text. Bound in full
modern calf. Blind tooled on spine. New endpapers. Arkway 22-13
1983 $975

BORRICHIUS, OLAUS   De ortu et progressu chemiae, dissertatio. Copenhagen: Matthias Godicchenus for Petrus Haubold, 1668.
Printer's device on title. 4to. Cont. French red morocco. Triple
gilt border line. Arms of Colbert on sides and his cipher in compartments on spine. With exlibris of Bibliothecae Colbertine on title-
page and bookplate of the Skene library. First edition. Fine.
Kraus 164-27 1983 $4,500

BORROW, GEORGE   The Bible in Spain; or the Journeys,
Adventures, and Imprisonments of an Englishman. London: Murray, 1843.
First editions. 3 vols. Cont. 3/4 calf, marbled boards. Covers
darkened and somewhat worn. Good. MacManus 277-589 1983 $100

BORROW, GEORGE   The Brother Avenged and Other Ballads.
London: Printed for Private Circulation, 1913. First edition. Small
4to. Orig. green printed wrappers. Limited to only 30 copies. Unopened. Very fine. MacManus 277-590 1983 $150

BORROW, GEORGE   Emelian the Fool. London: Printed for
Private Circulation, 1913. First edition. 8vo. Orig. green printed
wrappers. Limited to 30 copies. Unopened. Very fine. MacManus 277-
593 1983 $150

BORROW, GEORGE   The Giant of Bern and Orm Ungerswayne.
London: Printed for Private Circulation, 1913. First edition. 8vo.
Orig. printed green wrappers. Limited to 30 copies. Unopened. Very
fine. MacManus 277-594 1983 $150

BORROW, GEORGE   The Gold Horns. London: Printed for
Private Circulation, 1913. First edition. Intro. by Edmund Gosse, C.B.
Small 4to. Orig. green printed wrappers. Limited to 30 copies.
Unopened. Very fine. MacManus 277-595 1983 $150

BORROW, GEORGE   Grimhild's Vengeance. London: Printed
for Private Circulation, 1913. First edition. Intro. by Edmund Gosse,
C.B. Small 4to. Orig. printed green wrappers. Limited to 30 copies.
Unopened. Very fine. MacManus 277-596 1983 $150

BORROW, GEORGE   Lavengro. John Murray, 1851. First
edition, 3 vols. Half titles, front. vol. I. 32 pp ads. vol. I & III.
Orig. dull blue cloth, borders in blind, paper labels. Very good.
Jarndyce 30-306 1983 £78

BORROW, GEORGE   Lavengro. John Murray, 1851. First
edition, 3 vols. Half titles, 32 pp ads. vols. I & II. Orig. cloth
recased. Paper labels rubbed, otherwise very good. Jarndyce 30-307
1983 £38

BORROW, GEORGE   Marsk Stig. London: Printed for Private
Circulation, 1913. First edition. 8vo. Orig. green printed wrappers.
Limited to 30 copies. Unopened. Very fine. MacManus 277-597 1983
$150

BORROW, GEORGE   Romano Lavo-Liv. John Murray, 1874.
First edition. Half title, 16 pp ads. An unopened copy in orig. blue
cloth, paper label, sl. rubbed. Fine. Jarndyce 31-434 1983 £54

BORROW, GOERGE   The Sleeping Bard. John Murray, 1860.
First edition. 8vo, blue half morocco, gilt, t.e.g., by Root & Son.
Printed in 250 copies only. Hannas 69-13 1983 £45

BORROW, GEORGE   The Songs of Ranild. London: Printed
for Private Circulation, 1913. First edition. Small 4to. Orig. green
printed wrappers. Limited to 30 copies. Unopened. Very fine. Mac-
Manus 277-598 1983 $150

BORROW, GEORGE   The Tale of Brynild and King Valdemar and
His Sister. London: Printed for Private Circulation, 1913. First
edition. Small 4to. Orig. green printed wrappers. Limited to 30
copies. Unopened. Very fine. MacManus 277-599 1983 $150

BORROW, GEORGE   The Works. London: Constable & Co.,
1923. Norwich Edition. 16 vols. Orig. cloth with paper spine labels.
Dust jackets (several a trifle worn at the edges). Contains much
unpublished material. Near-fine. MacManus 277-601 1983 $350

BORROW, GEORGE   Young Swaigder or The Force of Runes and
Other Ballads. London: Printed for Private Circulation, 1913. First
edition. Small 4to. Orig. green printed wrappers. Limited to 30
copies. Unopened. Very fine. MacManus 277-600 1983 $150

BORROW, GEORGE   The Zincali. John Murray, 1843. 3rd
edition, 2 vols. Half titles, orig. dark green cloth, paper labels.
Very good. Jarndyce 30-305 1983 £26

BORSCH-SUPAN, HELMUT   Caspar David Friedrich. New York:
George Braziller, 1974. 120 illus. (57 tipped-in color). Large
4to. Cloth. Dust jacket. Ars Libri 32-227 1983 $85

BORSI, FRANCO   Leon Battista Alberti. Milano:
Electa, 1975. 386 illus. Stout square 4to. Cloth. Slipcase.
Ars Libri 33-3 1983 $100

BORST, MAX   Allgemeine Pathologie der malignen
Geschwuelste. Leipzig, 1924. 8vo, cloth-backed bds. 6 plates and
21 text illus. Argosy 713-68 1983 $75

BORTHWICK, J. DOUGLAS   History and Biographical Gazetteer
of Montreal to the Year 1892. Montreal: Printed & Published by
John Lovell & Son, 1892. 22 1/2cm. Many portraits. Rebound in
buckram, else a fine copy. McGahern 53-180 1983 $100

THE BORZOI 1925. New York: Alfred A. Knopf, 1925. First edition.
8vo. Illus. Orig. cloth-backed boards. One of 500 copies printed
on rag paper. Inscribed on the half-title by the publishers. Very
good copy. Jaffe 1-8 1983 $85

BOSANQUET, BERNARD   A Companion to Plato's Republic for
English Readers. London, 1895. 8vo, cloth. Salloch 385-681 1983
$35

BOSANQUET, BERNARD   Science and Philosophy. London: George
Allen & Unwin, (1927). First edition. Gach 95-56 1983 $27.50

BOSCANA, GERONIMO   Chinigchinich. Santa Ana, Fine Arts
Press, 1933. Folio. Illus. in color with linoleum cuts by Jean
Goodwin. Brown cloth over boards. Cloth slipcase. Fine. Houle 22-
1136 1983 $275

BOSE, EMIL   The Cretaceous and Tertiary of Southern
Texas and Northern Mexico. Austin: UT Press, 1912. First edition.
Plates, large folding map. Orig. grey printed wrappers. Fragile
backstrip reinforced with matching paper. Fine. Jenkins 152-309
1983 $75

BOSE, GEORG MATHIAS   Hypothesis Soni Perraultiana ac in eam Meditationes. Leipzig: Breitkopf, 1735. First edition. 4to. Boards. Gurney 90-21 1983 £40

BOSE, J. C.   Plant Autographs and their Revelations. 1927. Faded cloth. Wheldon 160-1495 1983 £12

BOSE, S. C.   The Hindoos as They Are. Calcutta, 1881. 8vo. Orig. cloth. Good. Edwards 1044-77 1983 £40

BOSKOVIC, RUDJER JOSIP   Dissertatio de Viribus Vivis. (Vienna), 1752. 12mo. Old sheep, creased and slightly wormed. 1 plate. Gurney 90-20 1983 £80

BOSSAGLIA, ROSSANA   La scultura italiana dall'Alto Medioeve alle correnti contemporanee. Milano, n.d. A cura di Rossana Bossaglio, Enzo Carli, Franco Russoli, Valentino Martinelli, Carlo Pirovani. 449pp. 244 plates (partly tipped-in color). Folio. Cloth. D.j. Ars Libri SB 26-36 1983 $100

BOSSANGE, HECTOR   Ma Bibliotheque Francaise. Paris, 1855. 1st ed., 8vo, cont. half morocco gilt, marbled boards, half-title, uncut copy, vignette tile. Hinges of rear cover repaired, but a very good copy. Trebizond 18-106 1983 $75

BOSSCHA, H.   Bibliotheca Classica. Deventer, 1825. Vellum gilt, 3rd edition. 8vo, cloth. Salloch 385-71 1983 $90

BOSSCHERE, JEAN DE   Christmas Tales of Flanders. N.Y.: Dodd, 1917. First edition. 4to. Blue cloth, extensive gilt decoration. Spine slightly faded. Full-page color plates (12) many full-page black & whites and 2-color illus. plus numerous smaller black & whites. Very good. Aleph-bet 8-80 1983 $70

BOSSERT, H.   The Art of Ancient Crete. 1937. 4to, cloth. Salloch 385-271 1983 $45

BOSSOM, ALFRED C.   Building to the Skies. The Studio Limited, 1934. First edition, with 72 plates, roy. 8vo, orig. cloth. Fenning 60-34 1983 £16.50

BOSSUET, JACQUES BENIGNE   An Exposition of the Doctrine of the Catholic Church in Matters of Controversie. Printed by Henry Hills, 1686. 4to, wrapper, a very good copy. Fenning 61-37 1983 £32.50

BOSSUET, JACQUES BENIGNE   Maximes et Reflexions sur la Comedie. Paris: Jean Annison, 1694. 1st ed., 12mo, modern full calf, spine gilt, a.e.g., inner dentelles gilt. Vignette title page, bookplate. A very fine copy of an uncommon title. Trebizond 18-107 1983 $225

THE BOSTON Directory. Boston, 1830. Folding map. Calf-backed printed boards (very worn, covers detached). Felcone 22-137 1983 $60

BOSWELL, JAMES   Boswell on the Grand Tour: Germany and Switzerland. London: 1953. Edited by Frederick A. Pottle. 4to, parchment-backed bds., leather label, slipcase. Illustrated. Bottom of spine bumped; a very fine copy. Perata 27-20 1983 $75

BOSWELL, JAMES   Boswell's Autobiography. Chatto & Windus, 1912. First edition, half title, front. Orig. green cloth. Jarndyce 30-901 1983 £20

BOSWELL, JAMES   Letters of James Boswell, addressed to the Rev. W.J. Temple. London: Bentley, 1857. First edition. 8vo. Orig. purple-brown cloth. Spine faded, inner hinges cracked. Ximenes 63-229 1983 $100

BOSWELL, JAMES   Letters of James Boswell. Oxford: At the Clarendon Press, 1924. First edition. Tall 8vo. Three-quarter creme buckram over antique marbled paper, paper spine label, t.e.g., others uncut. Limited to only 100 numbered copies signed by Tinker and Hackett of the Brick Row Bookshop. Minor cover wear. Oak Knoll 48-68 1983 $250

BOSWELL, JAMES   The Life of Samuel Johnson, LL.D. London: by Henry Baldwin, for Charles Dilly, 1791. First edition, first issue. 2 vols. 4to. Cont. calf, neatly rebacked with morocco labels, gilt. Engraved portrait by Heath and engraved plates of the Round-Robin and facsimile. Traylen 94-95 1983 £900

BOSWELL, JAMES   The life of Samuel Johnson, LL.D. Dublin: printed by John Chambers, for R. Cross, etc., 1792. First Irish edition. 3 vols. 8vo. Old half calf. With two folding plates. Spines scuffed, labels chipped, one label missing, a few minor stains. Ximenes 63-27 1983 $150

BOSWELL, JAMES   The Life of Samuel Johnson, LL.D. London: Henry Baldwin for Charles Dilly, 1793. 2nd ed., revised and augmented. 8vo, 3 volumes, cont. half calf, morocco labels, marbled boards. Frontis. portrait in Vol. 1, two folding plates, lacking the rare leaf of "Additional Corrections" in Vol. 1. A very clean copy, despite chipping of top edge of one spine. Trebizond 18-10 1983 $375

BOSWELL, JAMES   The Life of Samuel Johnson, LLD. London: Routledge, 1891. Illus. with port. by Sir Joshua Reynolds. 5 vols. Old half morocco. Bindings somewhat rubbed; a bit stained. MacManus 277-622 1983 $100

BOSWELL, JAMES   The Life of Samuel Johnson. London: J.M. Dent & Co., 1901. 3 vols. Thick roy. 8vo. Orig. light blue buckram, vellum label, gilt, uncut edges. Limited edition of 150 numbered copies on large paper, with 100 full-page and other illus. from line-drawings by Herbert Railton, 30 portrait in photogravure, and end-paper maps. Traylen 94-97 1983 £70

BOSWELL, JAMES   The Life of Samuel Johnson. Bath, 1925. 2 vols. 4to. Bound in half dark blue crushed levant morocco, gilt, gilt panelled spines, edges gilt, by Bayntun. 576 illus., facsimiles and maps, including 13 plates in photogravure. Traylen 94-98 1983 £75

BOSWELL, JAMES   Private Papers of James Boswell from Malahide Castle. New York, 1928-34. 18 vols. 4to. Full red boards, buckram spines, printed paper labels, preserved in the orig. slip-cases. Limited edition of 570 copies, designed by Bruce Rogers and printed by W.E. Rudge, with numerous facsimiles, illus. and a map. A mint set. Traylen 94-100 1983 £900

BOSWELL, JAMES   Reproductions of some of the Original Proof Sheets of Boswell's Life of Johnson. Buffalo: privately printed by R.B. Adam for his friends, 1923. Folio. Cloth-backed boards. 63 full page facsimiles of the corrected proof sheets. Signed by Adam. Spine ends show wear else very good copy. Oak Knoll 49-300 1983 $125

BOSWELL, P. G. H.   The Middle Silurian Rocks of North Wales. 1949. 37 folders and 25 plates, 8vo, cloth. Wheldon 160-1361 1983 £15

BOSWELL, PEYTON   George Bellows. New York: Crown, 1942. 112 plates. 4to. Cloth. Ars Libri 32-29 1983 $50

BOSWORTH, T. O.   Geology of the Tertiary and Quaternary Periods in the North-west part of Peru. 1922. 26 plates, 11 charts and 150 figures, 8vo, cloth (slightly marked). Wheldon 160-1362 1983 £20

BOTANIQUE Pratique. Suisse et Savoie. Geneva, 1885. 319 coloured plates, 2 vols., 8vo, original cloth. Very scarce. Spine of vol. 2 faded. Wheldon 160-1656 1983 £70

BOTELER, T.   Narrative of A Voyage of Discovery to Africa and Arabia. London, 1835. First edition. 4 engraved plates. 2 vols. Later quarter calf, gilt. 8vo. Good. Edwards 1044-78 1983 £225

BOTHWELL, JAMES, EARL OF   Les Affaires du Conte de Boduel. 1829. 4to, orig. boards with paper label, rubbed at the edges. Bickersteth 77-99 1983 £35

BOTSFORD, GEORGE W.   The Athenian Constitution. NY, 1893. 1/4 cl. 8vo. Salloch 385-212 1983 $20

BOTTARI, STEFANO   Antonello da Messina. Milano: Silvana,
1955. 45 tipped-in plates (39 color). 6 text illus. Folio. Cloth.
Dust jacket. Slipcase. Ars Libri 33-10 1983 $100

BOTTOMLEY, GORDON   Chambers of Imagery. London: Elkin
Mathews, 1907, 1912. First editions. Orig. wrappers. Second
series is a presentation copy, inscribed by Bottomley to Edward Thomas
on the half-title, dated April 14th, 1912, Cartmel. Very good pair.
MacManus 277-628 1983 $150

BOTTOMLEY, GORDON   Chambers of Imagery. London, 1912.
First edition. Wrappers. Author's signed autograph presentation
inscription to J. Guthrie, followd by the recipient's presentation
inscription. Very nice. Rota 230-90 1983 £25

BOTTOMLEY, GORDON   Laodice and Danae: Play in One Act.
n.p. (London). Printed for private circulation. 1909. 8vo. Wraps.
1st ed. Edges of wrappers are worn and chipped, otherwise vg-fine.
Seven pages of play bear annotations and deletions by author. In
addition, this copy bears three pages of manuscript inserted into
text at various places and the author has made the comment "insert
at". Signed by author. In Our Time 156-92 1983 $250

BOTTOMLEY, GORDON   Lyric Plays. London: Constable & Co.,
Ltd., 1932. First edition. Orig. cream buckram. Presentation copy,
inscribed on the front flyleaf. Covers somewhat dust-soiled. Good.
MacManus 277-630 1983 $85

BOTTOMLEY, GORDON   Lyric Plays. London, 1932. First edition. Wrappers over limp boards. Inscribed on flyleaf and also on
the verso of the contents leaf. A review of "Marsaili's Weeping" is
loosely inserted. Nice. Rota 230-91 1983 £30

BOTTOMLEY, GORDON   Poems of Thirty Years. London: Con-
stable & Co., 1925. First edition. Frontis. port. of the author by
Emery Walker. Orig. embossed cloth designed by Charles Ricketts.
Presentation copy to Edward Marsh, inscribed. Spine faded. Very good.
Unopened. MacManus 277-631 1983 $150

BOTTOMLEY, GORDON   The Riding to Lithend. Flansham,
Sussex: The Pear Tree Press, 1909. Small 4to, with 5 illus.
Presentation copy, signed by Guthrie on half-title in 1909. Linen
spine over boards; paper cover label. Boards a bit soiled. Some
foxing to endpaper. Karmiole 74-75 1983 $150

BOTTOMLEY, GORDON   Scenes and Plays. London: Constable &
Co., Ltd., 1929. First edition. Orig. decorated wrappers with printed
labels. Presentation copy, inscribed to Edward Marsh. Spine slightly
darkened. Label a bit rubbed. Scarce. Very good. MacManus 277-632
1983 $150

BOTTOMLEY, GORDON   Scenes and Plays. London: Constable &
Co. Ltd., 1929. First edition. Orig. decorated wrappers. Very fine.
MacManus 277-633 1983 $45

BOTTOMLEY, GORDON   A Vision of Giorgione. Portland, Maine:
Thomas B. Mosher, 1910. First edition. Orig. lavender boards with
paper labels, plain printed dust jacket (darkened & a little worn at
edges). Presentation copy, inscribed to Lascelles Abercrombie.
Boards faded. Slight foxing. Limited to 500 copies. Very good.
MacManus 277-634 1983 $85

BOUCHARD, CHARLES   A Study of Some Points in the Pathology
of Cerebral Haemorrhage. London, 1872. Cloth, (crudely rebacked);
ex-lib. 4 lithos, 1 partly colored. Argosy 713-69 1983 $65

BOUCHARD, CHARLES   Therapeutique des Maladies Infectieuses
Antisepsie Cours de Pathologie Generale... Paris, 1889. 8vo. Red
quarter-shagreen. First edition. Gurney JJ-47 1983 £12.50

BOUCHETTE, JOSEPH   The British Dominions in North America.
London: Longman, Rees, Orme, Brown, Green & Longman, 1832. 4to.
First edition, second issue. 3 vols. 31 plates, maps and plans,
including 2 folding. Orig. publishers green pebble cloth with paper
labels. A fine set. McGahern 53-9 1983 $1,350

BOUCHUT, EUGENE (1818-1891) Traite Des Signes de law Mort et Des
Moyens de Prevenir Les Enterrements Prematures. Paris: J. B.
Bailliere, 1849. 12mo. Ad leaf, titlepage. Contemporary leather-
backed boards, spine quite worn, library bookplate and label on rear
paste-down. First edition. John Ordronaux's copy, signed and dated
1861 with his occasional pencil lining. Gach 95-57 1983 $45

BOUDIER, E.   Icones Mycologicae ou Iconographie des
Champignons de France principalement Discomycetes. Lausanne, (1905-
11) 1982. 4 vols., 4to, art leather, 600 coloured plates. Wheldon
160-9a 1983 £380

BOUDINOT, ELIAS   A Star in the West. Trenton, 1816.
New half morocco, somewhat foxed, but nice. Reese 18-492 1983 $175

BOUGEOIS, LOUYSE   A Sketch of the Life and Writings of...
Phila., 1876. 8vo, pr. wrs., in board binder, ex-lib. Argosy 713-
70 1983 $75

BOUGHEN, EDWARD   An Account of the Church Catholick.
Printed by E. Cotes, for Richard Royston, 1653. First edition, 4to,
wrapper, the title-page just a little dusty, but otherwise a very good
copy. Fenning 61-38 1983 £18.50

BOUGUES, LUCIEN   La Musique et la vie Interieure. Paris &
Lausanne, 1921. 18 illus. Large folding plate. Thick 4to, new
buckram with leather label. Salloch 387-291 1983 $75

BOUILLAUD, J.   Traite Clinique du Rhumatisme Arti-
culaire... Paris, 1840. First edition. 8vo. Cont. boards, uncut,
largely unopened. Gurney 90-22 1983 £175

BOUILLET, M.   Traite des moyens de rendre les
rivieres navigables. Paris: chez Estienne Michaellet, 1693.
First edition. 8vo. Old half morocco. 12 engraved folding
plates. Binding worn, spine defective. Internally fine. Rare.
Ximenes 63-566 1983 $450

BOULE, MARCELLIN   Les Hommes Fossiles. Paris, 1921.
8vo. Orig. wrappers. Numerous illus. First edition. Gurney JJ-48
1983 $18

BOULENGER, G. A.   Catalogue of the Freshwater Fishes of
Africa. British Museum, 1909-16. Text-figures, 4 vols., imp. 8vo,
cloth. The rare original printing. A good ex-library copy. Wheldon
160-944 1983 £140

BOULENGER, G. A.   Contributions to the Ichthyology of
Lake Tanganyika. Zoo. Trans., 1899-1906. 24 plates, 3 parts, 4to,
wrappers. Wheldon 160-943 1983 £25

BOULGER, D. C.   The History of China. London, 1898.
New and revised edition. Folding map, 6 portraits. 2 vols. Thick
8vo. Uncut. Good. Edwards 1044-80 1983 £65

BOULGER, D. C.   The Life of Sir Stamford Raffles.
London, 1897. Frontis. 2 maps, 1 folding, folding facsimile, 14
plates. Worming in the first few pages. Uncut. Binders, cloth with
morocco label. 8vo. Good. Edwards 1044-79 1983 £50

BOULTON, ALFREDO   Imagenes del Occidente Venezolane.
(N. Y., 1940). Illus., square 4to, ringed pr. bds., foxed. One of
200 copies. Argosy 710-499 1983 $35

BOUN, ABRAHAM   The Pride and Avarice of the Clergie.
Printed for T.M. and are to be sold by Giles Calvert. 1650. 12mo,
orig. calf, rebacked. Orig. calf, rebacked. Old ink inscription on
the flies, and stamp of the Heber Library. Bickersteth 77-7 1983
£160

BOUQUET for BR, a Birthday Garland Gathered by the Typophiles.
New York: (The Typophiles), 1950. First edition. 12mo. Cloth-
backed decorated boards. Limited to 600 copies. Very fine copy.
Oak Knoll 38-338 1983 $50

BOURET, JEAN   Henri Rousseau. Greenwich: New
York Graphic Society, 1961. 232 illus. (50 color). Large square
4to. Cloth. Dust jacket. Ars Libri 32-593 1983 $75

BOURGERY, JEAN-BAPTISTE MARC Traite Complet de l'Anatomie de l'Homme
Comprenant la Medecine Operatoire...avec Planches Lithographiees
d'Apres Nature. C.A. Delaunay, Paris, 1831-54. First edition. 8vo,
folio, with 729 hand coloured lithographed plates; very occasional
light foxing but a fine set; cont. half crimson morocco, several
joints repaired. Quaritch NS 5-15 1983 $4,850

BOURJAILY, FANCE   The End of My Life. New York:
Scribner's, 1947. Printed wraps. Advance reading copy of the first
edition. A couple of slight creases, but a fine copy. Reese 20-141
1983 $125

BOURKE, JOHN G.   On the Border with Crook. New York:
Charles Scribner's Sons, 1891. Illustrations. Original pictorial
cloth, gilt. Some wear. Jenkins 153-57 1983 $175

BOURKE, JOHN G.   The Urine Dance of the Zuni Indians
of New Mexico... Privately printed, 1920. Wash., 1858. Half
morocco. First edition. Ginsberg 47-670 1983 $75

BOURKE-WHITE, MARGARET   Shooting the Russian War. New York,
1942. 1st ed. Photographs by author. 8vo, few light stains on
front cover. Morrill 288-559 1983 $42.50

BOURNE, GEORGE   The Picture of Quebec and Its Vicinty.
Quebec: P. & W. Ruthven, 1831. 18mo, 1/2 roan, pr. boards, 6 plates,
folding map. Worn, spine chipped. Argosy 710-46 1983 $300

BOURNE, GEORGE   The Spirit of the Public Journals.
Baltimore, George Dobbin & Murphy, 1806. 12mo. Contemporary calf.
1st ed. Lacks label and endleaves; hinges partly broken. Morrill
289-276 1983 $35

BOURNE, HENRY RICHARD FOX   English merchants: memoirs in illustrations of the progress of British commerce. London: Bentley,
1866. 2 vols. First edition. 8vo. Orig. blue cloth. Frontis.
in each vol., nine plates, and many illus. in the text. Fine copy.
Ximenes 63-593 1983 $70

BOURNE, JOHN C.   The History and Description of the Great
Western Railway. David Bogue, London, 1846. Folio, tinted lithographed title and 46 views on 33 plates, 2 hand-coloured maps and 1
plate of sections, and 3 vignettes. A good clean copy in the orig.
half green morocco, gilt spine, gilt edges. Joints repaired. First
edition. Quaritch NS 5-16 1983 $5,000

BOURNE, STEPHEN   Trade, population and food. London:
Bell, 1880. First edition. 8vo. Orig. olive-green cloth. Slightly
rubbed. Ximenes 63-594 1983 $85

BOUSSEAU, FRANCOIS-GABRIEL   Physiological Pyretology. Phila., 1832.
First American edition. 8vo, cont. calf, (worn) leather label; ex-lib.
Argosy 713-67 1983 $75

BOUTCHER, WILLIAM   A treatise on forest-trees. Edinburgh:
printed by R. Fleming, and sold by the author, 1775. First edition.
4to. Cont. calf, spine gilt. Subscriber's copy, with an additional
engraved title-page not issued with most copies; ownership inscription of John Pringle of Crichton, whose name appears in the 17-page
subscriber's list. Ximenes 63-177 1983 $350

BOUTELL, CHARLES   Boutell's Manual of Heraldry.
London (1931). Rev. & Illus. 32 color plates & text illus. G.t.,
ex-lib. Argosy 710-206 1983 $40

BOUTELL, H. S.   First Editions of Today... Berkeley:
Univ. of California Press, 1949. Third edition, revised and enlarged.
Small 8vo. Cloth. Jacket is worn. Oak Knoll 48-407 1983 $35

BOUVENNE, AGLAUS   Notes et souvenirs sur Charles Meryon.
Paris: Charavay Freres, 1883. 7 plates. 19 text ornaments. Large
4to. Wrappers. No. 277 of a limited edition of 335 copies on Marais.
Designed by Bracquemond. Dusty; spine torn. Ars Libri 32-448 1983
$150

BOVI, ARTURO   Caravaggio. Firenze: Edizioni d'Arte
Il Fiorino, 1974. 20 color plates. 111 illus. Large 4to. Cloth.
Dust jacket. Ars Libri 33-67 1983 $125

BOWDEN, HANNAH   Poetical Remains. A.W. Bennett, 1861.
2nd edition, half title, orig. brown cloth, sl. rubbed. Jarndyce 30-
651 1983 $12.50

BOWDICH, THOMAS EDWARD   Excursions in Madeira and Porto Santo...
London: George B. Whittaker, 1825. 4to. 23 plates (4 hand-colored).
Modern 1/4 brown calf, red label. Library blind stamp on title,
repairs to few pp. corners. Adelson Africa-15 1983 $400

BOWDITCH, HENRY P.   The Medical School of the Future.
1900. Offprint. Wrappers. 8vo. Fye H-3-49 1983 $20

BOWDITCH, NATHANIEL INGERSOLL   A History of the Massachusetts General Hospital. Boston, 1872. Second edition. 8vo. Orig. binding.
Many engr. plates. Spine chipped. Fye H-3-50 1983 $100

BOWDITCH, NATHANIEL INGERSOLL Memoir of Nathaniel Bowditch. Boston,
1839. 1st ed. Presentation from author to Professor Felton. 2
portraits. 4to, orig. boards, cloth back. Binding rubbed and
stained, few blank margins dampstained at bottom. Morrill 289-592
1983 $75

BOWDITCH, VINCENT   Life and Correspondence of Henry
Ingersoll Bowditch. Boston, 1902. 2 vols. First edition. 8vo.
Orig. binding. Ex-library. Fye H-3-692 1983 $40

BOWDLER, JANE   Poems and essays. Bath: printed by
R. Crutwell, 1786. First edition. 2 vols. 8vo. Cont. red morocco,
gilt, spines gilt, a.e.g. Bookplate of Lady Newdigate. A fine
copy. Ximenes 63-356 1983 $250

BOWEN, ELIZABETH   The Death of the Heart. London, 1938.
8vo, wraps.; worn; backstrip missing. Uncorrected proof. Argosy
714-71 1983 $50

BOWEN, ELIZABETH   The Hotel. NY, 1928. Near fine in fine
dustwrapper. Quill & Brush 54-125 1983 $35

BOWEN, ELIZABETH   The House in Paris. New York: 1936.
First American edition. Red cloth. Lightly worn dust jacket.
Bradley 66-59 1983 $27.50

BOWEN, ELIZABETH   Seven Winters. Dublin: Cuala Press,
1942. First edition. One of 450 numbered copies. Covers just a
little soiled. Stephen Gooden's signed autograph presentation inscription to Mona Gooden. Nice. Rota 230-92 1983 £60

BOWEN, F. C.   Sailing Ships of the London River.
London, 1936. First edition. 8vo. Orig. cloth. 40 plates from
drawings by P. Jones. Orig. dust jacket. Fine. Edwards 1042-12
1983 £18

BOWEN, F. C.   The Sea Its History and Romance. New
York, 1927. 4to. Orig. cloth. 4 coloured frontis. 58 coloured
plates (2 folding) and numerous other plates and illus., some in text.
4 vols. Spines slightly worn and soiled. Inner hinges strengthened.
Good. Edwards 1042-13 1983 £80

BOWEN, MARJORIE   Mary Queen of Scots, Daughter of
Debate. John Lane, the Bodley Head Ltd., (1934). 8vo, portrait.
Cloth, slightly soiled. First edition. Bickersteth 77-100 1983
£12

BOWER, BERTHA M.   A Collection of Her Works. 35 vols.,
many of which were illus. by Charles M. Russell. In fine bright
condition. Jenkins 155-108 1983 $600

BOWER, F. O.   The Origin of a Land Flora. 1908.
Trifle used, good ex-library copy. Wheldon 160-1496 1983 £15

BOWER, JOHN   Description of the Abbeys of Melrose
and Old Melrose with their Traditions. Printed for the author,
Edinburgh, 1827. Third edition improved, good ex-library, crisp copy,
orig. boards. K Books 301-27 1983 £25

BOWERS, FREDSON   The Red Badge of Courage: A Facsimile
Edition of the Manuscript, edited with an Introduction and Apparatus
by Fredson Bowers. Washington, D.C.: Bruccoli-Clark, (1973). 2
vols. 1st ed. limited to 1,000 numbered sets. Orig. red cloth,
labels, box. Fine set. Jenkins 155-265 1983 $85

BOWLES, ELLA SHANNON   Homespun Handicrafts. Philadelphia,
Lippincott, 1931. 1st ed. Presentation copy. Illus. 8vo. Morrill
288-43 1983 $22.50

BOWLES, PAUL   Collected Stories. L.A., 1979. Limited
to 60 numbered copies signed by author and Gore Vidal. Very fine.
Quill & Brush 54-126 1983 $125

BOWLES, PAUL   The Delicate Prey, and Other Stories.
N.Y., (1950). First edition. Argosy 714-75 1983 $20

BOWLES, PAUL   A Little Stone. London, 1950. First
edition. In Keith Vaughan dustwrapper with a small tear. Very fine.
Jolliffe 26-61 1983 £25

BOWLES, PAUL   A Little Stone. London, 1950. First
edition. Small stain on front board, in slightly buckled dustwrapper
with a small tear at head of spine. Gekoski 2-16 1983 £25

BOWLES, PAUL   The Sheltering Sky. (New York): A New
Directions Book, (1949). First American edition. 8vo. Orig. cloth.
Dust jacket. Fine copy. Jaffe 1-47 1983 $100

BOWLES, PAUL   The Sheltering Sky. (N.Y. 1949). First
American edition. Fine, in a slightly frayed dust wrapper. Argosy
714-77 1983 $20

BOWLES, SAMUEL   Across the Continent. Springfield, Ma.,
1865. Folded map. Orig. cloth. First edition, first issue. Ginsberg
48 502 1093 1983 $75

BOWLES, SAMUEL   Across the Continent. Springfield,
1865. First edition, 8vo, orig. cloth, (backstrip top mended).
Inscribed by Bowles. Argosy 716-539 1983 $75

BOWLES, SAMUEL   The Pacific Railroad-Open. Boston,
Fields & Osgood, 1869. First edition. Small 8vo, green cloth stamped
in gilt, (some rubbing, spine edges worn). Very good. Houle 22-
1028 1983 $85

BOWMAN, JAMES C.   Pecos Bill the Greatest Cowboy of All
Time. Chicago, 1937. First edition. Frontis. and illus. Jenkins
152-25 1983 $40

BOWMAN, JOHN G.   Nationality Rooms of the University of
Pittsburgh. Pittsburgh, 1947. 1st ed., limited. Water colors and
crayon drawings by Andrey Avinoff, etchings by Louis Orr. Folio,
orig. buckram. Fine plates. Morrill 289-497 1983 $37.50

BOWNAS, SAMUEL   An Account of the Life, Travels, and
Christian Experiences...of Samuel Bownas. Stanford, N.Y., 1805. Old
calf, very good. Reese 18-272 1983 $95

BOWNAS, SAMUEL   The Journals of the Lives and Travels
of Samuel Bownas, and John Richardson. Philadelphia: William Dunlap,
1759. Cont. calf, spine shabby and front hinge broken. First
American edition. Nantucket Starbuck family association copy.
This copy belonged to Daniel Starbuck and bears his signature and
date 1774 on the front endsheet. Tipped to this same endsheet is a
colored chart of the Starbuck family. Felcone 21-15 1983 $200

BOWREY, T.   A Geographical Account of Countries
Round the Bay of Bengal. Cambridge, 1905. Folding chart in pocket.
Numerous plates. Ex-library, some wear, spine faded. 8vo. Orig.
cloth. Good. Edwards 1044-81 1983 £40

BOWRING, JOHN   Minor Morals for Young People. London:
Whittaker, 1834-35. Edinburgh: William Tait, 1839 (for Vol. III).
1st ed., first state, 8vo, 3 vols., later calf gilt, spines gilt,
morocco labels, t.e.g., original paper labels bound in at end. 12
etchings signed by George Cruikshank, and 8 by William Heath. Uncut
copy with the half-titles. Despite wear to some hinges, a very good
copy. Trebizond 18-22 1983 $160

BOX, E. O.   Macroclimate and Plant Forms. The
Hague, 1981. 25 maps, 8vo, cloth. Wheldon 160-1497 1983 £42

BOXING Made Easy. New York: Dick & Fitzgerald, 1890? 8vo, with 10
plates in text; publishers' ads. Orig. printed green pictorial
wraps. (chipped). In orig. wraps. Rostenberg 88-64 1983 $45

BOYCE, THOMAS   A Specimen of Elegiac Poetry. London:
Printed for T. Becket...MDCCLXXIII. First and only edition. 4to,
small piece torn from corner of half-title, disbound. Quaritch NS
7-12 1983 $75

BOYD, JAMES   Drums. NY: Scribner's, (1928). Octavo.
First signed limited edition. 14 color plates and numerous b&w drawings by N. C. Wyeth. Signed by both Wyeth and Boyd with facsimilies
of correspondence between them bound-in. Extremely fine with large
pictorial label. Bromer 25-406A 1983 $225

BOYD, JAMES   Drums. N.Y., Scribner's, (1928). First
edition. 4to, illus. with 14 full page color plates, cover label,
endpapers, title page by Wyeth. Black cloth stamped in gilt with
cover label, very good. Houle 22-995 1983 $85

BOYD, JAMES   Drums. NY: Scribner's, (1928). Octavo.
First illus. trade edition. 14 color plates and numerous b&w drawings
by N. C. Wyeth. Very fine with slightly chipped pictorial dust wrapper.
Bromer 25-406B 1983 $75

BOYD, JOHN   Sir George Etienne Cartier, His Life
and Times. Toronto: Macmillan, 1914. 24cm. Photogravure frontis.
and 20 plates. Blue cloth. Very good to fine copy. McGahern 54-
191 1983 $45

BOYD, LYNN   To the People of the First Congressional
District of Kentucky. N.p., (1841). Dbd. First edition. Ginsberg
46-394 1983 $125

BOYD, THOMAS   Mad Anthony Wayne. New York, 1929.
1st ed. Portrait and maps. 8vo. Morrill 286-65 1983 $12.50

BOYD, THOMAS ALVIN   As I Remember It...Personal Recollections. (Detroit), n.p., n.d. Photos, cloth, very good. Contains
copies of personal pictures, etc. King 46-142 1983 $125

BOYD, THOMAS ALVIN   Looking Back On My Life After 30.
(Detroit), n.p., 1966. Library cloth. Very good. Includes
photo album filled with numerous personal pictures, etc.
King 46-143 1983 $350

BOYLE, ELEANOR VERE   Days and Hours in a Garden. London:
Elliot Stock, 1884. Third edition. Orig. tissue-covered stiff
wrappers. One of 50 copies on handmade paper. Cont. owner's inscription on half-title. All corners worn. Some edges frayed. Covers
slightly soiled. MacManus 277-639 1983 $20

BOYLE, FREDERICK   The Savage Life. A Second Series of
"Camp Notes". London, 1876. First edition, 8vo, original brown
cloth, neatly recased, new endpapers, corners repaired, slight
worming of cover. Deighton 3-50 1983 £48

BOYLE, G. E.   The Rifle Brigade Century. London, 1905.
Orig. cloth. 8vo. Signature on endpaper. Good. Edwards 1042-549
1983 £40

BOYLE, KAY   A Frenchman Must Die. London, (1946).
8vo. Cloth. 1st English ed. Fine in dj. In Our Time 156-94 1983
$35

BOYLE, KAY   Gentlemen I Address You Privately. Lon.,
(1934). Spine and edges faded, tiny tear at top spine edge, still
good or better, tight copy in slightly frayed and chipped dustwrapper.
Quill & Brush 54-132 1983 $60

BOYLE, KAY   Monday Night. NY, (1938). Spine edge
sunned, else very good in slightly chipped and worn still presentable
dustwrapper. Quill & Brush 54-133 1983 $50

BOYLE, KAY   Primer For Combat. NY, 1942. Very good
in slightly soiled, slightly chipped, else very good dustwrapper. Quill
& Brush 54-134 1983 $30

BOYLE, KAY   Primer for Combat. New York, 1942.
First edition. Bookplate. Very nice. Rota 230-95 1983 £15

BOYLE, KAY   Thirty Stories. NY, (1946). Review slip laid-in, front fly slightly skinned, still near fine in two very good dustwrappers. Quill & Brush 54-136 1983 $50

BOYLE, ROBERT   Medicinal Experiments. London: For Smith & Walford, 1696. 2 vols. in 1. Small 12mo, modern calf, third edition, vols. 1 & 2 complete; vol. 3 printed for J. Taylor, 1694, not present. Argosy 713-72 1983 $200

BOYLE, ROBERT   New Experiments and Observations Touching Cold. London: Richard Davis, 1683. Two folding plates. Disbound. Second edition. Felcone 21-16 1983 $250

BOYLE, ROBERT   Reasons why a Protestant Should not Turn Papist. Printed by H. Clark, for John Taylor, 1687. First edition, without the imprimatur leaf, 4to, wrapper, first and last page just a little dusty, but otherwise a very good copy. Fenning 61-40 1983 £55

BOYLE, ROBERT   Tentamina Quaedam Physiologica... Amsterdam: Elzevier, 1776. 12mo, boards. Rostenberg 88-78 1983 $325

BOYNE, WILLIAM   The Yorkshire Library, a Bibliography of Books... 1869. 4to, orig. cloth, spine faded, otherwise a bright crisp copy, limited to 150 copies for private distribution. K Books 307-30 1983 £55

BOYNTON, CHARLES B.   The History of the Navy. N.Y., 1867-68. First edition. 2 vols. Steel eng. portraits. Color litho plates of ships. Full calf. Ink inscriptions. Foxed. Covers rubbed. King 45-17 1983 $150

BOYNTON, EDWARD C.   History of West Point... New York, 1863. 1st ed. Maps and plates, including large folding tinted plate. 8vo, corners and ends of spine worn, inner front hinge slightly cracked. Morrill 288-44 1983 $75

BRACHET, A.   Traite d'embryologie des vertebres. Paris, 1935. Second edition, 603 figures, royal 8vo, cloth. Wheldon 160-464 1983 £20

BRACKENBURY, GEORGE   The Campaign in the Crimae. London, 1855-56. 2 vols., lithograph and printed titles and 79 tinted lithograph plates, imperial 8vo, a little foxed, some blank margins slightly frayed, orig. gilt-decorated cloth (by Digby Wyatt), backstrips neatly laid down. K Books 307-31 1983 £150

BRACKENRIDGE, HENRY M.   Views of Louisiana; Together with a Journal of a Voyage up the Missouri River in 1811. Pittsburgh, 1814. Orig. calf, red leather label, top of hinges starting, but internally tight. Reese 18-434 1983 $1,000

BRACKENRIDGE, HENRY M.   Views of Louisiana. Baltimore, 1817. Full cont. mottled calf. Usual foxing and slight browning, otherwise a near fine copy. Reese 18-511 1983 $300

BRACKENRIDGE, HENRY M.   Views of Louisiana; Containing Geographical, Statistical, and Historical Notices of that Vast and Important Portion of America. Baltimore, 1817. Contemp. tree calf with morocco label. Minor staining and repairs. Overall a nice copy. Jenkins 151-21 1983 $250

BRACKETT, ALBERT G.   History of the United States Cavalry... N.Y., 1865. Illus. Orig. cloth. First edition. Ginsberg 47-35 1983 $125

BRADBEER, WILLIAM W.   Confederate and Southern State Currency, Historical and Financial Data. Mt. Vernon, NY, 1945. Ltd. edition. Illus. Argosy 716-108 1983 $35

BRADBURY, RAY   The Aqueduct. 1979. Limited to 230 signed copies, paperwraps, mint in orig. envelope. Quill & Brush 54-152 1983 $100

BRADBURY, RAY   Dandelion Wine. GC, 1957. Edges slightly rubbed, corners lightly bumped, else very good in slightly chipped and frayed, very good dustwrapper. Quill & Brush 54-141 1983 $125

BRADBURY, RAY   Dark Carnival. Lon., (1948). Illus. by Michael Ayrton. Slightly cocked, light interior foxing, else very good in price clipped, slightly frayed and chipped, still presentable dust-wrapper. Quill & Brush 54-142 1983 $175

BRADBURY, RAY   Fahrenheit 451. N.Y., Simon & Schuster, (1967). First printing of the reissue with a new seven page intro. by author. Advance issue for review, with the pub.'s printed slip laid in. Fine in dust jacket. Houle 22-132 1983 $175

BRADBURY, RAY   Fahrenheit 451. N.Y., Limited Editions Club, 1982. Color illus. by Joseph Mugnaini. Tall 8vo, aluminum boards; boxed. Ltd. edition. Signed by the illustrator and by the author. Mint. Argosy 714-85 1983 $125

BRADBURY, RAY   The Golden Apples of the Sun. London: Rupert Hart Davis, 1953. First English edition. Boards. Very fine in dust jacket. Bradley 66-109 1983 $75

BRADBURY, RAY   The Last Circus and The Electrocution. Ca., 1980. Illus. by Mugnaini. One of 100 deluxe copies signed by Ray, Mugnaini, and Wm. F. Nolan. Mint in slipcase. Quill & Brush 54-157 1983 $125

BRADBURY, RAY   The Love Affair. Northridge: Lord John Press, 1982. Cloth. First edition. Illus. by Joe Mugnaini. One of 100 numbered copies, signed by the author and artist. Reese 20-145 1983 $75

BRADBURY, RAY   A Medicine for Melancholy. NY, 1959. Signed by author, fine in fine dustwrapper that is lightly rubbed at top spine edge. Quill & Brush 54-137 1983 $100

BRADBURY, RAY   The October Country. NY, (1955). Flys slightly soiled, edges lightly rubbed,else very good in slightly frayed and lightly chipped, soiled, still very good dustwrapper. Quill & Brush 54-160 1983 $125

BRADBURY, RAY   The Pedestrian. 1964. Paperwraps, limited to 280 copies, tipped-in illus. by Joe Mugnaini, signed, fine. Quill & Brush 54-161 1983 $125

BRADBURY, RAY   That Ghost, That Bride of Time. (N.p.), (1976). Limited to 150 numbered and signed copies, mint in orig. envelope, paperwraps. Quill & Brush 54-151 1983 $75

BRADBURY, RAY   Twice 22. GC, 1966. First edition. Fine in fine dustwrapper. Quill & Brush 54-164 1983 $100

BRADFIELD, WESLEY   Cameron Creek Village. Santa Fe, 1931. 108 plates. 1 folding map. 4to. Wrappers. Ars Libri 34-142 1983 $45

BRADFORD, GAMALIEL   The Writer: A Series of Original Essays, Moral and Amusing. Boston: Russell & Gardner, 1822. Orig. printed front board, wanting rear board, else a near fine, untrimmed copy. First edition. Reese 18-560 1983 $50

BRADFORD, ROARK   John Henry. New York, 1931. 8vo. Cloth. 25 woodcuts by J.J. Lankes. A very good-fine copy in lightly worn and soiled dj. In Our Time 156-96 1983 $30

BRADFORD, THOMAS LINDSLEY   The Bibliographer's Manual of American History... Philadelphia: Stan. V. Henkels, 1907-10. 5 vols., cloth, top edges gilt; covers a little marked, leather spine labels drying out. Dawson 470-42 1983 $75

BRADFORD, WILLIAM   An Enquiry How Far the Punishment of Death is Neccessary in Pennsylvania. London, 1795. Folding table, dsb., very good. Reese 18-199 1983 $150

BRADFORD, WILLIAM   The Excellent Privilege of Liberty and Property. Philadelphia: Philobiblon Club, 1897. First edition. 4to. Full vellum. Limited to 500 copies. Covers somewhat soiled. Oak Knoll 49-92 1983 $50

BRADFORD, WILLIAM J. A.   Notes on the Northwest. NY, 1846.
First edition. Blind-stamped cloth, (neatly rebacked with orig.
backstrip). Ex lib. Argosy 716-224 1983 $50

BRADLAUGH, CHARLES   In the High Court of Justice, June 18th
1877. (1883). 24 pp ads. Orig. brown cloth. Jarndyce 31-391 1983
£12.50

BRADLAUGH, CHARLES   Labor and Law. R. Forder, 1891.
First edition, orig. dark blue cloth. Jarndyce 31-104 1983 £20

BRADLEY, CUTHBERT   The Foxhound of the Twentieth Century.
G. Routledge, 1914. Sole edition, with 32 plates (16 coloured) and 93
other illus., roy. 8vo, pub.'s half red cloth. Fenning 60-36 1983
£42.50

BRADLEY, E. T.   Life Of The Lady Arabella Stuart...
London: Richard Bentley & Son, 1889. First edition. 2 vols. Orig.
green decorated cloth. Spines and covers worn and soiled. Inner
hinges weak. Former owner's small rubber stamp signature. Good set.
MacManus 277-659 1983 $22.50

BRADLEY, EDWARD   The Adventures of Mr. Verdant Green.
London: 1853-57. 4 vols. 12mo. Orig. printed wrappers, (some
soiling, a few spines repaired). First editions. All four copies,
despite the defects noted, are in unusually nice condition. MacManus
277-256 1983 $350

BRADLEY, EDWARD   Glencreggan: or, a Highland Home in
Cantire. London: Longman, Green, Longman, & Roberts, 1861. Illus.
with 3 maps, 8 chromolithographs, and 61 woodcuts, from the author's
drawings. 2 vols. Orig. green cloth. First edition. Fine copy.
MacManus 277-257 1983 $250

BRADLEY, EDWARD   Photographic pleasures. London:
Thomas McLean, 1855. First edition. 8vo. Orig. blue cloth.
Frontis., pictorial title, and 22 plates, all printed on plate
paper, after drawings by Bradley. Ends of spine rubbed, inner
hinge cracked. Ximenes 63-188 1983 $475

BRADLEY, ELIZA   An Authentic Narrative of the Shipwreck
and Sufferings of Mrs. Eliza Bradley... Ithaca, 1837. Folding frontis.
16mo, orig. printed and illus. boards. Part of backstrip lacking.
Morrill 286-69 1983 $25

BRADLEY, JOHN H.   Farewell Thou Busy World. Los Angeles:
Primavera Press, 1935. First edition. Small 8vo, half cloth over
boards, paper label. Illus. with woodcut decorations, and binding by
Paul Landacre. Printed by the Ward Ritchie Press. Very good. Houle
22-551 1983 $55

BRADLEY, RICHARD   A Philosophical Account of the Works
of Nature. 1739. 8vo, 29 folding plates, orig. calf, rebacked, new
end papers. Bickersteth 75-215 1983 £48

BRADLEY, WILLIAM ASPENWALL   French Etchers of the Second Empire.
Boston: Houghton Mifflin Co., 1916. First edition. 8vo. Cloth.
Prof. illus. Spine faded. Oak Knoll 49-93 1983 $25

BRADLEY-BIRT, F. B.   Bengal Fairy Tales. John Lane, 1920
4to. Colour frontis. 5 delicate colour plates. Green decorated cloth.
Greer 40-216 1983 $27.50

BRADLEY-BIRT, F. B.   Chota Nagpore. London, 1903. Folding
map, plates. Library stamp on title. Spine slightly soiled. 8vo.
Orig. cloth. Good. Edwards 1044-83 1983 £35

BRADSHAW, GEORGE   Map and Sections of the Railways of
Great Britain. George Bradshaw, Manchester, 1839. 8vo, engraved
hand-coloured map mounted on linen and folded; orig. morocco,
stamped in blind and gilt, rebacked with orig. spine laid down.
First edition. Quaritch NS 5-17 1983 $650

BRADSHAW, JOHN   Martin Ffrench. London: Sampson Low,
Marston, Searle & Rivington, 1886. First edition. Orig. decorated
cloth. Some offsetting to the title page of vol. 1. Slight foxing.
MacManus 277-661 1983 $350

BRADY, CYRUS TOWNSEND   The Conquest of the Southwest. New
York: Appleton, 1903. Plates and maps. Original blue pictorial cloth.
Fine. Jenkins 153-59 1983 $60

BRADY, CYRUS TOWNSEND   Indian Fights and Fighters. Garden
City, 1913. Maps, illus. Clark 741-300 1983 $36.50

BRADY, CYRUS TOWNSEND   Northwestern Fights and Fighters. New
York, 1907. 1st ed. Maps, illus. Stain on back cover. Clark 741-
301 1983 $28.50

BRADY, CYRUS TOWNSEND   Recollections of a Missionary in the
Great West. New York, 1900. Frontis. Light staining to text. Orig.
cloth. Nice copy. Jenkins 153-60 1983 $45

BRADY, WILLIAM   Glimpses of Texas. Houston, 1871.
Wraps., near fine. Reese 19-87 1983 $300

BRAGG, WILLIAM HENRY   Studies in Radioactivity. London:
Macmillan, 1912. First edition. 8vo. Orig. blue cloth. Stamped
presentation copy on title page. Ads. Zeitlin 264-58 1983 $65

BRAGT, T.J. VAN   Der Blutige Schau-Platz Oder Martyrer
Spiegel. Ephrata in Pennsylvania: Drucks & Verlags der Brueder-
schafft, 1748-9. 2 vols. in one. 1st ed. Orig. binding of calf
(mostly removed) over oaken boards, bosses and clasps. Between 1200
and 1300 copies were printed. A tight crisp copy. Jenkins 155-118
1983 $850

BRAHE, TYCHO   Epistolarum astronomicarum libri.
Uraniburg: Tycho Brahe, 1596. First edition. With 6 large woodcuts.
2 diagrams and the Uraniburg press mark. Small 4to. 18th-century
half calf. With ms. exlibris of Daniel Melanderhielm and F. Duarte,
and bookplate of Hans Ludendorff. Some marginalia in a small, very
neat, early hand. Kraus 164-30 1983 $12,000

BRAHMS, JOHANNES   Vierte Symphonie (E moll) fuer Grosses
Orchester. Berlin, Simrock, 1886. Folio, wrs. First edition of
this version. Salloch 387-30 1983 $75

BRAID, JAMES   Advanced Golf. Phila. (ca. 1910).
First American edition. 4to, with 88 diagrams and photos. Dust
jacket. Very good. Houle 21-378 1983 $45

BRAID, JAMES (1795-1860)   Observations on Trance: or, Human
Hybernation. London, 1850. First edition. 12mo. Orig. cloth.
Old inscription on title. Gurney 90-23 1983 £175

BRAID, JAMES (1795-1860)   Satanic Agency and Mesmerism Reviewed.
Manchester: Sims and Dinham, and Galt and Anderson, 1842. Later
marbled boards. With brief ink correction probably in Braid's hand.
Gach 95-58 1983 $3000

BRAIN, BELLE M.   The True Story of Marcus Whitman. (New
York: 1902). First edition. Illus., printed wrappers. Very good.
Bradley 66-630 1983 $50

BRAINARD'S Collection of Instrumental Music. Cleveland, Brainard,
1841. Oblong folio, blue 1/2 morocco over marbled boards (new binding),
orig. printed and decorated green wrs, with the title within woodcut
frame, bound in. First edition. Salloch 387-33 1983 $90

BRAINE, SHELIA   In Nursery Land. R. Tucj, n.d. 4to.
Colour frontis. Title vignette. 4 two-tone & 44 text illus. Colour
pictorial glazed boards, edges worn. Greer 40-233 1983 £45

BRAINE, SHEILA   To Tell the King the Sky Is Falling.
Blackie, nd (1897). Illus. by Alice B. Woodward. 85 b&w illus. &
decor. title page. Green buckram decor. fr. cvr., a.e.g. Some sl.
foxing & thumbing, contemp. insc. half title, vg. Hodgkins 27-14
1983 £15

BRAINERD, DAVID   Memoirs of...Missionary to the Indians
of North America. N.Y., 1884. Orig. cloth. Small library stamp on
title page. Ginsberg 46-66 1983 $25

BRAITHWAITE, WILLIAM STANLEY Lyrics of Love and Life. Boston: Turner & Co., 1904. Cloth and boards. First edition. Bookplate, and slight rubbing, but a very good to fine copy. Reese 20-112 1983 $100

BRAKE, HEZEKIAH   On Two Continents. Topeka: Crane & Company, 1896. Plates. Original cloth gilt. Spotting to spine. Scarce. Jenkins 153-61 1983 $65

BRAMSTON, JAMES   The Art of Politicks. London: Printed for Lawton Gilliver...MDCCXXIX. 8vo, engraved frontis., new wraps. Second London edition, "double-line" issue, with the engraved portrait of Homer in an oval frame on the title, a double rule over the imprint, and ten books advertised on the final leaf. Quaritch NS 7-14 1983 $200

BRAMSTON, JAMES   The Man of Taste. London: printed by J. Wright, for Lawton Gilliver, 1733. Folio, advertisemetns, engraved frontis. printed on the verso of the half title. A very fine copy, entirely uncut, disbound in wrappers. First or second edition. Pickering & Chatto 19-4 1983 $450

BRAMSTON, JAMES   The Man of Taste. London: Printed by J. Wright, for Lawton Gilliver...1733. Folio, with engraved frontis. A large copy, disbound. First edition. Quaritch NS 7-15 1983 $125

BRANAGAN, THOMAS   A Preliminary Essay on the Oppression of the Exiled Sons of Africa. Phila., 1804. Frontis., 16mo, modern linen-backed boards. Ex-lib. Argosy 710-22 1983 $85

BRANCH, DOUGLAS   The Cowboy and His Interpreters. New York, 1926. Cloth, very good. Illus. by Russell, De Yong, and Will James. Reese 19-89 1983 $60

BRANCH, DOUGLAS   The Cowboy and His Interpreters. N.Y.: D. Appleton & Co., 1926. First edition, with "(1)" at the end of the index. Page of ads. Cloth. Illus. by W. James, J. de Yong & C.M. Russell. Dawson 471-32 1983 $30

BRAND, DONALD D.   The Natural Landscape of Northwestern Chihuahua. Albuquerque, 1837. Illus., 5 maps, 3 charts, 10 plates. Orig. printed wraps. First edition. Ginsberg 46-522 1983 $25

BRAND, MAX   The Notebooks and Poems of Max Brand. New York: Dodd, Mead, 1957. 1st ed., 1 of 750 numbered copies. Orig. cloth, gilt, boxed. Very fine copy. Jenkins 155-125 1983 $75

BRAND, MILLEN   The Outward Room. New York: Simon and Schuster, 1937. First edition. 8vo. Orig. cloth. Dust jacket. Fine copy. Jaffe 1-48 1983 $25

BRANDE, WILLIAM THOMAS   A Dictionary of Science, Literature, and Art. London: Longmans, 1872. New edition. Prize binding. Full calf with gilt, red and green labels. Rehinged. 8vo. A near fine copy. Zeitlin 264-59 1983 $100

BRANDE, WILLIAM THOMAS   A Manual of Chemistry... London: John Murray, 1821. 3 vols. 8vo. Cont. olive green diced calf, rebacked in tan calf, original labels preserved. Extending frontis. and 3 plates (2 extending) and 11 wood engravings. Zeitlin 264-60 1983 $110

BRANDE, WILLIAM THOMAS   Outlines of Geology. 1817. 8vo, with coloured folding plate, slight spotting to title and plate only; cont. tree calf, rubbed, lacking label. Quaritch NS 5-18 1983 $385

BRANDI, CESARE   Quarantun disegni di Giacomo Manzu. Torino: Giulio Einaudi, 1961. 41 color facsimile plates each under passepartout loose in portfolio as issued. Embossed design by the artist on title page. Elephant folio. Cloth. Edition limited to 1250 numbered copies, initialled by the artist in pencil. Ars Libri 33-509 1983 $450

BRANDON, ISAAC   Fragmente in Yoricks Manier. London (i.e. Regensburg, Montag und Weiss), 1800. First German edition. 8vo, three plates, final errata leaf. Modern quarter sheep, uncut. Hannas 69-199 1983 £55

BRANDON, JAMES   The whole proceedings on a trial of an action brought by Henry Clifford, Esquire, against Mr. James Brandon, for an assault and false imprisonment. London: printed by E. Blackaderm and sold by Longman, etc., 1809. 8vo, disbound. First edition. Ximenes 64-574 1983 $50

BRANDT, J. F.   Symbolae ad Polypos Hyalochaetides Spectantes. St. Petersburg, 1859. 4 lithograph plates, folio, original wrappers. Some dustsoiling. Wheldon 160-1252 1983 £20

BRANGWYN, CHRISTIAN   The Bridge. London, 1926. First edition. Illus. in colour and black and white by F. Brangwyn. 4to. Spine a little faded. Frayed dust wrapper. Nice. Rota 230-99 1983 £35

BRANGWYN, FRANK   Eothen. Phila.: Lipp.; London: Sams. Low, 1913. 4to. Orange pictorial cloth. Covers slightly smudged. 12 tipped in color plates, many black & whites by Brangwyn. Very good. Aleph-bet 8-42 1983 $40

BRAQUE, GEORGES   Georges Braque. Papiers colles cubistes. Paris: Maeght, 1963. 11 plates with 29 illus. (3 color). Small folio. Wrappers, looser under boards, as issued. Slipcase. One of 150 numbered copies on uncut velin de Rives comprising the edition de tete. Ars Libri 32-59 1983 $125

BRASFIELD, JOHN C.   The Architectural Digest. Los Angeles, (ca.1922). Illus. Wrappers. Southern California Business edition. Dawson 471-33 1983 $20

BRASSEY, T. A.   The Naval Annual, 1904. Portsmouth, 1904. 5 plates. 5 coloured plans (2 folding), 1 diagram. 78 plates of ships plans and sections. Slightly worn and soiled. 4to. Orig. cloth. Ink ownership inscriptions on front paste-down endpaper. Top section of free endpaper cut away. Good. Edwards 1042-14 1983 £30

BRASSEY, T. A.   The Naval Annual, 1915. London, 1915. War edition. 8vo, orig. cloth. Frontis. 3 plates, 4 illus., 78 pages of ships and plans and sections. 10 pages of ads. at end, slightly worn and soiled. Endpapers browned. Ink signature on endpaper. Some ink annotation of text. Good. Edwards 1042-15 1983 £18

BRATHWAITE, RICHARD   The Arcadian princesse. London: printed by Thomas Harper for Robert Bostocke, 1635. First edition. 8vo. 19th-century full red morocco, gilt, spine gilt, a.e.g. Engraved frontis. A few leaves shaved a bit close at the top, but a fine copy. Ximenes 63-116 1983 $750

BRATT, JOHN   Trails of Yesterday. Chicago, 1921. Pictorial cloth, very good. Reese 19-92 1983 $200

BRATT, JOHN   Trails of Yesterday. Lincoln, 1921. 302pp. Frontis and illustrations. Original pictorial cloth. Fine copy of the first edition. Jenkins 151-22 1983 $100

BRATZ, DR.   Humor in Der Neurologie Und Psychiatrie. Berlin/Leipzig: Walter de Gruyter & Co., 1930. First edition. Ad leaf. Library stamps and bookplate. Library buckram, preserving orig. printed wrappers. Gach 95-59 1983 $27.50

BRAUN, JOSEPH   Der christliche Altar in seiner geschichtlichen Entwicklung. 2 vols. Munchen, 1924. xxiii, (1), 755, (1)pp.; xvi, 704 pp., 377 plates with 714 illus. (43 double-page). 130 test illus. Sm. stout 4to. Cloth. Rare. Ars Libri SB 26-38 1983 $525

BRAUNGART, RICHARD   Julius Diez. Munchen: D. & R. Bischoff, 1920. 15 hinged gravure plates, numerous text illis., printed in red and black. Large 4to, cloth. Edition limited to 1250 copies. Binding design and splendid endpapers (in green and gold) designed by the artist. Ars Libri 32-167 1983 $125

BRAUTIGAN, RICHARD   The Tokyo-Montana Express. NY, (1979). Limited to 350 signed copies, very fine in glassine wrapper. Quill & Brush 54-178 1983 $75

BRAY, ANNA ELIZA   Courtenay of Walreddon. London: Richard Bentley, 1844. First edition. Half-titles present. Bound in old 3/4 maroon calf over marbled boards, gilt-stamped spines. Outer hinges sl. rubbed in a few places. Bookplate. Karmiole 74-27 1983 $75

BRAY, ANNA ELIZA   De Foix; or, Sketches of the Manners and Customs of the Fourteenth Century. Longman, 1826. First edition. 3 vols. Half calf, sl. rubbing to heads of spine vol. I, otherwise very good. Jarndyce 30-310 1983 £48

BRAYBROOKE, PATRICK   Some Aspects of H. G. Wells. London: C.W. Daniel Co., (1928). First edition. Frontis port. Orig. cloth. Dust jacket. In a half-morocco slipcase. Near mint. MacManus 280-5502 1983 $45

BRAYLEY, ARTHUR W.   A History of the Boston Yacht Club. Boston, (1891). First edition. Illus. 8vo. Morrill 287-611 1983 $40

BRAZER, SAMUEL   Address Pronounced at Worcester, on May 12th, 1804. Worcester, Goodridge, 1804. Half calf. First edition, with the half-title. Ginsberg 46-416 1983 $250

BRAZIER, MARION H.   Stage and Screen. Boston, (1920). First edition, with over 80 halftones of early stage and screen personalities. Tan cloth (slight soiling), else very good. Inscribed and signed by the author: "Mrs. Ayer. My first subscriber representing the motion picture industry..." Houle 21-648 1983 $37.50

BREAKENRIDGE, WILLIAM M.   Helldorado. Boston, 1928. Cloth, very good. Reese 19-93 1983 $75

BREAKENRIDGE, WILLIAM M.   Helldorado: Bringing the Law to the Mesquite. Boston, 1928. 256pp. Frontis. First edition. Fine copy. Jenkins 151-5 1983 $40

BREAKENRIDGE, WILLIAM M.   Helldorado: Bringing the Law to the Mesquite. Boston, 1928. 1st ed. Illus. Argosy 710-12 1983 $35

BREAZEALE, J. F.   The Pima and His Basket. Tucson: Arizona Archaeological and Historical Society, 1932. 132 illus. Cloth. Ars Libri 34-144 1983 $37.50

BREBEUF, JEAN DE   Brebeuf's Travels and Sufferings among the Hurons of Canada... London: the Golden Cockerel Press, 1938. First English edition. Folio. Uncut in quarter red canvas over black cloth, black morocco label, gilt. Dougle title-page with 2 woodcut illus. and wood-engraved lettering by Eric Gill, endpapers printed with maps. Limited to 300 numbered copies. Traylen 94-101 1983 £295

BREBNER, JOHN BARTLETT   North Atlantic Triangle. New Haven: Yale Un. Press; Toronto: Ryerson Press; London: OUP, 1947. 24 1/2cm. Third printing. 38 maps (several folding). Spine dulled, else very good. McGahern 53-10 1983 $25

BREDIUS, A.   Jan Steen. Amsterdam: Scheltema & Holkema, n.d. 100 photogravure plates with titled tissue guards. Folio. Dramatic full vellum over boards, gilt and embossed. T.e.g. Finely printed on uncut rag paper watermarked with the artist's name. Ars Libri 32-643 1983 $675

BREDIUS, A.   The Paintings of Rembrandt. London: Phaidon, n.d. 2 vols. 630 gravure plates. Stout 4to. Portfolios. Cloth. All contents loose, as issued. No. 99 of a limited edition of 950 copies. Ars Libri 32-551 1983 $100

BREHM, ALFRED E.   From North Pole to Equator. Blackie & Son, 1897. With portrait and 83 full-page and other illus., roy. 8vo, orig. cloth, gilt, t.e.g. Fenning 61-42 1983 £38.50

BREHM'S Tierleben, allgemeine Kunde des Tierreichs. Leipzig, 1911-18. 633 plates (many coloured), 13 maps and 1803 text-figures, 13 vols., royal 8vo, original half cloth. A complete set of the last edition, which has been reprinted several times without change. Wheldon 160-465 1983 £120

BREMER, FREDERIKA   The Home... Longman, Brown (etc)., 1843. 1st ed. in English. 2 vols, 12mo, original cloth-backed boards and printed spine labels, uncut. A fine copy. Hill 165-12 1983 £65

BREMER, FREDRIKA   The Home. Longman, Brown, etc, 1843. 2 vols. Large 12mo, cont. half vellum, gilt. Hannas 69-103 1983 £15

BREMER, FREDERIKA   The Home. Longman, Brown, etc., 1843. 2nd edition, 2 vols. Half titles, ads. Orig. brown cloth, very good. Jarndyce 30-311 1983 £10.50

BREMER, FREDERIKA   The Neighbours... Longman, Brown (etc)., 1842. 1st ed. in English, 2 vols., 12mo, original cloth-backed boards and printed spine labels, uncut; inner joints of Vol. II split, else a very good copy. Hill 165-13 1983 £60

BREMER, FREDRIKA   The Neighbours. H.G. Clarke, 1844. First edition, without half-titles, 2 vols. in 1, 12mo, cont. half calf. Fenning 62-41 1983 £10.50

BREMER, FREDERIKA   The Neighbours. Longman, Brown, etc., 1843. 3rd edition, 2 vols., half titles, ads. Orig. brown cloth, very good. Jarndyce 30-312 1983 £10.50

BREMER, FREDRIKA   The Neighbours. London, Brown, etc, 1843. 2 vols. Large 12mo, cont. half vellum, gilt. Hannas 69-104 1983 £10

BREMER, FREDERIKA   The President's Daughters... Longman, Brown (etc), 1843. 3 vols., 12mo, original boards, cloth backs, printed labels, uncut. Hill 165-14 1983 £42

BREMER, FREDRIKA   The President's Daughters. Longman, Brown, etc, 1843. First English edition. 3 vols. Large 12mo, cont. half vellum, gilt. Hannas 69-105 1983 £40

BREMNER, C. S.   Education of Girls and Women in Great Britain. 1897. First edition. Half title, orig. half brown cloth, pink cloth boards. Jarndyce 31-153 1983 £14.50

BREMOND, SEBASTIEN   Le double-cocu. Histoire du tems. Paris (i.e. London): imprime pour Mrs. Jacques Magnes et Richard Bentley, 1678. First edition. 12mo. Old calf. Worn. Very rare. Ximenes 63-11 1983 $350

BRENAN, GERALD   Jack Robinson. London, 1935. First edition. Good. Rota 230-101 1983 £25

BRENDEL, FRANZ   Geschichte der Musik in Italien, Deutschland und Frankreich. Leipzig, 1903. 8vo, orig. decorated cloth. Art Nouveau design in two colors, gilt lettering. Salloch 387-293 1983 $40

BRENNER, ANITA   The Wind that Swept Mexico. New York: Harper, (1943). Cloth. 184 photos. arranged by G.R. Leighton. First edition. About fine in shelfworn dust jacket. Reese 19-215 1983 $95

BRENTON, E. P.   The Naval History of Great Britain. London, 1837. 8vo. Portrait frontis. 15 engraved portrait plates. 6 folding maps and battle plans. 2 vols. Cont. half calf, neatly rebacked. New morocco labels, marbled edges. Some very slight foxing throughout. Good. Edwards 1042-17 1983 £150

BRERETON, AUSTIN   Dramatic Notes. London: David Bogue, 1882-1883. First edition. Illus. Orig. printed wrappers. Spine worn and chipped (partially defective). Covers a bit spotted. In a half-morocco slipcase. Very good. MacManus 277-666 1983 $40

BRERETON, AUSTIN   Henry Irving. London: Anthony Treherne & Co., 1905. First edition. Orig. pictorial wrappers (slightly worn and soiled). Little foxing. Very good. MacManus 279-2938 1983 $35

BRERETON, AUSTIN   Henry Irving. London: Anthony Traherne and Co., 1905. Sm. 4to, original grey pictorial wrappers, 1st ed. With 5 plates. Fine copy. Ximenes 64-298 1983 $25

BRERETON, AUSTIN   The Life of Henry Irving. London: Longmans, Green, and Co., 1908. 2 vols., 8vo, original blue cloth (spines a little spotted). First edition, with 1 photogravure, 22 collotype plates, and other illus. Ximenes 64-299 1983 $30

BRESADOLA, J.   Iconographia Mycologica. (Milan, 1927-60), facsimile reprint, 1981-82. 1250 coloured plates, 26 vols. in 5, 8vo, leather. Wheldon 160-10 1983 £360

BRESADOLA, J.   Iconographia Mycologica. (Milan, 1940-41) Reprint, 1983. Supplement I. 60 coloured and 72 plain plates, 8vo, calf, gilt. Wheldon 160-1794 1983 £57.50

BRESADOLA, J.   Iconographia Mycologica. Trento, 1960. Supplement 2. 48 coloured plate, 8vo, calf. Wheldon 160-1795 1983 £66

BRESADOLA, J.   Iconographia Mycologica (Supplement III). Tridenti, 1980. 100 coloured plates of numerous figures, 2 vols., 8vo, calf, gilt. Atlas in a portfolio. Wheldon 160-1796 1983 £66

BRESDIN To Redon. Six letters 1870 to 1881. 1969. 8vo, printed in red and black, double portrait frontispiece etched by Baskin. 300 numbered copies, in quarter morocco gilt over marbled paper boards. Deighton 3-51 1983 £95

BRESSANY, R. P. F. - J.   Relation Abregee de Quelques Missions des Peres de la Compagnie de Jesus dans la Mouvelle France. Montreal, 1852. 1st ed. in French. Pictorial and printed title page, 9 plates (one tipped in), 3 maps (2 folding), one folding lake level tableau, illus. in text. Orig. brown calf, much worn and rebacked with cloth, portion of old leather spine laid down. Rare. Bradley 63-31 1983 $135

BRETT, DOROTHY   Lawrence and Brett. Phila., Lippincott, (1933). First edition. Color frontis. and 12 plates. Red cloth, a bit faded. Very good. Houle 21-535 1983 $40

BREUIL, HENRI   The White Lady of the Brandberg. Paris/London: The Trianon Press, 1966. 18 plates with 39 illus. Folio. Cloth. Edition limited to 2187 copies. Ars Libri 34-576 1983 $150

BREUNING, MARGARET   Maurice Prendergast. New York: Whitney Museum of American Art, 1931. 21 plates. 4to. Cloth. Ars Libri 32-540 1983 $50

BREVAL, JOHN DURANT   The Art of Dress. London: Printed for R. Burleigh...M.DCC.XVII. 8vo, with fine engraved frontis., lacking half-title, some staining, partly uncut copy in quarter polished calf. First edition, with "Apple-pye. A Poem" on pp. 27ff. A good copy. Quaritch NS 7-16 1983 $275

BREVAL, JOHN DURANT   The Rake's Progress: or the Humorous of Drury Lane... London: Chettwood, 1735. Late 19th century type-facsimile printed in a limited ed. Orig. 3/4 red morocco. Fine copy. Jenkins 155-128 1983 $20

BREWER, JAMES NORRIS   The Picture of England. London: Printed for Harris and Son, 1820. 1st ed., 2 vols, small 8vo, with the half-titles in each volume, 84 plates containing 252 engraved views, polished half calf, marbled boards, gilt backs, morocco labels gilt, one slightly defective. Deighton 3-52 1983 £65

BREWER, LUTHER ALBERTUS   Around the Library Table, an Evening with Leigh Hunt. Cedar Rapids: privately printed, 1920. First edition. Small 8vo. Parchment-backed boards. Limited to 225 copies printed by the Torch Press. Fine. Oak Knoll 49-95 1983 $45

BREWER, LUTHER ALBERTUS   Some Letters from my Leigh Hunt Port-folios. Cedar Rapids: Torch Press, 1929. First edition. 8vo. Cloth-backed boards. Limited to 300 copies. Bookplate. Oak Knoll 49-96 1983 $35

BREWER, WILLIAM   Up and Down California in 1960-1864. New Haven, 1930. Cloth, very good. Reese 19-94 1983 $150

BREWER, WILLIAM   Up and Down in 1860-1964, the Journal of William H. Brewer, Professor Agriculture in the Sheffield Scientific School from 1864 to 1903. New Haven, 1930. Frontis. and plates. First edition. Jenkins 151-23 1983 $125

BREWERTON, G. DOUGLAS   The War in Kansas A Rough Trip to the Border. New York: Derby & Jackson, 1856. Ads., frontis. and illus. Orig. cloth, gilt. Presentation from publisher Mr. Derby. Nice. Jenkins 152-28 1983 $65

BREWERTON, GEORGE   Overland with Kit Carson. N.Y., 1930. Folding map & illus. Argosy 716-611 1983 $45

BREWSTER, DAVID   The Life of Sir Isaac Newton. John Murray, London, 1831. First edition, first issue in its orig. Family Library binding. Small 8vo, with engraved portrait by W.C. Edwards after Kneller, woodcut vignette on title and woodcut text illus.; portrait foxed; orig. cloth titled The Family Library No. XXIV...MDCCCXXXI price five shillings" in black on upper board, spine faded and torn at head, joints split but sound. Quaritch NS 5-82 1983 $220

BREWSTER, DAVID   Memoirs of the Life, Writings and Discoveries of Sir Isaac Newton. Edinburgh: Constable, 1855. Two vols. Orig. cloth. Portraits. Portraits a bit foxed, and minor chipping at head and toes of spines, otherwise a very fine set. Reese 20-719 1983 $200

BRICKER, CHARLES   Landmarks of Mapmaking. New York: Crowell, 1976. Folio. Maps chosen and displayed by R.V. Tooley. Over 350 illus. and plates. Dust jacket. A fine copy. McGahern 54-176 1983 $85

BRIDENBAUGH, CARL   Peter Harrison. First American archi-tect. Chapel Hill: University of North Carolina Press, 1949. 41 illus. 4to. Cloth. Dust jacket. Ars Libri 32-302 1983 $50

BRIDGES, ROBERT   Achilles In Scyros, A Drama In A Mixed Manner. London: Edward Bumpus, 1890. First edition. Orig. printed wrappers. Printed on handmade paper with the Van Gelder watermark. Spine and covers slightly faded. Some foxing throughout. With the bookplate of A.J.A. Symons. Very good. MacManus 277-667 1983 $65

BRIDGES, ROBERT   Bramble Brae. New York, 1902. 8vo. Cloth. This copy bears the author's contemporary presentation on front flyleaf. Little rubbing to extremity of spine, else fine. In Our Time 156-97 1983 $50

BRIDGES, ROBERT   Collected Essays Papers & c. London, 1928. First edition. Inscribed by author to his cousin, dated Xmas 1928. With the recipient's bookplate, designed by W. Gill of the Omega Workshop. Rota 230-103 1983 £40

BRIDGES, ROBERT   Demeter. A Mask. Oxford: At the Clar-endon Press, 1905. First edition. Orig. wrappers. Very fine. MacManus 277-668 1983 $25

BRIDGES, ROBERT   Eden. An Oratorio Set to Music by C.V. Stanford. London: George Bell & Sons, 1891. One of 1015 copies. Bookplate. Covers slightly soiled. Engpapers slightly browned. Very good. MacManus 277-670 1983 $85

BRIDGES, ROBERT   Eden. An Oratorio. London: Geo. Bell & Sons, 1891. First edition. Orig. wrappers. One of 1015 copies. Wrappers a bit faded or soiled at the edges; front wrapper torn at the spine (tear is about 3" long). Good. MacManus 277-669 1983 $75

BRIDGES, ROBERT   The Feast of Bacchus. London: George Bell & Sons, (1894). Second edition. Orig. printed wrappers. Spine & covers faded and worn. With the bookplate of A.J.A. Symons. Very good. MacManus 277-671 1983 $45

BRIDGES, ROBERT   Humours of the Court. G. Bell & Sons, 1893. First edition. One of 100 copies. Full parchment. Covers soiled and endpapers foxed. Bookplate. Very good. Rota 231-90 1983 £40

BRIDGES, ROBERT   The Humours of the Court. London: George Bell & Sons, (1893). First edition. Orig. printed wrappers. Printed on hand-made laid paper with Van Gelder watermark. Spine and covers faded and slightly worn. Some foxing throughout. With the bookplate of A. J. A. Symons. Good. MacManus 277-672 1983 $65

BRIDGES, ROBERT   Nero. London: Edward Bumpus, (1885). First edition. Orig. printed wrappers. Printed on hand-made paper with watermarks. Spine and covers slightly faded. Near-fine. Mac-Manus 277-674 1983 $65

BRIDGES, ROBERT   New Verse written in 1921... Oxford:
At the Clarendon Press, 1925. First edition. Photogravure frontis.
port. 8vo. Orig. limp parchment. Dust jacket. One of 100 copies
signed by the Poet Laureate. Very fine. MacManus 277-676 1983 $100

BRIDGES, ROBERT   October and other poems. London, 1920.
First edition. One of 65 numbered copies on handmade paper, signed by
author. Lower corners a little bruised. Very nice. Rota 230-102
1983 £50

BRIDGES, ROBERT   Poems. Daniel, Oxford, 1884. First
edition. One of 150 numbered copies. Orig. quarter parchment. Spine
cracked at hinges. Corners a little rubbed and occasional light foxing.
Inscribed on flyleaf: "Bella (Fry) from her loving Bessie. 16 Feb. 85."
Bookplate of Margery Fry, designed by W. Gill of Omega Workshop.
Photograph of Bridges. Good. Rota 231-89 1983 £125

BRIDGES, ROBERT   The Return Of Ulysses. London: Edward
Bumpus, 1890. First edition. Orig. printed wrappers. Printed on
handmade paper with the Van Gelder watermark. Spine and covers faded
and slightly worn. With the bookplate of A.J.A. Symons. Very good.
MacManus 277-678 1983 $65

BRIDGES, ROBERT   The Shorter Poems of... London: Bell,
1896. Light blue cloth, gilt. Cloth slightly soiled, but a very good
copy. Reese 20-150 1983 $30

BRIDGES, ROBERT   The Tapestry Poems. Privately printed,
1925. 4to, marbled boards, sl. mark to spine, orig. black slip-case.
Ltd. to 150 copies. Jarndyce 31-978 1983 £20

BRIDGES, ROBERT   The Testament of Beauty. Oxford, 1929.
First edition. 4to. One of 250 copies on large paper. Torn dust
wrapper. Fine. Rota 230-104 1983 £30

BRIDGES, ROBERT   The Testament of Beauty. Lon., 1929.
Publisher's note on text bound in at rear, very good in slightly
soiled and darkened, very good dustwrapper with lightly chipped spine
edges. Quill & Brush 54-179 1983 $40

BRIDGES, ROBERT   The testament of Beauty. Oxford,
Clarendon Press, 1930. Sm. 4to, frontispiece, uncut in quarter
vellum gilt over marbled paper boards, corners slightly worn, but
an excellent unopened copy. Deighton 3-53 1983 £18

BRIDGES, ROY   From Silver to Steel. Melbourne:
George Robertson & Co. 1920. Large thick 8vo, 66 leaves of plates.
Frontis. Silver-stamped gray cloth. With previous owner's name
silver-stamped on cover and his bookplate. Karmiole 76-80 1983
$125

BRIDGES, ROY   From Silver to Steel. Melbourne, 1920.
1st ed. Illus. Large 8vo. Morrill 289-280 1983 $75

BRIDGMAN, THOMAS   Epitaphs From Copp's Hill Burial Ground.
Boston, 1851. First edition, with subscribers' list. Frontis,
cloth. Ink name, spine ends frayed. King 46-132 1983 $35

BRIDGMAN, THOMAS   Inscriptions on the Grave Stones in Grave
Yards of Northampton... Northampton, Mass.: Hopkins, Bridgman & Co.,
1850. First edition. Frontis. and portraits. Orig. cloth. Some
fading. Jenkins 152-700 1983 $35

BRIEF Biography of William Birch. Manchester, 1906.
Drawings, cloth, inner hinges loose, covers slightly speckled.
King 46-116 1983 $20

A BRIEF Sketch of the Morris Movement and of the Firm Founded by
William Morris. London: 1911. 12mo. Privately printed at Chiswick
Press. Several b&w photographic plates. Fine in printed wrappers.
Printed presentation card with handwritten note laid-in. Bromer 25-
254 1983 $95

BRIERLY, BEN   "Ab-O'th'-Yate" Sketches and Other Short
Stories. Oldham: Clegg, 1896. First edition. 3 vols. Illus. Orig.
cloth. Covers a trifle worn. Very good set. MacManus 277-683 1983
$100

BRIERRE DE BOISMONT, ALEXANDRE   Du Suicide et de la Folie Suicide
Considers. Paris: Bailliere, 1856. 1/4 leather, rubbed. Gach
95-60 1983 $75

BRIGGS, WALTER DE BLOIS   James Phillips, Jr. S.F., 1935. 8vo,
cloth-backed decorated boards, paper label. Title-page illus. One of
75 copies. Fine copy. Scarce. Perata 28-49 1983 $90

BRIGHAM, AMARIAH   Remarks on the Influence of Mental
Cultivation and Mental Excitement upon Health. 1844. Small 8vo,
cont. half calf, rubbed. Bickersteth 77-261 1983 £18

BRIGHAM, CLARENCE S.   History and Bibliography of American News-
papers, 1690-1820. Worcester, Mass., 1947. 2 vols. First edition.
Quarto. Over 1,500 pages of text and indexed. Covers a bit spotted.
Jenkins 151-24 1983 $100

BRIGHAM, CLARENCE S.   Paul Revere's Engravings. NY, 1969. 146
Illus., 3 color plates, 4to, dust wrappers. Argosy 710-96 1983 $75

BRIGHT, J.B.   The Brights of Suffolk, England.
Boston, 1858. 1st ed. Presentation copy. For private distribution.
Illus. 8vo. Ex-library; binding faded. Morrill 289-281 1983 $22.50

BRIGHT, JOHN   Speeches on Questions of Public Policy.
Macmillan, 1869. 2nd edition, 2 vols. Front. vol. I, half title,
56 pp ads. vol. II. Orig. brown cloth, fine. Jarndyce 31-105 1983
£24

BRIGHT, RICHARD   Clinical Memoirs on Abdominal Tumours and
Intumescence. New Sydenham Society, 1860. 8vo, text figures, orig.
cloth, rebacked. Bickersteth 77-272 1983 £20

BRIGHT, RICHARD   Fatal Epilepsy. London, 1836. First
edition. 8vo, cont. 1/2 calf; ex-lib. Argosy 713-75 1983 $150

BRIGHT, TIMOTHY   A Treatise of Melancholy. London:
John Windet, 1586. First edition. Small 8vo. 19th century half
morocco, gilt, t.e.g. Woodcut device on title and several other
woodcut initials and ornaments, errata leaf, title-page a little
soiled. Traylen 94-102 1983 £800

BRIGNOLI, P. M.   A Catalogue of the Araneae. Manchester,
1982. Royal 8vo, cloth. Wheldon 160-1253 1983 £46.50

BRILL, CHARLES J.   Conquest of the Southern Plains:
Uncensored Narrative of the Battle of the Washita and Custer's
Southern Campaign. Oklahoma City, 1938. Illus. Argosy 710-572
1983 $35

BRINCKERHOFF, R.   The Family of Joris Dircksen
Brinckerhoff. NY, 1887. Illus., thin 8vo, 1/4 red morocco, edges
worn, ex-lib. Argosy 710-170 1983 $40

BRINCKMANN, A. E.   Barock-Bozzetti. Frankfurt, 1923-1925.
Lg. 4to, marbled boards, 1/4 cloth. 4 vols. Parallel English and
German text. A complete set of the rare fundamental work. Ars Libri
SB 26-40 1983 $2,500

BRINCKMANN, A.E.   Barockskulptur. Berlin-Neubabelsberg,
1917. Entwicklungsgeschichte der Skulptur in den romanischen
und germanischen Landern seit Michelangelo bis zum Berginn des 18.
Jahrhunderts. (Handbuch der Kunstgeschichte.) viii, 427pp., 10
tipped-in plates. 437 text illus. 4to. Boards, 3/4 cloth. From
the library of Georg Swarzenski. Ars Libri SB 26-41 1983 $30

BRINE, PERCIVAL J.   The Revolution and Siege of Paris.
London: Lewis, 1871. 8vo, extra-illus. with 6 hand-colored plates.
Red rippled cloth stamped in bild on both covers, the back bearing
the statement in gilt: "The Colour Of The Auroras In Paris On Octr.
24th & 25th. 1870. Is Represented By The Binding Of This Book."
With blind-stamped cartouches & gilt edges. Presentation copy "From
the Author." Rostenberg 88-113 1983 $325

BRININSTOOL, E. A.   Fighting Red Cloud's Warriors. Columbus:
The Hunter-Trader-Trapper Co., 1926. Pictorial cloth. First edition.
Illus. Jenkins 152-29 1983 $30

BRINKERHOFF, JACOB   Military Posts on the Route to Oregon.
Wash., 1845. Later cloth. Jenkins 153-64 1983 $65

BRINKLEY, F.   Japan and China, their History. London,
1903-04. Library edition limited to 500 copies. Numerous coloured
and plain plates. 12 vols. Covers slightly soiled. 8vo. Orig.
cloth. Good. Edwards 1044-85 1983 £220

BRINKLEY, F   Oriental Series. Japan: Its History, Arts, and Literature. Boston, Millet, (1901-2). Orig. green cloth with onlaid white circular gilt stamped lotus design on front covers (faded on spines). Profusely illus. with color and tinted plates. T.e.g., uncut, 12 vols. One of 1000 copies. Very good. Houle 22-508 1983 $250

BRINLEY, GORDON   Away to the Canadian Rockies and British Columbia. N.Y., 1938. Illus. by D.P. Brinley. Cloth. Slight cover staining and wear. King 45-10 1983 $20

BRINNIN, JOHN MALCOLM   The Garden in Political. NY, 1942. Poor erasure and mark on top edge front end paper, otherwise very good plus in chipped dustwrapper. Quill & Brush 54-180 1983 $35

BRINSLEY, JOHN   Ludus Literarius or, The Grammar Schoole. London: Thomas Man, 1612. First edition. Small 4to. Old calf. Little staining in lower margins and small piece at top of title-page just affecting the lettering. Very scarce. Traylen 94-103 1983 £380

BRISSON, MATHURIN JACQUES   Pesanteur Specifique Des Corps. Paris: l'Imprimerie Royale, 1787. 4to. Cont. calf over boards. 2 engraved plates. First edition. Front cover detached, rubbed. Zeitlin 264-61 1983 $140

BRISSOT DE WARVILLE, JACQUES PIERRE   The Commerce of America with Europe. New York, 1795. First American edition. Later full morocco, gilt-stamped, portrait of the author bound in. Very good. Reese 18-200 1983 $150

BRISSOT DE WARVILLE, JACQUES PIERRE   New Travels in the United States of America, Performed in 1788. London: Printed for J. S. Jordan, 1792. First English edition. Errata. Folding table. Orig. cont. mottled calf with morocco label on spine. Jenkins 152-30 1983 $200

BRISTOL Theatre: a poem. Bristol: printed by S. Farley, 1766. 4to, quarter red morocco. First edition. Very rare. An uncut copy. Ximenes 64-61 1983 $750

BRISTOW, AMELIA   Emma De Lissau. London: Tilt, 1830. Third edition. 2 vols. Orig. boards. Fine. MacManus 277-684 1983 $85

BRISTOW, J. T.   The Old Overland Trail. Horton, Kans., 1937. Wrps. Clark 741-382 1983 $21

THE BRITISH constitution triumphant. London: Dean and Munday, n.d. (1820). First edition. 8vo. Disbound. 14 woodcut illus. Ximenes 63-479 1983 $45

BRITISH MUSEUM.   Catalogue of Printed Books. Jesuits. London, 1889. Cloth, top edge gilt, ex-library but fine. Dawson 470-36 1983 $20

BRITISH MUSEUM.   Catalogue of the Books Printed in Iceland from A.D. 1758 to 1880. London, 1885. Cloth, top edge gilt, ex-library but fine. Dawson 470-37 1983 $20

BRITISH MUSEUM.   Catalogue of the Collection of Birds' Eggs. 1901-12. 79 coloured plates, 5 vols., 8vo, cloth. Complete sets are scarce. Trifle used. Wheldon 160-658 1983 £85

THE BRITISH Novelists. London, 1820. 50 vols. 12mo. Cont. half dark blue calf, gilt, gilt decorated spines with crimson morocco, gilt, slightly rubbed. Traylen 94-104 1983 £385

THE BRITISH Poetical Miscellany. Huddersfield: by Sikes and Smart, n.d. (1820). Third edition. 12mo. Modern boards. 3 vignettes, (woodcuts). Heath 48-465 1983 £45

THE BRITISH Stage; or, the exploits of Harlequin: a farce. London: printed for T. Warner, 1724. 8vo, disbound, 1st ed. Half-title present, slight foxing but a very good copy. Rare. Ximenes 64-64 1983 $650

BRITTAIN, VERA   Testament of Friendship. N.Y., MacMillian, 1940. First American edition. Dust jacket (slight rubbing and small nicks). Signed and inscribed by the author. Good - very good. Houle 22-140 1983 $50

BRITTON, JOHN LE   Britton on the Laws of England. London, 1640. 2nd ed. Folios, irregular but complete. Foremargins of 2 leaves a bit trimmed, not affecting text, bound in full, contemp. calf, bit rubbed, covers in triple blind-ruled border, spine unlettered & double blind-ruled with 4 raised bands, clean & fresh copy. Boswell 7-31 1983 $400

THE BRITWELL Hand-List, or Short-Title Catalogue of the Principal Volumes from the Time of Caxton to the Year 1800. London: Bernard Quaritch, 1933. First (only) edition. 4to, 2 volumes, original cloth, spines gilt. Frontispieces. Lightly soiled but a very good copy. Trebizond 18-6 1983 $150

BROADFOOT, W.   The Career of Major George Broadfoot. London, 1888. Map, plan. Portrait frontis. Modern half blue morocco. 8vo. Good. Edwards 1044-86 1983 £60

BROCH, HERMANN   The Death of Virgil. London, 1946. First English edition. Dust wrapper designed by E. McKnight Kauffer. Fine. Rota 230-105 1983 £20

BROCHANT DE VILLIERS, ANDRE JEAN MARIE   De la Cristallisation consideree Geometriquement et Physiquement... Strasbourg: F.G. Levrault, 1819. 8vo. Cont. half green leather. 15 plates, lacking plate 10. Ownership inscription on title page. A very good copy. Zeitlin 264-62 1983 $100

BROCK, ALAN ST. H.   A History of Fireworks. London, 1949. First edition. Roy. 8vo. Orig. cloth. Coloured frontis. 7 coloured and 16 other plates, 6 illus. (2 full page). Very slightly worn. Good. Edwards 1042-287 1983 £70

BROCK, H. M.   Blackie's Boys' Annual. n.d. 4to. Colour frontis. 1 plate by N.M.B. 3 text illus. Other illus. Colour pictorial boards. Greer 39-50 1983 £15

BROCK, H. M.   The Great Book of School Stories for Boys. H. Milford, 1933. Sm. 4to. Colour frontis. by H.M.B. & 5 text illus. by H.M.B. Other illus. Colour pictorial boards. Excellent in tissue wrapper. Greer 39-51 1983 £15

BROCK, H. M.   Puss in Boots. F. Warne, n.d. (ca.1914). Large 4to. Mounted colour frontis. & 7 mounted colour plates. Green cloth gilt. Onlaid colour plate. Light wear. Greer 39-43 1983 £65

BROCK, H. M.   Thrilling Stories for Boys. Blackie, n.d. 4to. Colour frontis. Other colour plates. 1 text illus. by H.M.B. Colour pictorial boards. Greer 39-52 1983 £10.50

BROCK, SAMUEL   Injuries of the Skull, Brain, and Spinal Cord. Baltimore, 1940. First edition. Argosy 713-76 1983 $85

BROCKEDON, WILLIAM   Road-Book from London to Naples. 1835. Illus. with 25 views from drawings by Stanfield, Prout and Brockedon, engraved by W. and E. Finden. Half green calf, a little rubbed, some minor foxing. K Books 301-30 1983 £94

BROCKETT, PAUL   Bibliography of Aeronautics, 1909-1916. Wash., 1921. 1st ed. Jenkins 153-743 1983 $125

BRODEL, MAX   The Origin, Growth and Future of Medical Illustration at the Johns Hopkins Hospital... 1915. Offprint. 8vo. Wrappers. Fye H-3-51 1983 $40

BRODER, PATRICIA JANIS   Hopi Painting: The World of the Hopis. (N.Y., 1978). Illus., orig. cloth, boxed. First edition. Orig. colored print by Willard Lomahawa laid in. Limited to 150 numbered copies signed by the artist. Ginsberg 47-343 1983 $75

BRODERIP, FRANCES FREELING   Crosspatch. Griffith & Farran, 1865. Illus. by Tom Hood. 1st ed., later issue with frontis. & 5 other hand-col'd illus., 32 pp. adverts. Scarlet fine ribbed cloth with black & gilt decor. fr. cvr. & bkstrip, with titling on gilt panels, a.e.g., pale cream eps. Fine copy. Hodgkins 27-15 1983 £40

BRODIE, BENJAMIN C.   Lectures Illustrative of Certain Local Nervous Affections. 1837. 8vo, orig. boards with cloth spine and paper label. Cloth slit at joints and worn at head and foot of spine, label rubbed. First edition. Bickersteth 75-216 1983 £75

BRODIE, PETER BELLINGER   A History of the Fossil Insects in the Secondary Rocks of England. London, 1845. First edition. 8vo. Orig. cloth. 11 plates. Plates foxed. Gurney 90-25 1983 £32

BROGLIE, LOUIS DE   L'Electron Magnetique. Paris: Hermann et Cie, 1934. First edition. 8vo. Orig. printed paper wrappers. 2 plates. Wrappers loose. Very good. Zeitlin 264-64 1983 $150

BROGLIE, LOUIS DE   An Introduction to the Study of Wave Mechanics. London: Methuen, 1930. First English edition. Modern green cloth. Ads. Very good. Zeitlin 264-63 1983 $60

BROGLIE, MAURICE DE   Les rayons X. Paris: Journal de Physique, 1922. First edition. 5 photographic plates and large folding table. Orig. cloth. 8vo. Very good copy. Zeitlin 264-65 1983 $150

BROME, RICHARD   Dramatic Works... London, Pearson, 1873. First edition thus. Thick 8vo, frontis. portrait. Grey boards, red leather labels. Very good. 3 vols. Houle 21-166 1983 $55

BROMFIELD, LOUIS   Mr. Smith. N.Y., Harper (1941). First edition. Dust jacket, small nicks, else very good. One of 600 copies, signed by the author. Houle 21-167 1983 $30

BROMFIELD, LOUIS   Night in Bombay. NY, 1940. Light interior foxing, else very good in slightly frayed, very good dustwrapper. Quill & Brush 54-181 1983 $25

BROMFIELD, LOUIS   The Rains Came. NY, 1937. Very good in frayed, slightly soiled, very good dustwrapper with tear top rear panel. Quill & Brush 54-182 1983 $25

BROMFIELD, LOUIS   The Strange Case of Miss Annie Spragg. NY, 1928. Minor cover wear, else bright fine copy in slightly chipped, very good dustwrapper with faded spine. Quill & Brush 54-183 1983 $35

BROMFIELD, LOUIS   Tabloid News. New York, 1930. 8vo. Wrappers. 1 of 875 copies. A very good copy. In Our Time 156-100 1983 $25

BROMFIELD, LOUIS   Twenty-Four Hours. New York: Stokes, 1930. 1st ed. Orig. orange cloth. Near fine copy with ink inscrip. from Bromfield on half-title in year of publication. Jenkins 155-131 1983 $20

BROMFIELD, LOUIS   Twenty-Four Hours. New York: Stokes, 1930. Fine bright copy with six line ink inscription from Bromfield on half-title in year of publication. Jenkins 155-131-A 1983 $20

BROMLEY, WILLIAM   Remarks in the Grande Tour of France and Italy. Printed by E.H. for Tho. Basset, 1692. 8vo, quarter calf antique with marbled boards. First edition. Bickersteth 77-8 1983 £180

BRONAUGH, WARREN C.   The Younger' Fight for Freedom. Columbia, Mo.: E.W. Stephens Publishing, 1906. Illus. Orig. cloth. Jenkins 153-725 1983 $65

BRONGNIART, A.   Classification et Caracteres Mineralogiques des Roches Homogenes et Heterogenes. Paris, 1827. 8vo, original wrappers. Wheldon 160-1365 1983 £20

BRONGNIART, A.   Description de quelques plantes remarquables de la Nouvelle Caledonie. Paris, Nouv. Arch. du Mus., (1868-71). 21 plates, 2 parts, 4to, wrappers. Wheldon 160-1657 1983 £18

BRONSON, EDGAR BEECHER   The Red-Blooded. Chicago, 1910. Pictorial cloth, very good. Reese 19-96 1983 $40

BRONSON, EDGAR BEECHER   Reminiscences of a Ranchman. New York: The McClure Company, 1908. First edition. Scarce, fine copy. Jenkins 153-67 1983 $150

BRONSON, EDGAR BEECHER   Reminiscences of a Ranchman. New York, 1908. Cloth, very good. First edition. Reese 19-97 1983 $50

BRONTE, CHARLOTTE   The Complete Novels. Edinburgh, 1905. Thornton edition. 12 vols. 8vo. Orig. green cloth, gilt, t.e.g., others uncut. With plates after photographs. Traylen 94-110 1983 £130

BRONTE, CHARLOTTE   The Complete Novels. Edinburgh, 1924. Thornton edition. 12 vols. 8vo. Orig. green cloth, gilt. Traylen 94-111 1983 £130

BRONTE, CHARLOTTE   Jane Eyre. An Autobiography. London: Smith, Elder and Co., 1848. Third edition. 3 vols. Orig. cloth. Spines slightly faded, corners and edges very slightly worn. Covers a little scratched and waterspotted. In Vol. 1 there is a "Note to the Third edition," in which Ms. "Bell" denies the authorship of "Wuthering Heights" and "Agnes Grey." Good set. MacManus 277-686 1983 $650

BRONTE, CHARLOTTE   Jane Eyre. Leipzig, 1848- First Continental edition. 2 vols. Square 8vo, cont. quarter calf, some light foxing. Hannas 69-211 1983 £45

BRONTE, CHARLOTTE   Jane Eyre. Smith, Elder, 1848. 3rd edition, 3 vols., half titles; 2 pp ads. preceding half title vol. I, 8 pp ads. vol. III. All vols. a little loose. Orig. purple-brown cloth, generally dulled and rubbed. Jarndyce 30-313 1983 £45

BRONTE, CHARLOTTE   Jane Eyre. Paris, 1923. Large 4to. Bound in full blue Cape morocco, three-line gilt borders, fully gilt panelled spine, inner gilt dentelles, silk end-papers, t.e.g., others uncut, preserved in the orig. marbled boards slip-case. 17 lithographs by Ethel Gabain, printed in red and black on hand-made paper with the water mark "Jane Eyre". Limited edition of 450 numbered copies. Traylen 94-107 1983 £130

BRONTE, CHARLOTTE   Poems by Currer, Ellis and Acton Bell. London: Smith Elder & Co., 1846. First edition, second issue. 12mo. Orig. green cloth with blind stamped lyre on the upper board. Errata slip and ad. leaf. A trifle faded. Traylen 94-112 1983 £195

BRONTE, CHARLOTTE   Poems By Currer, Ellis, & Acton Bell. London: Smith, Elder & Co., 1846. First edition, second issue. Orig. green embossed cloth. Lacking the errata slip. Spine lightly faded. Extremities of spine worn. Inner hinges cracked. Bookplate. Good. MacManus 277-687 1983 $250

BRONTE, CHARLOTTE   The Professor, a Tale. London: Smith, Elder & Co., 1857. 2 vols. 8vo. Half calf, gilt spines with morocco labels, gilt, t.e.g. Half-titles and 26 pp. of pub's ads. Traylen 94-108 1983 £190

BRONTE, CHARLOTTE   The Professor. NY, 1857. First American edition. Orig. cloth that is very good, small bookplate on front pastedown. Quill & Brush 54-184 1983 $100

BRONTE, CHARLOTTE   Shirley. Smith, Elder, 1849. First edition, 3 vols. 16 pp cata. (Nov. 1849) vol. I, 3 pp ads. vol. III. Half dark green morocco by Riviere & Son, t.e.g. Jarndyce 30-314 1983 £130

BRONTE, CHARLOTTE   Thackeray and Charlotte Bronte. London: Privately Printed by Clement Shorter, January 1919. First edition. 4to. Orig. printed wrappers. One of 25 copies printed. Bookseller's catalogue entry pasted to front endsheet. Fine. MacManus 277-688 1983 $250

BRONTE, CHARLOTTE   Villette. London: Smith, Elder & Co., 1853. First edition. 3 vols. Orig. cloth. Covers a bit rubbed at extremities. Rear inner hinge of Vol. 1 partially cracked. Outer hinge of Vol. 3 torn. Former owner's signature on front flyleaves. Near-fine. MacManus 277-689 1983 $1,000

BRONTE, CHARLOTTE   Villette. London: Smith, Elder & Co., 1853. First edition. 3 vols. 8vo. Half brown calf, gilt, t.e.g. 12 pp. of ads. in vol. 1. Traylen 94-109 1983 £220

BRONTE, CHARLOTTE   Villette. Smith, Elder & Co., 1853. 3 vols., 8vo, no half titles, cont. half maroon calf, marbled boards with marbled end-papers, spines evenly faded. First edition. Bickersteth 75-112 1983 £185

BROOK, HARRY ELLINGTON   The Land of Sunshine. L.A., 1893. Illus., map, numerous plates. Orig. pictorial printed wraps. First edition. Ginsberg 46-83 1983 $100

BROOKE, FRANCES   The History of Lady Julia Mandeville. London: R. and J. Dodsley, 1763. Second edition. 2 vols. 12mo. Cont. calf, morocco labels, joints slighly worn and some light staining. Signature of D. Wynne on the title-pages. Traylen 94-115 1983 £25

BROOKE, FRANCES   The Siege of Sinope. London: For T. Cadell, 1781. First edition. 8vo. Cont. polished calf, gilt. Presentation copy from the Author to Mrs. Yates, an actress. Slight wear. Heath 48-246 1983 £175

BROOKE, HENRY   Gustavus Vasa, the deliverer of his country. London: printed for R. Dodsley, 1739. 8vo, wrappers, 1st edition. Subscribers list. A very good copy. Ximenes 64-63 1983 $100

BROOKE, HENRY   Gustavus Vasa, the deliverer of his country. A tragedy. London: printed for R. Dodsley, 1739. 8vo, wrappers, 1st ed. The trade issue, without the list of subscribers. Ximenes 64-64 1983 $40

BROOKE, HENRY   The last speech of John Good... London: John Ward, 1751. 8vo. Wrappers. Wanting a half-title, otherwise a very good copy. Ximenes 63-473 1983 $250

BROOKE, JOCELYN   December Spring. London, 1946. First English edition. Chipped, nicked, and slightly torn, internally repaired dustwrapper. Very good. Jolliffe 26-62 1983 £25

BROOKE, RUPERT   Democracy and the Arts. Lon., 1946. Fine in very good dustwrapper with top edge of spine and rear panel slightly chipped. Quill & Brush 54-187 1983 $40

BROOKE, RUPERT   Democracy and the Arts. London: Hart-Davis, 1946. 1st ed. Orig. cloth, gilt dj. Fine copy. Jenkins 155-132 1983 $25

BROOKE, RUPERT   Democracy and the Arts. Lon., 1946. Very good or better. Quill & Brush 54-186 1983 $25

BROOKE, RUPERT   Fragments Now First Collected. Hartford: 1925. First edition. Orig. parchment-backed boards, in tissue dust jacket. One of 99 copies. Fine. MacManus 277-694 1983 $250

BROOKE, RUPERT   John Webster & the Elizabethan Drama. London, Sidgwick & Jackson, 1916. First edition. Dust jacket (small chips, back a bit darkened), very good. Houle 22-141 1983 $145

BROOKE, RUPERT   John Webster & the Elizabethan Drama. London, 1916. First English edition. Spine a little faded and covers marked. Nice. Rota 230-106 1983 £12.50

BROOKE, RUPERT   Letters From America. N.Y.: Scribners, 1916. First edition. Intro. by Henry James. Orig. cloth. Very good. MacManus 277-695 1983 $35

BROOKE, RUPERT   Letters from America. N.Y., Scribner, 1916. First edition (preceded the English issue). Frontis. portrait. Orig. blue cloth stamped in gilt. This copy has no broken type. Very good. Houle 22-507 1983 $75

BROOKE, RUPERT   Lithuania. Chicago: The Chicago Little Theatre, 1915. First edition. Orig. brown pictorial wrappers designed by C. Raymond Johnson. 200 copies are said to have been printed. Mint. MacManus 277-696 1983 $400

BROOKE, RUPERT   1914 And Other Poems. London: Sedgwick & Jackson, Ltd., 1915. First edition. Frontis. port. Orig. cloth with paper label, dust jacket (covers and spine lightly worn and foxed, spine ends frayed, with a few small tears to the covers). One of 1000 copies printed. Rare in dust jacket. Bookplate. Very good. MacManus 277-698 1983 $350

BROOKE, RUPERT   Poems. London: Sidgwick & Jackson, 1911. First edition. 12mo. Orig. cloth. Paper label. Spine label discolored. In a half morocco case. 500 copies were printed. MacManus 277-699 1983 $300

BROOKER, WILLIAM H.   Texas an Epitome of Texas History from the Filibustering and Revolutionary Eras to the Independence of the Republic. Columbus, Ohio: Press of Nitschke Brothers, 1897. Frontis. portrait. Plates. Original pictorial cloth. Scarce. Jenkins 153-68 1983 $150

BROOKES, CHRISTOPHER   A New Quadrant, of More Naturall, Easie, and Manifold Performance... London, 1649. First edition. 12mo. Modern blue leather. From the library of the Earls of Kinnoul, Dupplin Castle. Kraus 164-31 1983 $1,250

BROOKES, IVESON L.   A Defence of Southern Slavery. Hamburg, S.C., 1851. Stitched. Uncut. Felcone 22-21 1983 $35

BROOKES, IVESON L.   A Defence of the South Against the Reproaches and Incroachments of the North. Hamburg, S.C., 1850. Stitched. Uncut. Foxed. Felcone 22-22 1983 $35

BROOKES, RICHARD   The Art of Angling. London: T. Lowndes. 1770. 12mo, engraved frontis. + 135 text woodcuts of fish. Old calf, worn, hinges cracked. Karmiole 73-42 1983 $175

BROOKES, RICHARD   The General Dispensatory... London, 1773. Third edition. 12mo. Old sheep worn. Gurney JJ-54 1983 £18

BROOKS, ALFRED H.   Mineral Resources of Alaska Report. Washington, 1911. Maps and illus. Orig. cloth. x-1 but minor. Jenkins 152-4 1983 $35

BROOKS, GWENDOLYN   A Street in Bronzeville. NY, 1945. Pgs. 34-35 slightly skinned, affecting text, spine and edges slightly rubbed, some minor wear to corners, else very good in slightly chipped, very good dustwrapper. Quill & Brush 54-188 1983 $150

BROOKS, HILDEGARD   The Larky Furnace. N.Y.: Holt, 1906. First edition. 8vo. Blue cloth, light soil. Title page, cover and 5 full-page black & whites by Newell. Very good. Aleph-bet 8-188 1983 $35

BROOKS, J. W.   Reply to....Mitchell Hindseill and Others. Detroit: Munger & Pattison, 1848. Printed wrappers. Stained internally. Bradley 66-591 1983 $22.50

BROOKS, JAMES G.   The Rivals of Este, and Other Poems. New York: J. & J. Harper, 1829. Orig. muslin-backed boards, paper label, edges untrimmed. First edition. Some scattered foxing, and last two leaves lightly stained, otherwise a very good copy. Reese 18-630 1983 $50

BROOKS, VAN WYCK   New England: Indian Summer, 1865-1915. (New York), 1940. 1st ed. Cloth. Very good in dj. Bradley 63-27 1983 $25

BROOKS, W. K.   Report on the Stomatopoda. 1886. 4to, new wrappers, 16 plates. Wheldon 160-300 1983 £15

BROOKS, WALTER R.   Wiggins for President. NY 1939. First ed. Cloth, very good in slightly frayed dw. Drawings by Kurt Wiese. King 46-446 1983 $25

BROOME, A.   History of the Rise and Progress of the Bengal Army. Calcutta, 1850. Folding map, 5 folding plans. Thick 8vo. Half morocco. Good. Edwards 1044-87 1983 £125

BROSTER, J.   Impediments of speech... Chester, 1824.
4to. Two leaves, folded. In fine condition. Ximenes 63-272 1983
$75

BROTHERHEAD, WILLIAM   Forty Years Among the Old Booksellers of
Philadelphia. Philadelphia: A.P. Brotherhead, 1891. 8vo, orig.
cloth with label (spine damaged). Pleadwell bookplates. Somewhat
shaken. Rostenberg 88-20 1983 $75

THE BROTHERS Dalziel. London: Methuen, 1901. Small quarto. First
edition. Profusely illus. in b&w. Slightly shaken but clean copy in
lightly rubbed covers. Bromer 25-164 1983 $185

THE BROTHERS Dalziel. Methuen, 1901. 1st edn. With selected pic. by
& autograph letters from J.E. Millais, E.J. Poynter, Holman Hunt, et
al. Numerous b&w illus. Pub's cloth, t.e.g. others uncut (some
bubbling of cloth on covers, corners sl. bruised), v.g. Hodgkins 27-
561 1983 £65

BROUGH, ROBERT B.   The Life of Sir John Falstaff. London:
Longman, Brown, Green, Longmans & Roberts, 1857-1858. First edition,
first issue. Illus. by Cruikshank. 10 parts, orig. printed wrappers.
Contains 20 full-page etchings by Cruikshank. With the exception of
the first part, whose wrappers are slightly soiled, worn and foxed,
with an expert repair to the backstrip, the entire set is near-fine.
In red, full morocco solander case. MacManus 277-1222 1983 $650

BROUGH, ROBERT B.   The Life of Sir John Falstaff. London,
Longman, et al., 1858. Illustrated by George Cruikshank. Large 8vo.
With 40 fullpage etchings, colored and uncolored, & 1 woodcut. Full
olive levant morocco (spine uniformly faded to brown), gilt-panelled
sides with several frames, fleurons, etc. Elaborately gilt-extra
spine, gilt inner dentelles, gt. 1st ed. with orig. cloth clovers
bound in. This copy has duplicate set of the 200 Cruikshank etchings
colored by hand. Fine. O'Neal 50-17 1983 $600

BROUGH, ROBERT B.   The Life of Sir John Falstaff. Longman,
etc., 1858. Illus. by George Cruikshank. Frontis. & 19 etchings.
Red morocco grain cloth, gilt vignette fr. cvr., cvrs. some marks,
recased & bkstrip repr'd top/bottom, eps. strengthened at hinges with
cloth tape, occasional foxing, bookpl. insc. 2nd ep., vg. Hodgkins
27-248 1983 £55

BROUGHAM, HENRY   Correspondence Between Robert McKerrell,
Esq. and Henry Brougham Esq. Liverpool: T. Kaye, printer, 1812.
First edition, stabbed pamphlet, sl. dusted. Jarndyce 31-116 1983
£20

BROUGHAM, HENRY   Historical Sketches of Statemen who
Flourished in the Time of George III. Charles Knight, 1839-43.
First editions. 3 vols. Tall 8vo, half titles, ports. Orig.
brown cloth, vol. I hinges fraying and tear across spine; vols. II and
III good. Jarndyce 30-914 1983 £18

BROUGHAM, HENRY   Lord Brougham's Reply to Lord John
Russell's Letter to the Electors of Stroud on the Principles of the
Reform Act. London, Ridgway, 1839. 3rd edition, 8vo, modern marbled
boards, paper label. Pickering & Chatto 21-10 1983 $50

BROUGHAM, HENRY   Lord Brougham's Speech...On the Corn
Laws. London, Ridgway, 1839. 2nd ed., 8vo, modern marbled boards,
paper label. Pickering & Chatto 21-9 1983 $55

BROUGHAM, HENRY   Opinions of Lord Brougham, on Politics,
Theology, Law, Science, Education, Literature. London: Henry
Colburn, 1837. 1st ed., 8vo, 2 advertisements, crisp and clean
throughout, cont. half calf, spine elaborately gilt, marbled boards
and edges, corners rubbed. Pickering & Chatto 21-12 1983 $65

BROUGHAM, HENRY   The Speech of Henry Brougham, Esq.
Before the House of Commons... Philadelphia, 1808. Very good.
Dsb. First American edition. Reese 18-301 1983 $45

BROUGHAM, HENRY   Speeches of Henry Lord Brougham, upon
questions relating to Public Rights, Duties, and Interests. Edinburgh, Adam and Charles Black, 1838. 4 vols., internally very
good, cont. half calf, spines gilt, marbled boards, spines rubbed
and corners worn, bookplate. Pickering & Chatto 21-11 1983 $95

BROUGHTON, BRIAN   Copse-Grove Hill. Printed by Wm. Nicol,
1829. First edition, 4to, sl. affected by damp in inner margins.
Orig. blue cloth a little worn. Jarndyce 30-653 1983 £28

BROUGHTON, RHODA   Alas! A Novel. London: Richard Bentley
& Son, 1890. First edition. Orig. decorated cloth. 3 vols. Covers
darkened, inner hinges cracking. Very good. MacManus 277-705 1983
$450

BROUGHTON, RHODA   Belinda. A Novel. London: Richard
Bentley & Son, 1883. First edition. 3 vols. Orig. smooth cloth.
Fine. MacManus 277-706 1983 $400

BROUGHTON, RHODA   Alas! Richard Bentley, 1890. First
edition, half titles, 6 pp ads. vol. III. Orig. light blue cloth,
elaborately dec. Spines sl. browned otherwise very good. Smith's
labels on pastedowns. Jarndyce 30-315 1983 £78

BROUGHTON, RHODA   Cometh Up As A Flower. London: Richard
Bentley, 1867. First edition. 2 vols. Orig. green cloth. Half-title
in Vol. 2 only (as issued). Foxing. Rare. Very good. MacManus 277-
707 1983 $750

BROUGHTON, RHODA   Cometh Up As A Flower. London: Richard
Bentley & Son, 1890. New Edition. Illus. Orig. embossed cloth. Inscribed on the title-page: "W.E. Norris, with the author's best regards, April 17th, '95." Some offsetting on title-page. Fine.
MacManus 277-708 1983 $85

BROUGHTON, RHODA   Dear Faustina. London: Richard Bentley
& Son, 1897. First edition. Orig. cloth. Former owner's signature.
Pages 7/8 torn across (no text disturbed). Good. MacManus 277-709
1983 $125

BROUGHTON, RHODA   The Game and The Candle. London: Macmillan & Co., 1899. First edition. Orig. cloth. Former owner's
signature in pencil erased from title-page. Fine. MacManus 277-711
1983 $150

BROUGHTON, RHODA   Mrs. Bligh. A Novel. London: Bentley,
1892. First edition. Orig. decorated cloth. Fine. MacManus 277-712
1983 $125

BROUGHTON, RHODA   Nancy. Richard Bentley and Son, 1873.
First edition, 3 vols., 8vo, titles printed in red and black. Cont.
half roan (spines rubbed and a little weakened). Title pages and
some other leaves foxed. Hannas 69-15 1983 £30

BROUGHTON, RHODA   Scylla or Charybdis? London: Richard
Bentley & Sons, 1895. First edition. Orig. cloth. Former owner's
signature on half-title. Front flyleaf slightly torn. Near-fine.
MacManus 277-714 1983 $150

BROUGHTON, RHODA   A Waif's Progress. London: Macmillan
& Co., 1905. First edition. Orig. cloth. Edges and corners worn.
Covers a little soiled. A touch of foxing. MacManus 277-715 1983
$50

BROUGHTON, T. D.   The Costume, Character, Manners, Domestic
Habits, and Religious Ceremonies, of the Mahrattas. London, 1813.
10 coloured plates. 4to. Endpapers spotted. Cont. panelled calf.
Painted on both boards with a landscape, slightly worn. Ornately
boardered with decorations gilt and blind, rebacked. Good. Edwards
1044-88 1983 £250

BROULHIET, GEORGES   Meindert Hobbema (1638-1709). Paris:
Firmin-Didot, 1938. 271 collotype plates with 590 illus. Large
stout 4to. Wrappers. Unopened. Edition limited to 1000 numbered
copies. Ars Libri 32-308 1983 $275

BROUSSAIS, F. J. V.   Principles of Physiological Medicine.
Phila., 1832. First American ed. Argosy 713-77 1983 $85

BROUWER, HENRICUS   De Jure Connubiorum Duo. 1714. Red
and black title, 4to, a little age-marked, some old ink-notes, worn
but sound old panelled calf. K Books 22-26 1983 £40

BROWN, ABBIE FARWELL   The Book of Saints and Friendly Beasts.
Boston: H.M., 1900. First edition. 8vo. Gold-gilt decorated cloth.
Light wear. Many intricate black and whites by Cory. Very good.
Aleph-bet 8-68 1983 $25

BROWN, ABRAM ENGLISH   Faneuil Hall and Faneuil Hall Market. Boston, 1900. 1st ed. Illus. 8vo. Morrill 288-638 1983 $25

BROWN, ALEXANDER   The First Republic in America... Boston: Houghton, Mifflin, 1898. Original cloth. First edition. Jenkins 153-69 1983 $45

BROWN, ALEXANDER   The Genesis of the United States. London, 1890. First British edition. 2 vols., 100 ports., maps & plans. G.t. Argosy 710-97 1983 $125

BROWN, ALFRED   Old Masterpieces in Surgery. Omaha, 1928. Privately printed. 8vo. Orig. binding. Uncut and untrimmed. 57 plates. Scarce. Fye H-3-52 1983 $100

BROWN, ALFRED   Old Masterpieces in Surgery. Omaha, 1928. 8vo. Orig. binding. Ex-library. Fye H-3-53 1983 $75

BROWN, ALICE   Children of Earth. New York, 1915. 8vo. Cloth. A fine copy in the uncommon dj. Jacket has some light wear. In Our Time 156-102 1983 $25

BROWN, ALICE   Fable and Song. Boston, 1939. 8vo. Cloth. A fine copy in plain dj as issued. In Our Time 156-103 1983 $25

BROWN, BOB   Let there be Beer! New York: Smith & Haas, 1932. Cloth. First edition. Slight soiling, but a very good copy in dust jacket, which lacks a small chip from the head of the spine. Reese 20-159 1983 $45

BROWN, BOB   Readies for Bob Brown's Machine. Cagnes-sur-Mer: Roving Eye Press, 1931. Orig. printed wraps. Plate. First edition. Slightest traces of wear and fading, else a fine copy. Reese 20-158 1983 $400

BROWN, CHARLES BROCKTON   An Address to the Government of the United States, on the Cession of Lousiana to the French. Phila., 1803. Cloth, leather label, fine. Reese 18-251 1983 $750

BROWN, DAVID L.   "Kit Carson," The Rob Roy of the Rocky Mountains. Hartford: Supplement to the Courant, December 12, 1846. Complete issue. Jenkins 153-119 1983 $100

BROWN, DAVID PAUL   The Forensic Speeches of David Paul Brown... Philadelphia, 1873. First edition. Mounted actual photo with David Brown's facsimile inscription below. Ex-Library. Hinges broken, writing on end papers, worn. King 46-89 1983 $20

BROWN, E. K.   Gants du Ciel. Montreal: Editions Fides, 1946. 23cm. Wrappers. Dust soiled else very good. McGahern 53-11 1983 $20

BROWN, EARLE B.   Basic Optics for the Sportsman. New York, Stoeger Arms Corp., 1949. First edition. Illustrated. 8vo. Morrill 290-45 1983 $25

BROWN, EVERETT S.   The Missouri Compromises and Presidential Politics, 1820-1825. St. Louis, 1926. 155pp. 1st ed. Scholarly edition. Notes and index. Jenkins 151-27 1983 $35

BROWN, EVERETT S.   William Plumer's Memorandum of Proceedings in the United States Senate, 1803-1807. N.Y.? 1923. 673pp. 1st ed. Excellent notes and index. Jenkins 151-28 1983 $40

BROWN, F. B. H.   Flora of Southeastern Polynesia. Honolulu, B. P. Bishop Mus., 1931-35. 65 plates, 3 parts in 2, 8vo, plain wrappers. Library stamp on title-pages, else a good copy. Wheldon 160-1658 1983 £30

BROWN, FREDRIC   The Bloody Moonlight. NY, 1949. Edges rubbed, else very good in lightly worn, slightly frayed and chipped but presentable dustwrapper, owner's name. Quill & Brush 54-192 1983 $60

BROWN, FREDRIC   The Screaming Mimi. NY, (1949). Top page edge foxed, else bright, very good in soiled but very good dustwrapper, owner's name. Quill & Brush 54-193 1983 $50

BROWN, GEORGE   Melanesians and Polynesians. 1910. Numerous illus., gilt cloth slightly chafed. K Books 307-34 1983 £38

BROWN, GEORGE W.   Reminiscences of Gov. R. J. Walker. Rockford, Ill., privately printed, 1902. Ports. 12mo. Clark 741-332 1983 $67.50

BROWN, H., OF AYRSHIRE   The Covenanters: and other poems. Glasgow: Symington, 1838. First edition. 8vo. Orig. purple figured cloth, printed paper label. Slight wear to label. Very good copy. Ximenes 63-436 1983 $60

BROWN, HARRY   The Beast in His Hunger: Poems. New York, 1949. 8vo. Cloth. A copy for review with slip from the publisher laid in. Fine copy in dj which is intact but rubbed. In Our Time 156-104 1983 $45

BROWN, HENRY   A Narrative of the Anti-Masonick Excitement, in the Western Part of the State of New-York, During the Years 1826, '7, '8, and a Part of 1829. Batavia, N.Y.: Printed by Adams & M'Cleary, 1829. Orig. paper over boards. Hinges a trifle weak, otherwise a fine copy. Reese 18-631 1983 $150

BROWN, HENRY COLLINS   New York of To-Day. NY: Old Colony Press, 1917. 16 cm. Colored frontis., including 67 plates, 3 colored, and the 16 x 29 inch folding supplement showing lower Manhatten. Orig. blue gilt-lettered limp cloth. A fine copy. Grunder 6-60 1983 $20

BROWN, JOHN   Horae Subsecivae. Edinburgh, 1882. 8vo, cont. crushed morocco, inner dentelles, g.e. Illus. Frontis. ports. Argosy 713-78 1983 $125

BROWN, JOHN   Horae Subsecivae. London, 1897. First edition, third series. 8vo. 3 vols. Half olive morocco, t.e.g. Gurney JJ-56 1983 £12

BROWN, JOHN   John Leech and other papers. Edinburgh: David Douglas, 1882. Fourth edition. 8vo. Orig. cloth, paper spine label. Cloth on cover is bubbled, label is rubbed. Oak Knoll 48-246 1983 $26

BROWN, JOHN ALLEN   The Chronicles of Greenford Parva; or, Perivale, Past and Present. London, by J. S. Virtue & Co. for the author, (ca. 1890). Large paper copy, 4to, with a map and 14 plates, original maroon cloth gilt, top edge gilt, cover stained corners little worn, inner joint weak, internally a clean copy. Deighton 3-57 1983 £55

BROWN, JOHN CROMBIE   The ethics of George Eliot's works. Edinburgh: Blackwood, 1879. First edition. Small 8vo. Orig. brown cloth. Fine copy. Ximenes 63-234 1983 $45

BROWN, JOHN CROUMBIE   Hydrology of South Africa. 1875. Half calf, ex-library copy. K Books 301-28 1983 £25

BROWN, K. R. G.   Heath Robinson at Home. Strand Magazine, November, 1935. 4to. 10 text illus. by W.H. Robinson. Other illus. Colour pictorial wrappers. Greer 39-109 1983 £12.50

BROWN, L.   The Birds of Africa. 1982. Vol. 1, 32 coloured plates by P. Hayman and M. Woodcock numerous line drawings and distribution maps, 4to, cloth. Wheldon 160-660 1983 £55

BROWN, LEONARD   Poems of the Prairies. Des Moines, 1865. Orig. cloth. First edition. Ginsberg 47-352 1983 $50

BROWN, MARY LOUISE   Rhode Island in Verse. (Providence): Roger Williams Press, 1936. 2 plates, port. Argosy 716-481 1983 $20

BROWN, O. P.   The Complete Herbalist. 1885. Portrait and text-figures, 8vo, cloth. Wheldon 160-2163 1983 £15

BROWN, PAUL   No Trouble at All. N.Y.: Scrib., 1940.
First edition. Orange cloth. Illus. throughout with line drawings
by Brown. Fine. Aleph-bet 8-44 1983 $20

BROWN, ROBERT   Passages in the Life of an Indian
Merchant. James Nisbet, 1867. Half title, front. Orig. red cloth.
Jarndyce 30-915 1983 £15

BROWN, SAMUEL R.   The Western Gazetteer. Auburn, N.Y.,
1817. Later leather and cloth, new endsheets. Title page stained
and worn on outer extremities, otherwise very good. Reese 18-512
1983 $300

BROWN, T. E.   The Manx Witch and Other Poems. London:
Macmillan & Co., 1889. First edition. Bookplate. Orig. cloth. Spine
faded. MacManus 277-717 1983 $40

BROWN, THOMAS   Illustrations of the Recent Conchology
of Great Britain and Ireland... London, Smith, Elder, 1844. Sm.
folio. With 62 hand-colored engraved plates. Orig. cloth. 2nd ed.,
greatly enlarged. Corner bumped, spine worn at extremities, first
few plates lightly browned. Very good copy. O'Neal 50-10 1983 $400

BROWN, THOMAS   Illustrations of the Conchology of Great
Britain and Ireland. 1844. Second edition, errata page, 62 hand-
coloured engraved plates, 4to, new quarter morocco. K Books 307-36
1983 £250

BROWN, THOMAS   Lectures on the Philosophy of the Human
Mind. Philadelphia: John Grigg, 1824. 3 vols. Nineteenth century
1/2 calf, marbled boards. Some edgewear, else very fresh and attractive set of first American edition. Gach 95-61 1983 $125

BROWN, THOMAS N.   Labour and Triumph. The Life and Times
of Hugh Miller. London & Glasgow: Richard Griffin, 1858. First
edition, half title. A little worn, half calf, rubbed. Jarndyce 30-
1080 1983 £18

BROWN, W. P.   An Epistle to Jew and Gentile from
Jerusalem. n.p., dated at end of text "Jerusalem. March 1897."
18 cm. Orig. yellow printed wraps. Creased, wraps. somewhat faded
with slight chipping; old file numbers on front wrapper. Grunder 6-
9 1983 $175

BROWN, WILLIAM H.   An Historical Sketch of the Early
Movement in Illinois for the Legalization of Slavery. Chicago, 1865.
Dsb., good. Reese 19-98 1983 $100

BROWN, WILLIAM H.   An Historical Sketch of the Early
Movement in Illinois for the Legalization of Slavery...Chicago, 1865.
1st ed. 8vo, orig. wrappers. Morrill 288-193 1983 $27.50

BROWN, WILLIAM H.   The History of the First Locomotives
in America. N.Y., 1871. Illus., many fine folded plates of
locomotives, etc. Orig. cloth. First edition. Ginsberg 46-67 1983
$125

BROWN, WILLIAM H   On the South African Frontier. New
York: Charles Scribner's Sons, 1899. 8vo. 2 folding maps. 32
plates. Orig. cloth. Lightly rubbed. Adelson Africa-17 1983
$100

BROWN, WILLIAM W.   Narrative of the Life of a Fugitive Slave.
Boston, 1848. Enlarged edition, later cloth. Morocco label, orig.
front printed wrapper bound in. Portrait, frontis. Jenkins 152-758
1983 $75

BROWNE, CHARLES FARRAR   Artemus Ward (His Travels). London:
J.C. Hotten, 1865. 12mo, orig. pr. wraps., gilt-
dec. spine, g.t. With an entrance ticket to Browne's lecture on
the Mormons laid across front wrapper. Signed binding by Birdsall.
Argosy 716-553 1983 $75

BROWNE, CHARLES FARRAR   Artemus Ward's Lecture. John Camden
Hotten; N.Y. G.W. Carleton, 1869. First edition, half title, front. &
tinted illus. from the Panorama, 12 pp ads. Lacking leading free
end paper and a trifle loose, otherwise v.g. in orig. blue cloth.
Jarndyce 31-447 1983 £12.50

BROWNE, E. GORDON   Nutcracker & Mouse-king. G.G. Harrap,
1916. 4to. Colour frontis. Title vignette. 3 full-page & 2 text
illus. Red boards. Onlaid colour plate. Greer 40-22 1983 £27.50

BROWNE, EDGAR   Phiz and Dickens. 1913. First edition,
tall 8vo, front. Orig. blue cloth, sl. rubbed. A few cuttings
loosely inserted. Jarndyce 30-145 1983 £22

BROWNE, EDWARD   Arabian Medicine. Cambridge, 1921.
8vo. Orig. binding. First edition. Fye H-3-54 1983 $50

BROWNE, GORDON FREDERICK   Nonsense for Somebody, Anybody or
Everybody. Gardner, Darton & Co., nd (1895). Illus. by A. Nobody.
Illus. title p., frontis. & 47 illus. page in colour, interleaved,
illus. eps. & cover design by author. Cream canvas cloth with titling
& designs on cvrs. in dark brown, a.e.g. Fr. free ep. frayed at
edges & broken at hinge, some interleaves chipped at edges & some pp.
sl. discolouration, sml. snag bkstrip & sl. mark fr. cvr., vg, scarce.
Hodgkins 27-16 1983 £30

BROWNE, ISAAC HAWKINGS   De Animi Immortalitate. Londini:
Impenses J. & R. Tonson & S. Draper. 1754. 4to, some sections of the
text very lightly browned, disbound. Inscribed by the author at the
top of the title to William Fellows, esq., of Shotesham Park, near
Norwich. First edition. Bickersteth 77-9 1983 £55

BROWNE, ISAAC HAWKINS   Poems upon Various Subjects, Latin and
English. London: J. Nourse and C. Marsh, 1768. First ed., 8vo,
cont. calf, leather label, frontis. portrait. A very good copy.
Trebizond 18-11 1983 $70

BROWNE, JAMES   A History of the (Scotish) Highlands
and of the Highland Clans; with an extensive selection from the un-
edited Stuart Papers. A Fullarton & Co. Edinburgh & London. n.d.
66 illustrative engravings and numerous woodcuts. 4 vols. Leather,
boards, a.e.g. Some scuffing to the leather spines, mainly a fine
set. In Our Time 156-105 1983 $450

BROWNE, JOHN HUTTON BALFOUR   The medical jurisprudence of insanity.
London: J. and A. Churchill, 1871. First edition. 8vo. Orig.
green cloth. Ximenes 63-273 1983 $150

BROWNE, JOHN ROSS   Report of the Debates in the Convention
of California on the Formation of the State Constitution in Sept. &
Oct. 1842. Washington: Towers, 1850. 8vo, calf antique. Occasional
browning. Publisher's presentation copy with inscription on first leaf.
First edition. Very fine. Jenkins 153-71 1983 $150

BROWNE, JOHN ROSS   Resources of the Pacific Slope. New
York: D. Appleton and Company, 1869. Original cloth. Spine neatly
repaired. Fine clean copy. Jenkins 153-72 1983 $125

BROWNE, M.   Practical Taxidermy. 1884. Second ed.,
plan, 4 plates and text-figures, cr. 8vo, original cloth, inner
joints loose. Wheldon 160-466 1983 $20

BROWNE, MAGGIE   The Surprising Adventures of Tuppy and
Tue. London: Cassell & Co. Limited, 1904. First edition. Colored
plates and other illus. by A. Rackham. Orig. decorated cloth. Bookplate. Former owner's signature on front free endpaper. Covers
darkened and slightly soiled. MacManus 280-4290 1983 $450

BROWNE, MAURICE   Zetetes and other poems. London, 1905.
First edition. Quarter parchment. Bookplates. Nice. Rota 230-107
1983 £15

BROWNE, O'DONEL T. D.   The Rotunda Hospital, 1745-1945.
Edinburgh, Livingstone, 1947. With 38 plates and a folding chart,
4to, orig. cloth, in dust wrapper. Fenning 62-43 1983 £18.50

BROWNE, THOMAS   Christian Morals. Cambridge: at the
University Press, 1716. First edition. Half-title. An extra
folding frontis., and the 3 pp. of ads. 12mo. Full antique calf,
morocco labels, gilt. Traylen 94-118 1983 £225

BROWNE, THOMAS   Hydriotaphia. Urne-Buriall, or a
Discourse of the Sepulchrall Urnes... London: for Henry Brown, 1658.
First octavo edition. Antique calf. 2 engraved plates, ad. leaf,
and longitudinal half-title at the end. Traylen 94-119 1983 £220

BROWNE, THOMAS   Pseudodoxia Epidemica: or, Enquiries
into very many received Tenents... London: by T.H. for Edward Dod,
1646. First edition. Small folio. Cont. panelled calf, morocco
label, gilt. Imprimatur leaf. Traylen 94-120 1983 £220

BROWNE, THOMAS   Browne's Religio Medici and Digby's
Observations. Oxford, 1909. 8vo. Orig. dustwrapper, chipped and
stained. Some soiling to white boards, but a fine copy. Fye H-3-57
1983 $100

BROWNE, THOMAS   Religio Medici and other Essays.
London, (1911). 8vo. 1/2 leather. Printed at the Ballantyne
Press on Aldwych hand-made paper. A very fine copy. Fye H-3-58
1983 $250

BROWNE, THOMAS   Works. London: T. Basset, etc.,
1686. First collected edition. Folio. Cont. calf, spine neatly
repaired with orig. backstrip laid down, morocco label, gilt.
Portrait by R. White. Title-page printed in red and black. 2
engraving in the text. Traylen 94-116 1983 £190

BROWNE, THOMAS   Works, including his Life and Correspondence. London: William Pickering, 1836. Portrait and 4 plates.
4 vols. 8vo. Cont. calf, gilt panelled spines with morocco labels,
gilt, some joints neatly repaired. Traylen 94-117 1983 £60

BROWNELL, L. W.   Photography for the Sportsman Naturalist.
N.Y.: MacMillan Co., 1904. Thick 8vo, 3/4 crushed blue morocco, raised
bands, in-lays of crimson morocco, gilt extra, t.e.g. Profusely illus.
One of 100 large paper copies. Fine. Perata 28-202 1983 $175

BROWNING, ELIZABETH BARRETT Aurora Leigh. London: Chapman and
Hall, 1857. First edition. 8vo. Orig. green cloth. A very fine
copy. Ximenes 63-437 1983 $250

BROWNING, ELIZABETH BARRETT Casa Guidi Windows. Chapman & Hall,
1851. First edition, half title, orig. blue cloth, v.g. Jarndyce
31-448 1983 £42

BROWNING, ELIZABETH BARRETT The Greek Christian Poets and the English
Poets. London: Chapman & Hall, 1863. First edition. 12mo. Orig.
cloth. Near-fine. MacManus 277-719 1983 $50

BROWNING, ELIZABETH BARRETT Letters to her Sister, 1846-1859.
John Murray, 1931. 2nd impressions. Half title, front. & illus.
Orig. green cloth. Jarndyce 30-917 1983 £10.50

BROWNING, ELIZABETH BARRETT Poems. London: Edward Moxon, Dover
Street, 1844. First edition. 2 vols. Orig. cloth. Author's first
set of collected poems. Spines slightly faded. In a quarter-morocco
slipcase. Cont. gift inscription on front free endpaper of vol. 1
dated September 1844. Fine. MacManus 277-721 1983 $1,500

BROWNING, ELIZABETH BARRETT Poems. London: Chapman and Hall,
1856. Fourth edition. 3 vols. 8vo. Orig. green cloth. Spines
evenly faded. Ximenes 63-438 1983 $75

BROWNING, ELIZABETH BARRETT Poems before Congress. Chapman and
Hall, 1860. First edition, ads. dated February, 1860. 8vo, orig.
red cloth, gilt. Binding lightly stained, but sound and a very good
copy. Fenning 62-44 1983 £32.50

BROWNING, ELIZABETH BARRETT Sonnets from the Portuguese. (London),
(1914). Cloth and boards, gilt. One of 1,000 copies printed on
handmade paper. Near ink name, otherwise about fine. Reese 20-824
1983 $60

BROWNING, ELIZABETH BARRETT Sonnets from the Portuguese. (London,
1914). 1 of 1000 copies on handmade Riccardi paper, printed in the
Riccardi Press font. 8vo, orig. boards, cloth back, nice. Morrill
287-47 1983 $30

BROWNING, ELIZABETH BARRETT Sonnets from the Portuguese. Bath:
Bayntun, 1922. Square octavo, frontis. & 12 full-page woodcuts.
Red & black letter. Full red gilt calf. Ltd. edition of 1,000 copies.
Rostenberg 88-56 1983 $25

BROWNING, ELIZABETH BARRETT Sonnets From the Portuguese. NY, 1948.
Limited Editions Club. Illus. by Valenti Angelo. Limited to 1500
numbered copies signed by illus. Spine and cover slightly stained,
else very good or better in sunned, very good slipcase. Quill & Brush
54-194 1983 $75

BROWNING, ELIZABETH BARRETT Two Poems by Elizabeth Barrett and
Robert Browning. London: Chapman & Hall, 1854. 20 cm. Orig.
printed wraps. stitched as issued. A very good copy. First edition.
Grunder 7-7 1983 $150

BROWNING, ELIZABETH BARRETT Two Poems. Chapman and Hall, 1854.
First edition, sm. 8vo, original printed buff wrappers, fine.
Deighton 3-58 1983 £58

BROWNING, HUGH H.   A Short Historical Account of the
Andersonian Professors of Chemistry... Glasgow: William Hodge,
1894. Slim 4to. Orig. cloth. Portraits. Inscribed by the
author. A very good copy. Zeitlin 264-66 1983 $40

BROWNING, OSCAR   Napoleon the First Phase... London,
1905. First edition. 8vo. Hlaf blue calf, gilt, gilt panelled
spine, t.e.g. 14 plates and a map. Traylen 94-629 1983 £20

BROWNING, ROBERT   Balaustion's Adventure. Smith, Elder,
1871. First edition, 8vo, orig. brown cloth, v.g. copy. Fenning
61-44 1983 £14.50

BROWNING, ROBERT   Bells and Pomegranates. Edward Moxon,
1841-46. First collected, 4 pp ads, half title. Orig. dark blue
cloth, v.g./fine. First editions of the original numbers.
Jarndyce 31-450 1983 £120

BROWNING, ROBERT   Christmas Eve and Easter Day. London:
Chapman & Hall, 1850. 1st ed., 1st binding. Orig. slate cloth,
gilt on spine only. From the library of H. Buxton Forman, with his
bookplate, signature, and date (1868). Light spine wear, else a
fine copy. Jenkins 155-1364 1983 $150

BROWNING, ROBERT   Christmas Eve and Easter Day. London:
Chapman & Hall, 1850. 1st ed., 2nd binding. Orig. bright green
cloth, gilt on front cover only. Slight bit of fraying to crown of
spine, else fine. Jenkins 155-1365 1983 $100

BROWNING, ROBERT   Christmas-Eve and Easter-Day. Chapman &
Hall, 1850. First edition, half title, 32 pp ads. Sl. cracking of
inner hinges, orig. dull brown cloth, v.g. Jarndyce 31-451 1983
£32

BROWNING, ROBERT   Christmas Eve and Easter Day. London:
Chapman & Hall, 1850. First edition. 12mo. Half title. Orig.
green cloth, gilt. Front e.p. removed, else fine copy. Heath 48-
248 1983 £30

BROWNING, ROBERT   Dramatic Idyls. Smith, Elder, 1879-80.
First editions, all published, 2 vols., 8vo, orig. straw and brown
cloth, name neatly cut from small blank portion of half-titles, otherwise nice copies. Fenning 61-45 1983 £28.50

BROWNING, ROBERT   Dramatic Idyls. London: Smith, Elder,
& Co., 1880. First edition. Orig. cloth. Good. MacManus 277-725
1983 $30

BROWNING, ROBERT   Dramatis Personae. London: Chapman &
Hall, 1864. First edition. Rebound in full brown morocco, gilt,
a.e.g. with marbled endpapers, by Bedford. Presentation copy, inscribed on the half-title to "Mr. & Mrs. Benzon from theirs affectionately, ever Robert Browning, May 25 '69." Fine. MacManus 277-726
1983 $950

BROWNING, ROBERT   Dramatis Personae, & Dramatic Romances &
Lyrics. Chatto & Windus, 1909. 4to. Mounted colour frontis., pictorial title. 9 mounted colour plates, full white vellum gilt,
browned. Edition limited to 260 copies, No. 184. Greer 40-51 1983
£35

BROWNING, ROBERT   Ferishtah's Fancies. London: Smith,
Elder, & Co., 1884. First edition. Orig. cloth. Bookplate. Good.
MacManus 277-727 1983 $25

BROWNING, ROBERT   The Inn Album. London: Smith, Elder, & Co., 1875. First edition. Orig. cloth. Presentation copy, inscribed on the half-title to "Mrs. Benzon, with RB's affectionate regards, Nov. 19, '75." Covers rubbed at edges. Inner hinges weak. Prelims foxed. Good. MacManus 277-728 1983 $950

BROWNING, ROBERT   The Inn Album. London: Smith, Elder, & Co., 1875. First edition. Orig. cloth. Good. MacManus 277-729 1983 $25

BROWNING, ROBERT   Letters from Robert Browning to T.J. Wise & Other Correspondents. London: Printed for Private Circulation, 1912. First edition. 8vo. Orig. printed buff wrappers. Limited to 30 copies. Mint. MacManus 277-733 1983 $175

BROWNING, ROBERT   Letters of...Collected by Thomas J. Wise, 1933. First edition, half title, front. port. & illus. Orig. green cloth, v.g. Jarndyce 31-453 1983 £20

BROWNING, ROBERT   Men and Women. Chapman and Hall, 1855. First edition, 2 vols., 8vo, orig. green cloth, a very good copy. Fenning 61-46 1983 £135

BROWNING, ROBERT   Pacchiarotto and How He Worked in Distemper. Smith, Elder, 1876. First edition, 8vo, orig. brown cloth, a very good copy. Fenning 61-47 1983 £12.50

BROWNING, ROBERT   Paracelsus. Lon., 1835. John Drinkwater's copy with his signature and date (1922) on front end-paper. Drinkwater's bookplate on front pastedown; Mark Holstein's bookplate. Front hinge appears to have had minor repair, otherwise very fine, uncut, orig. boards with paper label on spine showing only minor wear. Internally fine. Mark on back pastedown where another bookplate may have been removed. Enclosed in clam shell case with red leather spine with gold lettering. Quill & Brush 54-195 1983 $3500

BROWNING, ROBERT   The Pied Piper of Hamelin. Phila.: J.B. Lippincott Co., (1934). First American edition. Illus. by A. Rackham. Orig. cloth with pictorial panel. Dust jacket. Fine. MacManus 280-4291 1983 $150

BROWNING, ROBERT   The Pied Piper of Hamelin. London: Geo. Routledge, n.d. First edition. 35 illus. by Kate Greenaway. 4to. Orig. glazed pictorial boards (corners a little rubbed). Very good. MacManus 278-2377 1983 $225

BROWNING, ROBERT   The Poetical Works. London, 1888-94. 17 vols. Roy. 8vo. Brown buckram, printed paper labels, uncut edges. Limited edition of 250 copies, printed on handmade paper. Traylen 94-121 1983 £75

BROWNING, ROBERT   Prince Hohenstiel-Schwangau, Saviour of Society. London: Smith, Elder & Co., 1871. First edition. Orig. cloth. Very good. MacManus 277-734 1983 $35

BROWNING, ROBERT   Red Cotton Night-Cap Country. Boston, 1873. 16mo, orig. cloth; pages foxed. First American edition. Printed from advance sheets. Argosy 714-90 1983 $45

BROWING, ROBERT   The Ring and the Book. London: Smith, Elder, 1868. First edition, first issue. 4 vols. Orig. cloth. Small bookplates. Very fine. MacManus 277-735 1983 $250

BROWNING, ROBERT   The Ring and the Book. London: Smith, Elder & Co., 1868. First edition, second binding. 4 vols. Orig. cloth. Minor wear. Bookplates. Very good. MacManus 277-736 1983 $125

BROWNING, ROBERT   Robert Browning and Alfred Dornett. Smith, Elder, 1906. Half title, front. & two other ports. 2 pp. ads. Orig. green cloth, untrimmed, t.e.g. First edition. Jarndyce 30-918 1983 £10.50

BROWNSON, ORESTES A.   The American Republic. N.Y., (1866). New edition. Argosy 716-188 1983 $30

BROWNSON, ORESTES A.   Essays and Reviews Chiefly on Theology, Politics, and Socialism. NY, 1852. First edition. Cloth, ink inscription and scribbling. Very worn. King 46-494 1983 $25

BRUCE, C. G.   Twenty Years in the Himalaya. London, 1910. First edition. Folding map, 60 illus. 8vo. Orig. cloth. Good. Edwards 1044-91 1983 £85

BRUCE, CARLTON   Mirth and Morality. T. Tegg, 1834. First edition, finely bound in three-quarters brown calf by Bayntun, spine gilt, t.e.g., v.g. Jarndyce 31-455 1983 £45

BRUCE, CARLTON   Mirth and Morality. T. Tegg, 1834. First edition, half title, '20...cuts from drawings by George Cruikshank'. Orig. branch patterned drab cloth, black label, sl. chipped. Jarndyce 31-454 1983 £42

BRUCE, JAMES   Travels to discover the source of the Nile... Edinburgh: G.G.J. & J. Robinson, 1790. 5 vols. 4to. 3 maps. 59 plates. Orig. 1/2 calf gilt, marbled boards, rubbed. Adelson Africa-18 1983 $1,200

BRUCE, JOHN   Gaudy Century. N.Y., Random (1948). First edition. Dust jacket. Very good-fine. Signed by the author. Houle 21-1005 1983 $20

BRUCE, MICHAEL   Poems on Several Occasions... Edinburgh: Printed by J. Robertson...MDCCLXX. First edition. 8vo, cont. half red morocco, drab boards. Quaritch NS 7-17a 1983 $550

BRUCE, PHILLIP A.   Economic History of Virginia in the Seventeenth Century. New York, 1896. First edition. 2 vols. T.e.g. Folding map. Ex-library. Very good. Jenkins 152-32 1983 $45

BRUCE, ROBERT   The Fighting Norths and Pawnee Scouts. N.Y., 1932. Illus. Orig. printed folio wraps. Ginsberg 46-843 1983 $25

BRUCKNER, CHRISTIAN MELCHIOR Dissertationem inauguralem medico physicam de dentibus... Frankfurt a. O.: Officina Winteriana, 1747. Woodcut initial, head- and tail-pieces. Small 4to. Cont. paper backstrip. Kraus 164-49 1983 $175

BRUMIERES, JEAN   La Maison Hanser. Paris, 1927. 4 hand-coloured plates. 3 handcoloured text illus. White wrappers. Edition limited to 200 copies, No. 102. Greer 40-130 1983 £35

BRUNET, JACQUES-CHARLES   Manuel du libraire et de l'amateur des livres... Paris: Dorbon Aine, 1919. 6 vols. plus 2 vol. supplement, quarter brown morocco and marbled boards, very little worn. Dawson 470-44 1983 $300

BRUNET, JACQUES-CHARLES   Manuel du Libraire et de l'Amateur de Livres. Copenhagan, 1966-68. 9 vols. Reissue of 5th ed., complete with 3 supplementary vols. Boswell 7-13 1983 $300

BRUNKER, H. M. S.   Story of the Russo-Japanese War. London, 1909-11. 8vo. Orig. cloth. 14 folding maps (13 coloured). 2 vols. Very slightly worn and faded. Bookplates. Good. Edwards 1042-289 1983 £25

BRUNO, GUIDO   Frank Harris: In Memoriam. New York: Privately printed, 1933. Printed wraps. Portrait. First edition. One of 450 copies (this copy not numbered). Light soiling, else fine. Reese 20-165 1983 $20

BRUNO, GUIDO   The Sacred Band of Litany of Ingratitude. New York, 1921. Cloth backed floral boards, paper label. Illus. First edition. Reese 20-164 1983 $25

BRUNTON, LAUDER   On Disorders of Assimiliation, Digestion, etc. London, 1901. 8vo. Orig. cloth. First edition. Name on title. Gurney JJ-62 1983 £18

BRUNTON, MARY   Self-Control. Edinburgh, 1811. First edition. 2 vols. Small 8vo. Cont. half red morocco, gilt, marbled boards. Half-titles. Traylen 94-122 1983 £130

BRUSH, DANIEL H.   Growing Up with Southern Illinois, 1820-61. Chicago, Lakeside Press, 1944. Map, illus. 12mo, gilt top. Clark 741-285 1983 $21

BRUSH, GEROME   Boston Symphony Orchestra. (Merrymount Press), 1936. 109 plates. 4to, orig. boards with pictorial paper cover. Names on back fly leaf, otherwise fine. Salloch 387-294 1983 $30

BRUSSEL, I. R.   Anglo-American First Editions 1826-1900, East to West... (With:) Anglo-American First Editions, West to East. New York: Sol Lewis, 1981. 2 vols. 8vo. Cloth, slip-case. Limited to 500 numbered copies. Illus. and with plates printed on a yellow background just like the orig. edition. Oak Knoll 49-424 1983 $110

BRUZEN LA MARTINIERE, ANTOINE AUGUSTIN   Introduction a l'histoire de l'Asie, de l'Afrique, et de l'Amerique. Amsterdam: Zacharie Chatelain, 1735. 2 vols. 12mo. 2 frontis. 4 folding maps. Orig. calf. Gilt spines. Red labels. Adelson Africa-19 1983 $150

BRY, JOHANNE THEODOR DE   Dritter Theil Indiae Orientalis... Oppenheim, 1616. Second German edition. Engraved title, over 60 plates and maps, some double-page or large folding. Folio. Orig. 19th century maroon cloth over marbled boards, black morocco label. A.e.g. Carefully washed and two of the large folding maps expertly silked. Fine. Jenkins 152-612 1983 $950

BRYAN, DANIEL   The Mountain Muse. Harrisonburg: Printed for the author by Davidson & Bourne, 1813. Subscriber's list. Orig. calf. First edition. Scattered foxing and browning, else a near fine copy, with the half-title and subscriber's list. Reese 18-407 1983 $250

BRYAN, WILLIAM S.   A History of the Pioneer Families of Missouri. St. Louis: 1876. First edition. Illus., including portraits and woodcuts. Blue cloth. Fine copy. Bradley 66-594 1983 $225

BRYANT, EDWIN   Voyage en Californie... Bruxelles, 1849. 4 plates. Original pale blue pictorial boards, skillfully rebacked in matching paper. Fragile boards worn. First edition in French. Internally very fine. Very scarce. Jenkins 153-73 1983 $175

BRYANT, EDWIN   What I Saw in California. Santa Ana, CA: The Fine Arts Press, 1936. 4to, illus. with 8 plates including a color woodblock frontis. This copy inscribed by the editor. Quarter calf over boards. Edition ltd. to 500 copies. Spine a bit rubbed. Karmiole 74-30 1983 $150

BRYANT, JACOB   Observations upon a Treatise entitled a Description of the Plain of Troy by Monsieur le Chevalier. Eton: by M. Pore, 1795. First edition. 4to. Half green calf, gilt. Fine copy. Heath 48-593 1983 $50

BRYANT, WILLIAM CULLEN   A Discourse on the Life, Character & Genius of Washington Irving. New York, 1860. 8vo. Cloth. A large paper copy of the book. From the library of Stephen Wakeman with his bookplate. A fine copy. In our Time 156-107 1983 $100

BRYANT, WILLIAM CULLEN   Poems. Boston: 1834. Octavo. Double fore-edge paintings. Some faint foxing to paintings. About fine in orig. full calf, gilt-decorated on both covers, spine and dentelles; rubbed at extremities. Occasional foxing throughout. A.e.g. Owner's signature. In protective slip-case. Bromer 25-207 1983 $1750

BRYANT, WILLIAM CULLEN   Poems. New York: Appleton: 1855. 2 vols. 1st ed. thus. Orig. full publisher's morocco gift binding, raised bands, gilt, a.e.g. Fine set with 1854 owner's inscription. Jenkins 155-135 1983 $30

BRYANT, WILLIAM CULLEN   Thirty Poems. New York: Appleton, 1864. 1st ed., 2nd state. Orig. brown cloth, gilt. Inscribed by author on front free end paper in ink: "William Cullen Bryant, March, 1864." This copy was part of the Wakeman collection. Near fine copy. Jenkins 155-136 1983 $90

BRYCE, JAMES   The American Commonwealth. London: Macmillan and Co., 1888. First edition, first issue. 3 vols. 8vo. Half brown morocco, gilt, gilt panelled spines, t.e.g., by Riviere. Traylen 94-124 1983 £65

BRYCE, JAMES   The American Commonwealth. London: 1888. First edition. 3 vols. Blue cloth. Folding color map. Extremities worn, inner hinges starting, otherwise very good. Bradley 66-475 1983 $85

BRYCE, JAMES   The American Commonwealth. 1889. 2 vols., 8vo, orig. cloth. Good copy. Bickersteth 75-113 1983 £25

BRYCE, JAMES   A Sketch of the State of British India. Edinburgh, 1810. First edition. Half calf, by J. Edmond of Aberdeen, with his ticket. With the bookplate of the 7th Earl of Kintore and the ownership inscription of the 6th Countess. 8vo. Good. Edwards 1044-94 1983 £75

BRYDEN, H. ANDERSON   Gun and camera in Southern Africa. London: Edward Stanford, 1893. 8vo. Folding map. 35 plates. Orig. pictorial cloth. Lightly rubbed. Adelson Africa-21 1983 $130

BRYDEN, H. ANDERSON   Kloof and Karroo. London: Longmans, Green, 1889. 8vo. 17 plates. Orig. cloth. Rubbed, spine ends frayed. Adelson Africa-20 1983 $120

BRYDGES, EGERTON   The anti-critic for August 1821, and March 1822. Geneva: printed by W. Fick, 1822. First edition. 8vo. Cont. purple half calf. One of only 75 copies printed, this one numbered by Brydges "42 SEB" on the verso of the title. Spine faded, and a little rubbed. Ximenes 63-235 1983 $250

BRYDGES, EGERTON   Archaica. Containing a reprint of scarce old English prose tracts. London: printed by private press of Longman, etc., 1815. First edition. 2 vols. Large 4to. Half dark blue calf. Printed in an edition of 200 copies. Ximenes 63-254 1983 $175

BRYDGES, EGERTON   The Autobiography, Times, Opinions and Contemporaries. Cochrane & M'crone. First edition. 2 vols. Half titles, fronts. 4 pp ads. vol. II. Later dull green boards, paper labels, v.g. Extra-illustrated with 29 portraits. Jarndyce 30-919 1983 £42

BRYDGES, EGERTON   Human fate, and an address to the poets Wordsworth and Southey: poems. Totham: printed by Charles Clark at his private press, 1848. First edition. 8vo. Orig. printed wrappers. Somewhat soiled, spine slightly worn. Ximenes 63-439 1983 $200

BRYDGES, EGERTON   Letters on the character and poetical genius of Lord Byron. London: Longman, etc., 1824. First edition. 8vo. Half calf, spine gilt. Ximenes 63-43 1983 $200

BRYDONE, PATRICK   A Tour through Sicily and Malta. Printed for W. Strahan and T. Cadell, 1774. 2 vols, 8vo, cont. calf with red and green labels. Upper joint of first volume cracked, leather defective near the joint on upper cover of second volume, one label chipped. Bickersteth 75-9 1983 £26

BRYDONE, PATRICK   A tour through Sicily and Malta. Dublin: printed for the United Company of Booksellers, 1775. Third edition, corrected and enlarged. 2 vols. 12mo. Cont. calf, spines gilt, early prize stamp of Munster Academy on the front covers. A few ink splashes along the outer edges of one volume. Ximenes 63-616 1983 $50

BRYHER, WINIFRED   Civilians. Raint Chateau, Territet: Pool, (1927). Cont. marbled boards, paper label, orig. wraps. bound in. First edition. Carl Van Vechten's copy, with his bookplate. A fine copy. Reese 20-171 1983 $250

BRYMER, JOHN   Gammon & Spinach. Blackie, nd (1900). Pictures by Stuart Orr. 24 colour illus. printed by Edmund Evans on one side of page only, blanks also numbered. Cloth backed col. pic. bds. Oblong. Contemp. insc. fr. ep., cvrs. sl. worn, vg. Hodgkins 27-17 1983 £20

BUBSEY, HAMILTON   The Troting and Pacing Horse in America. N.Y., MacMillan, 1904. First edition. Thick 8vo, illus. with halftone frontis. and numerous plates. 3/4 green morocco over marbled boards, spine ruled and decorated in gilt, t.e.g., unopened, marbled endpapers. One of 100 copies on large paper. Fine as issued. Houle 22-1109 1983 $275

BUCHAN, ANNA   Unforgettable, Unforgotten. London: Hodder & Stoughton, (1945). First edition. Illus. Orig. cloth. Dust jacket (somewhat faded, worn, and slightly chipped at the spine ends). Spine and covers somewhat faded. Good. MacManus 277-754 1983 $20

BUCHAN, JOHN   Adventures of Richard Hannay. Boston, 1939. 8vo. Cloth. Contains 3 books by author. Jacket design by N.C. Wyeth. About fine in dj which is chipped on the rear flap. In Our Time 156-109 1983 $45

BUCHAN, JOHN   The African Colony. Edinburgh: William Blackwood & Sons, 1903. 8vo. 2 folding maps. Orig. cloth. Lightly rubbed. Adelson Africa-22 1983 $125

BUCHAN, JOHN   Greenmantle. London: Hodder & Stoughton, 1916. First edition. Orig. cloth. Signed by the author on the title-page. Spine and covers slightly faded and rubbed. Front inner hinge a trifle cracked. Good. MacManus 277-740 1983 $225

BUCHAN, JOHN   Greenmantle. T. Nelson, 1942. Sm. 8vo. Dark green buckram. Colour pictorial dust wrapper by H.M.B. Bookplate by D. Wheeler. Greer 39-45 1983 $10.50

BUCHAN, JOHN   The Half-Hearted. London: Isbister & Co. Ltd., 1900. First edition. Orig. pictorial cloth. Rubbed. Good. MacManus 277-741 1983 $85

BUCHAN, JOHN   The House of the Four Winds. Boston: Houghton Mifflin Co., (1935). First American edition. Orig. cloth. Very good. MacManus 277-742 1983 $20

BUCHAN, JOHN   The Island of Sheep. London: Hodder & Stoughton, (1936). First edition. Orig. cloth. Covers dusty. In chipped dust jacket. Good. MacManus 277-744 1983 $100

BUCHAN, JOHN   The Long Traverse. London: Hodder & Stoughton, (1941). First edition. Illus. Orig. cloth. Dust jacket (defective, with a small piece missing from the front cover; spine ends chipped; slightly soiled). Covers slightly spotted. Edges foxed. Rare in dust jacket. Good. MacManus 277-745 1983 $35

BUCHAN, JOHN   Memory Hold-the-Door. London: Hodder and Stoughton, 1940. First edition. Orig. cloth. Dust jacket (very slightly frayed and soiled). Fine. MacManus 277-746 1983 $35

BUCHAN, JOHN   The Rungates Club. Boston, 1928. 8vo. Cloth. A fine copy in the uncommon dj. In Our Time 156-108 1983 $85

BUCHAN, JOHN   Sick Heart River. London: Hodder & Stoughton, (1941). First edition. Orig. cloth. Dust jacket (darkened and worn). MacManus 277-749 1983 $50

BUCHANAN, C.   Christian Researchers in Asia. London, 1812. Mottled calf by A. Milne of Forres, with his stamp. 8vo. Good. Edwards 1044-95 1983 £65

BUCHANAN, DONALD W.   The Growth of Canadian Painting. London & Toronto, Collins, 1950. First edition, with 16 coloured and 64 other plates, roy. 8vo, orig. cloth. Fenning 60-39 1983 £55

BUCHANAN, DONALD W.   The Growth of Canadian Painting. London & Toronto: Collins, 1950. First edition. 24 1/2cm. 16 colour plates and 64 in monochrome, green cloth, bookplate, slightly faded, else very good. McGahern 54-21 1983 $45

BUCHANAN, GEORGE   An Appendix to the History of Scotland. Printed by Sam. Palmer, for S. Illidge; T. Corbet; and T. Payne, 1721. 8vo, engraved frontis. Cont. panelled calf, rubbed, lacking the label. Bickersteth 77-105 1983 £68

BUCHANAN, GEORGE   Rerum Scoticarum Historia. Edinburgi, Apud Alexandrum Arbuthnetum. Anno, 1582. Small folio, errata leaf, cont. calf with blind ornamental panel in the centre of each cover, rebacked some time ago, and upper joint again cracked. Clean tear in one leaf. Label chipped. First edition. Bickersteth 77-104 1983 £180

BUCHANAN, JAMES   The British grammar. London: printed for A. Millar, 1762. First edition. 12mo. Cont. calf, spine gilt. Slight soiling, but a very good copy. Ximenes 63-220 1983 $90

BUCHANAN, JAMES   The British Grammer... Boston: Nathaniel Coverly for John Norman, 1784. Full calf. Signature "Israel Bartlett's 1791." Very good. Felcone 20-77 1983 $60

BUCHANAN, JAMES   Sketches of the History, Manners and Customs, of the North American Indian, with a Plan for their Melioration. New York, 1824. Two vols. Orig. printed boards (dated 1825). Spines perished, but sewn cords still intact and strong. Scattered foxing, else a very good to fine set. Reese 18-571 1983 $175

BUCHANAN, JOHN   The Shire Highlands (East Central Africa). Edinburgh, 1885. Red decorated cloth, spine frayed, with the bookplate of Sir W.G. Gordon Cumming. K Books 301-31 1983 £45

BUCHANAN, ROBERT   The Ballad of Judas Iscariot. Reigate: The Priory Press; London: A.C. Fifield, 1904. First edition. Orig. pictorial wrappers. Fine. MacManus 277-755 1983 $40

BUCHANAN, ROBERT   The City of Dream. London: Chatto & Windus, 1888. First edition. Frontis. Orig. cloth. Endpapers foxed. Fine. MacManus 277-756 1983 $50

BUCHANAN, ROBERT   The Complete Poetical Works of Robert Buchanan. London: Chatto & Windus, 1901. First edition. 2 vols. Frontis. Orig. cloth. Covers and spine slightly worn. Contents a trifle shaken. Very good set. MacManus 277-757 1983 $65

BUCHANAN, ROBERT   The Fleshly School of Poetry and Other Phenomena of the Day. London: Strahan & Co., 1872. First edition. Full polished calf, gilt, marbled endpapers, t.e.g., with morocco labels on spine, by Bartlett of Boston, with orig. wrappers bound in. Fine. MacManus 277-758 1983 $450

BUCHANAN, ROBERT   Master-Spirits. London: Henry S. King & Co., 1873. First edition. Orig. cloth. Spine darkened. Front covers lighlty rubbed. Bookplate. Poor quality paper browning toward margins. Inner hinges strained. Very good. MacManus 277-759 1983 $45

BUCHANAN, ROBERT   Selected Poems. London: Chatto & Windus, 1882. First edition. Frontis. by Thomas Dalziel. Orig. cloth. Spine darkened. Bookplate. Inner hinges weak. Good. MacManus 277-760 1983 $35

BUCHANAN, THOMAS   Physiological Illustrations of the Organ of Hearing... London, 1828. First edition. 4to. Orig. boards, uncut. 3 adverts. 10 plates engraved after drawings by the author. Back torn. Library inscription on title. Fine copy. Gurney 90-26 1983 £120

BUCHNER, ERNST   Martin Schongauer als Maler. Berlin: Deutscher Verein fur Kunstwissenschaft, 1941. 104 plates (3 color). Small folio. Boards, 1/4 cloth. Rare. Ars Libri 32-621 1983 $200

BUCHOWIECKI, WALTHER   Der Barockbau der ehemaligen Hofbibliothek in Wien, ein Werk J.B. Fischers Von Erlach. Wien: Georg Prachner, 1957. 95 illus. hors texte. Large 4to. Cloth. Dust jacket. Ars Libri 32-220 1983 $75

BUCK, ALBERT H.   Growth of Medicine from the Earliest Times to about 1800. Yale Univ. Press, 1917. First edition. Argosy 713-80 1983 $85

BUCK, E. J.   Simla Past and Present. Bombay, 1925. Second edition. 2 maps, numerous illus. 8vo. Orig. cloth. Good. Edwards 1044-96 1983 £50

BUCK, FRANKLIN   A Yankee Trader in the Gold Rush... Boston, 1930. First edition. Frontis. and illus. Index. Fine. Jenkins 152-34 1983 $40

BUCK, FRANKLIN   A Yankee Trader in the Gold Rush. Boston, 1930. 1st ed. Illus. Clark 741-83 1983 $21

BUCK, HOWARD   The Tempering. New Haven: Yale, 1919. Printed wraps. over boards. First edition. A couple of short closed tears at corners, else fine. Reese 20-174 1983 $30

BUCK, J.H.   Old Plate. New York, Gorham Man. Co., 1903. New & Enlarged ed. Illus. 8vo. Buckram. Morrill 289-282 1983 $35

BUCK, MITCHELL S.   Book Repair and Restoration... Philadelphia: Nicholas L. Brown, 1918. Square 8vo. Cloth. Paper spine label. Limited to 1000 copies. Karl Kup's copy. Label chipped. Oak Knoll 48-44 1983 $45

BUCK, PEARL   The Good Earth. NY, (1931). First issue with flees' on line 17, page 100, covers soft and shaken, good, owner's name and address on half-title. Quill & Brush 54-199 1983 $25

BUCK, SOLON J.   Travel and Description, 1765-1865. Springfield, Illinois, 1914. First edition. Illus. Index. Jenkins 152-562 1983 $65

BUCKBEE, EDNA BRYAN   Pioneer Days of Angel's Camp. Angel's Camp: The Calaveras Californian, (1932). 1st ed. Illus. Gray pic. wrappers. Includes a chapter by Mark Twain. Bradley 63-127 1983 $40

BUCKBEE, EDNA BRYAN   The Saga of Old Tuolumne. N.Y.: Press of the Pioneers, 1935. 16 plates. Cloth in taped dust wrapper. Dawson 471-35 1983 $75

BUCKE, CHARLES   The Italians; or the fatal accusation: a tragedy. London: printed for G. and W. B. Whittaker, 1819. 8vo, wrappers, first edition. Half-title present. Very scarce. Ximenes 64-67 1983 $75

BUCKE, CHARLES   The Italians; or the fatal accusation: a tragedy. London: printed for G. and W. B. Whittaker, 1819. 8vo, disbound, 5th edition. Ximenes 64-68 1983 $40

BUCKE, CHARLES   On the Life, Writings, and Genius of Akenside. James Cochrane, 1832. First edition, half title, front. Half brown morocco. Jarndyce 30-878 1983 £20

BUCKINGHAM, GEORGE VILLIERS, DUKE OF   The rehearsal. London: printed for Thomas Dring, 1675. Sm. 4to, disbound, 3rd edition. Some stains, some headlines shaved. Ximenes 64-555 1983 $150

BUCKINGHAM, GEORGE VILLIERS, DUKE OF   The rehearsal. London: printed for T. Dring, and sold by Jacob Tonson, 1692. Sm. 4to, disbound, 6th edition. A few minor marginal stains, but a very good copy. Ximenes 64-556 1983 $75

BUCKINGHAM, GEORGE VILLIERS, DUKE OF   The rehearsal. London: printed for Richard Wellington; and sold by A. Bettesworth; and Jacob Tonson, 1701. Sm. 4to, disbound, 7th edition. Some light water-stains, a few margins trimmed a little close. Ximenes 64-557 1983 $75

BUCKINGHAM, GEORGE VILLIERS, DUKE OF   The rehearsal; a comedy. London: printed and sold by H. Hills, 1709. 12mo, wrappers. Ximenes 64-558 1983 $75

BUCKINGHAM, GEORGE VILLIERS, DUKE OF   The rehearsal...To which is added, a key, or critical view of the authors. London: printed for W. Feales, etc., 1735. 12mo, wrappers, 13th edition. With an engraved frontis. by Vander Gucht. Uncut copy. Ximenes 64-559 1983 $25

BUCKINGHAM, JAMES SILK   America: Historical, Statistic, and Descriptive. London, (1841). 3 vols. Port. Illus. Folding map. Cloth. First edition. Felcone 21-17 1983 $100

BUCKINGHAM, JAMES SILK   Travels in Assyria, Media, and Persia. London, 1830. Folding map. 26 plates. Half calf. 8vo. Good. Edwards 1044-97 1983 £230

BUCKINGHAM, JAMES SILK   Two letters, addressed to the honourable Court of Directors of the East India Company. London: printed by James Holmes, 1825. First edition. 8vo. Modern wrappers. Rare. Ximenes 63-200 1983 $125

BUCKINGHAM, JOHN SHEFFIELD, DUKE OF   Poems on Several Occasions. Glasgow, printed by Robert and Andrew Foulis, 1752. Small 8vo, cont. calf, short tear in two leaves without loss and binding worn at corners, but sound, a very good copy. Fenning 62-333 1983 £26.50

BUCKINGHAM, JOSEPH T.   Personal Memoirs and Recollections of Editorial Life. Boston, 1852. First edition. 2 vols. Frontis. Library bookplate inside covers. Nice. Felcone 20-17 1983 $25

BUCKLAND, F.   Curiosities of Natural History. 1873-75. 4 vols., cr. 8vo, cloth (trifle used and loose). Series 1-4. Wheldon 160-467 1983 £18

BUCKLAND, WILLIAM   Geology and Mineralogy. Philadelphia: Carey, Lea and Blanchard, 1837. First American edition. 705 engraved figures. In orig. cloth, stained; paper spine labels, a bit chipped. Some minor water-staining to lower right margin, not affecting text or plates. Karmiole 76-46 1983 $100

BUCKLAND, WILLIAM   Reliquiae Diluvianae. John Murray, 1823. 4to, folding table, 27 lithographed plates and maps, one of them folding, and three coloured, cont. half calf with marbled boards, rubbed, calf defective at top of upper joint on the upper cover. First edition. Bickersteth 77-263 1983 £140

BUCKLAND, WILLIAM   Reliquiae Diluvianae. London, 1823. First edition. 27 plates, including 2 hand-coloured geological maps, folding table, 4to, orig. cloth, neatly rebacked. K Books 307-37 1983 £120

BUCKLEY, HAROLD   Squadron 95. Paris: The Obelisk Press, 1933. Illus. with numerous photographic plates and drawings. Presentation copy, signed by the author, "from Buck". Bound in orig. blue cloth. 5 drawings by L.C. Holden. Karmiole 72-77 1983 $100

BUCKLEY, MICHAEL J.   Day at the Farm. SF, 1937. Lg 4to, linen-backed bds., paper label. First edition. A very nice copy with large decorative borders. Perata 28-113 1983 $27.50

BUCKLEY, WILFRED   The Art of Glass. N.Y., Oxford University, 1939. First edition. 4to, illus. with 180 fine gravures. Dust jacket (some rubbing and chips) else, very good. Houle 22-408 1983 $35

BUCKLYN, JOHN K.   Battle of Cedar Creek, Oct. 19, 1864. Providence, 1883. Orig. printed wraps. First edition. One of 250 copies. Ginsberg 46-769 1983 $20

BUCKMAN, GEORGE REX   Colorado Springs Colorado. (Colorado Springs), 1892. Orig. pictorial wrappers. Slight blemish on front. Profusely illus. Jenkins 152-57 1983 $35

BUCKMINSTER, JOSEPH   A Discourse Delivered in Portsmouth, Dec. 14, 1800: The Anniversary of the Death of Washington. Portsmouth, Chas. Peirce, Dec., 1800. 8vo., sewed, few pages foxed. Argosy 716-604 1983 $50

BUCKNER, J. P.   The Hoosier Doctor: A Medicated Story. Columbus, Ohio, 1881. First edition. Green cloth. Locating only the copy at the Huntington Library. Rare. Very good. Bradley 65-103 1983 $45

BUDDEN, MARIA ELIZABETH   Claudine: or, Humility, the Basis of all the Virtues. London: John Harris, 1835. Seventh edition. 12mo. Four engravings. Very fine copy in leather-backed marbled boards. Owner's inscription dated 1841. Bromer 25-323 1983 $85

BUDGE, E. A. WALLIS   The Gods Of The Egyptians Or Studies In Egyptian Mythology. 1904. 1st ed., 2 vols, small 4to, illus., original decorative embossed cloth, gilt, decorative gilt backs, worn and faded. Deighton 3-59 1983 £98

BUDGE, WILLIAM   The Gospel Message. Liverpool, 1879. First edition. Dbd. Ginsberg 47-593 1983 $25

BUDGELL, EUSTACE   Memoirs of the Life and Character of the Late Earl of Orrery and of the Family of the Boyles. 1732. Lacking portrait. K Books 301-32 1983 £34

BUDGELL, EUSTACE　　　　Verres and His Scribblers. London: Printed for C. Browne...MDCCXXXII. First and only edition. 8vo, title somewhat soiled, final page soiled and with a small hole affecting several words; plain wraps. Quaritch NS 7-18 1983 $225

BUECHER, KARL　　　　Arbeit und Rhythmus. Leipzig, 1909. 26 illus. on 14 plates, musical samples. 8vo, 1/2 morocco over marbled boards, spine gilt, with 5 raised bands. Orig. wrs. bound in. Fine copy. Salloch 387-295 1983 $50

BUECHNER, FREDERICK　　　　A Long Day's Dying. New York: Alfred A. Knopf, 1950. First edition. 8vo. Orig. cloth. Dust jacket. Very fine copy. Jaffe 1-49 1983 $75

BUEHLER, CHARLOTTE　　　　The Child and His Family. NY: Harper, 1939. First edition. Very good in worn dust jacket. Gach 95-62 1983 $25

BUEHLER, CHARLOTTE　　　　Kindheit Und Jugend. Leipzig: S. Hirzel, 1928. First edition. Bookplate removed, stamp on rear paste-down. Gach 95-63 1983 $30

BUEHLER, KARL　　　　The Mental Development of the Child. NY: Harcourt, Brace, 1930. First American edition, translated from the fifth German edition. Orig. green cloth, scratched and rubbed. Gach 94-528 1983 $25

BUELL, AUGUSTUS C.　　　　Paul Jones, Founder of the American Navy: A History. N.Y., 1900. Illus. & map. 2 vols. Pict. cloth, g.t. Argosy 716-252 1983 $30

BUERGER, LEO　　　　Circulatory Disturbances of the Extremities. Phila., 1924. 192 illus. some in color. Buckram. First edition. Argosy 713-81 1983 $50

BUFF, HEINRICH　　　　Lehrbuch der Physikalischen und Theoretischen Chemie. Braunschweig: Vieweg, 1857. First edition. 8vo. Cont. half calf (rubbed, front board detached, library stamps). Internally very good. Zeitlin 264-67 1983 $35

BUFFON, G. L. L.　　　　Istoria dell'Elefante. Venice: A. Milocco, 1774. 8vo. Old pasteboards, uncut. Folding plate. Gurney 90-27 1983 £45

BUFFUM, E. GOULD　　　　Six Months in the Gold Mines. Phila.: Lea and Blanchard, 1850. First edition. Ads. Orig. black cloth with title in gilt on spine. Some bumping and chipping. Jenkins 152-37 1983 $250

BUFFUM, GEORGE T.　　　　On Two Frontiers. Boston, (1918). Frontis. by Maynard Dixon. Illus. by Frank T. Merrill. Gilt pictorial cloth. Fine copy. Reese 19-100 1983 $50

BUFFUM, GEORGE T.　　　　Smith of Bear City and Other Frontier Sketches. New York, 1906. 1st ed. Illus., gilt top, rear cover slightly marred. Clark 741-243 1983 $31.50

BUGEAUD, THOMAS R.　　　　Memoirs of Marshal Bugeaud... London: Hurst & Blackett, 1884. 2 vols. 8vo. Portrait. Orig. red cloth. Spines faded, ex-lib. Adelson Africa-169 1983 $40

BUHLER, WILHELM　　　　Kupferstichalphabet des Meisters E.S. Strassburg: J.H. Ed. Heitz, 1934. 23 collotype plates. 4to. Portfolio. Wrappers. Text fascicle and loose plates, as issued. Ars Libri 32-432 1983 $60

BUKOWSKI, CHARLES　　　　At Terror Street and Agony Way. Black Sparrow Press, 1968. 8vo. Wraps. 1st issue, 1st ed. with the word "Street" misprinted as "Sreet". Fine. In Our Time 156-114 1983 $150

BUKOWSKI, CHARLES　　　　Burning in Water Drowning in Flame. SB, 1974. One of 300 numbered and signed copies, very fine. Quill & Brush 54-200 1983 $75

BUKOWSKI, CHARLES　　　　Crucifix in a Deathhand. (New Orleans: Loujon Press, 1965). Small folio printed by hand with handset Bulmer, Roman and Uncial types on ivory tinted paper and also other colored paper, with illus. by Noel Rockmore. Ltd. edition, designed, printed and hand-bound by Louise and John Webb, and signed by the author. Duschnes 240-35 1983 $75

BUKOWSKI, CHARLES　　　　The Curtains Are Waving and People Walk Through the Afternoon Here and in Berlin and in New York City and in Mexico. Black Sparrow Press, 1967. 8vo. Wraps. Total edition is 125 copies signed by author. This copy contains a drawing by Bukowski on the colophon page. A fine copy of this early title. In Our Time 156-111 1983 $250

BUKOWSKI, CHARLES　　　　The Curtains Are Waving... Black Sparrow Press, 1967. A proof copy of the book, with the original sheets for the book, unfolded, unnumbered and unsigned. A fine copy. In Our Time 156-112 1983 $150

BUKOWSKI, CHARLES　　　　The Days Run Away Like Wild Horses Over the Hills. Black Sparrow Press, 1969. 8vo. Cloth, boards. 1 of 50 copies signed by Bukowski with an orig. watercolor by same. Fine in acetate jacket. In Our Time 156-116 1983 $150

BUKOWSKI, CHARLES　　　　The Days Run Away Like Wild Horses Over the Hill. Los Angeles: Black Sparrow, 1969. Orig. printed wraps. First edition, trade issue. Inscribed presentation copy to Neeli Cherry. Follows a self-portrait, with bottle, signed "Buk." The inscription date is six days after publication. Wraps. very slightly used, near fine. Reese 20-180 1983 $75

BUKOWSKI, CHARLES　　　　Ham on Rye. Santa Barbara: Black Sparrow Press, 1982. Limited to 350 copies signed by Bukowski with small drawing. Mint in cloth-backed printed boards. Bromer 25-11 1983 $35

BUKOWSKI, CHARLES　　　　Poems and Drawings. Crescent City: Epos, 1962. Printed wraps. First edition. One of 500 copies (200 for sale; 300 distributed gratis to subscribers). Very slightest traces of soiling, else a fine copy. Reese 20-177 1983 $250

BUKOWSKI, CHARLES　　　　2 Poems. Black Sparrow Press, 1967. 8vo. Sewn wrappers. First and only edition. Total edition is 99 copies signed by the poet. A very fine copy. In Our Time 156-113 1983 $250

BUKOWSKI, CHARLES　　　　Women. Black Sparrow Press, 1978. 8vo. Cloth, boards. 1 of 75 copies signed with an original watercolor by same. Fine in acetate jacket. In Our Time 156-118 1983 $125

BUKOWSKI, CHARLES　　　　Women. Santa Barbara, Black Sparrow, 1978. First edition. One of 75 signed copies, with signed orig. painting by the author. Decorated cloth over printed boards. Acetate jacket. Houle 22-145 1983 $95

BUKOWSKI, CHARLES　　　　You Kissed Lilly. Santa Barbara, Black Sparrow, 1978. First edition. Half cloth. One of 10 author's presentation copies. Signed twice and inscribed by Bukowski to poet Steve Richmond. Fine. Houle 21-173 1983 $125

BULFINCH, THOMAS　　　　Oregon and Eldorado. Boston, 1866. Orig. cloth, first edition. Ginsberg 46-72 1983 $75

BULL, H. G.　　　　Notes on the Birds of Herefordshire. 1888. Portrait, 8vo, original decorated cloth, joints trifle rubbed, covers slightly marked. Wheldon 160-662 1983 £25

BULL, SIDNEY A.　　　　History of the Town of Carlisle, Massachusetts, 1754-1920. Cambridge, 1920. 1st ed. Illus. 8vo. Ends of spine frayed. Morrill 287-215 1983 $30

BULL, WILLIAM PERKINS　　　　From Brock to Currie. Toronto: Perkins Bull Foundation, 1935. 25cm. With 14 colour plates and over 300 illus. Half blue cloth and paper boards, paper label. Good to very good. McGahern 53-181 1983 $45

BULLEN, A. H.   Musa Proterva: Love-Poems of the
Restoration. Privately ptd., 1902. (no. 392 of 400). Half title,
orig. light green cloth, mock vellum spine, browned, t.e.g.
Jarndyce 31-459 1983 £10.50

BULLEN, FRANK T.   The Apostles of the South East.
London, 1901. First edition. 8vo, cloth. Argosy 714-92 1983 $35

BULLEN, FRANK T.   Beyond. Lon., 1909. Minor interior foxing, else very good. Quill & Brush 54-202 1983 $30

BULLEN, FRANK T.   The Cruise of the "Cachalot." London,
1898. First edition. 8vo. Orig. cloth. Frontis. 7 other plates.
Folding map. Slightly worn and soiled. Good. Edwards 1042-21 1983
£55

BULLEN, FRANK T.   The Cruise of the "Cachalot" Round the
World After Sperm Whales. London: Smith, Elder, 1898. First edition.
Orig. cloth. Illus. Some cover soiling. Inner hinges tightened,
a little worn. Good. MacManus 277-764 1983 $60

BULLEN, FRANK T.   Idylls of the Sea and Other Marine
Sketches. London: Richards, 1899. First edition. Orig. cloth.
Near-fine. MacManus 277-765 1983 $27.50

BULLEN, FRANK T.   The Log of a Sea Waif. London: Smith,
Elder, 1899. First edition. Illus. Orig. cloth. Good. MacManus
277-766 1983 $25

BULLEN, FRANK T.   Sea Puritans. London: Hodder & Stoughton, 1904. First edition. Illus. by Arhtur Twidle. Orig. pictorial
cloth. A little light foxing. Near-fine. MacManus 277-767 1983 $35

BULLEN, FRANK T.   Sea Spray. London, 1906. First
edition, 8vo, pict. cloth. Argosy 714-91 1983 $30

BULLEN, FRANK T.   Sea-Wrack. London: Smith, Elder & Co.,
1903. First edition. 8 illus. Orig. cloth. Edges and corners a bit
worn. A few leaves lightly foxed. Former owner's inscription. Good.
MacManus 277-768 1983 $30

BULLEN, FRANK T.   A Whaleman's Wife. London, 1902.
First edition. Illus. Argosy 714-93 1983 $40

BULLEN, HENRY LEWIS   Nicolas Jensen, Printer of Venice. San
Francisco: 1926. Folio. Limited to 207 copies printed by John Henry
Nash, each copy containing a leaf from Jensen's Plutarch of 1478.
Light foxing to title-page and wear to corners, else fine in marbled
boards and vellum spine. Bromer 25-259 1983 $200

BULLER, HENRY F.   Where Two Tides Meet. London: Hurst &
Blackett, 1896. First edition. 2 vols. Orig. maroon cloth (library
labels removed). Inner hinges cracked. Spines worn. Bookplate &
cont. owner's signature. Fair. MacManus 277-769 1983 $85

BULLER, W. L.   Birds of New Zealand. 1967. Coloured
facsimiles of the 48 plates of the second edition (of 1888), folio,
cloth. Wheldon 160-663 1983 £40

BULLIARD, P.   Dictionnaire elementaire de Botanique.
Paris, An VII (1798). 20 engraved plates, 8vo, contemporary calf,
gilt. Wheldon 160-1499 1983 £30

BULLIARD, P.   Herbier de la France. (Paris, 178-).
52 coloured plates, 4to, half calf (trifle rubbed). Wheldon 160-12
1983 £85

BULLIET, C. J.   Venus Castini. New York, 1928. Tall
8vo, cloth, boards. Illus. by Alexander King. A very good-fine copy.
In Our Time 156-470 1983 $35

BULLOCH, WILLIAM   The History of Bacteriology. London,
1938. 8vo. Orig. binding. First edition. Fye H-3-61 1983 $65

BULTMANN, BERNHARD   Oskar Kokoschka. New York: Abrams,
n.d. 50 tipped-in plates. 23 text illus. Large square 4to. Cloth.
Dust jacket. Ars Libri 32-375 1983 $75

BUNAU-VARILLA, PHIIPPE   Panama, the Creation, Destruction, and
Resurrection. London, 1913. Illus, 8vo, mod. buckram, ex-library.
Argosy 710-57 $45

BUNBURY, CHARLES J. F.   Journal of a residence at the Cape of
Good Hope. London: John Murray, 1848. 12mo. 3 adv. 5 plates.
Orig. cloth. Presentation copy signed by the author. Adelson Africa-
23 1983 $375

BUNBURY, HENRY   Narrative of some passages in the Great
War with France. London, 1927. 8vo. Bound in half red morocco,
gilt, t.e.g. 6 maps. Traylen 94-126 1983 £18

BUNIN, IVAN   The Gentleman from San Francisco.
Boston: Stratford, 1918. 1st American ed. Orig. printed boards.
Nice copy. Jenkins 155-141 1983 $25

BUNIN, IVAN   The Gentleman From San Francisco And
Other Stories. Richmond: The Hogarth Press, 1922. First edition.
8vo. Orig. decorated boards with paper label on spine. Complete
with the errata slip tipped-in before title-page. Label on spine
a little worn, but a fine copy. Jaffe 1-147 1983 $185

BUNIN, IVAN   The Well of Days. London: Hogarth
Press, 1933. First edition. Argosy 714-94 1983 $20

BUNIVA, MICHELE   Instruzione intorno alla Vaccinazione
(also): Discours Historique sur l'Utilite de la Vaccination...
Turin, 1803. 8vo. 2 vols. in one. Old quarter-sheep. 3 plates
(2 coloured). 1 folding table. Back worn. Gurney 90-28 1983 £60

BUNN, ALFRED   The Stage; both before and behind the
curtain. London: Richard Bentley, 1840. 3 vols., 12mo, original
purple cloth (spines evenly faded). 1st edition. Two errata slips
present. A very fine copy. Ximenes 64-69 1983 $250

BUNN, WILLIAM M.   Biennial Message of...Governor of
Idaho. Boise City, Idaho, Milton Kelly, Printer, 1884. Orig. blue
printed wraps. Ginsberg 46-321 1983 $85

BUNNELL, LAFAYETTE H   Discovery of the Yosemite and the Indian
War of 1851. Chicago: Fleming Revell, (1880). Portrait. Gray-brown
cloth. Orig. edition. Ex-library with bookplates. Inscribed "To
Mrs. Gertrude Gale with highest regards of The Author, July 27th, 1882."
Dawson 471-36 1983 $200

BUNNELL, LAFAYETTE H.   Discovery of the Yosemite. Chicago:
Revell, (1880). 1st ed. Map, port, plates & illus. Orig. dec. cloth.
Ex-library. Inscribed by the author. Argosy 710-32 1983 $125

BUNNER, HENRY CUYLER   Airs from Arcay and Elsewhere. New York:
Scribners, 1884. 1st ed. Orig. blue cloth, gilt, t.e.g. Fine copy.
Jenkins 155-142 1983 $25

BUNSEN, CHRISTIAN CHARLES   Christianity and Mankind, Their
Beginnings and Prospects. London, Longman, Brown, Green & Longmans,
1854. Frontis. 3/4 maroon calf over marbled boards, gilt stamped
spines, marbled edges. 7 vols. Fine. Houle 22-149 1983 $275

BUNTING, BASIL   Collected Poems. London, 1968. First
edition. One of 150 signed by the author. Dustwrapper very slightly
browned. Silkscreen print of dustwrapper missing. A fine copy.
Gekoski 2-20 1983 £60

BUNTING, BASIL   Poems: 1950. Galveston: The Cleaner's
Press, (1950). Boards. First edition. One of 1,000 copies. Fine
in slightly worn oversize dust jacket. Reese 20-1184 1983 $150

BUNTING, EDWARD   The Ancient Music of Ireland. Dublin:
Hodges & Smith, 1840. First edition, title in red and black and
dedication leaf in gold and colours, 4to, orig. cloth, gilt, by
Galwey of Dublin, with his ticket, a fine copy. Fenning 61-48
1983 £85

BUNYAN, JOHN   A book for boys and girls; or country
rhymes for children. Elliot Stock, 1889. First edition, sm. 8vo,
19th century style half calf, morocco labels, marbled paper boards,
fine uncut copy. Deighton 3-60 1983 £30

BUNYAN, JOHN   The Pilgrim's Progress from this
World to that which is to Come... Printed for J. and F. Rivington,
B. Law, W. Strahan, Hawes and Co., H. Woodfall, E. Johnston and R.
Baldwin, 1775. 8vo, errata leaf, portrait, 20 engraved plates, and
large folding plate "A Complete View of Christian's Travels", cont.
calf, rebacked and repaired. A good copy. Bickersteth 77-10 1983
£75

BUNYAN, JOHN   The Pilgrim's Progress... London: T.
Heptinstall, 1796. 2 parts in one vol. Full polished calf by Sangorski & Sutcliffe. Top of spine rubbed. Fine. MacManus 277-784 1983
$65

BUNYAN, JOHN   The Pilgrim's Progress. Exeter: Henry
Ranlet, 1804. 12mo, cont. calf (worn; quite foxed). 3 parts in 1.
Numerous crude full-page woodcuts. Argosy 710-65 1983 $85

BUNYAN, JOHN   The Pilgrim's Progress. Ward Lock, nd
(1875). Re-issue. 100 illus. by Thomas Dalziel. Blue sand grain
decor. cloth, bevelled boards, a.e.g. Bkstrip faded, corners of bds.
v. sl. worn, sl. wear top bkstrip, vg. Hodgkins 27-249 1983 £16.50

BUNYAN, JOHN   Pilgrim's Progress. Relig. Tract Soc.,
nd (ca. 1886). Frontis. & 12 plates printed in colours. Red sand
grain decor. cloth, bevelled bds., a.e.g. (tissues foxed, 2" split
top fr. joint, eps. cracking at hinges, occasional thumbing), v.g.
Hodgkins 27-358 1983 £15

BUNYAN, JOHN   The Pilgrim's Progress. London, John C.
Nimmo, 1895. Illus. by William Strang. 8vo. 14 fullpage etched
plates (including frontis. & extra-title). Full tan polished speckled
calf, gilt rules on sides, gilt-extra spine with 3 dark brown morocco
labels, gilt inner dentelles, marbled endpapers, gt. 1st ed. Bound
by Morrell. Fine. O'Neal 50-48 1983 $125

BUNYAN, JOHN   The Pilgrim's Progress. London, Oxford
University Press, 1903. 8vo, cloth illus. with 25 drawings on wood
by George Cruikshank from the collection of Edwin Truman. One of
1,000 copies printed on handmade paper and signed by Edwin Truman.
Duschnes 240-56 1983 $150

BUNYAN, JOHN   The Pilgrim's Progess. London: J.M.
Dent & Sons Ltd., 1912. First edition. Illus. with colored plates
by Frank C. Pape. Large 8vo. Orig. gilt-decorated cloth. Illustrator
has signed ten of the plates in full. Front inner hinge weak. Covers
a little marked and dull. In a green half-morocco slipcase. Very good.
MacManus 277-785 1983 $450

BUNYAN, JOHN   The Pilgrim's Progress. N.p., 1928.
2 vols., folio, black vellum, raised bands, gilt, t.e.g., others uncut,
slipcase. With 10 full-page wood-engr. by Gertrude Hermes and Blair
Hughes-Stanton. One of 195 copies printed by Bernard Newdigate at the
Shakespeare Head Press. Some cover wear, internally very fine. Perata
27-210 1983 $600

BUNYAN, JOHN   The Pilgrim's Progress. London, 1928.
Folio, black dyed vellum over boards by Sangorski & Sutcliffe,
slipcase. With ten full-page wood-engravings by Blair Hughes-
Stanton and Gertrude Hermes. One of 195 copies on Batchelor
handmade paper, printed by Bernard Newdigate at the Shakespeare Head
Press. With bookplate designed by Eric Gill and signed by him in
pencil. 2 vols. Duschnes 240-54 1983 $450

BUNYAN, JOHN   The Pilgrim's Progress. 1928. The Noel
Douglas Replicas - reproduction of the first edition of 1678, in
facs. Cream boards, spine browned. Jarndyce 31-980 1983 £15

BUNYAN, JOHN   The Pilgrim's Progress. (NY): The
Limited Editions Club, 1941. Folio. With mounted color plates.
Edition ltd. to 1,500 numbered copies, printed at the Spiral
Press. Green cloth, leather spine label. Without slipcase.
Illus. with 29 watercolor paintings by William Blake. Karmiole 76-72
1983 $75

BUNYARD, G.   The Fruit Garden. 1904. Lower corners
stained. Wheldon 160-1921 1983 £12

BUONAMICI, CASTRUCCIO   Commentaries of the Late War in Italy.
London: for A. Millar, 1753. First English edition. 8vo. Cont.
speckled calf, gilt, gilt panelled spine with crimson morocco label,
gilt. Traylen 94-128 1983 £38

BUONARROTI, MICHELANGELO   Le lettere di Michelangelo Buonarroti...
Firenze: Successori Le Monnier, 1875. Large 4to. Marbled boards.
1/4 leather. Presentation copy, inscribed by the editor, Gaetano
Milanesi. Binding slightly worn. Ars Libri 33-245 1983 $375

BURBANK, CALEB   Defence of Major General Caleb Burbank,
and the Arguments of the Complainants before his General Court-Martial.
Worcester: William Manning, Jan. 1819. 1st ed., 8vo, stitched as
issued; uncut copy. Title page stained, but a very good copy.
Trebizond 18-214 1983 $40

BURBERRY, H. A.   The Amateur Orchid Cultivator's Guide
Book. Liverpool, 1895. Second edition, 4 coloured plates and other
illus., 8vo, original cloth. Wheldon 160-2038 1983 £18

BURBURY, SAMUEL HAWKSLEY   A Treatise on the Kinetic Theory of
Gases. Cambridge, 1899. First edition. 8vo. Orig. cloth.
spine faded. Loose. Zeitlin 264-68 1983 $40

BURCH, JOHN P.   Charles W. Quatrell. (Vega, TX) Burch,
1923. First edition. Illus. Gilt stamped red cloth. Fine. Houle
21-1006 1983 $45

BURCH, JOHN P.   Charles W. Quantrell. Vega, Tx., 1923.
Illus. Orig. cloth. First edition. Ginsberg 47-809 1983 $25

BURCKHARDT, DANIEL   Albrecht Durer's Aufenthalt in Basel,
1492-1494. Munchen/Leipzig: G. Hirth, 1892. 49 collotype plates.
15 text illus. Large 4to. Boards, 1/4 leather. Ars Libri 32-174
1983 $100

BURCKHARDT, JOHN LEWIS   Travels in Nubia. London: John
Murray, 1822. Second edition. 4to. Portrait. 3 maps. Orig.
tree calf, rebacked, rubbed, internally very good. Adelson Africa-
24 1983 $300

BURCKHARDT, JOHN LEWIS   Travels in Arabia... London: Henry
Colburn, 1829. 2 vols. 8vo. Folding map. 4 plans. Modern 1/4
brown calf, red labels. Adelson Africa-25 1983 $400

BURDICK, USHER L.   Jim Johnson, Pioneer. (Williston, 1941).
1st ed. 1 of 300. Illus., wrappers. Bradley 63-99 1983 $25

BURDICK, USHER L.   Life and Exploits of John Goodall.
Watford City, N.D., 1931. 1st ed. Portraits, wrappers. Fine.
Bradley 63-96 1983 $25

BURDICK, USHER L.   Life and Exploits of John Goodall. Watford City, N. D.: 1931. First edition. Two plates, printed orange
wrappers. Fine copy. Bradley 66-596 1983 $22.50

BURDICK, USHER L.   Tragedy in the Great Sioux Camp. Baltimore: Proof Press, 1936. First edition. 2 full-page maps. Printed
stiff tan wrappers. Fine copy. Closed tear in blank margin of one
leaf. Bradley 66-666 1983 $75

BURDON, WILLIAM   The gentleman's pocket farrier.
Boston: Barrett, 1832. 12mo. Orig. pink printed wrappers. Frontis.
Very fine copy. Ximenes 63-185 1983 $40

BURG, MARGRET   Ottonische Plastik. Bonn/Leipzig,
1922. (Forschungen zur Kunstgeschichte Westeuropas. Vol. 3.)
112pp., 74 plates. Sm. 4to. Boards, 1/4 cloth. Intermittent
light foxing. Ars Libri SB 26-45 1983 $30

BURGES, TRISTAM   Solitude and Society Contrasted.
Providence, 1797. 2 leaves, dsb. Stain on title page. Good.
Reese 18-219 1983 $40

BURGESS, ANTHONY   Time for a Tiger. London, 1956. First
edition. Foxed dustwrapper, very slightly bumped at head and tail of
spine. Excellent. Gekoski 2-21 1983 £185

BURGESS, GELETT   The Lark No. 1. San Francisco, 1895.
First edition. Printed self wraps.; unopened. First issue, with
the Murdock imprint. A very good copy. Argosy 714-97 1983 $250

BURGESS, GELETT   The Lark Vol. 1 Nos. 1-12, May 1895 to April 1896. First edition, second state. Illus., pict. cloth, bookplate, covers darkened and a bit rubbed. King 46-447 1983 $85

BURGESS, GELETT   The Burgess Nonsense Book. N.Y., (1901). First edition. Pictorial cloth. Top of spine has been crushed; otherwise a fine copy. Argosy 714-95 1983 $75

BURGESS, GELETT   Vivette. Boston: Copeland & Day, 1897. First edition. 16mo, cloth; faded. Argosy 714-96 1983 $20

THE BURGHERS of New Amsterdam... New York, 1886. In the orig. pebbled buckram gilt, uncut, very nice. Boswell 7-127 1983 $35

BURGIN, G. B.   Gascoigne's Ghost. London: Neville Beeman, Ltd., 1896. First edition. Orig. decorated cloth. MacManus 277-786 1983 $45

BURGOYNE, JOHN   The Lord of the Manor, a comic opera. London: printed for T. Evans, 1781. 8vo, wrappers. 1st edition. Very good copy. Ximenes 64-72 1983 $75

BURKE, ANDREW   Burke's Descriptive Guide. Buffalo: Andrew Burke, 1851. 15 1/2cm. Frontis. and 4 plates (2 being folding litho. views) and numerous text illus. Orig. blind stamped cloth. Title and borders stamped in gilt on the upper cover. Fine. Scarce. McGahern 53-12 1983 $75

BURKE, BERNARD   The Book of Orders of Knighthood and Decorations of Honour of All Nations. London, 1858. Colored illus. of Insignias. Half leather. Index. Disbound but with all 100 color plates (few with minor edge fray). King 45-651 1983 $150

BURKE, BERNARD   The Rise of Great Families. London, 1873. Second edition. Cloth. Index. Top of spine badly frayed, hinges loose. King 45-587 1983 $20

BURKE, EDMUND   Portrait, after Reynolds. London, 1791. Stipple, in brown. Folio. Argosy 710-445 1983 $85

BURKE, EDMUND   An Account of the European Settlements in America. London: Printed for R. and J. Dodsley in Pall-Mall. MDCCLVII. (1757). 8vo, old folding map; one folding map. Bound in cont. calf. Double gold fillet on boards, worn. Scuffed at corners and hinges. Lacks first blank in volume two. A.E. Lownes bookplate. Apart from light toning, internally excellent. Arkway 22-17 1983 $325

BURKE, EDMUND   Correspondence of the Rt. Hon. Edmund Burke, 1744-1797. Francis & Rivington, 1844. First edition, 4 vols. Front. & 2 pp ads. vol. 1. Orig. brown cloth a little rubbed at heads and tails of spines. Signed presentation copy from Lord Fitzwilliam. Jarndyce 30-922 1983 £34

BURKE, EDMUND   The Epistolary Correspondence of the Rt. Hon. Edmund Burke, and Dr. French Lawrence. C. & J. Rivington, 1827. 3 pp ads. Uncut, orig. boards, paper label. A little bumped, otherwise v.g. Jarndyce 30-921 1983 £18

BURKE, EDMUND   A Letter from the Rt. Honourable Edmund Burke to His Grace the Duke of Portland, on the Conduct of the Minority in Parliament. London, 1797. Dsb. Very good. Reese 13-220 1983 $50

BURKE, EDMUND   A Letter from...to John Farr and John Harris...on the Affairs of America. London, 1777. Worn calf and boards, good. Reese 18-118 1983 $135

BURKE, EDMUND   Reflections on the Revolution in France. London: Printed for J. Dodsley, 1790. First edition, second impression. Full cont. calf with red morocco label. Top of spine very slightly worn. Cont. signature of William Beverley on front flyleaf, with occasional underlings in ink apparently in his hand. Very good. MacManus 277-787 1983 $750

BURKE, EDMUND   Reflections on the Revolution in France... Dublin: for W. Watson, etc., 1790. First Irish edition. 8vo. Cont. speckled calf, gilt spine with crimson morocco label. Traylen 94-129 1983 £75

BURKE, EDMUND   Reflexions Sur La Revolution De France. Paris: Chez Laurent; Londres: Chez Edwards, (1791). 8vo, cont. half calf, speckled boards, slightly rubbed, but a very good copy internally. Pickering & Chatto 21-13 1983 $75

BURKE, EDMUND   Speech of Edmund Burke, Esq. On American Taxation, April 19, 1774. London: J. Dodsley, 1775. 2nd ed., 8vo, title and last leaf slightly dust-soiled, else clean. Disbound. Pickering & Chatto 21-15 1983 $175

BURKE, EDMUND   Temperate Comments Upon Intemperate Reflections; Or, A Review of Mr. Burke's Letter. London: J. Walter, 1791. 1st ed., 8vo, disbound, spine reinforced. Pickering & Chatto 21-14 1983 $45

BURKE, EDMUND   Three Memorials on French Affairs. London: F. and C. Rivington, 1797. 1st ed., 2nd impression. 8vo, lacking the half-title, occasional pencilled marginalia, disbound. A good copy. Pickering & Chatto 21-16 1983 $150

BURKE, EDMUND   The Works of the Right Honourable Edmund Burke. London: J. Dodsley, 1792. First collected edition. 3 vols. 4to. Cont. half brown morocco. Some light usage internally. Heath 48-60 1983 £150

BURKE, EDMUND   The Works of the Right Honourable... Dublin: Printed for Messrs. R. Cross, 1792-93. First Irish edition. 3 vols., 8vo. Cont. mottled calf, gilt spines, with red and blue labels, a little rubbed at the corners, but thoroughly sound. Fenning 61-513 1983 £85

BURKE, JACKSON   Prelum to Albion. SF, 1940. A History of the Development of the Hand Press from Gutenberg to Morris. 12mo, linen-backed bds., vignette on upper cover, paper label. Illustrated. One of 250 copies printed by hand at the Press of Marie Louise & Jackson Burke. Signed, presentation from the author/printer. Presentation slip laid in. Perata 28-12 1983 $75

BURKE, JAMES HENRY   Days in the East. London: Smith, Elder, 1842. First edition. 8vo. Orig. blue-grey cloth. With a map. Slightly rubbed and faded. Ximenes 63-441 1983 $65

BURKE, JOHN   The Burden of the South. New York: (1864). First edition. Orig. printed wrappers. Soiled. Bradley 66-668 1983 $20

BURKE, JOSEPH   Hogarth: The Complete Engravings. New York: Abrams, n.d. 267 plates. Folio. Cloth. Dust jacket. Ars Libri 32-313 1983 $75

BURKE, MARIE LOUISE   Verse for Christmas. S.F., 1938. 8vo, stiff wrappers, French-fold, sewn. Printed in red & black. Minor foxing to covers; a very nice copy. One of 50 numbered copies printed by Jackson Burke. Perata 28-215 1983 $75

BURKE, THOMAS   The Bloomsbury Wonder. Lon., 1929. Edges slightly worn, few minor cover stains, else very good in slightly soiled, lightly chipped and frayed, very good dustwrapper. Quill & Brush 54-209 1983 $40

BURKE, THOMAS   The Bloomsbury Wonder. London: The Mandrake Press, 1929. First edition. 16mo. Orig. cloth-backed bds. with paper label on spine. Dust jacket (spine darkened). Crosby Gaige's copy with his bookplate. MacManus 277-788 1983 $25

BURKE, THOMAS   City of Encounters. London, (1932). First edition. D.w. Fine. Argosy 714-98 1983 $40

BURKE, THOMAS   East of Mansion House. London, 1928. First edition. 8vo, cloth. Fine, in a torn & chipped dust wrapper. Argosy 714-99 1983 $30

BURKE, THOMAS   The English Inn. London: Longmans, Green & Co., 1930. First edition. Orig. cloth. Dust jacket (slightly dust-soiled). Fine. MacManus 277-791 1983 $20

BURKE, THOMAS   The Flower of Life. London, 1929. First edition. 8vo, dec. linen; d.w. Argosy 714-100 1983 $40

BURKE, THOMAS   The Flower of Life. London, 1929. First edition. Corners a little bruised. Erasure from flyleaf. Author's autograph signature. Nice. Rota 230-109 1983 £15

BURKE, THOMAS   The Flower of Life. London: Constable & Co. Ltd., 1929. First edition. Orig. cloth. Dust jacket (top of spine slightly chipped, a bit soiled and worn). Bookplate of Crosby Gaige. Fine. MacManus 277-792 1983 $25

BURKE, THOMAS   Go, Lovely Rose. Brooklyn, N.Y.: Sesphra Library, 1931. First edition. 4to. Orig. cloth-backed bds. with paper label, in orig. publisher's box (damaged). Limited to 100 copies signed by author. Fine. MacManus 277-793 1983 $125

BURKE, THOMAS   Limehouse Nights. London: Grant Richards Limited, 1916. First edition. Orig. cloth. With a TLS, 1 page, 8vo. With the original envelope, with a note on it by Lemperly. With Lemperly's bookplate on the front endsheet. Front endpaper slightly stained where bookseller's catalogue entry has been pasted in. Very good. MacManus 277-794 1983 $150

BURKE, THOMAS   London Lamps. N.Y., McBride, 1919. First American edition (from English sheets). Tall 8vo, yellow cloth. Very good. Houle 21-177 1983 $20

BURKE, THOMAS   Nights In Town. London: George Allen & Unwin Limited, (1915). First edition. Orig. pictorial cloth. Dust jacket. Presentation copy, inscribed on the front flyleaf to "Crosby Gaige with kind regards Thos. Burke." Bound in purple cloth. On the spine, lettered in gilt, is a street lamp; same design reproduced on the jacket. Faintest wear to the jacket where it overlaps the edges of the boards. Preserved in a brown half-morocco slipcase. MacManus 277-795 1983 $500

BURKE, THOMAS   The Outer Circle. London: George Allen & Unwin Ltd., (1921). First edition. Orig. cloth. Dust jacket, scarce. Preserved in a half-morocco slipcase. Very fine. MacManus 277-796 1983 $250

BURKE, THOMAS   Pavements and Pastures. N.p.: n.d. (London: 1912). First edition. Orig. gray paper wrappers. Privately printed in an edition of 100 copies. Wrappers slightly dust-soiled. Preserved in a brown half-morocco slipcase. Fine. MacManus 277-797 1983 $350

BURKE, THOMAS   The Pleasantries of Old Quong. London, (1931). First edition. 8vo, orange cloth, (d.w.). Argosy 714-101 1983 $40

BURKE, THOMAS   The Real East End. London: Constable & Co. Ltd., (1932). First edition. Lithographs by Pearl Binder. Orig. cloth. Very good. MacManus 277-798 1983 $35

BURKE, THOMAS   The Real East End. Lon., (1932). Lithographs by Pearl Binder. Many pages uncut, edges slightly rubbed, else very good in slightly frayed and chipped, very good dustwrapper. Quill & Brush 54-210 1983 $25

BURKE, THOMAS   The Song Book of Quong Lee of Limehouse. London: George Allen & Unwin Ltd., (1920). First edition. Orig. decorated wrappers. Printed at The Curwen Press. Some offsetting from wrappers onto endpapers. Small tear from outer margin of front flyleaf. Fine. MacManus 277-799 1983 $50

BURKE, THOMAS   The Sun in Splendor. London, (1927). First edition. Argosy 714-102 1983 $40

BURKE, THOMAS   The Sun in Splendour. Lon., (1927). Spine edges frayed, flys lightly offset, spine faded, else very good in lightly chipped, very good dustwrapper with one tear. Quill & Brush 54-211 1983 $35

BURKE, THOMAS   The Sun in Splendour. London: Constable, (1927). First English edition. Orig. cloth. Slightly worn dust jacket. Very good. MacManus 277-800 1983 $25

BURKE, THOMAS   Twinkletoes. London: Grant Richards Limited, 1917. First edition. Orig. cloth. Presentation copy, inscribed on the front flyleaf from the author to Crosby Gaige. In a half-morocco slipcase. Fine. MacManus 277-801 1983 $175

BURKE, THOMAS   Verses. N.p.: n.d. (Guildford: 1910). First edition. 8vo. Orig. gray paper wrappers. Privately printed in an edition of only 25 copies. Author's own copy, with his bookplate on the front inner wrapper and a holograph inscription on the half-title. In a rubbed, red half-morocco slipcase. Very fine. MacManus 277-802 1983 $750

BURKE, THOMAS   Whispering Windows. London: Grant Richards Limited, 1921. First edition. Orig. cloth. Crosby & Hilda Gaige's copy, with their bookplate on the front endsheet. In a brown half-morocco slipcase. Near-fine. MacManus 277-803 1983 $125

BURKE, THOMAS   Whispering Windows. London, 1921. First edition. 8vo, cloth; rubbed. Argosy 714-103 1983 $25

BURKE, THOMAS   Will Someone Lead Me To A Pub? London: George Routledge & Sons, Ltd., 1936. First edition. Illus. by Frederick Carter. Orig. pictorial cloth. Dust jacket (somewhat worn). Presentation copy, inscribed by both author & illustrator to John Gawsworth. Burke's inscription appears on the half-title. Carter's inscription, on the front flyleaf. Illustration on page 41 signed by Gawsworth & Machen. Gawsworth has annotated his copy, with the dates of the separate inscriptions. Very good. MacManus 277-804 1983 $250

BURKE, THOMAS   The Wind and the Rain. London: Thornton Butterworth Limited, (1924). First edition. Orig. cloth. Dust jacket. Presentation copy to Crosby Gaige, inscribed "with kind regards" to him on the front flyleaf. With an ALS, 1 page. 4to. No date from Burke to Crosby Gaige. In a half-morocco slipcase. Very fine. MacManus 277-805 1983 $250

BURKE, THOMAS   The Wind and the Rain. London: Thornton Butterworth Limited, (1924). First edition. Orig. cloth-backed boards with leather label on spine. One of 110 copies signed by author. Author's complimentary card and an ALS laid in. Very fine. MacManus 277-807 1983 $75

BURKE, THOMAS   The Wind and the Rain. Lon., (1924). Small tear to paper covering front hinge, flys offset, small tears to margins of last few pages, else near very good in chipped and soiled dustwrapper. Quill & Brush 54-212 1983 $35

BURKE, THOMAS   The Wind and the Rain. London: Thornton Butterworth Limited, (1924). First edition. Orig. cloth. Dust jacket (chipped & tape repaired). Very good. MacManus 2-7-806 1983 $20

BURKE, ULICK RALPH   Loyal and Lawless. Chapman and Hall, 1880. 2 vols. bound as one, in orig. remainder red cloth, v.g. Jarndyce 30-318 1983 £52

BURKE, W. J.   American Authors & Books: 1640-1940. New York: (1943). Red cloth. Good copy. Bradley 66-41 1983 $40

BURKET, WALTER   Bibliography of William Henry Welch. Baltimore, 1917. 8vo. Orig. binding. Fye H-3-1020 1983 $40

BURKITT, M. C.   South Africa's Past in Stone & Paint. Cambridge: University Press, 1928. 8 plates. 30 text illus. Large 8vo. Cloth. Dust jacket. Ars Libri 34-580 1983 $40

BURKLEY, FRANK J.   The Faded Frontier. Omaha, 1935. Privately printed. Maps, illus. Spot on front cover, former owner's stamp inside front cover. Clark 741-358 1983 $27.50

BURLAMAQUI, JEAN-JACQUES   The Principles of Natural Law. London: Nourse, 1748-1752. 2 vols. Large 8vo, full gilt calf. First English Edition. First English edition. Fine. Rostenberg 88-114 1983 $325

BURLAND, C. A.   Codex Laud, Bodleian Library, Oxford. Graz: Akademische Druck- und Verlagsanstalt, 1966. Text: folding chart, 3 plates. Wrappers. Facsimile: Folding color facsimile plate. 4to. Clamshell box. Boards, 1/4 pigskin. English language text. Ars Libri 34-155 1983 $185

BURLAND, C. A.   Codex Edgerton 2895, British Museum London. Graz: Akademische Druck- und Verlagsanstalt, 1966. Text: Wrappers. Facsimile: Folding color facsimile plate, linen-backed. Large oblong 4to. Clamshell box. Boards, 1/4 leather. English-language text. Ars Libri 34-153 1983 $275

BURLAND, C. A.   Codex Fejervary-Mayer. 12014M, City
of Liverpool Museums. Graz: Akademische Druck- und Verlagsanstalt,
1971. Text: Wrappers. Facsimile: Folding color facsimile plate,
mounted at each end on boards. 4to. Clamshell box. Boards, 1/4
pigskin. English language text. Ars Libri 34-154 1983 $185

BURLEIGH, BENNET   Sirdar and Khalifa. Chapman and Hall,
1898. First edition, with a portrait, a folding map, 2 plates and
26 other illus. Half-title, 8vo, recent half calf, gilt.
Fenning 62-45 1983 £32.50

BURLEND, REBECCA   True Portrait of Emmigration. Chicago,
Lakeside Press, 1936. Portrait. 12mo. Clark 741-286 1983 $24

BURLESON, GEORGIA J.   The Life and Writings of Rufus C. Burleson
Waco, 1901. First edition. Jenkins 153-75 1983 $100

BURMAN, BEN L.   Rooster Crows for a Day. New York:
Dutton, 1945. 1st ed. Orig. cloth, dj. Very fine copy with inscrip.
from the author. Jenkins 155-144 1983 $20

BURMEISTER, H.   Beitrage zur Naturgeschichte der
Rankenfusser. Berlin, 1834. 2 plates, 4to, original boards.
Wheldon 160-1255 1983 £15

BURMEISTER, H.   The Organisation of Trilobites. Ray
Society, 1846. 6 plates, folio, original boards. Wheldon 160-1370
1983 £20

BURMEISTER, H.   Systematische Uebersicht der Thiere
Brasiliens. Berlin, 1854-56. 2 vols. in, 8vo, half morocco, slightly
worn and rubbed. Rare. Wheldon 160-352 1983 £90

BURN, PETER   English Border Ballads. Carlisle:
G.T. Coward, 1874. Half title, 8 pp ads., orig. brown cloth, first
edition. Jarndyce 30-658 1983 £10.50

BURN, ROBERT SCOTT   The Colonist's and Emigrant's Handbook
of the Mechanical Arts. Wm. Blackwood, 1854. First edition,
numerous illus., 16 pp ads. Orig. brown cloth; very small nick to
leading hinge, v.g. Jarndyce 31-118 1983 £72

BURN, ROBERT SCOTT   Practical ventilation as applied to
public, domestic, and agricultural structures... Edinburgh:
Blackwood, 1850. First edition. 8vo. Orig. green cloth. Very
slightly faded. Fine copy. Ximenes 63-567 1983 $90

BURN-MURDOCH, WILLIAM GORDON   From Edinburgh to India. London, (1898)
24 coloured plates, text illus. Pictorial cloth, 8vo., good. Edwards
1044-510 1983 £36

BURNABY, ANDREW   Travels Through the Middle Settlements
in North America... London: T. Payne, 1775. Second edition. 3/4
morocco. Hinges rubbed. Fine. Felcone 20-18 1983 $200

BURNABY, ANDREW   Travels Through the Middle Settlements
in North-America... London: T. Payne, 1798. Folding map and two
plates. Original marbled boards, neatly rebacked. Third edition,
revised, corrected, and greatly enlarged. Jenkins 153-76 1983 $200

BURNET, GILBERT   An Enquiry into the Reasons for
Abrogating the Test imposed on all Members of Parliament. (London,
1688). First edition, drop-title, 4to, wrapper, little dusty and two
page numerals shaved, otherwise a very good copy. Fenning 61-49
1983 £16.50

BURNET, GILBERT   History of His Own Time. Oxford, 1833.
Second edition. 6 vols. 8vo. Half brown morocco, gilt, gilt spines
with decorative ornaments, t.e.g. Vignette title-pages. Traylen
94-131 1983 £75

BURNET, GILBERT   A Sermon Preached at the Funderal of
the Honourable Robert Boyle. London: Chiswell, 1692. 4to, title
within mourning bands. Stitched. Rostenberg 88-79 1983 $115

BURNET, THOMAS   Homerides: or, a letter to Mr. Pope...
London: W. Wilkins, sold by J. Roberts, 1715. 8vo. Disbound.
First edition. Half-title present. Ximenes 63-474 1983 $275

BURNET, THOMAS   The Sacred Theory of the Earth. Printed
for J. Hooke, 1722. 2 vols., 8vo, portrait in vol. 1 rebacked,
vol. 2 joints cracked. Bickersteth 77-264 1983 £35

BURNET, THOMAS   A Second Tale of a Tub. Printed for J.
Roberts, 1715. 8vo, engraved frontis, imprimatur leaf at beginning.
Cont. panelled calf. First edition. Bickersteth 75-10 1983 £135

BURNET, THOMAS   The Theory of the Earth. London, R.N.
for Walter Kettilby, 1697. Third edition. 4to, full old calf,
joint cracked, tips a bit chipped. Engraved title and portrait
frontis. Illus. in the text and two engraved folding maps of the
earth. A fresh copy with only occasional light foxing. Heraldic
bookplates of the Duke of Kent and the Earl of Grey. 2 vols. in 1.
Houle 22-150 1983 $325

BURNETT, FRANCES HODGSON   Editha's Burglar, a Story for Children.
Boston: Jordan, March, 1888. 1st ed., 1st state. Orig. maroon
pictorial cloth, gilt. Not quite a fine copy. Jenkins 155-145 1983
$30

BURNETT, FRANCES HODGSON   Editha's Burglar, a Story for Children.
Boston: Jordan, March, 1888. 1st ed., 2nd state. Brown cloth. Fine.
Jenkins 155-145-A 1983 $20

BURNETT, FRANCES HODGSON   Editha's Burglar. Boston, Page (1925).
"Baby Peggy" movie edition. Gilt stamped brown cloth with large
label illustrating scenes from the film. Frontis. and 15 plates of
scenes. Very good. Houle 21-179 1983 $45

BURNETT, FRANCES HODGSON   Giovanni and the Other Children Who
Have Made Stories. New York: Scribners, 1892. Frontis., plates.
1st ed. Orig. pale green pictorial cloth, gilt. Fine copy. Jenkins
155-146 1983 $30

BURNETT, FRANCES HODGSON   In the Closed Room. N.Y.: McLure Phil.,
1904. First edition. 8vo. Cloth. Bottom edges slightly rubbed.
Decorative border on all pages. 8 color plates. Fine. Aleph-bet
8-238 1983 $55

BURNETT, FRANCES HODGSON   Little Lord Fauntleroy. NY, 1886. First
issue with Devine Press at end of text and 14 pages ads, hinges
cracked, cover rubbed, good, owner's name. Quill & Brush 54-213 1983
$75

BURNETT, FRANCES HODGSON   Little Saint Elizabeth. New York, 1890.
8vo. Cloth. Illus. by Reginald Birch. First American edition. About
fine. In Our Time 156-124 1983 $30

BURNETT, FRANCES HODGSON   Two Little Pilgrim's Progress. New
York, 1895. Tall 8vo. Cloth. With illustrations after drawings
by Reginald Birch. About fine. In Our Time 156-125 1983 $35

BURNETT, FRANCES HODGSON   Little Lord Faunteroy. Warne, 1887. 3rd
ed. Frontis., title vignette & 24 b&w illus. by Reginald Birch, 14
pp. adverts. Pub's decor. cloth, bevelled bds. Eps. cracked at
hinges, corners sl. worn, occasional foxing, vg. Hodgkins 27-18 1983
£12.50

BURNETT, FRANCES HODGSON   The Pretty Sisters of Jose. New York,
Scribner, 1889. Frontis. 7 11 engrs. by C.S. Reinhart, 8 pp. adverts.
Pub's decor. cloth. Bkstrip. sl. faded, name fr. ep. & contemp.
insc. 2nd ep., vg. Hodgkins 27-20 1983 £15

BURNETT, FRANCIS HODGSON   Sara Crew. N.Y., 1888. First edition.
Square 8vo, pictorial cloth. Argosy 714-104 1983 $40

BURNETT, FRANCES HODGSON   Surly Tim, and Other Stories. N.Y.,
1877. First edition. 16mo, terra cotta cloth. Argosy 714-105 1983
$20

BURNETT, FRANCES HODGSON   That Lass O'Lowrie's. N.Y., Scribner,
1877. First edition. Frontis. Decorative cloth. Cloth slipcase.
Very good. Houle 21-180 1983 $80

BURNETT, FRANK   Summer Isles of Eden. Sifton, Praed,
1923. First edition, with a folding map and 63 plates, 8vo,
orig. cloth, gilt. Fenning 61-50 1983 £16.50

BURNETT, GEORGE   A Book of Scottish Verse. London, 1932.
First edition. Frontis. by J.M. King. Frayed dust wrapper. Very nice.
Rota 230-326 1983 £25

BURNETT, W. R.   High Sierra. New York: Knopf, 1940.
First edition. Orig. cloth, d.j. Fine fresh copy in lightly worn d.j.
Jenkins 155-147 1983 $50

BURNETT, W. R.   Little Caesar. New York: Dial
Press, 1929. Cloth. First edition. Ink name, slight rubbing, but
a very good copy. Reese 20-194 1983 $35

BURNHAM, FREDERICK W. E.   Haemocytes and Haemic Infections.
226 Microphotograms. 4to, ex-lib. First edition. Argosy 713-82
1983 $75

BURNS, JOHN   Dissertations in Inflammation. Albany,
1812. 2 vols. in 1. 8vo. Contemporary calf, leather label. 1st
American ed. Rebacked; some rubbing. Morrill 289-31 1983 $25

BURNS, JOHN   Observations on Abortion: Containing
an Account of the Manner in Which It Takes Place, the Causes Which...
Troy, New York, 1808. 1st American ed. 16mo. Contemporary calf.
Rubbed; lacks label; hinges cracked. Morrill 289-30 1983 $35

BURNS, JOHN   Observations on Abortion. Springfield:
For Isaiah Thomas, Jr. 1809. 12mo, old calf, worn; spine chipped,
hinged cracked. Second American edition. Karmiole 73-71 1983 $60

BURNS, JOHN   The Principles of Surgery. London, 1838.
2 vols. bound in 1. 8vo, orig. cloth. Ex-lib. Argosy 713-83 1983
$60

BURNS, ROBERT   Burns in Dumfriesshire. Edinburgh:
Adam & Charles Black, 1870. 2nd edition, orig. green cloth, sl.
rubbed. Jarndyce 31-461 1983 £10.50

BURNS, ROBERT   The House That Jack Built. (Edinburgh):
1937. Folio. First edition. White printed boards with some sunning
on edges and bumping to corners, internally fine. Illus. Bromer 25-
324 1983 $85

BURNS, ROBERT   The Life and Works of Robert Burns.
Edinburgh and London: W & R Chambers, 1896. Four vols. Large post
8vo, 21-1/2 cm. Orig. green ribbed gilt-lettered cloth; 22 engraved
plates. Uncut, t.e.g. Some foxing but very good. First edition
thus. Grunder 7-8 1983 $100

BURNS, ROBERT   Poems. Edinburgh, 1798. Two vols.
bound in one, interior stained and yellowed, leather binding worn,
good or better, owner's name. Quill & Brush 54-216 1983 $60

BURNS, ROBERT   Poems & Songs. Kent, 1861. Illus. by
Birket Foster, C.W. Cope, Horsley, Harrison Weir, Archer, Edmonston,
etc. Blue morocco grain cloth gilt, bevelled boards, a.e.g. Contemp.
insc. fr. ep., sl. foxing prelims. Hodgkins 27-250 1983 £25

BURNS, ROBERT   Poems, Chiefly in the Scottish Dialect.
Printed for A. Straham; T. Cadell; and W. Creech, 1787. 8vo, half
title, portrait, t.e.g., other edges uncut, full crushed red morocco
by Riviere, gilt filets on the covers, gilt dentelles, spine gilt
in compartments. A little spotting on the half title, on which there
is a very pale ink inscription dated the year of publication. First
London edition. Bickersteth 75-11 1983 £230

BURNS, ROBERT   Poems, Chiefly in the Scottish Dialect.
London: Strahan, Cadell, and Creech, 1787. Frontis. 1st London ed.
Contemporary full calf, morocco label, gilt. Expertly rehinged.
This ed. is described as the 3rd ed. on the title-page, having been
preceded by the Kilmarnock and Edinburgh eds. Else a fine copy.
Jenkins 155-148 1983 $300

BURNS, ROBERT   Poems Chiefly in the Scottish Dialect.
Glasgow: David Bryce (ca. 1900). Reduced facs. of first edition
printed by John Wilson, Kilmarnock, in 1786. Lacquered plaid boards,
cloth spine, with gilt-stamped "Burns Poems First Edition 1786" on
cover. Slight rubbing to covers. A.e.g. Bookplate of Arthur A.
Houghton. (1 1/16 x 3/4; 26x20mm). Bromer 25-418A 1983 $200

BURNS, ROBERT   Poems, Chiefly In The Scottish Dialect.
A. Strahan, T. Cadell, & W. Creech, 1787. Third edition. Frontis.
port. Full morocco. Very good. MacManus 277-813 1983 $150

BURNS, ROBERT   The Poetical Works. London, 1866..
3 vols. Cr. 8vo. Dark blue calf, two-line gilt borders with corner
ornaments, gilt panelled spines with morocco labels, gilt. Portrait,
vignette title-pages. Traylen 94-133 1983 £45

BURNS, ROBERT   Songs from Robert Burns. London:
the Golden Cockerel Press, 1925. Roy. 8vo. Boards with linen
spine, gilt, uncut edges. Limited edition of 450 copies numbered.
Wood-engravings by Mabel M. Annesley. Traylen 94-135 1983 £45

BURNS, ROBERT   Tam O'Shanter. N.p.: Essex House,
1902. Octavo. Frontis. by William Strang. Limited to 150 copies,
all printed entirely on vellum. Elaborately hand-colored opening
initial plus other initials colored in text. About fine in vellum,
blind-embossed binding. Bromer 25-201 1983 $275

BURNS, ROBERT   The Works of Robert Burns. Phila.:
Printed by Budd and Bartram for Thomas Dobson, 1801. Engraved
frontis. of Burns in volume 1. Old tree calf; some internal stains
and foxing. Karmiole 71-34 1983 $200

BURNS, ROBERT   The Works... London, 1813. Vol. 3
(of 4) only of the 7th ed., in loose sheets, heavily edited and
revised, possibly for the 8th ed. Jenkins 155-149 1983 $75

BURNS, ROBERT   Works; with an account of his life...
London: T. Cadell & W. Davies, 1814. 5 vols. Cr. 8vo. Cont.
calf, gilt panelled sides, gilt spines with morocco labels, gilt.
Eighth edition. Engraved portrait after Stothard. Traylen 94-134
1983 £25

BURNS, ROBERT   Complete Works. Phila., Gebbie, 1896.
Ellisland edition. 4to, illus. with 60 etchings, woodcuts, maps and
facs. Bound in full brown morocco, spine decorated in gilt with
floral designs and scrolling, covers ruled in gilt, watered silk
doublures, t.e.g., uncut. Some minor chipping, else very good. 12
vols. One of 50 sets on handmade paper. Houle 21-181 1983 $300

BURNS, THOMAS   Poems. J.M. Carr, Newcastle-upon-Tyne,
1885. First edition, orig. brown cloth boards, rubbed. Jarndyce 30-
659 1983 £10.50

BURNS, WALTER N.   The Robin Hood of El Dorado. New York,
1932. Frontis. First edition. Jenkins 152-278 1983 $35

BURNS, WALTER N.   Tombstone: an Iliad of the Southwest.
N.Y., Doubleday, 1927. First edition. Cloth. Good-very good.
Houle 21-1007 1983 $25

BURNS, WALTER N.   Tombstone. New York, 1927. First
edition. Orig. cloth. Some soiling. Jenkins 152-545 1983 $25

BURNYEAT, JONATHAN   Some Account of the Gospel Labours of...
W. & F.G. Cash, 1857. First edition, with a frontis., large 12mo,
orig. cloth, gilt. Fenning 60-42 1983 £10.50

BURPEE, LAWRENCE J.   Among The Canadian Alps. New York,
London & Toronto: John Lane & Bell & Cockburn, 1914. 23cm. 49
plates (including 4 colour) and 5 maps. Orig. green decorated
cloth. A fine copy. McGahern 53-182 1983 $95

BURR, AARON   Reports of the Trials of Aaron Burr.
Phila., 1808. 2 vols., one uncut, 8vo, mod. fabricoid, foxed.
Argosy 710-252 1983 $100

BURR, ANNA R.   Weir Mitchell, His Life and Letters.
New York, 1929. First edition. 8vo. Orig. binding. Fye H-3-860
1983 $40

BURR, ANNA R.   Weir Mitchell, His Life and Letters.
New York, 1929. First edition. 8vo. Orig. binding. Backstrip
spotted, contents fine. Fye H-3-861 1983 $25

BURR, C. B.   Medical History of Michigan. Vol. 1.
Minneapolis, 1930. 8vo, orig. binding. Fye H-3-64 1983 $20

BURRAGE, HENRY S.   History of the Thirty-Sixth Regiment,
Massachusetts Volunteers, 1862-1865. Boston, 1884. First edition.
Brown cloth. Extremities worn, back inner hinge cracked. Bradley
64-39 1983 $25

BURRAGE, WALTER   A History of the Massachusetts Medical
Society... Boston, 1923. First edition. 8vo. Orig. binding.
Fye H-3-65 1983 $25

BURRIS-MEYER, ELIZABETH   Historical Color Guide: Primitive
to Modern Times... New York: William Helburn, (1938). 8vo.
Cloth. Over 100 color samples pasted in. Oak Knoll 49-106 1983
$115

BURROUGH, EDWARD   A Visitation of Love unto the King,
and Those Call'd Royalists. London, Robert Wilson, 1660. 4to,
new tan calf, inner margin of title torn and repaired, lower blank
tip mended, title dust-soiled, blank verso of last leaf dust-soiled.
A decent copy. First and only edition. Ravenstree 97-173 1983
$135

BURROUGHS, BURT E.   Legends and Tales of Homeland on the
Kankakee. Chicago: Regan Printing House, 1923. First edition.
Frontis. and portraits. Presentation copy from author. Fine. Jenkins
152-40 1983 $35

BURROUGHS, BURT E.   Tales of an Old "Border Town" and Along
the Kankakee. Fowler, Indiana: The Benton Review Shop, 1925. First
edition. Frontis. and illus. Fine. Jenkins 152-41 1983 $50

BURROUGHS, EDGAR RICE   The Girl from Hollywood. N.Y.,
Macauley, (1923). First edition (Currey "A" binding, Tarzan spelled
"Tarzon" on title page). Red coarse weave cloth stamped in light
green (front free endpaper lacking, inked number on spine), else,
very good. Houle 22-152 1983 $60

BURROUGHS, EDGAR RICE   The Illustrated Tarzan Books No. 1.
NY: G&D, (1929). First edition. Cloth spine, pict. boards,
covers worn, edges showing. 300 pictures by Harold Foster.
King 46-256 1983 $50

BURROUGHS, EDGAR RICE   Jungle Tales of Tarzan. Chicago, McClurg,
1919. First edition. Frontis. and 4 plates by J. Allen St. John.
Orig. orange cloth stamped in blue. Very good. Houle 22-154 1983
$75

BURROUGHS, EDGAR RICE   Jungle Tales of Tarzan. Chicago, 1919.
First edition. Green binding. Illus. by J. Allen St. John. Cloth.
Very good. Color reproduction dust jacket. King 46-448 1983 $25

BURROUGHS, EDGAR RICE   The Return of Tarzan. Chicago:
McClurg, 1915. Illus. 1st ed. Orig. green cloth, gilt. Fine
bright copy. Jenkins 155-150 1983 $150

BURROUGHS, EDGAR RICE   The Return of Tarzan. Chicago, 1915.
1st ed. Illus. 8vo. Few cover spots, otherwise a nice copy.
Morrill 286-579 1983 $75

BURROUGHS, EDGAR RICE   The Son of Tarzan. Chicago: McClurg,
1917. Illus. 1st ed. Orig. green cloth, gilt. Very fine fresh
copy. Jenkins 155-151 1983 $175

BURROUGHS, EDGAR RICE   The Son of Tarzan. Chicago, 1917. 1st
issue. Illus. 8vo, nice. Morrill 286-580 1983 $75

BURROUGHS, EDGAR RICE   Tarzan and The Ant Men. Chicago:
McClurg, 1924. 1st ed. Orig. tan cloth. Tiny spot, else a fresh
clean copy with minute signs of use. Jenkins 155-152 1983 $85

BURROUGHS, EDGAR RICE   Tarzan and the Forbidden City. Tarzana,
(1938). Illus., 8vo, blue cloth; d.w. First edition. Fine.
Argosy 714-106 1983 $200

BURROUGHS, EDGAR RICE   Tarzan and the Forbidden City. Ca.,
(1938). Illus. by John Coleman Burroughs. Endpapers very slightly
foxed, else fine in dustwrapper with few small chips. Quill & Brush
54-218 1983 $135

BURROUGHS, EDGAR RICE   Tarzan and the Forbidden City.
Tarzana: Burroughs, (1938). 1st ed. Orig. cloth, dj. Fine fresh
copy with fire label at front, but no signs of smoke. Jenkins
155-153 1983 $85

BURROUGHS, EDGAR RICE   Tarzan and the Foreign Legion.
Tarzana: Burroughs, (1947). 1st ed. Orig. cloth, dj. Very fine
fresh copy. Jenkins 155-154 1983 $35

BURROUGHS, EDGAR RICE   Tarzan And The Jewels Of Opar.
Chicago, 1918. First edition (color reproduction dust jacket).
Cloth, rear hinge loose, covers slightly spotted and worn. King 46-
449 1983 $35

BURROUGHS, EDGAR RICE   Tarzan and the Lost Empire. Tarzana:
Burroughs, (1948). 1st Tarzana ed. Orig. cloth, dj. Fine copy.
Jenkins 155-155 1983 $35

BURROUGHS, EDGAR RICE   Tarzan of the Apes. Chicago: McClurg,
1914. First edition, first printing. Orig. moroon cloth, gilt. Fine.
Orig. owner's inscription on the front endpaper dated June, 1914, the
same month the book was issued. Jenkins 152-575 1983 $1,000

BURROUGHS, EDGAR RICE   Tarzan of the Apes. Chicago, 1914.
1st issue, with acorn device at foot of spine. 8vo. Some very light
cover stains, but a good copy. Morrill 286-578 1983 $150

BURROUGHS, EDGAR RICE   Tarzan the Invincible. Tarzana:
Burroughs, (1931). 1st ed. Orig. cloth. Fine copy in near fine
dj. Jenkins 155-156 1983 $100

BURROUGHS, EDGAR RICE   The Warlord of Mars. Chicago, McClung,
1919. First edition, first issue (with W.F. imprint on copyright
page). Color frontis. by J. Allen St. John. Orig. gilt stamped
red cloth. Very good. Houle 22-155 1983 $150

BURROUGHS, EDMUND   A Declaration of the Sad and Great
Persecution and Martyrdom of the People of God, Called Quakers, in
New-England, for the Worshipping of God. London, 1660. Full calf,
very good. Reese 18-22 1983 $1,200

BURROUGHS, EDWARD   The Case of Free Liberty of Conscience
in the Exercise of Faith and Religion. London. 1661. Old leather
and boards, good. The author's name is misspelled on the title page,
actually not having a final 's'. Reese 18-23 1983 $325

BURROUGHS, JEREMIAH   An Exposition with Practical Observations
Continued upon the Eighth, Ninth, Tenth, Eleventh, Twelfth, and
Thirteenth Chapters of the Prophesy of Hosea. Printed by Peter Cole,
1654. Pagination erratic in plates, but complete, with the blank
leaves, 2 vols. in 1, 4to, cont. calf, neatly rebacked, some light
browning, but still a very good copy. Fenning 60-43 1983 £45

BURROUGHS, JOHN   Wake Robin. New York, 1871. 8vo.
Cloth. 1st ed., binding A. Some rubbing to the corners, else a
fine copy. This copy bears a presentation from author on front
flyleaf to Miss Cecilia N. French. In Our Time 156-129 1983 $150

BURROUGHS, JOHN   Wake-Robin. New York: Hurd &
Houghton, 1877. 2nd ed., enlarged by one chapter. Orig. mauve
cloth, gilt. First printed in 1871 this ed. first prints his
chapter on the bluebird. Jenkins 155-157 1983 $20

BURROUGHS, JOHN   Whitman. Boston, Houghton, Mifflin &
Co., 1896. Photogravure frontis. Green gilt-stamped cloth, spine
faded. The first edition; published as Volume X of the "Riverside
Edition. The Writings of John Burroughs", edition ltd. to 1,000
copies. Laid in is a 2 page letter, dated March 31, 1897, signed by
Burroughs. Karmiole 75-30 1983 $75

BURROUGHS, STEPHEN   Memoirs; with Notes & an Appendix.
Albany: B. D. Packard, 1811. 2 vols. in 1, thick 12mo, sheep,
covers loose. Enlarged, scarce ed. Argosy 710-253 1983 $50

BURROUGHS, WILLIAM   The Last Words of Dutch Schultz. Cape
Goliard, 1970. First edition. One of 100 numbered copies, signed
by author. Fine. Rota 231-94 1983 £45

BURROUGHS, WILLIAM   Roosevelt After Inauguration. (NY:
Fuck You Press, 1964). First edition. Approx. 500 copies printed.
Very fine copy in self-wrappers. Bromer 25-12 1983 $100

BURROUGHS, WILLIAM   The Ticket That Exploded. Paris:
Olympia Press, (1962). First edition. Signed on title-page by
Burroughs. Extremeties lightly rubbed, else fine in wrappers. Bromer
25-13 1983 $1000

BURROW, E. I.   Elements of Conchology. 1815.
28 plates, 8vo, contemporary calf, gilt, joints cracking, trifle
worn, plates waterstained. Wheldon 160-1200 1983 £24

BURROWS, JOHN WILLIAM   The Essex Regiment. Southend-on-Sea,
1932. 8vo. Orig. cloth. Coloured frontis. 3 coloured plates, 5
coloured maps (2 folding), 1 folding panorama, 5 other maps and 93
other plates. Slightly worn and faded. Good. Edwards 1042-543
1983 £15

BURRUS, ERNEST J.   Kino and the Cartography of North-
Western New Spain. Tucson, 1965. Illus., cloth, fine. Folio.
Reese 19-102 1983 $225

BURRUS, ERNEST J.   Kino and the Cartography of North-
western New Spain. Tucson, 1965. Illus., plates, figs., maps.
Orig. folio cloth. Ltd. to 75- copies printed and designed by
Lawton Kennedy. Ginsberg 46-75 1983 $175

BURRUS, ERNEST J.   Kino and the Cartography of North-
western New Spain. (Tucson), Ariz. Pion. Hist. Soc., Lawton Kennedy,
1965. Lim. edn. 1st edn. Maps, illus. Folio. Clark 741-333 1983
$160

BURT, ALFRED   Life Assurance. Effingham Wilson,
(1849). First edition, half title, errata slip, orig. blue cloth, sl.
rubbed, v.g. Jarndyce 31-119 1983 £64

BURT, C. E.   Study of Teiid Lizards Genus Cnemido-
phorus. Bull. U.S. Nat. Mus., 1931. 38 text-figures, 8vo, wrappers.
Wheldon 160-948 1983 £12

BURT, HENRY M.   The First Century of the History of
Springfield. Springfield, 1898-99. 1st ed. Map and text illus. 2
vols., 8vo, very nice. Morrill 287-216 1983 $55

BURT, NATHANIEL   Rooms in a House and Other Poems:
1931-1944. New York, 1947. 8vo. Cloth. Review copy with slip
laid in. Fine in dj. In Our Time 156-130 1983 $25

BURT, STRUTHERS   The Diary of a Dude Wrangler. N.Y.,
1934. 1st ed. Fine copy. Jenkins 153-77 1983 $35

BURT, STRUTHERS   Powder River Let 'Er Buck. New York,
1938. First edition. Original cloth. Spine faded as usual. Scarce.
Jenkins 153-78 1983 $40

BURT, THOMAS   A Great Labour Leader. Brown,
Langham, 1908. First edition, front. & illus. Orig. blue cloth,
t.e.g., v.g. Jarndyce 30-925 1983 £20

BURTON, A.R.E.   Cape Colony (South Africa) for the
Settler. London, 1903. 1st ed. Folding maps and many plates. 8vo,
pictorial front cover, ads. Scarce. Morrill 289-595 1983 $75

BURTON, CLARENCE M.   The City of Detroit, Michigan 1701-1922.
Detroit, 1922. 5 vols. Illustrated, green cloth. A nice set.
King 46-145 1983 $125

BURTON, ISABEL   The Life of Captain Sir Richard F. Burton.
London: Chapman & Hall, Ltd., 1893. First edition. Numerous port.,
illus., and maps. 2 vols. Orig. decorated cloth. Front outer hinge
of vol. 1 partially split at bottom of spine. Inner hinges strained.
Bookplate. Very good. MacManus 277-816 1983 $225

BURTON, ISABEL   The Life of Captain Sir Richard F.
Burton. 1893. 2 vols., numerous portraits, illus. and maps, orig.
gilt dec. black cloth, slightly rubbed but a good set. K Books 301-
33 1983 £50

BURTON, ISABEL   The romance of Isabel Lady Burton.
New York: Dodd, Mead, 1897. 2 vols. 8vo. 18 plates. Orig.
cloth. Rubbed. Adelson Africa-176 1983 $75

BURTON, JOHN   Lectures on Female Education and Manners.
Elizabeth Town: S. Kollock for Cornelius Davis, 1799. Calf, neatly
rebacked in cloth, preserving the orig. spine label. Very good.
Felcone 19-7 1983 $60

BURTON, JOHN   Monasticon Eboracense. York, 1758.
Sole edition, complete with the 3 folding maps and plans (one torn
without loss), folio, a little age marked and dusty but a good
large copy in 19th century half morocco (a little worn). K Books 307-
39 1983 £110

BURTON, JOHN   Trackless Winds. S.F., Jonck & Seeger,
1930. First edition. Frontis. gravure portrait by Ansel Adams.
Half blue cloth (corners rubbed), else very good. Inscribed by the
author on the frontis. Houle 21-187 1983 $85

BURTON, JOHN HILL   The Book-Hunter, etc. Wm. Blackwood,
1882. Half title, front. Illus. Untrimmed, orig. dark blue cloth,
v.g. Jarndyce 31-93 1983 £20

BURTON, RICHARD FRANCIS   Abeokuta and the Camaroons Mountains.
London: Tinsley Brothers, 1863. First edition. 2 vols. 12 mo.
Frontis. portrait. Folding map, 4 plates. New 1/2 red crushed
levant. Gilt spines. Adelson Africa-35 1983 $475

BURTON, RICHARD FRANCIS   Ananga-Ranga. Cosmopoli: Kama
Shastra Society, 1885. Small 4to. Full imitation vellum, hand-
made paper uncut. Covers rubbed. Adelson Africa-59 1983 $100

BURTON, RICHARD FRANCIS   The Book of the Sword. London: Chatto
and Windus, 1884. Royal 8vo. Numerous illus. in text. Orig.
pictorail grey cloth, rubbed. Adelson Africa-53 1983 $400

BURTON, RICHARD FRANCIS   The Book of the Sword. London, 1884.
First edition. Numerous illus. Roy.8vo. Decorative cloth. Fine.
Edwards 1044-101 1983 £225

BURTON, RICHARD FRANCIS   Camoens: His life and his Lusiads.
London: Bernard Quaritch, 1881. 2 vols. 12mo. Orig. gilt decorated
green cloth, rubbed, x-library. Adelson Africa-52 1983 $100

BURTON, RICHARD FRANCIS   Camoens: His life and his Lusiads.
London: Bernard Quaritch, 1881. Second issue. 2 vols. 12mo.
Orig. red cloth. Lightly rubbed. Adelson Africa-173 1983 $60

BURTON, RICHARD FRANCIS   The captivity of Hans Stade of Hesse...
London: The Hakluy Society, 1874. 8vo. Rebound in modern blue
cloth. Ex-library. Adelson Africa-45 1983 $85

BURTON, RICHARD FRANCIS   The City of the Saints and Across the
Rocky Mountains to California. London: Longman, Green, Longman, &
Roberts, 1861. First edition. Illus. Orig. Bookplate. Inner hinges
strained. Fine. MacManus 277-814 1983 $400

BURTON, RICHARD FRANCIS   The City of the Saints. London, Longmans,
1861. 8vo, old half calf rebacked in library cloth, library bookplate
canceled, number on title and spine, well-thumbed copy, library stamps
inside back cover. First edition. Ravenstree 97-119 1983 $145

BURTON, RICHARD FRANCIS   The City of the Saints... London:
Longman, Green, etc., 1862. Second edition. 8vo. Folding map,
folding plan, 8 plates. Orig. green pictorial cloth. rebacked.
Adelson Africa-34 1983 $300

BURTON, RICHARD FRANCIS   The City of the Saints and Across the
Rocky Mountains to California. New York, 1862. Orig. blue embossed
cloth. Two folding maps. First American edition. Extremities a bit
shelf-rubbed, else a very nice copy. Jenkins 151-30 1983 $200

BURTON, RICHARD FRANCIS   The City of the Saints and Across
the Rocky Mountains to California. NY, 1862. First American edition.
Fine. Argosy 716-554 1983 $175

BURTON, RICHARD FRANCIS   The City of Saints, and Across the
Rocky Mountains to California. N.Y., 1862. Illus., orig. cloth.
First American edition. Ginsberg 47-37 1983 $175

BURTON, RICHARD FRANCIS   The City of the Saints. New York,
1862. Illus. Folding map. Cloth, hinges weak, good. First
American edition. Reese 19-103 1983 $125

BURTON, RICHARD FRANCIS   Etruscan Bologna: A Study. London:
Smith, Elder, 1876. 8vo. Errata slip. Folding frontis. Orig.
blue cloth. Rubbed. Adelson Africa-47 1983 $100

BURTON, RICHARD FRANCIS   Explorations of the highlands of Brazil.
London: Tinsley Brothers, 1869. First edition, second issue. 2
vols. 8vo. Folding map. Orig. green cloth. Lightly rubbed, light
foxing to a few leaves. Adelson Africa-40 1983 $375

BURTON, RICHARD FRANCIS   Falconry in the Valley of the Indus.
London: John van Voorst, 1852. First edition. 8vo. Untrimmed
in orig. dark purple cloth, blind border, lettered in gilt. 4
tinted lithograph plates, publisher's Catalogue at end. Limited
to 500 copies. Very fine copy. Heath 48-580 1983 £425

BURTON, RICHARD FRANCIS   Falconry in the Valley of the Indus.
London, 1852. First edition. 4 tinted lithographs. 8vo. Orig. cloth.
Fine. Edwards 1044-99 1983 £350

BURTON, RICHARD FRANCIS   Falconry in the valley of the Indus.
London: John Van Voorst, 1852. 8vo. 8 adv. 4 tinted plates.
Orig. dark purple cloth, faded, small chip top of spine. Adelson
Africa-26 1983 $375

BURTON, RICHARD FRANCIS   First Footsteps in East Africa. London:
Longman, Brown, etc., 1856. First edition. 8vo, 2 maps, 4 colored
plates. Orig. violet cloth. Spine faded, dampstaining to cover and
plates. Adelson Africa-31 1983 $750

BURTON, RICHARD FRANCIS   First Footsteps in East Africa. London:
Tylston & Edwards, 1894. 2 vols. 8vo. 2 maps, 4 colored plates.
Orig. black cloth. Library labels inside front covers. Adelson
Africa-32 1983 $160

BURTON, RICHARD FRANCIS   GOA, and the Blue Mountains. London,
1851. First edition. Folding map, 4 tinted lithographs. Orig. cloth
skillfully repaired at spine. Frayed very slightly at hinges and
corners. 8vo. Good. Edwards 1044-100 1983 £195

BURTON, RICHARD FRANCIS   The Guide Book. A pictorial pilgrimage
to Mecca dn Medina. London: William Clowes & Son, 1865. 8vo.
Portrait. Orig. stiff, green paper covers, in new 1/4 tan morocco
slipcase. Covers rubbed, spine worn but intact. Adelson Africa-39
1983 $1,500

BURTON, RICHARD FRANCIS   The Jew The Gypsy and El Islam.
London: Hutchinson & Co., 1898. 8vo. Frontis. portrait of Burton.
Orig. red buckram boards, backed in red morocco. Adelson Africa-57
1983 $175

BURTON, RICHARD FRANCIS   The Journal of the Royal Geographical
Society. Volume the Forty-Ninth. London: John Murray, 1879. 8vo.
3 folding maps. Orig. blue cloth. A fine copy. Adelson Africa-62
1983 $200

BURTON, RICHARD FRANCIS   The Lake Regions of Central Africa.
London: Longman, Green, etc., 1860. First edition. 2 vols. 8vo.
Folding map. 12 tinted plates. Modern 1/4 dark green morocco, brown
labels. Adelson Africa-33 1983 $600

BURTON, RICHARD FRANCIS   The Lake Regions of Central Africa.
Longman, Green, 1860. First edition, with a folding map, 12
chromosyloglraph plates and 22 wood-cut illus., without the half-
titles, 2 vols., 8vo, cont. half pale brown calf over marbled
boards, fully gilt spines, with red and blue labels, particularly nice
copy. Fenning 61-51 1983 £295

BURTON, RICHARD FRANCIS   The Lake Regions of Central Africa.
1860. 2 vols., 12 tinted plates, 22 text illus., folding map, half
green morocco, rubbed, first edition. A little thumbed. K Books 301-
34 1983 £120

BURTON, RICHARD FRANCIS   The Lake Regions of Central Africa.
New York, 1860. First American edition. Folding map, wood-engraved
frontis. and illus., roy 8vo, a slightly shabby ex-library copy in
the orig. cloth. K Books 301-35 1983 £75

BURTON, RICHARD FRANCIS   The Land of Midian. London: C. Kegan
Paul & Co., 1879. 2 vols. 8vo. Folding map, 16 plates (6 colored).
Orig. pictorail yellow cloth. Lightly rubbed. Adelson Africa-49
1983 $385

BURTON, RICHARD FRANCIS   The Lands of Cazembe. London: Royal
Geog. Society, 1873. 8vo. Folding map. Orig. blue cloth, lightly
rubbed. Adelson Africa-44 1983 $185

BURTON, RICHARD FRANCIS   Letters from the battle-fields of
Paraguay. London: Tinsley Brothers, 1870. 8vo. Frontis., engraved
title. Folding map. Modern 1/4 red morocco. Leather labels.
Adelson Africa-42 1983 $550

BURTON, RICHARD FRANCIS   A Mission to Gelele, King of Dahome.
London: Tinsley Brothers, 1864. First edition. 2 vols. 8vo.
2 plates. 1/2 green morocco gilt, rubbed, lacks 1/2 titles.
Adelson Africa-37 1983 $475

BURTON, RICHARD FRANCIS   A Mission to Gelele, King of Dahome.
London: Tinsley Brothers, 1864. First edition. 2 vols. Illus.
Orig. cloth. Bookplates. Spines faded & slightly nicked, shaken.
Rear inner hings of Vol. 1 cracked. Good set. MacManus 277-815
1983 $350

BURTON, RICHARD FRANCIS   The Perfumed Garden of the Cheikh Nef-
zaoui. Cosmopoli: Kama Shastra Society, 1886. Second edition. 8vo.
Full imitation vellum, hand-made paper, uncut. Adelson Africa-60
1983 $300

BURTON, RICHARD FRANCIS   Personal narrative of a pilgrimage to
El-Medinah and Meccah. London: Longman, Brown, Green, 1855. First
edition. 3 vols. 8vo. 4 maps and plans. 14 plates (5 colored).
Orig. blue cloth. Hinges, edges, & corners rubbed, one hinge &
spine ends slightly frayed. Adelson Africa-27 1983 $1,250

BURTON, RICHARD FRANCIS   Personal narrative of a pilgrimage to
El-Medinah and Meccah. London: Longman, Brown, Green, 1855. First
edition. 3 vols. 8vo. 4 maps & plans. 14 plates (5 colored).
Modern 1/2 green crushed levant, t.e.g. A very good copy. Adelson
Africa-28 1983 $700

BURTON, RICHARD FRANCIS   Personal narrative of a pilgrimage to
El-Medinah and Meccah. London: Longman, Brown, Green, 1857. Second
edition. 2 vols. 12mo. 4 maps and plates, 14 plates (5 colored).
Orig. green cloth, gilt decorated spines and covers. Rubbed, spine
ends starting. Adelson Africa-29 1983 $250

BURTON, RICHARD FRANCIS   Personal narrative of a pilgrimage to
Al-Medinah & Meccah. London: Tylston and Edward, 1893. 2 vols.
8vo. Portrait. 4 maps and plans, 14 plates (5 colored). Orig.
black cloth. Bottom of spines starting. Adelson Africa-30 1983
$200

BURTON, RICHARD FRANCIS   Personal Narrative of a Pilgrimage
to El-Medinah and Meccah. New York: G.P. Putnam, 1856. 8vo.
Folding map, 2 plates. Orig. cloth. Rubbed, some light foxing.
Adelson Africa-170 1983 $125

BURTON, RICHARD FRANCIS   Priapeia or the sportive epigrams of
divers poets on Priapus... Athens: Erotika Biblion Society. 8vo.
1/2 modern blue calf. Adelson Africa-55 1983 $500

BURTON, RICHARD FRANCIS   Selected papers on anthropology, travel
and exploration. London: A.M. Philpot Ltd., 1924. 8vo. Number
74 of a limited edition of 100 copies. Orig. brown buckram, on
hand-made paper, uncut. Adelson Africa-63 1983 $150

BURTON, RICHARD FRANCIS   Sind Revisited: With notices of the Anglo-Indian Army... London: Richard Bentley, 1877. 2 vols. 8vo. Orig. grey cloth. Rubbed, corners and spine ends startin. Adelson Africa-48 1983 $500

BURTON, RICHARD FRANCIS   Sindh, and the Races that Inhabit the Valley of the Indus. London, 1851. Folding map, backed with canvas. Half calf. 8vo. Library stamp on title of the Atheneum, which was Burton's club. Good. Edwards 1044-98 1983 £220

BURTON, RICHARD FRANCIS   Ultima Thule; or, a summer in Iceland. London: William P. Nimmo, 1875. 2 vols. 8vo. 16 adv. 2 folding maps. 11 plates. Orig. blue cloth. Rubbed. Adelson Africa-46 1983 $425

BURTON, RICHARD FRANCIS   Wanderings in Three Continents. New York: Dodd, Mead & Co., 1901. 8vo. Portrait. 4 plates. Orig. blue cloth. Rubbed, worn. Adelson Africa-58 1983 $40

BURTON, RICHARD FRANCIS   Wanderings in West Africa from Liverpool to Fernando Po. London: Tinsley Bros., 1863. 2 vols. 8vo. Folding map, plate. Orig. cloth. Spines slightly faded. Adelson Africa-36 1983 $425

BURTON, RICHARD FRANCIS   Wit and Wisdom from West Africa. London: Tinsley Brothers, 1865. 8vo. Orig. plum-colored cloth. Rebacked, ex-library. Adelson Africa-38 1983 $600

BURTON, RICHARD FRANCIS   Zanzibar; City, Island, and Coast. London: Tinsley Brothers, 1872. 2 vols. 8vo. Folding map. 4 plans, 11 plates. 1/2 cont. calf, red labels, rubbed. Adelson Africa-43 1983 $475

BURTON, ROBERT   The Anatomy of Melancholy... Oxford: John Lichfield, 1621. First edition. Small 4to. Nineteenth century morocco, gilt, gilt edges. With the errata leaf, scored and mounted. From the library of the Earl of Southesk, with his bookplate. Traylen 94-137 1983 £5,500

BURTON, ROBERT   The Anatomy of Melancholy. Printed for H. Cripps and are to be sold at his Shop...and by E. Willis, 1660. Small folio, fine engraved title, preceded by leaf The Argument of the Frontispiece. Orig. calf, small chip at top of the spine, small hole at foot of the lower joint, but a fine copy. Bickersteth 75-12 1983 £30

BURTON, ROBERT   The Anatomy of Melancholy. Philadelphia, 1857. 8vo. Orig. binding. Engraved frontis. and engraved facsimile of the orig. frontis. Fye H-3-66 1983 $25

BURTON, WARREN   White Slavery. Worcester, 1839. 18mo, orig. cloth. Argosy 716-428 1983 $40

BURTON, WILLIAM   Josiah Wedgwood and His Pottery. New York and London, 1922. 1st ed. 1 of 500 copies for the United States (of an ed. of 1500). 32 tipped-in plates and 72 plates in black and white. Pictorial blue cloth, gilt, top edges gilt. Fine. Scarce. Bradley 63-29 1983 $250

BURTON, WILLIAM   Josiah Wedgwood and His Pottery. New York and London: 1922. First edition. 1/500 copies for United States. 32 tipped-in color plates, 72 b&w plates. Pictorial blue cloth, gilt, t.e.g. Fine. Bradley 66-406 1983 $225

BURTON, WILLIAM   A Pasquinade, on the performers of the York company. Leeds: printed by Edward Baines, for the author, 1801. 8vo, sewn, First edition. Very rare. Blank margins of title-page trimmed; some dust-soiling. Ximenes 64-74 1983 $200

BURTY, PHILIPPE   Lettres de Eugene Delacroix (1815 a 1863). Paris: A. Quantin, 1878. 11 plates (10 facsimile holographs and 1 folding chromolithograph by Lemercier). Frontis. Stout 4to. Splendidly bound in marbled boards, 1/2 blue morocco, finely gilt. T.e.g. Orig. wrappers and backstrip bound in. No. 24 of 50 on hollande, with etched portrait by Villot present in 2 states. With an ALS of Delacroix, dated 22 dec. 1851. Ars Libri 32-156 1983 $850

BURY, ADRIAN   Shadow of Eros. A biographical and critical study of the life and works of Sir Alfred Gilbert. Dropmore Press, 1952. 1st ed., 4to, 24 plates, half brown morocco gilt over cloth boards, t.e. tinted, others uncut, decorative endpapers by Biro. Very fine unopened copy in dusty dustwrappers. 247 numbered copies. Deighton 3-143 1983 £55

BURY, CHARLOTTE   Flirtation. Henry Colburn, 1834. 3 vols., half dark blue calf, red labels, very good. Jarndyce 30-320 1983 £48

BURY, CHARLOTTE   The History of a Flirt. Related by Herself. Henry Colburn, 1841. 2nd edition. 3 vols, 12mo, contemporary half blue calf. Hill 165-17 1983 £45

BURY, CHARLOTTE   Journal of the heart. London: Colburn and Bentley, 1830. First edition. 8vo. 19th-century green half calf. Wood-engraved frontis. and four plates (one folding). Spine a corners quite rubbed. Very scarce. Ximenes 63-118 1983 $80

BURY, CHARLOTTE   The Manoeuvring Mother. Henry Colburn, 1842. 1st ed., 3 vols, 12mo, original boards, uncut; new backstrips. 16 pp. of advertisements in vol. I, 6 in vol. II. Half-titles not called for. Hill 165-18 1983 £48

BURY, CHARLOTTE   Self-Indulgence; a Tale of the Nineteenth Century. Edinburgh: by Thomas Allan & Company, 1812. 2 vols. First edition, with the half-titles, early ownership inscription on title-pages. 12mo. Cont. half red morocco, gilt, marbled boards. Traylen 94-138 1983 £160

BURY, RICHARD DE   Philobiblon of Richard de Bury, Bishop of Durham. (San Francisco: The Book Club of California, 1925). Folio, double column text. Printed in red and black, with illuminated initials and illus. by Donald McKay. Edition ltd. to 250 numbered copies, printed at the Grabhorn Press. Prospectus laid in. Linen over boards; fray paper dust jacket. Fine copy. Karmiole 72-105 1983 $125

BUSBEY, HAMILTON   Trotting and Pacing Horse in America. N.Y., Macmillan, 1904. First edition, thick 8vo, illus. 3/4 green morocco over marbled boards, t.e.g., uncut; marbled endpapers. One of 100 deluxe copies, printed on large paper. Houle 21-1008 1983 $275

BUSHNAN, J. S.   The Natural History of Fishes. Edinburgh, 1840. Portrait, vignette, 32 coloured plates, post 8vo, original cloth (neatly repaired). First edition. Wheldon 160-949 1983 £30

BUSHNELL, HENRY   The History of Granville. Columbus, 1889. Illus. Cloth. Covers loose and heavily worn. King 45-129 1983 $35

BUSHNELL, MABEL CONE   Poems. Los Angeles: The Ward Ritchie Press, (1945). Title-page printed in brown & black. Signed by the author on title-page. Green cloth over marbled boards; matching slipcase. Fine copy. Karmiole 76-93 1983 $25

BUSIRI VICI, ANDREA   Giovanni Battista Busiri. Roma: Ugo Bozzi, 1966. 13 plates. 246 catalogue illus., text illus. Square 4to. Cloth. Dust jacket. Ars Libri 33-56 1983 $100

BUSIRI VICI, ANDREA   Jan Frans Van Bloemen Orizzonte... Roma: Ugo Bozzi, 1974. 243 plates. 444 reference illus. Large square 4to. Cloth. Dust jacket. Ars Libri 32-44 1983 $125

BUSTEED, H. E.   Echoes from Old Calcutta. London, 1908. Fourth edition. Maps and plates. Thick 8vo. Pictorial cloth. Good. Edwards 1044-104 1983 £20

BUTLER, A. G.   Foreign Birds for Cage and Aviary. (1908-10). Numerous black and white illus. from drawings, 2 vols., cr. 4to, cloth, trifle used. Wheldon 160-664 1983 £25

BUTLER, A. G.   Foreign Finches in Captivity. 1894. 60 hand-coloured plates by F. W. Frohawk, roy. 4to, original red cloth, gilt. A rare first edition. Internally a nice clean copy. Spine slightly faded. Wheldon 160-13 1983 £800

BUTLER, BENJAMIN F.   Outline of the Constitutional History
of New York. New York, 1848. 2nd series, vol. II. In orig. printed
wraps, uncut, covers somewhat dusty. Boswell 7-34 1983 $48

BUTLER, C. H.   The Little Messenger Birds. Broombridge,
n.d. (ca.1870). Colour printed frontis. Colour title vignette. 6
colour printed plates. Green pictorial cloth, gilt. Greer 40-136
1983 £22.50

BUTLER, CHARLES   The Life of Erasmus. London: John
Murray, 1825. First edition. 8vo. Half calf, rubbed. Heath
48-282 1983 £35

BUTCHER, DAVID   The Whittington Press. (Andoversford,
Gloucestershire): The Whittington Press. (1982). Folio. Illus.
with mounted photographic plates, text woodcuts and a large
folding tipped-in broadside. Index. This is one of 200 numbered
copies (from a total edition of 320). Brown buckram over marbled
boards. Fine. Karmiole 71-45 1983 $100

BUTLER, GEORGE H.   Thomas Butler and His Descendants.
NY, 1886. 8vo. later linen-backed boards, ex lib. Argosy 710-
171 1983 $37.50

BUTLER, HOWARD C.   The Story of Athens. NY, 1902. Illus.
8vo, cloth. Salloch 385-334 1983 $28

BUTLER, JAMES D.   Nebraska. N.p., (1873). Dbd.
Ginsberg 47-612 1983 $50

BUTLER, JOHN   A Sketch of Assam. London, 1847. Folding map, hand-coloured frontis. 15 hand-coloured plates, 1 black and
white. Illus. in text. Calf with morocco label, raised bands. Spine
gilt and boards ruled in gilt and in blind, gilt inner dentelles. Fine.
Edwards 1044-105 1983 £275

BUTLER, JOHN   Travels and Adventures in the Province
of Assam. London, 1855. Not in Abbey. 2 folding maps, folding plan.
8 plates. Calf with morocco label, raised bands. Spine gilt and
boards ruled in gilt and in blind, gilt inner dentelles. Fine.
Edwards 1044-106 1983 £220

BUTLER, JOSEPHINE   An Autobiographical Memoir. Bristol:
J.W. Arrowsmith, 1915. 3rd edition, half title. Orig. green cloth.
Jarndyce 30-927 1983 £9.50

BUTLER, MANN   A History of the Commonwealth of
Kentucky. Louisville, 1834. First edition. 8vo, mod. fabricoid,
(lacks port.). Argosy 716-231 1983 $100

BUTLER, SAMUEL   Erewhon Revisited. London, Grant
Richards, 1901. First ed., pres. copy inscribed to F.B. Bickley by
author. Inner hinges weak, very good copy, cloth slipcase, orig.
cloth. MacManus 277-818 1983 $400

BUTLER, SAMUEL   Erewhon Revisited. London, Grant
Richards, 1901. 8vo., orig. cloth, t.e.g., first ed. MacManus
277-819 1983 $75

BUTLER, SAMUEL   The Genuine Remains in Verse and Prose
of... London, Tonson, 1759. First ed., 2 vols., old calf, worn,
hinges broken. MacManus 277-820 1983 $50

BUTLER, SAMUEL   The Way of All Flesh. London, Grant
Richards, 1903. Orig. cloth, first ed., spine faded, inner hinges
weak, else very good copy. MacManus 277-828 1983 $350

BUTLER, SAMUEL (1612-1680)   Hudibras... London: Motte, 1726.
Early ed. with Hogarth's famous illus. Orig. full calf. Spine
ends rubbed, else a nice copy. Jenkins 155-564 1983 $100

BUTLER, SAMUEL (1612-1680)   Hudibras. Cambridge: 1744. 2 vols.,
8vo, portrait and 16 plates by Hogarth, 4 of them folding, cont.
calf, spines gilt, lacking labels, joints cracked, rubbed at edges,
top of second volume worn. First Edition edited by Grey. Bickersteth
75-13 1983 £45

BUTLER, SAMUEL (1612-1680)   Hudibras. Glasgow, printed by Robert and
Andrew Foulis, 1774. 2 vols., 12mo, orig. sheep (worn, joints
breaking, spine ends chipped, spines cracked) internally very nice
and clean. Ravenstree 94-106 1983 $47.50

BUTLER, SAMUEL (1612-1680)   Hudibras, a Poem. Lon, 1819. Two vols.
11 handcolored plates, full leather, interior moderately foxed, edges
rubbed, good or better. Quill & Brush 54-221 1983 $275

BUTLER, SAMUEL (1612-1680)   Hudibras. Charles & Henry Baldwyn, 1819.
In three vols. With vignette title-pages, 3 portraits and 5
plates, all on India paper, a series of 28 woodcuts illus. after
J. Thurston. 3 vols., half-titles, ad. leaf, 8vo. Full nineteenth
century dark blue morocco, gilt bordered sides, gilt ruled and lettered
spines, t.e.g., other edges uncut. Fine paper set. Fenning 62-47
1983 £85

BUTLER, SAMUEL (1612-1680)   Hudibras,... London: John Murray, 1835.
New edition. 2 vols. Extra-illus. with the addition of numerous
engraved port. & illus. from other editions. Full green morocco, gilt,
a.e.g., marbled endpapers. Fine. MacManus 277-817 1983 $260

BUTLER, WILLIAM F   The campaign of the Cataracts.
London: Sampson Low etc., 1887. 8vo. Folding map. 7 plates.
Orig. pictorail cloth. Lightly rubbed. Adelson Africa-65 1983
$150

BUTLER, WILLIAM F.   The Campaign of the Cataracts. Sampson
Low..., 1887. First edition, with a large folding map, 7 plates, and
a few other illus. from drawings by Lady Butler, 8vo, recent boards.
Fenning 60-45 1983 £24.50

BUTLER, WILLIAM F.   The Wild North Land. London, 1873.
Illus., folding map. Argosy 716-44 1983 $50

BUTSCHLI, O.   Untersuchungen uber Mikrostrukturen
des Erstarrten Schwefels. Leipzig, 1900. 4 plates and 6 text-figures.
4to, cloth. Wheldon 160-122 1983 £15

BUTT, ISAAC   The Irish People and the Irish Land.
Dublin: John Falconer, 1867. First edition, 8vo, orig. cloth, by
Falconer with his ticket, a few light pencil notes, a good to v.g.
copy. Fenning 61-52 1983 £28.50

BUTT, ISAAC   A Practical Treatise on the New Law of
Compensation to Tenants in Ireland. Dublin: John Falconer, 1871.
First edition, roy. 8vo, orig. cloth, by J. Falconer, with his
ticket, binding lightly stained and a little worn, but sound and
otherwise a very good copy. Signed by the author on the title-page.
Fenning 62-48 1983 £35

BUTTERFIELD, CONSUL W.   History of George Rogers Clark's Conquest
of the Illinois and the Wabash Towns. Columbus, Ohio, 1904. First
edition. A.e.g. Orig. 3/4 morocco. Portrait frontis. Jenkins 152-
792 1983 $40

BUTTERFIELD, JACK C.   Men of the Alamo Goliad and San Jacinto.
San Antonio, 1936. Stiff pictorial wrappers. Jenkins 153-80 1983
$35

THE BUTTERFLY. (London: 1893-1894). Vols. 1-11. First edition.
8vo. Illus. Orig. green cloth. Covers somewhat soiled. Spines
darkened. Former owner's signatures of flyleaves. MacManus 277-830
1983 $125

THE BUTTERFLY. (London: Grant Richards & The Idler Office, 1899-1900).
New Series. Vols. 1-11. 2 vols. Small 4to. Illus. Orig. cream
buckram, gilt. First edition. Covers dust-soiled, front outer hinge
of Vol. 1 splitting. MacManus 277-831 1983 $150

BUTTERWORTH, E.   Parrots and Cockatoos. 1981. 20
etchings, roy. 8vo, limp boards-together 2 vols., folio and roy. 8vo,
in a portfolio. Edition limited to 60 copies, numbered, dated, and
signed by the artist. The first ten copies were bound and are now
all sold. Wheldon 160-14 1983 £365

BUTTERWORTH, WILLIAM   Three Years Adventures of a Minor in
England, Africa, the West Indies, South Carolina and Georgia. Leeds,
1831. Half calf. Portrait frontis. Jenkins 153-81 1983 $175

BUTTERWORTH, WILLIAM   Table of roads from Madras to the principal towns and military stations under the presidency of St. George... Madras: printed at the Asylum Press, by G. Clader, and published by C. Phillips, n.d. (1833). 8vo. Cont. half roan, printed side-label. Signature of Frederick Parr, 54th Regiment, who has made extensive manscript notations and corrections. With a folding lithographed map (cut in two by the binder, with slight loss). Rubbed, spine slightly worn. Rare. Ximenes 63-201 1983 $200

BUTTS, MARY   The Crystal Cabinet. London, 1937. First edition. Frontis. from a sketch by J. Cocteau. Torn dust wrapper. Very nice. Rota 230-111 1983 £20

BUTTS, MARY   Imaginary Letters. Paris, Titus, 1928. First edition. Small 4to, beige silk, paper label, uncut and mostly unopened. One of 250 copies, illus. with five full page copper engravings after drawings by Jean Cocteau. Fine. Houle 21-188 1983 $150

BUTTS, MARY   Imaginary Letters. Paris: Edward W. Titus, 1928. First edition. Engravings on copper from the orig. drawings by Jean Cocteau. Orig. cloth with paper labels. Limited to 250 copies initialed by the publisher. Endpapers foxed. Unopened. Fine. MacManus 277-832 1983 $125

BUTTS, MARY   Imaginary Letters. Paris, 1928. Illus. by Jean Cocteau, limited to 250 copies (this is out of series), endpaper slightly foxed and some soiling to covers, very good. Quill & Brush 54-285 1983 $90

BUTTS, MARY   Imaginary Letters. Paris: Edward W. Titus, 1928. First edition. Copperlate engravings from drawings by J. Cocteau. One of 250 copies, this unnumbered. Endpapers a little foxed. Nice. Rota 230-112 1983 £40

BUTTS, MARY   Imaginary Letters. Paris: (1929). First edition. Illus. with 5 copper engravings. Limited to 250 copies. Very fine, partially unopened copy. Lightly chipped orig. glassine. Bromer 25-14 1983 $200

BUTTS, MARY   Last Stories. (London): Brendin Publishing Co., (1938). Cloth. First edition. A very fine copy in dust jacket, with a couple of tiny chips. Reese 20-199 1983 $85

BUTTS, MARY   Scenes from the Life of Cleopatra. London: William Heinemann Ltd., (1935). First edition. Orig. cloth. Dust jacket (faintly dust-soiled, a few short tears). Scarce. Fine. MacManus 277-833 1983 $165

BUTTS, MARY   Scenes from the Life of Cleopatra. London, 1935. First edition. Fore-edges lightly foxed, dustwrapper slightly frayed, soiled, and off-set onto spine, otherwise a very good copy. Gekoski 2-23 1983 £40

BUXTON, P. A.   Animal Life in Deserts. 1923. Illustrated, 8vo, cloth (trifle used). Wheldon 160-470 1983 £15

BUXTON, THOMAS FOWELL   Memoirs... 1884. First edition, tall 8vo, half title, front. 16 pp ads. Orig. purple cloth, faded and a little rubbed. Jarndyce 30-930 1983 £20

BUXTORF, JOHANNES   Lexicon Hebraicum et Chaldaicum. Basle, In Officina Episcopiana, 1735. Engraved portrait frontis., (slightly frayed), old vellum. K Books 301-36 1983 £50

BYERS, DOUGLAS S.   The Prehistory of the Tehuacan Valley. Austin/London: University of Texas Press, 1967-1972. 5 vols. Prof. illus. Large 4to. Cloth. Dust jacket. Ars Libri 34-161 1983 $150

BYFIELD, NATHANIEL   An Account of the Late Revolution in New England. London: Printed for Ric. Chiswell, 1689. Small quarto. Full red polished calf, elaborately gilt, a.e.g., by Zaehnsdorf. A fine copy. Reese 18-31 1983 $1,250

BYFIELD, NATHANIEL   An Account of the Late Revolution in New England. Together with the Declaration of the Gentlemen, Merchants, and Inhabitants of Boston... London: Printed for Ric Chiswell, at the Rose and Crown in St. Paul's Church-Yard. MDCLXXXIX (1689). 4to, modern red morocco binding. Title gold stamped on upper board and on spine. Elaborate gold dentelles. A.E. Lownes bookplate. Arkway 22-18 1983 $750

BYLES, JOHN BARNARD   Sophisms of Free-Trade and Popular Political Economy Examined. Seeleys, 1849. First edition, half title, 1 p ads. Orig. brown cloth, paper label, v.g. Jarndyce 31-121 1983 £25

BYNE, ARTHUR   Decorated Wooden Ceilings in Spain. NY: G.P. Putnam's Sons, (1920). Large cloth portfolio with ties. Containing 56 plates, some in colors. Karmiole 72-22 1983 $125

BYNNER, WITTER   The Beloved Stranger. New York, 1922. 8vo. Cloth, boards. 2nd printing. This copy inscribed by the poet to Alexander Laing and dated 1929. Vg-fine. In Our Time 156-133 1983 $25

BYNNER, WITTER   Grenstone Poems. New York, (1917). 8vo. Cloth, boards. Name of a reviewer on flyleaf, news photo of the poet on endboard, else very good copy. In Our Time 156-132 1983 $20

BYNUM, LINDLEY   The Record Book of the Rancho Santa Ana del Chino. Los Angeles, 1935. Wrps. Scarce. Clark 741-85 1983 $28.50

BYRD, RICHARD E.   Alone. N.Y., 1938. Signed by author. Cloth. Good. King 45-536 1983 $25

BYRD, RICHARD E.   Little America. New York & London, 1930. Portrait plates. Maps. Parchment and boards. A fine copy in orig. glassine (frayed and chipped). Ltd. to 1,000 numbered copies, printed on rag paper, specially bound, and signed by the author, and by the publishers. Reese 19-105 1983 $225

BYRD, RICHARD E.   Little America. NY, 1930. Author's autograph edition, limited to 1000 numbered and signed copies, cover and spine slightly soiled, fine. Quill & Brush 54-1684 1983 $75

BYRD, WILLIAM   Another Secret Diary of William Byrd of Westover 1739-1741. Richmond, Va., 1942. Illus. Orig. cloth, dust jacket. Ginsberg 46-771 1983 $25

BYRD, WILLIAM   The History of the Dividing Line, Between Virginia and North Carolina as Run in 1728-29. Richmond, Va., 1866. Two vols. Three-quarter morocco. Ex-library. Small stamp on title page, bookplate. Very good. Reese 19-106 1983 $200

BYRD, WILLIAM   William Byrd's Histories of the Dividing Line Betwixt Virginia and North Carolina. Raleigh, 1929. Illus., facs., map. Orig. cloth. Ginsberg 46-77 1983 $75

BYRD, WILLIAM   The Secret Diary, 1709-1712. AND: Another Secret Diary, 1739-41 with Letters & Literary Exercises 1696-1726. Richmond, 1941, 1942. 2 vols. Thick 8vo, d.w. Argosy 710-553 1983 $100

BYRD, WILLIAM   The Writings of "Colonel William Byrd of Westover in Virginia Esqr." New York, 1901. Vellum & boards. Cloth jacket. Uncut. Fine. One of an edition of 500 copies. Presentation copy by Anne H. Byrd. Bookplate of George H. Byrd. Reese 19-108 1983 $135

BYRD, WILLIAM   The Writings of "Colonel William Byrd of Westover in Virginia Esqr." N.Y., 1901. Illus. Orig. boards, vellum spine with paper label, dust jacket. First edition. One of 500 copies printed by the De Vinne Press. Ginsberg 46-773 1983 $125

BYRNE, BERNARD M.   An Essay To Prove the Contagious Character of Malignant Cholera; with Brief Instructions for Its Prevention and Cure. Philadelphia, 1855. 2nd ed., with additional notes by the author. 8vo. Morrill 289-33 1983 $25

BYRNE, DONN   Blind Raftery. NY, (1924). State A. Endpapers slightly offset, else very good or better in slightly soiled and frayed, still very good dustwrapper. Quill & Brush 54-223 1983 $50

BYRNE, DONN   Field on Honor. NY, (1929). Top page edge foxed, else bright, near fine in bright dustwrapper with internally reinforced tear on spine edge. Quill & Brush 54-224 1983 $50

BYRNE, DONN   O'Malley of Shanganagh. NY, (1925).
Bright, fine in slightly chipped, very good dustwrapper with darkened
spine. Quill & Brush 54-197 1983 $40

BYRNE, DONN   A Party of Baccarat. NY, (1930). Flexible leather binding, illus., fine in slightly soiled and lightly
chipped, very good dustwrapper. Quill & Brush 54-222 1983 $60

BYRNE, DONN   The Wind Bloweth. N.Y., 1922. First
edition. Illus. by George Bellows. Argosy 714-112 1983 $20

BYRNE, MRS. WILLIAM PITT   Flemish Interiors. Longman, (1856).
First edition, litho, front. & title. Half title, 24 pp ads. Orig.
red cloth, gilt sl. darkened, v.g. Jarndyce 31-122 1983 £25

BYRNE, MRS. WILLIAM PITT   Undercurrents Overlooked. Richard
Bentley, 1860. First edition, 2 vols. Inner hinges a little weak.
Orig. orange cloth. Inscribed presentation copy from the author.
Jarndyce 31-123 1983 £38

BYRNES, GENE   How to Draw Comics and Commercial Art.
N.Y., (1939). First edition. Pictorial spiral wraps. Blind-stamped
names. Moderately worn. King 45-384 1983 $25

BYROM, JOHN   Miscellaneous Poems. Manchester: J.
Harrop, 1773. First collected edition, 8vo, 2 vols., cont. calf,
spines gilt, morocco labels, half-titles. A fine copy, with the
bookplates of a prior owner. Trebizond 18-13 1983 $225

BYRON, GEORGE GORDON   The Age of Bronze; or, Carmen Seculare et
Annus Haud Mirabilis. London: Printed for John Hunt, 1823. First
edition. Rebound in later wrappers. Lacks the half-title. Good.
MacManus 277-834 1983 $75

BYRON, GEORGE GORDON   Beppo, a Venetian story. London:
Murray, 1818. First edition. 8vo. Old half morocco. One of 500
copies. Half-title present. Binding quite scuffed. Ximenes 63-44
1983 $250

BYRON, GEORGE GORDON   Bibliographical Catalogue of First
Editions, Proof Copies & Manuscripts of Books by Lord Byron.
London: printed for the First Edition Club, 1925. 4to. Black
buckram, gilt, t.e.g., others uncut. 14 illus. Limited edition
of 500 numbered copies. Traylen 94-144 1983 £35

BYRON, GEORGE GORDON   The Bride of Abydos. 1814. Sixth
edition. 8vo, wrapper, a very good copy. Fenning 60-47 1983 £10.50

BYRON, GEORGE GORDON   Cain; a mystery. London: printed
for the booksellers, by W. Benbow, 1822. 12mo. Orig. blue-grey
printed wrappers. Piracy. Very fine. Ximenes 63-45 1983 $125

BYRON, GEORGE GORDON   Cain, a Mystery. N.d. (c. 1822).
12mo, engr. title, uncut, orig. grey printed wraps. (tear from lower
corner of back wrapper), spine worn. Jarndyce 31-464 1983 £38

BYRON, GEORGE GORDON   Childe Harold's Pilgrimage. London:
John Murray, 1818. First edition. 8vo. Uncut in orig. boards.
Advertisers Catalogue dated August 1818. Heath 48-250 1983 £55

BYRON, GEORGE GORDON   The Corsair, a Tale. 1814. Including
half-title, 8vo, wrapper. A very good copy. The two leaves of Notes
(pp. 97-100) are bound following the four leaves of Poems (pp. 101-108).
Fenning 60-49 1983 £16.50

BYRON, GEORGE GORDON   The Corsair, a Tale. London: for
John Murray, 1814. First edition. 8vo. Modern wrappers. Traylen
94-142 1983 £15

BYRON, GEORGE GORDON   Don Juan. London: 1823; 1821-1824.
First editions. Demy 8vo. 6 vols. Later half-calf & drab boards.
"Small paper" or "common" issues of Cantos III-XVI; reprint of Cantos
I-II. Spines rubbed. Some foxing. MacManus 277-836 1983 $350

BYRON, GEORGE GORDON   Don Juan. 1826. Cantos I-XVI complete
in 2 vols., for the booksellers. Half red morocco, sl. rubbed.
Jarndyce 31-465 1983 £25

BYRON, GEORGE GORDON   Don Juan. London: Thomas Davison, 1828.
2 vols., engraved frontis., full diced calf, very good, titles inset
on black morocco, reprint. K Books 307-42 1983 £25

BYRON, GEORGE GORDON   Don Juan. London: Arthur L. Humphreys,
1906. 2 vols. 8vo. Full green morocco gilt. Spines faded to brown.
Bookplates. Fine. MacManus 277-835 1983 $75

BYRON, GEORGE GORDON   Don Juan. London: John Lane, The Bodley
Head, (1926). Illus. by John Austen. Orig. white decorated buckram.
First of this edition. Spine and covers soiled and a trifle faded.
Endpapers darkened. Good copy. MacManus 277-130 1983 $35

BYRON, GEORGE GORDON   The Giaour, a Fragment of a Turkish
Tale. 1814. Without the half-title, 8vo, wrapper, a very good copy.
Fenning 60-51 1983 £12.50

BYRON, GEORGE GORDON   Hours of idleness, a series of poems...
Newark: printed and sold by S. and J. Ridge, etc., 1807. First
edition. 8vo. 19th-century blue half calf, gilt, spine gilt, m.e.
Scuffed. Wanting the half-title, a few minor signs of use, but a
very good copy. Ximenes 63-46 1983 $275

BYRON, GEORGE GORDON   Hours of Idleness. Newark: S. & J.
Ridge, 1807. First edition. Cont. full morocco with marbled endpapers.
Lacking the half-title page. Spine edges slightly rubbed. Bookplate.
Very good. MacManus 277-838 1983 $150

BYRON, GEORGE GORDON   Hours of idleness. English bards
and Scotch reviewers. Glasgow: printed by James Starke, 1829.
12mo. Orig. printed boards. A bit worn, occasional stains.
Ximenes 63-47 1983 $40

BYRON, GEORGE GORDON   Lara, A. Tale. Jacqueline, A. Tale.
London: Printed for J. Murray, Albemarle-Street, By T. Davison,
Whitefriars, 1814. First edition. 8vo. Orig. paper-backed boards,
with label on spine. Spine a little worn. Bookplates. Very good.
MacManus 277-839 1983 $125

BYRON, GEORGE GORDON   Manfred, a dramatic poem. London:
Murray, 1817. First edition, third issue. 8vo. Orig. grey
wrappers. 4 pages of ads. Slight wear to spine, but a fine copy.
Ximenes 63-48 1983 $200

BYRON, GEORGE GORDON   Manfred, A Dramatic Poem. London: John
Murray, Albemarle Street, 1817. First edition, third issue. Cont.
quarter morocco with marbled boards. With two-line quote from "Hamlet"
on title-page. Bookplate. Very good. MacManus 277-840 1983 $85

BYRON, GEORGE GORDON   Manfred. London: John Murray, 1817.
8vo, old calf, gilt (rubbed). Lacks the half-title, and the printed
notes at the end of the text. With Henry Irving's bookplates.
Ximenes 64-294 1983 $75

BYRON, GEORGE GORDON   Marino Faliero, Doge of Venice. London:
Murray, 1821. First edition, first issue. Orig. boards (hinges broken;
spine rubbed). MacManus 277-841 1983 $100

BYRON, GEORGE GORDON   Marino Faliero, Doge Of Venice. London:
First edition, second issue. Cont. quarter-morocco with marbled boards.
Some foxing. Bookplate. Very good. MacManus 277-842 1983 $85

BYRON, GEORGE GORDON   Marino Faliero, Doge of Venice.
London: Murray, 1821. 1st ed., 2nd issue. Mid-nineteenth century
blue binder's cloth, gilt. Not quite a fine copy. Jenkins 155-163
1983 $65

BYRON, GEORGE GORDON   Marino Faliero, Doge of Venice. London:
John Murray, 1821. First edition, second issue. Contemporary boards
(recased), uncut. Very good copy. Brown cloth folding box, somewhat
worn. Bradley 66-67 1983 $45

BYRON, GEORGE GORDON   Ode to Napoleon Bonaparte. London:
Printed for John Murray, Albemarle-St., May, 1814. New York: Reprinted by John Low, 17 Chatham-St., 1814. Early American edition. Small
4to. Self-wrappers, lacking stitches. Worn, last leaf torn, slightly
affecting text. Cont. owner's signature on title. Half-morocco slipcase. MacManus 277-843 1983 $250

BYRON, GEORGE GORDON   The Poetical Works of Lord Byron. London: John Murray, 1855-56. 6 vols. 8vo. Full purple crushed levant morocco, decorative gilt borders on sides, fully gilt panelled spines, edges gilt. With 141 extra illus. of which 30 are in colour. Spines a little faded. Traylen 94-140 1983 £330

BYRON, GEORGE GORDON   The Poetical Works. John Murray, 1855-6. A new edition, 6 vols. Front. vol. I, half titles. 20pp/32pp ads. in vols. I & II. Orig. pink cloth a little mottled by damp. A good set. Jarndyce 31-468 1983 £38

BYRON, GEORGE GORDON   The Prisoner of Chillon, and Other Poems. 1816. First edition, first issue, including half-title and ad. leaf, 8vo, very faint old water stain on outer margin of first two leaves, but otherwise a nice copy in old brown paper wraps. With the ads. on the verso of the final leaf and the recto blank. Fenning 62-49 1983 £37.50

BYRON, GEORGE GORDON   The Prisoner of Chillon, and Other Poems. London: John Murray, 1816. First edition. Rebound in later wrappers. Lacking last leaf of ads. Wrappers badly torn. MacManus 277-844 1983 $75

BYRON, GEORGE GORDON   Sardanapalus, A Tragedy. London: John Murray, 1821. First edition. Cont. quarter-morocco with marbled boards. Spine edges and cover corners slightly rubbed. Bookplate. Very good. MacManus 277-845 1983 $125

BYRON, GEORGE GORDON   The Sardanapalus, a Tragedy. 1821. First edition, including half-title, 8vo, in cont. half green calf, gilt spine, with double red lettering pieces. Fenning 60-52 1983 £35

BYRON, GEORGE GORDON   The Siege of Corinth. London: Printed for John Murray, 1816. First edition. Orig. drab paper wrappers (bottom of spine worn). Uncut. Complete with half-title and two pages of Murray's advertisements, printed by Dove, bound in at the back. Folding cloth case. Fine. MacManus 277-846 1983 $200

BYRON, GEORGE GORDON   The Siege of Corinth. London: for John Murray, 1816. First edition. 8vo. Modern wrappers. Traylen 94-143 1983 £18

BYRON, GEORGE GORDON   Werner, a tragedy. London: Murray, 1823. First edition, first issue, with no imprint at the foot of p. 188. 8vo. Orig. grey wrappers. 7 pages of ads. Cont. owner's signature on both the front wrapper and the dedication page. A very fine copy Ximenes 63-50 1983 $325

BYRON, GEORGE GORDON   Werner, A Tragedy. London: John Murray, 1823. First edition, second issue. Orig. drab paper wrappers (split along outer hinge). Uncut. Good. MacManus 277-848 1983 $150

BYRON, GEORGE GORDON   Werner, A Tragedy. London: John Murray, Albemarle Street, 1823. First edition, second issue. Cont. quarter-morocco with marbled boards. Spine ends slightly rubbed. Bookplate. Very good. MacManus 277-847 1983 $85

BYRON, GEORGE GORDON   The Works. London, 1904-24. Definitive edition. 13 vols. 8vo. Half light brown calf, gilt, gilt panelled spines, t.e.g., by Sangorski and Sutcliffe. Frontis. to each vol., and other illus. Traylen 94-141 1983 £330

BYRON, JOHN   The Narrative of the Honourable John Byron. London: S. Baker & G. Leigh, and T. Davies, 1768. 1st ed., 8vo, later calf, spine richly gilt, gilt-embossed crests, engraved frontis. Half-title. Light offsetting of frontis., but a fine copy. Trebizond 18-131 1983 $450

BYRON, JOHN   The Narrative of...also an Account of the Loss of the Wager. Printed for C.J.G. & F. Rivington, 1831. With frontis., 12mo, cont. calf-backed marbled boards, some light thumbing, but a very good copy. Fenning 60-53 1983 £12.50

BYRON, MAY   The Garden of Love. Hodder & Stoughton, 1910. 4 plates (repeated with colour on endpapers) & 27 text illus. Red cloth pictorial gilt. Greer 40-55 1983 £14

BYRON, MAY   The Poor Dear Dollies. London: Hodder & Stoughton, n.d. (ca. 1908). Profusely illus., including 12 color plates. Green cloth over illus. color boards. Bookplate. Illus. by Rosa C. Petherick. Karmiole 72-27 1983 $45

BYRON, ROBERT   The Appreciation of Literature. London, 1932. First edition. Corners bruised. Very good. Jolliffe 26-76 1983 £18

BYRON, ROBERT   First Russia, Then Tibet. London, 1933. First edition. Pastedowns and edges slightly spotted. One corner bumped. Very good. Jolliffe 26-77 1983 £35

BYRON, ROBERT   Imperial Pilgrimage. London, 1937. First edition. Well-used wrappers. Very good copy. Gekoski 2-24 1983 £15

BYWATER, JOHN   An Essay on the History, Practice and Theory of Electricity... London: Printed for the author, 1810. Only ed., 8vo, title, 2 folding engraved plates; new grey boards. Pickering & Chatto 22-19 1983 $185

C

CABANILLIS, JUAN   Opera Omnia. Barcelona 1927-1941.
Only edition. 3 vols., 4to. Salloch 387-37 1983 $75

CABANIS, P. J. G.   Coup d'Oeil sur les Revolutions...
Paris, 1804. First edition. 8vo. Old half-cloth. Blank corner
of one leaf torn; last three leaves stained. Gurney 90-29 1983
£45

CABELL, JAMES BRANCH   Ballads From the Hidden Way. NY, 1928.
Fine in orig. tissue dustwrapper slightly darkened. Quill & Brush 54-
225 1983 $100

CABELL, JAMES BRANCH   The Cream of the Jest. New York:
McBride, 1927. Gilt cloth. First illus. edition, with plates and
decorations by Pape. Fine in dust jacket with tears in rear panel.
Reese 20-756 1983 $35

CABELL, JAMES BRANCH   The Eagle's Shadow. New York:
Doubleday, 1904. 1st ed., correct 1st state. Orig. red cloth,
gilt. Just short of fine, but a fresh copy. Jenkins 155-164 1983
$75

CABELL, JAMES BRANCH   Gallantry... New York & London:
Harper, 1907. Frontis., color plates. 1st ed., 2nd binding. Orig.
pale green cloth, stamped in dark green and white. Illus. by Howard
Pyle. Fine copy. Jenkins 155-165 1983 $30

CABELL, JAMES BRANCH   Jurgen. N.Y., Modern Library, (1934).
First edition thus (so stated). Small 8vo, dust jacket (small nicks,
trifle rubbed), very good. Houle 22-157 1983 $35

CABELL, JAMES BRANCH   Jurgen. (London, 1949). 8vo, bound
by Sangorski & Sutcliffe in full morocco with an inlay of purple
morocco embellished with abstract design in gilt, g.t. With 16
engravings by John Buckland-Wright. One of 100 copies specially
bound and one extra engraving. Signed by the artist on the colophon.
Duschnes 240-89 1983 $675

CABELL, JAMES BRANCH   The Line of Love. New York, 1905.
8vo, decorated cloth with mounted illus. on front cover. Text
printed within decorated borders throughout and ten illus. in
color by Howard Pyle. First edition. Duschnes 240-187 1983 $75

CABELL, JAMES BRANCH   The Line of Love. New York & London:
Harper & Brothers, 1905. Gilt pictorial cloth. Illus., in color,
by Howard Pyle. First edition. First state of the binding. Fine.
Reese 20-200 1983 $60

CABELL, JAMES BRANCH   Smirt. NY, 1934. Front endpapers offset from newspaper clipping laid-in, very minor cover stains, else
fine in slightly frayed dustwrapper. Quill & Brush 54-226 1983 $50

CABELL, JAMES BRANCH   Something About Eve. NY, 1927. Large
paper edition. Limited to 850 numbered and signed copies, spine
slightly stained, thin mark top page edge, else near fine in remnants
of slipcase. Quill & Brush 54-229 1983 $75

CABELL, JAMES BRANCH   Something about Eve. New York: McBride,
1929. Gilt cloth. First illus. edition, with plates by Pape.
Fine in very slightly used foil dust jacket. Reese 20-757 1983 $45

CABELL, JAMES BRANCH   Something About Eve. New York: McBride,
1930. Cloth and boards. First edition. One of 1295 numbered copies,
signed by the author. Fine in slightly worn slipcase. Reese 20-202
1983 $45

CABELL, JAMES BRANCH   These Restless Heads. NY, 1932. One of
410 numbered and signed copies, some pages uncut, spine slightly soiled
still very good in wearing slipcase. Quill & Brush 54-227 1983 $75

CABELL, JAMES BRANCH   The Way of Ecben. N.Y., McBride, 1929.
First edition. Decorations by Frank Pape. Half black cloth over
gilt marbled boards, top edge stained grey, uncut, unopened. Glassine
dust jacket (edges lightly foxed). Enclosed in pub.'s marbled box.
Very good. Houle 22-158 1983 $30

CABELL, JAMES BRANCH   The White Robe. London & New York,
1928. With 8 woodcut plates, small folio, orig. calf-backed boards,
edges uncut, a fine copy in the slip-case. Ltd. edition of 200
numbered copies on Italian hand-made paper at the Plimpton Press,
the whole designed by W.D. Orcutt. Fenning 62-50 1983 £32

CABLE, B.   A Hundred Year History of the P. & O.
London, 1937. First edition. Sq. 8vo. Coloured armorial frontis. 12
coloured and 6 other plates. 10 pages of silhouettes. Endpaper maps.
Slightly soiled. Orig. dust jacket. Edwards 1042-23 1983 £35

CABLE, GEORGE WASHINGTON   The Creoles of Louisiana. New York,
1884. Cloth, spine very lightly faded and rubbed at ends. First
edition. Felcone 22-126 1983 $25

CABLE, GEORGE WASHINGTON   Gideon's Band, A tale of the Mississippi.
NY, 1914. First edition, inscribed and signed on front end paper by
author. Cloth, spine with small spot, covers darkened and worn, front
inner hinge cracked. King 46-258 1983 $40

CABLE, GEORGE WASHINGTON   The Flower of the Chapdelaines. NY,
1918. First edition, inscribed and signed by the author on half-title.
Frontis. by F. C. Yohn. Cloth. Inner hinges cracked, moderately
worn. King 46-257 1983 $40

CABLE, GEORGE WASHINGTON   The Grandissimes. N.Y., 1880. First
edition. 8vo, gilt stamped blue cloth. Argosy 714-113 1983 $150

CABLE, GEORGE WASHINGTON   Lovers of Louisiana. NY, 1918. First
edition, inscribed & signed by the author on half-title. Cloth, covers
worn and spotted. King 46-259 1983 $35

CABLE, GEORGE WASHINGTON   Old Creole Days. 1879. First
edition, pict. cloth, somewhat rubbed & stained. First issue, with
no ads. Argosy 714-114 1983 $200

CABLE, GEORGE WASHINGTON   Strange True Stories of Louisiana.
New York, 1889. Plates. Cloth. Binding a trifle soiled. First
edition. Felcone 22-127 1983 $25

CACKLER, CHRISTIAN   "Recollection of an Old Settler." Kent,
1904. Illus. Modern cloth. Ginsberg 46-572 1983 $75

CADEL, P.   History of the Bombay Army. London,
1938. 11 maps, 2 coloured plates. Some occasional spotting, some
slight wear. 8vo. Orig. cloth. Good. Edwards 1044-108 1983 £40

CADET DE GASSICOURT, CHARLES LOUIS   Rapport...sur le concours
propose pour le perfectionnement des Sirops de Raisins... Paris:
l'Imprimerie Imperiale, 1813. 8vo. Orig. paper wrappers. 2
folding plates. Wrappers a little frayed. Zeitlin 264-69 1983
$80

CADY, HARRISON   The Raggedy Animal Book. Chicago: Rand.,
(1928). First edition. 4to. Green cloth. Pictorial paste-on.
Full-page color plates, full-page black & whites. Plus page decorations. Very good. Aleph-bet 8-47 1983 $45

CAESAR, GAIUS JULIUS   Commentaries of his Wars in Gaul...
London: by T. Wood, 1737. Sixth edition. 8vo. Cont. speckled calf,
gilt, gilt panelled spine with morocco label, gilt. Engraved frontis.,
title-page printed in red and black, 10 engraved plates, 9 of which
are folding, and 3 folding maps. Traylen 94-146 1983 £35

CAESAR, GAIUS JULIUS   Commentarii Rerum in Gallia Gestarum.
London, Medici Society, 1914. Ltd., numbered edition of 525 copies
only, 4to, 1/2 cloth. Salloch 385-490 1983 $75

CAESAR, GAIUS JULIUS   The Eight Bookes of Caius Julius
Caesar Conteyning His Martiall Exploits in the Realme of Gallia...
London, Thomas Este, 1590. 4to, old straight-grain morocco, quite
worn, rubbed, hinges cracked, title frayed about edges and with some
scribbling, last leaf of text soiled and with cont. scribbling as
well as having a blank strip torn from upper margin not touching any
text. Ravenstree 95-21 1983 $850

CAHOON, GUY F.   Sketches of Dallas. (Dallas), 1933.
Orig. pictorial stiff paper boards. Limited to 400 numbered copies.
Illus. Fine copy. Jenkins 153-597 1983 $35

CAHOON, HERBERT   Thanatopsis. NY: Printed at the
Banyan Press for The Tiger's Eye, 1949. 12mo, linen-backed bds.,
gilt. One of 200 copies (of 206) signed by the poet. Inscribed to
Ruthven Todd. Perata 28-3 1983 $75

CAIN, JAMES M.   Love's Lonely Counterfeit. N.Y., Knopf,
1942. First edition. Red cloth stamped in black, top edge
stained red; with the stamp of the Swanson Literary Agency. Very good.
Houle 22-159 1983 $40

CAIN, JAMES M.   The Magician's Wife. First edition.
Dust jacket (slight rubbing and small creases). Agent's copy with
stamp H.N. Swanson. Very good. Houle 22-160 1983 $40

CAIN, JAMES M.   The Moth. N.Y., Knopf, 1948. First
edition. Dust jacket. Fine. Houle 22-161 1983 $60

CAIN, JAMES M.   The Moth. NY, 1948. Very good in very
good but frayed dustwrapper. Quill & Brush 54-232 1983 $35

CAIN, JAMES M.   Our Government. N.Y., Knopf, 1930.
First edition. Orig. grey cloth stamped in black (bookplate, faded
on spine slightly) else, very good. Houle 22-162 1983 $85

CAIN, JULIEN   Chagall Lithographs... Monte Carlo &
Boston, 1960-69. 3 vols. Orig. lithographs by Chagall. Numerous
colored and other reproductions. Very fine in dj. Jenkins 155-200
1983 $2250

CAIN, JULIEN   Chagall Lithographe, 1962-1968. Monte
Carlo: Andre Sauret, 1969. 1 orig. color lithograph. 195 illus.
Large 4to, cloth, dust jacket with orig. lithograph. Vol. III of the
catalogue raisonne. Ars Libri 32-94 1983 $475

CAINE, HALL   The Bondman. London: Heinemann, 1890.
First edition. 3 vols. Orig. cloth (extremities rather worn; covers
considerably dampstained; soiled). Association copy inscribed "To
my friend Robert Leighton whose very early warm opinion of the 'Bondman' has since been ratified by the public. Hall Caine 17/Feb./90."
MacManus 277-850 1983 $200

CAINE, HALL   The Bondman. London: William Heinemann,
1890. First edition. 3 vols. Orig. cloth. With a 2 page ALS, dated
August 17, 1893, to a Mrs. Meade. Spines a little darkened and worn.
Endpapers foxed. Very good. MacManus 277-851 1983 $200

CAINE, HALL   The Bondman. Wm. Heinemann, 1890.
3rd edition, 3 vols., half titles, 8 pp ads. vol. I, bookplates
removed. Orig. red cloth, very good. Jarndyce 30-321 1983 £18

CAINE, HALL   The Bondman Play. London: The Daily
Mail, 1906. First edition. Illus. with photographs of the cast.
Presentation copy, inscribed in pencil on the front flyleaf: "To
Charles Sharp with best thanks Hall Caine." Some photo. signed by
actors. Good. MacManus 277-852 1983 $50

CAINE, HALL   Capt'n Davy's Honeymoon. London: William Heinemann, 1893. First edition. Orig. cloth. Presentation copy,
inscribed on the flyleaf: "To Edmund Yates with friendly greetings
Hall Caine, 48, Ashley Gardens, Westminster." Yates's bookplate on
front endsheet, and a note. W. Macdonald MacKay bookplate on the rear
pastedown. Cover a little soiled. MacManus 277-853 1983 $50

CAINE, HALL   The Christian. A Story. London: William Heinemann, 1897. First edition. Orig. cloth. Spine faded. Very
good. MacManus 277-856 1983 $25

CAINE, HALL   The Christian. A Drama in 4 Acts.
London: Collier, 1907. First edition. Orig. printed boards. Covers
a bit soiled. MacManus 277-855 1983 $25

CAINE, HALL   The Christian. London: Printed by
Horace Cox, n.d. First edition. Orig. printed wrappers. "Printed for
private circulation and the use of the actors only." Wrappers faded,
somewhat worn. Unopened. Very good. MacManus 277-854 1983 $75

CAINE, HALL   The Deemster. London: Chatto & Windus,
1887. First edition. 3 vols. Orig. decorated cloth. Some foxing.
Laid in is an ALS, 2 pages closely written, 29 Dec. 91, from Caine to
Colles (literary agent). MacManus 277-859 1983 $450

CAINE, HALL   The Drama of Three Hundred & Sixty-Five
Days. London: Heinemann, (1915). First edition. Orig. cloth.
MacManus 277-860 1983 $20

CAINE, HALL   The Eternal City. London: Heinemann,
1901. First edition. Orig. cloth. Inscribed by author. Half morocco
case. Very fine. MacManus 277-864 1983 $45

CAINE, HALL   The Eternal City. London: Heinemann,
1901. First edition. Orig. cloth. Presentation copy, inscribed,
"To E.T. Cook from Hall Caine." Very good. MacManus 277-863 1983
$30

CAINE, HALL   The Eternal City. London: Heinemann,
1901. First edition. Orig. cloth. Near-fine. MacManus 277-861 1983
$20

CAINE, HALL   The Manxman. N.Y.: D. Appleton & Co.,
1895. First American edition. Illus. 2 vols. Orig. gilt parchment.
Limited to 250 copies signed by author at end of preface. Parchment
a little spotted. Fine set. MacManus 866-50

CAINE, HALL   Pete. London: Collier & Co., 1908.
First edition. Orig. pictorial wrappers. Hall Caine's copy, with
numerous holograph annotations and revisions. Wrappers worn and
slightly dust-soiled. Good. MacManus 277-873 1983 $125

CAINE, HALL   The Prodigal Son. London: William Heinemann, 1904. First edition. Orig. cloth. Darkened. Good. MacManus
277-867 1983 $20

CAINE, HALL   The Woman of Knockoloe. London: Cassell
& Co., (1923). First edition. Orig. cloth. Presentation copy in-
scribed on the front free endpaper: "H.R. Saxton from Hall Caine."
Edges slightly worn (small nick in head of spine). Some light foxing.
Rear inner hinges cracking. Very good. MacManus 277-870 1983 $75

CAINE, HALL   The Woman Thou Gavest Me. London: Heinemann, 1913. First edition. Orig. cloth. Very fine. MacManus 277-872
1983 $20

CAIUS, JOHN   A Boke of Counseill Against the Disease
Called the Sweate (1552). New York, 1937. Facs. of the first English
book on sweating sickness. Argosy 713-85 1983 $40

CALDECOTT, RANDOLPH   The Fox jumps over the Parson's Gate.
Routledge, n.d. First edition. Oblong 4to. 6 colour plates & 17
text illus. Colour pictorial wrappers, light wear. Greer 40-76
1983 £12.50

CALDECOTT, RANDOLPH   R. Caldecott's Picture Books. London:
George Routledge & Sons, 1878-1882. First edition(s). 4 vols. Illus.
with black-and-white drawings and color plates by Caldecott. Orig.
pictorial wrappers. Some of the covers a trifle soiled. Scarce.
MacManus 277-874 1983 $300

CALDER, ALEXANDER   Three Young Rats. NY, 1944. 85 Calder
drawings. Dated and signed by Calder. Limited to 700 copies. Edges
worn, some staining to pages and cover, good to very good. Quill &
Brush 54-233 1983 $100

CALDICOTT, J.W.   The Values of Old English Silver and
the Sheffield Plate, from the XVth to the XIXth Centuries. London,
1906. 1st ed. Plates. 4to. Some occasional cover stains. Morrill
289-287 1983 $50

CALDWELL, CHARLES   Thoughts on the Spirit of Improvement...
Nashville: S. Nye, 1835. Later cloth. Morocco label. Jenkins 152-
445 1983 $65

CALDWELL, ERSKINE   All-Out on the Road to Smolensk. N.Y.,
(1942). First edition. Pencilled name. Slightly frayed dust wrapper.
Cloth. Very good. King 45-155 1983 $20

CALDWELL, ERSKINE   American Earth. New York, 1931. 8vo.
Cloth. About fine copy in dj which has some chipping at top edge of
spine. In Our Time 156-135 1983 $150

CALDWELL, ERSKINE   The Bastard. New York: Heron Press,
(1929). 1st ed., one of 200 numbered copies, signed by Caldwell and
illustrator Ty Mahon. Orig. lavender cloth, gilt, uncut. Fine copy.
Jenkins 155-171 1983 $225

CALDWELL, ERSKINE   Georgia Boy. New York, (1943). 8vo.
Cloth. Fine in dj. In Our Time 156-138 1983 $65

CALDWELL, ERSKINE   Journeyman. (N.Y., 1935). Ltd. first
edition. Boxed. Argosy 714-115 1983 $35

CALDWELL, ERSKINE   Kneel to the Rising Sun. New York:
Viking, 1935. 1st ed. Orig. cloth, dj. Fine copy. Jenkins 155-172
1983 $20

CALDWELL, ERSKINE   North of the Danube. N.Y., (1939).
First edition. Photos. by M. Bourke-White. Cloth. Slightly frayed
dust wrapper. Very good. King 45-368 1983 $75

CALDWELL, ERSKINE   Poor Fool. NY, 1930. Illus. by Alex.
Couard. Limited to 1000 copies, edges rubbed, light cover soiling,
few pages carelessly opened, good or better. Quill & Brush 54-235
1983 $125

CALDWELL, ERSKINE   Tenant Farmer. New York, (1935). 8vo.
Wraps. A fine copy. In Our Time 156-136 1983 $125

CALDWELL, ERSKINE   Trouble in July. New York, (1940).
8vo. Cloth. Price clipped, else fine in dj. In Our Time 156-137
1983 $40

CALDWELL, ROBERT G.   The Lopez Expeditions to Cuba, 1848-
1851. Princeton, 1915. Orig. printed wraps. First edition.
Ginsberg 46-213 1983 $25

THE CALEDONIAN Musical Repertory. Edinburgh, Oliver & Boyd, Caledonian
Press, 1811. Engraved frontis., engraved and printed titles, 8vo,
3/4 calf over marbled boards. Some foxing. Engraved frontis. and
the tile are by Mitchell. Engraved title has the imprint of B.
Crosby & Co. Salloch 387-38 1983 $75

CALESTANI, GIROLAMO   Delle Osservationi. Guinti, 1655.
4to, cont. vellum. 2 parts in 1 volume. Some margins frayed and
repaired; last leaf (verso blank) mounted. Argosy 713-86 1983 $100

CALHOUN, GEORGE R.   Report of the Consulting Surgeon on
Spermatorrhoea, or Seminal Weakness... Howard Association, Phil.,
1856. 12mo. Sewn. Morrill 289-34 1983 $22.50

CALHOUN, JANET   Reflecting Many Moods. San Francisco:
The Grabhorn Press, 1948. Edition ltd. to 250 copies. Linen over
boards; paper spine label. Paper dust jacket. Fine. Karmiole 72-
106 1983 $40

CALIFORNIA Gold Discovery. Centennial Papers on the Time, the Site and
Artifacts. S.F.: California Historical Society, 1947. Sm. 4to, red
cloth, gilt. Special Publication Number 21. Illustrated. A very good
copy with title-page vignette by Lowell Hecking. Perata 28-183 1983
$40

CALIFORNIA. Great Register of the County of Mono, State of California.
San Francisco: A. L. Bancroft, 1877. Wrappers, folded. Back wrapper
browned. Very fine. Dawson 471-198 1983 $125

CALIFORNIA: its Past; its Present History; its Present Position; its
Future Prospects... London, 1050. Colored map and two colored
plates. Orig. cloth, rebacked, with leather label. Reese 19-113
1983 $750

CALIFORNIA. LAWS.   The Practice Act of California.
San Francisco, 1856. Full calf, repaired. First edition. Ginsberg
46-106 1983 $125

THE CALIFORNIA Monopolists Against the Sutro Tunnel. (San F.,
1874). Self wrapper. First edition. Ginsberg 47-644 1983 $45

CALIFORNIA. SUPREME COURT   Rules of the Supreme Court of the State
of California. Sacramento: A.J. Johnston, 1892. Orig. cloth.
Jenkins 153-749 1983 $35

CALKINS, CLINCH   Some Folks Won't Work. NY, (1930). Flys
slightly offset from wrapper, light cover soiling, else very good in
lightly chipped and rubbed, internally reinforced dustwrapper, bookplate. Quill & Brush 54-236 1983 $35

CALKINS, EARNEST ELMO   The Lure of Little Ships. NY: 1927.
12mo, boards, paper label. Tipped-in frontis. illustration. One of
300 copies. Fine. Perata 27-206 1983 $30

CALKINS, ERNEST ELMO   The Lure of the Little Ships. New
York: privately printed, 1927. First edition. Square thin 8vo.
Boards. Limited to 300 numbered copies of which this is number 2.
Presentation copy. Tipped-in frontis. Oak Knoll 49-109 1983 $25

CALL, WILLIAM TIMOTHY   The Literature of Checkers... New
York: privately printed, 1908. Tall 12mo. Orig. cloth. Fine.
Oak Knoll 48-412 1983 $35

CALLAGHAN, MORLEY   No Man's Meat. Paris, 1931. Limited to
525 numbered and signed copies, t.e.g., many pages uncut, slightly
nicked, else fine glassine wrapper in wearing, split slipcase. Quill
& Brush 54-237 1983 $150

CALLAHAN, HARRY   Color: 1941-1980. Matrix Publications, R.I. (1980). Large folio. Cloth. Signed by Callahan on
half-title page. Fine copy in slipcase box which has some fading.
In Our Time 156-141 1983 $150

CALLANAN, MARTIN   Records of four Tipperary Septs.
Galway: O'Gorman, ltd., 1938. First edition, errata slip, 8vo, orig.
cloth, with printed paper label. Fenning 61-53 1983 £32.50

CALLAWAY, HENRY   A Memoir of James Parnell, with Extracts
from His Writings. Charles Gilpin, 1846. First edition, with
folding frontis., 12mo, orig. cloth, wanting a flyleaf and with
library label on endpaper, otherwise a nice copy. Fenning 60-54
1983 £10.50

CALLENDER, JAMES H.   Yesterdays in Little Old New York.
New York, 1929. Limited and signed ed., with a presentation from
author. Illus. 8vo, orig. limp leather. Morrill 286-355 1983
$20

CALLENDER, JAMES T.   British Honour and Humanity.
Philadelphia: Robert Campbell, 1796. Disbound. First edition.
Felcone 22-26 1983 $85

CALLIERES, FRANCOIS DE   The Art of Negotiating with Sovereign
Princes. London: for Geo. Strahan, etc., 1716. First English
edition. 12mo. Cont. panelled calf, joints cracking. Traylen
94-147 1983 £48

CALLIMACHUS   Hymni & Epigrammata. Berlin, 1882. Wrs.
8vo, cloth. Salloch 385-494 1983 $20

CALLWELL, C. E.   Military Operations and Maritime Pre-
ponderance. London, 1905. Thick 8vo. Orig. cloth. 3 full page and
9 other text maps. Very slightly worn and soiled. Small ink stamps
and library marks. Bookplate. Good. Edwards 1042-292 1983 £25

CALMEIL, LOUIS FLORENTIN (1798-1895)   De La Paralyse Consideree
Chez Les Alienes. Paris: J.-B. Bailliere, 1826. Half-title. Contemporary calf backed marbled boards, lightly foxed. Gach 95-66
1983 $375

CALVER, EDWARD KILLWICK   The Conservations and Improvement of Tidal Rivers. London, John Weale, 1853. 8vo, original cloth, gilt, large folding coloured lithograph (slightly torn at the fold), and woodcut illus. Deighton 3-64 1983 £21

CALVERT, ALBERT F.   The Discovery of Australia. London: Dean & Son, 1902. 4to, illus. with maps & plates. Index. Green cloth, gilt-stamped. Second edition. Karmiole 71-16 1983 $60

CALVERT, WALTER   Souvenir of Miss Ellen Terry. London: Henry J. Drane, n.d. (1897). 8vo, original pink printed wrappers (foxed). 1st edition, with numerous illus. Nice copy. Ximenes 64-522 1983 $30

CALVERT, WALTER   Souvenir of Sir Henry Irving. London: Henry J. Brane, Chant & Co., n.d. First edition. Illus. Orig. pictorial wrappers, darkened and a bit worn. Very good. MacManus 280-4294 1983 $185

CALVERT, WALTER   Souvenir of Sir Henry Irving. London: Henry J. Drane, Chant and Co., n.d. (1895). 8vo, original light green stiff printed wrappers, 1st edition. Many illus. Fine copy. Ximenes 64-301 1983 $30

CALVESI, MAURIZIO   Umberto Boccioni. Firenze: La Nuova Italia, 1973. 63 color plates (many folding). Folio. Cloth. Ars Libri 33-409 1983 $150

CALVIN, D. D.   A Corner of Empire. Cambridge: University Press, 1937. 22cm. Map, 12 plates and 2 text illus. Fine in dust jacket. McGahern 53-14 1983 $25

CALVIN, IRA   The Lost White Race. Brookline, Mass: Countway-White Publ., n.d. (circa 1920's). Cloth, very good in worn dw. King 46-10 1983 $25

CALVINO, ITALO   The Silent Mr. Palomar. New York: Targ Editions, 1981. Cloth and pictorial boards. First edition. One of 250 copies, printed at the Grenfell Press, and signed by the author. Mint as issued, in plain dust jacket. Reese 20-467 1983 $75

CALVO, CHARLES   Dictionnaire de Droit International Public et Prive. Berlin & Paris, 1885. 2 vols., ex lib. Orig. printed wrs. bound in. Argosy 710-254 1983 $50

CAMAC, C. N. B.   Counsels and Ideals from the Writings of Sir William Osler. Boston, 1906. Second impression. 8vo. Orig. binding. Fine. Fye H-3-874 1983 $40

CAMAC, C. N. B.   Counsels and Ideals from the Writings of Sir William Osler. Oxford, 1906. Second British impression. 8vo. Orig. binding. Fye H-3-875 1983 $40

CAMAC, C. N. B.   Counsels and Ideals from the Writings of Sir William Osler. Oxford, 1908. Fourth British impression. 8vo. Orig. binding. Fye H-3-876 1983 $40

CAMBERT, ROBERT   Les Peines et les Plaisirs de l'Amour. (1672). Paris, n.d. (19th century) (after 1880). With lithograph title and frontis., 4to, wrs. (covers rebacked). Pub.'s rubberstamp (Th. Michaelis, Paris) on title. Salloch 387-39 1983 $80

CAMBRELENG, CHURCHILL C.   Report of the Committee on the Commerce & Navigation of the United States. Washington: Published. Republished in London by John Miller, First London editions, 8vo, wrapper. Fenning 61-54 1983 £45

CAMBRIDGE, ADA   Fidelis. London: Hutchinson, n.d. (1895). First edition. 8vo. Orig. green cloth. 3 vols. Front flyleaves neatly renewed, otherwise a fine copy. Ximenes 63-142 1983 $400

CAMBRIDGE History of American Literature. New York: The Macmillan Co., 1933. 8vo. Cloth. 3 vols. Parts of dust jackets, (worn). Covers aged. Oak Knoll 48-93 1983 $35

CAMBRIDGE History of English Literature. Cambridge, 1932. 15 vols. 8vo. Cloth, gilt. Traylen 94-149 1983 £48

CAMDEN, WILLIAM   Remaines Concerning Britaine. London, Harper, 1636. Engraved portrait frontis. and 26 woodcut coats of arms. Full early panelled calf (rebacked, gatherings E, G, I, and K misbound). Very good. Houle 22-163 1983 $125

CAMERON, D. EWEN   Objective and Experimental Psychiatry. NY: Macmillan, 1941. Second edition. Ex-lib. Gach 94-304 1983 $20

CAMERON, VERNEY LOVETT   Across Africa. George Philip & Son, 1855. Large folding map in end pocket, and over 120 other illus. 8vo. Orig. cloth, t.e.g., inside joints neatly repaired. A very good copy. Fenning 61-55 1983 £55

CAMERON, VERNEY LOVETT   Across Africa. London: Daldy, Isbister & Co., 1877. 2 vols. 8vo. Folding map. 33 plates. Orig. blue pictorial cloth. Lightly rubbed. Adelson Africa-66 1983 $225

CAMERON, VERNEY LOVETT   Across Africa. New York, 1877. Large folding map in pocket and 33 plates, numerous text-illus., orig. gilt-decorated cloth. K Books 307-45 1983 £75

CAMERON, VERNEY LOVETT   Across Africa. New York: Harper, 1877. 8vo. Folding map. 33 plates. Orig. brown pictorial cloth. Lightly rubbed. Adelson Africa-177 1983 $60

CAMMELL, CHARLES R.   The Triumph of Beauty. Edinburgh: The Poseidon Press, 1945. Quarto. Stiff wraps. Ltd. to 250 numbered copies on handmade paper. This copy is inscribed by the author to Martin Secker, and signed. About fine. Reese 20-205 1983 $25

CAMOES, LUIZ VAZ DE   Os Lusiadas. London: Bernard Quaritch, 1880. 2 vols. 12mo. Errata leaf. Orig. gilt decorated green cloth. Rubbed, ex-library. Adelson Africa-51 1983 $100

CAMP, WALTER   American Football. New York, 1891. 31 photo. illus. Cloth, worn. Very good. Reese 19-228 1983 $100

THE CAMPAIGN in Virginia in 1781... London, 1888. 2 vols., first ed., t.e.g., extremely scarce. Jenkins 153-730 1983 $250

CAMPAIGNS of the Civil War. New York, 1882-84. 13 vols., 12mo, top half of front endleaves clipped out, tops of spines rubbed. Morrill 288-52 1983 $75

CAMPAN, JEANNE L. H.   Memoirs of the Court of Marie Antoinette. H.S. Nichols, 1895. With 2 portraits, 2 vols., 8vo, orig. cloth, gilt, a very good copy. Fenning 62-52 1983 £16.50

CAMPANELLA, TOMMASO   De Sensu rerum et magia. Frankfurt: Egenolph Emmel, 1620. First issue. Woodcut headpieces and inter-lace tailpiece, 3 woodcut initials. First issue of title-page without the engraved border, and with bothouter corners clipped off, to denote a cancel (tiny hole in top portion of fore-edge of first 3 leaves). 4to. Orig. vellum over boards. Kraus 164-33 1983 $2,850

CAMPBELL, A.   Santal Folk Tales. Pokhuira: Santal Mission Press, 1891. Some marginal worming. Binders cloth. Presentation copy from Author to Mr. R.M. Douglas. 8vo. Good. Edwards 1044-112 1983 £25

CAMPBELL, C. G.   Tales from the Arab Tribes. London, 1949. First English edition. Numerous full-page black and white drawings and chapter headings by John Buckland-Wright. The words "Complimentary Copy" embossed on the front free endpaper. Spine dull. Nicked dustwrapper slightly darkened at the spine. Very good. Jolliffe 26-63 1983 £25

CAMPBELL, CAMILLA   Galleons Sail Westward. Dallas, 1939. Bold Block prints by Ena McKinney, endpaper maps. First edition. Very fine Josey copy in d.j. Jenkins 153-113 1983 $45

CAMPBELL, DOROTHEA PRIMROSE   Poems. London: printed for the authoress, etc., 1816. Second edition. 8vo. Cont. half calf, spine gilt. In fine condition. Ximenes 63-394 1983 $90

CAMPBELL, DOUGLAS   The Puritan in Holland, England, and America. New York: Harper & Brothers, 1893. First edition. 2 vols. Orig. cloth. Fine. Jenkins 152-46 1983 $46

CAMPBELL, DUNCAN   Nova Scotia. Montreal, 1873. 8vo, cont. calf gilt, scratch on upper cover, small defective spot on lower cover. Bickersteth 75-116 1983 £32

CAMPBELL, DUNCAN   Secret Memoirs of the Late Mr. Duncan Campbell... London, J. Millan and J. Chrichley, 1732. 8vo, later calf gilt, from the library of Walter Wilson. First edition. Ravenstree 94-22 1983 $195

CAMPBELL, F. R.   The Language of Medicine. N.Y., 1888. First edition. Argosy 713-87 1983 $40

CAMPBELL, FRANCIS BUNBURY FITZGERALD   An index catalogue of bibliographical works (chiefly in the English language) relating to India. London: Library Bureau Co., Ltd., 1897. First edition. 8vo. Orig. pink printed wrappers. Trifle dusty, minor wear to spine. Ximenes 62-203 1983 $30

CAMPBELL, G.   India as It May be. London, 1853. 2 maps, rebacked. 8vo. Orig. cloth. Good. Edwards 1044-116 1983 £40

CAMPBELL, G.   Modern India. London, 1853. Second edition revised and corrected. Calf, heavily gilt spine. 8vo. Orig. cloth. Good. Edwards 1044-117 1983 £35

CAMPBELL, HARRY   Differences in the Nervous Organisation of Man & Woman. London, 1891. First edition. Several text illus. Ex-lib. Argosy 713-88 1983 $50

CAMPBELL, HELEN   Darkness and Daylight. Hartford, Conn., 1892. With 232 illus., 8vo, orig. cloth. A very good copy of the cheaper issue, from which the full-page plates were omitted. Fenning 61-56 1983 £18.50

CAMPBELL, HEYWORTH   Camera Around the World. N.Y., (1937). First edition. Mostly illus. Cloth. Blind-stamped names. Moderately worn. King 45-369 1983 $25

CAMPBELL, JAMES V.   Outlines of the Political History of Michigan. Detroit, 1876. Original cloth, first edition, inscribed and signed by the author. Jenkins 151-211 1983 $85

CAMPBELL, JAMES V.   Outlines of the Political History of Michigan. Detroit, 1876. 1st ed., presentation copy, 8vo, some rubbing. Morrill 289-437 1983 $25

CAMPBELL, JOHN (1708-1775)   Lives of the British Admirals. Alexander Donaldson, 1779. Fourth (?) edition. 8vo. Orig. cloth. 4 engraved frontis. 6 fine large folding engr. maps by J. Lodge. 4 vols. Full cont. calf. Red morocco labels on spines. Gilt. Red speckled edges. Some very slight foxing and offsetting. Cont. ink signatures on titles. 4 page publisher's list at end of vol. 4. Good. Edwards 1042-25 1983 £200

CAMPBELL, JOHN (1708-1775)   A Political Survey of Britain. London, for the Author, 1774. First edition, library stamps on titles, 2 vols, 4to, contemporary calf, gilt backs, with morocco labels, gilt spines, a little worn, lacking one label. Deighton 3-65 1983 £55

CAMPBELL, JOHN (1766-1840)   Travels in South Africa. London: London Missionary Society, 1822. 2 vols. 8vo. Folding map. 12 hand-colored plates. Orig. 1/2 tan calf. Rubbed, hinges worn but intact, map cloth backed. Adelson Africa-67 1983 $500

CAMPBELL, JOHN (1766-1840)   Travels in South Africa. London, 1822. First edition, 2 vols. in one, folding map and 12 hand-coloured aquatint plates, in old style half calf. K Books 307-44 1983 £230

CAMPBELL, JOHN FRANCIS   Frost and Fire, Natural Engines, Tool-Marks and Chips with Sketches taken at home and abroad by a Traveller. Edinburgh, 1865. 2 vols., 8vo, folding plate, map, numerous text illus., partly unopened, orig. cloth, gilt. First edition. Bickersteth 75-217 1983 £25

CAMPBELL, JOHN FRANCIS   My circular notes. London: Macmillan, 1876. First edition. 2 vols. 8vo. Orig. grey cloth. 43 wood-engraved plates. Some spotting. A bit rubbed and soiled, spines dark. Ximenes 63-601 1983 $125

CAMPBELL, JOHN W.   The Atomic Story. NY, (1947). Near fine in frayed, soiled, very good dustwrapper. Quill & Brush 54-238 1983 $40

CAMPBELL, JOSEPH   A Skeleton Key to Finnegan's Wake. New York: Harcourt, Brace, (1944). 1st ed. Orig. green cloth, dj. Fine copy. Scarce. Jenkins 155-732 1983 $65

CAMPBELL, JOSEPH   A Skeleton Key to Finnegan's Wake. Fine copy in lightly chipped dj. In Our Time 156-449 1983 $25

CAMPBELL, L.   The Life of James Clark Maxwell... London, 1882. 8vo. Orig. cloth. Portrait, 7 plates (5 colour) & 2 ms. facsimiles. Gurney JJ-263 1983 £20

CAMPBELL, MARIA   Revolutionary Service & Civil Life of General William Hull, Together with the History of the Campaign of 1812 & Surrender of the Post of Detroit. N.Y., 1848. Foxed. Argosy 716-458 1983 $50

CAMPBELL, MARIUS R.   Guidebook('s) of the Western United States. Washington, 1916-1933. 6 vols. Plates and maps. Later cloth. Some staining to text. Jenkins 152-47 1983 $125

CAMPBELL, PATRICK   Travels in the Inhabited Parts of North America... Toronto: The Champlain Society, 1937. 24 1/2cm. Plates. Limited to 550 copies, this being number 356. Red cloth, crested, largely unopened. Binding dust worn, else very good. McGahern 53-96 1983 $125

CAMPBELL, PATRICK   Travels in the Interior Inhabited Parts of North America... Toronton, 1937. Plates. 24cm. Limited to 550 copies, this being number 356. Red cloth. Crested, largely unopened, binding bit dust soiled on the boards else a very good copy. McGahern 54-40 1983 $125

CAMPBELL, ROY   Adamaster. New York, 1931. 8vo. Cloth, boards. From the library of Alexander Laing, signed by same on front fly. Spine faded and dulled, else very good. In Our Time 156-143 1983 $20

CAMPBELL, ROY   The Flaming Terrapin. London, 1924. First edition. Covers marked and two leaves discoloured. Name on flyleaf. Bookplate. Very good. Rota 231-95 1983 £18

CAMPBELL, ROY   The Flying Terrapin. New York, 1924. 8vo. Cloth, boards. Alexander Laing copy, signed by same. Very good copy. In Our Time 156-142 1983 $25

CAMPBELL, ROY   The Gum Trees. Ariel Poems, 1930. First edition. Drawings by D. Jones. One of 300 numbered copies on large paper, signed by author. Very nice. Rota 230-113 1983 £40

CAMPBELL, ROY   Pomegranates: A Poem. London: Boriswood Limited, 1932. First edition. One of 99 numbered copies signed by poet, this being copy No. 7. Drawings by James Boswell. Tan cloth. Very fine in acetate jacket. Bradley 65-40 1983 $200

CAMBPBELL, ROY   Talking Bronco. London, 1946. First edition. Dust wrapper. Author's signed autograph presentation inscription. Very nice. Rota 231-98 1983 £50

CAMPBELL, ROY   Talking Bronco. London, 1946. First edition. Frayed dust wrapper. Fine. Rota 231-97 1983 £15

CAMPBELL, RUTH   The Turtle Whose Snap Unfastened. Volland Pub., (1927). Probably first edition. 8vo. Pictorial boards. Cloth back. Light edgeware. Color illus. by. Ve Elizabeth Cadie. Fine. Aleph-bet 8-256 1983 $25

CAMPBELL, THOMAS   Gertrude of Wyoming. Printed by T. Bensley, published for the author, 1809. First edition, 4to, orig. boards, uncut, with printed paper label, without the inserted slip, a very nice copy. Fenning 62-53 1983 £21.50

CAMPBELL, THOMAS   Gertrude of Wyoming. London: Longman,
Hurst, Rees, and Orme, 1809. First edition. 4to. Orig. boards,
rebacked, uncut. Internally clean. Lacks the half-title, but has
the erratum slip. Lower hinge weak. Cloth slipcase. MacManus 277-
875 1983 $35

CAMPBELL, THOMAS   Letters from the south. London:
Henry Colburn, 1837. 2 vols. 8vo. Folding plan. 10 plates.
1/2 purple calf gilt. Boards rubbed, some foxing to plates.
Adelson Africa-68 1983 $150

CAMPBELL, THOMPSON   Union and Secession. Sacramento, 1863.
Double columns. Dbd. First edition. Ginsberg 47-51 1983 $35

CAMPBELL, W. D.   Beyond the Border. Archibald Constable,
1898. Title vignette. 42 plates & 124 text illus. Dark green cloth
pictorial gilt. 16pp of ads. "Cranford" style presentation.
Greer 40-211 1983 £25

CAMPBELL, WALTER S.   Writing: Advice and Devices. Garden
City: Doubleday, 1950. Cloth. First edition. Fine in dust jacket.
Reese 20-207 1983 $25

CAMPBELL, WILFRED   The Beauty, History, Romance and
Mystery of the Canadian Lake Region. Toronto (1910). Photos,
cloth with pict. label, t.e.g., extremities worn. King 46-31
1983 $35

CAMPBELL, WILLIAM C.   A Colorado Colonel and Other Sketches.
Topeka: Crane & Company, 1901. Illustrations. Original pictorial
cloth. First edition. Jenkins 153-114 1983 $55

CAMPBELL-BROWN, JAMES   A History of Chemistry from the
Earliest Times till the Present Day... London: Churchill, 1913.
First edition. 8vo. Orig. red cloth. Portrait, 106 illus. Cloth
slightly chipped, internally very good. Zeitlin 264-70 1983 $30

CAMPINI, DINO   Giunta Pisano Capitini e le croce
dipinti romaniche. Milano: Aldo Martello, 1966. 41 plates
(20 color). Large 4to. Cloth. Dust jacket. Ars Libri 33-284
1983 $150

CAMPION, THOMAS   Selected Songs of Thomas Campion.
Boston, 1973. Deluxe ed. Tall 8vo. Cloth, decorated boards. 1 of
250 copies. A fine copy in slipcase box. In Our Time 156-32 1983
$100

CAMPOS, JULES   Jose de Creeft. New York: Erich
S. Herrmann, 1945. 42 collotype plates. Illus. 4to. Cloth.
Dust jacket. Printed on fine paper in a limited edition of 700
copies. Presentation copy, boldly inscribed by the artist in red
oil paint to "Curt Valentin, may simpatico friend." Ars Libri
32-150 1983 $150

CAMUS, ALBERT   The Outsider. London: Hamilton,
(1946). 1st English ed. Orig. cloth. Very good. Jenkins 155-176
1983 $20

CAMUS, JEAN PIERRE   The loving enemie. London: printed
by J.G., sold by John Dakins, 1650. First edition in English. 8vo.
Cont. calf, rebacked and restored. One wormhole towards the end,
touching the occasional letter. Ximenes 63-119 1983 $325

CAMUS, JEAN PIERRE   Nature's Paradox. By J.G. for Edw. Dod,
and Nath. Ekins, 1652. First edition in English. 4to, frontis.
engraved by Vaughan. Title in red and black. Nouveau quarter
morocco, blind-tooled, gilt spine, by Henderson & Bissett. Inscribed
on end-paper, "To the Right Honourable H. Dalton, M.P....Christmas
1940". One small hole and two repairs. Some water-stains on first
and last few leaves. Hannas 69-23 1983 £250

CAMUS, JEAN PIERRE   Nature's Paradox. By J.G. for Edw. Dod,
and Nath. Ekins, 1652. Lacks frontis. and "The Minde of the Frontispiece" leaf. Cont. sheep (rather rubbed, with slight damage to
spine). One small worm-hole through book, with trifling loss, one
leaf neatly repaired with loss of a couple of words, a few margins
a little frayed. Hannas 69-24 1983 £85

CANADA. DEPARTMENT OF AGRICULTURE.   Farm Weeds of Canada.
Ottawa, 1909. 4to. Second edition, revised and enlarged. 76 full
colour chromo-litho plates, grey cloth, dust soiled else very good.
McGahern 54-25 1983 $45

CANADA. DEPARTMENT OF THE INTERIOR.   Description of & Guide to
Jasper Park. Ottawa: Dept. of the Interior, 1917. 25cm. 93 photo.
illustrations. Limp green cloth. Fine. McGahern 53-87 1983 $20

CANADA. GEOLOGICAL SURVEY.   Report of Progress, 1882-83-84.
Montreal: Dawson, 1885. Numerous charts, maps and views, some
folding. Half calf, raised bands, double leather labels. Very
good. McGahern 53-17 1983 $50

CANADA. GEOLOGICAL SURVEY.   Summary Report on the Operations of the
Geological Survey for the year 1898. Ottawa: S.E. Dawson, 1899-1900.
2 large folding maps. Rebound in green cloth. Hinges shaken else
very good. McGahern 53-18 1983 $35

CANADA. LAWS.   The King's Regulations and Orders for
the Canadian Militia, 1926. Ottawa: King's Printer, 1926. 21 1/2cm.
Printed red wrappers. Very good. McGahern 53-21 1983 $25

CANADA. NATIONAL GALLERY.   Lawren Harris, Painting 1910-1948.
Catalogue. Toronto, 1948. 16 full-page plates. Stiff illus'd.
wrappers. Fine. McGahern 54-82 1983 $25

CANADA RAILWAY NEWS CO.   All-Round Route and Panoramic Guide of
the St. Lawrence... Toronto, 1923. 20 1/2cm. Numerous illus. 6
folding maps, ads., stiff decorated wrappers. Fine. McGahern 54-31
1983 $35

CANADA. ROYAL COMMISSION.   Quebec Bridge Inquiry, Report.
Ottawa, 1908. 25cm. 4 folding illus. and numerous text drawings.
Green cloth. Very good. McGahern 53-24 1983 $25

CANADA. ROYAL COMMISION.   Report of the Royal Commision to Investi-
gate the Penal System... Ottawa: King's Printer, 1938. 24 1/2cm.
Blue printed wrappers. Fine. McGahern 54-28 1983 $35

CANADA. SENATE.   Report pursuant to Resolution of the
Senate...Relating to the Enactment of the British North America Act...
Ottawa: King's Printer, 1939. 25cm. Printed wrappers. Underlining
else very good. McGahern 53-25 1983 $20

CANAVAN, MYRTELLE M.   Elmer Ernest Southard and His Parents.
Cambridge, Mass., 1925. 1st ed., privately printed. 4to. Orig.
plain dust wrapper. 6 plates and descriptions, nice. Morrill 289-35
1983 $37.50

CANBY, HENRY SEIDEL   Whitman: An American. N.Y., 1943.
First edition. Illus., d.w. Review copy. Argosy 714-811 1983 $20

CANDEE, H. C.   Angkor the Magnificent. London, 1925.
Map. Numerous plates. 8vo. Orig. cloth. Good. Edwards 1044-121
1983 £18

CANDLER, EDMUND   The Long Road to Baghdad. London, 1919.
First edition. Roy. 8vo. Orig. cloth. Frontis. portraits, 1 other
portrait, 7 maps (1 folding and 1 repaired), 12 other maps in text,
13 other plates (1 reinserted). 2 vols. Spines faded and rubbed.
Lower covers slightly marked. Bookplates of the Signet Library on
front paste-down endpapers. Good. Edwards 1042-295 1983 £15

CANDLER, EDMUND   A Vagabond in Asia. Greening & Co.,
1900. First edition, half title, map, plates, 2 pp ads. Orig. red
cloth, t.e.g., v.g. Jarndyce 31-126 1983 £10.50

CANDOLLE, A. P. DE   Astragalogia. Paris, 1802. Roy. folio,
original boards, 50 engraved plates by Redoute. Very scarce Large
Paper edition. Binding worn, with original leather label still
intact. Internally a good clean copy except for a few small wormholes.
Wheldon 160-16 1983 £900

CANDOLLE, A. P. DE   Rapports sur les plantes rares cultivees
dans le Jardin Botanique de Geneve. Geneva and Paris, 1823-47.
28 plates (5 coloured), 10 parts, 4to, wrappers (part 1 unbound,
parts 2 and 4 supplied in xerox). Wheldon 160-1923 1983 £75

CANE, MELVILLE   A Wider Arc. New York, 1947. 8vo.
Cloth. Advance copy with slip from the publisher laid in. A fine
copy in lightly scuffed dj. In Our Time 156-144 1983 $25

CANEPARIO, PETRO MARIA   De Atramentis cujuscunque Generis...
London, 1660. 4to. Cont. calf, gilt back, worn. Lightly browned.
Gurney 90-31 1983 £95

CANEUON Cierog: Detholiad. London: the Gregynog Press, 1925. 4to.
Full orange morocco, gilt. 31 wood-engravings by Horace W. Bray and
R. Ashwin Maynard. Limited edition of 400 numbered copies. Traylen
94-150 1983 £175

CANNING, ALBERT S. G.   British Writers on Classic Lands.
London, 1907. 8vo, cloth. Salloch 385-336 1983 $22

CANNING, GEORGE   Poems. London: 1767. First edition.
Bound with A Translation of Anti-Lucretius by Canning. London: 1766.
Each vol. signed by Canning after dedication. Half-titles. Bound
together in full contemporary leather, spine gilt in six compartments,
red morocco lettering piece. Small piece of leather lacking from
front cover, some wear to edges and hinges. Internally fine. Bromer
25-15 1983 $200

CANNON, DOROTHY   Explorer of the Human Brain, the Life
of Santiago Ramon Y Cajal. New York, 1949. First edition. 8vo.
Orig. binding. Fye H-3-924 1983 $25

CANNON, FRANK J.   Under the Prophet in Utah. Boston:
C.M. Clarke Pub. Co., 1911. 19 cm. Frontis. portrait. Orig. orange
gilt-lettered cloth. Very good; one leaf torn without loss.
First edition in book form. Grunder 7-60 1983 $25

CANNON, MILES   Wailatpu: Its Rise and Fall, 1836-1847.
Boise, 1915. Illus. Orig. printed pictorial wraps. First edition.
Ginsberg 47-918 1983 $35

CANNON, WALTER B.   The Wisdome of the Body. N.Y.? (c. 1939).
Illus. 8vo, ex-lib. Cloth. Argosy 713-89 1983 $60

CANNON, WALTER B.   The Wisdom of the Body. NY: W. W.
Norton, (1939 (1932)). Second edition. Very good ex-library copy.
Gach 94-307 1983 $20

CANOVA, ANTONIO   Lettere inedite di Antonio Canova al
Cardinale Ercole Consalvi. Roma: Forzani & Co., 1888. 2 plates
(1 large folding). Small folio. Orig. wrappers. Ars Libri 33-424
1983 $55

CANTINELLI, RICHARD   Jacques-Louis David, 1748-1825. Paris/
Bruxelles (G. Van Oest), 1930. 90 heliotype plates, large 4to.
Wrappers, dust jacket. Uncut. Printed on fine laid paper. Ars Libri
32-146 1983 $275

CANTIQUES pour la Culte Public. Dordrecht, 1803. 8vo, cont. calf.
Authentication signed in manuscript by S. Geraud, Pasteur de
Rotterdam, Commissaire. Salloch 387-40 1983 $75

CANTON, EDWIN   On the Arcus Senilis. London, 1863.
First edition. Tall 8vo, blind-stamped cloth. Fine lithographic
plates. Argosy 713-90 1983 $65

CANTON, FRANK   Frontier Trails. Boston, 1930. 1st
ed. Plates. Clark 741-246 1983 $48.50

CANTON, FRANK   Frontier Trails. The Autobiography of...
Boston: Houghton, Mifflin, 1930. First edition. Frontis. Portraits.
Orig. cloth in chipped dust jacket. Lower back corner bumped. Jenkins
152-585 1983 $45

CANTON, WILLIAM   A Lost Epic and Other Poems. Edinburgh
and London: William Blackwood and Sons, 1887. 8vo, 17-1/2 cm. Orig.
gilt-decorated green cloth; bevelled boards. A very good copy.
First edition. Grunder 7-10 1983 $37.50

CANTUS, Songs and Fancies. Aberdeen, John Forbes, 1682. Oblong 8vo,
cont. panelled calf restored and rebacked. Woodcut title. Salloch
387-42 1983 $2,750

CANTWELL, ROBERT   Laugh And Lie Down. New York: Farrar &
Rinehart, Incorporated, (1931). First edition. 8vo. Orig. cloth.
Dust jacket. Fine copy. Jaffe 1-50 1983 $85

CANZONE a Ballo composte dal Magnifico Lorenzo de Medici et da M.
Agnolo Politano, & altri Autori. (Milan: Gamba, 1812). One of
one hundred copies of this facsimile reprint of the exceedingly
scarce edition of 1568. Original boards, vignette title page. Light
waterstaining of a few pages, but a very good copy. Trebizond 18-116
1983 $225

CAPEK, KAREL   The First Rescue Party. Lon., (1939).
Fine in very good dustwrapper with few small tears. Quill & Brush 54-
244 1983 $75

CAPEK, KAREL   Intimate Things. NY, 1936. Minor cover
wear, else bright, fine copy in price clipped, slightly chipped and
rubbed dustwrapper, inscription. Quill & Brush 54-240 1983 $30

CAPEK, KAREL   Krakatit. NY, 1925. Edges very slightly
rubbed, near fine in lightly frayed and skinned, very good dustwrapper,
owner's name. Quill & Brush 54-241 1983 $125

CAPEK, KAREL   Letters From England. GC, 1925. 4 page
edges offset from bookmark, bottom edges rubbed, else very good in
remnants of dustwrapper. Quill & Brush 54-242 1983 $30

CAPEK, KAREL   Meteor. NY, 1935. Reviews tipped-in on
front endpapers causing offsetting, else bright fine copy in good dustwrapper with tear mended inside rear cover. Quill & Brush 54-243 1983
$45

CAPEK, KAREL   An Ordinary Life. Lon., (1936). Light
blue cloth, spine and edges slightly discolored, very good in lightly
chipped very good dustwrapper. Quill & Brush 54-239 1983 $60

CAPERN, EDWARD   Ballads and Songs. W. Kent, 1858.
First edition, 4pp opinions of the press. Orig. light green cloth,
v.g. Jarndyce 31-858 1983 £12.50

CAPERN, EDWARD   Poems. London: Bogue, 1856. First
edition. 8vo. Orig. green cloth. Spine slightly faded. Ximenes
63-442 1983 $70

CAPERN, EDWARD   Poems by...Rural Postman of Bideford,
Devon. David Bogue, 1856. Half title, subscribers list, 4pp
opinions of the Press. Orig. light green cloth, v.g. 2nd edition.
Jarndyce 31-857 1983 £15

CAPES, BERNARD   Adventures of the Comte de La Muette.
Edinburgh: Blackwood, 1898. First edition. Orig. cloth. Bookplate.
MacManus 277-878 1983 $20

CAPES, BERNARD   A Castle in Spain. London: Smith, Elder
& Co., 1903. First edition. Orig. cloth. Binding very slightly soiled
and worn (one ocrner bumped). Few pages carelessly opened. Good.
MacManus 277-879 1983 $35

CAPITALS of Europe. London: W. Belch (ca. 1815-1825). Sm. octavo.
Eight leaves of very fine hand-colored plates. New marbled wrappers,
lacking orig. covers. Bromer 25-325 1983 $175

CAPOTE, TRUMAN   The Grass Harp. (N.Y., 1951). Pictorial
title-page. 8vo, cloth; d.w. First edition, first issue. Fine.
Argosy 714-116 1983 $100

CAPOTE, TRUMAN   In Cold Blood. New York, (1965). 8vo.
Cloth. The limited signed edition, being 1 of 500 copies signed by
the author. Fine copy in slipcase box. In Our Time 156-145 1983
$175

CAPOTE, TRUMAN   In Cold Blood. NY, (1965). Advance
reading copy, paperwraps, covers very lightly used, else fine. Quill
& Brush 54-245 1983 $125

CAPOTE, TRUMAN   Observations. NY, (1959). Photographs
by Richard Avedon. Cover lightly bowed and soiled, else very good,
owner's name. Quill & Brush 54-247 1983 $150

CAPOTE, TRUMAN   Other Voices, Other Rooms. New York:
Random House, (1948). First edition. 8vo. Orig. cloth. Dust
jacket. Very fine copy. Jaffe 1-51 1983 $150

CAPOTE, TRUMAN   Other Voices, Other Rooms. New York:
Random House, (1948). 1st ed. Orig. cloth. Near fine copy in
fresh dj. Jenkins 155-177 1983 $85

CAPOTE, TRUMAN   Other Voices, Other Rooms. New York:
Random House, (1948). 1st ed. Orig. cloth. No dj. Jenkins 155-178
1983 $25

CAPP, EDWARD H.   The Story of Baw-A-Ting.
Sault Sainte Marie, Canada 1904. Limited to 300 numbered copies,
signed by the author. Illus., cloth, with list of subscribers.
Slightly worn. King 46-146 1983 $100

CAPPER, JAMES   Observations on the winds and monsoons.
London: printed by C. Whittingham, sold by J. Debrett, etc., 1801.
4to. Cont. mottled calf, spine gilt. First edition. Folding map
of the world. A fine copy. Rare. Ximenes 63-301 1983 $400

CAPPER, JOHN   The Three Presidencies of India. Ingram,
Cooke, 1853. First edition, with 7 plates and 55 other illus., ads.
8vo, orig. cloth, gilt. Fenning 60-58 1983 £16.50

CAPPON, LESTER   Bibliography of Virginia History Since
1865. Univ., VA: Institute for Research in the Social Sciences,
1930. Wrappers browned and worn, internally fine. Dawson 470-51
1983 $20

CAPRON, ELISHA SMITH   History of California, from Its Discovery
to the Present Time... Boston: John P. Jewett, 1854. Original cloth
with minor chipping. Folding map by Colton of California with an inset
of San Francisco. Tear in map neatly repaired. Jenkins 153-89 1983
$125

CAPTAIN Herbert. London: Chapman and Hall, 1864. First edition.
3 vols. 8vo. Orig. green cloth. Slightly rubbed, minor wear to
the top of two joints. Ximenes 63-143 1983 $150

CAPTAIN Jones Expedition. N.Y., N.Y. Tribune Extra No. 14,
Scientific Extra, 1873. 6 columns per page. Map. Dbd. as issued.
Ginsberg 47-983 1983 $75

THE CAPTIVE of Valence. G. & J. Robinson, by W. Meyler, Bath, 1804.
First edition, 2 vols., fronts. 2 vols. bound as one. Mottled calf,
rubbed, hinges weak, black label. Jarndyce 30-272 1983 £90

CARANDENTE, GIOVANNI   Giacomo Serpotta. Torino: Edizioni
RAI Radiotelevisione Italiana, 1967. 32 tipped-in color plates.
75 text illus. Folio. Cloth. Dust jacket. Slipcase. Ars Libri
33-334 1983 $135

CARANDENTE, GIOVANNI   Mattia Preti a Taverna. Roma:
Associazione fra le Casse di Risparmio Italiane, 1966. 24 color
plates. 8 text illus. (2 tipped-in color). Folio. Boards,
1/4 cloth. Dust jacket. Ars Libri 33-292 1983 $75

CARBON, DAMIAN   Libro del arte de las Comadres, o
madrinas... Mallorca: Hernando de Cansoles, 1541. First edition.
Woodcut title, full-page woodcut of the author, woodcut title,
woodcut coat of arms at end, woodcut initials throughout. 4to.
Old vellum. Ms. exlibris of Juan Cerda. Bookplates of Alistair
Livingston Gunn and Alfred K. Hellman. Kraus 164-108 1983 $45,000

CARBONELL Y BRAVO, FRANCISCO Pharmaciae Elementa Chemiae Recentioris
Fundamentis Innix. Barcelona, 1796. Large 4to, old marbled wrs.
First edition, but lacking the title-page. Argosy 713-91 1983 $75

CARBONERI, NINO   L'architetto Francesco Gallo 1672-
1750. Torino: Bertello, 1954. 98 plates. 21 text illus. Large
4to. Boards. Dust jacket. Ars Libri 33-154 1983 $125

CARCEPHALUS, CHRISTOPHORUS   Duodecim Domiciliorum Coelestium Tabula
Nova, pro Inclinatione Spherae sive Altitudine Poli 51. Wratislaviae:
Ex Officina Typographica Georgij Bawmanni, 1600. Modern paper-backed
stiff wrappers. Fine armorial device on verso of title page. Old
library stamp. Extremely scarce. Fine. Trebizond 18-178 1983 $325

CARCOPINO, JEROME   Daily Life in Ancient Rome. New Haven,
1945. 8vo, cloth. Salloch 385-337 1983 $25

CARDAN, GIROLAMO   Contradicentium Medicorum liber...
Venetiis: Scoto, 1545. 8vo, cont. limp vellum. First edition,
lacking the last leaf of index. Argosy 713-92 1983 $600

CARDAN, GIROLAMO   Contradicentium Medicorum Libri Duo.
Paris: Jacobum Macaeum, 1565. 2 vols. in 1. Thick small 8vo, old
calf (rebacked). Argosy 713-93 1983 $650

CARDAN, GIROLAMO   In Septem Aphorismorum Hippocratis Par-
ticulas Commentaria. Basel: Henrichum Petri, 1564. First edition.
Folio, cont. vellum. Rare. Argosy 713-94 1983 $500

CARDAN, GIROLAMO   Opus Novum cunctis de Sanitate Tuenda.
Romae, 1580. First edition. Folio, cont. limp vellum; small exlibris on title. Engr. printer's device on title. Argosy 713-95
1983 $750

CARDELLINI SIGNORINI, IDA   Lorenzini Viani. Firenze: La Nuova
Italia, 1975. 61 color plates (several folding). Folio. Cloth.
Ars Libri 33-604 1983 $75

CARDOZO, BENJAMIN N.   Law is Justice. New York, 1938. First
of 20 copies, of which this is number 8, a special deluxe issue by the
Publisher, bound in full, dark 3/4 blue morocco, a bit worn, over
marbled boards, the spine gilt in compartments, gilt-lettered, top edge
gilt, marbled endpapers. Boswell 7-38 1983 $225

CARERI, J. F. GEMELLI   A Voyage Round the World. London, 1732.
About 40 full-page engraved plates by Picart (some folding). Text
engravings. Folio, three-quarter 19th century calf, spine with raised
bands and black morocco label. Some binding wear and first few leaves
stained in upper blank corner. Uncut edges. Plates with sharp impressions. Fine, tall copy. Jenkins 152-48 1983 $650

CAREW, BAMPFYLDE MOORE   An Apology for the Life of Mr.
Bampfylde Moore Carew. London, n.d. (1760?). Fifth edition.
Eng. frontis., full calf, ink names, hinges cracked, frontis
torn but repaired with thread, worn. King 46-261 1983 $125

CAREW, BAMPFYLDE-MOORE   Life and Adventures: ...with his
Travels twice through great Part of America. London, 1793. 16mo,
orig. blindstamped lea. Argosy 710-98 1983 $100

CAREY, HENRY   Amelia. London: printed for J. Watts,
1732. 1st edition, 8vo, advertisements, wood-engraved head- and
tail-pieces, a few stains in the lower margin towards the end, but a
good copy in modern red quarter morocco. Pickering & Chatto 19-5
1983 $450

CAREY, HENRY   Blunderella. London: Printed for A.
Dodd...MDCCXXX. Folio, largely uncut copy in later wraps. First
edition, with "speech" in line 7, page 8. Quaritch NS 7-19 1983
$750

CAREY, HENRY   The Dragon of Wantley. London: printed
for J. Shuckburgh, 1738. 14th edition, 8vo, pagination on two leaves
shaved, some waterstaining in margins not affecting text, disbound
in wrappers. Pickering & Chatto 19-6 1983 $200

CAREY, HENRY   The Dramatick Works of Henry Carey.
London: printed by S. Gilbert, 1743. 1st edition, 4to, subscribers
list, a little browned at the beginning and end, running-titles and
catchwords occasionally cropped, 19th century polished half calf,
spine gilt. Not a good copy, but a rare book. Pickering & Chatto
19-8 1983 $650

CAREY, HENRY   The Honest Yorkshire-Man. London:
printed for W. Feales...and the booksellers of London and Westminster,
1735. 1st edition, 12mo in sixes, engraved frontispiece, one title
page. A fine copy, uncut in marbled wrappers. Very rare. Pickering
& Chatto 19-7 1983 $2,000

CAREY, HENRY   The Tragedy of Chrononhotonthologos.
London: Printed, and Dublin, Reprinted by George Faulkner, 1735. First
Irish edition. 12mo, wrapper. Rare first Irish edition. Fenning
60-61 1983 £125

CAREY, HENRY C.   Reconstruction: Industrial, Financial,
and Political. Phila., 1867. 8vo, sewed, (rear wr. loose). Argosy
716-501 1983 $25

CAREY, MATHEW   Annals of Liberality, Generosity, Public Spirit, etc. (Phila., 1829). Dbd. First edition. Ginsberg 46-155 1983 $35

CAREY, MATHEW   The Dissolution of the Union a Sober Address to all those who have any Interest in the Welfare, the Power, the Glory, or the Happiness of the United States. Phila., 1832. First edition. Dbd. Ginsberg 46-156 1983 $35

CAREY, MATHEW   Essays Tending to Prove the Ruinous Effects of the Policy of the United States on the Three Classes, Farmers, Planters and Merchants. Phila., Skerrett, 1826. Dbd. First edition. Ginsberg 46-157 1983 $75

CAREY, MATHEW   Carey's General Atlas Improved and En-larged. Phila.: Published by M. Carey, No. 121, Chestnut Street, 1815. Folio. 58 maps, many double page, all with orig. outline color, wide margins. Some offsetting. A few centerfolds split. New endpapers. Bound in full orig. blue paper boards. Respined and cornered in modern morocco. Spine tooled with gold. Boards with some ink stains. Arkway 22-21 1983 $3,500

CAREY, MATHEW   Historical Sketch of, and Remarks upon Congressional Caucuses for President & Vice-President. Phila.: The author, 1816. Disbound. Very good. Felcone 20-20 1983 $20

CAREY, MATHEW   The Olive Branch, or Faults on Both Sides, Federal & Democratic. Boston, Feb. 1815. 12mo, later 1/2 linen, ex lib., some foxing. Enlarged and revised 3rd ed. Argosy 710-563 1983 $35

CAREY, MATHEW   The Olive Branch. Middlebury, Vt., 1816. Old calf. Some scattered foxing, but a very good copy. Reese 18-493 1983 $50

CAREY, MATHEW   The Olive Branch. Philadelphia, 1815. Orig. printed boards, cracking and wear to spine, boards rubbed, but overall very nice. Reese 18-469 1983 $50

CAREY, MATHEW   A Short Account of the Plague, or Malig-nang Fever Lately Prevalent in Philadelphia... London, 1794. Half leather and boards, fine. Reese 18-194 1983 $250

CAREY, PATRICK   Trivial Poems, and Triolets. John Murray, 1820. 4to, orig. half green morocco gilt, a little rubbed. First complete edition. Bickersteth 77-189 1983 £65

CAREY, ROSA NOUCHETTE   Lover or Friend? London: Richard Bent-ley & Son, 1890. First edition. 3 vols. Orig. decorated cloth. Extremities of spines slightly worn. Several inner hinges cracking. Good. MacManus 277-880 1983 $225

CARION, JOHN   The Thre (Sic) Bokes of Cronicles, Whyche John Carion (A Man Syngularly Well Sene in the Mathematical... London, 1550. Quarto, 279 leaves. 1st ed. Half morocco & old marbled boards, a.e.g. Woodcut initials. Some worming in margins of first 40 leaves else very good copy of a scarce ed. Jenkins 155-973 1983 $850

CARITA, ROBERTO   Pietro Francesco Guala. Torino: Soceita Piemontese d'Archeologia e di Belle Arti, 1949. 55 plates (3 color). Tall 4to. Wrappers. Ars Libri 33-179 1983 $125

CARLEN, EMILIE   The Rose of Tistelton. London: Printed for Longman, Brown, Green, and Longmans, 1844. First edition in English. 2 vols. Orig. cloth-backed boards with paper spine labels. Inscribed on the front free endpaper of Vol. 1: "Mrs. W. Moneypenny--with the translator's love. Edinburgh, April 23rd, 1844." All edges slightly worn; labels slightly soiled and frayed. A little light foxing. Very good to near-fine set. MacManus 277-882 1983 $250

CARLETON, GEORGE W.   Our Artist in Cuba. N.Y. & London, 1865. First edition. 12mo. Purple gilt cloth. Shelfwear. 50 cartoons with captions, printed on one side of paper. Very good. Aleph-bet 8-52 1983 $30

CARLETON, JAMES HENRY   Diary of an Excursion to the Ruins of Abo Quarra, and Gran Quivira. (Wash., 1853). First edition. Dbd. Ginsberg 46-161 1983 $75

CARLETON, JAMES HENRY   Diary of an Excursion to the Ruins of Abo, Quarra, and Gran Quivira, in New Mexico, under the Command of Major James Henry Carleton... (Washington), 1855. Cloth, very good. Reese 19-126 1983 $175

CARLETON, JOHN WILLIAM   Hyde Marston; Or, A Sportsman's Life. London: Henry Colburn, 1844. First edition. 3 vols. Orig. cloth-backed boards with paper spine labels (rather worn, darkened & slightly chipped). Spines and covers worn. Good. MacManus 277-883 1983 $300

CARLETON, WILL   City Legends. S. Low, etc., 1889. 20 b&w illus., 4pp adverts. Pale green fine ribbed pictorial cloth, bevelled boards, nice copy. Hodgkins 27-252 1983 £12.50

CARLETON, WILL   Drifted In. NY, 1908. Signed twice and inscribed by author, cover slightly rubbed, back board spotted, else very good. Quill & Brush 54-249 1983 $25

CARLETON, WILL   Farm Ballads. New York: Harper & Brothers, 1882. Frontis. and illus. Jenkins 152-586 1983 $30

CARLETON, WILL   Farm Legends. New York: Harper & Brothers, 1875. Ads. Illus. Orig. pictorial cloth. Jenkins 152-587 1983 $35

CARLETON, WILLIAM   The Black Prophet. Belfast: Simms & McIntyre, 1847. First edition. Orig. light green glazed boards printed in brown. Spine and covers slightly rubbed. Very good. MacManus 277-884 1983 $450

CARLETON, WILLIAM   The Squanders. London: Office of the Illustrated London Library, 1852. First edition. 2 vols. Illus. with 10 full-page wood engraved plates. Orig. silver decorated blue cloth. Covers and spines slightly mold-spotted and rubbed. Former owner's signature. Very good. MacManus 277-885 1983 $450

CARLI, ENZO   La scultura lignea italiana dal XII al XVI secolo. Milano, 1960. Lg. 4to, 90 tipped-in color plates, 131 text illus. Boards, d.j. Ars Libri SB 26-48 1983 $125

CARLI, ENZO   Le sculture del Duomo di Orvieto. (I Grandi Cicli Artistici.) Bergamo, 1947. 53, (3)pp., 70 gravure plates. Tall 4to. Wraps. (worn). Ars Libri SB 26-49 1983 $37.50

CARLI, ENZO   Miniature di Liberale da Verona dai corali per il Duomo di Siena. Milano: Aldo Martello, n.d. 24 tipped-in color plates with commentary. 4to. Cloth. Ars Libri 33-194 1983 $125

CARLI, ENZO   Sassetta e il Maestro dell'Osservanza. Milano: Aldo Martello, 1957. 215 plates (45 tipped-in color). Large 4to. Cloth. Dust jacket. Ars Libri 33-327 1983 $125

CARLI, ENZO   Il Sodoma. Vercelli: Cassa di Ris-parmio di Vercelli, 1979. 173 plates (40 color). 4to. Boards. Slipcase. Ars Libri 33-340 1983 $100

CARLILE, RICHARD   The Deist. London: R. Carlile. 1819-1826. 3 vols. Engraved frontis. in each volume. Each separately printed. Bound in half green calf, gilt, with red spine labels. Karmiole 71-37 1983 $250

CARLISLE, ANTHONY   An Essay on the Disorders of Old Age. London, 1818. Disbound, leather label, ex-lib. Second edition. 8vo, title in red and black. Argosy 713-96 1983 $100

CARLISLE, BILL   Bill Carlisle, Lone Bandit. Pasadena: Trail's End Publishing Co., 1946. Limited and signed by author. Illus. Dust jacket. Presented to the noted bookseller J.C. Dykes. Jenkins 152-588 1983 $50

CARLISLE, BILL   Bill Carlisle, Lone Bandit. Pasadena, (1946). First edition. Photos. Illus. by C.M. Russell. Cloth. Covers water stained. Dust wrapper tattered. Inscribed and signed by author. King 45-139 1983 $20

CARLISLE, BILL ..., Lone Bandit. Pasadena: (1946). First edition. Illus. Map end papers. Red cloth. Signed by author on dedication page. Good copy. Bradley 66-491 1983 $40

CARLISLE, GEORGE W. F. HOWARD, 7TH EARL OF Diary in Turkish and Greek Waters. Longman, Brown, 1854. 24 ads., 8vo. Recent boards, a very good copy. Fenning 61-210 1983 £18.50

CARLISLE, HARRY Darkness at Noon. N.Y., Liveright, 1931. First edition. Inscribed by the author to Norman Taurog. Brown cloth stamped in gilt and red. Spine faded. Good. Houle 22-167 1983 $25

CARLISLE, JOHN M. Red Arrow Men. Detroit, (1945). First edition. Inscribed & signed by author. Drawings by J. Ash. Cloth. Tattered dust wrapper. Very good. King 45-549 1983 $30

CARLYLE, JOHN NEWMAN Sour Music. London: Adam & Charles Black, 1903. First edition. Orig. pictorial cloth. Binding a bit faded and soiled. Inscription erased (carelessly) from front pastedown endpaper. Attractive pictorial design on the spine. Good. MacManus 277-886 1983 $35

CARLISLE, WILLIAM L. Bill Carlisle, Lone Bandit. Pasadena, 1946. Illustrations. First edition. Jenkins 153-117 1983 $30

CARLTON, ROBERT The New Purchase; or, Early Years in the Far West. New Albany, Ind., (1855). 4 plates (by Momberger). Cloth. Covers worn, interior rather foxed. Sound. Felcone 20-66 1983 $45

CARLTON, WILLIAM J. Charles Dickens, Shorthand Writer. 1926. First edition, half title, 12 illus., 2 pp ads. Orig. blue cloth, faded on spine. Jarndyce 30-146 1983 £12.50

CARLYLE, ALEXANDER Autobiography of the Rev. Dr. Alexander Carlyle, Minister of Inveresk. Edinburgh, 1860. 2nd edition, portrait, half black calf. K Books 301-40 1983 £30

CARLYLE, THOMAS Address At Edinburgh, April 1866. London: Chapman & Hall, 1866. First edition. Orig. printed wrappers. Loosely laid in is the pictorial front cover of "On the Choice of Books. An Address." Spine and covers lightly worn and soiled. Near-fine. Mac-Manus 277-899 1983 $125

CARLYLE, THOMAS Collected Works. London: Chapman & Hall, (1869-71). Reissue of the Library Edition. 34 vols. Profusely illus. with engravings and photo-mechanical full-page plates. 3/4 morocco with marbled boards and endpapers. With the additional 3 vols. of translations and an index, printed with large type on excellent paper, which contains an abundance of full plate illus. Spines and cover corners a trifle rubbed. MacManus 277-897 1983 $1,100

CARLYLE, THOMAS Early Letters (1814-1826). Macmillan, 1886. First edition, 2 vols. Front. Half titles, orig. dark olive cloth, v.g. Jarndyce 30-937 1983 £12.50

CARLYLE, THOMAS German Romance. Edinburgh: Wm. Tait, 1827. First edition, 4 vols. Half titles, engr. titles. Orig. grey boards, green cloth spines sl. rubbed, paper labels a little worn. Jarndyce 31-470 1983 £85

CARLYLE, THOMAS History of Friedrich II of Prussia. London: Chapman & Hall, 1858-1865. First edition. 6 vols. Illus. Three-quarter morocco with marbled boards. Frontis. stained in Vol. 5. Former owner's signature. Near-fine. MacManus 277-888 1983 $250

CARLYLE, THOMAS Jocelin of Brakelond, From Past to Present. N.Y.: William Edwin Rudge, 1923. 12mo. Orig. cloth. One of 500 copies printed by Bruce Rogers. Good. MacManus 277-890 1983 $25

CARLYLE, THOMAS Jocelin of Brakelond. New York: William Edwin Rudge, 1923. Black cloth. 1/510 numbered copies designed and printed by Bruce Rogers. Fine. Bradley 66-300 1983 $25

CARLYLE, THOMAS Latter-Day Pamphlets. Boston: Phillips, Sampson, 1850. 1st American ed. Bound from the 8 parts, without wrappers. Contemporary 3/4 sheep. Good tight copy with worn spine. Jenkins 155-180 1983 $60

CARLYLE, THOMAS Letters...to His Younger Sister. Chapman & Hall, 1899. First edition, orig. dark green cloth, ports. and other illus. Orig. dark green cloth, very good. Jarndyce 30-941 1983 £12.50

CARLYLE, THOMAS The Life of John Sterling. London: Chapman & Hall, 1851. First edition. Orig. cloth. Fine. MacManus 277-892 1983 $135

CARLYLE, THOMAS Life of Robert Burns. N.Y.: American Book Exchange, 1880. Orig. yellow printed wrappers (a bit split at top of spine). Fine. MacManus 277-891 1983 $20

CARLYLE, THOMAS On Heroes, Hero-Worship, and the Heroic in History. Chapman & Hall, 1852. 4th edition, orig. brown cloth, sl. rubbed. Jarndyce 31-472 1983 £14.50

CARLYLE, THOMAS On the Choice of Books. John Camden Hotten, 1866. First edition, two portraits. Disbound. Jarndyce 31-473 1983 £10.50

CARLYLE, THOMAS Past and present. London: Chapman and Hall, 1843. First edition. 8vo. Orig. blue cloth. Slight wear. Ximenes 63-343 1983 $125

CARLYLE, THOMAS Past and Present. Chapman & Hall, 1843. First edition, half title. Orig. blue cloth, inner hinges cracked, rubbing to head and tail of spine. Jarndyce 31-471 1983 £18.50

CARLYLE, THOMAS Reminiscences. London: Macmillan & Co., 1887. First edition. 2 vols. Maps. Orig. cloth. Bookplates. Very good. MacManus 277-894 1983 $75

CARLYLE, THOMAS Reminiscences. London: Longmans, Green & Co., 1881. First edition. 2 vols. Orig. cloth. Publisher's blind-stamped presentation copy. Good. MacManus 277-893 1983 $35

CARLYLE, THOMAS Reminiscences. Longmans, 1881. First edition, 2 vols. Front. vol. 1. Half titles, orig. green cloth. Jarndyce 30-935 1983 £16.50

CARLYLE, THOMAS Reminiscences of My Irish Journey in 1849. London: Sampson, Low, Marston, Searle, & Rivington, 1882. First edition. Orig. cloth. Very fine. MacManus 277-895 1983 $75

CARLYLE, THOMAS Reminiscences. Macmillan, 1887. First edition, 2 vols. Half titles, map fronts. 2 pp ads. in both vols. Orig. olive cloth. Jarndyce 30-938 1983 £16.50

CARLYLE, THOMAS Sartor Resartus. G. Bell, 1898. Frontis. 12 plates & 66 text illus., on Japanese vellum. Dusty cream linen. Edition limited to 150 copies, No. 149. Extra Plate. Greer 40-214 1983 £65

CARLYLE, THOMAS Sartor Resartus: the Life and Opinions of Herr Teufelsdroeckh. London: the Doves Press, 1907. 4to. Orig. vellum, gilt, uncut edges. Limited edition of 300 copies, printed in red and black. Traylen 94-153 1983 £180

CARLYLE, THOMAS Sartor resartus: the life and opinions of Herr Teufelsdrockh. London: Chapman and Hall, 1849. 8vo. Cont. half calf. Third English edition. Presentation copy, inscribed on the endpaper: "To Miss Williams Wynne with many kind regards: T. Carlyle. Chelsea, 12 Decr. 1848." Early photograph of Carlyle pasted to the flyleaf. Slight wear to calf. Slight browning. Ximenes 63-344 1983 $150

CARLYLE, THOMAS Shooting Niagara; And After? London: Chapman & Hall, 1867. First edition. 12mo. Orig. printed wrappers. Brittle wrappers & backstrip rather chipped. MacManus 277-896 1983 $20

CARLYLE, THOMAS Carlyle's Unpublished Lectures. Bombay: Curwen, Kane; London: T.G. Johnson "Times of India" Office. Half title, orig. pink cloth, sl. marked. Jarndyce 31-474 1983 £20

CARMAN, BLISS   Four Sonnets. Boston, (1916). 8vo. Stitched wrappers. Total edition is 438 copies printed for private distribution. Rear wrapper has a tiny chip at one corner, else a fine copy. This copy signed by author on the half-title page. In Our Time 156-146 1983 $150

CARMAN, BLISS   The Kinship of Nature. Bos., 1903. Signed inscription from Carmen on front fly, edges rubbed and slightly worn at top spine, very good. Quill & Brush 54-252 1983 $125

CARMAN, BLISS   Later Poems. Boston, Small, (1922). First edition. Dust jacket. Inscribed by the author: "For Harold Carew from his friend B.C., Sierra Madre, 5 April, 1903, Bliss Carman." Light soiling, else very good. Houle 21-197 1983 $250

CARMAN, BLISS   The Rough Rider. NY, 1909. Flexible covered boards, slightly rubbed and soiled, interior bright and clean, very good. Quill & Brush 54-253 1983 $100

CARMAN, BLISS   Sanctuary. NY, 1929. Fine bright copy in very good dustwrapper with few short tears, illus. by Whitman Bailey, owner's name. Quill & Brush 54-251 1983 $35

CARMAN, BLISS   Sappho: Lyrics. N.p., Privately printed, 1902. One of 60 copies. Stiff printed tan wraps., stitched. Some light soiling, else, very good. Presentation copy, inscribed: "To my friend, Laureus Maynard, New York, April, 1903, Bliss Carman." Houle 22-165 1983 $250

CARMAN, BLISS   A Vision of Sappho. N.p., privately printed, 1903. Tall 8vo, printed blue wraps. One of 60 copies. Inscribed by the author: "Laureus Maynard, from B.C." Very good copy. Houle 21-198 1983 $250

CARMAN, BLISS   Wild Garden. New York, 1929. 12 mo. Cloth. Fine in near perfect dj. In Our Time 156-147 1983 $20

CARMICHAEL, C. P.   Report on the Administration of the Police of the North-Western Provinces... Allahabad, 1872. 2 folding tables. Folio, half calf, rubbed. 8vo. C. P. Carmichael's own copy. Good. Edwards 1044-122 1983 £50

CARMICHAEL, C. P.   Report on the Administration of the Police of the North-Western Provinces... Allahabad, 1873. 2 folding tables. Folio, half calf, rubbed. 8vo. C.P. Carmichael's own copy. Good. Edwards 1044-123 1983 £50

CARMICHAEL, JOHN WILSON   Views on the Newcastle and Carlisle Railway, from Original Drawings by J. W. Carmichael. Currie and Bowman, Newcastle, Turnham, Carlisle, C. Tilt, London, 1836. First edition. 4to, steel engraved title and 23 steel engraved views, all printed on India paper and mounted; cont. half crimson morocco. Quaritch NS 5-20 1983 $2,250

CARMICHAEL, RICHARD   Essay on Venereal Diseases. Phila., 1825. First American edition. 5 colored fold. litho plates. 1/4 calf (top of title page cut out). Argosy 713-97 1983 $50

THE CARNATIC question stated. London: Stockdale, 1808. First edition. 8vo. Disbound. Ximenes 63-204 1983 $60

CARNE, JOHN   Letters from the East. London, 1826. Second edition. Coloured frontis. 2 vols. Sm.8vo. Half calf. Good. Edwards 1044-124 1983 £85

CARNE, JOHN   Letters from the East. 1826. Second edition, 2 vols., col'd litho frontis., half calf, minor rubbing. K Books 301-41 1983 £55

CARNES, JOSHUA A.   Journal of a voyage from Boston to the west coast of Africa. Boston: John P. Jewett, 1852. 12mo. Orig. red cloth, rubbed. Adelson Africa-69 1983 $100

CARNEVALLI, EMANUEL   A Hurried Man. (Paris): Contact Editions, (1925). Printed wraps. First edition. A very fine, unopened copy. Reese 20-222 1983 $175

CAROLI, FLAVIO   Lorenzo Lotto. Firenze: Edizioni d'Arte Il Fiorino, 1975. 16 color plates. 159 illus. Small folio. Cloth. Dust jacket. Ars Libri 33-202 1983 $125

CAROLINE OF BRUNSWICK, QUEEN   The Queen's letter to the King. London: Limbird, sold by T. Dolby, 1820. 8vo. Disbound. Ximenes 63-480 1983 $25

CARPENTER, ALFRED   Nature Notes for Ocean Voyages. London: Charles Griffin & Co., ltd. 1915. Tall 8vo, folding map. Index. Dark blue cloth, faded. Karmiole 75-96 1983 $35

CARPENTER, EDWARD   The Art of Creation. London, 1904. First edition. Presentation copy from the author, inscribed. T.e.g. Spine faded. Edges spotted. Very good. Jolliffe 26-80 1983 £45

CARPENTER, G. D. H.   A Naturalist on Lake Victoria. 1920. 2 coloured plates, a map, 7 charts and 87 illustrations. 8vo, original cloth, covers trifle stained. Wheldon 160-354 1983 £35

CARPENTER, WILLIAM   Principles of Mental Physiology. NY: Appleton, 1874. First American edition. Lacking front endpapers, else very good copy in publisher's decorative cloth. Gach 94-532 1983 $75

CARPENTRY and Contracting. Chicago, American Technical Society, 1920. Over 1500 illustrations. 5 vols., 8vo, original limp leatherette. Morrill 290-54 1983 $35

CARPI, ALDO   Via Crucis. Milano: Parrocchia di S. Maria del Suffragio, 1933. 19 plates. Large 8vo. Wrappers. Ars Libri 33-427 1983 $20

CARR, EMILY   The House of All Sorts. Toronto, London: Oxford University Press, 1944. 22 1/2cm. Second printing. 4 colour plates. Good to very good. McGahern 54-34 1983 $45

CARR, HARRY   The West is Still Wild. Boston: Houghton, Mifflin, 1932. First edition in dust jacket. Illus. Signed by author and illustrator. Jenkins 152-589 1983 $30

CARR, JOHN   Pioneer Days in California... Eureka, 1891. Portrait. Original cloth. Fine copy. Jenkins 153-118 1983 $150

CARR, JOHN   A Vulcan Among the Argonauts. San Francisco, 1936. Edn. lim. to 500 copies, signed by the editor. Illus. Clark 741-89 1983 $30

CARR, JOHN DICKSON   He Who Whispers. NY, (1946). Spine edges rubbed, else very good in lightly chipped and soiled, still presentable dustwrapper. Quill & Brush 54-256 1983 $35

CARR, JOHN DICKSON   The Life of Sir Arthur Conan Doyle. NY, (1949). Tiny tear at top spine edge, else very good or better in frayed and lightly chipped, price clipped, good dustwrapper. Quill & Brush 54-382 1983 $30

CARR, JOHN DICKSON   The Sleeping Sphinx. London, 1947. First English edition. Chipped and slightly torn and rubbed dustwrapper. Very good. Jolliffe 26-127 1983 £15

CARRA, MASSIMO   Carlo Carra. Firenze: La Nuova Italia, 1980. 62 color plates (partly folding). Folio. Cloth. Ars Libri 33-429 1983 $125

CARREL, ALEXIS   Transplantation in Mass of the Kidneys. N.Y., 1908. First edition. 8vo, new wrs. Argosy 713-98 1983 $200

CARRIERI, RAFFAELE   12 opere di Piero Marussig. Milano: Edizioni del Milione, 1942. 12 tipped-in color plates. Small folio. Wrappers. Ars Libri 33-520 1983 $20

CARRIGAN, MINNIE B.   Captured by the Indians. (Buffalo Lake, Minn., 1912). Orig. printed pictorial wraps. Ginsberg 46-472 1983 $75

CARRINGTON, J. F.   Talking Drums of Africa. London: Carey Kingsgate Press, 1949. Illus. Small 4to. Cloth. Dust jacket. Ars Libri 34-582 1983 $20

CARRISSO, L. W.   Conspectus Florae Angolensis. Lisbon, 1937-77. Maps, photographs and numerous line drawings, 4 vols. and index, in 8 parts, royal 8vo, wrappers. Vols. 1-3 pt. 1 are clean second-hand copies. Wheldon 160-1659 1983 £60

CARROLL, LEWIS, PSEUD.
Please turn to
DODGSON, CHARLES LUTWIDGE

CARROLL, H. BAILEY   The Texan Santa Fe Trail. Canyon, Texas, 1951. First edition. In slipcase. Illus. Maps. Index. Jenkins 152-788 1983 $85

CARROLL, JOHN M.   Eggenhofer: The Pulp Years. Fort Collins, 1975. 145pp. Illustrations by Nick Eggenhofer. Autographed edition limited to 250 copies signed by John Carroll and Jeff Dykes. Jenkins 151-33 1983 $125

CARROLL, WALTER   River & Rainbow. Forsyth Bros., n.d. (1934). 4to, colour pictorial top wrapper and pictorial title, dusty. Greer 40-179 1983 £12.50

CARRUTHERS, D.   Beyond the Caspain, a naturalist in Central Asia. 1949. Folding coloured map, 6 coloured and 15 plain plates, 8vo, cloth. Wheldon 160-355 1983 £38

CARRYL, GUY WETMORE.   Fables for the Frivolous. New York, 1904. 8vo. Decorated cloth. A new ed. of the work, with illus. by Peter Newell. Some light rubbing to extremities of the spine, bookplate. This copy contains an ALS from Newell. A fine copy. In Our Time 156-592 1983 $75

CARRYL, GUY WETMORE   Mother Goose for Grown-ups. N.Y., 1900. First edition. 5 plates by P. Newell and G. Verbeek. Pictorial cloth. T.e.g. Extremities worn (back cover spotted). King 45-413 1983 $45

CARRYL, GUY WETMORE   The Transgression of Andrew Vane. N.Y., 1904. First edition, 8vo, red cloth. Argosy 714-141 1983 $25

CARSE, ROLAND   Monarchs of Merrie England. Alf Cooke, n.d. 4 vols. 4to. 8 colour plates & 137 text illus. Colour pictorial wrappers with extra designs. Greer 40-195 1983 £45

CARSON, CHRISTOPHER   Kit Carson's Own Story of His Life. Taos, 1926. First edition. 13 plates. Decorated green wrappers. Nice. Bradley 64-35 1983 $35

CARSON, KIT   Autobiography. Chicago, Lakeside Press, 1935. Illus., gilt top. Clark 741-176 1983 $24.50

CARSON, RACHEL L.   The Sea Around Us. NY, 1951. First edition. 8vo, pict. boards, d.w. Presentation copy. Argosy 714-143 1983 $85

CARSON, RACHEL L.   The Sea Around Us. New York: Oxford Univ. Press, 1951. 1st ed. Orig. pictorial boards, dj. Very fine fresh copy. Jenkins 155-184 1983 $75

CARSON, RACHEL L.   The Sea Around Us. NY, 1980. Limited Editions Club. Limited to 2000 numbered copies. Photographs by Eisenstaedt, signed by Eisenstaedt, fine in glassine wrapper in fine slipcase. Quill & Brush 54-257 1983 $75

CARTER, CLARENCE E.   Territorial Papers of the U.S.: The Territory of Orleans, 1803-1812. Wash., 1940. Orig. cloth. First edition. Ginsberg 47-445 1983 $35

CARTER, ELIZABETH   Poems on Several Occasions. London: Printed for John Rivington...MDCCLXII. 8vo, later wraps. First edition, with signed dedication. Quaritch NS 7-20 1983 $275

CARTER, ELIZABETH   Poems on several occasions. London: Rivington, 1766. Second edition. 8vo. Cont. calf, gilt. Ximenes 63-357 1983 $175

CARTER, HENRY   Yellow Fever: An Epidemiological and Historical Study of its Place of Origin. Baltimore, 1931. 8vo. Orig. binding. First edition. Fye H-3-73 1983 $50

CARTER, HOSEA B.   Political Memorial of New Hampshire, 1876. East Hampstead, 1876. 3 colored maps on one sheet, 17 x 27 inches, contained in the original. 12mo, cloth, nice. Morrill 290-337 1983 $45

CARTER, JEAN   Annotated List of Labor Plays. New York: Affiliated Schools for Workers, Inc., 1938. 4to. Paper wrappers. Covers worn. Oak Knoll 48-411 1983 $20

CARTER, JOHN   A. E. Housman, An Annotated Check-List. London: The Bibliographical Society, 1940. Orig. printed wrappers. Presentation copy to Sir Sydney Cockerell inscribed on the front free endpaper: "For Sir Sydney Cockerell from John Carter, April 1941." Contains several holograph corrections in the text. Spine and covers slightly darkened and rubbed. Good. MacManus 279-2780 1983 $125

CARTER, JOHN   An enquiry into the nature of certain nineteenth century pamphlets. 1934. First edition, 8vo, 4 plates, t.e.g., cloth gilt, very good. Deighton 3-67 1983 £110

CARTER, JOHN   An Enquiry into the Nature of Certain Nineteenth Century Pamphlets. London, 1934. First edition. 8vo. Cloth. Orig. dustwrapper. 4 plates. A presentation copy, inscribed "for Roger from Margaret Furse and John Carter, April, 1937." Traylen 94-162 1983 £95

CARTER, JOHN   Printing and the Mind of Man... (New York & London, 1967). Cloth in dw, nearly new. Dawson 470-53 1983 $200

CARTER, JOHN   The progress of architecture... London: J.B. Nichols, 1830. First edition. 4to. Orig. drab boards. With 7 plates. Fine copy. Ximenes 63-11 1983 $125

CARTER, MARY E.   Mrs. Severn, A Novel. London: Richard Bentley & Son, 1889. First edition. 3 vols. Orig. red cloth. Spines and covers slightly faded and worn. Very good. MacManus 277-901 1983 $250

CARTER, MATTHEW   Honor Redivivus or an Analysis of Honor and Armory. Printed for Henry Heringman and are to be sold by Henry Herringman, 1660. Engraved frontis., engraved title-page, 7 plates and many woodcut coats of arms in the text, 8vo, cont. sheep, neatly rebacked, a very good copy. Fenning 60-62 1983 £65

CARTER, NATHANIEL H.   Pains of the Imagination, a Poem, Read Before the Phi Beta Kappa Society at Dartmouth College, August 19, 1824. New York, 1824. Later half morocco and boards, fine. Inscribed by the author to jurist Chancellor Kent, on the title page. Reese 18-572 1983 $85

CARTER, NELLIE PAGE   Persimmon Creek. N.Y.: Longmans, 1938. Advance Review Copy. 8vo. Cloth. Dust wrapper. Illus. in black & white. Fine. Aleph-bet 8-181 1983 $25

CARTER, T. D.   Mammals of the Pacific World. New York, 1945. 69 figures, 8vo, cloth. Ink stain on fore-edge, contents not affected. Wheldon 160-546 1983 $20

CARTER, THOMAS   Medals of the British Army. London, 1861. 8vo. Orig. cloth. 3 coloured frontis. and 15 coloured plates heightened in silver and gilt (some tarnished and faded), 5 illus. 3 vols. A.e.g. Slightly worn and faded. Bookplates. Good. Edwards 1042-297 1983 £80

CARTER, THOMAS J. P.   Kings College Chapel. (Cambridge): Macmillan, 1867. 1st edn. Mounted photo. frontis. & folding plan. Purple cloth, uncut (Binder's ticket of Burn & Co.) (fr. ep. broken at hinge, occasional fox mark, bkstrip darkened with sl. wear top/bottom), v.g. Hodgkins 27-345 1983 £25

CARTER, WILLIAM H.   Horses, Saddles and Bridles. Baltimore, 1906. 3rd ed., corrected and enlarged. Illus. 8vo, some darkening on perimeter of covers. Morrill 288-55 1983 $35

CARTERET, JOHN DUNLOE   A Fortune Hunter. Cincinnati, 1888.
First edition. Cloth. Fine copy. Bradley 66-662 1983 $45

CARTERET, JOHN DUNLOE   A Fortune Hunter. Cincinnati, 1888.
Orig. cloth. First edition. Ginsberg 47-213 1983 $35

CARTIER, JACQUES   Voyage au Canada: La Mission...
(Paris), 1935. Illus., 18 plates. 4to, orig. pictorial printed
wraps. First edition. Ginsberg 46-162 1983 $25

CARTIER-BRESSON, HENRI   The People of Moscow. N.Y., 1955. First
edition. Photos. Buckram, front hinge loose, slightly chipped and
torn dust wrapper. King 45-370 1983 $135

CARTIER-BRESSON, HENRI   The People of Moscow. New York: Simon &
Schuster, 1955. Quarto. Rough woven linen. Photographs by the
author. Spine very slightly tanned, else a fine copy, sans dust
jacket. Ink sentiment. Reese 20-226 1983 $85

CARTWRIGHT, EDMUND   Armine and Elvira. London: Printed
for J. Murray...MDCCLXXI. 4to, engraved vignette by Isaac Taylor
on title, lacking half-title, title-page a bit worn and mounted but
a good copy, disbound. First edition. Quaritch NS 7-21 1983 $65

CARTWRIGHT, THOMAS   A Confvtation of the Rhemists
Translation, Glosses and Annotations on the Nevv Testament. (Leyden:
Pilgrim Press), 1618. Small folio, quarter calf. David Gibson
ownership inscription, repeated. Lower corner of Bb3 torn with loss
of few letters of text; leaves CCCC1 and MMMM3-4 missing. Rostenberg
88-10 1983 $750

CARTY, JAMES   Bibliography of Irish History, 1912-1921.
Dublin: National Library of Ireland, 1940. 8vo, orig. cloth, a fine
copy. This is the second of two vols. Only 750 copies were printed.
Fenning 62-54 1983 £26.50

CARUS, C. G.   Psyche. Jena: Diederichs, 1926. Spine
tips very lightly worn. Gach 94-126 1983 $25

CARVALHO, SOLOMON N.   Incidents of Travel and Adventure in
the Far West. New York, 1856. Cloth-backed boards (worn, paper
spine label worn away). First edition. Felcone 22-27 1983 $75

CARVER, HARTWELL   A Memorial for a Private Carter. (Washington): J. & G. S. Gideon, printers, (January 1849). First edition.
Uncut and unbound. Library file numbers in ink at top of first page,
folded twice. Last leaf detached. Laid into folding cloth protective
case. Bradley 66-492 1983 $185

CARVER, RAYMOND   At Night the Salmon Move. Santa Barbara:
Capra Press, 1976. Cloth and pictorial boards. First edition. One of
100 numbered copies, specially bound and signed by the author. Fine.
Reese 20-228 1983 $75

CARVER, ROBIN   Anecdotes of Natural History. Boston,
1833. First edition. 120 woodcuts. 12mo. Argosy 716-227 1983
$75

CARY, JOHN   Cary's New Map of England and Wales,
with Part of Scotland. London: G & J Cary, May 1, 1824. 2nd ed.,
2nd impression, 4to, engraved title-page, coloured map,
advertisements, rebound in modern half calf, gilt, contemporary
marbled sides, endpapers, very slight foxing in upper margin
of 4 sheets, otherwise a fine copy. Deighton 3-69 1983 £155

CARY, JOHN   An Essay Towards Setling a National
Credit, in the Kingdom of England. London: printed by Freeman
Collins, to be sold by S. Crouch and E. Whitlock, 1696. First ed.,
small 8vo, headlines shaved but else a very good copy in modern grey
wrappers. Scarce. Pickering & Chatto 21-18 1983 $550

CARY, JOYCE   The African Witch. London: Victor
Gollancz Ltd., 1936. First edition. 8vo. Orig. cloth. Dust
jacket. Yellow jacket slightly faded, otherwise a fine copy. Jaffe
1-53 1983 $65

CARY, JOYCE   Aissa Saved. London: Ernest Benn
Limited, (1932). First edition. 8vo. Orig. cloth. A fine copy.
Rare. Jaffe 1-52 1983 $250

CARY, JOYCE   Aissa Saved. London, 1932. First
edition, second binding. Frayed late dust wrapper. Fine. Rota
231-99 1983 £15

CARY, JOYCE   An American Visitor. London, 1933.
First edition, first binding. Black cloth lettered in gilt. Nice.
Rota 231-100 1983 £35

CARY, JOYCE   Britain and West Africa. London, 1946.
First edition. Photographs. Wrappers. Fine. Tora 231-104 1983 £20

CARY, JOYCE   Castle Corner. London: Victor Gollancz,
Ltd., 1938. First edition. 8vo. Orig. cloth. Dust jacket. Jacket
slightly darkened and torn, but a very good copy. Jaffe 1-54 1983
$65

CARY, JOYCE   The Drunken Sailor. London, 1947.
First edition. 3 full-page black and white drawings by the author.
Dustwrapper. Fine. Jolliffe 26-86 1983 £30

CARY, JOYCE   A Fearful Joy. London, 1949. First
edition. Author's autograph presentation inscription and autograph
signature. Nice. Rota 231-106 1983 £40

CARY, JOYCE   A Fearful Joy. London, 1949. First
edition. Nicked dustwrapper. Fine. Jolliffe 26-87 1983 £15

CARY, JOYCE   The Horse's Mouth. London: Michael
Joseph, (1944). Cloth. First edition. Foxing of wartime paper,
otherwise near fine in dust jacket, with Book Society Wraparound
intact. Reese 20-229 1983 $45

CARY, JOYCE   Illustrations by Joyce Cary for The Old
Strife at Plant's. At the New Bodleian, Oxford, 1956. First edition.
One of 100 numbered copies, signed by Cary. Orig. grey wrappers. Fine.
Rota 231-108 1983 £50

CARY, JOYCE   Marching Soldier. London, 1945. First
edition. Dust wrapper. Fine. Rota 231-103 1983 £15

CARY, JOYCE   Power in Men. Liberal Book Club, 1939.
First edition. Covers marked and spine a little darkened. Author's
autograph signature on title-page and his autograph presentation
inscription on the flyleaf. Nice. Rota 230-115 1983 £50

CARY, JOYCE   Process of Real Freedom. London, 1943.
First edition. Wrappers a little frayed. Author's signed autograph
presentation inscription. Very good. Rota 231-102 1983 £40

CARY, JOYCE   Process of Real Freedom. London, 1943.
First edition. Wrappers. Fine. Rota 231-101 1983 £20

CASANOVA DE SEINGALT, GIACOMO GIROLAMO   Casanova's Escape from
the Leads. Casanova Society, 1925. With 3 plates, 8vo, orig.
cloth-backed boards, with printed paper label, a very good copy.
Fenning 62-55 1983 £10.50

CASANOVA DE SEINGALT, GIACOMO GIROLAMO   The Memoirs. Privately
printed for subscribers only, The Casanova Society, 1922. With frontis.
12 vols., 4to, orig. parchment-backed blue paper boards, t.e.g. A
fine set in the orig. tissues. Ltd. edition of 1,000 numbered
sets. Fenning 62-56 1983 £45

CASANOVA DE SEINGALT, GIACOMO GIROLAMO   The Memoirs of Jacques Casanova, an Autobiography. London & N.Y.: The Venetian Society, 1928.
12 vols. Portrait, highly gilt-dec. spines, t.e.g., cloth, minor
staining and wear. Loose hinges. Translated by Arthur Machen. Limited
to 666 sets. King 46-263 1983 $65

CASATI, MAJOR GAETANO   Ten years in Equatoria and the return
with Emin Pasha. London: Frederick Warne, 1891. 2 vols. 8vo.
60 plates. 4 maps. Orig. pictorial cloth. Spine starting vol. 1.
Adelson Africa-70 1983 $175

CASE, SHEELER   Revolutionary Memorials. New York,
1852. Cloth. Felcone 22-28 1983 $25

THE CASE of Charles Moore, late Master Cooper of the Victualing-Office. London: printed for the author, 1749. First edition. 8vo. Disbound. Ximenes 63-340 1983 $125

CASEMENT, ROGER　　　　Sir Roger Casement's Diaries. Munich: Arche, 1932. First edition, with 3 portraits and 3 facs., 8vo, orig. printed wraps., the wraps. just a little dusty, but a very good copy in orig. state. Fenning 61-59 1983 £28.50

CASEY, C.　　　　Riviera Nature Notes. Manchester, 1898. 5 plates, cr. 8vo, cloth. Wheldon 160-356 1983 £12

CASEY, C.　　　　Riviera Nature Notes. 1903. 2nd ed., 32 plates and 93 text-figures, 8vo, original decorated cloth. Wheldon 160-357 1983 £28

CASO, ALFONSO　　　　Urnas de Oaxaca. Mexico, 1952. 527 illus. Small folio. Cloth. Ars Libri 34-170 1983 $150

CASPER, JOHANN LUDWIG (1796-1864)　　A Handbook of the Practice of Forensc Medicine. London: The New Sydenham Society, 1861-1865. Four vols. Publisher's cloth, rebacked. Gach 95-67 1983 $150

CASS, LEWIS　　　　France, Its King, Court, and Government. New York, 1840. 1st ed. Portrait. 8vo. Ex-library, faded, slightly rubbed. Morrill 287-56 1983 $27.50

CASS, LEWIS　　　　Letter from...Transmitting Documents in Relation to Hostilities of Creek Indians. Wash., 1836. Half morocco. First edition. Ginsberg 46-209 1983 $125

CASS, LEWIS　　　　Sketch of the Life and Public Services of Gen. Lewis Cass. Washington: Printed at the Congressional Globe Office, 1848. Self wrappers. Light stain to text. Jenkins 152-49 1983 $35

CASS, LEWIS　　　　Speech of Hon...of Michigan, on the Collins Line of Steamers. Wash., 1852. Dbd. First edition. Ginsberg 46-163 1983 $25

CASS, LEWIS　　　　Substance of a Speech Delivered by Hon...of Michigan, in Secret Session of the Senate of the United States, on the Ratification of the Oregon Treaty with Additions. Detroit, ca. 1846. Double columns. Sewn as issued. First edition. Ginsberg 47-720 1983 $75

CASSERIUS, JULIUS　　　　Tabulae Anatomicae LXXIIX. Mathew Merian, Frankfurt, 1632. 4to, with 107 full page anatomical plates printed in the text; some slight browning; nineteenth century half vellum. Quaritch NS 5-21 1983 $1,450

CASSINI, JEAN DOMINIQUE DE　　Voyage fait par Ordre du Roi en 1768. Paris, 1770. 4to, with 1 folding engraved map, 3 folding engraved charts and views to the Voyage, and 6 folding engraved plates of clockwork mechanisms; cont. French mottled calf, the Leroy copy with bookplate. Quaritch NS 5-22 1983 $1,500

CASSIRER, ERNEST　　　　The Philosophy of Ernest Cassirer. Evanston, Ill.: The Library of Living Philosophers, Inc., 1949. Thick 8vo. First edition. Gach 95-68 1983 $35

CASSIUS DIO COCCEIANUS　　　　E Dione Excerptae Historiae Ab Ioanne Xiphilino. (Geneva,), Excudebat Henricus Stephanus, 1592. Folio, cont. calf rebacked, library stamp on title, minor damp-marking in inner upper blank gutter, but quite decent copy. Ravenstree 95-39 1983 $157.50

CASSOUS, JEAN　　　　Fernand Leger: Dessins et gouaches. Paris: Edition de Chene, 1972. 304 illus. Large 4to. Cloth. Dust jacket. Ars Libri 32-396 1983 $75

CASTAING, MARCELLIN　　　　Soutine. New York: Abrams, n.d. 59 illus. (34 tipped-in color plates). Folio. Cloth. Dust jacket. Ars Libri 32-641 1983 $75

CASTELLI, BENEDETTO　　　　Della Misura dell'Acque correnti. Rome: Francesco Cavalli, 1639. Second edition. Engraved frontis. Woodcut diagrams in text, arms of Urban VIII (dedicatee). Small 4to. Cont. limp vellum. Kraus 164-85 1983 $375

CASTELLI, BENEDETTO　　　　Risposta alle Opposizioni Del S. Lodovico delle Colombe... Florence: Cosimo Giunta, 1615. Small 4to. First edition. Leather. With exlibris of Giuseppe Martini and Pietro Ginori Conti. Two pages missing (further errata and printer's mark). Ink blot on one page. Kraus 164-84 1983 $1,500

CASTIGLIONI, ARTURO　　　　History of Medicine. N.Y., 1841. First American edition. 4to, buckram. Argosy 713-99 1983 $45

CASTIGLIONI, ARTURO　　　　A History of Medicine. New York, 1941. First edition. 8vo. Orig. binding. Ex-library. Fye H-3-78 1983 $85

CASTILLO, BERNAL DIAZ DEL
Please turn to
DIAZ DEL CASTILLO, BERNAL

CASTLE, EGERTON　　　　Schools and Masters of Fence. London, 1910. Illus, newer 1/2 lea., plates, very good. King 46-550 1983 $35

CASTLE, MELISSA A.　　　　Texas' Bloodless Revolution. Dallas, (1934). First edition. Illus. Jenkins 152-338a 1983 $45

CASTLEMAN, HARVEY N.　　　　The Texas Rangers. Girard, Kansas: Halderman-Julius Publications, 1944. Original printed wrappers. 1st ed. Jenkins 153-121 1983 $30

CASTLEMEN, RIVA　　　　Technics and Creativity. NY: Museum of Modern Art, (1971). Octavo. Exhibition catalog with small b&w reproductions of every piece in show, numerous large b&w and color plates. Very fine in pictorial wrappers. One of limited number of copies housed in molded plastic box together with separate orig. signed "multiple" by Jasper Johns. Box faintly soiled. Print extremely fine. Bromer 25-232 1983 $250

CASTRO E ALMEIDA, EDUARDO DE Inventario dos Documentos Relativos ao Brasil existentes no Archivo de Marinha e Ultramar de Lisboa... Rio de Janeiro: Biblioteca Nacional, 1913-14. Dawson 470-57 1983 $25

CASWELL, HARRIET S.　　　　Our Life Among the Iroquois Indians. Boston & Chicago, (1892). First edition. Illus. Small 8vo. Morrill 290-347 1983 $27.50

CATALOGUE of A Pickwick Exhibition. The Dickens Fellowship, 1936. Orig. green printed wraps. Very good. Jarndyce 30-169 1983 £20

CATALOGUE of Books & Manuscripts in the Estelle Doheny Collection. Los Angeles, 1940. The first of a 3 vol. set. Plates, some in color. Cloth, bookplate removed. 1 of 100 copies printed at the Ward Ritchie Press. Very good. Dawson 470-208 1983 $100

THE CATALOGUE of Books from the Libraries or Collections of Celebrated Bibliophiles and Illustrious Persons. NY: Grolier Club, 1895. Octavo. Numerous full-page b&w illus. Limited to 350 copies. Gilt-stamped covers slightly rubbed. Bookplate. Bromer 25-165 1983 $165

CATALOGUE of Connecticut Volunteer Organizations (Infantry, Cavalry and Artillery), in the Service of the United States, 1861-1865... Hartford, 1869. Large 8vo. Ends of backstrip torn. Morrill 289-599 1983 $35

A CATALOGUE of English and American First Editions 1911-1932 of D.H. Lawrence. New York: Harold Jay Snyder, 1932. Tall 8vo. Paper wrappers. Cover soiled. Oak Knoll 48-451 1983 $25

CATALOGUE of Some Five Hundred Examples of the Printing of Edwin and Robert Grabhorn 1917-1960 Two Gentlemen from Indiana now Resident in California. SF, 1961. Compiled by David Magee. Lg 4to, linen-backed decorated bds., paper label. Photographs byMarjory Farquhar. Perata 27-77 1983 $100

A CATALOGUE of such Testimonies in all Ages... (London), 1640. 4to. Wrappers. Small stain in margin of title. Heath 48-62 1983 £50

CATALOGUE of the American School of Osteopathy. Kirksville, Mo., 1897. 8vo. Orig. wrappers. Morrill 289-39 1983 $25

CATALOGUE of the Choice Books found by Pantagrual in the Abbey of Saint Victor. SF, 1952. Devised by Francois Rabelais. Translated and annotated by Walter Klinefelter. Sm 4to, cloth-backed bds., paper label. Ruled pages printed in three colors. Perata 27-73 1983 $145

A CATALOGUE of the Collection of Eighteenth-century Printed Books and Manuscripts Formed by Lord Rothchild. London: Dawson of Pall Mall, 1969. 2 vols. Large 8vo. Cloth. Some facsimiles. Oak Knoll 49-488 1983 $275

THE CATALOGUE of the Collection of Joseph T. Tower, Jr. Privately printed, 1933. Cloth, slight wear. One of 110 copies printed at the Merrymount Press. Dawson 470-59 1983 $40

CATALOGUE of the Extensive and Valuable Collection of Books forming the Library of the late John George Hargreaves. Durham: Geo. H. Proctor, (1893). 8vo. Stitched as issued. Heath 48-251 1983 £30

A CATALOGUE of the First Editions of First Books in the Collection of Paul S. Seybolt. Boston: privately printed, 1946. 8vo. Cloth. Illus. Lettering on spine faded. Minor soiling. Oak Knoll 48-428 1983 $35

A CATALOGUE of the Names of so many of those Commissioners... (London, 1660). 4to. Wrappers. Heath 48-63 1983 £60

CATALOGUE of the Plants, Indigenous and Exotic, cultivated in the Garden, Dalbeth, 1813. Glasgow: by William Lang, (1813). 12mo. Wrappers. Heath 48-2 1983 £30

CATALOGUE of the Printed Books in the Library of the University of Edinburgh. Edinburgh: Univ. Press, 1918-23. Cloth, bumped and lightly used. 3 vols. Dawson 470-60 1983 $125

CATALOGUE of the Valuable and Extensive Library of the Late John Scott, Esq. C.B. Halkshill, Largs, Ayrshire. 8vo, the price list with buyer's names being bound in at the end, boards, worn, with buckram spine. Bickersteth 77-191 1983 £20

CATALOGUE of the William Loring Andrews Collection of Early Books... New Haven: Yale Univ. Press, 1913. First edition. Tall 8vo. Cloth-backed boards. Limited to 300 copies. Small stamp indicating that this copy was discarded from Yale University Library. Oak Knoll 49-9 1983 $65

CATALOGUE of the William Loring Andrews Collection of Early Books in the Library of Yale University. New Haven, 1913. Ed. limited to 300 copies. Tall 8vo, orig. boards, cloth back. Morrill 289-588 1983 $37.50

CATALOGUE of the Works of Rudyard Kipling Exhibited at the Grolier Club from February 21 to March 30, 1929. New York, 1930. One of 325 copies. Portrait frontis. Facsimiles. Boards and cloth. Very good. Bradley 63-20 1983 $85

A CATALOGUE Raisonne of the Select Collection of Engravings of an Amateur. London: 1828. First edition. Illus. with 5 etchings by George Cruikshank. Cont. half-morocco. Spine and covers slightly worn and foxed. Bookplates. Very good. MacManus 277-1210 1983 $300

CATALOGUS Van De Verzameling Etsen van Rembrandt in het bezit van I. Bruijn en J.G. de Bruijn-van der Leeuz. 's-Gravenhage: Martinus Nijhoff, 1932. 2 plates. 4to. Boards, 1/4 cloth. Printed on fine laid paper. Slightly shaken. Ars Libri 32-552 1983 $85

CATCOTT, GEORGE SYMES   A Descriptive Account of a Descent Made into Penpark-Hole...in the Year 1775. Bristol: Printed by J. Rudhall, in Small-Street, 1792.Copper-plate engraving of cavern. Cont. boards. K Books 307-43 1983 £48

CATHER, WILLA   April Twilights. Boston: Richard G. Badger, The Gorham Press, 1903. 1st ed. Orig. boards, paper labels, uncut. Light wear at crown of spine and a couple of minute chips to spine label; a fine copy. Jenkins 155-185 1983 $550

CATHER, WILLA   Death Comes for the Archibishop. New York: Knopf, 1927. Cloth, first edition, trade issue. Ink name and evidence of bookplate removal, otherwise a fine, unfaded copy. In a slightly frayed dust jacket. Reese 20-233 1983 $125

CATHER, WILLA   Lucy Gayheart. NY, 1935. Spine and edges sunned, very good in lightly chipped and frayed, very good dust-wrapper, owner's name and date. Quill & Brush 54-259 1983 $40

CATHER, WILLA   Lucy Gayheart. New York: Knopf, 1935. First edition. Orig. cloth, labels, dj. Fine fresh copy in near perfect dj. Jenkins 155-186 1983 $40

CATHER, WILLA   My Antonia. Boston, 1918. First edition, first issue, with the illus. inserted, on glazed paper. The binding is rubbed, and there is minor dampstaining on the top edges of some pages. Argosy 714-145 1983 $100

CATHER, WILLA   My Mortal Enemy. New York: Knopf, 1926. First edition. One of 220 numbered and signed copies. Orig. linen-backed patterned boards, label, uncut, spare label at front, tissue dust dust jacket. Very fine fresh copy in rare dust jacket with small pieces lacking from some edges. Mostly unopened. Jenkins 155-187 1983 $200

CATHER, WILLA   Not Under Forty. New York, 1936. 8vo, cloth. Limited signed edition. One of 333 copies printed on Japan vellum and signed by Cather. Fine in box. In Our Time 156-149 1983 $200

CATHER, WILLA   O Pioneers. Boston, 1913. 8vo, tan ribbed cloth; binding rubbed & worn. First edition. Worn copy of the first issue. Argosy 714-146 1983 $50

CATHER, WILLA   Obscure Destinies: Three New Stories of the West. New York: Knopf, 1932. First edition. Orig. cloth, labels, dj. Fine fresh copy. Jenkins 155-188 1983 $45

CATHER, WILLA   Obscure Destinies. NY, 1932. Cover edges faded, else very good in internally mended, lightly chipped and worn price clipped dustwrapper. Quill & Brush 54-260 1983 $30

CATHER, WILLA   Obscure Destinies. NY, 1932. Later printing, signed by Cather on front fly, spine faded, photo of Cather tipped-in on front pastedown, very good. Quill & Brush 54-261 1983 $30

CATHER, WILLA   One of Ours. New York, 1922. First edition. One of 345 copies signed by the author, who has also in-scribed the book on the half-title. Inner hinge weak, corners bumped, lettering piece slightly chipped, but overall a very good copy. Gekoski 2-25 1983 £100

CATHER, WILLA   One of Ours. New York: Knopf, 1922. Cloth and batik boards, paper label. First edition. One of 310 numbered copies, specially printed on handmade paper, signed by the author. Bookplate neatly removed, else a fine copy, sans box. Reese 20-231 1983 $150

CATHER, WILLA   The Professor's House. New York: Knopf, 1925. Cloth and patterned paper over boards, paper label. First edition. One of 185 numbered copies, specially printed and bound, and signed by the author. Bookplate of Mrs. Linda (Cole) Porter, else a fine, unopened copy in slightly worn slipcase. Reese 20-232 1093 $225

CATHER, WILLA   Sapphira and the Slave Girl. New York: Knopf, 1940. First edition. Orig. green cloth, label, dj. Advance review copy, so imprinted on front free end paper in same type as text. Mint. Jenkins 155-190 1983 $65

CATHER, WILLA   Sapphira and the Slave Girl. New York: Knopf, 1940. First edition. Orig. cloth, labels. Very fine copy in like dust jacket. Jenkins 155-191 1983 $25

CATHER, WILLA   Shadows on the Rock. New York: Knopf, 1931. Orange vellum, gilt. First edition. One of 199 numbered copies, printed on Japon Vellum, specially bound, and signed by the author. Bookplate neatly removed, else a very fine copy in dust jacket and slipcase. Reese 20-234 1983 $385

CATHER, WILLA　　　　　　Shadows on the Rock.　New York: Knopf, 1931.　First edition.　Orig. cloth, labels.　Very fine copy in fine fresh dust jacket.　Jenkins 155-193　1983　$45

CATHER, WILLA　　　　　　The Troll Garden.　New York: McClure, Phillips, 1904.　1st ed., 1st binding.　Orig. red cloth, gilt.　Fine copy.　Jenkins 155-194　1983　$275

CATHER, WILLA　　　　　　Willa Cather on Writing.　New York: Knopf, 1949.　1st ed.　Orig. cloth, dj.　Fine fresh copy.　Jenkins 155-196　1983　$25

CATHERALL, SAMUEL　　　　An Essay on the Conflagration.　Oxford: Printed for Anthony Peisley...MDCCXX.　8vo, with frontis. portrait of Thomas Burnet and engraved view of Clarendon Printing House on title; later boards.　First edition.　Quaritch NS 7-22　1983　$225

CATHERWOOD, MARY HARTWELL　　Lazarre.　Indianapolis: Bowen-Merrill, (1901).　1st ed.　Orig. cloth, gilt.　Fine copy.　Jenkins 155-1370　1983　$20

CATHOLIC Builders of the Nation.　A Symposium on the Catholic Contribution to the Civilization of the United States.　Boston, Continental Press, 1923.　First edition.　Illus.　5 vols., 8vo.　Orig. leatherette. Ex-library, nice.　Morrill 286-82　1983　$20

CATHOLIC CHURCH. LITURGY & RITUAL. HOURS.　The Hours of Catherine of Cleves.　New York, (n.d.)　Fine in slipcase.　Quill & Brush 54-1661　1983　$30

THE CATHOLIC Encyclopedia.　New York: D. Appleton, 1907-14, 1922. 17 vols. including index and supplement.　Half leather, one volume worn at hinges, the others with very minor wear.　Dawson 470-61 1983　$100

CATHRALL, ISAAC　　　　Domestic Medicine; or, a Treatise on the Prevention and Cure of Diseases...　Philadelphia: Richard Folwell, 1799.　8vo.　Contemporary calf.　Rubbed; lacks label, few signatures pulled; lacks top inch of backstrip.　Morrill 289-23 1983　$40

CATLIN, GEORGE　　　　Catlin's Notes of Eight Years' Travels and Residence in Europe, with His North American Indian Collection. N.Y., 1848.　2 vols., 24 plates.　Blind-stamped stipple cloth (2nd t.p. margin stained).　First American edition.　Argosy 716-213　1983　$200

CATLIN, GEORGE B.　　　　The Story of Detroit.　Detroit 1926. Revised edition.　Inscribed and signed by the author.　Photos, buckram, very good.　King 46-148　1983　$35

CATLOW, A.　　　　Popular Conchology.　1854.　Second edition, numerous text-figures, cr. 8vo, cloth (slightly used). Wheldon 160-1201　19-3　£28

CATO, M. PORCIUS　　　　Cato's Farm Management.　N.p.: 1910. Privately printed at the Lakeside Press in Chicago.　First edition. Very good copy, lightly rubbed.　Bradley 66-407　1983　$40

CATON, JOHN DEAN　　　　The Antelope and Deer in America... New York, 1877.　Stamped cloth binding (with a moose), very good. Reese 19-133　1983　$150

CATTELL, J. M.　　　　Medical Research and Education.　New York, 1913.　First edition.　8vo.　Orig. binding.　Fye H-3-82　1983 $75

CATULLUS, GAIUS VALERIUS　　Catulli Carmina: The Poems of Catullus. The Piazza Press, issued to subscribers by Peter Davies, 1929.　With 8 plates, 8vo, orig. full vellum, t.e.g., a fine copy in the orig. slip-case.　Ltd. edition of 510 numbered copies on Itlaian mould-made paper.　Fenning 62-57　1983　£35

CATULLUS, GAIUS VALERIUS　　Opera.　Londini, Jacob Tonson & Johannis Watts, 1715.　Stout 12mo, covers detached, frontis. offset a bit onto title, some minor age-spotting.　Ravenstree 95-22　1983 $55

CAUDWELL, CHRISTOPHER　　　Poems.　London, 1939.　First edition. Very good.　Rota 231-109　1983　£15

CAUGHEY, JOHN W.　　　　Historian of the West.　Berkeley, 1946. Ports., plates.　Clark 641-55　1983　$35

CAUGHEY, JOHN W.　　　　Old is the Cornerstone.　Berkeley, 1948. First edition in dust jacket.　Illus.　Fine.　Jenkins 152-49　1983　$30

CAUNTER, H.　　　　The Oriental Annual.　London, 1835. Frontis.　Vignette on title.　Some plates slightly spotted.　Decorated morocco.　8vo.　Good.　Edwards 1044-125　1983　£50

CAUNTER, H.　　　　The Oriental Annual.　London, 1838. Orig. decorated morocco.　8vo.　Good.　Edwards 1044-126　1983　£50

CAUS, ISAAC DE　　　　New and Rare Inventions of Water-Works shewing the Easiest Waies to Raise Water...　London: printed by Joseph Moxon..., 1659.　First edition.　Folio.　Cont. calf, rebacked. Engraved title-page, with 26 copper engravings and 20 woodcuts in text.　Ownership inscription and price.　Early bookplate of Sir John Cope.　Folding plate repaired in outer margin, very slightly affecting a figure.　Fine copy.　Gurney 90-32　1983　£1,200

CAUWET-MARC, A. M.　　　Les Ombelliferes.　(Perignan, 1977), St. Louis, Mo., 1982.　8vo, paper.　Wheldon 160-1502　1983　£38

CAVALUCCI, J.　　　　Les Della Robbia.　Paris: J. Rouam, 1884.　Prof. illus.　Large 4to.　Marbled boards, 3/4 morocco.　Ars Libri 33-310　1983　$150

CAVE, F. O.　　　　Birds of the Sudan.　1955.　12 coloured plates, photographs and 2 maps, 8vo, original cloth.　Scarce. Wheldon 160-669　1983　£90

CAVE, HENRY W.　　　　Golden Tips.　Cassell, 1905.　Fourth edition, with a map and 234 full-page and other illus. from photos., 8vo, orig. cloth, gilt, edges gilt.　Fenning 61-62　1983　£24.50

CAVE, HENRY W.　　　　Golden Tips.　1905.　4th edition, numerous illustrations, 8vo, cloth.　A trifle waterstained.　Wheldon 160-358　1983　£12

CAVE, JANE　　　　Poems on Various Subjects... Bristol: by N. Biggs, 1794.　Fourth edition, corrected.　8vo. Cont. calf.　Engraved portrait.　Light wear.　Heath 48-253　1983 £60

CAVE, RODERICK　　　　The Private Press.　NY: (1971).　Octavo. First American edition.　Fine in dust wrapper.　Bromer 25-169　1983 $75

CAVE, WILLIAM　　　　A Discourse Concerning the Unity of the Catholick Church Maintained in the Church of England.　Printed for B. Tooke...and F. Gardner, 1684.　First edition, 4to, wrapper a very good copy.　Fenning 61-63　1983　£14.50

CAVE, WILLIAM　　　　Primitive Christianity: or the Religion of the ancient Christians in the first Ages of the Gospel.　London: printed by J. M. for Richard Chiswell, 1673.　First edition.　8vo, 3 parts in one vol., full morocco by Riviere, spine gilt, gilt gauffered edges.　Trebizond 18-182　1983　$150

CAVERSAZZI, CIRO　　　　Giovanni Carnovali detto il Piccio. Bergamo: Istituto Italiano d'Arti Grafiche, 1933.　186 illus. (6 color plates).　Large 4to.　Cloth.　Ars Libri 33-558　1983 $100

CAWEIN, MADISON　　　　The Republic, Little Book of Homespun Verse.　Cincinnati (1913).　First edition.　Cloth, minor cover staining, extremities slightly worn.　King 46-265　1983　$20

CAYLEY, ARTHUR　　　　Table of...　Read October 27, 1879. Orig. offprint, 4to, stab sewn in the orig. plain paper wrapper; inscribed "from the author," somewhat soiled and a piece torn from the upper cover.　Pickering & Chatto 22-20　1983　$65

CAYLEY, N. W.　　　　Australian Finches.　Sydney, 1932. 10 coloured plates and 16 other illustrations, 8vo, new cloth. Wheldon 160-670　1983　£30

CAYLEY, N. W.   Australian Parrots. Sydney, 1938.
11 coloured plates and 19 other illus., 8vo, cloth. Wheldon 160-671
1983 £45

CAZA, FRANCESCO   Tractato Vulgare de Canto Figurato.
(Milan, 1492). Facs. edition with German translation. Uncut, ltd.
numbered edition, 8vo, bds. (small chip on spine). Salloch 387-298
1983 $80

CECCHI, EMILIO   Giotto. Milano: Ulrico Hoepli,
1950. 200 plates. Small 4to. Cloth. Ars Libri 33-170 1983
$35

CECCHI, EMILIO   Pietro Lorenzetti. Milano: Fratelli
Treves, 1930. 143 plates. Large 4to. Cloth. Ars Libri 33-199
1983 $125

CECIL, E.   A History of Gardening in England. 1910.
3rd edition, 69 illus., 8vo, original cloth, gilt. Wheldon 160-219
1983 £40

THE CELEBRATED Opera Dances as performed at the King's Theatre in the
Haymarket, 1783. London, W. Forster, (1783). Engraved title,
engraved music. Oblong 8vo, new marbled boards. Salloch 387-28 1983
$135

CELEBRATED Trials of All Countries, and Remarkable Cases of Criminal
Jurisprudence.   Philadelphia: Jesper Harding, 1846. Blue cloth.
Foxed throughout, dime-sized hole through leaf 57-58, otherwise good
and solid copy. Bradley 66-410 1983 $45

CELENIA and Adrastes; With the Delightful History of Hyempsal, King of
Numidia; an Allegorical Romance. Dublin: Printed for Cor. Wynne...
1742. 2 vols., 12mo, contemporary calf, lacking labels. Hill 165-20
1983 £60

CELLARIUS, CHRISTOPHER   Geographia Antiqua. London, 1745.
26 large engraved folding maps. Engraved frontis. Cont. calf.
8vo. Salloch 385-338 1983 $250

CELLINI, BENVENUTO   The Life of Benvenute Cellini, a Florentine Artist. London: T. Davies, 1771. First edition, 8vo, 2 vols.
Cont. calf, spines gilt, morocco labels, engraved frontis. A very
fine copy. Trebizond 18-121 1983 $275

CELSUS, AULUS CORNELIUS   De medecina. Padua, 1750. 2 vols.
Portrait and 2 engravings. 8vo. 18th-century citron morocco. Gilt-
tooled panels on covers, rules and fleurons on backs, edges gilt.
Written on the flyleaf of vol. 1, in an 18th-century hand, is a
quotation of thirteen lines. Kraus 164-37 1983 $450

CENDRARS, BLAISE   Panama or the Adventures of My Seven
Uncles. New York, 1931. Large 8vo. Wraps. Fine. In Our Time
156-213 1983 $75

THE CENTENNIAL of Incorporation. (Charleston, 1884). 1st ed.
Folding maps, plans, plates, facsimiles, etc. 8vo. Some binding
stains. Morrill 289-540 1983 $25

CENTLIVRE, S.   The Works of the celebrated Mrs.
Centlivre. London: for J. Knapton..., 1761. First collected
edition. 3 vols. 8vo. Engraved portrait. Cont. calf. Heath
48-254 1983 £150

CENTO Salmi di David. Geneva, de Tournes, 1683. Tall 12mo, cont.
calf. Salloch 387-183 1983 $200

CENTRAL PACIFIC RAILROAD.   Report of the Chief Engineer on the
Preliminary Survey, Cost of Construction, and Estimated Revenue, of
the Central Pacific Railroad of California. Sacramento, 1862.
Orig. printed wraps. First edition. Ginsberg 46-105 1983 $175

CENTRAL PACIFIC RAILROAD   To the Bondholders of the Central
Pacific Railroad Company, Jan. 1, 1872. N.Y., Fisk and Hatch
Bankers, (1872). Orig. front printed wraps. First edition. Ginsberg
46-165 1983 $35

CENTRAL Park, a Guide. NY: A.O. Moore & Co., 1859. 2 text illus.
Folding map. Mod. wraps. Argosy 716-374 1983 $75

EL CENTRO Progress. San Diego & Arizona Railway edition, December 5th,
1919. Wrappers. Spine replaced with fabric tape. Dawson 471-72 1983
$50

CERIO, EDWIN   That Capri Air. Heinemann, (1929).
First edition, roy. 8vo, orig. cloth, gilt, t.e.g., a fine copy.
Ltd. edition of 530 numbered copies. The typography, cover design
and title-page ornament by Percy Smith. Fenning 62-58 1983 £21.50

CERONI, AMBROGIO   Amedeo Modigliani. Milano: Edizioni
del Milione, 1965. 222 plates, (numerous color). 5 text illus.
4to. Boards. Ars Libri 33-533 1983 $85

CERTON, PIERRE   Messes a Quatre Voix. Paris, 1925.
3 facs. plates. Editor's inscribed presentation copy. 4to, wrs.
Spine repaired. Salloch 387-130a 1983 $45

CERVANTES, ENRIQUE   Loza Blanca y azulejo de pueblas.
Mexico: Privately Printed, 1939. Prof. illus. Large 4to. Wrappers.
Edition limited to 1000 copies. Ars Libri 34-174 1983 $50

CERVANTES SAAVEDRA, MIGUEL DE (1547-1616)   The History of the Valor-
ous and Witty Knight-Errant, Don Quixote of la Mancha. London: Printed
for Edward Blount, 1620. 2 vols. First complete edition in English.
Full morocco gilt, a.e.g., by Bradstreet, in full morocco solander
case. Engr. titles lacking and title to vol. 1 in facs., else a very
fine set. Jenkins 155-199 1983 $1,950

CERVANTES SAAVEDRA, MIGUEL DE (1547-1616)   The Life and Exploits of
the Ingenious Gentleman Don Quixote of la Mancha. For J. and R. Tonson, and R. Dodsley, 1742. First edition of this translation. 2 vols.
4to, port. by Virtue, and 68 numbered plates. Cont. calf, gilt (heads
and tails of spines worn, lacks one label). Occ. minor stains. This
copy has the 'Supplement to the Translator's Preface", unsigned but
written by Bishop Warburton. There is no 'Finis' on leaf m1, but fly-
title on m2. Hannas 69-26 1983 £150

CERVANTES SAAVEDRA, MIGUEL DE (1547-1616)   The Life and Exploits of
the ingenious Don Quixote de la Mancha. London: for A. Millar, etc.,
1745. First edition of this translation. 2 vols. 28 copper-plate
engr. by Grignion, Scotin, Muller and Ravenet, from drawings by Francis
Hayman. 4to. Nineteenth century half brown morocco, gilt panelled
spines with crimson and black morocco labels, gilt. Traylen 94-166
1983 £250

CERVANTES SAAVEDRA, MIGUEL DE (1547-1616)   Don Quixote de la Mancha.
London: Printed for T. Cadell & W. Davies, 1818. 8 vols. Quarto.
Full green crushed levant, gilt, inner dentelles gilt, raised bands,
gilt compartments with windmill motifs on spine and covers, green silk
markers, t.e.g., others uncut. Extra-illus. set with engr. Orig.
etchings, color plates, orig. paintings. Also included are title pages,
prefaces, and frontis. of all major ed., and portraits of Cervantes et
al. Binding very fine. Jenkins 155-198 1983 $6,000

CERTANTES SAAVEDRA, MIGUEL DE (1547-1616)   The History of Don Quixote. London, (copyright 1864-67). Illus. by Gustave Dore. Full
leather, a.e.g., leather edges rubbed, else very good clean copy.
Bookplate. Quill & Brush 54-263 1983 $50

CERVANTES SAAVEDRA, MIGUEL DE (1547-1616)   The History of Don
Quixote. London: Cassell, Petter and Galpin (ca. 1890). Large 4to.
Cont. half calf. Title-page printed in red and black with 118 plates
and other illus. from drawings by Gustave Dore. Traylen 94-167 1983
£25

CERVANTES SAAVEDRA, MIGUEL DE (1547-1616)   The History of Don
Quixote. London: Cassell & Company, (ca. 1890). 4to. Half blue
calf, gilt spine with morocco label, gilt. With 118 plates and other
illus. from drawings by Gustave Dore. Traylen 94-168 1983 £20

CERTANTES SAAVEDRA, MIGUEL DE (1547-1616)   The History of the Ingenious Gentleman Don Quixote of La Mancha. Edingurgh, 1906. 4 vols.
Roy. 8vo. Cloth. Buckram spines, gilt, t.e.g., others uncut. Portrait and 36 plates from etchings by Lalauze. Traylen 94-169 1983
£20

CERVANTES, SAAVEDRA, MIGUEL DE (1547-1616)   Don Quixote de la Mancha.
Warne, n.d. (1926). Illus. by Arthur Boyd Houghton. Re-issue frontis.,
title vignette and numerous engr. Publisher's cloth, t.e.g., others
uncut, top corners slightly bumped. Very good copy. Hodgkins 27-265
1983 £12.50

CERVANTES SAAVEDRA, MIGUEL DE (1547-1616) Persiles and Sigismunda. For C. Ward and R. Chandler, etc, 1741. First edition of this translation. 2 vols. 12mo, portrait. Initial advert. leaf in vol. II. Mottled calf, gilt, by W. Nutt. Hannas 69-27 1983 £250

CERVANTES SAAVEDRA, MIGUEL DE (1547-1616) Persile and Sigismunda; a celebrated novel. London: C. Ward & R. Chandler, 1741. Second edition in English. 12mo. Two volumes. Cont. calf, rebacked, frontis. Adv. leaf. Tear to one leaf with loss of a catchword, else a very good copy. Trebizond 18-110 1983 $275

CHABERT, M. DE Voyage fait par ordre du roi en 1750 et 1751... Paris: De l'Imprimerie Royale, 1753. 4to. First edition. 6 folding maps, one folding diagram and one folding chart. Two engraved vignettes and several woodcut ornaments. Cont. calf binding, raised bands, gilt decorations in the panels. Edges rubbed. A fine copy. McGahern 54-42 1983 $1,100

CHADBOURN, J. H. Lynching and the Law. Chapel Hill: 1933. First edition. Cloth. Fine in mended jacket. Bradley 66-523 1983 $30

CHADOURNE, MARC China. N.Y., (1932). First American edition. Illus. by Miguel Covarrubias. Review copy. Argosy 714-192 1983 $40

CHADWICK, DANIEL The Life and Times of Daniel Defoe. John Russell Smith, 1859. First edition, half title, front. port. Orig. purple cloth, v.g. Jarndyce 30-968 1983 £24

CHADWICK, HENRY The American Game of Baseball. Philadelphia, 1888. Gaudy chromolithographed wraps., fine. Reese 19-39 1983 $175

CHADWICK, WILLIAM The life and times of Daniel De Foe. London: John Russell Smith, 1859. First edition. 8vo. Orig. magenta cloth. Portrait. Slight nick at top of spine, spine faded, unopened. Ximenes 63-28 1983 $40

CHAGALL, MARC The Lithographs of Chagall. NY: George Braziller, (1960). Large 4to, profusely illus., including many color plates, and with 12 orig. lithographs. Fine copy in dust jacket (a few very small chips along the dust jacket edges). Card-board slipcase. Karmiole 72-25 1983 $1,350

CHAILLE, STANFORD State Medicine and State Medical Societies. 1879. Extract. 8vo. Orig. binding. Folding charts. Fye H-3-83 1983 $20

CHALFANT, W. A. The Story of Inyo. Published by author, 1922. Folding map. Errata slip pasted inside back cover. Cloth. First edition. Dawson 471-43 1983 $30

CHALMERS, ALEX A History of the Colleges, Halls, and Public Buildings, attached to the University of Oxford. Oxford, 1810. 2 vols., 8vo, engraved frontis., engraved and printed titles, 30 other engraved plates, cont. half calf, spines gilt, rebacked preserving the spines. Illus. by a series of engravings. Bickersteth 75-117 1983 £80

CHALMERS, CHARLES Notes of Experiments... Edinburgh: Sutherland & Knox...London, Simpkin, Marshall, & Co., 1850. 1st ed., 8vo, inscribed "To the Royal Medical Society from the Author" and with their stamp on the title; disbound. Pickering & Chatto 22-21 1983 $50

CHALMERS, PATRICK R. A Peck O'Maut. Dublin: Maunsel, 1914. First edition. 12mo. Orig. cloth. Dust jacket (rather chipped). MacManus 277-909 1983 $20

CHALMERS, THOMAS A Series of Discourses on the Christian Revelation Viewed in Connection with the Modern Astronomy. Glasgow, 1817. Calf, gilt, crisp copy. K Books 301-44 1983 £15

CHAMBAUD, LEWIS A New Dictionary, English and French, and, French and English. London: Cadell and Davies, etc., 1805. 2 vols. 4to. Cont. diced calf, elaborately gilt decorated spines, marbled edges. Traylen 94-170 1983 £38

CHAMBAUD, LEWIS The Treasure of the French and English Languages. 1772. 8vo, orig. calf, a little worn. Bickersteth 75-17 1983 £14

CHAMBAUD, LEWIS Treasure of the French and English Languages. P. Vaillant, J. Rivington & Sons, T. Longman, 1790. Eighth edition. Half title, sheep, slight worm damage, otherwise v.g. Jarndyce 31-25 1983 £28

CHAMBERLAIN, ALEXANDER F. The Child. London: 1906 (1900). Second edition. Spine tips rubbed. Gach 95-69 1983 $25

CHAMBERLAIN, ALLEN Beacon Hill. Boston, 1925. One of 475 large paper copies. Illustrated. 8vo, original boards, cloth back. Lettering on spine partly effaced. Morrill 290-649 1983 $25

CHAMBERLAIN, ARTHUR B. Hans Holbein the Younger. London: George Allen, 1913. 2 vols. 95 plates in vol. 1, 54 plates in vol. 2. Large stout 4to. Cloth. Slightly shaken. Rare. Ars Libri 32-317 1983 $250

CHAMBERLAIN, BASIL HALL Letters from Basil Hall Chamberlain to Lafcadio Hearn. Tokyo: Hokuseido Press, 1936. With 11 plates. T.e.g. Fine copy in dust jacket and slipcase with printed labels. Karmiole 74-54 1983 $200

CHAMBERLAIN, I. Common Objects of the Riviera. 1913. 8 coloured plates of plants, 8vo, cloth, small tear in foot of spine. Wheldon 160-359 1983 £12

CHAMBERLAIN, M. A Catalogue of Canadian Birds. Saint John, 1887. Sm. 4to, cloth. Wheldon 160-673 1983 £12

CHAMBERLAIN, NEWELL D. The Call of Gold True Tales on the Gold Road to Yosemite. Mariposa, Calif.: Gazette Press, 1936. Illus. First edition. Privately printed for author, scarce. Jenkins 153-122 1983 $45

CHAMBERLAIN, NEWELL D. The Call of Gold. (Mariposa (CA.), Gazette, 1936. First edition. Illus. Dust jacket (a bit faded, small chips). Signed by the author on page 5. Very good. Houle 22-1031 1983 $35

CHAMBERLAIN, SAMUEL Fair is Our Land. New York, 1942. Cloth, very good. Illus. with Farm Security Administration photos. Reese 19-139 1983 $40

CHAMBERLAINE, JOHN Portrait of Illustrious Personages of the Court of Henry VIII. London: John Chamberlaine, 1828. 84 stipple-engraved color plates, many printed on pink paper. Small folio. Full red morocco. A.e.g. Inner dentelles. Front cover repaired at hinge. Intermittent foxing. Ars Libri 32-318 1983 $650

CHAMBERLAINE, WILLIAM Tyrocinium Medicum. London: printed for the author, 1819. Second edition. 12mo. Old sheep rubbed. Label engraving missing. Gurney JJ-68 1983 £20

CHAMBERLAND, MICHEL Histoire de Notre-Dame des Sept-Douleurs de Grenville. Montreal, 1931. 24 1/2cm. Maps and illus. Stiff wrappers. Very good. McGahern 53-32 1983 $25

CHAMBERLAYNE, HAM Ham Chamberlayne-Virginian, Letters and Papers of an Artillery Officer... Richmond, VA, 1932. First edition limited to 1000 numbered copies. Very good in torn and chipped dust wrappers. King 46-45 1983 $50

CHAMBERLAYNE, JOHN Magnae Britanniae Notitia: or, the Present State of Great Britain; with diverse Remarks upon the Ancient State thereof. 1743. 35th ed., 2 parts in one, engraved portrait-frontispiece, 8vo, contemporary calf, gilt, morocco label. Deighton 3-71 1983 £42

CHAMBERLIN, ETHEL CLERE The Romance of Old Glory. New York, (1930). 1st ed. Illus. by Harold M. Brett. 8vo. Morrill 288-59 1983 $25

CHAMBERLIN, J. C. The Arachnid order Chelonethida. Stanford Biol. Sci., 1931. 71 figures, royal 8vo, wrappers (trifle soiled). Wheldon 160-1257 1983 £15

CHAMBERLIN, RALPH V.   The Ethno-Botany of the Gosiute Indians of Utah. Lancaster, Pa.: The New Era Printing Co., 1911. Uncut & unopened. Orig. printed wrappers. Fine. Jenkins 152-133 1983 $35

CHAMBERS, ANDREW JACKSON   Recollections. N.p.: (ca. 1944). First edition. Plain white self-wrappers, stapled at side. Fine copy. Bradley 66-631 1983 $85

CHAMBERS, ANDREW JACKSON   Recollections by... N.p., ca. 1947. 12mo, half morocco. Small edition printed for the family. Ginsberg 46-166 1983 $125

CHAMBERS, E. K.   The Mediaeval Stage. Oxford, 1903. First edition. Frontis. 2 vols. 8vo. Cloth. In the orig. dust-wrappers. Traylen 94-173 1983 £24

CHAMBERS, EPHRAIM   Cyclopaedia. London, 1779-1786. 4 vols. plus vol. of 145 engraved plates (some folding). Full cont. calf. Covers dry and detached, else a fine, wide-margined set with the plates in perfect state. Felcone 21-22 1983 $275

CHAMBERS, HENRY E.   Mississippi Valley Beginnings... N.Y., 1922. First edition. Dust jacket. Illus. Maps. Index. Inscribed by author. Fine. Jenkins 152-790 1983 $25

CHAMBERS, JULIUS   The Book of New York: 40 Years' Recollections of the American Metropolis. NY, (1912). Ports. & illus., 4to, corners and 1 spot damaged. Argosy 710-373 1983 $30

CHAMBERS, ROBERT   A Biographical Dictionary of Eminent Scotsmen. Glasgow: Blackie, 1835. First edition. 4 vols. Front. vol. I, portraits, calf, gilt borders, brown and black labels. Fine. Jarndyce 31-366 1983 £78

CHAMBERS, ROBERT   Domestic Annals of Scotland... Edinburgh, 1858. 3 vols. 8vo. Cont. polished calf, gilt panelled spines, crimson and green morocco labels, gilt. 2 frontis. and 25 illus. Traylen 94-175 1983 £38

CHAMBERS, ROBERT W.   The Flaming Jewel. NY, (1922). Near fine in lightly worn and soiled dustwrapper. Quill & Brush 54-264 1983 $40

CHAMBERS, WILLIAM   Memoir of Robert Chambers with auto-biographic reminiscences of William Chambers. New York: Scribner, Armstrong and Co., 1872. First U.S. edition. 8vo. Orig. cloth. Covers faded with a chip at the head of the spine and wear along the back hinge. Scarce. Oak Knoll 48-99 1983 $45

CHAMBERS'S Cyclopaedia of English Literature. London, 1906. 3 vols. 4to. Boards, blue cloth spines, gilt. 287 portraits and facs. Traylen 94-174 1983 £15

CHAMBRE DE COMMERCE DE LYON   La Mission Lyonnaise d'exploration Commerciale en Chine 1895-1897. Lyon, 1898. Maps, plates and illustrations, 4to, wrappers (soiled). Wheldon 160-361 1983 £30

CHAMEROVZOE, LOUIS A.   Chronicles of The Bastile. London: T.C. Newby, 1845-1848. First complete edition of the first series and first edition of the second series. Illus. on steel by Robert Cruikshank. 2 vols. Profusely illus. with engravings. Full blue morocco, gilt, marbled endpapers, t.e.g., by Riviere. Bookplates. Rear outer hinge of Vol.I cracked toward top of spine. Fine. MacManus 277-911 1983 $250

CHAMIER, FREDERICK   The Arethusa. A naval story. London: Bentley, 1837. First edition. 3 vols. 12mo. Cont. half calf. Bound without half-titles; light waterstains affecting lower corners of first and last few leaves in each volume. A bit rubbed. Ximenes 63-120 1983 $100

CHAMIER, FREDERICK   Ben Brace. Richard Bentley, 1836. First edition. 3 vols. Large 12mo, lacks half-titles and final advertisement leaf, etc, where called for. Cont. cloth, with the label of S. Roberts, Oswestry. Hannas 69-29 1983 £30

CHAMIER, FREDERICK   The Life of a Sailor. Bentley, 1832. First edition, 3 vols., half title vol. I, half green calf, a little rubbed, black and brown labels. Jarndyce 30-323 1983 £85

CHAMISSO, A. VON   The Shadowless Man & The Cold Heart. Holden & Harding, n.d. (1912). 4to. Mounted colour frontis. Pictorial title. 19 mounted colour plates. 10 tinted plates & 6 chapter vignettes. White pictorial cloth gilt. Edition de Luxe. Limited to 100 copies. Signed by artist. Greer 39-112 1983 £60

CHAMPION, FREDERICK W.   With A Camera In Tiger-Land. Garden City 1928. First ed. Photos, cloth, bookplate, inner hinges broken, covers spotted, spine worn. King 46-552 1983 $25

CHAMPION, FREDERICK W.   With a Camera in Tiger-Land. Garden City, 1928. 1st ed. Illus. Royal 8vo. Clark 741-414 1983 $25

CHAMPNEY, J. WELLS   Scrapbook containing some 250 original pencil and pen drawings made through the South. (1873). Sq. 4to, blue 3/4 levant by the Atelier Bindery, back gilt, joints worn. Argosy 710-490 1983 $3,500

CHANDLER, FRANK W.   Modern Continental Playwrights. New York: Harper & Brothers, 1931. First edition. 8vo. Cloth. Dust jacket. Presentation from Chandler to his collaborator, Estelle hunt. Oak Knoll 49-114 1983 $25

CHANDLER, JOHN   The New Seaman's Guide and Coaster's Companion. Printed for P. Mason, 1800. Oblong 8vo, engraved frontis. and 15 woodcut text figures, orig. sail-cloth. A fine copy. Bickersteth 75-118 1983 £48

CHANDLER, JOHN   The Remarkable History of Chicken Little (1840-1940). South Lanc., Ma.: Privately Printed, (1940). 12mo. Cloth. Wood engravings from orig. edition. Bio. of Chandler and history of book. Fine. Aleph-bet 8-59 1983 $20

CHANDLER, LLOYD H.   A Summary of the Work of Rudyard Kipling. N.Y.: The Grolier Club, 1930. Ltd. first edition. Small 4to, linen backed bpards; unopened. One of 325 numbered copies. Argosy 714-447 1983 $150

CHANDLER, M. E. J.   Lower Teriary Floras of Southern England. British Museum, 1961-64. 92 plates and 118 text-figures, 4 vols. in 5, 4to, buckram. Wheldon 160-1372 1983 £73.50

CHANDLER, PELEG W.   American Criminal Trials. Boston, 1841-1844. 2 vols. Orig. cloth. First edition. Fine set. Jenkins 153-123 1983 $385

CHANDLER, RAYMOND   The Little Sister. Boston, 1949. First edition. D.w. Argosy 714-865 1983 $100

CHANDLER, RAYMOND   Spanish Blood: A Collection of Short Stories. Cleveland & New York, 1946. 8vo. Cloth. A fine copy in dj. In Our Time 156-151 1983 $50

CHANDLER, RAYMOND   Spanish Blood. Cleveland and New York, 1946. First American edition. Dustwrapper. Fine. Jolliffe 26-92 1983 £15

CHANDLER, RICHARD   Travels in Greece. Dublin, 1776. 8vo, cont. calf. Lacks front fly. Bickersteth 77-13 1983 £36

CHANDLER, STEPHANIE   The Arts in Belgian Congo and Ruanda-Urundi. N.p.: CID, Information and Documentation Center for Belgian Congo and Ruanda-Urundi, 1950. 98 plates. Small 4to. Wrappers. Ars Libri 34-583 1983 $45

CHANDLER, THOMAS B.   What Think ye of Congress Now? New York, 1775. Disbound, loss of paper to title, not affecting text, otherwise very good. Printed by James Rivington. Reese 18-109 1983 $225

CHANDLESS, WILLIAM   A Visit to Salt Lake. London, Smith, Elder, 1857. 8vo, orig. cloth, worn, folding map wrinkled, inner joints splitting, bookplates. First edition. Ravenstree 97-121 1983 $125

CHANDRA DAS GUPTA, DEBENDRA   Educational Psychology of the Ancient Hindus. University of Calcutta, 1949. Orig. wrappers. Gach 94-533 1983 $20

CHANG, S. T.   The Biology and Cultivation of Edible
Mushrooms. 1978. 8vo, cloth. Wheldon 160-1799 1983 £54

CHANLER, WILLIAM ASTOR   Through jungle and desert. New York:
Macmillan, 1896. 8vo. 2 portraits, 2 folding maps, 18 plates.
Orig. blue cloth, rubbed. Adelson Africa-71 1983 $175

CHANNELL, L. S.   History of Compton County... Cook-
shire, Quebec: The Author, 1896. 31 1/2cm. 200 illus. Orig.
cloth expertly restored. Fine. Rare. McGahern 54-36 1983 $165

CHANNING, WILLIAM E.   A Sermon, Delivered in Boston... Boston,
1814. Stitched, good. Reese 18-436 1983 $20

CHANNING, WILLIAM E.   A Sermon on War. Boston, 1816. Stitched,
good. Reese 18-494 1983 $25

CHANNING, WILLIAM E.   A Sermon, Preached in Boston...the
Day of the Publick Fast... Boston, 1812. Dsb. Foxed. Good. Reese
18-369 1983 $25

THE CHAPBOOK. London: The Poetry Bookshop. 1919-1925. 40 vols.
38 in the original pictorial wrappers and 2 in the original boards (one
with a chipped dust jacket). With the prospectus for No. 40 laid into
that vol., and a handwitten notice on the Poetry Bookshop's letterhead.
Covers slightly soiled. Bookplate and previous owner's signature in
one vol. Endpapers of two vol. browned. Wrappers on two or three vol.
a bit frayed. Very good. MacManus 277-912 1983 $1,000

CHAPELLE, H. I.   The History of American Sailing Ships.
New York, 1935. 4to. Orig. decorated cloth. Coloured title page.
16 double page plans, 7 plates, numerous illus., many full page. Good.
First trade edition. Edwards 1042-27 1983 £50

CHAPELLE, H. I.   The History of the American Sailing Navy.
New York, 1949. First edition. 4to, orig. decorated cloth. Coloured
frontis. 8 plates, 32 folding plans, numerous illus., many full page.
Very slightly worn. Good. Edwards 1042-28 1983 £50

CHAPIN, ANNA A.   The Everday Fairy Book. J. Coker, n.d.
Large 4to. Colour frontis. Title vignette & 6 colour plates. Colour
pictorial boards, bumped. Greer 39-118 1983 £25

CHAPIN, HAROLD   The Comedies. London: Chatto & Windus,
1921. An introduction by J.M. Barrie. Orig. cloth. Dust jacket.
First edition. Fine copy. MacManus 277-218 1983 $25

CHAPIN, J. P.   The Birds of the Belgian Congo. New
York, 1932-54. 73 plates (some coloured), 328 text-figures and a
map, 4 vols., royal 8vo, half cloth. Very scarce. A nice clean copy.
Wheldon 160-674 1983 $350

CHAPIN, WILLIAM   A Complete Reference Gazetteer of the
United States of North America... New York: Pub. by T.E.H. Ensign,
1845. Orig. cloth. Fine copy. Jenkins 153-750 1983 $100

THE CHAPLET; an Elegant Literary Miscellany. J. Harwood, (1845).
First edition, with additional engraved vignette title-page and
26 engraved plates, roy. 8vo, orig. pub.'s gilt and blindstamped
morocco, edges gilt. Front blank flyleaf is wanting and two small
sections are working loose. Fenning 62-61 1983 £28.50

CHAPMAN, ARTHUR   The Pony Express, The Record of a
Romantic Business. New York, 1932. Frontis. 1st ed. in dj. Fine.
Jenkins 153-440 1983 $45

CHAPMAN, ARTHUR   The Pony Express. New York, 1932. 1st
ed. Contemporary prints, photos. Clark 741-416 1983 $40

CHAPMAN, BIRD B.   Memorial of...With Accompanying
Papers and Depositions Contesting the Right of Fenner Ferguson to
His Seat as a Delegate from the Territory of Nebraska. Wash., 1857.
Dbd. First edition. Ginsberg 47-613 1983 $30

CHAPMAN, CHARLES   The Suez Canal. London, 1870. Second
edition. Large folding plan. Decorative cloth. 8vo. Good. Edwards
1044-130 1983 £40

CHAPMAN, EDMUND   An Essay on the Improvement of Midwifery. London, 1733. First edition. 8vo. Old calf, rebacked.
Ownership stamp on title. Some light foxing. Gurney 90-33 1983
£275

CHAPMAN, FRANK M.   The Warblers of North America. NY 1917.
3rd ed. Cloth, corners bumped, lower spine rather rubbed.
Color plates, drawings by Louis Agassiz Fuertes. King 46-508 1983
$20

CHAPMAN, GEORGE   The Comedies and Tragedies. London,
1873. 3 vols. 12mo. Binder's cloth. Traylen 94-176 1983 £16

CHAPMAN, GEORGE   The Works. London: Chatto & Windus,
1975. First edition with this introduction (by A. C. Swinburne).
Orig. cloth. Former owner's signature on half-title. A little light
foxing. Fine. MacManus 280-5020 1983 $25

CHAPMAN, HENRY SMITH   History of Winchester, Massachusetts.
Winchester, 1936. 1st ed. Illus. 8vo. Few cover spots. Morrill
287-217 1983 $25

CHAPMAN, ISAAC A.   A Sketch of the History of Wyoming.
Wilkesbarre, 1830. 1st ed. 12mo, contemporary calf. Some light
dampstains in text, otherwise nice. Morrill 286-667 1983 $65

CHAPMAN, NATHANIEL   Lectures on the More Important
Eruptive Fevers, Haemorrhages and Dropsies, and on Gout and
Rheumatism. Philadelphia, 1844. Ads. Full calf. Foxed. First
edition. Felcone 22-145 1983 $35

CHAPMAN, R. G.   Charles Darwin, 1809-1882, A Centennial
Commemorative. Wellington, 1982. 4to, half leather, slip case,
coloured and plain plates. Edition limited to 1000 copies. Wheldon
160-21 1983 £270

CHAPMAN, THOMAS   An Inquiry into the Rights of Appeal
from the Chancellor, or Vice-Chancellor, of the University of
Cambridge, in Matters of Discipline. Printed for J. Payne and J.
Bouquet, 1751. 8vo, disbound. Bickersteth 77-14 1983 £28

CHAPMAN, V. J.   Introduction to the Study of Algae.
Cambridge, 1941. 24 tables and 209 diagrams, 8vo, cloth. Wheldon
160-1800 1983 £15

CHAPMAN, WILLIAM   Observations On The Most Advisable
Measures To Be Adopted In Forming A Communication For The Transit
Of Merchandise And The Produce Of Land. Newcastle: Printed by
Edward Walker, 1824. First edition, 8vo, modern calf-backed marbled
boards, slightly foxed. Deighton 3-72 1983 £140

CHAPON, FRANCOIS   Rouault: Oeuvre grave. Monte-Carlo:
Andre Sauret, 1978. 2 vols. Most prof. illus. Small folio.
Cloth. Dust jacket. No. 27 of a limited edition of 220 copies,
containing an orig. aquatint by Rouault, signed and numbered in the
margins by Isabelle Rouault. Ars Libri 32-590 1983 $500

CHAPPE D'AUTEROCHE, JEAN-BAPTISTE   Voyage en Californie pour l'observation de passage de Venus sur le disque du soleil, le 3 Juin 1769.
Paris: Charles-Antoine Jombert, 1772. Folding map of Mexico City.
Plates and charts. Calf, rebacked. Orig. edition. Dawson 471-44
1983 $1,250

CHAPPE D'AUTEROCHE, JEAN-BAPTISTE   Voyage en Californie pour l'Observation Du Passage de Venus sur le disque du Soleil...MDCCLXXII.
(1772). 4to. Engr. folding map, folding table. 3 engr. plates.
Quarter modern calf, gilt stamped and tooled between raised bands.
Marbled paper covered boards, marbled endpapers. Half title margin
reinforced. Many leaves with deckled edges. Some light toning. A. E.
Lownes bookplate. Arkway 22-29 1983 $1,500

CHAPPUIS, ADRIEN   The Drawings of Paul Cezanne: A
Catalogue Raisonne. Greenwich: New York Graphic Society, 1973.
2 vols. Vol. 1: 168 illus. Vol. 2: 1223 illus. Large 4to.
Cloth. Slipcase. Ars Libri 32-87 1983 $150

CHARAKA CLUB.   The Proceedings of the Charaka Club.
New York, 1910. 8vo. Orig. binding. Limited edition of 370 copies.
Fye H-3-85 1983 $60

CHARAKA CLUB. The Proceedings of the Charaka Club. Vol. 7. New York, 1931. 8vo. Orig. binding. Limited edition of 575 copies. Fye H-3-86 1983 $60

CHARAS, MOISE Nouvelles Experiences sur la Vipere... Paris, 1672. Second French edition. 8vo. Vellum. Engraved frontis. and 3 folding plates. Library stamp on frontis. and title. Gurney 90-34 1983 £125

CHARCOT, J. M. Lectures on the Diseases of the Nervous System. London: New Sydenham Society, 1877. First edition in English. 8vo, cloth. Arogsy 713-100 1983 $60

CHARDON, FRANCIS T. Chardon's Journal at Fort Clark, 1834-1839. Pierre, S.D., 1932. Plates. Edges untrimmed, some water staining. Clark 741-264 1983 $30

THE CHARGE of the Scottish Commissioners against Canterburie and the Lieutenant of Ireland. London: for Nath Butter, 1641. 4to. Uncut, stitched as issued. Slightly frayed at blank corner. Heath 48-211 1983 £65

CHARKE, CHARLOTTE The Art of Management; or, tragedy expell'd. London: printed by W. Rayner, 1735. 8vo, polished calf, gilt, spine gilt. First edition. Last leaf mounted, a number of margins neatly renewed, not affecting the text (save for one or two shaved headlines); title dusty. Extremely rare. Ximenes 64-75 1983 $750

CHARKE, CHARLOTTE A Narrative of the Life of Mrs. Charlotte Charke. London: printed for W. Reeve; A. Dodd; and E. Cook, 1755. 12mo, full polished mottled calf, gilt spine and inner dentelles gilt, a.e.g. by Roger de Coverly (small rubbed spot on upper hinge). 1st ed., with a portrait; half-title present. A fine copy. Scarce. Ximenes 64-76 1983 $400

CHARLES, ELIZABETH Chronicles of the Schonberg-Cotta Family. T. Nelson & Son, 1886. 8vo, including engraved frontis., and engraved and printed titles, a.e.g., full brown morocco, ruled in blind, gilt dentelles. Bickersteth 77-192 1983 £12

CHARLES, ELIZABETH Diary of Mrs. Kitty Trevylyan. N.Y.: Dodd, 1864. First American(?) edition. With a preface by the author. Orig. cloth. Fine. MacManus 277-913 1983 $20

CHARLES' Wain. A Miscellany of short stories. London: Mallinson, (1933). First edition. 8vo. Frontis. by Nina Hamnett. Orig. cloth. Publisher's slipcase. One of only 95 copies signed by the 18 contributors. Spine a little darkened, otherwise a fine, unopened copy. Jaffe 1-12 1983 $275

CHARLES-ROUX, F. Bonaparte; Governor of Egypt. London, 1937. 8vo. Half red morocco, gilt, t.e.g. 16 plates and 2 maps. Traylen 94-630 1983 £24

CHARLESWORTH, MARIA LOUISA Ministering Children. Seeley, Jackson & Halliday, 1867. First edition. Half title, front. Engr. title, 2 pp ads. Orig. blue cloth, bevelled boards, v.g. Jarndyce 31-477 1983 £15

CHARLESWORTH, MARIA LOUISA Oliver of the Mill. Seeley, Jackson & Halliday, 1876. First edition. Front. engr. title. 3 pp ads. Orig. dark green dec. cloth, a little rubbed. Jarndyce 31-478 1983 £10.50

CHARLETON, WALTER Spiritus Gorgonicus Visua Saxipara Exutus, siv de Causis, Signis, & Sanatione Lithiaseos. 16mo, modern marbled boards. First edition. Argosy 713-101 1983 $300

CHARLEVOIX, PIERRE FRANCOIS XAVIER DE Histoire du Paraguay. Paris: Desaint, David & Durand, 1757. 2nd ed., 12mo, 6 vols., cont. calf and morocco labels. 7 folding maps and charts. Half-titles in four volumes; privilege leaf in vol. I. Minor wear to some outer hinges, some light dampstaining, nevertheless a fine, crisp copy. Trebizond 18-134 1983 $400

CHARLEVOIX, PIERRE FRANCIS-XAVIER DE Journal of a Voyage to North-America... London: Printed for R., and J. Dodsley, 1761. Two vols. Three quarter gilt morocco. Folding map. A very fine set, bound complete with the half-titles, and the ads in the second volume. Reese 18-73 1983 $1,200

THE CHARMS of Melody. Dublin, n.d. (1796?). Folio, 1/2 calf. Nos. 1-100 (Lacks issues 21-26; 36; 52 and one leaf each of Nos. 48 and 78). Title page reinforced. New binding. Salloch 387-44 1983 $150

CHARYN, JEROME Once upon a Droshky. New York: McGraw-Hill, (1964). Cloth and boards. First edition. Inscribed by the author on the front free endpaper. Reese 20-236 1983 $85

A CHART of Part of the Coast of Canada. Londono, (1794). Finely engraved map. Engraved by Thomas Jefferys. Argosy 710-49 1983 $200

CHARTERIS, LESLIE Call for the Saint. Lon., (1948). Very good in chipped, slightly soiled and worn, presentable dustwrapper. Quill & Brush 54-268 1983 $30

CHASE, PHILIP S. Service with Battery F, First Rhode Island Light Artillery in North Carolina. Providence, 1884. Orig. printed wraps. First edition. One of 250 copies. Ginsberg 46-550 1983 $25

CHASE, PHILIP S. Service with Battery F, First R.I. Light Artillery. Providence, 1889. Orig. printed wraps. Ginsberg 46-167 1983 $25

CHASE, SALMON P. Banks in the United States. Wash., 1863. Dbd. First edition. Ginsberg 46-47 1983 $35

THE CHASE. London: Daniel O'Conner, 1922. First edition. Frontis. by Claude Lovat Fraser. Orig. cloth. Dust jacket (spine and covers slightly soiled and worn at the margins, two very small tears to the rear cover, with a small chip missing from the front cover). Spine a trifle faded. Near-fine. MacManus 278-1986 1983 $125

CHAST, ROZ Last Resorts. (New York: Ink, Inc., 1979). Unbound folio leaves, laid into printed wrapper and folding cloth portfolio. One of 150 numbered copies, signed by the cartoonist, with one plate handcolored. Mint as issued. Designed and printed by Tom Whitridge. Reese 20-1125 1983 $200

CHATEAUBRIAND, FRANCOIS R. DE, VISCOUNT Celuta; or, The Natchez: an Indian Tale. Henry Colburn and Richard Bentley, 1832. Second edition. In three vols., without half-titles. Small 8vo, cont. half calf, gilt spines. "Atala" is added on pages 323-412 of the final volume. Fenning 62-62 1983 £32.50

CHATFIELD, R. An Historical Review of the Commercial, Political, and Moral State of Hindoostan. London, 1808. Folding map, slight spotting. 4to. Half blue morocco, spine faded. Good. Edwards 1044-121 1983 £125

CHATTERTON, EDWARD KEBLE Danger Zone. Boston, 1934. 1st ed. 40 plates & 3 maps. 8vo, partly torn dust wrapper. Morrill 287-531 1983 $25

CHATTERTON, EDWARD KEBLE King's Cutters and Smugglers, 1700-1855. Philadelphia, 1912. Colored frontispiece and 33 other illustrations. 8vo, half original leather. Rubbed, some light dampstains on bottom margin. Morrill 290-58 1983 $25

CHATTERTON, EDWARD KEBLE Old Sea Paintings. London, 1928. First edition. 4to. Orig. cloth. Coloured frontis. 14 coloured and 64 other plates. Slightly worn. Good. Edwards 1042-30 1983 £60

CHATTERTON, EDWARD KEBLE Old Ship Prints. New York, 1927. First U.S. edition. 4to. Orig. cloth. Coloured frontis. 14 coloured and 95 other plates. Uncut. Some very faint foxing. Review copy with printed slip tipped in at front endpaper. Good. Edwards 1042-31 1983 £60

CHATTERTON, EDWARD KEBLE Ship-Models. London, The Studio Ltd., 1923. Ed. limited to 1000 copies. 4to, plates. Morrill 288-63 1983 $100

CHATTERTON, EDWARD KEBLE The Ship Under Sail. London, 1926. First edition. Sq. 8vo. Orig. cloth. Frontis. 23 plates (1 folding). Spine faded, illus. endpapers. Good. Edwards 1042-33 1983 £35

CHATTERTON, EDWARD KEBLE   Steamship Models. London, 1924. Limited edition signed by author. 4to. Orig. blue buckram. Coloured mounted frontis. 7 coloured mounted plates, 120 plates and illus. Gilt. Lower cover slightly dampstained. Good. Edwards 1042-34 1983 £90

CHATTERTON, GEORGIANA   Aunt Dorothy's Tale. Richard Bentley, 1837. First edition, 2 vols. Half titles. Without the 'apology' slip mentioned by Sadleir. Half calf. Very good. Jarndyce 30-324 1983 £46

CHATTERTON, GEORGIANA   Memoirs... Hurst & Blackett, 1878. First edition, half title, 16 pp ads. Orig. green cloth, sl. rubbed. Jarndyce 30-945 1983 £24

CHATTERON, GEORGIANA   Oswald of Deira. Longmans, Green, 1867. First edition, half title, orig. cream cloth, spine sl. darkened. Jarndyce 30-664 1983 £10.50

CHATTERTON, THOMAS   Poems, supposed to have been written at Bristol... London: T. Payne and Son, 1777. First edition, second state. 8vo. Three-quarter 19th century leather binding. Front hinge weak and endpaper detached. Rare. Oak Knoll 49-116 1983 $350

CHATTERTON, THOMAS   The Works. London: by Biggs and Cottle, 1803. First collected edition. 7 engraved plates, inc. one folding. 3 vols. 8vo. 19th century full green morocco, gilt floral borders, gilt decorated spines, inner gilt dentelles, edges gilt, by James Toovey. Traylen 94-177 1983 £105

CHATTO, WILLIAM ANDREW   A Paper:--Of Tobacco. London: Chapman & Hall, 1839. First edition. Illus. by Phiz. Orig. pictorial boards. Boards worn. Front inner hinge cracked. Some foxing. Good. MacManus 277-919 1983 $50

CHATTO, WILLIAM ANDREW   A Treatise on Wood Engraving... London: Chatto and Windus, (1861). New edition. Thick small 4to. Half leather over pebbled cloth, t.e.g. Minor spotting of the front cover, else a fine copy. Oak Knoll 48-100 1983 $125

CHAUCER, GEOFFREY   The Canterbury Tales. Oxford: at the Clarendon Press, 1798. 2 vols, 4to, nineteenth century half red morocco, rubbed at the edges. Bickersteth 75-18 1983 £68

CHAUCER, GEOFFREY   The Canterbury Tales. Routledge, 1857. New edn. Illus. by Edward Corbould. Frontis. & 7 wood engrs. engr'd by Bros. Dalziel. Royal blue chain ribbed blind stamped cloth, gilt vignette fr. cvr., a.e.g. Name half title, eps. cracked at hinges, vg. Hodgkins 27-253 1983 £15

CHAUCER, GEOFFREY   The Canterbury Tales of Geoffrey Chaucer. London: the Riccardi Press, 1913. 3 vols. 4to. Orig. grey boards with canvas spines, printed paper labels, t.e.g., others uncut. 36 mounted coloured plates from drawings by W. Russell Flint. Limited edition of 500 numbered copies, printed on hand-made Riccardi paper. Traylen 94-180 1983 £180

CHAUCER, GEOFFREY   The Canterbury Tales of... N.Y.: Covici-Friede, 1930. 2 vols. Folio. Orig. cloth. One of 999 numbered and signed by the artist, Rockwell Kent. Small bookplate in each vol. Very good. MacManus 277-920 1983 $225

CHAUCER, GEOFFREY   Canterbury Tales. N.Y., (1934). First trade edition. Thick small 4to, dust jacket. Very good. Illus. with full page plates and vignettes by Kent. Houle 21-469 1983 $85

CHAUCER, GEOFFREY   The Canterbury Tale of the Miller. San Francisco: (Black Vine Press). 1939. Tall 8vo, with 3 woodcut illus. Printed in red & black by Lawton R. Kennedy, Harold N. Seeger and Albert A. Sperison. Bound in calf-backed blind-stamped boards. Spine gilt-stamped, but calf is a bit faded. Some slight foxing. Slipcase. Karmiole 76-15 1983 $60

CHAUCER, GEOFFREY   The Canterbury Tales. New York, 1946. Done into modern English by Frank Ernest Hill. Portraits in miniature by Arthur Szyk. 8vo., pigskin backed dec. paper over boards, slipcase, one of 1500 copies signed by the artist. Very nice copy. Perata 27-127 1983 $175

CHAUCER, GEOFFREY   The Poetical Works. London, 1866. 6 vols. Cr. 8vo. Dark blue calf, two-line gilt borders with corner ornaments, gilt panelled spines with morocco labels, gilt. Portrait, vignette title-pages. Traylen 94-181 1983 £80

CHAUCER, GEOFFREY   The Poetical Works. London, 1884-85. The Aldine edition. 6 vols. 12mo. Orig. green cloth, gilt, uncut edges. Traylen 94-182 1983 £15

CHAUCER, GEOFFREY   Selected Works. London, Scott, n.d. Ca., 1898. Small 8vo, half vellum over boards, brown leather spine label, the spine stamped in gilt with a floral motif, t.e.g. Fine. Houle 21-205 1983 $65

CHAUCER, GEOFFREY   Troilus and Cressida. N.Y., 1932. Vellum backed boards. Some cover soil and wear. Each page with wood engraving plus full page engravings by E. Gill. Good. King 45-401 1983 $25

CHAUCER, GEOFFREY   The Works of Our Ancient and Learned English Poet, Geoffrey Chaucer, Newly Printed. London: Printed by Adam Islip at the charges of Bonham Norton, 1598. Folio. First ed. edited by Speght, and the 5th ed. of Chaucer's collected works. Cont. panelled calf, label. Frontis. portrait. Fine crisp text and well-preserved binding. Ownership inscriptions of Judge Richard Newgate and his grandson Roger. Jenkins 155-202 1983 $1,000

CHAUCER, GEOFFREY   Works. Stratford-upon-Avon: the Shakespeare Head Press, 1928-29. 8 vols. 4to. Orig. holland-backed blue boards, uncut edges. Limited edition of 375 numbered copies, printed in red, blue and black, large initials in red and blue, paragraph vignette drawings supplied by hand, some full-page illus. and many smaller illus. and marginal vignette drawings, almost all coloured by hand. Traylen 94-919 1983 £595

CHAUNCY, CHARLES   Breaking of Bread in Rememberance of the Dying Love of Christ... Boston, 1772. Rough cloth binding, reinforced with printed waste sheets and newspapers. Reese 18-95 1983 $225

CHAUNCY, CHARLES   Nathanael's Character Displayed. (Boston), printed in the year 1733. Three quarter roan and boards. A fine, untrimmed copy, bound complete with the half-title. Reese 18-50 1983 $150

CHAUNCY, CHARLES   Seasonable Thoughts on the State of Religion in New-England, a Treatise in Five Parts... Boston, 1743. Leather. Front cover worn. Good. Reese 18-56 1983 $175

CHAVEAU, C.   Les Maitres de l'Ecole de Paris dans la periode pre-specialistique... Paris, 1908-10. 8vo. 2 vols. in one. Buckram, wrappers bound in. Gurney JJ-70 1983 £20

CHAVEZ, AGUSTIN VELAZQUEZ   Contemporary Mexican Artists. NY: Covici-Friede, (1937). Profusely illus. with full-page b/w plates. Brown cloth. Karmiole 76-78 1983 $40

CHAWNER, ROSA A.   Hits and Bits. Cheltenham F.C. Westly; London: Simpkin, Marshall, 1861. First edition, orig. pale mauve cloth, faded. Jarndyce 31-479 1983 £12.50

CHEADLE, W. W.   Cheadle's Journal of Trip Across Canada, 1862-1863. Ottawa: Graphic, 1931. 20cm. Illus. Rear folding map, limp fabrikoid. Very good copy. McGahern 54-37 1983 $40

CHEADLE, WALTER BUTLER   On Some Cirrhoses of the Liver. London, 1900. First edition. 12mo, cloth, (spine chipped). Argosy 713-102 1983 $40

A CHECK List of California Non-Documentary Imprints 1833-1855. San Francisco, 1942. 4to, orig. pr. wrs., rebacked with cloth. Argosy 710-42 1983 $35

CHECK List of Kansas Imprints, 1854-1876. Topeka: WPA Historical Records Survey Project, 1939. Thick 4to. Cloth. Oak Knoll 49-458 1983 $45

CHECK List of Kentucky Imprints, 1811-1820. Louisville: The Historical Records Survey, 1939. 4to. Cloth spine, paper wrappers. Cover wear. Oak Knoll 48-447 1983 $45

CHEESEMAN, T. F.   Illustrations of the New Zealand Flora. Wellington, 1914. 251 plates with descriptions, 2 vols., royal 4to, cloth. Signature on title-pages. Wheldon 160-1660 1983 £180

CHEESMAN, R. E.   In Unknown Arabia. Macmillan, 1906. First edition, with many plates, maps and plans, roy. 8vo, orig. cloth, gilt, t.e.g. A very good copy. Fenning 60-65 1983 £48.50

CHEETHAM, JAMES   Peace or War? New York: M. Ward, 1807. First edition. Later calf-backed boards. Argosy 716-596 1983 $50

CHEEVER, CHARLES A.   Extracts from (his) Writings. Boston, 1854. First edition. Fine. Argosy 713-105 1983 $100

CHEEVER, DAVID   A History of the Boston City Hospital from its Foundation until 1904. Boston, 1906. First edition. 8vo. Orig. binding. Fye H-3-88 1983 $50

CHEEVER, GEORGE B.   The American Common-Place Book of Poetry. Boston: Carter, Hendee, 1831. Frontis. 1st ed. New bright purple half-morocco and marbled boards, gilt label, tooling. Early appearances of Longfellow, Whittier, et al. Fine copy. Jenkins 155-854 1983 $65

CHEEVER, HENRY T.   The Island World of the Pacific. NY, 1851. Illus., fold-out map, interior foxed, cover worn, good or better, bookplate. Quill & Brush 54-1687 1983 $60

CHEEVER, HENRY T.   The Island World of the Pacific... Glasgow, William Collins, ca. 1860. 8vo, old style half calf. K Books 307-46 1983 £46

CHEEVER, JOHN   The Day the Pig Fell Into the Well. CA, 1978. One of 275 numbered and signed copies, fine. Quill & Brush 54-269 1983 $125

CHEEVER, JOHN   The Enormous Radio and Other Stories. N.Y., 1953. First edition. 8vo, cloth; backstrip lightly spotted. Argosy 714-148 1983 $50

CHEKHOV, ANTON   Voisins. Paris: Librairie Plon, (1927). Orig. printed wraps. First edition in French. Slight wear to spine, otherwise a near fine copy. Reese 20-238 1983 $50

CHELTENHAM: A Fragment. London Printed, and sold by G. Robinson; S. Harward, Tewkesbury, Glocester and Cheltenham, 1780. First edition. Rebound in hand-marbled boards, paper label. 4to, v.g. Jarndyce 31-8 1983 £60

CHELTENHAM in the Wrong. Tewkesbury: S. Harward, Glocester and Cheltham, 1781. First edition. 4to. Sl. close trimmed to final of imprint. Rebound in hand-marbled boards, paper label. Very good. Jarndyce 31-9 1983 £60

THE CHEMICAL SOCIETY.   Faraday Lectures 1869-1928. London: The Chemical Society, 1928. 8vo. Orig. blue cloth. Facsimile letter, folding table. 16 plates. Minor spotting of covers, internally very good. Zeitlin 264-72 1983 $50

THE CHEMICAL SOCIETY.   Memorial Lectures Delivered Before the Chemical Society 1893-1900. London: Gurney and Jackson, 1901. 8vo. Orig. cloth. Partially unopened. 13 portraits, 1 photographic plate. Facsimile letters. Rubbed. Zeitlin 264-73 1983 $75

THE CHEMICAL SOCIETY.   Memorial Lectures Delivered Before The Chemical Society 1893-1900. London: Gurney and Jackson, 1901. 8vo. Orig. cloth. 13 portraits, 1 photographic plate. Facsimile letters. Rubbed. Zeitlin 264-74 1983 $70

THE CHEMICAL SOCIETY.   Memorial Lectures delivered before The Chemical Society 1901-1913. London: Gurney & Jackson, 1914. 8vo. Orig. cloth. 14 portraits. First edition. A fine copy. Zeitlin 264-75 1983 $50

THE CHEMICAL SOCIETY.   Memorial Lectures Delivered Before The Chemical Society 1914-1932. London: The Chemical Society, 1933. 8vo. Orig. blue cloth. 5 plates with portraits. A very good copy. Zeitlin 264-76 1983 $50

THE CHEMICAL SOCIETY.   A Record of the Centenary Celebrations 1947. London: The Chemical Society, 1948. 4to. Orig. cardboard wrapper. 5 plates. Zeitlin 264-79 1983 $20

CHENEY, JOHN   Catalogue of the Engraved and Lithographed Work of John Cheney and Seth Wells Cheney. Boston, 1891. 1st ed. Portrait. 8vo, nice. Morrill 286-236 1983 $20

CHENEY, JOHN   The Caxton Club Scrap Book: Early English Verses, 1250-1650. 1st ed., limited to 250 copies. Orig. cloth-backed boards, uncut. Very good copy. Jenkins 155-204 1983 $30

CHENEY, O. H.   Supplementary Report of the Economic Survey of the Book Industry... New York: Employing Bookbinders of America, 1932. First edition. 8vo. Cloth. Oak Knoll 49-85 1983 $35

CHENEY, T. APOLEON   Historical Sketch of the Chemung Valley. New York: Watkins, 1866. Later wrappers. Presentation copy from author. Jenkins 152-295 1983 $50

CHENG, TSO-HSIN   China's Economic Fauna: Birds. Washington, USJPRS, 1964. 64 plates (35 coloured), 4to, half cloth. Wheldon 160-675 1983 £40

CHENU, J. C.   Encyclopedie d'Histoire Naturelle: Oiseaux. Paris (1852-54). 240 plates and 2081 text-figures, 6 vols. in 3, 4to, half calf (trifle worn). Scarce. The scarce "Table alphabetique" by Desmarest, which was published later, is not included. A few figures have been neatly coloured by a former owner; there is a little offsetting and dustsoiling, but the set is generally in good condition. Wheldon 160-676 1983 £85

LA CHERCHEUSE D'Esprit. Paris, chez la veuve Allouet, 1741. Woodcut vignette on title. Small 8vo, wrs. First edition. Salloch 387-164 1983 $45

CHERRY, RICHARD R.   The Irish Land Law and Land Purchase Acts, 1860 to 1891. Dublin, J. Falconer, 1893. Second edition. Roy. 8vo, orig. cloth, inside joints cracked but holding. A very good copy. Fenning 62-63 1983 £24.50

CHESNEL, PAUL   History of Cavelier de la Salle, 1643-1687... N.Y.: Putnam's, 1932. 1st ed. in dj. Fld. map. Nice copy. Jenkins 153-322 1983 $25

CHESNEY, ALLEN   Johns Hopkins Hospital and the Johns Hopkins University School of Medicine... Baltimore, 1943, 1958, 1963. Fye H-3-91 1983 $75

CHESNEY, ALLEN   The Johns Hopkins Hospital and the Johns Hopkins University School of Medicine... Vol. 1. Baltimore, 1943. 8vo. Orig. binding. First edition. Autographed by the author. Fye H-3-92 1983 $50

CHESNEY, ALLEN   The Johns Hopkins Hospital... Baltimore, 1943. 8vo. Orig. binding. First edition. Fye H-3-93 1983 $35

CHESNEY, ALLEN   The Johns Hopkins Hospital... Baltimore, 1943. 8vo. Orig. binding. Ex-library. Fye H-3-94 1983 $20

CHESSON, NORA   Selected Poems. London, 1916. First edition. Intro. by Ford Madox Hueffer. 5 vols. Wrappers. Very nice. Rota 231-218 1983 £20

CHESTERFIELD, PHILIP DORMER STANHOPE, FOURTH EARL OF   Letters...to his son, Philip Stanhope... London: For J. Dodsley, 1774. First edition. 2 vols., 4to. Cont. marbled boards, new calf spines with crimson and green morocco labels, gilt. Portrait, half-titles to each vol. Errata leaf at end of vol. 2. Traylen 94-184 1983 £225

CHESTERFIELD, PHILIP DORMER STANHOPE, FOURTH EARL OF   Letters.
London, 1845. Frontis. portraits. 4 vols., 8v . Bindings faded, tops
of spines frayed, minute tear on spine of vol. 4. Morrill 287-58 1983
$25

CHESTERFIELD, PHILIP DORMER STANHOPE, FOURTH EARL OF   Miscellaneous
Works... London: E. & C. Dilly, 1777. First edition. 2 vols., 4to.
Cont. calf, old rebacking. Portrait and frontis. to vol. 2 by Barto-
lozzi, half-titles. Traylen 94-187 1983 £160

CHESTERTON, CECIL   The Perils of Peace. London: T. Werner
Laurie, Ltd., (1916). First edition. Intro. by Hilaire Belloc. Orig.
cloth. Dust jacket (worn at edges). Pasted to the front flyleaf is an
APC, 1 page, no place, 16 November 1914, from the author to Holbrook
Jackson. Very good. MacManus 277-922 1983 $75

CHESTERTON, E.   The Wonderful Story of Dunder van Haeden.
London: Brimley Johnson, n.d. (1901). First edition. With illus.
by the author. Orig. red pictorial boards. Margins of boards a trifle
darkened. Fine. MacManus 277-923 1983 $85

CHESTERTON, GEORGE L.   Peace, War, and Adventure. London,
1853. 2 vols. bound in one. Full polished calf, gilt, with some
wear to hinges and extremities, otherwise very good. Reese 19-141
1983 $125

CHESTERTON, GILBERT KEITH   Alarms and Discursions. London, 1910.
First edition. Nice. Rota 230-118 1983 £12

CHESTERTON, GILBERT KEITH   All is Grist. N.Y., 1932. First
American edition. 8vo, d.w. Argosy 714-151 1983 $30

CHESTERTON, GILBERT KEITH   All Things Considered. London: Methuen
& Co., (1908). First edition. Orig. cloth. Covers a little rubbed.
Endpapers slightly soiled. Good. MacManus 277-924 1983 $25

CHESTERTON, GILBERT KEITH   All Things Considered. N.Y.: John Lane
Co., 1908. First American edition. Orig. cloth. Good. MacManus 277-
925 1983 $20

CHESTERTON, GILBERT KEITH   An Anthology of Recent Poetry. London,
Harrap, (1920). First edition. Small 8vo, blue cloth stamped in
black & gilt; cover border in blind (spine faded, small stain on
cover). Good - very good. Houle 22-214 1983 $37.50

CHESTERTON, GILBERT KEITH   Autobiography. London, (1936). First
edition, illus., d.w. Argosy 714-152 1983 $30

CHESTERTON, GILBERT KEITH   The Ball and The Cross. London: Wells,
Gardner, Darton & Co., Ltd., (1910). Orig. pictorial paper wrappers.
Unrecorded format: probably a remainder binding, rather than an
advance copy, being the second state of the text. Wrappers a little
worn at extremities of spine. Very good. MacManus 277-928 1983 $125

CHESTERTON, GILBERT KEITH   The Ballad of St. Barbara & Other Verses.
London: Cecil Palmer, (1922). First edition. Orig. cloth-backed
boards. In a half-morocco slipcase. Fine. MacManus 277-927 1983
$85

CHESTERTON, GILBERT KEITH   The Ballad of St. Barbara & Other Verses.
London, Cecil Palmer, (1922). First edition. Cloth over decorated
boards. Dust jacket (slight soiling, light foxing at edge of pages)
else, very good. Houle 22-189 1983 $65

CHESTERTON, GILBERT KEITH   The Ballad of The White Horse. London:
Methuen & Co. Ltd., (1911). First edition. Orig. cloth. Former
owner's signature on front flyleaf. Red half-morocco slipcase. Near-
fine. MacManus 277-926 1983 $85

CHESTERTON, GILBERT KEITH   Charles Dickens. 1906. First edition.
2 ports. Orig. brown cloth, library labels on inside covers. Jarndyce
30-147 1983 £10.50

CHESTERTON, GILBERT KEITH   Chaucer. London, 1932. Advance proof
copy. Wrappers. Pencilled notes on lower cover. Very good. Jolliffe
26-94 1983 £32

CHESTERTON, GILBERT KEITH   Christendom in Dublin. NY, 1933. Paperwraps, minor interior soiling, cover slightly skinned and dampstained
with title written in ink down spine, good, tight copy, owner's name
on fly and cover. Quill & Brush 54-270 1983 $30

CHESTERTON, GILBERT KEITH   The Collected Poems. London, Burns,
Oates & Washbourne, (1927). First edition, state B with title leaf
on a stub. Aqua cloth (slight rubbing) stamped in gilt. Very
good. Houle 22-193 1983 $30

CHESTERTON, GILBERT KEITH   Collected Poems. London, 1927. Roy.
8vo. Orig. quarter vellum over batik paper boards, t.e.g., others
uncut. Limited edition of 350 copies, numbered and signed by the
author. Traylen 94-188 1983 £65

CHESTERTON, GILBERT KEITH   Collected Poems. London, 1927. First
edition. One of 350 numbered copies, signed by author. Quarter parchment, batik boards. Spine just a little darkened. Very nice. Rota
230-119 1983 £35

CHESTERTON, GILBERT KEITH   The Coloured Lands. London: Sheed &
Ward, 1938. First edition, in a variant (all board) binding. 4to.
Illus. in color & black & white by the author. Orig. pale green bds.
Dust jacket with design not reproduced in text. Very fine. MacManus
277-929 1983 $100

CHESTERTON, GILBERT KEITH   The Coloured Lands. London, Shed &
Ward, 1938. First edition. 4to, light green boards, stamped in
red. 18 colored and b/w illus. by Chesterton. Pictorial dust
jacket. Houle 22-194 1983 $75

CHESTERTON, GILBERT KEITH   The Defendant. London: R. Brimley
Johnson, 1901. First edition. Orig. cloth. Pasted to the front endsheet is a holograph testimonial for R. Brimley Johnson by Chesterton,
one page, 8vo. Cloth a trifle rubbed. Very good. MacManus 277-930
1983 $275

CHESTERTON, GILBERT KEITH   The Defendant. London: R. Brimley
Johnson, 1901. First edition. Orig. cloth. Extremities of spine a
trifle rubbed. Near-fine. MacManus 277-931 1983 $125

CHESTERTON, GILBERT KEITH   Divorce versus Democracy. London: The
Society of SS. Peter & Paul, 1916. First edition. Orig. wrappers.
Very fine. MacManus 277-932 1983 $75

CHESTERTON, GILBERT KEITH   Eugenics and Other Evils. London,
Cassell, 1922. First edition. Brown cloth, top edge brown,
uncut. Dust jacket (small chips, but still nice) with portrait of
Chesterton. Very good - fine. Houle 22-195 1983 $85

CHESTERTON, GILBERT KEITH   Eyes of Youth. London: Herbert & Daniel,
n.d. (1910). First edition. Orig. holland-backed boards. Former
owner's signature on front flyleaf. Covers somewhat soiled. Good.
MacManus 277-933 1983 $25

CHESTERTON, GILBERT KEITH   Fancies Versus Fads. London: Methuen &
Co., Ltd., (1923). First edition. Orig. cloth. Dust jacket. In a
half-morocco slipcase. Very fine. MacManus 277-934 1983 $100

CHESTERTON, GILBERT KEITH   Five Types. London: Arthur L. Humphreys,
1910. First edition. 12mo. Illus. with engraved vignettes. Orig.
parchment wrappers in publisher's box (extremities worn). Very good.
MacManus 277-935 1983 $35

CHESTERTON, GILBERT KEITH   Five Types. London: Arthur Humphrey,
1910. Illus. 32mo wras. First edition. Boxed. Fine. Argosy 714-
154 1983 $25

CHESTERTON, GILBERT KEITH   The Flying Inn. London, Library Press,
(1926). Minerva edition, first edition thus. Small 8vo, full blue
simulated leather, leaf design stamped in blind on border, stamped
on gilt and green; marbled endpapers, t.e.g. Very good. Houle 22-
196 1983 $22.50

CHESTERTON, GILBERT KEITH   Four Faultless Felons. London, 1930.
First edition. Very nice. Rota 230-120 1983 £15

CHESTERTON, GILBERT KEITH   Four Faultless Felons. London, Cassell,
(1930). First edition, second impression October. Black cloth
stamped in gilt (slight rubbing). Good - very good. Houle 22-197
1983 $20

CHESTERTON, GILBERT KEITH   G. F. Watts. London: Duckworth & Co.,
1904. First edition. Orig. cloth. Extremities a bit rubbed. Very
good. MacManus 277-937 1983 $35

CHESTERTON, GILBERT KEITH   George Bernard Shaw. London: John Lane, The Bodley Head, 1910. First edition. Orig. cloth. Very good. MacManus 277-936 1983 $25

CHESTERTON, GILBERT KEITH   A Gleaming Cohort. London: Methuen & Co. Ltd., (1926). First edition. Orig. cloth. Very good. MacManus 277-938 1983 $25

CHESTERTON, GILBERT KEITH   Gloria in Profundis. N.Y.: William Edwin Rudge, 1927. First American edition, copyright issue. Orig. wrappers. Limited to 27 copies. Mint. MacManus 277-939 1983 $350

CHESTERTON, GILBERT KEITH   Greybeards At Play. London: R. Brimley Johnson, 1900. First edition. Orig. cloth-backed pictorial boards. Extremities of boards slightly worn. Spine a bit soiled. Very good. MacManus 277-940 1983 $500

CHESTERTON, GILBERT KEITH   Heretics. London & N.Y., John Lane, 1912. Seventh edition (printed in the U.S.A.). The title page is on a stub. Green cloth stamped in black. Good - very good. Houle 22-198 1983 $22.50

CHESTERTON, GILBERT KEITH   The Ignorance of the Educated. (Los Angeles, Philharmonic Auditorium, 1931). 4to, printed four page program for Chesterton's address given in Los Angeles, February 11, 1931. Signed by Chesterton on page three above the program announcement of his address. Houle 22-199 1983 $95

CHESTERTON, GILBERT KEITH   Irish Impressions. London: W. Collins Sons & Co. Ltd., (1919). First edition. Orig. cloth. In a red half-morocco slipcase. Fine. MacManus 277-942 1983 $85

CHESTERTON, GILBERT KEITH   The Judgement of Dr. Johnson. London: Sheed & Ward, (1927). First edition. Orig. cloth. Portion of orig. dust jacket pasted to front endsheet, front flyleaf partially stained. Good. MacManus 277-942 1983 $20

CHESTERTON, GILBERT KEITH   The Judgement of Dr. Johnson. N.Y., 1928. First American edition. 12mo, dust wrapper faded & chipped. Argosy 714-155 1983 $20

CHESTERTON, GILBERT KEITH   Magic. London: Martin Secker, n.d. (1913). First edition. Orig. boards with paper label on spine, tissue jacket. One of 150 copies printed on Japon paper and signed by author. John Quinn's copy, with his bookplate on the front endsheet. Red half-morocco slipcase. Very fine. MacManus 277-944 1983 $350

CHESTERTON, GILBERT KEITH   Magic: A Fantastic Comedy. London: Secker, (1921). Ninth printing, October 1921. Small 8vo, checkered printed boards (slight rubbing), paper label, good-very good. Houle 22-201 1983 $20

CHESTERTON, GILBERT KEITH   Magic: A Fantastic Comedy. London: Martin Secker, n.d. First edition. 16mo, cloth; paper label. Argosy 715-156 1983 $25

CHESTERTON, GILBERT KEITH   Manalive. London: Thomas Nelson & Sons, (1912). First edition. Orig. cloth. Fine. MacManus 277-945 1983 $65

CHESTERTON, GILBERT KEITH   A Miscellany of Men. London: Methuen & Co., (1912). First edition. Orig. cloth. Extremities of spine a bit rubbed. Very good. MacManus 277-946 1983 $35

CHESTERTON, GILBERT KEITH   The Napoleon of Notting Hill. London, Bodley Head, 1904. First edition. Illus. with 7 plates by W. Graham Robertson. Orig. green pictorial cloth stamped in green, black, and red, top edge green, others uncut (very light wear) else, very good. Houle 22-203 1983 $95

CHESTERTON, GILBERT KEITH   The Napoleon of Notting Hill. London, 1904. First English edition. Illus. Pictorial cloth. Very good. Rota 231-111 1983 £20

CHESTERTON, GILBERT KEITH   The Napoleon of Notting Hill. London: John Lane: The Bodley Head, 1914. First edition. With 7 full-page illus. by W. Graham Robertson and a map of the Seat of War. Orig. pictorial cloth. Covers dulled. Good. MacManus 277-947 1983 $50

CHESTERTON, GILBERT KEITH   The New Jerusalem. London: Hodder & Stoughton Limited, (1920). First edition. Orig. cloth. John Quinn's copy, with his bookplate on the front endsheet. Half-morocco slipcase. Near-fine. MacManus 277-948 1983 $85

CHESTERTON, GILBERT KEITH   The New Jerusalem. N.Y., Doran, (1921). An early American edition, blue cloth stamped in blind and gilt. Very good. Houle 22-205 1983 $20

CHESTERTON, GILBERT KEITH   Number Two Joy Street. N.Y.: Appleton, 1924. First American edition. Illus. with 8 color plates by various artists. Tan cloth decorated in blue. Very good. Houle 22-217 1983 $45

CHESTERTON, GILBERT KEITH   The Queen of Seven Swords. London: Sheed & Ward, (1926). First edition. Orig. cloth-backed boards with paper label. Inscription on front flyleaf. Fine. MacManus 277-949 1983 $35

CHESTERTON, GILBERT KEITH   The Queen of Seven Swords. London, Sheed & Ward, (1926). First edition. Orange cloth over purple boards (slight fading) label on front cover. Very good. Houle 22-206 1983 $35

CHESTERTON, GILBERT KEITH   The Ressurection of Rome. London: Hodder & Stoughton, Limited, (1930). First edition. Orig. cloth. Dust jacket (slightly dust-soiled). Former owner's signature on title-page. Fine. MacManus 277-950 1983 $45

CHESTERTON, GILBERT KEITH   The Resurrection of Rome. London, Hodder & Stoughton, (1930). First edition. Red cloth stamped in black and gilt, top edge stained blue-black. Very good. Houle 22-207 1983 $35

CHESTERTON, GILBERT KEITH   The Return of Don Quixote. London, Chatto & Windus, (1927). First edition. First state of binding, blue cloth stamped in gilt. Light foxing on edges, else, very good. Houle 22-208 1983 $60

CHESTERTON, GILBERT KEITH   The Return of Don Quixote. London: Chatto & Windus, (1927). First edition. Orig. cloth. Dust jacket (extremities of spine worn). Fine. MacManus 277-951 1983 $50

CHESTERTON, GILBERT KEITH   The Return of Don Quixote. London, (1927). First edition. Argosy 714-157 1983 $35

CHESTERTON, GILBERT KEITH   A Short History of England. London: Chatto & Windus, 1917. First edition. Orig. cloth. Dust jacket (slightly soiled & worn). Red half-morocco slipcase. Fine. MacManus 277-952 1983 $125

CHESTERTON, GILBERT KEITH   The Superstition of Divorce. London: Chatto & Windus, 1920. First edition. Orig. cloth. Half-morocco slipcase. Very good. MacManus 277-953 1983 $85

CHESTERTON, GILBERT KEITH   The Sword of Wood. London, Matthews & Marrot, 1928. First edition. Decorated boards. One of 530 copies signed by the author. Dust jacket (short tear). Fine. Houle 22-209 1983 $125

CHESTERTON, GILBERT KEITH   The Sword of Wood. London: 1928. Boards. First edition. 1/530 signed. Very fine in dust jacket. Bradley 66-71 1983 $110

CHESTERTON, GILBERT KEITH   The Thing. London, Sheed & Ward, 1931. Bright orange cloth stamped in blue and black (small stains on front). Very good. Houle 22-210 1983 $20

CHESTERTON, GILBERT KEITH   Tremendous Trifles. N.Y., Doss, Mead, 1909. First American edition. Red cloth stamped in gilt. Very good - fine. Houle 22-212 1983 $30

CHESTERTON, GILBERT KEITH   Trial of John Jasper. London: Chapman & Hall, 1914. First edition. Orig. wrappers. Front wrapper coming unglued. Previous owner's signature on half-title. Good. MacManus 277-954 1983 $75

CHESTERTON, GILBERT KEITH　　Twelve Types. London: Arthur L. Humphrey, 1902. First edition. Orig. cloth. Bookplate on front endsheet, front inner hinge slightly strained. Very good. MacManus 277-956 1983 $85

CHESTERTON, GILBERT KEITH　　What's Wrong with the World. London: Cassell & Co., 1910. First edition, first state. Orig. cloth, dust jacket (chipped). Jacket reinforced with tape. Half-morocco slipcase. Fine. MacManus 277-957 1983 $125

CHESTERTON, GILBERT KEITH　　Wine Water and Song. London: Methuen & Co., Ltd., (1915). First edition. Orig. wrappers (a bit dusty). Half-morocco slipcase. Fine. MacManus 277-958 1983 $75

CHETWOOD, WILLIAM RUFUS　　A General History of the State; from its origin in Greece down to the present time. Dublin: printed by E. Rider, for the author, and sold by Messieurs Ewing, Wilson, Esdall, and James, and Mr. Sullivan in Cork, 1749. 12mo, sewn, 1st edition. List of subscribers. With an engraved frontis. and a portrait. An uncut copy. Rare. Ximenes 64-78 1983 $650

CHEVALIER, M.　　Memoires et Observations sur les Effets des Eaux de Bourbonne-les-Bains, en Champagne... Paris, 1772. First edition. 8vo, cont. 1/4 morocco. Argosy 713-103 1983 $85

CHEW, BEVERLY　　Essays and Verses About Books. New York, 1926. 8vo, boards with marbled cloth backstrip, facs. title pages. One of 275 copies. Duschnes 240-149 1983 $75

CHEYNE, GEORGE　　An Essay of Health and Long-Life. London: George Strahan, 1724. First edition. Old calf; hinges rubbed & cracking, but still sound. Newspaper clippings pasted to the rear blanks. Eighteenth century bookplate of "John Butt, Surgeon, Warminster" on front and back pastedowns. Karmiole 74-68 1983 $175

CHEYNE, GEORGE　　An Essay on Health and Long Life. Printed for George Strahan; and J. Leake, 1725. 8vo, old calf, rebacked. First edition. Bickersteth 75-218 1983 £48

CHEYNEY, PETER　　The Stars are Cark. N.Y., Dodd, Mead, 1943. First edition. Dust jacket (trifle rubbed) else, very good - fine. Houle 22-225 1983 $37.50

CHICAGO AND ILLINOIS SOUTHERN RAILROAD　　Circular of the Chicago & Illinois Souther Railway. New York, 1872. Orig. printed wrappers. Jenkins 152-51 1983 $50

CHICAGO AND NORTHWESTERN RAILWAY COMPANY.　　Second Annual Report of the... N.Y., 1861. Orig. printed front wrapper. First edition. Ginsberg 46-173 1983 $85

CHICAGO AND NORTHWESTERN RAILWAY COMPANY.　　Third Annual Report of the Chicago and Northwestern Railway Co. Chicago, Dunlop, Sewell & Spalding, Printers, 1862. Illus., large folded map. Orig. printed wraps. Ginsberg 46-174 1983 $150

CHICHESTER, F. C.　　Solo to Sydney. London, c.1930. First edition. Orig. cloth. 8vo. Portrait frontis. 9 plates. Spine slightly faded. Good. Edwards 1042-581 1983 £15

CHICHESTER, HENRY MANNERS　　The Records and Badges of Every Regiment and Corps in the British Army. Aldershot, 1900. Second edition. Thick 8vo. Blue cloth backed orig. red cloth gilt. 24 fine coloured plates of uniform and colours, 6pp. of ads. at end. Good. Edwards 1042-302 1983 £150

CHICK, FRANK N.　　Kansas City First Mortgage Notes. Kansas City, Mo., 1889. Orig. wraps. First edition. Ginsberg 47-515 1983 $50

CHILD, ANDREW　　Overland Route to California. Los Angeles: N.A. Kovach, 1946. Folding map. Plates. Half morocco. Signed by editor and limited to 25 copies. Some wear. Jenkins 152-591 1983 $75

CHILD, CHARLES M.　　Physiological Foundations of Behavior. NY: Holt, 1924. First edition. Gach 94-534 1983 $25

CHILD, LYDIA MARIA　　The Frugal Housewife. Boston, 1830. 2nd ed. 12mo, orig. printed boards. Lacks backstrip; covers and signatures loose; rubbed. Morrill 286-87 1983 $25

CHILD, LYDIA MARIA　　Letters From New York. NY, 1843. 1st ed. Light foxing, ex library. Argosy 710-374 1983 $30

CHILD, LYDIA MARIA　　Philothea. Bos., 1836. Interior fine, half-title removed, edges worn and chipped, fair, owner's name. Quill & Brush 54-271 1983 $35

CHILD, THEODORE　　The Spanish-American Republics. New York, 1891. 1st ed. Illus. 4to, some rubbing at edges and corners. Morrill 288-66 1983 $27.50

THE CHILD from the Dove on the Cross. Day & Sons, nd (1863). 1st edn. 9 illuminated pages printed in colours & heightened in gold by Day & Sons from designes by Miss Ellice. Plum morocco grain cloth gilt (designed by W.R. Tymms), bevelled bds. (fr. cvr. faded & dust soiled, sl. wear to corners, lacks interleaves & title sl. foxed, fr. ep. broken at hinge). Inscribed on fr. free ep. "Hubt. Blair of Blair, May 1863...done by Miss Ellice Neice to the Rt. Hon. Edward Ellice, M.P." V.g. Hodgkins 27-360 1983 £40

THE CHILD of Thirty-Six Fathers. NY: Isaac Riley, 1809. 12mo, old calf over marbled boards; boards a bit shelfworn. Karmiole 75-36 1983 $100

CHILDERS, ERSKINE　　The H. A. C. in South Africa. London, 1903. First edition. Covers a little marked. Unopened. From the library of C(onstantance) Childers, the author's sister, bearing her autograph signature. Very nice. Rota 231-115 1983 £40

CHILDHOOD Valley: The Favourite Songs of Childhood. London: E. Nister (ca. 1895). Octavo. 12 full-page chromolithographs, numerous monochrome vignettes. Some very light occasional offsetting, else fine in cloth-backed boards with chromolithographed illus. Bromer 25-333 1983 $75

CHILDREN as They Are. Printed for Harvey & Darton, 1830. 5 engrs. Red lea. backed grey bds. with titling & vignette on fr. cvr. & vignette rear cvr., printed in black. Ink insc. dd. May 5th 1887 "Alfred Shayler, Present from Lady Churchill." Occasional thumb mark, worm patch top rear board, cvrs. some marks & corner sl. wear, vg. Hodgkins 27-39 1983 £35

CHILDREN Reclaimed for Life. Hodder & Stoughton, 1875. Half title, front. Illus. 3 pp ads. Orig. olive dec. cloth, v.g. Jarndyce 31-229 1983 £20

A CHILDREN'S Sampler. 1950. 4to. Edition ltd. to 375 copies. Yellow illus. Cloth; slipcase. Fine. 4to. Karmiole 72-45 1983 $100

CHILDS, ST. JULIEN R.　　Malaria and Colonization in the Carolina Low Country. Baltimore, 1940. First edition. 8vo. Wrappers. Fye H-3-96 1983 $50

THE CHILD'S Illuminated Fable Book. W. Smith, n.d. (ca.1860). Sm. 8vo. Decorated title. 11 colour printed illuminated pp & decorative borders to text. Lithography by Woods & Co. Lacks flyleaf. Pink cloth, rubbed. Onlaid colour printed label. Greer 39-58 1983 £25

THE CHILD'S Instructor. New York, Burtus, 1818. 12mo. Orig. boards, calf back. Binding worn; lacks back endleaf; small piece torn from p. 58 affecting a few words. Morrill 289-326 1983 $22.50

CHILVERS, HEDLEY A.　　Out of the Crucible. Cassell, 1929. Frontis. & 15 plates. Brick red cloth gilt. Dust wrappers. Very good. Greer 39-132 1983 £15

CHINN, GEORGE MORGAN　　Encyclopedia of American Hand Arms. Huntington, W.Va., 1942. First edition. Drawings. Cloth. Bookplate. Chipped dust wrapper. King 45-478 1983 $35

CHINTAMON, H.　　A Commentary on the Text of the Bhagavad-Gita. London, 1874. 8vo. Orig. cloth. Inscribed on title "With the Author's Compliments." Good. Edwards 1044-137 1983 £15

CHIPMAN, NATHANIEL   Sketches of the Principles of
Government. Rutland: From the Press of J. Lyon: Printed for the
author, 1793. Modern half morocco and boards, bound complete with
half-title. Scattered foxing, else very good. Reese 18-133 1983
$200

CHISHOLM, LOUEY   The Enchanted Land, Tales Told Again.
T.C. & E.C. Jack, 1906. 4to. Colour frontis. Title vignette & 29
colour plates. Some pp roughly opened. Brown decorated cloth gilt.
Onlaid colour plate. Greer 39-55 1983 £60

CHISHOLM, LOUEY   In Fairyland, Tales Told Again. T.C. &
E.C. Jack, 1904. 4to. Colour frontis. Title vignette & 29 colour
plates. Pictorial endpapers. White cloth gilt. Some damp. Onlaid
colour plate. Greer 39-54 1983 £65

CHITTENDEN, HIRAM M.   The American Fur Trade of the Far West.
New York, 1936. 2 vols., frontis., 1st ed. Folding map. Some
fading to spine else a nice copy. Jenkins 151-91 1983 $125

CHITTENDEN, HIRAM M   The American Fur Trade of the Far West.
N.Y.: Francis P. Harper, 1902. First edition. 3 vols. Green cloth.
Lacking maps in picket of Vol. 3. A few light pen marks by N. Loomis
in Vol. I. Dawson 471-45 1983 $125

CHITTENDEN, LUCIUS E.   Personal Reminiscences, 1840-1890.
New York, 1893. 1st ed. Illus., gilt top, slight stain on front
cover. Clark 741-95 1983 $21.50

CHOATE, FLORENCE   The Indian Fairy Book. Grant Richards,
1920. Colour frontis. 7 colour plates (1 creased). 15 text illus. &
pictorial endpapers. Brown pictorial cloth, gilt, rubbed. Greer 40-
77 1983 £15

CHOCTAW NATION. CONSTITUTION. Constitution and laws of the Choctaw
Nation. Dallas, Texas: John F. Worley, 1894. First edition in
Choctaw of the Durant Code. Orig. full sheep, red and black leather
labels. Rehinged. Fine. Jenkins 152-105 1983 $175

CHODAT, R.   Algues vertes de la Suisse. Berne,
1902. 264 figures, royal 8vo, buckram. Wheldon 160-1802 1983 $20

CHODERLOS DE LACLOS, P. A. F.   Dangerous Acquaintances. London,
(1924). 8vo. Half orange morocco, gilt, t.e.g. Traylen 94-189
1983 £28

CHODERLOS DE LACLOS, P. A. F.   Dangerous Acquaintances. London:
the Nonesuch Press, 1940. 4to. Decorated boards, buckram spine.
Coloured and other illus. by Charles Laborde. Traylen 94-190 1983
£25

A CHOICE Collection of Scots Poems. Edinburgh: Printed for Wal.
Ruddiman, Junior, 1766. 12mo, wormhole at outer edge of side margin
in final signature, old calf, rubbed, defective at top of the spine.
Bickersteth 77-15 1983 £45

CHOLMONDELEY, MARY   Notwithstanding. London: Eveleigh Nash
& Grayson, n.d. (1913). First edition. Orig. cloth. Very slight
offsetting to half-title and last page of text. Spine a bit faded.
Good. MacManus 277-963 1983 $45

CHOLMENDELEY, MARY   Red Pottage. London: Edward Arnold,
1899. First edition. Orig. maroon cloth. Spine and covers rubbed,
worn and slightly darkened. Good. MacManus 277-964 1983 $50

CHORIS, LOUIS   Voyage Pittoresque Auour Du Monde. Paris,
1822, 1826. 2 vols. in one. Collates complete with Lada-Mocarski
except for the dedication leaf to the Tzar in Vues which is usually
lacking. Including 3 maps on 2 sheets. Frontis. portrait. 128 colored
lithographed plates. Folio. Cont. marbled boards and 19th century
brown calf with leather label. Some shelf wear, light foxing. Uncut
copies in the preferred states. First edition, each book printed on
large velin paper. Jenkins 152-791 1983 $15,000

A CHOROGRAPHICAL and Statistical Description of the District of
Columbia. Paris, 1816. First edition. 8vo, cont. calf-backed
marbled boards. Argosy 716-139 1983 $350

CHOULANT, LUDWIG   Die Anatomischen Abbildungen des XV.
und XVI. Leipzig, 1843. First edition. Modern buckram; orig.
printed wrs. bound in. Argosy 713-108 1983 $75

CHRETIEN, DOUGLAS   The Battle Book of the O'Donnells.
Berkeley. University of California, 1935. First edition. Full vellum
stamped in gilt, green cloth ties. One of 25 copies on handmade
paper, signed by the author and printed by Samuel Farquhar. Fine copy.
Houle 22-226 1983 $150

CHRISTELLER, ERWIN   Atlas der Histotopographie. Leipzig,
1927. 182 colored figures, & other illus. Small folio, ex-lib.
Argosy 713-109 1983 $125

CHRISTENSEN, ERWIN O.   Primitive Art. New York: Bonanza,
n.d. 32 color plates. Numerous text illus. Large square 4to.
Boards. 1/2 cloth. Ars Libri 34-9 1983 $40

CHRISTIAN, ELEANOR E.   Recollections of Charles Dickens.
Extracted from Temple Bar, April 1888. Grey wraps. Jarndyce 30-148
1983 £14.50

CHRISTIAN, P.   L'Afrique Francaise. Paris: A. Barbier,
(1846). Royal 8vo. Folding map. 29 plates (10 hand-colored). New
1/4 red morocco, marbled boards, uncut. Some light foxing. Adelson
Africa-72 1983 $350

THE CHRISTIAN Calendar and New England Farmer's Almanack, 1827.
Boston, 1827. Illus., 16mo, modern wrappers. Used as date book by
Ezra Gannett. Argosy 710-68 1983 $75

THE CHRISTIAN Keepsake. Fisher, 1838. Frontis. portrait of Mrs.
Fletcher and 15 engravings, 10 pp. of ads, green morocco, a.e.g.
Leather faded in places, very good. Hodgkins 27-254 1983 £12

THE CHRISTIAN Year. Oxford, Parker, 1849. 58th edn. (1st edn. in
this form). 18 illuminated title pages printed in colour & heightened
in gold by Lemercier. Designed title page in green, gold & red, each
page text with double ruled red borders. Cream leather gilt, raised
bands, gilt dentelles, a.e.g. (leather some discol. with sl. damage top
left fr. corner of cvr., hand illuminated presentation page at front),
nice clean copy. Hodgkins 27-361 1983 £35

THE CHRISTIAN'S, Scholar's and Farmer's Magazine. Elizabeth Town:
Shepard Kollock. Volume I, April 1789-March 1790. All orig. printed
wrappers present. Bound in 3/4 burgundy morocco, gilt spine panels,
by Bennett. Very fine. Felcone 19-8 1983 $175

CHRISTIANSEN, PETER   Otto Bache. Kobenhavn, 1928. 162 plates.
Pictorial boards, lacks front fly. Spine tips beginning to fray.
Tattered dust wrapper. Good. King 45-325 1983 $35

CHRISTIE, AGATHA   The Mysterious Affair at Styles.
London, 1920. Advance review copy, blind-stamped on title page:
"Review Copy with John Lane's Compliments". Top edge slightly
faded, spine a little bumped at foot, a couple of trifling damp
spots, but a very good copy. Gekoski 2-27 1983 £950

CHRISTIE, AGATHA   Sparkling Cyanide. London, Crime
Club (1945). First edition. Green cloth. Dust jacket, very good.
Houle 21-218 1983 $20

CHRISTIE, JAMES   Northumberland: Its History, Its
Features, And Its People. Carlise, 1893. First edition, large paper
copy, 4 photographic plates, 4to, roan-backed cloth boards, gilt, a
little worn. Deighton 3-75 1983 £12

CHRISTINA; Or, Memoirs of a German Princess. Printed for Henry
Colburn... 1808. 2 vols., 12mo, contemporary calf; half-titles,
Colburn's advertisement leaf in vol. I. 1st English ed. Hill 165-
21 1983 £185

CHRISTINE DE PISAN   The Epistle of Othea to Hector...
London, 1904. 4to. Orig. quarter morocco. Limited edition,
printed for Members of the Roxburghe club only. Traylen 94-191
1983 £65

CHRISTMAN, ENOS   One Man's Gold. New York, 1930. 1st
ed. Ports., facsimiles. Half buckram, dj. Clark 741-96 1983 $25.50

CHRISTMAS Carols Ancient and Modern. NY, 1901. Etched frontis.,
with tissue guard. Title in red and black, with woodcut vignette.
4 plates, 8vo, uncut, green and gold decorated cloth. Inscription on
fly leaf. Salloch 387-46 1983 $35

A CHRISTMAS Play. Ditchling: St. Dominic's Press, 1924. 16mo, illus. wrappers slightly creased at one corner. Else fine. Bromer 25-296 1983 $85

CHRISTMAS Poems & Pictures. N.Y., Gregory, 1864. 1st American edn. Wood engrs. by John Gilbert, Birket Foster, etc. Each page text & illus. printed on tinted ground, engr'd frontis. & title page. Brown heavily embossed morocco, raised bands, a.e.g., gilt dentelles, blue moire eps., corners sl. rubbed. Colour printed bookpl. heightened in gold of Sir Campbell Stuart. Very nice copy. Hodgkins 27-257 1983 £45

CHRISTO   Valley Curtain. NY, (1973). Signed by Christo, limited to 1500 numbered copies, lavishly illus., fine. Quill & Brush 54-276 1983 $100

CHRISTOPHERSEN, E.   Flowering Plants of Samoa. Honolulu, B. P. Bishop Museum, 1935-38. 3 plates and 53 figures, 2 parts, 8vo, plain wrappers. Library stamp on title-pages. Wheldon 160-1662 1983 £20

CHRISTY, GEORGE   George Christy's Essence of Old Kentucky. New York, ca. 1865. Orig. pictorial wrappers. Jenkins 152-676 1983 $75

CHRISTY, HOWARD CHANDLER   The American Girl. N.Y., 1906. First edition. 16 full page color plates and other drawings by Christy. Cloth with color pictorial label. Ink inscription. Bookplate. Covers loose and slightly stained. Worn. One plate loose. King 45-385 1983 $35

CHRISTY, HOWARD CHANDLER   The Christy Book of Drawings, Pictures in Black and White and Color. N.Y., Moffat, Yard, 1908. Oblong folio. 57 illus. (4 in colors). Printed cloth-backed pictorial boards, with picture in colors on front, gt. 1st ed. With the orig. glassine jacket and the orig. box. Very fine. O'Neal 50-9 1983 $85

CHRISTY, HOWARD CHANDLER   Our Girls: An Anthology. N.Y.: Moffat & Yard, 1907. First edition. 4to. Green cloth. Pictorial paste-on. Light soil. 17 full-page color plates, text black & whites. Page decorations. Small tipped-in illus. Very good. Aleph-bet 8-60 1983 $50

CHRISTY, MILLER   The Silver Map of the World. London, 1900. 8vo, pict., silver-stamped cloth, illus. Argosy 710-130 1983 $45

THE CHRONICLE of Abomilech, King of the Isles... London: T. Dolby, 1820. First edition. 8vo. Disbound. Scarce. Ximenes 63-481 1983 $45

THE CHRONICLES of the Bastile. Newby, 1852. 3 vols. Illus. by Robert Cruikshank. 5th edn. Frontis. & 57 illus. Rebound in canvas backed slate blue boards, paper title labels, edges stained red. Unattractive copy with some marks cvrs., foxing contents. Hodgkins 27-258 1983 £20

CHRYSLER, WALTER P.   Life of an American Workman. N.Y., privately printed, 1937. Large 8vo, illus. with gravures. Bound in fine full red morocco, by Macdonald, the spine with gilt panels, covers ruled in gilt with author's facs. signature, t.e.g. Enclosed in a fleece lined cloth slipcase. One of 500 copies on rag paper. Printed by Wm. Rudge. Inscribed by the author: "To Dr. Benjamin Solzer with admiration and tratitude...W.P. Chrysler..." Houle 21-222 1983 $150

CHUBB, RALPH   Woodcuts. Block, printed at the Hawthorne Press, 1928. First edition, sq. 8vo, 12 woodcut illustrations, woodcut title and colophon, uncut in original marbled mauve paper, printed paper label, slight wear but a very good copy. 200 copies only of this issue. Deighton 3-76 1983 £60

CHUBB, THOMAS C.   The White God and Other Poems. New Haven: Yale, 1920. Printed wraps. over boards. First edition. Short closed tear, else about fine. Reese 20-240 1983 $20

CHUIKEVICH, PETER A.   Reflections on the War of 1812. Boston, 1813. Dsb., very good. Reese 18-408 1983 $125

CHURCH, ALFRED J.   Isis and Thamesis. Hours on the River from Oxford to Henley. London, Seeley & Co., 1886. First edition, roy. 8vo, vignette title-page, 12 sepia etched plates, 33 text illustrations, original green cloth, lettered and decorated in gilt on spine and upper cover, a.e.g., joints and corners worn, slight foxing on some text leaves. Deighton 3-77 1983 £35

CHURCH, RICHARD   Calling for a Spade. London, 1939. 29 black and white drawings, including 9 full-page, by Joan Hassall. With the bookplate of A.J.A. Symons. Small tear in fore-edge of page 75. Very good in nicked and slightly chipped, internally repaired dustwrapper. First edition. Jolliffe 26-245 1983 £45

CHURCH, RICHARD   The Collected Poems. London: J.M. Dent and Sons, (1948). First edition. Orig. wrappers. Advance proof. Wrappers slightly soiled and worn. Good. MacManus 277-966 1983 $50

CHURCH, RICHARD   Hurricane and Other Poems. London: Selwyn & Blount, 1919. First edition. Orig. wrappers with paper label. Presentation copy, inscribed on the dedication page "Au Tante anna mit vielen grussen Richard Church." Bottom of spine chipped, wrappers partially faded. Good. MacManus 277-970 1983 $85

CHURCH, RICHARD   Mary Shelley. N.Y.: The Viking Press, 1928. First American edition. Frontis. Rebound in 3/4 navy morocco & cloth. Ex-library copy, with preforations and marks on title page and copyright page. Fine. MacManus 280-4708 1983 $35

CHURCH, RICHARD   Mood without Measure. London, 1927. First edition, late binding. Unopened. Fine. Rota 231-117 1983 £20

CHURCH, RICHARD   Twelve Noon. London, 1936. Advance proof copy. Wrappers. Very nice. Rota 231-118 1983 £12.50

CHURCH, THOMAS   The History of Philip's War. Boston, 1827. Second edition with plates, engraved frontis. and 3 other plates, 12mo, some occasionally heavy foxing, cont. sheep rebacked. K Books 307-47 1983 £40

CHURCH, THOMAS   The History of Philip's War, Commonly Called the Great Indian War, of 1675 and 1676... also an Appendix... Boston, 1829. 2nd ed. with plates. Engraved plates. 12mo, contemp. calf, leather label. Hinges slightly cracked. Morrill 289-597 1983 $30

CHURCH OF ENGLAND.   Articles agreed upon by the Archbishops & Bishops of both Provinces and the whole Clergie... Savoy: by the Assigns of John Bill..., 1669. 4to. Half blue calf. Heath 48-87 1983 £45

CHURCH OF ENGLAND   The Book of Common Prayer... London: John Baskett, 1735. Title in red and black (bound with) The Whole Book of Psalms... London: John March, 1735. Folio, cont. full morocco, elaborately gilt. Margins of a few leaves neatly strengthened; binding worn, hinges broken. Felcone 21-12 1983 $175

CHURCH OF ENGLAND   The Book of Common Prayer...Together with the Psalter. London: Thomas Baskett, 1758. Small quarto. Gilt-stamped full blue, straight-grain morocco, rubbed at extremities, front cover expertly repaired. A.e.g. With clean and well-preserved fore-edge watercolor. Bookplate of George L. Lincoln. Bromer 25-204 1983 $575

CHURCH OF ENGLAND   Book of Common Prayer. Cambridge, 1771. Contemp. red morocco, gilt, a.e.g. Light rubbing. Jenkins 155-425 1983 $350

CHURCH OF ENGLAND   The Book of Common Prayer. London: Eyre & Spottiswoode, (ca. 1900). Nice copy in full black leather with hall-marked sterling silver plaque on front cover. First signature slightly loose, faint rubbing to extremities, but altogeth a clean and tight with plaque in excellent condition. A.e.g. Owner's signature. (2 1/8 x 1 7/8; 53x48mm). Bromer 25-414 1983 $185

CHURCH OF ENGLAND   The Book of Common Prayer. London: Charles Courtier & Sons, (ca. 1900). Together with Hymns Ancient and Modern. London: William Clowers (ca. 1900). Bound in slightly rubbed limp suede with loop to latch on toggle, which is lacking. Some slitting to inner hinges, but still near fine and very readable. A.e.g. (2 7/8 x 2 1/4; 72/57mm). Bromer 25-413 1983 $75

CHURCH OF ENGLAND.   The Book of Common Prayer and
Administration of the Sacraments and Other Rites and Ceremonies
of the Church...together with the Psalter, or Psalms of David.
Boston, 1928 (1930). Folio, full pub.'s red levant morocco, tooled
in blind, t.e.g., others uncut. One of 530 copies printed by
D.B. Updike, The Merrymount Press, in Janson type in red and black.
Duschnes 240-150 1983 $1,100

THE CHURCHILIAD: or, a few modest questions proposed to the Reverend
author of the Rosciad. London: printed for J. Williams; and T.
Lewis, 1761. 4to, wrappers, first edition. Very good copy. Rare.
Ximenes 64-87 1983 $350

CHURCHILL, CHARLES   The Author. A Poem. London: W.
Flexney, 1763. First edition, 4to, disbound, wanting half-title,
first owner's inscription. Foxing; verso of last leaf dusty, but a
very good copy. Trebizond 18-16 1983 $145

CHURCHILL, CHARLES   Poems. London: The King's Printers,
1933. 2 vols. Illus. Orig. cloth. Limited to 600 copies. Fine.
MacManus 277-972 1983 $50

CHURCHILL, CHARLES   The Poetical Works. London, 1866.
2 vols. Cr. 8vo. Dark blue calf, two-line gilt, borders with
corner ornaments, gilt panelled spines, morocco labels, gilt.
Traylen 94-192 1983 £30

CHURCHILL, CHARLES   The Rosciad. London: printed for the
author, and sold by W. Flexney, 1761. 4to, disbound, 1st edition.
Foremargin a bit trimmed; half-title foxed, last page of text browned,
but a sound copy. Ximenes 64-80 1983 $400

CHURCHILL, CHARLES   The Rosciad. London: printed for the
author, and sold by W. Flexney, 1761. 4to, wrappers, 2nd edition,
revised and corrected. A very good copy; half-title present, edges
browned. Ximenes 64-81 1983 $150

CHURCHILL, CHARLES   The Rosciad. London: printed for the
author, and sold by W. Flexney, 1741 (sic, for 1761). 4to, wrappers,
4th edition, revised and corrected. A very good copy, complete with
half-title. Ximenes 64-83 1983 $100

CHURCHILL, CHARLES   The Rosciad. London: printed for the
author, and sold by W. Flexney, 1761. 4to, disbound, 3rd edition,
revised and corrected. Last leaf mounted, and repaired on the verso
(no loss of text). Lacks the half-title. Ximenes 64-82 1983 $45

CHURCHILL, CHARLES   The Rosciad. London: printed for the
author, and sold by W. Flexney, 1762. 4to, wrappers, 6th edition,
revised and corrected, with additions. Ximenes 64-84 1983 $100

CHURCHILL, CHARLES   The Rosciad. London: printed for the
author, and sold by W. Flexney, 1763. 4to, disbound 7th edition.
Margins trimmed somewhat irregularly; small hole in several leaves,
affecting a few letters. Some stains; a fair copy. Ximenes 64-85
1983 $25

CHURCHILL, CHARLES   The Rosciad. London: printed for the
author, and sold by W. Flexney, 1765. 4to, disbound, 9th edition.
The final text, 1090 lines, with all names printed in full for the
first time. Wanting a half-title; rather foxed, several tears in the
last few leaves. An uncommon edition. Ximenes 64-86 1983 $50

CHURCHILL, RANDOLPH   Speeches...1880-1888. Longmans, Green,
1889. First edition, 2 vols. Half titles, 24 pp ads. (Nov. 1888),
vol. I. Orig. blue cloth. Jarndyce 31-128 1983 £24

CHURCHILL, WINSTON LEONARD SPENCER   All Clear Aft; episodes at sea.
London, 1936. First edition. Foreword by W.S. Churchill. Slightly
frayed dust wrapper. Very good. Rota 230-127 1983 £15

CHURCHILL, WINSTON LEONARD SPENCER   Churchill in Ottawa. N.d.
(ca. 1942). 19 1/2cm. 15 illus. (including 2 full and one double
page). Illus. wrappers. Fine. McGahern 53-33 1983 $20

CHURCHILL, WINSTON LEONARD SPENCER   Great Contemporaries. London,
1937. First edition. Illus. Spine faded, covers slightly marked.
Some foxing. Name of flyleaf. Good. Rota 230-124 1983 £30

CHURCHILL, WINSTON LEONARD SPENCER   Great Contemporaries.
New York, 1937. First American edition. Spine a little darkened.
Nice. Rota 230-125 1983 £20

CHURCHILL, WINSTON LEONARD SPENCER   A History of the English
Speaking Peoples. London, (1956-8). First editions. 4 vols.
D.w. Argosy 714-160 1983 $125

CHURCHILL, WINSTON LEONARD SPENCER   London to Ladysmith via Pretoria.
London: Longmans, Green, and Co., 1900. First edition. 8vo. Orig.
pictorial cloth, gilt spine. 4 maps and 4 plans. Traylen 94-193
1983 £90

CHURCHILL, WINSTON LEONARD SPENCER   Marlborough. London, Harrap,
(1949). Photogravure frontis., facs., maps and plans. 2 vols., 8vo.
Torn dust wrappers. Pasted on title of vol. I is a Churchill U.S.
5 cent stamp. Morrill 286-88 1983 $20

CHURCHILL, WINSTON LEONARD SPENCER   Painting as a Pastime. New
York, (1950). First American edition. Argosy 714-162 1983 $20

CHURCHILL, WINSTON LEONARD SPENCER   Savrola: A Tale of the Revolution in Laurania. New York, 1900. First edition. Orig. blue cloth,
gilt. Bright and fine, lightly worn at extremities, very light stains
on front pastedown and fore-edges. Protected in folding blue buckram
box. Bradley 66-72 1983 $750

CHURCHILL, WINSTON LEONARD SPENCER   The Second World War. New York,
1948-1953. First American edition. Maps and diagrams. 6 vols. 8vo.
Dust wrappers, some d/w's slightly frayed and torn. Morrill 290-615
1983 $25

CHURCHILL, WINSTON LEONARD SPENCER   The World Crisis. London,
Thorton Butterworth, 1923-31. First edition. Illus. with maps, some
folding, and photographs. Gilt stamped blue cloth. 6 vols. A few
vols. with light foxing at edges, else, a fine set. Houle 22-232 1983
$350

CHURCHMAN, JOHN   An Account of the Gospel Labours,
and Christian Experiences of a Faithful Minister of Christ, John
Churchman, Late of Nottingham in Pennsylvania, Deceased. Philadelphia:
Joseph Crukshank, 1779. Calf (covers warped). Some interior
waterspotting. First edition. Felcone 22-30 1983 $40

CIBBER, COLLEY   Another Occasional Letter from Mr. Cibber
to Mr. Pope. Glasgow: printed for W. Macpherson, n.d. (1744?).
8vo, disbound, 2nd edition. Half-title present. Ximenes 64-96 1983
$100

CIBBER, COLLEY   An Apology For The Life Of Mr. Colley
Cibber, Comedian, And Late Patentee Of The Theatre-Royal. London:
printed by John Watts, for the author, 1740. 4to, modern half morocco
and marbled boards. First edition. With a frontis. portrait. A
fine copy, entirely uncut; very scarce in this condition. Ximenes
64-88 1983 $350

CIBBER, COLLEY   An Apology for the Life of Mr. Colley
Cibber, Comedian, and Late Patentee of the Theatre-Royal. London:
printed by John Watts for the author; and sold by W. Lewis, 1740.
8vo, cont. calf, spine gilt (minor rubbing), 2nd edition. With the
signature and armorial bookplate of John Boyle, Earl of Orrery and
occasional marginal notes in his hand. A fine copy. Ximenes 64-89
1983 $175

CIBBER, COLLEY   An Apology for the Life of Mr. Colley
Cibber. Printed by John Watts for the author, 1740. 4to, portrait,
old half calf with marbled boards, rebacked, preserving the orig.
spine. First edition. Bickersteth 75-19 1873 £85

CIBBER, COLLEY   An Apology for the Life... R. & J.
Dodsley, 1756. Fourth edition, 12mo, in two vols. Front. port.
vol. I. Mottled calf, hinges rubbed, black labels. Jarndyce 31-16
1983 £38

CIBBER, COLLEY   An Apology for the Life of Mr. Colley
Cibber, Comedian and Patentee of the Theatre Royal. London: printed
for W. Simpkin and R. Marshall, 1822. 8vo, original blue boards,
drab paper backstrip, printed paper label. New edition, with a portrait. A very fine copy in original condition. Ximenes 64-90 1983
$150

CIBBER, COLLEY   An Apology for the Life of Colley
Cibber. Golden Cockerel Press, 1925. 2 vols. Roy. 8vo.
Boards, white buckram spines, uncut edges. Limited edition of 450 numbered
copies, printed in black and blue with Initial Letters by Eric
Gill. Traylen 94-196 1983 £38

CIBBER, COLLEY   The Egotist: or, Colley upon Cibber.
London: printed, and sold by W. Lewis, 1743. 8vo, disbound. 1st
edition. Tear in one blank margin, without surface loss, but a very
good copy of an uncommon pamphlet. Ximenes 64-91 1983 $350

CIBBER, COLLEY   A Letter from Mr. Cibber to Mr. Pope,
inquiring into the motives that might induce him in his satyrical
works, to be so frequently fond of Mr. Cibber's name. London: printed
and sold by W. Lewis, 1742. 8vo, wrappers, 1st edition. Half-title
present. Incorrect catchword on p. 39. Ximenes 64-92 1983 $150

CIBBER, COLLEY   A Letter from Mr. Cibber to Mr. Pope.
London: printed and sold by W. Lewis, 1742. 8vo, wrappers. A copy
of the first edition, with the correct catchword. Half-title present.
Ximenes 64-93 1983 $150

CIBBER, COLLEY   A Letter from Mr. Cibber, to Mr. Pope,
inquiring into the motives that might induce him in his satyrical
works, to be frequently fond of Mr. Cibber's name. Dublin: printed
by A. Reilly, for G. Ewing, 1742. 12mo, wrappers. First Irish
edition. A rare printing. Title dusty, else a very good copy.
Ximenes 64-94 1983 $125

CIBBER, COLLEY   A Letter from Mr. Cibber, to Mr. Pope,
inquiring into the motives that might induce him in his satyrical
works, to be frequently fond of Mr. Cibber's name. London: printed
in the year 1777. 8vo, wrappers, 4th edition, bound in (neatly
trimmed and inlaid) is a plate. Half-title present. Ximenes 64-95
1983 $75

CIBBER, SUSANNAH MARIA   An Account of the Life of the
Celebrated Actress. 1887. Front. Printed in brown throughout.
Orig. red cloth, fine. Jarndyce 30-947 1983 £10.50

CIBBER, THEOPHILUS   An Epistle from Mr. Theophilus Cibber, to
David Garrick, Esq. London: printed for R. Griffiths, and to be had
also of Mr. Cibber, 1755. 8vo, wrappers, 1st ed. Half-title present.
Very good copy of a rare pamphlet. Ximenes 64-99 1983 $450

CIBBER, THEOPHILUS   The Lives and Characters of the Most
Eminent Actors and Actresses of Great Britain and Ireland, From
Shakespear to the Present Time. London: printed for R. Griffiths,
1753. 8vo, original light blue boards, drab paper backstrip (bit
worn); in a cloth folding case. First edition. A fine copy in original condition, wholly uncut and largely unopened. Ximenes 64-100
1983 $425

CIBBER, THEOPHILUS   The Lover. London: printed for J.
Watts, 1730. 1st edition, 8vo, advertisements, title a little
spotted, wrappers. Pickering & Chatto 19-9 1983 $300

CIBBER, THEOPHILUS   Theophilus Cibber, to David Garrick,
Esq. London: printed for W. Reeves, and J. Phipps, 1759. 8vo, full
polished calf, gilt, spine and inner dentelles gilt, a.e.g. 1st ed.,
with a new title-page and new illustrations, with a frontispiece.
A fine copy; very scarce. Ximenes 64-102 1983 $450

CICCONI, GIOVANNI   Luigi Fontana e le sue opere. Fermo:
Stab. Cooperativo Tipografico, 1928. 86 plates. Large 4to. New
cloth. Ars Libri 33-466 1983 $85

CICERO, MARCUS TULLIUS   Cicero Against Catiline. London, T.N.
for Samuel Lowndes, 1671. 8vo, later sheep period style gilt,
hinges restored, a "Britwell" binding from the Christie-Miller Library
at Britwell Court, with the Britwell Court shelf mark on the
endleaf. First edition. Ravenstree 95-25 1983 $375

CICERO, MARCUS TULLIUS   Extracts from and observations on
Cicero's dialogues De Senectute and De Amicitia... Exeter: printed
for the author by E. Woolmer, etc., 1829. Translation by William
Danby. First edition. Slim 8vo. Orig. grey-green boards. With
Danby's own pencilled shelf-mark on the endpaper. A very fine copy.
Ximenes 63-65 1983 $85

CICERO, MARCUS TILLIUS   M. T. Ciceronis and Q. fratrem dialogi
tres de oratore. Crownfield: Cambridge, 1732. Second edition, 8vo,
calf, gilt spine. From the Duke of Devonshire's Chatsworth library.
K Books 307-50 1983 £28

CICERO, MARCUS TULLIUS   Marcvs Tullius Ciceroes three Bookes
of Duties to Marcus His Sonne. London, Thomas Este, 1596. 12mo,
cont. calf newly rebacked antique style, bookplates. Ravenstree 95-
34 1983 $375

CICERO, MARCUS TULLIUS   Marcus Tullius Cicero, his Three Bookes
of Duties to Marcus his Sonne... London: by Thomas Este, (1600?).
Small 8vo. Early vellum (recased). Light inkstain on title, else
good copy. Heath 48-259 1983 £150

CICERO, MARCUS TULLIUS   De Natura Deorum. London, 1896. 8vo,
boards. Salloch 385-506 1983 $20

CICERO, MARCUS TULLIUS   De Officiis Ad Marcum Felum Libri
Trex. Glasguae, Andreas Foulis, 1784. 8vo, cont. tree calf gilt,
hinges cracked, bookplate, the variant issue on less fine paper.
This copy has a faint impression of Hh2. Ravenstree 95-31 1983
$42.50

CICERO, MARCUS TULLIUS   De Officiis Marci Tullii Ciceronis.
Londini, J.M., 1674. Small 8vo, 18th century calf, front hinge
broken, 18th century signatures on title and back flyleaf, ink
stain on title, few notes through text. Right-hand margin of C5
torn away with loss of side notes, outer margin cut close shaving a
few side notes and some text of index. Ravenstree 95-27 1983 $35

CICERO, MARCUS TULLIUS   Opera Rhetorica. Lg, 1893. 3/4 morocco
(ex-library copy). 2 vols. in one. 8vo. Salloch 385-504 1983 $22

CICERO, MARCUS TULLIUS   M. Tvillii Cicernois Orationvm Volvmen
Prjmvm a Ioan. Londini, Thomas Vautrollerus, impensis I. Harison,
1587. 12mo, cont. sheep, restored, title and last leaf with few
minor age-spots. Ravenstree 95-33 1983 $450

CICERO, MARCUS TULLIUS   De Oratore. Oxford, 1892. Folding
plate. 8vo, cloth. Salloch 385-505 1983 $55

CICOGNARA, LEOPOLDO   Storia della scultura dal suo risorgi-
mento in Italia fino al secolo di Canova. Prato, 1823-1824. Second
edition. 7 vols. Sm. 4to, buckram (slightly worn). 185 engr. plates.
Folio. Boards, 3/4 calf (worn, spine torn). Ars Libre SB 26-54
1983 $450

CICOGNINI, JACOPO   Alla Sacra Maesta Cesarea dell'Imperatore
In lode del famoso Signor Galileo Galilei... Florence: Giovanni
Battista Landini, 1631. 4to. Cont. limp vellum. Very rare. Kraus
164-86 1983 $6,800

CICOGNINI, JACOPO   Lagrime di Gieremia Profeta. Florence:
Zanobi Pignoni, 1627. Small 4to. Cont. boards. Uncut. Backstrip
mostly gone. In a cloth case. First edition. On title-page are
the words "Dono dell'autore", in the handwriting of Galileo, as well
as marginal corrections on two the of the pages. Kraus 164-87 1983
$3,800

CIMAROSA, DOMENICO   Il Matrimonio Segreto. Paris, Imbault,
(c. 1806). Title, "Repertoire", plate #738. Thick folio, green 1/2
vellum. First edition. Salloch 387-49 1983 $700

CIRICI PELLICER, A.   Picasso antes de Picasso. Barcelona:
Iberia-Joaquin Gil, 1946. 273 illus. hors texte (17 tipped-in color).
4to. Cloth. Dust jacket. Ars Libri 32-516 1983 $75

THE CIRCLING Year. Relig. Tract Soc., nd (ca. 1868). Frontis. &
21 plates (18 being printed in colours by Kronheim, Edmund Evans,
Vincent Brooks, et al.), & numerous b&w text illus. Mauve pebble
grain decor. cloth gilt, a.e.g. (re-backed with orig. bkstrip, worn
at top/bottom, corners some bruising, covers faded). 1st edn. V.g.
Hodgkins 27-362 1983 £40

CIRLOT, JUAN EDUARDO   El arte de Gaudi. Barcelona:
Ediciones Omega, 1950. 68 plates (4 tipped-in color). Small 4to.
Boards, 1/4 cloth. Dust jacket. Ars Libri 32-241 1983 $37.50

CIST, CHARLES   Cincinnati in 1841. Cincinnati,
1841. Eight plates, orig. cloth. Head of spine chipped, and
scattered foxing, otherwise a near fine copy. With the signed
presentation inscription, dated 1843, of the author's son, Lewis J.
Cist. Reese 19-143 1983 $175

THE CITIZEN Soldiers at North Point and Fort McHenry, September 12 &
13, 1814. Baltimore, N. Hickman, n.d. (ca. mid-1800s). 12mo. New
cloth. 1st ed. Morrill 289-410 1983 $42.50

THE CITIZEN'S Daughter. Vernor and Hood, 1804. First edition,
half tan calf, gilt spines, drab boards. Jarndyce 31-408 1983 £150

CITRI DE LA GUETTE, SAMUEL   The History of the Triumvirates. London,
Charles Brome, 1686. 8vo, orig. calf, hinges cracked. The first
and only edition. Ravenstree 95-82 1983 $150

THE CITY College, Memories of 60 Years. NY, 1907. Illus., engr.
frontis, large 8vo, g.t. Argosy 710-380 1983 $35

CITY Men and City Manners. London: Goombridge & Sons, 1852.
First edition. 12mo. Orig. cloth. Heath 48-33 1983 £20

THE CITY of Orange, Texas: The Winter Garden of America. N.P.,
ca. 1920. Stiff orange printed wrappers. Several photos. Jenkins
151-260 1983 $25

THE CITY of the Saints, in Picture and Story.   Salt Lake City: The
Deseret News, 1906. Quarto. Illus., pictorial wrappers. First edition. Bradley 66-603 1983 $27.50

CLAGETT, WILLIAM   An Answer to the Representer's
Reflections upon the State and View of the Controversy. Printed for
Ric. Chiswell, 1688. First edition, with the imprimatur leaf, 4to,
wrapper, a very good copy. Fenning 61-67 1983 £21.50

CLAGETT, WILLIAM   A Discourse Concerning the Pretended
Sacrament of Extreme Unction. Printed for Richard Chiswell, 1687.
First edition, including imprimatur leaf, 4to, wrapper, v.g.
Fenning 61-68 1983 £14.50

CLAGETT, WILLIAM   A Discourse Concerning the Worship of
the Blessed Virgin and the Saints. Printed for Tho. Basset...and
Tho. Newborough, 1686. First edition, including imprimatur leaf, 4to,
wrapper, a very good copy. Fenning 61-69 1983 £14.50

CLAGETT, WILLIAM   A Second Letter from the Author of the
Discourse Concerning Extreme Unction, to the Vindicator of the Bishop
of Condom. Printed for Ric. Chiswell, 1688. First edition, 4to,
wrapper, first and last page dusty, but a very good copy. Fenning
61-70 1983 £12.50

CLAGETT, WILLIAM   The State of the Church of Rome when
the Reformation Began. Printed for William Rogers...and Samuel
Smith, 1688. First edition thus, including imprimatur leaf, 4to,
wrapper, a very good copy. Fenning 61-71 1983 £14.50

CLAGETT, WILLIAM   A View of the Whole Controversy Between
the Representer (Gother) and the Answerer. Printed for William
Rogers, 1687. First edition, 4to, wrapper, v.g. to nice. Fenning
61-72 1983 £16.50

CLAIRMONT, ROBERT   Quintillions. New York: Dial Press,
1928. 1st ed., 1 of 500 copies. Silver-coated covers somewhat
rubbed. Jenkins 155-1372 1983 $35

CLAPAREDE, EDOUARD (1873-1940)   Theorie Biologique du Sommeil et
de L'Hysterie. Geneva: Librarie Kundig, 1928. Orig. orange wrappers,
inscribed to Adolf Meyer. Gach 95-72 1983 $100

CLAPESATTLE, HELEN   The Doctors Mayo. Minneapolis, 1941.
8vo, illus., cloth. Bickersteth 77-266 1983 £14

CLAPP, WILLIAM   A Record of the Boston Stage. Boston,
1853. 8vo, orig. embossed cloth, spine chipped. Salloch 387-301
1983 $90

CLAPPERTON, HUGH   Journal of a second expedition into
the interior of Africa... London: John Murray, 1829. First edition.
4to. Portrait, 2 maps (1 folding). Orig. marbled boards. Rebacked
in tan calf, black label, ex-library. Adelson Africa-73 1983
$200

CLAPPERTON, ROBERT HENDERSON Modern Paper-Making. London: Waverley
Book Co., n.d. (1929). First edition. Small 4to. Cloth. 160 illus.
in text. Oak Knoll 49-310 1983 $75

CLARE, ALICE   Maui, A Few Facts about the Valley Isle.
(N.p.: Privately published. One front cover "1930"). Map. Cloth.
Dawson 471-48 1983 $60

CLARE, JOHN   Madrigals and Chronicles. London:
The Beaumont Press, 1924. First edition. Covers and decorations
by Randolph Schwabe. Hand made paper. Buckram-backed decorated
covers. Edges and covers slightly spotted. Very good indeed.
Jolliffe 26-95 1983 £65

CLARE, JOHN   Poems Descriptive of Rural Life and
Scenery. London, 1820. 3rd ed. Orig. full calf, nicely gilt.
Jenkins 155-206 1983 $40

CLARE, JOHN FITZGIBBON, EARL OF   The Speech of...in the House of
Lords of Ireland. Dublin: Printed...London: Reprinted for J. Wright,
1798. 8vo, old paper wrapper, a good to very good copy. Fenning 60-
115 1983 £24.50

CLARENDON, EDWARD HYDE   An answer to a pamphlet... (London):
printed for R. Royston, 1648. First edition. Small 4to. Disbound.
Ximenes 63-93 1983 $125

CLARENDON, EDWARD HYDE   A full answer to an infamous and tray-
terous pamphlet. (London): printed for R. Royston, 1648. First
complete edition. Ximenes 63-94 1983 $125

CLARIDGE, W.   Origin and History of the Bradford
Grammar School. Bradford, J. Green, 1882. First edition, front. and
illus. Orig. brown cloth, v.g. Signed presentation copy from the
author. Jarndyce 31-154 1983 £16.50

CLARK, A. H.   A Monograph of the Existing Crinoids,
Vol. 1, The Comatulids, Part 1. Washington, Nat. Mus. Bull., 1915.
17 plates, 4to, wrappers (rebacked). Wheldon 160-1259 1983 £15

CLARK, ALONZO   The Paris Will Case. Albany, 1860.
4to, wrs. (detached); ex-library. Laid in, Dr. John Watson's
extended criticism of Clark's opinion. Argosy 713-110 1983 $75

CLARK, ANDREW   The Colleges of Oxford. Methuen & Co.,
1891. 8vo, orig. cloth. Bickersteth 75-119 1983 £15

CLARK, ARCHIBALD   Memoir of Colonel John Cameron. Glasgow:
For Private Circulation, 1858. Imperial 8vo. Orig. green decorated
cloth. Sepia lithograph portrait frontis. and 2 sepia lithograph
plates (all with slight marginal foxing and staining). Gilt. A.e.g.
Very slightly soiled and faded. Bookplate. Good. Edwards 1042-293
1983 £60

CLARK, ARTHUR H.   The Clipper Ship Era. New York, 1912.
Illus. 8vo, lacks front blank endleaves. Morrill 288-67 1983 $25

CLARK, CUMBERLAND   Dickens and Democracy. First edition.
Privately printed at the Chiswick Press, 1926. Half title. Orig.
title. Orig. morocco-grained maroon cloth. Signed presentation copy
from the author. Jarndyce 30-149 1983 £18.50

CLARK, CUMBERLAND   The Story of a Great Friendship.
Chiswick Press, 1918. First edition, half title, orig. blue cloth,
mark to back board. Jarndyce 31-587 1983 £16.50

CLARK, DANIEL   Proofs of the Corruption of Gen. James
Wilkinson, and his Connexion with Aaron Burr. Philadelphia, 1809.
Half leather and boards, a fine copy. Reese 18-321 1983 $850

CLARK, EDWARD L.   Daleth or the homestead of the nations.
Boston: Ticknor & Fields, 1864. 8vo. 16 plates (8 colored).
Orig. green cloth. Rubbed. Adelson Africa-178 1983 $35

CLARK, GEORGE R.   The Conquest of the Illinois. Chicago,
1920. Frontis. Signed presentation copy from the editor, Milo
Quaife. Jenkins 152-165 1983 $30

CLARK, GILBERT   Oughtredus Explicatus, sive Commentarius
in eius Clavem Mathematicam. Milonis Flescher, L. London, for
Richard Davis, Oxford, 1682. First edition. Quaritch NS 5-23 1983
$950

CLARK, H. L.   North Pacific Ophiurans. U.S. Nat.
Mus. Bull., 1911. 144 figures, 8vo, wrappers. Wheldon 160-1260
1983 £12

CLARK, JAMES   Circular Address of James Clark and
Richard A. Buckner... (Lexington? or Frankfort? or Louisville? 1828).
First leaf lacks upper right corner, with some loss of text, and tear
across middle of leaf, otherwise good. Disbound. Reese 18-618
1983 $150

CLARK, JAMES   Observations upon the Shoeing of Horses.
Edinburgh: J. Balfour; London: T. Cadell, 1775. 2nd ed., greatly
enlarged from the 1770 ed., 8vo, cont. calf, spine gilt, morocco
label. Engraved folding plate. Light dampstaining of covers, but a
fine copy. Trebizond 18-183 1983 $300

CLARK, JOHN   The Amateur's Assistant. Printed for
Samuel Leigh, 1826. First edition, with 10 aquatint and line plates.
Ads., 4to, orig. green paper boards, with large engraved paper
label on the upper cover; the backstrip neatly renewed in a matching
style. Fenning 62-65 1983 £155

CLARK, JOHN HEAVISIDE   A Practical Illustration of Gilpin's
Day. London: 1811. Folio. First edition. Illus. Uncut, wash
borders for each plate, orig. tissues present. Bound in orig. plain
boards with printed, pink palette, dated 1812, which is chipped. Edges
rubbed, spine renewed. Altogether very nice copy. Bromer 25-181
1983 $1500

CLARK, JOSEPH B.   Leavening the Nation. N.Y., (1903).
Illus. Orig. cloth. First edition. Ginsberg 47-218 1983 $25

CLARK, JOSEPH G.   Lights and Shadows of Sailor Life.
Boston, 1848. Cloth, spine ends frayed, worn. King 46-744 1983
$50

CLARK, LEONARD   Alfred Williams, his life and work.
Bristol, 1945. First edition. Illus. Covers dull and some foxing.
Author's copy, with his autograph signature and bookplate. Good.
Rota 230-641 1983 £20

CLARK, LEONARD   Rhandanim. Leeds: Salamander Press,
1945. First edition. Drawings by I. Allam. One of 250 copies. Autograph signatures of poet and artist. Very nice. Rota 230-130 1983
£20

CLARK, LINCOLN   To the People of the Second Congressional
District of the State of Iowa. (Wash., 1852). Dbd. First edition.
Ginsberg 47-355 1983 $50

CLARK, OLYNTHUS B.   The Politics of Iowa During the Civil
War and Reconstruction. Iowa City, Iowa, 1911. Orig. printed
wraps. First edition. Ginsberg 47-356 1983 $25

CLARK, RICHARD   The Words of the Most Favourite Pieces,
Performed at the Glee Club, the Catch Club, and Other Public Societies.
London, Philanthropic Society, 1814. Engraved head vignette, two
engraved plates of music. Tall 8vo, cont. calf, rebacked, gilt
edges. Front hinge beginning to split. Salloch 387-50 1983 $65

CLARK, ROBERT CARLTON   The Beginnings of Texas, 1684-1718.
Austin, 1907. Orig. printed wrappers. 1st ed. Jenkins 153-563
1983 $125

CLARK, SAMUEL   A Mirrour or Looking-Glasse Both for
Saints, and Sinners... London, 1657. Orig. calf, much worn, hinges
cracked, but still sound. First engraved title repaired with tape,
otherwise internally quite sound throughout. Reese 19-149 1983
$300

CLARK, STEPHEN M.   Account of the Short Life and
Ignominious Death of Stephen Merrill Clark...May, 1821. Salem, 1921.
Self-wraps., foxed. Reese 18-551 1983 $90

CLARK, STERLING   How Many Miles From St. Jo? San
Francisco, priv. prntd, 1929. Illus., append. 12mo, cloth-backed
brds. Clark 741-97 1983 $35

CLARK, STERLING   How Many Miles from St. Jo?... San
Francisco, Privately Printed, 1929. Pictorial boards. First edition.
Near mint. Jenkins 153-125 1983 $25

CLARK, THOMAS BLAKE   Omai: First Polynesian Ambassador to
England. (SF), 1940. Sq 4to, linen-backed batik bds., paper
label. Portrait. One of 500 copies. A very nice copy.

CLARK, THOMAS D.   The Rampaging Frontier. Indianapolis,
1939. Signed by author. Jenkins 152-593 1983 $30

CLARK, WALTER VAN TILBURG   The Ox-Bow Incident. New York:
Random House, (1940). First edition. 8vo. Orig. cloth. Dust
jacket. Fine copy. Jaffe 1-56 1983 $185

CLARK, WALTER VAN TILBURG   The Track of the Cat. New York:
Random House, (1949). First edition. 8vo. Orig. cloth. Dust
jacket. Fine copy. Jaffe 1-57 1983 $75

CLARKE, ADAM   A Dissertation on the Use and Abuse of
Tobacco. London: Printed for G. Whitfield...1787. 8vo; disbound.
Pickering & Chatto 22-23 1983 $85

CLARKE, ARTHUR C.   Interplanetary Flight. London, 1950.
First edition. Covers slightly faded, in slightly browned dustwrapper chipped at head of spine, but very good. Gekoski 2-28 1983
£50

CLARKE, ARTHUR C.   Sands of Mars. New York: Gnome Press,
(1952). Cloth. First American edition. Fine in lightly used dust
jacket. Reese 20-245 1983 $75

CLARKE, ASA B.   Travels in Mexico and California.
Boston, 1582. First edition. Tall 12mo, later 1/2 morocco, slightly
cropped, new end-papers. Fine, in folding slipcase. Argosy 715-287
1983 $450

CLARKE, BENJAMIN   The Sentry System. Hampstead J. Newet-
son, 1875. Third edition. Jarndyce 31-342 1983 £10.50

CLARKE, CHARLES   Drawing the Corks. 1869. 4 pp inserted
ads. on blue paper (of 6?). Orig. blue printed wraps., v.g.
Jarndyce 31-565 1983 £15

CLARKE, EDWARD   The Romance of a Great Career, 1804-1881.
1926. First edition, half title, front. port. illus. 2 pp ads.
Orig. blue cloth. Jarndyce 30-976 1983 £14.50

CLARKE, EDWARD   The Tomb of Alexander. Cambridge:
Printed by R. Watts at the University Press, 1805. First edition,
with a coloured plate, 4 other plates and 1 engraved vignette,
including half-title, 4to, orig. boards, with printed paper label,
a little wear to spine but sound. Uncut. Fenning 61-73 1983
£48.50

CLARKE, EDWARD   A Tour through the South of England,
Wales and Part of Ireland, made during the Summer of 1791. London:
printed at the Minerva Press, 1793. First edition, 8vo, with a
folding plan and 10 folding aquatint plates, rebound in half calf,
gilt, with morocco label. Deighton 3-79 1983 £60

CLARKE, EDWARD H.   The Building of a Brain. Boston, 1874. 1st ed. 12mo. Morrill 289-42 1983 $20

CLARKE, FRANCIS G.   The American Ship-Master's Guide. Boston: Allen & Co., 1838. Second edition. Illus. 4 engraved plates (1 folding). Full calf. Covers rubbed. Good, tight copy. Felcone 20-21 1983 $150

CLARKE, HAROLD GEORGE   Baxter Colour Prints. London, Maggs Bros., 1920-1. Complete from the original twelve parts with the front wrappers bound in. Pictorially presented. 136 plates. 4to, half morocco. Morrill 290-63 1983 $125

CLARKE, HARRY   Faust by Goethe. London, Harrap, (1925). 4to, illus. with 21 full page plates and designs throughout by Harry Clarke. Pictorial endpapers. Vellum backed boards stamped in gilt, t.e.g., uncut. Bookplate. One of 1,000 numbered copies signed by the artist. Very good. Houle 22-234 1983 $325

CLARKE, HERMANN F.   John Coney, Silversmith: 1655-1722. Boston, 1932. Illus., 31 plates. Orig. cloth. x-l. First edition. One of 350 numbered copies. Ginsberg 46-195 1983 $125

CLARKE, HEWSON   The Saunterer, a Periodical Paper, in Two Volumes. London: Longman, hurst, 1808. 3rd ed., 8vo, cont. half calf gilt, morocco labels, marbled boards, errata leaf in vol. 2. Small stains on one spine, but a very good copy. Trebizond 18-77 1983 $100

CLARKE, JOHN   Memoir of Richard Merrick. Benjamin L. Green, 1850. First edition, orig. brown cloth, v.g. Jarndyce 30-1077 1983 £20

CLARKE, SAMUEL   A Collection of Papers, which Passed Between the Late Learned Mr. Leibnitz, and Dr. Clarke, in the Years 1715 and 1716. London: James Knapton, 1717. 2 pages of pub.'s ads. Cont. calf, rubbed; hinges cracked, but still sound. Karmiole 75-100 1983 $125

CLARKE, SAMUEL FESSENDEN   Samuel Fessenden Clarke as Revealed in Some of His Writings. New York, Privately Printed, 1932. Edition limited to 250 copies. Inserted are an ALS and TLS from Mrs. Clarke; also 2 photographs. Illustrated. Tall 8vo, original cloth, leather back, boxed. Backstrip rubbed and slightly chipped at top. Morrill 290-64 1983 $22.50

CLARKE, WILLIAM   Every night book; or, life after dark. London: T. Richardson, 1827. First edition. 8vo. Orig. drab boards. Ximenes 63-261 1983 $75

CLARKSON, L.   Indian Summer. London: Griffith & Far.; N.Y.: Dutton, 1881. Large 4to. Red gilt and pictorial cloth. Beveled edges. A.e.g. Many full-page chromoliths. with tissue guards. Fine. Aleph-bet 8-61 1983 $65

CLARKSON, THOMAS   An Essay on the Slavery and Commerce of the Human Species. London: printed by J. Phillips, and sold by T. Cadell and J. Phillips, 1786. 1st ed., 8vo, errata, uncut in original boards, rebacked in antique calf. A very good copy. Pickering & Chatto 21-19 1983 $385

CLARKSON, THOMAS   An Essay on the Slavery and Commerce of the Human Species. Philadelphia: Wiley, 1804. 8vo, orig. calf (scuffed). Rostenberg 88-3 1983 $85

CLARKSON, THOMAS   The History of the Rise, Progress, and Accomplishment of the Abolition of the African Slave-Trade by the British Parliament. London: Longman, Hurst, Rees and Orme, 1808. 1st ed., 8vo, folding engraved map and folding diagram, both repaired in places, cont. half calf, marbled boards, slightly rubbed. A very good, clean copy. Pickering & Chatto 21-20 1983 $325

CLARKSON, THOMAS   The History of the Rise, Progress and Accomplishment of the Abolition of the African Slave Trade, by the British Parliament. Wilmington, 1816. Old calf, very good. Reese 18-495 1983 $40

CLARKSON, THOMAS   The History of the Rise, Progress, and Accomplishment of the Abolition of the African Slave Trade... New York: John S. Taylor, 1836. 3 vols. 12mo, 3 plates. Orig. maroon cloth. Spines faded. Adelson Africa-179 1983 $60

CLARKSON, THOMAS   The History of the Rise, Progress and Accomplishment of the Abolition of the African Slave-Trade. Wilmington: R. Porter, 1816. 12mo, later cloth-backed boards. Ex-library. Abridged. Last page margin bit chipped, t.p. slight hole decay not affecting text. Argosy 710-23 1983 $45

CLARKSON, THOMAS   A Portraiture of Quakerism. For Longman, Hurst, 1806. First edition, 3 vols. 8vo, cont. half calf, the sides a little worn, but quite strong. Fenning 60-66 1983 £65

CLASSEN, ALEXANDER   Ausgewahlte Methoden der analytischen Chemie. Braunschweig: F. Vieweg & Sohn, 1901, 1903. 2 vols. 8vo. Orig. cloth backed boards. First edition. Numerous text illus., 3 color plates. One hinge split. Zeitlin 264-84 1983 $50

CLAUDE, GEORGES   Liquid Air, Oxygen, Nitrogen. London: J. & A. Churchill, 1913. First English edition. 8vo. Orig. cloth. 151 text figures, many photographs, some full page. Lacking half-title. A little rubbed. A very good copy. Zeitlin 264-85 1983 $50

CLAUDE, JEAN   An Account of the Persecutions and Oppressions of the Protestants in France. (London: Printed in the year 1686. First edition, including the initial blank leaf. 4to. Wrapper, clean tear, without loss, in final leaf. Fenning 61-74 1983 £21.50

CLAUDEL, PAUL   The Book of Christopher Columbus. New Haven: Yale University Press, 1930. 4to, with an orig. lithograph frontis. portrait of Columbus, signed by Charlot. Profusely illus., printed in blue, brown and black. Edition limited to 250 numbered copies, signed by Paul Claudel. Siver-stamped blue cloth. Karmiole 75-35 1983 $250

CLAUDIANUS, CLAUDIUS   Opera Qvam Diligentissime Castigata. (Venice, in Aedibus Aldi et Andreae Asvlani Soceri, 1523). 8vo, 18th century crimson straight-grained morocco gilt, small burn to lower cover, newly rebacked in red morocco gilt, a.e.g., the Duke of Devonshire--Henry Pilkinton copy, with the Pilkington bookplate. Ravenstree 95-35 1983 $695

CLAUSEN, R. T.   Sedum of North America. Ithaca, N.Y., 1976 102 plates, 8vo, cloth. Wheldon 160-1503 1983 £53

CLAVELL, JAMES   Noble House. NY, (1981). Limited to 500 numbered and signed copies, a.e.g., very minor cover wear, else fine in fine slipcase. Quill & Brush 54-281 1983 $150

CLAVERS, MARY PSEUD.
Please turn to
KIRKLAND, CAROLINE MATILDA

CLAWSON, H. PHELPS   By Their Works. Buffalo: Buffalo Society of Natural Sciences, 1941. Prof. illus. 4to. Cloth. Ex-library. Ars Libri 34-10 1983 $37.50

CLAY, ENID   The Constant Mistress. (London): Golden Cockerel Press, 1934. Octavo. First edition. Illus. with 5 full-page wood engravings by Eric Gill. Limited to 300 copies signed by Gill and Clay. Covers faded, else fine in cloth-backed boards. Internally pristine. Owner's signature and stamp on end-paper. Bromer 25-215 1983 $375

CLAY, HENRY   Farewell Speech to the Senate of the United States ... March 31, 1842. Phila.: J. Crissy, (18422). Broadside, printed on silk. 65 x 41 cm. Attractively framed. Fine. Felcone 20-23 1983 $225

CLAY, HENRY   Mr. Clay's Speech, at the Dinner at Noble's Inn, Near Lexington, July 12, 1827. Lexington, 1827. Dsb., pages separated, but good. Reese 18-613 1933 $50

CLAY, HENRY   Speech of Mr. Clay, of Kentucky, Establishing a Deliberate Design, on the Part of the Late and Present Execution of the United States... Washington, 1838. Unopened. Very good. Felcone 20-22 1983 $30

CLAY, HENRY   Works, Comprising His Life, Correspondence & Speeches. 10 vols. Thick large 8vo, brown 3/4 morocco, backs & tops gilt. Connoisseur's Federal edition, ltd. to 400 numbered sets. Argosy 716-430 1983 $500

CLAY, JOHN   My Life on the Range. New York, 1961.
Illus., port. Edn. limited to 750 num. copies. Re-issue of this
rare classic. Clark 741-198 1983 $54.50

CLAY, JOHN   Old Days Recalled. Chicago, 1915.
Illus. Orig. cloth. First edition. Ginsberg 47-220 1983 $150

CLAY, LADY   A Stranger in a Strange Land. London:
Sampson Low, Marston, Searle & Rivington, 1882. First edition. Mac-
Manus 277-980 1983 $300

CLAYTON, ELLEN C.   Female Warriors. London: Tinsley Bro.,
1879. First edition. 2 vols. ·Orig. cloth. Slightly rubbed. Inscriptions on flyleaves. Very good. MacManus 277-981 1983 $125

CLAYTON, DAVID   A Short but Thorough Search Into What
May Be the Real Cause of the Present Scarcity of Our Silver Coin.
London: printed for the author, 1717. 1st ed., 8vo, without the
final leaf, probably blank, disbound. Scarce. Pickering & Chatto
21-21 1983 $100

CLAYTON, POWELL   The Aftermath of the Civil War, in
Arkansas. NY, 1915. Argosy 716-10 1983 $27.50

CLEAVER, HYLTON   Captains of Harley. H. Milford, n.d.
Colour frontis. & 4 plates. Green cloth gilt, repousse pictorial.
Very good. Greer 40-59 1983 £15

CLEAVELAND, AGNES MORLEY   No Life for a Lady. Boston, (1941).
Illus. by Edward Borein. Clark 741-369 1983 $21

CLEGHORN, GEORGE   Observations on the Epidemical
Diseases in Minorca, 1744-9. 8vo, cont. calf, (hinges repaired; ex
lib.). Argosy 713-112 1983 $125

CLELAND, JAMES   Statistical Facts Descriptive of the
Former and Present State of Glasgow. Glasgow, printed by Bell and
Bain, 1837. First edition, 8vo, disbound. Pickering & Chatto 21-
22 1983 $100

CLELAND, ROBERT G.   The Place Called Sespe, the History of
a California Ranch. N.p., 1940. Folding map as frontis. Original
cloth with morocco label. Privately printed, in a small edition,
very scarce. Jenkins 153-126 1983 $100

CLELAND, THOMAS MAITLAND   The Decorative Work of T.M. Cleland.
N.Y., Pynson, 1929. First edition, small folio, frontis. lithograph
by Rockwell Kent. With over 90 color and b/w plates, some folding.
Dust jacket (small chips), else very good-fine. One of 1145 copies.
Houle 21-225 1983 $165

CLEMEN, RUDOLF ALEXANDER   The American Livestock and Meat Industry.
New York, 1923. First edition. Illustrated. 8vo. Morrill 290-631
1983 $25

CLEMENS, CLARA   My Husband Gabrilowitsch. N.Y., 1938.
First edition. Illus. Large 8vo, cloth. Presentation copy.
Argosy 714-763 1983 $30

CLEMENS, CYRIL   Josh Billings, Yankee Humorist. Webster
Groves, Missouri: Int'l Mark Twain Society, 1932. Photos. Drawings.
Cloth. Index. Slight soil and spotting. Good. King 45-200 1983
$20

CLEMENS, JEREMIAH   Bernard Lile: An Historical Romance,
Embracing the Period of the Texas Revolution and the Mexican War.
Philadelphia: Lippincott, 1857. 1st ed. Orig. black cloth, gilt.
This copy is the state with the author's name on the title (no
priority). Joints expertly strengthened, else a very good copy.
Jenkins 155-208 1983 $100

CLEMENS, SAMUEL LANGHORNE   Adventures of Huckleberry Finn. NY:
1884. First American edition. Rebound in full crushed green morocco
with representation of frontis. on front cover in various colored onlays with blind tooling. Spine with raised bands and gilt. A.e.g.
Orig. covers bound in. Very fine copy. Preserved in cloth slip-case.
Bromer 25-16 1983 $1350

CLEMENS, SAMUEL LANGHORNE   Adventures of Huckleberry Finn. New
York: Webster, 1885. Frontis., illus. 1st ed., early issue with
all the earliest textual points possible for cloth copies. Orig.
green pictorial cloth, gilt. pp. 13 and 57 are in state 1; no signature mark at p. 161; last 5 lacking in folio 155; p. 283 a cancel;
frontis in second state (this is an insert with no bearing on priority
of the sheets). Two tiny points of rubbing at lower tip of spine,
else a fine fresh copy. Jenkins 155-209 1983 $750

CLEMENS, SAMUEL LANGHORNE   Adventures of Huckleberry Finn. N.Y.:
Webster, 1885. First American edition, mixed issue. With 274 illus.
by E. W. Kemble. Bound in full dark green morocco by Bayntun, spine
decorated in gilt, gilt inner dentelles. Edges extra gilt, white
watered silk doublures, orig. cloth bound in. Fine copy enclosed in
a fleece-lined slipcase. Houle 22-907 1983 $650

CLEMENS, SAMUEL LANGHORNE   Adventures of Huckleberry Finn. N.Y.,
1885. First edition. Green pictorial cloth. Although the frontis.
and front flyleaf are missing, this is a very early issue, with "was"
for "saw," "Him & another man," the two cancel leaves, and the final
5 missing on p. 155. Argosy 714-751 1983 $350

CLEMENS, SAMUEL LANGHORNE   Adventures of Huckleberry Finn. New
York: Webster, 1885. Frontis., illus. First edition, later state.
Orig. green pictorial cloth, gilt. Light rubbing to spine tips and
corners, else a much better copy than usually encountered. Jenkins
155-210 1983 $250

CLEMENS, SAMUEL LANGHORNE   The American Claimant. N.Y., 1892.
First edition. 8vo, pict. cloth. Illus. by Dan Beard, A fine
copy. Argosy 714-752 1983 $100

CLEMENS, SAMUEL LANGHORNE   The American Claimant. NY, 1892. Name
of hospital stamp in small letters on endpaper, otherwise very good to
fine in grey/green cloth. Quill & Brush 54-1402 1983 $75

CLEMENS, SAMUEL LANGHORNE   The American Claimant. NY, 1892. Bookplate front pastedown, tannish cloth shows wear, particularly on
edges. Quill & Brush 54-1404 1983 $35

CLEMENS, SAMUEL LANGHORNE   The American Claimant. New York: 1892.
First edition. Illus. Pictorial gray-green cloth, stamped in gold
and black. Bookplate removed, presentation at first free end paper.
Very good tight copy, covers lightly worn. Bradley 66-343 1983 $30

CLEMENS, SAMUEL LANGHORNE   (An Autobiography). New York: The
Aldine, 1871. 1st printing as contained in a complete run of The
Aldine from January-December 1871. Orig. publisher's green cloth,
gilt. Folio, top of spine chipped, but very good copy of this
heavily illus. journal. Jenkins 155-211 1983 $100

CLEMENS, SAMUEL LANGHORNE   Mark Twain's (Burlesque) Autobiography.
NY, (1871). Second issue, cover slightly worn and stained, light
interior staining, good or better, bookplate. Quill & Brush 54-1394
1983 $60

CLEMENS, SAMUEL LANGHORNE   Mark Twain's Autobiography. NY, 1924.
First edition. 2 vols. Portrait, cloth, t.e.g., covers soiled,
rubbed. King 46-344 1983 $35

CLEMENS, SAMUEL LANGHORNE   Mark Twain's Autobiography. New York,
1924. 1st ed. Frontispiece portraits. 2 vols., 8vo. Morrill
286-584 1983 $30

CLEMENS, SAMUEL LANGHORNE   The Celebrated Jumping Frog of Calaveras
County. London: Routledge, 1867. First English edition. Later 3/4
brown calf and marbled boards, raised bands, gilt. This edition originally issued in glazed wrappers, is scarcer than the American edition of the same year. Fine copy. Jenkins 155-212 1983 $375

CLEMENS, SAMUEL LANGHORNE   The Celebrated Jumping Frog of
Calaveras County, and Other Sketches. NY: C.H. Webb, 1868. 12mo,
orig. rust cloth, with gilt lettering and frog on the front cover;
extremities a little frayed. Karmiole 73-104 1983 $100

CLEMENS, SAMUEL LANGHORNE   The Jumping Frog. NY, 1903. In English
and French, cover lightly worn, very good. Quill & Brush 54-1406
1983 $60

CLEMENS, SAMUEL LANGHORNE   A Champagne Cocktail and a Catastrophe. (New York, ca. 1930). 1st ed. Orig. self-wrappers, stapled as issued. The colophon, reads: "Printed from the original manuscript in the possession of Robin and Marian MacVicars...Xmas, 1930." Mint. Jenkins 155-213 1983 $100

CLEMENS, SAMUEL LANGHORNE   A Champagne Cocktail and a Catastrophe. 1930. 8vo. Wraps. Printed in a small ed. and issued as a holiday greeting. A fine copy. In Our Time 156-820 1983 $50

CLEMENS, SAMUEL LANGHORNE   Christian Science. N.Y., 1907. First edition. Red cloth, fine, unfaded copy. Early issue, with many of the points, including a 1906 date on the frontis. Argosy 714-753 1983 $100

CLEMENS, SAMUEL LANGHORNE   Christian Science. New York & London: Harper, 1907. 1st ed., 2nd state. Orig. red cloth, gilt. Fine bright copy, and scarce thus. Jenkins 155-214 1983 $50

CLEMENS, SAMUEL LANGHORNE   A Connecticut Yankee in King Arthur's Court. N.Y., Webster, 1889. First edition. Large 8vo, illus. by Dan Beard and others. 3/4 navy blue morocco by Bayntun of Bath, spine decorated in gilt, t.e.g., marbled endpapers. Fine copy. Houle 22-908 1983 $275

CLEMENS, SAMUEL LANGHORNE   A Connecticut Yankee in King Arthur's Court. New York: Webster, 1889. Frontis., illus. 1st ed., with the S-ornament present at p. 59, no half-title printed on recto of frontis, broken type at p. 72. Orig. green pictorial cloth, gilt, floral end papers. Copies of this book with the S-ornament present are equally rare to those with half-title. Jenkins 155-215 1983 $200

CLEMENS, SAMUEL LANGHORNE   A Connecticut Yankee in King Arthur's Court. NY, 1889. First issue, bright copy with edges slightly rubbed, slightly worn at corners and spine edges, front hinge starting, very good. Quill & Brush 54-1383 1983 $250

CLEMENS, SAMUEL LANGHORNE   A Connecticut Yankee in King Arthur's Court. New York: Webster, 1889. Frontis., illus. 1st ed, with the S-ornament present at p.59, no half-title printed on recto of frontis, broken type at p. 72. Orig. green pictorial cloth, gilt, floral end papers (earlier style). Rare with the S-ornament. Jenkins 153-819 1983 $200

CLEMENS, SAMUEL LANGHORNE   A Connecticut Yankee in King Arthur's Court. NY, 1889. No "S" on page 59 but perfect type on page 72, very bright, tight copy. Quill & Brush 54-1384 1983 $175

CLEMENS, SAMUEL LANGHORNE   A Connecticut Yankee in King Arthur's Court. New York, 1889. Illus. Cloth. First edition, with the plate at p. (59) in the earliest state. A near fine copy. Felcone 21-23 1983 $150

CLEMENS, SAMUEL LANGHORNE   A Connecticut Yankee in King Arthur's Court. New York: Webster, 1889. Frontis., illus. 1st ed., without the S-ornament at p. 59, without the half-title, and with perfect type at p. 72 (early state). Orig. pictorial green cloth, gilt, floral end papers. Minute wear, but a fine copy with less common end papers (usually geometric design on light blue rather than green floral design). Jenkins 155-216 1983 $150

CLEMENS, SAMUEL LANGHORNE   A Conversazione in the Year MDCI. N.p.: Privately printed on July 20, 1913. One of only 75 copies, on Japan vellum. Argosy 714-754 1983 $75

CLEMENS, SAMUEL LANGHORNE   The Curious Republic of Gondour. NY, 1919. Edges slightly worn, very good. Quill & Brush 54-1405 1983 $75

CLEMENS, SAMUEL LANGHORNE   Editorial Wild Oats. NY, 1905. Cover slightly soiled and spine lettering faded but still readable, otherwise very good. Quill & Brush 54-1388 1983 $50

CLEMENS, SAMUEL LANGHORNE   Editorial Wild Oats. N.Y., 1905. First edition. Illus., 8vo, pict. red cloth, uniformly faded. Argosy 714-757 1983 $30

CLEMENS, SAMUEL LANGHORNE   English as She Is Taught. Boston: Mutual Book Co., (1900). 1st ed., 2nd state with "five." Orig. green cloth. Very near fine copy. Jenkins 155-217 1983 $30

CLEMENS, SAMUEL LANGHORNE   Extract from Captain Stormfield's Visit to Heaven. N.Y., 1909. First edition. Pictorial red cloth. Argosy 714-758 1983 $40

CLEMENS, SAMUEL LANGHORNE   Extract from Captain Stormfield's Visit to Heaven. New York & London: Harper, 1909. Frontis., illus. 1st ed. Orig. pictorial cloth. This copy bulks 9/16". Very good copy. Jenkins 155-218 1983 $22.50

CLEMENS, SAMUEL LANGHORNE   Following the Equator. Hartford, American Publishing, 1897. First edition. Thick 8vo, frontis. portrait; illus. by A.B. Frost, Peter Newell, A.G. Reinhardt, et. al. Fine 3/4 gilt stamped brown morocco, t.e.g., marbled endpapers, by Bayntun of Bath. A fine copy. Houle 22-909 1983 $275

CLEMENS, SAMUEL LANGHORNE   Following the Equator. Ht., 1897. Cover slightly rubbed, very good. Quill & Brush 54-1390 1983 $90

CLEMENS, SAMUEL LANGHORNE   Following the Equator. Hartford: American Pub. Co., 1897. Frontis., plates. 1st ed., with preferred single imprint. Orig. blue cloth, gilt, inlaid panel on front cover. Very good copy. Jenkins 155-219 1983 $75

CLEMENS, SAMUEL LANGHORNE   Following the Equator. Hartford & New York, 1897. Frontis., plates. 1st ed., double imprint. Orig. blue decorated cloth, gilt. Copies with the double imprint are rarer by a ratio of ten to one. Fine bright tight copy of this scarce state. Jenkins 155-220 1983 $75

CLEMENS, SAMUEL LANGHORNE   A Horse's Tale. NY, 1907. Very good. Quill & Brush 54-1386 1983 $50

CLEMENS, SAMUEL LANGHORNE   A Horse's Tale. NY, 1907. Slightly faded on spine, white lettering still visible, good to very good, owner's name. Quill & Brush 54-1385 1983 $40

CLEMENS, SAMUEL LANGHORNE   How to Tell a Story. NY, 1897. Edges slightly rubbed, endpapers very slightly offset, very good. Quill & Brush 54-1391 1983 $150

CLEMENS, SAMUEL LANGHORNE   The Innocents Abroad. American Pub. Co., 1869. 8vo. Orig. publisher's sheep. Some wear along edge of spine, mainly a good-fine copy in slipcase box. In Our Time 156-812 1983 $350

CLEMENS, SAMUEL LANGHORNE   Innocents Abroad. Hartford, 1869. Illus. Thick 8vo, black cloth stamped in gilt & blind. First edition. Argosy 714-760 1983 $150

CLEMENS, SAMUEL LANGHORNE   The Innocents Abroad. Hartford, 1871. Early reprint from 1st ed. plates. Orig. black cloth, gilt. Very good. Jenkins 155-222 1983 $20

CLEMENS, SAMUEL LANGHORNE   The Innocents Abroad; or, the New Pilgrims Progress. Leipzig: Bernhard Tauchnitz, 1879. 12mo. 2 vols. Orig. paper wrappers. Later printing of the Tauchnitz edition. Fine, unopened copy. Oak Knoll 49-377 1983 $45

CLEMENS, SAMUEL LANGHORNE   Is Shakespeare Dead???? NY, 1909. State A, slight wear on spine ends, fine. Quill & Brush 54-1392 1983 $60

CLEMENS, SAMUEL LANGHORNE   Is Shakespeare Dead? New York: 1909. First edition, state A, without inserted note after title page. Two frontis. plates. Green cloth, stamped in gold, t.e.g. Bookplate. Nice, clean copy, very lightly rubbed at corners. Bradley 66-344 $45

CLEMENS, SAMUEL LANGHORNE   Jim Smiley and his Jumping Frog. Chicago: The Pocahontas Press, 1940. Sm. 12mo, green leather-backed patterned cloth boards, gilt. Illus. by John T. McCutcheon. Backstrip lightly rubbed. Perata 28-176 1983 $40

CLEMENS, SAMUEL LANGHORNE   Mark Twain's Letters. NY, (1917). Two vols., limited to 350 sets, covers slightly soiled and edges slightly rubbed, very good. Quill & Brush 54-1395 1983 $175

CLEMENS, SAMUEL LANGHORNE   The Letters of Quitus Curtius Snodgress. TX, 1946. Fine in lightly soiled dustwrapper. Quill & Brush 54-1407 1983 $40

CLEMENS, SAMUEL LANGHORNE   Life on the Mississippi. Boston: Osgood, 1883. Frontis., illus. 1st ed. 1st state, intermediate B. Orig. pictorial brown cloth, gilt. Minor wear at base of spine, else a fine bright copy. Jenkins 155-224 1983 $150

CLEMENS, SAMUEL LANGHORNE   Love Letters of Mark Twain. N.Y., Harper, 1949. First edition. Frontis. One of 155 copies of the deluxe edition, with a leaf signed by Twain, with his double signature. Very good-fine. Houle 21-882 1983 $60

CLEMENS, SAMUEL LANGHORNE   The Love Letters of Mark Twain. N.Y., 1949. First edition, d.w. Argosy 714-768 1983 $20

CLEMENS, SAMUEL LANGHORNE   Life on the Mississippi. London, 1883. 8vo. Cloth. Publisher's catalogue at rear dated March, 1883. This English ed. precedes the American. Some light spotting to cloth, mainly a fine bright copy. In Our Time 156-814 1983 $500

CLEMENS, SAMUEL LANGHORNE   Life on the Mississippi. Boston: 1883. First American edition, second state, without tailpiece on p. 441. 316 illus. Full pictorial brown cloth, stamped in black and gold. Solid copy, corners worn, spine ends frayed. Bookplate. Very good. Bradley 66-345 1983 $55

CLEMENS, SAMUEL LANGHORNE   Mark Twain's Library of Humor. NY, 1888. First edition, first issue. Illus. by E.W. Kemble. Dec. cloth, ink inscription (1888), a bit rubbed else a nice copy. King 46-345 1983 $100

CLEMENS, SAMUEL LANGHORNE   The Love Letters of Mark Twain. N.Y., Harper, 1949. First edition. Frontis. Dust jacket. One of 155 copies with a leaf signed by Twain with his double signature (Twain and Clemens). Pub.'s box. Fine. Houle 22-910 1983 $850

CLEMENS, SAMUEL LANGHORNE   More Tramps Abroad. London: Chatto & Windus, 1897. Gilt cloth. First British edition. Very slight rubbing, else about fine. Reese 20-248 1983 $75

CLEMENS, SAMUEL LANGHORNE   More Tramps Abroad. L, 1897. Edges rubbed, front hinge starting at top half title, good. Quill & Brush 54-1396 1983 $50

CLEMENS, SAMUEL LANGHORNE   The £1,000,000 Bank-Note. New York: Webster, 1893. Frontis. 1st ed. Orig. mustard pictorial cloth, gilt. Near fine copy with December 26, 1893 Denison, Texas owner's inscription. Jenkins 155-228 1983 $60

CLEMENS, SAMUEL LANGHORNE   Personal Recollections of Joan of Arc. London: Chatto & Windus, 1896. Frontis. 1st English ed. Orig. blue pictorial cloth, gilt, t.e.g., other uncut. Fine bright copy. March ads at end. Jenkins 155-229 1983 $150

CLEMENS, SAMUEL LANGHORNE   Personal Recollections of Joan of Arc. NY, 1896. First state, spine shows some light wear, hinge paper cracked at c page, slightly cocked, good or better. Quill & Brush 54-1397 1983 $125

CLEMENS, SAMUEL LANGHORNE   The Prince and the Pauper. Boston, 1882. 8vo. 1st American ed. Bound in the orig. publisher's calf binding. Some scuffing to the leather, otherwise a very good copy. In Our Time 156-813 1983 $350

CLEMENS, SAMUEL LANGHORNE   The Prince and the Pauper. B, 1882. State A, "Franklin Press" on copyright page, spine ends and corners worn, otherwise good. Quill & Brush 54-1409 1983 $225

CLEMENS, SAMUEL LANGHORNE   The Prince and the Pauper. Boston: Osgood, 1882. Illus. 1st ed., 1st binding. Orig. green pictorial cloth, gilt. Some rubbing at spine tips, but a bright little used copy otherwise. Jenkins 155-230 1983 $100

CLEMENS, SAMUEL LANGHORNE   The Prince and the Pauper. B, 1882. First issue with Franklin Press on copyright page, hinges cracked, cover edges worn, some interior staining, fair, owner's name. Quill & Brush 54-1408 1983 $60

CLEMENS, SAMUEL LANGHORNE   Pudd'nhead Wilson. L, 1894. Hinges cracked, cover worn, good. Quill & Brush 54-1398 1983 $75

CLEMENS, SAMUEL LANGHORNE   Roughing It. Hartford, 1872. First edition, later issue. In Modern quarter black calf gilt. K Books 301-183 1983 £30

CLEMENS, SAMUEL LANGHORNE   1601, or, a Fireside Conversation in Ye Time of Queen Elizabeth. S.F.: Privately printed, 1929. 12mo, parchment-backed boards, vignette in gilt on upper cover. 4 hand-colored illus. by W. R. Cameron. One of 40 illustrated copies. Perata 28-78 1983 $100

CLEMENS, SAMUEL LANGHORNE   1601, or Sociall Fireside Conversation in Ye Time of Ye Tudors. Louisville: Ye Blew Grasse Press, 1929. Uncut, square 8vo, boards. Fine. Ltd. numbered edition. Argosy 714-756 1983 $35

CLEMENS, SAMUEL LANGHORNE   1601. Louisville: Ye Blew Grasse Press, 1929. Limited ed. of 1,000 copies. Orig. printed boards, uncut. Nicely done on handmade paper. Fine. Jenkins 155-231 1983 $30

CLEMENS, SAMUEL LANGHORNE   "1601". Chicago, Black Cat Press, 1936. Ed. limited to 300 copies. Frontispiece. 8vo, orig. red leatherette. Morrill 286-93 1983 $30

CLEMENS, SAMUEL LANGHORNE   Mark Twain's Sketches, New and Old. Hartford: American Pub. Co., 1875. Frontis., illus. 1st ed., 2nd state without inserted slip and garbled footnote. Orig. blue decorated cloth, gilt. Spine tips slightly frayed and corner of front free end paper clipped, else a fresh clean copy. Jenkins 155-226 1983 $100

CLEMENS, SAMUEL LANGHORNE   Sketches of the Sixties. San Francisco, 1926. First edition. Tall 8vo, cloth backed boards. Frontis. Presentation copy, from John Howell, the publisher. Argosy 714-762 1983 $75

CLEMENS, SAMUEL LANGHORNE   The Stolen White Elephant, Etc. B, 1882. Cover shows some wear and soiled, good copy. Quill & Brush 54-1410 1983 $75

CLEMENS, SAMUEL LANGHORNE   The Stolen White Elephant. London: Chatto & Windus, 1897. Gilt cloth. Very slight rubbing, else about fine. Reese 20-247 1983 $25

CLEMENS, SAMUEL LANGHORNE   The $30,000 Bequest and Other Stories. NY, 1906. State 2 with ads on copyright page, hinge starting at title page, good to very good, owner's name. Quill & Brush 54-1399 1983 $60

CLEMENS, SAMUEL LANGHORNE   Three Aces, Jim Todd's Episode in Social Euchre, a Poem and a Denial. (New York, ca. 1930). 1st ed. Orig. self-wrappers, stapled as issued. The colophon reads: "Of this poem by Mark Twain, now for the first time published in book form, there have been printed but 50 copies for friends of Robin and Marian MacVicars,--in their studio at Westport-in-Connecticut. Christmas Season, MCMXXIX." Mint copy. Jenkins 155-232 1983 $100

CLEMENS, SAMUEL LANGHORNE   To the Person Sitting in Darkness and Concerning the Rev. Mr. Ament. Privately Printed, 1926. 1st ed., 1 of 250 numbered copies. Orig. brown printed wrappers, uncut. Very fine. Jenkins 155-1374 1983 $75

CLEMENS, SAMUEL LANGHORNE   Tom Sawyer Abroad. New York: Webster, 1894. 1st ed., binding A. Orig. white pictorial cloth, gilt. BAL describes the cloth as being tan, but fresh copies are white with tiny specks of green detectable in the threads as in this copy. But for a closed crack in the front end paper (hinge is firm) a fine fresh copy of an uncommon title, that is usually found rubbed and aged. Jenkins 155-233 1983 $200

CLEMENS, SAMUEL LANGHORNE   Tom Sawyer Abroad. London: Chatto & Windus, 1894. Frontis. 1st English ed., 1st binding. Orig. red pictorial cloth, gilt. Spine very slightly darkened, else a fine copy of this scarce ed. This copy has February, 1894 ads. Jenkins 155-234 1983 $125

CLEMENS, SAMUEL LANGHORNE   The Tragedy of Pudd'nhead Wilson and the Comedy of Those Extraordinary Twins. Hartford: American Pub. Co., 1894. First American edition. Title page in black and red. Portrait frontispiece, other illustrations in text. Decorated reddish-brown cloth, stamped in gold and black. Frontispiece in first state with Twain's signature. Previous owner's bookplate on front pastedown, his penciled signature on first flyleaf. Fine, tight copy with light rubbing on extremities. Bradley 64-173 1983 $225

CLEMENS, SAMUEL LANGHORNE   The Tragedy of Pudd'nhead Wilson and Those Extraordinary Twins. Ht., 1894. First state with sheets size and facsimile as called for, small chip out of top edge of spine, otherwise very good or better. Quill & Brush 54-1411 1983 $200

CLEMENS, SAMUEL LANGHORNE   The Tragedy of Pudd'nhead Wilson and the Comedy Those Extraordinary Twins. Hartford, 1894. Illus. Cloth. First American edition. A fine copy. Felcone 21-24 1983 $150

CLEMENS, SAMUEL LANGHORNE   A Tramp Abroad. Hartford: American Pub. Co., 1880. Frontis., illus. 1st ed., 1st state of sheets. Orig. black cloth, gilt. Sheets bulk 1-5/8"; 1st state of portrait; 2nd state of caption to frontis.; binding B (no sequence). But for some reddening of spine gilt, a very fine copy. Jenkins 155-235 1983 $125

CLEMENS, SAMUEL LANGHORNE   Travels with Mr. Brown. NY, 1940. Limited to 1795 copies, minute spot on front cover, else bright copy in slightly soiled, else fine dustwrapper, bookplate. Quill & Brush 54-1413 1983 $40

CLEMENS, SAMUEL LANGHORNE   An Unexpected Acquaintance. NY, (1904). Printed wrapper, cover slightly soiled and torn along spine, else very good. Quill & Brush 54-1387 1983 $75

CLEMENS, SAMUEL LANGHORNE   The Writings of Mark Twain. Hartford: 1899-1907. First edition. 25 vols. Edition De Luxe. Ltd. to 1000 copies signed by Twain/Clemens and Charles Dudley Warner. Full crushed morocco, marbled pattern. Onlaid border of burgundy morocco outlined in gilt. Painted vellum and gilt flowers on both covers. Gilt-tooled spine with 6 compartments. Gilt-decorated turn-ins, olive morocco doublures. Green silk free endpapers, a.e.g. Very fine set. Bookplate in each volume. Bromer 25-17 1983 $3500

CLEMENS, SAMUEL LANGHORNE   The Writings of Mark Twain. Hartford, Conn., 1899-1907. 25 vols. Ed. deluxe, 1 of 1000 sets printed. Bound in quarter morocco. This set specially signed by Twain on copyright page. Signed "SL Clemens/Mark Twain". Some scuffing to a few bindings, mainly a fine set. In Our Time 156-818 1983 $2500

CLEMENS, SAMUEL LANGHORNE   A Yankee at the Court of King Arthur. London, 1889. 8vo, cloth. First English edition. Illus. by Dan Beard. Ads on this copy read June, 1889. A fine copy. In Our Time 156-815 1983 $200

CLEMENS, SAMUEL LANGHORNE   A Yankee in King Arthur's Court. Toronto: G.M. Rose & Sons Co., (1899). Thick 8vo. 1st Canadian ed. of the work and uncommon. Front flyleaf has been repaired near hinge, otherwise a vg-fine bright copy. In Our Time 156-816 1983 $100

CLEMENS, WILLIAM M.   American Marriage Records Before 1699. NY, 1926. 4to, cloth, paper labels. Limited edition. Argosy 716-176 1983 $22.50

CLEMENT, ARTHUR W.   Our Pioneer Potters. New York, 1947. Ed. limited to 500 copies. Illus. 8vo, orig. boards, cloth back, very nice. Morrill 288-70 1983 $35

CLEMENT, JEAN MARIE BERNARD Anecdotes Dramatiques. Paris: chez la veuve Duchesne, 1775. 3 vols., 8vo, cont. mottled calf, spines gilt (some wear to spines). 1st edition. Half-titles present. Very scarce. Ximenes 64-104 1983 $275

CLEMENTS, L.   Shooting adventures, canine lore and sea-fishing trips. London: Chapman and Hall, 1879. First edition. 2 vols. 8vo. Orig. brown cloth. Trifle rubbed. Ximenes 63-553 1983 $125

CLEMSON, THOMAS G.   Observations on the La Motte Mines and Domain in the State of Missouri, with Some Account of the Advantages and Inducements there Promised to Capitalists. Wash., Blair & Rives, 1838. Half morocco. First edition. Ginsberg 47-516 1983 $100

CLENARDUS, NICHOLAS   Institvtiones Lingvae Graece. Londini, Robertus Robinsonus, 1594. 8vo, orig. calf wonr, loose in binding, contents trifle soiled and thumbed. Ravenstree 95-37 1983 $320

CLENDENING, LOGAN   A Handbook to Pickwick Papers. NY, 1936. First American edition. Photos, cloth backed boards. Very good in soiled dust wrapper. King 46-273 1983 $20

CLENDENING, LOGAN   Source Book of Medical History. N.Y., (c. 1942). 4to. Argosy 713-113 1983 $75

CLEPHAN, JAMES   The Bud and the Flower. Newcastle-upon-Tyne, 1856. First edition, printed for private distribution (by Thomas & James Pegg). Orig. brick-red-paper wraps., worn on spine. Signed presentation copy from the author to his sister. Jarndyce 30-665 1983 £20

CLEPHAN, JAMES   Finchdale, the Holy Isle. Newcastle-upon-Tyne by Thomas & James Pegg, 1857. Lacking wraps. Signed presentation copy from the author to his sister. Jarndyce 30-666 1983 £20

CLEPHAN, JAMES   Finchdale, the Holy Isle. Newcastle-upon-Tyne by Thomas & James Pegg, 1857. First edition. Orig. brick-red-wraps., v.g. Jarndyce 30-667 1983 £18.50

CLEPHAN, R. COLTMAN   The Tournament Its Periods and Phases. London, 1919. First edition. 8vo. Orig. cloth. Coloured frontis. 20 plates, extra illus., coloured pencil lines and annotations in text, folio. Gilt embossed design of tournament jouster on upper cover, fore-and lower-edges uncut. Spine faded. Fine. Edwards 1042-305 1983 £140

CLERK-MAXWELL, JAMES
Please turn to
MAXWELL, JAMES CLERK

CLERY, JEAN BAPTISTE   A Journal of The Occurences at the Temple, during the Confinement of Louis XVI, King of France. London: printed by Baylis, 1798. 1st English edition, 8vo, cont. linen-backed boards, morocco label. Half-title, engraved frontis., facsimile leaf, library bookplates. Spine chipped, but a good copy. Trebizond 18-192 1983 $50

CLEVELAND, GROVER   Message from the President of the U.S. Washington: SED20, 1895. First edition. Orig. red cloth. Jenkins 152-272 1983 $50

CLIFFORD, LADY
Please turn to
PEMBROKE, ANNE CLIFFORD, COUNTESS OF 1590-1676

CLIFFORD, CHARLES CAVENDISH Travels by 'Umbra'. Edinburgh: Edmonston & Douglas, 1865. First and apparently only edition, with engraved title-page and frontis., 8vo, cont. half calf. Rubbed but sound and a very good copy. Fenning 62-67 1983 £21.50

CLIFFORD, ETHEL   Love's Journey. London: John Lane, The Bodley Head, 1905. First edition. Orig. boards. Dust jacket. Fine. MacManus 277-982 1983 $25

CLIFFORD, ETHEL   Songs of Dreams. London: John Lane, The Bodley Head, 1903. First edition. Orig. boards. Dust jacket (a bit worn). Fine. MacManus 277-983 1983 $25

CLIFFORD, HUGH   The Downfall of the Gods. London: John Murray, 1911. First edition. Orig. cloth. Publisher's blind-stamped presentation copy. Spine faded. Good. MacManus 277-984 1983 $30

CLIFFORD, HUGH   A Free Lance of ToDay. London: Methuen & Co., 1903. First edition. Orig. cloth. Spine darkened. Good. MacManus 277-985 1983 $45

CLIFFORD, HUGH   The Gold Coast Regiment in the East
African Campaign. London: John Murray, 1920. First edition. Orig.
cloth. Covers a little spotted. Good. MacManus 277-986 1983 $25

CLIFFORD, HUGH   Heroes of Exile. London: Smith, Elder
& Co., 1906. First edition. Orig. cloth. Spine darkened. Endpapers
foxed. Good. MacManus 277-987 1983 $35

CLIFFORD, HUGH   In A Corner of Asia. London: T. Fisher
Unwin, 1899. First edition. Orig. cloth. Part of The Over-Seas
Library. Front endpapers put in upside-down. Covers a little soiled.
Very good. MacManus 277-988 1983 $50

CLIFFORD, HUGH   In Camp & Kampong. London & N.Y.: 1897-
1916. First editions. 8 vols. Uniformly bound in 3/4 morocco & cloth.
Lacking title-page in Bush-Whacking. Some wear to outer hinges. Very
good set. MacManus 277-989 1983 $175

CLIFFORD, HUGH   In Court & Kampong. London: Grant
Richards, 1897. First edition. Orig. decorated cloth. Covers darkened, soiled. Good. MacManus 277-990 1983 $75

CLIFFORD, HUGH   In Days That Are Dead. London: John
Murray, (1926). First edition. Orig. cloth. Covers partially faded.
Good. MacManus 277-991 1983 $35

CLIFFORD, HUGH   Saleh: A Sequel. Edinburgh: William
Blackwood & Sons, 1908. First edition. Orig. cloth. Covers faded.
Good. MacManus 277-994 1983 $45

CLIFFORD, ISIDORE   Crown, Bar, and Bridge-work. London,
1887. Colored litho. plates. "With the Author's compliments" on
fly-leaf. Lacks plates 5, 6, 8. Argosy 713-114 1983 $50

CLIFFORD, MARTIN   Notes upon Mr. Dryden's poems in four
letters. London: printed in the year 1687. First edition. Small
4to. Later wrappers. Title-page a trifle soiled. Ximenes 63-236
1983 $175

CLIFFORD, MARTIN   Notes upon Mr. Dryden's poems in four
letters. London: 1687. Sm. 4to, disbound. 1st edition, first
issue. Piece torn from upper inner margin of title, affecting the
ruled border and part of the first letter of "Notes." Ximenes 64-
105 1983 $150

CLIFFORD, W. K.   Mrs. Keith's Crime. London: T. Fisher
Unwin, 1897. Sixth edition, with a new Preface by the Author. Orig.
cloth. Frontispiece by Hon. John Collier. Edges and corners a bit
worn, endpapers browned. Previous owner's signature. Bookseller's
stamp. Good. MacManus 277-995 1983 $25

CLIFTON, VIOLET M.   The Book of Talbot. Faber & Faber,
1933. First edition, with 4 plates and 4 folding maps, 8vo, cloth,
gilt, t.e.g. With a long presentation inscription by the author.
Fenning 62-68 1983 £12.50

CLIFTON, VIOLET M.   Pilgrims to the Isles of Penance. John
Long, 1911. First edition. With a folding map and 54 illus. on 48
plates, errata slip. 8vo, orig. cloth, t.e.g. Small nick in headband, but otherwise a very good copy. Fenning 61-77 1983 £24.50

CLIFTON-SHELTON, A.   The Nursery Alphabet. Nelson, n.d.
(ca.1920). 4to. 26 colour text illus. Ink erasure on first page.
Colour pictorial boards, edges worn. Greer 40-17 1983 £17.50

THE CLIMATE of New Mexico and Las Vegas Hot Springs.   Chicago: 1883.
Full-page plate. Tan wrappers. Fine copy. Bradley 66-613 1983 $75

CLINCH, GEORGE   Mayfair and Belgravia. Truslove &
Shirley, 1892. First edition, 4to. Half title, numerous illus.
2 pp ads., orig. red cloth, gilt, v.g. Jarndyce 31-236 1983 £22

CLINCH, GEORGE   St. Marylebone and St. Pancros. Trus-
love and Shirley, 1890. Half title, num rous illus. Slightly loose.
Orig. dec. red cloth, slight wear to hinges and head of spine.
Jarndyce 31-235 1983 £20

CLINTON, DE WITT   An Introductory Discourse Delivered
Before the Literary and Philosophical Society of New-York. New York,
1815. Marbled wraps., foxed. Reese 18-470 1983 $50

CLINTON, HENRY   Authentic Copies of Letters Between Sir
Henry Clinton, D.B., and the Commissioners for Auditing the Public
Accounts. London, 1793. Stitched, an unopened copy. Reese 18-187
1983 $150

CLINTON, HENRY   Narrative relative to his Conduct...in
North America. Phila., 1866. 3 vols. in one, linen-backed chart.
Thick 8vo, buckram, ex library. 250 copies. Argosy 710-444 1983
$50

CLIVE, CATHERINE   The Case of Mrs. Clive submitted to the
Publick. London: printed for B. Dod, 1744. 8vo, blue half roan,
1st edition. A fine copy, complete with half-title. Ximenes 64-106
1983 $225

CLODD, EDWARD   The Story of Primitive Man. London:
George Newnes, 1895. First edition. Illus. Orig. pictorial cloth
and floral endpapers. Edges slightly worn. Former owner's signature
and pen markings on reverse on front free endpaper. Good. MacManus
277-998 1983 $25

CLOETTA, A.   Lehrbuch Der Arzneimittellehre Und
Arzneiverordnungslehre. Frieburg: J. C. B. Mohr, 1887. Fourth
revised edition. Contemporary leather-backed boards, worn. Adolf
Meyer's copy, signed on flyleaf. Gach 95-357 1983 $25

CLOPPER, EDWARD N.   An American Family. Cincinnati, Oh.,
1950. Orig. cloth, dust jacket. First edition. Ginsberg 47-858
1983 $20

CLOQUET, JULES   Atlas Anatomie. Bruxelles, 1834.
Oblong tall folio, cont. marbled boards, worn; some margins dampstained. 15 lithographed plates by A. Jaubert. Argosy 713-116
1983 $150

CLOUGH, ARTHUR H.   The Bothie of Toper-na-Fuosich.
Oxford: Francis MacPherson, 1848. First edition, second issue, roy.
8vo, orig. limp blue cloth, gilt. A slip bearing a presentation
inscription to William Wilkins, signed by Florence M. Clough, dated
1880, is mounted on the front flyleaf. Fenning 61-79 1983 £65

CLOUGH, ARTHUR H   The Poems and Prose Remains. Macmillan,
1869. First edition, 2 vols. Front. vol. I, half title vol. II,
2 pp ads. in both vols. Orig. green cloth dec., v.g. Jarndyce
31-481 1983 £58

CLOUSTON, J. STORER   The Adventures of M. D'Haricot. Edinburgh: William Blackwood and Sons, 1902. First edition. Inscribed
by Clouston: "To Miss Barbara Robertson from the translator. Oct. 8th,
1902." Edges very slightly worn. Endpapers browned. Very good.
MacManus 277-999 1983 $50

CLOUSTON, J. STORER   Court Bunker. Edinburgh: William Blackwood and Sons, 1906. First edition. Orig. cloth. Spine and covers
soiled. Corners and edges very slightly worn. Endpapers browned.
MacManus 277-1000 1983 $35

CLOUSTON, J. STORER   The Duke. London: Edward Arnold, 1900.
First edition. Orig. cloth. Inscribed by Clouston: "To Mrs. Robertson
from the author. 1 Nov. 1900." Spine faded, torn at the head. Corners
bumped. Endpapers browned. MacManus 277-1001 1983 $50

CLOUSTON, J. STORER   The Prodigal Father. London: Mills &
Boon, (1909). First edition. Orig. cloth. Inscribed by Clouston:
"To Barbara Robertson from the author. 28th Aug. 1909." Edges slightly
worn. Endpapers browned. Very good. MacManus 277-1003 1983 $50

CLOUZOT, HENRI   L'art negre et l'art oceanien. Paris:
Devambez, 1919. 40 plates. 4to. Marbled boards, 1/4 cloth. Orig.
wrappers bound in. Rare. Ars Libri 34-11 1983 $250

CLOVER, SAM T.   A Pioneer Heritage. Los Angeles, 1932.
1st ed. End maps, illus. Backstrip worn. Clark 741-98 1983 $36.50

CLOWES, G. S. LAIRD   Sailing Ships. London, 1932-6. Third
& second editions. 8vo. Blue cloth. 66 plates and illus., 11 text
illus. 2 parts in one. Good. Edwards 1042-35 1983 £55

CLOWES, G. S. LAIRD   The Story of Sail. London, 1936. 4to. Orig. cloth. 53 full page illus. by C.G. Trew. Slightly soiled. Good. Edwards 1042-36 1983 £15

CLOWES, W. L.   The Royal Navy. London, 1897-1903. Orig. edition. 4to. 667 illus. of which 35 are photogravure plates. Numerous maps. 7 vols. Very slightly worn & soiled. Printed on art paper, with half tone illus. and photogravure plates. Good. Edwards 1042-37 1983 £750

CLOWES, WILLIAM   Profitable and Necessarie Booke of Observations. New York, 1945. Facsimile of 1596 edition. 8vo. Orig. binding. Fye H-3-109 1983 $45

CLUB Internationale of Ensenada. Los Angeles: Printed by Young & Mc-Callister, (1926). 39 pages with photographs. Embossed boards. Chipped at spine and browned. Dawson 471-49 1983 $75

CLUM, WOODWORTH   Apache Agent. Boston: 1936. First edition. Portrait frontis. in color. Illus. Red cloth, printed white cloth, spine label. Fine copy. Bradley 66-454 1983 $65

CLUNES, J.   An Historical Sketch of the Princes of India... Edinburgh: Andrew Shortrede, 1833. First few pages spotted. Morocco ornately gilded, gilt edges. Slight wear at top of spine and hinges. Presentation copy "The Honourable Mr. Elphinstone with the author's best respects." With the Elphinstone Carberry Tower Library label. 8vo. Good. Edwards 1044-140 1983 £80

CLUSIUS, CAROLUS
Please turn to
L'ECLUSE, CHARLES DE

CLUTTON-BROCK, A.   Essays on Books. London: Methuen & Co. Ltd., (1921). Second edition of first vol., first edition of second vol. Orig. cloth. Dust jackets. Fine. MacManus 277-1005 1983 $25

CLUTTON-BROCK, A.   Shelley. The Man and the Poet. N.Y.: G.P. Putnam's Sons, 1909. First edition. 8 illus. Rebound in 3/4 moroon morocco & cloth. Fine. MacManus 280-4722 1983 $50

CLUVERIUS, PHILIPPUS   Introductionis in Universam Geographiam. Amsterdam: Elzeviriana, 1672. 12mo, engraved title page and 41 folding engraved maps and plates (although only 38 are called for in Willems). Bound in early 19th century calf, gilt. Front hinge cracked, but sound; extremities rubbed. A.e.g. The last four leaves of index have repaired missing portions, affecting about 20 percent of the text. Karmiole 75-50 1983 $175

CLYMER, MEREDITH   Epidemic Cerebro-Spinal Meningitis. Phila., 1872. First edition. Colored large folding map. Argosy 713-118 1983 $50

COALE, GRIFFITH BAILY   Victory at Midway. New York, (1944). 1st ed. Reproductions of the artist's paintings, some in color. 4to. Morrill 287-534 1983 $20

COALE, WILLIAM EDWARD   Hints on Health; with Familiar Instructions for the Treatment and Preservation of the Skin, Hair... Boston, 1852. Illus. 12mo. Ends of spine worn; lacks front fly-leaf. Morrill 289-43 1983 $22.50

COALITION, a farce; founded on facts, and lately performed, with the approbation, and under the joint inspection of the managers, of the Theatres-Royal. London: printed for D. Browne, 1779. 8vo, disbound. First edition. Title a bit dusty, else a very good copy. Ximenes 64-488 1983 $375

THE COAST Country of Texas...On the Line of the Southern Pacific Sunset Route. (Houston), ca.1895. Pictorial wrappers. Jenkins 152-53 1983 $65

COATES, ROBERT M.   All the Year Round. N.Y., (1943). First edition. 12mo, cloth, d.w. Presentation copy, signed "Bob." Fine, in slightly chipped dust wrapper. Argosy 714-164 1983 $50

COATES, ROBERT M.   The Bitter Season. New York, (1946). First edition. Presentation copy, signed "Bob." Argosy 714-165 1983 $35

COATES, ROBERT M.   The Eater of Darkness. (Paris): Contact Editions, (1926). Marbled wraps., paper label. First edition. But for slight traces of wear at the top and bottom of the spine, this is a fine, unopened copy. Reese 20-251 1983 $450

COATSWORTH, ELIZABETH J.   Atlas and Beyond. New York: 1924. First edition. Woodcuts by Harry Cimino. Green cloth, printed front cover label. Presentation copy signed. Very good. Bradley 66-73 1983 $25

COBB, ARTHUR STANLEY   Banks' Cash Reserves. Effingham Wilson, 1891. First edition, 24 pp ads. Orig. blue cloth, v.g. Jarndyce 31-130 1983 £20

COBB, HUMPHREY   Paths of Glory. New York: Viking, 1935. Cloth. First edition. Fine in dust jacket, which is slightly worn at the edges. Reese 20-252 1983 $35

COBB, LYMAN   Cobb's Juvenile Reader. Oxford, 1832. 18mo, orig. cloth-backed pr. boards, (lightly dampstained). Argosy 716-495 1983 $25

COBB, SANFORD H.   The Story of the Palatines. New York, 1897. 1st ed. 3 maps. 8vo. Morrill 288-72 1983 $40

COBB, THOMAS   The Castaways of Meadow Bank. London: Methuen & Co., n.d. First edition. 4 illus. by A.H. Buckland. Orig. pictorial cloth. The editor's copy, with his initials on the front free endpaper. Covers a bit soiled. Very good. MacManus 279-3379 1983 $50

COBB, MRS. WILTON P.   History of Dodge County. (Atlanta), 1932. First edition. Illus. Map. Jenkins 152-819 1983 $45

COBBAN, JAMES MACLAREN   The Iron Hand. London: John Long, 1904. First edition. Orig. cloth. Head and foot of spine a bit worn. One corner rather badly bumped. Back cover waterstained. Endpapers browned. Bookseller's stamp on front pastedown endpaper. MacManus 277-1006 1983 $35

COBBETT, WILLIAM   The Bloody Buoy. Paradise: Witmer, 1823. 8vo, quarter calf. "2nd Edition." Browned and foxed. Rostenberg 88-4 1983 $125

COBBETT, WILLIAM   Cottage Economy. London, 1926. First edition with this preface (by G.K. Chesterton). Very nice. Rota 230-121 1983 £12

COBBETT, WILLIAM   A French grammar. London: Charles Clement, 1824. First edition. 12mo. Orig. grey boards, printed paper label. Minor wear to joints. Short tear in title, but a fine copy in orig. condition. Ximenes 63-221 1983 $150

COBBETT, WILLIAM   Grammar of the English Language, in a Series of Letters. New York, 1818. Calf, front board detached, good otherwise. Reese 18-518 1983 $30

COBBETT, WILLIAM   A Grammar of the English Language. Anne Cobbett, 1836. Half calf, sl. rubbed, black label. Jarndyce 131-131 1983 £20

COBBETT, WILLIAM   A History of the Protestant 'Reformation' in England and Ireland. 1824. First edition, 12mo, some age-browning throughout, a few blind library stamps, half calf rebacked. K Books 307-52 1983 £45

COBBETT, WILLIAM   A History of the Protestant "Reformation" in England and Ireland. London, Clement, 1825, 1827. 3/4 plum morocco over marbled boards (rebacked, minor rubbing, soiling) else very good. Presentation copy with fine inscription on verso of leaf before title, "Kensington, 11 Oct., 1828. This book presented to his dear son James by his affectionate father, Wm. Cobbett." Houle 22-236 1983 $195

COBBETT, WILLIAM   Letters on the Late War Between the United States and Great Britain. NY: J. Belden and Co., 1815. First edition. Orig. boards, uncut. Spine extremities a bit chipped. Karmiole 72-101 1983 $100

COBBETT, WILLIAM   Letters on the Late War Between
the United States and Great Britain. New York: J. Belden and Co.,
1815. Calf. Endsheets foxed, first edition. Felcone 22-33 1983
$85

COBBETT, WILLIAM   Life and Adventures of Peter Porcupine,
with Other Records of His Early Career in England and America. The
Nonesuch Press, 1927. Half title, col. frontis. Uncut, orig. half
brown cloth, marbled boards. No. 183 of 1800 copies. Jarndyce 31-982
1983 £15

COBBETT, WILLIAM   Porcupine's Political Censor, for
November 1796. Philadelphia, 1796. Dsb., slight staining, good.
Reese 18-209 1983 $85

COBBETT, WILLIAM   Rural Rides. A. Cobbett, 1853. Front.
port. Orig. blue-green cloth, well re-cased, head of spine repaired.
Jarndyce 31-132 1983 £38

COBBETT, WILLIAM   Rural Rides in the Southern, Western
and Eastern Counties of England... London, 1930. 3 vols. Roy. 8vo.
Marbled boards with buckram spines, uncut edges. Limited edition
of 1,000 copies, with numerous vignettes by John Nash, and a map of
Cobbett's Country by A.E. Taylor. Traylen 94-198 1983 £110

COBBOLD, ELIZABETH   The Mince Pye. London: by Thomas
Bensley, 1800. First edition. 4to. Wrappers. 2 "etched" plates,
slightly cropped, corner cut from last leaf, very slight loss.
Heath 48-260 1983 £25

COBBOLD, ELIZABETH   Ode on the victory of Waterloo. Ipswich:
printed for the author by J. Raw, etc., 1815. First edition. 8vo.
Stitched. Plain front wrapper present. Scarce. Ximenes 63-397
1983 $85

COBBOLD, RICHARD   Valentine Verses. Ipswich: Printed
and sold by E. Shalders., 1827. Front. & Illus. by the author, (tear
to front. repaired). Half title, uncut, rebound in half dark green
morocco. Inscribed presentation copy: 'Presented to Mrs. Charlotte
Lewin, by the Author 1846'. Jarndyce 30-669 1983 £28

COBDEN, RICHARD   Ligue Contre Les Lois-Cereales et
Discours Politiques (1836-1864). Paris, Guillaumin, 1891. Small 8vo,
full-length portrait, uncut and unopened, original printed wrappers.
Pickering & Chatto 21-23 1983 $50

COBDEN, RICHARD   The Political Writings. Wm. Ridgway,
New York: D. Appleton, 1867. First edition, 2 vols. Inner hinges
weak, library marks at base of spine. Orig. blue cloth. Jarndyce
31-133 1983 £24

COBDEN-SANDERSON, THOMAS JAMES   The Book Beautiful. Printed for the
occasion of the visit of George W. Jones and William Edwin Rudge to the
Roxburghe Club, San Francisco, 1930. Octavo. Limited to 85 copies
signed by Jones and William Edwin Rudge. Minor stain to front cover of
vellum-backed boards, else fine. Bookplate carefully removed. Bromer
25-233 1983 $85

COBDEN-SANDERSON, THOMAS JAMES   Ecce Mundus: Industrial Ideals
and the Book Beautiful. Hammersmith: Hammersmith Publishing
Society, 1902. First edition. Thin 8vo. Vellum-backed brown
boards. Printed at the Chiswick Press. Oak Knoll 49-123 1983
$75

COBDEN-SANDERSON, THOMAS JAMES   The Journal... London, 1926.
2 vols. 4to. Cloth. Uncut edges, in the orig. dustwrappers.
Limited edition of 1050 numbered copies, portrait and 4 plates.
With presentation inscription from Annie Cobden-Sanderson, dated
September 7th, 1926. Traylen 94-199 1983 £120

COBHAM, A.   Skyways. London, 1925. First edition.
Frontis. portrait. 31 plates. Good. Edwards 1042-583 1983 £20

COBHAM, A.   My Flight to the Cape and Back. London,
1926. 8vo. Portrait frontis. Numerous illus, some full page. Orig.
orange decorated boards. Slightly worn and faded. Preliminaries
slightly foxed. Good. Edwards 1042-582 1983 £15

COBHAM, A   Twenty Thousand Miles In A Flying-Boat.
London (1930). 46 photos, folding map, cloth, ink name, minor wear.
King 46-714 1983 $25

COBIN, A.   Short and Plain Principles of Linear
Perspective. D.Steel, 1794. Fourth edition, revised and corrected.
Half-title, title. 3 pages of publishers ads. 5 folding copper plates
(1 slightly duststained). Blue wrappers, some slight foxing. Orig.
cloth. Good. Edwards 1042-39 1983 £50

COBLENTZ, STANTON   When the Birds Fly South. Mill Valley
& New York, 1945. First edition. Dust jacket. Inscribed by the
author to his English teacher: "...with kindest remembrance from
your student of years ago..." Houle 21-227 1983 $75

COBLENTZ, STANTON   Winds of Chaos. Wings Press, 1942. 8vo.
Cloth. Review copy with slip laid in, name of reviewer on fly. Front
panel of jacket has a blurb by Robert Nathan. Fine in dust jacket.
In Our Time 156-155 1983 $20

COCHRAN, D. M.   The Herpetology of Hispaniola. U.S.
Nat. Mus. Bull., 1941. 12 plates and 120 text-figures, 8vo, sewed.
Wheldon 160-950 1983 £25

COCHRANE, ALFRED   Collected Verses. London: Longmans,
Green & Co., 1903. First edition. Frontispiece by H.J. Ford.
12mo. Orig. cloth. Very fine. MacManus 277-1009 1983 $20

COCHRANE, THOMAS 10TH EARL OF DUNDONALD
Please turn to
DUNDONALD, THOMAS COCHRANE, 10TH EARL OF

COCKAYNE, THOMAS OSWALD   Spoon and sparrow... London: Parker,
etc., 1861. First edition. 8vo. Orig. brown cloth. Ximenes 63-
222 1983 $45

COCKAYNE, WILLIAM   The foundations of freedome,
vindicated. London: John Harris, 1649. First edition. Small
4to. Disbound. Ximenes 63-95 1983 $40

COCKBURN, HENRY   Works. Edinburgh and London, 1852-74.
6 vols. 8vo. Half dark brown morocco, gilt, t.e.g. Engraved
portraits. Traylen 94-200 1983 £130

COCKEL, EBERHARD   Enchiridion medico-practicum de Peste...
(and), Libellus Alter de Venenis. Augsburg, 1669. 2 vols. bound in
1. 8vo, cont. vellum; ex-lib. First editions. Separate titles and
paginations. Argosy 713-220 1983 $250

COCKERELL, DOUGLAS   Some Notes on Book-Binding. London:
Oxford University Press, 1929. Small 8vo, frontis., one plate + 29
text illus. 1/4 beige cloth over marbled boards. Karmiole 75-26
1983 $35

COCKERELL, MORGAN   An Atlas of Dermatology. 1905. Small
folio, 62 plates coloured, with explanatory text, orig. cloth, slightly
worn at edges. Bickersteth 77-271 1983 £40

COCKERELL, T. D. A.   Zoology of Colorado. Boulder, Colorado,
1927. 6 plates, 8vo, cloth (trifle stained.) Wheldon 160-364
1983 £15

COCKTON, HENRY   Stanley Thorn. London, 1841. 3 vols.
Half titles. Rebound in leather, boards. Illus. by George
Cruikshank. Bookplate. A fine set. In Our Time 156-156 1983
$150

COCORAN, MICHAEL   The Captivity of General Cocoran. Phila.,
1862. First edition. Orig. pictorial wrappers. Illus. Jenkins
152-600 1983 $100

COCTEAU, JEAN   A Call to Order. Lon., 1926. Frontis.
by author, very good or better in internally mended dustwrapper with
slight chipping and wear, bookplate. Quill & Brush 54-284 1983 $60

COCTEAU, JEAN   A Call to Order. Lon., 1926. Cover
slightly soiled, some spotting, top paperwraps edge soiled, good.
Quill & Brush 54-283 1983 $35

COCTEAU, JEAN   A Call to Order. London, 1926. First
English edition. 12mo, cloth, paper label. Argosy 714-168 1983 $25

COCTEAU, JEAN   The Infernal Machine. London, 1936.
First English edition. Argosy 714-169 1983 $20

COCTEAU, JEAN   Morceaux Choisis. Paris, 1932. First
edition. Frontis. by author. Wrappers. Author's signed autograph
presentation inscription to Sybil, Lady Colefax. Good reading copy.
Rota 231-123 1983 £40

COCTEAU, JEAN   Orphee. Paris: Librairie Stock, 1927.
First edition. With a long presentation inscription, signed by
Cocteau. Pink printed wraps. Karmiole 72-33 1983 $150

COCTEAU, JEAN   Theatre de Poche. (Paris, 1949).
First edition. Illus., 12mo, pr. wrs. Argosy 714-170 1983 $25

COCTEAU, JEAN   Thomas the Imposter. NY, 1925. Boards
and spine lettering rubbed, cover soiled, some interior staining,
chipped at top of some page edges, good. Quill & Brush 54-288 1983
$30

CODMAN, JOHN   Arnold's Expedition to Quebec. New
York, 1902. 2nd ed. Maps and illus. 8vo. Morrill 286-585 1983
$20

CODMAN, JOHN   An Oration on the Fiftieth Anniversary
of American Independence. Boston: Crocker & Brewster, 1826. Disbound. Half-title present. Very good. Felcone 20-24 1983 $20

CODMAN, JOHN   Sailors' Life and Sailors' Yarns.
NY, 1847. First edition, orig. pict. cloth (occasional light
foxing). Inscribed by the author. Argosy 716-157 1983 $22.50

CODRINGTON, ROBERT   The Life and Death of the Illustrious
Robert Earl of Essex, &c. Printed by F. Leach, for L. Chapman, 1646.
First edition, 4to, wrapper, a little dusty, but a very good copy.
Fenning 60-68 1983 £18.50

CODY, LOUISA F.   Memories of Buffalo Bill. N.Y., 1909.
Illus. Orig. cloth. First edition. Ginsberg 46-851 1983 $25

CODY, WILLIAM F.   An Autobiography of Buffalo Bill. New
York: Cosmopolitan Book Corp., 1920. First edition. Frontis. and
plates. Jenkins 152-35 1983 $30

CODY, WILLIAM F.   Life and Adventures of "Buffalo Bill."
Chicago, 1917. Illus. 8vo, stamped cloth with photo. First edition.
Argosy 716-613 1983 $45

COE, CHARLES H.   Juggling a Rope. Pendleton, Ore.: 1927.
First edition. Frontis., other illus. Blue cloth. Bradley 66-512
1983 $65

COE, MICHAEL D.   The Maya Scribe and His World.
New York: Grolier Club, 1973. 88 plates. Oblong folio. Cloth.
Edition limited to 1000 copies. Orig. edition. Ars Libri 34-185
1983 $100

COE, URLING   Frontier Doctor. New York, 1939. First
edition. Jenkins 152-55 1983 $35

COE, URLING   Frontier Doctor. New York, 1939.
Clark 741-258 1983 $27.50

COFFIN, CHARLES C.   The Great Commercial Prize. Boston: A.
Williams & Co., 1858. Half morocco and boards. Bradley 66-513 1983
$250

COFFIN, CHARLES C.   The Seat of Empire. Boston: 1870.
First edition. Frontis. and 4 other plates. Large folding map in
back pocket. Green cloth. Very fine copy. Bradley 66-514 1983
$65

COFFIN, JOSHUA   Sketch of the History of Newbury...
Boston, Samuel G. Drake, 1845. 1st ed. 8vo. Morrill 288-269 1983
$40

COFFIN, LEVI   Reminiscences, the Reputed President of
the Underground Railroad. Cincinnati, Western Tract Society, (1876).
1st ed. Portraits. 8vo. Rubbed, backstrip partly chipped and torn.
Morrill 287-69 1983 $25

COFFIN, ROBERT TRISTRAM   Primer for America. N.Y., 1943.
First edition. Illus. by the author. Lightly chipped. Presentation
copy, with an ink sketch. Argosy 714-172 1983 $40

COFFINBERRY, ANDREW   The Forest Rangers. Columbus, 1842.
Orig. boards, paper label on spine. First edition. Ginsberg 46-574
1983 $200

COGGESHALL, WILLIAM T.   The Poets and Poetry of the West.
Columbus, 1860. 1st ed. Large 8vo, orig. leather-backed cloth,
rubbed, some foxing. Morrill 288-73 1983 $20

COHEN, HENRY   Guide de l'Amateur de Livres a Figures...
Paris: P. Rouquette, 1876. Third edition. Small thick 4to. Modern
stiff paper wrappers with the orig. spine and part of the front cover
laid down. Covers worn. Oak Knoll 48-416 1983 $125

COHEN, MEYER M.   Notices of Florida and the Campaigns.
Charleston, S.C. and N.Y., 1836. Illus., folded map, port. Half
morocco. First edition. Ginsberg 46-259 1983 $150

COHEN, OCTAVUS ROY   Sound of Revelry. N.Y., 1943. First
edition. D.w. Argosy 714-174 1983 $25

COHN, ALBERT M.   A Bibliographical Catalogue of the
Printed Works Illustrated by George Cruikshank. London: Longmans,
Green, 1914. First edition. Tall 8vo. Cloth. Oak Knoll 48-420
1983 $150

COHN, FERDINAND   Blatter der Erinnerung zusammengestelt
von seiner Gattin Pauline Cohn. Breslau, 1901. 8vo. Orig. cloth.
With portrait and 3 plates. Gurney JJ-75 1983 £16

COILLARD, FRANCOIS   On the Threshold of Central Africa.
London, 1897. First English edition, 8vo, with plates and a folding
map, torn in margins, complete except for a piece missing from lower
left hand corner, frontispiece loose, original cloth, gilt. Deighton
3-82 1983 £55

COIT, DANIEL WADSWORTH   An Artist in El Dorado, 1848-1851.
SF, 1937. Edited, with a Biographical Sketch by Edith M. Coulter.
Folio, cloth-backed bds., paper labels. 8 full-page illustrations.
Perata 27-64 1983 $100

COIT, DANIEL WADSWORTH   The Drawings and Letters of... (San
Francisco): Book Club of California, 1937. Folio. Cloth and
boards, paper label. 8 plates, a fine copy. One of 325 copies
printed at the Grabhorn Press. Reese 19-152 1983 $125

COIT, DANIEL WADSWORTH   The Drawings and Letters of... San
Francisco: Grabhorn Press, 1937. Plates. Limited to 325 copies.
Fine. Jenkins 153-226 1983 $75

COKE, EDWARD   A Booke of Entries. London, 1614.
Folios, irregular but complete. 1st ed. Title page backed & repaired,
2 ownership inscriptions crossed out, fraying & wear to margins of
first & last leaves, some embrowning throughout, occasional lightish
dampstaining essentially marginal, bit of insignificant worming to
foremargin of latter part of vol, covers blind-ruled and spine unlettered, with 5 raised bands, ruled in blind, else clean, tall folio,
newly bound in full dark calf. Boswell 7-43 1983 $600

COKE, EDWARD   Le Quart... London, 1610, 1612 & 1607.
Folio. 4th, 5th & 6th parts, all early eds., including 1st ed. of part
6. Title page of part 4 & the next several leaves dampstained, occasional dampstaining, essentially marginal, elsewhere, a few marginal
tears, just affecting text (but not legibility) in 2 instances, some
insignificant worming to part 6, the 3 parts bound in 1 vol., in full
contemp. calf, worn, the initials "WS" in gilt on both covers, newly
rebacked. Clean & crisp copy. Boswell 7-44 1983 $700

COKE, EDWARD   Three Law Tracts. London, 1764.
Portrait. 8vo. Bit of occasional spotting, bit of chipping & fraying,
nicely rebound in 3/4 calf over marbled boards, spine double gilt-
ruled, with matching red leather labels, double gilt-ruled & lettered,
clean copy. Boswell 7-45 1983 $375

COKE, HENRY J.   A Ride Over the Rocky Mountains to Oregon and California... London: Richard Bentley, 1852. Frontis. portrait. Orig. brown embossed cloth with title gilt on spine. Spine neatly repaired. Jenkins 152-56 1983 $225

COKE, MARY   The Letters and Journals of Lady Mary Coke. Edinburgh: Privately Printed, 1889. 4 vols. 4to. Orig. buckram, gilt, t.e.g., others uncut. Limited edition of 100 numbered copies, with 4 plates. Traylen 94-201 1983 £50

COLANGE, L.   The American Dictionary of Commerce. Manufacturers, Commercial Law, and Finance. Boston, 1880-81. 2 vols. Many illus, thick 4to dec. cloth, ex-lib. Argosy 710-138 1983 $75

COLAS, RENE   Bibliographie Generale du Costume et de la Mode... Paris: Rene Colas, 1933. 2 vols., wrappers, fine. Dawson 470-67 1983 $100

COLASANTI, ARDUINO   Gentile Da Fabriano. Bergamo: Istituto Italiano d'Arti Grafiche, 1909. 2 tipped-in plates. 112 illus. 4to. Boards, 1/4 cloth. Covers detached. Ars Libri 33-156 1983 $45

COLASANTI, ARDUINO   Lorenzo e Jacopo Salimbeni da San-severino. Roma: E. Calzone, 1910. 10 plates (2 tipped-in). 23 text illus. 4to. New cloth. Orig. wrappers bound in. Presentation copy, inscribed by the author. Ars Libri 33-318 1983 $85

COLBURN, ZERAH   A Memoir of... Springfield, Mass.: C. & G. Merriam, 1833. 12mo, contemp. calf, rubbed, lacking front flyleaf and 1 page torn without loss of text. Gach 95-73 1983 $65

COLBURN, ZERAH   A Memoir of Zerah Colburn. Springfield, Mass., 1833. Port. Calf-backed boards (some cover wear), minor dampstaining. First edition. Felcone 22-34 1983 $30

COLBY, CHARLES L.   Wisconsin Central Railroad Lands. Milwaukee, Wic., 1886. Folded map. Orig. printed wraps. First edition. Ginsberg 46-822 1983 $75

COLCORD, ROSWELL   Bienniel Message of...Governor of Nevada. (Carson City), 1893. Orig. printed wraps. Ginsberg 46-515 1983 $45

COLDEN, CADWALLADER   The History of the Five Indian Nations of Canada. London, 1755. 2 vols., engr. map, 3rd edition, 12mo, full calf, (lightly worn, few pp. dampstained). Argosy 716-214 1983 $400

COLDEN, CADWALLADER   Letter and Papers of Cadwallader Colden, 1711-1775. NY, 1917-23. 7 vols., few lower corners dampstained. Argosy 710-347 1983 $75

COLE, CHARLES N.   A Collection of Laws which form the Constition of the Bedford Level Corporation... London: for W. Clarke, 1803. Second edition, corrected with additions. Thick 8vo. Cont. calf. Heath 48-564 1983 £65

COLE, F. J.   History of Comparative Anatomy from Aristotle to the 18th Century. London, 1949. Fine. Facs. Argosy 713-120 1983 $100

COLE, F. J.   A History of Comparative Anatomy from Aristotle to the Eighteenth Century. London, 1949. Ex-library. 8vo. Orig. binding. Fye H-3-111 1983 $35

COLE, GILBERT L.   In the Early Days Along the Overland Trail in Nebraska Territory. Kansas City, 1905. Portrait. Orig. gray cloth. Minor damp stain. Jenkins 153-128 1983 $40

COLE, H. N.   Heraldry in War. Aldershot, 1946. 8vo. Orig. cloth. Coloured frontis., 2 coloured and 2 other plates, numerous illus. Good. Edwards 1042-306 1983 £12

COLE, HARRY ELLSWORTH   Stagecoach and Tavern Tales of the Old Northwest. Cleveland, Arthur H. Clark Co., 1930. 1st ed. Map & illus. 8vo, uncut and unopened. Very fine copy. Morrill 288-74 1983 $25

COLE, JOHN WILLIAM   A Defence of the Stage, or an inquiry into the real qualities of theatrical entertainments, their scope and tendency. Dublin: Milliken and Son, 1839. 8vo, original dark green cloth, printed paper label (label rubbed). 1st edition. Very good copy. Ximenes 64-107 1983 $100

COLE, JOHN WILLIAM   The life and theatrical times of Charles Kean, F. S. A. London: Richard Bentley, 1859. 2 vols., 8vo, original purple striped moire cloth (slight wear to ends of spines). 1st ed. An excellent copy. Ximenes 64-108 1983 $125

COLE, PHILIP G.   Montana in Miniature. Kalispell, Montana, 1966. Illus., some in color. Limited and boxed edition of 300 copies and signed. Jenkins 151-226 1983 $175

COLE, RALPH D.   The Thirty-Seventh Division in the World War 1917-1918. Columbus, Ohio: The Thirty-Seventh Division Veterans Association, 1926; 1929. In two vols. Profusely illus. Blue cloth. Karmiole 73-109 1983 $40

COLE, TIMOTHY   Considerations on Engraving. New York: William Edwin Rudge, 1921. First edition. 8vo. Boards. Pencil signed engraved frontis. by Cole. Some spine chipping. Oak Knoll 49-125 1983 $30

COLEBROOKE, T. E.   Life of the Honourable Mountstuart Elphinstone. London, 1884. 2 vols. Folding map, 2 plans, 2 portraits. 2 vols. Elphinstone's Carberry Tower Library label, also a label on which is printed "From the Author." 8vo. Good. Edwards 1044-236 1983 £60

COLEMAN, BENJAMIN   Spiritualism in America. London: Pitman, 1861. First edition. Facsimiles of spirit drawings & writing. Covers worn. MacManus 277-1012 1983 $75

COLEMAN, J. WINSTON   A Bibliography of Kentucky History. Lexington, 1949. First edition. Dust jacket. Fine. Jenkins 152-783 1983 $100

COLEMAN, J. WINSTON   A Bibliography of Kentucky History. Lexington: Univ. of Kentucky Press, 1949. Frontispiece, cloth in lightly-worn dw. Dawson 470-69 1983 $37.50

COLEMAN, JOHN   Charles Reade, as I Knew Him. Treherne & Co., 1903. First edition, front. & illus. Half title, rebound in green moire-patterned cloth, label. Jarndyce 30-1109 1983 £15

COLEMAN, LEIGHTON   The Church in America. NY, (1895). Folding map. Argosy 716-60 1983 $22.50

COLEMAN, R. V.   The First Frontier. New York, 1948. First edition in dust jacket. Illus. and maps. Jenkins 152-596 1983 $30

COLEMAN, WILLIAM   A Collection of the Facts and Documents, Relative to the Death of Major-General Alexander Hamilton. New York: Hopkins and Seymour for I. Riley and Co., 1804. Full cont. calf. Top of front hinge cracked just slightly. First edition. Felcone 22-35 1983 $85

COLEMAN, WILLIAM   Remarks and Criticisms on the Hon. John Quincy Adam's Letter to the Hon. Harrison Gray Otis. Boston: J. Cushing, 1808. 8vo, uncut & unopened, sewed. Argosy 710-417 1983 $35

COLENSO, FRANCES E.   History of the Zulu War and its origin. London: Chapman and Hall, 1880. 8vo. 24 adv. Folding map. Orig. cloth. Lightly rubbed. Adelson Africa-74 1983 $200

COLENSO, JOHN WILLIAM   Ten weeks in Natal. Cambridge: Mac-millan & Co., 1855. 12mo. 16 adv. Folding map, 4 plates. Orig. cloth backed in modern tan calf. Adelson Africa-75 1983 $150

COLERIDGE, HARTLEY   Poems...with a Memoir of His Life, by His Brother. Moxon, 1851. 2nd edition, 2 vols. Front. vol. I, half titles, half calf, labels, v.g. Jarndyce 30-670 1983 £25

COLERIDGE, HENRY NELSON   Introduction to the Study of the Greek Classic Poets. Philadelphia: Carey & Lea, 1831. First American edition. Orig. cloth-backed boards, paper label. Near-fine. MacManus 277-1013 1983 $35

COLERIDGE, SAMUEL TAYLOR   Aids to Reflection in the Formation of a Manly Character. Taylor and Hessey, 1825. First edition. Half calf, well rebacked, retaining spine, labels. Stephen Coleridge's copy 1889, with his bookplate. Jarndyce 31-482 1983 £60

COLERIDGE, SAMUEL TAYLOR   Aids to Reflection in the Formation of Manly Character on the Several Grounds of Prudence, Morality, and Religion... London: Taylor and Hessey, 1825. Cont. calf, rebacked. First edition, bound without the ads. A very good copy. Reese 20-1186 1983 $75

COLERIDGE, SAMUEL TAYLOR   Biographia Literaria. N.Y.: Published by Kirk & Mercein, No. 22 Wall-street, 1817. First American edition. 2 vols. in one. Orig. paper-backed boards. Spine defective but cords sound. Boards worn at edges, light dampstaining to portion of text. Very good. MacManus 277-1014 1983 $250

COLERIDGE, SAMUEL TAYLOR   Kubla Khan. J. M. Dent, 1934. Sm. 4to. 13 sepia plates. Brown & white boards. Greer 40-232 1983 £15

COLERIDGE, SAMUEL TAYLOR   A Lay Sermon, addressed to the Higher and Middle Classes, on the existing Distresses and Discontents. London: Gale & Fenner, 1817. 1st ed., 8vo, orig. printed wrappers, expertly rebacked. Uncut copy with the half-title. Advertisements inside rear wrapper. A very fine copy and scarce in this original state. Trebizond 18-184 1983 $475

COLERIDGE, SAMUEL TAYLOR   Letters, Conversations and Recollections. Groombridge, 1858. 2nd edition, half title, orig. brown cloth. Jarndyce 30-954 1983 £12.50

COLERIDGE, SAMUEL TAYLOR   Poems on Various Subjects. London: Printed for G.G. and J. Robinson, and J. Cottle, Bookseller, Bristol. 1796. 8vo, half-title, errata, and ads.; orig. tree calf, spine very slightly scratched. First edition. Quaritch NS 5-23a 1983 $2,250

COLERIDGE, SAMUEL TAYLOR   Poems on Various Subjects. London & Bristol, 1796. 1st ed., complete with half-title, errata, and final ad leaf. Later full dark blue morocco, gilt, all edges uncut. Very fine. Rare. Jenkins 155-1376 1983 $1,650

COLERIDGE, SAMUEL TAYLOR   Poems On Various Subjects. Bristol: Printed for G. G. and J. Robinson, and J. Cottle, Bookseller, 1796. First edition. Full blue morocco with marbled endpapers. Spine and cover edges slightly rubbed. First collected set of Coleridge's poems. Uncut. Near-fine. MacManus 277-1015 1983 $850

COLERIDGE, SAMUEL TAYLOR   Selected Poems of Coleridge. London: the Nonesuch Press, 1935. 4to. Limp orange vellum, gilt. 3 illus. by Stefan Mrozewski and a vignette. Limited edition of 500 numbered copies. Traylen 94-202 1983 £48

COLERIDGE, SAMUEL TAYLOR   Zapolya: A Christman Tale. London: Printed for Rest Fenner, Paternoster Row, 1817. First edition. Half-morocco with marbled boards. Initially published against Coleridge's wishes. Bookplate. Near-fine. MacManus 277-1017 1983 $250

COLERIDGE, SARA   Memoir and Letters. Henry S. King, 1873. First edition, fronts., half calf, a little rubbed; red and green labels. Jarndyce 30-955 1983 £28

COLES, L. B.   Philosophy of Health. Boston: Ticknor, Reed & Fields, 1853 (1851). Cloth worn. Gach 95-74 1983 $25

COLES, MANNING   The Emperor's Bracelet. University of London Press, 1947. Colour frontis. 3 colour plates. 8 full-page & 20 text illus. Faded. Light blue cloth. Colour pictorial dust wrappers Greer 40-60 1983 £12.75

COLES, MANNING   They Tell No Tales. N.Y.: Doubleday, Doran, 1942. First edition. Dust jacket (small nicks), else very good-fine. Houle 22-239 1983 $45

COLESON, ANN   Miss Coleson's Narrative of Her Captivity Among the Sioux Indians! Philadelphia, 1864. Wraps., chipped and the both detached. On bad paper, some internal staining. Reese 19-153 1983 $275

COLETTE, SIDONIE GABRIELLE   Claudine at School. N.Y., Boni, 1930. First American edition. Illus. by H. Mirande. Dust jacket (small chips). Very good. Houle 22-243 1983 $65

COLETTE, SIDONIE GABRIELLE   La Femme Cachee. Paris, Flammarion, (1924). First edition. 3/4 brown morocco over vellum, yellow leather spine label, t.e.g., by Jean Duval. Inscribed by the author to actor Charles Boyer. Very good. Houle 22-240 1983 $395

COLETTE, SIDONIE GABRIELLE   De La Patte A L'Aile. Paris: Editions Correa, 1953. 8vo. Wraps. Drawings by Chastel. Total edition is 590 copies of which this is one of 320 on velin. Some light bumping to the corners, mainly a very fine copy. In Our Time 156-159 1983 $150

COLETTI, GIUSEPPE   Tomaso da Modena. Venezia: Neri Pozza, 1963. 158 plates (12 color). 4to. Cloth. Dust jacket. Ars Libri 33-371 1983 $75

COLIGNY, MARGARET   The Snipsnops and the Woo-Woo Bird. NY: Cupples & Leon, (1923). Octavo. Full-color illus. throughout. Small rectangle cut from top corner of front blank, covers slightly rubbed at corners, otherwise fine with large color pictorial label. Bromer 25-334 1983 $95

A COLLECTION of advertisements, advices, and directions... London: for H.M., sold by J. Whitlock, 1695. First edition. Small 4to. Disbound. Rare. Ximenes 63-595 1983 $450

COLLECTION of Poems. Elizabeth-town: Shepard Kollock for Cornelius Davis, 1797. Second title-page for Edw. Young's The Last Day. Argosy 716-416 1983 $45

A COLLECTION of Poems in Four Volumes. Printed by J. Hughes, for R. and J. Dodsley, 1755-1758. 6 vols. 8vo, cont. speckled calf with red labels, vol. 1 rebacked preserving the orig. spine, with new matching label. Bickersteth 77-24 1983 £30

A COLLECTION of Poems in Six Volumes. Printed by J. Hughs for J. Dodsley, 1766. 6 vols, small 8vo, cont. calf with maroon labels, the label for the author's name defective on vol. 1. Bindings a little rubbed, and some joints cracked, but sound. Bickersteth 75-26 1983 £30

A COLLECTION of poems: viz. The Temple of Death... London: printed for Ralph Smith, 1702. Second printing of the fourth "Temple of Death" miscellany. 8vo. Cont. panelled calf. Slight wear. Fine copy. Ximenes 63-376 1983 $250

A COLLECTION of the rights and priviledges of Parliament. London: Laurence Chapman, 1642. First edition. Small 4to. Disbound. First edition. Ximenes 63-96 1983 $40

COLLECTIONS Relative to the Funerals of Mary Queen of Scots. Edinburgh: Printed for W. and D. Laing, 1822. 8vo, 1 plate, old half morocco, rubbed, sewing a trifle loose. Bickersteth 77-109 1983 £20

COLLES, ABRAHAM   Selections from the Works of Abraham Colles. New Sydenham Scoiety, 1881. 8vo, portrait, orig. cloth, slight wear at top of the spine. Bickersteth 77-267 1983 £16

COLLES, ABRAHAM   Selections from the Works of Abraham Colles. London, 1891. 8vo. Orig. binding. First edition. Engraved portrait. Fye H-3-113 1983 $75

COLLES, JOHN M.   The Lunacy Acts and Orders. Dublin, W. McGee, 1887. New edition, 8vo, orig. cloth, with paper labels, a very good copy. Fenning 62-70 1983 £10.50

COLLIDGE, DANE   Old California Cowboys. N.Y., 1939. Illus. Orig. cloth, dust jacket. First edition. Ginsberg 47-55 1983 $35

COLLIER, J. PAYNE　　Extracts from the Registers of the Stationers' Company from 1557 to 1587. (London): Shakespeare Society, 1853. First edition. 8vo. Three-quarter leather over marbled boards, all edges marbled. Minor cover rubbing, else a fine copy. Oak Knoll 48-107 1983 $100

COLLIER, JEREMY　　Mr. Collier's dissuasive from the play-house; in a letter to a person of quality, occasion'd by the calamity of the tempest. London: printed for Richard Sare, 1703. 8vo, wrappers, 1st edition. Ximenes 64-114 1983 $225

COLLIER, JEREMY　　Essays upon Several Subjects. Printed for R. Sare and H. Hindmarsh, 1698. 2 vols. in 1, 8vo, cont. panelled calf, spine gilt, lower joint cracked, lacks label, rubbed. Bickersteth 77-17 1983 £58

COLLIER, JEREMY　　A short view of the immorality, and profaneness of the English stage. London: printed for S. Keble, R. Sare, and H. Hindmarsh, 1698. 8vo, cont. polished calf, gilt, spine gilt (a trifle rubbed, slight wear to top of spine). 1st ed. A fine copy, in exceptional condition. Ximenes 64-109 1983 $600

COLLIER, JEREMY　　A Short View of the Immorality and Profanes of the English Stage. London: for S. Keble, R. Sare, and H. Hindmarsh, 1698. Third edition. 8vo. Cont. mottled calf. Traylen 94-203 1983 £120

COLLIER, JEREMY　　A short view of the immorality and profaneness of the English stage. London: printed for S. Keble, R. Sare, and H. Hindmarsh, 1698. 8vo, cont. panelled cloth (a bit rubbed). 2nd ed, some foxing, else a very good copy. Ximenes 64-110 1983 $125

COLLIER, JEREMY　　A short view of the immorality and pro-faneness of the English stage. London: printed for S. Keble, R. Sare, and H. Hindmarsh, 1698. 8vo, cont. panelled calf, rebacked (corners renewed). 3rd edition. A paginary reprint, but the three pages of ads have been somewhat altered from the 2nd edition. Ximenes 64-111 1983 $100

COLLIER, JEREMY　　A short view of the profaneness and immorality of the English stage, etc. London: printed for Samuel Birt, and Thomas Trye, 1738. 8vo, early boards (spine soiled and somewhat worn). First collected edition, a re-issue of the 1730 sheets, with a new title-page. Entirely uncut; an excellent copy; scarce. Ximenes 64-112 1983 $175

COLLIER, JOHN　　The Art of Portrait Painting. Cassell and Company, 1905. First edition, with 41 plates (14 coloured), 4to, orig. cloth. Fenning 61-80 1983 £12.50

COLLIER, JOHN　　Defy The Foul Fiend or The Misadventures of a Heart. London: Macmillan and Co., Limited, 1934. First edition. 8vo. Orig. cloth. Dust jacket designed by John Farleigh. Slightly nicked dust jacket. Fine copy. Jaffe 1-64 1983 $135

COLLIER, JOHN　　The Devil And All. Nonesuch Press, 1934. First edition. 8vo. Frontis. by Blair Hughes-Stanton. Orig. green cloth. Gilt. Dust jacket. Limited to 1000 copies signed by the author. Mint. Rare. Jaffe 1-63 1983 $185

COLLIER, JOHN　　An Epistle To A Friend. London: The Ulysses Press, 1932. First edition. Frontis. by Helen Kapp. 8vo. Orig. green vellum. One of 99 copies signed by the author. Very fine copy. Jaffe 1-60 1983 $250

COLLIER, JOHN　　An Epistle To A Friend. London: The Ulysses Press, 1932. First edition. Frontispiece by Helen Kapp. Orig. limp green vellum. Limited to 99 copies signed by Collier. Fine. MacManus 277-1032 1983 $125

COLLIER, JOHN　　Gemini. London; Ulysses Press (1931). Tall 8vo, 1/2 boards. Ltd. edition. One of only 185 signed and numbered copies. Presentation copy to E.M. Forster. E.M. Forster's ownership label. Argosy 714-175 1983 $375

COLLIER, JOHN　　Gemini. Poems. London: Ulysses Press, (1931). First edition. 4to. Orig. cloth-backed boards. Limited to 185 copies signed by the author. Very fine copy. Jaffe 1-58 1983 $165

COLLIER, JOHN　　Gemini. Poems. London: Ulysses Press, (1931). First edition. Orig. cloth-backed boards. Limited to 185 copies signed by author. Fine. MacManus 277-1033 1983 $150

COLLIER, JOHN　　Gemini. Lon., (1931). Limited to 185 numbered and signed copies, some cover stains, flys slightly offset, else very good, inscription. Quill & Brush 54-290 1983 $125

COLLIER, JOHN　　Green Thoughts. London, 1932. First edition. One of 550 numbered copies signed by the author. Frontis. and endpiece by Edward Wolfe. Very good. Jolliffe 26-97 1983 £45

COLLIER, JOHN　　Green Thoughts. London: William Jackson (Books) Ltd., 1932. First edition. Frontis. by Edward Wolfe. 4to. Orig. cloth. Limited to 550 copies signed by Collier. With the Joiner & Steele, Ltd., slip tipped-in over the imprint. Very good copy. Jaffe 1-61 1983 $40

COLLIER, JOHN　　Just The Other Day. London: Hamish Hamilton, (1932). First edition. 8vo. Illus. Orig. cloth. Dust jacket. Jacket chipped, otherwise a very good copy. Scarce. Jaffe 1-66 1983 $50

COLLIER, JOHN　　Green Thoughts. William Jackson, 1932. First edition, roy. 8vo, orig. buckram, gilt, t.e.g., a fine copy. Ltd. edition of 440 copies, numbered and signed by the author. Fenning 62-71 1983 £16.50

COLLIER, JOHN　　No Traveller Returns. London: The White Owl Press, 1931. First edition. 8vo. Orig. decorated velvet. Limited to 210 copies signed by the author. A very fine copy. Jaffe 1-59 1983 $125

COLLIER, JOHN　　Tom's A-Cold. A Tale. London: Macmillan and Co., Limited, 1933. First edition. 8vo. Orig. cloth. Dust jacket. Fine copy. Jaffe 1-62 1983 $135

COLLIER, JOHN　　Variation on a Theme. London: Grayson & Grayson, 1935. First edition. 8vo. Orig. cloth. Dust jacket. Limited to 285 copies signed by the author. Fine copy. Jaffe 1-65 1983 $85

COLLIER, JOHN PAYNE　　A book of Roxburghe ballads. London: Longman, etc., 1847. First edition. Square 8vo. Orig. "Roxburghe-style" quarter roan. Rubbed, ends of spine slightly worn. Ximenes 63-255 1983 $60

COLLIER, JOHN PAYNE　　The History of English Dramatic Poetry to the time of Shakespeare: and annals of the stage to the Restoration. London: John Murray, 1831. 3 vols., 8vo, original purple cloth, morocco labels (spines evenly faded, a couple of very small tears). 1st edition. A fine fresh copy. Ximenes 64-120 1983 $175

COLLIER, JOHN PAYNE　　The poetical decameron, or ten conversations on English poets and poetry... Edinburgh: Constable, etc., 1820. First edition. 2 vols. 8vo, cont. polished calf, gilt. Very fine. Ximenes 63-256 1983 $150

COLLIER, JOHN PAYNE　　The Poetical Decameron, or the Conversations of English Poets and Poetry. London: Hurst, Robinson, 1820. First (only) edition, 8vo, two volumes, cont. half calf gilt, morocco labels, marbled boards. Half-titles. A good copy. Trebizond 18-19 1983 $60

COLLIER, WILLIAM ROSS　　Dave Cook of the Rockies. New York, 1936. First edition. Frontis. and plates. Jenkins 152-597 1983 $35

COLLIER, WILLIAM ROSS　　Dave Cook of the Rockies. New York, 1936. 1st ed. Ports., plates. Clark 741-249 1983 $22.50

COLLIER, WILLIAM ROSS　　The Reign of Soapy Smith Monarch of Misrule. Garden City, Doubleday, 1935. First edition. Illus. Dust jacket. Very good. Houle 22-1032 1983 $45

COLLIN, V.　　Manual for the Use of the Stethoscope. Boston, 1829. 12mo, orig. cloth-backed boards, paper label; uncut & partially unopened. 4 engraved plates. First edition in English. Argosy 713-121 1983 $350

COLLINGWOOD, HARRY   The Log of the "Flying Fish." Blackie,
n.d. (ca.1893). Frontis. & 5 plates. Light brown pictorial cloth
gilt. Greer 40-70 1983 £14

COLLINGWOOD, W. G.   The Life and Works of John Ruskin.
Methuen, 1893. First edition, 2 vols. Half titles, frontis., illus.
16 pp. ads. in vol. 1. Orig. olive cloth, v.g. Jarndyce 30-1119
1983 £42

COLLINGWOOD, W. G.   The Life of John Ruskin. Boston:
Houghton Mifflin, 1893. First edition. With port. and illus. 2 vols.
Cloth-backed boards with paper spine labels. One of 200 large-paper
copies. With bookplates designed by E.H. Blashfield. Spine labels
rather soiled and frayed. Spines darkened. Newsclippings tipped in
at the end. Good. MacManus 280-4436 1983 $65

COLLINS, CHARLES ALLSTON   A Cruise Upon Wheels. Warne & Routledge,
1863. 2nd edition, half title, front. Orig. red cloth, recased,
free end papers renewed. Jarndyce 31-484 1983 £22

COLLINS, DALE   Sea-Tracks of the Speejacks Round the
World. London: William Heinemann, 1923. With 95 plates. Green
gilt-stamped cloth. Karmiole 73-30 1983 $30

COLLINS, HUBERT E.   Warpath and Cattle Trail. New York,
1928. Illus. 1st ed. Clark 741-303 1983 $37.50

COLLINS, LEO C.   Hercules Seghers. Chicago: University
of Chicago Press, 1953. 111 gravure plates. Large 4to. Cloth, dust
jacket. Ars Libri 32-626 1983 $100

COLLINS, MICHAEL   THe Path to Freedom. Dublin: Talbot,
1922. First edition, with a portrait, 8vo, orig. cloth, a very good
copy in a soiled dust wrapper. Fenning 61-81 1983 £24.50

COLLINS, MORTIMER   The British Birds. Richard Bentley, 1878.
2nd edition, tall 8vo, orig. red cloth, a little rubbed. No. 71 of
250 copies. Jarndyce 30-671 1983 £10.50

COLLINS, MORTIMER   Miranda: A Midsummer Madness. London:
Henry S. King & Co., 1873. First edition. 3 vols. Orig. cloth.
Covers and spines somewhat worn and spotted, with some offsetting to
the endpapers. Very good. MacManus 277-1035 1983 $350

COLLINS, MORTIMER   Sweet and Twenty. London: Hurst &
Blackett, 1875. First edition. 3 vols. Orig. cloth. Presentation
copy, inscribed by Collins' wife, Frances, who collaborated in the
writing, on the title-page, "M.J. Jackson from F.P.C. 25/3/77."
Fine. MacManus 277-1036 1983 $350

COLLINS, MORTIMER   Sweet and Twenty. Hurst & Blackett,
1875. First edition, 3 vols. Half titles. Orig. green cloth, gilt.
Bevelled boards, sl. marked, a.e.g. A good copy. Jarndyce 31-485
1983 £85

COLLINS, MORTIMER   Sweet Anne Page. London: Hurst & Blackett, 1868. First edition. 3 vols. 3/4 morocco, t.e.g. With the
16-page catalogue normally found in vol. 3 bound at the end of vol. 2.
Bookplates of Michael Sadleir and John Croft Deverell. Very good.
MacManus 277-1037 1983 $650

COLLINS, MORTIMER   Thoughts in My Garden. London: Richard
Bentley & Son, 1880. First edition. 2 vols. Orig. decorated cloth.
Covers and spines a bit worn, preliminary leaves foxed. Former owner's
signature. Good. MacManus 277-1038 1983 $135

COLLINS, WILLIAM WILKIE   Antonina; or, The Fall of Rome. London:
Richard Bentley, 1850. First edition. 3 vols. Orig. cloth. Spines
and covers badly soiled, edges a bit worn. Bookplates. Newspaper
clipping about the book glued to fron free endpaper of Vol. 1. Good.
MacManus 277-1039 1983 $850

COLLINS, WILLIAM WILKIE   Antonina: or, The Fall of Rome. Richard
Bentley, 1850. First edition. 3 vols. Half titles in vols. II & III.
Tears to half title and title in vol. II repaired with no loss. Rebound in green moire-patterned cloth. Labels. Jarndyce 30-329 1983
£58

COLLINS, WILLIAM WILKIE   Armadale. Smith, Elder, 1866. 2 vols.,
vol. I, 2nd edition; vol. II, first edition. 20 illus. by George
H. Thomas, lacking front. vol. I. Library copy, rebound in red cloth.
Jarndyce 30-330 1983 £15

COLLINS, WILLIAM WILKIE   The Dead Alive. Boston: Shepard & Gill,
1874. First edition. Fully illus. Orig. green cloth. Covers a bit
worn. MacManus 277-1040 1983 $125

COLLINS, WILLIAM WILKIE   The Dead Secret. Gloucester: Davies &
Co., n.d. (c. 1895). Printed by Walter Scott. Half title, front.
16 pp ads. Orig. half dark green cloth, t.e.g. Jarndyce 31-488 1983
£10.50

COLLINS, WILLIAM WILKIE   The Law and the Lady. Chatto & Windus,
1875. First edition. 3 vols. Small lib. stamp on each title.
Rebound in moire-patterned green cloth, labels. Jarndyce 30-332 1983
£58

COLLINS, WILLIAM WILKIE   The Moonstone. London: Tinsley Brothers,
1868. First edition. 3 vols. Rebound in purple cloth. With half-
titles but lacking the ads in Vol, II, the ads in Vol. III detached.
Spines darkened. Corners and edges rubbed. Contents somewhat smudged
and dust-soiled. MacManus 277-1042 1983 $450

COLLINS, WILLIAM WILKIE   My Miscellanies. London: Sampson Low,
Sone and Co., 1863. First edition. 2 vols. Orig. cloth. Vol. II
torn at head of spine and chewed at top of front edges. Bookplates
(armorial); library blind-stamp on front free endpaper of Vol. I.
Good. MacManus 277-1043 1983 $450

COLLINS, WILLIAM WILKIE   My Miscellanies. London: Sampson Low,
1863. First edition. 2 vols. Orig. cloth. With a signed inscription
from Collins tipped-in. Spines rather chipped. Inner hinges cracked
and weak. Half-morocco slipcase (erroneously labelled "presentation
copy"). MacManus 277-1044 1983 $250

COLLINS, WILLIAM WILKIE   No Name. London: Sampson Low, 1862.
First edition. 3 vols. Orig. cloth. Inner hinges cracked and
tightened. Covers a bit faded. Slightly worn. MacManus 277-1045
1983 $400

COLLINS, WILLIAM WILKIE   The Poetical Works. London, 1858.
Cr. 8vo. Full dark blue calf, two-line gilt borders with corner
ornaments, gilt panelled spine, morocco label, gilt. Portrait,
vignette title-page. Traylen 94-205 1983 £16

COLLINS, WILLIAM WILKIE   Poor Miss Finch. Bentley, 1872. First
edition. 3 vols. Library copy, rebound in red cloth. Jarndyce 30-331
1983 £35

COLLINS, WILLIAM WILKIE   Rambles Beyond Railways. Richard
Bentley, 1852. 2nd edition, front. & illus. by Henry C. Grandling.
New 'advertisement' by the author. Orig. brown cloth, recased.
Jarndyce 31-486 1983 £48

COLLINS, WILLIAM WILKIE   Rambles Beyond Railways. London: Richard
Bentley, 1861. New edition. Orig. cloth. Spine and covers worn.
Former owner's signature. Good. MacManus 277-1046 1983 $185

COLLINS, WILLIAM WILKIE   The Stoken Mask. Philadelphia: T.B.
Peterson & Brothers, n.d. Peterson's Cheap Edition. Orig. pictorial
wrappers (worn and soiled). MacManus 277-1047 1983 $25

COLLINS, WILLIAM WILKIE   The Woman in White. London: Sampson
Low, Sons and Co., 1860. First English edition. 3 vols. 3/4 morocco
and marbled boards with marbled endpapers. All edges a bit rubbed.
Bookplates. All pages in vol. I slightly waterstained at the lower
edge (not affecting text). Good. MacManus 277-1048 1983 $450

COLLINS, WILLIAM WILKIE   The Woman in White. New York: Harper &
Bros.., 1869. Illus. by John McLenan, 4 pp ads. Orig. dull purple
cloth, sl. rubbing at extremities of spine, otherwise v.g. Jarndyce
31-487 1983 £18

COLLODI, CARLO, PSEUD.
Please turn to
LORENZINI, CARLO

COLLYER, JOSEPH   The Messiah. Elizabeth Town: Kollock, 1788. 16mo, cont. morocco, gilt fillets & dentelles, extra gilt back, (foxing, some waterstaining). Argosy 716-332 1983 $50

COLMAN, BENJAMIN   A Humble Discourse of the Incomprehensibleness of God. Boston: B. Green, for Samuel Gerrish, 1715. 12mo, cont. lea. Argosy 710-66 1983 $125

COLMAN, BENJAMIN   Some of the Glories of Our Lord and Saviour Jesus Christ, Exhibited in Twenty Sacramental Discourses, Preached at Boston... London: Printed by S. Palmer, for Thomas Nancock...at Boston...1728. Frontis. Errata sheet pasted to rear pastedown. Leather, worn, with outer and inner hinges weak. Internally very good. Reese 18-46 1983 $75

COLMAN, GEORGE   The Deuce is in Him. T. Becket and P.A. De Hondt, 1769. A new edition, rebound in blue boards. Jarndyce 31-59 1983 £15

COLMAN, GEORGE   Eccentricities for Edinburgh. Edinburgh: John Ballantyne, (1816). First edition, uncut. Orig. boards, paper label. Fine. Jarndyce 30-672 1983 £20

COLMAN, GEORGE   A full and accurate description of the popular romance of Blue-Beard. London: printed by J. D. Dewick, for T. and R. Hughes, 1808. 12mo, wrappers, 1st ed. Ximenes 64-126 1983 $20

COLMAN, GEORGE   The Iron Chest: a play; in three acts. London: printed by W. Woodfall, for Messrs. Cadell and Davies, 1796. 8vo, old calf (spine worn). 2nd ed., with a postscript. Very rare. Half-title present; a few stains. Ximenes 64-128 1983 $200

COLMAN, GEORGE   The Iron Chest: a play; in three acts. London: printed by W. Woodfall, for Messrs. Cadell and Davies, 1796. 8vo, modern wrappers, 1st ed. A fine copy, entirely uncut, complete with half-title. Ximenes 64-127 1983 $125

COLMAN, GEORGE   The Mountaineers. Dublin: Printed by T.M. 'Donnel, 1794. First Irish edition, ad. leaf with short tear without loss, 12mo, wrapper, a fine copy. Fenning 62-73 1983 £15

COLMAN, GEORGE   The Mountaineers; a play, in three acts. London: printed for J. Debrett, 1795. 8vo, cont. red straight-grained morocco, gilt, spine gilt, a.e.g. (some rubbing). First authorized edition. A fine copy. Ximines 64-129 1983 $175

COLMAN, GEORGE   The Oxonian in Town. T. Becket and R. Baldwin, 1770. Rebound in blue boards, v.g. Jarndyce 31-60 1983 £18.50

COLMAN, GEORGE   Poetical Vagaries. London: Printed for the author, 1812. 1st ed., 4to, cont. marbled boards, attractively rebacked. Half-title, bookplate. Inner margin of initial leaves repaired, but a very good copy. Trebizond 18-20 1983 $100

COLMAN, GEORGE   Poetical Vagaries. London: for the Author, 1812. First edition. 4to. Cont. diced calf, gilt, gilt panelled spine with morocco label. Half-title. From the library of Lord Leigh, Stoneleigh Abbey, with his bookplate. Traylen 94-206 1983 £55

COLMAN, GEORGE   Poetical Vagaries. 1814. 8vo, 13 text engravings, t.e.g., other edges uncut, polished calf gilt, spine gilt in compartments, by Bedford. Bickersteth 77-194 1983 £45

COLMAN, GEORGE   Prose on several occasions; accompanied with some pieces in verse. London: printed for T. Cadell, 1787. 3 vols., 8vo, 19th-cent. half morocco (some rubbing). 1st edition. Half-titles present; outer edges uncut. Very good copy. Ximenes 64-122 1983 $150

COLMAN, GEORGE   Random Records. London: Henry Colburn and Richard Bentley, 1830. Two vols., 12mo, original purple cloth (faded), printed paper labels (ends of one spine a little rubbed). 1st ed., with a portrait, a very good copy. Ximenes 64-130 1983 $125

COLMAN, GEORGE   Some particulars of the life of the late George Colman, Esq. London: printed for T. Cadell Jun. and W. Davies, 1795. 8vo, disbound, 1st ed. Scarce. Frontis. portrait, lacking a half-title, else a fine copy. Ximenes 64-123 1983 $225

COLMAN, GEORGE   The Spleen, or, Islington Spa; a comick piece, of two acts. London: printed for T. Becket, 1776. 8vo, disbound, 1st ed. Ximenes 64-124 1983 $45

COLMAN, HENRY   European Life and Manners; in familiar Letters to Friends. Boston: Little & Brown; London: Petheram, 1849. 1st ed., 12mo, 2 vols., orig. decorated cloth, spines gilt (sun faded). Half-titles. A fine copy. Trebizond 18-135 1983 $60

COLOMBAT DE L'ISERE, M.   A Treatise upon the Diseases and Hygiene of the Organs of the Voice. Boston, 1857. 12mo. Orig. cloth. With frontis. Rather heavily dampstained. Gurney JJ-76 1983 £15

COLOMBE, LODOVICO DELLE   Risposte piacevoli e curiose alle considerazioni di certa Maschera saccente nominata Alimberto Mauri... Florence: Gio. Antonio Caneo, e Raffaello Grossi compagni, 1608. First edition. 4to. Cont. limp vellum. Cont. exlibris of William van Thienen. Lower margin of first few leaves a little frayed. Kraus 164-88 1983 $3,500

COLOMBONI, ANGELO   Prattica Gnomonica... In Bologna, per gli Eredi di Domenico Barbieri 1669. 4to, bound in full vellum. Title in MS on spine. Occasional light foxing. A few leaves renewed at margins. No loss of text. Title page with two holes (library stamps) repaired. First edition. Arkway 22-68 1983 $375

COLQUHOUN, A. H. U.   Press, Politics and People. Toronto: MacMillan, 1935. 23cm. 3 portrait illus. Red cloth. Spine faded else very good. McGahern 54-44 1983 $25

COLQUHOUN, A. R.   Across Chryse. London, 1883. 3 maps, 2 folding. Woodcut plates. Text illus. 2 vols. Half calf, worn. 8vo. Good. Edwards 1044-143 1983 £85

COLQUHOUN, JAMES   Adventures in Red Russia. J. Murray, printed for private circulation, 1926. First edition, 16 plates, 8vo, orig. cloth. Inscribed by the author, engineer and managing director of the Causasus Copper Company. Fenning 62-74 1983 £18.50

COLSON, NATHANIEL   The Mariner's New Calendar... 1755. 4to. Cont. panelled calf. Woodcuts in text. Some light usage. Heath 48-491 1983 £75

COLSON, PERCY   Georgian Portraits. Williams and Norgate, (1938). Subscribers' edition. First edition, with 12 portraits, 4to, orig. white buckram, gilt, t.e.g., a fine copy in the slip-case. The portraits of the author and of Reginald Eves are both signed by their subjects. With a letter from the publishers, dated December 1938 enclosing the errata slip, loosely inserted. Fenning 62-75 1983 £16.50

COLT Revolvers and Automatic Pistols. Hartford, Conn.: Colt's Fire Arms Division, 1933. Illus. Orig. printed wrappers. Fine copy. Jenkins 153-755 1983 $30

COLTON, HAROLD S.   Hopi Kachina Dolls. Albuquerque: University of New Mexico Press, 1949. 20 plates (partly in color). 250 text figures. 4to. Cloth. Ars Libri 34-189 1983 $50

COLTON, WALTER   The Colton Diary... Oakland: Biobooks, 1948. Illustrations. Map. Limited to 1000 copies. Jenkins 153-135 1983 $30

COLTON, WALTER   Land and Lee in the Bosphorus and Aegean. NY 1851. Frontis, cloth, bookplate, ink inscriptions, foxed, spine ends and corners frayed. King 46-757 1983 $40

COLTON, WALTER   Land and Lee in the Bosphorus and Aegean. New York, 1851. First edition. Illus., 8vo. Morrill 290-66 1983 $27.50

COLT'S 100th Anniversary, Fire Arms Manual 1836-1936. Hartford, Conn. 1937. Illus, embossed fabrikoid, some wear but good. King 46-555 1983 $35

COLUM, PADRAIC   The Adventures of Odysseus and The Tale of Troy. N.Y.: MacMill., (1918). First edition. 8vo. Red pictorial cloth. Full-page color plates. Many full-page line illus. Fine. Aleph-bet 8-207 1983 $30

COLUM, PADRIAC   Creatures. NY, 1927. Illus. by Artzy-basheff. Limited to 300 copies signed by both author and illus., boards and lettering on spine slightly worn, otherwise very good in good slipcase. Quill & Brush 54-292 1983 $75

COLUM, PADRAIC   Creatures. N.Y., MacMillian, 1927. First edition. With 10 full page black and white drawings and text vignettes by Boris Artzybashef. Illus. endpapers. Half cloth over decorated boards. Very good. Houle 22-244 1983 $32.50

COLUM, PADRAIC   The Frenzied Prince. Phila., (1943). First edition, fine. Small 4to, cloth. Illus., some in color, by Willy Pogany. Argosy 714-177 1983 $35

COLUM, PADRAIC   The Golden Fleece and The Heroes Who Lived Before Achilles. N.Y.: Mac., (1921). 8vo. Red pictorial cloth. First edition. Color plates plus black & whites. Fine. Aleph-bet 8-208 1983 $30

COLUM, PADRAIC   Story of Lowry Maen. New York, Macmillan, 1937. First edition. Wood engravings by Sean O'Sullivan. Dust jacket. Fine. Houle 21-233 1983 $75

COLUM, PADRIAC   Wild Earth. Dublin, Maunsel, 1907. First edition, errata slip, small 8vo, orig. cloth-backed printed paper boards, a very good copy. Fenning 62-76 1983 £18.50

COLUM, PADRAIC   Wild Earth and other poems. New York, 1916. First American edition. Head and foot of spine a little rubbed. Author's autograph signature. Very good. Rota 230-131 1983 £25

COLUMBUS, CHRISTOPHER   The Letter of Columbus on the Discovery of America. New York: Lenox Library, 1892. First edition thus. 8vo. Cloth. From the library of Lee Edmonds Grove. Oak Knoll 49-132 1983 $35

COLVIN, VERPLANCK   Report on the Progress of the Adirondack State Land Survey to the Year 1886. Albany, 1886. Maps. Thick 8vo, orig. cloth, ex-library. Argosy 710-348 1983 $40

COMAN, EDWIN T.   Time, Tide and Timber. Stanford, (1949). Illus. Clark 741-100 1983 $22.50

COMBE, WILLIAM   Doctor Syntax's Three Tours. London: Chatto & Windus, n.d. 80 full page illus. drawn and coloured after the orig. by T. Rowlandson. Full red morocco, gilt, with marbled end-papers. Front free endpaper splitting near margin. Inner hinge strained. Fine. MacManus 277-1052 1983 $125

COMBE, WILLIAM   The First (Third) Tour of Doctor Syn-tax. London: Nattali & Bond, n.d. Ninth edition. Illus. with 80 plates by T. Rowlandson. 3 vols. Large 8vo. Cont. 3/4 calf and marbled boards. Marbled endpapers, with morocco labels on spines. New plates. Very good. MacManus 280-4420 1983 $350

COMBE, WILLIAM   The royal interview: a fragment. London: printed at the Logographic Press, etc., 1789. First edition. 8vo. Disbound. Ximenes 63-475 1983 $65

COMBE, WILLIAM   The Three Tours of Doctor Syntax... London: Nattali and Bond, 1855. 3 vols. Roy. 8vo. Orig. embossed green cloth, gilt. 81 hand-coloured plates from drawings by Row-landson. Traylen 94-209 1983 £250

COMBE, WILLIAM   The Tour of Doctor Syntax in Search of the Picturesque. (R. Ackermann's Repository of Arts, 1813). 8vo, coloured frontis., coloured title with vignette, and 29 coloured plates by T. Rowlandson, imprints on some plates shaved, orig. half morocco, spine gilt, rubbed at the edges. A good copy. Bickersteth 75-120 1983 £85

COMBE, WILLIAM   A Word in Season to the Traders & Manufacturers of Great Britain. N.p., 1792. 8vo, stitched. 7th edition. Rostenberg 88-126 1983 $60

COMBERMERE, MARY   Memoirs and Correspondence of Field-Marshal Viscount Combermere. London, 1866. First edition. 8vo. Orig. cloth. Portrait frontis. 2 vols. 2 engraved vignettes and 1 map. Spines faded. Some slight foxing of preliminaries and very slight worming of inner margin of title frontis. to Vol. I (not affecting text or illus). Fine. Edwards 1042-307 1983 £100

COMBS, LESLIE   Substance of Remarks Made by Col. Leslie Combs, a Member from Fayette... (Lexington, 1829). Disbound, good. Reese 18-637 1983 $75

COMENIUS, JOHN AMOS   The Orbis Pictus. Syracuse, NY, 1887. Woodcut facsimiles, cloth, inner hinges cracked, spine very worn and faded, top of covers heavily soiled. King 46-450 1983 $25

COMERFORD, MARY TERESA   Memoir of Rev. Mother...Foundress of the Convents of the Presentation Order on the Pacific Coast. San Francisco, 1882. Orig. cloth, cover beginning to warp. Ginsberg 47-53 1983 $35

COMFORT, ALEX   Elegies. London: Routledge, (1944). First edition. Orig. cloth-backed boards. Dust jacket. Former owner's small stamp on front endsheet. Very fine. MacManus 277-1054 1983 $50

COMFORT, J.W.   Thomsonian Practice of Midwifery, and Treatment of Complaints Peculiar to Women and Children. Philadelphia: Aaron Comfort, 1845. 1st ed. 8vo. Contemporary calf, leather label. Front hinge slightly cracked. Morrill 289-49 1983 $35

COMFORT, WILL   Trooper Tales. New York, (1899). Illus. Ads. Clark 741-342 1983 $25

THE COMIC Almanack: First Series, 1835-1843 and Second Series, 1844-1853. London: Chatto and Windus, n.d. Two vols. Crimson morocco and cloth. Few leaves in vol. II with faint dampstains. Fine set. Bradley 66-82 1983 $165

THE COMIC Novel. 1840. Orig. part III. Illus. in many styles, by the Artists Fun Society, H. Bailliere. Orig. printed wraps, v.g. Jarndyce 31-410 1983 £12.50

COMIC tales, in verse. London: W. Fearman, 1820. First edition. 8vo. Cont. half morocco. Hinges a bit rubbed. Very good copy. Ximenes 63-398 1983 $50

THE COMICAL Adventures of Beau Ogleby. Tilt and Bogue, n.d. (c. 1845). First edition, oblong 8vo, engraved throughout. Orig. purple cloth, v.g. Jarndyce 31-81 1983 £20

COMMAGER, HENRY STEELE   The Blue and the Gray. Indianapolis, (1950). First edition, 2 vols., illus. & maps. D.w., boxed. Argosy 716-75 1983 $35

THE COMMERCIAL Code of France, with the Motives, or Discourses of the Counsellors of State. (New York): Wiley, 1814. 8vo, linen & boards. Ownership stamp (repeated) and inked numbers on title-page. Rostenberg 88-127 1983 $65

COMMERCIAL Directory, Containing a Topographical Description, Extent and Productions of Different Sections of the Union. Phila., 1823. 4to, mod. buckram, (some soiling). Extra engr. title, engr. subtitles for 6 sections. Argosy 716-141 1983 $100

THE COMMON Cause. N.Y., Social Reform Press, 1912. Illus. Orig. cloth. First edition. Ginsberg 46-13 1983 $75

A COMPANION to the Theatre: or, a view of our most celebrated drama-tic pieces. London: printed for J. Nourse, 1747. 2 vols., 12mo, cont. mottled calf (spines rubbed, rather dry). 2nd edition, greatly expanded. With a preliminary advertisement leaf in each volume. Rare. Ximenes 64-132 1983 $350

A COMPLAINT to the House of Commons... Oxford: Leonard Lichfield, 1642. Small 4to. Disbound. Ximenes 63-97 1983 $40

THE COMPLEAT History of Bob and Lyn. London: Printed for Jacob Lock... (1741). Folio, largely uncut, disbound. First edition. Pub.'s ads. on the last page list two other political ballads. Very good copy. Quaritch NS 7-25 1983 $400

THE COMPLETE Anderson. NY: Limited Editions Club, (1949). Six octavo vols. Hand-colored illus. by Fritz Kredel throughout. Limited to 1500 copies signed by Kredel and translator, Jean Hersholt. Very fine set in rubbed orig. slip-case. Bromer 25-241 1983 $150

COMPLETE Guide to Ornamental Leather Work. Boston, 1854. 1st Am. ed. Text illus. 12mo. Morrill 286-102 1983 $35

A COMPLETE history of James Maclean, the gentleman highwayman... London: printed for Charles Corbett, n.d. (1750). Second edition. Portrait. Ximenes 63-77 1983 $125

COMPTON-BURNETT, IVY   Dolores. Edingurgh & London: Blackwood, 1911. Spine darkened and worn. Covers marked and rubbed. Erasure from flyleaf. Good. First edition. Rota 230-132 1983 £80

COMPTON-BURNETT, IVY   Manservant and Maidservant. London, 1947. First edition. Inscription on flyleaf. Nice. Rota 231-124 1983 £12.50

COMPTON-BURNETT, IVY   Men and Wives. London, 1931. First edition. Lower cover stained. Nice. Rota 230-133 1983 £30

COMPTON-BURNETT, IVY   Two Worlds and Their Ways. London, 1949. First edition. Covers a little marked and spine darkened and a little worn. Nice. Rota 231-125 1983 £12

CONARD, HOWARD LOUIS   "Uncle Dick" Wootton. Chicago: 1890. First edition. Frontis., other illus. Pictorial brown cloth. Bright copy, inner hinges weak. Bradley 66-519 1983 $135

CONDER, ARTHUR   Our Lady's Garland. De la More Press, 1911. Decorated title. 7 full-page & 2 text illus. Cream wrappers decorated, dusty. Presentation copy from J.M. King. Greer 40-123 1983 £60

CONE, ANDREW   Petrolia. N.Y., 1870. Illus. Orig. cloth. First edition. Ginsberg 46-589 1983 $250

CONEY, JOHN   Engravings of Ancient Cathedrals, Hotels de Ville and Other Public Buildings of Celebrity, in France, Holland, Germany and Italy... London: Henry G. Bohn, 1842. Folio, with a double-page frontis. and 32 double page plates mounted on paper guards. 3/4 calf over marbled boards, corners rubbed. Karmiole 71-8 1983 $250

CONFEDERATE STATES OF AMERICA. LAWS.   A Bill to be Entitled an Act to Define and Punish Conspiracy Against the Confederate States. (Richmond), 1864. Jenkins 152-60 1983 $25

CONFEDERATE STATES OF AMERICA. LAWS.   A Bill to be Entitled an Act to Establish a Bureau of Foreign Supplies in the War Department, with an Agency in the Trans-Mississippi. (Richmond), 1864. Jenkins 152-61 1983 $75

CONFEDERATE STATES OF AMERICA. LAWS.   A Bill to Provide for Keeping in Repair the Railroads of the Confederate States. (Richmond, 1863). Very good. Reese 19-158 1983 $60

CONGER, ROGER N.   Highlights of Waco History. Waco, 1945. Illus. 1st ed. Printed wrappers. Signed by author. Fine copy. Jenkins 153-612 1983 $50

A CONGRATULATORY Ode. London: Printed for John Warner...1744. Folio, largely uncut; disbound. First and only edition. A very good copy. Quaritch NS 7-26 1983 $250

CONGREVE, WILLIAM   Amendments of Mr. Collier's false and imperfect citations, etc. from the Old Batchelour, Double Dealer, Love for Love, Mourning Bride. London: printed for J. Tonson, 1698. 8vo, cont. mottled calf, spine gilt (slight wear to hinges). 1st ed., a large and thick paper copy. In fine condition. Ximenes 64-134 1983 $1,250

CONGREVE, WILLIAM   Amendments of Mr. Collier's False and Imperfect Citations, etc. London: printed for J. Tonson, 1698. 8vo, cont. mottled calf, spine gilt (some wear). 1st ed. An early issue, with the verso of the half-title blank, two errata on the verso of the title, and D6 uncancelled. Uncommon. Wanting a front flyleaf, else a very good copy. Ximenes 64-135 1983 $500

CONGREVE, WILLIAM   Amendments of Mr. Collier's false and imperfect citations, etc. London: printed for J. Tonson, 1698. 8vo, cont. quarter vellum and marbled boards (some wear). A copy of the first edition, with the verso of the half-title blank, two errata on the verso of the title, but D6 cancelled. A large copy, with the lower edges uncut. Ximenes 64-136 1983 $400

CONGREVE, WILLIAM   Amendments of Mr. Collier's false and imperfect citations, etc. London: printed for J. Tonson, 1698. 8vo, modern half green morocco. A copy of the first edition, with the "advertisement" added to the verso of the half-title, three errata on the verso of the title, and D6 cancelled. Ximenes 64-137 1983 $300

CONGREVE, WILLIAM   The Way of the World. London: Printed for Jacob Tonson, within Gray's-Inn Gate next Gray's-In-Lane, 1700. First edition. Full 19th century calf, a.e.g., by Riviere. Complete with half-title. Johnsonian bookplate of R.B. Adam and the Robert Honeyman bookplate on the front endsheet. Tiny institutional stamp in gutter of dedication leaf. Slightly foxed. Covers a bit rubbed. Very good. MacManus 277-1056 1983 $750

CONGREVE, WILLIAM   The Works of Mr. William Congreve. Dublin: by Theo Jones for George Risk..., 1736. 2 vols. Small 8vo. Cont. calf, gilt. Rare. Heath 48-264 1983 £65

CONGREVE, WILLIAM   The Works. Birmingham: Printed by John Baskerville; For J. & R. Tonson, in the Strand, 1761. First Baskerville edition. 6 engraved plates by Kneller, Hayman & Grignion. Full mottled calf with red & green morocco labels. Marbled endpapers, a.e.g., in the style of the period. A few expert marginal repairs to several leaves in the concellans. Fine. MacManus 277-1057 1983 $500

CONINGTON, JOHN   Miscellaneous Writings of John Conington, Late Corpus Professor of Latin in the University of Oxford. 1872. 8vo, 2 vols. Cont. calf, spines gilt. Bickersteth 75-121 1983 £14

CONKEY, JANE PHILLIPS   A Trip to Fairyland. Chicago: W.B. Conkey, (1905). 8vo. Half cloth, half pictorial boards. Printed on heavy coated paper. Illus. with full-page and small sepia tone plates by W. Carqueville. Very good. Aleph-bet 8-67 1983 $25

CONKLING, EDGAR   Benton's Policy of Selling and Developing the Mineral Lands and the Necessity of Furnishing Access to the Rocky Mountains by the Construction of the Northern and Central Pacific Railroads... Cincinnati, Clark, 1864. Double columns. Cloth, first edition. Ginsberg 47-773 1983 $125

CONNECTICUT. LAWS.   Acts and Laws of the State of Connecticut, in America. Hartford: Hudson and Goodwin, 1796, (1797). Full calf (dry, scuffed, hinges broken). Includes the Session Laws through May 1797. Very good. Felcone 20-25 1983 $65

CONNECTICUT. LAWS.   The Code of 1650, Being a Compilation of the Earliest Laws and Orders of the General Court of Connecticut... Hartford: Andrus & Judd, 1833. Frontis. (woodcut). Calf-backed boards. Dime-sized corner of frontis. lacking. Very good. Felcone 20-27 1983 $30

CONNELL, JOHN   W. E. Henely. London: Constable, (1949). First edition. Blue cloth. Very good. Houle 21-843 1983 $27.50

CONNELLEY, WILLIAM E.   John Brown. Topeka, 1900. 2 vols. Orig. issued as no. 10 and no. 11. Wrappers. Very scarce. Clark 741-71 1983 $30, set

CONNELLEY, WILLIAM E.   Quantrill and the Border Wards. Cedar Rapids, Iowa, 1910. Illus., maps. Orig. cloth. First edition. Ginsberg 46-651 1983 $75

CONNELLEY, WILLIAM E.   War with Mexico, 1846-1847: Doniphan's Expedition and the Conquest of New Mexico and California. Kansas City, Mo.: Bryant & Douglass, 1907. Illus. Orig. pictorial cloth. Folding maps. Fine copy. Jenkins 153-757 1983 $65

CONNELLEY, WILLIAM E   Wild Bill and His Era. The Life
and Adventures of James Butler Hickok. N.Y., Press of the Pioneers,
1933. First edition. Illus. with 12 plates. Red cloth stamped
in gilt, uncut (spine a bit faded) else very good. One of 200
numbered copies. Houle 22-1034 1983 $75

CONNELLEY, WILLIAM E   Wild Bill and his Ear. New York: Press
of the Pioneers, 1933. Plates, 1st ed., nice copy. A limited
edition. Scarce. Jenkins 151-124 1983 $65

CONNELLY, MARC   The Green Pastures. NY, 1930. Illus.
by Robt. E. Jones, limited to 550 large paper copies, signed by both
author and illus., edges of green boards slightly rubbed, else fine
in very good slipcase. Quill & Brush 54-296 1983 $125

CONNELLY, MARC   The Green Pastures. N.Y., 1930. First
illus. edition. 4to, green cloth; faded. Illus. by Robert Edmond
Jones. Argosy 714-181 1983 $35

CONNELY, WILLARD   Brawny Wycherley. London: Charles
Scriber's Sons, 1930. First edition. Frontis. Orig. cloth. Presentation copy, inscribed on the half-title to Miss Eleanore Boswell,
dated March 5, 1930. Very good. MacManus 280-5664 1983 $20

CONNOLD, E. T.   British Vegetable Galls. 1901. 130
plates and 27 text-figures, royal 8vo, cloth, trifle used. Wheldon
160-1504 1983 £20

CONNOLD, E. T.   Plant Galls of Great Britain. 1909.
354 illustrations, 8vo, cloth. Wheldon 160-1505 1983 £15

CONNOLLY, CYRIL   The Condemned Playground. NY, 1946.
Near fine in slightly frayed and rubbed, lightly soiled, very good
dustwrapper. Quill & Brush 54-297 1983 $40

CONNOLLY, CYRIL   The Condemned Playground. London: Routledge, (1945). First edition. Frontis. Orig. cloth. Very good.
MacManus 277-1058 1983 $20

CONNOLLY, CYRIL   Enemies of Promise. London, 1938.
First edition. With the pencilled ownership signature of Arctic explorer Charles Brocklehurst and with several pencilled annotations by
him to the text. Edges spotted. In scarce dustwrapper which is
chipped, browned at the spine, and missing a one-inch piece at the
head of the spine. Very good. Jolliffe 26-98 1983 £95

CONNOLLY, CYRIL   Enemies of Promise. London, 1938.
First edition. Covers just a little marked. Very nice. Rota 231-
129 1983 £50

CONNOLLY, CYRIL   The Evening Colonnade. London, 1973.
First edition. Dust wrapper. With autograph presentation inscription
from the author to Sonia Orwell. Fine. Rota 231-130 1983 £100

CONNOLLY, CYRIL   The Rock Pool. Paris: Obelisk Press,
1936. First edition. Wrappers rubbed at head and foot of the spine,
but a very good copy. Gekoski 2-29 1983 £185

CONNOLLY, CYRIL   The Rock Pool. NY, 1936. Cover very
slightly darkened, very good in lightly chipped and slightly soiled
dustwrapper. Quill & Brush 54-295 1983 $175

CONNOLLY, CYRIL   The Rock Pool. Paris: Obelisk Press,
1936. First edition. Wrappers. Backstrip a little darkened and worn.
Nice. Rota 230-135 1983 £105

CONNOLLY, CYRIL   The Unquiet Grave. Horizon, 1944 (i.e.
March, 1945). First edition. One of 1000 numbered copies on handmade
paper. Orig. blue cloth. Spine severely faded and corners bruised.
Internally very good. Rota 230-136 1983 £20

CONNOLLY, CYRIL   The Unquiet Grave. N.Y., 1945.
First American edition. Frontis., 12mo. Argosy 714-183 1983 $35

CONNOLY, JAMES   Labour in Ireland, Labour in Irish
History. Dublin: Maunsel, 1917. First collected edition, 8vo,
orig. cloth, a very good copy. Fenninh 60-69 1983 £10.50

CONNOLLY, JAMES B.   The Seiners. New York: Scribner,
1904. 1st ed. Orig. green pictorial cloth. Very good copy.
Jenkins 155-239 1983 $20

CONNOR, RALPH   The Patrol of the Sun Dance Trail.
London, Toronto, New York: Hodder & Stoughton, 1914. 19cm. First
edition. Ads. Red cloth, gilt titles on the spine, black titles
and decoration on the upper cover. Fine. McGahern 54-46 1983
$20

CONOVER, CHARLES T.   Thomas Burke, 1849-1925. Seattle,
1926. Illus. Orig. cloth. First edition. Ginsberg 46-793 1983
$30

CONRAD, JESSIE   Personal Recollections of Joseph
Conrad. London: Privately printed, 1924. Cloth, t.e.g., large
ink inscription on title, spine label frayed, cover cloth bubbled
and soiled. Limited to 100 numbered copies, signed by author.
(This is no. 100). King 46-269 1983 $45

CONRAD, JOSEPH   Almayer's Folly. London, Unwin, 1895.
First edition, first issue. Gilt stamped green cloth, t.e.g.,
uncut (spine faded, minor fraying), else very good. Houle 22-245 1983
$575

CONRAD, JOSEPH   Almayer's Folly... London, T. Fisher
Unwin, 1895. 8vo. Orig. green cloth, gt., other edges uncut. 1st
ed., 1st issue. Corners bumped, spine faded & slightly bubbled.
Very good. O'Neal 50-11 1983 $450

CONRAD, JOSEPH   Almayer's Folly. NY, 1895. Hinges
starting, endpaper foxed, cover rubbed and edges wearing, book
slightly rolled over, good, 600 copies. Quill & Brush 54-298 1983
$175

CONRAD, JOSEPH   Arrow of Gold. NY, 1919. Edges slightly
rubbed, else very good, bright copy. Quill & Brush 54-302 1983 $30

CONRAD, JOSEPH   Arrow of Gold. Lon., (1919). First
issue of English edition with A in Arrow page 67, front endpaper missing, edges slightly bumped, stain to fore edge, else very good. Quill
& Brush 54-301 1983 $25

CONRAD, JOSEPH   The Arrow of Gold. London: Unwin, 1919.
First English edition, earliest issue. Orig. cloth. MacManus 277-1059
1983 $20

CONRAD, JOSEPH   Chance, A Tale In Two Parts. New York:
Doubleday, Page & Co., 1913. First American edition. Orig. decorated
blue cloth. Spine and covers worn, inner hinges weak. Folding,
quarter-morocco slipcase (outer hinge worn). Good. MacManus 277-1060
1983 $350

CONRAD, JOSEPH   Chance. London, Methuen, (1914).
First edition (later issue), with title leaf a cancel. Gilt
decorated green cloth, uncut (slight foxing, mostly to edges). Very
good. Houle 22-246 1983 $175

CONRAD, JOSEPH   The Children of the Sea. New York,
1897. First edition. Pictorial boards. Fine. Scarce. Gekoski
2-30 1983 £225

CONRAD, JOSEPH   Conrad to a Friend: 150 Selected
Letters. London: 1928. First edition. Folding facsimile frontis.
Black cloth. Very fine in dust jacket. Bradley 66-74 1983 $75

CONRAD, JOSEPH   Conrad to a Friend. London: Sampson
Low, Marston & Co., 1928. First edition. Intro. by Richard Curle.
Covers waterspotted and slightly worn. Bookplate. Orig. cloth.
Good. MacManus 277-1061 1983 $20

CONRAD, JOSEPH   The Dover Patrol. Caterbury, 1922.
1st ed., 1 of 75 copies printed for Conrad's own use. Orig. printed
wrappers, uncut. In cloth folding case. Very fine copy, signed on
title-page by Conrad. Jenkins 155-1377 1983 $350

CONRAD, JOSEPH   Falk, Amy Foster, To-Morrow. N.Y.:
McClure, Phillips & Co., 1903. First separate edition. Orig. embossed
navy blue cloth. Spine ends a trifle rubbed. Inner hinges weak and
cracking. Full-morocco solander case. Former owner's signature.
Very good. MacManus 277-1063 1983 $150

CONRAD, JOSEPH   Five Letters Written to Edward Noble in 1895. London: Privately Printed, 1925. Orig. wrappers with glassine dust jacket (a bit frayed and stained). One of 100 copies numbered and signed by Noble. Cloth folder. Fine. MacManus 277-1064 1983 $350

CONRAD, JOSEPH   Fortune. (Paris): NRF/Gallimard, (1933). Orig. printed wraps. First edition in French. One of 230 numbered copies on velin pur fil Lafuma-Navarre. This copy bears a presentation inscription from the translator, Philippe Neel. Fine in glassine wrapper. Reese 20-273 1983 $125

CONRAD, JOSEPH   Laughing Anne & One Day More. London: John Castle, 1924. First edition. Intro. by John Galsworthy. Orig. cloth. Dust jacket (very slightly soiled & frayed). Covers slightly water-spotted. Half-morocco (rubbed) folding box. Very good. MacManus 277-1071 1983 $150

CONRAD, JOSEPH   Life and Letters. London, 1927. First edition. 2 vols. Bookplate. Fine set. Gekoski 2-36 1983 £25

CONRAD, JOSEPH   Lord Jim. N.Y.: Doubleday & McClure Co., 1900. First American edition. Orig. cloth. Endpapers a bit foxed & dust-soiled. Fine. MacManus 277-1080 1983 $150

CONRAD. JOSEPH   Mirror of the Sea. London, Methuen, (1906). First edition, ads dated August. Gilt stamped green cloth, t.e.g., uncut (corners slightly bumped), else very good. Houle 21-238 1983 $200

CONRAD, JOSEPH   The Nature of a Crime. London: Duckworth, (1924). 1st ed. Orig. apricot cloth, gilt. Fine copy in near fine dj, less often seen than the American ed. Jenkins 155-242 1983 $65

CONRAD, JOSEPH   The Nature of a Crime. Duckworth & Co., (1924). 8vo, orig. cloth in dust-wrapper. First edition. Bickersteth 77-196 1983 £25

CONRAD, JOSEPH   The Nigger of the Narcissus. Los Angeles, Limited Editions Club, 1965. First edition thus. 4to, illus. by Millard Sheets. 1/2 dark green morocco stamped in black and gilt with ship design, slipcase. One of 1500 printed by Ward Ritchie Press and signed by the illustrator. Fine. Houle 22-1191 1983 $75

CONRAD, JOSEPH   Nostromo. London, 1904. First edition. Previous owner's initials on end-paper, slight foxing, slightly bumped at head and tail of spine, but a fresh copy. Gekoski 2-33 1983 £120

CONRAD, JOSEPH   Nostromo. London, Harper, 1904. First edition. Blue cloth stamped in gilt and light blue (slight wear, trifle foxing on first few pages of text), else very good. Houle 21-239 1983 $200

CONRAD, JOSEPH   Nostromo, A Tale of the Seaboard. London: Harper, 1904. 1st ed.. remainder binding. Orig. bright blue cloth, gilt, edges sprinkled in red. This copy has smooth un-stamped covers, the spine stamped in gilt from brasses like those of the first binding, the sheets trimmed down slightly and sprinkled with red-orange ink. Rare state. Fine copy. Jenkins 155-240 1983 $150

CONRAD, JOSEPH   Nostromo. Paris: NRF/Gallimard, (1926). Two vols. Orig. printed wraps. First edition in French. One of 900 numbered sets, printed on velin pur fil Lafum-Navarre. Tiny nick in toe of the spine, otherwise a fine set in glassine wraps. Reese 20-272 1983 $65

CONRAD, JOSEPH   Notes On Life & Letters. London: J. M. Dent & Sons, 1921. First edition. Orig. cloth. Covers a trifle spotted. Some offsetting to the endpapers. Bookplate. Very good. MacManus 277-1084 1983 $25

CONRAD, JOSEPH   An Outcast Of The Islands. New York: D. Appleton and Company, 1896. First American edition. 8vo. Orig. decorated cloth. Very fine copy. Jaffe 1-68 1983 $425

CONRAD, JOSEPH   An Outcast of the Islands. London, Unwin, 1896. First edition. Gilt stamped green cloth, t.e.g., uncut, (fraying at hinges, corners bumped, inner hinges starting), else, good - very good. Houle 22-247 1983 $275

CONRAD, JOSEPH   An Outcast of the Islands. New York: Appleton, 1896. Orig. green decorated cloth, gilt. First American edition. Reese 20-271 1983 $135

CONRAD, JOSEPH   An Outcast of the Islands. NY, 1896. Spine slightly darkened, edges rubbed, cover slightly soiled, top corner edge of front fly torn off, good plus copy, owner's name. Quill & Brush 54-299 1983 $125

CONRAD, JOSEPH   A Personal Record. London, Dent, 1919. First edition thus, with a new 16pp preface by the author. Decorated olive green cloth, stamped in brown and gilt, top edges green (spine a bit darkened), else very good. Houle 21-241 1983 $125

CONRAD, JOSEPH   The Point of Honor. N.Y., 1908. First edition. Illus. pict. cloth. First issue, with "McClure" on backstrip. Argosy 714-186 1983 $125

CONRAD, JOSEPH   The Rescue. London, 1920. First English Published edition. Dust wrapper. Very nice. Rota 231-131 1983 £15

CONRAD, JOSEPH   The Rescue. London: J.M. Dent, 1920. Orig. cloth. First English trade edition. MacManus 277-1085 1983 $20

CONRAD, JOSEPH   Romance. London: Smith, Elder & Co., 1903. First edition. Orig. blue cloth. Spine ends and edges slightly rubbed. Quarter-morocco slipcase. Very good. MacManus 277-1087 1983 $250

CONRAD, JOSEPH   Romance. London, 1903. First edition. Bookplate. Front cover very slightly faded, but an excellent copy. Gekoski 2-32 1983 £65

CONRAD, JOSEPH   Romance. NY, 1904. Front hinge cracked, lightly stained at top corner edge of last 50 or so pages, corners slightly rubbed, bottom spine edge slightly frayed, bright, good or better, owner's name. Quill & Brush 54-300 1983 $75

CONRAD, JOSEPH   Romance. N.Y.: McClure, Phillips & Co., 1904. First American edition. Illus. by Charles R. Macauley. Orig. decorated blue cloth. Covers a bit soiled. Very good. MacManus 277-1086 1983 $65

CONRAD, JOSEPH   The Rover. London, Unwin (1923). First English edition. Gilt stamped green cloth, dust jacket (trifle soiled and rubbed), else very good-fine. Houle 21-242 1983 $125

CONRAD, JOSEPH   The Rover. London: T. Fisher Unwin, (1923). First English edition. Orig. cloth. Dust jacket (faded, worn and soiled, with a few small tears to the covers and spine ends). Loosely laid in is a 4-page publisher's prospectus for several books. Spine ends slightly worn, with some foxing to the endpapers and pre-liminary pages. Good. MacManus 277-1088 1983 $125

CONRAD, JOSEPH   Secret Agent. NY, 1907. Page edges slightly stained, front endpapers offset, covers slightly stained and darkened, good plus copy. Quill & Brush 54-303 1983 $50

CONRAD, JOSEPH   The Secret Agent. London: T. Werner Laurie, 1923. First edition. Orig. boards, paper label on spine. Dust jacket (soiled and faded, a bit frayed). One of 1000 copies signed by author. Edges very slightly worn. Very good. MacManus 277-1090 1983 $150

CONRAD, JOSEPH   A Set of Six. London, Methuen, (1908). First edition, second issue with the ads dated June, 1908; title and half title on a stub. Blue cloth stamped in gilt and dark red (spine faded, front and rear inner hinges repaired), else good-very good. Houle 21-243 1983 $150

CONRAD, JOSEPH   A Set of Six. London: Methuen, (1908). First edition. Orig. cloth. Covers faded. Large bookplate. MacManus 277-1091 1983 $50

CONRAD, JOSEPH   Shadow-Line. London, Dent (1907). First edition, first issue with 18pp. of ads. Light green cloth stamped in brown and gilt, top edge stained blueish green. Very good. Houle 21-244 1983 $150

CONRAD, JOSEPH   Some Reminiscences. London: Eveleigh Nash, 1912. First edition. Orig. cloth. Inner hinges cracking. Former owner's signature. Fine. MacManus 277-1092 1983 $125

CONRAD, JOSEPH   Suspense. Garden City, Doubleday, 1925. First regular edition. Dust jacket (small chip). Very good-fine. Houle 21-245 1983 $175

CONRAD, JOSEPH   Suspense. London: 1925. First English edition. Dark red cloth. Fine in very good dust jacket. Bradley 66-75 1983 $150

CONRAD, JOSEPH   Suspense. London, 1925. First English edition. 8vo, dark red cloth. Fine. Argosy 714-187 1983 $50

CONRAD, JOSEPH   Suspense. London: J.M. Dent, 1925. First English edition. 8vo. Orig. maroon cloth. MacManus 277-1093 1983 $20

CONRAD, JOSEPH   Tales of Hearsay. London, Unwin, (1925). First edition. Gilt stamped dark green cloth. Very good. Houle 21-246 1983 $65

CONRAD, JOSEPH   Tales of Hearsay. Garden City: Double-day, Page & Co., 1925. First American edition. Orig. cloth. Dust jacket (spine darkened, top of spine slightly chipped). Very good. MacManus 277-1094 1983 $45

CONRAD, JOSEPH   Tales of Unrest. London: Unwin, 1898. 1st ed. Orig. green cloth, gilt, t.e.g., others uncut. But for a repaired chip to crown of spine, a crisp clean copy. Jenkins 155-241 1983 $200

CONRAD, JOSEPH   Tales of Unrest. London, Unwin, 1898. First English edition. Title printed in red and black. Gilt stamped dark green cloth, t.e.g. (inner joints neatly repaired). Good-very good. Houle 21-248 1983 $150

CONRAD, JOSEPH   "To My Brethern of the Pen." Privately printed: 1927. First edition. Orig. decorated wrappers. One of 150 copies. Covers slightly worn, foxed, and soiled. Very good. MacManus 277-1097 1983 $125

CONRAD, JOSEPH   Twist Land and Sea Tales. London, Dent, 1912. First edition. Medium green cloth stamped in gilt and dark green, top edges stained red (slight darkening at top of spine), else very good. Houle 21-249 1983 $125

CONRAD, JOSEPH   Typhoon and Other Stories. London: William Heinemann, 1903. First English edition. Orig. decorated cloth. Variant title page lacking the Heinemann "windmill" emblem. Spine and covers slightly worn and faded. Some foxing to the endpapers and edges. Front inner hinges cracking. Good. MacManus 277-1099 1983 $185

CONRAD, JOSEPH   Typhoon and other stories. London, 1903. First Complete edition. First issue, with the publisher's windmill device on the title-page. One corner a little bruised and prelimin-aries slightly foxed. Nice. Rota 230-139 1983 £45

CONRAD, JOSEPH   Typhoon and Other Stories. London: Heinemann, 1903. First English edition. Orig. cloth. Covers a bit worn. Inner hinges cracked. Ex-library. Label removed from front cover. MacManus 277-1098 1983 $50

CONRAD, JOSEPH   Under Western Eyes. London, Methuen, (1911). First edition, first issue. Gilt stamped red cloth (rebacked, with orig. spine laid down; new endpapers). Very good. Houle 21-250 1983 $175

CONRAD, JOSEPH   Victory. Garden City, Doubleday, 1915. First edition. Gilt stamped blue cloth. Very good. Houle 21-251 1983 $75

CONRAD, JOSEPH   Victory. N.Y., Modern Library, (1932). First edition thus, (so stated). Small 8vo, dust jacket (spine darkened) else, very good. Houle 22-248 1983 $30

CONRAD, JOSEPH   Within the Tides. London, Dent, 1915. First edition. Gilt stamped medium green cloth. Very good-fine. Review tipped-in at end. Houle 21-252 1983 $175

CONRAD, JOSEPH   The Works. London, 1921-27. 20 vols. 8vo. Boards with buckram spines, uncut edges, in the orig. printed dustwrappers. Limited edition of 780 sets, numbered and signed by the author. Traylen 94-211 1983 £475

CONRAD, JOSEPH   The Works. London, 1923-29. The Uniform Edition. 22 vols. 8vo. Orig. pink cloth, gilt. Frontis. to each vol. Traylen 94-212 1983 £190

CONRAD, JOSEPH   The Works. Edinburgh, 1925. 20 vols. 8vo. Orig. blue buckram, gilt. Frontis. to each vol. Traylen 94-213 1983 £150

CONRAD, JOSEPH   Complete Works. Garden City, Doubleday, Page, 1926. Kent edition. Grey cloth stamped in blind with a design of a sailing ship; paper labels, t.e.g., uncut. Dust jacket (a few minor nicks and tears), else a fine, fresh and almost mint set. 26 vols. complete. Houle 21-237 1983 $475

CONRAD, JOSEPH   Youth: A Narrative, And Two Other Stories. Edinburgh & London: William Blackwood & Sons, 1902. First edition. Orig. decorated cloth. With the ads dating "10/02." Contains one of Conrad's most famous tales. Spine slightly darkened. Half-morocco folding case. Former owner's signature. Very good. MacManus 277-1101 1983 $250

CONRAD, JOSEPH   Youth: A Narrative and Two Other Stories. Edinburgh & London: William Blackwood & Sons, 1902. First edition. Orig. cloth. 32 pages of publisher's ads at the back, dated 11/02. Spine slightly darkened, bubbled. Former owner's signature. Very good. MacManus 277-1102 1983 $200

CONRAD, JOSEPH   Youth: A Narrative. London, 1902. First edition. Cloth a little worn at head of spine and bubbled at hinge of lower cover. Two slight markes on upper cover. Nice. Rota 230-138 1983 £60

CONRAD, JOSEPH   Youth. New York, 1903. First American edition, inscribed "W.P.W. from the author, 1903". Two stamped addresses of Walter P. Wright on front paste-down. Spine faded and frayed at top, hinges weak. Good. Gekoski 2-31 1983 £175

CONSIDERATIONS on the Nature, Origin and Institution of Tithes... London: by W. Strahan..., 1773. First edition. 8vo. Uncut in orig. grey covers. Heath 48-219 1983 £35

CONSIDERATIONS on the past and present state of the stage; with references to the late contests at Covent Garden. London: published by C. Chapple, 1809. 8vo, disbound, 1st ed. Scarce. Ximenes 64-139 1983 $100

CONSIDERATIONS Upon a Proposal for Lowering the Interest of all the Redeemable National Debts to Three Per Cent. per Ann. London: J. Purser, 1737. First edition. 8vo, blank, modern cloth. Pickering & Chatto 21-25 1983 $65

CONSTABLE, W. G.   Richard Wilson. London: Routledge & Kegan Paul, 1953. 160 plates. 4to. Cloth. Ars Libri 32-708 1983 $125

CONTEMPORARY American Sculpture. (New York, 1929). Illus. 4to, orig. boards. 1st ed. Morrill 286-105 1983 $25

CONTES De Perrault et de Mme. De. Beaumont. Paris, George Cres, 1914. Illus. by Charles Robinson. Col. frontis., b&w decor. title & 7 col. plates. Green cloth gilt, contemp. insc. fr. ep., gilt on bkstrip dull, vg. Hodgkins 27-160 1983 £12.50

CONTI, ANGELO   Giorgione. Studio. Firenze: Alinari, 1894. 2 photogravure plates. Numerous text illus. Small folio. Marbled boards, 1/4 cloth. Orig. wrappers bound in. Ars Libri 33-167 1983 $65

CONTI, ARMAND DE BOURBON, PRINCE OF   The Works...with a short
account of his life. London: printed by E. P. for W. Bray, 1711.
8vo, cont. panelled calf, spine stained black and gilt. First ed. in
English. With an engraved portrait. A fine copy, complete with 5
pages of ads at the end. Ximenes 64-58 1983 $275

THE CONTINENTAL Legal History Series. New York, 1968. 10 vols. Re-
issue of the 1912 edition. Boswell 7-154 1983 $225

THE CONTRAST to the Man of Honour. London: Printed for J. Morgan
in the Strand. 1737. Folio, disbound. First edition. A very good
copy. Quaritch NS 7-27 1983 $225

CONTRIBUTIONS to Medical and Biological Research Dedicated to Sir
William Osler. New York, 1919. 2 vols. 8vo. Orig. blue cloth,
gilt. Limited to 1600 copies. Fine set. Scarce. Fye H-3-904
1983 $125

CONTRIBUTIONS to the Fauna of Mergui and its Archipelago. 1889.
Vol. 1, 8vo, half morocco, 32 plates (7 coloured, 3 photographic).
Wheldon 160-321 1983 £12

CONWAY, HUGH, PSEUD.
Please turn to
FARGUS, FREDERICK JOHN

CONWAY, MARTIN   The Van Eycks and Their Followers.
New York: E.P. Dutton, 1921. 24 plates. Stout 4to. Cloth. Ars
Libri 32-211 1983 $75

CONWAY, MONCURE DANIEL   Life of Thomas Paine, with a History
of His Literary, Political & Religious Career in America, France &
England. NY, 1892. First edition, 2 vols., g.t. Argosy 716-431
1983 $75

CONWAY, MONCURE DANIEL   The Rejected Stone. Boston, 1862.
Cloth. Second edition. A presentation copy, inscribed by the
author. Felcone 22-40 1983 $20

CONWAY, WILLIAM MARTIN   Climbing in the Karakoram-Himalayas.
London, 1894. First edition. Folding map. Numerous illus. Thick
roy.8vo. Pictorial cloth. T.e.g. Uncut. Edwards 1044-145 1983
£185

CONWAY, WILLIAM MARTIN   The Woodcutters of the Netherlands in
the Fifteenth Century. Cambridge: Univ. Press, 1884. Cloth, bookplate, fine copy. Dawson 470-71 1983 $50

CONYBEARE, JOHN   A Defence of Reveal'd Religion against
the Exceptions of a Late Writer (Matthew Tindal). Dublin: Printed
by S. Powell, for Stearne Brock, 1732. First Irish edition (?),
ads., 8vo, cont. calf. Fenning 62-77 1983 £24.50

COOK, DUTTON   A Book of the Play: studies and illustrations of histrionic story, life, and character. London: Sampson
Low, etc., 1876. 2 vols., 8vo, original green cloth (very slightly
rubbed). 1st ed., presentation copy from the author to J. L. Toole.
Fine copy. Ximenes 64-140 1983 $90

COOK, DUTTON   Hours with the Players. London: Chatto
and Windus, 1881. 2 vols., 8vo, original dark green cloth (slight
wear, traces of labels removed from front covers). 1st ed. Old
library bookplates and blindstamps. Ximenes 64-141 1983 $45

COOK, EDWARD   The Life of Florence Nightingale.
Macmillan and Co., 1913. 2 vols., 8vo, portraits and facs., orig.
cloth, spines faded, short slit at top of spine of vol. 1. First
edition. Bickersteth 75-257 1983 £24

COOK, EDWARD WILLIAM   Views of the Old and New London Bridges.
Brown and Syrett etc., London, 1833. First edition. Folio, with
12 etched plates, all proof impressions printed on India paper and
mounted; orig. cloth with gilt lettering on upper board, rather
worn, rebacked. Internally a very good copy. Quaritch NS 5-24 1983
$1,200

COOK, ELIZA   Poems. Routledge, 1859. New edn. in
1 vol. Frontis. Portrait & 8 engrs. Dark blue bead grain blind
stamped cl. gilt vignette fr. cvr. & bkstrip, a.e.g., frontis. water
stained & one section sl. sprung, vg copy. Hodgkins 27-259 1983
£15

COOK, ELIZA   Poems. Routledge, 1861. Deluxe edn.
bound in full dark green morocco with heavily blind embossed design
both cvrs., raised bands, blind embossed decor. bkstrip., gilt titling,
a.e.g. guaffered edges, marbled eps., bevelled boards, frontis. foxed
& occasional foxing contents, fine copy. Hodgkins 27-261 1983
£35

COOK, ELIZA   Poems. Routledge, 1861. New edn. with
frontis. portrait & 81 illus. by John Gilbert, Wolf, H. Weir, Watson,
etc. Engr'd by Bros. Dalziel. Blue mor. grain cloth gilt, designed
by John Leighton, bevelled boards, a.e.g., sml. part of gilt rubbed
on fr. cvr., corners sl. rubbed & bruised, occasional foxing, vg.
Hodgkins 27-260 1983 £25

COOK, ELIZA   Poems. Routledge, 1862. New edn. in 1
vol. with frontis. portrait & 8 wood engrs. by Godwin, H. Weir, etc.
Engr'd by Bros. Dalziel. Royal blue blind stamped cloth, gilt vig.
fr. cvr. & gilt decor. bkstrip, bevelled boards, a.e.g., fr. ep.
cracking at hinge. With manuscript poem on verso fr. ep. addressed
to Major G.E. Brown Westhead, 1863. Very good. Hodgkins 27-262 1983
£40

COOK, ELLIOTT W.   Land Ho! The Original Diary of a
Forty-Niner. Baltimore, (1935). Orig. boards, paper labels on
spine and cover. First edition. Ginsberg 47-256 1983 $25

COOK, FREDERICK   Journals of the Military Expedition
of Major General John Sullivan Against the Six Nations of Indians in
1779. NY: Knapp, Peck & Thomson, 1887. Tall thick 8vo, illus.
with 4 steel engravings, 6 maps (3 folding) and 5 folding maps and
plans, laid inside front and rear pockets. Maroon gilt-stamped
cloth. Karmiole 73-31 1983 $50

COOK, JAMES   Bibliography of the Writings of Charles
Dickens. Frank Kerslake; Paisley: J.&J. Cook, 1879. First edition.
Front. orig. printed wraps. bound into half maroon calf, v.g.
Jarndyce 30-150 1983 £52

COOK, JAMES H.   Fifty Years on the Old Frontier... New
Haven, 1923. Frontis. and illus. Some wear but fairly nice copy.
Jenkins 153-138 1983 $65

COOK, JAMES H.   Fifty Years on the Old Frontier...New
Haven, 1923. 2nd prntg. Illus., front flyleaf replaced. Clark 741-
199 1983 $23.50

COOK, JAMES H.   Longhorn Cowboy. N.Y., Putnam, (1942).
First edition. Dust jacket. Very good - fine. Houle 22-1035 1983
$45

COOK, JAMES H.   Longhorn Cowboy. New York, 1942. Illus.
First edition. Jenkins 153-139 1983 $35

COOK, JIM LANE   Lane of the Llano. Boston, 1936. End
map, illus. Clark 741-201 1983 $22.50

COOK, JOEL   The Mediterranean and its Borderlands.
Philadelphia, ca. 1910. 2 vols., 50 photogravure plates, elaborate
gilt cloth, gilt tops. K Books 307-54 1983 £40

COOK, JOHN   A True Relation of Mr. John Cook's
Passage by Sea from Wexford to Kinsale in that Great Storm Ianuary 5.
Printed at Cork, and re-printed at London, and are to be sold by T.
Brewster and G. Moule, 1650. 4to, old paper boards, with label.
Fenning 60-71 1983 £125

COOK, JOHN R.   The Border and the Buffalo. Topeka:
Crane and Co., 1907. Cloth. One page rumpled. Dawson 471-50 1983
$60

COOK, JOHN R.   The Border and the Buffalo: An Untold
Story of the Southwest Plains. Chicago, 1938. Frontis, g.t., 16mo.
Argosy 710-518 1983 $25

COOK, JOSEPH W.   Diary and Letters of the Reverend...
Missionary to Cheyenne. Laramie, 1919. Portrait. Orig. printed
wrappers. 1st ed. Scarce. Jenkins 153-711 1983 $100

COOK, KENINGALE ROBERT   Purpose and Passion. 1870. First
edition, 4to, orig. blue cloth, rubbed. Jarndyce 30-673 1983 £10.50

COOK, REGINALD LANSING   The Concord Saunterer. Middlebury, Vt., 1940. First edition. Orig. letters by Thoreau, and check list of Thoreau items. 8vo, original boards, slightly torn dust wrappers, very nice. Morrill 290-535 1983 $20

COOKE, JACOB B.   Battle of Kelly's Ford, March 17, 1863. Providence, 1887. Orig. printed wraps. First edition. One of 250 copies. Ginsberg 46-776 1983 $25

COOKE, JOHN ESTEN   An Essay on the Invalidity of Presbyterian Ordination. Lexington, 1829. First edition. 8vo, cont. calf-backed bds., (inner front hinge strengthened). Argosy 713-123 1983 $150

COOKE, JOHN ESTEN   Henry St. John, Gentleman. New York: Harper, 1859. 1st ed. Orig. cloth, gilt. Very good copy. Jenkins 155-243 1983 $40

COOKE, JOHN ESTEN   The Last of the Foresters: or, Humors on the Border; A Story of the Old Virginia Frontier. New York: Derby & Jackson, 1856. 1st ed. Orig. cloth, gilt. Fine copy. Jenkins 155-244 1983 $50

COOKE, JOSIAH PARSONS   The New Chemistry. London: Henry S. King, 1874. 8vo. Orig. cloth. Second edition. Zeitlin 264-87 1983 $40

COOKE, JOSIAH PARSONS   Principles of Chemical Philosophy. London: Macmillan, 1882. Revised edition. 8vo. Orig. cloth. Partially uncut. Ownership inscription on title page. Zeitlin 264-88 1983 $60

COOKE, M. C.   British Desmids. 1887. 66 coloured plates, 8vo, original cloth. Neatly refixed in case. Tape marks on endpapers. Wheldon 160-1808 1983 £50

COOKE, M. C.   Fungi: their nature, influence, and uses. 109 text-figures, 8vo, cloth. Wheldon 160-1805 1983 £12

COOKE, M. C.   Introduction to Fresh-Water Algae. 1902. 13 plates, 8vo, cloth. Wheldon 160-1809 1983 £12

COOKE, M. C.   Rust, Smut, Mildew, and Mould. 1878. 4th edition, 16 plates including 269 coloured figures, 8vo, cloth. Wheldon 160-1806 1983 £20

COOKE, THOMAS   Essays. I. On Nobility...II. On the Ancient and Modern State of Britain... London: Printed and Sold by J. Huggonson...MDCCXXXVII. Folio, disbound. First edition. Only the Bodleian copy is recorded in England. A good large copy. Quaritch NS 7-28 1983 $300

COOKE, THOMAS   The Mournful Nuptials, or Love the Cure of all Woes, a tragedy. London: printed for T. Cooper, 1739. 8vo, wrappers, 1st ed. Ximenes 64-142 1983 $60

COOKE, THOMAS   The Triumphs of Love and Honour, a play. London: printed for J. Roberts, 1731. 8vo, disbound, 1st ed. Ximenes 64-143 1983 $125

COOLEY, THOMAS B.   Catalogue of the Books in the Library of the Incorporated Law Society of Ireland. Dublin, 1937. 8vo, orig. cloth, gilt. Fenning 62-204 1983 £24.50

COOKE, WILLIAM   The Elements of Dramatic Criticism. London: printed for G. Kearsly, 1775. 8vo, cont. calf (some wear). First edition. A very good copy, complete with half title. Ximenes 64-144 1983 $225

COOKE, WILLIAM   Memoirs of Charles Macklin, comedian. London: printed for James Asperne, by Thomas Maiden, 1804. 8vo, original green boards, white paper backstrip, rose printed paper label. 1st ed. With a portrait. A very fine copy in original condition. Ximenes 64-145 1983 $225

COOLIDGE, DANE   Fighting Men of the West. New York, 1932. 343pp. Illustrations. Nice copy in dust jacket. Inscribed by the author with a picture of the author laid in. Jenkins 151-45 1983 $75

COOLIDGE, DANE   Fighting Men of the West. New York, (1932). 1st ed. Illus. Light spot on back cover, small stain upper margin in first 35 pages. Clark 741-250 1983 $37.50

COOLIDGE, DANE   Hidden Water. Chicago: A.C. McClurg & Co., 1910. Illustrations by Maynard Dixon. Orig. pictorial cloth boards with cloth spine. Some bumping to corners, 1st ed. Nice copy. Jenkins 153-165 1983 $35

COOLIDGE, DANE   The Last of the Seris. New York, (1939). 1st ed. Illus. Clark 741-304 1983 $24.50

COOLIDGE, DANE   Texas Cowboys. New York, 1937. 162pp. Frontis illustrations. First edition. A very good copy. "Thin, but genuine...well illustrated by photographs. A scarce Collidge title. Jenkins 151-46 1983 $40

COOLIDGE, MARY R.   The Rain-Makers. Boston, 1929. 1st ed. End maps, plates. Clark 741-305 1983 $42

COOLIDGE, RICHARD   Statistical Report on the Sickness and Mortality in the Army of the United States... Washington, 1856. First edition. 4to. Rebound in 1/4 leather with raised bands. Fye H-3-114 1983 $125

COOLS, JACOB   Syntagma Herbarum Encomiasticum Abrahamo Ortelio quondam inscriptum. (Antwerp): ex officina Plantiniana Raphelengii, 1614. Printer's device on title. Small 4to. Cont. limp vellum, in a cloth case. Second edition. Kraus 164-44 1983 $450

COON, CHARLES L.   The Beginnings of Public Education in North Carolina: a Documentary History, 1790-1840. Raleigh, 1908. 2 vols., large 8vo, cloth, ex library. Argosy 710-389 1983 $40

COONEY, ROBERT   The Autobiography of a Wesleyan Methodist Missionary. Montreal, E. Pickup, 1856. Second thousand. 8vo. Morrill 290-74 1983 $47.50

COONEY, SEAMUS   The Black Sparrow Press: A Checklist. Black Sparrow Press, 1971. 8vo. Cloth, boards. 1 of 50 copies signed by Cooney and Kelly. Fine in acetate jacket. In Our Time 156-162 1983 $200

COOPER, ASTLEY   Short Account of Sir...Vital Restorative. 1864. 8vo, ad., orig. purple cloth blocked in blind and gilt, gilt edges. Pickering & Chatto 22-25 1983 $65

COOPER, BRANSBY BLAKE   The Life of Sir Astley Cooper... London, 1843. 8vo. 2 vols. Cloth (rebound). Gurney JJ-81 1983 £20

COOPER, COURTNEY RYLEY   Annie Oakley, Woman at Arms. N.Y.: Duffield & Co., 1927. Cloth. A little soiled. Intro. by Will Rogers. Dawson 471-52 1983 $25

COOPER, EIDTH   Joint Author with Katherine Harris Bradley
Please turn to
FIELD, MICHAEL, PSEUD.

COOPER, FRED G.   Letters and Cartoons from FGC to WIM... Boston, 1927. Edition limited to 100 copies signed by Cooper and Morse. Inserted is Morse's calling card with an inscription by him. Cartoon illustrations. Tall 8vo, original boards, cloth back. Lacks front endleaf. Morrill 290-75 1983 $30

COOPER, JAMES FENIMORE   The American Democrat, or Hints on the Social and Civic Relations of the United States. Cooperstown: Phinney, 1838. 1st ed. Orig. muslin, paper label. State B of label (no sequence). Very scarce. Some fading, but a fine copy. Jenkins 155-245 1983 $300

COOPER, JAMES FENIMORE   Autobiography of a Pocket-Handkerchief. Chapel Hill, 1949. 1st ed. in book form, 1 of 300 copies printed of which only 100 were for sale. Orig. cloth-backed boards, gilt. Privately printed. Fine copy. Jenkins 155-246 1983 $25

COOPER, JAMES FENIMORE　　The Bravo: A Venetian Story. Ph., 1831. Two vols, boards, spines chipped and very worn but still intact with most of the paper labels present, good, owner's name. Quill & Brush 54-306　1983　$200

COOPER, JAMES FENNIMORE　　The Bravo. A Venetian Story. London: Henry Colburn and Richard Bentley, 1831. First English edition. 3 vols. 8vo. Orig. blue-grey boards, paper spine with printed paper labels. Half-titles, ad. leaf at end of vols. 2 and 3. Joints worn. Traylen 94-215　1983　£95

COOPER, JAMES FENIMORE　　The Chainbearer. New York: Burgess, Stringer, 1845. 2 vols. bound in 1. 1st ed. Contemporary 3/4 black morocco, gilt, raised bands. Pieces chipped from spine ends, else a very good copy. Jenkins 155-247　1983　$45

COOPER, JAMES FENIMORE　　The Deerslayer. Richard Bentley, 1841. 2nd edition, 3 vols., half calf, dark brown labels, very good. Jarndyce 30-334　1983　£20

COOPER, JAMES FENIMORE　　Eve Effingham; or, Home. Richard Bentley, 1838. 3 vols, 12mo, original boards, uncut; new backstrips. 3 half-titles; 16 pp. of advertisements in vol. I. 1st London ed. Hill 165-22　1983　£30

COOPER, JAMES FENIMORE　　Home as Found. Ph., 1838. Two vols. in one, board in 3/4 leather which is rubbed and worn with front board detaching, ex-lib., foxed, good. Quill & Brush 54-305　1983　$50

COOPER, JAMES FENIMORE　　The Last of the Mohicans. W. Simpkin & R. Marshall, 1828. 2nd edition, 3 vols., half dark blue calf, red labels, v.g. Jarndyce 30-333　1983　£40

COOPER, JAMES FENIMORE　　The Last of the Mohicans. NY, 1932. Limited Editions Club. Illus. by Edw. A. Wilson. Limited to 1500 copies, signed by illus., very slight soiling to spine, very good plus in slipcase. Quill & Brush 54-308　1983　$65

COOPER, JAMES FENIMORE　　New York. N.Y., Payson, 1930. Frontis. Title page portrait, half cloth, paper labels, uncut and unopened. Pub.'s box. One of 765 numbered copies. Fine. Houle 21-259　1983　$22.50

COOPER, JAMES FENIMORE　　Oak-Openings; or, The Bee-Hunter. New York, 1848. 2 vols. bound in one. First edition. Contemporary 3/4 sheep and marbled boards. Fine copy, originally published in wrappers and rarely encountered thus. Jenkins 151-47　1983　$75

COOPER, JAMES FENIMORE　　The Pilot. John Miller, 1824. First English edition. 3 vols. 12mo, lacks half-titles in vols. II and III. Cont. half calf (lacks labels). Hannas 69-35　1983　£30

COOPER, JAMES FENIMORE　　The Spy. NY, 1929. Illus. by Wm. Cotton, printed by Rudge, three vols., limited to 1000 copies. Spine slightly faded, else fine in worn slipcase. Quill & Brush 54-309　1983　$50

COOPER, JAMES FENIMORE　　The Water Witch. London, 1830. 8vo. Rebound, cloth, boards, leather. 3 vols. 1st English edition. Bookplate, some scuffing to leather around the edges, otherwise a vg-fine copy. In Our Time 156-164　1983　$200

COOPER, JAMES FENIMORE　　The Water-Witch. Philadelphia: Carey & Lea, 1831. Two vols. Orig. paper and boards, paper labels. First American edition. Spine of volume two cracking, extremities a bit rubbed, otherwise a very good copy in orig. state. Reese 20-275　1983　$150

COOPER, JAMES FENNIMORE　　The Water-Witch. London: Henry Colburn and Richard Bentley, 1830. First English edition. 3 vols. 12mo. Cont. half calf, gilt. Traylen 94-216　1983　£48

COOPER, JAMES FENNIMORE　　Wyandotte; or, The Hutted Knoll. Paris: Baudry, 1843. Half title, half red morocco, tall 8vo. Jarndyce 31-491　1983　£10.50

COOPER, LANE　　An Aristotelian Theory of Comedy. NY, 1922. New cloth. 8vo. Salloch 385-78　1983　$35

COOPER, LANE　　A Bibliography of the Poetics of Aristotle. New Haven, Cornell Studies in English, 1928. Wrs. 8vo, cloth. Salloch 385-471　1983　$40

COOPER, MADISON　　Sironia, Texas. Boston: Houghton, Mifflin, 1952. 2 vols. 1st ed. Orig. cloth-backed boards, gilt, dj. Fine fresh set. Jenkins 155-250　1983　$75

COOPER, OSWALD BRUCE　　An Appreciation. Chicago: Society of Typographic Arts, 1949. Tall 8vo, cloth, portrait frontis. Printed in red and black, with many samples of type, ornaments, etc. Printed at the Lakeside Press. Duschnes 240-127　1983　$65

COOPER, SAMUEL　　Dizionario di Chirurgia Pratica. Milano, 1823. 4 vols., 8vo, vellum. First edition. Argosy 713-124　1983　$100

COOPER, SAMUEL　　Obstructions in the Sabine River. Wash., 1838. Fine folding map. Later wrappers. Jenkins 153-141　1983　$100

COOPER, T. P.　　With Dickens in Yorkshire. Ben Johnson, 1923. First edition, half title, illus. by E. Ridsdale Tate, orig. red cloth, spine sl. faded, v.g. Jarndyce 31-590　1983　£10.50

COOPER, T. T.　　Travels of a Pioneer. London, 1871. Folding map. Frontis. Numerous text illus. Calf, gilt spine. 8vo. Good. Edwards 1044-150　1983　£60

COOPER, THOMAS　　Tracts on Medical Jurisprudence. Phila., 1819. First edition. 8vo, cont. mottled calf. Argosy 713-125　1983　$100

COOPER, WILLIAM　　Three Marriages. London, 1946. First edition. Frayed dust wrapper. Nice. Rota 231-132　1983　£25

CO-OPERATIVE WORKING WOMEN　　Life as We Have Known It. L, 1931. Photos, interior foxed, else very good in chipped dustwrapper. Quill & Brush 54-1587　1983　$75

COOTE, HENRY CHARLES　　The Romans of Britain. 1878. First edition. K Books 307-204　1983　£32

COOVER, ROBERT　　The Origin of the Brunists. NY, (1966). Very good to fine in like dustwrapper with two small closed tears. Quill & Brush 54-311　1983　$125

COPE, E. D.　　The Crocodilians, Lizards and Snakes of North America. Washington, Rept. U.S. Nat. Mus., 1900. 36 plates and numerous text-figures, 8vo, cloth (spine defective). Wheldon 160-951　1983　£45

COPELAND, THOMAS　　Observations on Some of the Principal Diseases of the Rectum and Anus; Particularly Stricture of the... Philadelphia, 1811. 1st American ed. 12mo. Contemporary calf, leather label. Morrill 289-50　1983　$35

COPLAND, SAMUEL　　A history of the island of Madagascar... London: Burton & Smith, 1822. 8vo. Errata. Folding map. Full brown morocco. Rubbed. Adelson Africa-76　1983　$240

COPLESTONE, EDWARD　　A Reply to the Calumnies of the Oxford Review against Oxford... Oxford, 1810. First edition. 8vo. Green cloth. Heath 48-88　1983　£30

COPPARD, ALFRED EDGAR　　Collected Poems. London, 1928. First edition. Endpapers foxed, covers a little marked. Dust wrapper. Author's signed autograph presentation inscription. Nice. Rota 231-135　1983　£30

COPPARD, ALFRED EDGAR　　Count Stephen (Waltham St. Lawrence), Golden Cockerel Press, 1928. Illus. with woodcuts by Robert Gibbings. Cloth backed marbled boards. Dust jacket (short tape mended tear) else very good. One of 600 numbered copies. Zane Grey's copy with his stamp. Houle 22-410　1983　$125

COPPARD, ALFRED EDGAR   Count Stefan. (Waltham Saint Lawrence): The Golden Cockerel Press, 1928. First edition. Orig. cloth-backed marbled boards. Limited to 600 copies. Very good. MacManus 277-1116a 1983 $45

COPPARD, ALFRED EDGAR   Dunky Fitlow. London, 1933. First edition. One of 300 numbered copies, signed by author. Full vellum. Covers a little spring. Very nice. Rota 231-139 1983 £25

COPPARD, ALFRED EDGAR   Emergency Exit. N.Y.: Random House, (1934). First edition. Decorations by Warren Chappel. Orig. decorated cloth. One of 350 copies printed at the Spiral Press & signed by Coppard. Fine. MacManus 277-1117 1983 $45

COPPARD, ALFRED EDGAR   Fearful Pleasures. Sauk City, Wisconsin: Arkham House, 1946. Edition ltd. to 4000 copies. Dust jacket. Fine. Karmiole 74-37 1983 $40

COPPARD, ALFRED EDGAR   Fearful Pleasures. SC, 1946. Lightly soiled cover, very good in slightly dampstained dustwrapper. Quill & Brush 54-314 1983 $25

COPPARD, ALFRED EDGAR   The Field of Mustard. London, 1926. First edition. One of 85 numbered copies, signed by author. Full vellum. Lacks lettering-label. Very nice. Rota 231-134 1983 £21

COPPARD, ALFRED EDGAR   The Higgler. N.Y.: The Chocorua Press, (1930). First edition. 4to. Orig. cloth-backed boards, paper label. One of 39 copies printed on fine paper with a page of the orig. manuscript lain in at back. Slight dampstaining of outer page of front free endpaper, tape marks on endpaper. Bookplate. Fine. MacManus 277-1118 1983 $250

COPPARD, ALFRED EDGAR   The Hundredth Story. (Waltham Saint Lawrence): The Golden Cockerel Press, 1931. First edition. With engravings by Robert Gibbings. 4to. Orig. half-morocco and decorated boards. With the publisher's slip laid in. Spine faded and slightly worn. Jaffe 1-70 1983 $85

COPPARD, ALFRED EDGAR   The Hundredth Story. The Golden Cockerell Press, 1931. With engravings by Robert Gibbings. Ltd. edition of 1,000 numbered copies, roy. 8vo, orig. calf-backed patterned boards, t.e.g., by Sangorski & Sutcliffe, a fine copy. With ad. leaf regarding the extending of the limitation from 75- to 1,000 copies loosely inserted. Fenning 62-78 1983 £48.50

COPPARD, ALFRED EDGAR   The Hundredth Story of A.E. Coppard. London: the Golden Cockerell Press, 1931. Roy. 8vo. Orig. quarter morocco, decorated paper boards, t.e.g. Engravings by Robert Gibbings. Limited edition of 1,000 numbered copies. Traylen 94-217 1983 £35

COPPARD, ALFRED EDGAR   Nixey's Harlequin. Jonathan Cape, 1931. First edition, 8vo, full vellum, with leather spine label, t.e.g. Ltd. edition of 304 numbered copies on hand-made paper, signed by the author. Fenning 62-79 1983 £32.50

COPPARD, ALFRED EDGAR   Nixey's Harlequin. London, 1931. First edition. One of 304 numbered copies, signed by author. Full vellum. Lettering-label a little stained. Nice. Rota 231-138 1983 £25

COPPARD, ALFRED EDGAR   Nixey's Harlequin. London, (1931). 8vo. Cloth, boards. Fine copy in dj which has some light wear. In Our Time 156-166 1983 $25

COPPARD, ALFRED EDGAR   Nixey's Harlequin. London: Jonathan Cape (1931). First edition. Orig. cloth-backed marbled boards, paper label on spine. Dust jacket. Fine. MacManus 277-1119 1983 $20

COPPARD, ALFRED EDGAR   Pink Furniture. London: Jonathan Cape, (1930). First edition. 8vo. Orig. full vellum. Dust jacket, t.e.g. One of 250 copies signed by author. MacManus 277-1120 1983 $45

COPPARD, ALFRED EDGAR   Pink Furniture. London, 1930. First edition. Illus. One of 260 numbered copies, signed by author. Full vellum. Foxing throughout. Nice. Rota 231-137 1983 £25

COPPARD, ALFRED EDGAR   Polly Oliver. London, 1935. First edition. One of 50 numbered copies, signed by author. Full vellum. Endpapers a little discoloured. Very nice. Rota 231-140 1983 £30

COPPARD, ALFRED EDGAR   Silver Circus. London, 1928. First edition. One of 125 numbered copies, signed by author. Full vellum. Very nice. Rota 231-136 1983 £30

COPPARD, ALFRED EDGAR   The Writings of A.E. Coppard. The Ulysses Bookshop, 1931. Ltd. edition of 650 numbered copies, signed by Coppard, 8vo, orig. cloth-backed boards, with printed paper label. A fine copy. Fenning 62-80 1983 £21.50

COPPARD, ALFRED EDGAR   Yokohama Garland and other Poems. Philadelphia: Centaur Press, (1926). First edition. Vignettes by Wharton Esherick. 4to. Orig. cloth-backed boards with paper label on spine, in publisher's slipcase. Limited to 500 copies printed by the Pynson Printers and signed by both Coppard and Esherick. Covers a little dust-soiled, in slightly worn slipcase, otherwise a very good copy. Jaffe 1-69 1983 $125

COPPIER, ANDRE-CHARLES   Les eaux-fortes de Rembrandt. Paris: Armand Colin, 1922. Prof. illus. (heliogravure). Small folio. Boards, 1/2 leather. T.e.g. Orig. wrappers bound in. Ars Libri 32-553 1983 $150

COPWAY, GEORGE   The Life, Letters and Speeches of Kah-Ge-Ga-Gah-Gowh. New York, 1850. 224pp. Frontis portrait. Original cloth, with some fading. Fairly nice copy. Jenkins 151-48 1983 $50

COQUIOT, GUSTAVE   Rodin a l'Hotel de Biron et a Meudon. Paris: Ollendorff, 1917. 49 plates. Large 4to. Marbled boards, 3/4 cloth. Ars Libri 32-585 1983 $100

COQUIOT, GUSTAVE   Toulouse-Lautrec. Berlin: Wasmuth, n.d. 49 collotype plates. Folio. Boards, 1/4 vellum. Edition limited to 1000 copies. Ars Libri 32-665 1983 $85

CORBETT, J. S.   Official History of the Great War. London, 1920-31. 8vo, orig. cloth. 59 maps and plans (mostly coloured & folding) and 107 maps and plans (mostly colored & all folding) in the 4 separate map cases. 5 vols. in 9. Very slightly soiled and worn. Complete set, with map No. 2 in vol. 3 map case replaced with colored facsimile. Good. Edwards 1042-42 1983 £175

CORDELL, EUGENE   Medical Annals of Maryland. Baltimore, 1903. First edition. 8vo. Orig. cloth. Fye H-3-115 1983 $40

CORDELL, EUGENE   Medical Annals of Maryland. Baltimore, 1903. 8vo. Orig. cloth. Ex-library. Fye H-3-116 1983 $40

CORDIER, HENRI   Bibliotheca Japonica... Paris: Imprimerie Nationale, 1912 (1931 reprint). Cloth, fine in somewhat torn dw and worn slip case. Dawson 470-75 1983 $45

CORDIER, HENRI   Bibliotheca Sinica... New York: Burt Franklin, (1968). Deuxieme edition, six vols. in five, cloth. Reprint of the 1904-22 edition. Dawson 470-76 1983 $150

CORDINER, CHARLES   Remarkable Ruins, and Romantic Prospects, of North Britain. Published by I. & J. Taylor, 1795. 2 vols. in 1, 4to, engraved titles with vignettes, frontis. to vol. 1, and 97 other plates, each with a leaf of explanatory letter press, orig. calf, rubbed, rebacked preserving the orig. spine. Bickersteth 75-20 1983 £90

CORDINER, JAMES   A Description of Ceylon. London, 1807. Map, plan, 23 plates, 2 folding. 3 Cont. watercolour portraits of Ceylon characters tipped-in. 2 vols. 4to. Some offsetting, occasional spotting. This copy belonged to Sir Robert Mowbray and has his bookplate in each volume. Good. Edwards 1044-147 1983 £250

CORDINER, JAMES   A Description of Ceylon. 1807. 2 vols., 25 engravings, half calf, new title labels inset on red and black morocco, some foxing and browning throughout. K Books 307-55 1983 £130

CORDRY, DONALD BUSH   Costumes and Weaving of the Zoque Indians of Chiapas, Mexico. Los Angeles: Southwest Museum, 1941. Folding map. 39 illus. 4to. Wrappers. Ars Libri 34-192 1983 $27.50

CORDUS, VALERIUS   Das Dispensatorium. Mittenwald, 1934.
Facsimile of 1546 edition. 8vo. Quarter-parchment. With inscription on title. Gurney JJ-83 1983 £25

CORELLI, MARIE   Barabbas. Methuen, 1893. First edition,
3 vols., half titles. Orig. dark green remainder cloth, spine gilt.
Sl. stain to half title vol. II, otherwise very good. Jarndyce 30-335
1983 £30

CORELLI, MARIE   Boy. A Sketch. London: Hutchinson & Co.,
1900. First edition. Orig. red cloth. Edges of spine a little rubbed.
Publisher's tipped-in announcement facing the title-page. Very good.
MacManus 277-1125 1983 $40

CORELLI, MARIE   The Master-Christian. London: Methuen
& Co., 1900. First edition. Orig. cloth. Covers lightly dust-soiled.
Edges of spine worn. Former owner's signature on front flyleaf.
MacManus 277-1128 1983 $22.50

CORELLI, MARIE   The Murder of Delicia. London: Skeffington, 1896. First edition. Orig. cloth. Prelims foxed. Fine.
MaxManus 277-1129 1983 $20

CORELLI, MARIE   "Temporal Power". London: Methuen & Co.,
1902. First edition. Orig. cloth. Very good. MacManus 277-1130
1983 $30

CORELLI, MARIE   The Treasure of Heaven. London: Archibald Constable and Co., 1906. First edition. Orig. cloth. Edges a
bit worn. Some light foxing. Small stain on spine. Good. MacManus
277-1133 1983 $35

CORELLI, MARIE   The Treasure of Heaven. London: Archibald Constable and Co., 1906. First edition. Orig. decorated cloth.
Corners and edges very slightly worn. Endpapers browned. Little
minor foxing. Good. MacManus 277-1132 1983 $35

CORELLI, MARIE   Ziska. The Problem of a Wicked Soul.
N.Y.: Stone & Kimball, 1897. First American edition. Orig. cloth.
Fine. MacManus 277-1136 1983 $45

CORELLI, MARIE   Ziska. The Problem of a Wicked Soul.
N.Y.: Stone & Kimball, 1897. First American edition. Orig. decorated
cloth. Very good. MacManus 277-1134 1983 $30

COREY, ALBERT B.   The Crisis of 1830-1842 in Canadian-
American Relations. New Haven: Yale Un. Press; Toronto: Ryerson;
London: OUP, 1941. 25cm. 3 maps. Mapped endpapers. Very good.
McGahern 53-35 1983 $45

CORKE, H. E.   Wild Flowers as They Grow. 1912-14.
175 coloured plates from photographs, 7 vols., 8vo, cloth. Wheldon
160-1591 1983 £25

CORKERY, DANIEL   The Hidden Ireland. Dublin: M.H.
Gill, 1925. Second edition, 8vo, orig. cloth, in dust wrapper. Fenning
61-82 1983 £16.50

CORKERY, DANIEL   The Stormy Hills. London, (1929).
First edition, d.w. Argosy 714-189 1983 $20

CORLE, EDWARD   Burro Alley. New York: Duell, (1946).
Cloth and pictorial boards. One of 1,500 numbered copies, designed
by Merle Armitage, and signed by the author. A fine copy in very
slightly used dust jacket. Reese 20-45 1983 $50

CORLE, EDWIN   Burro Alley. New York, (1938). 1st
ed. Signed by author. Clark 741-370 1983 $24.50

CORLE, EDWIN   Burro Alley. New York, (1946). First
edition. One of 1,500 signed by Corle. 3-line presentation inscrip.
signed by Merle Armitage, who designed the book. Decorated yellow
boards and black cloth. Fine in worn jacket. Bradley 65-52 1983
$45

CORLE, EDWIN   The Royal Highway. Indianapolis,
(1949). 1st ed. End and other maps; illus. Autographed. Clark
741-103 1983 $25

CORNARO, LEWIS   Discourses on a Sober and Temperate
Life. Printed for Benjamin White, 1768. 8vo, calf antique with
morocco label. Bickersteth 75-219 1983 £30

CORNARO, LEWIS   Sure Methods of Attaining a Long and
Healthful Life. Edinburgh: Printed by A. Donaldson, 1777. 12mo,
cont. calf, joints cracked, spine worn at head and foot. Bickersteth
77-268 1983 £15

CORNELL, H.   Das Hogfeldt-Buch. Berlin: Neff, 1937.
Title vignette. 36 colour plates & 17 text illus. Light grey cloth,
slight stain. Colour pictorial dust wrappers. Greer 40-111 1983
£25

CORNER, GEORGE   The Autobiography of Benjamin Rush.
Princeton, 1948. First edition. 8vo. Orig. binding. Dust wrapper.
Fye H-3-936 1983 $40

CORNER, GEORGE   The Autobiography of Benjamin Rush.
Princeton, 1948. First edition. 8vo. Orig. binding. Ex-library.
Fye H-3-937 1983 $30

CORNFORD, F. MC DONALD   Plato's Cosmology. London, 1948.
8vo, cloth. Salloch 385-682 1983 $20

CORNFORD, FRANCES   Autumn Midnight. London: The Poetry
Bookshop, 1923. First edition. Illus. by Eric Gill. Orig. decorated
wrappers. Presentation copy, inscribed on the front inner wrapper to
"Walter de la Mare from Frances Cornford Xmas 1923." Wrappers slightly
dust-soiled. Printed at S. Dominic's Press, Ditchling, Sussex, on
hand-made paper. Fine. MacManus 277-1137 1983 $350

CORNFORD, FRANCES   Autumn Midnight. London: The Poetry
Bookshop, 1923. First edition. Orig. wrappers. Illus. by Eric Gill.
Fine. MacManus 277-1138 1983 $185

CORNFORD, FRANCES   Different Days. London: Published by
Leonard & Virginia Woolf at The Hogarth Press, 1928. First edition.
Orig. decorated boards. Presentation copy, inscribed on the verso
of the front free endpaper to "Walter de la Mare from Frances Cornford,
May 1928." Spine darkened. Fine. MacManus 277-1141 1983 $185

CORNFORD, FRANCES   Poems from the Russian. London: Faber
& Faber Ltd., (1943). First edition. Orig. cloth. Dust jacket.
From the library of Walter de la Mare. Fine. MacManus 277-1143 1983
$35

CORNFORD, FRANCES   Spring Morning. London: The Poetry
Bookshop, 1915. First edition. Woodcuts by Gwen Raverat. Orig.
pictorial wrappers (a bit worn). Fine. MacManus 277-1146 1983 $85

CORNFORD, FRANCES   Spring Morning. London: The Poetry
Bookshop, 1915. First edition. Woodcuts by G. Raverat. Orig. pict.
green wrappers. Walter de la Mare's copy, with his annotations for a
review in pencil on the last page of text: "true spring freshness,
quite rare gift,...she has something new to say, woodcuts." Wrappers
somewhat worn at edges. Good. MacManus 277-1145 1983 $75

CORNISH, F. T. W.   Letters and Sketches... Eton, 1902.
Portrait. 2 plates. Text illus. Boards, vellum spine. Good.
Edwards 1044-148 1983 £30

CORNISH, VAUGHAN   The Panama Canal and Its Makers. London,
1909. 8vo. Signet Library copy. 62 illus. on 31 plates. Folding
coloured map at end (3 small tears at fold, 1 repaired). Publisher's
ads. on verso of half-title. Slightly soiled. Spine faded. Uncut.
Orig. cloth. Good. Edwards 1042-43 1983 £15

CORNWAILE, JOHN   Yvonne. London: Thomas Burleigh, 1900.
First edition. Orig. wrappers (worn & soiled). A. C. Swinburne's
copy, with his bookplate on the inner wrapper, and a letter from the
author sending his book to Swinburne. Front cover nearly detached.
MacManus 280-5021 1983 $75

CORNWALL, BARRY   Mirandola. A Tragedy. London: John
Warren, 1821. First edition. Orig. grey wrappers with printed label.
Covers a bit worn. Spine partly deteriorated. Very good. MacManus
277-1151 1983 $135

CORNWALL, BRUCE   Life Sketch of Pierre Barlow Cornwall.
San F., 1906. Illus. Orig. half morocco, mended. First edition.
Ginsberg 47-257 1983 $150

CORNWALLIS, CAROLINE FRANCIS An Introduction to Practical Organic
Chemistry. London: Pickering, 1843. 8vo. Orig. green cloth with
paper label. Very good. Zeitlin 264-89 1983 $50

CORNISH, C. J.   Sir William Henry Flower KCB, a personal
memoir. 1904. 5 plates, 8vo, full green calf, gilt, front joint
slightly cracked. Wheldon 160-226 1983 £20

CORP, HARRIET   Cottage Sketches. London: for E.
Blackader..., 1812. First edition. 2 vols. 12mo. Cont. half calf,
one joint repaired, some wear. Heath 48-375 1983 £90

CORP, WILLIAM   An Essay on the Changes produced in
the Body by Operations of the Mind. London: James Ridgway, 1791.
First edition. 8vo. Cont. half-calf. Adverts. leaf. Gurney 90-
36 1983 £150

CORTESI, LUIGI   Iacopo da Balsemo miniature. Bergamo:
Edizioni "Monumenta Bergomensia", 1972. 181 illus. (partly in color).
Small folio. Leather. Ars Libri 33-187 1983 $85

CORRY, JOHN   The English Metropolis; or, London in
the Year 1820. London: Sherwood, Neely & Jones, 1820. First (only)
edition, 8vo, cont. half calf gilt, marbled boards. A very good
copy. A scarce title. Trebizond 18-40 1983 $175

CORSER, THOMAS   Collectanea Anglo-Poetica. Printed
for the Chetham Society, 1860-73. First (only) edition, 11 vols.,
4to, original decorated cloth, partly uncut copy. Wear to some spines,
otherwise a very good set. Trebizond 18-7 1983 $285

CORVINUS, LAURENTIUS   Cosmographia dans manuductionem in
tabulas Ptholomei. (Basel: Nicolaus Kesler, not before 1496).
Small 4to (196 x 135 mm). Old vellum. From the library of Harrison
D. Horblit, with his bookplate. Final blank not present. Closely
cut, shaving some side-notes. Last leaf slightly wormed. Kraus
164-45 1983 $5,800

CORVO, FREDERICK BARON, PSEUD.
Please turn to
ROLFE, FREDERICK WILLIAM

CORWIN, THOMAS   Oregon-Location of Seat of Government,
etc. Letter from...Transmitting Copies of Correspondence Between
that Department and E. Hamilton, Sec. of the Territory of Oregon.
Wash., 1852. First edition. Dbd. Ginsberg 47-723 1983 $25

CORWIN, THOMAS   Report of the Officers Constituting
the Light-House Board. Wash., 1852. Illus. 40 plates, mostly
folded. Orig. full calf. First edition. Ginsberg 46-407 1983
$125

CORY, ISAAC PRESTON   Metaphysical inquiry into the method,
objects and result of ancient and modern philosophy. London:
Pickering, 1833. First edition. 8vo. Orig. blue cloth. Printed
paper label. Spine faded. Ximenes 63-345 1983 $75

CORY, WILLIAM JOHNSON   Ionica. London: Allen, 1891. First
of this edition. Orig. cloth. With a transcript of Edmund Gosse's
essay on "Ionica" extracted from "Gossip in a Library" laid in.
Fine. MacManus 277-1152 1983 $45

CORYAT, THOMAS   Coryat's Crudites. London, 1776.
8 engravings. Woodcuts in text. A few gatherings miss sewn. 3 vols.
Speckled calf, rebacked, some slight wear. 8vo. Good. Edwards 1044-
151 1983 £225

CORYAT, THOMAS   Thomas Coriate Traveller for the English
Wits. (London, 1810?). Small 4to, fine large woodcut on the title.
2 other large text woodcuts, old half calf with marbled boards,
rubbed, joints cracked. Headlines of second leaf shaved, short tear
in title, no front or back free end papers. Bickersteth 77-18 1983
£80

CORWIN, NORMAN   Untitled and Other Radio Dramas. New
York, (1946). 8vo. Cloth. Presentation inscription by author. Fine
copy in near perfect dj. In Our Time 156-169 1983 $40

CORY, WILLIAM   Extracts from the Letters and Journals.
Oxford, printed for the subscribers, 1897. Front. port. Subscribers'
list. Orig. half green morocco, green cloth boards. Jarndyce 30-958
1983 £18

CORY, WILLIAM   Ionica. George Allen, 1891. First
collected edition. Erratum slip. Orig. light blue cloth, v.g.
Jarndyce 30-675 1983 £10.50

COSGRAVE, GEORGE   Early California Justice. San
Francisco, Grabhorn Press, 1948. First edition. 4to, 7 tipped-in
facs. plates. Orig. cloth, paper label. One of 400 copies. Very
good. Houle 22-1036 1983 $80

COSOMATI, ETTORE   La Calabria. Milan, 1928. Color
plates, many illus. Tall folio, wrs. Salloch 385-341 1983 $35

COSSA, A.   Ricerche Chimiche e Microscopiche su
Roccie e Minerali d'Italia . Turin, 1881. 12 plates (11 coloured),
4to, half morocco. Wheldon 160-1375 1983 £20

COSSERY, ALBERT   Men God Forgot. (CA, 1946). Boards,
cloth spine, cover slightly rubbed and lightly soiled, very good.
Quill & Brush 54-320 1983 $40

COSSLEY-BATT, JILL L.   The Last of the California Rangers.
New York, 1928. Illus. 1st ed. Scarce. Jenkins 153-142 1983 $45

COSSLEY-BATT, JILL L.   The Last of the California Rangers.
New York, 1928. 1st ed. Portrait frontispiece, pictorial end papers,
full-page illus. Blue cloth, gilt. Extremities lightly worn.
Scarce. Bradley 63-37 1983 $30

COSTANTINI, VINCENZO   Guido Reni. Milano: Alpes, 1928.
32 plates. Large 8vo. Wrappers. Ars Libri 33-304 1983 $27.50

COSTE, H.   Flore descriptive et illustree de la
France. Paris, (1901-06) 1937. 3 vols., royal 8vo, cloth, 4354
text-figures. Unchanged reprint of the original edition. The
coloured map is not present. Wheldon 160-1663 1983 £55

COSTELLO, LOUISA   Jacques Coeur, the French Argonaut, and
his Times. Richard Bentley, 1847. 8vo, portrait, text illus. Half
calf, spine gilt. Bickersteth 75-123 1983 £12

COSTELLO, LOUISA   The Queen's Poinsoner. Richard Bentley,
1841. First edition, half titles, orig. boards, blue cloth spines,
paper labels a little chipped. Jarndyce 30-336 1983 £60

COSTELLO, LOUISA   Specimens of the Early Poetry of France.
London: William Pickering, 1835. First edition. 8vo. Full polished
calf, three-line gilt border, fully gilt panelled spine with two
morocco labels, gilt, inner gilt dentelles, edges gilt, by Riviere.
4 hand-coloured plates, heightened with gold, done after the
style of an illuminated MSS., each plate accompanied by a black
and white proof. Traylen 94-218 1983 £135

COSTER, GEORGE T.   Lorrin, and Other Poems. W. Kent,
1859. First edition, 32 pp ads. Orig. green cloth, spine gilt,
v.g. Presentation inscription from 'J.C.?' Ms. poem loosely
inserted. Jarndyce 30-678 1983 £15

COSTIGAN, ARTHUR WILLIAM   Sketches of Society and Manners in
Portugal. London: T. Vernon, n.d. (1787). 1st ed., 8vo, 2 vols.,
cont. calf, morocco labels. Two owner's names on flyleaves; a fine
copy. Trebizond 18-136 1983 $175

COSTUMES Francais de 1200 a 1715. London, n.d. Gilt-dec. leather,
a.e.g., rebacked with orig. (chipped) spine laid onto cloth, inner
hinges reinforced. Drawn on stone by G. Scharf, with 100 aquatint
costume plates. King 46-426 1983 $350

THE COSTUMES of the Members of the University of Cambridge. London,
published by H. Hyde. (N.d., about 1840). Strip of paper 72 inches
long and 4-1/2 inches wide engraved on one side with 47 different
figures, hand coloured, folding concertina-wise into its original
cloth cover blocked in blind and gilt. Bickersteth 75-124 1983 £70

COTT, H. B.   Adaptive Coloration in Animals.
(1940). Coloured frontispiece, 48 half tone plates and numerous text-
figures. Royal 8vo, cloth. Wheldon 160-474 1983 £25

COTTERELL, HOWARD HERSCHEL   National Types of Old Pewter. Boston,
Antiques, Inc., 1925. Limited ed. 4to, orig. boards, cloth back.
Morrill 286-109 1983 $20

COTTERILL, H. B.   Ancient Greece. London, 1913. Maps.
Salloch 385-219 1983 $25

COTTING, JOHN RUGGLES   An Introcution to Chemistry...
Boston: Ewer, 1822. Roy. 12mo in sixes. Cont. tree calf. 5
plates, folding table. First edition. Worn, front cover detached.
A very good copy. Zeitlin 264-90 1983 $120

COTTLE, JOSEPH   Early Recollections... London, Longman,
et al., 1837. 2 vols. 12mo. 6 orig. plates, extra-illustrated with
21 fine portraits and views. 3/4 olive green crushed levant morocco
& marbled boards, spines fully gilt with floral pattern, marbled endpapers, aeg. 1st ed. Very fine binding. O'Neal 50-13 1983 $250

COTTON, CHARLES   The Genuine Poetical Works... London:
Bonwicke & Wilkin, 1725. Plates. 2nd ed. Contemporary calf, rebacked,
label, gilt. This ed. corrects the errors of the first. Very good
copy. Jenkins 155-252 1983 $45

COTTON, CHARLES   The Genuine Poetical Works of Charles
Cotton, Esq. 1765. Fifth edition, corrected. 9 copper engravings,
including the folded plate of Chatsworth. K Books 301-58 1983 £46

COTTON, CHARLES   Lyrical Poems. Cottingham Near Hull,
Editor, 1903. Ed. limited to 200 copies signed by Tutin, the editor.
Small 8vo. Orig. vellum. Lightly dust-soiled. Morrill 289-297
1983 $50

COTTON, CHARLES   Poems from the Works of Charles Cotton.
London: The Poetry Bookshop, (1922). First Limited edition. Newly
decorated by C. L. Fraser. Orig. white buckram. One of 300 copies
printed on hand-made paper. Cloth a little dust-soiled. Good. Mac-
Manus 278-1090 1983 $50

COTTON, EDWARD   A Voice from Waterloo. Brussels, 1895.
Eighth edition, revised and enlarged. Sm. 8vo. Orig. red decorated
cloth gilt. 2 frontis. plates, 2 other plates and 2 coloured maps
(1 folding), 7 text illus. Very slightly worn. Ink inscription on
front endpaper. Good. Edwards 1042-310 1983 £20

COTTON, EVAN   East Indiamen. London, 1949. Coloured
frontis. and 11 plates. 8vo. Orig. cloth. Good. Edwards 1044-153
1983 £30

COTTON, HENRY   A Typographical Gazetteer. Oxford:
University Press, 1831. Second edition. 8vo. Full leather,
gilt decorated spine, all edges marbled. Front and back covers
and the first few and last few pages are water stained. Oak Knoll
48-115 1983 $75

COTTON, WILLIAM   The Story of the Drama in Exeter,
During its Best Period, 1787 to 1823. London: Hamilton, Adams &
Co., 1887. Blue cloth, sl. stained and worn. Front free endpaper
loose. Bookplates, one of the American actor William Winter;
endpaper signed by Winter. Karmiole 72-94 1983 $35

COTTON States and International Exposition. (Portland, Me.: Leighton,
1895). Thin 8vo, dec. cloth, accordian-folding photographic illus.
Argosy 710-151 1983 $45

COTTRELL, LEONARD   Mountains of Pharoah. N.Y., Rinehart
(1956). First edition. Illus. with photographs and diagrams. 3/4
maroon morocco over marbled boards, edges gilt; gilt stamped pyramid
devices on spine. Fine. Houle 22-1209 1983 $95

COUCH, JONATHAN   A History of the Fishes of the British
Islands. 1877-78. 252 coloured plates, 4 vols., roy. 8vo, original
cloth. Spines worn and a little foxing, but a good set. Wheldon
160-18 1983 £250

COUCH, JONATHAN   Illustrations of instinct deduced from
the habits of British animals. London: John Van Voorst, 1847.
12mo. First edition. Orig. dark brown cloth. Very good copy.
Ximenes 63-520 1983 $45

COUCH, JONATHAN   Illustrations of Instinct. 1847.
Cr. 8vo, cloth (slightly worn, joints splitting). Wheldon 160-475
1983 £18

COULDREY, O. J.   South Indian Hours. London, 1924.
3 coloured and 19 other plates. Edges foxed. 8vo. Orig. cloth.
Good. Edwards 1044-155 1983 £16

COULOMB, C. A.   Theorie des Machines Simples... Paris:
Bachelier, 1821. 4to. Cont. half green straight-grained morocco.
10 folding plates. Fine copy. Gurney 90-37 1983 £150

COULTER, E. MERTON   The Civil War and Readjustment in
Kentucky. Chapel Hill: University of North Carolina Press, 1926.
First edition. Dust jacket. Fine. Jenkins 152-843 1983 $75

COULTER, E. MERTON   Georgia's Disputed Ruins. Chapel
Hill, 1937. Illus, dw. One of 750 copies with type melted thereafter.
Argosy 710-200 1983 $35

COUNTRY Dances, 1815. Printed by Goulding, (1815). With proper
figures & directions to each dance. Title-lead and 12-pages, narrow
oblong 12mo. Fenning 62-84 1983 £22.50

THE COUNTY. London: Smith, Elder, 1889. First edition. 2 vols.
8vo. Orig. dark blue-green cloth. A bit rubbed. Very good copy.
Ximenes 63-144 1983 $150

THE COUNTY Court Houses of America. Princeton, 1982. 2 vols. Each
vol. may be ordered separately at $275. Boswell 7-48 1983 $550

COUPLAND, R.   Kirk on the Zambesi. Oxford: Oxford
Univ. Press, 1928. 8vo. Map. 15 plates. Orig. red cloth in dustwrapper. Adelson Africa-180 1983 $50

COURNOS, JOHN   Wandering Women. New York: Boni Paper
Books, 1930. 8vo. Wraps. Fine copy. In Our Time 156-170 1983
$20

COURTHION, PIERRE   Courbet. Paris: Floury, 1931. 96
collotype plates. Large 4to. Wrappers. Dust jacket. Ars Libri
32-123 1983 $65

COURTILZ, GATIEN DE, SIEUR DE SANDRAS   The French Spy. For. R.
Basset, 1700. First English edition. 8vo., modern vellum. Title
foxed, many head-lines cut into. Hannas 69-38 1983 £95

THE COURTLAND F. Bishop Library. N.Y.: American Art. Assn., Anderson
Galleries, 1938. 4 vols. 4to, illus. Printed wraps. Complete set.
O'Neal 50-109 1983 $125

COURTNEY, JOSEPH W.   The Multiple Personality of Dr. Guy
Patin and Gabriel Naude, M.D. New York, 1924. 4to. Three-quarter
cloth over marbled boards. Presentation copy. Oak Knoll 49-136
1983 $20

COUSINS, FRANK   Colonial Architecture. Series I:
Fifty Salem Doorways. Garden City, 1912. Photographic plates,
loose as issued in cloth folder. Folio. Argosy 710-99 1983 $50

COUSSEMAKER, EDMOND   Histoire de l'Harmonie au Moyen Age.
Paris, 1852. 38 facs. plates in color and 44 pp. of transcriptions.
4to, cl. Binding new. Salloch 387-302 1983 $500

COUSTURIER, LUCIE   P. Signac. Paris: Editions des
"Cahiers d'Aujourd'hui"/G. Cres, 1922. 20 plates. Text illus.
4to. Wrappers. Ars Libri 32-635 1983 $65

COUTINHO, A. X. P.   Flora de Portugal. (Lisbon, 1939),
Facsimile Reprint, 1974. 8vo, cloth, second edition. Wheldon 160-
1664 1983 £52

COUTTS, FRANCIS   Musa Verticordia. London: John Lane,
The Bodley Head, 1905. First edition. Orig. cloth. Fine. MacManus
277-1154 1983 $35

COVARRUBIAS, MIGUEL   Island of Bali. N.Y., 1937. First
edition. Photos by R. Cavarrubias. Two-tone cloth. Slightly frayed
dust wrapper. Numerous drawings by author. Very good. King 45-393
1983. $45

COVENTRY, FRANCIS   The History of Pompey the Little,
or, the Life and Adventures of a Lap-Dag. Waltham Saint Lawrence,
1926. Introduction by Arundell Del Re. 8vo, linen-backed bds.
Wood-engravings by David Jones. One of 400 copies. A very nice
copy with the bookplate of Samuel Kahn, designed by Robert Gibbings.
Perata 27-48 1983 $150

COVERTE, ROBERT   The Travels of Captain Robert Coverte.
Philadelphia: Privately printed, 1931. Frontis. + folding map.
Edition ltd. to 150 numbered copies. Cloth spine over boards.
Karmiole 73-33 1983 $50

COWAN, BUD   Range Rider. New York, 1930. Illus.
Dust jacket. 1st ed. Fine copy. Jenkins 153-143 1983 $35

COWAN, ROBERT ELSWORTH
Please turn to
COWAN, BUD (1869-)

COWAN, ROBERT ERNEST   A Bibliography of the History of
California and the Pacific West... Columbus: Long's College Book
Co., 1952. Reprint of the 1914 ed. New ed. Cloth, lightly used.
Dawson 470-78 1983 $75

COWAN, ROBERT ERNEST   A Bibliography of the History of
California, 1510-1930. San Francisco, Nash, 1933. 3 vols. 4to,
linen backed orig. boards, paper labels. Second edition. Ginsberg
46-89 1983 $300

COWAN, ROBERT ERNEST   A Bibliography of the History of
California, 1510-1930. San F., Nash, 1933. 3 vols. bound in one.
Illus. Half morocco. Ginsberg 47-56 1983 $250

COWAN, SAMUEL   The Gowrie Conspiracy and its Official
Narrative. 1902. 8vo, frontis. and 2 folding plans, cloth.
Bickersteth 77-111 1983 £24

COWAN, SAMUEL   The Last Days of Mary Stuart and the
Journal of Bourgoyne her Physician. 1907. 8vo, 12 plates, cloth.
Bickersteth 77-112 1983 £18

COWAN, SAMUEL   Laurel Leaves. Belfast: M'Caw Stevenson
& Orr, 1885. First edition, large 12mo, orig. green cloth, gilt, a
fine copy. Fenning 61-83 1983 £16.50

COWAN, SAMUEL   Mary Queen of Scots and Who Wrote the
Casket Letters? 1901. 2 vols., 8vo, 19 plates, orig. cloth. First
edition. Bickersteth 77-110 1983 £22

COWARD, NOEL   Cavalcade. London, (1932). First
edition, illus., 8vo, yellow cloth; dust soiled. Argosy 714-194 1983
$25

COWARD, NOEL   Play Parade. N.Y.: Garden City Pub.
Co., Inc., (1933). First edition. Orig. cloth. Dust jacket (spine
faded, edges a bit worn). Bookplate. Very good. MacManus 277-1155
1983 $40

COWARD, NOEL   Present Indicative. GC, 1937. Fine in
very good, slightly soiled dustwrapper. Quill & Brush 54-322 1983
$35

COWARD, NOEL   Private Lives. Lon., 1930. Flys offset
from dustwrapper, spine slightly faded, very good in slightly frayed
and soiled, near very good dustwrapper. Quill & Brush 54-323 1983
$125

COWARD, NOEL   Sheet music: I'll See you Again.
London, 1939. 4to, pictorial colored wrap. Argosy 714-196 1983
$30

COWARD, NOEL   A Withered Nosegay. Lon., (1922). Drawings by Lorn MacNaughtan, near fine. Quill & Brush 54-321 1983 $60

COWDEN-CLARKE, MARY   My Long Life, an Autobiographic Sketch.
T. Fisher Unwin, 1896. First edition, half title, front. illus.
Orig. green cloth, a little faded, t.e.g. Jarndyce 31-492 1983
£20

COWDERY, CHARLOTTE   Island Leaflets. Longmans, 1871.
First edition, orig. brown cloth, rubbed. Inscribed presentation
copy from the author. Jarndyce 30-749 1983 £10.50

COWDRY, EDMUND V.   Human Biology and Racial Welfare. N.Y.,
1930. Argosy 713-126 1983 $75

COWLES, FLORENCE C.   Early Algona. Des Moines, 1929.
Illus. Orig. cloth. First edition. Ginsberg 47-359 1983 $50

COWLEY, ABRAHAM   Poemata Latina. In quibus Continentur... London: T. Roycroft, 1668. First collected edition.
8vo. Cont. calf, morocco label. Engraved portrait by Faithorne
(mounted on fly-leaf). Spine a little defective. Traylen 94-219
1983 £65

COWLEY, ABRAHAM   The Works of... Printed by J.M. for
Henry Herringman, 1672. Third edition. With an engraved portrait by
Faithorne, folio, cont. calf, neatly and recently rebacked, with
some very light signs of use, but a very good copy. Fenning 62-85
1983 £65

COWLEY, HANNAH   Albina, Countess Raimond; a tragedy.
London: printed by T. Spilsbury; for J. Dodsley, etc., 1779. 8vo,
disbound, 1st ed. Ximenes 64-148 1983 $75

COWLEY, MALCOLM   Blue Juniata. New York, 1929. First
edition. Top and tail of spine rubbed, otherwise an excellent copy.
Gekoski 2-37 1983 £25

COWLEY, MALCOLM   Blue Juniata. NY, 1929. Edges of spine
slightly worn, otherwise good or better. Quill & Brush 54-325 1983
$30

COWLEY, MALCOLM   Exile's Return. N.Y.: Limited
Editions Club, 1981. Large 8vo, printed boards, silk cloth back;
publisher's box. Illus. with cont. photographs by Berenice Abbott &
others. Limited edition, signed by Cowley & by Abbott. Argosy 714-
200 1983 $85

COWLING, MARY JO   Geography of Denton County. Dallas:
Banks Upshaw and Company, 1936. Illus. 1st ed. Scarce. Jenkins
153-601 1983 $85

COWPER, WILLIAM   Anatomia Corporum Humanorum centum et
Quatuordecim Tabulis...Curante Guilielmo Dundass. Arnold Langerak,
Leyden, 1739. Folio, with engraved title and 114 engraved plates;
cont. mottled calf, red and green morocco panels on spine, joints
repaired. First edition in Latin. Quaritch NS 5-26 1983 $2,000

COWPER, WILLIAM   The Diverting History of John Gilpin.
Routledge, n.d., (ca. 1888). Illus. by H. Rosa. Illus. title page
& numerous illus. in green, brown, black & white. Pages unnumbered,
printed on one side only. Gold cl. backed decor. bds. Contemp. insc.
fr. ep., fr. ep. creased, bds. sl. worn at corners & edges, bkstrip
worn top/bottom, vg. Hodgkins 27-51 1983 £20

COWPER, WILLIAM   John Gilpin. E. Nister, n.d. Colour
frontis. Title vignette. 7 colour plates. 3 full-page (1 double)
& 12 text illus., browned. Green pictorial cloth. Greer 40-106
1983 £12.75

COWPER, WILLIAM   Memoir of the Early Life. R. Edwards,
1816. 2nd edition, front. port. Uncut. Orig. blue boards, paper
spine and label. Sl. worn, v.g. Jarndyce 30-959 1983 £28

COWPER, WILLIAM   Poems... London, J. Johnson, 1782-1785.
2 vols. 8vo. Full polished tan calf, by Bedford, with elaborately
gilt spines, green morocco labels, gilt board edges & inner dentelles,
aeg. 1st eds., 1st issue. Rare half-title reading "Poems, vol. II"
is present in the 2nd vol., and with the rare preface by Newton in vol.
I. Very fine. O'Neal 50-14 1983 $1,500

COWPER, WILLIAM   Poems. London: Printed for J. Johnson
& Co., 1810. New edition. 2 vols. 8vo. Full red cont. morocco, gilt,
with marbled endpapers, a.e.g., with fore-edge paintings on each vol.
Cont. and later owner's signatures and annotation on flyleaves. Covers
a little rubbed. In an open-faced cloth slipcase. MacManus 278-1937
1983 $750

COWPER, WILLIAM   Poems. Printed for J. Johnson (by T.
Bensley), 1811. With the 8 Fuseli plates, 2 vols., 8vo, cont. diced
calf, gilt bordered sides, gilt spines, with double lettering pieces.
A very small area of worm in one joint, but thoroughly sound. Fenning
60-72 1983 £45

COWPER, WILLIAM   Poems, the Early Productions of
William Cowper. London: Baldwin, Cradock, 1825. 1st ed., 12mo,
original boards, rebacked, half-title not called for, uncut copy.
Some light soiling, but a very good copy. Trebizond 18-21 1983
$175

COWPER, WILLIAM   Table Talk, and Other Poems. John
Sharpe by C. Whittingham, 1817. First edition, 12mo, engr. title (a
little foxed). Calf, sl. rubbed, gilt borders and spine, maroon
labels. Jarndyce 31-493 1983 £20

COWPER, WILLIAM   The Task, a Poem. London: James Nisbet
& Co., 1855. First edition. Illus. by Birket Foster. Orig. decorated
cloth. Bookplate of John Lowe. Fine. MacManus 277-1156 1983 $185

COX, ANNIE F.   Baby's Kingdom. Boston, 1885. Designed
and illustrated by Annie F. Cox. Colored pictorial scenes. Square
8vo, orig. full morocco. Comprising colored plates, stanzas of
poetry, and blank leaves. Morrill 286-589 1983 $25

COX, EARNEST SEVIER   White America. White America Society.
Richmond, VA (1925). Cloth, very good in worn and soiled dw.
Special reprint for members of Congress. King 46-11 1983 $35

COX, EDWARD GODFREY   A Reference Guide to the Literature of
Travel. Seattle, 1938. First edition. Volume Two (of 3). 4to, fine.
Morrill 290-79 1983 $50

COX, H.   Journal of a Residence in the Burman
Empire. London, 1821. First edition. Folding coloured frontis.
4 coloured plates. Sion College Library Stamp on verso of title.
New quarter calf, morocco label. 8vo. Good. Edwards 1044-156 1983
£285

COX, HOMERSHAM   A History of the Reform Bill of 1866 &
1867. Longmans, Green, 1868. First edition, ads. Orig. green
cloth, spine darkened. Jarndyce 31-355 1983 £10.50

COX, ISAAC   The Annals of Trinity County. Eugene,
Oregon, John Henry Nash, 1940. 4to, 2 plates. Cloth-backed boards,
paper label. Acetate jacket. Slipcase. Ltd. to 350 copies.
Signed by John Henry Nash and Harold C. Holmes. Houle 22-1037 1983
$120

COX, JAMES   Historical and Biographical Record of
the Cattle Industry and Cattlemen of Texas and Adjacent Territory.
St. Louis, 1895. Colored frontispiece, repaired, numerous illus.
Small folio, orig. pictorial gilt leather, expertly rebacked. 1st ed.
Rare. Jenkins 153-758 1983 $4500

COX, JAMES   Historical and Biographical Record
of the Cattle Industry. N.Y., 1959. 2 volumes. Boxed. Folio.
Illus. Complete facsimile of the 1895 original. Limited to 500
copies. Fine introduction by J. Frank Dobie. One of the vaunted
"Big Four" cattle and range books. Jenkins 151-49 1983 $200

COX, JOHN EDMUND   Musical recollections of the last half-
century. London: Tinsley, 1872. First edition. 2 vols. 8vo.
Orig. blue cloth. A bit rubbed, spines a little dark. A very good
copy. Ximenes 63-327 1983 $75

COX, PALMER   The Brownies Around the World. New
York, (1894). 1st ed. 4to. Illus. by author. Orig. pictorial
boards. Binding rubbed; backstrip slightly torn; some pencil
scribbling in text. Morrill 289-298 1983 $25

COX, PALMER   Queer People. Griffith, Farran, nd
(ca. 1895). Illus. by author. 1st Eng. edn., unnumbered, numerous
b&w illus. Yellow glazed col. decor. bds. Bkstrip. some wear, corners
worn, 3 pp. have tear margin at bottom, vg. Hodgkins 27-52 1983
£25

COX, PALMER   That Stanley! New York: Art Printing,
1878. 1st ed. Stapled as issued, but lacking the wrappers and last
few pages chipped at lower corner, else a very good copy of a scarce
title. Jenkins 155-254 1983 $35

COX, RICHARD   Hibernia Anglicana. London, Clark,
1689-1690. Folio. Four parts in 1, including a letter to the author
and appendices. The second title in red and black. Repairs to title
page, damage to the dedication with loss of text, staining to text,
else good. Modern cloth. Houle 21-263 1983 $55

COX, SANDFORD C.   Recollections of the Early Settlement
of the Wabash Valley. Lafayette, Ind., 1860. Stamped cloth. Very
good. Reese 19-165 1983 $125

COX, W. H. M.   The Library of Edmund Gosse... London:
Dulau, 1924. Frontispiece, cloth, top edge gilt, a few leaves
roughly opened, slight use externally. Dawson 470-80 1983 $50

COX, WILLIAM   Crayon Sketches, by an Amateur.
NY: Conner & Cooke, 1833. 1st ed. 2 vols., 12mo, orig green
cloth, ex lib. Argosy 710-158 1983 $50.

COXE, JOHN REDMAN   The Philadelphia Medical Museum. Vol. VI.
Philadelphia: T. & G. Palmer, 1809. 8vo, full calf. Illus.
Argosy 713-127 1983 $50

COXE, TENCH   A View of the United States of America.
Philadelphia, 1794. Library buckram, ex. lib. Stamps on title,
otherwise a clean copy. Reese 18-195 1983 $150

COXE, WILLIAM   Memoirs of Horatio, Lord Walpole.
London, 1802. 1st ed., large paper copy. Portraits. Large heavy
4to, contemporary boards, calf back and corners. Ex-library; rubbed;
front hinge partly cracked. Morrill 286-110 1983 $32.50

COXE, WILLIAM   Travels in Poland, Russia, Sweden, and
Denmark. Printed for T. Cadell, 1802. With 14 folding engraved
maps by Kitchen and others. 12 engraved plates and 5 folding tables,
5 vols., 8vo, cont. diced calf, gilt bordered sides, gilt spines,
with double lettering pieces. Fenning 60-73 1983 £125

COY, OWEN C.   Guide to the County Archives of
California. Sacramento: California State Printing Office, 1919.
Signed presentation from author. Folding maps, cloth. Dawson 470-
81 1983 $45

COYER, GABRIEL FRANCOIS   A Supplement to Lord Anson's Voyage
Around the World. For A. Millar; and J. Whiston and B. White, 1752.
First English edition. 4to, modern mottled calf, old style. Hannas
69-39 1983 £160

COYTE, JOSEPH WILLIAM   A cockney's adventures... London:
Sherwood, Neely and Jones, 1811. First edition. 12mo. Cont.
quarter calf, spine gilt. With 3 hand-colored woodcut plates. Rare.
A little worn. Ximenes 63-399 1983 $80

COZZENS, FREDERICK S.   The Sparrowgrass Papers: or Living in
the Country. New York: Derby & Jackson, 1856. Frontis. 1st ed.,
1st printing. Orig. blue cloth, gilt. Fine bright copy. Jenkins
155-257 1983 $25

COZZENS, ISSACHAR   A Geological History of Manhattan or
New York Island. NY, 1843. Tables, hand-colored plates, lacks
map and plate 1. Mod. linen-backed boards, ex library. Argosy 710-
376 1983 $30

COZZENS, JAMES GOULD   The Just and the Unjust. New York, 1942.
First edition. Covers a little marked. Frayed dust wrapper. Loosely
inserted is the promotional leaflet reprinting Henry Canby's review.
Nice. Rota 230-145 1983 £12

CRABB, JAMES   The Gipsies' Advocate. Seeley, Westley and Davis, 1831. First edition, orig. green cloth, maroon leather label. Very good. Jarndyce 31-171 1983 £48

CRABB, JAMES   The Gipsies' Advocate. 1832. 12mo, orig. watered cloth, paper label on spine. Bickersteth 75-125 1983 £28

CRABBE, GEORGE   Tales. London: Printed for J. Hatchard, 1812. First edition. 8vo. Rebound in later 3/4 calf & marbled boards. With an ALS, 2 pages, 4to, Grantham, July 17, 1807, from author to an unnamed Lord. Former owner's signature on flyleaf, some foxing. Bookplate. Very good. Uncut. MacManus 277-1157 1983 $350

CRABBE, GEORGE   Tales of the Hall. John Murray, 1819. First edition. 2 vols. 8vo, final colophon leaf in vol. I, but lacking half-titles and advertisement leaf. Cont. binder's cloth. Three leaves torn and repaired. Hannas 69-40 1983 £20

CRABBE, GEORGE   The Works. John Murray, 1823. 8vo, cont. blue calf gilt, spine gilt with red labels, one label chipped. Bickersteth 77-197 1983 £65

CRACKANTHORPE, HUBERT   Vignettes. London: John Lane, 1896. First edition. 12mo. Orig. boards. Spine darkened at extremities. Tape stains on endpapers. MacManus 277-1158 1983 $45

CRACKANTHORPE, HUBERT   Wreckage; seven studies. London, 1893. First edition. Spine worn and lower corners a little bruised. Newspaper reproduction of a portrait of the author neatly mounted on verso of half-title page. Bookplate. Nice. Rota 230-146 1983 £30

CRACKANTHORPE, HUBERT   Wreckage. London: Heinemann, 1893. First edition. Orig. decorated cloth. Spine a little rubbed. Very good. MacManus 277-1159 1983 $85

CRADDOCK, THOMAS   Charles Lamb. Simpkin, Marshall; Liverpool: James Woollard, 1867. First edition, orig. green cloth, v.g. Jarndyce 30-1046 1983 £10.50

CRADDOCK, THOMAS   Literary Papers. London: Arthur Hall and Co., 1873. First edition. Orig. cloth. Spine slightly darkened. Covers a little soiled, worn at edges. Endpapers a bit stained by damp. Small nick in middle of spine. Good. MacManus 277-1160 1983 $50

CRADLEBAUGH, JOHN   Utah and the Mormons...Speech on the Admission of Utah as a State. Washington, 1863. Cloth, calf spine. Very good. Reese 19-166 1983 $300

CRADOCK, ZACHARY   A Sermon Preached before the King, February 10th, 1677/8. Printed for Richard Royston, 1678. Second edition. Wanting half-title, 4to, wrapper. Fenning 62-86 1983 £16.50

CRAIG, EDWARD GORDON   Bookplates Designed and Cut on Wood. Surrey: At the Sign of the Rose, 1900. 12mo. Limited to 350 copies. Fine in printed self-wrappers with ribbon ties. Bookplate. Bromer 25-183 1983 $275

CRAIG, GORDON   The Dome. London, Sign of the Unicorn, 1898-1900. Second series. 4to, illus. with numerous plates, gravures, music, etc. Pub.'s gilt stamped blue cloth, uncut. 7 vols. complete. Houle 22-252 1983 $475

CRAIG, GORDON   Gordon Craig's Paris Diary, 1932-1933. North Hills: Bird & Bull, 1982. Color plates. First edition. 1 of 350 numbered copies. Orig. half morocco and Japanese paper sides, morocco-tipped corners, morocco label, uncut. Mint. Jenkins 155-1362 1983 $200

CRAIG, J. D.   The 1st Canadian Division, in the Battles of 1918. London: Barrs & Co., 1919. 21 1/2cm. Maps & illus. Printed wrappers. A fine copy. Scarce. McGahern 54-47 1983 $45

CRAIG, JOHN R.   Ranching with Lords and Commons; or, Twenty Years on the Range... Toronto, 1903. Pictorial cloth, slight rubbing at joints, otherwise very good. Reese 19-167 1983 $275

CRAIG, R. MANIFOLD   The Weird of "The Silken Thomas." Aberdeen: Moran & Co., 1900. First edition. Orig. pictorial cloth. Covers a bit worn and soiled. Rear inner hinges cracking, all pages browned. Little foxing. Bookplate. MacManus 277-1163 1983 $35

CRAIG, R. S.   The Making of Carlyle. Eveleigh Nash, 1908. First edition, tall 8vo, half title, front. Orig. grey cloth. Jarndyce 30-943 1983 £12.50

CRAIGIE, PEARL MARY TERESA RICHARDS   The Ambassador. London: Unwin, 1898. First edition. Orig. cloth. MacManus 279-2666 1983 $20

CRAIGIE, PEARL MARY TERESA RICHARDS   A Bundle of Life. N.Y.: J. Selwin Tait & Sons, 1894. First American edition. Thin 8vo. Orig. moroon cloth. Fine. MacManus 279-2667 1983 $25

CRAIGIE, PEARL MARY TERESA RICHARDS   The Dream and the Business. London: Unwin, 1906. First edition. Orig. pictorial cloth. The cover design (in color) by Beardsley. Spine somewhat soiled. Covers slightly marked. MacManus 279-2669 1983 $35

CRAIGIE, PEARL MARY TERESA RICHARDS   The Dream and The Business. Toronto: The Copp Clark Co., Ltd, 1906. First Canadian edition. Orig. cloth with pictorial label designed by Beardsley. Front inner hinge weak. Good. MacManus 279-2668 1983 $25

CRAIGIE, PEARL MARY TERESA RICHARDS   The Flute of Pan. London: Unwin, 1905. First edition. Orig. cloth. MacManus 279-2670 1983 $25

CRAIGIE, PEARL MARY TERESA RICHARDS   The Gods, Some Mortals and Lord Wickenham. London: Henry & Co., 1895. First edition. Orig. cloth. Covers a bit worn & soiled. Good. MacManus 279-2671 1983 $25

CRAIGIE, PEARL MARY TERESA RICHARDS   Good Reading About Many Books Mostly By Their Authors. London: T. Fisher Unwin, 1894-5. First edition. Illus. with portraits. Thin 8vo. Orig. cloth. Very good. MacManus 279-2672 1983 $35

CRAIGIE, PEARL MARY TERESA RICHARDS   Osbern and Ursyne. London: John Lane, 1900. First edition. Orig. cloth. Pale covers soiled. Good. MacManus 278-2673 1983 $60

CRAIGIE, PERAL MARY TERESA RICHARDS   Robert Orange. London: Unwin, 1900. First edition. Orig. cloth. MacManus 279-2674 1983 $20

CRAIGIE, PEARL MARY TERESA RICHARDS   The Sinner's Comedy. London: T. Fisher Unwin, 1892. First edition. Orig. decorated boards. Extremities of spine rubbed. Spine faded. Good. MacManus 279-2676 1983 $45

CRAIGIE, PEARL MARY TERESA RICHARDS   The Vineyard. London: T. Fisher Unwin, 1904. First edition. Frontis. Orig. cloth. Cont. owner's inscription on front free endpaper. Endpapers foxed. Spine slightly faded. Very good. MacManus 279-2677 1983 $35

CRAIK, DINAH MARIA MULOCK   About Money And Other Things. London: Macmillan & Co., 1886. First edition. Orig. green cloth. Spine and covers worn. Front inner hinge cracking. Former bookseller's small rubbed stamp on the verso of the front free endpaper. Good. MacManus 279-3951 1983 $75

CRAIK, DINAH MARIA MULOCK   John Halifax, Gentleman. London: Hurst & Blackett, 1856. First edition, primary binding. 3 vols. Orig. blind-stamped cloth. Tipped into Vol. one is an ALS, 2 pages, 12mo, The Corner House, Shortlands, Kent, 16 Feb. '84 from the author to an unnamed gentleman. Cont. ownership signatures on flyleaves. Front inner hinge of Vol. one weak. In a fleece-lined half-morocco folding box. Very fine. MacManus 279-3952 1983 $850

CRAIK, DINAH MARIA MULOCK   John Halifax, Gentleman. London: Hurst & Blackett, 1856. 3 vols. 8vo. Cont. half calf gilt, rehinged, bit worn. First edition. Ravenstree 96-132 1983 $135

CRAIK, DINAH MARIA MULOCK   John Halifax, Gentleman. London: Hurst & Blackett, 1856. First edition. 3 vols. Orig. cloth (spines skillfully repaired). Covers worn. MacManus 279-3953 1983 $35

CRAIK, DINAH MARIA MULOCK   A Life for a Life. London: Hurst & Blackett, 1859. First edition. 3 vols. Orig. cloth (spines faded). MacManus 279-3954 1983 $125

CRAIK, DINAH MARIA MULOCK   A Life for a Life. London: Hurst & Blackett, 1859. 3 vols. 8vo. Orig. cloth, quite worn, faded. Spines chipped and defective, name on titles. Bookplate of Emily Maud Mulock. First edition. Ravenstree 96-133 1983 $75

CRAIK, DINAH MARIA MULOCK   A Noble Life. London: Hurst & Blackett, 1866. First edition. 2 vols. Orig. cloth. Inner hinges cracked. Very good. MacManus 279-3955 1983 $125

CRAIK, DINAH MARIA MULOCK   An Unsentimental Journey through Cornwall. London: Macmillan & Co., 1884. First edition. Illus. by C.N. Hemy. Small folio. Orig. pictorial blue cloth. Endpapers foxed. Covers slightly rubbed. Fine. MacManus 279-3956 1983 $85

CRAIK, DINAH MARIA MULOCK   A woman's thoughts about women. London: Hurst & Blackett, 1858. First edition. 8vo. Orig. purple cloth. Lacks an endpaper at back, but a fine copy. Ximenes 63-653 1983 $100

CRAIK, GEORGE L.   English Causes Celebres. London: Knight, 1844. Early edition. Illus. Orig. cloth. Inner hinges cracked. Slightly worn. MacManus 277-1164 1983 $20

CRAIK, GEORGIANA M.   Godfrey Helstone. London: Richard Bentley & Son, 1884. First edition. 3 vols. Orig. decorated cloth. Spines slightly faded and a trifle worn. Very good. MacManus 277-1165 1983 $450

CRAIK, GEORGIANA M.   Riverston. London: Smith, Elder, & Co., 1857. First edition. 3 vols. Orig. green embossed cloth. Very fine. MacManus 277-1166 1983 $650

CRAIK, JAMES   The Past and Present Position of the Church. Lexington, 1847. Dbd. First edition. Ginsberg 46-395 1983 $75

CRAIK, JAMES   The Union. Louisville, 1860. Dbd. First edition. Ginsberg 46-396 1983 $35

CRAKES, SYLVESTER   Five Years a Captive Among the Black-Feet Indians. Columbus, 1858. Frontis. plates. Orig. cloth. Corner of front blank torn away, closed tear in one leaf, with no loss, scattered foxing, and one signature starting, otherwise a very good copy. Reese 19-168 1983 $850

CRAM, THOMAS J.   Topographical Memoir of the Department of the Pacific. Wash., 1859. Cloth with leather label. First edition. Ginsberg 47-259 1983 $75

CRAMER, AUGUST (1860-?)   Die Hallucinationen. Freiburg: J. C. B. Mohr, 1889. First edition. Library buckram, retaining orig. wrappers. Gach 95-77 1983 $50

CRAMER, ZADOK   The Navigator, Containing Directions for Navigating the Monongahela, Allegheny, Ohio, and Mississippi Rivers... Pittsburgh, 1818. Plates. Later cloth, usual scattered foxing and light staining, discretely ex-library, otherwise a very good copy. Reese 18-520 1983 $600

CRAMP, S.   Handbook of the Birds of Europe, Vol. 2, Hawks to Bustards. (1980). 56 coloured plates, royal 8vo, cloth. Wheldon 160-740 1983 £41

CRAMP, S.   Handbook of the Birds of Europe, Vol. 3, Snipe to Gulls. 56 coloured plates, royal 8vo, cloth. Wheldon 160-741 1983 £51

CRANCH, CHRISTOPHER PEARSE   The Last of the Huggermuggers. Boston: Lee & Shep., 1889, (1859). Red gilt cloth. Spine faded. 8vo. Illus. with full-page & small black & whites. Very good. Aleph-bet 8-70 1983 $20

CRANE, AIMEE   Portrait of America. New York, 1945. Profusely illustrated, many in color. Jenkins 152-796 1983 $35

CRANE, FRANCES   The Shocking Pink Hat. N.Y., Random House, (1946). First edition. Dust jacket (small chip) else, very good-fine. Houle 22-253 1983 $30

CRANE, HART   The Bridge. New York: Horace Liveright, (1930). 1st American ed. Orig. blue cloth, gilt. Three very fine photographic illus. by Walker Evans. Fine copy. Jenkins 155-258 1983 $165

CRANE, HART   The Bridge. N.Y.: Limited Edtions Club, 1981. Photographic illus. by Richard Benson. Small folio, cloth; pub.'s box. Mint. Argosy 714-202 1983 $100

CRANE, HART   The Collected Poems of... New York: Liveright, (1933). Cloth. Portrait. First edition, third printing. A fine copy in very good dust jacket. Reese 20-281 1983 $35

CRANE, HART   Voyages: Six Poems from White Buildings. N.Y.: Museum of Modern Art, 1957. With wood engravings by Leonard Baskin, small oblong 4to, pr. wraps., in folding board slipcase. One of 975 copies, printed at the Gehenna Press, and signed by Baskin. Argosy 714-203 1983 $250

CRANE, HART   White Buildings. (N.Y.), Boni & Liveright, 1926. 12mo. Cloth-backed patterned boards. 1st ed., 1st issue (with Tate's name misspelled on integral title page). Spine bit dull, not quite fresh. Only about 500 copies were printed, of which very few are 1st issue (before title page was canceled). Very good copy. O'Neal 50-15 1983 $700

CRANE, HART   White Buildings: Poems. (NY): 1926. First edition, second state. 500 copies printed. Extremities lightly rubbed, else fine in cloth-backed batik boards. Bromer 25-18 1983 $300

CRANE, HART   White Buildings. (N.Y.): Boni & Liveright, 1926. First edition. Thin 8vo, cloth backed marbled boards, covers rubbed. Second issue, with Tate's name spelled correctly on title page. Argosy 714-204 1983 $200

CRANE, MUNROE   Recollections of Lincoln and Douglas Forty Years Ago. New York, Privately Printed, 1899. Edition limited to 200 copies. 2 portraits and plate. 12mo. Part of fore-edge margin of pp.11-14 torn off, otherwise nice. Morrill 290-80 1983 $37.50

CRANE, NATHALIA   The Janitor's Boy. New York, 1924. Second printing. Presentation inscription to Louis Untermeyer... dated 1925 on half title page. Three page holograph letter tipped in, plus one typed letter. Vg-fine. In Our Time 156-173 1983 $300

CRANE, NATHALIA   Lava Lane. New York, 1925. 8vo. Cloth. Very good copy. This copy inscribed by Crane. A review of the book laid in. In Our Time 156-174 1983 $100

CRANE, NATHALIA   Lava Lane. New York: Seltzer, 1925. Parchment and boards. First edition. One of 350 numbered copies, specially bound, and signed. One corner bruised, else a fine copy in the orig. glassine. Reese 20-282 1983 $50

CRANE, NATHALIA   Swear by Night. New York, 1936. 8vo. Cloth. Fine copy in dj. Laid into this copy is a long two page letter by Crane, two other holograph letters and two Christmas cards. In Our Time 156-176 1983 $250

CRANE, NATHALIA   Venus Invisible. New York, 1928. 8vo. Cloth. Tipped into this copy is a holograph postcard from Crane to Louis Untermeyer. Fine copy in tanned dj. In Our Time 156-175 1983 $75

CRANE, NATHALIA   Venus Invisible and Other Poems. New York: Coward, 1928. Cloth and boards. First edition. Fine copy in lightly worn dust jacket. Reese 20-283 1983 $25

CRANE, STEPHEN   Active Service. London: Heinemann, 1899. 1st English ed. Orig. decorated cream cloth. Spine slightly aged, else a crisp unrubbed copy. Jenkins 155-261 1983 $90

CRANE, STEPHEN   Active Service. NY, (1899). Hinges cracked, front fly missing, good. Quill & Brush 54-326 1983 $20

CRANE, STEPHEN   George's Mother. NY, 1898. Cover soiled and finish rubbed, some minor interior staining, good or better. Quill & Brush 54- 327 1983 $25

CRANE, STEPHEN   Killing His Bear. N.p., 1949. One of 100 copies printed for the Friends of Lee & Gabriel Engel. Argosy 714-205 1983 $40

CRANE, STEPHEN   Maggie. NY: Newland Press, (n.d., ca. 1940). Tall 8vo, with an orig. signed frontis. etching by Bernard Sanders + 2 other plates, all printed on blue paper. This is one of 100 numbered copies, with the orig. signed etching. Turquoise cloth. Karmiole 74-38 1983 $40

CRANE, STEPHEN   The Open Boat and Other Stories. London: Heinemann, 1898. 1st English ed., 1st issue. Orig. green cloth, gilt, uncut. Some faint spots to covers, but a bright unworn copy. Scarce ed. Jenkins 155-262 1983 $175

CRANE, STEPHEN   The Open Boat and Other Stories. London, 1898. 8vo. Cloth. 1st English ed. Name on flyleaf and endboard, else a fine copy. In Our Time 156-177 1983 $75

CRANE, STEPHEN   The Open Boat. NY, 1898. Hinges starting, edges rubbed, spine edges slightly frayed, good. Quill & Brush 54-329 1983 $60

CRANE, STEPHEN   The O'Ruddy. New York, 1903. First edition. Very nice. Rota 231-146 1983 £35

CRANE, STEPHEN   The Red Badge of Courage, an Episode of the American Civil War. New York: Appleton, 1896. Early ed., from the 1st ed. plates. Orig. decorated cream cloth, gilt. Some rubbing and aging, but very good copy. Jenkins 155-264 1983 $25

CRANE, STEPHEN   The Red Badge of Courage. New York: Random House, (1931). 1st ed., limited to 980 numbered copies. Orig. cloth-backed decorated boards, leather label, uncut. Decorations by Valenti Angelo. Very fine copy. Jenkins 155-263 1983 $125

CRANE, STEPHEN   A Stephen Crane Collection. Hanover: Dartmouth College, 1948. 1st ed., 1 of 350 copies printed at the Anthoensen Press. Orig. cloth, gilt. Very fine. Jenkins 155-1379 1983 $30

CRANE, STEPHEN   The Third Violet. NY, 1897. Covers slightly soiled, otherwise very good. Quill & Brush 54-331 1983 $60

CRANE, STEPHEN   War Is Kind. New York: Frederick A. Stokes Company, 1899. First edition. Drawings by Will Bradley. Pictorial gray boards. Designed and printed by Bradley. A fine, skillfully rebacked copy, without spine label, corners expertly restored. Bradley 65-54 1983 $285

CRANE, THOMAS   Abroad. Marcus Ward, nd, (ca. 1870s). Frontis., illus. title page & 46 col. illus. & many col. decorations. Blue cloth backed col. decor. boards, edges stained yellow, blue & white decor. eps. Corners sl. worn & edges sl. rubbed, name top fr. ep., some sl. foxing first & last pp., vg copy. Hodgkins 27-53 1983 £30

CRANE, WALTER   The Blue Beard Picture Book. London, George Routledge and Sons...New York, n.d. Illus. by Walter Crane. Printed in Colours by Edmund Evans. Tall 8vo, pictorial cover in gilt. Corners slightly rubbed. Morrill 287-558 1983 $45

CRANE, WALTER   Flora's Feast. London: Cassell and Company, 1890. First edition. 4to. Orig. pictorial boards, blue linen spine. Coloured title-page and 40 pages of coloured illus. by Walter Crane, 8 pp. of pub's ads. Traylen 94-221 1983 £28

CRANE, WALTER   Walter Crane's Hazelford Sketchbook. Cambridge: John Barn. Assoc., 1937. Tall 4to. Cloth backed pictorial boards. In orig. clear wrapper. First edition. Limited to 700 copies. Illus. in black & white. Aleph-bet 8-72 1983 $35

CRANE, WALTER   Hazelford Sketch Book. Cambridge, Mass.,: The John Barnard Assoc., 1937. First edition. 4to. Illus. Orig. cloth-backed pictorial boards. Fine. MacManus 277-1167 1983 $30

CRANE, WALTER   Ideals In Art. London: George Bell & Sons, 1905. First edition. Illus. Orig. decorated cloth. Inscription on half-title. Covers a bit rubbed and faded. Cover design and a number of illus. by Crane. Very good. MacManus 277-1168 1983 $100

CRANE, WALTER   A Masque of Days. London, 1901. First edition. 4to. Covers a little soiled. Bookplate on half-title page. Nice. Rota 231-147 1983 £45

CRANE, WALTER   A Masque of Days. London: Cassell and Company, 1901. First edition. 4to. Orig. pictorial boards, linen spine. Double-page coloured title, and 40 pp. of coloured illus. by Walter Crane (one page carelessly opened). Binding a little soiled. Traylen 94-222 1983 £25

CRANE, WALTER   The Romance of the Three Rs. Marcus Ward, 1886. Penned & pictured by Walter Crane. Printed in colour, each book having its own title page (dated). Brown & blue decor. boards designed by Crane, red & cream decor. eps., edges stained red. Corners sl. worn, bookpl. fr. ep., very nice copy. Hodgkins 27-54 1983 £135

CRANMER, THOMAS   Reformatio Legum Ecclesiasticarum. London, 1640. 2nd ed. Text surrounded by woodcut rules, with woodcut initials & decorations throughout; lightish dampstaining, primarily to upper margin, occasional embrowning, title page dusty, nicely & newly bound in full, dark calf, covers double blind-ruled, spine with brown morocco label, double gilt-ruled & lettered. With the signature of John Lightfoot, dated 1640, on title page. Well-preserved copy. Boswell 7-50 1983 $350

CRANWELL, JOHN PHILIPS   Notes on Figures of Earth. NY, 1929. Limited to 685 copies, pencil notations in margins, spine darkened, still very good. Quill & Brush 54-228 1983 $35

CRAUFURD, Q.   Sketches Chiefly relating to the History, Religion, Learning, and Manners, of the Hindoos. London, 1792. Second edition, enlarged. Folding plate. Engravings on titles. 2 vols. Calf rebacked, morocco labels, gilt. 8vo. Good. Edwards 1044-157 1983 £165

CRAWFORD, A.   Our Troubles in Poona and the Deccan. London, 1897. Numerous plates. 8vo. Orig. cloth. Good. Edwards 1044-158 1983 £45

CRAWFORD, CHARLES   Scenes of Earlier Days in Crossing the Plains to Oregon and Experiences of Western Life. Petaluma, Ca., 1898. Illus., frontis. Orig. gold stamped cloth. First edition. Ginsberg 46-207 1983 $200

CRAWFORD, DAVID   Poems, Chiefly in the Scottish Dialect. Edinburgh: Printed for the Author, by J. Pillans & Sons, 1798. First edition. Frontispiece port. & an engraving of Heriot's Hospital. Large 8vo. Orig. boards. Very slight wear to spine. Red half-morocco drop-down box. Uncut. Very fine. MacManus 277-1170 1983 $500

CRAWFORD, FRANCIS MARION   An American Politician. Chapman & Hall, 1884. First edition, 2 vols. Half titles. Half red roan, rubbed. Jarndyce 30-337 1983 £15

CRAWFORD, FRANCIS MARION   Corleone. Macmillan, 1897. First edition, 2 vols. Half titles, orig. blue cloth, fine copy. Jarndyce 30-344 1983 £38

CRAWFORD, FRANCIS MARION   Khaled. Macmillan, 1891. First edition, 2 vols. Half titles. Dark blue cloth, spine gilt, red labels. Jarndyce 30-342 1983 £26

CRAWFORD, FRANCIS MARION   Marion Darche. Macmillan, 1893. First edition. Half titles, 48 pp ads. vol. I. Orig. light blue cloth, standard binding. Jarndyce 30-343 1983 £28

CRAWFORD, FRANCIS MARION   Paul Patoff. Macmillan, 1888. Half titles, orig. blue cloth, 3 vols. Fine. Jarndyce 30-341 1983 £24

CRAWFORD, FRANCIS MARION   Saracinesca. Wm. Blackwood, 1887. First edition, 3 vols. Orig. salmon-brown cloth, blocked in dark brown and gilt, creasing of boards vol. II, otherwise a very fine copy. Half titles. Jarndyce 30-340 1983 £42

CRAWFORD, FRANCIS MARION   A Tale of a Lonely Parish. Macmillan, 1886. 2 vols., half titles, orig. blue cloth. Lacking leading f.e.p. vol. II, otherwise fine. First edition. Jarndyce 30-339 1983 £35

CRAWFORD, FRANCIS MARION   Zoroaster. 1885. First edition, 2 vols. Half titles. Orig. blue cloth. Fine, except for sl. splashing of upper cover vol. I. Jarndyce 30-338 1983 £36

CRAWFORD, HENRY S.   Handbook of Carved Ornament from Irish Monuments of the Christian Period. Dublin: R.I.A.S., 1926. With 51 plates and 23 other illus. Roy. 8vo, orig. cloth. Fenning 61-84 1983 £24.50

CRAWFORD, JACK   The Poet Scout. N.Y., 1886. Illus. Pict. cloth. Signed. Argosy 716-614 1983 $35

CRAWFORD, JOHN   Chinese Monopoly Examined. James Ridgway, 1830. First edition, wanting half-title, 8vo, wrapper. Fenning 61-85 1983 £55

CRAWFORD, JOSEPH U.   In Congress. The People of Southern Extension of the Central Pacific R.R.... Washington: National Repub. Printing House, 1878. Orig. printed wrappers. Fine copy. Jenkins 153-629 1983 $200

CRAWFORD, LEWIS   Badlands and Broncho Trails. Bismarck, N.D., Capital Book Co., 1922. Illus. Frontis. Orig. cloth. 1st ed. Scarce. Jenkins 153-145 1983 $45

CRAWFORD, LEWIS   Rekinling Camp Fires. Bismarck, N.D., 1926. First edition in dust jacket. Orig. blue cloth. Map and 10 plates. Jenkins 152-794 1983 $55

CRAWFORD, LEWIS   The Medora-Deadwood Stage Line. Bismarck, N.D., Capital Book Company, 1925. Orig. printed wrappers. Illus. Jenkins 153-146 1983 $35

CRAWFORD, MARY CAROLINE   The Romance of the American Theatre. Boston: Little, Brown & Co., 1913. Illus. Pictorial cloth. Dawson 471-318 1983 $20

CRAWFORD, MEDOREM   Journal of...an Account of His Trip Across the Plains with the Oregon Pioneers of 1842. Eugene, Ore., 1897. Stapled. Ginsberg 47-260 1983 $65

CRAWFORD, O. G. S.   Air-Photography for Archaeologists. London; Published by Order...H.M.S.O..., 1929-28. Second Edition, 4to, 2 vols. in 1, with 2 large folding maps and 40 plates, red cloth, printed paper label on upper cover, cover stained and faded, a little worn, internally a good copy. Deighton 3-87 1983 £75

CRAWFURD, OSWALD JOHN FREDERICK   Alix Fairford. London: Sampson Low, 1877. First edition. 2 vols, in one. Orig. cloth. Publisher's remainder binding. Recased with new endpapers. MacManus 278-1262 1983 $25

CRAWFORD, SAMUEL W.   History of the Fall of Ford Sumter. (NY, 1896). Illus, mod. buckram, ex lib. Argosy 710-80 1983 $35

CRAWFORD, THOMAS E.   The West of the Texas Kid. Norman, 1862. First edition in dust jacket. Illus. Fine. Jenkins 152-795 1983 $20

CRAWFURD, J.   History of the Indian Archipelago. Edinburgh, 1820. Folding map, 34 plates. 3 vols. Uncut. Orig. paper labels on spines, worn. Cloth slightly marked, spines faded, front joints of vols. 1 and 3 cracked. Good. Edwards 1044-780 1983 £195

CRAWHALL, JOSEPH   'Impresses Quaint.' Newcastle Upon Tine, 1889. Small quarto. Printed on one side only. First edition. Vignette wood engravings. Limited to 300 copies. Spine faded, else fine in cloth-backed printed boards. Bromer 25-336 1983 $475

CRAYON, GEOFFREY, PSEUD.
Please turn to
IRVING, WASHINGTON

THE CREAM of the Jest. Derby: Henry Mozley, (1826). First edition, Half title, hand-coloured front. and illus. by George Cruikshank. Mottled calf, gilt borders and spine, red label. Fine. With bookplate of Albert M. Cohn. Jarndyce 31-498 1983 £95

CREASSY, JAMES   Observations On The Means of Better Draining The Middle And South Levels of the Fenns. London: printed for T. Evans, 1777. First edition, 4to, folding engraved plate, wrappers. Deighton 3-88 1983 £68

CREASY, EDWARD   The Fifteen Decisive Battles of the World. London, 1915. 8vo. Orig. cloth. Illus. Ink inscriptions on endpaper. Good. Edwards 1042-312 1983 £12

CREASY, JOHN   The Toff Takes Shares. London, John Long, (ca. 1944). First edition. Dust jacket (a few chips) but still very good. Houle 22-258 1983 $60

CREBILLION, CLAUDE PROSPER JOLYOT DE   Ah, quel Conte! Conte politique et astronomique. Bruxelles: Freres Vasse, 1754. Second edition. 12mo. 8 parts in 4 vols. Cont. calf, spines gilt, morocco labels. Half-titles in all volumes. 16 engr. pages and 6 leaves of errata. Fine tight copy. Trebizond 18-111 1983 $200

CREBILLION, CLAUDE PROSPER JOLYOT DE   The Opportunities of a Night. London: Chapman & Hall Ltd., 1925. First edition. 8vo. Orig. cloth-backed decorated boards. Dust jacket. Limited to 1,000 copies. Slightly torn jacket. Very fine copy. Jaffe 1-189 1983 $25

CREECH, WILLIAM   Edinburgh Fugitive Pieces. Edinburgh: printed for William Creech; and T. Cadell (London), 1791. 8vo, cont. half black morocco (some rubbing and wear to corners). 1st ed. A very good copy; uncut. Scarce. Ximenes 64-150 1983 $350

CREEKMORE, HUBERT   The Long Reprieve and Other Poems from New Caledonia. New Directions, (1946). 8vo. Cloth. A fine copy in spotted dj. In Our Time 156-178 1983 $25

CREELEY, ROBERT   The Finger. Black Sparrow Press, 1968. 8vo. Cloth, boards. Scarce hardbound edition of the book, 1 of 50 copies clothbound and signed by author. With an original collage by Bobbie Creeley signed by same. Fine. In Our Time 156-179 1983 $150

CREIGHTON, MANDELL   Queen Elizabeth. London: 1896. Quarto, full calf. Frontis. portrait. 39 other plates and illus. 1/300 copies on Japan paper with duplicate set of plates. Some light off-setting from leather binding on borders of end leaves, including title page, minor wear, hinges strengthened. Very nice copy. Bradley 66-409 1983 $175

CREILING, JOHN CON.   Dissertatio Academica de Aureo Vellere aut Possiblitate Transmatationibus Metallorum. Tubingen, 1737. Also Dissertatio de Aureo Vellere, Sectio IV. Tubingen, 1739. 4to. 2 vols. Boards. Some dampstaining and underlining in the first part; the second part cut rather close. Gurney 90-38 1983 £45

CRELL, LORENZ FLORENZ FRIEDRICH VON   Die Neuesten Entdeckungen in der Chemie. Weygandschen Buchhandlung, Leipzig, 1781-86. 13 vols. 8vo, with 4 engraved plates plus 3 duplicates not called for; a fine set in cont. mottled sheep, gilt spines, spines worn and a few slightly defective. First edition. Quaritch NS 5-27 1983 $2,350

CRELLY, WILLIAM R.   The Painting of Simon Vouet. New Haven/London: Yale University Press, 1962. 193 illus. hors texte. 4to. Cloth. Dust jacket. Ars Libri 32-691 1983 $125

CRENSHAW, J. W.   Salt River Valley. (Phoenix?: Published by the author, 1908). Wrappers. Rubber stamp. Covers a little worn. Dawson 471-53 1983 $20

CRESSWELL, BEATRICE F.   The Royal Progress of King Pepito. London: Society For Promoting Christian Knowledge, n.d. (1889). First edition. Illus. by Kate Greenaway. Engraved & printed by Edmund Evans. Orig. boards (somewhat rubbed). Good. MacManus 278-2380 1983 $100

CRESSWELL, BEATRICE F.   The Royal Progress of King Pepito.
S.P.C.K., nd (1889). Illus. by D.G. Frontis. & 11 illus. printed in
colour by Edmund Evans. Pale cream bds. with col'd vignette & black
titling fr. cvr., black titling bkstrip, bkstrip delicate with most
of titling rubbed away corners of bds. worn, cvrs. sl. marked, free
eps. discol'd, sm. tear bottom margin of p. 39, good copy. Hodgkins
27-91 1983 £25

CRESSWELL, HENRY   Fair and Free. Smith, Elder, 1882.
First edition, 3 vols. 3 vols. bound as one. Half titles vols. II
and III. Orig. green cloth, inner hinges weakening. Jarndyce 30-345
1983 £30

CRESSWELL, HENRY   Sliding Sands. London: Hurst & Blackett,
1890. First edition. 3 vols. Orig. light-brown decorated cloth.
Spines and covers worn. Library labels removed from the pastedown endpapers. Cont. owner's inscription on rear covers. Good. MacManus
277-1172 1983 £225

CREUZBAUR, ROBERT   Route from the Gulf of Mexico and the
Lower Mississippi Valley to California and the Pacific Ocean... H.
Long & Brother, New York: Robert Creuzbaur, Austin, Texas, 1849.
Orig. cloth. Maps lacking as usual. First and only ed. Extremely
rare. Jenkins 153-147 1983 $3000

CRICHTON, ANDREW   History of Arabia, Ancient and Modern.
Edinburgh, 1834. Second edition, 2 vols., map, engravings, new
binders cloth, ex-library, unobtrusive blind stamps. K Books 301-52
1983 £38

CRICHTON, KYLE S.   Law and Order Ltd. Santa Fe: New Mexican Publishing, 1928. First edition. Plates. Dust jacket. Limited
signed edition without the number or signature. Jenkins 152-286 1983
$50

CRIMINAL and Miscellaneous Statistical Returns for the Year 1857 West
Riding Constabulary, from 1st January to 29th September. Wakefield,
printed by J. Stanfield. Jarndyce 31-136 1983 £28

CRIPPS, ERNEST C.   Plough Court. London, 1927. First
edition. Illus. Cloth. Argosy 713-128 1983 $35

CRISP, STEPHEN   A Memorable Account of the Christian
Experiences, Gospel Labours, Travels and Sufferings of... Printed
and sold by T. Sowle, 1694. First collected edition, 4to, cont.
calf, neatly and recently rebacked, a very good copy. Fenning 62-87
1983 £75

CRISPIN, EDMUND   Obsequies at Oxford. Phil., (1945).
Minor cover wear, else very good in chipped and worn but still presentable dustwrapper. Quill & Brush 54-333 1983 $30

CRISPOLTI, ENRICO   Lucio Fontana. Bruxelles: La
Connaissance, 1974. 2 vols. Prof. illus (numerous color plates).
Large 4to. Cloth. Ars Libri 33-465 1983 $100

CRISSEY, FORREST   Alexander Legge, 1866-1933. Chicago,
1936. First edition. Illus., cloth. Signed by author. Bradley
66-527 1983 $22.50

CRISTINELLI, GIUSEPPE   Baldassare Longhena. Padova: Marsilio,
1972. Prof. illus. Large square 4to. Cloth. Dust jacket. Ars
Libri 33-196 1983 $75

CRITCHELL, ROBERT S.   Recollections of a Fire Insurance Man.
Chicago, 1909. Illus., 12mo, orig. cloth. Signed by the author.
Argosy 710-81 1983 $35

A CRITICAL review of the publick buildings... London: printed by
C. Ackers, for J. Wilford and J. Clarke, 1734. First edition. 8vo.
Disbound. Folding table. Ximenes 63-267 1983 $90

A CRITICISM on the Foundling. London: printed for M. Cooper, 1748.
8vo, disbound, 1st ed. Scarce. Ximenes 64-152 1983 $400

CROASDAILE, HENRY E.   Scenes on Pacific Shores. The Town
& Country Publishing Company, 1873. First edition, with a frontis.,
errata slip, 8vo, orig. blue cloth, gilt. Fenning 61-88 1983 £28.50

CROCE, BENEDETTO   Aesthetic. London: Macmillan, 1909.
First edition in English. Lower spine tip frayed. Gach 95-79
1983 $37.50

CROCE, BENEDETTO   My Philosophy. London: George Allen
& Unwin, (1949). First edition in English. Gach 95-80 1983 $27.50

CROCE, G.   Chirurgiae Universalis Opus
Absolutum in quo quorumque affactum Universo corpori Humano
Obvenientium & ad Chirurgi curam Spectatium... Addita insu-per
Officina Chirurgica Venzia, 1596. Folio, cont. vellum binding.
A few small repairs to the last blank and to the margin of one
leaf. Arkway 22033 1983 $4,250

CROCKER, J. B.   A Complete and Comprehensive Treatise
on the Art of Crayon Portraiture in Black and White. Chicago, 1884.
1st ed. 16mo. Chicago ads, nice. Morrill 287-559 1983 $30

CROCKETT, DAVID   An Account of Col. Crockett's Tour to
the North and Down East. Phila., 1835. First edition. Orig. cloth,
paper label. Some slight foxing and wear. Jenkins 152-603 1983
$150

CROCKETT, DAVID   The Life of Martin Van Buren...
Philadelphia, 1835. 1st ed. 12mo. Paper label. Lacks pp. 173-174,
and leaf 175-176 loose. Label rubbed; covers stained. Morrill 289-
301 1983 $20

CROCKETT, SAMUEL RUTHERFORD The Banner of Blue. London: Hodder &
Stoughton, 1903. First edition. Orig. cloth. Edges and corners very
slightly worn. Very good to near-fine. MacManus 277-1173 1983 $35

CROCKETT, SAMUEL RUTHERFORD The Cherry Ribband. London: Hodder &
Stoughton, 1905. First edition. 4 illus. by Claude B. Shepperson.
Orig. pictorial cloth. Edges and corners slightly worn. Little foxing.
Back cover a bit soiled. Good. MacManus 277-1175 1983 $45

CROCKETT, SAMUEL RUTHERFORD Cinderella. London: James Clarke &
Co., 1901. First edition. Orig. decorated cloth. Endpapers browned
and a bit stained. Covers very slightly worn at the corners and edges.
All pages starting to turn brown. Very good. MacManus 277-1176
1983 $35

CROCKETT, SAMUEL RUTHERFORD Deep Moat Grange. London: Hodder &
Stoughton, 1908. First edition. Orig. pictorial cloth. Covers
slightly soiled. Edges very slightly worn. Former owner's signature
on front free endpaper. Very good. MacManus 277-1177 1983 $45

CROCKETT, SAMUEL RUTHERFORD The Firebrand. London: Macmillan & Co.,
1901. First edition. Orig. cloth. Covers a bit water-spotted. Inscription on front free endpaper. Good. MacManus 277-1178 1983 $35

CROCKETT, SAMUEL RUTHERFORD Flower-o'-the-Corn. London: James
Clark & Co., 1902. First edition. Orig. cloth. Head and foot of
spine slightly worn. Light soiling & foxing to some pages. Inscription on front free endpaper. Good. MacManus 277-1180 1983 $35

CROCKETT, SAMUEL RUTHERFORD Kit Kennedy: Country Boy. London: James
Clark & Co., 1899. First edition. Frontis. port. Orig. elaborate
gilt-decorated cloth. One of 100 copies printed on hand-made paper
and signed by author. Fine. MacManus 277-1181 1983 $75

CROCKETT, SAMUEL RUTHERFORD Maid Margaret of Galloway. London:
Hodder and Stoughton, 1905. First edition. Orig. pictorial cloth.
Edges and corners rather worn (small nick in base of spine). Some
light foxing. Good. MacManus 277-1183 1983 $45

CROCKETT, SAMUEL RUTHERFORD Me and Myn. London: T. Fisher Unwin,
1907. First edition. Orig. cloth. Corners very slightly worn,
signature of previous owner on front pastedown endpaper. Near-fine.
MacManus 277-1184 1983 $35

CROCKETT, SAMUEL RUTHERFORD Red Cap Adventures. London: Adam &
Charles Black. 1908. First edition. Illus. in color. Orig. pictorial
cloth. Very good. MacManus 277-1185 1983 $20

CROCKETT, SAMUEL RUTHERFORD The Silver Skull. London: Smith, Elder
& Co., 1901. First edition. Orig. cloth. Binding a bit worn and
soiled. Endpapers browned. Good. MacManus 277-1186 1983 $35

CROCKETT, SAMUEL RUTHERFORD   Vida, or the Iron Lord of Kirktown.
London: James Clarke & Co., 1907. First edition. 4 illus. Orig.
cloth. Spine very slightly faded. Previous owner's stamp on front
pastedown endpaper. Very good to near-fine. MacManus 277-1187 1983
$35

CROCKWELL, JAMES H.   Souvenir Album. Virginia City, Nevada,
1889. Printed title page (soiled). 130 orig. photographs. Cloth
covers. Presentation inscription in ink on title (March 1889), and
some interesting pencil noted by a former owner. Dawson 471-54 1983
$1,500

CROFT, HERBERT   The Legacy of...to His Diocess. Printed
for Charles Harper, 1679. First edition, ad. leaf, with separate
title-page to the Supplement, 4to, wrapper. Fenning 61-89 1983
£14.50

CROFT, HERBERT   A Short Narrative of the Discovery of
a College of Jesuits... London: T.N. for Charles Harper, 1679. 4to.
Wrappers. Heath 48-89 1983 £45

CROFUTT, GEORGE A.   Crofutt's New Overland Tourist and
Pacific Coast Guide... Vol. 2, 1979-80. Chicago: Overland Pub. Co.,
1879. 19 1/2cm. Ads. Numerous photo-engraved illus. Orig. brown
cloth. Very good. McGahern 54-48 1983 $30

CROGHAN, JOHN   Rambles In The Mammoth Cave, During
the Year 1844. Louisville, KY, 1845. Lithographs, lea. backed
cloth, inner hinges cracked, spine very worn. Errata slip present
but lacks map. First edition. 6 lithos on stone. King 46-126
1983 $35

CROKER, B. M.   Beyond the Pale. London: Chatto & Windus, 1897. First edition. Orig. decorated cloth. Binding worn and
soiled. Signature of previous owner on front free endpaper. Internally good. MacManus 277-1188 1983 $85

CROKER, B. M.   The Happy Valley. London: Methuen &
Co., (1904). First edition. Frontispiece. Orig. red cloth. Spine
ends worn and fraying, spine faded. Bookplate. Good. MacManus 277-
1189 1983 $45

CROKER, B. M.   Interference, A Novel. London: F.V.
White, 1891. First edition. 3 vols. Orig. cloth. Spine ends and
edges rather worn. Good. MacManus 277-1190 1983 $225

CROKER, B. M.   Married or Single? London: Chatto &
Windus, 1895. First edition. 3 vols. Orig. cloth. Spines darkened
and somewhat worn. Margins slightly rubbed. Covers soiled. Fair.
MacManus 277-1191 1983 $135

CROKER, JOHN WILSON   The Croker Papers. John Murray, 1885.
2nd edition, revised. 3 vols. Front. vol. 1. Orig. brown cloth,
presentation inscription from Wilson's daughter, Lady Barrow, 1895.
Fine. Jarndyce 30-961 1983 £34

CROKER, JOHN WILSON   Familiar Epistles to Frederick J----s,
Esq. on the present state of the Irish stage. Dublin: John Barlow,
1804. 12mo, half calf, 1st ed. Bound without an errata leaf at the
end, else a fine uncut copy. Ximenes 64-153 1983 $150

CROKER, JOHN WILSON   Familiar epistles to Frederick E.
Jones, Esq. on the present state of the Irish stage. Dublin: printed
by Graisberry and Campbell, 1805. 12mo, wrappers (torn). 4th ed.
With an errata leaf at the end. Ximenes 64-154 1983 $75

CROKER, THOMAS CROFTON   Fairy Legends, and Traditions of the
South of Ireland. John Murray, 1834. First edition, wood engravings
after Brooke, McClise and the Author. Orig. light brown printed
cloth. Following hinge sl. fraying, otherwise v.g. Jarndyce 31-494
1983 £20

CROLL, PAULINE   Just for You. Volland Pub., (1918).
Probably first edition. Sq. 8vo. Pictorial boards. Defective box.
Color illus. by M. Bassett. Fine. Aleph-bet 8-254 1983 $40

CROLY, GEORGE   The Angel of the World. John Warren,
1820. First edition, errata slip and ad. leaf, with the half-title,
8vo, orig. boards, uncut, with printed paper spine label, wanting
a small portion of backstrip at head of spine, but still a fine
copy in orig. state. Fenning 61-90 1983 £45

CROLY, GEORGE   Gems, Principally from the Antique.
1822. 8vo, uncut, frontis. and 20 plates, orig. boards with paper
label on the spine, lower piece of spine lacking. Bickersteth 77-198
1983 £35

CROLY, GEORGE   Gems, Principally from the Antique,
Drawn and Etched by Richard Dagley. Printed for Hurst, Robinson, 1822.
First edition, with additional engraved title-page and 20 plates,
including half-title, small 8vo, cont. half calf, by T. Painter of
Wrexham, with his ticket, the spine worn but the cords strong,
otherwise a nice copy. Fenning 61-91 1983 £21.50

CROLY, GEORGE   The Life of Luther. Ward Lock, 1858.
Illus. by engrs. from Gustav Konig. Engrs., portraits, etc. by
Gilbert, Clayton, Nicholson, Dalziel, etc. Frontis. & 79 engrs.
Dark green morocco, with gilt & black embossed "Grolier" style
decor. cvrs., marbled eps., a.e.g. Contemp. insc. fr. ep. with a
l.s. explaining presentation. Fr. ep. broken at hinge, foxing first
& last pp. Fine. Hodgkins 27-263 1983 £30

CROLY, GEORGE   Paris in 1815. John Murray, 1817.
First edition. Half red calf by Riviere & Son, t.e.g. Jarndyce 30-
676 1983 £28

CROLY, GEORGE   The Poetical Works. Henry Colburn &
Richard Bentley, 1830. Half green morocco, leading hinge vol. I a
little weak, otherwise v.g. Jarndyce 30-677 1983 £32

CROLY, GEORGE   Salathiel. Henry Colburn, 1829. 3 vols.,
2nd edition, half calf, marbled boards. Very good. Jarndyce 30-347
1983 £32

CROMARTY, GEORGE MAC KENZIE, 1ST EARL OF   A Vindication of Robert
III. Edinburgh: Heirs of Andrew Anderson, 1695. 4to, 19 cm. Modern
calf-backed marbled boards. Very good; ink smudge in upper margin of
title. Grunder 7-12 1983 $45

CROMPTON, RICHMAL   Miss Francis goes to stay with Friends.
Good Housekeeping, November, 1933. 4to. 2 double-page text illus. by
W.H. Robinson. Colour plate by G. Jones. Colour pictorial. Greer 39-
110 1983 £15

CRONIN, A. J.   The Citadel. London: Victor Gollancz
Ltd., 1937. First edition. 8vo. Orig. cloth. Dust jacket. Fine
copy. Jaffe 1-74 1983 $85

CRONIN, A. J.   The Keys of the Kingdom. Boston:
Little, Brown and Company, 1941. First edition. 8vo. Orig. cloth.
Dust jacket. Jacket slightly torn, but a fine copy. Jaffe 1-75
1983 $65

CRONIN, A. J.   The Stars Look Down. London: Victor
Gollancz Ltd., 1935. First edition. 8vo. Orig. cloth. Dust jacket.
Very good copy. Jaffe 1-73 1983 $65

CRONISE, TITUS FEY   The Natural Wealth of California. San
Francisco, 1868. 1st ed. Green cloth, front hinge cracked, otherwise
very good. Bradley 63-38 1983 $25

CROOK, GEORGE   General George Crook His Autobiography.
Norman, 1946. Illus. 1st ed. in dust jacket. Jenkins 151-50
1983 $40

CROOKE, W.   The North-Western Provinces of India...
London, 1897. Folding map, 16 plates. 8vo. Orig. cloth. Good.
Edwards 1044-162 1983 £55

CROOKES, WILLIAM   Select Methods in Chemical Analysis.
London: Longman, 1871. 8vo. Orig. cloth. Text illus. and
tables. Ads. First edition. Front cover detached, spine chipped,
rubbed. Zeitlin 264-92 1983 $40

CROOKS, WILL   The British Workman Defends His Home.
London: The Whitwell Press, 1917. First edition. Orig. pictorial
wrappers. Fine. MacManus 277-1194 1983 $45

CROQUEZ, ALBERT   L'oeuvre grave de James Ensor.
Geneve/Bruxelles: Pierre Cailler, 1947. 133 plates (8 color).
140 illus. 4to. Cloth. Ars Libri 32-204 1983 $100

CROSBY, CARESSE   Painted Shores. Paris: Editions
Narcisse, 1927. Quarto. Orig. printed wraps. First edition. Illus.
with three watercolors by Francois Quelvee. One of 222 numbered
copies on Velin d'arches, from a total of 246 copies. Very slight
chipping at head and toe of spine, otherwise a near fine copy,
with the author's card (a bit mussed) laid in. Reese 20-129 1983
$150

CROSBY, HARRY   Sleeping Together - A Book of Dreams.
Paris: The Black Sun Press, 1931. First edition. One of 500 sets
of sheets printed on uncut Navarre. Inscription. Spine slightly
faded. Edges slightly browned. Very good. Jolliffe 26-112 1983
£45

CROSCUP, GEORGE E.   History Made Visible, a Synchronic
Chart and Statistical Tables of United States History. NY, 1910.
Folding table with color (hinges reinforced), maps, tables, 4to,
buckram, ex lib. Argosy 710-181 1983 $35

CROSLAND, CAMILLA TOULMIN   Landmarks of a Literary Life. Sampson
Low, Marston, 1893. First edition, half title, front. port. Orig.
maroon cloth, v.g. Jarndyce 30-963 1983 £12.50

CROSLAND, T. W. H.   The Absent-Minded Mule And Other Occasional Verses. London: At the Sign of the Unicorn, 1899. First ed.
Orig. green wrappers (slightly dust-soiled). Very good. MacManus
277-1195 1983 $25

CROSLAND, T. W. H.   Last Poems. London: The Fortune Press,
n.d. First edition. Orig. cloth. Dust jacket (soiled, a little worn
at edges). One of 325 numbered copies printed on hand-made paper.
Fine. MacManus 277-1196 1983 $50

CROSLAND, T. W. H.   Literary Parables. London: The Unicorn
Press, 1898. First edition. Orig. cloth-backed boards. Fine.
MacManus 277-1197 1983 $35

CROSLAND, T. W. H.   The Rogue. London: Stanley Paul & Co.,
1926. First edition. Orig. cloth. Covers rather soiled. MacManus
277-1199 1983 $25

CROSLAND, T. W. H.   The Wild Irishman. London: T. Werner
Laurie, 1905. First edition. Orig. cloth. A bit faded. Very good.
MacManus 277-1200 1983 $35

CROSS, M. I.   Modern Microscopy. 1912. 4th ed.,
7 plates. Wheldon 160-129 1983 £15

CROSS, MARGARET B.   The Saffron Robe. London: Hurst &
Blackett, 1893. First edition. 3 vols. Orig. cloth. Very fine.
MacManus 277-1201 1983 $250

CROUCH, CARRIE   Young County... Dallas, 1937. Illus.
1st ed. Fine copy. Jenkins 153-148 1983 $100

CROUCH, E. A.   An Illustrated Introduction to Lamarck's
Conchology. 1827. 22 hand-coloured plates of figures, 4to, new
calf-backed boards. Coloured copies are very scarce. One plate
trifle creased. Slight foxing of the text. Wheldon 160-1205 1985
£120

CROUCH, E. A.   An Illustrated Introduction to Lamarck's
Conchology. 1827. 22 plain plates, 4to, original boards (neatly
rebacked). Boards somewhat used. Wheldon 160-1206 1983 £30

CROUCH, NATHANIEL   Historical Remarques, and Observations of
the Ancient and Present State of London... London: for Nath Crouch,
1681. 12mo. Woodcut plates and coats of arms. Cont. calf. Light
discolouring, small lib. stamps. Heath 48-90 1983 £80

CROUCH, WILLIAM   Posthuma Christiana. Printed and sold by
the Assigns of J. Sowle, 1712. First edition, 8vo, cont. sheep, with
label. Some light browning, but a very good copy. Fenning 60-74 1983
£45

CROUSAZ, JEAN PIERRE DE   A New Treatise of the Art of Thinking.
Printed for Tho. Woodward, 1724. First English edition. Small tear
to last leaf vol. II, sl. affecting advertisements. Calf, labels,
v.g. Jarndyce 31-17 1983 £185

CROWDER, WILLIAM   A Naturalist at the Seashore. New York &
London, 1928. First collected edition, with 52 plates (8 coloured).
8vo, orig. cloth, gilt, a very good copy. Fenning 61-93 1983
£10.50

CROWE, CATHERINE   The Night Side of Nature. T.C. Newby,
1848. First edition, 2 vols. Orig. brown cloth, rubbed at heads of
spines, 1848. Jarndyce 31-495 1983 £85

CROWELL, BENEDICT   America's Munitions 1917-1918. D.C.,
1919. Edges rubbed and lightly worn, slightly shaken, near very good,
photographs. Quill & Brush 54-1610 1983 $20

CROWELL, DAVE   Montana's Own. Missoura, (Montana),
1970. 4to, profusely illus. Orig. signed etching by Asa L. Powell.
Tan cloth stamped in brown. One of 250 numbered copies signed by
the author. Signed and inscribed by artists Fred Fellows and Shorty
Shope. With orig. ink sketches by A. Powell and Gary Schidt. Very
good. Houle 22-1039 1983 $200

CROWLEY, ALEISTER   Aceldama, a Place to Bury Strangers in.
London, Privately printed, 1898. First edition. Printed wraps.
(lightly soiled), else very good. One of 88 copies (of 100) on
handmade paper. Houle 21-264 1983 $550

CROWLEY, ALEISTER   The Book of Toth. (London), O.T.O.,
1944. Small 4to, illus. with a tipped in frontis. and 31 plates.
Half morocco over Egyptian patterned boards, the spine with gilt
mystical devices, t.e.g., uncut. One of 200 on large paper, signed
by the author. Cloth slipcase. Houle 22-260 1983 $495

CROWLEY, ALEISTER   The Poem. London, Privately printed,
1898. First edition. Only 10 copies issued. Printed Japan wraps.
(very small stains) else, very good. Houle 22-262 1983 $450

CROWNINSHIELD, BENJAMIN W.   A History of the First Regiment of
Massachusetts Cavalry Volunteers. Boston, 1891. 1st ed. Illus.,
map in back flap. 8vo. Morrill 287-219 1983 $47.50

CROWQUILL, ALFRED
Please turn to
FORRESTER, ALFRED HENRY

CROWTHER, JAMES ARNOLD   Ions, Electrons and Ionizing Radiations.
London: Edward Arnold, 1919. First edition. 8vo. Orig. cloth.
2 plates. Slightly rubbed and shook. Zeitlin 264-93 1983 $40

CROXTON, ARTHUR   Queen Alexandra Sanatorium Davos.
(London): Theatre Royal, Drury Lane, Tuesday, May 11th, 1909. Small
folio. Illus. with frontis. by Max Beerbohm. Orig. boards, linen
ties. First edition. Boards soiled. Spine neatly repaired at extremities. MacManus 277-177 1983 $40

CROZET, LEO   Manuel Pratique du Bibliothecaire.
Paris, Nourry, 1937. New edition, illus. Full red calf stamped
in gilt, blue leather spine labels, with a fleur de lys inlay on
spine and a small inlay of books on upper cover, marbled edges.
Cloth slipcase. Very good-fine. Houle 21-119 1983 $65

CROZIER, JOHN BEATTIE   My Inner Life being a chapter in Personal
Evolution and Autobiography. London: Longmans, Green & Co., 1898.
First edition. Orig. cloth. Unopened. Fine. MacManus 277-1203
1983 $20

THE CRUELTIES of the Algerine pirates... London: for W. Hone,
1816. First edition. 8vo. Half calf. Engraved tinted frontis.
by George Cruikshank (in two compartments). Slight spotting.
Ximenes 63-352 1983 $150

CRUGER, ALFRED   Report of the Experimental Survey for
the Central Railroad of Georgia from Savannah to Macon. Savannah:
Thomas Purse, 1835. Sewed. Very scarce early southern railroad
survey. Argosy 710-434 1983 $125

CRUIKSHANK, E. A.   The Government of Upper Canada and
Robert Gourlay. Ontario: Ontario Historical Society, Paper and
Records, 1926. Offprint. 25cm. Grey printed wrappers. Fine.
McGahern 54-49 1983 $20

CRUIKSHANK, GEORGE   "The Artist And The Author." (London:
Bell & Daldy, n.d.)(1872). First edition. 16-page pamphlet. Self-
wrappers. One very small tear to the side of the front cover. Near
fine. MacManus 277-1205 1983 $50

CRUIKSHANK, GEORGE   The Bachelor's Own Book... (London),
Designed, Etched and Published by G. Cruikshank, and Sold by D. Bogue,
August 1, 1844. Oblong 12mo. Pictorial title and 24 etchings, with
text, on 12 plates. Stiff printed wrappers. Bound in half morocco,
marbled boards, back gilt. 1st ed. Some light browning, few small
stains. Presentation copy with Cruikshank's inscription and signature
on first blank leaf. O'Neal 50-16 1983 $200

CRUIKSHANK, GEORGE   The Comic Almanack, For 1835(-1853).
London: Charles Tilt, ?David Bogue, 1835-1853. First edition, complete
Illus. with engravings (some in color). 6 vols. Rebound in full green
morocco, gilt, with marbled endpapers, by L. Broca of London.
Almost 200 engraving by Cruikshank. Very fine. MacManus 277-1212
1983 $1,000

CRUIKSHANK, GEORGE   George Cruikshank's Fairy Library.
London, n.d. (ca. 1853-1854). Nice 1/2 lea., gilt-dec. spine, a
bit rubbed. With 24 pages of etched plates by George Cruikshank.
King 46-428 1983 $150

CRUIKSHANK, GEORGE   George Cruikshank's Fairy Library.
London: David Bogue, et. al., 1854-1864. First editions, later
issues. Double-illus. with one set of the plates hand-colored. Gilt-
decorated full red morocco by Bedford. Orig. wrappers bound in.
Bookplate. Fine. MacManus 277-1225 1983 $1,250

CRUIKSHANK, GEORGE   George Cruikshank's Fairy Library.
N.d. (1854). Ed. & illus. with ten subjects, designed and etched on
steel., front. and 5 plates. Orig. light blue printed wraps., v.g.
Jarndyce 31-499 1983 £75

CRUIKSHANK, GEORGE   Forty Illustrations of Lord Byron.
J. Robins, 1824. First edition, engr. facs., front. port. and
woodcuts. Orig. pink printed wraps., a little dust marked, and
repair to lower outer corner of front wrap., otherwise v.g., bound
into full calf by Zaehnsdorf. Gilt borders and spine, label.
Jarndyce 31-497 1983 £85

CRUIKSHANK, GEORGE   The Glass And The New Crystal Palace.
London: J. Cassell, 1853. First edition. Illus. with woodcuts by
Cruikshank. Orig. decorated wrappers. Covers slightly soiled and
worn at the edges. Very good. MacManus 277-1215 1983 $125

CRUIKSHANK, GEORGE   The Humourist. Printed and published
by J. Robins and Co. Vol. 1, 1822. Vol. II, 1819. Vol. III, 1819.
Vol. IV, 1820. 4 vols. 12mo, each with engraved frontis., title,
and 8 plates by Cruikshank, cont. hand-coloured, uncut, orig. boards
with Cruikshank's design on the upper covers. All vols. rebacked with
plain paper spines and new end papers. A fine set. Bickersteth 75-
126 1983 £145

CRUIKSHANK, GEORGE   Illustrations of Time. London: 1827.
Oblong folio. Etched title and 6 etched plates by
Cruikshank. Colored copy with 6 plates colored, title-page in b&w.
Bound in full calf by Riviere with red lettering piece. Title in gilt
on both front cover and spine. Some wear to edges and marks to covers,
internally fine and clean copy. Bromer 25-184 1983 $400

CRUIKSHANK, GEORGE   George Cruikshank's Omnibus. Tilt &
Bogue, 1842. Illus. with 100 engrs. on steel & wood. Frontis. & 21
etchings & 78 wood cuts. Bound in full tan goat skin with pictorial
covers in gilt & black after design by Cruikshank from the Hampstead
Bindery, a.e.g., lea. some discol., vg. Hodgkins 27-264 1983 £160

CRUIKSHANK, GEORGE   George Cruikshank's Omnibus. London,
1842. 8vo. Full leather with a floral pattern on the spine. Illustrated with over one hundred engravings on wood and steel. Some
light foxing, mainly a fine copy. In Our Time 156-180 1983 $150

CRUIKSHANK, GEORGE   A Pop-Gun Fired Off By George Cruikshank.
London: W. Kent & Co., (1860). First edition. Illus. with woodcuts
by Cruikshank. Orig. green wrappers. Presentation copy from author
inscribed on the front wrapper. Back wrapper detached. Front wrapper
slightly soiled and worn at the spine. Small piece to each outer
corner of the front cover missing. Good. MacManus 277-1217 1983
$250

CRUIKSHANK, GEORGE   Scraps and Sketches. London: Published
by the Artist, 1828-1832; 1827,1826. First editions. Three separate
works bound together in 3/4 morocco & cloth, marbled endpapers. Slight
foxing to several plates. A number of short marginal tears neatly
repaired. Fine. MacManus 277-1229 1983 $600

CRUIKSHANK, GEORGE   Scraps and Sketches. London: 1828.
Oblong folio. First edition of 4 parts bound together. 24 plates.
Bound in full calf by Riviere with red lettering piece. Title in gilt
on front cover and spine. Some wear to edges, plates in very fine and
clean condition. Bromer 25-185 1983 $525

CRUIKSHANK, GEORGE   George Cruikshank's Table Book. London,
Bell & Daldy, 1869. New edition. Small 4to, illus. by Cruikshank.
12 steel plates, numerous woodcuts (light spot on one plate).
3/4 red morocco, gilt spine with raised bands (rubbed), t.e.g., uncut.
Presentation copy. Inscribed in Cruikshank's fine, bold hand at top
of title page: "To A. MacInnes with the best wishes of George
Cruikshank, March 2nd, 1877..." Good - very good. Houle 22-264 1983
$275

CRUIKSHANK, GEORGE   Cruikshank's Water Colours. London:
A. & C. Black, 1903. 68 color plates with tissue guards. 4to.
Cloth. With facsimile reproductsion of the 3 watercolor suites
of the artist. One plate loose. Binding slightly worn. Ars Libri
32-135 1983 $75

CRUIKSHANK, ROBERT   Sketches of pumps... London: D.
Bogue, 1846. First edition. 8vo. 19th-century half calf (orig.
printed wrappers bound in). Fine copy. Ximenes 63-194 1983
$60

CRULL, JODOCUS   Denmark Vindicated: being an Answer
to a late Treatise called "An Account of Denmark, as it was in the
Year 1692". London: Thomas Newborough and Edward Mory, 1694.
1st ed., 8vo, cont. panelled calf, initial and final blanks present.
Front cover chipped; top margin of title neatly excited, not affecting
text; a very good copy. Trebizond 18-137 1983 $190

CRUM, H. A.   Mosses of Eastern North America. New
York, 1980. Illustrated, 2 vols., 8vo, cloth. Wheldon 160-1813
1983 £60

CRUMBINE, SAMUEL J.   Frontier Doctor. Phila., (1948).
Orig. cloth, dust jacket. First edition. Ginsberg 46-384 1983 $35

CRUMMER, LEROY   An Introduction to the Study of Physic...
New York: William Heberden, 1929. 8vo. Orig. binding. Limited
edition of 230 copies. A very fine copy. Fye H-3-124 1983 $150

CRUSE, THOMAS   Apache Days and After. Caldwell, 1941.
Frontis. and plates. First edition in dust jacket. Fine Copy. A
very scarce Caxton title. Jenkins 151-4 1983 $125

CRUSIUS, LEWIS   The Lives of the Roman Poets....together
with an Introduction concerning the Origin and Progress of Poetry in
General. 1733. 2 vols., 12mo, frontis. and 6 plates in vol. 1,
mappe-monde and 5 plates in vol. 2, orig. calf with morocco labels.
Bickersteth 77-19 1983 £24

CRUTTWELL, MAUD   Andrea Mantegna. London: George Bell
& Sons, 1908. 40 plates. Small 4to. Cloth. Worn. Ars Libri 33-
218 1983 $27.50

CRUZ, MARTIN DE LA   Libellus de Medicinalibus Indorum
Herbis. Mexico: Instituto Mexicano del Seguro Social, 1964.
133 color facsimile plates. Large 4to. Full tooled leather.
Edition limited to 215 copies bound in leather. Ars Libri 34-199
1983 $250

CUBA; or the Policy of England, Mexico, and Spain, with Regard to
that Island. James Ridgway, 1830. First edition, wanting half-title,
8vo, wrapper. Fenning 61-95 1983 £65

CUBBON, WILLIAM   A Bibliographical Account of Works
Relating to the Isle of Man... Oxford & London: Published for The
Manx Museum and Ancient Monuments Trustees, 1933, 1939. 3 plates (2
folding). Cloth. Dawson 470-83 1983 $100

CUDWORTH, RALPH   Systema Intellectuale jugus Universi...
Lugd. Bat., 1773. 2 vols., 4to, cont. calf, gilt edges, joints
worn. K Books 301-54 1983 £80

CUEVAS, LUIS G.   Memoir of the Minister of Interior and Exterior Relations. Wash., 1849. Dsb., good. Reese 19-171 1983 $85

CULLEN, COUNTEE   The Black Christ. NY, 1929. Illus. by Chas. Cullen. Paper labels slightly rubbed and discolored, page edge foxed, else very good in very good dustwrapper with small chips. Quill & Brush 54-337 1983 $90

CULLEN, COUNTEE   Color. New York, (1925). First ed. Cloth-backed boards, paper labels. "F-A" on copyright. Covers soiled and worn. Bradley 64-46 1983 $20

CULLEN, COUNTEE   Copper Sun. New York: Harper, (1927). Cloth and boards. Decorations by Charles Cullen. First edition. Fine in the striking pictorial dust jacket, which lacks two small chips at the head and toe of the spine. Reese 20-288 1983 $50

CULLEN, COUNTEE   Copper Sun. NY, (1927). Signed "Cordially, Countee Cullen", sixth printing, edges slightly bumped, otherwise very good, owner's name. Quill & Brush 54-336 1983 $35

CULLEN, THOMAS   Dr. Howard A. Kelly, 1919. Offprint. 8vo. Wrappers. Scarce. Fye H-3-818 1983 $20

CULLEN, THOMAS   Henry Mills Hurd - The First Superintendent of the Johns Hopkins Hospital. Baltimore, 1920. First edition. 8vo. Orig. binding. Fye H-3-801 1983 $20

CULLEN, WILLIAM   First Lines of the Practice of Physics. Printed in Worcester, Massachusetts, by Isaiah Thomas. MDCCXC. (1790). 12mo, misnumbered. A blank is lacking. 19th century sprinkled leather. Title stamped on black leather label. Gold tooling around raised bands. "Geo. Howe" stamped in gold at foot of each spine. Joints weakening. A.E. Lownes bookplate. Apart from slight toning, internally excellent. Arkway 22-34 1983 $425

CULLEN, WILLIAM   Treatise of the Materia Medica. Phila., Carey, 1808. 2 vols. in 1. 8vo, cont. sheep, leather label, ex-lib. Argosy 713-129 1983 $125

CULLITON, JOHN T.   Assisted Emigration and Land Settlement. Montreal, n.d. (1928). 22cm. Stiff wrappers. Fine. McGahern 53-37 1983 $30

CULLUM, JOHN   The History and Antiquities of Hawsted, and Hardwick, In The County Of Suffolk. London, 1813. Second edition, limited to 230 copies, 4to, engraved frontispiece portrait, 10 engraved plates and 4 folding pedigrees, some spotting and offsetting, contemporary polished half calf, marbled boards, morocco label, gilt, a little worn. Deighton 3-91 1983 £105

CULPEPPER, NICHOLAS   The English Physician Enlarged. London: Peter Cole, 1656. Cont. panelled calf, hinges split, pages cropped, affecting some running heads. Bound in at the end are 32 manuscript pages in 3 separate hands, the first two apparently 17th century. Argosy 713-130 1983 $1,250

CULPEPPER, NICHOLAS   The English Physician Enlarged with 369 Medicines. London: Scatcherd et al, circa 1800. 12mo, modern brown 1/2 morocco. Argosy 713-131 1983 $100

CULVER, HENRY B.   The Book of Old Ships. New York, 1924. Limited edition. 4to. Illus. by G. Grant. Coloured frontis. (a little foxed in inner margin) and 1 plate. 60 full-page illus., 27 other illus. in Appendix at end, illus. endpapers. Orig. blue boards, slightly soiled. Spine a little faded, mounted illus. on upper cover. Uncut. Front inner hinge worn, pencil inscriptions on endpaper and limitation leaf. Good. Edwards 1042-45 1983 £80

CULVER, HENRY B.   Contemporary Scale Models of Vessels. New York: Book Collectors Society, 1954. Limited edition of which 100 were bound in morocco; first published in 1926. 8vo. Orig. cloth. 50 sepia photogravure plates, folio. Orig. full black morocco, gilt. T.e.g., marbled endpapers. Good. Edwards 1042-46 1983 £125

CULWICK, JAMES   The Distinctive Characteristics of Ancient Irish Melody. Dublin: E. Ponsonby, 1897. First edition, with music examples, roy. 8vo, orig. glazed printed paper wraps. Spine trifle worn and the lower wrapper slightly at foot, a very good copy. Fenning 60-75 1983 £16.50

CUMBERLAND, RICHARD   Calvary; or the Death of Christ. Burlington: Neale & Kammerer, June, 1795. Full calf. Nice. Felcone 19-10 1983 $45

CUMBERLAND, RICHARD   Calvary; or, the Death of Christ. London for Lackington: Allen & Co., 1805. 2 vols. 12mo. Cont. Spanish calf, gilt, gilt panelled spines with morocco labels. 9 engraved plates from drawings by W. Brown. Joints worn. Traylen 94-223 1983 £12

CUMBERLAND, RICHARD   John de Lancaster. Lackington, Allen, 1809. First edition, 3 vols., half titles, calf, spines rubbed, red and black labels (lacking one vol. No. label). Jarndyce 30-348 1983 £85

CUMBERLAND, RICHARD   The Mysterious Husband. Dublin: Printed by William Gilbert, 1783. First Irish edition, 12mo, wrapper. Fenning 60-76 1983 £14.50

CUMBERLAND, STUART   The Vasty Deep. Sampson, Low, 1889. First edition, 2 vols., half titles, 32 pp ads. in both vols. Orig. lilac dec. cloth, spines rubbed. Jarndyce 30-349 1983 £36

CUMING, FORTESCUE   Sketches of a Tour to the Western Country, through the States of Ohio and Kentucky... Pittsburgh, 1810. Writing on free endleaves and light foxing, but a very good copy in orig. calf. Reese 18-334 1983 $675

CUMINGS, HENRY   An Half-Century Discourse, Addressed to the People of Billerica... Cambridge, 1813. Disbound. Reese 18-410 1983 $20

CUMINGS, SAMUEL   The Western Navigator. Phila.: E. Littell, 1822. Vol. 2 only. Errata. Calf-backed printed boards. Very sound. Felcone 20-33 1983 $350

CUMING, CONSTANCE FREDERICA GORDON
Please turn to
GORDON-CUMMING, CONSTANCE FREDERICA

CUMMING, JOHN   Benedictions: or, the Blessed Life. J.F. Shaw, 1853. First edition, small 8vo, cont. half calf. Fenning 62-88 1983 £10.50

CUMMING, ROUALEYN GORDON   Five years of a hunter's life in the far interior of South Africa. London: John Murray, 1850. First edition. 2 vols. 8vo. Map. 2 vignettes, 14 plates. 1/2 green morocco. Rubbed. Adelson Africa-77 1983 $275

CUMMING, ROUALEYN GORDON   Five Years of a Hunter's Life in the Far Interior of South Africa. London: John Murray, 1850. 2nd ed., 2 vols. Cr. 8vo, with half-titles, vignette titles printed title page, map and 15 plates, rebound in light-brown cloth, spines lettered and ruled in gilt, orig. gilt decorated cloth upper bound in, occasional foxing. A very good copy. Deighton 3-92 1983 £75

CUMMING, ROUALEYN GORDON   A hunter's life among lions, elephants, and other wild animals of South Africa. New York: Derby & Jackson, 1857. 2 vols./one. 8vo. 7 plates. Orig. red pictorial cloth. Rebacked. Adelson Africa-181 1983 $75

CUMMING, W. F.   Notes of a Wanderer. London, 1839. Half morocco by Kerr and Richardson of Galsgow. Gilt edges. Folding map, frontis. to each volume. Occasional marginal corrections in author's hand. 8vo. Orig. cloth. Good. Edwards 1044-168 1983 £55

CUMMINGS, BRUCE FREDERICK   Enjoying Life and Other Literary Remains. London: Chatto & Windus, 1919. Orig. cloth. Paper label on spine. Dust jacket (worn). First edition. Very good copy. MacManus 277-154 1983 $35

CUMMINGS, BYRON   Kinishba: A Prehistoric Pueblo of the Great Pueblo Period, Tuscon (1940). First edition. Illus. with 33 halftones; 36 color plates of pottery; 3 maps; and drawings in the text. Dust jacket (small chip). Very good. Houle 22-1009 1983 $37.50

CUMMINGS, EDWARD ESTLIN   Anthropos. (NY, 1944). One of 222 copies, very good in damaged slipcase. Quill & Brush 54-338 1983 $75

CUMMINGS, EDWARD ESTLIN   Complete Poems. Macgibbon & Kee, (1968). 2 vols. 8vo. Wrappers. Definitive ed. These are the uncorrected proofs for the set. A fine set. In Our Time 156-183 1983 $200

CUMMINGS, EDWARD ESTLIN   Eimi. New York, (1933). 8vo. Cloth. 1 of 1381 copies signed by Cummings. A fine copy in almost flawless dj. In Our Time 156-182 1983 $200

CUMMINGS, EDWARD ESTLIN   Complete Poems 1913-1962. London, 1968. First edition. 2 vols. One of 150 numbered copies. Slipcase. Fine. Rota 231-149 1983 £60

CUMMINGS, EDWARD ESTLIN   Eimi. NY: 1933. First edition. Limited to 1381 copies signed by Cummings. Extremely fine in dust wrapper. Bromer 25-19 1983 $165

CUMMINGS, EDWARD ESTLIN   Eimi. NY, 1933. Limited to 1381 num- bered and signed copies, cover lightly soiled, else very good. Quill & Brush 54-339 1983 $90

CUMMINGS, EDWARD ESTLIN   Eimi. N.Y., Covici-Friede, 1933. First edition. Black stamped yellow cloth, uncut (soiled, tear at head of spine). Copy number 13 of the limited edition, signed by the author. Good. Houle 22-265 1983 $85

CUMMINGS, EDWARD ESTLIN   The Enormous Room. NY, (1922). Page 219 has offensive word blacked out, endpapers offset, very good, front portion of dustwrapper laid in. Quill & Brush 54-341 1983 $125

CUMMINGS, EDWARD ESTLIN   Him. NY: 1927. First edition. Limited to 160 copies signed by Cummings. Quarter-vellum and boards very fine except for some foxing to vellum spine. Orig. glassine torn and slip-case rubbed. Bromer 25-20 1983 $225

CUMMINGS, EDWARD ESTLIN   Him. New York: 1927. First edition. 1/160 signed by poet. Black boards, vellum spine. Vellum spotted and discolored, otherwise very good copy. Bradley 66-83 1983 $150

CUMMINGS, EDWARD ESTLIN   Him. New York: Boni & Liveright, 1927. 1st ed. Orig. cloth-backed boards with drawing by author reproduced on front cover. Fine copy without dj. Jenkins 155-269 1983 $50

CUMMINGS, EDWARD ESTLIN   Him. NY, (1927). Spine lettering slightly rubbed, minor cover wear and stains, else very good. Quill & Brush 54-340 1983 $30

CUMMINGS, EDWARD ESTLIN   95 Poems. New York, 1958. First edition. Author's compliment slip loosely inserted (this was Theodore Roethke's copy, but does not contain his ownership signature). Small stain on fore-edge. Slightly torn and chipped dustwrapper. Fine. Jolliffe 26-113 1983 £48

CUMMINGS, EDWARD ESTLIN   (No Thanks). (NY: Golden Eagle Press: 1935). First edition. Limited to 900 copies. Inscribed on copy- right page by Cummings. Very fine in chipped dust wrapper. Bromer 25-21 1983 $100

CUMMINGS, EDWARD ESTLIN   No Thanks. (New York: Golden Eagle Press, 1935). Cloth. First edition. One of 900 trade copies printed on Japanese paper. Fine in slightly darkened dust jacket. Reese 20-289 1983 $50

CUMMINGS, EDWARD ESTLIN   Santa Claus. N.Y., (1946). First edition. Small thin 4to, red & black cloth. First edition. Fine, in a chipped dust wrapper. Argosy 714-866 1983 $40

CUMMINGS, EDWARD ESTLIN   Tom. New York: Arrow Editions, 1935. First edition. Coloured frontis. by B. Shahn. Autograph presentation inscription of Marion Cummings, incorporating her husband's autograph signature. Very nice. Rota 230-147 1983 £60

CUMMINGS, EDWARD ESTLIN   Tom. New York: Arrow Editions, (1935). Cloth. Frontis. by Ben Shahn. Printed at the Rydal Press. A fine copy, in rather chipped dust jacket. Reese 20-290 1983 $85

CUMMINGS, EDWARD ESTLIN   Tom. (N.Y., Arrow Editions, 1935). Color frontis. by Ben Shahn. Printed by the Rydal Press, Santa Fe. Brown cloth stamped in silver. Very good. Houle 22-266 1983 $65

CUMMINGS, EDWARD ESTLIN   VV (Viva). New York, 1931. First trade edition. Large 8vo. Boards soiled. Internally very good. Rota 231- 148 1983 £35

CUMMINGS, SAMUEL   The Western Pilot, Containing Charts of the Ohio River, and of the Mississippi. Cincinnati, 1832. Original printed boards, spine repaired. Illus. with engraved plates. Jenkins 151-51 1983 $250

CUMSTON, CHARLES GREENE   Introduction to the History of Medicine. N.Y., 1927. Tall 8vo, d.w. 24 illus. Argosy 713-132 1983 $85

CUMSTON, CHARLES GREENE   An Introduction to the History of Medicine. New York, 1926. 8vo. Orig. binding. First American edition. Scarce. Fye H-3-128 1983 $75

CUNARD, NANCY   Negro Anthology 1931-1933. London: Published by Nancy Cunard at Wishart & Co., 1934. First edition. Many illus. Small folio, linen. Paul Robeson's copy, with his name on the flyleaf. Argosy 714-207 1983 $1,000

CUNARD, NANCY   Outlaws. London, Matthews, 1921. First edition. Black boards, uncut, (lightly rubbed), else very good. Houle 21-270 1983 $225

CUNARD, NANCY   Outlaws. Lon., 1931. Top 1/2 inch of spine missing, label slightly chipped, British Poetry Soc. copy with markings, balance of book very good. Quill & Brush 54-342 1983 $100

CUNDALL, JOSEPH   The Babes in the Wood. Cundall, 1849. Sm. folio, pictorial title & 9 plates. Light green boards, gilt, some wear. Greer 40-84 1983 £28

CUNDALL, JOSEPH   A Brief History of Wood-Engraving from Its Invention. London: 1895. Sm 8vo, green cloth, pictorial design on front cover, gilt, t.e.g. Illustrated throughout. Moderate shelf-wear. A very good copy. Perata 27-32 1983 $50

CUNHA, FELIX   Osler as a Gastroenterologist. San Francisco, 1948. 8vo. Orig. binding. Very fine. Scarce. Fye H-3-877 1983 $35

CUNNINGHAM, ALLAN   Paul Jones: A Romance. Edinburgh: Oliver and Boyd, 1826. 3 vols, contemporary half blue calf; no half- titles; a good copy. Hill 165-24 1983 $85

CUNNINGHAM, ALLAN   Paul Jones. Edinburgh: Oliver & Boyd; Longman, 1826. Half title, orig. boards, dark green cloth spines; rubbed, paper labels worn. Jarndyce 30-350 1983 £65

CUNNINGHAM, D. D.   Some Indian Friends and Acquaintances. 1903. 1903. 23 plates (1 coloured), 8vo, cloth. Wheldon 160-368 1983 £15

CUNNINGHAM, EUGENE   Famous in the West. El Paso, Texas: Hick-Hayward Co., 1926. Original pictorial wrappers, 1st ed. Rare. Most copies of the edition destroyed by the dealer. Jenkins 151-52 1983 $200

CUNNINGHAM, J. D.   A History of the Sikhs. London, 1849. 2 maps, 1 folding. Folding table, spine faded and repaired. Elphin- stone Carberry Tower Library label. 8vo. Orig. cloth. Good. Edwards 1044-169 1983 £95

CUNNINGHAM, J. T.   The Natural History of the Marketable Marine Fishes of the British Islands. 1896. Slight marginal stain on first few leaves. Wheldon 160-952 1983 £12

CUNNINGHAM, JOHN   Poems, chiefly Pastoral. London: for the Author, 1766. First edition. 8vo. Engraved frontis., list of Subscribers. Cont. polished calf. Heath 48-267 1983 £175

CUNNINGHAM, JOHN   Poems, Chiefly Pastoral. Newcastle:
Printed by T. Slack...MDCCLXXI. 12mo, pastoral frontis. neatly
backed with linen; cont. calf, rebacked. Second edition. Quaritch
NS 7-29 1983 $325

CUNNINGHAM, JOHN   Poems, Chiefly Pastoral. Newcastle:
Printed by T. Slack...MDCCLXXI. 12mo, pastoral frontis. neatly
backed with linen; cont. calf, rebacked. Second edition. Quaritch
NS 7-30 1983 $125

CUNNINGHAM, PETER   A Handbook for London, Past and Present.
John Murray, 1849. First edition. 2 vols. Half calf, slightly
rubbed, maroon labels. Jarndyce 31-238 1983 £38

CUNNINGHAM, PETER   Murray's Handbook for Modern London.
John Murray, 1851. First edition. Folding hand-coloured map, 24 pp
ads. (small section cut from one page), orig. pink cloth, v.g.
Jarndyce 31-240 1983 £20

CUNNINGHAM, PETER   The Story of Nell Gwyn and the Sayings
of Charles the Second. London: 1852. Sm 8vo, 3/4 crimson morocco,
raised bands, gilt extra, t.e.g. First edition. With 17 extra
portraits, including 4 hand-colored ones of Nell Gwyn. Bookplate.
A very nice copy. Scarce. Perata 27-33 1983 $175

CUNNINGHAME-GRAHAM, ROBERT BONTINE
Please turn to
GRAHAM, ROBERT BONTINE CUNNINGHAME

CUNTIRA, FRANCIS JOHANN   Dissertatio inauguralis medica de
viribus medicis nicotinae ejusque usu et abusu. Vienna: Johann
Thomas von Trattner, 1777. First edition. Small 8vo. Modern
boards. Kraus 164-230 1983 $180

CUPPLES, GEORGE   A Spliced Yarn. Some Strands from the
Life Cable of Bill Bullen. London: Gibbings & Co., Ltd., (1899).
Illus. by Frank Brangwyn. Orig. pictorial cloth. Covers a little
rubbed. First edition. Very good. MacManus 277-665 1983 $40

CUREAU, ADOLPHE LOUIS   Savage Man in Central Africa. London:
T. Fisher Unwin, (1915). With 23 plates, 9 text illus. and folding
map. Index. Blue cloth, gilt-stamped spine, slightly discolored.
Karmiole 75-1 1983 $75

CURIE, IRENE   La Projection de Noyaux Atomiques par
un Rayonnement tres penetrant. Paris: Hermann, 1932. First
edition. 8vo. Orig. printed wrappers. 3 photographic plates.
Inscribed presentation copy from the author. Near fine. Zeitlin
264-94 1983 $100

CURIE, MARIE SKLODOWSKA   L'Isotope et les Elements Isotopes.
Paris: Journal de Physique, 1924. 8vo. Orig. cloth. 3 photo-
graphic plates (2 on 1 page). Numerous text figures (1 full page).
Internally very good. Zeitlin 264-95 1983 $100

CURIE, MARIE SKLODOWSKA   Pierre Curie. N.Y., Doubleday, 1923.
First edition thus. Half black cloth over blue boards, lined and
stamped in gilt, uncut. Illus. with portrait of M. Curie opposite
limitation page, frontis. portrait of P. Curie, and 7 photographs.
One of 100 deluxe numbered copies, signed by M. Curie. Bookplate.
Very good - fine. Houle 22-270 1983 $750

CURIE, MARIE SKLODOWSKA   Pierre Curie. Paris: Payot, 1924.
8vo. Orig. printed paper wrappers, protective wrapper. Partially
unopened. Ads. Zeitlin 264-96 1983 $20

CURIE, MARIE SKLODOWSKA   Radioactivite. Paris: Hermann & Cie.,
1935. 8vo. Modern green cloth. Frontis. portraits of the Curies,
24 photographic plates, text illus. and diagrams. Very good.
Zeitlin 264-97 1983 $175

CURIE, MARIE SKLODOWSKA   Recherches sur Substances Radioactives...
Deuxieme Edition, Revue et Corrigee. Gauthier-Villars, Paris, 1904.
8vo, text diagrams; uncut in orig. printed wraps., a little frayed.
Quaritch NS 5-28 1983 $450

CURIE, MARIE SKLODOWSKA   Untersuchungen uber die radioaktiven
substanzen... Braunschweig: Vieweg, 1904. First German edition.
8vo. Half blue cloth. Text figures. A very good copy. Zeitlin
264-101 1983 $75

THE CURIOUS Book of Clampus, or, Gumshaniana. Yerbe Buena, Calif.,
1935. 8vo, bds., paper labels. Illustrated with vignettes
throughout. One of 200 copies printed by Lawton R. Kennedy &
John J. Johnck. A very fine copy. Perata 27-153 1983 $75

CURJEL, HANS   Hans Baldung Grien. Munchen: O.C.
Recht, 1923. 97 plates (3 color collotype). 66 illus. Large 4to.
Boards, 1/4 cloth. Edition limited to 1000 copies. From the library
of Jakob Rosenberg. Ars Libri 32-16 1983 $85

CURLE, RICHARD   Collecting American First Editions, Its
Pitfalls and its Pleasures. Indianapolis: Bobbs-Merrill, (1930).
Numerous photographic plates. 1st ed., limited to 1250 numbered and
signed copies. Orig. blue cloth, labels, t.e.g., others uncut. Very
fine copy. Jenkins 155-100 1983 $45

CURLE, RICHARD   Collecting American First Editions.
Indianapolis, Bobbs-Merrill (1930). First edition. 51 illus.
Blue cloth, t.e.g. Uncut. Slipcase. A little rubbed, else fine.
One of 1250 numbered and signed copies. Houle 21-121 1983 $45

CURLE, RICHARD   Corruption. Indianapolis: Bobbs Merrill,
(1933). First American edition. Orig. cloth. Presentation copy
inscribed to Ruth Moorhead, dated March 1933. Head of spine rather
worn, binding a bit water-stained and worn at the edges. Endpapers
slightly browned. MacManus 277-1252 1983 $35

CURLE, RICHARD   A Handlist of the Various Books, Pamphlets, Prefaces,...Written About Joseph Conrad. Pennsylvania: Privately
Printed, 1932. First edition. Orig. printed wrappers. One of 250
copies. Very slight tear to the first few pages. Bookplate. Very
good. MacManus 277-1110 1983 $85

CURLE, RICHARD   Joseph Conrad. Garden City, Doubleday,
1914. First American edition. Frontis. Blue cloth stamped in
orange, else very good. Houle 21-254 1983 $20

CURLE, RICHARD   The Last Twelve Years of Joseph Conrad.
London: 1928. First edition. Portrait frontis. 7 other full-page
plates. Black cloth. Very fine in dust jacket. Bradley 66-76 1983
$50

CURLING, HENRY   The Soldier of Fortune. London: G.
Routledge & Co., 1852. Second edition, abridged. Orig. green cloth.
Spine and covers slightly rubbed and spotted. Good. MacManus 277-
1293 1983 $35

CURLL, EDMUND   The Case of Seduction: being an Account
of the late Proceedings at Paris. London: E. Curll, 1726. Only
edition in English, 12mo, cont. calf gilt, morocco label, bookplate.
Edge of leaf B4 cropped, with loss of a few letters; else a very good
copy. Very scarce. Trebizond 18-186 1983 $400

CURLL, EDMUND   Faithful memoirs of the life, amours
and performances, of that justly celebrated actress of her time,
Mrs. Anne Oldfield. London: 1731. 8vo, disbound, 1st ed. With a
fine portrait. Ximenes 64-156 1983 $250

CURLL, EDMUND   The Life of that Eminent Comedian Robert
Wilks, Esq. London: printed for E. Curll, 1733. 8vo, disbound,
1st ed. Vignette portrait on the title-page, half-title present;
lacks two leaves of ads, else a good copy. Ximenes 64-157 1983 $250

CURRAN, M.P.   Life of Patrick A. Collins. Norwood,
Mass., 1906. Memorial ed. de luxe, 1 of 100 copies. Printed for
Frank G. Webster and inscribed by Curran. Illus. Large 8vo. Full
blue crushed levant morocco with gilt decorations and borders on
covers, raised bands, dentelles, marbled endpapers, gilt top, untrimmed. Fine. Morrill 289-304 1983 $47.50

CURRIE, BARTON   Booth Tarkington, A Bibliography.
Garden City: Doubleday, Doran & Company, 1932. First edition.
8vo. Cloth. Slipcase. Fine in worn slipcase. Oak Knoll 49-503
1983 $65

CURRY, GEORGE   Message of George Curry, Governor of
New Mexico, to the Legislature. Santa Fe, 1909. Contemp. full
morocco presentation binding. Jenkins 153-386 1983 $50

CURRY, J. C.   The Indian Police. London, 1932. First edition. Folding coloured map, spine slightly worn and soiled. Presentation bookplate from the publisher's to the R.U.S.I. 8vo. Orig. cloth. Good. Edwards 1044-165 1983 £25

CURSORY suggestions, on naval subjects... Ramsgate: printed by Burgess, Hunt and Carter, 1822. First edition. 8vo. Disbound. Large folding table. Ximenes 63-337 1983 $60

CURTIN, JEREMIAH   Irish Folk-Tales. Dublin: for the Folklore of Ireland Society, 1943. First collected edition, with a portrait, 8vo, orig. cloth. In dustwrapper. Fenning 60-77 1983 £16.50

CURTIS, ALVA   Lectures on Midwifery & the Forms of Disease. Columbus: Printed for the author, 1841. 25 illus. 8vo, leather backed boards. (Foxing, ex-lib.) Argosy 713-133 1983 $75

CURTIS, ALVA   Lectures on Midwifery and the Forms of Disease Peculiar to Women and Children... Columbus, 1841. 2nd ed. Corrected and enlarged. Illus. Small 8vo. Contemporary calf, leather label. Hinges cracked; rubbed. Scarce. Morrill 289-55 1983 $40

CURTIS, BENJAMIN R.   Opinion of the Hon...Relating to the Right of the Central Branch Union Pacific Railroad Company to Continue and Extend its Road to the Main Trunk. Wash., Gibson, 1869. Dbd. First edition. Ginsberg 47-889 1983 $40

CURTIS, EDWARD S.   Portraits from North American Indian Life. NY: Amer. Mus. Nat. Hist. & Outerbridge & Lazard, Co., (1972). Oblong folio, cloth-backed pict. boards. Argosy 710-219 1983 $75

CURTIS, GEORGE   Oration...Delivered at the Celebration of the Russian Victories. (Georgetown, 1813). Dsb., ex. lib., fair. Reese 18-411 1983 $20

CURTIS, GEORGE MUNSON   Early Silver of Connecticut and Its Makers. Meriden, International Silver Company, 1913. 1st ed. Plates. 8vo, new cloth, very nice. Morrill 287-72 1983 $75

CURTIS, GEORGE WILLIAM   Lotus-Eating. New York, 1854. Illus. Cloth. Covers a bit discolored, bookplate removed. Felcone 22-43 1983 $25

CURTIS, HERBERT P.   Arabian Days' Entertainments. Boston, 1858. Frontis., plates. 1st American ed. Orig. red cloth, gilt. Fine copy. Jenkins 155-270 1983 $20

CURTIS, NEWTON MARTIN   From Bull Run to Chancellorsville. New York, 1906. 1st ed. Autographed. Illus. 8vo. Ex-library with no external marks; fore-edge of back cover partly dented. Morrill 287-307 1983 $25

CURTIS'S Botanical Magazine. (1787), 1793-1804. 20 vols. in 19, 8vo, modern boards, fine hand-coloured plates. Some slight foxing here and there in a few volumes, but nowhere is this serious. Two plates in vol. 14 are library stamped, else a good, clean complete series. Wheldon 160-19 1983 £2,000

CURZON, ROBERT   Visits to Monasteries in the Levant. 1865. Fifth edition, numerous woodcuts, additional engraved title, old style half calf. K Books 307-60 1983 £35

CURZON, RONALDSHY   The Life of Lord Curzon... London, (1928). Numerous plates. 3 vols. Thick 8vo. Dust wrappers. Orig. cloth. Good. Edwards 1044-170 1983 £35

CUSHING, FRANK HAMILTON   My Adventures in Zuni. Santa Fe: The Peripatetic Press, (1941). Illus. with sketches, some in color, by Fanita Lanier. Cloth. Unobtrusively rebacked, with orig. backstrip laid down. A very good copy in marbled slipcase. Reese 19-172 1983 $425

CUSHING, FRANK HAMILTON   Zuni Breadstuff. N.Y., Heye Foundation, 1920. Illus. Orig. 12mo, cloth. First edition. Ginsberg 47-263 1983 $75

CUSHING, HARVEY   A Bio-Bibliography of Andreas Vesalius. New York, 1943. 8vo. Orig. binding. 1/2 leather. Minor scuffing of leather, cloth cover boards soiled, corners bumped, contents fine. Limited edition of 800 copies. Fye H-3-1030 1983 $250

CUSHING, HARVEY   Consecration Medici. 1926. Offprint. Wrappers. 8vo. Fye H-3-132 1983 $35

CUSHING, HARVEY   Consecratio Medici, & Other Papers. Boston, 1928. First edition. 8vo, cloth, ex-lib. Fine. Argosy 713-134 1983 $60

CUSHING, HARVEY   Consecratio Medici and other Papers. Boston, 1929. First edition, 3rd printing. 8vo. Orig. binding. Fye H-3-133 1983 $40

CUSHING, HARVEY   Laboratories: Then and Now. 1922. Offprint, wrappers. 8vo. Fye H-3-135 1983 $30

CUSHING, HARVEY   The Life of Sir William Osler. Oxford, 1925. First printing. 2 vols. 8vo. Orig. binding. Very fine. Fye H-3-878 1983 $150

CUSHING, HARVEY   The Life of Sir William Osler. Oxford, 1925. First printing. 2 vols. bound in four. 8vo. Fine. Fye H-3-879 1983 $125

CUSHING, HARVEY   The Life of Sir William Osler. Oxford, 1925. First printing. 2 vols. Vol. 2 was Simon Flexner's copy, with his autographed signature and occasional annotations. Fye H-3-880 1983 $100

CUSHING, HARVEY   The Life of Sir William Osler. Oxford, 1925. Second printing. 2 vols. 8vo. Orig. binding. Very fine. Fye H-3-881 1983 $125

CUSHING, HARVEY   The Life of Sir William Osler. Oxford, 1925. Second impression. 2 vols. 8vo. Orig. binding. Vol. 1 is Philip Bard's copy with minor binding wear. Vol. 2 is very fine. Fye H-3-882 1983 $75

CUSHING, HARVEY   The Life of Sir William Osler. Oxford, 1925. 3rd impression. Illus. 2 vols. 8vo. Pasted inside front cover of Vol. 1 is inscription "For Dr. Mather Cleveland...Harvey Cushing, Waldorf Astoria, Nov. 17, 1926." Below is a note by Cleveland. Morrill 289-56 1983 $150

CUSHING, HARVEY   The Life of Sir William Osler. Oxford, 1925. 3rd impression. 2 vols. 8vo. Morrill 289-57 1983 $40

CUSHING, HARVEY   The Life of Sir William Osler. Oxford, 1926. Fourth printing. 2 vols. 8vo, orig. binding, dust wrapper. Bound in green cloth and issued with green dust wrappers. Cushing's "Corrigenda and Addenda" bound in at the end of Vol. 2. Very fine. Scarce. Fye H-3-884 1983 $150

CUSHING, HARVEY   The Life of Sir William Osler. Oxford, 1926. Fourth printing. 2 vols. 8vo. Orig. binding. Very fine. Fye H-3-883 1983 $80

CUSHING, HARVEY   The Physician and the Surgeon. 1922. Offprint, wrappers. 8vo. Fye H-3-136 1983 $30

CUSHING, HARVEY   William Stewart Halsted. 1922. Offprint. 8vo. Orig. binding. Fye H-3-763 1983 $20

CUSHING, LUTHER STEARNS   Rules of Proceeding and Debate in Deliberative Assemblies. Boston: Reynolds, 1845. 1st ed., original full sheep, label, gilt. Rebacked in matching sheep with original label intact. Fine copy of a scarce work. 12mo. Jenkins 151-53 1983 $300

CUSHING, WILLIAM   Initials and Pseudonyms... Waltham: Mark Press, 1963. Reprint of the 1885 ed. 2 vols., cloth. Dawson 470-85 1983 $75

CUSHMAN, ROBERT   The Sin and Danger of Self-Love
Described, in a Sermon Preached at Plymouth, in New England, 1621.
Plymouth, 1785. Half leather, very good. Reese 18-152 1983 $500

CUSICK, DAVID   Sketches of Ancient History of the Six
Nations. Lockport, N.Y., 1848. 4 plates. Printed wraps. Felcone
22-44 1983 $40

CUSSANS, JOHN EDWIN   History of Hertfordshire, Containing an
Account of the Descents of the Various Manors. London: Chatto &
Windus, 1870-81. Eight vols. bound in three. Tall folio, 50-1/2 cm.
Six frontis., some colored; 21 lithographed plates and numerous
other illus., plans, text woodcuts, maps (some folding), portraits,
genealogical tables and coats of arms; some colored. Special title
pages for several vols. Blue morocco-backed boards, spines gilt.
Very good. No. 10 of 75 copies. Grunder 6-14 1983 $600

CUSTANCE, GEORGE   A Concise View of the Constitution
of England. Kidderminster, ca. 1808. 12mo, cont. mottled calf
gilt. K Books 307-61 1983 £45

CUSTANCE, OLIVE   The Inn of Dreams. London: John Lane,
The Bodley Head, 1911. First edition. Presentation copy to Olive
Grissell, dated 1914. Cover edges worn. Good. MacManus-277-1255
1983 $85

CUSTER, ELIZABETH B.   Following the Guidon. N.Y., 1890.
First edition. Illus. Pictorial-cloth. Presentation copy. Argosy
716-615 1983 $35

CUSTER, ELIZABETH B.   Following the Guidon. New York: 1890.
First edition. Illus. Cloth. Very good copy. Bradley 66-529 1983
$35

CUSTER, ELIZABETH B.   Tenting on the Plains. New York, 1889.
Illus. Leather, rubbed hinges weak, front cracked. Clark 741-210
1983 $90

CUTHBERTSON, BENNET   Cuthbertson's system, for the complete
interior management and oeconomy of a battalion of infantry. Bristol:
printed by Rouths and Nelson, for A. Gray(Taunton), etc., 1776.
8vo. Cont. calf. New edition. Spine a bit scuffed. Very good copy.
Rare. Ximenes 63-311 1983 $150

CUTHBERTSON, CATHERINE   Forest of Montalbano. London: G.
Robinson, 1810. First edition. 4 vols. 8vo. Cont. half calf,
red leather labels. A fine copy. Rare. Traylen 94-225 1983
£170

CUTHBERTSON, CATHERINE   Santo Sebastiano: or, the Young
Protector. George Robinson, 1806. In five vols. First edition.
Half titles, half blue calf, v.g. Jarndyce 30-351 1983 £160

CUTHBERTSON, CATHERINE   Santo Sebastiano; or, the Young
Protector. London: G. Robinson, 1806. First edition. 5 vols.
12mo. Cont. half calf, gilt decorated spines, morocco labels,
gilt. Some worming at beginning and end of vol. 1 affecting
some pages of text, but still a good copy. Rare. Traylen 94-226
1983 £85

CUTTER, BLOODGOOD H.   The Long Island Farmer's Poems, Lines
Written on the Quaker City Excursion to Palestine and Other Poems.
New York: Tibbals, (1886). Frontis., 1st ed. Orig. blue cloth,
gilt. Beneath a wood-engraving of Cutter's wife is an inscription.
Very good bright copy. Jenkins 155-271 1983 $75

CUTTER, BLOODGOOD H.   The Long Island Farmer's Poems. New
York, Author, (1886). 1st ed. Illus. 8vo. On cheap paper.
Title-page partly torn. Morrill 286-114 1983 $20

CUTTER, CHARLES   Cutter's Guide to the Hot Springs of
Arkansas. St. Louis, 1874. Orig. printed wraps. First edition.
Ginsberg 46-37 1983 $100

CUTTER, LELAND W.   Once Upon a Time. S.F., 1934. Lg. 4to,
cloth-backed decorated boards, paper label, slipcase. Signed presentation from the author. Fine copy with headpieces, large decorative
initials. Perata 28-111 1983 $35

CUTTMACHER, MANFRED S.   America's Last King. An Interpretation
of the Madness of George III. NY: Scribner's Sons, 1941. Dust
jacket. First edition. Gach 94-191 1983 $25

CUTTS, JAMES M.   Conquest of California and New Mexico...
1846-7. Phila., 1847. Eng. title and 4 maps and plans. Half
morocco. First edition. Ginsberg 47-265 1983 $600

CUTTS, JAMES M   The Conquest of California and New
Mexico by the Forces of the United States in the Years 1846 & 1847.
Philadelphia, 1847. Portraits. Maps. In a later half morocco
binding. Reese 19-174 1983 $475

CUTTS, JAMES M.   The Conquest of California and New
Mexico, by the Forces of the U.S., in the Years 1846 & 1847. Phila.,
Carey & Hart, 1847. 4 maps and plans, portrait, cont. full morocco.
A.e.g. 1st ed. Jenkins 151-58 1983 $450

CUVIER, GEORGES   Essay on the Theory of the Earth.
Edinburgh, 1827. Fifth edition, greatly enlarged. 8vo. Old
half-calf, rubbed. Plates. Gurney JJ-90 1983 £27

CUVIER, GEORGES   Funerailles de M. Le Chevalier Delambre.
(Paris, 1822). 1st ed., 8vo, drop head title, early inscription on
first leaf; uncut, disbound. Pickering & Chatto 22-28 1983 $65

CUVIER, GEORGES   Recherches sur les Ossemens Fossiles
de Quadruptedes... Paris, 1812. First edition. 4to. 4 vols. 19th
century cloth, stained, leather labels. With 154 plates and 1
coloured geological map. Some dampstaining in vol. 1. Some plates
trimmed, in a few cases affecting figures or lettering. Gurney 90-
39 1983 £700

CUVIER, GEORGES   Le Regne Animal. Paris, 1829-30.
Second edition, 20 engraved plates, 5 vols., 8vo, half calf, m.e.,
bindings worn and joints broken. Covers of vol. 1 detached. Some
slight foxing. Wheldon 160-476 1983 £80

CYPRESS, J., JR., PSEUD.
Please turn to
HERBERT, HENRY WILLIAM

CZWIKLITZER, CHRISTOPH   Werkverzeichnis der Picasso-Plakate.
Paris: Art-C.C., 1970. More than 300 plates (many color). 307
reference illus. Folio. Cloth. Dust jacket. Edition limited to
1000 numbered copies. Ars Libri 32-517 1983 $225

D

D.H., PSEUD.
Please turn to
DOOLITTLE, HILDA

DABBS, G. H. R.   From Her to Him. Charles Wm. Deacon, 1906. First edition, orig. limp green roan. Jarndyce 30-752 1983 £10.50

DABBS, G. H. R.   Poems. (Newport, I.o.W.), 1872. Orig. green cloth. Jarndyce 30-750 1983 £15

DABNEY, OWEN P.   True Story of the Lost Shackle or Seven Years with the Indians. (Salem, Ore., 1897). Frontis. Illus. Wraps. Very good. Reese 19-175 1983 $135

DABRY DE THIERSANT, PIERRE   La Medicine Chez Les Chinois. Paris: Henri Plon, 1863. 8vo. 1 large folding acupuncture plate with numerous figures (pp. 561-62 bound in upside down). Half morocco, gilt, orig. printed wrappers bound in, uncut. First edition. Fine copy. Gach 95-81 $250

DACIER, EMILE   Gabriel de Saint-Aubin. Peintre, dessinateur et graveur (1724-1780). Paris: G. Van Oest, 1929-1931. 2 vols. 40 plates and 41 plates. Large 4to. Orig. wrappers. Ars Libri 32-611 1983 $350

DACIER, EMILE   Jean de Julienne et les graveurs de Watteau au XVIIIe siecle. Paris: Societe Pour l'Etude de la Gravure Francaise, 1919-1922. 4 vols. Vol. 1: 119 illus. Vol. 2: 32 illus. Vol. 3: 4 illus. Vol. 4: 316 plates, loose, as issued, in portfolio. Large 4to. New marbled boards, 1/2 cloth. Orig. wrappers bound in. Ars Libri 32-695 1983 $300

DACIER, EMILE   L'oeuvre grave de Gabriel de Saint-Aubin. Paris: Imprimerie Nationale, 1914. 37 plates. 4to. Wrappers. Edition limited to 500 copies only, printed on uncut velin d'Arches. Slightly worn and smudged. Ars Libri 32-612 1983 $325

DACK, CHARLES   The Trial, Execution and Death of Mary Queen of Scots. Northampton: The Dryden Press: Taylor & Son, London: Elliot Stock, 1889. 4to, text illus. and 4 plates, orig. wraps., soiled, chipped at corners. Bickersteth 77-113 1983 £12

DACOSTA, JOHN   Selections from the Papers and Speeches of John D. DaCosta. Philadelphia, 1931. First edition. 8vo. Orig. binding. Fye H-3-138 1983 $40

DACRE, BARBARINA BRAND   Dramas, Translations and Occasional Poems. London: Privately Printed, John Murray, 1821. First edition. 2 vols. 8vo. Cont. vellum, two-line gilt borders on blue painted backgrounds inner wide gilt borders with centre lozenge shaped ornaments, gilt on blue painted backgrounds, full gilt decorated spines with black morocco labels, gilt, inner gilt dentelles, edges gilt. Half-titles. Presentation copy, with inscription. Stoneleigh Abbey bookplate. Traylen 94-227 1983 £110

DADDI, GIANPAOLO   Raffaello Sernesi. Oggiono: Paolo Cattaneo, 1977. 46 plates (12 color). 5 text illus. 4to. Cloth. Edition limited to 800 numbered copies. Ars Libri 33-585 1983 $85

DAFOE, JOHN W.   Clifford Sifton in relation to His Times. Toronto: Macmillan, 1931. 22cm. 8 portrait illus. Wine cloth. Fine. McGahern 54-192 1983 $30

DA GAMA, VASCO   A journal of the first voyage of Vasco Da Gama, 1497-1499. London: Hakluyt Soc., 1898. 8vo. 7 maps. Orig. cloth. Rubbed, spine chipped, ex-lib. Adelson Africa-182 1983 $30

DAGGETT, CARLEEN M.   Noah McCuistion, Pioneer Texas Cattleman. (Waco, 1975). Special edition limited to 25 signed and numbered copies bound in full leather, with slipcase. A.e.g. Illus. Jenkins 152-218 1983 $150

DAGGETT, DAVID   Count the Cost. Hartford: Hudson & Goodwin, 1804. Sewed; uncut. Argosy 716-119 1983 $35

DAGGETT, DAVID   Count the Cost. Hartford: Hudson & Goodwin, 1804. Stitched. Very good. Felcone 20-28 1983 $25

D'AGUILLAR, GEORGE C.   Observations on the Practice and the Forms of District, Regimental, and Detachment Courts Martial. Dublin, 1855. 8vo, orig. cloth. Very good. Fenning 61-97 1983 £14.50

DAHLBERG, EDWARD   Bottom Dogs. London, 1929. 8vo. Cloth. Name on inside flyleaf, else a fine copy in dj which has some light wear. In Our Time 156-186 1983 $250

DAHLBERG, EDWARD   Bottom Dogs. Lon., 1929. One of 520 numbered copies, very good to fine in chipped dustwrapper lacking 1/2 inch at top of spine and 1 1/2 inch at bottom of spine. Quill & Brush 54-345 1983 $125

DAHLBERG, EDWARD   Bottom Dogs. N.Y., S&S, 1930. First American edition. Dust jacket (small chips, old tape on verso), good-very good. Houle 21-536 1983 $95

DAHLBERG, EDWARD   The Confessions of Edward Dahlberg. New York, (1971). 8vo. Cloth. Limited signed edition. Fine in box. In Our Time 156-188 1983 $100

DAHLBERG, EDWARD   The Sorrows of Priapus. New Directions, 1957. 8vo. Clothboards. Limited signed ed., 1 of 150 copies signed by Dahlberg and Shahn. With an orig. lithograph laid in. Bookplate. Illus. by Ben Shahn. Fine copy in slipcase box. In Our Time 156-187 1983 $350

DAHLBERG. EDWARD   The Sorrows of Priapus. (NY): New Directions, 1957. First edition. Drawings by Ben Shahn. Limited to 150 copies signed by Dahlberg and Shahn. Laid-in is extra signed lithograph by Shahn. Mint copy in white boards. Slightly chipped glassine and slip-case. Bromer 25-22 1983 $325

DAHLBERG, EDWARD   Those Who Perish. NY, (1934). Very good in torn, slightly chipped and aged dustwrapper, owner's name. Quill & Brush 54-344 1983 $40

DAHLSTROM, GRANT   Type Specimen Book. Los Angeles: Ad-craft, n.d. Wrappers, some use. Lynton Kistler's signature on front cover. Dawson 471-58 1983 $50

DAHN, FELIX   A Struggle For Rome. London: Bentley, 1878. First edition in English. 3 vols. Orig. cloth. Good. Mac-Manus 278-1257 1983 $85

DAIBER, ALBERT   Mikroskopie der Harnsediments. Wiesbaden, 1906. 65 litho. plates, some partly colored. 8vo, cloth. Argosy 713-136 1983 $50

THE DAILY Advertiser Directory For The City of Detroit For The Year 1850. Duncklee, Wales & Co., 1850. Lea. backed printed boards, scuffed. King 46-150 1983 $75

DAIS, WILLIAM S.   The Influence of Wealth in Imperial Rome. NY, 1910. 8vo, cloth. Salloch 385-221 1983 $40

DAIX, PIERRE   Picasso: The Blue and Rose Periods. Greenwich: New York Graphic Society, 1967. More than 800 illus. (61 tipped-in color). Folio. Cloth. Ars Libri 32-518 1983 $175

DAKOTA Odowan. Dakota Hymns. N.Y., 1879. Orig. cloth. Ginsberg 46-820 1983 $100

DAKOTA TERRITORY. LAWS. General and Private Laws and Memorials and Resolutions of the Territory of Dakota... Yankton, D.T., Trask, 1862. Orig. printed wraps. First edition. Ginsberg 47-277 1983 $300

DALBIAC, P. H. History of the 45th. London, 1902. 8vo. Orig. cloth. Coloured frontis. of colours. 12 maps (1 folding) and plate of monument, arms and battle honours of the Regiment on upper cover. Slightly worn and soiled. Lacks front free endpaper. Good. Edwards 1042-544 1983 £45

DALBIEZ, ROLAND La Methode Psychanalytique et la Doctrine Freudienne. Paris: Desclee de Brouwer, (1936). First edition. Two volumes. Original wrappers. Gach 94-159 1983 $65

DALBIEZ, ROLAND Psychoanalytic Method and the Doctrine of Freud. London: Longmans, (1941). Two. vols. First edition in English. Fine in dust jackets. Gach 94-160 1983 $50

DALBY, FRANCIS Mr. Dalby's Case. (London, 1756?). Folio, folded. Very good. Reese 18-68 1983 $200

DALCQ, A. L'Oeuf et son Dynamisme Organisateur. Paris, 1941. Plates and text-figures, 8vo, cloth, ex-library. Wheldon 160-477 1983 £15

DALE, CLIFFORD H. The Ashley-Smith Explorations and the Discovery of a Central Route to the Pacific 1822-1829. Cleveland, 1918. Maps. Illus. Cloth, fine. Reese 19-177 1983 $100

DALE, EDWARD EVERETT Cow Country. Norman, 1945. Dust jacket. Jenkins 151-59 1983 $25

DALE, EDWARD EVERETT The Cow Country in Transition. N.p., 1937. Author's separate. Presentation copy from Dale to J.L. Rader. Jenkins 153-156 1983 $35

DALE, EDWARD EVERETT The Prairie Schooner and Other Poems. Guthrie, Oklahoma, 1929. Flexible stamped boards, very good. Presentation copy. Reese 19-178 1983 $100

DALE, EDWARD EVERETT The Range Cattle Industry. Norman: Univ. of Oklahoma, 1930. Maps and plates. 1st ed. Fine copy. Jenkins 153-157 1983 $225

DALE, EDWARD EVERETT The Range Cattle Industry. Norman: Univ. Oklahoma, 1930. Illus., maps, tall 8vo, backstrip discolored. Argosy 710-575 1983 $85

DALE, MAUD Modigliani. New York: Knopf, 1929. 51 plates. Frontis. 4to. Cloth. Ars Libri 33-535 1983 $35

D'ALEMBERT, JEAN LEROND
Please turn to
ALEMBERT, JEAN LEROND D'

DALHUSIE, JOHN H. The Salvation of Protestants Asserted and Defended. Printed for James Adamson, 1689. First edition in English, including imprimatur leaf, 4to, wrapper, lightly dampstained, a good sound copy. Fenning 61-98 1983 £12.50

DALI, SALVADOR The Secret Life of... NY: 1942. First edition. Illus. Presentation inscription dated 1943 from Dali. Owner's penned signature. About fine. Bromer 25-188 1983 $125

DALI, SALVADOR The Secret Life of Salvador Dali. New York, 1942. 1st American ed. Illus. 4to, dust wrapper. Morrill 286-591 1983 $37.50

DALLAS, ALEXANDER J. Features of Mr. Jay's Treaty. Phila.; Lang & Ustick, 1795. 1st ed. 12mo, later 3/4 green morocco, g.t., lacks orig. flyleaves. Argosy 710-139 1983 $100

DALLAS, BRETT R. History of British Aviation 1908-1914. London, c.1933. First edition. Frontis. 80 plates, numerous tables and appendices. Thick roy. 8vo. Good. Edwards 1042-584 1983 £50

DALLAS, G. A Vindication of the Justice and Policy of the Late Wars... London, 1806. 4to. Wrapper. Orig. cloth. Good. Edwards 1044-173 1983 £45

DALLAS, ROBERT CHARLES Correspondence of Lord Byron... Paris: A. and W. Calignani, 1825. First published (and first complete) edition. 3 vols. in one. 12mo. Cont. half calf, by Thurnham of Carlisle. Wanting half-titles. Worn binding. Ximenes 63-51 1983 $100

DALLAS, ROBERT CHARLES Ode to the Duke of Wellington, and Other Poems. John Murray, 1819. First edition. Half title, front. Half calf, a little rubbed. Jarndyce 30-681 1983 £10.50

D'ALLEMAGNE, HENRY RENE
Please turn to
ALLEMAGNE, HENRY RENE D'

DALLISON, CHARLES The royalists defence: vindicating the King's proceedings in the late warre made against him. N.p. (London): printed in the year 1648. First edition. Small 4to. Disbound. Errata leaf at the end. Minor tear in title. Slight marginal fraying of the last two leaves. Ximenes 63-98 1983 $45

DALRYMPLE, ALEXANDER A collection of English songs with an appendix of original pieces. Bennett, 1796. First edition, tall 8vo, uncut in original boards, later quarter calf spine with red morocco label, short tear in title and extreme margin of pages slightly browned, still a very good copy. Deighton 3-93 1983 £24

DALRYMPLE, JOHN Pathology of the Human Eye. London, 1852. Folio. Half-calf, new back and corners. 36 coloured engravings by W. Bagg after original water colours by W.H. Kearny and Leonard. Library stamp on title, dedication leaf and plates. Gurney 90-40 1983 £160

DALTON, C. The Blenheim Roll. London, 1899. Roy. 8vo. Orig. half red calf. Ad. leaf at end. Very slightly soiled. Good. Edwards 1042-315 1983 £45

DALTON, C. English Army Lists and Commission Registers, 1661-1714. Reprint 1960. Thick imperial 8vo. Orig. red cloth. 6 vols. in 3. Good. Edwards 1042-316 1983 £60

DALTON, C. George the First's Army 1714-1727. London, 1910-12. First edition. Imperial 8vo. Orig. red decorated cloth gilt. Portrait frontis., 3 double-page plates (1 folding), 35 other plates and 2 illus. 2 vols. Very slightly soiled and faded. Some very slight foxing. Inserted at the front endpapers of Vol. I is a four page ALS from Dalton dated Sept. 9th, 1911? to Major (M.L.) Ferrar. Plus a 2 page obituary of Dalton dated July 1913. Good. Edwards 1042-317 1983 £150

DALTON, C. The Scots Army 1661-1688. Edinburgh & London, 1909. Imperial 8vo. Orig. blue cloth gilt. Frontis., 6 double-page facsimiles, 14 plates, illus. T.e.g. Others uncut. First edition. Fine. Edwards 1042-318 1983 £150

DALTON, EMMETT When the Daltons Rode. N.Y., Doubleday, 1931. First edition. Illus. Brown cloth (spine a bit sunned), else very good. Signed and inscribed by Dalton, April 3, 1931. Houle 21-1019 1983 $300

DALTON, EMMETT When the Daltons Rode. New York, 1931. Illus., original pictorial cloth. Fine copy. 1st ed. Jenkins 151-60 1983 $45

D'ALTON, J. F. Roman Literary Theory and Criticism. NY, 1931. Salloch 385-84 1983 $20

DALTON, J. W. The Cape Cod Canal. (Boston, 1911). Illus. Oblong 8vo, orig. wrappers. Backstrip partly torn. Morrill 286-282 1983 $20

DALTON, JOHN   History of the College of Physicians
and Surgeons in the City of New York. New York, 1888. 8vo. Orig.
binding. First edition. Scarce. Fye H-3-139 1983 $40

D'ALTON, JOHN   The History of the County of Dublin.
Dublin, 1838. First and only edition, 8vo, slightly later calf-
backed boards, gilt, a very good copy. Fenning 61-99 1983 £55

D'ALTON, JOHN   Illustrations, Historical and Genealogical. London, 1861. Second edition enlarged. 2 vols. Cont. red cloth.
8vo. Rebacked in roan gilt. Black morocco labels. Good. Edwards
1042-319 1983 £65

D'ALTON, JOHN   The Memoirs of the Archbishops of
Dublin. Dublin, 1838. First and only edition, 8vo, slightly later
calf-backed boards, gilt, a very good copy. Fenning 61-99 1983
£55

D'ALTON, JOHN   The Memoirs of the Archbishops of
Dublin. Dublin, 1838. First and only edition, 8vo, orig. cloth,
neatly repaired. This copy has the additional pages v-xxi. Fenning
61-100 1983 £32.50

DALTON, JOHN   Meteorological Observations and Essays.
London, (1793). 8vo. Half morocco. First edition. Inner margin of
title slightly stained and with blind stamp. Gurney 90-41 1983
£285

DALTON, JOHN   Meteorological Observations and Essays.
Manchester, 1834. Second edition. 8vo. Orig. boards, cloth rebacked,
unopened. 2 adverts. Gurney 90-42 1983 £100

DALTON, JOHN EDWARD   Forges in Strong Fires. Caldwell, Ida.,
1948. Limited, signed edition. Illus. by Cecil Smith. Frontis. in
color. Facsimile, neatly inserted, otherwise fine copy. Clark 741-
202 1983 $32.50

DALTON, WILLIAM   Phaulcon the Adventurer. London: S.O.
Beeton, 1862. First edition. Frontis. port. Illus. with 8 color-
plates. Orig. decorated cloth. Spine a little faded. Very fine.
MacManus 278-1259 1983 $85

DALTON, WILLIAM   Phaulcon the Adventurer. London, 1862.
Portrait frontis. 8 coloured plates. Half calf, slight wear. 8vo.
Orig. cloth. Good. Edwards 1044-175 1983 £25

DALY, FREDERIC   Henry Irving in England and America,
1838-84. T. Fisher Unwin, 1884. First edition, half title, front.
port. 2 pp ads. Orig. maroon cloth, sl. rubbed. Jarndyce 30-1029
1983 £10.50

DALY, R. A.   Igneous Rocks. New York, 1933.
Second edition, text-figures, 8vo, cloth. Wheldon 160-1381 1983 £15

DAME, LAWRENCE   Yucatan. NY, 1941. 1st ed. Map, illus.
Argosy 710-58 1983 $30

DAME Wiggins of Lee, and Her Seven Wonderful Cats. London: A. K.
Newman, 1823. First edition. Hand-colored frontis., 16 colored
illus. Each page, including title, pasted onto heavy card stock by
early owner. Some foxing and pencilled underlinings. Bromer 25-388
1983 $140

DAME Wiggins of Lee, and Her Seven Wonderful Cats. Orpington,
George Allen, 1885. Illus. by Kate Greenaway. Woodcuts. 8vo. Top
of spine chipped. Morrill 289-305 1983 $47.50

D'AMICO, FRANCOISE DE P.   The Golden Age. Hutchinson, n.d.
Colour frontis. 8 colour plates (2 taped in) & 20 text illus, loose.
Library green cloth. Greer 40-61 1983 £12.50

DAMON, ETHEL M.   Koamalu. Honolulu: Privately
printed, 1931. 2 vols. Tall 8vo, profusely illus. Index. Cloth-
backed boards, a little rubbed. Karmiole 75-63 1983 $85

DAMON, GEORGE A.   Picturesque Pasadena. (Pasadena, Chamber
of Commerce and Civic Association, n.d.). Boards. Wearing at extremities. Dawson 471-59 1983 $45

DAMPIER, WILLIAM   A New Voyage Round the World. London,
1937. Port., maps. D.w. Argosy 710-532 1983 $20

DAMPIER-WHETHAM, W. C.   A History of Science and its relations
with Philosophy and Religion. Cambridge: University Press, 1929.
8vo. Cloth. First edition. Gurney JJ-92 1983 £15

DAMPMARTIN, PIERRE DE   De la Connoissance et Merveilles du
Monde et de l'Homme. (Paris): Thomas Perier, 1585. Woodcut
printer's mark on title, on the verso of which is an engraved poem,
within ornamental wreath. Fine woodcut headpieces and initials in
the text which is framed by ink rules. Folio. Cont. vellum with
gilt wreaths in centre of both sides. First edition. Kraus 164-46
1983 $2,300

DAMROSCH, FRANK   A Birthday Greeting and Other Songs.
N.Y.: Schirmer, (1918). 4to. Cloth backed boards, rubbed. Illus.
by H. Damrosch with 12 tipped in color plates on heavy stock. Aleph-
bet 8-76 1983 $30

DANA, DANIEL   A Discourse Delivered in Newburyport,
July 4, 1814. Newburyport, 1814. Dsb., very good. Reese 13-437
1983 $25

DANA, DANIEL   A Discourse on the Character and Virtues
of General George Washington... Newburyport: Angier March, (1800).
Stitched. Uncut. Marginal corner of title torn away. Felcone 20-186
1983 $45

DANA, DAVID D.   The Fireman: The Fire Departments of
the United States... Boston, 1858. First edition. Ads. 7 plates.
Cloth. Very good. Felcone 20-45 1983 $25

DANA, HENRY S.   History of Woodstock, Vt. Boston,
1889. Map & illus., tall 8vo, g.t., ex lib. Argosy 710-547 1983
$40

DANA, J. D.   Corals and Coral Islands. 1875. 2nd
ed., coloured frontispiece, 3 maps and numerous text-figures, 8vo,
original decorated cloth. Wheldon 160-304 1983 £35

DANA, JOHN COTTON   Notes on Bookbinding for Libraries.
Chicago: Library Bureau, 1906. First edition. 8vo. Cloth. Oak
Knoll 49-84 1983 $45

DANA, RICHARD   Remarks of...Before the Committee on
Federal Relations on the Proposed Removal of Edward G. Loring from
the Office of Judge Probate. Boston, 1855. First edition.
Ginsberg 46-225 1983 $35

DANA, RICHARD HENRY (1787-1879)   Poems and Prose Writings. New
York, 1850. 2 vols., 8vo., first ed., 2nd printing. Presentation
copy. Rubbed, ends of spines chipped, backstrip of vol. 1 partly
torn along hinge. Morrill 289-309 1983 $20

DANA, RICHARD HENRY (1815-1882)   To Cuba and Back. Boston, Ticknor
and Fields, 1859. First edition. Gilt and blind stamped blue cloth.
Ads dated May, 1859. Bookplate of Clifton Barrett. Very good.
Houle 22-280 1983 $55

DANA, RICHARD HENRY (1815-1882)   To Cuba and Back. Boston, 1859.
First ed. K Books 301-56 1983 £20

DANA, RICHARD HENRY (1815-1882)   To Cuba and Back. Boston, 1859.
First ed., 12mo., ends of spine slightly frayed. Morrill 287-83 1983
$25

DANA, RICHARD HENRY (1815-1882)   Two Years Before the Mast. New
York, 1840. Half morocco, very good. Second issue without the dot
over the i on the copyright page and with the broken type heading on
page 9. Reese 19-179 1983 $600

DANA, RICHARD HENRY (1815-1882)   Two Years Before the Mast. New York: Harper, 1840. First ed., second state with broken running head at page 9 and undotted "i" in copyright. Contemporary three quarter morocco and marbled boards, raised bands, gilt, fine, with author's signature tipped in. Jenkins 155-278 1983 $550

DANA, RICHARD HENRY (1815-1882)   Two Years Before the Mast. Boston, 1911. First edition, illus., fine with large pictorial label on front cover. Bromer 25-390 1983 $40

DANA, RICHARD HENRY (1815-1882)   Two Years Before the Mast. Chicago: Lakeside Press, 1930. First edition, one of 1000 copies, orig. linen backed dec. bds., gilt, t.e.g., others uncut, orig. box Color illus. by Edward A. Eillson. Mint copy in very fine box. Jenkins 155-279 1983 $150

DANA, RICHARD HENRY (1815-1882)   Two Years Before the Mast. Chicago, 1930. Tall 8vo., two-tone cloth, lettering & design in gilt, t.e.g., slipcase, color illus. by Edward A. Wilson. Very fine, uncut and unopened, one of 1000 copies. Perata 28-98 1983 $135

DANA, RICHARD HENRY (1815-1882)   Two Years Before the Mast... Los Angeles, Ward Ritchie Press, 1964. Slipcased, 2 vols. Jenkins 153-158 1983 $75

DANA, RICHARD HENRY (1815-1882)   Voyage a l'Ile de Cuba. (Paris, 1860). Wood engravings, small folio, wrappers. Argosy 710-125 1983 $30

DANA, SAMUEL W.   Speech of...on a Resolution Concerning Francis J. Jackson... Washington, 1810. Self-wraps., stitched, uncut. Good. Reese 18-335 1983 $40

DANBY, WILLIAM   Extracts from and Observations on Cicero's Dialogues De Senectute... Exeter: for the Author, 1829. First edition. Errata slip. 8vo. Orig. boards, uncut. Traylen 94-229 1983 £20

DANBY, WILLIAM   Extracts from Young's Night Thoughts... London, 1832. First edition. 8vo. Orig. cloth. Printed paper label. A presentation copy from the author. Traylen 94-230 1983 £20

DANBY, WILLIAM   Thoughts Chiefly on Serious Subjects. Vol I only. Exeter: for the author, 1822. Second edition. The author's own copy, interleaved throughout and with several manuscript notes in the author's hand. Thick 8vo. Cont. half calf. Traylen 94-231 1983 £25

D'ANCONA, PAOLO   Michelangelo. Architettura, pittura, scultura. Milano: Bramante, 1964. 274 illus. Large 4to. Leather. Dust jacket. Ars Libri 33-235 1983 $75

DANDY, WALTER E.   Benign, Encapsulated Tumors in the Lateral Ventricles of the Brain. Baltimore, 1934. First edition, mint. Illus. d.w. Argosy 713-139 1983 $100

DANE, CLEMENCE   Tradition and Hugh Walpole. London: William Heinemann Ltd., (1930). First edition. Orig. cloth. Dust jacket (spine darkened). Fine. MacManus 280-5372 1983 $20

D'ANGOULEME, MARGUERITE
Please turn to
MARGUERITE D'ANGOULEME

DANIEL, GABRIEL   Viaggio per lo Mondo di Caresio, con seco la sua continuazione. Venice, 1739. With 3 folding plates engraved by J. Filosi. 8vo. Cont. vellum. Kraus 164-64 1983 $160

DANIEL, GABRIEL   A Voyage to the World of Cartesius. Printed, and Sold by Thomas Bennet, 1692. 1st English ed., 8vo, new half calf antique; leaves somewhat age-browned. Hill 165-25 1983 £125

DANIEL, GEORGE   Garrick in the green room! London: James Webb, 1829. 8vo, disbound, 1st ed. Rare. With a folding frontispiece of the picture. Ximenes 64-158 1983 $75

DANIEL, GEORGE   Love's Last Labour Not Lost. London: Basil Montagu Pickering, 1863. First edition. Small 8vo. Three-quarters crushed levant red morocco, gilt, t.e.g. Half-title. Aldine device on title-page. Limited to 250 copies. Traylen 94-232 1983 £25

DANIEL, GEORGE   Merrie England in the Olden Time. London: Richard Bentley, 1842. First edition. Illus. by John Leech & Robert Cruikshank. 2 vols. Orig. cloth. Presentation copy inscribed: "To Mr. Edward Evans Great Queen Street these volumes are presented by his friend, George Daniel. 1848". Fine. MacManus 278-1263 1983 $450

DANIEL, J. F.   The Elasmobranch Fishes. Berkeley, 1934. Third edition, 270 illus., royal 8vo, cloth. Wheldon 160-953 1983 £35

DANIEL-ROPS, HENRY   The Misted Mirror. London: Martin Secker, 1930. First edition. Orig. cloth with paper spine label. Dust jacket (faded, worn and soiled). Some offsetting to the end-paper. Near-fine. MacManus 279-3913 1983 $50

DANIELL, EDWARD   The Woodland Muse. 1824. Small 8vo, uncut, orig. boards with printed paper label, slight wear at top of spine, paper peeling a little at the joints, but fine. Includes list of subscribers. First edition. Bickersteth 77-199 1983 £55

DANIELL, JOHN FREDERIC   An Introduction to the Study of Chemical Philosophy. London: John W. Parker, 1839. First edition. 8vo. Modern buckram. Numerous text illus. Ads. Very good copy. Zeitlin 264-107 1983 $170

DANIELL, JOHN FREDERIC   An Introduction to the Study of Chemical Philosophy... London: Parker, 1843. Second edition. 8vo. Cont. half calf. Numerous text illus. Rubbed, inside front hinge detached, internally very good. Zeitlin 264-109 1983 $80

DANIELL, JOHN FREDERIC   An Introduction to the study of Chemical Philosophy... London: Parker, 1843. Second edition. Modern buckram. 8vo. Numerous text illus. A very good copy. Zeitlin 264-108 1983 $80

DANIELS, MARK   Green Symbols. San Francisco: (Printed for Mark Daniels by) John Henry Nash, 1924. Folio, with a stipple-engraved initial. Decorations printed in green. Edition ltd. to 200 numbered copies. Pres. copy, signed by the author. Bound in marbled boards; paper spine label. Karmiole 73-76 1983 $75

DANIELSON, HENRY   Bibliographies of Modern Authors. London, 1921. First edition. Very nice. Rota 231-80 1983 £35

DANIELSON, RICHARD E.   Martha Doyle and Other Sporting Memories. NY: Derrydale Press, (1938). 4to, with 7 plates, edition ltd. to 1250 numbered copies. Red cloth; leather labels. Karmiole 73-38 1983 $60

DANNAY, FREDERIC
Please turn to
QUEEN, ELLERY, PSEUD.

DANNER, JOHN   Old Landmarks of Canton and Stark County. Logansport, Ind., 1904. Ports., some views, mor. (rubbed, rebacked), g.t., sm. thick 4to. Argosy 710-392 1983 $75

D'ANNUNZIO, GABRIELE
Please turn to
ANNUNZIO, GABRIELE D'

DANTE, ALIGHIERI   La Comedia. Venice: Marcolini, 1544. Thick 4to. 3 full-page & 84 large woodcuts. Gilt calf, with center cartouche on each cover. Presentation inscription of Lodovico Manin, Doge of Venice. Full-page woodcuts after the designs of Titian, Veronese and other Italian masters. Special font cast by Marcolini for this edition. Three lines in Purgatory, II, 64 were omitted. Lines added by hand printing. Rostenberg 88-103 1983 $2,500

DANTE, ALIGHIERI   The Commedia and Ganzoniere of... London: William Isbister, 1886-87. First edition. 2 vols. Roy. 8vo. Orig. illus. green cloth, gilt, t.e.g. 2 portraits. Traylen 94-233 1983 £16

DANTE, ALIGHIERI   La Divina Commedia or the Divine Version. London: the Nonesuch Press, 1928. In English and Italian. Folio. Full orange vellum, gilt, t.e.g., others uncut. 42 illus. after the drawings of Sandro Botticelli. Limited edition of 1475 numbered copies. Very fine. Traylen 94-234 1983 £240

DANTE, ALIGHIERI   The Comedy of Dante Alighieri. S.F.: 1958. 3 vols., 4 to, cream boards, lettering & design in gilt, decorated cloth slipcase. Printed in red & black. One of 300 sets. Perata 28-63 1983 $250

DANTE, ALIGHIERI   Delle Opere Di Dante Alighiere. Venezia, G. Pasquali, 1739-1741. 8vo. 5 vols. Old Calf, leather labels on spines. Little light wear to extremities of spine, mainly a fine copy. A rare work in the initial ed. In Our Time 156-191 1983 $500

DANTE, ALIGHIERI   The Inferno from La Divine Commedia of Dante. New York: Cheshire House, 1931. Folio, full blind-stamped sheepskin, g.t. Seven engr. on copper by William Blake. One of 1200 copies with orig. prospectus laid in. Duschnes 240-16 1983 $250

DANTE, ALIGHIERI   The vision; or, Hell, Purgatory and Paradise. London: Taylor and Hessey, 1814. First complete edition. 3 vols. 16mo. Cont. calf, spines gilt, a.e.g. Slight rubbing. Bound without half-titles, but a very good copy. Ximenes 63-395 1983 $300

DANTE, ALIGHIERI   The Vision of Purgatory and Paradise. Cassell and Co, ND. Large 4to, 60 illus., rebound in black cloth lettered in gilt, an excellent copy. Deighton 3-94 1983 £30

DANYSZ, J. JAN   These. Recherches Experimentales sur les Rayons Beta... Paris: Gauthier-Villars, 1913. 8vo. Modern buckram with orig. wrappers bound in. 2 plates. Very good copy. Zeitlin 264-110 1983 $80

DANZ, LOUIS   Persona Revolution and Picasso. N.Y., Longmans, 1941. First edition. Illus. with two page reproduction of Picasso's Guernica. Dust jacket (faded on spine). Very good. Houle 22-35 1983 $45

DANZEL, THEODOR-WILHELM   Codex Hammaburgensis. Hamburg, 1926. 7 plates (1 color). 41 text illus. 4to. Wrappers. Ars Libri 34-202 1983 $20

DARAN, JACQUES   Chirurgical Observations on the Disorders of the Urethra. London, 1750. First English edition. 8vo. Cont. calf, rebacked. 1 folding plate. Slightly worn. Gurney 90-43 1983 £120

D'ARBLAY, FRANCES BURNEY
Please turn to
ARBLAY, FRANCES BURNEY D' (1752-1840)

DARBY, WILLIAM   The Emigrant's Guide to the Western and Southwestern States and Territories. NY, 1818. Later linen-backed boards, ex lib., lacks maps, title-page loose. Argosy 710-576 1983 $30

DARBY, WILLIAM   Mnemonika. Baltimore, 1829. Modern cloth with leather label. First edition. Ginsberg 46-226 1983 $75

DARBY, WILLIAM   A Tour from the City of New-York, to Detroit, in the Michigan Territory... New York, 1819. 3 folding maps. Orig. boards, printed paper label. Spine worn, slight foxing, but a nice copy. Thomas Streeter's copy, with notes in his hand on the front fly leaf. Reese 18-529 1983 $375

DARBY, WILLIAM   View of the United States, Historical, Geographical, and Statistical. Philadelphia: Published by H. Tanner. 1828. 12mo, fourteen folding maps. Early hand color. In 1/2 red morocco with marbled paper covered boards. Lightly toned internally. Maps, &c. by William Darby. Arkway 22-39 1983 $475

D'ARCET, JEAN   Memoire sur l'action d'un feu egal... Paris: P.G. Cavelier, 1766. 8vo. Modern marbled boards (a little worn). Some minor foxing and spotting. A good copy. Zeitlin 264-10 1983 $175

DARDIS, PATRICK G.   The Occupation of Land in Ireland in the First Half of the Nineteenth Century. Dublin, 1920. First edition, 8vo, orig. parchment-backed boards. Fenning 61-102 1983 £18.50

D'ARLINCOURT, CHARLES VICTOR PREVOT, MARQUIS   Charles the Bold; or, the Recluse of The Wild Mountain. London: Printed for William Cole, n.d. (ca.1821). First edition in English. 8vo. Stitched as issued. Uncut. Illus. with colored folding frontispiece (detached). Marginal soiling. Fine. MacManus 278-1267 1983 $200

DARLING, JAMES   Cyclopeadia Bibliographica. London: James Darling, 1854. 2 vols. New cloth. MacManus 278-1268 1983 $35

DARLINGTON, WILLIAM   Memorials of John Bartram and Humphry Marshall. Philadelphia, 1849. First edition. Illustrated. 8vo. Worn; backstrip partly torn along hinges; some foxing and few damp-stains at back; occasional flower offprints. Morrill 290-87 1983 $40

DARLOW, BIDDY   Fifteen Old Nursery Rhymes. Bristol: Perpetua Press, 1935. 4to. Handcoloured pictorial title & 15 hand-coloured linocut plates. Handmade paper. Red cloth. Edition limited to 150 copies. Greer 40-86 1983 £27.50

DARROW, CLARENCE   Farmington. N.Y., Boni & Liveright, 1925. First Boni & Liveright edition. Half cloth over grey boards, stamped in gilt. Signed and inscribed by Darrow April 9th, 1928. Very good. Houle 22-283 1983 $125

DARROW, CLARENCE   Farmington. Chicago: McClurg, 1905. Pictorial cloth, first edition. Extremities rubbed slightly, else very good. Reese 19-181 1983 $35

DARROW, CLARENCE   This Story of My Life. N.Y., Scribner, 1932. First edition. Thick 8vo, illus. Dust jacket. Signed and inscribed to F.H. Schoolcraft, January 19, 1932. Very good - fine. Houle 22-284 1983 $250

DARTMOUTH OUTING CLUB   Dartmouth Outing Club Handbook. Hanover, n.d. (1920s). 1st issue. Illus. 16mo. Morrill 287-298 1983 $27.50

DARTON'S Scripture Alphabet. Darton n.d. (ca.1860). Oblong 8vo. Frontis. & title amateur hand tinted. 26 plates. Printed wrappers, quite dusty. Greer 39-6 1983 £10.50

DARWIN, BERNARD   The Dickens Advertiser. Elkin Mathews, 1930. With many illus., 8vo, orig. cloth, a very good copy. Fenning 61-112 1983 £10.50

DARWIN, CHARLES   The Beagle Record. (1979). Coloured and other photographs, royal 8vo, cloth. Wheldon 160-146 1983 £46.50

DARWIN, CHARLES   The Descent of Man, and Selection in Relation to Sex. John Murray, 1871. 2 vols., 8vo, orig. green cloth. Short slits in cloth at extreme end of the joints, covers a little rubbed. Sewing of two sections in vol. 1 loose. First edition. Bickersteth 75-222 1983 £75

DARWIN, CHARLES   The Descent of Man, and Selection in Relation to Sex. John Murray, 1871. 2 vols., 8vo, orig. green cloth, pale foxing on fly leaves and half titles. Bickersteth 75-223 1983 £18

DARWIN, CHARLES   The Descent of Man and Selection in Relation to Sex. London, Murray, 1885. Revised second edition. Illus. 3/4 gilt stamped green morocco, t.e.g., by Baynyun of Bath. Fine copy. Houle 22-286 1983 $165

DARWIN, CHARLES   The Descent of Man. London, Murray, 1888. Second, revised edition. Illus. Gilt stamped grey-green cloth, partially unopened. Very good. 2 vols. Houle 22-285 1983 $135

DARWIN, CHARLES   The Descent of Man. 1901. Reprint of the 2nd ed. of 1874. 8vo, cloth. Wheldon 160-131 1983 £15

DARWIN, CHARLES   Expression of the Emotions in Man and
Animals. NY: Appleton, 1873. First American edition. Publisher's
ads. 7 heliotypes and 21 text illus. Very good copy in publisher's
cloth. Gach 95-83 1983 $150

DARWIN, CHARLES   The Formation of Vegetable Mould.
John Murray, 1881. Third thousand. With 15 text woodcuts, ad. leaf,
with the errata slip, 8vo, orig. cloth, a light suggestion of foxing
on the end leaves, but otherwise a fine copy. Fenning 60-78 1983
£24.50

DARWIN, CHARLES   Formation of vegetable mould through
the action of worms. 1904. 10 plates, 8vo, cloth. Wheldon 160-133
1983 £12

DARWIN, CHARLES   Insectivorous Plants. 1888. 20 woodcuts, 8vo, original cloth, trifle used. Wheldon 160-1508 1983 £35

DARWIN, CHARLES   On the Origin of Species by Means of
Natural Selection. London, 1860. Thick 12mo, orig. green cloth,
gilt-lettered spine. There is a brown wrapper-style leaf preceding
the half-title and following the pub.'s catalogue. Argosy 713-140
1983 $350

DARWIN, CHARLES   On The Origin of Species By Means of
Natural Selection. London: John Murray, 1861. Third edition, with
additions and corrections. Orig. cloth. Front inner hinge cracked.
Rear inner hinge weak. Very good. MacManus 278-1269 1983 $375

DARWIN, CHARLES   On the Origin of Species by Means of
Natural Selection. John Murray, 1866. 4th edition, half titles,
illus. Orig. dark green cloth, v.g. Jarndyce 31-140 1983 £12.50

DARWIN, CHARLES   The Origin of Species. 1872. With a
folding diagram, cr. 8vo, orig. cloth, the inside joints skilfully
repaired, a very good copy. Sixth edition. Fenning 60-79 1983
£85

DARWIN, CHARLES   The Origin of Species by Means of Natural
Selection. London: John Murray, 1891. Sixth edition, with additions
and corrections. Illus. with one folding diagram. Orig. cloth. Covers
and spine slightly worn. Some foxing to the endpapers. Very good.
MacManus 278-1270 1983 $150

DARWIN, CHARLES   The Origin of the Species. London,
Murray, 1902. Frontis. portrait; folding diagram. 3/4 gilt stamped
green morocco, t.e.g. Fine copy. Houle 22-287 1983 $175

DARWIN, CHARLES   The Origin of Species. 1906. 6th ed.,
portrait, 8vo, cloth. Wheldon 160-130 1983 £15

DARWIN, CHARLES   On the Origin of Species. Watts & Co.,
1917. 8vo, orig. printed paper wrappers, a very good copy. Wrappers
lettered "Fifth Impression". Fenning 60-80 1983 £12.50

DARWIN, CHARLES   The Power of Movements in Plants.
New York, 1881. Illus., 8vo, cloth, slightly used. First American
edition. Name erased from flyleaf, old price and small blind stamp
on title-page, but a good copy. Wheldon 160-1507 1983 £40

DARWIN, CHARLES   The Zoology of the Voyage of H.M.S.
Beagle, under the command of Capt. Fitzroy, 1832-36. (1839-43) Facs.
Reprint, Wellington, N.Z., 1979. 5 parts in 3 vols., roy. 4to,
qtr. calf, cloth sides, coloured and plain plates. Edition limited
to 750 copies. Wheldon 160-20 1983 £400

DARWIN, ERASMUS   The Temple of Nature. London, 1803.
First edition. 4to. Orig. boards, rebacked, uncut. Engraved frontis.
and 3 plates engraved by Houghton from drawings by Fuseli. Plates
slightly foxed, and with slight tears in margin (not in frontis.).
Gurney 90-44 1983 £95

DARWIN, ERASMUS   The Temple of Nature. Baltimore:
Butler, 1804. 1st American ed., with fine copper-plate engravings
Tanner, Seymour, et al, after Blake. Contemp. calf, label. Jenkins
155-284 1983 $150

DARWIN, GEORGE HOWARD   Figures of Equilibrium of Rotating
Masses of Fluid. London: Pub. for the Royal Society by Trubner and
Co., 1887. Orig. offprint, 4to, 2 plates; disbound, orig. printed
upper wrapper retained and inscribed "J.J. Thomson from G.H.D.",
lacking lower wrapper. Pickering & Chatto 22-27 1983 $125

DASENT, GEORGE WEBBE   Annals of an Eventful Life. Hurst &
Blackett, 1870. 4th edition, revised. 3 vols., half titles, half
calf, red and blue labels. Fine. Jarndyce 30-352 1983 £30

DATTNER, BERNHARD   Kurzer Leitfaden Der Malariatherapie...
Lp/Wien: Franz Deuticke, 1927. Second edition. Gach 94-310 1983
$25

DAUBLER, THEODOR   Archipenko-Album. Potsdam: Gustav
Kiepenheuer, 1921. 33 illus. 4to. Wrappers. Light waterstaining
at extremities. Ars Libri 32-9 1983 $125

DAUDET, ALPHONSE   The Nabob. A story of Parisian life
and manners. London: Smith, Elder, 1878. First edition in English.
3 vols. in one. 8vo. Orig. brown cloth. Slightly rubbed. Pub's
remainder binding. Scarce. Ximenes 63-145 1983 $125

DAUDET, ALPHONSE   Sappho: Parisian Manners. Vizetelly,
1886. Ad. slip, half title, front. Engr. title and illus. 2 pp ads.
Orig. brown-grey dec. cloth, v.g. Jarndyce 31-143 1983 £14.50

D'AULAIRE, INGRI   The Lord's Prayer. N.Y.: Doub., 1934.
First edition. Folio. Cloth backed pictorial boards. Edges lightly
rubbed. Spine slightly faded. Color illus., much gilt accent.
Aleph-bet 8-77 1983 $30

D'AULAIRE, INGRI   Pocahontas. N.Y.: Doub., 1946. Folio.
Dust wrapper. Color illus. Fine. Aleph-bet 8-78 1983 $25

D'AULAIRE, INGRI   Sidsel Longskirt and Solve Suntrap.
Phila.: Winston, (1935). 8vo. Blue cloth, glossary, light cover
wear. Pictorial endpapers. 4 color plates & many black & whites
(some full-page). Very good. Aleph-bet 8-79 1983 $20

DAULTE, FRANCOIS   Alfred Sisley. Catalogue raisonne de
l'oeuvre peint. Lausanne: Editions Durand-Ruel, 1959. 898 illus.
(4 color). Folio. Cloth. Edition limited to 1200 numbered copies.
Inside front hinge slightly cracked. Rare. Ars Libri 32-637 1983
$1,300

DAUMER, GEORG FRIEDRICH (1800-1875)   Mittheilungen Ueber Kaspar
Hauser. Nuernberg: Heinrich Haubenstricker, 1832. Heft 1 & 2 bound
together. Contemporary drab boards. Gach 95-195 1983 $175

DAUN, BERTHOLD   Veit Stoss und seine Schule in Deutschland... Leipzig: Karl W. Hiersemann, 1903. 89 illus. Small 4to.
Marbled boards, 1/4 cloth. Ex-library. Ars Libri 32-648 1983 $40

DAU'S Detroit Society Blue Book and Ladies' Address Book.
Detroit, 1902. Cloth. Moderately worn. King 46-151 1983 $20

DAVAINE, C.   Memoire sur les Anomalies de l'oeuff.
Paris, 1861. 2 plates, 8vo, wrappers. Wheldon 160-478 1983 £25

DAVE, H. L.   A Short History of Gongal. Bombay, 1889.
Sm.8vo. Orig. cloth. Good. Edwards 1044-179 1983 £50

DAVENANT, CHARLES   Discourses on the Publick Revenues.
London: printed for James Knapton, 1698. 1st ed., vols. I of 2,
8vo, advertisements, half-title, separate titles to each part, 3 folding tables, cont. panelled calf, spine with raised bands. Pickering
& Chatto 21-29 1983 $250

DAVENANT, FRANCIS   Hubert Ellis. Ward, Lock, and Tyler,
(1866). First and apparently only edition, with additional
coloured litho title-page, coloured frontis. and 11 plates, 8vo, orig.
cloth, the spine neatly repaired. A very good copy. Fenning 62-89
1983 £14.50

DAVENANT, WILLIAM   The Dramatic Works. Edinburgh, 1872-74. 5 vols. 8vo. Half brown morocco, gilt, gilt panelled spines, t.e.g., other edges entirely uncut. Traylen 94-238 1983 £135

DAVENPORT, C. B.   Experimental Morphology. 1897-99 or 1908. Ex-library. Wheldon 160-147 1983 £12

DAVENPORT, CYRIL   The Book; its History and Development. London: Archibald Constable & Co., 1907. First edition. 8vo. Cloth. Prof. illus. Head of spine chipped. Book-plate removed. Oak Knoll 48-122 1983 $30

DAVENPORT, CYRIL   Byways Among English Books. New York: Frederick A. Stokes Co., n.d. (ca. 1920's). First U.S. edition. 8vo. Cloth. Illus. with sixty-one drawings and sixteen other illus. Bookplate and pocket. Very good. Oak Knoll 48-123 1983 $25

DAVENPORT, CYRIL   English Embroidered Bookbindings. London, 1899. 8vo, cloth, g.t. Colored frontis., illus. Duschnes 240-58 1983 $125

DAVENPORT, CYRIL   Mezzotints. London: Methuen and Co., 1904. First edition. 4to. Cloth. T.e.g. Fine. Oak Knoll 49-144 1983 $100

DAVENPORT, CYRIL   Royal English Book-Bindings. London: Seeley and Co. Ltd. 1896. Tall 8vo, illus. with 8 chromolithograph plates + 27 text illus. (most full-page). Red cloth. Karmiole 73-15 1983 $85

DAVENPORT, CYRIL   Royal English Bookbindings. London: Seeley and Co., 1896. First edition. 4to. Orig. cloth, t.e.g. 8 colored plates of bindings and many other illus. Minor fading of covers. Oak Knoll 48-51 1983 $85

DAVENPORT, CYRIL   Royal English Bookbindings. London, 1899. 8vo, cloth, g.t. Colored frontis., text illus., plates, backstrip darkened, bookplate of Karl Kup. Duschnes 240-59 1983 $185

DAVENPORT, EDWARD DAVIES   The golden age; or, England in 1822-3. London: James Ridgeway, 1823. First edition. 8vo. Disbound. Ximenes 63-400 1983 $75

DAVENPORT, FRANCIS G.   European Treaties Bearing on the History of the United States and Its Dependencies. Wash., 1917-37. 4 vols. Orig. cloth, faded, first edition. Ginsberg 46-227 1983 $75

DAVENPORT, HUMPHREY   Synopsis, or an Exact Abridgement of the Lord Cook's Commentaries upon Littleton. 1652. Portrait, 8vo, calf rubbed. K Books 301-111 1983 £40

DAVENPORT, JOHN   Aphrodisiacs and Anti-Aphrodisiacs. London, Privately Printed, 1869 (i.e., by J. C. Hotten, 1873). 1st ed. Frontispiece and 7 plates. Tall 8vo, uncut and unopened, in orig. sheets, never in a binding. Fine. Morrill 286-116 1983 $25

DAVENPORT, JOHN   Curiositates Eroticae Physiologiae. London, Privately Printed, 1875. 1st ed., only 250 copies printed. 8vo, uncut and unopened, in orig. sheets, never in a binding. Fine. Morrill 286-117 1983 $25

DAVENPORT, JOHN J.   The Wig and the Jimmy. N.Y., 1869. Orig. printed wraps. First edition. Ginsberg 46-536 1983 $35

DAVEY, F. H.   Flora of Cornwall. Penryn, 1909. Folding map and 6 portraits, 8vo, cloth. Very scarce. A tear in the folding map and binding used. Wheldon 160-1593 1983 £45

DAVEY, R.   The Sultan and his Subjects. London, 1897. Folding map and plan. 2 frontis., 1 folding. 2 vols. Some foxing on title of vol. I. 8vo. Orig. cloth. Good. Edwards 1044-180 1983 £60

DAVID, VILLIERS   The Guardsman and Cupid's Daughter, and Other Poems. The Cayme Press, 1930. Decorations by John Austen. First edition, 8vo, orig. green buckram, with coloured printed paper label on the upper cover, t.e.g., a fine copy. Ltd. edition of 500 numbered copies, signed by both the author and the artist. Printed at the Alcuin Press. Fenning 62-90 1983 £35

DAVID, VILLIERS   The Guardsman and Cupid's Daughter and other poems. (London): The Cayme Press, 1930. Illus. with decorations by John Austen. Orig. cloth with pictorial label. First edition. One of 500 copies signed by author and artist. Bookplate. Fine. MacManus 277-133 1983 $50

DAVID, VILLERS   The Guardsman and Cupids Daughter and Other Poems. London, Humphrey, 1930. First edition. Illus. by John Austen. One of 500 copies, signed by the author and illustrator. Green cloth with paper label (slight fading on spine), t.e.g., uncut. Houle 22-9 1983 $50

DAVID, VILLIERS   The Guardsman & Cupid's Daughter. Cayme Press, 1930. Frontis. Title vignette & 5 illus. Light green cloth. Onlaid plate. Edition limited to 500 copies on Japanese vellum. Signed by author & artist. Greer 40-37 1983 £25

DAVIDOFF, LEO M.   Brain Tumors. (1931). First separate edition. Illus. Argosy 713-141 1983 $100

DAVIDS, A.   Flowers - Rock Plants. Paris, Hyperion Press, 1939. 40 coloured plates, cr. folio. linen. Front inner joint broken. Wheldon 160-1930 1983 £15

DAVIDSON, ANDREW   Geographical Pathology. N.Y., 1892. Ex-lib. First edition. Argosy 713-142 1983 $45

DAVIDSON, D. J. D.   Diary of Travels and Adventures in Upper India. London, 1843. 2 vols. Labels, spine gilt. 8vo. Orig. cloth. Good. Edwards 1044-182 1983 £75

DAVIDSON, ELLIS A.   A Practical Manual of Home-Painting, Graining, Marbling and Sign-Writing. Crosby Lockwood, 1888. Half titles, ads. 5th edition, small ink stain to foredge. Orig. green cloth, bevelled boards, v.g. Jarndyce 31-144 1983 £24

DAVIDSON, GEORGE   Legend of Saint Swithin. London: Hamilton, Adams & Co., 1864. 4to. Orig. limp boards, cloth spine. Lithograph title-page and 12 lithograph plates by John Faed, R.S.A. Traylen 94-240 1983 £15

DAVIDSON, JOHN   Ballads & Songs. John Lane, 1894. Third edition. Spine faded and covers marked. Bookplate. Meatly tipped-in on the flyleaf is a cont. review of the book. Nice. Rota 230-662 1983 £15

DAVIDSON, JOHN   Ballads & Songs. London: John Lane; Boston: Copeland & Day, 1894. First edition. 12mo. Orig. decorated cloth. MacManus 278-1272 1983 $25

DAVIDSON, JOHN   Bruce. London: Wilson & McCormick, 1886. First edition. Orig. cloth-backed boards with paper spine label (faded & slightly rubbed, with one small chip to the top end). Inscribed on the front free endpaper: "With the author's compliments." Cover corners worn, with some offsetting to the endpapers. Scarce. Very good. MacManus 278-1274 1983 $500

DAVIDSON, JOHN   Bruce. Glasgow, 1886. First edition. Spine darkened, corners worn and covers marked. Good. Rota 230-660 1983 £40

DAVIDSON, JOHN   Fleet Street Eclogues. Elkin Mathews & John Lane, 1893. First edition. One of 300 copies. Spine darkened and a little rubbed and covers marked. Nice. Rota 230-661 1983 £25

DAVIDSON, JOHN   Fleet Street Eclogues. New York, 1895. First American edition. Covers a little marked. Inscription on flyleaf. Nice. Rota 230-152 1983 £20

DAVIDSON, JOHN   Fleet Street Eclogues. London: Elkin Mathews & John Lane, 1893. First edition. 12mo. Orig. buckram. 300 copies were printed. Fine. MacManus 278-1275 1983 $25

DAVIDSON, JOHN   God and Mammon. London, 1907. First edition. Nice. Rota 230-678 1983 £15

DAVIDSON, JOHN   Godfrida. John Lane, New York, 1898. First American edition. Spine faded and lower cover marked. Nice. Rota 230-670 1983 £20

DAVIDSON, JOHN   Godfrida. New York & London: John Lane (The Bodley Head), 1898. First edition. Orig. pictorial buckram, spine slightly darkened. Covers and spine a bit worn, with slight foxing to the endpapers. Very good. MacManus 278-1276 1983 $35

DAVIDSON, JOHN   Godfrida. New York & London: John Lane The Bodley Head, 1898. Gilt pictorial cloth. First American edition. Pencil erasure, else about fine. Reese 20-301 1983 $20

DAVIDSON, JOHN   Holiday & Other Poems. London: E. Grant Richards, 1906. First edition. Orig. buckram. Spine faded. Endpapers slightly foxed. Very good. MacManus 278-1277 1983 $25

DAVIDSON, JOHN   Holiday and other poems. London, 1906. First edition. Spine faded. Bookplate. Cont. review neatly mounted on flyleaf. Nice. Rota 230-677 1983 £15

DAVIDSON, JOHN   The Knight of the Maypole. London, 1903. First edition. Spine split and worn. Internally a nice copy. Rota 230-672 1983 £18

DAVIDSON, JOHN   The Man Forbid and other essays. Boston: The Ball Publishing Co., 1910. First edition. Intro. by Edward J. O'Brien. Orig. cloth. Spine a bit spotted. Fine. MacManus 278-1279 1983 $25

DAVIDSON, JOHN   The Man Forbid. Boston, 1910. First edition. Intro. by E.J. O'Brien. Spine and covers a little darkened. Bookplate. Nice. Rota 230-681 1983 £15

DAVIDSON, JOHN   New Ballads. John Lane, 1897. First edition. Spine darkened. Covers spotted and corner of rear endpaper defective. Name on flyleaf. Very good. Rota 230-668 1983 £20

DAVIDSON, JOHN   New Ballads. New York, 1897. First American edition. Spine faded. Nice. Rota 230-669 1983 £20

DAVIDSON, JOHN   New Ballads. London: John Lane The Bodley Head, 1897. Gilt pictorial cloth. First edition. Spine slightly sunned. Reese 20-300 1983 $30

DAVIDSON, JOHN   The Pilgrimage of Strongsoul. London, 1896. First edition of this selection. Spine darkened and marked. Corners and edges of covers bruised. Bookplate. Rota 230-665 1983 £25

DAVIDSON, JOHN   Plays. Elkin Mathews & John Lane, 1894. Second edition. Frontis. and cover device by A. Beardsley. Spine worn and covers faded and marked. Good. Rota 230-663 1983 £30

DAVIDSON, JOHN   A Queen's Romance. London, 1904. First edition. Spine and covers a little darkened. Rota 230-675 1983 £20

DAVIDSON, JOHN   A Queen's Romance. London: Grant Richards, 1904. Gilt cloth. First edition. About fine. Reese 20-303 1983 $20

DAVIDSON, JOHN   A Random Itinerary. Elkin Mathews & John Lane, 1894. First edition. Frontis. by L. Housman. One of 600 copies. Spine darkened and covers marked. Very good. Rota 230-664 1983 £25

DAVIDSON, JOHN   A Random Itinerary. London: Elkin Mathews & John Land; Boston: Copeland & Day, 1894. First edition. 12mo. Orig. buckram. Limited to 600 copies. Covers a bit soiled and worn. MacManus 278-1281 1983 $30

DAVIDSON, JOHN   A Rosary. London, 1903. First edition. Spine and covers faded and marked. Edges string-marked. From the library of H. Walpole, bearing his armorial and Brackenburn bookplates. Good. Rota 230-673 1983 £21

DAVIDSON, JOHN   A Rosary. New York, 1904. First American edition. Spine and covers a little darkened and marked. Nice. Rota 230-674 1983 £15

DAVIDSON, JOHN   A Second Series of Fleet Street Eclogues. John Lane, 1896. First edition. Spine darkened. Covers a little marked. Bookplate. Nice. Rota 230-666 1983 £25

DAVIDSON, JOHN   A Second Series of Fleet Street Eclogues. John Lane, 1896. Second edition. Spine faded and covers a little marked. Nice. Rota 230-667 1983 £15

DAVIDSON, JOHN   Sentences and Paragraphs. London, 1893. First edition. Foot of spine bruised and pages browned. Nice. Rota 230-151 1983 £30

DAVIDSON, JOHN   Smith; a tragedy. Glasgow, 1888. First edition. Wrappers. Foot of backstrip frayed. Unopened. Nice. Rota 230-150 1983 £40

DAVIDSON, JOHN   The Testament of a Prime Minister. London: Grant Richards, 1904. Cloth, gilt, first edition. Spine a bit sunned, else fine. Reese 20-302 1983 $20

DAVIDSON, JOHN   Testaments. No. 1, 2, & 3. London: Grant Richards, 1901-1902. First editions. 3 vols. Orig. printed wrappers. Very good. MacManus 278-1284 1983 $150

DAVIDSON, JOHN   Testaments. London, 1901-02. First edition. 3 vols. 4to. Wrappers darkened and frayed. Name of title page of Vol. I. Good. Rota 230-671 1983 £30

DAVIDSON, JOHN   The Theatrocrat. London: E. Grant Richards, 1905. First edition. Orig. cloth. Spine slightly faded. Covers a little marked. Good. MacManus 278-1282 1983 $35

DAVIDSON, JOHN   The Theatrocrat. London, 1905. First edition. Spine and covers faded and marked. Corners bruised. Nice. Rota 230-676 1983 £18

DAVIDSON, JOHN   The Triumph of Mammon. London: E. Grant Richards, 1907. First edition. Orig. cloth. Front inner hinge slightly cracked. Spine and covers very slightly worn. Very good. MacManus 278-1283 1983 $35

DAVIDSON, T.   A Monograph of the Carboniferous Brachiopoda of Scotland. 1860. 5 plates, 8vo, cloth. Plate 1 stained on reverse, spine repaired. Wheldon 160-1382 1983 £15

DAVIDSON, THOMAS   Aristotle and Ancient Educational Ideas. NY (The Great Educators), 1907. Salloch 385-472 1983 $45

DAVIE, O.   Methods in the art of Taxidermy. Philadelphia, 1894. 90 plates, royal 8vo, original cloth (neatly refixed), ex-library copy, a few margins defective. Wheldon 160-479 1983 £30

DAVIES, ACTON   Maude Adams. N.Y.: Frederick A. Stokes Co., (1901). Illustrated. Small 8vo. Orig. decorated cloth. First edition. Laid in is a package of four rotograph post cards picturing Maude Adams in "Peter Pan." Good copy. MacManus 277-25 1983 $25

DAVIES, CHARLES MAURICE   Mystic London. Tinsley Brothers, 1875. First edition, half title, 2 pp ads., orig. brown cloth, recased. Jarndyce 31-241 1983 £18

DAVIES, JOHN   The Original, Nature and Immortality
of the Soul. London: for W. Rogers, 1697. First edition. 8vo.
Cont. panelled calf. Half title. Very good copy. Heath 48-271
1983 £100

DAVIES, JOHN   Travels of Four Years and a Half in the
United States of America. London, 1803. First edition. 3/4 scarlet
morocco binding by Sangorski & Sutcliffe. Jenkins 152-610 1983 $750

DAVIES, K. G.   Documents of the American Revolution...
Dublin, 1972-81. 21 vols. Boswell 7-56 1983 $1120

DAVIES, RHYS   A Bed of Feathers. Mandrake Press,
(1929). First edition. 12mo. Dust wrapper. Author's signed autograph presentation inscription to E. Goldston. Rota 231-152 1983 £20

DAVIES, RHYS   Daisy Matthews and Three Other Tales.
Waltham Saint Lawrence: The Golden Cockerel Press, (1932). First
edition. 4to. Orig. half-morocco and decorated cloth. Limited to
325 copies signed by the author. Fine copy. Jaffe 1-76 1983 $150

DAVIES, RHYS   Honey and Bread. London, 1935. First
edition. Author's signed autograph presentation inscription. Very
good. Rota 231-154 1983 £15

DAVIES, RHYS   One of Norah's Early Days. London:
1935. Thin 8vo, cloth. One of 250 signed copies. Argosy 714-209
1983 $45

DAVIES, RHYS   One of Norah's Early Days. London:
Grayson & Grayson, 1935. First edition. Orig. cloth. Dust jacket
(lightly soiled). Limited to 285 copies signed by author. Very good.
MacManus 278-1287 1983 $25

DAVIES, RHYS   Rings on Her Fingers. London, 1930.
First edition. One of 175 numbered copies, signed by the author. In
cellophane dust wrapper and slipcase. Very nice. Rota 231-153 1983
£25

DAVIES, RHYS   The Song of Songs and other Stories.
London: E. Archer, n.d. (1927). First edition. Frontis. portrait
by William Roberts. One of 900 copies. Orig. wrappers. Very fine.
MacManus 278-1288 1983 $45

DAVIES, RHYS   The Song of Songs & Other Stories.
London, (n.d.). Limited to 1000 copies (100 signed), this copy being
unsigned. Very good plus in paperwraps. Quill & Brush 54-350 1983
$40

DAVIES, RHYS   Tale. London: E. Lahr, (1930). First
edition. Orig. wrappers. One of 100 copies signed by author. Fine.
MacManus 278-1289 1983 $35

DAVIES, RHYS   The Things Men Do. London, 1936. First
edition. Author's signed autograph presentation inscription. Very
good. Rota 231-155 1983 £15

DAVIES, THOMAS   Dramatic Miscellanies: consisting of
critical observations on several plays of Shakespeare. Dublin:
printed for S. Price, etc., 1784. 3 vols. 12mo, cont. calf, spines
gilt, contrasting morocco labels (a bit rubbed). First Irish edition.
A fine set. Ximenes 64-159 1983 $175

DAVIES, THOMAS   Memoirs of the life of David Garrick,
Esq. London: printed for the author, 1780. 2 vols., 8vo, original
boards, later paper spines and MS labels (ends of spines worn).
1st ed. With a frontis. portrait. Lacks one front flyleaf, slight
stain in upper margins near the end of Vol. I, but an uncut copy.
Ximenes 64-160 1983 $225

DAVIES, THOMAS   Memoirs of the life of David Garrick,
Esq. London: printed for the author, 1781. 2 vols., 8vo, cont. calf,
spines gilt (slight wear). 3rd edition. With a portrait. A very
good copy, complete with the half-title in vol. 2. Ximenes 64-161
1983 $125

DAVIES, THOMAS   Memoirs of the Life of David Garrick.
Printed for the author, 1781. 2 vols, 8vo, portrait, cont. calf.
Calf defective on the upper part of the upper joint of vol. 1 and at
the head and foot of both spines. Half title present in vol. 2.
Bickersteth 75-23 1983 £60

DAVIES, THOMAS   Memoirs of the life of David Garrick,
Esq. London: printed for the author, 1784. 2 vols., 8vo, cont.
mottled calf, spines gilt, contrasting morocco labels (spines rubbed).
4th edition, with a portrait, complete with the half-title in vol.
2. Ximenes 64-162 1983 $175

DAVIES, WILLIAM   Sermons on Religious and Moral
Subjects... Bristol: for the Author, 1754. First edition. 8vo.
Cont. panelled calf, gilt. Fine copy. Heath 48-546 1983 £45

DAVIES, WILLIAM HENRY   The Adventures of Johnny Walker, Tramp.
London: Jonathan Cape, (1926). First edition. Orig. buckram. One
of 125 copies signed by author. Spine and covers faded. Slight foxing
to the endpapers. Very good. MacManus 278-1291 1983 $65

DAVIES, WILLIAM HENRY   The Adventures of Johnny Walker, Tramp.
London: Jonathan Cape, (1926). First edition. Orig. cloth. Dust
jacket (faded, worn, and soiled, with one small tear to the front
cover). Some offsetting to the endpapers. Very good. MacManus 278-
1290 1983 $25

DAVIES, WILLIAM HENRY   Ambition and Other Poems. London:
Jonathan Cape, (1929). First edition. Orig. half-morocco & boards.
Dust jacket. Limited to 210 copies signed by author. Fine. MacManus
278-1293 1983 $50

DAVIES, WILLIAM HENRY   Beggars. London: Duckworth & Co., 1909.
First edition. Orig. cloth. Covers rather rubbed. MacManus 278-1295
1983 $25

DAVIES, WILLIAM HENRY   The Bird of Paradise and Other Poems.
London: Methuen & Co., Ltd., (1914). First edition. Orig. boards.
Inscribed to "Augustus John from W.H. Davies" on the front flyleaf.
Front cover stained. Good. MacManus 278-1296 1983 $40

DAVIES, WILLIAM HENRY   The Bird of Paradise and Other Poems.
London: Methuen & Co., (1914). First edition. Orig. printed boards.
Dust jacket (faded and worn; spine ends chipped). Edges foxed.
Very good. MacManus 278-1297 1983 $40

DAVIES, WILLIAM HENRY   The Birth of Song. London: Jonathan
Cape, (1936). First edition. Orig. decorated cloth. Dust jacket
(spine and covers faded, worn, and soiled). Endpapers a trifle foxed.
Near-fine. MacManus 278-1298 1983 $35

DAVIES, WILLIAM HENRY   Child Lovers and Other Poems. London:
A.C. Fifield, 1916. Second edition. Orig. grey printed wrappers.
Presentation copy from author inscribed: "Walter Sickert, from W.H.
Davies." Spine and covers faded, worn and rubbed, especially at the
margins. Fair. MacManus 278-1303 1983 $125

DAVIES, WILLIAM HENRY   Child Lovers and other poems. London:
A.C. Fifield, 1916. First edition. Orig. wrappers. Inscribed by
author to C.W. Beaumont. Light soiling around margin. Very good.
MacManus 278-1300 1983 $45

DAVIES, WILLIAM HENRY   Child Lovers And other Poems. London:
A.C. Fifield, 1916. First edition. Orig. wrappers (a little dust-
soiled). Very good. MacManus 278-1302 1983 $25

DAVIES, WILLIAM HENRY   Collected Poems. London: A.C. Fifield,
1916. First edition. Port. in collotype from pencil sketch by Will
Rothenstein, and facsimile of author's script. Orig. cloth. Presentation copy from author to publisher Elkin Mathews, inscribed on the
front free endpaper "C. Elkin Mathews, my first publisher and a good
one, from W.H. Davies." Covers dull. Very good. MacManus 278-1304
1983 $125

DAVIES, WILLIAM HENRY   Collected Poems. London: Jonathan
Cape, (1921). First edition, third impression. Frontispiece port.
Orig. vellum. Presentation copy from author to his publisher, in-
scribed: "What is this life if, full of care/We have no time to stand
and stare. Christmas 1921. To Jonathan Cape, from W.H. Davies."
Cover warped. Uncut. Near-fine. MacManus 278-1305 1983 $75

DAVIES, WILLIAM HENRY   Collected Poems: Second Series. London: Jonathan Cape, (1923). First edition, large paper copy. Frontispiece port. Orig. cloth-backed boards with paper spine and cover labels. One of 106 copies signed by author. Spine and covers faded, worn and rubbed at the margins. Slight offsetting to the endpapers. Bookplate. Good. MacManus 278-1307 1983 $65

DAVIES, WILLIAM HENRY   Dancing Mad. London: Jonathan Cape, (1927). First edition. Orig. cloth. Presentation copy, inscribed: "To Marjorie Pease, from W.H. Davies, Christmas 1927." Spine and covers slightly faded and worn. Slight foxing to the edges and preliminary pages. Good. MacManus 278-1314 1983 $50

DAVIES, WILLIAM HENRY   Farewell to Poesy And Other Pieces. London: A.C. Fifield, 1910. First edition. Orig. boards. Inscribed on the front flyleaf to "Augustus John from W.H. Davies." Spine darkened. Very good. MacManus 278-1320 1983 $50

DAVIES, WILLIAM HENRY   Farewell to Poesy, And Other Pieces. London: A.C. Fifield, (1910). First edition. Orig. printed boards. Dust jacket (spine quite faded, worn at margins & chipped at the ends; covers slightly worn and soiled). Bookplate. Near-fine. MacManus 278-1321 1983 $45

DAVIES, WILLIAM HENRY   Foliage. London: Elkin Mathews, Cork Street, 1913. First edition. Orig. cloth. Copy belonging to A.C. Fifield who was Davies's earlier publisher. Signed by Fifield, with the note "The MS alterations by W.H.D." Spine and covers faded and worn. Slight foxing to endpapers. Good. MacManus 278-1324 1983 $350

DAVIES, WILLIAM HENRY   Foliage. London: Elkin Mathews, 1913. First edition. 12mo. Orig. cloth. Presentation copy to John Freeman. Fine. MacManus 278-1326 1983 $125

DAVIES, WILLIAM HENRY   Foliage. London: Elkin Mathews, 1913. First edition. Orig. cloth. Inscribed to "Augustus John from W.H. Davies." Spine faded. Very good. MacManus 278-1325 1983 $60

DAVIES, WILLIAM HENRY   Foliage. London: Elkin Mathews, 1913. First edition. 12mo. Orig. cloth. Presentation copy to C.W. Beaumont. Very good. MacManus 278-1328 1983 $45

DAVIES, WILLIAM HENRY   Foliage. London: Elkins Mathews, Cork Street, 1913. First edition. Orig. cloth. Spine slightly faded. Near-fine. MacManus 278-1329 1983 $35

DAVIES, WILLIAM HENRY   Forty New Poems. London: A.C. Fifield, 1918. First edition. Orig. grey cloth. Copies were also issued in blue cloth without a blindstamp on the front cover. Former owner's signature. Good. MacManus 278-1332 1983 $20

DAVIES, WILLIAM HENRY   Forty-Nine Poems. London: The Medici Society, 1928. First edition. Selected & Illus. by Jacynth Parsons. Orig cloth. Dust jacket (slightly worn). Presentation copy, inscribed by Davies on the front flyleaf: "To John, Gertrude, Joy and Carl Freeman from William, Helen, Betty & Pharoah Davies, Best wishes for Xmas, 1928." Fine. MacManus 278-1327 1983 $125

DAVIES, WILLIAM HENRY   Forty-Nine Poems. London: The Medici Society, 1928. First edition. Selected & illus. by J. Parsons. Orig. cloth. Dust jacket (spine and covers slightly faded, with one very small tear to the back cover). One of 110 copies signed by author & artist. Some offsetting to the endpapers. Near-fine. MacManus 278-1334 1983 $75

DAVIES, WILLIAM HENRY   Forty-Nine Poems. London: the Medici Society, 1928. Roy. 8vo. Cloth. Mint in the orig. dust-wrapper. Coloured frontis. 50 illus., of which 8 are coloured by Jacynth Parsons. Traylen 94-241 1983 £20

DAVIES, WILLIAM HENRY   The Hour of Magic. London: Jonathan Cape, (1922). First edition. Illus. by William Nicholson. Orig. boards with decorated spine and cover labels (spine label slightly rubbed and darkened; cover label a trifle soiled). The author's own copy and signed by him on the half-title page. With one correction in the text in Davies's hand. Spine and covers worn, faded, and soiled. Bookplate. Good. MacManus 278-1322 1983 $165

DAVIES, WILLIAM HENRY   The Hour of Magic and other Poems. London: Jonathan Cape, (1922). First edition. Decorated by Wm. Nicholson. Orig. cloth-backed boards with paper labels. One of 110 large-paper copies signed by Davies & Nicholson. Label on spine worn. Fine. MacManus 278-1339 1983 $65

DAVIES, WILLIAM HENRY   The Hour of Magic and Other Poems. London: Jonathan Cape, (1922). First edition. Decorated by William Nicholson. 8vo. Orig. parchment boards with paper labels. Limited to 325 copies signed by the author. Fine copy. Jaffe 1-77 1983 $35

DAVIES, WILLIAM HENRY   In Winter. London: Privately Printed, 1931. First edition. Illus. & hand-colored by Edward Carrick. Orig. boards with paper cover label. Publisher's glassine jacket (quite chipped and worn at the spine). One of 15 copies printed on fine paper & signed by author & illus. Spine and covers faded. Good. MacManus 278-1341 1983 $135

DAVIES, WILLIAM HENRY   In Winter. London: Privately printed, 1931. First edition. Illus. Orig. printed boards. One of 290 copies signed by W. H. Davies. Presentation copy from John Gawsworth to Wilfred Gibson. Spine worn and faded, with two small tears. Spine margins slightly torn. Covers faded and worn. Good. MacManus 278-1323 1983 $40

DAVIES, WILLIAM HENRY   In Winter. London: Privately Printed, 1931. First edition. Illus. Orig. printed boards. One of 290 copies signed by Davies. Collates differently, having its free endpapers tipped in. Spine and covers faded and slightly worn. Bookplate. Good. MacManus 278-1340 1983 $30

DAVIES, WILLIAM HENRY   Later Days. London: Cape, (1925). First edition. Orig. cloth. Limited to 125 copies signed by author. Spine faded. Very good. MacManus 278-1346 1983 $65

DAVIES, WILLIAM HENRY   The Loneliest Mountain and Other Poems. London: Jonathan Cape, (1939). First edition, advance proofs. Orig. printed wrappers. Covers slightly faded. Very good. MacManus 278-1358 1983 $85

DAVIES, WILLIAM HENRY   The Loneliest Mountain and Other Poems. London: Jonathan Cape, (1939). First edition. Orig. decorated cloth. Dust jacket (somewhat faded, worn and soiled). Slight offsetting to the endpapers. Good. MacManus 278-1359 1983 $25

DAVIES, WILLIAM HENRY   Love Poems. London: Jonathan Cape, (1935). First edition. Illus. Orig. cloth. Dust jacket (faded, worn, and soiled, with one small tear to the spine). Spine a trifle faded, with slight foxing to the preliminary pages. Near-fine. MacManus 278-1360 1983 $20

DAVIES, WILLIAM HENRY   Moss and Feather. London: Faber & Gwyer Ltd. 1928. First edition. Drawings by Wm. Nicholson. Orig. boards. One of 500 copies signed by Davies. Fine. MacManus 278-1366 1983 $45

DAVIES, WILLIAM HENRY   Moss and Feather. (London: Faber & Gwyer, 1929). First edition. Illus. & designed by Nicholson. Orig. decorated wrappers. Signed by Nicholson in green ink, with several additions by him to the illustration on page 1 in the same color. Included is another copy of "Moss & Feather" without Nicholson's signature or additions to the illustration. Very fine. MacManus 278-1365 1983 $450

DAVIES, WILLIAM HENRY   Nature Poems And Others. London: A.C. Fifield, 1908. First edition. Orig. boards. Holbrook Jackson's copy, with his signature, dated 1908, and bookplate, on the front endpapers. With an ALS, 2 pages, 8vo, Weald, Near Sevenoaks, June 6th, 1909, from Davies to Jackson. Very good. MacManus 278-1371 1983 $75

DAVIES, WILLIAM HENRY   Nature Poems, And Others. London: A.C. Fifield, 1908. First edition. Orig. boards. Dust jacket (spine and covers somewhat faded and worn, rear cover spotte, spine ends slightly chipped). Near-fine. MacManus 278-1372 1983 $45

DAVIES, WILLIAM HENRY   Nature Poems. London: Fifield, 1908. First edition. Orig. boards. Covers slightly soiled. Very good. 12mo. MacManus 278-1373 1983 $20

DAVIES, WILLIAM HENRY   New Poems. London: Elkin Mathews, 1907. First edition. Orig. cloth. Signed by author on the front free end-paper, "William H. Davies, February 11, 1909." Spine and covers a trifle worn at the margins. Slightly foxed. Near-fine. MacManus 278-1376 1983 $45

DAVIES, WILLIAM HENRY   New Poems. London: Elkin Mathews, 1907. First edition. Orig. cloth. Publisher's glassine jacket (somewhat chipped). Publisher's bookplate. Endpapers slightly foxed. Near-fine. MacManus 278-1378 1983 $50

DAVIES, WILLIAM HENRY   New Poems. London: Elkin Mathews, 1907. First edition. 12mo. Orig. cloth. Mint. MacManus 278-1377 1983 $35

DAVIES, WILLIAM HENRY   Poems 1930-31. London: Jonathan Cape, (1932). First edition. Illus. Orig. parchment-backed cloth. Publisher's glassine jacket (a trifle faded and chipped). One of 150 copies signed by author. Covers very slightly faded. Near-fine. MacManus 278-1385 1983 $50

DAVIES, WILLIAM HENRY   Poems 1930-31. London: Jonathan Cape, (1932). First edition. Orig. decorated cloth, dust jacket (slightly faded). Pages slightly foxed. Very good. MacManus 278-1386 1983 $20

DAVIES, WILLIAM HENRY   A Poet's Alphabet. London: Jonathan Cape, (1925). First edition. Decorations by Dora M. Batty. Orig. vellum-backed boards. Dust jacket (slightly worn). One of 125 copies signed by author. Very good. MacManus 278-1388 1983 $35

DAVIES, WILLIAM HENRY   A Poet's Alphabet. London: Jonathan Cape, (1925). First edition. Illus. with vignettes by Dora Batty. Orig. decorated boards with paper spine and cover labels. Dust jacket (slightly faded, worn and soiled; a trifle chipped at top spine end). Slightly foxed throughout. Some offsetting to the endpapers. Very good. MacManus 278-1387 1983 $20

DAVIES, WILLIAM HENRY   A Poet's Calendar. London: Jonathan Cape, (1927). First edition. Orig. parchment-backed decorated boards. Dust jacket (faded and worn; margins and spine rubbed and slightly chipped). One of 125 copies signed by author. Uncut copy with the publisher's prospectus for The Song of Love loosely laid in. MacManus 278-1389 1983 $65

DAVIES, WILLIAM HENRY   A Poet's Calendar. London: Jonathan Cape, (1927). First edition. Orig. parchment-backed decorated boards. One of 125 copies signed by author. Corners a trifle bent. Slight foxing to the endpapers. Very good. MacManus 278-1390 1983 $65

DAVIES, WILLIAM HENRY   A Poet's Pilgrimage. London: Andrew Melrose, 1918. First edition. Orig. cloth. Dust jacket (somewhat faded, worn and soiled; spine ends slighlty chipped and fraying). Former owner's signature. Spine slightly faded and worn. Good. MacManus 278-1392 1983 $40

DAVIES, WILLIAM HENRY   Raptures, A Book of Poems. (London: Cyril William Beaumont Press, 1918). First edition. Orig. cloth-backed decorated boards with spine and cover labels (spine label quite faded and slightly worn). One of 250 copies printed on hand-made paper and bound by Sangorski & Sutcliffe. Near-fine. MacManus 278-1394 1983 $35

DAVIES, WILLIAM HENRY   Secrets. London: Jonathan Cape, (1924). First edition. Illus. with vignettes by Claud Lovat Fraser. Orig. parchment-backed decorated boards. Dust jacket (somewhat faded, worn, and slightly soiled, with one very small chip to the lower spine end). One of 100 copies signed by author. Slight offsetting to the endpapers. Near-fine. MacManus 278-1396 1983 $75

DAVIES, WILLIAM HENRY   The Song of Life and Other Poems. London: A.C. Fifield, 1920. First edition. Frontispiece from a port. by Laura Knight. Orig. cloth. Presentation copy, inscribed to "Augustus John with kind regards from W.H. Davies Oct. 1920." Very good. MacManus 278-1403 1983 $50

DAVIES, WILLIAM HENRY   The Song of Love. London: Jonathan Cape, (1926). First edition. Illus. Orig. parchment-backed boards. Dust jacket (slightly faded, worn and soiled, with one small tear to the front spine margin). One of 125 copies signed by author. Endpapers a trifle foxed. Near-fine. MacManus 278-1405 1983 $65

DAVIES, WILLIAM HENRY   Songs of Joy and others. London: A.C. Fifield, 1911. First edition. Orig. cloth. Inscribed on the front flyleaf to "Augustus John from W.H. Davies." Very good. MacManus 278-1401 1983 $60

DAVIES, WILLIAM HENRY   The Soul's Destroyer & Other Poems. (London): Privately Printed by the Author, (1905). First edition. Orig. printed wrappers. Spine and covers faded and worn, front spine margin torn. Some foxing throughout. Good. MacManus 278-1408 1983 $350

DAVIES, WILLIAM HENRY   The Soul's Destroyer and Other Poems. London: Alston Rivers Ltd., 1907. Later edition. Orig. printed wrappers. Presentation copy from Edward Thomas, one of Davies' close friends to E.S.P. Haynes, inscribed by Thomas on the half-title. Foxing. Very good. MacManus 280-5196 1983 $350

DAVIES, WILLIAM HENRY   The Soul's Destroyer & Other Poems. London: Alston Rivers, 1907. First abridged edition. Orig. printed wrappers. Spine and covers slightly worn at the margins, inner contents a bit foxed. Bookplate. Good. MacManus 278-1409 1983 $40

DAVIES, WILLIAM HENRY   The Soul's Destroyer & Other Poems. London: Alston Rivers, 1910. Second edition (?). Orig. printed wrappers. Presentation copy from the author to Harold & Laura Knight inscribed. Loosely laid in is an ALS, 1 page, London, 14 Great Russell Street, February 8, 1920, from Davies to Laura Knight. Spine and covers rather faded and worn at the margins. Spine chipped. Hinges weak. Fair. MacManus 278-1410 1983 $185

DAVIES, WILLIAM HENRY   The Soul's Destroyer & Other Poems. London: Alston Rivers Ltd., 1910. Later edition of Davies' first book. Orig. brown wrappers. Presentation copy from W.H. Davies to Richard Church. Wrappers a little worn. Light foxing. MacManus 278-1411 1983 $75

DAVIES, WILLIAM HENRY   True Travellers. London: Jonathan Cape, (1923). First edition. Illus. by Wm. Nicholson. Orig. cloth-backed decorated boards with paper spine and cover labels. Publisher's glassine jacket and box (jacket slightly worn and frayed; box quite worn, faded, with some corners broken). One of 100 copies signed by author and artist. Presentation copy to John Gawsworth inscribed. Some offsetting to the endpapers. Near-fine. MacManus 278-1419 1983 $150

DAVIES, WILLIAM HENRY   True Travellers. London, (1923). Sq. 8vo, printed boards; d.w. With decorations by William Nicholson. Fine. Argosy 714-210 1983 $45

DAVIES, WILLIAM HENRY   True Travellers. London: Jonathan Cape, (1923). First edition. Illus. by Wm. Nicholson. Orig. decorated boards. Dust jacket (quite faded, worn, and somewhat chipped at the top margin and spine end). A trifle foxed throughout. Very good. MacManus 278-1420 1983 $25

DAVIES, WILLIAM HENRY   A Weak Woman. London: Duckworth & Co., 1911. First edition. Orig. cloth. Spine and covers worn and slightly spotted. Good. MacManus 278-1423 1983 $40

DAVIS, CHARLES E.   Three Years in the Army. Boston, 1894. First edition. Special presentation binding. Full morocco, gilt extra. Inscribed by the president of the regimental society. Near mint. Jenkins 152-608 1983 $300

DAVIS, CHARLES G.   The Built-up Ship Model. Salem, Mass.: Marine Research Society, 1933. First edition. 8vo. Orig. cloth. Frontis. 37 plates. numerous illus. Orig. dust jacket. Fine. Edwards 1042-47 1983 £35

DAVIS, CHARLES G.   The Ship Model Builder's Assistant. Salem, Mass., 1926. 8vo. Orig. cloth. Numerous figures in text. Slightly faded. Orig. dust jacket. Good. Edwards 1042-48 1983 £35

DAVIS, CHARLES G.   Shipping & Craft in Silhouette. Salem: Marine Research Society, 1929. Imperial 8vo. Orig. cloth. Frontis. vignette on title, 101 illus. Occasional very slight foxing. Small ink stamp on title. Good. Edwards 1042-49 1983 £60

DAVIS, CHARLES G.   Shipping & Craft in Silhouette. Salem, Marine Research Society, 1929. 1st ed. Drawings by author. 4to, label removed from spine, top of spine frayed. Morrill 288-87 1983 $25

DAVIS, CHARLES G.   Shipping & Craft in Silhouette. Salem, Mass.: Marine Research Society, 1929. Drawings by author. Cloth. Minor wear and cover soil. King 45-526 1983 $25

DAVIS, CHARLES THOMAS   The Manufacture of Paper. Phila., 1886. Ads. Illus. Cloth. Felcone 21-28 1983 $100

DAVIS, GEORGE   Recollections of a Sea Wanderer's Life. N.Y., 1887. Illus. Orig. pictorial cloth. First edition. Ginsberg 47-58 1983 $150

DAVIS, GEORGE WESLEY   Sketches of Butte. Boston, 1921. Illus. Orig. cloth. First edition. Autograph presentation copy signed by Davis. Ginsberg 46-503 1983 $50

DAVIS, J. F.   The Chinese. London, 1836. Numerous woodcut plates. 2 vols. Calf, spines worn, labels chipped. 8vo. Good. Edwards 1044-196 1983 £50

DAVIS, JEFFERSON   Engagement Between United States Troops and Sioux Indians. Wash., 1855. Dbd. First edition. Ginsberg 46-692 1983 $50

DAVIS, JEFFERSON   Report of...Calling for Correspondence Relative to the Military Reservation at Fort Leavenworth. Wash., 1855. Dbd. First edition. Ginsberg 47-400 1983 $25

DAVIS, JEFFERSON   Report of...Communicating...a Copy of the Report of Lieut. Col. Cooke of the Part Taken by His Command in the Action at Bluewater, Nebraska Terr., with the Sioux Indians. Wash., 1855. Dbd. First edition. Ginsberg 47-836 1983 $25

DAVIS, JEFFERSON   The Rise and Fall of the Confederate Government. NY, 1881. 2 Vols. First edition. Slightly worn and soiled covers. King 46-48 1983 $75

DAVIS, JOHN   Travels of John Davis in the United States of America 1798 to 1802. Boston, 1910. 2 vols. Boards with vellum backstrip. Printed privately. Only 487 printed. Ginsberg 46-229 1983 $100

DAVIS, MATTHEW L.   Memoirs of Aaron Burr. NY, 1838. 2 ports., 2 vols., orig. cloth, (one vol. rebacked, lightly foxed, usual wear). Argosy 716-432 1983 $40

DAVIS, NATHAN   Carthage and Her Remains. New York, 1861. 8vo, 2 tinted plates, 21 engr. and other plates of which 2 are folding, 4 plans and maps and engr. illus. Orig. cloth, gilt vignette and paper library label on upper board, gilt, faded. Deighton 3-97 1983 £48

DAVIS, NATHAN   Carthage and her remains. New York: Harper & Bros., 1861. 8vo. 26 maps and plates. Orig. cloth. Rubbed, chipped, ex-lib. Adelson Africa-183 1983 $30

DAVIS, NATHAN S.   History of Medicine with the Code of Medical Ethics. Chicago, 1903. First edition. 8vo. Orig. binding. Very fine copy. Fye H-3-144 1983 $65

DAVIS, PARIS M.   An Authentick History of the Late War Between the United States and Great Britain, with a Full Account of Every Battle by Sea and Land... Ithaca, 1829. Worn cont. calf, internally very good. Reese 18-632 1983 $125

DAVIS, RICHARD HARDING   Cuba in War Time. N.Y., 1897. Illus. by Frederic Remington. 12mo, printed boards, g.t. First edition. Fine. First issue, with printer's slug on last page of text, & "Mr. Hearst" in Note, following list of illustrations. Argosy 714-211 1983 $125

DAVIS, RICHARD HARDING   Galleagher and Other Stories. NY: 1891. First edition, first printing. Covers rubbed at extremities. Tipped-in ALS dated 1901, from Davis to publisher R. H. Russell. Pencil markings on first page of letter, else very fine. Bromer 25-23 1983 $75

DAVIS, RICHARD HARDING   The Lion and the Unicorn. N.Y., 1899. First edition. Illus. by H.C. Christy. Fine. Laid in is a 2p. A.L.S. Argosy 714-212 1983 $50

DAVIS, RICHARD HARDING   Ransom's Folly. New York, 1902. 8vo. Cloth. Cloth sateen binding. Red cloth, gilt lettering. A fine copy. In Our Time 156-193 1983 $50

DAVIS, RICHARD HARDING   The Scarlet Car. New York, 1907. 8vo. Pictorial cloth. Illustrations by Frederic Steele. Some foxing, else a very good-fine copy. In Our Time 156-194 1983 $25

DAVIS, RICHARD HARDING.   Vera, the Medium. New York: Scribners, 1908. Frontis., plates. 1st ed. Orig. pictorial lavender cloth, gilt. Fine copy. Jenkins 155-288 1983 $20

DAVIS, RICHARD HARDING   The West from a Car-Window. New York: Harper, 1892. Frontis., plates. 1st ed., 1st state of binding. Orig. blue cloth, stamped in silver. Very fine fresh copy. Jenkins 153-159 1983 $65

DAVIS, ROBERT TYLER   Native Arts of the Pacific Northwest. Stanford: Stanford University Press, 1949. 5 color plates. Large 4to. Cloth. Ars Libri 34-204 1983 $85

DAVIS, WILLIAM HEATH   Reviews of "Sixty Years in California." N.p., ca. 1890. Orig. printed wraps. First edition. Ginsberg 46-845 1983 $75

DAVIS, WILLIAM HEATH   Seventy-Five Years in California. San Francisco: John Howell, 1929. Inserted plates, etc. Folding map. A fine copy in lightly worn dust jacket (a few small mends on verso). The "El Dorado Edition," Ltd. to 55 numbered copies, extra-illus., and signed by Douglas Watson, and John Howell. Reese 19-184 1983 $425

DAVIS, WILLIAM HEATH   Sixty Years in California. San Francisco: A.J. Leary, 1889. Cloth. Rehinged. Dawson 471-62 1983 $75

DAVIS, WILLIAM T.   History of the Town of Plymouth. Phila., 1885. First edition. Illustrated. 4to. Morrill 290-287 1983 $30

DAVIS, WILLIAM W. H.   El Gringo; or, New Mexico and Her People. New York, 1857. First edition. 13 plates, by J.H. Eaton and "F.A. Percy, Esq., of El Paso, Texas." Very good. Felcone 20-34 1983 $150

DAVIS, WINFIELD J.   History of Political Conventions in California, 1849-1892. Sacramento, 1893. Cloth, a fine copy. Reese 19-185 1983 $175

DAVISSON, JOHN   A Funeral Discourse setting forth the Loving Kindness of God... Bristol: by Henry Greep, 1719. 8vo. Modern boards, leather label. Heath 48-92 1983 £40

DAVY, EDMUND   On a New Acid and its Combinations... Dublin: R. Graisberry, 1829. First edition. 8vo. Half title, new quarter calf. Heath 48-496 1983 £60

DAVY, EDMUND   On a New Gaseous Compound of Carbon and Hydrogen. Dublin: Graiseberry, 1838. 4to. Orig. wrappers, loose. Presentation copy from author. Zeitlin 264-111 1983 $110

DAVY, HUMPHRY   Salmonia: or, Days of Fly Fishing. London, 1828. First edition. 8vo. Half-calf, t.e.g. 3 plates and woodcuts in text. Gurney 90-45 1983 £60

DAVY, HUMPHRY   Salmonia. London: John Murray, 1829. 16mo, illus. with 6 engraved plates + many text illus. Bound in 19th century 1/2 calf, sl. rubbed. Some foxing to plates. Karmiole 73-43 1983 $125

DAVY, JOHN   The angler in the Lake District. London: Longman, etc., 1857. First edition. Small 8vo. Orig. green cloth. A bit rubbed. Ximenes 63-554 1983 $65

DAWE, EDWARD A.   Paper and its Uses... London: Crosby Lockwood and Son, 1914. First edition. 8vo. Cloth. 34 specimens of paper bound-in at end with one page of explanatory text. Rebacked with orig. spine laid-down. Some foxing of specimens. Oak Knoll 49-312 1983 $50

DAWE, W. CARLTON   Kakemonos. London: John Lane: The Bodley Head, 1897. First edition. Orig. decorated cloth. Covers somewhat soiled. Good. MacManus 278-1430 1983 $45

DAWES, CHARLES G.   A Journal of the Great War. Boston 1921. 2 vols. Illus, cloth, t.e.g., extremities worn, minor cover stain, bookplates. Tipped into inside back cover of Vol. 1 is a blank French order of transport from the minister of war. King 46-776 1983 $25

DAWKINS, R. M.   The Monks of Athos. London, 1936. 8 drawings, folding map. 6 plates. 8vo, cloth. Salloch 385-343 1983 $20

DAWSON, HENRY B.   The Sons of Liberty in New York. New York, 1859. Three-quarter leather and boards, fine. Reese 19-187 1983 $75

DAWSON, HENRY P.   Current Fictions Tested by Uncurrent Facts. NY, 1864. Orig. pr. wraps. Argosy 716-433 1983 $20

DAWSON, J. WILLIAM   Fifty Years of Work in Canada. London and Edinburgh: Ballantyne, Hanson & Co., 1901. 19cm. Frontis. portrait. Black cloth. Fine. McGahern 53-39 1983 $25

DAWSON, J. WILLIAM   Handbook of Zoology. Montreal: Dawson, 1886. Third edition. 16 1/2cm. Numerous text illus. from engravings. Red cloth. Spine faded. Very good. Scarce. McGahern 53-40 1983 $65

DAWSON, K.   Marsh and Mudflat. 1931. 16 plates, royal 8vo, cloth. Illustrated from original dry-points and etchings by Winifred Austen. Wheldon 160-679 1983 £12

DAWSON, LIONEL   Flotillas: a Hard-Lying Story. Rich & Cowan, 1933. First edition, with 23 plates, 8vo, orig. cloth, a very good copy. Fenning 62-92 1983 £10.50

DAWSON, SAMUEL E.   The Voyages of the Cabots. Ottawa, James Hope & London: Bernard Quaritch, 1897. 25cm. Offprint. Ca. 33 maps (incl. 3 folding). Wrappers. Frayed on the bottom wrapper, else fine. Scarce. McGahern 54-50A 1983 $45

DAWSON, W. J.   London Idylls. London: Hodder & Stoughton, 1895. First edition. Orig. decorated cloth. Very good. MacManus 278-1433 1983 $20

DAWSON, WILLIAM L.   The Birds of Ohio. Columbus, 1903. 80 color plates plus over 200 halftones. Vol. 1 only (of 2), 4to, 1/2 mor., (backstrip lacks top 1/4). Argosy 716-389 1983 $35

DAY, ALBERT   Methomania: A Treatise on Alcoholic Poisoning. Boston: 1867. Wrappers. Gach 94-778 1983 $25

DAY, CLARENCE   Life With Mother. NY, 1937. One of 700 numbered copies printed on hand-made paper, fine in slightly torn dust-wrapper with darkened spine in worn slipcase. Quill & Brush 54-351 1983 $30

DAY, JACK HAYS   The Ustton-Taylor Feud. (San Antonio, 1937). Orig. printed wrappers. Illus. Jenkins 152-849 1983 $35

DAY, LEWIS F.   Alphabets Old and New for the Use of Craftsmen... London: B.T. Batsford, n.c. (1910). Third edition, revised and enlarged. 8vo. Cloth. 254 illus. Some cover rubbing, name in ink. Oak Knoll 48-125 1983 $20

DAY, LEWIS F.   Lettering in Ornament... London: B.T. Batsford, n.d. (ca. 1902). First edition. Small 8vo. Orig. cloth. Contains 186 illus. With the bookplate of the autograph collector, Charles Dexter Allen, signed by the author. Also inserted is the letter Day wrote Allen enclosing the bookplate. Fine copy. Oak Knoll 48-126 1983 $45

DAY, LEWIS F.   Nature and Ornament. Batsford, 1929. With many illus., 8vo, orig., a very good copy. Second edition. Fenning 60-82 1983 £14.50

DAY, LEWIS F.   Pattern Design. Batsford, 1903. First edition, with 285 illus., errata slip, 8vo, orig. cloth, gilt. A very good copy. Fenning 60-83 1983 £24.50

DAY, LEWIS F.   Penmanship of the XVI, XVII, & XVIIIth Centuries. London, (ca. 1913). 8vo, boards and cloth. Frontis. and 112 plates. Edges of covers worn, name on flyleaf. Duschnes 240-60 1983 $50

DAY, THOMAS   The Dying Negro. London: Printed for W. Flexney...1774. 4to, new wraps. Second edition, enlarged. Quaritch NS 7-31 1983 $350

DAY, THOMAS   The History of Sandford and Merton. Printed for F.C. and J. Rivington (etc., many others), 1818. 2 vols, 12mo, contemporary tree sheep, rebacked. Two frontispieces and two plates. Hill 165-26 1983 £42

DAY, W. C.   Street nuisances; a letter to Colonel E.Y.W. Henderson... London: William Tweedle, 1871. First edition. 8vo. Self-wrappers. Ximenes 63-262 1983 $35

DAY-LEWIS, CECIL   Beechen Vigil and other poems. London: The Fortune Press, (1925). First edition. Orig. green paper wrappers with paper label on upper cover. Presentation copy, inscribed on the front flyleaf. Later inscription on the title-page. Frederick Prokosch's copy, with his bookplate tipped to the front endsheet. Extremities of spine and yapped edges a little worn. Very good. MacManus 278-1434 1983 $250

DAY-LEWIS, CECIL   Beechen Vigil. Fortune Press, 1925. First edition. Wrappers. Yapped edges a little frayed. Unopened. Author's autograph signature. Very nice. Rota 231-156 1983 £125

DAY-LEWIS, CECIL   Collected Poems: 1929-1933. New York, (1935). 8vo. Cloth. From the library of Louis Untermeyer with multiple scoring and notes in the text by same. Accompanied by a four page ALS from Lewis dated 1935 and one short TLS dated 1935. With orig. envelopes. A very good copy, with reviews pasted onto the endpapers by Untermeyer. In Our Time 156-503 1983 $150

DAY-LEWIS, CECIL   Country Comets. London, 1928. First edition, first issue. Covers a little marked and some light foxing. L. Clark's bookplate. Author's autograph signature. Very good. Rota 231-157 1983 £50

DAY-LEWIS, CECIL   Country Comets. London: Martin Hopkinson & Co., 1928. First edition. Orig. boards with paper label on front cover. Spine very slightly faded. Very good. MacManus 279-3270 1983 $65

DAY-LEWIS, CECIL   Country Comets. London, 1928. First edition, second issue. Fine. Rota 230-153 1983 £12

DAY-LEWIS, CECIL   A Hope for Poetry. Oxford: Basil Blackwell, 1934. 1st ed. Orig. cloth, gilt. Fine copy in dj with split as hinge. Jenkins 155-792 1983 $20

DAY-LEWIS, CECIL   The Magnetic Mountain. London: The Hograth Press, 1933. First edition. Orig. boards. Plain brown paper dust jacket. Fine. MacManus 278-1435 1983 $65

DAY-LEWIS, CECIL   The Magnetic Mountain. Hogarth Press, 1933. First edition. Covers a little marked. Very nice. Rota 231-158 1983 £25

DAY-LEWIS, CECIL   Overtures To Death and Other Poems. London: Jonathan Cape, (1938). First edition. Orig. cloth. Dust jacket. Fine. MacManus 279-3271 1983 $50

DAY LEWIS, CECIL   The Otterbury Incident. London, 1948. First English edition. Numerous black and white drawings by Edward Ardizzone. Frayed and slightly torn, price-clipped dustwrapper by Ardizzone. Very good. Jolliffe 26-12 1983 £18

DAY-LEWIS, CECIL   Poems in Wartime. London, 1940. First edition. Wrapper and title-page decorations by J. Piper. One of 250 numbered copies. Fine. Rota 231-159 1983 £25

DAY LEWIS, CECIL   A Question of Proof. London: Published
for The Crime Club Ltd. by W. Collins Sons & Co. Ltd, (1935). First
edition. 8vo. Orig. cloth. Dust jacket. Bottom of spine and jacket
chipped, otherwise a fine copy. Jaffe 1-78 1983 $375

DAY LEWIS, CECIL   Revolution In Writing. London: The
Hogarth Press, 1935. First edition. 8vo. Orig. wrappers. 1500
copies printed. Fine copy. Jaffe 1-80 1983 $35

DAY-LEWIS, CECIL   Short is the Time: Poems 1936-42.
New York, 1945. 8vo. Cloth. Review copy with slip laid in, with
name of reviewer on fly. Endpapers browned, else fine in near perfect dj. In Our Time 156-504 1983 $35

DAY-LEWIS, CECIL   Ten Singers. London, 1925. First
edition. Wrappers. Unopened. Fine. Rota 231-161 1983 £25

DAY LEWIS, CECIL   A Time To Dance And Other Poems.
London: The Hogarth Press, 1935. First edition. 8vo. Orig. cloth.
Dust jacket. One of 750 copies printed. Very fine copy. Jaffe 1-79
1983 $100

DAYLESFORD. A poem. London: printed by J. Brettell, for Robert
Faulder, 1806. First edition. 4to. Disbound. Title and last
leaf dusty, spine a trifle frayed. Ximenes 63-401 1983 $50

DAYTON, FRED ERVING   Steamboat Days. New York, 1925. First
edition. Illustrated by John Wolcott Adams. 8vo. Morrill 290-89
1983 $25

THE DEAD Shot; Or, Sportsman's Complete Guide. NY (1873). Illus,
cloth, subliminal staining, moderately worn, front hinge loose.
King 46-561 1983 $25

DEADY, MATTHEW P.   Towns and Cities. Portland, 1886. Orig.
printed wraps. First edition. Ginsberg 46-597 1983 $75

DEAN, B.   Handbook of Arms and Armor. New York,
1915. 8vo. Red binders cloth. 65 plates. Slightly faded. Orig.
printed wrappers preserved at end. Limited edition, 1000 copies.
The Metropolitan Museum of Art (blind stamped on title). Good.
Edwards 1042-320 1983 £55

DEAN, HENRY CLAY   Address of...Delivered Before the Des
Moines Lecture Association... Des Moines, (1862). Dbd. First
edition. Ginsberg 47-360 1983 $50

DEAN, JOHN   Narrative of the Shipwreck of the
Nottingham Balley, etc. (London): n.p., 1738. Recent blue boards.
Karmiole 76-35 1983 $200

DEAN, SAMUEL   The New-England Farmer. Worcester,
1797. Lacks two leaves of contents pages in the front. Calf, worn,
hinge starting. The second edition. Reese 18-222 1983 $85

DEAN, WILLIAM   The China Mission. New York, 1859.
First edition. Ads. Orig. cloth. Jenkins 152-611 1983 $90

DEANE, MARY   Kinsfolk. London: Hurst and Blackett,
1891. First edition. 3 vols. Orig. decorated cloth. Bindings soiled
and worn (library labels removed from front covers). Hinges weak or
cracked. Covers of Vol. 3 badly waterstained. Internally good.
MacManus 278-1436 1983 $125

DEANE, SILAS   Papers. NY: NY Hist. Soc., 1887-1891.
5 vols., 8vo, stipple cloth, ex lib. Argosy 716-120 1983 $50

DEAN'S Historical Alphabet. Dean & Son, n.d. (ca.1855). Sm. 4to.
27 handcoloured images on 14pp. Blue wrappers, worn. Greer 40-13
1983 £27.50

DEARBORN, GEORGE VAN NESS (1869-1938)   Moto-Sensory Development.
Baltimore: Warwick & York, 1910. 12mo. Publisher's green cloth.
First edition. Gach 95-85 1983 $35

DEARBORN, H. A. S.   The Life of William Bainbridge of the
United States Navy. Princeton, 1931. 1st ed. Portrait and fac.
8vo, partly unopened. Morrill 286-122 1983 $20

DEARBORN, HENRY   Defence of Gen. Henry Dearborn, Against
the Attack of Gen. William Hull. Boston, 1824. Dsb., good. Reese
18-573 1983 $65

DEARBORN, HENRY   Report from...on the Petition of the
Officers of the Army Serving in Louisiana... Wash., 1806. Dbd.
First edition. Ginsberg 47-453 1983 $65

DEARBORN, N. S.   American Text Book for Letters, with a
Diagram of the...Alphabet. Boston, 1873. Illus. Oblong 8vo, orig.
boards, leather back. Plates. Rubbed, bottom portion of text dampstained. Morrill 287-87 1983 $40

DEARBORNE, FREDERICK   American Homeopathy in the World War.
Chicago, 1923. 8vo. Orig. binding. Ex-library. Fye H-3-145
1983 $20

DEARDEN, ROBERT R.   The Guiding Light on the Great Highway.
Philadelphia, (1929). First edition. Illustrations and facsimiles.
8vo, torn dust wrapper. Morrill 290-90 1983 $25

DEARDEN, ROBERT R.   Milestones on the Great Highway.
Philadelphia: United States Review Publishing Co., 1926. First
edition. 8vo. Cloth. Limited to 250 numbered copies, this copy
is not numbered. Presentation from Dearden. Oak Knoll 48-127
1983 $35

DEARDEN, ROBERT R.   An Original Leaf from the Bible of the
Revolution... San Francisco: Printed for John Howell by Edwin &
Robert Grabhorn, (1930). First edition. Small 4to. Leather
spine, boards. Limited to 580 numbered copies. Facsimiles of the
title page of the Aitken Bible, numerous portraits, a facsimile
of a Washington letter, and an orig. leaf of the Aitken Bible.
Chipping at spine ends. Oak Knoll 48-245 1983 $350

DEARMER, PERCY   The Little Lives of the Saints. Wells
Gardner Darton, 1900. Illus. by Charles Robinson. Frontis. & 25
illus., numerous head & tail pieces & decor. initial letters. Green
decor. cloth, eps. sl. foxed, cvrs. sl. rubbed, occasional thumb mark,
vg. Hodgkins 27-57 1983 £15

DEARMOND, ANNA JANNEY   Andrew Bradford, Colonial Journalist.
Newark: University of Delaware Press, 1949. First edition. 8vo.
Cloth. Oak Knoll 49-91 1983 $25

THE DEATH of General John H. Morgan and What Led Up to It... Wills
Point, Tex., (1904). 1st ed. Orig. printed wrappers. Port. of
author. Author's complimentary slip tipped in. Extremely scarce.
Jenkins 153-372 1983 $100

DEATH Valley, a Guide. Boston, 1939. Many illus., folding map. Pict.
wraps. Argosy 716-638 1983 $30

DE BEER, G. R.   Embryos and Ancestors. Oxford, 1940.
8vo, cloth. Wheldon 160-481 1983 £12

DE BEER, G.R.   Essays on Aspects of Evolutionary
Biology presented to Prof. Goodrich on his seventieth birthday.
Oxford, 1938. Portrait, 2 plates and illustrations, 8vo, cloth.
Wheldon 160-485 1983 £18

DEBENEDETTI, SALVADOR   L'ancienne civilisation de Barreales
du nord-ouest Argentin. Paris: G. Van Oest, 1931. 68 heliotype
plates. 20 text illus. 1 map. Folio. Wrappers. Ars Libri 34-205
1983 $250

DEBENHAM, MARY H.   The Whispering Winds. Blackie, nd, (ca.
1895). 25 illus. by Paul Hardy. 32pp. adverts. Slate blue col.
decor. cloth, bkstrip. sl. soiled, corners sl. bruised, occasional
foxing, vg. Hodgkins 27-58 1983 £12.50

DEBERLE, ALFRED J.   South America. Chicago, (1910). Orig.
1/2 blue mor., g.t. Illus., some pp. unopened. Argosy 716-508 1983
$40

DEBO, ANGIE   And Still the Waters Run. Princeton,
1940. Orig. cloth. First edition. Ginsberg 47-700 1983 $40

DEBO, ANGIE   The Cowman's Southwest Being the Reminiscences of Oliver Nelson. Glendale: The Arthur H. Clark Co.,
1953. Maps and illus. Fine copy of the 1st edition, uncut and
unopened. Quite scarce. Jenkins 151-62 1983 $75

DEBO, ANGIE   Oklahoma Foot-Loose and Fancy Free.
Norman, 1949. 1st ed. Illus. Jenkins 153-407 1983 $35

DEBO, ANGIE   The Road to Disappearance. Norman,
1941. Illus., 1st ed. Scarce. Jenkins 151-63 1983 $50

DE BOSSCHERE, JEAN
Please turn to
BOSSCHERE, JEAN DE

DE BOW, JAMES DUNWOODY BROWNSON   The Industrial Resources... of the
Southern and Western States. New Orleans, 1853. 3 vols. 1st ed.
Some outer wear. Jenkins 153-160 1983 $200

DE BRATH, STANLEY   Mysteries of Life. London: George Allen
& Unwin Ltd., (1915). First edition. Orig. cloth. Arthur C. Doyle's
copy, with his signature, dated 1919, on the title-page. Fine.
MacManus 278-1658 1983 $150

DE BURY, RICHARD
Please turn to
AUNGERVILLE, RICHARD

DEBUS, HEINRICH   On the Constitution of some Carbon
Compounds. London, 1866. First edition. 2 parts. Orig. orange
paper wrappers. 8vo. Inscribed presentation copies. Very good
copies. Zeitlin 264-114 1983 $40

DEBUS, HEINRICH   Ueber Einige Fundamental-Satze der
Chemie insbesondere das Dalton-Avogadro'sche Gesetz. Cassel: Gustav
Klaunig, 1894. 8vo. Orig. paper wrappers. Presentation copy to
Prof. Thorpe. Worn, front cover detached. Zeitlin 264-115 1983
$50

DEBUSSY, CLAUDE   Prelude a l'Apres-Midi d'un Faune.
Paris, E. Fremont, n.d. Folio, cloth-backed orig. wrs. Salloch 387-
51 1983 $100

DEBYE, PIERRE   Polar Molecules. New York: The
Chemical Society, 1929. 8vo. Orig. red cloth. First English
edition. Lightly rubbed. Very good copy. Zeitlin 264-116 1983
$65

DEBYE, PIERRE   Polar Molecules. New York: Dover
Publications, 1945. 8vo. Orig. black cloth with gilt. Ads.
Facsimile reprint. Very good copy. Zeitlin 264-117 1983 $45

DECAISNE, J.   Nouveaux genres et especes de plantes
de l'Arabie Heureuse. Paris, Ann. Sci. Nat., 1835. 2 plates, 2 papers,
8vo, wrappers. Wheldon 160-1667 1983 £12

DE CASSERES, BENJAMIN   Anathema! NY, 1928. Limited to 1250
signed copies, vellum spine slightly soiled, otherwise very good in
damaged slipcase. Quill & Brush 54-1025 1983 $25

DECCAN, HILARY   Light In The Offing. London: Hurst
& Blackett, 1892. First edition. 3 vols. Orig. green decorated cloth.
Spine ends slightly rubbed. Fine, bright set. MacManus 278-1439
1983 $350

DE CHARME, PAUL   Euripides and the Spirit of His Dramas.
NY, 1906. Salloch 385-531 1983 $25

DE CHASSEPOL, FRANCOIS   The History of the Grand Visiers,
Mahomet and Achmet Coprogli, of the Three Last Grand Signiors...
1677. Licence leaf, engraved frontis. (shaved), small 8vo, old calf.
K Books 307-64 1983 $95

DE CHATELAIN, CLARA   The Night Laundresses. Guben: Fechner,
(ca. 1850-60). 2 hand-colored illus. Vol. 4 of a set of 4 stories.
Text pages lightly foxed, else fine in embossed and decorated paper
over boards, slightly darkened at spine. Floral decal on front
cover. (3 3/8 x 2 3/16; 86x55mm). Bromer 25-446 1983 $50

DECKER, HEINRICH   Barockplastik in den Alpenlandern.
Wien, 1943. 86, (235), xvi pp. 308 illus. 4to. Boards, 1/4
cloth. Lucas p. 65. Ars Libri SB 26-55 1983 $95

DECKER, HUGO   Carl Rottmann. Berlin: Deutscher
Verein fur Kunstwissenschaft, 1957. 4 color plates. 347 illus.
hors texte. 14 figs. Large 4to. Cloth. Ars Libri 32-589 1983
$125

DECKER, MALCOLM   Benedict Arnold Sone of the Havens.
Tarrytown: William Abbatt, 1932. Illus. Orig. cloth. Ex-library.
First edition. 250 copies printed. Fairly nice. Jenkins 152-16
1983 $50

DECKER, PETER   Peter Decker's Catalogues of Americana.
Austin, 1979. 3 vols. Illus. Orig. cloth. First edition.
Ginsberg 47-302 1983 $145

DECORDOVA, JACOB   Lecture on Texas. Phila.: Printed by
Ernest Corzet, 1858. Orig. printed wrappers bound in. Later full
morocco gilt. Fine. Jenkins 152-453 1983 $145

DE CORDOVA, RAFAEL J.   A Prince's Visit. New York, 1861.
1st ed. Illus. by Stephens, Rosenberg, and J. D. Smillie. 8vo,
half leather. With notes. Bottom third of text dampstained.
Morrill 286-108 1983 $25

DECORUM, a Practical Treatise on Etiquette and Dress of the Best
American Society. NY: J.A. Ruth, 1879. 12mo, orig. dec. & pict.
cloth. With ruled blank pages at end for notes. Argosy 716-302
1983 $27.50

DE COSTER, CHARLES   The Glorious Adventures of Tyl Ulen-
spiegl. Holland, 1934. Limited Editions Club. Illus. by R. Floethe.
One of 1500 copies signed by illus., very good in damaged box. Quill
& Brush 54-352 1983 $40

DECREMPS, HENRI   La Magie Blanche Devoilee. Paris,
1792. 2 vols. in one, frontis. and 101 text figures, full calf,
gilt spine. K Books 307-65 1983 £185

DE CRESPIGNY, E. C.   A New London Flora. 1877. Post 8vo,
cloth. Wheldon 160-1594 1983 £15

DEDICATION of the New York State Monument on the Battlefield of
Antietam. Albany, 1923. 1st ed. Maps and illus. 4to. Morrill
286-357 1983 $27.50

DEEPING, WARWICK   Uther & Igraine. London: Grant Richards,
1903. First edition. Orig. decorated cloth. Covers somewhat rubbed
and darkened. Good. MacManus 278-1441 1983 $75

DEERFIELD Collection of Sacred Music. Northampton: S. & E. Butler
(Graves & Clap, pr.), (1807?). Calf-backed boards. Signature
"Adonijah Bidwell's bought 1808." Very good. Felcone 20-116 1983
$40

A DEFENCE of Edmund Kean, Esq. Being a reply to Mr. Buck's preface,
and remarks on his tragedy of the "Italians." London: printed for
John Lowndes, n.d. (1819). 8vo, half pigskin, 1st ed. Blank strip
clipped from top of the title, else a nice copy. Scarce. Ximenes
64-327 1983 $125

A DEFENSE of Southern Slavery. Hamburg, S.C., 1851. Stitched,
unopened, fine except for a tear to the top of the title leaf.
Reese 19-515 1983 $100

DEFOE, DANIEL   The Advantages of the Present Settlement... London: Ric. Chiswell, 1689. First edition. Small 4to.
Modern marbled wrappers. 38 pp. and ad. leaf. Traylen 94-245 1983
£145

DEFOE, DANIEL   An Answer to the Late K. James's Last Declaration, Dated at St. Germains. London, Richard Baldwin, 1693. 4to, disbound, half title trifle soiled, but a very good copy with many uncut fore-edges. First edition. Ravenstree 94-1 1983 $350

DEFOE, DANIEL   The Consolidator: or, Memoirs of sundry Transactions from the World in the Moon. London: Benjamin Bragg, 1705. First edition. 8vo, cont. panelled calf, bearing the crest of Algernon, 2nd Earl of Essex, in gilt. Spine gilt, morocco label. Half-title. Armorial bookplate. Hinges cracked, spine worn, some leaves age darkened, otherwise a very good copy. Trebizond 18-24 1983 $425

DEFOE, DANIEL   The Dyet of Poland, A Satyr. Printed at Dantzick, in the Year 1705. First edition. Small 4to. Later half-calf & marbled boards. Some foxing, with cont. identifications in the margins. The fine Herschel V. Jones copy. MacManus 278-1442 1983 $650

DEFOE, DANIEL   Faction Display'd. The second part. London: 1704. 1st edition, modern marbled boards, 4to, catchword on Elv and one word on Flv cropped. Pickering & Chatto 19-11 1983 $650

DEFOE, DANIEL   The Fortunes and Misfortunes of the Famous Moll Flanders. London: John Lane, The Bodley Head, (1929). First edition illus. by John Austen. Intro. by W.H. Davies. Orig. decorated buckram. Dust jacket (slightly soiled and worn). Free endpapers slightly foxed. Near-fine. MacManus 278-1331 1983 $65

DEFOE, DANIEL   An Historical Narrative of the Great and Tremendous Storm... London: for W. Nicoll, 1769. 8vo. Modern marbled boards. Slight foxing. Heath 48-469 1983 £75

DEFOE, DANIEL   The History of the Life and Adventures of Mr. Duncan Campbell. London, E. Curll, et al., 1720. 8vo, cont. calf newly rebacked period style, bookplate, new end-papers, very minor foxing, a rather fine copy complete with all the plates. Rare first edition. Ravenstree 94-2 1983 $465

DEFOE, DANIEL   A Hymn to the Pillory. London: Printed in the Year MDCCIII. 1703. 4to, half title. Affected by damp and marginal repairs to several leaves not affecting text. Half calf, rebacked. Jarndyce 31-18 1983 £65

DEFOE, DANIEL   Jure Divino: A Satyr. London: Printed in the Year, MDCCVI. 8vo, engraved portrait, extensive marginalia by an early owner (John Massey). Modern sheep antique, lettered in blind. First (pirated) edition. Quaritch NS 7-32 1983 $675

DEFOE, DANIEL   Jure Divino; A Satyr. London, Printed in the Year, 1706. Folio, cont. calf rebacked, the Vander Gucht frontis. portrait of Defoe and title a bit soiled, some quite minor stains throughout. First edition. Ravenstree 94-3 1983 $210

DEFOE, DANIEL   Jure Divino: A Satyr. London, 1706. Folio. Port. Early calf (spine broken). With the Jerome Kern book label. First edition. Felcone 21-29 1983 $150

DEFOE, DANIEL   A Letter from a Gentleman at the Court of St. Germains. London, printed 1710. 8vo, disbound, half title lightly soiled, good copy. First issue of the first edition. Ravenstree 94-4 1983 $250

DEFOE, DANIEL   The Life and Strange Surprising Adventures of Robinson Crusoe. 1766. 2 vols., 12mo, frontis. and 6 plates in vol. 1, mappe-monde and 5 plates in vol. 2, orig. calf with morocco labels. Bickersteth 77-20 1983 £95

DEFOE, DANIEL   The Whole Life and Surprising Adventures of Robinson Crusoe... London: at the Logographic Press, 1785. 2 vols. 8vo. Cont. tree calf, gilt spines with crimson morocco labels, gilt. 2 engraved frontis. From the library of John Rutherford, with booklabel in each vol. In very fine condition. Traylen 94-247 1983 £110

DEFOE, DANIEL   The History of Robinson Crusoe. Wood-stock, (Vt.), Printed by David Watson, 1819. 24mo. Vignette on front wrap, woodcut on back wrap, frontis., vignette on title, full-page alphabet, 11 text woodcuts. Orig. printed wrappers. Rare ed. Fine. O'Neal 50-19 1983 $225

DEFOE, DANIEL   The Life and Adventures of Robinson Crusoe. London: for T. Cadell & W. Davies, 1820. 2 vols. Roy. 8vo. Cont. straight-grained green morocco, wide gilt borders surrounding a central two-line panel with corner ornaments surrounding a blind-tooled panel, inner gilt dentelles, gilt panelled spines, edges gilt. Vignette title-pages and 20 plates, engraved by C. Heath from drawings by Thomas Stothard. Joints and spines a little rubbed. Traylen 94-248 1983 £135

DEFOE, DANIEL   Robinson Crusoe, Done With Slate Pencil. NY: McLoughlin Bros., (ca. 1880). Octavo. 12 full-page illus. Colored pictorial self-wrappers rubbed at extremities, else fine. Bromer 25-339 1983 $110

DEFOE, DANIEL   The Life of Robinson Crusoe. Phila., Lippincott, 1891. Illus. with 23 plates, including etchings by M. Moulleron, portrait by L. Flaming, and engravings after designs by T. Stothard. Fine 3/4 calf over marbled boards, contrasting red and blue leather labels, t.e.g., uncut. One of 250 numbered copies. 2 vols. Fine. Houle 22-289 1983 $200

DEFOE, DANIEL   The Life and Adventures of Robinson Crusoe. Ph., 1891. Limited to 250 copies, two vols., illus., edges of leather spine lightly worn and rubbed, else very good. Quill & Brush 54-353 1983 $50

DEFOE, DANIEL   The Life and Strange Surprising Adventures of Robinson Crusoe of York Mariner. London: Frederick Etchells & Hugh Macdonald, 1929. Orig. decorated cloth. Illus. by E. McKnight Kauffer. Limited to 535 numbered copies, with the illus. hand-colored by the pochoir process. Lower corner of front free endpaper torn away. Inner hinges cracking. Good. MacManus 279-3017 1983 $35

DEFOE, DANIEL   Robinson Crusoe. Seeley & Co., n.d. (Princes Library). Colour frontis. 3 colour plates & 8 black and white plates. Colour pictorial grey cloth designed by F. Gardner. Greer 39-46 1983 £15

DEFOE, DANIEL   Memoirs of a Cavalier. London, A. Bell, (1720). 8vo, cont. calf rebacked, front cover detached, armorial bookplate, few pages with minor stains at edges, else good copy of the first edition. Ravenstree 94-5 1983 $240

DEFOE, DANIEL   Memoirs of Capt. George Carleton, an English Officer. Ballantyne for Constable, 1808. 2nd printed ed., large 8vo, full contemporary speckled calf, red morocco label and small library paper label, speckled edges, trifling wear to head of lower joint, internally a little stained throughout, still a good copy. Deighton 3-98 1983 £68

DEFOE, DANIEL   The Memoirs of Cap. George Carleton. Tho. Astley, 1943. 8vo. Orig. cloth. Half sheep. Slightly worn. Last leaf repaired in margin. A reissue of the unsold sheets of the first edition, with a new title. With the erroneous dedication to Spencer Lord Campton, Baron of Wilmington. Good. Edwards 1042-321 1983 £95

DEFOE, DANIEL   Memoirs of Count Tariff, &c. London, John Morphew, 1713. 8vo, recent quarter morocco gilt, bookplate. Little age-browned but nice copy of the first edition. Ravenstree 94-6 1983 $375

DEFOE, DANIEL   Memoirs of the Church of Scotland. Matthews and T. Warner, 1717. 8vo, late 19th century polished tree calf gilt extra, hinges restored, a.e.g., fine. The first edition. Ravenstree 94-7 1983 $210

DEFOE, DANIEL   The Mock Mourners. London, 1702. The seventh edition corrected. 4to, bottom line of D2 (recto and verso) cropped by binder, also catchword on D3r, else a clean copy in modern marbled boards. Pickering & Chatto 19-10 1983 $200

DEFOE, DANIEL   A New Test of the Church of England's Loyalty. (London), printed in the year 1702. 4to, unbound, uncut, stitched as issued, minor spotting and dust soiling. Ravenstree 94-9 1983 $385

DEFOE, DANIEL   No Queen: Or, No General. London, the Booksellers, 1712. 8vo, unbound, uncut, stitched as issued and complete with half title, end sheets somewhat dust-soiled and lightly worn. The first edition. Ravenstree 94-10 1983 $295

DEFOE, DANIEL   The Novels and Miscellaneous Works...
London, 1872-85. 7 vols. Cr. 8vo. Half crimson morocco, gilt,
gilt panelled spines. Portrait. Corners of one vol. damaged.
Traylen 94-242 1983 £110

DEFOE, DANIEL   Novels and Miscellaneous Works. London,
1910-13. 7 vols. 8vo. Half blue morocco, gilt, gilt decorated
spines, t.e.g. Frontis., and textual illus. Traylen 94-243 1983
£140

DEFOE, DANIEL   Novels and Selected Writings. Oxford:
the Shakespeare Head Press, 1927-28. 14 vols. Small 8vo. Orig.
blue cloth, gilt. Limited edition of 750 sets. Traylen 94-244
1983 £220

DEGENHART, B.   Pisanello. Torinto: Chiantore, 1945.
170 plates. 7 tipped-in color. 4to. Boards. Ars Libri 33-281
1983 $35

DEFOE, DANIEL   The Political History of the Devil.
London, printed for T. Warner, 1726. 8vo, cont. calf, joints
broken, spine chipped, internally fine. Kern copy in slipcase.
First edition. Ravenstree 94-11 1983 $450

DEFOE, DANIEL   The Pretences of the French Invasion
Examined for the Information of the People of England. London, for
R. Clavel, 1692. 1st ed., sm. 4to, licence leaf, title with advts.
on verso, fine in modern quarter calf, marbled paper boards.
Deighton 3-99 1983 £180

DEFOE, DANIEL   The Pretences of the French Invasion
Examined. London, R. Clavel, 1692. 4to, modern boards, minor
waterstaining, good large copy complete with the Imprimatur leaf.
A collector has noted on the blank end-leaf, "Probably one of Defoe's
earliest works..." The first edition. Ravenstree 94-12 1983 $195

DEFOE, DANIEL   Reasons against the Succession of the
House of Hanover, with an Enquiry how far the Abdication of King James,
supposing it to be legal, ought to affect the Person of the Pretender.
London: J. Baker, 1713. 1st ed., 8vo, disbound. A very good copy.
Trebizond 18-187 1983 $150

DEFOE, DANIEL   The Secret History of the White-Staff...
London, J. Baker, 1714. 8vo, unbound, uncut, stitched as issued,
slight dust soiling, very minor wear. First edition. In orig.
condition. Ravenstree 94-14 1983 $285

DEFOE, DANIEL   Some Reasons Offered by the Late
Ministry in Defence of their Administration. London, J. Morphew,
1715. 8vo, unbound, uncut, stitched as issued, case number and
Latin note on title, trifle worn, slightly dust soiled, but a well
preserved copy complete with the blank final leaf. First edition.
Ravenstree 94-17 1983 $310

DEFOE, DANIEL   A Spectators Address to the Whigs...
(London) Printed in the Year 1711. 8vo, disbound, very fine copy,
preserved in folding cloth protective case. First edition.
Ravenstree 94-18 1983 $210

DEFOE, DANIEL   A Speech without Doors. London, A.
Baldwin, 1710. 8vo, old half calf gilt, inconsequential wormhole,
bit rubbed, some age-spotting and foxing throughout. Woburn Abbey
bookplate. First edition. Ravenstree 94-19 1983 $350

DEFOE, DANIEL   The Storm. Printed for G. Sawbridge,
and sold by J. Nutt, 1704. 8vo, folding table, cont. panelled calf,
rebacked, worn at foot of upper cover, corners renewed, new end
papers. First edition. Bickersteth 75-24 1983 £250

DEFOE, DANIEL   The Storm. London: for G. Sawbridge
and Sold by J. Nutt, 1704. First edition. 8vo. Folding table.
Half calf. Slight occasional discolouring. Rare with the folding
table. Heath 48-272 1983 £150

DEFOE, DANIEL   A Tour Thro' London about the Year
1725... London: B.T. Batsford, 1929. Folio. Full mottled antique
style calf, gilt panelled sides and spine with morocco labels, gilt,
t.e.g., others uncut. Endpaper maps, after Hollar, a portrait, 54
plates and 3 folding maps. Limited edition of 300 copies. Traylen
94-249 1983 £140

DEFOE, DANIEL   A Tour through the Island of Great
Britain. Dublin, 1779. Ninth edition, 12mo. In four vols. Tree
calf, gilt borders and spines, red and green labels. Very sl. rubbing.
Jarndyce 31-19 1983 £85

DEFOE, DANIEL   A True Collection of the Writings of
the Author of the True Born English-man. London, the Booksellers,
1703. 8vo, cont. calf rebacked period style, with the engraved
frontis. portrait of Defoe, light waterstaining, uneven foxing.
Ravenstree 94-20 1983 $335

DEFOE, DANIEL   A True Collection of the Writings of
the Author of the True Born English-man. London, the Booksellers,
1703. 8vo, bound without portrait in modern half tree calf gilt,
small mend to blank top of title, minor pinhole worming to outer
edge of last portion just touching some letters, some headlines and
page numerals shaved. Ravenstree 94-21 1983 $180

DEFOE, DANIEL   The Two Great Questions consider'd.
London, 1700. First edition. Small 4to. Modern marbled wrappers.
Title-page. A little foxing. Traylen 94-250 1983 £160

DE FOSSA, F.   Le Chateau Historique de Vincennes a
Travers les Ages. Paris, 1908. Ed. limited to 515 copies. 2 vols.,
4to, half morocco. Illus. and plans. Ex-library, some rubbing.
Morrill 286-159 1983 $37.50

DE GAURY, GERALD   Arabian Journey, and Other Desert
Travels. Harrap, 1950. First edition, plates, cr. 8vo, orig. cloth,
frayed dust wrapper. Fenning 60-85 1983 £10.50

DE GAURY, GERALD   Arabia Phoenix. Harrap, 1946. First
edition, many plates, cr. 8vo, orig. cloth, dust wrapper. Fenning 60-
86 1983 £10.50

DEGERING, HERMANN   Lettering... Berlin: Ernst Wasmuth,
(1929). First edition in English. 4to. Cloth. 240 full page
plates. Slight cover rubbing. Oak Knoll 48-128 1983 $55

DE GENLIS Madame la Comtesse. Dublin: Printed for W. Jones, 1794.
Third edition. Three vols., 12mo, calf, rubbed, maroon and green
labels. Jarndyce 31-20 1983 £38

DE GRAZIA, TED   De Grazia Paints the Yaqui Easter The
Forty Days of Lent in Forty Paintings with a Personal Commentary.
Tucson, 1968. Limited edition of 100 with an original sketch by
Ted De Grazia. Scarce. Jenkins 151-108 1983 $150

DE GROOT, HENRY   Recollections of California Mining
Life. San F., 1884. Illus. Orig. pictorial printed wraps. First
edition. Ginsberg 47-60 1983 $175

DE HAAS, JACOB   Theodor Herzl. New York, 1927. First
edition. With Sixty Illustrations. 2 vols., 8vo. Few minor cover
stains. Morrill 290-633 1983 $20

D'HARCOURT, R.   Arts de l'Amerique. Paris: Editions
du Chene, 1948. 4 color plates. 160 illus. Large 8vo. Boards.
Dust jacket. Ars Libri 34-268 1983 $30

DE HALSALLE, HENRY   The Romance of Modern First Editions.
Indianapolis, Bobbs-Merrill (1930). First American edition. Black
cloth (spine faded). Bookplate of Adrian Goldstone. Very good.
Houle 21-122 1983 $30

DE HALSALLE, HENRY   Treasure Trove in Bookland. London,
Laurie (1931). First edition. Gilt stamped purple cloth, a bit
faded, else good-very good. With the bookplate of Adrain Goldstone.
Houle 21-123 1983 $30

DE HELL, X. H.   Travels in the Steppes of the Caspian Sea.
London, 1847. Calf with raised bands, morocco label, rubbed. 8vo.
Good. Edwards 1044-184 1983 £100

DE HERIZ, PATRICK   La Belle O'Morphi. (London, 1947).
Slim 8vo, two-tone cloth, gilt. With illus. after Boucher. One of
750 copies. Duschnes 240-87 1983 $45

DEIGHTON, LEN   Billion Dollar Brain. London, 1966.
First edition. Wrappers. Advance proof copy. Covers slightly
rubbed and worn. Very good. Jolliffe 26-128 1983 £75

DEIGNAN, H. G.   The Birds of Northern Thailand.
Washington, 1945. 9 plates and 4 maps, 8vo, half cloth. Wheldon
160-680 1983 £20

DEIHM, C. F.   Merchants of Our Second Century.
NY, 1889. 2 vols. in one. 4to, cloth, full-page steel-engraved
ports. Argosy 710-140 1983 $40

DEILER, JOHN H.   Zur Geschicte Der Duetchen Kircengmein-
den in Staate Louisiana... New Orleans, 1894. 1st ed. Cloth.
Jenkins 153-338 1983 $125

DE KATZLEBEN, BARONESS   The Cat's Tail. London: William Blackwood & T. Cadell, 1831. First edition. Illus. with 3 etchings by
Cruikshank. Orig. printed wrappers. Spine and covers slightly worn
and soiled. Good. MacManus 277-1211 1983 $150

DEKKER, THOMAS   The Double PP. London: Thomas Creed,
sold by John Hodgets, 1606. First edition, first issue. Small 4to.
Modern red morocco, a little browned, but a fine copy. Traylen 94-
252 1983 £2,000

DEKKER, THOMAS   The Dramatic Works. Cambridge, 1964-
70. 4 vols. 8vo. Cloth. Traylen 94-251 1983 £70

DEKKER, THOMAS   The Magnificent Entertainment. London:
by Thomas Creede for Tho. Man the yonger, 1604. First edition.
Small 4to. Modern red morocco. Top margin of title-page is
cropped taking off the top of the word "The", else fine copy. Traylen 94-253 1983 £1,500

DEKKERS, FREDERIK   Exercitationes Practice circa Medendi
Methodum, Auctoritate, Ratione, Observationibusque Plurimis Confirmatae.
Naples, 1726. 6 engraved plates, 4to, cont. calf. Argosy 713-145
1983 $200

DE KOCK, CHARLES PAUL
Please turn to
KOCK, CHARLES PAUL DE

DEKOVEN, REGINALD   American Composer. NY 1901.
Inscribed and signed cabinet photograph. Sm. piece of paper affixed
to bottom margin, remnants of former backing still attached to
reverse, worn and soiled but not that bad. King 46-396 1983 $50

DE KRIEF, PAUL   Life Among the Doctors. New York,
1949. First edition. 8vo. Orig. wrappers. Autographed by the
author. Fye H-3-148 1983 $45

DE LA CIERVA, JUAN   Wings of Tomorrow. N.p. (1931). 1st ed.
Photos, cloth, minor wear and spot on spine else a nice copy.
King 46-717 1983 $25

DELACOUR, J.   Les Oiseaux de l'Indochine Francaise.
Paris, 1931. 4 vols., imp. 8vo, modern half cloth, maps and plates.
A fine copy. Wheldon 160-22 1983 £300

DELACOUR, J.   The Pheasants of the World. 1951.
16 coloured and 16 plain plates, 21 maps and diagrams, cr. 4to, cloth.
Very scarce first impression. Wheldon 160-681 1983 £100

DELACOUR, J.   The Waterfowl of the World. 1954-64.
66 coloured plates, numerous distribution maps and text-figures,
4 vols., cr. 4to, cloth. The original printing, out of print and
scarce. Wheldon 160-683 1983 £120

DELACRE, MAURICE   Histoire de la Chimie. Paris:
Gauthier-Villars, 1920. 8vo. Orig. red buckram. Text tables,
some full page. Spine defective, otherwise a good copy. Zeitlin
264-118 1983 $45

DELACRE, MAURICE   Recherches sur le role du dessin dans
l'iconographie de Van Dyck. Bruxelles: Hayez, 1932. 36 plates.
4to. Wrappers. Uncut. Edition limited to 100 numbered copies
on antique verge. Presentation copy, inscribed to Raphael Rosenberg.
From the library of Jakob Rosenberg. Ars Libri 32-194 1983 $100

DELACROIX, EUGENE   Journal de Eugene Delacroix. Paris:
Plon-Nourrit et Cie., 1893. 3 vols. 6 plates. Small 4to. Marbled
boards, 1/2 leather. Lightly rubbed. Ars Libri 32-157 1983 $100

DELAFIELD, FRANCIS   Studies in Pathological Anatomy. N.Y.,
1882. 2 vols., 4to, 1/2 mor. (rubbed); ex-lib. First edition.
Plate stamped on versos. Argosy 713-146 1983 $400

DE LA FONTAINE, JEAN
Please turn to
LA FONTAINE, JEAN DE

DELAGE, Y.   Traite de Zoologie Concrete, Vol. 2
part 1, Mesozoaires, Spongiaires. Paris, 1899. 15 coloured plates
and 274 text-figures, 8vo, new cloth. Wheldon 160-1263 1983 £15

DE LA MARE, WALTER   Alone. N.Y.: William Edwin Rudge, 1927.
First American edition, copyright issue, limited to 27 copies, of which
only 12 were for sale. Orig. wrappers. Mint. MacManus 278-1443a
1983 $350

DE LA MARE, WALTER   Alone. Ariel Poems, (1927). First
edition. Wood-engravings by B. Hughes-Stanton. Wrappers. Name on
verso of flyleaf. Author's initialled autograph presentation inscription on the upper wrapper. Very nice. Rota 230-160 1983 £15

DE LA MARE, WALTER   At First Sight. New York: Crosby Gaige,
1928. First edition. Orig. cloth-backed boards. Publisher's glassine
jacket (worn and chipped). One of 650 copies signed by author. Presentation copy from De La Mare to Siegfried Sassoon inscribed: "To S.S.
a novelete, from W.J., Christmas 1928." Very good. MacManus 278-1444
1983 $450

DE LA MARE, WALTER   The Burning-Glass. London, 1945. First
edition. Spine faded. Dust wrapper. Author's signed autograph
presentation inscription. Very nice. Rota 231-170 1983 £35

DE LA MARE, WALTER   Collected Poems. London, 1942. First
edition. Second Impression. Covers a little marked and bruised at
edges. Frayed dust wrapper. Author's initialled autograph presentation and an autograph manuscript poem. Very good. Rota 231-169
1983 £40

DE LA MARE, WALTER   The Connoisseur and Other Stories.
London: W. Collins Sons & Co. Ltd., (1926). First edition. Orig.
cloth-backed gilt-decorated boards. Dust jacket (worn & chipped).
Presentation copy, inscribed by author: "Walter de la Mare, with all
good wishes, June 1926." Former owner's signature in corner of front
endsheet. Very good. MacManus 278-1447 1983 $85

DE LA MARE, WALTER   The Connoisseur and Other Stories.
N.Y.: Alfred A. Knopf, 1926. First American edition, complimentary
advance copy in wrappers. Orig. wrappers. Very good. MacManus 278-
1445 1983 $40

DE LA MARE, WALTER   The Connoisseur and Other Stories.
London: W. Collins Sons & Co., (1926). First edition. Orig. cloth-
backed decorated boards. Endpapers foxed. Former owner's signature
and bookplate. Very good. MacManus 278-1446 1983 $20

DE LA MARE, WALTER   Crossings. (London: Beaumont Press,
1921). 8vo, decorated boards and cloth. Cover and illus. by
Randolph Schwabe. One of 330 copies. Bookplate. First edition.
Duschnes 240-61 1983 $75

DE LA MARE, WALTER   Desert Islands and Robinson Crusoe.
(1930). Author's corrected proofs, contains first trial setting on
this paper of pages 1-73 of the text without the Rex Whistler illus.,
with corrections throughout in the author's hand. With a complete set
of page proofs with the Rex Whistler illus., also containing corrections
throughout in de la Mare's hand. Preserved in a handsome grey buckram
folding case. MacManus 278-1448 1983 $1,250

DE LA MARE, WALTER   Desert Islands and Robinson Crusoe.
London: Faber & Faber Limited, 1930. First edition. With decorations
by Rex Whistler. 4to. Orig. green cloth, t.e.g. One of 650 copies
signed by author. Spine somewhat darkened. Very good. MacManus
278-1449 1983 $85

DE LA MARE, WALTER   Desert Islands and Robinson Crusoe.
London, 1930. First edition. Roy. 8vo. Orig. decorated green
cloth, gilt, t.e.g., others uncut. Engraved title-page and decorations by Rex Whistler. Traylen 94-254 1983 £20

DE LA MARE, WALTER   Ding Dong Bell. London: Selwyn & Blount
Ltd., 1924. First edition. Orig. cloth with paper label on spine.
Dust jacket. Presentation copy, inscribed by author on the front free
endpaper: "Walter de la Mare, with all good wishes, May 1924. Very
fine. MacManus 278-1452 1983 $85

DE LA MARE, WALTER   Ding Dong Bell. London, 1924. 8vo,
boards and cloth. One of 300 copies signed by the author. First
edition. Backstrip faded. Duschnes 240-62 1983 $85

DE LA MARE, WALTER   Ding Dong Bell. London, 1924. First
edition. One of 300 copies, this unnumbered and unsigned. Spine
darkened. Frayed dust wrapper. Nice. Rota 231-165 1983 £12

DE LA MARE, WALTER   Down-Adown-Derry. London, 1922. First
edition. Illus. in colour and black and white by D.P. Lathrop. Torn
dust wrapper. Nice. Rota 231-163 1983 £15

DE LA MARE, WALTER   Early One Morning In The Spring. London:
Faber & Faber, (1935). First edition. Illus. Orig. cloth. Presentation copy to Siegfried and Hester Sassoon inscribed: "S.S. & H.S. from
the compiler, May 16, 1935." Spine edges worn. Good. MacManus 278-
1453 1983 $350

DE LA MARE, WALTER   Early One Morning in the Spring.
London: Faber & Faber, (1935). Frontis., illus. 1st ed. Orig.
red cloth, gilt. Owner's inscription, else a nice copy. Jenkins
155-290 1983 $25

DE LA MARE, WALTER   The Fleeting and Other Poems. London:
Constable & Co., (1933). First edition. Orig. cloth. Presentation
copy to Siegfried Sassoon inscribed: "S.S. from W.J. dlm, 'And the stars
in his hair were SEVEN,' author unknown." Near-fine. MacManus 278-
1454 1983 $450

DE LA MARE, WALTER   The Fleeting and Other Poems. London:
Constable & Co. Ltd., (1933). First edition. Orig. cloth. Dust
jacket (head of spine worn; foxed). Endpapers foxed. Very good.
MacManus 278-1455 1983 $25

DE LA MARE, WALTER   Lewis Carroll. Faber, 1932. Limited
to 65 signed copies (copy no. 44). Red cloth, gilt titling, t.e.g.
other uncut, cvrs. sl. marked, vg. Hodgkins 27-32 1983 £70

DE LA MARE, WALTER   Lispet, Lispett and Vaine. London:
1923. 1/200 copies signed by author. 3 W. P. Robins woodcuts. Vellum,
uncut. Preserved in folding cloth wrapper and green half-morocco
slipcase. With Vincent Starrett's Sherlock Holmes bookplates on
front pastedown. Very fine. Bradley 66-87 1983 $85

DE LA MARE, WALTER   Lispet, Lispett and Vaine. London:
1923. 1/200 copies signed by author. 3 W. P. Robins woodcuts. Vellum,
uncut. Preserved in folding cloth wrapper and green half-morocco
slipcase. Bradley 66-86 1983 $85

DE LA MARE, WALTER   The Listeners and other poems. London,
1912. First edition. 12mo. Nice. Rota 230-158 1983 £30

DE LA MARE, WALTER   The Listeners and Other Poems. N.Y.:
Henry Holt, 1916. First American edition. Orig. cloth (ends of spine
rubbed, spine dull). MacManus 278-1456 1983 $25

DE LA MARE, WALTER   The Lord Fish. London: Faber & Faber,
n.d. (1933). First edition. Illus. by Rex Whistler. Orig. decorated
cloth. Dust jacket (slightly faded and worn, with a few small tears).
Includes four full-page, inserted illus. by R. Whistler. Covers and
spine slightly faded. Very good. MacManus 278-1457 1983 $35

DE LA MARE, WALTER   Love. London, 1943. First edition.
Illus. by B. Freedman. Corners bruised and spine a little faded.
Very nice. Rota 231-174 1983 £12

DE LA MARE, WALTER   Memoirs of a Midget. London, 1921.
First edition. Upper cover a little creased. Inscription on flyleaf.
Very good. Rota 231-162 1983 £15

DE LA MARE, WALTER   O Lovely England And Other Poems. London:
Faber & Faber, (1953). First edition. Orig. cloth. Dust jacket
(slightly worn and a trifle soiled). Presentation copy to Siegfried
Sassoon inscribed: "Seigfried with Love from WjDlm, Christmas 1953..."
Near-fine. MacManus 278-1459 1983 $450

DE LA MARE, WALTER   On the Edge. London, 1930. First edition. Wood-engravings by E. Rivers. Lower corners a little dampstained. Name on endpaper. Author's initialled autograph presentation inscription. Very good. Rota 231-167 1983 £40

DE LA MARE, WALTER   On the Edge. London, 1930. First
edition. Wood-engravings by E. Rivers. One of 300 numbered copies,
signed by author. One corner a little bruised. Slipcase. Bookplate.
Very nice. Rota 230-161 1983 £35

DE LA MARE, WALTER   Poems for Children. London: Constable
& Co. Ltd., (1930). First edition. Orig. holland-backed boards with
green leather lavel on spine. One of 8 lettered copies out of a total
edition of 133, signed by author. Bookplate on front endsheet.
Endpapers lightly foxed. Spine a little browned. Fine. MacManus 278-
1460 1983 $150

DE LA MARE, WALTER   Poems 1919 to 1934. London, 1935. First
edition. Dust wrapper. Fine. Rota 231-168 1983 £14

DE LA MARE, WALTER   The Return. London, 1910. First edition.
Head of spine badly worn. Bookplate. Author's signed autograph presentation inscription. Good. Rota 230-157 1983 £45

DE LA MARE, WALTER   Rupert Brooke and the Intellectual Imagination. London: Sidgwick & Jackson, 1919. First edition, first
issue. Orig. boards, dust jacket (a trifle worn, internally reinforced
at top & bottom of spine). Fine. MacManus 277-700 1983 $125

DE LA MARE, WALTER   Self to Self. London, 1928. First
edition. One of 500 numbered copies signed by the author. 2 wood
engravings by Blair Hughes-Stanton. Hand made paper. Covers very
slightly spotted. Spine slightly browned. Very good. Jolliffe
26-123 1983 £30

DE LA MARE, WALTER   Self to Self. Ariel Poems, 1928.
First edition. Wood-engravings by B. Hughes-Stanton. One of 500
numbered copies, signed by author. Nice. Rota 231-166 1983 £15

DE LA MARE, WALTER   Seven Short Stories. London: Faber &
Faber Limited, 1931. Author's revised proof for the Limited edition,
with numerous corrections throughout in the author's hand. Differences
between the proof and the published version, principally in the colophon. Printed on Italian hand-made paper and signed by both author
and artist. Over-lapping edges a trifle worn. Fleece-lined half-
morocco and buckram slipcase. Very fine. MacManus 278-1462 1983
$1,000

DE LA MARE, WALTER   Songs of Childhood. London: Longmans,
Green & Co., 1923. First of this revised illus. edition. Illus.
(some in color) by Estella Canziani. New edition. Orig. half-vellum
& boards. One of 310 large-paper copies signed by author, of which
this is No. 1, De La Mare's own copy, with his holograph emendations
and revisions throughout. Some darkening to spine and extremities of
boards. In blue fleece-lined half-morocco fall-down box. MacManus
278-1465 1983 $2,500

DE LA MARE, WALTER   Songs of Childhood. London, 1923. New
edition. Illus. by E. Canziani. One of 310 numbered copies, signed
by author. Half parchment. Edges of covers darkened and corners
rubbed. Nice. Rota 231-164 1983 £40

DE LA MARE, WALTER   Stuff and Nonsense, and So On. London:
Constable and Co., 1927. First edition. Illus. with woodcuts by Bold.
Orig. green cloth. Presentation copy to Siegfried Sassoon inscribed:
"S.S. from W.J. dLM with his respects and affection, June 15, 1927."
Spine slightly faded. Front cover to the dust jacket pasted neatly
to the front endpaper. Good. MacManus 278-1466 1983 $350

DE LA MARE, WALTER   Stuff and Nonsense and So On. London: Constable & Co., 1927. First edition. Illus. Orig. cloth. Dust jacket (spine and covers slightly worn and soiled, with a few small tears). Bookplate. Very good. MacManus 278-1467 1983 $25

DE LA MARE, WALTER   The Three Mulla-Mulgars. London: Duckworth & Co., 1910. First edition. Colored frontis. by Mansell. Orig. decorated cloth. Pictorial dust jacket (a little worn & chipped). Very fine. MacManus 278-1470 1983 $225

DE LA MARE, WALTER   The Three Mulla-Mulgars. Duckworth, n.d. 4to, colour frontis, title vignette. 11 plates (7 colour), 25 text illus. Pictorial endpapers. Bookplate of E. D. Baring Gould. Blue decorated cloth, gilt. Greer 40-125 1983 £35

DE LA MARE, WALTER   Thus Her Tale. Edinburgh: The Porpoise Press, 1923. First edition. Illus. by Wm. Ogilvie. Orig. decorated white wrappers. Presentation copy to Siegfried Sassoon inscribed on the front cover, dated March 1924. Spine edges a trifle darkened. Near-fine. MacManus 278-1468 1983 $450

DELAMAYNE, THOMAS HALLIE   The Patricians. Printed for G. Kearsly, 1773. 4to, half title, engraved vignette on title, new ornamental wraps. Bickersteth 77-22 1983 £26

DELAMAYNE, THOMAS HALLIE   The Senators. London: Printed for G. Kearsly...MDCCLXXII. 4to, with half-title and a vignette on title page; half-title and final page slightly dust-soiled, but a large copy in modern marbled boards. First edition. Quaritch NS 7-33 1983 $125

DELANO, ALONZO   Life on the Plains and among the Diggings. Auburn & Buffalo: Miller, Orton & Mulligan, 1854. 3 plates. New marbled boards. Leather spine. Vellum tips. Some marginal foxing. "Second thousand." Dawson 471-340 1983 $150

DELANO, AMASA   A Narrative of Voyages and Travels, in the Northern and Southern Hemispheres. Boston, 1817. Illus., folded map, 2 plates. Half morocco. First edition. Ginsberg 46-230 1983 $375

DE LA RAMEE, LOUISE   An Altruist. London: T. Fisher Unwin, 1897. Colonial edition. Orig. apple-green cloth. Front inner hinge cracked. Rear hinge cracking. Covers dust-soiled. MacManus 279-4099 1983 $35

DE LA RAMEE, LOUISE   Critical Studies. London: T. Fisher Unwin, 1900. First edition. Orig. cloth. Binding slightly soiled. Endpapers a little browned. Very good. MacManus 279-4100 1983 $60

DE LA RAMEE, LOUISE   A Dog of Flanders, and Other Stories. London: Chapman & Hall, 1872. First edition. 4 illus. by E. Mazzanti of Florence. Orig. cloth. A bit rubbed. Hinges tender. MacManus 279-4101 1983 $125

DE LA RAMEE, LOUISE   Guilderoy. London: Chatto & Windus, 1889. First edition. 3 vols. Orig. cloth. Extremities of spines a trifle rubbed. Near-fine. MacManus 279-4102 1983 $450

DE LA RAMEE, LOUISE   Folle-Farine. London: Chapman & Hall, 1871. First edition. 3 vols. Orig. cloth. Front inner hinge of Vol. one weak. Some minor foxing. Very good. MacManus 279-4103 1983 $350

DE LA RAMEE, LOUISE   Helianthus. London: Macmillan & Co., Limited, 1908. First edition. Orig. cloth. Extremities of spine slightly rubbed. Front inner hinge strained. Good. MacManus 279-4104 1983 $125

DE LA RAMEE, LOUISE   In A Winter City. London: Chapman & Hall, 1876. First edition. Orig. decorated cloth. Inner hinges cracked. Covers rubbed at edges. Good. MacManus 279-4105 1983 $300

DE LA RAMEE, LOUISE   In Maremma. London: Chatto & Windus, 1882. First edition. 3 vols. Orig. decorated blue cloth. Spines and covers worn and darkened. Good. MacManus 279-4106 1983 $200

DE LA RAMEE, LOUISE   The Massarenes. London: Sampson Low, Marston & Co., 1897. First edition. Orig. cloth. Former owner's signature on front endsheet. Cloth soiled. MacManus 279-4108 1983 $100

DE LA RAMEE, LOUISE   The Silver Christ. London: T. Fisher Unwin, 1898. Orig. cloth. First collected edition. Former owner's initials and date on front flyleaf. Very good. MacManus 279-4109 1983 $75

DE LA RAMEE, LOUISE   La Strega And Other Stories. London: Sampson Low, Marston & Co., 1899. First edition. Orig. cloth. Covers lightly worn. MacManus 279-4107 1983 $125

DE LA RAMEE, LOUISE   Wanda. London: Chatto & Windus, 1883. First edition. 3 vols. Orig. decorated cloth. All edges and corners rather worn. Covers a bit soiled and waterstained. Some light foxing. Good. MacManus 279-4110 1983 $150

DE LA RONCIERE, CHARLES   Jacques Cartier. Paris: Librairie Plon, 1931. 19cm. 5 illus. and a map. Printed wrappers. Frayed, else very good. McGahern 53-41 1983 $25

DELAVAN, EDWARD C.   A Report of the Trial of the Cause of John Taylor vs. Edward C. Delavan... Albany, 1840. 8vo, sewn. Morrill 287-314 1983 $20

DEL BRAVO, CARLO   Liberale da Verona. Firenze: Edizione d'Arte Il Fiorino, 1967. 230 plates (20 tipped-in color). Small folio. Cloth. Dust jacket. Ars Libri 33-195 1983 $125

DE LEE, JOSEPH BOLIVAR   The Newer Methods of Caesarian Section. Chicago, 1919. First edition. Vol. 3, no. 2. Tall 4to, sewn. Argosy 713-147 1983 $100

DE L'ESTOCART, PASCHAL   Premier Livres des Octonaires de la Vanite du Monde. Paris, 1929. 6 facs. plates. 4to, cloth. Salloch 387-131 1983 $40

DELEZENNE, M.   Notes sur la Polarisation. Lille: L. Daniel, 1835. 8vo. Orig. paper wrappers. 1 folding table, 2 folding plates. First edition. Minor dampstaining, lacking backstrip, front cover detached. Extract. Zeitlin 264-119 1983 $50

DELLA PIANA, GIOVANNI ORESTE Macrino d'Alba. Como: Pietro Cairoli, 1962. 29 tipped-in color plates. Large 4to. Cloth. Dust jacket. Ars Libri 33-205 1983 $85

DELLENBAUGH, FREDERICK S.   A Canyon Voyage. New Haven: Yale University Press, 1926. Plates. Light stain on title. A little marginal foxing. Inscription. Dawson 471-63 1983 $25

DELLENBAUGH, FREDERICK S.   A Canyon Voyage. New Haven, 1926. Photos. Cloth. Index. Covers dull with some soil. King 45-140 1983 $25

DELLENBAUGH, FREDERICK S.   Fremont and '49. New York, 1914. 1st ed. Illus., fldg. maps. Ink presentation inscription on front fly leaf. Clark 741-238 1983 $55

DELLENBAUGH, FREDERICK S.   The Romance of the Colorado River. N.Y. & London: G.P. Putnam's Sons, 1902. Plates and ads. Cloth. T.e.g. Dawson 471-64 1983 $90

DELLENBAUGH, FREDERICK S.   The Romance of the Colorado River. N.Y., 1909. Illus., folding maps, pict. cloth, g.t. Argosy 716-8 1983 $50

DELMAR, ALEX   The Great Paper Bubble. New York, 1864. Orig. printed wrappers. Jenkins 152-614 1983 $65

DELOGU, GIUSEPPE   Antologia della scultura italiana dall' XI al XIX secolo. Milano, 1956. clvii, (1), 345pp., 233 plates (19 color). Sm. 4to. Cloth. Ars Libri SB 26-57 1983 $85

DELOGU, GIUSEPPE   Tiziano. Bergamo: Istituto Italiano d'Arti Grafiche, 1950. 145 plates (3 tipped-in color). Square 4to. Cloth. Dust jacket. Ars Libri 33-368 1983 $35

DELONDRE, A.   Quinologie. Paris, 1854. Large 4to.
Old boards, cloth back. Map and 23 coloured plates. Signed presentation copy, inscribed by Delondre. The map was added to this copy.
Gurney 90-46 1983 £95

DELTEIL, LOYS   Le peintre graveur illustre (XIXe et
XXe siecles). Tome II. Charles Meryon. Paris: The Author, 1907.
1 orig. etching by Meryon. Prof. illus. Large 4to. Pastepaper
over boards, 3/4 morocco. T.e.g. Edition de tete: no. 19 of an
unspecified limitation printed on chine and initialled and numbered
by Delteil. Ars Libri 32-449 1983 $500

DELTEIL, LOYS   Le peintre graveur illustre (XIXe et
XXe siecles). Tome XIV/XV. Francisco Goya. Paris: The Author,
1922. 2 vols. in 1. 1 orig. etching by Goya. Prof. illus. Large
4to. New cloth. Ars Libri 32-265 1983 $950

DELTEIL, LOYS   Le peintre graveur illustre (XIXe et
XXe siecles). Tome XVII. Theodore Gericault. Paris: The Author,
1924. 104 illus. Large 4to. Orig. wrappers. Partly unopened.
Binding worn. Ars Libri 32-254 1983 $250

DELTEIL, LOYS   Le peintre-graveur illustre. (XIXe et
XXe siecles). Tome XX-XXIXbis: Honore Daumier. New York: Collectors
Editions/Da Capo Press, 1969. 10 vols. 4003 illus. Large 4to.
Cloth. Unabridged and authorized republication of the 1925-1930
Paris edition. Ars Libri 32-138 1983 $450

DELTEIL, LOYS   Le peintre graveur illustre (XIXe et
XXe siecles). Tome XXXI. Jean Frelaut. Paris: The Author, 1926.
1 orig. etching by Frelaut. Prof. illus. Large 4to. New cloth.
Ars Libri 32-226 1983 $250

DE LUE, WILLARD   The Story of Walpole... Norwood, 1925.
1st ed. Illus. 8vo, some stains on spine and few on front cover.
Morrill 288-273 1983 $20

DE MAN, HENRI   Joy in Work. London: George Allen &
Unwin, (1929). First edition in English. Dust wrappers. Gach 95-86
1983 $27.50

DE MARBOT, BARON   Memoirs. London, Longmans, 1892.
Illus., folding map. Full tan calf by Tout, spines ornately gilt
stamped with various designs, including an eagle, the imperial 'N,''
queen bee and other Napoleonic devices; red and blue leather labels,
t.e.g., very good. 2 vols. Houle 21-284 1983 $200

DEMARCAY, EUGENE   Spectres Electriques. Atlas. Paris,
1895. Folio. Orig. boards. 10 plates (photographs mounted on
stiff boards) loose. Missing spine. Gurney JJ-98 1983 £15

DEMOCRITUS JUNIOR
Please turn to
BURTON, ROBERT

DE MOLEYNS, THOMAS   The Landowner's and Agent's Practical
Guide. Dublin: E. Ponsonby, 1872. 8vo, cont. half calf, worn but
sound, very good copy. Fenning 62-93 1983 £18.50

DE MORGAN, MARY   On a Pincushion. Seeley, Jackson &
Halliday, 1877. Illus. by William de Morgan. 2nd edn. Frontis.
decor. title page & 31 illus. & decor. & initial letters, 4 pp Pub's
adverts. Dark green fine ribbed cloth with elaborate gilt & black
decor. fr. cvr., black titling thereon, gilt titling bkstrip, bevelled
bds., a.e.g., yellow eps., eps., some discol., name fr. ep., fine
copy. Hodgkins 27-61 1983 £35

DE MORGAN, MARY   The Windfairies. Seeley & Co., 1900.
Illus. by Olive Cockerell. Frontis. & 40 illus. & initial letters,
4 pp Pub's adverts. Lt. brown cloth with darker brown & gilt pic.
fr. cvr. & bkstrip, gilt titling, bevelled bds., a.e.g., contents foxed,
eps. sl. discol'd, vg copy, scarce. Hodgkins 27-62 1983 £25

DE MORGAN, WILLIAM   An Affair of Dishonour. London: William
Heinemann, 1910. First edition. Orig. cloth. Dust jacket (portion
of spine cut away, as issued?). Fine. MacManus 278-1471 1983 $25

DE MORGAN, WILLIAM   It Can Never Happen Again. London:
Heinemann, 1909. First edition. 2 vols. Orig. cloth. Dust jackets
(a bit torn). MacManus 278-1472 1983 $30

DE MORGAN, WILLIAM   Joseph Vance. London: William Heinemann,
1906. First edition. Orig. cloth. Covers faded and lightly soiled.
In green half-morocco slipcase. Bookplate. Good. MacManus 278-1473
1983 $75

DEMOSTHENES   On the Crown. Cambridge, 1901. 8vo,
cloth. Salloch 385-514 1983 $30

DEMOSTHENES   Several Orations of Demosthenes, to
Encourage the Athenians to Oppose the Exorbitant Power of Philip of
Macedon. London, Jacob Tonson, 1702. 8vo, orig. sheep, much worn and
spine defective, hinges breaking. Very fine Chippendale style bookplate
of Alexander Hamilton. First edition. Ravenstree 95-38 1983 $65

DEMPSEY & CARROLL ART STATIONERS.   Sunbeams by Dempsey & Carroll
Art Stationers. New York: Dempsey & Carroll, (1887). First
edition. Small 4to. Orig. red cloth stamped in gold, a.e.g.
Covers spotted, else very good. Oak Knoll 48-129 1983 $160

DE MUSSET, ALFRED
Please turn to
MUSSET, ALFRED DE

DE NAVARRO, ANTONIO   Offerings to Friends. London & N.Y.:
Country Life Limited, Charles Scribner's Sons, (1931). First edition.
Orig. cloth. Dust jacket (somewhat faded and worn, edges frayed, with
a few small tears). Presentation copy to John Masefield inscribed,
dated Dec. 3, '31. Very good. MacManus 278-1475 1983 $40

DENDY, WALTER COOPER   THe Philosophy of Mystery. Longman,
1841. First edition, tall 8vo, 32 pp ads. Orig. dark green cloth,
v.g. Jarndyce 31-146 1983 £34

DENDY, WALTER COOPER   The Philosophy of Mystery. NY: Harper
& Brothers, 1845. Orig. cloth, chipped at extremeties. Gach 95-87
1983 $50

DENHAM, DIXON   Narrative of travels and discoveries
in northern and central Africa... London: John Murray, 1826.
Second edition. 2 vols. 8vo. 12 plates (1 colored), 3 maps.
Orig. boards, uncut, rebacked in cloth, paper labels. Adelson
Africa-78 1983 $275

DENHAM, JOHN   Poems and Translations. London, H.
Herringman, 1668. 8vo, cont. calf newly rebacked period style, new
end-papers, name erased from top edge of title with slight damage
to blank edge, some cont. mss. corrections, blank tip of 2B torn
away without loss of text, generally a good copy. Ravenstree 94-23
1983 $370

DENHAM, JOHN   Poems and Translations, with the
Sophy. London: by J.M. for H. Herringman, 1684. Third edition.
Small 8vo. Cont. speckled calf, morocco label, gilt. Slightly
worn. Traylen 94-256 1983 £38

DENHOLM, JAMES   A Tour to the Principal Scottish and
English Lakes. Glasgow, 1804. 1st ed., 8vo, folding engraved
frontispiece map, map foxed and offset. A very good copy, contemporary
half calf gilt, marbled sides, neatly rebacked, black morocco label.
Deighton 3-100 1983 £58

DENISON, FREDERIC   Westerly and Its Witnesses, for Two Hundred and Fifty Years, 1626-1876. Providence, 1878. First edition.
Illus. & map. Small ink stain on frontis. Argosy 710-469 1983 $40

DENISON, GEORGE T.   The Struggle for Imperial Unity.
London, Toronto, New York: MacMillan, 1909. 20 1/2cm. Portrait
frontis., folding facsimiles, wine cloth. A fine copy. McGahern
54-51 1983 $35

DENISON, MARY A.   What Not. Phila., 1855. First edition.
Frontis., fore-title and 4 plates. Cloth (worn at extremities). Some
marginal red pencil checks. Illus. by G.G. White, engraved on wood by
W.H. Van Ingen. Very good. Felcone 20-42 1983 $25

DENISON, MERRILL   Harvest Triumphant: The Story of Massey-Harris. Toronto: M&S, 1948. 21 1/2cm. Colour frontis. and 30 pages of illus. and drawings. Red cloth. Fine. McGahern 53-42 1983 $20

DENNIS, JOHN   The Characters and Conduct of Sir John Edgar, call'd by himself sole monarch of the stage in Drury-Lane; and his three deputy-governors. London: printed for M. Smith, 1720. 8vo, disbound, 1st ed., half-title present (trifle dusty). Very rare. Ximenes 64-163 1983 $750

DENNIS, JOHN   An Essay on the Opera's after the Italian manner, which are about to be establish'd on the English stage. London: printed for, and are to be sold by John Nutt, 1706. Sm. 4to, disbound, (inner margins neatly strengthened). 1st ed. Very rare. Title and last page dusty, a few page numbers shaved, but a sound copy. Ximenes 64-165 1983 $675

DENNIS, JOHN   The nuptials of Britain's genius and fame. London: for R. Parker, etc., 1697. Folio. Disbound. First edition. Some foxing, otherwise a good copy. Uncommon. Ximenes 63-359 1983 $550

DENNIS, JOHN   Remarks Upon Cato, a tragedy. London: printed for B. Lintott, 1713. Sm. 4to, disbound, 1st ed. Light foxing, but a very good copy of an important piece of early dramatic criticism. Ximenes 64-164 1983 $600

DENNISTOUN, JAMES   Memoirs of Sir Robert Strange, Knt... London: Longman, etc., 1855. First edition. 2 vols. 8vo. Orig. bright blue cloth. Frontis. in each vol., and two plates. Slight wear to binding. Ximenes 63-12 1983 $125

DENNY, HENRY   Monographia Anoplourorum Britanniae... London: Bohn, 1842. First edition. 8vo. Orig. purple cloth. With 26 detailed hand-colored plates. Wanting a front endpaper, a bit rubbed, spine faded. Ximenes 63-521 1983 $150

DE NOGALES, RAFAEL   The Looting of Nicaragua. London (ca. 1932). Thick 8vo, lightly spotted, signed with carbon copy of typed letter. Argosy 710-59 1983 $27.50

DENON, VIVANT   Travels in upper and lower Egypt... London: Longman & Rees, & Phillips, 1803. 3 vols. 8vo. 2 folding maps, 59 plates. Orig. calf, red labels, rebacked. Adelson Africa-79 1983 $400

DENSLOW, W. W.   The Big Circus Book. Chicago: Donohue, n.d. Folio. Yellow stiff pictorial wrappers. Minor wear. Covers by Denslow. Full-page color illus. plus black & whites by C. White. Very good. Aleph-bet 8-82 1983 $40

DENT, H. C.   A Year in Brazil. 1886. 10 plates and 2 maps, 8vo, cloth, spine trifle faded. Wheldon 160-372 1983 £15

DENT, JOHN CHARLES   The Canadian Portrait Gallery. Toronto: Published by John B. Magurn, 1880. 4to. Four volumes. Numerous full page colour lithographed portraits. Brown cloth. Black and gilt stamped, all edges gilt. Very good to fine set. McGahern 54-52 1983 $75

DENTICE, LUIGI   Duo Dialoghi della Musica. Rome, Lucrino, 1553. Woodcut printer's device on title. 4to, bound in antiphonal vellum. First edition. Salloch 387-52 1983 $550

DENTON, SHERMAN F.   Incidents of a Collector's Rambles in Australia, New Zealand and New Guinea. Boston, 1889. First edition. Illustrated from sketches by the author. 8vo. Ex-library; nice. Morrill 290-95 1983 $30

DE PEYSTER, JOHN WATTS   Personal and Military History of Phillip Kearny. N.Y., 1849. First edition. Orig. pictorial cloth. Slight chipping to spine, expertly repaired. Corners bumped, otherwise a good tight copy. Jenkins 153-306 1983 $85

DE QUILLE, DAN (PSEUD.)
Please turn to
WRIGHT, WILLIAM

DE QUINCEY, THOMAS   Confessions of an English Opium Eater. London: for Taylor and Hessey, 1822. First edition. 12mo. Half-calf, gilt. Half-title. Traylen 94-257 1983 £190

DE QUINCEY, THOMAS   Confessions of an English Opium-Eater. London, printed for Taylor and Hessey, 1822. 8vo, bound without half title and ads in cont. cloth, small library stamp on front end-paper, else fair. First edition. Ravenstree 94-25 1983 $195

DEQUINCEY, THOMAS   Confessions of an Opium-Eater. London: Taylor & Hessey, 1823. Second edition. 12mo. Old 3/4 cloth, boards, leather label on spine. Lacks the half-title and ads. Covers soiled and a little worn. Uncut. MacManus 278-1477 1983 $50

DE QUINCEY, THOMAS   Confessions of an Opium Eater. Edinburgh: A. & C. Black, 1866. Front. port. Orig. blue cloth, v.g. Jarndyce 31-506 1983 £10.50

DEQUINCEY, THOMAS   Dr. Johnson and Lord Chesterfield. New York: Abramson, 1945. Quarto, facsimiles. 1st ed., 1 of 250 copies. Orig. cloth-backed patterned boards, gilt. Near fine copy with manuscript facsimile of the essay. Jenkins 155-292 1983 $25

DE QUINCEY, THOMAS   The Ecstasies of... N.Y.: Doubleday, Doran & Co., n.d. First American edition. Orig. cloth-backed boards. Dust jacket (a few small tears). Fine. MacManus 277-790 1983 $25

DE QUINCEY, THOMAS   An Essay on Novels. (San Francisco), Privately Printed, 1928. 1 of 100 copies printed at the Windsor Press. 12mo, orig. boards, vellum back, boxed, fine. Morrill 286-126 1983 $25

DERBY, GEORGE H.   Phoeniziana, a Collection of the Burlesque & Sketches of John Phoenix. Edited by Francis P. Farquhar. SF, 1937. 8vo, cloth-backed decorated bds., paper label. Illustrated. Perata 27-66 1983 $75

DERBY, PERLEY   The Foster Family. Boston, 1872. 8vo, 1/4 mor., g.t. One of 200 numbered, privately printed copies. Argosy 716-177 1983 $40

DERCUM, FRANCIS (1856-1931)   An Essay on the Physiology of the Mind. Philadelphia: W. B. Saunders, 1922. First edition. Orig. cloth, Arnold Gesell's copy. Gach 95-88 1983 $20

DERHAM, WILLIAM   Physico-Theology. London, printed and reprinted in Dublin, by and for Samuel Fairbrother, 1730. First Irish edition, with a plate. 8vo, cont. calf, a very good copy. Fenning 61-104 1983 £24.50

DERING, EDWARD HENEAGE   Sherborne; or, The House at the Four Ways. London: Smith, Elder & Co., 1875. First edition. 3 vols. Orig. decorated cloth. Presentation copy from the author, inscribed: "Mrs. Hamilton Marr, with the author's kind regards." All edges and corners a little worn. Covers a bit soiled. Good. MacManus 278-1478 1983 $300

DERLETH, AUGUST   H.P.L.: A Memoir. N.Y., Ben Abramson, 1945. First edition. Illus. with tipped-in halftone portrait of Lovecraft. Dust jacket (a few small chips). Very good. Houle 22-298 1983 $75

DERLETH, AUGUST   Shadow of Night. N.Y., Scribner, 1943. First edition. Dust jacket (a few tiny tears), else, fine. With the bookplate of Adrian Goldstone. Houle 22-291 1983 $65

DERLETH, AUGUST   Wind Over Wisconsin. N.Y., Scribner, 1943. Pictorial endpapers. Orig. black cloth stamped in gilt and blue (rubbed, a few spots), else very good. Signed and inscribed by the author to fellow author "M.P. Shiel- My most "Popular" novel, August Derleth." With the bookplate of M.P. Shiel and John Gawsworth. Houle 22-293 1983 $60

DE ROOS, JOHN FREDERICK FITZGERALD
Please turn to
DE ROS, JOHN FREDERICK FITZGERALD (1804-1861)

DE ROS, JOHN FREDERICK FITZGERALD   Personal Narrative of Travels in the United States and Canada in 1826. London: William Harrison Ainsworth, 1827. First edition. 22 1/2cm. 14 plates (incl. 2 plans and 12 litho plates, folding frontis.). Complete with half title. Bound in half brown calf and marbled boards, gilt titles and bands. Some foxing. Very good. McGahern 54-50b 1983 $250

DERRA DE MORODA, FREDERICA   The Dance Library. Munich, 1982. 32 plates, 8vo, 1/2 morocco. Salloch 387-305 1983 $100

DESAGULIERS, J. T.   A Course of Experimental Philosophy. London, 1734-44. 4 to. 2 vols. Cont. calf, rebacked. 78 folding copper-plates. First editions. Gurney 90-47 1983 £385

DESCHAMPS, CITOYEN   Memoire sur les Extraits... Lyon: J.T. Reymann et Cie, An 7, (1799). First edition. 8vo. Modern quarter calf over old boards. Folding table. Zeitlin 264-120 1983 $190

DESCHAMPS, PAUL   French Sculpture of the Romanesque Period: Eleventh and Twelfth Centuries. Firenze/Paris, 1930. Sm. folio, cloth, 1/4 leather. 96 hinged collotype plates with titled tissue guards. Slight intermittent foxing. Ars Libri SB 26-58 1983 $250

DESCHARNES, ROBERT   Auguste Rodin. New York: Viking, 1967. Most prof. illus. Large 4to. Cloth. Ars Libri 32-586 1983 $100

DESCHARNES, ROBERT   Gaudi the Visionary. New York: Viking, 1971. 228 illus. Large 4to. Cloth. Dust jacket. Ars Libri 32-242 1983 $75

DESCHARNES, ROBERT   The World of Salvador Dali. New York/Evanston: Harper & Row, 1962. Prof. illus. Large 4to. Cloth. Dust jacket. Ars Libri 32-136 1983 $75

DESCRIPTION of Banvard's Panorama of the Mississippi & Missouri Rivers, Extensively Known as the "Three-Mile Painting"... London, 1848. Later cloth, morocco label, orig. printed wrappers bound in. Scarce English ed., after the Boston 1847 orig. Wrappers slightly chipped. Jenkins 153-738 1983 $125

A DESCRIPTION of the Defeat of the French Army, under...Napoleon Bonaparte, by the Allied Armies, Commanded by...the Duke of Wellington, and...Prince Blucher, in Front of Waterloo. (London: Printed by J. Adlard), 1816. 8vo, a little stained but a very good copy in the orig. plain paper wraps. Fenning 60-89 1983 £18.50

DESCRIPTIVE Catalogue of the Pathological Series in the Hunterian Mueseum... Edinburgh, 1966-1972. First edition. 2 vols. 8vo. Orig. binding. Photographic plates. Fye H-3-1053 1983 $75

DE SEVERESKY, ALEXANDER P.   Victory through Air Power. N.Y., Simon & Schuster, 1942. Fifth printing. Illus. with halftone portrait of General William (Billy) Mitchell; 15 halftone plates. Dust jacket (small chips). Inscribed by the author to William Gillespie. Very good. Houle 22-61 1983 $37.50

DESFONTAINES, R.   Flora Atlantica. Paris, 1798-1800. 263 engraved plates, 4 vols. in 2, 4to, half morocco. Rare. Some slight marginal waterstaining. Wheldon 160-24 1983 £1,200

DE SHANE, BRIAN   De Sade...
Please turn to
EGAN, BERESFORD PATRICK

D'ESME, JEAN   Afrique Equatoriale. Paris: Duchartre, 1931. 152 plates. Large 4to. Wrappers. Worn. Ars Libri 34-593 1983 $45

DES MOUSSEAUX, GOUGENOT
Please turn to
GOUGENOT DES MOUSSEAUX, HENRI ROGER

DE STAEL, MME.
Please turn to
STAEL-HOLSTEIN, ANNE LOUISE GERMAINE NECKER, BARONNE DE

DESTREE, JULES   Roger de la Pasture van der Weyden. Paris/Bruxelles: G. Van Oest, 1930. 2 vols. 12 heliotype plates; 143 heliotype plates. Folio. Wrappers. Dust jacket. Ars Libri 32-701 1983 $200

DE STUERS, F. V. A.   Memoirs Sur La Guerre De l'Lle De Java de 1825 a 1830. Leiden, 1833. 2 maps and 3 lithograph portraits. Modern cloth, calf spine, some marginal water staining. 8vo. Good. Edwards 1044-676 1983 £160

DETMOLD, EDWARD J.   Fabres Book of Insects. N.Y.: Tudor, (1939, Dodd, 1921). 4to. Green cloth. Spine slightly faded, light wear. Illus. with 12 tipped in colored plates by Detmold with lettered tissue guards. Very good. Aleph-bet 8-84 1983 $40

DETMOLD, EDWARD J.   Twenty-Four Nature Pictures. J.M. Dent, n.d. Portfolio. 24 excellent mounted colour plates of birds, fish, crabs & c. Worn green portfolio. Edition limited to 500 copies. No. 229 signed by Detmold. Rare & Important Greer 39-60 1983 £850

DE TONNANCOUR, JACQUES G.   Roberts. Montreal: L'Arbre, 1944. 20 1/2cm. First edition. 20 plates, frontis. portrait. Stiff wrappers. Dust soiled else very good. McGahern 53-160 1983 $20

DE TOURZEL, DUCHESS   Memoirs of the Duchess de Tourzel... London: Remington & Co., 1886. 2 vols. 8vo. Bound in half crimson morocco, gilt, gilt panelled spines, t.e.g. Traylen 94-259 1983 £30

DETZER, KARL   Carl Sandburg: A Study in Personality and Background. N.Y., (1941). First edition. Advance review copy. 4 photos by Edw. Steichen, d.w. Argosy 714-654 1983 $30

DEULIN, CHARLES   Johnny Nut & The Golden Goose. Longmans, 1887. 1st Eng. edn. Illus. by A.M. Lynen. Frontis., title vignette & numerous illus. & decor. in margins. Turquoise fine ribbed cloth, gilt & black decor. fr. cvr. & bkstrip gilt titling, bevelled boards, t.e.g., contemp. insc. fr. ep. Binding designed by W. Reader. Nice. Hodgkins 27-63 1983 £25

DEUSSEN, P.   The Philosophy of the Upanishads. London, 1906. Spine slightly worn. 8vo. Orig. cloth. Good. Edwards 1044-187 1983 £35

DEUTSCH, BABETTE   Fire for the Night. New York, (1930). 8vo. Cloth. Spine is heavily faded and tiny tear at top edge of spine, else very good, internally fine copy. In Our Time 156-199 1983 $20

DEUTSCH, BABETTE   Walt Whitman: Constructor Para America. Mex., 1942. Paperwraps, edges show light wear, near fine. Quill & Brush 54-1530 1983 $35

DE VERE, AUBREY   The Fall of Rora. Henry S. King, 1877. Cr. 8vo, orig. green cloth, gilt, a light mark on spine but a nice copy. Fenning 61-109 1983 £9.50

DE VERE, AUBREY   The Legends of Saint Patrick. Henry S. King & Co., 1872. First edition, 8vo, orig. cloth, gilt, by Burn & Co., with their ticket. William Wilkins's copy, a very good copy. Fenning 61-110 1983 £18.50

DE VERE, AUBREY   The Legends of Saint Patrick. Henry S. King, 1872. First edition, half title. Orig. green cloth, bevelled boards, small chip from head of spine. Inscribed presentation copy to Lady Georgiana Fullerton, signed with initials A. de V. June 18 1872. Jarndyce 30-685 1983 £16

DE VERE, AUBREY   Legends and Records of the Church, and the Empire. Kegan Paul, Trench, 1887. First edition, half title, unopened. Orig. green cloth, bevelled boards. Sl. rubbed at head and tail of spine. Signed presentation copy, with 3rd person ALS affixed to verso of title, from Lady Molyneux, de Vere's cousin, presenting the book. Jarndyce 30-686 1983 £14.50

DE VERE, AUBREY   Recollections. Edward Arnold, New York and London, 1897. Front. half title, 32 pp ads. Orig. green cloth, v.g. Label and ticket of Bradford Library & Literary Society. Tall 8vo. Jarndyce 30-971 1983 £10.50

DE VERE, AUBREY   The Waldenses, or The Fall of Rora.
Oxford: John Henry Parker, 1842. First edition, complete with
tipped-in errata slip. Orig. cloth. Faded, extremities of spine
slightly worn. Bookplate. Very good. MacManus 278-1480 1983 $125

DEVERE, WILLIAM   Jim Marshall's New Planner and Other
Western Stories. New York: 1897. First edition. Illus. Cloth.
Bookplate. Nice and bright. Bradley 66-532 1983 $40

DE VIGNY, ALFRED   Cinq Mars. Boston, Little, Brown,
1889. Illus. with drawings by A. Dawant, etched by Gaujean. 3/4
brown morocco over marbled boards, spines decorated with gilt floral
designs, t.e.g.; marbled ends. Fine set. 2 vols. Houle 21-398
1983 $150

DEVILLE, J. J.   Memoire et Observations sur l'Epidemie
de Cholera Morbus qui a regne au Bengale pendent l'Ete de 1818.
Paris, 1819. First edition. Argosy 713-151 1983 $75

DEVINE, E. J.   Historic Caughnawaga. Montreal:
Messenger Press, 1922. 23 1/2cm. Folding map and 19 plates.
Uncut. Stiff grey wrappers. Fine. McGahern 53-183 1983 $50

DE VINNE, THEODORE   The First Editor: Aldus Pius Manutius.
(New York): Targ Edition, (1983). 1st ed., 1 of 250 copies signed
by the artist and the printer. Orig. linen-backed embossed boards,
uncut. Color woodcuts by Antonio Frasconi; printed by Leslie Miller
at the Grenfell Press on Rives Mouldmade paper. Boxed. Mint, at
published price. Jenkins 155-1035 1983 $100

DE VINNE, THEODORE   The Invention of Printing. New York:
Hart, 1978. Illus. 2nd ed. Orig. cloth, gilt, uncut. ALS from
the author on his DeVinne Press letterhead is tipped in. Front
hinge cracked, else very good little-used copy. Jenkins 155-1036
1983 $80

DE VINNE, THEODORE   The Plantin-Moretus Museum. The Grabhorn Press, 1929. 16mo. Full calf. Total edition is 425 copies.
This copy unnumbered. A presentation copy, inscribed by author. A
fine copy. In Our Time 156-326 1983 $250

DE VINNE, THEODORE   A Treatise on Title-Pages. New York,
Century Co., 1902. 1st ed., 8vo, c. 200 facsimile illus., original
buckram, leather label, very good. Deighton 3-103 1983 £45

DE VINNE PRESS.   Types of the De Vinne Press. New York,
1907. Thick 8vo, cloth, frontis. Type specimens, head bands, initial
letters, borders, tail-pieces, ornaments. Duschnes 240-64 1983
$125

DEVINNY, V.   The Story of a Pioneer. Denver: The
Reed Publishing Co., 1904. First edition in orig. pictorial cloth.
Plates. Jenkins 152-615 1983 $150

DE VITO BATTAGLIA, SILVIA   Correggio bibliografia. Roma, 1934.
4to. Wrappers. 1169 entries. Ars Libri 33-117 1983 $135

DEVOL, GEORGE H.   Forty Years a Gambler on the Mississippi.
Cincnnati, 1887. 1st ed., original cloth, illus. A good copy.
Jenkins 151-64 1983 $300

DEVOTO, BERNARD   Across the Wide Missouri... Boston:
Houghton, 1947. Orig. printed pictorial wraps. Plates, some in
color, after A.J. Miller, Bodmer and Catlin. Light rubbing at
edges, otherwise a fine copy. Advance reading copy. Reese 19-191
1983 $85

DEVOTO, BERNARD   Across The Wide Missouri. Boston, 1947.
First edition in dust jacket. Illus. by Alfred Jacob Miller, Carl Bodmer, and George Catlin. Jenkins 152-634 1983 $45

DE VOTO, BERNARD   The House of Sun-Goes-Down. Chicago:
White House, (1928). 1st ed. Orig. cloth, dj. Very fine copy.
Jenkins 155-293 1983 $30

DEVRIENT, PHILIPP EDUARD   My recollections of Felix Mendelssohn-
Batholdy, and his letters to me. London: Bentley, 1869. First
edition in English. 8vo. Orig. brown cloth. Portrait. Trifle
rubbed and soiled. Text lightly browned; pencilled corrections.
Ximenes 63-328 1983 $50

DE VRIES, HUGO
Please turn to
VRIES, HUGO DE

DEWAR, GEORGE   The Book of the Seasons. Geo. Allen,
(ca.1928). Mounted colour frontis. Decorated title. 11 colour
plates (3 mounted). Blue decorated cloth. Greer 40-218 1983 £18

DEWAR, GEORGE   Wild Life in Hampshire Highlands.
London: H.M. Dent & Co., 1899. First edition. Illus. Orig. decorated cloth. Rackham designed the endpapers and contributed pen-and-
ink vignettes. Covers a bit rubbed. Some foxing. Very good. Mac-
Manus 280-4296 1983 $85

DEWAR, GEORGE   Wild Life in Hampshire Highlands.
1899. 7 plates (2 coloured). Wheldon 160-373 1983 £12

DEWEES, WILLIAM P.   Practice of Physic. Phila., 1830.
2 vols., 8vo, cont. calf. Argosy 713-150 1983 $175

DEWEY, BERENICE   Poems. (N.Y.), 1933. Privately printed.
8vo, cloth. Argosy 714-214 1983 $35

DEWEY, JOHN (1859-1952)   Art as Experience. NY: Minton, Balch
& Co., (1934). First edition. Publisher's black cloth. Near fine
copy. Gach 95-91 1983 $35

DEWEY, JOHN (1859-1952)   Dewey's Suppressed Psychology.
Winchester, Mass.: Scudder Klyce, 1928. First edition. 4to.
Gach 95-94 1983 $50

DEWEY, JOHN (1859-1952)   Liebniz's New Essays Concerning the
Human Understanding. Chicago: S. C. Griggs & Co., 1888. Spine
tips rubbed. First edition. Gach 95-93 1983 $85

DEWEY, JOHN (1859-1952)   Psychology. NY: Harper & Brothers,
1887. First edition. Ads. Very good copy in publisher's pebbled
mauve cloth, minor wear to tips and joints. Gach 95-92 1983 $150

DEWEY, ORVILLE   The Old World and the New. New York:
Harper & Brothers, 1836. 1st ed., 12mo, 2 vols., original embossed
cloth, paper labels. Old library labels inside front covers. Some
foxing throughout but a very good copy. Trebizond 18-138 1983 $40

DE WOLF, GORDON   Flora Exotica. Boston: David Godine,
1972. Special edition. Folio. With 15 woodcut plates, each
printed in one color + an extra suite of 15 orig. woodcuts
printed directly from the block. This is one of 300 special copies
with the extra suite, and signed by the artist, Hnizdovsky. Fine
copy in cloth. The plates from the suite are laid inside a paper
portfolio. Slipcase. Karmiole 75-46 1983 $85

DE WOLFF, J. H.   Pawnee Bill (Major Gordon W. Lillie),
His Experiences and Adventures and the Western Plains. Pawnee Bill's
Historic Wild West Co., 1902. 1st ed. Illus., original colored
pictorial wrappers appliqued on new cloth, new endpapers, in slip
case. Clark 741-412 1983 $105

DEXTER, TIMOTHY   Life of... Boston, 1838. 16mo,
rebacked, (foxed). 1 illus. Argosy 716-268 1983 $35

DEXTER, WALTER   The Kent of Dickens. Cecil Palmer,
1924. First edition, half title, front. Orig. red cloth, spine
sl. faded, v.g. Jarndyce 31-594 1983 £10.50

DEXTER, WALTER   The Origin of Pickwick. Chapman &
Hall, 1936. First edition. Half title, illus. Orig. orange cloth,
spine sl. faded. Jarndyce 30-155 1983 £10.50

DEXTER, WALTER   Some Rogues and Vagabonds of Dickens.
Cecil Palmer, 1927. Half title, illus. 3 pp ads. Orig. blue cloth,
spine faded. Jarndyce 30-154 1983 £14

DE ZOGHEB, BERNARD   Le Sorelle Bronte. New York: Tibor
de Nagy Editions, 1963. 8vo. Wraps. Total ed. was 200 copies.
A fine copy. In Our Time 156-566 1983 $150

D'HULST, R.-A.   Jordaens Drawings. London/New York:
Phaidon, 1974. 4 vols. Vol 2, 8 plates; vol. 3, 272 plates;
vol. 4, 376 plates. 4to. Cloth. Dust jacket. Slipcase. Ars
Libri 32-346 1983 $275

THE DIABO-LADY: or, a match in hell. London: Fielding and Walker,
1777. First edition. 4to. Disbound. Lacks a half-title. Ximenes
63-358 1983 $30

DIARY of the American Revolution. N.Y., 1860. Steel engrs. & maps.
2 vols. Orig. stipple cloth. Ex lib. Argosy 716-465 1983 $40

DIAZ DEL CASTILLO, BERNAL   The True History of the Conquest of
Mexico. London: J. Wright, 1800. First complete edition in English,
4to, later half calf gilt, marbled boards, engraved frontis., errata
leaf. Despite rust stains on two leaves, a very clean copy.
Trebizond 18-139 1983 $525

DIAZ LOPEZ, GONZALO   Algunos estatuarios de los siglos
XV al XVII. Madrid, 1943. (Museo de Reproducciones Artisticas.)
Prologo de Jose Frances. 587 (5)pp., 43 plates, 1 folding plan.
Sm. 4to, Cloth, 1/4 leather. Orig. wraps. bound in. Ars Libri
SB 26-59 1983 $85

DIBBLE, CHARLES E.   Codex Hall. An ancient Mexican hieroglyphic picture manuscript. Santa Fe, 1947. Folding screen plate.
4to. Wrappers. Ars Libri 34-207 1983 $65

DIBBLE, CHARLES E.   Codice Xolotl. Mexico: Editorial Jus,
1951. 20 folding plates. Charts and diagrams hors texte. Large
4to. Wrappers. Backstrip torn at extremities. Edition limited
to 500 numbered copies. Ars Libri 34-208 1983 $150

DIBDIN, CHARLES   Henry Hooka. London: for C. Chapple,
1807. First edition. 3 vols. 12mo. Cont. boards with blue
morocco spines and corners, gilt, endpapers lightly stained. Traylen 94-260 1983 £150

DIBDIN, CHARLES   The High-mettled Racer. London: William
Kidd, 1831. First edition. 10 engravings on wood from designs by
Cruikshank. 12mo. Half morocco with marbled boards. Slight foxing.
Bookplate. Very good. MacManus 277-1241 1983 $75

DIBDIN, CHARLES   The Mirror; or, Harlequin Every-Where.
London: Printed for G. Kearsley, No. 46, Fleet Street, 1779. First
edition. Disbound, in a manila folder. Half-title and last page
dust-soiled. Half-title bears a bookseller's label. Several pages
unevenly cropped, corners worn. MacManus 278-1481 1983 $35

DIBDIN, CHARLES   The Musical Tour of Mr. Dibdin. Sheffield: printed for the author by J. Gales, 1788. 4to, old half
calf (hinges rubbed, some wear to top of spine), 1st ed. Subscriber's
list, and 15 leaves of engraved music. A scarce book. Ximenes 64-
168 1983 $400

DIBDIN, CHARLES   The Public Undeceived, written by Mr.
Dibdin; and containing a statement of all the material facts relative
to his pension. London: published for the author by C. Chapple;
printed by H. Reynell, n.d. (1807). 8vo, wrappers, 1st ed. Very
rare. Half-title present (dusty); uncut copy. Ximenes 64-169
1983 $150

DIBDIN, CHARLES   The Songs...and the Music. 1847.
2 vols., roy 8vo, half morocco, some minor rubbing. 5th edition.
K Books 301-59 1983 £35

DIBDIN, CHARLES   The Waterman; or, the first of August.
London: printed for R. Baldwin, 1783. 8vo, sewn. New edition.
Some soiling. Ximenes 64-170 1983 $125

DIBDIN, THOMAS   The Heart of Mid-Lothain. N.Y. & London:
Samuel French, n.d. French's Standard Drama edition. Orig. wrappers.
Very fine. MacManus 278-1482 1983 $45

DIBDIN, THOMAS   The Lady of the Lake. London: G.H.
Davidson, n.d. Cumberland's British Theatre edition. With a fine
engraving, by Mr. Bonner, from a drawing taken in the theatre, by
R. Cruikshank. 12mo. Orig. pictorial wrappers. Very fine. MacManus
278-1483 1983 $25

DIBDIN, THOMAS   The Sixes; or, The Devil's in the Dice!
London: John Cumberland, n.d. Cumberland's Minor Theatre edition.
With a fine engraving, by Mr. Bonner, from a drawing taken in the
theatre, by R. Cruikshank. Orig. wrappers (little worn). MacManus
278-1487 1983 $25

DIBDIN, THOMAS FROGNALL   A Bibliographical, Antiquarian and
Picturesque Tour in the Northern Counties of England, and In Scotland.
London, C. Richards, 1838. 2 vols. Large 8vos, cont. calf gilt,
rebacked preserving old spines, a.e.g., the Castlecraig-Todd copy
with bookplates. Illus. with plates. First edition. Ravenstree 94-
29 1983 $325

DIBDIN, THOMAS FROGNALL   The Bibliographical Decameron, or Ten
Days Pleasant Discourse upon Illuminated Manuscripts, and Subjects
connected with Early Engraving... London: Printed for the author
by W. Bulmer at the Shakespeare Press, 1817. First (only) edition,
tall 8vo, 3 vols., elaborately designed cont. calf gilt, a.e.g.;
carefully rehinged. Illus. with mezzotints, steel engravings and
woodcuts, some in color. All half-titles present. One front cover
spotted, but a very good copy. Trebizond 18-25 1983 $650

DIBDIN, THOMAS FROGNALL   Bibliomania; or Book Madness... London:
Printed for the Author, 1811. Frontis, illus., errata at end. Third
edition, the first complete edition with the third part here first
printed. Nineteenth century calf, rebacked. Some minor extra-illus.
at end by the Texas book collector (and author) Alexander Dienst.
Jenkins 155-101 1983 $100

DIBDIN, THOMAS FROGNALL   The Bibliomania, or Book-Madness.
Boston: The Bibliophile Society, 1903. Quarto, full green morocco,
4 vols. Four frontis. from orig. oil paintings by Howard Pyle.
One of 483 sets. 4 vols. enclosed in fleece-lined board slipcases.
Bound in full green morocco with floral spray in gilt and white
inlays on front and back cover, gilt fillet, decorated dentelles,
marbled endpapers. Spine with five raised bands, decorated
compartments in gilt. Duschnes 240-65 1983 $400

DIBDIN, THOMAS FROGNALL   Bibliophobia. London: Henry Bohn,
1832. First edition. Orig. boards, paper cover label. Front
cover is almost loose; part of spine is chipped away. Scarce.
Oak Knoll 48-136 1983 $275

DIBDIN, THOMAS FROGNALL   An Introduction to the knowledge of
Rare and Valuable editions of the Greek and Latin Classics. London:
for Harding & Lepard, 1827. Fourth edition, greatly corrected and
enlarged. 2 vols. 8vo. Half polished calf, gilt. Heath 48-278
1983 £50

DIBDIN, THOMAS FROGNALL   The Library Companion. London, Harding
et al., 1824. 8vo, two vols. in 1, cont. dark green morocco gilt,
a.e.g., trifle worn, slightly foxed. First edition. Ravenstree 94-
30 1983 $210

DIBDIN, THOMAS FROGNALL   Reminiscences of a Literary Life.
London: John Major, 1836. First edition. 2 vols. 8vo. Full
leather stamped in gilt, red and brown leather spine labels, a.e.g.
2 frontis. Index present. Contains an extra plate showing a
portrait of Dibdin as a frontis. to vol. one and a one page A.L.S.
from Dibdin to G. Lewis dated Feb. 13, 1821. From the library
of John Sheepshanks. Some rubbing along hinges, else fine. Oak
Knoll 48-138 1983 $400

DIBDIN, THOMAS FROGNALL   Reminiscences of a Literary Life.
London, John Major, 1836. 2 vols., large 8vos, cont. half calf
rehinged preserving orig. spines, which have new morocco gilt
numbering labels, Earl of Sefton copy with bookplate. First edition.
Ravenstree 94-31 1983 $320

DIBDIN, THOMAS FROGNALL   Reminiscences Of A Literary Life...
London: John Major, 1836. First edition. 2 vols. Illus. 3/4
morocco with marbled boards and endpapers. Spines and covers slightly
worn. Bookplate. Good. MacManus 278-1489 1983 $200

DICEY, EDWARD   The Story of the Khedivate. London,
1902. 1st ed., 8vo, original brown cloth, gilt, cover little soiled,
library label removed from front pastedown, library stamp on some
leaves. Deighton 3-106 1983 £22

DICK, EVERETT   Vanguards of the Frontiers. New York:
D. Appleton-Century, 1941. Frontis. & plates. 1st ed. Fine copy in
dust jacket. Jenkins 153-163 1983 $35

DICK, THOMAS   The Sidereal Heavens, and Other Subjects Connected with Astronomy. Thomas Ward, circa 1840. With portrait, plates and illus., small 8vo, orig. cloth, a very good copy. Fenning 61-111 1983 £12.50

DICKENS, CHARLES   American Notes for General Circulation. London: Chapman & Hall, 1842. First edition, first issue. 2 vols. Orig. cloth. Spines a bit faded and worn. MacManus 278-1491 1983 $450

DICKENS, CHARLES   American Notes for General Circulation. London, Chapman and Hall, 1842. 2 vols. 8vo, cont. blindstamped cloth gilt, little scuffed, spine ends chipped, hinges weak or cracking, bookplate partially scraped away, library classification number pencilled inside front covers; half titles and ads. First issue of the first edition. Ravenstree 94-32 1983 $270

DICKENS, CHARLES   American Notes for General Circulation. New York: New World Extra Nos. 32-3. 1st American ed., preceding the Harper book ed. Orig. self-wrappers, bound in a vol. of Extra numbers. Contemp. 3/4 green straight-grain morocco and marbled boards, gilt. The final leaf contains an ad for Whitman's Franklin Evans. Light rubbing, but a fine copy. Very scarce. Jenkins 155-295 1983 $200

DICKENS, CHARLES   American Notes for General Circulation. N.Y.: Harper & Bros., 1842. Tall thin 8vo, printed brown wraps.; backstrip chipped and repaired with tape. First American edition. Argosy 714-217 1983 $60

DICKENS, CHARLES   American Notes. Paris: A. & W. Galignani, 1842. Tall 8vo, half title, half black calf, sl. rubbed, v.g. Jarndyce 31-530 1983 £18.50

DICKENS, CHARLES   Barnaby Rudge. Chapman & Hall, 1841. Illus. by George Cattermole & H.K. Browne. 1st separate edn. with numerous text wood engrs. Mispaginated. Orig. green bead grain blind stamped cloth. Bkstrip faded, corners bruised, bookpl. v. sl. wear top/bottom bkstrip, scarce, vg. Hodgkins 27-267 1983 £50

DICKENS, CHARLES   Barnaby Rudge. Chapman & Hall, 1841. First separate edition, tall 8vo, illus. by Cattermole and H.K. Browne, half brown morocco. Jarndyce 30-34 1983 £42

DICKENS, CHARLES   Barnaby Rudge. Chapman & Hall, 1849. First cheap edition. Front. by Hablot Browne. Half black calf, a little rubbed. Jarndyce 30-35 1983 £14.50

DICKENS, CHARLES   The Battle Of Life, A Love Story. London: Bradbury & Evans, Whitefriars, 1846. First edition, second issue. Engraved frontispiece and title-page. Illus. Orig. decorated cloth. Small tear to the front cover well-repaired. Small bookplate. Fine. MacManus 278-1493 1983 $500

DICKENS, CHARLES   The Battle of Life. A Love Story. London: Bradbury & Evans, 1846. First edition, fourth issue. Full polished calf, gilt, marbled endpapers. Morocco labels on spine. Orig. cloth covers bound in, by Riviere. Fine. MacManus 278-1495 1983 $200

DICKENS, CHARLES   The Battle of Life. London: Bradbury & Evans, 1846. 1st ed., 4th issue. Orig. red cloth, gilt, a.e.g. Near fine copy. Jenkins 155-296 1983 $125

DICKENS, CHARLES   The Battle of Life. London: Bradbury & Evans, 1846. First edition, fourth issue. 12mo. Orig. gilt pictorial cloth. Spine ragged. MacManus 278-1494 1983 $40

DICKENS, CHARLES   The Battle of Life. Bradbury & Evans, 1846. First edition, fourth issue, with engraved frontis., additional engraved title-page and illus. by Maclise, Leech, and Doyle, with the half-title and the ad. leaf, 12mo, orig. crimson cloth, gilt, edges gilt. Fenning 60-90 1983 £21.50

DICKENS, CHARLES   The Battle of Life. Bradbury & Evans, 1846. Illus. First edition, 4th issue. Orig. red cloth, gilt. A.e.g., v.g. Jarndyce 30-57 1983 £20

DICKENS, CHARLES   Bleak House. London: Bradbury & Evans, 1852-3. First edition in the orig. parts. Orig. printed wrappers, 20 parts in 19. Slight soiling and foxing, light wear, and a few expert backstrip repairs. Most of the orig. ads. appear to be present. In a half-morocco solander case. Very good. MacManus 278-1496 1983 $1,000

DICKENS, CHARLES   Bleak House. London: Bradbury & Evans, 1853. First book edition. Illus. by H.K. Browne. Orig. cloth. Spine faded. A bit stained and cracked. In publisher's cloth. Small bookplate. Very good. MacManus 278-1497 1983 $450

DICKENS, CHARLES   Bleak House. Bradbury & Evans, 1853. First edition. Illus. by H.K. Browne. Half dark purple calf, faded on spine. Spine gilt, brown and black labels. V.g. Jarndyce 30-82 1983 £74

DICKENS, CHARLES   Bleak House. Bradbury & Evans, 1853. First edition, bound from the parts. Illus. by H.K. Browne. Occasional light foxing. Half green calf, marbled boards, spine gilt, brown label. A.e.g. Very good. Jarndyce 30-83 1983 £54

DICKENS, CHARLES   Bleak House. Bradbury and Evans, 1853. 8vo, lacking the half title, engraved frontis., title and 38 plates, old half calf, rebacked some time ago, preserving the orig. spine, rubbed at the edges and a little worn. Title and frontis. a little soiled, occasional spotting on plates, first edition. Bickersteth 77-201 1983 £22

DICKENS, CHARLES   Bleak House. Bradbury & Evans, 1853. Illus. by H.K. Browne. Plates foxed and stained in places. Half title, vellum, brown label. Jarndyce 30-84 1983 £20

DICKENS, CHARLES   Bleak House. Bloomsbury: Nonesuch Press, 1938. 8vo, buckram with leather label. Illus. by Hablot K. Browne (Phiz). One of 877 copies. Duschnes 240-71 1983 $100

DICKENS, CHARLES   Child's History of England. London, Bradbury & Evans, 1852, 53, 54. First edition, small 8vo, frontis. Orig. red cloth, stamped in gilt and blind (a few short tears and slight fading), marbled edges, else a very good set. Half blue leather slipcase. 3 vols. complete. Houle 21-290 1983 $750

DICKENS, CHARLES   A Child's History of England. Bradbury & Evans, 1852-3-4. 3 vols., half titles, engr. fronts. 1 p ads, vol. 1; 2 pp ads., vol. II, 1 p ads, vol. III. Orig. cloth, gilt. Spines a little dulled, and very sl. wear at heads and tails, but generally v.g. Jarndyce 30-81 1983 £220

DICKENS, CHARLES   A Child's History of England. Dent., 1902. Illus. by Patten Wilson. Frontis., title page, each with red decor. border & 97 b&w illus. Beige cloth with colour pictorial fr. cvr. & bkstrip, colour decor. rear cvr., t.e.g., others uncut. Binding designed by Patten Wilson. Contemp. insc. fr. ep., scarce, nice copy. Hodgkins 27-65 1983 £25

DICKENS, CHARLES   The Chimes. London: Chapman & Hall, 1845. First edition, first issue and first edition, second issue. 2 copies, 2 vols. Illus. Orig. decorated cloth. Spines and covers slightly faded and worn. Front inner hinge cracking on first edition, first issue. In a full-morocco slipcase. Near-fine. MacManus 278-1498 1983 $500

DICKENS, CHARLES   The Chimes. London: Chapman & Hall, 1845. First edition, later issue. Full polished calf, gilt, marbled endpapers. Morocco labels on spine. Orig. cloth covers bound in, by Riviere & Son. Fine. MacManus 278-1499 1983 $200

DICKENS, CHARLES   The Chimes: A Goblin Story. London: Chapman & Hall, 1845. 1st ed., 2nd issue. Orig. red cloth, gilt, a.e.g. Near fine copy. Jenkins 155-297 1983 $125

DICKENS, CHARLES   The Chimes. Chapman & Hall, 1845. First edition, 1st issue. 1 p ads. Half title, engr. front. and title (sl. ink marked). Orig. red cloth, gilt. Sl. rubbed, a.e.g., v.g. Jarndyce 31-544 1983 £78

DICKENS, CHARLES   The Chimes. Chapman & Hall, 1845. First edition, 1st issue. Half title, front. & engraved title. Illus. by Maclise, Doyle, Leech, etc. Following hinge sl. weak. Orig. red cloth, gilt, a.e.g. Very good. Jarndyce 30-54 1983 £72

DICKENS, CHARLES   The Chimes. London: Limited Editions
Club, 1931. First edition thus. Illus. by Arthur Rackham. 4to.
Polished buckram, t.e.g., slipcase. Limited to 1500 numbered copies
signed by Rackham and printed by George W. Jones at The Sign of the
Dolphin. Spine darkened, slipcase soiled. Oak Knoll 38-332 1983
$225

DICKENS, CHARLES   A Christmas Carol. London: Chapman &
Hall, 1843. First edition, second issue. Illus. by John Leech. Orig.
cloth. A bit shaken and worn. MacManus 278-1503 1983 $1,000

DICKENS, CHARLES   A Christmas Carol. London: Chapman &
Hall, 1843. First edition, third issue. Illus. by John Leech. Orig.
decorated cloth. Spine slightly faded. In a half-morocco slipcase.
Near-fine. MacManus 278-1500 1983 $850

DICKENS, CHARLES   A Christmas Carol. London: Chapman &
Hall, 1843. First edition. Illus. by John Leech. 12mo. Orig. decorated cloth. Yellow endpapers. Covers a bit soiled, extremities
chipped. Frontispiece loosening. MacManus 278-1504 1983 $600

DICKENS, CHARLES   A Christmas Carol. Chapman & Hall,
1843. First edition (stave one). Half title, 4 hand-coloured illus.
by Leech, 2 pp ads. Orig. salmon pink cloth gilt, a.e.g. Yellow
end papers. Small repairs to head and tail of spine. Jarndyce 31-
533 1983 £300

DICKENS, CHARLES   A Christmas Carol. Chapman & Hall,
1843. Half title, 4 hand-col. illus. by Leech. Yellow e.p.s. Orig.
salmon-pink cloth, skilfully recased, with repairs to spine.
Jarndyce 30-49 1983 £260

DICKENS, CHARLES   A Christmas Carol. Chapman & Hall,
1843. 2nd edition. Half title, 4 hand-coloured illus. by Leech.
Orig. salmon-pink cloth, skilfully recased with small repairs to head
and tail of spine. Jarndyce 30-51 1983 £200

DICKENS, CHARLES   A Christmas Carol. Chapman & Hall,
1843. Half title, front. and 3 illus. in colour by John Leech. A
little worn, half brown calf. Jarndyce 30-50 1983 £160

DICKENS, CHARLES   A Christmas Carol. London: Chapman &
Hall, 1844. "Trial" issue with green endpapers. Illus. by John
Leech. Orig. gilt-decorated tan cloth. Spine ends, covers and edges
worn, inner hinges weak. Bookplate. Contemporary owner's signature
on the front free endpaper. Very good. MacManus 278-1501 1983
$2,000

DICKENS, CHARLES   A Christmas Carol. Chapman & Hall,
1844. 5th edition. 4 hand-coloured illus. by Leech. Vignette
illus.; half title and 2 pp ads. Orig. pink cloth, some browning of
text, inner hinges cracked, otherwise v.g. Jarndyce 31-534 1983
£55

DICKENS, CHARLES   A Christmas Carol in Prose; The Chimes;
The Cricket on the Hearth. Leipzig: Bernard Tauchnitz, 1846. First
Tauchnitz collected edition. 3/4 vellum with marbled boards. Two
bookplates (one armorial) and a previous owner's signature on the front
endpapers. Spine a bit soiled; edges slightly worn. Good. MacManus
278-1505 1983 $75

DICKENS, CHARLES   A Christmas Carol. East Aurora, 1902.
3/4 brown morocco over marbled boards, gilt stamped scrolling on
spine, t.e.g., uncut. One of 100 copies on Japan vellum, signed by
Hubbard. Roycroft binding. Fine. Houle 22-758 1983 $175

DICKENS, CHARLES   A Christmas Carol. Chapman & Hall,
1903. Facs. of the orig. manuscript. 4to, orig. red cloth, sl.
marked. Jarndyce 31-542 1983 £18

DICKENS, CHARLES   A Christmas Carol. NY: Press of the
Woolly Whale, 1930. Folio. Printed in red and black. Dec. initial
letters designed by W.A. Dwiggins. Edition ltd. to 250 numbered
copies. Bound in 3/4 green morocco over marbled boards; dec.
gilt-stamped spine. T.e.g. In a plain paper dust jacket. Fine.
Karmiole 71-112 1983 $150

DICKENS, CHARLES   A Christmas Carol. Boston: Marrymount
Press, 1934. Octavo. Illus. by Gordon Ross. Limited to 1500 copies
signed by artist. Paper label on spine slightly rubbed, otherwise
extremely fine in cloth-backed pastepaper over boards. Slip-case
beginning to split at one edge. Bromer 25-243 1983 $50

DICKENS, CHARLES   A Christmas Carol. Chapman & Hall, n.d.
The "trial issue". Half title printed in green, title printed in red
and green. 4 hand-coloured plates by Leech (repairs with no loss to
front.) Inserted from another copy is sig. H. of text. 2 pp. ads.
Text generally rather worn. Finely rebound in dark green crushed morocco, gilt borders and spine. Signature on title of this copy "Farnham Maxwell-Lyte Jany. 10th 1844'. Jarndyce 31-531 1983 £380

DICKENS, CHARLES   A Christmas Carol. Phila.: J.B. Lippincott Co., n.d. Illus. by A. Rackham. 8vo. Orig. cloth. Very good.
MacManus 280-4320 1983 $50

DICKENS, CHARLES   The Cricket on the Hearth. London:
Printed and Published for the Author, By Bradbury & Evans, 1846. First
edition. Full polished calf, gilt, marbled endpapers. Orig. cloth
covers bound in, by Riviere. Fine. MacManus 278-1506 1983 $200

DICKENS, CHARLES   The Cricket on the Hearth. Boston,
1846. Illus. 1st American ed. Orig. printed wrappers. Some
creases and foxing, but a good copy of a very scarce ed. Jenkins
155-298 1983 $75

DICKENS, CHARLES   The Cricket on the Hearth. Printed &
pub. for the author, by Bradbury & Evans, 1846. Illus. by Maclise,
Doyle, etc. Half title, orig. red cloth, gilt, a.e.g. First edition.
Jarndyce 30-56 1983 £32

DICKENS, CHARLES   The Cricket on the Hearth. NY:
(1927). First American edition with these illustrations. Sq 8vo,
red cloth, lettering 7 design in gilt, pictorial d/w. With 8
color plates, b/w drawings & text illustrations plus decorative
endpapers by Bedford. An exceptional copy. Perata 27-11 1983
$65

DICKENS, CHARLES   A Curious Dance Round a Curious Tree.
(1860). Orig. pink wraps. Bound into cloth backed card wraps.,
bookplate. First edition, second issue. Jarndyce 30-112 1983 £80

DICKENS, CHARLES   A Curious Dance Round a Curious Tree.
Published in aid of St. Luke's Hospital, (1883). Orig. blue printed
paper wraps., v.g. Jarndyce 30-113 1983 £35

DICKENS, CHARLES   Dealings With The Firm of Dombey And Son.
London: Bardbury & Evans, 1848. First edition. Illus. by H.K. Browne
("Phiz"). Orig. green cloth. Spine and covers worn, small tear to
top spine-end repaired, inner hinges weak. Former owner's signature.
Good. MacManus 278-1507 1983 $450

DICKENS, CHARLES   Dealings With The Firm Of Dombey And Son.
London: Bradbury & Evans, 1848. First edition. Illus. by H.K. Browne,
with one set of the orig. wrappers bound in. Full, heavy-tooled
morocco. Finely bound in blue morocco by Tout, with decorated endpapers. Spine slightly faded. Some foxing throughout. Very good.
MacManus 278-1508 1983 $225

DICKENS, CHARLES   Dickens's Dictionary of London, 1896-
1897. (London): J. Smith, St. Bride St., E.C. (1896). 16mo, pict.
tan cloth; slightly blistered. With a new 1 page preface. Jarndyce
31-227 1983 $50

DICKENS, CHARLES   The Dickens-Kolle Letters. Boston:
The Bibliophile Society, 1910. Ltd. edition. One of 483 copies,
for members only. Argosy 714-219 1983 $40

DICKENS, CHARLES   Dickens v. Barabbas... London:
Charles F. Sawyer, 1930. First edition. Square 8vo. Polished
buckram, t.e.g. Limited to 200 numbered copies of which this
is one of the 90 printed on handmade paper. Covers faded. Oak
Knoll 48-139 1983 $75

DICKENS, CHARLES   Dombey and Son. London, 1848. Illus.
by H.K. Browne. 8vo, 1/2 calf; gilt back, marbled boards, first
edition. Argosy 714-868 1983 $200

DICKENS, CHARLES   Dombey and Son. London: Bradbury
and Evans, 1848. First book edition. 8vo. Green half calf, spine
gilt. Etched frontis. and title, and 38 plates by "Phiz." Errata
leaf present. Couple of corners of spine slightly worn. Bound
without half-title. Plates browned around the edges, but a very
good copy. Ximenes 63-146 1983 $125

DICKENS, CHARLES   Dombey and Son. Bradbury & Evans, 1848.
Illus. by H.K. Browne, and with a series of portrait extra illus.,
also by Browne. Half title, wraps. & some ads from part XIX-XX bound
in. Some light foxing. Half calf, spine gilt, black and maroon
labels. A fine copy. Jarndyce 30-73 1983 £76

DICKENS, CHARLES   Dombey and Son. Bradbury & Evans, 1848.
Illus. by H.K. Browne. Half title. Some foxing to plates. First
edition. Half green morocco, spine gilt, v.g. Jarndyce 30-74 1983
£54

DICKENS, CHARLES   Edwin Drood. Chapman & Hall, 1870.
First edition, bound from the parts. Front. port. engr. title,
and illus. by S.L. Fildes. 2 pp ads. Front wrapper to part VI,
bound in. Half dark green roan, sl. rubbed. Jarndyce 31-567 1983
£30

DICKENS, CHARLES   Edwin Drood. Chapman & Hall, 1870.
Front. port. and illus. by S. L. Fildes. A little foxing, half red
calf, rubbed. Jarndyce 30-122 1983 £20

DICKENS, CHARLES   (Edwin Drood). Boston: Osgood, 1870.
1st Am. printing. Orig. publisher's green cloth, gilt. Thick folio.
Spine ends chipped, but a solid copy. Jenkins 155-299 1983 $45

DICKENS, CHARLES   Edwin Drood. W.H. Allen, 1887. First
edition, 1st issue. Engr. front. 48 pp ads. Orig. dec. slate-grey
cloth, v.g. Jarndyce 31-569 1983 £48

DICKENS, CHARLES   Gone Astray. Chapman & Hall, 1912.
First edition, illus. by Ruth Cobb, from old prints and from photographs, by T.W. Tyrrell. Orig. light green cloth, neatly titled
in ink on spine, v.g. Jarndyce 31-575 1983 £38

DICKENS, CHARLES   Great Expectations. Chapman & Hall,
1861. Vols. I & II, 2nd edition, vol. III, first edition. Half
maroon calf, a little rubbed, spines gilt, green and brown labels.
Jarndyce 30-114 1983 £150

DICKENS, CHARLES   Great Expectations. London: Chapman &
Hall, 1861. Fourth edition of Vol. 1, second editions of Vols. 2 & 3.
3 vols. Orig. embossed cloth. Covers somewhat rubbed & soiled. Bookplates. Very good. MacManus 278-1510 1983 $250

DICKENS, CHARLES   Great Expectations. Philadelphia:
Peterson, (1861). Illus. 1st American ed. Orig. green cloth, gilt.
Near fine copy. Jenkins 155-1381 1983 $100

DICKENS, CHARLES   Great Expectations. Leipzig, Bernhard
Tauchnitz, 1861. Half title vol. 1 (vol. 547). Half green calf,
a little rubbed, red label. Jarndyce 30-115 1983 £18

DICKENS, CHARLES   Great Expectations. Edinburgh:
1937. Preface by Bernard Shaw. Thick 8vo, green cloth, gilt,
t.e.g. Illustrated by Gordon Ross. One of 1500 copies signed
by the artist. Backstrip darkened, else a fine copy in worn
slipcase. Perata 27-124 1983 $60

DICKENS, CHARLES   Hard Times, For These Times. London:
Bradbury & Evans, 1854. First edition. Full gilt-tooled morocco by
Emile Rouselle. Fine. MacManus 278-1511 1983 $350

DICKENS, CHARLES   Hard times. For these times. London:
Bradbury and Evans, 1854. First edition. 8vo. Orig. green fine-
ribbed cloth. Slightly rubbed and faded, very slight tear at foot
of spine, some cracking of the inner hinges. Ximenes 63-147 1983
$275

DICKENS, CHARLES   Hard Times. Bradbury & Evans, 1854.
First edition, half title. Orig. green cloth. Fine. Jarndyce 30-98
1983 £160

DICKENS, CHARLES   Hard Times. Bradbury & Evans, 1854.
First edition. Half titles. Half black morocco, sl. rubbed.
Jarndyce 30-99 1983 £95

DICKENS, CHARLES   Hard Times. For these Times. Bradbury &
Evans, 1854. First edition, half title, orig. green cloth, recased.
A good copy. Jarndyce 31-556 1983 £85

DICKENS, CHARLES   The Haunted Man and The Ghost's Bargain.
London: Bradbury & Evans, 1848. First edition. Full polished calf,
gilt, marbled endpapers. Orig. covers bound in, by Riviere. Fine.
MacManus 278-1513 1983 $200

DICKENS, CHARLES   The Haunted Man and the Ghost's Bargain.
London: Bradbury & Evans, 1848. 1st ed. Orig. red cloth gilt,
a.e.g. Tiny nick at base of spine. This copy has broken type in
folio 166 which has been incorrectly described as a rare 1st issue.
Near fine copy, bright. Jenkins 155-300 1983 $100

DICKENS, CHARLES   The Haunted Man. Bradbury & Evans,
1848. 2 pp ads. Orig. red cloth. Head and tail of spine worn,
lacks leading free e.p. Jarndyce 30-58 1983 £10.50

DICKENS, CHARLES   The Holly Tree. East Aurora: Roycroft
Shop, 1903. Octavo. Limited to 100 copies on Japan Vellum signed by
Elbert Hubbard. Hand-colored boards. Full, crushed apple-green
morocco by Louis H. Kinder. Gilt-decorated cover and spine. Gilt
lettering on front cover and spine. T.e.g. Binding executed at
Roycroft bindery, with their stamp, signed by Kinder. Edges slightly
faded and faint bumping to corners. Bookplate. Bromer 25-293 1983
$1200

DICKENS, CHARLES   The Holly Tree. East Aurora, 1903.
3/4 brown morocco, t.e.g., uncut, gilt stamped spine with floral
design by Roycroft bindery. One of 100 copies on Japan vellum signed
by Hubbard. Hand colored borders designed by Samuel Warner. Fine.
Houle 22-759 1983 $150

DICKENS, CHARLES   Hunted Down. (1870). Half title, ads.
Orig. green printed wraps. bound into half green calf by Bickers.
Sl. rubbed, t.e.g. Jarndyce 30-111 1983 £75

DICKENS, CHARLES   Hunted Down: a Story. John Camden
Hotten, (1871?). Small 8vo, vignette on title lacking half title,
cont. half vellum with marbled boards. First edition. Bickersteth
75-128 1983 £28

DICKENS, CHARLES   An Interesting Dickens Collection. Birmingham, 1887. 100 copies printed, 9th June 1887. Orig. grey wraps.,
fine. Jarndyce 31-578 1983 £30

DICKENS, CHARLES   The Letters. Chapman and Hall, 1880.
2 vols., 8vo, cont. half calf, rubbed at the edges. First edition.
Bickersteth 75-129 1983 £55

DICKENS, CHARLES   Letters of Charles Dickens to Wilkie
Collins, 1851-1870. 1892. First edition. Half title, orig. blue
cloth, sl. rubbed. Jarndyce 30-131 1983 £38

DICKENS, CHARLES   The Life and Adventures of Martin Chuzzel-
wit. London: Chapman & Hall, 1843-44. First edition, first issue,
with the reward notice on the signpost incorrectly worded. Will illus.
by Phiz. Orig. 20 parts in 19. Pictorial wrappers. Wrappers slightly
frayed and soiled. A few spines worn at the ends and a trifle chipped.
Housed in two fine full-morocco solander cases. Very good. MacManus
278-1516 1983 $1,250

DICKENS, CHARLES   Martin Chuzzlewit. London: Chapman &
Hall, 1843-44. First edition in the orig. monthly parts. Illus. by
"Phiz." Orig. printed wrappers. 20 parts in 19. Portrait frontis.
in second state. Wrappers generally worn; a few plates rather foxed.
Backstrips restored. In a cloth-folding box (spine faded). MacManus
278-1533 1983 $650

DICKENS, CHARLES   The Life and Adventures of Martin Chuzzlewit. London: Chapman & Hall, 1844. First edition, first issue.
Illus. by Phiz. Full red morocco, gilt, with marbled endpapers, a.e.g.,
by Chambolle-Duru. Bookplate. Very fine. MacManus 278-1515 1983
$450

DICKENS, CHARLES   The Life and Adventures of Martin
Chuzzlewit. London, 1844. First edition. Thick 8vo, tan calf;
gilt fillet borders, dentelles, & gilt back, by Root, a.e.g. Fine copy.
Errata & plate list. First issue engraved title page. Argosy 714-221
1983 $250

DICKENS, CHARLES   Martin Chuzzlewit. 1844. Illus. by
Phiz. Some foxing to plates, calf sl. rubbed, gilt borders, red label.
Jarndyce 30-61 1983 £58

DICKENS, CHARLES   The life and adventures of Martin
Chuzzlewit. London: Chapman and Hall, 1844. First edition. 8vo.
Cont. half black morocco, t.e.g., by W.J. Scopes of Ipswich. Frontis.
and engraved title (reading 100£) and 38 plates by H.K. Browne.
Slight rubbing of binding, some foxing, occasionally rather heavy.
Ximenes 63-148 1983 $75

DICKENS, CHARLES   Martin Chuzzlewit. Paris, A.W. Galignani,
1844. Half calf rubbed, black labels. 2 vols. Jarndyce 30-62 1983
£38

DICKENS, CHARLES   Martin Chuzzlewit. Leipzig, Bernh,
Tauchnitz Jun., 1844. Marbled boards, sl. variant red labels.
2 vols. Jarndyce 30-63 1983 £20

DICKENS, CHARLES   Martin Chuzzlewit. Chapman and Hall,
1850. First cheap edition. Front. by Frank Stone. Half black
calf, sl. rubbed. Jarndyce 30-64 1983 £15

DICKENS, CHARLES   The Life and Adventures of Martin Chuzzel-
wit. London: Chapman & Hall, Ld., n.d. Gadshill edition. Intro. &
notes by Andrew Lang. 2 vols. Orig. illus. Bound in 3/4 green
morocco and marbled boards, t.e.g., by Southeran & Co. Bookplates.
Fine. MacManus 278-1514 1983 $85

DICKENS, CHARLES   The Life and Adventures of Nicholas
Nickleby. London: Chapman & Hall, 1839. First book edition. Illus.
by Phiz. Orig. cloth. Front outer hinge slightly split near top of
spine, inner hinges expertly reinforced. Some offsetting from frontispiece. In a folding cloth box. Exceptionally fine. MacManus 278-
1517 1983 $1,000

DICKENS, CHARLES   The Life And Adventures of Nicholas
Nickleby. London: Chapman & Hall, 1839. First edition. Illus. by
Phiz. Frontispiece port. Full morocco with marbled endpapers.
Contains an extra set of plates including the portrait which bears the
Chapman & Hall imprint in each case. MacManus 278-1518 1983 $350

DICKENS, CHARLES   The Life and Adventures of Nicholas
Nickleby. Lon., 1839. Illus. by H. K. Browne. Spine restored, front
board and fly detached, rear hinge starting, good in folding box.
Quill & Brush 54-361 1983 $350

DICKENS, CHARLES   Nicholas Nickleby. Chapman & Hall,
1839. First edition, bound from the parts. Front. port. & illus.
by Phiz. With the extra-illustrations; two series, one by Peter
Palette, and portraits by Onwhyn. Calf, red & Black labels, sl.
rubbing. Jarndyce 31-528 1983 £72

DICKENS, CHARLES   Nicholas Nickleby. Chapman & Hall,
1839. First edition, front. port. & illus. by Phiz. Half title.
Crushed green morocco, gilt borders, spine, t.e.g., v.g. Jarndyce
31-529 1983 £68

DICKENS, CHARLES   Nicholas Nickleby. Chapman & Hall, 1839.
First edition. Bound into 2 vols., front. port. illus. by "Peter
Palette" (T. Onwhyn). Dark blue, straight-grained morocco, gilt
borders and spines, hinges rubbed. Jarndyce 30-28 1983 £65

DICKENS, CHARLES   Nicholas Nickleby. Chapman & Hall, 1839.
First edition, bound from the parts. Front. port. with illus. by Phiz.
Some foxing, half title, half dark blue calf, marbled boards a little
rubbed. Jarndyce 30-29 1983 £45

DICKENS, CHARLES   The Life of Our Lord. London, 1934.
4to. Vellum, gilt, t.e.g., others uncut. Printed in two colours
on hand-made paper, portrait, 8 plates and 3 facsimiles of the
orig. manuscript. Limited edition of 250 numbered copies. Traylen
94-269 1983 £20

DICKENS, CHARLES   The Life of Our Lord. London: Associated Newspapers Ltd., 1934. First English trade edition. 4to. Orig.
cloth. Dust jacket (a bit frayed and soiled). Fine. MacManus 278-
1520 1983 $25

DICKENS, CHARLES   The Life of Our Lord. 1934. First
published edition. Half title, front. port. Orig. maroon cloth.
Jarndyce 30-138 1983 £10.50

DICKENS, CHARLES   Little Dorrit. London: 1855-57. First
edition. Illus. by H. K. Browne. Some light foxing and marginal foxing to plates. Most spines repaired. Nice set in two red morocco,
fleece-lined solander cases, spines ornately extra gilted. Bromer
25-25 1983 $950

DICKENS, CHARLES   Little Dorrit. London: Bradbury & Evans,
1855-57. First edition, first issue with the errata slip at page 481.
Illus. by H.K. Browne. 20 parts in 19. Orig. pictorial wrappers.
General wear and foxing. Backstrips restored. MacManus 278-1521 1983
$850

DICKENS, CHARLES   Little Dorrit. Leipzig, 1856-7. 4
vols. Square 8vo, 20 plates. Orig. cloth. A fine set. Hannas 69-
213 1983 £65

DICKENS, CHARLES   Little Dorrit. London: Bradbury & Evans,
1857. First edition. Illus. by H.K. Browne. One of the orig. wrappers
bound in 3/4 morocco. Very good. MacManus 278-1522 1983 $200

DICKENS, CHARLES   Little Dorrit. Bradbury & Evans, 1857.
Half black calf, marbled boards, raised spines gilt, red label. Very
sl. damp stain to outer corner of some plates. Jarndyce 30-103 1983
£55

DICKENS, CHARLES   Little Dorrit. Philadelphia: Peterson,
(1857). Plates. 1st American ed. Orig. black cloth, gilt. Very
good copy with moderate rubbing and light stain to rear cover.
Jenkins 155-1382 1983 $60

DICKENS, CHARLES   Little Dorrit. Bradbury & Evans, 1857.
First edition, front. engr. title and illus. by H.K. Browne. Half
black calf, spine gilt in compartments. Jarndyce 31-558 1983 £42

DICKENS, CHARLES   Little Dorrit. Bradbury & Evans, 1857.
Illus. by H. K. Browne. First edition, bound from the parts. Some
foxing. Half green calf rubbed, maroon label, leading hinge a little
weak. Jarndyce 30-105 1983 £15

DICKENS, CHARLES   Master Humphrey's Clock. London: Chapman & Hall, 1840-1841. First edition. 88 weekly parts. Illus. by
G. Cattermole & H.K. Browne. Orig. decorated wrappers with a woodcut
design by Cattermole. Spines slightly worn, with some foxing on several
of the issues. In a half-morocco solander case. Near-fine. MacManus
278-1534 1983 $1,250

DICKENS, CHARLES   Master Humphrey's Clock. London,
Chapman & Hall, 1840. First edition. 4to, illus. Full polished
tan calf, raised bands, contrasting leather labels, a.e.g. Frontis.
Very good - fine. 3 vols. Cloth slipcase. Illus. throughout with
fine engravings by George Cattermole and Hablot Browne. Houle 22-
302 1983 $450

DICKENS, CHARLES   Master Humphrey's Clock. Chapman & Hall,
1840-1. First edition, 3 vols., frontis. vignette illus. by Phiz,
Cattermole, etc. Half calf, spines a little rubbed, black labels.
Jarndyce 30-32 1983 £42

DICKENS, CHARLES   The Mudfog Papers. Richard Bentley,
1880. Orig. red cloth, block in black and gilt. V.g. First edition.
Jarndyce 30-128 1983 £38

DICKENS, CHARLES   The Mudfrog Papers, etc. N.Y.: Henry
Holt & Co., 1880. Authorized edition. 12mo, cloth; spine darkened.
Argosy 714-222 1983 $20

DICKENS, CHARLES   Mugby Junction, the Extra Christmas
Number of All the Year Round. London: Chapman & Hall, 1866. 1st
ed. Orig. blue printed wrappers, stitched, as issued. Small piece
torn from one corner of front wrapper, else a nice copy. Jenkins
155-301 1983 $35

DICKENS, CHARLES   The Old Curiosity Shop. Chapman & Hall,
1841. Illus. by George Cattermole & H.K. Browne. 1st separate edn.
with many text wood engrs., mis paginated. Orig. green blind stamped
cloth. Top bkstrip repaired, top corners bruised & bkstrip faded
with some wear at bottom, bkplate, scarce, vg. Hodgkins 27-266 1983
£50

DICKENS, CHARLES　　　　The Old Curiosity Shop. Chapman & Hall, 1848. Front. by Cattermole. Half black calf, sl. rubbed. Jarndyce 30-33 1983 £10.50

DICKENS, CHARLES　　　　The Old Curiousity Shop. Hodder & Stoughton, n.d. 4to. Mounted colour frontis. Pictorial title. 20 mounted colour plates. Pictorial endpapers. Full white vellum pictorial gilt, some wear. Limited to 350 copies. Signed by Reynolds. Greer 39-102 1983 £90

DICKENS, CHARLES　　　　Oliver Twist. 1837-39. Illus. by George Cruikshank. Front. wrapper of part II of Bentley's Miscellany bound in. Modern half dark green morocco, t.e.g. Jarndyce 31-516 1983 £85

DICKENS, CHARLES　　　　Oliver Twist; Or, The Parish Boy's Progress. London: Bentley, 1838. First edition, first issue in the second binding. 3 vols. Illus. by G. Cruikshank. Orig. maroon cloth. Loosely laid, in Vol. 3, is a copy of the plate used for the second issue. Spines and covers slightly faded and worn. Some foxing to the preliminary pages. In three half-morocco slipcases. Very good. MacManus 278-1538 1983 $1,500

DICKENS, CHARLES　　　　Oliver Twist. Richard Bentley, 1839. 2nd edition, 3 vols. Half titles, illus. by George Cruikshank. Half green morocco, spines gilt. Jarndyce 31-517 1983 £90

DICKENS, CHARLES　　　　Oliver Twist. 1839. Illus. by Cruikshank. 3 vols., half title vols. I and II. 4 pp ads., vol. I. Orig. brown ribbed cloth, some foxing to plates. Jarndyce 30-22 1983 £72

DICKENS, CHARLES　　　　Oliver Twist. Paris, Baudry, 1839. Half title, lightly foxed. Half calf, worn but sound. Tall 8vo. Jarndyce 30-25 1983 £24

DICKENS, CHARLES　　　　The Adventures of Oliver Twist. London: for the Author, 1846. First octavo edition. 8vo. Full red crushed levant morocco, gilt rule borders with gilt vignette portrait within ornamental frame on top cover, and fac-simile signature in gilt in centre of back cover, fully gilt panelled spine, wide inner gilt dentelles, edges, gilt. 24 engraved plates by Cruikshank. Very rare. Traylen 94-268 1983 £225

DICKENS, CHARLES　　　　The Adventures of Oliver Twist; or, The Parish Boy's Progress. London: Bradbury & Evans, 1846. First Octavo edition. Illus. by G. Cruikshank. Orig. decorated cloth. Spine very faded and worn. Inner hinges cracked. MacManus 278-1490 1983 $350

DICKENS, CHARLES　　　　The Adventures of Oliver Twist. Bradbury & Evans, 1846. A new edition, 24 illus. by George Cruikshank. Some browning of plates, half calf, a little rubbed, label. Jarndyce 31-520 1983 £54

DICKENS, CHARLES　　　　Oliver Twist. 1939. Illus. by Barnett Freedman. 8vo, light brown cloth with dark brown stamping, title in gilt on spine, slipcase. Duschnes 240-68 1983 $22.50

DICKENS, CHARLES　　　　Oliver Twist. Chapman & Hall, 1841. 3 vols., illus. by George Cruikshank. Orig. green cloth, inner hinges a little weak. A good copy. Jarndyce 30-23 1983 £72

DICKENS, CHARLES　　　　Oliver Twist. Chapman & Hall, 1850. Front. by George Cruikshank. Half black calf. Sl. rubbed. Jarndyce 30-26 1983 £14

DICKENS, CHARLES　　　　Our Mutual Friend. London: Chapman & Hall, 1864-5. First edition in the original parts. Illus. by Marcus Stone. Orig. printed wrappers. 20 parts in 19. Wrappers ragged. Spines repaired. Most of the ads. appear to be present. In full morocco solander case. MacManus 278-1537 1983 $1,000

DICKENS, CHARLES　　　　Our Mutual Friend. London: 1864-65. First edition. Illus. by Marcus Stone. Some chipping to wrappers, spine repaired. Internally a clean and fine set. Enclosed in morocco-backed solander case. Bromer 25-26 1983 $775

DICKENS, CHARLES　　　　Our Mutual Friend. London: Chapman & Hall, May 1864-November 1865. First edition. 20 parts in 19. Orig. printed wrappers. Some spines repaired. Some chipping of the wrappers. In a full solander slipcase. MacManus 278-1539 1983 $650

DICKENS, CHARLES　　　　Our Mutual Friend. Chapman & Hall, 1865. Illus. by Marcus Stone. Half titles, e.ps. renewed. Orig. maroon cloth, a little rubbed. First edition. Jarndyce 30-118 1983 £65

DICKENS, CHARLES　　　　Our Mutual Friend. London: Chapman and Hall, 1865. First edition. 2 vols. 8vo. Orig. maroon sand-grain cloth. 40 engraved plates by Marcus Stone, half-titles and errata slip. Joints on one vol. neatly repaired. Traylen 94-270 1983 £65

DICKENS, CHARLES　　　　Our Mutual Friend. Chapman & Hall, 1865. First edition, 2 vols. Illus. by Marcus Stone. Additional engr. title vol. I. 2 vols. bound as one. Half calf, sl. rubbed maroon label, v.g. Jarndyce 31-560 1983 £58

DICKENS, CHARLES　　　　Our Mutual Friend. Chapman & Hall, 1865. Illus. by Marcus Stone. Half titles, e. ps. renewed, orig. maroon cloth, a little rubbed. 2 vols. First edition. Jarndyce 30-119 1983 £55

DICKENS, CHARLES　　　　Our mutual friend. London: Chapman and Hall, 1865. First book edition. 2 vols. 8vo. Black half morocco. Frontis. in each vol., and 38 plates by Marcus Stone. With the printed slip explaining the title tipped into Vol. 1. Binding neatly rebacked. Ximenes 63-149 1983 $50

DICKENS, CHARLES　　　　The Personal History of David Copperfield. London: Bradbury & Evans, 1850. First book edition. Illus. by H.K. Browne. Orig. cloth. Spine faded, edges frayed and slightly torn. Inner hinges cracking although webbing intact. Covers rubbed. With the binder's stamp on the front pastedown endpaper. Good. MacManus 278-1540 1983 $750

DICKENS, CHARLES　　　　The Personal History of David Copperfield. London: Bradbury & Evans, 1850. First edition. Illus. by H.K. Browne. 3/4 calf with heavy gilt tooling to the spine. Very good. MacManus 278-1541 1983 $250

DICKENS, CHARLES　　　　David Copperfield. Bradbury & Evans, 1850. First edition. Illus. by H.K. Browne. Half title, some wraps. and ads from the part issues bound in. Full calf by Grieve of Edinburgh, 1850. Gilt borders and spines, dark green labels, t.e.g. Fine. Jarndyce 30-77 1983 £130

DICKENS, CHARLES　　　　David Copperfield. Bradbury & Evans, 1850. First edition, bound from the parts. Illus. by H.K. Browne. Some browning of plates, half calf, sl. rubbed. Jarndyce 31-554 1983 £68

DICKENS, CHARLES　　　　The Personal History of David Copperfield. Westminster Press, ND (ca. 1910). 4to, pictorial title-page in colours, 20 mounted colour plates, original red cloth lettered in black and gilt, and with portrait silhouette in black and gilt, pictorial endpapers. A very fine copy in triflingly worn dustwrapper. Deighton 3-107 1983 £38

DICKENS, CHARLES　　　　David Copperfield. n.d. (c. 1910). Orig. 13 penny parts. Ads. Orig. wraps. sl. rubbed. Jarndyce 30-78 1983 £18

DICKENS, CHARLES　　　　David Copperfield. 1921. No. 93 of 275 copies reprinted from the privately ptd. edition of 1866. Half title, front. Uncut. Orig. grey boards, v.g. Jarndyce 30-80 1983 £20

DICKENS, CHARLES　　　　David Copperfield. New York: Heritage Press, 1935. 8vo, full tan leather binding, slipcase. Illus. by John Austen; frontis. signed by the artist. Duschnes 240-67 1983 $40

DICKENS, CHARLES　　　　David Copperfield. Westminster Press, n.d. Illus. in colour by Frank Reynolds. 4to. Orig. red cloth, blocked and lettered in black and gilt. Very good. Jarndyce 30-79 1983 £25

DICKENS, CHARLES   Pictures From Italy. London: Bradbury & Evans, 1846. First edition. 12mo. Illus. Full calf by Zaehnsdorf. Very good. MacManus 278-1546 1983 $150

DICKENS, CHARLES   Pictures from Italy. Bradbury & Evans, 1846. 2 pp ads. Half title, vignette illus. on wood by Samuel Palmer. Orig. blue cloth. Leading endpapers have been replaced. Fine. Jarndyce 30-68 1983 £65

DICKENS, CHARLES   Pictures from Italy. Bradbury & Evans, 1846. Vignette illus. by Samuel Palmer. Half title, 2 pp ads., orig. blue cloth a little rubbed at heads of hinges, lacking the preliminary ad leaf, otherwise v.g. Jarndyce 30-69 1983 £30

DICKENS, CHARLES   The Plays and Poems. 1882. First collected edition. 2 vols., half titles. Orig. blue cloth, v.g. Jarndyce 30-129 1983 £120

DICKENS, CHARLES   The Poor Traveller. London, 1858. 16mo, orig. green printed wraps., backstrip chipped. First edition in this form. Argosy 714-223 1983 $20

DICKENS, CHARLES   The Posthumous Papers of the Pickwick Club. London: Chapman & Hall, 1836. First edition. Illus. In the 19-20 orig. parts. Orig. pictorial wrappers. Wrappers a bit soiled and worn; backstrips repaired or torn. Plates very foxed. In a (defective) cloth case. MacManus 278-1549 1983 $750

DICKENS, CHARLES   The Posthumous Papers of the Pickwick Club. London: Chapman & Hall, 1837. First edition. Illus. by R. Seymour and Phiz. Orig. cloth (edges torn along the lower edge of each spine; a bit faded). Some plates are foxed. Good. MacManus 278-1548 1983 $1,000

DICKENS, CHARLES   The Pickwick Papers. London: Chapman & Hall, 1837. First edition. Illus. by "Phiz" and R. Seymour. Full decorated morocco with heavy gilt tooling on the spine. Marbled endpapers. Bound with a portrait of Dickens in gilt on the front cover and his signature in facsimile on the back cover. Near-fine. MacManus 278-1542 1983 $350

DICKENS, CHARLES   The Posthumous Papers of the Pickwick Club. London: Chapman & Hall, 1837. Frontis., engraved title, plates. 1st ed., early copy with 2 Buss plates, but with "Weller" engraved title, bound from the parts. Contemp. full diced calf, elaborately tooled and gilt, bands, label. Foxing to most of the plates, else a fine copy. Jenkins 155-303 1983 $300

DICKENS, CHARLES   Pickwick Papers. Chapman & Hall, 1837. Illus. by Seymour, Buss and Phiz. Plates in an early state, without captions; some foxing. Half calf, sl. rubbed, maroon label. Very good. Jarndyce 30-4 1983 £110

DICKENS, CHARLES   The Pickwick Papers. Chapman & Hall, 1837. First edition, bound from the parts. Half title, front. Engr. title and plates by R. Eymour and Phiz, and with the 2 Buss plates. "Veller" title and uncaptioned plates. Some browning and foxing to plates. Half dark green calf by Morrell, gilt spine, maroon labels, a.e.g. Jarndyce 31-507 1983 £140

DICKENS, CHARLES   The Posthumous Papers of the Pickwick Club. London: Chapman & Hall, 1837. Frontis., engraved title, plates. 1st ed., without the Buss plates, and "Weller" on engraved title. Contemp. half black morocco and marbled boards, raised bands, gilt compartments. Fine copy with some foxing to plates. Bound from the parts. Jenkins 155-304 1983 $165

DICKENS, CHARLES   Pickwick Papers. Chapman and Hall, 1837. Illus. by Seymour and Phiz. Plates without captions. Some foxing, but generally a good clean copy. Half black morocco, marbled boards rubbed. Jarndyce 30-5 1983 £72

DICKENS, CHARLES   The posthumous papers of the Pickwick Club. London: Chapman and Hall, 1837. First book edition. 8vo. Cont. dark green half morocco, spine gilt, a.e.g. Frontis., etched title (second state, reading "Weller"), and 41 plates by Seymour and H.K. Browne. Joints a little rubbed, some foxing, rather heavy in places. Ximenes 63-150 1983 $125

DICKENS, CHARLES   Pickwick Papers. Chapman & Hall, 1837. Illus. by Seymour and Phiz. Plates moderately foxed. Later maroon morocco, rubbed on hinges, and small repair to head of spine, a.e.g. Jarndyce 31-509 1983 £54

DICKENS, CHARLES   Pickwick Papers. Chapman & Hall, 1838. Illus. by Semour and Phiz. Some foxing. Calf, maroon and green labels, a good copy. Jarndyce 30-6 1983 £70

DICKENS, CHARLES   Pickwick Papers. Paris, Bauldry, 1838. Half dark blue calf, rubbed. 2 vols. Jarndyce 30-7 1983 £20

DICKENS, CHARLES   The Pickwick Papers. Chapman & Hall, 1847. Front. by C.R. Leslie. Half title, half black calf, a little rubbed. Jarndyce 30-10 1983 £14.50

DICKENS, CHARLES   Pickwick Papers. Chapman & Hall, n.d. (c. 1860). Orig. format, with half title and illus. by Semour and Phiz. Orig. green cloth, v.g. Jarndyce 30-11 1983 £18.50

DICKENS, CHARLES   The Pickwick Papers. Chapman & Hall, 1887. Illus. with India proofs of the orig. drawings by Seymour, Phiz, Buss and Leech. (One of 500 copies). Half titles. Untrimmed. Orig. dark green cloth, v.g. Jarndyce 30-12 1983 £42

DICKENS, CHARLES   The Posthumous Papers of the Pickwick Club. Oxford, Ltd. Editions Club, 1933. First edition thus. 4to, color illus. by John Austen. Gilt stamped brown cloth, uncut. Bookplates, else a fine set. 2 vols. One of 1,500 copies. Houle 21-214 1983 $85

DICKENS, CHARLES   Pickwick Papers. Heritage Press, 1936. 8vo, light brown cloth with dark brown stamping, title in gilt on spine, slipcase. Duschnes 240-69 1983 $22.50

DICKENS, CHARLES   Pickwick Papers. Westminster Press, n.d. 4to, orig. red cloth, blocked and lettered in black, gilt and white. Illus. in colour by Frank Reynolds. Sl. marking of upper cover, otherwise v.g. Jarndyce 30-13 1983 £22

DICKENS, CHARLES   Readings from the Works of Charles Dickens. Dublin: Carson Bros.... First edition. Half title; 16 pp ads and advertising e. ps. Yellow-back. Orig. yellow boards printed in black and red. Fine. Jarndyce 30-130 1983 £48

DICKENS, CHARLES   Sikes and Nancy. London: Henry Sotheran & Co., 1931. Illus. Orig. boards with paper spine label. One of 275 copies reprinted from a privately printed edition, formerly in the collection of Sir Henry Irving. Spine and covers slightly faded and worn. Bookplate. Near-fine. MacManus 278-1550 1983 $85

DICKENS, CHARLES   Sister Rose. Philadelphia: T.B. Peterson, (c. 1854). Orig. printed wraps., worn on margin of front cover. Jarndyce 31-557 1983 £20

DICKENS, CHARLES   Sketches by Boz. 1837. First series: 2 vols., 3rd edition; second series, first edition. 3 vols. in all. Illus. by George Cruikshank. Half calf, gilt spines, black labels. Green cloth boards. Very good. Jarndyce 30-1 1983 £150

DICKENS, CHARLES   Sketches, by Boz. Chapman & Hall, 1839. First one-volume edition, tall 8vo, 40 illus. by George Cruikshank. Finely bound by Riviere & Son; gilt borders, spines & dentelles; raised bands, dark green and black labels, t.e.g. Fine. Bound in is front wrapper to Part VII and orig. brown cloth. Jarndyce 31-515 1983 £140

DICKENS, CHARLES   Sketches Of Young Couples. London: Chapman & Hall, 1840. First edition. 6 illus. by "Phiz." Orig. pictorial boards. Spine rebacked, spine and covers worn. In a quarter-morocco slipcase. Former owner's inscription. Good. MacManus 278-1551 1983 $350

DICKENS, CHARLES   Sketches of Young Couples. Chapman & Hall, 1840. Half title (with Dickens Centenary Stamp), 6 illus. by Phiz, 4 pp ads. Orig. wraps bound into full red morocco. A.e.g. Internally a little worn, externally v.g. Jarndyce 30-37 1983 £78

DICKENS, CHARLES   Sketches of Young Couples. Chapman &
Hall, 1840. Illus. by "Phiz," first edition. Half title, 4 pp ads.
Orig. printed covers laid down on to matching boards, back cover
badly rubbed, and lacking free e.ps. Jarndyce 30-36 1983 £70

DICKENS, CHARLES   Sketches of Young Couples. Cassell,
Petter, and Galpin, (n.d.). Illus. by Phiz. 2 pp ads. Corner torn
from leading free e.p. Otherwise, fine, in orig. green cloth,
bevelled boards, blocked in gilt, red & black. Jarndyce 30-38 1983
£28

DICKENS, CHARLES   Sketches of Young Gentlemen. Chapman &
Hall, 1838. Second edition. Orig. printed blue card binding. Small
portion missing from the bottom of spine, otherwise very good. Six
illus. by Phiz. Jarndyce 30-17 1983 £30

DICKENS, CHARLES   Sketches of Young Gentlemen. Chapman &
Hall, 1838. Quarter red morocco, green cloth boards, illus. by Phiz.
Very good. Jarndyce 30-18 1983 £25

DICKENS, CHARLES   Sketchers of Young Ladies. London:
Chapman & Hall, 1837. First edition. 6 illus. by "Phiz." Orig.
pictorial boards. Spine very neatly repaired, spine and covers rubbed.
Small bookplate. Good. MacManus 278-1552 1983 $450

DICKENS, CHARLES   Sketches of Young Ladies. London:
Chapman & Hall, 1837. First edition. 6 illus. by Phiz. 12mo. Old
3/4 morocco. MacManus 278-1553 1983 $85

DICKENS, CHARLES   Sketches of Young Ladies. Chapman &
Hall, 1837. Illus. by Phiz. Quarter red morocco, green cloth boards.
V.g. Jarndyce 30-20 1983 £22

DICKENS, CHARLES   Speeches, Literary and Social. John
Camden Hotten, (1870). First collected edition, cont. green cloth,
v.g. Jarndyce 30-123 1983 £32

DICKENS, CHARLES   The Story of Little Dombey. Bradbury &
Evans, 1858. First edition. Half title. Half dark blue morocco,
a.e.g., v.g. Jarndyce 30-106 1983 £52

DICKENS, CHARLES   The Story of Little Dombey. Bradbury &
Evans, 1858. First edition. The orig. green printed wraps. are
bound in. 12mo, 1/2 green morocco, faded to brown; hinges worn.
Argosy 714-225 1983 $100

DICKENS, CHARLES   The Strange Gentleman. London: Chapman
& Hall, 1837 (actually 1871). First facsimile edition. Orig. lavender
wrappers. Frontispiece by Pailthorpe. Wrappers a bit soiled and
frayed. Good. MacManus 278-1554 1983 $45

DICKENS, CHARLES   The Strange Gentleman. London: Chapman
& Hall, 1837 (actually 1871). A perfact facsimile, minus the frontis.,
of the first edition. Orig. printed wrappers (slightly soiled and
frayed). Good. MacManus 278-1555 1983 $35

DICKENS, CHARLES   The Strange Gentleman. Chapman & Hall,
1837 (1871). Facs. reprint. Orig. printed wraps., a little worn.
Jarndyce 30-3 1983 £14.50

DICKENS, CHARLES   A Tale of Two Cities. Chapman and Hall,
1859. First edition, first issue, bound from the parts. Illus. by
H.K. Browne. Foxing to front. and engr. title, otherwise v.g. Green
morocco, a.e.g. Jarndyce 30-107 1983 £160

DICKENS, CHARLES   A Tale of Two Cities. Philadelphia:
Peterson, (1859). Ads, illus. 1st American ed. Orig. green cloth,
gilt. Scarce. Fine copy. Jenkins 155-305 1983 $200

DICKENS, CHARLES   A Tale of Two Cities. Chapman and Hall,
1859. First edition, second issue, bound from the parts. Illus. by
H.K. Browne. Some foxing to plates, half blue calf, a little rubbed.
Jarndyce 30-108 1983 £85

DICKENS, CHARLES   Tale of Two Cities. Heritage Press,
1938. 8vo, light brown cloth with dark brown stamping, title in gilt on
spine, slipcase. Duschnes 240-70 1983 $22.50

DICKENS, CHARLES   To be Read at Dusk, and Other Stories.
George Redway, 1898. Half title, front. Orig. dark green cloth, v.g.
Jarndyce 30-133 1983 £35

DICKENS, CHARLES   The Uncommercial Traveller. Chapman &
Hall, 1861. Rebound in half calf, marbled boards, maroon label, v.g.
First edition. Jarndyce 30-116 1983 £75

DICKENS, CHARLES   The Uncommercial Traveller. Chapman &
Hall, 1861, Second edition. Half title. Orig. lilac cloth, spine
faded, v.g. Jarndyce 30-117 1983 £48

DICKENS, CHARLES   The Works. London: Chapman and Hall,
1861-62. Library edition. 22 vols. 8vo. Full polished light tan
calf, three-line gilt borders on sides with centre arms and other
decorations, edges gilt. Orig. illus. Traylen 94-263 1983 £650

DICKENS, CHARLES   Works. London, 1865-67. 17 works
in 12 vols. Cr. 8vo. Half crimson calf, gilt spines with morocco
labels, gilt. Illus. Traylen 94-262 1983 £120

DICKENS, CHARLES   Works. A Collection of first and
early editions. London, 1865-88. 15 vols. in 13. 8vo. Half
black morocco, gilt, gilt panelled spines, marbled edges. Traylen
94-261 1983 £295

DICKENS, CHARLES   The Works of Charles Dickens. Chapman &
Hall, (1871-1879). 21 vols., tall 8vo, illus. throughout by F.
Barnard, etc. Orig. green dec. cloth. Sl. varying in colour,
generally v.g. Jarndyce 30-126 1983 £110

DICKENS, CHARLES   Complete Works. London: Chapman &
Hall, (1876-1889). Library edition. 30 vols. Roy. 8vo. Half
red calf, gilt panelled spines with black morocco labels, gilt,
t.e.g. Traylen 94-264 1983 £1,100

DICKENS, CHARLES   Works. London: Chapman and Hall,
1890-91. 17 vols. 8vo. Half dark blue morocco, gilt spines,
t.e.g. Illus. Traylen 94-265 1983 £330

DICKENS, CHARLES   Complete Works. London, 1897-99.
Gadshill edition. 34 vols. 8vo. Orig. red cloth, gilt, t.e.g.
Orig. illus. Spines faded and one vol. slightly damaged. Traylen
94-266 1983 £110

DICKENS, CHARLES   Works. London, Chapman and Hall, 1906-
1908. 40 vols. Large thick 8vo. Profusely illus. with hundreds of
mounted plates from the originals, drawings, facs, ports, wrappers, etc.
Full blue crushed levant morocco, gilt frame on sides with large flower
& leaf pattern in corners, backs gilt, raised bands, gilt board edges,
inner dentelles, marbled endpapers, gt. Finely bound set. 750 sets
only. Fine. O'Neal 50-21 1983 $3,000

DICKENS, CHARLES   The Works. London: the Nonesuch
Press, 1937-38. 25 vols. Roy. 8vo. Orig. different coloured
buckram, morocco labels, gilt, t.e.g. More than 800 illus. One
orig. woodcut by Marcus Stone. Limited edition of 877 sets. Traylen
94-267 1983 £1,800

DICKENS, HENRY F.   Memories of My Father. London, 1928.
8vo, blue cloth, gilt, d/w. Illustrated. One of 250 copies signed by
the author. Bookplate. Very nice. Parata 27-213 1983 $75

DICKENS, HENRY F.   Memories of My Father. 1928. First
edition. Front. & illus. Half title, orig. blue cloth. Jarndyce 30-
160 1983 £10.50

DICKENS, MAMIE   Charles Dickens. Cassell, 1885.
Front. port. 16 pp ads. Orig. mustard dec. cloth, v.g. Jarndyce
31-595 1983 £24

DICKENS, MAMIE   Charles Dickens, by His Eldest Daughter.
1911. 2nd edition, 4 full-page colour illus. by C.E. Brook. Half
title. Orig. turquoise cloth. V.g. Jarndyce 30-161 1983 £12.50

DICKENS, MAMIE   My Father as I Recall Him. Roxburghe
Press, n.d. (1897). First edition, half title, fronts. and illus.
4 pp ads. Untrimmed. Orig. red cloth, blocked and lettered in gilt.
Fine. Jarndyce 31-596 1983 £26

A DICKENS Library, Exhibition Catalogue of the Sawyer Collection of the Works of Charles Dickens. N.P.: Privately printed, 1936. Small 4to. Boards. Illus. Oak Knoll 49-433 1983 $55

DICKERSON, E. N.   Joseph Henry and the Magnetic Telegraph Address at Princeton. NY, 1885. Wrs. Argosy 710-141 1983 $20

DICKERSON, OLIVER M.   American Colonial Government 1696-1765. Cleveland, 1912. Frontis. Illus. Uncut. Fine. Reese 19-192 1983 $65

DICKERSON, PHILIP   History of the Osage Nation. Pawhuska: (1906). First edition. Illus. Pictorial wrappers. Map on inside of back cover. Inscribed presentation copy. Covers a little soiled and worn, but sound. Bradley 66-635 1983 $185

DICKERSON, PHILIP   History of the Osage Nation. Pawhuska: (1906). First edition. Illus. Pictorial wrappers. Map on inside of back cover. Covers a little soiled and worn, but sound. Bradley 66-636 1983 $150

DICKES, WILLIAM   Studies from the Great Masters. Hamilton Adams, nd. Prose illus. by Rev. B.G. Johns, 18 illus. printed in colours & engr'd by Wm. Dickes. Pub's dark green morocco gilt, gilt dentelles, marbled eps., a.e.g. (corners of cvrs. sl. bruised & worn, top/bottom bkstrip worn with some cracking of joints at top & bottom, sl. foxing first & last pp.), contents v. clean & nice, rare. Hodgkins 27-363 1983 £150

DICKEY, J. M.   Christopher Columbus and His Monument Columbia. Chicago, Rand, McNally, 1892. First edition. 8vo, orig. white boards. Light dampstain on part of back cover; lightly dust-soiled. Morrill 290-99 1983 $20

DICKEY, JAMES   Collection of His Works. 43 vols. Limited signed eds. All in fine condition. Jenkins 155-307 1983 $600

DICKEY, JAMES   Jericho. Birmingham, (1974). First edition. Oblong folio, cloth, d.w. Autographed by Dickey. Fine. Argosy 714-233 1983 $100

DICKEY, JAMES   Veteran Birth, the Gadfly Poems, 1947-1949. (n.p.): Palaemon Press, (1978). 1st ed., limited to 200 numbered copies, signed by the author. Orig. marbled wrappers. Illus. by Robert Dance. Flawed only by over-inking in the second color. Mint. Jenkins 155-312 1983 $35

DICKINSON, EMILY   Further Poems of Emily Dickinson. Boston, 1929. First edition. One of 465 numbered copies. T.e.g. Title label slightly browned. Bookplate. Slipcase disintegrating, else fine. Jolliffe 26-155 1983 £165

DICKINSON, EMILY   Further Poems of Emily Dickinson. Boston: Little, Brown, 1929. 1st ed. Orig. cloth, dj. Spine gilt darkened, but fine copy in slightly chipped dj. Jenkins 155-1383 1983 $35

DICKINSON, EMILY   Letters. Boston, 1894. First edition. 2 vols. First issue, in the green binding, with Roberts Brothers imprint on spine. Argosy 714-235 1983 $250

DICKINSON, EMILY   Poems. Third Series. Boston, Roberts Bros., 1896. 12mo. Gilt-stamped grey cloth. 1st ed., 1st binding. Fine. O'Neal 50-111 1983 $200

DICKINSON, EMILY   Riddle Poems. Northampton: Gehenna Press, 1957. 12mo. Wood engraving. Of 250, 1/25 preferred copies bound in quarter-morocco and Japanese paper over boards, signed by both Esther and Leonard Baskin. Very fine copy. Bromer 25-213 1983 $950

DICKINSON, EMILY   Selected Poems. London, 1924. First edition of this selection. Slightly torn dust wrapper. Name on end-paper. Very nice. Rota 231-176 1983 £22.50

DICKINSON, EMILY   Unpublished Poems. Boston: 1935. First edition. Limited to 525 copies. Mint in torn glassine and soiled slip-case. Bromer 25-28 1983 $85

DICKINSON, JOHN   An Essay on the Constitutional Power of Great Britain over the Colonies in America. Philadelphia: William and Thomas Bradford, 1774. Disbound. First edition. Felcone 21-35 1983 $200

DICKINSON, JONATHAN   Familiar Letters to a Gentleman. Newark: John Woods, 1797. Full calf (very worn, rear cover detached). Very good. Felcone 19-11 1983 $50

DICKINSON, JONATHAN   The True Scripture-Doctrine Concerning Some Important Points of Christian Faith. Eliazbeth Town: Shepard Kollock, 1793. Full calf. Signature "Joseph Beach's Book." Excellent. Felcone 19-12 1983 $60

DICKINSON, RODOLPHUS   Elements of Geography, or, an Extensive Abridgement Thereof. Boston, 1813. 1st ed., 8vo, 2 folding maps, linen-backed, later cloth-backed boards, ex lib. Argosy 710-195 1983 $60

DICKINSON, S. N.   The Boston Almanac for the year 1841. Boston: Thomas Groom, (1840). 16mo. Orig. cloth. With embossed card inserted advertising Dickinson's printing firm, list of Groom's books, example of gold printing by Dickinson. Slightly shaken. Oak Knoll 49-159 1983 $20

DICKSON, D. J. H.   Observations on the Prevalence of Fever in various parts of the United Kingdom... Bristol: Barry & Son, 1819. First edition. 8vo. Modern quarter calf. Heath 48-497 1983 £100

DICKSON, MABEL   The Saga of the Sea Swallow. Innes, 1896. Illus. by J.D. Batten & Hilda Fairbairn. Frontis. & 3 full page illus. & 29 decor. illus. & initial letters. Dark green vertical ribbed cloth gilt, t.e.g., vg. Hodgkins 27-66 1983 £20

A DICTIONARY of Polite Literature; or, Fabulous History of the Heathen Gods and Illustrious Heroes. (London): Proprietors, Scatchered & Letterman; etc., 1804. 2 vols. 12mo. Illus. with engraved title-pages & engraved plates. Cont. calf, gilt spines, with marbled endpapers. Some foxing, slight stain at inner margin of the first few leaves of Vol. 1. Outer hinges a little worn. MacManus 278-1566 1983 $40

DIDION, JOAN   Run River. New York, (1973). 1st ed., 1st printing. Green cloth. In dj. Bradley 63-42 1983 $80

DIEHL, CHARLES   Constantinople. Paris, 1935. 115 illus. 2nd edition. 4to, wraps. Salloch 385-345 1983 $20

DIEHL, EDITH   Bookbinding: Its Background and Technique. N.Y., Rinehart, 1946. First edition. Profusely illus. with 91 plates and 189 figures. Gilt stamped black cloth. Very good. 2 vols. Houle 22-119 1983 $165

DIEHL, EDITH   Bookbinding. New York, 1946. 8vo, buckram. 2 vols. 92 plates in vol. I; 189 figures in vol. II. Orig. edition, slipcase. Duschnes 240-73 1983 $150

DIEHL, EDITH   Bookbinding. NY: 1946. Two octavo vols. First edition. Illus. with 91 full-page plates in vol. 1 and numerous line drawings in vol. 2. Pages 145, 148, 149, 152, 153, 156, 157, 160 double-printed. Pages 146, 147, 150, 151, 154, 155, 158, 159 not printed at all. Xerox of text for these pages is supplied. Otherwise, near fine copy in rubbed slip-case. Bromer 25-150 1983 $100

DIEMERBROECK, YSBRAND VAN   Opera Omnia Anatomica et Medica. Ultrajecti, 1685. Double-col., thick folio, full cont. calf, back gilt. Fine copy. Folding copperplate portrait by Edeling. Argosy 713-153 1983 $1000

DIETEL, FRIEDRICH   Das Bettnaessen. Munich: J. F. Lehmanns, 1929. Gach 94-316 1983 $27.50

DIETRICH, B.   Nord- und Mittelamerika, Die Arktis, in Natur, Kultur und Wirtschaft. Potsdam, 1933. 30 coloured plates, 463 text-figures, 4to, cloth. Wheldon 160-374 1983 £12

DIETRICH, WALDEMAR   The Clay Resources and the Ceramic In-
dustry of California. Sacramento: Calif. State Printing Office, 1928.
First edition. Illus. with maps (some folding) and the halftones.
Brown cloth stamped in black. Very good. Houle 22-180 1983 $30

DIETTRICH-KALKHO, FRANZ   Geschichte der Notenschrift. 1907.
3 illus., 18 tables, frontis. in color. 8vo, orig. wraps., uncut.
Salloch 387-309 1983 $45

DIETZ, AMBROSE   For our Boys, A Collection of Original
Literary Offerings... San Francisco: A.L. Bankcroft, 1879. Orig.
pictorial cloth. Jenkins 153-164 1983 $85

DIEULAFAIT, L.   Diamants et Pierres Precieuses. Paris,
1871. 150 illustrations, sm. 8vo, original cloth, trifle used,
stamp on title-page. Wheldon 160-1388 1983 £15

THE DIFFERENCE Between Keeping and Marriage. London: Printed for W.
Webb...1743. Folio, a good large copy, disbound. First edition.
Quaritch NS 7-34 1983 $375

DIGBY, JOAN   A Sound of Feathers. NY: Red Ozier
Press, 1982. Octavo. First edition. Full-page collage illus. by
John Digby. Limited to 130 copies signed by author and illustrator.
Mint in illus. wrappers. Bromer 25-285 1983 $55

DIGGES, DUDLEY   An answer to a printed, intituled
Observations upon Some of His Majesties Late Answers and Expresses.
Oxford: Leonard Lichfield, 1642. A London counterfeit of the true
Oxford edition. Small 4to. Disbound. Slight stain to upper corners.
Ximenes 63-99 1983 $50

DIGGES, LEONARD   A Geometrical Practical Treatize
named Pantometria... London: Abell Jeffes, 1591. Second, and
enlarged edition. Errata leaf. With woodcut on title, arms of
Nicholas Bacon (dedicatee) on verso of title, and of Digges on
verso of p. 195. Numerous woodcut illus. and diagrams in the text.
Folio. 19th-century calf. With exlibris of Robert Napier and bookplate of Lord Napier of Merchiston. Lacking first blank. Kraus
164-65 1983 $2,400

DILKE, CHARLES WENTWORTH   Greater Britain. New York, 1869.
Illus., maps. Cloth (spine ends rubbed). Front endsheet wanting.
First American edition. Felcone 22-46 1983 $35

DILL, SAMUEL   Roman Society in the Last Century of
the Western Empire. London, 1905. 8vo, cloth. Salloch 385-222 1983
$45

DILLIARD, MAUD ESTHER   Old Dutch Houses of Brooklyn. New
York, 1945. First edition. Maps and illustrations from old prints
and photographs. 8vo. Morrill 290-350 1983 $20

DILLON, GEORGE   Boy in the Wind. New York, 1927.
8vo. Cloth, boards. Paper label on spine chipped, else only very
good. In Our Time 156-201 1983 $20

DILLON, GEORGE   The Flowering Stone. New York, 1931.
Cloth. From the library of Alexander Laing, signed by same with
note on front fly. Fine copy. In Our Time 156-202 1983 $20

DILLON, VISCOUNT   An Almain Armourer's Album. London,
1905. 34 coloured plates (1 double page, 1 folding), 1 other plate,
illus., folio. Orig. parchment, gilt. Very slightly worn and soiled.
T.e.g. Marbled endpapers (repaired). Some very slight foxing of
preliminaries. Good. Edwards 1042-323 1983 £300

DILWORTH, THOMAS   The Schoolmasters Assistant. NY: W.
Durell, 1792. The latest edition. Woodcut port. 12mo, disbound.
Argosy 716-496 1983 $35

DILWORTH, THOMAS   The Schoolmaster's Assistant. Brooklyn:
T. Kirk for Himself & S. Wood, 1811. 12mo, cont. mottled calf (worn);
foxed. Argosy 716-373 1983 $45

DIMOCK, A. W.   The Book of the Tarpon. New York,
1911. 1st ed. Illus. with photographs by Julian Dimock. 8vo.
Morrill 286-129 1983 $22.50

DIMSDALE, THOMAS J.   The Vigilantes of Montana. Virginia
City, 1882. Wraps., very good. Reese 19-193 1983 $150

DIMSDALE, THOMAS J.   The Vigilantes of Montana, or Popular
Justice in the Rocky Mountains. Butte, Mont., (n.d. but ca. 1900).
Pictorial wraps. Felcone 22-47 1983 $35

DINESEN, ISAK   Out of Africa. New York: Random
House, (1938). 1st ed. Orig. cloth-backed boards, gilt. Fine copy
in nice dj. Jenkins 155-318 1983 $60

DINESEN, ISAK   Out of Africa. NY, (1938). Very good
in slightly frayed, very good dustwrapper with few tiny chips. Quill
& Brush 54-367 1983 $40

DINESEN, ISAK   Seven Gothic Tales. New York:
Harrison Smith and Robert Haas, 1934. First American edition.
8vo. Orig. cloth and boards, dust jacket. Very fine copy.
Jaffe 1-81 1983 $150

DINESEN, ISAK   Seven Gothic Tales. New York: Smith
& Haas, 1934. 1st ed. Orig. 3/4 red cloth, gilt. Uncommon. Fine
fresh copy in lightly rubbed dj. Jenkins 155-319 1983 $85

DINESEN, ISAK   Winter's Tales. (New York:) Random
House, (1942). 1st ed. Orig. cloth. Fine in near perfect dj.
Jenkins 155-320 1983 $22.50

DIONIS, PIERRE   Cours d'Operations de Chirurgie,
Demontrees au Jardin Royale. Freres t'Serstevens and Antoine
Claudinot, Brussels, 1708. 8vo, with 61 engravings including a view
of a lecture theatre and 9 full-page plates, the rest printed in the
text; title slightly dust soiled but a very good copy in cont. unlettered panelled calf, slightly rubbed and head of spine frayed.
Quaritch NS 5-33 1983 $950

THE DIONNE Quintuplets, Growing Up. London: Putnam & Co., 1935.
Oblong. 21 x 28cm. 64 pages of photographs. Illustrated paper
over boards. Very good. McGahern 53-44 1983 $25

DIONYSIUS LONGINUS   Rhetoris Praestantissimi Liber de
Grandi Loquentia sive sublimi decendi genere Latine Redditus... G.L.
Oxonii, Gulielmi Webb, (1638). 8vo, cont. sheep rebacked, second
edition, complete with folding table. Ravenstree 95-41 1983 $52.50

DIOPHANTOS OF ALEXANDRIA   Arithmeticorum Libri Sex, et de numeris
multangulis liber unus. Paris: Sebastian Cramoisy, 1621. Large
engraved printer's device on title, title printed in black and red.
Woodcut diagrams in text (title mounted on stub, innermost edges
of next 5 leaves guarded with tissue). Folio. Modern vellum. Cont.
inscription on lower margin of title recording the donation of the
book by the dedicatee, Antoine-Favre, to the library of the Jesuit
College at Chambery, 1621. 1st edit. Kraus 164-66 1983 $4,500

DI PESO, CHARLES C.   Casas Grandes. Flagstaff: Northland
Press, 1974. 8 vols. Large 4to. Cloth. Ars Libri 34-210 1983
$250

DIPROSE, JOHN   Diprose's book of the stage and the
players. London: Diprose and Bateman, n.d. (1877). 12mo, original
white pictorial boards (slight rubbing). 1st ed. In excellent
condition. Ximenes 64-171 1983 $75

DIRAC, PAUL ADRIEN MAURICE   The Principles of Quantum Mechanics.
Oxford: University Press, 1930. Small 4to. Orig. buckram. Near
fine copy. Zeitlin 264-121 1983 $160

DIRECTIONS for Using the Hall's Rifle. Harpers-Ferry, Va.,
Gallaher and Daugherty, 1829. Stitched. Uncut. A very fine copy.
Felcone 21-50 1983 $600

DIRECTORY of the Marine Interests of the Great Lakes. Detroit: F.L.
Polk & Co., 1884. Orig. cloth, gilt. Some wear. Fine. Jenkins 152-
134 1983 $250

A DISCOURSE of the Laws Relating to Pirates and Piracies. London,
1726. 8vo. 1st & only ed. Attractively printed, title page in
double-ruled border & dusty, nicely rebound in 3/4 mottled calf over
marbled boards, bit rubbed, spine with brown morocco label, double
gilt-ruled & lettered, else clean. Boswell 7-132 1983 $500

DISCURSO del cometa del Ano de 1680. (Madrid), n.d. Woodcut tailpiece. Ornamental initial. Folio. Sewn. From the library of Sir Thomas Phillipps. Kraus 164-39 1983 $350

DISNEY, WALT   Ave Maria: An Interpretation from... "Fantasia". (NY: 1940). Octavo. First edition. Color and b&w reproductions of Disney illus. Fine with slightly chipped dust wrapper. Bromer 25-342 1983 $50

DISNEY, WALT   Dance of the Hours from..."Fantasia". NY: Harper (1940). Octavo. First edition. Numerous b&w and full-color illus. Very light stamp to title-page, else extremely fine in cloth-backed pictorial boards and slightly chipped dust wrapper. Bromer 25-343 1983 $75

DISNEY, WALT   Pastoral, from..."Fantasia". NY: Harper, (1940). Octavo. First edition. Illus. throughout in b&w and color. Cloth-backed pictorial boards lightly rubbed at extremities, else very fine with slightly chipped dust wrapper. Bromer 25-344 1983 $65

DISOBEDIENCE. A Novel. Printed for William Lane, at the Minerva Press, 1797. 1st ed., 4 vols, 12mo, contemporary half calf, marbled sides; all half-titles, and advertisements for Minerva publications at end of each volume. Scarce. Hill 165-28 1983 £325

DISPENSATORIUM Pro Pharmacopoeis Viennensibus in Austria. 1570. Berlin, 1938. 8vo. Cloth. Gurney JJ-102 1983 £20

DISRAELI, BENJAMIN   Anti-Coningsby. T.C. Newby, 1844. First edition, 2 vols. Rebound in green moire-patterned cloth, labels. Jarndyce 30-364 1983 £120

DISRAELI, BENJAMIN   Contarini Fleming & Alroy. London: Henry Colburn, 1846. "Second edition." 3 vols. Frontispiece port. in vol. 1. Half-calf with marbled boards. Presentation copy inscribed on the title-page "Wm(?) Milner Gibson with the kind regards of the author." Very outer edge of title-page inscription cut away when rebound. Spines slightly faded and rubbed. Very good. MacManus 278-1568 1983 $450

DISRAELI, BENJAMIN   Endymion. Longmans, Green, 1880. First edition. 3 vols. Half titles, full crushed green morocco, by Riviere, gilt dentelles, 1880. A.e.g., very sl. rubbing of hinges, v.g. Signed presentation inscription to his publisher: 'T. Norton Longman Esqr. With the very kind regards of Beaconsfield. Nov 22, 80'. Jarndyce 31-671 1983 £240

DISRAELI, BENJAMIN   Endymion. London: Longman, 1880. 1st ed., 8vo, 3 vols., original red cloth, silver-lettered spines. Half-titles, advertisement leaf. Waterspot on one front cover, another cover rubbed, else a very good copy. Trebizond 18-27 1983 $145

DISRAELI, BENJAMIN   Endymion. London, 1880. First edition. 3 vols. 8vo. Orig. red cloth, spines lettered in silver. 2 pp. of ads. in vols. 3. Slightly faded. Traylen 94-274 1983 £48

DISRAELI, BENJAMIN   Endymion. Longmans, 1880. First edition. 3 vols., half titles, orig. red cloth, a little dulled, v.g. Jarndyce 30-363 1983 £48

DISRAELI, BENJAMIN   Endymion. Longmans, Green, and Co, 1880. First edition, 3 vols. 8vo, has all 3 half-titles but lacks final blank leaf in vol. II, and final advert. leaf in vol. III. Cont. calf-backed boards, t.e.g. Hannas 69-42 1983 £20

DISRAELI, BENJAMIN   Endymion. New York: D. Appleton, 1881. First American edition, orig. green cloth, v.g. Jarndyce 31-672 1983 £20

DISRAELI, BENJAMIN   Endymion. Ch., 1881. Spine edges slightly frayed, corners slightly worn, cover slightly discolored, good or better copy. Quill & Brush 54-368 1983 $35

DISRAELI, BENJAMIN   The Letters of Disraeli to Lady Chesterfield & Lady Bradford. New York, D. Appleton, 1929. 2 vols. 8vo, orig. cloth, in slightly worn dust jackets. Ravenstree 94-35 1983 $47.50

DISRAELI, BENJAMIN   The Letters of Runnymede. London: John Macrone, 1836. First complete edition, 8vo, orig. cloth, spine gilt, half-title and advertisement leaf preceding title, advertisements. Fine early bookplate. A fine copy of this uncommon title. Trebizond 18-188 1983 $210

DISRAELI, BENJAMIN   Lord George Bentinck. London: Colburn & Co., 1852. First edition. Orig. cloth. Presentation copy inscribed: "The Marchioness of Londonderry, from her friend and servant the author." A few pages carelessly opened. Edges slightly worn. Very good. MacManus 278-1572 1983 $450

DISRAELI, BENJAMIN   Lord George Bentinck: a Political Biography. London: Colburn, 1852. First edition, 8vo, orig. cloth, spine gilt, uncut copy. Advertisements. A fine copy. Trebizond 18-189 1983 $250

DISRAELI, BENJAMIN   Lord George Bentinck. London, Colburn, 1852. 8vo, orig. cloth, worn, shaken, with all ads as called for in Sadlier's bibliography. First edition. Ravenstree 94-36 1983 $115

DISRAELI, BENJAMIN   Lothair. London: Longman, 1870. 1st ed., 8vo, 3 vols., original cloth, spines gilt. Half-titles, advertisements. Some very light foxing, but a very good copy. Trebizond 18-28 1983 $175

DISRAELI, BENJAMIN   Lothair. Longmans, Green & Co., 1870. First edition, 3 vols., half titles, 32 pp ads. vol. I; 2 pp ads vol. II; 2 pp ads vol. III. Orig. green cloth, a little rubbed. Jarndyce 30-361 1983 £35

DISRAELI, BENJAMIN   Lothair. London: Longmans, 1870. First edition. 3 vols. Orig. cloth. Extremities of spine worn. Inner hinges cracked. Good. MacManus 278-1569 1983 $50

DISRAELI, BENJAMIN   Lothair. London, 1870. Second edition. 3 vols. 12mo. Orig. green ribbed cloth, gilt. Half-titles. 32 pp. publisher's cat. at end of vol. 1, 2 pp. at end of vol. 2, 4 pp. at end of vol. 3. Traylen 94-275 1983 £28

DISRAELI, BENJAMIN   The Novels and Tales. London, 1870. Collected edition. 2 vols. 8vo. Half blue morocco, gilt, marbled edges. Engraved portrait. Traylen 94-272 1983 £165

DISRAELI, BENJAMIN   The Novels and Tales. London, 1926. The Bradenham edition. 12 vols. Roy. 8vo. Orig. black buckram, gilt, t.e.g., others uncut. Traylen 94-273 1983 £130

DISRAELI, BENJAMIN   The Speech of Mr. Disraeli, in the House of Commons, on Friday, 15th May, 1846. First edition, stabbed pamphlet, as issued, first and last pages dusted. Jarndyce 31-670 1983 £48

DISRAELI, BENJAMIN   Sybil. Henry Colburn, 1845. First edition, 3 vols. Half dark blue calf, red labels, boards a little rubbed, otherwise v.g. Jarndyce 30-356 1983 £120

DISRAELI, BENJAMIN   Sybil; or, The Two Nations. Henry Colburn, 1845. First edition. 3 vols. Half titles, vols. I & II; 2 pps. ads. vol. III. Half black calf, rubbed but sound. Jarndyce 31-669 1983 £70

DISRAELI, BENJAMIN   Tancred: or, the New Crusade. London: Henry Colburn, 1847. First edition, 8vo, 3 vols., original cloth-backed boards and paper labels. Advertisements, uncut copy. Binding labels worn, spot on one cover; a good copy. Trebizond 18-29 1983 $275

DISRAELI, BENJAMIN   Tancred. Henry Colburn, 1847. First edition, 3 vols. Calf, gilt borders and spines, red and blue labels by Riviere; a little rubbing to heads and tails, otherwise very good. Jarndyce 30-359 1983 £48

DISRAELI, BENJAMIN   Vindication of the English Constitution in a Letter to a Noble and Learned Lord. London, Saunders and Otley, 1835. 8vo, later green half morocco gilt, top edge, others uncut, by Riviere. Spine faded, bookplate, hinges cracked, else fine. Ravenstree 94-37 1983 $375

DISRAELI, BENJAMIN   Vivian Grey. London: Henry Colburn, 1826-27. 5 vols., 1st ed. of vols. 3-5, 2nd. ed. of Vols. I and 2. Original boards and paper labels. Entirely uncut throughout. Half-titles, advertisements. Spine of final volume partly chipped, front cover loose; minor chipping of some labels; a very clean copy. Very scarce in this original condition. Trebizond 18-30 1983 $475

DISRAELI, BENJAMIN   Vivian Grey. Henry Colburn, 1826-7. 5 vols., vols. I & II, new edition; vols. III, IV & V, first edition. Half calf, rebacked, black and red labels. A good set. Jarndyce 30-355 1983 £75

DISRAELI, BENJAMIN   The Young Duke. London: Henry Colburn & Richard Bentley, 1831. First edition. 3 vols. Orig. paper boards with paper labels on spines. Michael Sadleir's copy, with his small bookplate, and another's larger armorial bookplate, on the front end-sheets; cont. owner's signature on front flyleaf of Vol. 1, shelf no. on spine of Vol. I. Extremities of boards slightly worn. In a folding cloth box. Very fine. MacManus 278-1570 1983 $1,250

D'ISRAELI, ISAAC   The Curiosities of Literature. Newry: Printed by Alexander Wilkinson, 1817. 8vo, recent boards, a very good copy. Reprint of volume one of the fifth edition, without the author's name. Fenning 60-91 1983 £18.50

D'ISRAELI, ISAAC   Miscellanies; or, literary recreations. London: Cadell and Davies, 1796. First edition. 8vo. Old half calf and marbled boards. Presentation copy, inscribed on the title page by the author to James Anderson. Very good copy. Ximenes 63-237 1983 $275

D'ISRAELI, ISAAC   Narrative poems. London: printed for John Murray, 1803. First edition. 4to. Orig. printed boards. Very worn. Internally nice, uncut. A few pencilled annotations, in one case adding a couplet. Ximenes 63-402 1983 $150

DISARAELI, ISAAC   Quarrels of Authors. London, 1814. 8vo. Leather, boards. 3 vols. A very good-fine set. In Our Time 156-203 1983 $125

THE DISTINGUISHED Collection of Western Americana Formed by the late Herbert S. Auerbach. New York, 25-26 October 1948. 2 vols., wrappers, good. Dawson 470-227 1983 $20

DISTURNELL, JOHN   Great Lakes. New York: J. Disturnell, 1863. Frontis and illus. Orig. pictorial wrappers. Minor chipping. Lacking the map. Revised ed. Jenkins 153-763 1983 $50

DISTURNELL, JOHN   The New York State Guide. Albany, Disturnell, 1842. 1st ed. Large folding map. 16mo. Morrill 286-661 1983 $47.50

DITMAR, RUDOLF   Die Synthese des Kautschuks... Dresden und Leipzig: Steinkopff, 1912. 8vo. Cont. quarter green morocco with gilt. Frontis. portrait. A fine copy. Zeitlin 264-122 1983 $60

DIX, HENRY T.   The New Chancery Practice. Dublin: King, 1867. First edition, interleaved throughout with unused blanks, 8vo, cont. half calf, a very good copy. Fenning 62-95 1983 £18.50

DIX, JOHN A.   Speech of...President of the Mississippi and Missouri Railroad Co... New York, 1856. Printed wraps., fine. Reese 19-292 1983 $125

DIX, JOHN A.   Speeches and Occasional Addresses. NY, 1864. 2 vols., port., facs. letter. Thick 8vo, stipple cloth, ex lib. Argosy 716-347 1983 $40

DIX, MORGAN   A History of the Parish of Trinity Church in the City of New York. NY, 1898-1901. Letterpress edition of 750 copies; later expanded to 6 vols. 2 vols. Fine ports. & illus. Tall 8vo, g.t., (small stain on one vol.). Argosy 716-376 1983 $40

DIXIE, FLORENCE   Redeemed in Blood. London: Henry & Co., 1889. First edition. 3 vols. in one. Orig. publisher's remainder binding. Front inner hinge cracked. Spine faded. Covers a little rubbed. MacManus 278-1574 1983 $35

DIXON, CAMPBELL   This Way To Paradise. London: Chatto & Windus, 1930. First edition. 8vo. Orig. cloth. Dust jacket. Fine copy. Jaffe 1-190 1983 $100

DIXON, H.   Robert Blake Admiral and General at Sea. London, 1852. 8vo. Orig. cloth. Engraved frontis. portrait. Publishers ads. at end and on endpapers. Rebacked. Orig. spine (faded) laid down. Bookplate. Good. Edwards 1042-8 1983 £25

DIXON, H.   Robert Black Admiral and General at Sea. London, 1855. 8vo, orig. cloth. Mounted photographic portrait frontis. 9 mounted portrait photographic plates. 16 pp. ads. Orig. blue decorated cloth, gilt. Very slightly worn. A.E.G. Some very slight foxing. Good. Edwards 1042-9 1983 £15

DIXON, RICHARD WATSON   The Last Poems of... London: Henry Frowde, 1905. First edition. Preface by M.E. Coleridge. Frontispiece portrait. Orig. blue cloth. Spine edges slightly worn. Near-fine. MacManus 278-1575 1983 $45

DIXON, SARAH   Poems on several occasions. Canterbury: J. Abree, 1740. 8vo. Cont. calf. First edition. A bit worn. A few stains, but a very good copy. Very scarce. Ximenes 63-360 1983 $600

DIXON, THOMAS   The Traitor, a Story of the Fall of the Invisible Empire. New York: Doubleday, 1907. Frontis. 1st ed. Orig. presentation binding of 3/4 green morocco, gilt. Fine copy inscribed by author and signed in full. Jenkins 155-323 1983 $45

DIXON, WILLIAM HEPWORTH   New America. London, 1867. 2 vols. Plates. Cloth. Seventh edition. Felcone 22-48 1983 $35

DIXON, WILLIAM HEPWORTH   William Penn, an Historical Biography. Chapman & Hall, 1851. First edition, with a portrait, 8vo, orig. cloth. Fenning 61-345 1983 £45

DIXSON, ZELLA ALLEN   Concerning Bookplates; A Handbook for Collectors. Chicago: 1903. Octavo. First edition. Several b&w reproductions of bookplates. Fine. T.e.g. Bromer 25-159 1983 $85

DOANE, GILBERT H.   About Collecting Bookplates. N.p. 1941. 12mo, linen-backed decorated bds., paper label, slipcase. One of 360 copies with 16 plates in collotype. Perata 27-17 1983 $60

DOANE, GUSTAVUS C.   Report upon the so-called Yellowstone Expedition of 1870. (Wash.), 1873. 8vo, new buckram, mod. printed title inserted. Argosy 716-642 1983 $100

DOBBS, ARTHUR   An essay on the trade and improvement of Ireland. (with:) An essay on the trade of Ireland. Part II. Dublin: printed by A. Rhames, for J. Smith and W. Bruce, 1729 and 1731. 2 vols. in one. First edition of both parts. 8vo. Half calf. Very scarce. Ximenes 63-596 1983 $600

DOBELL, BERTRAM   Catalogue of Books printed for private circulation. London: privately printed, 1906. 8vo. Cloth. Paper spine label. Label chipped. Oak Knoll 49-161 1983 $20

DOBELL, BERTRAM   The Laureate of Pessimism, a Sketch of the Life and Character of James Thomson. London: Privately published, 1910. First edition. 8vo. Cloth. Endpapers are yellowed, else a fine unopened copy. Oak Knoll 48-146 1983 $30

DOBELL, BERTRAM   Rosemary and Pansies. 1901. 22 cm. Orig. buckram-backed boards, paper label on spine. Very good; label chipped and binding darkening. First edition, one of 75 copies printed by Dobell for private circulation. Inscribed by the author to Sir Arthur Quiller-Couch. Laid in is Dobell's presentation A.L.S. (a bit creased & discolored). Grunder 7-13 $65

DOBELL, BERTRAM   Rosemary and Pansies. London: Published by the author, 1904. First edition. Orig. cloth. Presentation copy, inscribed on the front flyleaf to "Mrs. Bradlaugh Bonner with the Author's compts. & respects Mar. 15, 1904." With an ALS, 1 page, 8vo. from the author to Mrs. Bonner, laid in. Covers faded and slightly soiled. MacManus 278-1577 1983 $35

DOBELL, MRS. HORACE   Dark Pages. Remington, 1882. First edition, 3 vols., 3 vols. bound as one. Orig. red remainder cloth, blocked in black, lettered in gilt, v.g. Jarndyce 30-365 1983 £38

DOBIE, FRANK J.   John C. Duval: First Texas Man of Letters. Dallas, Southwest Review, 1939. Illus. by Tom Lee. Brown cloth over tan, stamped in gilt and brown (stain on lower part of upper cover) else very good. One of 1,000 copies. This copy signed by the author of half title page. Houle 22-1045 1983 $95

DOBIE, JAMES FRANK   The Alamo's Immortalization of Words Christmas Remembrance. 1942. Paperwraps, signed inscription from Dobie, edges slightly frayed, else very good. Also contains Bertha Dobie's Old ALF. Quill & Brush 54-369 1983 $100

DOBIE, JAMES FRANK   Apache Gold & Yakui Silver. Boston: Little, Brown, 1929. 1st ed., illus. by Tom Lea, including many plates in color. The special "Sierra Madre" edition, limited to 265 numbered copies, signed by author and Lea. S. Dykes. Rare. Extremities of boards shelfworn, else a fine copy in a custom made slipcase. Jenkins 151-65 1983 $650

DOBIE, JAMES FRANK   Bob More, Man and Bird Man. Dallas: Encino Press, 1965. Limited to 550 numbered copies. Near mint slipcase. Jenkins 153-565 1983 $125

DOBIE, JAMES FRANK   A Collection of Stray Mavericks Caught, Roped, and Branded by Members of the "Big Corral"... Austin, Univ. of Texas, 1940. Mimeographed. Orig. stiff printed wrappers. Quite scarce. Fine copy. Jenkins 153-764 1983 $225

DOBIE, JAMES FRANK   Coronado's Children. Dallas: Neiman-Marcus, 1980. One of 300 copies; printed by the Arion Press. Printed in several colors including gold initials. Mexican bark paper sides. Pigskin spine, in slipcase. Folding map. Dawson 471-68 1983 $700

DOBIE, JAMES FRANK   Coronado's Children: Tales of Lost Mines & Buried Treasures of the Southwest. Dallas: Neiman-Marcus, 1980. Limited edition (300 copies printed). Folding colored map of Southwest. Portrait of Dobie (by Hoyem). Text-charts coloured. Title and chapter headings in red, initial gold letters. Folio, orig. tan goatskin over handmade Mexican bark paper. Very fine. Jenkins 152-89 1983 $700

DOBIE, JAMES FRANK   Do Rattlesnakes Swallow Their Young? Austin, 1946. Offprint from the Texas Folklore Society. Presentation copy from Dobie. Jenkins 152-802 1983 $85

DOBIE, JAMES FRANK   Guide to Life and Literature of the Southwest... Dallas: Special printing for Univ. Press and Southern Methodist Univ., 1943. Signed by Dobie on title page. Cloth. Dawson 470-90 1983 $25

DOBIE, JAMES FRANK   The Longhorns. Boston, 1941. Illus. First edition. Fine copy. Jenkins 153-168 1983 $50

DOBIE, W. HENRY   Recollections of Charles Kingsley. Arbroath: T. Buncle & Co., (1936). Illus. Orig. blue wraps. Jarndyce 30-1042 1983 £10.50

DOBLIN, ALFRED   Alexanderplatz Berlin. New York: The Viking Press, 1931. Two vols. Cloth. First edition in English. Fine copies in dust jackets (spines a trifle darkened, two tiny chips at corners), in slightly soiled slipcase. Reese 20-319 1983 $60

DOBLIN, ALFRED   Men Without Mercy. London, 1937. First English edition. Very nice. Rota 231-178 1983 £15

DOBROWOLSKI, TADEUSZ   Zit Stwosz: Oltarz Krakowski. Warszawa: Auriga/Oficyna Wydawnicza, 1964. 174 gravure and tipped-in color plates. Small folio. Cloth. Dust jacket. Ars Libri 32-649 1983 $100

DOBSON, AUSTIN   At the Sign of the Lyre. London, 1885. 8vo, new 1/2 crushed red levant, g.t. Ltd. first edition. Large paper edition. One of only 75 numbered and signed copies. Fine. Argosy 714-240 1983 $65

DOBSON, AUSTIN   At the Sign of the Lyre. New York, 1885. 8vo. Cloth. Initials of former owner on inside fly, else a fine copy. In Our Time 156-204 1983 $35

DOBSON, AUSTIN   At the Sign of the Lyre. London: Kegan Paul, 1890. 8vo, original cloth gilt; uncut. Frontis. Trebizond 18-31 1983 $25

DOBSON, AUSTIN   The Ballad of Beau Brocade and Other Poems. London: Kegan, Paul, 1892. First edition. Illus. by Hugh Thomson. Orig. pictorial cloth. Dust jacket. Fine. MacManus 278-1578 1983 $250

DOBSON, AUSTIN   Eighteenth Century Vignettes. NY, 1892. One of 250 numbered copies. Edges rubbed, cover soiled, very good with water-colors in margins added by owner. Quill & Brush 54-370 1983 $35

DOBSON, AUSTIN   Eighteenth Century Vignettes. Chatto & Windux, 1892. First edition, front. 1 p ads. Orig. dark blue cloth, t.e.g., v.g. Jarndyce 31-673 1983 £10.50

DOBSON, AUSTIN   Old English Songs. London: Macmillan & Co., 1894. First edition. Illus. by H. Thomson. Intro. by A. Dobson. Orig. pictorial cloth. Bookplates. Fine. MacManus 280-5226 1983 $20

DOBSON, AUSTIN   Old Kensington Place & Other Papers. London: Chatto & Windus, 1910. First edition. Orig. cloth. Presentation copy inscribed: "For Sir Henry Craik fr. Austin Dobson. 6:x:10." With Craik's bookplate. Edges very slightly worn. Very good. MacManus 278-1580 1983 $50

DOBSON, AUSTIN   Poems On Several Occasions. N.Y.: Dodd, Mead & Co., 1895. New edition (2nd) revised and enlarged. 2 vols. Illus. with etchings including a frontispiece portrait. Orig. Cloth-backed grey boards with decorated endpapers. One of 50 copies printed on Japan paper, the plates in two states, one set signed by the artist, and a frontis. port. of Dobson signed by both the artist (Wm. Strang), and the author himself. Spines and covers slightly worn, soiled and a trifle fox. Good. MacManus 278-1581 1983 $85

DOBSON, AUSTIN   Proverbs in Porcelain and Other Verses. London: Henry S. King, 1877. First edition. Orig. cloth. Inner hinges cracking, foxed. Good. MacManus 278-1582 1983 $35

DOBSON, AUSTIN   Proverbs in Porcelain, and Other Verse. Henry S. King, 1877. First edition, half title, 32 pp ads. Orig. brown cloth, v.g. Jarndyce 30-688 1983 £10.50

DOBSON, AUSTIN   Side-Walk Studies. London: Chatto & Windus, 1902. First edition. Presentation copy inscribed: "For Sir Henry Craik with the best regards of Austin Dobson. 4:x:1902." Orig. cloth. With Craik's bookplate. Edges slightly worn. Endpapers slightly browned. Good. MacManus 278-1584 1983 $50

DOBSON, AUSTIN   Side-Walk Studies. London: Chatto & Windus, 1902. First edition. Orig. cloth. Presentation copy inscribed: "H.(?) W. Lucy with the kind regards of Austin Dobson. 6:x:1902." Endpapers slightly browned. Edges slightly worn. Very good. MacManus 278-1583 1983 $50

DOBSON, AUSTIN   Story of Rosina and Other Verses. London, Kegan, 1895. First edition, 4to, frontis. and 49 full page plates printed on Japan vellum, by Hugh Thompson. One of 250 numbered copies printed on large paper. Very good. Houle 21-296 1983 $95

DOBSON, AUSTIN   The Story of Rosina and other Verses. N.Y.: Dodd, Mead & Co., 1895. First American edition. Illus. by H. Thomson. Orig. gilt-decorated green cloth. Fine. MacManus 280-5227 1983 $25

DOBSON, AUSTIN   The Story of Rosina and other Verse. London: Kegan Paul, Trench, Turbner & Co., 1895. First edition. Illus. by H. Thomson. Orig. pictorial cloth. Endpapers a little foxed. Fine. MacManus 280-5230 1983 $25

DOBSON, SUSANNAH   The Life of Petrarch. Printed for the author, 1776. 2 vols., 8vo, frontis. in vol. 1, cont. calf. Slight wear at top of spine. Bickersteth 77-23 1983 £34

DOBSON, SUSANNAH   The Life of Petrarch. Printed for the author, 1776. With a frontis. (engraved by Isaac Taylor), 2 vols. 8vo, orig. unlettered calf, bindings worn but sound, fine internally. Fenning 62-96 1983 £16.50

DOBYNS, WINIFRED S.   California Gardens. NY, 1931. 4to, (backstrip faded). 208 photos. Illus. Argosy 716-31 1983 $40

DOCKHAM, C. AUGUSTINE   A Directory of the City of Lawrence... Lawrence, 1855. 12mo. Ads. Few binding stains. Morrill 289-419 1983 $25

DOCTOROW, E. L.   Loon Lake. New York, 1980. 8vo, wraps. Uncorrected proof copy. Fine. In Our Time 156-205 1983 $100

DOCTOROW, E. L.   Loon Lake. New York, (1980). First ed. Printed red wrappers. Advance uncorrected proofs. Publisher's dated announcement slip affixed to front wrapper, publicity release and publisher's letter laid in. Bradley 65-56 1983 $110

DOCUMENTS Relating to the Organization of the Illinois Central Rail-Road Company.   New York: Geo. Scott Rue, 1852. Second edition. Printed wrappers. Wrappers soiled and chipped. Pencil marks and notes in text. Bradley 66-557 1983 $85

DOCUMENTS Relative to Central American Affairs... Washington, 1856. Map. 8vo. Morrill 286-130 1983 $30

DODD, ALFRED   The Ballad of the Iron Cross. London: Erskine MacDonald, (1918). First edition. Orig. boards. Dust jacket (defective). Presentation copy to Arthur Conan Doyle inscribed: "Sir Arthur Conan Doyle with the author's good wishes. Alfred Dodd 31.10.18." Near-fine. MacManus 278-1634 1983 $135

DODD, EDWARD   The Ring of Fire. New York: Dodd, Mead & Company, 1967. Prof. illus. Small folio. Cloth. Dust jacket. Ars Libri 34-796 1983 $85

DODD, J.   Journal of a Blockaded Resident in North Formosa. Hong Kong: For Private Circulation, 1888. Presentation copy. Half calf, worn. 8vo. Good. Edwards 1044-190 1983 £150

DODD, JAMES WILLIAM   Ballads of archery, sonnets, etc. London: for R.H. Evans, etc., 1818. First edition. 8vo. Cont. green straight-grained morocco, gilt, spine gilt with lyre tools, a.e.g. 33 pages of engraved music. From the library of Joseph Haslewood, with his book-label and cost code. A fine copy. Ximenes 63-555 1983 $125

DODD, WILLIAM   An epistle to a lady... London: printed for the author, and sold by Mr. Dodsley, etc., 1753. 4to. Modern quarter morocco. First edition. With a couple of library blindstamps. Ximenes 63-361 1983 $175

DODD, WILLIAM   Thoughts in Prison, in Five Parts. Boston: Robert Hodge, n.d. (1783). First American edition, 4to, cont. sheep, morocco label, Some foxing, but a very good copy. Trebizond 18-32 1983 $180

DODDERIDGE, JOHN   The History of the Ancient and Moderne Estate of the Principality of Wales... London, 1630. 8vo. Nicely rebound in 3/4 calf over marbled boards, spine gilt-lettered, lightish dampstaining throughout, occasional embrowning, top margins of title page & 2 other leaves repaired, not affecting text, foremargins cut bit close, affecting few letters of sidenotes-not legibility-occasional worming. Boswell 7-59 1983 $300

DODDRIDGE, JOSEPH   Notes on the Settlement and Indian Wars, of the Western Parts of Virginia & Pennsylvania, from the Year 1763 until the Year 1783 Inclusive. Wellsburgh, Va.: Printed at the Office of the Gazette, for the author, 1824. Orig. mottled calf. Some slight browning and staining. The Deering copy, enclosed in a full morocco, gilt, solander case. First edition. Reese 18-574 1983 $400

DODGE, J. R.   West Virginia: Its Farms and Forests, Mines and Oil-Wells. Philadelphia, 1865. 1st ed. Small 8vo. Morrill 286-508 1983 $50

DODGE, J. W.   A Wonderful City, Leading all Others in Washington, Oregon, Montana, Idaho and British Columbia. Seattle, 1890. Illus. Orig. printed wraps. First edition. Small embossed library stamp on title page. Ginsberg 47-921 1983 $150

DODGE, MARY ABIGAIL   Memorial Mrs. Hannah Stanwood Dodge. Cambridge: Printed at the Riverside Press, 1869. First edition. Inscribed to G. M. Dodge by author. Illus. with 9 orig. mounted photographs and a 2 page facs. letter. 8vo, orig. purple boards, leather shelfback. Some rubbing. Scarce. Morrill 287-92 1983 $100

DODGE, MARY MAPES   Along the Way. New York, 1879. 1st ed. in the gilt-extra binding. Inscription by author. 12mo. Morrill 289-314 1983 $30

DODGE, RICHARD IRVING   The Black Hills. N.Y., 1876. Illus., folded map, tinted plates. Orig. cloth. First edition. Ginsberg 47-303 1983 $100

DODGE, RICHARD IRVING   Our Wild Indians. Hartford, 1882. Orig. calf, cracking to hinges and spine, internally good. Reese 19-198 1983 $80

DODGE, RICHARD IRVING   The Plains of the Great West and Their Inhabitants Being a Description of the Plains, Game, Indians, etc. N.Y., 1877. Illus., map, plates. Orig. cloth. First edition. A few library stamps on the endpapers. Ginsberg 47-304 1983 $85

DODGE, WILLIAM E.   Old New York. N.Y., 1880. Illus. Orig. printed wraps. First edition. Ginsberg 46-865 1983 $25

DODGSON, CAMPBELL   The Etchings of Sir David Wilkie & Andrew Geddes. London: Print Collector's Club, 1936. 44 collotype plates. 4to. Boards, 1/4 cloth. No. 315 of a limited edition of 425 copies. Ars Libri 32-707 1983 $50

DODGSON, CAMPBELL   The Etchings of William Strang & Sir Charles Holroyd. London: The Print Collectors' Club, 1933. 17 collotype plates. 4to. Boards, 1/4 cloth. No. 369 of a limited edition of 500 copies. Ars Libri 32-651 1983 $50

DODGSON, CAMPBELL   Old French Colour-Prints. London, 1924. First edition. One of 1,250. Illustrated. Folio, half vellum and red cloth, vellum front cover label. Fine in dj. Bradley 65-13 1983 $135

DODGSON, CHARLES LUTWIDGE   Alice's Adventures in Wonderland. London, 1866. 8vo, full crushed levant, g.e., by Zaehsdorf. 42 illus. by John Tenniel. Second edition. Maurice Baring's copy, with his bookplate and autograph. The half-title, which also has Baring's name and address written over a partially eradicated inscription from 1866, is torn out, but present. Argosy 714-120 1983 $1,500

DODGSON, CHARLES LUTWIDGE   Alice's Adventures in Wonderland. London: MacMillan, 1884. Illus. Seventy Third Thousand. Orig. crimson cloth, gilt, a.e.g. Housed in fine half-morocco folding case. Minor rubbing; a bright copy with an inscription on the half-title by Dodgson, in purple ink: "Grace Denman, from the Author, Oct., 1884." Jenkins 155-183 1983 $850

DODGSON, CHARLES LUTWIDGE   Alice's Adventures in Wonderland. London and New York, Heinemann, (1907). First edition thus. Illus. with 13 color plates and 12 b/w drawings by Arthur Rackham. Full red morocco stamped in gilt with a design of the White Rabbit on upper cover, gilt devices on spine, raised bands, watered silk endpapers and doublures, a.e.g. Houle 22-168 1983 $450

DODGSON, CHARLES LUTWIDGE   Alice in Wonderland. Raphael Tuck, n.d. (ca.1911). Sm. 4to. Colour frontis. Decorated title. 11 colour plates. 71 text illus. & decorated endpapers. Cream colour pictorial glazed boards, worn. Greer 40-2 1983 £45

DODGSON, CHARLES LUTWIDGE   Alice's Adventures in Wonderland. Allen & Unwin, n.d. (1911). Sm. 4to. Colour frontis. Title pictorial. 5 colour plates. 7 full-page & 29 text illus. Pictorial endpaper. Red pictorial cloth. Greer 39-10 1983 £35

DODSON, CHARLES LUTWIDGE   Alice's Adventures in Wonderland. C. H.
Kelly, 1916. Colour frontis., title vignette. 5 colour plates, 7 full-
page & 12 text illus. Blue decorated cloth. Greer 40-7 1983 £28

DODGSON, CHARLES LUTWIDGE   Alice in Wonderland and Through the
Looking Glass. Chicago: Rand., (1916). Windermere Series. Blue
gilt cloth. Pictorial paste-on. Illus. with M. Winter's color plates.
Fine. Aleph-bet 8-55 1983 $35

DODGSON, CHARLES LUTWIDGE   Alice's Adventures in Wonderland, and,
through the Looking Glass... N.Y., Hurst, n.d., ca. 1920. Pictorial
maroon cloth, stamped in gilt, black and white. Illus. with six
chromolithographs and b/w plates after John Tenniel. Very good-fine.
Houle 21-199 1983 $65

DODGSON, CHARLES LUTWIDGE   Alice in Wonderland. N.Y.: Garden City
Pub., n.d. (ca. 1920). 8vo. Orange cloth. Pictorial paste-on.
Light spotting. 8 color plates & black & whites by A. E. Jackson.
Very good. Aleph-bet 8-56 1983 $28

DODGSON, CHARLES LUTWIDGE   Alice in Wonderland. Tuck, nd (1921).
Pictured by Mabel Lucie Attwell. Re-issue, with col. frontis. & 5
col. plates, numerous b&w illus. Red cloth backed col. pictorial
glazed bds., edges of bds. sl. wear, bkstrip faded, vg. Hodgkins 27-
26 1983 £10.50

DODGSON, CHARLES LUTWIDGE   Alice in Wonderland. Readers Library,
n.d. (1928). Frontis. Title vignette, 13 plates & 27 text illus.
Pictorial endpapers. Red cloth gilt. Greer 40-4 1983 £15

DODGSON, CHARLES LUTWIDGE   Songs from Alice in Wonderland. Methuen,
1932. Illus. by Tenniel. 1st edn. Black cloth backed bright yellow
pictorial fr. cvr. bds., red titling, d/w to match. Insc. fr. ep.,
some ink scoring through of music pp.23-27, d/w some wear, vg.
Hodgkins 27-27 1983 £10.50

DODGSON, CHARLES LUTWIDGE   Alice's Adventures in Wonderland. T.
Nelson, n.d. (1936). Frontis. 8 plates & 70 text illus. Blue leatherette gilt. Greer 39-12 1983 £15

DODGSON, CHARLES LUTWIDGE   Alice's Adventures in Wonderland & Through
the Looking Glass. A. Wingate, 1954. First edition. Frontis. Title
vignette. 25 full-page & 37 text illus. Blue cloth gilt, light wear.
Greer 40-6 1983 £48

DODGSON, CHARLES LUTWIDGE   Alice in Wonderland, Printed in Gregg
Shorthand. NY: n.d. Octavo. Numerous b&w vignettes. Pictorial
wrappers slightly rubbed, else fine. Signature of owner. Bromer
25-329 1983 $240

DODGSON, CHARLES LUTWIDGE   Alice in Wonderland & Through the Looking-
Glass. Odhams Press, n.d. Frontis. Decorated title & 21 full-page
illus. Brown buckram. Greer 40-9 1983 £20

DODGSON, CHARLES LUTWIDGE   Alice in Wonderland. Readers Library,
n.d. Frontis. Title vignette. 12 full-page & 26 text illus. Pictorial endpaper. Red cloth, gilt. Greer 39-11 1983 £16

DODGSON, CHARLES LUTWIDGE   Alice's Adventure in Wonderland. F.
Warne, n.d. Colour frontis. & 8 full-page illus. Red cloth. Tattered
colour pictorial dust wrapper, by D. Newsome. Greer 39-9 1983 £14

DODGSON, CHARLES LUTWIDGE   Alice's Adventures Under Ground.
London: Macmillan and Co., 1886. First edition. 8vo. Orig.
red cloth, triple-line gilt borders, gilt lettered with motif on
back cover, edges gilt. 37 illus. by the author. A fine copy.
Traylen 94-155 1983 £165

DODGSON, CHARLES LUTWIDGE   Alice's Adventures Under Ground. London:
Macmillan & Co., 1886. First edition. With 37 illus. by author.
Orig. red cloth. Spine a little darkened and worn, inner hinges
starting. Bookplate of Paul Lemperly. MacManus 278-1587 1983 $225

DODGSON, CHARLES LUTWIDGE   Alice's Adventures Under Ground.
London: Macmillan, 1886. First edition. 37 illustrations by author.
Original pictorial red cloth, gilt, all edges gilt. Facsimile of
the first draft of the original handwritten manuscript. Cover extremities lightly worn, small library label on front cover, pictorial
bookplate on front end paper, front hinge cracked. Good and sound copy.
Bradley 65-41 1983 $125

DODGSON, CHARLES LUTWIDGE   Doublets. London: Macmillan, 1879.
First published edition. 12mo. Orig. cloth (very slightly soiled,
some minor blistering). Fine. MacManus 278-1590 1983 $125

DODGSON, CHARLES LUTWIDGE   The dynamics of a particle... Oxford:
J. Vincent, 1865. Third edition. 8vo. Disbound. Some dampstains.
Ximenes 63-522 1983 $25

DODGSON, CHARLES LUTWIDGE   Eight or Nine Wise Words about Letter-
Writing. Emberlin & Son, Oxford, (c. 1910). Small format pamphlet.
Mint. Jarndyce 31-469 1983 £10.50

DODGSON, CHARLES LUTWIDGE   Feeding the Mind. London: Chatto &
Windus, 1907. First edition. Orig. wrappers. Former owner's
signatures on flyleaf. Almost fine. MacManus 278-1592 1983 $55

DODGSON, CHARLES LUTWIDGE   Feeding the Mind. London: Chatto &
Windus, 1907. 1st ed. Orig. white linen-backed printed boards.
Uncommon. Fine copy. Jenkins 155-330 1983 $45

DODGSON, CHARLES LUTWIDGE   The Game of Logic. London: Macmillan
and Co., 1887. First edition. 8vo. Orig. red cloth, gilt. Half-
title, publisher's ads. at end, and the loosely inserted envelope
containing boards and 8 (of 9) counters at end. A presentation
copy inscribed, "Helen Bell from the Author, Mar./87." Traylen 94-
918 1983 £295

DODGSON, CHARLES LUTWIDGE   The Hunting of the Snark. London: Macmillan & Co., 1876. First edition. 9 illus. by Henry Holiday. Orig.
pictorial cloth. Spine worn, front inner hinge cracked. Covers a bit
darkened and soiled. MacManus 278-1594 1983 $75

DODGSON, CHARLES LUTWIDGE   The Hunting of the Snark. New York &
London: Harper, 1903. Color frontis., plates. 1st ed. thus, with
illus. by Peter Newell. Orig. parchment boards, gilt, t.e.g., others
uncut. Very fine copy in orig. fabric-lined dj (small piece lacking
from base of spine). Jenkins 155-1367 1983 $165

DODGSON, CHARLES LUTWIDGE   The Hunting of the Snark. London, 1876.
First edition, 16mo, pictorial buff cloth, 9 illus. by Henry Holiday.
Argosy 714-122 1983 $150

DODGSON, CHARLES LUTWIDGE   The Hunting of the Snark and Other Poems.
N.Y. & London: Harp., 1903. First edition, publisher's binding. 8vo.
Red gilt dec. cloth. Short bios of Tenniel & Kredel laid into front
free flyleaf. Decorative border on each page of text. T.e.g. Fine.
Aleph-bet 8-53 1983 $50

DODGSON, CHARLES LUTWIDGE   The Hunting of the Snark. London, 1941.
First edition with these illus. (by M. Peake). Nice. Rota 230-464
1983 £25

DODGSON, CHARLES LUTWIDGE   The Hunting of the Snark. Catalpa
Press, 1974. Illus. by Byron Sewell. Limited to 250 numbered copies
signed by illustrator. With illus. title page, a 16 foot illus. pull-
out & 9 other illus., some folding. At rear of book is pocket containing drawings. Bound in black cloth, gilt titling bkstrip, fine.
Hodgkins 27-29 1983 £45

DODGSON, CHARLES LUTWIDGE   The Hunting of the Snark. Whittington
Press, 1975. Illus. by Harold Jones. Limited to 30 copies, signed
by the illustrator & bound in full black leather, gilt decor. &
titling fr. cvr., raised bands, gilt titling on bkstrip., t.e.g.,
others uncut, yellow marbled eps. with slip-case, fine copy. Hodgkins
27-30 1983 £60

DODGSON, CHARLES LUTWIDGE   Hunting of the Snark. New Rochelle,
Peter Pauper Press, n.d. First edition thus. Tall 8vo, text printed
on light green paper. Illus. by Edward A. Wilson. Half cloth,
t.e.g., uncut. One of 275 copies printed at the Walpole printing
office. Bookplate of Adrian Goldstone. Very good. Houle 21-200
1983 $35

DODGSON, CHARLES LUTWIDGE   An index to "In Memoriam." London:
Moxon, 1862. First edition. 12mo. Orig. purple-brown cloth.
Slight wear. Ximenes 63-443 1983 $75

DODGSON, CHARLES LUTWIDGE   The Lewis Carroll Picture Book. T. Fisher Unwin, 1899. First edition, with full-page and other illus. 8vo, orig. cloth, gilt, t.e.g. Inside joints weak, but a very good copy. Fenning 60-94 1983 £24.50

DODGSON, CHARLES LUTWIDGE   Logical Nonsense. N.Y., (1934). First edition. With a T.L.S. from Blackburn. Argosy 714-123 1983 $40

DODGSON, CHARLES LUTWIDGE   The principles of parliamentary representation. Supplement. Oxford: printed by E. Baxter, n.d. (1885). First edition. 8vo. Four leaves, folded. Very slightly browned and dusty. Scarce. Ximenes 63-463 1983 $125

DODGSON, CHARLES LUTWIDGE   The principles of parliamentary representation. London: Harrison and Sons, 1884. First published edition. 8vo. Stitched as issued. Slight browning, short marginal tear in last leaf. Ximenes 63-462 1983 $125

DODGSON, CHARLES LUTWIDGE   The Rectory Umbrella and Mischmasch. Cassell, 1932. First edition. 4to. Frontis. handcoloured & 74 text illus. Blue decorated cloth gilt, rubbed. Greer 40-11 1983 £15

DODGSON, CHARLES LUTWIDGE   Some Popular Fallacies about Vivisection. Oxford: Printed for private circulation only, 1875. First edition. Orig. wrappers. One of 150 copies. Back wrapper a bit browned and foxed. Very good. MacManus 278-1595 1983 $150

DODGSON, CHARLES LUTWIDGE   Sylvie And Bruno. London: Macmillan & Co., 1889 & 1893. First edition(s). 2 vols. Illus. by Harry Furniss. Orig. decorated cloth. Presentation copy inscribed: "Ruth Martin Woodhouse, from the Author. Feb. 6, 1894." Spine and covers faded and slightly worn. Rear inner hinge cracking. In a half-morocco case. MacManus 278-1596 1983 $500

DODGSON, CHARLES LUTWIDGE   Sylvie and Bruno. London: Macmillan, 1889, 1893. First edition. Illus. by Harry Furniss. 2 vols. Orig. cloth. Vol. 1, little soiled; vol. 2, fine with publisher's printed dust jacket and the "Advertisement Leaf" inserted at the front as issued. MacManus 278-1597 1983 $250

DODGSON, CHARLES LUTWIDGE   Sylvie and Bruno (with) Sylvie and Bruno Concluded. London, 1889-93. First editions, with frontis. and 92 illus. by Harry Furniss, ad. leaves at end of both works. 2 vols. 8vo. Orig. red cloth, triple-line gilt rule and gilt centre motif, gilt spines, gilt edges, black endpapers. Traylen 94-157 1983 £85

DODGSON, CHARLES LUTWIDGE   Sylvie & Bruno, and Sylvie & Bruno Concluded. Macmillan, 1889 & 1893. 2 vols. 46 illus. by Harry Furniss in each vol. Index & 3pp adverts, 5 pp. adverts. Scarlet cloth with circular gilt vignettes cvrs., a.e.g. black eps. Loosely inserted is advertisement sheet in 2nd vol., corners sl. bumped, bk-strips faded, some foxing prelims, vg. Hodgkins 27-24 1983 £30

DODGSON, CHARLES LUTWIDGE   Sylvie and Bruno. London, 1889. 8vo, red cloth; faded & slightly rubbed. First edition. At end, 3 pp of ads for Carroll's work. Argosy 714-124 1983 $50

DODGSON, CHARLES LUTWIDGE   Sylvie and Bruno Concluded. London, 1893. Illus. by Harry Furniss. Red cloth, first edition. First issue, with error in table of contents. Argosy 714-125 1983 $65

DODGSON, CHARLES LUTWIDGE   Sylvie and Bruno Concluded. London, 1893. First edition. 8vo. Orig. decorated red cloth, gilt. 46 illus., ad. leaf. Traylen 94-158 1983 £25

DODGSON, CHARLES LUTWIDGE   A Tangled Tale. London: Macmillan & Co., 1885. 6 illus. by Arthur B. Frost. Orig. red cloth with black endpapers. Presentation copy from Dodgson inscribed: "Enid Gertrude Stevens, with the Author's love. June 17, 1897." Spine a bit faded & covers slightly soiled. Hinges very slightly cracked. In a half-morocco slipcase. Good. MacManus 278-1599 1983 $1,000

DODGSON, CHARLES LUTWIDGE   Tangled Tale. London, 1885. 8vo, red cloth, first edition. 6 illus. by A.B. Frost. Argosy 714-126 1983 $185

DODGSON, CHARLES LUTWIDGE   A Tangled Tale. London: Macmillan and Co., 1885. First edition. 8vo. Orig. red cloth, front and back triple line border and centre motif, gilt, spine gilt, edges gilt, black endpapers. 6 illus. by Arthur B. Frost, half-title, ad. leaf. Traylen 94-159 1983 £75

DODGSON, CHARLES LUTWIDGE   The Three Cats. Berkely, Privately printed, 1937. First edition thus. Small 8vo, illus. with woodcuts. Pictorial orange wraps. stamped in black (trifle rubbed at edges). Privately printed by Ellen and Wilder Bentley. Very good. Houle 22-172 1983 $750

DODGSON, CHARLES LUTWIDGE   Through the Looking-Glass. London, 1872. First edition. 12mo, full crushed levant, by Zaehnsdorf g.e. 50 illus. by John Tenniel. First issue, with "wade" for "wabe", page 21. The advertisement leaf at end is present. Argosy 714-127 1983 $600

DODGSON, CHARLES LUTWIDGE   Through the Looking-Glass, and What Alice Found There. Boston & New York, 1872. 1st American ed. Illus. by John Tenniel. Small 8vo. Ends of spine rubbed, slight rubbing at corners, inner back hinge cracked, occasional light foxing. Morrill 287-561 1983 $225

DODGSON, CHARLES LUTWIDGE   Through the Looking-Glass, and What Alice Found There. London: Macmillan & Co., 1872. First edition. 8vo. Orig. red cloth, triple gilt rule, gilt vignettes of the Red Queen and the White Queen on the front and back covers, spine lettered gilt, gilt edges. Half-title, frontis., and 50 illus. by John Tenniel. Very slightly worn and spotted. Traylen 94-160 1983 £120

DODGSON, CHARLES LUTWIDGE   Through the Looking Glass and What Alice Found There. Boston: DeWolfe Fiske, n.d. (ca.1900). 12mo. Green pictorial cloth. Small hole in front gutter. 4 chromolithographs. Black & whites by Tenniel. Very good. Aleph-bet 8-57 1983 $30

DODGSON, CHARLES LUTWIDGE   Through the Looking Glass and What Alice Found There. N.Y., Cheshire House, 1931. First edition thus. 4to, illus. with seven full page color plates by Franklin Hughes. Bound in full white watered silk, top edge silvered. One of 1,200 numbered copies. Designed by Richard Ellis. Pub.'s silver foil slipcase, a bit rubbed. Houle 22-173 1983 $125

DODGSON, CHARLES LUTWIDGE   Through the Looking-Glass and What Alice Found There. NY: 1931. Small quarto. Mostly unopened. 8 full-page illus. Limited to 1200 copies. Spine slightly darkened, else extremely fine in white watered-silk over boards. Rubbed slip-case. Bromer 25-331 1983 $75

DODGSON, CHARLES LUTWIDGE   Through the Looking Glass and What Alice Found There. N.Y.: Limited Editions Club, 1935. 8vo. Full blue leather, gilt stamped. A.e.g. In orig. glassene wrap. Slipcase, with prospectus. No. 801 of 1500 copies printed by Rudge on all-rag Hurlbut paper. Cover design by F. Warde. Mint. Aleph-bet 8-54 1983 $150

DODGSON, CHARLES LUTWIDGE   Through the Looking Glass. Mount Vernon, Peter Pauper Press, nd. 50 illus. by John Tenniel. Limited to 1650 copies, illus. printed in green, colophon. Grey cloth backed col. patterned bds., paper title label bkstrip, uncut. Sml. stain top fore-edge first 13pp., corners sl. bruised & worn, bkstrip faded & title label discol'd, good copy. Hodgkins 27-25 1983 £10.50

DODGSON, CHARLES LUTWIDGE   The Wonderland Postage-Stamp Case. Emberlin & Son, Oxford, 1889. Postage stamp case in slipcase. 4 colour vignettes. Greer 40-10 1983 £25

DODGSON, CHARLES LUTWIDGE   The Wonderland Postage-Stamp Case. Oxford: Emberline & Son, n.d. Second edition. Orig. thin paper boards, folded, with the printed envelope. Slightly soiled and faded. Very good. MacManus 278-1600 1983 $35

DODINGTON, GEORGE BUBB   The diary of the late George Bubb Dodington... Salisbury: E. Easton, etc., 1784. First edition. 8vo. Cont. calf, gilt, spine gilt. Fine copy. Ximenes 63-460 1983 $125

DODSLEY, ROBERT   The Art of Preaching. London: Printed for R. Dodsley...(1738). Folio, disbound. First edition. Good copy. Quaritch NS 7-35 1983 $225

DODSLEY, ROBERT   The Art of Preaching: in Imitation of
Horace's 'Art of Poetry.' London: R. Dodsley, (1738). First edition, folio, disbound. A very good copy. Trebizond 18-33 1983 $145

DODSLEY, ROBERT   A Collection of Poems by Several Hands.
London: printed for R. Dodsley, 1748. 1st ed., 3 vols., 12mo,
engraved vignette on the three graces on each title page, a little
browned at the end of each volume, cont. calf, rebacked preserving
most of the original gilt spines. Pickering & Chatto 19-45 1983
$450

DODSLEY, ROBERT   Trifles: viz. The Toy Shop...
(London), 1745. First collected ediiton. 8vo. Modern half calf.
Vignette engraving on title, half title. Fine copy. Heath 48-283
1983 £60

DODSON, JAMES   The Calculator. For James Wilcox...
and James Dodson, London, 1747. 4to, ad. leaf at the end; a fine
copy in cont. calf, a little rubbed, head of joints split. Quaritch
NS 5-34 1983 $385

DODSWORTH, ANN   Fugitive pieces. Canterbury: printed
by Simmons and Kirkby, 1802. First edition. Small 8vo. Cont.
mottled calf, spine gilt. With a presentation inscription from
the author's husband to a George Morland. On the rear endpapers is
a 5-page manuscript poem. A bit worn, hinges tender, some light
dampstains, but a very good copy. Rare. Ximenes 63-403 1983
$100

DOE, JANET   A Bibliography of the Works of Ambroise
Pare. Chicago, 1937. First edition. 8vo. Orig. binding. Ex-
library. Fye H-3-1033 1983 $100

DOELL, EMIL   Das Schicksal Aller Utopien Oder
Socialen Charlatnieren. Leipzig: C. G. Naumann, (1879). Orig.
printed wrappers, detached and worn. Adolf Meyer's copy, signed on
front wrapper. Gach 95-358 1983 $25

DOGGETT, JOHN   The Great Metropolis: or New York in
1845. N.Y., (1844). 16mo. Argosy 716-378 1983 $45

DOHERTY, ANN   The Castles of Wolfnorth and Mont Eagle.
London: T. & E.T. Hookham, 1812. First (only) edition, 12mo, 4 vols.,
cont. calf, spines gilt, morocco labels. Five sepia plates. Half-
titles in Vols. 3 and 4. A very scarce novel. One cover detached
but present, others tender, otherwise a very good copy. Trebizond
18-46 1983 $300

DOLBY, GEORGE   Charles Dickens as I Knew Him. T.
Fisher Unwin, 1885. First edition, half title, 32 pp ads. Orig. red
cloth, v.g. Jarndyce 31-597 1983 £35

DOLBY, GEORGE   Charles Dickens as I Knew Him. T.
Fisher Unwin, (c. 1886). Half title. Orig. green cloth, t.e.g.
Jarndyce 31-598 1983 £12.50

DOLBY, GEORGE   Charles Dickens, as I Knew Him. T.
Fisher Unwin, 1887. Orig. red cloth, inner hinges sl. weak. Very
good. Jarndyce 30-167 1983 £12.50

DOLOMIEU, DEODAT GRATET DE   Voyages aux Iles de Lipari, fait en 1781.
Paris, 1783. 1st ed., 8vo, cont. panelled calf, spine gilt, morocco
label. Half-title. Edges of half-title time darkened, but a fine
copy. Trebizond 18-169 1983 $285

DOMENECH, EMMANUEL H. D.   Seven Years' Residence in the Great
Deserts of North America. London, 1860. 2 vols. Illus. map and
58 colored plates. Half calf. First edition. Ginsberg 46-236 1983
$275

DOMINGUIN, LUIS MIGUEL   Pablo Picasso: Toros y Toreros.
New York: Abrams, 1961. 134 color plates. Small folio. Cloth.
Slipcase. Binding and title-page designed by the artist. Ars
Libri 32-519 1983 $125

DOMSCHCKE, BERNHARD   Zwanzig Monate in Kriegs-Gesangenschaft
Erinnerungen. Milwaukee, 1865. 1st ed. Contemp. 3/4 morocco.
Library stamping. Extremely scarce. Jenkins 153-765 1983 $150

DONALD, JAY   Outlaws of the Border... Chicago:
Coburn & Newman Pub. Co., 1882. Frontis. and plates. Original pic.
cloth. First edition. Jenkins 153-173 1983 $125

DONALDSON, HENRY H.   Growth of the Brain. N.Y., 1914.
Illus. Argosy 713-155 1983 $100

DONALDSON, JOHN WILLIAM   Varronianus. John W. Parker, 1852.
With a folding map, 4 ads., 8vo, recently and neatly rebound cloth.
Second edition. Fenning 60-95 1983 £21.50

DONALDSON, THOMAS   Idaho of Yesterday. Caldwell, 1941.
Illus. Orig. cloth. First edition. Presentation copy signed by
the author. Ginsberg 47-347 1983 $40

DONALDSON, WALTER   Recollections of an actor. London:
John Maxwell and Co., 1865. Sm. 8vo, original yellow decorated
boards (rubbed, some wear to hinges). 1st edition. Very scarce.
Ximenes 64-172 1983 $75

DONATI, UGO   Carlo Maderno, architetto ticinese
a Roma. Lugano: Banco di Roma per la Svizzeria, 1957. 16 plates.
38 text illus. 4to. Cloth. Dust jacket. Edition limited to
2500 numbered copies. Ars Libri 33-206 1983 $85

DONATO, PIERO   Domenico Fiasella, "Il Sarzana."
Genova: Stringa, 1974. 74 plates (20 color). Small folio. Cloth.
Dust jacket. Ars Libri 33-141 1983 $95

DONLEAVY, J. P.   The Ginger Man. Paris, (1955). Paperwraps show some minor wear on edges, printed price scratched out and
small bookstore's stamp front endpaper, otherwise very good. Quill &
Brush 54-372 1983 $200

DONN, BENJAMIN   A Map Of The County Of Devon With The
City & County Of Exeter. (ca. 1765). Large folding engraved map,
some routes in colour, mounted on linen with an engraved vignette
title. 8vo, enclosed within a red morocco backed, cloth box.
Deighton 3-110 1983 £335

DONNE, JOHN   Biathanatos. London, Humphrey Moseley,
1648. Small 4to, cont. calf, rebacked using the orig. covers,
corners knocked, text a little age-browned. The first edition, second
issue. Ravenstree 94-45 1983 $750

DONNE, JOHN   Complete Poetry and Selected Prose.
London: the Nonesuch Press, 1929. Thick 8vo. Full light blue
morocco, gilt, top edges gilt, others uncut, preserved in the
orig. marbled slipcase. Limited edition of 675 numbered copies
printed on Pannekoek paper, the rule head-pieces by Paul Beaujon
specially printed in colour for this edition. Traylen 94-279
1983 £85

DONNE, JOHN   The Courtier's Library, or Catalogus
Librorum Aulicorum... (N.p.): Nonesuch Press, 1930. Paper over
boards, leather label. One of 950 copies printed in Fell types on
handmade paper. Backstrip slightly faded, else a very fine copy in
slipcase. Reese 20-727 1983 $45

DONNE, JOHN   Ignatius his conclave. London:
printed for John Marriott, sold by W. Sheares, 1635. Third
English edition, variant title. 12mo. Calf antique, by Middleton.
Some side-notes shaved, a couple of leaves at the beginning and
end somewhat rubbed and soiled. Ximenes 63-579 1983 $350

DONNE, JOHN   The Love Poems of John Donne. Boston,
1905. 12mo, vellum backed boards. Ltd. edition. One of 535 numbered
copies, designed by Bruce Rogers and printed at the Riverside Press.
Inscribed by Norton on the half-title. Argosy 714-637 1983 $60

DONNE, JOHN   Love Poems. Soho the Nonesuch Press,
1923. Front. Printed boards, vellum spine. 4to. Jarndyce 31-984
1983 £20

DONNE, JOHN   Paradoxes and Problemes. The Nonesuch
Press, 1923. Printed boards, spine darkened, label. No. 210 of 645.
Jarndyce 31-983 1983 £28

DONNE, JOHN   Poems, etc... In the Savoy: printed
by T.N. for Henry Herringman, 1669. 8vo. Cont. calf, rebacked.
Complete with the preliminary and final blanks. A couple of corners
torn, once touching an obvious letter or two, but a very good copy.
Ximenes 63-362 1983 $400

DONNE, JOHN   The Poems. Oxford: at the Clarendon
Press, 1912. 2 vols. 8vo. Orig. orange buckram, printed paper
labels, uncut edges. Traylen 94-281 1983 £28

DONNE, JOHN   X Sermons. London: the Nonesuch
Press, 1923. Small folio. Printed throughout in red and black,
boards, linen spine with printed paper label, uncut edges. Limited
edition of 725 numbered copies, printed by the Kynoch Press. Traylen 94-282 1983 £60

DONNE, JOHN   The Works of John Donne, D.D., Dean
of St. Paul's, 1621-1631. John W. Parker, 1839. Six vols. With an
engraved portrait, 6 vols., 8vo, orig. cloth, very light discolouration of the sides of one volume and the lower outer corners of the
same a little worn, but otherwise a fine set. Fenning 60-96 1983
£165

DONNELLY, EDWARD   The Confession of Edward Donnelly.
N.p.: Printed for the Purchasers, n.d. (1808). 16mo, self wraps.,
sewn & uncut as issued (last leaf frayed). Argosy 716-129 1983
$200

DONOHO, M. H.   Circle-Dot: A True Story of Cowboy
Life Forty Years Ago. Topeka, 1907. 1st ed. Frontispiece. Red
cloth. Fine copy. Very scarce. Bradley 63-123 1983 $65

DONOVAN, DICK, PSEUD.
Please turn to
MURDOCK, JOYCE EMERSON PRESTON

DONOVAN, E.   An Epitome of the Natural History of the
Insects of China. London: Printed for the Author, 1798. 50 fine
handcoloured plates. 4to. Cont. green straight grained half morocco,
gilt. Good. Edwards 1044-194 1983 £2,000

DONOVAN, E.   An Epitome of the Natural History of
the Insects of China. Printed for the author, 1798 (-1799).
50 hand-coloured engraved plates by the author, 4to, half calf, gilt,
m.e. Rare first edition. Binding slightly rubbed; tear in one plate
has been mended and a small piece has been torn from the lower blank
margin of a text leaf, else in nice condition, with the plates free
from blackening. Wheldon 160-25 1983 £1,600

DONOVAN, MICHAEL   Chemistry. London: Longmans, 1832.
Third edition. 8vo. Cont. half calf. Text illus. Engraved
additional title-page. Ownership inscription on title-page. A
very good copy. Zeitlin 264-123 1983 $70

DONOVAN, MIKE   The Roosevelt that I Knew: Ten Years
of Boxing with the President. N.Y., 1909. Pictorial cloth. Fine
copy. First edition. Scarce. Jenkins 151-296 1983 $45

DOOLITTLE, HILDA   The Flowering of the Rod. London:
Oxford, 1946. Stiff wrappers. First edition. Fine. Reese 20-326
1983 $50

DOOLITTLE, HILDA   Hedylus. Boston & New York, 1928.
8vo. Cloth, boards. Total ed. is 775 copies. Name on endpaper,
else a fine copy in the uncommon dj. Jacket has a few small chips.
In Our Time 156-207 1983 $250

DOOLITTLE, HILDA   Hedylus. Oxford, 1928. First edition.
One of 775 copies printed at the Shakespeare Head Press. Covers just
a little marked. Nice. Rota 231-309 1983 £55

DOOLITTLE, HILDA   Hippolytus Temporized. Boston,
Houghton, 1927. First edition. Tall 8vo, half black cloth. Very
good. One of 550 copies. Houle 21-299 1983 $200

DOOLITTLE, HILDA   Palimpsest. Paris, (1926). Paperwraps,
signed on front fly, cover slightly soiled, edges lightly chipped,
many pages uncut, good or better in slightly soiled, very good box.
Quill & Brush 54-374 1983 $300

DOOLITTLE, HILDA   Palimpeest. Boston, 1926. 8vo.
Cloth, boards. 1 of 200 copies. 1st American ed. A fine copy in
dj. In Our Time 156-206 1983 $250

DOOLITTLE, HILDA   Palimpsest. (Bos., 1926). Limited to
700 copies, edges and lettering lightly rubbed, front hinge just starting, good or better in lightly worn and chipped dustwrapper with chipped spine edges, owner's name. Quill & Brush 54-373 1983 $150

DOOLITTLE, HILDA   Tribute to the Angels. London: Oxford,
1945. Stiff wraps. First edition. Fine copy. Reese 20-325 1983
$50

DOOLITTLE, MARK   Historical Sketch of the Congregational
Church in Belchertown, Mass... Northampton, 1852. 1st ed. Pres.
copy. Small 8vo. Binding rubbed and lightly stained. Morrill 287-
221 1983 $25

DORAN, GEORGE H.   Chronicles of Barabbas, 1884-1934.
London: Methuen & Co., (1935). First English edition. Thick
8vo. Cloth. Dust jacket. Jacket slightly soiled, small hole in
paper covering of inside hinge. Oak Knoll 48-148 1983 $25

DORAN, JOHN   Sketches and Reminiscences. London:
S. Maunder, 1828. First edition. 8vo. Orig. boards (rebacked; new
label). Uncut. Internally fine. MacManus 278-1602 1983 $35

DORAN, JOHN   Their Majesties' Servants, or annals
of the English stage. London: Wm. H. Allen, 1865. 8vo, Victorian
calf, gilt, spine and inner dentelles gilt, a.e.g., by Roach (a little
rubbed). 2nd edition, revised, corrected and enlarged. 60 plates,
portraits, etc. inserted. A very good copy. Ximenes 64-174 1983 $75

DORAN, JOHN   "Their Majesties' Servants". New York,
1865. First American edition, 2 vols., titles printed in red and
black, half calf, gilt decorated spines. K Books 307-69 1983 £36

DORAN, JOHN   "Their Majesties' Servants," or annals
of the English stage, from Thomas Betterton to Edmund Kean. London:
John C. Nimmo, 1897. 8vo, original red cloth (dull). "People's
edition." With a frontispiece, and numerous other wood-engraved
illus. Ximenes 64-175 1983 $20

DORIA, ARNAULD   Louis Tocque. Biographie et catalogue
critiques. Paris: Les Beaux-Arts, 1929. 2 vols. 149 heliogravure
plates. Small folio. Bound in new cloth. Ars Libri 32-663 1983
$200

DORIA, BIAGIO   Bibliografia della penisola Sorrentina
e dell'isola di Capri... Napoli, 1909. Cloth, pretty good condition
but paper browning. Dawson 470-91 1983 $20

DORN, EDWARD   The North Atlantic Turbine. Lon.,
(1967). Limited to 100 numbered and signed copies, fine in slightly
yellowed else fine dustwrapper. Quill & Brush 54-376 1983 $75

DORNER, ALEXANDER   Meister Bertram von Minden. Berlin:
Rembrandt-Verlag, 1937. 9 plates (6 color; 3 folding). 33 text
illus. Square 4to. Wrappers. Chipped at edges. Ars Libri 32-
431 1983 $50

DORNHOFFER, FRIEDRICH   Albrecht Durers Fechtbuch. Wien/
Leipzig: F. Tempsky/G. Freytag), 1910. 78 collotype plates. 157
illus. Folio. Boards, 3/4 cloth. Uncut. Ars Libri 32-175 1983
$185

DORR, THOMAS   The Conspiracy to Defeat the Liberation
of Gov. Dorr. NY: John Windt, 1845. Orig. pr. wraps. Argosy 716-
482 1983 $35

DORSET, CATHERINE ANN   The Peacock at Home. London: Harris
(successor to Newbery), 1807. First edition. Sq. 16mo. Later boards.
Illus. with 6 fine copperplate engravings by W. Mulready. Very good to
fine. Aleph-bet 8-93 1983 $170

DORSEY, JOHN SYNG   Elements of Surgery for the Use of
Students. Phila., 1818. 27 plates, 2 vols., 8vo, orig. mottled
calf (vol. 1 mod. calf rebacking). Argosy 713-156 1983 $200

DORTORT, DAVID   The Post Honor. N.Y., McGraw Hill,
(1949). First edition. Dust jacket (some rubbing and nicking) else,
very good. Houle 22-309 1983 $45

DORTU, M. G.   Toulouse-Lautrec et son oeuvre. New
York: Collectors Editions, 1971. 6 vols. 5861 catalogue illus.,
323 documentary illus. Small folio. Cloth. Uncut. T.e.g.
Edition limited to 1500 numbered copies on velin, watermarked with
the artist's monogram. Ars Libri 32-666 1983 $500

DORVEAUX, PAUL   Les Pots de Pharmacie... Toulouse,
1923. Second edition. 8vo. Boards. 14 plates. Gurney JJ-104
1983 £15

DOS PASSOS, JOHN   The Big Money. NY: (1936). First
edition. Small bump to bottom rear cover, else very fine in slightly
chipped dust wrapper. Bromer 25-30 1983 $65

DOS PASSOS, JOHN   Chosen Country. Boston, 1951. Tall
8vo. Wraps. 2 vols. Spiral binding. Uncorrected proof copies.
Fine set. In Our Time 156-212 1983 $150

DOS PASSOS, JOHN   Facing the Chair. Boston, Sacco-
Vanzetti Defence Committee, 1927. First edition. 8vo, original
wrappers. Lacks bottom inch of backstrip. Morrill 290-103 1983
$75

DOS PASSOS, JOHN   1919. New York, (1932). 8vo. Cloth.
About fine in a near perfect and colorful dj. In Our Time 156-210
1983 $175

DOS PASSOS, JOHN   One Man's Initiation. London (1920).
12mo. Cloth. 1st issue. A fine copy in dj. In Our Time 156-209
1983 $350

DOS PASSOS, JOHN   State of the Nation. Boston,
Houghton, 1944. First edition. Illus. by F. Strobel. Dust
jacket. Fine. Houle 21-300 1983 $55

DOS PASSOS, JOHN   Three Plays. New York, (1934). 8vo.
Cloth. Fine copy in dj which has some tanning. In Our Time 156-211
1983 $150

DOS PASSOS, JOHN   Three Soldiers. NY, (1921). Fine in
3rd state, lightly chipped, very good dustwrapper. Quill & Brush 54-
378 1983 $75

DOS PASSOS, JOHN   Three Soldiers. NY, (1921). First
issue with "singing" vs. "signing" page 213, spine sunned, top edge
of spine nicked, else very good. Quill & Brush 54-377 1983 $30

DOSTOEVSKY, FYODOR   A Gentle Spirit. NY: 1931. Octavo.
Illus. with frontispiece and tailpiece by Christian Berard. Of 495
copies, 1/50 printed on Iridescent Imperial Japan vellum. Extremely
fine in vellum-backed boards. Slip-case starting to split at two
edges. Bookplate. Bromer 25-229 1983 $175

DOSTOEVSKY, FYODOR   A Gentle Spirit. Paris & New York:
Harrison of Paris & Minton, Balch and Company, (1931). Cloth. Illus.
by Christian Berard. First edition thus. One of 495 numbered copies,
designed by Monroe Wheeler. Fine in slipcase. Reese 20-488 1983
$100

DOSTOEVSKY, FYODOR   Poor Folk. London, Elkin Mathews and
John Lane, 1894. First ed., with intro. by George Moore, orig. pict.
cloth, little soiled. Very good. MacManus 278-1604 1983 $75

DOUBLEDAY, RUSSELL   Cattle Ranch to College. N.Y., Doubleday, 1899. First edition. Dark blue cloth, stamped in gilt. 24 halftone plates, marginal illus. by Ernest Seton Thompson and Janet Macdonald. Very good. Houle 21-1024 1983 $65

DOUGAL, WILLIAM H.   Off for California. Oakland, 1949.
Illus., folded plates. Cloth, long 8vo, first edition. Ltd. to 600
copies. Ginsberg 47-62 1983 $35

DOUGAL, WILLIAM H.   Off for California. Oakland: Biobooks,
1949. 22 plates. Sketches. Fine copy. Jenkins 153-174 1983 $35

DOUGHTY, ARTHUR G.   A Daughter of New France. Ottawa:
Mortimer Press, 1916. 18cm. Frontis. and 10 colour plates. Bound
in full blue crushed morocco, gilt titles and decorations on the
spine. T.e.g. Very good to fine. McGahern 53-45 1983 $35

DOUGHTY, CHARLES MONTAGU   Adam Cast Forth. London: Duckworth &
Co., 1908. First edition. Orig. cloth. Covers faded. Very good.
MacManus 278-1605 1983 $50

DOUGHTY, CHARLES MONTAGU   Arabia Deserta. Cambridge, University
Press, 1888. First edition, thick 8vo, plates and diagrams, some
folding. Complete copy with large folding map in pocket. Orig.
dark green cloth, uncut. A very good set. Cloth slipcase. 2 vols.
Houle 21-301 1983 $1,500

DOUGHTY, CHARLES MONTAGU   Mansoul (Or, The Riddle of the World).
London, 1920. First edition. Edges of leaves just a little foxed.
Bookplate. Very nice. Rota 230-164 1983 £15

DOUGHTY, CHARLES MONTAGU   Mansoul, or The Riddle of the World.
London: Jonathan Cape and the Medici Society, 1923. Limited edition.
Orig. vellum-covered boards. One of 500 copies. Presentation copy
inscribed: " Dr. H.K. Anderson, F.R.S., with Charles M. Doughty's kind
regards." With an ALS, 1 page, tipped in, dated June 9th, 1923.
Endpapers slightly browned, edges slightly soiled. MacManus 278-1607
1983 $225

DOUGHTY, CHARLES MONTAGU   Mansoul, or the Riddle of the World.
London, 1923. 8vo. Orig. cloth. Limited to 500 numbered and signed
copies. This copy belonged to R.L. Latimer of the Alcestis Press,
inscribed above the limitation. Vellum. Good. Edwards 1044-195
1983 £40

DOUGHTY, CHARLES MONTAGU   Mansoul or The Riddle of the World.
London: Jonathan Cape, 1923. New & revised edition. Orig. parchment.
Dust jacket. Limited to 500 copies, signed by author. Soiled.
MacManus 278-1608 1983 $30

DOUGHTY, CHARLES MONTAGU   Travels in Arabia Deserts. Cambridge,
1888. First edition. Large folding map in end-pocket, mounted on
linen. Numerous other illus. 2 vols. Thick 8vo. 1st vol. rebacked
with orig. spine laid down. Orig. decorative cloth. Good. Edwards
1044-197 1983 £975

DOUGHTY, CHARLES MONTAGU   Travels in Arabia Deserta. P.L. Warner,
Medici Society and J. Cape, 1921. Second printing of the new edition,
map in pocket, other maps, plates etc., 2 vols. 8vo, orig. cloth,
gilt. Spine worn and frayed, but joints sound and otherwise a nice
clean copy. Fenning 60-97 1983 £32.50

DOUGHTY, CHARLES MONTAGU   Travels in Arabian Deserts. London,
Reprinted 1943. New and Definitive edition. 2 large folding maps.
Numerous plates. 2 vols. Roy.8vo. Spines sunned. Good. Edwards
1044-198 1983 £65

DOUGHTY, THOMAS   The Cabinet of Natural History, and
American Rural Sports. Philadelphia, 1330-1332. 3 vols. bound in
two. Second two vols. are bound together. Uniform dark morocco,
slightly worn on edges. Plates clean and complete free of foxing.
Reese 19-200 1983 $12,000

DOUGLAS, A. C.   The Physical Mechanism of the Human
Mind. Baltimore: William Wood, 1933. First edition, American issue.
Library bookplate and stamp on rear paste-down. Smith Ely Jelliffe's
copy, signed on titlepage and front paste-down. Gach 95-96 1983
$27.50

DOUGLAS, ALFRED   The Autobiography. London: Martin
Secker, 1929. First edition. Illus. Orig. cloth. Inner hinges
cracked. Very good. MacManus 278-1609 1983 $35

DOUGLAS, ALFRED   The Collected Poems. Martin Secker,
1919. First collected edition, 8vo, orig. blue paper boards, with
printed paper spine label, a fine copy. One of 200 copies on Japon
paper, numbered and signed by the author. Fenning 62-97 1983 £35

DOUGLAS, ALFRED   The Collected Poems. Martin Secker, 1919. First collected edition, half title, front. 10pp 'Note' by the author, 2pp ads. Orig. green cloth, paper label. Jarndyce 31-985 1983 £15

DOUGLAS, ALFRED   The Complete Poems, including the Light Verse. Martin Secker, 1928. First edition, half title, front. Errata slip. Grey boards, mock vellum spine, t.e.g. Jarndyce 31-986 1983 £16.50

DOUGLAS, ALFRED   The Duke of Berwick and Other Rhymes. N.Y., 1925. First American edition. 8vo, cloth backed boards. Argosy 714-244 1983 $20

DOUGLAS, ALFRED   My Friendship with Oscar Wilde. N.Y.: Coventry House, 1932. First American edition. Illus. Orig. cloth with paper label on spine. Fine. MacManus 278-1610 1983 $25

DOUGLAS, ALFRED   Sonnets. London, 1909. First edition. Boards worn at spine. Inscribed: "Wilfrid Meynell with best wishes from Alfred Douglas. June 1909." Nice. Rota 230-165 1983 £65

DOUGLAS, ALFRED   Sonnets. (with) Lyrics. London: Rich and Cowan, 1935. Second edition of the first title; first edition of Lyrics. Each uniformly bound and limited to 50 copies signed by author. Covers a bit darkened and soiled. MacManus 278-1611 1983 $200

DOUGLAS, FRANCIS   A general description of the east coast of Scotland... Paisley: printed for the author, by Alexander Weir, 1782. First edition. 12mo. Cont. calf, spine gilt. Ximenes 63-618 1983 $200

DOUGLAS, FREDERICK   Indian Art of the United States. New York: Museum of Modern Art, 1941. Prof. illus. 4to. Cloth. Ars Libri 34-216 1983 $25

DOUGLAS, GEORGE A. H.   Sir William Wallace, and Other Poems. Glasgow, G.A.H. Douglas & Co., (1887?). First edition, 8vo, orig. blue cloth, gilt. Fenning 62-98 1983 £12.50

DOUGLAS, JAMES   Bombay and Western India. London, 1893. 2 maps, 1 folding. 15 plates, numerous maps and illus. in text. 2 vols. Roy.8vo. Spines faded. Orig. cloth. Good. Edwards 1044-199 1983 £60

DOUGLAS, JAMES   New England and New France. Toronto: Briggs & New York: Putnam's, 1913. 22cm. 44 illus. and maps, some folding. Quarter bound in linen, blue spine and white boards, gilt titles and decorations, t.e.g. A fine copy. Dust jacket. McGahern 53-46 1983 $45

DOUGLAS, JAMES   Old France in the New World. Cleveland, 1905. 1st ed. Autographed. Illus. 8vo. Ex-library. Morrill 287-93 1983 $27.50

DOUGLAS, JAMES   Theodore Watts-Dunton, Poet, Novelist. Hodder & Stoughton, 1904. First edition, tall 8vo, 24 illus. Half title. Orig. dark blue cloth, v.g. Jarndyce 30-1173 1983 £18

DOUGLAS, NORMAN   Birds and Beasts of the Greek Anthology. Privately Printed, (Florence), 1927. First edition. One of 250 numbered copies, signed by author. Slightly marked dust wrapper. With the slip bearing the publication address tipped-in on the front flap of the dust wrapper. With an autograph note, signed, from Douglas, 3rd May 1927, 1 page 4to. Fine. Rota 231-184 1983 £85

DOUGLAS, NORMAN   Birds and Beasts of the Greek Anthology. (Florence): Privately Printed, 1927. First edition. 8vo. Frontis. Orig. blue boards with paper label, dust jacket. Limited to 500 copies signed by the author. Jacket a little torn and soiled, otherwise a fine copy. Jaffe 1-83 1983 $100

DOUGLAS, NORMAN   D.H. Lawrence and Maurice Magnus. (Florence): Privately printed, 1924. First edition. 12mo, buff wrappers. Fine. Argosy 714-246 1983 $85

DOUGLAS, NORMAN   D.H. Lawrence and Maurice Magnus. (Florence): Privately printed, 1924. Printed wraps. Frontis. First edition, with the pink slip inserted. Slight wear at toe of spine, else fine. Reese 20-1214 1983 $50

DOUGLAS, NORMAN   D.H. Lawrence and Maurice Magnus... Florence, 1924. Fine. Scarce in first edition. Gekoski 2-39 1983 £25

DOUGLAS, NORMAN   Experiments. (Florence): Privately Printed, 1925. First edition. 4to. Orig. boards with paper label on spine, platin printed dust jacket (dust-soiled). Limited to 300 copies signed by author. Fine. MacManus 278-1612 1983 $150

DOUGLAS, NORMAN   Experiments. (Florence): Privately Printed, 1925. First edition. 4to. Orig. boards with paper label. Dust jacket. One of 300 copies signed by the author. Soiled. Jaffe 1-82 1983 $75

DOUGLAS, NORMAN   Experiments. London: Chapman & Hall, 1925. Cloth. Edges lightly foxed, else a fine copy in very slightly frayed dust jacket. Reese 20-329 1983 $35

DOUGLAS, NORMAN   How About Europe? Privately Printed, (Florence), 1929. First edition. One of 550 numbered copies, signed by author. Spine darkened and bumped. Author's signed autograph presentation inscription. Nice. Rota 231-187 1983 £80

DOUGLAS, NORMAN   How About Europe? Privately Printed, (Florence), 1929. First edition. One of 550 numbered copies, signed by author. Spine darkened. Nice. Rota 231-186 1983 £60

DOUGLAS, NORMAN   How About Europe? (Florence): Privately printed, 1929. First edition. One of 550 numbered and signed copies. Orig. decorated boards, gilt, label, uncut. Small piece torn from edge of very good d.j., bookplate and ownership inscription at front, else a fine copy with the binding unusually fresh and perfect. Scarce. Jenkins 155-355 1983 $75

DOUGLAS, NORMAN   How About Europe? (Florence): Privately Printed, 1929. First edition. Orig. paper-covered boards, label on spine. One of 550 copies, numbered and signed by author. Dust jacket (worn and faded). Good. MacManus 278-1613 1983 $60

DOUGLAS, NORMAN   In The Beginning. N.p. (Florence): Privately Printed, 1927. First edition. Orig. decorated boards with leather label on spine. Limited to 750 copies signed by author. Presentation copy, inscribed on the half-title "To Reggie (Turner) hoping he won't follow Symira's example in every respect from Norman Douglas, Florence 9 Dec 1927." Spine label a bit worn. Fine. MacManus 278-1614 1983 $375

DOUGLAS, NORMAN   In the Beginning. Privately Printed, (Florence), 1927. First edition. One of 700 numbered copies, signed by author. Patterned boards. Some slight foxing of preliminaries. Very nice. Rota 231-185 1983 £60

DOUGLAS, NORMAN   In The Beginning. London: Privately Printed, 1927. First edition. Orig. boards. Limited to 750 signed copies. Spine a bit darkened and worn. MacManus 278-1615 1983 $60

DOUGLAS, NORMAN   London Street Games. London, 1916. First edition. One of 1000 copies. T.e.g. Some faint internal spotting. Very good. Jolliffe 26-157 1983 £55

DOUGLAS, NORMAN   Nerinda. Florence, 1929. First edition. One of 475 numbered copies, signed by author. Sm. 4to. One corner rubbed and spine a little faded. Nice. Rota 230-167 1983 £60

DOUGLAS, NORMAN   Nerinda. Florence: G. Orioli, 1929. Roy. 8vo. Orig. orange boards, uncut edges. Limited edition of 475 copies, numbered and signed by the author. Boards slightly soiled. Traylen 94-284 1983 £50

DOUGLAS, NORMAN   Nerinda (1901). Florence: G. Orioli, 1929. First edition. Orig. paper-covered boards. One of 475 copies, numbered and signed by author. Covers dirty. MacManus 278-1616 1983 $55

DOUGLAS, NORMAN On the Herpetology of the Grand Duchy of Baden. London, 1894. First edition. Wrappers. Upper wrapper lightly foxed and staples rusted. Inscribed: "For Arthur Johnson with best wishes for 1948 from Norman Douglas. Capri Jan 1948." Nice. Rota 230-166 1983 £300

DOUGLAS, NORMAN One Day. Chapelle-Reanville: Hours Press, 1929. Boards. First edition. One of 300 numbered copies on Verges, from an edition of 500 copies. Very slight traces of rubbing, else a fine copy. Reese 20-525 1983 $100

DOUGLAS, NORMAN One Day. Chapelle-Reanville: Hours Press, 1929. Full crimson roan. First edition. One of 200 numbered copies, printed on Velin de Rives, and signed by the author, from a total edition of 500. Binding material rather worn. Internally, a fine copy. Reese 20-526 1983 $45

DOUGLAS, NORMAN One Day. Eure, France: Hours Press, 1929. Roy. 8vo. Orig. boards, uncut edges. Limited edition of 300 numbered copies, printed on Verge paper. Traylen 94-285 1983 £25

DOUGLAS, NORMAN Paneros. London, 1931. First English edition. Tall 8vo, dec. boards, buckram back, one of 650 numbered copies. Argosy 714-245 1983 $75

DOUGLAS, NORMAN Paneros. Some words on Aphrodisiacs and the Like. London, 1931. Roy. 8vo. Boards, buckram spine. Frontis. Limited edition of 650 numbered copies. Spine a little faded. Traylen 94-286 1983 £28

DOUGLAS, NORMAN Some Antiquarian Notes. Naples, 1907. First edition. One of 250 copies. Wrappers. Neatly rebacked and preliminaries lightly foxed. Inscribed to author's friend and publisher, dated Florence, 1924. Nice. Rota 231-181 1983 £300

DOUGLAS, NORMAN Some Limericks. 1928. Privately printed. Limited to 750 numbered copies, this copy unnumbered, covers soiled, some extra limericks pencilled in. Quill & Brush 54-379 1983 $30

DOUGLAS, NORMAN Some Limericks. N.p.: Privately Printed, 1928 (i.e. Philadelphia: Nathan Young & William Sterling, 1931). Second American edition. Orig. cloth. Limited to 750 copies. Bookplate. Fine. MacManus 278-1617 1983 $25

DOUGLAS, NORMAN South Wind. Chicago, Argus Books, 1929. Illustrated in color and black and white by John Austen. 2 vols., 8vo, dust wrappers, original box--partly cracked. Virtually fine. Morrill 290-105 1983 $42.50

DOUGLAS, NORMAN Summer Islands. N.Y.: The Colophon, 1931. First edition. Illus. with pen & ink drawings by H. Willard. 4to. Orig. decorated cloth, in publisher's slipcase. Limited to 550 copies signed by Douglas. Slipcase partially faded. Fine. MacManus 278-1619 1983 $125

DOUGLAS, NORMAN Summer Islands. NY, 1931. Limited to 550 numbered and signed copies, spine very slightly darkened, else very good or better in remnants of slipcase. Quill & Brush 54-380 1983 $50

DOUGLAS, NORMAN Three Monographs. Naples, July, 1906. First edition. One of 250 copies. Wrappers. Little wear at head and foot of backstrip and some foxing. Nice. Rota 231-180 1983 £125

DOUGLAS, NORMAN Together. London, 1923. First edition. One of 275 numbered copies, signed by author. Cloth a little bubbled and spotted. Torn dust wrapper. Nice. Rota 231-182 1983 £45

DOUGLAS, NORMAN Together. Cahpman & Hall, 1923. First edition, half title. Orig. maroon cloth, sl. marked. Jarndyce 31-988 1988 £16.50

DOUGLAS, ROBERT The Peerage of Scotland. Edinburgh: Printed by R. Fleming, 1764. 1st ed., folio, 10 plates containing 120 engraved coats of arms, contemporary calf, gilt, morocco label, joints cracked. Deighton 3-111 1983 £65

DOUGLAS, ROBERT B. Sophie Arnould. Paris: Charles Carrington, 1898. Gilt cloth. Illus. with seven copper-plate engravings by Adolphe Lalauze, and printed on Japan vellum. Very fine copy. One of 500 copies. Reese 20-224 1983 $50

DOUGLAS, STEPHEN M. Remarks of the Hon. Stephen A. Douglas, on Kansas, Utah, and the Dred Scott Decision. Chicago, 1857. Self-wraps., faint library stamp, very good. Reese 19-201 1983 $150

DOUGLAS, WALTER B. An Account of Manuel Lisa. St. Louis, 1911. 2 vols. Orig. printed wraps. First edition. Ginsberg 47-432 1983 $75

DOUGLAS, WILLIAM W. Relief of Washington, North Carolina, by the Fifth Rhode Island Volunteers. Providence, 1886. Orig. printed wraps. First edition. One of 250 copies. Ginsberg 46-551 1983 $20

DOUGLAS-LITHGOW, R. A. Dictionary of American-Indian Place and Proper Names in New England. Salem, 1909. First edition. Portrait. 8vo. Lacks front endleaf. Morrill 290-634 1983 $40

DOUGLASS, A. E. Climatic Cycles and Tree Growth, Vol. 3. Washington, 1936. Wrappers. Wheldon 160-2081 1983 £12

DOUGLASS, FREDERICK My Bondage and My Freedom. NY, 1855. First edition. Engr. port. 8vo, orig. stamped cloth (edges scuffed, neatly rebacked with orig. backstrip). Ex-lib. Argosy 716-18 1983 $50

DOUTHIT, MARY O. The Souvenir of Western Women. Portland, Ore., 1905. Illus., many by Charles M. Russell. Orig. printed pictorial wraps. First edition. Uncut. Ginsberg 47-307 1983 $125

DOUTHIT, MARY O The Souvenir of Western Women. Portland, 1905. Color frontis. Wrappers, creased. Unopened. Dawson 471-70 1983 $20

DOUTHWAITE, W. R. Gray's Inn. N.p., London, 1876. First edition. Half title, orig. brown cloth, sl. rubbed at head of spine. Jarndyce 31-243 1983 £14.50

DOVE, HEINRICH WILHELM The law of storms considered in connection with the ordinary movements of the atmosphere. London: Longman, etc., 1862. First edition in English. 8vo. Orig. purple-brown cloth. With four folding charts. Ownership stamp of Sir Joseph Hooker. A bit rubbed. Ximenes 63-302 1983 $125

DOW, DANIEL A Dissertation, on the Sinaitic and Abrahamic Covenants. Hartford: Peter B. Gleason & Co., 1811. Disbound. Very good. Felcone 20-74 1983 $30

DOW, GEORGE F. Every Day Life in the Massachusetts Bay Colony. Boston, 1935. Illus. diagrams, cloth-backed bds., ex-library. Argosy 710-101 1983 $35

DOW, JOY WHEELER American Renaissance. NY: William T. Comstock, 1904. 4to. Green cloth. Illus. by ninety-six half-tone plates. Karmiole 74-7 1983 $60

DOW, MOSES A Sermon Preached in Beverly...on Account of War with Great-Britain. Salem, 1813. Dsb., good. Reese 18-412 1983 $20

DOWELL, WILLIAM CHIPCASE The Webley Story, A History of Webley Pistols and Revolvers. Leeds (1962). Illus., cloth, very good in frayed dw. Signed by author. King 46-565 1983 $100

DOWNING, CLEMENT A Compendious History of the Indian Wars. London: For T. Cooper, 1737. 12mo. Full cont. straight-grain morocco. Panelled boards, gilt edges. Good. Edwards 1044-200 1983 £300

DOWNES, WILLIAM HOWE John S. Sargent. Boston, 1925. First edition. Illustrated. 4to. Former owner has installed thumb-index tabs on fore-edge; some underlining in text. Morrill 290-106 1983 $20

DOWNEY, FAIRFAX   Portrait of an Era as Drawn by C. D.
Gibson. New York, (1936). Illus. of Gibson's drawings. 8vo,
slightly torn and repaired dust wrapper. 1st ed. Presentation copy.
Morrill 287-94 1983 $20

DOWNIE, WILLIAM   Hunting for Gold. San Francisco: 1893.
First edition. Portrait, 70 other illus. Blue cloth. Very good.
Bradley 66-539 1983 $150

DOWNING, ANDREW JACKSON   A Treatise on the Theory and Practice
of Landscape Gardening. New York, 1884. 2nd ed., enlarged, revised,
newly illus. 8vo. Rubbed, spine partly torn, binding partly broken.
Morrill 287-562 1983 $25

DOWNMAN, HUGH   Tragedies. Exeter: by E. Grigg for
G.G.J. & J. Robinson, 1792. First collected edition. 8vo. Half
calf, worn. Heath 48-284 1983 £60

DOWSING, WILLIAM   The Journal of William Dowsing of
Stratford... Woodbridge, (Suffolk): by and for R. Loder, 1786.
First edition. Large 4to. Uncut in later cloth. Generally damp
affected, couple of small repairs. Very rare. Heath 48-590

DOWSON, ERNEST   Dilemmas. London: Elkin Mathews, 1895.
First edition. Orig. cloth. Bookplate. Very good. MacManus 278-
1620 1983 $85

DOWSON, ERNEST   The Poetical Works of Ernest Christopher
Dowson. London, 1934. First edition. Spine and covers a little
faded. Nice. Rota 231-183 1983 $20

DOYLE, ARTHUR CONAN   The Adventure of the Blue Carbuncle.
New York: Baker Street Irregulars, Inc., 1948. 8vo, cloth, slipcase.
Deluxe edition, one of 1,500 copies. First separate appearance.
Duschnes 240-75 1983 $75

DOYLE, ARTHUR CONAN   The Adventure of the Blue Carbuncle.
N.Y., 1948. First edition. D.w. Argosy 714-247 1983 $40

DOYLE, ARTHUR CONAN   The Adventure of the Blue Carbuncle.
N.Y.: The Baker Street Irregulars, 1948. First separate edition.
Orig. cloth. First book published by the Baker Street Irregulars.
Very good. MacManus 278-1623 1983 $30

DOYLE, ARTHUR CONAN   The Adventures of Gerard. N.Y.: McClure,
Phillips & Co., 1903. First American edition. Illus. by W.B. Wollen.
Orig. pictorial cloth. Illus. differ from the English edition. Erasure
on front flyleaf. Fine. MacManus 278-1624 1983 $35

DOYLE, ARTHUR CONAN   The Adventures of Sherlock Holmes.
George Newnes, 1893. 2nd edition, half title, vignette illus. Orig.
light blue dec. cloth, a.e.g., v.g. Jarndyce 31-674 1983 £35

DOYLE, ARTHUR CONAN   The British Campaign in France & Flanders,
1914. London: Hodder & Stoughton, 1916. First edition. Illus. with
maps. Orig. cloth. Covers slightly soiled. Very good. MacManus 278-
1627 1983 $45

DOYLE, ARTHUR CONAN   The British Campaign in France & Flanders,
1915. N.Y.: George H. Doran Co., (1917). First American edition.
Illus. with maps. Orig. cloth. Very good. MacManus 278-1626 1983
$35

DOYLE, ARTHUR CONAN   The British Campaign in France & Flanders,
1916. N.Y.: George H. Doran Co., (1918). First American edition.
Illus. with maps. Orig. cloth. Very good. MacManus 278-1625 1983
$35

DOYLE, ARTHUR CONAN   The Casebook of Sherlock Holmes.
London, 1927. First editon. Very slightly faded at the spine,
offsetting to end-papers, but a fine copy. Gekoski 2-40 1983
£110

DOYLE, ARTHUR CONAN   The Case Book of Sherlock Holmes. New
York: Doran, (1927). 1st American ed., 1st printing with Doran logo
on copyright page. Orig. tan cloth. Fine copy of extremely scarce
book. Jenkins 155-336 1983 $150

DOYLE, ARTHUR CONAN   The Case Book of Sherlock Holmes.
NY (1927). First American ed. Cloth, rubbed and soiled covers.
King 46-274 1983 $50

DOYLE, ARTHUR CONAN   The Case Book of Sherlock Holmes. NY,
(1927). First American edition. Cloth, reading copy only. King
45-590 1983 $20

DOYLE, ARTHUR CONAN   The Conan Doyle Stories. London: John
Murray, (1929). First one-volume edition. Orig. cloth. Thick 8vo.
Dust jacket. Covers somewhat mottled. Spine faded beneath jacket.
With a publisher's flyer laid in. Very good. MacManus 278-1643
1983 $60

DOYLE, ARTHUR CONAN   The Croxley Master and Other Tales. N.Y.:
George H. Doran Co., n.d. (c. 1919). First of this edition. Orig.
pictorial cloth. Dust jacket (a bit torn and worn). Fine. MacManus
278-1645 1983 $45

DOYLE, ARTHUR CONAN   Danger! London: John Murray, 1918.
First edition. Orig. gold cloth. Fine. MacManus 278-1647 1983 $65

DOYLE, ARTHUR CONAN   Danger! London: John Murray, 1918.
First edition. Orig. red cloth. Spine faded. Bookplate. MacManus
278-1646 1983 $60

DOYLE, ARTHUR CONAN   Danger! and other stories. London, 1918.
First edition. Name on flyleaf. Very nice. Rota 230-169 1983 £25

DOYLE, ARTHUR CONAN   A Desert Drama. Phila., 1898.
First American edition. Illus. pict. cloth. Argosy 714-248 1983
$40

DOYLE, ARTHUR CONAN   The Dooings of Raffles Haw. London:
Cassell, 1892. First edition. Orig. cloth. Covers a little marked.
Bookplate of Vincent Starrett. Very good. MacManus 278-1648 1983
$125

DOYLE, ARTHUR CONAN   A Duet. N.Y., 1899. First American
edition. Fine. Argosy 714-249 1983 $35

DOYLE, ARTHUR CONAN   The Exploits of Brigadier Gerard.
N.Y., 1896. Illus. First American edition. Argosy 714-250 1983
$35

DOYLE, ARTHUR CONAN   Ghost Stories & Presentiments. London:
George Redway, n.d. (c.1888). First edition, second issue. Orig.
light-blue decorated cloth. Spine and covers slightly worn and soiled.
Good. MacManus 278-1628 1983 $125

DOYLE, ARTHUR CONAN   The Great Boer War. London, 1900.
First edition. 8vo, cloth; inner hinges starting. Argosy 714-251
1983 $65

DOYLE, ARTHUR CONAN   The Green Flag and Other Stories of War
& Sport. N.Y.: McClure, Phillips & Co., 1900. First American edition.
Orig. decorated green cloth. Publisher's presentation copy, inscribed
on the flyleaf: "Compliments of McClure, Phillips & Co., Dec. 20. 1900."
Bookplate on front endsheet. Very good. MacManus 278-1629 1983 $40

DOYLE, ARTHUR CONAN   His Last Bow. London: Murray, 1917.
First edition. Orig. cloth. Spine dull. Small landscape picture
pasted to front flyleaf. MacManus 278-1649 1983 $85

DOYLE, ARTHUR CONAN   His Last Bow. N.Y., (1917). 8vo, cloth
faded. Argosy 714-253 1983 $20

DOYLE, ARTHUR CONAN   The Hound of the Baskervilles. London,
Newnes, 1902. First edition. Frontis. and 15 plates by Sidney Paget.
Fine full navy blue morocco binding by Bayntun, raised bands on spine
with gilt panels, covers ruled in gilt, gilt inner dentelles, a.e.g.,
marbled endpapers, orig. cloth bound in. Fine copy. Houle 22-315
1983 $550

DOYLE, ARTHUR CONAN   The Land of Mist. London, (1926).
First edition. 8vo, cloth. Fine. Argosy 714-252 1983 $50

DOYLE, ARTHUR CONAN   The Last Galley. London: Smith, Elder
& Co., 1911. First edition. Illus. by N.C. Wyeth (colored frontis.).
Orig. decorated cloth. Spine wrinkled. Bookplate. Good. MacManus
278-1650 1983 $50

DOYLE, ARTHUR CONAN   The Lost World. London: Hodder and
Stoughton, (ca. 1912). Gilt cloth. Frontis. First edition. A
couple of tiny nicks in rear joint, otherwise a fine copy. Reese 20-
331 1983 $85

DOYLE, ARTHUR CONAN   The Lost World. London: Hodder &
Stoughton, n.d. First edition. Illus. Orig. pictorial cloth. Covers
somewhat rubbed. Bookplate. Very good. MacManus 278-1652 1983
$150

DOYLE, ARTHUR CONAN   The Maracot Deep. Garden City: Doubleday, Doran & Co., 1929. First American edition. Orig. cloth. Former
owner's signature on flyleaf. With remnants of orig. dust jacket in
acetate jacket. Fine. MacManus 278-1654 1983 $25

DOYLE, ARTHUR CONAN   The Memoirs of Sherlock Holmes. London:
George Newnes, 1894. First edition. Illus. by Sidney Paget. Orig.
cloth. Much better than average copy. Fine. MacManus 278-1657
1983 $550

DOYLE, ARTHUR CONAN   The Memoirs of Sherlock Holmes. London:
Geo. Newnes, 1894. First edition. Illus. by Sidney Paget. Tall 8vo,
dec. blue cloth, inner joint cracked, bevelled edges, g.e. New
endpapers. Argosy 714-254 1983 $200

DOYLE, ARTHUR CONAN   Micah Clarke, His Statement. N.Y.:
A.L. Burt, n.d. (March 16, 1895). Early American reprint. Orig.
printed wrappers. Fine. MacManus 278-1655 1983 $25

DOYLE, ARTHUR CONAN   My First Book: The Experiences of.
London, 1894. 8vo. Cloth. A Little rubbing to cloth, else about
fine, partially unopened copy. 185 illus. In Our Time 156-216
1983 $100

DOYLE, ARTHUR CONAN   The Mystery of Cloomber. N.Y.: R.F.
Fenno & Co., 1903. Orig. stiff pictorial wrappers. Very good.
MacManus 278-1659 1983 $20

DOYLE, ARTHUR CONAN   The New Revelation. London: Hodder &
Stoughton, 1918. First edition. Orig. cloth. Stamped "For Review"
on half-title. Poor. MacManus 278-1660 1983 $20

DOYLE, ARTHUR CONAN   Pheneas Speaks. London: The Psychic
Press, n.d. (1927). First edition. Frontis. port. Orig. cloth.
Former owner's signature on flyleaf. Covers somewhat faded and soiled.
MacManus 278-1661 1983 $25

DOYLE, ARTHUR CONAN   The Poison Belt. London: Hodder &
Stoughton, (1913). First edition. 16 illus. by H. Roundtree. Orig.
pictorial cloth. Spine faded; shaken; and worn. MacManus 278-1662
1983 $125

DOYLE, ARTHUR CONAN   Rodney Stone. London: Smith, Elder,
1896. First edition. Illus. Orig. cloth. Good. MacManus 278-1665
1983 $60

DOYLE, ARTHUR CONAN   Rodney Stone. New York: Appleton,
1896. Frontis., plates. 1st American ed. Orig. maroon cloth,
gilt. Spine evenly faded, but a fresh copy. Jenkins 155-341 1983
$20

DOYLE, ARTHUR CONAN   Sir Nigel. London: Smith, Elder, 1906.
First edition. Orig. cloth. Spine faded. Good. MacManus 278-1667
1983 $35

DOYLE, ARTHUR CONAN   Songs of Action. N.Y.: Doubleday &
McClure Co., 1898. First American edition. Orig. cloth. Fine.
MacManus 278-1669 1983 $50

DOYLE, ARTHUR CONAN   Songs of Action. London: Smith, Elder,
1898. First edition. 12mo. Orig. cloth. MacManus 278-1668 1983
$50

DOYLE, ARTHUR CONAN   The Stark Munro Letters. London: Longmans, Green, & Co., 1895. First edition. Illus. Orig. cloth. Very
good. MacManus 278-1670 1983 $75

DOYLE, ARTHUR CONAN   The Stark Munro Letters. Longmans,
Green, 1895. First edition, half title, front. 24 pp ads. Orig.
dark blue cloth, lettered in gilt, bevelled boards, v.g. Jarndyce
31-675 1983 £40

DOYLE, ARTHUR CONAN   Strange Secrets. N.Y.: R.F. Fenno &
Co., (1895). First American appearance (?). Orig. pictorial cloth.
Spine a bit faded, a little dusty. Very good. MacManus 278-1671
1983 $65

DOYLE, ARTHUR CONAN   A Study in Scarlet. London: Ward, Lock
& Bowden Limited, 1893. New edition. 40 illus. by Geo. Hutchinson.
Orig. two-tone cloth. Recased, with spine repaired at top and bottom.
Covers somewhat dust-soiled & worn. In a blue half-morocco slipcase.
MacManus 278-1672 1983 $75

DOYLE, ARTHUR CONAN   Tales of Sherlock Holmes. N.Y.: Grosset
& Dunlap, n.d. (ca. 1920). Orig. decorated cloth. With photographic
illus. of stage performances of the Sherlock Holmes stories. Edges
slightly worn, a few pages opened carelessly. A trifle foxed. Good.
MacManus 278-1631 1983 $35

DOYLE, ARTHUR CONAN   Three of Them. London: Murray, 1923.
First edition. 12mo. Orig. cloth-backed boards. Dust jacket. With
the publisher's prospectus laid in. Fine. MacManus 278-1674 1983
$135

DOYLE, ARTHUR CONAN   Three of Them. London, 1923. First
edition. 16mo, cloth backed boards, rubbed. Argosy 714-255 1983
$30

DOYLE, ARTHUR CONAN   Through the Magic Door. London: Smith,
Elder & Co., 1907. First edition. 16 illus. Orig. red pictorial
cloth. Fine. MacManus 278-1675 1983 $65

DOYLE, ARTHUR CONAN   Through The Magic Door. London:
Smith, Elder & Co., 1907. First edition. 8vo. Red cloth. Contains
16 illus. Some rubbing. Oak Knoll 49-163 1983 $65

DOYLE, ARTHUR CONAN   Through the Magic Door. N.Y.: The
McClure Co., 1908. First American edition. Orig. gilt-decorated cloth.
Fine. MacManus 278-1676 1983 $50

DOYLE, ARTHUR CONAN   Through the Magic Door. London, 1907.
First edition. 8vo. Orig. red cloth, gilt. 16 illus. Spine faded.
Traylen 94-287 1983 £20

DOYLE, ARTHUR CONAN   Through the Magic Door. NY, 1908. Spine
slightly darkened and edges rubbed, marks on upper spine edges, very
good. Quill & Brush 54-381 1983 $30

DOYLE, ARTHUR CONAN   The Tragedy of the Korosko. London,
Smith, Elder, 1898. First edition. Illus. with 40 full page plates
by Sidney Paget. Gilt decorated red cloth (spine a bit faded, slight
foxing), uncut, else, very good. Houle 22-316 1983 $75

DOYLE, ARTHUR CONAN   The Tragedy of Korosko. London: Smith,
Elder, 1898. First edition. Illus. Orig. cloth. Back cover waterstained. MacManus 278-1677 1983 $35

DOYLE, ARTHUR CONAN   Uncle Bernac: A Memory of the Empire.
London, Smith Elder, 1897. First complete edition in book form.
12 illus. by Tauber. Gilt decorated red cloth (spine slightly faded,
inner hinges starting), else, very good. Houle 22-317 1983 $65

DOYLE, ARTHUR CONAN   Uncle Bernac. London: Smith, Elder,
1897. First published edition. Orig. cloth. Good. MacManus 278-
1678 1983 $50

DOYLE, ARTHUR CONAN   The Valley of Fear. N.Y., (1914).
8vo, red cloth. First edition. Argosy 714-256 1983 $100

DOYLE, ARTHUR CONAN   The War in South Africa, its Cause and
Conduct. Smith, Elder, 1902. First edition, half title, orig.
printed wraps. Some slight wear, but a good copy. Jarndyce 31-676
1983 £64

DOYLE, ARTHUR CONAN   The White Company. London: Smith, Elder,
1891. First edition. 3 vols. Orig. cloth. Ex-library copy, with
labels removed from the front covers. Recased with new endpapers in
vol. 2; lacking the blank leaves before the half-titles in vols. 2 & 3,
and the ads in vol. 2. Worn. MacManus 278-1680 1983 $250

DOYLE, JAMES E.   A Chronicle of England, BC. 55 - AD.
1485. Longman, etc., 1864. 1st edn. Illus. by author, engr'd &
printed in colour by Edmund Evans. Title page printed in red & black
& 81 colour illus. Plum pebble grain cloth gilt, bevelled boards,
a.e.g., red eps. (designed by John Leighton) (re-backed with orig.
bkstrip, eps. strengthened at hinges with cloth tape), v.g. Hodgkins
27-364 1983 £265

DOYLE, JAMES E.   A Chronicle of England, B.C. 55 -
A.D. 1485. London: Longman, Green, etc., 1864. First edition.
4to. Orig. dark brown morocco cloth ornately gilt with heraldic
design on covers, gilt decorated spine, edges gilt. Title-page
printed in red and black, colour-printed illus. in the text,
decorative initials in red and black. Half-title. Traylen 94-288
1983 £60

D'OYLEY, CHARLES   The European in India. London, 1813.
20 fine hand-coloured plates. Endpapers spotted and stained. 4to.
Full straight-grain morocco, richly gilt spine, gilt edges. Good.
Edwards 1044-204 1983 £235

D'OYLEY, CHARLES   Indian Sports. Behar: Amateur Litho-
graphic Press, n.d. (1828?). 12 engraved plates and engraved title.
Oblong folio. Half morocco, marbled boards. Bookplate of Archibald
Trotter. 8vo. Good. Edwards 1044-203 1983 £750

D'OYLEY, CHARLES   Original Commonplace Book. London, 1826.
Containing 80 orig. wash, pencil, pen and ink and watercolour drawings,
including some lithographs, probably from his own lithographic press,
beautifully executed and mostly signed and dated. Thick 4to. Blue
morocco, worn. This volume passed from D'Oyley to St. G. D. Showers,
whose name is stamped in gilt on the upper cover. Later it was in the
possession of Capt. E. W. Martindell, with his "Jungle Book" Kipling
Society bookplate. Good. Edwards 1044-202 1983 £3,650

D'OYLEY, CHARLES   Tom Raw, The Griffin. London, 1828.
First edition. 25 finely coloured plates. Occasional offsetting onto
text. Half marbled calf, morocco labels, spine gilt. 8vo. Good.
Edwards 1044-205 1983 £250

DRAGO, HARRY SINCLAIR   Following the Grass. New York: The
Macaulay Co., 1924. First edition in dust jacket. Frontis. Inscribed
by author. Jenkins 152-90 1983 $35

DRAGO, HARRY SINCLAIR   Outlaws on Horseback. N.Y., Dodd,
Mead, (1964). First edition. Illus. Full red morocco, t.e.g.
One of 150 numbered copies signed by the author. Pub.'s slipcase.
Houle 22-1049 1983 $125

DRAGO, HARRY SINCLAIR   Outlaws on Horseback. The History of
the Organized Bands of Bank and Train Robbers. New York, 1964.
Limited boxed edition of 150 copies and signed by the author. Illus.
Fine copy. A good work and scarce in the limited edition. Jenkins
151-66 1983 $85

DRAGO, HARRY SINCLAIR   Suzanna a Romance of Early California.
New York: The Macaulay Co., 1922. First edition. Frontis. Jenkins
152-100 1983 $35

DRAGO, HARRY SINCLAIR   Whispering Sage. New York: The Century
Co., 1922. First edition. Frontis. Fine. Jenkins 152-102 1983 $30

DRAGO, HARRY SINCLAIR   The Wild Bunch. N.Y., 1934. Orig.
cloth. First edition. Ginsberg 47-308 1983 $30

DRAGO, HARRY SINCLAIR   Wild, Woolly & Wicked. New York, 1960.
First edition. Limited to 250 copies, numbered and signed by author.
Fine. Jenkins 152-101 1983 $75

DRAGONE, ANGELO   Delleani. Biella: Cassa di Risparmio
di Biella, 1973-1974. 2 vols. 471 illus. (134 tipped-in color
plates). Large stout 4to. Cloth. Dust jacket. Slipcase. Small
numbered edition. Ars Libri 33-453 1983 $225

DRAKE, CHARLES D.   Drake's Victoria Speech. St. Louis,
1860. First edition. Dbd. Ginsberg 47-518 1983 $35

DRAKE, DANIEL   Memoirs of (his) Life and Services.
Cincinnati, 1855. First edition. 8vo, orig. cloth. Argosy 713-160
1983 $50

DRAKE, DANIEL   Natural and Statistical View...
Cincinnati, 1815. 2 folding maps. Orig. printed boards, stained,
chipped at head and tail of spine, some scattered foxing internally.
Reese 18-472 1983 $825

DRAKE, DANIEL   Pioneer Education and Life. Cedar
Rapids, Iowa: Torch Press, 1939. 1st edition. Privately printed.
Limited to 400 copies. Original glassline dust jacket. Jenkins
151-67 1983 $45

DRAKE, DANIEL   Pioneer Life in Kentucky. N.Y., (1948).
Illus. Tall 8vo, 1/4 cloth. One of 250 large-paper copies, printed
at the Golden Eagle Press. Argosy 713-157 1983 $125

DRAKE, FRANCIS   Eboracum: Or the History and Antiquities
of the City of York. London, William Bowyer for the Author, 1736.
Complete with all the fine maps, plans, plates and text-engravings,
folio, a good fresh copy in cont. calf. K Books 301-62 1983 £200

DRAKE, FRANCIS   Le Voyage de l'illustre Seigner et
Chevalier Francois Drach Admiral d'Angleterre... Paris: Jean
Gesselin, 1613. Woodcut title vignette. Headpieces, and decorative
initials. Small 8vo. Limp vellum. In a cloth box. First edition.
Kraus 164-67 1983 $18,500

DRAKE, FRANCIS S.   Tea Leaves. Boston: A.O. Crane, 1884.
4to, profusely illus. with full-page plates. Illus. brown cloth.
Karmiole 76-39 1983 $50

DRAKE, FRANCIS S.   The Town of Roxbury. Roxbury, Author,
1878. 1st ed. 8vo. Inner hinges partly cracked, otherwise nice.
Morrill 287-222 1983 $35

DRAKE, J. MADISON   Historical Sketches of the Revolutionary
and Civil Wars. NY: for the Author, 1908. Frontis. 1st ed.
Argosy 710-82 1983 $30

DRAKE, JAMES   The antient and modern stages survey'd.
London: printed for Abel Roper, 1699. 8vo, cont. calf (worn, front
cover loose). 1st ed. Some worming in the lower margin of the last
few leaves. Ximenes 64-179 1983 $225

DRAKE, JOSEPH RODMAN   The Culprit Fay and Other Poems. N.Y.:
1923. 8vo, parchment-backed boards, t.e.g. Illus. One of 300 copies.
Fine. Perata 28-71 1983 $60

DRAKE, NATHAN   Evenings in autumn. London: Longman,
etc., 1822. First edition. 2 vols. 8vo. Orig. blue boards, drab
paper spines, printed paper labels. Very fine copy. Ximenes 63-238
1983 $225

DRAKE, NATHAN   Literary Hours. London: Printed for
Longman, Hurst, Rees, Orme, and Brown, 1820. Fourth edition, corrected.
3 vols. Orig. boards with paper labels on spines. Bookplates. Tops
of spines, chipped. Very good. MacManus 278-1683 1983 $50

DRAKE, NATHAN   Shakespeare and His Times. Printed for
T. Cadell and W. Davies, 1817. 2 vols., 4to, portrait in each volume.
Cont. half calf, spines gilt. Tipped into the front of vol. 2 is
J. Britton's Remarks on the Monumental Bust of Shakespeare at
Stratford-upon-Avon... 1816. 8vo, inscribed by the author to R.
Drake at the top of the title. First edition. Bickersteth 75-131
1983 £40

DRAKE, NATHAN   Shakespeare and his Times. London:
T. Cadell and W. Davies, 1817. First edition. 2 vols. 4to. Half
calf, gilt spines with green morocco labels, gilt. Portrait and
frontis. (foxed). Joints weak. Traylen 94-732 1983 £38

DRAKE, S. C.   Black Metropolis: A Study of Negro
Life. NY, (1945). Errata slip present, endpapers slightly offset,
very good in slightly frayed dustwrapper. Quill & Brush 54-1597 1983
$60

DRAKE, SAMUEL A.   Nooks & Corners of the New England Coast.
N.Y.: Harper & Brothers, 1875. Illus. Orig. pictorial cloth. Fine.
Jenkins 152-103 1983 $40

DRAKE, SAMUEL G.   The History and Antiquities of Boston...
Boston, Luther Stevens, 1856. 1st ed. Plates, some folding, and
text illus. Large 8vo, half morocco, marbled sides. Very nice.
Morrill 287-223 1983 $60

DRANNAN, WILLIAM F.   Thirty-One Years on the Plains and in the
Mountains. Chicago: Rhodes & McClure Pub. Co., 1899. Illustrations.
Original cloth with silver gilting. Nice copy. Jenkins 153-174 1983
$150

DRAPER, JOHN C.   Text-Book on Anatomy, Physiology, &
Hygiene. N.Y., 1870. 8vo, 170 text illus. Ex-lib. Argosy 713-159
1983 $40

DRAPER, JOHN W.   A Century of Broadside Elegies...
London: Ingpen and Grant, 1928. Large 4to. Boards, buckram
spine, t.e.g., others uncut. Limited edition of 275 numbered
copies with 100 full-page facsimiles. Traylen 94-289 1983
£65

DRAPER, JOHN W   Human Physiology, Statistical &
Dynamical. N.Y., 1856. 8vo, 300 illus. Cloth (back crudely taped);
ex-lib. First edition. Argosy 713-158 1983 $100

DRAPER, LYMAN C.   Madison, the Capital of Wisconsin.
Madison: Calkins & Proudfit, 1857. Illus., with a map & a view
of the city, both on the back cover. Orig. printed wraps., soiled,
a round water stain affecting the first 25 pages. Karmiole 71-43
1983 $75

DRAPER, THEODORE   The 84th Infantry Division in the
Battle of Germany...New York, 1946. 1st ed. Maps and drawings by
Sgt. Walter H. Chapman; also photographs. 8vo. Morrill 287-535
1983 $27.50

DRAPER, WILLIAM R.   A Cub Reporter in the Old Indian
Territory. Girard, Kansas, 1946. Ptd. wrp. Jenkins 153-176 1983
$30

DRAPER, WILLIAM R.   Exciting Adventures Along the Indian
Frontier. Girard, Kansas, 1946. 1st ed. Ptd. wrp. Jenkins 153-177
1983 $25

DRAWING and Painting Exercises. N.p. (English, ca. 1880's). Oblong
octavo. Full-color illus. and b&w line drawings. Some very light
occasional foxing, otherwise nice copy in slightly rubbed monochrome
pictorial wrappers. Bromer 25-345 1983 $35

DRAYSON, ALFRED W.   Sporting Scenes Amongst the Kaffirs
of South Africa. 1858. Coloured frontis. and 6 coloured plates of
7 (plate to face page 193 lacking but a photo facsimile is present),
uncoloured plate to face page 50 present but not listed, bound in
new half calf. K Books 301-63 1983 £52

DRAYTON, MICHAEL   Nimphidia, the Count of Fayrie.
Stratford-upon-Avon, at the Shakespeare Head, 1921. Untrimmed.
Printed boards, vellum spine, labels a little darkened. Jarndyce 31-
989 1983 £12.50

DRAYTON, MICHAEL   Poly-Olbion, or a Chorographicall
Description of Tracts... London: by H. Lownes for Mathew Lownes...,
1613. Folio. Cont. calf, neatly rebacked with the orig. spine
laid down. Engraved title-page by W. Hole, printed title, and
18 fine engraved maps, wood-engraved head- and tail-pieces thoughout. Some tears and neat repairs, slight staining mainly confined
to the margins. Traylen 94-290 1983 £2,800

DREADFULL Newes: or a true relation of the great, violent and
late earthquake... London: printed by I. Okes, for R. Mab, 1638.
First edition. Small 4to. Disbound. Very good copy. Rare.
Ximenes 63-89 1983 $350

THE DREAMER'S Sure Guide. New York, Elton & Harrison, 1837. Woodcuts, some colored by former owner. 24mo, orig. printed and pic.
boards. Restitched along backstrip. Morrill 289-604 1983 $45

DREIER, KATHERINE S.   Shawn the Dancer. NY: A.S. Barnes
and Co. Inc., 1933. Large 4to, color frontis. + 42 photo plates.
Presentation copy, signed by Shawn in 1954. Black cloth over
boards. Karmiole 72-38 1983 $100

DREISER, THEODORE   Chains: Lesser Novels and Stories.
New York, 1927. 8vo. Cloth. Price clipped on dj. else a fine copy
in flawless dj. In Our Time 156-217 1983 $100

DREISER, THEODORE   Dawn. N.Y., (1931). Ltd. first
edition. One of 275 signed copies. Argosy 714-260 1983 $100

DREISER, THEODORE   Epitaph: A Poem. New York, (1929).
Illus. by Robert Fawcett. Large quarto, black Japanese silk, stamped
in silver. 1 of 200 on handmade Keijyo Kami paper, signed by Dreiser
and artist. In glassine jacket and slipcase. Very fine. Bradley 63-
44 1983 $200

DREISER, THOEDORE   Epitaph. NY, (1929). Illus. by Robt.
Fawcett. One of 200 numbered copies signed by both author and illus.,
printed on hand-made Keijyo Kami and bound in Japanese silk, near
fine, slightly worn. Quill & Brush 54-386 1983 $200

DREISER, THEODORE   Epitaph. New York: Heron Press, (1929).
Folio. Black Japanese silk. First edition. One of 200 numbered
copies, specially printed on handmade Keijyo Kami paper, and signed
by the author, and the artist Robert Fawcett, from a total edition of
1,100 copies. A very fine copy in orig. glassine (slightly chipped),
and gilt slipcase. Reese 20-334 1983 $150

DREISER, THEODORE   The Financier. NY, 1912. Front hinge
starting, else bright, very good copy. Quill & Brush 54-387 1983
$45

DREISER, THEODORE   The Financier. NY, 1912. Spine sunned,
spine edges frayed, otherwise good. Quill & Brush 54-388 1983 $40

DREISER, THEODORE   The Financier, a Novel. New York:
Harper, 1912. 1st ed. Orig. cloth, gilt. Spine slightly aged,
else nice copy. Jenkins 155-343 1983 $20

DREISER, THEODORE   Fine Furniture. New York, 1930. 8vo.
Wraps. 1 of 875 copies. Very good-fine copy. In Our Time 156-218
1983 $25

DREISER, THEODORE   A Gallery of Women. N.Y., 1929. First
edition. 2 vols., d.w., chipped. Argosy 714-261 1983 $25

DREISER, THEODORE   The "Genius." N.Y., 1915. First edition.
Earliest issue, with p. 497 numbered. 8vo, red ribbed cloth. Argosy
714-262 1983 $100

DREISER, THEODORE   Sister Carrie. New York: Limited
Editions Club, 1939. Cloth and boards. Illus. with crayon drawings
by Reginald Marsh. One of 1,500 numbered copies, printed at the
spiral press, and signed by Marsh. Light offset on edge, else fine
in slipcase. Reese 20-913 1983 $75

DREISER, THEODORE   The Symbolic Drawings of Hubert Davis
for an American Tragedy. (New York): Horace Liveright, n.d. Folio.
Cloth spine, gold and silver paper over boards. One of 525 copies.
This copy is marked Printers Copy and is not signed by the artist or
author. The metallic paper has a scuffed appearance, the tips are
worn. Scarce. Oak Knoll 49-164 1983 $45

DREISER, THEODORE   Tragic America. New York, 1931. 8vo.
Cloth. First ed., intermediate state. This copy bears the author's
signed signature. Small glue spot on front pastedown, else fine
copy in somewhat used and sunned dj. In Our Time 156-219 1983 $200

DREISER, THEODORE   Tragic America. New York: Liveright,
(1931). 1st ed., early issue with the "suppressed readings." Orig.
cloth, gilt. Light use, else fine. Jenkins 155-345 1983 $25

DRELINCOURT, CHARLES   The Christian's Defence Against the Fears
of Death. Trenton: James Oram, 1808. Engraved frontis. by Charles
Rollinson. Full calf (front hinge broken, spine ends chipped). Very
good. Felcone 20-36 1983 $40

DREPPARD, CARL W.   American Pioneer Arts & Artists.
Springfield, Pond-Ekberg, 1942. First edition. 4to, color frontis.
and over 75 illus. in b/w. Blue cloth, paper label on upper cover.
Very good. Houle 22-528 1983 $75

DRESSER, H. E.   A Manual of Palearctic Birds. 1902-03.
2 plates (1 coloured, by Wolf), 2 vols. in 1, 8vo, limp leather,
trifle used. A few annotations. Wheldon 160-690 1983 £40

DRESSER, PAUL   The Songs of Paul Dresser. New York:
Liveright, 1927. 1st ed. Orig. cloth-backed boards. Photographic
illus. Publisher's promo broadside laid in. Very good copy. Jenkins
155-346 1983 $25

DRESSLER, ALBERT   California's Pioneer Mountaineer of
Rabbit Creek. San Francisco, 1930. Privately printed. Illus. D.w.
Illus. Argosy 716-33 1983 $40

DREW, F.   The Northern Barrier of India. London,
1877. Folding map and 3 Woodbury types after Frith. 8vo. Embossed
cloth, spine faded. Good. Edwards 1044-206 1983 £70

DREW, S   An Essay on the Identity and General
Resurrection of the Human Body. Brooklyn; Th. Kirk, 1811. Mod.
1/4 linen, title-page edge dampstained and mended, affecting few
letters. Ex library. Argosy 710-377 1983 $50

DREW, S.   An Original Essay on the Immateriality
and Immortality of the Human Soul... Bristol: by Richard Edwards,
1803. Second edition, revised. 8vo. Half calf. Some wear. Heath
48-549 1983 £20

DREWITT, F. D.   The Romance of the Apothecaries' Garden
at Chelsea. 1924. Second edition. Wheldon 160-223 1983 £12

DRIFTING Clouds. E. Marlborough, Bath: Binns & Goodwin, n.d.
(c. 1875). First edition, 2 vols. 2 pp ads. vol. II. Inner hinges
a little weak, orig. green cloth sl. rubbed. Labels of the Birdwell
Working-Men's Institute and Circulating Library. Jarndyce 30-274
1983 £40

DRINKER, CECIL K.   Not so Long Ago. N.Y., 1937. First
edition. Argosy 713-161 1983 $30

DRINKWATER, H.   Fifty Years of Medical Progress 1873-
1922. New York, 1924. 8vo. Orig. wrappers. First edition. Ex-
library. Fye H-3-155 1873 $25

DRINKWATER, JOHN   Abraham Lincoln. London: Sidgwick &
Jackson, Ltd., 1918. First edition. Orig. wrappers with paper label
on spine. Inscribed on the front free endpaper at a later date, and
with an ALS, 1 page, 8vo, London, 26.5.19, from Drinkwater to the
editor of the Anglo-American Review. Bottom of spine of wrappers
deteriorated. In a full red solander slipcase. Good. MacManus 278-
1685 1983 $75

DRINKWATER, JOHN   Abraham Lincoln. London: Sidgwick &
Jackson, Ltd., 1918. First edition. Orig. wrappers with paper label
on spine. Presentation copy, inscribed on the half-title: "To Noel
Shammon from John Drinkwater 12.10.18 'I may tell you that I am not
unsympathetic.'" With an ALS, 1 page, 8vo, 1929, from Drinkwater laid
in. Bookplate on inner wrapper. In a cloth slipcase. Fine. MacManus
278-1684 1983 $65

DRINKWATER, JOHN   All about Me. W. Collins, 1928. Pictorial title & 110 text illus. Decorated endpapers. Orig. cloth gilt,
small snag. Pictorial dust wrapper. Signed by author on title-page.
Greer 40-62 1983 £15

DRINKWATER, JOHN   Bird in Hand. London: Sidgwick & Jackson, Ltd., 1927. Author's corrected proofs. Orig. hand-made floral
boards with paper label. With a slip pasted to the title-page signed
by author and dated London May 1928. With pencilled corrections
throughout the text and notes in the author's hand at the end. Fine.
MacManus 278-1687 1983 $150

DRINKWATER, JOHN   Christmas Poems. London, 1931.
First edition. Square 8vo, printed stiff wraps. Illus. by Ernest H.
Shepard. Frayed. Argosy 714-263 1983 $20

DRINKWATER, JOHN   The Collected Poems of John Drinkwater.
London, 1923. First edition. One of 230 numbered copies on handmade
paper, signed by author beneath the preface. 2 vols. Full white
buckram. Fine. Rota 231-190 1983 £15

DRINKWATER, JOHN   From the German. Sidgwick & Jackson,
1924. First edition, 8vo, orig. parchment-backed patterned boards,
with parchment label, t.e.g., a fine copy. Ltd. edition of 250
numbered copies. Signed by the author. Fenning 62-99 1983 £18.50

DRINKWATER, JOHN   The Lyric. London: Martin Secker,
(1915). First edition. Orig. wrappers. Fine. MacManus 278-1693
1983 $20

DRINKWATER, JOHN   Lyrical and Other Poems. Cranleigh:
The Samurai Press, (1908). First edition. Orig. cloth-backed boards.
Limited to 300 copies. Very good. MacManus 278-1694 1983 $35

DRINKWATER, JOHN   Poems 1908-1914. London: Sidgwick &
Jackson, Ltd., 1917. First edition. Frontis. port. by Wm. Rothenstein.
Orig. cloth with paper label on spine, dust jacket. Bookplate on
front endsheet. Fine. MacManus 278-1701 1983 $20

DRINKWATER, JOHN   Poems. Boston: Houghton Mifflin Co.,
(1919). First edition. Frontis. port. Orig. boards with paper label
on spine. Inscribed on the front flyleaf by the author at a later
date. Very good. MacManus 278-1702 1983 $30

DRINKWATER, JOHN   Poems of Men and Hours. London: David
Nutt, 1911. First edition. Orig. parchment boards. Foxed, boards
a bit dusty. Very good. MacManus 278-1703 1983 $20

DRINKWATER, JOHN   Preludes, 1921-1922. London: (The Morland Press), 1922. Proof copy for the first edition, eventually
printed on hand-made paper and bound in full vellum by The Morland
Press in an edition of 125 copies. Orig. green wrappers. Presentation
copy, inscribed on the front flyleaf "For Max Beerbohm....London, May
1923." Drinkwater's address is on the front wrapper in his hand.
Darkening at margins of wrappers. Very good. MacManus 278-1705 1983
$350

DRINKWATER, JOHN   Preludes. 1921-1922. London: Sidgwick
& Jackson, 1922. First edition. Orig. cloth. Dust jacket. Signed
by author on the title-page. In a half morocco slipcase. MacManus
278-1707 1983 $35

DRINKWATER, JOHN   Rupert Brooke. London: Printed for
the author at the Chiswick Press, 1916. First edition. Orig. boards
with printed label. One of 115 copies signed by author. Spine a bit
faded, with some offsetting to the endpapers. Very good. MacManus
278-1711 1983 $85

DRINKWATER, JOHN   Seeds of Time. London: Sidgwick &
Jackson, 1921. First edition. Orig. cloth. Dust jacket. Signed by
Drinkwater on the title-page. In a half morocco slipcase. MacManus
278-1712 1983 $35

DRINKWATER, JOHN   The World's Lincoln. New York, at the
Bowling Green Press, 1928. First edition, 8vo, orig. parchment-
backed boards, gilt. Fine copy. Ltd. edition of 800 copies.
Fenning 62-100 1983 £15

DROLL Doings. Blackie, nd (1905). Illus. by Harry B. Neilson. Col.
frontis. & title page & 39 col. illus., unnumbered. Red cloth backed
pictorial cvrs., contemp. insc. fr. ep., corners sl. wear, nice copy.
Hodgkins 27-67 1983 £30

DROST, WILLI   Adal Elsheimer und sein Kreis. Potsdam:
Athenaion, 1933. 14 plates (several tipped-in color). 122 illus.
Large 4to. Cloth. Scarce. Ars Libri 32-202 1983 $300

DRUCE, G. C.   The Flora of Berkshire. Oxford, 1897.
Map, 8vo, cloth. Wheldon 160-1595 1983 £40

DRUMMOND, GEORGE AURIOL HAY   A Town Eclogue. Edinburgh: For the
author by Oliver & Co. Sold by John Buchanan, 1804. First edition.
A little dusted, uncut. Later half dark green morocco, v.g.
Jarndyce 30-689 1983 £38

DRUMMOND, HENRY   The Greatest Thing in the World. New
York: James Pott, 1890. 1st ed. Orig. printed wrappers. Very good
copy. Uncommon. Jenkins 155-348 1983 $25

DRUMMOND, JAMES   Ancient Scottish Weapons. Edinburgh,
1881. 8vo. Decorative title, 54 fine chromolighographs, folio.
Orig. morocco-backed cloth boards. Very slightly worn and faded.
T.e.g. Bookplate of Pat Murray (late Curator of the Museum of Child-
hood in Edinburgh) and printed label, pasted onto endpaper. Fine.
Edwrads 1042-326 1983 £200

DRUMMOND, M.   Tripp's Buildings. Henry S. King, 1877.
First edition, half title, front. Ads., orig. green cloth, dec. in
gilt and black, v.g. Jarndyce 31-244 1983 £18

DRUMMOND, WILLIAM HENRY   Johnnie Courteau. New York & London:
Putnam, 1901. Frontis, plates. 1st ed. Orig. vellum-backed boards,
gilt, t.e.g., uncut. Illus. by Frederick Coburn. Presentation copy
inscribed by Drummond at time of publication. Very good. Jenkins
155-349 1983 $20

DRUMMOND, WILLIAM HENRY   The large game and natural history of
south and south-east Africa. Edinburgh: Edmonston & Douglas, 1875.
8vo. 1 colored & 12 tinted plates, map. Orig. green cloth, rubbed.
Adelson Africa-80 1983 $225

DRURY, ALAN   California. N.Y., Harper (1939). Illus.
with 52 halftone plates. Dust jacket. Signed by the author. Very
good. Houle 21-1026 1983 $22.50

DRURY, AUBREY   World Metric Standardization an Urgent
Issue. San Francisco, World Metric Standardization Council, (1922).
1st ed. Portraits. 8vo. Morrill 289-318 1983 $20

DRURY, JOHN   Old Chicago Houses. Chicago, (1941).
First edition. Map end papers, illustrated. Red cloth. Fine in
dj. Very good. Bradley 65-45 1983 $75

DRURY, JOHN   Old Chicago Houses. Chicago, (1941).
First edition. Map end papers, illustrated. Red cloth. Very good.
Bradley 65-46 1983 $50

DRURY, R.   Madagascar. London, 1829. First edition.
Large folding map, 6 plates. Cont. panelled calf, boards rebacked.
8vo. Good. Edwards 1044-207 1983 £220

DRURY, ROBERT   The Devil of a Duke: or, Trapolin's
Vagaries. London: printed for Charles Corbet...and John Torbuck,
1732. 1st edition, 8vo, half-title, 18 engraved pages, uncut, in
original wrappers. Pickering & Chatto 19-12 1983 $650

DRURY, W. P.   The Peradventures of Private Pagett.
London: Chapman & Hall, 1904. First edition. Illus. by A. Rackham.
Orig. pictorial cloth. Spine a bit rubbed. Some foxing throughout.
Bookplate. Good. MacManus 280-4297 1983 $85

DRURY, W. P.   The Tadpole of an Archangel. London:
Chapman & Hall, 1904. First edition. Orig. pictorial cloth. Foot
of spine slightly nicked. Very good. MacManus 278-1715 1983 $35

DRURY, WELLS   An Editor on the Comstock Lode. N.Y.,
Farrar, Straus, (1936). First edition. Illus. Dust jacket. Signed
and inscribed by the author's wife. Fine. Houle 11-1050 1983 $35

DRYDEN, CECIL   Up the Columbia for Furs. Caldwell,
Idaho: Caxton Printers, 1950. 23cm. Second printing. Illus.
by E. Joseph Dreany. Colour illus. Very good dust jacket. Fine.
McGahern 54-55 1983 $25

DRYDEN, JOHN   Albion and Albanius. London, Tonson,
1691. 4to, wrs. Salloch 387-53 1983 $225

DRYDEN, JOHN   Cleomenes, the Spartan Heroe...
London: for Jacob Tonson, 1692. First edition. 4to. Modern cloth.
Title paper discoloured, couple of leaves slightly cropped. Heath
48-287 1983 £65

DRYDEN, JOHN   Dramatic Works. London: the Nonesuch
Press, 1931-32. 6 vols. Roy. 8vo. Quarter green buckram, gilt,
over marbled boards, t.e.g., others uncut. Limited edition of 750
numbered sets. Traylen 94-291 1983 £160

DRYDEN, JOHN   An Evening's Love: or, the mock-
astrologer. London: printed for Henry Herrmingman, and are to be
sold by Richard Bentley, 1691. Sm. 4to, early wrappers (calligraph-
ically decorated in a contemporary hand; enclosed within later
wrappers). 4th ed. Some browning and stains, particularly in the
latter part of the text. Ximenes 64-183 1983 $850

DRYDEN, JOHN   Examen Poeticum: being the third part
of Miscellany Poems. London; R. E. for Jacob Tonson, 1693. 1st ed.,
2nd issue, thick 8vo, half-title and final blank leaf, contemporary
speckled calf panelled in blind, very neatly rebacked and recornered
in calf, new morocco label, 7 leaves stained, signature on title-page
inked over, otherwise very good. Deighton 3-113 1983 £120

DRYDEN, JOHN   Fables Ancient and Modern. Printed for
Jacob Tonson, 1721. 12mo, engr. frontis., orig. calf, joints cracked,
lacking labels. Bickersteth 77-25 1983 £22

DRYDEN, JOHN   The Kind Keeper; or, Mrs. Limberham.
London: Printed for R. Bentley, & M. Magnes, in Russell-Street in
Covent-Garden, 1680. First edition. Small 4to. Rebound in 3/4
blue morocco & marbled boards. Some foxing, faint dampstaining to one
corner, tiny institutional stamp in the gutter of dedication leaf.
Bookplates of Richard Honeyman, Thomas Jefferson McKee & Stanley
Kidder Wilson on endpapers. Very good. MacManus 278-1717 1983 $225

DRYDEN, JOHN   Notes and observations on the Empress
of Morocco. London: printed in the year 1674. Sm. 4to, disbound,
1st ed. Margins trimmed close, just touching the occasional page
number or catchword, else a sound copy. Paste-on errata slip present.
Ximenes 64-184 1983 $900

DRYDEN, JOHN   Of Dramatick Poesie. London, T. Warren
for Henry Herringman, 1693. 4to, disbound, some foxing and age-
spotting throughout. Ravenstree 94-46 1983 $285

DRYDEN, JOHN   Of Dramatick Poesie, an essay. London:
printed by T. Warren for Henry Herringman, and are to be sold by
R. Bentley, J. Tonson, F. Saunders, and T. Bennet, 1693. Sm. 4to,
wrappers. 3rd edition. Some stains on title, some spotting, light
marginal stains; a sound copy. Ximenes 64-182 1983 $125

DRYDEN, JOHN   The Poetical Works. London, 1866.
5 vols. Cr. 8vo. Dark blue calf, two-line gilt borders with
corner ornaments, gilt panelled spines, morocco labels, gilt.
Portrait, vignette title-pages. Traylen 94-292 1983 £70

DRYDEN, JOHN   Select Essays on the Belles Lettres.
Glasgow, Urie, 1750. 1st separate edition, 12mo, 3 advts., cont.
sheep, morocco label, worn and joints cracking, internally clean.
Deighton 3-114 1983 £20

DRYDEN, JOHN   Songs and Poems Chosen and Introduced
by Gwyn Jones. Golden Cockerel Press, 1957. Folio, 8 full-page
water colour illus. and 11 large pencil drawings, all reproduced by
collotype, quarter red morocco gilt over cloth boards, t.e.g., spine
triflingly faded, otherwise very fine. 400 numbered copies.
Deighton 3-115 1983 £110

DRYDEN, JOHN   Songs and Poems. Golden Cockerel
Press, 1957. Folio. Orig. orange quarter morocco, gilt, t.e.g.
19 plates by Lavinia Blythe, 8 of which are in colour. Limited
edition of 500 numbered copies. Traylen 94-293 1983 £105

DRYDEN, JOHN   Works. London, 1808. Notes, etc.,
by Sir Walter Scott. Best Library edition. 18 vols. Roy. 8vo.
Cont. polished calf, wide gilt borders with arms in gilt on sides,
gilt panelled spines, red, green and black morocco labels, gilt,
edges gilt. Portrait. One label missing. Traylen 94-294 1983
£225

DRYSDALE, CHARLES R.   The Life and Writings of Thomas R.
Malthus. Geo. Standring, 1892. 2nd edition, orig. brown printed
wraps., v.g. Jarndyce 30-1065 1983 £36

DUANE, WILLIAM   Experience the Test of Government.
Philadelphia, 1307. Dsb. Some chipping and staining, good.
Reese 18-293 1983 $85

DUANE, WILLIAM   A Hand Book For Infantry. Phila., 1812.
Scarce edition. 65 engraved plates and text diagrams. Cont. calf-
backed, marbled boards. Morocco spine label. Bookplate. Ink names.
Ex-Library, foxed, two plates defective. Worn copy. King 46-205
1983 $165

DUANE, WILLIAM   The Mississippi Question. Phila.:
Printed by W. Duane, 1803. Three quarter calf. Some wear. Untrimed
copy. Jenkins 152-104 1983 $300

DUANE, WILLIAM   Sampson Against the Philistines, or the
Reformation of Lawsuits... Phila.: B. Graves for W. Duane, 1805.
Second edition. Later wrappers. Uncut. Fine. Felcone 20-85 1983
$35

DUBE, PAUL   Le Medecin de Pauvres. Lyon: J.
Veyron, 1700. Small 12mo, calf (worn; backstrip chipped). Bound in,
with separate title & paging is Le Chirurgien des Pauvres. Argosy
713-162 1983 $125

DUBOIS, EDWARD   My Pocket Book. Printed for Vernor, Hood,
and Sharpe, 1808. With 5 tinted plates (1 folding), small 8vo, cont.
half calf, some light signs of use, but a very good copy. Fenning
61-117 1983 £38.50

DU BOIS, EDWARD   The Wreath. Bensley for White, Egerton,
Vernor & Hood, 1799. 1st ed., large paper 8vo, engraved frontis.,
cont. calf elegantly panelled in gilt, neatly rebacked retaining
original backstrip with morocco label, marbled endpapers, fine copy.
Deighton 3-116 1983 £70

DUBOIS, H.-M.   Monographie des Betsileo (Madagascar).
Paris: Institut d'Ethnologie, 1938. 10 plates. 2 folding maps.
190 text illus. Stout 4to. Cloth. Front inner hinge cracked.
Ars Libri 34-600 1983 $150

DUBOIS, PAUL (1848-1918)   Die Psychoneurosen. Bern: Verlag von
A. Francke, vorm. Schmid & Francke, 1905. First edition in Germany.
Cloth, spine tips snagged and worn, cloth lightly rubbed. Gach 95-
101 1983 $40

DUBOIS, PAUL (1848-1918)   Reason and Sentiment. NY: Funk &
Wagnalls, 1911. First edition in English. Front hinge weak. Gach
95-103 1983 $25

DU BOIS, W. E. B.   Some Notes on Negro Crime. Atlanta,
1904. Orig. wrs. No backstrip. Argosy 716-19 1983 $45

DU BOIS, W. E. B.   The Souls of Black Fold. Ch., 1903.
Cover slightly dampstained and rippled, small hole in cloth on front
cover, light cover wear, good, bookplate over owner's name. Quill &
Brush 54-391 1983 $125

DU BOIS, WILLIAM PENE   The Great Geppy. N.Y.: Vik., 1940.
First edition. 8vo. Striped cloth. Slightly worn dust wrapper.
Illus. with full-page color and black & whites. Fine. Aleph-bet 8-94
1983 $27

DUBREUIL, JEAN   The Practice of Perspective. Printed for
Tho. Bowles; and John Bowles, 1743. 4to, title in red and black, 2
folding plates, numbered in pairs with 150 full-page engraved plates
each with facing explanatory text. Cont. calf, worn at head and
foot of spine and joints cracked, but binding firm, and contents
fine. First edition. Bickersteth 77-26 1983 £190

DU CANE, FLORENCE   The Flowers and Gardens of Japan.
London: Adam & Charles Black, 1908. Large thick 8vo, with 50
colored plates, each with titled tissue guard. Illus. white cloth.
Bookplate. T.e.g. Karmiole 75-67 1983 $40

DU CHAILLU, PAUL B.   Explorations and adventures in Equatorial Africa. New York: Harper & Bros., 1868. 8vo. Folding
map. Many plates. Orig. cloth. Rubbed, worn. Adelson Africa-184
1983 $35

DU CHAILLU, PAUL B.   A journey to Ashango-Land. New York:
D. Appleton, 1867. 8vo. Folding map. 23 plates. Orig. pictorial
cloth. Spine faded. Rubbed. Adelson Africa-185 1983 $35

DU CHAILLU, PAUL B.   The Viking Age. New York, 1889. 2
vols., map, 1366 illus., roy 8vo, gilt-decorated cloth. K Books 301-
64 1983 £30

DUCHE, JACOB   The American Vine. Philadelphia:
James Humphreys, Jun., 1775. Disbound. Felcone 22-49 1983 $65

DUCHE, JACOB   The Duty of Standing Fast in Our
Spiritual and Temporal Liberties, a Sermon, Preached...July 7th, 1775.
Philadelphia: James Humphreys, Jun., 1774. Modern boards, cloth
spine. Cont. signature "Thomas Tucker's" on title. Felcone 22-50
1983 $85

DUCHE, JACOB   The Duty of Standing Fast in our Spiritual and Temporal Liberties. Phila.: James Humphreys, June, 1775.
3/4 morocco. Very minor foxing. Fine. Felcone 20-37 1983 $85

DUCHENE, CAPTAIN   The Mechanics of the Aeroplane.
London, 1912. 8vo. Cloth. Gurney JJ-106 1983 £15

DUCHESNE, JEAN   Musee Francais Recueil Des Plus Beaux
Tableaux. Paris, n.d. A.e.g. Bindings chipped, some detached.
Contents with some foxing but mostly to reverses of plates and text.
344 full page magnificent copper engravings (just a few repairs).
King 45-396 1983 $1,750

THE DUCHESS, PSEUD.
Please turn to
HUNGERFORD, MRS. MARGARET WOLFE HAMILTON

DUCK, STEPHEN   Poems on Several Subjects. London:
printed for J. Roberts, 1730. 7th edition, corrected. 8vo, engraved
frontispiece, last leaf slightly stained, in wrappers. Pickering &
Chatto 19-13 1983 $125

DUCLOS, CHARLES PINOT   Considerations sur les Moeurs de ce
Siecle. A Paris, 1764. 12mo, engraved frontis, cont. calf, rubbed.
Bickersteth 75-27 1983 £14

DU COLOMBIER, PIERRE   Albert Durer. Paris: Albin Michel,
1927. 59 phototype plates. 3 tipped-in text illus. 4to. Wrappers.
Edition limited to 1650 numbered copies. Ars Libri 32-176 1983
$100

DUDEVANT, AMANTINE LUCILLE AURORE DUPIN
Please turn to
SAND, GEORGE, PSEUD.

DUDIN, M.   The Art of the Bookbinder and Gilder...
Leeds: Elmete Press, 1977. First English edition. Small folio.
Full leather with raised bands and two red leather spine labels,
t.e.g. Limited to 490 numbered copies. Oak Knoll 48-34 1983 $275

DUDLEY, DOROTHY   Forgotten Frontiers: Dreiser and the
Land of the Free. New York, 1932. 8vo. Cloth. Blurb on rear jacket
by Carl Sandburg. A fine copy in worn dj. In Our Time 156-220 1983
$25

DUDLEY, ELIZABETH   Memoirs of... A.W. Bennett, 1861.
First edition, 8vo, orig. cloth. Fenning 62-101 1983 £14.50

DUDLEY, OWEN FRANCIS   The Coming of the Monster. London: Longmans, Green & Co., 1936. First edition. Orig. cloth. Dust jacket.
Fine. MacManus 278-1719 1983 $20

DUDLEY, OWEN FRANCIS   Pageant of Life. London: Longmans, Green & Co., 1932. First edition. Orig. cloth-backed boards. Dust jacket (a bit chipped). Fine. MacManus 278-1720 1983 $20

DUDLEY, OWEN FRANCIS   The Tremaynes and The Masterful Monk. Longmans, Green & Co., 1940. First edition. Orig. cloth. Dust jacket. Fine. MacManus 278-1721 1983 $20

DUDLEY, PAUL   An Essay on the Merchandise of Slaves and Souls of Men... London, 1732. Dsb., very good. Reese 18-49 1983 $150

DUERER, ALBRECHT   The Construction of Roman Letters. Cambridge: Dunster House, 1924. Ltd. edition. 12mo, boards. One of 350 copies printed by Bruce Rogers at the Printing House of Wm. Edwin Rudge. Backstrip label chipped. Argosy 714-634 1983 $25

DUERER, ALBRECHT   Records of Journeys to Venice and the Low Countries. Boston: The Merrymount Press, 1913. 4to. Boards, 1/4 cloth. Printed by D.B. Updike on fine laid paper, with title-page by W.A. Dwiggings. Ars Libri 32-178 1983 $75

DUFF, HENRIETTA A.   Honor Carmichael. London: Bentley, 1880. First edition. 2 vols. Orig. cloth. Inner hinge in vol. 2 cracked and loose. MacManus 278-1722 1983 $150

DUFFY, CHARLES G.   Thomas Davis. Kegan Paul, 1890. First edition, with a portrait, 8vo, orig. cloth, preliminary leaves lightly foxed, otherwise a nice copy. Fenning 61-103 1983 £28.50

DUFOUR, L.   Atlas des Champignons Comestibles et Veneneux. Paris, 1891. 80 coloured plates, 8vo, morocco. Some foxing and a few small marginal tears, but a good copy. Wheldon 160-1820 1983 £80

DU GARDIN, LOUIS   Alexiloemos sive de Pestis Natura, Causis, Signis, Prognosticis, Praecautione, et Curatione, Epitome Methodica per Conclusiones Distributa. Pierre Auroy, Douai, 1617. 8vo, with 3/4 page allegorical engraving on a4; cont. vellum, gilt, gilt edges. First edition. Quaritch NS 5-36 1983 $900

DUGDALE, FLORENCE E.   The Book of Baby Pets. H. Milford, 1938. 4to. Colour frontis. & 18 colour plates. Blue cloth, worn. Text browned. Greer 39-61 1983 £25

DUGDALE, WILLIAM   The Antiquities of Warwickshire illustrated. Birmingham: printed for Subscribers, 1891. Limited edition of 150 numbered copies signed by W. F. Carter (who added notes and additions), folio, subscribers list, plates and illus., half parchment, t.e.g., others uncut, cover soiled and a trifle chafed, internally a very good copy. Deighton 3-117 1983 £18

DUGMORE, ARTHUR RADCLYFFE   Camera adventures in the African wilds. London: William Heinemann, 1910. 4to. Map, numerous photographs. Orig. red pictorial cloth, rubbed. Adelson Africa-81 1983 $100

DUGMORE, ARTHUR RADCLYFFE   The Romance of the Newfoundland Caribou. Philadelphia, 1913. First American edition. Large folding map, illustrations from photographs made by the author from paintings and drawings. Quarto, original cloth, gilt. Very good copy. Bradley 65-58 1983 $75

DUGMORE, ARTHUR RADCLYFFE   The Romance of the Newfoundland Caribou. London: Heinemann, 1913. 4to. Colour frontis. and 72 illus. mostly full-page plates. 8 text illus. Rear folding maps. Blue cloth. Very good to fine copy. McGahern 53-48 1983 $65

DUGMORE, ARTHUR RADCLYFFE   The Romance of the Newfoundland Caribou. Philadelphia & London, 1913. 1st American ed. Illus. by author. 4to. Portions of covers, particularly around fore-edge, water-stained. Morrill 289-320 1983 $30

DUHAMEL, GEORGE   Maurice de Vlaminck. Paris: Les Ecrivains Reunis, (1927). Quarto. Three quarter crushed levant, t.e.g. Illus. with four orig. copper etchings by Vlaminck, and 24 plates in phototype. From an edition of 875 numbered copies, this is one of 850 on velin. Very fine copy, with the orig. wrappers bound in. Reese 20-1220 1983 $250

DUHEM, PIERRE-MAURICE-MARIE   Traite Elementaire de Mecanique Chimique Fondee sur la Thermodynamique... Paris: A. Hermann, 1897-1899. 4 vols. in 2. Orig. blue cloth with gilt. 8vo. First edition. Front hinge of the second volume split, otherwise a good set. Zeitlin 264-124 1983 $120

DUKE, BASIL W.   Reminiscences of General Basil W. Duke. New York, 1911. First edition. Orig. cloth. Portrait frontis. T.e.g. Jenkins 152-619 1983 $75

THE DUKE of Exeter; an Historical Romance. Printed for W. Lane, 1789. 3 vols, sm. 8vo, contemporary half sheep, marbled sides, sprinkled edges; a fine copy. 1st ed. Hill 165-29 1983 $235

DUKE-ELDER, W. STEWART   Text-Book of Opthalmology. Vol. I. The Development, Form and Function of the Visual Apparatus. St. Louis: C. V. Mosby Co., 1934. First edition. With 1,022 illus., including 7 color plates. Gach 94-704 1983 $30

DUKES, ASHLEY   Jew Suss. London: Martin Secker, 1929. Cloth. First edition. Very fine in dust jacket, which advertises the pocket edition of D.H. Lawrence on the rear panel. Reese 20-338 1983 $30

DULAC, EDMUND   Birmingham Printing School Booklet. 1927. Colour plate. Light blue wrappers. Light wear. Greer 39-67 1983 £12.50

DULAC, EDMUND   Edmund Dulac Fairy Book. London: Hodd. & Stought. 4to. Pictorial cloth. Occasional light foxing. 15 tipped in color plates. Very good. Aleph-bet 8-95 1983 $100

DULAC, EDMUND   Lyrics Pathetic and Humourous from A to Z. F. Warne, 1908. 4to. Decorated title & 24 colour plates. Green boards, worn. Paper label, marked. Seemingly a variant publishers binding. Greer 39-63 1983 £140

DULBERG, FRANZ   Frans Hals. Stuttgart: Paul Neff, 1930. 94 illus. 4to. Cloth. From the library of Jakob Rosenberg. Ars Libri 32-299 1983 $50

DUMAS, ALEXANDRE (1802-1870)   Celebrated Crimes. Boston, Knight, 1896. Probably first American ed., illus., 3 vols. Orig. dec. cloth. Very good. MacManus 278-1724 1983 $35

DUMAS, ALEXANDRE (1802-1870)   Pascal Bruno, A Sicilian Story. Henry Colburn, 1837. 8vo, contemp. half calf. First edition in English. Hill 165-30 1983 £40

DUMAS, JEAN BAPTISTE ANDRE   Essai de Statique Chimique des Etres Organises. Paris: Fortin & Masson, 1844. 8vo. New wrappers, orig. wrappers bound in. Ads. A good uncut copy. Zeitlin 264-125 1983 $60

DUMAS, JEAN BAPTISTE ANDRE   Lecons sur la Philosophie Chimique, Professees au College de France en 1836. Paris: Gauthiers-Villars, 1878. Second edition. 8vo. Orig. paper wrappers. Tape repairs to spine. Zeitlin 264-127 1983 $70

DUMAS, JEAN BAPTISTE ANDRE   Lecons sur la Philosophie Chimique professees au College de France... Paris: Ebrard, 1837. First edition, later issue. 8vo. Old half calf. Publisher's list dated 1839. Ads. Spine faded, rubbed. Zeitlin 264-126 1983 $100

DU MAURIER, DAPHNE   Frenchman's Creek. GC, 1942. Tipped-in Christmas Greeting page from Doubleday, Doran. Appears to be advance reading copy, near fine in slightly worn, very good dustwrapper with one small chip. Quill & Brush 54-392 1983 $35

DU MAURIER, GEORGE   An Appendix to Trilby. Richmond & Backus, Detroit, (1895). Front. Orig. printed wraps. Jarndyce 31-677 1983 £10.50

DU MAURIER, GEORGE   The Martian. London, 1898. Illus. by author, 8vo, pict. cloth; uncut. First English edition. Laid in is an A.L.S. declining an invitation. Argosy 714-264 1983 $40

DU MAURIER, GEORGE   The Martian. London: Harper & Brothers, 1898. First edition. Illus. by author. Orig. pictorial cloth. Good. MacManus 278-1726 1983 $20

DU MAURIER, GEORGE   Peter Ibbetson. London: James R. Osgood, McIlvain & Co., 1892. First English edition, in the secondary binding with all-black blocking and lettering. Illus. by G. Du Maurier. 2 vols. 8vo. Orig. cloth. E. Hubert Litchfield bookplate. In a cloth slipcase. Fine. MacManus 278-1727 1983 $90

DU MAURIER, GEORGE   Peter Ibbetson. London: Osgood, McIlvaine, 1892. First edition. Illus. by author. 2 vols. Orig. cloth (spines a trifle dark). First binding. Very good. MacManus 278-1728 1983 $85

DU MAURIER, GEORGE   Trilby. London: Osgood, McIlvaine, 1894. First edition. 3 vols. Orig. cloth (extremities and edges of spine worn; spines darkened). A few inner hinges cracked. Good. MacManus 278-1730 1983 $150

DU MAURIER, GEORGE   Trilby. Osgood, McIlvaine, 1894. First edition, 3 vols., half titles, 1p ads. vol. IV. Buff canvas, blocked in blue. Spines a little darkened and a little rubbing, otherwise v.g. Jarndyce 30-368 1983 £46

DU MAURIER, GEORGE   Trilby. London, 1895. First English edition. Illus. by the author. 8vo, gilt pict. cloth; uncut. Laid in is an A.L.S. Argosy 714-265 1983 $100

DU MAURIER, GEORGE   Trilby. London: Osgood, McIlvaine, 1894. "Seventh edition." 3 vols. Orig. cloth. Covers stained; inner hinges cracked in vol. 1. MacManus 278-1731 1983 $30

DU MAURIER, GEORGE   Trilby, a Novel. New York, 1895. Ed. limited to 600 copies. Illus. by author. 8vo, orig. white dec. boards, gilt top, untrimmed. Binding dust-soiled. Morrill 287-563 1983 $25

DUMBRILLE, DOROTHY   All This Difference. Toronto, (1945). 8vo. Cloth. Fine in dj. In Our Time 156-225 1983 $25

DUMESNIL, RENE   Histoire Illustree de la Musique. Paris, 1948. 104 illus. on fine gravure plates. 4to, orig. wrs. Salloch 387-312 1983 $35

DU MONCEL, THEODOSE ACHILLE LOUIS, COUNT   The telephone, the microphone and the phonograph. London: Kegan Paul, 1879. First edition in English. 8vo. Orig. dark red cloth. Ends of spine rubbed. Ximenes 63-568 1983 $75

DUMONT, H. J.   Rotatoria. Proceedings of the 2nd International Rotifer Symposium. The Hague, 1980. 8vo, cloth. Wheldon 160-1268 1983 £39

DUMORTIER, B. C.   Observations sur les Graminees de la Flore Belgique. Tournay: de J. Casterman, 1823. First edition. 8vo. Half title. Engraved plates. Uncut in orig. boards. Presentation inscription from the Author to Dr. St. George. Slight waterstains. Heath 48-20 1983 £35

DUMOURIEZ, C. F.   Campagnes Du Marechal De Schomberg. London, 1807. 12mo. Cont. half calf. Spine slightly rubbed. Small stamp on title. Orig. cloth. Good. Edwards 1042-327 1983 £30

DUNBAR, EDWARD E.   The Romance of the Age. New York, 1867. Port., 2 plates. Cloth (spine ends chipped); a good copy. First edition. Felcone 22-51 1983 $50

DUNBAR, G.   A History of India. London, 1949. Fourth edition, revised. Maps, plates. 2 vols. 8vo. Orig. cloth. Good. Edwards 1044-208 1983 £18

DUNBAR, H. FLANDERS   Emotions and Bodily Changes. NY: Columbia Univ. Press, 1938. Second edition. Dust jacket dusty. Gach 94-144 1983 $30

DUNBAR, PAUL L   Folks from Dixie. New York: Dodd, Mead, 1898. Frontis., plates. 1st ed. Orig. pictorial brown cloth, label, gilt. Illus. by E.W. Kemble. Minor rubbing but a near fine copy. Jenkins 155-350 1983 $60

DUNBAR, PAUL L.   Howdy Honey Howdy. NY, 1905. Photographs, edges slightly worn, minor cover stains, very good, owner's name. Quill & Brush 54-393 1983 $100

DUNBAR, PAUL L.   Li'l Gal. NY, 1904. Photographs, edges rubbed and lightly worn, light cover stains, minor interior staining, else near very good, gift inscription. Quill & Brush 54-394 1983 $50

DUNBAR, PAUL L   Li'L' Gal. NY, 1904. First edition. Pict. cloth, t.e.g., a soiled copy with covers stained, spine dull. King 46-279 1983 $50

DUNBAR, PAUL L   Lyrics of Lowly Life. London, 1897. Front. 16mo, cloth. First English edition. Paul Robeson's copy, with his autograph on the endpaper. Argosy 714-266 1983 $100

DUNBAR, PAUL L   Lyrics of Lowly Life. NY: 1896. First edition. Extremities lightly rubbed, some fading to covers. Owner's contemporary signature. Bromer 25-31 1983 $65

DUNBAR, PAUL L.   Lyrics of Lowly Life. NY, 1896. Dedication page slightly torn, title offset by tissue guard, edges rubbed, good or better, owner's name, bookplate. Quill & Brush 54-395 1983 $50

DUNBAR, PAUL L.   Lyrics of The Hearthside. NY, 1899. Cover stained, edges rubbed, title offset by tissue guard, good or better, owner's name. Quill & Brush 54-396 1983 $60

DUNBAR, PAUL L.   Poems of Cabin and Field. NY, 1899. Hinge cracking at half-title, spine slightly darkened and edges slightly frayed, page 47 torn and creased but still intact. Good or better, owner's name. Quill & Brush 54-397 1983 $60

DUNBAR, PAUL L.   When Malindy Sings. NY, 1903. Front hinge starting, edges slightly worn, cover slightly soiled, good or better, owner's name. Quill & Brush 54-398 1983 $75

DUNBAR, SEYMOUR   A History of Travel in America. Indianapolis: (1915). First edition. 2 maps, 12 colored plates, 400 other illus. 4 vols. Blue cloth. Fine copy, gilt worn off spine of Vol. 4, otherwise very good. Set once owned by Carl von Roden, bears his bookplate. Bradley 66-540 1983 $85

DUNCAN, DAVID DOUGLAS   Self-Portrait: U. S. A. NY, (n.d.). Very good in mended, good dustwrapper. Quill & Brush 54-399 1983 $30

DUNCAN, F.   History of the Royal Regiment of Artillery. London, 1872-3. 2 vols. Mounted photographic frontis. Slightly worn and soiled. Some very slight foxing. Good. Edwards 1042-552 1983 £20

DUNCAN, ISADORA   My Life. NY: Boni and Liveright, 1927. Tall 8vo, with 24 photo plates. The "Presentation Edition," ltd. to 650 numbered copies. Black cloth; leather spine label. In worn slipcase. Karmiole 71-104 1983 $60

DUNCAN, JONATHAN   The History of Guernsey. Longman, Brown, 1841. First edition, 8vo, fore-edge of one leaf defective affecting the page numeral only, with some very light browning, but still a very good copy in recent calf-backed marbled boards, gilt, with label. Fenning 61-122 1983 £75

DUNCAN, ROBERT   Epilogos. (Los Angeles): Black Sparrow Press, (1967). Oblong 12mo, printed wraps. First edition. One of 100 numbered copies (of 115), signed by the author, and decorated with an orig. drawing by him on the second blank. Very fine. Reese 20-342 1983 $200

DUNCAN, ROBERT   Heavenly City Earthly City. (Berkeley): Bern Porter, 1947. Pictorial boards. First edition. Very slightest traces of soiling to white boards, otherwise a fine copy, without the dust jacket. Reese 20-340 1983 $200

DUNCAN, ROBERT   Poems 1948-49. Berkeley. Miscellany Editions, (1950). 8vo. Wraps. 1st ed., 2nd issue. A fine copy. In Our Time 156-227 1983 $75

DUNCAN, ROBERT   A Selection of 65 Drawings. Black Sparrow Press, 1970. 8vo. Cloth, in folding slipcase box. First and only edition. Total edition is 326 copies signed by author. Fine copy. In Our Time 156-230 1983 $125

DUNCAN, WILLIAM HENRY   Dissertatio Physiologica Inauguralis De Ventris. Edinburgh: Excudebat Jacobus Walker, 1829. 1st ed., 8vo; old boards, new calf spine and corners. Pickering & Chatto 22-32 1983 $100

DUNCOMBE, THOMAS SLINGSBY   The Life and Correspondence. Hurst & Blackett, 1868. First edition, 2 vols. Front. vol. I, half titles, 16 pp ads. vol. II. Orig. green cloth. Jarndyce 31-152 1983 £28

DUNDONALD, THOMAS COCHRANE, 10TH EARL OF   The Autobiography of a Seaman. Hafton, 1860. First ed., 8vo., orig. cloth, half titles, sm. devices on titles, 4 folding maps, 2 vols., contemp. half calf, gilt, slightly worn, marbled boards, edges and endpapers. Some gatherings loose. Some sl. foxing. Bookplates of James Hunter. Good. Edwards 1042-53 1983 $50

DUNDONALD, THOMAS COCHRANE, 10TH EARL OF   The Autobiography of a Seaman. Bentley, 1860. 2nd edition, vol. I. First edition, vol. II. 2 vols., tall 8vo. Half titles, tan calf, gilt borders and spines, maroon and black labels, v.g. Jarndyce 30-978 1983 £20

DUNDONALD, THOMAS COCHRANE, 10TH EARL OF   The Autobiography of a Seaman. London, 1861. Small 8vo., orig. cloth, portrait, 4 engraved maps. Slightly worn and soiled, ink signature on endpaper. Good. Edwards 1042-54 1983 £25

DUNDONALD, THOMAS COCHRANE, 10TH EARL OF   Narrative of Services. London, 1859. 2 vols., half titles, orig. blue dec. cloth, gilt. Very slightly stained. Small library stamps in upper margins of titles. Good. Edwards 1042-55 1983 £180

DUNGLISON, ROBLEY   Address to the Medical Graduates of the Jefferson Medical College, 1837. 8vo, old wraps. 2-leaf prospectus. Argosy 713-164 1983 $30

DUNHAM, JACOB   Journal of Voyages. N.Y., 1851. Privately printed. Illus. (backstrip ends worn, blank portion on last p. cut away). Argosy 716-254 1983 $35

DUNHAM, JOHN MOSELEY   The Vocal Companion, and Masonic Register. Boston, 1802. 1st ed. In 2 parts. 12mo. Contemporary calf, leather label. Lacks frontispiece and few endleaves. Morrill 289-321 1983 $32.50

DUNKERLEY, WILLIAM ARTHUR   The Hidden Years. London: Longmans, Green & Co., 1928. New Impression. Orig. cloth. Dust jacket. Inscribed by the author on the front free endpaper. Fine. MacManus 279-4114 1983 $25

DUNKERLEY, WILLIAM ARTHUR   The Later Te Deums. London: Methuen & Co. Ltd., n.d. First edition. Orig. wrappers. Inscribed by the author on the front wrapper. Fine. MacManus 279-4115 1983 $35

DUNKERLEY, WILLIAM ARTHUR   A Little Te Deum of the Commonplace. London: Methuen & Co. Ltd., n.d. (1915). First edition. 12mo. Orig. wrappers. Inscribed by the author on the front wrapper. Fine. MacManus 279-4116 1983 $35

DUNKERLEY, WILLIAM ARTHUR   Mary All-Alone. London: Methuen & Co. Ltd., (1913). First edition. Frontispiece in color by P.B. Hickling. Orig. cloth. Pictorial dust jacket (slightly chipped). Inscribed by the author on the front free endpaper. Fine. MacManus 279-4117 1983 $35

DUNKERLEY, WILLIAM ARTHUR   The Sacraments of Fire. London: Methuen & Co. Ltd., n.d. (1920). First edition. Orig. wrappers. Inscribed by the author on the inside front wrapper. Fine. MacManus 279-4118 1983 $35

DUNKERLEY, WILLIAM ARTHUR   The Splendour of the Dawn. London: Longmans, Green & Co., 1930. First edition. Orig. cloth. Dust jacket (large chip at top of spine, a few other small tears). Presentation copy, inscribed on the front free endpaper to "Charles Wilson, with every good wish from John Oxenham, 13.ix.30." Very good. MacManus 279-4119 1983 $25

DUNKERLEY, WILLIAM ARTHUR   The Very Short Memory of Mr. Joseph Scorer. Edinburgh: Geo. A. Morton, 1903. Second edition. 12mo. Orig. wrappers. Inscribed by the author on the half-title. Fine. MacManus 279-4120 1983 $20

DUNLAP, HOPE   The Pied Piper of Hamelin. Chicago: Rand McN., (1910). First edition. 4to. Blue cloth. Pictorial inset. Illus. by Dunlap, with full-page and smaller illus. Decorative border on pages. Fine. Aleph-bet 8-97 1983 $40

DUNLAP, KNIGHT   Habits. NY: Liveright, (1932). First edition. Library bookplate, stamps on rear paste-down. Smith Ely Jelliffe's copy, signed on titlepage and paste-down. Gach 95-104 1983 $25

DUNLAP, WILLIAM   A History of the American Theatre. N.Y.: J & J Harper, 1832. 4 pages of ads. Orig. cloth, worn. Torn at top of backstrip. Dawson 471-321 1983 $125

DUNLAP, WILLIAM   The life of George Fred. Cooke. London: printed for Henry Colburn; sold by Bell and Bradfute (Edinburgh); and John Cumming (Dublin), 1815. 2 vols., 8vo, cont. cloth, morocco labels. 2nd ed., revised and improved. With a portrait; very good set. Ximenes 64-186 1983 $100

DUNLAP, WILLIAM   Memoirs of George Fred. Cooke, Esq. London: printed for Henry Colburn; sold by George Goldie (Edinburgh); and John Cumming (Dublin), 1813. 2 vols., 8vo, cont. half calf, spines gilt (hinges a little rubbed). First English edition. With a portrait, some light browning, but a very good copy. Ximenes 64-185 1983 $150

DUNLAP, WILLIAM   Memoirs of the Life of George Frederick Cooke, Esquire. N.Y.: Published by D. Longworth at the Shapespeare Gallery, 1813. 2 vols. Frontis. in each. Half red morocco, slightly chipped. Dawson 471-320 1983 $50

DUNLOP, J   The history of fiction. Edinburgh: printed by Ballantyne, for Longman, etc., 1816. Second edition, with additions. 3 vols. 8vo. Cont. maroon half calf. Bit rubbed, one label chipped. Wanting half-titles; a couple of leaves stained. Ximenes 63-239 1983 $85

DUNLOP, J   Memoirs of Spain during the Reigns of Philip IV and Charles II from 1621 to 1700. Edinburgh, Thomas Clark. London, Whittaker & Co., 1834. 2 vols., 8vo, orig. boards uncut, paper labels on the spines. Paper defective at top of both spines, and at foot of spine of vol. 1. Bickersteth 75-132 1983 £24

DUNLOP, J.   Mooltan, during and After the Siege. London, 1849. 21 tinted lithographs, after drawings made on the spot. Small marginal waterstain and some occasional spotting. Folio, re-backed. 8vo. Orig. cloth. Good. Edwards 1044-211 1983 £160

DUNN, ARTHUR WALLACE   Gridiron Nights, Humorous and Satirical Views of Politics and Statesmen. NY (1915). Gilt-pict. cloth, t.e.g., covers heavily soiled, some pencil underlining. King 46-438 1983 $25

DUNN, JOHN   History of the Oregon Territory and British North American Fur Trade. London, 1844. Folding map. Cloth. A fine copy. First edition. Felcone 21-36 1983 $500

DUNN, SAMUEL   The Theory and Practice of Longitude at Sea. Printed for the author, 1786. 4to, 10 single page engr. plates and 2 folded plates, one of them a map of the moon, cont. calf, re-backed. A fine, crisp copy. Bickersteth 77-265 1983 £186

DUNNE, EDMUND F.   Our Public Schools. San F., 1875. Orig. printed wraps. Second edition. Ginsberg 47-14 1983 $35

DUNNE, J. H.   From Calcutta to Pekin. London, 1861. Portrait frontis. Folding map. Sm.8vo. Orig. green coloured decorated boards, slightly worn, neatly rebacked. Booksellers ticket and bookplate on endpaper. Good. Edwards 1044-212 1983 £40

THE DUNNIAD: Being a Collection of Pieces, in Prose and Verse... Printed for the Compiler and sold by Him and John Lindley, Bookseller in Pontefract, (1769). 12mo, title rather soiled, 19th century quarter morocco. Bickersteth 75-28 1983 £18

DUNSANY, EDWARD JOHN MORETON DRAX PLUNKETT   The Chronicles of Rodriguez. London: Putnam, (1922). First edition. Frontis. by S.H. Sime. 4to. Orig. vellum-backed boards. Dust jacket (a little worn). Limited to 500 copies signed by both author and illustrator. Bookplate. Fine. MacManus 278-1734 1983 $185

DUNSANY, EDWARD JOHN MORETON DRAX PLUNKETT   The Compromise of the King of the Golden Isles. The Grolier Club, 1924. Large 8vo. Cloth, boards. Total ed. is 300 copies. Fine. In Our Time 156-231 1983 $45

DUNSANY, EDWARD JOHN MORETON DRAX PLUNKETT   The Curse of the Wise Woman. New York, 1933. Advance reading copy, paper wrappers, spine of printed cover lightly worn, endpapers and page edges slightly foxed, else very good. Quill & Brush 54-401 1983 $150

DUNSANY, EDWARD JOHN MORETON DRAX PLUNKETT   The Fourth Book of Jorkens. Sauk City, Arkham House, 1948. First American ed., cloth, mint in d.j. Bradley 66-116 1983 $42.50

DUNSANY, EDWARD JOHN MORETON DRAX PLUNKETT   If. London: G.P. Putnam's Sons, (1921). First edition. Orig. cloth. Covers slightly dust-soiled. Good. MacManus 278-1735 1983 $35

DUNSANY, EDWARD JOHN MORETON DRAX PLUNKETT   If, a Play in Four Acts. G.P. Putnam's Sons, 1921. First edition, orig. mustard cloth, sl. darkened. Jarndyce 31-991 1983 £10.50

DUNSANY, EDWARD JOHN MORETON DRAX PLUNKETT   The King of Elfland's Daughter. G. P. Putnam, 1924. Second edition. Frontis. by S. H. Sime. Blue cloth gilt. Greer 390116 1983 £15

DUNSANY, EDWARD JOHN MORETON DRAX PLUNKETT   My Talks with Dean Spanley. London, 1936. First edition. Frontis. by S.H. Sime. Some foxing throughout. Slightly frayed dust wrapper. Nice. Rota 231-191 1983 £12

DUNSANY, EDWARD JOHN MORETON DRAX PLUNKETT   A Night At An Inn. N.Y.: The Sunwise Turn, Inc., 1916. First edition. Orig. wrappers. Fine. MacManus 278-1736 1983 $65

DUNSANY, EDWARD JOHN MORETON DRAX PLUNKETT   The Old Folk of the Centuries. London: Elkin Mathews & Marrot, 1930. First edition. Orig. cloth-backed boards. Dust jacket (slightly darkened & worn). Limited to 900 copies. Fine. MacManus 278-1737 1983 $25

DUNSANY, EDWARD JOHN MORETON DRAX PLUNKETT   Seven Modern Comedies. London: G.P. Putnam's Sons, (1928). First edition. Orig. cloth. Limited to 250 copies. Good. MacManus 278-1738 1983 $35

DUNSAY, EDWARD JOHN MORETON DRAX PLUNKETT   Tales of Three Hemispheres. London: T. Fisher Unwin, Ltd., 1920. First English edition. Former owner's signature on front flyleaf. Good. MacManus 278-1739 1983 $35

DUNSANY, EDWARD JOHN MORETON DRAX PLUNKETT   Tales of Three Hemispheres. T. Fisher Unwin, 1920. First edition, half title, orig. half brown cloth, v.g. Jarndyce 31-990 1983 £10.50

DUNSANY, EDWARD JOHN MORETON DRAX PLUNKETT   Unhappy Far-Off Things. London: Elkin Mathews, 1919. First edition. Orig. cloth-backed boards. Good. MacManus 278-1741 1983 $35

DUNSTABLE, JOHN   Complete Works. London, 1953. 8 plates, folio, flexible boards. Salloch 387-54 1983 $90

DUNTON, JOHN   The Phenix: or, a Revival of Scarce and Valuable Pieces from the Remotest Antiquity... London: J. Morphew, 1707-1708. 2 vols. 8vo. Cont. calf rebacked with more modern leather, leather spine labels (one black and one red). First edition. Bookplate of Ruth and Chester Greenough in each vol. along with Chester Greenough's signature in vol. 2. Covers rubbed, a few marks in ink in the text. Scarce. Oak Knoll 49-167 1983 $225

DUNTON, JOHN   A Supplement to the Athenian Oracle. Printed for Andrew Bell, 1710. First edition, with engraved frontis., 8vo, cont. panelled calf, neatly rebacked, a very good copy. Fenning 60-99 1983 £85

DUPIN, CHARLES   Narratives of Two Excursions To The Ports of England, Scotland, and Ireland, in 1816, 1817, and 1818. London: printed for Richard Philips, (ca. 1820). Folding engraved sketch, coloured aquatint plate, 8vo, modern boards. Deighton 3-118 1983 £20

DUPIN, JACQUES   Miro. New York: Abrams, n.d. 46 tipped-in color plates. Stout 4to. Cloth. Dust jacket. Ars Libri 32-460 1983 $85

DUPLESSIS-MORNAY, PHILIPPE
Please turn to
MORNAY, PHILIPPE DE

DU PONCEAU, PETER S.   A Dissertation on the Nature and Character of the Chinese System of Writing. Philadelphia: American Philosophical Society, 1838. Tall 8vo, errata. With 10 engraved plates showing Chinese characters. Orig. black cloth over boards a bit soiled. Karmiole 76-30 1983 $100

DUPONT, EMILE   Original Sketchbook. France, Switzerland, Italy, 1859. Oblong 4to. Manuscript title & 47 leaves with sketches on one side. Pen & ink & brush & ink. Orig. leather-backed boards album. O'Neal 50-64 1983 $1200

DUPPA, RICHARD   A Journal of the Most Remarkable Occurrences That Took Place in Rome... London, 1799. 1st ed. 8vo, full polished calf, leather labels. Very nice copy. Morrill 286-133 1983 $90

DU PRE, ABBE   The monk unvail'd. London: Jonathan Edwin, 1678. First edition in English. 8vo. Cont. calf. Engraved frontis. Complete with half-title. Calf worn, spine defective. Ximenes 63-580 1983 $250

DUPUYTREN, GUILLAUME, BARON   Clinical Lectures on Surgery. N.Y., 1833. First edition in English. Orig. cloth, leather label. Argosy 713-165 1983 $175

DURAN SANPERE, AGUSTI   Los retablos de piedra. Barcelona, 1932-1934. Folio, cloth, uncut. 120 collotype plates. Edition limited to 275 copies. Rare. Ars Libri SB 26-62 1983 $600

DURAND, H. M.   The Life of Major-General Sir Henry Marion Durand. London, 1883. 3 folding maps, portrait. 2 vols. Orig. cloth. 8vo. Good. Edwards 1044-213 1983 £50

DURAND, JEAN BAPTISTE LEONARD   A voyage to Senegal. London: Richard Phillips, 1806. 8vo. Folding map. 7 plates. Modern cloth. Adelson Africa-82 1983 $350

DURAND, JOHN   The Life and Times of A. B. Durand. New York, 1894. 1 of 500 copies. Illus. Tall 8vo, orig. buckram, binding rubbed and with a few light stains, some lettering on backstrip partly effaced, inner hinges cracked. Morrill 286-134 1983 $37.50

DURANT, SAMUEL W.   History of Oakland County, Michigan. Philadelphia, 1877. Lithos., lea. spine, gilt stamped cloth. A.e.g. Covers very worn, signatures loose. King 46-152 1983 $125

DURBIN, WALTER   (My Life as a Texas Ranger and Lawman). Orig. Autograph Manuscript. Quarto and octavo. Rare unpublished manuscript. Jenkins 153-566 1983 $6500

DURER, ALBRECHT
Please turn to
DUERER, ALBRECHT

DURER Literatur in Ungarn, 1800-1928. Budapest: Kgl. Ungarische Universitatsdruckerei, 1928. Frontis. Wrappers. Ars Libri 32-173 1983 $50

DURET, THEODORE   Lautrec. Paris: Bernheim-Jeune, 1920. 38 plates, including 1 original color lithograph and 1 original drypoint. 4to. Wrappers over boards. No. 53 of 100 copies on japon, of a limited edition of 200 copies. Ars Libri 32-667 1983 $1,250

D'URFEY, THOMAS   The Campaigners. London: printed for A. Baldwin, 1698. Sm. 4to, disbound. Some headlines shaved, small repair to the last leaf, affecting a couple of words. Ximenes 64-188 1983 $250

D'URFEY, THOMAS   The English Stage Italianiz'd in a new dramatick entertainment called Dido and Aeneas. London: printed for A. Moore, 1727. First ed., wrappers. Pickering & Chatto 19-14 1983 $350

D'URFEY, THOMAS   New Opera's, with Comical Stories, and Poems on several Occasions. London: William Chetwood, 1721. 1st ed., 8vo, later calf antique, morocco label. Front cover rehinged; a very good copy. Trebizond 18-34 1983 $200

DURRELL, LAWRENCE   The Alexandria Quartet. NY: Justine, (1957). Four first American editions. Very good or better in like dustwrappers. Quill & Brush 54-403 1983 $150

DURRELL, LAWRENCE   Cities and Plains and People. London: Faber & Faber, (1946). 1st ed. Orig. yellow cloth, gilt, dj. Fine copy. Jenkins 155-1384 1983 $65

DURRELL, LAWRENCE   Cities Plains and People. London, 1946. First edition. Dust wrapper. Fine. Rota 231-193 1983 £35

DURRELL, LAWRENCE   Collected Poems. London: Faber and Faber, (1960). First edition. Orig. printed wrappers. Early proof copy, with the last three verses of "The Hanged Man" crossed out and the word "Summer" written at the top of p. 191 (all corrections in ink). Wrappers soiled and worn at the spine. Title and author of book written on the spine. Good. MacManus 278-1743 1983 $185

DURRELL, LAWRENCE   La Descente du Styx. Montpellier, France: La Murene, (1964). First edition. One of 250 copies signed. Stiff white wrappers. Fine. Bradley 65-59 1983 $135

DURRELL, LAWRENCE   La Descente du Styx. Montpelier, 1964. First French edition. Wrappers. One of 250 copies signed and numbered by the author. Near mint. Jolliffe 26-162 1983 £60

DURRELL, LAWRENCE   Lifelines - four poems. Edinburgh, Privately printed at the Tragara Press, 1974. Wrappers. One of 115 numbered copies. Hand-printed. Mint. Jolliffe 26-165 1983 £60

DURRELL, LAWRENCE   On Seeming to Presume. London: Faber & Faber, (1948). First edition. Orig. cloth. Dust jacket (a bit soiled). Near-fine. MacManus 278-1744 1983 $25

DURRELL, LAWRENCE   On Seeming to Presume. London, 1948. First edition. 8vo. Cloth in the orig. dustwrapper. Traylen 94-298 1983 £12

DURRELL, LAWRENCE   A Private Country. London, 1943. First edition. Slightly frayed dust wrapper. Fine. Rota 231-192 1983 £50

DURRELL, LAWRENCE   Prospero's Cell. London, 1945. First English edition. Slightly torn and nicked dustwrapper faded at the spine and with a small soiled spot on the upper panel. Near fine. Jolliffe 26-160 1983 £18

DURRELL, LAWRENCE   The Red Limbo Lingo. New York: Dutton, 1971. 1st ed., 1 of 100 numbered and signed copies for America. Orig. red cloth, gilt, box, glassine. Trade ed. consisted of 500 copies each for England and America. Mint copy. Jenkins 155-353 1983 $200

DUSART, CORNELIUS   Renversement de la Morale Chretienne Par les desordres du Monachisme. (Amsterdam, c. 1690). 4to, fold. front., 25 single page plates; two parts bound in one. Full cont. morocco binding. Triple gold fillet on both boards. Spine stamped with gold flowers between raised bands. Elaborate gold dentelles. Marbled endpapers. A.E.G. Excellent copy. Arkway 22-43 1983 $1,675

DUSS, A.   Flora phanerogamique des Antilles francaises (Guadeloupe et Martinique), avec annotations du Prof. E. Heckel sur l'emploi de ces plantes. Macon, 1897. Royal 8vo, cont. quarter roan (trifle used), original wrappers bound in. A few pencil annotations, but a good copy of this rare work. Wheldon 160-1670 1983 £60

DUTHIE, J. F.   The Orchids of the (North-) Western Himalayas. (Calcutta, Ann. Bot. Garden, 1906) Reprint, 1967. 58 plates, folio, cloth. Wheldon 160-2041 1983 £78

DUTHIE, WILLIAM   A tramp's wallet. London: Darton, 1858. First edition. 8vo. Orig. blue cloth. Rubbed. Ximenes 63-619 1983 $50

DUTT, R. C.   Open letters to Lord Curzon... London, 1900. 8vo. Orig. cloth. Presentation copy from author to A.H.L. Frater. Good. Edwards 1044-215 1983 £20

DUTTON, THOMAS   The Wise Man of the East; or, the apparition of Zoroaster, the son of Oromases. London: printed by J. Fricker, 1800. 8vo. Wrappers, 2nd edition. Very good copy. Rare. Ximenes 64-189 1983 $125

DUTTON, WARREN   The Present State of Literature: a Poem delivered in New-Haven, at the Public Commencement of Yale-College, September 10, 1800. Hartford: Hudson & Goodwin, 1800. First (only) edition, 8vo, modern boards. Vignette title page bearing early owner's signature. Foxed throughout, but a good copy. Trebizond 18-35 1983 $100

DUVAL, M.   Le Placenta des Carnassiers. Paris, 1895. Atlas of 13 plates, 2 vols., 4to, wrappers. Wheldon 160-554 1983 £20

DUVAL, PAUL   The Art of Glen Loates. Toronto: Cerebrus Publishing Co., 1978. Folio. 14 folding colour plates. Ca. 135 full-page plates in colour, ca. 60 plates and illus. in black and white and ca. 21 colour illus., coloured initials, and one lithograph signed and numbered by the artist and preserved separately in a cloth covered gilt stamped portfolio. Bound in full leather gilt, in linen slip case, boxed in cherry wood case with lock. Limited to 325 copies signed by artist and author. McGahern 54-58 1983 $2,000

DU VERNEY, J. G.   Oeuvres Anatomiques. Paris, 1761. 4to. 2 vols. Cont. calf. 30 folding plates. Gurney 90-48 1983 £200

DUYCKINCK, EVERT A.   National History of the War for the Union. N.Y., (1861). Vols. 1 & 2 (of 3). 46 fine steel engravings from paintings by A. Chappel and 1 by T. Mast. Full tooled lea. Raised bands. Hinges splitting. Plates nice. King 45-22 1983 $50

DVORAK, MAX   Das Ratsel der Kunst der Bruder Van Eyck. Wien/Leipzig: T. Tempsky/G. Freytag, 1904. 7 plates. 65 text illus. Folio. Boards, 3/4 cloth. Ars Libri 32-212 1983 $100

DWIGGINS, W. A.   Towards a Reform of the Paper Currency. N.Y.: Limited Editions Club, 1932. 4to, edition ltd. to 452 copies. Black calf spine over boards. A fine copy in slipcase. Karmiole 71-110 1983 $350

DWIGHT, EDWARD W.   Memoirs of Henry Obookiah, a Native of Owhyhee and a Member of the Foreign Mission School. Elizabeth-town, N.J., 1819. Illus., fort. frontis. Dbd. Ginsberg 46-857 1983 $50

DWIGHT, THEODORE   A Discourse on Some Events of the
Last Century, Delivered in the Brick Church in New Haven, On
Wednesday, January 7, 1801. New Haven, 1801. Disbound. Reese 18-
242 1983 $30

DWIGHT, THOMAS   Frozen Sections of a Child. New York,
1881. 1st ed. 15 drawings by H.P. Quincy, M.D. 4to. Slightly
rubbed at corners. Morrill 289-63 1983 $57.50

DWIGHT, TIMOTHY   The Conquest of Canaan. Hartford:
Printed by Elisha Babcock, 1785. Cont. sheep, red leather label
on spine. Ownership inscription, 1799. Occasional foxing, but a
very good copy, the binding in nice condition. First edition.
Grunder 6-17 1983 $185

DWIGHT, TIMOTHY   The Dignity and Excellence of the
Gospel, Illustrated in a Discourse, Delivered April 8, 1812. New
York: J. Seymour, printer, 1812. Octavo, orig. printed wraps. Sewn.
A fine, untrimmed copy. Reese 18-372 1983 $30

DWIGHT, TIMOTHY   A Discourse on Some Events of the
Last Century, Delivered in...New Haven... New Haven: Ezra Read,
1801. Disbound. Signature "John Backus' Book." Felcone 22-52 1983
$20

DWIGHT, TIMOTHY   A Discourse on Some Events of the Last
Century... New Haven: Ezra Read, 1801. Disbound. Signature "John
Backus' Book." Very good. Felcone 20-38 1983 $20

DWIGHT, TIMOTHY   Travels; in New-England and New-York.
New Haven, 1821. 4 vols. 3 maps. Orig. boards, uncut, with somewhat
later cloth spines, very nice. Reese 18-552 1983 $250

DWINELLE, JOHN W.   A Funeral Oration Upon David C.
Broderick, Late Senator from California. Rochester, 1859. Cloth.
First edition. Ginsberg 47-67 1983 $65

DYE, EVA E.   McLoughlin and Old Oregon A Chronicle.
Chicago: A. C. McClurg & Co., 1902. Frontis., 1st ed. Jenkins
151-93 1983 $35

DYER, GEORGE   Academic Unity. Printed for Longman,
1827. First edition, complete in spite of pagination jump, 8vo,
orig. boards, uncut, with printed paper label. Just a little wear to
spine. Inscribed by the author. Fenning 60-100 1983 £45

DYER, GEORGE   Four Letters on the English Constitution.
Printed for Longmans, 1817. Third edition, with additions. 8vo,
ad. leaf, orig. boards, uncut. Spine worn, very good. Inscribed by
the author. Fenning 60-101 1983 £32.50

DYER, ROBERT   Nine years of an actor's life. London:
Longman, etc., and Edward Nettleton (Plymouth), 1833. 8vo, original
green cloth, black paper label printed in gold (slight wear to spine,
label rubbed). First edition. Uncommon. Subscriber's list.
Ximenes 64-190 1983 $200

DYESS, WILLIAM E.   The Dyess Story. Toronto, (1944). 1st
Canadian ed. Maps and illus. Small 8vo, upside down in binding.
Morrill 288-563 1983 $25

DYKE, JEREMIAH   A Sermon Dedicatory. Printed by I.D.
for Nathanael Newbery, 1623. First edition, 4to, wrapper, v.g.
Fenning 62-103 1983 £35

DYKES, HANNAH S. B.   History of Richard Bourne and Some of
His Descendants. Cleveland, Privately Printed by Benjamin F.
Bourne, (1919). 1st ed. Illus. 8vo, very nice. Morrill 288-274
1983 $50

DYKES, W. R.   A handbook of Garden Irises. 1924.
24 plates, 8vo, cloth. Wheldon 160-1933 1983 £18

DYKES, W. R.   Notes on Tulip Species. 1930. 54
coloured plates, folio, original buckram, slight foxing on the reverse
of 4 of the plates and small marginal tear in plate 46 neatly repaired.
Binding very slightly used. Wheldon 160-1934 1983 £75

DYMOCK, CRESSY   An Invention of Engines of Motion
lately brought to perfection. London: Printed by I.C. For Richard
Woodnoth..., 1651. 4to. Old calf, rebacked. Title in woodcut
border. Small copy with top of border of title, some numerals and
signatures, and one line of text cut into. Very rare. Gurney 90-49
1983 £350

E

EAGEN, CHARLES   Statement of the Financial Condition of the Territory of Washington, from its Organization to Dec. 31, 1863. Olympia, 1864. Dbd. First edition. Ginsberg 47-922 1983 $100

EAGER, SAMUEL W.   An Outline History of Orange County. Newburgh: S.T. Callahan, 1846-7. First edition. Errata. Later morocco-backed marbled boards, (back-strip mended, prelim. pp. torn in upper margin, not effecting text). Argosy 716-348 1983 $100

EAGLES, JOHN   The Journal of Llewellin Penrose, A Seaman. Printed for Taylor and Hesse, 1825. A new edition. 8vo, original cloth; woodcut frontispiece and title-vignette. Hill 165-31 1983 £40

EAGLESTON, JOHN H.   Account of an Early California Voyage. Salem: Salem Press, 1874. Offprint from Essex Inst. Hist. Coll. 8vo. Orig. plain wrappers, sewn. Fragile wrappers strengthened. First separate ed. Fine. Jenkins 153-179 1983 $75

EARHART, AMELIA   The Fun of It. NY: Brewer, Warren & Putnam, 1932. With 31 photographic plates. This is the first printing, signed by Earhart on the front free endpaper. With a phonograph record of Amelia Earhart in rear pocket. Fine, in a somewhat chipped dust jacket. Karmiole 74-21 1983 $175

EARHART, AMELIA   20 Hrs. 40 Min.: Our Flight in the Friendship. N.Y., 1928. 61 illus., 8vo, 1/2 cloth. First edition. Author's autograph edition. One of 150 signed and numbered copies printed on Old Stratford Line, & containing small silk flag carried by Earhart in the "Friendship." Argosy 714-270 1983 $200

EARLAND, ADA   John Opie and His Circle. London: Hutchinson & Co., 1911. 51 plates. 4to. Cloth. Faded. Inside front hinge cracked. Ars Libri 32-496 1983 $125

EARLE, ALICE MORSE   Child Life in Colonial Days. N.Y.: MacMil., 1899. First edition. 8vo. Green cloth. Ads. Index. Very good. Aleph-bet 8-103 1983 $30

EARLE, ALICE MORSE   Child-Life in Colonial Days. New York, 1899. First edition. Illustrated from photographs and old prints. 8vo. Morrill 290-110 1983 $25

EARLE, ALICE MORSE   China Collecting in America. New York, 1892. 1st ed. Illus., 8vo, very nice. Morrill 286-135 1983 $25

EARLE, ALICE MORSE   Stage-Coach and Tavern Days. New York, 1900. First edition. 8vo, pictorial front cover. Illustrated. Virtually fine. Morrill 290-111 1983 $20

EARLE, E. M.   Makers of Modern Strategy. Princeton U.P., 1943. First edition. Roy. 8vo. Orig. cloth. Maps, some full page. Good. Edwards 1042-328 1983 £25

EARLE, EDWIN   Hopi Kachinas. NY: J.J. Augustin, (1938). Small folio, 28 leaves of color plates. Five text illus. Gold cloth. Karmiole 74-3 1983 $350

EARLE, THOMAS   A Treatise on Rail-roads and Internal Communications. Phila.: John Grigg, 1830. Illus. 4 plates (2 folding), 2 folding maps. Orig. linen-backed boards, paper spine label. Uncut and unopened. Foxed. Handsome copy. Felcone 20-39 1983 $450

EARLE, WILLIAM   Obi: Or, The History of Three-Fingered Jack. Worcester, Isaiah Thomas, Jr., 1804. New cloth, leather label, good. Reese 19-300 1983 $225

EARLY California Travels Series. Los Angeles, Dawson, 1951-1961. 50 vols., complete set of all published. 12mo, in full cloth, or boards with cloth spines in very nice condition. Clark 741-107 1983 $1,450

EARLY Children's Books and Their Illustrations. New York: The Pierpont Morgan Library, (1975). First edition. 4to. Cloth. Dust jacket. Printed at the Stinehour Press. Many illus., including some in color. Oak Knoll 49-429 1983 $75

EARLY Illinois: Parts I-IV. Chicago: Fergus, 1890, 1889, 1899, 1890. 4 vols., printed wrappers (complete). Spines of Parts 3 & 4 chipped, otherwise fine set. Bradley 63-67 1983 $35

EARNSHAW, SAMUEL   The Doctrine of Germs... Cambridge, 1881. 8vo. Maroon cloth, gilt. Inscribed "From the Author". Shaken. A fine copy. Zeitlin 264-129 1983 $37.50

EARP, F. R.   The Way of the Greeks. Oxford, 1930. 8vo, cloth. Salloch 385-102 1983 $20

EASDALE, JOAN ADENEY   Clemence And Clare. London: The Hogarth Press, 1932. First edition. Orig. yellow printed boards. Presentation copy to V. Woolf. Spine and covers faded and worn. Good. MacManus 280-5653 1983 $650

EASDALE, JOAN ADENEY   Clemence and Clare. London, 1932. First edition. One of 500 copies (of which 238 were pulped). Spine a little darkened. Nice. Rota 230-291 1983 £15

EAST London, Illustrated. East London, South Africa: Hebbes & Co., n.d. (ca. 1895). 28 leaves of photogravure plates, each with tissue guard with printed description. Bound in orig. blue gilt-stamped cloth. Karmiole 73-83a 1983 $50

EASTLAKE, WILLIAM   The Bronc People. New York, (1958). 8vo. Cloth. A fine copy in near perfect dj. In Our Time 156-234 1983 $85

EASTMAN, EDWIN   Captured and Branded by the Comanche Indians in the Year 1860. (Jersey City, Ca. 1876). Large woodcut of Indian on title, 8vo, sewed, (some dampstains). Argosy 713-166 1983 $50

EASTMAN, EDWIN   Edwin Eastman, Captured and Branded by the Comanche Indians in the Year 1860. N.p., (1872). Illus. 3 ports. Sewn as issued, slipcased. First edition. Ginsberg 46-354 1983 $250

EASTMAN, EDWIN   Seven and Nine Years Among the Camanches and Apaches. Jersey City: Clark W. Johnson, M. D., 1873. First (?) edition. Frontis. and other plates. Orange cloth. Printed signature beneath a portrait at head of Chapter 1. Foxed, covers badly stained and worn. Bradley 66-541 1983 $65

EASTMAN, MARY H.   Chicora and Other Regions of the Conquerors and the Conquered. Philadelphia, 1854. 21 plates. Gilt-stamped cloth, a fine copy. Reese 19-207 1983 $550

EASTMAN, MAX   Leon Trotsky, The Portrait of a Youth. NY 1925. First edition. Cloth, moderately worn. King 46-460 1983 $20

EASTON, JAMES   Human Longevity: Recording the Name, Age, Place of Residence, and Year, of the Decease of 1712 Persons, who attained a Century, & Upwards, from A.D. 66 to 1799. Salisbury, printed and sold by James Easton, 1799. 1st ed., 8vo, half-title, occasional leaf lightly spotted, original grey boards, paper label, spine slightly rubbed but generally a fine uncut copy. Pickering & Chatto 21-33 1983 $385

EAT California Fruit by One of the Eaters. SanF., Southern Pacific, 1904. Orig. pictorial printed wraps. First edition. Ginsberg 46-68 1983 $25

EATES, MARGOT   Paul Nash: The Master of the Image, 1889-1946. New York: St. Martin's Press, 1974. 144 illus. hors texte. Large 4to. Cloth. Dust jacket. Ars Libri 32-490 1983 $75

EATON, ALLEN H.   Handicrafts of the Southern Highlands. NY, (1939). Photo. illus, color frontis. Argosy 710-491 1983 $30

EATON, CHARLOTTE   At Home and Abroad. John Murray, 1831. First edition, 3 vols., half titles, half blue calf, brown labels, v.g. Jarndyce 30-369 1983 £84

EATON, DORMAN B.   Civil Service in Great Britain. NY, 1880. Ex lib. Argosy 716-191 1983 $40

EATON, JOHN H.   Candid Appeal to the American Public. Wash., 1831. Dbd. First edition. Ginsberg 46-241 1983 $75

EATON, JOHN H.   Leben des General-Majors Andreas Jackson... Reading, Pa.: Johann Ritter and Co., 1831. Port., folding map. Calf-backed boards. First German translation. Felcone 22-53 1983 $60

EATON, WILLIAM   The Life of the Late Gen. William Eaton. Brookfield (Mass.), 1813. 1st ed. Portrait. 8vo, contemp. calf, leather label. Morrill 287-360 1983 $50

EBBUTT, PERCY G.   Emigrant Life in Kansas. London, 1886. Illus., plates. Orig. cloth. First edition. Ginsberg 46-385 1983 $75

EBERHART, RICHARD   Brotherhood of Men. (Pawlet): Banyan Press, (1949). Printed wraps. First edition. From an edition of 226 copies, this is one of 26 lettered copies signed by the author. A fine copy. Reese 20-349 1983 $275

EBERHART, RICHARD   Burr Oaks; poems. New York, 1947. First edition. Frayed dust wrapper. Author's signed autograph presentation inscription to Andre de Bouchet. Nice. Rota 230-185 1983 £25

EBERHART, RICHARD   An Herb Basket. (N.p.): The Cummington Press, 1950. Small quarto. First edition. One of 150 copies, of which this is one of a few copies bound in variant decorated paper. Evidently a review copy, as it bears the stamp "The Tiger's Eye" on the front free endsheet. A fine copy. Reese 20-350 1983 $175

EBERHART, RICHARD   Reading the Spirit. New York, 1937. First American edition. With the pencilled initials of Theodore Roethke on the front free endpaper. Slightly chipped and very slightly soiled dustwrapper faded at the spine. Very good. Jolliffe 26-441 1983 £45

EBERLEIN, HAROLD DONALDSON   The English Inn Past and Present. Phila., 1926. First edition. Illus. Cloth. Index. Extremities worn. Good. King 45-338 1983 $35

EBERLEIN, HAROLD DONALDSON   Interiors, Fireplaces & Furniture of the Italian Renaissance. NY: The Architectural Book Publishing Co., (1927, "second printing"). Large 4to, 82 photo plates. Blue cloth. Karmiole 72-41 1983 $40

EBERLEIN, HAROLD DONALDSON   Manor Houses and Historic Homes of Long Island and Staten Island. Phila., 1938. 1st ed., limited ed. Illus., pict. cloth, thick 8vo, g.t. Argosy 710-351 1983 $35

EBERLEIN, HAROLD D.   The Manors & Historic Homes of the Hudson Valley. Phila., 1924. 82 illus. Pict. cloth, uncut, g.t. Argosy 716-349 1983 $35

EBERLEIN, HAROLD DONALDSON   The Practical Book of Interior Decoration. Philadelphia, 1919. 1st ed. 7 plates in color, 283 in double-tone, and chart. 8vo. Binding partly dust-soiled. Morrill 289-324 1983 $20

EBERS, GEORG   In the Fire of the Forge. London: Sampson Low, Marston & Co., (1895). First English edition, printed in America. 2 vols. Orig. cloth. Cont. owner's signatures. Edges a trifle rubbed. Fine. MacManus 278-1747 1983 $135

EBERSTADT, EDWARD   Americana Catalogue. N.Y., 1966. 4 vols. Ltd. to 75- sets. Ginsberg 47-309 1983 $165

EBERSTADT, EDWARD   The Annotated Eberstadt Catalogs of Americana. New York: Argosy-Antiquarian, 1965. 5 vols., cloth. One of 750 sets. Dawson 470-95 1983 $125

EBERSTADT, EDWARD   The Northwest Coast: Personal Narrative of Discovery, Conquest and Exploration: Catalogue No. 119. N.Y., 1941. Orig. printed wraps. First edition. Ginsberg 47-310 1983 $25

ECCLES, CAROLINE A.   The Princess Eloise. London: C.W. Daniel Co., (1931). First edition. Orig. cloth. Dust jacket (a little dust-soiled). Inscription on flyleaf. Very good. MacManus 278-1748 1983 $20

ECHARD, LAURENCE   The Roman History. 1724-1720. 5 vols. 8vo, cont. calf, a little rubbed, small chip at top of one spine, but sound. Bickersteth 69-30 1983 £45

ECHOS de France. Paris, n.d. (1909). Tall 4to, 1/2 calf with labels. Four vols. Salloch 387-159 1983 $110

ECILAW, ARY   The Romance Of A German Court. London: Remington & Co., 1886. First English edition. 2 vols. Orig. brown cloth. Spines and covers slightly worn. Very good. MacManus 278-1749 1983 $125

ECKEL, JOHN C.   The First Editions of the Writings of Charles Dickens. London and New York, 1932. With illus. and facs. 8vo, 3/4 morocco, dust-jacket, slipcase. One of 250 copies signed by the author. Duschnes 240-66 1983 $250

ECKEL, JOHN C.   The First Editions of the Writings of Charles Dickens, Their Points and Values... N.Y. & London, 1932. 4to. Frontis. & numerous plates, facs., illus. 3/4 leather, gt. 1 of 250 numbered copies, signed by Eckel. Best ed., revised & enlarged. Some scuffing to covers. Nice copy. O'Neal 50-110 1983 $175

ECKENRODE, H. J.   Jefferson Davis, President of the South. NY, 1923. First edition, with typed letter signed from author affixed to inside front cover. Covers, esp. spine, soiled. Extremities worn. King 46-50 1983 $25

ECKFELDT, JACOB R.   A Manual of Gold and Silver Coins of all Nations. Phila.: A. Hart, Late Carey & Hart, 1851. 11 of 16 plates. Orig. boards and cloth. Rebacked. Formerly Henry Wagner's copy. Jenkins 152-621 1983 $100

ECKLEY, JOSEPH   Divine Glory brought to View in the Condemnation of the Ungody. Boston: Robert Hodge, 1782. First (only) edition, 8vo, disbound, uncut copy. Title-page browned and torn in margins, not affecting text; otherwise a good copy of an uncommon title. Trebizond 18-190 1983 $50

ECKLEY, SOPHIA MAY   Minor chords. London: Bell and Daldy, 1869. First edition. 8vo. Orig. bright green cloth. Presentation copy, inscribed by the author to her friend Mrs. Tipping. Just a trifle rubbed. Ximenes 63-444 1983 $30

ECKSTEIN, GUSTAV   Noguchi. New York, 1931. First edition. 8vo. Orig. binding. Autographed by the author. Fye H-3-869 1983 $30

ECTON, JOHN   Thesaurus Rerum Ecclesiasticarum: Being an Account of the Valuations of All The Ecclesiastical Benefices In The Several Dioceses in England and Wales. London: printed for D. Browne, 1742. 4to, cont. calf, worn, joints weak. Deighton 3-120 1983 £18

ECTON, JOHN   Thesaurus Rerum Ecclesiasticarum. London: J. & P. Knapton, etc., 1754. Second edition. 4to. Cont. calf, gilt spine with morocco label, joints worn. Traylen 94-300 1983 £18

EDDISON, E. R.   The Mezentian Gate. London: The Curwen Press, 1958. First edition. Frontis. and decorations by Keith Henderson. Nicked and very slightly soiled dustwrapper with a minute tear. Fine. Jolliffe 26-168 1983 £45

EDDISON, E. R.   Mistress of Mistresses - a Vision of
Zimiamvia. London, 1935. First edition. Numerous black and white
decorations by Keith Henderson. With the bookplate of Montgomery
Evans II by S.H. Sime. Slightly torn and chipped dustwrapper missing
a piece from the head of the spine and slightly browned at the head
of the spine. Fine. Jolliffe 26-167 1983 £95

EDDISON, E, R,   The Worm Ouroboros. NY, 1926. Minor
cover soiling, edges slightly worn, else very good, bookplate. Quill
& Brush 54-411 1983 $35

EDDY, MARY BAKER (GLOVER)   Science and Health. Boston: Christian
Science Pub. Co., 1875. 1st ed., earliest state with errata slip
glued in at rear rather than bound in as in later copies. Orig.
terra cotta cloth, gilt. Rare 1st ed. in an ed. of 1,000. Some
spine & edge rubbing, but very good tight copy. Jenkins 153-354
1983 $1500

EDDY, RICHARD   Universalism in America, a History.
Boston, 1891. 2 vols., 8vo, cloth, (mismatched). Argosy 716-62
1983 $50

EDE. A Story. Remington & Co., 1889. First edition, 3 vols. bound
as one. Orig. remainder red cloth, leading inner hinge sl. weak.
Very good. Jarndyce 30-275 1983 £32

EDER, J. M.   Karl Kampmann. Wien: K.K. Graphische
Lehr- und Versuchsanstalt, 1918. 5 plates. 4to. Wrappers. Ars
Libri 32-352 1983 $125

EDGAR, J. D.   Canada And Its Capital. Toronto:
George N. Morang, 1898. 19 1/2cm. Frontis. portrait and 20 illus.
Printed wrappers. Fine. McGahern 54-59 1983 $25

EDGE, JOHN H.   An Irish Utopia. Dublin: Hodges, Figgis,
1906. First edition, cr. 8vo, orig. (?) unlettered paper wraps., a
very good copy. Fenning 61-24 1983 £14.50

EDGERTON, HENRY   State of the Union. Sacramento, 1861.
Dbd. First edition. Ginsberg 47-69 1983 $35

EDGEWORTH, MARIA   Belinda. For R. Hunter...and Baldwin,
Cradock and Joy, 1821. 3 vols., large 12mo, cont. half calf (a little
rubbed, lacks one label), gilt. Hannas 69-46 1983 £25

EDGEWORTH, MARIA   Comic Dramas. Printed for R. Hunter,
1817. 12mo, 3 pp. advertisements, orig. half calf, rubbed. First
edition. Bickersteth 75-133 1983 £32

EDGEWORTH, MARIA   Early Lessons. London: J. Johnson,
1815. 12mo, 2 vols., cont. half morocco, marbled boards. Binding
very worn, but internally a good copy. Treibzond 18-26 1983 $50

EDGEWORTH, MARIA   Essays on Practical Education.
J. Johnson, 1811. 3rd edition. 2 vols. 2 folding plates. Calf,
borders in blind and gilt, spines gilt. Fine. Jarndyce 31-156
1983 £110

EDGEWORTH, MARIA   Frank, a Sequel to Frank in Early
Lessons. Cambridge, 1822. 2 vols. 12mo, cont. mottled calf,
some pp. darkened. Argosy 710-157 1983 $40

EDGEWORTH, MARIA   Harrington, a Tale; and Ormond, a Tale.
R. Hunter & Baldwin, Cradock & Joy, 1817. First edition, 3 vols.,
orig. half calf, some rubbing, but a very good set. Jarndyce 30-370
1983 £55

EDGEWORTH, MARIA   Harry and Lucy Concluded. London:
Printed for R. Hunter,...Baldwin, Cradock, & Joy, 1825. First edition.
4 vols. Orig. boards. Uncut. Presentation copy, inscribed on the
front free endpaper of Vol.1 "Dr. Hope form the author." Bookplates
of The Hope Trust on front endsheets. Small labels removed from spines.
Extremities of spines worn. Very good. MacManus 278-1751 1983 $450

EDGEWORTH, MARIA   Harry and Lucy concluded: being the
last part of 'Early Lessons.' London: R. Hunter and Baldwin,
Craddock & Joy, 1825. 1st ed., 12mo, 4 vols., cont. half morocco
gilt, boards. Wanting advertisements in final volume, bookplates.
Despite excision of top margin of ten leaves (text unaffected), a
very good copy. Trebizond 18-37 1983 $100

EDGEWORTH, MARIA   Helen. Richard Bentley, 1834. First
edition. 3 vols. Large 12mo, lacks half-titles. Cont. half vellum,
gilt spines. Some slight browning. Hannas 69-48 1983 £35

EDGEWORTH, MARIA   Leonora. J. Johnson, 1806. First
edition, 2 vols. Orig. boards, well respined. Jarndyce 31-679 1983
£62

EDGEWORTH, MARIA   Patronage. London: Printed for J. Johnson & Co., 1814. First edition. 4 vols. Orig. boards and paper spine
labels. Spines rather worn at each head and foot and at the labels.
Covers a bit soiled and becoming detached (all cords still good).
Front cover of vol. I chewed at the lower edge. Good. MacManus
278-1752 1983 $150

EDGEWORTH, MARIA   Patronage. London: for J. Johnson
and Co., 1814. First edition. 12mo. Cont. grey boards, calf spines
and corners, gilt. Errata leaf at end of vol. 1. 4 vols. Traylen
94-303 1983 £48

EDGEWORTH, MARIA   Patronage. For J. Johnson and Co., 1814.
First edition. Has final errata slip, but lacks half-titles, cont.
half calf (heads of two spines slightly defective, lacks two labels.
Hannas 69-49 1983 £20

EDGEWORTH, MARIA   Patronage. J. Johnson, 1814. 2nd
edition, 4 vols. Half calf, wear to heads of spines and sl. defective
at base of spine vol. II. A good set. Jarndyce 30-373 1983 £48

EDGEWORTH, MARIA   Tales and Miscellaneous Pieces.
London, 1825. First collected edition. 14 vols. Cr. 8vo. Cont.
embossed blue morocco, gilt borders on sides, gilt panelled spines,
inner gilt dentelles, edges gilt. Vignette title-pages. Spines
rubbed. Very scarce. Traylen 94-301 1983 £180

EDGEWORTH, MARIA   Tales and Novels of Maria Edgeworth.
London: Baldwin and Cradock, 1832-33. Second collected edition.
18 vols. Cr. 8vo. Half green morocco, gilt, t.e.g. Engraved
frontis. and title-pages. A fine set. Traylen 94-302 1983 £220

EDGEWORTH, MARIA   Tales and novels. London: Baldwin
and Cradock, etc., 1832-3. Second collected edition. 18 vols.
12mo. Orig. maroon watered cloth. Engraved title and frontis.
in each vol. Slight wear to ends of a few spines, one lower joint
neatly repaired, otherwise good. Ximenes 63-649 1983 $200

EDGEWORTH, MARIA   Tales of Fashionable Life. J. Johnson,
1809/12. 6 vols. Vols. I-III first edition; vols. IV-VI 3rd
edition. Half titles vols. IV-VI. Calf a little rubbed, lacking 3
labels. Jarndyce 30-372 1983 £85

EDGEWORTH, RICHARD L.   Memoirs of Richard Lovell Edgeworth,
Esq. London, R. Hunter, 1820. 2 vols., 8vo, orig. boards, covers
detached to vol. 1 and spine broken; vol. 2 rebacked with orig.
printed paper label (chipped and browned) reattached. A large,
uncut set complete with all portraits. First edition. Ravenstree
94-57 1983 $90

EDGEWORTH, RICHARD L.   Practical Education. London, J. Johnson,
1798. 2 vols., 4to, orig. tree sheep, hinges cracked, name on titles,
folding plates, the rare leaf of corrections. Ravenstree 94-58 1983
$390

EDINBURGH Societies. Edinburgh, Printed by William Burness, 1842.
8vo, inscribed "for the Royal Medical Society"; disbound. Pickering &
Chatto 22-33 1983 $20

EDMONDS, GEORGE   Facts and Falsehood Concerning the War
on the South 1861-1865. Memphis, Tenn. (1904). Lacks front cover.
King 46-51 1983 $25

EDMONDS, WALTER D.   Chad Hanna. Bos., 1940. Signed, fine
in bright, near fine dustwrapper. Quill & Brush 54-412 1983 $40

EDMONDS, WALTER D.   Drums Along the Mohawk. Boston, Little
Brown, 1936. First edition. Laid in presentation note, signed by
the author. Dust jacket. Fine copy. Houle 22-328 1983 $60

EDMONDSON, MARY   The Lavender Garden. Warne, 1929.
Illus. by Charles Howard. Col. frontis., 3 col. plates, 18 b&w illus.,
col'd pictorial eps., lavender blue decor. cloth, t.e.g. others uncut.
Rear cvr. rubbed at middle, insc. half title, vg. Hodgkins 27-171
1983 £15

EDMONDSON, WILLIAM   An Epistle Containing Wholesome Advice
and Councel to all Friends. (London?), printed in the year 1701.
First edition, large 12mo, unbound, sewn as issued. Very good.
Fenning 62-105 1983 £32.50

EDMUNDSON, WILLIAM   A Journal of the Life, Travels,
Sufferings, and Labour...of...William Edmundson... Dublin: Printed by
Samuel Fairbrother...over against the Tholsel, 1715. First edition,
4to, some light signs of use but a very good copy in cont. panelled
calf, recently rebacked. Fenning 60-103 1983 £45

EDOUARD-JOSEPH   Dictionnaire Biographique des Artistes
Contemporains, 1910-1930. Paris: Art & Edition, 1930-1931-1934.
Tall 8vo. Cloth. Limited to 3000 numbered copies. Ex-library copy
with stamp on spine and bookplates. Oak Knoll 48-423 1983 $85

EDUCATORS of Michigan. Chicago, 1900. Folio, full morocco, gilt,
all edges gilt. Jenkins 151-212 1983 $100

EDWARD VI, KING OF ENGLAND   Literary Remains. London: for the
Roxburghe, 1857. 2 vols., 4to., orig. maroon boards, brown mor. spines,
gilt. 2 engraved title-pages and vignettes, title-pages printed in
red and black. With presentation inscription from E. P. Shirley.
Limited ed., printed for Members of the Roxburghe Club only. Traylen
94-304 1983 £75

EDWARD, DAVID B.   The History of Texas. Cincinnati: J.A.
James & Co., 1836. Folding map. Original cloth and printed paper
label. Some chipping and wear. Laid in folding cloth case. Jenkins
153-181 1983 $850

EDWARD Vischer's Drawing of the California Missions 1861-1878.
With a Biography of the Artist by Jeanne Van Nostrand. SF: 1982.
Introduction by Thomas Albright. Oblong 4to, cloth, gilt, plain
d/w. Containing 44 plates. One of 600 copies. Fine as issued.
Perata 27-5 1983 $250

EDWARDES, S. M.   Babur. London, (1935). 5 plates.
8vo. Orig. cloth. Good. Edwards 1044-225 1983 £16

EDWARDS, AMELIA R.   Hand and Glove. J. & C. Brown, n.d.
Half calf, maroon label, v.g. Jarndyce 31-680 1983 £12.50

EDWARDS, AMELIA B.   A thousand miles up the Nile.
London: Geo. Routledge, 1891. 4to. Frontis. Text engravings.
Orig. pictorial cloth. Adelson Africa-187 1983 $25

EDWARDS, DELTUS M.   The Toll of the Arctic Seas. NY:
Henry Holt and Co., 1910. Profusely illus., including one large
folding color map. Red cloth. Bookplate. Index. T.e.g. Karmiole
71-11 1983 $50

EDWARDS, E. I.   The Valley Whose Name Is Death.
Pasadena: San Pasqual Press, 1940. Cloth. Dawson 470-101 1983
$45

EDWARDS, FRED G.   Chemistry, An Exact Mechanical Philosophy. London: Churchill, 1900. First edition. 8vo. Orig.
cloth. 3 photographic plates, text illus. and diagrams. Ads. Very
good. Zeitlin 264-133 1983 $40

EDWARDS, H.   How to Pass the Winter... London, 1889.
Orig. printed wrappers, soiled. 8vo. Good. Edwards 1044-221 1983
£12

EDWARDS, H. B.   A Year on the Punjab Frontier. London,
1851. Folding map, 2 folding plans, portrait, spotted. 7 plates
including 3 coloured and 2 folding. 2 vols. Half calf. 8vo. Good.
Edwards 1044-223 1983 £95

EDWARDS, H. SUTHERLAND   The Missing Man. London: Remington &
Co., 1885. First edition. Orig. decorated wrappers. Wrappers slightly
worn and foxed. Small bookseller's blindstamp on the rear cover. Near
fine. MacManus 278-1753 1983 $125

EDWARDS, H. SUTHERLAND   Russian Projects against India...
London, 1885. First edition. Folding coloured map. Head of spine
slightly torn. 8vo. Orig. cloth. Good. Edwards 1044-220 1983 £35

EDWARDS, JOHN N.   John Edwards Biography, Memoirs...
Kansas City: Jennie Edwards, 1889. Illustrations. Original cloth,
gilt. New edition (with notes and additions). Jenkins 153-182 1983
$75

EDWARDS, JOHN N.   Noted Guerillas. St. Louis, 1877. 1st
ed. Rebound. Illus. (lacks 1 plate). Jenkins 153-183 1983 $75

EDWARDS, JOHN N.   Shelby and His Men. Cincinnati, 1867.
First edition. Illus. Folding map. Marginal wear. Jenkins 152-814
1983 $100

EDWARDS, JONATHAN   An Account of the Life of the Late
Reverend Mr. David Brainerd. Boston: D. Henchman, 1749. First edition
thus. Full calf. Covers detached. Front endsheet lacking. Signature
clipped from upper blank corner of title. Very good. Felcone 20-14
1983 $225

EDWARDS, JONATHAN   A Careful and Strict Inquiry into the
Modern Prevailing Notions of that Freedom of Will ... London: J.
Johnson, 1768. Third edition. Full calf (spine label wanting). Very
good. Felcone 20-40 1983 $50

EDWARDS, JONATHAN   A Faithful Narrative of the Surprising
Work of God in the Conversion of Many Hundred Souls in Northampton.
Elizabeth Town: Shepard Kollock, 1790. Full calf. Very good.
Felcone 19-13 1983 $125

EDWARDS, JONATHAN   The Salvation of All Men Strictly
Examined. New Haven: A. Morse, 1790. First edition. With list
of subscribers and Morse's Printing and Book-Binding ad. at end
listing in detail his services. Argosy 716-63 1983 $200

EDWARDS, JONATHAN   Some Thoughts Concerning the Present
Revival of Religion in New-England... Lexington (K.): Re-printed
by Joseph Charless, 1803. Orig. unlettered calf. A very good
copy. Reese 18-252 1983 $400

EDWARDS, JONATHAN   A Treatise Concerning Religious Affections, in Three Parts. Boston: Printed for S. Kneeland and T. Green,
1746. 8vo. Contemporary calf, rebacked with new label. Signed on
title page "Stephen Williams's Book 1765 return". Some foxing else
a vg-fine copy. In Our Time 156-239 1983 $350

EDWARDS, JONATHAN   A Treatise Concerning Religious
Affections... Boston printed; New York: Reprinted J. Parker,
for Garrat Noel, 1768. Calf. Blind-tooled cont. binding. Second
edition. Felcone 22-56 1983 $85

EDWARDS, JONATHAN   A Treatise Concerning Religious Affections. Elizabeth Town: Shepard Kollock for Robert Hodge, 1787. Full
calf. Old library stamp on title, hinges beginning to crack. Very
nice. Felcone 19-14 1983 $60

EDWARDS, JONATHAN   A Treatise Concerning Religious
Affections, in Three Parts. Phila.: M. Carey, Oct. 22, 1794.
12mo, mod. cloth-backed boards, slightly torn, mended, affecting
few letters. Ex-library. Argosy 710-67 1983 $75

EDWARDS, JOSEPH   Poems, Humorous and Philosophical.
Houlston & Sons; Bristol: J. Wright, n.d. (1875). A new edition,
orig. green cloth. Jarndyce 30-691 1983 £10.50

EDWARDS, LIONEL   Huntsmen Past and Present. London:
1929. 4to, vellum-backed cloth bds., gilt, t.e.g. Illustrated with
contemporary prints and from original watercolor drawings by the
author. One of 150 copies numbered & signed by the author. A fine
copy with 10 tipped-in color plates. Perata 28-25 1983 $250

EDWARDS, LIONEL   Reminiscences of a Sporting Artist.
London, (1947). 1st ed. Illus. by author. 8vo. Morrill 288-95
1983 $25

EDWARDS, LIONEL   Sketches in Stable and Kennel. London:
G.P. Putnam's Sons, (1933). First English edition. Illus. Half
vellum with cloth boards. Limited to 31 signed copies, with a fine,
orig. signed drawing by Edwards, inscribed "a leg", neatly tipped in.
Spine slightly rubbed. Some foxing throughout. Bookplates. Very
good. MacManus 278-1754 1983 $450

EDWARDS, MATILDA BETHAM   Through Spain to the Sahara. Hurst &
Blackett, 1868. First edition, half title, front. vignette title,
16 pp ads. Orig. brown cloth, gilt, bevelled boards, v.g. Jarndyce
31-681 1983 £35

EDWARDS, PHILIP L.   California in 1837. Diary of...Contain-
ing an Account of a Trip to the Pacific Coast. Sacramento: Johnston,
1890. Orig. printed wrappers. Laid in half morocco case. 1st ed.
Fine copy. Jenkins 153-766 1983 $225

EDWARDS, RICHARD   Edward's Great West and Her Commercial
Metropolis... St. Louis: Published at the Office of Edward's Monthly,
1860. Frontis. and illus. Orig. pictorial gilt morocco. A.e.g.
Metal clasp. Some wear to the spine with minor repairs. Presentation
copy from Richard Edwards to A.S. Abell the editor of the Baltimore Sun.
Jenkins 152-107 1983 $100

EDWARDS, S. M.   The Rise of Bombay. Bombay, 1902. 10
maps, 4 folding, 4 plans, 5 plates. Morocco spine, worn. Ex-library.
8vo. Good. Edwards 1044-224 1983 £25

EDWARDS, WILLIAM H.   Football Days. New York: Moffat,
Yard and Company, 1916. Profusely illus. Presentation copy,
signed by the author. Blue cloth, gilt-stamped. Small gouge on
front cover. Karmiole 71-44 1983 $40

EDWIN, JOHN PROSSER   An Appeal to the Public, relative to the
conduct of William M'Cready, Esq. Newcastle-upon-Tyne: printed for
the author, by S. Hodgson, 1807. 8vo, disbound, 1st ed. Title-page
dust-soiled (loose); one clean tear, without loss of text. Very
scarce. Ximenes 64-192 1983 $100

EDWIN, JOHN PROSSER   Candour versus calumny. Newcastle-
upon-Tyne: printed for the author by S. Hodgson, 1807. 8vo, disbound,
1st ed. Rare. Ximenes 64-193 1983 $150

EGAN, BERESFORD PATRICK   De Sade. The Fortune Press, (1929).
With a coloured frontis., a title-page vignette and 15 illus. by
Beresford Egan, large 4to, orig. pigskin, gilt, t.e.g. 1600 copies
were printed, this being copy number 6 of 100 copies on special
paper, signed by both the author and the artist. Fenning 62-94 1983
£125

EGAN, PIERCE   Pierce Egan's Book of Sports, and
Mirror of Life. London: Printed to T.T. & J. Tegg, 1832. First
edition. 8vo. Later 3/4 red morocco & marbled boards, marbled endpapers, t.e.g., with orig. pictorial wrappers bound in, by Tout.
Some foxing. Very good. MacManus 278-1755 1983 $250

EGAS, MONIZ, ANTONIO CAETANO DE ABREU FREIRE
Please turn to
MONIZ, EGAS 1874-

EGERTON, FRANCIS   Journal of a Tour in the Holy Land, in
May and June, 1840. London: printed by Harrison and Co. for
private circulation only, 1841. 1st ed., 8vo, 4 tinted lithograph
plates, original green cloth, blind, and gilt, slight foxing, with
binder's ticket of Remnant & Edmonds. Deighton 3-121 1983 £32

EGERTON, GEORGE   Symphonies. N.Y.: John Lane, 1897.
First American edition. Orig. cloth. Endpapers slightly spotted.
Very good. MacManus 278-1758 1983 $35

EGGELING BINDERY.   Bookbinding by Hand. New York: Eggeling Bookbindery, (1925). Thin 8vo. Cloth. Covers spoiled. Oak
Knoll 48-42 1983 $25

EGGLESTON, EDWARD   A History of the United States and Its
People. New York: D. Appleton and Company, 1888. Illus., 3 by
Frederic Remington. 1st ed. Fine copy. Jenkins 153-462 1983 $50

EGGLESTON, EDWARD   The Hoosier School-Master. New York:
Orange Judd, circa 1871. First edition in book form, with 29 full-
page and other illus., 8vo, orig. green cloth, some light fingermarks
in a few places, but still a very good copy. Fenning 61-126 1983
£14.50

EGGLESTON, EDWARD   The Hoosier-School Boy. NY, 1883.
Second issue with "Cousin Surey" as frontis., spine darkened, cover
rubbed and worn, spine edges chipped, else good. Quill & Brush 54-
413 1983 $35

EGGLESTON, EDWARD   Roxy. Chatto & Windus, 1878. 2 vols.,
vol. I, first edition; vol. II, 2nd edition. Half green calf.
Jarndyce 30-374 1983 £32

EGLE, WILLIAM H.   An Illustrated History of the Commonwealth of Pennsylvania. Harrisburg: 1876. First edition. Profusely
illus. Black leather. Rubbed, back inner hinge repaired. Very good
copy. Bradley 66-644 1983 $22.50

EGLESTON, THOMAS   Life of John Paterson. NY, 1894.
Tall 8vo, cloth, g.t., ex lib., stamped on versos, plates. Argosy
710-457 1983 $35

EGLINTON, JOHN, PSEUD.
Please turn to
MAGEE, WILLIAM KIRKPATRICK

EGMONT, JOHN PERCEVAL, SECOND EARL OF   A Proposal for Selling Part
of the Forest Lands and Chaces. London: T. Payne, 1763. 1st ed.,
4to, disbound. Pickering & Chatto 21-95 1983 $50

EHRENBERG, HERMAN   With Milam and Fannin. Dallas, 1935.
Illustrated. Original red cloth. First edition in English. Very
scarce. Very fine. Jenkins 153-184 1983 $75

EHRLICH, PAUL   Beitrage zur experimentellen Pathologie
und Chemotherapie... Leipzig: Akademische Verlagsgesellschaft,
1909. 8vo. Orig. half cloth. Ownership inscription cut off from
half-title, otherwise a very good copy. Zeitlin 264-135 1983 $170

EHRLICH, PAUL   Die Chemotherapie Des Spirillosen...
Sechzehntes Heft, 1911. Orig. offprint, 8vo, orig. printed paper
wrappers, rather frayed and torn. Pickering & Chatto 22-34 1983 $350

EHRMANN, JEAN   Antoine Caron, peintre a la cour
des Valois, 1521-1599. Geneve/Lille: Droz/Giard, 1955. 32 heliogravure plates with 48 illus. loose in portfolio. 4to. Wrappers.
Ars Libri 32-80 1983 $85

EICHWALD, E.   Die Physikalisch-Chemischen Grundlagen
der Biologie. Berlin, 1919. Good ex-library. Wheldon 160-150 1983
£12

EICKEMEYER, RUDOLF   Letters from the South-West. (NY: Pri-
vately printed for the author by Press of J. J. Little & Co.), 1894.
Tall 8vo, with 34 illus. (some full-page). Orig. grey cloth, soiled.
Karmiole 74-102 1983 $150

EIFFEL, G.   La Resistance De L'Air Et L'Aviation.
Paris, 1910. Orig. cloth. 28 double-page plates. 4to. Half cloth.
Slightly worn. Good. Edwards 1042-585 1983 £60

THE EIGHTEEN-Eighties. Cambridge: At the University Press, 1930.
First edition. 8vo. Orig. cloth. Dust jacket. Fine copy. Jaffe
1-9 1983 $35

EINSTEIN, ALBERT   Investigations on the Theory of the
Brownian Movement. London: (1926). First edition in English. Orig.
blue-green cloth. Very fine copy. Bookplate. Bradley 66-415 1983
$185

EINSTEIN, ALBERT   Relativity, the Special & General
Theory. Methuen & Co. ltd. (1920). 8vo, 8 page pub.'s catalogue,
portrait, orig. cloth, spine a little faded. First edition in
English. Bickersteth 75-224 1983 £30

EINSTEIN, ALBERT   Teorria Otndistel 'Nosti... Berlin:
Knigoizdatel'stvo, 1921. Frontispiece portrait of Einstein with
facsimile of his signature; text figures. Orig. grey printed wrappers. 1st ed. in Russian. No other known copy of this printing.
Fine. Jenkins 155-356-A 1983 $1850

EINSTEIN, ALFRED   The Italian Madrigal. Princeton, 1971.
Three vols. With illus. and music. Folio, cl. Salloch 387-313
1983 $200

EINSTEIN, CARL   Negerplastik. Munchen: Kurt Wolff,
1920. Second edition. 108 plates with 116 illus. 4to. Boards.
1/4 cloth. Ars Libri 34-603 1983 $100

EISEN, GUSTAVUS A.   The Great Chalice of Antioch. NY, 1923.
Two vols. Ltd., numbered ed. Tall folio, 1/2 mor. Salloch 385-279
1983 $350

EISENHOWER, DWIGHT DAVID   Crusade in Europe. Garden City, 1948.
1st ed., limited to 1426 numbered copies, signed by author. Illus,
cloth, t.e.g., very good. King 46-780 1983 $250

EISENHOWER, DWIGHT DAVID   The White House Years. GC, 1965. Signed
bookplate from Eisenhower farm, fine in slightly frayed and torn, very
good dustwrapper with 2 inch skinned spot on front panel. Quill &
Brush 54-1621 1983 $75

EISENSCHIML, OTTO   Why Was Lincoln Murdered? Boston,
1937. 1st ed. Illus. Argosy 710-259 1983 $35

EISLER, MAX   Gustav Klimt. Eine Nachlese. Wien
Oosterreichische Staatsdruckerei, 1931. 30 heliogravure plates
(15 color) tipped-in heavy stock. Square folio. Vorzugsausgabe:
one of 30 copies of the German-language edition (limited to 200
copies) bound in Goldleder (unornamented full leather, entirely gilt)
with moire doublures and endpapers. Slipcase. Uncut. Backstrip
rubbed. Ars Libri 32-371 1983 $1,650

EKART, T. P.   Synopsis Jungermanniarum. Coburg,
1832. 13 plates of 116 figures, 4to, cloth (worn). Somewhat foxed
throughout. Wheldon 160-1822 1983 £20

EL COMANCHO. The Old-Timer's Tale. Chicago, 1929. Illus.,
pr. pict. bds. Argosy 710-435 1983 $25

ELDER, WILLIAM   How the Western States Can Become the
Imperial Power in the Union. Phila., 1865. Sewn as issued. First
edition. Ginsberg 47-311 1983 $50

ELDREDGE, ZOETH S.   The Beginnings of San Francisco from the
Expedition of Anza, 1774 to the City Charter of April 15, 1860.
San Francisco, 1912. 2 vols. Illus., folded map. Orig. cloth.
First edition. Ginsberg 47-71 1983 $50

ELGOOD, G. S.   Some English Gardens. 1904. Second
edition, 50 coloured plates, folio, cloth. Wheldon 160-1936 1983 £30

ELGOOD, P. G.   Bonaparte's Adventures in Egypt.
Oxford, 1931. 8vo. Half red morocco, t.e.g. 17 illus. and 2
maps. Traylen 94-631 1983 £18

ELIBANK, PATRICK MURRAY, FIFTH BARON OF   Thoughts on Money, Circulation and Paper Currency. Edinburgh, printed by Hamilton Balfour
and Neill, 1758. 1st ed., 8vo, uncut in modern marbled boards,
edges a little dust-soiled. Scarce. Pickering & Chatto 21-84 1983
$85

ELIOT, ELLSWORTH   West Point In The Confederacy. NY, 1941.
First edition. Very good in discolored and torn dust wrappers.
King 46-52 1983 $40

ELIOT, GEORGE   Adam Bede. Wm. Blackwood, 1859. First
edition. 3 vols. Half title. Some light foxing, half calf, labels.
Vols. I & III have black vol. labels, vol. II brown, otherwise uniform.
Jarndyce 31-682 1983 £76

ELIOT, GEORGE   Adam Bede. Wm. Blackwood, 1859.
First edition, 3 vols. Half black calf, marbled boards, rubbed. A
good copy. Jarndyce 31-683 1983 £60

ELIOT, GEORGE   Agatha. London: Trubner & Co., 1869.
Orig. wrappers (very slightly soiled and bent at one corner). In a
cloth folder. Very good. MacManus 280-5590 1983 $250

ELIOT, GEORGE   Daniel Deronda. Edinburgh & London:
William Blackwood & Sons, 1876. First edition. 4 vols. in 8 parts.
Orig. printed paper wrappers. With all inserted ads and errata noted.
Unrecorded variant wrapper on Book II which bears no ads on the inside
front and back wrappers. Enclosed in a cloth slipcase (individual
wraparound cases worn). MacManus 278-1761 1983 $1,250

ELIOT, GEORGE   Daniel Deronda. Edinburgh & London:
William Blackwood & Sons, 1876. 4 vols. in 8. Orig.
purple cloth. Spines faded, extremities worn with some splitting at
outer hinges. A number of inner hinges carcking. Preserved in two
matching half-morocco slipcases. Good. MacManus 278-1762 1983 $750

ELIOT, GEORGE   Daniel Deronda. Edinburgh: Balckwood,
1876. First book edition. 4 vols. Orig. cloth. One signature
starting in vol. 4. Covers a little shaken and worn. Complete with
the errata slip in vol. 3. Very good. MacManus 278-1760 1983 $550

ELIOT, GEORGE   Daniel Deronda. William Blackwood and
Sons, 1876. First edition, first issue. 4 vols., 8vo, all 4 half-
titles but lacks final advert. leaf. Cont. red half calf, gilt.
Two leaves torn across corner, in margin only. A fine set. Errata
slip after p. 367, Vol. I, and another after p. 196. Hannas 69-50
1983 £85

ELIOT, GEORGE   Early Essays. N.p.: Privately printed,
1919. First edition. Orig. cloth. One of 220 copies. Fine.
MacManus 278-1763 1983 $85

ELIOT, GEORGE   Felix Holt the Radical. Edinburgh &
London, 1846. 3 vols. With half-titles. Rebound in morocco,
boards. Some scuffing to leather, else a vg-fine set. In Our Time
156-241 1983 $150

ELIOT, GEORGE   Felix Holt, the Radical. Edinburgh,
Blackwood, 1866. 1st ed., 3 vols, 8vo, 2 leaves of advts., uncut in
the original bright blue cloth decorated in black, spines lettered
and decorated in gilt, slight internal cracking, very slight wear to
head and foot of spines. Nevertheless a very fine and entirely
unopened copy . Extremely rare in this binding. Deighton 3-122
1983 £550

ELIOT, GEORGE   Felix Holt, the Radical. New York:
Harper, 1866. 1st American ed. Orig. brown cloth, gilt. Wear, but
solid copy. Jenkins 155-357 1983 $50

ELIOT, GEORGE   Impressions of Theophrastus Such.
Edinburgh: Blackwood, 1879. First edition. Covers slightly worn.
Very good. MacManus 278-1764 1983 $85

ELIOT, GEORGE   Impressions of Theoprastus Such.
Edinburgh, 1879. First edition. 8vo, cloth. With the tipped-in
pub.'s note explaining delay in publication. Argosy 714-271 1983
$50

ELIOT, GEORGE   The Life of Jesus, Critically Examined.
London: Chapman, Brothers, 1846. First edition. 3 vols. Orig. cloth.
Spines repaired. Very good. MacManus 278-1765 1983 $550

ELIOT, GEORGE   Middlemarch. Edinburgh & London:
William Blackwood & Sons, 1871-72. First edition. 4 vols. Orig.
decorated cloth. Rear outer hinge of Vol. I split at the top of the
spine. Inner hinges cracking in the same vol. Minor wear at extremities. Very good. MacManus 278-1766 1983 $1,500

ELIOT, GEORGE   The Mill on the Floss. Wm. Blackwood,
1858. First edition, 3 vols., half titles, 16 pp ads. vol. III.
Orig. orange-brown cloth. Very small nick from leading free end
papers, vol. I. Sl. rubbing at base of spines, otherwise a fine copy.
Jarndyce 30-376 1983 £140

ELIOT, GEORGE   The Mill on the Floss. Edinburgh:
Blackwood, 1860. First edition. 3 vols. Orig. cloth. Labels
expertly removed from two covers. MacManus 278-1767 1983 $275

ELIOT, GEORGE   The Mill on the Floss. NY, 1860. Cover
slightly rubbed and lightly worn, spine slightly faded, light interior
foxing, else near very good, owner's name. Quill & Brush 54-416 1983
$75

ELIOT, GEORGE   Romola. London: Smith, Elder and Co.,
1863. First edition. 3 vols. 8vo. Orig. dark green cloth, gilt.
Advert. leaf in vol. 2. Traylen 94-308 1983 £130

ELIOT, GEORGE   Romola. T. Fisher Unwin, 1907. 2 vols.
8vo, titles in red and black. 160 plates. Orig. gilt vellum, t.e.g.,
rest uncut. Hannas 69-51 1983 £20

ELIOT, GEORGE   Scenes of Clerical Life. Edinburgh:
Blackwood, 1858. First edition. 2 vols. Orig. cloth. A bit shaken
and worn. Very good. MacManus 278-1768 1983 $650

ELIOT, GEORGE   Scenes of Clerical Life. Blackwood,
1858. First edition, 2 vols., half titles. Half calf, sl. rubbed,
maroon labels, v.g. Jarndyce 30-375 1983 £120

ELIOT, GEORGE   Scenes of Clerical Life. Edinburgh &
London, Blackwood, 1858. 2 vols. 8vo, later dark brown half
morocco now scuffed, bit bumped, complete with half titles. First
edition. Ravenstree 94-60 1983 $365

ELIOT, GEORGE   Scenes of Clerical Life. London: Macmillan & Co., Limited, 1906. First of this illus. edition. Illus. in
color by Hugh Thomson. Orig. gilt-decorated cloth, a.e.g. Dust jacket
(defective). Very fine. MacManus 280-5228 1983 $250

ELIOT, GEORGE   Silas Marner: The Weaver of Raveloe.
Edinburgh & London: William Blackwood & Sons, 1861. First edition,
Carter's "A" binding. Orig. brown decorated cloth. Spine and covers
slightly worn and soiled. From the library of A. Edward Newton with
his bookplate on the front paste-down endpaper. Near-fine. MacManus
278-1769 1983 $350

ELIOT, GEORGE   Silas Marner. Edinburgh & London: William Blackwood & Sons, 1861. First edition. 8vo. Orig. cloth.
Presentation copy from the publisher, inscribed, "From Mr. Balckwood"
in ink on the half-title page. Publisher's catalogue present. Endpapers cracked along both inner hinges. Extremities of spine slightly
rubbed. MacManus 278-1770 1983 $225

ELIOT, GEORGE   The Spanish Gypsy. Edinburgh: Blackwood,
1868. First edition. Orig. cloth. Extremities and edges slightly
worn. MacManus 278-1771 1983 $75

ELIOT, GEORGE   The Spanish Gypsy. William Blackwood,
1868. First edition, 8vo, orig. blue cloth, gilt, by Burn & Co.,
with their ticket, a little wear at headband and top of spine, but
otherwise a very good copy. Fenning 61-127 1983 £28.50

ELIOT, GEORGE   Works. Boston, Estes, 1898. Holly
Lodge edition. Illus. Green cloth, leather labels, t.e.g., uncut.
One of 500 copies. 24 vols. complete. Very good - fine. Houle 22-1210
1983 $350

ELIOT, GEORGE   The Works. Edinburgh and London,
(ca. 1891). 10 vols. 8vo. Half brown morocco, gilt, gilt panelled
spines, edges gilt. Frontis. to each vol. Library edition.
Traylen 94-306 1983 £190

ELIOT, GEORGE   The Writings. Boston: Houghton Mifflin
Co., 1908. Large paper edition. 25 vols. Orig. cloth with paper
labels on spines. One of 750 copies. A few spines slightly faded.
Very good. MacManus 278-1772 1983 $350

ELIOT, JOHN   An Apology for Socrates and Negotium
Posterorum. Printed for Earl St. Germans and Private Circulation
only, 1881. 2 vols. 4to. Cloth. Orig. printed labels, uncut
edges. Large paper copy, limited to 100 sets, initialled by Grosart.
Traylen 94-309 1983 £36

ELIOT, JOHN   A Further Account of the Progresse of
the Gospel amongst the Indians in New-England. London, 1659. NY,
1865. Sabin's reprints quarto series, one of 250 copies, initialed by
Sabin. Thin, small 4to, printed wrappers. Argosy 710-102 1983 $35

ELIOT, RICHARD R.   Two Sermons Preached at Watertown.
Boston, 1810. Stitched, fair. Reese 18-336 1983 $20

ELIOT, SAMUEL A.   A Sketch of the History of Harvard
College and of its Present State. Boston, 1848. 12mo, orig. boards,
(backstrip darkened). Argosy 716-269 1983 $40

ELIOT, THOMAS STEARNS   Animula. (London: Faber & Faber
limited, n.d.). First eddition. Wood engravings by Gertrude
Hermes. 8vo. Orig. decorated wrappers. Fine copy. Jaffe 1-85
1983 $85

ELIOT, THOMAS STEARNS   Animula. (London, n.d.). First edition.
Illus. Printed wraps. Argosy 714-272 1983 $45

ELIOT, THOMAS STEARNS   (Ash Wednesday. London, 1930). First
edition. Printed in 16pt Baskerville on specially watermarked Curwen
Press paper. Blank p.(16) discoloured. Very nice, fresh state.
Rota 230-187 1983 £125

ELIOT, THOMAS STEARNS   The Chapbook, no. 22. London, 1921.
Printed wraps. (small chips), else very good. Houle 21-322 1983
$45

ELIOT, THOMAS STEARNS   Charles Whibley. (London: Oxford),
1931. Orig. printed wraps. First edition. A couple of minor
creases, else fine. Reese 20-357 1983 $75

ELIOT, THOMAS STEARNS   The Classics and the Man of Letters.
London: Oxford, 1942. Orig. printed wraps., wallet edges. First
edition. Spine slightly sunned, else fine. The 't' in the sixth
line of the title-page appears to be in an intermediate state of
vanishing. Reese 20-360 1983 $50

ELIOT, THOMAS STEARNS   The Classic and the Man of Letters.
London: Oxford Univ. Press, 1942. 1st ed. Orig. blue printed
wrappers. 2nd issue with "t" on title page broken but still clearly
visible. Very good. Jenkins 155-358 1983 $35

ELIOT, THOMAS STEARNS   The Classics and the Man of Letters.
London, 1942. First edition. Wrappers. Last leaf is franked: "Free
Copy Not For Sale." Very nice. Rota 230-193 1983 £12

ELIOT, THOMAS STEARNS   The Cocktail Party. London, 1950.
First edition, first issue. 8vo. Cloth. In the orig. dustwrapper.
Traylen 94-310 1983 £15

ELIOT, THOMAS STEARNS   The Cocktail Party. London, 1950.
First edition, first issue. 8vo. Orig. cloth. Gilt. Traylen
94-311 1983 £12

ELIOT, THOMAS STEARNS   Collected Poems of T.S. Eliot. New
York, (1936). 8vo. Cloth. 1st American ed. A copy for review with
stamp of the publisher on the front flyleaf giving date and price of
publication. Some light fading to spine, mainly a fine copy in near
perfect dj. In Our Time 156-242 1983 $175

ELIOT, THOMAS STEARNS   Commerce XXI. Paris, Autume, 1929.
First edition. Of 2900 numbered copies, this is one of 100 "sur
Hollande Van Gelder" paper. Wrappers. Unopened. Fine. Rota
230-198 ;093 $20

ELIOT, THOMAS STEARNS   Commerce XXIX. Paris, Winter, 1932.
First edition. One of 2900 copies. Wrappers. Unopened. Fine.
Rota 230-197 1983 £15

ELIOT, THOMAS STEARNS   Dante. London, Faber, (1929). First
edition. Small 8vo, pictorial boards & dust jacket illus. by Rex
Whistler (sm. chips) else, very good. Partly unopened. Houle 22-331
1983 $75

ELIOT, THOMAS STEARNS   Dante. London: Faber & Faber, (1929).
Pictorial boards. First trade edition, one of 2,000 copies issued
simultaneously with the 125 signed copies. Light offset on endsheets
from dust wrapper, otherwise a very fine copy, in the very fragile
jacket, which is backed at the folds, and slightly chipped and soiled
at the top edge. Reese 20-355 1983 $60

ELIOT, THOMAS STEARNS   The Dry Salvages. London: (1941).
First edition. Fine in faintly rubbed printed wrappers. Bromer 25-
32 1983 $40

ELIOT, THOMAS STEARNS   Elizabethan Essays. London: Faber &
Faber, (1934). Cloth, first edition, second state of three, with
the half-title a cancel. With the pencil signature of Louis
Kronenberger. A fine copy, in the fragile wrapper, which is slightly
chipped at the edges. Reese 20-358 1983 $45

ELIOT, THOMAS STEARNS   Essays Ancient and Modern. New York:
Harcourt, (1936). Cloth, first American edition, Pub.'s review
copy, with review notice and publication date stamped on front free
endsheet. A fine copy in dust jacket. Reese 20-359 1983 $85

ELIOT, THOMAS STEARNS   Ezra Pound: His Metric and Poetry.
New York, 1917. First edition. Marginal sunning to a couple of
spots on the spine. Plain tan dustwrapper is missing several small
chips on the spine and edges. Fine. Gekoski 2-41 1983 £300

ELIOT, THOMAS STEARNS   The Family Reunion. New York: Harcourt,
Brace, (1939). 1st Am. ed. Orig. black cloth, gilt. Contemp.
inscrip. by Lucy Ward Stebbins, dean of women at UC. 2500 copies
printed. Fine copy in slightly used dj. Jenkins 155-360 1983
$40

ELIOT, THOMAS STEARNS   The Family Reunion. London, 1939. First
edition. Torn dust wrapper. Very nice. Rota 231-198 1983 £15

ELIOT, THOMAS STEARNS   For Lancelot Andrewes. Garden City:
Doubleday, 1929. Cloth. First American Edition, one of 2,000 copies
printed. Very slight sunning at top edge, and small bookplate, else a
fine copy in lightly used dust jacket. Reese 20-354 1983 $50

ELIOT, THOMAS STEARNS   Four Quartets. London (1960). Small
folio, marbled boards with vellum back, t.e.g., slipcase. One of
290 copies printed on mould-made paper and set in Dante type.
Signed by the author. Duschnes 240-177 1983 $1,550

ELIOT, THOMAS STEARNS   Homage to John Dryden. London: The
Hogarth Press, 1924. Orig. pictorial wraps., after a design by
Venessa Bell. First edition, one of about 2,000 copies printed. Wraps.
slightly tanned, else about fine. Reese 20-353 1983 $85

ELIOT, THOMAS STEARNS   The Idea of a Christian Society. London,
1939. First edition. Spine darkened and corners bruised. Nice.
Rota 231-199 1983 £15

ELIOT, THOMAS STEARNS   The Idea of a Christian Society. New
York, 1940. First American edition. Dust wrapper. Very nice. Rota
230-191 1983 £12

ELIOT, THOMAS STEARNS   Journey of the Magi. New York, 1927.
First edition. One of 27 copies printed, of which only 12 were for
sale. Mint. Gekoski 2-42 1983 £475

ELIOT, THOMAS STEARNS   Journey of the Magi. (London, Curwen
Press, 1927). First edition. With two drawings by E.M. Kauffer.
Printed wraps. Fine. Houle 21-317 1983 $75

ELIOT, THOMAS STEARNS   Journey of the Magi. (London, Curwen
Press, 1927). Illus. with 2 drawings by E. McNight Kauffer. First
edition. Orig. yellow printed wraps. Fine. Houle 22-332 1983 $65

ELIOT, THOMAS STEARNS   Journey of the Magi. (London, n.d.).
First edition. 16mo, pr. wraps. Illus. by E. McKnight Kauffer.
Argosy 714-273 1983 $45

ELIOT, THOMAS STEARNS   Journey Of The Magi. (London: Faber &
Gwyer Limited, n.d.). First edition. Drawings by E. McKnight Kauffer.
8vo. Orig. decorated wrappers. Fine copy. Jaffe 1-84 1983 $25

ELIOT, THOMAS STEARNS   Little Gidding. Lon., (1942). Paperwraps, cover edges slightly faded, very good. Quill & Brush 54-417
1983 $35

ELIOT, THOMAS STEARNS   Little Gidding. London, Faber & Faber
(1942). 8vo, printed flexible wraps. First edition. Duschnes 240-
76 1983 $35

ELIOT, THOMAS STEARNS   The Little Review. New York, May and
September, 1917. First edition. 2 vols. Wrappers. Edges of wrappers
a little chipped. Nice. Rota 230-199 1983 $75

ELIOT, THOMAS STEARNS   The Music of Poetry. Glasgow:
Jackson, Son & Company, 1942. Orig. printed wraps. First separate
edition, one of 1,000 copies printed. A fine copy. Reese 20-361 1983
$60

ELIOT, THOMAS STEARNS   The Music of Poetry. Glasgow, 1942.
First edition. Wrappers. Nice. Rota 230-194 1983 £12.50

ELIOT, THOMAS STEARNS   The New Criterion. London, October,
1926 and January, 1927. First edition. 2 vols. Wrappers. Very good.
Rota 230-200 1983 £15

ELIOT, THOMAS STEARNS   Old Possum's Book of Practical Cats.
London, 1940. First illus. edition. Illus. by N. Bentley. Cloth
slightly spotted. Dust wrapper. Publisher's compliments slip bearing
the typed addition of the author's name. Very nice. Rota 230-192
1983 £40

ELIOT, THOMAS STEARNS   Poems, 1909-1925. London, Faber &
Gwyer, 1925. First edition. Blue cloth, paper label. Dust jacket.
Very good. Cloth slipcase. Houle 22-333 1983 $250

ELIOT, THOMAS STEARNS   Reunion by Destruction. (London: The
Pax House, 1943). Orig. printed wraps. First and only separate
edition. Very fine copy. Reese 20-362 1983 $50

ELIOT, THOMAS STEARNS   The Rock - a Pageant Play. London,
1934. First edition. Wrappers. One of 1000 copies in wrappers,
which were on sale at the premiere on 28th May, 1934. Pencilled
inscription. Spine and cover edges slightly browned. Very good.
Jolliffe 26-169 1983 £30

ELIOT, THOMAS STEARNS   The Rock. London, 1934. First edition.
Orig. boards. Spine a little discoloured and ink lines on upper
cover. Nice. Rota 230-190 1983 £25

ELIOT, THOMAS STEARNS   The Rock. New York: Harcourt, Brace,
(1934). 1st Am. ed. Orig. cloth. 1 of 1500 copies printed. Fine
copy in fine fresh dj with tear in fore-edge of rear panel. Jenkins
155-361 1983 $50

ELIOT, THOMAS STEARNS   The Sacred Wood. New York: Knopf,
1921. 1st Am. ed. Orig. blue cloth, gilt. 1 of 365 copies only,
issued with a new title-page, using the English sheets. Fine copy
of this rare ed. Jenkins 155-362 1983 $125

ELIOT, THOMAS STEARNS   Selected Essays, 1917-1932. London,
Faber (1932). First edition. Full gilt stamped blue vellum (spine
faded), t.e.g., uncut. Cloth slipcase. A fine copy. One of 115
deluxe copies, signed by Eliot. Houle 21-319 1983 $525

ELIOT, THOMAS STEARNS   Selected Essays 1917-1932. London, 1932.
First edition. Spine and edges of covers a little faded and some fox-
ing throughout. Inscribed by author and dated "6.ix.32." Very good.
Rota 230-189 1983 £165

ELIOT, THOMAS STEARNS   Selected Prose. Harmondsworth, 1953.
First edition of this selection. Wrappers. Inscribed by author:
"F(rank). V. M(orley). from T.S.E." Very nice. Rota 230-195 1983
£80

ELIOT, THOMAS STEARNS   A Sermon Preached in Magdalene College
Chapel... (Cambridge), (1948). Orig. printed wraps. First and
only edition, one of 300 copies printed for distribution to Members
of the College. A very fine copy. Reese 20-364 1983 $165

ELIOT, THOMAS STEARNS   A Song for Simeon. London, n.d. First
edition. Illus. by E. McKnight Kauffer. 16mo, pr. wraps. Argosy
714-276 1983 $50

ELIOT, THOMAS STEARNS   A Song for Simeon. (London, Curwen
Press, 1928). Illus. with 2 drawings by E. McNight Kauffer. First
edition. Orig. printed wraps. Fine. Houle 22-335 1983 $32.50

ELIOT, THOMAS STEARNS   Sweeney Agonistes. London, Faber &
Faber, (1932). First edition. Small 8vo, dust jacket (back faded,
large bookplate on endpaper) else, very good. Houle 22-336 1983
$85

ELIOT, THOMAS STEARNS   Sweeney Agonistes. London, 1932. First edition, late binding. Torn dust wrapper. Very good. Rota 231-197 1983 £24

ELIOT, THOMAS STEARNS   Triumphal March. (London, n.d.). First edition. Illus. by E. McKnight Kauffer. Printed wraps. First edition. Argosy 714-277 1983 $50

ELIOT, THOMAS STEARNS   Triumphal March. (London: Faber & Faber, 1931). Pictorial wraps., design by E. McKnight Kauffer. First edition, preceding the limited issue by three weeks. One of 2,000 copies. Fine. Reese 20-356 1983 $40

ELIOT, THOMAS STEARNS   The Undergraduate Poems of... (Cambridge), (1949). Printed wraps. First edition, one of about 1,000 copies published without authorization. Very fine. Reese 20-366 1983 $75

ELIOT, THOMAS STEARNS   The Waste Land. New York: Boni & Liveright, (1922). 2nd ed., 1 of 1,000 numbered copies. Orig. black cloth, gilt. The sheets from this ed. were printed from those of the 1st ed. Rare thus. Very fine copy in fine fresh dj which carries reviews on front flap, announcement of its winning the Dial's poetry prize that year, and a bio. of Eliot on rear flap. Jenkins 155-363 1983 $325

ELIOT, THOMAS STEARNS   What is a Classic. London: Faber & Faber, Ltd., (1940). Cloth. First public published edition. Fine copy in very slightly used dust jacket with some foxmarks on the rear panel. Reese 20-363 1983 $45

ELISA, SOL P.   Stories of the Stanislaus. Modesto, 1924. Fabricoid. A little wear. Endpapers browned. Signed by author on title page. Dawson 471-73 1983 $30

ELISOFON, ELIOT   The Sculpture of Africa. London: Thames and Hudson, 1958. 405 illus. Folio. Cloth. Dust jacket. Ars Libri 34-604 1983 $250

ELIZABETH, CHARLOTTE   The Siege of Derry. N.Y.: Taylor, 1841. First American edition, "from the seventh English edition." 3/4 calf. MacManus 278-1776 1983 $25

ELIZABETHAN Anthology. A garland of Elizabethan sonnets. Curwen Press for Leonard Parsons, 1923. Slim sq. 8vo, uncut in quarter linen, cream paper boards with a floral pattern in red and green, printed paper label, excellent. 500 numbered copies printed on hand-made paper. Deighton 3-123 1983 £25

ELKINS, JOHN M.   Indian Fighting on the Texas Frontier. (Amarillo, Texas: Russell & Cockrell, 1929). Orig. pictorial wrappers. Plates. Jenkins 152-108 1983 $75

ELLENBECKER, JOHN G.   The Jayhawkers of Death Valley. Marysville, Ks., 1938. Illus. Orig. printed stiff wraps. First edition. Ginsberg 47-72 1983 $75

ELLENBECKER, JOHN G.   The Jayhawkers of Death Valley. Marysville, Kansas, 1938. 23 cm. Illus. Orig. printed brown paper wraps. Wraps. and flyleaf a bit worn. Grunder 6-19 1983 $20

ELLENDT, F.   Lexicon Sophocleum. Koenigsberg, 1835. 2 vols., full calf, 8vo, cloth. Salloch 385-750 1983 $110

ELLICOTT, JOHN   A Description of Two Methods. London: Printed for R. Wilcock, 1753. 1st ed., 4to, 2 folding engraved plates; fore-edges uncut but a little brittle and frayed, prelims. slightly discoloured; disbound. Pickering & Chatto 22-36 1983 $350

ELLIOT, ANNE   Evelyn's Career. London: Bentley, 1891. First edition. 3 vols. Orig. patterned paper-covered cloth. Fine. MacManus 278-1777 1983 $175

ELLIOT, D. G.   A Monograph of the Paradiseidae, or Birds of Paradise. Printed for the subscribers, by the Author, 1873. Double elephant folio, cont. half morocco, gilt (trifle used), with 1 plain and 36 fine hand-coloured plates. Extremely rare, as there were only 50 subscribers. Plates by Joseph Wolf. Some very slight foxing, small blind stamp and small number stamped on title-page. Wheldon 160-26 1983 £12,000

ELLIOT, ROBERT H.   Written on Their Foreheads. London: Sampson Low, Marston, Searle & Rivington, 1879. First edition. 2 vols. Orig. cloth. Edges slightly worn. Foot of one spine rather worn. Hinges of Vol. 1 cracked; a few pages carelessly opened. MacManus 278-1778 1983 $150

ELLIOT, ROBERT H.   Written on their Foreheads. Sampson Low, 1879. First edition, 2 vols., half titles, orig. brown cloth, blocked in black, lettered in gilt, v.g. Jarndyce 30-377 1983 £58

ELLIOTT, B. F.   Experiences in the Gospel Work in Lower California, Mexico. La Paz, Baja (Lower) California: Published at the Office of "The Gospel", 1906. Tear in corner of title page. Orig. printed boards, worn. Cloth back strip. With a curious typographical map of Baja California. Dawson 471-74 1983 $300

ELLIOTT, RICHARD SMITH   Notes Taken in Sixty Years. St. Louis, 1883. Frontis., stamped cloth. Front hinge loosened, else very good. Reese 19-210 1983 $125

ELLIOTT, RICHARD SMITH   Notes Taken in Sixty Years. St. Louis, 1883. Cloth. Rear endsheets lacking. First edition. Felcone 22-58 1983 $45

ELLIS, CHARLES   Richmond and other Poems. London: Madden and Malcolm, 1845. First edition. Cr. 8vo. Orig. embossed green cloth, gilt. Coloured frontis. printed in oils by George Baxter after Warren, and 3 engraved views. Joints worn. Traylen 94-316 1983 £25

ELLIS, CLEMENT   The Protestant Resolved. Printed for William Rogers, 1688. First edition, including half-title, 4to, wrapper, v.g. Fenning 61-128 1983 £14.50

ELLIS, GEORGE   Specimens of Early English Metrical Romances. 1805. 3 vols., 8vo, cont. half calf, some joints cracked, but bindings sound. First edition. Bickersteth 75-134 1983 £35

ELLIS, GEORGE   Specimens of the Early English Poets. London, Printed for Edwards...1790. 8vo, cont. green morocco, gilt, spine gilt, a.e.g. Bookplate of Graham Pollard. First edition. Quaritch NS 7-36 1983 $225

ELLIS, GEORGE MERLE   Trapper Trails to California, 1826-1832. San Diego State College, August, 1954. Typed red cloth. Dawson 471-75 1983 $150

ELLIS, HAVELOCK   George Chapman. London: the Nonesuch Press, 1934. Orange boards, printed paper label, in a cloth folding case. Limited edition of 700 numbered copies, printed on Van Gelder paper. Traylen 94-317 1983 £21

ELLIS, HAVELOCK   Kanga Creek. NY, 1938. 17 wood engravings by Sleigh and I. Ellis. Limited to 250 copies, edges slightly worn, else very good in slightly soiled, very good dustwrapper with tiny chip out of spine edge bottom. Quill & Brush 54-423 1983 $35

ELLIS, HAVELOCK   View and Reviews 1884-1932. London, (1932). Two vols. Edges slightly rubbed, else very good in soiled, lightly chipped and frayed, very good dustwrappers with darkened spines. Quill & Brush 54-424 1983 $60

ELLIS, HENRY   Journal of the Proceedings of the Late Embassy to China. London, 1817. First edition. 2 maps, 1 folding and skillfully repaired. 7 fine engraved plates, coloured from drawings by Hon. Charles Abbot. 4to. Half calf. Good. Edwards 1044-229 1983 £250

ELLIS, HENRY   A Journal of the Proceedings of the Late Embassy to China. London, 1818. Second edition. 2 folding maps, some slight offsetting. Half calf, some wear. Labels removed from spine. 8vo. Good. Edwards 1044-228 1983 £120

ELLIS, HENRY S.   A Letter to the Directors of the Bristol and Exeter Railway Company. Exeter, (1869). 8vo. Stitched as issued. Heath 48-499 1983 £25

ELLIS, JOHN   Copies of Two Letters from John Ellis... London: by W. Bowyer and J. Nichols, 1771. First edition. 4to. 2 folding engraved plates. Modern half calf. Ink stain along top margin throughout. Heath 48-3 1983 £100

ELLIS, JOHN B.   Free Love and Its Votaries.   New
York, 1870. 12 plates. Cover cloth somewhat spotted, otherwise
fine. Reese 19-211 1983 $165

ELLIS, JOHN B.   Free Love and Its Votaries.   N.Y.,
(1870). Illus., orig. cloth. First edition. Ginsberg 46-244 1983
$125

ELLIS, L. ETHAN   Reciprocity 1911. New Haven: Yale
Un. Press; Toronto: Ryerson; London: OUP, 1939. 24 1/2cm.
Mapped endpapers. Blue cloth. Fine copy. McGahern 53-51 1983
$50

ELLIS, L. ETHAN   Reciprocity 1911. New Haven: Yale
Un. Press; Toronto: Ryerson; London: OUP, 1939. 24 1/2cm.
Mapped endpapers. Blue cloth. Ex-lib. with small call no. on
spine, else a very good copy. McGahern 53-52 1983 $45

ELLIS, RICHARD W.   Book Illustration. Kingsport, 1952.
First edition, 4to, illus. Half black cloth; boxed. Very good-fine.
Presentation copy, signed and inscribed in the book and on the box.
Houle 21-127 1983 $95

ELLIS, S. M.   George Meredith. His Life and Friends in
Relation to His Work. London: Grant Richards, 1919. First edition.
Illus. Orig. cloth. MacManus 279-3685 1983 $45

ELLIS, SARAH STICKNEY   The wives of England, their relative
duties... London: Fisher, n.d. (1843). First edition. 8vo.
Orig. rose cloth. A bit rubbed and faded. Ximenes 63-650 1983
$50

ELLIS, VIVIAN LOCKE   Collected Lyrical Poems. New York,
1947. 8vo. Cloth. Review copy with slip from publisher laid in.
Fine in dj. In Our Time 156-248 1983 $20

ELLIS, VIVIAN LOCKE   An English Ilian, Book I. Privately
Printed, 1906. First edition. Orig. blue wrappers (soiled and worn).
The author's copy (marked "our copy" in pencil on the front cover)
with ten holograph corrections in the text. Small indentation to the
outer edge. Good. MacManus 278-1779 1983 $65

ELLIS, WILLIAM   History of Madagascar. London: Fisher,
Sone & Co., 1838. 2 vols. 8vo. 10 plates. 2 folding maps. Orig.
black cloth. Rubbed, some foxing to plates, 1 vol. rebacked. Adelson
Africa-83 1983 $350

ELLIS, WILLIAM   Three visits to Madagascar during the
years 1853- 1854- 1856. London: John Murray, 1859. 8vo. Map,
14 plates. Orig. purple cloth. Rubbed, spine ends worn. Adelson
Africa-84 1983 $150

ELLIS, WILLIS D.   A Source Book of Gestalt Psychology. NY:
Harcourt, Brace, 1938. First American edition. Very good ex-library
copy. Gach 94-145 1983 $25

ELLISON, FRANK   A Journal of a Trip Down East. Waltham:
Ellison, 1858, (Dallas: Somesuch Press, 1981). First edition in
facsimile of the orig. edition. Orig. printed stiff wrappers. One of
200 numbered copies, signed by Stanley Marcus (Somesuch Press) and
Stephen Stinehaur (Meriden Gravure). Mint copy of a fine reprint of
the extremely rare orig. miniature book. Jenkins 152-707 1983 $45

ELLSON, HAL   Duke. New York: Scribners, 1949.
Cloth. First edition. Fine in dust jacket, which is slightly frayed
at edges. Reese 20-380 1983 $25

ELMHAM, THOMAS DE   Thomas de Elmham Vita & Gesta Henrici
Quinti Anglorum Regis... Oxonii, E. Theatro Sheldoniano, 1727.
8vo, orig. calf, joints slightly cracked. First edition. Ravenstree
94-193 1983 $95

ELPHINSTONE, M.   An Account of the Kingdom of Caubul.
London, 1815. First edition. 2 maps, 1 folding, 13 coloured plates,
1 uncoloured. 4to. Half morocco, raised bands. Good. Edwards 1044-
234 1983 £435

ELPHINSTONE, M.   An Account of the Kingdom of Caubul.
London, 1839. New and revised edition. Large folding map backed with
linen. 2 coloured frontis. 1 plate. 2 vols. Morocco. 8vo. Good.
Edwards 1044-235 1983 £180

ELPHINSTONE, M.   The History of India. London, 1899.
Seventh edition. Large folding map. 8vo. Orig. cloth. Good.
Edwards 1044-232 1983 £20

ELSBERG, CHARLES A.   Diagnosis & Treatment of Surgical
Diseases of the Spinal Cord & its Membrances. Phila., 1916. First
edition. Illus. 4to. Argosy 713-169 1983 $85

ELSE, JOSEPH   An Essay on the Cure of the Hydrocele...
London: Printed for John Wilkie, 1776. 8vo, half title, new calf
backed boards. Pickering & Chatto 22-37 1983 $200

ELSHOLTZ, JOHANN SIGISMUND   Destillatoria Curiosa... Berolini:
Volcheri, 1674. First edition. 8vo. Modern calf with gilt.
Lacking engraved title-page. Some wear to front hinge, otherwise
a very good copy. Zeitlin 264-138 1983 $150

ELTON, AMBROSE   Pipe Lights for the Piper by A.E.
Cambridge: Redin, (1891). 1st ed. Orig. printed wrappers. Light
dust-soiling, but nice copy. Jenkins 155-367 1983 $20

ELTON, CHARLES A.
Please turn to
HABINGTON, WILLIAM

ELUARD, PAUL   Medieuses: Poems. Paris, 1944.
Illus. by Valentine Hugo. Tall 8vo. Rebound in a library type
binding. 2nd ed. Presentation inscription by Eluard on inside
flyleaf. Name of the orig. recipient has been erased and a new
name inserted by the illus. Hugo... In Our Time 156-249 1983 $125

ELUARD, PAUL   Pablo Picasso. N.Y., Philosophical
Library, (1947). 4to, profusely illus. Dust jacket, very good - fine.
Houle 22-340 1983 $27.50

ELUARD, PAUL   Thorns of Thunder. Europa Press & Stanley
Nott, (1936). First edition. Frontis. by Picasso. One of 600 numbered copies. Covers soiled and faded. Fragile dust wrapper designed
by Max Ernst (torn and defective along upper edge). Very good. Rota
231-56 1983 £40

ELWOOD, LOUIE BUTLER   Queen Calafia's Land. SF, 1940.
8vo, pigskin-backed decorated bds. Illustrated in color. Perata 27-
68 1983 $65

ELY, ALFRED B.   American Liberty. N.Y., 1850. First
edition. Dbd. Ginsberg 46-592 1983 $25

ELYOT, THOMAS   The Image of Gouernaunce compiled of
the Actes and Sentances Notable, of the Most Noble Emperour Alexandre
Seuerus. (London, Thomas Berthelette), 1549. 8vo, old calf, badly
worn, old rebacking worn, chipped, cover detached, marginal wormhole
in blank edge of last few gatherings, signature of Thomas Hervey,
Esq. (1669-1775) at head of Preface leaf. Ravenstree 94-64 1983
$750

ELZE, KARL   Lord Byron. London: Murray, 1872. 8vo,
orig. orange-brown cloth. First edition in English. Fine. Ximenes
63-32 1983 $90

EMANUEL, HARRY   Diamonds and Precious Stones. J.C.
Hotten, 1867. With an additional coloured title-page, 5 plates and some
other illus., 8vo, orig. cloth, gilt. Some light finger marks, but
a sound and very good copy. Fenning 60-104 1983 £18.50

EMBROIDERY Lessons with Colored Studies, 1907. New London, Brainerd
& Armstrong, 1907. 8 colored plates and other illustrations. 8vo,
original colored pictorial wrappers, ads. Top right corner of front
cover torn off. Morrill 290-118 1983 $20

EMERSON, BROWN   The Causes and Effects of the War.
Salem, 1812. Dsb., very good. Reese 18-373 1983 $25

EMERSON, HAVEN   Selected Papers of Haven Emerson.
Battle Creek, 1949. First edition. 8vo. Orig. wrappers. Autographed by the author. Fye H-3-162 1983 $45

EMERSON, JAMES   Letters from the Aegean. New York:
Harper, 1829. 1st American Edition, tall 8vo, orig. cloth-backed
boards and paper label. Uncut copy. Advertisements. Trebizond 18-
141 1983 $100

EMERSON, RALPH WALDO   An Address Delivered in the Court-House
in Concord, Massachusetts. Boston: James Monroe and Company, 1844.
First edition. Disbound. Title page and last leaf dusty and stained,
corners chipped. Bradley 66-542 1983 $20

EMERSON, RALPH WALDO   The Complete Writings. Cambridge:
Riverside Press, 1903-4. Autograph Centenary Edition, limited to 600
copies signed by publisher with leaf of autograph manuscript by Emerson
bound in. 12 vols. Together with The Journals. Cambridge: Riverside
Press, 1909-14. Large paper edition. 10 vols. Limited to 600 copies,
almost completely unopened. Orig. brown buckram, paper labels. Very
fine set, some spines slightly darkened, chip from top of one. Bromer
25-34 1983 $1,000

EMERSON, RALPH WALDO   The Essay on Self-Reliance. East
Aurora: Roycroft Shop, 1905. Small octavo. One of 100 copies on
Imperial Japan Vellum signed by Elbert Hubbard. Bond in full brown
morocco with cream and tan onlays. Gilt-tooled boards, front cover.
Spine gilt, inner dentelles gilt. T.e.g. Binding executed at Roy-
croft bindery with their stamp, signed H.A. Extremely fine copy.
Bookplate. Bromer 25-292 1983 $650

EMERSON, RALPH WALDO   Essays, Lectures and Orations. Wm. S.
Orr, 1848. First edition, orig. purple cloth, spine faded, v.g.
Jarndyce 31-689 1983 £10.50

EMERSON, RALPH WALDO   The Essays of Emerson. London,
Humphreys, 1899. Small 4to, 3/4 brown morocco stamped in gilt with
starburst designs on spine, t.e.g. 2 vols. Very good - fine. Houle
22-344 1983 $225

EMERSON, RALPH WALDO   Letters and Social Aims. Boston:
Osgood, 1876. 1st ed., 1st printing. Orig. terra cotta cloth,
gilt. Light rubbing, but essentially a fine copy. Jenkins 155-
370 1983 $25

EMERSON, RALPH WALDO   Letters and Social Aims. Boston, 1876.
First edition. Cloth. Spine slightly sunned. Nice. King 45-174
1983 $25

EMERSON, RALPH WALDO   May-Day, and Other Pieces. Boston:
Ticknor & Fields, 1867. 1st ed. Orig. terra cotta cloth, gilt,
t.e.g. All known copies have so-called 1st issue point "flowers"
for "hours" on p. 184. Very good. Jenkins 155-371 1983 $45

EMERSON, RALPH WALDO   Nature. (East Aurora: Roycroft Shop,
1905). Small octavo. One of 100 copies on Imperial Japan Vellum
signed by Elbert Hubbard. Illus. by Dard Hunter. Full blue-green
morocco with gilt tooling. Spine gilt-lettered, t.e.g. Binding
executed at Roycroft Bindery with their mark, signed by H. A. Edges
faintly sunned, else very fine. Bookplate. Bromer 25-294 1983 $550

EMERSON, RALPH WALDO   Nature: An Essay. Aylott and Hones,
1845. Colour-printed half title in red, blue & gold. Orig. brown
cloth, v.g. First edition of this collection. Jarndyce 31-687 1983
£22

EMERSON, RALPH WALDO   Poems. Chapman, Bros., 1847. First
English edition. Half title, 24 pp ads. Orig. pale green cloth,
spine darkened to brown, sl. chipped at head of spine. With the
pub.'s compliments' inscribed on end paper. Jarndyce 31-688 1983
£48

EMERSON, RALPH WALDO   Representative Men. Boston: Phillips,
Samson, 1850. 1st ed., 2nd printing, 2nd binding. Orig. black cloth,
gilt. Front free end paper excised, else an average copy with some
spine wear. Jenkins 155-372 1983 $20

EMERSON, RALPH WALDO   The Works. London, 1898-1902. 6 vols.
Cr. 8vo. Full red crushed levant morocco, gilt, gilt panelled spines,
inner gilt dentelles, edges gilt, by Riviere. Traylen 94-318 1983
£75

EMLEN, SAMUEL   Extracts from the Diary of... London:
Harvey and Darton, 1830. 1st ed., 12mo; stitched in the orig. drab
wrapper. Pickering & Chatto 22-38 1983 $50

EMMET, BORIS   California and Hawaiian Sugar Refining
Corp. Palo Alto, Stanford, 1928. First edition. Very good. Houle
21-1083 1983 $22.50

EMMONS, WILLIAM   Biography of Martin Van Buren, Vice President of the United States. Washington: Jacob Gideon, Jr., 1835.
Second edition. Orig. paper boards with cloth spine. Printed paper
label on front cover. Fairly nice. Jenkins 152-39 1983 $40

EMORY, WILLIAM H.   Notes of a Military Reconnoissance
from Fort Leavenworth, in Missouri, to San Diego, in California...
Washington, 1848. 2 maps. Cloth, rear hinge cracking, some foxing,
otherwise very good. Reese 19-213 1983 $300

EMPIRE State: A History. (NY: Empire State, Inc.) 1931. Tall 4to,
profusely illus. with photographs and drawings. Boards. Karmiole
74-8 1983 $30

EMPSON, WILLIAM   Collected Poems. New York, 1949. 8vo.
Cloth. Advance copy with slip from publisher pasted on the front
flyleaf. Fine in DJ. In Our Time 156-250 1983 $35

EMPSON, WILLIAM   The Gathering Storm. London, 1940.
First edition. Partially defective dust wrapper. Very nice. Rota
231-201 1983 £25

EMPSON, WILLIAM   Poems. London, 1935. First edition.
Dust wrapper. Fine. Rota 231-200 1983 £55

EMPSON, WILLIAM   Seven Types of Ambiguity. London:
Chatto & Windus, 1930. First edition. Orig. cloth. Dust jacket
(spine faded, covers somewhat soiled, repaired). Presentation
copy to John Hayward inscribed: "John Hayward from William Empson in all
respect and affection." Some offsetting to the free endpapers.
Very good. MacManus 278-1783 1983 $450

ENCISO, JORGE   Sellos del antiguo Mexico. Mexico:
Privately Printed, 1947. 153 plates (partly in color). Large 4to.
Cloth. Ars Libri 34-228 1983 $100

ENCYCLOPEDIE de la Fleur. Paris, N. D. (c. 1900). 120 photographic
plates, index leaf, folio, in a trifle soiled portfolio. Wheldon
160-1511 1983 £16

ENDERBIE, PERCY   Cambria Triumphans, or Brittain in its
Perfect Lustre. London; reprinted, for Samuel Bagster, 1810. 2 vols.
in 1, folio, woodcut frontispiece, contemporary half morocco, worn,
upper section of backstrip defective. Deighton 3-124 1983 £50

ENDICOTT, WILLIAM C.   Letter from...Transmitting...Report
Relative to the Raising of Volunteer Troops to Guard Overland
and Other Mails from 1861 to 1866. Wash., 1889. Half morocco.
First edition. Ginsberg 47-766 1983 $60

ENDLE, S.   The Kacharis. London, 1911. Folding
map, coloured and other plates. 8vo. Orig. cloth. Good. Edwards
1044-238 1983 £36

ENFIELD, WILLIAM   Institutes of Natural Philosophy.
Boston: Isaiah Thomas and Ebenezer T. Andrews, 1802. Fifteen large
folding plates. Extremities slightly chipped, otherwise a near fine
copy. Cont. mottled calf. The first American edition, from the
second London edition. Reese 18-247 1983 $150

ENFIELD, WILLIAM   The Speaker, or Miscellaneous Pieces.
Boston: J. Larkin, 1808. 12mo, cont. sheep, worn, leather label.
Argosy 710-475 1983 $50

ENFIELD, WILLIAM   The Speaker. Belfast: Printed by Simms
and M'Intyre, 1811. Large 12mo, cont. sheep, worn but sound, good
copy. Fenning 61-130 1983 £18.50

ENGELBERTS, EDWIN   Georges Braque. Oeuvre graphique original. Geneve, 1958. Prof. illus. 4to. Wrappers. Designed by Braque. Dust jacket. Edition limited to 1500 copies. Ars Libri 32-60 1983 $75

ENGELHARDT, ZEPHYRIN   Mission San Luis Obispo in the Valley of the Bears. Santa Barbara, Mission Santa Barbara, 1933. First edition. Illus. Pictorial gilt stamped brown cloth. Very good - fine. Houle 22-1051 1983 $45

ENGLEHARDT, ZEPHYRIN   Santa Barbara Mission. San Francisco, Barry, 1923. First edition. Illus. with halftones and facs. Gilt stamped pictorial brown cloth. Signed by the author. Very good. Houle 22-1137 1983 $60

ENGELS, MATHIAS T.   Campendonk. Holzschnitte. Werk-verzeichnis. Stuttgart: Kohlhammer, 1959. 78 illus. Large 4to. Cloth. Dust jacket. Ars Libri 32-78 1983 $100

ENGLAND und die Antike. Leipzig, 1932. Thick 4to, wrs. Salloch 385-13 1983 $50

ENGLER, A.   Die Naturlichen Pflanzenfamilien, Teil 2 to 4. 1887-1908. 18 vols., royal 8vo, cloth, a little worn. A few vols. neatly rebacked or repaired. Wheldon 160-1517 1983 £250

ENGLISH, WILLIAM H.   Conquest of the Country Northwest of the River Ohio 1778-1783. Indianapolis, 1896. 1st ed., 25 illus., 2 vols, 8vo, gilt-pict. cloth. Argosy 710-393 1983 $125

THE ENGLISH Bijou Almanac for 1837. London, Schloss, 42 Gr. Russell St. (1837). Frontis. and 6 portraits, orig. gold-stamped paper boards, in matching slip-case, a little worn. Bickersteth 77-203 1983 £58

ENGLISH Folk Songs from the Southern Appalachiens. NY & London, 1917. 8vo, cl. Salloch 387-296 1983 $35

ENGLISH Garner. Westminster: Archibald Constable & Co., 1903. 10 vols. Orig. cloth. These ten volumes are complete in themselves; the missing volumes being Voyages and Travels mainly during the 16th and 17th centuries (2 vols.) with introductions by C. Raymond Beazley. Fine. MacManus 278-1784 1983 $125

AN ENGLISH Garner. London, 1909. Complete set. 12 vols. 8vo. Half blue morocco, gilt, t.e.g. Limited edition of 750 numbered sets. Traylen 94-920 1983 £160

THE ENGRAVED & Topographic Work of Rudolph Ruzicka: An Exhibition... New York: Grolier Club, 1948. 8vo. Paper wrappers. Limited to 500 copies signed by Ruzicka. With nine illus., including two in color. Oak Knoll 49-489 1983 $35

ENSKO, STEPHEN G.C.   American Silversmiths and Their Marks II. New York, Robert Ensko, 1937. 1st ed. Illus. 8vo. Morrill 289-327 1983 $95

EPHRON, WALTER   Hieronymus Bosch. Zwei Kreuztragungen. Zurich/Wien/Leipzig: Amalthea, 1931. 44 illus. hors texte. 2 plates inserted loose, as issued, under flap. 4to. Wrappers. From the library of Jakob Rosenberg. Ars Libri 32-52 1983 $60

EPICTETUS   Epicteti Enchiridion...cum Notis Merici Casauboni. Londini, Tho. Roycroft, 1659. 8vo, cont. French calf, good sound copy. Ravenstree 95-45 1983 $65

EPICTETUS   Epicteti Stoico Philosophi Enchridion... Cantabriglae, Ex celeberrimae Academiae Typographeco, 1655. 8vo, 18th century calf, rebacked, title in red and black, Greek and Latin in parallel columns. Ravenstree 95-43 1983 $110

EPICTETUS   Epicteti Stoici Philosophi Enchiridion. Londini, Typis Jacobi Flesher, prostant apud Guilielmum Morden, 1670. Stout 8vo, cont. calf, worn, cover loose, slight worming to blank inner margin of first few leaves. Two title pages are present, one printed in red and black and one in black only. Ravenstree 95-46 1983 $49

EPICTETUS   Epictetus His Morals, with Simplicius His Comment. London, Richard Sare, 1694. 8vo, cont. calf, rebacked, good sound copy. First edition of this translation. Ravenstree 95-47 1983 $65

EPICTETUS   All the Works of Epictetus... London, printed by S(amuel). Richardson et al., 1758. Stout 4to, orig. calf, joints cracked and breaking but cords firm, bookplate, of Robert Fellowes, a large, thick paper copy with list of subscribers. First edition in this translation. Ravenstree 95-48 1983 $295

EPICURUS   Epicurus's Morals collected... London: by W. Wilson for Henry Harringman, 1656. First English edition. 4to. Early panelled calf, gilt inlay, rebacked. Engr. portrait, inner margin of title reinforced. Heath 48-281 1983 £150

EPIGRAMS In Distich. London: Printed for J. Stagg, in Westminster-Hall. 1740. Folio, disbound. First and only edition. A good copy. Quaritch NS 7-37 1983 $275

EPISODES of Fiction. Edinburgh, W.P. Nimmo, 1870. Numerous illus. Engr'd on wood by R. Paterson. Frontis. 27 illus. by F. Barnard, Green, H. Weir, etc. White colour decor. cloth, a.e.g. Hodgkins 27-269 1983 £20

EPISTOLAE Indicae de Stvpendis et Praeclaris Rebvs, quasdiuina bonitas in India. Lovanii Apud Rutgerum Velpium, Bibliopol. Iura... Cum Priuileg...1566. 8vo, 3 pts. in 1 v. Bound in full vellum. Title in manuscript on spine. New endpapers. Title page repaired. Several leaves reinforced at margins. Some light browning. Good. Arkway 22-44 1983 $1,725

EPSTEIN, JACOB   Let There be Sculpture. (London): Michael Joseph, (1940). Full gilt vellum. Photographs. First edition. One of 100 numbered copies, specially bound, and signed by the author. Vellum slightly bowed, slight offsetting on endsheets, else about fine. Reese 20-381 1983 $250

EPSTEIN, JACOB   The Sculptor Speaks...to Arnold L. Haskell. New York, 1932. 1st American ed. Illus. 8vo. Ends of spine chipped. Morrill 287-103 1983 $20

EQUITABLE SOCIETY OF LONDON. The Plan of the Society for Equitable Assurances on Lives and Survivorships. London, printed in the year M.DCC.LXVI (1766). 19 x 13-1/2 cm. Guarded with Japanese tissue and resewn; age-darkened with loss of two corners (final two leaves). Recent linen-covered folder with printed paper label. Grunder 6-42 1983 $225

ERASMUS, DESIDERIUS   Vita...Edidit Pavllvs Mervlla. Leyden: Basson, 1607. 4to, device on title-page & circular woodcut of Erasmus on title verso. Stitched. Rostenberg 88-105 1983 $425

ERCKMANN-CHATRIAN, MADAME   The Conscript: A Tale of the French War of 1813. London: Smith, Elder & Co., 1870. First edition in English. Orig. pictorial cloth. Edges slightly worn, inner hinges cracking. Good. MacManus 278-1787 1983 $45

ERDMANN, JOHANN FRIDERIC   Utrum Aqua Per Electricitatem Columnae A Cel. Volta Inventae in Elementa sua Dissoluatur? Wittebergae Litteris Tzschiedrichii, (1802). 1st ed., 4to, 1 engraved plate; wax stain on title and several leaves of text, library stamp on verso of title; stab sewn. Rare. Pickering & Chatto 22-39 1983 $200

ERIN go bragh. London: John Murray, 1822. First edition. 8vo. Sewn, as issued. Trifle stained. Very good copy. Scarce. Ximenes 63-404 1983 $50

DIE ERKRANKUNGEN Des Weiblichen Genitales. Wien/Leipsig: Alfred Hoelder, 1912. First edition. Two vols. Thick 8vo. One-half leather (rubbed). Inscribed to Adolf Meyer by Frankl-Hochwart. Gach 95-142 1983 $50

ERLAM, D.   Ranks and Uniforms of the German Army, Navy and Air Force. London, (1940). 8vo. Orig. decorated cloth. Coloured frontis., 10 fine coloured plates, numerous text illus. Very slightly worn. Good. Edwards 1042-333 1983 £60

ERMAN, ADOLPH   Travels in Siberia... Philadelphia, 1850. Some foxing. K Books 301-70 1983 £50

ERNST, MARGARET S.   In a Word. NY, (1939). Atcheson L.
Hench's copy with review and pencilled notations, slight foxing, else
very good in frayed dustwrapper. Quill & Brush 54-1364 1983 $35

ERNST, MAX   Misfortunes of the Immortals. (N.p.):
The Black Sun Press, 1943. Quarto. Pictorial boards. First edition
in English. Illus. One of 500 copies, designed by Caresse Crosby,
and printed at the Gemor Press. This copy is inscribed and signed
by Max Ernst. Edges of the pages have tanned; a bit of shelfwear to
the edges of the boards, otherwise a near fine copy in rather worn
plain dust jacket. Reese 20-954 1983 $375

ERROLL, HENRY   An Ugly Duckling. London: Richard
Bentley & Son, 1887. First edition. 3 vols. Orig. decorated cloth.
Spines and covers very slightly spotted and worn, with a part torn
away from the rear free endpaper of vol. 1. Former owner's signature.
MacManus 278-1788 1983 $225

ERSKINE, JOHN E.   Journal of a Cruise Among the Islands
of the Western Pacific. Lon., 1853. Small tear in fold-out map,
4 color plates, rebound, very good, ink notations on title page.
Quill & Brush 54-1682 1983 $75

ERSKINE, S.   King Faisal of Iraq. London, 1933.
Plates. 2 small holes on spine. 8vo. Orig. cloth. Good. Edwards
1044-239 1983 £25

ERSKINE, THOMAS   A View of the Causes and Consequences
of the Present War with France. Boston, 1797. Dsb., good. Reese
18-223 1983 $40

ERSKINE, WILLIAM   The Entertaining Travels and
Adventures of Mademoiselle de Richelieu. Printed and sold by S.
Ballard at the Blue-Ball in Little-Britain, n.d. (ca. 1744). 3 vols.
12mo, cont. calf (rebacked, new end-papers), a few minor tears,
with no loss of text. Hannas 69-53 1983 £180

ESCHOLIER, RAYMOND   Daumier peintre et lithographe. Paris:
H. Floury, 1923. 169 illus. Many heliogravure and color plates
hors texte. 4to. Wrappers. Backstrip chipped. Ars Libri 32-139
1983 $125

ESCHOLIER, RAYMOND   Victor Hugo artiste. Paris: G. Cres,
1926. 46 plates (some color). 64 text illus. 4to. Orig. wrappers.
Dust jacket. Edition limited to 1050 numbered copies on velin Lafuma.
Ars Libri 32-333 1983 $100

ESCOUFLAIRE, R. C.   Ireland, an Enemy of the Allies?
John Murray, 1920. Half title, orig. green paper wraps. Jarndyce
31-197 1983 £10.50

ESDAILE, ARUNDELL   Autolycus' Pack and other Light Wares.
London: Grafton & Co., 1940. 8vo. Cloth. Fine copy. Oak Knoll
48-152 1983 $25

ESDAILE, ARUNDELL   A List of English Tales and Prose
Romances Printed before 1740. London: for the Bibliographical
Society, 1912. First edition. Small 4to. Orig. holland-backed
boards, spine soiled. Traylen 94-320 1983 £60

ESDAILE, ARUNDELL   A List of English Tales and Prose
Romances Printed Before 1740. London, Bibliographical Society, 1912.
Large 8vo, orig. cloth gilt, mint copy. Ravenstree 94-71 1983 $27.50

AN ESSAY on the Rationality of Brutes. With a philosophical comparison between Dr. Codgill Inspector General of Town-Island. London:
printed for J. Bouquet, n.d. (1752). 8vo, wrappers, 1st ed. Half-
title present (very small hole). Extremely rare. Ximenes 64-196
1983 $450

ESSAYS & Studies by members of The English Association. Oxford: At
the Clarendon Press, 1910-1914. First edition. Vols. I-V. Orig.
cloth. Dust jackets. A fine run of this important periodical. Very
fine. MacManus 278-1790 1983 $100

ESSAYS Honoring Lawrence C. Wroth. Portland, Maine, 1951. Frontis.
Cloth, top edge gilt. Dawson 470-105 1983 $150

ESSWEIN, HERMANN   Alfred Kubin. Der Kunstler und sein
Werk. Munchen: Georg Muller, (1911). 82 plates. Numerous text
illus. 4to. Calf. Front cover split at spine and somewhat worn.
Ars Libri 32-378 1983 $65

ESTE, CHARLES   A journey in the year 1793, through
Flanders, Brabant, and Germany... London: for J. Debrett, 1795.
First edition. 8vo. Cont. half calf, spine gilt. Fine copy.
Ximenes 63-620 1983 $175

ESTIENNE, CHARLES   L'Agriculture et Maison Rustique de
M.M. Charles Estienne et Jean Liebaust. Rouen: Chez Robert Vallentin,
1620. 4to. Numerous fine woodcut illus. Cont. vellum. From the
library of Andre Simon, with his bookplate. Heath 48-21 1983 £225

ESTIENNE, HENRI   Dictionarium medicum, vel Expositiones
Vocum medicinalium... (Geneva): H. Fugger, 1564. 8vo. Old calf.
Rebacked in morocco. First edition. Title slightly dust-soiled.
Good copy. Gurney 90-51 1983 £320

ETCHECOPAR, R. D.   Les Oiseaux de Chine. Paris, 1978-83.
44 coloured plates and numerous other illus. and maps, 2 vols.,
8vo, cloth. Wheldon 160-694 1983 £89

ETHERIDGE, R.   Catalogue of the Blastoidea. British
Museum, 1886. 20 plates, 4to, cloth, slightly worn ex-library copy.
Wheldon 160-1394 1983 £25

ETIENNE, M.   Traite de l'office. Paris: Laignier
(Vol. II: Careme), 1845-6. First edition thus. 2 vols. in one.
8vo. Cont. quarter calf. With four lithograph or aquatint plates.
Signed by the author. Binding slightly rubbed, lower cover scratched.
Plates rather foxed, one folding. Some foxing, a couple of leaves
torn (no loss). Ximenes 63-86 1983 $125

ETTING, FRANK   An Historical Account of the Old State
House of Pennsylvania Now Known as the Hall of Independence. Boston:
J. R. Osgood & Co, 1876. Illus., many plates, sq. 8vo, stamped
cloth with gilt pict., ex library. Argosy 710-400 1983 $50

EUCLIDES   Euclidis Elementorum Libri XV...a
Federico Commandino Urbinate, Huper in Latinum Conversi. Pisauri:
(Camillo Francischini), 1572. Folio. 255 numbered leaves. Illus.
Woodcut title page. Early vellum. Felcone 21-37 1983 $550

EULER, LEONHARD   Letters of Euler to a German Princess,
on Different Subjects in Physics and Philosophy. For the translator
and H. Murray, London, 1795. 8vo, with 20 engraved plates, leaf of
directions to the binder; engraved bookplate of Ralph Creyke Marton;
cont. polished calf, a little rubbed, head and tail of one spine
frayed. First edition in English. Quaritch NS 5-37 1983 $800

EURIPIDES   Alcestis. London: 1930. First edition.
Boards and cloth. 1/260 signed. Bradley 66-3 1983 $20

EURIPIDES   The Plays of Euripides. Newtown,
Montgomeryshire, 1931. 2 vols. Folio. Orig. linen bindings,
gilt, uncut edges. Wood-engravings by R.A. Maynard and H.W. Bray,
after Greek vase paintins. Limited edition of 500 copies on hand-
made paper. Traylen 94-321 1983 £220

EURIPIDES   Tragedies in English Verse. London,
1894-98. First edition. 3 vols. 8vo. Half dark blue morocco,
gilt, t.e.g. Traylen 94-322 1983 £60

EURIPIDES   Tragoediae XIX. Heidelbergae, Hieronymi
Commelini, 1597. 2 vols., 8vo, later polished sheet gilt, bit worn,
age-browned, first title bit soiled, two bookplates, good set.
Ravenstree 95-49 1983 $165

EVANS, A. H.   A Flora of Cambridgeshire. 1939.
Wheldon 160-1598 1983 £15

EVANS, ABEL   The Apparition. Printed in the Year
MDCCX. 8vo, complete with final blank. New wraps. First edition,
printed in Oxford. Quaritch NS 7-40 1983 $225

EVANS, ABEL   The Apparition. A Poem. (Oxford):
1710. First ed., 8vo, disbound, final blank leaf present. A very good
copy. Trebizond 18-38 1983 $140

EVANS, CHARLES   American Bibliography, A Chronological Dictionary of all books... New York: Peter Smith, 1941. 12 vols. Tall 8vo. Cloth. Very good condition. Oak Knoll 49-440 1983 $200

EVANS, CHARLES   American Bibliography. Metuchen: Mini-Print, 1967 and Worcester: American Antiquarian Society, 1959. Micro-print ed. of Vols. 1-13, regular ed. of Vol. 14. Cloth, fine. Dawson 470-106 1983 $125

EVANS, ELWOOD   Oration. Portland, 1865. Orig. printed wraps. First edition. Ginsberg 47-726 1983 $100

EVANS, ELWOOD   The State of Washington. (Tacoma, 1893). Illus. Orig. printed pictorial wraps. First edition. Ginsberg 47-923 1983 $45

EVANS, ELWOOD   The State of Washington, a Brief History. (Tacoma, 1893). Orig. pict. wraps. Numerous illus. Inscribed by the editor. Argosy 716-602 1983 $35

EVANS, GEORGE C.   History of the Town of Jefferson, New Hampshire, 1773-1927. Manchester, 1927. 1st ed. 8vo, back cover dampstained, otherwise nice. Morrill 288-333 1983 $22.50

EVANS, GEORGE G.   Illustrated History of the United States Mint... Philadelphia, 1892. New Revised Edition. 81st thousand. Photo illustrations and fine engravings of 32 plates of rare coins. 8vo. Some light cover stains. Morrill 290-122 1983 $20

EVANS, GEORGE W. B.   Mexican Gold Trail. San Marino, 1945. End maps, illus, dj. Clark 741-383 1983 $36.50

EVANS, GEORGE W. B.   Mexican Gold Trail, The Journal of a Forty-Niner. San Marino: The Huntington Library, 1945. Preface by R.G. Cleland. Illus. Cloth. Dawson 471-78 1983 $25

EVANS, JOHN   A Sketch of the Denominations of the Christian World. Boston, E.C. Beals for R. Lothian, 1807. 8vo, cont. tree calf worn and scuffed, a well used copy with pages thumbed, few stains, age-browning, frontis. has page numbers by the various portraits, several biographies plus accounts of the various religions and philosophies. First American edition. Ravenstree 94-75 1983 $21

EVANS, MARGIAD   Country Dance. London, 1932. First edition. 4 colour illus. by Peggy Whistler. Spine slightly darkened. Very slightly torn and rubbed dustwrapper. Very good. Jolliffe 26-176 1983 £45

EVANS, MARGIAD   The Old and the Young. London, 1948. First edition. Decorations by the author. Chipped and slightly worn dustwrapper. Very good. Jolliffe 26-177 1983 £18

EVANS, MARY ANN
Please turn to
ELIOT, GEORGE

EVANS, MONTGOMERY   Prodigal Sons or The Future of Caste. London: Kegan Paul, Trench, Trubner & Co., Ltd., 1928. First edition. 12mo. Orig. cloth-backed boards. Tissue jacket. Presentation copy, inscribed on the front flyleaf "For Thomas Burke, with profound apologies that I can not offer a better reminder of a pleasant excursion to pubs I had not seen. Sincerely, Montgomery Evans, July 13, 1939." Very good. MacManus 278-1791 1983 $35

EVANS, THOMAS   Old Ballads, historical and narrative, with some of modern date. London: T. Evans, 1777. First edition. 8vo, 2 vols., cont. gilt-bordered calf, morocco labels, spines richly gilt. Half-titles, ad. leaf in vol. I. Title vignettes engraved by Isaac Taylor. In excellent contemp. condition. Trebizond 18-39 1983 $260

EVANS, WALKER   American Photographs. New York: Moma, (1938). Oblong octavo. Cloth. First edition. Photos. Inscribed presentation copy from Evans. About fine in somewhat used dust jacket. Reese 20-383 1983 $300

EVANS, WILL F.   Border Skylines Fifty Years of "Tallying Out" on the Bloys Round-Up Ground. Dallas: Cicil Baugh, 1940. Frontis. portrait. Illustrations. First edition. Some shelf wear. Scarce. Jenkins 153-185 1983 $75

EVARTS, JEREMIAH   Essays on the Present Crisis in the Condition of the American Indians. Boston, 1829. First edition. Dbd. Ginsberg 46-355 1983 $75

EVARTS, WILLIAM M.   Letter of...Communicating... Correspondence and Papers Relative to the Case of the United States Vs. Vicente P. Gomez. Wash., 1869. Half morocco. First edition. Ginsberg 47-75 1983 $50

EVELYN, JOHN   Directions for the Gardiner at Says-Court. London: Nonesuch Press, 1932. Octavo. Limited to 800 copies. Faint corner rubbing, else very fine in marbled boards. Slightly chipped dust wrapper reinforced on inside with tape in a few spots. Bromer 25-264 1983 $75

EVELYN, JOHN   Fuminfugium. 1933. 8vo, woodcut on title of London Bridge, and woodcut portrait of Evelyn. Orig. buckram with paper label on upper cover. Bickersteth 75-135 1983 £12

EVELYN, JOHN   Navigation and Commerce, Their Original Progress. London: T. R. for Benj. Tooke, 1674. First edition, 8vo, final two leaves errata and advertisements, prelim. blank leaf preceding title, a number of marginal inscriptions, almost all in pencil. Printed on thicker paper than usual, cont. mottled calf, rebacked, rubbed, recent endpapers. A crisp and clean copy. Pickering & Chatto 21-34 1983 $1,600

EVELYN, JOHN   Silva. York, 1801. Third edition, revised, corrected, and enlarged. With the portrait by Bartolozzi and 45 engraved plates (2 folding), spines worn at one joint. Fenning 62-110 1983 £125

EVENTFUL Narratives. S.L.C., 1887. Orig. cloth. First edition. Ginsberg 47-596 1983 $35

EVENTS in Paris, During the 26, 27, 28, and 29 of July, 1830. Boston: Carter & Hendee, 1830. First American edition. First 72 pages on blue stock. Wrappers soiled and chipped. Bradley 66-416 1983 $30

EVERETT, ALEXANDER HILL   Address Delivered at Jefferson College, St. James Parish, La., June 30, 1841. New Orleans, 1841. Half morocco. First edition. Ginsberg 46-420 1983 $100

EVERETT, ALEXANDER HILL   Remarks on the Governor's Speech. Boston, 1814. Disbound, good. Reese 18-438 1983 $35

EVERETT, EDWARD   A Euology of the Life and Character of John Quincy Adams... Boston: Dutton and Wentworth, 1848. Orig. printed blue wrappers. Presentation copy from Edward Everett. Jenkins 153-1 1983 $40

EVERETT, GEORGE   The Path-way to Peace and Profit. Printed for the Author, 1694. Sm. 4to. Orig. cloth. Half calf. Good. Edwards 1042-59 1983 £250

EVERETT-GREEN, EVELYN   Olive Roscoe, or The New Sister. London: T. Nelson & Sons, 1901. A reprint of the 1895 first edition. 8 illus. Orig. decorated cloth. Corners slightly bumped. Bookplate. With an ornate gilt design on the spine and front cover. Very good. MacManus 278-1792 1983 $25

EVERMANN, B. W.   The Fishes of Porto Rico. Washington, 1902. 3 maps, 49 coloured plates and 112 text-figures, royal 8vo, cloth. A trifle loose and maps slightly creased, but a good copy. Wheldon 160-954 1983 £55

EVERS, HANS GERHARD   Rubens und sein Werk. Brussel: De Lage Landen, 1943. 370 illus. hors texte. Large 4to. Boards, 1/4 cloth. Front hinge cracked at foot. Ars Libri 32-598 1983 $150

EVERSON, WILLIAM OLIVER
Please turn to
ANTONINUS, BROTHER

EVERTS, TRUMAS C.　　　　Thirty-Seven Days of Peril. S.F., 1923. A Narrative of the Early Days of the Yellowstone. 12mo, linen-backed boards, gilt. Title-page & decorations by Joseph Sinel. One of 375 copies. Fine, unopened copy. Perata 28-40　1983　$65

EVERY Day Occurrences. Charles Knight, 1825. First edition, 2 vols. Half titles, half black calf, rubbed. Jarndyce 31-409　1983　£85

EVERYMAN. Chatto, 1914. 3rd imp., dec. title & 13 full page illus., designs by Ambrose Dudley. Brown decor. cloth uncut (free eps. sl. discol'd, bkstrip faded), v.g. Hodgkins 27-437　1983　£10.50

EWALD, H. F.　　　　The Story of Waldemar Krone's Youth. Edinburgh: Edmonston & Douglas, 1867. First English edition, 2 vols., half titles, orig. brown cloth, a little rubbed. Jarndyce 31-691　1983　£36

EWART, GAVIN　　　　Poems and Songs. London: The Fortune Press, n.d. (1939). First edition. Fine. Gekoski 2-46　1983 £30

EWING, J. A.　　　　Magnetic Induction in Iron and other Metals. London, (1900). Third edition. 8vo. Orig. cloth. With numerous illus. Gurney JJ-114　1983　£12

EWING, JAMES　　　　Neoplastic Diseases. Phila., 1919. First edition. Tall 8vo, orig. cloth. 479 illus. Argosy 713-171 1983　$100

EWING, JULIANA H.　　　　Daddy Darwin's Dovecot, A Country Tale. London: Soc. for Promoting Christian Knowledge, (n.d.). 1st ed. Orig. printed boards. Worn spine and some binding stains; text nice; a good copy. Jenkins 155-169　1983　$25

EWING, JULIANA H　　　　Jackanapes. NY: Oxford University Press, 1948. Small octavo. First edition. Numerous illus. Fine with slightly soiled dust wrapper. Bromer 25-399　1983　$65

EWING, THOMAS　　　　The Struggle for Freedom in Kansas. (N.Y., 1894). Orig. printed wraps. Ginsberg 47-401　1983　$25

AN EXAMEN of the new comedy, call'd The Suspicious Husband. London: printed for J. Roberts, 1747. 8vo, wrappers, 1st ed. Half-title present. Fine copy. Rare. Ximenes 64-197　1983　$400

EXERCISES, Instructive and Entertaining, in False English. Leeds: John Heaton, 1809. Thirteenth ed., 12mo., roan, very good. Jarndyce 31-82　1983　£20

EXLEY, FREDERICK　　　　A Fan's Notes. New York, (1968). 8vo. Wraps. Advance reading copy. Lightly rubbed at edges, else fine. In Our Time 156-257　1983　$100

THE EXORBITANT Grants of William III. London, 1703. 4to, stitched. Rostenberg 88-128　1983　$40

AN EXPOSITION of spiritualism. London: Manwaring, 1862. First edition. 8vo. Orig. black cloth, decorated with pink polka-dot spots. Ximenes 63-547　1983　$90

EXPOSITIONS of Raphael's Bible. Arthur Miall, 1868. 1st edn. Illus. by photographs taken by Dunmore. 12 mounted photographs, 4 pp. ads. Mauve sand grain cloth, bevelled boards (top/bottom bkstrip worn, cvrs. faded, occasional foxing contents), good sound copy. Hodgkins 27-346　1983　£18

EXTRA Binding at the Lakeside Press Chicago. Chicago: R.R. Donnelley & Sons Co., 1925. Small 4to. First edition. Decorated boards, paper cover label. 29 full page illus. of bindings executed by Donnelley including a full color frontis. Paper covering boards chipped in places. Oak Knoll 49-78　1983　$65

EYGES, THOMAS B.　　　　Beyond the Horizon. Boston: Free Group Society, 1944. Cloth. First edition. Near fine. Reese 19-216　1983　$35

EYRE, VINCENT　　　　The Military Operations at Cabul. John Murray, 1843. Second edition. With a folding plan, 8vo, half calf, a very good copy. Fenning 61-132　1983　£45

F

FABER, GEOFFREY   The Buried Stream. London: Faber &
Faber, (1941). Cloth, first edition. Fine copy in lightly used
dust jacket, with a couple of internal mends. Reese 20-389 1983
$35

FABER, GEORGE STANLEY   A Dissertation on the Mysteries of
the Cabiri. Oxford, 1803. 8vo. Calf, boards. 2 vols. Frontispiece
reinforced, else a fine set. In Our Time 156-258 1983 $100

FABER, KNUD   Nosography in Modern Internal Medicine.
New York, 1923. First edition. 8vo. Orig. wrappers. Fye H-3-166
1983 $45

FABER, MELCHIOR   These philosophicae de hominis aetate,
eiusque incremento et decremento. Marburg: Paul Egenolph, 1594.
Woodcut border and vignette on title. 4to. Boards. Kraus 164-70
1983 $200

FABES, GILBERT   Autobiography of a Book. London,
Elzevier, (1926). First edition. Dust jacket, very good. Signed
and inscribed by the author. Bookplate of Adrian Goldstone. Houle
21-128 1983 $37.50

FABES, GILBERT   Modern First Editions: Points and
Values. London: W. and G. Foyle Ltd., (1931). Second series.
Cloth in slightly-used dw. One of 1000 copies. Dawson 470-107 1983
$40

FABES, GILBERT   The First Editions of Ralph Hale
Mottram. London: Myers & Co., 1934. First edition. 8vo. Cloth.
Limited to 300 numbered copies. Fine in slightly chipped jacket.
Oak Knoll 49-477 1983 $45

FABRICZY, CORNELIUS VON   Brunelleschiana. Urkunden und
Forschungen zur Biographie des Meisters. Berlin: G. Grote, 1907.
Wrappers. Lacks front cover. Ars Libri 33-54 1983 $40

FABYAN, ROBERT   The Chronicle of Fabian... London,
John Kynsgton, 1559. 2 vols. in 1, folio, old calf, sometime
rebacked, repaired, worn and scuffed, hinges cracked, old soiling,
minor tears and stains. Final Elizabethan edition. Ravenstree 94-
78 1983 $975

FACCIO, CESARE   Giovan Antonio Bazzi "Il Sodoma."
Vercelli: Gallardi & Ugo, 1902. Prof. illus. 4to. Wrappers.
Worn. Ars Libri 33-341 1983 $85

FAGATELLI, GUISEPPE   Retta Linae Gnomonica... In Modona,
M.DC.LXXV, (1675). Per Viuiano Soliani Stampator Ducale... 4to,
eight folding tables or diagrams. Blue paper covered paperboards.
Spine in earlier paper, rubbed at head and tail of backstrip. Some
light waterstaining. Two of the folding diagrams browned. Very
good. Arkway 22-70 1983 $450

FAGG, WILLIAM   Miniature Wood Carvings of Africa.
Bath: Adam & Dart, 1970. 110 illus. 8 color plates. Square
4to. Cloth. Dust jacket. Ars Libri 34-611 1983 $45

FAGG, WILLIAM   Nigerian Images. The splendor of
African sculpture. New York: Praeger, 1963. Photographs by
Herbert List. 68 plates. 144 illus. Large 4to. Cloth. Dust
jacket. Ars Libri 34-612 1983 $125

FAGG, WILLIAM   Tribes and Forms in African Art.
New York: Tudor, 1965. 122 plates. Large square 4to. Cloth.
Dust jacket. Ars Libri 34-613 1983 $100

FAGIOLO DELL'ARCO, MAURIZIO Bernini. Roma: Mario Bulzoni, 1967.
187 plates, 364 illus. Stout sq. 4to. Cloth. Dust jacket. Ars Libri
33-29 1983 $125

FAIRBANKS, GEORGE R.   History of Florida From Its Discovery
by Ponce de Leon in 1512. Philadelphia, 1871. Cloth, lacks
real e.p., worn. First edition. King 46-95 1983 $35

FAIRBRIDGE, R. W.   Encyclopedia of Paleontology. New
York, 1980. Numerous illus., royal 8vo, cloth. Wheldon 160-1393
1983 £54

FAIRFAX, HENRY   An Impartial Relation of the Illegal
Proceedings Against St. Mary Magdalen Colledge in Oxon. Printed and
are to be sold by Richard Baldwin, 1689. 4to, wrapper, a very good
copy. Fenning 61-134 1983 £45

FAIRFAX, THOMAS   The Memoirs of General Fairfax.
Leeds: by J. Bowling..., 1776. 12mo. Cont. tree calf, rebacked.
Engraved portrait, 3 full page engravings. Very rare. Heath 48-112
1983 £140

FAIRFIELD, JOHN H.   Known Violin Makers. (New York: 1942).
First edition. Brown cloth. Some cover stains. Bradley 66-436 1983
$65

THE FAIRIES Return Or New Tales For Old By Several Hands. (London):
Peter Davies Limited, 1934. First edition. 8vo. Orig. cloth.
Dust jacket. Fine copy. Jaffe 1-14 1983 $100

FAIRLESS, MICHAEL   The Grey Brethren. London: Duckworth &
Co., 1905. First edition. Orig. cloth. Covers a bit stained.
Somewhat foxed. Former owner's signature on flyleaf. Good. MacManus
278-1870 1983 $20

FAIRLESS, MICHAEL   The Roadmender. London: The Medici
Society, 1920. Orig. cloth-backed boards. Limited to 1000 copies
printed on handmade paper. A little dust-soiled. Very good.
MacManus 278-1871 1983 $25

FAIRLIE, ROBERT F.   Railways or no Railways. 1872. First
edition, with 9 plates and 3 folding tables, 8vo, orig. cloth, gilt.
Fenning 61-135 1983 £38.50

FAIRLY Won. Tinsley Brothers, 1871. First edition, 3 vols. Half
calf, a little rubbed, otherwise very good. Jarndyce 30-276 1983
£48

FAIRY and Folk Tales of the Irish Peasantry. Scott, 1888. 6 pp. of
ads. Dark blue cloth, paper title label backstrip, uncut with
errata slip present, backstrip soiled, label soiled and chipped, top
and bottom of backstrip worn, name on front endpaper, very good.
Hodgkins 27-220 1983 £25

FAITHFULL, EMILY   Three Visits to America. New York,
(1884). Cloth. Fone signature disbound. First American edition.
Felcone 22-59 1983 $35

FAJANS, KASIMIR   Physikalisch-Chemisches Praktikum...
Leipzig: Akademische Verlag, 1935. 8vo. Orig. cloth. Ads. One
corner soiled, portion of pastedown torn away, otherwise a fine
copy. Zeitlin 264-139 1983 $40

FALB, RODOLFO   Il taccuino senese di Giuliano da
San Gallo. Siena: Luigi Marzocchi, 1899. 50 facsimili di disegni
d'architettura, scultura ed arte applicata. 49 plates loose in
portfolio as issued. Large oblong 4to. Boards, 3/4 cloth. Ties.
Ars Libri 33-320 1983 $150

FALCKNER, DANIEL   Curieuse Nachricht from Pennsylvania.
Lancaster, 1905. Illustrated. 8vo, new buckram. Morrill 290-401
1983 $25

FALCONAR, MARIA   Poems... London: Printed for J.
Johnson...and Messrs. MDCCLXXXVII. 12mo, orig. wraps., lacking
spine, uncut, with list of subscribers. First edition, fine.
Quaritch NS 7-42 1983 $285

FALCONBRIDGE, ALEXANDER   Account of the Slave Trade on the Coast of Africa. London: J. Phillips, 1788. Disbound. First edition. Felcone 21-38 1983 $100

FALCONER, HELEN   The Story of a Strange Marriage. Remington, 1885. First edition, 2 vols. bound as one. Orig. red remainder cloth. Mint. Jarndyce 30-378 1983 £58

FALCONER, THOMAS   Letters and Notes on the Texas Santa Fe Expedition 1841-1842. New York, 1930. Boards, uncut, a fine copy. Reese 19-217 1983 $100

FALCONER, THOMAS   On Surnames and the Rules of Law Affecting their Change. Charles W. Reynell, 1862. 2nd edition, orig. brown cloth, paper label, hand-lettered on spine. Inscribed presentation copy from the author. Jarndyce 31-161 1983 £14.50

FALCONER, THOMAS   Oregon Question. London, 1845. Folded map. Half morocco. Second edition. Ginsberg 47-727 1983 $100

FALCONER, WILLIAM   The Poetical Works. London, 1866. Cr. 8vo. Dark blue calf, two-line gilt borders with corner ornaments, gilt panelled spine, morocco label, gilt. Vignette title-page. Traylen 94-323 1983 £16

FALCONER, WILLIAM   The Shipwreck. Nelson, 1868. Re-issue with 30 illus. engr'd by Edmund Evans, Dalziel Bros. etc. & vignettes, initial letters designed by Henry Noel Humphreys & engr'd by Woods. Illus. by Birket Foster. Green pebble grain blind stamped cloth, a.e.g., vg. Hodgkins 27-270 1983 £12.50

FALCONER, WILLIAM   An Universal Dictionary of the Marine. London, 1776. 4to. Orig. cloth. 12 fine folding engraved plates. Full cont. speckled calf, gilt. Green morocco label on spine. Speckled edges. Some very slight foxing. Ink signature in upper margin of title. Good. Edwards 1042-60 1983 £400

FALK, BERNARD   Thomas Rowlandson: His Life and Art. New York: Beechhurst Press, 1952. 68 plates. (20 color). Large 4to. Cloth. Ars Libri 32-595 1983 $75

FALKINER, FREDERICK R.   The Foundation of the Hospital and Free School of King Charles II., Oxmantown, Dublin. Dublin: Sealy, Bryers, 1906. First edition, with 9 plates, 8vo, orig. cloth, gilt. Some marginal pencil notes, a good copy. Fenning 61-136 1983 £21.50

A FALLEN Angel. London: Tinsley Brothers, 1878. Orig green decorated cloth. First edition. Spines and covers slightly worn. A very good, clean set. MacManus 277-79 1983 $225

FALLOPPIO, G.   Tractatus de Vulneribus oculorum... Venice, 1569. 4to. Disbound. Gurney JJ-117 1983 £15

FALSE Appearances; or, Memoirs of Henry Auberville. Dublin: Printed by William Porter, 1803. 12mo, original boards uncut; waterstain in first few leaves. Hill 165-32 1983 £55

FALTA, WILHELM   The Ductless Glandular Diseases. Phila. (1915). First English trans. 101 text illus. Argosy 713-173 1983 $85

FAMILIEN Lieder und Haeusliche Gelegenheitsdichtungen. Leipzig, Loeschke, 1853. Ads., frontis. printed in gold on black ground, gold vignette on cover. 29 woodcuts by Richter. 8vo, orig. cloth-backed boards. Corners rubbed, some slight foxing. Salloch 387-62 1983 $175

FANE, H. E.   Five Years in India. London, 1842. 12 plates, some slight spotting. 2 vols. Half calf. 8vo. Presentation copy from author, inscribed on title. Good. Edwards 1044-241 1983 £95

FANNING, E.   Voyages and Discoveries in the South Seas. Salem, 1924. 32 plates, bottom edges worn, else very good in slightly chipped and stained good dustwrapper. Quill & Brush 54-1692 1983 $75

FANTONI, FILIPPO   De Ratione Reducendi Anni ad legitamam formam et numerum... Florence: Giunta, 1560. 2 full-page woodcut diagrams. Small 8vo. Limp vellum. From the Liechtenstein library ts bookplate. Blank corner of title mended. Kraus 164-71 1983 $285

FARADAY, CORNELIA BATEMAN   European and American Carpets and Rugs. Grand Rapids, Mich. 1929. First edition, more than 400 illus., dec. cloth, ex-library else a good copy. King 46-388 1983 $65

FARADAY, MICHAEL   Chemical Manipulation... London: Murray, 1830. New edition. 8vo. Orig. cloth. Text illus. Some foxing, backstrip missing. Zeitlin 264-140 1983 $160

FARADAY, MICHAEL   The Letters of Faraday and Schoenbein, 1836-1862... Basle: Schwabe; London: Williams & Norgate, 1899. 8vo. Orig. green cloth. Frontis. portraits of the correspondents. Slightly rubbed. First edition. Very good copy. Zeitlin 264-143 1983 $60

FARADAY, MICHAEL   The Subject Matter of a Course of Six Lectures on the Non-Metallic Elements. London: Longman, 1853. First edition. 8vo. Orig. cloth. Ads. Illus. and tables in text. Slight wear. A good copy. Zeitlin 264-142 1983 $160

FARAGO, L.   Abyssinia on the Eve. London, 1935. 4 maps, numerous illus. 8vo. Orig. cloth. Good. Edwards 1044-242 1983 £16

FARBER, EDUARD   Die Geschichtliche Entwicklung der Chemie. Berlin: Springer, 1921. First edition. 8vo. Orig. half leather. Ads. 4 photographic plates. A very good copy. Zeitlin 264-146 1983 $70

FARGO, FRANK F.   Speech of...on the Resolutions Upon the State of the Union. Sacramento, 1861. Dbd. First edition. Ginsberg 47-77 1983 $35

FARINGTON, JOSEPH   The Farington Diary. London, (1922-28). Roy. 8vo. Orig. blue cloth, gilt. Portrait and 16 other illus. Traylen 94-325 1983 £65

FARIS, JOHN T.   Old Churches and Meeting Houses in and around Philadelphia. Phila., 1926. 1st ed., ex library, 74 illus. Argosy 710-401 1983 $35

FARISH, THOMAS E.   History of Arizona. Phoenix, 1915. 2 vols. Illus. Orig. cloth, as new. First edition. Ginsberg 46-23 1983 $50

FARISH, THOMAS E.   History of Arizona. Phoenix. 1915. 2 vols., orig. cloth, very fine. Reese 19-25 1983 $45

FARJEON, BENJAMIN LEOPOLD   Aaron The Jew. London: Hutchinson & Co., 1894. First edition. 3 vols. Orig. red decorated cloth. Spines & covers rather worn and spotted. Some foxing to the preliminary pages of all three volumes. Former owner's signature in pencil. Fair. MacManus 278-1874 1983 $125

FARJEON, BENJAMIN LEOPOLD   Blade-o'-Grass. Golden Grain. N.Y.: Harper & Brothers, 1872, 1874, 1875. First American editions. Illus. 3 vols. in one. Cont. 3/4 morocco. Very good. MacMa us 278-1873 1983 $75

FARJEON, BENJAMIN LEOPOLD   The Clairvoyante. London: Hutchinson & Co., 1905. First edition. Orig. cloth. Spine and covers worn and spotted. Some offsetting to the endpapers. Good. MacManus 278-1875 1983 $65

FARJEON, BENJAMIN LEOPOLD   Jessie Trim. London: Tinsley Brothers, 1874. First edition. 3 vols. Orig. decorated cloth. Covers badly worn. Library stamps. MacManus 278-1876 1983 $125

FARJEON, BENJAMIN LEOPOLD   The Sacred Nugget. London: Ward & Downey, 1885. Second edition. 3 vols. Orig. decorated cloth. Presentation copy from Margaret J. Farjeon "To Edith Tombes with all good wishes...Christmas 1904." Fine. MacManus 278-1877 1983 $350

FARJEON, BENJAMIN LEOPOLD   Samuel Boyd of Catchpole Square. London: Hutchinson & Co., 1899. First edition. Orig. cloth. Extremities and edges a bit rubbed. Endpapers browned. Bookplate of Adrian Homer Goldstone. Good. MacManus 278-1878 1983 $125

FARJEON, ELEANOR   Pannychis. Shaftesbury: The High House Press, 1933. First edition. One of 225 numbered copies. Presentation copy from the author to Enid Faber. 2 wood-engravings by Clare Leighton. Very good. Jolliffe 26-180 1983 £36

FARJEON, ELEANOR   A Sussex Alphabet. Flansham, Sussex, 1939. Colour illus. by Sheila M. Thompson. 4to, pict. green boards, glassine d/w. Printed from lino-cuts and type by John Freeman on Arnold & Foster's hand-made paper. Prospectus laid in. One of 220 copies. Perata 28-122 1983 $165

FARMER, H. G.   Memoirs of the Royal Artillery Band. London, 1904. First edition. Portrait frontis. 7 portrait and 6 other plates. 8vo. Orig. cloth. Good. Edwards 1042-553 1983 £35

FARMER, JOHN   A Gazetteer of the State of New-Hampshire. Concord, 1823. First edition. 12mo, orig. mottled calf, lea. label. Folding map, (neatly repaired on verso). Engrs. by A. Bowen. Argosy 716-327 1983 $100

FARMER, JOHN S.   Americanisms Old and New. London, Privately Printed by Thomas Poulter & Sons, 1889. Ed. limited to 500 copies for England and 250 for America, signed by Farmer. 8vo, marbled boards, morocco back and corners. Bookplate, some rubbing. Morrill 287-111 1983 $75

FARMER, SILAS   History of Detroit and Wayne County and Early Michigan. Detroit, 1890. Third edition, revised & enlarged. 2 vols. Numerous illus., portraits, 1/2 lea. A.e.g. Vol. 1 with large chip out of spine (present), vol. 2 spine torn but basically a good set. King 46-154 1983 $125

FARMILOF, EDITH   Chapel Street Children Pictures and Stories. Grant Richards, 1900. First edition, half title, front. & illus. Orig. dark blue cloth a little rubbed. Jarndyce 31-245 1983 £10.50

FARMILOE, EDITH   Mr. Biddle and the Dragon. Skeffington, 1904. 4to. 20 plates. Red pictorial cloth. Greer 39-68 1983 £15

FARNHAM, ELIZA   Life in Prairie Land. New York: Harper, 1855. 8vo, orig. cloth (corners & top & bottom of spine reinforced). Ownership inscription on title-page: Georgiana B Kirby/Santa Cruz. The present copy was given to Kirby by the author during the feminists' residence in Santa Cruz. 2nd edition. Rostenberg 88-88 1983 $125

FARNHAM, JOSEPH E. C.   Brief Historical Data and Memories of My Boyhood Days in Nantucket. (Providence, 1923). Illus. 2nd ed. 8vo, some waterstaining at lower portion causing some slight text damage from leaves having been stuck together--mostly in blank margins. Morrill 288-275 1983 $25

FARNHAM, THOMAS JEFFERSON   Travels in California. Oakland: 1947. 8vo, fabrikoid, gilt. Title drawings and initial letters by William Kay, folding map. One of 750 copies. A fine copy. Perata 27-200 1983 $20

FARNOL, JEFFERY   My Lady Caprice. NY, 1907. Front hinge starting, spine edges bumped, otherwise very good. Quill & Brush 54-429 1983 $35

FARNSWORTH, SIDNEY   Illumination: And Its Development in the Present Day. London: n.d. (ca 1920). First edition. 8vo, cloth, gilt. Illustrated with Drawings & Diagrams by the Author. Inscription on title-page; a very nice copy. Scarce. Perata 27-44 1983 $75

FARQUHAR, GEORGE   The Works of the late Ingenious Mr. George Farquhar... London: for Bernard Lintott, (1711). Second edition. 8vo. 2 vols. in 1. Plates. Cont. calf gilt, some wear. Heath 48-290 1983 £50

FARQUHAR, WILLIAM H.   Annals of Sandy Spring. Baltimore: Cushings & Bailey, 1884. 12mo, purple cloth. Bookplate. Karmiole 72-44 1983 $30

FARRAGUT, DAVID G.   Regulations for the Government of Commanders and Pursers of the Vessels of the United States, and Recruiting Officers. Washington, 1838. Cont. calf (rubbed). Admiral Farragut's copy, signed "D.G. Farragut/U.S. Navy" on the titlepage. Felcone 21-39 1983 $125

FARRAGUT, LOYALL   The Life of David Glasgow Farragut. New York, 1879. 1st ed. Portraits, maps and illus. 8vo. Morrill 287-112 1983 $30

FARRAR, EDMUND   Portraits in Suffolk Houses. London, 1908. Limited edition of 400 numbered copies, thick 4to, title-page in red and black, 139 portraits illus., original boards, buckram spine, gilt, lower cover trifle spotted. Deighton 3-127 1983 £48

FARRAR, FREDERIC W.   Chapters on Language. Longmans, Green, 1865. First edition, calf, a little rubbed, gilt borders and spine, red label. Jarndyce 31-693 1983 £15

FARRAR, FREDERIC W.   Gathering Clouds: A Tale Of The Days Of St. Chrysostom. London: Longmans, Green & Co., 1895. First edition. 2 vols. Orig. blue decorated cloth. Spines and covers slightly worn and a trifle soiled. Cont. owner's signature. Very good. MacManus 278-1881 1983 $125

FARRAR, FREDERIC W.   Gathering Clouds. Longmans, Green, 1895. First edition, 2 vols. Half titles, 24 pp ads. vol. I. Orig. dark blue cloth, rubbed, ex-library copy, some lib. stamps. Jarndyce 30-379 1983 £15

FARRAR, FREDERICK W   Darkness and Dawn, or Scenes in the Days of Nero. London: Longmans, 1891. First edition, Colonial issue. 2 vols. Orig. cloth. Very good. MacManus 278-1880 1983 $65

FARRAR, JOHN CHAPMAN   Forgotten Shrines. New Haven: Yale, 1919. Printed wraps. over boards. First edition. Short closed tear, else fine. Reese 20-392 1983 $20

FARRELL, JAMES T.   Bernard Clare. NY: (1946). First edition. Presentation inscription from Farrell. Fine in dust wrapper. Bromer 25-35 1983 $60

FARRELL, JAMES T.   Bernard Clare. (New York): Vanguard Press, (1946). 1st ed. Orig. cloth, dj. Very fine copy. Jenkins 155-380 1983 $20

FARRELL, JAMES T.   Father and Son. NY, (1940). Cover slightly discolored, else very good in slightly frayed and soiled, very good dustwrapper. Quill & Brush 54-431 1983 $30

FARRELL, JAMES T.   Gas-House McGinty. NY, 1933. Small tear at hinge of front title, edges slightly rubbed, still very good in internally mended, slightly chipped dustwrapper. Quill & Brush 54-432 1983 $125

FARRELL, JAMES T.   Judgment Day. NY, 1935. Spine of red cloth slightly faded, endpapers slightly offset, else very good in frayed and lightly chipped, lightly worn, still presentable dustwrapper, bookplate front fly. Quill & Brush 54-433 1983 $125

FARRELL, JAMES T.   Literature and Morality. (New York): Vanguard Press, (1947). 1st ed. Orig. cloth. Fine copy in slightly used dj. Jenkins 155-381 1983 $20

FARRELL, JAMES T.   A Misunderstanding. New York, 1949. 1st ed., 1 of 300 numbered and signed copies. Orig. mustard cloth, gilt. Brief presentation inscription from Farrell to an individual. Fine copy. Jenkins 155-382 1983 $75

FARRELL, JAMES T.   A Note on Literary Criticism. NY: (1936). First edition. Presentation inscription, "To Fred Higgins, a poet from a prose writer Jim Farrell." Endpapers darkened, else fine in torn dust wrapper. Bromer 25-36 1983 $65

FARRELL, JAMES T.   Texas by the Potomac. Dallas: The Times Herald, 1940. Printed wrappers. Limited ed. Fine copy. Jenkins 153-796 1983 $30

FARRELL, JAMES T.   Young Lonigan. NY, 1935. Green cover faded especially on spine, otherwise very good. Quill & Brush 54-435 1983 $30

FARRELL, JAMES T.   The Young Manhood of Studs Lonigan. NY, 1935. Spine of red cloth slightly faded, endpapers slightly offset, else very good in frayed and lightly chipped, lightly worn, still presentable dustwrapper, bookplate front fly. Quill & Brush 54-434 1983 $125

FARREN, ROBERT   Time's Wall Asunder. Sheed & Ward, 1939. First edition, 8vo, orig. cloth. Signed by the author. Fenning 60-105 1983 £10.50

FARRER, JAMES ANSON   Books Condemned to be Burnt. London: Elliot Stock, 1892. First edition. Small 8vo. Half leather over cloth, t.e.g., others uncut. A larger paper copy in the orig. special binding. Covers rubbed. Oak Knoll 48-154 1983 $25

FARRER, R.   My Rock-Garden. 1907. Illus. from photographs, 8vo, original cloth, joints rubbed. First edition. Scarce. Publisher's advertisements dated October 1907 at end. Wheldon 160-1939 1983 £25

FARRER, R.   The Rock Garden. (1912). 8 coloured plates, 8vo, boards. Wheldon 160-1940 1983 £12

FARROW, G. E.   The Adventures of a Dodo. T. Fisher Unwin, n.d. (ca.1910). Frontis. Pictorial title. 36 full-page & 34 text illus. Pictorial endpapers. Blue pictorial cloth, gilt. Greer 39-97 1983 £35

FARROW, G. E.   Pixie Pickles. Skeffington, n.d. (ca. 1914). 4to. 20 two-colour plates. Pictorial boards, worn. Greer 40-150 1983 £38

FARWELL, WILLARD B.   Society of California Pioneers. San Francisco, 1862. Orig. printed wraps. First edition. Ginsberg 47-78 1983 $35

FASCISTS At Olympia. A Record of Eye-Witnesses and Victims. London: Victor Gollancz Ltd, 1934. First edition. 8vo. Orig. wrappers. Wrappers dust-soiled, otherwise a very good copy. Jaffe 1-191 1983 $85

FASHIONABLE amusement. London: Hatchard, 1827. First edition. 8vo. Orig. blue boards, drab paper backstrip, printed paper label. Foot of spine worn. A very good copy. Rare. Ximenes 63-110 1983 $60

FASOLO, VINCENZO   Michelangniolo architettor, poeta. Genova: Vitali e Ghianda, 1965. 324 illus. Large square 4to. Cloth. Dust jacket. Ars Libri 33-238 1983 $85

FAST, HOWARD   The American. N.Y., Duell, Sloan & Pearce, (1946). First edition. Dust jacket, fine copy. Houle 22-348 1983 $40

FAST, HOWARD   Departure and Other Stories. Boston, Little, Brown, 1949. First edition. Dust jacket. Fine copy. Houle 21-327 1983 $40

FAST, HOWARD   A Fable. N.Y., Random House (1954). First edition. Dark blue cloth. One of 1,000 deluxe copies, signed by Faulkner. Pub.'s box (soiled). Fine copy. Houle 21-330 1983 $285

FAULDING, G. M.   Old Man's Beard. J.M. Dent, 1909. Colour frontis. Colour pictorial title. 3 colour plates. 15 full-page & 30 text illus, some thumbing. Blue pictorial cloth. Greer 39-130 1983 £12.50

FAULKNER, G.   The White Elephant. N.Y.: Wise-Pars., (1929 Volland). 8vo. Pictorial cloth. Full-page & smaller color illus. by Richardson. Fine. Aleph-bet 8-225 1983 $20

FAULKNER, THOMAS P.   The Career of George Robert Fitzgerald. Dublin: Sealy Bryers & Walker, 1893. First edition, 8vo, orig. cloth, gilt. Very good copy. Inscribed by the author. Fenning 62-113 1983 £18.50

FAULKNER, WILLIAM   An Address by..., Oxford, Mississippi, at the Seventeenth Annual Meeting of Delta Council... Cleveland, Miss., (1952). First edition. Orig. green printed wrappers. A couple of faint spots to wrapper, but fine copy. Jenkins 153-770 1983 $3,000

FAULKNER, WILLIAM   Big Woods. NY, (1955). Gift inscription on front fly, near fine in very good dustwrapper that is lightly chipped and frayed at edges. Quill & Brush 54-441 1983 $75

FAULKNER, WILLIAM   Collected Stories. New York, (1951). 8vo, cloth. Price clipped from just jacket, else a fine copy in immaculate jacket. In Our Time 156-264 1983 $150

FAULKNER, WILLIAM   Collected Stories of William Faulkner. New York, (1950). First edition, first printing. Gray cloth. Very fine in dj. Bradley 65-63 1983 $125

FAULKNER, WILLIAM   Doctor Martino. NY, 1934. Limited to 360 numbered and signed copies, limitation page offset, spine and cover edges slightly faded, good or better. Quill & Brush 54-442 1983 $750

FAULKNER, WILLIAM   Doctor Martino and Other Stories. New York, 1934. 1st ed. Blue cloth. Fine in dj, which has small chip missing at top of spine. Bradley 63-46 1983 $295

FAULKNER, WILLIAM   Early Prose and Poetry. Lon., (1936). Illus., very fine in fine dustwrapper. Quill & Brush 54-443 1983 $40

FAULKNER, WILLIAM   A Fable. New York, 1954. 8vo. Cloth. Limited signed edition, being 1 of 1000 copies signed by Faulkner. Fine copy in acetate jacket and box. In Our Time 156-266 1983 $500

FAULKNER, WILLIAM   A Fable. NY, (1954). Limited to 1000 numbered and signed copies, fine, bright in glassine wrap in slightly soiled and stained, near fine slipcase. Quill & Brush 54-437 1983 $450

FAULKNER, WILLIAM   Go Down, Moses. London, 1942. First edition. Bookplate. Very slightly dusty dustwrapper. Fine. Gekoski 2-47 1983 £80

FAULKNER, WILLIAM   A Green Bough. NY: 1933. First edition. Limited to 360 copies signed by Faulkner. Illus. Cover and frontispiece wood engravings by Lynd Ward. Fine, partly unopened copy. Bromer 25-38 1983 $525

FAULKNER, WILLIAM   The Hamlet. NY, 1940. Top edges spotted, else very good in lightly worn dustwrapper with crease down front panel. Quill & Brush 54-455 1983 $225

FAULKNER, WILLIAM   The Hamlet. N.Y., 1940. First edition. Cloth. Rubbed. Good. King 45-175 1983 $45

FAULKNER, WILLIAM   Idyll in the Desert. New York: Random House, 1931. 1st ed. limited to 400 numbered and signed copies. Orig. marbled boards, paper label, uncut. Fine copy but for vestiges of neatly removed bookplate, unusual for this fragile binding. Jenkins 155-387 1983 $500

FAULKNER, WILLIAM   Intruder in the Dust. New York, 1948. 8vo. Cloth. As new in dj. In Our Time 156-263 1983 $250

FAULKNER, WILLIAM   Intruder in the Dust. New York: (1948). First edition, first printing. Dark blue cloth, top edges blue. Fine in the jacket. Bradley 66-157 1983 $185

FAULKNER, WILLIAM   Intruder in the Dust. N.Y., Random House (1948). First edition. Black cloth, stamped in blue and gilt. Good-very good. Houle 21-332 1983 $45

FAULKNER, WILLIAM   Light in August. NY, (1932). Very good
in dustwrapper that is lightly chipped on corners and with two closed
tears, internally mended, still very presentable dustwrapper. Quill &
Brush 54-444 1983 $400

FAULKNER, WILLIAM   Marionettes: A Play in One Act. (Char-
lottesville, 1975). First printed edition, limited to 100 copies.
Unopened sheets in solander case. Mint. Quill & Brush 54-445 1983
$400

FAULKNER, WILLIAM   Marionettes: A Play in One Act. (Yok-
napatawpha Press, 1979). First edition, second issue, limited to 320
copies, a facsimile edition. Boxed with separately bound paperwraps,
mint. Quill & Brush 54-446 1983 $125

FAULKNER, WILLIAM   Mirrors of Chartres Street. Minnesota,
(1953). 8vo. Cloth. Total edition is 1000 numbered copies. Very
fine in dj. Jacket has a small nick at spinal extremity. In Our
Time 156-265 1983 $250

FAULKNER, WILLIAM   Mississippi Poems. (1979). Advance
review copy, paperwraps, very good, inscribed by Joseph Blotner and
signed on title. Quill & Brush 54-447 1983 $75

FAULKNER, WILLIAM   Mosquitoes Moustiques. (Paris): Les
Editions de Minuit, (1948). Orig. printed wraps. First edition in
French. One of 200 on Alfa Mousse from an edition of 1,200. A mint,
wholly unopened copy. Reese 20-394 1983 $125

FAULKNER, WILLIAM   Mosquitoes. Lon., 1964. Fine in bright,
price clipped, dustwrapper that is only slightly frayed at edges.
Quill & Brush 54-448 1983 $100

FAULKNER, WILLIAM   Notes on a Horse Thief. Ms., 1950.
Limited to 975 numbered and signed copies, fine. Quill & Brush 54-
449 1983 $500

FAULKNER, WILLIAM   Pylon. NY, 1935. Limited to 310 numbered and signed copies, boards rubbed and small skinned area on front
cover, spine slightly faded, still good or better, tight. Quill &
Brush 54-451 1983 $450

FAULKNER, WILLIAM   Pylon. N.Y., Smith & Haas, 1935. First
edition. Dust jacket (a few small nicks; back a bit faded) else,
very good. Houle 22-352 1983 $225

FAULKNER, WILLIAM   Pylon. NY, 1935. Very good in slightly
chipped, still very good dustwrapper. Quill & Brush 54-452 1983 $225

FAULKNER, WILLIAM   Pylon. NY, 1935. 2nd printed, two small
tears at top spine edge, else very good in lightly frayed and aged
dustwrapper. Quill & Brush 54-450 1983 $25

FAULKNER, WILLIAM   The Reivers. New York, 1962. 8vo.
Cloth. Limited signed ed., being 1 of 500 numbered copies signed
by Faulkner. Some very light rubbing to the base of the spine, else
a fine copy in acetate jacket. In Our Time 156-267 1983 $500

FAULKNER, WILLIAM   Requiem for a Nun. NY, (1951). Limited
to 750 numbered and signed, specially bound copies. Marbled boards very
lightly rubbed, else fine. Quill & Brush 54-453 1983 $400

FAULKNER, WILLIAM   Requiem for a Nun. N.Y., Random, (1951).
First edition. 3/4 black cloth stamped in gilt over marbled boards
(spine faded, a bit rubbed at edges) else, very good. One of 750
numbered copies signed by Faulkner. Houle 22-354 1983 $395

FAULKNER, WILLIAM   Salmagundi...and a Poem. Milwaukee:
The Casanova Press, 1932. 1st ed., limited to 525 numbered copies.
Orig. printed wrappers, uncut, tipped in frontis. of Faulkner. Rear
wrapper prints Hemingway's poem, "Ultimately." Fine copy in lightly
rubbed box, seldom seen thus. Jenkins 155-391 1983 $500

FAULKNER, WILLIAM   Salmagundi. Milwaukee: Casanova Press,
1932. First edition. 1/525 copies. Tipped-in portrait of Faulkner.
Tan wrappers. Fine, trivial wear on spine. In board slipcase.
Bradley 66-158 1983 $535

FAULKNER, WILLIAM   Salmagundi. Milwaukee: Cassanova
Press, 1932. First edition. One of 525. Tipped-in portrait. Tan
wrappers. In board slipcase. Very light wear on spine. Bradley 65-
66 1983 $500

FAULKNER, WILLIAM   Salmagundi. Milwaukee: Casanova
Press, 1932. 1st ed. 1 of 525. Tipped-in portrait of Faulkner.
Title page in red and black, tan wrappers. Very slight wear on spine.
Bradley 63-47 1983 $475

FAULKNER, WILLIAM   Soldier's Pay. Horace Liveright,
(1931). 8vo. Cloth. Third printing. First printing under
Liveright Imprint. Blue dj. Reviews of book on rear flap. Vg-fine
copy in intact and near perfect dj. In Our Time 156-262 1983 $100

FAULKNER, WILLIAM   These Thirteen. New York, (1931). 8vo.
Cloth. Limited ed., signed by Faulkner. Tiny bookplate on inside
endboard, a fine bright copy. In Our Time 156-260 1983 $1200

FAULKNER, WILLIAM   These Thirteen. New York (1931). 8vo.
Cloth. 1st trade ed. Fine copy in mint dust jacket. In Our Time
156-261 1983 $1000

FAULKNER, WILLIAM   These Thirteen. London, 1933. First
English edition. One of 1500 copies. Spine dull. Name of flyleaf.
Very good. Rota 230-207 1983 £20

FAULKNER, WILLIAM   The Wishing Tree. New York, (1964).
8vo. Cloth. Limited issue, being 1 of 500 numbered copies on
specially made paper and specially bound. A fine copy in dj.
Original slipcase box has a few nicks. In Our Time 156-268 1983
$150

FAUNO, LUCIO   Compendio di Roma Antica. Venice:
(Michele Tramezzino). 1552. Small 8vo, large printer's devices on
title and on the verso of the final leaf. Old vellum. Karmiole 73-
41 1983 $150

FAUNTLEROY, JOSEPH   John Henry Nash Printer. Oakland:
Westgate Press, 1948. Octavo. Limited to 235 copies printed by
Alfred and Lawton Kennedy. Faint wear to corner, else fine in boards
with cloth spine. Bromer 25-258 1983 $150

FAUNTLEROY, JOSEPH   John Henry Nash: Printer. Oakland, 1948.
Sm. 8vo, linen-backed boards, paper label. With 2 tipped-in phogo-
graphs, hand-colored initial. Presswork by Alfred & Lawton Kennedy.
One of 235 copies. Fine. Perata 28-114 1983 $100

FAURE, ELIE   A. Derain. Paris: G. Cres, 1923.
60 plates. Text illus. 4to. Wrappers. Slightly worn. Ars Libri
32-164 1983 $50

FAURE, ELIE   Eugene Carriere, peintre et lithographe. Paris: H. Floury, 1908. 36 gravure plates. Illus.
4to. Marbled boards, 3/4 blue morocco. Orig. wrappers bound in.
Ars Libri 32-82 1983 $150

FAURE, GABRIEL   En Sicile. Illus. 8vo, cloth.
Salloch 385-347 1983 $20

FAUSSETT, GODFREY   Jewish History Vindicated from the Un-
scriptural View of it Displayed in The History of the Jews. Oxford:
Printed for the author, 1830. 8vo, wrapper. Fenning 61-137 1983
£28.50

FAUST, ALBERT BERNHARDT   The German Element in the U.S. NY,
1927. Many illus. & maps, 2 vols. in one. Argosy 716-149 1983
$35

FAVORITE Authors. Boston: Ticknor & Fields, 1863. Early ed. Orig.
lavender cloth, fully gilt, a.e.g. Very good unfaded copy of this
collection by Hawthorne, Tennyson, et al. Jenkins 155-531 1983
$25

FAWCETT, BENJAMIN   Murther Lamented and Improved. Shrewsbury: by J. Eddowes..., 1771. 8vo. Half title, modern boards.
Very scarce. Heath 48-113 1983 £65

FAWCETT, C. The First Century of British Justice in India. Oxford, 1934. Maps. 8vo. Orig. cloth. Good. Edwards 1044-244 1983 £25

FAWCETT, C. H. On Making, Mending and Dressing Dolls. N.Y., 1949. 8vo. Pink cloth. Frayed dust wrapper. 276 orig. drawings by author. Fine. Aleph-bet 8-91 1983 $20

FAWCETT, EDGAR Fantasy and Passion. Boston, Roberts Brothers, 1878. First edition, small 8vo, orig. reddish brown cloth, gilt (monogram on spine), slight wear to spine but a very good copy. Fenning 62-114 1983 £10.50

FAWCETT, HENRY Mr. Hare's Reform Bill simplified and explained. London: n.d. (1860). First edition. 8vo. Disbound. Inscribed on the first page "with the author's compliments." Very scarce. Ximenes 63-461 1983 £65

FAWCETT, JOHN Prospectus; with songs, choruses, etc. London: printed for the author, by T. Woodfall; and sold in the theatre, n. d. (1804). 8vo, disbound, 1st ed. Title soiled, last leaf repaired on the verso, without affecting text. Scarce. Ximenes 64-201 1983 $75

FAWKES, FRANCIS A Description of May. London. Printed for J. Whitson and B. White...A. Millar...and R. Dodsley...MDCCLII. 4to, complete with final glossary leaf; dark green morocco by Pratt, gilt, a.e.g., with the Christie-Miller arms in gilt in the centre of both covers. First edition. Quaritch NS 7-43 1983 $300

FAWKES, FRANCIS Original Poems and Translations. London: for the Author and sold by R. & J. Dodsley..., 1761. First edition. 8vo. Modern boards. Engraved vignette on title, errata slip. Slight foxing. Heath 48-469 1983 £65

FAXON, FREDERICK W. Literary Annuals and Gift Books, A Bibliography. Boston: Boston Book Co., 1912. 1st ed., 1 of 150 copies. Orig. cloth-backed boards, gilt. A little dusty, but nice copy. Scarce in the 1st ed. Jenkins 155-1358 1983 $35

FAY, CHARLES EDEY Mary Celeste. Salem, Peabody Museum, 1942. Ed. limited to 1000 copies. Tall 8vo. Illus. Morrill 289-328 1983 $25

FAY, ELIZA Original Letters From India. NY, (1925). Few marginal pencil notes, minor cover stains, very good, owner's name. Quill & Brush 54-507 1983 $30

FAYDEN, F. A. Historical Record of the 76th "Hindoostan" Regiment. Lichfield, 1908. 8vo, double page coloured frontis. of colours, 3 photogravure portraits and 1 coloured portrait, 7 folding maps (6 coloured). Slightly soiled. Signet Library bookplate. Good. Edwards 1042-541 1983 £55

FAYLE, C. E. Seaborne Trade. London, 1920-24. 8vo. Orig. cloth. 12 folding maps (2 coloured) and 14 tables (some folding, some coloured). 4 vols. Slightly worn and faded. Library labels and ink marks on spines of 2 vols. Good. Edwards 1042-62 1983 £45

FEARING, FRANKLIN Reflex Action. Baltimore, 1930. First edition. 8vo. Orig. wrappers. Scarce. Fye H-3-168 1983 $65

FEARING, FRANKLIN Reflex Action. A Study in the History of Physiological psychology. Baltimore: Williams & Wilkins, 1930. First edition. Ex-library copy. Gach 94-150 1983 $37.50

FEARING, KENNETH Poems. New York, 1935. First American edition. One of 1000 numbered copies. Without the ownership signature of Theodore Roethke, but on the lower panel of the dustwrapper a signed and dated sketch has been drawn of him. Spine faded. Very good in torn and chipped dustwrapper in two halves and missing two pieces. Jolliffe 26-442 1983 £45

FEARON, HENRY BRADSHAW Sketches of America. London, 1819. Lacking covers entirely, name clipped from top blank margin of title. Third edition. Felcone 22-61 1983 $50

FEARON, JAMES PETER Theatrical criticism. London: printed and published, (for the author) by Barker and Son, 1805. 8vo, disbound, 1st ed. Half-title present (dusty); leaf of ads at the end. Ximenes 64-203 1983 $150

FEATHERSTONHAUGH, GEORGE WILLIAM Excursion Through the Slave States ... London, 1844. 2 vols. Orig. cloth with paper labels. Folding map. Two tinted lithographic plates. First edition. Jenkins 153-191 1983 $300

FEATHERSTONHAUGH, GEORGE WILLIAM Excursion Through the Slave States from Washington on the Potomace to the Frontier of Mexico... New York, 1844. Printed wrappers, moderately foxed, else nice orig. copy in protective cloth box, worn and soiled, first American edition. King 46-12 1983 $125

FEATHERSTONHAUGH, GEORGE WILLIAM Excursion through the Slave States, from Washington on the Potomac to the Frontier of Mexico. New York, 1844. Disbound. Strip torn from blank margin of title, minor dogearing. First American edition. Felcone 22-62 1983 $60

FEDER, NORMAN American Indian Art. New York: Abrams, (1971). 302 plates (60 tipped-in color). Small oblong folio. Cloth. Dust jacket. Worn. Ars Libri 34-230 1983 $125

FEDOROVA, NINA The Family. Boston, Little Brown, 1940. First edition. Dust jacket (small nicks) else very good. Signed by the author. Houle 22-358 1983 $30

FEINBRUN-DOTHAN, N. Flora Palaestina, Vol. 3, Ericaceae to Compositae. Jerusalem, 1977-78. Text and Atlas. 2 maps (1 coloured), 757 full page line-drawings, 2 vols., royal 8vo, cloth. Wheldon 160-1674 1983 £46

FELIBIEN, JEAN FRANCOIS, SIEUR DES AVAUX Entretien sur Nicolas Poussin. Paris: Fernand Roches, 1929. 13 plates, 4to., full vellum over boards, t.e.g., uncut, slipcase, no. 86 of a limited ed. of 500 copies, on papier d'Auvergne. Ars Libri 32-534 1983 $75

FELL, MARGARET A Brief collection of Remarkable Passages and Occurrences Relating to the Birth, Education, Life, Conversion, Travels, Services, and Deep Suffering of... Margaret Fell. Printed and sold by J. Sowles, 1710. First edition, errata slip mounted on the final page of text, 8vo, wanting a blank front flyleaf, cont. panelled calf, just a little worn but thoroughly sound. A very good copy. Fenning 62-115 1983 £65

FELLOWES, E. H. The English Madrigal Composers. Oxford: at the Clarendon Press, 1921. 8vo. Cloth. Traylen 94-327 1983 £20

FELLOWES, WILLIAM D A Visit to the Monastery of La Trappe, in 1817. London: William Stockdale, 1818. 1st ed., 8vo, modern calf antique, spine gilt, 12 colored aquatints, two uncolored line engravings, text vignette. Margins of title and of first leaf in text carefully repaired, touching one work; occasional light foxing, but a very good copy. Trebizond 18-142 1983 $275

FELLOWES, WILLIAM D. A Visit to the Monestary of la Trappe, in 1817. London: Thomas M'Lean, 1823. Quarto. Full black straight-grain morocco, spine heavily and intricately gilt, heavily gilt borders, e.g. Illus. with fifteen full-page plates (14 colored). A fine, large copy, with only the barest traces of foxing touching the extreme edges of the margins of one or two plates. Reese 20-401 1983 $400

FELLOWS, CHARLES An Account of Discoveries in Lycia, Being a Journal Kept During a Second Excursion in Asia Minor. John Murray, 1841. First edition, with 2 maps, 37 plates, roy. 8vo, orig. cloth, gilt. Skillful repair to spine. Fenning 60-106 1983 £110

FELLOWS, CHARLES An Account of Discoveries in Lycia, being a Journal kept during a second Excursion in Asia Minor. London: John Murray, 1841. 1st ed., large 8vo, modern buckram (front cover original cloth; original spine label). Two maps, partly colored; 36 full-page engraved plates, one of them colored; text illus. Errata leaf. Verso of frontis. dusty, some foxing of plates, else a very good copy. Trebizond 18-143 1983 $175

FELLOWS, CHARLES Travels and researches in Asia Minor... London: John Murray, 1852. 8vo. 2 folding maps, 4 folding plates. Orig. green cloth. Rubbed, spine ends worn. Adelson Africa-85 1983 $150

FELLOWS, GEORGE   Arms, Armour and Alabaster round Nottingham. Nottingham; H. B. Saxton, 1907. 1st ed., 4to, subscribers list, partly printed in red, 20 plates and other illus., quarter white buckram, gilt, marbled sides, with gilt decoration on upper cover, t.e.g., others uncut, cover soiled and stained, marbled paper foxed, margins of some leaves trifle foxed. Loosely inserted is a signed mounted photo. of the author. Deighton 3-128 1983 £25

FELLOWS, GEORGE   History of the South Notts. Yeomanry Cavalry. Nottingham, 1895. Half-title, portrait frontis. 8 plates (1 with key). Imp. 8vo. Orig. blue and yellow cloth gilt. T.e.g., others uncut. Very fine. Edwards 1042-564 1983 £55

FELS, FLORENT   Ange-Jacques Gabriel, Premier Architecte du Roi. Paris: Emile-Paul, 1912. 44 heliogravure and other plates with titled tissue guards, 1 genealogical chart. Folio. Wrappers. Uncut. No. 268 of a limited edition of 300 copies only, printed on hollande. Intermittent pale foxing, not affecting plates. Rare. Ars Libri 32-234 1983 $750

FELS, FLORENT   James Ensor: Geneve: Pierre Cailler, 1947. 70 plates (7 color). 4to. Cloth. Ars Libri 32-205 1983 $45

FELTHAM, OWEN   Resolves a Duple Century ye 4th Edition. London, Imprinted (by Thomas Purfoot) for Henry Seile, 1631. 4to, orig. calf, 18th century rebacking, front joint cracked. The second complete edition, complete with the leaf before the title "The Face of the Booke vnmasked." Ravenstree 94-79 1983 $185

FELTON, CHARLES N.   A Contested Election in California. (new Almaden), ca. 1887. First edition. Illus. Half morocco. Ginsberg 46-95 1983 $150

FELTON, EDMOND   Engins invented to save much blood and moneyes... London: printed for Thomas Underhill, 1644. First edition. Small 4to. Disbound. Rare. Ximenes 63-312 1983 $600

THE FEMALE Faction: or, the gay subscribers, a poem. London: printed for J. Roberts, 1729. Folio, wrappers, 1st ed. Title shaved a trifle close at the top, but generally a very good copy. Ximenes 64-230 1983 $600

FENELON, FRANCOIS DE SALIGNAC DE LA MOTHE The Adventures of Telemachus, the Son of Ulysses. London: for the Author, 1768. 4to. Cont. calf, gilt, gilt panelled spine with morocco label, gilt. 24 engraved vignettes by Charles Grignion, numerous tail-pieces, and 2 pp. list of subscribers. Joints neatly repaired. Traylen 94-330 1983 £30

FENELON, FRANCOIS DE SALIGNAC DE LA MOTHE The Adventures of Telemachus, Son of Ulysses. New York: T. & J. Swords for David Longworth. (1796-97). 8vo., 2 vols., two frontispieces and 12 plates. Rebound in leather. Fine set. In Our Time 156-269 1983 $200

FENICHEL, OTTO   The Collected Papers of. NY: reprint edition. Two vols. Gach 94-326 1983 $20

FENICHEL, OTTO   Hysterien Und Zwangsneurosen. Wien: IPV, 1931. First edition. Fine in orig. cloth. Gach 94-327 1983 $50

FENICHEL, OTTO   Perversionen, Psychosen, Charakterstoerungen. Wien: IPV, 1931. First edition. Very good copy in orig. yellow printed wrappers. Gach 94-328 1983 $50

FENN, G. MANVILLE   The Cankerworn. London: Chatto & Windus, 1901. First edition. Orig. decorated cloth. Former owner's blind and ink stamps on front free endpaper. Fine. MacManus 278-1882 1983 $65

FENN, G. MANVILLE   Dutch the Diver; or, A Man's Mistake. London: Cassell & Co., Ltd., n.d. First edition. Orig. pictorial boards. Spine and covers somewhat worn. Very good. MacManus 278-1883 1983 $65

FENN, G. MANVILLE   Glyn Severn's School-Days. Edinburgh & London: W. & R. Chambers, Ltd., 1904. First edition. 8 drawings by Charles Pears. Orig. pictorial cloth. Front inner hinge starting. Fine. MacManus 278-1884 1983 $50

FENN, G. MANVILLE   In An Alpine Valley. London: Hurst & Blackett, 1894. First edition. 3 vols. Orig. embossed cloth. Near-fine. MacManus 278-1885 1983 $350

FENN, G. MANVILLE   The Kopje Garrison. London & Edinburgh: W. & R. Chambers, 1901. First edition. 8 illus. by W. Boucher. Orig. pictorial cloth. Inscription on flyleaf. Inner hinges cracked. Covers somewhat worn. Good. MacManus 278-1886 1983 $65

FENN, G. MANVILLE   Mahme Nousie. London: Hurst & Blackett, Ltd., n.d. First one-volume edition. Orig. cloth. Inner hinges cracked. Former owner's name label on front endsheet. Very good. MacManus 278-1887 1983 $85

FENN, G. MANVILLE   Walsh The Wonder-Worker. London: W. & R. Chambers, 1903. First edition. 8 illus. by W.H.C. Groome, R.B.A. Orig. pictorial cloth. Extremities lightly rubbed. Very good. MacManus 278-1888 1983 $35

FENN, JOHN   Original Letters, written during the Reigns of Henry VI, Edward IV, and Richard III... London, 1787-1823. First edition. 5 vols. 4to. 19th century half green calf, gilt, fully gilt panelled spines with morocco labels, gilt. 4 engraved frontis., 3 of which are coloured, and a lithographed frontis., vignette title-pages and 40 plates, 3 of which are coloured. Traylen 94-328 1983 £180

FENNER, DUDLEY   A Counter Poyson. At London: Printed by Robert Waldegrave, (1584). First edition, black letter, woodcut ornament at head of title-page, complete in spite of pagination jump, though possibly wanting two further blank leaves at end, small 8vo, cont. limp vellum. A small portion in the upper blank margin of title-page torn away just clean of ornament. Fenning 60-107 1983 £350

FENNER, DUDLEY   A Counter-Poyson... London: by Robert Waldegrave. First edition. Cr. 8vo. Printed in Black Letter, calf, gilt spine with morocco label, gilt. Some side-notes and a few headlines cut into. Traylen 94-331 1983 £220

FENNING, DANIEL   The universal spelling-book. Rotterdam: printed and sold by J. Hendriksen, 1806. 12mo. Orig. blue-grey stiff wrappers. Woodcut frontis. Backstrip missing. Ximenes 63-224 1983 $75

FENOLLOSA, ERNEST   Certain Noble Plays of Japan. Churchtown, Dundrum: the Cuala Press, 1916. 8vo. Boards, linen spine, uncut edges. Limited edition of 350 numbered copies. Traylen 94-329 1983 £90

FENOLLOSA, ERNEST   The Chinese Written Character as a Medium for Poetry. Stanley Nott, 1936. First edition. Covers just a little marked. Dust wrapper. Name on flyleaf. Very nice. Rota 231-486 1983 £65

FENTON, EDWARD   Soldiers and Strangers: Poems. New York, 1945. 8vo. Cloth. Review copy with slip laid in. Clipping about the book on inside endboard, fine in dj. In Our Time 156-270 1983 $25

FENTON, ELIJAH   An Epistle to Mr. Southerne, from Mr. El. Fenton. From Kent, Jan. 28. 1710/11. London: Printed for Benj. Tooke...and Bernard Lintott...1711. 8vo, complete with half-title. A bit dust-soiled but otherwise a good copy in new wraps. First edition. Quaritch NS 7-44 1983 $275

FENWICK, JOHN   The Proceedings Against Sir John Fenwick, Bar. (London:) Printed in the Year, 1698. First edition, 8vo, cont. panelled calf, neatly rebacked. Fenning 60-108 1983 £28.50

FEODOR Vladimir Larrovitch: An Appreciation of His Life and Works. New York: The Authors Club, 1918. 1st ed. Orig. cloth, label. Fine copy with memento mori photos, letters, memoirs, etc. Jenkins 155-562 1983 $25

FERBER, EDNA   Cimarron. Garden City: 1930. First edition. Tan cloth. Very good in chipped dust jacket. Bradley 66-162 1983 $30

FERBER, EDNA   A Peculiar Treasure. NY, 1939. Special bookseller's edition, limited to 500 copies, bright fine copy in very good dustwrapper. Quill & Brush 54-456 1983 $30

FERCHL, F.   Chemisch-Pharmazeutisches Bio-und-Bibliographikon. Mittenwald, 1937. Large 8vo. Wrappers. Gurney JJ-119 1983 £30

FERE, CHARLES (1852-1907)   The Pathology of the Emotions. London: The University Press, 1899. Tall 8vo. Publisher's maroon cloth. First edition in English. Ads. Gach 95-125 1983 $75

FERENCZI, SANDOR (1873-1933) Bausteine Zur Psychoanalyse. IPV, 1927 (Vols. 1 & 2); Bern: Huber, 1939 (Vols. 3 & 4). Vols. 1 & 2 in publisher's blue buckram (spines rubbed). Vols. 3 & 4 in orig. printed wrappers. Gach 95-126 1983 $150

FERENCZI, SANDOR (1873-1933) Contributions to Psycho-Analysis. Boston: 1916. First edition in English. Spine tips slightly rubbed. Gach 95-127 1983 $50

FERENCZI, SANDOR (1873-1933) The Development of Psycho-Analysis. NY: N. M. D. Pub. Co., 1925. First edition. Ad leaf. Orig. printed boards, edges shelfworn. Gach 95-128 1983 $65

FERENCZI, SANDOR (1873-1933) Introjection Und Uebertragung. Leipzig: Franz Deuticke, 1910. Fine in orig. wrappers. Gach 95-129 1983 $35

FERENCZI, SANDOR (1873-1933) Versuch Einer Genitaltheorie. IPV, 1924. Publisher's cloth-backed boards. Fine copy. Gach 95-130 1983 $150

FERGUSON, ADAM   An Essay on the History of Civil Society. Edinburgh: printed for A. Millar & T. Caddel and A. Kincaid, and J. Bell, 1767. 1st ed., 4to, a little light spotting here and there, cont. speckled calf, spine elaborately gilt in compartments, joints cracked but sound. A very good copy with large margins. Bookplate. Pickering & Chatto 21-35 1983 $750

FERGUSON, ADAM   The Morality of Stage-Plays seriously considered. Edinburgh: 1757. 8vo, wrappers, 1st ed. Title a bit foxed, else an excellent copy. Ximenes 64-205 1983 $425

FERGUSON, ALASTAIR MAC KENZIE   India Rubber and Gutta Percha. Cololbo, Ceylon: A.M. & J. Ferguson, (1887). 8vo. Orig. cloth. Second edition. Some marginalia. A good copy. Zeitlin 264-147 1983 $50

FERGUSON, ALBERT B.   Roentgen Diagnosis of the Extremities and Spine. N.Y., 1941. 8 illus. 4to, ex-lib. Argosy 713-174 1983 $50

FERGUSON, CHARLES D.   California Gold Fields. Oakland: Biobooks, 1948. Illustrations. Limited to 750 copies. Jenkins 153-91 1983 $30

FERGUSON, CHARLES D.   The Experiences of a Forty-Niner During Thirty Four Years Residence in California and Australia. Cleveland, 1888. Illus., orig. cloth. First edition. Ginsberg 46-255 1983 $100

FERGUSON, CHARLES D.   The Experiences of a Forty-Niner During a Third of a Century in the Gold Fields. Chico, Cal.: H.A. Carson, 1924. Plates. Frontis. Original pictorial blue wrappers. Minor chipping to spine. Signed presentation copy from author. Limited ed. Jenkins 153-192 1983 $55

FERGUSON, JAMES   A Plain Method of Determing the Parallax of Venus. London, Printed for, and sold by the author..., 1761. 1st ed., 4to, title-page, 4 folding engraved plates; disbound. Pickering & Chatto 22-41 1983 $450

FERGUSON, JAMES   Select mechanical exercises: shewing how to construct different clocks... London: Strahan and Cadell, 1773. First edition. 8vo. 19th-century black half morocco. With 9 folding plates. Slight wear. Very good copy. Ximenes 63-73 1983 $325

FERGUSON, JOHN   Some Aspects of Bibliography. Edinburgh: George P. Johnston, 1900. First edition. 8vo. Cloth. Paper spine label, t.e.g., others uncut. Limited to 300 copies. Label soiled, else a fine copy. Oak Knoll 48-155 1983 $85

FERGUSON, JOHN ALEXANDER   Bibliography of Australia. Sydney & London: Angus & Robertson, 1941-69. 7 vols. Cloth in dust wrappers, some use and browning to earlier vols., but generally fine. Dawson 470-108 1983 $500

FERGUSON, MAXWELL   State Regulation of Railroads in the South. N.Y., 1916. 1st ed., later cloth, morocco label, original printed wrappers bound in. Jenkins 151-74 1983 $45

FERGUSON, MUNGO   Printed Books in the Library of the Hunterian Museum... Glasgow, 1930. Folio. First edition. Orig. binding. Fye H-3-1035 1983 $85

FERGUSON, SAMUEL   Congal. Dublin: Edward Ponsonby, 1872. First edition, 4to, some light foxing of the preliminary leaves, but a very good copy in the orig. cloth, gilt, the spine neatly repaired. Fenning 60-109 1983 £45

FERGUSON, SAMUEL   Poems. Dublin: William McGee, 1880. First edition, first issue, with the "Fountain" badge leaf which was not in later issues, roy. 8vo, orig. blue cloth, gilt. With an inscription by the author, dated Dublin, July 1880. Fenning 60-110 1983 £55

FERGUSON, WILLIAM   Light of Paradise. Lincoln, MA: Penmaen Press, 1973. Octavo. First edition. Wood engravings by Michael McCurdy. Limited to 200 copies signed by poet and illustrator/printer. Near mint with very slightly chipped glassine. Bromer 25-278 1983 $95

FERGUSSON, ERNA   Murder & Mystery in New Mexico. Albuquerque, 1948. Frontis. by Peter Hurd. Fine copy of the first edition in dust jacket. Photographs. Jenkins 151-243 1983 $35

FERGUSSON, JAMES   History of Indian and Eastern Architecture. John Murray, 1910. With 2 folding maps, 65 plates and 512 full-page and other illus. 2 vols. 8vo, orig. cloth, t.e.g. Fenning 60-111 1983 £55

FERGUSSON, ROBERT   Poems... Edinburgh. Printed by Walter & Thomas Ruddiman. MDCCLXXIII. 12mo, title-vignette, other vignettes and two early portraits inserted, some foxing throughout, but a good copy. Early polished calf, joints rubbed. First edition. Quaritch NS 7-45 1983 $475

FERLINGHETTI, LAWRENCE   Pictures of the Gone World. San Francisco: City Lights (1955). Stiff wrappers. First ed. A fine copy. In Our Time 156-271 1983 $200

FERLINGHETTI, LAWRENCE   The Secret Meaning of Things. New York: New Directions, (1969). 1st ed., 1 of 150 numbered and signed copies. Orig. blue cloth, gilt, box with label. Mint copy. Jenkins 155-396 1983 $75

FERMI, ENRICO   Sui Momenti Magnetici dei Nuclei Atomici. Rome, 1930. 8vo. Orig. printed wrappers. Offprint. First edition. Kraus 164-72 1983 $500

FERMI, ENRICO   Sul Calculo degli Spettri degli Ioni. Rome, 1930. One blank leaf. 8vo. Orig. printed wrappers. Offprint. First separate edition. Kraus 164-73 1983 $250

FERNANDEZ, JUSTINO   Obras de Jose Clemente Orozco en la Coleccion Carrillo, Mexico. Mexico: Privately Printed, 1949. 119 plates (17 color). Large 4to. Cloth. Dust jacket. Edition limited to 1500 numbered copies. Ars Libri 32-497 1983 $125

FERRANDIS, JOSE   Marfiles arabes de Occidente. Madrid, 1935 - 1940. 2 vols. 116, (4)pp., 67 collotype plates; 305, (3)pp., 90 collotype plates. Numerous text illus. 4to. Cloth. 1/2 morocco. Edition limited to 800 copies. Ars Libri SB 26-69 1983 $225

FERRARI, GIULIO   I due Canaletto. Antonio Canal, Bernardo Bellotto, pittori. Torino: E. Celanza, 1914. 56 plates. 4to. Boards. Ars Libri 33-65 1983 $65

FERRARI, GIULIO   La tomba nell'arte italiana dal periodo preromano all'odierno. Milano, n.d. 38pp., 272 plates. Lrg. 4to. Cloth. Ars Libri SB 26-70 1983 $150

FERRARI, ORESTE   Luca Giordano. Napoli: Edizioni Scientifiche Italiane, 1966. 3 vols. 45 plates. 680 illus. Square 4to. Cloth. Dust jacket. Slipcase. Ars Libri 33-162 1983 $300

FERRARO, ARMANDO   Experimental Catalepsy. Utica, NY: State Hospitals Press, 1932. Library buckram. Bookplate and stamp on rear paste-down. Gach 94-330 1983 $25

FERRERO, GUGLIELMO   Characters and Events of Roman History from Caesar to Nero. NY, 1909. 8vo, cloth. Salloch 385-223 1983 $20

FERRERO, GUGLIELMO   Nouvelle Histoire Romaine. 3/4 blue calf, gilt top. Paris, 1936. 8vo. Salloch 385-225 1983 $30

FERRETI, F.   Diporti notturni dialoghi familiari con la dimonstratione digurale intagliata da Michel Aggelo Marrelli anconitano. Ancona, Saluioni, 1580. 12mo, 3 d-p plates; 2 s-p plates; 28 maps. Cont. vellum. Very slight browning. Arkway 22-49 1983 $4,500

FERRI, ARMANDO   Alessandro Magnasco. Roma, 1922. 40 plates. Large 8vo. Wrappers. Ars Libri 33-211 1983 $27.50

FERRIER, DAVID   Functions of the Brain. N.Y., 1876. First American edition. 8vo, illus. Argosy 713-176 1983 $250

FERRIER, DAVID   The Localization of Cerebral Disease. N.Y., 1879. Illus. Small 8vo, cloth. First American edition. Argosy 713-177 1983 $75

FERRIER, J. A.   The Franco-German War 1870-71. Chatam: Royal Engineers Institute, 1894. 8vo. Orig. cloth. 39 folding maps at end. Spine slightly worn and soiled. Small paper shelf label. Ink inscription on endpaper. Good. Edwards 1042-337 1983 £15

FERRIER, J. P.   History of the Afghans. London, 1858. First edition. 2 maps, 1 folding, shaken. 8vo. Orig. cloth. Good. Edwards 1044-245 1983 £185

FERRIER, SUSAN   Destiny; or, the Chief's Daughter. Edinburgh: Robert Cadell, 1831. First edition. 8vo. Cont. half calf, marbled boards, morocco labels, gilt. Half-titles, errata slip, and advert. leaf in vol 1. 3 vols. Traylen 94-333 1983 £150

FERRIER, SUSAN   Destiny. Edinburgh: Robert Cadell, 1831. First edition, 3 vols. Half titles, orig. grey boards, paper labels, uncut. Vols. I & II contain, attached to the inside of the leading board, the ticket of the Ambleside Book Society. Very good copy in orig. condition. Jarndyce 30-383 1983 £66

FERRIER, SUSAN   Destiny. Edinburgh, for Robert Cadell, etc., 1831. First edition. 3 vols. Large 12mo, half-titles. Cont. half calf (head-bands worn). Occasional foxing. Hannas 69-54 1983 £50

FERRIER, SUSAN   The Inheritance. Wm. Blackwood, 1824. First edition, 3 vols., half titles. Half calf, marbled boards, red and green labels, spines gilt, v.g. Jarndyce 30-382 1983 £38

FERRIS, BENJAMIN   A History of the Original Settlements on the Delaware, from Its Discovery by Hudson to the Colonization Under William Penn. Wilington, Wilson & Head, 1846. Illus., maps and plates. Three quarter morocco. Ginsberg 46-231 1983 $125

FERRIS, BENJAMIN   Utah and the Mormons. N.Y., 1854. 3 plates. Orig. cloth. First edition. Ginsberg 47-904 1983 $50

FERRIS, JOHN ALEXANDER   The Financial Economy of the U.S. Illustrated. San Francisco, 1867. Orig. cloth. First edition. Ginsberg 47-80 1983 $75

FERRIS, WARREN A.   Life in the Rocky Mountains 1830-35. Salt Lake City, (1940). Argosy 716-616 1983 $20

FERRISS, HUGH   The Metropolis of Tomorrow. N.Y., 1929. Full page drawings, mostly of buildings. Cloth. Ink name. Covers rubbed with some soil. 3 parts in one volume. King 45-322 1983 $75

FERRISS, HUGH   The Metropolis of Tomorrow. NY 1929. Cloth, bookplate, blind-stamped and ink stamped end papers, corners bumped, slightly rubbed. King 46-384 1983 $25

FERRY, ELISHA P.   Message of...Governor of Washington Territory, to the Legislative Assembly, Thurs. Oct. 9, 1873. Olympia, 1873. Orig. printed wraps. First edition. Ginsberg 47-924 1983 $75

FERRY, ELISHA P.   Message to the Legislative Assembly, Session of 1879. Olympia, 1879. Orig. printed wraps. First edition. Ginsberg 47-927 1983 $65

FESCA, FRIEDRICH ERNST   Ein Satz aus Dem 13. Psalm... Bonn & Coeln, N. Simrock, (1822). First edition. Fine set, from the Lowell Mason Collection. Salloch 387-59 1983 $100

FESSENDEN, THOMAS G.   Democracy Unveiled. Boston: Printed for David Carlisle, 1805. Old boards. A couple of signatures starting, otherwise a very good copy. Reese 13-273 1983 $175

FESTING, G.   When Kings Rode to Dheli. London, 1913. Plates. Thick 8vo. Orig. cloth. Good. Edwards 1044-246 1983 £18

THE FESTIVAL of Wit, being a Collection of Bon-Mots, Anecdotes, etc of the most exalted characters. Dresden: for C. & F. Walther, 1795. 12mo. Boards. Fine copy. Very rare. Heath 48-472 1983 £125

FETHERSTONEAUGH, MARIA GEORGINA   Alan Dering. London: Richard Bentley & Son, 1880. First ed., 2 vols., orig. dec. cloth, edges very slightly worn. One endpaper trifle discolored by an erasure. Near fine. MacManus 278-1889 1983 $225

FETHERSTONEHAUGH, MARIA GEORGIANA   Kingsdene. Londo : Bentley, 1878. First edition. 2 vols. 8vo. Orig. light blue cloth. Rather rubbed, inner hinges cracked. Ximenes 63-151 1983 $60

FEUILLEE, L.   Journal des observations physiques, mathematiques et botaniques faites par ordre du Roy sur les cotes orientales de L'Amerique meridionale. Paris, 1714-25. 31 maps and plates of view, 50 plates of medicinal plants, 3 vols., 4to, cont. binding (different styles). Vol. 3 does not include the 2nd section on medicinal plants and the title-page is that for vol. 2, while there is some warer-staining particularly in the lower margins. Rare. Wheldon 160-377 1983 £250

FEUILLET, OCTAVE   Vie de Polichinelle... Paris, Hetzel, nd, (ca. 1865). New edn. Illus. par Bertall. Frontis., title vignette & numerous b&w text illus. Royal blue fine ribbed cloth with central oval col'd picture within ornate gilt decor. frame, black decor. borders both cvrs., gilt titling, a.e.g., re-cased with new eps., sl. thumbing contents, vg. Hodgkins 27-69 1983 £18

FEULNER, ADOLF   Munchner Barockskulptur. Munchen, 1922. (Sammelbande zur Geschichte der Kunst und des Kunstgewerbes. Vol. I.). xii, 16pp., 96 plates. Sm. 4to. Boards, 1/4 cloth (slightly worn). Ars Libri SB 26-72 1983 $35

FEWKES, J. W.   Antiquities of the Mesa Verde National Park. Washington: BAE No.51, 1911. Map, numerous photo-illus. Orig. olive green cloth. Fine. Jenkins 152-245 1983 $45

FEYNES, FRANCOIS   Medicina Practica. Lyon, 1650. First edition. 4to, cont. vellum. Fine engraved title vignette, decorated initials. Argosy 713-178 1983 $175

FFOULKES, CHARLES   Sword, Lance & Bayonet. Cambridge, 1938.
First edition. Roy. 8vo. Orig. cloth. Frontis. portrait. 2 plates
and 80 illus. Spine slightly faded. Good. Edwards 1042-338 1983
£40

FIELD, B. RUSH   Medical Thoughts of Shakespeare. Easton,
Penn, 1885. Tall 8vo, pr. wraps; ex-lib. Argosy 713-180 1983 $45

FIELD, DAVID D.   The Genealogy of the Brainerd Family.
New York: 1857. First edition. Illus. Cloth. Worn, shaken, foxed.
Bradley 66-474 1983 $25

FIELD, EDWARD   Revolutionary Defences in Rhode Island.
Providence, 1896. 1st ed. Maps, plans, illus. 8vo. Ex-library
but nice. Morrill 289-517 1983 $20

FIELD, EUGENE   The Complete Tribune Primer. Boston:
Mutual Book Co., (1901). 75 drawings by F. Opper. 8vo, green cloth,
stamped in white. Fine. Argosy 714-290 1983 $25

FIELD, EUGENE   Dibden's Ghost and Boccacio. (Boston,
W.X. Bixby), 1922. Large red initials. Half black cloth stamped
in gilt over printed boards. One of 500 copies printed by D.B.
Updike at the Merrymount Press. Fine. Houle 22-362 1983 $45

FIELD, EUGENE   The Lullaby Book. Evanston: Schori
Press, 1963. Printed in blue on silver-flecked paper. Illus. stamped
in gold on both covers. Limited to 600 copies. Mint in full blue
morocco. A.e.g. (1 13/16 x 2 1/4; 46x54mm). Bromer 25-426 1983
$175

FIELD, EUGENE   Lullaby Land. Lane, 1898. Illus. by
Charles Robinson. Numerous b&w illus. Sage green vertical ribbed
cloth with gilt vignette & decor. by Robinson on cvrs., uncut,
bkstrip & top edge fr. cvr. faded, nice clean copy. Hodgkins 27-70
1983 £35

FIELD, EUGENE   Lullaby Land. Lane, 1898. 1st edn.
Blue suede with gilt titling, fr. cvr. & bkstrip, blue marbled eps.,
a.e.g., binding variant, suede faded & discol'd at bkstrip, sl. rubbed
at edges, insc. verso fr. ep., illus. by Charles Robinson, contents
nice. Hodgkins 27-71 1983 £25

FIELD, EUGENE   Poems of Childhood. London, 1904. First
English edition with these illus. (by Max Parrish). 4to. Covers just
a little faded and marked. Nice. Rota 230-462 1983 £50

FIELD, EUGENE   Two Poems... (Boston) Privately
printed for W.K. Bixby (1922). First edition thus. Facs. of the
orig. manuscripts. Half cloth over blue boards. One of 250 copies
printed by D.B. Updike at the Merrymount Press. Fine copy. Houle
21-335 1983 $45

FIELD, EUGENE   Verse and Prose... Boston: The
Bibliophile Society, 1917. Small 4to. Half parchment over cloth,
t.e.g., others uncut. With many full page facsimiles of Field's
manuscripts. Some cover soiling, else very good copy. Oak Knoll
49-179 1983 $30

FIELD, EUGENE   The Writings in Prose and Verse of...
London: Prepared by London Book Exchange, n.d. (Ca. 1901). 8vo, three
quarter blue leather, boards, t.e.g. Gilt lettering on the spine, with
three circular emblems on every spine. 12 vols. A fine set. In Our
Time 156-273 1983 $1,000

FIELD, HENRY M.   Gibraltar. London, 1889. First edition.
8vo. Orig. cloth. Frontis., 10 plates (1 folding), 1 map. Slightly
worn and soiled. Good. Edwards 1042-339 1983 £18

FIELD, HENRY M.   Our Western Archipelago. New York:
Charles Scribner's Sons, 1902. Illustrations. Original cloth.
Jenkins 153-194 1983 $40

FIELD, JOSEPH E.   Three Years in Texas. Austin, 1935.
Stock reissue of the 1836 rarity. Jenkins 152-850 1983 $35

FIELD, MICHAEL   A Selection from the Poems of Michael
Field. Poetry Bookshop, 1923. First edition. Repaired dust wrapper.
Very nice. Rota 231-203 1983 £15

FIELD, RACHEL   Time Out of Mind. New York: MacMillan,
1935. 1st ed. Orig. cloth, dj. Fine fresh copy with author's 4
page ALS laid in. Jenkins 155-401 1983 $20

FIELD, ROSWELL   The Bondage of Ballinger. Chicago:
Fleming H. Revell Co., 1903. First edition. 8vo. Orig. boards,
paper spine label, t.e.g., others uncut. Limited to only 212
numbered copies. Presentation copy. Paper covering on front hinge
slightly cracked. Scarce. Oak Knoll 49-180 1983 $65

FIELD, ROSWELL   The Bondage of Ballinger. Chicago,
Revell, 1903. Frontis. Title page in red and black. Boards, paper
spine label, t.e.g., uncut (spine faded and rubbed, hinges starting)
else, good - very good. One of 212 copies of the deluxe edition.
TN from the publisher attesting to this laid in loose. Houle
22-363 1983 $35

FIELD, SARA BARD   Vineyard Voices. S.F., 1930. 8vo, two-
tone boards. With hand-colored vignettes by Paula Norton. Presswork
and binding by Lawton & Freda Kennedy. One of 75 copies signed by
Johnck. Perata 28-76 1983 $90

FIELD, STEPHEN J.   Personal Reminiscences of Early Days
in California with Other Sketches. (Wash.), printed for a few
friends, not published, (1893). Orig. half morocco, hinges
strengthened, spine chipped at head and foot. Inscribed presentation
copy from Field to Hon. James C. Carter. Ginsberg 47-81 1983
$150

FIELD, STEPHEN J.   The Railroad Tax Case. N.p., (1882).
Dbd. Ginsberg 47-83 1983 $50

FIELD, THOMAS W.   The Battle of Long Island. Brooklyn,
(1869). Folding map, thick 8vo, mod. green buckram. One of 1000
copies. Argosy 710-352 1983 $35

FIELDING, H. B.   Sertum Plantarum. 1844. Plates, 8vo,
boards. Lacks the title-page. Wheldon 160-1521 1983 £45

FIELDING, HENRY   The Adventures Of Joseph Andrews.
London: James Cochrane & Co., 1832. First edition. Illus. by
Cruikshank. Full light blue morocco with marbled endpapers by
Zaehnsdorf. Spine a trifle faded. Near-fine. MacManus 277-1234
1983 $200

FIELDING, HENRY   Amelia. London, A. Millar, 1752.
4 vols., small 8vo, old calf, hinges broken, spines badly defective,
outer blank edges of few leaves in vol. 4 torn with no loss, complete
with advertisement leaf in vol. II. The J.P. Morgan (duplicate)
copy, with morocco gilt labels, of the first edition. Ravenstree 94-
81 1983 $450

FIELDING, HENRY   Amelia. London: 1752. First edition.
4 vols. Lacks final blank in first vol. Ad leaf in second vol.
Two signatures misbound in third vol. Nice copy in contemporary calf,
later lettering pieces. Beverly Chew copy with his leather bookplates.
Bromer 25-41 1983 $650

FIELDING, HENRY   Amelia. For A. Millar, 1752. First
edition. 4 vols., 12mo, final blank leaf in vol. I, and advertisement
leaf in vol. II. Cont. calf, gilt (worn). Early name on titles.
Hannas 69-56 1983 £200

FIELDING, HENRY   Don Quixote in England. London:
printed for J. Watts, 1754. 2nd edition, 8vo, title a little browned,
modern cloth. Bookplates. Pickering & Chatto 19-15 1983 $250

FIELDING, HENRY   An Enquiry into the Causes of the Late
Inscrease of Robbers... London, A. Millar, 1751. 8vo, modern half
calf antique style, single small wormhole in outer blank edge of
last few leaves, bookplate removed, some age-darkening and light
fraying; uncut copy complete with half title. Ravenstree 94-83
1983 $165

FIELDING, HENRY   The Fathers: or, the good-natur'd man.
London: printed for T. Cadell, in the Strand, 1778. First ed., 8vo,
advertisements, modern morocco-backed boards, spine lettered in gilt.
A nice copy. Pickering & Chatto 19-16 1983 $225

FIELDING, HENRY   The Historical Register for the year
1736. London: printed by J. Roberts. 8vo, last page a little dust-
soiled, in wrappers. 2nd edition. Pickering & Chatto 19-17 1983
$250

FIELDING, HENRY   The History of the Life of the Late
Mr. Jonathan Wild the Great. New York: Limited Editions Club,
1943. Illus. by T.M. Cleland. Small 4to. Cloth-backed marbled
paper covered boards, paper spine label, slipcase. Limited to
1500 numbered copies and signed by Cleland. Oak Knoll 49-267
1983 $45

FIELDING, HENRY   The History of Tom Jones. For A.
Millar, 1749. 6 vols., 12mo, final blank leaves in vols. I and III.
Cont. calf, gilt spines (minor wear at some heads and tails). Cont.
signature of Eliza: Tryon on each title. One gathering misbound in
vol. VI. Hannas 69-57 1983 £450

FIELDING, HENRY   The History of Tom Jones, a Foundling.
Edinburgh; Printed in the Year 1771. 3 vols, 12mo, contemporary
calf. Hill 165-33 1983 £45

FIELDING, HENRY   The History of Tom Jones, the Foundling
in His Married State. J. Barker, Russell-Court, Dryry Lane, 1786.
12mo. Calf, rebacked, maroon label. Very Good. Jarndyce 31-29 1983
£120

FIELDING, HENRY   Love in Several Masques. London:
John Watts, 1728. First edition. Title leaf a little soiled. Bound
in later half calf over marbled boards. Karmiole 75-53 1983 $175

FIELDING, HENRY   The Miser. London: printed for J.
Watts, 1733. First edition, 8vo, advertisement, modern morocco-
backed marbled boards, spine lettered in gilt. Pickering & Chatto
19-18 1983 $450

FIELDING, HENRY   The Miser. London, J. Watts, 1733. 8vo,
modern tan polished calf, gilt spine, by Sangorski & Sutcliffe, joints
rubbed, name on title, top edge cut close shaving and occasionally
bleeding rubbing headline and/or page numeral, some age spotting,
decent copy. First edition. Ravenstree 94-85 1983 $275

FIELDING, HENRY   The Modern Husband. London: printed
for J. Watts, 1732. First edition, 8vo, advertisements, title and
first and last leaves of text rather stained, corner of G1 torn off,
losing one word of text only. 19th century morocco-backed boards,
spine lettered in gilt. Very rare. Pickering & Chatto 19-19 1983
$850

FIELDING, HENRY   Pasquin. London: printed for J. Watts,
1736. First edition, 8vo, advertisements, title printed in red and
black, in recent red quarter morocco with marbled boards, gilt
lettering on spine. A fine copy. Pickering & Chatto 19-20 1983
$165

FIELDING, HENRY   A Proposal for Making an Effectual
Provision for the Poor... London, A. Millar, 1753. 8vo, half
morocco gilt, bookplate, title bit soiled with old marginal stab-
holes, short tear to blank margin of folding plan mended. Thick
paper copy of the first edition, first issue. Ravenstree 94-84 1983
$420

FIELDING, HENRY   The Temple Beau. London: printed for
J. Watts, 1730. 1st edition, 8vo, advertisement, modern morocco
backed boards, spine lettered in gilt. Pickering & Chatto 19-21
1983 $350

FIELDING, HENRY   The Tragedy of Tragedies. London:
Printed, and Dublin Re-printed and sold by George Faulkner, at the
Pamphlet-shop (sic) in Essex Street, pposite (sic) to the Bridge.
Circa 1731. First Irish edition, 12mo, wrapper, a very good copy.
Fenning 60-112 1983 £165

FIELDING, HENRY   Tragedy of tragedies, or Tom Thumb the
Great. Cambridge, very privately printed for the 10th Dinner
of the Spenser Society of Pembroke-hall, 1925. 8vo, uncut in quarter
white cloth over paper boards, two red paper labels, fine. 500
numbered copies (this copy unnumbered). Deighton 3-129 1983 £18

FIELDING, HENRY   The Wedding Day. London, printed for
A. Millar, 1743. First edition, 8vo, small portion missing from top
of L4 affecting a few words, else a good copy in modern morocco-backed
marbled boards, spine lettered in gilt. Pickering & Chatto 19-23
1983 $250

FIELDING, HENRY   The Works of Henry Fielding, Esq. London:
Printed for A. Millar, opposite Catharine-Stree, in the Strand, 1762.
First collected edition. 4 vols. Frontis. port. by Hogarth. Cont.
calf, rebacked with matching calf, morocco labels. Bookplates on
front endsheets. Occasional foxing. Covers rubbed. Very good.
MacManus 278-1891 1983 $750

FIELDING, HENRY   The Works. London, 1771. 8 vols.
8vo. Cont. calf, gilt panelled spines with red and green morocco
labels, gilt. Engraved portrait. Traylen 94-334 1983 £195

FIELDING, SARAH   The Adventures of David Simple. For
A. Millar, 1744. First edition. 2 vols. 12mo, cont. calf, gilt.
Hannas 69-58 1983 £200

FIELDING, SARAH   The Adventures of David Simple.
Printed for A. Millar, 1744. 2nd ed., revised and corrected.
2 vols, 12mo, contemporary calf. Hill 165-34 1983 £95

FIENNES, NATHANAEL   A Speech in Answere to the Third
Speech of the Lord George Digby. (London) Printed in the yeare 1641.
4to, disbound, cont. manuscript date on title of 9, Feb; 40, the
day of the speech. First edition. Ravenstree 94-86 1983 $55

FIERENS, PAUL   Gino Severini. Paris/Milano: Chroniques du Jour/Ulrico Hoepli, 1936. 35 gravure plates. 4to. Wraps.
Ars Libri 33-586 1983 $60

FIERENS, PAUL   Les Le Nain. Paris: Floury, 1933.
96 plates. Large 4to. Wrappers. Dust jacket. Ars Libri 32-400
1983 $100

FIFTH Annual Convention of the Independent Order of Odd Fellows of
Arizona. Phoenix: Herald Print, 1888. Wrappers. Back cover lacking.
Front cover loose. Badly worn and stained. Dawson 471-7 1983 $300

A FIFTH Collection of Papers Relating to the Present Juncture of
Affairs in England. Printed, and are to be sold by Rich Janeway,
1688. First edition, complete thus, 4to, wrapper. Fenning 62-118
1983 £24.50

FIFTY Years in Brown County Convent. Cincinnati, McDonald & Co.,
1895. First edition. Illustrated. 8vo. Morrill 290-384 1983 $20

FIGGIS, DARRELL   The Mount of Transfiguration. Dublin &
London: Maunsel & Co. Ltd., 1915. First edition. Orig. parchment-
backed boards. Dust jacket. Fine. MacManus 278-1893 1983 $35

FIGGIS, DARRELL   The Paintings of William Blake. New
York: Charles Scribner's Sons, 1925. 100 collotype plates (5
color). Captioned tissue guards. 4to. Boards, 1/4 cloth. Edition
limited to 1150 copies. Ars Libri 32-39 1983 $150

FILLMORE, MILLARD   Message from...Requesting Information
in Regard to the Fisheries on the Coasts of the British Possessions
in North America. Wash., 1852. Sewn and uncut as issued. First
edition. Ginsberg 46-140 1983 $50

FILLMORE, MILLARD   Message of the President...the
Correspondence in Relation to the Seizure of the British Ship Albion,
in Oregon, for a Violation of the Revenue Laws. Wash., 1851. First
edition. Dbd. Ginsberg 47-728 1983 $25

FILLMORE, MILLARD   Oregon Territory. Wash., 1852.
Dbd. First edition. Ginsberg 47-729 1983 $45

FILMER, EDWARD   A Defence of plays: or, the stage
vindicated. London: printed for Jacob Tonson, 1707. 8vo, cont. calf,
slightly stained, later paper label on spine. 1st ed. Wanting
flyleaves, but an excellent copy, complete with half-title. Ximenes
64-207 1983 $350

FILMER, ROBERT   The Free Holders Grand Inquest Touching
Our Soveraigne Lord the King and His Parliament. (London): printed
(1648). 4to, new half calf gilt by Sangorski & Sutcliffe, stabholes
in blank inner margin, few small spots, very fine large uncut copy.
First edition. Ravenstree 94-87 1983 $350

THE FINANCIAL house that Jack built. London: J.M. Richardson, 1819. First edition. 8vo. Disbound. Scarce. Ximenes 63-482 1983 $50

FINBERG, ALEXANDER J.   The Drawings of David Cox. London: George Newnes, n.d. 44 plates (4 tipped-in color). Large 4to. Boards, 1/4 cloth. Slightly worn. Ars Libri 32-126 1983 $45

FINCH, ANNE   Miscellany Poems, On Several Occasions. London, Printed by J.B. and Sold by Benj. Tooke, et al., 1713. 8vo. Cont. panelled calf, gold title lettering, extremities of spine worn. 1st ed. With usual cancels. Very nice, clean copy. O'Neal 50-22 1983 $400

FINCH, HENRY   Law. London, 1678. 8vo. 4th & last printing of the 17th century. Lightish embrowning throughout, tears to margins of 2 leaves, just affecting a few words, bound in later full sheep, neatly rebacked, spine gilt-ruled & lettered, blind decorated. Clean copy. Boswell 7-76 1983 $350

FINDLEY, PALMER   The Story of Childbirth. Garden City, 1934. First edition. 8vo. Orig. wrappers. Fye H-3-171 1983 $20

FINDLEY, WILLIAM   Observations on "The Two Sons of Oil". Pittsburgh, 1812. Errata slip. Old calf, front board detached, a very good copy. Reese 18-375 1983 $75

FINE, ALVIN I.   In Loving Memory of Mae Swig, June 12, 1895. October 15, 1957. (San Francisco: The Grabhorn Press, 1958). Large 4to, tipped-in photo on title-page. Printed in magenta and black. Edition ltd. to 100 copies. Black cloth spine over dec. boards; leather spine label. Karmiole 76-52 1983 $75

FINE, ORONCE   La Theorique des Cielz. Paris: Simon Du Bois for Jean Pierre de Tours, 31 August 1528. 47 woodcuts by the author, one on f.42v signed with his monogram. Folio. 18th-century half-calf over marbled boards, gilt-stamped title label on spine. First edition. Kraus 164-74 1983 $4,200

THE FINE Book, A Symposium. Pittsburgh: Laboratory Press, 1934. Octavo. Limited to 225 copies. Bound by Grabau in full leather with gilt-stamped covers and spine, which has five raised bands. Extremely fine. T.e.g. Bromer 25-168 1983 $250

FINERTY, JOHN F.   War-Path and Bivouac... Chicago, (1890). Plates. Folding map. Full brown morocco, gilt extra, a.e.g., a pub.'s deluxe or presentation binding. Lower inner edge of title-page cracking, lower corners rubbed, otherwise a fine copy. Reese 19-220 1983 $275

FINLAY, GEORGE IRVING   Colorado Springs. Colorado Springs: The Out West Co., (1906). Double-page map. Orig. green cloth. Karmiole 76-32 1983 $40

FINLAY, JOHN H.   Thucydides. Cambridge, 1942. 8vo, cloth. Salloch 385-782 1983 $30

FINLAYSON, ARCHIBALD W.   A Trip to America. Glasgow, 1879. Orig. cloth. First edition. Inscribed on flyleaf "To Mr. C.W. Loring-with Arch. W. Finlayson's compliments, January, 1880..." Ginsberg 46-257 1983 $100

FINLAYSON, JOSEPH   The Voice of Facts from the Convent of S. Joseph, Ranelagh, Dublin. Edinburgh: William Blackwood, 1824. First and apparently only edition, including half-title, large 12mo, orig. boards, uncut. A very good copy. Fenning 61-140 1983 £45

FINNEY, CHARLES G.   The Circus of Dr. Lao. N.Y.: Limited Editions Club, 1982. 4to, patterned cloth; boxed. Argosy 714-291 1983 $125

FINNEY, CHARLES G.   The Circus of Doctor Lao. New York: Abramson, 1946. Illus. by Artzybasheff. Orig. cloth. Very good copy in chipped and torn dj. Jenkins 155-402 1983 $25

FINNEY, CHARLES G.   Past the End of the Pavement. New York: Holt, (1939). Cloth. First edition. Fine in lightly soiled dust jacket, which has been reinforced on the verso. Reese 20-405 1983 $50

FINSCH, O.   Beitrag zur Fauna Centralpolynesiens. Ornithologie der Viti-, Samoa- und Tonga-Inseln. Halle, 1867, 14 coloured plates, royal 8vo, half cloth. Wheldon 160-702 1983 £100

FINSCH, O.   Die Papageien. Leyden, 1867-68. Folding map, 1 plain and 5 coloured plates and 6 tables of geographical distribution, 2 vols., 8vo, qtr. morocco (slightly rubbed). Some foxing and a few corners affected by damp, but on the whole a good copy. A classic work. Wheldon 160-701 1983 £200

FIOCCO, GIUSEPPE   Bernard Strozzi. Roma, 1921. 24 plates. Small 4to. Wrappers. Ars Libri 33-349 1983 $20

FIOCCO, GIUSEPPE   Giambattista Crosato. Padova: "Le Tre Venezie", 1944. Second edition. 72 plates. Small 4to. Wrappers. Dust jacket. Ars Libri 33-127 1983 $75

FIOCCO, GIUSEPPE   Guardi. Milano: ERI. Edizioni RAI. Radiotelevisione Italiana, 1965. 40 color plates under passepartouts. 60 text illus. Small folio. Cloth, 1/4 calf. Slipcase. Edition limited to 1600 copies, printed for the Amici della Sipra. Ars Libri 33-183 1983 $125

FIOCCO, GIUSEPPE   Le pitture del Mantegna. Torino: ERI. Edizioni RAI. Radiotelevisione Italiana, 1951. 30 color plates each under passepartout. 25 text illus. Folio. Cloth. 1/4 vellum. Slipcase. Ars Libri 33-220 1983 $85

FIRBANK, RONALD   The Artificial Princess. London, 1934. First edition. One of 2000 copies. Intro. by C. Kennard. Lower cover stained. Good. Rota 231-205 1983 £12

FIRBANK, RONALD   Inclinations. Lon., 1916. 500 copies, edges slightly rubbed and spine lightly sunned, bottom edge of boards slightly creased, else very good. Quill & Brush 54-458 1983 $75

FIRBANK, RONALD   Odette D'Antrevernes and A Study in Temperament. London: Elkin Mathews, 1905. First edition. Orig. seagreen wrappers. One of 500 copies. Edges very slightly frayed and faded. Very good. MacManus 278-1895 1983 $300

FIRBANK, RONALD   Odette - A Fairy Tale for Weary People. London, 1916. First separate printing. Slightly spotted wrappers. Slightly bumped and with a small tear at foot of spine. Fine. Gekoski 2-48 1983 £25

FIRBANK, RONALD   Odette. London, 1916. First Separate and first illus. edition. One of 2000 copies. Wrappers. Edges of wrappers a little darkened and some light foxing on lower wrapper. Very nice. Rota 231-204 1983 £20

FIRBANK, RONALD   Santal. London, 1921. First edition. One of 300 copies. Wrappers. Edges of wrappers a little faded and chipped. Nice. Rota 230-210 1983 £50

FIRBANK, RONALD   Sorrow in Sunlight. London, (1924). First English edition of "Prancing Nigger." One of 1000 numbered copies. Cloth rubbed at head and foot of spine. Very nice. Rota 230-211 1983 £30

FIREBAUGH, ELLEN   The Physician's Wife and the Things that Pertain to Her Life. Philadelphia, 1894. First edition. 8vo. Orig. wrappers. Fye H-3-172 1983 $60

FIRST Book of Records of the Town of Pepperellborough. Portland, 1896. 1st ed. Small light cover stain. 8vo. Morrill 288-251 1983 $35

FIRST Help in Accidents and in Sickness. Boston, Alexander Moore, 1871. 1st ed. 12mo. Morrill 289-70 1983 $25

FIRST Time in America: A Selection of Poems Never Before Published in the U.S.A. New York, 1948. 8vo. Cloth. Review copy with slip laid in. Vg-fine in rubbed dj. In Our Time 156-26 1983 $25

FIRTH, RAYMOND   Art and Life in New Guinea. London: The Studio, 1936. 8 tipped-in plates. Numerous text illus. 4to. Cloth. Ars Libri 34-800 1983 $60

FISCHER, EMIL HERMANN   Exercises in the Preparation of Organic Compounds... Glasgow: Wm. Hodge & Co., 1895. 8vo. Orig. blue cloth. 20 text figures. Slightly rubbed. A very good copy. Zeitlin 264-148 1983 $45

FISCHER, EMIL HERMANN   Organische Synthese und Biologie. Berlin: J. Springer, 1908. 8vo. Orig. printed wrappers. First edition. A fine copy. Zeitlin 264-149 1983 $85

FISCHER, EMIL HERMANN   Untersuchungen aus Berschiedenen Gebieten... Berlin: Springer, 1924. 8vo. Orig. blue cloth. Ads. Spotted and marked. A good copy. Zeitlin 264-152 1983 $80

FISCHER, EMIL HERMANN   Untersuchungen uber Kohlenhydrate und Fermente. Berlin: Springer, 1909-1922. 2 vols. 8vo. Orig. paper wrappers. First Collected edition. Slightly worn and spotted. Zeitlin 264-153 1983 $120

FISCHER, OTTO   Hans Baldung Grien. Munchen: F. Bruckmann, 1939. 68 plates (4 color). 39 illus. 4to. Cloth. From the library of Jakob Rosenberg. Ars Libri 32-18 1983 $40

FISH, HENRY C.   Freedom or Despotism. Newark, 1856. First edition. Dbd. Ginsberg 47-402 1983 $50

FISH, HOWARD   The Wrongs of Man. Sherwood, Neely & Jones, 1819. First edition, half title. Uncut. Orig. grey wraps., v.g. Jarndyce 30-693 1983 £48

FISHBEIN, MORRIS   Doctors and Specialists... Indianapolis, 1930. First edition. 8vo. Orig. wrappers. Fye H-3-174 1983 $25

FISHENDEN, R. B.   The Penrose Annual, Review of the Graphic Arts. London 1940. Cloth, numerous illus., slightly soiled else good in tattered dw. King 46-379 1983 $25

FISHER, A. H.   Through India and Burma with Pen & Brush. London, (1910). Coloured frontis. Numerous plates. Pictorial cloth. 8vo. Good. Edwards 1044-248 1983 £20

FISHER, ALFRED YOUNG   The Ghost in the Underblows. Los Angeles, Ward Ritchie Press, 1940. First edition. Illus. with drawings by Alvin Lustig. Black cloth stamped in gilt and blind. One of 300 copies. This is the "printer's copy." Very good. Houle 22-1157 1983 $75

FISHER, GEORGE   The American Instructor... Phila.: B. Franklin and D. Hall, 1748. Ninth edition revised and corrected. 4 (of 6) calligraphic plates. Full morocco (front hinge broken). First American edition of this famous compendium for farmer, merchant and ailing planter, revised and largely rewritten by Franklin to suit American needs. Plates contain the first American calligraphic models. Very good. Felcone 20-53 1983 $350

FISHER, HOWELL   Report on the Agricultural and Mineral Resources of Virginia and West Virginia. N.Y., 1871. Dbd. First edition. Ginaberg 46-258 1983 $50

FISHER, JOHN   The political plough that Jack built. London: printed by Wm. Shackell, etc., 1820. First edition. 8vo. Disbound. With 10 woodcut illus. Ximenes 63-483 1983 $60

FISHER, JOHN D.   Description of the Distinct, Confluent, and Inoculated Small Pox, Varioloid Disease, Cow Pox, and Chicken Pox. Boston, 1834. 2nd ed. 13 colored plates. Small folio, orig. boards, cloth back, paper label. Binding rubbed and partly stained; backstrip partly torn. Morrill 289-71 1983 $95

FISHER, PAYNE   A Synopsis of Heraldry. London, L. Curtis and T. Simmons, 1682. 8vo, cont. calf newly rebacked, blindstamped crest on upper cover, signature of Simon Griebelin on endpaper, bookplate, one plate mended in blank portion. First and only edition. Ravenstree 94-90 1983 $325

FISHER, SAMUEL   The Bishop Busied Beside the Businesse. (London,), printed in the month, called August, in the year 1662. 4to, disbound, last portion wormed at upper edge, sometime straying into text but not affecting legibility; some age-browning, light soiling, minor spotting. First edition. Ravenstree 94-91 1983 $87.50

FISHER, SAMUEL   Christ the Refuge of His People. (Morristown? 1812). Dsb. Good. Reese 18-376 1983 $25

FISHER, VARDIS   Children of God. New York: 1939. First edition. Brown cloth, yellow cloth spine. Near fine in jacket. Bradley 66-164 1983 $35

FISHER, VARDIS   Children of God. New York, 1939. Cloth and boards. About fine, wanting dust jacket. Reese 19-223 1983 $30

FISHER, VARDIS   City of Illusion. Caldwell, Idaho: The Caxton Printers, ltd., 1941. Orig. gilt-stamped dark green sheep, top edge gilt. A fine copy. First edition. No. 69 of 100 copies, and signed by Fisher. Grunder 6-22 1983 $135

FISHER, VARDIS   City of Illusion. Caldwell: Caxton Printers, 1941. 1st ed., limited to 1000 unsigned copies. Orig. cloth. Fine copy in fresh dj with two tears. Jenkins 155-404 1983 $45

FISHER, VARDIS   City of Illusion. Caldwell: Caxton Printers, 1941. 1st trade ed. Orig. cloth, dj. Fine copy. Jenkins 155-405 1983 $25

FISHER, VARDIS   A Goat for Azazel. Denver, Swallow, (1956). First edition. Dust jacket (some soiling and spotting), else, very good. One of 200 numbered copies signed by Fisher. Houle 22-365 1983 $95

FISHER, VARDIS   The Golden Room. N.Y., Vanguard, 1944. First edition. Dust jacket (a trifle nicked), else very good. Houle 21-339 1983 $35

FISHER, VARDIS   In Tragic Life. Caldwell, Caxton, 1937. First edition. Dust jacket (light fading, small nicks). Very good. Houle 22-366 1983 $65

FISHER, VARDIS   Toilers of the Hills. Boston, Houghton Mifflin, 1928. First edition. Brown cloth stamped in green. Very good - fine. Houle 22-367 1983 $45

FISHER, VARDIS   We Are Betrayed. Caldwell, Idaho & New York, (1935). 1st trade ed. Orig. brown cloth, gilt. Fine copy inscribed by Fisher to friend, with date and place, the dj torn and cracked but complete. Jenkins 155-407 1983 $60

FISHER, WALTER M.   The Californians. London, 1876. Orig. cloth. First edition. Ginsberg 47-84 1983 $45

FISHER, WILLIAM   The Petrel. Henry Colburn, 1850. First edition, 3 vols. 2pp/4pp inserted ads. vol. I. Orig. boards, purple-brown cloth spines, paper labels. Inner hinges a little weak. Langport Subscription Library labels on end papers. Jarndyce 31-695 1983 £48

FISHMAN, JOSEPH F.   Sex in Prison. Nat'l. Library Press, (c. 1934). Illus. Argosy 713-182 1983 $25

FISK, JAMES   The Life of Col. James Fisk, Jr.... Togher with a Sketch of the Grand Duke Alexis, of Russia. Chicago, etc., 1872. Illus. Folding plate (lacking half). Cloth, good. Reese 19-224 1983 $175

FITCH, JOHN   Annals of the Army of the Cumberland... Philadelphia, 1863. 1st ed. Map and illus. 8vo, all edges gilt. Morrill 286-151 1983 $30

FITCHETT, JOHN   Bewsey, a Poem. Warrington: Printed by W. Eyres...MDCCXCVI. 4to, half-title dusty, stains on several leaves not obliterating text; with five-page list of subscribers, modern boards. First edition. Quaritch NS 7-47 1983 $150

FITT, MARY   Requeim for Robert. Lon., (1942). Vincent Starrett's copy with his signature and bookplate, edges rubbed, else very good in slightly chipped and frayed, soiled, good dustwrapper. Quill & Brush 54-460 1983 $30

FITTON, E.   Conversations on Botany. 1828. 21 plain plates, post 8vo, original boards, joints worn, some pencil underlining. Wheldon 160-1522 1983 £12

FITZ-ADAMS, ADAM   The World. Dublin 1756-7. 4 vols. Vols. 1 and 2 are 3rd ed., other two appear to be 1st Irish. Old rebacked calf, with new labels, bookplates, names. King 46-285 1983 $85

FITZCLARENCE, GEORGE A.   Journal of a route across India... London: John Murray, 1819. 4to. 2 maps. 17 plates (9 hand-colored). Full tan calf, gilt. Rubbed, lacks 1/2 title, but internally excellent. Adelson Africa-86 1983 $550

FITZGERALD, EDWARD   Agamemnon. London: Bernard Quaritch, 1876. First edition. 4to. Full brown morocco, gilt, by Zaehnsdorf. With a holograph revision on page 74 in the author's hand. Small bookplate removed from front endpaper. Fine. MacManus 278-1897 1983 $225

FITZGERALD, EDWARD   Euphranor. London: Pickering, 1851. First edition. 12mo. Orig. green cloth. Extremities of spine a trifle rubbed. Fine. MacManus 278-1898 1983 $375

FITZGERALD, EDWARD   Letters and Literary Remains. Macmillan, 1889. First edition, 3 vols. Half title and front. in all vols.; 2 pp ads. vol. I. Orig. red cloth, spines sl. faded. Jarndyce 30-993 1983 £38

FITZGERALD, EDWARD   Letters from Edward Fitzgerald to Bernard Quaritch, 1853 to 1883. Bern. Quaritch ltd., 1926. Front. & plates, orig. dark blue cloth. Untrimmed, t.e.g. Jarndyce 30-996 1983 £14

FITZGERALD, EDWARD   Miscellanies. London: Macmillan & Co., 1900. First edition. Orig. cloth. Dust jacket (torn). Fine. MacManus 278-1900 1983 $25

FITZGERALD, EDWARD   Two Dramas from Calderon. (Bungay: John Childs & Son, 1865). First edition. Orig. wrappers. Issued without title-page. One of about 100 copies printed. H. Buxton Forman's copy, with his bookplate on front inner wrappers. Wrappers expertly rebacked. In a half-morocco slipcase. Fine. MacManus 278-1902 1983 $400

FITZGERALD, EDWARD   The Two Generals. N.p.: n.d. (ca.1865). First edition. Small 4to. 8 pages, unbound as issued. Fine. MacManus 278-1903 1983 $400

FITZGERALD, FRANCIS SCOTT KEY   All the Sad Young Men. New York, (1926). 8vo. Cloth. A fine copy in dj. In Our Time 156-277 1983 $950

FITZGERALD, FRANCIS SCOTT KEY   All the Sad Young Men. New York, Scribners, 1926. First edition, dark green cloth stamped in blind and gilt, spine bit faded, some foxing within, else good to very good. Houle 22-368 1983 $125

FITZGERALD, FRANCIS SCOTT KEY   All The Sad Young Men. NY, 1926. First edition, first printing, edges very slightly rubbed, minor cover wear, else near fine in lightly frayed and chipped dustwrapper with 1 1/2 inch slit at bottom front spine gutter. Owner's name and address. Wrapper appears to be early issue. Quill & Brush 54-462 1983 $850

FITZGERALD, FRANCIS SCOTT KEY   All The Sad Young Men. NY, 1926. First issue, corners and spine edges very slightly rubbed, very good. Quill & Brush 54-461 1983 $175

FITZGERALD, FRANCIS SCOTT KEY   All the Sad Young Men. New York: 1926. First edition, first issue. Dark green cloth. Name in ink on front free end paper. Very good. Bradley 66-165 1983 $125

FITZGERALD, FRANCIS SCOTT KEY   The Beautiful and the Damned. New York: Scribners, 1922. 1st ed., 1st printing. Orig. green cloth, gilt. Mint copy in dj with only slightest signs of use. Jenkins 155-410 1983 $900

FITZGERALD, FRANCIS SCOTT KEY   The Beautiful and Damned. N.Y., 1922. First edition, first issue. 8vo, cloth. Fine copy, in a first issue dust jacket, with black lettering. Dust jacket is chipped and has been strengthened on the verso with tape. Argosy 714-292 1983 $850

FITZGERALD, FRANCIS SCOTT KEY   The Beautiful and the Damned. NY, 1922. Bright copy in dustwrapper with half inch chip on front corner, front edge (on fold) worn, other minor chipping, still good copy. Quill & Brush 54-468 1983 $750

FITZGERALD, FRANCIS SCOTT KEY   The Beautiful and the Damned. New York, 1922. 1st issue. 8vo. Morrill 286-596 1983 $40

FITZGERALD, FRANCIS SCOTT KEY   The Crack-Up. (NY: 1945). First edition. Fine in cloth-backed boards, slightly rubbed at corners. Chipped dust wrapper. Owner's signature. Bromer 25-42 1983 $65

FITZGERALD, FRANCIS SCOTT KEY   Dearly Beloved. Iowa, 1969. Graphics by Byron Burford, limited to 300 copies, first 30 copies signed by artist (no. 25), large boards and cloth, spine slightly rubbed on ends, otherwise fine. Quill & Brush 54-463 1983 $175

FITZGERALD, FRANCIS SCOTT KEY   F. Scott Fitzgerald's Ledger. D.C., (1972). Limited to 1000 copies, fine to new in slipcase. Quill & Brush 54-464 1983 $75

FITZGERALD, FRANCIS SCOTT KEY   The Great Gatsby. New York: Charles Scribner's Sons, 1925. First edition, first issue. 8vo. Orig. cloth. Fine copy. Jaffe 1-88 1983 $250

FITZGERALD, FRANCIS SCOTT KEY   The Great Gatsby. New York: Scribners, 1925. 1st ed., 1st printing with all six orig. readings. Orig. cloth, gilt. Fine copy. Jenkins 155-411 1983 $200

FITZGERALD, FRANCIS SCOTT KEY   The Mystery of the Raymond Mortgage. NY, 1960. Promotional material distributed by Random House, not for sale, limited to 750 copies, fine in paperwraps. Quill & Brush 54-471 1983 $175

FITZGERALD, FRANCIS SCOTT KEY   Poems, 1911-1940. Bloomfield Hills: Bruccoli Clark, 1891. 1st ed., 1 of 100 copies numbered and signed by James Dickey, who wrote the foreword. Orig. cloth, gilt, dj. Mint, at published price. Jenkins 155-412 1983 $25

FITZGERALD, FRANCIS SCOTT KEY   The Price Was High: The Last Uncollected Stories of F. Scott Fitzgerald. New York, 1979. 8vo. Wraps. Uncorrected proof copy. A fine copy. In Our Time 156-279 1983 $150

FITZGERALD, FRANCIS SCOTT KEY   Tales of the Jazz Age. Toronto: The Copp Clark Company, 1922. 8vo. Cloth. First Canadian ed., with title page insertion and incorporating the Scribner sheets. Error on copyright page "1902". Name of former owner on front flyleaf, some flaking to lettering on spine, otherwise a very good plus copy. In Our Time 156-276 1983 $200

FITZGERALD, FRANCIS SCOTT KEY   Tales of the Jazz Age. New York, (1922). 8vo. Cloth. Fine copy. In Our Time 156-275 1983 $100

FITZGERALD, FRANCIS SCOTT KEY   Taps at Reveille. NY, 1935. First edition, second state, tiny hole in rear spine hinge, else fine, bright copy in dustwrapper showing wear on edges and slight soiling but still very good. 5100 copies in total edition. Quill & Brush 54-466 1983 $650

FITZGERALD, FRANCIS SCOTT KEY   Tender is the Night. New York, 1934. 8vo. Cloth. A bright copy of the book in the uncommon dj which is worn though largely intact but with heavy tape mending on interior. Short holograph note on last blank flyleaf. Signed by author on second inner flyleaf. In Our Time 156-278 1983 $1250

FITZGERALD, FRANCIS SCOTT KEY   This Side of Paradise. N.Y., 1920. First edition. 8vo. First printing, with "published April, 1920" and publishers seal on copyright page. Fine copy, except for owner's rubber stamp on copyright page. Argosy 714-296 1983 $200

FITZGERALD, FRANCIS SCOTT KEY   The Vegetable. New York, Charles
Scribner's Sons, 1923. First ed., green cloth, blind stamped on upper
cover, stamped in gilt on spine, else very good. Houle 22-370 1983
$125

FITZGERALD, FRANCIS SCOTT KEY   The Vegetable. NY, 1923. Aside from
minor cover wear and faint circular stain on front board, very good.
Quill & Brush 54-473 1983 $75

FITZGERALD, GEOFFREY   Rockets in the Afternoon. New York:
Fine Editions Press, (1946). 8vo. Cloth. Review copy with slip
laid in. Fine in dj. Clipping on endboard. In Our Time 156-280
1983 $20

FITZGERALD, GEORGE ROBERT   The Riddle of the Late Unhappy George-
Robert Fitzgerald... London: for the Editor and sold by R. Jameson,
(1787?) Sole edition. 4to. Cont. half calf. Title browned and
waterstained, waterstains to about half of the work. Light wear to
binding. Heath 48-296 1983 £275

FITZGERALD, PERCY   Beauty Talbot. Richard Bentley, 1870.
First edition, 3 vols., bound as one. Orig. green remainder cloth,
rubbed, spine creased. Jarndyce 30-381 1983 £20

FITZGERALD, PERCY   The Life of Charles Dickens. Chatto &
Windus, 1905. First edition, 2 vols., half titles, front. Orig. (?)
red cloth, v.g. Jarndyce 30-185 1983 £20

FITZGERALD, PERCY   The Life of George Borrow. John
Murray, 1912. Second edition, frontis. and 12 other illus. Half
title, 4 pp ads, orig. green cloth, t.e.g. Jarndyce 30-899 1983
£16.50

FITZGERALD, PERCY   The Life of Laurence Sterne. London:
Chapman & Hall, 1864. First edition. Illus. from drawings by author.
2 vols. Orig. cloth. Inner hinges weak. Very good. MacManus 280-
4885 1983 $40

FITZGERALD, PERCY   The Life of Mrs. Cahterine Clive. London:
A. Reader, 1888. First edition. Frontispiece port. Orig. buckram
with printed spine label. Spine faded, front inner hinge cracking.
In a half-morocco slipcase. Very good. MacManus 278-1904 1983 $85

FITZGERALD, PERCY   The Pickwickian Dictionary and
Cyclopaedia. (1900). Orig. dark blue cloth, half title and front.
Orig. dark blue cloth, paper label. Very good. With W. Miller's
bookplate, and signed presentation inscription to Miller from the
publisher W.T. Spencer. Jarndyce 30-184 1983 £40

FITZGERALD, PERCY   Pickwickian Manners and Customs. First
edition, Roxburghe Press, (1897), Half title, front. 4 pp ads.
Uncut. Orig. maroon cloth, very good. Jarndyce 30-182 1983 £12.50

FITZGERALD, PERCY   Pickwickian Studies. New Century Press,
1899. Large 8vo, half title, 8 pp ads. Untrimmed, orig. maroon cloth,
sl. rubbing to following board, otherwise very good. Jarndyce 30-183
1983 £14.50

FITZGERALD, PERCY   Principals of comedy and dramatic
effect. London: Tinsley Brothers, 1870. 8vo, cont. half calf (rather
scuffed). 1st ed. Old library stamp on title. Ximenes 64-209
1983 $20

FITZGERALD, PERCY   Recreations of A Literary Man or Does
Writing Pay. London: Chatto & Windus, 1882. First edition. 2 vols.
Orig. cloth. Front outer hinge of Vol. 2 partially split at bottom.
Covers darkened. Institutional stamps on title-page. MacManus 278-
1905 1983 $35

FITZGIBBON, A.   Canadian Wild Flowers. Montreal, 1869.
Roy. 4to, original cloth, coloured title-page and 10 hand-coloured
plates. First edition. Rare. A little foxing and dust-soiling
and binding a trifle used, but a good copy. Wheldon 160-29 1983 £330

FITZGERALD, PERCY   Recreations of a Literary Man, or,
Does Writing Pay? Chatto & Windus, 1883. Orig. dull olive dec.
cloth. Jarndyce 31-696 1983 £10.50

FITZHERBERT, ANTHONY   La Novvelle Natura Breuiu... Londini,
in aedibus Richardi Tottelli, 1533. (Colophon dated 1560). 8vo,
cont. calf rebacked, inner margin of title restored. Ravenstree 94-
92 1983 $410

FITZPATRICK, THOMAS   The Bloody Bridge, and Other Papers
Relating to the Insurrection of 1641. Dublin: Sealy, Bryers, 1903.
First edition, 8vo, orig. cloth, t.e.g. Fenning 61-141 1983 £16.50

FITZPATRICK, THOMAS   Letter of Thomas Fitzpatrick, Indian
Agent, Upper Platte and Arkansas... Washington, 1847. Later wrappers.
Jenkins 153-771 1983 $150

FITZPATRICK, WALTER   The Great Conde and the Period of the
Fronde. T. Cautley Newby, 1873. First edition, including half-titles
& errata slips in both vols., 2 vols., 8vo, orig. cloth, by Leighton
Son & Hodge with their ticket, binding dull but thoroughly sound and
internally fine copies. Fenning 61-142 1983 £14.50

FIVE Cotton States and New York, or...Social & Economic Aspects of
the Southern Political Crisis. (N.p.), 1861. Orig. pr. wrs. Argosy
716-109 1983 $27.50

FLADER, LOUIS   Achievement in Photo-Engraving and
Letter Press Printing. Chicago, Illinois, 1927. 4to. Multiple
plates, many in color. Some restoration to leather binding. One
plate in text has some scuffing from having stuck to the opposite
leaf, otherwise a very good-fine copy. In Our Time 156-282 1983
$200

FLAGG, CHARLES A.   A Guide to Massachusetts Local History.
Salem, (1907). 1st ed. 8vo. Corners rubbed. Morrill 287-224
1983 $25

FLAGG, EDMUND T.   The Far West... New York, 1838. Two
vols., orig. plum cloth, paper labels. In a folding cloth case.
Reese 19-225 1983 $500

FLAGG, JARED B.   The Life and Letters of Washington
Allston. New York: Charles Scribner's Sons, 1892. 18 plates.
Stout 4to. Cloth. Slightly worn. From the library of James
Thrall Soby. Ars Libri 32-3 1983 $125

FLAGG, WILSON   Analysis of the Female Beauty.
Boston, 1834. First edition. 12mo, orig. cloth-backed boards.
Argosy 716-418 1983 $30

FLAHERTY, ROBERT   The Captain's Chair. London, 1938.
First edition. Cloth bubbled and small tear at head of spine. Author's
signed autograph presentation inscription. Good. Rota 230-212 1983
£12

FLAMSTEED, JOHN   Atlas Coelestis. London, 1729. First
edition. With engraved portrait of the author, and 27 double folio
engraved star charts. Large folio. Half calf. With ms. exlibris
of William Barclay and J.W. Streeter. Bookplate of the Franklin
Institute, all on the front endleaf. Kraus 164-76 1983 $4,250

FLAMSTEED, JOHN   Atlas Coelestis... 1781. Folio, with
engraved portrait by Vertue after Gibson, engraved vignette of
title, engraved initial, head and tailpiece, and 27 double-page
engraved star-maps on 28 sheets, faint marginal dampstaining on a
few sheets. A large copy in cont. quarter calf and marbled boards.
Third folio issue. Quaritch NS 5-40 1983 $6,000

FLAMSTEED, JOHN   Historiae Coelestis Britannicae...
1725. 3 vols., folio, with engraved portrait by Vertue after Gibson,
8 engraved plates and one full-page engraving on recto of letterpress,
engraved headpieces, some faint dampstaining in vol. I, some gatherings browned, margins of a few leaves of tables just shaved affecting
a few figures, but withal a good copy in cont. mottled French calf,
joints and corners repaired. Quaritch NS 5-41 1983 $6,500

FLAMSTEED, JOHN   Historia Coelestis Britannicae.
Londoni: Typis H. Meere. M.DCC.XXV. (1725). Folio, 3v., half
title, title. Errata, engraved portrait, six plates. Two engraved
plates. Cont. calf, rebacked, worn; blind stamped boards; library
stamp on t-p; minor staining and toning, generally clean internally;
very good. Arkway 22-50 1983 $2,850

FLANDRAU, GRACE   A Glance at the Lewis and Clark Expedition. N.p., ca.1920's. Frontis. portrait. Stiff printed wrappers.
Fine. Jenkins 152-687 1983 $30

FLANNER, HILDEGARD   A Tree in Bloom. S.F., Lantern Press,
1924. First edition. 4to, light blue boards, paper label. One of
500 printed by the Grabhorn Press. Houle 21-346 1983 $65

FLANNER, WILLIAM   A Brief Memoir of Stillwater Quarterly Meeting. Mountpleasent, Ohio, 1860. Orig. yellow printed wrappers. Jenkins 152-724 1983 $35

FLAT, PAUL   Le Musee Gustave Moreau. L'artiste, son oeuvre, son influence. Paris: Societe d'Edition Artistique, (1899). 18 fine heliogravure plates. Large 4to. Portfolio. Cloth, silk ties. Contents loose, as issued. Finely printed. Ars Libri 32-474 1983 $100

FLATMAN, THOMAS   Poems and Songs. London: S. & B.G. for Benjamin Took, 1674. First edition. Small 8vo. Cont. calf. Cancel title-page. John Drinkwater's copy with his signature and the date 1920, his elegant nude gold and black bookplate and in his hand, a precise bibliographical note correcting the errors of a former owner. Joints weak. Traylen 94-338 1983 £210

FLAUBERT, GUSTAVE   Bouvard and Pechuchet. London: H.S. Nichols, 1896. First English translation. Illus. Orig. pictorial cloth. Bookplate. Very good. MacManus 278-1906 1983 $125

FLAUBERT, GUSTAVE   Madame Bovary. Paris: Revue de Paris, 1856. Cont. three quarter red morocco, t.e.g., others untrimmed. Very slight occasional foxmarks, otherwise a fine copy, in a morocco faced slipcase. Reese 20-409 1983 $4,000

FLAUBERT, GUSTAVE   Madame Bovary. Paris, Michel Levy, 1857. 2 vols., 12mo, orig. printed paper wraps., minor wear and light chipping, faint traces of slight foxing, uncut, and preserved in folding cloth case. First edition. Ravenstree 94-98 1983 $3,950

FLAUBERT, GUSTAVE   Madame Bovary. NY: 1950. Quarto. Full-page color illus. by Pierre Brissaud engraved in wood by Theo Schmied. Limited to 1500 copies signed by Brissaud. Near mint with slightly rubbed slip-case. Bromer 25-247 1983 $75

FLAUBERT, GUSTAVE   Madame Bovary. NY, (n.d.). Illus. by Richard Lindner, spine slightly darkened, otherwise very good in worn slipcase. Quill & Brush 54-476 1983 $30

FLAUBERT, GUSTAVE   Salammbo. Paris: Collection Francaise, 1928. Orig. printed pictorial wraps. Illus., in color, by S. R. Lagneau. One of 965 numbered copies on Rives. Wraps. very slightly foxed, otherwise a fine copy. Reese 20-411 1983 $30

FLAUBERT, GUSTAVE   Salammbo. New York, The Brown House, 1930. Edition limited to 800 copies. 4to, orig. full leather. Spine slightly faded and with a few inkstains, in orig. box. Illus. by Alexander King. Morrill 287-114 1983 $25

FLAUBERT, GUSTAVE   Sentimental Education. London: H.S. Nichols Ltd., 1898. First edition in English. 2 vols. Orig. pictorial cloth. Illus. Top of spines worn. Very good. MacManus 278-1907 1983 $135

FLAUTAU, EDWARD   Atlas des Menschlichen Gehirns und des Faserverlaufes. Berlin, 1899. Small folio, 1/2 morocco (lacks backstrips). Argosy 713-184 1983 $75

FLAVEL, JOHN   Husbandry Spiritualized; or, The Heavenly Use of Earthly Things. Elizabeth Town: Shepard Kollock, 1794. Full calf. Signature L is misnumbered H. Very nice. Felcone 19-15 1983 $45

FLAVEL, JOHN   Husbandry Spiritualized; or, The Heavenly Use of Earthly Things. Elizabeth Town: Shepard Kollock, 1795. Full calf (shabby, covers detached). Very good. Felcone 19-17 1983 $40

FLAXMAN, JOHN   Lectures on Sculpture. London, John Murray, 1829. 8vo, cont. green calf gilt, a.e.g., little foxing, front joint broken; the plates (52 in all) in fine condition. Ravenstree 94-100 1983 $115

FLECHSIG, PAUL (1847-1929) Die Koerperlichen Grundlagen Der Geistesstoerungen. Liepzig: Von Veit, 1882. Orig. printed wrappers, chipped. Unopened copy. Gach 95-132 1983 $65

FLECKER, JAMES ELROY   The Bridge of Fire. London: Elkin Mathews, 1907. First edition. Orig. wrappers. Edges a bit worn. Very good. MacManus 278-1908 1983 $150

FLECKER, JAMES ELROY   Bridge of Fire. London, 1907. Orig. red wrappers frayed and a little bruised, otherwise an excellent copy. First edition. Gekoski 2-49 1983 £40

FLECKER, JAMES ELROY   The Collected Poems. London: Martin Secker, (1916). First edition. Frontis. port. Orig. cloth with paper label on spine. Fine. MacManus 278-1909 1983 $35

FLECKER, JAMES ELROY   Forty-Two Poems. London: J.M. Dent & Sons, Ltd., 1911. First edition. Orig. cloth. Dust jacket. Very fine. MacManus 278-1910 1983 $150

FLECKER, JAMES ELROY   The King of Alsander. London, 1914. First edition, first issue. Red cloth. Spine faded and covers badly stained. Very good. Rota 231-212 1983 £40

FLECKER, JAMES ELROY   The Letters of J. E. Flecker to Frank Savery. Beaumont Press, 1926. First edition. One of 310 numbered copies. Half parchment, patterned boards. Fine. Rota 231-213 1983 £25

FLECKER, JAMES ELROY   The Old Ships. London: The Poetry Bookshop, (1915). First edition. Orig. pictorial wrappers (torn). MacManus 278-1911 1983 $50

FLECKER, JAMES ELROY   The Old Ships. London: The Poetry Bookshop, 1915. Second Thousand. Orig. pictorial wrappers. Very good. MacManus 278-1912 1983 $20

FLECKER, JAMES ELROY   Some Letters from Abroad. London, 1930. First edition. Numerous photographs. Edges spotted. Chipped, frayed, and slightly torn, internally repaired dustwrapper. Very good. Jolliffe 26-181 1983 £45

FLEG, EDMUND   The Wall of Weeping. L, 1929. One of 750 numbered copies signed by both author and translator, Humbert Wolfe. Spine edges bumped, otherwise very good in chipped dustwrapper. Quill & Brush 54-1571 1983 $40

FLEG, EDMOND   The Wall of Weeping. London: Victor Gollancz Ltd.; N.Y.: E.P. Dutton & Co., Inc., 1929. First edition, American issue. Orig. cloth. Dust jacket (chipped, dust-soiled). Limited to 750 copies, of which 250 are for America. Signed by author and translator. Very good. MacManus 280-5620 1983 $20

FLEMING, ALEXANDER   On the antibacterial action of cultures of a penicillium... London: H.K. Lewis & Co., 1929. Orig. offprint. 3 blank pages. 4 illus. and text-tables. 4to. Orig. orange printed wrappers. From the library of the Medical Research Council, Hampstead, with its acquisition stamp, dated 9 Aug. 1929, in upper right corner of front cover. In a morocco-backed case. Kraus 164-77 1983 $8,500

FLEMING, ALEXANDER   Penicillin: Its Practical Application. London: Butterworth, 1946. Plates. 1st ed. Orig. blue cloth, gilt. A scarce book in unworn condition. Fine copy. Jenkins 155-419 1983 $175

FLEMING, ALEXANDER   Penicillin. Its Practical Application. London: Butterworth, 1946. 8vo. Orig. green cloth. First edition. Numerous text figures. Slightly rubbed, shook. A very good copy. Zeitlin 264-154 1983 $80

FLEMING, ALEXANDER   Penicillin. London, 1946. First edition. Illus. 8vo, cloth. Argosy 713-185 1983 $75

FLEMING, ANDREW   Blood Stains in Criminal Trials. Pittsburgh, 1861. 1st separate ed. Presentation from author. 8vo. Half of spine lacking. Morrill 289-72 1983 $20

FLEMING, CLINT   When The Fish Are Rising. New York: Duell, Sloan & Pearce, 1947. 21cm. Frontis. portrait. Mapped endpapers. Frayed dust jacket. Fine. McGahern 53-54 1983 $25

FLEMING, DAVID HAY   Mary Queen of Scots. London: Hodder & Stoughton, 1897. Orig. cloth. First edition. From the library of J.M. Barrie, with his signature on the half-title and bookplate on the front endpaper. Spine darkened. Front hinge cracking. A good copy. MacManus 277-217 1983 $25

FLEMING, FRANCIS   Kaffraria and Its Inhabitants. London, 1853. 1st ed., small 8vo, vignette title-page, 9 plates, one loose and one repaired, folding map coloured in outline, original blue decorative cloth, faded, gilt back, neat library stamp on 2 leaves. Deighton 3-134 1983 £70

FLEMING, IAN   Casino Royale. London, 1953. First edition. Bookplate. Very slightly chipped dustwrapper, wrinkled and very slightly stained on inner flap. Very good copy. Gekoski 2-50 1983 £425

FLEMING, IAN   Diamonds are Forever. London: Cape, (1956). 1st ed. Orig. black cloth, stamped in silver. Very fine copy in very fine dj. Scarce. Jenkins 155-414 1983 $300

FLEMING, IAN   Diamonds are Forever. Lon., (1956). Light cover soiling, minor stains to top page edge, else very good in slightly frayed and stained, very good (later issue) dustwrapper. Quill & Brush 54-477 1983 $100

FLEMING, IAN   The Diamond Smugglers. Lon., (1957). Rear fly slightly skinned from piece of tape, else fine in dustwrapper with very minor wear to spine edges, else fine. Quill & Brush 54-481 1983 $75

FLEMING, IAN   Goldfinger. Lon., (1959). Bright, very good in lightly frayed and chipped, slightly soiled dustwrapper with price neatly inked over on flap. Quill & Brush 54-478 1983 $100

FLEMING, IAN   Live and Let Die. London, 1954. First edition. Bookplate. Worn and reinforced dustwrapper, missing a piece from the top of the spine. Very good. Gekoski 2-51 1983 £80

FLEMING, IAN   The Man With The Golden Gun. London (1965). First edition. Boards, pocket on r.e.p. else very good in slightly worn dust wrapper. King 46-286 1983 $100

FLEMING, IAN   Moonraker. London, 1955. First edition. Slightly worn, rubbed, and chipped dustwrapper with a small tear. Very good. Jolliffe 26-131 1983 £75

FLEMING, IAN   On Her Majesty's Secret Service. Lon., (1963). Very good or better in slightly chipped and soiled, very good dustwrapper. Quill & Brush 54-480 1983 $75

FLEMING, IAN   The Spy Who Loved Me. Lon., (1962). Tiny tear to front spine gutter, else very good, bright copy in slightly worn, price clipped dustwrapper. Quill & Brush 54-483 1983 $100

FLEMING, IAN   Thunderball. London, Cape (1961). First edition. Dust jacket. Very good. Houle 21-347 1983 $80

FLEMING, J.   A History of British Animals. Edinburgh, 1828. 8vo, cloth. Wheldon 160-379 1983 £25

FLEMING, J. WILMINGTON   The deserted cottage. London: printed for the author, by E. Spragg, etc., 1816. First edition. 8vo. Disbound. Half-title present; outer edges uncut. Ximenes 63-405 1983 $40

FLEMING, WALTER L.   Documentary History of Reconstruction: Political, Military, Social, Religious, Educational, and Industrial. Cleveland: Arthur Clark, 1906. 2 volumes, first edition, t.e.g. Fine set in slipcase. Illus. Jenkins 151-280 1983 $150

FLEMWELL, G.   Alpine Flowers and Gardens. 1910. 20 coloured plates from paintings by the author, 8vo, cloth. Wheldon 160-1942 1983 £12

FLESCHE, HERMAN   Tilman Riemenschneider. Bilder von Gunther Beyer und Klaus Beyer. Dresden: Verlag der Kunst, 1957. 180 plates. Large 4to. Cloth. Ars Libri 32-580 1983 $75

FLETCHER, ALICE C.   The Hako. Wash., 1904. Color plates, musical scores, text illus., 4to, later buckram. Argosy 716-215 1983 $35

FLETCHER, C. R. L.   Gustavus Adolphus. New York, 1890. First edition, large paper edition of 250 copies. 8vo. Orig. cloth. Portrait frontis., 27 plates, 1 folding, 1 folding coloured map, 3 text illus. Orig. paper label on spine. Very slightly soiled. Bookplate. Good. Edwards 1042-340 1983 £30

FLETCHER, DANIEL COOLEDGE   Reminiscences of California and the Civil War. Ayer, Mass., 1894. First edition. Portrait. Red cloth. Ex-library. Bradley 65-69 1983 $85

FLETCHER, F. MORLEY   Wood-block Printing. A description based on the Japanese practice. Hogg, Artistic Crafts Series, 1916. 1st ed., sm. 8vo, 7 collotype plates, original colour woodblock printed on Japanese hand-mader paper. Original holland-backed boards. Excellent copy. Deighton 3-135 1983 £30

FLETCHER, F. MORLEY   Wood-Block Printing. London: Sir Isaac Pitman & Sons, n.d. (ca. 1910). 8vo. Cloth-backed boards, dust jacket. Drawings and illus. by the author and A.W. Seaby. Spine of dust jacket is missing. Very good. Oak Knoll 48-158 1983 $22.50

FLETCHER, GILES   Christ's Victory and Triumph, In Heaven, and Earth, Over and After Death. Cambridge, Roger Daniel, for Richard Royston, 1640. Sm. 4to. 4 engraved pictorial plates. Full red morocco, aeg. 4th ed. Fine Huth copy with bookplate. O'Neal 50-23 1983 $400

FLETCHER, HERBERT P.   The St. Louis Exhibition, 1904. Batsford, 1905. First edition, with 15 plates and some other illus. 4to, orig. cloth, gilt. A very good copy. Fenning 60-118 1983 £18.50

FLETCHER, J. S.   Ballads of Revolt. London: John Lane, The Bodley Head, 1897. First edition. Orig. cloth. Contains an ALS from the author, 4 pages to C. H. Leversham of Adelphia College, Brooklyn. Spine faded, front inside hinge cracking. Former owner's signature. Good. MacManus 278-1913 1983 $50

FLETCHER, J. S.   God's Failures. N.Y. & London: John Lane, The Bodley Head, 1897. First American edition. Orig. cloth. Fine. MacManus 278-1914 1983 $45

FLETCHER, J. S.   Life in Arcadia. London: John Lane, The Bodley Head, 1896. First edition. Illus. by Patten Wilson. Orig. cloth-backed decorated boards. With a 3-2/3 page ALS, June 23rd, 1925, from the author to an editor, tipped in at the front. Extremities of spine worn. Good. MacManus 278-1915 1983 $65

FLETCHER, J. S.   The Yorkshire Moorland Murder. New York: Alfred A. Knopf, 1930. First edition. 8vo. Cloth. Cover wear, spotted. Oak Knoll 48-132 1983 $25

FLETCHER, JAMES C.   Brazil and the Brazilians portrayed in historical and descriptive sketches. Boston: Little, Brown & Co., 1867. 8vo. Folding map. 18 plates. Orig. green cloth. Lightly rubbed. Adelson Africa-61 1983 $150

FLETCHER, JAMES PHILLIPS   The Autobiography of a Missionary. Hurst & Blackett, 1853. Half titles, half brown morocco-grained cloth, labels on upper covers. Jarndyce 30-384 1983 £45

FLETCHER, JOHN   A dreadful phenomenon described and improved. Shrewsbury: J. Eddowes, etc., 1773. First edition. 12mo. Disbound. Ximenes 63-90 1983 $75

FLETCHER, JOHN W.   American Patriotism Farther Confronted with Reason, Scripture, and the Constitution. Shrewsbury, 1776. Title and half-title trimmed, not affecting the text. Calf and boards, overall good. Reese 18-113 1983 $125

FLETCHER, PHINEAS   The Purple Island. Cambridge, 1633. 3 parts in one. Small 4to, title in red & black. Blind-impressed calf. First edition. Rostenberg 88-57 1983 $750

FLETCHER, R. A.   Warships and Their Story. London, 1911. First edition. Thick roy. 8vo. Orig. blue decorated cloth. Coloured frontis. and 79 plates. Coloured illus. mounted on upper cover. Slightly worn and soiled. T.e.g. Some slight foxing. 3 large ink signatures on pages 50-51. Good. Edwards 1041-64 1983 £35

FLETCHER, WILLIAM Y.   English Book Collectors. London, 1902. 8vo, cloth, g.t. Illus. Duschnes 240-77 1983 $75

FLETCHER, WILLIAM Y   English Book Collectors. London: Kegan Paul, Trench, Trubner, 1902. First edition. Square 8vo. Green buckram, t.e.g. Illus. Allen Hazen's copy. Spine faded else very good. Oak Knoll 48-159 1983 $75

FLEURY, CLAUDE   A Short Historical Catechism. Detroit: Theophilus Mettez, 1812. Cont. mottled calf. In very fine condition. Presentation copy from Father Richard to Bishop John Carroll, [...] Fine. Felcone 21-40 1983 $3,000

FLEXNER, ABRAHAM   Daniel Coit Gilman Creator of the American Type of University. New York, 1946. First edition. 8vo. Orig. binding. Autographed by Flexner. Dust wrapper. Fye H-3-747 1983 $65

FLEXNER, ABRAHAM   Daniel Coit Gilman Creator of the American Type of University. New York, 1946. First edition. 8vo. Orig. binding. Fye H-3-748 1983 $25

FLEXNER, ABRAHAM   From the Report on the Johns Hopkins Medical School. (1910). 8vo. Orig. binding. Rear wrapper soiled. Very rare. Fye H-3-177 1983 $150

FLEXNER, ABRAHAM   I Remember - The Autobiography of Abraham Flexner. New York, 1940. First edition. 8vo. Orig. binding. Fye H-3-740 1983 $35

FLEXNER, ABRAHAM   Medical Education a Comparative Study. New York, 1925. First edition. 8vo. Orig. binding. Fye H-3-178 1983 $30

FLEXNER, ABRAHAM   Medical Education in Europe. New York, 1912. First edition. 8vo. Orig. printed wrappers. Scarce. Fye H-3-179 1983 $50

FLEXNER, ABRAHAM   Medical Education in the United States and Canada. New York, 1910. 8vo. Orig. cloth. Ex-library. Binding worn. Fye H-3-180 1983 $125

FLEXNER, ABRAHAM   Prostitution in Europe. New York, 1914. First edition. 8vo. Orig. binding. Fye H-3-182 1983 $35

FLEXNER, ABRAHAM   Universities American English German. 1931. Second edition. 8vo. Orig. binding. Fye H-3-183 1983 $25

FLEXNER, SIMON   William Henry Welch: and the Heroic Age of American Medicine. N.Y., 1941. First edition. Illus. Argosy 713-565 1983 $40

FLEXNER, SIMON   William Henry Welch and the Heroic Age of American Medicine. New York, 1941. 8vo. Orig. binding. Dust wrapper. Autographed by Flexner and co-author James T. Flexner. Fye H-3-993 1983 $30

FLICK, ALEX   History of the State of New York. NY: 1933-37. 1st ed. 10 vols., illus., maps. Blue buckram, g.t., ex library. Argosy 710-353 1983 $125

FLICKINGER, ROY C.   The Greek Theatre & Its Drama. Chicago, 1926. 4to, cloth. Salloch 385-107 1983 $25

FLINN, FRANK M.   Campaigning with Banks in Louisiana. Lynn, Mass., 1887. First edition. Extremely nice. Jenkins 152-626 1983 $175

FLINT, ABEL   A Discourse, Occasioned by the News of Peace...1815. Hartford, 1815. Dsb., library stamp, good. Reese 18-473 1983 $20

FLINT, F. S.   Otherworlds. Poetry Bookshop, 1950. First edition. Spine neatly repaired. Head and foot of spine and corners bruised. Author's signed autograph presentation inscription to R. Church. Nice. Rota 231-217 1983 £40

FLINT, TIMOTHY   A Condensed Geography and History of the Western States, or the Mississippi Valley... Cincinnati, 1828. 2 vols., leather and marbled boards, hinges weak. Good. Reese 18-621 1983 $175

FLINT, TIMOTHY   Recollections of the Last Ten Years... Boston: Cummings, Hilliard, and Co., 1826. Orig. mottled calf. Traces of foxing, otherwise a fine copy. Reese 18-596 1983 $300

FLINT, WILLIAM RUSSELL   Models of Propriety. London: Michael Joseph, (1951). First edition. Illus. Orig. cloth. One of 500 copies signed by the artist. Spine very slightly faded. Bookplate. Near-fine. MacManus 278-1916 1983 $185

FLINT, WILLIAM RUSSELL   Works of Sir William Russell Flint, R.A. London: Royal Academy of the Arts, 1962. First edition. Orig. boards. One of 200 copies signed by the artist. Bookplate. Near-fine. MacManus 278-1917 1983 $85

FLINTOFT'S Collection of the British Ferns in the English Lake District. (Keswick, c. 1830). 4to cloth album. Scarce. Title from cover. Cover somewhat worn and a few specimens slightly defective, but on the whole a good copy. Wheldon 160-1824 1983 £35

FLORA Malesiana, Series 2, Pteridophyta. The Hague, 1982. Portrait and 20 text-figures, 8vo, wrappers. Complete Series 2, Vol. I and is supplied with the binding case. Wheldon 160-1825 1983 £44

THE FLORAL World. Groombridge, 1879. 1st edn. 12 col'd plates (some folding) & wood engrs. Pub's green sand grain cloth with gilt decor. fr. cvr., a.e.g. (bkstrip soiled, eps. broken at hinges & contemp. insc. fr. ep., some foxing & thumbing), vg. Hodgkins 27-367 1983 £20

THE FLORAL World and Garden Guide. 1866. 2 vols., 8vo, orig. cloth gilt, a.e.g. Later volume containing 6 fine coloured plates. Bickersteth 75-227 1983 £15

FLORENZ, KARL   White Aster. Tokyo: T. Hasegawa. n.d. (Circa 1897). Printed on creped paper. Profusely illus. with color woodblock illus. Housed in a folding slipcase, clasps missing. Otherwise a fine copy. Karmiole 72-58 1983 $60

FLORIAN, J. P. CLARIS DE   Eleazar and Naphtaly, an Hebrew Tale. Joseph John Leathwick, 1827. 12mo, contemporary calf. Hill 165-35 1983 £25

FLORIAN, J. P. CLARIS DE   Gonsalva of Cordova; or, Granada Reconquered. Printed for J. Johnson, 1793. 3 vols, 12mo, contemporary tree calf, fully gilt backs, gilt borders, green title- and volume-labels; with all half-titles; owner's name "Marcus Gage" on titles; 1st ed. in English; slight waterstain at foot of first few leaves of Vol. I, but a fine copy. Hill 165-36 1983 £225

FLORKIN, M.   Chemical Zoology. 1978. Vol. 10, text-figures, 8vo, cloth. Wheldon 160-706 1983 £38

FLORUS, LUCIUS ANNAEUS   Epitome of Roman Things. London, 1822. 3 vols. Leather, all edges gilt. Some foxing in text, otherwise a nice set. In Our Time 156-287 1983 $150

FLORUS, LUCIUS ANNAEUS   Rerum Romanarum Epitome. Londini, R. Clavell, N. Mortlock, & S. Smith, 1692. 8vo, orig. paneled calf, quite worn, joints broken, notes on flyleaf. Ravenstree 95-50 1983 $35

FLORUS, LUCIUS JULIUS
Please turn to
FLORUS, LUCIUS ANNAEUS

FLOURENS, M. J. P.   Vorlesungen uber Befruchtung und Ei- Bildung des Menschen und der Thiere... Leipzig, 1838. 8vo. Old half-calf. Gurney JJ-122 1983 £60

FLOWER, FRANK A.   The Eye of the North-West. (Milwaukee): 1890. Illus., including large folding map. Oblong, printed boards. Bradley 66-699 1983 $40

FLOWER, J. CYRIL   An Approach to the Psychology of Religion. NY: Harcourt, Brace & Co., 1927. First American edition. Dust jacket a bit worn. Gach 95-133 1983 $25

FLOWER, W. H.   An Introduction to the Study of Mammals, living and extinct. 1891. 357 figures, 8vo, original cloth, gilt design on front cover. Original issue. Stamp on title and half-title. Wheldon 160-556 1983 £25

THE FLOWER-PIECE: A Collection of Miscellany Poems. London: Printed for J. Walthoe...MDCCXXXI. 12mo, wanting final signature of pub.'s ads. Cont. panelled calf, joints repaired. First edition. Quaritch NS 7-48 1983 $650

FLUCKIGER, F. A.   Pharmacographia. A history of the principal Drugs of vegetable origin met with in Great Britain and British India. 1879. Second edition, 8vo, orig. half leather (rubbed). Wheldon 160-2169 1983 £45

FLUGEL, JOHN CARL (1884-1955) The Psychoanalytic Study of the Family. London/Vienna/NY: International Psycho-Analytical Press, 1921. Rebound ex-library copy, paper browned. First edition. Gach 95-134 1983 $25

THE FLYING Burgomaster. F. Morley Invt. et Sculpt., 1832. Frontis., title vignette & 14 lithographs, plates. Red bead grain blind stamped cloth, a.e.g. Cvrs. mottled frontis. & plates sl. foxed & discol'd, scarce, vg. Hodgkins 27-271 1983 £30

FLYNN, P. J.   Irrigation Canals and Other Irrigation Works Including the Flow of Water in Irrigation Canals and Open and Closed Channels Generally... San F., 1892. Illus., orig. cloth. First edition. Ginsberg 47-387 1983 $125

FOGACCIA, PIERO   Cosimo Fanzago. Bergamo: Istituto Italiano d'Arti Grafiche, 1945. 111 plates. Folio. Boards, 1/4 cloth. Ars Libri 33-135 1983 $175

FOGAZZARO, ANTONIO   Eden Anto. S.F., 1930. 4to, boards, paper label, silk ties, slipcase. Illus. by Rene Gockinga. Bookplate on slipcase. One of 250 copies printed for the Roxburghe Club of San Francisco. A fine copy. Perata 28-43 1983 $125

FOGAZZARO, ANTONIO   Eden Anto. San Francisco: The Roxburghe Club, 1930. Quarto, facsimiles. 1st ed., 1 of 250 copies printed at the Grabhorn Press. Orig. flexible boards, silk ties, paper spine label. Inscribed by Kock. Mint copy. Jenkins 155-488 1983 $85

FOGERTY, J.   Lauterdale. London: Strahan & Co., 1893. First edition. 3 vols. Orig. cloth. Corners a little bumped. Foot of each spine very slightly worn. Binder's ticket. Very good. MacManus 278-1919 1983 $200

FOGG, WALTER   One Thousand Sayings of History Presented as Pictures in Prose. Boston, 1929. First edition. Presen. copy. 8vo. Morrill 290-131 1983 $20

FOLARD, JEAN CHARLES DE   Abrege des Commentaires sur l'Histoire de Polybe. Paris: Veuve Gaudouin, 1754. 1st ed., large 4to, 3 vols. Cont. speckled calf, spines gilt, copperplates and maps, many folding. Half-titles and errata leaves in all volumes. A crisp copy. Trebizond 18-206 1983 $475

FOLEY, HENRY   Records of the English Province of the Society of Jesus. 1883. With folding chart and 6 portraits, 8vo, orig. cloth, a very good to nice copy. Fenning 61-143 1983 £18.50

FOLGER, CHARLES J.   Trade Between Mexico and the United States. Letter from...Transmitting...Information in Regard to... the Traffic Over the Railroads Connecting the Two Countries. Wash., 1884. Illus., large folded map. Dbd. First edition. Ginsberg 47-498 1983 $35

FONBLANQUE, ALBANY   How We are Governed. F. Routledge, 1858. First edition, orig. purple cloth, v.g. Jarndyce 31-164 1983 £14.50

FONT, PEDRO   The Anza Expedition of 1775-1776. Diary of... Berkeley, 1913. Illus. Orig. printed wraps. Ginsberg 47-85 1983 $25

FONTAINE, SIEUR DE LA   The Military Duties of the Officers of Cavalry. Robert Harford, 1687. Sm. 8vo. Orig. cloth. 2 folding plates. Modern maroon morocco. Text slightly browned. Good. Edwards 1042-341 1983 £200

FONTEYN, NICHOLAS   Responsium & Curationum medicinalium liber unus. Amsterdam, 1639. 12mo, cont. limp vellum, first edition. Argosy 713-187 1983 $100

FONTINAS, ANDRE   La Peinture de Daumier. Paris: G. Cres, 1923. 47 heliogravure plates. 4to. Cloth, 3/4 leather. Orig. wrappers bound in. One of 50 copies on paper Gaspard-Maillol, of 60 copies only. Front cover detached. Ars Libri 32-140 1983 $100

FOOT, JESSE   The Life of Arthur Murphy, Esq. London: printed for J. Faulder, by John Nichols and Son, 1811. 4to, cont. red straight-grained morocco, gilt, spine gilt, a.e.g. (some rubbing, but sound; corners bruised). 1st edition. Some dampstaining in the margins. Ximenes 64-210 1983 $225

FOOTE, ANDREW H.   Africa and the American Flag. New York, 1854. 1st ed. Lithograph plates by Sarony, some tinted (or lightly colored). 8vo. Back cover bit spotted; corners rubbed. Morrill 289-331 1983 $57.50

FOOTE, ANDREW H.   Africa and the American Flag. New York: D. Appleton, 1854. 8vo. Map. 7 tinted plates. Orig. brown cloth. Rubbed, spines starting. Adelson Africa-188 1983 $40

FOOTE, HENRY S.   Casket of Reminiscences. Wash., 1874. Cloth, fine. Reese 19-229 1983 $200

FOOTE, HENRY STUART   Texas and the Texans; or, Advance of the Anglo-Americans to the Southwest. Phila., 1841. 2 vols., complete. Fine set in original cloth. First edition. Jenkins 151-79 1983 $500

FOOTE, HENRY STUART   Texas and the Texans. Philadelphia: Thomas Cowperthwait & Co., 1841. First edition. 2 vols. Dark green cloth, spines gilt, large gilt star at foot of each spine. Light foxing, minor wear at corners. Fine set. Bradley 66-545 1983 $535

FOOTE, JOHN TAINTOR   Angler's All. N.Y., Appleton-Century (1947). First edition. 11 illus. by Milton Weiler. Dust jacket (a few small nicks) very good. Houle 22-1053 1983 $27.50

FOOTE, JOHN TAINTOR   Dumb-Bell and Others, The Great Dog Stories of... NY (1946) 1st ed. Cloth, minor wear else very good in chipped dw. King 46-569 1983 $20

FOOTE, JOHN TAINTOR   Jing. New York: Derrydale Press, (1936). Plates by Aiden L. Ripley. 3/4 cloth. Uncut. One of 950 numbered copies. Felcone 21-31 1983 $85

FOOTE, SAMUEL   A Letter from Mr. Foote, to the reverend author of the Remarks, Critical and Christian, on the Minor. London: printed for T. Davies; T. Becket; and J. Coote, 1760. 8vo, wrappers. 1st ed. Half-title present. A very good copy. Ximenes 64-214 1983 $175

FOOTE, SAMUEL   The Lyar. A comedy in three acts. London: printed for P. Vaillant, J. Rivington, R. Baldwin, and S. Bladon, 1769. 8vo, disbound. Ximenes 64-215 1983 $150

FOR Our Boys, A Collection of Original Literary Offerings by Popular Writers at Home and Abroad. San Francisco: A.L. Bancroft, 1879. Orig. pictorial cloth. Brief note and the final lines of "The Chambered Nautilus" enclosed by O.W. Holmes. Jenkins 155-317 1983 $85

FORBERG, ROBERT   Zerzeichnis des Musikalien Verlages von Robert Forberg in Leipzig. Leipzig, 1894. 8vo, cl. Salloch 387-358 1983 $45

FORBES, ALEXANDER   California: A History of Upper and
Lower California... San F., Nash, 1937. Illus., map, frontis. 2
facs. Orig. boards. One of 650 copies. Ginsberg 47-86 1983
$100

FORBES, ALEXANDER   California: A History of Upper and
Lower California. SF, 1937. 4to, cloth-backed marbled boards, paper
label, d/w. Illus., folding map. One of 650 copies. Fine reprint of
the work first published in 1839. Perata 27-138 1983 $100

FORBES, ALEXANDER   California: A History of Upper and
Lower California. San Francisco: John Henry Nash, 1937. Small
folio, with 13 plates, including a folding color map. In addition,
there are dec. headpieces and a text illus. Edition ltd. to 650
copies. Cloth spine over marbled boards; paper spine label.
Karmiole 75-95 1983 $85

FORBES, BRYAN   Truth Lies Sleeping. London, Methuen,
(1950). First edition. Presentation copy: signed and inscribed
on the title page by the author to film director Bob Angus. Dust
jacket (chips), else good-very good. Houle 22-376 1983 $125

FORBES, E.   A History of British Mollusca and their
Shells. (1848-) 1853. 4 vols., roy. 8vo, original cloth, 203 plates,
(201 hand coloured). Rare Large Paper edition. Some slight foxing
of a few plates and the binding trifle used, but generally a good
copy. Wheldon 160-31 1983 £575

FORBES, E.   A History of British Mollusca and their
shells. (1848-) 1853. 203 plain plates, 8vo, 4 vols., cont.
full calf, gilt (neatly rebacked), g.e. Some slight foxing but a
nice copy. Wheldon 160-1208 1983 £200

FORBES, E.   A History of British Starfishes. 1841.
Numerous woodcuts, 8vo, cloth, ex-library copy. Covers slightly
stained but contents clean and sound. Wheldon 160-1280 1983 £18

FORBES, F. E.   Five Years in China. London, 1848.
Map. Coloured lithograph frontis. 20 vignettes. Half calf. 8vo.
Good. Edwards 1044-252 1983 £120

FORBES, H. O.   A Handbook to the Primates. 1896-97.
41 coloured plates, 8 folding maps, 2 vols., cr. 8vo, cloth, spines
faded. Wheldon 160-557 1983 £30

FORBES, HARRIETTE MERRIFIELD New England Diaries, 1602-1800.
(Topsfield, Mass.), Privately Printed, 1923. Ed. limited to 300
copies. 8vo. Morrill 288-598 1983 $35

FORBES, JOHN   Of Nature and Art in the Cure of
Disease. London, 1858. 8vo. Orig. cloth. Gurney JJ-123 1983
£15

FORBES, R. J.   Short History of the Art of Distillation
from the beginnings... Leiden, 1948. 8vo. Cloth. Dust wrapper.
With many illus. Gurney JJ-124 1983 £15

FORBES, WILLIAM CAMERON   As to Polo. N.P. (1911). 1st ed. 23
plates. 8vo. Scarce. Morrill 288-599 1983 $30

FORBURY Hill: a poem. London: printed by Law and Gilbert, for
Rivington, 1813. First edition. 8vo. Stitched, as issued. A
fine copy. Ximenes 63-406 1983 $80

FORBUSH, EDWARD HOWE   Birds of Massachusetts and Other New
England States. (Boston), 1928, 1927, 1929. Illus. 3 vols., 4to,
stain on front cover of vol. 3. Morrill 288-276 1983 $125

FORBUSH, EDWARD HOWE   A History of the Game Birds, Wild Fowl
and Shore Birds of Massachusetts and Adjacent States. Mass. State
Board of Agriculture, 1916. 2nd ed. Illus, cloth, inner hinges
cracked, covers very rubbed. King 46-570 1983 $35

FORBUSH, EDWARD HOWE   Useful Birds and Their Protection.
1913. 4th ed. Illus., cloth, extremities worn. King 46-511 1983
$20

FORD, CHARLES HENRI   The Garden of Disorder. Lon., (1938).
One of 500 numbered copies, cover stains, interior very good. Quill
& Brush 54-489 1983 $30

FORD, CHARLES HENRI   Sleep in a Nest of Flames. New
Directions, (1949). First edition. Thin tall 8vo, boards; foxed.
Argosy 714-300 1983 $25

FORD, FORD MADOX   Between St. Dennis and St. George. L.,
1915. Cover darkened, some minor interior staining, else very good.
Quill & Brush 54-646 1983 $25

FORD, FORD MADOX   Buckshee. Pym-Randall Press, (1966).
8vo, cloth. Fine in just jacket. In Our Time 156-290 1983 $200

FORD, FORD MADOX   Buckshee. Cambridge: Pym-Randall Press,
(1966). First separate edition. Of 300 clothbound copies, 1/50 signed
by Lowell and Rexroth. Mint in dust wrapper. Bromer 25-43 1983
$150

FORD, FORD MADOX   The Critical Attitude. London, 1911.
First edition, late binding. Some faint foxing of the preliminaries.
Nice. Rota 230-216 1983 £15

FORD, FORD MADOX   The Fifth Queen. London, 1906. First
edition. 8pp. of ads. Spine faded and slightly torn at head. Very
good. Rota 230-215 1983 £45

FORD, FORD MADOX   Great Trade Route. NY, 1937. First
issue with illus., name on title, page edges slightly foxed, few pages
slightly soiled, else very good in lightly worn and chipped, very good
dustwrapper. Quill & Brush 54-490 1983 $75

FORD, FORD MADOX   Great Trade Route. N.Y.: Oxford University Press, 1937. First edition, precedes English edition. Color
frontispiece & vignettes by Biala. Orig. cloth. Dust jacket. Very
fine. MacManus 278-1921 1983 $75

FORD, FORD MADOX   Great Trade Route. NY, 1937. Interior
foxing, very good in chipped and frayed dustwrapper. Quill & Brush
54-491 1983 $40

FORD, FORD MADOX   The Heart of the Country. London:
Alston Rivers, Ltd., 1906. First edition. Orig. cloth. Apart from a
holograph quatrain penned in the margin of page 89, probably not in
Ford's hand, a fine copy. MacManus 278-1922 1983 $135

FORD, FORD MADOX   Joseph Conrad, a Personal Remembrance
Duckworth, 1924. First edition, half title, front. orig. dull olive
cloth. Jarndyce 31-489 1983 £10.50

FORD, FORD MADOX   Ladies Whose Bright Eyes. London:
Constable & Co. Ltd., 1911. First edition. Orig. cloth. Presentation
copy from Richard Garnett to Olive Garnett, inscribed on the front
free endpaper. Spine a little rubbed. Very good. MacManus 278-1923
1983 $185

FORD, FORD MADOX   Last Post. London: Duckworth, (1928).
First edition. Orig. cloth. Dust jacket (a few short tears, dust-
soiled). Very good. MacManus 278-1924 1983 $125

FORD, FORD MADOX   Last Post. London, 1928. First English
edition. Spine darkened. Very nice. Rota 230-217 1983 £40

FORD, FORD MADOX   Last Post. London: Duckworth, (1928).
First edition. Orig. cloth. MacManus 278-1925 1983 $30

FORD, FORD MADOX   The Last Post. NY, 1928. Front hinge
starting at half title, slightly rubbed cover, cover dulled, good or
better, owner's name. Quill & Brush 54-492 1983 $20

FORD, FORD MADOX   The Last Post. N.Y.: Albert & Charles
Boni, 1928. Second American edition, preceded by the Literary Guild
edition. Orig. green cloth. Decorated endpapers. Very good. Mac-
Manus 278-1926 1983 $20

FORD, FORD MADOX.   A Little Less Than Gods. London, (1928).
8vo. Cloth. A fine copy in perfect dj. In Our Time 156-289 1983
$200

FORD, FORD MADOX   A Man Could Stand Up--A Novel. London:
Duckworth, (1926). First edition. Orig. cloth. Presentation copy
inscribed: "To Mop, from F.M.F. 17 September MCMXXVI." Spine and covers
faded and slightly worn. Very good. MacManus 278-1928 1983 $250

FORD, FORD MADOX   A Man Could Stand Up. London: Duckworth,
(1926). First edition. Orig. cloth. Dust jacket (defective). Fine.
MacManus 278-1929 1983 $125

FORD, FORD MADOX   A Man Could Stand Up. London: Duckworth,
(1926). First edition. Orig. cloth. Very good. MacManus 278-1927
1983 $25

FORD, FORD MADOX   A Mirror To France. London: Duckworth,
(1926). First edition. Color frontispiece. Orig. cloth. Dust
jacket (slightly worn at edges). Fine. MacManus 278-1930 1983 $200

FORD, FORD MADOX   Mister Bosphorus and The Muses. London:
Duckworth & Co., (1923). First trade edition, after an edition of
70 copies. Decorated with designs engraved on wood by Paul Nash. 4to.
Orig. cloth-backed pictorial boards. Dust jacket (a few minor tape-
repairs inside). Fine. MacManus 278-1931 1983 $385

FORD, FORD MADOX   No More Parades. London: Duckworth,
(1925). First edition. Orig. cloth. Very fine. MacManus 278-1932
1983 $75

FORD, FORD MADOX   The Panel. London, 1912. First English
edition. Bookplate. Hinges cracked, covers slightly marked and rubbed.
Edges spotted. Very good. Jolliffe 26-271 1983 £15

FORD, FORD MADOX   Portraits from Life. N.Y., 1937. First
American edition. Robert Lowell's copy, with his autograph, and the
date, May 1937, on the flyleaf. Backtrip & edges rubbed. Argosy 714-
479 1983 $75

FORD, FORD MADDOX   The Rash Act. N.Y., Long & Smith, 1933.
First edition. Dust jacket (bright). Slight foxing at edges, but
a fine copy. Houle 22-378 1983 $225

FORD, FORD MADOX   Rosetti: A Critical Essay on His Art.
Ch., (1915). Front hinge cracked at title, edges slightly rubbed,
else very good. Quill & Brush 54-647 1983 $40

FORD, FORD MADOX   The Shifting of the Fire. London: T.
Fisher Unwin, 1892. First edition. Orig. decorated cloth. Spine
and covers slightly rubbed. Very good. MacManus 278-1933 1983 $850

FORD, FORD MADOX   Some Do Not. Not More Parades. A Man
Could Stand Up. Last Post. London: Duckworth & Co., (1924, 1925,
1926, 1928). First edition, with the exception of the last vol.,
which was originally published in America. 4 vols. 8vo. Orig.
cloth. Dust jackets (very slightly worn). Fine. MacManus 278-1934
1983 $1,750

FORD, FORD MADOX   The Soul of London. London, 1905.
First edition. Spine faded and covers marked. Very good. Rota 230-
214 1983 £35

FORD, FORD MADOX.   When Blood Is Their Argument. New York
& London, 1915. 8vo. Cloth. Some light spotting to the cloth,
otherwise a very good-fine copy. Presentation inscription by author.
In Our Time 156-288 1983 $200

FORD, FRANK R.   Diseases of the Nervous System in Fancy.
Springfield, Ill., 1937. First edition. Profusely illus. Thick 8vo.
Argosy 713-188 1983 $35

FORD, GEORGE H.   The Pickersgill Letters. Toronto:
Ryerson, 1948. 20 1/2cm. Frontis. portrait and 6 illus. Fine.
McGahern 54-62 1983 $25

FORD, GERALD   Global Stability. Northridge: Lord
John Press, 1982. 1st ed., 1 of 100 slipcased Deluxe copies.
Jenkins 155-421 1983 $125

FORD, GERALD   Global Stability. Northridge: Lord
John Press, 1982. 1st ed., 1 of 400 signed copies. Orig. cloth-
backed boards. Mint, at published price. Jenkins 155-420 1983
$40

FORD, GERALD   A Time to Heal. (N.Y.) Harper (1979).
First edition. Illus. with halftones. Blue cloth. Pub.'s slipcase.
One of 250 specially bound and signed by the author. Houle 22-1212
1983 $225

FORD, GERALD   A Time To Heal. (New York): Harper,
(1979). 1st ed., limited to 250 numbered and signed copies. Orig.
blue cloth, gilt, boxed. Mint copy. Jenkins 155-422 1983 $150

FORD, GERALD   A Vision for America. Northridge, 1980.
Limited to 100 leather bound, numbered and signed copies, fine, in
slipcase. Quill & Brush 54-494 1983 $125

FORD, HORACE A.   Archery: its theory and practice.
London: Buchanan, etc., 1856. First edition. 8vo. Orig. green
cloth, gilt. With a frontis. and five other plates. Some wear
to ends of spine. Wanting a front endpaper. Ximenes 63-556 1983
$125

FORD, JOHN   Memoir of Thomas Pumphrey, for Twenty-
Seven Years Superintendent of Ackworth School. A.W. Bennett, 1864.
First edition, portrait, large 12mo, orig. cloth, v.g. copy. Fenning
60-339 1983 £18.50

FORD, LAUREN   The Ageless Story. N.Y.: Dodd, 1939.
First edition. Sq. 4to. Dust wrapper. 4-color plus gilt illus.
Printed on coated paper. Color border on each page. Fine. Aleph-bet
8-109 1983 $40

FORD, LESLIE   Murder in the Open. NY, 1942. Gutters
slightly soiled, covers lightly rubbed, else very good in chipped and
worn dustwrapper. Quill & Brush 54-495 1983 $25

FORD, LESLIE   The Murder of the Fifth Columnist. NY,
1941. Edges slightly rubbed, corners slightly bumped, book slightly
cocked, else very good in lightly chipped and frayed, slightly soiled
still presentable dustwrapper. Quill & Brush 54-498 1983 $35

FORD, LESLIE   Road to Folly. Lon., (1941). Orange
cover edges slightly faded, very good in slightly stained and frayed
dustwrapper. Quill & Brush 54-496 1983 $30

FORD, LESLIE   Siren in the Night. NY, 1943. Cover
lightly soiled, second front free endpaper slightly torn, else very
good in bright, very good dustwrapper with inner flaps lightly skinned.
Quill & Brush 54-497 1983 $25

FORD, PAUL LEICESTER   A Checked Love Affair. N.Y., 1903.
First edition, with 5 photogravures by H. Fisher. Cover and decorations by G. W. Edwards. Nicely decorated covers. T.e.g., illus.
loose, minor wear. King 45-398 1983 $20

FORD, PAUL LEICESTER   The Great K & A Robbery. New York:
Dodd Mead, 1897. Frontis. 1st ed., 1st state. Orig. pictorial
blue cloth, gilt, t.e.g., uncut. Fine copy. Jenkins 155-424 1983
$20

FORD, RICHARD   Gatherings from Spain. John Murray,
1851. 8vo, orig. red cloth, blocked in blind, "Murray's Colonial &
Home Library" in the centre of each cover, lettered gilt on the spine.
Slits just beginning at end of the joints, bookplate and inscription
inside front cover, but a good copy. Bickersteth 75-137 1983 £85

FORD, SIMON   The Conflagration of London: Poetically
Delineated. Sq. Gellibrand, 1667. Small 4to, rebound in half calf,
hand marbled boards, label on front cover, v.g. Jarndyce 31-4 1983
£95

FORD, THOMAS   History of Illinois, 1818-1847. Chi.,
Lakeside Press, 1945-46. Maps, illus. 2 vols. 12mo, gilt tops.
Clark 741-352 1983 $47.50, set

FORD, THOMAS   A History of Illinois from its
Commencement as a State in 1818 to 1847. Chicago, 1945, 6. Illus.
& maps, 1 colored folding. 2 vols., 16mo, g.t. Argosy 710-209
1983 $30

FORD, WORTHINGTON CHAUNCEY   George Washington. New York, 1900.
2 vols. Colored frontis., numerous plates. Red pub.'s 3/4 levant,
spine elaborately gilt in compartments with eagle motif. One of
25 numbered presentation copies. Felcone 22-255 1983 $60

FORDE, GERTRUDE   In The Old Palazzo. London: White,
1885. First edition. 3 vols. Orig. cloth. Presentation copy,
inscribed, "John Leach, from the Author,: in each vol. Pencilled note
on the flyleaf in vol. one. Very good. MacManus 278-1935 1983 $285

FORDHAM, ELIAS PYM   Personal Narrative of Travels in
Virginia, Maryland, Pennsylvania, Ohio, Indiana, Kentucky. Cleveland,
Arthur H. Clark Co., 1906. 1st ed. 4 plates, 1 text sketch map.
8vo. Morrill 286-597 1983 $47.50

FORDUN, JOHN   Johannis de Fordun Scotichronichon
Genuinum Una cum ejusdem Supplemento ac Continuatione... Oxonii,
E Theatro Sheldoniano, 1722. 5 vols., 8vo, orig. calf, worn, spine
labels lacking; all plates are present. First edition. Ravenstree
94-194 1983 $185

FORDYCE, GEORGE   Five Dissertations on Fever. Boston:
Bradford & Read, 1815. First American edition. Argosy 713-189 1983
$85

FOREL, AUGUST (1848-1931)   Alkohol Und Venerischen Krankheiten.
Vienna: Verlag von Moritz Perles, 1901. Orig. printed wrappers
(chipped). First edition. Gach 95-136 1983 $35

FOREL, AUGUST (1848-1931)   Die Berechtigung Der Vergleichende
Psychologie. Leipzig: J. A. Barth, 1912. Orig. printed orange
wrappers. Inscribed to Adolf Meyer and with Professor and Madame
Forel's calling card inserted and initialed by Forel. Gach 95-137
1983 $125

FOREL, AUGUST (1848-1931)   Die Hypnose Ver Der Aerztekammer.
Munich: Verlang von J. F. Lehmann, 1903. Orig. printed wrappers,
detached. With several inked corrections in Forel's hand. Gach
95-138 1983 $50

FOREL, AUGUST (1848-1931)   La Psychologie et la Psychotherapie A
L'Universite. Leipzig: J. A. Barth, 1910. Orig. printed orange
wrappers (dusty). Inscribed (to Adolf Meyer) "V. Verf." Gach 95-
139 1983 $45

FOREL, AUGUST (1848-1931)   Sensation Des Insectes. Como: Romco
Longatti, 1901. Orig. printed orange wrappers (worn and detached).
Inscribed to Adolf Meyer. Gach 95-140 1983 $65

FOREL, AUGUST (1848-1931)   Senuelle Ethik. Munich: E. Reinhardt,
1906. Orig. printed wrappers. First edition. Near fine copy.
Enclosed in cloth folder and slipcase. Inscribed to Adolf Meyer.
Gach 95-141 1983 $85

FOREMAN, CAROLYN THOMAS   Oklahoma Imprints 1835-1907... Norman:
Univ. of Oklahoma, 1936. Frontispiece, plates. Cloth in slightly-
worn dw. Dawson 470-112 1983 $45

FOREMAN, GRANT   The Adventures of James Collier. Chicago:
Black Cat Press, 1937. Cloth, a little used. One of 250 copies.
Dawson 471-86 1983 $25

FOREMAN, GRANT   Marcy & the Gold Seekers. Norman,
1939. Illus., 1st edition in dust jacket. Fine copy. Jenkins 151-
82 1983 $40

FOREMAN, GRANT   A Pathfinder in the Southwest. Norman,
1941. First edition. Folding map and illus. Nice. Jenkins 152-115
1983 $45

FOREMAN, GRANT   Sequoyah. Norman, 1938. 1st ed.,
illus., nice copy. Jenkins 151-308 1983 $40

FOREMAN, JOHN   The Philippine Islands...and its
Political Dependencies. NY, 1899. Photo, plates, map in rear
pocket, 8vo, pict. cloth, 2nd ed, revised & enlarged. Argosy
710-410 1983 $50

FOREST Flowers. J. Paul, 1867. First edition. Orig. maroon cloth,
v.g. Jarndyce 30-615 1983 £10.50

FORESTER, CECIL SCOTT   The African Queen. London: William
Heinemann Ltd, (1935). First edition. 8vo. Orig. cloth. Dust
jacket. Chipped dust jacket. A fine copy. Rare. Jaffe 1-89 1983
$775

FORESTER, CECIL SCOTT   Beat to Quarters. Boston, 1937. Later
printing. 8vo, cloth. Specially signed by Forester on the half-title
page. A fine copy in just jacket. In Our Time 156-291 1983 $45

FORESTER, CECIL SCOTT   The Captain from Connecticut. London,
(1941). 8vo. Cloth. A fine copy in near perfect dj. In Our Time
156-292 1983 $65

FORESTER, CECIL SCOTT   The Happy Return. (London): Michael
Joseph Ltd., (1937). First edition. 8vo. Orig. cloth. Dust
jacket. Two-inch chip out of back panel of jacket, otherwise a
very good copy. Jaffe 1-90 1983 $60

FORESTER, CECIL SCOTT   A Ship of the Line. (London): Michael
Joseph Ltd., (1938). First edition. 8vo. Orig. cloth. Dust jacket.
Back panel of jacket a little soiled and worn, otherwise a very good
copy. Jaffe 1-91 1983 $85

FORESTER, FRANK
Please turn to
HERBERT, HENRY WILLIAM

FORESTER, THOMAS   Rambles in the Islands of Corsica and
Sardinia. 1858. First edition, coloured map, 2 chromolithograph and
6 lithograph plates. Roy. 8vo, red morocco, gilt dec. spine, lacking
free endpapers, otherwise a nice copy free from foxing. K Books
307-76 1983 £130

FORKEL, J. N.   Life of John Sebastian Bach. London:
T. Boosey, 1820. First edition in English. 8vo. Orig. boards,
printed paper label. Three folding plates of music at the end.
Spine worn. Scarce. Ximenes 63-329 1983 $125

FORMULAE Selectae. New York, 1818. 1st ed. 8vo. Contemporary
marbled boards, calf back and corners. Rubbed; hinges cracked; lacks
label; some text stained. Morrill 289-76 1983 $50

FORREST, BERNARD   Not Meaning Not To See. Black Sparrow
Press, N.p., n.d. 16mo. Wrappers. Total edition is 70 copies signed
by poet. Fine. In Our Time 156-294 1983 $200

FORREST, C. R.   A Picturesque Tour Along the Rivers
Ganges and Jamna. London, 1824. Folding map, 24 fine hand-coloured
aquatint plates. Folio. Half blue morocco. T.e.g. by Sangorski &
Sutcliff. Large paper copy with very little offsetting. 8vo. Good.
Edwards 1044-255 1983 £1,500

FORREST, EARLE R.   Lone War Trail of Apache Kid. Pasadena,
1947. Illus., limited deluxe edition of 250 copies signed by the
authors. Dust jacket. Jenkins 151-83 1983 $75

FORREST, EARLE R.   Lone War Trail of Apache Kid. Pasadena:
(1947). First edition. Color plates, other illus. Map end papers.
Blue cloth. Nice copy in chipped dust jacket. Bradley 66-455 1983
$47.50

FORREST, EDWIN   Case of Catharine N. Forrest, Plaintiff,
Against Edwin Forrest, Defendant... New York, 1863. 1st ed. 2 vols.
Tall 8vo, contemporary calf, leather labels. Morrill 288-600 1983
$45

FORREST, H. E.   A Handbook to the Vertebrate Fauna of
North Wales. 1919. 8vo, cloth. Wheldon 160-381 1983 £15

FORRESTER, ALFRED HENRY   Phantasmagoria of Fun. London: Richard
Bentley, 1843. First edition. 2 vols. Illus. Orig. cloth. Extremities of spines a bit rubbed. Very good. MacManus 277-1202 1983
$125

FORRESTER, IZOLA   This One Mad Act. Boston, 1937. 1st
ed. Illus. 8vo. Morrill 289-332 1983 $20

FORSBECK, FILIP A.   New Upsala, the First Swedish
Settlement in Wisconsin. Milwaukee, Wisc.: no pub. 1936. (Illus).
Edition ltd. to 200 copies. This is a "complimentary" copy,
inscribed by the author. Blue cloth. Karmiole 71-46 1983 $30

FORSHAW, J.   Parrots of the World. Melbourne, 1973.
imp. 4to, cloth, 158 coloured plates. Original edition, now out of
print and very scarce. Wheldon 160-32 1983 £170

FORSTER, EDWARD MORGAN   Abinger Harvest. London: Edward
Arnold & Co., (1936). First edition, first impression. Large 8vo.
Orig. cloth. Dust jacket. One of 2000 copies printed. Clean one-
inch tear at head of spine of jacket, otherwise a fine copy. Jaffe
1-99 1983 $165

FORSTER, EDWARD MORGAN   Alexandria: A History And A Guide.
Alexandria: Whitehead Morril Limited, 1922. First edition. 8vo.
Illus. Folding maps. Orig. buff boards. Very fine copy. Rare.
Jaffe 1-93 1983 $500

FORSTER, EDWARD MORGAN   Anonymity. Hogarth Press, 1925. First
edition. Upper cover a little marked. Very nice. Rota 231-220 1983
£35

FORSTER, EDWARD MORGAN   Aspects Of The Novel. London: Edward
Arnold & Co., 1927. First edition. 8vo. Orig. cloth. Dust jacket
(torn). Fine copy. Jaffe 1-96 1983 $75

FORSTER, EDWARD MORGAN   The Celestial Omnibus. London, 1911.
First edition. One of 1000 copies. Spine a little darkened and lower
cover marked. Nice. Rota 231-219 1983 £40

FORSTER, EDWARD MORGAN   The Development Of English Prose
Between 1918 and 1939. First edition. 8vo. Orig. wrappers. One
of 1000 copies printed. Very fine copy. Jaffe 1-100 1983 $75

FORSTER, EDWARD MORGAN   The Development of English Prose
Between 1918 and 1939. Glasgow, 1945. First edition. Loosely
inserted is a 36 word A.L.S., dated November 7th, 1951, from the
author. Very good. Jolliffe 26-182 1983 £18

FORSTER, EDWARD MORGAN   England's Pleasant Land. London, 1940.
First edition. Spine a little faded. Nice. Rota 230-219 1983 £12

FORSTER, EDWARD MORGAN   The Eternal Moment and other Stories.
London: Sidgwick & Jackson, Ltd., 1928. First edition. 8vo.
Orig. cloth. Dust jacket. Slightly nicked jacket. A very fine
copy. Rare. Jaffe 1-97 1983 $225

FORSTER, EDWARD MORGAN   The Eternal Moment, and Other Stories.
London, 1928. First binding. First edition. Argosy 714-301 1983
$60

FORSTER, EDWARD MORGAN   The Eternal Moment. London, 1928.
First edition, first binding. Name of flyleaf. Book-label. Good.
Rota 230-218 1983 £30

FORSTER, EDWARD MORGAN   The Eternal Moment and Other Stories.
1928. 8vo, orig. cloth, lettered in gilt. First edition.
Bickersteth 77-204 1983 £25

FORSTER, EDWARD MORGAN   Goldsworthy Lowes Dickinson. London:
Edward Arnold & Co., 1934. First edition. Large 8vo. Illus. Orig.
cloth. Dust jacket. One of 2050 copies printed. Dust-soiled jacket.
Fine copy. Jaffe 1-98 1983 $150

FORSTER, EDWARD MORGAN   Howards End. London: Edward Arnold,
1910. First edition, first issue. 8vo. Orig. cloth. Spine slightly
darkened and rubbed, but a very good copy. Jaffe 1-92 1983 $450

FORSTER, EDWARD MORGAN   Howards End. NY, 1910. 1500 copies in
2 states, 2nd state with extra leaves in rear and front cover decoration, corners and spine slightly rubbed, very good. Quill & Brush 54-
506 1983 $75

FORSTER, EDWARD MORGAN   The Longest Journey. Edinburgh & London:
William Blackwood & Sons, 1907. First edition. Orig. cloth. One of
1587 copies printed. Covers a little dull and very slightly rubbed at
extremities of spine. Very good. MacManus 278-1941 1983 $450

FORSTER, EDWARD MORGAN   The Longest Journey. N.Y.: Alfred A.
Knopf, 1922. First American edition. Orig. cloth. Dust jacket (spine
darkened, edges a bit chipped). One of 2100 copies printed. Former
owner's neat signature on front free endpaper. Fine. MacManus 278-
1940 1983 $225

FORSTER, EDWARD MORGAN   The Longest Journey. London, 1941.
First edition. Reprint. Author's signed autograph presentation inscription to J. Morris. Very nice. Rota 231-223 1983 £35

FORSTER, EDWARD MORGAN   Marianne Thornton. 1797-1887. London:
Edward Arnold, (1956). First edition. Illus. Orig. cloth. Dust
jacket (slightly faded with a small tear). Probably a presentation
copy, signed by Forster below his crossed out printed name on the title
page, and also signed by Siegfried Sassoon on the front free endpaper:
"Siegfried May 1956." Fine. MacManus 278-1942 1983 $375

FORSTER, EDWARD MORGAN   A Passage To India. London: Edward
Arnold & Co., 1924. First edition. Large 8vo. Orig. cloth-backed
boards with paper label on spine. One of 200 copies signed by the
author. Faint darkening of boards, but a fine copy. Jaffe 1-95
1983 $850

FORSTER, EDWARD MORGAN   A Passage to India. London: Edward
Arnold & Co., 1924. First edition. Orig. cloth. Signed by author on
the title-page. Edges rather worn, covers slightly soiled. A bit
foxed. MacManus 278-1943 1983 $450

FORSTER, EDWARD MORGAN   A Passage to India. London: Arnold,
1924. First edition. Orig. cloth. Front cover a little worn. Inner
hinge cracked. MacManus 278-1944 1983 $100

FORSTER, EDWARD MORGAN   A Passage to India. NY (1924). Spine
slightly faded, front hinge starting, otherwise very good. Quill &
Brush 54-505 1983 $50

FORSTER, EDWARD MORGAN   Pharos and Pharillon. Richmond: The
Hogarth Press, 1923. First edition, first state. 8vo. Orig. cloth-
backed decorated boards with paper label on spine. One of 900 copies
printed. Very fine copy. Jaffe 1-94 1983 $250

FORSTER, EDWARD MORGAN   Pharos and Pharillon. N.Y.: Alfred A.
Knopf, 1923. First American edition. Orig. cloth. Very good.
MacManus 278-1945 1983 $20

FORSTER, EDWARD MORGAN   What I Believe. Hogarth Press, 1939.
First edition. Wrappers. Pages browned. Very good. Rota 231-222
1983 £12.50

FORSTER, J. R.   Characteres generum plantarum quas in
itinere ad insulas maris australis collegerunt. 1776. 78 engraved
plates, 4to, modern half calf, rare. Crease and small repaired tear
in title-page. Wheldon 160-1676 1983 £480

FORSTER, JOHN   The Life and Times of Oliver Goldsmith.
Bradbury and Evans, 1854. 2 vols., 8vo, orig. cloth. Inside joints
weak, but still a very good copy. Fenning 61-164 1983 £28.50

FORSTER, JOHN   The Life of Charles Dickens. Chapman &
Hall, 1872/3/4. 3 vols., vol. 1, 9th edition; vols. II & III, first
editions. Half titles, fronts. illus., 6 pp ads. Orig. purple cloth,
faded on spines, very good. Jarndyce 30-186 1983 £42

FORSTER, JOHN   The Life of Charles Dickens. Phila.:
J.B. Lippincott, 1872-4. Half calf, fronts. illus. 10 pp ads. vol.
II. Orig. maroon cloth, bevelled boards, sl. rubbed. Jarndyce 31-
601 1983 £34

FORSTER, JOHN   The Life of Charles Dickens. New
York: The Baker and Taylor Company, 1911. 2 vols. Thick 4to.
Cloth. T.e.g. Memorial Edition with 500 portraits, facsimiles
and other illus. Each vol. has the Centenary Testimonial stamp
pasted inside front cover. Inner hinges cracked at title page,
covers rubbed. Oak Knoll 49-158 1983 $45

FORSTER, JOSEPH   Studies in Balck and Red. London: Ward
& Downey, 1896. First edition. Orig. pictorial cloth. MacManus
278-1946 1983 $30

FORSTER, OTTO H.   Stefan Lochner. Ein Maler zu Koln. Frankfurt: Prestel, 1938. 137 plates. 4to. Boards, 1/4 cloth. Dust jacket. From the library of Jakob Rosenberg. Ars Libri 32-410 1983 $75

FORSTER, THOMAS   Researches About Atmospheric Phaenomena. London, Baldwin, Cradork, Joy, 1815. Second edition, enlarged. Frontis. and 5 tinted plates of cloud formations. Cont. boards (rebacked) uncut. Light soiling and staining, else good - very good. Houle 22-1060 1983 $125

FORSTER, WILLIAM   Memoirs of William Forster. A.W. Bennett, 1865. First edition, 2 vols. 8vo, orig. cloth, by Hanbury & Simpson, with their ticket, a fine copy. Fenning 62-122 1983 £26.50

FORSYTH, DOUGLAS   Autobiography and Reminiscences. London, 1887. First edition. Folding coloured map, frontis. 8vo. Orig. cloth. Good. Edwards 1044-257 1983 £75

FORSYTH, JAMES W.   Report of an Expedition up the Yellowstone River, Made in 1875. Washington, 1875. 5 plates. Large folding map. Minor splitting. Original printed wrappers bound in. Half morocco and boards. Jenkins 153-200 1983 $300

FORSYTH, JOHN   Address to the People of Georgia. Fredericksburg, Va., 1840. Marbled wrappers. Inscribed by author. Jenkins 152-116 1983 $50

FORSYTH, WILLIAM   Idylls and Lyrics. Blackwood, 1872. First edition, half title, 4 pp ads. Orig. dark green cloth, v.g. Jarndyce 30-696 1983 £10.50

FORSYTH, WILLIAM   A Treatise on the Culture and Management of Fruit Trees... Phila.: J. Morgan, 1802. 13 engraved plates (11 folding). Full calf. Covers very shabby and in need of rebinding. Internally nice. Felcone 20-48 1983 $85

FORSYTH, WILLIAM   A Treatise on the Culture and Management of Fruit-Trees. London, 1803. Lacks half title, 13 engraved plates (mostly folding), 8vo, half dark blue calf, gilt spine. Second edition. K Books 307-77 1983 £42

FORTESCUE, JOHN   A Learned Commendation of the Politique Lawes of England. London, Thomas Wight and Bonham Norton, 1599. 8vo, orig. calf, little worn. Last Elizabethan edition. Ravenstree 94-102 1983 $335

FORTIER, ALCEE   A History of Louisiana. New York, 1904. 4 vols. Special ed. limited to 1000 numbered copies. T.e.g. Few faint library stamps. Rebound in maroon cloth, black morocco labels. Solid set. Jenkins 153-339 1983 $150

A FORTNIGHT'S tour amongst the Arabs on Mount Lebanon... London: Nisbet, 1876. First edition. 8vo. Orig. green cloth. 4 mounted photographs. A bit rubbed and darkened. Ximenes 63-604 1983 $75

THE FORTSAS Catalogue; a Facsimile. (Philadelphia): Philobiblion Club, 1970. 4to. Cloth spine, marbled paper over boards. 16 page 8vo., facsimile of the orig. Fortsas Catalogue laid-in a pocket in the inside rear cover. One of 250 numbered copies, this one of the 160 copies for members of the Club. The project was designed and printed by Henry Morris at The Bird & Bull Press. Fine. Oak Knoll 39-39 1983 $325

FOSBROKE, THOMAS DUDLEY   British Monachism. 1843. 8vo, portrait and 12 plates, orig. cloth, faded. Plates spotted. Bickersteth 77-205 1983 £12

FOSCA, FRANCOIS A.
Please turn to
TRAZ, GEORGES DE

FOSSI, MAZZINO   Bartolomeo Ammannati architetto. Firenze: Morano, nd. 167 illus. 4to. Wrappers. Ars Libri 33-5 1983 $85

FOSTER, BIRKET   Pictures of English Landscape. Routledge, 1881. De luxe large paper ed., limited to 1000 copies (copy 860) with 30 proof wood engrs. on India paper engr'd by Bros. Dalziel, text on hand-made paper. Full white parchment decor. in brown, red & gold, bevelled boards, uncut. 6" crack top of front joint, rear cvr. scuffed, fr. cvr. rubbed with sml. red stain, vg. Hodgkins 27-315A 1983 £75

FOSTER, BIRKET   Pictures of Rustic Landscape. Nimmo, 1896. 1st edn. thus. Frontis. portrait & 30 b&w wood engrs. by Bros. Dalziel. Green cloth, gilt titling, bevelled bds., green & gold decor. eps., a.e.g., fine copy. Hodgkins 27-316 1983 £40

FOSTER, CHARLES   Letter from...Transmitting Several Reports of Special Agents to the Seal Islands. Wash., 1893. Illus., 6 maps and plates, many folded. Dbd. Ginsberg 46-20 1983 $45

FOSTER, E. M.   The Duke of Clarence. London: for William Lane at the Minerva Press, 1795. First edition. 4 vols. 12mo. Cont. marbled boards, red morocco spines and coners, gilt. Traylen 94-341 1983 £330

FOSTER, EDMUND   A Sermon Preached before His Excellency the Governor...May 27, 1812. Boston, 1812. Dsb. Reese 18-377 1983 $20

FOSTER, GEORGE G.   The Gold Regions of California... New York: DeWitt & Davenport, 1848. 3 ads, frontispiece woodcut map. Bound into later cloth, green calf label (no wraps). Few holes in map (not affecting image) and ink diagram on blank recto of map, upper corner of title missing and a few stains. Second edition. Jenkins 153-201 1983 $125

FOSTER, HANNAH   The Cocquette. Newburyport: Thomas & Whipple, 1811. Orig. boards, rebacked at an early date. Margin of title frayed, two leaves repaired, otherwise a good, completely untrimmed copy. Reese 18-344 1983 $45

FOSTER, JOHN   Annual Report of the Board of Trade of Evansville, for 1867. Evansville, 1868. Map, several plates, ads. Argosy 716-212 1983 $20

FOSTER, JOHN LESLIE   An Essay On The Principle of Commercial Exchanges. London: J. Hatchard, 1804. 1st ed., 8vo, lacking the half title, later half calf, green cloth sides, slightly rubbed, spine gilt, raised bands, bookplate and shelf mark of H. M. Treasury. Pickering & Chatto 21-37 1983 $125

FOSTER, JOSEPH   Some Feudal Coats of Arms. Oxford and London, James Parker, 1902. 1st ed., chromolithographed frontispiece, numerous illus., some printed in color, 4to, original cloth, gilt. Deighton 3-136 1983 £48

FOSTER, JOSEPH C.   The Uncertainty of Life. Brattleboro, 1849. Dbd. First edition. Ginsberg 47-87 1983 $35

FOSTER, MICHAEL   Claude Bernard. London, 1899. First edition. 8vo. Orig. binding. Fye H-3-677 1983 $45

FOSTER, MICHAEL   Lectures on the History of Physiology. Cambridge, 1901. First edition. 8vo. Orig. binding. Fye H-3-187 1983 $60

FOSTER, MORRISON   My Brother Stephen. Indianapolis, 1932. Privately printed, 8vo, cl. Salloch 387-318 1983 $20

FOSTER, STEPHEN C.   Catalogue of First Editions of Stephen C. Foster. Washington, GPO, 1915. 1st ed. Tall 8vo. Morrill 288-530 1983 $25

FOSTER, STEPHEN C   Willie We Have Missed You. NY: Firth, Pond, & Co., 1854. Oval lithogr. plate on cover, large 4to, sewn. 1st ed. Argosy 710-324 1983 $50

FOSTER, VERE   Vere Foster's Simple Lessons in Water-Color. London, 1884. 8vo. Morrill 287-120 1983 $20

FOSTER, WILLIAM   Hoplocrismaspongus. London: Thomas Cotes, for John Grove, 1631. First edition. Small 4to. Disbound. Some catchwords cropped. Ximenes 63-275 1983 $250

FOSTER, WILLIAM   A Society for the Special Study of Political Economy, the Philosophy of History, and The Science of Government. Boston: Mudge, 1857. 8vo, stitched. Rostenberg 88-129 1983 $45

FOTHERGILL, JESSIE   The First Violin. Richard Bentley, 1878. First published edition, 3 vols. Orig. half calf, rubbed, maroon and green labels. A good copy. Jarndyce 30-386 1983 £48

FOTHERGILL, JESSIE   From Moor Isles. London: Bentley, 1888. First edition. 3 vols. Orig. half cloth. Decorated boards. Covers somewhat stained and worn. A bit foxed. Sound copy. MacManus 278-1947 1983 $200

FOTHERGILL, JESSIE   Peril. London: Bentley, 1884. First edition. 3 vols. 8vo. Orig. dark blue cloth. (Slight rubbing and just a trifle marked by damp). A fine copy. Ximenes 63-152 1983 $200

THE FOTHERGILL Omnibus. London: Eyre & Spottiswoode, 1931. First edition. Full green morocco. One of 250 copies on special paper, signed by each of the contribution authors. Spine & extremities faded. Slightly worn. MacManus 278-1948 1983 $165

FOTTRELL, GEORGE   Practical Guide to the Land Purchase Acts (Ireland). Dublin: M.H. Fill, 1889. Second edition. Cr. 8vo, orig. cloth, a very good copy. Fenning 62-123 1983 £14.50

FOULKE, ROY A.   The Sinews of American Commerce. NY: Dun & Bradstreet, Inc., 1941. Illus., fine copy boxed. 1st ed. Jenkins 151-84 1983 $50

FOUNTAIN, PAUL   The Great North-West and the Great Lake Region of North America. London: Longmans, Green & Co., 1904. 22cm. Wine cloth. Some wear else a very good copy. McGahern 53-55 1983 $30

FOUNTAIN, PAUL   The River Amazon From Its Sources To The Sea. London, 1914. 1st ed., 8vo, with a frontispiece and other plates from photographs, original cloth. Deighton 3-137 1983 £18

FOUQUET, MARIE   Suite du Recueil des Remedes Faciles et Domestiques, choisis, Experimentez & Approuvez... Dijon; Ressayre, 1689. Argosy 713-192 1983 $150

FOUR Kings of Canada. (London: Garratt, 1891). 16mo, pr. wrs., some pp. unopened. One of 250 copies reprinted from the London, 1710 edition. Argosy 716-46 1983 $50

A FOUR months tour through France. London: G. Kearsly, 1775. First edition. 2 vols. 12mo. Cont. calf, spines gilt. Fine copy. Ximenes 63-630 1983 $175

FOURCROY, ANTOINE FRANCOIS DE   Elements of Chemistry and Natural History... Edinburgh: Longman & Rees and J. Johnson, 1800. Fifth edition. 3 vols. Cont. half calf. 8vo. 9 folding tables bound at end of vol. III. Lacking titles to vol. II, marginal repair end of vol. II. Zeitlin 264-155 1983 $160

FOURNIER, LESLIE T.   Railway Nationalization in Canada. Toronto: Macmillan, 1935. 23cm. Blue cloth. About fine. McGahern 54-64 1983 $50

A FOURTH Collection of Papers Relating to the Present Juncture of Affairs in England. Printed, and are to be sold by Ric. Janeway, 1688. First edition, 4to, wrapper. Fenning 62-124 1983 £24.50

FOWKE, GERARD   Archaeological History of Ohio. Columbus, 1902. 1st ed. Illus. 8vo, inner front hinge slightly cracked. Morrill 287-632 1983 $35

FOWLER, EDWARD   An Answer to the Paper delivered by Mr. Ashton... London: for Robert Clavell, 1690. 4to. Wrappers. Heath 48-114 1983 £35

FOWLER, G. H.   Science of the Sea. Oxford, 1928. 2nd edition, 220 illustrations and 11 charts, 8vo, cloth, spine faded. Wheldon 160-311 1983 £15

FOWLER, GENE   Beau James: The Life and Times of Jimmy Walker. N.Y., Viking, 1949. First edition. Illus. with halftones. Dust jacket (light nicking). Inscribed and signed by the author. Good - very good. Houle 22-383 1983 $45

FOWLER, GENE   A Solo in Tom-Tom's. N.Y., Viking, 1946. First edition. Dust jacket (slight rubbing and soiling) else very good. With signed presentation inscription tipped in and numbered 73. Houle 22-384 1983 $45

FOWLER, O. S.   Creative & Sexual Science. N.Y., (c. 1875). 8vo, orig. cloth. Port. frontis., many text wood engr. Argosy 713-193 1983 $75

FOWLER, W. W.   The Roman Festivals of the Period of the Republic. London, 1916. 8vo, cloth. Salloch 385-109 1983 $30

FOWLER, W. W   Social Life at Rome in the Age of Cicero. NY, 1916. 8vo, cloth. Salloch 385-227 1983 $50

FOWLES, JOHN   The Aristos. London, 1965. First English edition. Inscription. Dustwrapper faded at spine and edges. Fine. Jolliffe 26-183 1983 £180

FOWLES, JOHN   The Aristos. Boston: Little, Brown & Co., (1964). First American edition. Orig. boards. Dust jacket. Very fine. MacManus 278-1949 1983 $175

FOWLES, JOHN   The Collector. Boston, (1963). 8vo. Wraps. Advance reading copy of the first American ed. In Our Time 156-297 1983 $350

FOWLES, JOHN   The Collector. Boston, Little Brown, (1963). First American edition. Inscribed by Fowles: "With the author's kind wishes-John Fowles. Los Angeles 18. vi.1969." Very good - fine. Houle 22-385 1983 $300

FOWLES, JOHN   The Collector. Boston: Little, Brown & Co., (1963). Advance copy of the first American edition. Orig. pict. printed wrappers. Spine slightly darkened. Fine. MacManus 278-1956 1983 $250

FOWLES, JOHN   The Collector. Boston: Little, Brown & Co., (1963). First American edition. Orig. cloth. Dust jacket. Former owner's signature. Fine. MacManus 278-1955 1983 $150

FOWLES, JOHN   The Collector. Boston: Little, Brown, (1963). Cloth, first American edition. Fine in dust jacket. Reese 20-415 1983 $100

FOWLES, JOHN   Daniel Martin. Sweden, (1977). 8vo, cloth. First Swedish edition. This copy signed by Fowles on the title page. Fine copy in dust jacket which is rubbed around the extremities. In Our Time 156-299 1983 $100

FOWLES, JOHN   The French Lieutenant's Woman. Boston: Little, Brown & Co., (1969). First American edition. Orig. cloth. Dust jacket (a few short tears). Very fine. MacManus 278-1961 1983 $125

FOWLES, JOHN   The Magus. London, Cape (1966). First edition. Dust jacket (a few small nicks; ink signature on endpaper), else very good. Houle 21-353 1983 $225

FOWLES, JOHN   Mantissa. Boston, (1982). 8vo. Cloth. Limited signed ed., being 1 of 510 copies signed by Fowles. A fine copy in slipcase box. In Our Time 156-300 1983 $100

FOWLES, JOHN   Shipwreck. Boston: Little, Brown & Company, (1974). First American edition. Photography by the Gibsons of Scilly. Oblong 4to. Orig. cloth-backed boards, dust jacket. Very fine copy. Jaffe 1-101 1983 $100

FOWLIE, WALLACE   Mallarme as Hamlet: A Study of Igitur. Yonkers: Alicat Bookshop, 1949. First edition. Frontis. by Picasso. Tan wrappers. Bradley 66-168 1983 $20

FOWNES, GEORGE   Chemistry, as exemplifying the Wisdom and Beneficence of God... London: Churchill, 1844. First edition. 8vo. Orig. red stamped cloth. Half title. Spine soiled, some wear, some inserted ad. leaves removed. Zeitlin 264-156 1983 $60

FOWNES, GEORGE   A Manual of Elementary Chemistry Theoretical and Practical... London: Churchill, 1854. 8vo. Orig. cloth. Errata. Zeitlin 264-157 1983 $50

FOX, ARCHIBALD DOUGLAS   Follow Up! London: Brown, Langham & Co., 1908. First edition. Orig. cloth. Presentation copy inscribed to H.A. Vachell, dated 21. 3. 1908. Edges a bit worn, a little foxing. Good. MacManus 278-1968 1983 $50

FOX, ARTHUR W.   Ye Legende of St. Brade. Oldbury: J. Morgan, n.d. (1896). First edition. Illus. Orig. blue cloth gilt, v.g. Signed presentation copy from the editor, Henry McKean. Jarndyce 30-697 1983 £12.50

FOX, CHARLES   A Series of Poems. Bristol: Printed by Bulgin and Rosser, for J. Cottle...1797. 8vo, cont. speckled calf, somewhat worn. First edition. Quaritch NS 7-49 1983 $550

FOX, CORNELIUS B.   The Disposal of the Slop Water of Villages. J. and A. Churchill, 1875. Disbound. Jarndyce 31-343 1983 £12.50

FOX, GEORGE   A Collection of Many Select and Christian Epistles, Letters and Testimonies. Printed and sold by T. Sowle, 1698. First edition, 3Y4 being a cancel, folio, cont. panelled calf, neatly rebacked. A very good copy. Fenning 62-125 1983 £250

FOX, JOHN   A Cumberland Vendetta... New York, 1896. First issue. Inscr. by Fox, Dec. 23, 1895. Illus. 8vo. Morrill 288-127 1983 $35

FOX, JOHN   The Little Shepherd of Kingdom Come. New York: 1903. First edition, first printing. Illus. Red cloth. Fine and bright. Bradley 66-169 1983 $30

FOX, SAMSON   A Description of the Water-Gas Plant at Leeds Forge, Leeds. Whitehead, Morris & Lowe, printers, 1889. First edition, with 2 plages, 8vo, disbound, with the upper orig. printer paper wrapper. Fenning 62-126 1983 £24.50

FOX, UFFA   The Beauty of Sail. Peter Davies, (1938). First edition, with over 100 plates, 4to, orig. cloth, a very good copy in a slightly chipped dust wrapper. Fenning 62-127 1983 £18.50

FOXE, ARTHUR   Plague - Laennec (1782-1826) Inventor of the Stethescope... New York, 1947. First edition. 8vo. Orig. binding. Fye H-3-824 1983 $40

FOXON, DAVID F.   English Verse 1701-1750. Cambridge, 1975. 2 vols. 4to. Buckram, preserved in a slip-case. Traylen 94-342 1983 £60

FRACASTOR, HIERONYMUS   Contagion, Contagious Diseases, and their Treatment. New York, 1930. 8vo. Orig. binding. Dust wrapper. First English edition. Fye H-3-193 1983 $30

FRACASTOR, HIERONYMUS   Syphilis.from the Original Latin. St. Louis, 1911. 8vo. Orig. binding. Fye H-3-192 1983 $50

FRAENKEL, G. S.   The Orientation of Animals. Oxford, 1940. Illustrations, 8vo, cloth. Wheldon 160-483 1983 £18

FRAENKEL, HERMAN   Ovid, a Poet Between Two Worlds. 1945. 8vo, cloth. Salloch 385-636 1983 $22

FRANCE, ANATOLE   Crainquebille. New York: LEC, 1949. Quarto. 1st ed., 1 of 1500 numbered copies, signed by the artist, Bernard Lamotte. Orig. pink burlap, slipcased. Light wear to slipcase with one area of fading. Fine. Jenkins 155-810 1983 $40

FRANCE, ANATOLE   The Crime of Sylvestre Bonnard. NY, 1890. First edition, second state. Front hinge cracked, spine label and edges rubbed, good, owner's name. Quill & Brush 54-622 1983 $40

FRANCE, ANATOLE   Penguin Island. NY, 1947. Translated by A. W. Evans. Introduction by Carl Van Doren. Tall 8vo, leather-backed decorated silk bds., gilt. With drawings by Malcolm Cameron. One of 1500 copies signed by the artist. A very nice copy in rubbed slipcase. Perata 27-128 1983 $50

FRANCESCO D'ASSISI, SAINT   I. Fioretti Del Glorioso Poversello Di Christo S. Francesco De Assisi. The Ashendene Press, 1922. 4to. Orig. limp vellum with green silk ties, uncut edges. Printed on hand-made paper, initials in red and blue, woodcuts by J. Swain after C.M. Grere. Limited edition of 240 copies. Traylen 94-343 1983 £330

FRANCHERE, GABRIEL   Journal of a Voyage on the North West Coast of North America During the Years 1811, 1812, 1813, and 1814. Toronto, 1969. Illus. Orig. cloth. One of 825 numbered copies. Ginsberg 47-317 1983 $150

FRANCHERE, GABRIEL   Narrative of a Voyage to the Northwest Coast of America... New York: Redfield, 1854. 3 plates. Original green cloth. First English translation. Fine. Jenkins 153-210 1983 $300

FRANCHINI GUELFI, FAUSTA   Alessandro Magnasco. Genova: Cassa di Risparmio di Genova e Imperia, 1977. 60 color plates. 270 illus. Large 4to. Cloth. Dust jacket. Ars Libri 33-212 1983 $300

FRANCIS OF ASSISI
Please turn to
FRANCESCO D'ASSISI, SAINT

FRANCIS, ERIC T. B.   The Anatomy of the Salamander. Oxford: Claredon Press, 1934. Tall 8vo, with a color frontis. Black cloth. Karmiole 74-109 1983 $75

FRANCIS, GEORGE WILLIAM   Chemical Experiments... London: G. Berger, 1842. First edition. 8vo. Modern half calf over old boards. Numerous engravings of apparatus. Title written over in Cont. hand. Zeitlin 264-158 1983 $60

FRANCIS, JOHN   History of the Bank of England. Willoughby & Co., 1848. 3rd edition, 2 vols. Half titles, 6 pp 'Notices of the Press' vol. II. Orig. dull purple cloth, v.g. Jarndyce 31-165 1983 £46

FRANCIS, PHILIP   Speeches in the House of Commons... London: Ridgway, 1805. First edition. 8vo. Disbound. Scarce. Ximenes 63-206 1983 $50

FRANCIS, SAMUEL F.   Report of Professor Valentine Mott's Surgical Cliniques in the University of New York, Session 1859-60. New York, 1860. Illus. 12mo. 1st ed. Morrill 289-77 1983 $60

FRANCKLIN, WILLIAM   Observations made on a tour from Bengal to Persia... London: T. Cadell, 1790. First English edition. 8vo. Cont. tree calf, spine gilt. Fine copy. Ximenes 63-603 1983 $225

FRANCL, JOSEPH   The Story of...: Across the Plains to California in 1854. Cedar Rapids: 1928. Blue cloth, leather spine label, gilt. Laid in is long typed letter, signed, written in 1929 relating specifics about publication of the journal. Very good copy. Bradley 66-638 1983 $300

FRANCOIS, CITOYEN DE NEUFCHATEAU   Rapport sur le Perfectionnement des Charrues... Paris, An IX (1801). First edition. 8vo. Orig. wrappers. Very good copy. Heath 48-22 1983 £65

FRANK, JOHANN PETER   De Curandis Hominum Morbis Epitome...
Vienna, 1810-21. 8vo, orig. calf backed boards; ex-lib. 7 vols. in
5. Argosy 713-194 1983 $250

FRANK, LEONARD   Carl and Anna. New York: Putnam,
1930. Illus. with woodcuts. 1st ed. in English. Orig. cloth-
backed veneer-covered boards, boxed. Fine copy. Jenkins 155-438
1983 $20

FRANK, PHILIPP   Between Physics and Philosophy.
Cambridge, Harvard University, 1941. First edition. Inscribed and
signed by the author. Red cloth (slight rubbing). Very good.
Houle 22-388 1983 $45

FRANK, WALDO   The Bridegroom Cometh. NY, 1939. Special Bookseller's Edition. Limited to 251 numbered and signed copies,
darkening to spine gutter, very good in frayed and worn dustwrapper.
Quill & Brush 54-516 1983 $35

FRANK, WALDO   City Block. Darien, Conn., 1922. Published by author. One of 1225 numbered copies. Lower corners a little
rubbed. Flyleaf bears the signature of M. Reynolds. Nice. Rota 230-
221 1983 £40

FRANKAU, GILBERT   Everywoman. London: Hutchinson & Co.,
(1934). First English edition. Orig. cloth. Dust jacket (slightly
faded and worn). Presentation copy to Dennis Wheatley inscribed on
the title-page: "Gilbert Frankau for Dennis Wheatley." Slight foxing
to the endpapers and edges. Wheatley's bookplate on the front paste-
down endpaper. Near-fine. MacManus 278-1977 1983 $65

FRANKAU, GILBERT   Farewell Romance. London: Hutchinson &
Co., (1936). First edition. Orig. cloth. Dust jacket (spine and
covers slightly faded and a trifle worn). Presentation copy to Dennis
Wheatley inscribed on title-page: "Inscribed for his friend, Dennis
Wheatley, Gilbert Frankau, June 1936." Bookplate of Dennis Wheatley.
Near-fine. MacManus 278-1978 1983 $65

FRANKAU, GILBERT   More of Us. London: Hutchinson & Co.,
1937. First edition. Orig. cloth. Dust jacket (spine and covers
slightly faded and worn). Presentation copy to Dennis Wheatley
inscribed on the title-page: "Inscribed for his friend, Dennis Wheatley
with every good wish, Gilbert Frankau, June 1937." Spine faded and
slightly rubbed. With Wheatley's bookplate. Very good. MacManus
278-1979 1983 $65

FRANKAU, GILBERT   The Poetical Works. London: Chatto &
Windus, 1923. First edition. 2 vols. Photogravure frontispiece port.
Orig. cloth. Dust jackets (spines and covers faded and a trifle rubbed)
Edges slightly foxed. Some offsetting to the endpapers. Near-fine.
MacManus 278-1980 1983 $45

FRANKAU, GILBERT   Self-portrait. London: Hutchinson &
Co., (1940). First edition. Orig. cloth. Dust jacket (somewhat worn
and rubbed, spine ends slightly frayed, stains from tape repair).
Presentation copy to Dennis Wheatley inscribed: "With every good wish
for Dennis Wheatley, Gilbert Frankau, X'mas 1939." Preliminary pages
and edges slightly foxed. Wheatley's bookplate on the front paste-
down endpaper. Very good. MacManus 278-1981 1983 $65

FRANKAU, GILBERT   Winter of Discontent. London: Hutchinson & Co., (1941). First edition. Orig. cloth. Dust jacket (slightly
faded, worn and soiled, with one small tear to the rear cover). Presentation copy to Dennis Wheatley inscribed X'mas 1941. Endpapers and
edges slightly foxed. Wheatley's bookplate on the front paste-down
endpaper. Near-fine. MacManus 278-1982 1983 $65

FRANKENBURGER, MAX   Beitrage zur Geschichte Wenzel Jamnitzer
und seiner Familie. Strassburg: J.H. Ed. Heitz, 1901. Wrappers.
Ars Libri 32-342 1983 $45

FRANKLIN, BENJAMIN   The Autobiography. San Francisco:
Limited edition Club, 1931. Port. & borders by Wm. Wilke. Folio,
vellum-backed boards, (hinge slightly worn). One of a ltd. numbered
ed., signed by the printer, John Henry Nash. Argosy 716-171 1983
$40

FRANKLIN, BENJAMIN   A Collection of the Familiar Letters
and Miscellaneous Papers of Benjamin Franklin. Boston: Charles
Bowen, 1833. Linen cloth, paper spine label. First edition thus.
Felcone 22-69 1983 $20

FRANKLIN, BENJAMIN   Experiences et Observations sur l'
Electricite. Paris: Durand, 1752. With one finely engraved folding
plate. Calf. With bookplates of Mildred & Robert Woods Bliss/
Dumbarton Oakds/& ownership inscription: "ex lib. j.f. barailon m.d."
Rostenberg 88-82 1983 $1,850

FRANKLIN, BENJAMIN   Experiments and Observations on
Electricity, Made at Philadelphia in America...to which are Added,
Letters and Papers on Philosophical Subjects. London, 1769. 7
plates, 10 illus. in text. Orig. marbled boards, leather spine,
some cracking at the hinges. Completely uncut and partially
unopened, an extremely fine copy. Reese 18-88 1983 $4,500

FRANKLIN, BENJAMIN   Frankliniana, ou Recueil d'Anecdotes,
bon Mots... Paris: Chez Tiger, (ca.1818). Disbound. Portrait lacking. Very good. Felcone 20-51 1983 $25

FRANKLIN, BENJAMIN   The Life of... Cincinnati, 1830.
Port., extra engr. title, 24mo, calf-backed boards, (lightly
foxed). Argosy 716-172 1983 $35

FRANKLIN, BENJAMIN   Memoirs of the Life and Writings of
Benjamin Franklin... London: Colburn, 1818-9. 6 vols. Frontis.
portrait, facsimile of letter, 6 engraved plates of 7, and folding
map. 8vo. Old sheep. Rubbed, chipped. Defect to spine of vol.
IV. Zeitlin 264-159 1983 $140

FRANKLIN, BENJAMIN   Memoires de la Vie Privee de Benjamin
Franklin. Paris: Chez Buisson, 1791. Two parts bound in one vol.
as issued. 1st ed. Contemporary half calf and mottled boards, gilt.
Spine ends worn and some minor foxing of first and last leaves, else
a very good crisp copy. Jenkins 155-439 1983 $800

FRANKLIN, BENJAMIN   A Narrative of the Late Massacres, in
Lancaster County... (Phila.: Anthony Armbruster), 1764. Disbound.
One leaf supplied from another copy, last leaf (containing but two
sentences, otherwise blank) lacking. Felcone 20-49 1983 $400

FRANKLIN, BENJAMIN   Poor Richard: The Almanacs. 1964.
Proofs of the titlepage, 3 attempts in black, final printed version in
red & black. Proofs are corrected and annotated by hand by Richard
Ellis who designed the book. 16 pages of specification sheets, corres.
with suppliers, etc. O'Neal 50-73 1983 $75

FRANKLIN, BENJAMIN   Satires & Bagatelles. Detroit: Fine
Book Circle, 1937. Cloth backed boards. Ink name. Chipped and
slightly stained dust wrapper. Limited to 1000 numbered copies,
collected, designed and illus. by P. McPharlin. Very good. King 45-
177 1983 $20

FRANKLIN, BENJAMIN   Some Account of the Pennsylvania
Hospital from its First Rise to the Beginning. Phila., Office of the
U.S. Gazette, 1817. Tall 8vo, cont. boards; uncut, bookplate.
Argosy 713-195 1983 $150

FRANKLIN, BENJAMIN   The Way to Wealth. Newipswich:
Simeon Ide, 1816. Later cloth, orig. wraps. bound in. Felcone
22-67 1983 $35

FRANKLIN, BENJAMIN   The Way to Wealth, or Poor Richard
improved. Paris: Ant. Aug. Renouard, 1795. 1st ed. bearing this
title, large paper copy, cont. calf, spine gilt, morocco label.
Engraved frontis. portrait, half-title. Hinges rubbed but firm;
a fine copy. Trebizond 18-191 1983 $325

FRANKLIN, BENJAMIN   The Way to Wealth or Poor Richard
Improved (& Other Works). Paris: Renouard, 1795. 5 parts in one.
8vo, with frontis. portrait of Franklin & with 31-page catalogue of
books printed by Bodoni & sold by Renouard. Boards Ownership
entry of Jules Brunet. One of 6 copies printed on large paper.
Rostenberg 88-130 1983 $350

FRANKLIN, BENJAMIN   Oeuvres. 1773. 2 vols. in 1, 4to,
portrait, 12 plates, light waterstain at the beginning of vol. 1
and on the plates at the end of vol. 2, cont. mottled calf, upper
joint cracked, slight wear at foot of the spine, spine gilt, but
binding firm. First edition in French. Bickersteth 77-272 1983
£200

FRANKLIN, BENJAMIN   Oeuvres. Paris, 1773. 2 vols.,
finely engr. port., 12 plates, half-titles, 4to, orig. paper wraps.
4th edition. Argosy 716-173 1983 $350

FRANKLIN, BENJAMIN   Works of the Late Dr. Benjamin Franklin: Consisting of His Life, Written by Himself. Humtingdon (Pa.): The proprietor, 1800. Full calf. Lacks portrait frontis. Felcone 22-68 1983 $75

FRANKLIN, JOHN   Narrative of a Journey to the Shores of the Polar Sea, in the Years 1819, 20, 21, and 22. Phila., 1824. Illus., engraved frontis. of Esquimos, folded map. Half morocco. First American edition. Ginsberg 47-318 1983 $250

FRANKLIN, JOHN   Narrative of a Second Expedition to the Shores of the Polar Sea. London, 1828. Illus., 6 maps. 31 plates. Cont. half morocco. First edition. Ginsberg 47-319 1983 $875

FRANKLIN, THOMAS   Matilda. London, T. Cadell, 1775. 8vo, boards, title and end-leaf bit dust-soiled, else good. First edition. Ravenstree 94-121 1983 $42

FRANKLYN, THOMAS   A Dissertation on Ancient Tragedy. (London), 1768. First edition. 12mo. Half roan morocco. Engraved frontis. Some wear to binding. Heath 48-306 1983 £45

FRANKS, J. M.   Seventy Years in Texas. Gatesville, 1924. First edition. Portrait. Orig. green printed wrappers. Fine Josey copy. Jenkins 152-119 1983 $85

FRANZ, SHEPHERD IVORY   Handbook of Mental Examination Methods. NY: N.M.D. Pub. Co., 1912. A rebound ex-library copy. Gach 94-338 1983 $20

FRASCHETTI, STANISLAO   Il Bernini. Milano: Ulrico Hoepli, 1900. 270 illus. Stout 4to. Marbled boards, 3/4 calf. Orig. wrappers bound in. Rare. Ars Libri 33-30 1983 $550

FRASER, CLAUD LOVAT   The Apple (of Beauty & Discord). London: Printed by The Morland Press, April 1920. First edition. Illus. with decorations by C.L. Fraser and others. Orig. pictorial wrappers. Spine and covers rather worn at margins, separated from inner contents. Spine badly torn. Inner pages unharmed. MacManus 278-1983 1983 $25

FRASER, CLAUD LOVAT   Catalogue of the Memorial Exhibition of Works. London: Ernest Brown & Phillips, The Leicester Galleries, December 1921. First edition, second issue. 12mo. Illus. Orig. pictorial wrappers (a little rubbed and stained). Very good. MacManus 278-1985 1983 $150

FRASER, CLAUD LOVAT   Designs. London: The Morland Press, (1922). First edition. Illus. Orig. cloth-backed boards. One of 7 copies printed on hand-made paper. Spine and covers faded, slightly worn, and spotted. Some offsetting to the endpapers. Very good. MacManus 278-1992 1983 $750

FRASER, CLAUD LOVAT   Designs by Claud Lovat Fraser (1890-1921). London: The Morland Press, (1922). First edition. Illus. Orig. cloth-backed boards. One of 25 copies. Spine and covers slightly faded, worn and soiled. Very good. MacManus 278-2009 1983 $450

FRASER, CLAUD LOVAT   A Garland of New Songs. London: A.T. Stevens for Flying Fame, 1913. First edition. 8-page folded leaf, in black and white. Near-fine. MacManus 278-1994 1983 $65

FRASER, CLAUD LOVAT   Nursery Rhymes. London: T.C. & E.C. Jack, (1919). First edition. Illus. by C.L. Fraser. Orig. pictorial cloth-backed boards. Dust jacket (spine and covers faded and worn; front cover badly torn). Covers slightly faded. Near-fine. MacManus 278-2015 1983 $150

FRASER, CLAUD LOVAT   Nursery Rhymes. N.Y.: Knopf, n.d. Printed in Great Britain. 4to. Blue cloth. Slight smudging on covers. Illus. in color on almost all pages. Very good. Aleph-bet 8-110 1983 $55

FRASER, CLAUD LOVAT   Pirates. London: Jonathan Cape, (1921). First edition, second issue. Illus. Orig. cloth-backed decorated boards. Paper spine label (slightly chipped, faded). Inscription on front free endpaper: "To Edward Penfield with the great appreciation of William A. Kittridge, 1922." Spine and covers faded and slightly worn at the margins, spine ends slightly frayed, with some offsetting to the endpapers. Good. MacManus 278-2017 1983 $125

FRASER, GORDON   Poems. Wigtown: Gordon Fraser and the Booksellers. 1885. Front. photographic port. Orig. brown cloth, v.g. Jarndyce 30-698 1983 £12.50

FRASER, JAMES BAILLIE   The Kuzzilbash. Henry Colburn, 1828. First edition. 3 vols. Large 12mo, half-titles, two advertisement leaves at end. Later paper boards, uncut. Marginal stain on two leaves. Hannas 69-63 1983 £55

FRASER, JAMES BAILLIE   The Highland Smugglers. Henry Colburn and Richard Bentley, 1832. 1st ed., 3 vols, lge. 12mo, contemporary half calif, gilt backs; a good copy. Hill 165-37 1983 £75

FRASER, JAMES BAILLIE   The Highland Smugglers. London: H. Colburn and R. Bentley, 1832. First edition. 3 vols. 8vo. Orig. boards, paper labels, uncut edges. Spines defective. Traylen 94-344 1983 £25

FRASER, W. M.   Rings from a Chota Sahib's Pipe. Calcutta, 1901. Sm.8vo. Decorated cloth. Good. Edwards 1044-269 1983 £15

FRASER, WILLIAM   Disraeli and His Day. Kegan Paul, Trench, 1891. 2nd edition, half title, orig. brown cloth, v.g. Jarndyce 30-974 1983 £16.50

FRAUENKNECHT, JOHANN JACOB   Dissertatio inauguralis medico-chemica de Genuinis Viribus Tabaci ex principiis eius constitutiuis. Halle-Magdeburg, 1746. First edition. Decorative woodcut headpiece and initials. Small 4to. Modern boards. Kraus 164-231 1983 $220

FRAXI, PISANUS   Bibliography of Printed Books. New York: Jack Brussel, 1962. First printing of DeLuxe Edition. 3 vols. Buckram. 1/1,000 sets. Largely unopened, in publisher's board slipcase. Bradley 66-33 1983 $150

FRAZER, JAMES GEORGE   The Golden Bough... London: MacMillan, 1911-15. 12 vols. 3rd ed., much revised and enlarged. Orig. green cloth, gilt, uncut. Good sturdy set. Jenkins 153-823 1983 $225

FRAZER, JAMES GEORGE   Man, God and Immortality. New York, Macmillan, 1927. First American ed., ads., very good in worn dust jacket. Gach 95-143 1983 $25

FRAZER, JAMES GEORGE   Pausanias and Other Greek Sketches. London, 1900. 8vo, cloth. Salloch 385-349 1983 $35

FREASE, W. M.   The Recollections of a Tea Planter. London, (c.1935). Map. Spine faded. 8vo. Orig. cloth. Good. Edwards 1044-268 1983 £25

FRECHETTE, LOUIS   Voix de Noel. SF, 1936. 4to, stiff wrappers. One of 200 copies printed for Leon Gelber & Theodore Lilienthal. A very good copy. Perata 27-216 1983 $25

FREDERIC II, KING OF PRUSSIA   Posthumous Works. London, 1789. 4 vols., 8vo., contemporary tree calf, gilt spines with crimson and blue mor. labels, gilt. Engraved portrait, folding map. Traylen 94-349 1983 £38

FREDERICK, JAMES V.   Ben Holladay The Stagecoach King. Glendale, 1940. 1st ed. Illus., large fldg. map. Edges untrimmed, gilt top. Clark 741-396 1983 $125

FREDERICK, WILLIAM   A Declaration of His Electoral Highness the Duke of Brandenburgh... London: for Richard Chiswell, 1689. 4to. Wrappers. Heath 48-115 1983 £30

FREDERICKSON, A. D.   Ad Orientem. London, 1889. 14 coloured natural history plates, 12 lithograph plates, 6 coloured, and other illus. 8vo. Pictorial cloth gilt, slightly soiled. Good. Edwards 1044-270 1983 £45

A FREE Examination of a Modern Romance. Printed for W. Webb, 1746. 8vo, speckled calf gilt, a.e.g. First edition. Bickersteth 77-49 1983 £28

FREE Man's Companion. Hartford, Abel Brewster, 1827. 1st ed. 8vo, contemporary calf, leather label. Morrill 287-122 1983 $35

FREEBETTER, EDMUND   The New England Almanack, and Gentlemen and Ladies Diary, for ... 1787. New London: T. Green, (1786). Stitched. Very good. Felcone 20-2 1983 $35

FREEDLEY, EDWIN T.   Leading Pursuits and Leading Men. Philadelphia, Edward Young, (1856). Ads, some illus. Frontispiece. 8vo. Rubbed, some foxing. Morrill 287-123 1983 $40

FREEDMAN, RALPH   Divided. N.Y., Dutton, 1948. First edition. Dust jacket (chips) else very good. Inscribed by the author December 15, 1948. Houle 22-389 1983 $35

FREEDOM: A Journal of Realistic Idealism. Sea Breeze, Fla., March 1, 1899. Single issue. Folio. Vol. 6, no. 38. Jenkins 153-772 1983 $20

FREEMAN, DON   It Shouldn't Happen. (N.Y.), Harcourt, (1945). First edition. Dust jacket (small chips). Illus. by author. Good - very good. Houle 22-390 1983 $55

FREEMAN, DOUGLAS SOUTHALL   George Washington: A Biography. New York: 1948-57. First edition. Illus. 7 vols. Blue cloth. Fine set. First 6 vols. contained in four board slipcases, vol. 7 in dust jacket without slipcase. Bradley 66-548 1983 $435

FREEMAN, DOUGLAS SOUTHALL   Lee's Lieutenants. New York, 1945, 1944, 1945. 3 vols. 8vo. Mismatched set--vol. 1 in blue cloth and vols. 2 & 3 in black. Morrill 286-164 1983 $25

FREEMAN, DOUGLAS SOUTHALL   R. E. Lee, A Biography. NY, 1943. 4 Vols. Pulitzer Prize edition. Fancy dec. cloth, small note in text, ink inscription else very good set. King 46-53 1983 $65

FREEMAN, EDWARD AUGUSTUS   An essay on the origin and development of window tracery in England. Oxford: Parker, 1851. First edition. 8vo. Orig. purple-brown cloth. 74 plates, one gathering pulled. Ximenes 63-13 1983 $75

FREEMAN, G. E.   Practical Falconry. 1869. 8vo, original cloth. Very scarce. Wheldon 160-708 1983 £45

FREEMAN, GEORGE D.   Midnight and Noonday. Caldwell, Dan., 1892. Cloth, very good. Reese 19-232 1983 $200

FREEMAN, GEORGE WASHINGTON   A Biography. New York, 1948. 1st ed. Maps and illus. 8vo, boxed, nice. Morrill 286-165 1983 $20

FREEMAN, H. W.   Down In The Valley. London: Chatto & Windus, 1930. First edition. Orig. cloth-backed patterned boards. One of 132 copies signed by author. Very good. MacManus 278-2027 1983 $35

FREEMAN, H. W.   Down In The Valley. London: Chatto & Windus, 1930. First edition. Orig. cloth. Dust jacket (slightly faded and worn). Spine and covers slightly faded, edges a trifle foxed. Very good. MacManus 278-2026 1983 $25

FREEMAN, HARRY C.   A Brief History of Butte, Montana. Chicago: Henry O. Shepard Co., 1900. 4to, profusely illus. with photographs of the city, the mining industry, the shops, etc. Orig. brown dec. cloth, a bit soiled (primarily on back cover). Karmiole 75-94 1983 $50

FREEMAN, JAMES W.   Prose and Poetry of the Live Stock Industry of the United States. N.Y., 1949. Facsimile of the 1890 original. Large quarto. Limited to 500 numbered copies bound in half morocco, slipcased. Jenkins 151-85 1983 $200

FREEMAN, JAMES W.   Prose and Poetry of the Live Stock Industry of the U.S. New York, 1959. Edn. ltd. to 500 numbered copies. Facs. edn. Many illus., ports., 4to, half leather, gilt top, boxed. Clark 741-207 1983 $150

FREEMAN, JAMES W.   Prose and Poetry of the Live Stock Industry. N.Y., 1959. Illus. Orig. cloth, boxed. Limited edition of 750 copies. Ginsberg 47-320 1083 $100

FREEMAN, JOHN   A Portrait of George Moore in a Study of His Work. London: T. Werner Laurie, Ltd., 1922. First edition. 8vo. Frontis. Orig. cloth. Dust jacket. Fine copy. Jaffe 1-257 1983 $45

FREEMAN, JOHN   A Portrait of George Moore in a Study of his Work. London, 1922. First edition. One of 600 numbered copies, signed by author. Half parchment. Dust wrapper. Nice. Rota 231-432 1983 £18

FREEMAN, JOHN   A Portrait of George Moore in a Study of His Work. London: Privately Printed, 1922. First edition. Orig. boards. Dust jacket (spine slightly faded and worn). One of 600 copies signed by author. Near-fine. MacManus 279-3841 1983 $35

FREEMAN, LEWIS R.   By Waterways to Gotham. New York, 1926. 1st ed. Illus. 8vo, dust wrapper. Morrill 286-166 1983 $30

FREEMAN, LEWIS R.   The Colorado River Yesterday, Today, and Tomorrow. New York: Dodd, Mead and Co., 1923. Frontis. and plates. Light foxing to text. Fairly nice copy overall. Jenkins 152-122 1983 $75

FREEMAN, LEWIS R.   Down the Yellowstone. New York, 1922. Plates. First edition. Some wear. Ramon Adams's personal copy. Nice copy. Jenkins 153-202 1983 $40

FREEMAN, MARGARET B.   Herbs for the Mediaeval household for cooking... New York: Metropolitan Museum of Art, 1943. Large 8vo. Boards. Printed in red and black, and illustrated throughout. Gurney JJ-129 1983 £15

FREEMAN, R. AUSTIN   As a Thief in the Night. London, n.d. (1928). First edition. Inscription. Free endpapers spotted. Spine faded. Very good. Jolliffe 26-136 1983 £25

FREEMAN, R. AUSTIN   The Case of Oscar Brodski. NY, (1923). Paper-covered boards have slight wear, near very good, owner's name. Quill & Brush 54-518 1983 $35

FREEMAN, R. AUSTIN   Felo De Se. London, 1937. First edition. Blue covers faded and a little soiled. Soiled dustwrapper with a few closed tears. Very good. Gekoski 2-57 1983 £65

FREEMAN, R. AUSTIN   Felo de Se? London, 1937. First edition. Spine faded. Inscription on title-page. Very good. Jolliffe 26-140 1983 £20

FREEMAN, R. AUSTIN   For the Defence: Dr. Thorndyke. London, 1934. First edition. Edges spotted. Spine faded. Very good. Jolliffe 26-138 1983 £25

FREEMAN, R. AUSTIN   The Penrose Mystery. London, 1936. First edition. Edges slightly spotted. Pastedowns discoloured. Spine faded. Very good. Jolliffe 26-139 1983 £20

FREEMAN, R. AUSTIN   Pontifex, Son and Thorndyke. London, 1931. First edition. Edges spotted. Spine faded and slightly worn at the head and tail. Very good. Jolliffe 26-137 1983 £25

FREEMAN, R. AUSTIN   The Stoneware Monkey. London, 1938. Inscription. Edges slightly spotted. First edition. Very good. Jolliffe 26-141 1983 £25

FREEMAN, WALTER   Psychosurgery. Springfield, Il.: Charles C. Thomas, 1942. First edition. Near fine copy in dust jacket. Gach 95-144 1983 $75

FREIND, JOHN   An Account of the Earl of Peterborow's Conduct in Spain. Printed for Johan Bowyer, 1707. 8vo, cont. calf, lower margin and lower half of the side margins of many leaves soiled, and a few brittle from damp with small holes or pieces missing from margin, but text unaffected. Calf binding sound, with remains of old paper label at top of spine. Author's name added in an early hand in ink to the title. Bickersteth 69-31 1983 £28

FREIND, JOHN   Emmenologia; in qua Fluxus Muliebris
Menstrui Phaenomena Periodi... London, 1717. Second edition. 8vo.
Old vellum. Title torn, with large piece missing from lower outer
corner (restored). Heavily browned. Gurney JJ-130 1983 £15

FREIRE DE ANDRADE, JACINTO   The Life of Dom John de Castro, the
Fourth Vice-Roy of India. Printed for Henry Herringman, 1664. First
edition in English, with a fine impression of the engraved portrait
frontis. by Faithorne, a double-page engraved plan and an engraved
plate, folio, cont. calf, the spine neatly repaired retaining the
orig. label. Fenning 60-121 1983 £245

FREISE, KURT   Rembrandts Handzeichnungen. Parchim
i.M.: Hermann Freise, 1912-1914. 2 vols. 57 tipped-in plates.
176 tipped-in plates. Large 4to. Boards. Light wear. Ars Libri
32-554 1983 $175

FREKE, JOHN   An Essay to Shew the Cause of Electricity. London, Printed for W. Innys, 1746. 1st ed., 8vo, title page,
possibly lacks a half title; title a little soiled; disbound in a
modern paper wrapper. Pickering & Chatto 22-43 1983 $225

FREMANTLE, LIEUTENANT COLONEL   Three Months in the Soutnern States:
April-June, 1863. NY, 1864. Foxed, covers worn. First American edition. King 46-54 1983 $50

FREMONT, JOHN CHARLES   Geographical Memois upon Upper California,
an Illustration of His Map of Oregon and California. Wash., 1849.
Illus., large folding map. Half morocco. Ginsberg 47-322 1983 $250

FREMONT, JOHN CHARLES   Life of Col. Fremond. (NY: Greeley &
M'Elrath, 1856). Illus. Port. Argosy 716-35 1983 $27.50

FREMONT, JOHN CHARLES   Memoirs of My Life. Chicago: Belford,
Clarke & Co., 1887. Marginal stains. Maps & illus. including folding
map at end. Orig. half leather. Gilt stamped, some wear. Dawson 471-
90 1983 $175

FRENCH, ALLEN   The First Year of the American Revolution. Boston, 1934. Maps. Argosy 710-446 1983 $30

FRENCH, GILBERT J.   The Life and Times of Samuel Crompton
of Hall-in-the-Wood. Manchester, Charles Simms, 1862. With a
portrait and 9 illus., small 8vo, cont. calf, gilt, label
supplied, a very good copy. Fenning 61-92 1983 £32.50

FRENCH, GILBERT J.   The life and times of Samuel Compton
of Hall-in-the-Wood. Manchester: Simms, 1862. Third edition.
12mo. Orig. printed wrappers. Frontis., and several full-page
wood-engravings. Dusty, slight wear. Ximenes 63-569 1983 $27.50

FRENCH, HERBERT   An Index of Differential Diagnosis
of Main Symptoms by Various Writers. New York, 1913. 8vo. Orig.
binding. First American edition. Fye H-3-197 1983 $50

FRENCH, HOLLIS   The Thatcher Maqoun. Cambridge, (1936).
Second impression. Illustrated. 8vo, original boards, cloth back,
paper label, very nice. Morrill 290-134 1983 $20

FRENCH, JOSEPH L.   The Pioneer West Narratives of the
Westward March of Empire. Boston, 1923. Frontis. Original pic.
cloth. First edition. Fine copy. Jenkins 153-207 1983 $30

FRENEAU, PHILIP   American Poems, Selected and Original.
Litchfield (Ct.): Collier & Buel, (1793). First edition. Complete
with two blanks between contents and text, list of subscribers, and
the errata at end. Orig. sheep, red morocco label, gilt. Jenkins 152-
631 1983 $150

FRENEAU, PHILIP   Poems Written Between the Years 1768 &
1794. Monmouth, (N.J.): Printed at the Press of the Author, at Mount
Pleasant, near Middletown Point, 1795. Full calf. Spine very poor and
glue-covered. Half-title. Very clean, good. Felcone 19-18 1983 $250

FRENEAU, PHILIP   Some Account of the Capture of the Ship
"Aurora". New York: Mansfield, (1899). First edition. Several
plates and facsimilies. Orig. cloth-backed printed boards, uncut.
Obviously a limited edition, although not stated. Fine. Jenkins
155-444 1983 $35

FRENZEL, H. K.   Ludwig Hohlwein. Berlin: Phonix,
1926. 289 plates (66 color). Large 4to. Cloth. Colored brochure
designed by Hohlwein loosely inserted. Very scarce. Ars Libri 32-
316 1983 $500

FRERE, EDOUARD   Manuel du Bibliographe Normand... New
York: Burt Franklin, n.d. 2 vols. Cloth. Reprint of the 1858-60
ed. Dawson 470-114 1983 $24.98

FRERE, JOHN HOOKHAM   John Hookham Frere's National Poems.
1867. First edition, 2 vols. 8pp inserted ads., fronts. and half
titles in both vols. Orig. pink cloth, paper labels. Largely uncut,
v.g. Jarndyce 31-699 1983 £80

FRERE, M.   Old Deccan Days. London, 1868. 4 chromolithograph plates. Cloth faded and worn. 8vo. Inscribed on the front
endpaper from Author also "for Dear Amy with love from her affectionate
M. & C. Frere, February 29th 1868." Good. Edwards 1044-271 1983 £40

FRESENIUS, CARL REMIGIUS   Anleitung zur Qualitativen Chemischen
Analyse fur Anfanger und Gebutere... Braunschweig: Vieweg, 1895.
8vo. 3/4 morocco over boards. Folding color plate, text illus.
Water damaged, minor dampstaining of endleaves, otherwise a good
copy. Zeitlin 264-160 1983 $50

FRESENIUS, CARL REMIGIUS   Elementary Instruction in Chemical
Analysis... London: Churchill, 1843. First English edition.
8vo. Orig. blind stamped cloth. Ads. Very good copy. Zeitlin
264-162 1983 $60

FRESERNIUS, CARL REMIGIUS   Qualitative Chemical Analysis...
London: Churchill, 1897. Tenth edition. 8vo. Orig. stamped
cloth. Extending colored frontis. Publisher's list. A little
aged but a very good copy. Zeitlin 264-163 1983 $45

FRESHFIELD, MRS. HENRY   A Summer Tour in the Grisons and
Italian Valleys of the Bernina. London: Longman, Green, Longman
and Roberts, 1862. Illus. with 4 color lithograph plates and 2
folding color maps. Bound in cont. full polished calf; elaborately
gilt spine with leather spine label. Binding by "Dickens" of London.
Bookplate. Karmiole 72-72 1983 $125

FREUD, ANNA   Das Ich und die Abwehrmechanismen.
Wien, 1936. 1st ed. 8vo. Morrill 289-78 1983 $25

FREUD, ANNA   Psychoanalysis for Teachers and Parents.
NY: Emerson Books, 1935. First American edition. Good copy. Gach
95-145 1983 $25

FREUD, SIGMUND   An Autobiographical Study. London:
Hogarth, 1935. First British edition. First separate appearance in
English. Ad leaf. Orig. green cloth. Good copy, endpapers foxed.
Gach 95-146 1983 $35

FREUD, SIGMUND   Aus den Anfaengen der Psychoanalyse.
London, (1950). First edition. 8vo, cloth. Argosy 713-197 1983
$100

FREUD, SIGMUND   Das Ich Und Das Es. IPV, 1923. Ad
leaf. First edition. Very good copy in orig. wrappers. Gach 95-
148 1983 $185

FREUD, SIGMUND   Dream Psychology. NY: The James A.
McCann Co., 1920. First edition. Publisher's green cloth. Gach
95-147 1983 $35

FREUD, SIGMUND   The Future of an Illusion. London:
The Hogarth Press, 1928. First edition. Dark green cloth. Some
pencil underscoring, otherwise a very good copy. Bradley 66-417
1983 $125

FREUD, SIGMUND   Inhibition, Symptoms and Anxiety.
London: Hogarth, 1936. First edition in English of third translation. First edition published in Britain. Orig. green cloth, very
good in dust jacket. Gach 95-149 1983 $65

FREUD, SIGMUND   The Interpretation of Dreams. New York:
Macmillan, 1913. 8vo, erratum slip, orig. cloth. First edition in
English. Argosy 713-198 1983 $250

FREUD, SIGMUND   Introductory Lectures on Psycho-
Analysis... 1922. First English edition, frontis, covers dull.
K Books 307-78 1983 £30

FREUD, SIGMUND   Moses and Monotheism. London: Hogarth,
1939. First edition in English. Very good copy in worn dust jacket.
Gach 95-151 1983 $75

FREUD, SIGMUND   Moses and Monotheism. N.Y., Knopf,
1939. First American edition. Dark blue cloth stamped in gilt.
Very good. Houle 22-392 1983 $27.50

FREUD, SIGMUND   Moses and Monotheism. NY: Knopf, 1939.
First American edition. Very good in worn and taped dust jacket.
Gach 95-151a 1983 $20

FREUD, SIGMUND   Psychoanalytische Studien. IPV, 1924.
Ads. First edition. Very good copy in orig. printed yellow linen.
Gach 95-153 1983 $135

FREUD, SIGMUND   Studies in Hysteria. NY: N. M. D.
Pub. Co., 1936. First complete edition. Boards. Fine copy. Gach
95-155 1983 $125

FREUD, SIGMUND   Three Contributions to the Sexual
Theory. N.Y., 1910. First edition in English. 8vo, orig. pr. wrs.
(worn & chipped). Argosy 713-199 1983 $35

FREUD, SIGMUND   Wit and its Relation to the Unconscious.
NY: Moffat, Yard, 1916. Very good copy in publisher's red cloth.
Gach 95-157 1983 $100

FREUD, SIGMUND   Zur Psychopathologie Des Alltagslebens.
Berlin: S. Karger, 1912. Fourth edition, revised. Ads. Modern grey
cloth with leather label. Gach 95-154 1983 $50

FREUND, IDA   The Study of Chemical Composition.
Cambridge: University Press, 1904. First edition. 8vo. Orig.
cloth. Numerous text diagrams and tables (1 folding). Lightly
rubbed. Very good copy. Zeitlin 264-164 1983 $70

FREUNDLICH, HERBERT   Kapillarchemie. Leipzig, 1922. Illus.
Argosy 713-210 1983 $100

FREUNDLICH, HERBERT   Kapillarchemie, eine Darstellung der
Chemie der Kolloide und verwandter Gebiete. Leipzig: Akad. Verlag,
1909. First edition. 8vo. Orig. cloth. Spine chipped slightly,
minor spotting boards. Zeitlin 264-165 1983 $45

FREWEN, MORETON   Melton Mowbray, and Other Memories.
London: Herbert Jenkins Limited, 1924. First edition. Frontis.
Orig. cloth. Minor wear to spine. Jenkins 152-123 1983 $200

FREY, CAROLL   Bibliography of the Writings of H.L.
Mencken. Phila., Centaur, 1924. Half black cloth, gold labels,
uncut (a bit rubbed), one of 300 copies. Very good. Houle 21-1201
1983 $135

FREY, KARL   Die Handzeichnungen Michelagniolos
Buonarroti. Berlin: Julius Bard, 1909-1911. 3 vols. 300 superb
collotype plates (partly in color) loose in 2 portfolios as issued.
Small folio. Cloth. Edition limited to 400 numbered copies. Light
intermittent foxing. From the library of Vittorio Emanuele III,
King of Italy. Ars Libri 33-240 1983 $1,800

FRIDGE, IKE   Life of Ike Fridge. Electra, (1927).
Illus. wrps. Scarce. Clark 741-204 1983 $297.50

FRIED, ERICH   Gedichte. Hamburg, 1958. First
edition. Presentation copy from the author, inscribed to Theodore
Roethke. Cellophane over wrappers nicked and loosening, otherwise
fine. Jolliffe 26-443 1983 £40

FRIEDE, DONALD   The Mechanical Angel. N.Y., Knopf,
1948. First edition. Dust jacket. Very good. Houle 22-828 1983
$25

FRIEDENWALD, HARRY   Jewish Luminaries in Medical History...
Baltimore, 1946. First edition. 8vo. Orig. binding. Dust wrapper.
Fye H-3-1038 1983 $30

FRIEDENWALD, JONAS S.   Pathology of the Eye. N.Y., 1929.
First edition. 252 illus. Argosy 713-202 1983 $50

FRIEDLAENDER, LUDWIG   Sittengeschichte Roms. Vienna, 1934.
8vo, cloth. Salloch 385-229 1983 $80

FRIEDLAENDER, PAUL   Platon. Berlin & Lg, 1928-1930. 8vo,
cloth. 2 vols., cl. Salloch 385-683 1983 $90

FRIEDLAENDER, WALTER   Claude Lorrain. Berlin: Paul Cassirer,
1921. Prof. illus. 4to. Cloth. From the library of Jakob Rosenberg.
Ars Libri 32-110 1983 $50

FRIEDLAENDER, WALTER   Nicolas Poussin. Die Entwicklung
seiner Kunst. Munchen: R. Piper, 1914. 137 plates (4 tipped-in
hors texte). 4to. Cloth. From the library of Jakob Rosenberg.
Ars Libri 32-535 1983 $125

FRIEDLANDER, GERALD   The Jewish Fairy Book. N.Y.: Stokes,
(1920). 8vo. Green pictorial cloth. Illus. with 8 color plates by
G. Hood. Very good. Aleph-bet 8- 119 1983 $20

FRIEDLANDER, MAX J.   Albrecht Altdorfer. Berlin: Bruno
Cassirer, (1923). 111 illus. Large 4to. Boards, 1/4 cloth. From
the library of Jakob Rosenberg. Ars Libri 32-4 1983 $85

FRIEDLANDER, MAX J.   Albrecht Durer der Kupferstecher und
Holzschnittzeichner. Berlin: Julius Bard, 1919. 67 superb facsimile plates. 40 text illus. Folio. Boards. Edition limited to
500 numbered copies. Ars Libri 32-177 1983 $275

FRIEDLANDER, MAX J.   Die Gemalde von Lucas Cranach. Berlin:
Deutscher Verein fur Kunstwissenschaft, 1932. 368 plates. Large
4to. New Cloth. Ars Libri 32-130 1983 $300

FRIEDLANDER, MAX J.   Die Zeichnungen von Matthias Grunewald.
Berlin: G. Grote, 1927. 33 plates. Large 4to. Boards, 1/4 cloth.
Edition limited to 2000 copies. Ars Libri 32-293 1983 $50

FRIEDLANDER, MAX J.   The Paintings of Lucas Cranach. Ithaca:
Cornell University Press, 1978. Revised edition. 486 plates. 14
text illus. 4to. Cloth. Dust jacket. Ars Libri 32-131 1983 $100

FRIEDMANN, H.   Birds Collect-d by the Childs Frick
Expedition to Ethiopa and Kenha Colony. Washington, 1930-37. Two
coloured plates of birds and 24 plates of views, 2 vols., 8vo, orig.
wrappers. Wheldon 160-709 1983 £30

THE FRIEND. A Religious and Literary Journal. Philadelphia: Printed
by Adam Waldie, October 7, 1837-September 29, 1838. Demy 4to, 28-1/2
x 23 cm. Nineteenth-century half roan and marbled boards. Scuffed,
some internal staining with a few leaves chipped into lower margin,
but a solid and generally very good copy. Grunder 7-30 1983 $125

FRIEZE, JACOB   A Concise History of the Efforts To
Obtain an Extension of Suffrage in Rhode Island. Providence, 1842.
1st ed. 12mo, orig. boards, cloth back, paper label, some foxing.
Morrill 288-423 1983 $20

FRISBIE, BARNES   The History of Middletown, Vermont...
Rutland, 1867. 1st ed. 8vo, half morocco, orig. wrappers bound in.
Morrill 287-472 1983 $22.50

FRISWELL, LAURA H.   James Hain Friswell: a Memoir. George
Redway, 1898. First edition, with 3 plates, 8vo, orig. cloth, gilt.
Very good. Fenning 60-122 1983 £12.50

FRISWOLD, CARROLL   Marching with Custer. Glendale: The
Arthur H. Clark Company, 1964. Colored frontis. Illus. 1st ed.
of this issue; limited to 300 copies. Scarce. Jenkins 151-55 1983
$75

FRITH, HENRY   Jack O'Lanthorn, a Tale of Adventure.
Blackie & Son, n.d. (c. 1895). Half title, front. & illus. 32pp ads.
Orig. light brown cloth, pic. blocked in black and gilt. Fine.
Jarndyce 31-701 1983 £10.50

FRITH, W. P.   My Autobiography and Reminiscences.
Richard Bentley, 1887. 2nd edition, 2 vols. Front. Half titles.
Orig. green cloth, artist's palette imprint on leading boards, v.g.
Jarndyce 30-1001 1983 £12.50

FRITZ, PERCY STANLEY   Colorado; the Centennial State. New
York, 1941. 1st ed. Illus., fldg. map. Clark 741-185 1983 $23.50

FROBENIUS, LEO   The Childhood of Man. London: Seeley
& Company, 1909. 415 illus. Small stout 4to. Cloth. Ars Libri
34-18 1983 $50

FROBENIUS, LEO   Hadschra Maktuba. Urzeitliche Fels-
bilder Kleinafriias. Munchen: Kurt Wolff, 1925. 160 plates. 55
color. 11 maps. Folio. Cloth. Ars Libri 34-627 1983 $250

FROBENIUS, LEO   Prehistoric Rock Pictures in Europe
and Africa. New York: Museum of Modern Art, 1937. 38 illus.
Frontis. in color. 4to. Cloth. Ars Libri 34-626 1983 $25

FROEBEL, JULIUS   Seven Years' Travel in Central
America, Northern Mexico, and the Far West of the United States.
London, 1859. Orig. full gilt calf, very good. Reese 19-236 1983
$375

FROEBEL, JULIUS   Seven Years' Travel in Central America.
London: Richard Bentley, 1859. 8 plates. Cloth. A.e.g. Hinges
repaired. Rather worn and faded. Few marginal notes. Dawson 471-92
1983 $150

FROEBES, JOSEPH   Lehrbuch Der Experimentellen Psychologie.
Breisgau: Herder & Co., 1923. Two vols. Second and third editions
revised. Library bookplates, stamps on rear paste-downs. Gach
94-551 1983 $30

FROHAWK, F. W.   Varieties of British Butterflies.
1938 (1946). Second issue, 48 coloured plates, royal 8vo,
original cloth. Good copy with dust jacket. Wheldon 160-1076 1983
£40

FROHLICH-BUM, L.   Ingres. Sein Leben und sein Stil.
Wien/Leipzig: Manz Verlag, 1924. 80 plates with captioned tissue-
guards. Frontis. Large 4to. Marbled boards, 3/4 red morocco.
Ars Libri 32-336 1983 $275

FROISSART, JEAN   Chronicles. Here begynneth the first
volum... London: Richard Pynson, 1523-25. First edition in
English, variant issue with Pynson's name spelt with a "y". 2 vols.
Black Letter. Folio. Gull red morocco, gilt over wooden boards,
gilt panelled sides and spines, gilt edges, by Bedford. Title
in each vol. within woodcut border, full-page woodcut arms of Henry
VIII on verso of both titles, full-page arms of Richard Pynson
at end of each vol. Traylen 94-346 1983 £5,500

FROISSART, JEAN   Chronicles of England, France, Spain
and the Adjoining Countries... London, 1808. 13 vols. 8vo. Cont.
diced calf, neatly rebacked with morocco labels, gilt, (plates
vol. in cont. half calf, neatly rebacked to match). 58 aquatint
plates, 57 of which are double-page, and a map. Traylen 94-347
1983 £95

FROISSART, JEAN   Froissart's Chronycles. Oxford: the
Shakespeare Head Press, 1927-28. 8 vols. Roy. 8vo. Grey boards
with canvas backs, printed paper labels. 6 maps. Devices of the
lords and knights in the margins hand-coloured. Limited edition of
350 numbered sets, printed in Caslon type on Batchelor hand-made
paper. Traylen 94-348 1983 £420

FROISSART, JEAN   Forssardi, Nobilissimi Scriptoris
Gallici, Historiarum opus omne. Parisiis, Ex officina Iacobi
Dupuys, 1562. 12mo, cont. calf, rebacked, new endpapers, small repair
to upper blank corner of title. Ravenstree 94-122 1983 $175

FROLICH-BUM, LILI   La Journee de Mademoiselle Lili. Paris,
Hetzel, nd. 3rd edn. Frontis., title vignette & 20 illus. Red cloth
backed cream glazed bds. with title page design repeated on fr. cvr.,
bkstrip worn top/bottom, corners worn & fr. cvr. broken across affecting part of design, repaired, new eps., some thumbing contents, good.
Hodgkins 27-74 1983 £25

FROM HELL Gate to Portland, The Story of the Race Across the American
Continent in Oldsmobile Runabouts. (Detroit 1905). Profusely
illustrated by photographs, wraps, minor cover wear and soil. King
46-736 1983 $20

FROMAGET, NICOLAS   Le Cousin de Mahomet. Constantiople
(i.e. Paris) 1742. 1st ed., 12mo, cont. panelled calf, spine gilt.
2 vols. in 1. Vignette title pages, 6 engraved plates, headpieces.
A very good copy despite wear to binding. Trebizond 18-114 1983
$225

FROME, DAVID   Two Against Scotland Yard. NY, (1931).
Bright, near fine in slightly frayed, soiled, very good dustwrapper.
Quill & Brush 54-520 1983 $50

FRONT, ROBERT   Mountain Interval. NY, (1916). Light
dampstain to top edge of cover and pages, else near fine, owner's name,
date. Quill & Brush 54-522 1983 $75

FROST, JOHN   The Book of the Army of the United States.
New York: D. Appleton & Co., 1845. Illus. Orig. cloth. Pictorial
spine gilt. Nice. Jenkins 152-125 1983 $100

FROST, JOHN   History of the State of California.
Auburn, 1850. First edition. 15 (of 16) plates, text illus. Blind-
stamped mor., gilt-dec. spine, (foxed, some pp dampstained).
Argosy 716-36 1983 $65

FROST, JOSEPHINE C.   Records of the Town of Jamaica Long
Island, New York 1657-1751. Brooklyn: Long Island Hist. Soc., 1914.
3 vols., 8vo, green cloth. Argosy 710-354 1983 $65

FROST, ROBERT   American Poetry-A Miscellany. New
York, (1922). 8vo. Cloth. Tipped into this copy is a telegram
from Frost. Spine is dulled and book is lightly worn at the extremities, mainly a very good-fine copy. In Our Time 156-306 1983
$150

FROST, ROBERT   A Boy's Will. London: 1913. Fourth
binding. Fine copy in cream wrappers. Bromer 25-44 1983 $250

FROST, ROBERT   A Boy's Will. London: David Nutt,
1913. Printed wraps. First edition. Spine slightly tanned, but a
fine copy. Reese 20-424 1983 $175

FROST, ROBERT   Collected Poems, 1939. NY: (1939).
Very fine in lightly chipped dust wrapper. Signed by Frost, Boston
1939. Bromer 25-45 1983 $85

FROST, ROBERT   The Complete Poems of Robert Frost.
London, (1951). 8vo. Cloth. 1st English ed. A fine copy in almost
flawless dj. In Our Time 156-307 1983 $100

FROST, ROBERT   From Snow to Snow. New York, (1936).
8vo. Green cloth (faded around the front edges). Second ed. Total
edition of the new printing was 3000 copies. Presentation inscription by Frost on the front flyleaf. Accompanying the volume is the
orig. mailing envelope to the recipient of the book, addressed in
holograph by Frost. Also present, a one page holograph letter from
Frost. In Our Time 156-304 1983 $450

FROST, ROBERT   A Further Range. New York, 1936. 8vo.
Cloth. Signed by Frost on the front flyleaf. This copy has present
the original band from the publisher that was put on remaining
copies in stock that the book had won the Pulitzer Prize. A fine
copy in dj. In Our Time 156-305 1983 $275

FROST, ROBERT   In the Clearing. NY: (1962). First
edition. Limited to 1500 copies signed by Frost. Mint in slipcase. Bromer 25-46 1983 $100

FROST, ROBERT   The Lone Striker. N.Y., (1933). First
edition. 16mo, pict. wraps. In the orig. mailing envelope. Argosy
714-307 1983 $45

FROST, ROBERT   The Lovely Shall Be Choosers. New
York, 1929. First edition. One of 475. Pictorial tan wrappers.
Very fine. Bradley 65-75 1983 $65

FROST, ROBERT   A Masque of Mercy. N.Y., (1947).
Tall thin 8vo, 1/4 buckram; boxed. Ltd. first edition. One of 751
copies, printed at the Spiral Press, and signed by Frost. Fine.
Argosy 714-308 1983 $120

FROST, ROBERT   A Masque of Mercy. New York: Holt,
(1947). Cloth and boards. First edition. One of 751 numbered
copies, printed at the Spiral Press, and signed by the author. Fine
copy in orig. tissue and slipcase. Reese 20-914 1983 $85

FROST, ROBERT   A Minor Bird. N.Y., Schirmer, 1949.
Pictorial wraps. Presentation: "From Robert Frost, Celius & Vincent,"
is not in Frost's handwriting. Argosy 714-309 1983 $35

FROST, ROBERT   Mountain Interval. NY: (1916). First
issue. Inscribed by Frost to Charles Wallis. Fine copy. Small bookplate of Harry Bacon Collamore. Bromer 25-47 1983 $1100

FROST, ROBERT   North of Boston. N.Y.: Henry Holt, n.d.
(1919). 8vo, cloth backed boards; gold label on front cover worn.
Second American edition. Only 500 copies were printed. Argosy 714-
310 1983 $100

FROST, ROBERT   Steeple Bush. N.Y., 1947. Thin
8vo, cloth backed boards; boxed. Ltd. first edition. One of 751
copies, printed at the Spiral Press, and signed by Frost. Argosy 714-
311 1983 $120

FROST, ROBERT   Triple Plate. (NY: Spiral Press, 1939).
First edition. Of 1825 copies, 1/150 with printed holiday greeting
from Ann & Joseph Blumenthal. Decorations by Fritz Eichenberg. Very
fine in illus. wrappers. Bromer 25-48 1983 $50

FROST, ROBERT   West-running Brook. N.Y., (1928).
First edition, first state, lacking "First edition". Woodcut frontis.
Cloth backed boards with paper label. Slight denting to top of front
cover and some pp. Extremities wearing, in worn and soiled dust
wrapper that has a few tears and crease marks. King 45-180 1983 $35

FROST, ROBERT   A Witness Tree. N.Y., (1942). First
Trade edition. Portrait. Cloth. Frayed dust wrapper. Very good.
King 45-181 1983 $25

FROST, S. ANNIE   The Ladies' Guide to Needle Work, Embroidery, Etc. N.Y., (1870's?). Woodcuts. Decorated cloth. Index.
Bookplate. Spine faded, covers moderately worn. King 45-356 1983
$35

FROST, THOMAS   In Kent with Charles Dickens. Tinsley
Brothers, 1880. First edition, half title, orig. blue cloth, v.g.
Jarndyce 30-189 1983 £32

FROTHINGHAM, RICHARD   Songs of the Sea & Sailors' Chanteys.
Cambridge, 1924. First edition. 12mo, original boards, cloth back.
Morrill 290-136 1983 $22.50

FROUDE, JAMES ANTHONY   The Two Chiefs of Dunboy, or An Irish
Romance of the Last Century. London: Longmans, etc., 1889. First
edition. Orig. cloth. Slight wear along the spine. Good. MacManus
278-2029 1983 $35

FROUDE, JAMES ANTHONY   The Two Chiefs of Dunboy. Longmans,
Green, 1889. First edition. 8vo, orig. cloth, gilt. Very good.
Fenning 60-123 1983 £14.50

FRY, CHRISTOPHER   Thor, with Angels. London, 1948.
Friends of Canterbury Cathedral (Acting) edition. One of 750 copies.
Wrappers. Fine. Rota 231-232 1983 £16

FRY, EDWARD   England, China and Opium. Edward
Bumpus, 1878. First edition, disbound, retaining front printed wrap.
Jarndyce 31-107 1983 £25

FRY, ELIZABETH   Memoirs of the Life of Elizabeth Fry.
Charles Gilpin, 1847. First edition, with 2 portraits, 2 vols., 8vo,
orig. cloth, inside joints of second volume a little wek, but still
a very good copy. Fenning 62-130 1983 £38.50

FRY, ELIZABETH   Memoir of the Life...from Her Journals
and Letters. John Hatchard, 1848. 2nd edition, 2 vols. Fronts.
Half titles. Orig. purple cloth, faded, otherwise v.g. Jarndyce 30-
1002 1983 £16.50

FRY, HENRIETTA J.   Portraits in Miniature. Charles
Gilpin; Daniel Vickery, Bristol, 1848. Front. and ports. (water stains
in top margins), half title. Orig. green cloth, water stain to top
of upper cover, otherwise very good. Jarndyce 30-700 1983 £10.50

FRY, JAMES B.   New York and the Conscription of 1863.
New York, 1885. 1st ed. Small 8vo, orig. limp cloth. Slightly
rubbed. Morrill 289-461 1983 $20

FRY, JOHN   Bibliographical Memoranda: in Illustration of Early English Literature. Bristol, 1816. Sole edition.
4to. Cont. half calf. Privately printed, limited to 100 copies.
Some interleaving with Mss. notes. Calf worn. With the ownership
plate of Albert Wallis. Heath 48-307 1983 £180

FRY, LOUISE S.   A Glimpse of Fairyland. Hutchinson, n.d.
Sm. 4to. Colour frontis. Pictorial title. 3 colour plates & 32
text illus. Red cloth gilt, light wear. Greer 40-42 1983 £14

FRY, ROGER   Cezanne. Hogarth Press, 1927. First
edition. 54 illus. Sm. 4to. Fine. Rota 231-234 1983 £40

FRY, ROGER   Duncan Grant. London: Hogarth Press,
1923. Inscription on end-paper, corners bumped, spine sunned, but
very good. Gekoski 2-58 1983 £40

FRY, ROGER   Flemish Art - a Critical Survey. London,
1927. First edition. Numerous black and white plates. Name stamp
on front free endpaper. Bottom corners bruised. Very good. Jolliffe
26-195 1983 £35

FRY, ROGER   Flemish Art. London, 1927. First
edition. Illus. Small 4to, cloth backed pictorial boards. Argosy
714-315 1983 $40

FRY, ROGER   Flemish Art. London, 1927. First
edition. Illus. Sm. 4to. Boards, the upper cover bearing a design
by the author. Corners rubbed. Nice. Rota 230-224 1983 £20

FRY, ROGER   Henri-Matisse. London, 1941. First
edition. Inscription by previous owner. Pictorial boards slightly
bowed, but a better than very good copy. Gekoski 2-59 1983 £45

FRY, ROGER   Last Lectures. Cambridge, 1939.
First edition. 346 black and white reproductions. Nicked and frayed,
slightly torn, internally repaired dustwrapper. Fine. Jolliffe 26-
197 1983 £65

FRY, ROGER   A Sampler of Castile. London: the
Hogarth Press, 1923. 4to. Orig. decorated boards, cloth spine.
16 plates. Limited edition of 550 numbered copies. Traylen 94-
350 1983 £65

FRYER, A.   The Potamogetons of the British Isles.
(1898-) 1915. 60 hand-coloured plates mostly by R. Morgan, 4to,
original cloth. Very scarce. Wheldon 160-1600 1983 £35

FRYER, MARY ANN   John Fryer of the "Bounty." London,
1939. Small folio, blue sailcloth, backstrip faded. Eleven wood
engravings by Averil Mackenzie Grieve. One of 300 copies. First
edition. Duschnes 240-84 1983 $250

FUCHS, EDUARD   Der Maler Daumier. Munchen: Albert
Langen, 1930. 358 plates. 108 text illus. Folio. Cloth. From
the library of Jakob Rosenberg. Ars Libri 32-142 1983 $75

FUERTES, L. A.   Artist and Naturalist in Ethiopia.
New York, 1936. Map and 16 coloured plates, 4to, original cloth,
slightly used. Wheldon 160-382 1983 £70

FUESS, CLAUDE M.   Daniel Webster. Boston, 1930. 2 vols.,
illus. 8vo, cloth, g.t. Argosy 716-434 1983 $50

FUGATE, FRANCIS   The Spanish Heritage of the Southwest.
El Paso: Carl Hertzog/Texas Western Press, 1952. Folio. Cloth
and "adobe-block" boards. Illus. by Jose Cisneros. First edition.
One of 525 numbered copies, signed by Cisneros and Carl Hertzog,
the designer. Fine in very lightly rubbed dust jacket. Reese 19-269
1983 $775

FUGITIVE Pieces on Various Subjects by Several Authors. London, R.
and J. Dodsley, 1761. 2 vols., 8vo, cont. calf, old rebacking,
spines worn, joints cracked, blank flyleaf missing in vol. 2. First
edition of this collection. Ravenstree 94-44 1983 $85

FUHRMANN, ERNST   Africa. Sakralkulte. Vorgeschichte
der Hieroglyphen. Hagen/Darmstadt: Folkwang-Verlag, 1922. 121
plates. Text illus. 4to. Boards. Head of spine chipped. Ars
Libri 34-629 1983 $37.50

FUHRMANN, ERNST   Reich der Inka. Hagen: Folkwang,
1922. 2 vols. 196 plates. Large 4to. Boards. Ars Libri 34-241
1983 $85

FULCHER, GEORGE WILLIAMS   Life of Thomas Gainsborough, R.A.
London: Longman, etc., 1856. First edition. Small 8vo. Orig.
green cloth. Frontis., engraved title, and two plates. Fine
copy. Ximenes 63-14 1983 $60

FULKE, WILLIAM   A Briefe Confutation, of a Popish
Discourse. London, George Byshop, 1581. 4to, new calf antique
style, interior age-darkened with minor spotting, light soiling, some
blank edges frayed, few minor mends to blank edges, last few leaves
have wormhole in blank tip. First and only edition. Ravenstree 94-
123 1983 $425

FULKE, WILLIAM   A Defense of the Sincere and True
Translations of the Holie Scriptures in the English tong... At
London, Henrie Bynneman, 1583. 8vo, orig. calf, fly leaf loose,
some slight water-marking and staining. First and only Elizabethan
edition. Ravenstree 94-124 1983 $375

A FULL Report of the Trial of James Blomfield Rush.   London: W. M.
Clark, (ca. 1849). Title page portrait of Rush, 4 full-page plates,
text illus. Green cloth. Clippings and engraved bookplate on end
papers. Extremities worn but good and sound copy. Bradley 66-411
1983 $35

FULLARTON, W. F.   A View of the English Interests in India.
London, 1788. Second edition. Folding map and plan. Calf, rebacked,
with orig. spine laid down. Crest in gilt on upper and lower covers.
8vo. Good. Edwards 1044-273 1983 £60

FULLER, ANDREW   A Sermon on the Importance of a Deep
and Intimate Knowledge of Divine Truth. Elizabeth Town: Shepard
Kollock, for Cornelius Davis, (1796). Modern cloth. Very good.
Felcone 19-20 1983 $40

FULLER, EDWARD N.   From the Press of Tacoma, Washington,
to... Tacoma, 1896. Illus. Orig. printed wraps. First edition.
Ginsberg 47-928 1983 $45

FULLER, EMILINE L.   Left by the Indians or Rapine, Massacre
and Cannibalism on the Overland Trail in 1860. N.Y., 1936. Reprint
of Mr. Vernon, Ia., 1892. Orig. printed wraps. Illus. Edition
ltd. to 200 copies. Ginsberg 47-325 1983 $25

FULLER, FRANCIS   Medicina Gymnastica. London: Robert
Knaplock, 1711. 8vo, cont. calf; hinges mended. Thomas Fuller's copy
with his signature & bookplate. Argosy 713-203 1983 $125

FULLER, GEORGE N.   Historic Michigan. National Historical
Assoc. n.d. (1924). 3 vols. Illus., cloth, rubbed with minor
staining and foxing. Vol. 3 hinges loose. King 46-156 1983 $85

FULLER, GEORGE N.   Messages of the Governors of Michigan.
Lansing, 1925-27. 4 vols. Illus. Orig. cloth. First edition.
Ginsberg 46-459 1983 $50

FULLER, HENRY B.   Gardens of this World. New York:
Knopf, 1929. 1st ed. Orig. cloth, dj. Limited to 2,000 copies.
Review copy. Very fine. Jenkins 155-453 1983 $30

FULLER, J. F. C.   Grant & Lee, A Study in Personality and
Generalship. London, 1933. First English edition. Covers slightly
stained else good in frayed and stained dust wrappers. King 46-55
1983 $35

FULLER, J. F. C.   Memoirs of an Unconventional Soldier.
London, 1936. 8vo. Orig. cloth. First edition. Portrait frontis.
8 plates, 5 folding maps, 11 full page diagrams. Spine slightly faded.
Good. Edwards 1042-346 1983 £25

FULLER, M. B.   The Wrongs of Indian Womanhood. London,
1900. Plates, slight wear. 8vo. Orig. cloth. Good. Edwards 1044-
274 1983 £18

FULLER, NICHOLAS   The Argument of Nicholas Fuller...
London, 1641. 2nd ed. Lightish embrowning, neatly bound in modern
boards, with paper label, clean copy. Boswell 7-80 1983 $200

FULLER, THOMAS   The Right Honourable Cecil John Rhodes.
London: Longmans, Green, 1910. 8vo. 13 plates. Orig. blue cloth.
Adelson Africa-189 1983 $20

FULLER, THOMAS   Truth maintained, or positions delivered
in a sermon at the Savoy. Oxford: printed 1643. First edition.
Ximenes 63-100 1983 $125

FULLER, WILLIAM   Architecture of the Brain. Grand
Rapids, Mich., 1896. First edition. 38 illus. 4to. Argosy 713-
204 1983 $50

FULLER, WILLIAM PARMER   Ninety Years. San Francisco, 1939.
Illus. Royal 8vo, half cloth boards. Clark 741-110 1983 $25

FULLERTON, GEORGIANA   Ellen Middleton. Edward Moxon, 1844.
First edition, 3 vols. Half maroon calf, spines gilt, black labels.
Very good. Jarndyce 30-390 1983 £48

FULLERTON, GEORGIANA   The Inner Life of... Burns & Oates,
(1899). First edition, front. orig. blue cloth, v.g. Jarndyce 31-
704 1983 £10.50

FULLERTON, GEORGIANA   Lady-Bird. Edward Moxon, 1852.
First edition, 3 vols. Half green calf, spines gilt, maroon labels,
v.g. Jarndyce 31-702 1983 £58

FULLERTON, GEORGIANA   Too Strange Not to be True. Richard
Bentley, 1864. First edition, 3 vols. Half green calf, spines gilt,
maroon labels. Very good. Jarndyce 31-703 1983 £65

FULOP-MILLER, R.   Triumph over Pain. London, 1938.
8vo. Cloth. 32 plates. Rubbed. Gurney JJ-131 1983 £12

FULTON, AMBROSE C.   A Life's Voyage. New York: Published
for Author, 1898. Frontis. portrait and illus. Signed by author.
Fine. Jenkins 152-632 1983 $100

FULTON, JOHN   Functional Localization in Relation to
Frontal Lobotomy. N.Y., 1949. Illus. First edition. Argosy 713-
205 1983 $75

FULTON, JOHN   Harvey Cushing a Biography. Springfield, 1946. First edition. 8vo. Orig. binding. Fye H-3-718
1983 $40

FULTON, JOHN   Harvey Cushing a Biography. Oxford, 1946. 8vo. Cloth. Dust wrapper. Plates. First edition; London issue. An Osler Club Annual Dinner menu, signed among others by J.F. Fulton enclosed. Gurney JJ-89 1983 £15

FULTON, JOHN   Muscular Contraction and the Reflex Control of Movement. Baltimore, 1926. 8vo. Orig. cloth. Illus in text, 2 adverts. Inscribed "E.G.T.L. from J.F.F.", with the Fulton Book Found Yale Medical Library bookplate, and the ownership inscriptions on flyleaf and title of "E.G.T. Liddell, Trinity College, Oxford." First edition. Fine copy. Gurney 90-52 1983 £115

FULTON, JOHN   Physiology of the Nervous System. London: Oxford Univ. Press, 1938. Publisher's blue cloth. First edition. Gach 95-161 1983 $85

FULTON, JOHN H. W.   With Ski in Norway & Lapland. Philip Lee Warner, 1911. First edition, map and many plates, 8vo, orig. cloth, bilt, binding just a little dull, but a very good copy. Fenning 61-144 1983 £21.50

FULTON, ROBERT   A Treatise on the Improvement of Canal Navigation; Exhibiting the Numerous Advantages to be Derived from Small Canals. London: I. and J. Taylor, 1796. Frontis. and 17 plates. Three-quarter morocco. Some bumping to corners. Title facsimile. Else a fine copy. Jenkins 151-87 1983 $450

THE FUNNY Alphabet. London: E. Wallis (ca. 1820's). Octavo. Some internal soiling and covers faded, still tight copy. Bromer 25-315 1983 $150

FURLONG, LAWRENCE   The American Coast Pilot. Newburyport, 1804. Maps and charts, some folding. Orig. calf, worn with hinges cracking, but sound. Reese 18-257 1983 $100

FURNAS, ROBERT W.   Arbor Day. Lincoln, Neb., 1888. Illus. Orig. gold stamped cloth. First edition. Autograph presentation copy from J. Sterling Morton. Ginsberg 47-618 1983 $100

FURNESS, WILLIAM H.   An Address Delivered Before a Meeting of the Members and Friends of the Pennsylvania Anti-Slavery Society. Phila., 1850. Disbound. Felcone 20-165 1983 $25

FURNESS, WILLIAM H.   An Address Delivered before the Art Union of Philadelphia in the Academy of Fine Arts. Phila., 1848. Disbound. Very good. Felcone 20-3 1983 $25

FURNESS, WILLIAM H.   A Discourse Occasioned by the Boston Fugitive Slave Case... Phila., 1851. Disbound. Felcone 20-166 1983 $25

FUTRELLE, JACQUES   Elusive Isabel. Ind., (1909). Edges slightly rubbed, minor cover stains, else near very good. Quill & Brush 54-523 1983 $40

FUTRELLE, JACQUES   The High Hand. Ind., (1911). Edges rubbed, else near fine. Quill & Brush 54-524 1983 $60

FYFE, ANDREW   Elements of Chemistry. Edinburgh: Black, 1827. First edition. 2 vols. 8vo. Orig. boards, rebacked. Some spotting. Zeitlin 264-167 1983 $130

FYFE, THOMAS ALEXANDER   Charles Dickens and the Law. Edinburgh and Glasgow, Wm. Hodge; London, Chapman & Hall, (1910). First edition, half title, 3 pp ads. Orig. light blue cloth. Jarndyce 31-603 1983 £20

G

GABILLOT, C.   Hubert Robert et son temps. Paris: Librarire de l'Art, 1895. 12 sanguine plates. 57 reproductive plates in text. 4to. Marbled boards, 3/4 leather. Orig. wrappers bound in. T.e.g. A bit browned internally. Ars Libri 32-582 1983 $75

GABRIEL, ESTRIK L.   A Summary Catalogue of Microfilms of one Thousand Scientific Manuscripts in the Ambrosiana Library, Milan. Notre Dame, Indiana, 1968. With 10 plates, roy. 8vo, orig. cloth, fine in d.w. Fenning 62-131 1983 £18.50

GADDIS, WILLIAM   JR. New York: Alfred A. Knopf, 1975. First edition. Large 8vo. Orig. cloth. Dust jacket. Signed by Gaddis on the front free endpaper. A very fine copy. Jaffe 1-103 1983 $85

GADOLIN, J.   Dissertatio Chemica de Cupro Albo Sinenesi... Abo: (Turku), 1810. 4to. 3 vols. in 1. Modern boards. Ownership stamps on titles, light waterstaining of the third part, otherwise very good. Zeitlin 264-169 1983 $110

GAFFE, RENE   Giorgio de Chirico le voyant. Bruxelles: La Boetie, 1946. 24 plates. Wrappers. Loose. Edition limited to 1500 numbered copies. Ars Libri 33-440 1983 $35

GAGE, JOHN   The History and Antiquities of Hengrave, in Suffolk. London: James Carpenter, Joseph Booker and John Deck, 1822. Folio. With 30 mounted engr. India-proof plates (6 hand-colored, 3 double-page tables). Index. Large paper copy. In cont. gilt-ruled calf, a bit rubbed, rebacked with gilt-stamped spine. New end-papers. A.e.g. Karmiole 74-110 1083 $200

GAGE, THOMAS   The History of Rowley...Boston, 1840. 1st ed. 8vo, rubbed and faded, some foxing. Morrill 288-277 1983 $45

GAGE, WILLIAM C.   "Chicago to the Sea." Battle Creek, 1883. First edition. Numerous illustrations. 8vo, original wrappers, several pages of ads. Morrill 290-139 1983 $50

GAGNON, MAURICE   Pellan. Montreal: L'Arbre, 1943. 20 1/2cm. 20 pages of illus. Portrait frontis. Stiff wrappers. Signed by Pellan. Very good. McGahern 53-57 1983 $45

GAGNON, PHILEAS   Essai de Bibliographie Canadienne... Quebec, 1895 and Montreal, 1913. 2 vols., library cloth, paper becoming brittle in first volume. Dawson 470-115 1983 $50

GAILEY, C. M.   The Classic Myths in English Literature & Art. NY, 1911. 8vo, cloth. Salloch 385-15 1983 $20

GAILHABAUD, JULES   L'Architecture...Et Les Arts Qui En Dependent. 4 vols. plus atlas volume. Paris, 1858. 302 engraved plates, some in color, including 45 folio plates. Half red leather. Blind-stamped names, spines frayed. Moderately foxed. (Atlas vol. includes chromo-lithographs of stained glass windows). King 45-323 1983 $350

GAILLARD, HONORE GABRIEL   Eloge de Rene Descartes. Paris: Regnard, 1765. 8vo, wrappers. First edition. Rostenberg 88-80 1983 $75

GAINE, HUGH   The Journals of...Printer. N.Y., 1902. 2 vols. Illus. Orig. cloth, faded, first edition. One of 350 sets published. Ginsberg 46-264 1983 $85

GAINSBOROUGH, THOMAS   The Letters of Thomas Gainsborough. London: Lion and Unicorn Press, 1961. 12 collotype plates with 26 illus. Large 4to. Boards, 1/4 leather. No. 166 of a limited edition of 400 copies only. Ars Libri 32-238 1983 $150

GALARZA, JOAQUIN   Lienzos de Chiepetlan. Mexico, 1972. 95 plates. Stout 4to. Cloth. Dust jacket. Ars Libri 34-243 1983 $100

GALASSI, GUISEPPE   La scultura fiorentina del Quattrocento (Collezione "Valori Plastici.") Milano, 1949. Lg. 8vo, 300 plates, cloth. Ars Libri SB 26-79 1983 $60

GALE, GEORGE   Upper Mississippi. Chicago, 1867. Green cloth, slight dampstain, overall very good. Reese 19-237 1983 $165

GALE, GEORGE   Upper Mississippi. Chicago, 1867. Illus. Orig. cloth. First edition. Ginsberg 46-265 1983 $150

GALE, NORMAN   The Candid Cuckoo. Old Briton, England: Privately printed, n.d. First edition. Orig. cloth. One of 100 copies. Presentation copy inscribed: "Given to Arnold Gridley by Norman Gale, With Gridley's bookplate. Endpapers browned. Front cover a bit waterspotted. Back cover slightly soiled. MacManus 278-2035 1983 $65

GALE, NORMAN   A June Romance. Rugby: Printed & Published by George E. Over, (1892). Large-paper edition. Orig. parchment wrappers. Limited to 23 copies, signed by the publisher. With a MS poem entitled "Alice Ellaby," 1 page, 8vo, signed in full by the author, tipped-in. Bookplate of W. MacDonald MacKay tipped to inner wrapper. In a ref half-morocco slipcase. Very fine. MacManus 278-2036 1983 $200

GALE, NORMAN   Orchard Songs. London, 1893. First edition. Covers marked and faded. Initials on flyleaf. Good. Rota 230-226 1983 £12

GALE, NORMAN   Songs for Little People. Archibald Constable, 1896. Pictorial title. 8 plates & 109 text illus. Brown cloth pictorial gilt, little worn. Greer 40-212 1983 £22.50

GALE, T.   Electricity, or Ethereal Fire... Troy (N.Y.), 1802. First edition. 12mo, contemporary calf. Lacks 3 of 4 blank leaves front and back. Very scarce. Morrill 290-140 1983 $150

GALE, ZONA   Wisconsin Plays. New York: B.W. Huebsch, 1914. 8vo. Cloth. Some spotting to cloth, otherwise very good-fine copy. In Our Time 156-310 1983 $35

GALE, ZONA   Yellow Gentians and Blue. New York, 1927. 8vo. Cloth. A new copy in dj. In Our Time 156-309 1983 $35

GALILEI, GALILEO   Discorso delle Comete. Florence: Pietro Cecconelli, Alle Stelle Medicee, 1619. Last leaf blank. Woodcut printer's mark on title, two woodcut diagrams in text. Small 4to, half leather. With exlibris of Hans Ludendorff, and Piero Ginori Conti. First edition. Kraus 164-82 1983 $4,800

GALILEI, GALILEO   De Proportionum Instrumento a se invento... Strassburg: Karl Kieffer for Johann Carolus, 1612. 1 engraved folding plate. Woodcut text diagrams, tables. Small 4to. Modern vellum. First edition. Kraus 164-81 1983 $2,850

GALILEI, GALILEO   Sidereus Nuncius Magna, longeque Admirabilia Spectacula pandens. Venice: Thomas Baglioni, 1610. Five text engravings on the surface of the moon, three woodcuts (1 double-page) and 67 diagrams. Small 4to. Cont., probably original vellum, multiple line borders in blind and gilt, corner and center ornaments, gilt edges. With engraved bookplate (18th cent.) of the Durazzo family. In a half morocco case. First edition. Kraus 164-80 1983 $65,000

GALINDO, CATHERINE   Mrs. Galindo's Letter to Mrs. Siddons: being a circumstantial detail of Mrs. Siddon's life for the last seven years. London: printed for the authoress, sold by M. Jones; W. N. Jones, printed, 1809. 8vo, wrappers, 1st ed. Lacks a half-title. Very scarce. Ximenes 64-218 1983 $150

GALLATIN, ALBERT   Georges Braque. Essay and bibliography. New York: George Wittenborn, 1943. 12 gravure plates.
Frontis. in color pochoir. 4to. Cloth. Printed in an edition of
450 copies only. Ars Libri 32-61 1983 $85

GALLATIN, ALBERT   Letters of...on the Oregon Question.
Wash., 1846. Folded sheets, uncut. First edition. Ginsberg 47-730
1983 $50

GALLATIN, ALBERT   The Oregon Question. N.Y., 1846.
Pr. wraps., (wraps. dust-soiled, internally fine). Argosy 716-394
1983 $25

GALLATIN, ALBERT   Peace with Mexico. N.Y., 1847.
Pr. wraps. Argosy 715-288 1983 $25

GALLATIN, ALBERT   Report of...on the Subject of Public
Roads and Canals. Wash., Weightman, 1808. Half morocco. First
edition. Ginsberg 46-269 1983 $85

GALLATIN, ALBERT   Writings. N.Y., 1960. 3 vols.
Orig. cloth, boxed. Folded tables. Ginsberg 46-270 1983 $75

GALLENGA, ANTONIO   History of Piedmont. London: Chapman
& Hall, 1855. First edition. 3 vols. Orig. cloth. Front cover of
Vol. 1 slightly waterspotted. Corners a trifle worn. Near-fine.
MacManus 278-2038 1983 $150

GALLIAN, MARCELLO   Eduardo Gordigiani. Firenze:
Edizioni "S.T.E.T.", 1948. 32 color plates. 111 monochrome
plates. Small folio. Boards, 1/4 cloth. Edition limited to
700 copies. Ars Libri 33-487 1983 $150

GALLOE, O.   Natural History of the Danish Lichens.
Copenhagen 1927-72. 1397 plates (some coloured) of 7004 figures,
10 vols., 4to, original wrappers. A complete copy. Wheldon 160-
1829 1983 £160

GALLON, TOM   The Charity Ghost. Hutchinson, 1902.
Sq. 8vo. Frontis. 13 full-page & 13 text illus. Foxing. Green
pictorial cloth gilt. Greer 40-71 1983 £12.50

GALLOWAY, JOSEPH   A Reply to the Observations of Lieut.
Gen. Sir William Howe, on a Pamphlet, Entitled Letters to a Nobleman.
London, 1780. Stitched, a fine copy. Reese 13-134 1983 $225

GALLUP, JOSEPH A.   Sketches of Epidemic Diseases in the
State of Vermont. Boston, 1815. Orig. boards, leather spine. First
edition. Ginsberg 46-763 1983 $200

THE GALLYNIPPER in Yankeeland. London, 1882. Frontis. Cloth (spine
very slightly faded). First edition. Felcone 22-73 1983 $25

GALOPIN, AUGUSTIN.   Le Tabac. L'Absinthe et la Folie.
Paris: Librarie Illustree, (1885). 12mo. Orig. printed wrappers,
front cover creased. Gach 94-787 1983 $35

GALSWORTHY, JOHN   Addresses in America. London: Heinemann,
1919. First edition. Frontis. port. Orig. boards. Dust jacket.
Fine. MacManus 278-2039 1983 $20

GALSWORTHY, JOHN   Another Sheaf. London: Heinemann,
(1919). First edition. Orig. boards. Dust jacket. Small bookplate.
Fine. MacManus 278-2040 1983 $20

GALSWORTHY, JOHN   Author and Critic. N.Y.: House of
Books, 1933. First edition. Orig. cloth. One of 300 copies. Near-
fine. MacManus 278-2041 1983 $35

GALSWORTHY, JOHN   Awakening. London: Heinemann, n.d.
(1920?). First edition. 4to. Illus. by R.H. Sauter. Orig. boards,
with gilt silhouette. Dust jacket. Fine. MacManus 278-2042 1983
$20

GALSWORTHY, JOHN   The Bells of Peace. Cambridge: W.
Heffer & Sons Ltd., 1921. First edition. Orig. wrappers. Limited to
1000 copies. In a green half-morocco slipcase. Fine. MacManus 278-
2043 1983 $50

GALSWORTHY, JOHN   Beyond. London: William Heinemann,
(1917). First edition. Orig. cloth. Presentation copy to author's
sister, inscribed on the front free endpaper: "B.L.S. With Love from
J.G., September 1917." Spine and covers faded, worn, and spotted,
inner hinges weak, with offsetting to the endpapers. Good. MacManus
278-2044 1983 $85

GALSWORTHY, JOHN   Captures. London: William Heinemann,
1923. First edition, second issue with the front free endpaper missing.
Orig. blue cloth. Presentation copy to author's sister, inscribed on
a small piece of paper pasted to the dedication page: "B.L.S. with
love, J.G." Very good. MacManus 278-2048 1983 $225

GALSWORTHY, JOHN   Carmen: An Opera in Four Acts.
London, 1932. Cloth-backed boards. Dust jacket. Bookplate.
Nearly fine. First edition, one of 650 numbered copies signed by John
and Ada Galsworthy. Felcone 21-46 1983 $125

GALSWORTHY, JOHN   A Commentary. London: The Richards
Press, 1930. First of this edition. Orig. buckram. One of 275
numbered copies. Presentation copy to John Drinkwater inscribed:
"John Drinkwater from John Galsworthy Nov. 5, 1930." With Drinkwater's
bookplate. Spine faded and spotted. Endpapers a bit foxed. Good.
MacManus 278-2053 1983 $135

GALSWORTHY, JOHN   A Commentary. London, 1930. New edition.
One of 275 numbered copies, signed by author. Foot of spine faded.
Very nice. Rota 230-235 1983 £15

GALSWORTHY, JOHN   A Commentary. London: Grant Richards,
1908. First edition. Orig. cloth. Very good. MacManus 278-2052
1983 $20

GALSWORTHY, JOHN   The Country House. London: William
Heinemann, 1919. Cheap edition. Orig. boards. Pictorial dust jacket.
Fine. MacManus 278-2054 1983 $20

GALSWORTHY, JOHN   The Creation of Character in Literature.
Oxford: The Clarendon Press, 1931. First edition. One of 250 copies
printed on handmade paper and signed by author. Near-fine. MacManus
278-2055 1983 $50

GALSWORTHY, JOHN   The Creation of Character in Literature.
Oxford, 1931. First edition. One of 250 numbered copies, signed by
author. Wrappers. Unopened. Fine. Rota 230-236 1983 £15

GALSWORTHY, JOHN   The Creation of Character in Literature.
Oxford: At the Clarendon Press, 1931. First edition. Orig. wrappers.
Fine. MacManus 278-2056 1983 $20

GALSWORTHY, JOHN   The Dark Flower. London, 1913. First
edition. Spine a little spotted. Nice. Rota 230-229 1983 £12

GALSWORTHY, JOHN   Five Tales. London, 1918. First English
edition. Nice. Rota 230-230 1983 £15

GALSWORTHY, JOHN   The Forsyte Saga. London: William
Heinemann Ltd., 1922, 1929. First editions. 2 vols. Orig. cloth.
Dust jackets (chipped and worn on the second title). Fine. MacManus
278-2066 1983 $150

GALSWORTHY, JOHN   Four Forsyte Stories. New York:
Fountain Press, 1929. 1st ed., 1 of 850 numbered and signed copies.
Orig. cloth-backed red boards, uncut. Fine copy. Jenkins 155-459
1983 $25

GALSWORTHY, JOHN   The Freelands. London: William Heinemann, (1915). First edition. Orig. cloth. Presentation copy to the
Sauters, inscribed on a slip tipped to the front free endpaper: "B.L.
& J.G.S. from J.G., August 19, 1915." Edges a trifle foxed. Near-
fine. MacManus 278-2068 1983 $125

GALSWORTHY, JOHN   In Chancery. London: William Heinemann, 1920. First edition, first issue. Orig. cloth. Presentation
copy to author's sister, inscribed on the front free endpaper: "B.L.S.
With love from J.G., October 22, 1920." Edges a trifle foxed. Near-
fine. MacManus 278-2072 1983 $125

GALSWORTHY, JOHN   The Inn of Tranquility. London: William
Heinemann, 1912. First edition. Orig. cloth. Very good. MacManus
278-2073 1983 $20

GALSWORTHY, JOHN   International Thought. Cambridge: W. Heffer & Sons Ltd., 1923. First edition. Orig. wrappers. Folding cloth box. Fine. MacManus 278-2074 1983 $25

GALSWORTHY, JOHN   The Island Pharisees. London: William Heinemann, (1927). First Grove edition. Orig. full calf. Presentation copy to author's relatives, the Sauters, inscribed: "For Rudi & Vi with my love, J.G., May 12, 1927." Spine faded. Edges a trifle worn. Good. MacManus 278-2075 1983 $65

GALSWORTHY, JOHN   Loyalties. London, 1930. 4to. Orig. buckram, gilt, t.e.g., others uncut. 8 plates by S. Van Abbe. Limited edition of 315 numbered copies, signed by the author. Traylen 94-354 1983 £30

GALSWORTHY, JOHN   Maid in Waiting. London: William Heinemann, 1931. First edition. Orig. decorated vellum. One of 525 copies signed and numbered by the author. Presentation copy inscribed on the front free endpaper: "For Rudy & Vi (Sauter) with love from J. G., November 2, 1931". Fine. MacManus 278-2082 1983 $150

GALSWORTHY, JOHN   Maid in Waiting. London: William Heinemann, 1931. First edition. Orig. green cloth. Dust jacket (worn at the edges, a trifle soiled). Presentation copy to author's relatives, the Sauters, inscribed: "Rudy & Vi with love, J. G." Near-fine. MacManus 278-2081 1983 $135

GALSWORTHY, JOHN   Maid in Waiting. London, 1931. First edition. One of 525 numbered copies, signed by author. Half parchment. Covers a little sprung. Very nice. Rota 230-237 1983 £20

GALSWORTHY, JOHN   A Man of Devon. Edinburgh & London: William Blackwood & Sons, 1901. First edition of Galsworthy's pseudonymously published fourth book. Orig. blue cloth. 1050 copies printed. Covers rubbed. Good. MacManus 278-2085 1983 $300

GALSWORTHY, JOHN   The Man of Property. London: William Heinemann, 1906. First edition. Orig. cloth. Presentation copy to author's protege, Ralph Hale Mottram, inscribed on the front flyleaf "Ralph Mottram from the Author, March 22: 1906." Newspaper reviews pasted in at the back. Covers soiled. Front inner hinge cracking. Preserved in a half-morocco folding box. Fine association item. MacManus 278-2086 1983 $650

GALSWORTHY, JOHN   The Man of Property. London: William Heinemann, 1906. First edition. Orig. cloth. A trifle worn. In a half-morocco slipcase. Very good. MacManus 278-2087 1983 $150

GALSWORTHY, JOHN   Memorable Days. London, Privately printed, 1924. First edition. Small 8vo, boards (trifle soiled, light foxing), else very good. Half green morocco slipcase. One of 60 copies, printed by the Curwen Press. Inscribed by Galsworthy. Houle 21-357 1983 $350

GALSWORTHY, JOHN   Memories. W. Heinemann, 1920. 4to. Mounted colour frontis. Title vignette. 3 mounted colour plates. 23 other plates. Decorated endpaper printed on Japanese vellum. Brown decorated boards. Orig. dust wrappers. Presentation inscription from Galsworthy on flyleaf. Very good. Greer 40-97 1983 £45

GALSWORTHY, JOHN   Mistaken Rhapsody. Kansas City, Privately printed, 1942. First edition thus. Facs. of Galsworthy's Manuscripts along with printed text. One of 30 copies. With two inscriptions by the publisher. Very good. Houle 21-359 1983 $200

GALSWORTHY, JOHN   The Mob. London: Duckworth & Co., 1914. First edition. Orig. cloth. Dust jacket. Small bookplate. Fine. MacManus 278-2088 1983 $20

GALSWORTHY, JOHN   A Modern Comedy. London: William Heinemann, 1929. First edition. Orig. vellum. One of 1030 copies signed by the author with a short quotation. Presentation copy inscribed: "Rudy & Vi (Sauter) with best love. J.G., August 15, 1929." Fine. MacManus 278-2090 1983 $150

GALSWORTHY, JOHN   A Modern Comedy. N.Y.: Charles Scribner's Sons, 1929. First American edition. Orig. cloth. Dust jacket. Tiny chip at top of jacket. Bookplate. Very fine. MacManus 278-2089 1983 $35

GALSWORTHY, JOHN   A Modern Comedy. London: Heinemann, 1929. First edition. Orig. cloth. Dust jacket (chipped). Very good. MacManus 278-2091 1983 $20

GALSWORTHY, JOHN   A Modern Comedy. London, 1929. 8vo. Limp vellum. Limited edition of 1030 numbered copies signed by the author. With a presentation inscription by the author. Traylen 94-355 1983 £18

GALSWORTHY, JOHN   Moods, Songs, & Doggerels. London: William Heinemann, 1912. First edition. Frontis. port. Orig. cloth with paper label. Covers slightly rubbed. In a half-morocco slipcase. Bookplate. Very good. MacManus 278-2092 1983 $75

GALSWORTHY, JOHN   Over the River. London: Heinemann, (1933). First edition. Orig. cloth. Dust jacket. Fine. MacManus 278-2096 1983 $25

GALSWORTHY, JOHN   The Patrician. London: William Heinemann, 1911. First edition. Orig. cloth. MacManus 278-2097 1983 $20

GALSWORTHY, JOHN   The Plays. London: Duckworth, (1929). First edition. 3/4 morocco with decorated boards. Spine a trifle faded. Near-fine. MacManus 278-2100 1983 $50

GALSWORTHY, JOHN   The Plays of John Galsworthy. London, 1929. First Collected edition. One of 1275 numbered copies, signed by author. Fine. Rota 230-234 1983 £18

GALSWORTHY, JOHN   The Plight of the Miners. London: Society of Friends, (1928). First separate publication. 4 pages. Reprinted from the Manchester Guardian, October 5th, 1928. Paper-clip mark on the top front page. Near-fine. MacManus 278-2101 1983 $25

GALSWORTHY, JOHN   The Rocks. Kansas City, Privately printed, 1837. First edition thus, 4to, facs. of the orig. manuscript, along with the printed text. Boards, uncut. One of 60 numbered copies. Fine. Houle 21-360 1983 $125

GALSWORTHY, JOHN   Saint's Progress. N.Y., Scribner, 1919. Advance copy of the first edition issued for the American Booksellers's Association, 5/15/19. Blue cloth over boards. Very good. Houle 21-361 1983 $37.50

GALSWORTHY, JOHN   Saint's Progress. London: Heinemann, 1919. First edition. Orig. cloth. Dust jacket (faded & torn). Fine. MacManus 278-2103 1983 $30

GALSWORTHY, JOHN   A Sheaf. London: Heinemann, (1916). First edition, first binding. Orig. boards. Very good. MacManus 278-2104 1983 $20

GALSWORTHY, JOHN   The Silver Spoon. London: William Heinemann, n.d. (11 November 1926). First edition. Orig. blue buckram. Dust jacket (slightly faded, worn and soiled, with a few small tears to the covers). One of 265 large paper copies numbered and signed by author. Endpapers very slightly foxed. Fine. MacManus 278-2107 1983 $350

GALSWORTHY, JOHN   The Silver Spoon. London: William Heinemann, (1926). First large paper edition. Orig. blue buckram. One of 265 copies signed by Galsworthy. Presentation copy, inscribed: "Rudi and Vi with love, J.G." Spine faded. Very good. MacManus 278-2106 1983 $150

GALSWORTHY, JOHN   The Silver Spoon. London: William Heinemann Ltd., n.d. First edition. Orig. cloth. Dust jacket (slightly worn & dust-soiled). One of 265 copies signed by Galsworthy. In a green half-morocco slipcase (a little rubbed). Fine. MacManus 278-2108 1983 $75

GALSWORTHY, JOHN   The Silver Spoon. London, (1926). 8vo. Orig. blue buckram, gilt, t.e.g., others uncut. Limited edition of 265 copies, numbered and signed by the author. Traylen 94-356 1983 £25

GALSWORTHY, JOHN   The Slaughter of Animals for Food. London: Royal Society for the Prevention of Cruelty to Animals, n.d. (1913). First edition. Orig. wrappers. In a cloth case. Bookplate. Fine. MacManus 278-2111 1983 $50

GALSWORTHY, JOHN   Soames and the Flag. London: Heinemann, 1930. First edition. Orig. full vellum. One of 1025 copies signed by the author. Vellum a little warped. Slipcase. MacManus 278-2112 1983 $35

GALSWORTHY, JOHN   Soames and the Flag. N.Y.: Scribner's Sons, 1930. First American edition. Orig. cloth-backed boards. In publisher's box. One of 680 copies signed by author. Fine. MacManus 278-2113 1983 $25

GALSWORTHY, JOHN   Swan Song. London: William Heinemann, (1928). First edition. Orig. green cloth. Dust jacket (slightly worn at the edges with a small tear to the rear cover). Presentation copy to author's relatives, the Sauter, inscribed: "For Rudi & Vi with my love, J.G., July 12, 1928." Near-fine. MacManus 278-2117 1983 $150

GALSWORTHY, JOHN   Swan Song. London: William Heinemann, 1928. First edition. Orig. blue buckram. Presentation copy to Rudi and Vi (Sauter), inscribed on the front free endpaper: "For Rudi & Vi with the best wishes(?) of J.G., July 12, 1928." One of 525 copies signed by Galsworthy. Spine faded. Very good. MacManus 278-2115 1983 $150

GALSWORTHY, JOHN   Swan Song. London: William Heinemann, Ltd., (1928). First edition. Orig. cloth. Dust jacket (a bit worn). Inscribed by author on the half-title. In a green half-morocco slip-case (a little rubbed). Fine. MacManus 278-2116 1983 $75

GALSWORTHY, JOHN   Swan Song. London, 1928. 8vo. Orig. blue buckram, gilt, t.e.g., others uncut. Limited edition of 525 copies, numbered and signed by the author. Traylen 94-357 1983 £25

GALSWORTHY, JOHN   Swan Song. London, 1928. First English edition. One of 525 numbered copies, signed by author. Spine slightly faded. Very nice. Rota 230-233 1983 £25

GALSWORTHY, JOHN   Tatterdemalion. London: William Heinemann, 1920. First edition. Orig. cloth. Presentation copy to author's sister, Blanch Lillian Sauter, inscribed: "B.L.S. With love from John Galsworthy, April 3, 1920." Top front cover corner slightly bent. Some offsetting to the free endpapers. Very good. MacManus 278-2122 1983 $125

GALSWORTHY, JOHN   Tatterdemalion. London, 1920. First edition. Very nice. Rota 230-232 1983 £15

GALSWORTHY, JOHN   To Let. London: William Heinemann, 1921. First edition. Orig. cloth. Presentation copy to author's sister, inscribed on the front free endpaper: "For all at Freeland. With my dear love. J.G. October 1921." Slight offsetting to the end-papers. Near-fine. MacManus 278-2123 1983 $125

GALSWORTHY, JOHN   To Let. London: William Heinemann, 1921. First edition. Orig. cloth. Dust jacket (chipped). Very good. MacManus 278-2127 1983 $25

GALSWORTHY, JOHN   Two Forsyte Interludes. London: William Heinemann, 1927. First edition. Orig. printed wrappers. Presentation copy to author's nephew R.G. Sauter, inscribed: "Dec. 16, 1927. Rudi and Vi, with love from J.G." Wrappers very slightly soiled and frayed. Very good. MacManus 278-2124 1983 $125

GALSWORTHY, JOHN   Verses New And Old. London: William Heinemann, 1926. First edition. Frontispiece port. Orig. blue cloth. Presentation to author's relatives, the Sauters, inscribed: "Rudi & Vi with best love, J.G., November 25, 1926." Near-fine. MacManus 278-2128 1983 $125

GALSWORTHY, JOHN   Villa Rubein. London: Duckworth, 1900. First edition. Orig. cloth, with labels. First issue. Covers soiled. In a half-morocco case (rubbed). Good. MacManus 278-2130 1983 $225

GALSWORTHY, JOHN   The White Monkey. London: William Heinemann, n.d. (11 November 1926). First edition. Orig. blue buckram. Dust jacket (faded, worn and soiled, with a small piece missing from the front cover). One of 265 large paper copies numbered and signed by author. Galsworthy's copy, signed by him on the front free endpaper: "Author's copy, November 7, 1926." Spine a trifle faded. Endpapers slightly foxed. Near-fine. MacManus 278-2132 1983 $350

GALSWORTHY, JOHN   The White Monkey. London: William Heinemann, (1926). First large paper edition. Orig. blue buckram. One of 265 copies signed by author. Presentation copy to the Sauters, inscribed: "Rudi and Vi with love, J.G." Spine faded. Very good. MacManus 278-2131 1983 $150

GALSWORTHY, JOHN   The White Monkey. London: William Heinemann Ltd., (1924). First edition. Orig. cloth. Presentation copy to R.H. Mottram. Good. MacManus 278-2134 1983 $85

GALSWORTHY, JOHN   The White Monkey. London: William Heinemann Ltd., (1924). First edition. Orig. cloth. Inscribed by author. In a half-morocco slipcase. Fine. MacManus 278-2133 1983 $85

GALSWORTHY, JOHN   The White Monkey. London, (1924). 8vo. Orig. blue buckram, gilt, t.e.g., others uncut. Limited edition of 265 copies, numbered and signed by the author. Traylen 94-358 1983 £25

GALSWORTHY, JOHN   The Works. London, 1923-37. Manaton edition. 30 vols. 8vo. Half parchment, gilt spines, uncut edges. Author's bookplate in vol. 1, with a portrait, plates and facsimiles. Limited to 530 numbered sets. Signed by the author. Traylen 94-352 1983 £475

GALT, JOHN   The Ayrshire Legatees; or, the Pringle Family. Edinburgh: for William Blackwood, 1821. First edition. Cr. 8vo. Half antique calf, crimson morocco label, gilt. Half-title. Traylen 94-360 1983 £35

GALT, JOHN   The Entail: or The Lairds of Grippy. Edinburgh: Blackwood, 1823. First edition. 3 vols. Orig. 3/4 boards. Printed paper labels. One signature loose in vol. one. Fine. MacManus 278-2146 1983 $175

GALT, JOHN   The Entail: or the Lairds of Grippy. Edinburgh: William Blackwood, 1823. First edition. 3 vols. Cr. 8vo. Half antique calf, crimson morocco labels, gilt. Half-titles in vols. 2 and 3. Traylen 94-361 1983 £60

GALT, JOHN   The Last of the Lairds. Edinburgh: William Blackwood, 1826. First edition. 8vo. Half antique calf, crimson morocco label, gilt. Half-title, 8 pp. of ads. Traylen 94-362 1983 £35

GALT, JOHN   The Lives of the Players. London: Henry Colburn and Richard Bentley, 1831. 2 vols., 12mo, cont. purple cloth (spines faded), morocco labels. 1st ed. A very good copy, with a half-title in vol. 1. Ximenes 64-219 1983 $125

GALT, JOHN   The Members: an Autobiography. London: James Fraser, 1832. First edition. Cr. 8vo. Half antique calf, crimson morocco label, gilt. Traylen 94-363 1983 £30

GALT, JOHN   Ringan Gilhaize. Edinburgh: Oliver and Boyd, etc., 1823. 3 vols. 12mo. Cont. lilac calf, gilt, spines gilt. First edition. Half-titles present. A fine copy. Ximenes 63-121 1983 $200

GALT, JOHN   Ringan Galhaize; or the Covenanters. Edinburgh: Oliver & Boyd, 1823. 3 vols. 12mo. Orig. boards, uncut, printed paper labels. First edition. Half-title in each vol. Spines slightly worn. Traylen 94-364 1983 £90

GALT, JOHN   Ringan Gilhaize. Edinburgh: Oliver & Boyd, 1823. First edition, 3 vols. Half titles, half blue calf, maroon labels, v.g. Jarndyce 30-393 1983 £70

GALT, JOHN   Ringan Galhaize; or the Covenanters. Edinburgh: Oliver and Boyd, 1823. First edition. 3 vols. 12mo. Half antique calf, crimson morocco labels, gilt. Half-title in each vol. Traylen 94-365 1983 £55

GALT, JOHN   Sir Andrew Wylie, of that Ilk. Edinburgh: William Blackwood, 1882. First edition. 3 vols. Cr. 8vo. Half antique calf, morocco labels, gilt. Half-title in each vol. Traylen 94-367 1983 £60

GALT, JOHN　　　　　　Sir Andrew Wylie of the Ilk. Wm.
Blackwood and T. Cadell, 1822. Half dull purple calf, green labels.
Fine. Jarndyce 30-392 1983 £46

GALT, JOHN　　　　　　The Spaewife. Edinburgh: Oliver and
Boyd, 1823. First edition. 3 vols. Cr. 8vo. Cont. half calf,
printed paper labels. Half-title in each vol. Traylen 94-366 1983
£48

GALT, JOHN　　　　　　The Spaewife. Edinburgh: Oliver &
Boyd, 1823. First edition, 3 vols. Half titles, half olive green
calf, a little rubbed. Jarndyce 30-394 1983 £45

GALT, JOHN　　　　　　The Works. Edinburgh, 1936. First
collected edition. 10 vols. 8vo. Cloth. In the orig. dustwrappers.
Illus. by C.E. Brock. Traylen 94-359 1983 £85

GALTON, FRANCIS　　　　　　Hereditary Genius. London: Macmillan
& Co., 1869. Ad leaf. Orig. mauve cloth, shelfworn. Good copy.
First edition. Gach 95-163 1983 $325

GALTON, FRANCIS　　　　　　Hereditary Genius. 1892. 8vo, 2
ad. leaves, orig. cloth. Bickersteth 75-230 1983 £38

GALTON, FRANCIS　　　　　　Inquiries Into Human Faculty and its
Development. NY: Macmillan, 1883. First American edition. Very
good copy. Gach 95-164 1983 $125

GALTON, FRANCIS　　　　　　Natural Inheritance. NY: Macmillan
and Co., 1894 (1889). Spine faded and endpapers torn at top inner
seams. Gach 95-165 1983 $40

GALTON, FRANCIS　　　　　　Noteworthy Families. London: John
Murray, 1906. Ad leaf. First edition. Fine copy in modern cloth.
Gach 95-166 1983 $65

GALTON, FRANCIS　　　　　　Noteworthy Families (Modern Science).
London, 1906. First edition. 8vo. Orig. binding. Fye H-3-209
1983 $30

GAMBA, CARLO　　　　　　Botticelli. Milano: Ulrico Hoepli,
1936. 200 plates. Small 4to. Cloth. Light pencilling. Ars
Libri 33-46 1983 $35

GAMBA, PETER　　　　　　A narrative of Lord Byron's last
journey to Greece. London: Murray, 1825. First edition. 8vo.
Cont. half red morocco, spine gilt, slightly rubbed. Corners of
a few leaves ink-stained, and lacking the half-title. Ximenes
63-53 1983 $275

GAMBOA, FRANCISCO XAVIER DE　　Commentarios a las Ordenanzas de Minas.
Madrid: Joachin Ibarra, 1761. First edition. Large paper copy.
3 large folding plates. Folio. Cont. Spanish mottled calf, spine
elaborately gilt. Inscribed on half title "A mi amigo Sam. B. Knight,
J.H. Ramirez, 8 agosto, '94" with embossed stamp of Jose H. Ramirez.
Corners rubbed. Back repaired. Kraus 164-98 1983 $3,600

GAMGEE, J. SAMPSON　　　　　On the Treatment of Wounds and
Fractures. London, 1883. 44 wood engravings. Ex-lib. Argosy 713-
208 1983 $75

GAMMER Grethel's Fairy Tales. Simpkin Marshall, nd (ca. 1910). Illus.
by George Cruikshank & others. Re-issue numerous b&w illus. Lt.
blue cloth with pictorial fr. cvr. & bkstrip in red, black & brown,
titling in red & black, uncut, lower bottom fr. corner bumped,
bkstrip faded, corners sl. bruised, some pp. carelessly opened, scarce,
vg. Hodgkins 27-75 1983 £18

GANAWAY, LOOMIS M.　　　　　New Mexico and the Sectional Controversy,
1846-1861. Albuquerque, 1944. Hist. Soc. of New Mexico, vol. XII.
Illus. Argosy 710-343 1983 $25

GANAY, SOLANGE DE　　　　　Les devises des Dogon. Paris: Musee
de l'Homme, 1941. 9 plates. Large 4to. Wrappers. Ars Libri 34-
632 1983 $75

GANILH, CHARLES　　　　　An Inquiry into the Various Systems
of Political Economy. 1812. 8vo, cont. calf. First edition in
English. Bickersteth 77-206 1983 £90

GANILH, CHARLES　　　　　An Inquiry Into the Various Systems of
Political Economy. NY 1812. First American ed. Old calf, stained
and worn copy, lacks rear end paper. King 46-470 1983 $65

GANNETT, HENRY　　　　　A Dictionary of Altitudes in the U. S.
Washington, 1906. 4th ed, 3/4 morocco. Argosy 710-196 1983 $45

GANNETT, LEWIS　　　　　John Steinbeck: Personal and Bibliographical Notes. NY, (1939). Paperwraps, first issue with frontis
by "Stjernstrom", cover lightly soiled, else fine. Quill & Brush 54-
1286 1983 $30

GANTT, W. HORSLEY　　　　　Volume of 13 papers authored or co-
authored by Gantt. Inscribed to Adolf Meyer. Gach 95-167 1983
$27.50

GANZ, PAUL　　　　　The Drawings of Henry Fuseli. New
York: Chanticleer Press, 1949. 107 plates (1 color). Large 4to.
Cloth. Ars Libri 32-231 1983 $65

GANZ, PAUL　　　　　Les dessins de Hans Holbein le Jeune.
Geneve: Fred. Boissonas, (1911-1926), 1939. Text volume and 8
portfolios of plates. Text: Small folio. Wrappers. Printed on
fine uncut laid paper. Plates: 643 collotype facsimiles to exact
scale (predominantly in color) on 400 mounts, loose as issued, in
folding portfolio cases (decorated boards, 1/4 vellum). Large folio.
Rare. Ars Libri 32-319 1983 $3,000

GANZ, PAUL　　　　　Hans Holbein D.J. Stuttgart/Leipzig:
Deutsche Verlags-Anstalt, 1912. 252 illus. 4to. Cloth. Ars
Libri 32-320 1983 $75

GANZ, PAUL　　　　　The Paintings of Hans Holbein. London:
Phaidon, 1956. Complete edition. Enlarged edition. 13 tipped-in
color plates. 300 illus. Large 4to. Cloth. Dust jacket. Ars Libri
32-321 1983 $100

GARAS, KLARA　　　　　Franz Anton Maulbertsch, 1724-1796.
Budapest: Verlag der Ungarischen Akademie der Wissenschaften,
(1960). 257 plates with 332 illus. (16 tipped-in color plates).
Large stout 4to. Cloth. Ars Libri 32-442 1983 $250

GARAS, KLARA　　　　　Franz Anton Maulbertsch. Salzburg:
Galerie Welz, 1974. 136 illus. (48 full-page color). Small folio.
Cloth. Ars Libri 32-443 1983 $150

GARCIA, MANUEL　　　　　Garcia's Schule, oder Die Kunst des
Gesanges. Maniz, Schott, n.d. Folio, 1/2 leather, rubbed. Salloch
387-60 1983 $75

GARCIA Y BELLIDO, ANTONIO　　Esculturas romanicas de Espana Y Portugal. Madrid, 1949. 4to, 2 vol. 352 plates, text illus, cloth, 1/2
morocco. Orig. wraps. bound in. Ars Libri SB 26-81 1983 $275

GARD, WAYNE　　　　　Sam Bass. Boston, Houghton, 1936.
First edition. Illus. Dust jacket. Very good-fine. With a typed
letter from the author laid in. Houle 21-1040 1983 $95

GARDANE, JOSEPH JACQUES DE　　Maniere Sure et Facile de Traiter les
Maladies Veneriennees. Paris, 1773. 12mo, cont. mottled calf.
First edition. Argosy 713-209 1983 $75

THE GARDEN of the Night. Andoversford, 1979. Twenty-six Sufi
Poems translated by Iftikhar Azmi. Illustrations by Richard
Kennedy. Folio, cloth-backed pictorial bds., slipcase. One of
200 copies signed by the translator & artist. A fine copy.
Prospectus laid in. Perata 27-186 1983 $90

GARDENER, WALTER H.　　　　The Perfect Advertisement, or, The
Biography of Humphrey Hangapple. N.p., n.d. Sm 8vo, two-tone
bds. A very nice copy. Perata 27-133 1983 $25

GARDINER, ALAN H.　　　　The Theory of Speech and Language.
Oxford: At the Clarendon Press, 1932. First edition. Gach 95-168
1983 $25

GARDINER, ALLEN FRANCIS   Narrative of a journey to the Zoolu Country... London: William Crofts, 1836. First edition. 8vo. 2 folding maps. 26 plates (3 hand-colored). Orig. blue cloth. Spine faded, rubbed. Adelson Africa-87 1983 $400

GARDINER, CHARLES F.   Doctor at Timberline. Caldwell: Caxton Printers, 1939. Frontis. and illustrations. First edition. Nice. Jenkins 153-217 1983 $45

GARDINER, CHARLES F   Doctor at Timberline. Caldwell, Idaho: Caxton Printers, 1938. First edition. Argosy 713-210 1983 $40

GARDINER, HOWARD C.   In Pursuit of the Golden Dream. Stoughton, Ma., 1970. Illus., folded map, plates. Orig. half leather with box. First edition. Ginsberg 47-90 1983 $300

GARDINER, HOWARD C.   In Pursuit of the Golden Dream. Stoughton, Mass.: Western Hemisphere, Inc., 1970. Frontis., illus. and maps, handsome half morocco. A special edition limited to 100 copies and signed by editor Dale Morgan. Jenkins 151-100 1983 $200

GARDINER, JOHN   Discourse on the Day of Publick Fast in Mass. Boston, 1812. Sewed. Argosy 716-598 1983 $20

GARDINER, O. C.   The Great Issue. N.Y., 1848. Printed wraps. Covers frayed and loose. Inscribed and signed by author (with his initials). King 45-58 1983 $45

GARDNER, ERNEST A.   A Handbook of Greek Sculpture. London, 1920. 8vo, cloth. Salloch 385-284 1983 $20

GARDNER, ERNEST ARTHUR   Ancient Athens. NY, 1902. Illus. 8vo, cloth. Salloch 385-350 1983 $40

GARDNER, JOHN   Grendel. New York: 1971. First edition. Purple cloth. Fine in dust jacket. Bradley 66-173 1983 $145

GARDNER, JOHN   Grendel. New York: Knopf, 1971. Cloth. First edition. A fine copy in dust jacket, with only the slightest sign of sunning of the spine. Reese 20-429 1983 $100

GARDNER, JOHN   The Resurrection. (NY, 1966). Signed inscrip. from Gardner on title, signed d/w blurb tipped-in on front fly, small piece of paper with Gardner's name and professional title tipped-in on ded. page, cover worn, good in slightly frayed and stained, very good dustwrapper. Quill & Brush 54-529 1983 $600

GARDNER, JOHN   Vlemk, The Box-Painter. Northridge, ca. 1979, Limited to 100 numbered and signed copies, bound in leather, orig. drawing by Gardner, mint. Quill & Brush 54-531 1983 $125

GARDNER, JOHN   Vlemk the Box-Painter. Northridge: Lord John Press, 1979. 1st ed. 1 of 100 specially bound deluxe copies, numbered and signed by author, and with an original drawing in ink by Gardner. Mint as issued, at publication price. Jenkins 155-468 1983 $125

GARDNER, JOHN   Collection of His Works. 23 vols. All in fine condition. Jenkins 155-463 1983 $550

GARDNER, MARSHALL B.   A Journey to the Earth's Interior or have the Poles Really Been Discovered. Aurora, IL: The Author, 1920. Illus., including some color plates. Maroon gilt-stamped cloth. Profusely illus. Karmiole 72-46 1983 $30

GARDNER, ROBERT EDWARD   Five Centuries of Gunsmiths, Swordsmiths and Armourers 1400-1900. N.p. 1948. Illus, boards, very good in worn dw. King 46-572 1983 $50

GARDNER, WILLOUGHBY   Ancient Defensive Earthworks of Warwickshire. 1904. Author's copy, 35 diagrams, a folding map, newspaper cuttings reviewing the work mounted at end, with pencilled notes in the author's hand, cloth, folio. Deighton 3-138 1983 £22

GARDINER, MARGUERITE POWER FARMER, COUNTESS OF BLESSINGTON
Please turn to
BLESSINGTON, MARGUERITE POWER FARMER GARDINER, COUNTESS OF

GARDYNE, C. GREENHILL   The Life of a Regiment. Edinburgh, 1901-3. 8vo. Orig. cloth. Half-titles, 2 coloured frontis., vignette on title vol. 1. 6 other coloured plates of uniform, numerous other plates, maps (some folding and coloured). 2 vols. Silver embossed Regimental breastplates on upper covers. Spines slightly worn and soiled. Ink inscription on front endpaper vol. I. Good. Edwards 1042-546 1983 £50

GARESCHE, LOUIS   Biography of Lieut. Col. Julius P. Garesche, Assistant Adjutant-General, U. S. Army. Philadelphia, 1887. 1st ed. Illus. 8vo. Ex-library. Morrill 286-600 1983 $32.50

GARLAND, HAMLIN   The Book of the American Indian. N.Y., Harper, 1923. First edition. 4to, color frontis. and 34 plates by Frederic Remington. Dust jacket, large color pictorial label on upper cover (slight nicking at top edge). Fine copy. Houle 22-1063 1983 $225

GARLAND, HAMLIN   Jason Edwards: an Average Man. Bos., 1892. Inscription by Garland, front right bottom corner frayed and faded, otherwise cover slightly worn but good plus. Quill & Brush 54-532 1983 $60

GARLAND, HAMLIN   The Light of the Star. New York, 1904. 8vo. Wraps. An advance copy in wrappers. Some chipping to wraps at the extremities, else a very good-fine copy. In Our Time 156-313 1983 $150

GARLAND, HAMLIN   Main-Travelled Roads... Boston, Arena Pub. Co., 1891. 12mo. Orig. grey cloth. 1st ed. With an ALS from Garland laid in. Near fine. O'Neal 50-24 1983 $100

GARLAND, HAMLIN   Main-Travelled Roads: Six Mississippi Valley Stories. Boston: Arena Pub. Co., 1891. 1st ed., 1st state with sheets bulking 5/8". Orig. grey cloth, gilt. Fine copy, and scarce thus. Jenkins 153-776 1983 $150

GARLAND, HAMLIN   Main-Travelled Roads: Six Mississippi Valley Stories. Boston: Arena Pub. Co., 1891. 1st ed., 1st state with sheets bulking 5/8". Orig. grey cloth, gilt. Fine copy and scarce. Jenkins 155-471 1983 $150

GARLAND, HERBERT   A Bibliography of the Writings of Sir James Matthew Barrie. London: the Bookman's Journal, 1928. 8vo. Blue cloth. T.e.g. Facsimile title-pages. Limited edition of 520 numbered copies. Traylen 94-56 1983 £20

GARNEAU, JOSEPH   Nebraska. Omaha, 1893. Orig. printed wraps. First edition. Ginsberg 47-619 1983 $50

GARNER, BESS ADAMS   Windows in an Old Adobe. Claremont, 1939. 1st ed. Photos., end maps. Author's inscription. Clark 741-111 1983 $52.50

GARNER, JAMES W.   The United States. Chicago, (1910). 2 vols. Illus. Thick 8vo, orig. blue mor., g.t. Argosy 716-192 1983 $45

GARNETT, ALGERNON S.   A Treatise on the Hot Springs of Arkansas. St. Louis, 1874. Orig. printed wraps. First edition. Ginsberg 46-38 1983 $125

GARNETT, DAVID   Beany-Eye. London: Chatto & Windus, 1935. First edition. Orig. cloth. Dust jacket (faded and slightly worn; price neatly clipped from front inner leaf). Near-fine. Mac-Manus 278-2148 1983 $50

GARNETT, DAVID   Beany-Eye. London: Chatto & Windus, 1935. First edition. 8vo. Orig. marbled cloth. Dust jacket. Very good copy. Jaffe 1-105 1983 $35

GARNETT, DAVID   Go She Must! London: Chatto & Windus, 1927. First edition. Orig. cloth with leather label on spine. One of only 160 copies signed by author. Very good. MacManus 278-2150 1983 $45

GARNETT, DAVID   The Grasshoppers Come. London, 1931. Ltd. to 210 copies, signed by the author. Fine. Argosy 714-317 1983 $85

GARNETT, DAVID   The Grasshoppers Come. Lon., 1931. Very good in slightly frayed, slightly skinned dustwrapper with one tear at corner flap. Quill & Brush 54-533 1983 $30

GARNETT, DAVID   Lady Into Fox. London: Chatto & Windus, 1922. First edition. Illus. with wood engravings by R.A. Garnett. Orig. cloth. Presentation copy inscribed: "Clementinia Black with love from David Garnett." Covers and spine faded and slightly worn. Some offsetting to the endpapers. Good. MacManus 278-2151 1983 $135

GARNETT, DAVID   A Man in the Zoo. London, 1924. First edition. Presentation copy from the author. T.e.g. Spare title label. Sporadic internal foxing. Spine faded. Very good. Jolliffe 26-200 1983 £45

GARNETT, DAVID   A Man in the Zoo. London: Chatto & Windus, 1924. First trade edition. Illus. with wood engravings by R.A. Garnett. Orig. patterned cloth with paper label. Dust jacket. Fine. MacManus 278-2152 1983 $20

GARNETT, DAVID   No Love. London: Chatto & Windus, 1929. First edition. 8vo. Orig. marbled cloth. Dust jacket. Very good copy. Jaffe 1-104 1983 $35

GARNETT, DAVID   A Rabbit in the Air. London, 1932. First edition. Fore-edge slightly spotted. Chipped and slightly rubbed dustwrapper with a small tear. Very good. Scarce. Jolliffe 26-201 1983 £40

GARNETT, DAVID   The Sailor's Return. New York, 1925. 8vo, cloth boards. From the library of Rudolph Ruzicka with his bookplate and with a presentation inscription to him on the front flyleaf from a friend. Label on spine is darkened and spine dulled, else very good copy. In Our Time 156-314 1983 $20

GARNETT, DAVID   War in the Air. London, 1941. First edition. Torn, chipped, and rubbed dustwrapper. Very good. Jolliffe 26-203 1983 £12.50

GARNETT, EDWARD   The Breaking Point. London: Duckworth & Co., 1907. First edition. Orig. cloth. Spine slightly darkened. Little foxing. Good. MacManus 278-2155 1983 $45

GARNETT, JOHN   Garnett's Craven Itinerary. Skipton: John Garnett, 1853. Fourth edition. 4 litho plates and 1 woodcut plate. Large 12mo, orig. cloth-backed limp printed paper boards. Fenning 60-127 1983 £18.50

GARNETT, RICHARD   English Literature. N.Y.: Macmillan, 1903. 4 vols. bound in 8. 3/4 red morocco. Profusely illus., t.e.g. Good. MacManus 278-2156 1983 $300

GARNETT, RICHARD   Poems. London: Elkin Mathews & John Lane, 1893. First edition. Orig. cloth. One of 350 copies. MacManus 278-2157 1983 $50

GARNETT, RICHARD   The Twilight of the Gods and Other Tales. London: John Lane, (1924). Elaborately gilt pictorial cloth. Illus. with full-page plates by Henry Keen. First edition with the plates and the introduction. A very fine copy in dust jacket. Reese 20-607 1983 $125

GARNETT, THOMAS   Popular Lectures on Zoonomia. London, 1804. 1st ed. Portrait. 4to. New cloth. Some stains on a few leaves, otherwise nice. Morrill 289-80 1983 $50

GARNIER, JOSEPH   Elements De L'Economie Politique. Paris, Guillaumin et Cie., 1848. Small 8vo, uncut in original printed wrappers. A fine copy. Pickering & Chatto 21-38 1983 $160

GARRETT, A. E.   The Periodic Law. London: Kegan Paul, 1909. First edition. 8vo. Orig. red stamped cloth. 3 folding tables. Ads. A very good copy. Zeitlin 264-170 1983 $45

GARRETT, JULIA K.   Green Flag over Texas: a Story of the Last Years of Spain in Texas. NY, 1939. Argosy 710-524 1983 $35

GARRETT, PAT FLOYD   Authentic Life of Billy the Kid. New York, 1927. 1st issue of 1st ed. Illus., spine label missing, covers dull. Clark 741-60 1983 $37.50

GARRICK, DAVID   The Fribbleriad. London: printed for J. Coote, 1761. 4to, wrappers, 1st ed. With an engraved frontis.; half-title present. A fine copy of one of the rarest Garrick first editions. Ximenes 64-227 1983 $850

GARRICK, DAVID   An Ode upon Dedicating a Building, and Erecting a Statue, to Shakespeare, at Stratford upon Avon. London: printed for T. Becket, and P. A. De Hondt, 1769. 4to, wrappers, 1st ed. Minor blemish in the outer margins, else a very good copy. Ximenes 64-228 1983 $275

GARRICK, DAVID   Pineapples of the Finest Flavour. A Selection of Sundry Unpublished Letters of David Garrick. Cambridge, 1930. 4to, cloth, paper label. One of 300 copies with 3 letters in facs. Bookplate. Spine lightly sunned. Nice copy. Perata 28-106 1983 $50

GARRICK, DAVID   The poetical works. London: Kearsley, 1785. First edition. 2 vols. 8vo. Early 19th-century calf, spines gilt. Rubbed. Wanting half-titles. Ximenes 63-363 1983 $150

GARRICK, DAVID   The Sick Monkey, a fable. London: printed for J. Fletcher, 1765. 4to, wrappers, 1st ed. A very good copy, complete with half-title, and an allegorical frontis. Rare. Ximenes 64-229 1983 $650

GARRIOCH, A. C.   First Furrows. Winnipeg, 1923. 20 1/2cm. Photo. and text illustrations. Green fabrikoid. Limited edition, this being no. 87. Spine dulled, else very good to fine copy. McGahern 54-67 1983 $45

GARRISON, FIELDING   An Introduction to the History of Medicine... Philadelphia, 1914. First edition. Second printing. 8vo. Orig. binding. Fye H-3-213 1983 $60

GARRISON, FIELDING   An Introduction to the History of Medicine... Philadelphia, 1917. Second edition. 8vo. Orig. binding. Fye H-3-214 1983 $45

GARRISON, FIELDING   An Introduction to the History of Medicine. Philadelphia, Saunders, 1924. 3rd ed., revised and enlarged. Illus. 8vo. Morrill 289-81 1983 $40

GARRISON, FIELDING   An Introduction to the History of Medicine... Philadelphia, 1929. Fourth edition, revised and enlarged. 8vo. Cloth. With numerous illus. Gurney JJ-134 1983 £15

GARRISON, FIELDING   John Shaw Billings a Memoir. New York, 1915. First edition. 8vo. Orig. binding. Fye H-3-685 1983 $50

GARRISON, FIELDING   Revised Students' Check-List of Texts Illustrating the History of Medicine. 1933. 8vo. Wrappers. Scarce. Fye H-3-1042 1983 $35

GARRISON, WILLIAM LLOYD   The New "Reign of Terror" in the Slave-holding States... New York, American Anti-Slavery Society, 1860. 1st ed. 12mo, sewn. Morrill 288-603 1983 $22.50

GARSIDE, ALSTON HILL   Cotton Goes to Market. NY: A. Stokes Co., 1935. Tall 8vo, dust jacket. Karmiole 74-48 1983 $35

GARTH, SAMUEL   The Dispensary. Printed: and Sold by John Nutt, 1706. 8vo, engraved frontis., orig. panelled calf, rubbed, upper joint cracked at head and foot. Bickersteth 75-231 1983 £18

GARVAN, JOHN M.   The Manobos of Mindanao. Washington: Government Printed Office, 1931. 14 plates with captioned tissue guards. Large 4to. New marbled boards, 1/4 cloth. Ars Libri 34-801 1983 $85

GARVEN, JOHN   Military Drill and Rifle Instruction Book for the Use of the Canadian Volunteers Under the Sanction of Colonel Dyde. Montreal, 1862. Orig. gold stamped cloth, first edition. Ginsberg 46-141 1983 $200

GARVEY, MICHAEL ANGELO   The silent revolution... London: Cash, etc., 1852. First edition. Small 8vo. Orig. violet cloth. Spine evenly faded. Very good copy. Ximenes 63-570 1983 $65

GARZELLI, ANNAROSA   Sculture toscane del Dugento e nel Tre-
cento. Firenze, 1969. 4to, boards, d.j. 424 illus. Ars Libri SB
26-82 1983 $75

GASCOYNE, DAVID   Holderlin's Madness. London, (1938).
First edition. Endpapers a little foxed. A free adaptation of poems
from the German of Holderlin, linked with five orig. poems. Nice.
Rota 231-242 1983 £50

GASCOYNE, DAVID   Poems 1937-1942. Poetry London, 1943.
First edition. Cover design & coloured illus. by G. Sutherland.
Boards rubbed and front hinge weak. Very good reading copy. Rota
231-243 1983 £15

GASCOYNE, DAVID   A Short Survey of Surrealism. London,
1935. First edition. Illus. Gilt device on upper cover by Y. Tanguy.
Spine darkened and covers marked. Internally nice. Rota 231-241
1983 £75

GASK, LILIAN   The Fairies and the Christmas Child.
Harrap, n.d. (ca.1912). Sm. 4to. Colour frontis. Pictorial title.
7 colour plates. 47 full-page & 34 text illus. Grey pictorial cloth,
gilt. Very good. Greer 39-96 1983 £85

GASKELL, ELIZABETH CLEGHORN   Cranford. Chapman & Hall, 1855.
Half calf, rubbed but sound. Cheap edition. Jarndyce 31-705 1983
£10.50

GASKELL, ELIZABETH CLEGHORN   Cranford. London: Macmillan & Co.,
1891. First of this edition. Preface by Anne Thackeray Ritchie.
Illus. by Hugh Thomas. Orig. decorated cloth. Blind-stamped presentation copy. Former owner's signature on half-title. Slight foxing.
Very good. MacManus 278-2158 1983 $35

GASKELL, ELIZABETH CLEGHORN   North And South. London: Chapman &
Hall, 1855. First edition. 2 vols. Orig. brown cloth. Recased with
new endpapers, spine and covers worn. Good. MacManus 278-2159 1983
$225

GASKELL, PHILIP   A Bibliography of the Foulis Press.
London: Rupert Hart-Davis, 1964. First edition. 8vo. Cloth.
Dust jacket. Fine copy. Oak Knoll 48-431 1983 $85

GASKILL, NELSON B.   Imprints from the Press of Stephen C.
Ustick. Washington, 1940. Frontis. Wrappers. Very good. Felcone
19-64 1983 $35

GASKINS, JOHN   Life and Adventures of John Gaskins,
in the Early History of Northwest Arkansas. Eureka Springs, 1893.
Printed wraps., very fine. In a folding cloth box, tied. Reese
19-240 1983 $275

GASPARIN, AGENOR DE   America Before Europe. New York,
1862. Cloth. First edition in English. Felcone 22-74 1983
$25

GASS, PATRICK   A Journal of the Voyages and Travels
of Capt. Lewis and Capt. Clarke. Pittsburgh, 1807. First edition.
Original three quarter calf, marbled boards, morocco label on spine.
A good copy, slipcased. Jenkins 151-181 1983 $750

GASS, PATRICK   Journal of the Voyages and Travels of a
Corps of Discovery Under the Command of Capt. Lewis and Capt. Clarke...
Phila.: Mathew Carey, 1812. Orig. calf. 6 plates. Map in fac. 4th
ed. Jenkins 153-777 1983 $200

GASSIER, PIERRE   The Drawings of Goya. New York:
Harper & Row, 1975. 407 illus. 9 color plates. Small folio.
Cloth. Ars Libri 32-266 1983 $100

GASSIER, PIERRE   The Life and Complete Work of Francisco
Goya. New York: Reynal, 1971. 2148 illus. (48 tipped-in color).
Small stout folio. Cloth. Dust jacket. The orig. English-language
edition. Ars Libri 32-267 1983 $125

GASTINEAU, HENRY   Wales Illustrated In A Series Of Views.
London, 1830. 4to, engraved vignette title-page, some offsetting and
a small library stamp, 142 engraved views by Radclyffe, Adlard,
Varrall and others. Some spottings, half polished blue calf, gilt,
marbled endpapers and edges. Deighton 3-139 1983 £215

GASTON, WILLIAM   An Address Delivered Before the
American Whig and Cliosophic Societies of the College of New Jersey.
Princeton, 1835. Dbd. First edition. Ginsberg 46-863 1983 $75

GASTON, WILLIAM   Speech of the Hon. William Gaston, of
North Carolina, on the Bill to Authorize a Loan of Twenty-Five
Millions of Dollars. Georgetown, 1814. Dsb. Good. Reese 18-439
1983 $30

GASTON-DREYFUS, PHILIPPE   Catalogue raisonne de l'oeuvre peint
et dessine par Nicolas-Bernard Lepicie (1735-1784). Paris: Armand
Colin, 1923. 9 plates. Large 8vo. Wrappers. Ars Libri 32-402
1983 $65

GATES, GEORGINA S.   The Modern Cat: Her Mind & Manners.
NY: Macmillan, 1928. First edition. Gach 94-22 1983 $20

GATES, JOSEPHINE SCRIBNER   Live Dolls in Wonderland. Chicago: Don.,
(1912:Bobbs). 8vo. Red cloth. Pictorial paste-on. 3 pinholes in
gutter. Full-page half-tones plus black & whites by V. Keep. Very
good. Aleph-bet 8-90 1983 $35

GATES, SUSA YOUNG   THe Life Story of Brigham Young.
NY, 1931. Many illus. D.w. 2nd edition, with port. of Brigham
Young varying from the 1st. Argosy 716-556 1983 $30

GATFORD, LIONEL   A Petition for the Vindication of the
Publique use of the Book of Common-Prayer. London, printed for John
Williams, 1655. 4to, disbound, title soiled, bit dust-soiled
throughout. Earl of Selborne copy. Ravenstree 94-127 1983 $75

GATSCHET, ALBERT S.   A Dictionary of the Atakapa Language.
Washington, 1932. Printed wrappers. Jenkins 152-818 1983 $30

GATTI PERER, MARIA LUISA   Carlo Giuseppe Merlo architetto.
Milano: Edizioni La Rete, 1966. 347 illus. Large 4to. Cloth.
Dust jacket. Ars Libri 33-234 1983 $125

GATTY, ALFRED   Domestic Pictures and Tales. Bell &
Daldy, 1866. First edition, half title, front. & illus. Small tear
with no loss, to half title, orig. blue cloth. Jarndyce 31-707 1983
£25

GATTY, ALFRED   Sheffield: Past and Present.
Sheffield and London, 1873. Engravings, cloth gilt, a bright copy.
K Books 301-74 1983 £38

GATTY, MARGARET   British Sea-Weeds. London, Bell &
Dalby, 1872. 2 vols., 80 coloured plates showing 384 specimens,
roy. 8vo, half morocco gilt, gilt tops. K Books 307-81 1983 £125

GAUDEN, JOHN   A Discourse of Artifical Beauty...
London, R. Royston, 1662. 8vo, cont. black morocco or sheep,
rebacked, fine, complete with frontis. Ravenstree 94-128 1983 $385

GAUDEN, JOHN   The Love of Truth and Peace. Printed by
G.M. for Andrew Crooke, 1641. 4to, wrapper. Fenning 62-133 1983
£24.50

GAUDEN, JOHN   The Religious & Loyal Protestation
Against the Present Declared Purposes and Proceedings of the Army and
Others... London, Richard Royston, 1648. 4to, disbound, few minor
stains. First edition. Ravenstree 94-129 1983 $65

GAUDRY, A.   Recherches scientifiques en Orient.
Paris, 1855. 8 plates (1 coloured), folding coloured map, royal
8vo, half morocco, gilt (trifle rubbed). Wheldon 160-2117 1983 £30

GAUGER, NICOLAS   Fires Improved: or, a New Method of
Building Chimnies... London: J. Senex & E. Curll, 1736. 8vo.
Cont. calf, repaired. 1 advert. leaf, with 10 folding plates.
Gurney 90-54 1983 £145

GAUGER, NICOLAS   La Mechanique du Feu... Amsterdam:
Henri Schelte, 1714. 8vo. Cont. mottled calf, gilt borders, gilt
fleurons in compartments of spine. Added engraved title by J.
Goeree and title-page printed in red and black with a woodcut device.
12 folding engraved plates. Morocco label chipped off, upper joint
defective, internally a fine copy with armorial bookplate. Rare.
Zeitlin 264-171 1983 $150

GAUGUIN, PAUL   Le "Sourire" de Paul Gauguin. Paris:
G.-P. Maisonneuve, 1952. Portfolio. 10 facsimile mss. (most 4pp.
in length), 5 plates with 8 comparative illus. All contents loose,
as issued. Small folio. Wrappers, with tipped-in facsimile. Test
on Marais. Edition limited to 1000 copies. Ars Libri 32-247 1983
$275

GAUGUIN, PAUL   Paul Gauguin. NY: Hammer Galleries.
(1962). 12mo, 3 vols. 2 in paper wraps., 1 clothbound; housed in
a slipcase. Edition ltd. to 1,000 numbered copies. Fine set.
Karmiole 75-55 1983 $75

GAUGUIN, POLA   Grafikeren Edvard Munch. Trondheim:
F. Bruns, 1946. 2 vols. in 1. 65 illus. (2 color). Large 4to.
Boards, 3/4 leather. From the library of Jakob Rosenberg, with his
copy of the mimeographed exhibition catalogue of "The Graphic Art
of Edvard Munch" from the Fogg Art Museum (1946), loosely inserted.
Ars Libri 32-483 1983 $200

GAUGUIN, POLA   My Father, Paul Gauguin. N.Y.: Alfred
Knopf, 1937. First edition. Illus. Orig. cloth. Presentation
copy from Blanche Knopf, wife of the publisher, to Ada Galsworthy, wife of
the author inscribed: "A.G. with love from Blanche Knopf, January
1937." In a worn dust jacket. Near-fine. MacManus 278-2139 1983
$35

GAULTIER, BON   The Book of Ballads. Edinburgh & London:
William Blackwood, 1903. New edition. 8vo. Blue cloth, beveled
edges, gilt dec., a.e.g. Plus 32pp catalogue. Illus. throughout with
black & whites by Doyle, Leech & Crowquill. Very good to fine.
Aleph-bet 8-24 1983 $40

GAULTIER, CAMILLE   Magic Without Apparatus. Berkeley
Heights, New Jersey: Fleming Book Co., 1945. Illus. with 216
text figures. Index. Fine copy in dust jacket. Karmiole 72-67
1983 $50

GAUNT, WILLIAM   London Promenade. London, 1930. First
edition. Illus. by author. 4to. Covers marked, endpapers soiled.
Some plates slightly foxed. Inscription on front endpaper. Very good.
Rota 230-239 1983 £15

GAUSE, HARRY T.   A Detailed Description of the Scenes and
Incidents Connected with a Trip Through the Mountains and Parks of
Colorado. (Wilmington: James & Webb, 1871). Three quarter. Corners
bumped with some wear. Scarce. Jenkins 153-218 1983 $300

GAUSS, KARL FRIEDRICH   Disquisitiones Arithmeticae. Gerhard
Fleischer Jr., Leipzig, 1801. 8vo, light foxing in a few gatherings;
a fine uncut copy, unopened from p. 201 to the end. Cont.
decorative wraps., buckram case. First edition. Quaritch NS 5-43
1983 $4,500

GAUSS, KARL FRIEDRICH   Recherches Arithmetiques. Courcier,
Paris, 1807. 4to, cont. sprinkled calf, gilt device of the College
Royal de St. Louis, spine rubbed. First edition in French. Quaritch
NS 5-44 1983 $950

GAUTHIER, MAXIMILIEN   Achille et Eugene Deveria. Paris:
H. Floury, 1925. 36 plates Numerous text illus. 4to. Marbled
boards, 3/4 leather. Orig. wrappers bound in. Ars Libri 32-166
1983 $100

GAUTIER, THEOPHILE   One of Cleopatra's Nights. Chicago:
Privately printed 1929. 1st ed. thus, 1 of 150 numbered copies.
Orig. vellum-backed decorated boards, gilt. Fine copy in chipped
box. Jenkins 155-540 1983 $45

GAUTIER, THEOPHILE   Theatre. Paris: Charpentier et cie.
1872. Brown calf over marbled boards. Orig. printed wraps. bound
in. Karmiole 72-47 1983 $75

GAUTIER, THEOPHILE   The Works. New York: the Jenson
Society. 24 vols. 8vo. Half red morocco, gilt, gilt panelled
spines, t.e.g. Portrait and 100 etchings by A. Mongin and others.
Privately printed for subscribers only. Traylen 94-369 1983 £175

GAUTRUCHE, PIERRE   The Poetical Histories. London, W.G.,
sold by M. Pitt, 1674. 8vo, orig. calf, joints cracked, lower blank
tip of G7 torn away, paper flaw in edge of 2E6 affects 2 words in the
marginal note. Ravenstree 95-51 1983 $210

GAVARNI in London: sketches of life and character. London: David
Bogue, 1849. Large 8vo. Orig. blue-grey cloth. Engraved title and
23 plates of life in London drawn on wood by Gavarni, and engraved
by Henry Vizetelly. Slightly rubbed, spine faded. Very good copy.
Ximenes 63-196 1983 $100

GAVIN, ANTONIO   A Master-Key to Popery. Newport: Solomon Southwick, 1773. First American edition. Full calf. Endsheets
lacking. Sound. Felcone 20-56 1983 $75

GAWSWORTH, JOHN   Fifty Years of Modern Verse. London,
Secker, (1938). First edition. Dust jacket. Very good. Signed
and inscribed by Gawsworth, with an eight line holograph poem.
Also signed by fourteen of the contributors. According to a note
by the editor this is one of 8 copies, with the top edge blue.
Houle 21-370 1983 $125

GAY, CLAUDIO   Historia fisica y politica de Chile.
Paris and Santiago, 1844-71. 28 vols. of texts and 2 atlas vols.
With 315 lithographed plates and maps. 8vo. Cont. marbled boards
with green leather backs. Some plates with marginal repairs, affecting
edges of plate in a very few cases. Light foxing on many plates.
4 vols. in slightly different binding. Occasional light wear. Scarce.
Kraus 164-99 1983 $7,500

GAY, EBENEZER   Well-Accomplish'd Soldiers, a Glory to
their King... Boston: T. Fleet for Daniel Henchman, 1738. Stitched.
Uncut. Half-title present (a bit soiled). Very good. Felcone 20-106
1983 $75

GAY, JOHN   The Beggar's Opera. London: printed
for John Watts, 1728. Second edition, issue with the "ouverture",
2 advertisements on the verso of the title-page, 8vo, uncut, edges
frayed especially at bottom corner, titlepage soiled and repaired
with tissue in two plates, in original wrappers. Pickering & Chatto
19-25 1983 $450

GAY, JOHN   The Beggar's Opera. London: printed
for John Watts, 1728. 2nd edition, issue without the "ouverture", 8vo,
1 advertisement on the verso of the title-page. Heavy foxing on pages
20-29, disbound. Pickering & Chatto 19-24 1983 $300

GAY, JOHN   The Beggar's Opera. London: printed
for John Watts, 1733. 3rd octavo edition, some waterstaining at
inner margins, first few leaves slightly browned, tear in B2 affecting a few bars of music, in modern wrappers. Pickering & Chatto
19-26 1983 $300

GAY, JOHN   The Beggars's Opera. Published by
Daniel O'Connor, 1922. Imperial 8vo, 28 plates, t.e.g., other
edges uncut, boards with buckram spine. Twenty-eight plates in colo-
type and a facs. title of the first edition. Bickersteth 75-141 1983
£12

GAY, JOHN   The Beggars Opera. Paris: Limited Editions Club, 1937. 4to. 15 lithographs by Lydis. Blue decorated
cloth, in buff slipcase. Edition limited to 1500 copies, signed by
M. Lydis. Greer 40-134 1983 £65

GAY, JOHN   Fables. John Stockdale, 1793. 2 vols. in
one. Tall 8vo. First edition, first issue. 70 plates (12 engraved by
Blake). Subscribers list & adverts. Cont. calf, rebacked. Greer 40-
50 1983 £175

GAY, JOHN   Fables... London: for John Stockdale,
1793. 2 vols. Roy. 8vo. Cont. speckled calf, wide gilt borders, gilt
decorated spines with black morocco labels, gilt plates illus. three
fables, from engr. by William Blake, etc. Engr. title-page, with
vignette, and engr. frontis. Traylen 94-372 1983 £135

GAY, JOHN   The Fables of Mr. John Gay. York:
Wilson, Spence and Mawman, 1797. 18mo, frontis. and 100 cuts and vignettes. 19th cent. calf, worn. Head of spine chipped. Karmiole
75-23 1983 $100

GAY, JOHN   Fables... London: by C. Whittingham,
1808. Cr. 4to. Cont. calf, gilt borders, gilt decorated spine.
Engraved vignette title-page and 70 head-piece illus. Traylen 94-
373 1983 £18

GAY, JOHN   Plays Written by Mr. John Gay. Printed
for W. Strahan, 1772. With a portrait, 12mo, cont. calf, neatly
rebacked, a very good copy. Fenning 61-146 1983 £32.50

GAY, JOHN   Trivia: or, the art of walking the streets of London. London: Lintott, n.d. (1716). First edition. 8vo. Disbound. The small paper issue. A bit browned. Ximenes 63-364 1983 $150

GAY, THERESSA   James W. Marshall: The Discoverer of California Gold. Georgetown, Ca., 1967. Illus., plates, facs. in pocket. Half leather, boxed. First edition. One of 250 numbered copies containing inserts in back cover pocket. Ginsberg 46-441 1983 $75

GAYA, LOUIS DE   A Treatise of the Arms and Engines of War. Robert Harfold, 1678. First English edition. Small 8vo, orig. cloth. Engr. frontis. and 19 engr. plates of armour, swords, pikes, muskets, long and cross bows, shields, mortars, flags & musical instruments, etc. Cont. sprinkled sheep. From the library of J. Evelyn, with press-mark in his hand deleted in upper margin of frontis. Good. Edwards 1042-350 1983 £750

GAYLORD, HARVEY R.   The Principles of Pathological Histology. Phila., (1901). 40 plates & 81 text illus. 4to, cloth (inner front mended); ex-lib. Argosy 713-213 1983 $75

GAYLORD, REUBEN   An Address Delivered on the Occasion of Laying the Foundation of the Building for the Prepatory Department of Nebraska University, at Fontelle, N.T., July 27, 1858. Omaha City, Republican, 1858. Orig. printed wraps. First edition. Ginsberg 47-620 1983 $125

GAYTON, A. H.   The Uhle Pottery Collections from Nazca. Berkeley: University of California Press, 1927. 21 plates. 12 text illus. Small 4to. Wrappers. Ars Libri 34-246 1983 $25

GEDDES, MICHAEL   Several Tracts against Popery: together with the Life of Don Alvaro de Luna. London: Bernard Lintott, 1715. 1st ed., 8vo, cont. calf, half-title. Advertisement page. Trebizond 18-212 1983 $100

GEDDIE, JOHN   The Lake Regions of Central Africa. T. Nelson, 1881. First edition, with a double-page map and 32 plates (some double-page), ads., cr. 8vo, orig. cloth, gilt. Fenning 61-147 1983 £28.50

GEE, EDWARD   An Answer to the Compiler of the Nubes Testium. Printed for Henry Mortlock, 1688. First edition, 4to, wrapper, two short tears in blank portion of imprimatur leaf, otherwise a very good copy. Fenning 61-148 1983 £16.50

GEE, EDWARD   An Answer to the Compiler of the Nubes Testium. Printed for Henry Mortlock, 1688. First edition, 4to, a fine copy. Fenning 62-134 1983 £12.50

GEE, EDWARD   An Exercitation concerning Usurped Powers... (London), 1650. 4to. Wrappers. Heath 48-117 1983 £30

GEE, EDWARD   A Vindication of the Principles of the Author of the Answer to the Compiler of the Nubes Testium from the Charge of Popery. Printed for Henry Mortlock, 1688. First edition, 4to, wrapper, a very good copy. Fenning 61-149 1983 £12.50

GEER, WALTER   Campaigns of the Civil War. NY, 1926. T.e.g., inner hinges cracked, else good. King 46-56 1983 $25

GEER, WALTER   Napoleon and His Family. London, 1928. Roy. 8vo. Orig. cloth. Portrait frontis. 14 plates, 2 full page plans. Slightly faded. Bookplate. Good. Edwards 1042-427 1983 £12

GEFFROY, GUSTAVE   Constantin Guys. L'historien du Second Empire. Paris: G. Cres, 1920. 37 fine heliotype plates (4 color). 4to. Wrappers. Edition limited to 1100 copies. Ars Libri 32-298 1983 $40

GEFFROY, GUSTAVE   Sisley. Paris: G. Cres, 1927. 60 plates. 4to. Cloth. Orig. wrappers bound in. Ars Libri 32-638 1983 $50

GEFFS, MARY L.   Under Ten Flags... Greeley, Colo., 1938. Fairly scarce. Jenkins 153-129 1983 $50

GEHLER, JOHANN KARL   Ordinis medicorum in Academia Lipsiensi. Liepzig: Officina Saalbachia, 1786. Engraved plate. Small 4to. Cont. paper backstrip. Rare. Kraus 164-50 1983 $250

GEIGER, BENNO   Alessandro Magnasco. Wien: Krystall-Verlag, 1923. 48 plates. 4to. Boards, 1/4 cloth. Shaken. Ars Libri 33-213 1983 $50

GEIGER, BENNO   Antonio Carneo. Udine: "La Panarie", 1940. 128 plates. 4to. Cloth. T.e.g. Slipcase. Edition limited to 450 copies. Ars Libri 33-86 1983 $135

GEIGER, CHRISTOPHER   These de quaestione illa: Utrum masticatio species concoctionis sit? Herborn: Christopher Corvin, 1593. Woodcut vignette on title. 4to. Boards. Kraus 164-100 1983 $125

GEIGER, VINCENT   Trail to California. The Overland Journal of... New Haven, 1945. Frontis., charts, map. Jenkins 153-442 1983 $25

GEIKIE, ARCHIBALD   Annals of the Royal Society Club. 1917. 8vo, cloth, 39 portraits. Wheldon 160-229 1983 £20

GEIKIE, ARCHIBALD   Annals of the Royal Society Club. London, 1917. First edition. 8vo. Cloth. 39 portraits. Gurney JJ-353 1983 £15

GEISTREICHE Gesaenqe und Lieder. Schweidnitz, 1725-1726. 125 engraved plates by M. Rentz and J.A. Montalegre. Oblong folio, bound in antiphonal vellum-leaf. Parts 1-5 are not included. Salloch 387-61 1983 $950

GELLER, HUGO   Comrade Gulliver. N.Y.: Put., (1935). 4to. Cloth. Worn dust wrapper. Each page of text faces full-page charcoal illus. Fine. Aleph-bet 8-120 1983 $27

GELLERT, G. R.   Geistliche Oden und Lieder, mit Melodien von Carl Phillipp Emanuel Bach. Berlin, Winter, 1764. Title within ornamental woodcut border, woodcut vignette. Square folio, calf-backed boards. Salloch 387-7 1983 $450

GELLHORN, MARTHA   The Wine of Astonishment. N.Y., Scribner, 1948. First edition. Dust jacket (slight rubbing and nicking) else very good. Houle 22-402 1983 $35

GENERA Insectorum. Hymenoptera: fasc. 18. Brussels, 1904. 2 coloured plates, 4to, wrappers. Wheldon 160-1078 1983 £15

GENERA Insectorum. Hymenoptera: fasc. 54, 76, 94, 107, 124. Brussels, 1907-11. 12 plates (3 coloured), 5 parts in 1 vols., 4to, cloth. Wheldon 160-1079 1983 £35

GENERA Insectorum. Hymenoptera: fasc. 107. Brussels, 1910. 3 plates (1 coloured), 4to, wrappers. Wheldon 160-1081 1983 £12

GENERAL Index to the First Thirty-Three Volumes of the Medico-Chirurgical Transactions. London, 1851. 8vo. First edition. Orig. binding. Scarce. Fye H-3-1043 1983 $45

THE GENERAL Stud-Book, Containing Pedigress of Race Horses. Printed for James Weatherby, 1808. First edition, 8vo, cont. calf, little rubbed, but quite sound and otherwise a nice copy. Fenning 61-150 1983 £45

THE GENEROUS Usurer Mr. Nevell in Thames Street... London: for Salomon Johnson, 1641. 4to. Woodcut vignette pasted onto title. Cont. half calf. Title soiled, some wear. Very rare facsimile. Heath 48-143 1983 £65

GENET, JEAN   Our Lady of the Flowers. Paris, Morhien, 1949. Tan boards with drawing by Jean Cocteau (cracked at joint, lacking front free endpaper), else good-very good. One of 500 copies. Houle 21-371 1983 $30

THE GENETIC and Endocrinic Basis for Differences in Form and Behavior. Philadelphia: Wistar Inst. of Anatomy and Biology, 1941. Cloth rubbed and with a few minor defects, else a good copy. Gach 94-74 1983 $40

GENIN, THOMAS H.   The Napolead, in Twelve Books.
St. Clairsville: H. J. Howard, 1833. Thick 18mo, disbound. 1st ed.
Argosy 710-394 1983 $30

GENLIS, STEPHANIE FELICITE DUCREST DE SAINT AUBIN   The Duchesse de
la Valliere. London, for John Murray, 1804. First English ed.,
2 vols., 12mo., contemp. half green mor., gilt, marbled boards, 2pp.
of ads in vol. 2. Traylen 94-374 1983 £65

GENLIS, STEPHANIE FELICITE DUCREST DE SAINT AUBIN   The Kings of the
Swan; Or, The Court of Charlemagne. Printed for J. Johnson, 1796.
3 vols, 12mo, contemporary tree calf, red and green labels; three
half-titles, advertisement leaf in Vol. III. 1st ed. in English.
Hill 165-38 1983 £165

GENLIS, STEPHANIE FELICITE DUCREST DE SAINT AUBIN   Petrarch and
Laura. Printed for Sir Richard Phillips, 1820. 12mo, original
roan-backed boards; half-title. Hill 165-39 1983 £48

GENLIS, STEPHANIE FELICITE DUCREST DE SAINT AUBIN   The Siege of
Rochelle; Or, The Christian Heroine. Printed by Cox, Son and Baylis
(vol. II P. Da Ponte; Vol. III R. Juigne) for B. Dulau and J. Hughes,
1808. 3 vols., 12mo, contemp. tree calf; lacking labels. Good. Three
half-titles, and 7 pp. of advertisements in Vol. III. First edition
in English. Hill 165-40 1983 £135

GENLIS, STEPHANIE FELICITE DUCREST DE SAINT AUBIN   Tales of the
Castle... London, for G. G. J. & J Robinson, 1787. Third ed., 5
vols., small 8vo., contemp. calf, lightly rubbed. Heath 48-376 1983
£125

GENLIS, STEPHANIE FELICITE DUCREST DE SAINT AUBIN   Tales of the
Castle: Or, Stories of Instruction and Delight. Dublin: Printed
for Messrs. Price, Moncrieffe, etc., 1785. 4 vols, 12mo, contemporary
calf, lacking two labels. Four half-titles. Hill 165-41 1983 £55

GENTHE, ARNOLD   As I Remember. NY, (1936). Third
printing, 112 photographic illus., very good. Quill & Brush 54-1636
1983 $50

GENTHE, ARNOLD   The Book of the Dance. NY: Mitchell
Kennerley, 1916. First edition. Large 8vo. 95 half-tone plates, 5 in
color. Green cloth. This copy with an orig. photo signed by Genthe,
laid in. Karmiole 73-36 1983 $200

GENTHE, ARNOLD   Impressions of Old New Orleans. N.Y.,
(1926). First edition. Full page photo plates. Cloth backed boards.
Covers a little loose, corners bumped. King 45-96 1983 $95

GENTHE, ARNOLD   Old Chinatown. N.Y., Mitchell
Kennerley, 1913. Second edition, with additional photos. 8vo,
black cloth stamped in red and gilt, acetate wrapper. Very good. 91
halftone photographs of San Francisco's Chinatown by Genthe. Houle
22-1064 1983 $150

GENTLEMAN, FRANCIS   The Dramatic Censor; or, Critical Companion. London: printed for J. Bell, and C. Etherington, 1770. 2
vols., 8vo, cont. calf, spines gilt (a couple of corners a little
worn). 1st ed, 2 plates, half-titles present. A fine set. Ximenes
64-232 1983 $375

GENTLEMAN, FRANCIS   Sejanus, a tragedy. London: printed
for R. Manby, and H. S. Cox, 1752. 8vo, wrappers, 1st ed. Ximenes
64-233 1983 $125

GENLTEMAN, FRANCIS   The Theatres. A Poetical Dissection.
London: printed for John Bell, and C. Etherington (York), 1772. 4to,
disbound, 1st ed. A very good copy, complete with half-title (errata
slip mounted on the verso) and final leaf of ads. Scarce. Ximenes
64-234 1983 $400

GENTLEMAN, FRANCIS   The Theatres. A Poetical Dissection.
London: printed for John Bell; and C. Etherington (York), 1772.
4to, red quarter morocco, 2nd ed. Title-page slightly dusty. Scarce.
Ximenes 64-235 1983 $175

THE GENTLEMAN, Merchant, Tradesman, Lawyer and Debtor's Pocket Guide
in Cases of Arrest. Bath: by W. Gye, (ca. 1785). 8vo. Cont.
quarter calf, vellum corners, marbled sides. Very rare. Heath 48-
224 1983 £125

THE GENTLEMAN'S Magazine Extraordinary. London: printed by E. Cave,
(1735). 8vo, small portion torn from the upper corner of pp. 447-8
(affecting the parliamentary reports only), 18th cent. half calf,
rebacked, internally a clean copy. Pickering & Chatto 19-46 1983
$450

THE GENTLEMAN'S Toilet. London: Rock Bros. & Payne, (ca. 1845).
12mo. Title vignetts and 9 other hand-colored plates, each of which
includes a hinged flap with another picture or words beneath it.
Binding loose, one flap of two on one of plates missing, otherwise
fine in gilt-decorated red morocco. A.e.g. Early, undated owner's
signature. Bromer 25-347 1983 $350

GENTRY, HELEN   Chronology of Books & Printing, 300
BC - AD 1032. San Francisco: Helen Gentry, 1933. First edition.
Tall 12mo. Orig. boards with new cloth spine with orig. spine laid
down on it. Decorations by Hilda Scott. Fine. Oak Knoll 49-191
1983 $40

THE GENUINE Account of the Trial of Eugene Aram for the Murder of
Daniel Clark, late of Knaresbrough, in the County of York. Leeds:
Printed by Thomas Wright; and sold by E. Hargrove, Knaresbrough,
(1780?). 12mo, later half morocco, rubbed. Title soiled and inner
hinge strengthened. Argosy 713-32 1983 £16

A GENUINE Collection of O. P. Songs, Whimsical and Satirical. London:
printed by W. Glindon, and published by R. Mace, n. d. (1810). 8vo,
disbound, 1st ed. Rare. Ximenes 64-236 1983 $90

GEOFFROY, GUSTAVE   Charles Meryon. Paris: H. Floury,
1926. 32 heliogravure plates. Prof. illus. 4to. Wrappers. Dust
jacket. Ars Libri 32-450 1983 $125

GEOLOGIC Atlas of the U.S. Portions Covering Arkansas and Missouri.
Washington, 1900's. Atlas folio, pr. wrs. Argosy 716-11 1983
$25

GEOLOGIC Atlas of the U.S. Portions Covering California. Washington,
1900's. Atlas folio, pr. wrs. Argosy 716-37 1983 $25

GEOLOGIC Atlas of the U.S. Portions Covering Illinois and Indiana.
Washington, 1900's. Each with several maps in color, several
photographic views, and explanatory text. Atlas folio, pr. wraps.
Argosy 716-209 1983 $25

GEOLOGIC Atlas of the U.S. Portions Covering Maryland, Pennsylvania,
and West Virginia. Washington, 1900's. Atlas folio, pr. wraps.
Argosy 716-257 1983 $25

GEOLOGIC Atlas of the U.S. Portion Covering Utah. Washington, 1900's.
With several maps in color, several photo. views. Atlas folio, pr.
wraps. Argosy 716-557 1983 $25

GEOLOGY of the European Countries. 1982. Illustrated, 4 vols., 4to,
cloth. Vols. 1 and 2 are in English, Vols. 3 and 4 in French.
Wheldon 160-1398 1983 £113

GEORGE, HENRY   A Perplexed Philosopher. New York:
Webster, 1892. 8vo, orig. cloth, worn, front flyleaf gone, name
on endpaper. Rare first edition. Ravenstree 94-131 1983 $43

GEORGE, HENRY   Progress and Poverty. San Francisco:
Wm. M. Hinton, 1879. 1st ed., 8vo, original cloth, spine faded
and repaired. Pickering & Chatto 21-39 1983 $550

GEORGE, HENRY   Progress and Poverty. New York, D.
Appleton, 1881. 8vo, orig. printed paper wraps., bit worn and lightly
soiled. A presentation copy inscribed by George; preserved in quarter
red morocco gilt slip-case with inner protective wraps. Ravenstree
94-133 1983 $120

GEORGE, HENRY   Progress and Poverty. New York, D.
Appleton, 1881. 8vo, orig. printed paper wraps., spine and wraps.
worn, top wrapper loose, note on blank endpaper. Ravenstree 94-132
1983 $35

GEORGE, HENRY   Progress and Poverty. Kegan Paul, Trench,
1882. First English edition. Half title, 32 pp. ads. Orig. maroon
cloth, spine faded. Jarndyce 31-168 1983 £20

GEORGE, HENRY   Protection or Free Trade. New York:
Henry George & Co., 1886. 1st ed., 8vo, margins slightly browned,
original brown cloth, upper hinge cracked, several small stains
on covers. Pickering & Chatto 21-40 1983 $65

GEORGE, HENRY   Protection or Free Trade? (Washington):
1892. Self wrappers. Jenkins 153-219 1983 $75

GEORGE, JOHN B.   Shots Fired in Anger. Plantersville,
S. C. (1947). Illus., cloth, spine dull else very good. King 46-782
1983 $75

GEORGE, K. E.   Ausfuehrliches Lateinisch Deutsches
Handwoerterbuch. N.p., n.d. 2 vols., very thick 4to, buckram.
Salloch 385-91 1983 $65

GEORGE, KING   The Annals of King George, Year of the
First... London: A. Bell, etc., 1716-21. 6 vols. 8vo. Cont.
mottled calf, wide gilt borders with fleur-de-lys, etc., gilt
panelled spines with red and green morocco labels, gilt, inner
gilt edges. Portrait. Very fine. Traylen 94-375 1983 £135

GEORGE, MILTON   The Western Rural Year Book, A Cyclopedia of Reference. Chicago, 1886. Illustrated, cloth,
extremities worn. King 46-2 1983 $20

GEORGE, WALDEMAR   Dessins et gouaches (1919-1925) de
Roger De La Fresnaye. Paris: Librairie de France, 1927. 30 plates
with 46 tipped-in facsimile illus. (numerous color pochoir). Folio.
Portfolio. Boards, 1/4 cloth. Contents loose, as issued. Edition
limited to 300 copies. Ars Libri 32-383 1983 $175

GEORGE, WALDEMAR   Gromaire. Paris: Edition des Chroniques
du Jour, 1928. 29 gravure plates. 4to. Wrappers. One of 500
numbered copies on velin, of a limited edition of 560 copies only.
Backstrip worn. Ars Libri 32-289 1983 $85

GEORGE, WALDEMAR   Picasso dessins. Paris: Quatre
Chemins, 1926. 64 plates. 4to. Boards. Printed by Ducros et
Colas. Boards dull. Ars Libri 32-520 1983 $75

GEORGE, WILLIS   Surreptitious Entry. N.Y., D. Appleton-
Century, (1946). First edition. 9 illus. Dust jacket (back faded).
Very good. Houle 22-403 1983 $20

GEORGES, KARL E.   Lexikon der Lateinishchen Wortformen.
Leipzig, 1889. First edition, roy. 8vo, cont. half morocco, gilt,
t.e.g. Fenning 62-135 1983 £24.50

GEORGES-MICHEL, MICHEL   Left Bank. New York: Horace Liveright
(1931). Illustrated by the Montparnassians: Modigliana, Picasso,
Man Ray, J. Gris, Picabia et al. 8vo. Cloth, boards. A bleeder.
The last 31 pages have been chewed at the corners, some flaking to
Liveright name at base of spine, else very good copy in worn dj. In
Our Time 156-497 1983 $25

GEORGIAN Stories. N.Y.: G.P. Putnam's Sons, 1925. First American
edition. Illus. with photographic portraits of the authors. Orig.
cloth-backed boards. Fine. MacManus 278-2160 1983 $20

GEORGIEVICS, G. VON   A Text-Book of Dye Chemistry...
London: Scott, 1920. Second English edition. 8vo. Orig. cloth.
Very good copy. Zeitlin 264-173 1983 $40

GERARD, ALEXANDER   An Essay on Taste. Philadelphia, 1804.
4pp. of subscribers. Leather and boards, very good. Reese 18-258
1983 $250

GERARD, E.   Letters in Rhyme. Liverpool: Rushton &
Melling, 1825. First edition, uncut. Rebound in blue bds. Cream
cloth spine, label. Jarndyce 30-701 1983 £30

GERARD, E. D.   Beggar My Neighbour. Edinburgh: William
Blackwood & Sons, 1882. First edition. 3 vols. Orig. cloth. Former
owner's signature torn from title-page in each volume. Near-fine.
MacManus 278-2161 1983 $150

GERARD, JOHN   Gerard's Herball. London: Gerald
Howe, 1927. 4to, illus. throughout with woodcuts reproduced from
the 1636 edition. Notes. Index. Edition ltd. to 150 copies,
printed on handmade paper. In full vellum, a little soiled.
Karmiole 71-103 1983 $200

GERARD, JOHN   The Herball or Generall Historie of
Plants. (London 1597), Amsterdam, 1975. Engraved title-page,
portrait, 2146 woodcuts of plants, bound in 2 vols., folio, cloth.
Excellent full-size facsimile of the first edition. Wheldon 160-
2171 1983 £130

GERBIER, BALTHAZAR   Counsel and advise to all builders.
London: printed by Thomas Mabb, 1663. First edition. 8vo. Calf
antique, gilt, spine gilt. Two signatures of dedications bound out
of order at the beginning, errata leaf present at the end; a few
minor marginal repairs, but a sound copy. Ximenes 63-15 1983 $1,200

GERHARDI, WILLIAM   Eva's Apples: A Story of Jazz and
Jasper. New York, 1928. 8vo. Cloth. A fine copy in colorful dj
which is chipped and worn. In Our Time 156-315 1983 $20

GERHARDI, WILLIAM   Futility. London: Richard Cobden-Sanderson, (1922). First edition. Orig. cloth. Presentation copy,
inscribed on the title-page to "Dennis Wheatley from William Gerhardi,
this first of my books." With Wheatley's paper bookplate on the front
endsheet. Fine. MacManus 278-2162 1983 $175

GERHARDI, WILLIAM   The Polyglots. London, 1925. First
edition. Lower cover marked. Nice. Rota 231-247 1983 £12.50

GERMAIN, H.   Flore des Diatomees Diatomophycees eaux
douces et saumatres du Massif Armoricain et des contrees voisines
d'Europe occidentale. Paris, 1981. 169 plates of 2125 microphotographs,
8vo, cloth. Wheldon 160-1833 1983 £42

GERMAN Glee Book. New York, American Musical Institute, 1848. Small
folio, orig. printed boards, spine repaired. Some foxing and light
stains. From the library of Lowell Mason. Salloch 387-64 1983 $35

GERMAN Romance: Specimens of its chief Authors. Edinburgh: William
Tait; London: Charles Tait, 1827. First edition. 8vo, 4 vols., later
half morocco gilt boards by Bayntun. Uncut copy, vignette title pages
and half-titles in all volumes. An exceptionally fine copy. Trebizond
18-109 1983 $300

GERMANISCHES Museum. Nurnberg, 1890. Katalog der im Germanischen
Museum Befindlichen Originalsculpturen. Foreword by Hans Bosch.
92, (2)pp., 16 plates. 4to. Wraps. (slightly worn). Ars Libri
SB 26-162 1983 $40

GERNSHEIM, HELMUT   Lewis Carroll Photographer. London,
1949. 64 black and white photographs taken by Lewis Carroll reproduced. Slightly torn, rubbed and frayed dustwrapper. Very good.
Jolliffe 26-81 1983 £55

GERSHWIN, GEORGE   An American in Paris. Los Angeles:
Philharmonic Orchestra, 1931. Stiff printed wraps. Signed in ink by
Gershwin, beneath his name in the program. Fine. Houle 22-404 1983
$550

GERSHWIN, GEORGE   Porgy and Bess. New York: Random House,
1935. Quarto, full red morocco, silvered top, grass cloth slipcase
worn. Frontis. and title vignette in color by George Biddle. One of
250 copies signed by George Gershwin, Ira Gershwin, DuBose Heyward and
Rouben Mamoulian. First edition. Duschnes 240-81 1983 $1,000

GERSON, HORST   Rembrandt Paintings. New York:
Reynal, 1968. More than 730 illus. (80 color plates). Folio.
Cloth. Dust jacket. Orig. edition. Ars Libri 32-555 1983
$75

GERSON, JEAN CHARLIER DE   De pollutione nocturna, cum forma
absolutionis sacramentalis. (Cologne: Ulrich Zell, c. 1466).
First edition of the first printed book on a medical subject. 4to.
Eighteenth-century calf-backed boards. From the library of Eric
Sexton. Top of spine a little worn. Kraus 164-102 1983 $9,500

GERSTAECKER, FRIEDRICH   Wild Sports in the Far West. Boston,
1860. Colored plates after Harrison Weir. Cloth. Rebacked with
orig. spine laid down. A worn copy, with some signatures pulled.
Felcone 22-79 1983 $40

GERVAIS, F. L. P.   Zoologie et Paleontologie Generales.
Paris, 1876. 12 plates, 4to, original wrappers. Second series.
Scarce. Unfinished series 2. Only plates 1-5, 7-10, 12, 13 and 25
were issued, while the text breaks off in the middle of a sentence.
Wheldon 160-1399 1983 £15

GESNER, ABRAHAM   New Brunswick. London, 1847. 5 plates,
vignette t.p. Blind-stamped cloth. Map mentioned in illus. index
is not present. Argosy 716-47 1983 $100

GESNER, CONRAD   On the Admiration of Mountains. S.F.,
1937. 4to, title page printed in red and black. Initials in text
by Dorothy Grover. With eight illus. from 16th century engravings
of Hans Schaufelin. Half cloth. One of 325 copies, signed by Ed &
Robert Grabhorn. Very good-fine. Houle 21-654 1983 $150

GESSLER, CLIFFORD   Kanaka Moon. 1927. 8vo. Cloth.
Illustrated by A.S. Macleod. Signed and dated by the poet on the
front flyleaf. A fine copy in dj. In Our Time 156-316 1983 $25

GESSNER, SALOMON   The Works... Liverpool, printed by
J.M.'Creery, 1802. First collected edition in English, with an
engraved portrait and 15 engraved plates by Cromek after Thomas
Stothard. Without half-titles, 3 vols., 8vo, cont. mottled calf,
the spines worn and joints cracked, otherwise very good. Fenning 60-
130 1983 £28.50

GETLEIN, FRANK   Harry Jackson Monograph - Catalogue.
New York: Kennedy Galleries, 1969. Deluxe edition limited to 300
numbered copies and signed by the artist. Original signed print
laid in. Full calf, boxed. Very fine copy. Profusely illustrated,
many in color. Jenkins 151-101 1983 $175

GETZ, JOHN   The Woodward Collection of Jades and
Other Hard Stones. (New York), Privately Printed, 1913. 1st ed.
Illus. 8vo. Ex-library. 1st ed. Morrill 287-578 1983 $45

GHIDIGLIA QUINTAVALLE, AUGUSTA   Il Bertoja. Parma: Cassa di
Risparmio di Parma, 1963. 44 plates (partly in color). 88 text
illus. Folio. Boards. Dust jacket. Ars Libri 33-32 1983 $100

GHIDIGLIA QUINTAVALLE, AUGUSTA   La Stufetta del Parmigianino nella
Rocca di Fonatnellato. Parma: Privately Printed, 1960. 27 orig.
color photographs by Bruno Maghi mounted on heavy boards. Folio.
Boards, 1/4 vellum. No. 30 of an unspecified limitation. Ars Libri
33-264 1983 $135

GHIRARDELLI, YNEZ   The Artist H. Daumier: Interpreter of
History. SF, 1940. Folio, maroon cloth, leather label. With 20
full-page examples of the work of Daumier. Very light fading to
covers; a very nice copy. Perata 28-53 1983 $250

GHISELIN, BREWSTER   Against the Circle. New York, 1946.
8vo. Cloth. A copy for review with slip from publisher laid in.
Newspaper clipping about the book under rear flap of fly, else fine
in dj which is chipped on the spine. In Our Time 156-317 1983 $50

GHOSE, SUDHIN N.   Folk Tales and Fairy Stories from
India. London: the Golden Cockerel Press, 1961. Full brown
crushed levant morocco, gilt, t.e.g., others uncut, in a slip-case.
6 illus. and vignettes on title-page endpapers. Limited edition
of 100 numbered copies, printed throughout in black and sepia.
Traylen 94-377 1983 £160

GHOST Towns of Colorado. NY, (1947). Profusely illus. with photos.
Thin 12mo, d.w. Argosy 716-639 1983 $25

GIARD, A.   Oeuvres Diverses. Paris, 1911-13.
2 volumes, 8vo, wrappers. Wrappers trifle worn. Wheldon 160-313
1983 £18

GIBB, GEORGE SWEET   The Whitesmiths of Taunton. Cambridge,
Harvard, 1943. 1st ed. Illus. 8vo, few binding stains. Morrill
288-604 1983 $20

GIBBES, R. W.   Monograph of the Fossil Squalidae of
the United States. Philadelphia, 1948-49. 7 plates, 2 parts, 4to,
new wrappers, contents trifle dustsoiled. Wheldon 160-1400 1983 £15

GIBBINGS, ROBERT   Blue Angels and Whales. London: J.M.
Dent & Sons, 1946. Second edition, revised & enlarged. In a rare
unrecorded publisher's binding. Bookplate. Near-fine. MacManus 278-
2164 1983 $45

GIBBINGS, ROBERT   John Graham (Convict) 1824. London,
1937. First edition. 40 wood-engravings by the author. Presentation
copy from the author in the week of publication, inscribed on the
front free endpaper. Tipped in on the front pastedown is an A.L.S.
from the author to the presentee. Chipped, repaired dustwrapper
slightly darkened at the spine. Near fine. Jolliffe 26-205 1983
£65

GIBBINGS, ROBERT   The Wood Engravings... London: J.M.
Dent, 1959. Frontispiece. Cloth, as new. Dawson 470-118 1983
$100

GIBBON, EDWARD   The History of the Decline and Fall
of the Roman Empire. London: for A. Strahan and T. Cadell, 1777-
1789. First edition of vols. 4-6, third edition of vol. 1, new
edition of vols. 2 & 3. 6 vols. 4to. Orig. boards, uncut.
Engraved portrait and 3 engraved maps. Spines worn and joints
weak. Traylen 94-379 1983 £180

GIBBON, EDWARD   The History of the Decline and Fall
of the Roman Empire. London: for W. Strahan and T. Cadell, 1782-
88. First edition of vols. 2-6, second edition of vol. 1. 6 vols.
4to. Cont. tree calf, neatly rebacked with the orig. spines laid
down, gilt, morocco labels, gilt. Engraved portrait front. and
3 folding engraved maps by Thomas Kitchin. From the library of
Lord Leigh, Stoneleigh Abbey. Traylen 94-378 1983 £160

GIBBON, EDWARD   The History of the Decline and Fall
of the Roman Empire. London, 1862. 8 vols. 8vo. Full polished
calf, gilt, gilt panelled spines. Portrait and folding maps.
Spines a little worn. Traylen 94-380 1983 £75

GIBBON, EDWARD   The History of the Decline and Fall of
the Roman Empire. 1817. 12 vols., 8vo, portrait, orig. boards with
cloth spines and paper labels, uncut. Spines evenly faded, and
labels rubbed and a little defective at the edges. Bickersteth 75-
142 1983 £35

GIBBON, EDWARD   The History of the Decline and Fall of
the Roman Empire. John Murray, 1881. With a portrait and 14 maps
(12 folding), 8 vols., 8vo, cont. black morocco-backed marbled
boards, gilt. Fenning 61-151 1983 £25

GIBBON, EDWARD   The Decline and Fall of the Roman
Empire. London: Warne & Co., n.d. 4 vols. Cr. 8vo. Half red
calf, gilt, marbled edges. Traylen 94-381 1983 £38

GIBBON, EDWARD   Miscellaneous Works, with Memoirs
of his Life and Writings... London, 1796-1815. First edition.
3 vols. 4to. Cont. calf (vol. 3 not quite uniform), neatly
rebacked with the orig. gilt decorated spines laid down, morocco
labels, gilt. Silhouette portrait. Traylen 94-382 1983 £150

GIBBON, EDWARD   Miscellaneous Works. Printed for A.
Strahan, 1796. First edition, with the silhouette portrait frontis.
Errata & ad. leaf, 2 vols. 4to, cont. sheep, gilt, rubbed at corners,
but a very good copy. Fenning 62-136 1983 £145

GIBBON, EDWARD   Miscellaneous Works. Dublin: Printed
for P. Wogan, 1796. First Irish and first 8vo edition, with the
silhouette portrait, with the half-titles in the second and third
vols., 3 vols., 8vo, cont. tree calf, gilt ruled spines, with red
and blue labels. Fine copy. Fenning 61-152 1983 £85

GIBBON, JOHN MURRAY   The Romantic History of the Canadian
Pacific. NY, 1935. 1st ed. Illus., & maps, some folding and in
color. D.w. Argosy 710-436 1983 $35

GIBBON, JOHN MURRAY   The Romantic History of the Canadian
Pacific. NY, 1937. Illus, dw. Argosy 710-47 1983 $30

GIBBON, JOHN MURRAY   The Romantic History of the Canadian
Pacific. New York: Tudor, 1937. 23 1/2cm. 16 colour plates and
ca. 125 illus. Mapped endpapers, spine dull, else very good copy.
McGahern 54-193 1983 $25

GIBBON, MONK   The Branch of Hawthorn Tree. Grayhound Press, 1927. 1st ed., tall 8vo, large vignette woodcut designs printed in colour, uncut in cream card wrappers printed in sepia and with coloured design. Fine. Publisher's presentation copy inscribed "To Stanley Baldwin with sincerest greetings from The Grayhound Press 10 May 1929". 460 numbered copies. Deighton 3-141 1983 £40

GIBBS, ARCHIBALD R.   British Honduras. Sampson, Law, 1883. Half title, 32 pp ads., orig. olive green cloth. First edition. V.g. Jarndyce 31-115 1983 £16.50

GIBBS, EDWARD J.   England and South Africa. London: Longmans, Green, & Co., 1889. First edition. Henry Haggard's copy, with his hieroglyphic bookplate on the front endsheet, and several pencil notes in his hand on the verso of the front free endpaper. Covers somewhat soiled and rubbed, but a goood copy. MacManus 278-2450 1983 $165

GIBBS, GEORGE   Memoirs of the Administrations of Washington and John Adams, ed. from the Papers of Oliver Wolcott. NY, 1846. 2 vols., orig. cloth, (edges slightly rubbed). Argosy 716-435 1983 $50

GIBBS, JOSIAH   Mountain Meadows Massacre. Salt Lake City, Tribune Publ co., 1910. First edition. Illus. Pictorial wraps. (small nicks), else very good. Houle 21-1043 1983 $45

GIBBS, JOSIAH WILLARD   Thermodynamische Studien... Leipzig: Engelmann, 1892. First German edition. 8vo. Orig. buckram. 33 text illus. Errata leaf. Half-title soiled. Zeitlin 264-174 1983 $120

GIBBS, MAY   Boronia Babies. Sydney: Angus & Robertson, 1922. Colour frontis. Pictorial title. 11 plates & text decorations. Brown wrappers. Extra onlaid colour plate. Corners turned. Greer 40-100 1983 £22.50

GIBBS, MAY   Little Ragged Blossom. Sydney: Angus & Robertson, n.d. Sm. 4to. Colour frontis. Pictorial title. Colour plate. 20 full-page & 27 text illus. Some tears. Pictorial endpapers. Pictorial grey boards, small onlaid plate. Greer 40-101 1983 £28

GIBBS, PHILIP   The Germans on the Somme. London: Darling & Son, Ltd., 1917. First separate edition, reprinted from The Daily Chronicle. Orig. wrappers. Slightly dust-soiled. Very good. MacManus 278-2166 1983 $255

GIBBS, VICARY   Covent Garden Theatre. The Speech...on moving for a rule to shew cause why a criminal information sould not be filed against Henry Clifford, Esq. and others. London: printed by W. Flint; for J. Ridgway, 1809. First edition. 8vo, disbound, half-title present. Rare. Ximenes 64-237 1983 $75

GIBELLINO KRASCENINNICOWA, MARIA   Guglielmo della Porta. Roma: Palombi, 1944. 42 plates. 4to. Boards. Spines taped. Ars Libri 33-290 1983 $45

GIBSON, CHARLES DANA   London as Seen by Charles Dana Gibson. NY: Scribner's, 1897. Oblong folio. Profusely illus. with full-page plates. Edition ltd. to 250 numbered copies, each accompanied by a loose proof of one of the illus., printed on Japanese paper, and signed by Gibson in pencil on the proof and also after the statement of limitation. Two-tone cloth, sl. soiled. Karmiole 75-57 1983 $250

GIBSON, CHARLES DANA   London as Seen by Charles Dana Gibson. New York, 1897. First edition. Numerous illustrations. Oblong folio, original boards with pictorial front cover, white cloth shelf-back. Small, light, insignificant stains on front cover; otherwise very nice. Morrill 290-639 1983 $55

GIBSON, CHARLES DANA   Sketches and Cartoons. N.Y., 1898. First edition. With 135 full page drawings by Gibson. Cloth spine. Pictorial boards. Blind-stamped names, rubber stamped names. Extremities frayed. Covers soiled. King 45-399 1983 $65

GIBSON, CHARLES DANA   A Widow and Her Friends. N.Y., 1901. Cloth spine. Pictorial boards. Blind-stamped names, rubber stamped names. Lacks front endpaper. Front inner hinge detached. Lacks few plates, few colored in, sold for illus. only. 66 full page drawings by Gibson. King 45-400 1983 $35

GIBSON, EDMUND   Chronicon Saxonicum. Oxford, 1692. Folding map, 4to, parallel text in Anglo-Saxon and Latin with notes, new old style half calf, rebacked, hinges strengthened, small ink stamps on Imprimatur page and verso of titlepage, catalogue number stamped in gold on spine, leather boards worn at corners, text good. K Books 307-82 1983 £110

GIBSON, FRANCIS   Streanshall Abbey. Whitby, 1800. 2nd edition, wood engraved title vignette by Thomas Bewick, 2 orig. drawings of Streanshall Abbey and Mulgrave Castle bound in, a green leather binding with gilt tooling. K Books 301-77 1983 £70

GIBSON, J. F.   Brocklebanks 1770-1950. Liverpool, 1953. 8vo. Orig. cloth. Frontis. 24 plates (8 coloured). 1 folding table. 2 vols. Orig. dust jackets. Fine. Edwards 1042-66 1983 £55

GIBSON, JEWEL   Joshua Beene and God. New York: Random House, (1946). Cloth. First edition. Half-page presentation inscription from the author. Fine in dust jacket. Reese 20-980 1983 $20

GIBSON, STRICKLAND.   Early Oxford Bindings. Oxford: The Bibliographical Society, 1903. 4to, 40 plates. Half red calf, a bit rubbed, over marbled boards. Bookplate removed. Karmiole 71-24 1983 $250

GIBSON, WALTER B.   Houdini's Magic. New York, 1932. First edition. Illus. Jenkins 152-658 1983 $45

GIBSON, WALTER M.   The Prison of Weltevreden. Boston, C.H. Brainard, 1857. Illus. 8vo. Printed label pasted on. Corners bit rubbed; some cover stains. Morrill 289-338 1983 $37.50

GIBSON, WILFRID WILSON   Borderlands. London, 1914. First edition. Covers a little marked. Inscribed by author to E. Marsh. Nice. Rota 230-241 1983 £35

GIBSON, WILFRED WILSON   The Early Whistler. N.Y.: William Edwin Rudge, 1927. First edition of this "Ariel Poem." Orig. printed wrappers. One of 27 copies printed for copyright purposes in America. Mint. MacManus 278-2169 1983 $125

GIBSON, WILFRED WILSON   The Early Whistler. (London: Faber & Gwyer, n.d.). First edition. Drawings by John Nash. Orig. decorated boards. One of 350 copies on hand-made paper. Fine. MacManus 278-2167 1983 $25

GIBSON, WILFRID WILSON   Home: A Book of Poems. Westminster: Beaumont Press, 1920). Octavo. Color woodcuts on title page and endpapers by Ethelbert White. Limited to 295 copies. Very fine in cloth-backed decorated boards. Bromer 25-140 1983 $85

GIBSON, WILFRED WILSON   The Nets of Love. London: Elkin Mathews, 1905. First edition. Orig. decorated wrappers. With an inscription: "The Revd. Frank Walters from Elizabeth Gibson Mat 1905." Spine and covers faded and worn. In a folding cloth case. Good. MacManus 278-2171 1983 $85

GIBSON, WILFRED WILSON   The Nets of Love. London: Elkins Mathews, 1905. First edition. Bookplate facing title-page. Spine faded. Good. MacManus 278-2172 1983 $45

GIBSON, WILFRID WILSON   On the Threshold. Samurai Press, 1907. First edition. One of 500 copies. Nice. Rota 230-240 1983 £12.50

GIBSON, WILFRID WILSON   The Stonefolds. Cranleigh: The Samurai Press, 1907. Ltd. edition of 500 copies, ad. leaf, 8vo, orig. printed paper boards, with printed paper spine label, uncut. The label a little rubbed, a very good copy. Fenning 61-153 1983 £18.50

GIBSON, WILFRID WILSON   Urlyn The Harper and Other Songs. London: Elkin Mathews, 1902. First edition. Orig. decorated wrappers. Spine and covers slightly faded. In a folding cloth case. Fine. MacManus 278-2174 1983 $135

GIBSON, WILFRID WILSON   The Web of Life. A Book of Poems. Samurai Press, 1908. 1st ed., sm. 4to, uncut in original buckram-backed boards with paper label, binding a little soiled and corners worn. Presentation copy from author's wife, "Esther Fletcher from Elizabeth Gibson. Summer 1909". Deighton 3-142 1983 £32

GIBSON, WILLIAM　　　　　　The Farrier's New Guide. Printed by
S. Palmer, for William Taylor, 1722. With a folding engraved
frontis. and 6 engraved plates, 8vo, light old water stain in places,
in cont. calf, gilt. Third edition. Fenning 62-137 1983 £75

GIBSON, WILLIAM　　　　　　The Institutes and Practice of
Surgery. Philadelphia, 1827. 23 plates, some in color, 2 vols.,
orig. calf, leather labels, ex-lib. Argosy 713-217 1983 $85

GIBSON, WILLIAM　　　　　　The Institutes and Practice of
Surgery: Being the Outlines of a Course of Lectures. Philadelphia,
1824-25. First ed., engraved plates, few partly in color, 2 vols.,
8vo., contemp. calf, leather labels, some rubbing and foxing. Morrill
289-83 1983 $85

GIDDINGS, JOSHUA R.　　　　The Exiles of Florida. Columbus, 1858.
Illus., lightly foxed. 1st ed. Argosy 710-168 1983 $40

GIDDINGS, JOSHUA R.　　　　The Exiles of Florida. Columbus: 1858.
First edition. Illus. Cloth. Very good copy, lightly foxed. Bradley 66-664 1983 $75

GIDDINGS, LUTHER　　　　　Sketches of the Campaign in Northern
Mexico. New York, 1853. Orig. ornately gilt pictorial cloth,
a.e.g. A fine copy. Bound in a presentation binding, and with the
author's signed presentation inscription. Reese 19-243 1983 $150

GIDE, ANDRE　　　　　　　Incidences. Paris: NRF, (1924).
Orig. printed wraps. First edition. One of 1050 numbered copies,
printed on velin pur fil Lafuma-Navarre. Very slight traces of
scattered foxing, otherwise a fine copy, enclosed in a half-vellum
slipcase. Reese 20-440 1983 $75

GIDE, ANDRE　　　　　　　The Journals of Andre Gide Translated
From the French. NY, 1947-49. 3 vols. Portrait, cloth, good in
worn and soiled dust wrappers. First American edition.
KIng 46-291 1983 $65

GIDE, ANDRE　　　　　　　Montaigne. London: The Blackamore
Press, 1929. Two parts. Sq. 12mo, full buckram. One of 800 copies,
signed by the author. Fine, in a darkened dust wrapper; owner's
signature on flyleaf. Argosy 713-323 1983 $35

GIEDION-WELCKER, CAROLA　　　Constantin Brancusi. New York:
George Braziller, 1959. Over 100 plates. Large 4to. Cloth.
Ars Libri 32-58 1983 $100

GIES, WILLIAM　　　　　　Dental Education in the United States
and Canada... New York, 1926. First edition. Wrappers. 8vo.
Fye H-3-221 1983 $25

GIFFARD, AMBROSE HARDINGE　　　Poems, political and miscellaneous.
London, 1843. First edition. 2 parts in one vol. 8vo. Cont.
brown morocco. Gilt. Presentation copy, inscribed at the front
by the editor Edward Giffard, to his mother. With a number of
manuscript corrections. A bit rubbed. Rare. Ximenes 63-446 1983
$90

GIFFORD, EDWARD W.　　　　California Indian Nights Entertainment.
Glendale: Arthur H. Clark Co., 1930. First edition. Frontis., fold-
ing map, plates and a drawing. Red cloth. Fine unopened copy.
Bradley 66-481 1983 $50

GIFFORD, MRS. GEORGE　　　　King's Baynard. London: Hurst and
Blackett, 1866. First edition. 3 vols. Orig. cloth. Dedicated to
J.A. Froude. Edges a bit worn, covers slightly soiled. Good. Mac-
Manus 278-2175 1983 $250

GIGLIOLI, EDOARDO H.　　　　Giovanni da San Giovanni. Firenze:
Edizioni "S.T.E.T.", 1949. 104 plates. Small folio. Cloth.
Edition limited to 1000 numbered copies. Ars Libri 33-217 1983
$150

GIHON, JOHN H.　　　　　　Geary and Kansas. Philadelphia, 1857.
Cloth. Marginal waterstain in text; a good copy. Felcone 22-80
1983 $20

GILBERT, GROVE K.　　　　The San Francisco Earthquake and Fire,
April 18, 1906. Washington, 1907. 55 plates and folding map. Orig.
grey wrappers, chipped. Fine copy. Jenkins 153-220 1983 $75

GILBERT, H. F.　　　　　Traite des Prairies Aritificielles...
Paris: chez Madame Huzard, 1826. Sixth edition, revised. 8vo.
Half title, cont. half calf, light wear. Heath 48-23 1983 £40

GILBERT, JOHN　　　　　　An Answer to the Bishop of Condom.
Printed by H.C. for R. Kettlewel and R. Wells, 1686. First edition,
with the preliminary ad. leaf, 4to, wrapper, a very good copy.
Fenning 61-154 1983 £16.50

GILBERT, JOHN　　　　　　The Historic Literature of Ireland.
Dublin: W.B. Kelly, 1851. First separate edition, ads., 8vo,
orig. wraps. a little dusty, but a very good copy. Fenning 61-155
1983 £28.50

GILBERT, LINNEY　　　　　Russia Illustrated. N.d. (c. 1850).
Tall 8vo, 25 steel engravings after drawings by Alfred George Vickers.
Orig. brown cloth, v.g. Jarndyce 31-364 1983 £68

GILBERT, PAUL　　　　　　Chicago & Its Makers, A Narrative of
Events. Chicago, 1929. Illus., 4to, cloth, g.t., small blind-stamp
on title. Limited, numbered ed. Argosy 710-210 1983 $125

GILBERT, T.　　　　　　　The Writing Reader, Comprising in the
Different Handwritings of the Present Day... New York: D. & J.
McLellan, 1858. Elaborately embossed cloth. A.e.g. Waterstain at
lower corner of all pages. Presentation inscription from the pub-
lishers. Printed entirely by lithography from handwritten copy.
Very good. Felcone 20-89 1983 $100

GILBERT, THOMAS　　　　　The First Satire of Juvenal Imitated.
London: Printed for H. Goreham next the Leg-Tavern in Fleet-Street.
MDCCXL. Folio, title-page a bit worn but a good copy, disbound.
First edition. Quaritch NS 7-51 1983 $250

GILBERT, WILLIAM　　　　　De Numo nostro sublunari Philosophia
nova. Amstelodami, Apud Ludovicum Elzevirium, MDCLI (1651). 4to,
orig. vellum binding, somewhat scuffed. Boards warping. Title
in MS on paper label. Title page with some light scattered foxing.
Arkway 22-53 1983 $2,750

GILBERT, WILLIAM SCHWENCK　　　The "Bab" Ballads. London: John Camden
Hotten, Piccadilly, 1869, (1873). First editions. 2 vols. Illus.
by author. Full decorated morocco. Hand-tooled figures modeling the
texts on both front and back covers. Spines faded. Spine and cover
edges rubbed and worn. Good. MacManus 278-2176 1983 $250

GILBERT, WILLIAM SCHWENCK　　　The Bab Ballads. London: Hotten, Routledge, 1869, (1873). First editions. Illus. by author. 2 vols.
Orig. pictorial cloth. Covers darkened along the spines. Covers worn.
Inner hinges cracked. In two half morocco slipcases. MacManus 278-
2177 1983 $225

GILBERT, WILLIAM SCHWENCK　　　The "Bab" Ballads. London: John
Camden Hotten, 1869. First edition. 8vo, green cloth. First
issue. Illus. by the author. Argosy 714-324 1983 $175

GILBERT, WILLIAM SCHWENCK　　　The Babs Ballads...with 350 Illustrations
by the Author. London & New York: Routledge, 1898. Illus. 3rd ed.
Orig. pictorial linen, gilt, t.e.g. Faint soiling to spine, else a
fine copy. Jenkins 155-474 1983 $50

GILBERT, WILLIAM SCHWENCK　　　Foggerty's Fairy and Other Tales. London,
1890. 12mo, red cloth. First edition. Argosy 714-326 1983 $40

GILBERT, WILLIAM SCHWENCK　　　"His Excellency." London: Chappell &
Co., 1894. First edition, with the imprint of Henderson & Spalding
(Limited). Orig. printed wrappers. Slight, wrapper wear. Fine.
MacManus 278-2179 1983 $85

GILBERT, WILLIAM SCHWENCK　　　The Mikado. New York: H. Grau, (1885).
1st American ed. Orig. printed wrappers. Some creases in upper
right corner, and a couple of minor nicks to edge of wrapper, else
a well-preserved copy of a scarce ed. Jenkins 155-476 1983 $90

GILBERT, WILLIAM SCHWENCK　　　More "Bab" Ballads. London, n.d. (1873).
First edition. Sq. 12mo, gilt-pict. cloth. Illus. by the author.
Argosy 714-327 1983 $60

GILBERT, WILLIAM SCHWENCK   The Pinafore Picture Book. Bell, 1908.
Edition de luxe with mounted col. frontis., illus. title in red & black,
& 15 col. plates mounted & 12 b&w text illus., illus. by Alice B.
Woodward. White decor. cloth, t.e.g. others uncut (fine in discol'd
& worn d/w). Hodgkins 27-443 1983 £40

GILBERT, WILLIAM SCHWENCK   Randall's Thumb. N.Y. & London: T.H.
French, Samuel French, n.d. French's Standard Drama edition. Orig.
wrappers. Fine. MacManus 278-2180 1983 $50

GILBERT, WILLIAM SCHWENCK   Songs of a Savoyard. London: Routledge, (1890). Illus. 1st ed. Orig. pink pictorial cloth, gilt.
Illus. by the author. Jenkins 155-475 1983 $100

GILBERT, WILLIAM SCHWENCK   Songs of a Savoyard. London, (1890).
Tall 8vo, pict. cloth; rubbed; inner hinges split, g.e. First
edition. Argosy 714-328 1983 $50

GILBERT, WILLIAM SCHWENCK   The Wicked World. N.Y. & London: Samuel
French, n.d. (1873). First edition. Orig. orange wrappers. Very fine.
MacManus 278-2181 1983 $85

GILBEY, WALTER   George Morland. His life and works.
London: Adam and Charles Black, 1907. 50 color plates. 4to.
Cloth. Ars Libri 32-479 1983 $65

GILCHRIST, EBENEZER   The Use of Sea Voyages in Medicine.
T. Cadell, 1771. 8vo. Orig. cloth. Cont. calf, slightly worn. Good.
Edwards 1042-67 1983 £100

GILCHRIST, JOHN B.   Dialogues, English and Hindoostanee.
London, 1820. Third edition. Half calf, joints worn. 8vo. Orig.
cloth. Good. Edwards 1044-277 1983 £50

GILCHRIST, JOHN B.   A New Theory and Prospectus of the
Persian Verbs. Calcutta: Printed by Thomas Hollingbery, Hircarrah
Press, 1801. First edition thus, with 2 large folding tables, errata
and subscription list leaves, 4to, clean uncut copy. Lower wrapper
and the first dozen leaves at the end have been nibbled, literally.
Fenning 60-131 1983 £65

GILCHRIST, M.   The Story of the Great Lakes. N.Y.:
Harp., (1942). Large sq. 4to. Cloth backed pictorial boards. Color
lithos. Fine. Aleph-bet 8-87 1983 $27

GILCHRIST, OCTAVIUS   A Letter to William Gifford, Esq. on
the late edition of Ford's plays. London: printed for John Murray,
1811. 8vo, disbound, 1st ed. Presentation copy, inscribed on the
half-title to "Mr. John Fry, with the author's Compts." Ximenes 64-
238 1983 $75

GILDER, RODMAN   The Battery. Boston, 1936. First ed.
Illustrated. 8vo. Morrill 290-351 1983 $25

GILDON, CHARLES   The Complete Art of Poetry. In six
parts. London: printed for Charles Rivington, 1718. 2 vols., 12mo,
cont. mottled calf, gilt, spines gilt (spines rubbed). 1st ed.
Ximenes 64-239 1983 $450

GILDON, CHARLES   The Laws of Poetry... London: for
W. Hinchliffe and J. Walthoe, jun. 1721. First edition. 8vo.
19th Century half roan, some wear. With half title. Very scarce.
Heath 48-309 1983 £125

GILDON, CHARLES   The Life of Mr. Thomas Betterton, the
late eminent tragedian. London: printed for Robert Gosling, 1710.
8vo, cont. panelled calf, rebacked, original spine laid down (stained,
corners rubbed). 1st ed. Waterstained, especially at the beginning
and end. Ximenes 64-240 1983 $100

GILDON, CHARLES   Phaeton: or, the fatal divorce. A
tragedy. London: printed for Abel Roper, 1698. Sm. 4to, modern
quarter morocco, first edition. Title and last leaf a bit creased
and dust-soiled, but an uncut copy. Ximenes 64-241 1983 $375

GILDON, CHARLES   The Post Man Robb'd of his Mail...
London: for A. Bettesworth..., 1719. First edition. 12mo.
Cont. vellum. Ad. leaf. Heath 48-310 1983 £125

GILDON, CHARLES   The Stage-Beaux toss'd in a blanket: or,
hypocrisie alamode. London: printed, and sold by John Nutt, 1704.
Sm. 4to, quarter calf (spine rubbed), 1st ed. Tears across the middle
of the half-title, title and following four leaves (partly repaired);
margins of signature B shaved close, touching some letters but legible
throughout. Not a very good copy, but a rare play. Ximenes 64-242
1983 $250

GILES, DAPHNE S.   East and West. NY, 1853. First edition.
18mo, orig. cloth. Argosy 716-159 1983 $25

GILES, ERNEST   Australia Twice Traversed. New York,
ca 1889. 2 vols., 5 of 6 maps present, lacking map to face page
131 in vol. 2, illus., orig. pictorial cloth, spine faded and boards
slightly cockled in vol. i, ex-library. K Books 301-78 1983 £100

GILES, G. M.   A Handbook of the Gnats. 1900.
8 plates, royal 8vo, cloth (trifle used). Wheldon 160-1083 1983
£20

GILES, ROESNA A.   Shasta County. Oakland, Ca., 1949.
Folded map. Orig. cloth. First edition. Ltd. to 1,000 copies.
Ginsberg 47-93 1983 $30

GILES, ROSENA A.   Shasta County, California. Oakland,
1949. 1st ed. Illus., fldg. map. Royal 8vo. Clark 741-112 1983
$30

GILES, ROSENA A.   Shasta County, California... Oakland:
Lederer, Street & Zeus Press, 1949. First edition. Large quarto.
Edition of 1000 copies. Illus. Large fld. map. Jenkins 153-93 1983
$30

GILES, WILLIAM B.   Political Miscellanies. (Richmond,
1829). Various paginations. New cloth, leather label, some foxing,
very good. Reese 18-633 1983 $250

GILIFILLAN, ARCHER B.   Sheep. Boston, 1929. Cloth, fine.
Reese 19-244 1983 $45

GILL, C. S.   The Old Wooden Walls. London, 1930.
8vo. Orig. cloth. Frontis. 30 plates (16 folding). Orig. dust
jacket. Fine. Edwards 1042-68 1983 £30

GILL, D. S.   Steel's Elements of Mastmaking, Sailmak-
ing and Rigging. London, 1932. 4to, orig. blue buckram. Frontis.
Gilt. 5 double-page plans, 53 plates. Spine very slightly faded.
T.e.g. Orig. dust jacket. Fine. Edwards 1042-69 1983 £40

GILL, ERIC   Art & Love. Bristol: 1927. Octavo.
First edition. Illus. Limited to 260 copies printed by Robert
Gibbings at the Golden Cockerel Press and signed by Gill. Rubbed
at extremities, else fine. Owner's stamp and signature on front
endpaper. Bromer 25-214 1983 $325

GILL, ERIC   Christianity and Art. Albergavenny,
1927. Frontis. engraved by David Jones. Narrow 12mo, cloth. One
of 200 copies, printed at the Shakespeare Head Press. Signed by Eric
Gill & David Jones. Argosy 714-870 1983 $375

GILL, ERIC   Clothing Without Cloth. Waltham,
St. Lawrence, England: Golden Cockerel Press, 1931. Narrow 8vo,
4 leaves of orig. wood-engraved plates (incl. frontis.) Edition ltd.
to 500 numbered copies. Red cloth, gilt-stamped. A.e.g. Karmiole 74-
50 1983 $250

GILL, ERIC   Clothing without Cloth. Waltham St.
Lawrence, Golden Cockerel Press, 1931. Tall narrow 8vo. Orig. gilt
stamped red cloth, top & foredge gilt. One of 500 copies. 4 full
page engravings by the author. Spine a little faded, else fine.
Houle 22-411 1983 $225

GILL, ERIC   Drawings from Life. London, 1940.
First edition. 36 full-page black and white drawings by Eric Gill.
Nicked dustwrapper. Very good. Jolliffe 26-209 1983 £45

GILL, ERIC   The Lord's Song. London, 1934. Slim
8vo, cream buckram, gilt. Wood-engr. frontis. by Gill. One of 500
copies printed on Arnold hand-made paper. Perata 28-30 1983 $225

GILL, ERIC   Unemployment. London, 1933. First
edition. Wood-engraving by author. Wrappers. Very nice. Rota
230-242 1983 £20

GILL, ERIC   Wood-engravings. Ditchling: S.
Dominic's Press, 1924. Sq. quarto, linen. With 37 wood-engravings
(original wood-engravings printed from the blocks and not reproductions). One of 150 copies on handmade paper. Spot in the margin
of several pages far removed from illus. Duschnes 240-81A 1983
$900

GILL, RONALD   Club Route in Europe. Hannover, 1946.
Imperial 8vo. Orig. cloth. Frontis. 13 plates, 14 folding coloured
maps. Slightly faded. Gilt boar on upper cover. Library bookplate
and ink stamp on endpapers. Good. Edwards 1042-352 1983 £18

GILL, WILLIAM F.   The Life of Edgar Allan Poe. New
York: Widdleton, 1878. Illus. Facsimiles. 4th ed., revised and
enlarged. Orig. 3/4 calf and marbled boards. Presentation copy
from the author to George Eliot, inscribed in ink on front flyleaf:
"Mrs. George H. Lewes, with the compliments of the author." A fine
assoc. vol. Jenkins 155-1386 1983 $550

GILLET, C. C.   Les Hymenomycetes. Alencon, 1874(-93).
8vo, text in wrappers (spine broken), plates loose, 426 plates
(nearly all hand-coloured). A very rare work. Privately printed.
A few plates have margins or corners frayed but most are in good
condition. Wheldon 160-34 1983 £260

GILLETT, CHARLES RIPLEY   Catalogue of the McAlpin Collection
of British History and Theology. New York: Union Theological
Seminary, 1927-1930. 5 vols. 8vo. Cloth. A fine set. Oak Knoll
48-456 1983 $180

GILLETT, JAMES B.   Six Years with the Texas Rangers,
1875 to 1881. 1921. Portrait, orig. gilt cloth. Front inner
hinge cracking slightly, otherwise a very fine, bright copy. Reese
19-245 1983 $150

GILLETT, JAMES B.   Six Years with the Texas Rangers, 1875
to 1881. Austin, 1921. 1st ed., 1st issue. Illus. Original green
cloth, gilt. Fine copy. Very scarce. Jenkins 151-104 1983
$150

GILLIAT, EDWARD   Asylum Christi: A Story of the Dragon-
nades. London: Sampson Low, Marston, Searle & Rivington, 1877. First
edition. 3 vols. Orig. cloth. Spines and covers a trifle worn.
Near-fine. MacManus 278-2184 1983 $350

GILLIES, H. CAMERON   Regimen Sanitatis the Rule of Health.
A Gaelic Medical Manuscript of the Early Sixteenth Century... Glas-
gow: University Press, 1911. Large 8vo. Cloth. 15 plates.
Gurney JJ-338 1983 £25

GILLILAND, THOMAS   The Dramatic mirror: containing the
history of the stage, from the earliest period to the present time.
London: printed for C. Chapple, by B. McMillan, 1808. 2 vols., 12mo,
original grey boards, printed paper labels (some wear to spines).
1st ed, with 17 plates. Despite the binding wear an excellent copy
in original condition. Ximenes 64-243 1983 $300

GILLILAND, THOMAS   Elbow room, a pamphlet; containing
remarks on the shameful increase of the private boxes of Covent Garden.
London: printed for the author, and sold by Chapple; Jordan and
Maxwell; Tegg, 1804. 8vo, disbound, 1st ed. A very good copy, with
a leaf of errata at the end. Uncommon. Ximenes 64-244 1983 $150

GILLILAND, THOMAS   Jack in office; containing remarks on
Mr. Braham's address to the public. London: printed for and sold
by C. Chapple; and T. Ostell, n.d. (1805). 8vo, disbound, 1st ed.
A very good copy, complete with half-title. Scarce. Ximenes 64-
245 1983 $90

GILLILAND, THOMAS   The Trap. London: Printed for T. Goddard, 1808. First edition. 2 vols. Frontispieces. Later 3/4 red
morocco & marbled boards. Half-title in Vol. one, none in vol. two.
Last few leaves of Vol. two slightly wormed. Fine. MacManus 278-
2185 1983 $250

GILLINGHAM, ROBERT CAMERON   The Rancho San Pedro. (Los Angeles:
Cole-Holmquist Press), 1961. Illus. Cloth. Dust wrapper. Dawson
471-98 1983 $175

GILLISS, WALTER   Recollections of the Gilliss Press
and Its Work... New York: The Grolier club, 1926. First
edition. 8vo. Leather-backed boards, t.e.g., others uncut.
Limited to 300 copies printed on hand-made paper. 13 plates and
2 illus. Bookplate; wear at spine ends and spotting of cover.
Oak Knoll 48-169 1983 $55

GILLMORE, PARKER   The Hunter's Arcadia. London: Chapman
& Hall, 1886. 8vo. 18 plates. Orig. brown pictorial cloth. Rubbed.
Spine starting. Adelson Africa-190 1983 $75

GILLMORE, PARKER   Leaves from a Sportsman's Diary. W. H.
Allen, 1893. First edition, with a portrait, 8vo, orig. cloth.
Fenning 60-132 1983 £12.50

GILLMORE, PARKER   Prairie Folk. London, 1872. 1st ed.,
2 vols., small 8vo, 2 engraved frontispieces and 2 vignette title-
pages, printed in red and black, quarter calf, gilt, marbled sides,
new endpapers. Deighton 3-144 1983 £30

GILLMORE, PARKER   Through Gasa Land, and the scene of
the Portuguese aggression. London: Harrison & Sons, (1890). 8vo.
Folding map. Orig. pictorial cloth. Spine faded, ex-lib. Adelson
Africa-191 1983 $60

GILLY, W. O. S.   Narratives of Shipwrecks. London, 1850.
First edition. 8vo. Orig. cloth. 4 pages of ads. at end. Bookplate.
Good. Edwards 1042-70 1983 £50

GILLY, WILLIAM STEPHEN   A Memoir of Felix Neff, Pastor of the
High Alps. 1832. Folding map, ad. leaf, orig. cloth with paper
label. First edition. Bickersteth 77-207 1983 £26

GILLY, WILLIAM STEPHEN   Narrative of an Excursion to the Mountains of Piemont... London, 1826. Third edition, 2 folding maps,
3 folding plates, binders cloth. K Books 307-83 1983 £45

GILMAN, BRADLEY   The Kingdom of Coins. Boston: Roberts,
1889. First edition. Pictorial boards. Spine and edges worn. Very
good. Aleph-bet 8-121 1983 $30

GILMAN, M. D.   The Bibliography of Vermont...
Burlington: Free Press Association, 1897. Cloth; ex-library, title
loose, card pocket. Dawson 470-119 1983 $30

GILMORE, HUGH   The Black Diamond. London: Joseph Toul-
son & Halilton Adams, n.d. (c. 1890). Possibly the first edition.
Illus. Orig. pictorial cloth. Spine edges a trifle rubbed. Near-fine.
MacManus 278-2186 1983 $35

GILPIN, HENRY   Miscellaneous Poems. Longman, Newcastle:
John Hare, 1863. Half title, orig. brown cloth, v.g. Signed
presentation copy from the author's wife. First edition. Jarndyce
30-702 1983 £10.50

GILPIN, THOMAS   Exiles in Virginia. Philadelphia,
Published for the Subscribers, 1848. First edition. Folding plate--
slightly torn. 8vo, rubbed and foxed; rebacked; new endpapers.
Morrill 290-561 1983 $40

GILPIN, WILLIAM   Observations on Several Parts of England.
1808. Third edition, 2 vols. in one, 30 aquatint plates or hand
coloured plans, new old style quarter calf. K Books 307-84 1983
£45

GILPIN, WILLIAM   Observations on the Western Parts of
England. Printed for T. Cadell jun. and W. Davies, 1798. 8vo,
18 aquatint plates, orig. calf, spine gilt, a little rubbed, but
sound. First edition. Argosy 713-34 1983 £85

GILPIN, WILLIAM   Observations, relative chiefly to
Picturesque Beauty, made in the Year 1772. Printed for R. Blamire,
1788. 2 vols., 8vo, with 29 tinted aquatint plates, and 3 maps, cont.
mottled calf, a little rubbed in places, lacking the label on vol. 1,
and top of spine on this volume defective. Argosy 713-35 1983 £85

GILPIN, WILLIAM   Remarks on Forest Scenery, and Other
Woodland Views. Printed for R. Blamire, 1794. 2 vols., 8vo, with
32 tinted plates and a double-page map, orig. calf, spine gilt,
rubbed, lacking labels, joints cracked, but binding sound. Argosy
713-36 1983 £85

GILPIN, WILLIAM   Remarks on Forest Scenery, and Other
Woodland Views. Edinburgh, 1834. 2 vols., 8vo, 20 plates, orig.
cloth, vol. 2 rebacked, preserving orig. spine, with paper labels,
partly defective. Bickersteth 77-208 1983 £24

GINGOLD, HELENE A.   Steyneville; or, Fated Fortunes. London:
Remington & Co., 1885. First edition. 3 vols. Orig. cloth and pat-
terned endpapers. All edges and corners a bit worn. Front cover of
Vol. two rather soiled. Good. MacManus 278-2187 1983 $165

GINSBERG, ALLEN   Howl for Carl Solomon. (San Francisco):
Grabhorn-Hoyem, (1971). Quarto. Pictorial cloth. One of 275 copies,
signed by the author on the title-page. Printed in Goudy Modern
on handmade paper. Very fine, with the prospectus laid in. Reese 20-
444 1983 $175

GIOLLI, RAFFAELLO   Emilio Gola. Milano: Anonima
Editrice Arte, 1929. 26 plates (2 color). Large 4to. Wrappers.
Ars Libri 33-485 1983 $37.50

GIOLLI, RAFFAELLO   Ranzoni. Milano: "L'Esame", 1926.
24 plates. 4to. Boards. Spine defective. Paper somewhat browned.
Ars Libri 33-568 1983 $20

GIOLLI, RAFFAELLO   Sandro Biazzo. Milano: Grandi
Edizioni Artistiche, 1928. 16 plates (2 color) loose in portfolio,
as issued. 4to. Paper folder. Ars Libri 33-403 1983 $20

GIORDA, JOSEPH   Syzmmeie-S Christ. St. Ignatius Print,
Monta, 1880. Part one only. Jenkins 153-283 1983 $50

GIORDANI, TOMMASO   Fourteen Preludes or Capricios and Eight
Cadences for the Piano Forte, Harpsichord, harp, or organ. Printed for
Longman and Broderip, ca. 1785. Oblong folio, disbound. Fenning 61-
156 1983 £24.50

GIOSEFFI, DECIO   Scultura altomedioevale in Fruili.
Milona, n.d. Folio, 25 color plates, 64 text illus. (partly tipped-
in color). Boards. Dust jacket. Ars Libri SB 26-87 1983 $75

GIPSON, FRED   Hound-Dog Man. New York: Harper, 1949.
First edition. Dust jacket. Author's signed presentation copy.
Jenkins 152-640 1983 $45

GIRALDUS, CAMBRENSIS   Pontici Virunnii Viri Doctissimi
Britannicae Historiae Libri Sex... Londini, Apud Edmundum Bollifantum,
1585. 8vo, 18th century brown morocco gilt, rebacked, title
soiled and E7 has a diagonal paper flaw across lower third of
page running across the text and cutting some words; otherwise a good
copy. Ravenstree 94-136 1983 $450

GIRARD, C.   Contributions to the Natural History
of the Fresh Water Fishes of North America. Washington, 1851.
3 plates, 4to, modern buckram. Scarce. A nice copy. Wheldon 160-
958 1983 £25

GIRARD, RAFAEL   Los Chortis ante el problema Maya.
Mexico: Robredo, 1949. 124 plates. Text illus. 4to. Wrappers.
Slightly worn. Presentation copy, inscribed by the author. Ars
Libri 34-251 1983 $125

GIRONIERE, PAUL P.   Twenty Years in the Philippines.
N.Y., 1854. Mod. wraps., illus. Argosy 716-412 1983 $25

GIROUARD, DESIRE   Lake St. Louis, Old and New. Montreal:
Printed by Poirer, Bessette & Co., 1893. 4to. 26cm. 97 maps and
illus. (many full-page). Hinges cracked. Former owners signatures
on title page else very good. Rare. McGahern 54-68 1983 $125

GIRTY, G. H.   The Carboniferous Formations and Faunas
of Colorado. Washington, U. S. Geol. Survey, 1903. 10 plates,
4to, wrappers. Wheldon 160-1401 1983 £18

GISBORNE, THOMAS   Poems, sacred and moral. London:
Cadell and Davies, 1798. First edition. 8vo. Cont. tree calf,
spine gilt. Slight rubbing. A fine copy. Ximenes 63-365 1983
$125

GISBORNE, THOMAS   The Principles of Moral Philosophy
Investigated, and Briefly Applied to the Constitution of Civil
Society. London: Printed by T. Bensley for B. White & Son, 1790.
Second edition, corrected and enlarged. Modern cloth, inscribed
"from the author". Gach 95-169 1983 $50

GISSESPIE, S. M.   A Manual of the Principles and Practice
of Road-Making. New York, 1848. 2nd ed., with additions. Text illus.
8vo, backstrip worn at ends & slightly torn. Morrill 288-136 1983
$30

GISSING, ALGERNON   The Dreams of Simon Usher. London:
Chatto & Windus, 1907. First edition. Orig. cloth. MacManus 278-
2189 1983 $50

GISSING, ALGERNON   A Moorland Idyl. Hurst & Blackett,
1891. First edition, 3 vols. Half titles, 16pp ads. vol. III.
Orig. dark brown cloth, v.g. Jarndyce 31-708 1983 £85

GISSING, ALGERNON   At Society's Expense. London: Hurst &
Blackett, Limited, 1894. First edition. 3 vols. Orig. cloth.
Library labels removed from front endpapers. Inner hinges cracked.
Bookplates. Good. MacManus 278-2188 1983 $450

GISSING, GEORGE   Born in Exile. London: Adam & Charles
Black, 1892. First edition. 3 vols. Orig. cloth. Circulating
Library labels on endsheets. Library labels neatly removed from front
covers. Covers dull, contents somewhat shaken. Good. MacManus 278-
2190 1983 $400

GISSING, GEORGE   Born in Exile. London & Edinburgh: Adam
and Charles Black, 1892. Three vols. 8vo, orig. purple cloth.
Very much rubbed, inner hinges badly cracked. Library stamps on verso
of titles, endpapers damaged. First edition. Grunder 6-25 1983
$50

GISSING, GEORGE   Brownie. N.Y.: Columbia University
Press, 1931. First edition. Orig. cloth-backed boards. Dust jacket
(soiled and frayed, repaired with scotch tape). One of 500 copies.
Edges very slightly worn, a trifle foxed. Very good to near-fine.
MacManus 278-2191 1983 $50

GISSING, GEORGE   By the Ionian Sea. London: Chapman &
Hall, Ltd., 1901. First edition. 8 illus. in color by Leo de Littrow
& others in black and white. 4to. Orig. white cloth. Foxed. Bookplate on front endsheet. Very good. MacManus 278-2192 1983 $150

GISSING, GEORGE   Charles Dickens, a Critical Study.
Blackie & Son, 1898. First edition, 2 pp ads, half title, orig.
maroon cloth, v.g. Jarndyce 31-604 1983 £30

GISSING, GEORGE   Charles Dickens. London: Blackie &
Son, 1898. First edition, orig. dark red cloth, sl. shelfworn.
Karmiole 75-58 1983 $45

GISSING, GEORGE   The Crown of Life. London: Methuen &
Co., 1899. First edition. Orig. cloth. Very fine. MacManus 278-
2193 1983 $150

GISSING, GEORGE   Demos. London: Smith, Elder, & Co.,
1886. First edition. 3 vols. Orig. cloth. Bookplates. Inner hinges
in Vol. three weak. Fine. MacManus 278-2194 1983 $1,000

GISSING, GEORGE   Demos. London: Smith, Elder, & Co.,
1886. First edition. 3 vols. Orig. cloth. Prelims foxed, slightly
worn. Enclosed in a half-morocco folding box. Fine. MacManus 278-
2195 1983 $1,000

GISSING, GEORGE   Denzil Quarrier. London: Lawrence &
Bullen, 1892. First edition. Orig. cloth. Spine slightly dull.
Very good. MacManus 278-2196 1983 $125

GISSING, GEORGE   Denzil Quarrier. New York: Macmillan,
1892. First American edition. Half title, 8 pp. ads. A little trimmed
in functional half green calf. Jarndyce 31-710 1983 £28

GISSING, GEORGE   Denzil Quarrier. N.Y.: Macmillan & Co.,
1892. First American edition. Orig. cloth. Dust-soiled. Rear inner
hinge cracking. MacManus 278-2197 1983 $35

GISSING, GEORGE   The Emancipated, A Novel. London:
Richard Bentley & Son, 1890. First edition. 3 vols. Orig. cloth-
backed decorated boards. Spine ends and edges and cover corners worn.
Some foxing to the preliminary pages. Former owner's small rubber
stamp. Good. MacManus 278-2198 1983 $650

GISSING, GEORGE   The Immortal Dickens. London: Cecil
Palmer, (1925). First edition. Frontis. port. of Dickens at the age
of 31. Orig. cloth with paper spine label (slightly foxed). Endpapers, preliminary pages and edges foxed. Very good. MacManus
278-2203 1983 $45

GISSING, GEORGE   The Immortal Dickens. Cecil Palmer,
1925. First edition, half title, front. port. Orig. purple cloth,
paper label, spine faded, v.g. Jarndyce 31-605 1983 £14.50

GISSING, GEORGE   In the Year of Jubilee. Lawrence and
Bullen, 1894. 2nd edition. Half title. Orig. maroon cloth, v.g.
This copy is dated 1894 and has 'A.H. Bullen' at base of spine.
Additionally, it does not have 'New Edition' on the title. Jarndyce
31-711 1983 £42

GISSING, GEORGE   A Life's Morning. London: Smith, Elder
& Co., 1888. First edition. 3 vols. Orig. cloth. Bookplates. Ex-
tremities of spines rubbed. Inner hinges weak with evidence of repair.
Very good. MacManus 278-2207 1983 $450

GISSING, GEORGE   A Life's Morning. London: Smith, Elder,
1892. Early "cheap" edition. Orig. cloth. Fine. MacManus 278-2208
1983 $35

GISSING, GEORGE   The Nether World. London: Smith, Elder,
1889. First edition. 3 vols. Orig. decorated cloth. Covers a bit
worn. Library labels neatly removed from front covers. With John
Quinn's bookplate. Half-morocco slipcase. Very good. MacManus 278-
2210 1983 $2,000

GISSING, GEORGE   New Grub Street. London: Smith, Elder
and Co., 1891. First edition. 3 vols. Orig. cloth. Bookplates.
Hinges cracked, edges and corners worn. Covers soiled. MacManus 278-
2110a 1983 $350

GISSING, GEORGE   New Grub Street. London: Smith, Elder
& Co., 1891. Reissue of the first edition. 3 vols. Orig. cloth.
Slight foxing. Very fine. MacManus 278-2211 1983 $250

GISSING, GEORGE   New Grub Street. Smith, Elder, 1891.
2nd edition, 3 vols. Half titles, 2 pp ads. vol. I. Orig. dark
green cloth, spines very sl. faded. Fine. Jarndyce 30-398 1983
£110

GISSING, GEORGE   The Private Life of Henry Maitland.
London, 1912. First edition. Preliminaries a little foxed. Very
good. Rota 231-257 1983 £20

GISSING, GEORGE   The Private Papers of Henry Ryecroft.
Westminster: Constable, 1903. First edition. Orig. cloth. Publisher's blind presentation stamp on the title page. Very good. MacManus
278-2213 1983 $125

GISSING, GEORGE   The Private Papers of Henry Ryecroft.
Portland, Maine: Thomas Bird Mosher, 1921. 8vo. White parchment
spine, boards, paper cover label, slipcase. Limited to 700 copies.
Printed on Van Gelder hand-made paper. Slipcase worn. Oak Knoll
49-197 1983 $40

GISSING, GEORGE   Sins of the Fathers and other tales.
Chicago: Pascal Covici, 1924. First edition. Large 8vo. Orig. cloth.
Limited to 550 copies. Former owner's inscription on flyleaf. Very
good. MacManus 278-2217 1983 $65

GISSING, GEORGE   The Town Traveller. Methuen & Co., 1898.
First edition. Half title, 40 pp. ads. Orig. red cloth, spine slightly
faded. Very good. Jarndyce 31-712 1983 £38

GISSING, GEORGE   The Unclassed. London: Chapman & Hall
Limited, 1884. First edition, remainder issue, without half-titles to
second and third volumes. 3 volumes in one. Orig. blue cloth.
Minor soiling and wear. Good. MacManus 278-2219 1983 $1,500

GISSING, GEORGE   Veranilda. London: Archibald Constable
& Co., 1904. First edition. Orig. cloth. Good. MacManus 278-2221
1983 $35

GISSING, GEORGE   A Victim of Circumstances and other
stories. London: Constable & Co., Ltd., 1927. First edition. Orig.
cloth. Dust jacket (rare; a trifle worn, one tape repair). Fine.
MacManus 278-2222 1983 $125

GISSING, GEORGE   The Whirlpool. London: Lawrence &
Bullen, 1897. First edition. Orig. cloth. Covers worn; shaken.
Good. MacManus 278-2223 1983 $75

GISSING, GEORGE   The Whirlpool. N.Y.: Frederick A.
Stokes, (1897). First American edition. Orig. decorated cloth.
Covers soiled. MacManus 278-2224 1983 $50

GISSING, GEORGE   Will Warburton: A Romance of Real Life.
Lon., 1905. (First with 16 ad pages in rear). Spine sunned, edges
rubbed, some interior foxing, over-zealous erasure of name front paste-
down, good, owner's name. Quill & Brush 54-539 1983 $60

GISSING, GEORGE   Will Warburton. London: Constable,
1905. First edition. Orig. cloth. Endpapers foxed, a bit worn.
Very good. MacManus 278-2225 1983 $45

GISSING, GEORGE   Workers in the Dawn. Garden City:
Doubleday, Doran & Co., Inc., (1935). First American edition. 2 vols.
Frontis. port. Orig. cloth. Very good. MacManus 278-2226 1983 $50

GISSING, GEORGE   A Yorkshire Lass. N.Y.: Privately
Printed, 1928. First edition. Orig. decorated boards, tissue jacket.
One of 93 copies printed. Fine. MacManus 278-2227 1983 $250

GISSING, GEORGE   A Yorkshire Lass. NY: Privately
printed, 1928. 12mo, edition limited to 93 numbered copies. Dec.
boards with paper cover label. Fine. Karmiole 76-49 1983 $75

GLADSTONE, IAGO   Behind the Sulfa Drugs. N.Y., 1943.
First edition. Argosy 713-206 1983 $30

GLADSTONE, THOMAS H.   Kansas. London, 1857. Illus., frontis.
Folded map. Orig. cloth. First edition. Small embossed library
stamp on title page. Ginsberg 47-405 1983 $125

GLADSTONE, WILLIAM EWART   Address to the Electors of Midlothian.
Edinburgh: Andres Elliot, 1885. First edition, unbound, as issued.
Fenning 62-139 1983 £14.50

GLADSTONE, WILLIAM EWART   Catalogue of the Valuable Collection
of English and Foreign Pottery... London, 1875. Tall 8vo. Partly
priced, with several newspaper cuttings. Orig. mauve printed
wrappers. Heath 48-594 1983 £75

GLADSTONE, WILLIAM EWART   Homeric Synchronism. 1876. First
edition, ads. dated Jan. 1875. 8vo, orig. brown cloth, gilt. Fenning
61-158 1983 £9.50

GLADSTONE, WILLIAM EWART   Speeches on the Irish Question in 1886.
Edinburgh: Andrew Elliot, 1886. Revised edition, tall 8vo, half
title, orig. brown cloth, v.g. Jarndyce 31-175 1983 £14.50

GLADSTONE, WILLIAM EWART   Substance of a Speech on the Motion of
Lord John Russell...with a View to the Removal of the Remaining Jewish
Disabilities... John Murray, 1848. First edition. Recent black cloth,
v.g. Jarndyce 31-173 1983 £16.50

GLAISTER, JOHN   Medico-Legal Aspects of the Ruxton Case.
172 illus. Ex-lib. First American edition. Argosy 713-218 1983
$50

GLANDORP, MATTHIAS   Opera Omnia. Londini, 1729. 4to,
old calf-backed bds., uncut; ex-lib. First collected edition. On
title, signature of Ezra Stiles, 1795. Argosy 713-219 1983 $150

GLANVIL, BARTHOLOMAEUS
Please turn to
BARTHOLOMAEUS ANGLICUS

GLASCOCK, WILLIAM NUGENT   Sailors and Saints. Henry Colburn,
1829. First edition. 3 vols. Large 12mo, lacks half-title (only
called for in vol. I). Binder's cloth, (spines faded). Occasional
slight stains. Hannas 69-74 1983 £30

GLASER, CURT   Edvard Munch. Berlin: Bruno Cassirer,
1917. Orig. etching by Munch as frontis. 78 plates in text. 4to.
Cloth. From the library of Jakob Rosenberg. Cloth. Backstrip partly
detached. Ars Libri 32-484 1983 $250

GLASER, CURT   Lukas Cranach. Leipzig: Insel-Verlag,
1923. 121 illus. 4to. Cloth. Slightly worn. Ars Libri 32-132
1983 $50

GLASGOW, ELLEN   Voice of the People. N.Y., 1900.
First edition. 12mo, buckram. First issue binding. Argosy 714-330
1983 $75

GLASS, SAMUEL   An Essay on Magnesia Alba wherein
its History is attempted... Oxford: for R. Davis..., 1764.
First edition. 8vo. Uncut in boards. Waterstain on title.
Heath 48-502 1983 £60

GLASSE, HANNAH   The Art of Cookery, Made Plain and Easy.
W. Strahan, J. Rivington & Sons, L. Davies, 1784. A new edition.
Rebound in half calf, hand-marbled boards, maroon label, v.g.
Jarndyce 31-30 1983 £120

GLAUBRECHT, FRANZ ERNST   Analecta de odontalgia ejusque remediis
variis praecipue magnete... Strassburg: Jonas Lorenz, 1766. Woodcut initial, head- and tail-piece. Small 4to. Boards. A few pages
closely trimmed on fore-edge. Rare. Kraus 164-51 1983 $200

THE GLEANER, or Cirencester Weekly Magazine, for the year 1816...
Cirencester: by T.S. Porter, (1816). First collected edition.
8vo. orig. half calf, early reback, now worn. Inner margin of
a couple of leaves reinforced. Very rare. Heath 48-311 1983
£125

GLEESON, JOHN   History of the Ely O'Carroll Territory
or Ancient Ormond...Ireland. Dublin, 1915. Reprinted, Kilkenny,
1982. With maps, plates and other illus., 2 vols., 8vo, orig. cloth.
New in matching slip-case. Ltd. edition of 1,000 numbered sets.
Fenning 60-133 1983 £50

GLEGG, W. E.   A History of the Birds of Essex. 1929.
Map and 20 plates from photos., 8vo, cloth, spine faded. Wheldon
160-717 1983 £45

GLEIG, GEORGE R.   The Campaigns of the British Army at
Washington and New Orleans...1814-1815. J. Murray, 1847. Small
8vo, wrapper. Fenning 60-134 1983 £18.50

GLEIG, GEORGE R   Chelsea Hospital and its Traditions.
Richard Bentley, 1838. First edition. 3 vols. Orig. calf, brown
labels, raised bands, gilt, v.g. Jarndyce 30-400 1983 £58

GLEIG, GEORGE R   The Chelsea Pensioners. Henry Colburn,
1829. First edition. 3 vols. Large 12mo, half-titles. Final advert.
leaves in vols. I and III. Half calf (corners worn, rebacked), uncut.
One leaf detached. Hannas 69-75 1983 £40

GLEIG, GEORGE R   The Country Curate. Henry Colburn and
Richard Bentley, 1830. First edition. 2 vols. Vol. II a little
loose, otherwise a very good copy in black half calf, brown labels.
Jarndyce 30-399 1983 £28

GLEIG, GEORGE R.   The Hussar. Henry Colburn: A.K. Newman,
1844. Including half-titles, 2 vols., 8vo, a very good uncut copy
in recent boards. Fenning 60-135 1983 £48.50

GLEIG, GEORGE R.   The Leipsic Campaign. Longman, Brown,
1852. First edition, small 8vo, strongly bound in cont. cloth. A
very good copy. Fenning 61-159 1983 £9.50

GLEIG, GEORGE R.   A Narrative of the Campaigns of the
British Army at Washington and New Orleans, Under Generals Ross,
Pakenham, and Lambert... London, 1826. Old calf and boards, spine
worn, internally good. Reese 18-598 1983 $75

GLENN, THOMAS ALLEN   Some Colonial Mansions and Those Who
Lived in Them. Philadelphia: Henry T. Coates & Co., 1899-1900.
In two vols. Profusely illus. Green cloth, orig. linen dust-covers.
Fine set. Karmiole 73-45 1983 $100

GLIEBE, FRANCIS DE SALES   The Planting of the Cross. Santa
Barbara, 1913. Illus. Orig. pictorial wraps. First edition.
Ginsberg 47-94 1983 $35

GLIMPSES of the Great Pleasure Resorts of New England. Portland,
G.W. Morris, n.c. (1890s). Illus., ads. Oblong 8vo. Morrill 287-
607 1983 $20

GLINSKI, A. J.   Polish Fairy Tales. John Lane, 1920.
4to. Colour frontis. 19 colour plates. 9 text illus. & decorated
endpapers. Blue cloth, gilt. Greer 40-234 1983 £35

GLISSON, FRANCIS   Anatomia Hepatis cui praemittuntur
Quaedam ad rem Anatomicam universe spectantia... Amsterdam:
Joannis Ravesteinii, 1659. Second edition. 16mo. Cont. vellum.
Engraved and printed title. Plates. Heath 48-503 1983 £200

GLISSON, FRANCIS   De Rachitide... London: Thomas
Roycroft for Lawrence Sadler, 1660. Second edition. Text woodcuts.
12mo. Cont. blind-stamped panelled calf. From the library of the
Royal College of Physicians, with their bookstamp and release stamp.
Kraus 164-104 1983 $1,450

GLOVER, JOHN M.   "Dark Lantern Dick." Wash., Polkinhorn,
1887. Half morocco. First edition. Ginsberg 47-521 1983 $85

GLOVER, RICHARD   Leonidas, a poem. London; printed for
R. Dodsley 1737. First edition, 4to, errata, including the preliminary blank, engraved vignette on title-page, a few wormholes in the
lower margin towards the end, cont. mottled calf gilt, upper joint
cracked and the lower cover a little scuffed. Large and fresh copy.
Pickering & Chatto 19-28 1983 $350

GLOVER, RICHARD   London: or, the Progress of Commerce.
Printed for T. Cooper, 1739. 4to, slight dusting of title and last
page. Rebound in half calf, hand-marbled boards, v.g. First
edition. Jarndyce 31-31 1983 £85

GLOVER, RICHARD   Medea. A Tragedy. London: H. Woodfall,
1761. First edition, 4to, disbound. External leaves somewhat soiled
but otherwise a fine copy. Trebizond 18-41 1983 $100

GLOVER, T. R.   Virgil. London, 1928. 8vo, cloth.
Salloch 385-800 1983 $32

GLOVER, WILLIAM   The Memoirs of a Cambridge Chorister.
Hurst & Blackett, 1885. First edition, 2 vols. Half red roan,
v.g. Jarndyce 30-107 1983 £24

GLUCK, CHRISTOFFORO   Aminta. Florence, 1939. Illus. Small
folio, parchment paper boards. Salloch 387-65 1983 $35

GLUCK, CHRISTOPH WILLIBALD   Echo et Narcisse. Paris, Des Lauriers,
(1779). First edition. Engraved title, folio, dark blue 1/2 morocco.
Salloch 387-66 1983 $900

GLUCK, CHRISTOPH WILLIBALD   Iphigenie en Aulide. Paris, Des Lauriers,
(1783?). Engraved title, engraved music. Folio, cont. suede-backed
boards, spine chipped. The word "Royale" (after Academie) has
been erased from the title page. Salloch 387-67 1983 $400

GLUCK, CHRISTOPH WILLIBALD   Iphigenie en Aulide. Paris, Des Lauriers.
(1801). Engraved title, engraved music. Folio, cont. green vellum.
A maroon leather label on the front cover. Salloch 387-68 1983 $400

GLUCK, CHRISTOPH WILLIBALD   Orphee et Euridice. Paris, Des Lauriers.
(c. 1783). Full score, all engraved. Title. Folio, red half-morocco,
spine gilt. Second edition. Salloch 387-69 1983 $350

GLUCK, GUSTAV　　　　Van Dyck. Des Meisters Gemalde.
Stuttgart/Berlin: Deutsche Verlags-Anstalt, 1931. 571 illus.
4to. Cloth. Ars Libri 32-195 1983 $125

GLYN, ELINOR　　　　Three Weeks. London, 1907. First
edition. Covers marked and some foxing throughout. Very good.
Rota 230-245 1983 £12.50

GNOLI, UMBERTO　　　　Pietro Perugino. Spoleto: Claudio
Argentieri, 1923. 52 plates. Large 4to. Boards. Edition limited
to 1000 numbered copies. Spine defective. Ars Libri 33-267 1983
$85

GNUDI, CESARE　　　　Vitale da Bologna. Milano: Silvana,
1962. 137 plates (48 color). 55 text illus. Folio. Boards.
Dust jacket. Ars Libri 33-387 1983 $85

GNUDI, MARTHA TEACH　　　　The Life and Times of Gaspare Taglia-
cozzi... New York, (1950). First edition. 8vo. Orig. binding.
Limited edition. Inscribed and autographed by Jerome Webster, the
co-author. Very scarce. Fye H-3-973 1983 $175

GOBEL, GERT　　　　Langer Als Ein Menschenleben in Missouri.
St. Louis: Wiebusch und sohn, 1877. Original printed wrappers.
Minor chipping. Jenkins 153-222 1983 $250

GOBIN, MAURICE　　　　Daumier sculpteur 1808-1879. Geneva:
Pierre Cailler, 1952. 150 plates. Small square 4to. Boards. Dust
jacket. Ars Libri 32-143 1983 $100

GOBRIGHT, L. A.　　　　Recollection of Men and Things At Washington, During the Third of a Century. Phila.: Claxton, Remsen &
Haffelfinger, 1869. Second edition. Frontis. of the Capitol. Orig.
green cloth. Title in gilt on spine. Nice. Jenkins 152-131 1983
$40

GODCHARLES, FREDERIC A.　　　　Pennsylvania. New York, American
Historical Society, (1933). Portraits and illus. 5 vols., 4to,
orig. half leather, gilt tops, nice. Morrill 289-496 1983 $57.50

GODDARD, FREDERICK B.　　　　Where To Emigrate and Why. New York:
Frederick B. Goddard, Publisher, 1869. Frontis and maps. Original
cloth worn. Light stains to text. Jenkins 153-223 1983 $75

GODDARD, HAROLD　　　　W. H. Hudson: Bird-Man. New York:
Dutton, (1928). First edition. Orig. cloth-backed boards. Good.
Jenkins 152-833 1983 $20

GODDARD, JULIA BACHOPE　　　　The search for the Gral. London:
Cassell, etc., n.d. (1868). First edition. Small 8vo. Orig. brown
cloth. Presentation copy, inscribed on the endpaper to "cousin
Sarah May from Julia Goddard." Fine copy. Ximenes 63-153 1983
$45

GODDARD, PAUL B.　　　　The Anatomy, Physiology and Pathology
of the Human Teeth. Phila., 1844. 4to, orig. cloth (worn, rebacked in
cloth); ex-lib. First edition. Argosy 713-221 1983 $350

GODDARD, WILLIAM G.　　　　An Address, In Commemoration of the
Death of...(William H. Harrison). Providence, 1841. Orig. printed
wraps. First edition. Ginsberg 46-294 1983 $35

GODDEN, RUMER　　　　The Dolls' House. London: Michael
Joseph Ltd., (1947). First edition. Pictures by Dana Saintsbury.
Orig. cloth, dust jacket (a trifle worn). Fine. MacManus 278-2241
1983 $20

GODDEN, RUMER　　　　The River. London: Michael Joseph Ltd.,
(1946). First edition. Orig. cloth. Dust jacket (internally tape-
repaired at bottom of spine). Very good. MacManus 278-2244 1983
$20

GODFREY, AMBROSE　　　　Proposals for Printing by Subscription...
4to. Modern boards, leather label. Engraved plate. Heavy ink
stain at top of work, slightly cropped. A poor copy. Very rare.
Heath 48-504 1983 £45

GODFREY, ELIAZBETH　　　　Cornish Diamonds. London: Richard
Bentley & Son, 1895. First edition. 2 vols. Orig. cloth-backed
decorated boards. Presentation copy inscribed: "Mrs. Terrybrurer with
the author's love, Christmas, 1894." Front inner hinge cracked in
vol. one. Spines and covers worn. Some foxing to the preliminary
pages. Good. MacManus 278-2245 1983 $225

GODKIN, GEORGINA SARAH　　　　The Monastery of San Marco. Florence
(Italy), 1890. 1st ed. Illus. with 10 orig. photographs. 12mo.
Orig. vellum boards, gilt decorations. Morrill 289-340 1983 $40

GODLEE, RICKMAN, JOHN　　　　Lord Lister. Oxford, 1924. Third
edition. 8vo. Orig. binding. Very fine copy. Fye H-3-834 1983
$50

GODMAN, JOHN D.　　　　Addresses delivered on Various Public
Occasions, with a Brief Explanation of the Injurious Effects of Tight
Lacing. Phila., 1829. 8vo, orig. cloth-backed bds. (worn); uncut.
Ex-lib. Library stamps and perforations throughout. Hand written
index on front flyleaf. Argosy 713-222 1983 $100

GODON, JULIEN　　　　Painted Tapestry... Lechertier, Barbe
Co., 1879. 1st Eng. edn. with 5 colour plates printed by J. Marie &
1 b&w plate, 26pp illus. pub's adverts. Crimson cloth, uncut & unopened (cvrs. some fading), fine copy. Hodgkins 27-369 1983 £25

GODOY, JOSE F.　　　　Porfirio Diaz, President of Mexico.
NY, 1910. First edition. Illustrated, cloth, sm. label on spine
else very good. Reprinted for $59.95. King 46-134 1983 $20

GODREY, E. L. B.　　　　History of the Medical Profession of
Camden County, N.J. Philadelphia, 1896. First edition. 8vo.
Orig. binding. Ex-library. Scarce. Fye H-3-223 1983 $60

GODSAL, P. T.　　　　The Conquests of Ceawlin. London: John
Murray, 1924. First edition. Illus. Orig. cloth. With an armorial
bookplate of A.C. Doyle on the front pastedown endpaper. Covers and
spine somewhat worn and spotted. Good. MacManus 278-1644 1983 $65

GODWIN, GEORGE　　　　Another Blow for Life. Wm. H. Allen,
1864. 41 illus. Half title, laid down on to end paper. 2 pp
'Reviews'. Orig. green cloth, bevelled boards, gilt, v.g. Jarndyce
31-247 1983 £68

GODWIN, MARY (WOLLSTONECRAFT) (1759-1797)　　　　An Historical and Moral
View of the Origin and Progress of the French Revolution; and the
Effect it has Produced in Europe. Dublin: printed for Pat. Byrne,
etc., 1795. First Dublin edition, 8vo, cont. tree calf, spine gilt,
red morocco label. A very good copy. Pickering & Chatto 21-135
1983 $385

GODWIN, MARY (WOLLSTONECRAFT) (1759-1797)　　　　Letters written during a
short Residence in Sweden, Norway and Denmark. London, 1796. First
edition. 8vo, cont. gilt-bordered calf, rebacked. Ad. leaf. Light
foxing throughout, otherwise a very good copy. Trebizond 18-173 1983
$500

GODWIN, MARY (WOLLSTONECRAFT) (1759-1797)　　　　Letters Written During a
Short Residence in Sweden, Norway, and Denmark. Wilmington. 1796.
Old calf. Binding rather chipped and worn, ownership stamp, otherwise
a very good copy, internally fine. Reese 18-217 1983 $275

GODWIN, MARY (WOLLSTONECRAFT) (1759-1797)　　　　A Vindication of the
Rights of Woman. Dublin: printed by J. Stockdale, for James Moore,
1793. First Dublin edition, 8vo, cont. tree calf, spine gilt, red
morocco label slightly rubbed. A very good copy. Pickering &
Chatto 21-136 1983 $500

GODWIN, WILLIAM　　　　The Adventures of Caleb Williams; or,
Things As They Are. London: Colburn & Bentley, 1832 (frontispiece
reads 1831). First of this edition. Memior by the author. 12mo.
Cont. 3/4 calf, marbled boards. Covers worn. Good sound copy.
MacManus 278-2246 1983 $75

GODWIN, WILLIAM　　　　Caleb Williams. Colburn and Bentley,
1831. Engr. front. and title, series title. Half maroon calf,
rubbed. Jarndyce 31-716 1983 £10.50

GODWIN, WILLIAM   The Enquirer. Philadelphia, for Robert
Campbell & Co. by John Bioren, 1797. 8vo, orig. tree sheep, joints
cracked, ends of spine chipped, name marked out on title. First
American edition. Ravenstree 94-137 1983 $185

GODWIN, WILLIAM   Essay on Sepulchres. London, W.
Miller, 1809. Small 8vo, old quarter cloth gilt, boards, little
worn, frontis. and first few leaves a bit waterstained. First and
only edition. Ravenstree 94-138 1983 $160

GODWIN, WILLIAM   Fleetwood: Or, The New Man of Feeling.
Printed for Richard Phillips, 1805. 3 vols, 12mo, contemporary
tree calf, a fine copy. Half-titles in Vos. I and II; advertisement
leaf but no half-title in Vol. III. 1st edition. Hill 165-42
1983 £325

GODWIN, WILLIAM   History of the Commonwealth of England.
London, Colburn, 1824-1828. 4 vols. 8vo, cont. diced calf gilt
(hinges cracked), bound by G. Cannon with his ticket in each volume.
First editions of all vols. Ravenstree 94-139 1983 $275

GODWIN, WILLIAM   The History of the Life of William
Pitt, Earl of Chatham. London: for the Author, 1783. Second
edition. 8vo. Cont. calf, gilt, slight wear. Heath 48-595 1983
£45

GODWIN, WILLIAM   Lives of the Necromancers. London:
Frederick J. Mason, 1824. First edition. 8vo. Orig. boards, printed
paper label, uncut edges. Spine worn. Traylen 94-385 1983 £135

GODWIN, WILLIAM   Lives of the Necromancers. London,
Frederick J. Mason, 1834. 8vo, bound without ads in later boards,
cloth spine good large copy complete with half title and preserved in
quarter calf gilt slipcase. First edition. Ravenstree 94-140 1983
$250

GODWIN, WILLIAM   Mandeville. A Tale of the Seventeenth
Century in England. Edinburgh: Printed for Archibald Constable,
1817. 3 vols, 12mo, 19th-century full mottled calf gilt, t.e.g.,
many other edges uncut; spines attractively tooled; with all half-
titles. First edition. Hill 165-43 1983 £225

GODWIN, WILLIAM   Mandeville. Edinburgh, for Archibald
Constable and Co. etc, 1817. First edition. 12mo, lacks half-titles.
Cont. half calf. Tiny hole in one leaf, some slight foxing. Hannas
69-76 1983 £200

GODWIN, WILLIAM   Mandeville. Edinburgh, Constable;
London, Longman (et al.), 1817. 3 vols., 8vo, cont. red quarter
morocco gilt, rather scuffed and worn, some marbling torn from front
cover of vol. 3, slight damage to foredge of approximately first 30
leaves of vol. 2, preliminaries rather foxed, traces of foxing
throughout, bookplate, with half titles. First edition. Ravenstree
94-141 1983 $275

GODWIN, WILLIAM   Mandeville. Edinburgh: Constable, 1817.
First edition, 3 vols. Sl. foxing, recently rebound in half calf,
labels, v.g. Jarndyce 30-401 1983 £85

GODWIN, WILLIAM   St. Leon: A Tale of the Sixteenth
Century. Dublin: Printed for P. Wogan (etc.), 1800. 2 vols, 12mo,
contemporary tree sheep, red and green labels; hinges wearing,
some chips to spines; a good copy. Old names on title-pages. First
Dublin edition. Hill 165-44 1983 £75

GOEBEL, JULIUS   The Law Practice of Alexander Hamilton.
New York, 1981. Vol. 5. Boswell 7-88 1983 $75

GOEBEL, K.   Outlines of Classification and Special
Morphology of Plants. Oxford, 1887. 407 text-figures, royal 8vo,
half morocco, slightly rubbed. Wheldon 160-1525 1983 £25

GOEDART, J.   Metamorphosis Naturalis. Middelburg,
(1660?). Engraved title-page, 8 plates, 12mo, cont. half calf,
slightly worn. Wheldon 160-1084 1983 £80

GOELDI, E. A.   Album de Aves Amazonicas. Zurich, 1900-
1906. 48 coloured plates, 3 parts, 4to, original paper portfolios
(somewhat worn). Very scarce. Slight waterstain in the blank margin
of plate 1 and slight tear of tissue of plates 13 and 16. Wheldon
160-35 1983 £200

GOEPPERT, H. R.   Ueber Einschlusse im Diamant. Haarlem,
Nat. Ver. Weten., 1864. 7 plates (3 coloured), 4to, boards. Marginal
staining of plates. Wheldon 160-1402 1983 £20

GOETHE, JOHANN WOLFGANG VON   Faust: A Dramatic Poem... London:
Edward Moxon, 1833. 8vo, 22 cm. Nineteenth-century black half
morocco. First edition of this translation. Inscribed to "T.P. Hayes
Esq: from the Translator A.H." Very good. Grunder 7-35 1983
$200

GOETHE, JOHANN WOLFGANG VON   The Sorrows of Werter. . Dodsley, 1784.
New edition, 2 vols. Half titles, sheep, a little rubbed. Jarndyce
31-32 1983 £32

GOETHE, JOHANN WOLFGANG VON   The Sorrows of Werter. Printed and sold
by Dean and Munday, 1815. 12mo, frontis. and additional engraved title
(a little stained). 2 ad. leaves. Cont. sheep, with slip-case.
Hannas 69-77 1983 £10

GOETHE, JOHANN WOLFGANG VON   Works. London, 1903. Best English
edition. 14 vols. 8vo. Orig. buckram with crimson morocco labels,
gilt. 73 plates. Slightly worn. Traylen 94-386 1983 £95

GOFF, RICHARD   Century in the Saddle. Denver, 1967.
Cloth, fine in dust jacket. Reese 19-248 1983 $75

GOGARTY, OLIVER ST. JOHN   The Collected Poems. (N.Y.): The Devin-
Adair Co., (1954). First American edition. Frontis. port. Orig.
cloth. Dust jacket. Presentation copy, inscribed "Dear Witter
(Bynner) These do you heartily, from Oliver." With a verse written
beneath by Bynner, and his holograph notes in the text and on the back
endpapers. Very good. MacManus 278-2247 1983 $85

GOGARTY, OLIVER ST. JOHN   Elbow Room. Dublin: The Cuala Press,
1939. First edition. Orig. cloth-backed boards. Paper label on
spine. Limited to 450 copies. Fine. MacManus 278-2248 1983 $110

GOGARTY, OLIVER ST. JOHN   Elbow Room. Dublin: The Cuala
Press, 1939. First edition, 8vo, orig. cloth-backed printed
paper boards, with printed paper spine label, an excellent unmarked
copy in the tissue. Ltd. edition of 450 copies. Fenning 61-160
1983 £48.50

GOGARTY, OLIVER ST. JOHN   Elbow Room. Dublin: Cuala Press, 1939.
First edition. One of 450 copies. Boards a little creased. Orig.
glassene wrapper. Unopened. Very nice. Rota 230-246 1983 £40

GOGARTY, OLIVER ST. JOHN   Elbow Room. N.Y.: Duell, Sloan & Pearce,
(1942). First edition. Orig. cloth. Presentation copy, inscribed
"For the most intellectual of living poets, For Witter Bynner from
Oliver St. J. Gogarty,...New York, N.Y. November 10th, 1947." Covers
partially faded. Fine. MacManus 278-2249 1983 $125

GOGARTY, OLIVER ST. JOHN   James Augustine Joyce. Dallas: Times
Hearlad, 1949. 1st ed., 1 of 1050 copies designed by Carl Hertzog.
Orig. printed wrappers, uncut. Fine copy. Jenkins 155-733 1983
$35

GOGARTY, OLIVER ST. JOHN   An Offering of Swans. Corrected page
proofs of the Cuala Press edition of 1924. Autograph letter, signed,
from Gogarty to G. Redding, Dublin, 11th October 1923. Gogarty has
added or substituted some 47 words as well as three complete poems.
Rota 231-258 1983 £350

GOGARTY, OLIVER ST. JOHN   An Offering of Swans. Dublin: The
Cuala Press, 1923. First edition, 8vo, orig. holland-backed printed
boards. The binding a little dusty, but sound and a very good copy.
300 copies were printed. Fenning 60-137 1983 £45

GOGARTY, OLIVER ST. JOHN   An Offering of Swans and Other Poems.
London: Eyre & Spottiswoode, Ltd., n.d. Later edition. Frontis. by
August John. Orig. cloth. With an ALS, 1 page, 8vo. From Gogarty
to Witter Bynner tipped to the front flyleaf, and with Bynner's bookplate on the front endsheet. Spine faded. Very good. MacManus 278-
2250 1983 $85

GOGARTY, OLIVER ST. JOHN   An Offering of Swans, and Other Poems.
Eyre & Spottiswoode, (1924). First English edition, with a portrait,
8vo, orig. cloth, gilt, a very good copy. Fenning 62-140 1983
£14.50

GOGARTY, OLIVER ST. JOHN   Selected Poems. New York, 1935. First
edition. Spine dull. Author's signed autograph presentation inscription. Nice. Rota 231-259 1983 £40

GOGARTY, OLIVER ST. JOHN   Tumbling in the Hay. London, 1939.
First edition. Neatly repaired dust wrapper. Author's signed autograph presentation inscription to Martha Smith. Fine. Rota 230-
247 1983 £50

GOGARTY, OLIVER ST. JOHN   Unselected Poems. Baltimore, Maryland:
Contemporary Poetry, 1954. First edition. Orig. cloth. Dust jacket.
Inscribed by the author for "Witter Bynner, greatfully by Oliver St.J.
Gogarty, January 20th, 1955. The way is high and very far." Bynner's
bookplate on the front endsheet. Fine. MacManus 278-2251 1983 $85

GOGOL, NIKOLAI   The Gamblers. NY, (1927). Spine edges
slightly soiled with tiny tear at bottom spine edge, front fly removed,
else very good in lightly chipped, very good dustwrapper. Quill &
Brush 54-540 1983 $35

GOGOL, NIKOLAI   The Overcoat. The Government Inspector.
The Meriden Gravure co. for The Limited Editions Club, 1976. 8vo,
19 illus., two title-pages with abstract decoration in pastel
colours, green and brown cloth divided horizontally, lettered in
silver, green boards slip-case silver, fine. Edition limited to
2,000 numbered copies signed by Saul Field, who created the
engravings. Deighton 3-145 1983 £48

GOINES, DAVID LANCE   A Constructed Roman Alphabet. Boston:
David R. Godine. (1982). Folio. With 157 plates (one folding).
Printed in red and black. Bound in blue cloth. The deluxe edition,
ltd. to 225 numbered copies, signed by Goines and with the separate
suite of 51 plates of the letters and numerals. Sheets laid loose
inside slipcase. Both parts housed in marbled boards slipcase with
paper label. Karmiole 74-49 1983 $150

GOLBERRY, SYLVAIN MEINRAD XAVIER DE   Fragmens d'un voyage en
Afrique... Paris: Treuttel & Wurtz, 1802. 2 vols. 8vo. 3 folding
maps, 4 plates. 19th century 1/4 green calf, gilt, marbled boards.
Adelson Africa-88 1983 $300

GOLDBERG, ISAAC   The Man Mencken. N.Y., 1925. First
edition. Illus. Cloth. Index. T.e.g. Ink name. Spine darkened.
Very good. King 45-224 1983 $20

THE GOLDEN Cockerel Greek Anthology. London: the Golden Cockerel
Press, 1937. Folio. Orig. quarter morocco, cloth sides, t.e.g.,
others uncut. 14 line-engravings on zinc by Lettice Sandford.
Limited edition of 206 numbered copies, printed in Greek and English.
Traylen 94-387 1983 £150

THE GOLDEN Gift. W.P. Nimmo, 1874. Re-issue, colour printed half
title & wood engr'd title p. Illus. by Clark Stanton, H. Weir,
MacWhirter, Halswelle, Lawson, Cameron, etc. Engr'd on wood by R.
Paterson. Green sand grain decor. cloth, bevelled boards, a.e.g.
Gilt school stamp rear cvr. & prize label fr. ep., some sl. thumbing
& foxing, corners sl. bruised, vg. Hodgkins 27-274 1983 £15

GOLDEN Light. Routledge, 1865. 80 illus. by A.W. Bayes, engr'd by
Bros. Dalziel. 4pp adverts. Green ribbed cloth gilt. Some sl.
thumbing & gilt sl. rubbed. ALS from A.W. Bayes of 13 lines dd. 1904
to Mr. Dalziel, inserted. Also inscribed to J. Newton Dalziel from
Papa Xmas 1864 with E. Dalziel's bookplate. Very good. Hodgkins 27-
275 1983 £35

THE GOLDEN Staircase. Jack, 1906. Pictures by M. Dibdin Spooner,
Color frontis. and 16 color plates. Maroon cloth gilt, t.e.g.,
others uncut, backstrip faded, contemporary inscription, nice copy.
Hodgkins 27-47 1983 £18

GOLDEN Thoughts from Golden Fountains. Warne, nd (ca. 1880). Arr. in
52 divisions, with illus. by A.B. Houghton, Dalziel Bros., Lawson,
Wolf, Burton, Pinwell, etc. Engr'd by Bros. Dalziel (73 illus.), 2pp
adverts. Red sand grain decor. cl. repr'd, 2 section sl. sprung,
foxing prelims., vg. Hodgkins 27-276 1983 £20

THE GOLDEN Treasury of the best songs... Cambridge: Macmillan and
Co., 1861. First edition. 12mo. Orig. green cloth, gilt. Vignette
on title-page. Slightly marked. Traylen 94-388 1983 £25

GOLDENWEISER, ALEXANDER   History, Psychology and Culture. NY:
Knopf, 1933. First edition. Gach 94-187 1983 $25

GOLDER, FRANK A.   The March of the Mormon Battalion from
Council Bluffs to California. New York, 1928. Frontis and illus.
Jenkins 153-224 1983 $45

GOLDER, FRANK A   The March of the Mormon Battalion.
N.Y.: The Century Co., (1928). Cloth with dust wrapper. Dawson 471-
99 1983 $40

GOLDING, HARRY   The Brownies Birthday. Ward Lock, n.d.
(ca.1915). 12mo. Colour frontis. & 26 colour plates. Colour pictorial
endpapers, light wear. Brown boards, rebacked. Onlaid colour plate.
Greer 39-81 1983 £22.50

GOLDING, HARRY   Tick, Tack, and Tock. Ward Lock, n.d.
(ca. 1915). 12mo. Colour frontis. & 26 colour plates. Colour pictorial endpapers. Brown boards, rebacked. Onlaid colour plate. Greer
39-82 1983 £22.50

GOLDING, LOUIS   Day of Atonement. London: Chatto &
Windus, 1925. First edition. Orig. cloth, with paper label on spine.
Presentation copy, inscribed "To Bessie (Moult) because it's about
Russia, and Tom, because it's about Doomington, and Joy Sylvia because
it's about Hellas, affectionately to all from Louis, London May 18,
1925." Spine faded. MacManus 278-2254 1983 $25

GOLDING, LOUIS   Five Silver Daughters. London: Victor
Gollancz, 1934. First edition. Orig. cloth. Dust jacket (spine and
covers faded and slightly soiled and worn). Presentation copy to
Dennis Wheatley inscribed: "For Dennis W. from the golding father of
the silver ladies, Louis G., December 1937." Loosely laid in is an
ANS, 1 page, 16 Hamilton Terrace, 19 xII '37, from Louis Golding to
Dennis Wheatley. Edges a trifle foxed. Wheatley's bookplate. Near-
fine. MacManus 278-2255 1983 $85

GOLDING, LOUIS   Five Silver Daughters. London: Victor
Gollancz Ltd., 1934. First edition. Orig. cloth. Dust jacket (faded
and chipped). With a TLS, 1 page, 4to, 13, Cambridge Street, London,
27th November 1933, from Golding to Tom (Moult) laid in. Very good.
MacManus 278-2256 1983 $50

GOLDING, LOUIS   The Glory of Elsie Silver. London:
Hutchinson & Co., (1945). Publisher's advance copy of the first Eng-
lish edition. Orig. wrappers. Presentation copy inscribed: "For
Dear Aloa and Dear Harry--Oh what a sight for sad eyes on a dull
October day! Louis with love October 1945." Spine very slightly faded.
Near-fine. MacManus 278-2260 1983 $125

GOLDING, LOUIS   The Glory of Elsie Silver. London:
Hutchinson & Co. Ltd., (1945). Proof copy. Orig. wrappers. Inscribed
on the half-title: "For Tom (Moult, Elsie in gingham who moves in this
tale from satin to sackcloth and ashes, affectionately Louis, Nov. 28,
1945." Very good. MacManus 278-2258 1983 $75

GOLDING, LOUIS   The Glory of Elsie Silver. N.Y.: Dial
Press, 1945. First edition. Orig. cloth. Dust jacket (faded, worn
at edges). Presentation copy, "For Tom & Constance (Moult)...who know
what happened next, Louis...with love, May 1950." Good. MacManus
278-2259 1983 $45

GOLDING, LOUIS   The Glory of Elsie Silver. London: The
Book Club, (1946). Book Club edition. Orig. cloth. Dust jacket (a
little worn). Presentation copy, inscribed on the front free endpaper:
"Louis and Elsie to Constance, with obeisances, April 11th, 1947,
London." Very good. MacManus 278-2261 1983 $30

GOLDING, LOUIS   The Jewish Problem. Harmondsworth:
Penguin Books Limited, (1938). First edition. 33 illus. Orig.
wrappers. Presentation copy, "To Tom (Moult) to round off his collection (and Constance may want to chip in too) Love, Louis, Nov. 1, 1954
(and what a long time after publication! shame!)." Top of spine defective. Good. MacManus 278-2262 1983 $65

GOLDING, LOUIS   The Jolly Gentlemen. London: Hutchinson & Co. Ltd., (1947). First edition. Orig. cloth. Dust jacket (a
bit worn). Presentation copy, inscribed on the front free endpaper:
"For Young Tom (Moult) from old Louis, two jolly gentlemen on the
birthday of these three competitors, 4 Dec. 47." Very good. MacManus
278-2278 1983 $45

GOLDING, LOUIS   Magnolia Street. London: Victor Gollancz Ltd., 1932. First edition. Orig. cloth. Dust jacket (faded and
chipped). Presentation copy, inscribed on the front flyleaf "For
Tommie and Bessie (Moult) who have an idea about Magnolia Street, and
Joy, who must wait a bit till she acquires one, Louis, with love, Jan.
4, 32." Very good. MacManus 278-2265 1983 $50

GOLDING, LOUIS   The Miracle Boy. London: Alfred A.
Knopf, 1927. First edition. Orig. decorated cloth, in publisher's
cloth. One of 50 copies printed on rag paper and signed by the author.
Fine. MacManus 278-2267 1983 $100

GOLDING, LOUIS   Mr. Emmanuel. London: Rich & Cowan,
Ltd., (1939). First edition. Orig. cloth. Dust jacket (worn at
edges). Presentation copy, inscribed on the title-page: "Tom & Bessie
(Moult) from their unswerving Louis, 24 April 1939." With a brief
autograph postcard from Golding laid in. Very good. MacManus 278-
2269 1983 $65

GOLDING, LOUIS   Poems Drunk and Drowsy. London: Privately Printed, (1934). First edition. Orig. printed wrappers.
Presentation copy inscribed: "For R. Cobden Sanderson, early in the
year, Louis Golding--Saluli! 1933." One of 100 copies. Covers faded.
Very good. MacManus 278-2271 1983 $85

GOLDING, LOUIS   The Prince of Somebody. London: Alfred
A. Knopf, (1929). First edition. Orig. cloth. Presentation copy,
inscribed: "For Bessie For Joy For Tom (Moult), London, 2 June 29, And
still they come...-- Love, Louis." Spine faded. Good. MacManus
278-2272 1983 $25

GOLDING, LOUIS   The Prince or Somebody. London: The
Gibson Press, n.d. Reissue. Orig. cloth. Dust jacket (chipped).
Inscribed: "For Constance (Moult) this early novel with my late and
early love, Louis, April 11th (say) 1947." Very good. MacManus 278-
2273 1983 $25

GOLDING, LOUIS   The Pursuer. London: Hutchinson & Co.,
(1936). First edition. Orig. cloth. Inscribed on the front free
endpaper "For Tom (Moult) each the pursuer, each the pursued, Louis,
May 1950." Good. MacManus 278-2275 1983 $25

GOLDING, LOUIS   Sorrow of War. London: Methuen & Co.
Ltd., (1919). First edition. Orig. grey paper boards with paper
label on spine. Dust jacket (worn). Fine. MacManus 278-2277 1983
$150

GOLDING, LOUIS   Sorrow of War. London: Methuen & Co.
Ltd., (1919). First edition. Orig. boards with paper label on spine.
Presentation copy, inscribed "To Thomas Moult (who is Tom McKellen)
best of friends and poets and to Bessie and to both, in gratitude for
'23' His first from Louis Golding 2.2.19." Boards dust-soiled. Label
slightly rubbed. Good. MacManus 278-2276 1983 $125

GOLDING, LOUIS   Sorrow of War. Lon., (1919). Very good
to fine in dustwrapper. Quill & Brush 54-543 1983 $100

GOLDING, LOUIS   Three Jolly Gentlemen. London: Hutchinson & Co., (1947). Proof copy. Orig. wrappers. Inscribed "For
Constance (Moult) who (I arrogantly assert) would have thrown both
arms around me, had she been here--not because of this novel, but
because of another, unwritten, with love, Louis, 1947." Fine.
MacManus 278-2279 1983 $75

GOLDING, WILLIAM   The Inheritors. London, 1955. First
edition. Slightly faded spine, dustwrapper having one tiny chip from
head and tail of spine. Bookplate. Excellent. Gekoski 2-62 1983
£75

GOLDING, WILLIAM   Lord of the Flies. London, 1954.
First edition. Inscribed presentation copy, undated. Light fading
to front board, otherwise a nice copy. Golding inscriptions very
scarce. Gekoski 2-61 1983 £275

GOLDING, WILLIAM   Lord of the Flies. N.Y.: Coward-McCann,
Inc. (1955). First American edition. Orig. cloth. Dust jacket.
Very fine. MacManus 278-2282 1983 $250

GOLDING, WILLIAM   Lord of the Flies. New York: Coward-
McCann,(1955). Cloth and boards. First American edition. Slightly
smudged ink name, else about fine in dust jacket. Reese 20-451
1983 $175

GOLDING, WILLIAM   Rites of Passage. London: Faber &
Faber, 1980. Proof copy of the first edition. Orig. wrappers. Dust
jacket. Fine. MacManus 278-2286 1983 $135

GOLDING, WILLIAM   Rites of Passage. N.Y.: Farrar Straus
Giroux, 1980. Uncorrected Proof of the first American edition.
Tall thin 4to. Orig. wrappers. Very fine. MacManus 278-2284 1983
$85

GOLDING, WILLIAM   The Scorpion God. London, 1971.
First edition. Dustwrapper. Signed by the author on front endpaper.
Fine. Gekoski 2-65 1983 £45

GOLDMAN, EMMA   The Social Significance of the Modern
Drama. Boston (1914). Covers, esp. spine, soiled and worn.
Reprinted for $69.95. King 46-87 1983 $25

GOLDMAN, WILLIAM   The Temple of Gold. New York, 1957.
8vo. Cloth. A fine copy in dj. In Our Time 156-321 1983 $100

GOLDMARK, JOSEPHINE   Pilgrims of '48: One Man's Part in the
Austrian Revolution of 1848. New Haven, 1930. Illus. Argosy 710-
147 1983 $35

GOLDONI, CARLO   The Liar. London: Selwyn and Blount
Ltd., (1922). First trade edition. Decorations by C.L. Fraser. Intro.
by E. Gordon Craig. Small 4to. Orig. cloth-backed boards with paper
labels. Covers a bit rubbed and worn. MacManus 278-1996 1983 $35

GOLDINI, CARLO   The Liar. London: Selwyn & Blount,
(1922). First edition. Intro. by Gordon Craig. Orig. decorated
buckram. Dust jacket (spine and covers a bit faded and soiled and
torn). One of 260 copies printed on special paper. Fine. MacManus
278-1995 1983 $175

GOLDONI, CARLO   Ninette a la Cour. Amsterdam, Hupkies,
1761. Small 8vo, wraps. Salloch 387-168 1983 $35

GOLDRING, DOUGLAS   Streets. London: Max Goschen, 1912.
First edition. Orig. cloth. Dust jacket (small portion of rear panel
lacking at corner). Unopened. Very fine. MacManus 278-2288 1983
$60

GOLDSCHMIDT, ADOLPH   Die deutschen Bronzeturen des fruhen
mittelalters. Marburg, 1926. (Die Fruhmittelalterlichen
Bronzeturen. Vol. 1.) 43pp., 6 plates + 103 collotype plates
loose in portfolio as illued. Folio. Cloth. Slipcase.
Ars Libri SB 26-88 1983 $325

GOLDSCHMIDT, ADOLPH   Gotische Madonnenstatuen in Deutschland.
Augsburg, 1933. 4to, 20 plates with 39 illus. Lg. 4to, wraps. Ars
Libri SB 26-89 1983 $37.50

GOLDSCHMIDT, E. P.   The Printed Book of the Renaissance.
Cambridge: The University Press, 1950. First edition. 4to.
Cloth, dust jacket. 10 plates. One of seven hundred and fifty
copies. Jacket chipped. Oak Knoll 49-199 1983 $110

GOLDSCHMIDT, MEIR A.   Jacob Bendixen, the Jew. Colburn and
Co, 1852. First edition of this translation. 3 vols. 8vo, orig.
boards, cloth spine, paper label (rubbed), uncut. Hannas 69-106
1983 £45

GOLDSMITH, LEWIS   The Crimes of Cabinets. Printed for,
and sold by, the author, 1801. First edition, including half-
title, 8vo, cont. half calf, a very good copy. Fenning 61-163 1983
£65

GOLDSMITH, LEWIS   Exposition of the Conduct of France
Towards America. London, 1810. 3rd edition. 12mo. Argosy 716-
599 1983 $40

GOLDSMITH, OLIVER   The Beauties of English Poesy. London:
William Griffin, 1767. First edition, 12mo, two volumes, cont.
calf, spines gilt, morocco labels, lacking the half-titles. Foredges
of leaves sun-darkened, but a very good copy. In a handsome morocco-
backed slipcase. Trebizond 18-42 1983 $425

GOLDSMITH, OLIVER   The Bee. London: W. Lane, (1800).
Cr. 8vo. Cont. tree calf, gilt spine with morocco label. Engraved
vignette title-page, after Page. Joints worn. Traylen 94-390
1983 £20

GOLDSMITH, OLIVER   The Citizen of the World. London: for R. Whiston, etc., 1776. 2 vols. 12mo. Cont. mottled calf, gilt panelled spines with morocco labels, gilt. Traylen 94-391 1983 £38

GOLDSMITH, OLIVER   The Comedies of... Allen, 1896. 1st edn. 24 b&w illus. by Chris Hammond, frontis. Dark green decor. cloth gilt, a.e.g. (insc. half title, one illus. creased across top corner, v. sl. wear corners), v.g. copy. Hodgkins 27-445 1983 £12.50

GOLDSMITH, OLIVER   Dalziel's Illustrated Goldsmith. Ward Lock, 1865. 100 illus. drawn by G.J. Pinwell, engr'd by Bros. Dalziel, 2pp adverts. Half blue sand grain cloth with blue morocco grain sides. Gilt vignette fr. cvr., gilt decor. bkstrip., cvrs. sl. marked, vg copy. Hodgkins 27-278 1983 £25

GOLDSMITH, OLIVER   The Deserted Village. London: Harper & Brothers, 1902. First edition with these illus. by E.A. Abbey, R.A. 4to. Orig. cloth. Fine. MacManus 278-2290 1983 $45

GOLDSMITH, OLIVER   An Enquiry into the Present State of Polite Learning in Europe. London, R. and J. Dodsley, 1759. 12mo, modern citron morocco gilt, a.e.g. by Riviere, hinges rubbed, the James Cox Brady-Robert Hoe copy with bookplates, complete with half title. First edition. Ravenstree 94-142 1983 $510

GOLDSMITH, OLIVER   An Enquiry into the Present State of Polite Learning in Europe. London: R. & J. Dodsley, 1759. 1st ed., 8vo, cont. panelled calf, rebacked in antique style with morocco label. Vignette title page. Half-title. A very good copy. Trebizond 18-43 1983 $400

GOLDSMITH, OLIVER   An Enquiry into the Present State of Polite Learning in Europe. London: for R. & J. Dodsley, 1759. First edition. Small 8vo. Polished tree calf, gilt. Half title. One joint weak. Heath 48-313 1983 £235

GOLDSMITH, OLIVER   Essays. London: W. Griffin, 1765. 12mo. Cont. sheep. Printed title. Minor wear. Scarce. Ximenes 63-240 1983 $225

GOLDSMITH, OLIVER   The Good Natur'd Man. London: for W. Griffin, 1768. First edition. 8vo. Modern half calf. Half title. Light at inner margin of a few leaves. Heath 48-314 1983 £200

GOLDSMITH, OLIVER   The Grecian History, from the Earliest State, to the Death of Alexander the Great. Philadelphia, 1818. 2 vols. in one, worn calf, front hinge broken. Reese 18-522 1983 $20

GOLDSMITH, OLIVER   The Life of Richard Nash of Bath, Esq. London, J. Newbery and W. Frederick, 1762. Octavo, new half calf period style, engraved portrait soiled, with verses on recto; verso of title inscribed, some age-darkening throughout, a.e.g. First edition. Ravenstree 97-2 1983 $240

GOLDSMITH, OLIVER   The Martial Review. London, J. Newbery, 1763. 8vo, cont. sheep, quite worn, hinges broken, blank end-leaves gone, title soiled, lightly frayed about edges, age, dust and thumbing throughout. First edition. Ravenstree 94-143 1983 $295

GOLDSMITH, OLIVER   Miscellaneous Works. London, 1812. 4 vols. 8vo. Cont. diced calf, gilt. Portrait and 13 engraved plates. Spine of vol. 1 neatly repaired. Traylen 94-389 1983 £35

GOLDSMITH, OLIVER   Poems for Young Ladies. In Three parts. Devotional, Moral and Entertaining. London: E. Johnson, 1785. Second, enlarged edition, 12mo., early 19th cent. half calf gilt, marbled boards, half-title, bookplate. Some light soiling, but a very good copy of this uncommon title. Trebizond 18-44 1983 $225

GOLDSMITH, OLIVER   The Poems of... Routledge, nd (1885). Frontis. & 49 col'd illus & many b&w designs by Birket Foster & Henry Noel Humphreys printed in colours by Edmund Evans. Each page within single ruled border. Cloth backed col'd pictorial boards, black titling bkstrip (free eps. discol'd, foxing of contents, fr. corners repaired), nice copy. Hodgkins 27-371 1983 £35

GOLDSMITH, OLIVER   The Poems of... Routledge, 1877. New edn. with frontis. & 49 col'd illus. & many b&w designs by Birket Foster & Henry Noel Humphreys printed in colours by Edmund Evans. Each page within single ruled border. Red diagonal grained decor. cloth, bevelled boards, a.e.g. (foxing contents, top/bottom bkstrip repr'd name verso of title), v.g. Hodgkins 27-370 1983 £35

GOLDSMITH, OLIVER   Poetical Works. Whittingham for Cadell and Davies, 1805. 1st ed., sm. 8vo, engraved portrait and title, 6 engraved plates after Wheatley and Hamilton, contemporary tree calf, red morocco label, some wear and joints cracked, some light foxing. Deighton 3-146 1983 £28

GOLDSMITH, OLIVER   The Foetical Works of... Kent, 1859. Complete edn., 1st thus, frontis. & 36 illus. by Absolon, Birket Foster, Godwin, Harrison Weir, 2pp adverts. Red sand grain cloth gilt, a.e.g. Re-cased with new eps., corners bumped, cvrs. sl. soiled & discol'd, occasional foxing, vg. Hodgkins 27-277 1983 £12.50

GOLDSMITH, OLIVER   The Poetical Works. London, 1846. Small 4to. Cont. full red morocco, gilt, wide gilt borders on sides, gilt panelled spine, inner gilt dentells, edges gilt, by Hayday. With wood-engravings from the drawings of C.W. Copy, etc. Traylen 94-392 1983 £25

GOLDSMITH, OLIVER   Poetical Works. Griffin, 1866. Engrs. by Stanfield, Unwins, Leslie, Stothard, D. Roberts, Boxall, etc., 4pp adverts. Blue sand grain cloth gilt, bevelled boards, a.e.g. Foxing prelims, 3 centre sections v. sl. sprung, top/bottom bkstrip sl. wear, contemp. insc. 2nd ep., vg. Hodgkins 27-279 1983 £16

GOLDSMITH, OLIVER   Retaliation. London: Printed for G. Kearsly...MDCCLXXIV. 4to, with half-title, engraved portrait on title-page, some faint marginal staining. New wraps. Second edition. Quaritch NS 7-52 1983 $165

GOLDSMITH, OLIVER   Retaliation: a Poem. London: G. Kearsley, 1774. 4th ed., second issue, but containing a poetical "Postscript" of 28 lines, never before published. 4to, disbound, half-title present but detached. Half-title and title lightly stained, otherwise a very good copy. Trebizond 18-45 1983 $125

GOLDSMITH, OLIVER   Retaliation. London: Printed for G. Kearsly...MDCCLXXIV. 4to, with half-title, engraved portrait on title-page, new wraps. Seventh edition. Quaritch NS 7-53 1983 $85

GOLDSMITH, OLIVER   The Roman History, From the Foundation of the City of Rome, To the Destruction of the Western Empire. London: Printed for S. Baker & G. Leigh, in York-Street; T. Davies, in Russel-Street, Convent Garden; & L. Davis, in Holborn, 1769. First edition. 2 vols. Orig. blue-grey paper boards (spines slightly defective). Entirely uncut. In a half-morocco case. Jerome Kern-William Stock-hausen copy, measuring 8-3/4" × 5-2/3". Very fine. MacManus 278-2293 1983 $850

GOLDSMITH, OLIVER   The Roman history abridged for the use of schools. London: W. Owen, etc., 1786. Fourth edition. 12mo. Cont. tree calf, spine gilt, red morocco prize label on front cover. Frontis. and three other copperplates. Ximenes 63-470 1983 $125

GOLDSMITH, OLIVER   The Traveller. London: Printed for J. Newbery...MDCCLXV. 4to, half-title genuine, but supplied, and slightly shorter than the rest of the text, which has been carefully washed and sized; lacking final leaf of ads.; dark blue morocco by Riviere, spine gilt, a.e.g. First edition, third state. Quaritch NS 7-54 1983 $200

GOLDSMITH, OLIVER   The Traveller, or a Prospect of Society. London: Printed for J. Newbery...MDCCLXV. 4to, with half-title, new wraps. Third edition. A fine copy. Quaritch NS 7-55 1983 $135

GOLDSMITH, OLIVER   The Vicar of Wakefield. For F. Newbery, 1766. 2 vols., 12mo, lacks final blank leaf in vol. 1. Modern blind-tooled calf, a.e.g. Clement K. Shorter bookplate. Small hole in one leaf not affecting text, some trifling stains. Printed by Strahan in 1,000 copies. Hannas 69-79 1983 £150

GOLDSMITH, OLIVER   The Vicar of Wakefield. London: Printed for, & sold by H.D. Symonds, Paternoster Row, 1793. "New edition." Full cont. calf with red morocco label on spine. Corners of endpapers slightly torn. Some foxing. Cont. ownership signature on title-page. Good. MacManus 278-2291 1983 $65

GOLDSMITH, OLIVER   The Vicar of Wakefield. London: 1843. Octavo. Illus. by William Mulready. Heavily gilt-decorated full brown morocco. Raised bands on spine, gilt-decorated. A.e.g. Signed binding (Sangorski & Sutcliffe) in pristine condition. Some very light occasional foxing to interior. Bookplate. Bromer 25-157 1983 $700

GOLDSMITH, OLIVER   The Vicar of Wakefield. London: John van Voorst, 1843. First edition with illus. by Mulready. Large 8vo. Orig. salmon cloth. 32 wood-engraved vignette illus. by William Mulready. Spine slightly faded and marked. Ximenes 63-195 1983 $60

GOLDSMITH, OLIVER   Vicar of Wakefield. E.E. Barrett, 1875. 12 steel engrs. on India paper laid on card by Sangster. Emerald green decor. cloth gilt, a.e.g. bevelled boards. Corners sl. worn, top/bottom bkstrip sl. worn, eps. cracking at hinges, scarce, vg. Hodgkins 27-280 1983 £38

GOLDSMITH, OLIVER   The Vicar of Wakefield. Macmillan, 1890. 1st edn. Illus. - Hugh Thomson. Frontis., 6pp adverts. Dark green decor. cloth gilt, a.e.g. (bookpl. fr. ep., corners sl. bruised, sl. foxing title & eps), nice copy. Hodgkins 27-444 1983 £16.50

GOLDSMITH, OLIVER   The Vicar of Wakefield. London: Macmillan & Co., 1891. Second edition. Illus. by H. Thomson. Orig. gilt-decorated cloth, a.e.g. Dust jacket (chipped, spine torn). Very fine. MacManus 280-5231 1983 $75

GOLDSMITH, OLIVER   The Vicar of Wakefield. London: Henry Frowde, (ca. !905). Frontis. portrait. Fine in slightly faded full green leather. T.e.g. Bookplate. (2 1/4 x 1 7/8; 54x47mm). Bromer 25-430 1983 $110

GOLDSMITH, OLIVER   The Vicar of Wakefield. Constable, 1914. 1st edn. Frontis. & 15 colour plates, 48 b&w illus. by E.J. Sullivan. Sage green vertical ribbed decor. cloth, t.e.g. others uncut, fine. Hodgkins 27-446 1983 £25

GOLDSMITH, OLIVER   The Vicar of Wakefield. London, 1929. 4to. Full light grey crushed levant morocco with elaborate inlaid coloured design on front cover, t.e.g. 12 coloured plates and other illus. by Arthur Rackham. Traylen 94-393 1983 £80

GOLDSMITH, OLIVER   The Vicar of Wakefield. London: George G. Harrap & Co., (1929). First edition. Illus. by A. Rackham. 4to. Orig. cloth. Dust jacket (rather chipped). Bookplate. Very good. MacManus 280-4323 1983 $135

GOLDSTEIN, KURT   Language and Language Disturbances. NY: Grune & Stratton, 1948. First edition. Inscribed ex-library copy. Gach 95-171 1983 $40

GOLDTWURM, CASPAR   Kirchen Calender om Welchem nach Ordnung gemeyner Allmanach die Monat, Tag, und Fuernembsten rest der gantzen Jars. Franckfurt am Meyn: C. Egenolffs Erben, 1564. 8vo, over 85 woodcut illus. Full cont. vellum. Tittle in MS on spine. Toned especially in early leaves. Title in red and black. Two small repairs on title page, slight loss of printed surface. Very good. Arkway 22-54 1983 $875

GOLL, YZAN   Four Poems of the Occult. (Kentfield, CA): The Allen Press, 1962. Folio. Loose signatures, within 5 wrappered portfolios. Edition ltd. to 130 copies printed on mould made all-rag Rives paper from France. Border decorations and initials by Mallette Dean; initials are colored by hand. Housed in a linen folder and linen slipcase. Fine. Karmiole 75-5 1983 $650

GOMEZ, ROBLEDO, A.   The Bucareli Agreements and International Law. Mexico, 1940. Orig. printed wrappers. Jenkins 152-310 1983 $75

GOMEZ-MORENO, MANUEL   El Greco (Dominico Theotocopuli). Barcelona: Ediciones Selectas, 1943. 63 tipped-in plates. 4to. Boards. Dust jacket. Ars Libri 32-283 1983 $85

GOMME, ALICE B.   Children's Singing Games. Nutt, 1894. Second Series. Sm. 4to. Pictorial title. 8 full-page & 28 text illus. Decorated borders. Light brown pictorial cloth, worn. Greer 40-207 1983 £18

GOMME, GEORGE LAURENCE   The London Council. David Nutt, 1888. First edition, orig. brown cloth, v.g. Jarndyce 31-248 1983 £10.50

GOMME, GEORGE LAURENCE   London in the Reign of Victoria (1837-1897). Blackie & Son, 1898. First edition. Half title. Orig. red cloth, v.g. Jarndyce 31-249 1983 £12.50

GOMME, GEORGE LAURENCE   The Story of London Maps. Pub. by the Royal Geographical Society and Edward Stanford, 1908. Plans and sketches printed in text; folding col. map, showing the growth of London. Well bound in green cloth. Jarndyce 31-250 1983 £16

GOMPERTZ, MAURICE   Corn from Egypt. London: Gerald Howe, (1927). First edition. Orig. pictorial cloth. Presentation copy from Howe inscribed "To John Galsworthy Esq. with the gratitude & admiration of the author." Binding very slightly worn and soiled. Very good. MacManus 278-2140 1983 $35

GONCOURT, EDMOND   Debucourt. Etude contenant deux dessins graves a l'eau-forte. Paris: E. Dentu, 1866. 2 orig. etchings by Jules de Goncourt, printed by Delatre. 4to. Marbled boards, 3/4 leather. T.e.g. Orig. wrappers bound in. Edition limited to 200 copies only, on fine laid paper. A few annotations in pencil. Ars Libri 32-149 1983 $150

GONFREVILLE, M. D.   Art de la Teinture des Laines en Toison, en Fil et en Tissu. Paris, n.d. (1850). 8vo. Old quarter-leather worn. Signed by the author. Light foxing and some stains. Gurney JJ-141 1983 £25

GONTARD, J. A.   Lecons de Chymie de l'Universite de Montpellier... Paris: Cavelier, 1750. 8vo. Modern boards with label. Light marginal dampstain. Zeitlin 264-176 1983 $160

GOOCH, BERNARD   The Strange World of Nature. London, 1950. First edition. Numerous woodcuts by Joan Hassall. Covers slightly marked. Free endpapers slightly spotted. Slightly spotted dustwrapper. Very good. Jolliffe 26-249 1983 £14

GOOCH, RICHARD   The Cambridge Tart: Epigrammatic and Satiric-Poetical Effusions... London: by James Smith, 1823. First edition. Cr. 8vo. Half calf, gilt spine with morocco label, gilt. Traylen 94-394 1983 £30

GOOD, JOHN J.   Cannon Smoke: The Letters of Captain John J. Good... (Hillsboro, 1971). Limited to 50 copies signed and numbered. Illustrations. Jenkins 153-196 1983 $75

GOODALL, WALTER   An Examination of the Letters, said to be Written by Mary Queen of Scots, to James Earl of Bothwell. Edinburgh: Printed by T. and W. Ruddiman, 1754. 2 vols., 8vo, cont. calf, rubbed, slightly worn at top of spines, upper joints cracked, but sound. First edition. Bickersteth 77-117 1983 £80

GOODE, G. B.   American Fishes. Boston, 1903. 6 coloured plates and numerous text-figures. Royal 8vo. Wheldon 160-959 1983 £20

GOODELL, WILLIAM   The Old and The New. N.Y., 1853. Portrait plus 7 color plates. Cloth. Ink names. Foxed. Spine ends frayed, covers worn. King 45-542 1983 $45

GOODEN, ORVILLE T.   The Missouri and North Arkansas Railroad Strikes. N.Y., 1926. Orig. printed wraps. First edition. Ginsberg 46-279 1983 $20

GOODEN, STEPHEN   The Poet's Cat. London, 1946. First edition. One of 110 numbered copies on large paper, signed by Mona and Stephen Gooden. 2 cooper-engravings (one being the title-page design) by S. Gooden. Half black calf. Upper corners a little bruised. Some light foxing of the preliminaries. Nice. Rota 231-261 1983 £55

GOODISON, WILLIAM   A historical and topographical essay upon the islands of Corfu... London: Underwood, 1822. First edition. 8vo. Orig. blue boards, drab paper spine, printed paper label. 4 maps, and 8 lithographed views. A bit worn. Ximenes 63-621 1983 $200

GOODLAND, ROGER   A Bibliography of Sex Rites and Customs. London: George Routledge & Sons, Ltd. Karmiole 76 1983 $65

GOODMAN, DANIEL CARSON   Sad, Sad Lovers. New York, 1931. 8vo. Cloth. Fine in dj which is chipped on the spine. In Our Time 156-322 1983 $35

GOODMAN, NATHAN   Benjamin Rush Physician and Citizen. Philadelphia 1934. First edition. 8vo. Orig. binding. Fye H-3-939 1983 $45

GOODMAN, PAUL   Stop-Light. Harrington Pk., 1941. First edition. Small 8vo, drawings by Percival Goodman, with both the plain and later printed dust jackets. Fine. Houle 21-379 1983 $60

GOODRICH, LLOYD   Edward Hopper. New York: Abrams, n.d. 246 illus. (88 color). Oblong folio. Cloth. Dust jacket. Ars Libri 32-331 1983 $175

GOODRICH, LLOYD   Kenneth Hayes Miller. New York: The Arts Publishing Co., 1930. 65 plates. 4to. Boards, 1/4 cloth. Slightly worn. Ars Libri 32-454 1983 $50

GOODRICH, LLOYD   Thomas Eakins. New York: Whitney Museum of American Art, 1933. 72 plates. Large 4to. Cloth. Ars Libri 32-198 1983 $125

GOODRICH, MARCUS   Delilah. New York: Farrar, 1941. Printed wraps. Advance reading copy. Light rubbing, but a very good copy. Reese 20-982 1983 $20

GOODRICH, SAMUEL GRISWOLD   Recollections of a Lifetime, or Men and Things I Have Seen. NY, 1857. Engrs., 2 vols., later fabricoid. Argosy 710-326 1983 $35

GOODRICH, SAMUEL GRISWOLD   Recollections of a Lifetime... New York: Miller, Orton and Mulligan, 1857. Thick 8vo. Orig. cloth. 2 vols. Covers worn; frontis. crudely rehung. Oak Knoll 48-171 1983 $25

GOODSPEED, CHARLES E.   Nathaniel Hawthorne and the Marine Museum of the Salem East India Marine Society. Boston: The Club of Odd Volumes. 1946. Illus. Edition ltd. to 99 copies, printed by the Southworth-Anthoensen Press. Black cloth over dec. boards; gilt-stamped spine. Karmiole 71-106 1983 $50

GOODWIN, CARDINAL   John Charles Fremont, an Explanation of his Career. Stanford Univ., 1930. Folding map, backstrip faded. Argosy 710-33 1983 $25

GOODWIN, GERAINT   Conversations with George Moore. London: Ernest Benn, 1929. First edition. Orig. 3/4 morocco and decorated boards. One of 110 copies signed by author and Moore. Spine a bit rubbed. Very good. MacManus 279-3842 1983 $35

GOODWIN, HENRY K.   The Official Report of the Trial of... Boston, 1887. 1st ed. 8vo, contemporary calf, leather label. Morrill 288-650 1983 $20

GOODWIN, THOMAS   Transubstantiation a Peculiar Article of the Roman Catholick Faith. Printed in the year, 1688. First edition, 4to, wrapper, a very good copy. Fenning 61-165 1983 £14.50

GOODWIN, WILLIAM B.   The Truth About Leif Ericsson and the Greenland Voyages. Boston, 1941. 1st ed. Illus. Large 8vo, partly torn dw, very nice. Morrill 288-137 1983 $37.50

GOODWIN, WILLIAM WATSON   Syntax of the Moods and Tenses of the Greek Verb. London, 1897. 8vo, cloth. Salloch 385-118 1983 $45

GOODY Two Shoes: The Sick Robin & Mary the Maid of the Inn. J. March, nd (ca. 1845). 26 hand-col'd woodcuts. Printed on one side of page only. Magenta wrappers lettered in black. Traces of over-stitching along bkstrip, resewn, sl. wear edges of cvrs. & some sl. thumbing & marks contents, scarce, vg. Hodgkins 27-78 1983 £35

GOOUCH, THOMAS   Plain Truth Vindicated and Asserted. Waterford: Printed by S. Smith & Son, 1830. First edition, 8vo, orig. unlettered paper boards. Fenning 60-141 1983 £32.50

GOOUCH, THOMAS   The Poor Man's Claim to a Part in the Land of Life for Evermore. Waterford: Printed for the author by John Bull, 1817. First edition, errata leaf, 8vo, orig. boards, uncut. Little wear to spine. Fenning 62-142 1983 £35

GOPEL, ERHARD   Max Beckmann. Katalog der Gemalde. Bern: Kornfeld & Cie., 1976. 2 vols. Numerous illus. 321 plates (18 color). Large stout 4to. Cloth. Dust jacket. Edition limited to 1500 copies. Ars Libri 32-25 1983 $850

GORDIMER, NADINE   Face to Face. Johannesburg, 1949. First edition. Bookplate. Covers slightly bumped at the spine and bottom corners. Rubbed and slightly torn, internally repaired, price-clipped dustwrapper slightly chipped at the head and tail of the spine. Very good. Jolliffe 26-218 1983 £165

GORDON, ARMISTEAD C.   In the Picturesque Shenandoah Valley. Richmond, (1930). First edition. Photographs, some in color. Jenkins 152-768 1983 $35

GORDON, BENJAMIN LEE   Medieval & Renaissance Medicine. N.Y., (1959). Illus. First edition. Argosy 713-223 1983 $85

GORDON, CHARLES   Events on the Taeping Rebellion. London, 1891. Folding coloured facsimile map. 2 plates. Covers marked, spine faded. 8vo. Good. Edwards 1044-281 1983 £65

GORDON, DON   Civilian Poems/The Glass Mountain and Other Poems. New York: Beechhurst Press, (1946). 8vo. Cloth. Clippings about the books on the endboards, else fine in intact but lightly worn dj. In Our Time 156-324 1983 $20

GORDON, DUFF   Letters from the Cape. London: Humphrey Milford, 1927. 8vo. 20 plates. Orig. cloth. Rubbed. Adelson Africa-192 1983 $20

GORDON, ELIZABETH   More Really So Stories. Volland, (1929). Probable first edition. 8vo. Cloth backed pictorial boards. Full-page color illus. plus black & whites. Fine. Aleph-bet 8-217 1983 $38

GORDON, GRANVILLE   Sporting Reminiscences. London, 1902. 1st ed. Illus. in half-tone, & four in photogravure from drawings by Harington Bird, J.G. Millais, & Archibald Thorburn. 8vo. Morrill 288-138 1983 $25

GORDON, H. R.   Pontiac, Chief of the Siege of Detroit. NY (1897). First edition. Illus., nice blue 1/2 lea., marbled boards and end papers, nicely gilt-stamped spine. Original cloth covers bound in at back. Very good. King 46-159 1983 $50

GORDON, JAMES   A Request to Roman Catholicks to Answer the Queries Upon these Their Following Tenets. Printed for Brab, Aylmer, 1687. First edition, 4to, wrapper, a fine copy. Fenning 60-142 1983 £14.50

GORDON, JOHN B.   Reminiscences of the Civil War. New York, 1904. First edition. With an orig. letter from General Gordon inserted, one page, quarto, 1890. Illus. Orig. pictorial cloth. Extremely fine, near-mint copy. Jenkins 152-641 1983 $165

GORDON, JOHN J. H.   The Sikhs. London, 1914. 8vo. Orig. cloth. Coloured portrait frontis. 15 plates. Very slightly worn and faded. Small library stamps. Good. Edwards 1042-345 1983 £25

GORDON, LINDSAY   Poems of Adam Lindsay Gordon. London: Constable & Co., (1928). First edition. Orig. cloth. Dust jacket (slightly faded, worn and soiled). Presentation copy to John Galsworthy inscribed: "To John Galsworthy with the regard and admiration of Douglas Sladen." Near-fine. MacManus 278-2141 1983 $65

GORDON, MARY   Chase of the Wild Goose. Hogarth Press,
1936. First edition. Spine and covers a little marked and worn.
Internally nice. Rota 231-319 1983 £18

GORDON, MAURICE   Aesculapius Comes to the Colonies.
Ventnor, 1949. First edition. 8vo. Orig. binding. Dust wrapper.
Fye H-3-224 1983 $35

GORDON, S.   The Charm of Skye. 1929. 4 coloured
plates, 16 photographs and other illustrations, 8vo, cloth. A little
light foxing. Wheldon 160-386 1983 £20

GORDON, S.   Hill Birds of Scotland. (1915), 1930.
35 photographic illus., 8vo, cloth (trifle foxed). Wheldon 160-720
1983 £18

GORDON, S.   The Immortal Isles. (1926), 1936.
Coloured frontispiece, 5 coloured and 31 plain plates, 8vo, cloth.
Wheldon 160-385 1983 £20

GORDON, S.   In Search of Northern Birds. (1941).
19 photographic illus. and 1 plate of figures, 8vo, cloth. Wheldon
160-723 1983 £12

GORDON, S.   The Land of the Hills and the Glens.
1920. 57 illustrations, 8vo, cloth. Wheldon 160-384 1983 £25

GORDON, THOMAS F.   A Gazetteer of the State of New Jersey
(bound with) The History of New Jersey. Trenton: Daniel Fenton, 1834.
Colored folding map (tears mended on verso). Full calf. Very good.
Felcone 20-122 1983 $125

GORDON, WILLIAM JOHN   Perseus the Gorgon Slayer. S. Low,
nd (ca. 1885). Illus. by T.R. Spence. 20 chromolithograph plates
with decor. borders in col. to nearly every page. Brown cloth backed
glazed col'd pictorial bds., pink edges green patterned eps., corners
some wear, edges chipped, sl. thumbing, vg. Hodgkins 27-79 1983
£25

GORDON of Duncairn. London: Richard Bentley, 1858.
Orig. cloth. First edition. Edges very slightly worn and faded.
Corners slightly bumped. A near-fine, internally perfect, set.
MacManus 277-80 $135

GORDON-CUMMING, CONSTANCE FREDERICA   From the Hebrides to the Himalayas... London, 1876. 27 plates and numerous text illus. 2 vols.
Pictorial cloth, gilt. Inscribed on both titles "Jane E. Gordon Cumming with love from C. F. Gordon Cumming." 8vo. Good. Edwards 1044-
167 1983 £58

GORE, CATHERINE GRACE FRANCES MOODY   The Heir of Selwood. Henry
Colburn, 1838. First edition, 3 vols., half titles, half red calf,
little rubbed, green and brown labels, very good. Jarndyce 30-402
1983 £95

GORE, CATHERINE GRACE FRANCES MOODY   The Inundation; or, Pardon and
Peace. London: Fisher, Son & Col., n.d. First edition. Illus. by
George Cruikshank. Orig. gilt dec. red cloth, a.e.g., covers somewhat
soiled. Very good. MacManus 278-2295 1983 $85

GORE, CATHERINE GRACE FRANCES MOODY   Memoirs of a Peeress, or the
Days of Fox. Henry Colburn, 1837. 3 vols. bound in 2, 12mo., contemp.
half green calf, without half titles or ads, good copy of the first
ed. Hill 165-46 1983 £70

GORE, CATHERINE GRACE FRANCES MOODY   Mrs. Armytage; or, Female
Domination. Henry Colburn, 1836. 3 vols., 12mo., contemporary half
cloth, printed paper labels, grey board sides, uncut, very fair copy,
first ed. A scarce "silver fork" novel. Hill 165-47 1983 £65

GORE, CATHERINE GRACE FRANCES MOODY   Mothers and Daughters. London,
Henry Colburn and Richard Bentley, 1830. First ed., 3 vols., 12mo.,
contemporary half calf, mor. labels, gilt, 4 pp. of ads, some foxing
and vol. 1 a little sprung. Traylen 94-395 1983 £38

GORE, CATHERINE GRACE FRANCES MOODY   New Year's Day, a Winter's
Tale. London, Fisher, Son & Co., n.d. (1846). First edition, illus.
by George Cruikshank. Orig. gilt dec. cloth, covers slightly soiled.
Bookplate. Very good. MacManus 278-2296 1983 $125

GORE, CATHERINE GRACE FRANCES MOODY   The Sketch Book of Fashion.
Bentley, 1833. First ed., 3 vols., half red mor., little rubbed at
heads and tails of spines. Jarndyce 31-717 1983 £68

GORE, CATHERINE GRACE FRANCES MOODY   Sketches of English Character.
Richard Bentley, 1848. 2 vols. in 1, 12mo., 19th century half calf,
half title of vol. 1. Hill 165-48 1983 £35

GORE, CATHERINE GRACE FRANCES MOODY   The Snow Storm. London,
Fisher, Son & Co., n.d. First edition, illus. by George Cruikshank,
orig. gilt dec. red cloth, a.e.g., bookplate, covers lightly soiled,
very good. MacManus 278-2297 1983 $85

GORE, F. ST. J.   Lights and Shades of Hill Life in the
Afgan & Hindu Highlands... London, 1895. Folding map. Numerous
plates. Front cover slightly marked. 8vo. Orig. cloth. Good.
Edwards 1044-283 1983 £50

GORE-BROWNE, ROBERT   Lord Bothwell. 1937. 16 plates, 3 maps,
front of dust jacket mounted on fly, cloth, short slit at top of spine.
Bickersteth 77-118 1983 £16

GORER, G.   Himalayan Village. London, 1938.
32 plates. Thick 8vo. Orig. cloth. Good. Edwards 1044-284 1983
£40

GOREY, EDWARD   The Listing Attic. N.Y., (1954). First
edition. Thin 12mo, pict. boards; d.w. Argosy 714-336 1983 $125

GOREY, EDWARD   The Unstrung Harp. N.Y., Boston; Duell,
Sloan, Pearce & Little Brown; 1953. First edition. Small 8vo,
illus. by Gorey. Dust jacket (a trifle rubbed). Fine. Houle 22-428
1983 $150

GOREY, EDWARD   The Unstrung Harp; or, Mr. Earbrass
Writes a Novel. New York & Boston, 1953. First edition. Dust
wrapper. Small ink mark on flyleaf. Very nice. Rota 231-262 1983
£45

GOREY, EDWARD   THe Unstrung Harp. N.Y., (1953).
First edition. Thin 12mo, d.w. A child's inscription covers the
whole front flyleaf. Argosy 714-337 1983 $75

GOREY, EDWARD   The Unstrung Harp. NY, (1953). Very
good or better in lightly worn dustwrapper with name on inside flap and
corner clipped, very good. Quill & Brush 54-552 1983 $75

GORGAS, MARIE   William Crawford Gorgas, His Life and
Work. New York, 1924. First edition. 8vo. Orig. binding. Fye
H-3-751 1983 $25

GORGAS, WILLIAM CRAWFORD   Sanitation of the Tropics with Special
Reference to Malaria and Yellow Fever. Chicago, 1909. First edition.
Argosy 713-225 1983 $150

GORHAM, GEORGE C.   The Story of the Attempted
Assassination of Justice Field by a Former Associate on the Supreme
Bench of California. (N.Y.?, 1895). Cont. half calf. First
edition. Ginsberg 46-97 1983 $100

GORHAM, MAURICE   Back to the Local. London, 1949. First
English edition. Numerous full page black and white drawings by
Edward Ardizzone. Chipped and nicked dustwrapper slightly faded at
the spine. Near fine. Jolliffe 26-13 1983 £20

GORIS, JAN-ALBERT   Rubens in America. New York:
Pantheon, 1947. 11 plates. Large 4to. Cloth. Ars Libri 32-599
1983 $65

GORKY, MAXIM   A Confession. London: Everett & Co.,
1910. Gilt decorated cloth. First English edition. A fine copy.
Reese 20-457 1983 $40

GORKY, MAXIM ·   Reminiscences of Leonid Andreyev.
London, 1931. First English edition. One of 750 numbered copies.
Nice. Rota 230-387 1983 £18

GORKY, MAXIM   Twenty-Six and One. New York: Taylor, 1902. 1st American ed. Orig. red cloth, stamped in black. Uncommon. Fine copy. Jenkins 155-486 1983 $30

GORST, HAROLD E.   The Fourth Party. Smith, Elder, 1906. First edition, half title, front. and facs. letter. 2 pp ads. Orig. dull purple cloth. Jarndyce 31-177 1983 £16.50

GORTON, DAVID ALLYN (1832-1916)   An Essay on the Principles of Mental Hygiene. Philadelphia: J. B. Lippincott & Co., 1873. Ads. Publisher's pebbled brown cloth. First edition. Gach 95-172 1983 $35

GOSLING, W.G.   Labrador: Its Discovery, Exploration, and Development. London, 1910. 1st ed. Illus. and folding map. 8vo. Morrill 289-343 1983 $40

GOSNELL, HAROLD F.   Boss Platt and His New York Machine. Chicago, 1924. First edition in dust jacket. Frontis. Jenkins 152-296 1983 $30

GOSNELL, HARPUR ALLEN   Before the Mast in the Clippers. New York: The Derrydale Press, 1937. Illus. including 6 folding maps & a color frontis. Edition ltd. to 950 copies. Bookplate removed. Karmiole 71-41 1983 $100

GOSNELL, HARPUR ALLEN   Before the Mast in the Clippers. N.Y., 1937. Numerous illus. Half cloth. Covers heavily fire stained (esp. spine). Limited to 950 numbered copies. Good. King 45-480 1983 $40

GOSSE, EDMUND   The Augustan Books of Modern Poetry. London: Ernest Benn, Ltd, n.d. (1926?). First edition. Orig. printed wrappers. One of 18 copies printed on thick paper (so noted in pencil on the front cover). Presentation copy to Siegfried Sassoon inscribed on the front cover. Covers slightly darkened and soiled. Very good. MacManus 278-2299 1983 $350

GOSSE, EDMUND   The Autumn Garden. London: William Heinemann, 1909. First edition. Orig. cloth-backed boards. Paper label on spine. Label a bit worn. Very good. MacManus 278-2300 1983 $25

GOSSE, EDMUND   British Portrait Painters and Engravers of the 18th Century. Paris, London, N.Y., Berlin, 1906. First edition. Limited to 400 copies printed on fine, thick paper. Copy No. 251. 100 beautiful engravings after orig. works of art, 2 in full brilliant color, the other 98 in sepia tones, a few text illus. Folio. Orig. printed wrappers bound in cont. 3/4 crimson levant morocco and marbled boards. Uncut. Fine. Jenkins 152-642 1983 $225

GOSSE, EDMUND   Cecil Lawson. London: The Fine Art Society, Limited, 1883. First edition. Illus. by Hubert Herkomer, A.R.A. Folio. Orig. blue cloth. One of 200 large-paper copies containing original etchings by Herkomer and and Whistler. Small bookplate removed from front pastedown. Very good. MacManus 278-2301 1983 $450

GOSSE, EDMUND   The Collected Poems. London: William Heinemann, 1911. First edition. Frontispiece port. Orig. decorated cloth. Presentation copy inscribed: "Lady Dorothy Nevill from her affectionate Friend, the Author." Edges and endpapers slightly foxed. Front inner hinge starting. Newspaper clipping reviewing this book tipped to the front free endpaper. Near-fine. MacManus 278-2302 1983 $135

GOSSE, EDMUND   Coventry Patmore. London: Hodder & Stoughton, 1905. First edition. Frontis. port. Orig. cloth. Dust jacket. Very fine. MacManus 278-2304 1983 $25

GOSSE, EDMUND   English Odes. London: Kegan Paul, Trench & Co., 1884. Frontis. Handsomely rebound in 3/4 navy morocco & cloth. Fine. MacManus 278-2306 1983 $45

GOSSE, EDMUND   Gray. N.Y.: Harper & Brothers, n.d. Orig. cloth. From the library of J.B. Yeats, with his signature. Piece from the first preliminary page torn away. Spine and covers worn and spotted. Good. MacManus 280-5685 1983 $50

GOSSE, EDMUND   Hypolympia or The Gods in the Island. London: William Heinemann, 1901. First edition. Orig. parchment. Soiled. MacManus 278-2308 1983 $25

GOSSE, EDMUND   In Russet & Silver. Chicago: Stone & Kimball, 1894. First American edition. Orig. buckram. Paper label. One of 75 large paper copies. Covers a little soiled. Small newsclipping tipped to front endpaper. MacManus 278-2309 1983 $152

GOSSE, EDMUND   The Jacobean Poets. London: John Murray, 1894. First edition. Orig. cloth. Mint. MacManus 278-2310 1983 $20

GOSSE, EDMUND   The Life of Algernon Charles Swinburne. London: Macmillan, 1917. First edition. Orig. cloth. Covers worn. Presentation copy from C.L. Fraser to his wife, Grace, signed and dated, "Christmas, 1919." MacManus 278-2002 1983 $65

GOSSE, EDMUND   The Life of Algernon Charles Swinburne. London: Macmillan and Co., 1917. First edition. 8vo. Cloth. Illus. Covers are somewhat rubbed; bookplate and ink inscription. Oak Knoll 49-202 1983 $30

GOSSE, EDMUND   Life of William Congreve. London: William Heinemann, Ltd., 1924. Second impression, revised and enlarged. Orig. cloth. Presentation copy, inscribed on the flyleaf to "William S. McCormick from his affectionate friend the author, Camusdarrock, Sept, 11, 1924." Very good. MacManus 278-2312 1983 $35

GOSSE, EDMUND   Robert Browning. London: T. Fisher Unwin, 1890. First edition. Frontis. port. 8vo. Orig. parchment (soiled). MacManus 278-2313 1983 $25

GOSSE, EDMUND   Silhouettes. London: William Heinemann, 1925. First edition. Orig. cloth. Dust jacket (somewhat worn and soiled). Endpapers slightly foxed. Bookplate. Good. MacManus 278-2314 1983 $35

GOSSE, EDMUND   Silhouettes. London: William Heinemann, 1925. First edition. 8vo. Orig. brown cloth. Inscription, not in Gosse's hand on flyleaf. Very good. MacManus 278-2315 1983 $20

GOSSE, EDMUND   Studies In The Literature of Northern Europe. London, 1879. First edition. Frontis etched by L. Alma Tadema. Half green morocco, marbled boards and end papers, raised bands. T.e.g., spine brown, extremities worn else a good binding. King 46-293 1983 $35

GOSSE, EDMUND   Swinburne. (Edinburgh): Printed for private circulation, 1925. First edition. Orig. cloth-backed marbled boards. Limited to 125 copies. Spine a bit soiled and worn. MacManus 278-2316 1983 $45

GOSSE, PHILIP HENRY   Actinologia Britannica. A History of the British Sea-Anemones and Corals. 1860. 11 coloured and 1 plain plate, 8vo, original cloth. Plates coloured by W. Dickes. Head of spine trifle worn. Wheldon 160-1282 1983 £45

GOSSE, PHILIP HENRY   The Canadian Naturalist. 1840. 44 engravings, cr. 8vo, original cloth, head and foot of spine slightly defective. Very scarce. An ex-library copy; contents in good condition. Wheldon 160-387 1983 $65

GOSSE, PHILIP HENRY   Evenings at the Microscope. New York, 1883. 8vo, cloth, trifle used. Wheldon 160-157 1983 £15

GOSSE, PHILIP HENRY   Evenings at the Microscope. 1884. New edition, numerous illus., 8vo, cloth (trifle used). A few margins slightly stained. Wheldon 160-158 1983 £12

GOSSE, PHILIP HENRY   Evenings at the Microscope. S.P.C.K., N.d. Woodcuts, 8vo, prize morocco, gilt, g.e. Lacks final leaf. Wheldon 160-156 1983 £30

GOSSE, PHILIP HENRY   An Introduction to Zoology. London: Society for Promoting Christian Knowledge, n.d. (1844). First edition. 2 vols. Orig. cloth. Fine. MacManus 278-2317 1983 $175

GOSSE, PHILIP HENRY   Life in its lower, intermediate, and higher forms. 1857. First edition, plates and text-illus., 8vo, original blue cloth, joints close. Some crayon scribbling and colouring of some illus. Wheldon 160-154 1983 £15

GOSSE, PHILIP HENRY   Life in its lower, intermediate and
higher forms. 1857. Post 8vo, cloth, 6 plates, 2nd ed. Wheldon 160-
155 1983 £15

GOSSE, PHILIP HENRY   The Ocean. 1846. Cr. 8vo, cloth, 56
illustrations, binding worn. Reprint of the first edition of 1845.
Wheldon 160-314 1983 £20

GOSSE, PHILIP HENRY   The Ocean. (1860). Cr. 8vo, original
cloth, gilt. Wheldon 160-315 1983 £20

GOSSLER, J. C.   Lebensgeschichte Napoleon Bonaparte's,
des Ersten Kaisers der Franzosen... Reading, Pa.: Carl A. Bruckman,
1822. 3 engraved plates (1 folding), one by G. Gilbert. Portrait
frontis. lacking. Calf-backed boards. Excellent. Felcone 20-58
1983 $30

GOSSUIN OF METZ   Mirrour of the World or thymage of
the same. Westminster: William Caxton, 1481). First English
edition. First scientific book in English and the first English
illustrated book with the first English printed map. 11 woodcuts
and 25 (of 26) diagrams. Chapter initials supplied in red. Folio
(275 x 210 mm. 18th-century English calf, gilt and blind-tooled.
From the collections of T. Skeffyngton, with his ms. exlibris, and R.
Weller. Trasl. by Caxton. Kraus 164-36 1983 $145,000

GOTHER, JOHN   An Amicable Accommodation of the
Difference Between the Representer (John Gother) and the Answerer
(Sm. Sherlock). Printed by H. Hills, 1686. First edition, including
the initial leaf blank, 4to, wrapper, a very good copy. Fenning
61-167 1983 £16.50

GOTHER, JOHN   A Papist Mis-Represented and Represented.
(London:) printed, 1685. 4to, wrapper, light old marginal
staining, but a good sound copy. Fenning 61-168 1983 £21.50

GOTHER, JOHN   The Pope's supremacy asserted, from the
considerations of Some Protestants, and the practice of the
Primitive Church. Printed by Henry Hills, 1688. First edition. 4to,
wrapper. Fenning 61-169 1983 £28.50

GOTHER, JOHN   Reflections upon the Answer. (London,
1686). First edition, drop-title, 4to, wrapper. Fenning 61-170
1983 £21.50

GOTHER, JOHN   Reflections upon the answer to the
Papist Mis-Represented, &c. (London, 1686). First edition, drop-
title, 4to, wrapper, a fine copy. Fenning 62-141 1983 £21

GOTTHEIL, RICHARD J. H.   Zionism. Philadelphia, 1914.
First edition. Cloth, minor staining and wear. King 46-118 1983
$20

GOTTI, AURELIO   Vita di Michelangelo Buonarroti.
Firenze: Gazzetta d'Italia, 1875. 2 vols. bound in 1. 7 folding
tables and facsimile plates. Woodcut illus. in text. Small 4to.
Marbled boards, 1/4 leather. Ars Libri 33-241 1983 $185

GOTTSCHE, GERTRUD   Wolfgang Heimbach. Ein norddeutscher
Maler des 17. Jahrhunderts. Berlin: Deutscher Verein fur Kunst-
wissenschaft, 1935. 78 collotype illus. hors texte. Large 4to.
Cloth. Ars Libri 32-305 1983 $225

GOUBE, CITOYEN   Traite de la Physique Vegetale des
Bois... Paris, An IX, (1801). First edition. 8vo. Folding
table. Loose in half calf, worn. Light waterstains. Heath 48-
24 1983 £35

GOUCH, RICHARD   The Cambridge Tart. 1823. 8vo, t.e.g.,
other edges uncut, half red morocco, spine gilt. Bickersteth 77-209
1983 £58

GOUDIMEL, CLAUDE   Messes a Quatre Voix. Paris, 1928.
3 facs. plates, 4to, wrs. Salloch 387-132 1983 $35

GOUDY, FREDERIC W.   The Alphabet. New York: Mitchell
Kennerley, 1918. Folio, cloth, gilt. With 15 designs drawn and
arranged with explanatory text and illus. by the author. 26 full-
page plates and 30 figures in the text. Text set by Bertha M. Goudy
at The Village Press with types designed by the author; printed by
William E. Rudge. First edition. Corners worn. Duschnes 240-98
1983 $75

GOUDY, FREDERIC W.   The Capitals from the Trajan Column
at Rome. New York: Oxford University Press, 1936. First edition.
8vo. Cloth-backed boards. Very fine copy. Oak Knoll 48-173
1983 $75

GOUGAUD, LOUIS   Gaelic Pioneers of Christianity. Dublin:
Gill, 1923. First collected English edition. Cr. 8vo, orig. cloth.
Fenning 62-143 1983 £24.50

GOUGENOT DES MOUSSEAUX, HENRI ROGER   Des Proletaires, Necessite et
Moyens D'Amelior leur Sort. Paris, Mellior Freres et Lyon, Guyot
Pere et Fills, 1846. 1st ed., 8vo, uncut and in places unopened,
later morocco backed marbled boards, original printed wrappers bound
in, a very good copy. Extremely rare. Pickering & Chatto 21-41 1983
$1,250

GOUGH, H.   Old Memories. London, 1897. Plates.
8vo. Orig. cloth. Some slight spotting. Good. Edwards 1044-285
1983 £12

GOUGH, RICHARD   Anecdotes Of British Topography.
London: printed by W. Richardson and S. Clark, 1768. 1st ed, 4to,
contemporary speckled calf gilt, binding worn and joints broken.
Deighton 3-147 1983 £65

GOUGH, RICHARD   British Topography Or, An Historical
Account Of What Has Been Done For Illustrating The Topographical
Antiquities Of Great Britain And Ireland. London: printed for T.
Payne and Son, 1780. 2 vols, 4to, engraved vignette title-pages
and folding maps and plates, contemporary calf, morocco labels,
worn. Deighton 3-148 1983 £150

GOULD, BENJAMIN A.   Report to the Smithsonian Institution,
on the History of the Discovery of Neptune. Washington, 1850. Printed
wraps., very good. Reese 19-503 1983 $65

GOULD, DAVID   Life of Robert Morris. Boston, 1834.
Calf-backed boards. Very good. Felcone 20-60 1983 $25

GOULD, F. CARRUTHERS   "Who Killed Cock Robin?" Westminster
Gazette, 1896. Numerous b&w illus. Red cloth backed green pictorial
cloth, a.e.g. Re-cased, bkstrip soiled & fr. ep. cracked at hinge,
some thumbing. Told in pen & pencil by F.C.G. Scarce. Very good.
Hodgkins 27-93 1983 £15

GOULD, FREDERICK JAMES   The Pioneers of Johnson's Court...
London: Watts & Co., (1929). First edition. 8vo. Cloth. Spine
faded. Oak Knoll 49-204 1983 $30

GOULD, GEORGE   Borderland Studies... Philadelphia,
1896. First edition. 8vo. Orig. binding. Inscribed by the
author. Fye H-3-226 1983 $40

GOULD, GEORGE L.   Historical Sketch of the Paint, Oil,
Varnish and Allied Trades of Boston Since 1800 A.D. (Boston), For
Private Circulation, (1914). 1st ed. 8vo. Scarce. Morrill 286-
291 1983 $35

GOULD, GEORGE M.   Righthandedness and Lefthandedness.
Philadelphia: Lippincott, 1908. First edition. Publisher's green
cloth, worn. Illus. with plates. Gach 95-174 1983 $25

GOULD, GERALD   Monogamy. A series of dramatic lyrics.
Pelican Press for Allen and Unwin, 1918. 1st ed., sm. 8vo, title
within decorative border in red, typographic headlines, decorative
colophon, uncut in original paper wrappers over boards, wrappers
with repeated border in black and colophone, near fine copy of a
fragile book. Printed on japon. Deighton 3-149 1983 £35

GOULD, JOHN   A Century of Birds from the Himalaya
Mountains. 1832. Imp. folio, cont. full green morocco, gilt, ducal
arms on sides, 80 hand-coloured plates. Exceptionally clean copy.
Binding very skilfully rebacked. Wheldon 160-36 1983 £5,000

GOULD, JOHN   Europaische Vogel - Australische Vogelwelt - Vogelwelt Asiens - Vogelwelt von Neuguinea - Vogelwelt von
Sudamerika. Gorssel, 1966-71. 10 volumes, coloured plates, royal
8vo, cloth. Wheldon 160-728 1983 £125

GOULD, JOHN　　　　　Handbook to the Birds of Australia.
1865. 2 vols., 8vo, original green cloth, gilt. Revised edition of
the text to the folio "Birds of Australia." Wheldon 160-727 1983
£130

GOULD, JOHN　　　　　Icones Avium. 1837-38. 2 parts, 18
hand-coloured plates, 2 vols., imp. folio, original wrappers, in a
modern cloth book-box backed with green morocco. Very rare. Part 1
is neatly rebacked with the wrappers a trifle soiled. A good copy.
Wheldon 160-38 1983 £3,000

GOULD, JOHN　　　　　A Monograph of the Odontophorinae or
Partridges of America. 1850. Imp. folio, cont. half morocco, gilt,
32 fine hand-coloured plates. Some of the tissues are foxed slightly
affecting several plates; corner of one leaf of text and one plate very
slightly defective; title-page and frontis. slightly foxed. Wheldon
160-39 1983 £4,000

GOULD, JOHN　　　　　A Monograph of the Trogonidae or family
of Trogons. (1835-) 1838. 36 fine hand-coloured plates, imp. folio,
19th century half morocco, gilt back, raised bands, t.e.g. Flyleaves
are somewhat foxed, the last leaf of text creased, and there is some
slight offsetting, but generally a good clean copy in an attractive
binding. Wheldon 160-37 1983 £4,000

GOULD, JOHN M.　　　　　History of the First-Tenth-Twenty-
Ninth Main Regiment...1861...1866. Portland, 1871. 1st ed., illus.,
fine copy. Jenkins 151-107 1983 $150

GOULDSBURY, CULLEN　　　　　The Great Plateau of Northern Rhodesia.
Edward Arnold, 1911. First edition, with a folding map and 40 plates,
8vo, orig. cloth, gilt. The inside joints neatly strengthened.
Very good. Fenning 61-171 1983 £45

GOURLIE, JOHN H.　　　　　An Address, Delivered Before the
Mercantile Library Association, at its Eighteenth Annual Meeting.
New York, 1839. Disbound. Felcone 22-162 1983 $20

GOURMONT, REMY DE　　　　　Colours. New York: Blue Faun Publications, The Renaissance Series, (1929). Illus. Orig. cloth-backed
decorated boards with paper spine and cover labels. Publisher's slipcase (a trifle foxed). First of this edition. Handsomely bound and
printed. 3 illus. by Aubrey Beardsley. Bookplate. Very Fine. Mac-
Manus 277-233 1983 $35

GOURMONT, REMY DE　　　　　The Natural Philosophy of Love. London,
1926. First English edition. One of 1500 numbered copies, this copy
having Roman capitals at the foot of the spine. 4to. Corners rubbed
and covers somewhat soiled. Bookplate. Very good. Rota 230-480
1983 £25

GOVE, JESSIE A.　　　　　The Utah Expedition, 1857-1858. Letters
of... Concord: New Hampshire Historical Society, 1928. Original
cloth backed boards with paper label. Minor bumping to corners. 1
of 50 copies on large paper. Fine copy. Jenkins 153-225 1983 $175

GOWANLOCK, THERESA　　　　　Two Months in the Camp of Big Bear.
Parkdale, 1885. Illus., orig. cloth. First edition. Ginsberg 46-
142 1983 $150

GOWER, FOOTE　　　　　Sketch of the Materials for a New
History of Cheshire... Chester: by Mr. Lawton, 1771. 4to.
Wrappers. Repair at top of title, slight marginal worming, title
dusty. First edition. Heath 48-567 1983 £45

GOWER, JOHN　　　　　Confessio Amantis... London: Bell &
Daldy, 1857. 3 vols. 8vo. Later 3/4 brown morocco & marbled boards,
t.e.g. Front outer hinge of vol one a little rubbed. Bookplates.
Fine. MacManus 278-2318 1983 $75

GOWERS, WILLIAM R　　　　　A Case of Tumour of the Spinal Cord.
London, 1888. First edition. 8vo, cloth.' Photo. plate. Several
large folding tables. Argosy 713-229 1983 $250

GOWERS, WILLIAM R.　　　　　Clinical Lectures on Diseases of the
Nervous System. Philadelphia, P. Blakiston, 1895. First American
ed., worn copy, lib. stamp and spine label. Gach 95-175 1983 $40

GOWERS, WILLIAM R.　　　　　Diagnosis of Diseases of the Brain and
of the Spinal Cord. 1 color plate & 32 wood-engravings. Fine copy.
Argosy 713-226 1983 $100

GOWERS, WILLIAM R.　　　　　Diagnosis of Diseases of the Spinal Cord.
London, 1884. Illus. Third edition. Argosy 713-227 1983 $85

GOWERS, WILLIAM R　　　　　A Manual of Diseases of the Nervous
System. London, 1899. 374 text illus. 2 vols. 8vo, buckram.
Argosy 713-228 1983 $250

GOWERS, WILLIAM R.　　　　　A Manual of the Diseases of the Nervous
System. Philadelphia: Blakiston, 1903. 2 vols., 8vo., publisher's
blue cloth, worn ex-library copy. Vol. 1 is third ed., vol. 2 is
second edition. Gach 95-176 1983 $85

GOWERS, WILLIAM R.　　　　　Syphillis and the Nervous System.
Philadelphia, P. Blakiston, 1892. First American ed., fair ex-lib.
copy. Gach 95-177 1983 $22.50

GOWING, EMELIA AYLMER　　　　　By Thames and Tiber. London: Long,
1903. First edition. Orig. cloth. MacManus 278-2319 1983 $20

GOZMANY, L.　　　　　Septemlingual Dictionary of the Names
of European Animals. Budapest, 1979. 2 vols., royal 8vo, cloth.
Wheldon 160-486 1983 £110

GRABHORN, EDWIN　　　　　Ukiyo-E, "The Floating World". San
Francisco: Printed for The Book Club of California, 1962. Limited
to 400 copies. Illus. by 28 rare examples of Japanese woodblock prints.
28 color plates. Two-tone cloth. Minor rubbing. Small spot on front
cover. Nice. King 45-611 1983 $350

THE GRABHORN Press: A Catalogue of Imprints in the Collection of Henry
R. Wagner. Los Angeles, 1938. 8vo, linen-backed boards, paper label,
d/w. Frontis. illus. A pristine copy. Perata 28-178 1983 $85

GRACE'S Fortune. Strahan, 1868/7. First edition. 3 vols., bound as
one. Half title vol. I. Orig. green remainder cloth, rubbed.
Jarndyce 30-277 1983 £15

GRACIE, ARCHIBALD　　　　　The Truth About the Titanic. New York,
1913. 1st ed. Illus. 8vo. Morrill 286-607 1983 $20

GRAEFE, FELIX　　　　　Jan Sanders van Hemessen und seine
Identification mit dem Braunschweiger Monogrammisten. Leipzig:
Karl W. Hiersemann, 1909. 24 collotype plates with 28 illus. 4to.
Cloth. Ars Libri 32-306 1983 $250

GRAEFER, JOHN　　　　　A Descriptive Catalogue of upwards of
Eleven Hundred Species and Varieties of Herbaceous or Perennial Plants.
London: J. Smeeton, (1789). First edition. 8vo. Early half calf,
gilt. Heath 48-4 1983 £85

GRAESSE, JEAN GEORGE THEODORE　　　　　Tresor des livres rares et
precieux... Milano: Gorlich, (1950). 8 vols. including supplement.
Cloth, lettering on spines somewhat scuffed, paper browning, but a
good, tight set. Dawson 470-122 1983 $400

GRAETZ, LEO　　　　　Recent Developments in Atomic Theory.
London: Methuen, 1923. First edition. 8vo. Orig. green cloth.
Folding table, 39 text illus. and diagrams. Front cover slightly
rubbed, otherwise fine. Zeitlin 264-178 1983 $45

GRAF, A. B.　　　　　Exotica, Series 4. E. Rutherford, N.J.,
1982. 16,600 (405 coloured) illustrations, 2 vols., 4to, cloth.
Wheldon 160-1945 1983 £115

GRAFF, REGNIER DE　　　　　Opera Omnia... Lugd. Batav. Ex
Officina a Hackiana 1677. 8vo, engraved title page, portrait, 41
plates, mostly folding. Bound in full cont. vellum. Title in MS
on spine, some staining on upper board. Extensive notes in MS (of
Davidson) on front free endpaper. Tears in two or three folding
plates, without loss of text. Signature and stamp of J. Budge. Label
of Howard A. Kelly. A.E. Lownes bookplate. First collected edition.
Very good. Arkway 22-57 1983 $1,000

GRAFTON, RICHARD　　　　　A Chronicle at large and meere History
of the Affayres of Englande and Kinges of the same... London:
Henry Denham for R. Tottle and H. Toy, 1569. Second edition. 2
vols. in 1, printed in Black Letter. Thick folio. 18th century
reversed blind panelled calf, spine neatly repaired, orig. blind-
stamped calf preserved as doublures. Titles within woodcut borders,
woodcuts and woodcut initials, woodcut device on last leaf. Bookplate. A very good copy. Traylen 94-396 1983 £900

GRAHAM, G.   Life in the Mofussil. London, 1878.
First edition. 2 vols. Sm.8vo. Pictorial cloth worn and marked.
Ex-library. Good. Edwards 1044-286 1983 £40

GRAHAM, G. F. I.   The Life and Work of Syed Ahmed Khan.
Edinburgh & London, 1885. Frontis. Worn. 8vo. Orig. cloth. Good.
Edwards 1044-287 1983 £18

GRAHAM, GEORGE EDWARD   Schley and Santiago. Chicago, Conkey,
(1902). 1st ed. Illus. with photographs taken by author. 8vo.
Morrill 288-141 1983 $25

GRAHAM, GERALD S.   The Walker Expedition to Quebec, 1711.
Toronto, 1953. 24cm. 4 maps, limited to 550 copies, out of series,
and a further 550 copies for the Navy Records Society. Red cloth,
crested. Very good. McGahern 54-41 1983 $125

GRAHAM, JAMES   The Life of General Daniel Morgan, of
the Virginia Line of the Army of the U. S.. NY, 1856. 1st ed.
Port. Argosy 710-449 1983 $35

GRAHAM, JOHN W.   Naeva. A Tale of Ancient Rome. Macmillan, 1886. First edition. 2 vols., tall 8vo, half titles, ex-
library copy. Orig. dark blue cloth. Jarndyce 30-403 1983 £20

GRAHAM, JOSEPH A.   The Sporting Dog. N.Y., MacMillian,
1904. First edition. Illus. with frontis. and numerous plates and
illus. 3/4 green morocco over marbled boards, spine ruled and
decorated in gilt, t.e.g., marbled endpapers, unopened. One of 100
copies on large paper. Fine as issued. Houle 22-1071 1983 $295

GRAHAM, M.   Journal of a Residence in India. London,
1813. Second edition. Coloured frontis. 15 plates, 2 folding. 4to.
Modern half blue morocco. T.e.g. Good. Edwards 1044-290 1983 £160

GRAHAM, M.   Letters on India. London, 1814. Folding
map, 9 plates. Waterstain on title page. A few of the plates spotted.
Cont. half red calf. 8vo. Good. Edwards 1044-289 1983 £60

GRAHAM, ROBERT BONTINE CUNNINGHAME   Bibi. London, N.d. First edition. Orig. cloth. Dust jacket, a little worn. One of 250 copies
signed by the author. Very good. MacManus 277-1247 1983 $35

GRAHAM, ROBERT BONTINE CUNNINGHAME   Bibi. London, 1929. No. 155
of 250 signed, numbered copies, spine strip very spotted, else very
good. Quill & Brush 54-555 1983 $30

GRAHAM, ROBERT BONTINE CUNNINGHAME   Brought Forward. London, 1916.
First edition. Spine a little faded. Very nice. Rota 230-253 1983
£12

GRAHAM, ROBERT BONTINE CUNNINGHAME   The Conquest of the River Plate.
London, 1924. First edition. Illus. Spine faded. Nice. Rota 231-
265 1983 £15

GRAHAM, ROBERT BONTINE CUNNINGHAME   Doughty Deeds. London:
Heinemann, 1925. First edition, first issue, with publisher's wind-
mill device on back cover. Title page printed in red and black.
Illustrated. Brown cloth. Fine copy. Bradley 64-47 1983 $22.50

GRAHAM, ROBERT BONTINE CUNNINGHAME   Father Archangel of Scotland
and other essays. London, 1896. Second issue. Spine a little faded.
Nice. Rota 230-251 1983 £20

GRAHAM, ROBERT BONTINE CUNNINGHAME   The Horses of the Conquest.
Norman, University of Oklahoma Press, 1949. First American ed., 4to.,
orig. pictorial cloth, lightly used d.j., very fine. Jenkins 152-
643 1983 $65

GRAHAM, ROBERT BONTINE CUNNINGHAME   The Horses of the Conquest.
London, 1930. First edition. Illus. Covers marked and spine faded.
From the library of P. Lindsay, with his bookplate. Very good. Rota
231-266 1983 £12.50

GRAHAM, ROBERT BONTINE CUNNINGHAME   Portrait of a Dictator. London,
1933. First edition. Illus. Some foxing throughout. Inscription
on flyleaf. Nice. Rota 231-267 1983 £15

GRAHAM, ROBERT BONTINE CUNNINGHAME   Success. London: Duckworth &
Co., 1902. First edition. 12mo. Orig. wrappers. Spine slightly
chipped and faded. In a cloth slipcase. Very good. MacManus 277-1249
1983 $45

GRAHAM, ROBERT BONTINE CUNNINGHAME   Success. London: Duckworth &
Co., 1902. First edition. Orig. green cloth. MacManus 277-1240 1983
$27.50

GRAHAM, ROBERT BONTINE CUNNINGHAME   Thirty Tales & Sketches. London,
1929. First English edition. Very nice. Rota 230-254 1983 £12.50

GRAHAM, STEPHEN   Russia and the World. Cassell & Co.,
1915. First edition, with 8 plates, 8vo, orig. cloth, gilt. Binding
lightly spotted, but a very good copy. Fenning 62-144 1983 £10.50

GRAHAM, THOMAS   A Chemical Catechism... London: for
the Author, 1829. First edition. 8vo. Old sprinkled calf. Plate.
Text illus. Plate spotted, calf rebacked with repairs to edges.
A good copy. Zeitlin 264-179 1983 $120

GRAHAM, THOMAS   Chemical Reports and Memoirs, on
Atomic Volume... London: Printed for the Cavendish Society, 1848.
First edition. 8vo. Orig. green stamped cloth, gilt. 2 folding
plates, text figures. Defects to spine. Good, uncut copy. Zeitlin
264-180 1983 $75

GRAHAM, THOMAS   Chemical Reports and Memoirs, on
Atomic Volume... London: The Cavendish Society, 1848. First
edition. 8vo. Orig. cloth. 2 folding plates, text table.
Marginal waterstaining of plates, affecting images. Zeitlin
264-181 1983 $60

GRAHAM, THOMAS   Chemical Reports and Memoirs, on
Atomic Volume... London: The Cavendish Society, 1848. First
edition. 8vo. Orig. cloth. Inside front cover detached, spine
worn, lacking the two folding plates. Zeitlin 264-182 1983 $50

GRAHAM, THOMAS   Observations on Disorders of the Mind
and Nerves. London, 1848. 1st ed. 8vo. Orig. boards, cloth back,
paper label. Morrill 289-86 1983 $25

GRAHAM, THOMAS   Sure Methods of Improving Health, and
Prolonging Life. Printed for the author, 1827. First edition, large
12mo, orig. boards, uncut, with printed paper label, the spine
defective but boards holding and otherwise a fine copy. Illus.
Fenning 62-146 1983 £36

GRAHAM, W. A.   Siam. London, 1912. Second edition.
Folding map, plates. Thick 8vo. Pictorial cloth gilt. Good.
Edwards 1044-291 1983 £30

GRAHAM, WILLIAM   Last Links with Byron, Shelley, and
Keats. London: Leonard Smithers and Co., 1898. First edition.
8vo. Orig. dark green cloth. Rubbed. Ximenes 63-54 1983 $75

GRAHAM, WILLIAM   Last Links with Byron, Shelley, and Keats.
London: Leonard Smithers & Co., 1898. First edition. Rebound in 3/4
green morocco & cloth. Fine. MacManus 278-2321 1983 $65

GRAHAM, WILLIAM SYDNEY   Cage without Grievance. London:
Parton Press, 1942. First edition. Slightly rubbed at the corners.
Fine. Gekoski 2-67 1983 £40

GRAHAM, WILLIAM SYDNEY   2nd Poems. London: PL Editions Poetry,
1945. First edition. Slight pulling between one pair of gatherings,
spine faded, bookplate on front endpaper, very slightly used dustwrapper, otherwise a very good copy. Gekoski 2-68 1983 £70

GRAHAM, WINSTON   The Stranger from the Sea. London:
Collins, 1981. First edition, uncorrected advance proofs. Spine and
covers slightly worn. Very good. MacManus 278-2322 1983 $75

GRAHAME, JAMES   The Birds of Scotland. Edinburgh:
Wm. Blackwood, etc., 1806. First edition. Uncut, recently rebound
in half calf, black label. Jarndyce 30-705 1983 £28

GRAHAME, KENNETH   Dream Days. London & N.Y., (1902).
Pictorial cloth. T.e.g., covers heavily worn, back cover spotted. Ten
full page plates by M. Parrish. King 45-417 1983 $35

GRAHAME, KENNETH   Dream Days. New York & London, 1899.
First edition. Spine slightly darkened and worn. Bookplate designed
by A. Rackham. Nice. Rota 231-274 1983 $50

GRAHAME, KENNETH   Dream Days. Lane, nd (1898). Illus.
by Maxfield Parrish. Frontis. & pictorial title p. & 8 full page
photogravure illus. Brown vertical ribbed cloth with blue, green &
red pictorial fr. cvr. pale orange eps. designed by Parrish, uncut &
unopened, fine copy. Hodgkins 27-80 1983 £40

GRAHAME, KENNETH   Dream Days. New York & London, 1899.
First English edition. Yellow buckram lettered and decorated in blue
on spine and upper cover. Bookplate. Rota 231-277 1983 £30

GRAHAME, KENNETH   Dream Days. New York & London, 1899.
First English edition. Lavender watered silk cloth, lettered in blue
on spine and upper cover. Bookplate by A. Rackham. Good. Rota 231-
276 1983 £20

GRAHAME, KENNETH   Fun O' The Fair. Lon., (1929). Paperwraps, edges slightly creased and split with slit down spine, very good.
Quill & Brush 54-556 1983 $30

GRAHAME, KENNETH   Fun O'The Fair. London: J.M. Dent,
(1929). First edition. Illus. by Roberta F.C. Waudby. Orig. pictorial
wrappers. Covers faded, a little worn. MacManus 278-2324 1983 $25

GRAHAME, KENNETH   The Golden Age. London: Lane, 1895.
First edition. Orig. cloth. Covers a little worn. Very good.
MacManus 278-2325 1983 $85

GRAHAME, KENNETH   The Golden Age. Lane, 1900. Illus.
by Maxfield Parrish. Frontis. & pictorial title, 17 illus. Very
good copy. Hodgkins 27-81 1983 £40

GRAHAME, KENNETH   The Golden Age. London & N.Y., 1900.
Gilt-decorated cloth. T.e.g. Etched bookplate. Front inner hinge
loose, covers heavily worn. 18 full page plates plus title by M.
Parrish. King 45-418 1983 $50

GRAHAME, KENNETH   The Golden Age. London: The Bodley
Head, 1900. Illus. by Maxfield Parrish. Orig. decorated cloth, t.e.g.
Spine stained. MacManus 278-2326 1983 $30

GRAHAME, KENNETH   The Golden Age. London, 1895. First
English edition. Good copy only. Rota 231-273 1983 £12

GRAHAME, KENNETH   The Headswoman. N.Y. & London: John
Lane, 1898. First edition. Orig. decorated wrappers. Cover design
by Will Bradley. Covers a bit worn. Fine. MacManus 278-2327 1983
$85

GRAHAME, KENNETH   The Headswoman. London & New York,
The Bodley Head, 1898. 12mo. Wraps. Inscription on fly, some
light chipping to wraps, else very good-fine. In Our Time 156-327
1983 $35

GRAHAME, KENNETH   Pagan Papers. Elkin Mathews and John
Lane, 1894. First edition. One of 450 copies. Spine and edges of
covers faded. Bookplate, with 2 ALS, & one autograph postcard, signed,
from author to his publishers. Very good. Rota 231-272 1983 £250

GRAHAME, KENNETH   The Wind in the Willows. London: Methuen
and Co., (1908). First edition. With a frontispiece by Graham Robertson. Orig. gilt-pictorial cloth. Enclosed in a cloth box with a
leather label. Very good. MacManus 278-2328 1983 $1,250

GRAHAME, KENNETH   The Wind in the Willows. N.Y.: The
Heritage Press, (1940). First of this edition. Illus. by A. Rackham.
Orig. pictorial cloth. Dust jacket (a bit worn, spotted). With 12
full-page color plates by Rackham. Fine. MacManus 280-4300 1983
$85

GRAHAME, KENNETH   The Wind in the Willows. NY: Heritage
Press, (1940). Cover lightly soiled, near fine in slightly stained,
very good slipcase. Quill & Brush 54-557 1983 $50

GRAHAME-WHITE, CLAUDE   Flying. London: Chatto and Windus, 1930.
With 40 plates, index. Blue cloth. Karmiole 76-12 1983 $50

GRAINGER, JACOBO   Historia Febris Anomalae Batavae,
Annorum 1746... Edinburgh, 1753. 1st ed. 8vo. Contemporary
boards, calf back, leather label. Rubbed; hinges cracked. Morrill
289-87 1983 $37.50

GRAINGER, RICHARD DUGARD   Observatons on the Cultivation of
Organic Science. London, 1848. First edition. Author's presentation
copy, inscribed on title. Argosy 713-230 1983 $85

GRAND, W. JOSEPH   Illustrated History of the Union
Stockyards. Chicago (1901). Numerous photos, cloth, moderately
worn, covers dull. King 46-233 1983 $35

GRANDEAU, LOUIS   Instruction Pratique Sur L'Analyse
Spectrale... Paris, Mallet-Bachellier, 1863. 1st ed., 8vo, folding
chromolithograph, 2 folding engraved plates; contemp. quarter crimson
morocco, a little rubbed. Pickering & Chatto 22-44 1983 $185

GRANDIDIER, A.   Histoire Physique, Naturelle et
Politique de Madagascar. Lepidopteres. Paris, 1885-86. Atlas
of 63 plain plates, 4to, new buckram. Small hole in first 8
leaves of text. Wheldon 160-1087 1983 £85

GRANDMAMMA'S Easy Travels of Matty Macaroni the Organ Boy. Dean, nd
(ca. 1850). New Pictorial Toy Books series. 9 hand col'd engrs.
White wrappers with black pictorial decor. fr. cvr., cvrs. some
rubbing & stains, etc., resewn, occasional fox mark, vg. Hodgkins
27-82 1983 £42

GRANDVILLE, J.   Vie Privee et Publique des Animaux.
Paris, 1867. Numerous illustrations, royal 8vo, new cloth, gilt.
Slight signs of use internally. Wheldon 160-487 1983 £45

GRANGE, W.   The Battles and Battle Fields of Yorkshire. York, 1854. Sm. 8vo. Orig. cloth. Frontis. map. Spine faded.
Slightly worn. Good. Edwards 1042-356 1983 £25

GRANT, ANNE   Letters From The Mountains. London:
Longman, Hurst, Rees & Orme, 1806. First edition. 3 vols. Orig.
boards with volume number imprinted on spine. Spine ends and edges
slightly chipped. Hinges weak although cords intact. Covers slightly
soiled. MacManus 278-2330 1983 $350

GRANT, ANNE   Letters from the Mountains. London:
Longmans, etc., 1807. Second edition. 3 vols., 12mo. Cont. marbled
boards, blue morocco spines, gilt. Half-titles. Traylen 94-397 1983
£16

GRANT, ANNE   Memoirs of an American Lady. London:
Longmann etc., 1808. First edition. 2 vols. 12mo. Orig. boards,
uncut. Paper spines. 2 pp. of ads. in vol. 1 and 36 pp. in vol. 2.
Spines a little defective. Traylen 94-398 1983 £95

GRANT, ANTHONY   An Historical Sketch of the Crimea.
Bell & Daldy, 1855. First edition. 32 pp ads. Orig. mustard-brown
cloth, v.g. Jarndyce 31-137 1983 £12.50

GRANT, BLANCHE C.   Taos Indians. Taos, New Mexico, 1925.
Plates. Original stiff printed wrappers. First edition. Fine copy.
Jenkins 153-229 1983 $75

GRANT, C.   Observations on the State of Society.
London: Privately printed, (1813). 4to. Half morocco. Good.
Edwards 1044-292 1983 £135

GRANT, EMMA F.   Remembrances of a Pioneer Woman. San
F., 1926. Portrait. Orig. 12mo, boards with paper label. First
edition. Privately printed. Ginsberg 47-96 1983 $35

GRANT, GEORGE MUNRO   The Easternmost Ridge of the Continent. Chicago, 1899. 1st ed. Illus. by wood engravings from orig. drawings by A.B. Frost, et al. 4to. Some rubbing. Morrill 287-132 1983 $35

GRANT, GEORGE MUNRO   The Easternmost Ridge of the Continent. Chicago: Belford and Co., 1899. 4to. 30cm. Extensively illus. Brown decorated cloth. Fine. McGahern 54-69 1983 $65

GRANT, GEORGE MUNRO   Picturesque Spots of the North. Chicago: Belford & Co., 1899. 4to. 30cm. Extensively illus. Green decorated cloth, fore-edges on the boards damp-stained else a very good copy. McGahern 54-70 1983 $45

GRANT, JAMES   The Bench and the Bar. London: Henry Colburn, 1837. First edition. 2 vols. 8vo. Cont. half calf, gilt, some wear. Heath 48-226 1983 £40

GRANT, JAMES   The Great Metropolis. Saunders & Otley, 1837. First edition, 2 vols. 16 pp inserted ads., vol. I, 4 pp ads. vol. II. Orig. boards, purple-brown cloth spines, paper labels. Jarndyce 31-252 1983 £28

GRANT, JAMES   Jane Seton. G. Routledge, 1853. First edition, 2 vols. Engr. front and title in both vols. 2 pp ads. vol. II. Orig. brown cloth, v.g. Jarndyce 30-404 1983 £65

GRANT, JAMES   The Master of Aberfeldie. London: Hurst & Blackett, 1884. First edition. 3 vols. Orig. cloth. Presentation copy to author's brother inscribed on the half-title page of vol. one: "To his brother John; with the best love of the author, 10th May 1884." Inner hinges weak. Bookplate. Fine. MacManus 278-2331 1983 $1,000

GRANT, JAMES   Memoirs and Adventures of Sir William Kirkaldy of Grange, Knight, Commander of French Horse... William Blackwood, 1849. 8vo, orig. cloth, blocked in blind, worn at head and foot of spine, cloth slit at joints. Bickersteth 77-119 1983 £20

GRANT, JAMES   Miss Cheyne of Essilmont. London: Hurst & Blackett, 1883. First edition. 3 vols. Orig. cloth. Fine. MacManus 278-2332 1983 $225

GRANT, JAMES   Only an Ensign. Tinsley Brothers, 1871. First edition. 3 vols., bound as one. Small stamps on titles. Half dark blue morocco. Jarndyce 30-405 1983 £24

GRANT, JAMES   Shall I Win Her? London: Tinsley Brothers, 1874. First edition. 3 vols. Orig. cloth. Several inner hinges cracking. Covers somewhat soiled. Good. MacManus 278-2333 1983 $150

GRANT, JAMES   Sketches in London. London: Thomas Tegg, 1840. Second edition. 24 humourous illus. by "Phiz," and others. Orig. cloth. With engraved title-page dated 1838. Shelf-number pasted to front endsheet. Cont. owner's signature on title-page. Very good. MacManus 278-2334 1983 $75

GRANT, JAMES   Sketches in London. W.S. Orr, 1838. First edition, front. engr. title and illus. by "Phiz", and others. Some foxing to plates, half calf, a little rubbed. Jarndyce 31-253 1983 £40

GRANT, JAMES   Sketches of London. Phila.: Carey & Hart, 1839. First American edition. 2 vols. 8vo. Orig. cloth. Spines faded. Labels a trifle worn. Very good. MacManus 278-2335 1983 $50

GRANT, JAMES   Vere of Ours, The Eighth of King's. London: Tinsley Brothers, 1878. First edition. 3 vols. Orig. cloth. Presentation copy inscribed: "To his brother John; with the best love of the author; 4th September 1878." Spines and covers very slightly rubbed. Bookplate. Former owner's signature. Fine. MacManus 278-2336 1983 $1,000

GRANT, JAMES HOPE   Incidents in the China War of 1860. Edinburgh: W. Blackwood, 1875. First edition, with 3 folding maps, half title neatly removed, 8vo, orig. cloth, a very good copy. Fenning 62-147 1983 £24.50

GRANT, JOHN CAMERON   The Ethiopian. Paris: Charles Carrington, 1900. American Issue. Name on title-page. Bookplate. Good. Rota 230-500 1983 £30

GRANT, U. S.   Catalogue of the Marine Pliocene and Pleistocene Mollusca of California and Adjacent Regions. San Diego, 1931. Wheldon 160-1404 1983 £40

GRANT, WILLIAM LAWSON   Principal Grant. Toronto: Morang & Co., 1904. 23cm. Photo-gravure frontis. portrait. Rag paper, green cloth. Very good. McGahern 54-71 1983 $30

THE GRANTA and Its Contributors. London: Constable, 1924. First edition. 4to. Orig. cloth-backed boards. Printed by the Chiswick Press. Spine worn. MacManus 278-2337 1983 $30

GRANTS of Land to the Minnesota and Pacific R.R. Co. and Others... St. Paul: Goodrich, Somers & Co., Printers, 1857. Half morocco. Very rare. Jenkins 153-368 1983 $25

GRANVIK, H.   Contributions to East African Ornithology: Birds. Berlin, Jnl. f. Orn., Sonderheft, 1923. Map and 10 plates (5 coloured), 8vo, morocco (trifle rubbed). Wheldon 160-732 1983 £20

GRANVILLE, CHARLES   Sir Hector's Watch. London: John Murray, 1887. First edition. Orig. cloth-backed boards. Title-page torn at lower corner. Foxing. Inner hinges weak. Covers slightly worn and dust-soiled. Good. MacManus 278-2338 1983 $20

GRANVILLE, JOSEPH MORTIMER (1833-1900)   Common Mind-Troubles. Salem, Mass.: S. E. Cassino/NY: Orange Judd Co., 1879. Orig. publisher's printed cloth, spine tips rubbed. Gach 95-178 1983 $35

GRANVILLE, R.   The King's General in the West. London, 1908. 8vo. Orig. cloth. Frontis. 8 plates (2 folding). Orig. brown cloth backed grey boards. Uncut. Some slight marginal foxing. Good. Edwards 1042-357 1983 £15

GRANVILLE-BARKER, HARLEY   The Marrying of Ann Leete. London: Sedgwick & Jackson, 1909. First edition. Orig. vellum-backed boards. One of 50 copies on handmade paper, each signed by author. With an inscription by the author. Binding a bit soiled. Endpapers browned. Good. MacManus 278-2339 1983 $100

GRANVILLE-BARKER, HARLEY   The Secret Life. London: Chatto & Windus, 1923. First edition. Orig. cloth. Paper spine label (a trifle darkened). Presentation copy to John Galsworthy inscribed: "J.G. from H.G.-B., 12.9.23." Spine and covers slightly darkened and scratched. Good. MacManus 278-2340 1983 $75

GRANVILLE-BARKER, HELEN   The Locked Book. London: Sidgwick & Jackson Ltd., (1936). Third edition and the first to be revised by Gray. 3/4 morocco and marbled boards, with marbled endpapers. Contains the first publication of the last stanza on page 11 before the Epitaph. Bookplate of H. Buxton Forman. Few neat annotations in a cont. hand in the margins of the text. Edges slightly rubbed. Fine. MacManus 278-2350 1983 $1,250

GRASSE, P. P.   Traite de Zoologie, Vol. 1, Phylogenie, Protozoaires. Paris, 1952-53. 3 coloured plates and 1663 text figures, 2 vols., royal 8vo, orig. boards. A clean second-hand copy. Wheldon 160-1283 1983 £90

GRASSI, ORAZIO   Libra Astronomica ac Philosophica qua Galilaei Galilaei Opiniones de Cometis a Mario Guidicio... Perugia: Marcus Naccarinus, 1619. Small 4to. Cont. vellum. Woodcut diagrams. First edition. Kraus 164-89 1983 $2,500

GRATTAN, THOMAS COLLEY   The Heiress of Bruges. Henry Colburn and Richard Bentley, 1830. First edition. 4 vols. 12mo, lacks 2 ad. leaves, cont. polished calf, blind-stamped and gilt, black and green labels, with the ticket of Tho. Brown, Bookseller, Arcade, Newcastle). A fine set. Hannas 69-80 1983 £100

GRATTAN, THOMAS COLLEY   Jacqueline of Holland. Henry Colburn and Richard Bentley, 1831. First edition. 3 vols. Large 12mo, half-title in vol. I, possibly lacking in the other two. Cont. half calf. Hannas 69-82 1983 £60

GRATTAN, THOMAS COLLEY   Traits of Travel. Henry Colburn, 1829.
First edition. 3 vols., large 12mo, cont. cloth, with the ticket of
S. Roberts, Oswestry. Inner margin of title and two following leaves
in vol. III torn and repaired. Hannas 69-81 1983 £35

GRATTON, JOHN   A Journal of the Life of... First
edition, 8vo, cont. calf, worn but sound, wanting label, some light
signs of use, a good sound copy. Fenning 60-144 1983 £21.50

GRAU, SHIRLEY ANN   The Black Prince and Other Stories.
New York: Knopf, 1955. Cloth and boards. First edition. A fine
copy in dust jacket which shows the slightest traces of use. Reese
20-461 1983 $75

GRAUNT, JOHN   Natural and Political Observations.
Oxford: John Martyn and James Allestry, 1665. 4th ed., small 8vo,
2 folding tables, slight browning to edges, 18th cent. panelled
sheep, rebacked in morocco, corners worn but a crisp copy. Pickering
& Chatto 21-42 1983 $550

GRAUTOFF, OTTO   Nicolas Poussin. Munchen: Georg
Muller, 1914. 2 vols. bound in 1. Vol. 1: 29 plates, 81 text
illus. Vol. 2: Hand-colored color chart, 160 plates (keyed by
numbered areas to color chart on tissue guards), 24 text illus.
Large stout 4to. Marbled boards, 3/4 leather. Ars Libri 32-536
1983 $250

GRAVENHORST, J. L. C.   Vergleichende Uebersicht des Linneischen
und Einiger Neuern Zoologischen Systeme. Gottingen, 1807. 8vo,
contemporary boards. Very rare. Wheldon 160-488 1983 £60

GRAVES, CHARLES L.   More Hawarden Horace. London: Smith,
Elder, & Co., 1896. First edition. Orig. cloth. Very good. Mac-
Manus 279-3380 1983 $35

GRAVES, JOHN   Goodbye to a River. New York: Knopf,
1960. 1st ed. Orig. cloth, dj. Fine copy inscribed by Graves with
four line inscription, 1980. Jenkins 155-1389 1983 $85

GRAVES, JOHN   The Last Running. Austin: The Encino
Press, (1974). Oblong quarto. Half morocco and cloth, paper label.
Illus. by John Groth. First edition. One of 300 numbered copies,
specially bound, and signed by the author, artist and designer,
and with an orig. ink sketch by Groth. Very fine in slipcase. Reese
20-986 1983 $75

GRAVES, RICHARD   The Festoon. London: Printed for
Mess. Robinson and Roberts...and W. Frederick at Bath. 1767. 12mo,
crimson straight grain morocco, gilt; g.e.; errata slip tipped onto
A12v; 3pp. of pub.'s ads.; bookplate of Charles Tennant. Second
edition. A fine copy. Quaritch NS 7-57 1983 $425

GRAVES, RICHARD   The Reveries of Solitude. Bath: by
R. Cruttwell..., 1793. First edition. 8vo. Modern boards. Vignette
on title, small hole in title, some light usage. Heath 48-316 1983
£75

GRAVES, ROBERT   Adam's Rib. (NY, 1958). Limited to 100
numbered copies signed by author and illus., James Metcalf. Very good
in torn and chipped, aged dustwrapper. Quill & Brush 54-559 1983
$90

GRAVES, ROBERT   But It Still Goes On. London, 1930.
First State. Dust wrapper. Fine. Rota 230-259 1983 £35

GRAVES, ROBERT   But it Still Goes on. N.Y., (1931).
First American edition. 8vo, cloth; rubbed. Argosy 714-339 1983
$35

GRAVES, ROBERT   Claudius The God and his wife Messaline.
London: Arthur Barker, 1934. First edition. Large 8vo. Orig. cloth.
Dust jacket, slightly worn and partially soiled. Fine copy. Jaffe
1-113 1983 $125

GRAVES, ROBERT   Claudius the God and His Wife Messalina.
London, Barker, 1934. First edition. Fold-out diagram. Dust
jacket. Very good. Houle 21-383 1983 $45

GRAVES, ROBERT   Colophone to Love Respelt. Privately
Printed, 1967. First edition. One of 386 numberd copies, signed by
author, this unnumbered and marked "Out of Series." Stiff wrappers.
Dust wrapper. Fine. Rota 231-287 1983 £40

GRAVES, ROBERT   Country Sentiment. Lon., (1920). Edges
slightly faded, flys lightly offset, very good in lightly chipped and
rubbed, slightly soiled dustwrapper. Quill & Brush 54-560 1983 $125

GRAVES, ROBERT   The Feather Bed. Hogarth Press, 1923.
First edition. Orig. pink decorated boards designed by William
Nicholson (some rubbing and light soiling), else good-very good. One
of 250 numbered copies, signed by the author. Houle 22-443 1983
$350

GRAVES, ROBERT   The Green-Sailed Vessel. (London):
Privately printed, 1971. Ltd. edition. One of 500 signed copies.
Argosy 714-340 1983 $75

GRAVES, ROBERT   Hercules, My Shipmate. NY, (1945). Very
good in slightly frayed and chipped, very good dustwrapper with price
inked out. Quill & Brush 54-561 1983 $40

GRAVES, ROBERT   Hercules, My Shipmate. NY, (1945). Very
good in frayed, very good dustwrapper, owner's name. Quill & Brush
54-562 1983 $30

GRAVES, ROBERT   Impenetrability or The Proper Habit
of English. London: The Hogarth Press, 1926. First edition. 12mo.
Orig. boards. Boards a little rubbed and soiled at edges, otherwise a
very good copy. Jaffe 1-109 1983 $65

GRAVES, ROBERT   Impenetrability - or The Proper Habit
of English. London: The Hogarth Press, 1926. First edition.
Front free endpaper slightly spotted. Spine slightly worn and faded.
Very good. Jolliffe 26-224 1983 £20

GRAVES, ROBERT   King Jesus. London, 1946. First edition.
Frayed dust wrapper. Nice. Rota 231-283 1983 £15

GRAVES, ROBERT   Lawrence and The Arabs. London:
Jonathan Cape, (1927). First edition. Illus. edited by Eric
Kennington, maps by Herry Perry. 8vo. Orig. cloth. Dust jacket.
Badly torn, but very scarce, jacket, otherwise a fine copy. Jaffe
1-111 1983 $45

GRAVES, ROBERT   Mrs. Fisher. Lon., 1928. Edges rubbed,
book slightly bowed, else near very good in soiled and lightly chipped,
internally mended, good dustwrapper. Quill & Brush 54-564 1983 $125

GRAVES, ROBERT   Poems (1914-1926). London: William
Heinemann, Ltd., 1927. First edition. 8vo. Orig. decorated cloth
with paper labels. One of 1000 copies printed. Fine copy. Jaffe
1-110 1983 $150

GRAVES, ROBERT   Poems (1926-1930). Lon., 1931. Limited
to 1000 copies, light interior foxing, cover rubbed and lightly worn,
spine label slightly chipped (extra laid-in), good or better, owner's
name. Quill & Brush 54-567 1983 $60

GRAVES, ROBERT   Poems 1926-1930. London, 1931. First
edition. One of 1000 copies. Torn and repaired dust wrapper. Very
nice. Rota 230-260 1983 £35

GRAVES, ROBERT   Poems 1929. Seizin Press, 1929. First
edition. One of 225 numbered copies, signed by author. Orig. green
buckram. Spine and edges of covers a little faded. Names and untidy
deletions on flyleaf. Nice. Rota 230-258 1983 £75

GRAVES, ROBERT   Poetic Unreason And Other Studies.
(London): Cecil Palmer, (1925). First edition. 8vo. Orig. cloth
with paper label on spine. Fine copy. Jaffe 1-107 1983 $150

GRAVES, ROBERT   Proceed Sergeant Lamb. New York, (1941).
8vo. Cloth. Inscription on front fly, else as new copy in dj.
In Our Time 156-329 1983 $45

GRAVES, ROBERT   The Real David Copperfield. London:
Arthur Barker, Ltd., (1933). First edition. 8vo. Orig. cloth.
Dust jacket, trifle nicked. Very fine copy. Jaffe 1-112 1983
$250

GRAVES, ROBERT   Sergeant Lamb Of The Ninth. London:
Methuen & Co., Ltd., (1940). First edition. 8vo. Frontis. Orig.
cloth. Dust jacket designed by John Aldridge, slightly worn. Very
fine copy. Jaffe 1-114 1983 $125

GRAVES, ROBERT   Sergeant Lamb of the Ninth. London,
1940. First edition. Inscription. Slightly rubbed dustwrapper
chipped at the head and tail of the spine. Very good. Jolliffe
26-226 1983 £25

GRAVES, ROBERT   Sergeant Lamb's America. New York
(1940). 8vo. Wraps. An advance copy in wrappers of the 1st
American ed. In the published dj of the book. Jacket has some
light wear near the top edge of the front flap, else about fine. In
Our Time 156-328 1983 $300

GRAVES, ROBERT   The Shout. London, 1929. First edition.
One of 530 numbered copies, signed by author. Dust wrapper. Rota
231-281 1983 £75

GRAVES, ROBERT   The Shout. Lon., 1929. Limited to 530
numbered and signed copies, flys slightly offset from wrapper, else
very good in lightly chipped, slightly soiled, very good dustwrapper.
Quill & Brush 54-569 1983 $125

GRAVES, ROBERT   Welchman's Hose. London: The Fleuron,
1925. First edition. Illus. with wood engravings by Paul Nash.
Limited to 525 printed at the Curwen Press. Fine in cloth-backed
boards with very small bump to one top edge. Bookplate. Bromer 25-
51 1983 $200

GRAVES, ROBERT   Welchman's Hose. London: The Fleuron,
1925. First edition. Wood engravings by Paul Nash. 8vo. Orig.
cloth-backed decorated boards. One of 525 copies printed. Fine
copy. Jaffe 1-108 1983 $175

GRAVES, ROBERT   Whipperginny. London: William Heinemann, Ltd., (1923). First edition. 8vo. Orig. decorated boards.
One of 1000 copies printed. Head of spine worn, outer hinge starting,
otherwise a good copy. Jaffe 1-106 1983 $84

GRAVES, ROBERT   The White Goddess. New York, 1948.
8vo. Cloth. A fine copy in perfect dj. In Our Time 156-330 1983
$125

GRAVES, WILLIAM   History of the Kickapoo Mission and
Parish, the First Catholic Church in Kansas. St. Paul, Ks., 1938.
Illus. Orig. wraps. First edition. Ginsberg 47-406 1983 $30

GRAVES, WILLIAM   Life and Letters of Fathers Ponziglione,
Schoenmakers, and Other Early Jesuits at Osage Mission. St. Paul,
Ks., 1916. Crudely printed. Illus. Orig. wraps. First edition.
Ginsberg 47-407 1983 $50

GRAY, ALONZO   Elements of Chemistry... New York:
Dayton & Newman; Boston: Saxton and Peirce, 1842. 12mo. Cont.
sheep. Numerous text illus. Front cover detached, back partially
so. Very good internally. Zeitlin 264-186 1983 $45

GRAY, ANDREW B.   Survey of a Route for the Southern
Pacific R.R. an the 32nd Parallel. Cincinnati, 1856. Errata slip.
33 lithographed plates. Final leaf of text and large folding map
neatly supplied in facs. Wraps. wanting. Scattered foxing. In a
cloth portfolio and slipcase. Felcone 21-48 1983 $400

GRAY, CHARLES   Poems by...of the Royal Marines.
Cupar: R. Tullis, 1811. Half title, black straight-grained morocco,
spine gilt, a.e.g., v.g. Inscribed presentation copy from the author.
Jarndyce 30-708 1983 £38

GRAY, DAVID   Gallops I, Gallops II; Mr. Carteret.
N.Y., 1929. Gilt stamped red cloth, t.e.g., uncut, (spines a bit
faded), one of 750 copies. Signed by the author in volume I. 3
vols. Good - very good. Houle 22-299 1983 $150

GRAY, DAVID   Gallops. New York, 1899-1903. 2nd and
1st eds. Pasted into vol. 1 is a 5-line inscription by author. 2
vols., 12mo. Backstrips faded. Morrill 287-133 1983 $35

GRAY, EDWARD F.   Leif Eriksson, Discoverer of America,
A.D. 1003. NY, 1930. Illus. Argosy 710-131 1983 $20

GRAY, G. R.   The Genera of Birds. 1844-49. 3 vols.,
imp. 4to, contemporary half morocco, gilt, 186 hand-coloured plates and
152 plain plates. Very scarce. A few very minor creases in vol. 1
and the plain plates are foxed. Wheldon 160-41 1983 £5,500

GRAY, G. R.   List of Specimens of Birds in the
British Museum. 1848-68. Parts 1-5, together 8 parts in 5 vols.,
12mo, 3 vols cloth (good ex-library), 3 vols. wrappers. Wheldon
160-733 1983 £40

GRAY, JOHN CHIPMAN   War Letters, 1862-1865. Boston, 1927.
First edition, 1275 copies printed. 8vo. Morrill 290-640 1983 $20

GRAY, PETER   People of Poros. NY, 1942. Illus.
8vo, cloth. Salloch 385-353 1983 $20

GRAY, THOMAS   Designs by Mr. R. Bentley for six
Poems by Mr. T. Gray. London: for J. Dodsley, 1775. 4to. Cont.
straight-grained red morocco, wide gilt borders on sides with
decoration, gilt panelled spine, inner gilt dentelles, edges gilt.
Engraved portrait, vignette title-page, 6 full-page plates, 13
vignettes, and 6 initials, engraved by J.S. Muller and C. Grignion
after designs by Bentley. From the library of Charles Tennent
with his bookplate. Traylen 94-402 1983 £15

GRAY, THOMAS   Designs by R. Bentley, For Six Poems by
Mr. T. Gray. London: Printed for R. Dodsley, in Pall-Mall, 1753.
Third edition, published in the same year as the first. Folio. Full
cont. calf, rebacked with remainder of orig. spine laid down.
Lacks half-title. The A.E. Newton copy, with his bookplate and one other on
the front endsheet. Light foxing throughout. Small nick at fore-edge
of most leaves, not affecting text. Good. MacManus 278-2351 1983
$175

GRAY, THOMAS   An Elegy Written in a Country Church Yard.
London: Printed for R. Dodsley in Pall-Mall; and sold by M. Cooper
in Pater-noster Row. 1751. Quarto, disbound and uncut, with orig.
stab-holes in the inner margins. A clean tear extending half-way across
the title, not affecting any printed surface, a minor marginal
waterstain to B1, and the letter "F" in "FINIS" at the end of the
text is punched out. In a folding case. Quaritch NS 7-59 1983 $750

GRAY, THOMAS   An Elegy Written in a Country Church
Yard. London: R. Dodsley, 1752. "Seventh edition, corrected."
Later wrappers (slightly frayed and soiled; with "Elegy of Gray.
Seventh Edition. 1752" written on the front wrapper in a recent hand.
Early owner's signature on the title-page. Some pages slightly soiled.
Very good. MacManus 278-2350a 1983 $150

GRAY, THOMAS   Elegia... Cambridge: sold by the
editor, and J. Deighton, 1782. First edition of this translation.
Large 8vo. Modern wrappers. Uncut copy. Ximenes 63-366 1983
$90

GRAY, THOMAS   Elegy. Longmans, 1846. 1st edn.
Illuminated by Owen Jones. Brown repousse calf, heavily embossed
covers, gilt dentelles, a.e.g. (Binder's ticket of Remnant & Edmonds)
(eps. discol'd at edges & some cracking of hinges, top/bottom bkstrip
repr'd), v.g. Hodgkins 27-372 1983 £120

GRAY, THOMAS   An Elegy. S. Low, etc. 1869 with 16
illus. from drawings by R. Barnes, R.P. Leitch, E.M. Wimperis, et al.,
printed in colours by Cooper, Clay & Co., 4 facs. (text printed on one
side only). 1st edn. Green sand grain cloth gilt, bevelled boards,
a.e.g. (contents foxed, eps. broken at hinges one inch crack at top
fr. joint, sml. mark fr. cvr., one plate sml. tear top margin), v.g.
Hodgkins 27-373 1983 £45

GRAY, THOMAS   Elegy Written in a Country Churchyard.
(SF), 1928. 8vo, parchment-backed boards. Decorations by W. R. Cameron. Presswork by Lawton Kennedy. Perata 27-93 1983 $40

GRAY, THOMAS   Elegy Written in a Country Churchyard.
London: Raven Press, 1938. Octavo. Illus. with numerous full-page
wood engravings by Agnes Miller Parker. Limited to 1500 copies
signed by Parker and printed for members of Limited Editions Club.
Spine faded, else extremely fine. Bromer 25-276 1983 $75

GRAY, THOMAS   Gray's Elegy Written in a Country
Church-Yard. London: Golden Cockerel Press, 1946. Octavo. Illus.
with 6 full-page wood engravings by Gwenda Morgan. Limited to 750
copies. Very fine in clothbacked marbled boards. Postcard format
announcement laid-in. T.e.g. Bromer 25-219 1983 $175

GRAY, THOMAS   Odes by Mr. Gray. Printed at
Strawberry-Hill, for R. and J. Dodsley, 1757. Disbound without
half title, very clean crisp copy of the first issue of the first
edition of the first book printed at Horace Walpole's Strawberry-Hill
Press. Ravenstree 94-148 1983 $375

GRAY, THOMAS   Poems & Letters. Chiswick Press, 1863.
1st edn. Mounted photographic portrait frontis. & 3 oval mounted
phot. views. Notes, decor. head & tail pieces, ornaments & initial
letters. Bound in full tan calf, gilt tooled bkstrip, raised bands,
brown lea. title label, marbled eps., a.e.g. (Lea. sl. marked, foxing
prelims. & occasional spotting contents.), nice copy. Hodgkins 27-
347 1983 £45

GRAY, THOMAS   The Poems of Mr. Gray. York: A.
Ward, 1775. Large paper copy. 4to. Cont. mottled calf, gilt,
neatly rebacked with morocco label, gilt. Engraved portrait
mounted by James Basire. Traylen 94-401 1983 £48

GRAY, THOMAS   Poetical Works. S. Low, nd (ca. 1859).
Frontis. & 7 full page illus. by Birket Foster engr'd by W. Palmer &
E.M. Wimperis & ornamental head & tail pieces by W. Harry Rogers engr'd
by Edmund Evans. Full calf, red lea. title label, raised bands,
marbled eps., edges stained red, insc. 2nd ep., foxing some pp., vg.
Hodgkins 27-282 1983 £15

GRAY, THOMAS   The Poetical Works. London, 1866.
Cr. 8vo. Dark blue calf, two-line gilt borders with corner ornaments
gilt panelled spine, morocco label, gilt. Portrait, vignette title-
page. Traylen 94-399 1983 £16

GRAY, THOMAS   Works. London, 1807. Third edition.
2 vols. 8vo. Cont. calf, morocco labels, gilt. From the library
of John Rutherfurd, of Edgerston, with his book-label. Traylen
94-400 1983 £20

GRAY, THOMAS   The Works of Thomas Gray. London:
William Pickering, 1835-1843. In five vols. 12mo, uniformly bound
in full black calf with London, 1836, gilt-stamped on spine. A.e.g.
Extremities sl. rubbed. Karmiole 75-105 1983 $125

GRAYDON, ALEXANDER   Memoirs of a Life Passed Chiefly in
Pennsylvania, within the Last Sixty Years... Harrisburg, 1811.
Three quarter morocco, fine. Reese 18-345 1983 $100

GRAZIA, VINCENZO DI   Considerazioni...sopra 'l Discorso di
Galileo Galilei intorno alle cose che stanno su l'acqua. Florence:
Zanobi Pignoni, 1613. First edition. 4to. Vellum. Two title-pages.
Kraus 164-90 1983 $2,800

GRAZIA, VINCENZO DI   Considerazioni...sopra 'l Discorso di
Galileo Galilei. Florence: Zanobi Pignoni, 1613. First edition.
With only the printed title. Boards with the exlibris of Pietro Ginori
Conti. Mends on title, not affecting the print. Some stains. Kraus
164-91 1983 $2,500

GRAZZINI, A. F.   The Story of Doctor Manente. Florence,
1929. 8vo. A fine copy in dj. In Our Time 156-489 1983 $75

GRAZZINI, A. F.   The Story of Doctor Manente being the
Tenth And Last Story from the Suppers... Florence: G. Orioli,
(1929). First edition. 8vo. Frontis. Orig. parchment boards.
One of 1000 copies on Lombardy paper. Very good copy. Jaffe 1-223
1983 $25

GREARD, M.O.   Meissonier. Ricordi e colloqui,
preceduti da uno studio sulla vita e sulle opere. Milano:
Corriere della Sera, 1898. 11 color plates. 280 illus. Large
4to. Boards (somewhat worn). Ars Libri 32-446 1983 $100

GREAT BRITAIN. PARLIAMENT. Act to continue an Act...for allowing
the Importation of Salted Beef, Pork, Bacon, and Butter. London:
Basket, 1768. Folio, wrs. Argosy 710-142 1983 $25

GREAT Cities & Remarkable Places. N.Y.: P.J. Cozans, ca. 1850.
Sq. 16mo, gilt-pict. red cloth. Title & frontis., and 30 full-page
woodcuts, all hand-colored. Argosy 716-540 1983 $100

A GREAT Man's Speech in Downing-Street Against the Enquiry. London:
Printed for W. Webb...MDCCXLIII. Folio, disbound. First edition.
Quaritch NS 7-60 1983 $300

GREAT Short Stories. New York: P. F. Collier & Son, 1906. Very good-
fine copy. In Our Time 156-642 1983 $20

GREATHEED, BERTIE   The Regent. 1788. Second edition.
8vo, wrapper, a fine copy. Fenning 60-145 1983 £14.50

GREAVES, JESSIE HOPPER   I Remember I Remember. S.F.: Privately
printed, 1939. 8vo, cloth-backed boards, paper label. Tipped-in
portrait frontis. Top of boards darkened; a fine copy. Perata 28-210
1983 $35

GREAVES, JOHN   A Discovrse of the Romane Foot, and
Denarivs. London, M.F. for William Lee, 1647. 8vo, new quarter
calf, boards, signature of Robert Davies (1684-1728). Folding
engraved plate, minor marginal tears, at page 88, and with numerous
diagrams etc. in the text. First and only edition. Ravenstree 94-
149 1983 $285

THE GREEK Genius and its Influence. Ithaca, 1917. First edition.
8vo. Salloch 385-10 1983 $45

THE GREEK Romances of Heliodorus, Longus, Achilles Tatius. London,
1889. Salloch 385-545 1983 $30

GREELEY, HORACE   A History of the Struggle for Slavery
Extension or Restriction in the United States... New York, 1856.
Cloth, ink inscription, covers worn, spine repaired, some
staining. King 46-13 1983 $35

GREELEY, HORACE   An Overland Journey from New York to
San Francisco in 1859. New York: C.M. Saxton, 1860. Ads. Orig.
cloth, gilt. Some wear to spine but nice copy. Jenkins 153-230 1983
$75

GREELEY, HORACE   A Political Text-Book for 1860. NY:
Tribune Assoc., 1860. 8vo, 23 cm. Orig. black blind-stamped cloth;
gilt-lettered spine. Fine, a corner tip worn. Grunder 7-37 1983
$35

GREEN, ALBERT R.   From Bridgeport to Ringgold by Way of
Lookout Mountain. Providence, 1890. Orig. printed wraps. First ed.
One of 250 copies. Ginsberg 46-283 1983 $25

GREEN, ALICE S.   The Making of Ireland and its Undoing.
Dublin: Maunsel, 1920. 8vo, orig. cloth. Fenning 61-173 1983
£10.50

GREEN, ANNA KATHARINE   Hand and Ring. NY, 1883.
First edition. Cloth, minor wear. Newsp. obits present.
King 46-295 1983 $35

GREEN, ANNA KATHERINE   The Leavenworth Case. New York & London:
Putnam, 1889. Orig. pictorial printed wraps. Reprint, issued as the
first title in the "Knickerbocker Novels" series. A few corners
turned. Reese 20-462 1983 $20

GREEN, ANNA KATHARINE   A Strange Disappearance. NY, 1880.
First edition. Cloth, bookplate, extremities worn. King 46-296
1983 $35

GREEN, ANNA KATHARINE   XYZ, A Detective Story. NY, 1883.
First edition. Wraps, sm. chip from bottom of cover at spine
bottom. Back cover chipped at foredge. Minor soil else a nice
copy. King 46-297 1983 $50

GREEN, ARTHUR G.   A Systematic Survey of the Organic Colouring Matters... London: Macmillan, 1908. Third edition. Folio. Orig. cloth. Ads. Very good copy. Zeitlin 264-187 1983 $30

GREEN, BEN K.   Back to Back. Austin: Encino Press, 1970. First edition, limited to 850 copies of which this is No.270. Signed by author. Frontis. portrait. Oblong 12mo. Orig. red boards with paper label. Orig. slipcase. Very fine. Jenkins 152-135 1983 $125

GREEN, BEN K.   Back to Back. Austin: Encino Press, 1970. 1st ed., limited to 850 numbered and signed copies. Orig. maroon pictorial boards, boxed. Mint copy. Jenkins 155-496 1983 $125

GREEN, BEN K.   The Color of Horses... Flagstaff: Northland Press, 1974. First edition. Limited deluxe edition, No.68 of 150 copies signed by author and illustrator. Frontis. portrait. 34 full-color paintings by Carol Dickinson. Large 4to. Orig. green leatherette over black buckram. Orig. slipcase. Very fine. Jenkins 152-645 1983 $250

GREEN, BEN K.   The Color of Horses. (Flagstaff, Northland Press, 1974). Deluxe edition of 150 copies. Signed by Green and Darol Dickinson who provided the illustrations. Jenkins 153-232 1983 $150

GREEN, BEN K.   The Last Trail Drive Through Downtown Dallas. Flagstaff: Northland, 1971. First trade edition. Limited to 1740 copies. Illus. by Joe Beeler. Oblong 8vo. Orig. red linen over brown buckram. Dust jacket. Very fine. Jenkins 152-646 1983 $85

GREEN, BEN K.   The Shield Mares. Austin: Encino Press, 1967. First edition, limited to 750 copies of which this is No.338. Signed by author. Small 4to. Orig. decorated beige boards. Orig. slipcase. Very fine. Jenkins 152-136 1983 $250

GREEN, BEN K.   Some More Horse Tradin'. New York: Knopf, 1972. First edition, limited to 350 numbered and signed copies. Illus. by Joe Beeler. Orig. cloth-backed boards, gilt. Mint copy in orig. printed box. Jenkins 155-499 1983 $150

GREEN, BEN K.   Wild Cow Tales. New York, 1969. First edition. Illus. Beige linen. 1/300 signed by author. Mint in slipcase. Bradley 66-551 1983 $185

GREEN, HENRY   Back. London: The Hogarth Press, 1946. First edition. 8vo. Orig. cloth. Dust jacket designed by Vanessa Bell. General browning of jacket and contents owing to poor quality paper, otherwise a fine copy. Jaffe 1-115 1983 $125

GREEN, HENRY   Doting. Lon., 1952. Fine in near fine dustwrapper. Quill & Brush 54-570 1983 $75

GREEN, HENRY   Loving. NY, 1949. Very good to fine in dustwrapper that is lightly worn on edges. Quill & Brush 54-571 1983 $35

GREEN, HENRY   Pack My Bag. London, 1940. First edition. Slight bruising to rear board and small area of fraying on front end-paper. Dustwrapper a little bumped along top edge and has a small chip missing from foot of browned spine. Previous owner's signature on foot of inner fold of dustwrapper. Gekoski 2-69 1983 £75

GREEN, HENRY   A Ramble to Ludchurch. Manchester: John Heywood, 1871. First edition, orig. purple cloth. Jarndyce 30-709 1983 £12.50

GREEN, JAMES S.   Letter of...of Missouri. Wash., 1849. Dbd. First edition. Ginsberg 47-523 1983 $45

GREEN, JOHN B.   Diving with & without Armor. Buffalo, 1859. Pictorial wraps. Felcone 22-81 1983 $85

GREEN, JOHN RICHARD   Letters... Macmillan, 1901. First edition, half title, front. & 2 other ports. Orig. maroon cloth. Jarndyce 30-1010 1983 £10.50

GREEN, JOSEPH HENRY   A letter to Sir Astley Cooper... London: Sherwood, etc., 1825. First edition. 8vo. Orig. drab wrappers, printed paper side-label. Spine slightly worn. Ximenes 63-277 1983 $65

GREEN, JULIAN   The Dark Journey. N.Y., 1929. First edition. D.w. Fine. Argosy 714-341 1983 $35

GREEN, JULIAN   The Pilgrim on the Earth. The Blackmore Press, 1929. First edition, 4to, orig. parchment-backed buckram, gilt, t.e.g. Ltd. edition of 410 numbered copies. 12 wood engravings in colour by Rene Ben Sussan. Fenning 62-148 1983 £32

GREEN, MASON A.   Springfield, 1636-1886. Springfield, 1888. 1st ed. Illus. 8vo. One corner rubbed. Morrill 287-227 1983 $30

GREEN, MATTHEW   The Spleen. London: by A. Dodd, 1738. Third edition, corrected. 8vo. Orig. grey boards, stitched. Heath 48-474 1983 £65

GREEN, MATTHEW   The Spleen, and Other Poems. T. Cadell, Junr. & W. Davies, 1796. Half title, 1 p. ads. 3 plates by Stothard, cont. vellum binding, blue line borders, blue spine label, marbled end papers. A.e.g. Jarndyce 31-33 1983 £30

GREEN, N. W.   Mormonism. Its Rise, Progress and Present Condition. Hartford, 1870. 1st ed. Illus. 12mo, covers little rubbed and edges worn. Clark 741-353 1983 $45

GREEN, PAUL   Salvation on a String and Other Tales of the South. New York: Harper, (1946). First edition. Orig. cloth, dust jacket. Fine. Jenkins 155-500 1983 $25

GREEN, SAMUEL A.   A List of Early American Imprints Belonging to the Library of the Massachusetts Historical Society. Boston, 1895-1903. First and last item being one of 200 copies reprinted from Proc. of Mass. Hist. Soc. Last item autographed. 8vo, first three items bound in cloth, last item in original wrappers. Morrill 290-152 1983 $47.50

GREEN, SAMUEL A.   The Story of a Famous Book. Boston, 1871. Cont. 1/4 straight-grained mor. Argosy 716-174 1983 $35

GREEN, THOMAS M.   The Spanish Conspiracy. Cincinnati, 1891. Orig. cloth. First edition. Ginsberg 47-330 1983 $250

GREEN, THOMAS M   The Spanish Conspiracy. Cincinnati, 1891. First edition. Green cloth. Hinges cracked, some cover spots, few marginal notes in pencil. Very scarce. Bradley 65-85 1983 $95

GREENAWAY, KATE   Almanack for 1883. London: Routledge. First edition. 16mo. Orig. glazed pictorial boards. Near-fine. MacManus 278-2354 1983 $100

GREENAWAY, KATE   Almanack for 1883. Routledge, 1883. Illus. in col. throughout. Yellow backed yellow glazed bds. with col. pictorial both cvrs. Dark green eps., cvrs. v. sl. marked, nice. Hodgkins 27-86 1983 £35

GREENAWAY, KATE   Almanack for 1884. Routledge, 1884. Variant binding of lime green morocco stamped cvrs., with gilt vig. & titling fr. cvr., a.e.g. Presentation binding, fine. Hodgkins 27-89 1983 £40

GREENAWAY, KATE   Almanack for 1884. Routledge, 1884. Variant binding of lime green morocco stamped cvrs., with gilt vig. & titling fr. cvr., a.e.g. Presentation binding, fine. Hodgkins 27-88 1983 £40

GREENAWAY, KATE   Almanack for 1884. Routledge, 1884. Illus. in col. throughout. White card cvrs. with pictorial col. decor. both cvrs., fine. Hodgkins 27-87 1983 £35

GREENAWAY, KATE   Almanack for 1885. London: Routledge. First edition. 16mo. Orig. cloth-backed glazed pictorial boards. Almost fine. MacManus 278-2356 1983 $100

GREENAWAY, KATE   Almanack for 1885. Routledge, 1885.
Illus. in col. throughout. Cream imitation morocco card cvrs. with 3
gilt rules bordering cvrs., gilt titling fr. cvr., orange eps., a.e.g.
Presentation binding, fine. Hodgkins 27-90 1983 £45

GREENAWAY, KATE   Almanack for 1886. London: George
Routledge & Sons, 1886. First edition. 24mo. Illus. Orig. cloth-
backed glazed pictorial boards. Foxed. Good. MacManus 278-2357
1983 $150

GREENAWAY, KATE   Almanack for 1887. London: Routledge,
(1887). First edition. Oblong 16mo. Orig. pictorial glazed boards.
Very good. MacManus 278-2358 1983 $100

GREENAWAY, KATE   Almanack for 1891. (London): George
Routledge & Sons, Limited, 1890. First edition. 12mo. Illus. Orig.
pictorial boards. Tissue jacket. Presentation copy, inscribed on the
half-title: "The Hon. Gerald Ponsonby from Kate Greenaway Dec. 1890."
Tipped in at the back is an orig. bill from Edmund Evans, the printer,
to Kate Greenaway, for a drawing for this almanac. In a red half-morocco slipcase. Very fine. MacManus 278-2359 1983 $850

GREENAWAY, KATE   Almanack for 1894. London: Routledge,
(1894). First edition. 16mo. Orig. cloth-backed glazed pictorial
boards. MacManus 278-2360 1983 $100

GREENAWAY, KATE   Almanack for 1895. (London): George
Routledge & Sons, 1895. First edition. 24mo. Orig. cloth-backed
pictorial glazed boards. Near-fine. MacManus 278-2361 1983 $150

GREENAWAY, KATE   Almanack for 1924. London: Frederick
Warne & Co. Ltd., 1924. Reissue of the illustrations to the 1883
almanack, with 1924 text inserted. 24mo. Orig. cloth-backed pictorial
boards. Printed tissue jacket. Fine. MacManus 278-2362 1983 $125

GREENAWAY, KATE   Almanack for 1925. Warne, 1925. Exact
copy of 1887 Almanack with year dates altered, oblong, fine copy.
Hodgkins 27-92 1983 £20

GREENAWAY, KATE   Almanack for 1926. (London): Frederick
Warne & Co. Ltd., 1926. Reissue of the illustrations of the 1890
almanack with the 1926 text inserted. 24mo. Orig. cloth-backed pictorial boards. Tissue jacket. Fine. MacManus 278-2363 1983 $125

GREENAWAY, KATE   Almanack for 1927. (London): Frederick
Warne & Co., 1927. Reissue of the illustrations to the 1891 almanack
with 1927 text inserted. 12mo. Orig. cloth-backed pictorial boards.
Printed tissue jacket. Fine. MacManus 278-2364 1983 $125

GREENAWAY, KATE   Alphabet. Routledge, nd (1885).
Frontis., 26 col'd pp. Green backed yellow glazed colour pictorial
bds, fine copy. Hodgkins 27-84 1983 £20

GREENAWAY, KATE   A Day in a Child's Life. London:
George Routledge, (1881). Quarto, color illus. 1st ed. Orig.
cloth-backed glazed color pictorial boards. Light edge-wear, else
fine copy. Jenkins 155-1391 1983 $150

GREENAWAY, KATE   A Day In A Child's Life. London: George
Routledge & Sons, n.d. First edition. Illus. by author. 4to. Illus.
in color. Orig. cloth-backed boards. Covers a little worn. Very good.
MacManus 278-2369 1983 $145

GREENAWAY, KATE   Language of Flowers. London: Routledge,
n.d. First edition. 12mo. Orig. cloth-backed glazed pictorial boards.
Very good. MacManus 278-2373 1983 $70

GREENAWAY, KATE   Marigold Garden. London: George Routledge & Sons, n.d. First edition. Printed in colors by Edmund Evans.
4to. Orig. cloth-backed decorated boards. Tipped-in ia an ALS, 3 pages
8vo, 11 Pemberton Gardens, Holloway, N., 8 May 1882, from author to an
unnamed Madam. Very good. MacManus 278-2374 1983 $350

GREENAWAY, KATE   Marigold Garden. London: Frederick
Warne & Co., n.d. 4to. Illus. in color. Orig. pictorial cloth-backed
boards. Some wear to edges. Very good. MacManus 278-2375 1983 $35

GREENAWAY, KATE   Pictures from the Originals... Warne,
1921. 1st edn. Mounted frontis. portrait & 18 mounted colour plates
on hand-made paper, printed interleaves. Cream canvas backed olive
green cloth, uncut (sml. mark bottom fr. cvr. & sl. wear top rear
corner), v. nice copy. Hodgkins 27-447 1983 £120

GREENAWAY, KATE   Under the Window. Routledge, nd (1879).
1st edn., 1st issue. Numerous col'd pictures printed by Edmund Evans.
Dark green cloth backed col'd pictorial glazed bds., edges stained
yellow, green eps. Contemp. insc. fr. ep., some sl. thumbing & foxing, some repairs to sewn edge of pages, re-cased, sl. wear corners
& bkstrip, vg. Hodgkins 27-85 1983 £50

GREENAWAY, KATE   Under the Window. London: George Routledge & Sons, (1878). First edition. Engraved & printed by Edmund
Evans. Illus. in color. Orig. pictorial boards. Rear inner hinges
cracked. Extremities worn. MacManus 278-2382 1983 $75

GREENBERG, CLEMENT   Joan Miro. New York: 1948 (actually
1949). Quarto, yellow boards. First edition, first state. Frontis.,
text illus. Small break near top of spine. Dust jacket soiled and
worn. Bradley 419 1983 $85

GREENBERG, SAMUEL   Poems. New York, 1947. 8vo. Cloth.
A copy for review with slip from the publisher laid in. Fine copy
in dj. In Our Time 156-332 1983 $65

GREENE, ALBERT G.   Old Grimes. Providence, R. I.
Sidney S. Rider, 1867. Small 4to, 14 leaves, each with engraved
illus. by Hoppin (engraved by N. Orr & Co.) Orig. elaborately
gilt-stamped brown cloth, spine faded. Karmiole 75-61 1983 $45

GREENE, ASA   The Perils of Pearl Street. New York:
Betts & Anstice, and Hill. 1834. 8vo, orig. cloth. Rostenberg 88-
132 1983 $125

GREENE, DANIEL H.   History of the Town of East Greenwich
(R.I.) and Adjacent Territory, from 1677-1877. Dec. cloth. Argosy
716-483 1983 $35

GREENE, GRAHAM   Another Mexico. NY, 1939. Spine slightly
faded and spattered, very good. Quill & Brush 54-574 1983 $35

GREENE, GRAHAM   British Dramatists. Lon., 1942. 8 color
plates, 26 b&w illus., cover slightly stained, edges rubbed and slightly
yellowed, else very good in frayed, mended dustwrapper. Quill & Brush
54-575 1983 $40

GREENE, GRAHAM   A Burnt-Out Case. London, 1961. First
edition. Proof copy with the label of Rosica Colin Ltd. Literary
Agents on title. Unprinted flimsy brown wrappers. Very good.
Gekoski 2-71 1983 £125

GREENE, GRAHAM   The Confidential Agent. NY, 1939. Front
fly removed, cover soiled, good. Quill & Brush 54-583 1983 $25

GREENE, GRAHAM   Doctor Fisher of Geneva or the Bomb
Party. New York: Simon & Schuster, 1980. 1st ed., 1 of 500
numbered and signed copies. Orig. cloth, gilt, boxed. Mint copy.
Jenkins 155-501 1983 $135

GREENE, GRAHAM   Doctor Fischer of Geneva or the Bomb.
New York, 1980. 8vo. Wraps. Uncorrected proofs. Little bumping
at the corner, mainly fine. In Our Time 156-335 1983 $100

GREENE, GRAHAM   The Great Jowett. London, 1981. Slim
12mo, cloth. One of 525 copies signed by the author. First edition.
Duschnes 240-109 1983 $75

GREENE, GRAHAM   The Heart of the Matter. New York,
1948. 8vo. Cloth. An advance copy being 1 of 750 copies issued
in advance of the regular ed. With a letter from the publisher
laid into the book. Spine faded, else a fine copy. In Our Time
156-333 1983 $100

GREENE, GRAHAM   The Heart of the Matter. NY, 1948.
Corners slightly rubbed, cover lightly stained, else very good in
stained and slightly nicked, lightly rubbed dustwrapper. Quill & Brush
54-584 1983 $35

GREENE, GRAHAM   How Father Quixote Became a Monsignor. L.A., 1980. First edition. Red cloth, one of 330 copies. Acetate jacket. Fine copy. Houle 21-387 1983 $75

GREENE, GRAHAM   Introductions to Three Novels. Stockholm, 1962. Wrappers. Spine slightly darkened. Nearly fine. Jolliffe 26-230 1983 £55

GREENE, GRAHAM   It's a Battlefield. New York: Doubleday, 1934. 1st American ed. Orig. cloth stamped in black. Nice copy. Jenkins 155-1392 1983 $60

GREENE, GRAHAM   Journey Without Maps. GC, 1936. Shallow ridge across top corner of front cover, else near fine in lightly frayed and chipped, very good dustwrapper. Quill & Brush 54-579 1983 $225

GREENE, GRAHAM   Labyrinthine Ways. N.Y., Viking, 1940. First American edition. Blue cloth (a few stains), else very good. Houle 21-388 1983 $30

GREENE, GRAHAM   The Little Fire Engine. (London: Max Parrish & Co. Ltd., n.d. (1950). First edition. Illus. by Dorothy Craigie. Oblong 4to. Orig. pictorial boards. Dust jacket. First of Greene's children's books to bear his name. Presentation copy, inscribed on the front free endpaper "For John Carter, with awe and affection from Graham Greene." Fine. MacManus 278-2391 1983 $2,000

GREENE, GRAHAM   The Little Horse Bus. London: Max Parrish, (1952). First edition. Illus. by Dorothy Craigie. 4to. Orig. gilt-decorated red cloth, dust jacket. Mint copy. Rare. Jaffe 1-117 1983 $650

GREENE, GRAHAM   The Little Steamroller. London: Max Parris, (1953). First edition. Illus. by Dorothy Craigie. 4to. Orig. gilt-decorated blue cloth. Dust jacket. Mint copy. Jaffe 1-118 1983 $650

GREENE, GRAHAM   The Man Within. London: William Heinemann Ltd., (1929). First edition. 8vo. Orig. cloth. Dust jacket. Fine. Jaffe 1-116 1983 $1,250

GREENE, GRAHAM   May We Borrow Your Husband? London: The Bodley Head, (1967). First edition. Orig. cloth-backed patterned boards. In acetate jacket. One of 500 specially printed and bound copies signed by author. Very fine. MacManus 278-2393 1983 $175

GREENE, GRAHAM   May We Borrow Your Husband? Lon., (1967). Limited to 500 specially bound, numbered and signed copies. Fine. Quill & Brush 54-581 1983 $150

GREENE, GRAHAME   The Ministry of Fear. London, Heinemann, (1943). First edition. Yellow cloth (lightly soiled). Very good. Houle 22-445 1983 $90

GREENE, GRAHAM   Ministry of Fear. London, Heinemann, (1943). First edition. Yellow cloth (lightly soiled), very good. Houle 21-389 1983 $95

GREENE, GRAHAM   The Ministry of Fear. N.Y., 1943. First American edition. Fine, in a slightly worn dust wrapper. Argosy 714-871 1983 $75

GREENE, GRAHAM   Our Man in Havana. London, 1958. 8vo, cloth, dust-jacket. Cont. dated inscription on fly-leaf. First edition. Duschnes 240-106 1983 $75

GREENE, GRAHAM   The Quiet America. London, (1955). First edition. D.w. Fine. Argosy 714-343 1983 $100

GREENE, GRAHAM   The Quiet American. NY, 1956. Review slip laid-in, very good or better in slightly frayed, chipped, very good dustwrapper. Quill & Brush 54-585 1983 $75

GREENE, GRAHAM   The Return of A. J. Raffles. The Bodley Head, 1975. 8vo, cloth. 1 of 250 copies signed by the author. Very fine in just dacket. In Our Time 156-334 1983 $200

GREENE, GRAHAM   A Visit to Morin. London, 1959. First edition. Very slightly dusty dustwrapper. Limited to 250 copies, not for sale. Fine. Gekoski 2-70 1983 £150

GREENE, GRAHAM   Ways of Escape. New York, 1981. 8vo. Wraps. Uncorrected proof copy. Note by publisher on the front wrapper, a fine copy. In Our Time 156-336 1983 $100

GREENE, J.W.   Dental Information for the People... St. Louis, 1870. 1st ed. 12mo. Corners rubbed. Morrill 289-88 1983 $25

GREENE, LAURENCE   The Filibuster: The Career of William Walker. Indianapolis, 1937. 1st ed. Near mint in dj. Jenkins 153-664 1983 $45

GREENE, LORENZO J.   The Negro in Colonial New England, 1620-1776. NY, 1942. Nice copy. Jenkins 151-109 1983 $40

GREENE, MAX   The Kanzas Region. N.Y., 1856. First edition. Illus., map. Orig. cloth. Ginsberg 47-331 1983 $150

GREENE, ROBERT   Greene's Groats-Worth of Wit. B.H. Blackwell, Oxford, 1919. Untrimmed, printed boards, cloth spine, labels, a little darkened. Jarndyce 31-992 1983 £10.50

GREENE, SAMUEL D.   The Broken Seal. Chicago, 1873. Ex lib. Argosy 716-262 1983 $45

GREENE, TALBOT   American Night's Entertainments: Compiled from Pencilings of a United States Senator... Jonesborough, Tenn., 1860. Orig. cloth. 1st ed. Jenkins 155-503 1983 $125

GREENE, W. T.   Parrots in Captivity. 1884. Vol. 1 (of 3), 27 fine coloured plates by B. Fawcett after A. F. Lydon, roy. 8vo, cloth. Wheldon 160-42 1983 £135

GREENER, WILLIAM   Gunnery in 1858. Smith, Elder, 1858. First edition, with 5 plates and 37 other illus. 8vo, orig. blue cloth, by Westleys, with their ticket. Fenning 60-146 1983 £85

GREENHOW, ROBERT   The History of Oregon and California, and the Other Territories on the North-West Coast of North America. Boston, 1844. Large folding map. 3/4 calf. Binding rubbed, map detached and browned along one fold. Felcond 22-83 1983 $100

GREENHOW, ROBERT   Memoir, Historical and Political, on the Northwest Coast of North America... Washington: Blair and Rives, Printers, 1840. 22cm. Large folding map. Bound in grey paper boards and paper label. Fine. Rare. McGahern 54-72 1983 $225

GREENHOW, ROBERT   Memoir, Historical and Political on the Northwest Coast of North America. Wash., 1840. Illus., folded map. Dbd. In cloth case. First edition. Ginsberg 46-284 1983 $200

GREENLY, ALBERT H.   Camels in America. New York: Biblio. Society of America, 1952. Original printed wrappers. First edition. "Author's Edition," limited to 100 numbered copies, signed by author. Mint as issued. Jenkins 153-110 1983 $75

GREENSFELDER, ELMER   Broomsticks, Amen! NY, 1932. Paper-wraps, signed, cover slightly faded, else very good. Quill & Brush 54-587 1983 $25

GREENWELL, DORA   Poems. William Pickering, 1848. First edition, half title. Leading free end paper laid down and torn, orig. green cloth. This copy marked up, possibly by the author. Jarndyce 30-710 1983 £20

GREENWOOD, JAMES   Journeys through London. Ward, Lock & Tyler, n.d. (c. 1880). Half title, double-page front. & illus. 16 pp ads. Orig. blue dec. cloth, bevelled boards, a.e.g. Jarndyce 31-255 1983 £22

GREENWOOD, JAMES   The London Vocabulary, English and Latin.
1807. 12mo, 26 large woodcuts in the text, orig. calf, slight wear
at the top of the spine, but a fine copy. Bickersteth 75-143 1983
£40

GREENWOOD, JAMES   Odd People in Odd Places. Fredk. Warne,
n.d. (c. 1870). Cont. maroon cloth, a little marked. Jarndyce
31-256 1983 £42

GREENWOOD, JAMES   Odd People in Odd Places. Fredk. Warne,
n.d. (c. 1880). Orig. red dec. cloth, v.g. Jarndyce 31-257 1983
£30

GREENWOOD, JAMES   The Seven Curses of London. Stanely
Rivers & Co., n.d. 2 pp ads. Half calf, black labels. Jarndyce 31-
258 1983 £20

GREENWOOD, JAMES   Unsentimental Journeys. Ward, Lock &
Tyler, 1867. First edition, half title, double-page front. & plates,
4 pp ads. Orig. green dec. cloth, bevelled boards. Jarndyce 31-254
1983 £42

GREENWOOD, ROBERT   California Imprints 1833-1862. Los
Gatos: Talisman Press, 1961. One of 50 copies printed on special
paper, numbered and signed by Greenwood, extra-illustrated with six
facsimiles, and bound in black leather. Dawson 470-127 1983 $100

GREENWOOD, THOMAS   Edward Edwards, the Chief Pioneer of
Municipal Public Libraries. Scott, Greenwood, 1902. First edition,
half title, orig. maroon cloth, t.e.g. Jarndyce 30-981 1983
£18.50

GREENWOOD, THOMAS   Edward Edwards, the Chief Pioneer of
Municipal Public Libraries. London: Scott, Greenwood and Co., 1902.
First edition. 8vo. Cloth. Covers rubbed with some fading of
extremities. Oak Knoll 49-209 1983 $35

GREENWOOD, W. E.   The Villa Madonna, Rome. London, 1928.
103 plates, some in color. 4to, boards. Salloch 385-354 1983 $30

GREG, PERCY   The Devil's Advocate. London: Trubner,
1878. First edition. 2 vols. Orig. cloth. Fine. MacManus 278-2406
1983 $250

GREG, ROBERT PHILLIPS   Manual of mineralogy of Great Britain
and Ireland. London: John Van Voorst, 1858. First edition. 8vo.
Orig. dark brown cloth. Ximenes 63-523 1983 $100

GREG, WALTER W.   A Bibliography of the English Printed
Drama to the Restoration. London: for the Bibliographical Society,
1939-59. 4 vols. 4to. Orig. boards with buckram spines. 137 full-
page facsimiles. Traylen 94-405 1983 £110

GREG, WALTER W.   A Bibliography of the English Printed
Drama to the Restoration. London: The Bibliographical Society, 1970.
Thick 4to. Cloth. Oak Knoll 49-446 1983 $140

GREGG, JOSIAH   Diary & Letters. Norman: University of
Oklahoma Press, 1941-44. 2 vols. Cloth. Dawson 471-104 1983 $50

GREGG, JOSIAH   Diary & Letters of... Norman, 1941. 1st
edn. Jenkins 153-233 1983 $45

GREGOR, ADALBERT   Leitfaden Der Experimentellen Psycho-
pathopathology. Berlin: S. Karger, 1910. First edition. Ads.
Gach 95-181 1983 $30

GREGOR, JOSEPH   Wiener Szenische Kunst. Zuerich, 1925.
4 color plates, 21 colored and 234 monochrome illus. on plates. Folio,
1/2 morocco. Salloch 387-321 1983 $75

GREGOROVIUS, FERDINAND   Siciliana. London, 1914. 8vo, cloth.
Salloch 385-357 1983 $20

GREGORY, DAVID   Astromiae Physicae & Geometricae
Elementa. Oxoniae, e Theatro Sheldoniano, 1702. First edition,
large engraved vignette on title and many mathematical figures in
text, folio, light old water stain in lower margin. In cont. panelled
calf, neatly rebacked. Fenning 60-147 1983 £245

GREGORY, GEORGE   The Economy of Nature. 1798. 3 vols.,
8vo, 56 engraved plates, cont. speckled calf with black labels.
Bickersteth 75-233 1983 £65

GREGORY, ISAAC   Rough Notes on the Silver Crisis and on
the Debased Money of India. Effingham Wilson, 1879. First edition.
Orig. printed wraps., v.g. Jarndyce 31-179 1983 £14.50

GREGORY, ISABELLA AUGUSTA PERSSE   The Image & Other Plays.
N.Y.: G.P. Putnam's Sons, 1922. First American edition. Orig. cloth.
Bookseller's small rubber stamp on front free endpaper. Very good.
MacManus 278-2407 1983 $40

GREGORY, ISABELLA AUGUSTA PERSSE   Irish Folk-History Plays.
N.Y.: G.P. Putnam's Sons, 1912. First American editions. 2 vols. Orig.
holland-backed boards with paper labels on spines. Mint. MacManus
278-2408 1983 $65

GREGORY, ISABELLA AUGUSTA PERSSE   The Kiltartan Moliere.
Dublin: Maunsel & Co., (1911). First edition. Orig. cloth-backed boards.
Spine slightly darkened. Cover corners worn. Former owner's signature.
Good. MacManus 278-2409 1983 $35

GREGORY, ISABELLA AUGUSTA PERSSE   The Kiltartan Poetry Book.
N.Y.: G.P. Putnam's Sons, 1919. First edition. Orig. cloth with paper spine
label. Dust jacket (defective; torn). Spine slightly darkened. Very
good. MacManus 278-2410 1983 $35

GREGORY, ISABELLA AUGUSTA PERSSE   Kincora. New York: Privately
printed, 1905. First American edition. One of 50 copies signed by the
author. Fine. MacManus 278-2411 1983 $450

GREGORY, ISABELLA AUGUSTA PERSSE   Poets and Dreamers. New York:
Charles Scribner's Sons, 1903. First edition. Orig. canvas-backed
boards. MacManus 278-2412 1983 $125

GREGORY, ISABELLA AUGUSTA PERSSE   Poets and Dreamers. Dublin,
New York, 1903. Minor stains and shelf wear to edges with some pages
poorly opened, endpaper offset, good or better. Quill & Brush 54-
589 1983 $30

GREGORY, ISABELLA AUGUSTA PERSSE   Spreading the News. New York:
Privately printed, 1904. Orig. printed wraps. First edition. One of
50 copies signed by the author. Front cover slightly spotted, otherwise a very good copy. MacManus 278-2413 1983 $450

GREGORY, JOHN   Idyls of Labour. Simpkin, Marshall,
(1871). First edition, small 8vo, orig. green cloth, gilt, a fine
copy. Inscribed "To the Generous Author of Beautiful Actaeon
W. Wilkins Esqr., from his ever obliged J. Gregory, the singing
Shoemaker, August 24th, 1877". Fenning 61-175 1983 £28.50

GREGORY, JOSEPH W.   Gregory's Guide for California Travellers.
San Francisco: Reprinted by the Book Club of Califronia, 1949. Cloth.
Dawson 471-105 1983 $20

GREGORY, OLINTHUS   Memoirs of the Life, Writings, and
Character, Literary, Professional, and Religious, of the Late John
Mason Good, M.D. Boston, 1829. 1st American ed. 8vo. Orig.
boards, cloth back, paper label. Morrill 289-89 1983 $32.50

GREGORY, SAMUEL   Letter to Ladies, in Favor of Female
Physicians. Boston, 1850. 1st ed. 8vo. Orig. wrappers. Morrill
289-90 1983 $22.50

GREGORY, WILLIAM   Letters to a Candid Inquirer or Animal
Magnetism. Phila., 1851. 12mo, orig. cloth; ex-lib. First edition.
Argosy 713-231 1983 $50

GREGORY, WILLIAM   Paddiana. Richard Bentley, 1848.
2nd edition, 2 vols., front., half titles, 1 p ads. Vol. I. orig.
green cloth, v.g. Jarndyce 30-408 1983 £32

GREGORY, WILLIAM   A Visible Display of Divine Providence.
London, 1801. 2nd edition, 7 engr. Plates. Sheep-backed boards,
ex lib. Argosy 716-52 1983 $45

GRELOT, W. J.   A Late Voyage to Constantinople. London,
1683. First edition. Plan. 8 folding plates. Frontis. 4 full-page
engravings. Sm.8vo. Calf, worn. Good. Edwards 1044-298 1983 £150

GRENTZENBACH, RUTGER   Disputatio physica de officina sanguinis. Herborn: Christopher Corvin, 1593. Woodcut vignette on title. 4to. Boards. Kraus 164-106   1983 $650

GRESHAM, WILLIAM L.   Nightmare Alley. New York: Rinehart, (1946). Cloth. First edition. About fine in modestly worn and chipped dust jacket. Reese 20-468   1983 $45

GRESSET (JEAN-BAPTISTE DE)   Ver-Vert, Suivi de La Chartreuse, L'Abbaye et Autre Pieces. Paris: Fonderie Typographique, 1855. Orig. printed wrappers. Slight slitting at spine, else fine. (2 3/8 x 1 5/8; 61x43mm). Bromer 25-432   1983 $150

GRESSIT, J. L.   Biogeography and Ecology of New Guinea. 1981. 330 figures and 64 tables, 2 volumes, 8vo, cloth. Wheldon 160-388   1983   £112

GRETRY, ANDRE ERNEST MODESTE   Colinette a la Cour, ou la Double Epreuve. Paris, Houbaut, n.d. First edition, full score, all engraved. Engraved title (imprime par Basset), dedication leaf to the Comte de Vaudreil. Engraved music. Folio, cont. 1/2 calf over green vellum. On the front cover, in gilt letters: "A Madame la Contesse de Salles". Salloch 387-84   1983 $400

GRETRY, ANDRE ERNEST MODESTE   La Fausse Magie. Cassell, J.F. Estienne, 1777. Woodcut vignette on title. Small 8vo, wrs. Salloch 387-79   1983 $60

GRETRY, ANDRE ERNEST MODESTE   Le Magnifique. Paris, (original imprint pasted over by) Mlle Castagnery. First edition, engraved title, dedication page to the Duke of Alba, engraved music. Folio, cont. red 1/2 calf, spine gilt. Small crack in top of front hinge. Salloch 387-78   1983 $350

GRETRY, ANDRE ERNEST MODESTE   Les Mariages Samnites. Paris, Houbaut, n.d. (1776). First edition. Full score. Engraved title, engraved music. Folio, cont. red 1/2 morocco, spine gilt. Salloch 387-80   1983 $300

GRETRY, ANDRE ERNEST MODESTE   Memoires ou Essais sur la Musique. Paris, Imprimerie de la Republique, an V (1797). Three vols., 8vo, cont. boards, rebacked with leather, red labels. First edition of vols. II and II; second edition of vol. 1. Pencil underlinings and marginal notes throughout. Salloch 387-86   1983 $150

GRETRY, ANDRE ERNEST MODESTE   Panurge dans l'Isle des Lanternes. Paris, chez Mlle Jenny Gretry, n.d. Full score, engraved title, engraved music. Rubber stamp (faded) of Jenny Gretry on title, also two stamps of a Paris music dealer. Folio, cont. red 1/2 calf. Salloch 387-85   1983 $200

GRETRY, ANDRE ERNEST MODESTE   Partition de l'Amant Jaloux. Paris, n.d. First edition. All engraved. Folio, full cont. calf, with gilt armorial vignette on covers. Salloch 387-82   1983 $250

GRETRY, ANDRE ERNEST MODESTE   Partition des Evenements Imprevus. Paris, Houbaut, n.d. Engraved title, folio, cont. green 1/2 vellum over marbled boards, top and bottom of spine chipped. Salloch 387-83   1983 $200

GRETRY, ANDRE ERNEST MODESTE   Silvain. Paris, aux Addresses Ordinaires, &c. First edition. Engraved title, dedication page, engraved music. Folio, cont. red 1/2 calf, spine gilt. A few scratches on front cover, otherwise fine. Old name on first page inked out. Salloch 387-76   1983 $350

GRETRY, ANDRE ERNEST MODESTE   Le Tableau Parlant. Paris, aux Addresses Ordinaires de Musique, n.d. First edition. All engraved, title, dedication leaf to the Duc de Choiseul, 135 leaves engraved music, full score. Folio, cont. green, 1/2 vellum over marbled boards. Top of spine chipped, otherwise fine. On the inside front-cover a large ad. label of Duvinage, Marchand Papetier. Salloch 387-75   1983 $350

GRETRY, ANDRE ERNEST MODESTE   Zemire et Azore. Paris, Houbaut, n.d. Engraved title, with autograph signature of Gretry. Engraved music. Folio, maroon 1/2 calf. Salloch 387-77   1983 $275

GRETTON, G. LE M.   The Campaigns and History of The Royal Irish Regiment. Edinburgh, 1911. Frontis. 3 plates, 1 double-page facsimile and 8 coloured maps (1 folding). Thick imp. 8vo. Orig. publisher's blue morocco gilt. A.e.g., very slightly worn. Rarely seen in this binding. Fine. Edwards 1042-537   1983   £60

GREVILLE, CHARLES C. F.   Memoirs. London, 1874-87. Second edition. 8 vols. 8vo. Orig. blue cloth. Worn. Traylen 94-406   1983   £28

GREVILLE, R. K.   Scottish Cryptogamic Flora. Edinburgh, 1823-28. 6 vols., roy. 8vo, cont. boards (rebacked in cloth), 360 hand-coloured plates. Very scarce. Some isolated offsetting but otherwise a nice copy. Wheldon 160-43   1983   £875

GREW, NEHEMIAH   The Anatomy of Plants. Printed by W. Rawlins, for the author, 1682. Small folio, 83 engraved plates (5 of them double page), old calf, joints cracked, but binding firm. Title a little dusty with old ink inscription, margins of some plates a little soiled, margin of one plate frayed at the edge. First edition. Plate 15 numbered 6. Bickersteth 75-234   1983   £340

GREW, NEHEMIAH   Musaeum Regalis Societatis. London: W. Rawlins for the author, 1681. Folio, 31 copper-plate engravings. Frontis. portrait of Daniel Colwal. Contemporary calf, spine re-backed, bookplate of John Cuitton, small stamp excised on bottom of title (not affecting print), inner tear on upper front two blanks and portrait, not affecting image. Else very clean and beautiful copy. First edition. Gach 95-182   1983 $550

GREY, ANCHITELL   Debates of the House of Commons... London: for D. Henry and R. Cave, 1763. First collected edition. 10 vols. 8vo. Cont. calf. Fine. Heath 48-120   1983   £225

GREY, C.   European Adventures of Northern India. Lahore, 1929. Plates. 8vo. Orig. cloth. Inscribed "With the Editor's Compts." Good. Edwards 1044-300   1983   £25

GREY, HERACLITUS   In Vain. Hurst & Blackett, 1868. First edition, 3 vols., half title. Orig. brown cloth. Fine. Jarndyce 30-409   1983   £110

GREY, HERBERT   The voyage of the Lady. London: Hurst and Blackett, 1860. First edition. Small 8vo. Orig. blue cloth. Presentation copy, inscribed by the author to E.E. Stahl-schmidt. Cloth a little rubbed. Ximenes 63-154   1983 $275

GREY, RICHARD   Memoria Technica. London: King, 1730. First edition. 12mo, cont. calf (hinges repaired; stain on lower margin, pp. 1-30). Copper engr. head and tail pieces. Title in red and black. Argosy 713-232   1983 $175

GREY, RICHARD   Memoria Technica or Method of Artificial Memory... London: W. Lowndes, 1812. 12mo. Cont. calf, gilt. A trifle worn. Traylen 94-407   1983   £12

GREY, ZANE   Arizona Ames. N.Y., Harper, 1932. First edition. Dust jacket with the rare wrap around band announcing the "New 1932 Zane Grey Novel." With Zane Grey's blind library stamp. Houle 21-1048   1983 $175

GREY, ZANE   Arizona Ames. N.Y., Harper, 1932. First edition "I-F". Beige cloth stamped in red. Pictorial endpapers. Very good. Houle 22-1072   1983 $45

GREY, ZANE   The Arizona Clan. London, Hodder & Stoughton, (1958). First English edition (reset and printed in England). With the Zane Grey estate stamp. Fine. Houle 22-1073   1983 $95

GREY, ZANE   Blue Father. N.Y., Harper, (1961). First edition. Dust jacket. Signed and inscribed by Grey's son Romber; with a four line inscription. Very good. Houle 21-1050   1983 $125

GREY, ZANE   Boulder Dam. London, Hodder & Stoughton, (1965). First English edition (reset and printed in England). Dust jacket. With the Zane Grey estate stamp. Fine. Houle 22-1076   1983 $85

GREY, ZANE   The Call of the Canyon. N.Y., Harpers, 1924. First edition. "K-X." Illus. with 4 plates by H.R. Bellinger. Dust jacket (small nicks, small abrasion on front) else very good. Houle 22-1077   1983 $135

GREY, ZANE   Captives of the Desert. N.Y., Harper, (1952). First edition "B-B". Dust jacket. Very good - fine. Houle 22-1078 1983 $85

GREY, ZANE   Fighting Caravans. N.Y., Harper, 1929. First edition. Dust jacket (trifle rubbed at edges). Signed by Zane Grey. From Grey's library with his stamp. Very good-fine. Houle 21-1053 1983 $425

GREY, ZANE   Forlorn River. N.Y., Harpers, 1927. First edition "H-B". Illus. with numerous decorations by Robert Amick. Dust jacket (a trifle nicked at edges) else fine. Signed and inscribed by the author to his son "To Loren, from Dad, Zane Grey." Also signed by Loren Grey. Houle 22-1079 1983 $600

GREY, ZANE   Forlorn River. New York: 1927. First edition. Illus. Cloth. Very good. Bradley 66-183 1983 $30

GREY, ZANE   Hash Knife Outfit. London, H&S, 1923. First English edition, reset and printed from new plates in England. Dust jacket. Presentation copy from the author to his son - "To Loren from Dad, Zane Grey." Also signed signed by Loren Grey. Houle 21-1057 1983 $550

GREY, ZANE   The Hash Knife Outfit. N.Y., Harper, 1933. First edition, "G-H." Dust jacket (slight nicking, trifle soiled). Very good. Houle 22-1080 1983 $150

GREY, ZANE   Heritage of the Desert. N.Y., Harper, (1910). Early issue, Y-Y, Feb., 1924. From Zane Grey's library, with blind stamp. Houle 21-1058 1983 $85

GREY, ZANE   Knights of the Range. N.Y., Harper, 1939. First edition "M-N". Pictorial endpapers. Dust jacket (small nicks). Very good - fine. Houle 22-1081 1983 $125

GREY, ZANE   The Light of Western Stars. N.Y., Harper, (1914). Later issue, "B-Y", Feb, 1924. From Zane Grey's library, signed in purple ink by Grey, and with his library stamp. Very good - fine. Houle 22-1082 1983 $225

GREY, ZANE   Lost Wagon Train. N.Y., Harper, 1936. First edition. Dust jacket (small chips), else very good. Houle 21-1061 1983 $125

GREY, ZANE   The Man and His Work. N.Y., Harper, 1928. First edition. Illus. Gilt stamped leatherette. With Zane Grey's library stamp. Fine. Houle 21-1062 1983 $125

GREY, ZANE   Nevada: A Romance of the West. N.Y., Harper, 1928. First edition "B-C". Illus. endpapers and jacket by Stockton Muford. Dust jacket (trifle rubbed). Signed by Grey on the front endpaper in purple ink. Houle 22-1083 1983 $425

GREY, ZANE   Nevada. Berlin, Knaur, n.d., ca. 1928. First edition in German? Yellow cloth, stamped in brown. The dust jacket has a few small chips and is very good. Zane Grey's copy with his library stamp and signature in purple ink on front endpaper. Houle 22-1084 1983 $175

GREY, ZANE   Riders of the Purple Sage. N.Y., Harper (1912). Early printing. Blue cloth, stamped in black. Fine. From Grey's library, with his blind library stamp. Houle 21-1064 1983 $45

GREY, ZANE   Rogue River Feud. N.Y., Harper, (1948). First edition "C-X". Dust jacket (tape in verso, rubbed) else very good. Houle 22- 1085 1983 $65

GREY, ZANE   Tales of Fishes. NY, (1919). Edges rubbed and slightly frayed, rear hinge starting, cover dulled, good. Quill & Brush 54-590 1983 $50

GREY, ZANE   Tales of Fresh Water Fishing. N.Y., Harper, 1928. First edition "F-C" 4to, bound in 3/4 green morocco over green cloth boards, spine with raised bands and gilt ornamentation, covers ruled in gilt, t.e.g., uncut. Cloth slipcase. One of only a few uncut presentation copies bound by the publisher for Zane Grey's use. This copy bears his personal library stamp. Houle 22-1086 1983 $1,250

GREY, ZANE   Tales of Lonely Trails. NY, (1922). Rear hinge cracked, page after front fly missing, edges rubbed and just starting to wear, good or better. Quill & Brush 54-591 1983 $40

GREY, ZANE   30,000 on the Hoof. N.Y., Grosset & Dunlap (1940). Dust jacket. Very good-fine. With the Zane Grey estate stamp. Houle 21-1066 1983 $45

GREY, ZANE   Thunder Mountain. N.Y., Harper, 1935. First edition. Dust jacket, with the circular label "The New 1935 Zane Grey Novel." Fine copy. From Zane Grey's library and signed by him. Houle 21-1067 1983 $450

GREY, ZANE   Trail Driver. N.Y., Harper, 1936. First edition. Dust jacket, with the "New 1936 Zane Grey Novel," sticker. Zane Grey's copy and with his stamp. Fine copy. Houle 21-1069 1983 $350

GREY, ZANE   Under the Tonto Rim. N.Y., Harper's, 1926. First edition "F-A". Dust jacket (small nicks). Very good. Houle 22-1088 1983 $175

GREY, ZANE   Under the Tonto Rim. N.Y., Harper's, 1926. First edition "F-A". Dust jacket (slight rubbing, 1" x 2" chip on front cover) else very good. Houle 22-1087 1983 $65

GREY, ZANE   Valley of Wild Horses. N.Y., Harper (1947). First edition. Dust jacket (slight wear); previous owner's inscription. Very good. Houle 21-1070 1983 $85

GREY, ZANE   Vanishing American. N.Y., Harper, 1925. First edition. Four plates by Frank Street. Dust jacket with illus. by W.R. Leigh (few small nicks), else very good-fine. Presentation copy inscribed by the author to his sister, November 17, 1925. Houle 21-1071 1983 $650

GREY, ZANE   The Vanishing American. New York: 1925. First edition. Frontis. Cloth. Very good. Bradley 66-184 1983 $45

GREY, ZANE   The Vanishing American. N.Y., Harper, 1925. First edition "I-Z". 4 illus. by Frank Street. Brick cloth stamped in blue. Very good. Houle 22-1090 1983 $45

GREY, ZANE   The Vanishing American. N.Y., 1925. Illus. First edition. Argosy 714-344 1983 $40

GREY, ZANE   Wanderer of the Wasteland. N.Y., Harper, 1923. First edition, second printing, December. Three illus. by W.H. Dunton. Dust jacket. Zane Grey's copy, signed by him in purple ink, and with his library stamp. Fine. Cloth slipcase. Houle 21-1072 1983 $275

GREY, ZANE   The Vanishing American. New York: Harper, 1925. 1st ed. Orig. cloth. Fine copy with publisher's slip laid in. Jenkins 155-505 1983 $20

GRIAULE, MARCEL   Arts de l'Afrique Noire. Paris: Editions du Chene, 1947. 108 illus. Small 4to. Boards. 1/4 cloth. Ars Libri 34-642 1983 $30

GRIAULE, MARCEL   Folk Art of Black Africa. New York: Tudor, 1950. 107 illus. Small 4to. Cloth. Ars Libri 34-643 1983 $35

GRIAULE, MARCEL   Jeux Dogons. Paris: Institut d'Ethnologie, 1938. 12 plates. 128 text illus. 4to. Cloth. Ars Libri 34-644 1983 $85

GRIBBLE, FRANCIS   The Romantic Life of Shelley and the Sequel. N.Y.: G.P. Putnam's Sons, 1911. First edition. Bound in 3/4 moroon morocco & cloth. Fine. MacManus 4724 1983 $50

GRIBBLE, LEONARD   Riley of the Special Branch. First edition. With tissue seal intact. Chipped dustwrapper missing a third of the upper panel. Very good. Jolliffe 26-142 1983 £20

GRIEN, HANS BALDUNG   Holzschnitte des Hans Baldung Grien. Munchen: Allgemeine Verlagsanstalt, 1924. 50 plates. Large 4to. Boards, 1/4 cloth. From the library of Jakob Rosenberg. Front hinge broken. Ars Libri 32-17 1983 $40

GRIERSON, FRANCIS   The Valley of the Shadows. London, 1909. First English edition. Signed by author. Jenkins 152-137 1983 $65

GRIERSON, JOHN   Jet Flight. London, c.1945. Portrait frontis. Numerous illus. and diagrams. Illus. endpapers. Very slightly soiled. Good. Edwards 1042-589 1983 £12

GRIESINGER, WILHELM   Mental Pathology and Therapeutics. London, New Sydenham Society, 1867. 1st English ed. 8vo. Lacks front endleaf; top of spine frayed. Morrill 289-91 1983 $87.50

GRIEVE, CHRISTOPHER MURRAY   Autran Blads. Glasgow: William Maclellan, 1943. First edition, roy. 8vo, orig. blindstamped cloth, in dust wrapper. Fenning 61-271 1983 £21.50

GRIEVE, CHRISTOPHER MURRAY   The Islands of Scotland. London, 1939. First edition. Photographs. Spine faded and spotted, and upper cover a little marked. Bookplate on half-title page. Very good. Rota 231-398 1983 £12

GRIEVE, CHRISTOPHER MURRAY   A Kist of Whistles. Glasgow: Poetry Scotland Series, 1947. Frayed dust wrapper. Very nice. Rota 231-399 1983 £15

GRIEVE, CHRISTOPHER MURRAY   Penny Wheep. Edinburgh & London, 1926. First edition. Covers a little marked. Nice. Rota 231-396 1983 £40

GRIEVE, CHRISTOPHER MURRAY   To Circumjack Cencrastus. Edinburgh & London, 1930. First edition. Ex-library copy. Very good. Rota 231-397 1983 £25

GRIFFIN, APPLETON P. C.   A List of Books on Samoa and Guam. Washington: GPO, 1901. Cloth, very good. Dawson 470-130 1983 $20

GRIFFIN, BENJAMIN   The Humours of Purgatory. London: printed for A. Bettesworth and Sold by J. Graves, 1716. 1st ed., 12mo, half-title, advertisements, uncut, in modern wrappers. Pickering & Chatto 19-29 1983 $450

GRIFFIN, ERNEST FREELAND   Westchester County and Its People. N.Y., (1946). Illus., 4to, 3 vols. Fine. Argosy 716-350 1983 $35

GRIFFIN, GERALD   Holland Tide; Aylmers; Hand & Word; Barber of Bantry. Dublin: Duffy, ND. Sm. 8vo, engraved frontis., bound without printed title in original red cloth with blind-stamped lyre, spine gilt, bindings a bit dulled, lacks front free endpaper. Good copy of a fragile and scarce book. Deighton 3-152 1983 £35

GRIFFIN, HOWARD   Cry Cadence: A Book of Poems. New York, 1947. 8vo, cloth. A review copy with slip from the publisher laid in. Fine copy in dust jacket which has a small tear. Scarce. In Our Time 156-340 1983 $75

GRIFFIN, JAMES B.   Archeology of Eastern United States. Chicago (1952). Plates, cloth, ex-library, moderately rubbed. King 46-7 1983 $75

GRIFFIN, JOHN HOWARD   Land of the High Sky. Midland: First National Bank of Midland, 1959. Cloth. First edition. With the author's presentation inscription to some close friends on the front free endsheet. Fine in the Cokesbury jacket, which is a bit faded, and with a few chips. Reese 20-988 1983 $75

GRIFFITH, A.   Mysteries of Police and Crime. Cassell, n.d. Special edition. 3 vols., 4to. 15 Rackham text illus. and many other illus. Green cloth gilt. Greer 40-180 1983 £45

GRIFFITH, DAVID WARK   The Rise and Fall of Free Speech in America. Los Angeles, 1916. Signed "compliments of author". Scarce. Drawings, boards with pict. label, covers frayed, loose, worn and soiled. King 46-392 1983 $125

GRIFFITH, ELIZABETH   A Wife in the Right: a comedy. London: printed for the author, and sold by Mess. E. and C. Dilly; J. Robson; and J. Walter, 1772. 8vo, wrappers, 1st ed. Half-title present. Ximenes 64-247 1983 $225

GRIFFITH, FRANK CARLOS   Mrs. Fiske. NY: Neale Publ. Co., 1912. Portraits, cloth ex-library, extremities worn. King 46-408 1983 $35

GRIFFITH, GEORGE C.   Olga Romanoff. Simpkin, Marshall, Hamilton, Kent & Co., 1897. First edition with these illus., 16 plates, 8vo, orig. blue cloth, a very good copy. Fenning 61-177 1983 £18.50

GRIFFITH, JOHN W.   An Elementary Text-book of the Microscope. J. van Boorst, 1864. First edition, with 12 coloured plates, 16 ads.(dated Jan. 1863). Small 8vo, orig. cloth, front free flyleaf neatly removed. Fenning 62-150 1983 £28.50

GRIFFITH, REGINALD H.   The Great Torch Race, An Address Delivered at the Dedication of the Wrenn Library. Austin: Univ. of Texas, (1921). Quarto. 1st ed. Orig. wrappers. Good copy. Jenkins 153-704 1983 $45

GRIFFITH, RICHARD   Variety; a comedy, in five acts. London: printed for T. Becket, 1782. 8vo, disbound, 1st ed., lacks a half-title. Ximenes 64-248 1983 $25

GRIFFITH, THOMAS W.   Sketches of the Early History of Maryland. Baltimore: Printed and Published by Frederick G. Schaeffer, 1821. Three quarter morocco by Ruperti. Frontis. A fine copy, with three corrections all in the same hand. Reese 18-554 1983 $150

GRIFFITH, W.   Journals of Travels in Assam, Burman... Calcutta: Bishop's College, 1847. Map repaired at fore-edge. 17 plates, some slightly stained and frayed. Small marginal worm hole in the early leaves. Half morocco. 8vo. Good. Edwards 1044-302 1983 £100

GRIFFITH, WILLIAM   A Treatise on the Jurisdiction and Proceedings of Justices of the Peace. Newark: John Woods, for the author, 1737. Second and revised edition. Full calf (shabby, covers detached). Very good. Felcone 19-21 1983 $40

GRIFFITHS, ACTON FREDERICK   Bibliotheca Anglo-Poetica. London: for the Proprietors of the Collection, 1851. 1st ed., 8vo, cont. half calf gilt, marbled boards. Woodcut frontis., vignette title page, text illus. Uncut copy with the half-title. Hinges and boards rubbed, but a very good copy. Trebizond 18-48 1983 $135

GRIFFITHS, ANSELM JOHN   Impressment fully considered, with a view to its gradual abolition. Cheltenham: printed for the author, 1826. First edition. 8vo. Cont. half calf, gilt, spine gilt. Rubbed, covers a little marked by damp. Scarce. Ximenes 63-338 1983 $125

GRIFFITHS, ANSELM JOHN   Observations on some points of seamanship... Cheltenham: printed by J.J. Hadley, Minerva Press, 1824. First edition. 8vo. Cont. half calf, gilt, spine gilt. Trifle rubbed. Ximenes 63-339 1983 $250

GRIFFITHS, ARTHUR   Wellington & Waterloo. London, 1898. Coloured portrait plate, 47 full page portraits, 27 full page illus. Numerous illus. 4to. Cont. half calf, slightly worn. Good. Edwards 1042-506 1983 £30

GRIFFITHS, THOMAS   Recreations in Chemistry. London: John W. Parker, 1841. First edition. 8vo. Orig. blindstamped cloth. Frontis., 11 plates. Ads. Cloth dampstained. Zeitlin 264-188 1983 $40

GRIFFITHS, WILLIAM H.   The Story of American Bank Note Company. (New York: American Bank Note Company, 1959). First edition. Small 4to. Cloth spine, paper over boards paper label. Fine. Oak Knoll 48-180 1983 $85

GRIGSBY, MELVIN   The Smoked Yank. (N.p., 1888). Illus. Cloth, very fine. A presentation copy. Reese 19-252 1983 $70

GRIGSON, GEOFFREY   The Harp of Aeolus and other essays...
London, 1948. First edition. 20 black and white illus. Slightly
torn dustwrapper slightly darkened at the spine. Very good.
Jolliffe 26-235 1983 £20

GRIGSON, GEOFFREY   The Isles of Scilly. London, 1946.
First edition. Inscription. Slightly torn dustwrapper, by John
Craxton, chipped at the head and tail of the spine. Very good.
Jolliffe 26-234 1983 £24

GRIGSON, GEOFFREY   The Isles of Scilly. London, 1946.
First edition. Partially defective dust wrapper. Very nice. Rota
231-289 1983 £15

GRIGSON, GEOFFREY   Palmer: the Visionary Years. London,
Kegan Paul, (1947). First edition. Illus. with 68 b/w and 2 color
plates of the artists work. Dust jacket (slight rubbing). Very
good. Houle 22-711 1983 $45

GRIGSON, GEOFFREY   Under the Cliff and other poems.
London, 1943. First edition. Slightly torn and marked dustwrapper.
Very good. Jolliffe 26-233 1983 £35

GRIMES, J. STANLEY   The Mysteries of Human Nature Explained
by a New System of Nervous Physiology. Buffalo, 1857. 1st ed. 8vo.
Illus. Morrill 289-92 1983 $35

GRIMES, JAMES   Governor's Message Delivered to the
Seventh General Assembly of the State of Iowa. Des Moines, Iowa,
1858. Dbd. First edition. Ginsberg 47-364 1983 $100

GRIMM, THE BROTHERS   Fairy Tales from Grimm. N.Y.: G & D,
n.d. (ca. 1930). 4to. Cloth backed pictorial boards, tips rubbed.
4 full-page color plates, 4 full-page pen drawings. Pictorial endpapers plus page decorations by Betts. Fine. Aleph-bet 8-37 1983
$45

GRIMM, THE BROTHERS   Household Stories. Macmillan, 1882.
First edition. Illus. by Walter Crane, 2 pp. adverts. Olive green
decor. cloth (designed by Crane), endpapers designed by Crane (endpapers cracked at hinges, corners slightly bruised, slight foxing at
prelims.), very good copy, scarce. Hodgkins 27-448 1983 £45

GRIMM, THE BROTHERS   Household Tales. Eyre & Spottiswoode,
1946. Sq. 8vo, double colour pictorial title, 4 colour plates. 17
full-page & 42 text illus. Yellow cloth. Greer 40-164 1983 £22

GRIMM, WILHELM   Grimm's Marchen. Vienna: M. Munk,
(n.d.). First edition. Cloth-backed marbled boards. Illus. by
H. Lefler & A.J. Urban. 12 color-plate illus., rebound with the
orig. wraps. Spine very slightly faded, otherwise a very good copy.
Bookplate. MacManus 268-2414 1983 $185

GRIMM, WILHELM   Grimm's other tales. London: Golden
Cockerel Press, 1956. 8vo. Full purple morocco, gilt design on
front cover, t.e.g. 10 wood-engravings by Gwenda Morgan. Limited
edition of 75 numbered copies, signed by the artist and specially
bound. Traylen 94-408 1983 £135

GRIMSTONE, MARY LEMAN   Louisa Egerton, or Castle Herbert.
George Virtue, 1830. First edition, front. engr. title, plates.
Half black calf, boards rubbed. Jarndyce 31-719 1983 £32

GRIMWOOD, ETHEL ST. C.   My Three Years in Manipur. London, 1891.
Third edition. Plan, illus. 8vo. Orig. cloth. Good. Edwards 1044-
303 1983 £35

GRINDLAY, R.   Scenery, Costumes and Architecture,
chiefly on the Western Side of India. London, 1826. Coloured engraved
title, uncoloured lithograph title to part II on India Paper. 36
magnificent hand-coloured aquatint plates. Folio. Half red morocco.
T.e.g. by Sangorski & Sutcliffe. An exceptionally large copy, the
plates in an early state, with no offsetting. 8vo. Good. Edwards
1044-304 1983 £1,500

GRINDON, LEO H.   Country Rambles and Manchester Walks and
Wild Flowers. Manchester: Palmer & Howe, 1882. With plates, 8vo,
orig. cloth, gilt. Inscribed by the author to Rosa E. Grindon.
Fenning 61-178 1983 £21.50

GRINDON, LEO H.   Lancashire. Seeley and Co., 1892.
First edition, with 40 full-page and other illus., cr. 8vo, orig.
cloth, gilt. Fenning 61-180 1983 £32.50

GRINDON, LEO H.   The Trees of old England. 1868.
Wheldon 160-2084 1983 £12

GRINNELL, GEORGE BIRD   American Game-Bird Shooting. NY (1910).
First ed. Color plates, cloth, ink and stamped name, inner hinges
broken, covers rubbed and darkened. King 46-579 1983 $35

GRINNELL, GEORGE BIRD   The Fighting Cheyennes. NY, 1915.
1st ed., maps & plans. Argosy 710-221 1983 $40

GRINNELL, GEORGE BIRD   The Indians of To-Day. N.Y.: Duffield
& Co., 1906. Illus. with full-page portraits of living Indians. Cloth,
worn and darkened. Dawson 471-342 1983 $60

GRINNELL, JOSEPH   Gold Hunting in Alaska. Elgin, Ill.,
(1901). Illus. Double-column measure. Boards and cloth. 1st ed.
Covers worn. Bradley 63-2 1983 $30

GRISCOM, ACTON   The Historia Regum Britanniae of
Geoffrey of Monmouth. London 1929. Photos, cloth, stamped name
on end papers, edges, etc., slightly worn. 1st ed. King 46-761
1983 $25

GRISEBACH, A. H. R.   Flora of the West Indian Islands.
(1864), reprint 1977. 8vo, cloth. Wheldon 160-1689 1983 £52

GRISEBACH, LUCIUS   Willem Kalf, 1619-1693. Berlin:
Gebr. Mann, 1974. 199 illus. hors texte. 4to. Cloth. Dust
jacket. Ars Libri 32-350 1983 $75

GRISENTHWAITE, W.   A Refutation of every Argument brought
against the Truth of Christianity and Revealed Religion... London:
G.B. Whittaker..., 1825. First edition. 8vo. Orig. quarter cloth.
Slight discolouring, one joint cracked. Heath 48-389 1983 £55

GRISIER, A.   Les Armes Et Le Duel. Paris, 1847.
Plates, newer 1/2 lea., foxed, else good. 2nd ed. King 46-580 1983
$35

GRISWOLD, ROGER   Message of His Excellency Governour
Griswold, to the General Assembly, at their Special Session, August
25, 1912. New Haven, 1812. Dsb., very good. Reese 18-378 1983
$60

A GROAN from the throne. London: Fairburn, 1820. First edition.
8vo. Disbound. Large woodcut on the title-page by George Cruikshank. Missing the ads. Scarce. Ximenes 63-484 1983 $75

THE "GROANS" of India: a voice and a visitor from Hindostan.
Boston: D.S. King, 1843. First edition. 12mo. Orig. pink
printed wrappers. With several woodcut illus. Fine copy.
Ximenes 63-208 1983 $45

GROBER, KARL   Schwabische Skulptur der Spatgotik.
Munchen, 1922. (Sammelbande zur Geschichte der Kunst und des
Kunstgewerbes. Vol. 2.) 16pp., 96 plates. 4to. Boards, 1/4
cloth (slightly worn). Ars Libri SB 26-91 1983 $25

GROEBER, KARL   Children's Toys of Bygone Days. New
York: (1928). First American edition. Profusely illus. Bright
orange cloth. Former owner's name on flyleaf. Fine in dust jacket.
Boxed. Bradley 66-420 1983 $110

GROHMANN, WILL   The Drawings of Paul Klee. New York:
Curt Valentin, 1944. 72 facsimile plates loose in portfolio as
issued. Large 4to. Cloth. Edition limited to 700 copies. Ars
Libri 32-365 1983 $125

GROHMANN, WILL   Wassily Kandinsky: Life and Work.
New York: Abrams, (1958). 920 illus. (41 color). Large 4to.
Cloth. Ars Libri 32-352 1983 $125

GROHMANN, WILL   Das Werk Ernst Ludwig Kirchners.
Munchen: Kurt Wolff, 1926. 100 collotype plates. 6 orig. woodcuts
by Kirchner, printed in blue (including those on binding). 26 illus.
Large oblong 4to. Orig. cloth. No. 226 of a limited edition of
850 copies. Ars Libri 32-362 1983 $950

GROHNE, ERNST   Die bremischen Truhen mit reforma-
torischen Darstellungen und der Ursprung ihrer Motive. Bremen,
1936. (Schriften der Bremer Wissenschaftlichen Gesellschaft.
Reihe D. Abhandlungen und Vortrage. Vol. 10 2.) 88pp. 38 plates.
Sm. 4to. Wraps. Ars Libri SB 26-92 1983 $65

GROLIER CLUB   Description of the Early Printed Books
Owned by the Grolier Club. NY: Grolier Club, 1895. Small quarto.
Includes 25 facs. of pages from books described. Limited to 400 copies
printed at the De Vinne Press. Very fine in slightly rubbed quarter-
leather and cloth-covered boards. Bromer 25-166 1983 $85

GROLIER CLUB   The Grolier Club of the City of New
York. (New York), 1907. Ed. limited to 500 copies. 12mo. Orig.
boards, vellum back. Some light spotting on covers. Morrill 289-
345 1983 $40

GROMAIRE, FRANCOIS   L'oeuvre grave de Marcel Gromaire.
Lausanne/Paris: La Bibliotheque des Arts, 1976. 2 vols. Prof.
illus. Large 4to. Cloth. Dust jacket. No. 204 of 650 copies
on velin, of a limited edition of 700 copies only. Ars Libri 32-
290 1983 $225

GROOMBRIDGE, WILLIAM   Sonnets. Canterbury: Printed for
the Author, by Simmons and Kirkby...MDCCLXXXIX. 4to, lacks half-
title, otherwise complete, in modern half leather. First edition.
Quaritch NS 7-61 1983 $150

GROSE, FRANCIS   The Antiquities of Ireland. London,
1791. First edition, 2 vols., engr. titles, frontis. and 268 views on
261 engr. plates, 4to, minor foxing. Russia gilt. K Books 307-86
1983 £150

GROSE, FRANCIS   The Olio. London, 1796. Portrait
frontis., lacks half-title, minor foxing and a few minor repairs,
half calf. Second edition. K Books 301-81 1983 £35

GROSS, CHARLES   A Bibliography of British Municipal
History... New York: Burt Franklin, n.d. Cloth. Reprint of the
1897 ed. Dawson 470-135 1983 $25

GROSS, MILT   He Done Her Wrong. N.Y., 1930.
First edition. Sq. 8vo, cloth, slightly rubbed. Argosy 714-345 1983
$75

GROSS, MILT   He Done Her Wrong: The Great American
Novel, and Not a Word in it Too.., New York, 1930. 8vo. Cloth. Name
of former owner on front flyleaf, some cocking for this bulky book,
otherwise about fine. In Our Time 156-344 1983 $35

GROSS, MILT   Nize Baby. N.Y., (1926). First
edition, fine. Argosy 714-346 1983 $100

GROSS, SAMUEL D.   Autobiography of Samuel D. Gross, M.D.
Philadelphia, 1887. 2 vols. First edition. 8vo. Backstrips faded,
stained. Contents very fine. Ex-library. Very scarce. Fye H-3-755
1983 $50

GROSSMITH, GEORGE   The Diary of a Nobody. London, 1892.
First edition. Short A.L.S. from Grossmith loosely inserted. Illus.
by Weedon Grossmith. Tail of spine worn. Very good. Jolliffe 26-
236 1983 £225

GROSVENOR, G.   The Book of Birds. Washington, 1937.
905 coloured illustrations, 2 vols., royal 8vo. Wheldon 160-735
1983 £25

GROTE, GEORGE   A History of Greece. London, 1918.
12 vols. 8vo, cloth. Salloch 385-235 1983 $120

GROTH, JOHN   Studio: Europe. NY, (1945). Near very
good in chipped, wearing dustwrapper. Quill & Brush 54-631 1983 $35

GROTIUS, HUGO   De Ivre Belli ac Pacis Libri Tres.
Amsterdam: Blaeu, 1631. Folio. Title in red & black. Title
vignette. Calf, blind-impressed armorial device on both covers showing
Griffin with staff below crown. 2nd edition. Rostenberg 88-115
1983 $1,750

GROTIUS, HUGO   De La Verite de la Religion Chrestienne.
Paris, Chez Pierre Le Petit, 1659. 16mo, contemporary calf, leather
label, raised bands with 5 tiny crown-like ornaments in gilt. Morrill
290-160 1983 $60

GROULX, LIONEL   Notre Maitre Le Passe. Montreal:
Librairie Granger, 1944-46. 20 1/2cm. 3 vols. Printed wrappers.
Very good. McGahern 53-61 1983 $25

GROVE, F. C.   The Frosty Caucasus. London, 1875.
Map. Frontis. 6 illus. engraved by E. Whymper. 8vo. Orig. cloth.
Good. Edwards 1044-305 1983 £78

GROVE, GEORGE   Grove's Dictionary of Music and
Musicians. New York, 1911. Illus. 5 vols. 8vo. Few gashes on
back hinge of vol. 5. Morrill 289-348 1983 $35

GROVES, J.   The British Charophyta. Ray Society,
1920-25. 4t plates, 2 vols., 8vo, cloth. Wheldon 160-1836 1983 £50

GROVES, J. PERCY   With the Green Jackets. London, c.1891.
Thick sm. 8vo. Orig. green decorated cloth. Frontis. 7 plates, 32
pages of ads. Very slightly worn and soiled. A.e.g. Ink inscription
on endpaper. Good. Edwards 1042-358 1983 £40

GROVE, WILLIAM ROBERT   The Bakerian Lecture on Certain
Phenomena of Voltaic Ignition... London: R. and J.E. Taylor,
1847. 4to. 1 plate. Inscribed presentation copy. Extract.
Zeitlin 264-189 1983 $45

GROVER, LA FAYETTE F.   Report of Governor Grover to General
Schofield on the Modoc War. Salem, Oregon: Mart. V. Brown, State
Printer, 1874. 20 cm. Later cloth. Fine; some faint staining
to title. First edition. From the library of Robert S. Ellison,
with his small leather bookplate. Grunder 6-64 1983 $75

GROVER, WILLIAM   Selections from the Letters and Other
Papers of William Grover. Printed for Harvey and Darton, 1829. Large
12mo, wrapper. Fenning 60-149 1983 £10.50

GRUBB, JOHN   The British Heroes. London: printed
and sold by John Morphew and H. Clements in Oxford, 1707. 1st ed.,
4to, modern marbled boards. Pickering & Chatto 19-30 1983 $350

GRUBB, N. H.   Cherries. 1949. 12 coloured plates and
16 plates from 40 photographs, royal 8vo, cloth. Wheldon 160-1948
1983 £12

GRUBB, SARAH   A Selection from the Letters of the
Late Sarah Grubb. Sudbury, J. Wright, 1848. First edition,
erratum slip, 8vo, orig. cloth, by Remnant & Edmonds, with their
ticket. Fenning 62-151 1983 £16.50

GRUBB, SARAH   Some Account of the Life and Religious
Labours of Sarah Grubb. Trenton: Isaac Collins, 1795. Full calf,
fine. Felcone 19-22 1983 $45

GRUBB, SARAH   Some Account of the Life and Religious
Labours of... Belfast: William Robinson, 1837. Errata slip, small
8vo, orig. cloth. Fenning 60-150 1983 £16.50

GRUBBE, EMIL   X-Ray Treatment. St. Paul, 1949.
First edition. 8vo. Orig. binding. Fye H-3-232 1983 $30

GRUENDER, HUBERT   Psychology Without a Soul. St. Louis:
B. Herder, (1921). First edition. Gach 95-183 1983 $27.50

GRUYTER, W. JOSEPH DE   A New Approach to Maya Hieroglyphs.
Amsterdam: H.J. Paris, 1946. One large folding plate with 154
figures. Small 4to. Boards. Ars Libri 34-260 1983 $35

GUALTIERI, GUIDO   Relationi della venuta de gli ambasciatori giaponesi a Roma, sino alla partita di Lisbona... In Venetia MDLXXXVI (1586). 8vo, new vellum backstrip. Title and author in MS on spine. Paper covered boards. New endpapers. A few corners of pages renewed, no loss of text. Arkway 22-59 1983 $1,800

GUARINI, GIOVANNI B.   The Faithful Shepherd, a Pastoral Tragi-Comedy... London: for Richard Montagu..., (1734?). 8vo. Modern quarter morocco. Engraved frontis. Titles and text in Italian and English. Heath 48-475 1983 £75

GUBBINS, M. R.   An Account of the Mutinies of Oudh. London, 1858. 8vo. Orig. cloth. 4 folding maps, 4 plates, 1 plan. Rebacked. Orig. spine laid down. Slightly worn. Good. Edwards 1042-359 1983 £80

GUDIOL, JOSE   Goya, 1746-1828. Barcelona: Ediciones Poligrafa, 1970. 4 vols. 1022 plates with 1295 illus. Large square 4to. Leatherette. Dust jacket. Ars Libri 32-268 1983 $250

GUE, BENJAMIN F.   History of Iowa from the Earliest Times to the Beginning of the 20th Century. NY, (1903). 4 vols. Many illus. 8vo, cloth, g.t. Ex lib. With errata slip. Argosy 716-225 1983 $85

GUE, GURNEY C.   Background of Iowa Territorial Pioneers as Exemplified by the Ancestry of Francis Parker and His Wife Rhoda Chaplin. N.p., 1945. Orig. cloth. First edition. Ginsberg 47-365 1983 $25

GUEDALLA, PHILIP   The Hundred Years. London: Hodder and Stoughton, (1936). First edition. One of 250 copies signed by the author. Covers very slightly soiled, end-papers a trifle browned, otherwise a very good copy. MacManus 278-2416 1983 $75

GUEDALLA, PHILIP   Metri Gratia: Verse and Prose. Oxford: B.H. Blackwell, 1911. First edition. Wrappers slightly frayed and soiled at the edges, otherwise a very good copy. MacManus 278-2417 1983 $40

GUEDALLA, PHILIP   The Two Marshalls. London: Hodder & Stoughton, 1943. Illus., orig. cloth, dust jacket (slightly faded, worn and soiled, with one very small tear to the spine margin). First edition. Near-fine. MacManus 278-2418 1983 $25

GUELLETTE, THOMAS S.   Peruvian Tales. Dublin: Printed by T. Henshall, for the United Company of Booksellers, 1784. 5th ed. 2 vols, 12mo, contemporary tree calf; lacks number-labels. Hill 165-49 1983 £50

GUENYVEAU, A.   Manuel d'Exploitation des Mines de Houille... Lyon & St. Etienne: J.B. Kindelem, 1812. First edition. 12mo. Boards. A few minor stains. Gurney 90-55 1983 £50

GUERANGER, EDOUARD   Lecons de Chimie appliquees a l'Agriculture... Paris: Julien, 1850. First edition. 8vo. Publisher's orig. morocco backed cloth. A few stains on cover. A very good copy. Zeitlin 264-190 1983 $60

GUERNON, CHARLES   Aristocracy in America. New York, 1928. Ed. limited to 100 privately printed copies. Decorative illus. 12mo, orig. full leather, boxed, very nice. Morrill 287-136 1983 $20

GUERNSEY, CHARLES A   Wyoming Cowboy Days. New York, 1936. First edition in dust jacket. Frontis. and plates. Jenkins 152-138 1983 $55

GUERNSEY, CHARLES A.   Wyoming Cowboy Days. NY, 1936. 1st ed. Illus., binding stained. Argosy 710-624 1983 $35

GUERNSEY, ORRIN   History of Rock County, and Transactions of the Rock County Agricultural Society and Mechanics' Institute. Janesville, Wis., 1856. Illus., 5 plates. Orig. cloth. First edition. Presentation copy from "the author." Ginsberg 46-825 1983 $150

GUERRA, CAMILLO   La vita e le opere del pittore napoletano Camillo Guerra... Napoli: L'Arte Tipografica, 1960. Prof. illus. Large square 4to. Boards, 1/4 cloth. Ars Libri 33-491 1983 $150

GUERRISI, MICHELE   Discorsi su la scultura. Torino, 1930. 216pp., 32 plates. Sm. 4to. Wraps. (slightly worn). Light intermittent foxing. Ars Libri SB 26-93 1983 $22.50

GUEST, MONTAGUE   The Royal Yacht Squadron. John Murray, 1903. First edition, with 48 plates, 8vo, orig. cloth, gilt, t.e.g. Wanting a blank flyleaf, otherwise a very good copy. Fenning 60-151 1983 £32.50

GUEST, MOSES   Poems on Several Occasions. Cincinnati, 1823. Foxed. Modern leather and buckram. Very good. Reese 18-567 1983 $175

GUEST, RICHARD   A Compendious History of the Cotton-Manufacture. Printed by Joseph Pratt, Manchester, 1823. First edition. 4to, with 3 lithographed and 9 engraved plates; wraps. Quaritch NS 5-48 1983 $850

GUEVARA, ANTONIO DE   The Dial of Princes... (London), Richarde Tottill and Thomas Marshe, 1568. Folio, cont. blind tooled and roll-stamped calf, rebacked period style, clasps reattached and present, name on title, some age-stains, title and last leaf washed and sized. Ravenstree 94-155 1983 $1,350

GUEVARA, ANTONIO DE   Golden Epistles... Imprinted at London by Ralph Newberie, 15 Octobris, 1582. 4to, full tan morocco blind and gilt tooled, few side-notes trimmed, minor water and damp marks through lower edge. Final Elizabethan edition. Ravenstree 94-157 1983 $450

GUGGISBERG, F. G.   "The Shop". London, 1902. Second edition. 8vo. Orig. blue decorated cloth. Frontis. 8 coloured and 9 other plates, 2 folding plans, numerous illus. Very slightly worn and stained. T.e.g. Good. Edwards 1042-360 1983 £15

GUGLIELMI FALDI, CARLA   Tiepolo alla Scuola dei Carmini a Venezia. Milano: Associazione fra le Casse di Risparmio Italiane, 1960. 24 color plates. 9 text illus. (1 tipped-in color). Folio. Boards, 1/4 cloth. Dust jacket. Ars Libri 33-355 1983 $75

GUIART, JEAN   The Arts of the South Pacific. New York: Golden Press, 1963. 417 illus. (partly in color). Large 4to. Cloth. Ars Libri 34-803 1983 $125

GUICCIARDINI, FRANCESCO   Two Discourses of Master Frances Guicciardin... London, William Ponsonbie, 1595. 4to, new quarter morocco gilt, title soiled, chipped at edges with small hole in blank inner edge, some old faded underlining; a polyglot edition with text in four columns. Ravenstree 94-160 1983 $540

GUICHARD, AUGUST C.   Dissertation Historique sur les Communes de France. Paris, chez Delaunay, 1819. First edition, including the half-title, 8vo, wrapper. Fenning 61-183 1983 £14.50

GUIDEBOOK of the Western United States. Washington: 1915-16. 4 vols. Illus., including numerous folding maps in color. Printed wrappers. Covers chipped, otherwise very good set. Bradley 66-693 1983 $37.50

GUIDOTT, THOMAS   A Collection of Treatises relating to the City and Waters of Bath... London: for J. Leake, 1725. First collected edition. 8vo. Cont. calf, gilt. Engraved plates. Very slight marginal worming at end, light wear to calf. Very rare. Heath 48-565 1983 £125

GUIDOTT, THOMAS   Gideon's Fleece. London: Sam Smith, 1684. First edition. Small 4to, cont. calf, (rebacked). Upper margins trimmed close, with the loss of "Gideon's Fleece" on the title. Argosy 713-233 1983 $175

GUIDOTTI, ALBERTO   Metodo facile Performare Qualunque Sia sorta Di Vernici Della Cina, e del Giappone Praticato In Francia, ed in Inghiterra Secondo gli Sperimenti di accreditati Prosessori... In Fuligno 1784. Per Giovanni Tomassini Stampator Fescevile. (1784). 8vo, 2 full page copper plates. 19th century MS notes bound in. Attached to lower board 12mo. In Venezia MDCCLXVIII with 1 sheet of notes attached. Bound in quarter morocco. 19th century marbled paper covered boards. Arkway 22-60 1983 $675

GUIFFREY, JULES   Antoine Van Dyck. Paris: A. Quantin, 1882. 28 engraved and heliogravure plates. 91 text illus. Folio. Cloth. Printed on fine uncut wove paper. Ars Libri 32-196 1983 $75

GUIFFREY, JEAN   P.P. Prud'hon. Peintures, pastels et dessins, Musee du Louvre. Paris: Albert Morance, 1924. 47 plates loose in portfolio as issued. Small 4to. Boards, 1/4 cloth. Head of spine chipped. Ars Libri 32-541 1983 $50

GUILD, JO. C.   Old Times in Tennessee. Nashville, 1878. First edition. Orig. cloth. Minimal outer wear only. Inscribed and signed by author. Jenkins 152-448 1983 $200

GUILLAUME, C. E.   Les Rayons X. Paris: Gauthier-Villars, 1896. Second edition. 8vo. Modern paper wrappers. 10 plates, plates VII & VIII appear twice. A good copy. Zeitlin 264-190 1983 $60

GUILLAUME, PAUL   La sculpture negre primitive. Paris: G. Cres, (1928). 43 plates. Large 8vo. Wrappers. Spine torn. Ars Libri 34-645 1983 $65

GUILLEMIN, AMEDEE   The Forces of Nature. Macmillan, 1873. Second edition, with 11 coloured plates and 455 full-page and other illus., roy. 8vo, orig. cloth, gilt, t.e.g. Inside joints neatly repaired. Fenning 62-152 1983 £32.50

GUILLET, EDWIN C.   Cobourg 1798-1948. Oshawa: Good-fellow Pub. Co., 1948. 25 1/2cm. 390 illus. Mapped endpapers. Very good copy. McGahern 54-74 1983 $35

GUILLIMEAU, JACQUES   Child-Birth or, the Happy Deliverie of Women. A. Hatfield, London, 1612. 4to, 3 woodcuts of instruments and 11 of the foetus in utero; ink blot on verso of title, blank upper corners of first 8 leaves repaired, otherwise a good copy; nineteenth century calf, rebacked. First edition in English. The woodcuts of the foetus in utero are copied from Roesslin with the addition of the umbilical cord. Quaritch NS 5-49 1983 $1,600

GUINAN, JOSEPH   The Soggarth Aroon. Dublin: James Duffy, 1905. First edition in book-form, 8vo, ads. Orig. cloth. Fenning 62-153 1983 £10.50

GUINNESS, ARTHUR   Alice Aforethought: Guinness Carrolls for 1938. (Dublin: Arthur Guinness), 1938. Octavo. Illus. Fine in colored pictorial self-wrappers. Publisher's printed presentation card laid-in. Bromer 25-326 1983 $65

GUIZOT, FRANCOIS P. G.   The Fine Arts. Thomas Bosworth, 1855. With 14 plates and 3 other illus., 8vo, orig. cloth, gilt, t.e.g., by Westley & Co., with their ticket, a very good copy. Fenning 61-184 1983 £16.50

GULDINUS, PAULUS   De centro gravitatis Trium speciorum Quantitatis continuae. Vienna: Gregor Gelbhaar, 1635. First edition. With one folding engraved plate and numerous text diagrams. Engraved title vignette. Small folio. Cont. vellum, green ties. Author's inscription on half-title. Kraus 164-107 1983 $800

GULICK, SIDNEY L.   Evolution of the Japanese: Social and Psychic. New York, London...F.H. Revell Company, (1903). First edition, 8vo, half calf, t.e.g. Fenning 61-186 1983 £10.50

GULL, CYRIL ARTHUR EDWARD RANGER   Miss Malevolent. London: Greening & Co., ltd., 1899. Orig. pictorial cloth. First edition, covers a little rubbed, otherwise a very good copy. MacManus 278-2420 1983 $25

GULLY, JAMES MANBY   The Water Cure in Chronic Disease. 1856. Small 8vo, orig. cloth, blocked in blind. Bickersteth 77-275 1983 £12

GULSTON, JOSEPHA   The Life and Death of Silas Barnstarke. London: Smith, Elder, & Co., 1853. Orig. cloth with paper spine label. First edition. With ads. dated June, 1853, but without the binder's ticket). Spine label slightly soiled and chipped, otherwise a very good copy, with the covers slightly waterspotted. MacManus 278-2423 1983 $135

GUMILLA, JOSEPH   Historia Natural civil y Geografica de las Naciones situadas en las Riveras Del Rio Orinoco. Barcelona: En la Imprenta de Carlos Gibert y Tuto Ano M DCCLXXXXI (1791). 8vo, in early mottled leather. Scuffed corners and hinges. Leather labels. Marbled endpapers. Bookplate and cancelled stamp from Princeton University. Very clean internally. Arkway 22-61 1983 $675

GUMMERE, SAMUEL R.   Definitions and Elementary Observations in Astronomy. Philadelphia, 1830. Diagrams. Calf-backed boards. Spine ends damaged. Felcone 22-6 1983 $35

GUNDOLF, F.   The Mantle of Caesar. NY, 1928. 8vo, cloth. Salloch 387-20 1983 $20

GUNN, DONALD   History of Manitoba. Ottawa: Maclean, Roger & Co., 1880. 21 1/2cm. Wanting the frontis. portrait, title page clipped, front hinge tape repaired. Orig. cloth. Good. McGahern 53-67 1983 $45

GUNN, FREDERICK WILLIAM   The Master of the Gunnery. NY, 1887. Tall 4to, gilt-pict. cloth, backstrip chipped, a.e.g., ex-library. Argosy 710-116 1983 $50

GUNN, MOSES   Memorial Sketches of... Chicago, 1889. First edition. Illus. Ex-lib. Argosy 713-235 1983 $35

GUNN, NEIL M.   Back Home. Glasgow: Walter Wilson & Co. Limited, 1932. First edition. 12mo. Orig. boards. Fine copy. Jaffe 1-120 1983 $65

GUNN, NEIL M.   Butcher's Broom. Edinburgh: The Porpoise Press, (1934). First edition. 8vo. Orig. cloth. Dust jacket. Fine copy. Jaffe 1-122 1983 $45

GUNN, NEIL M.   Hidden Doors. Edinburgh: The Porpoise Press, 1929. First edition. 8vo. Orig. cloth. Dust jacket. Fine copy. Jaffe 1-119 1983 $45

GUNN, NEIL M.   Highland River. Edinburgh: The Porpoise Press, (1937). First edition. 8vo. Orig. cloth. Dust jacket. Fine copy. Jaffe 1-123 1983 $45

GUNN, NEIL M.   The Lost Glen. Edinburgh: The Porpoise Press, (1932). First edition. 8vo. Orig. cloth. Dust jacket. Slightly chipped jacket. Fine copy. Jaffe 1-121 1983 $45

GUNN, THOM   Fighting Terms. Oxford: Fantasy Press, 1954. Signature of former editor of the Fantasy Press on free endpaper. Very slightly faded spine and tiny snag to edge of rear board. Very scarce. Fine. Gekoski 2-74 1983 £275

GUNS, Ammunition, and Tackle. N.Y., Macmillan, 1904. Thick 8vo, illus. with three color plates of flies and 20 b/w plates on other subjects. 3/4 green morocco over marbled boards, t.e.g., unopened. One of 100 deluxe copies, printed on large paper. Fine copy. Houle 21-1111 1983 $300

GUNTHER, A.   Andrew Garrett's Fische der Sudsee. (1873-1916). Reprint, 1966. 180 plates, 3 vols. in 1, 4to, cloth. Wheldon 160-965 1983 £95

GUNTHER, A.   Catalogue of the Fishes in the British Museum. 1859-70. 8 vols., original cloth. The original issue. An ex-library copy. Vols. 1-3 have been neatly repaired, the rest used but sound, the contents in good condition. Wheldon 160-964 1983 £150

GUNTHER, PAUL   Wilhelm Ostwald 2.9.1853 - 4.4.1932. Berlin: Verlag Chemie, 1932. Offprint. 8vo. Orig. printed paper wrappers. Presentation copy from the author. Slight soiling, internally near fine. Zeitlin 264-359 1983 $25

GURDON, P. R. T.   The Khasis. London, 1914. Coloured and
other plates. Pictorial cloth gilt. 8vo. Inscribed on endpaper "A.C.
Triminger from the author." Good. Edwards 1044-308 1983 £38

GURNEY, JOSEPH J.   Essays on the Evidences, Doctrines, and
Practical Operation, of Christianity. Published by J. and A. Arch,
1825. First edition, without half-title, 8vo, recent boards.
Fenning 60-152 1983 £28.50

GUTHRIE, DOUGLAS   A History of Medicine. Philadelphia,
1946. First American edition. 8vo. Orig. binding. Fye H-3-234
1983 $30

GUTHRIE, G. J.   A Treatise on Gun-Shot Wounds. London,
1827. 5 litho. plates, 8vo, crudely rebacked. Old signature on title;
upper margin of title cut out. Argosy 713-236 1983 $175

GUTHRIE, GEORGE C.   A Letter to the Honourable Geo.
Tierney, MP, on the Bank Restriction Act. R. Carlile, 1819. First
edition, modern blue boards, v.g. Jarndyce 31-180 1983 £20

GUTHRIE, JAMES CARGILL   Rowena. Hodder & Stoughton, 1871.
First edition. Front. 4 pp ads. Orig. green cloth, bevelled boards.
Jarndyce 30-713 1983 £10.50

GUTHRIE, RAMON   Trobar Clus. Ma., 1923. Limited to 250
signed and numbered copies, fine in tissue jacket. Quill & Brush 54-
593 1983 $60

GUTHRIE, STUART   A Little Anthology of Hitherto Uncollected Poems... Flansham, 1922. First English edition. Edges
spotted. Endpapers darkened and slightly spotted. In torn tissue
dustwrapper. Jolliffe 26-404 1983 £45

GUTHRIE, THOMAS ANSTEY   Baboo Jabberjee. London: J.M. Dent &
Co., 1897. Illus. by J. Bernard Partridge. Original pictorial cloth.
First edition. Edges and corners a little worn. Endpapers starting
to brown. Former owner's signature. Very good. MacManus 277-93
1983 $50

GUTHRIE, THOMAS ANSTEY   Love Among the Lions. London: J.M. Dent
& Co., n.d. (1898). Original cloth. First edition. Edges and corners
a little worn. Endpapers browned. Front cover faded at top edge.
A good copy. MacManus 277-94 1983 $50

GUTHRIE, THOMAS ANSTEY   Mr. Punch's Model Music-Hall Songs &
Dramas. London: Bradbury, Agnew & Co., 1892. Illus. Original decorated cloth. First edition. Spine and covers slightly worn, soiled
and faded. A very good copy. MacManus 277-95 1983 $50

GUTHRIE, THOMAS ANSTEY   Paleface and Redskin. London: Grant
Richards, (1898). Illus. by Gordon Browne. Orig. pictorial cloth.
First edition. Spine slightly darkened and worn at head and foot.
Corners bumped. Covers soiled. MacManus 277-96 1983 $60

GUTHRIE, THOMAS ANSTEY   The Pariah. London: Smith, Elder & Co.,
1889. 3 vols. Orig. grey cloth (library labels removed). First
edition. Spines and covers rather worn. Hinges weak. Bookplate.
A fair copy. MacManus 277-97 1983 $125

GUTHRIE, THOMAS ANSTEY   The Tinted Venus. London & New York:
Harper & Brothers, 1898. Illus. by Bernard Partridge. Orig. decorated
cloth. First edition. Covers rubbed at edges. Inner hinges weak.
MacManus 277-98 1983 $25

GUTHRIE, THOMAS ANSTEY   The Travelling Companions. London,
1892. First edition. Cloth at edge of spine torn. Covers marked.
Good. Rota 230-29 1983 £12

GUTHRIE, WILLIAM NORMAN   The Call and A Queen's Sending. Chicago:
Alderbrink Press, 1907. 12mo. Printed in blue and black with a series
of double-spreads. Printed wrappers slightly soiled, light rubbing to
spine, otherwise fine and internally pristine. Bromer 25-131 1983
$95

GUYTON, MORVEAU, L. B.   Traite des moyens de Desinfecter l'Air...
Paris: Bernard, 1801. First edition. 8vo. Boards. Old inscription on title. Gurney 90-57 1983 £80

GWILT, JOSEPH   Rudiments of a Grammar of the Anglo
Saxon Tongue. London: William Pickering. 1829. With an 8 page
catalog of Pickering's books in the front. Orig. cloth; paper
cover label. Karmiole 76-73 1983 $75

GWILT, JOSEPH   A treatise on the equilibrium of arches
... London: John Weale, 1839. Third edition. 8vo, cont. half calf,
spine gilt. Large folding engraved frontis. 4 engraved plates.
Binding rubbed. Ximenes 63-16 1983 $90

GWINETT, AMBROSE   The Life and Unparalleled Voyages and
Adventures of Ambrose Gwinett. London: Printed by W. Roberts, n.d.
(ca. 1770). Later 3/4 calf & marbled boards. Pages 17-20 cropped
with some loss of text. MacManus 278-2421 1983 $60

GYLDENSTOLPE, N.   Zoological Results of Swedish Expedition
to Central Africa 1921: Birds. K. Svensk. Vet. Handl., 1924.
Map, 2 coloured plates and 16 text-figures, roy. 8vo, half cloth.
Wheldon 160-737 1983 £18

GYNECOLOGICAL and Obstetrical. New York, Appleton, 1921-28. Illus.,
some in color. 16 vols. 8vo. Orig. blue cloth, nice. Morrill 289-
93 1983 $75

GYSIN, BRION   To Master-A Long Goodnight. New York:
Creative Age Press, (1946). 8vo. Cloth. A very good-fine copy in
lightly worn dj. In Our Time 156-349 1983 $100

GYSIN, BRION   To Master, A Long Goodnight. NY, (1946).
Some wear to edges, otherwise very good or better in lightly worn,
very good dustwrapper. Quill & Brush 54-594 1983 $50

H

HAAGENSEN, C. D.　　　　A Hundred Years of Medicine. N.Y., (1943). 42 plates. 8vo, cloth. First American edition. Argosy 713-237　1983　$85

HAAK, BOB　　　　Rembrandt. His life, his work, his time. New York: Abrams, n.d. 612 illus. (109 tipped-in color). Folio. Cloth. Dust jacket. Ars Libri 32-557　1983　$75

HAAS, ARTHUR ERICH　　　　Atomic Theory, An Elementary Exposition. London: Constable, 1927. First English edition. 8vo. Text illus. Orig. cloth. Zeitlin 264-192　1983　$40

HAAS, ROBERT BARTLETT　　　　A Catalogue of the Published and Unpublished Writings of Gertrude Stein. New Haven: Yale University Library, 1941. First edition. 8vo. Paper wrappers. Covers faded. Oak Knoll 48-481　1983　$25

HABBERTON, JOHN　　　　The Chautauquans. New York: Bonner, 1891. 1st ed. Orig. pictorial wrappers, uncut. Some chips at base of spine but a fine copy of this fragile volume. Jenkins 155-507　1983　$45

HABERLY, LOYD　　　　Anne Boleyn and Other Poems. Newton, Wales, 1934. Sq. 8vo, full brown morocco, gilt extra, t.e.g., others uncut. Printed in red, green and black on hand-made paper. Bookplate of R. R. Donnelley & Sons. One of 300 copies. Fine. Perata 28-69　1983　$350

HABERLY, LOYD　　　　The Crowning Year and Other Poems. Stoney Down, Corfe Mullen, Dorset; printed and bound by Lloyd Haberly, 1937. 1st ed., sm. 4to, wood-engraved title and colophon, printed throughout in red and black, hand drawn initials in green, quarter brown morocco gilt, decorative green and russet cloth boards, t.e.g., others uncut. A fine copy. 150 copies only on hand-made paper and printed in Paradise. Deighton 3-153　1983　£78

HABINGTON, WILLIAM　　　　The Brothers, a Monody; and Other Poems. Baldwin, Cradock & Joy, 1820. Calf, gilt, v.g. Jarndyce 30-692　1983　£28

HACHMEISTER, CARL　　　　Der Meister des Amsterdamer Cabinets und sein Verhaltnis zu Albrecht Durer. Berlin: Mayer & Muller, 1897. Boards. Slightly worn. Ars Libri 32-436　1983　$45

HACKETT, MARIA　　　　A popular account of St. Paul's Cathedral. London: printed by Nichols, Son, and Bentley, 1818. 8vo. Disbound. New edition. Frontis. Ximenes 63-263　1983　$25

HACKETT, W. T. G.　　　　A Background of Banking Theory. Toronto: Canadian Bankers' Assn., 1945. 23cm. Blue wrappers. Very good. McGahern 53-63　1983　$20

HADAMARD, JACQUES　　　　The Psychology of Invention in the Mathematical Field. Princeton: Princeton Univ. Press, 1945. First edition. Label chipped. Gach 95-184　1983　$20

HADATH, FLORENCE GUNBY　　　　Pamela. Collins, 1938. Frontis. & 4 full-page illus. Green cloth. Signed by author. Greer 40-56　1983　£15

HADDOCK, C. MARSTON　　　　"Idle Hours". Bradford: J.S. Toothill, 1896. First edition, half title, orig. half maroon morocco. Jarndyce 30-714　1983　£12.50

HADDOCK, J. W.　　　　Somnolismus und Psychelsmus. Leipzig, 1852. First edition in German. 8 woodcuts on 2 folding sheets. 8vo, cont. black boards (some foxing). Argosy 713-238　1983　$45

HADDOCK, JOHN A.　　　　A Souvenir of the Thousand Islands of the St. Lawrence River... New York, 1896. 22cm. Second edition, revised and corrected. With 34 full-page illus. and numerous text illus. Blue cloth. Silver titles. Fine. Scarce. McGahern 54-76　1983　$100

HADEN, FRANCIS-SEYMOUR　　　　L'oeuvre grave de Rembrandt. Etude monographique. Paris: Gazette des Beaux-Arts, 1880. 4to. Wrappers. Light wear. Ars Libri 32-558　1983　$50

HADER, BERTA　　　　Jamaica Johnny. N.Y.: Mac., 1935. First edition. Sq. 8vo. Frayed dust wrapper. Full color illus. Many black & whites. Fine. Aleph-bet 8-133　1983　$30

HADFIELD, JOSEPH　　　　An Englishman in America, 1785. Toronto, 1933. First edition. Portrait. 8vo. Morrill 290-162　1983　$25

HADFIELD, ROBERT　　　　Faraday and his Metallurgical Researches. London, 1931. First edition. Large 8vo. Cloth. Frontis., 53 plates and illus. in text. Gurney JJ-118　1983　£20

HADLEY, ARTHUR　　　　Railroad Transportation, Its History and Its Laws. NY, 1885. Ex lib. Argosy 716-450　1983　$30

HADLEY, GEORGE　　　　Grammatical Remarks on the Practical and Vulgar Dialect of the Inostan Language... London: for T. Cadell, 1772. First edition. 8vo. Early 19th Century half calf, full gilt spine. Blank margin at foot of title repaired, margins of a couple of leaves frayed, no text loss. Heath 48-584　1983　£90

HAEBLER, CONRADO　　　　Bibliografia Iberica del Siglo XV: Enumeracion de todos los libros impresos... New York: Burt Franklin, n.d. 2 vols., cloth. Reprint of the 1903-17 ed. Dawson 470-138　1983　$50

HAECKEL, ERNST　　　　Die Lebenswunder. Leipzig, 1925. New edition. Portrait frontispiece, 8 full-page plates, including 5 in full color, 2 tinted, and 2 in black and white. Decorated green boards and cloth. Scarce. Bradley 64-67　1983　$25

HAECKEL, ERNST　　　　Naturliche Schopfungs-Geschichte. Berlin, 1926. Illustrated, including 30 full-page plates (some tinted), and with folding map in color at end. Green cloth. Corners worn; otherwise good copy. Bradley 64-68　1983　$25

HAESAERTS, PAUL　　　　James Ensor. New York: Abrams, 1959. More than 400 illus. (57 tipped-in color). Large 4to. Cloth. Dust jacket. Ars Libri 32-206　1983　$100

HAFEN, LEROY　　　　Broken Hand. Denver, 1973. Cloth, fine in slipcase. One of 200 copies specially bound, printed by the Northland Press. Reese 19-253　1983　$150

HAFEN, LEROY　　　　Colorado Gold Rush. Glendale, 1941. 1st ed. Ports., plates, fldg. map. Deckle edges, gilt top, unopened. Clark 741-186　1983　$65

HAFEN, LEROY　　　　The Life of Thomas Fitzpatrick: Mountain Man, Guide and Indian Agent. Denver, 1973. Illus. Limited to 200 signed copies. Boxed. Mint as issued. 1st revised ed. Jenkins 151-94　1983　$75

HAGEDORN, HERMAN　　　　The Bomb That Fell on America. Pacific Coast Publishing Co. California, 1946. 8vo. Wraps. Advance copy, bound in plain white stapled wrappers, with publishing note. Fine copy. In Our Time 156-351　1983　$35

HAGEDORN, HERMAN　　　　Roosevelt in the Badlands. Cambridge, 1921. Cloth, very good. Reese 19-254　1983　$50

HAGEN, VICTOR WOLFGANG VON   The Aztec and Maya Papermakers. New York: J.J. Augustin, 1944. 41 plates. Frontis. in color. Text figures. Small 4to. Cloth. Dust jacket. Ars Libri 34-264 1983 $85

HAGEN, VICTOR WOLFGANG VON   Jungle in the Clouds. (1945). 8vo., cloth, numerous photos. Wheldon 160-389 1983 £12

HAGER, JOHN S.   The Louisiana Case. Wash., 1875. Dbd. First edition. Ginsberg 47-459 1983 $25

HAGER, WERNER   Die Ehrenstatuen der Papste. Leipzig, 1928. 4to, 44 collotype plates, cloth. Ars Libri SB 26-95 1983 $175

HAGERTY, FRANK H.   The State of North Dakota. Aberdeen, S.D., 1889. Orig. printed wraps. First edition. Ginsberg 47-281 1983 $125

HAGERTY, FRANK H.   The Territory of Dakota. Aberdeen, S.D., 1899. Printed wraps., chipped. First edition. Ginsberg 46-219 1983 $100

HAGERTY, HARRY J.   The Jasmine Trail. Boston: Lothrop, Lee & Shepard, 1936. 8vo. Cloth. A very good-fine copy in lightly worn and highly colorful jacket. In Our Time 156-352 1983 $35

HAGGARD, ELLA   Life and Its Author. London: Longmans, Green & Co., 1890. Second edition. Henry Haggard's own copy, with his signature on the verso of the flyleaf and his bookplate on the front endsheet. Covers partially stained, otherwise a very good copy. MacManus 278-2452 1983 $250

HAGGARD, HENRY RIDER   Allan Quatermain. London, 1887. First edition. Illus. Spine a little faded. One gathering loose. Very nice. Rota 230-268 1983 £30

HAGGARD, HENRY RIDER   Allan's Wife and Other Tales. London: Spencer Blackett, 1889. First edition. Illus. Orig. cloth. Slightly shaken and loose, but a fine, bright copy. MacManus 278-2425 1983 $75

HAGGARD, HENRY RIDER   Allan's Wife and Other Tales. Spencer Blackett, 1889. First edition, half title, 34 illus. by Maurice Greiffenhagen and Charles Kerr. 32pp ads. Orig. brown cloth, lined in black, lettered in gilt. Sl. rubbing of spine, otherwise v.g. Jarndyce 31-722 1983 £30

HAGGARD. HENRY RIDER   The Ancient Allan. London: Cassell & Company, (1920). Orig. cloth, dust jacket (somewhat soiled and worn). First edition. Some offsetting to the endpapers, otherwise a near-fine copy in the rare dust jacket. Former owner's signature. MacManus 278-2428 1983 $85

HAGGARD, HENRY RIDER   Cetwayo and His White Neighbors. London: Trubner & Company, 1888. Orig. cloth. Second edition, with added material. Spine and covers a bit worn, inside hinges weak, with some foxing and staining to the edges and endpapers. MacManus 278-2429 1983 $85

HAGGARD, HENRY RIDER   Church and State New Style. (London: 1895). 12mo, orig. printed wraps. First edition. Covers creased, somewhat foxed. MacManus 278-2430 1983 $350

HAGGARD, HENRY RIDER   Cleopatra. London: Longmans, Green, & Co., 1889. Orig. cloth. Illus. First edition. Presentation copy, inscribed on the half-title "To W.E. Henley from H. Rider Haggard, 24 June, 1889." Covers a bit rubbed, some foxing, but a very good copy. MacManus 278-2433 1983 $750

HAGGARD, HENRY RIDER   Cleopatra. Longmans, Green, 1889. First edition, half title, front. illus. 16pp ads. Orig. blue cloth, bevelled boards, v.g. Jarndyce 31-723 1983 £38

HAGGARD, HENRY RIDER   Colonial Quaritch, V.C. London: Longmans, Green & Company, 1888. First edition, 3 vols. Orig. red cloth. Spines slightly faded, ends a trifle worn. MacManus 278-2431 1983 $350

HAGGARD, HENRY RIDER   Eric Bright Eyes. Longmans, Green, 1891. First edition, half title, illus. by Lancelot Speed. 16pp ads. Inscribed on leading blank. Orig. navy-blue cloth lettered in gilt, bevelled boards, v.g. Jarndyce 31-725 1983 £25

HAGGARD, HENRY RIDER   Eugene Howard Lewis 1852-1907. N.p.: n.d. (Wisconsin? 1907?) Illus. Orig. limp leather. First edition. Haggard's own copy, with his hieroglyphic bookplate laid in. Fine copy. MacManus 278-2432 1983 $125

HAGGARD, HENRY RIDER   Getywayo and his White Neighbours. London, 1882. First edition. Prelims. slightly foxed, corners bumped, but a fine copy. One of 750. Gekoski 2-76 1983 £200

HAGGARD, HENRY RIDER   Heu-Heu, or The Monster. London: Hutchinson & Co., (1924). Orig. cloth. First edition. Covers partially faded, but a good copy. MacManus 278-2435 1983 $60

HAGGARD, HENRY RIDER   King Solomon's Mines. Cassell & Co., 1885. Half title, folding col. map front. 16pp ads. Orig. red cloth, blocked in black, lettered in gilt and black. Very small mark on leading hinge. This copy has ads dated '8.85'. Jarndyce 31-720 1983 £140

HAGGARD, HENRY RIDER   King Solomon's Mines. Cassell, (ca.1907). Sq. 8vo, colour frontis., 3 colour plates & folding map. Blue pictorial cloth, rubbed. Greer 40-140 1983 £14

HAGGARD, HENRY RIDER   Lysbeth; a tale of the Dutch. London, 1901. First English edition. Illus. Bookplate. Nice. Rota 231-299 1983 £12

HAGGARD, HENRY RIDER   The Mahatma and the Hare. London: Longmans, Green & Company, 1911. Orig. cloth, dust jacket (spine and covers faded and slightly worn). Illus. by W.T. Horton and H.M. Brock. First edition. Spine slightly faded, with some offsetting to the endpapers, otherwise a very good copy in the scarce dust jacket. MacManus 278-2436 1983 $275

HAGGARD, HENRY RIDER   Maiwa's Revenge. Longmans, Green, 1888. First edition, 8vo, orig. pale green boards, printed in red, the covers just a little marked. Fine copy. Fenning 62-157 1983 £16.50

HAGGARD, HENRY RIDER   Mary of Marion Isle. London: Hutchinson & Co. Limited, n.d. (1929). Orig. cloth, pictorial dust jacket. First edition. The author's own copy, with his hieroglyph bookplate tipped in. Jacket a trifle dust soiled and worn, but a very fine copy. MacManus 278-2437 1983 $300

HAGGARD, HENRY RIDER   Mr. Meeson's Will. London, 1888. First edition. Illus. Rota 230-269 1983 £15

HAGGARD, HENRY RIDER   Morning Star. London, 1910. First edition. Illus. 8vo, red cloth. Argosy 714-347 1983 £45

HAGGARD, HENRY RIDER   A Note on Religion. London: Longmans, Green & Co. Ltd., 1927. Orig. wraps. First edition. Fine copy. MacManus 278-2439 1983 $250

HAGGARD, HENRY RIDER   The People of the Mist. Longmans, Green, 1894. First edition, half title, front. & illus. by Arthur Layard. 24pp ads. Orig. blue cloth, bevelled boards, sl. rubbed. Jarndyce 31-726 1983 £25

HAGGARD, HENRY RIDER   The Poor and the Land. Longmans, Green, & Co., 1905. Twelve illus. Orig. cloth. First edition. Inscription on free endpaper, bookseler's stamp on front endsheet, otherwise a good copy. MacManus 278-2440 1983 $55

HAGGARD, HENRY RIDER   Queen Sheba's Ring. Longon: Eveleigh Nash, 1910. Illus. with colored frontis. by Cyrus Cuneo. Orig. cloth. First edition. Slightly soiled, otherwise a very good copy. MacManus 278-2441 1983 $35

HAGGARD, HENRY RIDER   Queen Sheba's Ring. London, 1910. First edition. Spine slightly darkened. Bookplate. Very nice. Rota 231-300 1983 £18

HAGGARD, HENRY RIDER   Regeneration. London: Longmans, 1910.
Orig. cloth. First edition. MacManus 278-2442 1983 $27.50

HAGGARD, HENRY RIDER   Regeneration. London, 1910. First
edition. Covers a little marked. Bookplate. Nice. Rota 231-301
1983 £15

HAGGARD, HENRY RIDER   Smith and the Pharaohs and Other Tales.
Bristol: J.W. Arrowsmith Ltd., 1920. First edition. Former
owner's signature on front flyleaf, otherwise a very good copy.
MacManus 278-2443 1983 $125

HAGGARD, HENRY RIDER   Stella Fregelius. London: Longmans,
1904. Orig. cloth. First English edition. Almost fine. MacManus
278-2445 1983 $35

HAGGARD, HENRY RIDER   The Wanderer's Necklace. London:
Cassell & Company, ltd., 1914. Orig. cloth. With four illus. in
color by A.C. Michael. First edition. Spine faded, bookplate,
ink stamp on front-flyleaf, otherwise a very good copy. MacManus
278-2446 1983 $85

HAGGARD, HENRY RIDER   The Witch's Head. London: Hurst &
Blackett, 1885. First edition. Library label removed from cover
of vol. I, partially removed from cover of vol. II, and present
on the cover of vol. III; covers worn, contents soiled and
shaken, inner hinges cracking. MacManus 278-2447 1983 $750

HAGGARD, HENRY RIDER   The Witch's Head. Hurst and Blackett,
1885. First edition, 3 vols. Half maroon roan, marbled boards a
little rubbed. Jarndyce 30-411 1983 £65

HAGGARD, HENRY RIDER   Works. London, 1894-1934. 57
vols. Cr. 8vo. Uniformly bound in half maroon morocco, gilt.
Traylen 94-410 1983 £335

HAGGARD, HOWARD   The Lame, the Halt, and the Blind.
New York, 1932. 8vo. Orig. binding. Dustwrapper. Fye H-3-235
1983 $25

HAGNER, LILLIE M.   Alluring San Antonio Through the Eyes
of an Artist. San Antonio, 1947. Illus. Dust jacket. Jenkins 153-
590 1983 $25

HAHNEMANN, SAMUEL   Organ in the Art of Healing. Phila.,
1900. 8vo, cloth; ex-lib. Argosy 713-240 1983 $50

HAIEN, JEANNETTE MICHAEL   Rip Van Winkle's Dream: A Narrative
Poem. New York, 1947. 8vo. Cloth. Review copy with slip laid in.
Jacket flap has a blurb by Conrad Aiken. Fine copy in lightly worn
dj. In Our Time 156-353 1983 $25

HAILE, BERNARD   A Manual of Navaho Grammar. St.
Michael's, Arizo., 1926. Orig. printed wraps. First edition.
Ginsberg 46-25 1983 $35

HAIMAN, MIECISLAUS   Polish Past in America, 1608-1865.
Chicago, Polish Roman Catholic Union, 1939. First edition. 66
illustrations and 2 maps. Morrill 290-163 1983 $32.50

HAIRPIN Calendar for 1906. (Tokyp: T. Hasegawa). Small octavo.
Crepe-paper book. Illus. Very fine in colored pictorial self-wrappers
sewn at one corner. Bromer 25-355 1983 $65

HAKE, ALFRED EGMONT   Regeneration! NY: G. P. Putnam's Sons,
1896. 8vo. Publisher's green cloth. Library bookplate and stamp
on titlepage. Gach 95-185 1983 $20

HAKE, THOMAS   The Life and Letters of Theodore Watts-
Dunton. London: T.C. & E.C. Jack, 1916. First edition. 2 vols.
Orig. cloth. Dust jackets (frayed and soiled). Edges slightly worn.
Endpapers a little foxed. Very good. MacManus 280-5433 1983 $25

HAKLUYT, RICHARD   The Principal Navigations, Voyages...
Glasgow: Hakluyt Society, Estra Series 1-12, 1903-5. Numerous maps
and illus. 12 vols. Spines soiled. 8vo. Orig. cloth. Good.
Edwards 1044-309 1983 £220

HAKLUYT, RICHARD   The Principal Navigations, Voyages...at
Any Time Within the Compass of these 1600 Years. London, etc.: Dent,
1927. 10 vols. Complete, numerous maps, plates, portraits. Orig.
gilt decorated blue cloth. Slightly used dust jackets. Very fine.
Jenkins 152-140 1983 $200

HAKLUYT, RICHARD   The Principal Navigations, Voyages,
Traffiques & Discoveries of the English Nation...London, Dent, 1927-
1928. Drawings by T. Derrick. Repro. from contemporary portraits,
engravings, etc. 10 vols, 8vo, dust wrappers. Some dust wrappers
partly torn. Morrill 286-176 1983 $90

HAKLUYT, RICHARD   The Principal Navigations, Voyages,
Traffiques and Discoveries of the English Nation. Edinburgh:
Goldsmid, 1889. 21 1/2cm. 2 vols. in one. Half wine morocco,
raised bands, marbled boards and endpapers. Very good. McGahern
53-64 1983 $25

HAKUSUI, INAMI   Nippon-To, The Japanese Sword.
Tokyo (1948). Illus, boards, spine chipped, in badly chipped dw.
King 46-584 1983 $50

HALACSY, E. VON   Conspectus Florae Graecae. (Leipzig,
1901-12), reprint Lehre, 1968. 3 vols. and 2 supplements, in 2 vols.,
8vo, cloth. Wheldon 160-1692 1983 £155

HALDANE, JOHN S.   Organism and Environment Illustrated
by the Physiology of Breathing. Yale University Press, 1917.
Argosy 713-241 1983 $35

HALDEMAN-JULIUS, E.   My First 25 Years. Kansas, (1949).
8vo. Wraps. Fine. In Our Time 156-714 1983 $25

HALDEMAN-JULIUS, E.   My Second 25 Years. Kansas, (1949).
8vo. Wraps. Fine. In Our Time 156-715 1983 $25

HALDEMAN-JULIUS, MARCET   Reviewer's Library. Kansas, (1936).
8vo. Wraps. Corners of wrappers chipped (not affecting text), else
vg-fine. In Our Time 156-716 1983 $20

HALE, EDWARD E.   June to May. Boston: Roberts, 1881.
1st ed. Orig. cloth, gilt. Presentation copy, inscribed by Hale
to a woman in 1882. Very good. Jenkins 155-1393 1983 $20

HALE, EDWARD E   Philip Nolan's Friends. New York:
Scribner, Armstrong, 1877. 5 plates. Original green decorated cloth.
First edition. Fine copy. Jenkins 153-236 1983 $85

HALE, EDWARD E.   The Queen of California, the Origin of
the Name of California. San Francisco: Colt Press, 1945. Folding
colored map, linen-backed boards, paper label. No. 4 of 500 copies
of Colt Press Series of Calif. Classics. Argosy 710-34 1983 $40

HALE, EDWIN M.   The Characteristics of the New Remedies.
Detroit, 1873. 1/2 mor., (rubbed); ex-lib. Third edition. Argosy
713-242 1983 $35

HALE, MATTHEW   Contemplations Moral and Devine. London,
Shrewsbury, 1679. Two parts in one with two title pages. Frontis.
portrait engraved by Hone. Later 3/4 brown morocco over marbled
boards (old signature on title page, tiny pin holes in first few
leaves) else very good. Houle 22-455 1983 $125

HALE, MATTHEW   Contemplations Moral and Divine. London,
William Shrowsbury and Charles Harper, 1695. 8vo, orig. calf,
worn, ends of spine and one corner of upper cover cellotaped, else
good copy. Ravenstree 94-165 1983 $75

HALE, T.   An Account of Several New Inventions
and Improvements. James Astwood, 1691. Sm. 8vo. Orig. cloth. Cont.
calf, slightly worn, some slight staining throughout. Some cont.
marginal ink notes. Bound in at end is the rare broadside, A Survey
of the Buildings and Encroachments on the River of Thames, 2 leaves,
folio, folded, small tears along folds. Good. Edwards 1042-72 1983
£220

HALES, JOHN GROVE　　Maps of the Street-Lines of Boston. Boston, 1894. Repro. of the orig. drawings by Hales. Maps. Folio, ex-library, 3 small gashes on spine, clean and sound. Morrill 288-279 1983 $65

HALES, STEPHEN　　An Account of a Useful Discovery... London: Printed for Richard Manby...1756. 1st ed., 8vo, list of books by Hales and 1 engraved plate; disbound in a recent wrapper. Pickering & Chatto 22-45 1983 $500

HALES STEPHEN　　An Account of Some Experiments and Observations on Mrs. Stephens's Medicines for Dissolving the Stone. Printed for T. Wood, (1740?). 8vo, folding engraved plate, recent calf antique, new end papers, lettered gilt on the spine. First edition. Bickersteth 77-277 1983 £120

HALES, STEPHEN　　Philosophical Experiments. For W. Innys, R. Manby and T. Woodward, London, 1739. 8vo, with 1 engraved plate and the ad. leaf M6; uncut in cont. calf-backed boards, joints cracked but sound; engraved bookplate of Robert Hunter of Thurston. First edition. A very good copy. Quaritch NS 5-50 1983 $1,300

HALES, STEPHEN　　Statical Essays: containing Vegetable Staticks...Haemastaticks. 1731-33. Engraved plates, 2 vols, 8vo, cont. calf (very neatly rebacked). Rare first edition. A nice copy. Wheldon 160-161 1983 £725

HALEY, J. EVETTS　　The Alamo Mission Bell. Austin: published for the Nita Stewart Haley Memorial Library, Midland, by the Encino Press, 1974. Half calf, paper label. Illus. 1st ed., one of 250 copies numbered, specially bound, and signed by the author. Mint as issued. Jenkins 151-111 1983 $150

HALEY, J. EVETTS　　Charles Goodnight, Cowman. Boston, 1936. Frontis. and illus. by Harold Bugbee. Fine copy of the first edition. Jenkins 151-106 1983 $85

HALEY, J. EVETTS　　Earl Vandale on the Trail of Texas Books. Canyon, Texas: Palo Duro Press, 1965. Limited to 500 copies. Fine. Jenkins 152-650 1983 $125

HALEY, J. EVETTS　　George W. Littlefield. Texan. Norman, 1943. First edition. Illus. by Harold D. Bugbee. Jenkins 151-183 1983 $40

HALEY, J. EVETTS　　Jeff Milton A Good Man with a Gun. Norman, 1948. Maps and illus. Original cloth. 1st edition in dust jacket with John Campbell Greenway printed upside down in the index. Signed by the author. Jenkins 151-113 1983 $65

HALEY, J. EVETTS　　Jeff Milton A Good Man with a Gun. Norman, 1948. Maps and illus. Orig. cloth. First edition, second issue. Jenkins 152-141 1983 $45

HALEY, J. EVETTS　　Rough Times -- Tough Fiber a Fragmentary Family Chronicle. Canyon, Texas: Palo Duro Press, 1976. Half morocco. Limited to 150 copies. Boxed. Jenkins 151-114 1983 $200

HALF Hours in the Wide West. London: Wm. Isbister Ltd., 1880. 17 1/2cm. Over 100 full-page and text illus. from engravings, map. Bound in half red calf, raised bands, gilt borders and decorations on the spine, marbled endpapers and edges. Label chipped, some light wear at the edges else a very good copy. McGahern 53-65 1983 $45

HALFORD, HENRY　　Essays and Orations, Read and Delivered at the Royal College of Physicians... London, John Murray, 1831. 8vo, cont. half calf, rubbed, the 4th Earl Tyrconnel copy with Sarah Tyrconnel's signature on title. First edition. Ravenstree 94-166 1983 $65

HALFORD, HENRY　　Oration in Collegii Regalis Medicorum Londiniensis Aedibus Novis habita Die Dedicationis Junii XXV, 1825. Ex Officina Johannis Nichols, 1825. 4to, disbound. Bickersteth 75-235 1983 £12

HALFPENNY, WILLIAM　　Practical Architecture, or a Sure Guide to the True Working According to the Rules of that Science. Printed for & sold by Tho. Bowles, 1736. Fifth edition. Engraved title-pages, leaf of dedication (neatly backed) and 48 numbered engraved plates, 12mo, old marbled paper boards, light signs of use, but a very good copy. Fenning 60-157 1983 £48.50

HALHED, N. B.　　A Code of Gentoo Laws. London, 1776. 8 plates. 4to. Boards, calf spine, worn. Good. Edwards 1044-310 1983 £150

HALIBURTON, THOMAS CHANDLER　　The Americans At Home... London: Hurst and Blackett, n.d. 19cm. Green cloth, gilt titles. A fine copy. McGahern 54-77 1983 $35

HALIBURTON, THOMAS CHANDLER　　The Clockmaker. Richard Bentley, 1838. 4th edition, 3 vols. Illus. plates foxed. Calf, labels (2 defective). Jarndyce 30-412 1983 £14

HALIBURTON, THOMAS CHANDLER　　The Clockmaker: or the Sayings and Doings of Sam Slick. Concord: Boyd, 1839. 3rd American ed. Orig. cloth, label. Good copy. Jenkins 155-510 1983 $20

HALIBURTON, THOMAS CHANDLER　　An Historical and Statistical account of Nova-Scotia. Halifax: Published for Joseph Howe, 1829. 22cm. 2 vols. 6 engraved maps and plans (2 folding) and engraved views. 3 folding tables. Cont. half calf, gilt dec. in the panels, black leather labels, expertly rebacked, marbled boards. A fine set. McGahern 54-78 1983 $500

HALIBURTON, THOMAS CHANDLER　　The Letter-Bag of the Great Western. Philadelphia, 1840. 1st ed. Orig. cloth-backed boards, label. Rear joint torn, but a good copy. Jenkins 155-511 1983 $30

HALIBURTON, THOMAS CHANDLER　　The Old Judge. Henry Colburn, 1849. First edition, ads., 2 vols., 8vo, orig. cloth by Westley & Co., with their ticket, the spines evenly faded. Fenning 61-190 1983 £135

HALIBURTON, THOMAS CHANDLER　　Sam Slick's Wise Saws and Modern Instances. London: Hurst and Blackett, 1853. Plus a 24pp pub.'s catalog. Orig. green cloth, gilt-stamped spines. Vol. 2 has a moderate water stain affecting the first half of the text. Bookplates. Karmiole 71-51 1983 $50

HALIFAX, GEORGE SAVILE, MARQUESS OF　　A Second Letter to a Dissenter, upon Occasion of His Majesties Late Gracious Declaration of Indulgence. Printed for John Harris, 1687. Small 4to, disbound. First edition. Argosy 713-39 1983 £20

HALIFAX, and its Gibbet-Law Placed in a True Light. Halifax: printed by P. Darby, (1761). Engr. frontis., separate title to Revenge upon Revenge. 12mo, foxed and a few minor repairs, sheep neatly rebacked. K Books 307-89 1983 £55

HALKETT, JOHN　　Statement Respecting the Earl of Selkirk's Settlement Upon the Red River in North America. London, Murray, 1817. Illus., folded map. Orig. boards, paper label on spine. Ginsberg 46-143 1983 $600

HALKETT, S.　　A Dictionary of the Anonymous and Pseudonymous English Literature of Great Britain... Edinburgh: 1926-56. New and enlarged edition. 8 vols. 4to. Cloth. Traylen 94-411 1983 £330

HALL, ALAN　　Observations on the Weather. Mansfield: by B. Robinson, 1807. Third edition. 8vo. Orig. wrappers. Wood-cuts. Very fine copy. Very rare. Heath 48-506 1983 £45

HALL, ANNA MARIA FIELDING　　The Buccaneer. Richard Bentley, 1832. First edition, 3 vols., 12mo. Lacks all half-titles and advertisement leaves. Cont. half calf, gilt spines. A few slight stains. Hannas 69-83 1983 £35

HALL, ANNA MARIA FIELDING　　Midsummer Eve. Longman, Brown, 1848. First edition in book form, with decorative title, 12 plates and some 180 illus. by Maclise, Stanfield, Creswick, War, Frost, Paton, Landseer and others. Roy. 8vo, orig. pub.'s gilt-stamped red calf, edges gilt, some very light spotting in a few places, but still a very good to nice copy. Fenning 61-191 1983 £36.50

HALL, ANNA MARIA FIELDING   Pilgrimages to English Shrines. Arthur Hall, 1850. First edition, with 91 vignette illus., 8 ads. 8vo, orig. green cloth, gilt, edges gilt. A little wear at headbands, but still a very good copy with the binder's ticket of Bone & Son. Fenning 60-154 1983 £18.50

HALL, ANSEL F.   Guide to Yosemite. (Yosemite, US National Park Service, 1920). Inscribed by the author, Yosemite Valley, 1923. Small 8vo, three maps. Stiff wraps. Fine. Houle 21-1193 1983 $55

HALL, ANSEL F.   Handbook of Yosemite National Park. N.Y., Putnam, 1921. First edition. Green pictorial cloth. Illus. with 27 full page halftones; fold-out map. Inscribed by the editor, Yosemite Valley, 1923. Fine copy. Houle 21-1194 1983 $75

HALL, BASIL   Account of a Voyage. London, 1818. 5 maps, 8 hand coloured aquatints. 2 other plates. 4to. Cont. calf, rebacked with the orig. labels. A fine copy of the first edition, with unworn clearly coloured plates, and little offsetting. Edwards 1044-311 1983 £225

HALL, BASIL   Forty Etchings, from Sketches Made with the Camera Lucida, in North America, in 1827 and 1828. Edinburgh and London, 1829. No pagination. Folding map. Orig. boards, some wear to backstrip, but very good. Reese 18-634 1983 $550

HALL, BRADLEY   United States Land Office, San Francisco, Ca. in the Contested Case of John Buchanan, VS. F. E. & E. F. Brady. San F., ca. 1864. Orig. printed wraps. Ginsberg 47-99 1983 $50

HALL, CHARLES E.   An Ancient Ancestor. London: Skiffington & Son, 1893. First edition. 3 vols., orig. maroon cloth. Spine ends and cover corners slightly worn, otherwise a very good copy. MacManus 278-2456 1983 $250

HALL, EDWARD   The Hudson-Fulton Celebration, 1909. Colored & other illus., folding ship plans at end. 2 vols. Thick 4to, pict. buckram, ex lib. Argosy 716-351 1983 $45

HALL, EDWARD H.   The Great West. N.Y., D. Appleton & Co., 1865. Ads. Folded map. Orig. cloth. First edition. W.J. Holliday's copy. Ginsberg 47-333 1983 $450

HALL, FRANCIS   Travels in Canada, and the United States, in 1816 and 1817. London, 1818. Folding map, later half morocco and cloth, very good. Reese 18-523 1983 $225

HALL, G. STANLEY   Adolescence. NY: Appleton, 1904. First edition. Two vols. Good, sound set, rear hinge of Vol. I cracked. Gach 94-559 1983 $50

HALL, G. STANLEY   Founders of Modern Psychology. NY: Appleton & Co., 1924 (1912). Gach 94-193 1983 $35

HALL, G. STANLEY   Life and Confessions of a Psychologist. NY: D. Appleton & Co., 1923. First edition. Lower spine tip frayed. Gach 94-194 1983 $25

HALL, H. R.   The Civilization of Greece in the Bronze Age. London, 1928. 2 maps, 4to. Cloth. Salloch 385-236 1983 $20

HALL, HENRY   Heaven Ravished. (London:) Printed by J. Raworth, for Samuel Gellibrand, 1644. First edition, 4to, wrapper, a few sidenotes just touched. A very good copy. Fenning 62-158 1983 £14.50

HALL, HENRY MARION   Woodcock Ways. NY, 1946. Illus. by Ralph Ray. First edition. Bottom of book and lower margins badly stained. Richard E. Bishop's copy containing his stamped signature and autograph. King 46-585 1983 $35

HALL, J. B.   Distribution and Ecology of Vascular Plants in a Tropical Rain Forest. The Hague, 1981. Distribution maps, 8vo, cloth. Wheldon 160-1693 1983 £57

HALL, J. SPARKES   The Book of the Feet... With Illus.... New York, 1847. 1st American ed. 4 colored plates. Small 8vo. Binding rubbed and dampstained; some light dampstains in text. Morrill 289-351 1983 $50

HALL, JAMES   A Memoir of the Public Services of William Henry Harrison, of Ohio. Philadelphia, 1836. 1st ed. Portrait. 16mo, paper label, backstrip slightly torn along hinges & slight rubbing at corners, sound. Morrill 288-153 1983 $35

HALL, JAMES   Sketches of History, Life, and Manners, in the West. Phila.: Harrison Hall, 1835. 2 vols, three quarter calf, morocco labels and marble boards. Fairly nice set. Frontis. First complete edition with volume two. Jenkins 151-115 1983 $300

HALL, JAMES   The West: Its Soil, Surface, and Productions. Cincinnati, 1848. Reissue of the 1836 orig. Later half calf over orig. marbled boards. Jenkins 152-822 1983 $65

HALL, JAMES   The Wilderness and the War Path. New York, 1846. Orig. printed wraps. Spine neatly restored, else a fine copy. First edition, first printing. In a cloth folding case. Felcone 21-49 1983 $250

HALL, JAMES NORMAN   The Friends. The Prairie Press, Iowa, 1939. 8vo. Cloth. Total ed. is 380 copies printed by Carroll Coleman. Orig. glassine jacket has some light wear. Fine copy. In Our Time 156-355 1983 $45

HALL, JAMES NORMAN   Kitchener's Mob, the Adventures of an American in the British Army. Boston: Houghton Mifflin Co., 1916. First edition. 8vo. Cloth. Fine copy. Oak Knoll 48-185 1983 $37.50

HALL, JOHN A.   The Great Strike on the "Q". Chicago and Philadelphia: Elliott & Beezley, 1889. Original cloth, 1st ed. Fine copy. Jenkins 151-116 1983 $45

HALL, JOSEPH   Christ Mysticall. London, printed by M. Flesher, sold by William Hope, Gabriel Beadle, and Nathaniel Webbe, 1647. 12mo, cont. calf, front cover loose, first and only edition. Ravenstree 94-167 1983 $95

HALL, JOSEPH   Episcopacie by Divine Right, Asserted. London, printed by R.B. for Nathanael Butter, 1640. 4to, orig. calf, some worming to outer upper blank corner, few waterstains, otherwise a fine large copy. First edition. Ravenstree 94-168 1983 $250

HALL, JOSEPH   An Humble Remonstrance to the High Covrt of Parliament, by a Dutifull Sonne of the Church. London, printed by M.F. for Nathaniel Butter, 1640. 4to, disbound. First issue of the first edition. Ravenstree 94-171 1983 $125

HALL, JOSEPH   A Recollection of such Treatises as haue bene hereto fore seuerally Published and are nowe Reuised, Corrected, Augmented... London, printed for Hen. Fetherstone (1617). Folio, cont. calf gilt rebacked in 19th century morocco, badly rubbed, name snipped from flyleaf, a very few miniscule rust holes in text, complete with the engraved general title-page by Elstrack. Ravenstree 94-173 1983 $87.50

HALL, JOSEPH   Resolvtions and Decisions of Divers Practicall Cases of Conscience in Continuall Use Amongst Men... London, N.B., 1650. 12mo, orig. vellum, from the Eveyln family library. Ravenstree 93-174 1983 $164

HALL, JOSEPH   The Shaking of the Olive-Tree. London, printed by J. Cadwel for J. Crooke, 1660. 4to, bound without frontis. in cont. calf rebacked, names on title, good large copy. Ravenstree 94-175 1983 $92

HALL, JOSEPH   A Short Answer to the Tedious Vindication of Smectymnvvs. London, printed for Nathaniel Butter, 1641. 4to, new boards, title little soiled, paper flaw in leaf L1 affecting six letters. A good copy of the first and only edition. Ravenstree 94-176 1983 $150

HALL, LAURENCE C.   Minutes of the Curfew Club. Pasadena, Val Trebz Press, 1941. First edition. Illus. chapter headings by James Hawkins. Half maroon cloth over dark blue cloth, printed in blue and orange, unopened. One of 100 copies. Fine. Houle 22-1186 1983 $45

HALL, MARSHALL   A Descriptive, Diagnostic and Practical Essay on Disorders of the Digestive Organs and General Health... London, 1820. 1st ed. 8vo. Contemporary calf, leather label. Ex-library; hinges cracked. Morrill 289-96 1983 $60

HALL, MARSHALL   A Letter Addressed to the Earl of Ross. London: November, 1848. 2nd ed., 8vo, half title and title; disbound. Pickering & Chatto 22-46 1983 $65

HALL, RADCLYFFE   Adam's Breed. N.Y.: Jonathan Cape & Harrison Smith, (1929). Orig. cloth, dust jacket (head of spine chipped, a bit rubbed). In a half-morocco slipcase. MacManus 278-2457 1983 $35

HALL, RADCLYFFE   The Master of the House. Jonathan Cape, 1932. First edition, roy. 8vo, orig. vellum-backed buckram, gilt, t.e.g., small mark from a paper clip on the first two leaves, but otherwise a fine copy in the orig. slip-case. Ltd. edition of 172 copies, signed by the author. Fenning 62-159 1983 $75

HALL, RADCLYFFE   The Well of Loneliness. Paris: The Pegasus Press, (1928). Black cloth. First Continental edition. Slight rubbing at toe of spine, else a near fine copy. Pencil ownership signature, dated Paris. Reese 20-475 1983 $75

HALL, ROBERT   An apology for the freedom of the press... London: printed for G.G.J. and J. Robinson, etc., 1793. First edition. 8vo. Disbound. Ximenes 63-173 1983 $250

HALL, SAMUEL   Samuel Hall's Patent Improvements on Steam Engines. Nottingham: printed by S. Bennett, n.d. First edition, 8vo, 2 large folding lithograph plates, head of title-page cut away and neatly repaired, not affecting text, occasional manuscript note and correction in the text, paper wrappers, slight wear, stitched as issued. Deighton 3-154 1983 £48

HALL, MRS. SAMUEL CARTER
Please turn to
HALL, ANNA MARIA FIELDING

HALL, SAMUEL CARTER   Ireland: Its Scenery, Character, &c. Virtue and Co., circa, 1850. With additional engraved vignette title-pages, 101 engraved plates, 17 coloured maps and many text illus. 3 vols., roy. 8vo, orig. pub.'s green morocco, gilt extra, edges gilt. Light marginal foxing of most the plates. Fenning 62-160 1983 £145

HALL, SAMUEL CARTER   Retrospect of a Long Life. Richard Bentley, 1883. First edition, 2 vols. Half titles, fronts. Half red morocco, gilt, v.g. Jarndyce 30-1014 1983 £38

HALL, SAMUEL CARTER   The trial of Sir Jasper. London: Virtue, etc., n.d. (1873). First "large-paper" edition. Small 4to. Orig. purple cloth. 25 wood-engraved plates by various artists, and with a signed mounted photograph portrait of the author. Presentation copy, inscribed on the endpaper by Hall to Mrs. James Jardine. Ximenes 63-447 1983 $75

HALL, SAMUEL R.   Lectures on School-Keeping. Boston, Richardson, Lord and Holbrook, 1829. 12mo. Orig. muslin-backed boards, paper label. 1st ed. Aside from few minor blemishes, a fine copy. O'Neal 50-25 1983 $100

HALL, SAMUEL R.   Lectures on School Keeping. Boston, 1830. Cloth band boards, foxed, else very good. Reese 18-647 1983 $75

HALL, SAMUEL R.   Lectures on School-Keeping. Boston, 1830. Cloth-backed boards (spine label worn); foxing. Second edition. Felcone 22-54 1983 $40

HALL, THOMAS CUMING   The Religious Background of American Culture. Boston, 1930. Argosy 710-69 1983 $25

HALL, WILLIAM H.   The Nemesis in China. Henry Colburn, 1846. Third edition. With 4 folding maps, 3 engraved plates and 7 other illus. 8vo, recent boards, a very good copy. Fenning 60-156 1983 £42

HALL, WILLIAM M.   The Aparian. New Haven, 1840. Orig. plain blue wraps. First edition. Ginsberg 46-290 1983 $75

HALLENBECK, CLEVE   The Journey of Fray Marcos de Niza. Dallas: University Press, 1949. 4to, cloth, lettering and design in gilt, d/w. Illus. and decorations by Jose Cisneros. One of 1065 copies. Very fine. Perata 28-208 1983 $175

HALLER, ALBRECHT VON   Description courte et abregee des Salines du Gouvernement d'Aigle au Canton de Berne... Lausanne: J.H. Pott, 1782. 8vo. Old boards. Gurney 90-58 1983 £80

HALLER, ALBRECHT VON   First Lines of Physiology. For Charles Elliot, Edinburgh, 1779. 8vo, cont. tree calf, gilt spine, bookplate of Richard Prime. First complete English edition. A fine copy. Quaritch NS 5-51 1983 $750

HALLER, ALBRECHT VON   De musculis diaphragmatis dissertatio. Berne: Emanuel Hortin for Nicolas Emanuel Haller, 1733. First edition. 1 plate. Woodcut title vignette and tail-pieces. 4to. Cont. boards. Kraus 164-123 1983 $750

HALLEY, ANNE   Between Wars and Other Poems. Northampton: Gehenna Press, 1965. Octavo. First edition. Illus. Limited to 500 copies. Mint in slightly darkened dust wrapper. Bromer 25-211 1983 $75

HALLEY, EDMUND   Astronomical Tables with Precepts Both in English and Latin for Computing the Places of the Sun, Moon, Planets and Comets. London, Printed for William Innys in Paternoster Row. MDCCLII (1752). Large 4to, engr. portrait, 195 unnumbered leaves. Bound in 18th century sprinkled calf. Double gold fillet on boards and between raised bands. Upper hinge cracked, corners rubbed, boards somewhat scuffed. Lightly foxed, otherwise very good. A.E. Lownes bookplate. Arkway 22-62 1983 $325

HALLEY, EDMUND   Miscellanea Curiosa. Printed by J.B. for Jeffery Wale; and John Senex, 1705. 8vo, folding map, and four plates numbered 1, 3, 4, 5. Cont. speckled calf. First edition. Bickersteth 75-236 1983 £110

HALLIWELL, JAMES ORCHARD   A Dictionary of Archaic and Provincial Words, Obsolete Phrases, Proverbs, and Ancient Customs, from the Fourteenth Century. John Russell Smith, 1847. First edition, 2 vols. 2 vols. bound as one. Half red morocco, t.e.g., v.c. Jarndyce 31-658 1983 £32

HALLOCK, CHARLES   Our New Alaska. N.Y., 1886. Illus. Folded map, frontis. Orig. cloth, spreckled. First edition. Ginsberg 46-8 1983 $35

HALM, PHILIPP MARIA   Erasmus Grasser. Augsburg: Benno Filser, 1928. 96 plates with 177 illus. Large 4to. Cloth. Ars Libri 32-282 1983 $125

HALPIN, NICHOLAS J.   Oberon's Vision in the Midsummer-Night's Dream. Printed for the Shakespeare Society, 1843. Illus. by a comparison with Lylie's Endymion. First edition, corrigenda slip, 8vo, cont. green morocco, gilt, edges gilt, a very good copy with a signed inscription by the author. Fenning 60-158 1983 £16.50

HALPIN, WILLIAM H.   The Cheltenham Mail Bag. John Warren, 1820. First edition, small 8vo, orig. boards, uncut, with printed paper label. Fenning 62-161 1983 £28.50

HALPINE, CHARLES G.   The Poetical Works... New York: Harper, 1869. Frontis. 1st ed. Orig. green cloth, extra gilt. Fine copy. Jenkins 155-512 1983 $20

HALSEY, DON P.   A Sketch of the Life of Capt. Don P.
Halsey of the Confederate States Army. Richmond, 1904. Orig. grey
printed wrappers. Jenkins 152-142 1983 $35

HALSEY, R. T. H.   The Homes of Our Ancestors as Shown in
the American Wing of the Metropolitan Museum of Art... New York,
1925. 1st ed. Illus. 4to, orig. marbled boards, cloth back, paper
label, dust wrapper. Very nice copy and scarce with dust wrapper.
Morrill 287-139 1983 $30

HALSTEAD, B. W.   Poisonous and Venomous Marine Animals
of the World. Princeton, 1978. Revised edition, 283 pp. of illus.
(some coloured), 4to, cloth. Wheldon 160-317 1983 £47

HALSTEAD, MURAT   Life and Achievements of Admiral Dewey
from Montpelier to Manila... (Chicago, 1899). Illus. Tall 8vo.
With the signature of William T. Dewey, Montpelier, Vt., July/99,
inside front cover. Morrill 287-140 1983 $25

HALTER, ERNEST J.   Collecting First Editions of Franklin
Roosevelt. Chicago, Privately Printed for Subscribers, (1949). 8vo.
Morrill 289-352 1983 $40

HAMADY, WALTER   Papermaking by Hand; a Book of Sus-
picions. (Mt. Horeb): The Perishable Press, 1982. 8vo. Cloth.
9 leaves of paper samples (three in front and six in the rear). One
of 200 numbered copies, signed by Hamady beneath a plate on page 19.
Woodcut drawings by Jim Lee. Fine. Oak Knoll 49-319 1983 $450

HAMANN, RICHARD   Die Holztur der Pfar-kirche zu St. Maria
im Kapitol. Marburg, 1926. Lg. 4to, 45 heliogravure plates loose in
portfolio as published. Boards, 1/4 cloth, slipcase. Ars Libri SB
26-98 1983 $100

HAMEL, GUSTAV   Flying Some Practical Experiences.
London, 1914. Orig. cloth. 8vo. Frontis. and numerous plates.
Signet Library bookplate on front paste-down endpaper. Good. Edwards
1042-590 1983 £35

HAMER, S. H.   Why & Other Whys. Cassell, 1907. 4to.
Frontis. Title vignette. 18 plates & 46 text illus., loose. Colour
pictorial boards, edges worn. Greer 40-149 1983 £27.50

HAMERTON, PHILIP GILBERT   Harry Blount. London: Seeley,
Jackson & Halliday, 1875. Frontis. Old half red calf, spine
ornately gilt. Karmiole 72-51 1983 $50

HAMERTON, PHILIP GILBERT   Wenderholme. Edinburgh: William
Blackwood and Sons, 1869. Bound in half red calf, ornately gilt,
over marbled boards (binding circa 1900). Half-titles preserved.
Karmiole 72-52 1983 $125

HAMILTON, ALEXANDER   Colonel Hamilton's Second Letter, from
Phocion to the Considerate Citizens of New-York, on the Politics of
the Times... Philadelphia: Robert Bell, 1784. 3/4 levant morocco.
With the Depuy and one other bookplate. A fine copy. Felcone 22-84
1983 $75

HAMILTON, ALEXANDER   The Farmer Refuted. New York: James
Rivington, 1775. First edition. 3/4 morocco by Sangorski & Sutcliffe.
A fine copy. Felcone 21-51 1983 $750

HAMILTON, ALEXANDER   Letter from Alexander Hamilton,
Concerning the Public Conduct and Character of John Adams, Esq.
New York: George F. Hopkins for John Lang, 1800. Disbound. First
edition. Felcone 21-52 1983 $125

HAMILTON, ALEXANDER   Observations on Certain Documents
Contained in No. V & VI of "The History of the United States for the
Year 1796." Philadelphia: Pro bono publico, 1800. 3/4 morocco.
With the signature of George Shea. Felcone 21-53 1983 $175

HAMILTON, ALEXANDER   Observations on Certain Documents.
Philadelphia: Fenno, 1797. 8vo, calf & boards. "Author's Edition".
Rostenberg 88-133 1983 $130

HAMILTON, ALEXANDER   Observations on Certain Documents
Contained in... Phila.: Printed Pro Bono Publico, 1800. Sewed,
laid in mod. cloth-backed boards. Argosy 716-436 1983 $125

HAMILTON, ALLAN M.   Recollections of an Alienist. NY: 1916.
First edition. Gach 94-198 1983 $25

HAMILTON, ANTHONY   Memoirs of Count Grammont. Phil., 1889.
1 of 780 copies for England and America. Portrait of author and
etchings by L. Boisson on India paper from orig. compositions by C.
Delort. 4to. Front endleaf torn. Morrill 287-583 1983 $20

HAMILTON, ARTHUR WARREN   Scrabble of the Fairchilds. Boston,
James H. Earle, (1895). First edition. Illustrated. 8vo. Morrill
290-167 1983 $25

HAMILTON, D.   Sketches of the Shevaroy Hills. War
Office, 1865. Vignette on title, 29 tinted lithograph plates. Large
folio. Half morocco, title label on upper cover. 8vo. Good.
Edwards 1044-312 1983 £350

HAMILTON, ELIZABETH   The Cottagers of Glenburnie. Edinburgh,
by James Ballantyne and Co., for Manners and Miller, etc, 1808. First
edition. 8vo, half-title. Cont. calf, slightly finger-marked.
Hannas 69-84 1983 £35

HAMILTON, ELIZABETH   The Cottagers of Glenburnie.
Edinburgh; Printed by James Ballantyne, 1808. 3rd edition, 8vo,
contemporary tree calf, with half-title. Hill 165-52 1983 £30

HAMILTON, ELIZABETH   Memoirs of the Life of Agrippina.
Bath, by R. Cruttwell; for G. and J. Robinson, 1804. First edition,
3 vols. 8vo, half-titles. Cont. mottled calf with "Tree calf"
lozenges on all covers (one head-band worn). Final gathering in two
vols. heavily foxed. Hannas 69-86 1983 £40

HAMILTON, F.   An Account of Asam. Annals of Oriental
Literature, (1820). Some slight spotting at end. Half calf. 8vo.
Good. Edwards 1044-313 1983 £32

HAMILTON, F.   An Account of the Fishes found in the
River Ganges. Edinburgh, 1822. Atlas of 39 engraved plates, 2 vols.,
4to and oblong 4to, newly rebound in marbled boards, leather spines.
Rare. Slight foxing and offsetting of the plates. The first plate
is creased but in general a good copy, with the text uncut.
Wheldon 160-966 1983 £300

HAMILTON, F. W.   The Origin and History of the First or
Grenadier Guards. London, 1874. 3 portrait frontis. 14 portrait
plates, 4 coloured plates of uniform and 3 coloured plates of badges.
1 plate of Horse Guards building, 76 plans on 67 sheets, 4 of which are
folding. 3 vols. Spines faded and label missing from vol. I. Good.
Edwards 1042-531 1983 £100

HAMILTON, G. V.   An Introduction to Objective Psychopathology. St. Louis: C. V. Mosby, 1925. First edition. Gach
95-186 1983 $25

HAMILTON, G. V.   A Research in Marriage. NY: Albert &
Charles Boni, 1929. First edition. Very good ex-library copy in torn
dust jacket. Gach 95-187 1983 $25

HAMILTON, GAIL PSEUD.
Please turn to
DODGE, MARY ABIGAIL

HAMILTON, HENRY S.   Reminiscences of a Veteran. Concord,
N.H., 1897. Illus. Orig. cloth. First edition. Autograph
presentation copy from Hamilton. Ginsberg 46-291 1983 $75

HAMILTON, IAN   Now and Then. London: Methuen, (1926).
Cloth and boards. First edition thus, with an etched frontis. by
William Strang. Pencil note, otherwise fine in lightly used dust
jacket. Reese 20-479 1983 $30

HAMILTON, JAMES   Observations on the Utility and
Administration of Purgative Medicines in Several Diseases. Phil.,
1829. From the 5th Edinburgh ed. 8vo. Contemporary calf. Morrill
289-97 1983 $20

HAMILTON, JAMES   Wanderings in North Africa. London:
John Murray, 1856. 12mo. Mpa, 8 plates. 1/2 dark green calf, black
label. Adelson Africa-193 1983 $75

HAMILTON, JOHN   The Catechisme. St. Andrews: John
Scot, 29 August, 1552. First edition. Black letter. Small 4to.
17th century calf. Preserved in a full morocco pull-off case. Title
within woodcut border of typographical ornaments, woodcut on U3,
woodcut devices on two leaves, woodcut initials. Cont. ownership
inscription on title, and 17th century inscription. Very rare.
Traylen 94-412 1983 £3,500

HAMILTON, MYRA   Kingdoms Curious. Heinemann, 1905.
Frontis. 31 plates (6 by A. Rackham, 2 by W.H. Robinson), foxing.
Brown pictorial cloth, gilt. Worn & spotted. Greer 40-181 1983
£38

HAMILTON, N. R.   Through Wonderful India and Beyond.
London, 1915. Coloured frontis. Plates. 8vo. Orig. cloth. Good.
Edwards 1044-314 1983 £15

HAMILTON, ROWAN   The Last of the Cornets. London: F.V.
White & Company, 1890. 2 vols., orig. blue cloth. First edition.
Spines and covers slightly worn at the ends and edges, rear cover
to volume II slightly dampstained, otherwise a good set. MacManus
278-2459 1983 $135

HAMILTON, SCHUYLER   History of the National Flag of the
United States of America. Phila.: Lippincott, Grambo, and Co.,
1852. Original cloth. Fine copy with colored plates. Scarce.
Jenkins 151-117 1983 $150

HAMILTON, THOMAS M.   The Young Pioneer When Captain Tom Was
a Boy. Washington, 1932. First edition. Fine copy. Jenkins 153-240
1983 $45

HAMILTON, THOMAS M.   The Young Pioneer. Wash., (1932).
Illus. Orig. cloth. First edition. Ginsberg 46-292 1983 $40

HAMILTON, WALTER   The East India Gazeteer. London, 1815.
3 extra plates tipped in. Thick 8vo. Slight marginal worming. Orig.
cloth. Good. Edwards 1044-315 1983 £75

HAMILTON, WILLIAM   Letters concerning the northern coast
of the county of Antrim. Dublin: George Bonham, etc., 1790. Second
edition. 8vo. Cont. tree calf, spine gilt. With a large folding
map and three folding plates. A couple of margins browned. Ximenes
63-524 1983 $175

HAMILTON, WILLIAM R.   My Sixty Years on the Plains. New
York, 1905. Cloth, pictorial cover, very good. Reese 19-260 1983
$200

HAMLEY, E. B.   The Operations of War. London, 1872.
Third edition. Sq. roy. 8vo. Orig. cloth. 19 folding maps, text
maps. Rebacked. Orig. spine laid down. Worn and faded. Some slight
foxing to preliminaries. Inscription on half title "Major G.P. Colley
from the Author, January 1873". Good. Edwards 1042-363 1983 £25

HAMLIN, PAUL M.   Supreme Court of Judicature of the
Province of New York, 1691-1704. New York, 1959. 3 vols. Orig.
green cloth, gilt, very nice. Boswell 7-128 1983 $75

HAMM, MARGHERITA ARLINA   Eminent Actors in their Homes. N.Y.:
James Pott & Co., 1902. Illus. Cloth. Dawson 471-324 1983 $20

HAMMER, VICTOR   Engravings and Woodcuts. Lexington,
Anvil Press, 1979. Tall 4to, boards, paper label, d/w. 36 engr. by
Hammer. One of 50 copies. Fine. Perata 28-198 1983 $250

HAMMER CREEK PRESS   Type and Stick at the Hammer Creek
Press. (N.P.: Hammer Creek Press), 1951. First edition. 12mo.
Stiff paper wrappers, paper cover label, paper slipcase. Printed
by John Fass at his Hammer Creek Press. Oak Knoll 49-216 1983
$75

HAMMETT, DASHIELL   The Thin Man. N.Y., Knopf, 1934.
First edition. Blue-green cloth (some fading) stamped in blue-red.
Very good. Houle 22-456 1983 $150

HAMMOND, GEORGE P.   Coronado's Seven Cities. Albuquerque,
1940. Wrps. Clark 741-457 1983 $21

HAMMOND, JABEZ D.   The History of Political Parties in
the State of New York, From the Ratification of the Federal Constitution to...1847. Albany, 1842-1852. 3 vols., 1st ed. 19th-cent.
three-quarter morocco, gilt extra. T.e.g. Illus. Jenkins 151-249
1983 $125

HAMMOND, JAMES   Love Elegies. London: Printed for G.
Hawkins...MCCLVII (sic, i.e. 1757). 4to, new wraps. Fourth edition.
A good copy. Quaritch NS 7-62 1983 $35

HAMMOND, JOHN   The practical surveyor... London:
Heath, 1731. Second edition. 8vo. Cont. calf. With a number
of inserted diagrammatic plates and slips, and an engraved frontis.
Slight wear to binding. Ximenes 63-564 1983 $350

HAMMOND, WILLIAM A.   Spiritualism and Allied Causes and
Conditions of Nervous Derangement. N.Y., 1876. Argosy 713-245 1983
$60

HAMOR, RAPHE   A True Discourse of the Present State
of Virginia...till the 18 of June, 1614. London, 1615 (reprint
ca. 1900). 4to, full red mor., black lea. inlays, gilt dec., a.e.g.
Few pages lightly foxed. One of 200 copies on large paper, privately
printed. Argosy 710-555 1983 $200

HAMPER, WILLIAM   Observations on certain pillars of
memorial, called hoar-stones. Birmingham: William Hodgetts, etc.,
1820. First edition. 4to. Orig. yellow printed boards. Presentation copy, inscribed on the title-page from the author to Sir
Thomas Phillipps. Bookplate of A.N.L. Munby. Very fine. Ximenes
63-5 1983 $225

HAMPSON, JOHN   Man about the House. London, 1935.
First edition. One of 285 numbered copies, signed by author. Dust
wrapper. Fine. Rota 230-271 1983 £15

HAMPSON, JOHN   Saturday Night at the Greyhound. Hogarth
Press, 1931. First edition. Covers faded and some light foxing. Name
on flyleaf. Nice. Rota 230-270 1983 £15

HAMPSON, JOHN   Strip Jack Naked. London: William
Heinemann Ltd., (1934). First edition. 8vo. Orig. cloth. Dust
jacket. Spine of jacket darkened, otherwise a fine copy. Jaffe
1-124 1983 $65

HANAFORD, W. G.   Lectures on Chemistry, with familiar
directions for performing experiments... Boston: Richardson,
Lord and Holebrook, 1831. First edition. 8vo. Modern quarter
calf over old boards. Some marginal waterstaining. Zeitlin 264-
193 1983 $80

HANCKE, ERICH   Max Liebermann. Berlin: Bruno
Cassirer, 1923. 1 orig. etching by Liebermann, signed in pencil.
305 illus. Large 4to. Calf. T.e.g. No. 54 of a limited edition
of 100 copies. Binding dusty. Ars Libri 32-405 1983 $375

HANCOCK, H. IRVING   Physical Training for Women by Japanese
Methods. London: G.P. Putnam's Sons; the Knickerbocker Press, 1905.
19-1/2 cm. Orig. yellow cloth with black & white illus. onlay.
Shaken, with some soiling. Grunder 6-30 1983 $65

HANCOCK, J.   The Herons of the World. 1978. Maps,
linedrawings and 64 coloured plates. 4to, half leather, gilt.
Published in a signed, limited edition of 150 copies. Wheldon 160-44
1983 £165

HANCOCK, J.   The Herons of the World. 1978. Maps,
line drawings and 64 full colour plates. 4to, cloth. Wheldon 160-738
1983 £46

HANCOCK, THOMAS   Elegy, Supposed to be Written on a Field
of Battle. John & Arthur Arch., 1818. Uncut, t.e.g. Some sl.
foxing, half red calf by Riviere & Son, v.g. First edition. Jarndyce
30-716 1983 £28

A HAND-BOOK for the Ball-Room and Evening Parties. NY: Leavitt & Allen, 1853. 12mo. Frontis. drawing and 3 small b&w illus. Occasional foxing, piece torn from rear end blank. Pictorially gilt-stamped and embossed boards. A.e.g. Bromer 25-189 1983 $45

THE HAND-BOOK of Games. London: Henry G. Bohn, 1850. Illus. with many diagrams and figures. Half calf over marbled boards. Karmiole 73-47 1983 $60

A HAND-BOOK of Iowa. N.p., 1893. Illus. Orig. printed wraps. First edition. Ginsberg 46-359 1983 $75

A HAND Book of Iowa, or the Discovery, Settlement, Geographical Location, Topography, Natural Resources, Geology, Climatology, Commercial Facilities...of the State of Iowa. (Chicago, 1893). Illus. Stiff wraps., good. Reese 19-293 1983 $75

HANDBUCH der Katholischen Kirchenmusik. 8vo, 1/2 cl. Salloch 387-344 1983 $25

HANDCOCK, A. G.   The Seige of Delhi in 1857. Allahabad, 1897. Second and revised edition. Folding map. Orig. printed wrappers, worn and chipped. 8vo. Good. Edwards 1044-316 1983 £14

HANDEL, GEORGE FREDERICK   Anthem in Score. London, c. 1790. Engraved title, engraved music, folio, unbound. Salloch 387-87 1983 $60

HANDEL, GEORGE FREDERICK   The Messiah: An Oratorio, Composed in the Year 1741. Boston, (Wilkins, Carter & Co.), 1846. Tall folio, new cloth with label. Between the front flyleaves, a page of cont. reviews has been bound in. Salloch 387-89 1983 $80

HANDEL, GEORGE FREDERICK   Otto und Theophano (Ottone). Bergedorf b. Hamburg, Chrysander, 1925. Folio, wrs., paper getting age-brown. Salloch 387-90 1983 $45

HANDEL, GEORGE FREDERICK   The sacred oratorios, as set to music... London: printed for T. Heptinstall, etc., 1799. 2 vols. 12mo. Cont. tree calf, spines gilt. 3 plates. One front endpaper removed, but a fine set. Ximenes 63-330 1983 $90

HANDEL, GEORGE FREDERICK   The Songs in the Ode Wrote by Mr. Dryden for St. Cecilia's Day, set by Mr. Handel. London, J. Walsh, (ca. 1739). Engraved title, engraved music. Marginal repair in lower corner of title, affecting a few words of the imprint which are replaced in manuscript facs. Otherwise fine. In a pigskin-backed linen box. First edition. Salloch 387-91 1983 $400

HANDEY, WILLIAM H.   Political Equilibrium. Hagers-town, 1842. Orig. cloth, expertly rebacked. First edition. Ginsberg 46-444 1983 $75

HANDLEY, JAMES   Colloquia Chirurgica. For Charles Bates and Arthur Bettesworth, London, 1705. 8vo, cont. unlettered sheep, G.O. Mitchell bookplate. First edition. A good copy. Quaritch NS 5-52 1983 $450

HANDLEY, M. A.   Roughing it in Southern India. London, 1911. Plates, some spotting. Press cuttings stuck to endpapers. 8vo. Orig. cloth. Good. Edwards 1044-317 1983 £20

HANDLIN, OSCAR   Commonwealth: A Study of the Role of Government in the American Economy: Massachusetts, 1776-1861. N.Y., 1947. Cloth. First edition. Ginsberg 46-447 1983 $25

HANDY, W. C.   Blues: An Anthology. New York, 1926. 4to, cloth, illus. by Miguel Covarrubias. Lettering on spine is faded, tiny tear to edge of introductory page, otherwise very good-fine. In Our Time 156-357 1983 $75

HANEY, JOHN LOUIS   A Bibliography of Samuel Taylor Coleridge. Philadelphia, printed for private circulation, 1903. 8vo, orig. cloth gilt. Ravenstree 94-178 1983 $25

HANIGHEN, FRANK C.   Santa Anna the Napoleon of the West. New York, 1934. Plates. 1st ed. Fine copy. Jenkins 153-242 1983 $85

HANKEY, THOMSON   The Principles of Banking, its Utility and Economy. Effingham Wilson, 1873. Half title, 20 pp ads. Small library stamp on verso of title. Orig. maroon cloth, v.g. 2nd edition. Jarndyce 31-181 1983 £18.50

HANKIN, E. H.   Animal Flight. 1914. Text-figures, 8vo, cloth, trifle used. Wheldon 160-489 1983 £18

HANKINSON, THOMAS EDWARDS   Poems. J. Hatchard, 1844. First edition, calf, sl. rubbed, maroon label, v.g. Jarndyce 30-719 1983 £16

HANKS, HENRY G.   State Mining Bureau. Sacramento, 1881. Orig. printed wraps. First edition. Ginsberg 47-100 1983 $35

HANLEY, JAMES   Aria & Finale. London: Boriswood Limited, 1932. First edition. 8vo. Orig. cloth. Dust jacket designed by James Boswell. Slightly torn jacket. Fine copy. Jaffe 1-126 1983 $65

HANLEY, JAMES   At Bay. London, 1935. 8vo. Cloth. 1 of 250 copies numbered and signed by the author. A fine copy. In Our Time 156-358 1983 $100

HANLEY, JAMES   Captain Bottell. Boriswood, 1933. First edition, 8vo, orig. buckram-backed cloth, t.e.g. A fine copy. Copy number 20 of a ltd. numbered edition of 99 copies on mediaeval rag paper, signed by the author. Fenning 62-162 1983 £75

HANLEY, JAMES   Captain Bottell. Boriswood, 1933. First edition. One of 99 copies, this unnumbered, signed by author. Light foxing of the endpapers. Very nice. Rota 231-304 1983 £50

HANLEY, JAMES   Captain Bottell. London, 1933. First edition. Cloth a head of spine a little rubbed. Nice. Rota 230-272 1983 £15

HANLEY, JAMES   Ebb and Flood. London: John Lane The Bodley Head Ltd., (1932). Folding frontis. designed by Alan Odle. Orig. cloth-backed boards with paper label on spine. First edition. One of only 105 copies printed on specially made rag paper and signed by the author. Fine copy. MacManus 278-2460 1983 $150

HANLEY, JAMES   Ebb and Flood. London: John Lane the Bodley Head Ltd., (1932). First trade edition. 8vo. Orig. cloth. Dust jacket designed by Alan Odle. Slightly torn jacket. Fine copy. Jaffe 1-127 1983 $75

HANLEY, JAMES   The Furys. A Novel. London: Chatto & Windus, 1935. First edition. 8vo. Orig. cloth. Dust jacket. Slightly nicked jacket with the orig. Book Guild wraparound band quoting J.C. Powys. A fine copy. Jaffe 1-129 1983 $100

HANLEY, JAMES   The German Prisoner. Privately printed by the author, (1903). First edition, with a frontis. by William Roberts, 8vo, orig. red buckram, gilt, t.e.g. A fine copy. Ltd. edition of 500 copies, numbered and signed by the author. Fenning 62-163 1983 £28.50

HANLEY, JAMES   The German Prisoner. (London): Privately printed by the author, n.d. First edition. Frontis. by William Roberts. Orig. cloth, acetate jacket. Ltd. to 500 copies for sale to subscribers, this being a presentation copy, inscribed by the author "For Brian W. Marrott with the author's compliments, James Hanley," Fine copy. MacManus 278-2461 1983 $85

HANLEY, JAMES   Herman Melville. Loughton: The Dud Noman Press, 1971. Orig. decorated wraps. First edition. Presentation copy from the author inscribed: "For Barbara & Hazel with love from James. 15.9.71." With the galley proofs for the same book laid in. Wrappers slightly soiled, otherwise a good copy. MacManus 278-2462 1983 $185

HANLEY, JAMES   The Last Voyage. London, 1931. First edition. One of 550 copies, signed by author. Spine and edges of covers faded and upper cover marked. Very good. Rota 231-302 1983 £25

HANLEY, JAMES　　　　　Men in Darkness. London: John Lane the Bodley Head Ltd., (1931). Frontis. by Alan Odle of his design for the dust jacket of the ordinary edition. Orig. cloth-backed boards with paper label on spine. First edition. One of 105 large-paper copies printed on specially made rag paper and signed by the author. Fine copy. MacManus 278-2463　1983　$150

HANLEY, JAMES　　　　　Men in Darkness. London: John Lane The Bodley Head Ltd., (1931). First trade edition. 8vo. Orig. cloth. Dust jacket designed by Alan Odle. Jacket trifle nicked. Fine copy. Jaffe 1-125　1983　$85

HANLEY, JAMES　　　　　The Ocean. New York: William Morrow & Company, 1941. Advance Copy in wrappers of the first American edition, with stamp on front free endpaper giving details of publication. 8vo. Orig. pictorial wrappers. Wrappers a bit rubbed, but a fine copy. Jaffe 1-130　1983　$125

HANLEY, JAMES　　　　　Quartermaster Clausen. London: Arlan at the White Owl Press, 1934. Orig. boards, dust jacket. First trade edition. Fine. MacManus 278-2464　1983　$65

HANLEY, JAMES　　　　　Quartermaster Clausen. London: Arlan Ath The White Owl Press, 1934. First edition, first binding. 8vo. Orig. grey boards, dust jacket. Slightly worn jacket. Fine copy. Jaffe 1-128　1983　$50

HANLEY, JAMES　　　　　Quartermaster Clausen. Arlan at the White Owl Press, 1934. First Trade edition. Covers just a little soiled. Very nice. Rota 230-273　1983　$21

HANLEY, JAMES　　　　　Sailor's Song. London: Nicholson & Watson, (1943). Orig. bright yellow cloth, dust jacket (inch-long tear at front). First edition, third state. Fine copy. MacManus 278-2465　1983　$65

HANLEY, JAMES　　　　　The Secret Journey. New York, 1936. 8vo. Cloth. Dust jacket has a chip on the front jacket and has some light wear. A fine copy. In Our Time 156-359　1983　$50

HANLEY, JAMES　　　　　Stoker Haslett. London: Joiner, 1932. Orig. cloth. One of 350 copies signed by Hanley. Fine. MacManus 278-2466　1983　$65

HANLEY, JAMES　　　　　Stoker Haslett. London, 1932. First edition. One of 350 numbered copies, signed by author. Orig. glassene wrapper. Exceptionally fine. Rota 231-303　1983　£40

HANLEY, JAMES　　　　　Stoker Haslett, a Tale. Joiner and Steel, 1932. First edition, 8vo, orig. white buckram, gilt, t.e.g. Fine. Ltd. edition of 350 copies, numbered and signed by the author. Printed at the Alcuin Press. Fenning 62-164　1983　£35

HANLEY, MILES L.　　　　Word Index to James Joyce's Ulysses. Madison, Wis.: 1937. First edition. Offset typescript, printed brown wrappers, rebacked with canvas. Covers worn. Bradley 66-217　1983　$47.50

HANNAY, JAMES　　　　　The History of Acadia. St. John, N.B.: Printed by J. & A. McMillan, 1879. 21cm. First edition. Orig. green cloth, black and gilt stamped on the upper cover. A fine copy. McGahern 53-68　1983　$75

HANNAY, JAMES　　　　　Satire and satirists. London: David Bogue, 1854. First edition. 8vo. Orig. green cloth. Spine faded. Ximenes 63-476　1983　$45

HANNEMA, FR.　　　　　Gerard Terborch. Amsterdam: "De Gulden Ster", 1943. 8 tipped-in color plates. 46 text illus. Large 4to. Boards, 1/4 cloth. Slightly worn. Ars Libri 32-660　1983　$75

HANNON, J.-D.　　　　　Essai Sur L'Hypochondrie. Bruxelles: N.-J. Gregoir, 1849. Orig. printed yellow wrappers. Unopened copy. Inscribed. First edition. Gach 95-191　1983　$65

HANOTEAU. J.　　　　　Memoirs of General de Caulaincourt. London, 1935. Thick 8vo. Orig. cloth. Portrait frontis. Slightly worn and soiled. Bookplate. Good. Edwards 1042-299　1983　£25

HANSON, JOSEPH M.　　　　Frontier Ballads. Chicago: A.C. McClurg & Co., 1910. Orig. pictorial boards. Illus. by Maynard Dixon. Fine. Jenkins 152-143　1983　$45

HANSON, L. W.　　　　　Contemporary Printed Sources for British and Irish Economic History 1701-1750. Cambridge: Univ. Press, 1963. Cloth in dw, pretty good copy. Dawson 470-143　1983　$75

HANSON, PAULINE　　　　The Forever Young. Denver: Alan Swallow, (1948). Boards. First edition, ltd. to 300 copies. Inscribed by the author to another poet: "For Bill, Polly." About fine in a lightly soiled dust jacket. Reese 20-481　1983　$35

HANWAY, JONAS　　　　　A Journal of Eight Days Journey from Portsmouth to Kingston Upon Thames. Printed by H. Woodfall, 1756. 4to, rebound in half claf, hand-marbled boards, maroon label. First edition. Jarndyce 31-37　1983　£140

HANWAY, JONAS　　　　　Reflections, Essays and Meditations on Life and Religion with a Collection of Proverbs. 1761. 2 vols., first edition, engraved frontis., full calf, one title label lacking o/w a very good set. K Books 307-207　1983　£68

HANWAY, THOMAS　　　　A Journal of Eight Days Journey from Portsmouth to Kingston Upon Thames. London: by H. Woodfall, 1756. First edition. 2 parts in 1 vol. 4to. Newly bound in half calf with morocco label, gilt. 2 engraved frontis. Traylen 94-413　1983　£165

HARADA, JIRO　　　　　The Lesson of Japanese Architecture. London: The Studio Ltd. (1936). 4to, profusely illus. with photographic plates. Dust jacket (chipped). Karmiole 73-53　1983　$65

HARBORD, JAMES G.　　　　The American Army in France, 1917-1919. Boston, Little Brown, 1936. First edition. Thick 8vo, color frontis. Illus. with photos and maps. Dust jacket (trifle rubbed). Fine. Houle 22-1203　1983　$30

HARBOUR, JENNIE　　　　The Fairy Tale Book. Rapheal Tuck, n.d. (inscr.1938). 4to. Colour frontis. Title vignette & 39 text illus. Green boards. Onlaid extra colour plate. Greer 39-73　1983　£28

HARCOURT, HELEN　　　　Florida Fruits and How To Raise Them. Louisville, 1886. Revised and Enlarged Edition. 8vo. Ex-library. Morrill 290-129　1983　$27.50

HARCOURT, HELEN　　　　Home Life in Florida. Louisville, 1889. First edition. Few illustrations. 8vo. Corners rubbed. Morrill 290-130　1983　$20

HARCUS, WILLIAM　　　　South Australia. Lon., 1876. Illus., folding maps, cover slightly stained, edges rubbed, very good. Quill & Brush 54-1685　1983　$150

HARDACRE, BENJAMIN　　　　Miscellanies in Prose and Verse. Simpkin, Marshall; Bradford: T. Brear & W. Morgan, 1874. Orig. blue cloth, v.g. First edition. Jarndyce 30-721　1983　£15

HARDAKER, ALFRED　　　　A Brief History of Pawnbroking. Jackson Ruston and Keeson, 1892. First edition. Half title. Presentation slip. Orig. dark green dec. cloth. Very good. Jarndyce 31-332　1983　£20

HARDCASTLE, EPHRAIM　　　　Wine and Walnuts; or After Dinner Chit-Chat. London, 1823. 8vo. Leather, boards. 2 vols. A fine set. In Our Time 156-360　1983　$125

HARDEN, RALPH W.　　　　St. John's Monkstown. Dublin: Hodges, Figgis, 1911. First edition, 10 plates, errata slip, 8vo, orig. cloth. Fenning 60-161　1983　£14.50

HARDIE, JAMES   An Account of the Malignant Fever.
N.Y., 1799. Cont. calf, first edition. Argosy 713-246 1983
$250

HARDIE, JAMES   The American Remembrancer, and Universal
Tablet of Memory... Philadelphia, 1795. Folding table. Half
morocco, hinge worn, but good. Reese 18-202 1983 $100

HARDIE, MARTIN   Charles Meryon and His Eaux-Fortes sur
Paris. London: The Print Collectors' Club, 1931. 22 plates. 4to.
Boards, 1/4 cloth. No. 236 of a limited edition of 500 copies only.
Ars Libri 32-451 1983 $50

HARDIE, MARTIN   English Coloured Books. New York:
G.P. Putnam, Co., (1906). First U.S. edition. Thick 4to. Gilt-
decorated cloth. With colored illus. Minor cover rubbing, endpaper
chipped, with inside hinges cracked. Oak Knoll 49-217 1983 $75

HARDIE, MARTIN   Frederick Goulding. Master printer of
copper plates. Stirling: Eneas MacKay, 1910. 6 plates (including
two original etchings by Goulding and R.W. Macbeth, and 4 photogravures). 4 illus. Large 4to. Boards. T.e.g. Uncut. No. 308 of
a limited edition of 350 copies on fine wove paper. Front hinge
damaged at foot. Ars Libri 32-264 1983 $250

HARDIE, MARTIN   The Liber Studiorum Mezzotints of
Sir Frank Short after J.M.W. Turner. London: The Print Collectors'
Club, 1933. 48 collotype illus. 4to. Cloth. Edition limited
to 510 copies in all. This is no. 89 of 110 copies on handmade
paper with a frontis. printed from part of the original copper-
plate of the artist's "Kingston Bank, No. 2," after Turner, signed
in pencil by Short. Ars Libri 32-633 1983 $75

HARDIN, JOHN WESLEY   The Life of John Wesley Hardin, from the
Original Manuscript. Seguin, Texas: Smith & Moore, 1896. Original
printed wrappers. First edition. Fine copy. Jenkins 153-243 1983
$100

HARDIN, JOHN WESLEY   The Life of John Wesley Hardin, from
the Original Manuscript. Seguin, Texas, Smith & Moore, 1896. 12mo.
Vignettes, 4 illus., one of which is repeated on back wrap. Orig.
printed wrappers. 1st ed., 1st issue. Near fine. O'Neal 50-112
1983 $80

HARDIN, MARTIN D.   Reports of Cases Argued and Adjudged in
the Court of Appeals of Kentucky, from Spring Term 1805, to Spring
Term 1808. Frankfort: Printed by Johnston and Pleasants. 1810.
Orig. full calf, calf a bit rubbed, but a very good copy, internally
fine. Reese 18-339 1983 $275

HARDING, E.   Naval Biography. John Scott, 1805. First
edition. 8vo, orig. cloth. 2 engr. frontis. 2 vols. 39 engraved
portrait plates. Cont. half calf, gilt, neatly rebacked and orig.
spines laid down. Marbled boards. Speckled edges. Some slight foxing and offsetting throughout. Well-illustrated. Fine. Edwards
1042-75 1983 £150

HARDINGE, BELLE (BOYD)   Belle Boyd in Camp and Prison, Written
by Herself. NY, 1865. 1st American edition. Nice copy of this
scarce memoir. Jenkins 151-119 1983 $75

HARDINGE, C. S.   Recollections of India. London, 1847.
26 tinted lithograph plates. Some slight foxing. Folio. Half
morocco, worn, recased. 8vo. Good. Edwards 1044-318 1983 £350

HARDMAN, WILLIAM   A Mid-Victorian Pepys. Cecil Palmer,
1923. 2nd edition, half title, front. port. illus. Orig. green cloth.
Jarndyce 30-1015 1983 £12.50

HARDWICK, HUMPHREY   The Difficulty of Sions Deliverance
and Reformation. Printed by I.L. for Christopher Meredith, 1644.
First edition, 4to, wrapper, a very good copy. Fenning 62-165 1983
£21.50

HARDY, ALLISON   Wild Bill Hickok, King of the Gun-
Fighters. Girard, Kansas: Haldeman-Julius, 1943. Original printed
grey wrappers. First edition. Scarce. Jenkins 153-244 1983 $30

HARDY, E. STUART   The Fire Engine Book. Nister, n.d.
(ca.1915). Oblong 4to. 9 colour plates (one double). 3 full-page
& one text illus. Colour pictorial limp wrappers, repaired. Greer
40-105 1983 £27.50

HARDY, FLORENCE EMILY   The Early Life of Thomas Hardy, 1840-
1891. New York: The Macmillan Co., 1928. First edition. 8vo.
Cloth. Illus. including facsimiles of manuscripts. Name in ink
on front free endpaper else very good. Oak Knoll 48-192 1983

HARDY, FLORENCE EMILY   The Later Years of Thomas Hardy, 1892-
1928. N.Y., 1930. D.w. First American edition. Review copy. Argosy
714-349 1983 $25

HARDY, MARY ANNE   The Two Catherines. Cambridge:
Macmillan, 1862. First edition, 2 vols. Half titles. Orig. dark
green grained cloth, spines gilt lettered. Jarndyce 31-727 1983
£56

HARDY, PHILIP D.   Hardy's Tourist's Guide. Simpkin and
Marshall, circa, 1860. With engraved frontis., folding coloured map
and 2 full-page illus., 12mo, orig. green cloth, gilt. Fenning 61-192
1983 £18.50

HARDY, THOMAS   A Changed Man. London: Macmillan &
Co., 1913. Orig. cloth. Frontis. First edition. Review copy,
with pub.'s printed slip, dated S.2.9.13. On the back endsheet is
stamped "This Book is the Property of the Field." Covers a trifle
rubbed, somewhat shaken, but a very good copy. MacManus 278-2470
1983 $250

HARDY, THOMAS   A Changed Man and Other Tales. L., 1913.
Top edge gilt, flys slightly offset, very good or better in lightly
chipped, very good dustwrapper. Quill & Brush 54-603 1983 $200

HARDY, THOMAS   A Changed Man. London: Macmillan &
Co., 1913. Frontis. Orig. cloth, dust jacket (chipped at
extremities, tape repaired). First edition, head of spine torn,
else a very good copy. Scarce in dust jacket. MacManus 278-2471 1983
$75

HARDY, THOMAS   A Changed Man and Other Tales. London:
Macmillan, 1913. Orig. cloth. First edition. MacManus 278-2469
1983 $25

HARDY, THOMAS   The Dynasts. London: Macmillan, 1927.
3 vols. 4to, orig. vellum-backed boards, dust jackets (a little worn).
One of 525 large paper copies signed by Hardy. Very fine.
MacManus 278-2475 1983 $500

HARDY, THOMAS   The Dynasts. London, 1927. 3 vols.
4to. Orig. quarter vellum over batik paper boards, with the orig.
printed dustwrappers. Title-pages printed in red and black. Cont.
etched portrait of Hardy signed in pencil by the artist, Frances
Dodd. Limited large paper edition of 525 copies, signed in vol. 1
by Thomas Hardy. Traylen 94-415 1983 £260

HARDY, THOMAS   The Dynasts. London, 1904-08. First
edition, second issue of part 1. 3 vols. 8vo. Orig. green cloth,
gilt. Traylen 94-414 1983 £65

HARDY, THOMAS   The Famous Tragedy of the Queen of Cornwall at Tintagel in Lyonnesse. London: 1923. First edition. Frontis.
and one other plate. Pictorial green boards. Fine in chipped and
soiled dust jacket. Bradley 66-189 1983 $35

HARDY, THOMAS   The Famous Tragedy of the Queen of
Cornwall. London: Macmillan & Co., 1923. 8vo, orig. cloth,
first edition, almost fine. MacManus 278-2476 1983 $20

HARDY, THOMAS   The Famous Tragedy of the Queen of
Cornwall... London, 1923. First edition. 4to. Orig. decorated
green cloth, gilt. Frontis and plate by Hardy. Traylen 94-416
1983 £14

HARDY, THOMAS   Far From the Madding Crowd. Cambridge:
University Press, 1958. Octavo. Illus. with wood engravings by
Agnes Miller Parker. Limited to 1500 copies signed by artist for
members of the Limited Editions Club. Very fine in leather-backed
decorated boards with defective glassine and slip-case, with one
edge partially split. Separate orig. engraving by Parker laid-in.
Bromer 25-277 1983 $125

HARDY, THOMAS   Far from the Madding Crowd. Sampson
Low, Marston, 1893. Half title, front. port. Lacking leading free
end paper. New and cheaper edition. Orig. maroon cloth. Jarndyce
31-734 1983 £15

HARDY, THOMAS   A Group of Noble Dames. London: Osgood,
McIlvaine, (1891). Orig. cloth. First edition. First binding.
Covers a bit soiled. MacManus 278-2478 1983 $65

HARDY, THOMAS   The Hand of Ethelberta. Sampson Low,
1890. Blue printed end papers. Orig. red dec. cloth. Jarndyce 31-
732 1983 £15

HARDY, THOMAS   Human Shows Far Phantasies. L., 1925.
Some pages unopened, fine in dustwrapper with small chip at edges of
spine. Quill & Brush 54-604 1983 $75

HARDY, THOMAS   Human Shows and Far Phantasies, Songs,
and Trifles. London, 1925. First edition. 8vo. Orig. green cloth,
gilt. Traylen 94-417 1983 £25

HARDY, THOMAS   Human Shows Far Phantasies Songs, and
Trifles. London: Macmillan, 1925. Orig. cloth, dust jacket. First
edition. Fine copy. MacManus 278-2480 1983 $35

HARDY, THOMAS   Human Shows Far Phantasies. L., 1925.
Edges lightly worn, good to very good. Quill & Brush 54-605 1983
$30

HARDY, THOMAS   Human Shows Far Phantasies. Macmillan
and Co., 1925. 8vo, 3 pages advertisements, orig. cloth gilt, with
dust wrapper slightly defective at top of spine, uncut and unopened.
First edition. Bickersteth 75-145 1983 £16

HARDY, THOMAS   Jude the Obscure. (L., 1896). First
issue with "Osgood" on title and spine. Gilt lettering bright, front
endpapers slightly rumpled and starting, minor foxing, good to very
good. Quill & Brush 54-606 1983 $125

HARDY, THOMAS   Jude the Obscure. (London: Osgood,
McIlvaine & Company, 1896). Illus. with an engraved frontis. by H.
MacBeth-Raeburn, orig. decorated cloth. First edition. Spine and
covers worn, inner hinges cracked, with slight offsetting to the
front endpapers, otherwise a good copy. Former owner's signature.
MacManus 278-2481 1983 $65

HARDY, THOMAS   A Laodicean. London: Sampson Low,
Marston, Searle & Rivington, 1881. In three vols. Orig. cloth. First
English edition, first binding. Library labels removed from upper
covers, inner hinges cracked, some foxing. MacManus 278-2484 1983
$350

HARDY, THOMAS   Late Lyrics and Earlier, with many other
verses. London, 1922. First edition. 8vo. Orig. green cloth, gilt.
Traylen 94-418 1983 £25

HARDY, THOMAS   Late Lyrics and Earlier. London:
Macmillan & Company, 1922. First edition. One very small tear to the
top spine end, otherwise a very good copy. Orig. cloth. MacManus
278-2483 1983 $20

HARDY, THOMAS   Life and Art. N.Y.: Greenberg, 1925.
Orig. cloth, dust jacket (worn). First American edition. MacManus 278-
2485 1983 $25

HARDY, THOMAS   Life's Little Ironies. London: Osgood,
(1894). Orig. decorated cloth. First edition. Inner hinges cracked;
worn. MacManus 278-2486 1983 $35

HARDY, THOMAS   Life's Little Ironies. London, 1894.
First edition. 8vo. Orig. sage-green sand-grain cloth, blocked
in brown and lettered in gold. Half-title. Traylen 94-419 1983
£20

HARDY, THOMAS   The Mayor of Casterbridge. Sampson
Low, Marston, n.d. Half title, orig. maroon cloth. Jarndyce 31-728
1983 £14.50

HARDY, THOMAS   Moments of Vision. Macmillan, 1917.
Orig. cloth, dust jacket (spine browned). First edition. A fine
copy and rare in dust jacket. MacManus 278-2487 1983 $75

HARDY, THOMAS   Moments of Vision. L. 1917. Uncut,
edges slightly rubbed, else near fine. Quill & Brush 54-607 1983
$60

HARDY, THOMAS   Old Mrs. Chundle. New York: Crosby
Gaibe, 1929. Orig. cloth-backed decorated boards. First edition.
One of 742 copies printed by D.B. Updike at the Merrymount Press.
Spine ends a trifle worn, otherwise a very good copy. MacManus 278-
2488 1983 $25

HARDY, THOMAS   The Oxen. Hove: Private Circulation
Only, 1915. Orig. printed wraps. First Separate edition. Fine copy
in cloth base. MacManus 278-2491 1983 $150

HARDY, THOMAS   A Pair of Blue Eyes. New York:
Harper & Brothers, 1895. Frontis. Orig. decorated cloth. MacManus
278-2492 1983 $20

HARDY, THOMAS   The Play of 'Saint George' as Aforetime
Acted by the Dorsetshire Christmas Mummers Based on the Version in 'The
Return of the Native,' and Completed from Other Versions, and from
Local Tradition. Cambridge: University Press, 1921. Orig. wraps.
First edition. One of 25 copies, each numbered and initialed by
Florence Hardy. Wraps. very slightly soiled and worn. A fine copy.
MacManus 278-2493 1983 $450

HARDY, THOMAS   Poems of the Past and The Present.
(London: Harper & Brothers, 1902). Orig. decorated green-ribbed
cloth. First edition. Spine and covers slightly worn and dusty,
otherwise a good copy. MacManus 278-2494 1983 $150

HARDY, THOMAS   Programme. Dorchester: Ling, 1924.
Orig. wraps. First edition. One of 25 copies. Front wrapper
slightly scratched, otherwise a very good to near-fine copy.
MacManus 278-2496 1983 $185

HARDY, THOMAS   A Quotation from the Works of Thomas
Hardy for Every Day in the Year. London: Cecil Palmer, (1921).
Frontis. portrait, orig. decorated wraps. First edition. Spine and
covers slightly worn and soiled, otherwise a very good copy. Former
owner's signature. MacManus 278-2497 1983 $135

HARDY, THOMAS   The Return of the Native. London, 1929.
First edition with these illus, English issue. Woodcuts by C. Leighton.
One of 1500 copies, signed by artist. Spine a little soiled. Book-
plate. Nice. Rota 230-274 1983 £45

HARDY, THOMAS   The Return of the Native. New York,
harpers, 1929. American issue, thick roy. 8vo, 12 mounted woodcut
illus., many woodcut vignettes, uncut in quarter natural buckram
over blue paper boards, paper label, trifling wear to couple of
corners, a very good copy. Illustrations by Clare Leighton. American
issue of 1,000 numbered copies signed by Clare Leighton. Deighton
3-155 1983 £38

HARDY, THOMAS   Satires of Circumstance. London:
Macmillan, 1914. Orig. cloth, dust jacket (edges a bit chipped).
First edition. Endpapers browned, otherwise a very good copy.
Scarce in dust jacket. MacManus 278-2499 1983 $185

HARDY, THOMAS   Selected Poems. London: the Ricardi
Press, 1921. 4to. Boards with holland back, printed paper labels,
t.e.g., others uncut. Portrait and vignette title-page engraved
by William Nicholson. Limited edition of 1,000 numbered copies.
Traylen 94-420 1983 £55

HARDY, THOMAS   Selected Poems. London: The Medici
Society Ltd., 1921. Orig. cloth-backed boards with paper label, dust
jacket (partially faded & stained). With portrait & title-page
design engraved on the wood by William Nicholson. Ltd. to 1000
copies. Covers and edges a little faded and stained, else a very good
copy. MacManus 278-2500 1983 $75

HARDY, THOMAS   Song of the Soldiers. Hove: (E.
Williams), 1915. Printed wraps. Fine. Reese 20-483 1983 $30

HARDY, THOMAS   Tess of the d'Urbervilles, a Pure Woman.
(London: James R. Osgood, McIlvaine & Company, 1891). First edition,
first impression. 3 vols., orig. tan gilt-decorated cloth. Spines
and covers slightly worn and soiled, inner hinges to vols. II and III
weak, otherwise a very good copy in a tan, quarter-morocco folding
case. MacManus 278-2501 1983 $1,850

HARDY, THOMAS   The Three Wayfarers. Dorchester: Henry
Ling, 1935. Orig. wraps. First English edition. Ltd. to 250
copies. Very good. MacManus 278-2503 1983 $25

HARDY, THOMAS   Time's Laughing-stocks and Other Verses.
London: Macmillan, 1909. Orig. cloth. First edition. Spine faded,
inner hinges partly cracked. MacManus 278-1504 1983 $50

HARDY, THOMAS   Time's Laughingstocks and other Verses.
London, 1909. First edition. 8vo. Orig. green cloth, gilt. 4 pp.
of ads. Traylen 94-421 1983 £15

HARDY, THOMAS   The Trumpet Major. London: Smith,
Elder, 1880. First edition, secondary binding. 3 vols. Orig. cloth.
Library labels on front covers; shaken and worn. In a half morocco
slipcase. MacManus 278-2506 1983 $185

HARDY, THOMAS   The Trumpet Major. London: Smith,
Elder, 1880. 3 vols., orig. cloth (recased; labels removed; orig.
spines laid down). First edition. First binding. MacManus 278-2505
1983 $125

HARDY, THOMAS   Two on a Tower. New York: Henry Holt &
Co., 1882. Orig. pictorial cloth. First American edition. Covers
a bit soiled, bookplate, otherwise a very good copy. MacManus 278-2507
1983 $100

HARDY, THOMAS   Two on a Tower. Sampson Low, 1883.
3rd edition, half title, 32 pp ads. Orig. red dec. cloth, bevelled
boards. Jarndyce 31-729 1983 £22

HARDY, THOMAS   Under the Greenwood Tree. N.Y.,
MacMillian, 1940. First American edition. 4to, illus. with 62
woodengravings by Leighton. Dust jacket with design by Leighton
(a little rubbed) else very good. Houle 22-585 1983 $45

HARDY, THOMAS   Under the Greenwood Tree. New York:
Harper & Brothers, 1896. Orig. decorated cloth. Frontis. First
revised edition, American issue. Very good copy. MacManus 278-2508
1983 $20

HARDY, THOMAS   The Well-Beloved. London: Osgood,
McIlvaine, (1897). Orig. cloth. First edition. Heaf of spine torn
away, else very good. MacManus 278-2509 1983 $25

HARDY, THOMAS   Wessex Poems and Other Verses. (London:
Harper & Brothers, 1898). Orig. gilt-decorated green cloth, printed
dust jacket (lacking portions of spine). First edition. A fine copy.
MacManus 278-2510 1983 $450

HARDY, THOMAS   Winter Words. London: Macmillan, 1888.
2 vols., orig. cloth. First edition. MacManus 278-2512 1983 $450

HARDY, THOMAS   Winter Words, in Various Moods and Metres.
New York: The Macmillan Company, 1928. First American edition. Orig.
boards, pub.'s glassine jacket (spine ends and cover margins chipped,
few small tears to the spine). One of 500 copies. Spine a trifle
faded, otherwise a near-fine copy. MacManus 278-1514 1983 $125

HARDY, THOMAS   Winter Words. NY, 1928. Very good to
near fine in dustwrapper with small chip on front panel and on bottom
of spine. Quill & Brush 54-609 1983 $35

HARDY, THOMAS   Winter Words in various moods and
metres. London, 1928. First edition. 8vo. Orig. green cloth,
gilt. Traylen 94-422 1983 £18

HARDY, THOMAS   The Woodlanders. London: Macmillan,
1887. 3 vols., orig. cloth. First edition, secondary binding. A
fine copy. MacManus 278-2515 1983 $1,000

HARDY, THOMAS   The Woodlanders. Macmillan, 1887. Half
title, following inner hinge weakening, orig. dark green cloth. First
one-volume edition. Jarndyce 31-731 1983 £24

HARDY, THOMAS   The Woodlanders. New York: Harper &
Brothers, 1896. Orig. pictorial cloth. Early American edition.
MacManus 278-2516 1983 $20

HARDY, THOMAS   The Works of Thomas Hardy. London,
1919. 8vo. Cloth. 37 vols. The Mellstock ed. 1 of 500 sets
signed by Hardy. Fine In Our Time 156-361 1983 $3000

HARDY, THOMAS   Yuletide in a Younger World. New York,
1927. First edition. One of only 27 copies printed, of which only
12 were for sale. Mint. Gekoski 2-77 1983 £190

HARE, AUGUSTUS J. C.   The Story of Two Noble Lives. London:
George Allen, 1893. 3 vols., illus., cont. cloth-backed marbled
boards. First edition. Spines and covers slightly worn at the
edges, some foxing to the preliminary pages, otherwise a good set.
MacManus 278-2527 1983 $50

HARE, FRANCIS AUGUSTUS   The Last of the Bushrangers. London:
Hurst and Blackett, 1892. Ads. With 8 plates, orig. red gilt-
stamped cloth; stained on back cover and spine sl. soiled. Karmiole
75-17 1983 $75

HARE, KENNETH   Three Poems. London: A.T. Stevens,
Martins Lane, 1916. First edition. Illus. by C.L. Fraser. Orig.
decorated wrappers. Contains five decorations by Fraser including the
cover designs. With the publisher's advertisement slip, also designed
by Fraser, loosely laid in. Very fine. MacManus 278-1997 1983 $150

HARE, WILLIAM H.   Another Letter from Bishop Hard to the
Children of the Church. (Yankton, Dakota, 1874?). Illus. Orig.
wraps. First edition. Ginsberg 47-282 1983 $35

HARGRAVE, CATHERINE PERRY   A History of Playing Cards and a
Bibliography of Cards and Gaming. Boston: Houghton Mifflin Co.,
1930. First edition. Tall 4to. Cloth. Some cover rubbing;
stain on top edge of pages not affecting the internal book. Oak
Knoll 49-450 1983 $200

HARINGTON, JOHN   The Metamorphosis of Aiax. Lon.: Fanfrolico Press, (1927). Limited to 450 numbered copies, cover soiled
and wearing, good. Quill & Brush 54-596 1983 $40

HARINGTON, JOHN   The School of Salernum. New York,
1920. First edition with additions by Packard & Garrison. 8vo.
Orig. binding. Rear inner hinge cracked. Fye H-3-238 1983 $40

HARKNESS, H.   A Description of a Singular Aboriginal
Race... London, 1832. 4 engraved plates, spotted. 2pp. of text
stained in margin. Roy.8vo. Half calf, rebacked, corners bumped.
Good. Edwards 1044-320 1983 £235

HARLAN, JACOB W.   California, 1846 to 1888. San Francisco:
The Bancroft Company, 1888. Portrait. Original pictorial cloth, gilt.
Some staining and wear to cloth. Nice. Jenkins 153-245 1983 $100

HARLAN, RICHARD   Fauna Americana. Philadelphia, 1825.
Orig. boards, some splitting to hinge. Unobtrusive library stamp.
Overall quite good. Reese 18-587 1983 $250

HARLAND, HENRY   Comedies & Errors. John Lane, 1898.
First issue, with ads. dated 1897. Endpapers cracking at hinge. Initials on flyleaf. From the library of Martin Secker, bearing his
bookplate. Good. Rota 230-275 1983 £25

HARLBUTT, FRANK   Old Derby Porcelain. London, T. Werner
Laurie, 1928. First edition, second impression. Illus. with 60
plates. Illus. dust jacket (small nicks). Very good. Houle 22-727
1983 $85

HARLER, C. R.   The Culture and Marketing of Tea. 1933.
2 maps and 8 plates, 8vo, cloth. Wheldon 160-2118 1983 £15

HARLEY, GEORGE DAVIES   An authentic sketch of the life, education, and personal character of William Henry West Betty, the
celebrated Young Roscius. London: printed for Richard Phillips; sold
by H. D. Symonds, etc., 1804. 8vo, disbound, 1st ed. With a
frontis. portrait (very small piece torn from blank margin). Very
scarce. Ximenes 64-254 1983 $150

HARLEY, GEORGE DAVIES   An authentic sketch of the life, education, and personal character of William Henry West Betty, the celebrated Young Roscius. London: printed for Richard Phillips; sold by
H. D. Symonds, etc., 1804. 8vo, wrappers, 4th edition, with a
portrait. Very good copy. Ximenes 64-255 1983 $75

HARLEY, JOHN   The veteran, or forty years in the
British service. London: Colburn, 1838. First edition. 2 vols.
12mo. Orig. lilac cloth. Spines evenly faded. A fine copy.
Ximenes 63-313 1983 $60

HARLOW, ALVIN F.   Old Bowery Days. New York, 1931. 1st
ed. Illus. 8vo, some binding stains. Morrill 288-340 1983 $20

HARLOW, ALVIN F.   Old Waybills... New York, 1934. First
edition. Illus. Jenkins 153-246 1983 $65

HARLOW, ALVIN F.   Old Waybills: the Romance of the
Express Companies. NY, 1934. Illus, d.w. Argosy 710-581 1983 $35

HARLOW, FREDERICK PEASE   The Making of a Sailor. Salem, Mass.:
Marine Research Society, 1928. Roy. 8vo. Orig. cloth. Frontis. &
25 plates. Spine slightly soiled, some slight foxing. Good. Edwards
1042-76 1983 £30

HARLOW, NEAL   Maps and Surveys of the Pueblo Lands
of Los Angeles. Los Angeles, 1976. Limited edition, numbered and
signed. 1st ed. Fldg. maps in back pocket, other fldg. maps, illus.
Cloth-backed decorated boards. Clark 741-119 1983 $165

HARLOW, NEAL   Maps & Surveys of the Pueblo Lands of
Los Angeles. Los Angeles: Dawson's Book Shop, 1976. Map and views.
Printed by Grant Dahlstrom. Dawson 471-110 1983 $100

HARLOW, NEAL   The Maps of San Francisco Bay. (San
Francisco): Book Club of California, 1950. One of 375 copies, printed
at the Grabhorn Press. Folding maps. Boards. Leather spine. Dawson
471-111 1983 $450

HARLOW, VINCENT T.   A History of Barbados, 1625-1685.
Oxford (Eng.), 1926. Map. 8vo, ex-library. Morrill 288-608 1983
$20

HARMAN, FRED   The Great West in Paintings. Chicago,
Swallow Press, (1969). First edition. Small oblong folio. Ltd.
edition. One of 500 copies. Signed and inscribed with an orig.
ink drawing of a bucking horse on the limitation page. Pub.'s
slipcase. Fine. Houle 22-1101 1983 $125

HARMAN, THOMAS   A Caveat or Warning for Common
Cursetors, Vulgarly called Vagabonds. 1814. Woodcuts, 4to, new
half calf, tear on page 70 not affecting text, the 1814 reprint of
the Middleton Edition of 1573, limited edition of 100 copies. K Books
301-83 1983 £48

HARMER, S. F.   Cambridge Natural History. (1895-1909),
Reprint 1958-60. 10 vols., 8vo, cloth, numerous illustrations.
Wheldon 160-471 1983 £75

HARMON, DANIEL W.   A Journal of Voyages and Travels in the
Interiour of North America, between the 47th and 58th Degrees of
North Latitude... Andover, 1820. Folding map. Portrait. Orig.
mottled calf. Usual browning and slight offsetting, otherwise a
fine copy, without the errata slip found in some copies. Reese 18-
544 1983 $850

HARMON, GEORGE D.   Sixty Years of Indian Affairs Political,
Economic, and Diplomatic 1789-1850. Chapel Hill, 1941. 1st ed.
Jenkins 151-118 1983 $40

HARMON, R. W.   Bibliography of Animal Venoms. Gaines-
ville, 1943. First edition. 8vo. Orig. binding. Fye H-3-1049
1983 $20

THE HARMONY of Divine and Heavenly Doctrines. London, 1795. Third
edition. 18mo, later cloth-backed boards, foxed, ex-library. Argosy
710-74 1983 $35

HARNED, THOMAS B.   The Letters of Anne Gilchrist and
Walt Whitman. New York: Doubleday, 1918. 1st ed. Orig. cloth,
gilt. Fine copy with presentation inscription from Harned on front
end paper, Oct. 26, 1918. Jenkins 155-1311 1983 $25

HARNEY, RICHARD J.   History of Winnebago County Wisconsin,
and Early History of the Northwest. Oshkosh, 1880. Illus., 79
views. Orig. three quarter morocco, gilt. Ginsberg 46-826 1983
$200

HARNEY, RICHARD J.   History of Winnebago County Wisconsin.
Oshkosh, 1880. First edition. Numerous old lithos, 1/2 lea., a.e.g.,
heavily rubbed. Signatures loose. King 46-243 1983 $75

HARPER, FRANCIS P.   Colored Plate Books and their values...
Princeton: Francis P. Harper, 1913. First edition. 12mo. Cloth.
Some cover rubbing. Oak Knoll 49-218 1983 $50

HARPER, HENRY H.   Random Verses. Boston: privately
printed, 1914. 8vo. Three-quarter parchment over boards. Presentation copy. Letter from the author to Mr. Harold Pierce loosely
inserted. Oak Knoll 49-224 1983 $20

HARPER, HENRY H.   The Story of a Manuscript. Boston:
privately printed, 1914. 8vo. Three-quarter parchment over boards,
slipcase. Presentation copy. Spine sunned, slight staining at top
of pages. Oak Knoll 49-226 1983 $30

HARPER, HENRY H   The Tides of Fate, A Novel.
Boston: Privately Printed, 1918. Original copperplate
etchings by W.H.W. Bicknell. Cloth backed boards, t.e.g.,
bookplate, rubbed. King 46-298 1983 $20

HARPER, IDA HUSTED   The Life and Work of Susan B. Anthony.
Indianapolis: Bobbs-Merrill Co. 1898-1908. In three vols.
Profusely illus. Orig. green cloth. Karmiole 71-96 1983 $85

HARPER, ROBERT GOODLOE   A Letter from... Portsmouth, N.H.:
Charles Peirce, 1801. Stitched. Very good. Felcone 20-61 1983 $25

HARPER, ROBERT GOODLOE   Speech of...at the Celebration of
the Recent Triumphs in the Cause of Mankind, in Germany. New Haven,
1814. Dbd. About fine. Reese 18-440 1983 $30

HARPER, THOMAS   Some serious remarks on a late pamphlet
entitled, The Morality of Stage-Plays Seriously Considered. Edinburgh: printed in the year 1757. 8vo, wrappers, 1st ed. Very good
copy. Ximenes 64-256 1983 $325

HARPER'S New York and Erie Rail-road Guide Book. New York, (1851).
Ads. Illus. Plates. Cloth (rubbed). Front endpaper lacking.
First edition. Felcone 22-86 1983 $35

HARRADEN, BEATRICE   The Fowler. Edinburgh: William
Blackwood & Sons, 1899. First edition. Orig. cloth. Very good copy.
MacManus 278-2528 1983 $35

HARRADEN, BEATRICE   Ships that Pass in the Night. London:
Lawrence & Bullen, 1893. First edition. Orig. cloth. Hinges
cracking, covers rubbed, but a good copy. MacManus 278-2529 1983
$45

HARRAL, THOMAS   The Infant Roscius; or, an inquiry
into the requisites of an actor. London: printed and published by
M. Allen; sold also by J. Whitaker, n.d. (1804). 8vo, disbound.
Fine copy of a scarce pamphlet. Ximenes 64-257 1983 $200

HARRIES, CARL DIETRICH   Untersuchungen uber das Ozon und
seine Einwirkung auf Organische Verbindungen, 1903-1916. Berlin:
Julius Springer, 1916. First edition. 8vo. Orig. half calf.
18 text illus. Ads. A little shaken. A very good copy. Zeitlin
264-194 1983 $50

HARRINGTON, CHARLES N.   Branch of the American Family.
Chicago, Privately printed, 1934. Illus., g.t. Argosy 710-174
1983 $35

HARRINGTON, JAMES   The Oceana of James Harrington, and
his other Works. London, 1700. First collected edition. Folio.
Cont. panelled calf, gilt panelled spines with morocco label, gilt.
Spines worn. Traylen 94-424 1983 £90

HARRINGTON, JOHN W.   The Adventures of Admiral Frog. N.Y.:
Russell, 1902. 8vo. Cloth backed pictorial boards. Edges worn.
Illus. by W.B. Price with full-page 2-color line drawings. Very good.
Aleph-bet 8-136 1983 $35

HARRINGTON, THOMAS   The Harvard Medical School. New York,
1905. 3 vols. 8vo. 1/2 leather. Bindings scuffed, some hinges
cracked, small tears at top of backstrip, contents very fine. Fye
H-3-240 1983 $125

HARRIS, BERNICE KELLY   Purslane. Univ. of North Carolina,
(1939). 8vo. Cloth. A fine copy in lightly used but intact dj. In
Our Time 156-362 1983 $50

HARRIS, CHARLES TOWNSEND   Memories of Manhattan in the Sixties &
Seventies. Derrydale Press, 1928. Limited ed., many plates,
cloth-backed boards, paper label, corner bumped. Argosy 710-378
1983 $45

HARRIS, FRANK   The Bomb. London: John Long, (1908).
1st ed. Orig. red cloth, gilt. Presentation copy inscribed by
Harris: "To Miss Monica-----from the author/Frank Harris." Fine
copy. Jenkins 155-513 1983 $75

HARRIS, FRANK   Contemporary Portraits, Second Series.
NY: Published by the author, 1919. First edition, inscribed and
signed by the author, "from Frankie, the author...". Covers worn
and heavily soiled. With a portrait of Bernard Shaw by Himself.
King 46-299 1983 $25

HARRIS, FRANK   Joan La Romee. London: The Fortune
Press, (1926). First edition. Orig. cloth. With a prefatory letter
by Shaw to Harris. Limited to 350 copies signed by author. Preserved
in a half morocco slipcase. Fine. MacManus 280-4680 1983 $135

HARRIS, FRANK   Joan La Romee. Nice: Imp. Nicoise,
(1926). First edition, 8vo, orig. printed paper wraps., the wraps.
little dusty and the spine worn, but internally a clean copy.
Fenning 61-193 1983 £18.50

HARRIS, FRANK   Joan la Romee. London, (1926). First
edition. Backstrip partially defective. Good copy only. Rota 230-
276 1983 £15

HARRIS, FRANK   My Life and Loves. Paris: Privately
Printed, 1922, (1925, 1927). 3 vols. First edition. Each volume with
various limitations from 425 to 1000 copies. Modern 3/4 morocco.
Very good. Jenkins 152-653 1983 $250

HARRIS, FRANK   Oscar Wilde: His Life and Confessions.
New York: Printed and published by the author, 1918. 2 vols. 1st
ed. Orig. green cloth, gilt. Fine and uncommon set. Jenkins 155-
514 1983 $75

HARRIS, G. D.   Oil and Gas in Louisiana. Wash., 1910.
First edition. Photographic illus. and color folding maps. Jenkins
152-691 1983 $65

HARRIS, HENRY E.   Essays and Photographs. London: R.H.
Porter, 1901. 55 leaves of plates. Index. Blue gilt-stamped cloth.
Karmiole 75-97 1983 $60

HARRIS, ISAAC   Harris' Pittsburgh Business Directory,
for 1837. Pittsburgh, 1837. Adv., thick 12mo, disbound, heavily
dampstained. Argosy 710-402 1983 $30

HARRIS, J. MORRISON   A Paper upon California, March, 1849.
8vo, orig. wrs. bound in bds., title backed. Argosy 716-38 1983
$40

HARRIS, JAMES   Philological Inquiries in Three Parts.
London: for C. Nourse, 1781. 2 vols. 8vo. Cont. tree calf, gilt
borders on sides, fully gilt panelled spines with crimson and green
morocco labels, gilt. First edition. Half-titles, engraved frontis.,
portrait by Bartolozzi, and engraved plate. From the Broughton
Baptist Library with pink printed labels. A very fine copy. Traylen 94-425 1983 £135

HARRIS, JAMES   Three Treatises. Printed by H. Woodfall,
jun. for J. Nourse, and P. Vaillant, 1744. First edition, 8vo, cont.
calf, gilt, neatly rebacked, a very good copy. Fenning 60-162 1983
£95

HARRIS, JOEL CHANDLER   Aaron in the Woods. Boston and New
York: Houghton, Mifflin, 1897. Illus. 1st ed., 1st printing.
Orig. yellow pictorial cloth, gilt. Very good bright copy.
Jenkins 155-515 1983 $35

HARRIS, JOEL CHANDLER   The Bishop and the Boogerman. New York:
Doubleday, 1909. Frontis., plates. First edition. Original red
cloth, gilt. Bookplate of Frederick W. Skiff. Inscribed by Harris on
front end paper to Skiff. Rare. Fine copy. Jenkins 153-248 1983

HARRIS, JOEL CHANDLER   Mr. Rabbit at Home. Boston & New
York: Houghton, Mifflin, 1895. 1st ed. Orig. tan pictorial cloth,
gilt. Spine slightly darkened but very good copy. Jenkins 155-517
1983 $22.50

HARRIS, JOEL CHANDLER   On the Wing of Occasions. New York:
Doubleday, 1900. Frontis., plates. 1st ed., special issue. Orig.
green cloth, gilt. Near fine copy in the scarce "Special Edition"
binding. Jenkins 155-518 1983 $45

HARRIS, JOEL CHANDLER   Uncle Remus, His Songs and his Sayings.
New York: Appleton, 1881. Frontis., plates, illus. First edition,
3rd state. Original mustard pictorial cloth, gilt. Some foxing
on the tissue guards, else a fine copy. Jenkins 151-120 1983 $150

HARRIS, JOEL CHANDLER   Uncle Remus. N.Y., 1910. Illus. by
A.B. Forst. Pict. red cloth. Argosy 714-305 1983 $50

HARRIS, JOHN   Lexicon Technicum: or, An Universal
English Dictionary of Arts and Sciences. For Dan Brown etc., London,
1708-10. 2 vols., folio with a frontis. portrait of the author by
G. White and 14 folding engraved plates and numerous woodcuts in the
text; some foxing and browning; cont. panelled calf, joints cracked.
Second edition of vol. I, first edition of vol. II. Quaritch NS 5-
53 1983 $1,250

HARRIS, JOHN   Navigantium atque Itinerantium Bibliotheca. Printed for Thomas Bennet; John Nicholson; and Daniel
Midwinter, 1705. 2 vols., folio, with 9 engraved maps by Moll, two
frontis. each with 4 portraits of English explorers, a portrait of
Drake, and 20 other engraved plates, cont. panelled calf, lacking
label on both vols. and upper joints of both vols. just beginning to
crack at the top. A fine, complete copy. First edition. Argosy
713-40 1983 £780

HARRIS, JOHN   Wonders of the World. (?) John Harris,
1821. 16 handcolored plates. Dutch floral boards, thus eliminating
the title. Very good. Greer 39-74 1983 £95

HARRIS, M.   An exposition of English Insects. 1782.
4to, modern half calf (antique style), hand-coloured frontis., a plain
anatomical plate and 50 hand-coloured plates. 2nd ed., 1st issue.
Wheldon 160-45 1983 £300

HARRIS, RENDEL   The Ascent of Olympus. Manchester,
England: The University Press, 1917. First edition. Cloth a little
scratched. Gach 95-192 1983 $40

HARRIS, ROBERT   Remarks On Heaving Down A Seventy-Two
Gun Ship, Shewing The Strain To Be Resisted. Portsea: W. Woodard,
Printer, (1841). 1st ed., 4to, lithograph frontispiece by W. Brown,
5 lithograph plates, a lithograph plate with a volvelle device,
some slight spotting of frontispiece, stitched as issued within a
fitted cloth box, morocco label, gilt. Deighton 3-157 1983 £295

HARRIS, T. Y.   Wild flowers of Australia. Sydney,
1949. 4th edition, revised, 68 coloured plates, small 4to, cloth.
Wheldon 160-1708 1983 £15

HARRIS, THADDEUS MASON   Discourses, Delivered on Public Occasions, Illustrating the Principles, Displaying the Tendency, and Vindicating the Design, of Free Masonry. Charlestown, Etheridge, 1801. Illus. Half morocco. First edition. Ginsberg 46-263 1983 $75

HARRIS, THOMAS   A Letter from T. Harris, to G. Colman, on the affairs of Covent-Garden Theatre. London: printed for J. Fletcher and Co.; and sold by J. Walter; and J. Robson, 1768. 4to, wrappers, 1st ed. Uncommon. A fine copy. Ximenes 64-258 1983 $400

HARRIS, THOMAS LAKE   The Foy Bringer. (Santa Rosa, Ca., 1886). Orig. cloth. First edition. Ginsberg 47-104 1983 $150

HARRIS, THOMAS LAKE   The New Republic. Santa Rosa, Ca., 1891. Orig. printed wraps. First edition. Ginsberg 47-105 1983 $100

HARRIS, WALTER   A description of the King's royal palace and gardens at Loo. London: printed by E. Roberts, and sold by J. Nutt, 1699. First edition. Small 4to. Disbound. Folding engraved view of the gardens. Slightly shaved. Ximenes 63-178 1983 $300

HARRIS, WILLIAM   The History of the Radical Party in Parliament. Kegan Paul, Trench, 1885. First edition, half title, 32 pp ads. Orig. maroon cloth, spine a little faded. Jarndyce 31-182 1983 £16.50

HARRIS, WILLIAM CORNWALLIS   The Highlands of Ethiopia. London: Longman, Brown, etc., 1844. 3 vols. 8vo. Folding map, 4 plates, 3 vignettes. Modern 1/4 tan morocco. Repairs to map. Adelson Africa-91 1983 $350

HARRIS, WILLIAM CORNWALLIS   The wild sports of southern Africa. London: Henry G. Bohn, 1852. Fifth edition. Royal 8vo. Engraved title, folding map, 25 colored plates. Orig. red pictorial cloth. Backed in red morocco, a.e.g. Adelson Africa-90 1983 $600

HARRIS, WILLIAM CORNWALLIS   The wild sports of southern Africa. London: John Murray, 1839. First edition. 8vo. Folding map. 7 plates. Orig. green pictorial cloth. Rubbed, chipping to spine. Adelson Africa-89 1983 $275

HARRIS, WILLIAM CORNWALLIS   The Wild Sports of Southern Africa. London, 1839. 8vo, folding map, 3 tinted lithograph plates, 4 wood engraved plates, original cloth, title and gilt vignette border, a little worn, some staining. Second edition. Deighton 3-158 1983 £125

HARRIS, WILLIAM THADDEUS   Epitaphs from the Old Burying Ground in Watertown. Boston, 1869. 1st ed. Tall 8vo. Morrill 287-229 1983 $20

HARRISON, BENJAMIN   Message from...with an Agreement of the Comanche, Kiowa, and Apache Indians for the Cession of Certain Lands in the Territory of Oklahoma. Wash., 1893. Dbd. Ginsberg 47-703 1983 $25

HARRISON, MRS. BURTON
Please turn to
HARRISON, CONSTANCE (CARY)

HARRISON, CANON F.   Treasures of Illumination. (c. 1250 to 1400). London: The Studio, 1937. Quarto. Pictorial boards. First edition. Tipped-in color facs. Pencil signature, otherwise a fine copy in dust jacket (a few closed tears). Reese 20-486 1983 $85

HARRISON, CONSTANCE CARY   Bric-a-Brac Stories. New York: Scribners, 1885. Frontis., plates. 1st ed. Orig. pictorial tan cloth, with cover designs by Walter Crane (signed) who did the illus. in the book. Nice copy with little rubbing. Jenkins 155-520 1983 $45

HARRISON, CONSTANCE CARY   Woman's Handiwork in Modern Homes. (N.Y.), 1882. Illus. incl. 2 color lithos by L.C. Tiffany. Decorated cloth. Index. Bookplate. Front hinge loose. Frayed spine, a bit foxed. Well worn. King 45-357 1983 $65

HARRISON, FLORENCE   In The Fairy Ring. Blackie, n.d. (ca. 1908). 4to, colour frontis., decorated title. 23 colour plates (2 creased). Pictorial boarders and text illus. Pictorial endpapers. White cloth pictorial gilt. Greer 40-107 1983 £35

HARRISON, FLORENCE   The Pixy Book. London: Blackie (ca. 1910). Small quarto. Illus. 12 full-color plates. Cloth-backed boards with large color pictorial label very slightly soiled and rubbed, otherwise fine. Owner's signature. Bromer 25-348 1983 $95

HARRISON, GABRIEL   John Howard Paine. Philadelphia, 1885. Engraved frontis. portrait, folding facs. plate, text illus. Tall 8vo, gilt-decorated orig. cloth. Salloch 387-327 1983 $40

HARRISON, GEORGE L. (1811-1885)   Chapters on Social Science as Connected With the Administration of State Charities. Philadelphia: privately published, 1877. 8vo. 3/4 leather, top edge gilt. Rubbed, front joint very weak. Gach 95-193 1983 $35

HARRISON, JIM   Selected and New Poems. (NY, 1982). Limited to 250 numbered and signed copies, as new in slipcase. Quill & Brush 54-611 1983 $100

HARRISON, JIM   Warlock. (NY, 1981). One of 250 signed and numbered copies, mint in mint slipcase. Quill & Brush 54-612 1983 $100

HARRISON, JIM   Warlock. (New York): Delecorte, (1981). Cloth, a.e.g. First edition. One of 250 numbered copies, specially bound, and signed by the author. Very fine in slipcase. Reese 20-487 1983 $75

HARRISON, JOSEPH T.   The Story of the Dining Fork. Cincinnati: The C.J. Krehbiel Co., 1927. First edition. Limited. Illus. Fine. Jenkins 152-606 1983 $75

HARRISON, MARY ST. LEGER KINGSLEY   The Carissima. London: Methuen & Co., 1896. First edition. Orig. cloth. Bookplate. Spine faded. Very good. MacManus 279-3486 1983 $25

HARRISON, MARY ST. LEGER KINGSLEY   The Carissima. Chicago: Herbert S. Stone, 1896. First American edition. Orig. cloth. Inner hinges cracked. MacManus 279-3485 1983 $20

HARRISON, MARY ST. LEGER KINGSLEY   Colonel Enderby's Wife. London: Kegan Paul, Trench & Co., 1885. First edition. 3 vols. Orig. cloth. Spines darkened. Covers a little soiled. A few rear inner hinges cracked. MacManus 279-3487 1983 $250

HARRISON, MARY ST. LEGER KINGSLEY   The Far Horizon. London: Hutchinson, 1906. First edition. Orig. cloth. Front inner hinge cracked. MacManus 279-3488 1983 $35

HARRISON, MARY ST. LEGER KINGSLEY   The Gateless Barrier. London: Methuen & Co., 1900. First edition. Orig. red cloth. Spine faded. Endpapers a trifle foxed. Good. MacManus 279-3490 1983 $25

HARRISON, MARY ST. LEGER KINGSLEY   The History of Sir Richard Calmady. London: Methuen, 1901. First edition, second issue. 2 vols. Orig. cloth. MacManus 279-3493 1983 $50

HARRISON, MARY ST. LEGER KINGSLEY   The History of Sir Richard Calmady. London: Methuen, 1901. First edition, first issue. 8vo. Orig. red cloth. Slightly worn. 2 vols. Former owner's signature on flyleaf. MacManus 279-3492 1983 $25

HARRISON, MARY ST. LEGER KINGSLEY   Little Peter. London: Kegan Paul, Trench, Turbner, & Co., Ltd., 1890. Third edition. Orig. pictorial cloth. Covers worn & soiled, shaken. Good. MacManus 279-3494 1983 $25

HARRISON, MARY ST. LEGER KINGSLEY   Mrs. Lorimer. London: Macmillan & Co., 1883. Later (second?) edition. 2 vols. Orig. cloth. Spine and covers slightly worn and soiled. Inner hinges weak. With slight foxing to the preliminary pages & edges. Good. MacManus 279-3495 1983 $65

HARRISON, MARY ST. LEGER KINGSLEY   The Score. London: Murray,
1909. First edition. Orig. cloth. MacManus 279-3496 1983 $20

HARRISON, MARY ST. LEGER KINGSLEY   The Wages of Sin. London: Swan
Sonnenschein & Co., 1891. First edition. 3 vols. Orig. cloth. Presentation copy from the author's sister, inscribed: "C.M. Hallett
from Lucas Malet's sister. Jan. 23/91." Edges and corners slightly
worn. Very light foxing. Very good. MacManus 279-3497 1983 $450

HARRISON, T.   The Bookbinding Craft and Industry...
London: Sir Isaac Pitman, n.d. (ca. 1930). Second edition. Small
8vo. Cloth. Prof. illus. Fine. Oak Knoll 48-41 1983 $35

HARRISON, TONY   Continuous - 50 Sonnets... London,
1981. First edition. One of 100 numbered copies signed by the
author. Mint in slipcase. Jolliffe 26-239 1983 £45

HARRISON, WILLIAM HENRY   A Discourse on the Aborigines of the
Valley of the Ohio... Cincinnati, 1838. Folding map. Orig.
printed wraps., fine, laid in a folding half-morocco box. Reese
19-262 1983 $675

HARRISON, WILLIAM HENRY   A Sketch of the Life and Public Services
of... Albany, 1836. Printed wrappers. A bit worn and foxed.
Felcone 20-63 1983 $35

HARRISSE, HENRY   Bibliotheca Americana Vetustissima...
New York: Geo. P. Philes, 1866 and Paris: Librairie Tross, 1872.
The first volume is printed offset and is apparently a reprint; the
second volume is a first printing. 2 vols., the first in half leather;
some wear. The second in wrappers, larger format, moderately worn
and browned. Dawson 470-148 1983 $135

HARROW, BENJAMIN   From Newton to Einstein. New York,
1920. Portraits and illustrations. 12mo, original boards. Top of
spine worn. Morrill 290-170 1983 $22.50

HARRY, JOSEPH E.   The Greek Tragic Poets. Wrs. 8vo,
cloth. Salloch 385-123 1983 $30

HART, ALBERT B.   The Monroe Doctrine, an Interpretation.
Boston, 1916. Colored map. Argosy 710-185 1983 $25

HART, C. P.   Repertory to the New Remedies. N.Y.,
1876. First edition. Small 8vo, cloth, (joints mended); ex-lib.
Argosy 713-247 1983 $35

HART, CHARLES HENRY   Catalogue of the Engraved Portraits of
Washington. New York, The Grolier Club, 1904. Many engr. illus.
Folio, fine, bound in boards with a vellum spine, fine in orig. dust
wrapper. With the small library stamp of Max Safron, the orig. subscriber. Orig. prospectus laid in. Slipcase. Reese 19-578 1983
$350

HART, FANNY   Silver Wings and Golden Scales.
Cassell, nd (1877). Frontis & numerous illus., some within decor.
borders, 8pp adverts. Red sand grain decor. cloth, a.e.g. Early
insc. fr. ep., rear cvr. sl. mottled, free eps. sl. discol'd, nice.
Hodgkins 27-284 1983 £30

HART, FRED H.   The Sazerac Lying Club. San F.,
1878. Illus. Orig. cloth. First edition. Ginsberg 47-646 1983
$65

HART, JAMES D.   The Oxford Companion to American
Literature. New York, Oxford University Press, 1941. Large stout
8vo, orig. cloth gilt, in worn dust jacket, good copy. Ravenstree
94-181 1983 $25

HART, JAMES D.   The Private Press Ventures of Samuel
Lloyd Osbourne and R. L. S. SF, 1966. 4to, cloth, vignette on upper
cover, gilt. Illustrated, 11 facs. contained in pocket in rear cover.
One of 500 copies. Bookplate. Very fine. Prospectus laid in. Perata
27-110 1983 $85

HART, JOHN   A Description of the Skeleton of the
Fossil Deer of Ireland. Dublin: R. Graisberry, 1830. Second edition.
With 2 engraved plates, including half-title, 8vo, unbound, sewn as
issued. A very good copy. Fenning 60-164 1983 £10.50

HART, JOSEPH   Hymns. Elizabeth Town: Shepard Kollock;
likewise sold by R. Hodge, (1787?). Full calf. Endsheets lacking.
Very good. Felcone 19-23 1983 $60

HART, MOSS   You Can't Take it With You. NY, (1937).
Spine faded, else very good in slightly frayed, very good dustwrapper.
Quill & Brush 54-613 1983 $40

HART, OLIVER   A Gospel Church Portrayed. Trenton:
Isaac Collins, 1791. Disbound. Very good. Felcone 19-24 1983 $60

HART, SCOTT   The Moon is Waning. NY, (1939). Illus.
by Edwin Megargee. Limited to 950 numbered copies, bright, very good
or better, bookplate. Quill & Brush 54-614 1983 $50

HART, WILLIAM S.   Pinto Ben. NY, (1919). Edges slightly
rubbed, otherwise near fine. Quill & Brush 54-615 1983 $30

HART House. University of Toronto. Toronto: Rous & Mann, 1921.
4to. Illus. from photographs by G.D. Haight. 28 1/2cm. 40 pp.
of illus. Blue cloth. Very good to fine. McGahern 54-81 1983
$35

HART-DAVIS, RUPERT   A Catalogue of the Caricatures of Max
Beerbohm. Cambridge: Harvard University Press, 1972. Orig. cloth.
Dust jacket. First American edition. Fine copy. MacManus 277-278
1983 $27.50

HARTCLIFFE, JOHN   A Discourse Against Purgatory. Printed
for Brabazon Aylmer, 1685. First edition, 4to, wrapper. Fenning
61-194 1983 £14.50

HARTE, BRET   Clarence. Boston, 1895. 12mo. Cloth.
1st American ed. Some glue marks on inside endboard, else a very
good-fine copy. In Our Time 156-364 1983 $20

HARTE, BRET   Cressy. Macmillan, 1889. First
edition, 2 vols. Half titles, 6 pp ads. vol. II. Ex-library copy,
orig. blue cloth rubbed. Jarndyce 30-415 1983 £15

HARTE, BRET   A First Family of Tasajara. Macmillan,
1891. First edition, 2 vols. Half titles, ex-library copy, orig.
blue cloth, rubbed. Jarndyce 30-414 1983 £14

HARTE, BRET   The Heathen Chinee. Chicago: Rock
Island Pacific & Pacific Railroad, (1873). Early printing, an
unrecorded variant. Orig. pale green printed wrappers, sewn, as
issued. Fine copy. Jenkins 155-526 1983 $125

HARTE, BRET   How Santa Claus Came to Simpson's Bar.
L.A., Ward Ritchie, (1941). First edition thus. Half red cloth.
Slipcase. One of 500 copies. Four woodcuts by Landacre. Fine.
Houle 21-498 1983 $45

HARTE, BRET   The Luck of the Roaring Camp. Boston:
Fields, Osgood, 1872. Folio, illus. 1st illus. ed. Orig. green
pictorial cloth, gilt. Spine tips rubbed, else a very good copy.
Jenkins 155-525 1983 $75

HARTE, BRET   The Luck of Roaring Camp, and Other
Sketches. Boston: Fields, Osgood, 1870. Gilt cloth, second
expanded edition. Very slight traces of rubbing, else a fine copy.
Reese 19-264 1983 $75

HARTE, BRET   The Luck of the Roaring Camp. Boston:
Fields, Osgood, 1870. 2nd ed., with the added story. Orig. cloth,
gilt. Fine copy. Jenkins 155-524 1983 $75

HARTE, BRET   The Luck of Roaring Camp... Boston,
1872. Illus. by Eytinge. Small folio, all edges gilt, front endleaf & fly-leaf partly torn. Morrill 288-158 1983 $20

HARTE, BRET   In Memoriam: Thomas Starr King. New
York n.d. (1864). 8vo. Wraps. (Back wrapper restored with new one.)
A fine copy. In Our Time 156-365 1983 $100

HARTE, BRET   Poems. Boston: R. Osgood, 1871.
Half title, orig. brown cloth, bevelled boards. Fine. Jarndyce 30-
725 1983 £12.50

HARTE, BERT   The Queen of the Pirate Isle. London:
Chatto & Windus, n.d. First edition. 8vo. Brown pictorial cloth.
A.e.g. Color illus. Very good. Aleph-bet 8-123 1983 $100

HARTE, BRET   The Queen of the Pirate Isle. Boston:
Houghton Mifflin, 1887. First American edition. Illus. by Kate
Greenaway. Covers soiled. Good. MacManus 278-2384 1983 $75

HARTE, BRET   The Right Eye of the Commander.
Berkeley, 1937. 8vo, decorated cloth. Illustrated by Hans.
One of 75 copies (of 350) hand-colored & signed by the artist
and printers. A fine copy. Perata 27-198 1983 $85

HARTE, BRET   The Right Eye of the Commander.
Berkeley, 1937. 8vo, pictorial cloth, Illustrated by Hans. One
of 350 copies signed by the artist & printers. Occasional foxing.
A very good copy. Perata 27-3 1983 $20

HARTE, BRET   Salomy Jane's Kiss. N.Y., Grosset &
Dunlap, (1915). Photoplay edition. Illus. with 12 halftone photos
of scenes from the film. Dust jacket (several chips) else very good.
Houle 22-458 1983 $45

HARTE, BRET   The Complete Works. London, 1891-1900.
10 vols. 8vo. Cont. half calf, gilt, gilt panelled spines with
morocco labels, gilt. Traylen 94-425 1983 £110

HARTE, WALTER   The History of the Life of Gustavus
Adophus, King of Sweden. 1767. 2 vols., 8vo, portrait, and 4 folding
plans, orig. calf. Bickersteth 77-27 1983 £60

HARTERT, E.   Die Vogel der Palaarktischen Fauna.
Berlin, 1903-22. Text-figures, 3 vols., royal 8vo, half morocco
(spines faded). The rare original printing. Two supplements were
issued but are not included. Wheldon 160-745 1983 £130

HARTING, JAMES E.   British Animals Extinct within Historic
Times. 1880. 36 illustrations by Wolf, Whymper and others, 8vo,
original cloth. A little foxing. Wheldon 160-562 1983 £30

HARTING, JAMES E   British Animals Extinct within
Historic Times. Boston: J.R. Osgood and Co., 1880. With 36 illus.
Brown dec. cloth. T.e.g. Karmiole 71-107 1983 $40

HARTING, JAMES E.   Hints on the Management of Hawks.
Horace Cox, 1884. First edition, with 8 illus., 8vo, orig. paper
boards, with printed paper label on upper cover, the spine worn but
sound, otherwise a very good copy. Fenning 62-167 1983 £45

HARTLAUB, G.   Die Vogel Madagascars. Halle, 1877.
Plate of Dodo, 8vo, half cloth. Very scarce. Wheldon 160-747
1983 £70

HARTLEY, DAVID   A View of the Present Evidence for and
Against Mrs. Stephen's Medicines, as a Solvent for the Stone. 1739.
8vo, modern calf antique, new end papers, lettered gilt on the spine.
First edition. Bickersteth 77-278 1983 £110

HARTLEY, L. P.   Eustace and Hilda. London, 1947. First
edition. Spine slightly faded. Dust wrapper. Inscribed by author:
"Darling Ethel with love from Leslie Aug. 1947." Very nice. Rota
231-306 1983 £50

HARTLEY, L. P.   Simonetta Perkins. L., (1925). Signed
and dated by Hartley, cover slightly worn, book cocked, good or better,
owner's name. Quill & Brush 54-616 1983 $40

HARTLIB, SAMUEL   Legacy of Husbandry Wherein are
Bequeathed to the Common-wealth of England... London, Printed by
J.M. for Richard Wodnothe...1655. 4to, recent brown calf. Scuffed
at hinges. Blind tooled on spine and board. Title stamped in
gold between raised bands. T.E.G. Some light foxing and general
toning; border on title page and subsequent leaf somewhat browned.
A.E. Lownes bookplate. Very good overall. Arkway 22-63 1983 $400

HARTMAN, C. V.   Archaeological Researches in Costa
Rica. Stockholm: Ivar Haeggstrom, 1901. 87 plates, (partly in
color). 486 text illus. Large stout folio. Marbled boards, 3/4
red morocco. Rare. Ars Libri 34-273 1983 $650

HARTMANN, F.   Dr. Caspari's Homeopathic Domestic
Physician. Philadelphia: Rademacher & Sheek, 1852 (1851). Contemporary leather-backed boards, worn. Gach 95-194 1983 $30

HARTMANN, ROBERT   Die Nigritier. Eine Anthropologisch-
Ethnologische Monographie. Berlin, 1876. Royal 8vo, 52 tinted
lithograph plates, half calf gilt, marbled sides, crimson morocco
label, slight cracking of joints at head and foot of back.
Deighton 3-159 1983 £65

HARTNOLL, PHYLLIS   The Grecian Enchanted. London: the
Golden Cockerel Press, 1952. Folio. Full grey and pink crushed
levant morocco, with gilt design on front cover, gilt spines, t.e.g.,
others uncut. 8 engraved plates from drawings by John Buckland-
Wright, and a second set of the eight illus., and an extra one, all
printed by hand from the copper-plates, enclosed in pocket at end.
One of 60 numbered and specially bound copies, signed by the author
and illustrator. Traylen 94-427 1983 £180

HARTPENCE, WILLIAM R.   History of the Fifty-First Indiana
Veteran Volunteer Infantry. Harrison, Ohio, Author, 1894. 1st ed.
Illus. 8vo. Bookplate removed, front cover partly stained. Morrill
287-165 1983 $65

HARTSHORNE, CHARLES   The Philosophy and Psychology of Sensation. Chicago: Univ. of Chicago Press, (1934). First edition.
Very good in worn dust jacket. Gach 94-720 1983 $25

HARTSOEKER, NICOLAS   Essay de Dioptrique. Jean Anisson,
Paris, 1694. 4to, with an engraved plate of the surface of the moon
with accompanying leaf of text, and woodcut diagrams in the text;
waterstain in upper inner margin; signature of William Molyneux
on title and bookplates of the Earl of Bute, on end paper and verso
of title; cont. calf, rebacked. First edition. Quaritch NS 5-54
1983 $1,500

HARTWIG, G.   The Subterranean World. 1881. New
edition, 3 maps, 8 plates and numerous wood-engravings, 8vo, original
cloth (trifle used). Wheldon 160-1411 1983 £12

HARTZELL, CHARLES   A Short & Truthful History of Colorado
During the Turbulent Reign of "Savis the First." Denver, 1894.
Illus. Orig. pictorial wraps., worn. Ginsberg 47-237 1983 $35

A HARVARD Alphabet. Cambridge: Harvard Co-operative Society, 1902.
Small quarto. Frenchfold. Illus. Fine in patterned boards, slightly
rubbed at extremities. Bromer 25-316 1983 $45

HARVARD College, The Tercentenary. Cambridge, 1937. Illus., color
frontis. D.w. Argosy 710-282 1983 $25

HARVARD UNIVERSITY   Historical Register, 1636-1936. Cambridge, 1937. Buckram, dust wrappers. Argosy 710-284 1983 $25

HARVEY, E. N.   Living Light. Princeton, 1940.
Coloured frontispiece and 88 other illustrations, 8vo, cloth.
Wheldon 160-491 1983 £18

HARVEY, E. N.   The Nature of Animal Light. Philadelphia,
1920. Wheldon 160-490 1983 £15

HARVEY, GIDEON   The family-physician, and the house-
apothecary. London: printed for M.R., 1678. Second edition.
8vo. Cont. calf, rebacked. Old library bookplate. Rare. Ximenes
63-278 1983 $350

HARVEY, JAMES M.   Annual Message of...Governor to the
Legislature of the State of Kansas, 1871. Topeka, 1871. Orig.
printed wraps. First edition. Ginsberg 47-408 1983 $50

HARVEY, JOSEPH   The Banner of Christ Set Up. Elizabeth-
town, N.J., 1819. Dbd. First edition. Ginsberg 46-858 1983 $50

HARVEY, MARY C.   A Memorial of Mary Christy Harvey.
(Dublin), privately printed, (1858). First edition, with an orig.
photograph portrait frontis., 8vo, orig. cloth, a very good copy.
Fenning 62-168 1983 £18.50

HARVEY, W. K.   Coin's Financial School. Chicago,
(1894). 1st ed. Illus. Small 8vo, orig. wrappers. Morrill 288-165
1983 $22.50

HARVEY, WILLIAM   London Scenes and London People.
1880. 4th edition, illus. Orig. dark maroon cloth, by Leighton,
blocked in blind and gilt. Fine. Jarndyce 31-259 1983 £15

HARVEY, WILLIAM (1578-1657)   An Anatomical Disquisition on the
Motion of the Heart and Blood in Animals. London, (1907). 8vo.,
orig. cloth. Fye H-3-244 1983 $30

HARVEY, WILLIAM (1578-1657)   Exercitatio Anatomica - De Motu
Cordis.. Springfield, 1928. 8vo., orig. cloth, facsimile of the
first ed. Fye H-3-245 1983 $50

HARVEY, WILLIAM (1578-1657)   The Works of William Harvey, M.D.
London, 1847. First ed. of the translation by Robert Willis. 8vo.,
orig. binding. Library bookplate and small stamp on title. Minor
chipping on top of spine, else very fine. Fye H-3-247 1983 $175

HARVEY, WILLIAM HENRY   Flora Capensis. 1859-1927. 7 vols. in
10, 8vo, cloth. Out of print. Wheldon 160-1710 1983 £120

THE HARVEY Cushing Collection of Books and Manuscripts. New York,
1943. First edition. 8vo. Orig. binding. Fye H-3-1050 1983
$50

HARZBERG, HILER   Slapstick and Dumbell. (Paris, 1924).
1st ed. With Harzberg's signature pasted in. Illus. by Harzberg,
et al. 4to. Orig. boards, paper label, 38 unnumbered pages. Binding
partly worn; few pieces of paper covering lacking from front cover;
back cover partly wrinkled; lacks front fly-leaf. Morrill 289-355
1983 $22.50

HASELOFF, ARTHUR   Pre-Romanesque Sculpture in Italy.
Firenze/Paris, 1930. Sm. folio, 80 collotype plates with captioned
tissue-guards. Boards, 1/2 leather. Ars Libri SB 26-99 1983 $275

HASENCLEVER, RICHARD   Die Grundzuege der Esoterischen Harmonik
des Alterthums. Cologne, 1870. 4to, orig. printed wrs, spine repaired.
Salloch 387-92 1983 $25

HASKINS, CHARLES H.   Studies in the History of Mediaeval
Scence. Cambridge: Harvard University Press, 1924. First edition.
8vo. Cloth. Gurney JJ-164 1983 £25

HASLERIG, ARTHUR   Sir Arthur Haslerigg, His Speech in
Parliament. Printed for John Wright, 1642. Device on title, 4to,
wrapper, a very good copy. Fenning 60-165 1983 £24.50

HASLEWOOD, JOSEPH   Green room gossip; or, gravity gallinipt:
a gallimaufry, consisting of theatrical anecdotes. (London): given
in gimman, under the guidance of J. Barker, 1809. 12mo, half citron
morocco, gilt, spine gilt, t.e.g. First edition. A fine uncut
copy; scarce. Ximenes 64-259 1983 $175

HASLUCK, PAUL N.   Bookbinding. London: Cassell, 1902.
Small octavo. First edition. Illus. throughout. Front inside hinges
very slightly started, covers lightly soiled. Bromer 25-148 1983
$60

HASSE, C.   Roger van Brugge, der Meister von
Flemalle. Strassburg: J.H. Ed. Heitz, 1904. 8 collotype plates.
4to. Wrappers. Unopened. Ars Libri 32-435 1983 $100

HASSE, C.   Roger van der Weyden und Roger van
Brugge mit ihren Schulen. Strassburg: J.H. Ed. Heitz, 1905. 15
plates. 4to. Wrappers. Ars Libri 32-702 1983 $65

HASTINGS, FRANK   A Ranchmans Recollections... Chicago,
1921. Cloth, fine. Reese 19-265 1983 $125

HASTINGS, FRANK   A Ranchman's Recollections. Chicago:
1921. First edition. Frontis. Illus. Pictorial tan cloth. Light
wear at extremities. Bradley 66-494 1983 $100

HASTINGS, FREDERICK   Back Streets and London Slums. N.d.
(1889). 16 pp ads. Orig. red dec. cloth. Jarndyce 31-260 1983 £45

HASTINGS, THOMAS   Musica Sacra, or Utica and Springfield
Collections United... Utica: William Williams, 1834. Tenth Revised
edition. Full calf. Cont. hand-stitched paper cover, inscribed "A.G.
Bidwell / Hillsdale / Octr 29th 1834." Very good. Felcone 20-117
1983 $30

HASTINGS, THOMAS   The New York Choralist. NY, 1847.
Oblong 12mo, orig. lea.-backed boards, (crudely rebacked, scuffed,
foxed). Argosy 716-319 1983 $40

HASTINGS, WARREN   The History of the Trial of...Containing
the whole of the Proceedings and Debates in Both Houses...Feb. 7,
1786. Printed for J. Debrett, 1796. With a portrait and a folding
plate, 8vo, with a few neat library stamps, but still a very good
copy in recent boards. Fenning 60-166 1983 £45

HATCH, W. J.   The Land Pirates of India. London, 1928.
Folding map, plates. 8vo. Orig. cloth. Good. Edwards 1044-322
1983 £40

HATCH, WILLIAM STANLEY   A Chapter of the History of the War of
1812 in the Northwest. Cincinnati, 1872. First edition. 12mo, contemporary calf, leather label. Morrill 290-171 1983 $37.50

HATCHER, JULIAN S.   Textbook of Firearms Investigation.
Onslow County, N.C. (1935). Illus, cloth. A good copy. King 46-
587 1983 $45

HATCHER, MATTIE A.   Letters of an Early American Traveller:
Mary Austin Holley, Her Life and Works, 1784-1846. Dallas, (1933).
First edition. Illus. Jenkins 152-823 1983 $35

HATFIELD, EDWIN F.   The Night No Time For Labor. NY 1850.
8vo, pr. wrs., mended, light dampstain and spots. Argosy 710-143
1983 $30

HATIN, JULIUS   Manual of Practical Obstetrics. Phila.,
1828. First edition. Mottled calf (crudely rebacked, foxed).
Argosy 713-251 1983 $125

HATT, J. ARTHUR H.   The Colorist. New York, 1908. 1st ed.
2 color charts. 8vo. Morrill 288-167 1983 $20

HATTON, JOSEPH   To-Day In America. Studies For The Old
World And The New. London, 1881. 1st ed., 2 vols, 8vo, modern half
calf, marbled sides, brown and blue morocco labels, new endpapers.
Deighton 3-160 1983 £30

HATTON, JOSEPH   Under the Great Seal. Hutchinson,
1893. First edition, 3 vols. Half titles. Orig. yellow cloth,
dusted, red 'great seal' removed from 2 covers. Royal library labels.
Jarndyce 31-736 1983 £24

HATTON, R. G.   The Craftsman's Plant Book. 1909.
Coloured frontispiece, 1083 facsimile reproductions, 4to, cloth.
Scarce original edition. Wheldon 160-2172 1983 £60

HATTON, THOMAS   An introduction to the mechanical part
of clock and watch work. London: Longman, etc., 1773. First edition.
8vo. 19th-century half calf. With 18 folding engraved plates; half-
title present. Spine rubbed. Very rare. Ximenes 63-74 1983 $800

HAUEY, RENE   Notes sur la Datholite et le Zoysite.
(Paris), 1806. Offprint. 8vo. Wrappers. One plate. Gurney 90-59
1983 £25

HAUG, E.   Traite de Geologie. Paris, (1907-11),
1920-27. 135 plates and 485 text-figures, 2 vols. in 3, royal 8vo,
half morocco (not uniform). Wheldon 160-1412 1983 £20

HAUGHTON, G. C.   Rudiments of Bengali Grammar. London,
1821. 4to. Half morocco. Good. Edwards 1044-323 1983 £90

HAUGUM, J.   A Monograph of the Birdwing Butterflies.
Klampenborg, 1978-79. 4 coloured photos., 12 coloured plates,
277 text-figures, royal 8vo, boards. Published in three parts,
the edition is limited to 350 numbered copies. Wheldon 160-1091
1983 £51

HAUNTED School-House at Newburyport, Mass. Boston: Loring, (1873).
Illus. Pr. wraps. Argosy 716-270 1983 $20

HAUSENSTEIN, WILHELM   Barbaren und Klassiker. Munchen: R.
Piper, 1922. 177 plates, large 4to. New cloth. Ars Libri 34-21
1983 $75

HAUSENSTEIN, WILHELM   Rene Beeh. Zeichnungen, Briefe,
Bilder. Munchen: R. Piper, 1922. 29 collotype plates. Text
illus. Large 4to. Boards, 1/4 cloth. Ars Libri 32-26 1983
$65

HAUSENSTEIN, WILHELM   Romanische Bildnerei. Munchen, 1922.
(Das Bild. Atlanten zur Kunst. Vol. V/VI.) 29, (3)pp., 135 plates.
4to. Boards. Ars Libri SB 26-100 1983 $25

HAUSMANN, B.   Albrecht Durer's Kupferstiche, Radi-
rungen, Holzschnitte und Zeichnungen... Hannover: Hahn, 1861.
9 plates. 4to. Wrappers. Worn at extremities. Ars Libri 32-179
1983 $100

HAUVETTE, HENRI   Ghirlandaio. Paris: Plon-Nourrit,
n.d. (1907). 24 plates. Small 4to. Cloth. Ars Libri 33-158
1983 $35

HAUY, L'ABBE   Extrait d'un Memoir sur la structure
des Crystaux de Grenat... Paris, 1782. Extract. 4to. Orig.
stitched paper wrappers. 2 plates. Light waterstaining. Zeitlin
264-195 1983 $130

HAVE at them. Tallyho!... Edinburgh: printed by Duncan Stevenson,
etc., 1820. First edition. 8vo. Modern wrappers. Very scarce.
Ximenes 63-485 1983 $45

HAVELL, E. B.   Benares the Sacred City. London, 1905.
Frontis. 8vo. Orig. cloth. Good. Edwards 1044-324 1983 £30

HAVELL, E. B.   The Ideals of Indian Art. London, 1911.
22 plates. Sm.4to. Orig. cloth. Good. Edwards 1044-325 1983 £40

HAVELL, E. B.   Indian Architecture Its Psychology...
London, 1927. Second edition. Frontis. and numerous plates. Illus.
in the text. 8vo. Orig. cloth. Good. Edwards 1044-326 1983 £85

HAVEN, CHARLES T.   A History of the Colt Revolver...New
York, 1940. 1st ed. Illus. 4to, box partly worn and chipped, nice
boxed. Morrill 288-109 1983 $75

HAVILTON, JEFFREY   George Pulls it Off. Blackie, n.d.
Frontis. & 5 plates. Beige pictorial cloth. Greer 40-64 1983 £14

HAVILTON, JEFFREY   Harold comes to School. Blackie, n.d.
Frontis. & 2 plates. Blue cloth. Greer 40-65 1983 £12.50

HAVILTON, JEFFREY   The Luck of Study Thirteen. Blackie,
n.d. Frontis. & 3 plates. Lacks front free endpaper. Faded orange
cloth. Greer 40-66 1983 £12.50

HAVRE, G. C. M. VAN   Les Oiseaux de la faune Belge.
Brussels, 1928. 124 figures, royal 8vo, wrappers. Wheldon 160-748
1983 £20

HAWEIS, H. R.   Old Violins and Violin Lore.
London, n.d. Illus, cloth, ex-library, covers very discolored.
King 46-397 1983 $25

HAWEIS, T.   The Path to Happiness. Newark: Pennington & Dodge, for Cornelius Davis, 1798. Full calf (worn, front cover
detached). Very good. Felcone 19-44 1983 $45

HAWK, JOHN   The Murder of a Mystery Writer.
Garden City, 1929. First edition. Cloth, bookplate, slight stain
at bottom part of covers else good. Slightly chipped dust wrapper.
King 46-300 1983 $20

HAWK, PHILIP B.   Off the Racket. NY: American Lawn
Tennis, Inc. 1937. Cartoons by Blythe Wilson. Folding chart, 33
plates & many text illus. Blue gilt-stamped cloth. Karmiole 73-94
1983 $25

HAWKE, CASSANDRA   Julia de Grammont. Printed by T.
Bensley, 1788. 2 vols, sm. 8vo, old mottled calf, gilt, rather
rubbed, rebacked; half-titles, two errata leaves. Presentation copy
inscribed "Elizabeth Leigh given by the Authoress". The only edition.
Hill 165-54 1983 £285

HAWKER, ROBERT S.   Echoes from Old Cornwall. London:
Joseph Masters, 1846. 3/4 morocco with marbled boards and marbled
endpapers. First edition. With a photo. of Hawker pasted to the
front free endpaper, along with a small slip of paper bearing
this inscription by Hawker: "For Monday. R.S.H." With the
bookplates of Lord Rosebery's library at the Durdans, and J.R. Nicholas
Ross. A fine copy. MacManus 278-2534 1983 $225

HAWKER, ROBERT S.   Footprints of Former Men in Far
Corwall. London & NY: John Lane, 1903. 8vo, 20 cm. 19 plates.
Orig. deeply embossed brown cloth, very good. Monastic stamp in
lower margin of title. Grunder 6-32 1983 $25

HAWKES, ERNEST WILLIAM   The "Inviting-In" Feast of the Alaskan
Eskimo. Ottawa: Government Printing Bureau, 1913. 13 plates with
titled tissue guards. 4 text illus. Large 8vo. Wrappers. Ars
Libri 34-275 1983 $30

HAWKES, JOHN   The Cannibal. (Norfolk: New Directions, 1949). First edition, first binding. Boards. Very good.
Bradley 66-191 1983 $50

HAWKES, JOHN   The Goose on the Grave. (N.Y.), New
Directions, (1954). First edition. Signed and inscribed by the author.
Dust jacket (short tear), else fine. Houle 22-460 1983 $85

HAWKESWORTH, JOHN   Almoran and Hamet. Dublin: Printed
for W. Smith (etc), 1761. 2 vols. in 1, 12mo, contemporary calf.
First Dublin edition. Hill 165-55 1983 £45

HAWKESWORTH, JOHN   Almoran and Hamet. Dublin: Printed for
W. Smith, H. Saunders, R. Watts, H. Bradley, J. Potts, and T. and J.
Whitehouse, 1761. 2 vols. in 1, 12mo., with continuous pagination
and signatures, contemp. calf. Top quarter of half title cut away.
Apparently first Dublin ed. Argosy 713-41 1983 £38

HAWKESWORTH, JOHN   Amphitryon. J. Payne, 1756. First
edition. Rebound in blue boards, v.g. Jarndyce 31-61 1983 £32

HAWKINS, ALFRED   Hawkins's Picture of Quebec. Quebec:
Printed for the Proprietor by Neilson & Cowan, 1834. 17 1/2cm.
Folding engraved map, one engraved plate and 13 lithographed plates
by Sproule after drawings by A.J. Russell. Author's presentation
copy to Col. Cockburn. Expertly rebound in full tan calf, raised
bands, blind ruled, with red morocco label. Fine. McGahern 54-83
1983 $450

HAWKINS, ANTHONY HOPE   The Adventures of The Lady Ursula. N.Y.:
R.H. Russell, 1898. First edition. Illus. Orig. decorated cloth.
With 3 A.Ls.S., 4 pages, 8vo, 27th Oct. & 5th Nov. 1897 & 13th Dec.
1898. Springfield, Mass., New York, & London, from author to his
publisher Russell. Inner hinges cracking. Covers somewhat rubbed.
Very good. MacManus 279-2746 1983 $100

HAWKINS, ANTHONY HOPE   The prisoner of Zenda. Bristol:
Arrowsmith, n.d. (1894). First edition, later issue. 8vo. Orig.
claret cloth (trifle faded, short nick at tope of spine). Very good
copy. Ximenes 63-155 1983 $45

HAWKINS, ANTHONY HOPE   The Prisoner of Zenda. Bristol, J.W.
Arrowsmith, n.d. (1895). First edition, 2 pp ads, orig. pink cloth.
Jarndyce 31-748 1983 £12.50

HAWKINS, ANTHONY HOPE   Why Italy is with The Allies.   London:
Richard Clay & Sons, Ltd., 1917.   First edition.   Orgi. wrappers.
Dust-soiled.   Very good.   MacManus 279-2752   1983 $75

HAWKINS, BENJAMIN WATERHOUSE   A Companarative View of the Human and
Animal Frame.   Chapman and Hall, London, 1860.   Folio, with 10
double page tinted lithograph plates; plates and text lightly foxed
but a good copy in orig. cloth gilt.   Quaritch NS 5-55   1983 $150

HAWKINS, BENJAMIN WATERHOUSE   Comparative View of the Human and
Animal Frame.   London, 1860.   Folio, moder cloth, 10 fine double page
tinted lithograph plates after the author's own drawings.   Argosy
713-242   1983 $125

HAWKINS, JEAN   Ghost Stories and Tales of the Supernatural.   Boston: Boston Book Company, 1909.   8vo.   Cloth.   Some
staining of covers.   Oak Knoll 49-452   1983 $55

HAWKINS, JOHN PARKER   Memoranda Concerning Some Branches
of the Hawkins Family and Connections.   (Indianapolis, 1913).   Illus.
Orig. cloth.   First edition.   Clipped signature and calling card
of author tipped in front.   Ginsberg 46-310   1983 $100

HAWKINS, LAETITIA MATILDA   The Countess and Gertrude.   For F.C. and
J. Rivington, by Law and Gilbert, 1811.   First edition, 4 vols.,
8vo, cont. calf.   Tears in two leaves, with no loss of text.   Hannas
69-87   1983   £80

HAWKINS, LAETITIA-MATILDA   Memoirs, Anecdotes, Facts, and
Opinions.   London: Longman, etc., 1824.   First edition.   2 vols.
12mo.   Cont. half calf, gilt, gilt panelled spines with morocco
labels, gilt.   From the library of Lord Suffield with his bookplate.   Traylen 94-430   1983   £35

HAWKINS, LAETITIA-MATILDA   Rosanne; or A Father's Labour Lost.
London: F. C. & J. Rivington, 1814.   First edition.   3 vols., 8vo.
Cont. blue calf, wide gilt borders with inner blind-tooled and gilt
borders, gilt panelled spines, marbled edges.   Printed label inside
each cover.   Very fine.   Very rare.   Traylen 94-431   1983   £330

HAWKINS, LAETITIA MATILDA   Rosanne; or, a Father's Labour Lost.
For F. C. and J. Rivington, 1814.   First edition.   3 vols.   8vo, half-
titles and final leaves (blank errata respectively) in vol. II and III.
Cont. half calf.   Name on title, or half-titles.   Hannas 69-88   1983
£90

HAWKINS, T.   The Book of the Great Sea-Dragons.
1840.   30 plates, folio, contemporary half calf (worn, spine partly
defective).   Very scarce.   Some foxing and dustsoiling.   Outer
margins towards end slightly waterstained.   Wheldon 160-1414   1983
£60

HAWKINS, T.   Memoirs of Ichthyosauri and Plesiosauri.
1834.   28 plates, folio, original cloth with paper label on side,
slightly worn, rebacked.   Scarce.   Subscribers list.   Some foxing and
a few marginal waterstains.   Tear in one plate repaired.   Dedication
to W. Buckland.   Wheldon 160-1413   1983   £45

HAWKINS, THOMAS   The Origin of the English Drama.
Oxford, Clarendon Press for S. Leacroft, et al., 1773.   3 vols.,
8vo, cont. calf, bit worn, rebacked, joints weak, labels chipped,
bookplates, few pages loose, fair to decent set.   Illus. with woodcuts.   First edition.   Ravenstree 94-183   1983 $285

HAWKINS, WILLARD   The Cowled Menace.   New York, (1930).
8vo.   Cloth.   Fine in dj.   In Our Time 156-366   1983 $30

HAWKS, FRANCIS L.   Narrative of the Expedition of an American
Squadron to the China Seas and Japan.   Washington, 1856.   Numerous
maps, plans and tinted lithograph plates, including the famous "Bathing
Plate".   3 vols.   Thick 4to.   Some slight fading.   Good.   Edwards 1044-
562   1983   £550

HAWKS, FRANCIS L.   Narrative of the Expedition of an
American Squadron to the China Seas and Japan...   New York, 1856.
Maps and illustrations.   Tall 8vo, half leather.   Rubbed.   Morrill
290-173   1983 $25

HAWKSLEY, ENID DICKENS   Charles Dickens Birthday Book.   London,
1948.   First English edition.   14 black and white drawings by Edward
Ardizzone.   Inscription.   Slightly rubbed and price-clipped dustwrappers.   Very good.   Jolliffe 26-11   1983   £35

HAWTHORNE, JULIAN   Hawthorne and his Circle.   New York:
Harper & Brothers, 1903.   First edition.   8vo.   Half calf, gilt
panelled spine with morocco label, gilt, t.e.g.   15 plates.   Traylen
94-433   1983   £18

HAWTHORNE, JULIAN   Nathaniel Hawthorne, and His Wife.
Chatto & Windux, 1885.   First edition, 2 vols.   Front. plates.   Orig.
dark green cloth, worn.   Jarndyce 30-1017   1983   £10.50

HAWTHORNE, NATHANIEL   Doctor Grimshawes Secret.   Boston,
1883.   First edition.   Pictorial cloth.   Fine.   Argosy 714-352   1983
$150

HAWTHORNE, NATHANIEL   Doctor Grimshawe's Secret.   Boston:
Osgood, 1883.   Facsimile of ms.   1st ed., 1st binding, 1st printing.
Orig. pictorial grey cloth, gilt.   Some minor foxing on end papers
(found in most copies due to paste used by publisher's binder) else
a fine bright copy.   Jenkins 155-528   1983 $50

HAWTHORNE, NATHANIEL   The Golden Touch.   S.F., 1927.   8vo,
vellum-backed decorated boards, gilt, slipcase.   Drawing by Valenti
Angelo.   A fine, uncut & unopened copy.   One of 240 copies.   Perata
28-42   1983 $145

HAWTHORNE, NATHANIEL   The House of the Seven Gables.   Boston:
Ticknor, Reed & Fields, 1851.   1st ed.   Orig. brown cloth, gilt.
Light rubbing.   BAL's binding D (with September, 1853 ads inserted at
front), a rare but later binding variant using 1st ed. sheets.   Fine
copy.   Jenkins 153-824   1983 $350

HAWTHORNE, NATHANIEL   The House of the Seven Gables.   Boston:
Ticknor, Reed & Fields, 1851.   1st ed.   Orig. brown cloth, gilt.   Light
rubbing.   Binding E.   No ads.   Bright copy.   Jenkins 153-825   1983 $30
$300

HAWTHORNE, NATHANIEL   Life of Franklin Pierce.   Boston:
Ticknor, Reed & Fields, 1852.   Frontis.   1st ed.   Orig. black wavy-
grained TR cloth, gilt.   Rear free end paper wanting.   Very good
copy in a less common color than the usual brown cloth.   Jenkins
155-532   1983 $65

HAWTHORNE, NATHANIEL   The Marble Faun.   B., 1860.   2 vols.
First issue without conclusion, spine edges chipped and edges slightly
worn, good or better, bookplate.   Quill & Brush 54-617   1983 $100

HAWTHORNE, NATHANIEL   The Marble Faun.   Boston: Ticknor and
Fields, 1860.   Half titles, 16 pp ads.   vol. II.   Orig. brown cloth.
Jarndyce 30-416   1983   £10.50

HAWTHORNE, NATHANIEL   Our Old Home.   Smith, Elder, 1863.
2 vols., half titles, 4 pp ads.   Orig. green cloth, v.g.   First
English edition.   Jarndyce 30-418   1983   £48

HAWTHORNE, NATHANIEL   Passages from the English Notebooks.
Boston: Fields, Osgood, 1870.   2 vols.   1st ed.   Orig. green cloth,
gilt.   Close to a fine set.   Jenkins 155-1394   1983 $100

HAWTHORNE, NATHANIEL   Passages from the American Note-Books.
London, 1868.   2 vols, small 8vo, original brown cloth gilt, backs
darkened.   Deighton 3-161   1983   £25

HAWTHORNE, NATHANIEL   Peter Parley's Universal History.
Boston: American Stationers, 1838.   2 vols.   1st ed., 3rd printing.
Orig. half black morocco and diamond cloth, gilt.   Some scattered
foxing and a couple of spots to cloth, else a fine set of an
extremely rare book.   Jenkins 155-533   1983 $300

HAWTHORNE, NATHANIEL   The Scarlet Letter.   Boston: Ticknor,
Reed & Fields, 1850.   1st ed.   Orig. brown cloth, gilt, with March
catalogue.   Some rubbing of spine ends and corners, but a much
better than usual copy.   Jenkins 155-534   1983 $650

HAWTHORNE, NATHANIEL   The Scarlet Letter. London, 1920.
4to. Orig. decorated blue cloth, gilt, t.e.g. 31 mounted coloured
plates from drawings by Hugh Thomson. Traylen 94-432 1983 £38

HAWTHORNE, NATHANIEL   The Scarlet Letter. NY: Heritage Press,
1935. Illus. and designed by W. A. Dwiggins. Frontis. signed by
Dwiggins, full red leather, spine slightly scuffed, else very good in
skinned slipcase. Quill & Brush 54-406 1983 $50

HAWTHORNE, NATHANIEL   Tanglewood Tales. Boston: 1853. First
American edition, first issue. Engraved title page, printed title, 8
plates. Orig. green cloth. Boston Stereotype Foundry entry only on
copyright page, July ads. Shaken, spine ends and corners frayed,
otherwise sound copy. Bradley 66-193 1983 $45

HAWTHORNE, NATHANIEL   Tanglewood Tales. Duckworth, 1914. 1st
edn. Illus. by Milo Winter, col. frontis. & 9 colour plates. Dark
blue decor. cloth designed by Winter (some occasional foxing), v.g.
copy. Hodgkins 27-449 1983 £10.50

HAWTHORNE, NATHANIEL   Transformation: or the Romance of
Monte Beni. Leipzig: Bernhard Tauchnitz, 1860. 12mo, illus. with
100 mounted orig. photographs. Bound in 3/4 vellum; gilt-stamped
spines. Small chip to upper spine extremity of volume I. Karmiole
76-87 1983 $75

HAWTHORNE, NATHANIEL   A Wonder Book. London: Hodder &
Stoughton, n.d. (1922). 4to. White cloth. Gold pictorial stamping.
Gilt lettered spine. T.e.g. Rear cover light soil. Limited to 600
copies, signed by A. Rackham. Illus. with 24 full-page tipped in
color illus. with lettered tissue guards. 20 black & white drawings.
Pictorial endpapers. Very good to fine. Aleph-bet 8-212 1983 $625

HAY, DAVID   Diary in the Form of a Letter written to
his Mother during the Siege of the Residency at Lucknow, 1857. Edinburgh: For Private Circulation, 1911. Sm.8vo. Orig. cloth. Good.
Edwards 1044-329 1983 £20

HAY, JOHN   Jim Bludson of the Prairie Belle and
Little Breeches. B., 1871. Paperwraps bound in three quarter leather,
very good to fine. Quill & Brush 54-619 1983 $90

HAY, JOHN   A Private History. New York, 1947.
8vo. Cloth. Review copy with slip from publisher laid in. Fine
in dj. In Our Time 156-367 1983 $25

HAY, ROBERT   Geology and Mineral Resources of Kansas.
Topeka, 1893. Illus., folding map, plate with 3 views, orig. pr.
wrs. World's Fair ed. Argosy 710-247 1983 $27.50

HAY, SARAH HENDERSON   This My Letter. New York: Knopf,
1939. Cloth. First edition. One of 1,000 numbered copies.
Inscribed presentation copy from the author. Very fine in printed and
glassine dust jacket. Reese 20-1190 1983 $45

HAY, THOMAS R.   Hood's Tennessee Campaign. N.Y.: Neale,
1929. 1st edition. Fld. maps. Jenkins 151-236 1983 $100

HAYDN, HIRAM C.   Western Reserve University: From
Hudson to Cleveland, 1878-1890. (Cleveland), Western Reserve, 1905.
Illus. Orig. cloth. First edition. Ginsberg 46-576 1983 $25

HAYDN, JOSEPH   Allmaechtiger, Preis dir und Ehre.
Leipzig, Breitkopf & Haertel, (1812). Oblong folio, unbound. First
edition. Salloch 387-93 1983 $150

HAYDN, JOSEPH   The Creation. Boston, Thomas Badger,
1818. From the London edition. 1 page damaged at upper corner, old
waterstains, 4to, cont. calf-backed marbled boards. Salloch 387-96
1983 $40

HAYDN, JOSEPH   Die Sieben Worte des Erloesers am
Kreutz. Bonn & Coeln, Simrock, plate #1876, n.d. (1822). Small tear
in cover, some foxing, otherwise fine copy. Engraved title and music,
uncut, orig. pink covers with ornamental border. Salloch 387-95 1983
$90

HAYDN, JOSEPH   Walte Gnaedig, O Ew'ge Liebe. Leipzig,
Breitkopf & Haertel, n.d. (1813). Oblong folio, unbound. First
edition. Salloch 387-94 1983 $135

HAYDOCK, ROGER   A Collection of the Christian Writings,
Labours, Travels and Sufferings of...to which is Added, an Account of
His Death and Burial. Printed and sold by T. Sowle, 1700. First
collected edition, ad. leaf, small 8vo, cont. unlettered mottled
calf, four leaves cut close without loss. Fenning 60-167 1983 £35

HAYDON, ARTHUR L.   The Trooper Police of Australia.
Andrew Melrose, 1911. Second impression. With 5 maps, 43 plates, 8vo,
orig. cloth. In a very slightly worn dust wrapper. Fenning 62-170
1983 £35

HAYDON, BENJAMIN ROBERT   The Autobiography and Memoirs. G. Bell,
1927. First edition, front. port. Illus. Half title, orig. blue
cloth. Jarndyce 30-1018 1983 £15

HAYES, BENJAMIN   Pioneer Notes from the Diaries of Judge
Benjamin Hayes 1849-1875. Los Angeles: Privately Printed, 1929.
Frontispiece and illustrations. Issued in a small edition. Fine.
Jenkins 153-249 1983 $75

HAYES, CHARLES WELLS   The Diocese of Western New York:
History & Recollections. Rochester, 1904. Illus. Argosy 716-352
1983 $25

HAYLEY, WILLIAM   Epistle to a Friend, on the Death of
John Thornton, Esq. London: Printed for J. Dodsley...MDCCLXXX. 4to,
complete with half-title; modern boards. Second edition, corrected,
published the same year as the first. Quaritch NS 7-64 1983 $75

HAYLEY, WILLIAM   An Essay on History. London, J. Dodsley,
1780. 4to, bound with half title in cont. tree sheep newly rebacked.
First edition. Ravenstree 94-184 1983 $80

HAYLEY, WILLIAM   The Life of Milton, in Three Parts.
London, T. Cadell and W. Davies, 1796. 4to, old half sheept, worn,
name on title, title trifle wrinkled. Ravenstree 94-185 1983 $165

HAYLEY, WILLIAM   A Philosophical, Historical, and Moral
Essay on Old Maids. London, Printed for T. Cadell, 1785. 3 vols.,
8vo, orig. quarter calf, quite worn, covers loose, some preliminary
pages loose, working copy. First edition. Ravenstree 94-186 1983
$95

HAYLEY, WILLIAM   Plays of Three Acts. London, 1784. 4to.
Rebacked in leather, boards. With half-title. Edges of the boards
scuffed, else a very good-fine copy. In Our Time 156-370 1983 $125

HAYLEY, WILLIAM   The Triumphs of Temper. London,
Printed for J. Dodsley, 1781. 4to, new boards, a smallish copy, with
the half title and errata. First edition. Ravenstree 94-187 1983
$55

HAYMOND, CREED   Pacific Railroads. N.p., (1888).
Dbd. First edition. Ginsberg 47-778 1983 $50

HAYNE, PAUL HAMILTON   Sonnets and Other Poems. Charleston:
Harper & Calvo, 1857. 1st edition, original full black morocco,
fully gilt, raised bands, gilt compartments, a.e.g., cover edges
and inner dentilles gilt. Presentation copy inscribed by author on
front end paper in ink. Some foxing else a fine copy. Jenkins
151-121 1983 $475

HAYNE, PAUL HAMILTON   Sonnets, and Other Poems. Charleston:
Harper & Calvo, 1857. 1st ed. Orig. full black morocco, fully gilt,
raised bands, gilt compartments, a.e.g., cover edges and inner
dentilles gilt. Presentation copy inscribed by Hayne on front end
paper in ink: "A.B. Mayer--From his friend--P.H. Hayne--March 26th,
1857." Jenkins 155-1395 1983 $300

HAYWARD, ABRAHAM   The Art of Dining. London, 1852. 1st
ed. 12mo, marbled boards, calf back & corners, ex-library with no
external marks. Morrill 288-168 1983 $40

HAYWARD, ARTHUR L.   The Dickens Encyclopaedia. Routledge,
1924. First edition. Half title, front. illus. Orig. red cloth.
Jarndyce 30-193 1983 £14.50

HAYWARD, ARTHUR L.   The Dickens Encyclopaedia. Routledge &
Kegan Paul, (1924). D.w., v.g. Jarndyce 31-607 1983 £10.50

HAYWARD, GEORGE   Surgical Reports and Miscellaneous
Papers on Medical Subjects. Boston, 1855. First collected edition.
Argosy 713-254 1983 $150

HAYWARD, GERTRUDE M.   Dulcibel. Hurst & Blackett, 1890.
First edition, 3 vols. Half titles, 6 pp ads. vol. III. Orig.
maroon cloth, sl. marking of upper cover vol. I, which is a little
duller than vols. II and II. Jarndyce 30-419 1983 £42

HAYWARD, H. RICHARD   In the Kingdom of Kerry. Dundalk,
1946. First edition, with 109 illus. and a folding map in an end
pocket, 8vo, orig. cloth backed boards, gilt, a very good copy.
Fenning 61-198 1983 £10.50

HAYWARD, H. RICHARD   Love in Ulster, and Other Poems. Dublin:
Talbot Press, 1922. First edition, cr. 8vo, orig. cloth, a very
good copy. Fenning 61-197 1983 £16.50

HAYWARD, JOHN   English Poetry: A Catalogue of First
& Early Editions... London: The National Book League, 1947. First
edition. 8vo. Printed wrappers. Oak Knoll 49-485 1983 $40

HAYWARD, JOHN   The First Part of the Life and Raigne
of King Henrie the IIII. London, Iohn Wolfe, 1599. 4to, old
quarter calf, boards, little rubbed, bookplate; internally fine,
clean copy. Ravenstree 94-188 1983 $310

HAYWARD, JOHN   A Gazetteer of the United States of
America... Hartford, 1853. 1st ed. Folding map, partly torn, and
text engravings. 8vo, contemporary calf, leather label. Some
rubbing, hinges cracked. Morrill 286-190 1983 $30

HAYWARD, JOHN   The Religious Creeds and Statistics of
Every Christian Denomination in the United States and British
Provinces. Boston, Author, 1836. 1st ed. 12mo, paper label.
Binding stained, some foxing. Morrill 287-144 1983 $25

HAYWOOD, A. L.   Indiscretions of A Prefect of Police.
London, 1929. First edition. 8vo. Orig. cloth. Frontis. 7 plates.
Slightly worn and stained. Some very slight foxing. Good. Edwards
1042-365 1983 £15

HAYWOOD, ELIZA   The invisible spy. London: H. Gardner,
1773. Second edition. 2 vols. 12mo. Later calf. Spine gilt.
Slight wear to hinges. Ximenes 63-122 1983 $150

HAYWOOD, ELIZA   Mary Stuart, Queen of Scots. Printed
for D. Browne Junior; S. Chapman; and J. Woodman and D. Lyon, 1725.
T.e.g., modern speckled calf antique, spine gilt. First edition.
Bickersteth 77-120 1983 £140

HAYWOOD, ELIZA   The secret history of the present
intrigues of the court of Caramania. London, 1727. Second edition.
8vo. Cont. calf. A later hand has filled the half-title and the
margins of the title-page with notes identifying the various characters. Quite worn, covers detached. Ximenes 63-124 1983 $150

HAYWOOD, ELIZA   A Wife to be Lett. London: printed for
W. Feales; and sold by J. Osborn, 1735. Fourth edition, 12mo, engraved
frontis., uncut in old marbled wrappers. Pickering & Chatto 19-31
1983 $350

HAYWOOD, HELEN   The Mouse that Ran. F. Warne, 1926.
Sm. 8vo. Colour frontis. Title vignette. 25 colour plates. Pictorial endpapers. Small hole in rear endpaper. Grey boards, small
onlaid colour plate. Greer 40-109 1983 £22.50

HAZEN, HENRY A.   History of Billerica, Massachusetts...
Boston, 1883. 1st ed. Map and illus. 8vo. Ex-library, lacks
endleaves. Morrill 287-232 1983 $25

HAZEN, W. B.   General Hazen's Reply to the Second
Comptroller. Wash., 1886. Cloth. First edition. Ginsberg 46-311
1983 $75

HAZEN, W. B.   Our Barren Lands. Cincinnati, 1875.
Orig. printed wraps., rubber stamps on front wraps. and several pages.
First edition. Ginsberg 47-335 1983 $400

HAZLITT, WILLIAM   Characters of Shakespear's Plays.
London, C.H. Reynell for R. Hunter et al., 1817. 8vo, orig. boards,
paper spine, bit worn, hinges cracked, little soiled, name on title,
uncut copy. First edition. Ravenstree 94-189 1983 $195

HAZLITT, WILLIAM   Essays on the Principles of Human
Action. John Miller, (1835). 12mo, orig. cloth, worn, with old
paper rebacking of the spine, with the cloth backstrip laid down on
the paper. Bickersteth 77-212 1983 £28

HAZLITT, WILLIAM   Lectures on the English Poets.
London: Taylor & Hessey, 1818. First edition, 8vo, half morocco
gilt, uncut copy with half-title, advertisements, bookplate. Hinges
tender, but a very good copy. Trebizond 18-52 1983 $200

HAZLITT, WILLIAM   Lectures on the English Comic Writers.
London: Taylor & Hessey, 1819. 1st ed., 8vo, gilt-bordered calf,
spine gilt, t.e.g., morocco label by Riviere. Uncut copy, bookplate,
half-title not called for. A fine copy. Trebizond 18-50 1983 $200

HAZLITT, WILLIAM   Lectures on the English Comic Writers.
Philadelphia: M. Carey & Son, 1819. First American edition, 8vo,
cont. calf, spine gilt, morocco label, bookplate, half-title not
called for. Some light foxing, but a fine copy. Trebizond 18-51
1983 $110

HAZLITT, WILLIAM   Lectures on the English Poets...
London: for Taylor and Hessey, 1818. First edition. 8vo. 19th
century half green morocco, gilt, gilt panelled spines, t.e.g.,
others uncut. Half-title, 4 pp. of ads., dated May 1,1818. Spine
faded. Traylen 94-434 1983 £80

HAZLITT, WILLIAM   Lectures on the English Poets.
Philadelphia: Thomas Dobson & Son, 1818. 1st American ed., 8vo,
original grey boards, recently rebacked. Uncut copy. Light foxing,
staining of initial leaves, but a very good copy. Trebizond 18-53
1983 $85

HAZLITT, WILLIAM   Lectures on the English Comic Writers.
John Templeman, 1841. 3rd edition, orig. green cloth. Jarndyce 31-
740 1983 £24

HAZLITT, WILLIAM   Liber Amoris. London, John Hunt, 1823.
8vo, bound without half title in full citron morocco gilt extra,
a.e.g., bit rubbed, joints cracked, light foxing, the W.K. Bixby-
Alfred Nathan copy with bookplates. First edition. Ravenstree 94-190
1983 $125

HAZLITT, WILLIAM   Liber Amoris. Privately printed, 1894.
Ltd. edition. Sq. tall 8vo, buckram; uncut and partially unopened.
One of 400 copies. Fine, except that several pages have been
carelessly opened, resulting in marginal tears. Argosy 714-353 1983
$85

HAZLITT, WILLIAM CAREW   Old Cookery Books and Ancient Cuisine.
London: Elliot Stock, 1893. Second edition. 12mo. Cloth-backed
boards. Front endpaper missing, else very good. Oak Knoll 48-195
1983 $20

HAZLITT, WILLIAM   The Plain Speaker: Opinions on Books,
Men, and Things. London: Henry Colburn, 1826. First edition. 2
vols. 8vo. Newly bound in orange buckram. Traylen 94-435 1983
£85

HAZLITT, WILLIAM   Political Essays, with Sketches of
Public Characters. Wm. Hone, 1819. First edition, small tear to
title, well repaired. Modern French combed-pattern boards, black
leather label, v.g. Jarndyce 31-737 1983 £52

HAZLITT, WILLIAM   Table-Talk. London, John Warren, 1821.
8vo, cont. half calf, quite worn, covers gone, the 4th Earl
Tyrconnel copy with his wife Sarah Tyrconnel's signature on title.
First edition. Ravenstree 94-191 1983 $35

HAZLITT, WILLIAM   A Reply to Z. Curwen Press for the First
Editions Club, 1923. 1st ed., tall 8vo, typographic ornaments in red,
quarter scarlet buckram over blue buckram, t.e.g., others uncut,
free endpapers darkened, fine in dustwrappers. 300 numbered copies
in Baskerville on hand-made paper. Deighton 3-166 1983 £25

HAZLITT, WILLIAM   A Reply to Z. London, printed for the
First Edition Club, 1923. 8vo, two-tone cloth, gilt, t.e.g. One of
300 copies. Bookplate. End papers browned. A very nice copy.
Perata 28-16 1983 $75

HAZLITT, WILLIAM CAREW   The Confessions of a Collector.
London: Ward & Downey, 1897. First edition. 8vo. Cloth. Covers
lightly rubbed. Oak Knoll 48-194 1983 $30

HAZLITT, WILLIAM CAREW   The Confessions of a Collector. Ward &
Downey, 1897. First edition, orig. pink cloth, spine faded. Jarndyce
31-94 1983 £18

HAZLITT, WILLIAM CAREW   A Manual for the Collector of Old
English Plays. London: 1892. First edition. New blue buckram.
1/250 copies. Bradley 66-49 1983 $50

HEAD, C. F.   Eastern & Egyptian Scenery. London, 1833.
3 folding maps, 1 coloured, 22 lithograph plates on India paper, some
occasional, marginal spotting. Oblong folio. Modern half morocco gilt,
title label on upper cover. 8vo. Good. Edwards 1044-330 1983 £400

HEAD, FRANCIS   A fortnight in Ireland. London:
Murray, 1852. First edition. 8vo. Orig. green cloth. Folding
map. Ximenes 63-622 1983 $80

HEAD, FRANCIS   A Narrative... London, 1839. Cloth,
spine faded, else a fine copy. Reese 19-267 1983 $300

HEAD, FRANCIS   Rough Notes Taken During Some Rapid
Journeys Across the Pampas and Among the Andes. J. Murray, 1846.
Wanting half-title, small 8vo, wrapper. Fenning 60-168 1983 £12.50

HEAL, AMBROSE   The English Writing-Masters and Their
Copybooks, 1570-1800. Hildesheim: Georg Olms Verlagsbuchhandlung,
1962. 4to. Cloth. Prof. illus. Oak Knoll 49-453 1983 $225

HEAL, AMBROSE   London Tradesmen's Cards of the XVIII
Century. London, 1925. 8vo, boards and cloth. 102 plates. Duschnes
240-110 1983 $125

HEALD, WILLIAM MARGETSON   The Brunoniad: An Heroic Poem in Six
Cantos. Printed for G. Kearsley, 1790. 4to, disbound. First edition.
Bickersteth 75-237 1983 £35

HEALD, WILLIAM MARGETSON   Moscow: an ode. London: Ridgway,
etc., 1813. First edition. 8vo. Disbound. Outer edges uncut;
bit dusty. Ximenes 63-407 1983 $45

HEALES, ALFRED   The Architecture of the Churches of
Denmark. Kegan Paul, 1892. First edition, with 10 plates and 63
other illus., roy. 8vo, orig. cloth, gilt, t.e.g. A small snag in
spine, otherwise a very good copy. Fenning 60-169 1983 £21.50

HEANEY, SEAMUS   Bog Poems. (London): The Rainbow
Press, 1975. First edition. Illus. by Barrie Cooke. 4to. Orig.
maroon morocco and marbled boards. T.e.g. By Sangorski & Sutcliffe,
in publisher's cloth slipcase. One of 150 copies printed on Italian
paper and signed by the author. Mint copy. Jaffe 1-133 1983 $350

HEANEY, SEAMUS   A Boy Driving His Father to Confession.
Frensham: The Sceptre Press, (1970). Orig. white wraps. First edition. One of 150 copies. Mint. MacManus 278-2539 1983 $250

HEANEY, SEAMUS   Death Of A Naturalist. London: Faber
and Faber, Ltd, (1966). First edition. 8vo. Orig. cloth. Dust
jacket. Very fine copy. Jaffe 1-131 1983 $375

HEANEY, SEAMUS   Death of an Naturalist. London, 1966.
Dustwrapper with fading to the pink lower half. A fine copy.
Gekoski 2-79 1983 £125

HEANEY, SEAMUS   Death of a Naturalist. London, 1966.
First edition. Inscription in red crayon. Rubbed and soiled dustwrapper faded at the spine and edges. Fine. Jolliffe 26-258 1983
£95

HEANEY, SEAMUS   Door into the Dark. London, 1969. First
edition. Dust wrapper. Fine. Rota 231-311 1983 £75

HEANEY, SEAMUS   Eleven Poems. Belfast: Festival
Publications, (1965). First edition, second state, with the larger,
black sun on the front covers. Signed by the author. Fine. Scarce.
Gekoski 2-78 1983 £200

HEANEY, SEAMUS   Eleven Poems. Belfast, 1966. First
edition. Wrappers. The second state printed on wove paper and with
the cover device redrawn and printed in a near black purple. Fine.
Jolliffe 26-257 1983 £75

HEANEY, SEAMUS   Field Work. London: Faber & Faber,
(1979). Orig. wraps. Uncorrected proof copy of the first edition.
Fine copy. MacManus 278-2541 1983 $150

HEANEY, SEAMUS   Hedge School. Ten sonnets from Glanmore.
Janus Press, 1979. Slim royal 8vo, thick pale brown paper with 6
woodcuts printed in colours, text in black and sepia, uncut in dark
brown card wrappers lettered in blind. A fine copy. 285 numbered
copies signed by author and Claire Van Vliet, who created the woodcuts.
Deighton 3-167 1983 £36

HEANEY, SEAMUS   A Lough Neagh Sequence. Phoenix
Pamphlet Poets Press, 1969. Signed by the author on title page and
dated October 1969. With a Phoenix prospectus loosely inserted.
A very fine copy. Gekoski 2-81 1983 £80

HEANEY, SEAMUS   North; poems. London, 1975. First
edition. One of 25 copies, specially bound in green canvas by B.
Dickson and signed by author in 1981. Fine. Rota 231-312 1983 £100

HEANEY, SEAMUS   North. London, 1981. First edition,
second issue. Mint. Gekoski 2-82 1983 £80

HEANEY, SEAMUS   Poems and a Memoir. New York: Limited
Editions Club, (1982). Quarto, full leather with decoration stamped
in blind, g.t., slipcase. With eight illus. by Henry Pearson.
First edition. One of 2,000 copies signed by Heaney, Flanagan and
Pearson. Duschnes 240-111 1983 $150

HEANEY, SEAMUS   Poems and A Memoir. London: Limited
Editions Club, 1982. One of 2,000 copies, signed by Heaney, the illus.
Pearson, and the author of the introduction, Thomas Flanagan. Bound
and cased by Robert Burien and Son. Mint. Gekoski 2-83 1983 £100

HEANEY, SEAMUS   Poems 1965-1975. N.Y.: Farrar Straus
Giroux, (1980). Uncorrected proof copy of the first American
edition, with pub.'s information laid in giving details of publication.
Mint copy. MacManus 278-2542 1983 $150

HEANEY, SEAMUS   Preoccupations. New York: Farrar,
Straus & Giroux, (1980). Orig. printed wraps. Uncorrected page
proofs of the first edition. Fine. MacManus 278-2543 1983 $125

HEANEY, SEAUMUS   Selected Poems. New York: Limited
Editions Club, 1982. Illus. by Henry Pearson. Signed by the author
and the artist. Mint. Argosy 714-354 1983 $125

HEARD, FRANKLIN FISK   Report of the Trial of Leavitt Alley,
Indicted for the Murder of Abijah Ellis. Boston, 1875. Reddish-brown
cloth. First edition. The text of the trial is a presentation copy,
inscribed by Alley's lawyer, Gustavus A. Somerby, to Professor Horsford of Harvard. Spine ends worn, but good copy. Bradley 64-171
1983 $50

HEARN, LAFCADIO   Chin Chin Kobakama. (Tokyo: Hasegawa,
1903). 1st ed., state C (no priority). Orig. color wrappers,
printed in color woodblocks throughout, creped after printing, and
bound Japanese style. Stain to front cover and some margins, still
a very good copy. Jenkins 155-535 1983 $50

HEARN, LAFCADIO   Chita: A Memory of the Last Island.
New York: Harper, (1889). 1st ed., 2nd state. Orig. rust cloth,
gilt. Very good copy with pencilled inscription to Doyle: "Dr.
Conan Doyle From Geo. M. Millard. Chicago. Oct. 14, 1894."
Jenkins 155-536 1983 $185

HEARN, LAFCADIO   Editorials. B., 1926. Spine lettering
and edges very slightly rubbed, flys slightly offset from dustwrapper,
near fine in lightly chipped and rubbed, very good dustwrapper. Quill
& Brush 54-621 1983 $40

HEARN, LAFCADIO   Essays in European and Oriental
Literature. N.Y., 1923. First edition. Argosy 714-355 1983 $35

HEARN, LAFCADIO   "Ghombo Zhebes." New York: Will
Coleman, 1885. Quarto. Gilt decorated cloth. First edition. Ink
ownership inscription, and bookplate removed, otherwise a very good
copy. Reese 20-492 1983 $150

HEARN, LAFCADIO   Glimpses of Unfamiliar Japan. Boston,
1894. 8vo. Cloth. 2 vols. Immaculate set. In Our Time 156-372
1983 $100

HEARN, LAFCADIO   Interpretations of Literature. N.Y.,
Dodd, 1916. First edition, second ptg. Red cloth, paper labels.
Frontis. 2 vols. Good-very good. Houle 21-399 1983 $30

HEARN, LAFCADIO   A Japanese Miscellany. B., 1901. Green
pic. cover slightly soiled, edges rubbed, very good. Quill & Brush 54-
620 1983 $75

HEARN, LAFCADIO   Karma. N.Y., Boni, 1918. First
edition. Dust jacket, uncommon thus. Very good. Houle 21-400 1983
$75

HEARN, LAFCADIO   Kokoro. Harper & Brothers, 1898. First
English edition, orig. maroon cloth, t.e.g. Jarndyce 31-183 1983
£20

HEARN, LAFCADIO   Kwaidan. Tokyo: The Limited Editions
Club, 1932. Profusely illus., including 3 hand-colored plates.
Edition ltd. to 1500 numbered copies, signed by the illustrator,
Yasumasa Fugita. Printed cloth, stabbed and tied Japanese style.
In three-paneled beige slipcase with ivory slaps. Paper cover label.
Karmiole 75-64 1983 $150

HEARN, LAFCADIO   Out of the East: Reveries and Studies
in New Japan. London: Kegan Paul, Trench, Trubner, (1895). 1st
English ed. Orig. blue cloth, gilt. Using American sheets and
binding brasses. Nice. Scarce. Jenkins 155-538 1983 $50

HEARN, LAFCADIO   The Romance of the Milky Way. London:
Archibald, Constable, 1905. 1st English ed. Orig. black cloth,
stamped in red in the style of the American ed. The sheets of this
ed. were printed in the U.S.A. Light wear to spine, else bright.
Uncommon. Jenkins 155-539 1983 $45

HEARN, LAFCADIO   Selected Writings. N.Y., Citadel (1949).
First edition thus. Dust jacket. Very good. Houle 21-403 1983
$22.50

HEARN, LAFCADIO   Some Chinese Ghosts. Boston: Roberts
Brothers, 1887. Yellow cloth, stamped in brown. First edition.
The front board is a trifle spotted, and a bookplate removed, and
another present, but a very good copy. Reese 20-493 1983 $85

HEARN, LAFCADIO   The Soul of the Great Bell. San Francisco (Marjorie and Paul Bissinger), 1939. First edition thus. 4to,
text printed in black and green with red initials. Half brown cloth
over patterned boards, paper label (tiny chip). Title page illus.,
one half-page illus., and initials by Essie Lowenstein. One of only
15 copies on Anvil paper. Houle 22-462 1983 $275

HEARNE, SAMUEL   A Journey from Prince of Wales's Fort
in Hudson's Bay, to the Northern Ocean. London, Strahan and Cadell,
1795. Large 4to. 2 ads & directions to binder. 9 maps (plates (8
folded)). Cont. diced calf, gilt rules on sides, expertly rebacked &
elaborately gilt-tooled, morocco label. 1st ed. Some plates mod.
browned, corners cumped. Nice copy. O'Neal 50-26 1983 $2,000

HEARNE, THOMAS   A Vindication of those who take the
Oath of Allegiance to his Present Majestie from Perjurie, Injustice,
and Disloyaltie. Printed in the Year 1731. 8vo, orig. calf.
Bickersteth 75-42 1983 £20

HEARNE, THOMAS   The Works of Thomas Hearne. Printed
for Samuel Bagster in the Strand, 1810. 4 vols. 8vo. Leather,
decorated boards. A fine copy. In Our Time 156-373 1983 $150

THE HEART of man the temple of the Lord... Calcutta: July, 1839.
First edition. 12mo. Orig. light green printed wrappers. 10
lithographs. One of 1000 copies. Fine copy. Ximenes 63-209
1983 $200

HEARTMAN, CHARLES F.   American Primers Indian Primers Royal
Primers and Thrity-Seven Other Types of Non-New-England Primers
Issued prior to 1830. Highland Park, N.J., 1935. Cloth, illus.
Fine. Reese 19-62 1983 $100

HEATH, AMBROSE   The Country Life Cookery Book.
London, 1937. First edition. 13 wood engravings by Eric Ravilious.
Top and fore-edges faintly spotted. Spine edges very slightly
rubbed. Very good. Jolliffe 26-429 1983 £40

HEATH, G.   Musae Etoneneses: Seu Carminum Delectus
Nunc Primun In Lucem Editus. London: G. Strafford, 1795. 2 vols.
Decorated with fore-edge paintings on both vols. Full vellum with
orig. paintings on both covers of each vol. Contains six orig. paintings. Near-fine. MacManus 278-1938 1983 $1,250

HEATH, J. B.   Some Account of the Worshipful Company
of Grocers... London: privately printed by the Chiswick Press,
1869. Large 8vo. Full brown morocco, arms in gilt on sides, gilt
dentelles, t.e.g., slightly rubbed. With 8 plates. Gurney JJ-165
1983 £45

HEATH, WILLIAM   Memoirs of Major-General William
Heath. Boston: I. Thomas and E.T. Andrews, Aug. 1798. Later 3/4
morocco (very slightly rubbed at extremities). Book label of Dean
Sage. First edition. Felcone 21-54 1983 $125

HEATH, WILLIAM   Memoirs. New York, William Abbatt,
1901. Edition limited to 500 copies. 8vo. Ex-library. Morrill
290-174 1983 $30

HEATON, ISAAC E.   New and Decisive Evidence of the Mode
of Baptism. Fremont, Neb., 1878. Orig. printed wraps. Second
edition. Ginsberg 47-621 1983 $65

HEBARD, GRACE R.   The Bozeman Trail. Cleveland, 1922.
2 vols. Illus. Orig. cloth, small paper labels on spine. First
edition. Ginsberg 46-312 1983 $125

HEBENSTREIT, W.   Dictionarium Ditionum... Vindobonae:
C. Arbrusteri, 1828. First edition. 8vo. Later three-quarter calf
over marbled boards, t.e.g. Name in ink on title page along with a
library stamp. Cover rubbed. Oak Knoll 49-454 1983 $85

HEBER, REGINALD   A Ballad. N.d. (c. 1825). Oblong 4to,
lithographed by W. Crane, Chester. Eight full page plates. Orig.
pink wraps., v.g. Jarndyce 30-729 1983 £20

HEBER, REGINALD   Narrative of a Journey through the Upper
Provinces of India... London, 1828. First edition. 10 engraved
plates. 2 vols. 4to. Half calf, spines faded. Vols. misnumbered,
some rubbing. Good. Edwards 1044-331 1983 £150

HEBER, REGINALD   Narrative of a Journey through the Upper
Provinces of India... London, 1828. Second edition. 28 wood en-
graved plates. 3 vols. Half calf, wear to corners and hinges. 8vo.
Good. Edwards 1044-332 1983 £75

HEBER, REGINALD   Narrative of a Journey through the Upper
Provinces of India... London, 1843. 2 vols. Half calf, by J. Carss
& Co., with their ticket. 8vo. Good. Edwards 1044-333 1983 £50

HECHT, BEN   Cutie! Ch., 1924. No. 23 of 200 copies.
Edges wearing, otherwise near very good. Quill & Brush 54-623 1983
$45

HECHT, BEN   The Great Magoo. New York, (1938).
8vo. Cloth. Some spotting to the very top edge of the front endpaper, else a fine copy in the uncommon dj. Jacket is chipped on
the front flap. In Our Time 156-374 1983 $85

HECHT, BEN   To Quito and Back. NY, (1937). Cover
soiled, otherwise near very good in slightly chipped, soiled dustwrapper. Quill & Brush 54-624 1983 $30

HECKMANN, HERMANN   M.D. Poppelmann als Zeichner. Dresden: Verlag der Kunst, 1954. 111 plates. 4to. Cloth. Ars Libri 32-528 1983 $75

HEDGE, LEVI   Elements of Logick. Cambridge, 1816. 1st ed. 12mo, contemporary calf, leather label. Bookplate removed. Morrill 286-191 1983 $40

HEDGE, MARY ANN   Affection's Gift to a Beloved God-Child. Baldwin, Cradock, and Joy, 1821. With engraved frontis., including half-title, two ad. leaves at end, 8vo, orig. boards, uncut, with printed paper label. Fenning 61-200 1983 £21.50

HEDIN, SVEN   Jehol, City of Emperors. London, (1932). Map and illus. Roy.8vo. Cloth. Good. Edwards 1044-335 1983 £30

HEDIN, SVEN   Through Asia. London, 1898. 2 large folding maps, 2 portrait frontis., numerous illus. Thick 8vo. Library cloth binding. Good. Edwards 1044-334 1983 £45

HEDIN, SVEN   The Wandering Lake. London, 1940. 10 maps, 1 folding, repaired, plates and illus. Ex-library, some wear. 8vo. Orig. cloth. Good. Edwards 1044-336 1983 £18

HEDRICK, ULYSSES PRENTISS   The Small Fruits of New York. Albany, 1915. Full-page colored plates. 4to. Lower portion of text and covers lightly dampstained. Morrill 286-361 1983 $47.50

HEER, O.   The Primaeval World of Switzerland. 1876. Folding coloured geological map, 19 plates and 372 text-figures, 2 vols. in 1, 8vo, half calf (slightly rubbed). A little minor foxing. Wheldon 160-1415. 1983 £35

HEGGEN, THOMAS   Mister Roberts. N.Y., (1948). First edition. Argosy 714-359 1983 $50

HEGI, G.   Illustrierte Flora von Mitteleuropa, Band 2, Teil I. Berlin, 1967-80. 17 (12 coloured) plates and 231 text-figures, royal 8vo, cloth. Wheldon 160-1711 1983 £65

HEGNER, ULRICH   Hans Holbein der Jungere. Berlin: G. Reimer, 1827. Engraved frontis. portrait. 4to. Wrappers. Uncut. Unopened. Foxed. Ars Libri 32-322 1983 $65

HEHN, V.   The Wanderings of Plants and Animals from their first home. 1888. 8vo, cloth. Wheldon 160-162 1983 £25

HEIDEGGER, JOHN JAMES   Heydegger's Letter to the Bishop of London. London: printed for N. Cox, 1724. Folio, wrappers, 1st edition. Title a bit soiled. Rare. Ximenes 64-261 1983 $450

HEIDEGGER, MARTIN   Kant Und Das Problem Der Metaphysik. Bonn: Friedrich Cohen, 1929. First edition. Modern black cloth, orig. wrappers preserved. Rudolf Allers' copy, signed on front wrapper. Gach 95-197 1983 $85

HEIDENHAIN, M.   Plasma und Zelle. Jena, 1907. 2 vols., royal 8vo, cloth, one joint torn. Wheldon 160-163 1983 £15

HEIDRICH, ERNST   Geschichte des Durerschen Marien-bildes. Leipzig: Karl W. Hiersemann, 1906. 26 illus. 4to. Wrappers. Ars Libri 32-180 1983 $60

HEIGERAN, JOHANN ALEX   Disputatio physica in qua examinatur ista quaestio... Herborn: Christopher Corvin, 1593. Woodcut vignette on title. 4to. Boards. Kraus 164-124 1983 $185

HEILBRONNER, KARL   Ueber Gewoehnung. Wiesbaden: J. F. Bergmann, 1912. Library bookplate, else a fine, unopened copy in orig. blue printed wrappers. Gach 95-198 1983 $25

HEILMANN, G.   Danmarks Fugleliv. Copenhagen 1928-30. 92 coloured plates and 458 illus., 3 vols., 4to, original half morocco, gilt. A nice copy. Wheldon 160-749 1983 $75

HEILNER, VAN CAMPEN   Our American Game Birds. Garden City, 1941. Paintings & drawings by L.B. Hunt. Cloth. First edition. Blind-stamped names, rubber stamped names. 1 illus. loose. Shattered dust wrapper. Very good. King 45-488 1983 $35

HEINE, ALBRECHT-FRIEDRICH   Asmus Jakob Carstens und die Entwick-lung des Figurenbildes. Strassburg: J.H. Ed. Heitz, 1928. 26 plates. 4to. Wrappers. Covers dusty. Ars Libri 32-84 1983 $75

HEINE, HEINRICH   Book of Songs. Chapman & Hall, 1856. First edition, orig. green cloth, v.g. Jarndyce 31-741 1983 £20

HEINE, HEINRICH   Florentine Nights. London, Howe, 1931. Illus. by Frederick Carter. Half red cloth. Printed glassine dust jacket, very good. One of 1,000 copies. Houle 21-203 1983 $37.50

HEINROTH, JOHANN CHRISTIAN AUGUST (1773-1843)   Die Luege. Leipzig: Friedrich Fleischer, 1834. First edition. Orig. mottled boards, paper label. Attractive copy. Gach 95-199 1983 $250

HEISENBERG, WERNER   The Physical Principles of the Quantum Theory... Chicago: The University of Chicago Press, (1930). 8vo. Orig. red cloth. 19 text illus. Spine darkened. Otherwise a good copy. Zeitlin 264-196 1983 $100

HELD, JULIUS   Durers Wirkung auf die niederlandische Kunst seiner Zeit. Den Haag: Martinus Nijhoff, 1931. 8 plates. Small 4to. Wrappers. Ars Libri 32-181 1983 $85

HELD, JULIUS   Rubens: Selected Drawings. Garden City: Phaidon, 1959. 2 vols. 66 illus. (5 tipped-in color). 180 plates (1 tipped-in color). Large 4to. Cloth. Ars Libri 32-600 1983 $100

HELIODORUS   Historiae AEthiopicae libri decem, nunquam antea in lucem editi. Basileae, in Officina Hervagiana, 1534. 4to, full modern red morocco gilt, early collector's stamp on title, few slight damp marks, minor spotting, large crisp and fine copy. Ravenstree 94-52 1983 $750

HELLEKESSEL, HEINRICH   De Digitalis Purpureae Usu in curra Phthiseos Pulmonalis per Metasyncrisin Absolvenda. Bonnae, (1819). Large 8vo, cont. red boards. Argosy 713-256 1983 $50

HELLER, JOSEPH   Catch-22. New York: Simon and Schuster, 1961. First edition. 8vo. Orig. cloth. Dust jacket. Front of jacket wrinkled, otherwise a very fine copy. Jaffe 1-136 1983 $350

HELLER, JOSEPH   Good as Gold. New York, (1979). First edition. One of 500 copies in special binding and signed by author. Dark blue cloth, decorated with white stars. Mint in acetate dj and bright yellow slipcase. Bradley 65-89 1983 $115

HELLER, JOSEPH   Good as Gold. New York: (1979). First edition. Dark blue cloth. 1/500 signed by author. Mint in acetate jacket and slipcase. Bradley 66-196 1983 $100

HELLER, JOSEPH   Good as Gold. New York: Simon & Schuster, (1979). 1st ed., 1 of 500 numbered and signed copies. Orig. star-spangled cloth, printed yellow box, glassine. Mint copy in near perfect box. Jenkins 155-541 1983 $100

HELLER, JOSEPH   Good as Gold. NY, (1979). No. 269 of 500 numbered, specially bound and signed copies, very fine in very fine slipcase. Quill & Brush 54-625 1983 $75

HELLER, JOSEPH   Something Happened. New York: Knopf, 1974. 1st ed., 1 of 350 numbered and signed copies. Orig. cloth, gilt, uncut, dj, printed box. Very fine copy. Jenkins 155-542 1983 $175

HELLER, JOSEPH   Something Happened. New York: (1974). Black cloth. First edition. 1/350 signed by author. Fine in dust jacket and slipcase. Bradley 66-197 1983 $135

HELLER, JOSEPH   Something Happened. (NY, 1974). No. 198 of 350 specialy bound, numbered and signed copies, printed on special paper, very fine in dustwrapper in lightly soiled and scuffed near fine slipcase. Quill & Brush 54-626 1983 $100

HELLER, JULES   Papermaking: The White Art. Scottsdale: Scorpio Press, 1980. 8vo, leather-backed cloth boards, gilt, slipcase. Orig. signed frontis lithograph by Heller, numerous paper samples from different contemporary papermakers. One of 185 copies signed by author. Fine. Perata 28-213 1983 $300

HELLMAN, LILLIAN   Three: An Unfinished Woman, Pentimento, Scoundrel Time. Boston: Little, Brown, (1979). 1st ed., 1 of 500 numbered and signed copies. Contains new commentaries by author. Orig. green cloth, gilt, box with label. Mint copy. Jenkins 155-543 1983 $75

HELLMAYR, C. E.   The Birds of Chile. Chicago, Field Mus. Nat. Hist., 1932. 8vo, half cloth. Wheldon 160-751 1983 £30

HELLMAYR, C. E.   A Contribution to the Ornithology of Northeastern Brazil. Chicago, 1929. Map, 8vo, half cloth. Wheldon 160-750 1983 £30

HELLON, HENRY GEORGE   Lord Harrie and Leila. Provost, 1869. First edition, orig. green cloth, bevelled boards, gilt, v.g. Jarndyce 30-754 1983 £15

HELL'S Angels Movie Program. (Los Angeles 1930). Photos, cloth backed boards, a bit loose and worn. King 46-393 $35

HELM, MACKINLEY   John Marin. Boston: Institute of Contemporary Art, 1948. 9 color plates. 64 plates in text. 4to. Cloth. Dust jacket. Slightly worn. Ars Libri 32-428 1983 $50

HELME, ELIZABETH   The Pilgrim of the Cross... Brentford: by and for P. Norbury..., 1805. First edition. 4 vols. Small 8vo. Cont. half calf, rebacked. A little general usage. Very rare. Heath 48-377 1983 £325

HELME, ELIZABETH   The pilgrim of the cross. Brentford: printed by and for P. Norbury, etc., 1805. First edition. 4 vols. 12mo. Cont. tree calf, gilt, spines gilt. Trifle rubbed, slight chipping of the labels. Bound without half-titles, but a very good copy. Scarce. Ximenes 63-125 1983 $275

HELMHOLTZ, HERMANN VON   Popular Lectures on Scientific Subjects. London, 1893. 2 vols. Orig. cloth. Gurney JJ-166 1983 £20

HELMHOLTZ, HERMANN VON   Victor Masson et fils. Paris, 1868. 8vo., 57 wood engravings in the text, early pencil underlining and neat marginal annotations, contemporary roan backed boards, head of spine repaired. First French ed. Quaritch NS 5-57 1983 $500

HELMHOLTZ, HERMANN VON   Vortrage und Reden... Braunschweig: Vieweg, 1896. Fourth edition. 2 vols. Orig. cloth. Frontis. portrait. Numerous text illus., some colored. Some small ink stains. Near fine set. Zeitlin 264-197 1983 $80

HELMONT, JEAN BAPTISTE VAN   Deliramenta cattarhi: or, the incongruities, impossibilities, and absurdities couched under the vulgar opinion of defluxions. London: printed by E.G. for William Lee, 1650. First edition in English. Small 4to. Disbound. Light browning, a few minor stains; several lower edges trimmed a bit close. Ximenes 63-279 1983 $300

HELMS, ANTOINE- ZACHARIE   Voyage dans l'Amerique Meridionale, commencant par Buenos-Ayres et Potosi jusqu'a Lima. Paris, Galignani, 1812. First French edition, 8vo, 2 folding engraved maps, qtr. vellum, marbled sides, vellum-tipped corners, green morocco label foxed. Deighton 3-168 1983 £125

HELMS, LUDVIG V.   Pioneering in the Far East... London: W.H. Allen, 1882. 48 pages of ads. Illus. Orig. pictorial cloth, gilt. Minor wear. Nice. Jenkins 152-150 1983 $75

HELPS, ARTHUR   The Claims of Labour. Wm. Pickering, 1845. 4 pp ads. Orig. brown cloth, paper label, v.g. Jarndyce 31-184 1983 £28

HELPS, ARTHUR   Friends in Council. London: Parker, 1859. 2 vols., orig. cloth. First edition. MacManus 278-2544 1983 $30

HELPS, ARTHUR   The Spanish Conquest in America... London, 1855-61. 1st ed. 4 vols., 8vo, ends of spines torn, some inner hinges bit cracked, some rubbing. Morrill 288-172 1983 $30

HELPS, ARTHUR   Thoughts in the Cloister and the Crowd. London: For Henry Wix, 1835. 8vo, 16-1/2 cm. Later dark brown three-quarter morocco, spine gilt, by Zaehnsdorf. A.e.g. First edition, inscribed by the author. Grunder 7-39 1983 $100

HELPS, ARTHUR   Thoughts Upon Government. Bell and Daldy, 1872. First edition, half title, 2 pp ads. Inner hinges weakening, orig. brown cloth rubbed. Jarndyce 31-185 1983 £10.50

HELVETIUS, ADRIEN   La Kinakina, e le di servirsene, in tutte le Febbri... Parma: G. Dall'Oglio & F.R. Rosati, 1694. 8vo. Old vellum. Folding armorial frontis. Ownership stamp on half-title; outer margin of title cut close. Gurney 90-112 1983 £135

HEMANS, FELICIA   Poems. Wm. Blackwood, 1849. Front. and engr. title. Red morocco, gilt, a.e.g. Fine. Jarndyce 30-736 1983 £12

HEMANS, FELICIA   Records of Woman: with other poems. Edinburgh: William Blackwood; London: T. Cadell, 1828. 1st ed., 12mo, cont. half calf, marbled boards. Inscribed by Mary Russell Mitford, the novelist and essayist, on half-title. A very good copy. Trebizond 18-54 1983 $175

HEMANS, FELICIA   The restoration of the works of art to Italy: a poem. Oxford: printed by W. Baxter; for R. Pearson, etc., 1816. First edition. 8vo. Later boards. Buxton Forman's copy, with his bookplate and pencilled note: "wants fly-title, I fancy." Scarce. Ximenes 63-408 1983 $60

HEMANS, FELICIA   Scenes and Hymns of Life. Blackwood, 1834. First edition, very good. Jarndyce 30-737 1983 £10

HEMANS, FELICIA   The Siege of Valencia; a Dramatic Poem. The Last Constantine: with other Poems. London: John Murray, 1823. 1st (only) ed., 8vo, original boards and paper label. Uncut and unopened. Advertisement page. A fine copy, with minor wear to spine. Trebizond 18-55 1983 $120

HEMANS, FELICIA   The Siege of Valencia. John Murray, 1823. First edition, tall 8vo, rebound in half calf, v.g. Jarndyce 30-733 1983 £10.50

HEMANS, FELICIA   The Siege of Valencia. John Murray, 1823. First edition, 8 pp. ads. Uncut, orig. boards, spine worn. Jarndyce 30-732 1983 £9.50

HEMANS, FELICIA   Songs of the affections, with other poems. Edinburgh: Blackwood, etc., 1830. Orig. blue boards. Grey paper backstrip, printed paper label. Buxton Forman's copy. Slight wear to spine. Ximenes 63-409 1983 $65

HEMANS, FELICIA   Songs of the Affections. Phila., 1868. 3 engr. plates. 12mo, (backstrip faded), gilt-dec. cloth, a.e.g. Argosy 716-419 1983 $25

HEMINGWAY, ERNEST   Across the River and into the Trees. New York, 1950. 8vo. Cloth. A fine copy in dj. In Our Time 156-381 1983 $100

HEMINGWAY, ERNEST   Across the River and into the Trees. London: Cape, (1950). Cloth, first edition. A fine, bright copy in dust jacket. Reese 20-506 1983 $65

HEMINGWAY, ERNEST   Cinquante Mille Dollars. Paris, (1928). 8vo, wraps. First French edition (small paper). Fine. In Our Time 156-375 1983 $125

HEMINGWAY, ERNEST   The Collected Poems of... N.p., n.d.
Unauthorized edition. Frontis. and photo back cover of Hemingway,
near fine. Quill & Brush 54-633 1983 $35

HEMINGWAY, ERNEST   Death in the Afternoon. NY, 1932. Edges
rubbed and slightly frayed, spine lettering lightly rubbed, front hinge
cracked, good, owner's name. Quill & Brush 54-629 1983 $25

HEMINGWAY, ERNEST   A Farewell to Arms. New York:
Scribners, 1929. 1st ed., 1st issue. Orig. black cloth, gold
labels. Fine fresh copy in slightly rubbed dj. Jenkins 155-546
1983 $425

HEMINGWAY, ERNEST   A Farewell to Arms. New York, 1929.
8vo. Cloth. Dust jacket has some chipping to the top and bottom
edge of the spine. A fine copy. In Our Time 156-376 1983 $350

HEMINGWAY, ERNEST   A Farewell to Arms. N.Y., Scribner,
1929. First edition, second issue with legal disclaimer. Dust
jacket (slight rubbing & tiny nicks) very good - fine. Houle 22-465
1983 $350

HEMINGWAY, ERNEST   A Farewell To Arms. New York: Charles
Scribner's Sons, 1929. First edition, first issue. 8vo. Orig.
cloth. Dust jacket. Slightly worn and dust-soiled jacket. Very
good copy. Jaffe 1-139 1983 $250

HEMINGWAY, ERNEST   A Farewell to Arms. New York, 1948.
8vo. Cloth. Illustrations by Daniel Rasmusson. 1st illus. ed.
(bound in grey cloth, paper label on spine-rubbed). Minus rubbing
to label a fine copy in lightly nicked slipcase box. In Our Time
156-380 1983 $100

HEMINGWAY, ERNEST   A Farewell to Arms. N.Y., 1948. First
illus. edition (by D. Rasmusson). Cloth. Label presenting book glued
to inside front cover. Newspaper clipping taped to rear fly. Paper
spine label wearing along edges. Slipcase a little worn and darkened.
King 45-197 1983 $50

HEMINGWAY, ERNEST   The Fifth Column and the First Forty-
Nine Stories. New York, 1938. 8vo. Cloth. This copy for review
with slip from publisher laid in. A vg-fine copy in rubbed but intact dj. In Our Time 156-378 1983 $375

HEMINGWAY, ERNEST   For Whom the Bells Toll. New York,
1940. 8vo. Cloth. Jacket is intact with some rubbing around the
edges. A fine copy in 1st issue jacket. In Our Time 156-379 1983
$150

HEMINGWAY, ERNEST   For Whom the Bell Tolls. N.Y.,
Scribner, 1940. First edition, first issue. Dust jacket (first
state), a few short tears and nicks, else very good. Houle 21-409
1983 $125

HEMINGWAY, ERNEST   For Whom the Bell Tolls. NY, 1940.
First state, endpapers slightly stained, spine slightly soiled, else
good or better in worn, chipped, first state dustwrapper, owner's
name. Quill & Brush 54-630 1983 $50

HEMINGWAY, ERNEST   For Whom the Bell Tolls. New York:
Scribners, 1940. 1st ed. Orig. cloth, dj. Dj in first state with
photographer's name absent; tape marks on dj flaps, some edge repairs. Jenkins 155-547 1983 $40

HEMINGWAY, ERNEST   For Whom the Bell Tolls. New York:
Scribners, 1940. 1st ed. Dj quite chipped. Jenkins 155-548 1983
$30

HEMINGWAY, ERNEST   Green Hills of Africa. N.Y., Scribner,
1935. First edition. Green cloth extremely fresh with only very
trifling evidence of fading. Dust jacket (light rubbing). Zane
Grey's copy with his stamp. Fine. Houle 22-467 1983 $425

HEMINGWAY, ERNEST   Green Hills of Africa. New York:
Charles Scribner's Sons, 1935. First edition. 8vo. Orig. cloth.
Dust jacket. Decorations by Edward Shenton. The usual slight
fading at spine, otherwise a fine copy. Jaffe 1-140 1983 $225

HEMINGWAY, ERNEST   In Our Time. Paris: Three Mountains
Press, 1924. Quarto. Orig. printed boards. First edition. One of
only 170 numbered copies. A toe of the spine reattached. One corner
is somewhat bruised. Near fine copy. Reese 20-503 1983 $3,500

HEMINGWAY, ERNEST   In Our Time. London, 1926. First
edition. Light foxing to edges, spine of dustwrapper very slightly
sunned, but a fine copy. Gekoski 2-84 1983 £325

HEMINGWAY, ERNEST   In Our Time. New York: Boni & Liveright, 1925. First edition. 8vo. Orig. cloth. Dust jacket.
Heavily tape-repaired jacket. A very good copy. Jaffe 1-137 1983
$450

HEMINGWAY, ERNEST   Islands in the Stream. London, 1970.
8vo. Wraps. 1st English ed. Uncorrected proof copy in the published dj. Jacket has some light wear, else fine. In Our Time
156-382 1983 $275

HEMINGWAY, ERNEST   The Old Man and The Sea. New York:
Charles Scribner's Sons, 1952. First edition. 8vo. Orig. cloth.
Dust jacket. Mint copy. Jaffe 1-143 1983 $125

HEMINGWAY, ERNEST   The Old Man and The Sea. NY, 1952.
Cover has few very minor stains, edges very slightly rubbed, else fine
in very bright dustwrapper, fine but for chip out of bottom right edge
of front panel. Dustwrapper has drawing by "A", with blue photograph
of Hemingway on rear panel. Quill & Brush 54-634 1983 $100

HEMINGWAY, ERNEST   The Spanish Earth. Cleveland: The J. B.
Savage Company, 1928. First edition, first issue with the "banner"
endpapers. 8vo. Orig. pictorial cloth, glassine dust jacket. Out of
a total edition of 1000 copies, 50-100 copies were issued with pictorial
endpapers. Jacket a trifle rubbed, otherwise a mint copy. Jaffe 1-142
1983 $850

HEMINGWAY, ERNEST   Spanish Earth. Cleveland, Savage,
1938. First edition, second issue (plain endpapers). Pictorial tan
cloth. Illus. by Fredrick Russell. Very good - fine. Houle 22-1213
1983 $225

HEMINGWAY, ERNEST   To Have and Have Not. New York:
Charles Scribner's Sons, 1937. First edition. 8vo. Orig. cloth.
Dust jacket. Fine copy. Jaffe 1-141 1983 $225

HEMINGWAY, ERNEST   To Have and Have Not. London, (1937).
First English edition. 8vo, blue cloth. Argosy 714-366 1983 $35

HEMINGWAY, ERNEST   The Torrents of Spring. New York:
Charles Scribner's Sons, 1926. First edition. 8vo. Orig. cloth.
Dust jacket. Former owner's bold signature on front free endpaper,
extremities of jacket slightly chipped, otherwise a very good copy.
Jaffe 1-138 1983 $450

HEMINGWAY, ERNEST   The Torrents of Spring. NY, 1926. Book-
dealer's stamp on front fly and rear pastedown, cover lightly soiled
and stained, very good. Quill & Brush 54-636 1983 $200

HEMINGWAY, ERNEST   Winner Take Nothing. N.Y., Scribner,
1923. First edition. Dust jacket (lacking about 2 inch piece at
lower corner of front). Some light foxing at edges, else a very good
copy with the gold labels on spines. Houle 22-468 1983 $175

HEMINGWAY, ERNEST   Winner Take Nothing. New York, 1933.
8vo. Cloth. Jacket is intact but some light scuffing. A fine copy
in dj. In Our Time 156-377 1983 $375

HEMINGWAY, ERNEST   Winner Take Nothing. NY, 1933. Bright
in bright, very good or better dustwrapper that is slightly rubbed and
frayed along edges and lightly skinned at rear panel. Quill & Brush
54-638 1983 $300

HEMINGWAY, ERNEST   Winner Take Nothing. N.Y., Scribners,
1923. First edition. Dust jacket (lacking a 2" piece at lower
front corner). Occasional light foxing. The gold labels bright.
Houle 21-411 1983 $175

HEMINGWAY, ERNEST   Winner Take Nothing. NY, 1933. First
edition. Cloth, sm. ink name and address. Bottom edge of covers
paint-stained, spine label a bit rubbed else very good. In rather
chipped dust wrapper. King 46-301 1983 $150

HEMINGWAY, JOSEPH   Panorama of the Beauties, Curiosities, and Antiquities of North Wales. R. Groombridge, 1845. With a folding coloured engraved map and 4 engraved plates, large 12mo, orig. cloth, gilt, a fine copy. Fenning 61-201 1983 £26.50

HEMON, LOUIS   Maria Chapdelaine. Montreal: Editions La Fregate, 1969. 4to. 29cm. 25 plates from drawings by Suzor Cote, limited to 250 copies. Bound in full linen with colour plates laid down on the upper cover, in wood folder with leather ties and oval see-through on the upper boards, the whole enclosed in cloth folder box. Fine. Scarce. McGahern 54-84 1983 $300

HEMPEL, WALTHER   Gasanalytische Methoden. Braun-schweig: Vieweg, 1890. Second edition. 8vo. Cont. half morocco. Numerous wood engraved illus. Errata leaf. Spine worn, inter-nally a very good copy. Zeitlin 264-199 1983 $50

HENDERSON, ARCHIBALD   Bernard Shaw. New York & London: Appleton, 1932. Photographs. First edition. Cloth. Spine slightly dull, else a very good copy. Reese 20-882 1983 $20

HENDERSON, GEORGE F. R.   Stonewall Jackson. London, 1898. First edition. 8vo, orig. cloth. Portrait frontis. in vol. 1, port. plate and 33 maps (31 folding). 2 vols. Spines faded. Some very light foxing. Good. Edwards 1042-217 1983 £90

HENDERSON, GEORGE F. R.   Stonewall Jackson and the American Civil War. London, 1898. Portraits, maps, plans. 2 vols., 8vo. 1st ed. Ex-library, endpapers loose. Morrill 286-611 1983 $55

HENDERSON, GEORGE WYLIE   Jule. NY, (1946). Cover very slightly stained, very good in lightly frayed and chipped dustwrapper. Quill & Brush 54-639 1983 $40

HENDERSON, JOHN   Letters and Poems, by the late Mr. John Henderson. London: printed for J. Johnson, 1786. 8vo, cont. calf (rubbed, covers stained). 1st edition. Errata leaf at the end. Half-title present; light waterstains. Ximenes 64-262 1983 $200

HENDERSON, JOHN   Letters and Poems by the late Mr. John Henderson. Dublin: printed for Messrs. Byrne, Lewis, Jones, and Moore, 1786. 12mo, old boards (loose). First Irish edition. Rare. An uncut copy. Ximenes 64-263 1983 $150

HENDERSON, KEITH   Letters to Helen. London, 1917. First edition. 12 tissue-guarded colour plates by the author. Corners bruised. Very good. Jolliffe 26-262 1983 £25

HENDERSON, ROBERT   State of the Union. Sacramento, 1861. Dbd. First edition. Ginsberg 47-107 1983 $35

HENDERSON, T. F.   The Casket Letters and Mary Queen of Scots. Edinburgh, 1890. 8vo, cloth. Bickersteth 77-121 1983 £20

HENDERSON, T. F.   Mary Queen of Scots, her Environment and her Tragedy, a Biography. 1905. 2 vols., 8vo, 102 plates, orig. cloth gilt, slightly soiled. Bickersteth 77-122 1983 £24

HENDERSON, WILLIAM   Notes and reminiscences of my life as an angler. London: Spottiswoode, 1876. First edition, printed "for private circulation only." 8vo. Orig. orange-brown cloth. With a mounted photograph frontis., and five plates, engraved by Edmund Evans after illus. by Clement Burlison. Ximenes 63-558 1983 $80

HENDRICKS, GORDON   The Photographs of Thomas Eakins. New York: Grossmann, 1972. 291 photographs. Oblong 4to. Cloth. Ars Libri 32-199 1983 $100

HENEBRY, RICHARD   A Handbook of Irish Music. Cork, 1928. First edition, with portrait and many music examples, roy. 8vo, orig. cloth. Fenning 60-170 1983 £35

HENEFREY, ARTHUR   Outlines of the Natural History of Europe. 1852. First edition, with a folding map, 8vo, orig. green cloth, gilt, by Remnant & Edmonds, with their ticket. Fenning 60-171 1983 £10.50

HENEKER, DOROTHY A.   The Seigniorial Regime in Canada. 1927. 18 1/2cm. Brown cloth. Very good copy. McGahern 54-85 1983 $25

HENING, WILLIAM WALTER   The Statutes at Large. New York, Richmond, and Philadelphia, 1819-1823. 8vo, cont. full calf, spines generally worn; some leaves in 2 vols. brittle at fore-edges. 13 vols. Argosy 716-591 1983 $450

HENKEL, M. D.   Catalogue van de nederlandsche Teekeningen in het Rijksmuseum te Amsterdam. 's-Gravenhage: Algemeene Landsdrukkerij, 1943. 179 plates. 4to. Cloth. Ars Libri 32-559 1983 $175

HENLEY, J.   An Introduction to an English Grammar... London: J. Roberts, 1726. First edition. 8vo. 19th Century calf Russia. Heath 48-40 1983 £75

HENLEY, WILLIAM ERNEST   A Century of Artist. Glasgow, 1889. First edition. One of 215 lagre paper copies, with the plates on japanese. Folio. Preliminaries a little foxed. Very nice. Rota 230-215 1983 £52

HENLEY, WILLIAM ERNEST   Hawthorn and Lavender. N.Y.: Harper & Brothers, 1901. Orig. decorated cloth. First American edition. Presentation copy from the author to his son-in-law, inscribed on the front free endpaper "W.E.H. to W.B. (To show him what he must never do). 3/3/1902." Fine copy. MacManus 278-2548 1983 $100

HENLEY, WILLIAM ERNEST   Hawthorn and Lavender. London: David Nutt, 1901. Orig. cloth. First edition. MacManus 278-2547 1983 $25

HENLEY, WILLIAM ERNEST   London Voluntaries. London: David Nutt, 1893. First edition. Orig. cloth. Spine a bit worn, with some fading to the free endpapers, otherwise a very good copy. MacManus 278-2549 1983 $20

HENLEY, WILLIAM ERNEST   Song of Speed. London: David Nutt, 1903. Orig. decorated cloth. First edition. Spine slightly faded, with some foxing to the first few pages, otherwise a very good copy. MacManus 278-2550 1983 $45

HENNEDY, R.   The Clydesdale Flora. Glasgow, 1878. 4th edition, portrait, 8 plates, cr. 8vo, cloth. Wheldon 160-1603 1983 £12

HENNING, HANS   Ernst Mach. Leipzig: J. A. Barth, 1915. First edition. Library bookplate. Gach 94-233 1983 $30

HENNINGSEN, CHARLES FREDERICK   Revelations of Russia. 1844. 2 vols., 2 engraved plates, folding map, good ex-library copy, spine of volume 1 relaid. K Books 307-96 1983 £46

HENOT, GEORGE   The Battles of Life. London: Wyman, 1884. First edition in English. 3 vols. Orig. cloth. This copy in red publisher's cloth and taller than the usual brown cloth sets. Very good. MacManus 279-4054 1983 $75

HENOT, GEORGE   The Battles of Life. London: Wyman, 1884. 3 vols., orig. cloth. First edition in English. Bindings a bit rubbed; otherwise a good set. MacManus 278-2551 1983 $50

HENRY VIII, KING OF ENGLAND   Miscellaneous Writings of... The Golden Cockerel Press, 1924. Frontis. Vellum backed boards. Uncit. Corners bumped, covers heavily soiled. Limited to 365 numbered copies. King 45-183 1983 $65

HENRY, ALEXANDER   Travel and Adventures in Canada and the Indian Territories, Between the Year 1760 and the Year 1776. New York, 1809. Portrait, half leather and boards. Very good. Reese 18-323 1983 $875

HENRY, F.   A Guide from the English Language to the French or a French Grammar... Bristol: by Biggs & Cottle, 1799. First edition. 8vo. Cont. sheep. Slight damage at corner of title. Heath 48-323 1983 £45

HENTY, GEORGE ALFRED   Battles of the Nineteenth Century.
Cassell, n.d. (ca.1901). 7 vols. 4to. Colour plates & a vast number
of illus. Little loose. Green cloth pictorial gilt. Rubbed. Special
edition, available by subscription only. Greer 39-76 1983 £45

HENRY, JOHN JOSEPH   An Accurate and Interesting Account of
the Hardships and Sufferings of that Band of Heroes, who traversed
the Wilderness in the Campaign against Quebec in 1775. Lancaster:
William Greer, 1812. 1st ed., 12mo, orig. calf, morocco label.
Copyright notice pasted on verso of title page. Discreet private
library stamp on final leaf of text. Text age-browned as usual.
Catalogue entry neatly pasted inside front cover, else an exceptionally
good copy. Trebizond 18-132 1983 $475

HENRY, JOHN JOSEPH   An Accurate and Interesting Account
of the Hardships and Sufferings of that Band of Heroes...1775.
Lancaster, 1812. Calf, expertly rebacked, good. Reese 18-379 1983
$225

HENRY, MATTHEW   S. History of the Lehigh Valley...
Easton, Pa., 1860. Numerous plates. Binding rubbed at extremities.
Some foxing, particularly on plates. First edition. Felcone 22-188
1983 $85

HENRY, O., PSEUD.
Please turn to
PORTER, WILLIAM SYDNEY

HENRY, PATRICK   The Bank Dinner, an Expose of the Court
Party in Kentucky, and the Curtain Drawn from the Holy Alliance of
America. Frankfort, (Ky).: Amos Kendall, 1824. 1st edition,
half morocco. Jenkins 151-164 1983 $150

HENRY, ROBERT M.   The Evolution of Sinn Fein. Dublin:
The Talbot Press, 1920. First edition, 8vo, orig. cloth. Fenning 60-
172 1983 £12.50

HENRY, ROBERT SELPH   "First With The Most" Forrest.
Indianapolis (1944). First edition, Bedford edition, limited
and signed. Good in shattered dust wrapper. King 46-57 1983 $25

HENRY, ROBERT SELPH   The Story of the Confederacy.
Indianapolis (1931). Inscribed and signed by the author on the
dedication page. Spine tips frayed and stained, else good.
Shattered dust wrappers. King 46-58 1983 $25

HENRY, STUART O.   Conquering Our Great American Plains.
New York, (1930). Plates and map. First edition. Light wear to
spine. Jenkins 153-250 1983 $40

HENRY, WILLIAM   An Epitome of Chemistry, in Three
Parts. Edinburgh: Ballantyne, 1806. Fourth edition. 8vo.
Cont. polished calf. 8 folding engraved plates. Very good copy.
Zeitlin 264-200 1983 $160

HENRY, WILLIAM WIRT   Patrick Henry, Life, Correspondence,
and Speeches. NY 1891. First edition, limited to 1100 sets. 3 vols.
Cloth, t.e.g., light wear. King 46-103 1983 $75

HENRY ERKINS STUDIOS   New York Plaisance. (New York, 1908).
Illustrated series. 4to, fine ads. Morrill 290-366 1983 $75

HENRY STEVENS SONS AND STILES.   Catalog No. 4, relating to the
United States, Canada... London, 1928. Numerous illus. and biblio-
graphical annotations. Orig. wrappers, few marginal pencil notations.
Clark 741-69 1983 $50

HENSHALL, JAMES A.   Bass, Pike, Perch and Others. N.Y.,
1903. First edition. 4to, illus. with 20 plates. 3/4 green morocco
over marbled boards, spine stamped and decorated in gilt, covers
ruled in gilt. One of 100 numbered deluxe copies on large paper.
T.e.g., marbled endpapers, uncut and unopened. Fine copy. Houle 22-
1054 1983 $300

HENSLOW, G.   The Origin of Floral Structures. 1888.
8vo, cloth, 88 illustrations. Wheldon 160-1529 1983 £12

HENSLOWE, LEONARD   Things Have Changed. London, 1930.
First English edition. Edges slightly spotted. Nicked and slightly
dusty dustwrapper darkened at the spine. Very good. Jolliffe 26-580
1983 £45

HENTSCHEL, WALTER   Peter Breuer. Eine spatgotische
Bilschnitzerwerkstatt. Berlin: Union Verlag, 1952. Second edition.
120 illus. 4to. Boards, 1/4 cloth. Ars Libri 32-66 1983 $50

HENTY, GEORGE ALFRED   At Agincourt. London, 1897. First
edition. Good reading copy. Rota 231-314 1983 £15

HENTY, GEORGE ALFRED   Condemned as a Nihilist. London, 1893.
First English edition. Orig. green cloth. Covers faded and marked.
A few leaves slightly soiled. Inscription on half-title page. Very
good. Rota 230-285 1983 £30

HENTY, GEORGE ALFRED   A Knight of the White Cross. New York,
1895. First edition. Extremities a little rubbed. Hinges weak.
Inscriptions on flyleaf. Very good. Rota 230-286 1983 £30

HENWOOD, GEO   Four Lectures on Geology and Mining...
London, 1855. 8vo. Orig. cloth. Large folding plate. Signature
of John Phillips on the flyleaf at the end. Gurney JJ-169 1983
£20

HEPWORTH, THOMAS CRADOCK   The Book of the Lantern. London, 1888.
1st ed. Illus. Small 8vo, ads for lanterns. Morrill 288-610 1983
$65

HERAUD, J. A.   Tottenham; a Poem. Printed for the
author, 1820. First edition, half title. Uncut. Modern half dark
blue morocco, blue cloth boards. Jarndyce 31-860 1983 £42

HERBERT, ALAN PATRICK   Big Ben. London: Methuen & Co., Ltd.,
(1946). Orig. wraps. First edition. Presentation copy, inscribed on
the title-page "To A.E.W. Mason with salutes from A.P. Herbert July 17,
1946." Fine copy. MacManus 278-2557 1983 $65

HERBERT, ALAN PATRICK   Double Demon (in) Four One-Act Plays.
Oxford: Basil Blackwell, 1923. First edition. One of only 50 copies
printed on Kelmscott hand-made paper and signed by Herbert. F. Sladen
Smith, Beatrice Mayor, and Helen Simpson have also signed the book.
MacManus 278-2562 1983 $75

HERBERT, ALAN PATRICK   Fat King Melon and Princess Caraway.
London: Oxford University Press, (1927). Orig. wraps. First
edition, very good copy. MacManus 278-2563 1983 $25

HERBERT, ALAN PATRICK   Fat King Melon & Princess Caraway.
London, n.d. 12mo. Wraps. As new copy. In Our Time 156-387 1983
$25

HERBERT, ALAN PATRICK   Half-Hours at Helles. Oxford: B.H.
Blackwell, 1916. Orig. wraps. First edition. Wraps. a bit worn, but
a good copy. MacManus 278-2564 1983 $40

HERBERT, ALAN PATRICK   Helen. London, (1932). 8vo. Cloth.
A fine copy in lightly spotted dj. In Our Time 156-386 1983 $35

HERBERT, ALAN PATRICK   The House by the River. London: Methuen
& Co., Ltd., (1920). Orig. cloth, dust jacket (a bit worn). First
edition. Inscribed on the title-page by the author. Fine copy in
dust jacket. MacManus 278-2567 1983 $45

HERBERT, ALAN PATRICK   Laughing Ann and Other Poems. London:
T. Fisher Unwin Ltd., (1925). Orig. cloth, dust jacket (chipped).
First edition. Inscribed on the half-title "All good wishes from
A.P. Herbert." Fine copy. MacManus 278-2570 1983 $30

HERBERT, ALAN PATRICK   Light Articles Only. London: Methuen &
Co., Ltd., (1921). Illus. by Geo. Morrow. Orig. cloth. First edition.
Inscribed by the author. Very good copy. MacManus 278-2575 1983
$25

HERBERT, ALAN PATRICK   More Misleading Cases. London: Methuen & Co., (1930). 12mo, orig. cloth, dust jacket (a little worn). First edition, presentation copy, inscribed on the title-page to "Edgar Wallace from A.P. Herbert, October 1930." Very good copy. MacManus 278-2579 1983 $60

HERBERT, ALAN PATRICK   No Boats on the River. London, 1932. First edition. Inscribed on the title-page to Stanley Baldwin, the Prime Minister. On the front paste-down a bookplate states that this copy is sent with the compliments of the author; on it Herbert has written "As this is not about beer I hope you will lead your party united to the boats and support me! A.P.H." Internally very good, but covers are very worn, bumped and soiled. Gekoski 2-85 1983 £75

HERBERT, ALAN PATRICK   The Old Flame. London: Methuen & Co. Ltd., (1925). Orig. cloth, dust jacket (a little soiled, top of spine chipped). First edition. Inscribed on the title-page "All good wishes from A.P. Herbert." Fine copy. MacManus 278-2582 1983 $35

HERBERT, ALAN PATRICK   Plain Jane. London, 1927. 8vo. Cloth. A vg-fine copy. In Our Time 156-384 1983 $25

HERBERT, ALAN PATRICK   Play Hours with Pegasus. Oxford: B.H. Blackwell, (1912). 12mo, orig. wraps. First edition. Lightly soiled, but a good copy. MacManus 278-2583 1983 $50

HERBERT, ALAN PATRICK   Poor Poems and Rotten Rhymes. Winchester: P. & G. Wells, Booksellers to Winchester College, 1910. First edition. A few tiny tears to back wraps., otherwise an exceptionally fine copy. MacManus 278-2584 1983 $150

HERBERT, ALAN PATRICK   The Red Pen. London: The Cornwall Press, (1927). Orig. wraps., first edition, very good copy. MacManus 278-2585 1983 $20

HERBERT, ALAN PATRICK   She-Shanties. London: T. Fisher Unwin Ltd., (1926). Illus. by A. K. Zinkeisen. Orig. cloth. First edition. Very good. MacManus 278-2587 1983 $20

HERBERT, ALAN PATRICK   "Tinker Tailor..." London: Methuen & Co., (1922). Illus. by George Morrow. Orig. cloth-backed pictorial boards. First edition. Extremities very slightly worn, but a fine copy. MacManus 278-2590 1983 $25

HERBERT, ALAN PATRICK   Topsy Turvey. London, (1947). 12mo. Cloth. A fine copy in dj which has some minimal wear. In Our Time 156-388 1983 $25

HERBERT, ALAN PATRICK   Topsy, M.P. London: Ernest Benn Limited, (1929). Orig. cloth. First edition. Presentation copy, inscribed on the half-title to "H.G. Wells with respect from Alan Herbert April 26th 1929." With Well's tiny bookplate on the front endsheet. Covers a little soiled, but a good copy. MacManus 278-2591 1983 $65

HERBERT, ALAN PATRICK   The Water Gipsies. London, (1930). Very good in slightly chipped dust wrapper. Quill & Brush 54-640 1983 $30

HERBERT, ALAN PATRICK   The Water Gipsies. London (1930). 8vo. Cloth. Jacket has some light fading on the spine. A fine copy. In Our Time 156-385 1983 $30

HERBERT, ALAN PATRICK   The Water Gypsies. London: Methuen, (1930). 1st ed. Bright green cloth. Fine in red and yellow dj. Very scarce. Bradley 63-61 1983 $30

HERBERT, ALAN PATRICK   The Wherefore and the Why. London: Methuen & Co., (1921). Illus. by Geo. Morrow. Orig. cloth-backed pictorial boards. First edition. Boards a little faded, rubbed as usual, but a good copy. MacManus 278-2597 1983 $25

HERBERT, CHARLES   Italy and Italian Literature. For Sherwood, Gilbert & Piper, 1835. First edition. Errata slip, 8vo. Orig. cloth-backed boards, with printed paper spine label. Small snag in headband, otherwise a nice copy. Fenning 60-173 1983 £38.50

HERBERT, FRANK   God Emperor of Dune. NY, (1981). Limited to 750 specially bound, numbered and signed copies, fine in fine slipcase. Quill & Brush 54-641 1983 $90

HERBERT, GEORGE   Facsimile of The Temple. Gresham Press for T. Fisher Unwin, 1883. Facsimile reprint of the First Edition. Fourth Edition. Small 8vo, contemporary binding by Riviere of mottled calf gilt, spine gilt and with morocco label, marbled endpapers, a.e.g., slight rubbing, inscription. Deighton 3-169 1983 £36

HERBERT, GEORGE   Poetical Works. Nisbet, 1856. Illus. by Birket Foster, John Clayton & Henry Noel Humphreys, engr'd by Edmund Evans, Dalziel Bros. & H.N. Woods. Ornamentation by Henry Noel Humphreys. Brown morocco grain cloth gilt, bevelled boards, a.e.g., vg. Hodgkins 27-285 1983 £25

HERBERT, GEORGE   The Temple, Sacred Poems and Private Ejaculations. Nonesuch Press, 1927. Front. Tapestry cloth. No. 1355 of 1,500. Jarndyce 31-993 1983 £30

HERBERT, GEORGE   Works. Oxford, Clarendon Press, 1941. Thick 8vo, facs. frontis. Full navy morocco by Gaston Pilon, spine decorated in gilt, cover ruled in gilt, wide, extra-gilt inner dentelles, t.e.g., marbled endpapers. Fine. Houle 22-472 1983 $95

HERBERT, HENRY   A fortnight's journal. London: Swale, 1838. First edition. 8vo. Orig. purple cloth. Folding lithographed frontis. Ximenes 63-624 1983 $75

HERBERT, HENRY ARTHUR   The Life of Edward, Lord Herbert of Cherbury. London: J. Dodsley, 1770. 4to, with a folding engraved frontis. of the author. Later calf, worn, over marbled boards; with a one inch chip at top of spine. Outer hinges cracked. Karmiole 72-54 1983 $85

HERBERT, HENRY WILLIAM   American Game in Its Seasons. New York, 1853. First edition. Illustrated by author. Cloth. Lightly rubbed at corners, few small spots on covers. Bradley 65-72 1983 $85

HERBERT, HENRY WILLIAM   Frank Forester's Field Sports of the United States. New York, ca. 1875. New edition. 2 vols., illus. Orig. cloth, gilt-decorated spines. K Books 307-97 1983 £35

HERBERT, HENRY WILLIAM   Frank Forester's Fish and Fishing of the United States and British Provinces of North America. NY: W.A. Townsend & Co., 1859. With 12 plates, (one color) and dozens of text wood engravings. Orig. dec. gilt-stamped cloth. Karmiole 74-45 1983 $85

HERBERT, HENRY WILLIAM   Frank Forester's Fish and Fishing of the United States and British Provinces of North America. New York, 1850. Plates by the author. Cloth, marginal waterstain in upper corner of about half the text. First edition. Felcone 21-55 1983 $85

HERBERT, HENRY WILLIAM   Frank Forester's Horse and Horsemanship of the United States and British Provinces of North America. N.Y., Stringer & Townsend, 1857. 2 vls. 4to. Extra engraved vignette titles in each vol., 14 engraved plates (all on India paper & mounted), 10 inserted double-page pedigress. Orig. pictorial cloth, stamped in gold & blind. 1st ed. Nice, bright condition. O'Neal 50-27 1983 $125

HERBERT, HENRY WILLIAM   The Quorndon Hounds. Philadelphia, 1852. Frontis. and 3 plates. No ads. Later 3/4 morocco. Some wear to extremities and scattered foxing. First edition. Felcone 21-56 1983 $150

HERBERT, ISAAC   Robert the Deuyll. A metrical romance, from an illuminated manuscript. London: printed for I. Herbert, 1798. Slim 8vo. 19th-century calf, gilt. 14 full-page aquatint plates. Joints slightly worn. A little browned. Ximenes 63-257 1983 $180

HERBERT, JOHN ALEXANDER   Illuminated Manuscripts. London, (1911). 1st ed. 51 plates. Tall 8vo. Ex-library; rebacked with typewritten label; inner hinges repaired. Morrill 289-359 1983 $30

HERBERT, PAUL   Stray Leaves. London: John Lane, The
Bodley Head, 1906. First edition. Orig. cloth. Dust jacket (faded
and slightly worn, with a few small tears). Fine. MacManus 278-
1775 1983 $25

HERBERT, THOMAS   Some Years Travels into Divers Parts
of Africa, and Asia the Great. London: R. Scot, T. Basset, J.
Wright and R. Chiswell, 1677. Folio. With an engraved title,
2 full-page plates and 55 engraved text illus., including maps,
pictures of birds, fish, people, etc. Index. Bound in old calf,
rebacked. Red leather spine label. Binding sl. rubbed. Karmiole
76-104 1983 $650

HERBERT, THOMAS   Theodore Roosevelt Typical American.
Atlanta: R.L. Phillips Pub. Co., 1919. Orig. cloth with illus.
Tipped in the front is a notice on "How to Sell the Life of Theodore
Roosevelt." Jenkins 152-364 1983 $35

HERBERT, WILLIAM   Helga. A Poem in Seven Cantos.
Murray, 1815. First edition, tall 8vo, advt. leaf, errata leaf,
uncut in near contemporary publishers cloth, manuscript label, slight
spotting throughout, but a very good tall copy. Deighton 3-170
1983 £48

HERDING, J. F.   Elemente der Experimentalchemie...
Hamburg & Leipzig: L. Voss, 1898. 8vo. Orig. printed wrappers.
Back cover detached, defect to spine, internally very good copy.
Rare. Zeitlin 264-201 1983 $80

HEREDIA, PEDRO MAGUEL   Opera Medica. Lugduni: Borde et al,
1665. 4 parts in 2 vols. Thick folio, cont. vellum, leather backs,
(bindings worn). First edition. Argosy 713-259 1983 $250

HERE'S New England. Boston, 1939. Map, illus., backstrip faded.
Clark 741-8 1983 $21

HERFORD, OLIVER   Artful Anticks. Gay & Bird, 1894.
Frontis. & numerous text illus. by author. Ochre illus. cloth, back-
strip sl. faded, free eps. sl. discol'd, foxing pp.97-99, nice copy.
Hodgkins 27-96 1983 £15

HERFORD, OLIVER   Overheard in a Garden. N.Y., Scribner,
1900. Col. frontis. & numerous b&w illus.
Colour pictorial bds., t.e.g. others uncut, bkstrip discol'd & corners
sl. rubbed, very good. Hodgkins 27-100 1983 £10.50

HERGESHEIMER, JOSEPH   Java Head. New York: Knopf, 1946.
Cloth. First this edition, with typography, design, binding, and
vignettes by Dwiggins. Dust jacket. Reese 20-346 1983 $25

HERGESHEIMER, JOSEPH   The Presbyterian Child. New York, 1923.
8vo, decorated boards and cloth, slipcase. One of 950 copies
printed by William E. Rudge and signed by the author. First edition.
Duschnes 240-191 1983 $50

HERIOT, ARCHIBALD   Memoirs of George Heriot, Jeweller to
King James VI... Edinburgh, 1822. Small 8vo. Old calf, repaired.
Frontis. and 4 plates. Gurney JJ-170 1983 £30

HERIOT, GEORGE   Travels through the Canadas. London:
Printed for Richard Phillips, 1807. 4to. 26 1/2cm. First edition.
With 27 uncoloured aquatint plates by Stadler and Lewis after Heriot
(6 being double folding) and a folding coloured map. Some offsetting
from the plates as usual. Orig. titsue guards. Bound in full cont.
calf boards, rebacked, with green crushed morocco label. McGahern
54-86 1983 $2,500

HERMANIN, FEDERICO   Giambattista Piranesi, architetto ed
incisore. Torinto: E. Celanza, 1915. 50 plates. 4to. Wrappers.
From the library of Helen, Queen of Italy. Ars Libri 33-278 1983
$55

HERMANIN, FEDERICO   Gli artisti italiani in Germania. Vol.
II: Gli scultori, gli stuccatori, i ceramisti. (L'Opera del Genio
Italiano all'Estero. Serie prima.) Roma, (1935). Lg. 4to, text
illus., 186 plates. Wraps, d.j. Edition limited to 500 copies.
Ars Libri SB 26-101 1983 $-25

HERMANIN, FEDERICO   Luigi Galli pittore. Torino: E.
Celanza, 1924. 42 plates. 4to. Boards. Ars Libri 33-477 1983
$45

HERMANIN, FEDERICO   Il mito di Giorgione. Spoleto:
Claudio Argentieri, 1933. 66 illus. 4to. Cloth. Ars Libri
33-168 1983 $40

HERNDON, WILLIAM H.   Herndon's Lincoln. Chicago, (1889).
1st ed, many illus. & ports., 3 vols, orig. cloth, pict. spine,
g.t. Argosy 710-261 1983 $175

HERNDON, WILLIAM L.   Exploration of the Valley of the Amazon.
Washington: Taylor & Maury, 1854. Folding map, many lithos.,
blindstamped cloth, lightly foxed. Argosy 710-502 1983 $45

HERO and Leander. London, (1949). 8vo., two-toned buckram, gilt
top, eleven copper engravings by John Buckland Wright. One of 400
copies, spine faded. Duschnes 240-88 1983 $125

HERODIAN   Herodiani Historiarum Libri 8,
Recogniti & notis illustrata. Oxoniae, E Theatro Sheldoniano, 1678.
8vo, cont. calf, rebacked in morocco, without frontis. Ravenstree
94-53 1983 $25

AN HEROIC Address to old Drury, from a new renter. London: printed
for Becket and Porter, 1812. 4to, disbound, 1st ed. Fine copy. Rare.
Ximenes 64-264 1983 $150

AN HEROIC epistle to the Right Honourable Lord Viscount Sackville.
London: Kearsley, 1783. First edition. 4to. Disbound. Ximenes
63-367 1983 $90

HEROLD, JACQUES   Louis-Marin Bonnet (1736-1793). Catalogue de l'oeuvre grave. Paris: Maurice Rousseau, 1935. 32 heliotype plates with 68 illus. 9 text illus. 4to. Wrappers. Uncut.
Ars Libri 32-49 1983 $250

HEROLD, M.   Exercitationes de Animalium Vertebris
Carentium in Ovo Formatione. Marburg, 1824. Part 1. 2 coloured
plates and 2 duplicates plain, folio, half morocco. Wheldon 160-
1287 1983 £20

HERRERA, ANTONIO DE   The General History of the Vast Continent and Islands of America... London, 1724-26. 6 vols., complete,
with 3 folding engraved maps. 3 portraits, 13 engraved plates, titles
printed in red and black. Full contemp. gilt armorial calf (2 vols.
expertly rebacked). Interiors crisp and clean. First English ed.
Jenkins 153-251 1983 $2000

HERRERA, ANTONIO DE   The General History of the Vast Continent
and Islands of America. London: Printed for Wood & Woodward, 1740.
Second English edition. 6 vols. 18 plates. Last 3 vols. include a
leaf of ads. Old sprinkled calf, expertly rebacked. Internally nearly
pristine with the folding plates untorn and clean. Dawson 471-114
1983 $1,250

HERRERA, GABRIEL A. DE   Agricultura General de Gabriel Alonso
de Herrera... Madrid: a la Imprenta Real, 1818-9. 4 vols. Small 4to.
Cont. tree calf gilt. Heath 48-5 1983 £90

HERRICK, CLARENCE LUTHER (1858-1904)   The Metaphysics of a
Naturalist. Granville, Oh.: 1910. Tall 8vo. Orig. boards.
Library bookplate and label. Gach 95-201 1983 $20

HERRICK, JAMES B.   Memories of Eighty Years by James B.
Herrick. Chicago, 1949. First edition. 8vo. Orig. binding.
Inscribed and autographed by the author. Dust wrapper. Fye H-3-
782 1983 $50

HERRICK, JAMES B.   Memories of Eighty Years by James B.
Herrick. Chicago, 1949. 8vo. Orig. binding. Ex-library. Fye
H-3-783 1983 $20

HERRICK, JUDSON   George Ellett Coghill. Chicago: Univ.
of Chicago Press, 1949. First edition. Dust jacket a bit yellowed.
Gach 94-14 1983 $20

HERRICK, ROBERT   Chrysomela. A selection from the
lyrical poems. London: Macmillan, 1877. First edition as edited
by F.T. Palgrave. 12mo. Cont. red morocco. Presentation copy,
inscribed by Palgrave to Catherine Milnes. Hinges rubbed. Ximenes
63-456 1983 $27.50

HERRICK, ROBERT   Hesperides. G. Newnes, n.d. (ca.1902).
2 vols. Frontis. & pictorial titles & 24 plates. Quarter white
parchemnt, gilt. Edition limited to 106 copies, No. 3, signed by
Savage. Greer 40-201 1983 £45

HERRICK, ROBERT   Robert Herrick: The Hesperides &
Noble Numbers... London & New York: 1891. 2 vols. 1st ed. thus.
Orig. light blue cloth, pictorial gilt, t.e.g., uncut. Fine set.
Jenkins 155-1193 1983 $45

HERRIES, JOHN MAXWELL   Historical Memoirs of Mary Queen of
Scots and a Portion of the Reign of James the Sixth. Printed at
Edinburgh, 1831. 4to, orig. cloth, worn at foot of the spine,
remains of a paper label at top of spine. Bickersteth 77-123 1983
£34

HERRING, RICHARD   Paper & Paper Making, Ancient and Modern.
Longman, Brown, Green, and Longmans, 1855. 8vo, including list of
subscribers, 4 lithographed plates and 25 specimens of different kinds
of paper bound in at the end, orig. cloth, rubbed and faded, but
sound. First edition. Fine copy. Bickersteth 77-280 1983 £165

HERRING, THOMAS   A Sermon Preach'd at the Cathedral Church
of York, September the 22nd, 1745. 1745. Modern grey wraps.
Jarndyce 31-38 1983 £24

HERRLINGER, ROBERT   History of Medical Illustration from
Antiquity to 1600. 32 plates, many in color. 4to, linen, boxed.
Argosy 713-260 1983 $40

HERSEY, JOHN   A Bell for Adano. N.Y., Knopf, 1944.
First edition. Dust jacket (nicked at edges). Very good. Houle 22-
473 1983 $50

HERSEY, JOHN   A Bell for Adano. New York: Alfred
A. Knopf, 1944. First edition. 8vo. Orig. cloth. Dust jacket,
slightly torn. Very good copy. Jaffe 1-144 1983 $25

HERSEY, JOHN   Hiroshima. New York: Knopf, 1946.
Blue cloth. First edition in cloth. About fine in dust jacket.
Reese 20-515 1983 $30

HERSKOVITS, MELVILLE   The Anthropemetry of the American Negro.
NY: Columbia Univ. Press, 1930. 1st edition. Jenkins 151-123
1983 $35

HERSKOVITS, MELVILLE   Rebel Destiny: among the Bush Negroes
of Dutch Guiana. N.Y., 1934. Illus. Argosy 710-503 1983 $35

HERTWIG, O.   Lehrbuch der Entwicklungsgeschichte
des Menschen und der Wirbelthiere. Jena, 1888. Half morocco, good
ex-library. Wheldon 160-493 1983 £15

HERTZ, DAVID   Valdemar. NY: Longmans Green and
Co., 1938. 4to, color illus. throughout. Presentation copy,
signed by Merle Armitage. Bound in colored boards. In dust jacket.
Karmiole 72-9 1983 $75

HERTZ, HEINRICH   Electric Waves, being Researches on
the propagation of Electric Action... London: Macmillan, 1900.
Second English edition. 8vo. Orig. cloth. A very good copy.
Zeitlin 264-202 1983 $60

HERTZ, HEINRICH   Miscellaneous Papers... London:
Macmillan, 1896. First English edition. 8vo. Orig. cloth.
Frontis. portrait, text figures, large folding diagram. Partially
unopened. Zeitlin 264-203 1983 $100

HERTZ, HEINRICH   The Principles of Mechanics Presented
in a New Form. London: Macmillan, 1899. First English edition.
8vo. Orig. green cloth. Somewhat dampstained, otherwise very good.
Zeitlin 264-204 1983 $100

HERTZ, HEINRICH   Untersuchungen uber die Ausbreitung
der elektrischen Kraft. Leipzig, 1892. 8vo. Half-morocco, wrappers.
First edition. Ownership stamp on title, and a few elsewear.
Wrappers torn. Gurney 90-60 1983 £375

HERTZ, RUDOLF   Congregational Woope. Santee, Neb.,
1926. Orig. 12mo, printed wraps. First edition. Ginsberg 47-337
1983 $50

HERTZKA, THEODOR   Freeland A Social Anticipation.
London: Chatto & Windus, 1891. First English edition, 8vo, adver-
tisements at end, uncut, a fine copy. Original cloth. Pickering &
Chatto 21-44 1983 $65

HERTZLER, ARTHUR E.   The Horse and Buggy Doctor. New York,
1938. 8vo, illus., cloth, spine faded. Bickersteth 77-281 1983 £12

HERVEY, MAURICE H.   The Reef of Gold. London: Edward
Arnold, 1894. Orig. pictorial cloth. First edition. Inner hinges
cracked, in elaborately decorated binding of red, black and gold.
MacManus 278-2600 1983 $35

HERZFELD, L.   Handelsgeschichte der Juden des
Altertums. Brunschweig, 1894. 2nd edition. 1/2 cloth. 8vo.
Salloch 385-240 1983 $60

HERZFELDE, WIELAND   John Heartfield. Dresden: VEB
Verlag der Kunst, 1962. Prof. illus. 4to. Cloth. Dust jacket.
First edition. Ars Libri 32-303 1983 $125

HERZOG, RUDOLF   Kie Wunderheilungen Von Epidauros.
Leipzig: Dieterich'sche Verlagsbuchhandlung, 1931. First edition.
Orig. printed wrappers. Gach 94-205 1983 $20

HESKETH-PRICHARD, H.   Sniping in France. London, c.1920.
First edition. 8vo. Orig. cloth. Frontis. 23 plates. Good.
Edwards 1042-366 1983 £30

HESLOP, D. G.   Through Jungle Bush and Forest. London,
(1928). Orig. cloth. 8vo. Numerous plates. Good. Edwards 1044-
338 1983 £20

HESS, H.   Die Gletscher. Braunschweig, 1904.
Maps, text-figures, 8vo, cloth, 8 plates. Wheldon 160-1416 1983 £15

HESSE, HERMANN   Zehn Gedichte. (Bern: Stampfli &
Cie., n.d. (1939). 22 cm. Orig. printed wraps. soiled and separating;
some corners wearing. Inscribed by the author "Gruss von H Hesse"
in pencil on the half title. Privately printed. Grunder 7-40 1983
$85

HESSE, R.   Ecological Animal Geography. New York,
1937. 135 figures, 8vo, cloth, front cover slightly dampstained.
Wheldon 160-494 1983 £15

HET Groote Tafereel Der Dwaasheid. The Great Mirror of Folly, showing
the Rise, Progress and Downfall of the Bubble in Stocks and Windy
Speculation...in the year 1720. (Amsterdam, 1720). Folio, engraved
title, printed title in red and black, 76 engraved plates, 8 smaller
plates mounted on two leaves, otherwise mostly double-page. Cont.
Dutch calf, panelled sides and central gilt ornament, spine elaborately
gilt in compartments, red morocco label, armourial bookplate. Rare.
Pickering & Chatto 21-121 1983 $3,000

HEUGLIN, M. T. VON   Ornithologie Nordost-Afrika's, der
Nilquellen und Kusten Gebiete des Rothen Meeres und des nordlichen
Somal-Landes. Cassel 1869-74 (-75). 1 vol., bound in 2 vols., roy.
8vo, half morocco, folding map, plain and coloured plates. Wheldon
160-46 1983 £450

HEUHAS, EUGEN   The Art Exposition. San Francisco,
Paul Elder, (1915). Illus. with tipped-in plates. Marbled endpapers.
Tan cloth stamped in gilt. Very good. Houle 22-1147 1983 $25

HEVELIUS, JOHANNES   Selenographia. Danzig: Hunefeld for
Hevelius, 1647. First edition. Engraved title, author's portrait.
109 plates (of 111). 24 text engravings. Folio. Cont. vellum with
blind stamped center ornament on both covers. Calf-rebacked. Orig.
vellum label preserved. Corners worn. Kraus 164-126 1983 $6,500

HEVESY, GEORG VON   A Manual of Radioactivity. Oxford:
University Press, 1926. First English edition. 8vo. Modern
buckram. 7 plates. Zeitlin 264-208 1983 $50

HEWARD, CONSTANCE   Ameliaranne Goes Touring. G.G. Harrap,
1941. Sq. 8vo. First edition. Colour pictorial title. 28 colour
plates (4 tears repaired). Some 50 text illus. Colour pictorial bds.
Greer 40-166 1983 £12.50

HEWETT, EDGAR L.   Ancient Life in the American Southwest.
Indianapolis: (1930). First edition. Frontis., other illus., map
end papers. Cloth. Small break at top of spine, otherwise very good
in soiled jacket. Bradley 66-565 1983 $45

HEWITT, EDWARD RINGWOOD   Secrets of the Salmon. New York, 1925.
Illus. from photographs and drawings by author. 8vo. Morrill 287-149
1983 $20

HEWITT, GIRART   Minnesota: Its Advantages to Settlers.
1868. St. Paul, Minn., 1868. Original printed wrappers. Fine copy.
8 pp. of ads. Second edition. Jenkins 151-219 1983 $175

HEWITT, GRAILY   Lettering for Students and Craftsmen.
London: n.d. Octavo. First edition. Slightly shaken, else very
fine with near mint dust wrapper. Bromer 25-177 1983 $65

HEWITT, GRAILY   The Pen and Type Design. London: First
Editions Club, 1928. Sm. 4to, full crimson morocco, gilt extra,
t.e.g. Printed in Treyford type. One of 250 copies. An unusually
fine copy. Prospectus laid in. Scarce in this condition. Perata
28-203 1983 $275

HEWITT, GRAILY   The Pen and Type Design. London: The
First Editions Club, 1928. Tall 8vo, full crushed morocco, geometric
design in gilt upper and lower covers, t.e.g. With plates and
figures. One of 250 copies printed on Barcham Green handmade paper
at the Oxford University Press. Duschnes 240-114 1983 $250

HEWITT, RANDALL H.   Across the Plains and Over the Divide.
N.Y., (1906). Illus., plates, folded map. Orig. pictorial cloth.
Ginsberg 47-338 1983 $150

HEWLETT, MAURICE   Artemision, Idylls, and Songs. London,
Elkin Mathews, 1909. First edition. Small 8vo, blue cloth stamped
in gilt. Very good. Houle 22-475 1983 $22.50

HEWLETT, MAURICE   Artemision. London: Elkin Mathews,
1909. Orig. cloth. First edition. Fine copy. MacManus 278-2602
1983 $20

HEWLETT, MAURICE   Bendish. N.Y.: Charles Scribner's Sons,
1913. First American edition. Orig. cloth. With a 2 page ALS from
Hewlett, dated 21 July 1913, tipped in. Fine. MacManus 278-2604
1983 $35

HEWLETT, MAURICE   Earthwork out of Tuscany. London:
J.M. Dent & Co., 1895. Orig. cloth, t.e.g. First edition. Very
small bookplate, spine slightly faded & worn, 500 copies were
printed. MacManus 278-2606 1983 $85

HEWLETT, MAURICE   Earthwork Out of Tuscany. London,
1895. Small 8vo, cloth; slightly rubbed. One of 500 copies. Argosy
714-369 1983 $50

HEWLETT, MAURICE   Extemporary Essays. Oxford: Humphrey
Milford, Oxford University Press, 1922. Orig. cloth, dust jacket.
First edition. Very good copy. MacManus 278-2608 1983 $20

HEWLETT, MAURICE   Fond Adventures. London: Macmillan &
Co., 1905. Orig. cloth, dust jacket. First edition. Good copy
and rare in dust jacket. MacManus 278-2611 1983 $25

HEWLETT, MAURICE   The Fool Errant. London: William
Heinemann, 1905. Orig. pictorial cloth, first edition, covers a
little soiled, but a good copy. MacManus 278-2612 1983 $20

HEWLETT, MAURICE   The Forest Lovers. London: Macmillan
& Co., 1898. First edition. Orig. decorated cloth. Covers a little
rubbed; hinges cracking, cloth slipcase. MacManus 278-2613 1983
$20

HEWLETT, MAURICE   In a Green Shade. London: G. Bell
& Sons, 1920. Orig. cloth, dust jacket. First edition. Very fine
copy. MacManus 278-2620 1983 $25

HEWLETT, MAURICE   Last Essays. London: William Heinemann,
Ltd., (1924). First edition. Orig. cloth, dust jacket (a little dust-
soiled). Fine copy. MacManus 278-2621 1983 $20

HEWLETT, MAURICE   Letters to Sanchia upon Things As They
Are. London: Macmillan & Co., 1910. Orig. parchment-wraps., dust
jacket (worn at edges). First published edition. Very good.
In dust jacket. MacManus 278-2624 1983 $35

HEWLETT, MAURICE   The Life and Death of Richard Yea-and-
Nay. N.Y.: Charles Scribner's Sons, 1909. Orig. cloth. Later
edition, but with an ALS from Hewlett, dated Oct. 1913, pasted to
the front endsheet. A fine copy. MacManus 278-2626 1983 $20

HEWLETT, MAURICE   The Light Heart. London: Chapman &
Hall, Ltd., 1920. First edition. Orig. cloth. Fine copy. MacManus
278-2628 1983 $20

HEWLETT, MAURICE   Little Novels of Italy. Leipzig:
Bernhard Taughnitz, 1899. Copyright edition. With an ALS, 8vo,
7, Northwick Terrace, N.W. (London), 20 June 1900, to the French
translator of his works. Very good copy. MacManus 278-2630 1983
$20

HEWLETT, MAURICE   A Masque of Dead Florentines.
London: J.M. Dent & Co., 1895. Oblong 8vo, printed in red & black.
Frontis. and numerous illus. by Batten. Bound in full polished
brown calf, gilt spine, by "Arthur S. Colley, bookbinder". Karmiole
72-55 1983 $75

HEWLETT, MAURICE   New Canterbury Tales. N.Y.: Macmillan
Co., 1901. Orig. cloth. First American edition. With an ALS
from Newlett, dated 27 Nov. 1913. Fine copy. MacManus 278-2640
1983 $25

HEWLETT, MAURICE   Pan and the Young Shepherd. London &
N.Y.: John Lane, 1898. First edition. Orig. cloth. Presentation
copy to Arthur Conan Doyle inscribed: "To A. Conan Doyle with the best
regards, M.H. 14xi.98." Spine a bit faded. Inside hinges cracking,
with very slight offsetting to the free endpapers. Good. MacManus
278-1636 1983 $250

HEWLETT, MAURICE   The Works. London and New York,
1905-06. 10 vols. Roy. 8vo. Orig. green satin cloth, gilt
medallion on front covers, gilt decorated spines, t.e.g., others
uncut. Edition-de-Luxe, limited to 500 sets. Traylen 94-438
1983 £110

HEWLETT, SAMUEL MUDWAY   The Cup and Its Conqueror. Boston,
(1862). 1st ed. Portrait. 12mo. Lacks endleaves. Morrill 287-150
1983 $25

HEWLITT, J.   The Description and Use of a Quadrant...
London: Printed for the Author, 1665. First edition. Blank leaf.
Folded engraved plate, and a woodcut. Small 8vo. Calf. From the
library of the Earls of Kinnoul, Dupplin Castle. Manuscript formula
on blank. Kraus 164-127 1983 $1,500

HEWSON, WILLIAM   The Works of William Hewson, F.R.S.
London, 1846. 8vo. Orig. binding. First collected edition.
Very fine. Scarce. Fye H-3-256 1983 $150

HEYLYN, P.   Cosmographie in Foure Books. London:
Printed for Anne Seile, 1669. Fifth edition, corrected and enlarged.
4 folding maps. 4to, mottled calf, rebacked, with orig. spine laid
down, recornered. Good. Edwards 1044-781 1983 £535

HEYWARD, DU BOSE   The Half Pint Flask. New York:
Farrar, 1929. 1st ed. Orig. cloth, dj. Illustrations by Joe
Sandford. Fine copy. Jenkins 155-559 1983 $25

HEYWARD, DU BOSE   Mamba's Daughter: A Play. New York,
1939. 8vo, cloth. Inscription on front fly, else fine in dust jacket.
In Our Time 156-393 1983 $45

HEYWOOD, THOMAS   The Actor's Vindication, containing,
three brief treatises, viz. I. Their antiquity. II. Their antient
dignity. III. The true use of their quality. London: printed by
G. E. for W. C., n.d. (1658). Sm. 4to, half green morocco, 2nd ed.
revised. Neat repair to a tear in the title-page, without loss of
surface, but an excellent copy of a very rare theatrical pamphlet.
Ximenes 64-265 1983 $3,500

HEYWOOD, THOMAS   The Life of Merlin... London, J. Okes,
sold by Jasper Emery, 1641. 4to, 19th century diced calf, joints broken
and the frontis. backed, tear in B4 repaired with no loss, some minor
stains. First edition. Ravenstree 94-201 1983 $420

HIATT, CHARLES   Henry Irving. A record and review.
London: George Bell and Sons, 1899. 8vo, original cloth (cover
designed by Gordon Craig; a little dull). First edition. With a
frontis. and 54 plates. Bookplate. Ximenes 64-303 1983 $40

HIBBEN, TERTIUS N.   A Dictionary of the Chinook Jargon.
Victoria, B.C., Hibben, (1871). Orig. pictorial printed wraps.
First edition. Ginsberg 46-617 1983 $375

HIBBERD, S.   The Amateur's Rose Book. 1878. New
edition, 5 coloured plates, tape marks in 2 inner margins. Wheldon
160-1953 1983 £12

HICHBORN, PHILIP   Report on European Dock-Yards. Washington, 1889. First edition. Many folding maps, plans, and plates. Orig.
3/4 morocco. Jenkins 152-280 1983 $125

HICKENS, GASPAR   The Glory and Beauty of Gods Portion.
Printed by G.M. for Christopher Meredith, 1644. First edition,
4to, wrapper, a few side notes just touched, a very good copy.
Fenning 62-174 1983 £16.50

HICHENS, ROBERT   Dr. Artz. London: Hutchinson & Co.,
(1929). First edition. Orig. cloth. Dust jacket (somewhat worn and
chipped; front inner leaf torn loose). Spine slightly faded, with very
slight foxing to the preliminary pages and edges. Very good. MacManus
279-2661 1983 $20

HICHENS, ROBERT   The God Within Him. London: Methuen &
Co., (1926). First edition. Orig. cloth. Dust jacket (somewhat worn
and soiled, with a few very small tears to the spine edges). Spine
slightly faded. Edges a trifle foxed. Very good. MacManus 279-2662
1983 $35

HICHENS, ROBERT   The Near East. NY, 1913. Illus. by
Jules Guerin, edges rubbed, few pencil notations, good or better.
Quill & Brush 54-1689 1983 $30

HICHENS, ROBERT   A Spirit in Prison. London: Hutchinson
& Co., 1908. First edition. Illus. Orig. cloth. Spine a bit faded.
Covers and spine slightly spotted. Very good. MacManus 279-2663 1983
$35

HICKENLOOPER, FRANK   An Illustrated History of Monroe County,
Iowa. Albia, Iowa, 1896. First edition. Frontis. and illus. Folding
map of county. Orig. cloth. Ads. Fine. Jenkins 152-171 1983 $50

HICKERINGILL, EDMUND   Gregory, Father-Greybeard, with his
Vizard off. London: by Robin Hood, at the Sign of the He-Cow,
1673. First edition. Small 8vo. Orig. sheep, repaired. Traylen
94-439 1983 £75

HICKES, GEORGE   An Apologetical Vindication of the
Church of England. Printed for Walter Kettilby, 1687. First edition,
including imprimatur leaf, 4to, wrapper, v.g. Fenning 61-202 1983
£26.50

HICKMAN, BILL   Brigham's Destroying Angel. NY, 1872.
First edition. 12mo, orig. dec. cloth. Argosy 716-559 1983 $125

HICKMAN, BILL   Brigham's Destroying Angel. Salt Lake
City, Shepard, 1904. First edition thus. Illus. Pictorial colored
wraps. (trifle worn). Very good. Houle 22-1105 1983 $45

HICKMAN, BILL   Brigham's Destroying Angel. Salt Lake
City: Shepard Publishing Co., 1904. Ads. Cloth. Later edition.
Dawson 471-115 1983 $40

HICKS, ELIAS   Journal: Life & Religious Labours.
New York, 1832. Second edition, calf. Argosy 710-70 1983 $35

HICKSON, S. J.   A Naturalist in North Celebes. 1889.
2 maps, coloured frontispiece and plates, 8vo, cloth. Wheldon
160-392 1983 £45

HIEROCLES   Hierocles Upon the Golden Verses of the
Pythagoreans. Glasgow, printed and sold by Robert & Andrew Foulis,
1756. 8vo, orig. calf (joints broken, light smudge on title page,
few pages with light smudges) good large copy of the first and only
Foulis Press edition. Ravenstree 94-108 1983 $65

HIFFERNAN, PAUL   Dramatic genius. In five books. London:
printed for the author, 1770. 4to, wrappers, 1st ed, half-title
present. A very good copy. Rare. Ximenes 64-266 1983 $375

HIFFERNAN, PAUL   Dramatic Genius. In five books. London:
printed for T. Becket and P. De Hondt, 1772. 8vo, early half calf
and marbled boards (spine worn). 2nd edition, wanting a half-title.
Ximenes 64-267 1983 $150

HIFFERNAN, PAUL   The Tuner. London: printed and sold
by M. Cooper, 1754. 8vo, half calf, 1st ed. Rare. Ximenes 64-268
1983 $150

HIGGINSON, ELLA   Alaska: the Great Country. NY, 1917.
Illus. & folding map. 8vo. Pict. cloth. New edition. Argosy 710-
6 1983 $35

HIGGINSON, THOMAS WENTWORTH   Out-Door Papers. Boston: Ticknor &
Fields, 1863. 1st ed., stamping A. Orig. brown cloth, gilt.
Jenkins 155-561 1983 $25

HIGGS, HENRY   Bibliography of Economics 1751-1775.
New York and Cambridge: Macmillan and the Univ. Press, 1935. Cloth,
tear at top of spine repaired. Dawson 470-152 1983 $20

HIGGS, PAGET   The Electric Light in its Practical
Application. E. & F.N. Spon, 1879. First edition, with 94 illus.,
8vo, orig. cloth, gilt. A very good copy. Fenning 60-176 1983
£45

HIGHAM, CHARLES FREDERICK   The Story of Royal Worcester China and
Some Notes on A Visit to the Ancient City of Worcester. (Worcester),
n.d. (1920's?). 8 color plates. Each page with two-color border.
Includes 4 related booklets and typescript. Well worn. King 45-319
1983 $20

HIGHET, GILBERT   The Classical Tradition. NY, 1949. 8vo,
cloth. Pencil marks. Salloch 385-23 1983 $22

HIGHSMITH, PATRICIA   Eleven. London, 1970. Wrappers.
Uncorrected proof copy. Covers slightly rubbed and marked. Very
good. Jolliffe 26-264 1983 £60

HILAIRE, GEORGES   Derain. Geneve: Pierre Cailler, 1959.
210 plates (numerous tipped-in color). Folio. Boards. No. 76
of a limited edition of 100 copies with 1 orig. color lithograph
and 3 orig. drypoint etchings by Derain on BFK Rives, loosely
inserted. Ars Libri 32-165 1983 $250

HILDEBRAND, S. F.   A Descriptive Catalogue of the Shore
Fishes of Peru. Washington, U. S. Nat. Mus. Bull., 1946. 95 text-
figures, 8vo, wrappers. Wheldon 160-967 1983 £20

HILDEBRANDT, ADOLPH M.   Heraldic Bookplates. London: H.
Grevel & Co., 1894. Twenty-five ex-libris. 25 leaves of plates
(several in color). Red buckram, badly faded. Karmiole 71-102
1983 $40

HILDEBRANDT, HANS   Alexander Archipenko. Berlin-
Schoneberg: Ukrains'ke Slowo, 1923. 67 plates (1 color). 4to.
Boards, 1/4 cloth. Ars Libri 32-10 1983 $125

HILDEBURN, CHARLES R.   Sketches of Printers and Printing in Colonial New York. New York: Dodd, Mead & Co., 1895. First edition. Small 8vo. Half parchment, boards, paper spine label, slipcase. Limited to 375 numbered copies printed at the DeVinne Press. With 31 illus. Slipcase is worn, spine spotted. Oak Knoll 49-235 1983 $55

HILDRETH, RICHARD   The History of the United States of America. New York, Harper (1877-1880). Revised ed. 6 vols., 8vo, ex-library. Morrill 288-611 1983 $22.50

HILDRETH, RICHARD   Japan as it was and Is. Boston: Phillips, Sampson & Co., 1855. First edition. With a folding map. Orig. dark brown cloth; spine extremities fraying. Rear free endpaper lacking. Karmiole 73-54 1983 $60

HILDRETH, RICHARD   The People's Presidential Candidate. Boston, 1839. 1st ed. 16mo, paper label. Ends of spine worn. Morrill 286-192 1983 $20

HILGARD, EUGENE   The Culture of the Grape. N.p., ca. 1880. Dbd. First edition. Ginsberg 47-108 1983 $50

HILL, AARON   The fatal vision: or, the fall of Siam. A tragedy. London: printed for Edw. Nutt, n.d. (1716). Sm. 4to, wrappers, 1st ed. Half-title present. A fine copy of a scarce play. Ximenes 64-269 1983 $275

HILL, AARON   The Tragedy of Zara. London: printed for J. Watts, 1736. 8vo, wrappers, 1st ed. Very good copy. Ximenes 64-270 1983 $75

HILL, ARCHIBALD VIVIAN   Lectures on Certain Aspects of Bio-chemistry. London: University of London Press, 1926. 8vo. Orig. green cloth with gilt. Various text illus., folding plate. Very good copy. Zeitlin 264-211 1983 $45

HILL, CHARLES L.   The Guernsey Breed. Waterloo, Iowa, 1917. 1st ed. Illus. 8vo, half leather. Top of spine chipped. Morrill 287-151 1983 $30

HILL, FRANK PIERCE   Books, Phamphlets and Newspapers Printed at Newark, New Jersey, 1776-1900. (N.p.), 1902. Cloth. 300 copies printed. Very good. Felcone 19-65 1983 $35

HILL, FREDERIC S.   Twenty-Six Historic Ships...Famous Vessels of War and their Successors. N.Y.: Putnam's, 1903. 1st ed., t.e.g., illus. Jenkins 151-125 1983 $40

HILL, GEORGE   An Historical Account of the MacDonnells of Antrim. Belfast, 1873. First edition, 4to, orig. cloth, neatly repaired, very good copy. Fenning 61-510 1983 £65

HILL, GEORGE BIRKBECK   Talks about Autographs. T. Fisher Unwin, 1896. First U.K. edition, with 27 plates, 8vo, orig. cloth, gilt, t.e.g., a good copy. Fenning 61-204 1983 £10.50

HILL, HAMNETT P.   History of Christ Church Cathedral, Ottawa. Ottawa: Runge Press, 1932. 23cm. 26 illus. Green cloth. Very good to fine. McGahern 54-89 1983 $30

HILL, J. L.   Passing of the Indian and Buffalo. Long Beach, n.d. Illus. Orig. wrps. Clark 741-309 1983 $25

HILL, JOHN   The actor: or, a treatise on the art of playing. London: printed for R. Griffiths, 1755. 12mo, cont. calf, gilt (bit rubbed, old shelf sticker on spine). 1st ed, with two leaves of ads at the end. A couple of old library stamps, but a very good copy of an important book. Ximenes 64-271 1983 $400

HILL, JOHN   The Family Herbal. Bungay, 1822. 54 hand-coloured plates of numerous figures, 8vo, contemporary calf. Signs of use. Wheldon 160-2173 1983 £50

HILL, JOHN   The Family Herbal. Bungay, J. & R. Childs, 1822. 54 hand-coloured plates, generally thumbed and dusty, old style half calf. K Books 307-98 1983 £80

HILL, JOHN   A Review of the Works of the Royal Society of London... London: for R. Griffiths, 1751. First edition. 4to. Half calf. Couple of small brown marks, else good. Heath 48-508 1983 £125

HILL, JOHN   The Usefulness of a Knowledge of Plants. London: for R. Baldwin and J. Jackson, 1759. First edition. 8vo. Wrappers. Title lightly dust soiled. Heath 48-6 1983 £125

HILL, JOSEPH J.   The History of Warner's Ranch and Its Environs. L.A., privately printed, 1927. Orig. boards with paper label on spine. First edition. One of 300 numbered copies for presentation. Ginsberg 46-99 1983 $100

HILL, OCTAVIA   Employment, or, Alms-Giving. 1871. Sewn as issued, title sl. dusted. Jarndyce 31-262 1983 £32

HILL, S. C.   Three Frenchmen in Bengal... London, 1903. 2 maps, 3 plans. 8vo. Orig. cloth. Good. Edwards 1044-339 1983 £35

HILL, S. C.   Yusuf Khan, the Rebel Commandant. London, 1914. Folding map, others in text. Plates. 8vo. Orig. cloth. Good. Edwards 1044-340 1983 £16

HILL, ROBERT T.   Cuba and Porto Rico. New York, 1898. 1st ed. Map and illus. 8vo. Morrill 287-152 1983 $25

HILL, WALTER H.   Historical Sketch of the St. Louis University. St. Louis, 1879. Illus. Orig. cloth. First edition. Ginsberg 47-525 1983 $30

HILLHOUSE, JAMES   Propositions for Amending the Constitution of the United States. New Haven, 1808. Self-wrappers, stitched, fine, uncut. Reese 13-306 1983 $45

HILLIARD, A. R.   Outlaw Island. New York (1942). 8vo, cloth. A fine copy in lightly rubbed just jacket. In Our Time 156-394 1983 $25

HILLICK, M. C.   Practical Carriage and Wagon Painting. Chicago 1903. 3rd ed. Illus., cloth, covers darkened and heavily rubbed. King 46-473 1983 $35

HILLS, ERNEST M.   The Song of the Sleep of Our Sweet. I.o.W. Observer Office. H. Butler, Ryde, n.d. (c. 1870). First edition. Orig. green cloth, inscribed presentation copy from the author. Jarndyce 30-755 1983 £10.50

HILL'S Yankee Story Teller's Own Book. Philadelphia & New York, Turner & Fisher, (1836). Frontispiece. 16mo, orig. wrappers, taped into plain wrappers, ex-library. Morrill 288-176 1983 $32.50

HILLYER, ANTHONY   Elizabeth's Irregular Humorist: Sir John Falstaffe. N.Y., 1943. Slim 12mo, printed wrappers, sewn. One of 150 copies printed for Private Distribution. A very good copy. Perata 28-164 1983 $22.50

HILLYER, ROBERT SILLIMAN   Sonnets and Other Lyrics. Cambridge: 1917. First edition. Boards, paper labels. Presentation copy signed and inscribed. Covers worn. In plain dust jacket. Bradley 66-202 1983 $20

HILSOP, HERBERT R.   An Englishman's Arizona. Tucson, 1965. Cloth, fine. Reese 19-271 1983 $85

HILTON, JAMES   Good-Bye Mr. Chips. (Boston): Little, Brown, 1935. Vellum and boards. First illus. edition. Illus. by H.M. Brock. One of 600 numbered copies, specially bound, and signed by the author and illustrator. Fine in slightly worn slipcase. Reese 20-519 1983 $85

HILTON, JAMES   Good-bye Mr. Chips. (London): Hodder & Stoughton, 1934. First edition. 8vo. Orig. cloth. Dust jacket. Chipped jacket, otherwise a fine copy. Jaffe 1-145 1983 $65

HILTON, JAMES   The Story of Dr. Wassell. Boston,
Little Brown, 1943. First edition. Signed by Hilton and Dr. Wassell.
Dust jacket (slight rubbing and nicking) else very good. Houle 22-477
1983 $35

HILTON, JAMES   We Are Not Alone. L., 1937. Fine,
bright copy with light foxing top page edge in very good, slightly
frayed dustwrapper with tear at top edge of spine and slightly rubbed
at edges. Quill & Brush 54-649 1983 $40

HILTON, JAMES   We Are Not Alone. London: Macmillan
and Co., Limited, 1937. First edition. 8vo. Orig. cloth. Dust
jacket. Fine copy. Jaffe 1-146 1983 $25

HILZINGER, JOHN G.   Treasure Land. Tucson, 1897. Illus.
Gild cloth. Inscribed presentation copy from the author. Ginsberg
46-26 1983 $150

HILZINGER, JOHN G.   Treasure Land. Tucson, 1897. Illus.
Cloth. First edition. Ginsberg 47-15 1983 $75

HIMROD, JAMES L.   Johnny Appleseed the True Story of Jonathan Chapman 1775-1846. Chicago: Chicago Historical Society, 1926.
Orig. pictorial wrappers. Frontis. and illus. Jenkins 152-9 1983
$30

HINCHLIFFE, THOMAS W.   Over the Sea and Far Away. Longmans,
Green, 1876. First edition, with 14 plates, roy. 8vo, orig. cloth,
gilt. A very good copy. Fenning 62-176 1983 £18.50

THE HINCHMAN Conspiracy Case. Philadelphia, 1849. 1st ed. 12mo,
orig. wrappers, bound into a stiff wrapper binder. Lacks back wrapper.
Morrill 289-613 1983 $45

HINCKLEY, EDITH PARKER   Frank Hinckley. Claremont, Saunders,
1946. Folding frontis. and 16 illus. Dust jacket (lightly soiled).
One of 500 copies. Designed by Ruth Saunders. Very good. Houle
21-1087 1983 $45

HINCKS, THOMAS   A History of the British Hydroid Zoophytes. 1868. 67 plates and a frontispiece, 2 vols., 8vo, new
cloth. Wheldon 160-1289 1983 £35

HINCKS, THOMAS   A History of the British Marine
Polyzoa. 1880. 2 vols., 83 plates, orig. cloth. Good. K Books 301-
91 1983 £40

HIND, ARTHUR   The Drawings of Claude Lorrain.
London/New York: Halton & Truscott Smith/Minton, Balch & co., 1925.
72 plates. 4to. Boards, 1/4 cloth. From the library of Jakob
Rosenberg. Ars Libri 32-111 1983 $75

HIND, ARTHUR   Rembrandt's Etchings. London:
Methuen, 1912. 2 vols. 16 plates; 240 plates. 4to. Cloth. Ars
Libri 32-560 1983 $175

HIND, HENRY YOULE   Narrative of the Canadian Red River
Exploring Expedition of 1857 and of the Assiniboine and Saskatchewan
Exploring Expedition of 1858. London, 1860. 2 vols. Illus., 20
plates, 3 plans and one profile. Orig. cloth. First edition.
Ginsberg 47-339 1983 $650

HIND, HENRY YOULE   Narrative of the Canadian Red River
Exploring Expedition of 1857. London: Longman, Green, Longman,
and Roberts. 1860. Two vols. Seven maps, two folding, all
partially colored. 20 colored plates. Folding leaf of profiles.
Full nineteenth century polished calf, spines gilt extra. A fine
set, unfoxed, and with the plates in fine state. Reese 19-272 1983
$600

HIND, HENRY YOULE   North-West Territory. Report of
Progress. Toronto: Printed by John Lovell, 1859. Small folio.
4 folding maps and 3 plates. Rear folding map is in facsimile.
Text illus. Crudely rebacked with library tape. Very good.
McGahern 53-72 1983 $75

HIND, HENRY YOULE   Report on a Topographical & Geological
Exploration of the Canoe Route Between Fort William, Lake Superior, and
Fort Garry, Red River... Toronto, 1858. First edition. Half
morocco slipcase. Ginsberg 46-314 1983 $300

HINDLE, E.   Flies in Relation to Disease.
Cambridge, 1914. Wheldon 160-1092 1983 £12

HINDLEY, CHARLES   Tavern Anecdotes and Sayings. Tinsley
Brothers, 1875. Half title, front. Orig. green cloth, spine gilt,
a little rubbed. Jarndyce 31-186 1983 £34

HINDMARCH, W. M.   A Treatise on the Law relating to Patent
Privileges. Harrisburg, 1847. 1st American ed. Bound in full,
contemp. sheep, well rubbed but sound, contrasting red & black leather
labels, double gilt-ruled & lettered, bit of spotting throughout,
moreso to preliminaries, but altogether decent copy. Boswell 7-130
1983 $125

HINKLE, BEATRICE M.   The Re-Creating of the Individual. NY:
Harcourt, Brace, (1923). First edition. Floyd Allport's copy, signed
and with his occasional notes. Gach 95-203 1983 $25

HINKSON, KATHERINE TYNAN   Ballads and Lyrics. London: Kegan,
Paul, Trench, Trubner & Co., 1891. First edition. Orig. boards.
Covers slightly soiled. Edges slightly worn. Rear free endpaper
lightly browned. Bookplate. Very nice. MacManus 280-5322 1983 $50

HINKSON, KATHERINE TYNAN   The Flower of Peace. London: Burns and
Oates, 1914. 8vo, 17 cm. Frontis. Uncut. Full limp gilt-decorated
vellum. Fine in cardboard slipcase. A few ornaments in red; top
edge gilt. Grunder 7-73 1983 $20

HINKSON, KATHERINE TYNAN   Shamrocks. London, 1887. First edition.
Covers a little soiled and marked. Very good. Rota 230-606 1983
£20

HINSHELWOOD, CYRIL NORMAN   The Kinetics of Chemical Change in
Gaseous Systems. Oxford: Clarendon, 1933. Third edition. 8vo.
Orig. cloth. Slightly rubbed. Very good copy. Zeitlin 264-212
1983 $30

HINTS on Advocacy as to Opening a Case. Waterlow Bros. & Layton,
1879. First edition, orig. brown cloth. Jarndyce 31-215 1983
£12.50

HIPPOCRATES   Opera, quae apud nos extant omnia.
Parisiis: Carolum Guillard & Guillielmum Desbois, 1546. Very thick
small 8vo, cont. stamped calf over boards, (repaired); ex-lib. Argosy
713-261 1983 $450

HIPPOCRATES   Upon Air, Water, and Situation. London,
1734. First edition. Title in red and black. 8vo, cont. calf.
Argosy 713-262 1983 $250

HIPPOCRATES   The Genuine Works of Hippocrates
translated from the Greek... London, 1849. 2 vols. Orig. cloth.
8vo. Two inch tear in outer hinge of each volume, wear to head
of spine, else a fine set. Fye H-3-258 1983 $150

HIPPOCRATES   The Genuine Works of Hippocrates
translated from the Greek... New York, 1886. 2 vols. 8vo. Orig.
cloth. Very fine set. Fye H-3-259 1983 $100

HIPPOCRATES   The Genuine Works of Hippocrates
translated from the Greek... New York, (1929). 8vo. Orig. cloth.
Fye H-3-260 1983 $50

HIRSCHFELD, MAGNUS   Sexualpathologie. Bonn, 1920-2. Illus.
3 vols. Tall 8vo, boards. Argosy 713-266 1983 $100

HISLOP, HERBERT R.   An Englishman's Arizona The Ranching
Letters of Herbert R. Hislop 1876-1878. Tucson, 1965. 74pp.
Frontis and illustrations. Limited to 510 copies and designed by
Carl Hertzog. First edition. Fine copy. Jenkins 151-6 1983
$75.

HISLOP SMITH, G.   Stephen Hislop Pioneer Missionary and
Naturalist. London, 1888. Map, portrait plates. Cover slightly
marked. 8vo. Good. Edwards 1044-344 1983 £30

HISTORIC Montreal: Past and Present. Montreal (ca. 1920). Full page
illus., many color. 4to. Argosy 710-52 1983 $35

AN HISTORICAL Description of the Cathedral and Metropolitical
Church of Christ, Canterbury. Canterbury: Printed and sold by T.
Smith & Son, 1772. Front. 19th Century half dark green calf, sl.
rubbed maroon label. Jarndyce 31-14 1983 £34

AN HISTORICAL Relation of Several Great and Learned Romanists who
Did Imbrace the Protestant Religion. Printed and are to be sold by
Richard Baldwin, 1688. First edition, 4to, wrapper. Fenning 61-206
1983 £18.50

AN HISTORICAL Sketch of Madison University. Hamilton: Waldron & Baker,
Printers, 1852. Later wrappers. Jenkins 152-297 1983 $45

HISTORICAL Sketches of Peterborough, New Hampshire. Peterborough,
1938. 1st ed. Illus. 8vo. Morrill 288-655 1983 $25

THE HISTORY and Antiquities of Winchester. Winston: Printed and sold,
by J. Wilkes, 1773. First edition, with 13 engraved plates, complete
in spite of pagination jump, 2 vols., large 12mo, full polished
calf, gilt, gilt spines, with contrasting spine labels and silk
markers by Riviere. Fenning 60-446 1983 £145

THE HISTORY, Commercial Advantages, and Future Prospects of Bay City,
Michigan. Bay City, Mich.: Henry S. Dow., 1875. Map and illus.,
1st ed. Original green cloth. Jenkins 151-213 1983 $125

HISTORY Getting Right, on the Invention of the American Electro-
Magnetic Telegraph. N.p., 1872. Sewn as issued. With a letter,
signed, small 4to, from Prof. Gale. Manuscript corrections throughout
text. Jenkins 153-252 1983 $150

THE HISTORY of a Man. Arthur Hall, Virtue, 1856. First edition,
half title, 24 pp ads. Orig. brown cloth, v.g. Jarndyce 31-414 1983
£20

THE HISTORY of a Sandal Wood Box. Privately Printed, nd (ca. 1847).
Engr'd dedication page by George Measom. Printed by Bell & Bain,
Glasgow. Brown vertical ribbed blins stamped cloth, re-cased with
new eps., bkstrip re-laid, ALS dated 1847 from husband of author (name
torn from bottom of letter). Loosely inserted is an obituary of
Sheriff Bell dated 1874. Very good. Hodgkins 27-97 1983 £20

HISTORY of Alameda, California, Including its Geology, Topography,
Soil and Productions. Oakland, Wood, 1883. Illus. Old cloth
with leather labels. First edition. Autograph presentation
inscription from the Publisher on front endpaper. Ginsberg 47-109
1983 $175

THE HISTORY of Bookbinding 525-1950. Baltimore: Walter Art Gallery,
1957. First edition. 4to. Cloth. Limited to 3,000 copies. 56 pages
of plates. Spine faded. Oak Knoll 49-81 1983 $95

THE HISTORY of Chesterfield. London and Chesterfield, (printed by
Thomas Ford, Chesterfield, 1839). 22 steel engravings, half roan,
some foxing. K Books 301-46 1983 £65

THE HISTORY of Fairford Church in Gloucestershire. Cirencester:
by S. Rudder, 1772. Sixth edition. 8vo. Modern quarter morocco.
Woodcut border to title. Heath 48-568 1983 £35

HISTORY of Livingston Co., Michigan. Philadelphia, 1880.
Numerous lithos, lea. spine. Gilt-stamped cloth. A.e.g. Bottom
of spine torn. I illus. loose and slightly trimmed. Loose and
worn. King 46-162 1983 $85

THE HISTORY of Miss Sommervile. For Newbery and Carnan, 1769.
First edition. 2 vols. Small 8vo, half-titles. Orig. paper boards
(very worn, spines defective). Corner of final leaf torn off, with
loss of seven or eight words. Hannas 69-89 1983 £230

THE HISTORY of Mr. Byron and Miss Greville. Printed for Francis Noble
and John Noble, 1767. 2 vols. in 1, 12mo, contemp. calf. Foot of
spine chipped, corners worn. Advertisement for Noble's Libraries
facing title, and for two other novels on final leaf of each volume.
Rare. Hill 165-57 1983 £325

A HISTORY of North American Birds. Land birds. (and) Water Birds.
Boston: Little, Brown, 1874 & 1884. Together 5 vols. 4to, lithographed plates and woodcuts. Orig. uniform green cloth, gilt, g.t.
First edition, first issue, with plain plates. Fine set. O'Neal
50-2 1983 $425

THE HISTORY of Pews. Cambridge: University Press, 1841. 8vo.
Modern boards. Heath 48-27 1983 £20

HISTORY of Psychology in Autobiography. Worcester, Mass.: Clark
Univ. Press, 1932. Vol. II. First edition. Gach 95-204 1983 $30

HISTORY of Queens County (Long Island), New York, with Illustrations...
New York, W.W. Munsell, 1882. 4to, orig. cloth, calf back, all edges
gilt, backstrip worn, chipped and partly torn, fore-edge of front
cover partly worn, otherwise clean and sound. Morrill 288-341 1983
$75

THE HISTORY of Singing Birds. Edinburgh, printed for Silvester Doig,
1791. 12mo, engraved title, 24 engraved plates of birds, orig. calf,
upper joint cracked, defective spots in calf at foot of spine and
upper cover. Bickersteth 75-240 1983 £28

HISTORY of Sioux City, Iowa, from Earliest Settlement to January,
1892. (Boston, 1892). Plain printed wraps. First edition. Ginsberg
47-367 1983 $35

HISTORY of Suffolk County, New York, with Illustrations, Portraits,
Sketches of Prominent Families and Individuals. New York, W. W.
Munsell, 1882. 4to, orig. cloth, leather back. Worn, lacks part of
backstrip, hinges cracked, as is. Morrill 286-362 1983 $25

THE HISTORY of Susanna Taken Out Of Context. N.P.: Stanton Press,
1923. 12mo. Decorated paper covered boards, paper cover label.
Limited to 228 numbered copies, printed by hand by Richard and
Elinor Lambert, with illus. and a spread title page designed by
Agnes Lambert and cut on wood by Elinor Lambert. Minor wear at spine
extremities, else a fine copy. Oak Knoll 48-352 1983 $30

HISTORY Of The American Physiological Society Semicentennial.
Baltimore, 1938. 8vo. Orig. binding. Numerous portraits. Fye
H-3-261 1983 $40

HISTORY of the First Troop Philidelphia City Calvary. (Phila., 1875).
First edition. 4to. Orig. 3/4 morocco, outer wear only. T.e.g.
Illus. with numerous engraved portraits, and color plates of flags.
Jenkins 152-322 1983 $75

THE HISTORY of the Life and Reign of Queen Elizabeth. London: F.
Noble, 1740. 3rd ed., greatly enlarged. 8vo, 2 vols., cont. calf,
morocco labels. 4 engraved plates. One cover partly detached, else
a very fine copy. Trebizond 18-195 1983 $275

THE HISTORY of the Life of Nader Shah, King of Persia. London:
J. Richardson for T. Cadell, 1778. First edition in English.
8vo. 19th century blue calf, gilt, morocco labels, t.e.g., others
uncut, marginal repair to B4, not affecting printed surface.
Traylen 94-625 1983 £70

THE HISTORY of the siege of Damascus, by the Saracens, in the year
633. London: printed and sold by J. Brotherton and W. Meadows, etc.,
1720. 8vo, disbound, 1st ed. Scarce. Ximenes 64-272 1983 $200

HISTORY of the Town of Houlton, (Maine) from 1804 to 1883.
Haverhill, Mass., 1884. Illus. Frontis. of village. Orig. printed
wraps. First edition. Ginsberg 46-429 1983 $30

HITCHCOCK, A. S.   The Grasses of Ecuador, Peru, and
Bolivia. U. S. Nat. Mus., 1927. 8vo, wrappers. Wheldon 160-1712
1983 £15

HITCHCOCK, EDWARD   First Anniversary Address Before the
Association of American Geologists, at their Second Annual Meeting.
New Haven, 1841. Orig. printed wraps. First edition. Ginsberg 46-
839 1983 $35

HITCHCOCK, EDWARD   Ichnology of New England. Boston, 1858.
Full-page lithograph plates by Bradford. 4to. Morrill 286-292
1983 $50

HITCHCOCK, ENOS   Memoirs of the Bloomsgrove Family.
Boston: Thomas and Andrews, 1790. Orig. calf. Two leaves torn,
with no loss, otherwise a very good copy. Reese 18-167 1983 $175

HITCHCOCK, HENRY-RUSSELL   Frank Lloyd Wright. Paris: Editions
"Cahiers d'Art", 1928. 44 plates. 4to. Wrappers. Ars Libri 32-
711 1983 $85

HITLER, ADOLF   Mein Kampf... London: Hutchinson,
Hurst & Blackett, n.d. (1940?). Numerous illus. Orig. red and yellow
wraps. 25 cm. Very good; backstrip of first wrapper reinforced,
the war-time paper slightly darkened. Contained in a folding cloth
box. Grunder 7-42 1983 $75

HITT, THOMAS   A Treatise of Fruit Trees. London:
for the Author, 1757. Second edition. 8vo. Cont. calf. 7 large
folding plates. Slight wear. Heath 48-591 1983 £65

HITTELL, JOHN S.   The Commerce and Industries of the
Pacific Coast of North America. San Francisco, 1882. Illus.,
folded maps, plates. Orig. cloth. First edition. Ginsberg 46-316
1983 $125

HITTELL, JOHN S.   The Prospects of Vallejo. Vallejo,
1871. First edition. Illus., large folding map. Orig. printed
wraps. Ginsberg 46-100 1983 $175

HITTELL, JOHN S.   The Resources of California. San
Francisco, 1866. Orig. cloth. Second edition. Ginsberg 46-101
1983 $50

HITTELL, THEODORE H   The Adventures of James Capen Adams.
Boston: Crosby & Ainsworth; N.Y.: Oliver S. Felt, 1867. Later
printing. Plates. Later fabricoid. Some marginal staining. Dawson
471-117 1983 $25

HITTELL, THEODORE H.   George Bancroft and His Services to
California. San Francisco, 1893. Orig. printed wraps., worn.
First edition. Ginsberg 47-110 1983 $25

HITTELL, THEODORE H   History of California. San Francisco: N.
J. Stone & Co., 1898. 4 vols. Orig. sheep, repaired. Dawson 471-118
1983 $325

HOADLY, BENJAMIN   Three Lectures on the Organs of
Respiration. London: Printed for W. Wilkins, 1740. 1st ed., 4to,
20 and 3 engraved plates, 1 folding; cut close in upper margin and
first word of title, a few headlines and plates shaved; disbound.
Pickering & Chatto 22-47 1983 $250

HOADLY, CHARLES J.   Records of the Colony and Plantation of
New Haven, from 1638 to 1649. Hartford, 1857, 1858. 2 vols.,
thick 8vo, cont. 3/4 mor., gilt-stamped spines, (2nd vol. partly
foxed). Argosy 716-123 1983 $85

HOADLY, CHARLES J.   Records of the Colony or Jurisdiction
of New Haven, from May, 1653, to the Union. Hartford, 1858. 1st ed.
8vo. Corners bit rubbed. Morrill 287-74 1983 $20

HOAGLAND, HENRY WILLIMSON   My Life. Privately printed (Pomona,
Progress-Bulletin), 1940. Half green morocco. One of 100 copies.
Very good. Houle 22-1106 1983 $125

HOAR, GEORGE FRISBIE   Woman Suffrage Essential to the True
Republic. Boston: Woman's Journal, 1873. 12mo. Ads at beginning.
Stitched. Rostenberg 88-90 1983 $40

HOBAN, RUSSELL   Pilgerman. London, 1983. Wrappers.
Uncorrected proof copy. Covers very slightly rubbed. Fine.
Jolliffe 26-268 1983 £75

HOBART, NOAH   An Attempt to Illustrate and Confirm
the Ecclesiastical Constitution of the Consociated Churches...
New Haven: Printed by B. Mecom., 1765. Printed self wraps., sewn,
edges rough trimmed. Two light stamps, else a very good copy.
Reese 18-80 1983 $125

HOBART, NOAH   An Attempt to Illustrate and Confirm the
Ecclesiastical Constitution of the Consociated Churches... New Haven:
B. Mecom, 1765. Stitched. Early library stamp on title. Inscription
on title "Joseph Woodbridge / Donatur a Napthali Daggett". Very good.
Felcone 20-29 1983 $35

HOBBES, JOHN OLIVER, PSEUD.
Please turn to
CRAIGIE, PEARL MARY TERESA RICHARDS

HOBBES, THOMAS   Leviathan, or the Matter, Forme and
Power of a Common-Wealth Ecclesisaticall and Civill. London: Andrew
Crooke, 1651. Folio. Full cont. calf, rebacked in cont. style,
gilt label. Engraved title and folding chart. Some slight browning,
and marginal repairs to two leaves, not affecting text. A very good
copy. Reese 20-1192 1983 $2,500

HOBBES, THOMAS   Leviathan, Sive de Materia, Forma, &
Potestate Civitatis Ecclesiasticae et Civilis. Amstelodami, Apud
Joahannem Blaev, 1670. 4to, orig. claf, minor wormhole in lower
margin occasionally dipping into text with no loss. First Latin
edition. Ravenstree 94-206 1983 $365

HOBBES, THOMAS   Quadratura Circuli, Cubatio Sphaerae,
Duplicatio Cubi, Breveter demonstrata. London: J(ohn) C(rooke) for
Andreas Crooke, 1669. First edition. Folding plate. Small 4to.
Unbound, in blue morocco box. From the libraries of the Colonna
family (stamp on title), the 5th Earl of Guilford, and Sir Thomas
Phillipps. Some edges uncut. Inner margins of plate waterstained.
Kraus 164-128 1983 $4,800

HOBBS, H.   The Romance of the Calcutta Sweep.
Calcutta: Published by the Author, 1930. Upper joint worn. 8vo.
Orig. cloth. Good. Edwards 1044-346 1983 £25

HOBHOUSE, C. P.   Some Account of the Family of Hobhouse
and Reminiscences. Leicester, (1909). 2 orig. photographs in text.
Folding pedigree. 8vo. Orig. cloth. Good. Edwards 1044-347 1983
£35

HOBHOUSE, MARY   Letters from India 1872-1877. London:
Printed for Private Circulation, 1906. Portrait frontis. A few pages
carelessly opened. 8vo. Orig. cloth. Good. Edwards 1044-348 1983
£30

HOBSON, G. D.   English Binding Before 1500.
Cambridge: University Press, 1929. First edition. Folio. Cloth.
T.e.g. 55 full page plates. Covers rubbed; light foxing. Oak
Knoll 48-47 1983 $450

HOBSON, G. D.   Thirty Bindings... London: The
First Edition Club, 1926. First edition. 4to. Red buckram stamped
in gilt. 30 full page plates. Limited to 600 copies. T.e.g.
Oak Knoll 48-56 1983 $225

HOBSON, J. A.   John Ruskin, Social Reformer. James
Nisbet, 1899. 2nd edition, half title, front. port. 4 pp ads., orig.
black cloth, paper label. Jarndyce 30-1120 1983 £15

HOCH, AUGUST (1868-1919)   Benign Stupors. NY: Macmillan Co.,
1921. First edition. Bookplate expunged, stamp on rear paste-down.
Gach 95-206 1983 $35

HOCH, AUGUST (1868-1919)   New York Psychiatric Society. In
Memorium Dr. August Hoch. 4to. 18 unnumbered pages printed on rag
paper. Gach 95-208 1983 $20

HOCH, AUGUST (1868-1919)   Ueber Due Wirkung Der Theebestandheile.
Leipzig: Engelmann, 1895. Wrappers. Gach 95-207 1983 $35

HOCHREUTINER, B. P. G.   Catalogus Bogoriensis novus. Buitenzorg, Bull. Inst. Bot., 1904-05. 2 parts, royal 8vo, wrappers. Wheldon 160-1713 1983 £12

HOCKEN, EDWARD O.   A Treatise on Amaurosis & Amaurotic Affections. Phila., 1842. 8vo, mod. 1/2 cloth; ex-lib. First American edition. Argosy 713-267 1983 $50

HOCKLEY, WILLIAM BROWNE   Pandurang Hari. Geo. B. Whittaker, 1826. First edition, 3 vols. Rebound in half calf, bands, hand-marbled boards, v.g. Jarndyce 30-420 1983 £62

HOCKLEY, WILLIAM BROWNE   Pandurang Hari. London, 1877. Frontis. Half calf, spine slightly rubbed. 8vo. Good. Edwards 1044-349 1983 £35

HODDER, GEORGE   Memories of My Time. Tinsley, 1870. First edition, half title. Orig. blue cloth, v.g. Jarndyce 30-1019 1983 £20

HODDER, GEORGE   Sketches of Life and Character. Sherwood & Bowyer, 1845. First edition. Front. & illus. by Meadows, Leech, Hinge, etc. Orig. blue cloth a little rubbed. Jarndyce 31-263 1983 £24

HODDER, JAMES   Hodder's arithmetic or, that necessary art made most easie. London: printed by T.H. for Ric. Chiswell, and Thomas Sawbridg (sic), 1678. Twelfth edition. 12mo. Cont. calf. A bit rubbed, some wear to corners, wanting a front flyleaf, but a fine copy. Ximenes 63-525 1983 $300

HODDER, JAMES   Hodder's Arithmetick or, the Necessary Art made most Easie... London: for D. Midwinter..., 1739. 27th edition. 16mo. Early quarter calf, some wear. Little browned. Heath 48-509 1983 £21

HODGE, HIRAM C.   Arizona as It Is; or, The Coming Country. New York: 1877. First edition. Illus. Terra-cotta cloth, covers worn. Bradley 66-456 1983 $100

HODGES, JOHN G.   Report of the Trial of William Smith O'Brien. Dublin: Alexander Thom, 1849. First edition, roy. 8vo, orig. cloth-backed boards, with printed paper label, by R. Pilkington of Dublin, with his ticket. Fenning 61-321 1983 £85

HODGES, NATHANIEL   Liomologia. Printed for E. Bell: and J. Osborn, 1720. 8vo, folding table, old calf, spine gilt, slight wear at head and foot of the spine, label chipped. First edition in English. Bickersteth 77-282 1983 £120

HODGES, RALPH   The Bull. London: A.T. Stevens, 1913. First edition. Illus. by Lovat Fraser. Orig. pictorial wrappers. Covers a bit faded and worn. Spine. torn. Good. MacManus 279-2682 1983 $45

HODGES, SYDNEY   When Leaves Were Green. London: Chatto & Windus, Piccadilly, 1896. First edition. 3 vols. Orig. decorated cloth. Spines slightly darkened and soiled. One small tear to the top edge of vol. two. Covers a trifle worn, spotted. Inner hinges weak on vol. one & two. With some offsetting to the endpapers. Good. MacManus 279-2680 1983 $185

HODGES, W.   Travels in India... London, 1793. Folding map, 14 plates slightly spotted. Faint marginal dampstaining in last 12 leaves. 4to. Half calf. Good. Edwards 1044-350 1983 £185

HODGKIN, THOMAS   On Some Morbid Appearances of the Absorbent Glands and Spleen. Baltimore, 1937. Pr. wrs. Argosy 713-268 1983 $150

HODGMAN, EDWIN R.   History of the Town of Westford... Lowell, 1883. 1st ed. Illus. 8vo. Corners rubbed. Morrill 287-233 1983 $35

HODGSON, ADAM   Letters from North America written during a Tour in the United States and Canada. London: Hurst, Robinson, & Co., 1824. 2 vols., later cloth, folding map and plate. Errata slips. Some foxing to title. With the Postscript not in all copies. Jenkins 151-126 1983 $300

HODGSON, FRED T.   Architect. New York, 1902. 2nd ed., revised & enlarged. Scale drawings & other illus. 12mo. Morrill 288-177 1983 $20

HODGSON, G. H.   Thomas Parry. Madras, 1938. Coloured frontis. Plates. Thick 8vo. Spine soiled. Orig. cloth. Good. Edwards 1044-553 1983 £20

HODGSON, RALPH   The Bull. London: A.T. Stevens for Flying Fame, 1913. First edition. Orig. hand-colored decorated wraps. Large paper copy. Signed by author on the title-page: "With best wishes, Ralph Hodgson." Included is a copy of the first edition, regular issue, with the same bookplate as the copy above. Spine and covers slightly faded and worn. In a quarter-morocco slipcase. Very good. MacManus 279-2681 1983 $185

HODGSON, RALPH   Eve and Other Poems. Westminster: Printed by A.T. Stevens...at the Sign of Flying Fame, 1913. First edition, ordinary issue. Small 8vo. Decorations by C.L. Fraser. Orig. wrappers. With the publisher's slip advertising large-paper copies of this title tipped to the title-page. With browning and offsetting from the publisher's slip. MacManus 279-2683 1983 $150

HODGSON, RALPH   Eve and Other Poems. London: A.T. Stevens for Flying Fame, 1913. Second edition. Illus. by C.L. Fraser. Orig. hand-colored decorated wrappers. Large paper copy. Spine and covers slightly faded and worn. One small chip missing from the top spine end. Near-fine. MacManus 279-2684 1983 $85

HODGSON, RALPH   The Last Blackbird And Other Lines. London: Allen, 1907. First edition, first issue. 12mo. Orig. cloth. Fine. MacManus 279-2709 1983 $75

HODGSON, RALPH   The Last Blackbird And Other Lines. London: George Allen, 1907. First edition, second issue with trimmed edges. Orig. cloth. Slight foxing. Fine. MacManus 279-2710 1983 $25

HODGSON, RALPH   The Mystery and Other Poems. London: A.T. Stevens for Flying Fame, 1913. First edition. Illus. by C.L. Fraser. Origl hand-colored decorated wrappers. Large paper copy. Spine and covers slightly faded and worn. Slight offsetting to the rear cover. Near-fine. MacManus 279-2712 1983 $135

HODGSON, RALPH   The Mystery and Other Poems. London, 1913. 8vo. Wraps. Decorations by Lovet Fraser. The large paper copy of this book with the decorations hand colored. A fine copy. In Our Time 156-395 1983 $100

HODGSON, RALPH   Poems. London: Macmillan & Co., 1917. First English edition. Orig. cloth. Dust jacket (slightly faded, worn and soiled, with a few small tears). Spine ends a trifle rubbed. Near-fine. MacManus 279-2713 1983 $45

HODGSON, RALPH   Silver Wedding & Other Poems. Minerva: Privately Printed by the Boerner Printing Co., 1941. First edition. Illus. by author. Orig. decorated wrappers. One of 300 copies with hand colored decorations designed by author. Spine very slightly faded. Near-fine. MacManus 279-2714 1983 $45

HODGSON, RALPH   The Skylark and other poems. Printed for Colin Fenton, 1958. First edition. Wood-engravings by Reynolds Stone. One of 350 numbered copies, signed by artist. Tall 8vo. Black buckram, gilt. Very nice. Rota 230-290 1983 £50

HODGSON, RALPH   The Song of Honour. London: A.T. Stevens for Flying Fame, 1913. First edition. Illus. by C.L. Fraser. Orig. hand-colored decorated wrappers. Large paper copy. Spine and covers slightly faded and worn. Near-fine. MacManus 279-2719 1983 $75

HODGSON, RALPH   The Song of Honour. London: A.T. Stevens, 1913. First edition. Illus. by Lovat Fraser. Orig. pictorial wrappers. Covers a bit faded. Some offsetting to the free endpapers. Very good. MacManus 279-2720 1983 $50

HODGSON, RALPH   Songs to Our Surnames. (Cerne Abbas: George Tee, 1960). First edition. Orig. wrappers with printed label. One of 50 copies. Label very slightly spotted. Near-fine. MacManus 279-2721 1983 $100

HODGSON, W. EARL   Salmon Fishing. London 1906. 1st ed. Illus, gilt-dec. cloth, t.e.g., spine slightly frayed, covers darkened. King 46-591 1983 $50

HODGSON, WILLIAM HOPE   The House of the Borderland. WI, 1946.
Cover shows some wear and soiling, endpaper slightly offset, good or
better in fine dustwrapper. Quill & Brush 54-650 1983 $125

HODGSON, WILLIAM HOPE   The House on the Borderland and Other
Novels. Sauk City: Arkham House, 1946. Cloth. First collected
edition. Very fine in lightly worn dust jacket. Bradley 66-121
1983 $185

HODIN, J. P.   Barbara Hepworth. Boston: Boston
Book and Art Shop, 1961. 128 plates. Large 4to. Cloth. Dust
jacket. Ars Libri 32-307 1983 $100

HODSON, WILLIAM   Zoraida: a tragedy. London: published
by W. Richardson, for G. Kearsly, 1780. 8vo, wrappers, 1st ed.
Very good copy. Ximenes 64-273 1983 $75

HOEBER, FRITZ   Peter Behrens. Munchen: Georg Muller
und Eugen Rentsch, 1913. 245 illus. Frontis. portrait (orig.
lithograph) by Max Liebermann. Large 4to. Cloth. Typography and
binding designed by Behrens. Rare. Ars Libri 32-27 1983 $450

HOENIG, F.   Inquiries Concerning the Tactics of the
Future. London, 1889. 8vo. Orig. cloth. 3 large folding maps.
Spine soiled. Very slight worn. Small library stamps. Good. Edwards
1042-368 1983 £12

HOFF, EBBE C.   A Bibliography of Aviation Medicine.
Springfield, 1942. First edition. 8vo. Orig. binding. Dust
wrapper. Fye H-3-1052 1983 $25

HOFF, JOHANN FRIEDRICH   Adrian Ludwig Richter, Maler und
Radierer. Dresden: J. Heinrich Richter, 1877. Collotype frontis.
portrait. 4to. Marbled boards, 3/4 cloth. Ars Libri 32-578 1983
$125

HOFFMAN, PROFESSOR   Modern Magic. A Practical Treatise on
The Art of Conjuring. Philadelphia, n.d. American Edition.
Illus., cloth, moderately worn. King 46-417 1983 $20

HOFFMAN, FREDERICK   Freudianism and the Literary Mind. Baton
Rouge: Louisiana State Univ. Press, 1945. First edition. Very good
in worn dust jacket. Gach 94-169 1983 $25

HOFFMAN, FREDERICK   The Statistical Experience Data of the
Johns Hopkins Hospital... 1916. Extract. 8vo. Orig. binding.
Fye H-3-266 1983 $25

HOFMANN, AUGUSTUS WILHELM   Chemische Erinnerungen aus der Berliner
Vergangenheit. Berlin: Hirschwald, 1882. 8vo. Cont. half morocco,
with orig. wrappers bound in. Inscribed presentation copy. A very
good copy. Zeitlin 264-213 1983 $80

HOFFMAN, AUGUSTUS WILHELM   On Ammonia and its Derivatives.
London: Walton & Maberly, 1859. First edition. 8vo. Orig.
wrappers. Front cover detached, otherwise a good copy. Zeitlin
264-218 1983 $60

HOFMANN, E.   The Young Beetle-Collector's Handbook.
1908. Third edition, 20 coloured plates, 8vo, original cloth.
Wheldon 160-1094 1983 £12

HOFFMANN, E. T. A.   The Devil's Elixir. Edinburgh:
Blackwood. London: Cadel, 1824. First and only translation, 8vo, 2
vols., cont. half calf gilt, marbled boards. A very fine copy.
Trebizond 18-116 1983 $300

HOFFMANN, E. T. A.   The Devil's Elixir. Edinburgh: William
Blackwood, 1824. First edition in English. 2 vols. Orig. boards
with paper labels on spines. Spines defective. Good. MacManus 279-
2723 1983 $125

HOFMANN, FRIEDRICH H.   Johann Peter Melchior, 1742-1825.
Munchen/Berlin/Leipzig: F. Schmidt, 1921. 46 plates (several
color facsimile). 4to. Boards. Ars Libri 32-447 1983 $100

HOFFMANN, G. F.   Plantarum Umbelliferarum Genera.
Moscow, 1816. Vol. I, coloured vignette title and 5 engraved plates,
8vo, contemporary straight grained morocco, gilt, trifle rubbed,
g.e. Scarce. A nice copy.

HOFFMANN, HEINRICH   Bastian der Faulpetz. Frankfort: a.M.,
n.d. Small quarto. Printed on one side only. Later printing of orig.
edition. Each page with half-page, color-printed illus. Nice copy
in color-printed boards, cloth spine. Bromer 25-350 1983 $110

HOFFMANN, HEINRICH   The English Struwwelpeter. Frankfort:
Rutten & Loening, n.d. (ca.1890). 47th edition. Sm. 4to. 34 hand-
coloured images on 24pp. One corner torn. Colour pictorial boards,
rebacked. Greer 40-110 1983 £15

HOFFMANN, HEINRICH   Der Struwwelpeter...Frankfurt am Main,
Rutten & Loning, n.d. Illus. in color. 4to, orig. boards, cloth
back, on heavy paper, nice. Morrill 288-178 1983 $27.50

HOFFMANN, HEINRICH   Der Struwwelpeter. Stuttgart: F. Carl,
n.d. (ca.1900). Orig. edition. 4to. Cloth backed pictorial boards.
Tips rubbed. Color illus. throughout. Printed on stiff-board.
Very good to fine. Aleph-bet 8-140 1983 $25

HOFFMANN, RICHARD   Bayerische Altarbaukunst. Munchen,
1923. xxxvii, (3), 307, (1)pp. 275 illus. 4to. Cloth. Ars Libri
SB 26-103 1983 $65

HOFMANN, JULIUS   Die Kupferstiche des Meisters. Wien:
Gesellschaft fur Vervielfaltigende Kunst, 1911. 8 collotype plates
Folio. Boards, 1/4 cloth. Ars Libri 33-254 1983 $85

HOFMANN, KURT   Die Erstdrucke der Werke von Johannes
Brahms. Tutzing, 1975. 8vo, cl. Reproduction of 209 title pages.
Salloch 387-292 1983 $100

HOFMANN, R.   Otto von Bismarck. Berlin: A. Hofman,
1897. 4to.(oblong). 40 colour plates. Green pictorial cloth.
Greer 40-198 1983 £27.50

HOFLAND, BARBARA   The Son of a Genius. London: J.
Harris, 1822. Engraved frontis. Orig. half calf over boards.
Karmiole 72-28 1983 $50

HOFMEISTER, W.   On the Germination, Development and
Fructification of the Higher Cryptogamia. Ray Society, 1862. 65
plates, 8vo, original cloth, used. Wheldon 160-1841 1983 £30

HOGABOAM, JAMES J.   The Bean Creek Valley. Hudson, Mich.:
Jas. M. Scarritt, Publisher, 1876. First edition. Printed green
wrappers. Aside from very few light stains, fine copy. Bradley 66-
592 1983 $52.50

HOGAN, JOHN JOSEPH   On the Mission in Missouri, 1857-68.
Kansas City, 1892. Argosy 710-322 1983 $50

HOGAN, JOHN JOSEPH   On the Mission in Missouri 1857-1868.
Kansas City, Mo., 1892. Orig. cloth. First edition. Ginsberg 47-
526 1982 $50

HOGARTH, DAVID G.   Arabia. Oxford, 1922. First edition,
folding map, cr. 8vo, orig. cloth. Fenning 60-178 1983 £12.50

HOGARTH, DAVID G.   The Life of Charles M. Doughty. N.Y.:
Doubleday, 1929. Orig. cloth. Illus. MacManus 278-1606 1983 $20

HOGARTH, DAVID G.   The Life of Charles M. Doughty. O.U.P.,
1928. First edition, map & plates, roy. 8vo, orig. cloth, spine
faded and wanting a blank flyleaf. Fenning 60-179 1983 £24.50

HOGARTH, DAVID G.   The Nearer East. H. Frowde, Regions of
the World Series, 1905. First edition, maps, plans, etc. 8vo, orig.
cloth, gilt. Fenning 60-180 1983 £32.50

HOGARTH, DAVID G.   The Penetration of Arabia. Lawrence and
Bullen, Story of Exploration series, 1904. First edition, maps, plates,
8vo, orig. cloth, gilt. Fenning 60-181 1983 £48.50

HOGARTH, DAVID G.   A Wandering Scholar in the Levant. John
Murray, 1896. Second edition, with folding map and 13 plates,
8vo, orig. cloth, gilt. Fenning 61-207 1983 £14.50

HOGARTH, WILLIAM   The Works of William Hogarth. Lon.,
1822. Elephant folio, complete but lacking suppressed plates, interior lightly foxed, nice in rubbed binding. Quill & Brush 54-651
1983 $750

HOGENDORP, G. K. VAN   Memorie Over Den Tegenwoordigen Staat.
Amsterdam, 1804. Cont. marbled paper over boards, cloth spine. 8vo.
Good. Edwards 1044-351 1983 £125

HOGG, JAMES   The Jacobite Relics of Scotland.
Edinburgh: for William Blackwood, 1819. First edition. 2 vols.
8vo. Full green crushed levant morocco, three-line gilt borders,
fully gilt panelled spines, inner gilt dentelles, edges gilt, by
James Toovey. With musical scores. From the library of Thomas
Gaysford, Dean of Christchurch, with his bookplates. Traylen
94-443 1983 £450

HOGG, JAMES   The Jacobite relics of Scotland.
Edinburgh: Blackwood, etc., 1819-21. First edition. 2 vols.
Later half calf, spine gilt. First edition. Slightly rubbed.
Very good copy. Ximenes 63-544 1983 $50

HOGG, JAMES   The Mountain Bard. Edinburgh: Oliver
& Boyd, 1821. 12mo, half title. Half calf, a little rubbed. Jarndyce
31-744 1983 £28

HOGG, JAMES   The Pilgrims of the Sun. Edinburgh,
1815. 8vo, uncut, modern boards. Some pages a little soiled at the
outer edges. First edition. Bickersteth 77-214 1983 £48

HOGG, JAMES   The Poetic Mirror, or the Living Bards
of Britain. 1817. 12mo, name in ink at top of the title, and name
"J. Hogg" below the title, but not in the author's autograph,
speckled calf by A. Milne of Forres, with his ticket. Bickersteth 77-
213 1983 £58

HOGG, JAMES   The Queen's Wake. Glasgow, 1871. 6
tipped-in photographs. K Books 301-93 1983 £25

HOGG, R.   The Vegetable Kingdom and its Products.
1858. Text-figures, 8vo, cloth. Wheldon 160-1532 1983 £12

HOGG, THOMAS JEFFERSON   Shelley at Oxford. London: Methuen &
Co., 1904. First separate edition. Orig. parchment-backed boards
with paper label. Paper label on spine worn. Corners bumped. With
the extra label tipped in at back. Good. MacManus 280-4726 1983
$25

HOHMAN, ELMO PAUL   The American Whaleman. New York, 1928.
1st ed. Illus. 8vo. Morrill 288-179 1983 $35

HOLBEIN, HANS   The Family of Sir Thomas More.
London/New York: Johnson Reprint Co., 1977. 8 collotype plates
(facsimile) as issued, loose. Folio. Portfolio. Cloth. Ars
Libri 32-325 1983 $85

HOLBERG, LUDVIG   A Journey to the World Underground.
Printed for T. Astley and B. Collins, 1742. 12mo, contemporary calf
rebacked; former owner's name cut from corner of title-page. 1st
English edition. Hill 165-58 1983 £285

HOLBERG, LUDVIG   A Journey to the World Under-Ground.
For T. Astley, and B. Collins, 1742. First English edition. 12mo,
cont. calf (rebacked). Tear in blank corner of title crudely repaired,
some finger-marks and traces of use. This copy has the 6 advert.
leaves at end. They bear their own signature (an asterisk). Hannas
69-92 1983 £180

HOLBROOK, ANN CATHERINE   The Dramatist; or, memoirs of the stage.
Birmingham: printed by Martin and Hunter, 1809. 8vo, sewn, as
issued. 1st edition. A bit dust-soiled at the beginning and end,
corners slightly rounded, but an uncut copy. Ximenes 64-274 1983
$200

HOLBROOK, J. E.   North American Herpetology. (1842),
facsimile reprint, 1976. Second edition with a coloured portrait and
147 plates (20 coloured), 5 vols. in 1, 4to, buckram. Wheldon
160-968 1983 £41

HOLBROOK, JACKSON   The Fear of Books. London: Curwen
Press, 1932. One of 48 copies signed by the author. Bound in full
dark green morocco. Fine. Gekoski 2-15 1983 £225

HOLBROOK, SAMUEL   Threescore Years: An Autobiography...
Boston, 1857. Illustrations. Jenkins 153-254 1983 $125

HOLCROFT, THOMAS   The man of ten thousand: a comedy.
London: printed for G. G. and J. Robinson, 1796. 8vo, modern half
calf, 1st ed. Presentation copy, inscribed by author on the title-
page: "Miss Pope from the author." Ximenes 64-275 1983 $200

HOLCROFT, THOMAS   Memoirs of the Late Thomas Holcroft.
Longman, Hurst, 1816. First edition, 3 vols. Half titles. Uncut.
Orig. blue boards, drab paper spines, labels. Leading hinge vol. I
sl. weak. Jarndyce 30-1020 1983 £160

HOLCROFT, THOMAS   The Road to Ruin. Dublin: Printed by
W. Porter, for T. Wilkinson, 1792. First Irish edition, 12mo,
wrapper. Fenning 62-177 1983 £10.50

HOLCROFT, THOMAS   Seduction: a comedy. London: printed
for G. G. J. and J. Robinson, 1787. 8vo, wrappers, 1st ed. Very
good copy. Ximenes 64-276 1983 $60

HOLCROFT, THOMAS   The Theatrical Recorder. London:
printed by C. Mercier and Co., and published for the author by H. D.
Symonds, 1805-6. 2 vols., 8vo, half maroon morocco, gilt, spines
gilt, t.e.g., by Lloyd, Wallis and Lloyd. 30 plates. A fine set.
Ximenes 64-277 1983 $550

HOLD, EDWIN BISSELL (1873-1946)   Animal Drive and the Learning
Process. NY: Henry Hold, (1931). First edition. Cloth lightly
flecked and very slight damp-staining to text. Generally very good
copy. Gach 95-217 1983 $30

HOLDEN, CURRY   Hill of the Rooster. New York: Holt,
(1956). Cloth and boards. First edition. Fine in very slightly
worn dust jacket. Reese 19-273 1983 $175

HOLDEN, EDWARD S.   List of Recorded Earthquakes in
California, Lower California, Oregon and Washington Territory.
Sacramento, 1887. Orig. printed wraps. bound in half morocco.
Embossed library stamps. Ginsberg 47-341 1983 $75

HOLDEN, JOHN ALLAN   Private Book Collectors in the
United States and Canada. New York: R.R. Bowker, 1931. 25 1/2cm.
Half bound in green cloth, paper over boards. Good to very good.
Scarce. McGahern 53-73 1983 $75

HOLDEN, RAYMOND   The Arrow at the Heel: Poems. New
York, (1940). 8vo. Cloth. A fine copy in lightly rubbed dj. In
Our Time 156-397 1983 $35

HOLDEN, WILLIAM C.   Alkali Trials or Social and Economic
Movements of the Texas Frontier 1846-1900. Dallas: Southwest
Press, 1903. Fine copy. Former owners stamp on title else a fine
copy. Jenkins 151-127 1983 $125

HOLDER, CHARLES FREDERICK   All About Pasadena and its Vicinity.
Boston: Lee & Shepard, 1889. Wrappers. Some browning. Dawson 471-
121 1983 $100

HOLDER, CHARLES FREDERICK   An Isle of Summer. L.A., (1892).
Illus., folded map. Orig. printed wraps. First ediiton. Ginsberg
47-111 1983 $50

HOLDER, CHARLES FREDERICK   Big Game at Sea. N.Y., Outing, 1908.
First edition. Illus. with 45 views and halftone photos. Fine
pictorial blue cloth stamped in gilt, black and light blue with
deepwater angling scene (minor waterstaining to first 10 pp of text
in upper right corner) else very good - fine. Houle 22-1107 1983
$85

HOLDER, CHARLES FREDERICK   The Big Game Fishes of the United States. N.Y., 1903. First edition. Thick 8vo, color frontis. with many other plates, several in color. 3/4 green morocco over marbled boards, spine ruled and decorated in gilt, t.e.g., one of 100 numbered deluxe copies on large paper. Marbled endpapers, unopened. Fine. Houle 22-1055 1983 $350

HOLDER, CHARLES FREDERICK   The Game Fishes of the World. London: Hodder & Stoughton, (1913). Plates. Cloth. Dawson 471-122 1983 $50

HOLDER, CHARLES FREDERICK   Life in the Open. N.Y., Putnam, 1906. First edition. Illus. Pictorial cloth, t.e.g. Very good-fine. Houle 21-1089 1983 $65

HOLDER, CHARLES FREDERICK   Mr. Punch with Rod and Gun. London, n.d., ca. 1880. 8vo, with 193 illus. by John Leech and others. Tan pictorial cloth, with design of Mr. Punch. Enclosed in a half morocco slipcase. Houle 21-1038 1983 $135

HOLDER, CHARLES FREDERICK   Southern California. Los Angeles: Times-Mirror Co., 1888. 8 folding woodcuts. Wrappers, delicate, some page corners broken off not affecting text. Dawson 471-123 1983 $150

HOLDICH, T. H.   India. London, (1904). Numerous maps and diagrams. 8vo. Orig. cloth. Good. Edwards 1044-352 1983 £18

HOLDSWORTH, JOHN THOM   The First and Second Banks of the United States. Wash., 1910. Orig. printed wraps. Rebacked in cloth. First edition. Ginsberg 46-48 1983 $25

HOLDSWORTH, WILLIAM S.   Charles Dickens as a Legal Historian. New Haven, Yale University Press, 1928. First edition, d.w. Sl. torn, otherwise v.g. Jarndyce 31-608 1983 £20

HOLE, HUGH MARSHALL   The Making of Rhodesia. London: Macmillan and Co. Ltd., 1926. With 14 photographic plates and 5 maps. (4 color maps, 1 folding, and 1 b/w folding map). Blue cloth. Karmiole 73-3 1983 $50

HOLE, S. R.   A Book about Roses. 1880. 7th edition, coloured plate, 8vo, original cloth, trifle used. Wheldon 160-1954 1983 £12

THE HOLKHAM Bible Picture Book. The Dropmore Press, 1954. Folio, buckram, cloth. The 2nd ed. printed on Arnold & Foster mould made vellum and bound in half red niger morocco with leather fore edge and parchment sides. Very fine. In Our Time 156-224 1983 $200

HOLLAND, CLIVE   A Writer of Fiction. Westminster: Archibald Constable & Co., 1897. First edition. Orig. cloth. Endpapers slightly foxed. Fine. MacManus 279-2727 1983 $35

HOLLAND, HENRY   Chapters on Mental Physiology. London: Longman, Brown, Green and Longmans, 1852. Publisher's blind-blocked brown cloth, rebacked with paper label. Library stamp on titlepage. Gach 95-211 1983 $75

HOLLAND, HENRY   Recollections of Past Life. NY: D. Appleton, 1872. First American edition. Spine tips very worn. Gach 94-210 1983 $27.50

HOLLAND, JOHN   The History and Description of Fossil Fuel, the Collieries, and Coal Trade of Great Britain. Whittaker and Co., 1835. 8vo, ad. leaf, numerous text illus., orig. cloth with paper label, slightly worn at top of the spine, top of upper joint slit. First edition. Bickersteth 75-241 1983 £48

HOLLAND, JOSIAH GILBERT   History of Western Massachusetts. Springfield, 1855. 1st ed. Map. 2 vols., 8vo. Bookplates. Morrill 287-234 1983 $60

HOLLAND, RICHARD   Globe Notes. (Oxford?), 1666. First edition. Small 8vo. Cont. calf. A slip with 11 lines of text laid in between pp. 14 and 15. From the library of the Earls of Kinnoul, with ms. exlibris "Dupplin Castle", and shelf mark. Binding rebacked. Eight contemporary pen corrections in the text. Kraus 164-129 1983 $1,850

HOLLAND, ROBERT   Account of the Late Aeronautical Expedition from London to Weilburg... New York, Theodore Foster, 1837. 1st American ed., small 8vo, modern calf backed marbled boards. Pickering & Chatto 22-48 1983 $500

HOLLANDER, BERNARD (1864-1934)   The Mental Functions of the Brain. London: Grant Richards, 1901. Publisher's green cloth. Inscribed by Hollander to the Bartholomew Hospital Library with their bookplate and stamp on titlepage. Gach 95-212 1983 $75

HOLLANDER, BERNARD (1864-1934)   Mental Symptoms of Brain Disease. NY: Rebman Co., (1910). First American edition. Library bookplate, tear to front flyleaf, hinges cracked. Gach 95-213 1983 $22.50

HOLLANDER, EUGEN   Askulap und Venus - Eine Kultur... Berlin, 1928. First edition. 4to. Orig. binding. Prof. illus. Scarce. Fye H-3-268 1983 $125

HOLLANDER, EUGEN   Plastik und Medizin. Stuttgart, 1903. Illus. 4to, orig. pict. wrs. in cloth-backed bd. Folder tied. First edition. Argosy 713-270 1983 $150

HOLLEY, GEORGE W.   The Falls of Niagara. New York, 1883. 1st ed. Illus. 8vo, all edges gilt. 2 small worn spots on spine. Morrill 286-196 1983 $27.50

HOLLEY, MARY AUSTIN   Texas. Austin: The Overland Press, 1981. Folio. Three quarter calf and cloth, gilt, t.e.g. Folding map. One of 325 numbered copies, printed on Arches Musee paper, after a design by Tom Whitridge, and signed by Ron Tyler. Mint as issued, in plain dust jacket. Reese 20-1129 1983 $240

HOLLEY, MARY AUSTIN   Texas: Observations Historical, Geographical and Descriptive in a Series of Letters. Austin, Overland, 1981. Illus., map. Three quarter leather. One of 325 copies, numbered and signed by the printer and author of the forward, Tom Whitridge and Ron Ryler. Ginsberg 47-863 1983 $240

HOLLICK, FREDERICK   Outlines of Anatomy & Physiology, Illustrated by a New Dissected Plate of the Human Organization (in color), and by Separate Views. Philadelphia, 1846. 1st ed. 4to. Orig. boards, roan back. Plate and text illus. Binding rubbed and stained; lacks blank endleaves. Morrill 289-101 1983 $47.50

HOLLIDAY, P.   Fungus diseases of Tropical Crops. 1980. Tables, 8vo, cloth. Wheldon 160-2119 1983 £61.50.

HOLLINGSHEAD, JOHN   Ragged London in 1861. Smith, Elder, 1861. First edition, half title, 1 p + 16 pp ads. Extensive pencil marginalia and underlining. Lacks following end paper. Orig. lilac cloth. Jarndyce 31-264 1983 £38

HOLLINGSHEAD, JOHN   The Story of Leicester Square. Simpkin, Marshall, 1892. First edition. Numerous illus. by Faustin, Russell, Phil May, etc. & facs. reproductions. 2 pp ads, front. port. 24 pp ads. Orig. printed lilac wraps. bound into modern blue cloth, v.g. Jarndyce 31-265 1983 £15

HOLLINGSWORTH, JOHN MC HENRY The Journal of...of the First New York Volunteers. San Francisco Historical Society: 1923. First edition. 1/300. Color frontis. Boards and vellum. Fine copy, covers a little dusty. Bradley 66-483 1983 $150

HOLLINGSWORTH, JOHN MC HENRY The Journal of Lieutenant...of the First New York Volunteers. San Francisco, Ca. Hist. Soc., 1923. Illus. Orig. boards. Ltd. edition of 50 large paper copies. Ginsberg 46-452 1983 $75

HOLLINGWORTH, HARRY LEVI (1880-1956)   The Influence of Caffein on Mental and Motor Efficiency. NY: The Science Press, 1922. Some pencilling, good copy in orig. cloth. Gach 95-214 1983 $25

HOLLINGWORTH, HARRY LEVI (1880-1956)   The Sense of Taste. NY: Moffat, Yard, 1917. First edition. Cloth soiled. Library bookplate and stamp. Gach 95-216 1983 $20

HOLLISTER, HIEL   Pawlet for One Hundred Years. Albany, Munsell, 1867. 1st ed. Small 8vo. Rubbed, backstrip partly torn. Morrill 287-473 1983 $35

HOLLISTER, PAUL M.   Dwiggins: A Characterization.
Cambridge, MA: Cygnet Press, 1929. Octavo. Unopened. Very fine
in printed wrappers. Bromer 25-195 1983 $85

HOLLOWAY, W.   The minor minstrel; or, poetical
pieces... London: for W. Suttaby, etc., 1808. First edition.
12mo. Cont. black morocco, gilt, spine gilt, a.e.g. Frontis.
Slightly rubbed. Very good copy. Ximenes 63-411 1983 $80

HOLMAN, BARBARA   The Letters of a Young Miner Covering
the Adventures of Jasper S. Hill During the California Goldrush,
1849-1852. San Francisco: John Howell Books, 1964. Plus map.
Limited to 475 copies. Mint copy. Jenkins 155-572 1983 $75

HOLMAN, DAVID   Buckskin and Homespun: 1820. Austin,
Wind River, (1979). Illus. by Pat Massey. Orig. cloth, dust wrapper.
First edition. Ltd. to 450 numbered copies, signed by Holman.
Ginsberg 47-864 1983 $200

HOLMAN, DAVID   Letters of Hard Times in Texas, 1840-
1890. Austin: Roger Beacham, 1974. 1st ed. Limited to 295
numbered copies, of which this is 1 of 90 special copies printed
on large handmade paper, and bound in cloth-backed marbled paper
over boards. Jenkins 155-565 1983 $175

HOLMAN, WILLIAM R.   Library Publications. San Francisco:
Roger Beacham, (1965). Folio, illus., inserts, samples in pocket
at back. 1st ed., 1 of 350 copies printed. Orig. cloth-backed
marbled boards, label, uncut. Fine copy. Jenkins 155-578 1983
$450

HOLMAN, WILLIAM R.   Library Publications. San Francisco:
Roger Beacham, (1965). First edition. Folio. Cloth spine, marbled
boards, paper spine label. Limited to 350 copies. Conts 16 tipped-in
examples of fine printing in text, and additional 16 examples
inserted in a pocket in the rear of the book. Oak Knoll 49-236
1983 $285

HOLMAN, WILLIAM R.   Library Publications. San Francisco:
Roger Beacham, (1965). 67 pages with separate samples laid into pocket
in back. Boards. Cloth spine. One sample offsetting on text.
Dawson 471-124 1983 $150

HOLME, C.   Touring the Ancient World with a Camera.
London, 1932. Illus. 4to, cloth. Salloch 385-361 1983 $20

HOLME, GEOFFREY   Caricature of To-Day. New York &
London (printed in London), 1928. 4to. Plates. Binding partly
faded, bookplate removed. Morrill 288-180 1983 $37.50

HOLME, GEOFFREY   Decorative Art 1930. N.Y., n.d. Numer-
ous photots of homes, interiors, furniture, etc. Cloth. T.e.g.
In frayed dust wrapper. Ads printed separately and are present.
Very good. King 45-344 1983 $85

HOLMES, ABIEL   American Annals; or a Chronological
History of America, 1492-1806. Cambridge: W. Hilliard, 1805.
1st ed, 2 vols., 8vo, orig. mottled calf, backstrips only slightly
worn. Argosy 710-186 1983 $150

HOLMES, EDMOND   The Triumph of Love. London: John Lane,
1903. First edition. Orig. decorated cloth. Presentation copy.
MacManus 279-2731 1983 $25

HOLMES, EDMOND   What is Poetry? London: John Lane,
1900. Small quarto. Gilt decorated cloth. First edition. Covers
slightly darkened, else near fine. Reese 20-523 1983 $20

HOLMES, J. H.   Way Back in Papua. London, 1926.
Frontis. 3 plates. 8vo. Orig. cloth. Good. Edwards 1044-353 1983
£40

HOLMES, JOHN   Address to the Living. New York,
(1937). 8vo. Cloth. Blurb on jacket by Robert Frost. This copy
inscribed by the poet. A vg-fine copy in rubbed dj. In Our Time
156-398 1983 $35

HOLMES, JOHN   Fair Warning. New York, (1939). 8vo,
cloth. Decorations by Henry Kane. Some fraying to the top of the
spine, else fine copy in lightly worn dust jacket. This copy inscribed
by the poet to a noted collector and dated 1957. In Our Time 156-399
1983 $35

HOLMES, JOHN   Map of My Country. New York, (1943).
8vo. Cloth. Name of a book reviewer on front flyleaf, else fine
copy in chipped dj. In Our Time 156-400 1983 $20

HOLMES, OLIVER WENDELL (1809-1894)   The Autocrat of the Breakfast
Table. Boston, Phillips, Sampson & Co., 1858. First ed., large paper
copy. Illus. Reddish brown cloth, all edges gilt, author's signature
(clipped from a letter) tipped in. Spine ends little worn, "Boston"
gilt gone on spine. Very good. Bradley 66-204 1983 $75

HOLMES, OLIVER WENDELL (1809-1894)   The Autocrat of the Breakfast
Table. B., 1858. First ed., second printing, covers worn and frayed,
some interior stains, otherwise good. Quill & Brush 54-653 1983
$35

HOLMES, OLIVER WENDELL (1809-1894)   The Autocrat of the Breakfast
Table. Boston: Phillips, Sampson, 1858. First ed., second printing,
binding A. Orig. brown cloth, gilt, first state of the endpapers.
Spine tips chipped, but brighter than usual for this cloth color.
Jenkins 155-580 1983 $20

HOLMES, OLIVER WENDELL (1809-1894)   The Autocrat of the Breakfast
Table. Boston, 1889. 2 vols., 8vo., orig. binding. Fye H-3-269 1983
$20

HOLMES, OLIVER WENDELL (1809-1894)   Before the Curfew and Other
Poems. London, (1888). Cloth, 8vo., first English ed., fine. In Our
Time 156-403 1983 $25

HOLMES, OLIVER WENDELL (1809-1894)   Border Lines of Knowledge.
Boston, 1862. Second issue with Houghton Mifflin on spine, ex-
lib. with all markings, corners worn and spine edges chipped, front
fly loose, good. Quill & Brush 54-654 1983 $25

HOLMES, OLIVER WENDELL (1809-1894)   Currents and Counter-Currents
in Medical Science... Boston, 1861. 8vo., orig. binding, first ed.,
minor chipping at head and tail of spine, else fine. Gye H-3-270
1983 $100

HOLMES, OLIVER WENDELL (1809-1894)   A Dissertation on Acute Peri-
carditis. Boston, 1937. First ed., 12mo., uncut, bound in white
vellum, very fine. Fye H-3-271 1983 $45

HOLMES, OLIVER WENDELL (1809-1894)   Homoeopathy, and Its Kindred
Delusions.. Boston, 1842. First ed., 12mo., orig. boards, rubbed,
lacks part of backstrip and part of label, lacks blank leaf before
title. Morrill 289-102 1983 $35

HOLMES, OLIVER WENDELL (1809-1894)   Mechanism in Thought and
Morals. Boston, Osgood, 1871. First ed., first printing, orig.
green cloth, gilt. The Frank Maier copy with bookplate and some old
catalogue descriptions pasted in on end papers. Very good copy, with
correction of a very important word in Holmes' hand at p. 23.
Jenkins 155-581 1983 $75

HOLMES, OLIVER WENDELL (1809-1894)   Memorial Bunker Hill. Boston,
(1875). First ed., illus., pictorial gray wrappers. Fine. Bradley
66-205 1983 $40

HOLMES, OLIVER WENDELL (1809-1894)   A Mortal Antipathy. Boston,
1885. First ed., 8vo., green cloth. Argosy 714-873 1983 $30

HOLMES, OLIVER WENDELL (1809-1894)   Our Hundred Days in Europe.
Boston & New York, Houghton, Mifflin, 1887. First ed., binding A.
Orig. light green pictorial cloth, gilt, t.e.g., no priority between
bindings A and B, but the pictorial cloth is much scarcer of the two.
owner's inscription. Fine. Jenkins 155-582 1983 $50

HOLMES, OLIVER WENDELL (1809-1894)   Over the Teacups. B., 1891.
First ed., later issue without ads, spine and corners sl. rubbed,
front flys sl. offset, else near fine. Quill & Brush 54-655 1983 $25

HOLMES, OLIVER WENDELL (1809-1894)   The Poetical Works. Boston, 1895. 8vo., orig. binding, with an engraved portrait of Holmes, very fine. Fye H-3-274 1983 $25

HOLMES, OLIVER WENDELL (1809-1894)   Professor at the Breakfast Table. Boston, Ticknor, 1860. First ed., orig. brown cloth, glazed endpapers, very good to fine. Houle 21-416 1983 $75

HOLMES, OLIVER WENDELL (1809-1894)   Songs in Many Keys. Boston, Ticknor & Fields, 1862. First ed. with period lacking at p. 42. Orig. purple cloth, gilt. Pres. copy inscribed by Holmes to fellow author F. S. Cozzens. Holmes has also made a textual correction in ink at p. 133 (not noted in other pres. copies of this vol.) Cloth faded but a very good unworn copy. Jenkins 155-585 1983 $150

HOLMES, OLIVER WENDELL (1809-1894)   Songs in Many Keys. Boston, Ticknor & Fields, 1862. First ed., orig. lavender cloth, gilt, t.e.g. From the lib. of Waldo Higginson, a correspondent of Holmes. Spine evenly faded, but fresh tight copy. Jenkins 155-586 1983 $20

HOLMES, OLIVER WENDELL (1809-1894)   Songs of Many Seasons. Boston, James Osgood, 1875. 8vo., cloth, some rubbing at base of spine, else fine. In Our Time 156-404 1983 $25

HOLMES, OLIVER WENDELL (1809-1894)   Urania. Boston, Ticknor, 1846. First ed., orig. printed wrapper. Rear wrapper wanting, else fine copy. Jenkins 155-590 1983 $40

HOLMES, OLIVER WENDELL (1809-1894)   Urania. Boston, Ticknor, 1846. First ed., lacks wrappers, fine. Jenkins 155-591 1983 $22.50

HOLMES, OLIVER WENDELL (1809-1894)   Works. Boston, Houghton & Mifflin, (1892-1896). Artist's ed., illus. with over 100 steel engrav-ed portraits and photogravures, drawings by Julian Scott, Alfred Kappes, William L. Sheppard, Frank T. Merrill, and five plates by Howard Pyle. Three quarter gilt stamped white vellum over red silk boards, t.e.g., uncut, mostly unopened, some light rubbing at corner, else fine. 15 vols., one of 750 sets. Houle 22-478 1983 $795

HOLMES, OLIVER WENDELL (1841-1935)   Speeches. Boston: Little Brown, 1891. First ed., orig. printed boards, uncut. Very nice copy with less than the usual aging of the paper boards and no rubbing. Jenkins 155-588 1983 $85

HOLMES, OLIVER WENDELL (1841-1935)   Speeches. Boston, Little Brown, 1900. Orig. printed boards, uncut, very lightly used copy. Jenkins 155-589 1983 $50

HOLMES, T. R.   A History of the Indian Mutiny. London, 1904. Fifth edition, revised throughout and slightly enlarged. Fold-ing maps and plans. Thick 8vo. Orig. cloth. Good. Edwards 1044-354 1983 £18

HOLMES, THOMAS J.   Cotton Mather. Cambridge, 1940. 3 vols. Half morocco and cloth, fine, with the stamp of the Bibliographical Center for Research on the verso of the title page, but otherwise unmarked. Reese 19-64 1983 $300

HOLMES, THOMAS J.   Increase Mather. Cleveland, 1931. 2 vols. Half morocco and cloth, fine, except for stamp of the Bibliographical Center for Research on the verso of the titlepage. Reese 19-65 1983 $250

HOLMES, WILLIAM H.   Ancient Art of the Province of Chiriqui, Colombia. Washington, 1888. 285 illus. 4to. New boards. 1/4 cloth. Ars Libri 34-280 1983 $40

HOLST, CHRISTIAN VON   Francesco Granacci. Munchen: Bruck-mann, 1974. 171 illus. Square 4to. Cloth. Dust jacket. Ars Libri 33-177 1983 $125

HOLT-WHITE, A. E.   The Butterflies and Moths of Teneriffe. 1894. 4 coloured plates, sm. 4to, original cloth (trifle rubbed). Inscription on half-title, which is slightly browned. Wheldon 160-1095 1983 £40

HOLUB, EMIL   Seven years in South Africa. Boston: Houghton, Mifflin, 1881. 2 vols. 8vo. Map. Numerous plates. Orig. pictorial cloth. Rubbed. Adelson Africa-194 1983 $120

HOLYOAKE, GEORGE JACOB   John Stuart Mill, as Some of the Working Classes Knew Him. Trubner, 1873. First edition. Rebound in moire-patterned green cloth, v.g. Jarndyce 31-323 1983 £28

HOLYOAKE, GEORGE JACOB   Sixty Years of an Agitator's Life. T. Fisher Unwin, 1893. 2nd edition, 2 vols. Half title vol. II. Orig. blue cloth, v.g. Jarndyce 30-1021 1983 £18.50

HOLZT, ALFRED   Die Schule des Elektrotechnikers. Leipzig, (1896). Illus. and diagrams, 17 double-page plates, partly in color. 3 vols., 4to. Some stains on back cover of vol. 2, otherwise nice. Morrill 289-197 1983 $27.50

HOME, EVERARD   A Dissertation on the Properties of Pus. London: Printed by John Richardson, Printer to the Society, 1788. 1st ed., 4to, engraving on title; disbound. Pickering & Chatto 22-49 1983 $300

HOME, EVERARD   Practical Observations on the Treatment of Ulcers of the Leg. Phila., 1811. First American edition. Argosy 713-273 1983 $85

HOME, EVERARD   Practical Observations on the Treatment of Strictures in the Urethra. Printed for George Nichol; and J. Johnson, 1795. 8vo, old marbled boards with calf spine, rebacked, ink inscription of the Edinburgh Medical Society on the title, and the words "Vol. I" added in ink. First edition. Bickersteth 77-283 1983 £25

HOME, JOHN   Agis: a tragedy. Dublin: printed for G. and A. Ewing, etc., 1758. 12mo, modern quarter morocco. First Dublin edition. Very scarce. Ximenes 64-278 1983 $125

HOME, JOHN   Douglas: a tragedy. Dublin: printed for G. Faulkner, etc., 1757. 12mo, disbound, First Dublin edition. A very scarce edition. Ximenes 64-281 1983 $75

HOME, JOHN   Douglas: a tragedy. Edinburgh: printed for G. Hamilton and J. Balfour, W. Gary and W. Peter, 1757. 8vo, disbound, 1st Edinburgh edition. Half-title present (soiled); short tears in the blank inner margins. Ximenes 64-280 1983 $75

HOME, JOHN   Douglas: a tragedy. London: printed for A. Millar, 1757. 8vo, wrappers. First London edition. Half-title present. Ximenes 64-279 1983 $75

HOME, MASSINGBERD   Carstairs. Chapman & Hall, 1876. First edition, 3 vols. Half title vol. I, 3 vols. bound as I. Orig. brown cloth, rubbed, inner hinges weakening. Jarndyce 30-422 1983 £17.50

THE HOME Affections Pourtrayed by the Poets. Routledge, 1866. New edn. Illus. with 100 engrs. by Birket Foster, J. Gilbert, H. Weir, Absolon, Harvey, Pickersgill, Tenniel, T. Dalziel, Millais, Godwin, Sleigh, etc., engr'd by Bros. Dalziel. Green sand grain cloth gilt, bevelled boards, a.e.g., extremities of cvrs. sl. wear, contemp. insc. pasted fr. ep., contents foxed, vg. Hodgkins 27-287 1983 £25

HOME of American Statesmen. New York, 1854. 8vo. Full leather, a.e.g. First American book to be illustrated with a mounted photo-graph. Some light wear to the spine, mainly a fine copy. In Our Time 156-405 1983 $350

HOMER, HENRY   An Enquiry into the Means of Preserving and Improving the Publick Roads of This Kingdom. Oxford, Printed for S. Parker...1767. 1st ed., 8vo, ad.; early annotations on verso of title and dedication; disbound. Pickering & Chatto 22-50 1983 $300

HOMERUS   The Iliad of Homer. London: W. Bowyer for Bernard Lintott, 1715-20. First folio edition, with engraved frontis., 4 plates and a map. 6 vols. Folio. Cont. half calf, gilt spines, morocco labels, gilt, joints cracked. Traylen 94-672 1983 £350

HOMERUS   Iliad. Glasguae, in AEdibus Academicis Excudebant Robertus et Andreas Foulis, 1747. 2 vols., bound in 1, 4to, cont. green morocco gilt, worn, faded, light foxing, bookplate of Charles Hoare, archdeacon of Surrey. Rare quarto edition. Ravenstree 95-56 1983 $375

HOMERUS The Iliad and Odyssey of Homer. London, printed for J. Johnson, 1791. 2 vols., 4to, orig. russia, hinges cracked, bookplates removed. A very well-preserved copy. One of 175 copies on large, fine paper. First edition. Ravenstree 95-57 1983 $350

HOMERUS The Iliad of Homer Engraved from the Compositions of Iohn Flaxman R.A. London, Longman, Hurst, 1805. Oblong folio of 39 plates and engraved title, cont. cloth, now worn, soiled, faded, hinges broken and spine defective. Some light foxing and a little dust-soiling about outer edges, the plates in good condition. Piroli and Blake were the engravers. Ravenstree 94-99 1983 $225

HOMERUS The Iliad... London, John Murray, 1865. 2 vols., 8vo, cont. purple prize calf, worn, gilt supra-libros and prize bookplate, spine rubbed. Ravenstree 95-58 1983 $35

HOMERUS Odyssey. Ingram, Cooke, 1853. Illus. with Flaxman's designs and other engravers. Frontis. and decor. title page. Blue morocco grain blind stamped cloth, gilt decor. backstrip, cover design by W. Harry Rogers, a.e.g. Nice. Hodgkins 27-288 1983 £15

HOMERUS The Odysseys of Homer. London, John Russell Smith, 1857. 2 vols. 12mo. Unopened. Bindings lightly faded, top of spines slightly frayed. Nice. Morrill 289-614 1983 $20

HOMERUS The Odyssey of Homer. London, 1932. Translated by T.E. Lawrence. 4to. Full black niger morocco, gilt, t.e.g., others uncut. Limited edition of 530 copies, printed and published by Sir Emery Walker, Wilfred Merton and Bruce Rogers, with rondels printed in black and gold from decorations on Greek vases drawn by Bruce Rogers. Traylen 94-514 1983 £200

HOMERUS The whole works of Homer; Prince of Poetts, in his Iliads and Odysses. Stratford-upon-Avon: Shakespeare Head Press, 1930-31. 5 vols. 4to. Uncut in the orange half orange morocco, gilt. Numerous full-page wood-engraved illus. by John Farleigh. Limited edition of 450 numbered copies. Traylen 94-921 1983 £285

HONE, JOSEPH The Love Story of Thomas Davis told in the Letters of Annie Hutton. Dublin, the Cuala Press, 1945. Ltd. edition of 280 numbered copies, with the erratum slip, 8vo, orig. cloth-backed printed boards, with printed paper spine label, fine. Fenning 62-178 1983 £28.50

HONE, PERCY F. Southern Rhodesia. London, 1909. First edition, 8vo, 2 folding maps, other plates, original cloth, gilt. Deighton 3-175 1983 £25

HONE, PHILIP Diary, 1828-1851. New York, 1889. 1st ed. Portrait. 2 vols., 8vo, nice. Morrill 286-614 1983 $50

HONE, WILLIAM Buonapartephobia. The origin of Dr. Slop's name. London: Hone, 1820. Ninth edition. 8vo. Disbound. With a reproduction of David's portrait of Napoleon on the title-page. Date on title slightly shaved. Ximenes 63-486 1983 $20

HONE, WILLIAM Facetiae and Miscellanies. London, 1827. First edition. 8vo. Cont. half morocco, gilt, t.e.g. 120 engravings by George Cruikshank. Traylen 94-447 1983 £80

HONE, WILLIAM The man in the moon. London: Hone, 1820. Second edition. 8vo. Disbound. 15 woodcut illus. by George Cruikshank. Ximenes 63-487 1983 $45

HONE, WILLIAM "Non mi ricordo!" London: Hone, 1820. First edition. 8vo. Disbound. 3 woodcuts by George Cruikshank. Ximenes 63-488 1983 $75

HONE, WILLIAM Non Mi Ricordo... London: Hone, 1820. 16th ed. Orig. plain wrappers, uncut, as issued. Illus. by Hone. Jenkins 155-592 1983 $25

HONE, WILLIAM Plenipo and the devil! London: J. Johnston, 1820. 8vo. Disbound. With a humourous woodcut on the title-page. Scarce. Ximenes 63-494 1983 $60

HONE, WILLIAM The political "A, Apple-pie;" or, the "Extraordinary Red Book" versified... London: printed for the author; and sold by J. Johnston, 1820. Third edition. 8vo. Disbound. 23 woodcuts by George Cruikshank. Ximenes 63-489 1983 $40

HONE, WILLIAM The political queen that Jack loves. London: Roach and Co., n.d. (1820). Third edition. 8vo. Disbound. With 13 woodcut illus. by George Cruikshank. Ximenes 63-490 1983 $60

HONE, WILLIAM The Queen and Magna Charta... London: T. Dolby, 1820. First edition. 8vo. Disbound. With woodcut illus. by I.R. Cruikshank. Very scarce. Ximenes 63-492 1983 $45

HONE, WILLIAM The Queen that Jack found. London: Fiarburn, 1820. Third edition. 8vo. Disbound. 13 woodcuts, 12 of which are by George Cruikshank. Ximenes 63-493 1983 $40

HONE, WILLIAM The Queen's matrimonial ladder... London: Hone, 1820. First edition. 8vo. Disbound. The illus. are by George Cruikshank. Also present, mounted in two parts on a leaf facing the title-page, is the "ladder" itself, designed by Cruikshank as well, and printed on cardboard. Ximenes 63-491 1983 $85

THE HONEST informer or Tom-Tell-Troth's observations. N.p. (London): printed in the yeare 1642. First edition. Small 4to, disbound. Some light browning, but a very good copy. Ximenes 63-101 1983 $75

HONEY, W. B. Dresden China. Troy, N.Y., David Rosenfeld, 1946. First edition. 61 plates illustrating 175 pieces. 8vo. Morrill 290-183 1983 $25

HONEY, W. B. German Porcelain. London, (1947). Illus., of which 4 are in color. 8vo. 1st ed. Morrill 286-198 1983 $12.50

HOOD, EDWIN PAXTON The Maid of Nuremberg, and Other Voluntaries. Chas. Messent, 1878. First edition, sq. 8vo, orig. green cloth, v.g. Signed presentation copy from the author, June 1879. Jarndyce 30-743 1983 £10.50

HOOD, THOMAS The Haunted House. Lawrence & Bullen, 1896. 1st edn. thus. 70 b&w illus. by Herbert Railton, unpaginated. Grey decor. cloth (bookpl. fr. ep., eps. sl. foxed), v.g. Hodgkins 27-453 1983 £12.50

HOOD, THOMAS Hood's Own. A.H. Baily, 1839. First edition. Front. port. vignette woodcuts throughout. Inner hinge cracked, repaired. Orig. purple-brown cloth. Jarndyce 31-746 1983 £28

HOOD, THOMAS Memorials. Edward Moxon, 1860. First edition, 2 vols. Half titles, front. 8 pp Moxon cata. vol. I, dated June 1860. 1 p ads. vol. II. Orig. purple cloth, blocked in blind and gilt. 'London, Edward Moxon & Co' at base of spine, v.g. Jarndyce 30-1022 1983 £20

HOOD, THOMAS Miss Kilmansegg & Her Precious Leg. Moxon, nd (ca. 1875). 60 illus. by Thomas Seccombe engr'd by Joubert. Numerous b&w illus, 2pp adverts. Green sand grain decor. cloth. Binder's ticket of Leighton, Son & Hodge, a.e.g., free eps. broken at hinge & water stain lower joint corner of fr. ep., contemp. insc., vg. Hodgkins 27-291 1983 £18

HOOD, THOMAS National Tales. William H. Ainsworth, 1827. First edition. 2 vols. 12mo, 8 lithographic plates by T. Dighton, printed by Hullmandel. Blue half calf, gilt (a little rubbed), t.e.g., others uncut, by Riviere. Hannas 69-94 1983 £20

HOOD, THOMAS The Plea of the Midsummer Fairies, Hero and Leander, Lycus the Centaur, and other Poems. 1827. 8vo, uncut and ad. leaf, orig. cloth, cracked and partly defective on the spine, orig. paper label chipped and rubbed, but a very good copy. First edition. Bickersteth 77-216 1983 £48

HOOD, THOMAS   Poems. Moxon, 1872. Second series. Illus. by Birket Foster. 22 illus. engraved on steel by William Miller, 4 pp. ads. Green decor. cloth, bevelled boards, a.e.g. Top/bottom backstrip very slightly worn, occasional slight foxing and corners of boards very slightly bruised. Very good. Hodgkins 27-289 1983 £40

HOOD, THOMAS   Poems. Moxon, nd (ca. 1875). 1st & 2nd series complete in 1 vol. Illus. by Birket Foster. Large paper copy with 44 illus. engr'd by W. Miller. Half crimson lea. backed red pebble grain cloth bds. Pub's binding, a.e.g., leather rubbed at edges, fr. ep. cracked at hinge, name fr. ep., vg copy. Hodgkins 27-290 1983 £45

HOOD, THOMAS   Poems... London: Macmillan & Co., 1897. First of this edition. 2 vols. 8vo. Orig. cloth. Fine. MacManus 279-2733 1983 $20

HOOD, THOMAS   The Serious Poems of Thomas Hood. London: George Newnes Limited, 1901. Illus. by H. Granville Fell. Small 8vo. Full red morocco, elaborately gilt, with silk panels on endsheets and silk endpapers, by Morrell. Fine. MacManus 279-2734 1983 $350

HOOD, THOMAS   The Serious Poems of... Newnes, 1901. Edn. de luxe, limited to 100 signed & numbered copies. Frontis. & 17 illus. by H. Granville Fell, printed on hand-made paper. Jap vellum backed bds., eps. designed by Garth Jones, uncut & unopened (bkstrip & free eps. discol'd, occasional foxing foreedge), fine copy. Hodgkins 27-454 1983 £35

HOOD, THOMAS   The Works, Comic and Serious. London, 1869-72. 10 vols. 8vo. Cont. half green morocco, gilt, edges gilt. Engraved portrait and numerous illus. Traylen 94-448 1983 £105

HOOK, JAMES   Percy Mallory. Edinburgh: William Blackwood, 1824. First edition. 3 vols. Cont. half-calf with marbled boards and endpapers. Spines and covers rubbed. Some foxing to the preliminary pages. Good. Bookplate. MacManus 279-2736 1983 $225

HOOK, JAMES   Percy Mallory. Wm. Blackwood, Edinburgh, and T. Cadell, 1824. First edition, 3 vols. Half titles. Half olive green calf. Jarndyce 30-424 1983 £52

HOOK, THEODORE   Adventures of an actor: comprising a picture of the French stage during a period of fifty years. London: Henry Colburn, 1842. 2 vols., 12mo, original yellow-green cloth (bit faded). "Second edition." Very good copy. Ximenes 64-285 1983 $75

HOOK, THEODORE   The Humorist. Philadelphia: E.L. Carey & A. Hart, 1837. First (American?) edition. 8vo. Orig. cloth-backed boards with paper label on spine. Foxing. Label on spine a little worn. Very good. MacManus 279-2737 1983 $125

HOOK, THEODORE   The French Stage and the French People, as illustrated in the memoirs of M. Fleury. London: Henry Colburn, 1841. 2 vols., 12mo, original yellow-green cloth (bit faded). First edition in English. Faint waterstains, else a very good copy. Uncommon. Ximenes 64-284 1983 $100

HOOK, THEODORE   Killing no murder: a farce in two acts. London: printed by W. Flint, for Samuel Tipper, 1809. 8vo, disbound, title dusty. First edition. Ximenes 64-283 1983 $60

HOOK, THEODORE   Killing No Murder. London: G.H. Davidson, n.d. Cumberland's British Theatre edition. Orig. decorated wraps. Fine. MacManus 279-2738 1983 $35

HOOK, THEODORE   Love and Pride. Whittaker & Co., 1833. First edition, 3 vols. Half green calf, brown labels, v.g. Jarndyce 30-424 1983 £52

HOOK, THEODORE   Sayings and Doings, or Sketches from Life. London: Colburn, 1825. First edition. Second series. 3 vols. Orig. boards. Paper labels. MacManus 279-2742 1983 $350

HOOK, THEODORE   Sayings and Doings: or Sketches from Life. London: Colburn, 1828. First edition. Third series. 3 vols. Orig. boards. Paper labels. MacManus 279-2741 1983 $350

HOOK, THEODORE   Sayings and Doings. London: Printed for Henry Colburn, 1824. First edition. 6 vols. Cont. 3/4 calf & marbled boards. Bookplates. Endpapers a little foxed. Some minor wear to bindings. Very good. MacManus 279-2739 1983 $150

HOOK, THEODORE   Sayings and Doings. Henry Colburn, 1834. Complete in 9 vols. Half calf, marbled boards, black labels, fine. Jarndyce 30-425 1983 £85

HOOK, THEODORE   Sayings and Doings. London: Colburn, 1824. First edition. 3 vols. Orig. boards. Paper labels. Hinges cracked with some repair. Spines a little defective. Good. MacManus 279-2740 1983 $85

HOOK, THEODORE   Sayings and Doings: Or Sketches from Life. London: Colburn, 1828. First edition. Third series. 3 vols. Cont. 3/4 calf. Binding rubbed. The half-titles are wanting. Sound set. MacManus 279-2743 1983 $65

HOOK, THEODORE   Sayings and Doings. For Henry Colburn, 1824. First edition. 3 vols. Large 12mo, half vellum. Occasional slight stains. Hannas 69-95 1983 £30

HOOK, THEODORE   Sayings and Doings. Henry Colburn, 1824. First edition, 3 vols. Half green calf, v.g. Jarndyce 30-426 1983 £15

HOOKE, ANDREW   An Essay on the National Debt, and National Capital. London: printed for W. Owen and sold by B. Hickey and J. Palmer, 1750. 1st ed., 8vo, disbound. Pickering & Chatto 21-45 1983 $150

HOOKE, ROBERT   An Attempt To Prove the Motion of the Earth... London, Printed by T.R. for John Martyn...1674. 1st ed., 4to, 1 folding plate at the end, margins stained throughout and a few corners frayed, tear in the plate repaired; partially uncut, modern half calf, fair copy. Pickering & Chatto 22-51 1983 $1,250

HOOKER, J. D.   Himalayan Journals. London, 1854. 2 folding maps, 12 tinted lithograph plates, including a folding panorama, numerous woodcuts in the text. Some slight spotting, mainly at the beginning and ends of the vols. 2 vols. Orig. pictorial cloth, gilt, spines browned. 8vo. Good. Edwards 1044-355 1983 £250

HOOKER, J. D.   Illustrations of Himalayan Plants. London, 1855. Coloured title, soiled in the margin, and 30 fine hand-coloured lithograph plates. Folio. Orig. printed boards, soiled and slightly worn, rebacked with buckram. 8vo. Good. Edwards 1044-357 1983 £2,250

HOOKER, J. D.   Journal of a Tour in Marocco and the Great Atlas. 1878. Folding map, 9 plates and 13 text-figures, 8vo, cloth, slightly used. Wheldon 160-393 1983 £60

HOOKER, J. D.   The Rhododendrons of Sikkim-Himalaya... London, 1849-51. 30 fine hand-coloured lithograph plates. Folio. Orig. cloth boards, strongly rebacked with morocco. 8vo. Good. Edwards 1044-356 1983 £2,750

HOOKER, LEROY   The Africaners. Chicago: Rand, McNally, 1900. 12mo. Folding map. 16 plates. Orig. green pictorial cloth. Slightly rubbed. Adelson Africa-195 1983 $25

HOOKER, W. J.   The Botany of Captain Beechey's Voyage. (1841) Facsimile Reprint, 1965. 94 plates, 4to, cloth. Wheldon 160-1717 1983 £42

HOOKER, W. J.   The British Flora. 1830. 8vo, cont. half calf, used. Wheldon 160-1604 1983 £18

HOOKER, W. J.   Flora Boreali-Americana Facsimile Reprint. (London 1840), 1980. Text 2 vols. in 1, royal 8vo, atlas of 238 plates, 1 vol., 4to - together 2 vols., cloth. Folding map is included in the text vol. Wheldon 160-1716 1983 £65

HOOKER, W. J.   Icones Filicum. Figures and descriptions
of Ferns. (1829)-31. 2 vols., folio, half morocco, 240 fine hand-
coloured plates. Rare. A nice copy. Subscribers' list. Small
tear in inner margin of slightly creased title-page to vol. 1 neatly
repaired. Binding neatly repaired with new cloth sides. Wheldon 160-
47 1983 £1,650

HOOKER, W. J.   Icones Plantarum. (1837)-1972. Vols.
1-37 part 2, 3548 plates, 8vo, cloth, wrappers. Very scarce. In
this set vols. 1-10 (in 2 vols.) and 21 are facsimile reprints 1967-
72, the remainder are original editions, in parts as issued. Wheldon
160-1533 1983 £350

HOOKER, W. J.   Niger Flora. (1849) Reprint 1966.
52 plates, 8vo, cloth. Wheldon 160-1718 1983 £39

HOOKER, W. J.   Species Filicum. (1844-64), facsimile
reprint, 1971. 304 plates, 5 vols. in 2, 8vo, cloth. Wheldon 160-
1842 £129

HOOLE, JOHN   Jerusalem Delivered; An Heroic Poem.
London: Printed for R. & J. Dodsley, P. Vaillant, T. Davies, J.
Newvery, & Z. Stuart, 1764. Second edition. 2 vols. Small 8vo.
Engraved title-pages by Walker. Full cont. calf. Spines a little
worn. Former owner's signature on title-pages. Bookplate. Very good.
MacManus 279-2745 1983 $75

HOOPER, JOHN   Agricultural Statistics, 1847-1926.
Dublin, 1928. Roy. 8vo, cont. cloth. Fenning 61-208 1983 £24.50

HOOPER, JOSEPH   A Discourse on the Best Means of Improving the Science of Medicine. London: Published by order of the
society, and printed by J. Phillips, 1788. 1st ed., 8vo; in the orig.
marbled wrappers, stitching broken, inscribed "To E. C. May with Mr.
Hooper's love." Pickering & Chatto 22-52 1983 $165

HOOPES, PENROSE R.   Connecticut Clockmakers of the
Eighteenth Century. Hartford & New York, 1930. 1st ed., 1000 copies
printed. Frontispiece, illus. Large 8vo, slightly torn dw, very
nice. Morrill 288-78 1983 $90

HOOTON, CHARLES   Colin Clink. London: Richard Bentley,
1841. 1st ed., 8vo, 3 vols., later half morocco gilt, marbled boards,
uncut copy with all half-titles. Etched plates, 15 by John Leech and
one by George Cruikshank. Bookplate. Very scarce. A very good copy.
Trebizond 18-59 1983 $175

HOOTON, CHARLES   Colin Clink. London, 1844. Illustra-
tions by Leech. 8vo. 3 vols. Rebound in modern leather, boards.
With all three half-titles. Bindings scuffed, else a vg-fine set.
In Our Time 156-406 1983 $100

HOOTON, HENRY   A Bridle for the Tongue. London:
for W. Taylor, 1709. First edition. 8vo. Cont. panelled calf,
rebacked. Heath 48-328 1983 £90

HOOVER, DOROTHY   J.W. Beatty. Toronto: Ryerson, 1948.
18cm. First edition. Colour frontis., portrait and 8 illus. (one
colour). Blue cloth. Spine slightly faded else very good. McGahern
53-26 1983 $30

HOOVER, HERBERT   Addresses upon the American Road. New
York, Van Nostrand, 1946. 8vo. First edition. Dust wrapper. Inscr.
by Herbert Hoover. D/w partly torn along some edges and with evidence
of removal of some scotch tape. Morrill 289-365 1983 $45

HOOVER, HERBERT   The Challenge to Liberty. New York,
1934. Cloth, d.j., fine copy. First edition, inscribed on the fly
leaf by the author. Jenkins 151-128 1983 $135

HOOVER, HERBERT   Challenge to Liberty. N.Y., Scribner,
1934. First edition. Signed and inscribed by Hoover. Dust jacket.
Fine. Houle 22-480 1983 $125

HOOVER, HERBERT   The Challenge to Liberty. New York,
1934. 8vo. 1st ed. Presentation copy. Morrill 286-299 1983
$47.50

HOOVER, HERBERT   The Challenge to Liberty. New York:
1934. First edition. Blue cloth. Presentation copy, inscribed.
Bradley 66-553 1983 $40

HOOVER, HERBERT   The Memoirs of Herbert Hoover. New
York, 1952. Portrait. Cloth. Inscribed and signed by Hoover on the
front endsheet. Very good in weary dust jacket. Reese 19-431 1983
$125

HOOVER, HERBERT   The Ordeal of Woodrow Wilson. NY:
1958. First edition. 8vo, buckram, slipcase. Illustrated.
Signed by Hoover. Perata 27-88 1983 $75

HOPE, ANTHONY, PSEUD.
Please turn to
HAWKINS, ANTHONY HOPE

HOPE, BERYL   The Shadow of a Life. W. H. Allen,
1800. First edition, 3 vols. 3 vols. bound as one. Orig. brown
remainder cloth lettered. Jarndyce 30-427 1983 £18.50

HOPE, JAMES   A Treatise on the Diseases of the Heart
and Great Vessels, and on the Affections which may be Mistaken for
Them. Phila., 1846. 8vo, disbound. Argosy 713-275 1983 $100

HOPE, STANLEY   A New Godiva. Richard Bentley, 1876.
First edition. 3 vols., 4 pp. ads. vol. III. Orig. olive green cloth,
spines gilt. Slight nick at head of spine in vol. II. Fine. Jarndyce
30-428 1983 £85

HOPKINS, GERALD MANLEY   Poems. London: Humphrey Milford,
(1918). First edition. Orig. cloth-backed boards. Backstrip a bit
dusty. Endpapers slightly darkened. Very good. MacManus 279-2755
1983 $850

HOPKINS, GERARD MANLEY   Poems. London, 1930. Second edition.
Inscription. Nicked and slightly dusty, price-clipped dustwrapper
darkened at the spine. Jolliffe 26-269 1983 £35

HOPKINS, KENNETH   Love and Elizabeth. London, 1944.
First edition. One of 1200 copies. Dust wrapper. Author's signed
autograph presentation inscription. Very nice. Rota 230-298 1983
£12

HOPKINS, MATTHEW   The Discovery of Witches. London:
for R. Royston, at the Angell in Ivie Lane, 1647. First edition.
Small 4to. Full red morocco, gilt, by Sangorski and Stucliffe.
Woodcut frontis. Rare. Traylen 94-449 1983 £1,800

HOPKINS, R. THURSTON   H. G. Wells. London: Cecil Palmer,
(1922). First edition. Illus. by E. Harries. Orig. cloth. Dust
jacket. In a half-morocco slipcase. Very fine. MacManus 280-5503
1983 $45

HOPKINS, R. THURSTON   Sheila Kaye-Smith and the Weald Country.
(London): Cecil Palmer, (1925). First edition. Illus. from photo.
by the author. Orig. cloth. Inscribed by author on the front flyleaf,
with an ALS from Hopkins laid in. Good. MacManus 279-3029 1983 $20

HOPKINS, SARAH WINNEMUCCA   Life Among the Piutes. Boston, 1883.
1st ed. 12mo, orig. cloth, small spot on lower edge of spine. Very
scarce. Clark 741-310 1983 $150

HOPKINS, TIGHE   For Freedom. London: Ward & Downey,
1888. First edition. Orig. red decorated cloth. Spine and covers
slightly worn and soiled. Very good. MacManus 279-2756 1983 $135

HOPKINS, WILLIAM   A Sermon Preached before the...Lord
Mayor, Aldermen and Citizens of...London. Printed for Walter
Kettilby, 1683. First edition, 4to, wrapper. Fenning 62-180 1983
£21.50

HOPPE, E. O.   Picturesque Great Britain. NY, (1926).
304 plates, spine and edges slightly sunned, top right corner edge
slightly worn, else very good in remnants of dustwrapper. Quill &
Brush 54-657 1983 $60

HOPPE, J. Californien, dets Nutid og Fremtid. Copenhagen: Chr. Steen & Sons Forlag, 1850. Folding map of Alta & Baja California. Wrappers, some wear and staining. Rare Danish imprint on California. Dawson 471-343 1983 $125

HOPPER, NORA Under Quicken Boughs. London: John Lane, The Bodley Head, 1896. First edition. Woodcut title-page. Orig. decorated cloth. Endpapers foxed. Fine. MacManus 279-2757 1983 $60

HOPPIN, JAMES MASON Life of Andrew Hull Foote. New York, 1874. 1st ed. Portrait and illus. 8vo. Ex-library. Morrill 287-158 1983 $30

HOPPUS, MARY A Great Treason. London: Macmillan & Co., 1883. First edition. 2 vols. 8vo. Orig. cloth. Very good. MacManus 279-2758 1983 $150

HOPPUS, MARY A Great Treason. London: Macmillan, 1883. 2 vols. in one. Orig. cloth. First edition. In the publisher's remainder binding. Very good. MacManus 279-2759 1983 $45

HORACE
Please turn to
HORATIUS FLACCUS, QUINTUS

HORAK, E. Entoloma (Agaricales) in Indomalaya and Australasia. Beih. Nov. Hed., 1980. 8 plates and 234 figures, 8vo, boards. Wheldon 160-1843 1983 £39

HORAN, JAMES D. The Life and Art of Charles Schreyvogel. New York, 1969. 35 color plates, with additional unnumbered black and white plates. Oblong folio, as new. One of the ltd. edition of 249, signed by Horan, and with four additional color plates. Reese 19-274 1983 $150

HORATIUS FLACCUS, QUINTUS Ad Lectiones Probatiores Diligenter Emendatus... Glasquae, in Aedibus Academicis, Excudebat Robertus Foulis, 1744. 12mo, orig. straight-grained red morocco gilt, a.e.g., bookplate. Few blank tips mended, blank leaf S2 has early verse translation of Horace's Epistola ad Pisones, few waterstains. First 12mo issue. Ravenstree 94-110 1983 $295

HORATIUS FLACCUS, QUINTUS The odes of Horace... London: John W. Parker and Son, 1860. First edition. 8vo. Orig. brown cloth. Fine copy. Ximenes 63-66 1983 $35

HORATIUS FLACCUS, QUINTUS The Odes and Epodes. NY & London, 1907. 8vo, cloth. Portraits. Salloch 385-581 1983 $22

HORATIUS FLACCUS, QUINTUS The Odes and Satyrs of Horace... London, Tonson, 1721. 8vo, cont. red morocco gilt extra, light wear and minor age-browning. Sotheby-Graham Pollard book label. Ravenstree 95-65 1983 $175

HORATIUS FLACCUS, QUINTUS Opera Omnia. Oxford, 1896. 2 vols. 8vo, cloth. Salloch 385-577 1983 $20

HORATIUS FLACCUS, QUINTUS The Poems of Horace... London: by A.C. for W. Lee, T. Collins, H. Herringman, and H. Brome, 1671. Second edition with Alterations, imprimatur leaf. 8vo. Cont. panelled sheep, neatly rebacked with morocco label, gilt. Traylen 94-450 1983 £30

HORATIUS FLACCUS, QUINTUS Quinti Horatii Flacci Poemata... Londini, Apud Tho. Harperum, 1637. 12mo, 18th century boards, newly rebacked in calf, various names and a few inkstains on title and final blank page, few headlines shaved. Ravenstree 95-64 1983 $85

HORATIUS FLACCUS, QUINTUS Satiren. Berlin, 1910. 8vo, cloth. Salloch 385-582 1983 $20

HORATIUS FLACCUS, QUINTUS The Works of... Murray, 1849. 1st edn. 8 colour title pages & coloured borders edging each page & other designs inc. eps. by Owen Jones. Full pub's morocco with blind stamped decor. both cvrs. & bkstrip, gilt titling bkstrip, raised bands, royal blue & gold patterned eps., guaffered edges, a.e.g. (foxing of contents re-backed with orig. bkstrip, small tear foredge pp. 167/171), scarce. Hodgkins 27-365 1983 £65

HORGAN, PAUL Archbishop Juan Bautista Lamy of Santa Fe. His Life and Times. New York, (1975). Ltd. edn. of 500 large paper copies, numbered and signed. 12 full-color illus., 20 black & white illus., maps. Slip case, gilt top, cloth-backed marbled boards. Clark 741-459 1983 $127.50

HORGAN, PAUL The Centuries of Santa Fe. New York, 1956. Illus.; limited edition of 350 copies signed by the author; inscribed. Boxed. T.e.g. Fine work. Jenkins 151-244 1983 $145

HORGAN, PAUL The Centuries of Santa Fe. New York: Dutton, 1956. Illus. 1st ed., 1 of 350 numbered and signed copies. Orig. 3/4 brown morocco, boxed. Fine copy with presentation inscrip. from Horgan on front end paper. Jenkins 155-593 1983 $145

HORGAN, PAUL Great River. New York: Rinehart, 1954. Two vols. Cloth. First edition. One of 1,000 sets, specially bound, with extra color plates after watercolors by the author, and signed by him. Long presentation inscription signed "Paul," probably not in Horgan's hand. Fine in slightly worn slipcase, which is cracking at the joints. Reese 20-994 1983 $200

HORGAN, PAUL Lamy of Santa Fe His Life and Times. New York, 1975. Boxed. Colored illus. Limited to 490 copies and signed by the author. Jenkins 151-129 1983 $150

HORGAN, PAUL Lamy of Santa Fe. NY, (1975). Limited to 500 large paper, numbered and signed copies, t.e.g., very fine in fine slipcase. 12 plates by Horgan. Quill & Brush 54-658 1983 $125

HORGAN, PAUL The Return of the Weed. New York: Harper, 1936. First edition, 1 of 350 numbered copies, of which 250 were for sale, signed by both Horgan and illustrator Peter Hurd. Original green cloth, paper label, box with label. Presentation insc. from Horgan on front end paper, seven lines, dated 1936. Scarce. Fine copy in tape-repaired (otherwise very good) box. Jenkins 153-257 1983 $500

HORGAN, PAUL The Return of the Weed. New York & London: Harper, 1936. First edition. Limited to 350 numbered copies signed by Horgan and Hurd. Orig. green cloth, label, box. Aside from tape repair to one edge of box, a fine copy with an additional presentation inscription from Horgan on the front endpaper dated at time of publication. Illus. with orig. lithographs by Hurd, tastefully printed in Baskerville types on Starthmore paper. Jenkins 152-824 1983 $500

HORGAN, PAUL The Return of the Weed. New York: Harper & Brothers, 1936. Quarto. Cloth. First edition. Illus. with orig. lithographs by Peter Hurd. One of only 350 numbered copies (250 for sale), signed by the author and the artist, and with orig. printings of the lithos. Cloth a trifle faded at edges, presentation note from a friend of the author and the artist tipped in, else a very good, internally fine copy. Reese 20-524 1983 $400

HORLOCK, KNIGHTLY WILLIAM The Master Of The Hounds. London: Hurst & Blackett, 1859. First edition. 3 vols. Frontispiece. Orig. brown cloth. Spines and covers faded and worn. Inner hinges cracked in vols. one and three. Preliminary pages foxed. Good. MacManus 279-2761 1983 $125

HORN, ELDER The Annals of Elder Horn Early Life in the Southwest. New York: Richard R. Smith, 1930. First edition. Frontis. Light foxing. Nice. Jenkins 152-155 1983 $35

HORN, STANLEY F. The Army of Tennessee, A Military History. Indianapolis (1941). First edition. Couple corners bumped, slight fade at top of spine else good. Defective dw. King 46-60 1983 $25

HORN, STANLEY F. Invisible Empire: The Story of the Ku Klux Klan, 1866-71. Boston, 1939. Illus., dw. Argosy 710-24 1983 $30

HORNBECK, ROBERT Roubidoux's Ranch in the 70's. Riverside, Press Printing Co., 1913. First edition. Illus. with 12 plates. Orig. yellow cloth stamped in black (soiled, front free endpaper pulling away) else good - very good. Presentation copy: signed and inscribed by the author "To my Old Friend...Feb. 16-1914." Houle 22-1108 1983 $125

HORNBY, G.   The Long Ago Book. N.p.: L.B. Fisher,
(1944). Cloth backed pictorial boards. Shape: 18" x 6" high.
Illus. by Florian. Very good. Aleph-bet 8-108 1983 $20

HORNE, CHARLES F.   The World and Its People. New York,
Ira R. Hiller (1924-1925). Illus. In the 85 orig. parts, tall 8vo,
orig. wrappers, very nice. Morrill 288-183 1983 $35

HORNE, HERBERT T.   The Binding of Books. London: Kegan
Paul, 1894. Octavo. Full brown morocco, elaborately gilt, by
Sarah T. Prideaux, signed "S.T.P. 1900," a.e.g., rebacked, orig.
backstrip laid down else a fine copy. Reese 20-798 1983 $225

HORNE, J. M.   The Adventures of Naufragus. London,
1828. Second edition. Calf, rebacked. Presentation copy to Viscount
Combermere. 8vo. Good. Edwards 1044-358 1983 £65

HORNE, MELVILLE   Letters on Missions. Schenectady:
C.P. Wyckoff, 1797. First American edition. Original paper-covered
wooden boards calf spine. Severely foxed and water-stained. Covers
worn and chipped. Rare imprint. Bradley 65-97 1983 $135

HORNE, RICHARD HENGIST   Orion. An epic poem in three books.
London: Miller, 1843. First edition. 8vo. Disbound. Presentation copy, inscribed by Horne on the fly-title in 1843 to John
Edmund Reade. Some soiling; first and last leaves spotted. Ximenes
63-448 1983 $50

HORNEMAN, FREDERICK   The Journal of Frederick Horneman's
Travels from Cairo to Mourzouk...1797-8. Two folding maps by Rennell
(tears in folds repaired), 4to, modern morocco. K Books 307-100
1983 £130

HORNER, CHARLES F.   The Life of James Redpath and the
Development of the Modern Lyceum. New York, (1926). First edition.
Illustrated. Dark green silk-moire cloth with printed green paper
label on cover and spine. Very good. Bradley 64-141 1983 $20

HORNUNG, CLARENCE P.   Treasury of American Design. New York,
Harry N. Abrams, n.d. Illus., some in color. 2 vols., 4to, very
fine. Morrill 288-184 1983 $75

HORNUNG, ERNEST WILLIAM   Mr. Justice Raffles. London: Smith,
Elder, 1909. First edition. Orig. pictorial cloth. Fine. MacManus
279-2764 1983 $200

HORNUNG, ERNEST WILLIAM   Mr. Justice Raffles. London, 1909.
First edition. Signs of a label having been removed from the rear
pastedown. Inscriptions. Upper hinge cracked. Corners slightly
bruised. Tail of spine slightly worn. Covers slightly rubbed and
marked. Very good. Jolliffe 26-143 1983 £35

HORNUNG, ERNEST WILLIAM   Peccavi. London: Grant Richards, 1900.
First edition. Orig. cloth. Very good. MacManus 279-2765 1983 $50

HORNUNG, ERNEST WILLIAM   Tiny Luttrell. London: Cassell, 1893.
First edition. 2 vols. Orig. cloth. Covers very worn. Library
labels on front covers. MacManus 279-2766 1983 $75

HORREBOW, NIELS   The Natural History of Iceland. London:
Printed for A. Linde in Catherine-Street...MDCCLVIII. (1758). Folio,
one engraved folding map. Bound in full 18th century calf. Worn.
Scuffed at corners. Hinges cracked, sometimes splitting. Spine
gilt stamped. Title on red morocco title piece. Lightly toned,
some scattered foxing. Armorial bookplate of Albert Davis Mead.
Letter from G. Adler Blumer M.D. 15 April 1914 presenting the book
to Dr. Mead, tipped in. Arkway 22-75 1983 $475

HORRIDA bella. Pains and penalties versus truth and justice.
London: G. Humphrey, 1820. First edition. 8vo. Disbound. With
an etched title-page, and 24 etched plates. Rare. Ximenes 63-495
1983 $125

HORSFORD, EBEN NORTON   The Landfall of Leif Erikson...
Boston, 1892. 1st ed. Maps & illus. 4to, nice copy. Morrill 288-
185 1983 $25

HORSWELL, JANE   Bronze Sculpture of "Les Animaliers."
Clopton, Woodbridge, 1971. Reference and price guide. (10),
iv, 339pp. Prof. Illus. Lrg. 4to. Leather. Ars Libri SB 26-104
1983 $75

HORT, JOHN JOSIAH   The Horse Guards. London: J. & D.A.
Darling, 1850. First edition. 12 colored illus. Orig. pictorial
boards. With bookplate of Duff Cooper. Covers and spine worn and
soiled. Good. MacManus 279-2767 1983 $150

HORTON, GEORGE   Home of Nymphs and Vampires.
Indianapolis, 1929. Illus. 8vo, cloth. Salloch 385-363 1983
$35

HORTON, GEORGE   In Argolis. Chicago, 1902. 15 plates,
8vo, cloth. Salloch 385-362 1983 $25

HORTON, GEORGE   Modern Athens. NY, 1901. 31 illus.
8vo, cloth. Salloch 385-364 1983 $30

HOSACK, JOHN   Mary Queen of Scots and Her Accusers.
William Blackwood, 1870-1874. 2 vols., 8vo, portrait, 3 folding
facs. plates, orig. cloth. Bickersteth 77-124 1983 £36

HOSACK, JOHN   Mary Stewart. 1888. 8vo, cloth gilt.
Bickersteth 77-125 1983 £14

HOSKING, E.   Birds of the Night (Owls). 1945. 86
photographs, royal 8vo, cloth (trifle used). Wheldon 160-760 1983
£15

HOSKINS, GEORGE ALEXANDER   Visit to the Great Oasis of the Libyan
Desert. London: Longman, Rees, etc., 1837. 8vo, folding map, 20
plates. 1/2 dark green morocco, marbled boards. Adelson Africa-92
1983 $150

HOSKINS, KATHERINE   A Penetential Primer. (Cummington,
Mass.): Cummington Press, 1945. Edition ltd. to 330 copies. Orig.
brown wraps.; paper label. Karmiole 73-34 1983 $60

HOSMER, FRANCIS J.   A Glimpse of Andersonville and Other
Writings. Springfield, Mass., 1896. 1st ed. Presentation from
author. Illus. 8vo, orig. wrappers, ex-library, spine partly repaired with transparent tape. Morrill 288-186 1983 $35

HOSMER, RALPH S.   Genealogy of that Branch of the Irwin
Family in New York. Ithaca, 1938. Illus. Ex lib. Argosy 716-179
1983 $35

HOSMER, WILLIAM   Slavery and the Church. Auburn (N.Y.),
William J. Moses, 1853. Second Thousand. 12mo. Morrill 288-614
1983 $25

HOSPITALIER, EDOUARD   Polyphased Alternating Currents.
H. Alabaster, (1895). First edition of this anonymous translation,
with 31 illus., 8vo, orig. cloth, gilt. A good to very good copy.
Fenning 60-184 1983 £26.50

HOSTE, WILLIAM   Memoirs and Letters. Richard Bentley,
1833. First edition, 2 vols. Half title, front. vol. I. Ex-library
copy, lib. stamps. Rebound in maroon moire-patterned cloth, labels.
Jarndyce 30-1027 1983 £22

THE HOT Springs of Arkansas. (St. Louis), 1877. Illus., folded
maps, orig. printed wraps. First edition. Ginsberg 46-39 1983
$85

HOTCHKIN, JAMES H.   A History of the Purchase and Settlement
of Western New York, and of the Rise, Progress, and Present State
of the Presbyterian Church in that Section. New York: M. W. Dodd,
Brick Church Chapel, 1848. Frontis. Half calf with morocco labels.
Rehinged. Nice copy overall. Jenkins 151-131 1983 $85

HOTMAN, JEAN   Gasparis Colinii Castellonii, Magni
Qvondam Franciae Amiralii, Vita. N.p., 1575. 8vo, boards. With
stamp on title-page and 3 stamps on title verso. Few marginal
repairs at end. Browned. Rostenberg 88-106 1983 $600

HOTTEN, JOHN CAMDEN   The Original Lists of Persons of
Quality... London, 1874. First edition. 4to, cloth, paper label.
Label partly worn. Morrill 290-187 1983 $75

HOUARD, C.   Les Zoocecidies des Plantes d'Europe
et du bassin de la Mediterranee. Paris, 1908-14. 8 portraits,
3 plates and 1566 figures, 3 vols., royal 8vo, half cloth. Very
scarce. Preliminates to vols. 1 and 2 misbound. Wheldon 160-1097
1983 £75

HOUGH, EMERSON   The Covered Wagon. New York, 1932.
Frontis. by W.H.D. Koerner. First edition. Original cloth. TLS
from Hough to Carlyle Ellis. Very good copy. Jenkins 153-258 1983
$100

HOUGH, EMERSON   The Firefly's Light. New York: Trow
Press, (1916). 1st ed., reprinted. Orig. half morocco. Very fine
copy in the orig. tissue dj. Scarce. Jenkins 155-596 1983 $45

HOUGH, EMERSON   The King of Gee-Whiz. Indianapolis:
Bobbs-Merrill, (1906). Color frontis., plates. 1st ed., 2nd
printing with pp. 26 and 140 correctly placed. Orig. pictorial
cloth. Illus. by Oscar Cesare. Fine copy. Jenkins 155-597 1983
$50

HOUGH, EMERSON   Out of Doors. NY, 1915. Near fine in
green cloth with gold design. Quill & Brush 54-661 1983 $25

HOUGH, EMERSON   The Singing Mouse Stories. Indianapolis:
(1910). Illus. Green cloth. Signed and dated by Hough at Chicago
December 19, 1911. Very good copy. Bradley 66-206 1983 $125

HOUGH, EMERSON   The Sowing. Winnipeg, 1909. 19cm.
30 illus. Green cloth, gilt titles and colour illus. mounted on
the upper cover. Fine copy. McGahern 53-75 1983 $25

HOUGH, EMERSON   The Story of the Cowboy. Gay and Bird,
1897. First U.K. edition, with 10 plates by W.L. Wells and C.M.
Russell, 8vo, orig. cloth, a very good copy. Fenning 62-181 1983
£21.50

HOUGH, EMERSON   The Story of the Outlaw, A Study of the
Western Desperado. New York, 1907. Frontis. and plates. Original
cloth and boards. First edition, second issue. Quite scarce in the
1st ed. Jenkins 153-259 1983 $40

HOUGH, EMERSON   The Way to the West. Ind., (1903).
Minor interior foxing, covers stained, otherwise good tight copy.
Illus. by Remington. Quill & Brush 54-662 1983 $30

HOUGH, EMERSON   The Web. Chicago: Reilly & Lee,
(1919). 1st ed., special issue. Orig. tan cloth. One of the
few copies with the inserted certificate at front (no. 101)
certifying this as a special member's ed., with facsimile signatures
and badges pictured. Fine. Jenkins 155-600 1983 $40

HOUGH, HORATIO GATES   Diving, or an Attempt to Describe upon
Hydraulic and Hydrostatic Principles, a Method of Supplying the
Diver with Air Under Water. Hartford: Printed by John Russell, 1813.
Disbound. First edition. A near fine copy, laid into a folding half
morocco case. Reese 18-413 1983 $175

HOUGHTON, CLAUDE, PSEUD.
Please turn to
OLDFIELD, CLAUDE HOUGHTON

HOUGHTON, CLYDE   Three Fantastic Tales. (L), 1934.
Limited to 275 numbered and signed copies, ALS from author to pub.
tipped-in, cover slightly stained at inner edges, else near fine in
mended slipcase. Quill & Brush 54-663 1983 $125

HOUGHTON, ELIZA P. (DONNER) The Expedition of the Donner Party and
its Tragic Fate. Cleveland: The Arthur H. Clark Company, 1920.
Portraits, original cloth, fine copy. Jenkins 151-132 1983 $40

HOUGHTON, ROBERT   Stray Verses. London: John Murray, 1891.
First edition. Orig. cloth. Possibly from the library of Lionel
Johnson, with an inscription on the front free endpaper. With the
publisher's blind presentation stamp on the first preliminary leaf.
Spine somewhat darkened. Very good. MacManus 279-2773 1983 $45

HOUGHTON, STANLEY   The Works of Stanley Houghton. London:
Constable & Co. Ltd., 1914. 3 vols. Orig. cloth with paper labels
on spines, extra labels tipped in at the backs. First edition. Max
Beerbohm's own copy: signed on the front flyleaf "Max Beerbohm,
Rapallo," and with his orig. caricature of Houghton redrawn beneath
the frontispiece in vol. II, with the caption: "What a wretched stiff
feeble painstaking drawing! This is slightly better. Max, 1930."
MacManus 277-279 1983 $750

HOUGHTON, WILLIAM   British Fresh-Water Fishes. London:
William MacKenzie (1879). Folio. 2 vols. 41 hand-colored plates.
Orig. brick cloth, gilt. A.e.g. Illus. with a coloured figure
of each species drawn from nature by A.F. Lydon, and numerous
engravings. Karmiole 71-55 1983 $500

HOUGHTON, WILLIAM A.   History of the Town of Berlin, Worcester
County, Mass., from 1784 to 1895. Worcester, 1895. First edition.
Illustrated. 8vo. Morrill 290-651 1983 $47.50

HOULT, NORAH   Time Gentlemen! Time! London: William
Heinemann Ltd., 1930. First edition. Orig. cloth. In publisher's
box. One of 265 copies signed by author. Very fine. MacManus 279-
2774 1983 $35

HOURS of Day & Spirits of Night. Joseph Cundall, 1847. Pictorial
title page. Illus. Unpaginated. Blue pictorial wrappers, red eps.,
a.e.g., bkstrip some wear with part missing, covers mottled, title
foxed & edges of pp. foxed. Illus. are signed "M.E.T." inv. & "H.F.T."
del., lithographed by F. Dangerfield. Rare. Hodgkins 27-101 1983
£45

HOURS with the Leslies; A Tale for Children. London: Hope & Co.,
1853. Orig. plum cloth. First edition. Former owner's bookplate and
signature on front endpapers. Spine slightly faded. Very good copy.
MacManus 277-81 1983 $65

HOURST, EMILE A. L.   French Enterprise in Africa. New York:
E.P. Dutton, 1899. 8vo. Portrait. Folding map. Text illus. Orig.
blue cloth. Slightly rubbed. Adelson Africa-196 1983 $50

HOUSATONUC Bookshop Catalog.   Salisbury, CT: (ca. 1938). Printed
at Cantina Press. Very fine copy. Wrappers. Bromer 25-33 1983
$75

HOUSE, HOMER D.   Wild Flowers. New York, 1934. First
popular (one-volume) edition. 364 color illustrations. Tan buckram.
Edward L. Ryerson's gift copy to the Ryerson Nature Library. Very
good. Bradley 65-98 1983 $32.50

HOUSE, HOMER D.   Wild Flowers of New York. Albany, 1918.
2 vols. 264 color plates plus text illus. 4to, ex lib. Argosy
716-353 1983 $75

HOUSE, HOMER D.   Wild Flowers of New York. New York,
1921. 264 coloured plates, 4to, original cloth. Enclosed in a book
box. Wheldon 160-1719 1983 £25

A HOUSE Party, an Account of the Stories Told at a Gathering of
American Authors... Boston: Small, Maynard, 1901. 1st ed., with
coupon attached. Orig. red cloth, gilt. Very good copy. Jenkins
155-724 1983 $25

THE HOUSE that Queen Caroline built. London: printed for the author,
1820. First edition. 8vo. Disbound. Rare. Ximenes 63-496 1983
$60

HOUSEHOLD, GEOFFREY   Rogue Male. London: Chatto & Windus,
1939. First edition. 8vo. Orig. cloth. Dust jacket, chipped.
Fine. Jaffe 1-158 1983 $35

HOUSEHOLD, GEOFFREY   The Salvation of Pisco Gabar and Other
Stories. London: Chatto & Windus, 1938. First edition. 8vo.
Orig. cloth. Dust jacket. Fine copy. Jaffe 1-157 1983 $50

HOUSEHOLD, GEOFFREY   The Spanish Cave. Boston: Little,
Brown, and Company, 1936. First American edition. Illus. by Henry
C. Pitz. 8vo. Orig. cloth. Dust jacket. Very good copy. Jaffe
1-156 1983 $75

THE HOUSEHOLD Treasure, or the Young Housewife's Companion. Phila.:
Published by J. Thomas Huey & Co., 1871. Illus. with color engravings. Ads. Dawson 471-127 1983 $85

HOUSMAN, ALFRED EDWARD   Last Poems. Alcuin Press, 1929.
Tall 8vo, title-page, initials and shoulder titles printed in red,
uncut in qtr. linen over paper boards, printed paper label, fine copy.
325 copies on hand-made paper. Deighton 3-178 1983 £40

HOUSMAN, ALFRED EDWARD   Last Poems. London: Grant Richards,
1922. Gilt cloth. First edition, the state without the two semi-
colons on page 52. Fine in slightly soiled dust jacket, with two
closed nicks. Reese 20-527 1983 $40

HOUSMAN, ALFRED EDWARD   Last Poems. London: Grant Richards
Ltd., 1922. First edition. Orig. cloth. Dust jacket. Fine. Mac-
Manus 279-2775 1983 $25

HOUSMAN, ALFRED EDWARD   An Order of Service. Trinity College,
Cambridge, 4 May, 1936. First edition. One of 300 copies. Single
leaf, folded. Some light foxing. Very nice. Rota 230-300 1983 £25

HOUSMAN, ALFRED EDWARD   A Shropshire Lad. New York: John Lane,
The Bodley Head, 1897. First edition. American issue, with the "B"
label. Orig. parchment, paper boards. Covers a little rubbed and
finger-marked. Bookplate. In a green cloth book-form box. Of 500
copies of the first edition, this is one of 150 copies for America,
with a cancel title in black and red with imprint as above. Nice.
Rota 231-321 1983 £500

HOUSMAN, ALFRED EDWARD   A Shropshire Lad. London: Kegan Paul
etc., 1896. First edition. 12mo. Orig. boards. Paper label.
Covers a bit stained or discolored. Corners slightly rubbed. Label
defective. In a half-morocco slipcase. Very good. MacManus 279-
2778 1983 $750

HOUSMAN, CLEMENCE   The Were-Wolf. London: John Lane at
The Bodley Head; Chicago: Way & Williams, 1896. First edition,
second binding. 6 illus. by Laurence Housman. Orig. brown cloth.
Fine. MacManus 279-2784 1983 $135

HOUSMAN, LAURENCE   All-Fellows. London: Kegan Paul, 1896.
First ediition. Illus. 8vo. Orig. decorated cloth. Spine darkened
and worn. Covers a bit rubbed. MacManus 279-2785 1983 $25

HOUSMAN, LAURENCE   Arthur Boyd Houghton. A selection from
his work in black and white... London: Kegan Paul, Trench, Trubner,
and Co., 1896. 89 plates (5 heliogravure). Large 4to. Cloth.
Uncut. Ars Libri 32-332 1983 $135

HOUSMAN, LAURENCE   As Good As Gold. N.Y.: Samuel French,
(1916). Samuel French Series. Orig. printed wrappers. Spine and
covers a trifle worn. Near-fine. MacManus 279-2786 1983 $20

HOUSMAN, LAURENCE   Bethlehem. London: Macmillan & Co.,
1902. First edition. Orig. decorated boards. Spine and covers faded
and slightly worn. Good. MacManus 279-2787 1983 $35

HOUSMAN, LAURENCE   An Englishwoman's Love-Letters. London:
John Murray, 1900. First edition. Orig. vellum (soiled). Wallet
edges. Ties broken. MacManus 279-2788 1983 $35

HOUSMAN, LAURENCE   The Field of Clover. Kegan Paul, 1898.
1st edn., 2nd issue. Illus. by author, frontis., engr'd by Clemence
Housman, decor. initial letters. Sage green decor. cloth designed by
author, uncut (free eps. discol'd, bkstrip faded & titling rubbed,
some foxing of plates). A.J.A. Symons' copy with his signature,
author's signature also fr. ep. Very good copy. Hodgkins 27-455
1983 £65

HOUSMAN, LAURENCE   The Field of Clover. Kegan Paul, 1898.
Frontis. Pictorial title & 10 plates. Green pictorial cloth, gilt.
Good, tight copy. Greer 40-112 1983 £30

HOUSMAN, LAURENCE   Ironical Tales. London: Jonathan Cape,
(1926). First edition. Orig. cloth. Dust jacket (spine darkened).
Fine. MacManus 279-2789 1983 $25

HOUSMAN, LAURENCE   The Life of H. R. H. London: Jonathan
Cape, (1928). First edition. Illus. Orig. cloth. Dust jacket (spine
darkened). Very good. MacManus 279-2790 1983 $25

HOUSMAN, LAURENCE   The Love Concealed. London: Sidgwick
& Johnson, 1928. First edition. Orig. cloth. Fine. MacManus 279-
2791 1983 $25

HOUSMAN, LAURENCE   Of Aucassin and Nicolette. N.Y., Dial,
1930. Full Japanese vellum, uncut. Pub.'s slipcase. Very good-fine
copy. Houle 21-421 1983 $37.50

HOUSMAN, LAURENCE   The Return of Alcestis. N.Y.: Samuel
French, (1916). Samuel French Series. Orig. printed wrappers. Spine
and covers a trifle worn. Near-fine. MacManus 279-2793 1983 $20

HOUSMAN, LAURENCE   Stories from The Arabian Nights...
London, Hodder & Stoughton, n.d. Illus. in color by Edmund Dulac.
4to. Morrill 288-94 1983 $50

HOUSMAN, LAURENCE   The Story of Seven Young Goslings.
Blackie, nd (1899). Illus. by Mabel Dearmer. Re-issue with 6 full
page col'd illus., illus. title, p. 9 two tone illus. & 5 b&w illus.,
plates. White linen backed col. pictorial bds., sl. thumbed, bds.
sl. rubbed & soiled, insc. fr. ep., scarce. Hodgkins 27-102 1983
£16.50

HOUSSAYE, ARSENE   Men and women of France, during the last
century. London: Richard Bentley, 1852. First edition in English.
3 vols. 8vo, orig. dark green cloth. Small nick in top of one spine.
Old library stamps on titles, but a fine set. Ximenes 63-30 1983
$45

HOUSSE, E.   Les Oiseaux du Chili. Paris, 1948.
25 text-figures, royal 8vo, wrappers. Wheldon 160-762 1983 £25

HOUSTON, SAM   Speech of Mr. Houston, of Tennessee...
Washington, 1826. First edition of Sam Houston's first apperance in
print. Jenkins 152-825 1983 $250

HOUSTON A History and Guide. Houston, 1942. First edition with dust
jacket. Illus. Jenkins 152-455 1983 $35

HOVER, OTTO   Das Eisenwerk, Die Kunstformen des
Schmiede-eisens vom Mittelalter bis zum Ausgang des 18. Jahrhunderts.
Berlin, n.d. Photos, cloth, ex-library, covers rough. King 46-390
1983 $35

HOVEY, ALVAH   A Memoir of the Life and Times of the
Rev. Isaac Backus. Boston, 1859. 1st ed. Small 8vo. Morrill 286-
202 1983 $25

HOVEY, RICHARD   Dartmouth Lyrics. N.H., (1938). 8vo.
Cloth. A fine copy. In Our Time 156-410 1983 $20

HOVGAARD, WILLIAM   The Voyages of the Norsemen to
America. N.Y., 1914. 83 illus. & 7 maps, some folding (backstrip
somewhat spotted). Argosy 716-136 1983 $20

HOW, LOUIS   The Other Don Juan. New York Harbor
Press, 1932. Illus. by Steele Savage. Tall 8vo, orig. boards,
leather back, nice. Morrill 287-160 1983 $30

HOWARD, ANNIE HORNADY   Georgia Homes and Notable Georgians.
Atlanta, n.d. (ca. 1940). First edition. Portraits and illustrations.
4to. Morrill 290-147 1983 $27.50

HOWARD, GEOFFREY ELIOT   Early English Drug Jars. London:
The Medici Society, 1931. 4to, this copy with the signature of
the English book illustrator, John Austen. With 2 plates in colour
and 21 monochrome. Karmiole 76-56 1983 $75

HOWARD, H. E.   Territory in Bird Life. 1948. New edition, 13 illus., 8vo, cloth. Wheldon 160-763 1983 £12

HOWARD, HAMILTON GAY   Civil-War Echoes, Character Sketches and State Secrets. Washington, Howard Publishing Co., 1907. First edition. The author's own copy with numerous notes, additions, changes, deletions, etc., throughout text and on covers. Illustrated by V. Floyd Campbell. 8vo. Morrill 290-189 1983 $85

HOWARD, JOHN   Histoire des Prinpaux Lazarets de l'Europe. Paris, 1801. 8vo, mod. bds. Argosy 713-272 1983 $150

HOWARD, OLIVER O.   My Life and Experiences Among Our Hostile Indians. Hartford, Ct., (1907). First edition. Illus. with 48 plates, including 10 in color, and 9 by Frederic Remington. Jenkins 152-156 1983 $200

HOWARD, OLIVER O.   My Life and Experiences Among Our Hostile Indians. Hartford, (1907). Frontis. Illus. Cloth, rebacked in leather, internally fine. Reese 19-275 1983 $125

HOWARD, ROBERT   The duell of the stags: a poem. London: for Henry Herringman, 1668. First edition. Small 4to. Half morocco. Trimmed a little close. Ximenes 63-368 1983 $200

HOWARD, ROBERT   The great favourite, or, the Duke of Lerma. In the Savoy: printed for Henry Herringman, 1668. Sm. 4to, disbound. 1st edition. A fine copy. Ximenes 64-286 1983 $450

HOWARD, THOMAS   On the Loss of Teeth. Simpkin and Marshall, London, 1857. Small 8vo, with frontis.; orig. cloth. Quaritch NS 5-59 1983 $100

HOWARD, THOMAS   On the Loss of Teeth and Loose Teeth. London, 1862. Frontispiece; also plate with 5 colored drawings. 16mo. Morrill 289-113 1983 $25

HOWARD, WILLIAM TRAVIS   Public Health Administration and the Natural History of disease in Baltimore, Maryland 1797-1920. Washington, 1924. Wrappers. First edition. Ex-library. Scarce. Fye H-3-278 1983 $45

HOWE, EDGAR WATSON   Plain People. New York: Dodd, Mead, 1929. Frontis. First edition. Orig. cloth, gilt. Not fine, but nice copy. Jenkins 155-601 1983 $20

HOWE, EDGAR WATSON   The Story of a Country Town. Atchison, Kan.: Howe & Co., 1883. First edition. Illus. Dark brown cloth. Deep dark brown binding. Inscribed on front free end paper by "one of the 'dedicatees'". Library stamp on front free end paper, bookplate and catalogue entry inside front cover. News clips about Howe pasted on four blank pages before frontis, fading and browning resulting. Some slight wear, otherwise very good copy. Bradley 66-207 1983 $75

HOWE, HENRY   Historical Collections of the Great West. Cincinnati, 1851. 1st ed., illus. & maps, engr. 1/2 title, calf (rubbed). 2 vols. in 1. Argosy 710-586 1983 $50

HOWE, JAMES VIRGIL   The Amateur Guncraftsman. NY, 1928. First edition. Illus., two-tone cloth, bookplate, rubbed. King 46-592 1983 $20

HOWE, JAMES VIRGIL   The Modern Gunsmith. New York, (1944). Revised ed. Illus. 2 vols., 4to, boxed-partly broken. Morrill 288-110 1983 $45

HOWE, JULIA WARD   Later Lyrics. Boston: 1866. First edition, first printing. Plum-colored cloth. 8 ad pages at back. Very good copy. Bradley 66-208 1983 $75

HOWE, MARK ANTHONY DE WOLFE   The Boston Symphony Orchestra. Boston, (1914). Ed. limited to 535 copies. Illus. Tall 8vo, orig. boards, buckram back, uncut and unopened, spine partly dampstained, slightly affecting adjoining leaves, otherwise nice. Morrill 288-282 1983 $20

HOWE, MAUD   Laura Bridgman. Boston: Little, Brown, 1903. First edition. Ads. Spine tips frayed. Gach 95-218 1983 $25

HOWE, OCTAVIUS   American Clipper Ships 1833-1858. Salem, Mass.: Marine Research Society, 1926-7. Two vols. 26 cm. Orig. blue cloth. Very good; light foxing. Colored frontis. and the 112 black & white plates of ships. Grunder 7-82 1983 $175

HOWE, OCTAVIUS   Argonauts of '49... Cambridge, 1923. Illus. Some wear. Fine study. Jenkins 153-261 1983 $40

HOWE, OCTAVIUS   Argonauts of '49. Cambridge: Harvard University Press, 1923. Second printing. Illus. Cloth. Dust wrapper. Dawson 471-125 1983 $25

HOWE, P. P.   J. M. Synge. A Critical Study. N.Y.: Mitchell Kennerley, 1912. First edition. Frontis. port. Orig. decorated cloth. Spine a bit darkened and slightly rubbed. Very good. MacManus 280-5070 1983 $35

HOWE, SAMUEL GRIDLEY (1801-1876)   A Letter to the Governor of Massachusetts. Boston: Tickor & Fields, 1857. Orig. grey printed wrappers. Gach 95-219 1983 $27.50

HOWELL, GEORGE   The Bimetallic League. P.S. King; Manchester, J. Heywood, 1889. First edition, orig. blue cloth, v.g. Jarndyce 31-187 1983 £15

HOWELL, GEORGE   The Conflicts and Labour Historically and Economically Considered. Macmillan, 1890. 2nd & revised edition, 60 pp ads. Orig. brown cloth. Jarndyce 31-188 1983 £16

HOWELL, JAMES   Dendrologia. (London), printed by T.B. for H. Mosely, 1640. Folio, new full polished calf with inner dentelles, text a little browned, first plate little browned, backed, one other plate frayed at edge, edge strengthened. With a cont. 4-page manuscript key to the characters. Ravenstree 94-209 1983 $250

HOWELL, JAMES   Epistolae Ho-Elianae. London, printed for Humphrey Moseley, 1645. 4to, cont. calf newly rebacked, inner blank edge of frontis. lightly strengthened, some minor soiling throughout, but a very good copy. First editions. Ravenstree 94-210 1983 $450

HOWELL, JAMES   Lustra Ludovici. London, printed for Humphrey Moseley, 1646. Folio, orig. sheep, joints broken, marginal glosses in cont. hand, first and only 17th century edition. Ravenstree 94-211 1983 $175

HOWELL, JAMES   S.P.Q.V. London, Richard Lownes, 1651. Folio, 19th century half calf, first edition, with the engravings in very fine condition. Ravenstree 94-213 1983 $135

HOWELL, JAMES   Som Sober Inspections Made into the Cariage and Consuits of the Late-Long Parlement. London, printed by E.C. for Henry Seile, 1655. 12mo, cont. mottled calf gilt, sometime restored and now with hinges cracked, title and preliminaries as well as last few leaves a bit frayed about edges. The Earl of Shelbourne copy with his signature on end-paper. First edition. Ravenstree 94-214 1983 $185

HOWELL, WILLIAM T.   The Hudson Highlands. NY, 1933. 2 vols. Many photo. illus. by author. One of 200 numbered copies presented at the Fresh Air Club. Argosy 716-354 1983 $25

HOWELLS, JOHN MEAD   Lost Examples of Colonial Architecture. NY: William Helburn, 1931. Folio. Edition ltd. to 1,000 numbered copies. Blue gilt-stamped cloth. In defective slipcase. Karmiole 74-104 1983 $150

HOWELLS, WILLIAM DEAN   A Hazard of New Fortunes. Edinburgh: David Douglas, 1889. First English edition. 2 vols., lacks free end papers vol. I, ex-library copy, orig. maroon cloth rubbed. Jarndyce 30-430 1983 £15

HOWELLS, WILLIAM DEAN   Italian Journeys. Boston, 1901. 8vo.
1st illustrated ed. Illustrations by Joseph Pennell. A fine copy
in the uncommon dj and slipcase box. In Our Time 156-412 1983 $125

HOWELLS, WILLIAM DEAN   The Rise of Silas Lapham. Boston:
Ticknor & Fields, 1885. 1st ed., 1st state with ads reading "Works."
Orig. tan cloth, gilt. Battered type at p. 176. Close to fine copy.
Jenkins 155-603 1983 $100

HOWELLS, WILLIAM DEAN   Their Wedding Journey. Boston & New
York: Houghton, Mifflin, (1913). Illus. Revised ed. Orig. red
cloth, gilt. Very fine copy inscribed by Howells on front end
paper: "W.D. Howells, Cambridge 1870, St. Augustin, 1916."
Jenkins 155-605 1983 $75

HOWELLS, WILLIAM DEAN   The Undiscovered Country. Boston:
Houghton, Mifflin, 1880. 1st ed., 1st printing, 1st binding. Orig.
decorative brown cloth, gilt. Near fine copy. Jenkins 155-606
1983 $30

HOWELLS, WILLIAM DEAN   The Undiscovered Country. Boston:
Houghton, Mifflin, 1880. 1st ed., 1st printing, 1st binding. Orig.
decorative green cloth. Near fine. Jenkins 155-609 1983 $30

HOWELLS, WILLIAM DEAN   The Undiscovered Country. Boston:
Houghton, Mifflin, 1880. 1st. ed., 1st printing, 1st binding. Orig.
decorative purple cloth. Very good. Jenkins 155-608 1983 $25

HOWELLS, WILLIAM DEAN   Venetian Life. Boston & New York:
HMCo., 1907. Frontis., color plates. 1st ed. thus. Orig. linen-
backed patterned boards, t.e.g., uncut. Illus. by Edmund Garrett.
Jenkins 155-610 1983 $20

HOWES, WILLIAM B.   Protection and Free Trade, Compared...
Salem: Printed at the Gazette Office, 1846. Sewn. First edition.
Jenkins 153-180 1983 $35

HOWES, WRIGHT   U.S.iana (1650-1960)... New York:
Bowker, 1962. Cloth, revised and enlarged ed., fine. Dawson 470-156
1983 $75

HOWITT, EMANUEL   Selections from Letters Written During
a Tour though the United States, in the Summer and Autumn of 1819.
Nottingham: Dunn, (1820). 8vo, orig. boards (joints somewhat cracked).
First edition. Sion College Library withdrawal stamp at end.
Rostenberg 88-7 1983 $325

HOWITT, EMANUEL   Selections from Letters Written During a
Tour Through the United States in the Summer and Autumn of 1819.
Nottingham: J. Dunn, (1820). Cloth, leather label. First edition.
Jenkins 153-262 1983 $150

HOWITT, SAMUEL   A New Work of Animals... London, Edward
Orme, 1811. 4to. 100 hand-colored plates etched by Howitt. Full red
straight-grained morocco wide gilt border on sides, built-up blind
border, finely rebacked with slightly raised gilt bands. 1st ed. One
of the rare colored copies, with the large paper plates and text
slightly smaller. Fine. O'Neal 50-28 1983 $2,000

HOWITT, WILLIAM   The Hall and the Hamlet. Henry
Colburn, 1848. First edition. 2 vols. Lacks leading free end paper
vol. I. Orig. green cloth. Jarndyce 30-432 1983 £30

HOWITT, WILLIAM   Land, Labor and Gold. Bos., 1855. Two
vols., spine edges chipped, cover slightly worn and stained, page edges
slightly stained, else good. Quill & Brush 54-1683 1983 $200

HOWITT, WILLIAM   Ruined Abbeys and Castles of Great Britain and Ireland. 1864. Second series, 26 tipped-in photographs by
Thompson, Sedgefield, Ogle and Hemphill. Small 4to, embossed coth
with inlaid photographic illus. K Books 307-101 1983 £60

HOWITT, WILLIAM   The Ruined Abbeys of Yorkshire.
Alfred W. Bennett, 1865. 1st edn. 5 mounted photographic illus. by
Sedgefield & Ogle, ads. Brown morocco grain blind stamped cloth,
a.e.g. (v.sl. foxing prelims. top/bottom of fr.jt. half inch split,
corners sl. bruised), nice copy. Hodgkins 27-348 1983 £65

HOWITT, WILLIAM   The Rural Life of England. London:
Longman, 1838. First edition. 2 vols. 3/4 morocco. Very good.
MacManus 279-2799 1983 $65

HOWITT, WILLIAM   Visits to Remarkable Places. Longman,
Orme, 1840-42. First edition of the second volume, with engraved
frontis., vignette title-pages and some 84 vignette illus. by
Samuel Williams, 2 vols. 8vo, cont. brown calf, gilt, gilt panelled
sides, gilt spines. Fenning 60-188 1983 £65

HOWITT, WILLIAM   Woodburn Grange. Phila.: T.B. Peterson
Brothers, n.d. First American edition. Orig. cloth. 3 vols. in one.
Spine slightly worn. Good. MacManus 279-2800 1983 $25

HOWS, JOHN A.   Forest Pictures in the Adirondacks.
New York: James B. Gregory, 1865. 1st ed., 4to, orig. embossed
morocco gilt, spine gilt, a.e.g., 16 engraved plates. A fine copy.
Trebizond 18-145 1983 $75

HOWSON, JOHN   A Sermon preached at Paule's Crosse the
4 of December 1597. London, Th. Adams, 1597. 4to, disbound, some
small holes to inner blank margin of title, some marking and underlining. Ravenstree 94-215 1983 $195

HOY, WILLIAM   The Chinese Six Companies. SF, 1942.
Sm 4to, blue cloth, vignette in red on front cover. Typography
by Harold N. Seeger. Illustrated. Perata 27-100 1983 $50

HOYLAND, FRANCIS   Poems and Translations. London: for
W. Bristow and C. Etherington, 1763. First edition. 4to. Uncut
in orig. grey wrappers. Trifle dusty. Heath 48-329 1983 £55

HOYLAND, JOHN   A Historical Survey of the Customs,
Habits & Present Stage of the Gypsies. York, 1816. First edition,
orig. boards, amateur rebacking, contents good. K Books 301-84 1983
£45

HOYLE, EDMOND   Breve tratado do jogo do whist...
Lisbon: na Typographia Rollandiana, 1818. Small 8vo. Disound.
Unopened. Ximenes 63-57 1983 $40

HOYT, EPAPHRAS   Antiquarian Researches. Greenfield,
Mass.: Ansel Phelps, Dec. 1824. Engraved fore-title, folding
plate, orig. boards, uncut. Binding worn and covers loose, some
foxing. Felcone 22-88 1983 $50

HOYT, HENRY F.   A Frontier Doctor. Boston, 1929.
Frontis and plates. First edition. Nice copy. Jenkins 151-136
1983 $50

HOZIER, HENRY M.   The Franco-Prussian War. William
Mackenzie, (1870-72). With the topography and history of the Rhine
Valley, by W.H. Davenport Adams. With an additional engraved title-
page, 27 engraved plates of views, 25 portraits, 4 other plates of
weapons, and 24 maps and plans, in the orig. 7 parts as issued, 4to,
orig. red cloth, gilt, a.e.g., a very good copy. Plates by Birkett
Forster. Fenning 62-182 1983 £250

HRDLICKA, A   Physiological and Medical Observations
among the Indians... Washington, 1908. 8vo. Orig. binding. First
edition. Fye H-3-279 1983 $40

HRDLICKA, A.   Recent Discoveries Attributed to Early
Man in America. Washington: BAE 66, 1918. First edition. Photo-
plates. Orig. olive green cloth. Mint. Jenkins 152-158 1983 $35

HUARTE DE SAN JUAN, JUAN   Examen de Ingenios para las sciencias.
(Antwerp): Officina Plantiniana, 1603. Printer's device on title.
12mo. Cont. limp vellum. Small piece missing from fore-margin of
front cover. Kraus 164-130 1983 $180

HUARTE Y NAVARRO, JUAN
Please turn to
HUARTE DE SAN JUAN, JUAN

HUBAUX, JEAN   Le Mythe du Phenix dans la Litterature
Grecque et Latine. 1939. Wrs. 8vo, cloth. Salloch 385-126 1983
$35

HUBBARD, ARTHUR   Neolithic Dew-Ponds and Cattle-Ways. Longmans, 1916. Third edition. With full-page and other illus. Roy. 8vo, orig. cloth, gilt. Fenning 60-189 1983 £21.50

HUBBARD, ARTHUR   Neolithic Dew-Ponds and Cattle-Ways. 1907. 8vo, cloth, 2nd edition, illus. Wheldon 160-237 1983 £15

HUBBARD, ELBERT   The Appreciation of Ali Baba of East Aurora... East Aurora: Roycrofter, (1894). 1st ed., 1 of 620 copies signed by author and by the illuminator, Anna McMillan (with her mark). Very fine copy. Jenkins 155-612 1983 $20

HUBBARD, ELBERT   Hollyhocks and Goldenglow. (Roycrofters, 1912). Portrait. Blind-stamped limp leather. T.e.g. Rubbed (esp. spine). King 45-640 1983 $20

HUBBARD, ELBERT   James Oliver. East Aurora, 1909. 1st ed. Orig. linen-backed printed boards, uncut. Presentation copy inscribed by Hubbard to Cyrus McCormick. Fine. Jenkins 155-611 1983 $35

HUBBARD, ELBERT   Little Journeys to the Homes of Good Men and Great. East Aurora, 1908. Sm. thick 4to, with gravures of thirteen authors; large color initials. Half pigskin, stamped in blind with Roycroft insignia, strap (lacking the buckle; scuffed), good-very good. Houle 21-758 1983 $45

HUBBARD, ELBERT   Little Journeys to the Homes of the Great. East Aurora, 1931. Memorial Ed. Portraits. 14 vols. 8vo. Paper labels. Morrill 289-370 1983 $37.50

HUBBARD, ELBERT   The Man of Sorrow. East Aurora, 1905. 3/4 brown morocco, small green leather oval inlays on spine, t.e.g, uncut. One of 100 copies on Japan vellum, signed by Hubbard. Hand colored initial letters throughout. Roycroft binding. Very good. Houle 22-760 1983 $175

HUBBARD, ELBERT   A Message to Garcia and Thirteen Other Things. East Aurora, 1901. 3/4 red morocco over marbled boards, t.e.g., uncut. One of 50 copies on Japan vellum, signed by Hubbard and the illuminator, Emma Johnson. Fine Roycroft bindery. Houle 22-761 1983 $250

HUBBARD, ELBERT   So Here Cometh White Hyacinths. (East Aurora: The Roycrofters, 1907). First edition. Small 8vo. Half suede over boards, leather spine label. Many color designs by Dard Hunter including a spread title page, initials and a front cover design. Some rubbing of cover. Oak Knoll 48-215 1983 $65

HUBBARD, ELBERT   Song of Songs. East Eurora, 1896. Full red levant morocco, t.e.g., uncut, by the Roycroft bindery. One of 600 copies, signed by Hubbard. Laid in are 2 ALS from an early Roycroft collector. Very good. Houle 22-762 1983 $150

HUBBARD, ELBERT   Time and Chance. East Aurora: Roycrofter, 1899. 2 vols. 1st ed. Orig. 3/4 cheesecake leather. One spine label mostly ripped away by William Morris, else fine set. Jenkins 155-613 1983 $30

HUBBARD, FREEMAN   Railroad Avenue. N.Y., McGraw-Hill, (1945). First edition. Illus. Pictorial dust jacket by Frederick Blakeslee (small nicks) else very good. Houle 22-1110 1983 $25

HUBBARD, JOHN N.   Sketches of Border Adventures in the Life and Times of Major Moses Van Campen. Bath, N.Y., 1842. Illus., folded maps, plates. Orig. cloth. First edition. Ginsberg 46-316 1983 $125

HUBERT, ELBERT   Justinian and Theodora. East Aurora: The Roycrofters, 1906. 8vo. Limp suede, leather cover label. With spread title page, chapter headings, initial letters and running heads designed by Dard Hunter. Only minor wear to covers. Oak Knoll 48-208 1983 $85

HUBERT, GERARD   La sculpture dans l'Italie napoleonienne. Paris, 1964. 532 pp. 225 illus. hors texts. Lar. 4to. Wraps. Ars Libri SB 26-105 1983 $135

HUBNER, J.   Sammlung Exotischer Schmetterlinge. Brussels, 1894-1912. New English Facsimile edition, hand colored plates, 4 vols., 4to, half green morocco, panelled backs, emblematically tooled. Limited to about 50 copies. A fine clean copy. Wheldon 160-48 1983 £3,200

HUC, M.   The Chinese Empire. London, 1855. Second edition. Folding map. Library stamp on titles and map. 2 vols. Library cloth bindings. Good. Edwards 1044-359 1983 £60

HUDDESFORD, GEORGE   Salmagundi. T. Bensley, 1791. First edition, errata leaf, additional engraved title, 4to, some foxing at the beginning but good in old style half calf. K Books 301-97 1983 £40

HUDSON, CHARLES   Speech of Mr....of Mass., on the Wheat Trade of the Country. Washington: J. & G. S. Gideon, 1846. Uncut. Edges dusty but a very good copy. Bradley 66-695 1983 $27.50

HUDSON, CHARLES   Speech on the Annexation of Texas. (Wash., 1845). Mod. wraps. Argosy 716-534 1983 $25

HUDSON, D. (1752-1819)   Memoir of Jemima Wilkinson, Preacheress of the Eighteenth Century. Bath, N.Y.: 1844. 16mo. Calf, rebacked. Foxed, but nice copy. Gach 95-536 1983 $85

HUDSON, DEREK   Arthur Rackham, His Life and Work. London: Heinemann, (1960). 4to, with 33 tipped-in color plates, 8 tipped-in b/w plates and numerous text illus. Bound in an exhibition binding, signed by Margaret Levy. Binding is full maroon morocco with an abstract design in gray and black on both covers; gilt-stamped spine. A.e.g. With gilt tooled inner dentelles, azure blue fine suede endpapers and with orig. illus. endpapers by Rackham used as flyleaves. Karmiole 74-24 1983 $850

HUDSON, DEREK   Arthur Rackham. His life and work. London: William Heinemann, 1960. 69 illus. (predominantly tipped-in; many color). 4to. Cloth. Ars Libri 32-543 1983 $150

HUDSON, G. V.   The Butterflies and Moths of New Zealand. Wellington, 1928. 9 plain and 53 coloured plates, 4to, original half morocco. A good copy of this very scarce work. Wheldon 160-1099 1983 £120

HUDSON, J. K.   Letters to Governor Lewelling. Topeka: The Topeka Capital Co., 1893. Orig. cloth. First edition. Author's presentation copy. Jenkins 152-840 1983 $65

HUDSON, MARIANNE SPENCER   Almack's. A Novel. Saunders and Otley, 1826. 3 vols, lge. 12mo, original boards uncut; with all half-titles; advertisement leaf in Vol. III; backstrips worn, labels defective (missing on Vol II); some pages rather roughly opened; a clean and unpressed copy. Scarce First Edition. Hill 165-59 1983 £120

HUDSON, MARIANNE SPENCER   Almack's. Saunders and Otley, 1827. 3 vols., large 12mo, cont. half calf, the bindings a little rubbed but thoroughly sound and otherwise a very good copy with the half-titles. Fenning 60-191 1983 £38.50

HUDSON, MARIANNE SPENCER   Almack's. Saunders and Otley, 1826. 3 vols. 12mo, lacks half-titles and final advert. leaf. Cont. half calf. 4 leaves loosening, but a very good set. Hannas 69-107 1983 £25

HUDSON, STEPHEN   Celeste & Other Sketches. Blackamore Press, 1930. 6 woodcuts. Green cloth, gilt, ex-libris copy. Edition limited to 700 copies, No. 118. Greer 40-148 1983 £25

HUDSON, WILLIAM HENRY   Adventures Among Birds. London: Hutchinson & Co., 1913. First edition. Orig. cloth. Fine. MacManus 279-2807 1983 $75

HUDSON, WILLIAM HENRY   Afoot in England. NY, 1922. Spine slightly rubbed, covers rumpled, else very good. Quill & Brush 54-666 1983 $20

HUDSON, WILLIAM HENRY   Birds and Man. London: Longmans, Green, & Co., 1091. First edition. Orig. cloth. Bookplate of William Henry Allen on the front endsheet. Fine. MacManus 279-2814 1983 $75

HUDSON, WILLIAM HENRY   Birds and Man. London: Duckworth & Co., 1915. Second edition. Mounted color frontis. Orig. cloth. Extensively revised. Two new chapters. Very good. MacManus 279-2812 1983 $45

HUDSON, WILLIAM HENRY   Birds in a Village. London: Chapman & Hall, Ltd., 1893. First edition, binding variant 3. Orig. terra cotta cloth. Covers soiled. MacManus 279-2815 1983 $35

HUDSON, WILLIAM HENRY   Birds in a Village. London: Chapman & Hall, Ltd., 1893. First edition, binding variant 3. Orig. terra cotta cloth. Covers soiled. MacManus 279-2816 1983 $35

HUDSON, WILLIAM HENRY   Birds in London: London: Longmans, Green, & Co., 1898. First edition. Illus. by B. Hook & A.D. McCormick. Orig. cloth. Good. MacManus 279-2817 1983 $75

HUDSON, WILLIAM HENRY   Birds of la Plata. London, Dent, 1920. First edition. 4to, with 22 color plates by Gronvold. Dust jackets, small nicks, else very good-fine. 2 vols. One of 1,500 sets. Houle 21-424 1983 $195

HUDSON, WILLIAM HENRY   Birds of La Plata. 1920. 22 coloured plates by H. Gronvold, 2 vols., royal 8vo, original half buckram. Scarce. Wheldon 160-766 1983 £75

HUDSON, WILLIAM HENRY   The Book of a Naturalist. London: Hodder & Stoughton, (1919). First edition. Orig. cloth. Covers a bit faded and worn. MacManus 279-2820 1983 $45

HUDSON, WILLIAM HENRY   The Book of a Naturalist. New York: Doran, (1919). First American edition. Orig. green cloth, gilt. Short of fine. Jenkins 152-827 1983 $25

HUDSON, WILLIAM HENRY   British Birds. London: Longman, Green & Co., 1895. First edition. 8 colored plates. Orig. decorated cloth. Covers a little rubbed. Very good. MacManus 279-2822 1983 $75

HUDSON, WILLIAM HENRY   British Birds. 1902 or 1911. New edition, 8 coloured plates by Thorburn, slightly used. Wheldon 160-765 1983 £12

HUDSON, WILSON HENRY   A Crystal Age. London: T. Fisher Unwin, 1887. First edition. Rebound in 3/4 calf & marbled boards. Marbled endpapers. With an APC, 1 page, 40 St. Lukes Road, W.11, (London), Aug 8, 1921, from Hudson to Messrs. Birrell & Garnett. Extremities somewhat rubbed. Good. MacManus 279-2824 1983 $350

HUDSON, WILLIAM HENRY   A Crystal Age. London: Unwin, 1887. First edition. Orig. cloth. Covers worn and marked. Inner hinges cracked. In a half morocco case. Good. MacManus 279-2823 1983 $175

HUDSON, WILLIAM HENRY   A Crystal Age. London: T. Fisher Unwin, 1906. Second, revised edition. Orig. decorated cloth. Author's name on title-page. Very good. MacManus 279-2825 1983 $35

HUDSON, WILLIAM HENRY   A Crystal Age. N.Y.: Dutton, (1917). First American edition. Intro. by C. Smyth. Orig. decorated cloth. Near-fine. MacManus 279-2826 1983 $30

HUDSON, WILLIAM HENRY   Dean Man's Plack. NY/L, 1920. Near fine in chipped dustwrapper. Quill & Brush 54-667 1983 $50

HUDSON, WILLIAM HENRY   El Ombu. London: Duckworth & Co., 1902. First edition. Orig. green paper wrappers. One of 1250 copies issued. David Garnett's copy, with his bookplate on the front endsheet. Spine faded. Wrappers worn. Enclosed in a custom-made half-morocco box. MacManus 279-2827 1983 $75

HUDSON, WILLIAM HENRY   El Ombu. L, 1902. Paperwraps, spine chipped and flaking, small circular stain on front cover, else good in solander case. Quill & Brush 54-668 1983 $50

HUDSON, WILLIAM HENRY   El Ombu. London, 1902. First edition. Spine a little darkened. Nice. Rota 230-301 1983 £17.50

HUDSON, WILLIAM HENRY   Famous Missions of California. N.Y., Dodge (1901). Color frontis. and numerous halftone plates. Pictorial boards. With dust jacket. Very good. Houle 21-1091 1983 $125

HUDSON, WILLIAM HENRY   Far Away and Long Ago. Buenos Aires, 1943. Quarto. Laced bleached calf and horsehide (with the hair still intact). Near fine. The Ltd. Editions Club; one of 1,500 numbered copies, illus. with lithographs by Raoul Rosarivo, and signed by him. Reese 19-277 1983 $125

HUDSON, WILLIAM HENRY   Far Away and Long Ago. London: Dent, 1918. First edition. Orig. cloth. Very good. MacManus 279-2828 1983 $25

HUDSON, WILLIAM HENRY   Green Mansions. London: Duckworth & Co., 1904. Gilt cloth. First edition, earliest state of the binding without the publ's monogram blindstamp. Ink name and scattered foxing to endsheets, otherwise about fine. Reese 20-533 1983 $275

HUDSON, WILLIAM HENRY   Green Mansions. London: Duckworth, 1904. First edition; the state without the publisher's blind device on the back cover. Orig. cloth. Front inner hinge partly cracked. In a half-morocco slipcase. Fine. MacManus 279-2830 1983 $250

HUDSON, WILLIAM HENRY   Green Mansions. London: Duckworth & Co., 1904. First edition. Orig. cloth. Slightly soiled. Very good. MacManus 279-2829 1983 $250

HUDSON, WILLIAM HENRY   Green Mansions. London: Duckworth, 1926. Frontis., plates. 1st illus. ed. Orig. green cloth, gilt. Fine bright fresh copy in chipped dj. Uncommon thus. Jenkins 155-615 1983 $45

HUDSON, WILLIAM HENRY   Green Mansions. L, 1926. Illus. by K. Henderson. Green and gold dec. boards with green cloth spine, near fine in near fine dustwrapper slightly worn along edges. First illus. edition. Quill & Brush 54-669 1983 $40

HUDSON, WILLIAM HENRY   Green Mansions. NY, 1904. Ex-lib., well worn on edges, bookplate and small perforation title page, stamp on copyright page, otherwise good tight copy. Quill & Brush 54-670 1983 $35

HUDSON, WILLIAM HENRY   Green Mansions. New York, 1944. First edition. Coloured illus. by E.M. Kauffer. Corners worn. Nice. Rota 230-302 1983 £12

HUDSON, WILLIAM HENRY   Hampshire Days. London: Longmans, Green, & Co., 1903. First edition, second issue. Illus. Orig. cloth. Bookplate. Very good. MacManus 279-2835 1983 $65

HUDSON, WILLIAM HENRY   A Hind in Richmond Park. L, 1922. Minor interior foxing, flys offset, edges slightly bumped, very good in slightly frayed and aged dustwrapper, review laid in. Quill & Brush 54-664 1983 $50

HUDSON, WILLIAM HENRY   A Hind in Richmond Park. 1922. 1st ed., 8vo, original cloth, relevant newscuttings pasted to endpapers. Wheldon 160-165 1983 £18

HUDSON, WILLIAM HENRY   A Hind in Richmond Park. New York: Dutton, (1923). First American edition. Limited to 1550 copies, of which 1500 were for sale. Frontis. Orig. red cloth, label. Very good. Jenkins 152-828 1983 $25

HUDSON, WILLIAM HENRY   A Hind in Richmond Park. London: J.M. Dent & Sons Ltd., 1922. First edition. Dust jacket. MacManus 279-2838 1983 $25

HUDSON, WILLIAM HENRY   Idle Days in Patagonia. London: Chapman & Hall, 1893. First edition. Illus. Orig. cloth (spine faded). Presentation copy, inscribed, "To G.E. Fritchie with greetings from W.H. Hudson. Feb. 3rd, 1893." Front inner hinge cracked. Good. MacManus 279-2839 1983 $250

HUDSON, WILLIAM HENRY   Idle Days In Patagonia. London: Chapman & Hall, Ltd., 1893. First edition. Illus. by A. Hartley & J. Smit. Orig. decorated cloth. One of 1750 copies printed. Foxing. Bookplates on front endsheet. Fine. MacManus 279-2840 1983 $125

HUDSON, WILLIAM HENRY   The Land's End. London: Hutchinson & Co., 1908. First edition. 49 illus. by A.L. Collins. Orig. decorated cloth. Bookplate. Very good. MacManus 279-2841 1983 $65

HUDSON, WILLIAM HENRY   Letters on the Orithology of Buenos Ayers. Ithaca: Cornell University, (1941). First edition. Orig. cloth. Glassine dust jacket, boxed. Fine. Jenkins 152-829 1983 $20

HUDSON, WILLIAM HENRY   A Linnet for Sixpence! London: Royal Society for the Protection of Birds, (1907). Second edition. Illus. with color reproduction. Self-wrappers, folded. Fine. MacManus 279-2846 1983 $35

HUDSON, WILLIAM HENRY   A Little Boy Lost. London: Duckworth & Co., 1905. First edition. Illus. by A.D. M'Cormick. Orig. pictorial cloth. Inscribed by the author on the front flyleaf. Covers soiled. Good. MacManus 279-2847 1983 $175

HUDSON, WILLIAM HENRY   A Little Boy Lost. London: Duckworth, 1905. First edition. Illus. by A.D. M'Cormick. Orig. cloth. Covers a bit darkened. Bookplates. Very good. MacManus 279-2848 1983 $55

HUDSON, WILLIAM HENRY   A Little Boy Lost. L, 1905. Cover shows some soiling, good or better copy. Quill & Brush 54-665 1983 $25

HUDSON, WILLIAM HENRY   A Little Boy Lost. N.Y.: Alfred A. Knopf, 1918. First American edition. Illus. by A.D. M'Cormick. Orig. cloth. First appearance of Hudson's letter to Knopf. Covers dull. Good. MacManus 279-2849 1983 $25

HUDSON, WILLIAM HENRY   Lost British Birds. N.p.: 1894. First edition, third printing. Illus. Orig. wrappers. Very good. MacManus 279-2852 1983 $65

HUDSON, WILLIAM HENRY   Lost British Birds. London: Chapman & Hall, Ltd., 1894. First edition, second printing. 15 drawings by by A.D. McCormick. Orig. printed wrappers. Former owner's signature on front cover. Wrappers rather dusty & worn at edges. Some foxing. MacManus 279-2851 1983 $50

HUDSON, WILLIAM HENRY   Lost British Birds. Soc. Protection of Birds, 1894. Text-figures, 8vo, wrappers. Rare. Third printing of the first edition. A trifle soiled and back wrapper slightly frayed at edges, first and last leaves a trifle foxed. Wheldon 160-764 1983 £20

HUDSON, WILLIAM HENRY   Men, Books and Birds. London: Eveleigh Nash & Grayson, 1925. First edition. Orig. cloth. Bookplate and stamp of A.A. Brill on front endsheet. Very good. MacManus 279-2855 1983 $50

HUDSON, WILLIAM HENRY   Men, Books and Birds. London: Eveleigh Nash, (1925). First edition. Orig. green cloth, gilt. Near fine. Jenkins 152-830 1983 $25

HUDSON, WILLIAM HENRY   The Naturalist in La Plata. London: Chapman & Hall, 1892. "Second edition." Illus. Orig. decorated cloth. Presentation copy, inscribed "To G.E. Fritche from W.H. Hudson. July 26th, 1892." Very good. MacManus 279-2856 1983 $125

HUDSON, WILLIAM HENRY   The Naturalist in La Plata. London-New York, 1895. 8vo. Cloth. 3d ed., with illustrations by J. Smit. From the library of William James with his penned signature on the half-title page and with one holograph comment on the last endpaper of the book. A vg-fine copy. In Our Time 156-435 1983 $100

HUDSON, WILLIAM HENRY   The Naturalist in La Plata. London: Chapman & Hall, Ltd., 1892. First edition. Illus. Orig. pictorial cloth. Front inner hinge cracking. Very good. MacManus 279-2857 1983 $85

HUDSON, WILLIAM HENRY   Nature in Downland. London: Longmans, 1900. First edition. Illus. Orig. cloth. Spine darkened and worn. MacManus 279-2858 1983 $35

HUDSON, WILLIAM HENRY   On Liberating Caged Birds. London: Royal Society for the Protection of Birds, (1914). First edition. Illus. with color reproduction. Self-wrappers, folded. Fine. MacManus 279-2859 1983 $75

HUDSON, WILLIAM HENRY   153 Letters. London: The Nonesuch Press, 1923. First edition. One of 1000 numbered copies. Spare title label. Small tear in margin pf P.183. Very good. Jolliffe 26-270 1983 £45

HUDSON, WILLIAM HENRY   153 Letters from... Soho: Nonesuch Press, 1923. First edition. One of 1000 numbered copies. Orig. cloth, label. Uncut. Dust jacket. Very fine. Jenkins 152-831 1983 $60

HUDSON, WILLIAM HENRY   153 Letters. (London): The Nonesuch Press, 1923. First edition. Tall 8vo, buckram. Argosy 714-373 1983 $30

HUDSON, WILLIAM HENRY   Le Pays Pourpre. Paris: Librairie Plon, 1927. First French edition. Orig. wrappers. Spine darkened. Very good. MacManus 279-2842 1983 $45

HUDSON, WILLIAM HENRY   The Purple Land That England Lost. London: Sampson Low, Marston, Searle, and Rivington, 1885. First edition. 2 vols. Orig. cloth. Covers very worn and faded. Labels partly removed from front covers. Inner hinges cracked. In a half-morocco slipcase. MacManus 279-2861 1983 $450

HUDSON, WILLIAM HENRY   The Purple Land That England Lost. London: Sampson Low, 1885. First edition. 2 vols. Orig. cloth. Inner hinges partly cracked. Head of spine on volume two defective. Very good, sound copy. MacManus 279-2860 1983 $450

HUDSON, WILLIAM HENRY   The Purple Land. London: Duckworth & Co., (1911). Readers' Library edition. Orig. cloth. Presentation copy, inscribed on the front flyleaf "To Violet Hunt from W.H. Hudson." Fine. MacManus 279-2862 1983 $150

HUDSON, WILLIAM HENRY   Ralph Herne. N.Y.: Alfred A. Knopf, 1923. First separate American edition. Orig. cloth-backed boards with paper label on spine. One of 950 copies designed by B. Rogers and printed by W.E. Ridge. Corners bumped. MacManus 279-2864 1983 $20

HUDSON, WILLIAM HENRY   Rare Vanishing & Lost British Birds. London: J.M. Dent & Sons Ltd., 1923. First edition. 25 colored plates by H. Gronvold. Orig. cloth. Good. MacManus 279-2865 1983 $20

HUDSON, WILLIAM HENRY   Sea-Sickness: Its Cause, Nature, and Prevention... Boston, 1883. 12mo. 1st ed. Morrill 289-114 1983 $25

HUDSON, WILLIAM HENRY   Shepherd's Life. London: Methuen & Co. Ltd., (1910). First edition. Illus. by B.C. Cotch. Bookplate. Fine. MacManus 279-2866 1983 $85

HUDSON, WILLIAM HENRY   A Shepherd's Life. N.Y.: E.P. Dutton & Co., 1910. First American edition. Illus. by B.C. Gotch. Color frontis. Orig. decorated cloth. Bookplate on front endsheet. Very good. MacManus 279-2867 1983 $25

HUDSON, WILLIAM HENRY   Tales of the Pampas. New York: Knopf, 1916. First American edition. Orig. green cloth. Dust jacket (few minor edge chips). Very fine. Jenkins 152-832 1983 $125

HUDSON, WILLIAM HENRY   Three Water Birds. London: Royal Society for the Protection of Birds, (1926). First edition. Illus. in color by R. Green. Self-wrappers, folded. Fine. MacManus 279-2869 1983 $75

HUDSON, WILLIAM HENRY   A Thrush that Never Lived. London: Royal Society for the Protection of Birds, (1911). First edition. Illus. with color reproduction. Self-wrappers, folded. Upper corners expertly repaired. Fine. MacManus 279-2870 1983 $65

HUDSON, WILLIAM HENRY   A Tired Traveller. London: Royal Society for the Protection of Birds, (1921). First edition. Illus. with color reproduction. Self-wrappers, folded. Near-fine. MacManus 279-2871 1983 $75

THE HUDSON River Route. New York, Taintor Brothers, 1869. Maps and views. 12mo, orig. wrappers. Morrill 288-342 1983 $25

HUEFFER, FORD MADOX
Please turn to
FORD, FORD MADOX

HUET, PIERRE D.   De Imbecillitate Mentis Humanae.
Amsterdam: H. du Sauzet, 1738. First edition. 12mo. Uncut,
half calf. Engraved portrait. Heath 48-510 1983 £40

HUET, PIERRE D   Traite Philosophique de la Foiblesse de
l'Esprit humain. Amsterdam, 1723. 12mo. Old calf. With portrait.
Gurney JJ-183 1983 £20

HUFELAND, C. W.   The Art of Prolonging Life. London,
1797. First English edition. 8vo. 2 vols. Orig. boards, uncut.
Advert. leaf. Very fine copy. Gurney 90-61 1983 £100

HUFELAND, OTTO   A Check List of Books, Maps, Pictures and
other printed matter relating to the Countries of Westchester and
Bronx. N.p.: Privately printed, 1929. 8vo, buckram, gilt. First
edition. Fine. Perata 28-209 1983 $65

HUG-HELLMUTH, HERMINE VON   A Young Girl's Diary. London: George
Allen, 1921. First English edition. Orig. grey cloth. Preface by
Sigmund Freud. Fine copy. Gach 95-158 1983 $30

HUGEL, C.   Travels in Kashmir... London, 1845.
Large folding map in endpocket, repaired, Portrait and 4 plates. Roy.
8vo. Half blue morocco. Good. Edwards 1044-360 1983 £95

HUGHES, C. E.   Above and Beyond...London, 1930. Folding
map. Numerous illus. 8vo. Orig. cloth. Good. Edwards 1044-361
1983 £15

HUGHES, ELIZABETH   The California of the Padres. San
Francisco, 1875. Orig. printed wraps. First edition. Ginsberg 47-
113 1983 $45

HUGHES, GEORGE   Rhymes, by a Poetaster. Saunders and
Otley, 1846. First edition, tall 8vo, orig. green cloth rubbed at
top of hinges. Inscribed presentation copy from the author, 1849.
Jarndyce 30-744 1983 £10.50

HUGHES, GRIFFITH   The Natural History of Barbados.
London: The author, 1750. Folio, 30 plates. Later 3/4 morocco.
Hinges just beginning to crack. First edition. Wide-margined
copy. Felcone 21-57 1983 $350

HUGHES, HECTOR S. J.   Select Cases in Registration of title
in Ireland. Dublin: E. Ponsonby, 1916. First edition, 8vo, orig.
cloth. Fenning 62-183 1983 £26.50

HUGHES, JOHN   Horae Britannicae. 1818. 2 vols.
bound as one, portrait, new half calf, uncut. K Books 301-98 1983
£30

HUGHES, JOHN T.   Doniphan's Expedition. Cincinnati,
(1847). Double columns. Illus. Orig. printed wraps. Fine copy.
Ginsberg 47-344 1983 $600

HUGHES, JOHN T.   Doniphan's Expedition: Containing an
Account of the Conquest of New Mexico. Cincinnati, 1848. Ports.,
8vo, mod. wrs., very light foxing, lacking map. Argosy 710-519
1983 $100

HUGHES, JOHN T.   Doniphan's Expedition; Containing an
Account of the Conquest of New Mexico. Cincinnati: U.P. James,
(ca. 1851). Illustrations. Original printed pictorial wrappers.
Unopened, very slight fraying to heel of spine. A fine copy. Jenkins
151-137 1983 $300

HUGHES, KATHERINE   The Black-Robe Voyageur. New York,
1911. 1st ed. Illus., marginal stains on two leaves, otherwise
very good. Clark 741-173 1983 $37.50

HUGHES, LANGSTON   An African Treasury. L, 1961. Fine in
price clipped, slightly soiled near fine dustwrapper with minor wear.
Quill & Brush 54-671 1983 $30

HUGHES, LANGSTON   The Big Sea, An Autobiography. NY:
1940. Contemporary inscription on front fly by Hughes. Very fine
in lightly chipped and spotted dust wrapper. Bromer 25-52 1983
$125

HUGHES, LANGSTON   The Big Sea. N.Y., 1940. First
edition. 8vo, cloth; somewhat worn & soiled. Presentation copy.
Argosy 714-874 1983 $60

HUGHES, LANGSTON   Fields of Wonder. N.Y., 1947. First
edition. Presentation copy. Fine in a chipped dust wrapper. Argosy
714-375 1983 $85

HUGHES, LANGSTON   Fields of Wonder. New York: Knopf,
1947. Cloth. First edition. A fine copy in dust jacket, with one
short, closed nick. Reese 20-534 1983 $60

HUGHES, LANGSTON   One-Way Ticket. New York: Knopf,
1949. Cloth and boards. First edition. Illus. by Jacob Lawrence.
Evidently a review copy, as it bears the light ownership stamp of
"The Tiger's Eye," with date of receipt. Fine in dust jacket with
one short nick. Reese 20-535 1983 $50

HUGHES, LANGSTON   Sheet Music: African Dance, 1939.
Pictorial wrap. Argosy 714-374 1983 $40

HUGHES, LANGSTON   Simple Speaks His Mind. (New York,
1950). First edition. Argosy 714-376 1983 $45

HUGHES, LANGSTON   Simple Speaks His Mind. (N.Y.), Simon &
Schuster, (1950). "Readers edition", 8vo. Stiff printed wraps.
(slight rubbing and nicking) else good - very good. Signed by Hughes
on front free endpaper. Houle 22-484 1983 $30

HUGHES, LANGSTON   The Ways of White Folks: Stories.
N.Y., 1934. First edition. Review copy. Fine, except that the
dust wrapper is sunned on the spine, and slightly chipped. Gladys
Rockmore Davis's copy, with her autograph. Argosy 714-377 1983
$75

HUGHES, LANGSTON   The Weary Blues. NY: 1926. First
edition. Light occasional foxing. Cloth-backed boards slightly
rubbed at extremities. Bromer 25-53 1983 $75

HUGHES, RICHARD   Confessio Juvenis. London, 1926.
First edition. One of 55 numbered copies signed by the author.
T.e.g. Pages unopened. Upper cover slightly spotted. Chipped
and nicked dustwrapper by Pamela Bianco. Very good. Jolliffe
26-273 1983 £95

HUGHES, RICHARD   Confessio Juvenis. London: Chatto &
Windus, 1926. First trade edition. Orig. cloth. Dust jacket with
illus. by Pamela Bianco. Jacket very slightly rubbed along spine.
Fine. MacManus 279-2877 1983 $45

HUGHES, RICHARD   A High Wind in Jamaica. L, 1929. Limited to 150 numbered and signed copies, corners worn, very good. Quill
& Brush 54-675 1983 $150

HUGHES, RICHARD   A High Wind in Jamaica. L, 1929. Cover
lightly faded, very good in slightly darkened and frayed dustwrapper
with wraparound blurb still present. Quill & Brush 54-674 1983 $125

HUGHES, RICHARD   A High Wind in Jamaica. Chatto &
Windus, 1929. First edition, 8vo, orig. buckram-backed patterned
boards, t.e.g. A fine copy. Ltd. edition of 150 numbered copies,
signed by the author. Fenning 62-184 1983 £75

HUGHES, RICHARD   In Hazard. A Sea Story. London:
Chatto & Windus, 1938. First edition. 8vo. Orig. cloth. Dust
jacket, trifle nicked. Fine copy. Jaffe 1-161 1983 $65

HUGHES, RICHARD   The Innocent Voyage. New York:
Harper, 1929. 1st ed. Orig. cloth-backed decorated boards, gilt.
Dust jacket panels laid in. Very good copy, signed by Hughes on
half-title. Jenkins 155-616 1983 $45

HUGHES, RICHARD   The Sisters' Tragedy. Oxford: Basil
Blackwell, 1922. First edition. Orig. decorated wrappers. Printed at
The Shakespeare Head Press, Stratford-Upon-Avon. **Fine.** MacManus 279-
2879 1983 $85

HUGHES, RICHARD   The Sisters' Tragedy. Oxford: The
Shakespeare Head Press, 1922. First edition. Wrappers. Very good.
Jolliffe 26-272 1983 £16

HUGHES, RICHARD   The Spider's Palace and other stories.
London, 1931. First edition. 11 full-page illus., 4 in colour, by
George Charlton. Chipped dustwrapper faded at the spine and missing
a piece from the head of the spine. Very good. Jolliffe 26-274
1983 £20

HUGHES, SUKEY   Washi: The World of Japanese Paper.
Tokyo, 1978. Thick quarto, heavy boards, cloth back. With over
100 original samples of handmade paper tipped in + 236 photographic
illus. of which 27 are in color and numerous text illus. Enclosed
in sturdy cloth-covered folding box. One of 1,000 copies. Duschnes
240-184 1983 $225

HUGHES, TED   Crow; poems. London, 1973. First
edition. Drawings by L. Baskin. One of 400 numbered copies, signed
by author and artist. 4to. Slipcase. Fine. Rota 231-328 1983 £75

HUGHES, TED   Crow. London, 1973. First illus.
edition. With 12 full-page black and white drawings by Leonard
Baskin. One of 400 numbered copies signed by the author and artist.
In slipcase with a small rubbed patch. Near mint. Jolliffe 26-
282 1983 £55

HUGHES, TED   A Few Crows. Exeter: Rougemont Press,
1970. First edition. Illus. by Reiner Burger. One of 75 copies
signed by Hughes. Fine. Gekoski 2-88 1983 £80

HUGHES, TED   Five Autumn Songs for Children's Voices.
London: Bow, Crediton, 1968. First edition. Wrappers. One of 25
copies, numbered from 12 to 37, each having one verse of the poem
"Who's Killed the Leaves?" in the author's manuscript and signed and
dated by the author. Fine. Jolliffe 26-280 1983 £65

HUGHES, TED   The Hawk in the Rain. L, (1957). Minor
interior foxing, else fine in slightly frayed and rubbed, very good
dustwrapper. Quill & Brush 54-676 1983 $175

HUGHES, TED   Meet My Folks. London, 1961. First
edition. Numerous black and white drawings and decorated covers by
George Adamson. Slightly torn, price-clipped dustwrapper by Adamson.
Fine. Jolliffe 26-277 1983 £45

HUGHES, TED   Moortown Elegies. London: The Rainbow
Press, 1978. First edition. One of 175 numbered copies signed by
the author. Designed and printed by Will Carter at The Rampant Lions
Press, Cambridge, on Barcham Green hand-made paper. Full limp white
goat vellum covers. T.e.g. Lower cover partially yellowed, o/w
near mint in slipcase. Jolliffe 26-283 1983 £75

HUGHES, TED   Oedipus. London, 1969. First edition.
Orig. wrappers. Inscribed by author to L. Clark, dated 12 Jan. 71.
Very nice. Rota 231-329 1983 £45

HUGHES, TED   Prometheus on His Crag. 21 Poems.
Rainbow Press, 1973. First edition, sq. 8vo, frontis. and small
coloured colophon, title in red and black, bound by Zaehnsdorf in
full crushed purple morocco lettered in gilt, t.e.g., others uncut,
mint in slip-case. 160 numbered copies signed by author. Deighton 3-
180 1983 £85

HUGHES, TED   Spring Summer Autumn Winter. The
Rainbow Press, (1973). 8vo. Leather. Total ed. is 140 copies
signed by Hughes. Fine in slipcase box. In Our Time 156-416 1983
$200

HUGHES, THOMAS   Early Memories For Children. London:
Thomas Burleigh, 1899. First edition. 12mo. Orig. wrappers. Mac-
Manus 279-2881 1983 $65

HUGHES, THOMAS   History of the Society of Jesus in
North America, Colonial and Federal. London, 1908-1917. 4 vols.,
maps, illus. Cloth, fine. Reese 19-278 1983 $200

HUGHES, THOMAS   James Fraser, Second Bishop of
Manchester. London, 1887. First edition. Portrait. Full brown
calf. Very good. Houle 21-427 1983 $37.50

HUGHES, THOMAS   Memoir of Daniel Macmillan. Macmillan,
1882. First edition, front. port. Half title. Orig. dark green
cloth, v.g. Jarndyce 30-1063 1983 £15

HUGHES, THOMAS   Memoir of Daniel Macmillan. London:
Macmillan, 1882. First edition. Orig. cloth. Front inner hinge
cracked. Fine. MacManus 279-2882 1983 $27.50

HUGHES, THOMAS   Mental furniture: or, the adaptation
of knowledge for man. London: Hamilton, Adams, 1857. 8vo. First
edition. Orig. ochre cloth. Rubbed, one endpaper renewed. Ximenes
63-298 1983 $90

HUGHES, THOMAS   Scouring of the White Horse. Cambridge,
1859. Illus. by Richard Doyle. First edition. 12mo, full crushed
blue morocco, raised bands, gilt extra, a.e.g. Orig. cloth covers
bound in. Perata 27-89 1983 $275

HUGHES, THOMAS   The Scouring of the White Horse. Cambridge: Macmillan & Co., 1859. First edition. Illus. by R. Doyle.
Orig. gilt pictorial cloth. Presentation copy inscribed on the half-
title to Mrs. Conway, dated Feby. 4th, 1864. Head and foot of spine
worn. Corners bumped. Hinges starting to crack. Good. MacManus
279-2884 1983 $225

HUGHES, THOMAS   The Scouring of the White Horse.
Cambridge: Macmillan & Co., 1859. First edition. Illus. by R. Doyle.
Orig. gilt-decorated cloth. Spine ends and cover edges slightly worn.
Rear cover rubbed in one small area. Bookplate. MacManus 279-2883
1983 $200

HUGHES, THOMAS   The Scouring of the White Horse; or,
the Long Vacation Ramble of a London Clerk. Cambridge: Macmillan,
1859. 1st ed., orig. pictorial cloth gilt, spine gilt, a fine copy.
Trebizond 18-56 1983 $85

HUGHES, THOMAS   Tom Brown at Oxford. Boston: Houghton,
Osgood, 1878. 2 vols. Early American ed. Orig. terra cotta cloth,
gilt. Presentation copy inscribed by Hughes in both vols.: "Earl T.
Mason with the authors best wishes, Thos Hughes, Nov. 1880." Some
spotting to binding. Jenkins 155-618 1983 $90

HUGHES, THOMAS   Tom Brown's School-days. Boston: LeRoy
Phillip, 1912. Colour frontis. Title vignette. 1 colour plate.
40 full-page & 45 text illus. Dark blue cloth. Onlaid extra colour
plate. Greer 40-222 1983 £65

HUGHES, THOMAS   Tom Brown's School Days. Macmillan,
1858. 6th edn. (with preface pub. here for first time), pub's adverts.
Blue morocco grain blind stamped cloth, gilt titling bkstrip, insc.
top of title p., corners bruised & extremities of cvrs. sl. rubbed,
cloth sl. marked, occasional foxing, vg. Hodgkins 27-104 1983 £25

HUGO, VICTOR   Hans of Iceland. London: J. Robins
& Co., 1825. First English edition. 8vo. Orig. cloth. 4 engraved
plates by George Cruikshank, one loose, small signature on title.
Early repairs to cloth. Heath 48-378 1983 £45

HUGO, VICTOR   Les Miserables. Hurst & Blackett, 1862.
2nd edition, 3 vols. Half titles, 8 pp ads. vol. III. Orig. purple
cloth blocked in blind, gilt spines, v.g. Jarndyce 30-433 1983
£18.50

HUGO, VICTOR   Notre-Dame de Paris. Boston, Estes &
Lauriat, (1888). Edition de Grand Luxe, limited to 100 copies in
English for America. Illustrated by Bieler, Rossi and De Myrbach. 2
vols., 8vo, original wrappers. Morrill 290-191 1983 $25

HUGO, VICTOR   Quatrevingt-Treize... Paris: Levy,
1874. 3 vols., complete. 1st ed. Contemporary half brown hard-
grain morocco and marbled boards. Very fine. Jenkins 155-619
1983 $400

HUGO, VICTOR   Toilers of the Sea. S. Low, 1867. 1st
Eng. illus. edn. with 2 illus. by Gustave Dore. Green sand grain
blind stamped cloth, gilt titling bkstrip, top corner torn from half
title, v. sl. foxing prelims, corners sl. bruised, scarce, vg.
Hodgkins 27-105 1983 £48

HUGO, VICTOR   Toilers of the Sea. Sampson Low, Son &
Marston, 1866. First edition, 3 vols. 2 + 16 pp ads. dated March and
Feb. 1866. Orig. green cloth, spines a little rubbed, otherwise
very good. Jarndyce 30-434 1983 £20

HUGO Helbing. Munchen, 1911 Sammlung des Herrn Universitats-
professors Dr. Robert Piloty, Wurzburg. Antiquitaten, besonders
Schmuck, Miniaturen, Kleinplastik. Holzskulpturen, Mobel,
Textilien, Geralde, Stiche und Bucher. Sale, Nov. 14-16, 1911
(6), 64pp., 30 plates. Lrg. 4to. Wraps. D.j. Ars Libri SB
26-149 1983 $35

THE HUGUENOT. A Tale of The French Protestants. N.Y.: Harper &
Brothers, 1839. 2 vols. Orig. cloth with paper labels on spines.
First American edition. Foxing, labels rubbed. Very good copy.
MacManus 277-82 1983 $25

HUGUIER, P.-C.   Memoire sur les Allongements Hyper-
trophiques du Col de l'Uterus... Paris: Bailliere, 1860. Large
4to. Orig. wrappers, uncut. 13 large folding lithographs. Wrappers
torn. Gurney JJ-184 1983 £45

HUISH, MARCUS   The American Pilgrim's Way in England
to Homes and Memorials of the Founders of Virginia. London: Fine
Arts Soc., 1907. Thick 4to, 1/4 buckram, ex lib. Many illus.,
mounted color plates by Eliz. Chettle. Argosy 716-96 1983 $40

HUISH, MARCUS   Birket Foster. Virtue, 1890. 1st edn.
List of books illus., orig. etching, 2 plates & numerous text illus.,
16pp adverts at front. Decor. wrappers (cvrs. spotted with sl. wear
edges & bkstrip, foxing prelims.), v.g. Hodgkins 27-567 1983
£17.50

HULBERT, ARCHER B.   The Call of the Columbia Iron Men.
Denver, 1934. First edition. Maps and illus. Fine. Jenkins 152-
315 1983 $100

HULBERT, ARCHER B   Forty-Niners: The Chronicle of the
California Trail. Boston, Little Brown, 1931. First edition. Illus.
Dust jacket. Fine. Houle 22-1111 1983 $25

HULBERT, ARCHER B.   Southwest on the Turquoise Trail. Denver,
c.1933. Frontis. Orig. cloth. Fine. Jenkins 152-159 1983 $100

HULBERT, ARCHER B.   Where Rolls the Oregon Prophet and
Pessimist Look Northwest. Denver: Denver Public Library, 1933.
Frontis., maps, illus. Fine copy. Jenkins 153-270 1983 $100

HULL, E. C. P.   The European in India. London, 1974.
Second edition, with additions. Sm.8vo. Half calf, some rubbing at
corners and hinges. Good. Edwards 1044-362 1983 £45

HULL, EDWARD   The Coal-Fields of Great Britain.
1905. Map in pocket, 12 other maps, plates, orig. cloth. Fifth
edition. K Books 307-102 1983 £25

HULL, LINDLEY M.   A History of Central Washington
Including the Famous Wenatchee, Entiat, Chelan and the Columbia
Valleys... (Spokane), privately printed, 1929. Illus. Orig.
cloth. First edition. Ginsberg 47-929 1983 $75

HULL, ROBERT   A Few Suggestions on Consumption.
London: Churchill, Norwich: Stevens and Matchett, (1849). 12mo,
orig. cloth. Bickersteth 75-243 1983 £12

HULL, THOMAS   The Royal Merchant: an opera. London:
printed for William Griffin, 1768. 8vo, cont. calf, gilt (very worn,
front cover detached). 1st edition. A fine presentation copy
inscribed from the author. Aside from the binding, in very good
condition. Ximenes 64-287 1983 $250

HULL, WILLIAM   Defence of Brigadier General William
Hull, Delivered Before the General Court Martial... Boston, 1814.
Worn calf spine and boards, old library stamps. Reese 18-442 1983
$90

HULL, WILLIAM   Memoirs of the Campaign of the North
Western Army of the United States. Boston, 1824. Recent half calf
and cont. boards, a very good copy. Reese 18-575 1983 $125

HULL, WILLIAM   Report of the Trial of Brig. General
William Hull. New York, 1814. First edition. 8vo, marbled boards,
calf back and corners, leather label. Bookplate; very slightly rubbed
but nice copy. Morrill 290-192 1983 $65

HULLAH, JOHN   The history of modern music. London:
Parker, etc., 1862. First edition. 8vo. Orig. bright green cloth.
Presentation copy, inscribed on the title-page from the author to
Lady Belper. A fine copy. Ximenes 63-331 1983 $100

HULLS, JONATHAN   A Description and Draught of a New-
Invented Machine... London, for the author, 1737. 1st ed., 12mo,
folding engraved frontispiece, title and final leaf dust-soiled, a few
leaves lightly spotted, 19th century calf, spine and corners rubbed,
library plate of the Royal Artillery, Woolwich. Pickering & Chatto
22-54 1983 $3,500

HULME, F. E.   Familiar Wild Flowers. N. D.-1920. 320
coloured plates, 8 vols., 8vo, original cloth. Wheldon 160-1606
1983 £40

HULME, F. E.   Familiar Wild Flowers. (1877-85).
Series 1-4, 160 coloured plates, 4 vols., 8vo, original decorated
cloth, gilt. First edition on thick paper. Coloured figures on front
covers. A little minor foxing and soiling and two frontispieces
stuck in with tape, else a nice set. Wheldon 160-1605 1983 £30

HULME, F. E.   Familiar Swiss Flowers. 1908. 100
coloured plates, 8vo, cloth (trifle used). Wheldon 160-1720 1983
£20

HUMBOLDT, ALEXANDER VON   Experiences sur le Galvanisme...
Paris: Didot jeune, 1799. 8vo. Old boards. Errata leaf. 8
folding plates. Gurney 90-62 1983 £145

HUMBOLDT, ALEXANDER VON   A Geognostical Essay on the Superposition
of Rocks in both Hemispheres. 1823. First English edition. Rare.
8vo, calf, rebacked. Wheldon 160-1421 1983 £65

HUMBOLDT, ALEXANDER VON   A Geognostic Essay on the Super-position
of Rocks in both Hemispheres. London: Longmans, &c., 1823. 8vo.
Old half-calf, rebacked. First English edition. Lacks half-title.
Gurney 90-63 1983 £60

HUMBOLDT, ALEXANDER VON   Researches, Concerning the Institutions
& Monuments of the Ancient Inhabitants of America. London: Longman,
et al., 1814. First English edition. 2 vols. Complete, engraved
title-pages with plates of Cotopaxi and Cholula. 19 fine engraved
plates, mostly of Mexican and Peruvian antiquities, including 5 hand-
colored plates from codices. 3/4 19th century levant morocco (neatly
rebacked, spines preserved). A few tears repaired. Plates bright and
clean. Fine. Jenkins 152-160 1983 $450

HUMBOLDT, FRIEDRICH, BARON VON   Aspects of nature, in different
lands and different climates. London: Longman, etc., 1850. First
edition. 2 vols. in one. 8vo. Orig. purple cloth. A very fine
copy. Ximenes 63-526 1983 $80

HUME, A. O.   Contributions to Indian Ornithology.
1873. Roy. 8vo, new cloth, hand-coloured plates. Narrow waterstain
on margins of some of the plates. Wheldon 160-49 1983 £120

HUME, A. O.   Nests and Eggs of Indian Birds. 1889-
90. Second edition, 12 portraits, 3 vols., royal 8vo, cloth.
Wheldon 160-768 1983 £40

HUME, DAVID   Essays and Treatises on Several Subjects. London: printed for A. Millar and A. Kincaid and A. Donaldson,
1758. 4to, cont. speckled calf, spine elaborately gilt, red morocco
label, bookplate, slightly rubbed but a fine copy. The first one
volume edition of Hume's works and the first in quarto. Pickering
& Chatto 21-46 1983 $650

HUME, DAVID   Four Dissertations. London: printed
for A. Millar, 1757. First edition, 12mo, stubs showing, without the
inserted leaf M9 with half-title and advertisement on verso, cont.
calf with label, a fine copy. With the four leaves of dedication.
Pickering & Chatto 21-47 1983 $1,200

HUME, DAVID   The Philosophical Works. Edinburgh: Adam Black & Wm. Tait; and Charles Tait, London, 1826. Front. port. vol. I. Half titles. Uncut. Orig. purple cloth, faded and a little rubbed, inner hinges a little weak, paper labels. Jarndyce 31-190 1983 £120

HUME, EDGAR E.   Victories of Army Medicine. Philadelphia, 1943. First edition. 8vo. Orig. binding. Fye H-3-280 1983 $30

HUME, FERGUS   Aladdin in London. London: A. & C. Black, 1892. First edition. Orig. cloth. MacManus 279-2886 1983 $40

HUME, FERGUS   Crazy Quilt. London: Ward, Lock, 1919. First edition. Illus. Orig. cloth. MacManus 279-2887 1983 $25

HUME, FERGUS   The Expedition of Captain Flick. London: Jarrold, 1896. First edition. Orig. decorated cloth. Ex-library. MacManus 279-2888 1983 $40

HUME, FERGUS   The Expedition of Captain Flick. L, 1896. Cover slightly soiled, else very good. Quill & Brush 54-677 1983 $40

HUME, FERGUS   The Man With a Secret. London: F. V. White, 1890. First edition. 3 vols. Orig. cloth. All edges slightly worn. A few endpapers somewhat browned. Covers a little soiled. Very good. MacManus 279-2890 1983 $250

HUME, FERGUS   The Turnpike House. London: John Long, (1902). First edition. Orig. pictorial cloth. Some foxing. Front inner hinge cracked. Very good. MacManus 279-2891 1983 $85

HUME, FRANCIS   The Story of the Circle of Chalk. London: The Rodale Press, n.d. One of 1000 numbered copies. 6 full-page, tissue-guarded coloure plates by John Buckland-Wright. Slightly worn slipcase. Fine. Jolliffe 26-64 1983 £32

HUME, H. H.   Gardening in the Lower South. New York, (1924) 1948. 49 plates, 8vo, cloth. Cuttings from dust-jacket pasted in at front. Wheldon 160-1956 1983 £12

HUME, MARTIN   The Love Affairs of Mary Queen of Scots. 1903. 8vo, 3 ports., orig. cloth gilt, inner joints weak. Bickersteth 77-126 1983 £20

HUME, S   An Exhortation to the Inhabitants of the Province of South Carolina, to Bring their Deeds to the Light of Christ... Philadelphia: Printed by William Bradford, (1747-8). Modern cloth. Margins of first and last leaves reinforced, marginal worming of Px-V2, affecting a few letters, somewhat browned, but a good copy. Reese 18-62 1983 $250

HUME, S   An Exhortation to the Inhabitants of the Province of South Carolina... Bristol: by Samuel Farley, 1751. First edition. Uncut in modern boards. Lightly discoloured. Heath 48-552 1983 £85

HUMPHREY, MABEL   Children of the Revolution. NY: Stokes, 1900. Octavo. 12 full-color plates. Small area of light browning to one text spread, otherwise internally near mint. Cloth-backed color pictorial boards slightly rubbed at corners, else fine. Contemporary owner's signature. Bromer 25-353 1983 $450

HUMPHREY, W. D.   Hazeldale. A Poem. Bristol: for the Author by George T. Wright, 1867. First edition. 8vo. Orig. green cloth, gilt. 4 photograph plates, one loose. Library ownership on e.p. Slight wear at spine. Heath 48-332 1983 £25

HUMPHREY, ZEPHINE   Cactus Forest. N.Y., Dutton, 1938. First edition. Dust jacket. Very good - fine. Houle 22-486 1983 $25

HUMPHREYS, ARTHUR L.   Old Decorative Maps and Charts. London, 1926. Sm folio. Illus. with 79 full page plates (19 tipped in color plates). Half vellum, t.e.g., uncut. Deluxe edition on large paper. One of 100 copies. Fine. Houle 21-1092 1983 $450

HUMPHREYS, ELIZA MARGARET J. Countess Daphne. London: Paul, (1912). Second edition. Orig. cloth. MacManus 280-4364 1983 $20

HUMPHREYS, ELIZA MARGARET J. Diana of the Ephesians. London: Eveligh Nash & Grayson, n.d. New and Revised edition. Presentation copy, inscribed on the front flyleaf "To Margaret Hatstan (My Mrs. Gordon) In very grateful appreciation of a most delightful performance, August 15th, 1927, From 'Rita'". Very good. MacManus 280-4365 1983 $45

HUMPHREYS, ELIZA MARGARET J. A Gender in Satin. London: T. Fisher Unwin, 1895. First edition. Orig. decorated cloth. Edges very slightly worn. Endpapers a little browned. Previous owner's signature on front free endpaper. Very good. MacManus 280-4369 1983 $75

HUMPHREYS, ELIZA MARGARET J. The Laird O'Cockpen. London: F.V. White & Co., 1891. First edition. 3 vols. Orig. cloth. Library labels removed from front covers. Covers faintly stained. Very good. MacManus 280-4366 1983 $185

HUMPHREYS, ELIZA MARGARET J. The Masqueraders. London: Hutchinson & Co., 1904. First edition. Orig. cloth. Subscription Library label on front endsheet. Very good. MacManus 280-4367 1983 $25

HUMPHREYS, ELIZA MARGARET J. The Prince Errant and Other Stories. London: Hutchinson & Co., (1928). First edition. Orig. cloth. Dust jacket (worn). Inscribed on the front flyleaf: "To John Coghlan In gratitude For much appreciative criticism of a grateful author, 'Rita' March 5th 1935." Very good. MacManus 280-4368 1983 $45

HUMPHREYS, ELIZA MARGARET J. Souls. London: Hutchinson & Co., 1903. First edition. Orig. decorated cloth. Former owner's signature on front flyleaf. Very good. MacManus 280-4370 1983 $25

HUMPHREYS, ELIZA MARGARET J. The Ungrown-Ups. London: G.P. Putnam's Sons, Ltd., (1923). First edition. Orig. cloth. Former owner's name erased from front flyleaf. Bookseller's stamp on endsheet. Fine. MacManus 280-4371 1983 $45

HUMPHREYS, HENRY NOEL   The Art of Illumination and Missal Painting. Bohn, 1849. 1st edn. 12 plates printed in colours & heightened in gold & 12 duplicate plates printed in outline & many decor. head & tail pieces, initial letters, etc. by Charles Whittingham. White calf with black decor. border on cvrs., & central colour printed illumination on fr. cvr., gilt titling on bkstrip, a.e.g. (re-cased, new eps., gilt titling on bkstrip almost rubbed away, bookpl. fr. ep.), rare, v.g. Hodgkins 27-376 1983 £75

HUMPHREYS, HENRY NOEL   The Butterfly Vivarium, or Insect Home. William Lay, 1858. Handcoloured frontis. 7 handcoloured plates. Red decorated cloth, gilt. Spine light worn. Greer 40-116 1983 £45

HUMPHREYS, HENRY NOEL   The Coinage of the British Empire. Griffin, 1868. 4th edn. with frontis. & 12 plates chromolithographed in gold, silver, copper & 12 b&w plates. Brown sand grain blind stamp. cloth with gold & silver vignette fr. cvr., bevelled boards, a.e.g. (top/bottom of bkstrip some wear, bookpl. fr. ep., fr.ep. cracked at hinge, corners sl. worn & title p. sl. foxed), v.g. copy. Hodgkins 27-378 1983 £65

HUMPHREYS, HENRY NOEL   The Miracles of our Lord. London: Longman & Co., 1848. First edition. Small 8vo. Papier mache binding, all edges gilt. Binding chipped around the corners. Oak Knoll 49-130 1983 $375

HUMPHREYS, HENRY NOEL   Parables of Our Lord. Longman, etc., 1847. with 32 pages illuminated in colours & heightened in gold, printed on card. 1st edn. Black elab. embossed 'papier mache' covers, with black leather embossed bkstrip, marbled eps., a.e.g. (designed by H.N. Humphreys). Hodgkins 27-375 1983 £100

HUMPHREYS, HENRY NOEL   Parables of Our Lord. Longman, 1847. 30pp of chromolighographed illuminations, loose. Moulded black papiermache binding. Very good. Greer 40-117 1983 £75

HUMPHREYS, HENRY NOEL   Rome, and its Surrounding Scenery. London: Charles Tilt, 1840. 4to, 26-1/2 cm. 19th century blind- and gilt-stamped red morocco, a.e.g. Light foxing, extremities worn. With 30 engraved plates and vignette title. Grunder 7-44 1983 $130

HUMPHREYS, HENRY NOEL   Ten Centuries of Art. Grant & Griffith, 1852. 1st edn. 10 plates printed in colour & heightened in gold & silver & 2 plates printed on tinted ground, elab. half title printed in gold & silver by Day & Son. Red morocco grained cloth, a.e.g., bev. bds. (re-backed with new bkstrip & title label, eps. strengthened at hinges with cloth, 2 plates badly water stained & 3 plates sl. water stained at lower edges, last 5 leaves also affected, foxing & rear cvr. marked), good sound copy. Hodgkins 27-377 1983 £20

HUMPHREYS, JENNETT   Laugh & Learn. Blackie, 1897. New edn. with frontis., title vignette & many illus. Slate blue pictorial cloth, occasional thumb mark, vg. Hodgkins 27-107 1983 £10.50

HUMPHRIES, ROLFE   The Wind of Time. New York, 1949. 8vo. Cloth. A fine copy in dj which has some light wear at the edge of the flaps. In Our Time 156-417 1983 $35

HUMPHRIES, WINIFRED   Wog & Wig. Franklyn Ward & Wheeler, Leicester, n.d. Colour frontis. 4 colour plates & 5 text illus. Colour pictorial boards bearing extra design. Colour pictorial dust wrapper. Greer 40-200 1983 £15

HUMPHRY, G. M.   Observations on the Limbs of Vertebrate Animals. Cambridge, 1860. 3 plates, 4to, wrappers, plates foxed. Wheldon 160-495 1983 £15

HUMPHRY, WILLIAM WOOD   Contributory Remarks on a General Registry. Stevens and Sons, 1830. First edition, with a folding table, 8vo, wrapper. Fenning 61-213 1983 £35

HUNEKER, JAMES   Melomaniacs. New York: Scribner, 1902. 1st ed. Orig. red pictorial cloth, gilt, t.e.g., uncut. Bright copy. Jenkins 155-629 1983 $25

HUNGARY. Budapest, 1910. Illus. from photographs by Erdelyi. Large 4to, ex-library, some rubbing at corners, nice. Morrill 288-189 1983 $25

HUNGERFORD, EDWARD   Wells Fargo: Advancing the American Frontier. N.Y., Random, (1949). First edition. Illus., dust jacket. Very good - fine. Houle 22-1112 1983 $35

HUNGERFORD, EDWARD   Wells Fargo: Advancing the American Frontier. N.Y., (1949). 1st ed. Illus. Maps. Jenkins 153-263 1983 $20

HUNGERFORD, MARGARET WOLFE HAMILTON   Portia; or, "By Passions Rocked". Smith, Elder, 1883. First edition. 3 vols. Half titles, some light foxing. Orig. purple cloth. Very good. Jarndyce 30-285 1983 £62

HUNNEWELL, JAMES F.   A Century of Town Life. Boston, 1888. 1st ed. Presentation copy. 8vo. Morrill 288-283 1983 $35

HUNT, CECIL   Paddy For News. London: Hodder & Stoughton, 1933. First edition. Orig. cloth. Dust jacket (faded and worn). Presentation copy to Dennis Wheatley inscribed; "For Dennis Wheatley with pleasure, Cecil Hunt, July 1933." Spine slightly faded and a trifle foxed. Wheatley's bookplate on the front paste-down endpaper. Very good. MacManus 279-2893 1983 $40

HUNT, CORNELIUS E.   The Shenandoah. New York, 1867. First edition. Frontispiece. Small 8vo. Lacks blank endleaves. Morrill 290-193 1983 $95

HUNT, ELVID   History of Fort Leavenworth, 1827-1927. Fort Leavenworth, Kans., 1937. 2nd ed. Illus., fldg. maps and plates. Clark 741-262 1983 $40

HUNT, FRAZIER   The Long Trail from Texas: The Story of Ad Spaugh, Cattleman. New York, 1940. Frontis. map. First edition. Fine copy. Jenkins 153-265 1983 $45

HUNT, FREEMAN   The Merchants "Magazine" the Gold Region of California. New York, Volume XX January, 1849. No. 1. The complete issue. Frontis. Original pictorial brown wrappers. Jenkins 153-94 1983 $75

HUNT, HENRY M.   The Crime of the Century. N.p.: (1889). First edition. Illus. Blue cloth. Front inner hinge repaired, cover lettering faded, but sound copy. Bradley 66-524 1983 $22.50

HUNT, JOHN   The Conquest of Everest. N.Y., Dutton, 1954. First edition. Illus. Signed by Hillary, George Lowe, and Charles Evans. Dust jacket (trifle rubbed). Very good - fine. Houle 22-1140 1983 $75

HUNT, LEIGH   The Autobiography of Leigh Hunt. N.Y.: Harper & Brothers, 1850. First American edition. Frontis. port. Rebound in 3/4 maroon morocco & cloth. Some foxing. Fine. MacManus 279-2895 1983 $100

HUNT, LEIGH   The Autobiography... N.Y.: Harper & Brothers, 1850. First American edition. 2 vols. Frontis. Orig. cloth. Extremities of spine a trifle worn. Fine. MacManus 279-2894 1983 $25

HUNT, LEIGH   The Companion. London: Hunt & Clarke, 1828. First edition. 3/4 morocco, t.e.g. Fine. MacManus 279-2896 1983 $150

HUNT, LEIGH   Essays. London: J.M. Dent & Co., 1891. First edition. Small 8vo. Rebound in 3/4 navy morocco & cloth. Fine. MacManus 279-2897 1983 $75

HUNT, LEIGH   The feast of the poets, with notes, and other pieces in verse. London: Cawthorn, 1814. 8vo. Old half morocco. First edition. Rubbed. Lacks a half-title and a final leaf of ads. Ximenes 63-412 1983 $45

HUNT, LEIGH   A Jar of Honey From Mount Hybla. London: Smith, Elder, & Co., 1848. First edition. Illus. by R. Doyle. Orig. decorated yellow boards. Extremities of spine and corners rubbed. In a folding cloth box. Fine. MacManus 279-2898 1983 $250

HUNT, LEIGH   The Liberal. London, John Hunt, 1822-23. 2 vols., 8vo, cont. quarter calf, boards, badly worn, hinges broken, some minor staining, light foxing, minor watermark to vol. 2, signature of John Shelley, dated 1830, on both title-pages. First edition. Ravenstree 94-217 1983 $145

HUNT, LEIGH   The Old Court Suburb. London: Free-mantle & Co., 1902. 2 vols. 4to. Orig. gilt-decorated vellum. Limited to 150 large-paper copies signed by all three illustrators. Vellum buckling and a little darkened. Very good. MacManus 279-2899 1983 $125

HUNT, LEIGH   Poems of... London: J. M. Dent & Co., 1891. 2 vols. Etchings. Three quarters crimson calf and marbled boards. 1/75 copies of Large Paper Edition for sale in America. Nice set with engraved bookplates of Abraham Goldsmith laid in. Bindings slightly rubbed. Bradley 66-396 1983 $275

HUNT, LEIGH   The Poetical Works. London, Edward Moxon, 1832. 8vo, boards, joints worn. First collected edition. Ravenstree 94-218 1983 $115

HUNT, LEIGH   Stories from the Italian Poets. London: Chapman & Hall, 1896. First edition. 2 vols. Orig. cloth. Very fine. MacManus 279-2900 1983 $125

HUNT, LEIGH   Stories from the Italian Poets. London, Chapman & Hall, 1846. 2 vols., cont. mauve calf, few scratches, marbled edges, gilt spine. Signature on fly, paper trifle browned. First edition. Ravenstree 94-219 1983 $67.50

HUNT, LEIGH   Stories from the Italian Poets... London: Chapman & Hall, 1846. First edition. 2 vols. 8vo. Orig. grey blue cloth, gilt. Slight foxing. Heath 48-333 1983 £40

HUNT, LEIGH   Table-Talk... London: Smith, Elder and Co., 1851. First edition. Small 8vo. Cloth publisher's binding, a.e.g. With the July 1850 advertisements in the rear. Presentation copy from Hunt to his daughter. Recased. Oak Knoll 49-238 1983 $450

HUNT, LEIGH   The Town. London: Smith, Elder &
Co., 1848. First edition. 2 vols. Illus. Orig. light brown cloth.
Inner hinges weak and cracked although webbing still intact. Spine
and covers slightly worn and soiled. Bookplate. Good. MacManus
279-2901 1983 $100

HUNT, LEIGH   The Town. London, Smith, Elder, 1848.
2 vols., 8vo, orig. cloth gilt, somewhat worn and trifle soiled, bit
bumped, an above-average copy. First edition. Ravenstree 94-220
1983 $65

HUNT, LEIGH   Wit and Humour. London, Smith, Elder,
1846. 8vo, orig. cloth gilt, soiled, joints torn and cracked,
corners a little knocked. First edition. Ravenstree 94-222 1983
$45

HUNT, MEMUCAN   The Public Debt and Lands of Texas.
(New Orleans, 1849). Half morocco. Jenkins 153-785 1983 $150

HUNT, P. F.   The Country Life Book of Orchids. 1978.
Coloured frontispiece and 34 coloured illus., imp. 4to, cloth,
slipcase. Wheldon 160-2045 1983 £41

HUNT, R. N. CAREW   Unpublished Letters from the Collection
of John Wild. London: Philip Allan & Co., (1930). First edition.
8vo. Half cloth over boards, paper spine label. Oak Knoll 48-205
1983 $25

HUNT, ROBERT   A descriptive guide to the Museum of
Practical Geology... London: Eyre and Spottiswoode, 1867. Third
edition. 8vo. Disbound. Orig. grey printed wrappers. Ximenes
63-528 1983 $30

HUNT, THOMAS STERRY   A New Basis for Chemistry. Boston:
Cassino, 1888. Second edition. 8vo. Orig. cloth. Presentation
copy from the author. A little rubbed. Zeitlin 264-220 1983
$40

HUNT, VIOLET   The Tiger Skin. London: William Heinemann, 1924. First separate edition. Orig. blind-stamped cloth.
Presentation copy to Lennox Robinson, dated July 1925. Edges worn
and dampstained. Endpapers browned. MacManus 279-2902 1983 $135

HUNTER, DARD   My Life with Paper. New York:
Alfred A. Knopf, 1958. First edition. 8vo. Cloth, dust jacket.
58 illus. With two specimens of paper. Fine. Oak Knoll 48-211
1983 $100

HUNTER, DARD   Papermaking. New York, 1943. 8vo,
buckram, dust-jacket. 162 illus. and folding plate. First edition.
Duschnes 240-115 1983 $150

HUNTER, DARD   Papermaking by Hand in America.
Chillicothe: Mountain House Press, 1950. Thick folio. Limited to
210 copies signed by Hunter. Near mint in half-cloth and patterned
paper over boards and leather-backed hinged box. With orig. mailing
box. Bromer 25-230 1983 $4850

HUNTER, DARD   A Papermaking Pilgrimage to Japan, Korea
and China. New York: Pynson Printers, 1936. First edition. 4to.
Half-leather over paper covered boards, slipcase. 50 tipped-in specimens of paper. Limited to 370 numbered copies signed by Dard Hunter
and the designer Elmer Adler. With 68 photogravure illus. by Hunter.
Book is in fine condition. Slipcase is worn. Oak Knoll 48-214 1983
$1,850

HUNTER, DARD   Papermaking: The History and Technique of an Ancient Craft. New York: Alfred A. Knopf, 1943.
First edition. Thick 8vo. Cloth. Dust jacket. 162 illus. Bookplate (foxed). Tipped in is a letter from Hunter. Fine in lightly
worn dust jacket. Oak Knoll 48-213 1983 $185

HUNTER, DARD   Romance of Watermarks. Cincinnati,
Ohio: The Stratford Press of E.F. Gleason. n.d., (circa 1940).
Small 8vo, frontis. & title page illus. Edition ltd. to 210
copies. Glassine, slipcase. Fine copy. Karmiole 71-57 1983 $250

HUNTER, GEORGE   Reminiscences of An Old Timer. San
Francisco: H.S. Crocker & Co., 1887. First edition. Frontis. & illus.
Orig. pictorial cloth. Fairly nice. Jenkins 152-163 1983 $125

HUNTER, GEORGE   Reminiscences of an Old Timer.
Battle Creek, Mich: Review and Herald, 1888. Frontis., illustrations.
Original red pictorial cloth, gilt. Fine copy of the 3rd edition
Jenkins 151-138 1983 $75

HUNTER, JOHN   A Treatise on the Blood, Inflammation,
and Gun-Shot Wounds. Printed by John Richardson, for George Nicol.
1794. 4to, portrait and 9 plates, lettered on the upper cover in
gilt "St. Thomas's Hospital. Demonstrators Prize to Walter Raleigh
1825". Recently rebacked with new label. Mounted on the inside front
cover is a portrait of Raleigh. Inscribed "With Mr John T South's
best wishes" at top of the title page. Light grey spotting on 3
pages in text. First edition. Bickersteth 75-244 1983 £640

HUNTER, JOHN   Treatise on the Blood, Inflammation,
and Gunshot Wounds. Phila., 1817. Plates. Mod. 1/2 calf. Argosy
713-279 1983 $175

HUNTER, JOHN   A Treatise on the Venereal Disease.
London, 1810. 4to, cont. 1/2 mor. Argosy 713-280 1983 $175

HUNTER, JOHN   A Treatise on the Venereal Disease.
Phila.: J. Webster, 1818. First American edition. Tall 8vo, cont.
tree calf, leather label. Argosy 713-281 1983 $150

HUNTER, JOHN   The White Phantom. NY, 1935. Wraps,
advance reading copy, edges slightly rubbed, else near fine. Quill &
Brush 54-679 1983 $30

HUNTER, JOHN MARVIN   The Album of Gun-Fighters. (Baandera,
Texas, 1951). 1st ed., limited ed. Argosy 710-587 1983 $125

HUNTER, JOHN MARVIN   The Trail Drivers of Texas. Nashville,
1925. 2nd ed. revised. Illus. Ink obliteration marks on title and
last pages, small rubber stamp number on several pages, and mid-spine
discoloration. Good sound copy, with few defects. Clark 741-424
1983 $92.50

HUNTER, LOUIS C.   Steamboats on the Western Rivers.
Cambridge, 1949. Illus. D.w. Argosy 710-271 1983 $30

HUNTER, MARVIN   Canadian Wilds. Columbus, Ohio, (1907).
1st ed. 12mo. Morrill 286-205 1983 $25

HUNTER, ROBERT HANCOCK   The Narrative of...Describing in His
Own Manner His Arrival in Texas in 1822 & His Participation in Events
of the Texas Revolution... Austin: Encino Press, 1966. Cloth and
pictorial boards. A fine copy in glassine dust jacket. One of 640
numbered copies. Reese 19-279 1983 $35

HUNTER, ROBERT HANCOCK   Narrative of...1813-1902. Austin, 1936.
Orig. printed wraps. First edition. Ginsberg 46-734 1983 $30

HUNTER, ROGER   A peep into the cottage at Windsor.
London: Benbor, 1820. First edition. 8vo. Disbound. Ximenes
63-497 1983 $45

HUNTER, WILLIAM C.   Frozen Dog Tales and Other Things.
Boston: Everett Press Co., 1905. 18 cm. All pages with margin
illus.; illus. title. Orig. decorated cloth. First edition. Very
good. Grunder 7-84 1983 $35

HUNTER, WILLIAM S.   Hunter & Pickup's Panoramic Guide from
Niagara Falls to Quebec. Montreal, 1866. Illus. Wraps. Covers
a bit soiled. Felcone 22-89 1983 $35

HUNTER, WILLIAM S.   Hunter's Ottawa Scenery... Ottawa City:
Published by William S. Hunter, 1855. One plate, frontis. Engraved
title page with vignette, folding map and 13 plates. Expertly cleaned
and restored. Some light spotting on the first plate else a fine
copy. McGahern 54-94 1983 $1,000

HUNTER, WILLIAM WILSON   The Annals of Rural Bengal. London,
1868. Half calf, spine gilt. Limited to 675 copies. 8vo. Good.
Edwards 1044-365 1983 £95

HUNTER, WILLIAM WILSON   Bombay 1885-1890. London, (1892). First edition. Spine frayed at head and tail. Ex-library. 8vo. Orig. cloth. Good. Edwards 1044-367 1983 £45

HUNTER, WILLIAM WILSON   The Thackerays in India. London, 1897. Sq.8vo. Uncut. Orig. cloth. Good. Edwards 1044-366 1983 £20

HUNTER, WILLIAM WILSON   The Thackerays in India, and Some Calcutta Graves. Henry Frowde, 1897. First edition, half title, 4pp ads. Inscription on end papers. Orig. blue cloth, bevelled boards, t.e.g. Jarndyce 31-943 1983 £18.50

HUNTINGTON, DAVID C.   The Landscapes of Frederic Edwin Church. New York: George Braziller, 1966. 8 color plates. 116 illus. Small oblong 4to. Cloth. Dust jacket. Ars Libri 32-109 1983 $75

HUNTINGTON, ELLSWORTH   The Red Man's Continent. New Haven, 1921. Plates. Gilt cloth. Fine. Reese 19-280 1983 $20

HUNTINGTON, NATHANIEL G.   A System of Modern Geography. Hartford, 1835. Rev. & improved. Illus., 12mo, calf-backed orig. pr. bds. Argosy 710-197 1983 $35

HUNTINGTON, WILLARD V.   Oneonta Memories and Sundry Personal Recollections of the Author. San Francisco, 1891. 1st ed. Portrait. 8vo, orig. leather, some rubbing at corners. Morrill 288-343 1983 $20

HUNTLEY, HENRY   Observations in Morbos Nautarum... Londini: impensis authoris, 1733. 2nd ed., 8vo, title-page a little soiled and a small portion of a blank corner torn away, modern quarter calf, extremely rare, good copy. Pickering & Chatto 22-55 1983 $650

HUNTLEY, HENRY V.   California: Its Gold and Its Inhabitants. London, 1856. First edition, 2 vols., bound in 1. Thick 8vo, rebound in buckram using orig. cloth, orig. backstrip laid in. Argosy 716-39 1983 $300

HUNTOON, JOHN   Report of the Territorial Treasurer of Idaho. Boise City, Kelly, 1882. Orange printed wraps. Ginsberg 46-323 1983 $35

HURD, ARCHIBALD   The Reign of the Pirates. N.Y., 1925. Illus. Cloth backed boards. Index. Bookplate. Extremities worn. King 45-530 1983 $22.50

HURD, HENRY   The Institutional Care of the Insane in the United States and Canada. Volume 4. Baltimore, 1917. First edition. 8vo. Orig. binding. Fye H-3-284 1983 $50

HURD, PETER   Peter Hurd Portfolio of Landscapes and Portraits. Albuquerque, 1950. Portfolio, eight prints. Minor repairs to the spine else a nice set. Jenkins 151-139 1983 $200

HURD, PETER   Peter Hurd Sketch Book. Chicago, 1971. Illus. with most in color. Special edition of 26 copies numbered and signed by the artist. Copy number 1. Bound in three-quarter morocco. Jenkins 151-140 1983 $250

HURDIS, JAMES   The Favorite Village. Bishopstone, Sussex, 1800. Printed at the Author's Own Press. First edition. 4to. Cont. tree calf, rebacked. Slight worming to few leaves of lower margin, some light usage. Very rare. Heath 48-335 1983 £250

HURET, JULES   En Amerique: De New-York a la Nouvelle Orleans. Paris: 1904. Orig. printed wraps., spine neatly recovered. Felcone 22-90 1983 $30

HURLBURD, PERCY   In Black and White. London: Ward & Downey, 1889. First edition. 3 vols. Orig. parchment-backed cloth. Spines darkened. Very good. MacManus 279-2903 1983 $125

HURST and Hanger. London: Kegan Paul, Trench & Company, 1886. 3 vols. Orig. cloth. First edition. Spines and covers slightly worn, soiled and rubbed at the margins. A good sound set. MacManus 277-83 1983 $150

HURTLEY, THOMAS   A Concise Account of Some Natural Curiosities, in the Environs of Malham, in Craven, Yorkshire. Printed at the Logographic Press, by J. Walter, 1786. First edition, with 3 engraved plates (2 folding) by W. Skelton after Devis, including the half-title and the 12 page subscriber list, 8vo, cont. half calf, the joints rubbed but sound. Fenning 61-214 1983 £48

HURTON, WILLIAM   Vonved the Dane. Richard Bentley, 1861. First edition, 2 vols. Half dark green morocco by Cedric Chivers; raised bands, spines gilt with red embellishments, green morocco grained boards, a.e.g., v.g. Jarndyce 30-435 1983 £68

HUSMANN, GEORGE   American Grape Growing and Wine Making. N.Y., Judd, 1880. First edition. Illus. with full page plates and diagrams in the text. Gilt stamped pictorial brown cloth. Fine. Houle 22-1113 1983 $85

HUSSEY, CHRISTOPHER   The Life of Sir Edward Lutyens. Country Life, 1953. Second edition, with a portrait and 178 plates, 4to, orig. cloth, a fine copy in the dust wrapper. Fenning 61-518 1983 £65

HUSSEY, CHRISTOPHER   Tait McKenzie. London: Country Life, 1929. 29cm. First edition. 93 plates. 14 text illus. Dust jacket. Very good to fine. McGahern 53-77 1983 $125

HUSSEY, SAMUEL M.   The Reminiscences of an Irish Land Agent, Being those of S.M. Hussey. Duckworth, 1904. First edition, with 2 portraits, roy. 8vo, orig. cloth, gilt, t.e.g., a very good copy. Fenning 60-193 1983 £14.50

HUSSLA, A.   Melodien zu Dr. Heinrich Hoffmanns Struwwelpeter. Frankfurt, Ruetten & Loening, n.d. (after 1876). 4to, orig. pictorial boards with color picture. Salloch 387-98 1983 $125

HUTCHESON, ARCHIBALD   Some Considerations relating to the Payment of the Publick Debts... London, 1717. First edition. 4to. Orig. wrappers, stitched. Heath 48-126 1983 £45

HUTCHINGS, J. M.   In the Heart of the Sierras: the Yosemite Valley. Oakland, 1886. Illus. and maps (one mounted on linen), later cloth-backed boards, ex-library. Backstrip top worn. Argosy 710-35 1983 $35

HUTCHINS, GABRIEL   The United States Almanac, for ... 1798. Elizabeth Town: Shepard Kollock, (1797). Stitched. Cloth folding case. The variant with Kollock's name alone in the imprint. Excellent. Felcone 19-54 1983 $75

HUTCHINSON, ARTHUR STUART M. This Freedom. London: Hodder & Stoughton, 1922. First edition. Orig. cloth. Dust jacket (torn). Presentation copy, inscribed to "Michael Sadlier who did what I shall always think the noblest action...August 1922." With an ALS by Hutchinson laid in. Several tiny worm holes along front outer hinge. MacManus 279-2907 1983 $40

HUTCHINSON, HENRY N.   Creatures of Other Days. 1894. Text-figures, 24 plates, 8vo, cloth, trifle used. Relevant newscutting pasted to endpaper. Wheldon 160-1422 1983 £12

HUTCHINSON, HENRY N.   Extinct Monsters. Chapman & Hall, 1892. First edition, with 24 plates by J. Smith and 38 full-page and other illus., 8vo, orig. cloth, gilt. Fenning 60-194 1983 £15

HUTCHINSON, HENRY N.   Extinct Monsters. 1897. Fifth edition, 26 plates, slightly used. Wheldon 160-1423 1983 £12

HUTCHINSON, J.   The Families of Flowering Plants. (Oxford 1973), authorized reprint Koenigstein, 1979. Third edition, 450 text-figures, royal 8vo, rexine. Wheldon 160-1534 1983 £50

HUTCHINSON, JANE C.   The Master of the Housebook. New York: Collectors Editions, 1972. 123 illus. Large 4to. Cloth. Ars Libri 32-437 1983 $100

HUTCHINSON, THOMAS   The History of the Province of Massachusetts Bay, From 1749-1774. London, 1828. 8vo, cont. bds., rebacked, flyleaves dampstained. Argosy 710-288 1983 $40

HUTCHINSON, THOMAS JOSEPH   Narrative of the Niger, Tshadda, &
Binue Exploration. Longman, Brown, 1855. First edition, with a
folding map, small 8vo, some light soiling and signs of use, but
a good copy in recent half calf, gilt. Fenning 61-215 1983 £45

HUTCHINSON, W. M. L.   Orpheus with his lute. Longmans, Green,
1926. Colour frontis. 10 plates. Pictorial endpapers. Black decorated cloth. Greer 39-134 1983 £16

HUTCHINSON, WILLIAM N.   Dog Breaking. John Murray, 1869.
Fifth edition. With full-page and other illus., 8vo, orig. roan-backed
cloth, gilt. Headbands chipped and inside joints weak, a sound clean
copy. Fenning 62-188 1983 £12.50

HUTCHINSON, WILLIAM T.   Cyrus Hall McCormick Seed-Time, 1809-
1856. New York: The Century Co., 1930. Frontis and plates, 1st.
ed. A fine copy. Jenkins 151-198 1983 $45

HUTH, HANS   Abraham und David Roentgen und ihre
Neuwieder Mobelwerkstatt. Berlin: Deutscher Verein fur Kunst-
wissenschaft, 1928. 120 photogravure plates. Frontis. Large 4to.
Cloth. Ars Libri 32-587 1983 $100

HUTTON, CLARKE   A Country ABC. N.Y.: OUP, n.d. (ca.
1930). Printed in Britain. 4to. Cloth. Fine in dust wrapper. Full
color illus. on each page. Printed on one side of paper. Aleph-bet
8-4 1983 $30

HUTTON, F. W.   Index Faunae Novae Zealandiae. 1904.
8vo, cloth, good ex-library. Wheldon 160-394 1983 £16

HUTTON, J. H.   The Angami Nagas. London, 1921. 4 folding maps, coloured frontis. and numerous plates. Cloth, slightly worn.
8vo. Good. Edwards 1044-373 1983 £40

HUTTON, J. H.   The Sema Nagas. London, 1921. Folding
map, chart, folding pedigrees. Coloured frontis, plates. 8vo. Good.
Edwards 1044-374 1983 £45

HUTTON, JOSEPH   Perry's Victory. Philadelphia, 1814.
Very good. Reese 18-456 1983 $250

HUTTON, LAURENCE   Curiosities of the American Stage.
Harper & Brothers, 1891. Illus. Cloth. Dawson 471-325 1983 $25

HUTTON, PETER A.   Greek Cities. London, 1932. 64 plates
from photos. 8vo, cloth. Salloch 385-366 1983 $20

HUTTON, R. N.   Five Years in the East. London, 1847.
2 vols. 2 frontis. Library stamp in corner of both frontis. Quarter
calf. 8vo. Good. Edwards 1044-375 1983 £35

HUTTON, WILLIAM   The History of the Roman Wall. Printed
by and for John Nichols and Son, 1802. 8vo, folding engraved map
(short tears at folds), 7 engraved plates, other small engraved plans
and figures in the text, cont. half calf with marbled boards, lower
joint cracked. First edition. Bickersteth 75-146 1983 £48

HUTTON, WILLIAM   A Journey to London. J. Nichols, Son &
Bentley, 1818. 2nd edition, 2 pp inserted ads. Uncut, largely
unopened. Orig. blue boards, drab paper spine, paper label. Fine.
Jarndyce 31-266 1983 £42

HUTTON, WILLIAM   The Life of William Hutton... London:
for Baldwin, Cradock..., 1817. Second edition, with additions. 8vo.
Half calf, worn. Foxed throughout. Heath 48-128 1983 £45

HUTTON, WILLIAM R.   California 1847-1852. San Marino: The
Huntington Library, 1942. Oblong 8vo, boards. Color plates. Slight
bumping to boards. Limited to 700 copies and printed at the Grabhorn
Press. Fine copy. Jenkins 153-95 1983 $50

HUXHAM, JOHN   Medical & Chemical Observations upon
Antimony. London, 1756. 8vo, later brown 1/2 mor. First edition.
With half-title and page of ads. Argosy 713-284 1983 $200

HUXHAM, JOHN   Observationes de Aere et Morbis Epidem-
ics. 1728-37. Londini, 1752. 2 vols. in 1. Cont. mottled calf, back
gilt, leather label. Argosy 713-285 1983 $200

HUXLEY, ALDOUS   After Many a Summer Dies the Swan.
New York: Harper, 1939. 1st American ed. Orig. cloth, gilt, dj.
Fine in frayed dj. Jenkins 155-630 1983 $20

HUXLEY, ALDOUS   Along the Road. London: Chatto &
Windus, 1925. First edition. 8vo. Orig. cloth with paper label.
Dust jacket. Fine copy. Jaffe 1-173 1983 $100

HUXLEY, ALDOUS   Antic Hay. London: Chatto & Windus,
1923. First edition. 8vo, orig. cloth with paper label. Dust jacket.
Jacket chipped at head of spine, otherwise a very good copy. Jaffe
1-168 1983 $125

HUXLEY, ALDOUS   Antic Hay. London: Chatto & Windus,
1923. 1st ed. Orig. yellow cloth, label, uncut. Fine. Jenkins
155-632 1983 $35

HUXLEY, ALDOUS   Ape and Essence. New York: Harper,
1948. 1st American ed. Orig. cloth, gilt. With fresh gold dj.
Jenkins 155-633 1983 $22.50

HUXLEY, ALDOUS   Arabia Infelix, and Other Poems.
N.Y. & London, 1929. First edition. Thin 8vo, boards. Ltd. to
692 copies signed by Huxley. Owner's inscription on flyleaf. Argosy
714-379 1983 $100

HUXLEY, ALDOUS   Arabia Infelix And Other Poems. New
York: The Fountain Press; London: Chatto & Windus, 1929. First
edition. 4to. Orig. cloth-backed boards. Glassine dust jacket.
Limited to 692 copies signed by the author. Torn jacket. Very fine
copy. Jaffe 1-178 1983 $100

HUXLEY, ALDOUS   Arabia Infelix and other Poems. N.Y.:
The Fountain Press, 1929. First edition. Orig. cloth-backed boards.
Limited to 692 copies signed on the half-title by author. Covers
rather soiled. Front inner hinge cracked. MacManus 279-2909 1983
$75

HUXLEY, ALDOUS   Beyond The Mexique Bay. London:
Chatto & Windus, 1934. First edition. 8vo. Illus. Orig. cloth.
Dust jacket. Chipped jacket. Fine copy. Jaffe 1-183 1983 $50

HUXLEY, ALDOUS   Beyond the Mexique Bay. London, 1934.
First edition. Frontis. and 29 plates. 8vo. Orig. cloth. Traylen
94-452 1983 £25

HUXLEY, ALDOUS   Brave New World. London: 1932. First
edition. Limited to 324 copies signed by Huxley. Spine slightly
darkened, else a fine copy. Bromer 25-54 1983 $750

HUXLEY, ALDOUS   Brave New World. London: Chatto &
Windus, 1932. Cloth, morocco label, t.e.g., others untrimmed. First
edition. One of 324 numbered copies, specially printed and bound,
and signed by the author. A fine copy. Reese 20-543 1983 $750

HUXLEY, ALDOUS   Brave New World. London: Chatto &
Windus, 1932. 1st ed., limited to 324 numbered and signed copies.
Orig. binder's cloth (red) lettered in black on spine, uncut,
unnumbered, and unsigned. This set of sheets of the limited ed.
was retained and protected in binding for such file copies.
Important and unique copy. Fine. Jenkins 155-636 1983 $1,350

HUXLEY, ALDOUS   Brave New World. L, 1932. Edges slightly
rubbed, very good bright copy in chipped and slightly frayed dustwrapper, name embossed on title and half-title. Quill & Brush 54-680 1983
$200

HUXLEY, ALDOUS   Brave New World. London: Chatto &
Windus, 1932. First edition. Orig. cloth, (badly chipped). Very good.
MacManus 279-2910 1983 $200

HUXLEY, ALDOUS   Brave New World. London, 1932. First
edition. D.w. Lightly chipped dust wrapper; owner's name on flyleaf.
Argosy 714-380 1983 $200

HUXLEY, ALDOUS   Brave New World. London, 1932. First
edition. Spine a little darkened and creased. Erasure from flyleaf.
Very good. Rota 231-332 1983 £30

HUXLEY, ALDOUS   Brave New World. London, Chatto & Windus,
1932. First edition. 3/4 gilt stamped dark blue morocco by Bayntun
of Bath. Fine copy. Houle 22-488 1983 $30

HUXLEY, ALDOUS   Brief Candles. London: Chatto &
Windus, 1930. First edition. 8vo. Orig. cloth. Dust jacket.
Jacket slightly soiled, but a fine copy. Jaffe 1-179 1983 $85

HUXLEY, ALDOUS   Brief Candles. New York: Doubleday,
Doran, 1930. 1st American ed., 1st printing with the Doran seal on
copyright page. Orig. green cloth, gilt. Fine fresh copy in tape-
repaired dj. Jenkins 155-638 1983 $30

HUXLEY, ALDOUS   The Burning Wheel. Oxford: B.H. Blackwell, 1916. First edition. Orig. buff wrappers with paper labels.
Very fine. MacManus 279-2913 1983 $850

HUXLEY, ALDOUS   The Cicadas and Other Poems. London:
Chatto & Windus, 1931. First edition. Orig. cloth-backed boards.
One of 160 signed copies. About fine. MacManus 279-2914 1983 $150

HUXLEY, ALDOUS   The Cicadas And Other Poems. London:
Chatto & Windus, 1931. First edition. 8vo. Orig. cloth with paper
label. Dust jacket (slightly faded). Fine copy. Jaffe 1-180 1983
$85

HUXLEY, ALDOUS   The Cicadas. Lon., 1931. Near fine in
chipped and sunned dustwrapper. Quill & Brush 54-686 1983 $75

HUXLEY, ALDOUS   The Cicadas. London, 1931. First
edition. Cloth backed patterned boards. Bookplate. No. removed from
spine. Appears to be ex-library, minor staining to spine. Moderately
worn. Limited to 160 numbered copies, signed by author. King 45-201
1983 $65

HUXLEY, ALDOUS   The Cicadas. London, 1931. First
edition. Spine just a little faded. Torn dust wrapper. Very nice.
Rota 231-331 1983 £15

HUXLEY, ALDOUS   Crome Yellow. London: Chatto & Windus,
1921. First edition. 8vo. Orig. cloth with paper label. Dust
jacket, fragmentary. Fine copy. Jaffe 1-166 1983 $100

HUXLEY, ALDOUS   The Defeat of Youth. Oxford, (1918).
First edition. Orig. stiff green printed boards, paper labels, (a
bit rubbed at joints), else good - very good. Uncut and partly
unopened. Houle 22-490 1983 $175

HUXLEY, ALDOUS   The Defeat of Youth & Other Poems.
(Oxford: B.H. Blackwell, 1918). First edition. 8vo. Orig.
decorated wrappers with paper labels. Wrappers slightly rubbed and
darkened, but a very good copy. Jaffe 1-165 1983 $100

HUXLEY, ALDOUS   The Defeat of Youth & Other Poems.
Oxford: Blackwell, (1918). 1st ed. Orig. patterned stiff wrappers,
label, uncut. Outer layer of fragile spine paper peeled from upper
half of spine, else clean fresh copy. Jenkins 155-641 1983 $75

HUXLEY, ALDOUS   The Discovery. London: Chatto & Windus,
1924. First edition. 8vo. Orig. cloth-backed decorated boards
with paper label on spine. Dust jacket. One of 210 copies printed
on Italian hand-made paper. Partially faded and torn jacket. A fine
copy. Jaffe 1-171 1983 $175

HUXLEY, ALDOUS   Do What You Will. London: Chatto &
Windus, 1930. First edition. Tan cloth. Soiled and chipped dust
jacket. Bradley 66-211 1983 $37.50

HUXLEY, ALDOUS   Do What You Will: Essays. London,
1949. First edition. Tan cloth. Fine in dj which is mended
internally. Bradley 64-78 1983 $30

HUXLEY, ALDOUS   An Encyclopedia of Pacifism. London:
Chatto & Windus, 1937. First edition. 8vo. Orig. wrappers. Fine
copy. Jaffe 1-188 1983 $65

HUXLEY, ALDOUS   Essays New And Old. London: Chatto &
Windus, At The Florence Press, 1926. First edition. 4to. Orig.
cloth-backed marbled boards. Dust jacket. Limited to 650 copies
signed by the author. Chipped and dusty jacket, but very fine copy.
Jaffe 1-174 1983 $100

HUXLEY, ALDOUS   Eyeless in Gaza. London: Chatto &
Windus, 1936. First edition. 8vo. Orig. cloth. Dust jacket.
Small piece missing from rear panel of jacket, otherwise a fine
copy. Jaffe 1-184 1983 $65

HUXLEY, ALDOUS   The Gioconda Smile. London: Chatto
& Windus, 1938. First separate edition. Small 8vo. Orig. decorated
boards. Dust jacket. Fine copy. Jaffe 1-185 1983 $100

HUXLEY, ALDOUS   Heaven and Hell. New York, (1956).
8vo. Cloth. Signed by Huxley on the front flyleaf. Fine in chipped
dj. In Our Time 156-425 1983 $125

HUXLEY, ALDOUS   Heaven and Hell. N.Y.: Harpers, (1956).
First edition. Orig. cloth. Dust jacket. Presentation copy to
Mildred and Robert Bliss. With a note by Bliss on the front paste-
down regarding the book and the Dumbarton Oaks bookplate. MacManus
279-2917 1983 $125

HUXLEY, ALDOUS   Jesting Pilate. Lon., 1926. Illus.,
portions of cover lightly sunned, edges just starting to wear, very good
in torn and chipped, still presentable dustwrapper. Quill & Brush 54-
681 1983 $75

HUXLEY, ALDOUS   Jesting Pilate. The Diary of a Journey.
London: Chatto & Windus, 1926. First edition. 8vo. Illus. Orig.
cloth. Dust jacket, chipped. Fine copy. Jaffe 1-175 1983 $45

HUXLEY, ALDOUS   Leda. NY, (1920). Cover slightly soiled
and faded, edges slightly rubbed with slight wear to corners, paper
labels slightly soiled with spine label slightly chipped. Very good,
owner's name. Quill & Brush 54-682 1983 $40

HUXLEY, ALDOUS   Little Mexican & Other Stories. London:
Chatto & Windus, 1924. First edition. 8vo. Orig. cloth with paper
label. Dust jacket. Jacket a little rubbed, but a fine copy. Jaffe
1-170 1983 $100

HUXLEY, ALDOUS   The Little Mexican and Other Stories.
London: Chatto & Windus, 1924. 1st ed. Orig. apricot cloth, label.
Tiny nick to spine, but fine fresh copy in the scarce dj marred only
by a one inch long narrow piece missing from spine. Jenkins 155-642
1983 $60

HUXLEY, ALDOUS   Mortal Coils. London, Chatto, 1922.
First edition. Dust jacket. A fine copy. Houle 21-430 1983 $175

HUXLEY, ALDOUS   Mortal Coils. London: Chatto & Windus,
1922. First edition. 8vo. Orig. cloth with paper label. Dust
jacket, partially torn, but a near-fine copy. Jaffe 1-167 1983
$100

HUXLEY, ALDOUS   Music at Night and Other Essays. NY,
1931. Limited to 842 numbered and signed copies, front hinge starting
at title, else very good. Quill & Brush 54-683 1983 $100

HUXLEY, ALDOUS   Music at Night and Other Essays. N.Y.:
Fountain Press, 1931. First edition. Orig. cloth-backed boards.
One of 842 signed copies. Bookplate. Former owner's inscription on
flyleaves. Very good. MacManus 279-2920 1983 $85

HUXLEY, ALDOUS   Music at Night and Other Essays. Lon.,
1931. Corners slightly bumped, else very good in slightly frayed and
sunned, very good dustwrapper. Quill & Brush 54-684 1983 $75

HUXLEY, ALDOUS   On The Margin. London: Chatto &
Windus, 1923. First edition. 8vo. Orig. cloth with paper label.
Dust jacket. Fine copy. Jaffe 1-169 1983 $100

HUXLEY, ALDOUS   On the Margin. NY, (1923). Spine
stained and edges slightly worn, good or better in soiled and chipped
dustwrapper, owner's name. Quill & Brush 54-685 1983 $30

HUXLEY, ALDOUS   On the Margin. London: Chatto & Windus,
1923. First edition. Orig. cloth. Paper label on spine (darkened).
Dust jacket (stained & worn). Covers spotted and stained. MacManus
279-2921 1983 $20

HUXLEY, ALDOUS   The Perennial Philosophy. New York,
(1945). 8vo. Cloth. Fine copy in dj which has a chip at the
spinal extremity. Signed by Huxley on the front flyleaf. In Our
Time 156-422 1983 $125

HUXLEY, ALDOUS   Point Counter Point. London: Chatto &
Windus, 1928. First edition. Orig. cloth. Dust jacket (repaired).
Presentation copy, inscribed on the flyleaf "To Anna Haslip with
affectionate good wishes from Aldous Huxley October 1928." Soiled and
worn. MacManus 279-2925 1983 $250

HUXLEY, ALDOUS   Point Counter Point. London: Chatto &
Windus, 1928. First edition. Orig. cloth. Limited to 256 copies
signed by author. Hinges cracked, a bit shaken. Very good. Mac-
Manus 279-2924 1983 $185

HUXLEY, ALDOUS   Point Counter Point. London: Chatto &
Windus, 1928. First edition. Orig. cloth. Dust jacket (somewhat
frayed; badly defective). Very good. MacManus 279-2923 1983 $75

HUXLEY, ALDOUS   Proper Studies. London: Chatto &
Windus, 1927. 1st ed., 1 of 260 numbered copies, signed by Huxley.
Orig. maroon cloth-backed marbled boards, t.e.g., others uncut.
Minor fading of spine, but bright fresh copy. Jenkins 155-644 1983
$150

HUXLEY, ALDOUS   Proper Studies. London: Chatto &
Windus, 1927. First edition. 8vo. Orig. cloth. Dust jacket.
Slightly spotted jacket. Fine copy. Jaffe 1-177 1983 $85

HUXLEY, ALDOUS   Science Liberty and Peace. New York,
1946. Signed by Huxley on the half-title page. 8vo. Cloth. Fine
in dj. In Our Time 156-423 1983 $125

HUXLEY, ALDOUS   Science, Liberty & Peace. N.Y.: Harper
& Brothers, 1946. First American edition. Orig. cloth. Dust jacket
(a bit soiled & chipped). Very good. MacManus 279-2926 1983 $20

HUXLEY, ALDOUS   Selected Poems. Oxford: Blackwell,
1925. Printed boards, paper label. First edition. Very slight wear
at ends of spine, otherwise a fine copy. Reese 20-540 1983 $65

HUXLEY, ALDOUS   Texts and Pretexts. London: Chatto &
Windus, 1932. Cloth and paper over boards. First edition. One of
214 numbered copies, specially printed and bound, and signed by
the author. Edges of boards very slightly darkened, else a fine copy.
Reese 20-542 1983 $165

HUXLEY, ALDOUS   Texts & Pretexts. London: Chatto &
Windus, 1932. First edition. 8vo. Orig. cloth. Dust jacket.
Fine copy. Jaffe 1-182 1983 $75

HUXLEY, ALDOUS   Themes and Variations. New York,
(1950). 8vo. Cloth. Signed by Huxley on front flyleaf. Fine in
lightly chipped dj. In Our Time 156-424 1983 $125

HUXLEY, ALDOUS   Those Barren Leaves. Lon., 1925. Hinge
starting at page 112, bottom spine edge bumped, else very good in
internally mended, slightly chipped and frayed, very good dustwrapper.
Quill & Brush 54-687 1983 $75

HUXLEY, ALDOUS   Those Barren Leaves. London: Chatto
& Windus, 1925. First edition. 8vo. Orig. cloth with paper label.
Dust jacket. Slightly darkened jacket but a fine copy. Jaffe 1-172
1983 $75

HUXLEY, ALDOUS   Those Barren Leaves. London: Chatto &
Windus, 1925. First edition. Orig. cloth with paper label. Dust
jacket (a bit soiled & torn). Very good. MacManus 279-2927 1983
$25

HUXLEY, ALDOUS   Time Must Have a Stop. New York,
1944. 8vo. Cloth. Fine in dj. Signed by Huxley on the front flyleaf. In Our Time 156-421 1983 $125

HUXLEY, ALDOUS   Tomorrow and Tomorrow and Tomorrow and
Other Essays. New York, (1956). 8vo. Cloth. Signed copy. Fine
in dj. In Our Time 156-426 1983 $125

HUXLEY, ALDOUS   Two Or Three Graces and Other Stories.
London: Chatto & Windus, 1926. First edition. Orig. blue cloth.
Dust jacket (a little soiled & worn). Presentation copy "To Sydney
Schiff in friendship and in homage to Stephen Hudson, Aldous Huxley,
June 1926." Spine and covers slightly worn and soiled. With three
pencil notations in the text in Hudson's hand. Good. MacManus 279-
2928 1983 $275

HUXLEY, ALDOUS   Two Or Three Graces And Other Stories.
London: Chatto & Windus, 1926. First edition. 8vo. Orig. cloth.
Dust jacket. Fine copy. Jaffe 1-176 1983 $100

HUXLEY, ALDOUS   A Virgin Heart. Toronto, n.d. (Ca. 1925).
8vo, cloth. First Canadian edition. Some light spotting to cloth,
mainly a fine copy in the uncommon dust jacket. In Our Time 156-427
1983 $125

HUXLEY, ALDOUS   What Are You Going To Do About It? The
Case for Constructive Peace. London: Peace Pledge Union, (1937).
1st ed. Orig. yellow printed wrappers. Fine copy. Jenkins 155-649
1983 $25

HUXLEY, ALDOUS   Words and Their Meanings. Los
Angeles: The Ward Ritchie Press, (1940). First edition. 8vo.
Orig. decorated boards. Dust jacket (lightly soiled and darkened).
A fine copy. Jaffe 1-186 1983 $150

HUXLEY, ALDOUS   The World of Light. London: Chatto &
Windust, 1931. First edition. 8vo. Orig. cloth. Dust jacket.
Slightly chipped dust jacket, but a fine copy. Jaffe 1-181 1983
$65

HUXLEY, J.   The Elements of Experimental Embryology.
Cambridge, 1934. 221 text-figures, 8vo, original cloth. The rare
original printing. Wheldon 160-496 1983 £30

HUXLEY, J.   Evolution the modern synthesis. 1942.
First issue of the first edition, 8vo, original cloth. Wheldon 160-
165 1983 £18

HUXLEY, THOMAS HENRY   Collected Essays. (1893-94), 1895-
1904. 9 vols., cr. 8vo, original red cloth. Wheldon 160-169 1983
£60

HUXLEY, THOMAS HENRY   The Crayfish. (1880). 82 figures, cr.
8vo, cloth (trifle worn). Wheldon 160-1292 1983 £15

HUXLEY, THOMAS HENRY   Lay Sermons, Addresses, and Reviews.
London, Macmillan, 1870. Orig. blind blocked mauve cloth, hinges
cracked. Very good copy. First ed. Gach 95-223 1983 $75

HUXLEY, THOMAS HENRY   Lessons in Elementary Physiology.
London, 1945. 8vo. Cloth. Woodcuts in text. First edition.
Gurney JJ-187 1983 £15

HUXLEY, THOMAS HENRY   Life and Letters of... NY: D. Appleton
& Co., 1901 (1900). Two vols. Publisher's gilt-stamped beige cloth,
hinges cracked, else a very good set. Gach 94-213 1983 $37.50

HUXLEY, THOMAS HENRY   National Association for the Promotion
of Technical Education. Pub. by the National Association, 1887. 1st
ed., orig. printed paper wrapper. Pickering & Chatto 22-56 1983 $85

HUXLEY, THOMAS HENRY   The Oceanic Hydrozoa. Ray Society,
1859. 12 plates by the author, folio, original boards (trifle worn).
Slight foxing. Wheldon 160-1291 1983 £36

HUYGENS, CHRISTIAAN   Kosmotheoros... The Hague: A Moetjens,
1698. First edition. 5 engraved plates and variant state of plate
4. 4to. Cont. calf. From the library of Andrew Fletcher of Saltoun.
Fine copy. Kraus 164-131 1983 $1,800

HUYGENS, CHRISTIAAN   Zvlichemii, Cont. F. Horologivm Oscillatorivm. Parisiis, Apud F. Muguet...MDCLXXIII (1673). Cvm Privilegio Regis. Small folio, bound in full new calf, blind stamped and tooled. Signature of "Willoughby M.D." on front free endpaper. Title page and early leaves lightly foxed. Lightly toned throughout. Arkway 22-76 1983 $4,250

HYDE, CHARLES L.   Pioneer Days: The Story of an Adventurous and Active Life. New York, 1939. Illus. 1st ed. Nice copy. Jenkins 153-271 1983 $45

HYDE, FREDERICK A.   A Miscellaneous Collection of Songs, Ballads, Canzonets, Duets, Trios, Glees, & Elegies. Printed by Clementi, circa 1798. Two vols. With engraved frontis. in each vol. Folio, cont. half calf, the marbled sides lifted but the bindings strong. Fenning 62-189 1983 £55

HYDE, HENRY   A True Copy of Sir Henry Hide's Speech on the Scaffold. London, Peter Cole, 1650. 4to, disbound, age-darkened, little frayed, uncut copy of the rare first and only edition. Ravenstree 94-224 1983 $32

HYDE, JAMES N.   Early Medical Chicago. Chicago, 1879. First edition. 8vo. Wrappers. Illus. with engravings and woodcuts. Rare. Fye H-3-286 1983 $45

HYDE, JOHN   Wonderland; or, The Pacific Northwest and Alaska. St. Paul: 1888. Illus., color map on inside front wrapper. Pictorial wrappers. Wrappers chipped, front cover detached. Bradley 66-705 1983 $60

HYDE, LAURENCE   Southern Cross. Los Angeles: Ward Ritchie Press, 1951. Sq. 8vo. First edition. With ca. 230 wood engraved illus. Red linen backed black paper over boards. Glassine wrapper. Fine. McGahern 53-78 1983 $100

HYMAN, HAROLD THOMAS   An Integrated Practice of Medicine. Philadelphia: W.B. Saunders, (1946). First edition. 1184 illus., 305 in color; 319 differential diagnosis tables. 5 vols., cloth. Fine set. Bradley 65-100 1983 $150

HYMAN, L. H.   Comparative Vertebrate Anatomy. Chicago (1942). Second edition, 136 text-figures, royal 8vo, cloth. Wheldon 160-497 1983 £12

HYMAN, L. H.   The Invertebrates, Vol. 1. 1940. 221 text-figures, 8vo, cloth. Wheldon 160-1294 1983 £20

HYMAN, L. H.   The Invertebrates, Vols. 1-4. 1940-55. 4 vols., 8vo, cloth, numerous text-figures. Out of print. Wheldon 160-1293 1983 £85

HYMNS to the Supreme Being. London: J. Nichols, 1780. Octavo. Fine in slightly rubbed full red leather with gilt-ornamented spine and dentelles. A.e.g. Fore-edge painting. Owner's signature. Bookplate of George Lincoln. Bromer 25-206 1983 $485

HYNE, CUTLIFFE   Adventures of Captain Kettle. London: C. Arthur Pearson, 1898. First edition. Illus. Orig. decorated cloth. Spine and covers slightly faded and worn. Contents a bit shaken, endpapers browned. Former owner's signature. Very good. MacManus 279-2930 1983 $75

HYNE, CUTLIFFE   Sandy Carmichael. Phila.: J.B. Lippincott Co., 1908. First American edition? Illus. Orig. pictorial cloth. Fine. MacManus 279-2932 1983 $25

HYRTL, JOSEPH   Handbuch der Topographischen Anatomie. Wien, 1853. 2 vols., tall 8vo, orig. prs. wrs. Foxed, dampstains, light pencilling. Argosy 713-287 1983 $125

HYSLOP, JAMES H. (1854-1920) Borderland of Psychical Research. Boston: Herbert B. Turner, 1906. First edition. Fine, bright copy. Orig. straight-grained blue cloth, gilt lettering and top edge. Gach 95-228 1983 $40

I

I Was Just Thinking. New York, (1959). 8vo, cloth. Wood engr. by Claire Leighton. From the library of Rudolph Ruzicka. With a letter from the publisher to same laid in. Fine in dust jacket. In Our Time 156-498 1983 $25

IBSEN, HENRIK   Peer Gynt. N.Y.: Doubleday, 1929. First edition. 4to. Cloth backed boards. Light wear. Illus. by MacKinstry with full-page color illus. plus black & whites. Very good. Aleph-bet 8-167 1983 $40

IBSEN, HENRIK   The Works of... N.Y., Scribner, 1917. Viking edition. Illus. with 41 plates (the frontis. on Japan vellum). Maroon cloth stamped in gilt, t.e.g., partially unopened, uncut. Complete in 13 vols. Very good. Houle 22-492 1983 $175

ICKIS, ALONZO FERDINAND   Bloody Trails Along the Rio Grande. Denver: 1958. First edition. Tipped-in portrait frontis. Large folding map. Cloth. 1/500 copies signed by editor, Nolie Mumey. Very good in chipped dust jacket. Bradley 66-608 1983 $100

ICKIS, ALONZO FERDINAND   Bloody Trails Along the Rio Grande. Denver, 1958. Frontis. and folding map. Limited to 500 numbered and signed copies. Fine copy in dj. Jenkins 153-375 1983 $75

ICKS, ROBERT J.   Tanks and Armored Vehicles. N.Y., (1945). First edition. Numerous photos. Blind-stamped names on endpapers. Minor stain on front cover. Frayed and chipped dust wrapper. Good. King 45-553 1983 $25

IDE, JOHN JAY   The Portraits of John Jay (1745-1829). N.Y.; NY Hist. Soc., 1938. Ports., repros., 8vo, dec. cloth, g.t., ex library. Argosy 710-423 1983 $30

IDE, SIMEON   The Conquest of California. Oakland: Biobooks, 1944. Folding map and illus. Cloth and boards. Printed at the Grabhorn Press. Dawson 471-131 1983 $40

IHARA, U.   Picasso. Tokyo: Atelier-Sha, 1936. 37 plates (6 color). 4to. Boards. Ars Libri 32-522 1983 $37.50

IHLE, J. E. W.   Leerboek der Vergelijkende Ontleedkunde van de Vertebraten. Utrecht, 1924. Numerous illustrations, 2 vols., royal 8vo, cloth. Wheldon 160-498 1983 £20

IHLSENG, M. C.   A Manual of Mining. New York, 1892. 1st ed. Illus. 8vo. Morrill 288-616 1983 $35

IHRE, JOHANN   Dissertatio Gradualis de Imputatione Actionum in Somno Patratarum... Westeras (Sweden), 1743. Small 4to. Modern wrappers. Kraus 164-132 1983 $180

IIAMS, THOMAS M.   Notes on the Causes and Prevention of Foxing in Books. London: H.W. Edwards, 1937. Square 8vo. Cloth, paper cover label. 4 illus. Fine copy. Scarce. Oak Knoll 49-241 1983 $65

IKBAL ALI SHAH, SIRDAR   Afghanistan of the Afghans. London: The Diamond Press Ltd., (1928). Illus., including a folding map. Green cloth, gilt-stamped. Karmiole 71-58 1983 $35

ILLANOS GUTIERREZ, VALENTIN   Don Esteban; or, Memoirs of a Spaniard. Henry Colburn, 1825. First and apparently only edition, without the half-titles, 3 vols., large 12mo, cont. half calf, gilt ruled and lettered spines. Fenning 62-209 1983 £75

ILLINOIS. GENERAL ASSEMBLY. SENATE.   Journal of the Senate of the Tenth General Assembly of the State of Illinois, at A Special Session, Begun and Held in Vandalia, July 10, 1837. Vandalia, Ill.: Printed by William Walters, Public Printer, 1837. Orig. wrappers. Some foxing. Very good. Jenkins 152-166 1983 $200

ILLINOIS. LAWS   The City Charter and Ordinances of the City of Galena. Galena: Printed at the Galena "Democrat" Office, 1865. Printed blue wrappers. Wrapper edges and spine chipped. Gen. J.G. Smith's copy with his signature in ink. Rare. Bradley 65-102 1983 $85

THE ILLUMINATED Gems of Sacred Poetry. Philadelphia: Lindsay and Blakiston, n.d. (ca. 1847). First edition. 4to. Orig. full red leather with an intricate stamped design in gold and in blind, all edges gilt. With a chromolithographic title page, 26 illuminated capitals. Covers worn with some of the lower spine chipped away and a crack in the front hinge. Internally, a bright copy. Oak Knoll 48-108 1983 $150

ILLUMINATED Manuscripts, Incunabula and Americana from the famous Libraries of the Marquis of Lothian. New York: American Art Association, 1932. Only edition, 4to, original printed wrappers. Edges of wrappers worn, one margin stained; internally a fine copy. Trebizond 18-2 1983 $45

THE ILLUMINATIONS of Arthur Rimbaud. New Directions, (1943). 8vo, stiff wrappers in dust jacket. This copy is inscribed by Auden on the front flyleaf. With the Newton bookplate. A fine copy. In Our Time 156-34 1983 $250

THE ILLUSTRATED Book of Nursery Rhymes & Songs. Nelson, 1876. Illus. by Keeley Halswelle. Frontis. & numerous b&w illus. Red decor. cloth, corners sl. bruised, occasional thumb marks, scarce, vg. Hodgkins 27-108 1983 £25

ILLUSTRATED Catalogue of the Remarkable Collection of Ancient Chinese Bronzes... New York: American Art Association, 1914. Tall 8vo. Stiff paper wrappers. Many illus. Oak Knoll 48-415 1983 $20

THE ILLUSTRATED exhibitor... London: Cassell, 1851. First edition, bound from the orig. 30 parts. Large 8vo. Orig. bright blue cloth. Illus. throughout with many hundreds of wood-engraved plates (some folding) and text illus. Very fine copy. Rare. Ximenes 63-571 1983 $250

THE ILLUSTRATED London Almanac for 1873. With 6 pictures printed in colour by Leighton Bros. & many b&w wood engrs, adverts. 1st edn. Colour printed decor. wrappers (top of bkstrip damaged), v.g. Hodgkins 27-580 1983 £15

THE ILLUSTRATED London Almanac for 1875. 1st edn. 6 pictures printed in colour by Leighton Bros. & many b&w wood engrs., adverts. Colour printed decorated wrappers (some water staining to foredge margin of plates & to covers), v.g. Hodgkins 27-578 1983 £12.50

THE ILLUSTRATED London Almanac for 1876. 1st edn. 6 pictures printed in colour by Leighton Bros. & many b&w text wood engrs., adverts. Colour printed decorated wrappers (waterstaining to foredge margin of plates & to covers, sml. piece missing top/bottom bkstrip), v.g. Hodgkins 27-579 1983 £12.50

THE IMAGES of a verye Chrysten bysshop... N.p. (London): printed by Robert Wyer for William Marshall, n.d. First edition. 8vo. 17th-century calf, spine gilt. Hinges a bit worn, one blank lower margin clipped, some faint marginal waterstains, but a fine copy. Very rare. Ximenes 63-581 1983 $2,250

AN IMPARTIAL enquiry into the advantages and losses than England hath received since the beginning of the present war with France. London: Richard Baldwin, 1693. First edition. Small 4to. Disbound. Some soiling of title, light waterstains. Scarce. Ximenes 63-597 1983 $150

AN IMPARTIAL History of Michael Servetus. London: Ward, 1724. 8vo, calf. John G. Lorimer 1837 inscription. Rostenberg 88-86 1983 $400

IMPARTIAL Reflections on the Principles, Character and Conduct of His Royal Highness the Prince of Wales. Worcester: by T. Eaton..., 1810. First edition. 8vo. Orig. quarter red roan. Some wear. Very scarce. Heath 48-148 1983 £35

AN IMPORTANT Enquiry; or, the Nature of a Church Reformation fully Considered. Printed in the Year 1751. 8vo, cont. calf, upper joint cracked. First edition. Bickersteth 75-44 1983 £12

IN and About Historic Boston. Portland: Nelson Co., 1904. Photos, oblong 8vo, pr. pict. wrs., spine mended. Argosy 710-30 1983 $30

IN MEMORIAM Samuel Colt and Caldwell Hart Colt. N.p., 1898. Plates. Original cilt decorated cloth. T.e.g. Fine copy. Jenkins 153-134 1983 $150

IN SOUTH Cheyenne Canon with Pen and Camera. (Colorado Springs, 1895?). Illus. Orig. pictorial printed wraps. Ginsberg 47-343 1983 $35

INCH Kenneth, a Poem. Dublin: Richard Moore Tims, 1830. First edition, half title. Uncut, orig. dark green cloth, paper label, v.g. Inscribed presentation copy from the author. Jarndyce 31-855 1983 £24

INCHBALD, ELIZABETH   The British Theatre. London, 1808. 12mo. 25 vols. Cont. half red morocco, gilt, marbled boards. Frontis to each play. A fine set. Traylen 94-453 1983 £195

INCIDENTS and Sketches Connected with the Early History and Settlement of the West. Cincinnati: U.P. James, (1847). Illus. Later cloth. 1st ed. Jenkins 153-786 1983 $60

INDIAN MUSEUM.   Records of the Indian Museum. Calcutta, 1914-20. Vols. 9-20, with plates and illustrations, 12 vols., 8vo, vols. 14, 17 and 20 original wrappers, remainder bound in cloth. Wheldon 160-395 1983 £85

INDIANA Geological Survey. Indianapolis, 1869-76. First to seventh annual reports, with plates and folding maps, 7 vols., 8vo, original cloth. Wheldon 160-1424 1983 £25

INDIANAPOLIS AND MADISON RAILROAD COMPANY   Report of the President of the...to the Bond and Stockholders. Madison, Wisc., 1862. Orig. printed wraps. First edition. Ginsberg 46-350 1983 $75

INGALLS, RUFUS   Reports by Captain Rufus Ingalls on the March from Fort Leavenworth to Salt Lake City... (Washington, 1855). Cloth, very good. Reese 19-287 1983 $125

INGELOW, JEAN   Poems. London, 1888. 2 vols. Cr. 8vo. Cont. polished calf, gilt, gilt panelled spines with morocco labels, gilt. Traylen 94-454 1983 £12

INGEMANN, BERNHARD SEVERIN   The Childhood of King Erik Menved. Bruce and Wyld, 1846. First English edition. 8vo, double column. Orig. cloth, uncut. Hannas 69-108 1983 £20

INGEMANN, BERNHARD SEVERIN   Waldemar. Saunders and Otley, 1841. First English edition. 3 vols. Large 12mo, orig. cloth (faded), uncut. Hannas 69-109 1983 £20

INGERSOLL, CHESTER   Overland to California in 1847. Chicago: Black Cat Press, 1937. Limited to 350 copies. Jenkins 152-169 1983 $75

INGERSOLLE-SMOUSE, FLORENCE   Joseph Vernet, peintre de marine. Paris: Etienne Bignou, 1926. 2 vols. 152 plates. Large 4to. New cloth. Orig. wrappers bound in. Edition limited to 500 numbered copies, printed by Firmin-Didot. Ars Libri 32-688 1983 $485

INGERSOLL-SMOUSE, FLORENCE   Pater. Biographie et catalogue critiques. Paris: Les Beaux-Arts, 1928. 230 illus. Large 4to. Wrappers. Ars Libri 32-505 1983 $200

INGLIS, CHARLES   The True Interest of America Inpartially stated. Philadelphia: James Humphreys, Jun., 1776. Disbound. Felcone 21-58 1983 $100

INGLIS, H. D.   Rambles in the Footsteps of Don Quixote. Whittaker and Co., 1837. First edition, 2 pp ads., half title, illus. by George Cruikshank. Orig. cloth bound into crushed green morocco by Hyman Zucker, gilt borders and dentelles and spine. Fine in cloth slip-case. Pencil inscription on blank 'From the Douglas Collection'. Jarndyce 31-501 1983 £110

INGLIS, JAMES   Tent Life in Tigerland. 1892. 24 coloured plates, roy 8vo, neatly recased in the orig. gilt-decorated cloth. K Books 307-103 1983 £35

INGOLDSBY, THOMAS, PSEUD. Please turn to BARHAM, RICHARD HARRIS

INGRAHAM, JOSEPH HOLT   The South-West. New York: Harper and Brothers, 1835. Two vols. Orig. cloth. Paper labels. First edition. The T.W. Streeter copy, with his book label and notes. Reese 19-288 1983 $500

INGRAM, J. S.   The Centennial Exposition...Phila., (1876). 1st ed. Illus. 8vo, rubbed. Morrill 288-201 1983 $20

INGRAM, JOHN G.   A Dictionary of the Scottish Language. Glasgow: David Bryce; Fredk. A. Stokes, New York, 1897. Brown cloth, leather label: 'A Guide Scotch Dictionary'. T.e.g., v.g. Jarndyce 31-659 1983 £12.50

INGRAM, JOHN H.   The Haunted Homes and Family Traditions of Great Britain. London: Allen, 1884. First editions. 2 vols. Orig. decorated cloth. Bindings a bit soiled. Good. MacManus 279-2936 1983 $75

INGRAM, REX   Mars in the House of Death. N.Y., Knopf, 1935. First edition. With 23 line drawings and a frontis. by Carlos Ruano Llopis. Typography, design and dust jacket by W.A. Dwiggins. Very good. Houle 22-493 1983 $45

INMAN, HENRY   The Great Salt Lake Trail. Topeka: Crane and Company, 1899. 8 plates including frontis. photo. of authors. Folding map. Handsome three-quarter morocco over marbled boards. Spine nicely decorated in gilt. Fine condition. Jenkins 151-145 1983 $100

INMAN, HENRY   The Old Santa Fe Trail: The Story of a Great Highway. New York: The Macmillan Co., 1898. Illus. Frontis. Pictorial cloth. Fairly nice copy. Jenkins 153-787 1983 $75

INMAN, HENRY   The Ranche on the Oxhide. N.Y., MacMillian, 1898. First edition. Illus. with 6 b/w plate drawings by Charles Bradford Hudson. Pictorial red cloth stamped in brown and gilt (spine lightly faded) with a design of three buffaloes. Zane Grey's copy. Houle 22-1114 1983 $55

INMAN, HENRY   Stories of the Old Santa Fe Trail. Topeka: Crane & Co., 1898. Plates and map. Expanded edition. Fine copy in pictorial cloth. Jenkins 153-275 1983 $125

INNES, ARTHUR D.   Seers and Singers. A.D. Innes & Co., 1893. First edition, half title, orig. green cloth, gilt, t.e.g., v.g. Jarndyce 31-749 1983 £10.50

INNES, JOHN   A Short Description of the Human Muscles, Arranged as they Appear on Dissection. NY: Collins & Co., 1818. Illus. with 17 plates, index. Orig. boards, uncut. Spine chipped; extremities rubbed. Karmiole 74-69 1983 $85

INNES, MC LEOD   Lucknow & Oude in the Mutiny. London, 1895. Folding maps and plans, plates. 8vo. Orig. cloth. Good. Edwards 1044-380 1983 £25

INNES-SMITH, R. W.   English Speaking Students of Medicine at the University of Leyden. Edinburgh & London, 1932. 8vo. Cloth. Portrait. Gurney JJ-190 1983 £15

INNIS, HAROLD A.   Political Economy in the Modern State. Toronto: Ryerson, 1946. 23cm. Blue cloth. Spine faded else very good. Scarce. McGahern 53-79 1983 $50

INNIS, HAROLD A.   Select Documents in Canadian Economic History, 1733-1885. Toronto: University of Toronto Press, 1933. 23cm. First edition. Red cloth. Fine copy. Scarce. McGahern 53-80 1983 $85

INNIS, VICTOR   Exposing the Twelve Great Secrets of the Modern Card Shark. L.A., Sturdevant & McCarrell, 1937. Small 8vo, stiff printed wraps. Very good. Houle 21-362 1983 $75

THE INQUISITION. Printed for Vernor and Hood, (1797). 2 vols, sm. 8vo, contemporary qtr. sheep, marbled sides; half-titles; a fine copy. Hill 165-60 1983 £285

INSALL, A. J.   Days on the Wing. Aviation Bookclub, c.1930. Portrait frontis. 7 plates. Spine slightly faded. Good. Edwards 1042-592 1983 £15

INSLEY, WILLIAM   Random Recollections of an Old Publisher. Simpkin Marshall, Bournemouth Bright's Ltd., 1900. First edition, 2 vols. Orig. green cloth; vol. II rather rubbed and darkened. Jarndyce 30-1157 1983 £28

INSTRUCTIONS to the Envoys Extraordinary and Ministers Plenipotentiary from the United States of America to the French Republic. Philadelphia: W. Ross, (1798). Disbound. Felcone 22-98 1983 $25

THE INTERNATIONAL Cyclopedia of Monograms, Alphabets, Initials, Cyphers, Types, Crests... Chicago, G. P. Engelhard, 1910. Illus. 4to. Morrill 286-652 1983 $47.50

INTERNATIONAL PAPER COMPANY   International Paper Company. 1898-1948, Np. 1948. Folio. 34cm. Extensively illus. Very good to fine. McGahern 54-97 1983 $25

THE INTERTYPE, a Book of Instruction... Brooklyn: Mergenthaler Linotype Co., (1940). First edition. 8vo. Cloth. Name in ink. Oak Knoll 48-366 1983 $35

THE INTERVIEW; or Jack Falstaff's ghost. A poem. London: printed for the author, and sold by S. Bladon; and F. Blyth, 1766. 4to, disbound, 1st ed. Half-title present. Rare. Ximenes 64-288 1983 $350

THE INTRACOASTAL Waterway, Norfolk to Key West. Wash., 1937. Photos., folding map, pict. wrs. Argosy 710-621 1983 $25

INWARDS, RICHARD   The Temple of the Andes. London: Privately Printed, 1884. 19 lithographic plates. Frontis. 4to. Cloth. Presentation copy, inscribed by the author. Ars Libri 34-287 1983 $100

IOTEYKO, JOSEFA   La Fatigue. Paris, 1920. 8vo. Orig. wrappers. Manuscript account of the author found at the beginning of the volume. Wrappers torn. Gurney JJ-191 1983 £15

IOWA. CONSTITUTION.   Constitution of Iowa...Adopted in Convention, Nov. 1, 1844. Wash., 1845. Dbd. Ginsberg 47-358 1983 $35

IOWA. LAWS.   Laws of the State of Iowa in Relation to Corporations for Railroad Purposes. Davenport, 1853. Orig. wraps. Ginsberg 46-364 1983 $150

IPSEN, LUDVIG SANDOE   The Book-Plates of Ludvig Sandoe Ipsen. Boston: Troutsdale Press, 1904. 31 leaves of plates (some printed in color). In addition, there is one orig. engr. plate. Bound in 1/2 parchment over boards; paper cover label. Karmiole 73-17 1983 $50

IREDALE, T.   Birds of Paradise and Bower Birds. Melbourne, 1950. 4to, original half leather, coloured plates and a map. Wheldon 160-50 1983 £140

IRELAND, JOHN   Hogarth Illustrated from his own Manuscripts. London: Boydell, 1812. 3rd ed., 8vo, 3 vols., bookplates of Sir Robert Peel. Fine Regency gilt-bordered morocco binding, spines gilt, a.e.g. Engraved and printed title pages; full-page engraved plates; text illus. Initial leaves of one volume dampstained, some light foxing of plates. Trebizond 18-198 1983 $350

IRELAND, JOHN   Hogarth Illustrated. London: J. & J. Boydell, 1793-1798. Second edition, corrected. 3 vols. Vol. 1: 46 engraved plates. Vols. 2 & 3 each: 44 engraved plates. 4to. Full red straight-grain morocco. Inner dentelles. Intermittent light foxing. A fine copy. Ars Libri 32-314 1983 $225

IRELAND, JOSEPH N.   Records of the American Stage from 1750 to 1860. N.Y.: T.H. Morrell, 1866-1867. Later cloth. Cone of sixty sets on large paper. Dawson 471-326 1983 $125

IRELAND, WILLIAM   Stultifera Navis. Wm. Miller, 1807. First edition, half title, folding hand-coloured front. by John Augustus Atkinson. Early cloth, maroon label. Jarndyce 30-746 1983 £28

IRELAND, WILLIAM HENRY   An Authentic Account of the Shakesperian Manuscripts, etc. London: Printed for J. Debrett, 1796. 1st ed. Contemporary three-quarter calf, labels, gilt, marbled sides. Fine copy, with an extra-illustrated portrait of Ireland. Jenkins 155-1125 1983 $300

IRELAND, WILLIAM-HENRY   The Confessions of William-Henry Ireland, containing the particulars of his fabrication of the Shakespeare Manuscripts... London: Thomas Goddard, 1805. First edition. Tall 12mo. Cont. three-quarter calf over marbled boards, red leather spine label. With two plates. Covers rubbed; a bookplate has been removed. Scarce. Oak Knoll 49-244 1983 $150

IRELAND, WILLIAM HENRY   The Confessions. London, 1805. Facsimile reprint, large 12mo, engraved frontispiece and 4 folding facsimiles, qtr. morocco gilt, over cont. cloth boards, marbled endpapers, t.e.g., occasional light foxing, corners rubbed otherwise a very good copy. Deighton 3-261 1983 £45

THE IRISH-CANADIAN Rangers. Montreal, 1916. 1st ed. Portraits and illus. 8vo. Morrill 288-550 1983 $25

IRISH Fairy Tales. 1892. Illus. by Jack B. Yeats. Backstrip discoloured, front cover stained, water stain lower corner of frontis., else very good. Hodgkins 27-46 1983 £30

THE IRISH Friend. Belfast, 1837. 4 vols. in 1, 4to, contemporary boards, calf back and corners. Rubbed, backstrip chipped, front hinge cracked. Very scarce. Morrill 286-213 1983 $50

THE IRISH Musical Repository. London, B. Crosby & Co., n.d. (1808). Frontis., engraved and printed titles. Rebacked. Small stain on front cover, paper foxed, ex-library copy, with bookplate and release. Salloch 387-101 1983 $60

THE IRISH Widow. Dublin: R.M. Tims, 1828. 12mo, wrapper, a very good copy. Fenning 60-201 1983 £12.50

IRVINE, F. R.   The Fish and Fisheries of the Gold Coast. 1947. 217 text-figures, 8vo, cloth. Wheldon 160-971 1983 £25

IRVINE, WILLIAM   The Farmers in Politics. Toronto: McClelland & Stewart, 1920. 19cm. First edition. Brown cloth. Authors' signed presentation copy. A fine copy. Rare. McGahern 53-81 1983 $125

IRVING, B. A.   The Theory and Practice of Caste. London, 1853. Cloth, frayed at head and tail of spine. Bookplate of the Marquess of Tweeddale. 8vo. Good. Edwards 1044-382 1983 £45

IRVING, HENRY   English Actors. Their characteristics and their methods. Oxford: at the Clarendon Press, 1886. 12mo, original light blue printed wrappers (bit dusty). 1st edition; a nice copy. Ximenes 64-291 1983 $30

IRVING, JOHN   The Hotel New Hampshire. New York: Dutton, (1981). Full red textured semi-leather, t.e.g., others rough-trimmed. First edition. One of 550 numbered copies, specially bound and signed by the author. Mint in slipcase. Reese 20-548 1983 $100

IRVING, JOHN   The Water-Method Man. New York: Random House, (1972). 1st ed. Orig. cloth, dj. Very fine copy. Jenkins 155-1396 1983 $100

IRVING, JOHN   The Water-Method Man. N.Y., (1972).
D.w. First edition. Fine. Argosy 714-383 1983 $85

IRVING, JOHN   The World According to Garp. New York,
(1978). 1st ed. Stiff white wrappers printed in red. Advance reading copy with promotional blurb from the editor, Henry Robbins, laid
in. Very good. Bradley 63-73 1983 $135

IRVING, JOHN B.   The South Carolina Jockey Club.
Charleston, 1857. Engraved plate. Modern buckram. Some waterspotting and foxing of text. Felcone 21-59 1983 $90

IRVING, JOHN TREAT   Indian Sketches. Philadelphia, 1835.
2 vols. Cloth, somewhat worn, good. Reese 19-293 1983 $175

IRVING, PIERRE M.   The Life and Letters of Washington
Irving. New York: Putnam's, 1883. Memorial ed. 1 of 300 copies.
Full-page engravings. 3 vols., brown cloth, paper spine labels, uncut.
Tipped in at front is check made out to author for $100 and signed
by publisher, G.P. Putnam. Covers worn, extremities frayed, labels
scuffed, but internally very good. Bradley 63-74 1983 $60

IRVING, W.   Saxifrages or rock-foils. (1914).
Wheldon 160-1961 1983 £12

IRVING, WASHINGTON   Adventures of Captain Bonneville, or
Scenes Beyond the Rocky Mountains of the Far West. London, 1837.
1st Eng. edition, 3 vols., cont. calf, gilt spine, lea. labels,
marbled edges. Argosy 710-588 1983 $200

IRVING, WASHINGTON   Adventures of Captain Bonneville.
Paris, 1837. Half morocco. First French edition. Ginsberg 47-388
1983 $100

IRVING, WASHINGTON   The Alhambra. Macmillan, 1896. 1st
edn. Illus. by Joseph Pennell. Dark green cloth gilt, a.e.g. (eps.
sl. cracked at hinges), nice copy. Hodgkins 27-458 1983 £15

IRVING, WASHINGTON   Astoria; or, Enterprise Beyond the
Rocky Mountains. London, 1836. 1st English ed. 3 vols., cont.
full calf, gilt spines, lea. labels, marbled edges. Argosy 710-398
1983 $200

IRVING, WASHINGTON   Bracebridge Hall. N.Y.: G.P. Putnam's
Sons, 1896. First of this edition. Illus. by A. Rackham (among others)
2 vols. Orig. gilt cloth. Extremities of spines worn. Good. Mac-
Manus 280-4326 1983 $50

IRVING, WASHINGTON   Bracebridge Hall. Macmillan, 1877. 1st
edn. Illus. by Randolph Caldecott, frontis, 4pp adverts. Dark green
cloth gilt designed by Caldecott, a.e.g. (partly erased contemp.
insc. 2nd ep., bookpl, occasional foxing, corners sl. bruised), v.g.
copy. Hodgkins 27-457 1983 £16

IRVING, WASHINGTON   Christmas at Bracebridge Hall. Dent,
1906. 24 coloured illus. by C.E. Brock. 1st edn. Pale green cloth
gilt, t.e.g. others uncut (2" split top fr. joint repaired, free eps.
sl. discol'd). Inscribed to "Nephew Fred" with visiting card of
J.M. Dent which is inscribed "For Brother Fred." V.g. Hodgkins 27-
460 1983 £16

IRVING, WASHINGTON   A History of New York... Glasgow:
Wylie, 1821. 4th English ed. Contemporary 3/4 calf & marbled boards.
Very good. Jenkins 155-665 1983 $40

IRVING, WASHINGTON   History of the Life and Voyages of
Christopher Columbus. NY, 1831. 2 vols. New ed., rev. & corr.
8vo, 1/4 lea. Argosy 710-132 1983 $75

IRVING, WASHINGTON   The Life and Voyages of Christopher
Columbus. John Murray, 1849. With 2 folding maps and a plate, 3 vols.
8vo, orig. cloth. Fenning 61-216 1983 £21.50

IRVING, WASHINGTON   The Legend of Sleepy Hollow. Philadelphia: McKay, (1928). Small quarto. 8 tipped-in color plates
and numerous b&w illus. by Arthur Rackham. Limited to 250 copies
signed by artist. Very fine in gilt-stamped full-vellum, slightly
rubbed at extremities. Bromer 25-282 1983 $675

IRVING, WASHINGTON   The Legend of Sleepy Hollow. Ph.,
(1928). Illus. by Arthur Rackham. 8 colored illus., corners and
spine edges worn and frayed, else very good. Quill & Brush 54-1132
1983 $60

IRVING, WASHINGTON   The Legend of Sleepy Hollow. SF,
1930 8vo, textured bds. Borders & woodcuts by Judson L. Starr.
One of 229 copies. A very fine copy. Perata 27-43 1983 $35

IRVING, WASHINGTON   The Life and Letters... Richard Bentley,
1862. First edition, 4 vols. Half title vol. I, port. vol. II.
Orig. green cloth, v.g. Jarndyce 30-1030 1983 £48

IRVING, WASHINGTON   Lives of Mahomet and His Successors.
London: John Murray, 1850. First English edition. 2 vols. Tall
8vo, 1/2 brown morocco. Argosy 714-384 1983 $75

IRVING, WASHINGTON   The Lives of Mahomet and His Successors.
John Murray, 1850. 2 vols., 8vo, orig. cloth, blocked in blind,
spines faded, top of spine of vol. 2 repaired, top of spine and
lower joint of vol. 1 repaired. With 2 16-page pub.'s catalogues,
one at the end of vol. 1 dated January 1850, one at the end of vol. 2
dated April 1850. First edition published in England. Bickersteth
75-147 1983 £18

IRVING, WASHINGTON   New-Year Civilities. N.Y.: Privately
printed; Christmas, 1912. Marbled wraps. over boards. Argosy 714-385
1983 $25

IRVING, WASHINGTON   Old Christmas. Macmillan, 1876. 1st
edn. Illus. by Randolph Caldecott. Frontis. Dark green cloth gilt
designed by Caldecott, a.e.g. (lower corner sl. bumped, insc. verso
frontis.), v.g. copy. Hodgkins 27-456 1983 £16.50

IRVING, WASHINGTON   Rip Van Winkle. London: William Heinemann, 1905. First edition. Folio. Illus. by A. Rackham. Orig.
decorated vellum. One of 250 copies signed by Rackham. Ties torn off.
Endpapers a trifle foxed. In a cloth clipcase. Very good. MacManus
280-4327 1983 $1,200

IRVING, WASHINGTON   Rip Van Winkle. London: William Heinemann; N.Y.: Doubleday, Page & Co., 1905. First edition, second impression. Drawings by A. Rackham. 4to. Orig. pictorial cloth.
Signed by Rackham on the half-title. Bookplates on front endsheet.
Very good. MacManus 280-4304 1983 $450

IRVING, WASHINGTON   Rip Van Winkle. N.Y.: Dodd, 1895. 8vo.
Gilt pictorial vellum. Limited to 150 copies. Illus. with photogravures on Japan paper. Very good. Aleph-bet 8-143 1983 $30

IRVING, WASHINGTON   The Rocky Mountains. Philadelphia,
1837. 2 vols. 2 folding maps, orig. cloth, paper spine labels.
One label a bit rubbed, light foxing, else a very good set. First
edition. Felcone 22-101 1983 $300

IRVING, WASHINGTON   Selections from The Sketchbook. NY:
Crowell, (ca. 1905). Printed on fine, thin india paper. Bound in
blind and gilt-stamped suede. Fine. (2 1/4 x 1 5/8; 56x40mm).
Bromer 25-443 1983 $45

IRVING, WASHINGTON   The Sketch Book of Geoffrey Crayon...
No. III. New York: Van Winkle, 1819. Part Three only. 1st ed.,
state B of p. 240; wrapper state 2. Orig. tan printed wrappers,
uncut. Piece torn from corner of rear blank wrapper, some soiling
and chipping to spine and edges, else very good. Jenkins 155-667
1983 $100

IRVING, WASHINGTON   The Sketch-Book of Geoffrey Crayon.
N.Y.: G.P. Putnam's Sons, 1895. "Westminster Edition." 2 vols. Orig.
full leather with morocco spine labels and floral endpapers. One of
175 copies with proofs on India paper. Some of the illus. by Rackham.
Spines and covers rubbed and slightly soiled. Good. MacManus 280-
4329 1983 $150

IRVING, WASHINGTON   The Sketch-Book of Geoffrey Crayon.
N.Y.: G.P. Putnam's Sons, 1895. Van Tassel edition. 2 vols. Illus.
Orig. decorated cloth. Cloth dust jackets (rubbed). Illus. by
Rackham and others. Cont. inscription on front flyleaf of Vol. I.
White covers somewhat foxed. Very good. MacManus 280-4328 1983 $125

IRVING, WASHINGTON   The Sketch Book. Newnes, 1902 in 2 vols.
Edn. de luxe, limited to 100 signed & numbered copies with 2 frontis.
& 18 illus. by Edmund J. Sullivan. Jap. vellum backed boards, eps.
designed by Garth Jones, t.e.g. others uncut (free eps. discol'd,
bkstrips sl. discol'd), v.g. Hodgkins 27-459 1983 £40

IRVING, WASHINGTON   Tales of a Traveller. N.Y. & London:
G.P. Putnam's Sons, 1895. First of this edition. 2 vols. Illus.,
with several plates by A. Rackham. Orig. decorated cloth. Cloth dust
jacket (spines faded, covers a bit soiled and worn). Bookplate. Fine.
MacManus 280-4305 1983 $125

IRVING, WASHINGTON   A Tour on the Prairies. London, 1835.
8vo, fine calf, gilt spine with leather labels, marbled edges. First
edition. Argosy 710-536 1983 $125

IRVING, WASHINGTON   A Tour on the Prairies. Paris, 1835.
Second edition. Half morocco. Ginsberg 46-373 1983 $20

IRVING, WASHINGTON   Wolfert's Roost. And Other Papers Now
First Collected. New York: Putnam, 1855. Frontis. 1st ed., 1st
binding, later issue. Orig. green cloth, gilt. Presentation copy
with ink inscription on title: "F.J. Bush with compts of the Author."
Does not appear to be in Irving's hand. Gilt vignette on front
cover, no "Works" statement on spine, and publisher's address of
10 Park Place on title. Fine. Jenkins 155-664 1983 $125

IRVING, WASHINGTON   Works. N.Y., Putnam, n.d. (ca. 1890).
Hudson edition with the author's revisions. Illus. 3/4 brown
morocco over marbled boards, blind ruled spine, with gilt stamped
thistles. Fine. 27 vols. Houle 22-494 1983 $650

IRWIN, EYLES   Saint Thomas's Mount. London: Printed
for J. Dodsley...MDCCLXXIV. 4to, with half-title, new wraps. First
edition. Quaritch NS 7-65 1983 $225

IRWIN, EYLES   A series of adventures in the course of
a voyage up the Red Sea... London: J. Dodsley, 1787. Third edition.
2 vols. 8vo. 5 folding maps, 7 plates. Full red morocco gilt, a.e.g.
Rubbed, proof portrait added. Adelson Africa-93 1983 $375

IRWIN, WILL   The House that Shadows Built. Garden
City, Doubleday, 1928. First edition. Frontis. portrait and 14
plates. Pictorial dust jacket (small nicks). Very good - fine. Zane
Grey's copy with his library stamp. Houle 22-672 1983 $75

ISAACS, NICHOLAS PETER   Twenty Years Before the Mast. N.Y.,
1845. Orig. cloth. First edition. Ginsberg 46-374 1983 $65

ISABELLA: A Novel. London, 1823. 3 vols. 8vo. Rebound in cloth,
boards. Bookplate by Lord Gray in each vol. A vg-fine set. In Our
Time 156-25 1983 $100

ISARD, A. P.   The Model Shipbuilder's Manual. London,
1939. 8vo. Orig. cloth. Frontis. 2 plates, numerous illus. Orig.
dust jacket. Fine. Edwards 1042-84 1983 £18

ISBELL, F. A.   Mining & Hunting in the Far West 1852-
1870. Burlingame: 1948. 8vo, linen backed pictorial boards, paper
label. Upper corners lightly bumped. Perata 28-68 1983 $75

ISCHLONDSKY, NAUM EFIMOVICH (1896-?)   Neuropsychose Und Hirnrinde.
Berlin: Urban & Schwarzenberg, 1930. Two vols. 54 illus. Library
buckram, bookplates removed, stamp on rear paste-down. Gach 95-229
1983 $50

ISELLA, DANTE   Milano capitale nelle vedute di
Gasparo Galliari... Miladno: Edizioni Il Polifilo, 1975. 28
double-page color plates. Folio. Boards, 3/4 leather. Slipcase.
Printed at the Stamperia Valdonega. Ars Libri 33-153 1983 $85

ISHAM, NORMAN MORRISON   Early American Houses. N.p.: The
Walpole Society, 1928. Illus. with text diagrams & 33 plates.
Edition ltd. to 175 copies. Gray cloth over marbled boards;
paper spine label. Boards a bit shelf rubbed. Karmiole 71-59
1983 $75

ISHERWOOD, CHRISTOPHER   The Berlin Stories. (NY, 1945). Light
staining to cover and endpapers, else good in slightly frayed and
chipped still good dustwrapper that is rubbed along edges and has few
holes on rear panel. Quill & Brush 54-689 1983 $40

ISHERWOOD, CHRISTOPHER   Christopher and his Kind: 1929-1939.
London, 1977. First English edition. Slightly frayed dust wrapper.
Inscribed by author for B. Lehmann, dated Easter 1977. Very nice.
Rota 231-340 1983 £110

ISHERWOOD, CHRISTOPHER   The Condor and the Cows. L, (1949).
Edges slightly rubbed, otherwise very good in chipped and slightly
soiled dustwrapper. Quill & Brush 54-690 1983 $40

ISHERWOOD, CHRISTOPHER   Down There on a Visit. New York, 1962.
First edition. Dust wrapper. Author's later signed autograph inscription "for Nancy, with my best wishes". Very nice. Rota 231-337 1983
£60

ISHERWOOD, CHRISTOPHER   Journey to a War. New York, 1939.
First American edition, first binding. Covers somewhat worn and
shaken. Labels removed from front endpapers and rear endpapers
cracked at hinge. With Isherwood's autograph signature on the title-
page and his inscription "for Peter from Chris his gurubhai - April
1973." Good. Rota 231-335 1983 £50

ISHERWOOD, CHRISTOPHER   Lions and Shadows. London: The
Hogarth Press, 1938. First edition. 8vo. Frontis. Orig. cloth.
Dust jacket. Very fine copy. Jaffe 1-196 1983 $350

ISHERWOOD, CHRISTOPHER   Lions and Shadows. London: The Hogarth
Press, 1938. Blue cloth, printed in black. First edition, first
state of the binding. Slight offset from dust jacket, otherwise a very
fine copy in the first state dust jacket, which shows only the
slightest traces of use. Reese 20-549 1983 $225

ISHERWOOD, CHRISTOPHER   Lions and Shadows. Norfolk, Conn., 1947.
First American edition. Lower corners a little bruised. Frayed dust
wrapper. Very nice. Rota 230-309 1983 £15

ISHERWOOD, CHRISTOPHER   A Meeting by the River. New York, 1967.
First edition. Slightly frayed dust wrapper. Inscribed by author to
his brother, dated March 9 1967. Nice. Rota 231-339 1983 £180

ISHERWOOD, CHRISTOPHER   The Memorial; portrait of a family.
Hogarth Press, 1932. First edition. Orig. pale pink linen. Slightly
worn and frayed dust wrapper (designed by J. Banting). Pasted onto
the flyleaf is a slip bearing the typed legend "With the Aughor's
Compliments"; above the slip is the author's autograph inscription
(to his mother). Very good. Rota 231-333 1983 £475

ISHERWOOD, CHRISTOPHER   The Memorial. N, (1946). Top edge of
spine slightly sunned, very good or better in torn and moderately worn,
good dustwrapper. Quill & Brush 54-691 1983 $40

ISHERWOOD, CHRISTOPHER   The Memorial. Portrait of a Family.
London: The Hogarth Press, 1932. First edition. 8vo. Orig. cloth.
Dust jacket designed by John Banting. Very fine copy. Jaffe 1-193
1983 $350

ISHERWOOD, CHRISTOPHER   Mr. Norris Changes Trains. London,
1935. First edition. Head and tail of spine faded, outer hinges
slightly rubbed, prelims. lightly foxed, in a strengthened dustwrapper showing signs of wear on the edges and lacking small portions
at head and tail of spine. Very scarce in dustwrapper. Gekoski
2-89 1983 £225

ISHERWOOD, CHRISTOPHER   Mr. Norris Changes Trains. London:
The Hogarth Press, 1935. First edition. 8vo. Orig. cloth. Dust
jacket. Chipped and a tape-repaired jacket. Rare. Fine copy.
Jaffe 1-194 1983 $385

ISHERWOOD, CHRISTOPHER   On the Frontier. London, Faber &
Faber, (1938). First edition. Dust jacket (slight nicking and
soiling) else, very good. Houle 22-495 1983 $125

ISHERWOOD, CHRISTOPHER   A Penny for the Poor. New York, 1938.
First American edition. Isherwood's autograph signature on the title-
page. Very nice. Rota 231-342 1983 £70

ISHERWOOD, CHRISTOPHER   Prater Violet. New York, 1945. First edition. Covers somewhat faded and stained. Inscribed: "For John Michel from Christopher Isherwood." Internally a nice copy. Rota 231-336 1983 £75

ISHERWOOD, CHRISTOPHER   Sally Bowles. London: The Hogarth Press, 1937. First edition. Small 8vo. Orig. cloth. Dust jacket. 2040 copies printed. A few short tears to jacket, otherwise a fine copy. Rare. Jaffe 1-195 1983 $650

ISHERWOOD, CHRISTOPHER   Sally Bowles. Hogarth Press, 1937. First edition. Spine a little faded and rubbed. Author's cont. autograph signature on title-page. Very good. Rota 231-334 1983 £90

ISHERWOOD, CHRISTOPHER   A Single Man. New York, 1964. First edition. Slightly worn dust wrapper. Inscribed by author "for Ronny", dated June 1964. Nice. Rota 231-338 1983 £150

ISIDORUS HISPALENSIS   Entimologiae. (Augsburg): Gunther Zainer, 19 November 1472. Ff. (128), (145-154), (216), (223), and (263) are genuine cancels. Full-page woodcut table of ancestry, two full-page genealogical trees (all folded), and small woodcut world map. Initials supplied in red, the first one in blue. Folio, old calf. Worn. A few margins insignificantly stained. From the library of Harrison D. Horblit. Kraus 164-133 1983 $28,000

ISNARD, MAXIMIM   Isnard & Freron. Paris: de l'Imprimerie Du Pont, AN IV (1796). First edition. 8vo, wrapper, very good. Fenning 61-217 1983 £12.50

ISOUARD, NICOLO   Les Rendez-Foux Bourgeois. Paris, Brandus & Cie, n.d. (1869). 2 leaves, engraved music, plate #5198. Tall 4to, new wrs. Salloch 387-102 1983 $140

ISSAVERDENS, J.   Armenia and the Armenians. Venice: Armenian Monastery of St. Lazarus, 1874. First edition. Sm.8vo. Orig. printed wrappers. Good. Edwards 1044-383 1983 £85

ISTVANFFI, G.   A Clusius Codex Mykologiai Meltatasa - Etudes et commentaires sur le Code de l'Escluse. Budapest, privately printed, (18938) 1900. Folio, cloth, original front wrapper bound in, coloured plates. Rare. Wheldon 160-51 1983 £185

THE ITALIAN in America. NY, 1905. Illus. Ex lib. Argosy 716-150 1983 $25

IVANOFF, NICOLA   Francesco Maffei. Padova: "Le Tre Venezie", 1942. 65 plates. Small 4to. Cloth. Ars Libri 33-208 1983 $40

IVANOVSKY, ELIZABETH   Deux Contes Russes. Paris, n.d., (ca. 1931). Sq. 4to. Cloth backed pictorial boards. Covers somewhat soiled. Faint stain in blank margin of first few pages. Each page illus. with color lithographs. Very good. Aleph-bet 8-144 1983 $35

IVES, CHARLES   Chips from the Workshops, Parnassus... and Other Poems. New Haven, 1843. 12mo, orig. stamped cloth, (lightly foxed). Argosy 716-420 1983 $35

IVES, CHARLES   Second Pianoforte Sonata. New York, 1947. 2nd edition, folio, wrs. Salloch 387-103 1983 $75

IVISON, BLAKEMAN   The New States. N.Y., 1889. Folded colored map. Orig. wraps. bound in cloth. Ginsberg 47-390 1983 $75

IVY, ROBERT H.   Interpretations of Dental & Maxillary Roentgenorgrams. St. Louis, 1918. First edition. 259 illus., many from orig. x-rays. Thin 8vo, cloth. Argosy 713-290 1983 $30

IZCUE, ELENA   El Arte Peruano en la Escuela, L'Art perunvien a l'ecole. (Paris, 1926). Many plates, some in color. Thin 4to, loose pages in pr. pict. bds., tied. 1st ed. Argosy 710-504 1983 $45

J

JACK and the queen killers. London: T. Dolby; J. Fairburn, 1820. First edition. 8vo. Disbound. Engraved portrait, and several woodcuts. Ximenes 63-498 1983 $45

JACKSON, A. Y. The Far North. Toronto: Raus & Mann, nd (c. 1928). 17 plates. Limited to 1000 copies. Jacket over boards. Binding poor, edges water stained, working copy. McGahern 53-82 1983 $25

JACKSON, ALFRED Tints from an Amateur's Palette. 1849. First edition. Orig. red cloth sl. rubbed. Jarndyce 30-157 1983 £12.50

JACKSON, ALFRED T. Diary of a Forty-Niner. Boston, 1920. 2nd ed. Map. Clark 741-88 1983 $35

JACKSON, ANDREW Correspondence Between...on the Seminole War. Wash., 1831. Sewed, (very closely cropped fore-edge but legible). Argosy 716-437 1983 $100

JACKSON, ANDREW Messages. Concord, N.H., 1837. 1st ed. Portrait. Small 8vo. Ex-library with no external marks, end of spine frayed. Morrill 286-214 1983 $27.50

JACKSON, ANDREW Seminole Hostilities. Wash., 1836. Cloth with leather label. First edition. Ginsberg 46-684 1983 $100

JACKSON, CHARLES JAMES English Goldsmiths and Their Marks. London, 1921. Facs. 2nd ed. Revised & enlarged. 4to. Morrill 288-619 1983 $50

JACKSON, CHARLES T. Report Upon the Property of the Abercrombie Gold Mining Co. Boston, 1863. Orig. printed wraps. First edition. Ginsberg 46-849 1983 $50

JACKSON, CHARLES T. Second Annual Report on the Geology of the Public Lands, Belonging to the Two States of Maine and Massachusetts. Augusta, 1838. Illus. 8vo, later buckram, plates. Morrill 286-637 1983 $25

JACKSON, CHARLES T. Third Annual Report on the Geology of the State of Maine. Augusta, 1839. Text illus. 8vo, orig. wrappers. Scotch tape marks on spine. Morrill 286-269 1983 $20

JACKSON, CHEVALIER The Life of Chevalier Jackson - An Autobiography. New York, 1938. First edition. 8vo. Orig. binding. Dust wrapper. Autographed by the author. Fye H-3-804 1983 $45

JACKSON, DONALD Johann Amerbach. Iowa City: The Prairie Press, 1956. Small 4to. 4to. 2 vols. One of a few sets bound in Rives China, handmade in France. Orig. page printed by Amerbach taken from Lectura Super Quinque Libros Decretalium... Fine. Oak Knoll 48-10 1983 $75

JACKSON, GEORGE PULLEN White Spirituals in the Southern Uplands. Chapel Hill: University of North Carolina Press, 1933. Illus. with 34 plates. This copy with a long presentation inscription to "Mrs. Franklin D. Roosevelt," signed by Jackson. And with Eleanor Roosevelt's engraved bookplate and her library bookplate. Red cloth. T.e.g. With small markin on spine from Mrs. Roosevelt's library. Karmiole 71-108 1983 $100

JACKSON, HELEN HUNT Ramona, A Story. Boston: Roberts Bros., 1884. First edition. 4 pages of ads. Red decorated cloth. Dawson 471-132 1983 $100

JACKSON, HELEN HUNT Ramona. Limited Editions Club, 1959. Special ed., limited to 1500 copies printed at the Plantin Press, and signed by the illustrator, E.G. Jackson. Very scarce to rare. Fine copy in publisher's slipcase. Jenkins 155-811 1983 $125

JACKSON, HELEN HUNT Ramona. Boston, Little Brown, 1900. First edition thus. Color frontis. and 23 plates on Japan vellum by Henry Sandham. Half green morocco over suede, spines ornately decorated in art deco style with floral motifs, suede covers decorated to match, t.e.g., uncut, (spines faded to a lustrous brown). One of 500 deluxe copies. 2 vols. Very good-fine. Houle 22-500 1983 $95

JACKSON, HOLBROOK The Anatomy of Bibliomania. London: The Soncino Press, 1931. First edition. 8vo. Red cloth. 2 vols. Dust jackets. Limited to 1048 copies. Jackets slightly soiled, chipped at spine ends. Oak Knoll 48-226 1983 $275

JACKSON, HOLBROOK The Anatomy of Bibliomania. London: Soncino Press, 1931. Two vols. Cloth. First edition. One of 1,000 sets. Some scattered foxing, and residue of private bookplates, still a very good to fine set. Reese 20-550 1983 $135

JACKSON, HOLBROOK The Anatomy of Bibliomania. NY: Scribner's, 1932. Third edition. Thick 8vo, fine copy in dust jacket. Karmiole 73-18 1983 $40

JACKSON, HOLBROOK The Anatomy of Bibliomania. Faber, 1950. 8vo, orig. cloth. Fenning 62-190 1983 £10.50

JACKSON, HOLBROOK The Fear of Books. London, 1932. First edition. One of 2000 numbered copies. Repaired and worn dust wrapper. ALS dated April 1944, from Jackson, in which he describes Oxford in wartime. Fine. Rota 231-345 1983 £40

JACKSON, HOLBROOK The Printing of Books. London, 1938. First edition. Illus. Repaired dust wrapper. Author's signed autograph presentation inscription, dated 23rd November 1938. Fine. Rota 231-346 1983 £45

JACKSON, HOLBROOK The Reading of Books. London, Faber & Faber, (1946). First edition. Dust jacket (slight rubbing). Very good. Houle 22-499 1983 $35

JACKSON, HOLBROOK Town. London: A.T. Stevens for Flying Fame, 1913. First edition. Illus. by C.L. Fraser. Orig. decorated wrappers. Spine and covers slightly faded and worn. Near-fine. MacManus 279-2947 1983 $35

JACKSON, HOLBROOK William Morris, Craftsman and Socialist. London: A.C. Fifield, 1908. First edition. 8vo. Cloth-backed boards. Inscription in ink on front free endpaper, else fine. Scarce. Oak Knoll 49-246 1983 $50

JACKSON, JAMES A Memoir... Boston, 1835. First edition. 8vo. Orig. binding. Ex-library. Fine. Fye H-3-807 1983 $125

JACKSON, JAMES Memoir. Boston, 1836. 1st ed. Early American embossed binding, signed by B(enjamin) Bradley, Boston bookbinder. 12mo. Orig. embossed cloth binding. Spine faded. Morrill 289-118 1983 $30

JACKSON, JOHN Case of John Jackson, patentee of the Edinburgh Theatre-Royal. (Edinburgh: 1786). Folio, wrappers, 1st edition. A little dusty at the beginning and end. Very rare. Ximenes 64-318 1983 $375

JACKSON, JOHN Reflections on the commerce of the Mediterranean... London: Clarke, 1804. First edition. 8vo. Cont. half calf, spine gilt. Slightly rubbed. Ximenes 63-598 1983 $225

JACKSON, JOHN HUGHLINGS Neurological Fragments. Oxford, 1925. Tall 8vo, cloth, bottom of spine chewed. Argosy 713-291 1983 $75

JACKSON, JOHN HUGHLINGS Selected Writings. London, 1931-2. First edition. Argosy 713-292 1983 $125

JACKSON, JOSEPH HENRY   Anybody's Gold, the Story of California's
Mining Towns. NY (1941). Illus by E. H. Suydam. Dw. Argosy 710-36
1983 $35

JACKSON, JOSEPH HENRY   Bad Company: The Story of
California's Legendary and Actual Stage Robbers, Bandits, Highwaymen,
and Outlaws... N.Y., Harcourt, (1949). First edition. Illus. Dust
jacket. Signed by the author. Very good - fine. Houle 22-1115 1983
$45

JACKSON, JOSEPH HENRY   Gold Rush Album. New York: Charles
Scribner's Sons, 1949. Illus. 1st ed. Jenkins 153-279 1983 $35

JACKSON, JOSEPH HENRY   A History of "The Grapes of Wrath."
New York: Limited Editions Club, (1940). First edition, second
printing. With Thomas Hart Benton illustrations. One of 3,000. Four
times as scarce as the first printing. Fine. Bradley 65-176 1983
$50

JACKSON, JOSEPH HENRY   Tintypes in Gold. N.Y., MacMillian,
1939. First edition. Decorations by Giacomo Patri. Dust jacket.
Signed and with lengthly inscription by the author, 8/31/1939. Fine.
Houle 22-1116 1983 $50

JACKSON, JOSEPH HENRY   Tintypes in Gold Four Studies in
Robbery. New York, 1939. Illus. 1st ed. Jenkins 153-280 1983 $35

JACKSON, JOSEPH HENRY   Tintypes in Gold. New York, 1939.
Clark 741-124 1983 $21

JACKSON, MARY ANNA   Memoirs of Stonewall Jackson. Louisville, Ky., 1895. First edition. Thick imperial 8vo. Orig. green
decorated cloth. Portrait frontis., 15 plates, 5 full page and 9 other
illus. Gilt. Very slightly soiled and faded. Good. Edwards 1042-
218 1983 £60

JACKSON, MARY CATHERINE   Word-sketches of the sweet south.
London: Bentley, 1873. First edition. 8vo. Orig. brown cloth.
A fine copy. Ximenes 63-626 1983 $45

JACKSON, MASON   The Pictorial Press. Its Origin and
Progress. Hurst and Blackett, 1885. First edition, large 8vo,
150 facsimile woodcut illustrations, uncut in original green cloth
gilt, fore-edges spotted, upper inner hinge tender, otherwise an
excellent copy. Deighton 3-182 1983 £45

JACKSON, THOMAS W.   On a Slow Train Through Arkansas.
Chicago, (1903). 1st ed. Later cloth, morocco label. Pictorial
wrappers present in facsimile. Illus. Jenkins 153-18 1983 $45

JACKSON, THOMAS W.   Through Missouri on a Mule: "Worse
than Arkansas" All Knew. Chicago, 1904. 1st ed. Original pictorial
wrappers (lacks back wrapper). Illus. Jenkins 151-224 1983 $35

JACKSON, WILLIAM   The Deliverance of Israel from Babylon.
London, Sacred Music Warehouse J. Alfred Novello, n.d. (1845?).
Title page advertises the availibility of single parts for voices and
instruments, but no full score. Engraved title, 4 pp. contents and
text of the oratorio, engraved music. Folio, new cloth with leather
label. Salloch 387-104 1983 $150

JACKSON, WILLIAM   Eulogium, on the Character of General
Washington... Phila.: John Ormrod, 1800. 3/4 calf, by Baynton.
Fine. Felcone 20-187 1983 $75

JACOB, GILES   The Law-Dictionary. New York: I. Riley;
Phila.: P. Byrne (Fry & Kammerer, pr.), 1811. First American edition.
6 vols. Full calf (broken and in need of rebinding). Felcone 20-86
1983 $50

JACOB, GILES   The Poetical Register. London: for
E. Curll, 1719. First edition. 8vo. Cont. speckled calf, gilt.
Traylen 94-455 1983 £48

JACOB, GILES   A Treatise of Laws. T. Woodward & J.
Peele, 1721. Calf, leading hinge slightly weakened, maroon label,
v.g. Jarndyce 31-44 1983 £46

JACOB, HILDEBRAND   The Fatal Constancy. London; printed
for J. Tonson, 1723. 1st ed., 8vo, advertisements, a good copy
in wrappers. Pickering & Chatto 19-32 1983 $350

JACOB, JOHN J.   A Biographical Sketch of the Life of the
Late Captain Michael Cresap. Cincinnati, 1866. Large paper edition.
Modern black pebbled cloth. Very fine. Bradley 66-522 1983 $100

JACOBI, CARL   Revelations in Black. Sauk City: Arkham House, 1947. First edition. Cloth. Very fine copy in dust
jacket. Bradley 66-122 1983 $35

JACOBI, CHARLES T.   Some Notes on Books and Printing.
Chiswick Press, 1892. First edition, tall 8vo, uncut in original
straw buckram lettered in red, binding a bit soiled and upper hinge
with split. Author's presentation copy inscribed: "W. Stirling Esq.
from the Author". Deighton 3-183 1983 £55

JACOBS, JOSEPH   Celtic Fairy Tales. David Nutt, 1892.
Sq. 8vo. Frontis. Title vignette. 7 plates & 65 text illus. Green
decorated cloth. Greer 39-25 1983 £25

JACOBS, JOSEPH   The Jews of Angevin England. New York,
1893. Illus. Small 8vo, ex-library. Morrill 288-203 1983 $25

JACOBS, JOSEPH   More Celtic Fairy Tales. David Nutt,
1894. Frontis. 7 plates & 55 text illus. Green decorated cloth.
Greer 39-24 1983 £25

JACOBS, WILLIAM WYMARK   Deep Waters. London: Hodder & Stoughton, (1919). First edition. Orig. pictorial cloth. Fine. MacManus
279-2950 1983 $20

JACOBS, WILLIAM WYMARK   The Skipper's Wooing. London: Pearson,
1897. First edition. Orig. cloth. MacManus 279-2958 1983 $25

JACOBY, HELMUT   Architectural Drawings. Thames and
Hudson, 1967. Second impression, with 80 full-page, double-page
and other illus. 4to, orig. cloth. Fenning 62-191 1983 £15

JACOMB, THOMAS   The Active and Publick Spirit Handled
in a Sermon Preached at Paul's October 26th, 1656. London, T.R. for
Philemon Stephens, 1657. Small 4to, errata slip pasted on verso of A
(4). 3/4 brown morocco in cont. style, spine stamped in gilt. Very
good. Houle 22-502 1983 $85

JACOPO Palma Il Giovane. Milano: Istituto Editoriale Italiano,
1963. 121 plates. 4 text illus. Small folio. Cloth. Ars Libri
33-262 1983 $45

JACQUE, FREDERIC   Le livre d'or de J.-F. Millet par un
ancien ami. Paris/London: A. Ferroud/E. Benezit-Constant/ Harry
G. Dickens, 1891. 12 orig. etchings by Jacque. 5 etched illus.
in text. Tissue guards. Large 4to. Wrappers. Uncut. No. 52,
on hollande teinte, of a limited edition of 500 copies only. Light
external wear. Backstrip reinforced. Ars Libri 32-456 1983 $285

JACQUES, FLORENCE PAGE   Canoe Country. Minneapolis: Un.
Minnesota Press, (1938). 4to. Illus. from wood-cut illus. by
Francis Lee Jacques. Very good in frayed dust jacket. McGahern
53-85 1983 $25

JACQUIN, N. J.   Examen Chemicum Doctrinae Meyerianae
de Acido Pingui... Vienna: J.P. Kraus, 1769. 8vo. Stitched,
uncut. Gurney 90-65 1983 £80

JAEGER, JOSEPH NICOLAUS   Seelenheilkunde Gestuetzt Auf Psycho-
logische Grundsaetze. Leipzig: F. A. Brockhaus, 1846. Second edition.
Orig. boards, leather label, library bookplate and spine label. Adolf
Meyer's copy inscribed in his hand on front flyleaf "(?) Meyeri
libris". Gach 95-231 1983 $75

JAEGER, WERNER   Aristotle. Oxford, 1934. 8vo, cloth.
Salloch 385-476 1983 $35

JAEGER, WERNER   Paideia. Berlin, 1936. Second edition.
4to, cloth. Salloch 385-127 1983 $20

JAEGER, WERNER   Paideia. NY, 1943-1944. Vols. II & III.
8vo, cloth. Salloch 385-128 1983 $32

JAFFE, BERNARD   Crucibles. The Lives and Achievements
of the Great Chemists. London, 1931. 8vo. Cloth. 24 plates.
Gurney JJ-193 1983 £15

JAHRBUCH Fuer Psychoanalytische und Psychopathologische Forschungen.
Leipzig/Vienna: Deuticke, 1910. Two parts. Band II Modern cloth
retaining orig. wrappers. Gach 95-232 1983 $150

JAHRBUCH Fuer Psychoanalytische und Psychopathologische Forschungen.
Vienna/Leipzig: Deuticke, 1912. Band IV. Orig. wrappers, detached
and worn. Unopened copies. Gach 95-233 1983 $125

JAHRBUCH Fuer Psychoanalytische und Psychopathologische Forschungen.
Leipzig/Vienna: Deuticke, 1913. Band V. Modern cloth, preserving
orig. wrappers. Front wrapper detached to first volume in fine,
unopened condition. Gach 95-234 1983 $150

JAHRBUCH Fuer Psychoanalytische und Psychopathologische Forschungen.
Leipzig/Wien: Deuticke, 1914. Band VI. Very good copy rebound in
modern black cloth, orig. front wrapper preserved. Gach 95-235 1983
$150

JAKOB, CHRISTFRIED   Atlas of the Nervous System. Phila.,
1901. 112 colored lithograph figures & 139 other illus., many in
color. Thick 8vo, first edition in English. Argosy 713-293 1983
$45

JAKOB, CHRISTFRIED   An Atlas of the Normal and Pathological
Nervous System. NY: William Wood & Co., 1896. Thick 12mo. Publisher's green cloth. First edition in English. Library bookplate
and spine lable. 78 lithographed plates, many in color. Gach 95-230
1983 $30

JALAS, J.   Atlas Florae Europeae, Distribution of
Vascular Plants in Europe. Helsinki, 1972-80. Vols. 1 to 5,
numerous maps, 4to, sewed. Wheldon 160-1647 1983 £45

JAMES II, KING OF ENGLAND   His Majesties Gracious Declaration...
London: by Charles Bill..., 1687. Folio. Wrappers. Heath 48-132
1983 £25

JAMES, ANNA B.   Sketches in Canada... London: Longman,
Brown, Green and Longmans, 1852. 12cm. Bound in half dark green
crushed morocco, gilt titles and blind dec. on the spine, marbled
boards and endpapers. A fine copy. McGahern 53-84 1983 $85

JAMES, F. L.   The Wild Tribes of the Soudan. London,
1884. Second edition. Folding map, 21 plates. Sm.8vo. Ex-library.
Orig. cloth. Good. Edwards 1044-385 1983 £40

JAMES, GEORGE PAYNE RAINSFORD   Attila: A Romance. New York, 1837.
2 vols. 1st American ed. Paper label on vol. 1 is worn, else very
good. In Our Time 156-430 1983 $20

JAMES, GEORGE PAYNE RAINSFORD   Charles Tyrrell. Richard Bentley,
1839. First ed., with engraved portrait, possibly wanting half title,
large 12mo., contemporary half green calf, with red label. Fenning
61-219 1983 £24.50

JAMES, GEORGE PAYNE RAINSFORD   The Commissioner. Dublin, W. Curry,
1843. First ed., with 28 plates by Phiz, 8vo., orig. green cloth,
binding little rubbed but sound, little foxing of the plates, very
good. Fenning 60-203 1983 £24.50

JAMES, GEORGE PAYNE RAINSFORD   La Coquetterie. T. & W. Boone,
1832. First edition, 3 vols., half green calf, a little rubbed and
small nick from following hinge vol. III. Generally very good.
Jarndyce 30-436 1983 £48

JAMES, GEORGE PAYNE RAINSFORD   Forest Days. Saunders and Otley,
1843. First ed., without the half-titles, 3 vols., 8vo., contemporary
half calf, gilt spines, spines little worn, sound and otherwise very
good copy, with binder's ticket of I. N. Pearce of Liverpool in each
vol. Fenning 60-204 1983 £32.50

JAMES, GEORGE PAYNE RAINSFORD   The Gipsy. Longman, etc., 1835.
First edition, 3 vols. Half blue calf, brown labels, v.g. Jarndyce
30-437 1983 £48

JAMES, GEORGE PAYNE RAINSFORD   Henry Masterton. Henry Colburn and
Richard Bentley, 1832. First ed., 3 vols., 12mo., has all half titles
but lacks final leaf of vol. III. Contemporary half calf, gilt spines,
by Mackenzie. Hannas 69-113 1983 £30

JAMES, GEORGE PAYNE RAINSFORD   A History of Richard Coeur-de-Lion
King of England. London, Saunders & Oatley, 1842-49. First edition.
Half titles. 3/4 crimson calf over marbled boards, spines richly
decorated in gilt, contrasting plum and green leather spine labels,
t.e.g., marbled endpapers. 4 vols. Very good. Houle 22-503 1983
$200

JAMES, GEORGE PAYNE RAINSFORD   History of the Life of Edward the
Black Prince. London, Longman, 1836. First ed., folding map, bound to
match Houle cat. number 21-443 in three quarter red calf over marbled
boards. 2 vols. very good. Houle 21-444 1983 $200

JAMES, GEORGE PAYNE RAINSFORD   A History of the Life of Edward the
Black Prince. London, Longman, et. al., 1836. First edition. Folding
map, 3/4 crimson calf over marbled boards, spine richly decorated
in gilt, contrasting plum and green leather spine labels, t.e.g.,
marbled endpapers (lightly rubbed). 2 vols. Very good. Houle 22-504
1983 $125

JAMES, GEORGE PAYNE RAINSFORD   Memoirs of Great Commanders. London,
1832. 3 vols., 8vo., orig. cloth, contemporary half calf, marbled
boards. Slightly scuffed. Joints worn. Ownership inscriptions on
front pastedown endpapers. Occasional slight foxing. Good. Edwards
1042-372 1983 £60

JAMES, GEORGE PAYNE RAINSFORD   Morley Ernstein. Saunders & Otley,
1842. First edition, 3 vols., half title, 2 pp ads. vol. I, 4 pp
ads. vol. II. Orig. boards, blue cloth spines, paper labels, v.g.
Jarndyce 30-438 1983 £68

JAMES, GEORGE PAYNE RAINSFORD   Rose D'Albret. Richard Bentley,
1844. First edition, 3 vols. Half titles. Orig. boards, cloth
spines, paper labels. Some wear to boards, otherwise v.g.
Jarndyce 30-439 1983 £48

JAMES, GEORGE WHARTON   Date Culture in Southern California.
Los Angeles: Out West, n.d. (after 1912). Wrappers. One margin
damaged during binding. Dawson 471-159 1983 $20

JAMES, GEORGE WHARTON   Fremont in California. Los Angeles:
Fremont Hotel, 1903. Illus. Wrappers. Dawsons 471-135 1983 $25

JAMES, GEORGE WHARTON   The Grand Canyon of Arizona. London:
T. Fisher Unwin, 1911. Plates and maps, some folding. Cloth, somewhat used. Pencil notes. Endpapers browned. English issue with cancel title, title page blindstamped "Presentation." Dawson 471-136
1983 $20

JAMES, GEORGE WHARTON   Heroes of California. Boston: Little,
Brown, 1910. Plates. Cloth. Dawson 471-137 1983 $25

JAMES, GEORGE WHARTON   In & Around the Grand Canyon. Boston:
Little, Brown, 1911. Plates and maps. Cloth. Call number effaced
from spine. Bookplate and rubber stamp of the Theosophical University
Raja Yoga Library, Point Loma, California. Dawson 471-139 1983 $20

JAMES, GEORGE WHARTON   In and Out of the Missions of California.
Boston: Little, Brown, 1906. 66 plates and page of ads. Cloth.
T.e.g. Signed and inscribed by author. Dawson 471-140 1983 $35

JAMES, GEORGE WHARTON   Indian Basketry. NY: Henry Malkan,
1902. Tall 8vo, green gilt-stamped cloth, lightly soiled. Some
foxing to half-title and final page of index. Karmiole 76-59 1983
$50

JAMES, GEORGE WHARTON   Indian Basketry and How to Make Indian
and Other Baskets. Boston: Privately Printed, 1903. 2 vols. in 1.
Ca. 600 illus. Small 4to. Cloth. Slightly worn. Ars Libri 34-290
1983 $85

JAMES, GEORGE WHARTON   Indian Blankets and Their Makers.
Chicago: A. C. McClurg & Co., 1920. (ca. 1914). 4to, 254 illus.
Orig. dec. cloth. Karmiole 76-60 1983 $100

JAMES, GEORGE WHARTON   Indian Blankets and Their Makers.
New York: Tudor, 1937. 254 illus. (partly in color). 4to. Cloth.
Ars Libri 34-291 1983 $85

JAMES, GEORGE WHARTON   The Indians of the Painted Desert Region.
Boston: Little, Brown, 1903. Plates. Cloth. Few margins stained.
Very good. Dawson 471-141 1983 $30

JAMES, GEORGE WHARTON   Mount Lowe Railway. Pasadena: Mount
Lowe Railway, (1893). Wrappers. Outer leaves detached and chipped.
Dawson 471-144 1983 $75

JAMES, GEORGE WHARTON   The 1910 Trip of the H.M.M.B.A. San
Francisco: Press of Bolte & Braden Co., 1911. Ads. Cloth. Stamped
in gold on front cover, "Compliments of the Palace and Fairmont Hotels,
San Francisco." Dawson 471-145 1983 $25

JAMES, GEORGE WHARTON   Old Missions and Mission Indians of California. Los Angeles: B.R. Baumgardt, 1895. Cloth. A little soiled.
Dawson 471-146 1983 $45

JAMES, GEORGE WHARTON   The Old Missions of California. Kansas
City: Fred Harvey, n.d. (ca.1906). Wrappers, a little soiled. Some
marginal tears repaired with tape. Dawson 471-147 1983 $25

JAMES, GEORGE WHARTON   Our American Wonderlands. Chicago: A.C.
McClurg, 1920. Reprint. Plates. Cloth. Dawson 471-148 1983 $30

JAMES, GEORGE WHARTON   Picturesque Pala. Pasadena: Radiant
Life Press, 1916. Plates (one present in duplicate). Wrappers,
a little soiled, foxed and chipped. Dawson 471-149 1983 $25

JAMES, GEORGE WHARTON   Quit Your Worrying! Pasadena: Radiant
Life Press, 1916. Ads. Cloth in somewhat used dust wrapper. Dawson
471-150 1983 $20

JAMES, GEORGE WHARTON   The Story of Scraggles. Boston: Little,
Brown, 1906. Plates. Cloth. Dawson 471-154 1983 $20

JAMES, GEORGE WHARTON   What the White Race May Learn from the
Indian. Chicago: Forbes & Co., 1908. Cloth in tattered dust wrapper.
Inscription signed by James. Dawson 471-156 1983 $50

JAMES, GEORGE WHARTON   Winter Sports at Huntington Lake Lodge
in the High Sierras. Pasadena: Radiant Life Press, 1916. Plates.
Wrapper, chipped. Dawson 471-158 1983 $25

JAMES, GEORGE WHARTON   The Wonders of the Colorado Desert...
Its Rivers and Its Mountains, Its Canyons and Its Springs. Boston:
Little, Brown, and Co., 1907. 2 vols., t.e.g., profusely illustrated.
Jenkins 151-147 1983 $75

JAMES, GRACE   Green Willow & Other Japanese Fairy Tales.
MacMillan, 1910. 4to. Mounted colour frontis. 39 mounted colour
plates. Blue cloth pictorial, gilt. Greer 40-102 1983 £60

JAMES, HENRY   Abstracts of the Principal Lines of
Spirit Levelling in England and Wales. London: by Order of the Secretary of State for War, 1861. First ed., 2 vols., 4to, engr. map,
24 double-page engr. plates, orig. blue embossed cloth, lettered in
gilt on spines, some chaffing of cover of volume 1, cover of plates
volume little faded and stained. Deighton 3-184 1983 £175

JAMES, HENRY   Abstracts of the Principal Lines of
Spirit Levelling in Scotland. London: by Order of the Secretary
of State for War, 1861. First edition, 1 vol. only (lacks the plates
volume), 4to, engraved front. map, original blue embossed cloth,
lettered in gilt on spine, head of spine defective. Deighton 3-185
1983 £50

JAMES, HENRY   The Ambassadors. Methuen, 1903.
First edition, half title, 38 pp cata. Orig. scarlet cloth, v.g.
Jarndyce 31-750 1983 £20

JAMES, HENRY   The American Novels and Stories of
Henry James. N.Y., 1947. First edition. Argosy 714-386 1983
$25

JAMES, HENRY   The Aspern Papers. London & New York:
MacMillan, 1888. First American edition. Orig. blue cloth, gilt.
Bottom of spine lightly frayed, else a nice copy. Jenkins 155-669
1983 $90

JAMES, HENRY   The Better Sort. London, 1903. First
edition. Remainder binding in blue cloth. Edges of leaves a little
foxed. Very nice. Rota 230-312 1983 £20

JAMES, HENRY   The Bostonians. London, 1886. Second
(first One-Volume) edition. Front hinge weak and covers a little
stained. Good. Rota 230-311 1983 £40

JAMES, HENRY   Charles W. Eliot President of Harvard
University 1869-1909. Boston, 1930. 2 vols. First edition. 8vo.
Orig. binding. Backstrip faded. Fye H-3-736 1983 $35

JAMES, HENRY   The Complete Plays. Phila., (1949).
First edition. Argosy 714-388 1983 $25

JAMES, HENRY   Confidence. Boston: Houghton, Osgood,
1880. First edition, first binding. Orig. green cloth, gilt. Very
fine with the exception of light tape stains at upper and lower edges
of free end papers. Jenkins 155-700 1983 $165

JAMES, HENRY   Daisy Miller... London, Macmillan, 1879.
2 vols. 12mo. ads. Orig. blue cloth. 1st English ed., state 2 of
vol. II. Corners bumped, extremities of spines chipped, few spots on
front cover of vol. II, endleaves bit browned. Good copy of this
scarce ed. O'Neal 50-113 1983 $100

JAMES, HENRY   Embarrassments. N.Y., 1896. First
American edition. Red cloth, somewhat rubbed. Clipped signature
of James, with a few words from a letter, pasted on front flyleaf.
Argosy 714-389 1983 $75

JAMES, HENRY   The Europeans. Boston: Houghton,
Osgood, 1879. 1st ed., 1st printing. Orig. light green cloth,
gilt. Some ink stains on lower portion of front cover, else very
good. Jenkins 155-701 1983 $125

JAMES, HENRY   French Poets and Novelists. London,
1878. First edition. 8vo, cloth; minor binding wear; inner hinge
frayed; owner's bookplate & signature. Argosy 714-390 1983 $75

JAMES, HENRY   Great Streets of the World. New York:
Scribners, 1892. Frontis., illus. 1st ed., 1st binding. Orig.
blue cloth, gilt, t.e.g. Extremely fine copy. Jenkins 155-711 1983
$110

JAMES, HENRY   In the Cage. Chicago & New York:
Herbert S. Stone, 1898. 1st American edition. A very fine copy.
Trebizond 18-58 1983 $125

JAMES, HENRY   In the Cage. Chicago: Herbert S.
Stone & Co., 1898. First edition. In orig. dec. gilt-stamped gray
cloth. T.e.g. Karmiole 74-61 1983 $50

JAMES, HENRY   In the Cage. Chicago: Herbert Stone,
1898. 1st American ed. Orig. slate cloth, fully gilt, t.e.g.,
others uncut. A very fine copy. Jenkins 155-702 1983 $125

JAMES, HENRY   Julia Bride. New York & London: 1909.
1st ed. Orig. red cloth, gilt, t.e.g., uncut. Fine copy of this
separate printing in the first state of binding. Jenkins 155-703
1983 $50

JAMES, HENRY   A Letter to Mrs. Linton. (Cambridge,
n.d.). Sq. 16mo, decorative wraps. Privately printed by G.P.
Winship. Argosy 714-391 1983 $75

JAMES, HENRY   Master Eustace. New York, 1920. 8vo.
Cloth. This copy stamped "review copy" on the front flyleaf. A vg-
fine copy. In Our Time 156-432 1983 $150

JAMES, HENRY   Master Eustace. N.Y., 1920. First
edition. Argosy 714-393 1983 $40

JAMES, HENRY   A Most Unholy Trade. (n.p.): Scarab
Press, Privately Printed, 1923. 1st ed., 1 of 100 copies. Orig.
cloth-backed pictorial boards, tissue dj, with complimentary pres.
card laid in. Frontispiece and cover design by Waldo Murray. Seldom
seen with the dj and card present. Mint copy of very rare book.
Jenkins 155-704 1983 $300

JAMES, HENRY   "A Most Unholy Trade" Being Letters on
the Drama. (Cambridge, Mass.), Scarab Press, Privately Printed, 1923.
16mo. Tipped-in portrait of James by Waldo Murray, who also designed
the cover. Cloth-backed pictorial boards. 1st ed., 1st state. 1 of
100 numbered copies. Some chipping to paper at top of front board.
Very good. O'Neal 50-114 1983 $150

JAMES, HENRY   Notes and Reviews. Cambridge: Dunster
House, 1921. 1st trade ed. Orig. cloth-backed boards, gilt, uncut.
Fine copy. Jenkins 155-705 1983 $50

JAMES, HENRY   Notes on Novelists with Some Other
Notes. N.Y., 1914. First American edition. Thick 8vo, sateen cloth,
g.t. Argosy 714-394 1983 $40

JAMES, HENRY   Novels and Tales. N.Y., Scribner,
1907-1917. New York edition. Frontis. gravures by Alvin Langdon
Coburn. Orig. plum cloth (spines a bit faded), t.e.g., uncut.
A very good set complete in 26 vols. Houle 21-446 1983 $1,450

JAMES, HENRY   The Novels and Tales. N.Y., 1907-9.
Limited first edition. Thick 8vo, cream 1/2 buckram, paper sides;
leather labels. One of 156 copies, on handmade paper. Argosy 714-
395 1983 $850

JAMES, HENRY   The Portrait of a Lady. N.Y., Modern
Library, (1936). First edition thus (so stated). Small 8vo, dust
jacket (slight rubbing and nicking) else, very good. Houle 22-505
1983 $30

JAMES, HENRY   The Prefaces of Henry James. Paris:
Jouve, 1931. First edition, half title, front. Orig. cream printed
wraps., end papers strengthened. Jarndyce 31-751 1983 £14.50

JAMES, HENRY   The Reverberator. London & New York,
1888. 8vo. Cloth. 1st American and 1st one vol. ed. An exlibrary
copy with bookplate on inside endboard and pocket removed from back
endboard. Just a good to very good copy. In Our Time 156-431 1983
$150

JAMES, HENRY   Roderick Hudson. Boston: James R.
Osgood, 1876. 1st ed., 1st binding. Orig. terra cotta cloth, gilt.
This copy has an early owner's inscription dated December 27, 1875
on flyleaf. Of the 1,572 copies printed, this was one of the first
to get into circulation. Fine copy. Jenkins 155-707 1983 $350

JAMES, HENRY   The Sense of the Past. London, 1715.
First edition. Portrait. 8vo. Orig. cloth, gilt. Traylen 94-456
1983 £20

JAMES, HENRY   A Small Boy and Others. N.Y., 1913.
First edition. 8vo, cloth, g.t., uncut. Argosy 714-396 1983 $40

JAMES, HENRY   The Soft Side. N.Y., 1900. First
edition. 8vo, cloth; rubbed; extremes of backstrip worn. Argosy
714-397 1983 $30

JAMES, HENRY   The Spoils of Poynton. London, 1897.
First edition. 8vo, blue cloth; rubbed. "Presentation copy"
blindstamped on flyleaf. Jean Stafford Lowell's signature on front
endpaper. Argosy 714-398 1983 $175

JAMES, HENRY   Terminations. N.Y., 1895. First
edition. 12mo, dec. cloth. Argosy 714-399 1983 $50

JAMES, HENRY   Theatricals. N.Y., 1894. First
American edition. 8vo, green cloth; front cover spotted; unopened.
Argosy 714-400 1983 $75

JAMES, HENRY   Theatricals: Second Series. New York:
Harper, 1895. 1st ed., American issue (1 of 550 copies). Orig.
green cloth, gilt. Some fading, but fresh unworn copy of this scarce
book. Jenkins 155-710 1983 $75

JAMES, HENRY   Transatlantic Sketches. Boston:
Osgood, 1875. 1st ed., 1st binding. Orig. maroon cloth, gilt.
1,578 copies printed. Very fine. Jenkins 155-709 1983 $350

JAMES, HENRY   Washington Square. N.Y., 1881. First
edition. 12mo, gilt pict. cloth. Illus. by George DuMaurier. Fine.
Argosy 714-401 1983 $75

JAMES, HENRY   What Maisie Knew. Chicago & N.Y.,
H.S. Stone, 1897. First American edition. Gilt stamped grey cloth,
t.e.g., uncut (a little rubbed) else, good-very good. Houle 22-506
1983 $80

JAMES, HENRY   The Yellow Book. London: Bodley Head,
January, 1897. Vol. 12. 1st ed. Orig. pictorial yellow cloth.
Partly unopened. Fine copy. Jenkins 155-713 1983 $30

JAMES, ISAAC   Providence Displayed: or the Remarkable Adventures of Alexander Selkirk of Largo in Scotland...
Bristol: by Biggs & Cottle, 1800. First edition. 8vo. 19th
Century cloth. Engraved map. 24 woodcuts in text. Grease stain
affecting four leaves, slight usage. Very rare. Heath 48-275
1983 £125

JAMES, JAMES ALTON   Chicago, a History in Block Prints.
Chicago: (Consolidated Book Publishers Inc.) 1934. 4to, profusely
illus. with woodcuts. Presentation copy, signed by MacGowan. Illus.
Red stiff wraps. Block prints executed by the Advanced Class in
Design under the direction of Clara MacGowan, Assistant Professor
of Art, Northwestern University. Karmiole 71-61 1983 $60

JAMES, JOHN   My Experiences with Indians. Austin,
1925. Cloth, fine. Reese 19-301 1983 $85

JAMES, L.   The Indian Frontier War. London, 1898.
8vo. Orig. cloth. Frontis. Numerous maps, plans and plates. Spine
faded. Lower cover worn. Good. Edwards 1042-373 1983 £55

JAMES, MONTAGUE R.   The Five Jars. Edward Arnold, 1922.
Frontis. Title vignette & 6 plates. Red cloth faded. Head of spine
nicked. Greer 39-78 1983 £30

JAMES, MONTAGUE R.   The Five Jars. Edward Arnold, 1922.
Frontis. Title vignette. 6 plates. Red cloth faded, snag in spine.
Greer 40-119 1983 £28

JAMES, NORAH C.   Sleeveless Errand. Paris, 1929. First
edition. Prelims and edges slightly spotted. Some sporadic internal
foxing. Slightly torn dustwrapper missing a small piece at the head
of the spine and with the very scarce original wraparound band. Very
good. Jolliffe 26-285 1983 £45

JAMES, PHILIP   Children's Books of Yesterday. London:
The Studio, 1933. Folio. With over 100 b/w illus. 8 color plates.
In dust jacket, a bit discolored and chipped. Karmiole 75-28 1983
$45

JAMES, THOMAS H.   Rambles in the United States and
Canada During the Year 1845. London, 1846. Cloth (somewhat worn).
Frontis. lacking, though apparently never bound in. First edition.
Felcone 22-102 1983 $50

JAMES, WILL   Flint Spears. N.Y., Scribner, 1938.
First edition. Illus. with photos and drawings by the author.
Dust jacket. Very good-fine. Houle 21-1093 1983 $75

JAMES, WILL   Lone Cowboy: My Life Story. New York,
(1939). 8vo. Cloth. Envelope (from author) glued to the frond endpaper, else a fine copy in dj which has a few minimal tears. In Our
Time 156-434 1983 $50

JAMES, WILL   Sand. New York, 1929. Cloth. Illus.
by the author. First edition, first printing. A fine copy in
dust jacket. Reese 19-303 1983 $75

JAMES, WILL   Young Cowboy. N.Y., Scribner, 1935.
First edition. Oblong 8vo, with five color and 22 b/w plates by
the author. Dust jacket (light soiling and short tears) else very
good. Houle 22-1117 1983 $50

JAMES, WILLIAM (1842-1910)   The Laws of Habit. NY: D. Appleton &
Co., 1887. Contemporary 1/2 leather, sound copy (joints worn).
Gach 95-236 1983 $50

JAMES, WILLIAM (1842-1910)   The Letters of... Boston: Atlantic
Monthly Press, (1920). First edition. Two vols. Large paper, cloth
spines, paper labels, boards. Limited to 600 sets. Gach 95-237 1983
$100

JAMES, WILLIAM (1842-1910)   Letters. Boston, (1920). Illus. 2
vols. Large 8vo, cloth backed boards. Ltd. edition. Argosy 714-
404 1983 $50

JAMES, WILLIAM (1842-1910)   The Letters of... Boston: Atlantic
Monthly Press, (1920). Two volumes. An early printing, but not first.
Gach 94-216 1983 $35

JAMES, WILLIAM (1842-1910)   Pragmatism. New York: Longmans, Green
and Co., 1907. Cloth, paper label. First edition. Label a trifle
soiled, but a fine copy. Reese 20-553 1983 $50

JAMES, WILLIAM (1842-1910)   The Principles of Psychology. London:
Macmillan & Co., 1890. Two vols. First British edition. Orig.
blue cloth. Very good set. Top of Vol. II shelfworn, hinges
cracked. Gach 95-238 1983 $100

JAMES, WILLIAM (1842-1910)   Talks to Teachers on Psychology. New
York: Henry Holt, 1899. 1st ed. Orig. grey cloth, gilt, t.e.g.,
other uncut. Fine copy. Jenkins 155-714 1983 $30

JAMESON, ANNA BROWNELL   Characteristics of Women. London:
Saunders & Otley, 1858. Second edition. Illus. from the author's
designs. 2 vols. Orig. bright blue cloth. Fine. MacManus 279-2959
1983 $35

JAMESON, ANNA BROWNELL   The History of Our Lord as Exemplified
in Works of Art. Longmans, Green, 1892. With 31 plates and other
illus., 2 vols., 8vo, orig. green cloth, gilt, t.e.g., a fine
copy. Fenning 61-220 1983 £18.50

JAMESON, ANNA BROWNELL   Legends of the Madonna as Represented in
the Fine Arts. Longmans, Green, 1890. With 27 plates and 165
other illus., 8vo, orig. green cloth, a fine copy. Fenning 61-221
1983 £10.50

JAMESON, ANNA BROWNELL   Sacred and Legendary Art. Longmans,
Green, 1898. With 19 plates and 187 other illus., 2 vols., 8vo,
orig. green cloth, gilt, t.e.g., fine copy. Fenning 61-222 1983
£16.50

JAMESON, JAMES SLIGO   Story of the Rear Column of the Emin
Pasha Relief Expedition. R.H. Porter, 1890. First edition, with
portrait, a large folding map, 2 folding plates, 2 other plates,
and many full-page and other illus., 8vo, a very good copy in recent
calf-backed marbled boards, gilt, with label. Fenning 61-223
1983 £65

JAMESON, JAMES SLIGO   The story of the rear column of the
Emin Pasha Relief Expedition. New York: U.S. Book Co., (1891).
8vo. Facs. Folding map. 16 plates. Orig. pictorial cloth. Rubbed.
Adelson Africa-197 1983 $65

JAMESON, STORM   Civil Journey. London, 1939. First
edition. Upper cover marked and creased. Author's signed autograph
presentation inscription to G. Bullett. Very good. Rota 231-347
1983 £12

JAMESON, STORM   The Moon is Making. London, (1937).
First edition, d.w. Argosy 714-405 1983 $20

JAMIESON, JOHN   An Etymological Dictionary of the
Scottish Language. Edinburgh: at the University Press, 1808-25.
4 vols. 4to. Half brown morocco, gilt, gilt panelled spines, t.e.g.
Includes the supplement volume. Traylen 94-457 1983 £110

JAMOT, PAUL   Auguste Ravier. Etude critique...
Lyon: H. Lardanchet, 1921. 35 plates (10 tipped-in color). 4to.
Buckram. No. 135 of a limited edition of 200 copies. Neat ex-library
copy. Ars Libri 32-545 1983 $100

JAMOT, PAUL   Dunoyer de Segonzac. Paris: Floury,
1929. 10 color facsimile plates, 1 original etching by Segonzac.
Most prof. illus. 4to. New cloth. Orig. wrappers bound in. Photo-
types and facsimiles printed by Jacomet. Light wear. Ars Libri
32-627 1983 $185

JANE, FRED T.   The British Battle Fleet. London, 1914.
Roy. 8vo. Orig. cloth. Title in red and black, coloured frontis.
24 other coloured plates of ships, 16 ship photographs, 9 portraits,
25 illus. Head of spine very slightly worn. Good. Edwards 1042-86
1983 £40

JANE, FRED T.   Fighting Ships 1914. London, 1914.
First edition. Oblong 4to. Orig. cloth. Numerous illus, diagrams and
silhouettes. Neatly rebacked, remains of orig. spine laid down.
Slightly worn and faded, inner hinges repaired with tape. Last ad.
leaf torn, repaired. Good. Edwards 1042-87 1983 £120

JANE, FRED T.   Fighting Ships 1914. London, 1914.
Third edition, with one page addenda. Oblong 4to. Orig. cloth.
Numerous illus., silhouettes, maps, etc. Slightly soiled, rebacked,
orig. spine laid down. Good. Edwards 1042-88 1983 £85

JANE, FRED T.   Fighting Ships 1914. London, 1914.
Fourth edition. Oblong 4to. Orig. cloth. Numerous illus., drawings,
silhouettes, ads. Rebacked, orig. spine laid down, inner hinges
repaired with tape. Slightly soiled. Good. Edwards 1042-89 1983
£100

JANE, FRED T.   Fighting Ships 1918. London, 1918.
Oblong 4to. Orig. cloth. Numerous illus. etc. Faded, slightly worn
and stained. Neatly rebacked with orig. spine laid down. Inner
hinges strengthened. Last 2 leaves with neatly repaired tears in lower
outer corner. Good. Edwards 1042-90 1983 £80

JANE, FRED T.   Fighting Ships 1919. London, 1919.
First uncensored edition of Jane's to be published after W.W.I.
Oblong 4to. Orig. cloth. Frontis. of H.M.S. Hood, numerous illus.,
diagrams and silhouettes. 38 pages of ships lost in the war at end.
Very slightly worn. Good. Edwards 1042-91 1983 £100

JANE, FRED T.   Fighting Ships 1935. London, 1935.
Oblong 4to. Orig cloth. Numerous illus. etc., including the addition-
al pp. 56a and 85a. Ink signature on endpaper. Orig. dust jacket.
Mint. Edwards 1042-92 1983 £95

JANE, FRED T.   Fighting Ships 1939. London, 1939.
Oblong 4to. Orig. cloth. Numerous illus. etc., including 7pp.
addenda at end. Slightly worn and soiled. Good. Edwards 1042-93
1983 £55

JANE, FRED T.   Fighting Ships 1940. London, 1941.
Oblong 4to. Orig. cloth. Numerous illus. and diagrams. Very slightly
faded. Good. Edwards 1042-94 1983 £50

JANE, FRED T.   Fighting Ships 1942. New York, 1943.
Oblong 4to. Orig. cloth. Numerous illus., drawings, silhouettes, etc.
Slightly faded. American edition on non-gloss paper. Endpaper ads.
pasted down, not in keeping with other U.S. editions. Some relevant
newspaper cuttings. Good. Edwards 1042-95 1983 $45

JANE, FRED T.   Fighting Ships 1943-4. New York, 1944.
American edition on non-gloss paper. Endpaper ad. leaves free. Ob.4to.
Numerous illus., drawings, silhouettes, etc. Good. Edwards 1042-96
1983 £45

JANE, FRED T.   Fighting Ships 1946-47. London, 1947.
Oblong 4to. Orig. cloth. Numerous illus. and diagrams. Very slightly
stained. Good. Edwards 1042-97 1983 £65

JANE, FRED T.   Fighting Ships 1950-51. London, 1950.
Oblong 4to. Orig. cloth. Numerous illus, drawings, etc. Mint.
Edwards 1042-98 1983 £55

JANES, THOMAS   The Beauties of the Poets... London:
at the Cicero Press, 1788. First edition. 12mo. Cont. mottled calf,
gilt, rubbed. Heath 48-338 1983 £65

JANET, PAUL   A History of the Problems of Philosophy.
London: Macmillan, 1902. Two vols. Ex-library, bindings worn.
Gach 95-239 1983 $25

JANET, PIERRE (1859-1947)   L'Automatisme Psychologique. Paris,
1889. First edition. 8vo. Old quarter-goat. Gurney 90-66 1983
£40

JANET, PIERRE (1859-1947)   Les Debuts de L'Intelligence. Paris:
(1935). First edition. Orig. wrappers, very good. Inscribed from
Janet to L. Vernon Briggs. Gach 95-243 1983 $75

JANET, PIERRE (1859-1947)   De L'Angoisse a L'Extase. Paris:
Felix Alcan, 1926. Two vols. 3 color plates, 37 text figures. Contemporary cloth-backed marbled boards. First edition. Gach 95-242
1983 $75

JANET, PIERRE (1859-1947)   L'Intelligence Avant le Langage. Paris:
1936. First edition. Orig. wrappers, very good. Inscribed from
Janet to L. Vernon Briggs. Gach 95-244 1983 $75

JANET, PIERRE (1859-1947)   The Major Symptoms of Hysteria. NY:
Macmillan, 1907. First edition. Ads. Publisher's blue cloth, worn
and recased. Gach 95-245 1983 $40

JANET, PIERRE (1859-1947)   Mental State of Hystericals. N.Y., 1901.
First American edition. Argosy 713-294 1983 $75

JANET, PIERRE (1859-1947)   Principles of Psychotherapy. NY:
Macmillan, 1924. First American edition. Gach 95-246 1983 $37.50

JANET, PIERRE (1859-1947)   Les Troubles de la Personnalite Sociale.
Paris: Masson et Cie, 1937. 8vo. Orig. green printed wrappers.
Inscribed in Janet's hand to A. Roback. First separate edition.
Gach 95-247 1983 $75

JANSEN, MURK   Feebleness of Growth and Congenital
Dwarfism. London, 1921. 4to, cloth, ex-lib. Illus. Argosy 713-295
1983 $25

JANTZEN, HANS   Deutsche Bildhauer des dreizehnten Jahrhunderts. (Deutsche Meister.) Leipzig, 1925. 4to, cloth, 147 illus.
Ars Libri SB 26-106 1983 $65

JANVIER, THOMAS A.   The Aztec Treasure-House. NY, 1890.
Illus by Frederick Remington. Edges very slightly rubbed, very good.
Quill & Brush 54-1142 1983 $100

JAQUET, JAMES   Rosalba et Autres Contes. Paris, (1922).
4to. Cloth backed pictorial boards. Paper slightly browning, light
wear. Illus. with silhouettes surrounding the text. Very good.
Aleph-bet 8-116 1983 $35

JARAMILLO-ARANGO, JAIME   Relacion Historica Del Viage A Los
Reynos Del Peru Y Chile. Madrid, 1952. 2nd ed., rev. & corr. 2
vols, 4to, port., 22 plates, mostly colored folding plans. Argosy
710-505 1983 $85

JARDINE, ALFRED   Pike and Perch. London: George
Routledge and Sons, n.d. (ca. 1890). Karmiole 71-105 1983 $30

JARDINE, DAVID   Criminal Trials. Charles Knight, 1832.
2 vols., 12mo, orig. pebble cloth, rebacked, preserving the orig.
spine of vol. 1 and the upper half of the orig. spine of vol. 2.
First edition. Bickersteth 77-219 1983 £20

JARDINE, W.   Monkeys. Jardine's Naturalist's
Library, Edinburgh, 1833. Portrait, coloured vignette and 30 coloured
plates, 8vo, new cloth. Wheldon 160-563 1983 £35

JARDINE, W.   Ruminantia Part 1, Deer, Antelopes,
Camels. Jardine's Naturalist's Library, Edinburgh, 1839. Portrait,
coloured vignette, 31 coloured and 2 plain plates, sm. 8vo, new cloth.
Wheldon 160-565 1983 £35

JARDINE, W.   Ruminantia, Part 2, Goats, Sheep,
Oxen. Jardine's Naturalist's Library, Edinburgh, Lizars, 1836.
Portrait, vignette and 31 coloured plates, sm. 8vo, original cloth.
Wheldon 160-566 1983 £35

JARDINE, W.   Thick-Skinned Quadrupeds. Jardine's
Naturalist's Library, Edinburgh, 1836. Portrait, vignette, 4 plain
and 30 coloured plates, sm. 8vo, original brown cloth (neatly fixed).
Wheldon 160-564 1983 £35

JARRELL, RANDALL   Blood for a Stranger. London, 1942.
First edition. Hinges slightly browned. Chipped dustwrapper with
a 1 1/2 inch tear. Near fine. Jolliffe 26-286 1983 £90

JARRELL, RANDALL   Little Friend, Little Friend. NY:
1945. First edition. Some fading to cloth covers. Bromer 25-55
1983 $50

JARRELL, RANDALL   Pictures from an Institution. New
York, 1954. 8vo. Wraps. Advance reading copy. A fine copy. In
Our Time 156-436 1983 $250

JARRELL, RANDALL   Poetry and the Age. London, 1955.
First edition. Dustwrapper. Fine. Jolliffe 26-287 1983 £40

JARRELL, RANDALL   Selected Poems. London, 1956. First
edition. Dustwrapper with a single nick and faded at the spine.
Near fine. Jolliffe 26-288 1983 £45

JARRETT, FRED   Postage Stamps of Canada. Brockville,
Ont: "Canadian Stamp Collector", 1923. 20cm. Many illus. Printed
grey stiff wrappers. Very good. Scarce. McGahern 53-86 1983
$50

JARRETT, ROBERT FRANK   Occoneechee, the Maid of Mystic Lake.
New York, Shakespeare Press, 1916. 1st ed. Illus. from photographs.
8vo. Morrill 288-206 1983 $25

JARRY, ALFRED   Ubu Roi. Paris: Marcel Sautier,
1947. Folio. Orig. lithographed wraps., unbound signatures laid in.
Illus. with orig. color lithographs by Edmond Heuze. One of 20
numbered copies on pur chiffon de Lana, with an additional suite of
the lithographs printed in black on Malacca, from a total edition of
200. Very fine in lightly rubbed slipcase. Reese 20-555 1983 $250

JARVIS, C. S.   Yesterday and To-Day in Sinai. Edinburgh
& London, 1931. Folding map. Frontis. and 27 illus. 8vo. Orig.
cloth. Good. Edwards 1044-386 1983 £15

JASTROW, JOSEPH   The House that Freud Built. NY: Greenberg, (1932). First edition. Dust jacket. Inscribed to Adolf Meyer.
Gach 94-168 1983 $35

JAY, CHARLES W.   My New Home in Northern Michigan,
and Other Tales. Trenton, 1874. First edition. Felcone 22-104
1983 $35

JAY, JOHN   Some Conversations of Dr. Franklin and
Mr. Jay. New Haven, The Three Monks Press, 1936. Edition limited to
247 copies. 8vo, original boards, paper label, nice. Morrill 290-202
1983 $25

JAY, WILLIAM   An Inquiry into the Character and
Tendency of the American Colonization and American Anti-Slavery
Societies. New York, 1835. 1st ed. 12mo, paper label, foxed,
binding partly faded & with few light stains. Morrill 288-207 1983
$45

JAYNE, WALTER   The Healing Gods of Ancient Civilizations. New Haven, 1925. First edition. 8vo. Orig. binding. Fye
H-3-293 1983 $65

JEAN-AUBRY, G.   Joseph Conrad. Life & Letters. N.Y.:
Doubleday & Co., 1927. First edition. 2 vols. Illus. Orig. cloth.
Bookplate. MacManus 277-1111 1983 $20

JEANS, JAMES HOPWOOD   Atomicity & Quanta, being the Rouse
Ball Lecture delivered on May 11, 1925. Cambridge: University
Press, 1926. First edition. 8vo. Orig. printed boards. Very
good copy. Zeitlin 264-225 1983 $30

JEANS, JAMES HOPWOOD   The Dynamic Theory of Gases. Cambridge: University Press, 1904. First edition. 8vo. Orig. cloth. Spine a little chipped. Very good copy. Zeitlin 264-226 1983 $70

JEBB, JOSHUA   A practical treatise on strengthening and defending outposts... (With): A practical treatise on the attack of military posts... Chatham: Burril, etc., 1836-7. First edition. 2 vols. 8vo. Orig. green cloth. 15 lithographed plates in Part I, and 5 in Part II. Minor wear to ends of spines. Second part rare. Ximenes 63-314 1983 $200

JEBB, R. C.   Homer: An Introduction to the Iliad and the Odyssey. Boston, 1902. 8vo, cloth. Salloch 385-567 1983 $20

JEBB, SAMUEL   The History of the Life and Reign of Mary Queen of Scots, and Dowager of France. Printed for J. Woodman and D. Lyon, and C. Davis, 1725. 8vo, engraved portrait by Vertue, cont. panelled calf, worn at top of the spine. Cont. panelled calf, worn at top of the spine. Bickersteth 77-127 1983 £85

JEDER Topf Find't Seinen Deckel. Magdeburg, 1775. 8vo, marbled boards. Salloch 387-173 1983 $25

JEDLICKA, GOTTHARD   Henri de Toulouse-Lautrec. Berlin: Bruno Cassirer, 1928. 3 fine color facsimile plates. 161 illus. (4 color). Large square 4to. Cloth. Edition limited to 1000 copies. Ars Libri 32-670 1983 $85

JEDLICKA, GOTTHARD   Henri de Toulouse-Lautrec. Berlin, 1929. 7 coloured plates, 157 other illus., no. 459 of a limited edition of 1000 copies, 4to, decorated cloth, slightly spotted. K Books 307-105 1983 £38

JEFFERIES, RICHARD   After London; or, Wild England. Cassell & Co., 1886. First edition, half title, orig. red cloth, black borders on front cover, gilt lettering on spine. Sl. fading of spine, otherwise v.g. Jarndyce 31-754 1983 £85

JEFFERIES, RICHARD   After London; or, wild England. London: Cassell, 1885. First edition. 8vo. Orig. grey cloth. Rubbed and soiled, spine dark. Ximenes 63-157 1983 $75

JEFFERIES, RICHARD   Bevis, the Story of a Boy. Sampson Low, Marston, Searle & Rivington, 1882. Half title, vol. I. Orig. green cloth, blocked on front covers in black and gilt, spines gilt-lettered, end papers fragile with careful repairs to inner hinges. Jarndyce 31-753 1983 £220

JEFFERIES, RICHARD   The Dewy Morn. London: Richard Bentley and Son, 1884. First edition. 2 vols. Orig. cloth. All edges worn. Inner hinges cracked. Library labels removed from front covers. Covers a bit soiled. Bookseller's ticket on front pastedown endpaper of vol. one. Good. MacManus 279-2960 1983 $250

JEFFERIES, RICHARD   The Dewy Morn. London: Richard Bentley and Son, 1884. First edition. 2 vols. 8vo. Orig. green pebble-grain cloth, neatly recased. Traylen 94-458 1983 £105

JEFFERIES, RICHARD   Field and Hedgerow. London: Longmans, Green & Co., 1889. First edition. Large 8vo. Orig. 3/4 parchment, t.e.g. One of 200 large paper copies. Good. MacManus 279-2963 1983 $125

JEFFERIES, RICHARD   Field and Hedgerow. London & Redhill: Lutterworth Press, (1948). First edition. Wood engravings by Agnes M. Parker. Orig. cloth. Dust jacket. Fine. MacManus 279-2961 1983 $35

JEFFERIES, RICHARD   The Gamekeeper at Home. London: Smith, Elder, 1878. First edition. Orig. cloth. MacManus 279-2962 1983 $60

JEFFERIES, RICHARD   Hodge and his Masters. London: Smith, Elder, & Co., 1880. First edition. 2 vols. Orig. pictorial cloth. Bookplates (armorial). Former owner's signature on title-pages. Edges a bit worn. Very good to near-fine. MacManus 279-2964 1983 $250

JEFFERIES, RICHARD   Hodge and His Masters. London: Smith, Elder, 1880. First edition. 2 vols. Small 8vo. Orig. brown cloth, blocked in black and gilt, with steam engine on front cover of vol. 2. Blank preceeding the half-title in each vol., and 4 pp. of publishers advertisements. Traylen 94-922 1983 £120

JEFFERIES, RICHARD   The Life of the Fields. London: Chatto & Windus, 1884. First edition. Orig. pictorial cloth. Top of spine a trifle nicked. Fine. MacManus 279-2965 1983 $125

JEFFERIES, RICHARD   The Old House at Coate. Cambridge, Mass.: Harvard University Press, 1948. First American edition. Wood engravings by A.M. Parker. Orig. cloth. Dust jacket. Fine. MacManus 279-2966 1983 $25

JEFFERIES, RICHARD   The Spring of the Year. London: Lutterworth Press, (1946). First edition. Wood engravings by A.M. Parker. Orig. cloth. Dust jacket (a bit chipped). Very good. MacManus 279-2968 1983 $30

JEFFERIES, RICHARD   The Story of My Heart. London, 1883. First edition. Some slight stains from gum of bookplate on front endpapers. Bookplate. Nice. Rota 230-312 1983 £100

JEFFERIES, RICHARD   T.T.T. Arthur Young, Wells, 1896. First edition. One of 100 copies. Wrappers. Foxed throughout. Nice. Rota 230-314 1983 £85

JEFFERIES, RICHARD   Wild Life in a Southern County. London: Smith, Elder, 1879. First edition. Orig. cloth. Hinges cracked. Covers a bit worn. MacManus 279-2969 1983 $75

JEFFERIES, RICHARD   Wood Magic. Cassell, Petter, Galpin, 1881. Half titles, 8 pp ads. in both vols. Orig. green cloth, dec. in black, lettered in gilt, a little rubbed; library labels removed from inner covers, small stamps on verso of titles. A very good set. Jarndyce 30- 440 1983 £62

JEFFERS, ROBINSON   Californians. NY, 1916. Title page perforatted with advance review copy notice, 4 pages carelessly opened, edges slightly rubbed, else bright copy. Quill & Brush 54-699 1983 $250

JEFFERS, ROBINSON   Californians. NY, 1916. Some interior foxing, blank page after ads missing, some interior pencil underlining, good or better, bookplage. Quill & Brush 54-700 1983 $175

JEFFERS, ROBINSON   Dear Judas. N.Y., Liveright, 1929. Tall 8vo, vellum backed boards, unopened, uncut. Pub.'s box a bit rubbed, else a fine, fresh copy. This is copy number 2 of 375, signed by the author, and is probably one of 25 for presentation. Houle 21-450 1983 $225

JEFFERS, ROBINSON   Dear Judas and Other Poems. New York: Liveright, 1929. Small quarto. Vellum backed boards. 1st ed. 1 of 375 numbered copies, printed on large-paper, specially bound, and signed by author. Vellum slightly foxed, else very fine. Jenkins 155-717 1983 $175

JEFFERS, ROBINSON   Dear Judas. NY, 1929. Fine in slightly chipped dustwrapper. Quill & Brush 54-702 1983 $75

JEFFERS, ROBINSON   Dear Judas. NY, 1929. One of 375 numbered and signed copies, vellum spine stained, front pastedown has small 3 inch lightly skinned tape stain, good or better. Quill & Brush 54-701 1983 $125

JEFFERS, ROBINSON   Dear Judas. N.Y., Liveright, 1929. First edition. Dust jacket (faded at back, nicks). Very good. Houle 22-510 1983 $80

JEFFERS, ROBINSON   Descent to the Dead. NY, (1931). One of 500 numbered and signed copies, paper covered boards and vellum spine, spine lightly darkened, cover lightly rubbed, near fine in slightly soiled, mended very good slipcase. Quill & Brush 54-703 1983 $275

JEFFERS, ROBINSON   Descent to the Dead. NY, 1931. Poems written in Ireland and Great Britain. First edition. 4to, vellum-backed Tokugawa bds., matching slipcase. Title & initials in burnt sienna. Signed by the poet. Perata 27-92 1983 $225

JEFFERS, ROBINSON   Flagons and Apples. Los Angeles, Grafton, 1912. First edition. Half cloth, paper label on cover and spine (a little rubbed). Enclosed in a cloth slipcase. Zane Grey's copy. Very good. Houle 22-511 1983 $750

JEFFERS, ROBINSON   Give Your Heart to the Hawks. New York: Random House, 1933. 1st ed. Orig. brown cloth, gilt. Fine copy in nice dj with slight chips at upper corners. Jenkins 155-718 1983 $50

JEFFERS, ROBINSON   Medea. N.Y., (1946). Thin 8vo, second printing, but inscribed by Judith Anderson. Argosy 714-410 1983 $20

JEFFERS, ROBINSON   Solstice. NY, 1935. First trade edition, spine slightly faded. Very good or better in slightly chipped dustwrapper with lower 2 1/2 inch portion of dustwrapper spine missing. Quill & Brush 54-704 1983 $50

JEFFERS, ROBINSON   Solstice and Other Poems. N.Y., 1935. First edition. Argosy 714-411 1983 $35

JEFFERS, ROBINSON   Themes in My Poems. San Francisco, Book Club of California, 1956. First edition. 4to. Half cloth over decorated boards, paper label. Prospectus laid in loose, cloth slipcase. One of 350 copies, printed and decorated with woodcuts by Mallette Dean. Fine. Houle 22-512 1983 $275

JEFFERS, ROBINSON   Themes in my Poems. San Francisco: Book Club of California, 1956. Quarto. Cloth and patterned boards. First edition. One of 350 copies printed, with woodcuts, by Mallette Dean. Mint as issued. Reese 20-556 1983 $225

JEFFERS, ROBINSON   Tragedy has Obligations. (Santa Cruz, Ca.): Lime Kiln Press, 1973. With an orig. full-page woodcut by Alison Clough and a tipped-in plate reproducing a page from Jeffers' holographic manuscript. Printed in red and black on handmade paper. Edition ltd. to 200 numbered copies, signed by William Everson, printer at the Lime Kiln Press, and Alison Clough. 1/4 leather; gilt-stamped spine. Prospectus laid in. Fine copy. Karmiole 73-56 1983 $175

JEFFERS, ROBINSON   Two Consolations. San Mateo: Quercus, 1940. 4to. Rose colored boards. 1st and only ed. Total ed. is 250 copies. Issued without dj. A fine copy. In Our Time 156-438 1983 $300

JEFFERS, ROBINSON   The Women at Point Sur. N.Y., Boni & Liveright, 1927. First edition. Dust jacket (some light foxing), uncut, t.e. black. Very good. Houle 22-513 1983 $95

JEFFERSON, THOMAS   Convention Between His Most Christian Majesty and the United States of America, for the Purpose of Defining and Establishing the Functions and Priviledges of Their Respective Consuls and Vice-Consuls. (Paris: Clousier, 1788). Disbound, very good. Reese 18-159 1983 $3,500

JEFFERSON, THOMAS   Documents Relating to the Purchase & Exploration of Louisiana. Boston, 1904. First edition. Limited to 550 numbered copies. Orig. cloth, paper label. Large folding map. Portraits. Jenkins 152-852 1983 $150

JEFFERSON, THOMAS   Memoir, Correspondence, and Miscellanies from the Papers of Thomas Jefferson. Boston, 1830. Four vols. Portrait, after Gilbert Stuart. Orig. cloth, paper labels. Some slight chipping and foxing, otherwise a nice set. Reese 18-648 1983 $125

JEFFERSON, THOMAS   Message from...Communicating Discoveries Made in Exploring the Missouri, Red River and Washita, by Capts. Lewis and Clark, Doctor Sibley, and Mr. Dunbar... Wash., Way, 1806. Illus. 2 folded tables. Cont. marbled boards, leather spine. First edition, first (House) issue. Ginsberg 47-431 1983 $2,500

JEFFERSON, THOMAS   Message from...Transmitting a Report on the Subject of the Military Academy Established at West Point. Wash., 1808. Dbd. First edition. Ginsberg 46-803 1983 $50

JEFFOLD, WALTER   Thomas Hood: His Life and Times. London: Alston Rivers, Ltd., 1907. First edition. Illus. Orig. cloth. Spine faded. Endpapers browned. Good. MacManus 279-2735 1983 $20

JEFFREYS, GEORGE W.   A Series of Essays on Agriculture & Rural Affairs. Raleigh: Joseph Gales, 1819. Illus. Calf (worn, tape stain, cover detached). Felcone 22-105 1983 $85

JEFFREYS, J. G.   Land and Freshwater Shells of Great Britain. 1904. Coloured frontispiece and 8 plates, 8vo, cloth. Blue pencil line down a few margins. Wheldon 160-1213 1983 £16

JEFFRIES, B. JOY   Color-Blindness. Boston, 1880. Cloth binding, 8vo. Tip of spine chipped. Presentation from Paul Dudley White on fly-leaf. Argosy 713-297 1983 $60

JEFFRIES, DAVID   A Treatise on Diamonds and Pearls. London: C. Clarke, for R. Lea and J. Nunn, 1800. Thirty plates. Orig. paper-covered boards, uncut. Spine completely broken; internally fine. Third edition. Felcone 21-61 1983 $175

JEHL, FRANCIS   Menlo Park Reminiscences. Dearborn, Mich.: Edison Institute, 1936. Photos. Stiff wraps. Minor cover soil. Presentation copy, inscribed and signed by the author. King 45-108 1983 $20

JELLIFE, SMITH ELY (1866-1945)   Psychopathology of Forced Movements and the Oculogyric Crises of Lethargic Encephalitis. NY/Washington: N. M. D. Pub. Co., 1932. First edition. Boards. Gach 95-248 1983 $35

JELLINEK, E. M.   Effects of Alcohol on the Individual. Vol. One. Alcohol Addiction & Chronic Alcoholism. New Haven, Ct.: Yale Univ. Press, 1942. Dust jacket worn. Gach 94-793 1983 $20

JEMMAT, CATHERINE   Miscellanies in Prose and Verse. London, 1771. Second edition. 4to. Cont. calf, gilt. Half title. Fine copy. Heath 48-340 1983 £90

JENKINS, EDWARD   The Devil's Chain. Strahan, 1876. First edition, half title, orig. brown cloth dec. in black and gilt. Sl. foxing of edges, fine. Jarndyce 31-756 1983 £82

JENKINS, H.   A Manual of Photoengraving... Chicago: Inland Printer Co., 1902. Second edition, revised. 8vo. Orig. cloth. Five colored illustrations on five separate plates in the front. Minor cover soiling. Oak Knoll 49-248 1983 $65

JENKINS, JAMES   The Martial Achievements of Great Britain and Her Allies from 1799 to 1815. London, Jenkins, 1814-15. Folio. Cont. half morocco. Colored engraved vignette title, dedication with coat-of-arms, engraved title, and 51 hand colored engraved plates of military scenes. All plates are on paper water marked no later than 1815, and are in a very clean state. Ginsberg 46-378 1983 $2,250

JENKINS, JAMES   The Martial Achievements of Great Britain and Her Allies; From 1799 to 1815. London: printed for Js. Jenkins by L. Harrison & L. C. Leigh, 1814-1815. 4to, uncoloured engraved vignette title-page, coloured aquatint frontis., coloured aquatint amorial dedication leaf and 51 fine coloured aquatint plates, finely bound in red half morocco, gilt line borders, matching boards, gilt panelled back, decorative tooling in compartments, marbled endpapers, gilt edges. Deighton 3-186 1983 £1,050

JENKINS, JEFF   The Northern Tier. Topeka, 1880. Orig. cloth. First edition. Ginsberg 47-411 1983 $125

JENKINS, JOHN H.   The Most Remarkable Texas Book. Austin, 1980. Facs. of title page. Cloth with leather backstrip. With a leaf from the orig. printing in pocket. Ltd. to 64 numbered copies, signed by the author. Ginsberg 47-865 1983 $125

JENKINS, JOHN H.   The Papers of the Texas Revolution, 1835-1836. Austin, 1973. 10 vols. Ginsberg 47-866 1983 $115

JENKINS, STEPHEN   The Old Boston Post Road. New York, 1913. 1st ed. Maps and illus. 8vo. Ex-library, no external marks. Morrill 287-170 1983 $22.50

JENKINS, THORNTON A.   The United States Naval Signal Code. Washington, 1867. 56 plates (should be 58), of which several are in color. 8vo, marbled boards, leather back and corners. Rubbed, spine partly torn. Plates 1 & 2 never bound in. Morrill 289-616 1983 $50

JENKS, ALBERT ERNEST   The Bontoc Igorot. Manila: Bureau
of Public Printing, 1905. 154 plates. 4to. New buckram. Ars
Libri 31-807 1983 $75

JENKS, JEREMIAH W.   Road Legislation for the American
State. (Baltimore), May, 1889. 4 large fold-out tables. Printed
red wrappers. Wrapper edges chipped. Bradley 65-105 1983 $35

JENKS, WILLIAM   The Explanatory Bible Atlas and
Scripture Gazetteer. Boston, Charles Hickling, 1847. 1st ed. 4to,
contemporary half morocco. Rubbed. Morrill 287-171 1983 $25

JENNER, CHARLES   Town Eclogues... London: Printed
for T. Cadell...1772. 4to, new wraps. First edition. Quaritch
NS 7-66 1983 $185

JENNER, EDWARD   An Inquiry into the Causes and Effects
of the Variolae Vaccinae. London, 1798 (i.e. Milan, 1923). Edition
ltd. to 500 copies. Argosy 713-298 1983 $60

JENNEY, WALTER P.   The Mineral Wealth, Climate and
Rainfall, and Natural Resources of the Black Hills of Dakota. Wash.,
1876. Folding map. Orig. printed wraps., loose. Stitched.
Internally very good. Reese 19-304 1983 $150

JENNEY, WALTER P.   The Mineral Wealth, Climate and Rain-
Fall, and Natural Resources of the Black Hills of Dakota. Wash.,
1876. Large folded map. Orig. printed wraps. Ginsberg 47-285
1983 $85

JENNINGS, AL   Through the Shadows with O. Henry.
New York, (1921). First edition. Illustrated, including frontispiece
in color. Pictorial cloth. Fine in chipped jacket. Bradley 65-106
1983 $35

JENNINGS, ELIZABETH   Poems. Oxford: Fantasy Press, 1953.
First edition. Slightly rubbed on spine, with a small mark at the
bottom of the front cover. Inscribed. A very good copy. Gekoski
2-90 1983 £45

JENNINGS, H. S.   Behavior of the Lower Organisms. New
York, (1906) 1931. 144 text-figures, 8vo, original cloth. Small
library stamp on reverse of title-page, but a good copy.
Wheldon 160-1299 1983 £15

JENNINGS, HERMAN A.   Chequocket. Yarmouthport, 1885.
With errata tipped in. Pr. wraps. Argosy 716-271 1983 $20

JENNINGS, ISAAC   Memorials of a Century. Boston, 1869.
1st ed. Map and plates. 8vo. Very nice copy. Morrill 286-493
1983 $47.50

JENNINGS, JOHN   Discoures. Boston, 1740. Sewed wrappers.
Title and dedication leaf with parts of margins cut off. Some foxing
and wear. Lacks cover and blanks. King 45-461 1983 $40

JENNINGS, N. A.   A Texas Ranger. Dallas, (1930). "Dobie"
edition. Orig. cobalt blue cloth. Jenkins 152-855 1983 $50

JENTSCH, RALPH   Hans Meid. Das Graphische Werk.
Esslingen: Kunstgalerie Esslingen, 1978. Prof. illus. Large 4to.
Cloth. Dust jacket. Edition limited to 650 copies. Ars Libri
32-445 1983 $150

JENTSCH, RALPH   Richard Seewald. Esslingen:
Verlag Kunstgalerie Esslingen, 1973. Folio. 200 pages of illus.
Edition ltd. to 600 numbered copies. Beige cloth, mounted color
illus. on front cover. Dust jacket. Karmiole 76-47 1983 $150

JENTSCH, RALPH   Richard Seewald. Das graphische Werk.
Esslingen: Kunstgalerie Esslingen, 1973. 493 illus. Large 4to.
Cloth. Dust jacket. Edition limited to 600 copies. Ars Libri 32-
625 1983 $125

JENYNS, SOAME   Miscellaneous Pieces in Verse and Prose.
J. Dodsley, 1770. Third edition, tall 8vo, calf. Very good.
Jarndyce 31-36 1983 £42

JENYNS, SOAME   A View of the Internal Evidence of the
Christian Religion... Philadelphia, 1780. Dsb. Foxed. Good.
Reese 18-131 1983 $30

JEPHSON, A. J. MOUNTENEY   Emin Pasha and the rebellion at the
equator. London: Sampson Low, etc., 1890. 8vo. Folding map.
Facs. 22 plates. Orig. pictorial cloth. Rubbed, starting, ex-
lib. Adelson Africa-198 1983 $75

JEPHSON, PHILIPPA PRITTIE   An April Day. F.V. White, 1883. 8 pp
ads. vol. II. Orig. turquoise cloth, blocked in black, lettered in
gilt, sl. rubbed, otherwise v.g. Jarndyce 30-441 1983 £30

JERABEK, ESTHER   A Bibliography of Minnesota Territorial
Documents. St. Paul, 1936. 8vo, pr. wrs. Argosy 710-318 1983 $35

JERDAN, WILLIAM   Men I Have Known. Routledge, 1866.
First edition, half title. Facs., 1 pp ads. Orig. maroon cloth,
bevelled boards. Sl. rubbed. Jarndyce 30-1032 1983 £24

JERDON, T. C.   The Mammals of India. 1874. Royal 8vo,
new cloth. London reprint with corrections. Wheldon 160-567 1983
£35

JERNINGHAM, EDWARD   Fugitive Poetical Pieces. London:
Printed by Scott for J. Robson...MDCCLXXVIII. 8vo, some foxing but
otherwise a very good, partly uncut copy in later half morocco. First
edition. Erratic collation beginning with a singleton title-page
but without a half-title. Quaritch NS 7-68 1983 $325

JERNINGHAM, EDWARD   The Peckham Frolic. Printed for J.
Hatchard, 1799. Half calf, spine sl. worn. First edition. Jarndyce
31-62 1983 £24

JERNINGHAM, EDWARD   Poems. London: J. Robson, 1786. 2
vols. 8vo. Cont. mottled calf, spine gilt. Tiny chip at top of
one spine. Fine copy. Ximenes 63-370 1983 $125

JERNINGHAM, EDWARD   Poems on various subjects. London:
printed for J. Robson, 1767. First edition. 12mo. Cont. tree
calf. Spine a bit worn. Very good copy. Ximenes 63-369 1983
$150

JEROME, JEROME K.   Fennel. N.Y. & London: Samuel French,
n.d. French's Acting edition. Orig. wrappers. Very fine. MacManus
279-2975 1983 $35

JEROME, JEROME K.   The Passing of The Third Floor Back.
London: Hurst & Blackett, Ltd., 1907. First edition. Orig. cloth.
Letter on spine rubbed. Very good. MacManus 279-2977 1983 $25

JEROME, JEROME K.   Sunset. N.Y. & London: Samuel French,
n.d. French's Acting edition. Orig. wrappers. Very fine. MacManus
279-2979 1983 $35

JERROLD, BLANCHARD   A brage-breaker with the Swedes.
London: Nathaniel Cooke, 1854. First edition. 8vo. Orig. blue
cloth. Wood-engraved frontis. and numerous other illus. Fine
copy. Ximenes 63-627 1983 $60

JERROLD, BLANCHARD   The Disgrace to the Family. London:
Darton & Co., (1847). First edition. 12 illus. by Phiz. In orig.
six parts. Orig. pictorial wrappers (dust-soiled). Marginal restorations. Back wrapper of last part torn along hinge. In a blue half-
morocco pull-off case. Very good. MacManus 279-2987 1983 $400

JERROLD, DOUGLAS   The Brownrigg Papers. London: John
Camden Hotten, 1860. First edition. Coloured illus. by. G. Cruik-
shank. Orig. cloth. Spine faded. Bookplate on front endsheet. Fine.
MacManus 279-2980 1983 $125

JERROLD, DOUGLAS   Cakes and Ale. London: How and Parsons,
1842. First edition. Small 8vo, 2 vols. Each volume with an
engraved frontis. and title-page by George Cruikshank. This set has
bound in to each volume an orig. holograph letter, signed by
Jerrold. Both of the letters are mounted and are 8 lines in length.
Bound by Alfred Matthews in (circa 1900) 3/4 brown morocco over
marbled boards, with gilt-stamped spines. Bookplate. A fine set.
Karmiole 73-57 1983 $125

JERROLD, DOUGLAS   The Chronicles of Clovernook. London:
Published at The Punch Office, 1846. First edition. Frontis. Orig.
gilt-decorated cloth. Small bookplate removed from front endsheet.
Very good. MacManus 279-2981 1983 $85

JERROLD, DOUGLAS   Fifteen Years of A Drunkard's Life.
N.Y. & London: Samuel French, n.d. French's Standard Drama edition.
Orig. wrappers. Very fine. MacManus 279-2983 1983 $35

JERROLD, DOUGLAS   Mr. Caudle's Curtain Lectures. London:
Bradbury & Evans, 1866. First edition. Illus. by C. Keene. 4to.
Full tan polished calf. Marbled endpapers, a.e.g., with morocco
labels on spine, by Zaehnsdorf. Covers slightly rubbed. Foxing.
Former owner's signature on flyleaf whited-out. Orig. cloth covers
bound in at the back. Very good. MacManus 279-2982 1983 $75

JERROLD, DOUGLAS   Sally In Our Alley. London: John
Cumberland, n.d. Cumberland's British Theatre edition. Orig. wrappers.
Fine. MacManus 279-2985 1983 $35

JERROLD, DOUGLAS   The White Milliner. London: John
Duncombe & Co., n.d. Cumberland's British Theatre edition. 12mo.
Engraved frontis. Orig. wrappers. Frontispiece stained. MacManus
279-2986 1983 $25

JERROLD, WALTER   The Big Book of Fables. Blackie, 1912.
4to, mounted colour frontis. Title vignette, 27 mounted colour plates,
100 other plates and over 200 text illus. White pictorial cloth, gilt.
Worn. Edition de Luxe, with all plates mounted. Greer 40-188 1983
£95

JERROLD, WALTER   Douglas Jerrold and 'Punch'. Macmillan,
1910. First edition, half title, front. port. Illus. Orig. dark blue
cloth, spine gilt, v.g. Jarndyce 31-759 1983 £20

JERROLD, WALTER   Thomas Hood: His Life and Times.
Alston Rivers, 1907. First edition, tall 8vo, half title, front.
illus. 12 pp ads. Orig. maroon cloth, v.g. Jarndyce 30-1024 1983
£30

JERROLD, WILLIAM BLANCHARD
Please turn to
JERROLD, BLANCHARD

JERVIS, H.   Narrative of a Journey to the Falls of
the Cavery. London, 1834. 12 engraved plates, inscription erased
from title. Calf, morocco label, spine gilt. 8vo. Good. Edwards
1044-387 1983 £225

JESSE, J. H.   Literary and Historical Memorials of
London. London: Bentley, 1847. First edition. 2 vols. Orig. cloth.
Quite faded and worn. Inner hinges carcked. MacManus 279-2988 1983
$25

JESSE, J. H.   The Works. London, 1901. 30 vols.
8vo. Choicely bound in half dark red morocco, gilt, gilt panelled
spines, t.e.g., others uncut. Engraved frontis. and numerous
engraved plates and portraits. Library edition. Traylen 94-459
1983 £450

JESSEL, GEORGE   So Help Me. NY, (1943). Very good in
slightly chipped and soiled dustwrapper worn along edges. Quill &
Brush 54-1194 1983 $35

JESSOP, GILBERT   Arthur Peck's Sacrifice. Nelson, n.d.
Colour frontis. & 3 colour plates. Some ink markings. Colour pictorial cloth, rubbed. Greer 40-68 1983 £14

JESTER, GEORGE   The Collected Verses. New York, 1941.
8vo, cloth, slipcase. Duschnes 240-135 1983 $$25

JESTY, SIMON   'Ye Drunken Damozel'. Boriswood, 1932.
First edition, 8vo, orig. buckram-backed cloth, t.e.g. A fine
copy. Copy number 2 of twenty-five numbered copies on mould-made
paper, signed by the author. Fenning 62-193 1983 £45

JEVONS, W. STANLEY   Pure Logic. Edward Stanford, 1864.
First edition. Half title, ad. slip. Orig. blue cloth, paper
labels, v.g. Jarndyce 31-208 1983 £75

JEVONS, W. STANLEY   The Theory of Political Economy.
London: Macmillan and Co., 1911. 4th ed., 8vo, original brown
cloth, a fine copy. Pickering & Chatto 21-49 1983 $125

JEWETT, SARAH ORNE   The Country of the Pointed Firs.
Boston & New York: Houghton, Mifflin, 1896. 1st ed., 1st printing.
Ed. consisted of 2,524 copies. Orig. green cloth, gilt. Near fine
copy. Jenkins 155-720 1983 $75

JEWETT, SARAH ORNE   The Country of the Pointed Firs. B,
1896. Front hinge starting, clippings and picture tipped-in on front
endpapers causing offset, owner's lengthy inscription, minor cover
spotting, edges slightly frayed, good. Quill & Brush 54-707 1983
$50

JEWETT, SARAH ORNE   The Country of the Pointed Firs.
Boston, 1896. First edition. Small 8vo, very nice. Morrill 290-203
1983 $25

JEWETT, SARAH ORNE   Deephaven. Boston: Osgood, 1877.
1st ed., 2nd printing. Orig. mauve cloth, gilt. Spine ends worn,
but good copy. Uncommon. Jenkins 155-721 1983 $65

JEWETT, SARAH ORNE   The Life of Nancy. B, 1895. Light cover
staining, edges slightly rubbed, else very good, owner's name and in-
scription. Quill & Brush 54-708 1983 $40

JEWETT, SARAH ORNE   A Native of Winby and Other Tales. B,
1893. Bright copy in remnants of orig. dustwrapper. Quill & Brush
54-706 1983 $125

JEWETT, SARAH ORNE   Tales of New England. Boston & New
York: Houghton, Mifflin, 1895. Frontis. Orig. green cloth, gilt,
t.e.g. Just short of fine, with inscription in Jewett's hand at
front: "For Lucy J. Voshell, With affectionate wishes from, Sarah
Orne Jewett, Boston, May, 1904." Jenkins 155-1398 1983 $125

JEWETT, SARAH ORNE   The Tory Lover. Boston, Houghton
Mifflin, 1901. First edition. Halftones after paintings by Marcia
and Charles Woodbury. Blue cloth stamped in gilt with coat of arms
on front. Good-very good. Houle 22-516 1983 $45

JEWETT, SARAH ORNE   The Tory Lover. B, 1901. Edges slightly
rubbed, minor cover soiling and wear, else very good, owner's name.
Quill & Brush 54-709 1983 $40

JEWETT, SARAH ORNE   The Tory Lover. Boston & New York:
Houghton, Mifflin, 1901. 1st ed., 1st printing. Orig. red cloth,
gilt. Fine copy. Jenkins 155-722 1983 $20

JEWETT, SARAH ORNE   A White Heron and Other Stories.
Boston & New York: Houghton, Mifflin, 1886. 1st ed., state 2.
Orig. two-tone cloth, gilt, t.e.g. Nice copy with early owner's
inscription. Jenkins 155-723 1983 $50

JEWISH Activities in the United States. Dearborn, 1921. Vols. 2 & 3
of The International Jew. Wraps, disbound, slightly water stained.
Scarce. King 46-734 1983 $25

JEWITT, LLEWELLYN   The Wedgewoods. London, Virtue, 1865.
First edition. Frontis. portrait and woodcuts throughout. 3/4 brown
morocco over cloth, marbled endpapers and edges (slight rubbing).
Very good. Houle 22-940 1983 $145

JEWSBURY, GERALDINE ENDSOR   Selections from the Letters of...to
Jane Welsh Carlyle. Longmans, Green, 1892. First edition, half
title, 24 pp ads. Orig. green cloth, v.g. Jarndyce 30-1033 1983
£15

JEWSBURY, MARIA JANE   Phantasmagoria; or, sketches of life
and literature. London: Hurst, Robinson and Co., etc., 1825. First
edition. 2 vols. 8vo. Cont. black half calf, spines gilt. Some-
what rubbed. Some foxing and stains, a few gatherings pulled.
Ximenes 63-243 1983 $150

JIANOU, IONEL   Zadkine. Paris: Arted, 1964. 97
plates. Large 4to. Cloth. Presentation copy, inscribed by the
artist to Sam Salz. Ars Libri 32-713 1983 $75

JINMAN, G.   Winds and their courses: or a practical exposition of the laws which govern the movemetns of hurricanes... London printed, Calcutta: reprinted by P.M. Cranenburgh, Bengal Printing Co., Ltd., 1863. 8vo. Orig. limp green cloth, printed paper side-label. Folding lithographed frontis. and eight litho-graphed plates (2 folding). Minor wear. Ximenes 63-303 1983 $65

JOAD, C. E. M.   The Adventures of the Young Soldier in Search of the Better World. L, (1943). Drawings by Mervyn Peake, very good in slightly torn and creased, very good dustwrapper. Quill & Brush 54-1069 1983 $60

JOAD, C. E. M.   Matter, Life and Value. Cambridge: Oxford Univ. Press, 1929. First edition. Dust jacket. Gach 95-250 1983 $35

JOCELYN, J. R. J.   The History of the Royal Artillery. London, 1911. Orig. cloth. Photogravure portrait frontis. 1 photo-gravure and 11 other plates (1 double page), 7 folding coloured maps, 3 text maps, numerous illus. Thick 8vo. Spine faded. Slightly worn. T.e.g. Good. Edwards 1042-554 1983 £30

JOCKNICK, SIGNEY   Early Days on the Western Slope of Colorado. Denver, 1913. First edition. 25 plates. Inscribed by Otto Mears Pathfinder of San Juan. Ginsberg 46-190 1983 $150

JOHANSEN, H.   Die Vogelfauna Westsibiriens. Journal fur Ornithologie, 1943-61. 8 coloured plates and 2 folding maps, 8vo, half cloth. Wheldon 160-777 1983 £75

JOHN, C. S.   The Gods of the East Indies. Hull, c.1815. Woodcut of idols on verso of title, title soiled. Small tear repaired. Sm.8vo. Wrapper. Good. Edwards 1044-388 1983 £40

JOHN McCutcheon's Book. Chicago, Caxton Club, 1948. First edition, one of 1000 copies. Illustrated. Buckram. Edward L. Ryerson's gift copy to Ryerson Nature Library with discard slip. Bradley 65-44 1983 $20

JOHN P. LOVELL ARMS CO.   Lovell Diamond Cycles. Boston, 1895. Illustrations. Oblong 8vo, original pictorial wrappers. Morrill 290-627 1983 $30

JOHNSON, A. E.   The Russian Ballet. Constable, 1913. 4to. Colour frontis. 11 colour plates. 24 full-page & 62 text illus. (4 colour). Light wear. Reddish brown cloth, gilt, worn. Greer 40-75 1983 £35

JOHNSON, A. J.   Johnson's New General Cyclopaedia and Copper-Plate Hand-Atlas...New York, A.J. Johnson & Co., 1885. 1st ed. Maps & illus. 2 vols., 4to, half orig. leather. Morrill 288-209 1983 $47.50

JOHNSON, A. M.   Taxonomy of the Flowering Plants. (New York, 1931), Reprint, Lehre, 1977. 478 text-figures, 8vo, cloth. Wheldon 160-1537 1983 £39

JOHNSON, A. T.   A woodland garden. 1937. Illustrated from photos, 8vo, cloth. Wheldon 160-1970 1983 £15

JOHNSON, AMANDUS   The Swedes On The Delaware 1638-1664. Phila., 1914. Vol. 1 of 4 vols. of The Swedes in America 1638-1900. Illus., cloth, ink name, extremities worn. King 46-235 1983 $40

JOHNSON, ANDREW   Trial of Andrew Johnson...on Impeach-ment...Washington, 1868. 1st ed. 3 vols., 8vo, minute pieces chipped from covers and backstrips. Morrill 288-210 1983 $50

JOHNSON, B. S.   Albert Angelo. London, 1964. First edition. Dust wrapper. Author's signed autograph presentation inscription to L. Clark (1967). Fine. Rota 231-349 1983 £75

JOHNSON, B. S.   Christie Malry's Own Double-Entry. London, 1973. First English edition. Presentation copy from the author to the poet Asa Benveniste. Bottom corners bumped. Dust-wrapper. Fine. Jolliffe 26-301 1983 £75

JOHNSON, B. S.   Statement against Corpses. London, 1964. First edition. Signed by Johnson. Presentation copy from co-author Zulfikar Ghose to Colin Franklin. Slightly marked and nicked dust-wrapper with a very small tear. Fine. Jolliffe 26-300 1983 £55

JOHNSON, CECIL JAMES   A Printer's Garland. (San Francisco, 1935). First edition. Small 8vo, pink printed boards over white. One of 300 copies. Very good. Houle 22-1199 1983 $25

JOHNSON, CHARLES   A General History of the Pirates. Kensington: Printed & sold by Philip Sainsbury at The Cayme Press, 1925-1927. 4to. 2 vols. in one. Orig. 3/4 blue morocco & cloth. Limited to 500 copies. Spine faded. Fine. MacManus 279-2990 1983 $85

JOHNSON, CHARLES   The tragedy of Medea. London: printed for R. Francklin, 1731. 8vo, disbound, 1st ed. Very good copy. Ximenes 64-319 1983 $225

JOHNSON, CHARLES B.   Letters from North America. (Phila?): Hall, 1821. Ads. Paper-backed boards. Map lacking. Ex-library copy. Broken spine. Very good. Felcone 20-72 1983 $35

JOHNSON, CHARLES PLUMPTRE   The Early Writings of William Makepeace Thackeray. London: Elliot Stock, 1888. First edition. Illus. Full morocco. Fine. MacManus 280-5139 1983 $30

JOHNSON, CLIFTON   Old Time Schools and School Books. N.Y. & London: Macmil., 1917. 8vo. Brown pictorial cloth. Illus. with photos & drawings. Fine. Aleph-bet 8-222 1983 $30

JOHNSON, HANNIBAL A.   The Sword of Honor. Worcester, (1906). Enlarged ed. Presentation from author. Portraits. 12mo. Morrill 288-621 1983 $22.50

JOHNSON, JAMES   Excursions to the principal mineral waters of England... London: S. Highley, 1843. First edition. 8vo. Orig. purple-brown cloth. Rather faded. Ximenes 63-280 1983 $80

JOHNSON, JAMES SYDNEY   Nocturne in St. Gauden's. San Francisco: The Windsor Press, 1929. Illus. with an orig. mounted wood-engraving by Howard Simon. Edition ltd. to 700 copies. In two-tone boards. This copy with a long presentation inscription from the author, dated 1929. Karmiole 71-94 1983 $45

JOHNSON, JAMES SYDNEY   Nocturne in St. Gauden's. S.F., 1929. Sm. 8vo, parchment-backed decorated boards, paper label. One of 700 copies with an original wood-engraving by Howard Simon. A fine copy. Perata 28-192 1983 $50

JOHNSON, JAMES WELDON   Saint Peter Relates an Incident. New York: Viking, 1935. Cloth. First edition. Two smudges on front free endsheet, otherwise fine in dust jacket. Reese 20-118 1983 $45

JOHNSON, JOHN   Poetica Typographia Johnsonia. Piedmont: Golden Key Press, 1959. Printed stiff brown wraps. Tipped-in is an illustrated leaf from the 1824 first edition of Johnson's "Typographia." One of 75 copies. Very good. Houle 22-120 1983 $85

JOHNSON, JOHN   Typographia, or the Printer's Instructor. 1824. 2 vols., royal 8vo, largest paper or Roxburghe copies, 5-1/2 x 8-3/4 inches, portrait in each volume, and additional engraved title pages, text within typographical ornamental borders throughout, t.e.g., other edges uncut, modern half dark brown crushed morocco, raised bands on the spines, lettered gilt on spines, new endpapers. A very fine copy. Bickersteth 75-148 1983 £285

JOHNSON, JOHN B.   An Oration on Union, Delivered in the ... City of New York... New York: John Buel, 1794. Disbound. Very good. Felcone 20-73 1983 $20

JOHNSON, JOSEPH   George MacDonald. Pitman, 1906. Fron-tis. portrait. Publisher's cloth, t.e.g., others uncut. Rubber name stamp verso frontis., slight foxing foreedge, name front endpaper. Very good. Scarce. Hodgkins 27-288 1983 £15

JOHNSON, JOSEPH   George Macdonald, a Biographical and Critical Appreciation. Pitman, 1906. Half title, front. port. Orig. maroon cloth. Jarndyce 31-799 1983 £14.50

JOHNSON, KENNETH M.   The Sting of the Wasp. San Francisco:
The Book Club of California, 1967. 20 lithographs reproduced in the
brilliant colors of the originals. Book has been designed and printed
by Saul and Lillian Marks at the Plantin Press. Fine. Jenkins 153-96
1983 $75

JOHNSON, LIONEL   The Gordon Riots. London, n.d. (1890's).
8vo. Wraps. 1st ed. Enclosed in foldover case. A fine copy. In
Our Time 156-440 1983 $350

JOHNSON, LIONEL   Poems. London & Boston: Elkin Mathews
& Copeland & Day, 1895. First eidtion. Orig. boards. One of 750
copies printed at the Chiswick Press, uncut, with a hand-lettered
title page. Spine and covers slightly rubbed and soiled. Offsetting
to the free endpapers from binder's paste. Former owner's signature
written in pencil. Very good. MacMansu 279-2991 1983 $125

JOHNSON, LIONEL   Selections from The Poems of Lionel
Johnson. London: Elkin Mathews, 1908. First edition. Orig. wrappers.
Elkin Mathews catalogue laid in at the back. Tape-stains on endpapers.
Very good. MacManus 279-2992 1983 $50

JOHNSON, LIONEL   Twenty-One Poems. Portland, 1908.
First American edition. One of 950 copies. Endpapers and edges
slightly spotted. Very good. Jolliffe 26-303 1983 £26

JOHNSON, LYNDON BAINES   The Vantage Point: Perspectives of the
Presidency, 1963-1969. N.Y., 1971. Mint in dust jacket. First edition, autographed by the President. Jenkins 151-149 1983 $125

JOHNSON, MARGARET   A Bunch of Keys. Chambers, nd, (ca.
1900). Illus. by Jessie Walcott. Frontis., 8 full page plates &
numerous other illus. Grey col'd illus. bds. Oblong. Free eps.
discol'd, sl. wear top/bottom rear joint, corners sl. worn, some red
stains rear cvr., vg. Hodgkins 27-113 1983 £20

JOHNSON, MELVIN M.   Automatic Weapons of the World. NY 1945.
Illus, cloth, very good in badly chipped dw. King 46-595 1983 $35

JOHNSON, MERLE   High Spots of American Literature. N.Y.,
Bennet, 1929. Tall 4to, 3/4 blue morocco over marbled boards,
t.e.g. Very good-fine. One of 700 numbered copies. Houle 21-133
1983 $85

JOHNSON, OVERTON   The Route Across the Rocky Mountains.
Princeton, 1932. Illus. Nice copy. Jenkins 153-290 1983 $30

JOHNSON, REVERDY   Remarks on Popular Sovereignty, as
Maintained and Denied Respectively by Judge (Stephen A.) Douglas,
and Attorney-General (Jeremiah S.) Black. Baltimore: Murphy & Co.,
1859. 23-1/2 cm. Self-wraps., side-stitched. Some stains & soiling;
creased horizontally. First edition. On the front wrapper is the
light pencil signature of G. (eorge) A. Smith. Grunder 6-37 1983
$65

JOHNSON, ROBERT   Enchiridion Medicum, or a Manual of
Physick. London: Heptinstall for Aylmer, 1684. 8vo, old calf,
repaired. On flyleaf, signature of "John Syer, 1689). The 6p. "Interpretation of certain hard Words" is present. Argosy 713-301 1983
$400

JOHNSON, ROBERT UNDERWOOD   Battles and Leaders of the Civil War.
New York, 1884-88. Orig. edition. Rebound copy. 4 vols. 4to. Green
cloth. Frontis. Numerous illus., maps, some full page. Good.
Edwards 1042-374 1983 £95

JOHNSON, ROBERT UNDERWOOD   Battles and Leaders of the Civil War.
N.Y., 1887-1889. First edition. Later cloth, morocco labels. Bound
in 4 vols. Indexed. Illus. Jenkins 153-286 1983 $125

JOHNSON, ROBERT UNDERWOOD   Battles and Leaders of the Civil War.
New York, (1884-1888). Grant-Lee Ed. Maps and illus. 4 vols. in 8,
4to, leather labels, nice. Morrill 286-219 1983 $60

JOHNSON, ROSSITER   Campfire & Battle-Field: History of
the Campaigns & Conflicts of the Great Civil War. NY (1894).
Many illus., some by Brady, & maps. 4to, gilt & blind stamped calf,
a.e.g. Argosy 710-87 1983 $100

JOHNSON, SAMUEL   An Argument Proving, that the
Abrogation of King James by the People of England from the Regal
Throne, and the Promotion of the Prince of Orange...In Opposition
to all the False and Treacherous Hypotheses... Printed for the
author, 1692. 4to, wrapper, a very good copy. Fenning 61-224 1983
£18.50

JOHNSON, SAMUEL   The Critical Opinions. Princeton:
Princeton University Press, 1926. First edition. 2 vols. Orig.
cloth-backed boards with paper spine labels. On of 25 copies on
Swedish handmade paper. With the bookplates of Barton Currie. Bindings a bit soiled and faded. Good. MacManus 279-2994 1983 $250

JOHNSON, SAMUEL   A Diary of a Journey into North Wales,
in the Year 1774. London: for Robert Jennings, 1816. Cr. 8vo.
Cont. boards, new paper spine with printed paper label. First
edition. Traylen 94-461 1983 £90

JOHNSON, SAMUEL   A dictionary of the English language.
London: printed for J. Knapton, etc., 1760. Second octavo edition.
2 vols. 8vo. Cont. calf, spines gilt, contrasting morocco labels.
Spines and edges rubbed, joints slightly tender. Ximenes 63-225
1983 $300

JOHNSON, SAMUEL   A Dictionary of the English Language.
London: by W. Strahan, etc., 1765. Third edition. 2 vols. Folio.
Cont. calf, gilt, neatly rebacked with orig. spines laid down,
crimson and green morocco labels, gilt. Traylen 94-462 1983 £450

JOHNSON, SAMUEL   A Dictionary of the English Language.
London: by W. Strahan, for W. Strahan, J. and F. Rivington, etc.,
1773. Fourth edition. 2 vols. Folio. Cont. polished calf, joints
and corners neatly repaired, gilt panelled spines with crimson and
green morocco labels, gilt. Title-pages printed in red and black.
Traylen 94-463 1983 £420

JOHNSON, SAMUEL   A Dictionary of the English Language.
J.F. & C. Rivington, L. Davis, T. Payne & Son, 1785. Seventh edition.
Folio, rebound in half calf, hand-marbled boards, retaining orig.
label and end papers. Signed on end paper by Arthur Hill-Trevor,
second Lord Dungannon. Jarndyce 31-27 1983 £380

JOHNSON, SAMUEL   A Dictionary of the English Language.
London, Rivington et al., 1785. 2 vols. 4to. Portrait, and half-
title in vol. I. Cont. calf, rebacked, red morocco labels. 6th ed.
Bit rubbed, but nice copy. O'Neal 50-29 1983 $300

JOHNSON, SAMUEL   A Dictionary of the English Language.
J.F. & C. Rivington, L. Davis, T. Longman, 1790. Ninth edition.
Rebound in half calf, hand-marbled boards, retaining orig. red label.
Very good. Jarndyce 31-28 1983 £85

JOHNSON, SAMUEL   A Dictionary of the English Language.
Montrose: Printed by D. Buchanon, sold by J. Fairbairn, C. Dickson,
1802. 12th edition, rebound in half calf, hand-marbled boards,
maroon label, v.g. Jarndyce 31-661 1983 £68

JOHNSON, SAMUEL   Dictionary of the English Language.
London, 1806. Ninth edition, revised and corrected. Large 4to,
full old diced calf, (expertly rebacked), contrasting leather labels;
marbled edges. Slipcase. 2 vols. A fine set. Houle 22-517 1983
$495

JOHNSON, SAMUEL   A Dictionary of the English Language.
Phil. Published by Moses Thomas. J. Maxwell printer. 1818. The
First American Edition of this work, published from the 11th London
edition. 2 vols. Thich 4to., mottled calf tooled in gilt, newly
rebacked with the orig. spines laid in. Lightly foxed. In Our Time
156-441 1983 $650

JOHNSON, SAMUEL   A Dictionary of the English Language...
London: for Longman, etc..., 1818. 4to. 4 vols. Cont. calf, gilt.
Neatlye rebacked at an early date in vellum with crimson morocco
labels, gilt. Engraved portrait frontis., 4 pp. of ads., and the
half-titles. Calf worn. Traylen 94-464 1983 £120

JOHNSON, SAMUEL   Johnson's Pocket Dictionary of the
English Language. Thomas Tegg, 1844. Small 8vo, front. port.
(sl. waterstained). Orig. dull green cloth, a.e.g. Jarndyce 31-662
1983 £15

JOHNSON, SAMUEL   The History of Rasselas. London:
Printed for John Sharpe, 1818. Small 8vo. Illus. with engravings
by Westall after Heath. Full cont. paneled calf, gilt, marbled endpapers. Bookplate. Light foxing. Covers a bit rubbed. Very good.
MacManus 279-2996 1983 $35

JOHNSON, SAMUEL   The Idler... London: for J. Rivington
and Sons, etc., 1783. Fourth edition. 2 vols. 12mo. Cont. speckled
calf, morocco labels, gilt, joints cracking. Traylen 94-465 1983
£28

JOHNSON, SAMUEL   A journey to the western islands of
Scotland. Dublin: printed for A. Leathley, J. Exshaw, et al., 1775.
2 vols. in one. 12mo. Cont. calf, spine gilt. Joints slightly
cracked, ends of spine a little worn, label missing. Ximenes 63-628
1983 $225

JOHNSON, SAMUEL   A Journey to the Western Islands of
Scotland. London: Printed for W. Strahan; and T. Cadell in the Strand,
1775. First edition, second issue. 8vo. Full cont. calf with morocco
label & marbled endpapers. With 6 line errata. Some foxing. Hinges
broken but cords sound. MacManus 279-2997 1983 $150

JOHNSON, SAMUEL   Julian the Apostate. London, printed
for Langley Curtis, 1682. 8vo, disbound, title a bit soiled and
worn, else good. Ravenstree 94-230 1983 $67.50

JOHNSON, SAMUEL   Letters To and From... Strahan and Cadell, published from the original manuscript in her possession by Hester
Lynch Piozzi, 1787. First edition, 2 vols, tall 8vo, cont. mottled
calf, spines gilt and with triple morocco labels, 3 labels lacking,
joints crackedq Deighton 3-188 1983 £100

JOHNSON, SAMUEL   Letters of Dr. Samuel Johnson...
Edinburgh: Bell and Bradfute, 1822. 12mo. First edition. Cont.
calf. Portrait. Slightly rubbed. Uncommon. Ximenes 63-230
1983 $75

JOHNSON, SAMUEL   The Lives of the Most Eminent English
Poets. 1781. 4 vols., 8vo, portrait in vol. 1, advertisement leaf
at the end of vol. 4 followed by leaf with the paper labels for each
volume, cont. calf with red morocco labels. Slight wear at top of
two spines, upper joint of vol. 1 cracked, small defective spot
on upper cover of vol. 4 by the joint, but a very good set. First
separate London edition. Bickersteth 75-45 1983 £180

JOHNSON, SAMUEL   The Lives of the most Eminent English
Poets. London, 1781. First London edition. 8vo. Cont. calf,
neatly rebacked, gilt. 4 vols. Engraved portrait in vol. 1, but
without the rare ad. leaf in vol. 4. Traylen 94-466 1983 £105

JOHNSON, SAMUEL   The Lives of the Most Eminent English
Poets. London: for C. Bathurst, J. Buckland and others, 1783. 4
vols. 8vo. Cont. calf, gilt spines (neatly repaired), crimson
morocco labels, gilt. New edition. Engraved portrait. Traylen
94-467 1983 £85

JOHNSON, SAMUEL   The Poetical Works of Samuel Johnson.
London: for the Editory, 1785. First edition, second issue. Small
8vo. Cont. tree calf, gilt rule, crimson morocco label, gilt,
joints neatly repaired. 4 pp. of publisher's ads. Traylen 94-469
1983 £135

JOHNSON, SAMUEL   The Poetical Works. Dublin: Printed
for L. White, 1785. First Irish edition, large 12mo, cont. sheep,
binding worn but cords holding, a very good copy. Fenning 62-194
1983 £65

JOHNSON, SAMUEL   Prayers and Meditations... London:
for T. Cadell, 1775. First edition. 8vo. Cont. marbled boards,
calf spine. Some marginal staining of last few leaves and ten
leaves severely foxed. Traylen 94-470 1983 £135

JOHNSON, SAMUEL   The Preface to Johnson's Dictionary of
the English Language. Cleveland: The Rowfant Club, 1934. First
separate edition. Orig. cloth-backed marbled boards. One of 110
copies. Printed by D.B. Updike at the Merrymount Press. Front cover
slightly scratched. Bookplate. Very good. MacManus 279-2998 1983
$125

JOHNSON, SAMUEL   Rasselas. London: 1823. Small octavo.
Engraved and printed title-page. Engravings in text. Double fore-
edge paintings. Full brown calf with gilt rules and gold designs.
Blind-embossed at center of covers. Red leather labels to spine and
gilt decoration, dentelles gilt. A.e.g. Very fine copy with binding
in especially fine condition. Bookplate of George L. Lincoln. Bromer
25-208 1983 $675

JOHNSON, SAMUEL   Sermons, on Different Subjects, left
for Publication by John Taylor. Pub. by the Rev. Hayes, 1795. Third
edition, 2 vols. Half titles. Tree calf; apart from chipped label
vol. II, a fine copy. Jarndyce 31-40 1983 £130

JOHNSON, SAMUEL   The Triple Wreath. Newtown, Pa., 1844.
Port. Cloth. Title foxed. First edition. Felcone 22-189 1983
$20

JOHNSON, SAMUEL   The Works of the English Poets. London:
John Nichols, 1790. 75 vols. Cr. 8vo. Cont. mottled calf, gilt,
neatly rebacked in 19th century vellum, gilt, red morocco labels,
gilt. Engraved portraits. Traylen 94-471 1983 £495

JOHNSON, SAMUEL   The Works. For F.C. & J. Rivington,
G. & W. Nicol, T. Egerton, 1823. Front. port. vol. I. Half calf,
marbled boards and edges, gilt bands and lettering on spines. Sl.
rubbing. A very good set, in 12 vols. Jarndyce 31-760 1983 £180

JOHNSON, SAMUEL ROOSEVELT   California: A Sermon Preached in St.
John's Church. N.Y., 1849. First edition. Dbd. Ginsberg 46-847
1983 $60

JOHNSON, SUSANNAH WILLARD   A Narrative of the Captivity of Mrs.
Johnson. Windsor, Vermont: Printed by Alden Spooner, 1807. 14-1/2
cm. Cont. calf-backed boards quite worn with wooden board edges
exposed. Foxed; portion torn from front free endpaper. Grunder 7-
46 1983 $150

JOHNSON, THEODORE T.   Sights in the Gold Region. New York:
Baker and Scribner, 1849. First edition. Orig. cloth, gilt. Some
wear to the extremities. Jenkins 152-177 1983 $175

JOHNSON, W. BOLINGBROKE   The Widening Stain. New York: Alfred
A. Knopf, 1942. First edition. 8vo. Cloth. Very good copy. Oak
Knoll 49-152 1983 $30

JOHNSON, WALTER R.   A Report to the Navy Department of the
United States on American Coals Applicable to Steam Navigation and
to Other Purposes. Wash., 1844. Folded maps. Cloth. First
edition. Ginsberg 46-380 1983 $35

JOHNSON, WARREN B.   From the Pacific to the Atlantic, being
an Account of a Journey Overland from Eureka, Humboldt Co., California.
Webster, Mass.: John Cort, Printer, 1887. Original cloth. 1st ed.
Jenkins 151-150 1983 $85

JOHNSON, WILLIAM   Lexicon Chymicum. William Nealand
for G. D., London, 1660. 8vo, 2 parts in 1 volume, worming affecting
headlines and a few words in the text, browned; cont. calf with gilt
arms on sides and ciphers in corners and on spine, joints repaired,
new endpapers. Third edition. Quaritch NS 5-61 1983 $500

JOHNSON, WILLIAM SAMUEL   Glamourie. N.Y. and London: Harper &
Brothers Publishers, 1911. First edition. Orig. cloth. Presentation
copy to Arthur Conan Doyle inscribed: "To Sir Arthur Conan Doyle with
the grateful regards of Wm Sam. Johnson. Apr. 19, 1922." Contains
Doyle's signature on the title-page and his armorial bookplate on the
front paste-down endpaper. Spine and covers slightly worn. Very good.
MacManus 278-1637 1983 $150

JOHNSON, WILLIS FLETCHER   "My Country, 'Tis of Thee!" Philadelphia: W.W. Houston & Co., 1892. 8vo. Cloth. Salesman's dummy
of this book with leather sample cover pasted to inside front cover
and reproductions of many illus. Minor cover wear. Oak Knoll 38-
343 1983 $20

JOHNSTON, A. B.   Marching with the Army of the West,
1846-48. Glendale, 1936. 1st ed. Ports., plates, fldg. map. Gilt
top, deckle edges, unopened. Clark 741-263 1983 $75

JOHNSTON, ALEX   The Life and Letters of Sir Harry
Johnston, Jonathan Cape, 1929. First edition, with 8 plates, 8vo,
orig. cloth, a very good copy, inscribed by the author. Fenning
61-226 1983 £10.50

JOHNSTON, ALEXANDER KEITH   A school atlas of astronomy... Edinburgh: Blackwood, 1856. First edition. Small folio. Orig. pub's
black half morocco. 18 striking double-page plates, color-printed
in blue, yellow and brown, and finished by hand. Slight rubbing.
Ximenes 63-189 1983 $175

JOHNSTON, CHARLES   A Narrative of the Incidents Attending
the Capture, Dentention, and Ransom of Charles Johnston... New York,
J.&J. Harper, 1827. 1st ed. in orig. boards. Illus. 8vo, cloth
back, paper label, all edges untrimmed. Fine copy. Morrill 287-173
1983 $150

JOHNSTON, CHARLES   Travels in Southern Abyssinia. London,
1844. First edition. Folding map and 2 tinted lithograph frontis.
2 vols. New quarter calf, gilt. 8vo. Good. Edwards 1044-390 1983
$235

JOHNSTON, EDWARD   Writing and Illuminating and Lettering.
Pitman, 1929. 16th ed., thick 8vo, 24 plates, diagrams and illus.,
orig. holland-backed paper boards a little darkened, still very good.
Deighton 3-190 1983 £20

JOHNSTON, ELLEN   Autobiography, Poems and Songs.
Glasgow: Wm. Love, 1867. Subscribers list. Orig. brown cloth,
a little rubbed. Jarndyce 30-767 1983 £15

JOHNSTON, G.   Asiatic Magnolias in Cultivation. London,
1955. 14 coloured and numerous other plates. Buckram leather label.
8vo. Good. Edwards 1044-392 1983 £160

JOHNSTON, G.   A History of the British Zoophytes.
1847. Second ed., 73 plates, 2 vols., 8vo, cloth. A good ex-library.
Wheldon 160-1301 1983 £40

JOHNSTON, HARRY H.   George Grenfell and the Congo.
Hutchinson, 1908. First edition, with 2 large folding maps, 2 plates,
496 full-page and other illus. and maps, 2 vols., roy. 8vo, orig.
cloth, t.e.g., a very good copy. Fenning 61-225 1983 £85

JOHNSTON, HARRY H.   The Uganda Protectorate. London:
Hutchinson & Co., 1902. 2 vols. 8vo. 48 colored plates. 9 maps.
505 black and white illus. Orig. blue cloth. Rubbed. Adelson
Africa-94 1983 $275

JOHNSTON, HARRY H.   The Uganda Protectorate. Hutchinson,
1902. First edition, with 9 folding maps, 48 coloured plates, 1
other plate, and 506 full-page and other illus. 2 vols., 4to,
orig. cloth, gilt, t.e.g., a little weakness in the inside joints
but otherwise a fresh copy. Fenning 62-195 1983 £85

JOHNSTON, HARRY V.   The Last Roundup. (Minneapolis, 1942).
First edition. Frontis. and illus. Jenkins 152-178 1983 $30

JOHNSTON, HARRY V.   My Home on the Range. St. Paul: (1942).
First edition. Profusely illus. Pictorial cloth. Very good copy.
Bradley 66-531 1983 $40

JOHNSTON, HENRY PHELPS   Nathan Hale, 1776: Biography and
Memorials. NY; Devinne Press, privately printed, 1901. Plates,
map, 8vo, uncut, g.t. One of 400 privately printed copies.
Argosy 710-450 1983 $60

JOHNSTON. J. P.   Twenty Years of Hus'ling. Chicago:
Thompson & Thomas, (1900). First edition. Illus. Pictorial tan
cloth. Printed on newsprint. Bright copy, inner hinges starting.
Bradley 66-570 1983 $45

JOHNSTON, JAMES DALE   The Detroit City Directory and Advertising Gazetteer of Michigan, For 1855-6. Detroit, 1855. Lea.
backed printed boards. Worn, minor staining. In a nice brown
leather backed cloth solander case, with the (detached) map which
is seldom found in these directories. King 46-165 1983 $100

JOHNSTON, JAMES FINLAY WEIR   The Chemistry of Common Life...
Edinburgh & London: Blackwood, 1854-5. 2 vols. First edition.
8vo. Orig. cloth. Worn, defect to spine vol. 1. A good set.
Zeitlin 264-227 1983 $65

JOHNSTON, JAMES FINLAY WEIR   Notes on North America Agricultural,
Economical and Social. Edinburgh & London, William Blackwood and Sons,
1851. 2 vols., folding map, three quarter mor., t.e.g. Jenkins 153-
288 1983 $150

JOHNSTON, JAMES FINLAY WEIR   Notes on North America. Edinburgh,
1851. 2 vols., folding map, cloth, first ed. Felcone 21-62 1983
$100

JOHNSTON, JOSEPH E.   Narrative of Military Operations...
NY, 1874. First edition. Rubbed, spine ends slightly frayed,
covers soiled, front hinge loose. Dec. cloth. King 46-51 1983 $75

JOHNSTON, MARY   Cease Firing. Boston: Houghton Mifflin
Co., 1912. First trade edition. Orig. grey pictorial cloth, gilt.
Fine. Jenkins 152-671 1983 $45

JOHNSTON, MARY   To Have and to Hold. Boston, Houghton,
1900. First edition. Illus. with eight plates by Howard Pyle, and
others. Decorated tan cloth. Very good. Houle 21-456 1983 $50

JOHNSTON, MARY   To Have and to Hold. B, 1900. Illus.
by Pyle. Dated inscription from author, front hinge starting, front
flys slightly offset, else very good. Quill & Brush 54-712 1983
$25

JOHNSTON, NATHANIEL   The King's Visitatorial Power Asserted.
Printed by Henry Hills, 1688. First edition, 4to, wrapper, some
light old damp staining, a good copy. Fenning 61-229 1983 £26.50

JOHNSTON, R. F.   Lion and Dragon in Northern China.
London, 1910. Folding map, numerous plates, slight foxing. Thick
8vo. Slight wear. Orig. cloth. 8vo. Good. Edwards 1044-391 1983
£22

JOHNSTON, WILLIAM G.   Overland to California. Oakland, 1948.
Reissue of the 1892 orig. Illus. Fld. map. Jenkins 153-291 1983
$45

JOHNSTON, WILLIAM P.   The Life of Gen. Albert Sidney Johnston.
N.Y., 1878. 1st ed. Jenkins 153-287 1983 $85

JOHNSTONE, CATHERINE LAURA   Tyrants of today; or, the secret society.
London: Tinsley, 1883. First edition. 3 vols. 8vo. Orig. dark
red cloth. Very fine copy. Rare. Ximenes 63-158 1983 $375

JOHNSTONE, CHARLES   Chrysal. For T. Becket, 1760. First
edition. 2 vols. 12mo, cont. speckled calf, gilt (rebacked). Hannas
69-114 1983 £70

JOHNSTONE, CHARLES   Chrystal; or the Adventures of a
Guinea. London, Hector McLean, 1821. New edition. Thick 8vo,
illus. with 15 aquatint plates by Barney, engraved by Maddocks. 3/4
red morocco over red cloth (a little foxing) else very good. Three
vols. bound in one, includes all three title pages. Houle 22-518
1983 $195

JOHNSTONE, CHARLES   The History of John Juniper, Esq.
R. Baldwin, 1781. 3 vols., 12mo, half titles, 2 pp ads. vol. I & II.
Calf, spines gilt, red and green labels. Sl. rubbed, v.g. First
edition. Jarndyce 31-41 1983 £160

JOHNSTONE, G. H.   Asiatic Magnolias in cultivation. 1955.
14 coloured and 20 plain plates, 4to, original buckram, slightly
used. Wheldon 160-2089 1983 £110

JOHNSTONE, J.   Conditions of Life in the Sea.
Cambridge, 1908. 8vo, cloth (worn), chart and 31 illustrations.
Wheldon 160-319 1983 £15

JOHNSTONE, J.   The Philosophy of Biology. Cambridge,
1914. Wheldon 160-170 1983 £15

JOHNSTONE, W. G.   The Nature-Printed British Sea-Weeds.
1859-60. 4 vols., 4oy. 8vo, original cloth, plain and coloured plates,
4 coloured title-vignettes. Some foxing. Bindings neatly refixed.
Wheldon 160-53 1983 £225

JOHONNOT, JACKSON   The Remarkable Adventures of...
Greenfield, MA, 1816. Folded, some tears and stains, but overall a
good copy. Reese 18-497 1983 $300

JOHONNOT, JACKSON   The Remarkable Adventures of Jackson
Johonnot. Greenfield: Printed by Ansel Phelps, 1816. Sewn. Rare.
Bradley 65-107 1983 $150

JOKAI, MAURUS   The New Landlord. London: Macmillan &
Co., 1868. First edition in English. 2 vols. Orig. cloth. All edges
very slightly worn and soiled. Endpapers of Vol. one a little dampstained. Covers slightly soiled. Very good. MacManus 279-3003 1983
$135

JOKAI, MAURUS   Timar's Two Worlds. Edinburgh: Blackwood, 1888. First edition in English. 3 vols. Orig. cloth. Spines
worn; recased. MacManus 279-3004 1983 $35

JOLAS, EUGENE   Vertical. N.Y.: Gotham Bookmart Press,
(1941). First edition. Orig. decorated cloth designed by A. Calder.
One of 100 copies printed on special rag paper at The Walpole Printing
Office and signed by Jolas. Fine. MacManus 279-3004 1983 $35

JOLIET in Photographs. Joliet, 1909. 1st ed. Illus., including
maps. Square gray wrappers. Bradley 63-69 1983 $35

JOLLY, THOMAS WILLIAM   Description of the New Patent Steering
Machine. London, (1779). 4to. Title plus 6 pages plates containing
3 diagrams. Small tear in outer margins repaired throughout. Modern
boards. Orig. wrappers preserved. Orig. cloth. Good. Edwards 1042-
112 1983 £65

JOLOWICZ, H. F.   Historical Introduction to the Study of
Roman Law. Cambridge, 1972. 3rd ed. Boswell 7-101 1983 $79

JOLY, N.   Memoire sur deux genres nouveaux de
Monstres Celosomiens... Toulouse, 1845. 8vo. Wrappers. 3 folding
plates. Signed presentation copy. Offprint. First leaf dust soiled.
Gurney JJ-201 1983 £12

JONAS, KLAUS W.   A Bibliography of the Writings of W.
Somerset Maugham. South Hadley: privately printed, 1950. Small
8vo, Cloth. One of 700 numbered copies. Oak Knoll 49-467 1983
$35

JONES, ALEXANDER   Historical Sketch of the Electric
Telegraph... New York, 1852. 1st ed. Text illus. 8vo. Some
foxing. Morrill 289-377 1983 $75

JONES, ANDREW A.   Jones's Digest. New York, 1835. 1st
ed. 8vo. Rubbed, faded and occasionally foxed; top blank inch of
spine lacking. Morrill 287-176 1983 $20

JONES, ARTHUR B.   The Salem Fire. Boston, Gorham Press,
1914. 1st ed. Illus. from photographs. 8vo. Morrill 288-639 1983
$27.50

JONES, ARTHUR EDWARD   "8Endake Ehen" or Old Huronia.
Toronto: Fifth Report of the Bureau of Archives..., 1909. 25cm.
Numerous illus., plates and maps, 2 rear folding maps, (some plates
in colour). Printed blue wrappers. Fine. McGahern 54-99 1983
$25

JONES, BENNETT MELVILL   Aerial Surveying by Rapids Methods.
Cambridge University Press, 1925. Large 8vo, illus., folding charts
in back pocket. K Books 301-104 1983 £25

JONES, CECIL K.   Hispanic American Bibliographies...
Baltimore: Hispanic American Historical Review, 1922. Frontis.,
wrappers, short tears. Dawson 470-167 1983 $25

JONES, CHARLES C.   Historical Sketch of the Chatham
Artillery During the Confederate Struggle for Independence. Albany,
1867. 1st edition, illus. A superb copy. Jenkins 151-152 1983
$250

JONES, CHARLES C.   Indian Remains in Southern Georgia.
Savannah, 1859. Orig. printed wraps. First edition. Ginsberg 46-
275 1983 $50

JONES, CHARLES C.   Jr. Brigadier General Robert Roombs.
Augusta, 1886. Pr. wrs. Argosy 716-111 1983 $22.50

JONES, CHARLES C.   The Siege of Savannah in December, 1864,
and the Confederate Operations in Georgia and... Albany, 1874. 1st
ed. Privately printed. Orig. printed wrappers bound in cloth, morocco
label. Issued in a small printing. Jenkins 153-779 1983 $125

JONES, CHARLES H.   Africa. New York: Henry Holt, 1875.
8vo. Folding map. 29 plates. Orig. maroon cloth. Rubbed. Adelson
Africa-200 1983 $55

JONES, CHARLES H.   Appleton's Hand-Book of American Travel.
New York, Appleton, 1874. Revised for Autumn of 1879. Folding maps.
Small 8vo, original limp cloth. Edges slightly rubbed. Morrill 290-
205 1983 $25

JONES, CHARLES INIGO   Memoirs of Miss O'Neill; containing her
public character, private life, and dramatic progress, from her
entrance upon the stage. London: printed for D. Cox, 1816. 8vo,
original light blue boards, drab paper backstrip (spine somewhat worn,
front cover almost loose). First edition. With a hand-coloured
frontis. portrait. Rare. Ximenes 64-321 1983 $200

JONES, DAVID   Anathemata. London, 1952. First
edition. Slightly frayed dustwrapper with one short tear. Ownership
signature on free endpaper. Fine. Gekoski 2-95 1983 £80

JONES, DAVID   Libellus Lapidum. N.d., (1924).
15 Woodcuts by David jones, in variant red and green decorated
cream wrapper. A fine copy. Gekoski 2-94 1983 £40

JONES, EDWARD   The Bardic Museum. London, 1802. Folio,
1/2 calf. Engraved frontis. by Rowlandson. Salloch 387-105 1983
$250

JONES, EDWIN GODDEN   An Account of the Remarkable Effects
of the Eau Medicinale d'Husson. London, 1810. First edition. 8vo.
Orig. boards, rebacked, uncut. Gurney 90-64 1983 £75

JONES, ERNEST (1879-1958)   Essays in Applied Psycho-Analysis.
London & Vienna, 1923. First edition. Frontis. 8vo, cloth. Argosy
713-302 1983 $50

JONES, ERNEST (1879-1958)   Essays in Applied Psycho-Analysis.
London/Vienna: IPP, 1923. First edition. Ads. Front hinge glued,
crown shelfworn. Gach 95-251 1983 $30

JONES, ERNEST (1879-1958)   The Life and Work of Sigmund Freud.
NY: Basic Books, (1953, 1955, 1957). Publisher's brown buckram,
painted label to Vol. 1 rubbed, minor stain to front board of Vol.
3, else fine set in original box. First editions, limited to 250
sets autographed by Jones. Gach 95-253 1983 $200

JONES, ERNEST (1879-1958)   The Precise Diagnostic Value of Allo-
chiria. London: John Bale, 1908. Orig. green wrappers. Inscribed
"With best compliments E.M." Gach 95-256 1983 $45

JONES, ERNEST (1879-1958)   Treatment of the Neuroses. London:
Bailliere, Tindall & Cox, 1920. First edition. Publisher's green
cloth. Gach 95-260 1983 $40

JONES, FREDERIC W.   The Matrix of the Mind. 1928. First
edition. Argosy 713-303 1983 $35

JONES, GWYN   The Green Island. (London), 1946.
Tall 8vo, two tone cloth, t.e.g., ten wood-engravings by John Petts.
One of 500 copies printed on mould-made paper. Christopher Sandford
signature on endleaf. Duschnes 240-85 1983 $65

JONES, H. BENCE   On Animal Chemistry in its Application
to Stomach & Renal Diseases. London, 1850. Thin 8vo, cont. cloth
(spine expertly mended). First edition. Argosy 713-299 1983 $85

JONES, HENRY   The Earl of Essex. R. Dodsley, 1753.
First edition, 8vo,. Fenning 62-196 1983 £24

JONES, HENRY ARTHUR   The Goal. Privately Printed, 1898.
First edition. Wrappers. Upper wrapper slightly ink-spotted. Nice.
Rota 231-355 1983 £25

JONES, HENRY ARTHUR   Michael and His Lost Angel. Macmillan,
1896. First edition, cr. 8vo, orig. cloth. Fenning 61-230 1983
£16.50

JONES, HENRY ARTHUR   My Dear Wells. London: Eveleigh Nash &
Grayson, (1921). First edition. Orig. cloth. Dust jacket. In a
half-morocco slipcase. Very fine. MacManus 280-5504 1983 $65

JONES, HERBERG G.   Maine Memories. Portland, 1940. One
of 1000 autographed copies. Sketches by the author. 8vo, torn dw.
Morrill 290-257 1983 $22.50

JONES, HERSCHEL V.   Adventures in Americana, 1492-1897. N.Y.,
1964. 3 vols. Orig. cloth. Ginsberg 47-392 1983 $75

JONES, IRA   King of Air Fighters. London, 1934.
First edition. Frontis. portrait (not called for in list of plates),
portrait plate of author and 15 other plates. Cont. calf backed cloth.
Speckled edges. Library marks on spine. Fine. Edwards 1042-601
1983 £35

JONES, J. P.   Flora Devoniensis. 1829. 8vo, cloth,
library stamp on reverse of title page. Wheldon 160-1610 1983 £40

JONES, J. T.   Journals of the Sieges. London, 1814.
8vo. Orig. cloth. 9 folding engraved maps at end. Cont. half calf,
marbled boards, joints repaired. Slightly worn, some slight foxing
throughout. Ink signature on title. Good. Edwards 1042-375 1983
£60

JONES, JAMES   From Here To Eternity. New York:
Charles Scribner's Sons, 1951. First edition. Thick 8vo. Orig.
cloth. Dust jacket. Back panel of jacket slightly dust-soiled,
but a fine copy. Jaffe 1-197 1983 $150

JONES, JAMES   From Here to Eternity. N.Y., Scribners,
1951. First edition. Thick 8vo, black cloth. Dust jacket (small
chips, rubbed) else very good. Houle 22-520 1983 $85

JONES, JOHN GALE   An invocation to Edward Quin, Esq.
London: printed for the author, and sold by R. Bagshaw, etc., n.d.
(1803). First edition. 8vo. Disbound. Title-page dusty. Uncut.
Ximenes 63-414 1983 $45

JONES, JOSEPH SEAWELL   A Defence of the Revolutionary History
of the State of North Carolina from the Aspersions of Mr. Jefferson.
Boston, 1834. Orig. cloth, expertly rebacked. Library label removed
from title page. Inscribed presentation copy from "the author."
Ginsberg 46-552 1983 $175

JONES, LE ROI   Raise Race Rays Raze, Essays Since
1965. New York: Random House, (1971). 1st ed., advance proof
copy in green printed wrappers. Fine copy of uncorrected proofs.
Jenkins 155-726 1983 $75

JONES, LEWIS T.   An Historical Journal of the British
Campaign on the Continent, in the Year 1794. Birmingham: Printed
for the author, by Swinney & Hawkins, 1797. First edition, with 5
folding maps (some coloured in outline), including the 4-page subscriber
list, 4to, cont. calf, gilt, neatly rebacked, a very good copy.
Fenning 60-208 1983 £55

JONES, RUFUS M.   Spiritual Reformers in the 16th and
17th Centuries. London, 1914. 8vo. Cloth. Traylen 94-474 1983
£12

JONES, S.   Fishes of the Laccadive Archipelago.
Trivandrum, 1980. 619 text-figures, cr. 4to, cloth. Wheldon 160-
972 1983 £55

JONES, S.   Introduction to Floral Mechanism.
1939. 77 illus., 8vo, cloth, trifle used. Wheldon 160-1538 1983
£12

JONES, SAMUEL MASTERMAN   The Practical Accountant. Birmingham:
for the Author, 1843. 2nd edition, rev. and imp. Orig. dark green
cloth, v.g. Jarndyce 31-210 1983 £25

JONES, STACY   The Medical Genius. Phila., 1887.
First edition. Ex-lib. Argosy 713-304 1983 $30

JONES, THOMAS   A companion to the Mountain Barometer,
consisting of tables... London: printed by Richard and Arthur
Taylor, for the author, 1817. First edition. 8vo. Modern wrappers.
Neatly pasted over his name on the title-page (and most of the
imprint) is the cont. engraved trade card of another firm. Ximenes
63-304 1983 $75

JONES, W. H. S.   Medical Writings of Anonymous
Londinensis. Cambridge: University Press, 1947. Argosy 713-305
1983 $50

JONES, WILLIAM   The Catholic Doctrine of a Trinity...
London: for J. Rivington, etc., 1767. Third edition. 8vo. Cont.
speckled calf, gilt, gilt panelled spine. Traylen 94-475 1983
£20

JONES, WILLIAM   Finger-Ring Lore. London, 1877. 1st
ed. Illus. Small 8vo, half morocco, marbled sides, orig. covers
bound in. Morrill 287-592 1983 $40

JONES, WILLIAM   Poems, consisting Chiefly of Translations from the Asiatick Languages... London: by W. Bowyer and J.
Nichols, 1777. Second edition, with additions. 8vo. Cont. polished
calf, morocco label, gilt. Traylen 94-476 1983 £65

JONES, WILLIAM   Poeseos Asiaticae Commentariorum.
Libri Sex... Londini: Richardsoniano..., 1774. First edition.
8vo. Later half calf. Small library stamp. Good copy. Heath
48-343 1983 £45

JONES, WILLIAM   Poikilographia. London, ca. 1830.
Folio, boards with leather back, orig. pictorial label on front
cover. Portrait frontis., title page and 20 specimen plates, all
engraved. Binding worn, foxing. Duschnes 240-36 1983 $175

JONGHE, C. H. DE   Paulus Moreelse. Portret- en Genre-
schilder te Utrecht, 1571-1638. Assen: Van Gorkum, 1938. 70
plates. Large 4to. Cloth. Ars Libri 32-477 1983 $300

JONNES, A. M. DE   Adventures in Wars of the Republic and
Consulate. London, 1920. 8vo. Orig. cloth. Full page map. Spine
faded, slightly worn. Library marks on endpapers. Good. Edwards
1042-376 1983 £12

JONSON, BEN   The Masque of Queenes. London, 1930.
Folio, red parchment, gilt, t.e.g. One of 350 copies with plates from
drawings by Inigo Jones & Ms. facs. Fine. Perata 28-96 1983 $150

JONSON, BENJAMIN   The Poems. Oxford: the Shakespeare
Head Press, 1936. Roy. 8vo. Orig. orange cloth, gilt. Portrait
and facsimile. Limited edition of 750 copies. Traylen 94-478 1983
£18

JONSON, BEN   The Workes. Imprinted at London by
Will Stansby, 1616. Folio in sixes. Engraved title by Hole. 1st
collected ed. Nineteenth century 3/4 tan morocco & marbled boards.
Engraved title mounted, light edge wear to covers. With contemporary
owner's inscription (Eliz. Finch) at head of engraved title and verso
of last leaf. In the presumed earliest state. Fine copy. Jenkins
155-727 1983 $750

JONVEAUX, EMILE   Two years in East Africa. London:
T. Nelson & Sons, 1875. 12mo. 2 folding maps. Text illus. Orig.
pictorial green cloth. Adelson Africa-95 1983 $100

JOPLING, LOUISE   Twenty Years of My Life. L, (1925).
Illus., covers bowed, else good or better in remnants of dustwrapper.
Quill & Brush 54-717 1983 $60

JORDAN, CORNELIA J. M.   Richmond: Her Glory and Her Graves.
Richmond, 1867. Orig. printed wraps. First edition. Ginsberg 46-
780 1983 $75

JORDAN, DENHAM   On Surrey Hills. London, 1891. First edition. Spine faded and worn and covers marked. Name on endpaper. Very good. Rota 230-317 1983 £15

JORDAN, DOROTHY   Public and Private Life of that Celebrated Actress, Miss Bland, Otherwise Mrs. Ford, or Mrs. Jordan. N.d. (1886?) Orig. cream boards, red leather label. Jarndyce 31-382 1983 £12.50

JOSEPHSON, MATTHEW   Portrait of the Artist as American. New York: Harcourt, (1930). Cloth. First edition. Inscribed presentation copy from the author. A very good in somewhat chipped and darkened dust jacket. Reese 20-561 1983 $50

JOSEPHSON, MATTHEW   Union House Union Bar the History of the Hotel and Restaurant Employees and Bartenders International Union AFL-CIO. New York: Random House, (1956). Cloth, first edition. Fine copy in crisp dust jacket, with very slightest traces of rubbing. Reese 20-562 1983 $25

JOSEPHUS, FLAVIUS   The Famous and Memorable Works of Josephus... London: for Thomas Adams, (colophon: printed by J. Lownes), 1620. Third English edition, 2 parts in 1 vol. Folio. Half antique calf, gilt. Vignette title-page and numerous decorate head and tail-pieces. Traylen 94-479 1983 £135

JOUBIN, L.   Les Memertiens. Paris, 1894. 4 coloured plates, 8vo, qtr. leather, Faune francaise. Wheldon 160-1302 1983 £18

JOUFFROY, ALAIN   Le nouveau Nouveau monde de LAM. Pollenza-Macerata: Nuova Foglio, 1975. Prof. illus. Folio. Cloth. Dust jacket. Printed in an edition of 1000 copies, on Ingres Cover Fabriano. Ars Libri 32-385 1983 $150

JOUIN, HENRY   Antoine Coyzevox. Sa vie, son oeuvre, et ses contemporains. Paris: Didier & Cie., 1883. Marbled boards. 1/2 leather. With catalogue raisonne and documents. Ex libris Ogden Codman, Jr. Ars Libri 32-127 1983 $75

JOURDAIN, AMABLE LOUIS M. M. B.   La Perse, ou Tableau de L'Histoire ... Paris, Ferra & Imbert, 1814. 5 vols. 16 mo. 39 engraved plates (7 folded). Cont. speckled calf & marbled boards, raised bands, red leather labels. 1st ed., nicely illustrated and very scarce. O'Neal 50-30 1983 $125

JOURNAL of the Ministry at Large. Boston, 1841. 12 numbers issued. Contributions by Dr. Walter Channing, Mrs. Sigourney, Longfellow, etc. 6 issues, 8vo, orig. wrappers. Wrappers of No. 1 chipped and loose. Morrill 286-222 1983 $25

JOURNAL of The Proceedings of the Congress, Held at Philadelphia, September 5, 1774. Phila.: William & Thomas Bradford, at the London Coffee House, 1774. First edition, first issue of the first official journal of Congress. Half morocco slipcase. Full cont. calf, spine with raised bands and orig. gilt-stamping. Upper spine cover almost detached and some binding wear. Orig. endpapers, half title, and cont. signature on upper cover of Thomas Wm. Pittman. Woodcut on title. Jenkins 152-602 1983 $5,000

JOURNAL UNIVERSEL D'ELECTRICITE, REVUE SCIENTIFIQUE ILLUSTREE   La Lumiere Electrique. Paris, 1880. Vol. 10. Illus., lea. spine, marbled boards, spine ends chipped and frayed, hinges loose, ex-technical library. King 46-510 1983 $50

JOYANT, MAURICE   Henri de Toulouse-Lautrec, 1864-1901. Paris: H. Floury, 1926. 55 plates, each present in two states (8 tipped-in color), 3 original drypoint etchings, each present in two states. 138 text illus. Square 4to. Marbled boards, 3/4 morocco. Orig. illus. wrappers bound in. T.e.g. No. 14 of a limited edition of 175 copies on japon. Ars Libri 32-671 1983 $1,500

JOYANT, MAURICE   Henri de Toulouse-Lautrec, 1864-1901. Paris: H. Floury, 1926-1927. 2 vols. 102 plates (22 color). 2 original drypoint etchings. Prof. illus. 4to. Orig. wrappers. Glassine dust jacket. Ars Libri 32-672 1983 $750

JOYCE, FREDERICK   Practical Chemical Mineralogy... London: for Knight and Lacey, 1825. Large 12mo. Modern boards. Engraved frontis. and title, inner margin of frontis. silked. Ads. Good copy. Zeitlin 264-228 1983 $140

JOYCE, JAMES   Anna Livia Plurabelle. Colum., NY: 1928. Limited to 800 copies signed by Joyce. End of spine slightly rubbed, else fine. Bromer 25-58 1983 $675

JOYCE, JAMES   Anna Livia Plurabelle. N.Y.: Crosby Gaige, 1928. First edition. Orig. cloth. One of 800 copies, signed by author. Fine. MacManus 279-3008 1983 $500

JOYCE, JAMES   Chamber Music. New York, 1923. 8vo. Cloth. The second authorized American printing of the work. Name on front flyleaf, edges of the spine have some wear, else a very good copy. Jacket is worn. In Our Time 156-442 1983 $200

JOYCE, JAMES   Chamber Music. Boston (1918). First American edition. Fine with chipped glassine. Bromer 25-59 1983 $150

JOYCE, JAMES   Collected Poems. Black Sun Press, 1936. 12mo. Parchment boards. 1 of 800 copies. From the library of Pearl Buck. Bookplate in the rear signed by her daughter. Some light foxing, else a fine copy. In Our Time 156-444 1983 $300

JOYCE, JAMES   Collected Poems. N.Y., 1937. First edition. Portrait. Owner's inscription on endpaper. Argosy 714-412 1983 $20

JOYCE, JAMES   The Dead, from Dubliners. N.p.: Kulgin D. Duval and Colin H. Hamilton (1982). Small folio. 4 etchings inserted. Edition limited to 150 numbered copies printed on Magnani hand-made paper at the Officina Bodoni in Verona, Italy. Signed by Pietro Annigoni. With the printer's device on the colophon leaf. Bound in green morocco over yellow paper-covered boards. Housed in a paper-covered slipcase. Fine. Karmiole 72-78 1983 $450

JOYCE, JAMES   The Dead, from Dubliners. K.D. Duval and C.H. Hamilton, 1982. Printed at the Officina Bodoni in Verona. Folio. Boards, green morocco spine, gilt, t.e.g., others uncut. Preserved in a slip-case. 4 etchings by Pietro Annigoni, printed on hand-made paper. Limited edition of 150 numbered copies, signed by the artist. Traylen 94-480 1983 £165

JOYCE, JAMES   Exiles: A Play in Three Acts. New York: B.W. Huebsch, 1924. 8vo. Cloth, boards. The second printing of a book which by 1921 the publisher had only sold 388 copies of the orig. ed. Tiny bookplate on inside endboard, else a fine copy in near perfect dj. Some minor binding changes. In Our Time 156-443 1983 $200

JOYCE, JAMES   Exiles. NY, 1951. Bright, fine copy in fine dustwrapper. Quill & Brush 54-719 1983 $125

JOYCE, JAMES   Finnegan's Wake. London, 1939. 8vo. Cloth. Limited signed ed., being 1 of 425 copies signed by Joyce. Orig. cloth slipcase box is soiled. A fine copy. In Our Time 156-447 1983 $1800

JOYCE, JAMES   Finnegans Wake. London & N.Y., 1939. Large 8vo. Rose buckram, gilt, gt., other edges uncut. 1st ed. 1 of 425 numbered copies, signed by Joyce. Fine, unopened copy in soiled orig. yellow cloth box. O'Neal 50-31 1983 $1,500

JOYCE, JAMES   Finnegans Wake. London: Faber and Faber Limited, (1939). First edition, regular issue. Large 8vo. Orig. cloth. Dust jacket. Price neatly clipped from front inner flap of jacket, otherwise an almost perfect copy. Jaffe 1-200 1983 $750

JOYCE, JAMES   Finnegans Wake. London: Faber and Faber, 1939. 4to. Red buckram gilt, t.e.g., others uncut, preserved in the orig. slip-case. Limited edition fo 425 numbered copies, this copy out-of-series but inscribed and signed on the half-title, "Best wishes, James Joyce." Traylen 94-481 1983 £450

JOYCE, JAMES   Finnegans Wake. London, 1939. First edition. Perforation stamp on page 627 notes "Complimentary Copy Not For Sale". Laid in is an advance review slip from Faber and Faber announcing date of publication. Slightly chipped and darkened dust-wrapper lacking a small piece at foot of spine. Fine. Gekoski 2-97 1983 £375

JOYCE, JAMES   Finnegans Wake. London, 1939. First edition. Roy. 8vo. Cloth, uncut edges, in the orig. dustwrapper (a little worn). Traylen 94-482 1983 £160

JOYCE, JAMES   Finnegans Wake. N.Y.: Viking, 1939. First American edition. Orig. cloth. Dust jacket (chipped). Bookplate. Very good. MacManus 279-3009 1983 $150

JOYCE, JAMES   Haveth Childers Everywhere. Paris: Henry Babou and Jack Kahane, 1930. Folio. Printed in green & black. This is one of 500 copies on hand-made paper. Orig. stiff wraps. and glassine; glassine sl. chipped. Karmiole 75-69 1983 $165

JOYCE, JAMES   Haveth Childers Everywhere. London, (1931). 12mo, first English edition, issued as no. 26 of the Criterion Miscellany. Argosy 714-413 1983 $25

JOYCE, JAMES   The Mime of Nick, Nick and the Maggies. The Hague: The Servire Press; London: Faber and Faber Ltd., (1933). First edition. 8vo, initial letter, tail-piece and cover designed by Lucia Joyce. Orig. decorated wrappers. Silver slipcase with paper label. Limited to 1,000 copies. Very fine. Jaffe 1-109 1093 $175

JOYCE, JAMES   Pomes Penyeach. Paris: Shakespeare & Co., 1927. First edition. 12mo. Spine and covers just a little faded. Very nice. Rota 231-357 1983 £60

JOYCE, JAMES   Pomes Penyeach. Paris: Shakespeare & Co., 1927. 1st ed. Orig. pale green printed boards. Some spots on rear cover, but much nicer copy than usually found with cover not faded to tan, and with delicate spine paper wholly intact. Jenkins 155-729 1983 $100

JOYCE, JAMES   Pomes Penyeach. Paris. Shakespeare & Co., 1927. First edition. Orig. boards. 16mo. With the errata slip. Lightly soiled. Backstrip a little worn. MacManus 279-3011 1983 $100

JOYCE, JAMES   Pomes Penyeach. Paris: Shakespeare & Co., 1927. Small thin 24mo. Orig. printed boards. Backstrip chipped. With the errata slip. Argosy 714-414 1983 $75

JOYCE, JAMES   Pomes Penyeach. Paris: Shakespeare & Co., 1933. First English edition. Wrappers just a little marked. Very nice. Rota 231-358 1983 £20

JOYCE, JAMES   A Portrait of the Artist as a Young Man. The Egoist, (1917). First English edition (from American sheets). Cloth at head and foot of spine torn. T. Bosanquet's copy, with her autograph signature. Good. Rota 231-356 1983 £45

JOYCE, JAMES   Stephen Hero. (New York): New Directions, (1944). Cloth and boards. Portrait. Facs. First American edition. Top edge a trifle dusty, one minor internal repair to dust jacket, else about fine. Reese 20-563 1983 $90

JOYCE, JAMES   Storiella As She Is Syung. (London): Corvinus Press, (1937). First edition. Large 4to. Illuminated capital by Lucia Joyce. Full orange limp vellum, gilt, in publisher's paper slipcase. One of 175 copies printed on Arnold hand-made paper. Very scarce, though damaged, slipcase. Pristine. Jaffe 1-199 1983 $1,475

JOYCE, JAMES   Tales Told of Shem and Shaun. Paris: Black Sun Press, 1929. Limited to 500 copies. Fine in wrappers, glassine and gilt slip-case. First edition. Bromer 25-61 1983 $350

JOYCE, JAMES   Two Tales of Shem and Shaun. London, (1932). 8vo. Cloth. 1st English ed. Dust jacket has a chip on the rear flap. A fine copy. In Our Time 156-445 1983 $125

JOYCE, JAMES   Two Tales of Shem and Shaun. London: Faber & Faber, (1932). First English edition. Orig. pale green boards. Dust jacket (spine faded, badly worn). Good. MacManus 279-3012 1983 $45

JOYCE, JAMES   Two Tales of Shem and Shaun. London, 1932. First English edition. Covers a little spotted. Slightly frayed dust wrapper. Nice. Rota 231-359 1983 £20

JOYCE, JAMES   Ulysses. Paris: Shakespeare and Co., 1922. First edition, 4to, 1 of 750 copies printed on handmade paper. Bound in 3/4 blue calf, with gilt "Ulysses" and "J. Joyce" on spine. Orig. blue wraps. bound in at back. Karmiole 75-70 1983 $1,850

JOYCE, JAMES   Ulysses. Paris: Shakespeare & Co., 1927. Ninth printing. Orig. blue wrappers. Bookplate. Wrappers darkened toward edges and on spine. Spine a little worn and cracking. Unopened. Very good. MacManus 279-3013 1983 $100

JOYCE, JAMES   Ulysses. New York: Random House, 1934. 8vo. Cloth. 1st authorized American ed. Laid into this copy is the brochure from Random House "How To Enjoy Ulysses." Cloth is tanned, else a fine tight copy. In Our Time 156-446 1983 $75

JOYCE, JAMES   Ulysses. N.Y.: Limited Editions Club, 1935. Illus. by Henri Matisse. Out of 1250 copies signed by Matisse. Fine, in mended pub.'s box. Argosy 714-415 1983 $800

JOYCE, JAMES   Ulysses. London: The Bodley Head (1936). Large thick quarto, green buckram with gilt bow on front and back covers (the binding and lettering designed by Eric Gill), t.e.g., dust-jacket. One of 900 copies printed on japon vellum. First English edition. Duschnes 240-118 1983 $650

JOYCE, JAMES   Ulysses. John Lane, The Bodley Head, 1936. First edition printed in England. One of 900 numbered copies on japon vellum. Bound in green buckram with a cover design in gilt by E. Gill. 4to. Spine faded, covers a little bubbled. G. Fay's copy with his autograph signature on a preliminary. Nice. Rota 230-318 1983 £200

JOYCE, JAMES   Ulysses: A Facsimile of the Manuscript. Philadelphia & New York: Rosenbach Foundation & Farrar, Straus, (1975). 3 vols. 1st ed. thus. Orig. blue cloth, boxed. Mint set. Jenkins 155-731 1983 $175

JOYCE, JAMES   James Joyce Ulysses; A Facsimile of the Manuscript... New York: Octagon Books, (1975). First edition. Folio. Cloth. Slipcase. One of 1775 numbered sets. Fine. Oak Knoll 49-252 1983 $150

JOYCE, JEREMIAH   Scientific Dialogues intended for the Instruction & Amusement of Young People. Phila., 1815. Corrected & improved ed. of Vol. 3 only. 8 detailed copperplates by J. Bower. Thick 18mo, cont. calf, joints cracked. Argosy 710-477 1983 $75

JUARROS, DOMINGO   A Statistical and Commercial History of the Kingdom of Guatemala in Spanish America. London: Hearne, 1823. First edition in English. 2 folding maps. Full cont. polished calf. Sides and spine stamped in gilt and blind (skillfully rebacked, orig. spine preserved). Maps foxed. Two cont. ms. leaves tipped in. Fine. Jenkins 152-673 1983 $300

JUDD, ALFRED   Derry of Dunn's House. Blackie, n.d. Frontis. & 3 plates. Grey pictorial cloth. Very nice. Greer 40-69 1983 £12.75

JUDD, EBEN W.   The United States Almanac, for ... 1791. Elizabeth Town: Shepard Kollock, (1790). Stitched. Verso of last leaf soiled. Cloth folding case. Very good. Felcone 19-52 1983 $75

JUDD, EBEN W.   The United States Almanac, for ... 1793. Elizabeth Town: Shepard Kollock, (1792). Lacking final two leaves. Signature and marginal notes of Jemima Scudder. Very good. Felcone 19-53 1983 $30

JUDD, SYLVESTER   History of Hadley...Northampton, 1863. 1st ed. With family genealogies by Lucius M. Boltwood. 8vo. Morrill 289-422 1983 $65

JUDD, SYLVESTER   History of Hadley... Springfield, 1905. 1st ed. Illus. 8vo. Inner hinges slightly cracked. Morrill 287-236 1983 $50

JUDGEMENT of the Judicial Committee of Her Majesty's most Honourable Privy Council... Gloucester: J.E. Lea, 1841. 8vo. Stitched. Heath 48-229 1983 £20

JUDGEMENT pronounced by Vice Chancellor Wigram, on Saturday 4th Nov. 1843... Gloucester: J.E. Lea, 1844. 8vo. Stitched. Heath 49-230 1983 £25

JUETTNER, OTTO   Daniel Drake and His Followers. Cincinnati, (1909). Photos. Cloth. Index. Minor wear and soil. King 45-466 1983 $35

JULIA De Vienne. For Henry Colburn, 1811. First edition. 4 vols. 12mo, half-titles in vols. II and III. Final ad. leaf in vol. I. List of subscribers. Ownership stamp on titles, with the crowned Garter ribbon round the letters A.F. A few tiny holes, some foxing and browning. Hannas 69-115 1983 £150

JULIEN, HENRI   Henri Julien Album. Montreal, 1916. 1st ed. Small folio. Morrill 286-223 1983 $75

JULIUS, SECUDUS, PSEUD.
Please turn to
ERASMUS, DESIDERIUS

JUNG, CARL   Psychological Analysis of Nietzsche's Zarathustra Part 3. (N.p.), (N.d.). Quarto. Cloth and boards. Mechanically reproduced typescript. Spine slightly flecked, else fine. Reese 20-566 1983 $125

JUNGFLEISCH, EMILE   Theses, presentees a la faculte des sciences de Paris... Paris: Gauthier-Villars, 1868. 4to. First edition. Orig. printed wrappers. Presentation copy from the author. Frayed, spine strengthened. Zeitlin 264-229 1983 $100

JUNKIN, GEORGE   The Baccalaureate in Miami University. Rossville, Ohio, 1842. Orig. green printed wrappers. Jenkins 152-725 1983 $75

JUSSIM, ESTELLE   Slave to Beauty: The Eccentric Life and Controversial Career of F. Holland Day... Boston: David R. Godine, (1981). Edition Deluxe, produced by James Cummins Bookseller. One-quarter black morocco with marbled paper over boards. Limited to 60 copies, this being 1 of 50 numbered copies signed by the author and the binder, Gray Parrot. Illus. with many photographs. Oak Knoll 49-147 1983 $100

JUSTICE and generosity against malice, ignorance, and poverty: or, an attempt to shew the equity of the new prices at the Theatre Royal, Covent Garden. London: printed for Sherwood, Neely, and Jones, 1809. 8vo, disbound, 1st edition. Half-title present. Very rare. Ximenes 64-323 1983 $75

JUSTIZ und NS-Verbrechen, The German War Trials... Amsterdam, 1968-81. 23 vols. Boswell 7-83 1983 $2,200

JUVENAL, DECIMUS JUNIUS   The satires of Juvenal. London: printed by T. Bensley; for Payne and MacKinlay, 1807. Translated and illustrated by Francis Hodgson. First edition. 4to. Cont. pale blue half calf and pink marbled boards, armorial crest on spine. With a 4-page list of subscribers; errata slip. Occasional foxing, but a fine copy. Ximenes 63-67 1983 $125

JUVENALIS, DECIMUS JUNIUS   Thirteen Satires. Cambridge, 1853. 8vo, cloth. Salloch 385-600 1983 $30

THE JUVENILE Mirror. Edward Lacey, nd (ca. 1840). Frontis., title p. woodcut & 5 full page wood engrs. Orig. black vertical ribbed blind stamped cloth, gilt decor. bkstrip, new eps., some foxing & sl. thumbing of contents, corners of cvrs. sl. bruised, vg. Hodgkins 27-114 1983 £20

K

KABERRY, C. J.　　　Our Little Neighbours: Animals of the Farmyard and the Woodland. London: Humphrey Milford (1921). Quarto. Illus. Some very faint foxing to fore-edge only, else extremely fine with pictorial dust wrapper, lightly rubbed at edges. Bromer 25-341 1983 $400

KAEMTZ, L. F.　　　A Complete Course of Meteorology. London: H. Bailliere, 1845. 12mo. Orig. cloth, recased. Coloured frontis. and 14 folding plates. Gurney JJ-203 1983 £20

KAFKA, FRANZ　　　The Great Wall of China, Stories and Reflections. New York: Schocken, (1946). 1st American ed. Orig. cloth, dj. Very fine copy. Jenkins 155-1402 1983 $30

KAFKA, ROGER　　　Warships of the World. New York, 1946. Imperial 8vo. Orig. cloth. Numerous illus, drawings and silhouettes. Ads. in text. 56-page chronology of the 1939-45 war (with separate index), as well as the details of the ships and war losses. Fine. Edwards 1042-113 1983 £35

KAGAN, SOLOMON　　　Contributions of Early Jews to American Medicine. Boston, (1934). 18 illus. 8vo. Orig. wrappers. 1st ed. Morrill 289-122 1983 $37.50

KAGAN, SOLOMON　　　Jewish Contributions to Medicine in America (1656-1934)... Boston, 1943. 8vo. First edition. 1/4 leather. Fye H-3-646 1983 $50

KAHLBAUM, KARL (1828-1899　　　Die Gruppirung Der Psychischen Krankheiten Und Die Eintheilung Der Seelenstoerungen. Danzig: Verlag von A. W. Kagemann, 1863. Ad leaf. Modern leatherette. Library bookplate and rear stamps. First edition. Gach 95-266 1983 $125

KAHN, EDGAR M.　　　Bret Harte in California. San Francisco, Privately printed, 1951. First edition. Hand colored frontis. portrait signed in pencil by the artist, William Wilke. Linen over boards, paper label. Very good. The artist's copy with a presentation inscription and small drawing on endpaper; signed on the frontis. Houle 22-459 1983 $135

KAHN, EDGAR M.　　　Cable Car Days in S.F. Palo Alto, Stanford, (1940). First edition, 4to, illus. Dust jacket. Fine. Houle 21-1096 1983 $20

KAHNWEILER, DANIEL-HENRY　　　Juan Gris. His life and work. New York: Abrams, n.d. Revised edition. 184 illus. (24 tipped-in color). Large 4to. Cloth. Dust jacket. Ars Libri 32-288 1983 $75

KALER, JAMES OTIS　　　The Life Savers. New York, 1899. 1st ed. Illus. from photographs. 8vo, pictorial front cover and back-strip, nice. Morrill 287-177 1983 $22.50

KALLIR, OTTO　　　Egon Schiele. The graphic work. New York: Crown, 1970. 66 illus. Large 4to. Cloth. Dust jacket. Ars Libri 32-616 1983 $150

KALLOCH, ISAAC S.　　　A Faint Idea of a Terrible Life. (San Francisco, 1879). Orig. printed yellow wrappers bound in 3/4 morocco. Listed as the 4th ed. Jenkins 153-294 1983 $100

KANE, ELISHA KENT　　　Arctic Explorations. Philadelphia, 1856. 1st ed. Illus. 2 vols., 8vo, backstrips bit faded. Morrill 288-625 1983 $40

KANE, ELISHA KENT　　　Arctic Explorations. Philadelphia, 1856. 1st ed. Maps and illus. 2 vols., 8vo. Corners rubbed. Morrill 286-224 1983 $40

KANE, ROBERT　　　Elements of Chemistry... Dublin: Hodges and Smith, 1846. 8vo. Orig. stamped cloth. Title-page indicates 1841 (variant). Spine faded, some wear. Otherwise a good copy. Zeitlin 264-230 1983 $100

KANE, ROBERT　　　Elements of Chemistry... Dublin: Hodges and Smith, 1849. Second edition. 8vo. Orig. stamped cloth. Spine faded, somewhat worn. Zeitlin 264-231 1983 $65

KANE, THOMAS L　　　The Private Papers and Diary of Thomas Leiper Kane A Friend of the Mormons. San Francisco: Gelber-Lilienthal, Inc., 1937. Frontis. and illus. Fine copy. Limited to 500 copies. Jenkins 151-153 1983 $85

KANE, THOMAS L.　　　The Private Papers and Diary of... San Francisco: Gelber-Lilienthal, 1937. Cloth and boards, paper label. Portrait. Corners very slightly bumped, otherwise a fine copy. One of 500 copies printed at the Grabhorn Press. Reese 19-309 1983 $75

KANN, EDUARD　　　The Currencies of China. Shanghai: Kelly & Walsh, 1927. Tall thick 8vo, with color frontis., map. 9 plates and folding chart. Black gilt-stamped. Second edition. Karmiole 76-28 1983 $75

KANNER, LEO　　　Child Psychiatry. Springfield: Charles C. Thomas, 1935. First edition. Fine copy in worn dust jacket. Gach 95-268 1983 $75

KANNER, LEO　　　Folklore of the Teeth. NY: Macmillan, 1933 (1928). Fine copy, with a 14 page bibliography. Gach 95-269 1983 $45

KANSAS. HISTORICAL SOCIETY.　　　Transactions of the Kansas State Historical Society. Topeka, 1886. Orig. cloth. Some spotting to cloth. Jenkins 152-842 1983 $45

KANT, IMMANUEL (1724-1804)　　　Religion Within the Boundary of Pure Reason. Edinburgh: Thomas Clark, 1838. 8vo. Modern paper-backed boards, paper label. Unopened and untrimmed copy. First English edition. Gach 95-270 1983 $185

KANTOR, MC KINLAY　　　Andersonville. World Publishing Co., (1955). 8vo. Cloth. Limited signed ed., signed by Kantor on the colophon page. Advance copy of the book, inscribed by Kantor to his editor. With the Bill Targ bookplate. Laid into the book is a flyer from World noting that the book will be published in November. One page ALS from Kantor to Targ. The letter with pencil is framed just as it was sent to Targ. Fine copy in slipcase box. In Our Time 156-450 1983 $500

KAPPEL, A. W.　　　Beetles, Butterflies, Moths, and other Insects. 1893. 12 coloured plates, royal 8vo, cloth (trifle used). Wheldon 160-1105 1983 £15

KAPPEL, A. W.　　　British and European Butterflies and Moths (macrolepidoptera). (1895). 30 coloured plates of numerous figures, 4to, original decorated cloth (somewhat worn), g.e. Wheldon 160-1106 1983 £38

KAPPERT, H.　　　Handbuch der Pflanzenzuchtung. Berlin and Hamburg, 1958-62. Second edition, many illus., 6 vols., royal 8vo, cloth (with dust-jackets). Clean second-hand copy. Wheldon 160-2123 1983 £80

KAPPIS, JOANNES JACOBUS　　　Theses inaugurales medicae primas linea odontitidis. Tubingen: Typis Reissianis, April 1794. Woodcut head-piece. Small 4to. Cont. paper backstrip. Kraus 164-53 1983 $80

KARPF, FAY B.　　　American Social Psychology. NY: McGraw-Hill, 1932. First edition. Gach 94-222 1983 $25

KARPINSKI, L　　　Bibliography of the Printed Maps of Michigan 1804-1880. Lansing 1931. Folding maps, etc., cloth, index. Covers dull with some staining to spine, moderately rubbed. Important association copy. King 45-109 1983 $100

KARPINSKI, L   Bibliography of Mathematical Works
Printed in America Through 1850. Ann Arbor, 1940. Presentation copy,
inscribed & signed by author. Facsimile title pp. Cloth. Index.
Dust wrapper. Very nice. King 45-467 1983 $325

KARR, ALPHONSE   The Alain Family: A Tale of The Norman
Coast. London: Ingram, Cooke, & Co., 1853. First English edition.
8 illus. by Anelay. Orig. embossed cloth, with gilt decorated spine.
Former owner's inscription on flyleaf. Some foxing and smudging of
pages. Very fine. MacManus 279-3016 1983 $75

KARR, JEAN   Zane Grey: Man of the West. Kingswood,
The World's Work, (1951). First English edition. Illus. with
halftones. Dust jacket (small nicks) else very good. Houle 22-1093
1983 $75

KARSH, YOUSUF   Faces of Destiny. Chicago, (1946).
Second printing. 75 full-page Karsh photographs. Light cover wear.
Scarce. Bradley 64-89 1983 $20

KAUFMAN, GEORGE S.   Beggar on Horseback. New York, (1924).
First edition. Inscribed by Kaufman and Connelly. 8vo, paper labels.
A play in two parts. Morrill 290-207 1983 $75

KAUP, J. J.   Description d'ossements fossiles de
mammiferes. Darmstadt, 1832-33. Parts 1 and 2 (of 5), 11 plates,
4to, half calf (trifle worn, text of part 1 loosely inserted). A
little foxing and soiling and 1 plate repaired, small library stamp
on title-pages and plates. Wheldon 160-1428 1983 £25

KAVANAGH. JULIA   Seven Years and Other Tales. London:
Hurst and Blackett, 1860. First edition. 3 vols. Orig. cloth. Bindings a bit worn and soiled (library numbers removed from spines). Some
endpapers a little soiled. Amorial bookplates. Corners bumped. Good,
tight set. MacManus 279-3018 1983 $250

KAY, GERTRUDE ALICE   The Book of Seven Wishes. N.Y.: Moff
& Yard, 1917. First edition. 8vo. Blue cloth, normal wear. 4 color
plates, many black & whites in text. Tipped into front free fly is a
handwritten letter from Kay to a fan, 8vo, written 2 sides. Very good.
Aleph-bet 8-145 1983 $80

KAY, GERTRUDE ALICE   Us Kids at the Circus. Volland, (1927,
3rd print). 8vo. Cloth backed pictorial boards. Light wear. Full-
page & in text color illus. throughout. Very good. Aleph-bet 8-147
1983 $20

KAYE, J. W.   Christianity in India. London, 1859.
Half calf, morocco label. Bookplate of the Marquess of Tweeddale.
8vo. Good. Edwards 1044-399 1983 £50

KAYE, J. W.   A History of the Sepoy War in India.
London, 1875. 2 folding maps, 4 folding plans. 3 vols. Thick 8vo.
Some spotting, cloth worn. Dust jacket, spines faded. Good. Edwards
1044-400 1983 £75

KAYE, J. W.   History of the War in Afghanistan. London, 1851. 2 vols. Some spotting at the beginning and end of the
volumes. Half red morocco by Birdsall. Spines with raised bands.
Gilt compartments enclosing arms and crest of Sir Andrew Agnew, also
with the family bookplate. 8vo. Good. Edwards 1044-398 1983 £135

KAYE, J. W.   The Life and Correspondence of Charles,
Lord Metcalfe. London, 1858. New and Revised edition. Engraved
frontis., foxed. 2 vols. 8vo. Orig. cloth. Good. Edwards 1044-490
1983 £36

KAYE, J. W.   The Life and Correspondence of Henry St.
George Tucker. London, 1854. First edition. The Elphinstone copy
inscribed by author, with the Tucker arms on boards. Scored calf,
spine gilt. A.e.g. Slightly rubbed. 8vo. Good. Edwards 1044-724
1983 £50

KAYE, J. W.   The Life and Correspondence of Major-General Sir John Malcolm. London, 1856. Portrait, dampstained. 2 vols.
Spines faded and slightly frayed. 8vo. From the Earl of Ellenborough's
library and with his bookplate. Good. Edwards 1044-470 1983 £40

KAYE, J. W.   Lives of Indian Officers. London, 1889.
New edition. Frontis. 2 vols. 8vo. Orig. cloth. Bookplate of the
Hon. Mr. Justice H.D. Cornish, Madras. Good. Edwards 1044-402 1983
£48

KAYE-SMITH, SHELIA   The George and the Crown. London:
Cassell & Co., Ltd., (1925). First edition. Orig. cloth. Dust jacket.
Preserved in a cloth slipcase with morocco labe. Very fine. MacManus
279-3023 1983 $65

KAYE-SMITH, SHEILA   Iron and Smoke. London: Cassell & Co.,
(1928). First edition. Orig. cloth. Dust jacket. Very fine. Mac-
Manus 279-3026 1983 $20

KAYE-SMITH, SHEILA   Joanna Godden. London, 1921. First
edition. Repaired dust wrapper. Very nice. Rota 230-319 1983 £20

KAYE-SMITH, SHEILA   John Galsworthy. London: Nisbet & Co.
Ltd., (1916). First edition. Frontis. port. Orig. cloth. Half-
morocco case. Fine. MacManus 278-2144 1983 $50

KAYE-SMITH, SHEILA   Sussex Gorse. London: Nisbet & Co.,
(1916). First edition. Orig. cloth. Spine and covers worn. Slight
foxing to the preliminary pages. Former owner's signature. Good.
MacManus 279-3027 1983 $50

KAYE-SMITH, SHEILA   The Village Doctor. London: Cassell &
Co., Ltd., (1929). First edition. Orig. cloth. Katharine de B.
Parsons' copy, with her bookplate on the front endsheet. Cloth slip-
case. Fine. MacManus 279-3028 1983 $50

KAYSER, H.   Die Dispersion der Luft. Berlin, 1893.
Offprint. 4to. Orig. wrappers. Gurney 90-134 1983 £25

KAYSER, H.   Ueber die Spectren der Elemente.
Berlin, 1888-1893. First edition. 4to. 7 vols. Orig. boards.
With plates. Fifth part in orig. wrappers, back missing, front
partly cut away. Gurney 90-135 1983 £145

KAYSER, JACQUES   The Dreyfus Affair. N.Y., Covici &
Friede, (1931). First American edition. Illus. Pictorial dust
jacket (small nicks and one taped tear) else very good. Houle 22-
524 1983 $35

KEANE, AUGUSTUS HENRY   The Boer States. Land and People.
London: Methuen, 1900. 8vo. Folding map. Orig. cloth. Spine
faded, ex-lib. Adelson Africa-201 1983 $35

KEANE, JOHN F.   Three years of a wanderer's life.
London: Ward and Downey, 1887. First edition. 2 vols. 8vo.
Orig. brown cloth. A very good set. Ximenes 63-606 1983 $125

KEARTON, CHERRY   Through Central Africa, from East to
West. Cassell, 1915. First edition, with a folding map, coloured
frontis. and 169 illus. on 118 plates, roy. 8vo, orig. pictorial
cloth, v.g. Fenning 60-213 1983 £35

KEATE, GEORGE   The Monument in Arcadia. London:
Printed for J. Dodsley...MDCCLXXIII. 4to, a very fine thick paper
copy complete with half-title and dedication leaf; new wraps.
First edition. Quaritch NS 7-69 1983 $175

KEATE, GEORGE   Sketches from nature; taken and coloured
in a journey to Margate. Published for J. Dodsley, 1779. 1st ed.,
2 vols. in 1, sm. 8vo, half-titles, contemporary mottled calf, morocco
label, a little rubbed, joints cracked but secure, internally a very
clean and crisp copy. Deighton 3-192 1983 £45

KEATING, J. M.   History of the Yellow Fever. Memphis,
1879. 4to, orig. cloth. Argosy 713-307 1983 $50

KEATING, WILLIAM H.   Narrative of an Expedition to the Source
of St. Peter's River Lake Winnepeek, Lake of the Woods, &C Performed
in the Year 1823. London: printed for Geo. B. Whittaker, Ave-Maria-
Lane 1825. 2 vols., full morocco, gilt. Fine copies. A.e.g. Large
folding map. Plates. First English edition. Jenkins 151-155
1983 $500

KEATING, WILLIAM H.   Narrative of an Expedition to the
Source of St. Peter's River. London: Geo. B. Whittaker, 1825. 23cm.
2 vols. First London edition. Half titles. Folding map & 8 plates.
Orig. boards, expertly rebacked, with paper labels. A fine copy.
McGahern 53-88 1983 $400

KEATS, JOHN   Endymion: A Poetic Romance. London,
Taylor and Hessey, 1818. 8vo. Full maroon levant morocco by Zaehnsdorf, with all-over gilt tooled pattern, richly gilt inner dentelles,
silk endpapers, gt. 1st ed., 2nd state, with 5-line errata. Signed
binding. Fine. O'Neal 50-32 1983 $1,200

KEATS, JOHN   The Eve of St. Agnes. Chicago: Ralph
Fletcher Seymour, (1900). Octavo. Illus. Of 820 copies, 1/800 on
handmade paper, fine in slightly rubbed cloth-backed boards, together
with 1/20 copies on Japanese vellum; unopened and very fine in full
vellum. Bromer 25-298 1983 $385

KEATS, JOHN   Isabella; or, The Pot of Basil. Edinburgh and London, (1907). First edition with these illus. 6 full-
colour plates and a black and white decoration by J.M. King. Tall 12mo.
Orig. cloth. Covers a little faded. Inscription on flyleaf. Nice.
Rota 230-327 1983 £30

KEATS, JOHN   The Letters of... (Oxford): Oxford
University Press, 1931. Two vols. Cloth, paper labels. Photogravure frontis. portraits by Emery Walker. First edition. Fine
set, in slightly worn dust jackets. Reese 20-570 1983 $50

KEATS, JOHN   The Letters of John Keats. Oxford,
1935. Second edition. Roy. 8vo. Gilt. Frontis. Traylen 94-
483 1983 £12

KEATS, JOHN   The Odes of John Keats. G. Bell, 1901.
Carillon Series. Sq. 8vo, frontis. Decorated title, 3 full-page & 14
text illus. Full green morocco gilt, faded. Greer 40-26 1983 £18

KEATS, JOHN   Poems. Bell, 1898. 2nd edn., revised
with new illus. Illus. by Robert Anning Bell. Beige decor. cloth
(designed by Bell), t.e.g. others uncut, orig. d/w (d/w repaired, sl.
foxing prelims., prize label fr. ep.), very nice copy. Hodgkins 27-
463 1983 £18

KEATS, JOHN   Poems. N.Y., Brentano's, (1928). Full
gilt stamped dark green morocco by Bayntun, gilt stamped decorative
floral lozenges on all covers, edges gilt, marbled endpapers. Fleece
lined slipcase. 2 vols. Fine. Houle 22-526 1983 $425

KEATS, JOHN   Poems of... Philadelphia, Jacobs, nd.
1st edn. Coloured illus. by Edmund J. Sullivan, col'd frontis., 7
col'd plates. Green decor. cloth, t.e.g. others uncut (mounted picture on fr. cvr. sl. chipped), v.g. Hodgkins 27-464 1983 £12.50

KEATS, JOHN   Poetical Works and Other Writings.
(AND) Poetry and Prose... London, Reeves & Turner, 1883-90. 5
vols. 8vo. Illus., ports., facs. 3/4 red morocco, spines elab.
gilt, gt., other edges uncut, orig. cloth covers bound into vol. I.
1st Forman ed. Fine binding. O'Neal 50-33 1983 $325

KEATS, JOHN   The Poetical Works of John Keats.
London: Reeves & Turner, 1889. Third edition. Orig. pictorial cloth.
Inner hinges cracked. Clipping glued to front free endpaper. Book-
plate. Good. MacManus 279-3030 1983 $35

KEBLE, JOHN   Hymns for Holy Weeks and Easter from
the Christian Year. (no date--about 1850?). 4to, 28 leaves of stiff
paper mounted on guards, each illuminated in gold and colours on one
side of the leaf only, a.e.g., full morocco gilt, spine gilt in
compartments. Light foxing on the title, and the subsequent two
leaves a little foxed at the edges, but the other pages clean and
bright. Bickersteth 77-221 1983 £60

KEDDIE, HENRIETTA   Citoyenne Jacqueline. London: Alexander
Strahan, 1866. First edition. 3 vols. Orig. green cloth. Vol. I
shaken. Rear hinge to vol. II cracked. Spines and covers rather worn.
Fair. MacManus 280-5324 1983 $150

KEELER, HARRY S.   The Case of the Transposed Legs. NY,
(1948). Inscription from author to his wife, corrections in text in
same ink as inscription, small tear to paper covering front hinge,
else near fine in frayed and lightly chipped, good dustwrapper with
rear panel skinned. Quill & Brush 54-724 1983 $40

KEELER, HARRY S.   The Case of the Jeweled Ragpicker. NY,
(1948). Presentation copy to author's wife, dated day of publication.
Slightly frayed and soiled dustwrapper. Very good. Quill & Brush
54-723 1983 $35

KEELER, RALPH   Vagabond Adventures. Boston, 1870.
First edition. Presentation to W.H.H. Murray from the author.
Small 8vo. Morrill 290-208 1983 $27.50

KEELEY, CECIL J. H.   A Book of Bungalows and Modern Homes.
Batsford, 1928. First edition, profusely illus., 8vo, orig. cloth.
Fenning 60-214 1983 £10.50

KEELY, ROBERT N.   In Arctic Seas. Philadelphia, 1892.
1st ed. Maps, portraits and photographic views. 8vo. Morrill 287-
595 1983 $35

KEEN, EDWIN HENRY   Songs, Sonnets and Verses. Edinburgh:
The University Press, 1912. First edition. 12mo. Orig. cloth.
Presentation copy with a four-line verse inscription from author to
Nathan Hasekll Dole on flyleaf. With two lengthy autograph letters
from author to Dole laid in. 12mo. Orig. cloth. Very fine. Mac-
Manus 279-3034 1983 $35

KEEN, WILLIAM W.   The Surgical Operations on President
Cleveland in 1893. Ph., (1917). Signed, dated inscription from Keen,
minor cover wear and skinning, very good. Quill & Brush 54-1667 1983
$40

KEEN, WILLIAM W.   The Surgical Operations on President
Cleveland in 1893. Philadelphia, (1928). 1st ed. Small 8vo. Dust
wrapper. Morrill 289-123 1983 $20

KEENAN, HENRY F.   Trajan: The History of a Sentimental
Young Man. London: Cassell & Co., 1885. First English edition. Orig.
cloth. Presentation copy, inscribed on the half-title by the author.
Inner hinges cracked. Covers a little dampstained. Good. MacManus
279-3035 1983 $45

KEENE, H. G.   Ex Eremo, Poems Chiefly Written in India.
Wm. Blackwood, 1855. First edition, 16pp ads. Orig. orange cloth,
v.g. Jarndyce 31-861 1983 £12.50

KEENE, H. G.   A Servant of "John Company." London,
1897. Frontis. stained. 6 plates. 8vo. Orig. cloth. Good. Edwards
1044-403 1983 £25

KEES, WELDON   The Fall of the Magicians. New York:
Reynal & Hitchcock, (1947). Cloth. First edition. A fine copy in
slightly chipped dust jacket. Reese 20-571 1983 $100

KEES, WELDON   The Fall of the Magicians. N.Y., (1947).
Thin 8vo, d.w. First edition. Argosy 714-416 1983 $50

KEGLEY, MAX   Rodeo the Sport of the Cow Country.
New York, 1942. First edition. Illus. Dust jacket. Fine. Jenkins
152-183 1983 $30

KEIGHTLEY, THOMAS   The Fairy Mythology. H.G. Boyn,
1860. With a frontis., 8vo, orig. green cloth, gilt. A little dull,
but a very good copy. New edition. Fenning 62-197 1983 £14.50

KEIL, JAMES   An Account of Animal Secretion, the
Quantity of Blood in the Humane Body, and Muscular Motion. Printed
for George Strahan, 1708. 8vo, orig. panelled calf, rebacked,
preserving the orig. label. First edition. Bickersteth 77-288 1983
£190

KEITH, ALEXANDER   Evidence of the Truth of the Christian
Religion. 1864. Thirty-eighth edition. With 8 plates, wanting a
blank flyleaf, 8vo, cont. divinity style calf, edges gilt, a very
good copy. Fenning 60-215 1983 £12.50

KEITH, ARTHUR B.   Responsible Government in the Dominions.
Oxford: at the University Press, 1912. 22cm. 3 vols. Orig. wine
cloth. A very good set. McGahern 53-89 1983 $50

KEITHLEY, RALPH   Buckey O'Neill...He Stayed with 'em While
He Lasted. Caldwell, Idaho: Caxton Printers, 1949. First edition in
dust jacket. Illus. Fine. Jenkins 152-184 1983 $45

KELEHER, WILLIAM A.   The Fabulous Frontier; Twelve New
Mexico Items. Santa Fe: The Rydal Press, 1945. Illus. 1st ed.
in dust jacket. Scarce. Jenkins 151-245 1983 $85

KELEHER, WILLIAM A.   The Fabulous Frontier. Santa Fe,
Rydal, (1945). Illus. Orig. cloth, small discoloration on spine.
First edition. "Inscribed for Estelle Walton Springer with kind
regards and best wishes-William A. Keleher..." Ltd. to 500 copies.
Ginsberg 47-672 1983 $75

KELEHER, WILLIAM A.   Maxwell Land Grant, a New Mexico
Item. Santa Fe, N.M., 1942. Illus. Orig. cloth. First edition.
Ginsberg 47-673 1983 $200

KELEMAN, PAL   Battlefield of the Gods. London:
George Allen & Unwin, 1937. 61 plates. Cloth. Presentation copy.
Inscribed by the author. Ars Libri 34-297 1983 $30

KELEMEN, PAL   Medieval American Art. NY: Macmillan,
1943. 2 vols. 4to, both vols. signed by author on verso of title-
page. Red cloth. Newspaper clippings pasted on rear blanks. Karmiole
75-107 1983 $100

KELLAND, CLARENCE   The Cat's Paw. New York, 1934. 8vo.
Cloth. This copy is inscribed by author. A very good copy. In Our
Time 156-453 1983 $25

KELLAND, CLARENCE   Dreamland. New York, (1935). 8vo.
Cloth. This copy is inscribed by author. A very good copy. In
Our Time 156-454 1983 $25

KELLER, GOTTFRIED   A Selection of His Tales. London: Unwin,
1891. First edition in English. Orig. cloth. MacManus 279-3036
1983 $20

KELLER, HELEN   Midstream. N.Y., 1929. First
edition. 8vo, full leather; front hinge broken. Argosy 714-419
1983 $150

KELLER, HELEN   My Key of Life. N.Y.: Crowell, (1926).
Small 8vo, boards; pictorial label, d.w. Presentation copy.
Argosy 714-420 1983 $100

KELLER, HELEN   The Song of the Stone Wall. New York,
1910. 8vo. Decorated boards. Some light rubbing along the spine,
else a fine copy. In Our Time 156-455 1983 $45

KELLER, HELEN   The World I Live In. London: Methuen &
Co. Ltd., (1933). First of this edition. Frontispiece. Orig. cloth.
Dust jacket (top of spine slightly nicked). Fine. MacManus 279-3381
1983 $45

KELLER, MARTHA   Brady's Bend and Other Poems. Rutgers
U.P., 1946. 8vo. Cloth. Review copy with slip laid in, plus name
of reviewer on flap. A fine copy. In Our Time 156-456 1983 $25

KELLER-DORIAN, GEORGES   Antoine Coysevox (1640-1720). Paris:
Privately Printed, 1920-(1921). 162 hinged heliotype plates. 1
tipped-in text illus. Large square 4to. 2 vols. Cloth. Orig.
wrappers bound in. Ars Libri 32-128 1983 $400

KELLEY, GEORGE H.   Legislative History. (Phoenix, 1926).
A very fine copy in orig. cloth. Reese 19-26 1983 $35

KELLEY, WILLIAM D.   The New Northwest: An Address. (Philadelphia: 1871). First edition. Buff wrappers. Map on verso of back
wrapper. Stains at edges. Bradley 66-575 1983 $85

KELLOGG, W. M.   The Ape and the Child. A Study of En-
vironmental Influence Upon Early Behavior. NY: 1933. First edition.
Spine tips frayed, rear hinge cracked. Gach 94-37 1983 $20

KELLWAYE, SIMON   A Defensative against the Plague...
London: John Windet, 1593. First edition. Wide title border of
fleurons, woodcut arms of Robert Devereux, Earl of Essex, on verso of
title. Decorative woodcut initials and head- and tail-pieces. Small
4to. Modern wrappers, in brown half-leather box. Ms. exlibris of
Edward Howes on title and on A4-5. A few running headlines trimmed,
occasional ink spots. Small piece torn from bottom margin of 2 leaves.
Early marginalia. Kraus 164-140 1983 $2,500

KELLY, CHARLES   Holy Murder the Story of Porter Rockwell.
New York: Minton, Balch & Co., 1934. First edition. Frontis. and
plates. Presentation from author. Frayed at extremities of spine.
Jenkins 152-185 1983 $45

KELLY, CHARLES   Holy Murder. N.Y., Minton, Blach,
(1934). First edition. Illus. Red cloth stamped in gilt and
black (spine a bit darkened) else very good. Houle 22-1123 1983 $30

KELLY, CHARLES   The Outlaw Trail..."Butch" Cassidy
and his Wild Bunch. Salt Lake City, 1938. Plates. 1st ed. in dust
jacket. Fine copy. Rare. Privately printed book, limited to 1,000
copies. Jenkins 151-156 1983 $125

KELLY, CHARLES   Salt Desert Trails: A History of the
Hastings Cutoff and Other Early Trails... Salt Lake City: Western
Printing Co., 1930. Orig. cloth. 1st ed. Illus. Jenkins 153-308
1983 $85

KELLY, HOWARD   Some American Medical Botanists.
Troy, 1914. First edition. 8vo. Orig. binding. Very fine.
Scarce. Fye H-3-315 1983 $75

KELLY, HOWARD   The Vermiform Appendix & Its Diseases.
Phila. & London, 1905. 4to, cloth (inner joints worn, some water-
staining to margins, not affectint text); ex-lib. First edition.
Argosy 713-308 1983 $100

KELLY, HUGH   Thespis: or, a critical examination
into the merits of all the principal performers belong to Covent-
Garden Theatre. Book the second. London: printed for G. Kearsly,
1767. 4to, disbound, 1st edition. Half-title present; very good
copy. Rare. Ximenes 64-330 1983 $400

KELLY, HUGH   Thespis: or, a critical examination
into the merits of the principal performers belong to Drury-Lane
Theatre. London: printed for G. Kearsly, 1766. 4to, disbound, 1st
edition. Wanting a half-title; the blank at the end is present, with
a mounted errata slip (loose). Rare. Ximenes 64-329 1983 $350

KELLY, HUGH   A Word to the Wise, a comedy. London:
printed for the author, and sold by J. Dodsley; J. and E. Dilly;
G. Kearsly; and T. Cadell, 1770. 8vo, cont. marbled wrappers (worn,
spine defective). 1st edition. Edges slightly dusty, but a very
good uncut copy; errata slip pasted to front inner wrapper. Ximenes
64-331 1983 $75

KELLY, ISABEL   The Archaeology of the Autlam-
Tuxcacuesco Area of Jalisco. II: The Tuxcacuesco-Zapotitlan
Zone. Berkeley/Los Angeles: University of California Press,
1949. 34 plates. 106 text illus. 41 tables. Large 8vo.
Wrappers. Ars Libri 34-299 1983 $35

KELLY, ISABEL   Excavations at Culiacan, Sinaloa.
Berkeley/Los Angeles: University of California Press, 1945.
17 plates (2 color). 1 folding map. 22 tables, 77 text figures.
Large 8vo. Wrappers. Ars Libri 34-300 1983 $35

KELLY, JAMES   A Complete Collection of Scotish
Proverbs Explained and made Intelligible to the English Reader.
Printed for William and John Innys, and John Osborn, 1721. 8vo,
cont. calf, cracks beginning at head and foot of joints, label
chipped, wear at head of spine, but binding firm. First edition.
Bickersteth 77-32 1983 £85

KELLY, LUTHER S.   Yellowstone Kelly: The Memoirs of
Luther S. Kelly. New Haven, 1926. Frontis. and plates. First ed.
Fine copy. Jenkins 151-157 1983 $75

KELLY, MICHAEL   The Green Spot that Blooms on the Desert
of Life. N.d. (c. 1800?). Engraved music, folio, unbound. Slight
tear in margin. With rubberstamp signature of Michael Kelly. This
is one (#3) of a set of 4 ballads. Salloch 387-107 1983 $45

KELLY, MICHAEL   Reminiscences of Michael Kelly, of the
King's Theatre, and Theatre Royal Drury Lane. London: Henry Colburn,
1826. 2 vols., 8vo, cont. half calf, spines gilt (bit rubbed).
First edition. With a portrait; bound without half-titles, but a
very good copy. Ximenes 64-333 1983 $100

KELLY, MICHAEL   Reminiscences of Michael Kelly, of the
King's Theatre, and Theatre Royal Drury Lane. London: Henry Colburn,
1826. 2 vols., 12mo, early dark green cloth, original printed paper
labels (labels darkened, and a bit chipped). 2nd edition, same year
as the first. With a portrait (spotted). Ximenes 64-334 1983 $40

KELLY, ROBERT   Finding the Measure. Black Sparrow
Press, 1968. 8vo. Cloth. 1 of 50 bound copies signed by the poet.
A fine copy. Issued without dj. In Our Time 156-458 1983 $100

KELLY, ROBERT   A Joining: A Sequence for H.D. Black
Sparrow Press, 1967. 8vo. Wraps. An advance copy, the unbound
signatures of the book (laid flat) in publisher's cover jacket for
the book. Some light bumping at the edges, else fine. In Our Time
156-457 1983 $75

KELLY, ROBERT   Raleigh. The Black Sparrow Press,
1972. 4to. Marbled paper wrappers, paper labels. Printed at the
Plantin Press. 1 of 26 bound copies lettered and signed by the
poet, each of the lettered copies containing a holograph poem by
the poet. Fine in acetate jacket. In Our Time 156-461 1983 $125

KELLY, ROBERT   Sonnets (1967). Black Sparrow Press,
1968. 1 of 65 copies bound in cloth, boards and signed by the poet.
Each of these copies has a holograph poem by the poet. In this copy
Kelly has written out a full page description covering the poem/
drawing. Fine copy. In Our Time 156-459 1983 $125

KELLY, ROBERT   Statement. Black Sparrow Press, 1968.
8vo. Boards. The uncommon hardbound ed., being 1 of 26 copies
lettered and signed by Kelly. Issued without dj. Fine. In Our
Time 156-460 1983 $100

KELLY, THOMAS ALEXANDER ERSKINE, 6TH EARL OF   Minuets. Edinburgh,
1836. Engraved portrait, title vignette, engraved music. Ltd.
edition of 60 copies only. 4to, cl. Salloch 387-57 1983 $225

KELLY, THOMAS W.   Myrtle leaves. London: Sherwood,
Jones and Co., etc., 1824. First edition. 8vo. Polished calf,
gilt, spine and inner dentelles gilt, t.e.g., by Morrell. Presentation copy, inscribed by Kelly on the title-page to M. de Jeaufres.
A fine uncut copy. Ximenes 63-415 1983 $75

KELLY, MRS. TOM   Time and Chance. Hurst & Blacket, 1882.
2nd edition, 3 vols. Half titles, 16 pp ads. vol. III. Orig.
black cloth, sl. rubbing to heads and tails of spines, otherwise v.g.
Inscribed presentation copy: 'To Francis Murphy Esq. From the Author
"Time and Chance happeneth to them all".' Jarndyce 30-443 1983 £28

KELLY, WAYNE SCOTT   Lariats and Chevrons or Corporal Jack
Wilson. Guthrie, 1905. Orig. dec. cloth. Argosy 716-619 1983 $75

KELLY, WILLIAM   A Stroll Through the Diggings of Cal.
Oakland: Biobooks, 1940. Illus. Limited to 750 copies. Jenkins 153-
309 1983 $35

KELM, HEINZ   Kunst vom Sepik. Berlin: Museum
fur Volkerkunde, 1966-1968. 3 vols. I: 4 color plates. 500
illus. hors texte. 1 folding map loose in rear pocket. II: 243
illus. hors texte. III: 8 color plates. 550 illus. hors texte.
4to. Wrappers. Ars Libri 31-810 1983 $125

KELSEY, D. M.   History of Our Wild West and Stories of
Pioneer Life. N.p., 1901. Illus. Orig. pictorial cloth depicting
Buffalo Bill on front cover. Jenkins 152-186 1983 $30

KELSEY, DANA H.   Report of the U.S. Indian Inspector
for the Indian Territory of the Secretary of the Interior for
the Year Ended June 30, 1905. Wash., 1905. Orig. printed wraps.,
frayed. First edition. Ginsberg 47-704 1983 $35

KELSEY, HENRY   The Kelsey Papers. Ottawa: Public
Archives, 1929. 26 1/2cm. Frontis. and rear folding maps. Stiff
printed wrappers. A fine copy. McGahern 54-101 1983 $75

KELTERBORN-HAEMMERLI, ANNA   Die Kunst des Hans Fries. Strassburg:
J.H. Ed. Heitz, 1927. 29 collotype plates. 4to. Wrappers. Slightly
worn. Ars Libri 32-228 1983 $65

KELTY, MARY A.   The Favourite of Nature. G.W. B.
Whittaker, 1821. 2nd edition, 3 vols. Half dark maroon morocco,
spines extra gilt, v.g. Jarndyce 30-444 1983 £38

KELVIN, WILLIAM THOMSON   Elements of Natural Philosophy...
Cambridge: University Press, 1879. Second edition. 8vo. Orig.
cloth. Ads. 2 small defects to spine. Zeitlin 264-233 1983
$50

KELVIN, WILLIAM THOMSON   Elements of Natural Philosophy...
Cambridge: University Press, 1894. 8vo. Orig. cloth. Text
illus. Zeitlin 264-234 1983 $50

KELVIN, WILLIAM THOMSON   The Molecular Tactics of a Crystal...
Oxford: Clarendon Press, 1894. 8vo. Orig. wrappers. 20 illus.
A little worn. Zeitlin 264-235 1983 $60

KELVIN, WILLIAM THOMSON   Popular Lectures and Addresses.
London: Macmillan, 1889-1894. 3 vols. 8vo. Orig. green cloth.
Numerous text illus. and 1 folding plate. Slightly rubbed,
internally a good set. Zeitlin 264-236 1983 $120

KELVIN, WILLIAM THOMSON   Treatise on Natural Philosophy.
Cambridge: University Press, 1912. 2 vols. 8vo. Orig. green
cloth. A good set. Zeitlin 264-237 1983 $120

KEMBLE, ADELAIDE
Please turn to
SARTORIS, ADELAIDE KEMBLE

KEMBLE, EDWARD CLEVELAND   Yerba Buena - 1846 (Sketched Through
a Loophole). SF, 1935. 12mo, cloth-backed bds., pictorial paste
label. Illustrated in color. Signed by Johnck & Lawton Kennedy.
Perata 27-95 1983 $75

KEMBLE, FRANCES ANNE   Journal. London: John Murray, 1835.
First edition. 12mo. 2 vols. Cont. half calf gilt, morocco labels,
marbled boards. A good copy. Trebizond 18-130 1983 $150

KEMBLE, FRANCES ANNE   Journal of a Residence on a Georgian
Plantation in 1838-1839. Longman, Green, 1863. First edition,
half title, 32 pp ads. Orig. brown cloth, a little mottled. Split
in following hinge, sometime repaired. A good copy. Jarndyce 31-763
1983 £60

KEMBLE, FRANCES ANNE   Journal of a Residence on a Georgian
Plantation in 1838-1839. New York, 1863. Ads. Cloth. Covers
drab; bookplate. First American edition, first issue. Felcone 22-
114 1983 $35

KEMBLE, FRANCES ANNE   Record of a Girlhood. London: Richard
Bentley & Son, 1878. First edition. 3 vols. Cont. 3/4 morocco and
marbled boards. Bookplate. Bindings worn. MacManus 279-3040 1983
$75

KEMBLE, FRANCES ANNE   Records of a Girlhood. N.Y.: Henry Holt,
1879. First American edition. Orig. cloth. Very good. MacManus
279-3041 1983 $25

KEMBLE, JOHN HASKELL   The Panama Route, 1848-1869. Berkeley:
University of Califronia Press, 1943. Cloth with dust wrapper.
Dawson 471-167 1983 $75

KEMBLE, JOHN PHILIP   Fugitive Pieces. York: Printed by
W. Blanchard and Co. for the Author, and sold by Fielding and
Walker, London; and T. Wilson and Son, and N. Frobisher, York,
MDCCLXXX. 8vo, half-title (dusty), partly uncut, in early nineteenth-
century green straight-grain morocco gilt, three scrapes on upper top
cover; gilt edges. First edition, with an autograph correction
by Kemble on p. vi, with recipient's note that alteration is in
John Kemble's hand-writing. Quaritch NS 7-70 1983 $875

KENDALL, AMOS   Letters to John Quincy Adams, Relative
to the Fisheries and the Mississippi... Lexington, Ky.: William
Tanner, 1823. Dbd. Uniformly foxed. Reese 18-568 1983 $275

KENDALL, EDWARD A.   Travels through the Northern Parts of
the United States in the Years 1807 and 1808. New York, 1809. 3 vols.
Three-quarter morocco and boards. Uncut. Fine. Reese 18-325 1983
$250

KENDALL, GEORGE W.   Narrative of Texan Santa Fe Expedition.
Chicago, Lakeside Press, 1929. Fldg. map, illus. 12mo, gilt top,
small light stains, bottom and margins of first several pages, former
owner's bookplate. Clark 741-458 1983 $26.50

KENDALL, HENRY   Songs from the Mountains. Sydney: William Maddock, 1880. First edition. 8vo. Orig. cloth, gilt. Traylen 94-486 1983 £75

KENDALL, PERCY FRY   Geology of Yorkshire. Printed for the authors, 1924. Illus., roy. 8vo. K Books 307-108 1983 £40

KENDERDINE, THADDEUS S.   A California Tramp and Later Footprints. Newtown, 1888. Portrait and illus. Orig. pictorial cloth, gilt. Light spotting. Jenkins 153-310 1983 $150

KENEALY, EDWARD VAUGHAN   Poems and Translations. Reeves & Turner, 1864. First edition. Orig. blue cloth, v.g. Inscribed presentation copy from the author, Nov. 10, 1863. Jarndyce 30-768 1983 £14.50

KENLY, JOHN R.   Memoirs of a Maryland Volunteer. Phil., Lippincott, 1873. Orig. brown cloth. 1st ed. Extremely fine copy. Jenkins 153-311 1983 $85

KENNARD, MRS. EDWARD   The Catch of the County. London: F.V. White & Co., 1894. First edition. 3 vols. Orig. cloth. Stamped "With the Publisher's Compliments." Extremities worn, with small tear to spine of Vol. one. A bit soiled and stained. Good. MacManus 279-3042 1983 $100

KENNARD, NINA H.   Lafcadio Hearn. Eveleigh Nash, 1911. First edition, half title, front., illus. Orig. red cloth, v.g. Jarndyce 30-1026 1983 £38

KENNEDY, CHARLES RANN   The Servant in the House. New York, (1908). First edition. Purple cloth. Illustrated with portraits. Laid in is typewritten letter, signed, dated at Los Angeles August 31, 1946. Both the letter and book, which is worn and frayed, bear tape marks. Bradley 64-90 1983 $25

KENNEDY, DOROTHEA   Patchwork Dreams. The Decker Press, Prairie City, Illinois, 1948. 8vo. Cloth. A fine copy in dj. Signed by the poet on the front flyleaf. In Our Time 156-197 1983 $45

KENNEDY, HUGH A.   Waifs and Strays. L. Booth, 1862. First edition, 12mo, wrapper, v.g. Some light signs of use. Recent boards. Fenning 61-233 1983 £28.50

KENNEDY, JAMES   Essays Ethnological and Linguistic. London, 1861. 8vo, 1/2 mor., ex lib. Argosy 716-217 1983 $45

KENNEDY, JOHN FITZGERALD   As We Remember Joe. Cambridge, MA: Privately printed, University Press, 1945. Prof. illus. with photographs of the entire Kennedy family. Red cloth, extremities lightly rubbed. An almost fine copy. Karmiole 75-72 1983 $750

KENNEDY, JOHN FITZGERALD   As We Remember Joe. Cambridge, Mass., privately printed, 1945. Thin 8vo, cloth. Mint copy in orig. glassine wrapper, of the second issue, with the aviator's wings in black rather than red. Argosy 714-422 1983 $175

KENNEDY, JOHN FITZGERALD   Why England Slept. L, (n.d.). First English edition, spine slightly faded, otherwise very good. Quill & Brush 54-728 1983 $40

KENNEDY, MARY   A Surprise to the Children. N.Y.: Doub., 1933. First edition. Cloth backed pictorial boards. Edges rubbed. Illus. with color plates, black & white text drawings by J.H. Dowd. Very good. Aleph-bet 8-149 1983 $27

KENNEDY, R. EMMET   Black Cameos. NY, 1924. Near fine in very lightly frayed near fine dustwrapper, unobtrusive bookplate. Quill & Brush 54-729 1983 $60

KENNEDY, R. H.   Narrative of the Campaign of the Army of the Indus. London, 1840. 2 vols. 8vo. 5 lithographic plates, illus. Half calf, spines gilt. Good. Edwards 1044-405 1983 £150

KENNEDY, W. P. M.   Documents of the Canadian Constitution, 1795-1915. Toronto: Oxford Univ. Press, 1918. 22cm. Title page clipped with loss of text, personal lib. stamps, hinges tender, else a good working copy. McGahern 53-90 1983 $25

KENNEDY, WILLIAM   Fitful Fancies. Edinburgh: Oliver & Boyd, and Geo. B. Whittaker, 1827. Later half maroon calf, v.g. Jarndyce 31-862 1983 £24

KENNETT, BASIL   The Lives and Characters of Ancient Grecian Poets. London, Abel Swall, 1697. 8vo, orig. calf, few signatures have slight worming at blank lower edge. Copper engr. are of Homer (full-page frontis.). First edition. Ravenstree 95-67 1983 $142

KENNETT, BASIL   The Lives and Characters of the Ancient Grecian Poets. London, Abel Swall, 1697. 8vo, orig. calf, hinges cracked, decent copy. First edition. Ravenstree 94-236 1983 $120

KENNEY, CHARLES L.   A Memoir of Michael William Balfe. Tinsley Brothers, 1875. First and apparently only edition, with a port., plate and folding facs. Includes half title but wanting a blank flyleaf. Roy. 8vo, orig. green cloth, gilt. A very good copy. Fenning 62-15 1983 £24.50

KENNEY, CHARLES L   The new actress and the new play at the Adelphi Theatre. London: W. S. Johnson and Co., 1863. 8vo, sewn, as issued. First edition. Title dusty, upper margins dog-eared; last leaf a bit chipped. Very scarce. Ximenes 64-338 1983 $75

KENNEY, JAMES   False alarms; or, my cousin, a comic opera, in three acts. London: printed for Longman, etc., by C. Stower, 1807. 8vo, wrappers, 2nd edition. Last page soiled. Ximenes 64-339 1983 $20

KENNEY, JAMES   A House out at Windows. C. Chapple, 1817. First edition, half calf. Jarndyce 31-849 1983 £10.50

KENNY, DANIEL J.   The American Newspaper Directory and Record of the Press. New York: Watson & Co., 1861. First edition. 8vo. Orig. cloth. Oak Knoll 49-254 1983 $125

KENRICK, WILLIAM   The American Silk Grower's Guide. Boston, 1835. Cloth, covers a bit worn and spotted, and internal foxing, but a good copy. First edition. Felcone 22-115 1983 $30

KENRICK, WILLIAM   The Duellist, a comedy. London: printed for T. Evans, n.d. (1773). 8vo, wrappers. 1st edition. Half-title present; very good copy. Ximenes 64-340 1983 $75

KENT, CHARLES   Charles Dickens as a Reader. Chapman & Hall, 1872. First edition, orig. green cloth a little rubbed. Jarndyce 30-195 1983 £32

KENT, CHARLES   The Humour and Pathos of Charles Dickens. Chapman & Hall, 1884. First edition, half title, front. port. 2 pp. ads. Orig. green cloth. Very good. Jarndyce 30-196 1983 £12.50

KENT, EDWIN C.   The Isle of Long Ago. New York, 1933. Edition limited to 1000 copies. Frontispiece. 8vo. Light dampstains on blank margins of last several leaves. Morrill 290-209 1983 $25

KENT, JAMES   The Charter of the City of New-York, with Notes Thereon. N.Y., 1836. Orig. cloth boards. First edition. Small rubber library stamp on title page. Ginsberg 46-537 1983 $75

KENT, ROCKWELL   A Birthday Book. New York: Random House, 1931. First edition. Small 4to. Cloth. 20 plates. Limited to 1850 copies numbered and signed by Kent. Some fraying of silken endpapers and cover wear along edges. Oak Knoll 48-237 1983 $50

KENT, ROCKWELL   The Bookplates and Marks of... NY: Random House, 1929. Octavo. Frenchfold. First edition. Of edition of 1250 copies signed by Kent, this is an unnumbered copy. Spine very slightly faded, else extremely fine with slightly faded printed dust wrapper. Two bookplates, including that of Sally and Rockwell Kent. Bromer 25-238 1983 $185

KENT, ROCKWELL   A Northern Christmas. NY (1941). Pict.
boards, title pg. slightly soiled else very good. In frayed dw.
First ed. No. one in a series. Illustrated by author and signed
on half-title page by author. King 46-437 1983 $50

KENT, ROCKWELL   Of Men and Mountains. Ausable Forks,
NY: Asgaard Press, 1959. Octavo. First edition. Limited to 250
copies. Inscription by Kent at later date on rear endpapers. Fine
copy in marbled boards, cloth spine with orig. glassine. Bromer 25-
239 1983 $110

KENT, ROCKWELL   On Earth Peace. N.Y., (1942). First
edition. Illus. by the author. Thin small 12mo, pict. boards.
Argosy 714-424 1983 $30

KENT, ROCKWELL   Rockwellkentiana. New York, 1933. 8vo.
Cloth. Inscribed by Kent on the front flyleaf. A fine copy in dj
which is chipped at the base of the spine. In Our Time 156-463
1983 $125

KENT, ROCKWELL   Salamina. N.Y., (1935). First edition.
Tall 8vo, cloth, d.w. Presentation copy. Fine. Argosy 714-425
1983 $125

KENT, ROCKWELL   Salamina. New York: Harcourt, Brace,
1935. Frontis., plates. 1st ed. Orig. blue decorated cloth. Fine
copy with illustrations by author, in dj with piece lacking (2'')
from foot of spine. Jenkins 155-736 1983 $40

KENT, WILLIAM   Reminiscences of Outdoor Life. San
Francisco: A.M. Robertson, 1929. Illus. Orig. cloth and paper bds.
Fairly nice copy. Jenkins 153-312 1983 $50

KENT, WILLIAM SAVILLE   A Manual of the Infusoria. David
Bogue, 1880-1881. First and only edition, coloured frontis. and 52
plates, with leaf of letterpress to each plate, 3 vols., roy. 8vo,
orig. cloth, t.e.g., a little weakness in the inside joints of
one volume, but otherwise a fine copy. Fenning 61-234 1983 £185

KENTUCKY. LAWS.   An Act to Incorporate the City of
Lexington. (Lexington, KY: Finnell & Herndon, 1831). 1st ed., half
morocco. Jenkins 151-161 1983 $350

KENYON, C. R.   The Argonauts of the Amazon. W. & R.
Chambers, 1901. Frontis. 5 plates. Blue pictorial cloth, gilt,
rubbed. Greer 40-182 1983 £45

KENYON, JOHN   Rhymed plea for tolerance. London:
Moxon, 1839. Second edition. 8vo. Cont. calf, spine gilt.
Presentation copy, inscribed in 1852 on the half-title from
Kenyon to Mrs. F.H. Goldsmid. Slightly rubbed. Ximenes 63-450
1983 $50

KEP, LEONARD   California Sketches with Recollections
of the Gold Mines. Los Angeles, 1946. Map and plates. Dust jacket.
Jenkins 152-578 1983 $45

KEPES, GYORGY   Language of Vision. (Chicago, 1944).
First edition. Illus. Cloth. Endpapers blind-stamped. Rubber
stamp. Minor wear and soil. King 45-313 1983 $25

KEPLER, JOHANNES   Dissertatio cum Nuncio Sidereo.
Florence: Gio Antonio Caneo, 1610. Second edition. Vellum.
Kraus 164-141 1983 $3,500

KEPLER, JOHANNES   Narratio de Observatis a se quatuor
Iovis satellitibus erronibus... Florence: Cosimo Giunta, 1611.
Small 4to. Paper mends, slightly affecting the print. Kraus 164-
142 1983 $2,500

KEPPEL, H   The Expedition to Borneo of 'H.M.S.
Dido' for the Suppression of Piracy. London: Chapman & Hall, 1846.
2nd ed., 8vo, 2 vols., orig. cloth, spines gilt, eleven lithographed
plates, six maps and plans; table. Uncut with half-titles. Some
offsetting and soiling but a very good, bright copy. Trebizond 18-
149 1983 $400

KEPPEL, H.   A Visit to the Indian Archipelago.
London, 1853. Folding map in end pocket, 8 tinted lithograph plates.
Some slight spotting. Roy.8vo. Bright blue cloth, with a gilt
picture of a war canoe on the upper covers. Vol. I is without the
half title. Good. Edwards 1044-406 1983 £320

KER, HENRY   Travels through the Western Interior of
the United States, from the Year 1808 up to the Year 1816. Elizabeth-
town, N.J., 1816. Orig. calf, some light foxing throughout text, but
overall very good. The first issue, with the list of subscribers in
the back. Reese 18-498 1983 $675

KER, ROBERT   St. George's Parish Church, St. Catharines. St. Catharines: Ont. Star Print., (1891). 21cm. Illus. Blue
cloth. Black and gilt stamped on the upper cover. Fine. Scarce.
McGahern 54-102 1983 $50

KERCHEVAL, SAMUEL   A History of the Valley of Virginia.
Winchester, (Va.): Samuel H. Davis, 1833. First edition. Cont.
3/4 morocco, expertly rebacked. Orig. leather label present. Jenkins
152-488 1983 $450

KERNAHAN, MRS. COULSON   More Tales of Our Village. London: The
Epworth Press, (1929). First edition. Orig. cloth. Dust jacket
(spine and covers slightly faded and worn). Former owner's signature.
Near-fine. MacManus 279-3047 1983 $25

KERNER VON MARILAUN, A.   The Natural History of Plants. 1894-95.
16 coloured plates and about 2000 text-figures, 2 vols. in 4, imp.
8vo, cloth. Title-page of vol. 4 foxed. Wheldon 160-1539 1983 £35

KEROUAC, JACK   The Dharma Bums. N.Y., 1958. First
edition. D.w. Fine. Argosy 714-427 1983 $100

KEROUAC, JACK   The Dharma Bums. New York: 1958. First
edition. Cloth. First printing. Fine in dust jacket. Bradley 66-
218 1983 $85

KEROUAC, JACK   Lonesome Traveler. N.Y., (1960).
First edition. 8vo, cloth backed boards. The dust wrapper is
slightly rubbed, with a chip at the top of the spine. Argosy 714-428
1983 $75

KEROUAC, JACK   On the Road. N.Y., Viking, 1957.
First edition. Dust jacket a trifle rubbed, else very good-fine.
Houle 21-473 1983 $250

KEROUAC, JACK   On the Road. New York: Viking Press,
1957. 1st ed. Orig. black cloth, sans dj. Fine copy. Jenkins
155-737 1983 $75

KEROUAC, JACK   On the Road. London, 1958. First
English edition. Covers dull. Spine slightly faded. Inscription.
Stamp on front free endpaper. Nicked and dusty, price-clipped dust-
wrapper by Len Deighton. Very good. Jolliffe 26-305 1983 £40

KEROUAC, JACK   The Subterraneans. New York, (1958).
Cloth-backed boards. First edition. One of 100 numbered copies.
A fine copy. Felcone 21-63 1983 $300

KEROUAC, JACK   The Town and the City. NY, (1950).
Edges slightly rubbed, very good, bright copy in frayed, slightly
chipped and creased dustwrapper. Quill & Brush 54-737 1983 $225

KEROUAC, JACK   The Town and the City. NY, (1950). Very
good in slightly worn dustwrapper that is lightly chipped and creased
with two tears at folds in front cover. Quill & Brush 54-738 1983
$200

KERR, J. M. MUNRO   Historical Review of British Obstetrics
and Gynaecology 1800-1950. Edinburgh, 1954. First edition. 8vo.
Orig. binding. Backstrip faded. Fye H-3-318 1983 $75

KERRY, EARL OF   The First Napoleon. London, 1925.
First edition. Coloured portrait frontis. 8vo. Orig. cloth. 13
plates, 2 facsimiles. 1 map. T.e.g. Others uncut. Very slightly
worn and faded. Good. Edwards 1042-430 1983 £15

KESSEY, KEN   The Day After Superman Died. CA, 1980.
Limited to 50 deluxe, numbered and signed copies, mint without dustwrapper. Quill & Brush 54-742 1983 $100

KESTEVEN, WILLIAM BEDFORD   The microscopical anatomy of the brain
and spinal cord... Lewes: Bacon, 1870. First edition. 8vo. Disbound. Orig. tan printed wrappers preserved. Presentation copy,
inscribed by the author on the title-page. Offprint. With a plate.
Ximenes 63-281 1983 $30

KETT, HENRY   Emily. For Messrs. Rivingtons; Payne;
Lunn, etc, 1809. First edition. 2 vols. 8vo. cont. calf (covers
rubbed). Hannas 69-116 1983 £45

KETTILBY, MARY   A Collection of about Three Hundred
Receipts in Cookery, Physick and Surgery...To which is added a Second
Part, containing Receipts for Preserving and Conserving Sweet Meats &c.
London: printed for Mary Kettilby, 1724. 3rd (second complete) ed.,
8vo, cont. panelled calf, rebacked. Advertisement leaf. Two parts in
one volume. Pervasively foxed, otherwise a very good copy. Trebizond
18-201 1983 $350

KEULEMANS, T.   Feathers to Brush. Deventer, 1982.
4to, half morocco, 24 coloured plates, 4 portraits, text figures.
Edition limited to 500 copies signed by authors. Wheldon 160-241
1983 £75

KEY, A. C.   A Narrative of the Recovery of H.M.S.
Gorgon. London, 1847. 8vo. Orig. cloth. Folding tinted lithographic
frontis., 5 folding and 11 other plates, 1 folding map. 36 pp. publishers ads. at end. Very slightly worn and faded. Some very slight
foxing, ms. note relating to H.M.S. Gorgon and the author pasted on to
front endpaper. Good. Edwards 1042-116 1983 £140

KEY, FRANCIS SCOTT   The Harleian Miscellany. London,
1745. Quarto. Vol. 5 only. Old calf. With Key's signature at
the head of the title-page and his notation that this book was a gift
from a Dr. Scott. Jenkins 155-739 1983 $125

KEY, FRANCIS SCOTT   The Star Spangled Banner. NY, (1861).
Sq. 8vo, cont. lea.-backed marbled boards, orig. wraps. bound in.
Argosy 716-320 1983 $50

KEYES, FRANCES PARKINSON   Along a Little Way. New York, (1940).
12mo. Cloth. Signed by the author on the front flyleaf. Very
good-fine copy. In Our Time 156-467 1983 $20

KEYNES, GEOFFREY   Bibliography of Jane Austen. R & R
Clark for the Nonesuch Press, 1929. First edition, sm. 8vo, 4 collo-
types and numerous facsimiles, uncut in original two-colour paper
boards, label, fine in dustwrappers and with errata leaf. 875
numbered copies. Deighton 3-15 1983 £75

KEYNES, GEOFFREY   A Bibliography of Sir Thomas Brown. Cambridge: Univ. Press, 1924. One of 500 numbered copies. Plates, cloth,
t.e.g. One corner a little bumped, endpapers and half-title lightly
browned, bookplate. In moderately-used dust wrapper missing a couple
of small pieces. Printed on hand-made paper with fine gravure plates.
Dawson 470-169 1983 $100

KEYNES, GEOFFREY   John Ray: A Bibliography. London:
Faber and Faber, (1951). Cloth in dw (the latter very slightly used).
One of 650 copies. Dawson 470-170 1983 $75

KEYNES, GEOFFREY   The Portraiture of William Harvey.
London, 1949. First edition. 8vo. Orig. binding. Numerous
plates. Fye H-3-774 1983 $40

KEYNES, GEOFFREY   William Blake's Engravings. London:
Faber and Faber, 1950. Plates. 4to. Cloth. Ars Libri 32-41 1983
$45

KEYNES, JOHN MAYNARD   The Economic Consequences of Mr.
Churchill. 1925. First edition, Orig. green wraps. sl. worn.
Jarndyce 31-995 1983 £20

KEYNES, JOHN MAYNARD   The Economic Consequences of the Peace.
London: Macmillan and Co., 1919. 1st ed., 8vo, original blue
cloth, ownership inscription on the title, a very good copy.
Pickering & Chatto 21-51 1983 $250

KEYNES, JOHN MAYNARD   The Economic Consequences of the Peace.
London: Macmillan, 1919. Cloth, gilt. First edition. Pencil
inscription on title-page, else a near fine copy. Reese 20-575 1983
$250

KEYNES, JOHN MAYNARD   The Economic Consequences of the Peace.
Macmillan and Co., 1919. 8vo, ownership inscription in ink upside
down on the rear fly, orig. cloth. Good copy. Review of the book
from The Times, January 5th, 1920, loosely inserted. First edition.
Bickersteth 75-150 1983 £55

KEYNES, JOHN MAYNARD   The Economic Consequences of the Peace.
London, 1920 (reprint). 8vo. Orig. cloth. Slightly worn and soiled.
Signet Library copy. Good. Edwards 1042-382 1983 £15

KEYNES, JOHN MAYNARD   The General Theory of Employment,
Interest and Money. London: Macmillan and Co., 1936. 1st ed.,
8vo, advertisement, original blue cloth, a fine copy. Pickering &
Chatto 21-52 1983 $450

KEYNES, JOHN MAYNARD   Revision Des Friedensvertrages.
Munich and Leipzig, Duncker and Humbolt, 1922. First German edition,
8vo, publisher's advertisements, uncut in original printed wrappers.
Pickering & Chatto 21-55 1983 $75

KEYNES, JOHN MAYNARD   A Revision of the Treaty being a
sequen to The Economic Consequences of the Peace. London: Macmillan
and Co., 1922. 1st ed., 8vo, 6 publisher's advertisements, original
blue cloth. Pickering & Chatto 21-54 1983 $110

KEYNES, JOHN MAYNARD   A Revision of the Treaty. London, 1922.
First edition. 8vo. Orig. cloth. Signet Library copy. 6 pages of
publisher's ads. at end. Slightly worn. Good. Edwards 1042-383
1983 £45

KEYNES, JOHN MAYNARD   Sysselsattningsproblemet. Stockholm,
Tidens, 1945. First Swedish ed., 8vo, uncut and unopened in the
original printed wrappers. Pickering & Chatto 21-53 1983 $150

KEYNES, JOHN MAYNARD   A Tract on Monetary Reform. London:
Macmillan and Co., 1923. 1st ed., 8vo, advertisements, original
blue cloth, bookplate, a fine copy. Pickering & Chatto 21-56 1983
$175

KEYSER, CHARLES E.   A List of Norman Tympana and Lintels,
with figure or symbolical sculpture still or till recently existing
in the churches of Great Britain. London, 1904. 1xxix, 65,
(1)pp. 155 illus. hors texte. 4to. Cloth. With 2 autograph
letters by the author loosely inserted. Ars Libri SB 26-108 1983
$100

KEYSLER, JOHANN GEORG   Travels through Germany, Bohemia,
Hungary, Switzerland, Italy and Lorrain... London, A. Linde, 1756-
57. 4 vols., 4to, cont. sprinkled calf, joints breaking and spines
of vols., 3-4 broken, little age-spotting, worn, bookplates. The
first English edition, complete with all the plates. Ravenstree
94-236 1983 $195

KHAN, M. F.   A History of Administrative Reforms in
Hyderabad State. Secunderabad, 1935. 2 plates. 8vo. Orig. cloth.
Good. Edwards 1044-410 1983 £16

KHAVCHINSKY, SERGYEI MIKHAILOVICH   King Stork and King Log. London:
Downey, 1895. First edition. 2 vols. Orig. cloth. With labels from
"Mudie's Select Library" on the front cover of each volume. Very good.
MacManus 280-4881 1983 $60

KHOMIAKOVA, ALEKSEI STEPANOVICH   Stikhotvoreniia (Poems).
Moscow: Bakhmetev, 1861. 1st ed. Orig. morocco-backed cloth-
covered boards, raised bands, gilt. Censor's statement on verso
of title. A couple of old Russian library stamps (title and rear
end paper) but very nice copy of rare book. Jenkins 155-740 1983
$250

KHUEN, JOHANN   Cor Contritum et Humiliatum. Munich,
1640. First edition. 12mo, cont. vellum. Salloch 387-109 1983
$3,200

KIBBE, WILLIAM C.   The Volunteer. Sacramento: B.B. Redding,
State Printer, 1855. Woodcut of a musket with parts labeled. Cloth.
Ownership inscriptions on front cover and endpapers. Foxed. Dawson
471-170 1983 $300

KIDD, DONALD M.   Bookcraft, A New Industrial Art
Subject... Syracuse: Gaylord Bros., 1928. 8vo. Paper wrappers.
Nine samples tipped in. Oak Knoll 49-74 1983 $65

KIDD, DUDLEY   Savage Childhood. London: Adam &
Charles Black, 1906. Illus. from photographs by the author. With
thirty-two full-page illus. Orig. cloth. First edition. Henry
Haggard's copy, with his hieroglyphic bookplate, and numerous pencil
annotations in his hand on the verso of the front free endpaper
and on the half-title. Very good copy. MacManus 278-2453 1983 $350

KIDD, DUDLEY   Savage Childhood. 1906. 32 plates.
K Books 301-107 1983 £19

KIDDER, ALFRED V.   Archaeology of Northwestern Venezuela.
Cambridge, 1944. 18 plates. 4to. Wrappers. Ars Libri 34-302
1983 $30

KIDDER, ALFRED V.   The Artifacts of Uaxactun, Guatemala.
Washington: Carnegie Institution, 1947. 87 illus. Partly hors texte.
4to. Cloth. Ars Libri 34-303 1983 $30

KIDDER, ALFRED V.   Excavations at Kaminaljuyu, Guatemala.
Washington: Carnegie Institution, 1946. 2 maps. 3 tables. 207
illus. (partly in color) hors texte. 4to. Wrappers. Ars Libri
34-304 1983 $45

KIDDER, ALFRED V.   An Introduction to the Study of
Southwestern Archaeology with a Preliminary Account of the Excavations
at Pecos. New Haven, 1924. Profusely illus., folding frontis.
4to, ex lib. Argosy 716-338 1983 $60

KIDDER, DANIEL P.   Mormonism and the Mormons. New York,
1842. Calf (worn, hinges and spine damaged). First edition.
Felcone 22-153 1983 $50

KIDDER, FREDERIC   History of the Boston Massacre, March 5,
1770. Albany: Joel Munsell, 1870. Plates. Map. 3/4 calf, spine
gilt in panels. Felcone 22-118 1983 $35

KIDDER, RICHARD   The Judgment of Private Discretion in
Matters of Religion Defended. Printed for Brabazon Aylmer, 1687.
First edition, 4to, wrapper, line border to title just cropped in fore-
edge, without other loss, otherwise a nice copy. Fenning 61-235
1983 £18.50

KIERAN, JOHN   The American Sporting Scene. N.Y., 1941.
4to, two-tone cloth, gilt, glassine d/w, slipcase. With pictures by
Joseph W. Golinkin (many in color). One of 500 copies signed by the
author and artist. Fine. Perata 28-95 1983 $90

KIERKEGAARD, SOREN   Either/Or. Princeton: Princeton
University Press, 1944. First English Language edition, 2 vols.
Indexes. Karmiole 75-101 1983 $45

KIERKEGAARD, SOREN   Journals and Papers. Bloomington:
Indiana University Press, 1967-1975. Four thick vols. Cloth. Very
fine in dust jackets. Reese 20-577 1983 $125

KIERNAN, R. H.   The Unveiling of Arabia. Harrap, 1937.
First edition, map & plates, 8vo, orig. cloth. Fenning 60-217 1983
£30

KIESLINGER, FRANZ   Die mittelalterliche Plastik in
Osterreich. Wien/Leipzig, 1929. Ein Umriss ihrer Geschichte.
165, (3)pp., 46 plates. 46 text illus. Sm. 4to. Boards, 1/4
cloth. Presentation copy, inscribed by the author. Ars Libri SB
26-109 1983 $35

KILBOURNE, PAYNE KENYON   Sketches and Chronicles of the Town of
Litchfield, Connecticut, Historical, Biographical, and Statistical.
Hartford, 1859. Plates. 8vo. 1st ed. Morrill 286-586 1983
$30

KILLENS, JOHN O.   Youngblood. NY, 1954. Minor cover
soiling, else near fine in bright, near fine dustwrapper with light
wear to edges. Quill & Brush 54-745 1983 $100

KILLIAN, H.   Facies Dolorosa. Leipzig, 1934. First
edition. Photos. Thin 4to, cloth (back mended). Argosy 713-309
1983 $75

KILLIAS, E.   Die Flora des Unterengadins. Chur,
1887-88. 8vo, wrappers. Wheldon 160-1727 1983 £12

KILLIGREW, THOMAS   Comedies and Tragedies. London: Printed
for Henry Herringman, at the Sign of the Anchor in the Lower Walk of
the New-Exchange, 1664. First collected edition. Folio. Frontis.
engraving by Faithorne. Full cont. calf, rebacked with brown morocco,
retaining orig. marbled endpapers. Robert Harley's copy, with his
signature overlaid with gilt on the title-page and his bookplate on
the verso of the title-page, with holograph annotations in the text.
Broadhead on the front endsheet. MacManus 279-3049 1983 $450

KILLIGREW, THOMAS   The Prisoners. London: T. Cotes for
Andrew Cooke, 1641. First edition. 12mo. Cont. sheep, rebacked.
General title and two sub-titles, the six preliminary leaves bound
at end. Traylen 94-487 1983 £450

KILMER, ANNIE KILBURN   Memories of My Son, Sergeant Joyce
Kilmer. New York, (1920). 1st ed., limited. Illus. 8vo. Morrill
287-182 1983 $22.50

KILMER, JOYCE   Summer of Love. New York, 1911. 3/4
calf (dry, hinges breaking). First edition. Felcone 21-64 1983
$350

KILMER, JOYCE   Trees and Other Poems. New York:
Doran, (1914). 1st ed., 2nd binding as usual. Orig. boards, labels.
Fine copy, not often seen thus. Jenkins 155-741 1983 $20

KILMER, JOYCE   Yanks, A Book of A.E.F. Verse. France:
1918. 1st ed. Orig. brown printed wrappers, uncut. 1st printing.
Inscription from A.E.F. Private to his pal. January, 1919. 1st
state of the wrapper. Fine copy and very scarce thus due to the
quality of paper used for text and wrapper. Jenkins 155-742 1983
$65

KILNER, DOROTHY   The Rational Brutes. London: J.
Harris. 1807. Engraved frontis. Cont. half morocco over boards,
sl. rubbed, otherwise a very nice copy. Karmiole 72-29 1983 $60

KILPATRICK, JACK F.   Sequoyah of Earth & Intellect. Austin:
Encino Press, 1965. Quarto. Cloth. Paper label. One of 550
numbered copies, signed by the author. Mint in slipcase, as issued.
Reese 19-315 1983 $75

KILPATRICK, JAMES A.   Literary Landmarks of Glasgow. Glasgow:
Saint Mungo Press, 1898. First edition, with frontis. and 87 other
illus., 8vo, orig. vellum-backed cloth, gilt, t.e.g., binding little
dull but sound, a very good copy. No. 8 of 50 copies printed, signed
by the author. Fenning 60-219 1983 £28.50

KILVERT, B. CORY   The Kite Book. N.Y.: Dodd, 1909. First
edition. 4to. Cloth. Pictorial paste-on. Covers finger smudged.
Some smudging inside. Printed on heavy coated stock. Full-page color
illus. Good to very good. Aleph-bet 8-151 1983 $30

KIMBALL, RICHARD B.   Virginia Randall; or To-Day in New York.
London: Bentley, 1870. First English edition. 2 vols. in one. Orig.
publisher's cloth. In the publisher's remainder binding. Covers
partially dampstained. Inner hinges cracked. Good. MacManus 279-
3050 1983 $85

KIMBER, SIDNEY A.   Cambridge Press Title-Pages, 1640-
1665. Takoma Park: Privately printed, (1954). First edition.
4to. Cloth. Dust jacket. Signed by Kimber. Fine in spotted
wrapper. Oak Knoll 49-255 1983 $75

KIMBER, SIDNEY A.   The Story of an Old Press. Cambridge,
Mass.: University Press, (1937). Small 8vo, numerous illus.
Printed in blue and black. Edition ltd. to 1,000 numbered copies.
Cloth over boards; orig. glassine. Karmiole 73-86 1983 $25

KIMBER, WILLIAM B.   Memoir of William B. Kimber. G. Glipin,
1852. 12mo, orig. cloth. Library label on endpaper. Fenning 60-220
1983 £10.50

KIMBLE, STEPHEN   Papers. NY, 1883. 2 vols. Green
textured cloth. Argosy 716-356 1983 $35

KIMBROUGH, EMILY   We Followed Our Hearts to Hollywood.
N.Y., Dodd, 1943. First edition. Signed by the author. Illus. by
Helen Hokinson. Dust jacket. Fine. Houle 22-673 1983 $45

KIMES, WILLIAM F.   John Muir: A Reading Bibliography.
Palo Alto: William P. Wreden, 1977. One of 300 copies, printed by
Grant Dahlstrom, signed by the authors and the printer. Quarter
cloth. Dawson 470-171 1983 $200

KINAHAN, DANIEL   An Outline of a Plan for Relieving
the Poor of Ireland by an Assessment on Property. Dublin: Richard
Milliken, 1829. First edition, without half-title, 8vo, wrapper.
Fenning 61-236 1983 £28.50

KINCAID, C. A.   The Land of 'Ranji' and 'Duleep'.
London, 1931. Plates. 8vo. Orig. cloth. Good. Edwards 1044-412
1983 £15

KINCAID, D.   The Grand Rebel. London, 1937. 8vo.
Orig. cloth. Good. Edwards 1044-413 1983 £15

KINDERSLEY, EDWARD C.   The Very Joyous, Pleasant and Refreshing
History of the Feats, Exploits, Triumphs, and Achievements of the
Good Knight... New York: Dodd, Mead, 1884. Frontis., plates,
illus. 1st ed. thus. Orig. 3/4 scarlet morocco and marbled boards,
raised bands, gilt compartments, t.e.g. Very fine copy with presentation inscription to Field on front flyleaf and manuscript on rear
flyleaf in pencil in Field's hand (in Greek). Jenkins 155-399 1983
$50

KINDERSLEY, N. E.   Specimens of Hindoo Literature. London,
1794. 5 folding engravings. Half calf, morocco label. Joints weak.
8vo. Good. Edwards 1044-408 1983 £60

KING, AUSTIN   Message of the Governor of Missouri.
Jefferson City, James Lusk, 1850. Dbd. Ginsberg 46-492 1983 $125

KING, CHARLES   Captain Blake. Philadelphia, Lippincott,
1891. First edition. Illus. by A.F. Halmer. Orig. blue cloth cloth
stamped in gilt and black. Fine. Houle 22-529 1983 $45

KING, CHARLES   Foes in Ambush. Philadelphia, Lippincott,
1893. First edition. Orig. gilt and black stamped blue cloth. Very
good - fine. Houle 22-530 1983 $45

KING, CHARLES   Foes in Ambush. Phila., Lippincott,
1893. First edition. Blue cloth. Very good-fine. Houle 21-475
1983 $45

KING, CHARLES   The General's Double. Philadelphia,
Lippincott, 1898. First edition. Illus. with frontis. and four
plates by J. Stepple Davis. Orig. gilt and blue stamped blue cloth.
Very good. Houle 22-531 1983 $35

KING, CHARLES   The Medal of Honor. New York: The H.B.
Claflin Co., 1905. Illus. Fine copy in orig. pictorial binding.
Jenkins 153-161 1983 $30

KING, CHARLES   A Trooper Galahad. Phila., Lippincott,
1899. First edition, frontis. Blue cloth. Fine. Houle 21-478
1983 $45

KING, CHARLES   Trooper Ross and Signal Butte.
Philadelphia, Lippincott, 1896. First edition. Frontis., 5 plates,
and vignettes by Charles Stephens. Orig. pictorial blue cloth stamped
in gilt and blue. Very good - fine. Houle 22-533 1983 $75

KING, CHARLES   Under Fire. Philadelphia, Lippincott,
1895. First edition. Illus. by C.B. Cox. Orig. blue cloth
stamped in gilt and black. Very good. Houle 22-534 1983 $45

KING, CHARLES   Waring's Peril. Philadelphia,
Lippincott, 1894. First edition. Orig. gilt and black stamped blue
cloth. Very good - fine. Houle 22-535 1983 $35

KING, CLARENCE   The Helmet of Mambrina. SF, 1938.
Introduction by Francis P. Farquhar. 12mo, parchment-backed
decorated bds., gilt, slipcase. One of 350 copies printed at the
Univ. of California Press. Bookplate. Perata 28-8 1983 $40

KING, CLARENCE   Mountaineering in the Sierra Nevada.
New York, (1935). Plates. Very light water spotting on covers, few
pages lightly damp warped but clean throughout. Clark 741-126 1983
$22.50

KING, EDWARD   Remarks on stones said to have fallen
from the clouds... London: printed for G. Nicol (by Bulmer), 1796.
First edition. 4to. Disbound. With a frontis. Very good copy.
Ximenes 63-305 1983 $150

KING, FRANCIS   To the Dark Tower. London, 1946. First
edition. Pages browned. Very nice. Rota 231-363 1983 £15

KING, FRANK M.   Mavericks the Salty Comments of An Old-
Time Cowpuncher. Pasadena: Trail's End Publishing Co., 1947. First
edition in dust jacket. Illus. by C.M. Russell. Presentation copy
inscribed by author. Jenkins 152-190 1983 $40

KING, FRANK M.   Pioneer Western Empire Builders.
Pasadena, 1946. 1st ed. Illus. Some illus. by Charles M. Russell.
Light fading to spine. Jenkins 153-316 1983 $35

KING, FRANK M.   Wranglin' the Past Being the Reminiscences of Frank King. Los Angeles, 1935. Illus., 1st edition of the
limited edition privately published for his friends. Limited to
300 copies. Scarce. Jenkins 151-167 1983 $75

KING, G.   The Orchids of the Sikkim-Himalaya.
Calcutta, 1898. 4 vols., folio, cont. half roan (worn, joints
cracked), 453 hand-coloured plates. Slightly foxed, and the binding
is in poor condition. 300 copies printed. Rare. Wheldon 160-53a
1983 £1,250

KING, G.   The Orchids of Sikkim Himalaya.
(Calcutta, Ann. Bot. Garden, 1898) Reprint 1967. 543 plates,
folio, cloth. Wheldon 160-2046 1983 £129

KING, JEFF   Where the Two Came to their Father.
New York, (1943). Two vols., one quarto in wraps., one large folio,
18 loose plates laid into cloth folder, ties. Portfolio, slightly
soiled, but a very good set. Reese 19-316 1983 $875

KING, JESSIE M.   The Grey City of the North. Edinburgh,
1914. First edition. Stiff wrappers. Upper wrapper a little stained.
Very good. Rota 230-324 1983 £25

KING, JOHN   Lectvres Vpon Ionas... Printed at
Oxford, by Joseph Barnes, 1597. 4go, orig. vellum, few light stains
and marginal glosses. First edition. Ravenstree 94-237 1983
$472.50

KING, LEONARD   Port of Drifting Men. San Antonio, 1945.
Illus. Dj. Jenkins 153-595 1983 $25

KING, MARTHA B.   Deer Stories. Chicago: Dickery, (1936).
Small quarto. 6 photographs printed in red and black which, when
viewed through colored cellophane glasses, appear to be three-
dimensional. Printed wrappers slightly rubbed at extremities. Two
sets of ortho-scopes (glasses) in pocket inside front cover. Bromer
25-373 1983 $45

KING, MAUDE EGERTON   Round About a Brighton Coach Office.
Lane, 1896. 1st edn. Frontis. & decor. title p. & 30 illus. by Lucy
Kemp Welch, 16pp adverts. Dark green backed beige decor. cloth
designed by Patten Wilson, t.e. stained green others uncut (couple of
marks rear cvrs. & sml. stain lower fr. cvr., some foxing). Very
good. Hodgkins 27-466 1983 £12.50

KING, MOSES   Harvard and its Surroundings.
Cambridge, 1884. Photos, illus., square 12mo, gilt dec. cloth,
a.e.g. subscription ed. (6th). Argosy 710-289 1983 $40

KING, NEPHEW W.   The Story of the Spanish-American War
and the Revolt in the Philippines. NY, 1900. Illus. by paintings &
photos., some color. Oblong 4to, buckram, endleaf & frontis. wrinkled.
Argosy 716-500 1983 $75

KING, PETER   An Enquiry into the Constitution,
Discipline, Unity & Worship, of the Primitive Church. London,
Jonathan Robinson and John Wyat, 1691. 8vo, orig. calf, joints
cracked, bit worn but good copy. First edition. Ravenstree 97-3
1983 $63

KING, RUFUS   A Variety of Weapons. GC, 1943. Edges
very slightly rubbed, nick to bottom edge of front board, else near
fine in frayed and lightly chipped dustwrapper. Quill & Brush 54-747
1983 $35

KING, STEPHEN   Cujo. NY, (1981). One of 750 numbered
and signed, specially bound copies. Very fine in very fine slipcase.
Quill & Brush 54-748 1983 $125

KING, T. BUTLER   Steam Communication with China, and
the Sandwich Islands. Wash., 1848. First edition. Illus., large
folded map. Ginsberg 46-303 1983 $40

KING, THOMAS STARR   My Vacation Among the Sierras. S.F.,
1962. Illus. Half cloth over boards. One of 400 copies. Printed
by Ward Ritchie. With prospectus. Fine. Houle 21-1097 1983 $75

KING, VALENTINE   Land Claims-Between the Rio Hondo and
the Sabine...Report of... Wash., 1836. Dbd. First edition.
Ginsberg 47-462 1983 $50

KING, WILLIAM   An Answer to the Considerations which
Obliged Peter Manby. Printed for R. Taylor, 1687. Without the
license leaf, 4to, wrapper, first and final leaf evenly dusty,
but otherwise a very good copy. Fenning 61-237 1983 £48

KING, WILLIAM   The Furmetary. London: printed, and
sold by A. Baldwin, 1699. 1st ed., 4to, marbled boards. Pickering
& Chatto 19-33 1983 $600

THE KING in a pickle! London: printed for the author, 1820.
First edition. 8vo. Modern wrappers. Ximenes 63-499 1983 $75

THE KING the avowed enemy of the queen. London: T. Dolby, 1820.
First edition. 8vo. Disbound. Folding frontis. by J.R. Cruikshank
(split in fold, without loss). Rare. Ximenes 63-500 1983 $100

KINGDON-WARD, F.   Commonsense Rock Gardening. 1948.
First edition, 12 plates and 8 figures, 8vo, cloth. Wheldon 160-
1973 1983 £12

KINGLAKE, ALEXANDER WILLIAM Eothen, or Traces of Travel brought home
from the East. London: John Olliver, 1844. 1st ed., 8vo, orig.
pictorial cloth gilt, skilfully rebacked. 2 hand-colored lithographs,
one of them folding. Uncut copy with the half-title. Bookplate.
A fine copy. Trebizond 18-150 1983 $250

KINGLAKE, ALEXANDER WILLIAM Eothen, or Traces of Travel Brought
Home from the East. London, Ollivier, 1844. First edition. Hand-
colored folding frontis. and one handcolored plate showing a view
of Jordan. Cont. tan calf (rebacked), spine decorated in gilt,
red leather spine label. Presentation copy; inscribed on title page
to "J.W. Colvile with the author's kind regards." Very good.
Houle 22-536 1983 $200

KINGLAKE, ALEXANDER WILLIAM Eothen. London, 1845. Fourth edition.
Frontis. and 1 plate. Decorative. 8vo. Good. Edwards 1044-414
1983 £45

KINGLAKE, ALEXANDER WILLIAM Eothen. George Newnes, 1898. Frontis.
16 full-page and 23 text illus. Blue decorated cloth gilt, rubbed.
Greer 39-85 1983 £16

KINGLAKE, ALEXANDER WILLIAM Eothen. S. Low, nd (ca. 1910). 1st
edn. 12 coloured plates & many b&w head pieces. Illus. by Frank
Brangwyn. Rust col'd cloth, uncut. Hodgkins 27-467 1983 £15

"THE KINGS of the East"; an Exposition of the Prophecies. Seeleys,
1849. Cr. 8vo, orig. cloth, some neat annotations & binding dull but
sound, with label on spine, very good copy. Fenning 60-222 1983
£10.50

KINGSBURY, BENJAMIN   The Justice of the Peace. Portland, 1860.
Full calf. Second edition. A very fine copy. Felcone 22-133 1983
$20

KINGSFORD, WILLIAM   The Canadian Canals. Toronto: Rollo
and Adam, 1865. 21cm. Orig. blind stamped pebbled cloth. Fine.
McGahern 54-104 1983 $85

KINGSFORD, WILLIAM   The Early Bibliography of the Province
of Ontario... Toronto & Montreal, 1892. 18 1/2cm. Orig. cloth.
Author's presentation copy to McLeod Stewart. McGahern 53-91 1983
$30

KINGSFORD, WILLIAM   The Early Bibliography of the Province
of Ontario... Toronto and Montreal: Rowsell & Hutchison and Eben
Picken, 1892. Cloth, front fly detached, overall a bit dusty and
faded. Dawson 470-172 1983 $20

KINGSLEY, CHARLES   Alton Locke. Chapman & Hall, 1851.
2nd edition, 2 vols. Orig. salmon-pink cloth, sl. rubbed.
Jarndyce 30-445 1983 £36

KINGSLEY, CHARLES   Alton Locke. Leipzig, Bernhard
Tauchnitz, 1857. 8vo, cont. cloth, name on half title, else good
copy of the first Tauchnitz edition. Ravenstree 96-1 1983 $30

KINGSLEY, CHARLES   Alton Locke. London, 1884. New
edition. 3/4 brown morocco over marbled boards, spine gilt decorated
with scolling roses, t.e.g., marbled ends. Fine. Houle 21-483
1983 $65

KINGSLEY, CHARLES   Andromeda and Other Poems. London:
John W. Parker & Son, 1858. First edition. Orig. cloth. Corners
slightly bumped. Spine slightly soiled or faded. Very good. Mac-
Mancu 279-3051 1983 $75

KINGSLEY, CHARLES   Andromeda and Other Poems. London,
John W. Parker, 1858. 8vo, orig. cloth now worn, bubbled, shaken,
bookplate, name on fly-leaf. A workable copy of the first edition.
Ravenstree 96-2 1983 $39

KINGSLEY, CHARLES   At Last. London: Macmillan, 1871.
First edition. Illus. 2 vols. Orig. cloth. Covers slightly worn.
Good. MacManus 279-3052 1983 $125

KINGSLEY, CHARLES   Glaucus; or The Wonders of the Shore.
Cambridge, MacMillan, 1855. 8vo, orig. cloth, somewhat rubbed
and worn. First edition. Ravenstree 96-3 1983 $35

KINGSLEY, CHARLES   Glaucus; or, The Wonders of the Shore.
Cambridge: Macmillan & Co., 1859. Fourth edition, corrected and
enlarged. Small 8vo. Illus. with colored plates. Orig. cloth.
Presentation copy, inscribed on the half-title to "Miss Dickinson
from the Author, Eversley Sept. 11/59." In a red half-morocco slipcase (spine damaged). Fine. MacManus 279-3054 1983 $275

KINGSLEY, CHARLES   Hereward, the Last of the English.
Boston, Ticknor and Fields, 1866. 8vo, orig. cloth gilt, little
facing, minor age darkening, name on end-paper, but a respectable
copy in very good condition. First American edition. Ravenstree 96-
4 1983 $85

KINGSLEY, CHARLES   Hereward. N.Y., Macmillan, 1885. New
edition. 3/4 morocco bound en suite with the above. Fine. Houle
21-484 1983 $65

KINGSLEY, CHARLES   Hereward the Wake. Macmillan, 1866.
First edition, 2 vols. 2 pp. ads. in both vols. Orig. red cloth,
rubbed on hinges. Half titles. Jarndyce 30-448 1983 £32

KINGSLEY, CHARLES   The Hermits. London, MacMillan (The
Sunday Library for Household Reading), n.d. (1868). 8vo, orig.
cloth gilt, somewhat worn, name on series half-title. First edition.
Ravenstree 96-5 1983 $45

KINGSLEY, CHARLES   His Letters and Memories of His Life.
Henry S. King, 1877. First edition, 2 vols. Front. ports. plates.
Half titles. Orig. brown cloth. Jarndyce 30-1041 1983 £14.50

KINGSLEY, CHARLES   Hypatia: or, New Foes with an Old Face.
London: John W. Parker & Son, 1853. First edition. 2 vols. Orig.
cloth. With an 8-page ALS from Kingsley to one of the editors of The
Leader tipped in (four pages in each vol.), dated Eversley Nov. 19,
1851, Kingsley explains his attitude towards The Leader. Covers a
little worn. Several hinges weak. Each vol. enclosed in a half-
morocco slipcase. Very good. MacManus 279-3055 1983 $750

KINGSLEY, CHARLES   Hypatia: or, New Foes With an Old Face.
London: Parker, 1853. First edition. 2 vols. Orig. cloth. Spines
chipped and frayed. Good, sound copy. MacManus 279-3056 1983 $125

KINGSLEY, CHARLES   Hypatia; or, New Foes with and Old Face.
London, John W. Parker, 1853. 2 vols., 8vo, spines neatly repaired,
slightly worn, name on endpaper, good copy. Ravenstree 96-6 1983
$95

KINGSLEY, CHARLES   Hypatia; or, New Foes with and Old Face.
London, John W. Parker, 1853. 8vo, 2 vols., cont. half calf gilt,
without half titles, quite worn. The Lord Belper copy. Ravenstree
96-7 1983 $75

KINGSLEY, CHARLES   Hypatia. N.Y., Macmillan, 1885. 3/4
brown morocco. Fine. Houle 21-485 1983 $65

KINGSLEY, CHARLES   Plays and Puritans, and Other Historical
Essays. London, MacMillan, 1873. 8vo, orig. cloth, worn, inner
hinges breaking and spine ends frayed. First edition. Ravenstree 96-
9 1983 $35

KINGSLEY, CHARLES   Prose Idylles, New And Old. London,
MacMillan, 1873. 8vo, orig. cloth gilt, bit worn, inner hinges
cracked, "With the Publisher's Compliments" blind stamped on half-
title. Ravenstree 96-10 1983 $35

KINGSLEY, CHARLES   The Roman and the Teuton. Cambridge,
MacMillan, 1864. 8vo, orig. cloth, rather worn and rubbed, spine
ends worn, hinges weak. The first edition. Ravenstree 96-11 1983
$45

KINGSLEY, CHARLES   Two Years Ago. Cambridge, MacMillan,
1857. 3 vols., 8vo, cont. half morocco gilt, somewhat rubbed and
worn, bookplate, signature on front fly leaves. First edition.
Ravenstree 96-12 1983 $65

KINGSLEY, CHARLES   Two Years Ago. N.Y., Macmillan, 1884.
3/4 brown morocco. Houle 21-486 1983 $65

KINGSLEY, CHARLES   Two Years Ago. Macmillan, 1857.
2nd edition, 3 vols. Half titles, 1 p ads. front of vols. II and III.
Orig. half calf, spines gilt, red and blue labels. Rubbing to leading
hinge vol. I, otherwise v.g. Signed on leading end paper. Jarndyce
30-447 1983 £16

KINGSLEY, CHARLES   The Water-Babies. London & Cambridge,
MacMillan, 1863. Square 8vo, newly bound without half title and
ads in full blue morocco gilt, some light age-marking, waterstaining
and soiling throughout. First issue of the first edition, with the
rare "L'Envoi" leaf present. Ravenstree 96-13 1983 $165

KINGSLEY, CHARLES   The Water-Babies. London & Cambridge:
Macmillan, 1863. Second issue. 4to. Orig. cloth (ends of spine,
upper joint, and corners rather rubbed). Lacking the "L'envoi" leaf.
Pasted-in on the half-title is a slip of paper with the autograph
of the author. Hinges cracked. Good. MacManus 279-3057 1983 $80

KINGSLEY, CHARLES   The Water Babies. Boston: deWolf Fiske,
n.d. (ca.1900). 12mo. Grey pictorial cloth. Worn dust wrapper.
4 chromolithographs plus black & whites by L. Sambourne. Very good.
Aleph-bet 8-152 1983 $25

KINGSLEY, CHARLES   The Water-Babies. MacMillan, 1927.
Sm. 4to. Colour frontis. 15 colour plates. Red cloth, gilt. Greer
40-103 1983 £16

KINGSLEY, CHARLES   The Water Babies. N.Y.: Macmil., 1878.
Orig. edition. 12mo. Green gilt and black stamped cloth. Spinal
extremities worn. Illus. by J. Noel Paton. Very good. Aleph-bet
8-152 1983 $20

KINGSLEY, CHARLES   Westward Ho! Cambridge: Macmillan &
Co., 1855. First edition. 3 vols. Orig. cloth. Covers a bit worn.
Enclosed in cloth dust jackets and slipcase. The Katharine Parsons
copy, with her bookplates. Very good. MacManus 279-3058 1983 $500

KINGSLEY, CHARLES   Westward Ho! Cambridge, MacMillan,
1855. 3 vols., 8vo, orig. cloth quite worn, soiled and shaken, "From
the Author" inscribed on half title to vol. 1. Ravenstree 96-14
1983 $225

KINGSLEY, CHARLES   Westward Ho! Boston, Ticknor & Fields,
1855. 8vo, orig. cloth gilt, now worn and faded, names on flyleaf,
minor stains, few signatures sprung. First American edition.
Ravenstree 96-15 1983 $83

KINGSLEY, CHARLES   Westward Ho! N.Y., MacMillan, 1885.
3/4 brown morocco over marbled boards, spines decorated with gilt
stamped roses within gilt scrolled borders, t.e.g., marbled endpapers.
Fine. Houle 22-537 1983 $95

KINGSLEY, CHARLES   Westward Ho! New York: The Limited
Editions Club, 1947. 2 vols. Illustrated by Edward A. Wilson. 1
of 1500 numbered copies, signed by the illustrator. Slipcase. Fine
set. Jenkins 155-814 1983 $65

KINGSLEY, CHARLES   The Works. London, 1890-1901. 11
vols. 8vo. Cont. half polished calf, gilt decorated spines with
floran ornaments, t.e.g. Traylen 94-489 1983 £110

KINGSLEY, CHARLES   Yeast. London, Macmillan, 1883.
3/4 brown morocco. Fine. Houle 21-487 1983 $65

KINGSLEY, HENRY   Tales of Old Travel. London: Macmillan
& Co., 1869. First edition. Orig. pictorial cloth. Edges a little
worn. Covers slightly soiled. Bookplate and previous owner's inscription (partially erased). Bookseller's ticket. Very good. MacManus
279-3059 1983 $85

KINGSLEY, MARY H.   West African Studies. London, 1899.
First edition, thick 8vo, with plates, original red cloth gilt, back
faded and trifle worn at head and foot, one or two leaves at end
trifle torn. Deighton 3-193 1983 £35

KINGSLEY, MARY H.   West African Studies. Macmillan, 1901.
With a folding map, a portrait and 22 plates, 8vo, orig. cloth, a
very good copy. Fenning 62-199 1983 £24.50

KINGSLEY, NELSON   Diary of Nelson Kingsley: A California
Argonaut of 1859. Berkeley, 1914. Orig. printed wrappers. Jenkins
153-317 1983 $30

KINGSTON, WILLIAM H. G.   In the Wilds of Africa. T. Nelson,
1871. Front. & illus. Orig. red cloth, blocked in gilt and black,
bevelled boards, v.g. Jarndyce 31-765 1983 £16.50

KINGSTON, WILLIAM H. G.   Will Weatherhelm. Griffith & Farran,
1860. First edition, front. & illus. by Georg. H. Thomas, 1860.
36pp ads. Orig. green cloth, spine gilt, a.e.g., v.g. Jarndyce 31-
764 1983 £38

KINGTON, W. J.   Thirty Letters on the Trade of
Bristol... Bristol: John Wright, 1834. First edition. 8vo.
Orig. printed cloth. Folding engraved table. Cloth darkened and
some wear. Heath 48-36 1983 £40

KINGZETT, CHARLES THOMAS   Animal Chemistry. London, 1878. 8vo,
cloth. First edition. Argosy 713-310 1983 $40

KINKEAD, A. S.   Landscapes of Corsica and Ireland.
London, 1921. First edition. With foreward by Joseph Conrad.
Orig. gray wrappers. Fine. Very scarce. Gekoski 2-34 1983
£120

KINKEAD, A. S.   Landscapes of Corsica and Ireland.
London: The United Arts Gallery, 1921. First edition. Forward by
Joseph Conrad. 4-page folded leaf with orig. printed wrappers. Folding
cloth slipcase. Near-fine. MacManus 277-1070 1983 $150

KINNELL, GALWAY   Body Rags. Boston: Houghton Mifflin Co.,
1968. First edition. Orig. cloth-backed boards. Dust jacket. Review
copy, with the publisher's slip laid in. Signed by Kinnell on the
title-page. Very fine. MacManus 279-3061 1983 $75

KINNELL, GALWAY   The Book of Nightmares. Boston:
Houghton Mifflin Co., 1971. First edition. Self-wrappers. Outer
wrappers slightly worn, soiled, and frayed, with a tear at the fold.
Ends curled. Good. MacManus 279-3063 1983 $175

KINNELL, GALWAY   First Poems: 1946-1954. The
Perishable Press, 1970. 8vo. Leather backed decorated boards.
Total ed. is 150 copies of which this is 1 of 40 author's copies
issued hors commerce. This copy signed by Kinnell. A fine copy.
In Our Time 156-472 1983 $300

KINNELL, GALWAY   What a Kingdom It Was. Boston, 1960.
8vo. Cloth. Signed by Kinnell on the title page. A fine copy in
soiled and lightly worn dj. In Our Time 156-471 1983 $100

KINSELLA, THOMAS   The Messenger. Dublin. (1978). 8vo.
1 of 50 copies bound in vellum and printed on hand-made paper,
signed by the poet. Each of the 50 copies contain a page of holograph manuscript bound in. A fine copy in slipcase box. In Our
Time 156-473 1983 $300

KINZIE, JULIETTE A.   Wau-Bun, the "Early Day" in the North-
West. New York, 1856. Cloth, some internal staining, but a good
copy. Reese 19-317 1983 $250

KINZIE, JULIETTE A.   Wau-Bun, the "Early Day" in the
North-West. Chicago, 1932. 16mo, g.t., cloth very lightly spotted.
Argosy 710-211 1983 $30

KINZIE, JULIETTE A.   Wau-Bun, The Early Days in the Northwest.
Chicago, Lakeside Press, 1932. Illus. 12mo, gilt top. Clark 741-371
1983 $21

KIP, LAWRENCE   Army Life on the Pacific. New York,
1859. First edition. Brown cloth. Very good, solid copy. Bradley
65-110 1983 $300

KIPLING, RUDYARD   The Absent-Minded Beggar. Daily Mail
Pub. Co., 1899. First edition, a little torn along one fold. Jarndyce
31-767 1983 £10.50

KIPLING, RUDYARD   Address. Garden City: Doubleday, 1923.
First American edition and American copyright issue. 12mo. Orig.
wrappers. Fine. MacManus 279-3065 1983 $125

KIPLING, RUDYARD   An Almanac of Twelve Sports. London:
William Heinemann, 1898. First edition. Thin 4to. Orig. illus.
boards, canvas spine, corners slightly worn. 12 full-page coloured
woodblock illus. by William Nicholson. Traylen 94-491 1983 £75

KIPLING, RUDYARD   Around the World with Kipling. Garden
City, Doubleday, 1926. First edition. Illus. with halftones and
folding map. Dust jacket (moderate chips) else good. Houle 22-542
1983 $35

KIPLING, RUDYARD   Ballads & Barrack-Room Ballads. N.Y.,
1892. First American edition. Argosy 714-432 1983 $45

KIPLING, RUDYARD   A Book of Words. London, 1928. First
edition. Fine. Argosy 714-433 1983 $25

KIPLING, RUDYARD   The Brushwood Boy. London, 1907.
Illus. by F.H. Townsend. 8vo, cloth. First edition with these
illus. Argosy 714-434 1983 $30

KIPLING, RUDYARD   The Brushwood Boy. NY, 1890. Illus. by
Orson Lowell. Dec. cover, edges slightly bumped, else fine. Quill &
Brush 54-755 1983 $35

KIPLING, RUDYARD   Captains Courageous. London, 1897.
8vo. Cloth. Tiny inscription on second flyleaf, otherwise a fine,
bright copy. In Our Time 156-474 1983 $175

KIPLING, RUDYARD   Captains Courageous. London: Macmillan,
1897. First edition. Orig. pictorial cloth, a.e.g. Minor foxing.
Fine. MacManus 279-3066 1983 $110

KIPLING, RUDYARD   Captains Courageous. N.Y., 1897.
First edition. Pict. cloth. Argosy 714-435 1983 $50

KIPLING, RUDYARD   Captains Courageous. London, Macmillan,
1897. 8vo, orig. pictorial cloth, gilt, worn, name and date on
half title. The first edition. Ravenstree 96-16 1983 $37.50

KIPLING, RUDYARD   Captains Courageous. NY, 1897. Spine
slightly soiled, else very good, small tear at top of spine, owner's
name. Quill & Brush 54-749 1983 $30

KIPLING, RUDYARD   A Choice of Songs from the Verse of
Rudyard Kipling. London: Methuen & Co., Ltd., (1925). First English
edition. Orig. yellow wrappers. Very fine. Unopened. MacManus 279-
3067 1983 $25

KIPLING, RUDYARD   The City of Dreadful Night and Other
Places. Allahabad, 1891. Orig. printed wraps. (chipped at extremities
with small pieces missing). First published edition. Felcone 21-
65 1983 $400

KIPLING, RUDYARD   Collected Dog Stories. N.Y.: Doubleday,
Doran & Co., 1934. First limited American edition. Illus. with
drawings by N. Kirmse. Orig. decorated boards with leather label,
publisher's glassine jacket and slipcase (box and jacket somewhat
worn, faded, and chipped). One of 450 copies. Contains an orig.
pencil drawing. Signed and numbered by the artist. Fine. MacManus
279-3068 1983 $350

KIPLING, RUDYARD   Collected Works. London: Macmillan &
Co., 1902-1911. First of this edition. 24 vols. Illus. 3/4 red
morocco. Spine and covers slightly faded and rubbed. Very good.
MacManus 279-3095 1983 $1,100

KIPLING, RUDYARD   The Day's Work. London: Macmillan,
1898. First edition. Orig. cloth. MacManus 279-3069 1983 $25

KIPLING, RUDYARD   The Day's Work. London, MacMillan,
1898. 8vo, orig. cloth gilt, trifle soiled, spine worn, top edge
gilt, name and blind stamp on fly leaf, decent copy. First English
edition. Ravenstree 96-18 1983 $20

KIPLING, RUDYARD   Departmental Ditties and Other Verses.
Lahore: The Civil and Military Gazette Press, 1886. First edition.
Tall, narrow 8vo. Orig. wrappers (in the form of an envelope).
Wrappers a bit chipped and worn. In a half morocco case. Fine.
MacManus 279-3070 1983 $1,250

KIPLING, RUDYARD   Departmental Ditties, and Other Verses.
Calcutta: Thacker, Spink, 1888. 3rd edition, half title, 40 pp illus.
ads. Orig. brown cloth, gilt, v.g. Jarndyce 31-766 1983 £15

KIPLING, RUDYARD   Destroyers at Jutland. N.Y., Doubleday,
1916. Printed wraps. Very good. One of a few copies issued for copyright. Houle 21-490 1983 $200

KIPLING, RUDYARD   Destroyers at Jutland. Garden City:
Doubleday, Page & Co., 1916. First edition. In 4 orig. parts. Orig.
printed wrappers. American copyright issue. Fine. MacManus 279-
3071 1983 $185

KIPLING, RUDYARD   The Elephants Child. (Berkeley,
Archtype Press, 1938). First edition thus. Illus. by Wilder Bentley
II, and Margaret Bentley. Stencilled green wraps. One of 135
copies printed by the artists for private circulation. Houle 22-
538 1983 $50

KIPLING, RUDYARD   The Feet of the Young Men. Garden
City, 1920. Photographically illustrated by Lewis R. Freeman. 1st
ed. Parchment-backed boards. Edition limited to 337 signed copies.
This is No. 12 of 20 copies especially set aside for Mr. Freeman,
and signed by Kipling. Mint copy. Clark 741-335 1983 $350

KIPLING, RUDYARD   The Five Nations. Lon., 1903. Front
hinge starting at half-title, cover edges worn and spine sunned, good
or better, gift bookplate. Quill & Brush 54-756 1983 $40

KIPLING, RUDYARD   The Five Nations. London: Methuen &
Co., 1903. First English edition, first issue. Orig. cloth. MacManus
279-3073 1983 $20

KIPLING, RUDYARD   A Fleet in Being. 1898. Macmillan and
Co. Ltd. 1898. 8vo, orig. blue pictorial wraps., bookplate on the
inner side of the upper wrapper. Slight wear at the head and foot
of the spine. First edition, first issue. Later issues were bound in
cloth. Bickersteth 75-151 1983 £38

KIPLING, RUDYARD   France at War on the Frontier of
Civilization. New York: Doubleday, 1915. 1st American ed. Orig.
boards, labels, dj. Fine copy. Jenkins 155-746 1983 $20

KIPLING, RUDYARD   Fringes of the Fleet. N.Y., Doubleday
1915. Printed wraps. Very good. One of a few copies issued for
American copyright. Houle 21-491 1983 $300

KIPLING, RUDYARD   The Fringes of the Fleet. Garden
City, 1915. First American edition. 16mo, bds., paper labels;
d.w. Argosy 714-436 1983 $20

KIPLING, RUDYARD   From Sea to Sea. N.Y., 1899. First
edition. 2 vols. First issue, with the errors on pp 90 and 153
of vol. II. Argosy 714-437 1983 $45

KIPLING, RUDYARD   Gipsy Trail. Boston, Bartlett, 1909.
First edition. Frontis. by W.A. Dwiggins. Stiff green wraps.,
uncut and unopened. Enclosed in a red half morocco slipcase. Houle
21-489 1983 $150

KIPLING, RUDYARD   The Gipsy Trail. Boston: Alfred
Bartlett, (1909). 12mo. Contains frontispiece and title-page decora-
tons by William A. Dwiggins. Near fine in wrappers with slightly
chipped spine. Bromer 25-196 1983 $45

KIPLING, RUDYARD   Great-Heart. Garden City: Doubleday,
Page & Co., 1919. First edition. Orig. wrappers. American copyright
issue. Fine. MacManus 279-3074 1983 $125

KIPLING, RUDYARD   The Irish Guards. Garden City: Doubleday, Page & Co., 1918. First edition. Orig. wrappers. American copyright issue. Very fine. MacManus 279-3075 1983 $125

KIPLING, RUDYARD   The Irish Guards in the Great War.
London, 1923. 2 coloured frontis. double-page maps, 2 folding coloured
maps and 7 other coloured maps, 8vo. Orig. cloth. T.e.g. Spines
slightly worn. Small labels removed from upper covers. With Signet
Library bookplate on front paste-down endpaper. Good. Edwards 1042-
532 1983 £20

KIPLING, RUDYARD   The Jungle Book. The Second Jungle Book.
London: Macmillan & Co., 1894. First editions. 2 vols. Orig. pictorial cloth. In a half-morocco slipcase. Very good. MacManus 279-
3076 1983 $650

KIPLING, RUDYARD   The Jungle Book. The Second Jungle Book.
London: Macmillan & Co., 1894. First edition. 2 vols. Full decorated morocco. Bound by Riviere & Sons of London. Hand-tooled colored
decorations. Spines slightly faded. Spine ends and outer hinges
slightly chipped and weak. Good. MacManus 279-3078 1983 $450

KIPLING, RUDYARD   The Jungle Book. N.Y.: The Century Co.,
1894-1895. First American editions. Decorated by J.L. Kipling.
2 vols. Orig. decorated green & terra cotta cloth. Covers somewhat
rubbed & dull. In a green half-morocco slipcase. Very good. Mac-
Manus 279-3077 1983 $135

KIPLING, RUDYARD   The Jungle Books. Lunenburg, Limited
Editions Club, 1968. First edition thus. 4to, illus. by David
Gentleman. Half cloth over marbled boards, printed in gilt, slipcase,
fine. One of 1,500 printed by the Stinehour Press and signed by
the illustrator. Houle 22-540 1983 $60

KIPLING, RUDYARD   Kim. New York, Doubleday, Page, 1901.
8vo, orig. pictorial cloth gilt, bookplate, shaken spine worn, ends
chipped. First edition. Ravenstree 96-19 1983 $55

KIPLING, RUDYARD   Kim. London: Macmillan and Co.,
1901. First edition. 8vo. Orig. decorated red cloth, gilt,
t.e.g. Frontis., 9 plates, and 2 pp. of ads. Traylen 94-492
1983 £15

KIPLING, RUDYARD   Kim. NY, 1912. Sm. 4to, red embossed
cloth, lettering & design in gilt, t.e.g. With 10 tipped-in color
plates plus decorative borders by J. L. Kipling. Fine. Perata 27-116
1983 $35

KIPLING, RUDYARD   King Albert's Book. (London): The
Daily Telegraph, etc., (1914). First edition. 4to. Illus. with
tipped-in colored plates by Rackham, Nielsen, etc. Orig. cream
cloth. Dust jacket (a little worn). In a green half-morocco slipcase. Bookplate. Fine. MacManus 279-3079 1983 $250

KIPLING, RUDYARD   Land and Sea Tales for Scouts and Guides.
L, 1923. Fine. Quill & Brush 54-750 1983 $40

KIPLING, RUDYARD   Letters of Travel (1892-1913). L, 1920.
Fine and bright in dustwrapper with slightly frayed spine. Quill &
Brush 54-751 1983 $35

KIPLING, RUDYARD   Letters of Travel (1892-1913). London:
Macmillan, 1920. First edition. Orig. cloth. Dust jacket. Fine.
MacManus 279-3080 1983 $20

KIPLING, RUDYARD   The Light That Failed. Philadelphia:
Lippincott, January 1891. First edition. Orig. printed wrappers.
Covers a bit chipped and soiled. MacManus 279-3081 1983 $50

KIPLING, RUDYARD   The Light that Failed. London and New
York, MacMillan, 1891. 8vo, orig. cloth gilt, spine faded and worn,
corners bumped, little shaken, hinges tender, name on half title.
First English edition. Ravenstree 96-20 1983 $45

KIPLING, RUDYARD   Limits and Renewals. N.Y., Scribner,
1932. Gravure frontis. portrait. Fine 3/4 green morocco by Bayntun,
spine decorated with gilt stamped naimal designs, edges extra gilt.
One of 204 numbered copies on Japan vellum, signed by Kipling.
Houle 22-541 1983 $325

KIPLING, RUDYARD   Limits and Renewals. Garden City:
Doubleday, Doran & Co., 1932. First American edition. Orig. cloth.
Dust jacket (very slightly frayed). Fine. MacManus 279-3082 1983
$35

KIPLING, RUDYARD   Many Inventions. NY, 1893. First American edition, spine edges starting to wear, very good. Quill & Brush
54-752 1983 $40

KIPLING, RUDYARD   Many Inventions. London and New York,
MacMillan, 1893. 8vo, orig. cloth gilt, spine worn, inner hinges
cracked, little shaken. First edition. Ravenstree 96-21 1983 $25

KIPLING, RUDYARD   Mesopotamia. Garden City: Doubleday,
Page & Co., 1917. First edition, American copyright issue. Orig.
wrappers. Very fine. MacManus 279-3083 1983 $125

KIPLING, RUDYARD   The Neutral. Garden City: Doubleday,
Page & Co., 1916. First edition, American copyright issue. Orig.
wrappers. Very fine. MacManus 279-3084 1983 $125

KIPLING, RUDYARD   The Phantom Rickshaw and Other Eerie
Tales. London & Allahabad: Sampson Low, (1888). 1st English ed.
Orig. printed wrappers. Although 10,000 copies were supposedly
printed, a very scarce book, esp. in this condition. Jenkins 155-
748 1983 $275

KIPLING, RUDYARD   A Pilgrim's Way. Garden City: Doubleday,
Page & Co., 1918. First edition, American copyright issue. Orig.
wrappers. Very fine. MacManus 279-3085 1983 $125

KIPLING, RUDYARD   Plain Tales from the Hills. Calcutta,
Thacker, Spink & Co., 1888. 8vo, orig. pictorial cloth, badly
soiled, worn and shaken, hinges split but holding, clean tear half
way through one leaf with no loss, one leaf badly chipped and tipped
in, front fly leaf gone. First edition, with December 1887 ads.
Ravenstree 96-22 1983 $75

KIPLING, RUDYARD   Puck of Pook's Hill. N.Y.: Doubleday,
1906. First edition. Illus. by A. Rackham. Orig. cloth. Spine a
bit rubbed. Some offsetting to endpapers. Bookplate. MacManus 279-
3086 1983 $85

KIPLING, RUDYARD   Puck of Pook's Hill. N.Y.: Doubleday,
1906. First edition. Orig. cloth. Illus. by A. Rackham. Covers
wrinkled. MacManus 279-3087 1983 $75

KIPLING, RUDYARD   Puck of Pook's Hill. London: Macmillan,
1906. First English edition. Orig. cloth. Covers a bit worn.
MacManus 279-3088 1983 $20

KIPLING, RUDYARD   Sea Warfare. L, 1916. Some pages uncut,
very good. Quill & Brush 54-754 1983 $25

KIPLING, RUDYARD   The Second Jungle Book. NY, 1895. Edges
rubbed and slightly worn, good or better. Quill & Brush 54-757 1983
$35

KIPLING, RUDYARD   The Seven Seas. London: Methuen & Co.,
1896. First English edition. Illus. with title-page vignette.
Bookplate. Good. MacManus 279-3089 1983 $20

KIPLING, RUDYARD   The Song of the Lathes. Garden City:
Doubleday, Page & Co., 1918. First edition, American copyright issue.
Orig. yellow wrappers. Fine. MacManus 279-3090 1983 $125

KIPLING, RUDYARD   Stalky and Co. London: Macmillan,
1899. First English edition. Orig. cloth. In a half-morocco slipcase. MacManus 279-3091 1983 $135

KIPLING, RUDYARD   Tales of East and West. (The Connecticut
Printers of Bloomfield, for) The Limited Editions Club, 1973. 4to,
8 colour plates and 20 line drawings, blue and green cloth divided
horizontally, gilt, similar boards slip-case, fine. Edition limited
to 2,000 numbered copies signed by Charles Raymond, illustrator.
Deighton 3-194 1983 £55

KIPLING, RUDYARD   Tales of the Trade. N.Y., Doubleday,
1961. Printed wraps. Very good. 3 vols. One of a few copies
issued for American copyright. Houle 21-492 1983 $175

KIPLING, RUDYARD   Thy Servant a Dog. London: 1930.
Told by Boots. Sq 12mo, red cloth, lettering & design in black.
First edition. Illustrated by G. L. Stampa. Bookplate. A very
nice copy. Perata 27-117 1983 $20

KIPLING, RUDYARD   Under the Deodars. New York: United
States Book Co., (1890). 1st American ed. Contemporary half
leather. Rubbed, but very good copy, scarcer than English ed.
Jenkins 155-751 1983 $30

KIPLING, RUDYARD   The Vampire and Other Poems. New
York: Street & Smith, (ca. 1897-8). Frontis. 1st ed. thus, with
Street & Smith cancel title-page. Orig. pictorial brown cloth,
gilt, t.e.g. Fine copy of this scarce ed. Jenkins 155-752 1983
$30

KIPLING, RUDYARD   Verse. Inclusive edition 1885-1918.
London: Hodder and Stoughton, 1919. First collected edition. 3
vols. 8vo. Full crimson morocco, two-line gilt borders, gilt
panelled spines, edges gilt. Traylen 94-493 1983 £48

KIPLING, RUDYARD   Wee Willie Winkie and Other Child
Stories. Allahabad: A.H. Wheeler & Co., n.d. (1888). First edition,
second issue. Orig. pictorial wrappers (soiled and rather worn at the
spine). Part of backstrip missing. Good. MacManus 279-3093 1983
$250

KIPLING, RUDYARD   We Willie Winkie and Other Child
Stories. Allahabad, A.H. Wheeler, n.d. (1888). 8vo, orig. printed
paper wraps., worn, soiled and chipped, spine perished; this is
number 6, the final number of the "Indian Railway Library". This
is the second state of the front wrapper, having a period after the
"A" and "H", the first edition. Ravenstree 96-24 1983 $85

KIPLING, RUDYARD   With the Night Mail. NY, 1909. Illus.
by Frank Leyendecker and H. Reuterdahl, edges rubbed, hinges starting,
else would be very good. Quill & Brush 54-758 1983 $40

KIPLING, RUDYARD   Works in Prose and Verse. London,
1913-38. Bombay edition. 31 vols. Roy. 8vo. Boards, canvas
backs with printed paper labels, t.e.g., others uncut. Printed
on hand-made paper, with initials printed in blue. Vol. 1, signed
in full by the author. Traylen 94-490 1983 £550

KIPLING, RUDYARD   The Years Between. London: Methuen,
(1919). First edition. 12mo. Orig. buckram. MacManus 279-3094
1983 $20

KIRBY, CHARLES F.   The adventures of an Arcot rupee.
London: Saunders, Otley, 1867. First edition. 3 vols. 8vo.
Orig. blue cloth. A little rubbed, spines a trifle dull. Scarce.
Ximenes 63-159 1983 $175

KIRBY, W. E.   The Butterflies and Moths of Europe.
(1903). 1 plain and 54 coloured plates, 4to, original decorated
cloth (repaired). A completely revised edition. Wheldon 160-1109
1983 £80

KIRBY, W. E.   Butterflies and Moths in Romance and
Reality. 1913. 28 coloured plates, 8vo, cloth (spine faded).
Wheldon 160-1110 1983 £15

KIRBY, W. E.   Familiar Butterflies and Moths. 1901.
18 coloured plates of 216 figures, cr. 4to, original decorated
cloth (trifle used). Wheldon 160-1108 1983 £25

KIRBY, W. E.   List of Hymenoptera. 1882.
Vol. 1, cloth, neatly repaired. Wheldon 160-1107 1983 £15

KIRBY, WILLIAM   An Introduction to Entomology. 1843.
2 vols., 8vo, 5 coloured plates, modern buckram, cloth beginning to
slit at the joints. Bickersteth 75-246 1983 £16

KIRCHER, A.   China Mounummentis. Amsterdam, 1767.
2 folding maps, engraved title, portrait, 23 plates including 3 folding,
1 repaired. 59 text illus., some marginal worming in the first few
leaves, some very slight spotting. Folio. Cont. vellum, slightly
soiled. 8vo. Good. Edwards 1044-409 1983 £675

KIRK, CHARLES   Recollections of Charles Kirk, Late of
Warminster, Pennsylvania. Philadelphia, 1892. Frontis. and plate.
Original cloth. Jenkins 151-169 1983 $35

KIRK, ELISHA   Memoirs of the Life of... Phila.,
1834. First edition. Dbd. Ginsberg 46-860 1983 $45

KIRKBRIDE, THOMAS S.   On the Construction. Phila., 1880.
Tall 8vo, cloth; ex-lib. Argosy 713-311 1983 $100

KIRKHAM, SAMUEL   English Grammer in Familiar Lectures...
Cincinnati, 1826. 3rd ed. 12mo, contemporary calf, lacks label and
blank endleaf at end. Morrill 288-235 1983 $22.50

KIRKLAND, CHARLES P.   Liability of the Government of Great
Britain for the Depredations of Rebel Privateers on the Commerce
of the U.S. N.Y., 1863. Wraps., (edges stained). Argosy 716-112
1983 $25

KIRKLAND, JOSEPH   The Story of Chicago. Chicago, 1892.
Illus. with ports. & views, many photos, 4to, orig. pict. cloth,
ex lib. Argosy 710-212 1983 $50

KIRLICKS, JOHN A.   Sense and Nonsense in Rhyme. (Houston:
Rein & Sons, 1913). Frontis., plates. 1st ed. Orig. blue cloth,
gilt. Fine copy. Scarce. Jenkins 155-1375 1983 $75

KIRKPATRICK, JOHN E.   Timothy Flint Pioneer, Missionary,
Author, Editor 1780-1840. Cleveland: The Arthur H. Clark Company,
1911. Frontis and plates, 1st ed., fine copy. Unopened. Jenkins
151-77 1983 $50

KIRKWOOD, SAMUEL J.   Special Message of Governor...in Reply
to a Resolution of Inquiry, Passed by the House of Representatives...
1860. Orig. printed wraps. First edition. Ginsberg 47-369 1983
$125

KIRMSE, MARGUERITE   Dogs in the Field. New York: Derry-
dale Press, (1935). Twenty-four plates + orig. drypoint etching
as frontis., signed by the artist. Oblong 4to, 3/4 cloth.
Accompanied by a portfolio of six plates. Engraved sporting bookplate.
In as new condition, in the orig. glassine and pub.'s box.
One of 685 numbered copies. Felcone 21-32 1983 $550

KIRSTEIN, LINCOLN   Elie Nadelman. New York: The Eakins
Press, 1973. 215 illus. Large 4to. Cloth. Dust jacket. Slipcase.
Printed in an edition of 3075 copies, designed by Martino Mardersteig
and printed at the Stamperia Valdonega. Ars Libri 32-488 1983 $85

KIRWAN, RICHARD   Elements of Mineralogy. Printed by
J. Nichols, for P. Elmsly, 1794. 2 vols., 8vo, errata leaf and 6
folding tables in the second vol., cont. tree calf with red morocco
labels, spines rubbed, lacking the label for the volume number on vol.
2, small defective patch in the calf in the centre of the upper cover
by the joint, but a good copy. Bickersteth 75-247 1983 £110

KISSELBACH, BALTHASAR   Disputatio medica de odontalgia...
Basel: Georg Decker, 1660. Cont. annotations in lavender ink.
8vo. Cont. paper backstrip. Ink stain along top edge. Kraus
164-54 1983 $180

KISSINGER, HENRY   White House Years. Boston: Little,
Brown & Co., 1979. Plates. Slipcased. Limited and signed edition.
Very fine. Jenkins 152-192 1983 $75

KISSINGER, HENRY   Years of Upheaval. Boston: Little,
Brown & CO., 1982. Plates. Slipcased. Special edition limited to
1500 copies and signed by Kissinger. Very fine. Jenkins 152-193 1983
$75

THE KITCHEN Directory, and American Housewife. New York, (1841).
Illus. 2 plates. Printed wraps. (rear lacking). Worn and dog-
earned; foxed. Felcone 22-41 1983 $50

KITCHINER, WILLIAM   The Art of Invigorating and Prolonging
Life. 1821. 2nd edition, 12mo, calf neatly rebacked. K Books 301-
109 1983 £36

KITCHINER, WILLIAM   The Economy of the Eyes. Boston:
Wells and Lilly, 1824. First American edition. 12mo, with 2 folding
plates & a couple of text illus. Orig. boards, uncut, with paper
spine label. Karmiole 76-76 1983 $125

KITCHINER, WILLIAM   Observations on Vocal Music. Printed
for Hurst, Robinson and Co., 1821. First edition, with an engraved
plate, including the half-title, large 12mo, orig. boards, uncut,
recently and neatly rebacked, a very good copy. Fenning 62-200
1983 £38.50

KITSON, C. H.   The Art of Counterpoint. Oxford, 1924.
2nd edition. 8vo, cl. Salloch 387-336 1983 $25

KITTON, F.   Charles Dickens. 1902. First edition,
half title, front. and illus. Orig. red cloth, v.g. Jarndyce 30-201
1983 £14

KITTON, F   Charles Dickens by Pen and Pencil.
London: Frank T. Sabin, 1889-1892. First edition. 100 illus. on
copper, steel and wood. In the orig. 14 parts. Orig. printed wrappers.
With a six-page catalogue laid in of books for sale by Sabin. Wrappers
of 3 parts soiled. Front wrapper on one part detached. Wrapper edges
slightly frayed in all parts. Very good. MacManus 278-1561 1983
$450

KITTON, F   Dickens and His Illustrators. 1899.
First edition, 4to, 22 portraits and facs. of 70 orig. drawings.
Half title, uncut. Orig. green cloth, rubbed, t.e.g. Jarndyce 30-198
1983 £85

KITTON, F   The Dickens Country. A. & C. Black,
1905. First edition, half title, front. 50 full-page photo. illus.
4 pp ads. Orig. dark green cloth, t.e.g., v.g. Jarndyce 31-610 1983
£15

KITTON, F   Dickensiana. George Redway, 1886.
Half titles, front. port. First edition (500 copies only). Orig.
green cloth, v.g. Jarndyce 30-197 1983 £42

KITTON, F   John Leech, Artist and Humourist.
George Redway, 1884. New edition, revised. 1 p ads. Half title,
4 pp ads. Orig. printed wraps., sl. rubbed. Jarndyce 30-1052 1983
£12.50

KITTON, F   The Minor Writings. Elliot Stock, 1900.
Endpapers browned. Orig. olive green cloth, bevelled boards, sl.
marking of upper cover as a result of label removal. Jarndyce 30-200
1983 £24

KITTON, F'   Phiz. W. Satchell, 1882. First
edition, front. port. and illus. Orig. grey printed wraps., a little
worn. Jarndyce 30-916 1983 £15

KITTREDGE, GEORGE L.   The Old Farmer and His Almanack.
Cambridge, 1920. Illus. Argosy 710-327 1983 $35

KITTRELL, NORMAN G.   Governors Who Have Been and Other Public
Men of Texas. Houston, 1921. First edition. Portrait frontis.
Covers a bit worn. Biographical sketches. Jenkins 152-845 1983 $40

KIYOSU, Y.   The Birds of Japan. Tokyo, 1952.
700 photographic illus. (a few coloured), coloured plates, 3 vols.,
royal 8vo, original half calf (trifle rubbed). Wheldon 160-780
1983 £75

KJERSMEIER, CARL   Afrikanske Negerskulpturer. / African
Negro Sculptures. New York: Wittenborn, Schultz, Inc., n.d. 40
plates. Large 4to. Boards. 1/4 cloth. Parallel text in Danish
and English. Ars Libri 34-664 1983 $100

KLAGES, LUDWIG   Vom Kosmogonischen Eros. Munich:
Georg Mueller, 1926. First edition. Cloth-backed boards. Library
bookplate, stamp on rear paste-down. Gach 95-273 1983 $25

KLAPKA, G.   The War in the East. London, 1855. 8vo.
Orig. cloth. Folding map. Good. Edwards 1044-415 1983 £40

KLEE, PAUL   Paul Klee. Paintings, watercolors,
1913-1939. New York: Oxford, 1941. 65 collotype plates. 2 tipped-
in reproductive color serigraphs in text. Large 4to. Heavy wrappers,
GBC-bound. Typography by H.K. Poster. Ars Libri 32-366 1983 $125

KLEINSCHMIDT, O.   Die Singvogel der Heimat. Leipzig,
1921. Third edition, 100 plates, 8vo, boards. Wheldon 160-782
1983 £12

KLIGER, ISRAEL J.   The Epidemiology & Control of Malaria
in Palestine. Chicago, (1939). Numerous illus., charts & maps,
8vo, buckram; ex-lib. First edition. Argosy 713-312 1983 $40

KLINEFELTER, WALTER   A Bibliographical Check-List of Christ-
mas Books. Portland: Southworth-Anthoensen Press, 1937. Octavo.
Limited to 1500 copies. Extremely fine in cloth-backed boards.
Together with More Christmas Books. Portland: Southworth-Anthoensen
Press, 1938. Octavo. Including index to both vols. Limited to 500
copies. Extremely fine. Bromer 25-180 1983 $95

KLINEFELTER, WALTER   More Christmas Books. Portland, Maine,
1938. 8vo, red buckram, gilt, illus., index. One of 500 copies. Very
fine. Perata 27-118 1983 $50

KLING, JOHANN PETER VON   Der Tabacksbau. Mannheim, 1778. First
edition. Uncut. 12mo. Modern boards. Kraus 164-232 1983 $240

KLOBIUS, JUSTUS   Ambrae Historiam ad Omnipotentis
Dei Gloriam et Hominum Samtatem exhibet, Justus Fidus Klobius D.
In Academ. Witteb. Wittenbergae, Sumptibus Haered. D. Tobiae Mevii &
Elerdi Schumacheri Typis Matthaei Henckelii Anno M.D.C.LXVI. (1666).
4to, 3 plates and one map. Full new vellum. Title in MS on spine.
Small wormholing at head of spine and 1-1/2 inch tear at base of
hinge, some loss of vellum exposing board. Toned through, plates
with lighter browning. Good. Arkway 22-77 1983 $475

KLOET, G. S.   A Check List of British Insects.
Stockport, privately printed, 1945. 8vo, cloth (inner joints
taped). Wheldon 160-1111 1983 £20

KLONDIKE, The Chicago Record's Book for Gold Seekers. Chicago, 1897. Illustrated, pict. cloth, heavily rubbed covers, pencil marks in text. King 46-4 1983 $25

KLOPSTEG, PAUL E. Turkish Archery And the Composite Bow. Evanston, Ill., 1947. Illus, cloth, minor wear. King 46-600 1983 $20

KLOPSTOCK, F Memoirs... R. Cruttwell, Bath, 1808. First edition, lacks leading free end paper. Tree calf, a little rubbed. Jarndyce 30-1044 1983 £12.50

KLOPSTOCK, F . The Messiah. Elizabeth Town: Shepard Kollock, 1788. Full calf. Signature "John Ogden Esqu. / His Book / July ye 7th. 1788 / price Six Shillings." Very good. Felcone 19-25 1983 $50

KLUEVER, HEINRICH Visual Mechanisms. Vol. VII of Biological Symposia. Lancaster, Pa.: Jacques Cattell Press, 1942. Gach 94-731 1983 $20

KLUMPKE, ANNA Rosa Bonheur. Paris: Ernest Flammarion, 1908. 7 heliogravure plates. Most prof. illus. Small folio. Wrappers. Ars Libri 32-46 1983 $325

KNAPP, F. H. The Botanical Chart of British Plants and Ferns. Bath, 1846. 8vo, original cloth, 2 ownership stamps. Wheldon 160-1612 1983 £20

KNAPP, FRIEDRICH Italienische Plastik vom funfzehnten bis achtzehnten Jahrhundert. Munchen, 1923. 130pp., 160 plates. Lrg. 4to. Boards, 1/4 cloth (light wear; a little waterstaining). Ars Libri SB 26-110 1983 $65

KNAPP, J. L. Gramina Brittanica. 1842. 2nd ed., 4to, new cloth, 118 hand-coloured plates. Inscription from author on fly-leaf, which is creased. A good clean copy. Wheldon 160-54 1983 £150

KNAPP, SAMUEL L Lectures on American Literature; with Remarks on some Passages of American History. (NY), 1829. 8vo, orig. linen, paper label, uncut, backstrip neatly mended, dampstained. Argosy 710-165 1983 $50

KNAPP, SAMUEL L. An Oration Delivered Before the Associated Disciples of Washington. Newburyport, 1812. Dsb., good. Reese 18-380 1983 $20

KNAPP, WILLIAM I. Life, Writings, and correspondence of George Borrow. London: John Murray, 1899. First edition. Port. & illus. 2 vols. Orig. cloth. Bookplates. Labels removed from front covers leaving faint trace. Very good set. MacManus 277-602 1983 $85

KNEELAND, GEORGE J. Commercialized Prostitution in New York. New York, The Century Co., 1913. Half title. Orig. maroon cloth, v.g. Jarndyce 31-212 1983 £18.50

KNEELAND, SAMUEL An American in Iceland. Boston, 1876. First edition. With the signature, S. Kneeland. Map and illustrations. 8vo. Morrill 290-213 1983 $25

KNEELAND, SAMUEL The Wonders of the Yosemite Valley and of California. Boston: Moore, 1871. 10 orig. photographs by John P. Soule. 4to, orig. gilt-stamped green cloth. Other than occas. spotting, with orig. tissue guards. 1st ed. Fine. Jenkins 153-722 1983 $500

KNICKERBOCKER, DEIDRICH, PSEUD.
Please turn to
IRVING, WASHINGTON

KNIGHT, CHARLES Knight's Cyclopaedia of London, 1851. Charles Knight, 1851. Front. and illus. Half maroon calf, hinges rubbed, spine gilt, green label. Jarndyce 31-268 1983 £38

KNIGHT, CHARLES Once Upon a Time. London: Murray, 1854. First edition. 2 vols. 12mo. Orig. cloth. Covers a tirfle worn. Inner hinges reglued in vol. one. MacManus 279-3098 1983 $50

KNIGHT, CHARLES Shadows of the Old Booksellers. Bell & Daldy, 1865. First edition, orig. brown cloth, v.g. Jarndyce 31-213 1983 £42

KNIGHT, ELLIS CORNELIA Dinabras; a Tale. Printed for C. Dilly, 1790. 12mo, uncut, orig. grey boards with calf spine, lower joint cracked, short tear in side margin of title and dedication leaf, but a fine copy. First edition. Bickersteth 75-47 1983 £110

KNIGHT, HENRY GALLY The Ecclesiastical Architecture of Italy. London, published by Henry Bohn, 1843. Folio, chromolithograph title-page by Owen Jones, 40 coloured and tinted lithograph plates, some slight spotting, half morocco, buckram boards, original label on upper board, new endpapers.

KNIGHT, LANDON The Real Jefferson Davis. Battle Creek, Mich., 1904. First edition. Illus. Jenkins 152-609 1983 $20

KNIGHT, N. R. Gold Horizon. Seattle, 1937. Illus. Clark 741-403 1983 $21.50

KNIGHT, NEHEMIAH R. Gov. Knight's Address to the Farmers of Rhode-Island, Oct. 1832. Providence, (1832). Sewed. Argosy 716-485 1983 $20

KNIGHT, RICHARD P. A Discourse on the Worship of Priapus. London: The Dilettanti Society, (ca. 1930), privately printed. 1/625 copies. Gach 95-274 1983 $30

KNIGHT, RUTH ADAMA Dr. Christian's Office. N.Y., Random, (1944). First edition. Pictorial dust jacket (slight rubbing and creases). Signed and inscribed by Hersholt, Christmas 1944. Houle 22-543 1983 $30

KNOLLES, RICHARD The Turkish History, from the Original of that Nation, to the Growth of the Ottoman Empire. 1687-1700. 3 vols., folio, with 25 portraits and one other plate, cont. mottled calf, upper joint of vol. 1 cracked and cracks at head and foot of some other joints and slight wear at head of spines, small defective spot in leather in spine of vol. 3, but generally bindings sound. Bickersteth 75-48 1983 £185

KNIGHT, T. A. A treatise on the culture of the Apple and Pear. Ludlow, 1801. Second edition, post 8vo, original boards (backstrip missing), uncut. Wheldon 160-1975 1983 £35

KNIGHT, THOMAS A. The Strange Disappearance of William Morgan. Brocksville, OH; for the author, (1932). Illus., rubber-stamped, ex lib. Argosy 710-276 1983 $30

KNIGHT, WILLIAM ALLEN The Song of Our Syrian Guest. Boston, (1903). First issue of the separate edition with the name of the printer on the last page. Reprinted from "The Congregationalist." 16mo, original self-wrapper. Morrill 290-215 1983 $35

KNIGHTS, ARTHUR E. Notes by the Way in a Sailors' Life. San Francisco: A.M. Robertson, 1905. Plate. Frontis. Boards and cloth. Worn and water-stained. Signed presentation from author. Dawson 471-173 1983 $20

KNIP, PAULINE Les Pigeons. Paris, 1811. Imp. folio, cont. full straight grained morocco, gilt (rubbed and neatly repaired), 87 fine coloured-printed plates, g.e., the Napoleonic crowned eagle gilt on both covers. Rare. Some foxing, mostly confined to the margins, and a few plate numbers and legends have been trimmed by the binder. Wheldon 160-55 1983 £9,000

KNOPF, ALFRED A. The Random Recollections... New York: The Typophiles, 1949. Small 8vo. Cloth. Mailing box. Limited to 1250 copies. With Christmas greeting loosely inserted. Oak Knoll 49-256 1983 $30

KNOWER, DANIEL The Adventures of a Forty-Niner. Albany: Week-Parsons, 1894. 11 half-tone plates. 12mo, orig. 3/4 dark brown morocco and cloth, spine gilt. Spinal extremities chipped. 1st ed. One of the few copies in a special binding. Very fine. Jenkins 153-319 1983 $50

KNOWLES, HORACE   Countryside Treasures. London: (Chiswick Press, 1946). Octavo. Illus. Printed from calligraphy. One corner slightly bumped, else fine. Bromer 25-240 1983 $85

KNOWLES, LEES   The British in Capri 1806-1808. First edition. 8vo. Orig. cloth. Frontis. 2 coloured mounted portraits. 1 tinted and 23 other plates. Double page map. 2 illus. T.e.g. Others uncut. Very slightly worn and soiled. Inscription from Lady Knowles to the Library of the Lancashire Fusiliers at Wellington Barracks, Bury. Good. Edwards 1042-385 1983 £45

KNOWN Signatures. London: Rich & Cowan Ltd., (1932). First edition. Fine copy. Jaffe 1-11 1983 $150

KNOX, C. H.   Harry Mowbray. London: John Ollivier, 1843. First edition. Illus. Orig. cloth. Slightly foxed. Fine. MacManus 279-3100 1983 $125

KNOX, DUDLEY W.   Naval Sketches of the War in California. NY, 1939. Folio, marbled boards, white lea. backstrip (rubbed), scarlet mor. label. 28 color repros of drawings by Wm. Meyer made in 1846-7. Ltd. edition. Printed at the Grabhorn Press. Argosy 716-255 1983 $150

KNOX, JOHN   An Historical Journal of the Campaigns in North-America... London: Printed for the Author, 1769. 4to. 2 vols. First edition. Engraved frontis. portraits. Large engraved folding map, wood-ornaments and initials. Bound in full cont. tree calf, raised bands, gilt stamped decorations in the panels, double leather labels (red and green). A fine set. McGahern 53-92 1983 $1,750

KNOX, JOHN   The History of the Reformation in Scotland. 1905. 8vo, portrait, cloth. Bickersteth 75-128 1983 £26

KNOX, JOHN   United States Notes: A History of the Various Issues of Paper Money by the Government of the United States. London, 1885. Illus. (facs.). Orig. cl. 2nd ed., revised. Jenkins 151-170 1983 $100

KNOX, KATHLEEN   Fairy Gifts; or, A Wallet of Wonders. London: Griffith & Farran, n.d. (1874). First edition. Illus. by Kate Greenaway. Orig. cloth-backed pictorial boards. Worn; shaken. MacManus 278-2371 1983 $150

KNOX, KATHLEEN   Poor Archie's Girls. London: Smith, Elder & Co., 1882. First edition. 3 vols. Orig. decorated cloth. Spine ends lightly rubbed. Some foxing to the preliminary pages. Near-fine. MacManus 279-3101 1983 $250

KNOX, ROBERT   The races of man: a fragment. London: Renshaw, 1850. First edition. 8vo. Orig. dark olive green cloth. Wood-engraved illus. throughout. Fine copy. Ximenes 63-529 1983 $200

KNOX, THOMAS   Business and Family Directory of Springfield, Illinois, for 1881-82. Springfield, 1881. Illus., 2 ad. plates. Orig. cloth. First edition. Ginsberg 46-330 1983 $85

KNOX, THOMAS W.   The Boy Travellers on the Congo. Sampson Low, 1888. First edition, with full-page and other illus., 8vo, orig. pictorial cloth, gilt. Some light finger marks but a sound and very good copy. Fenning 61-421 1983 £16.50

KNOX, THOMAS W.   Teetotaler Dick: ...A Temperance Story. NY (1890). 6 plates, dec. cloth. Argosy 710-159 1983 $35

KNOX, THOMAS W.   The Underground World. Hartford, 1880. Illus. 8vo. Top of spine torn. Morrill 286-234 1983 $25

KNOX, VICESIMUS   Epistles, Elegant, Familiar & Instructive... London, 1791. First edition. 2 vols. Roy. 8vo, cont. calf, gilt, fully gilt panelled spines with red and green morocco labels, gilt. Engr. vignette title-page after Corbould. Traylen 94-495 1983 £20

KNOX, VICESIMUS   The Spirit of Despotism. Morris Town: Jacob Mann, 1799. Full calf (worn, early rebacking). Early library label. First book printed in Morristown. Very good. Felcone 19-26 1983 $150

KNOX, VICESIMUS   The Spirit of Despotism. Morristown. (New Jersey). 1799. Leather and boards. Foxed. Bibl. note pasted on front endpaper. Very good. Reese 18-235 1983 $100

KOBBE, GUSTAV   New York and Its Environs. New York, 1891. 1st ed. Maps and illus. 12mo. Morrill 287-309 1983 $22.50

KOBERT, RUDOLF   Compendium der Praktischen Toxologie. Stuttgart: Ferdinand Enke, 1887. Second edition. Orig. yellow printed wrappers, very worn. Adolf Meyer's copy, signed on front wrapper. Gach 95-359 1983 $25

KOBUTORI. Kobunsha, Tokyo. No. 7. 9 col'd illus. (some double page). Col'd pictorial cvrs., vg. Hodgkins 27-111 1983 £18

KOCH, CARL   Die Zeichnungen Hans Baldung Griens. Berlin: Deutscher Verein fur Kunstwissenschaft, 1941. 283 collotype plates. Large 4to. Cloth. Slightly worn. Ars Libri 32-19 1983 $175

KOCH, ERNST   Valentin Lendenstreich und andere Saalfelder Maler um die Wende des Mittelalters. Jena: Gustav Fischer, 1914. Small 4to. Wrappers. Ars Libri 32-401 1983 $37.50

KOCH, ROBERT   The Aetiology of Tuberculosis. N.Y., 1932. 4to, cloth. Illus. Argosy 713-313 1983 $85

KOCH, ROBERT   The Aetiology of Tuberculosis. New York, 1932. First English translation. 8vo. Orig. binding. Ex-library. Fye H-3-325 1983 $35

KOCH, W. D. J.   Synopsis Florae Germanicae et Helveticae. Leipzig, 1857. Third edition, 2 vols. in 1, 8vo, half leather. Wheldon 160-1729 1983 £20

KOCK, CHARLES PAUL DE   Works. Boston, Frederick J. Quinby (1903). Gregory edition. Illus. with 12 etchings and 6 photogravures from drawings by John Sloan, 2 etchings and 11 gravures by William Glackens, 2 etchings and 3 gravures by George Luks, 3 etchings by Charles White, 4 etchings and 3 gravures by Louis Meynell and one etching by Jacques Reich; 8 other gravures. Green cloth stamped in gilt on spine, t.e.g., uncut. 23 vols. One of 1,000 sets. Houle 22-290 1983 $400

KODIS, J.   Zur Analyse Des Apperceptionsbegriffes. Berlin: S. Calvary & Co., 1893. First edition. Orig. printed wrappers, spine erose, inscribed to Adolf Meyer. Gach 95-275 1983 $28.50

KOECHEL, L.   Chronologische Thematisches Verzeichnis Saemtlicher Tonwerke Wolfgang amade Mozarts. Ann Arbor, 1947. Thick 4to, cl. Salloch 387-354 1983 $90

KOECHLIN, J.   Flore et Vegetation de Madagascar. Braunschweig, Flora et Vegetatio Mundi, 1974. Text-figures, maps and 189 plates, 8vo, cloth. Wheldon 160-1730 1983 £65

KOECHLIN, RAYMOND   Les ivoires gothiques francias. Paris, 1968. 3 vols., 4to. 231 plates. Cloth. Reprint of the Paris 1924 edition. Ars Libri SB 26-111 1983 $175

KOEGL, JOHANN EV. ABRAHAM   Dissertatio inauguralis medica de Usu, et Abusu Nicotianae, vulgo Tabaci... Inssbruck: Johann N. Wagner, 1772. First edition. Decorative woodcut head- and tail-pieces, printer's ornaments at top of each page, woodcut. Small 8vo. Boards. Kraus 164-233 1983 $480

KOEGLER, HANS   Niklaus Manuel Deutsch. Basel: Urs Graf Verlag, n.d. 124 plates. Frontis. in color. Folio. Boards, 1/4 cloth. Ars Libri 32-424 1983 $125

KOEHLER, R.   An Account of the Shallow-Water Asteroidea. Calcutta, 1910. 20 plates, 4to, wrappers. Wheldon 160-1307 1983 £20

KOELLIKER, A.   Elemens d'Histologie Humaine. Paris, 1856. First French edition. 8vo. Quarter-leather. Numerous illus. in text. Gurney JJ-209 1983 £20

KOELLINKER, A.   Manual of Human Microscopic Anatomy. London, 1860. 8vo, orig. cloth (inner joints expertly mended); ex-lib. Argosy 713-314 1983 $100

KOENIG, A.   Avifauna Spitzbergensis. Bonn, 1911. 4to, original cloth-backed boards, coloured and heliogravure plates, a folding map in cover-pocket. Very scarce. Wheldon 160-56 1983 £400

KOENIG, A.   Die Vogel am Nil. Vol. 2, Die Raubvogel. (Bonn, 1936). 4 plain and 52 coloured plates, 4to, original wrappers. The only volume published. Privately printed and very scarce. Wheldon 160-783 1983 £85

KOENIG, EDMUND   W. Wundt. Stuttgart: Fr. Frommanns Verlag, 1901. First edition. Ads. Gach 95-500 1983 $27.50

KOENIG, HEINRICH   Georg Forster's Lebin in Haus und Welt. Leipzig, 1858. 8vo. 2 vols. Orig. wrappers. Stamp on titles; one quire in vol. 2 loose. Gurney JJ-125 1983 £15

KOENIGSMARCK, H.   The Markhor Sport in Cashmere. London, 1910. First English edition. 9 plates. Sm.8vo. Pictorial front cover. Orig. cloth. Good. Edwards 1044-416 1983 £36

KOERTE, ALFRED   Hellenistic Poetry. NY, 1929. 8vo, cloth. Salloch 385-133 1983 $30

KOESTLER, ARTHUR   Darkness at Noon. New York: MacMillan, 1914. 1st ed. Orig. blue cloth. Fine copy in lightly used dj. Jenkins 155-756 1983 $25

KOHL-LARSEN, LUDWIG   Felsmalereien in Innerafrika. Stuttgart: Strecker und Schroder, 1938. 32 plates. 3 maps. 46 text illus. Small folio. Wrappers. Dust jacket. Ars Libri 34-667 1983 $100

KOHLER, CARL   A History of Costume. Philadelphia: David McKay Co., n.d. (ca. 1927). With sixteen plates in colour and about 600 other illus. and patterns. Dust jacket. Fine copy. Karmiole 73-32 1983 $30

KOHLER, W.   The Mentality of Apes. (1925). Second edition, 9 plates, 8vo, cloth. Wheldon 160-569 1983 £12

KOIZUMI, SETSU
Please turn to
HEARN, SETSU KIOZUMI

KOLB, PETER   The Present State of the Cape of Good-Hope....Together with a Short Account of the Dutch Settlement at the Cape... London, for W. Innys, 1731. First edition in English, 2 vols., frontis, folding map, and 28 unusual copper-plates, some occasional age-marking and a few smudges library stamps but good in old style calf. K Books 307-109 1983 £320

KOLBEN, PETER
Please turn to
KOLB, PETER

KOLLER, JOSEPH VON   Nordamerikanische Schilderungen (1855-1865). Hilpolstein, 1880. First edition. Later cloth, morocco label. Orig. printed wrappers bound in (somewhat chipped). Ex-library. Jenkins 152-846 1983 $150

KOLLIKER, RUDOPH ALBERT VON Manual of Human Histology. Sydenham Society, London, 1853-54. 2 vols., 8vo, with 513 text-illus., very occasional minor spotting; orig. cloth, a little worn, t.e.g. First English edition. Quaritch NS 5-63 1983 $150

KOLLONITZ, PAULA   The Court of Mexico. Saunders, Otley, and Co., 1867. 8vo, 32 page pub.'s catalogue, orig. blue cloth, blocked in blind, slightly worn at head and foot of spine. First English edition. Bickersteth 75-152 1983 £65

KOOP, ALBERT J.   Early Chinese Bronzes. NY: Charles Scribner's Sons, 1924. Folio, 110 fine full-page collotype plates (a few plates in color). Orig. grey cloth. Karmiole 73-77 1983 $175

KORAN   The Koran, Commonly called the Alcoran of Mohammed. London, C. Ackers for J. Wilcox, 1734. 4to, orig. calf, old rebacking now worn, joints cracked, name on title, ends of spine chipped. First complete edition in English. Ravenstree 97-6 1983 $250

KORAN   The Koran, commonly called the Alcoran of Mohammed. London: by C. Ackers, 1734. Translated by George Sale. First edition. 4to. Cont. mottled calf, gilt, gilt panelled spine with morocco label, gilt. Title-page printed in red and black, engraved folding map and 3 folding plates. A little worn. Traylen 94-496 1983 £130

KORDA, T.   Photography Year Book 1935. London. Mostly illus. Cloth spine. Pictorial boards. Rubber and blind-stamped names. Spine frayed. Extremities frayed. No. 1. King 45-373 1983 $35

KORNFELD, EBERHARD W.   Verzeichnis der Kupferstiche, Radierungen und Holzschnitte von Marc Chagall. Bern: Kornfeld und Klipstein, 1970. Band I: 1922-1966. 123 illus. (17 color). Large 4to. Cloth. Dust jacket. One of 1500 copies. Presentation copy inscribed by the author to Bernard Karpel. Ars Libiri 32-97 1983 $175

KORTRIGHT, FRANCIS H.   The Ducks, Geese and Swans of North America. Washington, D.C., 1942. Drawings. Cloth. Index. Lacks front endpaper. First edition. Good. King 45-491 1983 $25

KORTRIGHT, FRANCIS H.   The Ducks, Geese and Swans of North America. Washington, American Wildlife Institute, 1942. 1st ed. Inscription by Josephine Gibson Knowlton. Illus. in color & black & white by T.M. Shortt. 8vo, orig. leatherette. Morrill 288-228 1983 $25

KOSINSKI, JERZY   The Future is Ours, Comrade. New York, 1960. 8vo. Cloth. A fine copy in lightly rubbed dj. In Our Time 156-475 1983 $450

KOSINSKI, JERZY   No Third Path. New York, 1962. 8vo. Cloth. Fine copy in lightly rubbed dj. In Our Time 156-476 1983 $400

KOSINSKI, JERZY   No Third Path. GC, 1962. Cover slightly stained, else very good in frayed and lightly chipped, lightly stained dustwrapper. Quill & Brush 54-760 1983 $125

KOSTELETZKY, V. F.   Allgeneine Medizinisch-Pharmazeutische Flora. Prag, 1831-6. 6 vols. 8vo, cont. black boards. First edition. Argosy 713-316 1983 $250

KOTSUJI, ABRAM SETSUZAU   The Origin and Evolution of the Semitic Alphabets. Tokyo: Kyo Bun Kwan, 1937. 4to, presentation copy, signed by the author. Red cloth. Karmiole 76-64 1983 $30

KOTTENKAMPF, FRANZ   Der Unabhangigkeitskampf Der Spanisch-Amerikanischen Colonien. Stuttgart, 1838. First edition. Marbled boards, moderately foxed, rubbed. King 46-127 1983 $50

KOTZEBUE, AUGUST   The Most Remarkable Year in the Life of:... New York, 1802. 1st American ed. 12mo. Contemporary calf. Morrill 289-384 1983 $25

KOTZEBUE, AUGUST   The natural son; a play, in five acts. London: printed for R. Phillips; sold by H. D. Symonds; Carpenter and Co., etc., 1798. 8vo, wrappers. First edition. Ximenes 64-342 1983 $40

KOTZEBUE, MORITZ VON   Narrative of a Journey into Persia, in the Suite of the Imperial Russian Embassy, in the Year 1817. London: Longman, 1819. 1st ed. in English, 8vo, cont. half calf gilt, morocco label, marbled boards. Five uncolored aquatints. Foxing of text, else a very good copy. Trebizond 18-157 1983 $375

KOURNAKOFF, SERGEI N.   Russia's Fighting Forces. NY (1942). Pict. wraps, covers show wear, edges spotted. King 46-794 1983 $20

KOURY, MICHAEL J.   Military Posts of Montana. Bellevue:
The Old Army Press, 1970. Maps and illus. Full morocco, gilt, boxed.
Limited to 50 copies, signed by author and illustrator. Also an orig.
drawing by Derek FitzJames. Jenkins 153-371 1983 $150

KOUWENHOVEN, JOHN A   The Columbia Historical Portrait of New
York. New York, 1953. First edition. Hundreds of fine illustrations,
a few in color, from old prints, photographs, etc. 4to, slightly torn
dust wrapper. Morrill 290-657 1983 $75

KRAENZLIN, F.   Orchidacearum Genera et Species.
(Berlin, 1901-04), reprint 1969. 16 plates, 2 vols. in 1, 8vo.
Wheldon 160-2047 1983 £52

KRAEPELIN, EMIL   Lectures on Clinical Psychiatry. NY:
Wood, 1906 (1904). Second edition in English. Ex-Library copy,
joints and spinal extremities worn. Gach 94-380 1983 $50

KRAEPELIN, EMIL   Lectures on Clinical Psychiatry. NY:
William Wood, 1913. Third edition in English. Orig. blue cloth,
shelfworn, good ex-library copy. Gach 95-279 1983 $50

KRAEPELIN, EMIL   Manic-Depressive Insanity and Paranoia.
Edinburgh: E. & S. Livingstone, 1921. Publisher's blue cloth. Fine,
bright copy. First English edition. Gach 95-280 1983 $160

KRAEPELIN, EMIL   Psychiatrie: Ein Lehrbuch fuer
Studierende und Aerzte. Lp: Johann Ambrosius Barth, 1909, 1910.
First printings of the 8th edition (last edition published in
Kraepelin's lifetime). Lacking final two vols. Publisher's brown
cloth, top of spine to Vol. II worn, else a very good ex-library
copy. Gach 94-381 1983 $50

KRAEPELIN, EMIL   Psychiatrie. Leipzig: J. A. Barth,
1909, 1910, 1913. Three vols. (lacking fourth vol.). Ads. Very
good ex-library set in publisher's brown cloth. Gach 95-281 1983
$100

KRAFFT-EBING, RICHARD VON (1840-1902)   An Experimental Study in
the Domain of Hypnotism. NY: G. P. Putnam's Sons, 1889. Ad leaf.
Publisher's black cloth. First edition in English. Very good,
shelfworn copy. Gach 95-225 1983 $175

KRAITSIR, CHARLES V.   The Poles in the United States of
America, Preceded by the Earliest History of the Slavonians and by
the History of Poland. Philadelphia, Kiderlen and Stollmeyer, 1837.
1st ed. 16mo. Paper label. Binding faded. Morrill 289-385 1983
$35

KRAKEL, DEAN   James Boren A Study in Discipline.
Flagstaff, 1968. Limited to 200 copies with an original watercolor
sketch by James Boren. Boxed. Jenkins 151-171 1983 $575

KRAMER, SIDNEY   A History of Stone & Kimball...
Chicago, (1940). 1st trade ed. Illus. 8vo, text dampstained,
binding partly so. Morrill 288-229 1983 $45

KRAMER, WILHELM   The Aural Surgery of the Present Day.
London, New Sydenham Society, 1863. Small 8vo, orig. cloth. Ex-lib.
First edition. Argosy 713-318 1983 $50

KRATKOE Izlozhenie Prav I Obiazannostei Krest'Ian I Dvorovykh
Liudei... St. Petersburg, 1861. Orig. self-wrappers, stitched.
Fragile wraps, lightly dust soiled, untrimmed and uncut. 1st and
only ed. Extremely rare. Fine. Jenkins 153-812 1983 $300

KRAUS, H. P.   The Ninetieth Catalogue... New York,
n.d. Numerous tipped-on plates, boards, cloth spine. Dawson 470-
176 1983 $75

KRAUSE, GREGOR   Bali. Hagen: Folkwang-Verlag,
1922. Second edition. 207 plates. 4to. Boards. Worn. Ars
Libri 31-816 1983 $37.50

KRAUSOLD, JOHANNES ERNESTUS Disputationem medicam inauguralem,
de dentitione infantum. Jena: Literis Nisianis, 1678. Woodcut
initial and head-piece. Small 4to. Cont. paper backstrip. Kraus
164-55 1983 $180

KRAUSS, FRIEDRICH S.   Anthropophyteia. Leipzig: Ethnolo-
gischer Verlag, 1904, 1905, 1907, 1908, 1910. Vols. 1, 2, 4, 5 (of
10). 4to. Orig. cloth-backed boards and red cloth. Two vols. quite
worn, pp. k99-202 lacking in vol. 5 (not bound in). Gach 95-283
1983 $225

KRAUTHEIMER, RICHARD   Lorenzo Ghiberti. Princeton:
Princeton University Press, 1956. 176 collotype plates. Large
4to. Cloth. Original edition, with superior plates. Ars Libri
33-157 1983 $200

KREFFT, J. L. G.   The Mammals of Australia. (Sydney,
1871), Melbourne, 1979. 16 plates, folio, half leather. A facsimile
reprint with a new forward. Edition limited to 350 copies, numbered
and signed by Basil Marlow, writer of the foreword. Wheldon 160-
571 1983 £80

KREIDOLF, ERNST   Das Hundefest. Zurich: Rotapfel, 1928.
Oblong octavo. First edition. 12 full-page, full-colored illus.
Fine in quarter-cloth and pictorial boards, lightly rubbed at extre-
mities. Bromer 25-358 1983 $65

KREMERS, EDWARD   History of Pharmacy. Phila., 1845.
30 illus. Argosy 713-319 1983 $85

KREMERS, EDWARD   History of Pharmacy... Philadelphia,
(1940). First edition. 30 illustrations. Blue cloth. Fine copy.
Bradley 65-111 1983 $35

KRESS, CLAUDE W.   The Point System of Wing Shooting.
N.p. (1937). 2 Vols. Vol. 2 all illus, spiral bound pict. wraps.
Vol. 2 cover slight tear, a bit worn in rubbed box, bookplates,
and 2 pp of carbon copy info. from author. King 46-605 1983 $85

KREYMBORG, ALFRED   How do you do Sir? New York: Samuel
French, 1934. Printed wraps. First edition. Inscribed by the
author on the half-title in the year following publication. One
corner chipped, ink name, light spotting on front wrap, a very good
copy. Reese 20-585 1983 $48

KREYMBORG, ALFRED   Our Singing Strength. N.Y., McCann,
1929. First edition. Half tan cloth. Signed and inscribed by
the author, Nov. 14, 1929. Very good. Houle 22-547 1983 $65

KRIEGER, KURT   Westafrikanische Plastik. Berlin:
Museum fur Volkerkunde, 1965-1969. 3 vols. 1 folding map. 272
illus. hors texte. 1 folding map. 313 illus. hors text. 1 folding
map. 358 illus. hors texte. Small 4to. Wrappers. Ars Libri 34-
668 1983 $150

KRIS, ERNST   Catalogue of Postclassical Cameos in
the Milton Weil Collection. Vienna, Schroll, 1932. Stiff grey
wraps. with paper labels (a bit bumped, bookplate) else, very good.
Illus. with 40 plates. Houle 22-164 1983 $85

KROEBER, A. L.   Archaeological Explorations in Peru.
Part II: The Northern Coast. Chicago, 1930. 18 plates. 3 text
illus. Small folio. Wrappers. Ars Libri 34-309 1983 $25

KROEBER, A. L.   Archaeological Explorations in Peru.
Part IV: Canete Valley. Chicago, 1937. 22 plates. Small folio.
Wrappers. Ars Libri 34-310 1983 $25

KROEBER, A. L.   The Uhle Pottery Collections from
Ica. Berkeley: University of California Press, 1924. 16 plates.
17 text illus. Small 4to. Wrappers. Ars Libri 34-317 1983
$25

KROEBER, A. L.   The Uhle Pottery Collections from
Moche... Berkeley: University of California Press, 1925. 30
plates. 5 text illus. Small 4to. Wrappers. Ars Libri 34-315
1983 $30

KROEBER, A. L.   The Uhle Pottery Collections from
Moche... Berkeley: University of California Press, 1926. 11
plates. 26 text illus. Small 4to. Wrappers. Ars Libri 34-314
1983 $25

KRONTHAL, PAUL   Der Schlaf Des Andern. Halle: Carl
Marhold, 1907. First edition. Modern cloth. Gach 95-284 1983 $30

KRUEGER, KURT   I was Hitler's Doctor. N.Y., (1943).
First edition. Frontis. Argosy 713-321 1983 $30

KRUSSMAN, G.   Die Baumschule. Berlin, 1981.
5th revised edition, 376 illustrations, 8vo, cloth. Wheldon 160-2092 1983 £50

KRUTCH, JOSEPH WOOD   Edgar Alan Poe. N.Y., Knopf, 1926.
First edition. Illus. Half vellum over decorated boards, uncut.
One of 150 large paper copies signed by Krutch. Very good. Houle 22-548 1983 $145

KUAS, HERBERT   Die Naumburger Werkstatt. Berlin, 1937.
Lg. 4to, 130 plates, cloth. Ars Libri SB 26-114 1983 $250

KUELPE, OSWALD   Outlines of Psychology. London: Swan
Sonnenschein, 1901 (1895). Ex-library rebound in buckram. Gach 94-583 1983 $27.50

KUHN, ALFRED   Die Neuere Plastik von achtzehnhundert
bis zur gegenwart. Munchen, 1922. 4to, boards, 77 plates, 19 text
illus. Ars Libri SB 26-115 1983 $50

KUHN, HERBERT   Die kunst der Primitiven. Munchen:
Delphin-Verlag, 1923. 215 plates. Square 4to. Cloth. Backstrip
loose. Ars Libri 34-27 1983 $125

KUME, YASUO   Tesuki Wahsi Shuhu, Fine Handmade
Papers of Japan. Tokyo: Yushodo, 1980. 3 vols., folding case. 1st
ed., 1 of 200 sets produced. Very fine copy. Mint set. Jenkins
155-992 1983 $1,000

KUNGLE, CHARLES H.   State of the Union. Sacramento, 1861.
First edition. Dbd. Ginsberg 47-123 1983 $35

KUNHARDT, DOROTHY   Now Open the Box. N.Y.: HB, 1934.
First edition. Oblong 8vo. Cloth backed pictorial boards. Slight
marking on covers. Color illus. Very good. Aleph-bet 8-154 1983
$20

KUNZ, GEORGE FREDERICK   Catskill Aqueduct Celebration
Publications. N.Y., 1917. Illus. 8vo, cloth. Argosy 716-357
1983 $20

KUPRIN, ALEXANDRE   Yama. New York: Privately printed
for Subscribers only, 1922. Cloth and boards, paper label. One of
1225 numbered copies. First edition in English. Slight soiling
and traces of rubbing at edges of boards, else fine. Reese 20-587
1983 $20

KUPRIN, ALEXANDRE   Yama: The Pit. London, 1930. First
edition. Covers somewhat used. Very good. Rota 230-329 1983 £12.50

KURLBAUM-SIBERT, MARGARETE   Mary Queen of Scots. (1928). 8vo,
portraits, cloth. Bickersteth 77-129 1983 £12

KUTZ, C. R.   War on Wheels. London, 1942. Sm. 8vo.
Orig. cloth. 6 full page and 8 sketch maps. Slightly worn, spine
faded. Good. Edwards 1042-386 1983 £12

KUTZING, F. T.   Tabulae Phycologicae. (1846-71)
Facsimile reprint, 1977. 20 vols., each with 100 plates and descriptive text, in 4 vols., 8vo, cloth. Wheldon 160-1848 1983 £388

KUYKENDALL, IVAN LEE   Ghost Riders of the Mogollon. San
Antonio, 1954. Cloth, fine in dust jacket. Reese 19-313 1983 $500

KYSHE, JAMES WILLIAM NORTON   The History of the Laws and Courts of
Hongkong. London & Hongkong, 1898. First and apparently only edition,
with 9 plates, 2 vols. Roy. 8vo, cont. half calf, the spines worn
but holding and joints cracked, but otherwise a nice copy. Fenning
60-225 1983 £10.50

L

LA BILLARDIERE, J. J. H. DE   Novae Hollandiae Plantarum Specimen. (Paris, 1904-06). Reprint 1966. 265 plates, 2 vols. in 1, 4to, cloth. Wheldon 160-1734 1983 £62

LABILLIERE, FRANCIS P.   The Political Organisation of the Empire. 1881. First edition. Disbound, retaining front printed wrapper. Jarndyce 31-109 1983 £20

LABORDE, A. DE   Les Principaux Manuscrits a Peintures Conserves dans l'Ancienne Bibliotheque Imperiale... Paris: Societe francaise de Reproductions de Manuscrits a Peintures, 1936, 1938. First edition. 4to. Folder containing signatures of text and plates. 86 plates. The folders are worn through the text, and the plates are in fine condition. Oak Knoll 48-224 1983 $125

LABRIE, JACQUES   Les Premiers Rudimens de la Constitution Britannique. Montreal: Chez James Lane, 1827. 21c. Errata. Blue-grey plain wrappers. Very good. McGahern 54-106 1983 $75

LABRUNIE, GERARD
Please turn to
GERARD DE NERVAL

LA CALPRENEDE, GAUTHIER DE COSTES   Cassandra. London, Humphrey Moseley, 1652. Folio, new calf antique style, short tear to 4P4 with no loss; large, fresh copy with the signature of the collector Francis Wolfreston on title. A fine copy of the first edition in English. Ravenstree 96-26 1983 $385

LACEPEDE, B.-G.-E.   Histoire Naturelle de l'Homme... Paris, 1827. 8vo. Old quarter-calf. Portrait and 1 folding plate. First edition. Half-title and title foxed. Some slight foxing else-where. Gurney 90-68 1983 £40

LACHAISE, GASTON   Gaston Lachaise. Sixteen reproductions in collotype of the sculptor's work... New York: E.P. Dutton, 1924. 16 collotype plates in text. 4to. Boards, 1/4 cloth. Printed by D.B. Updike at the Merrymount Press in a limited edition of 400 copies only. With the ex-libris of the "Fifty Books of 1925" collections of the American Institue of Graphic Arts. Ars Libri 32-381 1983 $175

LACKINGTON, JAMES   The confessions of J. Lackington... London: printed by Richard Edwards, for the author, 1804. 12mo. 19th-century half calf, spine gilt. First edition. Ximenes 63-32 1983 $150

LACKINGTON, JAMES   Memoirs of the first forty-five years of the life of James Lackington... London: printed for and sold by the author, n.d. (1791). First edition. 8vo. 19th-century half calf, spine gilt. Portrait. Bookplate of Lord Derby. Trifle scuffed. Ximenes 63-31 1983 $175

LACONICS: or, New Maxims of State and Conversation Relating to the Affairs and Manners of the Present Times. Thomas Hodgson, 1701. Mottled calf, panelled, with gilt borders. Spine sl. rubbed and slight splitting of hinges. Bookplate of the Rt. Hon. Wm. Lord North. Jarndyce 31-6 1983 £180

LACORDAIRE, T.   Introduction a l'Entomologie. Paris, 1834-38. 24 plain plates, 2 vols. and atlas in 2 vols., 8vo, new cloth. Some slight foxing. Wheldon 160-1112 1983 £25

LACOSTE, HENRI DE   Washington, ou Les Represailles, Fait Historique en 3 Actes et en Prose. Paris, 1813. Leather backed marbled boards, leather label. With early copperplate, 4 extra engr. portraits laid in of Clinton, Asgill, Marie Antoin, & Louis 6th. Also pages at end with excerpts from various works copied in manuscript. Argosy 716-605 1983 $75

LACROIX, PAUL   History of Prostitution Among all the Peoples of the World. Chicago, 1926. 3 vols. Frontis., ltd. edition. K Books 301-150 1983 £38

LACROIX, PAUL   Manners, Customs, and Dress During the Middle Ages, and During the Renaissance Period. London: Chapman & Hall, 1874. Large quarto. Illus. with 15 full-page chromolithographs and hundreds of wood engravings. Three quarter plum crushed morocco, t.e.g., foredge untrimmed. Spine evenly faded to dark brown, a fine copy. Reese 20-589 1983 $100

LACROIX, PAUL   Science and Literature in the Middle Ages and at the Period of the Renaissance. London: Bickers & Sons, 1878. Large quarto. Illus. with 13 full-page chromolithographs, and several hundred wood engravings. Three quarter plum crushed morocco, t.e.g. Spine evenly faded to dark brown, a fine copy. Reese 20-591 1983 $125

LACROIX, PAUL   Science and Literature in the Middle Ages... London, 1878. Large 8vo. Orig. cloth, rebacked. 13 coloured plates and many illus. in text. Gurney JJ-213 1983 £15

LACTANTIUS, LUCIUS FIRMIANUS Opera, Quae Extant. Oxonii, E Theatro Sheldoniano, 1684. 8vo, orig. calf sometime restored and rebacked, now worn, hinges broken, canceled library bookplate, few holes in blank portions of title due to removal of early bookplate. A fair copy of the first edition to be printed in England. Ravenstree 95-68 1983 $67.50

LACTANTIUS, LUCIUS FIRMIANUS Opera, Quae extant Omnia. Hayes, 1685. 8vo, cont. calf, hinges broken. Second edition printed in England. Ravenstree 95-69 1983 $35

LACY, JOHN   The Steeleids, or the tryal of wit. London: printed and sold by J. Morphew, 1714. 1st ed., 8vo, title printed in red and black, leaf H1 misbound, modern boards. Pickering & Chatto 19-34 1983 $650

LADD, GEORGE TRUMBULL (1842-1921)   Elements of Physiological Psychology. New York, Scribner's 1894 (1887). Gach 94-584 1983 $27.50

LADD, GEORGE TRUMBULL (1842-1921)   Intimate Glimpses of Life in India. Boston: Richard G. Badger, (1919). First edition. Gach 95-290 1983 $27.50

LADD, GEORGE TRUMBULL (1842-1921)   Knowledge, Life and Reality. NY: Dodd, Mead & Co., 1909. First edition. Very good. Gach 95-292 1983 $27.50

LADD, GEORGE TRUMBULL (1842-1921)   Philosophy of Knowledge. NY: Charles Scribner's, 1897. First edition. Very clean ex-library copy. Gach 95-293 1983 $27.50

LADD, GEORGE TRUMBULL (1842-1921)   Philosophy of Mind. NY: Scribner's, 1905 (1895). First edition. Front hinge cracked. Gach 95-294 1983 $25

LADD, GEORGE TRUMBULL (1842-1921)   The Philosophy of Religion. London: 1906. First British edition. Two vols. Cloth a bit rubbed. Gach 95-295 1983 $30

LADD, GEORGE TRUMBULL (1842-1921)   Primer of Psychology. NY: Scribner's (1894), later printing. Gach 95-296 1983 $20

LADD, GEORGE TRUMBULL (1842-1921)   The Teacher's Practical Philos-ophy. New York, Funk & Wagnalls, 1911. First edition, fine, orig. green cloth. Gach 95-297 1983 $25

LADENBURG, ALBERT   Lectures on the History of the Development of Chemistry. Edinburgh: for the Alembic Club, 1900. First English edition. 8vo. Orig. cloth. Ads. Inside hinges split. Zeitlin 264-244 1983 $50

LADENBURG, ALBERT   Lectures on the History of the
Development of Chemistry. Edinburgh: for the Alembic Club, 1905.
Revised edition. 8vo. Orig. cloth. Very good copy. Zeitlin
264-245 1983 $40

LADENDORF, HEINZ   Andreas Schluter. Berlin: Rembrandt-
Verlag, 1937. Second edition. 172 illus. 4to. Wrappers. Ars
Libri 32-619 1983 $55

LA DEVIZE, ABEL DE   The Life and Death of Monsieur Claude.
London, Thomas Dring, 1688. 4to, disbound, first and only edition.
Ravenstree 97-9 1983 $45

LADIES' Manual of Art. Philadelphia & Chicago, American Mutual
Library Association, 1887. 1st ed. Illus. 8vo. Morrill 286-238
1983 $30

LADURIE, EMMANUEL LE ROY   Montaillou: Cathars and Catholics in a
French Village 1294-1324. London, 1978. Signed by Graham Greene on
verso of half title, and with Greene's underlinings and occasional
marginal notes. Head and Tail of dustwrapper very slightly worn,
otherwise fine. Gekoski 2-73 1983 £125

THE LADY and the saints. London: Edward Bull, 1839. First edition.
8vo. 19th-century half calf. Ten vignettes, designed by R. Cruikshank. A bit rubbed. Orig. cloth covers and spine bound in.
Ximenes 63-416 1983 $40

LADY Jane Grey: An Historical Tale. Printed for William Lane, at
the Minerva, Leadenhall-Street, 1791. 1st ed., 2 vols, sm. 8vo,
contemporary qtr. calf, marbled sides, uncut; small chips to spines,
but a very good copy. With both half-titles. Hill 165-61 1983 £285

LA FAILLE, J.-B. DE   L'oeuvre de Vincent Van Gogh. Catalogue
raisonne. Paris/Bruxelles: G. Van Oest, 1925. 4 vols. 446 collotype plates with more than 1600 illus. Supplement bound in. Folio.
New cloth with leather labels. Orig. edition. Ars Libri 32-259
1983 $850

LA FARGE, OLIVER   Laughing Boy. Cambridge, Houghton,
1929. First edition. Dust jacket (short tears and small chips),
else very good. Houle 21-496 1983 $85

LAFAYE, GEORGE DE   Principes de Chirurgie. Paris, 1749.
12mo, cont. calf, (bottom of backstrip chipped). Argosy 713-323
1983 $150

LAFOND, PAUL   Degas. Paris: H. Floury, 1918-1919.
2 vols. 17 plates. 84 illus. 76 plates. 4to. Marbled boards,
3/4 leather. T.e.g. Orig. wrappers bound in. The hors texte
plates include numerous tipped-in color facsimiles and gravures.
Ars Libri 32-153 1983 $400

LAFONTAINE, AUGUST HEINRICH JULIUS   Clara Duplessis and Clairant:
The History of a Family of French Emigrants. Printed for T. N. Longman, 1797. 3 vols., 12mo, contemp. qtr. calf, marbled sides; slight
wear to covers, one label lacking, but a very fair copy; half-titles
in vols. I and II, 3 pp. of advertisements in Vol. III. First edition
in English. Hill 165-62 1983 £195

LA FONTAINE, JEAN DE   Fables from La Fontaine in English
Verse. London: John Murray, 1820. 8vo. Cont. straight-grained
green morocco, blind tooled and wide gilt borders on sides with
floral ornaments, gilt panelled spine, inner gilt dentelles, edges
gilt. First edition of this translation by John Matthews. Traylen
94-498 1983 £48

LA FONTAINE, JEAN DE   Fables. Boston, Elizur Wright, Jr., &
Tappan and Dennet, 1841. First American edition. Numerous illus. by
J.J. Grandville. 2 vols., 8vo, contemporary calf, leather labels.
Few small stains and scratches on cover, otherwise nice. Morrill 290-
223 1983 $60

LA FONTAINE, JEAN DE   Tales: imitated in English Verse.
London: for C. Chapple, 1814. 2 vols. 12mo. 19th century crimson
morocco, two-line gilt borders with corner ornaments, elaborately
gilt panelled spines, inner gilt borders, t.e.g., others uncut.
Extra-illustrated with engraved portrait and 83 plates, including
7 in duplicate, from an 18th century French edition, the plates
unsigned. From the library of Charles Tennant with bookplates.
Traylen 94-499 1983 £195

LA FONTAINE, JEAN DE   Tales and Novels in Verse... Edinburgh: Samuel Humphreys, 1762. Small 8vo. Cont. calf. Heath
48-347 1983 £55

LAFORGUE, RENE   The Defeat of Baudelaire. London:
Hogarth Press/IPP, 1932. First edition in English. Very good in
dust jacket. Gach 95-298 1983 $50

LAFORGUE, RENE   The Relativity of Reality. NY: N. M. D.
Publishing Co., 1940. Orig. printed boards, spine rubbed. Gach 95-
300 1983 $25

LAFORGUE, RENE   Le Reve et la Psychanalyse. Paris:
(1926). First edition. Orig. wrappers. Gach 95-301 1983 $35

LAGO, MARIO   Angelo Zanelli. Roma: G. Romagna,
1911. 32 plates. 4to. Wrappers. Ars Libri 33-608 1983 $30

LA GRANGE, JACQUES   Clipper Ships of America and Great
Britain 1833-1869. 4to, orig. cloth. Coloured frontis., illus. title,
36 coloured plates from wood engr. by J. LaGrange. 23 full-page
illus., 1 double-page plan, 1 double-page chart, 7 illus., endpaper
charts. Orig. decorated green cloth, slightly faded. Good. Edwards
1042-117 1983 £45

LAHARPE, BENARD DE   Journal Historique De L'Etablissment Des
Francais A LA Louisiane. New Orleans, 1831. First edition (printed
in Paris). Half calf. Slight wear and foxing. Jenkins 152-197
1983 $500

LAIGNEL-LAVASTINE, M. P. M.   Histoire generale de la Medecine...
Paris, 1936-49. 4to. 3 vols. Half-morocco, t.e.g. Numerous
coloured plates and illus. in text. Binding slightly worn. Gurney
JJ-215 1983 £85

LAING, G. BLAIR   Memoirs of an Art Dealer. Toronto:
M&S, 1979. 25 1/2cm. Frontis. and 64 laid in colour plates.
Maroon cloth. Maroon cloth box with gilt titles and colour plate
laid down on the upper cover. A fine copy. McGahern 53-93 1983
$75

LAIRD, M.   Narrative of an Expedition. London,
1837. 2 vols. 8vo. Folding map, 6 plates, slight water staining.
Library stamp on the title of vol. I. New half calf, marbled boards.
Morocco labels. Good. Edwards 1042-387 1983 £140

LAKE, E.   Journals of the Sieges of the Madras Army.
London, 1825. 17 folding plans, 5 folding plates. Half maroon morocco
by Henderson & Bisset. 8vo. Good. Edwards 1044-419 1983 £95

LAL, MOHAN   Life of the Amir Dost Mohammed Khan.
London, 1846. 2 vols. 19 lithograph portraits on India paper. Green
calf, contrasting labels. Spines gilt, sunned. 8vo. Good. Edwards
1044-420 1983 £140

LALANDE, JOSEPH-JEROME LE FRANCAIS DE   Exposition du Calcul Astronomique. Paris: Imprimerie Royale, 1762. First edition. 3 folding
plates. 8vo. Modern brown half morocco over marbled boards, gilt-
stamped title on spine. Kraus 164-144 1983 $340

LALANNE, LUDOVIC   Dictionnaire Historique de la France...
New York: Burt Franklin, (1968). 2 vols., cloth. Reprint of the
1877 ed. Dawson 470-180 1983 $80

LALOUETTE, PIERRE   Nouvelle Methode de traiter les
Maladies Veneriennes par la Fumigation. Paris, 1776. 3 fine folding
copperplates. 8vo, modern black 1/2 calf. First edition; with the
half-title and Approbation. Old library bookplate. Argosy 713-324
1983 $175

LAM, WIFREDO   Wifredo Lam. Dessins. Paris:
Editions Galilee-Dutrou, 1975. 122 color plates. Small folio.
Cloth. Dust jacket. Ars Libri 32-387 1983 $45

LAMAR, CHARLES A. L.   The Reply of...of Savannah, Georgia,
to the Letter of Hon. Howell Cobb, Secretary of the Treasury of the
United States. Charleston, S.C., 1858. Dbd. First edition.
Ginsberg 46-276 1983 $50

LAMARCK, JEAN B. DE   An Illustrated Introduction to Lamarck's Conchology. Printed for Longman, Rees, 1827. With 22 coloured litho plates containing many figures. Errata slip, large 4to, orig. pictorial litho printed boards, uncut, neatly rebacked and upper blank portion of title-page neatly cut away, a very good copy. Fenning 61-240 1983 £145

LA MARTELIERE, PIERRE DE   An Argument of Mr. Peter de la Marteliere, Advocate in the Court of Parliament of Paris. Printed for James Adamson, 1689. 4to, wrapper, a very good copy. Fenning 61-241 1983 £21.50

LAMARTINE, ALPHONSE DE   Souvenirs, Impressions, Pensees et Paysages. Bruxelles, Ad. Wahlen, 1835. 3 vols. 12mo, bound in 2, portrait, half calf, rubbed. Bickersteth 75-153 1983 £12

LAMB, CAROLINE   Ada Reis, a Tale. John Murray, 1823. First edition, 3 vols. Half title, 4 pp music vol. II. Rebound in half calf, maroon label, v.g. Jarndyce 30-450 1983 £220

LAMB, CAROLINE   Glenarvon. Printed for Henry Colburn, 1816. 3 vols, 12mo, new qtr. calf, marbled sides; three fly-titles, and half-titles in Vos. I and III with printer's name on versos; no half-title called for in Vol. II. Two leaves of music in Vol. II. First edition. Hill 165-63 1983 £325

LAMB, CAROLINE   Glenarvon. London: printed for Henry Colburn, 1816. 3 vols., 12mo. Early 19th-century cloth. Minor wear. Bound without half-titles, but a very good copy. Ximenes 63-126 1983 $400

LAMB, CAROLINE   Glenarvon. Henry Colburn, 1816. 2nd edition, 3 vols. Half dark blue calf, lacks labels, some foxing and sl. rubbing. Jarndyce 31-774 1983 £68

LAMB, CHARLES   The Adventures of Ulysses. London, printed by T. Davision for the Juvenile Library, 1808. 8vo, orig. boards, now worn, covers detached, somewhat soiled, faint stain at foot of last few leaves, uncut copy and with the signature T. Hughes (the author?) several times on blank end-leaves; complete with frontis. and engraved as well as printed title, plus the ads at end. First edition, preserved in quarter morocco gilt slip-case. Ravenstree 97-11 1983 $435

LAMB, CHARLES   The Adventures of Ulysses. London, printed by T. Davison for the Juvenile Library, 1808. 8vo, modern tan polished calf gilt, a.e.g., by Bedford, except for slight wear and some minor age or dust spotting, very fine and complete with frontis. and engraved as well as printed title. First edition. Ravenstree 96-28 1983 $325

LAMB, CHARLES   The Book of the Ranks and Dignities of British Society. London: Cape, 1924. First of this edition. Illus. with an intro. note by C. Shorter. 12mo. Orig. cloth-backed boards. Dust jacket (torn). With an inscription from "the finder," presumably Shorter, on the copyright page. Fine. MacManus 279-3105 1983 $30

LAMB, CHARLES   A Dissertation Upon Roast Pig. (Concord, MA: Sign of the Vine, ca. 1902). 12mo. Unopened. Produced by Will Bradley. Printed in red and black, contains a frontispiece, title-page border decorations, ornamental initial and head and tail-pieces. Near mint in boards. Bromer 25-173 1983 $85

LAMB, CHARLES   Elia and The Last Essays of Elia. Newtown, Mont: Gregynog Press, 1929. 2 vols. 8vo. Orig. buckram. Wood-engravings adapted from cont. prints. Limited edition of 285 numbered copies. Traylen 94-501 1983 £90

LAMB, CHARLES   The Essays of Elia. London: Edward Moxon, 1853. "New Edition." Engraved frontis. port, illus, 3/4 morocco with marbled endpapers. Engraved port. and scenes by G. Cruikshank and others. One very small mar on the front cover. Near-fine. MacManus 279-3106 1983 $150

LAMB, CHARLES   The Essays of Elia, Mrs. Leicester's School, Poems, Plays and Essays. London, 1883-84-85. 8vo. Cloth. 3 vols. Library duplicate stamp. The editor's copies of the books, signed in each volume by Ainger. With some textual corrections by Ainger in each of the volumes. One volume is inscribed by Ainger; also included is a holograph letter from Ainger. Spines worn at the extremities, else good-very good copies, internally fine. Enclosed in a slipcase box. In Our Time 156-479 1983 $200

LAMB, CHARLES   The Essays of Elia. Methuen, 1902. 1st edn. Illus. by Garth Jones, frontis. portrait. Green decor. cloth gilt designed by Jones, t.e.g. others uncut (free eps. discol'd, corners sl. worn, fr. ep. cracked at hinge, occasional foxing & cvrs. sl. rubbed), v.g. Hodgkins 27-470 1983 £10.50

LAMB, CHARLES   John Woodvil, a Tragedy. London, T. Plummer for G. and J. Robinson, 1802. 8vo, cont. half green morocco gilt, bit worn, joints cracked, title trifle soiled, few spots, and uncut copy from the Viscount Esher collection, with the Oliver Brett bookplate. First edition. Preserved in full blue morocco gilt solander case. Ravenstree 97-12 1983 $425

LAMB, CHARLES   Mrs. Leicester's School. J.M. Dent, n.d. Sm. 4to. Colour frontis. Colour pictorial title. 18 colour plates. 21 text illus. Foxing. Grey pictorial cloth, worn. Greer 40-104 1983 £15

LAMB, CHARLES   Rosamund Gray. London, Edward Moxon, 1835. 8vo, orig. boards, new spine, minor soiling and spotting, decent copy. First edition. Ravenstree 97-13 1983 $210

LAMB, CHARLES   Seven Letters from Charles Lamb to Charles Ryle. Oxford University Press for Milford, 1931. Slim sm. 4to, uncut in qtr. linen over marbled paper boards, paper label, boards slightly faded along edges, very good. 250 copies only. Deighton 3-197 1983 £24

LAMB, CHARLES   Specimens of the English Dramatic Poets, who Lived about the Time of Shakespeare. London, Longman et al., 1808. 8vo, later calf gilt by Cecil and Larkins, rebacked preserving old gilt spine, without half-title, bit chipped and trifle worn, internally fine. First edition. Ravenstree 97-14 1983 $250

LAMB, CHARLES   A Tale of Rosamund Gray and Old Blind Margaret. For Lee and Hurst, 1798. First edition, London title page. Small 8vo, initial and final blank leaves. Modern crushed, black, morocco, gilt old style, by Middleton, orig. upper, blue, wraps.,end-papers bound in, one with signature of Elizabeth Haines. Hannas 69-120 1983 £650

LAMB, CHARLES   A Tale of Rosamund Gray and Old Blind Margaret. London: Printed for Lee & Hurst, No. 32, Pater-Noster Row, 1798. First edition. Small 8vo. Full green morocco, gilt, with marbled endpapers, a.e.g., by Sangorski & Sutcliffe. Upper right-hand corner of title-page expertly reapired. In a marbled board slipcase. Bookplate. Fine. MacManus 279-3110 1983 $750

LAMB, CHARLES   A Tale of Rosamund Gray and Old Blind Margaret. London: Frank Hollings, 1928. First Golden Cockerel Press edition. Limited to 500 numbered copies. Fine condition. Oak Knoll 49-261 1983 $37.50

LAMB, CHARLES   Tales from Shakespear. London: Printed for Thomas Hodgskins, at the Juvenile Library,...1807. First edition, first issue. Embellished with copper-plates. 2 vols. Full blue morocco, gilt, with marbled endpapers, t.e.g., by Wood of London. In a blue half-morocco folding box. MacManus 279-3111 1983 $1,000

LAMB, CHARLES   Tales from Shakespeare. London & N.Y.: J.M. Dent & Co., 1909. First of this edition. Illus. by A. Rackham. Orig. decorated cloth. Spine and covers very slightly worn and faded. Some foxing to the endpapers. Very good. MacManus 280-4306 1983 $85

LAMB, CHARLES   The Works. London, C. and J. Ollier, 1818. 2 vols., 12mo, orig. quarter cloth, boards, worn, joints splitting and chipped; internally a nice set of the first edition. Ravenstree 97-10 1983 $243

LAMB, CHARLES   The Works of Charles Lamb. New York: A. C. Armstrong and Son, 1881. Five vols. in three. With a portrait, 8vo, cont. half calf, gilt lettered spines, a neat library set. Fenning 60-229 1983 £28.50

LAMB, CHARLES   Works. London, 1899. 12 vols. Roy. 8vo. Orig. blue satin-cloth, gilt, gilt decorated spines, uncut edges. Portraits. Edition-de-Luxe, limited to 675 sets. Traylen 94-500 1983 £110

LAMB, JOHN   Memoir of the Life and Times of Isaac Q. Leake. Albany, 1850. 1st ed., port., 4 maps, 8vo, 1/2 calf, gilt spine, lea. label. Argosy 710-452 1983 $65

LAMB, MARY MONTGOMERY   Anthony Babbington. London: Chapman and Hall, 1877. First edition. 8vo. Cont. blue morocco, gilt, spine gilt, a.e.g. Presentation copy, inscribed on the half-title. Bookplate of poet Frederic W.H. Myers on front pastedown. Ximenes 63-445 1983 $50

LAMBARDE, WILLIAM   Archion, or, a Commentary upon the High Courts of Ivstice in England. London, Daniel Frere, 1635. 8vo, orig. sheep, quite worn, joints broken, spine ends chipped, bookplate, minor worming to blank outer margins, preserved in quarter morocco slip-case with folding inner wraps. First edition. Ravenstree 97-15 1983 $475

LAMBARDE, WILLIAM   A Perambulation of Kent. London, Edm. Bollifant, 1596. 4to, 18th century calf rebacked, 18th century portrait of the author inserted as frontis. Ravenstree 97-16 1983 $850

LAMBERT, ARTHUR W.   Modern Archery. New York, 1929. 1st ed. Presentation copy. Illus. with photographs and drawings by author. 8vo. Morrill 287-14 1983 $20

LAMBERT, C   Printing in California 1846-1856. N.p., n.d. Sm 8vo, cloth, lettering & design in gilt. Portrait frontis, folding plate. One of 100 copies printed for private distribution. Perata 28-88 1983 $100

LAMBERT, C.   The Story of Alaska. N.Y.: Harpers, (1940). Large sq. 4to. Cloth backed pictorial boards. Dust wrapper. Color illus, full-page and smaller. Fine. Aleph-bet 8-85 1983 $27

LAMBERT, M.   Contribution a l'etude des poils de l'homme et des animaux. Paris, 1910. 34 plates, 4to, modern buckram, paper slightly browned. A good copy. Wheldon 160-572 1983 £18

LAMBERT, W. HUMBERTO   The Ghost of Dunboy Castle. London'' Simpkin, Marshall & Co., 1889. First edition. 2 vols. Orig. decorated cloth. Presentation copy to Lord Leigh with an ALS, 3 pages (one folded leaf), Islington Square, Liverpool, December 4th, 1888. Spines and covers worn and slightly soiled. Inner hinges cracked. Good. MacManus 279-3113 1983 $250

LAMBOTTE, HENRI   Etablissements de Produits Chimiques. Bruxelles, 1855. 8vo, folding table, orig. blue printed wraps., entirely uncut and unopened, a mint copy. Bickersteth 75-249 1983 £95

LAMBOURNE, ALFRED   The Pioneer Trail. Deseret News, 1913. Illus. Orig. cloth. Ginsberg 47-907 1983 $35

LAMME, BENJAMIN GARVER   Electrical Engineering Papers. East Pittsburgh, Westinghouse Electric & Mfg. Co., 1919. First edition. Illustrated. 8vo. White lettering on backstrip effaced. Morrill 290-224 1983 $25

LAMONT, JAMES   Seasons with the Sea-Horses. New York, 1861. First American edition, ads., title-vignette, frontis., folding

LAMOTHE, H.   Excursion au Canada et a la Riviere Rouge du Nord, 1873. (Paris, 1875). Illus with wood-engrs, small folio, wrs. Argosy 710-50 1983 $35

LA MOTTE, ELLEN N.   The Ethics of Opium. NY: The Century Co., (1924). Publisher's orange cloth, very good. Gach 95-304 1983 $20

LA MOTTE FOUQUE, FRIEDRICH DE   Undine, a Romance. For W. Simpkin and R. Marshall, 1818. First English ed., 12mo., half title, final blank leaf, orig. boards, paper label, uncut. Hannas 69-61 1983 £35

LAMPSON, ROBIN   Laughter out of the Ground. N.Y., Scribner, 1935. First edition. Gilt stamped black cloth. Signed by the author on the title page. Very good. Houle 22-550 1983 $35

LAMPSON, ROBIN   The Mending of a Continent. Berkeley, Archetype, 1937. First edition. Large 8vo, stiff grey wraps. printed in blue with illus. by Chiura Obata. Stitched, uncut. One of 500 signed copies. Very good - fine. Houle 22-29 1983 $37.50

LAMSON, MARY SWIFT   Life and Education of Laura Dewey Bridgman, the Deaf, Dumb and Blind Girl. Boston: New England Pub. Co., 1879 (1878). 12mo. Frontis. portrait. Publisher's decorative cloth. Gach 94-119 1983 $25

LANCASTER, JOSEPH   The British System of Education. Washington: Pub. by William Cooper; and by Joseph Milligan, Georgetown, 1812. 12mo. Woodcut frontis., 5 woodcut plates (1 folded), text charts. Cont. calf, label. 1st ed. Nice copy. O'Neal 50-34 1983 $125

LANCASTER, NATHANIEL   The pretty gentleman: or, softness of manners vindicated from the false ridicule exhibited under the character of William Fribble, Esq. London: printed for M. Cooper, 1747. 8vo, disbound, 1st edition. A very good copy. Ximenes 64-343 1983 $275

LANCASTER, OSBERT   Progress at Pelvis Bay. London, 1936. First edition. Illus. by author. Torn dust wrapper. Very nice. Rota 230-331 1983 £20

LANCIANI, R.   The Roman Forum. Rome, 1910. Map. 4to, cloth. Salloch 385-293 1983 $25

LANCTOT, GUSTAVE   New Documents by Lahontan concerning Canada and Newfoundland. Ottawa: King's Printer, 1940. 24 1/2cm. 7 plates, one folding. Grey printed wrappers. Fine. McGahern 53-95 1983 $20

LANDAUER, BELLA C.   Early American Trade Cards. New York: William E. Rudge, 1927. Small quarto, cloth- fold-out frontis. and 44 plates. Duschnes 240-128 1983 $125

LANDE, LAWRENCE   The Lawrence Lande Collection of Canadiana in the Redpath Library of McGill University. Montreal, 1965. Plates and facs. Folio. Quarter pigskin and cloth, fore- and bottom-edges untrimmed. Extremely fine in slipcase. One of 950 numbered copies, printed on various Italian and English and mould made papers in Monotype Bulmer, and specially bound. Reese 19-67 1983 $375

LANDER, RICHARD   Journal of an Expedition to Explore the Course and Termination of the Niger. London: John Murray, 1832. 1st ed., 3 vols, 12mo, half-title in vol. 3, 2 engraved maps (one of which is folding), 2 engraved portraits, some foxing, 5 engraved plates, cont. calf, gilt and blind, marbled edges, backs of two vols. repaired at head, lacks double morocco labels. Deighton 3-199 1983 £78

LANDER, RICHARD   Journal of an Expedition to Explore the Course and Termination of the Niger. Thomas Tegg, 1838. With 2 portraits, a map, 5 plates and a few text illus. 2 vols., small 8vo, cont. polished calf, gilt, gilt spines with double labels, bound. Fenning 60-230 1983 £65

LANDIS, CHARLES SINGER   .22 Caliber Rifle Shooting. Marines, N.C., (1932). 1st ed. Illus. 8vo. Small stain on front cover. Morrill 288-111 1983 $35

LANDOLT, HANS HEINRICH   Handbook of the Polariscope and its Practical Applications... London: Macmillan, 1882. First English edition. 8vo. Numerous text illus. Ads. Partially unopened. Zeitlin 264-247 1983 $70

LANDON, T. D.   Narrative of a journey through India. Westminster: printed by Thomas Brettell, 1857. First edition. 8vo. Orig. blue cloth. With a hand-colored lithographed frontis. Ximenes 63-210 1983 $125

LANDOR, A. HENRY SAVAGE   Across widest Africa. London: Hurst & Blackett, 1907. 2 vols. 8vo. Folding map. 160 photographs. Orig. blue cloth. Rubbed, some light foxing. Adelson Africa-96 1983 $185

LANDOR, WALTER SAVAGE   Citation and Examination of William Shakespeare, Euseby Treen, Joseph Carnaby and Salas Gough... London, Saunders and Otley, 1834. 8vo, half calf gilt, nice. First edition. Ravenstree 96-29 1983 $125

LANDOR, WALTER SAVAGE   Dry Sticks, Fagoted. Edinburgh: James Nichol, 1858. First edition, 8vo, orig. green cloth, with a library label on the front endpaper, but nonetheless a nice copy. Fenning 60-231 1983 £42.50

LANDOR, WALTER SAVAGE   Imaginary Conversations of Literary Men and Statesmen. London: H. Colburn, 1826-28. Second edition, corrected and enlarged (first edition of vol. 1). 3 vols. 8vo. Half grey calf, gilt, blue cloth sides, t.e.g. Bound at the end of each vol. is some additional material by the author, with numerous manuscript corrections. Traylen 94-505 1983 £35

LANDOR, WALTER SAVAGE   Imaginary Conversations of Greeks and Romans. London, Moxon, 1853. 8vo, orig. cloth gilt, bit worn, 2 bookplates, good copy of the first edition. Ravenstree 96-31 1983 $45

LANDOR, WALTER SAVAGE   Imaginary Conversations... London: Printed for J.M. Dent & Co., 1891. 6 vols. Frontis. Orig. green cloth, gilt-decorated spines. Endpapers foxed. Inner hinges weak. Covers slightly rubbed. MacManus 279-3114 1983 £65

LANDOR, WALTER SAVAGE   Imaginary Conversations. Mardersteig, Officina Bodoni for Limited Editions Club, 1936. Royal 8vo, title-page printed in red and black within typographic border, typograph-ically decorated chapter headings, decorative cloth boards, t.e. tinted, others uncut, fine in dustwrappers and slightly worn slip-case. 1500 numbered copies signed by Mardersteig. Deighton 3-200 1983 £65

LANDOR, WALTER SAVAGE   The Last Fruit Off an Old Tree. London: Moxon, 1853. First edition. Orig. cloth. Covers faded. Fine. MacManus 279-3115 1983 $85

LANDOR, WALTER SAVAGE   The Last Fruit off an Old Tree. Edward Moxon, 1853. First edition, 8vo, orig. cloth, the spine evenly faded, but still a nice copy. With 8-pages ads. dated January, 1852 tipped in at front. Fenning 60-232 1983 £38.50

LANDOR, WALTER SAVAGE   Letters, and Other Unpublished Writings. Richard Bentley, 1897. First edition, half title. 4 ports. Orig. dark green cloth; library label removed from upper cover, otherwise v.g. Jarndyce 30-1050 1983 £10.50

LANDOR, WALTER SAVAGE   Pericles and Aspasia. London: Saunders & Otley, 1836. First edition. Spines a little worn & soiled. Book-plate. Very good. MacManus 279-3116 1983 $150

LANDOR, WALTER SAVAGE   Pericles and Aspasia. London, Saunders & Otley, 1836. 2 vols., bound without half title to vol. in cont. half morocco gilt, note on endpaper, names on title, somewhat worn. First edition. Ravenstree 96-32 1983 $135

LANDOR, WALTER SAVAGE   Pericles and Aspasia. London, Saunders & Otley, 1836. 2 vols., 8vo, modern boards with cloth spines, book-plates, good copy, with ads at front of vol. 1. First edition. Ravenstree 97-17 1983 $95

LANDOR, WALTER SAVAGE   Pericles and Aspasia. Saunders & Otley, 1836. First edition, with the half-title in the second volume only. 2 vols. bound in 1, large 12mo, cont. half calf, a very good copy. Fenning 60-233 1983 £55

LANDOR, WALTER SAVAGE   The Sculptured Garden. Dropmore Press, 1948. 4to, 18 wood engraved illus., uncut in publishers half brown morocco gilt, cream cloth boards, fine in dustwrappers and worn slip-case. 300 numbered copies on hand-made paper. Deighton 3-201 1983 £44

LANDOR, WALTER SAVAGE   Works. London: Edward Moxon, 1853. First collected edition. 2 vols. Roy. 8vo. Orig. embossed black cloth, gilt. Traylen 94-503 1983 £20

LANDOR, WALTER SAVAGE   The Complete Works. London and New York, 1969. 16 vols. 8vo. Green buckram. Portrait. Traylen 94-504 1983 £48

LANDSBOROUGH, DAVID   A Popular History of British Sea-Weeds. Reeve, Benham, and Reeve, 1849. First edition, with 20 coloured and 2 other plates, by Fitch, roy. 16mo, cont. half calf, gilt ruled spine, with label, a fine copy. Fenning 61-243 1983 £24.50

LANDSBOROUGH, D.   A Popular History of British Seaweeds. 1857. Third edition, 20 coloured and 2 plain plates, post 8vo, calf gilt, trifle rubbed. Some foxing and pencil annotations; front free endpaper removed. Wheldon 160-1849 1983 £20

LANDSBOROUGH, D.   A Popular History of British Zoophytes, or Corallines. 1852. 20 coloured plates, 4to, wrappers. Wheldon 160-1307 1983 £20

LANDSEER, JOHN   A Descriptive, Explanatory, and Critical Catalogue of Fifty of the Earliest Pictures Contained in the National Gallery of Great Britain. Printed for Richard Glynn, 1834. First edition, all published, wanting half-title, 8vo, cont. half calf, gilt. Little rubbed but sound. Very good to nice. Fenning 61-244 1983 £65

LANDSTEINER, KARL   The Specificity of Serological Reactions. Cambridge, Mass., 1947. 8vo, cloth, d.w. Argosy 713-325 1983 $50

LANDWEHR, JOHN   Studies in Dutch Books with Coloured Plates Published 1662-1875. The Hague: Dr. W. Junk B.V., 1976. 4to. Cloth. Dust jacket. Fine. Oak Knoll 48-450 1983 $125

LANE, MARGARET   The Tale of Beatrix Potter. Warne, 1946. 4 colour plates, 16 b&w plates. Pub's cloth, d/w sl. soiled & worn, vg. Hodgkins 27-177 1983 £15

LANE, MARY CROWIN   Index to the Fragments of the Greek Elegiac & Iambic Poets. Ithaca, 1908. 8vo, cloth. Salloch 385-135 1983 $20

LANE, RICHARD J.   Life at the Water Cure. Longman, Brown, 1846. First edition, folding front. Numerous illus. 32 pp ads. Orig. blue-green cloth, v.g. Jarndyce 31-214 1983 £48

LANE, THOMAS   The Student's Guide. Printed by I. Gold, for Thomas Lane, 1803. First edition, with engraved vignette title-page, subscriber list, 8vo, later half cloth. Fenning 60-234 1983 £45

LANE, WILLIAM COOLIDGE   A.L.A. Portrait Index... New York: Burt Franklin, n.d. 3 vols., cloth. Reprint of the 1906 ed. Dawson 470-182 1983 $45

LANG, A.   Die Experimentelle Vererbungslehre in der Zoologie seit 1900. Jena, 1914. Vol. 1, imp. 8vo, wrappers. Wheldon 160-500 1983 £12

LANG, A.   Text-book of Comparative Anatomy. 1891-96. 856 text-figures, 2 vols., 8vo, cloth. Wheldon 160-1309 1983 £30

LANG, MRS. ANDREW   The All Sorts of Stories Book. London: Longmans, Green, & Co., 1911. First edition. 5 colored plates and numerous other illus. by H. J. Ford. Orig. gilt-pictorial red cloth. Dust jacket (corners chipped). Very fine. MacManus 279-3135 1983 $350

LANG, MRS. ANDREW   The Book of Princes and Princesses. Lon-don: Longmans, Green, & Co., 1908. First edition. 8 colored plates and numerous illus. by H. J. Ford. Orig. pictorial cloth. Very fine. MacManus 279-3136 1983 $225

LANG, MRS. ANDREW   The Book of Princes and Princesses. NY, 1908. Illus. by Ford. Gilt stamped pic. cover, edges slightly worn, near very good, owner's name and inscription. Quill & Brush 54-763 1983 $40

LANG, ANDREW   Ballades in Blue China. London: C. Kegan Paul & Co., 1881. First edition. Engraved frontispiece. Orig. decorated wrappers. Covers and spine slightly worn and soiled. Full morocco slipcase. Near-fine. MacManus 279-3119 1983 $75

LANG, ANDREW   Ban and Arriere Ban. London: Longmans, Green & Co., 1894. First edition. Orig. parchment-backed boards with paper label on spine. One of 70 large paper copies. Covers soiled and a little worn at the edges. Some browning to the endpapers. MacManus 279-3120 1983 $85

LANG, ANDREW   The Blue Poetry Book. The Green Fairy
Book. London: Longmans, Green, & Co., 1891-1896; 1898-1899; 1901-1911;
Bristol; Arrowsmith; London: Simpkin, Marshall, 1895. First editions.
20 vols. 8vo. Orig. gilt-pictorial cloth (six in) dust jackets.
Bookplates in a few volumes. Very fine. MacManus 279-3122 1983
$5,500

LANG, ANDREW   The Blue Poetry Book. London: Longmans,
Green, & Co., 1891. First edition. Illus. by H.J. Ford and L. Speed.
Orig. gilt-pictorial blue cloth. Prelims and endleaves, including
title-page, foxed. Fine. MacManus 279-3121 1983 $225

LANG, ANDREW   The Book of Dreams and Ghosts. London,
1897. First edition. Cover design by P. Woodroffe. Bookplate. Nice.
Rota 231-365 1983 £35

LANG, ANDREW   The Book of Romance. N.Y., London,
Bomb.: Longmans, 1902. First edition. 8vo. Blue cloth. Elaborate
gilt decoration. Lacks frontis. A.e.g. Illus. by H.J. Ford with 7
color plates, 35 black & whites. Cover by Ford. Very good to fine.
Aleph-bet 8-155 1983 $35

LANG, ANDREW   Books and Bookmen. New York: George
J. Coombes, 1886. First edition. 8vo. Orig. cloth. 14 illus.
Fine. Oak Knoll 48-243 1983 $25

LANG, ANDREW   Books and Bookmen. London, 1887. Eng.
edition, with contents differing from the American edition. Illus.
Boards and cloth. Beverly Chew's copy, with his engraved bookplate.
Some cover soiling but a fine copy. Bradley 65-31 1983 $35

LANG, ANDREW   Books and Bookmen. London: 1887. Illus.
Boards and cloth. Beverly Chew's bookplate. Covers soiled. Bradley
66-48 1983 $30

LANG, ANDREW   The Brown Fairy Book. London: Longmans,
Green, & Co., 1904. First edition. 8 colored plates and numerous
illus. by H.J. Ford. Orig. gilt-pictorial brown cloth. Inscription
on verso of front free endpaper. Fine. MacManus 279-3124 1983 $225

LANG, ANDREW   The Disentanglers. London, 1902. First
edition. Illus. by H.J. Ford. Pictorial cloth. Spine dull and worn
at foot. Endpapers cracking hinges. Bookplate. Good. Rota 230-333
1983 £30

LANG, ANDREW   The Gold of Fairnilee. Bristol: J.W.
Arrowsmith, (1888). Large 4to, with 14 chromolithograph plates + a
few text illus., dec. initials and headpieces. A numbered ltd.
edition, though number of copies not specified. Orig. 3/4 beige
boards over cloth. Boards rubbed, and a 2" piece missing from top
of spine. Karmiole 74-34 1983 $50

LANG, ANDREW   Grass of Parnassus. London: Longmans,
Green & Co., 1888. First edition. Orig. decorated cloth. Spine and
covers a bit worn. Very good. MacManus 279-3125 1983 $35

LANG, ANDREW   The Green Fairy Book. London: Longmans,
Green, & Co., 1892. First edition. Illus. by H.J. Ford. Orig. gilt-
pictorial green cloth. Endpapers foxed. Very fine. MacManus 279-
3126 1983 $225

LANG, ANDREW   James VI and the Gowrie Mystery. 1902.
8vo, pub.'s catalogue, coloured frontis., 12 plates, 3 text figures,
orig. buckram gilt, a little rubbed. First edition. Bickersteth 77-
131 1983 £22

LANG, ANDREW   John Knox and the Reformation. 1905.
8vo, 5 plates, cloth, a little soiled. First edition. Bickersteth
77-132 1983 £18

LANG, ANDREW   Life, Letters, and Diaries of Sir
Stafford Northcote, First Earl of Iddesleigh. Edinburgh: Blackwood,
1890. First edition, with 4 plates, 2 vols., 8vo, orig. cloth, gilt.
Fenning 61-316 1983 £28.50

LANG, ANDREW   The Most Pleasant and Delectable Tale of
the Marriage of Cupid and Psyche. London: David Nutt, 1887. Illus.
Full pale blue morocco, gilt, by Riviere. Limited to 500 copies.
Bookplates on front flyleaves. Inner hinges weak. Silk front flyleaf
rubbed. Rear outer hinge strained. MacManus 279-3128 1983 $125

LANG, ANDREW   The Mystery of Mary Stuart. 1901.
8vo, pub.'s catalogue, frontis. and 18 plates, orig. cloth, slightly
rubbed. First edition. Bickersteth 77-130 1983 £22

LANG, ANDREW   Old French Title Pages. SF: 1924.
16mo, vellum-backed batik bds. Illustrated. One of 725 copies.
Printed presentation slip from Edwin Grabhorn. A very nice copy.
Perata 27-57 1983 $75

LANG, ANDREW   Old French Title Pages. S.F.: 1924.
16mo, vellum-backed batik boards. Illus. Presentation slip from Ed
Grabhorn. Bookplate. One of 725 copies. Perata 28-41 1983 $65

LANG, ANDREW   The Olive Fairy Book. London: Longmans,
Green, & Co., 1907. First edition. 8 colored plates and numerous
illus. by H.J. Ford. Orig. gilt-pictorial olive cloth. Fine.
MacManus 279-3129 1983 $150

LANG, ANDREW   The Orange Fairy Book. N.Y., 1907.
First American edition. 8 color plates & other illus. by H.J. Ford.
Gilt-pictorial cloth. A.e.g. Bookplate. Ink inscription. Rear end-
paper defective. Well worn covers, some pp torn. King 45-626 1983
$20

LANG, ANDREW   Prince Charles Edward. Paris and
London: Goupil & Co., 1900. Edition-de-Luxe. 4to. Full green
morocco, gilt ornaments on covers with white rose at each corner,
spines similarly tooled, inner edges gilt, cream silk linings, t.e.g.
Frontis. in 2 states, on hand-coloured, 39 plates and other illus.,
each in two states, and 3 facsimiles of hand-writing. Limited to
350 numbered copies, printed on Japanese vellum. Traylen 94-506
1983 £180

LANG, ANDREW   Prince Charles Edward. London:
Goupil & Co., 1900. 4to. Full red morocco, four-line gilt
borders with floral corner pieces, three-line centre panel with
gilt decoration and the initials CE inlaid in green and blue
morocco, gilt panelled spine in six compartments, t.e.g. Hand-
coloured frontis. and 39 plates and other illus., and 3 facsimiles
of hand-writing. Limited edition of 1500 numbered copies. Traylen
94-507 1983 £150

LANG, ANDREW   Rhymes a la Mode. London: Kegan Paul,
Trench & Co., 1885. First edition. Frontispiece. Orig. decorated
cloth. Spine and covers very slightly worn. Some offsetting to the
free endpapers. Near-fine. MacManus 279-3131 1983 £35

LANG, ANDREW   Tales of a Fairy Court. Collins, n.d.
(ca.1908). Colour frontis. Colour pictorial title. 11 colour plates
& colour decorative borders to all pages. Green pictorial cloth gilt.
Rubbed. Attractive. Greer 39-62 1983 £30

LANG, ANDREW   The True Story Book. London: Longmans,
Green & Co., 1893. First edition. Illus. Orig. pictorial cloth.
Very good. MacManus 279-3133 1983 $75

LANG, ANDREW   The True Story Book. London: Longman's,
Green, & Co., 1893. First edition. Illus. Orig. pictorial cloth.
Bookplate; signature. Outer hinges neatly re-colored. Fine. Mac-
Manus 279-3132 1983 $50

LANG, ANDREW   The Valet's Tragedy and Other Studies.
1903. 8vo, 3 plates, orig. cloth gilt, a little stained, inner joints
weak. First edition. Bickersteth 77-133 1983 £16

LANG, ANDREW   The Yellow Fairy Book. Longmans, 1894.
1st edn. Frontis. & title vignette & many b&w illus. by H.J. Ford,
leaf adverts. Yellow pictorial cloth gilt, a.e.g. (contemp. insc.
recto fr. ep., bkstrip v. sl. discol'd), nice copy. Hodgkins 27-504
1983 £38

LANG, LINCOLN A.   Ranching with Roosevelt. Philadelphia &
London. 1925. Gilt cloth. Frontis. Plates. Light spotting of
rear cover. Reese 19-320 1983 $50

LANG, LINCOLN A.   Ranching with Roosevelt. Philadelphia:
Lippincott, 1926. First edition. 24 illustrations. Pictorial
green cloth, gilt. Very fine in dj. Bradley 64-97 1983 $35

LANG, PAUL HENRY   Music in Western Civilization. NY, 1941.
25 plates, 3 maps. Thick tall 8vo, cl. First edition. A few underlinings and marginal notes in light pencil. Salloch 387-341 1983
$25

LANGAARD, JOHAN H.   Edvard Munchs Selvportretter. Oslo:
Gyldendal Norsk, 1947. 72 plates in text. Large 4to. Boards,
1/4 cloth. Ars Libri 32-485 1983 $75

LANGBAINE, GERARD   The lives and characters of the English
dramatic poets. London: printed for Nich. Cox, and William Turner,
1699. 8vo, cont. calf (worn, front hinge weak). First edition.
The imprint in this copy is a very rare variant. Leaf of ads present
at the end. Ximenes 64-344 1983 $500

LANGBAINE, GERARD   Momus triumphans: or, the plagiaries
of the English stage. London: printed for N. C. and are to be sold
by Sam. Holford, 1688. Sm. 4to, wrappers, 1st edition. Trimmed
just a little close at the top, but a very good copy. Ximenes 64-
345 1983 $500

LANGBRIDGE, FREDERICK   Poets at Play. London: Eyre and Spottiswoode, n.d. (1890). First edition. 2 vols. Orig. cloth. MacManus
279-3137 1983 $20

LANGDON, EMMA F.   The Cripple Creek Strike. Denver:
Great Western Pub. Co., 1905. Illus. (incl. folding plate). Orig.
maroon gilt-stamped cloth. Karmiole 76-33 1983 $60

LANGDON, EMMA F.   The Cripple Creek Strike. Denver:
Great Western Publishing Co., (1905). Cloth. Soiled. Lacks portrait.
With rubber stamps of the Goldfield Miners Union No. 220. Dawson 471-
176 1983 $30

LANGDON, JOHN E.   American Silversmiths in British North
America 1776-1880. Toronto, 1970. 25cm. Limited to 350 copies,
of which this is no. 147. Rag paper. Cloth backed boards, marbled
endpapers, boxed. Dustwrapper. Fine. McGahern 54-108 1983 $225

LANGDON-DAVIS, J.   Behind the Spanish Barricades. London,
1937. 8vo. Orig. cloth. Plate. Some very slight marginal foxing.
Good. Edwards 1042-390 1983 £12

LANGE, ALGOT   In the Amazon Jungle. New York & London,
Putnams, 1912. First edition. 2 folding maps and 86 full-page illus.
8vo, orig. cloth, gilt, t.e.g. Fenning 61-246 1983 £18.50

LANGE, CARL GEORGE (1834-1900)   Ueber Gemuethsbewegungen. Leipzig:
Verlag von Theodor Thomas, 1887. First edition in German. Modern
black linen preserving orig. wrappers. Gach 95-307 1983 $125

LANGE, KARL   Apperception. Boston: D. C. Heath &
Co., 1894 (1893). Gach 95-306 1983 $25

LANGERHANS, PAUL   Contributions to the Microscopic
Anatomy of the Pancreas. Baltimore, 1937. First English translation.
8vo. Orig. binding. Fye H-3-332 1983 $25

LANGFORD, JOHN ALFRED   Pleasant Spots and Famous Places.
London: William Tegg, (1862). 1st ed. Orig. red and black polka-
doted cloth. Spine rubbed, but very good copy. Jenkins 155-1119
1983 $35

LANGFORD, NATHANIEL P.   Diary of the Washburn Expedition to the
Yellowstone and Firehole Rivers in the Year 1870. N.p., 1905. Illus.
Orig. dark blue pictorial cloth, gilt. 1st ed. T.e.g. Fine copy.
Jenkins 153-321 1983 $50

LANGFORD, NATHANIEL P.   Vigilante Days and Ways. The Pioneers
of the Rockies. Boston: J. P. Cupples, 1890. Three quarter
morocco with marbled boards. A.e.g. Nice set. Scarce. Jenkins
151-173 1983 $150

LANGFORD, NATHANIEL P   Vigilante Days and Ways. Boston: 1890.
First edition. Illus. 2 vols. Pictorial cloth. Covers worn. Bradley 66-600 1983 $110

LANGFORD, NATHANIEL P.   Vigilante Days and Ways. Chicago, 1912.
15 plates. Cloth. Jenkins 153-791 1983 $45

LANGFORD, T.   Plain and full instructions to raise
all sorts of fruit-trees that prosper in England. London: Richard
Chiswell, 1696. Second edition, enlarged. 8vo. Cont. calf. 2
plates. Spine worn. Ximenes 63-179 1983 $150

LANGHORNE, JOHN   Letters between Theodosius and
Constantia. Printed for T. Becket and P.A. De Hondt, 1770. 2 vols.,
small 8vo, engraved frontis. in each volume, orig. calf. Bickersteth
77-33 1983 £30

LANGLAND, WILLIAM   The Vision of William Concerning Piers
the Plowman. New Rochelle: Elston Press, 1901. Quarto. Limited to
210 copies. Printed in red and black with wood-engraved illus. and
initial words by H. M. O'Kane. Cloth-backed boards slightly darkened
and rubbed at extremities; internally very fine. Bromer 25-197 1983
$350

LANGLES, L.   Monuments Anciens et Moderne de l'Hindou-
stan. Paris: P. Didot, 1821. 3 maps, 144 plates some hand-coloured
and some on tinted paper. 3 vols. Folio. Cont. French red morocco
spines, gilt. Red morocco style papered boards. 8vo. Good. Edwards
1044-422 1983 £900

LANGRISH, BROWNE   The Modern Theory and Practice of
Physic... London, 1764. Third edition. 8vo. Cont. calf. Some
insignificant worming in the lower margin. Gurney 90-69 1983
£65

LANGSON, WILLIAM J.   Twenty-Fourth Annual Report of the
Trade and Commerce of Milwaukee. Milwaukee: The Sentinel Co., 1882.
Large folding map. Jenkins 153-700 1983 $50

LANGSTAFF, JOHN   Doctor Bard of Hyde Park. New York,
1942. First edition. 8vo. Orig. binding. Fye H-3-666 1983
$25

LANGTOFT, PETER   Peter Langtoft's Chronicle from the
Death of Cadwalader to the end of K. Edward the First's Reign.
Oxford, printed at the theater, 1725. 2 vols., 8vo, orig. calf gilt,
spine ends chipped, hinges cracked. A fine copy, one of 50 on large
paper, of the first edition. Ravenstree 94-195 1983 $190

LANGTON, ANNE   A Gentlewoman in Upper Canada. Toronto:
Clark, Irwin, 1950. 21 1/2cm. 14 plates (frontis. in colour).
Fine in good dustjacket. McGahern 54-109 1983 $25

LANGTON, JOHN   Early Days in Upper Canada. Toronto:
Macmillan, 1926. 21 1/2cm. First edition. Frontis. and 16 illus.
Mapped endpapers, wine cloth. Small dent on the bottom cover else
a fine copy. McGahern 54-110 1983 $100

LANGTON, ROBERT   Charles Dickens and Rochester. Chapman &
Hall, 1880. With numerous illus. Blue cloth. Inscribed presentation
copy: 'Mr William Dinsmere with the writers regards'. Jarndyce 30-
205 1983 £25

LANGTON, ROBERT   The Childhood and Youth of Charles
Dickens... Manchester, 1883. Half title, front. numerous illus.
Orig. green cloth, v.g. Jarndyce 30-206 1983 £10.50

LANGUI, EMILE   Frits Van Den Berghe, 1883-1939.
Antwerp: Mercatorfonds, 1968. 129 tipped-in color plates. 80
illus. 23 figures. Small folio. Cloth. Dust jacket. Slipcase.
Ars Libri 32-32 1983 $100

LANGWORTHY, EDWARD   Memoirs of the Life of the Late Charles
Lee, Esq. ... Dublin, 1792. Full calf (spine worn, broken). Very
good. Felcone 20-84 1983 $85

LANIER, HENRY WYSHAM   The First English Actresses. NY:
The Players, 1930. Edition ltd. to 75- numbered copies, signed
by the author. In cloth (faded) over dec. boards. Karmiole 71-91
1983 $60

LANIER, SIDNEY   Selected Poems. New York, 1947. 8vo.
Cloth. Review copy with slip laid in. Fine in lightly torn dj. In
Our Time 156-482 1983 $35

LANKESTER, E. R.   Extinct Animals. 1905. Portrait and
218 illustrations, 8vo, cloth, (head of spine trifle frayed).
Wheldon 160-1433 1983 £12

LANKESTER, E. R.   A Treatise on Zoology, Part II the
Porifera and Coelentera. 1900. 8vo, cloth, trifle used. Wheldon
160-1311 1983 £12

LANKESTER, E. R.   A Treatise on Zoology, Part IV The
Platyhelmia, Mesozoa, and Menertini. 1901. 8vo, buckram, text-
illustrations. Wheldon 160-1313 1983 £12

LANKHEIT, KLAUS   Franz Mark: Katalog der Werke. Koln:
M. DuMont Schauberg, 1970. 917 illus. Folio. Cloth. Dust jacket.
Slipcase. Ars Libri 32-426 1983 $250

LANKHEIT, KLAUS   Die Zeichnungen des kurpfalzischen
Hofbildhauers Paul Egell. Karlsruhe: G. Braun, 1954. 68 plates.
Large 4to. Cloth. Dust jacket. Ars Libri 32-201 1983 $150

LANMAN, CHARLES   Adventures in the Wilds of North
America. London, 1854. Two parts, orig. printed wraps. of "The
Traveller's Library," with title page bound in the back. One rear
wrap. detached, else a very good set. Reese 19-321 1983 $250

LANMAN, CHARLES   Dictionary of the United States
Congress... Washington, 1864. 1st ed. 8vo. Ex-library, no external marks. Morrill 286-241 1983 $25

LANMAN, CHARLES   Dictionary of the United States Congress.
Washington, GPO, 1866. Third Edition, Revised. 8vo. Morrill 290-642
1983 $25

LANMAN, JAMES H.   History of Michigan. NY, 1839.
First edition. Library cloth, ink name, foxed else very good.
Lacks map. King 46-166 1983 $75

LANMAN, JAMES H.   History of Michigan, from Its Earliest
Colonization to the Present Time. New York, 1841. Orig. cloth. Nice
copy. Jenkins 153-367 1983 $65

LANNING, JOHN T.   The Spanish Missions of Georgia.
Chapel Hill, N.C., (1935). Illus. Orig. cloth. First edition.
Ginsberg 46-277 1983 $35

LANQUET, THOMAS   An Epitome of Cronicles Conteining
the Whole Discourse of the Histories... Imprinted at London in the
House of Thomas Berthelet, Anno. M.D. XLIX. 4to, full 18th century
calf, spine ends chipped and hinges cracked, uppermost sidenotes
shaved in last portion of volume with very slight loss; last 5
leaves frayed at upper blank edge and repaired with only minor loss
to a few sidenotes. Very rare first edition. Ravenstree 97-18 1983
$1,250

LANSBERG, PHILIPP   Commentationes in Motum Terrae Terrae
Diurnum & Annuum et in Verum Ad Spectabilis Caeli Typym...
Middelburgi...1630. 4to, one folding plate. Illus. within text.
Woodcut initials. Bound in full cont. vellum. MS title on spine.
Arkway 22-78 1983 $575

LANSDOWNE, J. F.   Birds of the Eastern Forest. 1968-70.
112 coloured plates, 2 vols., 4to, cloth. Wheldon 160-788 1983 £52

LANSTON MONOTYPE CORP.   Fournier, A Specimen of a Classic
Old Face... London: Lanston Monotype, 1927. Small 8vo. Limp
decorated paper covered boards, paper cover label. From the
library of Grant Dahlstrom with his name in ink. Oak Knoll 49-381
1983 $20

LANZAS, PEDRO T.   Relacion Descriptiva de los Mapas,
Planos, etc. Madrid, 1903. Folding illus. 16mo, orig. pr. wrs.,
(wrs. only foxed). Argosy 716-54 1983 $25

LAPHAM, I. A.   A Documentary History of the Milwaukee
and Rock River Canal. Milwaukee, Wisc., 1840. Later cloth, morocco
label. Three leaves in facsimile. Jenkins 152-528 1983 $85

LAPINER, ALAN   Pre-Columbian Art of South America.
New York: Abrams, 1976. 910 illus. (225 tipped-in color). Small
folio. Cloth. Dust jacket. Ars Libri 34-327 1983 $125

LA PLACETTE, JEAN   Of the Incurable Scepticism of the
Church of Rome. Printed for Ric. Chiswell, 1588. First edition
of this translation. 4to, wrapper. Fenning 61-248 1983 £10.50

LA PLACETTE, JEAN   Six Conferences Concerning the Eucharist.
Printed for Richard Chiswell, 1687. First English edition, including
half-title, 4to, wrapper. Light old marginal damp stain, a good
copy. Fenning 61-249 1983 £12.50

LAPPARENT, A. DE   Traite de Geologie. Paris, 1906.
5th (last) edition, 883 text-figures, 3 vols., royal 8vo, buckram.
Wheldon 160-1435 1983 £20

LAPPARENT, A. DE   Traite de Geologie. Paris, 1909.
850 text-figures, 3 vols., royal 8vo, half morocco. Wheldon 160-1434
1983 £15

LA RAMEE, LOUISE DE
Please turn to
DE LA RAMEE, LOUISE

LARDNER, RING   Bib Ballads. Chicago, (1915). First
edition. 12mo, illus. Fine copy. Laid in is a clipped signature.
Owner's inscription reads, "Niles, Michigan, Home of Ring Lardner."
Argosy 714-451 1983 $125

LARDNER, RING   June Moon. New York, 1930. 8vo.
Cloth. Paper label on spine. Some very light fading to cloth,
mainly a fine copy in dj. In Our Time 156-483 1983 $150

LARDNER, RING   Round Up. NY, 1929. Edges very slightly
rubbed, else fine, bright copy in moderately worn and chipped dustwrapper. Quill & Brush 54-764 1983 $100

LARDNER, RING   Treat 'Em Rough. Indianapolis, (1918).
First edition, first issue. 8vo, cloth; pictorial label; dust
soiled. Illus. by Frank Crerie. Argosy 714-452 1983 $50

LARDNER, RING   Treat ' em Rough. Ind., (1918). First
issue, light paper stain on front end paper, dustwrapper badly chipped
on spine and rear panel. Quill & Brush 54-766 1983 $35

LARDNER, RING   What of It? NY, 1925. First issue, near
fine. Quill & Brush 54-767 1983 $40

LARGE, E. C.   The Advance of the Fungi. (1940).
6 plates, 8vo, cloth. Wheldon 160-1850 1983 £15

LARKIN, EDWARD   Speculum Patrum: A Looking-Glasse of
the Fathers. London, Henry Eversden, 1659. 8vo, orig. sheep, now
worn and chipped, joints and spine broken, few pencilled notes, slit
in C2 not removing any text. First and only edition. Ravenstree 97-
23 1983 $187.50

LARKIN, PHILIP   Aubade. Salem, Oregon, 1980. First
edition. One of 250 numbered copies initialled by the author and
the printer and illustrator, Kathleen Gray Schallock. Printed on
Fabriano, Richard de Bas, and Japanese hand-made papers. In antique
silver lined envelope. Mint. Jolliffe 26-313 1983 £45

LARKIN, PHILIP   High Windows. London, 1974. First
edition. Inscribed to Harold Pinter. Dustwrapper. Fine. Gekoski
2-104 1983 £275

LARKIN, PHILIP   The Less Deceived. The Marvell Press,
1955. Lightly bumped, in a slightly sunned dustwrapper lackings
chips at head and tail. Ownership signature. First edition, first
issue. Gekoski 2-100 1983 £140

LARKIN, PHILIP   The Whitsun Weddings. London, 1964.
First English edition. Dustwrapper. Fine. Jolliffe 26-308 1983
£45

LARNED, CHARLES W.   History of the Battle Monument at West
Point. West Point, 1898. Ed. limited to 1000 copies. Illus. 8vo,
orig. boards, cloth shelfback, gilt top, untrimmed, slightly dust-
soiled. Morrill 288-493 1983 $20

LAROCQUE, FRANCOIS A.   Journal of...from the Assiniboine to the
Yellowstone 1805. Ottawa, 1910. Orig. printed wraps. Ginsberg 46-402
1983 $85

LA ROERIE, G.   Navires et Marins de la Rame a l'Helice.
Paris, (1930). First edition. Numerous fine illustrations, a few in
color, from old prints and photographs. 2 vols., 4to. Ex-library;
rebound in library buckram; rubbed. Morrill 290-218 1983 $55

LARPENTEUR, CHARLES   Forty Years a Fur Trader on Upper
Missouri, 1833-1872. Chicago, Lakeside Press, 1933. Fldg. map,
illus., gilt top. Clark 741-268 1983 $22.50

LARROVITCH, FEODOR VLADIMIR   Jahkst Orbytor Dopon. St. Petersburg:
1859. 1st ed. Orig. diced calf, gilt. Illustrated with two crude
woodcuts. Extremely rare. Jenkins 155-769 1983 $135

L'ARTE di Augusto Grassi, 1904-1926. Roma: Danesi, 1927. 65 plates
(11 tipped-in color). Frontis. Large 4to. Boards, 1/4 cloth. Ars
Libri 33-488 1983 $50

LARWOOD, JACOB   The History of Signboards. London: n.d.
Sixth edition. Frontis. in color, 19 full-page black and white plates.
Old marbled boards and calf (rubbed), Bradley 66-427 1983 $30

LA SALLE DE L'ETANG, SIMON-PHILIBERT   Manuel D'Agriculture pour le
Laboureur, pour le Proprietaire et pour le Gouvernement. Paris: Chez
P. Fr. Didot le Jeune, 1768. 2nd ed., 8vo, frontis. portrait, a fine
and crisp copy with very wide margins, cont. mottled calf, spine
gilt in compartments, red morocco label. Pickering & Chatto 21-58
1983 $250

LASATER, LAWRENCE M.   The Lasater Philosophy of Cattle
Raising. El Paso: Texas Western Press, 1972. Illus. Limited to
295 copies signed by the author and Carl Hertzog. Cowhide spine.
Boxed. Jenkins 151-174 1983 $100

LASCELLES, JOHN   Local Government and Sanitary Law
Reform. Simpkin, Marshall, 1874. Disbound. Jarndyce 31-345 1983
£10.50

LASHLEY, KARL S.   The Behavioristic Interpretation of
Consciousness I & II. Orig. printed wrappers. Inscribed on wrapper
of first pamphlet "compliments of K. S. Lashley." Gach 95-310 1983
$20

LASHLEY, KARL S.   Brain Mechanisms and Intelligence. A
Quantitative Study of Injuries to the Brain. Chicago: Univ. of
Chicago Press, (1929). First edition. Six black and white plates.
Very good ex-library copy. Gach 94-588 1983 $25

LASKOWSKI, SIGISMOND   Anatomie Normale du Corps Humain.
Geneva, 1894. First edition. 16 large chromolithographic plates.
Elephant folio, buckram (plates brittle, margins chipping; hinges
weak). Argosy 713-327 1983 $350

LASSAIGNE, JACQUES   Chagall. (Paris): Maeght Editeur,
(1957). First edition. Small 4to, profusely illus. with 14 orig.
lithographs (12 in color, of which 4 are folding plates, + cover),
100 full-page plates (many in color) and numerous text illus. The
color lithographs were printed by Mourlot Freres. Fine copy in
stiff wraps. with orig. color lithograph covers. Karmiole 73-25
1983 $300

LASSAIGNE, JACQUES   Toulouse Lautrec. Paris: 1939. First
edition. Folio, cloth. Text illus. plus 127 other plates and reproductions. Fine in dust jacket. Bradley 66-401 1983 $85

LASSUS, ORLANDE DE   Premier Fascicle des Melanges. Paris,
1894. 3 facs. plates, 4to, wrs., spine repaired. Salloch 387-133
1983 $40

THE LAST Letter of Mary Queen of Scotland Addressed to her brother
in law Henry III King of France. Chelsea, the Swan Press, 1927.
4to, uncut, cloth gilt, a little soiled on the cover, no. 46 of
500 copies on hand-made paper. Bickersteth 77-134 1983 £12

LATHAM, J.   A General Synopsis of Birds. 1781-1801.
3 vols. in 6 parts and 2 volume supplements, bound in 8 vols., 4to,
cont. calf, fully gilt spines, red and green leather labels, 8 hand-
coloured title-page vignettes, 142 hand-coloured plates. Very scarce
as only 500 copies were printed. A little minor foxing and offsetting
and neat repair to margin of 1 plate, but in general a clean set with
excellent original colouring. Wheldon 160-58 1983 £1,300

LATHAM, ROBERT G   Descriptive Ethnology. London: John
Van Voorst, 1859. 1st ed., 8vo, two vols., orig. cloth, spines gilt.
Half-titles; uncut copy; advertisements. Bookplates carefully excised, small library stamp at end of text; in all other respects a
fine copy. Trebizond 18-202 1983 $175

LATHAM, ROBERT G.   The Nationalities of Europe. Wm. H.
Allen, 1863. First edition, ad. leaf, 2 vols., 8vo, orig. cloth,
the spines neatly repaired, a very good copy. Fenning 60-238 1983
£45

LATHBURY, MARY   The Birthday Week. N.Y.: Worthington,
1884. 8vo. Cloth backed pictorial boards. Covers stained. Victorian colorplate book illus. by author with chromoliths. Decorative
borders. Very good. Aleph-bet 8-156 1983 $30

LATHOM, FRANCIS   Men and Manners. Printed by J. Davis for
J. Wright and H. D. Symonds, 1800. 4 vols., contemp. qtr. calf, marbled sides; spines rubbed, otherwise a fine copy; with the four half-
titles; signature B of Vol. III misbound but complete. Hill 165-65
1983 £85

LATHROP, AMY   Tales of Western Kansas. Norton, 1948.
Illus. 1st ed. Jenkins 153-298 1983 $20

LATHROP, DOROTHY   Animals of the Bible. N.Y.: Stokes,
1937. 4th printing. 4to. Cloth. Dust wrapper. Illus. with many
full-page black & whites. Fine. Aleph-bet 8-158 1983 $25

LATHROP, GEORGE   Memoirs of a Pioneer. Lusk, Wy., (1929).
Illus. Orig. printed wraps. Ginsberg 47-992 1983 $60

LATHROP, JOHN   A Discourse, in Two Parts, Preached at
the Commencement of the Nineteenth Century. Boston, 1801. Disbound.
Reese 13-244 1983 $25

LATHROP, JOHN H.   Wisconson... (Madison, 1853?). Sewn.
First edition. Ginsberg 46-829 1983 $85

LATIMER, HUGH   Frvitfvll Sermons. London, reprinted
by Valentine Sims, 1596. 4to, later calf, joints cracked, minor
soiling and spotting, names marked out on title, water stain to
lower portion of first of book, early marginalia, few headlines
shaved, 18th century bookplate of Hugh Rose of Kilravick, and with
his signature on endpaper. Ravenstree 97-24 1983 $565

LATIMER, ROBERT S.   Dr. Baedeker: and His Apostolic Work in
Russia. Morgan & Scott, 1907. First edition, with 2 maps and 14
plates, 8vo, orig. cloth, gilt, a very good copy. Fenning 60-239
1983 £10.50

LATROBE, BENJAMIN H.   The Journal of Latrobe: Being the Notes
& Sketches of an Architect. NY, 1905. Illus., uncut, g.t., good.
Argosy 710-537 1983 $45

LATROBE, CHRISTIAN I.   Journal of a visit to South Africa...
London: L.B. Seeley, 1821. Second edition. 8vo. Folding map.
4 plates. 1/2 calf gilt, marbled boards. Rubbed. Lacks 1/2 title.
Adelson Africa-97 1983 $175

LATROBE, JOHN H. B.   The First Steamboat Voyage on the
Western Waters. Baltimore, 1871. Orig. printed wrappers. 1st ed.
Uncut copy, near mint. Jenkins 153-323 1983 $45

LATROBE, JOHN H. B.   The History of Mason and Dixon's Line. (Philadelphia), 1855. Disbound. First edition. Felcone 22-136 1983 $20

LATROBE, JOHN H. B.   The History of Mason and Dixon's Line... Phila., 1855. First edition. Orig. printed wrappers. Jenkins 152-680 1983 $20

LATTA, JAMES W.   History of the First Regiment Infantry, National Guard of Pennsylvania (Gray Reserves), 1861-1911. Phil., 1912. First edition. 12 full page plates, black and white frontis., 20 other full-page black and white plates. Blue cloth, gilt, top edges gilt. Very good. Bradley 64-133 1983 $45

LATTA, ROBERT R.   Reminiscences of Pioneer Life. Kansas City, Mo., Franklin Hudson Pub. Co., 1912. Illus. Orig. pictorial cloth. Ginsberg 47-429 1983 $125

LATTIMORE, ELEANOR HOLGATE   Turkish Reunion. New York, (1934). 8vo, cloth, cloth faded on spine, else very good. This copy inscribed by author. In Our Time 156-485 1983 $20

LATTIMORE, RICHARD   Themes in Greek & Latin Epitaphs. Urbana, 1942. 4to, cloth. Cloth-backed bds. Salloch 385-136 1983 $40

LAUD, WILLIAM   A Relation of the Conference between William Lawd...And Mr. Fisher the Jesuite. Printed by Richard Badger, 1639. Small folio, nineteenth century ink notes on the flies, cont. speckled calf, top of spine a little worn. First edition. Bickersteth 77-34 1983 £35

LAUDER, THOMAS DICK   Lochandu. Elgin: James Watson, Glasgow: Thomas D. Morison, n.d. Half title, 16 pp ads. Orig. dark green cloth, differently blocked to previous item, v.g. Jarndyce 31-777 1983 £12.50

LAUDERDALE, JAMES MAITLAND, 8TH EARL OF   Letters to the Peers of Scotland. Printed for G.G. and J. Robinson, 1794. 8vo, errata leaf, disbound. Bickersteth 77-35 1983 £30

LAUGHLIN, JAMES   New Directions in Prose & Poetry 1941. Norfolk: New Directions, (1941). Cloth, paper label. Illus. About fine in slightly used dust jacket. Reese 20-596 1983 $50

LAUPAUZE, HENRY   Ingres. Sa vie et son oeuvre... Paris: Georges Petit, 1911. 11 heliogravure plates. 389 illus. Small folio. Marbled boards, 3/4 vellum. Ars Libri 32-337 1983 $350

THE LAUREAT: or, the right side of Colley Cibber, Esq. London: printed for J. Roberts, 1740. 8vo, disbound, 1st edition. Ximenes 64-97 1983 $375

LAURENCE, JOHN   A New System of Agriculture...and Gardening. London, Woodward, 1726. First edition, folio, engraved frontis. Two full page engraved plates. Full cont. tan calf (rebacked, corners restored). Very good. Houle 21-502 1983 $295

LAURENTS, ARTHUR   Home of the Brave. N.Y., Random, (1946). First edition. Dust jacket (small nicks) else, very good. Signed and inscribed by the author. Houle 22-555 1983 $30

LAURENTY, J. S.   Les Sanzas du tongo. Tervuren, 1962. 2 vols. 43 plates. 4 maps. Folio. Wrappers. Ars Libri 34-675 1983 $75

LAURIER, WILFRID   1871-1890. Wilfrid Laurier on the Platform. Collection of the principal speeches... Quebec, 1890. 22cm. Frontis. portrait. Presentation copy from Laurier. Purple cloth. Hinge cracked, else very good. McGahern 54-189 1983 $100

LAUT, AGNES C.   The Blazed Trail of the Old Frontier. N.Y., McBride, 1926. Illus. from drawings by Charles M. Russell. 8vo. Folded colored map, 33 plates, text illus. Pictorial maroon buckram, gilt, fore & bottom edges uncut. 1st ed. 200 numbered copies, signed by author. Very fine. O'Neal 50-43 1983 $200

LAUT, AGNES C.   The Blazed Trail of the Old Frontier. New York: Robert M. McBride and Co., 1926. Illus. by Charles Russell. Large folding map. Jenkins 152-681 1983 $45

LAUT, AGNES C.   Enchanted Trails of Glacier Park. New York: Robert M. McBride & Co., 1926. First edition. Frontis. and illus. Fine. Jenkins 152-200 1983 $30

LAVATER, J.   Essays on Physiognomy... London, n.d. (ca. 1800). 12mo. Orig. boards, rebacked, uncut, with 7 plates (each with 6 portraits), and vignette on title. Gurney JJ-220 1983 £20

LAVATER, J   Secret Journal of a Self-Observer. London: for T. Cadell, (1795). First English edition. 2 vols. 8vo. Bound by the Edwards of Halifax Bindery in cont. "Etruscan" calf, giltouter borders, gilt, decorated centre panels, gilt panelled spines with black morocco labels, gilt, and blind-tooled decorat, edges gilt. Presentation inscription on front end-leaf from Mr. Wilberforce to Mary Gisborne. Traylen 94-510 1983 £400

LAVEIRIERE, JULES   Ascension du Mont Popocatepetl, 1857. (Paris, 1861). Wood-engrs., small folio, wrs., 1st printing. Argosy 710-305 1983 $30

LAVENDER, DAVID   The Big Divide. New York, 1949. Map on endpapers. Plates. Dust jacket. Fine. Jenkins 152-201 1983 $30

LAVER, JAMES   Cervantes. Oxford: Blackwell, (1921). Printed wraps. First edition. Edges of wraps. slightly used, else a near fine copy. Reese 20-597 1983 $50

LAVER, JAMES   Forty Drawings by Horace Brodzky. London: William Heinemann, 1935. 40 plates. Large 4to. Cloth. Dust jacket. Presentation copy, inscribed by the artist. Ars Libri 32-67 1983 $50

LAVER, JAMES   French Painting and the Nineteenth Century. Batsford, 1937. First edition, with 112 plates (11 coloured), 4to, orig. cloth, a very good copy in the dust wrapper. Fenning 61-511 1983 £12.50

LAVER, JAMES   Ladie's Mistakes. Bloomsbury, The Nonesuch Press, 1933. First edition. Nine illus. by Thomas Lowinsky. Full green morocco stamped in gilt, t.e.g., uncut, marbled endpapers. One of 300 copies printed at the Fanfare Press. Houle 22-556 1983 $165

LAVER, JAMES   The Literature of Fashion: An Exhibition. London: National Book League, 1947. 8vo. Paper wrappers. 4 plates. Oak Knoll 49-461 1983 $30

LAVER, JAMES   Macrocosmos. London: Heinemann, 1929. First edition. 4to. Orig. pictorial boards. One of 775 copies signed by author. Presentation copy. Very good. MacManus 279-3140 1983 $40

LAVER, JAMES   Macrocosmos. N.Y.: Knopf, 1930. First edition. 4to. Orig. pictorial boards (somewhat soiled & worn). One of 500 copies signed by author. MacManus 279-3139 1983 $27.50

LAVER, JAMES   Macrocosmos: A Poem. Heinemann, 1929. First edition, large 4to, orig. printed boards. Ltd. edition of 775 numbered copies, signed by the author. A fine copy. Fenning 62-203 1983 £14.50

LAVER, JAMES   Wesley. N.Y.: D. Appleton & Co., 1933. First American edition. Frontispiece port. Orig. cloth. Dust jacket (a bit soiled and worn). Presentation copy "For A.J.A. this story of another traveller from James Laver." Covers slightly water-spotted. Good. MacManus 279-3141 1983 $50

LAVIN, MARY   The Becker Wives and other stories. London, 1946. First English edition. Very slightly dusty dust-wrapper. Fine. Jolliffe 26-314 1983 £16

LAVOISIER, ANTOINE-LAURENT (1743-1794)   Traite Elementaire de Chimie. A Paris, Chez Cuchet. M.DCC.LXXXIX (1789). 2 vols., 8vo, two folding tables. Thirteen folding plates, some closely trimmed, affecting running title though not surface of engraving. Bound in 1/4 vellum. Marbled paper covered boards. Title stamped in gold on orange morocco title piece. New endpapers. First edition. Good. Arkway 22-80 1983 $1,800

LAW, JOHN   The Colonial History of Vincennes. Vincennes: 1858. First edition. Orig. gray-green cloth. Nice copy. Bradley 66-558 1983 $150

LAW, JOHN   The Colonial History of Vincennes. Vincennes, 1858. Autograph presentation copy from the author, signed "John." Ginsberg 46-346 1983 $100

LAW, WILLIAM   The absolute unlawfulness of the stage entertainment fully demonstrated. London: printed for G. Robinson, 1773. 8vo, cont. half calf (spine worn, front hinge loose). 6th ed. Title-page a bit soiled. Ximenes 64-346 1983 $30

LAW, WILLIAM   A Serious Call to a Devout and Holy Life. London, Printed for William Innys, 1729. 8vo. Cont. paneled calf, bumped, hinges bit cracked but firm, spine chipped at top & bottom, new label. 1st ed. Very clean & crisp copy. O'Neal 50-35 1983 $400

LAW Books, 1876-1981. Bowker, 1981. 4 vols. Quadruple-columned. Boswell 7-16 1983 $375

LAWALL, CHARLES   Four Thousand Years of Pharmacy. Philadelphia, 1927. First edition. 8vo. Orig. binding. Fye H-3-333 1983 $55

LAWES, J. B.   Report of experiments on the Growth of Barley. 1873. 8vo, original wrappers. Wheldon 160-2125 1983 £15

LAWES, LEWIS E.   Man's Judgment of Death. NY: G. P. Putnam's Sons, 1924. First edition. Gach 95-312 1983 $20

LAWRENCE, ABBOT   Letters from...To the Hon. William Rives of Virginia. Boston, 1846. Orig. printed wrappers. Jenkins 152-489 1983 $45

LAWRENCE, ADA   Young Lorenzo. Florence: G. Orioli, (1931). First edition. Illus. Orig. vellum boards. Dust jacket. Limited to 750 copies. Very fine. MacManus 279-3170 1983 $175

LAWRENCE, ADA   Young Lorenzo; early life of D.H. Lawrence. Florence, 1931. First edition. One of 740 copies, this unnumbered. Dust wrapper. Contains hitherto unpublished letters from Lawrence. Nice. Rota 230-347 1983 £50

LAWRENCE, ADA   Young Lorenzo: Early Life of D.H. Lawrence. Florence, 1931. 8vo. Vellum. Dust jacket has some soiling. A fine copy, partially unopened. In Our Time 156-494 1983 $85

LAWRENCE, DAVID HERBERT   Aaron's Rod. London: Martin Secker, (1922). Gilt cloth. First British edition, postdating the American edition by two months. Bright copy in tattered and mended dust jacket. Reese 20-1197 1983 $40

LAWRENCE, DAVID HERBERT   Aaron's Rod. London, 1922. First English edition. Inscribed in an unknown hand "E.P.H. from D.H.L." Rota 231-367 1983 £40

LAWRENCE, DAVID HERBERT   Aaron's Rod. London, 1922. First English edition. Erasure from flyleaf. Bookplate. Nice. Rota 230-337 1983 £20

LAWRENCE, DAVID HERBERT   Amores. London, 1916. First edition. 900 printed. Faded along edge of front and rear cover, in scarce dustwrapper missing a piece at top of spine. Very good copy. Gekoski 2-109 1983 £130

LAWRENCE, DAVID HERBERT   Amores. London, 1916. First edition. Later issue. Chipped dustwrapper missing a piece at foot of spine. Very good. Gekoski 2-110 1983 £80

LAWRENCE, DAVID HERBERT   Apocalypse. Florence: G. Oriolo, 1931. First edition. Orig. red paper boards. Leather label on spine. Dust jacket. One of 750 copies printed. The green paper jacket is evenly darkened. Unopened. Very fine. MacManus 2 9-3142 1983 $450

LAWRENCE, DAVID HERBERT   Apocalypse. Florence: G. Orioli, 1931. Ltd. first edition. Fine, in a chipped dust wrapper. Argosy 714-453 1983 $175

LAWRENCE, DAVID HERBERT   Apocalypse. Florence: G. Orioli, 1931. Boards. First edition. Photographic frontis. One of 750 numbered copies. A bright copy, in the fragile jacket, which is slightly chipped and used. Reese 20-1209 1983 $150

LAWRENCE, DAVID HERBERT   Apocalypse. London, 1932. First trade edition. Bearing the ownership signature of Q.D. Leavis, but with textual notes and underlinings by F.R. Leavis. Orig. cloth slightly nicked at head and foot of spine. Small stain to rear cover, but a very good copy. Gekoski 2-212 1983 £80

LAWRENCE, DAVID HERBERT   Apocalypse. London, Secker, (1932). First English edition. Gilt stamped medium blue cloth, t.e. blue, uncut. Dust jacket (lightly soiled). Very good. Houle 22-558 1983 $95

LAWRENCE, DAVID HERBERT   Apocalypse. New York: The Viking Press, 1932. First American edition. 8vo. Orig. cloth. Dust jacket. Very slightly worn and darkened jacket, but a fine copy. Jaffe 1-216 1983 $75

LAWRENCE, DAVID HERBERT   Assorted Articles. London, 1930. 8vo. Cloth. Bookplate on inside endboard. Orig. dj is chipped. A fine copy. In Our Time 156-490 1983 $125

LAWRENCE, DAVID HERBERT   Assorted Articles. London: Martin Secker, 1930. Cloth. First edition. About fine in fragile jacket, which is a bit chipped and darkened. Reese 20-1207 1983 $75

LAWRENCE, DAVID HERBERT   Assorted Articles. London: Secker, 1930. 1st ed. Orig. cloth, gilt. 3700 copies printed. Fine copy, mostly unopened, in tape-reinforced dj. Jenkins 155-770 1983 $50

LAWRENCE, DAVID HERBERT   Assorted Articles. L, 1930. Minor cover spotting, else very good in chipped and aging dustwrapper. Quill & Brush 54-769 1983 $40

LAWRENCE, DAVID HERBERT   Bay: A Book of Poems. London: The Beaumont Press, 1919. 8vo. With illustrations by Anne Estelle Rice. The vellum ed. of the book which was limited to 30 copies printed on Japan vellum and signed by Lawrence and Rice. On this copy there is a note from the publisher that it is "One of three copies specially printed for presentation. Enclosed in a morocco-backed slipcase. A fine copy in vellum backed cloth wrapper. In Our Time 156-486 1983 $4000

LAWRENCE, DAVID HERBERT   Bay. (N.p.: The Beaumont Press, 1919). Cloth and patterned boards. First edition. One of 120 numbered copies, printed on handmade paper, from a total edition of 200. Very slight rubbing at edges, else a fine copy. Reese 20-1194 1983 $300

LAWRENCE, DAVID HERBERT   Birds, Beasts and Flowers. London, 1930. Small folio, Cockerell marbled boards with vellum backstrip, t.e.g., wood-engravings by Blair Hughes-Stanton. One of 500 copies. First illustrated edition. Duschnes 240-55 1983 $250

LAWRENCE, DAVID HERBERT   Birds, Beasts and Flowers. London: Martin Secker, (1923). First English edition. 8vo. Orig. cloth-backed.boards with paper label. Dust jacket. One of 1000 copies printed. Rare, but worn, jacket. Very good copy. Jaffe 1-207 1983 $85

LAWRENCE, DAVID HERBERT   Birds, Beasts and Flowers. London, Secker, (1923). First English edition. Half black cloth, paper label, uncut. 1,000 copies were printed. Very good. Houle 21-505 1983 $55

LAWRENCE, DAVID HERBERT   The Boy in the Bush. London: Martin Secker, (1924). Cloth. First edition, one of 2,000 copies printed. Foredge very lightly foxed, otherwise a fine copy in dust jacket, which is slightly chipped at top edges. Reese 20-1198 1983 $150

LAWRENCE, DAVID HERBERT   The Boy In The Bush. New York: Thomas Seltzer, 1924. First American edition. 8vo. Orig. cloth. Dust jacket designed by Dorothy Brett. Chipped jacket, but fine. Jaffe 1-221 1983 $125

LAWRENCE, DAVID HERBERT   The Boy in the Bush. N.Y.: Thomas Seltzer, 1924. First Americna edition. Orig. cloth. Very good. MacManus 279-3143 1983 $35

LAWRENCE, DAVID HERBERT   The Boy in the Bush. London, (1924). First edition. 8vo, cloth; rubbed. Argosy 714-454 1983 $30

LAWRENCE, DAVID HERBERT   The Boy in the Bush. NY, 1924. Edges rubbed, rear hinge starting, good or better. Quill & Brush 54-777 1983 $40

LAWRENCE, DAVID HERBERT   The Captain's Doll. N.Y.: Thomas Seltzer, 1923. First American edition. Orig. cloth. Worn. MacManus 279-3144 1983 $25

LAWRENCE, DAVID HERBERT   Collected Poems. New York: Jonathan Cape and Harrison Smith, 1929. First American edition. 2 vols. 8vo. Orig. cloth. Tissue jackets. In publisher's slipcase. Slightly worn slipcase, but very fine set. Jaffe 1-212 1983 $100

LAWRENCE, DAVID HERBERT   The Collected Poems of D. H. Lawrence. London, 1928. First edition. 2 vols. Covers just a little marked. Very nice. Rota 231-368 1983 £35

LAWRENCE, DAVID HERBERT   Collected Poems. New York, 1929. First American edition. 2 vols. With the ownership signature of Theodore Roethke in Volume 2. Inscription in Volume 1. Hinges split. Covers slightly rubbed. Very good. Jolliffe 26-446 1983 £25

LAWRENCE, DAVID HERBERT   Collected Poems. N.Y.: Jonathan Cape & Harrison Smith, 1929. First American edition. 2 vols. Orig. cloth. Spines and covers slightly worn. Very good. MacManus 279-3145 1983 $35

LAWRENCE, DAVID HERBERT   Collected Poems. London, Secker, 1932. First one volume edition. Frontis. portrait. Dust jacket (some chipping and light soiling). Very good. Houle 21-506 1983 $75

LAWRENCE, DAVID HERBERT   David. N.Y., Knopf, 1926. First edition. Color frontis. and decorations by DHL. Stiff wraps., glassine jacket. Pub.'s box. One of 450 copies. Fine. Houle 21-509 1983 $350

LAWRENCE, DAVID HERBERT   David. London: Martin Secker, (1926). 8vo. Orig. cloth. Dust jacket. First edition. Limited to 500 copies. Chipped jacket. A fine copy. Jaffe 1-209 1983 $150

LAWRENCE, DAVID HERBERT   David. London: Martin Secker, (1926). Cloth. First edition. One of 500 copies only. Light residue of early bookplate, otherwise a fine copy, in dust jacket with two chips at top edge and some reinforcement on the verso. Reese 20-1200 1983 $150

LAWRENCE, DAVID HERBERT   England My England. N.Y.: Thomas Seltzer, 1922. First edition. Orig. cloth. Very good. MacManus 279-3147 1983 $45

LAWRENCE, DAVID HERBERT   England, My England. L, (1924). Good to very good. Quill & Brush 54-770 1983 $30

LAWRENCE, DAVID HERBERT   England, My England. London: Martin Secker, (1924). First English edition. Orig. cloth. First few leaves lightly foxed. Fine. MacManus 279-3148 1983 $25

LAWRENCE, DAVID HERBERT   The Escaped Cock. Paris: The Black Sun Press, 1929. First edition. 4to. Orig. parchment wrappers. Tissue jacket. In publisher's marbled board slipcase. One of 450 copies on Holland Van Gelder. Very fine copy. Jaffe 1-215 1983 $450

LAWRENCE, DAVID HERBERT   The Escaped Cock. Paris, Black Sun, 1929. First edition. Color frontis. and text decorations by Lawrence. Stiff wraps., glassine jacket. One of 450 copies. Pub.'s box (a trifle rubbed). Fine. Houle 22-561 1983 $350

LAWRENCE, DAVID HERBERT   The Escaped Cock. Paris: The Black Sun Press, 1929. Quarto. Printed wraps. Decorations in color by the author. First edition. One of 450 numbered copies, printed on Holland Van Gelder Zonen. Reese 20-1205 1983 $350

LAWRENCE, DAVID HERBERT   Etruscan Places. London: Martin Secker, 1932. First edition. Illus. Orig. cloth. Dust jacket (a little chipped). One of 3070 copies printed. Spine faded. Lagely unopened. Fine. MacManus 279-3149 1983 $250

LAWRENCE, DAVID HERBERT   Etruscan Places. London: Martin Secker, 1932. First edition. 8vo. Illus. Orig. cloth. Dust jacket chipped along edges, otherwise a fine copy. Jaffe 1-217 1983 $100

LAWRENCE, DAVID HERBERT   Fantasia of the Unconscious. N.Y.: Thomas Seltzer, 1922. First edition. Orig. cloth. Dust jacket (top of spine chipped). Bookplate. Fine. MacManus 279-3150 1983 $150

LAWRENCE, DAVID HERBERT   Fantasia of the Unconcious. N.Y., Selftzer, 1922. First edition. Gilt stamped blue cloth (slightly frayed at head of spine), else good-very good. Houle 22-562 1983 $145

LAWRENCE, DAVID HERBERT   Fantasia of the Unconscious. NY, 1922. Spine lettering slightly rubbed, else fine. Quill & Brush 54-772 1983 $50

LAWRENCE, DAVID HERBERT   Fantasia of the Unconscious. NY: 1922. Spine lettering oxidized, else very fine copy. First edition. Bromer 25-62 1983 $45

LAWRENCE, DAVID HERBERT   Fantasia of the Unconscious. NY, 1922. Soiled and slightly shaken, good. Quill & Brush 54-771 1983 $20

LAWRENCE, DAVID HERBERT   Fire and Other Poems. (San Francisco): Printed at the Grabhorn Press for the Book Club of California, 1940. Canvas over boards, label. First edition. One of 300 copies. A very fine copy. Prospectus laid in. Issued in a plain wrapper, not here present. Reese 20-1211 1983 $275

LAWRENCE, DAVID HERBERT   Gentleman from San Francisco. N.Y., Seltzer, 1923. First American edition. Marbled boards, paper labels (spine faded, short tear), else good-very good. Houle 21-530 1983 $55

LAWRENCE, DAVID HERBERT   Georgian Poetry 1920-1922. First edition. Dust jacket (back faded), t.e.g., uncut. Very good. Houle 21-531 1983 $55

LAWRENCE, DAVID HERBERT   Glad Ghosts. London: Ernest Benn, 1926. First edition, first issue. Orig. yellow printed wrappers. Presentation copy to Mabel Dodge Luhan inscribed: "Mabel from D.H. Lawrence." One of 500 copies. Bottom spine edge slightly torn and spot-glued. Covers slightly worn and soiled. Some foxing to the last few pages. In a folding cloth case. Good. MacManus 279-3151 1983 $1,500

LAWRENCE, DAVID HERBERT   Glad Ghosts. London: Ernest Benn Ltd., 1926. "Second impression, October 1926." Orig. yellow wrappers. Presentation copy, inscribed on the free endpaper "Merry Christmas to you Miss Pearn from D.H. Lawrence." Wrappers a bit dust-soiled. Good. MacManus 279-3152 1983 $750

LAWRENCE, DAVID HERBERT   Glad Ghosts. London, Benn, 1926. First edition. Yellow wraps. printed in black. Enclosed in a half morocco slipcase. One of 500 copies. Fine. Houle 22-563 1983 $235

LAWRENCE, DAVID HERBERT   Glad Ghosts. London: Ernest Benn Ltd., (1926). Cloth. First edition. One of 500 copies only. Slightest traces of soiling, else a fine copy. Reese 20-1201 1983 $100

LAWRENCE, DAVID HERBERT   Jack im Buschland. Berlin, 1925. First German edition. Yellow cloth (faded and slightly frayed), good-very good. Houle 21-511 1983 $37.50

LAWRENCE, DAVID HERBERT   Kangaroo. N.Y., Seltzer, 1923. First American edition, reset and printed in USA. Blue cloth (several pages creased in printing; covers soiled). Good. Houle 21-512 1983 $30

LAWRENCE, DAVID HERBERT   Lady Chatterly's Lover. (Florence), Privately Printed, 1928. First edition. Mulberry colored boards, paper label, uncut and mostly unopened. Plain cream colored dust wrapper. One of 1,000 copies, signed by Lawrence. Enclosed in a fine cloth slipcase. A fine copy. Houle 22-564 1983 $1,250

LAWRENCE, DAVID HERBERT   Lady Chatterley's Lover. (Paris, 1929). Third edition "reproduced photograhically from the first edition." This edition is first with introduction "My Skirmish with the Jolly Roger." Paperwraps, chipped and frayed along edges, some waterstaining, good. Quill & Brush 54-773 1983 $75

LAWRENCE, DAVID HERBERT   The Ladybird: The Fox: The Captain's Doll. London: Martin Secker, (1923). First edition. 8vo. Orig. cloth. Dust jacket. Jacket a little chipped, but a near-fine copy. Jaffe 1-206 1983 $150

LAWRENCE, DAVID HERBERT   The Ladybird. London, (1923). First edition. 8vo, brown cloth; slightly rubbed. Argosy 714-455 1983 $30

LAWRENCE, DAVID HERBERT   The Ladybird. London: Martin Secker, (1923). First edition. Orig. cloth. MacManus 279-3153 1983 $30

LAWRENCE, DAVID HERBERT   Last Poems. Florence: G. Orioli, 1932. First edition. Orig. boards with paper label on spine. Dust jacket (remnants thereof, glued onto a new jacket made of brown paper). One of 750 copies. Head of spine slightly soiled. Very good. MacManus 279-3154 1983 $125

LAWRENCE, DAVID HERBERT   The Letters of... London: Heinemann, (1932). First edition. Full vellum stamped in black. Contained in a brown cloth slipcase with red morocco spine label. One of 525 copies. Very good-fine. Houle 22-566 1983 $275

LAWRENCE, DAVID HERBERT   Letters. London: William Heinemann, Ltd., 1932. 8vo. Full vellum, letter in black, the orig. slipcase with portrait of Lawrence. Limited edition of 525 numbered copies, printed on thin paper. A mint copy. Traylen 94-512 1983 £85

LAWRENCE, DAVID HERBERT   The Letters. London: William Heinemann, Ltd.; New York: The Viking Press, Inc., (1932). First edition. Limited to 525 copies. 8vo. Orig. vellum. Tissue jacket, in publisher's slipcase. Glassine jacket torn, otherwise a very fine copy. Jaffe 1-218 1983 $150

LAWRENCE, DAVID HERBERT   The Letters of D. H. Lawrence. London, 1932. First edition. One of 525 numbered copies. Full parchment. Slipcase. Fine. Rota 231-369 1983 £75

LAWRENCE, DAVID HERBERT   Letters. N.Y., 1932. Illus. First edition. Argosy 714-456 1983 $40

LAWRENCE, DAVID HERBERT   Look! We Have Come Through! London, 1917. First edition. One of 500 copies, inscribed by the author to Madge Dunlop. Somewhat mottled and bumped on boards, bookplate on endpaper causing creasing, but a very good copy. Gekoski 2-111 1983 £275

LAWRENCE, DAVID HERBERT   Look! We Have Come Through! London: Chatto & Windus, 1917. Salmon cloth, paper label. First edition, one of 500 copies. Cloth slightly bubbled, spine sunned, a very good, internally fine copy. Reese 20-599 1983 $85

LAWRENCE, DAVID HERBERT   The Lost Girl. London: Martin Secker, (1920). Gilt cloth. First edition, first state, with pages 256 and 268 in their unexpurgated state. Light cracking of rear hinge, and offsetting from wrapper, otherwise a very fine copy in lightly worn second state dust jacket. Enclosed in a folding cloth box. Scarce in first state. Reese 20-1196 1983 $600

LAWRENCE, DAVID HERBERT   The Lost Girl. London (1920). 8vo, cloth. First edition, first issue. Duschnes 240-130 1983 $175

LAWRENCE, DAVID HERBERT   Love Among the Haystacks & Other Pieces. London: Nonesuch Press, 1930. 8vo. Cloth. 1 of 1600 copies. Bookplate on front endboard, a fine copy in dj. In Our Time 156-491 1983 $150

LAWRENCE, DAVID HERBERT   Love Among the Haystacks. London, Nonesuch, 1930. First edition. Yellow and tan cloth. Ltd. edition printed at the Curwen Press on handmade paper. Very good-fine copy. Houle 21-517 1983 $150

LAWRENCE, DAVID HERBERT   Love Among the Haystacks. Nonesuch Press, 1930. First edition. One of 1600 numbered copies. Covers just a little soiled. Very nice. Rota 230-340 1983 £35

LAWRENCE, DAVID HERBERT   Love Among the Haystacks & Other Places. London: Nonesuch Press, 1930. Limited to 1600 copies. Corners very slightly bumped, else very fine. Owner's pencilled signature. First edition. Bromer 25-63 1983 $75

LAWRENCE, DAVID HERBERT   Love Among the Haystacks. Girard, Kansas: Haldeman-Julius Publications, n.d. First Separate edition. Wrappers very slightly faded. Text a little browned. Very nice. Rota 230-346 1983 £21

LAWRENCE, DAVID HERBERT   Love Poems and Others. London, 1913. First edition. Offsetting to endpapers. Dustwrapper browned and rubbed, missing a couple of very small chips. A fine copy. Gekoski 2-105 1983 £200

LAWRENCE, DAVID HERBERT   Love Poems and Others. London: Duckworth & Co., 1913. 8vo, blue buckram, gilt, t.e.g. First edition. Duschnes 240-129 1983 $125

LAWRENCE, DAVID HERBERT   Love Poems. N.Y., Kennerly, 1915. First American edition, second printing (?). Gilt stamped purple cloth (spine faded), else good. Houle 21-518 1983 $37.50

LAWRENCE, DAVID HERBERT   The Lovely Lady. London: Martin Secker, (1932). First edition. 8vo. Orig. cloth. Dust jacket. Slightly chipped jacket, else fine copy. Jaffe 1-219 1983 $185

LAWRENCE, DAVID HERBERT   The Man who Died. London: Martin Secker, 1931. Cloth. First British edition, and first edition under this title. One of 2,000 copies. There is some slight darkening of the endsheets, otherwise a fine copy in slightly chipped dust jacket, with a small stain at the toe of the spine. Reese 20-1206 1983 $85

LAWRENCE, DAVID HERBERT   The Man Who Died. London: Martin Secler, 1931. Tall 8vo, cloth, gilt, t.e.g. One of 2,000 copies. First English edition. Duschnes 240-132 1982 $50

LAWRENCE, DAVID HERBERT   The Man Who Died. 1931. Royal 8vo, t.e.g., others uncut, green cloth gilt, some fading and blanks rather browned otherwise a very good copy. Edition limited to 2,000 copies. Deighton 3-204 1983 £32

LAWRENCE, DAVID HERBERT   The Man Who Died. L, 1931. Limited to 2000 copies, spine slightly discolored, offset on endpapers, else near fine. Quill & Brush 54-778 1983 $40

LAWRENCE, DAVID HERBERT   A Modern Lover. NY, 1934. Edges lightly faded, corners worn, else near very good in chipped, good dustwrapper. Quill & Brush 54-768 1983 $30

LAWRENCE, DAVID HERBERT   Mornings in Mexico. London, 1927. First edition. Dustwrapper with two short tears and a minor crease. Fine. Gekoski 2-114 1983 £100

LAWRENCE, DAVID HERBERT   Mornings in Mexico. New York, 1927. 8vo. Cloth. A fine copy in near perfect dj. In Our Time 156-488 1983 $150

LAWRENCE, DAVID HERBERT   Mornings in Mexico. London: Martin Secker, 1927. First edition. 8vo. Orig. cloth. Dust jacket. Design by the author. One of 1000 copies printed. Partially soiled jacket. Fine copy. Jaffe 1-210 1983 $100

LAWRENCE, DAVID HERBERT   Movements in European History. Oxford:
University Press, Humphrey Milford, 1925. First illus. edition, large
paper issue. Illus. Orig. blue cloth. Dust jacket (slightly worn).
First issue with the suppressed plate on page 271. In a half-morocco
slipcase. Fine. MacManus 279-3156 1983 $750

LAWRENCE, DAVID HERBERT   Movements in European History. Oxford,
1925. First illustrated edition. Fine. Gekoski 2-113 1983 £30

LAWRENCE, DAVID HERBERT   My Skirmish With Jolly Roger. New
York: Random House, 1929. First edition. 8vo. Orig. boards with
paper label. Limited to 600 copies. Errata slip. Very good copy.
Jaffe 1-214 1983 $45

LAWRENCE, DAVID HERBERT   My Skirmish with Jolly Roger. New
York: Random House, 1929. Paper boards, label. First edition, one
of 600 numbered copies (actually 700). The head of the very fragile
spine is chipped, otherwise this is a fine copy, with the errata
slip laid in. Reese 20-1203 1983 $45

LAWRENCE, DAVID HERBERT   Nettles. London, (1930). Pr. wrs.
Argosy 714-457 1983 $20

LAWRENCE, DAVID HERBERT   Paintings of D.H. Lawrence. London,
Mandrake Press, (1929). First edition. Folio. Illus. 3/4 dark
brown morocco over green boards, t.e.g., uncut. Pub.'s box (cracked).
Fine. One of 500 on arches paper. Houle 21-519 1983 $850

LAWRENCE, DAVID HERBERT   Pansies. London, Privately printed,
1929. Frontis. portrait. Full orig. blue leather (a bit faded and
spotted), t.e.g., uncut. Pub.'s box, rubbed. One of 50 copies printed
on Japan vellum, signed by Lawrence. Very good. Houle 21-520 1983
$795

LAWRENCE, DAVID HERBERT   Pansies. London: Martin Secker, (1929).
First edition. Orig. vellum-backed decorated boards. Dust jacket
(worn at edges). One of 250 copies signed by Lawrence. Bookplate.
Fine. MacManus 279-3159 1983 $650

LAWRENCE, DAVID HERBERT   Pansies. N.Y.: Alfred A. Knopf, 1929.
First American edition. Orig. cloth. Dust jacket (very slightly worn).
Fine. MacManus 279-3158 1983 $125

LAWRENCE, DAVID HERBERT   Pansies. Poems. London: Martin
Secker, (1929). First edition, ordinary issue. 8vo. Orig. cloth-
backed decorated boards. Fine clean copy. Jaffe 1-213 1983
$65

LAWRENCE, DAVID HERBERT   Pansies. Poems. New York: Knopf,
1929. Cloth. First American trade edition. A very fine copy in
slightly faded dust jacket. Reese 20-600 1983 $45

LAWRENCE, DAVID HERBERT   The Plumed Serpent. London: Secker,
(1926). 1st ed. Orig. brown cloth, gilt. One of 3,000 copies
printed. About fine. Jenkins 155-772 1983 $50

LAWRENCE, DAVID HERBERT   The Plumed Serpent. N.Y., Knopf, 1926.
First edition, second printing, February, 1926. Dust jacket designed
by Dorothy Brett (chipped) but still a very good copy. Houle 22-570
1983 $45

LAWRENCE, DAVID HERBERT   Pornography and Obscenity. London:
Faber & Faber, (1929). 1st ed. Orig. printed orange wrappers. 5,000
copies printed. Fine copy. Jenkins 155-773 1983 $40

LAWRENCE, DAVID HERBERT   Pornography and Obscenity. London,
Faber (1929). First edition. Printed orange wraps. Very good.
Houle 21-522 1983 $30

LAWRENCE, DAVID HERBERT   Pornography and Obscenity. London:
Faber & Faber Ltd., (1929). First edition. Orig. wrappers. MacManus
279-3160 1983 $25

LAWRENCE, DAVID HERBERT   Pornography and Obscenity. N.Y., 1930.
First American edition. Striped boards. Argosy 714-458 1983 $20

LAWRENCE, DAVID HERBERT   Pornography and So On. London, (1936).
8vo. Wraps. Paper label on the spine. A proof copy of the book.
Light wear to spinal extremity, mainly fine. In Our Time 156-492
1983 $350

LAWRENCE, DAVID HERBERT   A Prelude... Surrey: The Merle
Press, 1949. Calf and boards. First edition. One of 160 numbered
copies, of which this is copy no. 2. A fine copy. Reese 20-1212
1983 $100

LAWRENCE, DAVID HERBERT   A Propos of Lady Chatterly's Lover.
London, Mandrake, 1930. First edition. Dust jacket (trifle rubbed),
else very good-fine. Houle 21-504 1983 $60

LAWRENCE, DAVID HERBERT   A Propos of Lady Chatterley's Lover.
London: Mandrake Press, 1930. Cloth. First edition thus, revised.
A fine copy in lightly used dust jacket. Reese 20-1204 1983 $50

LAWRENCE, DAVID HERBERT   A Propos of Lady Chatterley's Lover.
Mandrake, Press, 1930. First edition. Small tear in flyleaf. Dust
wrapper. Very nice. Rota 230-339 1983 £18

LAWRENCE, DAVID HERBERT   Psychoanalysis and the Unconscious.
London, Secker, (1923). First English edition. Red cloth, paper
label (slight wear), very good. Houle 21-524 1983 $95

LAWRENCE, DAVID HERBERT   The Rainbow. New York: Huebsch,
1916. 1st American ed. Orig. tan cloth. Fine copy. Jenkins 155-
774 1983 $50

LAWRENCE, DAVID HERBERT   The Rainbow. New York, 1916. First
American edition. Hinges clumsily reinforced with stiff paper.
Good. Rota 230-336 1983 £20

LAWRENCE, DAVID HERBERT   Rawdon's Roof. London: Elin Mathews &
Marrot, 1928. Boards. First edition. One of 530 numbered copies,
signed by the author, of which this is one of 30 copies reserved
for presentation. There is some slight offsetting to the endpapers
from the dust jacket, and some slight browning of the lower extreme
margin of the free endsheet and first leaf, otherwise a very fine copy
in dust jacket. Reese 20-1202 1983 $250

LAWRENCE, DAVID HERBERT   Reflections on the Death of a Porcupine.
Philadelphia: Centaur Press, 1925. First edition. Orig. marbled,
cloth-backed, boards. One of 925 copies. Fine. MacManus 279-3161
1983 $135

LAWRENCE, DAVID HERBERT   Reflections on the Death of a Porcupine
and Other Essays. London: Simpkin, Marshall, Hamilton, Kent & Co.,
1925. 1st ed., 1 of 475 numbered copies printed for England at the
Centaur Press in Philadelphia, whose imprint is obscured by printed
blue slip tipped in. Orig. linen-backed marbled boards, uncut. Very
fine copy of the scarcest form of this title. Jenkins 153-389 1983
$125

LAWRENCE, DAVID HERBERT   Reflections On The Death Of A Porcupine
And Other Essays. Philadelphia: The Centaur Press, 1925. First
edition. 8vo. Orig. holland-backed marbled boards, in publisher's
slipcase. One of 425 copies intended for England out of a total
edition of 925 copies. Mint copy. Jaffe 1-208 1983 $125

LAWRENCE, DAVID HERBERT   Reflections on the Death of a Porcupine
and Other Essays. Ph., 1925. Edges very slightly rubbed, spine
slightly darkened, very good or better. Quill & Brush 54-775 1983
$125

LAWRENCE, DAVID HERBERT   Reflections on the Death of a
Porcupine. Philadelphia: The Centaur Press, (1925). Canvas backed
boards. First edition, the unrecorded issue for Great Britain, with
the slip tipped in, and the limitation page indicating this as one
of 475 copies for England. Hinges cracking slightly, tips slightly
bruised, else a fine copy. Wants slipcase. Reese 20-1199 1983 $125

LAWRENCE, DAVID HERBERT   Reflections on the Death of a Porcupine
and other Essays. Philadelphia: the Centaur Press, 1925. First
edition. 8vo. Orig. decorative paper boards with cloth spine.
Limited to 475 numbered copies. A trifle browned. Traylen 94-513
1983 £60

LAWRENCE, DAVID HERBERT   St. Mawr, Together With the Princess.
London: Secker, (1925). First edition. Orig. cloth. Slightly
chipped and soiled dust jacket. Fine. MacManus 279-3162 1983 $65

LAWRENCE, DAVID HERBERT   Sea And Sardinia. New York: Thomas
Seltzer, 1921. First edition. Eight pictures in color by Jan Juta.
4to. Cloth-backed boards with paper label. Dust jacket. Jacket
badly chipped, but scarce. A very good copy. Jaffe 1-205 1983 $150

LAWRENCE, DAVID HERBERT   Sea and Sardinia. NY, 1921. Illus. by Jan Juta. Map loose, front hinge cracked, endpapers stained and cover worn, good. Quill & Brush 54-776 1983 $40

LAWRENCE, DAVID HERBERT   Ship of Death and Other Poems. London, Secker, (1933). Tall 8vo, first collected edition. 14 woodcuts by Blair Hughes-Stanton. Full black morocco, the upper cover stamped in blind with a large ship design, the title boldly stamped in large letters, t.e.g. uncut. A fine designer binding. Houle 21-527 1983 $395

LAWRENCE, DAVID HERBERT   The Ship of Death and Other Poems. L, (1933). 1500 copies, very good. Quill & Brush 54-779 1983 $50

LAWRENCE, DAVID HERBERT   Sons and Lovers. London, 1913. First edition. An advance copy, with publisher's stamp on the title page reading" "To be published on 29th May, 1913". Spine and hinges professionally restored, some bumping, otherwise very good. Gekoski 2-106 1983 £125

LAWRENCE, DAVID HERBERT   Sons and Lovers; a facsimile of the manuscript. Berkeley, 1977. First edition. New copy. 4to. Rota 230-345 1983 £52.50

LAWRENCE, DAVID HERBERT   Studies in Classic American Literature. New York, 1923. First edition. Slightly faded and bumped boards. Reinforced dustwrapper (designed by Lawrence) is missing two chips at corners and is slightly frayed at head of spine. Fine. Gekoski 2-112 1983 £85

LAWRENCE, DAVID HERBERT   Tortoises. New York, 1921. 8vo. Pictorial boards. In the highly uncommon plain dj. Jacket has some minimal wear. Some light wear at the spinal extremities and a few tape impressions on flyleaves, otherwise a fine copy. In Our Time 156-487 1983 $200

LAWRENCE, DAVID HERBERT   Tortoises. New York: Thomas Seltzer, 1921. First edition. 4to. Orig. pictorial boards with paper label on spine. Spine label defective, otherwise a fine copy. Jaffe 1-204 1983 $65

LAWRENCE, DAVID HERBERT   Touch and Go. London: C.W. Daniel, Ltd., 1920. First edition. Orig. orange wrappers with blue paper label. Printed dust jacket (slightly worn). Fine. MacManus 279-3165 1983 $125

LAWRENCE, DAVID HERBERT   Touch & Go. London: C.W. Daniel, ltd., (1920). Stiff wraps., paper labels. First edition. Tiny nick in head of backstrip, else a fine copy in the very fragile wrapper, which lacks a small chip from top back edge. Reese 20-1195 1983 $100

LAWRENCE, DAVID HERBERT   Touch and Go. London: C.W. Daniel, Ltd., 1920. First edition. Orig. wrappers. Paper label on spine worn. Largely unopened. Fine. MacManus 279-3164 1983 $60

LAWRENCE, DAVID HERBERT   Touch and Go. New York: Thomas Seltzer, 1920. First American edition. 8vo. Orig. pictorial boards. Dust jacket. Lightly chipped jacket, but a fine copy. Jaffe 1-203 1983 $50

LAWRENCE, DAVID HERBERT   The Triumph of the Machine. London: Faber, 1931. Boards. First edition. One of 400 numbered copies, printed on handmade paper. Some slight wear along the spine, otherwise a near fine copy. Reese 20-1210 1983 $50

LAWRENCE, DAVID HERBERT   The Triumph of the Machine. London, Faber & Faber, (1931). First edition. Printed at the Curwen Press. Illus. with drawings by Althea Willoughby. Pictorial green wraps. Very good - fine. Houle 22-573 1983 $35

LAWRENCE, DAVID HERBERT   Triumph of the Machine. London, Faber (1931). First edition. Color illus. by Althea Willoughby. Green pictorial wraps. Houle 21-527 1983 $30

LAWRENCE, DAVID HERBERT   Twilight in Italy. London, 1916. Advance copy, with publisher's stamp on title page, "To be published on 1st June, 1916." Covers faded, some foxing, and rubbing around spine, but very good. Bookplate. Gekoski 2-108 1983 £110

LAWRENCE, DAVID HERBERT   Twilight in Italy. N.Y.: B.W. Huebsch, 1916. First American edition. Orig. cloth. Tissue wrappers. Bound from the English sheets. Mint. MacManus 279-3166 1983 $150

LAWRENCE, DAVID HERBERT   Twilight in Italy. NY, 1916. Near fine. Quill & Brush 54-781 1983 $75

LAWRENCE, DAVID HERBERT   Virgin and the Gipsy. Florence, Orioli, 1930. First edition. White boards, paper label, uncut. One of 810 copies. Houle 21-528 1983 $295

LAWRENCE, DAVID HERBERT   The Virgin and The Gipsy. Florence: G. Orioli, 1930. First edition. Orig. white boards with paper label on spine. Dust jacket (slightly faded). Limited to 810 copies. Bookplate. Near-fine. MacManus 279-3167 1983 $200

LAWRENCE, DAVID HERBERT   The Virgin and the Gipsy. Florence: G. Orioli, 1930. Boards, paper label. First edition. One of 810 numbered copies. Corners are badly bruised, otherwise a fine copy, in slightly chipped and mended dust jacket. Reese 20-1208 1983 $125

LAWRENCE, DAVID HERBERT   The Virgin and the Gipsy. London: Martin Secker, (1930). First English edition. Orig. cloth. Very good. MacManus 279-3168 1983 $25

LAWRENCE, DAVID HERBERT   We Need One Another. New York: Equinox, 1933. First separate edition. Illus. with drawings by John P. Heins. 8vo. Orig. cloth. Dust jacket. Fine copy. Jaffe 1-220 1983 $75

LAWRENCE, DAVID HERBERT   When I Went to the Circus. N.P.: Cecily Dunham, 1979. Small folio, paper wrappers, cloth portfolio. 5 separate etchings. One of 15 copies. The book and each plate are signed and numbered by the artist. Printed on Rives paper with the five separate etchings and a sixth on the title page colored by the pochoir method. Oak Knoll 49-262 1983 $300

LAWRENCE, DAVID HERBERT   The Widowing of Mrs. Holroyd. London, 1914. Some fading of the spine, dustwrapper browned on spine, with some small chips at top and bottom and a 1 1/2" tear at top front edge. An advance copy: publishers stamp on title page reads "To be published 17th April, 1914". Gekoski 2-107 1983 £110

LAWRENCE, DAVID HERBERT   The Widowing of Mys. Holroyd. NY, 1914. Edges very slightly rubbed, else near fine. Quill & Brush 54-780 1983 $100

LAWRENCE, DAVID HERBERT   Woman who Rode Away. London, Secker, (1928). First edition. Dust jacket (short tear, a little soiled), else fine. Houle 21-529 1983 $185

LAWRENCE, DAVID HERBERT   The Woman Who Rode Away and other stories. London: Martin Secker, (1928). First edition. 8vo, orig. cloth, dust jacket. Slightly worn jacket, but fine copy. Jaffe 1-211 1983 $185

LAWRENCE, DAVID HERBERT   Women on Love. NY, 1920. Limited to 1250 copies, new endpaper, few page edges chipped, cover rubbed, good. Quill & Brush 54-782 1983 $75

LAWRENCE, FRIEDA   Not I, but the Wind... Santa Fe: Privately printed by the Rydal Press, (1934). Cloth and boards, paper label. First edition. One of 1,000 copies, signed by the author. Very fine copy (corners unbruised), in slightly used dust jacket. Reese 20-845 1983 $200

LAWRENCE, FRIEDA   Not I But the Wind. N.Y., Viking, 1934. First trade edition. Illus. Dust jacket (back faded), very good-fine. Houle 21-537 1983 $50

LAWRENCE, FRIEDA   "Not I, but the Wind..." New York: The Viking Press, 1934. Cloth and boards. First trade edition. A very good copy, with a large bookplate signed by Frieda inserted. Reese 20-1215 1983 $25

LAWRENCE, GEORGE ALFRED   Anteros, A Novel. London: Chapman & Hall, 1871. First edition. 3 vols. Orig. brown decorated cloth. Presentation copy from the publisher with the Chapman & Hall small blindstamp on the title-page of vol. one. Spines and covers slightly worn and soiled. Good. MacManus 279-3173 1983 $275

LAWRENCE, GEORGE ALFRED   Barren Honour. London: Parker, Son, & Bourn, 1862. First eidtion. 2 vols. Orig. cloth. Rubbed. Good. MacManus 279-3174 1983 $125

LAWRENCE, GEORGE ALFRED .   Barren Honour. Parker, Son & Bourn, 1862. First edition, 2 vols. 2 pp ads. in both vols. Half red morocco. Very good. Jarndyce 30-451 1983 £45

LAWRENCE, GEORGE ALFRED   A Bundle of Ballads. London: Tinsley, 1864. First edition. Orig. cloth. Very good. MacManus 279-3175 1983 $75

LAWRENCE, GEORGE ALFRED   Guy Livingstone; or, 'Thorough.' London: John W. Parker, 1857. First edition. Orig. cloth. Covers a little worn and soiled. Rear inner hinge starting. Bookplate of Douglas C. Ewing. MacManus 279-3176 1983 $250

LAWRENCE, GEORGE ALFRED   Sans Merci; or, Kestrels and Falcons. London: Tinsley Brothers, 1866. First edition. 3 vols. Orig. blue cloth. Bookplates (library labels?) neatly removed from front paste-downs. Near-fine. MacManus 279-3177 1983 $450

LAWRENCE, GEORGE ALFRED   Silverland... London, 1873. Orig. cloth. First edition. Ginsberg 47-126 1983 $75

LAWRENCE, H. M. L.   Adventures of an Officer in the Punjaub. London, 1846. Second edition. 2 vols. 2 frontis. 8vo. Orig. cloth. Good. Edwards 1044-423 1983 £95

LAWRENCE, JAMES   An Account of the Funeral Honours Bestowed on the Remains of Capt. Lawrence and Lieut. Ludlow... Boston: Joshua Belcher, 1813. Stitched. Very good. Felcone 20-87 1983 $25

LAWRENCE, ROASMUND   Indian Embers. Oxford, (1949). Plates. Pictorial dust wrapper and pictorial endpapers, by author. 8vo. Orig. cloth. Good. Edwards 1044-425 1983 £15

LAWRENCE, THOMAS EDWARD   A Brief Record of the Advance of the Egyptian Expeditionary Force. Cairo: Palestine News, 1919. First edition. 4to. Orig. wrappers. Working copy only. Rota 231-371 1983 £55

LAWRENCE, THOMAS EDWARD   The Letters of... London: (1938). First edition. Illus., including 4 maps. Tan cloth. Fine in dust jacket. Bradley 66-223 1983 $50

LAWRENCE, THOMAS EDWARD   The Letters of ... London, 1938. Maps and plates. Thick 8vo. Spines slightly sunned. Orig. cloth. Good. Edwards 1044-427 1983 £25

LAWRENCE, THOMAS EDWARD   The Letters of T. E. Lawrence. London, 1938. First edition. Illus. Torn dust wrapper. Very nice. Rota 230-350 1983 £15

LAWRENCE, THOMAS EDWARD   The Mint. London: Jonathan Cape, (1955). First edition. One of 2,000. Half blue morocco and cloth. In original slipcase. Bradley 65-114 1983 $110

LAWRENCE, THOMAS EDWARD   Revolt in the Desert. N.Y.: George H. Doran Co., 1927. First American edition. Large 4to. Illus. with color plates. Orig. blue buckram with morocco label on spine. One of 250 large-paper copies. Label on spine a trifle worn. Very fine. MacManus 279-3179 1983 $350

LAWRENCE, THOMAS EDWARD   Revolt in the Desert. London: Jonathan Cape, 1927. First trade edition. Illus. Orig. cloth. Bookplate. Very good. MacManus 279-3178 1983 $35

LAWRENCE, THOMAS EDWARD   Secret Dispatches from Arabia. (N.p.): Golden Cockerel Press, (1939). Quarto. Full white pigskin, gilt, by Sangorski & Sutcliffe. Portrait. First edition. One of 30 numbered copies, specially bound, and with a facs. of several pages of the manuscript of Seven Pillars bound in. Laid in is a typed letter from the press. Spine very slightly darkened, otherwise fine in slightly soiled slipcase. Reese 20-606 1983 $1,250

LAWRENCE, THOMAS EDWARD   Seven Pillars of Wisdom. London, 1935. Thick quarto, 3/4 russett morocco, cockerell sides and endleaves, gilt decorated spine with two black leather lettering pieces, illus., folding map, enclosed in cloth slipcase. First edition. Duschnes 240-133 1983 $150

LAWRENCE, THOMAS EDWARD   Seven Pillars of Wisdom, London, Jonathan Cape, n.d. (1935). Large 4to, orig. cloth gilt, somewhat shaken, trifle worn, little faded, scratch on cover, name on end-paper, uncut copy of the first (trade) edition. Ravenstree 97-25 1983 $95

LAWRENCE, THOMAS EDWARD   Seven Pillars of Wisdom, a triumph. London, 1938. 4to. Half orange morocco, panelled spine with green morocco labels, gilt, t.e.g. 46 full-page portraits and views, 4 folding maps, and other illus. Traylen 94-515 1983 £48

LAWRENCE, THOMAS EDWARD   Seven Pillars of Wisdom. New York: Doubleday, 1935. 1st American trade ed. Orig. cloth, gilt. Fine copy in very good dj. Jenkins 155-777 1983 $45

LAWRENCE, THOMAS EDWARD   Seven Pillars of Wisdom. N.Y.: Double-day, 1935. First American trade edition. 4to. Orig. cloth. Dust jacket, (worn; wrinkled). Very good. MacManus 279-3180 1983 $35

LAWRENCE, THOMAS EDWARD   Seven Pillars of Wisdom. London, 1935. 4 folding maps. Numerous plates. Roy.8vo. Orig. cloth. Good. Edwards 1044-426 1983 £25

LAWRENCE, THOMAS EDWARD   T. E. Lawrence to His Biographer, Robert Graves (and) T. E. Lawrence to His Biographer, Liddell Hart. New York, 1938. First editions. One of 500 sets for America. The Graves volume is signed by Graves and the Liddell Hart volume by Liddell Hart. 2 vols., buckram, each with frontispiece. Fine in dust jackets. Boxed. Bradley 65-115 1983 $235

LAWRENCE, W. R.   The India We Served. London, 1928. Fore-edge spotted. 8vo. Orig. cloth. Good. Edwards 1044-428 1983 £15

LAWRENCE, WILLIAM   Album of Coloured Photographic Views of Dublin. Dublin: Published by William Lawrence Photographer, circa 1895. Title-page, 18 coloured views on 12 plates and leaf of letter-press, oblong, 4to, orig. green cloth, gilt. Fenning 60-241 1983 £35

LAWRENCE, WILLIAM   The Life of Gustavus Vaughan Brooke, Tragedian. Belfast: W. & G. Baird, 1892. First edition, with portrait, roy. 8vo, orig. cloth, t.e.g., the preliminaries very lightly foxed, otherwise a very good copy. Ltd. edition of 500 numbered copies, signed by the author. Fenning 60-242 1983 £28.50

LAWSON, C.   Memories of Madras. London, 1905. Map, plates. Arms of the East India Company in gilt on upper cover. 8vo. Orig. cloth. Presentation copy from author to William Foster. Good. Edwards 1044-430 1983 £30

LAWSON, C.   A Private Life of Warren Hastings. London, 1895. 3 photogravure portraits. Numerous other plates. 8vo. Orig. cloth. Good. Edwards 1044-429 1983 £30

LAWSON, JAMES A.   Hymni Usitati Latine Redditi. Kegan Paul, 1883. First edition, small 8vo, orig. parchment, t.e.g., by Burn & Co., with their ticket. A very good copy. Fenning 61-250 1983 £21.50

LAWSON, P.   Synopsis of the Vegetable Products of Scotland. Edinburgh, 1852. Frontispiece, sm. 4to, original cloth, slightly used. Wheldon 160-2126 1983 £20

LAWSON, R.   What I Saw in India... Paisley: J. & R. Parlane, 1889. Folding map. 18 illus. Sm.8vo. Orig. cloth. Good. Edwards 1044-431 1983 £18

LAWSON, ROBERT   Fabulous Flight. Boston, Little, Brown, 1949. First edition. Tall 8vo, illus. by the author. Dust jacket (small nicks), very good. Houle 21-554 1983 $35

LAWSON, ROBERT   Mr. Revere and I. Boston: (1953).
Octavo. First edition. Numerous b&w drawings and silhouette illus.
by Lawson. Presentation copy "E" from special edition limited to 500
copies signed by author/artist, with extra suite of 8 illus. printed
on separate sheets and contained in an envelope. Extremely fine with
slightly faded slip-case. Bromer 25-360 1983 $150

LAWSON, THOMAS   Two Treatises of Thomas Lawson
Deceased. Printed and sold by T. Sowle, 1703. First collected edition,
including the preliminary ad. leaf, 12mo, some light browning but a
very good copy in a slightly later calf, worn but sound. Fenning
62-205 1983 £55

LAWSON, WILLIAM   A New Orchard & Garden, or the Best Way
for Planting. The Cresset Press, 1927. 4to, boards with parchment
spine. No. 217 of an edition of 650. Reproducing the 17th century
woodcuts of the orig. edition. Bickersteth 77-291 1983 £12

LAYARD, A. H.   The Monuments of Nineveh. London, 1849.
100 plates, 6 coloured, elephant folio. Occasional light spotting.
Cont. brown calf, glit. Panelled and diced in gilt. Slightly rubbed
by a strong binding. 8vo. Good. Edwards 1044-782 1983 £150

LAYARD, E. L.   The Birds of South Africa. Cape Town,
1867. Frontispiece, 8vo, original cloth. The rare first edition.
Wheldon 160-790 1983 £85

LAYARD, GEORGE SOAMES   The Life & Letters of Charles Keene.
S. Low, 1892. 1st edn. Frontis., 30 plates & 52 text illus. Maroon
buckram, t.e.g. others uncut (bkstrip & edges of cvrs. much faded,
bookpl. fr. ep., fr. ep. cracking at hinge, some foxing), v.g.
Hodgkins 27-569 1983 £25

LAZARUS, EMMA   The Poems of... Boston & New York:
Houghton, Mifflin, 1889. 2 vols. Limited to 1,012 copies. 1st
ed. Orig. green cloth, gilt. Fine set. Scarce. Jenkins 155-778
1983 $50

LAZZARONI, MICHELE   Filarete, scultore e architetto del
secolo XV. Roma: W. Modes, 1908. 24 plates. 130 illus. Folio.
Vellum wrappers. Dust jacket. Worn. Ars Libri 33-142 1983 $275

LEA, TOM   The Brave Bulls. Boston: Little,
Brown and Company, 1949. First edition. Title page painting and
decorative drawings by the author. 8vo. Orig. decorated cloth.
Dust jacket. Fine copy. Jaffe 1-228 1983 $100

LEA, TOM   The Brave Bulls. Boston: Little,
Brown and Co., 1949. First edition. Color frontis. and some text
illus. Presentation copy, signed by Lea. Cloth worn at the bottom
of the spine. Dust jacket. Karmiole 73-62 1983 $50

LEA, TOM   The Brave Bulls. Boston: Little,
Brown, 1949. 1st ed. Orig. cloth, dj. Fine unfaded copy in very
good dj. Jenkins 155-779 1983 $35

LEA, TOM   The Hands of Bantu. Boston & Toronto:
Little, Brown & Co., (1964). Full brown crushed levant, raised
bands, t.e.g. by Harcourt Bindery. Illus. by the author. First
edition. One of only 100 numbered copies, specially printed on
mouldmade Arches paper, and signed by the author. Accompanied by a
signed and dated print by Lea. Mint in the pub.'s cloth slipcase.
Reese 19-322 1983 $1,850

LEA, TOM   The King Ranch. Boston: Little,
Brown, (1957). 2 vols. 1st ed., 1st printing. Orig. two-tone
cloth. Maps and drawings by Lea. Designed by Hertzog. Fine copy
in the orig. box. Jenkins 155-780 1983 $125

LEA, TOM   The King Ranch. Boston: Little, Brown,
(1957). First edition, first printing. 2 vols. Orig. two-tone cloth.
Maps and drawings by Lea. Designed by Hertzog. Fine copy. Jenkins
155-781 1983 $100

LEA, TOM   The Land of the Mustang. (Austin?).
(Ca. 1967). Small quarto. Full rough calf, stamped in blind.
Plates in color, after paintings by the author. First edition thus.
One of 25 numbered copies, specially bound of which this is copy no.
16. Fine copy. Reese 19-323 1983 $400

LEA, TOM   Peleliu Landing. El Paso: Carl
Hertzog, 1945. Small folio. Orig. herringbone twill Marine
dungaree cloth. A fine copy. First edition, the special deluxe
issue, one of 500 numbered copies, printed in Rogers' Centaur type on
English handmade paper, and signed by the author. Illus. with Lea's
drawings, and with his accompanying text. Inscribed on the colophon
by Carl Hertzog, the designer/printer. Reese 20-831 1983 $2,000

LEA, TOM   Peleliu Landing. El Paso: Carl
Hertzog, 1945. Small folio. Orig. herringbone twill Marine dungaree
cloth. A very fine copy. Special deluxe edition, one of 500
numbered copies, printed in Rogers' Centaur Type on English handmade
paper, and signed by the author. Illus. with Lea's drawings. This
copy inscribed to Lea/Hertzog collectors Dorothy and Cling Josey.
Laid in front is 8pp. supplement from _Life_. Prospectus laid in.
Reese 19-324 1983 $1,250

LEA, TOM   A Picture Gallery: Paintings and
Drawings by Tom Lea, with Text by the Artist. Boston, 1968. 2 vols.,
large folio. Slipcased. Jenkins 151-176 1983 $150

LEA, TOM   A Selection of Paintings and Drawings
from the Nineteen-Sixties. San Antonio, (1969). Illus. Orig.
printed boards, boxed. First edition. Rio Bravo edition of 200
numbered copies specially bound and signed by Tom Lea, Harry Ranson,
Al Lowman and Wm. Witliff. Ginsberg 46-404 1983 $100

LEA, TOM   Tom Lea. San Antonio, (1969). Small
quarto. Cloth and boards. Illus. Mint in slipcase. The "Rio
Braco" edition, ltd. to 200 numbered copies, specially bound, and
signed by Lea, Harry Ransom. Reese 19-326 1903 $125

LEACH, ADONIRAM J.   Early Stories: The Overland Trail,
Animals and Birds That Lived Here... Norfold, Neb., (1916). Illus.
1st ed. Jenkins 153-325 1983 $75

LEACH, FRANK A.   Recollections of a Newspaperman. San
Francisco: Samuel Levinson, 1917. Cloth. Dawson 471-177 1983 $20

LEACH, HENRY   The Happy Golfer. London: Macmillan
and Co., ltd. 1914. Green cloth. Karmiole 76-50 1983 $30

LEACH, MAUD SHIPLEY   Hill 7. Chicago, Privately Printed,
1935. 1st ed. Illus. 8vo, fine, boxed. Morrill 286-701 1983
$25

LEACOCK, STEPHEN   How To Write. London: John Lane The
Bodley Head, 1944. 18 1/2cm. First edition. Red cloth. Very
good. McGahern 53-97 1983 $30

LEACOCK, STEPHEN   Sunshine Sketches of a Little Town. NY,
1922. Small mended tear in half title, cover slightly stained and
rubbed, else very good in worn and soiled, internally mended dustwrapper. Quill & Brush 54-789 1983 $30

LEADBEATER, MARY   Biographical Notices of Members of the
Society of Friends. Printed by Harvey & Darton, 1823. First edition,
12mo, cont. half calf, spine neatly repaired. Fenning 60-243 1983
£38.50

LEADBEATER, MARY   Biographical Notices of Members of the
Society of Friends, who were Resident In Ireland. Printed by Harvey
and Darton, 1823. First ediiton, large 12mo, cont. half calf, very
good. Fenning 62-206 1983 £35

LEADBEATER, MARY   Memoirs and Letters of Richard and
Elizabeth Shackleton Late of Baltimore, Ireland, Compiled by their
Daughter. Charles Gilpin, 1849. 8vo, orig. cloth. Fenning 60-244
1983 £28.50

LEADER, JOHN DANIEL   Mary Queen of Scots in Captivity.
London: George Bell & Sons, 1880. 8vo, 4 portraits, orig. cloth,
faded, inner joints weak. Bickersteth 77-135 1983 £20

THE LEADING Businessmen of Dakota Cities. Minneapolis, 1883. Brittle.
Printed wraps. First edition. Ginsberg 46-220 1983 $125

LEAF, MUNRO   Noodle. N.Y., 1937. First edition.
Oblong 4to. Argosy 714-460 1983 $65

A LEAF from a 15th Century Flemish Book of Hours. San Francisco, 1938. 12mo, decorated boards with linen back. Title page printed in black, red and blue; other initials and paragraph marks in red and blue. Vellum leaf tipped in. One of 120 copies. Orig. prospectus laid in. Duschnes 240-101 1983 $150

A LEAF From the Letters of St. Jerome. London and Los Angeles: Hm. M. Fletcher/Zeitlin & Ver Brugge, 1981. One of 300 copies. Folio. Vellum spine, marbled paper over boards. Plus a folio leaf laid-in. Fine. Oak Knoll 49-264 1983 $250

LEAN, THOMAS   Historical treatment of the improvements made in the duty performed by the steam engines... London: Simpkin, Marshall, 1839. First edition. 8vo. Orig. purple cloth, pink printed paper side-label. Fine copy. Ximenes 63-573 1983 $80

LEAR, EDWARD   Illustrations of the Family of Psittacidae, or Parrots. New York, 1978. Folio, half leather, gilt, 42 coloured plates. A slightly reduced facsimile, accompanied by a 16 page illustrated booklet. Edition limited to 530 copies. Wheldon 160-57 1983 £825

LEAR, EDWARD   Journal of a Landscape Painter in Albania, &c. London: Richard Bently, 1851. 1st ed., 8vo, orig. decorated cloth, spine gilt. Frontis. map; 20 tinted lithographs. Hinges and extremities of spine worn, spot on front cover; internally a very clean copy. Trebizond 18-151 1983 $475

LEAR, EDWARD   Later Letters of Edward Lear. New York: Duffield, 1911. Frontis., plates. 1st American ed. Orig. cloth, gilt. Nice copy. Jenkins 155-782 1983 $20

LEAR, EDWARD   Letters of Edward Lear to Chichester Fortescue...and Frances, Countess Waldegrave. T. Fisher Unwin, 1907. First edition, front. illus. (some in colour), half title. Uncut. Orig. green cloth, t.e.g. Jarndyce 30-1051 1983 £22

LEASKI, J. C.   The Regimental Records of the Royal Scots. Dublin: Alexander Thom & Co. Ltd., 1915. Photogravure portrait frontis. 1 photogravure portrait plate, 14 fine coloured plates (12 of uniform, 2 of colours), 31 other plates and 15 text illus. Thick imp. 8vo. Orig. dark blue calf, very slightly worn and faded. T.e.g., others uncut. Decorative endpapers. Good. Edwards 1042-534 1983 £160

LEATHAM, EDWARD A.   Charmione, a Tale of the Great Athenian Revolution. London: Bradbury and Evans, 1858. First edition. 2 vols. Orig. cloth. Spine and covers a bit soiled. All edges slightly worn. Bookplates. Good. MacManus 279-3183 1983 $225

LEAVITT, SHELDON (1848-?)   Psycho-Therapy. Chicago: Garner-Taylor Press, 1903. Publisher's red cloth, dull, front joint broken. Gach 95-314 1983 $40

LEBERT, H.   Ueber die Pilzkrankheit der Fliegen nebst Bemerkungen uver andere pflanzlich-parasitische Krankheiten der Insekten. (Zurich), 1856. 4to. Orig. wrappers. 3 plates (one partly coloured). Presentation inscription to Prof. Wurz. Gurney JJ-222 1983 £15

LE BLANC, M.   The Engineer & Machinist's Drawing Book. London, Blackie & Son, 1881. Drawings & engravings. Folio, half later morocco. Fine. Morrill 288-97 1983 $95

LEBLANC, M   The Extraordinary Adventures of Arsene Lupin, Gentleman-Burglar. Chicago, Donohue, (1910). Frontispiece. 8vo, pictorial front cover, nice. Morrill 286-618 1983 $20

LE BOSSU, RENE   Treatise of the Epick Poem. London, J. Knapton and H. Clements, 1719. 2 vols., 8vo, cont. sheep, rebacked, joints cracked, early bookplate of William Wynne. Ravenstree 97-27 1983 $210

LEBRET, ANDRE   Observations sur la Cure Radicale de Plusieurs Polypes de la Matrice, de la Gorge et du Nez. Paris, 1749. 6 folding copperplates. Thick 8vo, cont. mottled calf, back gilt. First edition. Argosy 713-334 1983 $175

LEBZELTER, VIKTOR   Rassen und Kulturen in Sudafrika. Leipzig: Karl W. Hiersemann, 1930-1934. 2 vols. 48 plates. 55 text illus. 26 plates. 111 text illus. Folio. Boards. Ars Libri 34-676 1983 $250

LE CARON, HENRI   Twenty-five Years in the Secret Service. Wm. Heinemann, 1892. 3rd edition, tall 8vo, ports. and facs. Orig. green cloth. Jarndyce 30-1053 1983 £10.50

LE CAT, C.-N.   Traite des Sens. Rouen, 1740. 8vo. Old calf, rebacked. 17 plates and 2 vignettes. Title with library stamp and slightly torn; a few minor stains and some foxing. Gurney 90-70 1983 £85

LECLAIR, A.   Les Bolets. Paris, 1968. 8 plain plates, 4to, parchment, 64 coloured plates. Wheldon 160-1851 1983 £41

LECLERC, DANIEL   Histoire de la Medecine... The Hague, 1729. New edition. 4to. Cont. half-calf. 2 plates and folding table. Binding slightly worn. Lacks frontis. Gurney JJ-223 1983 £80

LECLERC, JEAN   The Life of the famous Cardinal-Duke de Richelieu, principal Minister of State of Lewis XIII, King of France and Navarr. London: M. Gillyflower, 1695. 1st ed. in English, 2 vols., 8vo, cont. panelled calf, spines gilt. Frontis. engraved portraits. Minor wear to hinges, but a fine copy. Trebizond 18-203 1983 $200

LECLERC, PAUL   Autour de Toulouse-Lautrec. Paris: Floury, 1921. 8 heliogravure plates. Marbled boards, 1/2 cloth. Orig. wrappers bound in. Presentation copy, inscribed by the author to Ludwig Charrell, with a TLs from the author loosely inserted. Ars Libri 32-673 1983 $100

LE CLERC, SEBASTIAN   Pratique de la Geometrie... Amsterdam: Pierre Mortier, 1691. 12mo. Modern old style calf. Engraved vignette on title, over 80 very fine full page engraved plates. Heath 48-512 1983 £140

LE CLERC, SEBASTIEN   Traite de Geometrie. Paris: J. Jombert, 1690. 8vo. Cont. calf. With engraved frontis., plate and numerous engravings and diagrams in text. Tear in one leaf, slightly affecting text. A few leaves dampstained. Some minor stains and old ink scribbles. Gurney JJ-224 1983 £20

LECLERCQ, JULES   Le Colorado. Paris: Bureaux De La Revue Britannique, 1877. Half morocco. Jenkins 153-132 1983 $125

L'ECLUSE, CHARLES DE   Rariorum Plantarum Historia. Antwerp, 1601. Folio, cont. vellum, engraved title-page and numerous woodcuts. Wheldon 160-17 1983 £1,350

LE COLONIE, JEAN MARTIN DE   The Chronicles of an Old Campaigner J. de la Colonie, 1692-1717. John Murray, 1904. First edition in English. 5 folding maps and 10 plates, 8vo, a little light foxing in places, but a nice copy in half red calf, t.e.g. Fenning 61-238 1983 £12.50

LE COMTE, LOUIS D.   Memoirs and Remarks Geographical, Historical, Topographical, Physical, Natural... Printed by J. Hughes, 1737. With engraved frontis., 2 double-page plates, 1 other plate, a folding table and one text engraving, 8vo, small library stamp in three plates, otherwise a very good copy in calf-backed marbled boards. Fenning 62-207 1983 £75

LE COUTEUR, JOHN   On the varieties, properties and classification of wheat. London: Shearsmith, 1836. 8vo. Orig. blue boards (rebacked in green cloth). Five plates, and a folding table. Endpapers, removed. Uncut. First edition. Ximenes 63-1 1983 $150

A LECTURE Upon Partnership Accounts, with a Chapter Upon Balance. B. Law and J. Wilkie, 1769. Second edition, 16mo, half title, calf, spine rubbed, black label. Jarndyce 31-7 1983 £65

LEE, ARTHUR   An Appeal to the Justice and Interests of the People of Great Britain, in the Present Disputes with America. London: J. Almon, 1776. Disbound. Fourth edition. Felcone 21-66 1983 $150

LEE, CHARLES   Memoirs of the Life of the Late Charles
Lee, Esq. New York, 1793. Leather, rubbed, blank leaves missing.
Fair. Reese 18-184 1983 $50

LEE, CHAUNCEY   The Trial of Virtue, a Sacred Poem...
Hartford: Printed by Lincoln and Gleason, 1806. Orig. calf, first
edition. Some slight browning and chipping of the crown of spine,
else a very good copy. Reese 18-279 1983 $65

LEE, FRANCIS BAZLEY   New Jersey as a Colony and as a State.
NY, 1903. Illus. & Ports. 4 vols., g.t., uncut. Argosy 710-336
1983 $60

LEE, HANNAH FARNHAM   The Huguenots in France and America.
Cambridge, Mass.: John Owen, 1843. First American edition. 2 vols.
Orig. cloth. MacManus 279-3185 1983 $25

LEE, HARRIET   Canterbury Tales. Richard Bentley,
1834. Revised, corrected. 2 vols, sm. 8vo, 19th-cent. half calf,
gilt backs (slightly worn). Frontispieces, additional engraved
titles with vignettes. Hill 165-66 1983 £30

LEE, HENRY   Caleb Quotem and his wife! Or, paint,
poetry, and putty! London: published by John Roach; printed (for
the author) by W. Syle (Barnstaple), n.d. (1809). 8vo, wrappers,
1st edition. Frontispiece. Very scarce. Ximenes 64-347 1983 $125

LEE, HENRY   The Campaign of 1781 in the Carolinas.
Phila., 1824. 1st ed, thick 8vo, pp. uncut, bds., paper label,
backstrip worn. Argosy 710-453 1983 $80

LEE, HENRY   Memoirs of the War in the Southern
Department of the United States. Philadelphia, 1812. Two vols. Orig.
calf, worn, hinges cracked. One signature in facs. Fair, internally
very good. Reese 18-381 1983 $95

LEE, HENRY W.   The Christian Ministry. Davenport,
Ia., 1865. Orig. printed wraps. First edition. Ginsberg 47-370
1983 $50

LEE, HOLME, PSEUD.
Please turn to
PARR, HARRIET

LEE, LAURIE   The Bloom of Candles. Lehmann, 1947.
First edition. Nice. Rota 231-374 1983 £12.50

LEE, LAURIE   The Sun My Monument. London, 1944.
First edition. Small tear in margin of flyleaf repaired. Dust
wrapper. Very nice. Rota 231-373 1983 £15

LEE, LAURIE   The Sun My Monument: Poems. New
York, 1947. 8vo. Cloth. Fine in dj. Review copy with slip laid
in. In Our Time 156-496 1983 $25

LEE, LAURIE   The Voyage of Magellan. London, 1948.
First edition. Presentation copy from the author. Numerous drawings
by Edward Burra. Slightly soiled and torn dustwrapper missing a very
small piece at the head of the spine. Very good. Jolliffe 26-316
1983 £16

LEE, ROBERT E.   Recollections and Letters of...
New York, 1905. First edition. 8vo. Orig. grey decorated cloth.
Photogravure portrait frontis. 3 photogravure portrait plates.
Slightly stained and faded. Good. Edwards 1042-224 1983 £25

LEE, SAMUEL   The Joy of Faith. Boston, Samuel Green,
1687. 8vo, cont. sheep rebacked preserving old spine, name on title,
orig. blank endpapers covered with early names and dates. The
front and back pastedowns covering orig. wooden boards are from the
first edition of Cotton Mather's Decennium Luctuosum, Boston, 1699.
First edition. Ravenstree 97-28 1983 $2,300

LEE, SIDNEY   A Life of William Shakespeare. N.Y.:
The Macmillan Co., 1909. "New and Revised edition." Illus. with many
port. and scenes, including actors and actresses, writers, and other
personnages from the 16th through the 19th centuries. 3/4 morocco with
cloth endpapers. Edges slightly rubbed. Bookplate. Very good.
MacManus 280-4651 1983 $250

LEE, SOPHIA   The Recess; Or, A Tale of Other Times.
Dublin: Printed for G. Burnet, P. Byrne (etc), 1791. 2 vols, cont.
tree sheep, red and green labels. Hill 165-67 1983 £65

LEE, THOMAS   Election Clubs, late Riot at Bristol
on the day of Election... Bristol: by George Routh..., (1807).
Third edition. 8vo. Uncut, stitched as issued. Heath 48-134
1983 £45

LEE, VERNON, PSEUD.
Please turn to
PAGET, VIOLET

LEE-HAMILTON, EUGENE J.   Sonnets of the Wingless Hours.
Elliot Stock, 1894. First edition, small 8vo, orig. paper boards,
with printed paper spine label, wanting small portion of backstrip,
otherwise nice. Fenning 61-251 1983 £24.50

LEECH, ARTHUR B.   Irish Riflemen in America. London,
1875. Illus., 11 plates, 7 colored insignias, woodcuts in text,
folded map. Orig. gold stamped cloth. First edition. Ginsberg 46-
405 1983 $75

LEECH, JOHN   The Comic Latin Grammar. London:
Charles Tilt, 1840. First edition. Numerous illus. Orig. cloth.
With two bookplates (one armorial) and a bookseller's ticket on the
front endpapers. Covers slightly soiled. Corners a bit worn. Good.
MacManus 279-3199 1983 $125

LEECH, JOHN   Pictures of Life and Character. N.Y.:
D. Appleton & Co., 1884. First edition. Illus. Small 8vo. Orig.
printed wrappers. Dust-soiled. MacManus 279-3200 1983 $20

LEECH, JOHN   Portraits of Children of the Mobility.
R. Bentley, 1875. 1st edn. thus, with frontis. portrait of artist &
letter from John Ruskin & 6 full page drawings. Facsimile hand written
text. Dark olive green cloth with gilt vignette & titling by Leech.
pp.34 printed on one side only, eps. foxed & discol'd, vg. Hodgkins
27-295 1983 £17.50

LEECH, SAMUEL   Thirty Years from Home, or a Voice from
the Main Deck. Boston: Charles Tappan, 1844. 2nd ed., 12mo. orig.
cloth, spine gilt. Frontis. and 3 other engravings. A good copy.
Trebizond 18-152 1983 $50

LEEMANN-VAN ELCK, P.   Salomon Gessner. Sein Lebesbild...
Zurich/Leipzig: Orell Fussli, 1930. 16 plates. Prof. illus.
Large 4to. Wrappers. Dust jacket. Edition limited to 650 copies.
Ars Libri 32-255 1983 $175

LEEPER, DAVID R.   The Argonauts of 'Forty-Nine. South
Bend, Ind., 1894. Illus. Orig. cloth. First edition. Ginsberg
46-107 1983 $75

LEEPER, DAVID R   The Argonauts of 'Forty-Nine. South
Bend, Ind.: 1894. First edition. Illus. Orig. brown cloth.
Tipped-in errata slip. Light wear and trivial cover stain. Bradley
66-579 1983 $75

LEEPER, JANET   Edward Gordon Craig, Designs for the
Theatre. London: Penquin Books. (1948). First edition. Illus.
Orig. decorated boards. Contains a chronology of the designer written
by himself. Spine and covers slightly faded, rubbed, and worn at the
margins. Good. MacManus 277-1162 1983 $25

LEERS, J. D.   Flora Herbornensis. Berlin, 1789.
16 plates, 8vo, contemporary calf, neatly rebacked. Wheldon 160-
1735 1983 £35

LEES, JOHN   Journal of J.L., of Quebec, Merchant.
Detroit, 1911. 1st ed. Folding map. 8vo. Nice. Morrill 289-621
1983 $25

LE FANU, JOSEPH SHERIDAN   The Evil Guest. London: Downey, (1895).
First separate edition. Illus. by B. Le Fanu. Orig. decorated cloth.
Extremities of spine worn. Inner hinges cracked. MacManus 279-3202
1983 $175

LE FANU, JOSEPH SHERIDAN   The Fortunes of Colonel Torlogh O'Brien. Dublin: James McGlashan, 1847. First book edition, first binding in the blue variant. Illus. by H.K. Browne. Orig. cloth. Cont. owner's signature on front free endpaper. Inner hinges a little weak. Fine. MacManus 279-3203 1983 $450

LE FANU, JOSEPH SHERIDAN   Ghost Stories and Tales of Mystery. Dublin, McClashin, 1851. First edition. Small 8vo, title and half title printed in red and blue. Frontis. and three engraved plates by "Phiz." 3/4 green morocco over marbled boards, spine decorated in gilt with raised bands, covers ruled in gilt, a.e.g., marbled endpapers (minor rubbing). Cloth slipcase. Very good. Houle 22-582 1983 $395

LF FANU, JOSEPH SHERIDAN   Ghost Stories and Tales of Mystery. Dublin: James McGlashan, 1851. Illus. by Phiz. Half title and title printed in red and blue. Orig. red cloth, rubbed, rebacked, a.e.g. First edition. Jarndyce 31-778 1983 £18.50

LE FANU, JOSEPH SHERIDAN   Green Tea and Other Ghost Stories. Sauk City, Wisconsin: Arkham House, 1945. First edition. Orig. cloth. Spine dull; a little soiled. MacManus 279-3204 1983 $50

LE FANU, JOSEPH SHERIDAN   Guy Deverell. London: Richard Bentley, 1865. First edition. 3 vols. Orig. carmine sand-grain cloth. Spines and covers slightly worn and a trifle darkened. Very good. MacManus 279-3205 1983 $1,250

LE FANU, JOSEPH SHERIDAN   The House by the Church-Yard. Richard Bentley, 1897. 4pp ads. Orig. black cloth, sl. rubbed; Payn's Library, Jersey. Labels on front. cover and end paper. Jarndyce 31-789 1983 £18.50

LE FANU, JOSEPH SHERIDAN   Uncle Silas. Richard Bentley, 1865. First one-volume edition. Half title, front. & vignette title. Orig. green cloth blocked in blind, spine gilt lettered. Jarndyce 31-779 1983 £80

LE FANU, JOSEPH SHERIDAN   Uncle Silas. L, (1947). Bright near fine in frayed and lightly stained, very good dustwrapper. Quill & Brush 54-786 1983 $25

LE FANU, WILLIAM   A Bio-Bibliography of Edward Jenner, 1749-1823. London, 1950. 8vo. Orig. binding. Limited to 1000 copies. Fye H-3-1060 1983 $60

LEFEBURE, VICTORE   The Riddle of the Rhine. W. Collins, 1921. With 5 plates, 8vo, orig. cloth, a very good copy. Fenning 60-245 1983 £10.50

LEFEVRE, G. SHAW   Irish Members and English Gaolers. Kegan Paul, Trench, 1889. First edition, orig. pink cloth. Jarndyce 31-198 1983 £20

LEFEVRE, GEORGE (1798-1846)   An Apology for the Nerves. London: Longman, Brown, Green and Longmans, 1844. Inserted ads. Publisher's embossed brown cloth, front joint broken, spine chipped, library spine labels. First edition. John Ordronaux's copy, signed on flyleaf. Gach 95-315 1983 $50

LEFEVRE, THEOTISTE   Guide Pratique du Compositeur. Paris: Librairie de Firmin Didot Freres, 1855. First edition. 8vo. Cont. half leather over marbled paper covered boards. 26 wood engr. Some foxing. Covers show wear especially at spine extremities. Oak Knoll 48-247 1983 $75

LEFFINGWELL, ALBERT   An Ethical Problem or Sidelights upon Scientific Experimentation... New York, 1916. Second edition. 8vo. Orig. binding. Inscribed and autographed by the author's wife. Fye H-3-336 1983 $25

LEFFINGWELL, WILLIAM BRUCE   Wild Fowl Shooting. Chicago, 1888. 1st ed. Illus, gilt-pict. cloth, ink inscription, minor staining, spine ends frayed, rubbed. King 46-607 1983 $45

LE GAL, EUGENE   School of the Guides. New York, Van Nostrand, 1862. Illus. 16mo, orig. cloth wrappers. Morrill 287-187 1983 $25

LEGAL protection of dogs from the increasing evil of dog stealers and receivers. London: printed for the author, 1845. First edition. 8vo. Orig. dark green cloth. Very fine copy. Ximenes 63-80 1983 $60

LE GALLIENNE, RICHARD   The Book-Bills of Narcissus. London: John Lane, Vigo St. New York: G.P. Putnam's Sons, 1895. First edition. Frontispiece by R. Fowler. Orig. cloth. Inscribed on the half-title "O mes lettres, j'amour, de vertu, de jeunesse! Richard Le Gallienne." In a half-morocco slipcase. Near-fine. MacManus 279-3209 1983 $135

LE GALLIENNE, RICHARD   The Book-Bills of Narcissus. Derby, Leicester & Nottingham: Frank Murray, 1891. First edition. Orig. printed wrappers. One of 100 large-paper copies. Bookplate. Extremities of spine a bit rubbed. Wrappers a bit dust-soiled. Very good. MacManus 279-3208 1983 $100

LE GALLIENNE, RICHARD   English Poems. London: Elkin Mathews & John Lane,...1892. First edition. Orig. boards with paper label on spine. Limited to 800 copies printed. Presentation copy, inscribed with a verse by Le Gallienne on the half-title, dated June '97. Book-plates of Dodge and Francis Kettaneh on the front endsheet. Book-seller's catalogue entry for this book pasted to front free endpaper. Front inner hinge strained. Very good. MacManus 279-3212 1983 $225

LE GALLIENNE, RICHARD   English Poems. London: Elkin Mathews & John Lane at the Bodley Head, 1892. First edition. Orig. boards with paper label on spine. One of 800 copies. Presentation copy inscribed to Charles Strachey. Bookplate of Francis Kettaneh. Edges rather worn. Binding a bit soiled. MacManus 279-3211 1983 $135

LE GALLIENNE, RICHARD   English Poems. London: Elkin Mathews & John Lane at the Bodley Head, 1892. First edition. Orig. boards. Paper label on spine. One of 150 copies on large paper. Signed by author. Bookplate of Francis Kettaneh. Endpapers slightly browned. Binding rather soiled. MacManus 279-3210 1983 $75

LE GALLIENNE, RICHARD   English Poems. London: John Lane; Boston: Copeland & Day, 1895. Fourth (first revised) edition. Orig. cloth. First edition published jointly by Lane and Copeland & Day. MacManus 279-3213 1983 $25

LE GALLIENNE, RICHARD   George Meredith. London: Elkin Mathews, 1890. First edition. Large 8vo. Rebound in half brown morocco and marbled boards. Marbled endpapers, t.e.g. One of 75 large-paper copies printed on hand-made paper and signed by author. John Lane's copy, with his editorial corrections to the text and with his revisions to his bibliography of Meredith on interleaved sheets bound in at the back. Edges a bit rubbed. Bookplate. Fine. MacManus 279-3216 1983 $750

LE GALLIENNE, RICHARD   A Jongleur Strayed. Garden City: Doubleday, Page & Co., 1922. First edition. Orig. cloth-backed boards, paper label on front covers. Presentation copy inscribed: "To Mary and Will - with the love of Irma & Richard. New Year, 1923." Bookplate of Francis Kettaneh. Edges a bit worn. Covers slightly soiled. Spine dull. MacManus 279-3218 1983 $85

LE GALLIENNE, RICHARD   Limited Editions. London: Privately printed for Richard Le Gallienne, Elkin Mathews, John Lane, and Their Friends: Christmas, 1893. First edition. Orig. wrappers. Presenta-tion copy, inscribed "To Philip Moeller, true lover of books, in rem-embrance of, I fear, a public attempt to make a Paterian of our friend Herts--From Richard Le Gallienne, A May Day, 1911." Wrappers repaired at spine. Outer edges somewhat frayed. MacManus 279-3219 1983 $125

LE GALLIENNE, RICHARD   Little Dinners with the Sphinx. London: John Lane, 1909. First edition. Orig. cloth. Covers a little soiled. MacManus 279-3220 1983 $20

LE GALLIENNE, RICHARD   The Lonely Dancer and Other Poems. Lon-don: John Lane, et al 1914. First edition. Frontispiece port. by Irma Le Gallienne. Orig. cloth. Presentation copy, inscribed on the front free endpaper with a verse by Le Gallienne to 'Jack' McMartin, dated April, 1914. Frontispiece detached. Extremities of spine rubbed. Good. MacManus 279-3221 1983 $185

LE GALLIENNE, RICHARD   The Lonely Dancer and Other Poems. London: John Lane, 1914. First edition. Illus. with a frontispiece port. by Irma Le Gallienne. Near-fine. MacManus 279-3222 1983 $25

LE GALLIENNE, RICHARD   My Ladies' Sonnets. (Liverpool):
Privately printed, 1887. First edition. Orig. parchment-backed boards.
Presentation copy, in pencil to Mrs. Jameson, dated Sept. 20th, 1987.
Bookplate of Francis Kettaneh. Covers a bit soiled. Edges of spine
cracked. MacManus 279-3223 1983 $450

LE GALLIENNE, RICHARD   New Poems. London: John Lane, 1910.
Second edition. Orig. cloth. Presentation copy, inscribed on the
half-title "To Edward J. Wheeler, Friend of Poets, & the particular
good friend of one lonely muse, with the warm regard of Richard Le
Gallienne, Christmas, 1911." Spine slightly faded. Fine. MacManus
279-3224 1983 $135

LE GALLIENNE, RICHARD   Odes from the Divan of Hafiz. N.Y.:
Privately Printed, 1903. First edition. Orig. vellum-backed boards.
One of 35 copies on Japan vellum. Signed by author. With the book-
plate of Francis Kettaneh. Covers slightly soiled. Very good. Mac-
Manus 279-3225 1983 $450

LE GALLIENNE, RICHARD   Odes from the Divan of Hafiz. N.Y.:
Privately printed, 1903. First edition. 3/4 red morocco, with red
cloth endpapers. One of 300 copies. Signed by author. With the orig.
manuscript (2 pages) of Ode 16 tipped in. Bookplate of Francis
Kettaneh. Fine. MacManus 279-3226 1983 $300

LE GALLIENNE, RICHARD   An Old Country House. N.Y.: Harper &
Brothers, 1902. First edition. 3/4 brown morocco with chocolate-
colored cloth endpapers. Presentation copy inscribed to Mrs. Winship,
dated, December, 1902. Bookplate of Francis Kettaneh. Spine edges
rather rubbed. Small spot on front cover. Very good. MacManus 279-
3227 1983 $135

LE GALLIENNE, RICHARD   Omar Repentant. London: Grant Richards,
1908. First English (?) edition. Orig. vellum-covered boards. Bookplate of Francis Kettaneh. Binding rather rubbed ans soiled. Good.
MacManus 279-3228 1983 $25

LE GALLIENNE, RICHARD   Omar Repentant. London, 1908. First
English edition. Oblong 8vo. Full parchment (darkened and a little
marked, particularly on lower cover). Name on flyleaf. Very nice.
Rota 231-376 1983 £15

LE GALLIENNE, RICHARD   Painted Shadows. Boston: Little, Brown,
& Co., 1904. Orig. decorated cloth. First edition. Very good.
MacManus 279-3229 1983 $45

LE GALLIENNE, RICHARD   The Philosophy of Limited Editions.
(Weston, Conn., 1933). Thin 8vo, full blue leather. Ltd. edition.
One of only 100 copies for the friends of Helen & George Macy, hand
set with a new Goudy typeface. Argosy 714-463 1983 $60

LE GALLIENNE, RICHARD   Prose Fancies. London: Mathews & John
Lane, 1894. First edition. Orig. boards with paper label on spine.
One of 100 copies on hand-made paper. Signed by author. Bookplate of
Francis Kettaneh. Endpapers rather browned. Covers a bit soiled.
Good. MacManus 279-3230 1983 $125

LE GALLIENNE, RICHARD   Prose Fancies. Chicago: Herbert S.
Tone, 1896. First American edition. Orig. decorated cloth. Binding
designed by F. Hazenplug. Very good. MacManus 279-3232 1983 $55

LE GALLIENNE, RICHARD   Prose Fancies. London: Elkin Mathews &
John Lane, 1894. First edition. Orig. cloth. Signed by author. News-
clipping tipped in at the back. Covers somewhat worn. Good. MacManus
279-3231 1983 $45

LE GALLIENNE, RICHARD   Prose Fancies. London, John Lane, 1896.
8vo, orig. cloth gilt, little faded and soiled; uncut copy of the
first edition, and mainly unopened. Ravenstree 96-34 1983 $25

LE GALLIENNE, RICHARD   The Religion of a Literary Man. London:
Elkin Mathews & John Lane,...1893. First edition. Orig. cloth. One
of 250 large-paper copies printed on hand-made paper. Fine. MacManus
279-3236 1983 $50

LE GALLIENNE, RICHARD   The Religion of a Literary Man. N.Y.:
G.P. Putnam's Sons...1895. First edition. Orig. cloth. Inscribed
with a quotation by author on the front free endpaper:\"'This was thy
only task, to learn that man is small, and not forget that man is
great.' Richard Le Gallienne." Extremities of spine worn. Good.
MacManus 279-3234 1983 $45

LE GALLIENNE, RICHARD   The Religion of A Literary Man. London:
Elkin Mathews and John Lane, 1893. First edition. Orig. cloth. Small
bookplate. Very good. MacManus 279-3235 1983 $25

LE GALLIENNE, RICHARD   Retrospective Reviews. London: Bodley
Head, 1896. First edition. 2 vols. Orig. cloth. Covers a bit
stained. MacManus 279-3237 1983 $35

LE GALLIENNE, RICHARD   Retrospective Reviews: A Literary Log.
London, 1896. First edition. 2 vols. Covers a little marked. Bookplate in Vol. I. Nice. Rota 231-375 1983 £15

LE GALLIENNE, RICHARD   Robert Louis Stevenson. London: John
Lane, 1895. First edition. Etched title-page by D.Y. Cameron. Orig.
cloth. MacManus 279-3238 1983 $30

LE GALLIENNE, RICHARD   The Romance of Perfume. N.Y. & Paris:
R. Hudnut, 1928. Colour title vignette & 8 colour plates. White pictorial boards, tissue wrappers. At end in pocket a 10 pp. booklet with
4 colour plates about the publishers and a letter from the publishers.
Fine. Greer 40-40 1983 £45

LE GALLIENNE, RICHARD   The Romantic '90s. London, 1926. First
English edition. Frontis. by M. Beerbohm. Spine darkened. Very nice.
Rota 230-355 1983 £25

LE GALLIENNE, RICHARD   Sleeping Beauty and Other Prose Fancies.
London: John Lane, 1900. First edition. Orig. cloth. Very good.
MacManus 279-3240 1983 $22.50

LE GALLIENNE, RICHARD   Volumes in Folio. London: C. Elkin
Mathews, 1889. First edition. Orig. parchment-backed boards with
paper label on spine. Limited to 250 copies printed. Presentation
copy, inscribed on the front free endpaper "To Rogers Rees, with warm
regard, from his friend, Richard Le Gallienne, 12.3.'89." With
Le Gallienne's bookplate on the front endsheet. Spine darkened.
Spine label chipped. Very good. MacManus 279-3242 1983 $350

LE GALLIENNE, RICHARD   War. N.Y.: Press of the Woolly Whale,
1929. First edition. Orig. cloth-backed boards and glassine jacket
(a bit frayed). One of 50 copies. With an ALS by Le Gallienne, dated
April 28th, 1930, to Milbert Cary, the printer of "War" (3 pages).
Near-fine. MacManus 279-3243 1983 $350

LE GALLIENNE, RICHARD   The Worshipper of the Image. London,
John Lane, 1900. 8vo, orig. cloth gilt, little faded and soiled;
uncut copy of the first edition, and mainly unopened. Ravenstree 96-
35 1983 $25

LE GALLIENNE, RICHARD   Young Lives. N.Y. & London: John Lane,
The Bodley Head, 1899. First American edition. Orig. decorated cloth
designed by Will Bradley. Spine somewhat darkened. Very good.
MacManus 279-3244 1983 $75

THE LEGEND of Mary, Queen of Scots, and Other Ancient Poems.
Printed for Longman, Hurst, Rees, and Orme, 1810. 8vo, leaf with
subscribers' names, leaf with errata, a.e.g., 19th century red morocco
gilt, spine gilt, gilt dentelles, by Kerr and Richardson, Glasgow.
First edition. Bickersteth 77-136 1983 £35

LEGENDARY Ballads. Chatto, 1908. 1st edn. Col'd frontis. & 9 col'd
plates, b&w illus. by Byam Shaw. Red cloth, gilt vignette fr. cvr.,
t.e.g. others uncut (pp.35/37 sl. damage at foreedge due to binding
fault), nice copy. Hodgkins 27-472 1983 £15

LEGER, CHARLES   Courbet. Paris: G. Cres, 1929. 64
heliogravure plates. 61 plates in text. 4to. Marbled boards, 3/4
leather. Orig. wrappers bound in. Binding slightly rubbed. Ars
Libri 32-124 1983 $100

LEGER, JACQUES NICOLAS   Haiti, Her History and Her Detractors.
New York & Washington, Neale, 1907. 1st ed. Illus. 8vo. Morrill
287-188 1983 $35

LEGGE, ARTHUR E. J.   Land And Sea Pieces: Poems. London:
John Lane, The Bodley Head, 1904. First edition. Orig. cloth. Fine.
MacManus 279-3246 1983 $20

LEGGE, ARTHUR E. J.   The Silver Age. London: John Lane, The
Bodley Head, N.Y., John Land Co., 1911. First edition. Orig. cloth.
Dust jacket (bottom of spine chipped, dusty, torn in half). Fine.
MacManus 279-3247 1983 $20

LEGH, THOMAS   Narrative of a Journey in Egypt and the
Country beyond the Cataracts. London: John Murray, 1817. 2nd ed.,
but the 1st illus. ed., 8vo, cont. half calf, gilt, marbled boards.
Folding map; eleven uncolored aquatints. Half-title. Light foxing
and soiling of some leaves, but with plates in very fine condition;
a very good copy of a scarce title. Trebizond 18-140 1983 $285

LEGISLATIVE Blue Book of Arizona. N.p.: n.d., (1912-13). Wrappers.
A little soiled and chipped. Spine repaired with tape. Dawson 471-8
1983 $40

LEGRAIN, DR.   Les Folies a Eclipse. Paris: Librarie
Bloud & Cie, 1910. First edition. Orig. printed wrappers. Library
bookplate and label, else very good. Gach 95-316 1983 $20

LEGRAND, EDY   Petite Histoire de LaFayette. Paris:
Tolmer, n.d. (ca.1930). Oblong 4to. Cloth backed pictorial boards.
Frayed glassine wrapper. Color illus. throughout. Very good.
Aleph-bet 8-160 1983 $30

LE GRAND, JULIA   The Journal of Julia LeGrand, New
Orleans, 1862-1863. Richmond, 1911. 1st ed. Illus. 8vo, nice.
Morrill 286-257 1983 $35

LEGRE, L.   La Botanique en Provence au XVIe Siecle.
Marseille, 1900. 8vo, wrappers. Wheldon 160-246 1983 £15

LEGUAT, FRANCOIS   The voyage of Francois Leguat of Bresse...
London: Hakluyt Soc., 1891. 2 vols. 8vo. 23 plates and maps. Orig.
cloth. Spines darkened, ex-lib. Adelson Africa-203 1983 $30

LE GUIN, URSULA K.   Gwilan's Harp. CA, 1981. Limited to 50
numbered and signed copies, mint in cloth binding. Quill & Brush 54-
788 1983 $75

LEHMANN, C. G.   Lehrbuch der physiologischen Chemie.
Leipzig, 1850-52. Second, revised edition. 8vo. 3 vols. Half-
sheep, slightly rubbed. Gurney JJ-225 1983 £15

LEHMANN, C. G.   Physiological Chemistry... London:
Cavendish Society, 1851-4. 3 vols. 8vo. Orig. cloth. A little
rubbed, paper aged. Otherwise a good set. Zeitlin 264-256 1983
$80

LEHMANN, JOHN   Evil Was Abroad. London: The Cresset
Press, 1938. First English edition. Very good. Very scarce.
Jolliffe 26-318 1983 £35

LEHMANN, LOTTE   My Many Lives. N.Y., Boosey & Hawkes,
(1948). First edition. Halftones. Dust jacket (chips), very good.
Houle 21-694 1983 $20

LEHMANN, ROSAMOND   The Weather in the Streets. London:
Collins, 1936. First edition. Orig. cloth. Dust jacket (a little
rubbed at edges). Occasional foxing. Fine. MacManus 279-3249 1983
$100

LEHR, FRITZ HERBERT   Die Blutezeit romantischer Bildkunst.
Marburg: Kunstgeschichtliches Seminar, 1924. 42 plates with 69
illus., 1 folding facsimile. Frontis. Small 4to. Boards. Ars
Libri 32-512 1983 $85

LEIBER, FRITZ   Night's Black Agents. Sauk City: Arkham House, 1947. First edition. Cloth. Very good in dust jacket.
Bradley 66-125 1983 $75

LEIBIG, JUSTUS   Animal Chemistry... London, 1842.
8vo. Old half-calf. First English edition. Rubbed. Gurney
JJ-234 1983 £25

LEIBOWITZ, ADOLPHE   Japanese Prints and Their Creators.
The Shoreline Press, 1935. 1st ed. Presentation copy. 5 plates.
12mo. Orig. boards, cloth back, paper label. Morrill 289-392 1983
$25

LEIDEN UNIVERSITY   Catalogus rerum memorabilium quae in
theatro anaatomico academiae... Leiden: Diwer vander Boxe, 1721.
Woodcut title vignette. 4to. Boards. Marginalia. Kraus 164-145
1983 $650

LEIDY, JOSEPH   An Elementary Treatise on Human Anatomy.
Phila., 1861. 8vo, sheep; ex-lib. 392 text wood-engrs. First
edition. Argosy 713-329 1983 $85

LEIGH, GERARD   The Accedens of Armory. (Colophon:
Imprynted at London by Rychard Tottel, An. 1568). 4to, old vellum,
without front blank flyleaf, armorial bookplate, joints breaking,
some age-browning and slight fraying (no text touched), few cont. mss.,
and underlining; complete with the rare last leaf with the full-page
woodcut, and with "The way to vnderstande Tryckyng" on the verso.
Ravenstree 97-29 1983 $850

LEIGH, HOWARD   Planes of the Great War. London, 1934.
50 mounted colletype plates, imp. 8vo. Slightly soiled. Decorated
dust jacket (worn). Some slight foxing. Good. Edwards 1042-599
1983 £25

LEIGHTON, CLARE   Four Hedges. A Gardener's Chronicle.
New York, Macmillan, 1935. First American edition, 4to, 86 woodcut
illus., green cloth gilt, small mark on spine, otherwise a fine
presentation copy. Inscribed on half-title: "For Jean Cooke McCurdy
from Clare Leighton. Rochester, November 16 1939". Deighton 3-205
1983 £55

LEIGHTON, CLARE   Growing New Roots. (San Francisco),
1976. First edition. With fourteen wood engravings by the author.
Cloth. One of 500 copies, signed by Leighton. Houle 21-557 1983
$75

LEIGHTON, G. R.   The Life-history of British Lizards.
1903. 32 illus., cr. 8vo, cloth (trifle stained). Wheldon 160-977
1983 £15

LEIGHTON, G. R.   The Life-history of British Serpents.
1901. 50 illus., 8vo, cloth. Wheldon 160-976 1983 £15

LEIGHTON, JOHN   The Life of Man. Longmans, etc., 1866.
Illus. by Leighton, numerous wood engrs., some printed in black & red.
Green morocco gilt, raised bands, a.e.g. marbled eps., corners sl.
bruised, some foxing some pp., some thumbing & cvrs. sl. discol'd,
de luxe binding, vg copy. Hodgkins 27-296 1983 £35

LEIGHTON, JOHN   Madre natura versus the moloch of
fashion. London: Chatto and Windus, 1874. Fourth edition. 8vo.
Orig. grey decorated cloth. With many wood-engraved illus. by the
author. A bit rubbed and soiled. Ximenes 63-111 1983 $25

LEIGHTON, JOHN   Moral Emblems. Longmans, etc., 1865.
3rd edn. Illus. by J.L. Frontis. & numerous wood engrs., red &
black printed title p. Crimson sand grain decor. cloth designed by
J.L., bevelled boards, a.e.g. Top/bottom bkstrip some wear & corners
sl. wear, col'd illuminated insc. fr. ep. cvrs. sl. soiled, vg.
Hodgkins 27-297 1983 £35

LEIRIS, MICHEL   Joan Miro Lithographe. Paris, (1972).
11 colored plates. Cloth. Slightly soiled dust wrapper. Very good.
King 45-613 1983 $150

LEIRIS, MICHEL   The Prints of Joan Miro. New York:
Curt Valentin, 1947. Text fascicle: 6 plates. 42 plates,
loose, as issued (2 in color pochoir, 40 gravure). 4to. Cloth
portfolio. Edition limited to 1500 copies. Ars Libri 32-461 1983
$100

LEIRIS, MICHEL   Wifredo Lam. Milano: Fratelli
Fabbri, 1970. 197 plates (numerous color). Text illus. Large
4to. Cloth. Dust jacket. Slipcase. Ars Libri 32-386 1983
$85

LELAND, CHARLES G.   The English Gipsies and their Language.
1893. Green cloth. Fourth edition. Bright crisp copy. K Books
307-206 1983 £30

LELAND, CHARLES G   The Hundred Riddles of the Fairy Bellaria.
Fisher Unwin, 1892. Sq. 8vo. Orig. drawing by Artist-Author as
frontis. 101 text illus. Grey cloth label, worn. Edition limited to
100 copies on handmade paper. Greer 40-127 1983 £48

LELAND, JOHN   The Intinerary of John Leland the
Antiquary. Oxford, 1769-70. Third edition. 8vo. Cont. calf,
gilt spines with morocco labels, gilt. Engraved vignette title-
page and illus. in the text. 9 vols. in 5. Traylen 94-518 1983
£80

LELAND, JOHN   A Storke at the Branch. Hartford:
Elisha Babcock, 1801. Disbound. Very good. Felcone 20-88 1983 $20

LELAND, THOMAS   History of the Life and Reign of Philip
King of Macedon. London, Thomas Harrison, 1758. First edition. 4to.
Frontis.; large folding map. Full old calf, leather labels (rubbed,
joints starting), else very good. 2 vols. Houle 21-560 1983
$85

LEMAIRE, C. L.   Histoire naturelle des Oiseaux etrangers.
Paris, 1845. 2nd ed., 8vo, half morocco (trifle rubbed), plain and
coloured plates. Scarce. A nice copy, almost free from foxing, but
lacking the last 4 plates. Wheldon 160-59 1983 £320

LE MAOUT, E.   Lecons Elementaires de Botanique. Paris,
1857. 50 coloured illus., numerous text-figures, 8vo, half-calf,
slightly worn, a little foxing. Wheldon 160-1542 1983 £20

LEMERY, NICOLAS   A Course of Chymistry... London:
printed by R.N. for Walter Kettilby, 1686. Second edition. 8vo.
Cont. calf. 3 plates. A few leaves slightly wormed in the bottom
margin. Very good copy. Gurney 90-71 1983 £200

LE MIRE, AUBERT   Elogia Illvstrivm Belgii Scriptores.
Antwerp: Beller, 1602. 8vo, title device. Vellum. Rostenberg 88-
29 1983 $325

LEMLEY, JOHN   Autobiography and Personal Recollections
of,... Rockford, Ill., 1875. Orig. cloth, (slightly scuffed, foxed).
First complete edition. Argosy 716-210 1983 $200

LEMLEY, JOHN   Autobiography and Personal Recollections
of... Rockford, Illinois: 1878-8. Orig. cloth. Frontis. Front fly
excised. 1st complete narrative. Jenkins 153-327 1983 $250

LEMOINE, ALBERT   Du Sommeil au point de vue
Physiologique et Psychologique. Paris, 1855. 12mo, orig. pr. wrs.
First edition. With 36 pages of pub.'s ads. Argosy 713-330 1983
$50

LEMOINE, HENRY   Typographical Antiquities. London:
S. Fisher, 1797. First edition. Small 8vo. Early 19th century
cloth. Fine copy. Oak Knoll 49-266 1983 $250

LEMOINE, J. M.   The Explorations of Jonathan Oldbuck.
Quebec: Printed by L.J. Demers & Frere, 1889. 21cm. Frontis. view
and one illus. Red morocco backed marbled boards. Very good.
McGahern 54-114 1983 $25

LEMOISNE, P.-ANDRE   Eugene Lami, 1800-1890. Paris:
Goupil & Cie., 1912. 60 plates printed on papier chine blanc
(5 color) with captioned tissue guards printed on papier teinte.
Small folio. Marbled boards, 1/2 red morocco. Slipcase. No.
87 of a limited edition of 500 copies. Ars Libri 32-388 1983
$325

LEMON, MARK   The Enchanted Doll. T.C. & E.C. Jack,
n.d. Sm 4to. Colour frontis. 3 colour plates & 4 text illus. Green
boards. Onlaid extra colour plate. Head of spine, knocked. Greer 39-
137 1983 £28

LEMON, MARK   Gwynneth Vaughan. N.Y. & London: Samuel
French, n.d. French's Standard Drama edition. Orig. wrappers.
Brittle wrappers chipped. MacManus 279-3251 1983 $25

LEMON, MARK   A Moving Tale. London: Thomas Hailes
Lacy, n.d. Lacy's Acting edition. Orig. wrappers. Fine. MacManus
279-3252 1983 $35

LEMON, MARK   The Pach's Bridal! London: J. Duncombe
& Co., n.d. Duncombe's Acting edition. Orig. wrappers. A bit worn.
Very good. MacManus 279-3253 1983 $25

LEMON, MARK   Up and Down the London Streets.
Chapman & Hall, 1867. First edition, half title, vignette illus.
Orig. blue cloth, sl. rubbed, v.g. Jarndyce 31-269 1983 £32

LEMON, MARK   Wait for the End. Bradbury & Evans,
1863. First edition, 3 vols. 2 pp ads. vol. III. Orig. maroon cloth,
recased. Signed presentation copy from the author. Jarndyce 30-454
1983 £70

LEMON, ROBERT   Catalogue of a collection of printed
broadsides in the possession of the Society of Antiquaries of London.
London: published by the Society of Antiquaries, 1866. Large 8vo.
Orig. brown cloth. Numerous woodcut illus. Cloth rubbed, spine
slightly worn. Ximenes 63-258 1983 $75

LENIN, NIKOLAI
Please turn to
LENIN, VLADIMIR IL'ICH (1870-1924)

LENIN, VLADIMIR IL'ICH (1870-1924)   Chto Delta'? Nabolevshie
Voprosy Nashego Dvizhenia... Stuttgart, 1902. Bound in contemp. blue
cloth, first edition, very fine copy. Jenkins 153-809 1983 $2500

LENIN, VLADIMIR IL'ICH (1870-1924)   L'Imperialisme Derniere Etape
Du Capitalisme. Paris: Librairie de l'Humanite, 1923. 1st ed. in
French, 8vo, cont. half calf, marbled boards, spine gilt. A very
good copy. Pickering & Chatto 21-61 1983 $300

LENIN, VLADIMIR IL'ICH (1870-1924)   La Revolution Proletarienne et
le Renegat Kautsky. Paris, Bibliotheque Communiste, 1921. First
edition in French, publisher's advertisement, cont. half calf, marbled
boards, a very good copy. Pickering & Chatto 21-62 1983 $250

LENIN, VLADIMIR IL'ICH (1870-1924)   The State and Revolution.
London: The British Socialist Party and the Socialist Press, Glasgow,
1919. First ed. in English, 8vo, advertisements, a few pages soiled,
original printed wrappers, slightly soiled. Pickering & Chatto
21-63 1983 $100

LENIN, VLADIMIR IL'ICH (1870-1924)   Will the Bolsheviks Maintain
Power? London: The Labour Publishing Company, 1922. 1st ed. in
English, small 8vo, original brown cloth, upper free endpaper torn
away. Pickering & Chatto 21-64 1983 $85

LENNOX, WILLIAM PITT   Fashion Then and Now. Chapman & Hall,
1878. First edition, 2 vols. Half titles, orig. green cloth,
v.g. Jarndyce 31-221 1983 £40

LENNOX, WILLIAM PITT   Merrie England: its sports and
pastimes. London: Newby, 1857. First edition. 8vo. Orig.
blue cloth. Spine a trifle dull. Ximenes 63-559 1983 $80

LENNOX, WILLIAM PITT   Plays, players and playhouses at home
and abroad. London: Hurst and Blackett, 1881. 2 vols., 8vo, original
dark blue cloth (very slight wear). 1st edition. Fine set.
Ximenes 64-348 1983 $60

LENOBLE, JULES   La Traite des Glanches et le Congres
du Londres de 1899. Paris, 1900. Orig. wraps. K Books 301-152 1983
£20

LE NORMAND, CAMILLE   The Unerring Fortune-Teller. New York:
Dick & Fitzgerald, (c. 1866). 8vo, publishers' catalogue at beginning
& end. Orig. color pictorial boards. Rostenberg 88-66 1983 $60

LENSKI, LOIS   Bayou Suzette. N.Y.: Stokes, 1943.
First edition. 8vo. Cloth. Worn dust wrapper. Full-page and in
text black & whites. Very good. Aleph-bet 8-164 1983 $20

LENSKI, LOIS   Cinderella. N.Y.: Platt & Munk, 1922.
Folio. Stiff pictorial wrappers. Light wear. Full-page color illus.
plus black & whites by Lenski. 6-page handwritten letter by Lenski
8vo, 3 sheets written both sides, includes envelope. Very good.
Aleph-bet 8-162 1983 $85

LENTHAL, WILLIAM   Mr. Speakers Speech, with His Majesties
Speech to Both Houses of Parliament. Printed in the Yeare, 1641.
First edition, 4to, wrapper. Fenning 60-248 1983 £35

LENTINI, ROCCO   Le scolture e gli stucchi di Giacomo
Serpotta. Torino: C. Crudo, (1911). 65 heliogravure plates loose
in portfolio as issued. Folio. Boards, 1/4 cloth. Ties. Ars
Libri 33-337 1983 $150

LENTULO, SCIPIO   An Italian Grammar written in Latin...
London: T. Vautrollier, 1575. Second edition. 8vo. Cont. limp
vellum. Printer's device on title and final leaf. Owned by a cont.
student who has contributed extensive Ms. notes in the margins of
some pages. Cont. signatures. Upper cover defective, corners
creased, title stained. Traylen 94-519 1983 £350

LENYGON, FRANCIS, PSEUD.
Please turn to
JOURDAIN, MARGARET

LEO, F.   Geschichte der Roemischen Literature I.
New Buckram, Leipzig, 1913. Salloch 385-138 1983 $55

LEO, JOANNES   The history and description of Africa...
London: Hakluyt Soc., 1896. 3 vols. 8vo. 4 folding maps. Orig.
blue cloth. Spines darkened, ex-lib. Adelson Africa-204 1983 $60

LEON, FRANCISCO DE P.   Los esmaltes de Uruapan. Mexico:
D.A.P.P., 1939. 51 color plates. 4to. Wrappers. Ars Libri
34-334 1983 $50

LEON, NICOLAS   Codice Sierra. Mexico: Museo Nacional
de Arqueologia, Historia y Etnografia, 1933. 2 plates hors texte.
62 color facsimile plates loose in pocket as issued. Tall 4to.
Buckram. Ars Libri 34-335 1983 $200

LEONARD, FRED E.   Guide to the History of Physical
Education. Phila., 1947. 99 illus. Tall 8vo; ex-lib. Argosy 713-
331 1983 $75

LEONARD, JOHN W.   The Gold Fields of the Klondike.
Chicago, 1897. Wraps., somewhat chipped with part of spine lacking,
otherwise good. Reese 19-10 1983 $125

LEONARD, WILLIAM E.   The Fragments of Empedocles. Chicago:
1908. 1st ed. Orig. cloth-backed boards. Fine copy. Jenkins
155-787 1983 $20

LEONARD, WILLIAM E   A Son of Earth: Collected Poems. New
York: 1928. First edition. Blue cloth, paper spine label. Spine
faded, otherwise fine. Bradley 66-226 1983 $25

LEONARD, ZENAS   Adventures of...Fur Trader and Trapper,
1831-1836. Cleveland, 1904. Illus., folded map. Orig. cloth.
Ginsberg 47-430 1983 $100

LEONARD, ZENAS   Narrative of Adventures as Fur-Trader
& Trapper, 1831-1836. Chicago, Lakeside Press, 1934. Fldg. map.
Clark 741-269 1983 $25

LEONARDO Bistolfi. Milano: Bestetti & Tumminelli, n.d. 50 collotype plates loose in portfolio as issued. Folio. Cloth. Worn.
Ties. Ars Libri 33-405 1983 $75

LE PAGE, G.   De Cyferkonste item de Grondtregels
der Geometrie met de Landtmeteyre als oock de Wynroeyers-Konste...
Loven: Joan Franc van Overbeke, 1760. First edition. 8vo. Cont.
mottled calf, gilt. Folding engraved plates. Heath 48-513 1983
£35

LEPAGE, P.-C.   La decoration primitive afrique.
Paris: Librairie des Arts Decoratifs, (1922). 42 collotype
plates (6 color). Small folio. Portfolio. Boards. 1/4 cloth.
Contents loose as issued. Ex-library. Spine torn. Ars Libri
34-678 1983 $150

L'EPEE, CHARLES-MICHEL, ABBE DE   Institution des sourds et muets,
par la voie des signed methodiques... Paris: Nyon, 1776. First
edition. 12mo. Modern quarter calf. Ximenes 63-282 1983 $375

LEPPER, JOHN H.   History of the Grand Lodge of Free and
Accepted Masons of Ireland. Dublin: Lodge of Research, 1925.
First edition, with very many plates and illus., roy. 8vo, orig.
cloth, gilt. Fenning 61-517 1983 £32.50

LE PRINCE DE BEAUMONT, JEANNE MARIE   The New Clarissa: A True
History. Dublin: Printed for J. Exshaw and J. Potts, and J.
Williams, 1769. 2 vols, 12mo, cont. mottled sheep; slight wear to
covers, but a very fair copy. First Dublin edition. Hill 165-68
1983 £120

LEPSIUS, RICHARD   Letters from Egypt, Ethiopia, and the
Peninsula of Sinai. London: Henry G. Bohn, 1853. 12mo. Colored
frontis. 2 folding maps. Orig. cloth. Backed in new green morocco.
Adelson Africa-98 1983 $100

LE QUEUX, WILLIAM   Zoraida. London: Tower, 1895. First
edition. Illus. Orig. pictorial cloth. Covers worn. Inscription on
flyleaf. MacManus 279-3256 1983 $35

LERMONTOV, MIKHAIL YURIEVITCH   A Hero of Our Time. London, 1928.
First edition of this translation. Edge of upper cover soiled. Name
on flyleaf. Translated by R. Merton. Nice. Rota 230-356 1983
£12.50

LERMONTOV, MIKHAIL YURIEVITCH   A Song about Tsar Ivan Vasilyevitch.
Aquila Press, 1929. First edition. One of 750 numbered copies on
Maillol handmade paper, printed in red and black, using English black-
letter types. Bound in full morocco, the upper cover blind-tooled and
inlaid with a design in black, brown and white morocco. Covers a
little soiled and rubbed. Name of flyleaf. Nice. Rota 230-441 1983
£55

LEROUX, GASTON   The Man With the Black Feather. Bos.,
(1912). Very minor rubbing to edges, else bright, fine copy in slightly
soiled and frayed dustwrapper with one small chip. Quill & Brush 54-
790 1983 $125

LEROUX, GASTON   The Masked Man. NY, (1929). Bottom
corners slightly bumped, else bright, near fine in slightly worn and
frayed dustwrapper with price clipped and few short tears. Quill &
Brush 54-791 1983 $60

LEROUX, GASTON   The Octopus of Paris. NY, (1927). Spine
edges slightly rubbed and spine lightly faded, else very good or
better. Quill & Brush 54-792 1983 $35

LEROUX, GASTON   The Secret of the Night. NY, (1914).
Flys offset, edges worn, good or better. Quill & Brush 54-793 1983
$30

LE ROW, CAROLINE   English as She is Taught. London, 1887.
First edition. Small 8vo, orig. embossed cloth. Argosy 714-765 1983
$175

LE ROY DE BOSROGER, M.   Principes elementaires de la tactique...
Paris: Prault, 1768. First edition. 8vo. Cont. mottled calf,
spine gilt. 12 folding plates of military formations. Minor rubbing.
Fine copy. Ximenes 63-316 1983 $90

LE SAGE, ALAIN RENE   The Adventures of Gil Blas De Santillane.
London, 1819. 3 vols. 8vo. Full mottled calf, gilt, gilt panelled
spines with morocco labels, gilt, edges gilt. 15 hand-coloured
aquatint plates by J. Clarke. Traylen 94-520 1983 £75

LE SAGE, ALAIN RENE   The Adventures of Gil Blas of Santillane.
London: J.J. Dubochet, Charles Tilt, and H. Hopper, 1836. 2 vols.,
8vo, with 600 woodcut text illus. by Gigoux, uncut, orig. cloth with
title in gilt on spines with gilt cartouche, a little spotting on the
covers, but a fine uncut copy. First edition. Bickersteth 77-224
1983 £60

LE SAGE, ALAIN RENE   Asmodeus or the Devil upon Two Sticks.
London: J.C. Nimmo & Bain, 1881. First of this edition. Four orig.
etchings by R. de Los Rios. Cont. 3/4 brown morocco & marbled boards.
Limited to 100 copies with proof etchings on Whatman paper. Fine.
MacManus 279-3257 1983 $75

LE SAGE, ALAIN RENE   Le Diable Boiteux: or, the Devil upon
Two Sticks. Printed for Jacob Tonson, 1708. 8vo, engraved frontis.,
ad. leaf, orig. calf, rebacked, lightly foxed or spotted. First
edition in English. Bickersteth 77-38 1983 £120

LESBAZEILLES, E.   Tableaux et Scenes de la Vie des Animaux.
Paris, 1877. 20 woodcut plates, royal 4to, half morocco. A little
light foxing, but a good copy. Illustrations by J. Wolf. Wheldon
160-529 1983 £40

LESLIE, FRANK   Frank Leslie's Illustrated History of the
Civil War. N.Y., (1895). Numerous woodcuts. Recent rebound cloth.
Nice. King 45-33 1983 $85

LESLIE, SHANE   Jutland, a fragment of epic. London:
Ernest Benn Limited, 1930. First edition. Orig. cloth. Presentation
copy, inscribed to "Anne from Shane, with love for Xmas 1930 and a
thousand thoughts of gratitude." Bookplate. Very good. MacManus
279-3258 1983 $35

LESTER, CHARLES EDWARDS   The Life of Sam Houston. NY, 1855.
Maps & plates, 12mo, orig. cloth, spotted, pp. lightly foxed.
Argosy 710-527 1983 $50

LESTER, E. EDWARDS   The Glory and Shame of England. London:
Richard Bentley, 1844. Later edition. 2 vols. Orig. cloth-backed
boards with paper labels on spines. In Orig. binding. Very Good.
MacManus 279-3259 1983 $75

LESTER, J. R.   Tank Warfare. London, 1943. First
edition. Sm. 8vo. Orig. green cloth-backed yellow printed boards.
Portrait frontis. and 5 portrait plates. Very slightly worn and
soiled. Bookplate. Good. Edwards 1042-395 1983 £15

LESTER, JOHN E.   The Atlantic to the Pacific. Boston,
Shepard & Gill, 1873. First edition. Map and leaf of ads. Gilt
stamped green cloth (lacking front free endpaper), else good-very good.
Houle 21-1195 1983 $125

LESTER, PAUL   The Great Galveston Disaster. N.p.,
(1900). Embellished with photos. Woodpulp paper. Argosy 710-526
1983 $40

L'ESTRANGE, HAMON   The Alliance of Divine Offices
Exhibiting all the Liturgies of the Church of England Since the
Reformation... London, Henry Broom, 1659. Folio, cont. sheep
newly rebacked, new endpapers, minor offsetting and some age-spotting,
large copy. First edition. Ravenstree 97-31 1983 $165

L'ESTRANGE, ROGER   An Answer to a Letter to a Dissenter.
London, R. Sare, 1687. 4to, disbound, first edition. Ravenstree 97-
32 1983 $25

L'ESTRANGE, ROGER   A Fox & A Sick Lion... (Bloomington,
Indiana): Corydon Press, 1944. Folio. Half-cloth over boards,
paper cover label, dust jacket with paper cover label. With an
orig. wood-cut by Joseph Low, hand-colored and signed by Low.
Limited to 180 copies. Some foxing, jacket chipped. Oak Knoll
48-114 1983 $50

LETACQ, A. L.   Materiaux Pour Servir a la Faune des
Vertebres du Departement de l'Orne. Caen and Alencon, 1896-1904.
6 papers, 8vo, half morocco. Wheldon 160-402 1983 £18

LETANG, JEAN   Gall et Son Oeruvre. Paris: Maloine,
1906. Author's holograph letter on front flyleaf. Gach 94-182 1983
$30

LETHBRIDGE, ALAN   West Africa the Elusive. London: John
Bale, Sons & Danielsson. N.d., (ca. 1935). Illus. including a folding
map. Orange cloth, spine faded. Karmiole 71-4 1983 $50

LETI, GREGORIO   The Life of Donna Olimpia Maldachini...
London, printed by W. Godbid, sold by R. Littlebury, 1667. Small 8vo,
orig. sheep, little worn. Ravenstree 97-34 1983 $125

LETI, GREGORIO   The Life of Donna Olimpia Maldachini.
By W.G., sold by Robert Littlebury, 1667. Small 8vo, lacks final
blank leaf. Modern speckled calf, gilt spine. Title slightly
defective at fore-edge, laid down, with border rules restored in ink,
fore-edge of first few leaves strengthened. Hannas 69-121 1983
£50

LETI, GREGORIO   Il Nipotismo de Roma: Or, the History
of the Popes Nephews... London, printed for John Starkey, sold by
Thomas Archer, 1673. 8vo, 2 parts in one volume, orig. sheep, spine
ends and corners bit worn. Ravenstree 97-35 1983 $95

LETSCH, JOHANN T.   Annuente numine, Gratiosissime Medicae
Facultatis consensu, de Tabaco... Frankfurt a.d. Oder, 1695. First
edition. 4to. Modern boards. Kraus 164-234 1983 $220

A LETTER concerning the Disabling Clauses lately offered to the
House of Commons... London: by Randal Taylor, 1690. 4to. Wrappers.
Heath 48-136 1983 £25

A LETTER from Dick Estcourt, the comedian, to the Spectator. London:
printed for J. Baker, 1713. 8vo, half roan (rubbed). 1st ed. A
very rare pamphlet. Some foxing, else a very good copy. Ximenes 64-
349 1983 $600

A LETTER to a certain patentee: in which the conduct of managers is
impartially considered. London: printed for H. Mumford, n.d. (1747).
8vo, wrappers. First edition. Rare. Ximenes 64-350 1983 $600

A Letter to David Garrick, Esq; occasioned by the intended representa-
tion of the Minor at the Theatre-Royal in Drury-Lane. London: sold by
Mr. Field; Mr. Flexney; Mr. Hurd, 1760. 8vo, disbound, 1st ed.
Fine copy of a rare pamphlet. Ximenes 64-216 1983 $325

A LETTER to His Grace the Duke of N***... London: R. Griffiths,
n.d. (1761). First edition. 8vo. Orig. plain grey wrappers.
Half-title and final leaf dusty. Ximenes 63-464 1983 $35

A LETTER to the author of the burletta called Hero and Leander.
London; printed for G. Kearsley, 1787. 8vo, wrappers, 1st ed.
Presentation copy (inscription trimmed by the binder). Half-title
present (dusty). Very rare. Ximenes 64-351 1983 $425

LETTERING of To-day. London: The Studio Limited, (1949). 4to.
Cloth. Dust jacket. Prof. illus. Slight chipping of jacket,
else fine. Oak Knoll 48-89 1983 $35

LETTERS From a father to his son... Carmarthen: printed by William
Evans, 1833. First edition. 12mo. Cont. half calf, spine gilt.
Ximenes 63-317 1983 $65

LETTERS from Golden Latitudes. (St. Paul, 1885). Orig. printed
wraps. First edition. Illus., map on rear cover. Ginsberg 47-286
1983 $60

LETTERS from several parts of Europe, and the East. London:
for L. Davis, etc., 1753. First edition. 2 vols. 8vo. Cont.
calf. Slight wear. Very good copy. Ximenes 63-625 1983 $275

LETTERS from the United States of America, Exhibiting the Workings
of Democracy in that Country for the Last Twenty Years. London,
1844. Orig. printed wraps. First edition. Ginsberg 46-406 1983
$100

LETTS, JOHN M.   A Pictorial View of California. N.Y.:
Published by Henry Bill, 1853. 1 page of ads. 48 lithographed plates.
Orig. cloth, rebacked. Frontis. and title stained. Dawson 471-178
1983 $350

LETTSOM, JOHN COAKLEY   The Natural History of the Tea-Tree.
London, printed for Edward and Charles Dilly, 1772. 1st ed. in
English, 4to, coloured engraved frontispiece, orig. grey wrappers,
neatly repaired, signature F. Lloyd 1772 on title, small piece torn
from lower fore edge of frontispiece with slight loss, wrappers a
little soiled but very good uncut copy. Pickering & Chatto 22-58
1983 $500

LEUBA, JAMES HENRY (1868-1946)   The Psychology of Religious
Mysticism. NY: Harcourt, 1926. First American edition. Gach 95-
317 1983 $25

LEUBE, WILHELM   Specielle Diagnose der Inneren Krankheiten. Leipzig: F. C. W. Vogel, 1889. First edition. Orig.
wrappers, very worn, spine broken. Adolf Meyer's copy, initialed
on front wrapper. Gach 95-360 1983 $20

LEUCKART, R.   Zur Kenntniss des Generationswechsels
und der Parthenogenesis bei den Insekten. Frankfurt, 1858. 8vo,
folding plate, wrappers (foxed). Wheldon 160-1114 1983 £15

LE VAYER DE BOUTIGNY, ROLAND The Famous Romance of Tarsis and Zelie.
London, Nathanael Ponder, 1685. Folio, cont. calf rebacked, little
worn, small piece gone from foot of engraved frontis. removing part
of the printer, Nathanael Ponder's Name, paper flaw in D1 results in
loss of few letters but text is legible, blank tip of X1 gone, few
spots, minor foxing, two bookplates, one being that of Richard Brinsley
Sheridan. First and only edition in English. Ravenstree 96-36 1983
$185

LEVENS, HENRY C.   A History of Cooper County, Missouri.
St. Louis, 1876. Orig. printed boards. First edition. Ginsberg
47-532 1983 $125

LEVER, CHARLES   Arthur O'Leary. London, Henry Colburn,
1844. 3 vols., 8vo, later brown morocco gilt, edges uncut, very
slight wear, minor spotting. Rare first edition. Ravenstree 96-37
1983 $275

LEVER, CHARLES   Arthur O'Leary. London, Henry Colburn,
1845. 8vo, orig. cloth, recased, old spine laid down with some
portions missing at top and bottom, worn. Ravenstree 96-38 1983
$35

LEVER, CHARLES   Barrington. London: Chapman & Hall,
1862-63. First edition. Orig. 13 parts in 12, in pictorial wrappers
(very slightly frayed and soiled). Rather soiled cloth folding box.
Very good to near-fine. MacManus 279-3260 1983 $450

LEVER, CHARLES   Barrington. London: Chapman & Hall,
1863. 1st ed., 13 parts in 12. Orig. pink printed wrappers, uncut.
Some small chips to spine. Half-morocco slipcase. Fine set.
Jenkins 155-788 1983 $400

LEVER, CHARLES   Barrington. London, Chapman & Hall,
1863. 8vo, later citron half morocco gilt extra, t.e.g., slight wear,
bookplate, light water-marking, but generally a good copy. First
edition, bound up from the orig. parts, with the front wrapper to the
first part preserved. Ravenstree 96-39 1983 $85

LEVER, CHARLES   Charles O'Malley the Irish Dragoon.
Dublin, Curry, 1841. 2 vols., 8vo, cont. half calf, worn, spine
faded, plates foxed. This copy has the "L'Envoy," as well as the
poem to G.P.R. James and James' letter in reply. Vol. 2 has the
inset dedication to the Marquess of Douro. First edition, bound from
the orig. parts. Ravenstree 96-39 1983 $83

LEVER, CHARLES   Charles O'Malley the Irish Dragoon.
Dublin, William Curry, 1841. 2 vols., cont. half calf, plates age-
browned. First (book) edition. Ravenstree 97-36 1983 $67.50

LEVER, CHARLES   Charles O'Malley the Irish Dragoon.
London, Chapman and Hall, 1857. 2 vols., 8vo, orig. cloth gilt,
somewhat faded, soiled, spine ends worn, but sound; few very minor
smudges and spots of foxing through text. First London edition (?),
with a new preface for this edition by Lever. Ravenstree 96-40 1983
$25

LEVER, CHARLES   The Confessions of Harry Lorrequer.
Dublin, Curry, 1839. Tall 8vo, later dark green half morocco gilt,
orig. cloth blinding preserved, t.e.g. First edition. Ravenstree
96-43 1983 $175

LEVER, CHARLES   The Confessions of Harry Lorrequer.
Dublin, William Curry, 1839. 8vo, cont. half calf, worn, plates
foxes, bookplate, name on end-paper. First edition. Ravenstree 97-
37 1983 $135

LEVER, CHARLES   The Confessions of Harry Lorrequer.
Dublin, William Curry, Jun, and Company, etc, 1839. First edition.
8vo, frontis., additional engraved title and 20 plates (a little
spotted). Two ad. leaves in front. Orig. green cloth (joints
splitting, loose), uncut. Hannas 69-123 1983 £20

LEVER, CHARLES   The Daltons. London, Chapman & Hall,
1852. 2 vols., 8vo, orig. cloth gilt, spine ends worn, corners
bumped, few signatures sprung, spines sunned, light soiling, decent
set in the orig. cloth. First edition. Ravenstree 96-44a 1983
$85

LEVER, CHARLES   Davenport Dunn. London: Chapman & Hall,
July (1858) through April (1859). First edition. Illus. with 42 full-
page plates by Phiz. 22 parts in 21. Orig. printed pink wrappers.
Spines expertly repaired. Covers a trifle rubbed and faded. Maroon,
full morocco solander case. MacManus 279-3262 1983 $500

LEVER, CHARLES   Davenport Dunn; a Man of Our Day.
London, Chapman & Hall, 1859. 8vo, cont. maroon half calf gilt,
now worn, joints cracking, minor foxing, few old smudges, first
edition, bound from the orig. parts. Ravenstree 96-46 1983 $110

LEVER, CHARLES   Davenport Dunn. London: Chapman & Hall,
1859. First edition. Illus. by Phiz. Thick 8vo. Orig. cloth. Spine
faded. Small tear at head of spine. MacManus 279-3263 1983 $75

LEVER, CHARLES   Davenport Dunn. London, Chapman & Hall,
1859. 8vo, later green half calf gilt, a.e.g., little worn, trifle
faded, bookplate. First (book) edition. Ravenstree 97-38 1983
$75

LEVER, CHARLES   The Dodd Family Abroad. London,
Chapman & Hall, 1852-54. 8vo, the orig. 20 parts in 19, orig.
printed paper wraps., bit worn, soiled, little foxed, the orig.
spines present but chipped at ends, decent set. Preserved in trifle
worn full green morocco gilt solander case with inner protective
wraps. First edition. Ravenstree 96-47 1983 $95

LEVER, CHARLES   The Dodd Family Abroad. London, Chapman
& Hall, 1854. 8vo, full dark maroon contemporary calf, tooled in blind
and gilt, bit rubbed and worn, plates a trifle foxed, but a decent
copy. First edition. Ravenstree 97-39 1983 $85

LEVER, CHARLES   The Fortunes of Glencore. London,
Chapman & Hall, 1857. 3 vols., 8vo, orig. cloth gilt, lightly
worn and slightly shaken, name in pencil on titles, but a good set.
In orig. cloth. First edition. Ravenstree 96-49 1983 $275

LEVER, CHARLES   The Knight of Gwynne. London, Chapman &
Hall, 1847. 8vo, cont. maroon half calf gilt, the engraved title,
frontis. and plates foxed, good sound copy. First edition. Ravenstree
97-40 1983 $82.50

LEVER, CHARLES   The Knight of Gwynne. London, Chapman &
Hall, 1847. 8vo, bound in cont. half calf, boards, lightly worn,
frontis., engraved title, and most plates slightly foxed, but a
better than average copy. First edition. Ravenstree 96-50 1983
$67.50

LEVER, CHARLES   Lord Kilgobbin. London, Smith Elder,
1872. 3 vols., 8vo, 3/4 crimson morocco gilt, t.e.g. by Tout,
very slight wear, first edition. Ravenstree 96-51 1983 $275

LEVER, CHARLES   Luttrell of Arran. London, Chapman &
Hall, (1864-65). 8vo, the orig. 16 parts in 15, orig. printed paper
wraps., but worn and trifle soiled, most paper spines skillfully
renewed. First printings of all the orig. monthly parts, preserved
in little worn full green morocco gilt solander case with folding
protective inner wraps. First edition. Ravenstree 96-52 1983 $485

LEVER, CHARLES   Luttrell of Arran. London, Chapman &
Hall, 1865. 8vo, orig. cloth, rebacked with orig. spine laid down,
worn, armorial bookplate, some minor foxing, first edition. Ravenstree
96-53 1983 $85

LEVER, CHARLES   Luttrell of Arran. London, Chapman &
Hall, 1865. 8vo, later green half calf gilt, t.e.g., few minor
restorations to a blank edge here and there, some old age-darkening,
generally a good copy of the first edition. Ravenstree 97-41 1983
$63

LEVER, CHARLES   The Martins of Cro'Martin. London,
Chapman & Hall, 1854-1856. 8vo, the orig. 20 monthly parts in 19,
orig. printed paper wraps., somewhat soiled trifle frayed, worn, light
foxing, decent set. Preserved in folding cloth case, label chipped.
First edition. Ravenstree 96-54 1983 $495

LEVER, CHARLES   The Martins of Cro'Martin. London:
Chapman & Hall, December 1854 through June 1855. First edition. Illus.
with 39 full-page plates by Phiz. 20 parts in 19. Orig. printed pink
wrappers. Spines neatly reapired. Covers slightly rubbed and somewhat
faded. In a maroon, full morocco solander case. MacManus 279-3264
1983 $400

LEVER, CHARLES   The Martins of Cro'Martin. London,
Chapman & Hall, 1856. 8vo, orig. cloth gilt, now worn and skillfully
recased, plates foxed. First edition. Ravenstree 96-55 1983 $65

LEVER, CHARLES   The O'Donoghue; a Tale of Ireland
Fifty Years Ago. Dublin, William Curry, 1845. 8vo, orig. scarlet
cloth gilt, trifle soiled and worn, inner joint cracked, slight
foxing to plates. First edition, first issue binding. Ravenstree
96-58 1983 $125

LEVER, CHARLES   One of Them. London, Chapman & Hall,
n.d. (1859-61). 8vo, the orig. 15 parts in 14, orig. printed paper
wraps., little soiled, bit worn, few covers loose, good set of the
orig. monthly parts. Preserved in slightly worn full green morocco
gilt solander case with protective folding inner wraps. First
edition. Ravenstree 96-60 1983 $465

LEVER, CHARLES   One of Them. London: Chapman & Hall,
1861. 1st ed., 15 parts in 14. Orig. pink printed wrappers, uncut.
Slipcase, morocco label. Fine set. Scarce. Jenkins 155-790 1983
$450

LEVER, CHARLES   One of Them. London: Chapman & Hall,
(1859-61). Illus. by Phiz. First edition. Origl 14 parts in pictorial
wrappers (a bit frayed and soiled). A bit chipped and worn at the
spine. One ad. page in Part XIII torn out; shelf numbers on front
wrappers of two parts; Part XII reads "No. XIV" and is dated "March"
instead of reading "No. XII" and bearing the date of "November." In
a shabby, faded, cloth folding box. Good. MacManus 279-3266 1983
$250

LEVER, CHARLES   One of Them. London, Chapman & Hall,
1861. Illus. by Phiz. 8vo, later dark red half morocco gilt,
t.e.g., one orig. wrapper preserved at front, bookplate; clean copy.
First edition, bound from the orig. parts. Ravenstree 96-61 1983
$75

LEVER, CHARLES   Our Mess. Dublin. 1843-44. With a
portrait of the author and numerous illustrations on wood and steel
by Phiz. 3 vols. 8vo. Old half straight grain morocco. First eds.
of "Jack Hinton", "The Gardsman" and "Tom Burke". Some foxing,
mainly fine copies. In Our Time 156-500 1983 $150

LEVER, CHARLES   Our Mess. Dublin, William Curry Jr.,
1843-44. 3 vols.: Volume I in later 3/4 green morocco gilt, gilt
extra, plates age-browned and foxed. Volumes II and III in cont.
half calf, quite worn, plates quite age-browned and foxed, without
half titles. First editions. Ravenstree 96-63 1983 $75

LEVER, CHARLES   Roland Cashel. London, Chapman & Hall,
1850. Stout 8vo, cont. half calf gilt, bit worn. First edition.
Ravenstree 96-64 1983 $85

LEVER, CHARLES   St. Patrick's Eve. London: Chapman &
Hall, 1845. First edition, first binding. Illus. by Phiz. Orig. gilt
pictorial cloth. Corners and edges a bit worn. Covers slightly soiled
and dampstained. Plates slightly foxed. Good. MacManus 279-3267
1983 $85

LEVER, CHARLES   St. Patrick's Eve. New York, Harper,
1845. Tall, slim 8vo, orig. printed paper wraps., time and water
stains throughout, wraps. worn. First American edition. Ravenstree
96-67 1983 $72

LEVER, CHARLES   St. Patrick's Eve. London, Chapman &
Hall, 1845. Square 8vo, orig. cloth pictorially gilt, blind
stamped (Sadleir's primary binding), edges gilt; worn and lightly
soiled. First edition. Ravenstree 96-65 1983 $65

LEVER, CHARLES   St. Patrick's Eve. London, Chapman &
Hall, 1845. Illus. by Phiz. Square 8vo, orig. pictorial cloth gilt,
worn, shaken, inner hinges broken, top of spine split, few quires
sprung, light foxing. This copy is in Sadleir's primary binding
(there are two later bindings known), with the proper gilt edges,
gilt stamping and the necessary four harps blind stamped on front
and back cover corners. First edition. Ravenstree 97-42 1983
$53

LEVER, CHARLES   St. Patrick's Eve. London: Chapman &
Hall, 1845. First edition, in a later publisher's binding that does
not have the gilt pictorial design on the front cover. Illus. by Phiz.
Orig. light free, blind-stamped cloth. Binding faded and a little
waterspotted. Signature on front free endpaper. A Little light foxing.
Good. MacManus 279-3268 1983 $35

LEVER, CHARLES   Sir Brook Fossbrooke. Edinburgh and
London, Blackwood, 1866. 3 vols., later full crushed dark green
levant, now faded to brown, ends of spines, rubbed, tops bit worn,
as are hinges, some minor pencil markings, outer edge of last leaf
of second vol. has small repair to blank edge, corners bumped, t.e.g.,
vol. 1 bound without half title. First edition. Ravenstree 96-68
1983 $195

LEVER, CHARLES   Tom Burke of "Ours." Dublin, Curry, n.d.
Illus. by H.K. Browne. 2 vols. Orig. cloth. Later edition (ca.1850's).
Very good. MacManus 279-3269 1983 $20

LEVER, CHARLES   Tony Butler. Edinburgh and London,
Blackwood, 1865. 3 vols., 8vo, orig. cloth, somewhat worn, bookplate,
spine extremities worn, minor foxing and spotting, decent set. First
edition. Ravenstree 96-69 1983 $350

LEVERMORE, CHARLES HERBERT   Forerunners and Competitors of the
Pilgrims and Puritans. Brooklyn, 1912. 1st ed. 2 vols., tall 8vo.
Corners and ends of spines rubbed; few inner hinges bit cracked.
Morrill 286-247 1983 $40

LEVERSON, H. A.   The Hunting Grounds of the Old World.
London, 1860. First Series. 7 tinted lithographs, spotted. Decorative cloth frayed at top of spine, shaken. 8vo. Good. Edwards 1044-
432 1983 £25

LEVERTOV, DENISE   The Double Image. London: The Cresset
Press, 1946. First edition, cloth. Fine copy in lightly tanned dust
jacket. Reese 20-609 1983 $175

LEVERTOV, DENISE   The Double Image. London, Cresset, 1946.
First edition. Small 8vo, dust jacket. Signed and inscribed with
both variants of her name. Fine. Houle 21-562 1983 $65

LEVERTOV, DENISE   The Sorrow Dance. London, 1968. First
English edition. Wrappers. Advance proof copy. Very fine. Jolliffe
26-320 1983 £45

LEVERTOV, DENISE   Three Poems. Mt. Horeb: Perishable
Press, 1968. Octavo. Limited to 250 copies. Near mint in printed
wrappers. Bromer 25-281 1983 $75

LEVIN, HARRY   James Joyce. New Directions, (1941).
12mo. Cloth. Fine copy in dj. In Our Time 156-448 1983 $20

LEVIN, MEYER   Reporter. NY, (1929). Cover slightly
stained and edges slightly rubbed, top spine edge slightly frayed, good
or better. Quill & Brush 54-798 1983 $35

LEVINREW, WILL   Death Points a Finger. N.Y.,
Mystery League, 1933. First edition. Dust jacket (a few nicks)
else good - fine. Houle 22-589 1983 $45

LEVINSON, ANDRE   Bakst. New York: Brentano's, 1922.
Folio. With 68 numbered mounted color plates, each with a printed
tissue guard, and dozens of other smaller mounted plates throughout.
The American edition, ltd. to 250 numbered copies. Bound in full
vellum. Karmiole 75-78 1983 $750

LEWES, CHARLES LEE   Comic sketches; or, the comedian his
own manager. London: printed for H. D. Symonds, 1804. 12mo, cont.
half morocco, spine gilt (spine worn). 1st ed., with a frontis.
Ximenes 64-352 1983 $125

LEWES, CHARLES LEE   Memoirs of Charles Lee Lewes. London:
printed for Richard Phillips, by T. Gillet, 1805. Four vols., sm. 8vo,
original light blue boards, drab paper backstrips, printed paper
labels (spines a little worn). 1st edition. A fine set in original
condition. Ximenes 64-353 1983 $250

LEWES, GEORGE HENRY   On actors and the art of acting.
London: Smith, Elder, 1875. 8vo, original green cloth (trifle rubbed,
spine dull). First edition. Ximenes 64-354 1983 $45

LEWES, GEORGE HENRY   The Physiology of Common Life. Edinburgh,
London, William Blackwood, 1859, 1850. 2 vols. Polished morocco,
joints trifle rubbed, very good to fine set. Gach 95-320 1983 $75

LEWES, VIVIAN BYAM   Service Chemistry: being a Short Manual of Chemistry... London: Glaisher, 1895. 8vo. Orig. gilt stamped blue cloth. A few minor stains, drawing on half title. Zeitlin 264-259 1983 $50

LEWIN, EVANS   Subject Catalogue of the Library of the Royal Empire Society. London: Dawson's, 1967. Reprint of the 1930-37 ed. 4 vols., cloth, just a little bumped and stained. Dawson 470-188 1983 $100

LEWIN, J. W.   A natural history of the Birds of New South Wales. (1838), Melbourne, 1978. New edition, 26 fine coloured plates, folio, full leather, in a book-box. Limited edition of 500 copies for sale and 10 copies for presentation. Wheldon 160-60 1983 £135

LEWIN, KURT   A Dynamic Theory of Personality. NY: McGraw Hill, 1935, later printing. Gach 94-593 1983 $25

LEWIN, L.   Die Gifte in Der Weltgeschichte. Berlin: Julius Springer, 1920. First edition. Cloth spine and tips, boards. Gach 95-322 1983 $30

LEWIN, M.   The Way to Lose India. London, 1857. Second edition. Wrappers. Title slightly soiled. 8vo. Good. Edwards 1044-433 1983 £20

LEWIN, THOMAS HERBERT   Hill Proverbs of the Inhabitants of the Chittagong Hill Tracts. Calcutta: Bengal Secretariat Press, 1873. Folio. Printed in Bengali and English. Orig. printed wraps; spine badly chipped. Karmiole 74-59 1983 $30

LEWIS, ALBERT BUELL   Decorative Art of New Guinea. Chicago, 1925. 52 plates. Frontis., 2 text illus. Large 4to. Wrappers. Ars Libri 34-829 1983 $35

LEWIS, ALFRED HENRY   A Collection of His Works. 8 vols, very good to fine condition, some with illus. by Remington and Wyeth. Jenkins 155-791 1983 $200

LEWIS, ALFRED HENRY   Wolfville Days. New York: Frederick A. Stokes Company, 1902. Frontis. by Frederic Remington. Orig. pic. cloth. 1st ed. Very good copy. Jenkins 153-463 1983 $125

LEWIS, ALFRED HENRY   Wolfville Nights. New York: (1902). First edition, first binding. Frontis. Pictorial black cloth. Wolf design against blind-stamped blue field on spine and front cover. Covers lightly worn. Bradley 66-228 1983 $45

LEWIS, C. T. COURTNEY   The Picture Printer of the Nineteenth Century, George Baxter, 1804-1867. First edition. Thick large 8vo. Cloth with colored pictorial inlay on the front cover, t.e.g., others uncut. With many full page color plates of Baxter's prints. Some foxing of preliminary pages, else a very good copy. Oak Knoll 49-29 1983 $300

LEWIS, CECIL DAY
Please turn to
DAY-LEWIS, CECIL

LEWIS, CLIVE STAPLES   A Grief Observed. London, 1961. First English edition. Slightly nicked and chipped dustwrapper slightly faded at the spine and edges. Fine. Scarce. Jolliffe 26-322 1983 £55

LEWIS, DAVIS   Philip of Macedon. Dublin: Printed by S. Powell, 1727. First Irish edition, 12mo, wrapper, a very good copy. Fenning 60-250 1983 £35

LEWIS, DIOCLESAN   Our Girls. N.Y., 1871. First edition. Illus. Ex-lib. Argosy 713-335 1983 $35

LEWIS, EDWARD   The Patriot King Displayed: in the Life and Reign of Henry VIII King of England. Printed for Edward and Charles Dilly, 1769. 12mo, cont. calf, spine gilt. First edition. Bickersteth 77-39 1983 £28

LEWIS, EDWARD   Precious Bane. A Play... London: Samuel French, 1932. First edition. 8vo. Orig. printed wrappers. Inserted is a long typewritten letter, signed by Edward Lewis. Traylen 94-860 1983 £20

LEWIS, F.   Sixty-four Years in Ceylon. Colombo, 1926. 14 plates, edges foxed. 8vo. Orig. cloth. Good. Edwards 1044-434 1983 £25

LEWIS, GEORGE C   An Historical Survey of the Astronomy of the Ancients. Parker, Son, and Bourn, 1862. First edition, 8vo, a very good copy in cont. half calf, gilt ruled spine with label. Fenning 61-252 1983 £35

LEWIS, GEORGE C   A treatise on the methods of observation and reasoning in politics. London: Parker, 1852. First edition. 2 vols. 8vo. Cont. calf, spines gilt, contrasting morocco labels. Fine copy. Ximenes 63-465 1983 $175

LEWIS, GILBERT NEWTON   Valence and the Structure of Atoms and Molecules. New York: The Chemical Catalog., 1923. First edition. 8vo. Orig. cloth. Text illus. and diagrams. Spine worn, chipped, shelf mark, very good internally. Zeitlin 264-260 1983 $45

LEWIS, GRACE HEGGER   Half a Loaf. N.Y., Morace Liveright, (1931). First edition, second printing. Magenta cloth stamped in black and gilt. Spine a bit faded. Signed and inscribed by the author. Very good. Houle 22-592 1983 $25

LEWIS, H. C.   Papers and Notes on the Glacial Geology of Great Britain and Ireland. 1894. 10 maps and numerous figures, 8vo, half leather (rubbed). Some slight foxing. Wheldon 160-1436 1983 £25

LEWIS, JOHN   Printed Ephemera, the Changing Uses of Type and Letterforms in English and American Printing. Ipswich: W.S. Cowell (1962). First edition. 4to. Cloth. Dust jacket. Some chipping of dust jacket and tear at head of spine of jacket. Oak Knoll 48-249 1983 $75

LEWIS, LLOYD   Captain Sam Grant. Boston, 1950. D.w. Argosy 716-204 1983 $25

LEWIS, MATTHEW GREGORY   The Bravo of Venice, a Romance. London: D.N. Shury for J.F. Hughes, 1805. First edition. 8vo. Cont. half calf. Errata leaf and ads. Slightly loose with light wear to calf. Heath 48-379 1983 £150

LEWIS, MATTHEW GREGORY   The Bravo of Venice. Published by J. Clements, 1839. 12mo, original green blind-stamped cloth, gilt-titled on cover; fine copy, partly unopened.

LEWIS, MATTHEW GREGORY   The Isle of Devils. London: 1912. Square Quarto. Worn marbled boards. Large paper edition. 1/20 copies. Bradley 66-127 1983 $40

LEWIS, MATTHEW GREGORY   Raymond and Agnes. N.Y. & London: Samuel French, n.d. French's Standard Drama edition. Orig. wrappers. A bit chipped. Fine. MacManus 279-3272 1983 $35

LEWIS, MERIWETHER   History of the Expedition Under the Command of Captains Lewis and Clark... Philadelphia: Published by Bradford and Inskeep, 1814. Two vols. Orig. mottled calf, morocco labels, large folding map in vol. I, 5 in-text maps. Very early ownership signatures, otherwise a fine set, with the orig. binding in fine condition. Reese 18-443 1983 $10,000

LEWIS, MERIWETHER   History of the Expedition under the Command of Captains Lewis and Clark... Philadelphia & Dublin, 1817. Two vols. Orig. mottled calf, spines gilt extra. Folding map in vol. I, 5 in-text maps and a view. Trifling wear at the edges, otherwise an unusually fine, clean set. Reese 18-514 1983 $3,500

LEWIS, MERIWETHER   History of the Expedition, 1804-5-6. Chicago, 1905. Reprinted from the edition of 1814. Portraits, maps, 2 vols., gilt tops. Clark 741-336 1983 $60

LEWIS, MERIWETHER   Travels to the Source of the Missouri River... London: Printed for Longman, Hurst, Rees Orme and Brown, 1814. 4to. 27 1/2cm. First English edition. Engraved folding frontis. map, and 5 charts on 3 sheets. Corner repaired on the title page, in cont. full brown calf, raised bands, blind and gilt decorations in the panels, blind stamped decorations in borders of boards, marbled endpapers and edges, expertly rebacked. A fine copy. McGahern 54-115 1983 $1,500

LEWIS, MERIWETHER   The Travels of Capts. Lewis and Clarke, From St. Louis by way of the Missouri and Columbia Rivers to the Pacific Ocean. London: printed for Longman, Hurst, Rees, and Orme, 1809. Folding map. Linen backing, half morocco, spine gilt. Unauthorized or counterfeit edition. Scarce. Jenkins 151-180 1983 $1,250

LEWIS, MERIWETHER   Travels to the Source of the Missouri River and Across the American Continent to the Pacific Ocean. London: printed for Longman, Hurst, Rees, Orme, and Brown, 1814. 4 maps. Original calf, gilt, rehinged, and some wear. A fine clean copy. Jenkins 151-179 1983 $2,250

LEWIS, NOLAN D. C.   The Constitutional Factors in Dementia Precox. N.Y., 1923. Illus. Thin 8vo, pr. wrs. (chipped); unopened. Argosy 713-336 1983 $30

LEWIS, OSCAR   From Land's End to the Ferry. San Francisco, Black Vine Press, (1942). First edition. Blue cloth over boards, spine stamped in gilt. One of 200 copies. Very good. Houle 22-1126 1983 $45

LEWIS, OSCAR   Silver Kings. New York: 1947. First edition. Illus. In worn jacket. Bradley 66-610 1983 $20

LEWIS, OSCAR   The Wonderful City of Carrie Van Wie. SF, 1963. Folio, linen-backed decorated bds., paper label. With 21 color plated & title-page. Perata 27-78 1983 $85

LEWIS, PERCIVAL   Historical inquiries concerning forests and forest laws... London, 1811. Engraved frontis. and folding map. Large 4to. Modern boards. Inscribed to John Gardiner, 20 April, 1853, on Contents page. Kraus 164-147 1983 $150

LEWIS, PERCY WYNDHAM
Please turn to
LEWIS, WYNDHAM

LEWIS, SAMUEL   A Topographical Dictionary of England. Published by S. Lewis & Co., 1831. 1st ed., 4 vols, large 4to, subscribers list, folding engraved map, (slightly torn without loss), 16 other folding engraved maps (2 slightly torn but without loss), 28 engraved maps, some foxing and offsetting, half green morocco, gilt, marbled boards, and endpapers, binding rather worn. Deighton 3-206 1983 £175

LEWIS, SINCLAIR   Ann Vickers. Garden City, Doubleday, 1933. First edition on rag paper. Dust jacket (nicked at edges, trifle soiling, top edge soiled) else very good. Houle 22-593 1983 $85

LEWIS, SINCLAIR   Arrowsmith. N.Y., Modern Library, (1933). First edition thus (so stated). Small 8vo, dust jacket (a few nicks) else, very good. Houle 22-594 1983 $30

LEWIS, SINCLAIR   Babbitt. NY, (1922). First issue, slight dent to edge of rear board, minor cover wear and soiling, bright very good in chipped, still presentable dustwrapper. Quill & Brush 54-800 1983 $125

LEWIS, SINCLAIR   Babbitt. NY, (1922). First issue, edges slightly rubbed, else very good or better. Quill & Brush 54-799 1983 $75

LEWIS, SINCLAIR   Cheap and Contented Labor. New York, (1929). 8vo. Wraps. 1st issue with no quotation mark before Dodsworth. One page in text has a margin tear (mended, not affecting text) else a fine copy. In Our Time 156-506 1983 $125

LEWIS, SINCLAIR   Cheap and Contented Labor. New York, 1929. First edition, second issue. Few illustrations. 8vo, orig. wrappers. Morrill 290-231 1983 $27.50

LEWIS, SINCLAIR   Elmer Gantry. N.Y., Harcourt, (1927). First edition, first issue with "Cantry" on spine. Dust jacket (small chips) but very good. Houle 22-595 1983 $150

LEWIS, SINCLAIR   Elmer Gantry. New York (1927). 8vo, cloth. First ed., 1st issue with the "G" looking like a "C" on the spine. In later dust jacket which has reviews. In Our Time 156-505 1983 $100

LEWIS, SINCLAIR   Elmer Gantry. NY, (1927). Second issue, bright, very good copy in slightly soiled, moderately chipped dustwrapper. Quill & Brush 54-801 1983 $100

LEWIS, SINCLAIR   Elmer Gantry. New York: Harcourt, Brace, (1927). 1st ed. Orig. blue cloth. Fine copy. Jenkins 155-794 1983 $20

LEWIS, SINCLAIR   John Dos Passos' Manhattan Transfer. New York: Harper, 1926. Cloth and boards. First edition. Frontis. One of 975 numbered copies only. Fine in slightly chipped glassine. Reese 20-616 1983 $175

LEWIS, SINCLAIR   Kingsblood Royal. N.Y., (1947). Ltd. edition. One of 1050 copies, signed by the author. Fine, in publisher's box. Argosy 714-466 1983 $85

LEWIS, SINCLAIR   The Man Who Knew Coolidge. N.Y., Harcourt Brace, (1928). First edition. Dust jacket. Fine - mint. Houle 22-596 1983 $225

LEWIS, WILLIAM   Memoirs of the Life and Religious Experience of William Lewis, Late of Bristol. Bristol: Printed for the Editors, by Wansbrough and Saunders, 1820. Large 12mo, wrapper. Fenning 60-251 1983 £14.50

LEWIS, WYNDHAM   America and Cosmic Man. London: Nicholson & Watson Ltd., (1948). First edition, second binding. Orig. blue cloth. Dust jacket (price clipped from front inner flap). Fine. MacManus 279-3275 1983 $65

LEWIS, WYNDHAM   The Apes of God. London: The Arthur Press, 1930. Illus. 1st ed., 1 of 750 copies, signed by author. Orig. cloth, dj. Moderately used dj has been expertly backed, faint stain to front cover, repair to front pastedown. Boxed. Excellent. Jenkins 155-1404 1983 $400

LEWIS, WYNDHAM   The Apes of God. L, 1930. Limited to 750 numbered and signed copies, page edges and bottom edge of cover dampstained, else very good. Quill & Brush 54-803 1983 $100

LEWIS, WYNDHAM   The Apes of God. Nash and Grayson, (1931). First trade edition. Black and white decorations by author. Cloth a little foxed. Nice. Rota 230-358 1983 £20

LEWIS, WYNDHAM   Blast. London, Lane, 1914-1915. First edition. Folio. Illus., boards (the pictorial wraps. are bound in; one illustrated by Lewis). Some light foxing, a few short tears, else good-very good. Houle 21-568 1983 $350

LEWIS, WYNDHAM   Blasting & Bombardiering. London: Eyre & Spottiswoode, 1937. First edition, first binding. Illus. Orig. cloth. Dust jacket (lightly dust-soiled). Fine. MacManus 279-3277 1983 $200

LEWIS, WYNDHAM   Blasting and Bombardiering. London, 1937. First edition. 8vo. Orig. orange cloth. 20 plates. Traylen 94-526 1983 £25

LEWIS, WYNDHAM   The Caliph's Design. Architects! Where is your Vortex? London: The Egoist Ltd., 1919. First edition. 8vo. Orig. marbled wrappers over boards. One of 1000 copies. Wrappers worn and faded at extremities, otherwise a very good copy. Jaffe 1-229 1983 $185

LEWIS, WYNDHAM   The Caliph's Design. The Egoist Ltd., 1919. First edition. Stiff wrappers. Head of backstrip worn. List of Egoist Press publications loosely inserted. Nice. Rota 230-357 1983 £90

LEWIS, WYNDHAM   The Childermass. London: Chatto & Windus, 1928. First edition. Orig. cloth. One of 225 copies signed by author. Light foxing and soiling. Unopened. Very good. MacManus 279-3278 1983 $150

LEWIS, WYNDHAM   Count Your Dead: They Are Alive! London: Lovat Dickson Ltd., (1937). First edition. Orig. cloth. Dust jacket, with decorations by author. 1500 copies printed. Very fine. MacManus 279-3279 1983 $400

LEWIS, WYNDHAM   The Demon of Progress in the Arts. London, 1954. Inscribed on front end-paper by the author. Nicked dustwrapper with one or two very short creases. Very good. Gekoski 2-120 1983 £80

LEWIS, WYNDHAM   The Diabolical Principle and The Dithyrambic Spectator. London: Chatto & Windus, 1931. First edition. Orig. cloth. Dust jacket (a little soiled, chipped). Very good. MacManus 279-3281 1983 $50

LEWIS, WYNDHAM   Doom of Youth. London: Chatto & Windus, 1932. First English edition. Orig. cloth. Presentation copy, inscribed on the front free endpaper to Augustus John, dated July 1932. One of 550 copies extant after 1934 owing to the book's being withdrawn after publication for reasons of libel. Covers somewhat rubbed and dampstained. Good. MacManus 279-3282 1983 $750

LEWIS, WYNDHAM   The Enemy. London: The Arthur Press, 1927-1929. First editions. 3 vols. Illus. 4to. Orig. decorated wrappers designed by author. Wrappers of vol. one worn. Good. MacManus 279-3283 1983 $350

LEWIS, WYNDHAM   The Old Gang and The New Gang. London: Desmond Harmsworth, 1933. First edition, first binding. Orig. cloth. Dust jacket (slightly dust-soiled). One of 1000 copies printed. Unopened. Fine. MacManus 279-3284 1983 $350

LEWIS, WYNDHAM   One Way Song. London, 1933. Very slightly used dustwrapper. Very good. Gekoski 2-118 1983 £60

LEWIS, WYNDHAM   The Roaring Queen. London: Secker & Warburg, (1973). First edition. Illus. with an orig. etching (signed) by Michael Ayrton. Orig. cloth, in publisher's box. One of 100 copies. Mint. MacManus 279-3286 1983 $200

LEWIS, WYNDHAM   Self-Condemned. Chicago: Henry Regnery Co., (1955). First American edition. Advance Review Copy, with publisher's slip pasted to front endsheet giving details of publication. Orig. cloth. Dust jacket. Mint. MacManus 279-3288 1983 $100

LEWIS, WYNDHAM   Tarr. London: The Egoist Ltd., 1918. First English edition. Orig. orange cloth. Cont. owner's signature on half-title. Minor wear to extremities of spine. Very good. MacManus 279-3290 1983 $185

LEWIS, WYNDHAM   Tarr. London: Chatto & Windus, (1928). First revised edition. Orig. cloth. Dust jacket (slightly worn & foxed). With a new preface by the author. Very good. MacManus 279-3289 1983 $85

LEWIS, WYNDHAM   The Wild Body. London: Chatto & Windus, 1927. First edition. Orig. cloth-backed marbled boards. One of 79 copies numbered and signed by Lewis. Spine faded. Corners slightly bumped. Near-fine. MacManus 279-3292 1983 $450

LEWIS, WYNDHAM   The Writer and the Absolute. London, 1952. Advance proof copy. With the date "June 19" in ink on front cover (the book was published on June 26). Very good. Gekoski 2-119 1983 £125

LEWISOHN, LUDWIG   The Case of Mr. Crump. Paris: Edward Titus, 1926. Orig. printed wrappers. 1st ed., limited to 500 copies for America. This copy unnumbered and inscribed by author: "Gear Guide...L.L." Early review copy. Some soiling of wrappers, else fine copy. Jenkins 155-1411 1983 $225

LEWISOHN, LUDWIG   The Last Days of Shylock. N.Y.: Harp., 1931. Stated first edition. 8vo. Cloth. Dust wrapper frayed. Illus. with black & whites by Szyk, intricate design. Fine. Aleph-bet 8-248 1983 $25

LEWISOHN, LUDWIG   The Romantic. Paris: Edward Titus at the Sign of the Black Manikin, 1931. Canvas and boards, paper label. First edition. One of 500 numbered copies on Verge de Rives, signed by the author. About fine in broken slipcase. Reese 20-128 1983 $50

LEYBURN, JOHN   A Reply to the Answer Made upon the Three Royal Papers. Printed for Matthew Turner, 1686. First edition. Without the preliminary blank leaf, 4to, wrapper, a very good copy. Fenning 61-254 1983 £28.50

LEYDA, JAY   The Melville Log: A Documentary Life of Herman Melville, 1819-1891. New York: Harcourt, Brace, (1951). 2 vols. 1st ed. Orig. blue cloth, gilt. Fine set. Jenkins 155-921 1983 $85

LEYDEN, E. VON   Handbuch der Ernahrungstherapie und Diatetik. Leipzig, 1903. 8vo. 2 vols. Half-leather. Gurney JJ-232 1983 £25

LEYLAND, FRANCIS A.   The Bronte Family, with Special Reference to Patrick Branwell Bronte. Hurst and Blackett, 1886. First edition, 2 vols. Half titles. Orig. brown cloth, sl. rubbing, v.g. Jarndyce 31-444 1983 £45

LEYMARIE, JEAN   The Jerusalem Windows. New York, (1962). Large quarto, cloth, dust-jacket. Most of the 210 pages are illus. by Marc Chagall. These include two orig. lithographs, 36 prefatory color designs, some of which are in 20 colors and transferred to stone under the direction of the artist. Printed in France. Duschnes 240-44 1983 $300

LEYMARIE, JEAN   Marc Chagall. The Jerusalem Windows. New York: George Braziller, 1962. 2 orig. color lithographs. Prof. illus. Large 4to, cloth, dust jacket. Printed by Mourlot Freres. Ars Libri 32-98 1983 $275

LEYMARIE, JEAN   Les Pastels, Dessins et Aquarelles de Renoir. Paris, Fernand Hazan, (1949). 24 plates of which several are in color. 12mo, orig. wrappers. Backstrip slightly cracked. Morrill 286-19 1983 $25

LEYMARIE, M. A.-LEO   Catalogue Illustre. Paris: Societe d'Editions Geographique, Maritimes et Coloniales, 1929. 24cm. 137 plates. Printed wrappers. Fine. McGahern 54-116 1983 $25

LEYS, JOHN K.   The Lindsays. London: Chatto & Windus, 1888. First edition. 3 vols. Orig. decorated cloth. Former owner's signature partially erased from endpapers. Fine. MacManus 279-3294 1983 $350

LIBER Scriptorum: The First Book of the Author's Club. New York: Printed by Theodore De Vinne, 1893. Folio, orig. stamped leather. First and only edition. Total edition is 251 copies signed by all the contributors. Bookplate. Most of the copies are shoddy due to the leather used by the binder. A fine copy. In Our Time 156-822 1983 $1,200

THE LIBERAL Way. Toronto/Vancouver: J.M. Dent, 1933. 22cm. Illus. Very good. McGahern 53-186 1983 $20

LIBERATI, FRANCESCO   La Perfettione del Cavallo Libri Tre Di Francesco Liberati Romano. In Roma Per Michele Hercole, 1669. 4to, one large folding plate. Bound in full new, polished vellum. New endpapers. Lightly toned throughout. Small wormhole on title page, slight loss of text. Otherwise very good. Arkway 22-82 1983 $825

LIBERMAN, ALEXANDER   Greece, Gods and Art. NY, 1968. Folio. 121 color pl. 8vo, cloth. Salloch 385-296 1983 $75

THE LIBERTY Bell, by Friends of Freedom. Boston: National Anti-Slavery Bazaar, 1853. 1st ed. Orig. black cloth, gully gilt, a.e.g. Uncommon annual with Turgueneff's French letter, and contributions by Higginson, Martineau, et al. Chipped copy, good only. Jenkins 155-1220 1983 $25

LIBRARY Catalogue, A descriptive list with prices of the various articles of furniture and equipments for libraries and museums. (Boston) 1903. Photos, cloth, ex-library, covers a bit rubbed, with loose inner hinges. King 46-372 1983 $35

LICHNOWSKY, PRINCE   My Mission to London, 1912-1914. N.Y.:
George H. Doran Co., n.d. First American edition. Orig. wrappers
(dust-soiled). Good. MacManus 279-3968 1983 $25

LICHTWARK, ALFRED   Meister Franke. Hamburg: Kunsthalle,
1899. 22 plates. Large square 8vo. Cloth. Ars Libri 32-433 1983
$50

LIEB, FREDERICK G.   The Detroit Tigers. N.Y., (1946).
First edition. Cloth. Spine and back cover moderately stained.
Autographed by author, Chas. Gehringer & Harry Heilmann. King 45-
492 1983 $37.50

LIEB, NORBERT   Hans Holbein der Altere. Munchen/
Berlin: Deutscher Kunstverlag, 1960. 384 illus. hors texte. 3
tipped-in color plates in text. 4to. Cloth. Dust jacket. From
the library of Jakob Rosenberg. Ars Libri 32-323 1983 $75

LIEBER, FRANCIS   Manual of political ethics. London:
Smith, 1839. First English edition. 8vo. Cont. half calf. Half-
title present. Quite rubbed. Ximenes 63-466 1983 $60

LIEBERKUEHN, J. N.   Dissertatio Anatomico-Physiologica de
Fabrica... Amsterdam: J. Schreuder & P. Mortier, 1760. 4to. Old
limp boards, uncut. 3 folding plates and 1 engraving in text. Second
issue. Gurney 90-72 1983 £90

LIEBERKUEHN, J. N.   Dissertatio Medica Inauguralis de
Valvula Coli et Usu processus Vermicularis. Leiden: C. Wishoff,
1739. 4to. Boards. Gurney 90-73 1983 £40

LIEBERKUHN, SAMUEL   The History of Our Lord and Savior
Jesus Christ. New York: Saniel Fanshaw, 1821. Modern full
morocco, blind-tooled. First edition. A fine copy. Felcone 22-
45 1983 $125

LIEBIG, JUSTUS   Animal Chemistry. London, 1842. First
edition in English. 8vo, orig. cloth. Argosy 713-337 1983 $250

LIEBIG, JUSTUS   Letters on Modern Agriculture. 1859.
First English edition, cr 8vo, half calf, very good. K Books 307-117
1983 £34

LIEBIG, JUSTUS   Researches on the Chemistry of Food,
and the Motion of the Juices in the Animal Body. Lowell (Mass.), 1848.
12mo. 1st American ed. Morrill 289-131 1983 $95

DAS LIEBLICHSTE Geschenk Fuer Damen. Regensburg, n.d. (19th century).
5 parts in one volume. Engraved title with vignette (printed in
green) and engraved music. Oblong 4to, cont. gilt-decorated red 1/4
morocco, tinted adges. Corners a little rubbed. Salloch 387-63
1983 $150

LIEGEOIS, JULES   De la Suggestion et du Somnambulisme
dans leurs Rapports avec la Jurisprudence et la Medecine Legale.
Paris, 1889. 8vo, orig. pr. wrs. (mended). First edition. Argosy

LIEGEOIS, JULES   L'Hypnotisme et Les Suggestions
Criminelles. Brussels: Maison Severeyns, 1898. Orig. green printed
wrappers. Inscribed to Bergson. Gach 95-226 1983 $75

LIEURE, J.   J. Callot. Paris: Editions de la
Gazette des Beaux-Arts, 1924-1929. 2 parts in 5 vols. (bound in 6).
Part I: 2 vols. 148 hinged heliogravure plates with 306 illus.
Part II: Catalogue. 1428 illus. hors texte (hinged heliogravure
plates). 62 illus. in text. Small folio. Marbled boards, 3/4
leather. This set with a letter from Lieure loosely inserted.
Catalogue printed on pur fil Lafuma, with plates by Jacomet. Very
rare. Watermarks in vol. 2. Ars Libri 32-75 1983 $2,000.

LIEUTAUD, JOSEPH   Essais anatomiques, contenant l'histoire
exacte de toutes les parties qui composent le corps d l'homme. Paris:
Huart, 1742. Thick 8vo. Cont. quarter vellum. First edition. 6
folding plates. A fine uncut copy. Rare. Ximenes 63-283 1983 $800

THE LIFE and actions of Lewis Dominique Cartouche... London:
J. Roberts, 1722. First edition. 8vo. Disbound. Ximenes 63-79
1983 $85

LIFE and Adventures of Robert, the Hermit of Massachusetts,...
Providence, Trumbull, 1829. First edition. Frontispiece. 12mo,
old wrappers. Restitched; foxed; 2 minute tears repaired on title,
no loss of text. Morrill 290-546 1983 $50

LIFE and Adventures of Sam Bass the Notorious Union Pacific and Texas
Train Robber... Austin, n.d. Blue wrappers. Some staining. Printed
by John A. Norris. This issue has become scarce. Jenkins 153-740
1983 $35

THE LIFE and character of Marcus Portius Cato Uticensis. London:
printed for Bernard Lintott, 1713. 4to, wrappers, first edition.
Fine copy of a scarce pamphlet. Ximenes 64-534 1983 $250

THE LIFE and Death of Ralph Wallis the Cobler of Glocester. London:
by E. Okes for William Whitwood, 1670. First edition. 4to. 19th
Century half calf. Browned, damage to bottom margin of last few
leaves, a few words lost. Heath 48-200 1983 £75

LIFE and Public Services of George G. Meade. Philadelphia, (1864).
First edition, orig. pictorial wrappers, virtually mint. Jenkins
152-703 1983 $65

THE LIFE and Travels of Mungo Park. NY, 1840. Illus., interior foxed,
very good, rebound. Quill & Brush 54-1688 1983 $75

LIFE and Works of Charlotte Bronte and Her Sisters. London: Smith,
Elder & Co., 1877. 7 vols. Illus. 3/4 morocco with marbled boards
and endpapers. An early collected edition, well illus. Spines and
covers slightly faded and worn. Handsomely bound. Very good set.
MacManus 277-693 1983 $350

THE LIFE of John Metcalf... York: by E. & R. Peck, 1795. First
edition. 8vo. Engraved portrait. Modern half calf. Some browning.
Very rare. Heath 48-139 1983 £150

THE LIFE of Mrs. Abington, celebrated comic actress. London: Reader,
1888. 8vo, original parchment boards (waterstained, spine defective).
1st edition. With a portrait (light stain). Ximenes 64-2 1983
$30

THE LIFE of Mr. James Quin, comedian. London: printed for S. Bladon,
1766. 12mo, contemporary calf, gilt, neatly rebacked, spine gilt.
First edition. Frontispiece portrait; very good copy. Ximenes 64-
446 1983 $400

THE LIFE of Mr. James Quin, comedian. London: Reader, 1887. 8vo,
original white parchment boards, morocco label (a bit rubbed, slightly
soiled). First edition thus; a reprint of the 1766 edition, with a
substantial supplement added. With a portrait. Ximenes 64-447 1983
$35

THE LIFE of Mr. John Dennis, the renowned critick. London: printed
for J. Roberts, 1734. 8vo, disbound, 1st ed. Half-title present.
Very rare. Ximenes 64-167 1983 $750

THE LIFE of William Henry Harrison... Philadelphia, 1840. 2nd ed.
16mo. Lacks back endleaf. Morrill 289-612 1983 $22.50

LIGER, L.   Amusemens de la Campagne. A Paris
chez Claude Prudhomme...M.DCCIX, (1709). 12mo, bound in full
cont. mottled calf. Elaborately tooled and stamped in gold on
spine. Hinges worn, slightly cracked. 18th century marbled endpapers.
Gauffered edges. Numerous woodcut illus. including within the
text. Arkway 22-83 1983 $575

LIGHT, ALFRED W.   Bunhill Fields. C.J. Farncombe, 1913.
First edition, front. illus. & chart of the grounds. Orig. green
cloth. Signed presentation copy from the author. Jarndyce 31-270
1983 £14.50

LIGHT-HOUSES. London, Printed by W. Clowes & Sons, 1849. 8vo, title-
page, orig. blue wrapper, worn. Pickering & Chatto 22-59 1983 $120

LIGHTFOOT, JOHN   The Chemical History and Progress of
Aniline Black. Burnley, Lancashire: by the Author, 1871. 8vo.
Orig. blind stamped black cloth. Very good copy. Rare. Zeitlin
264-261 1983 $150

LIGHTFOOT, JOHN   Ervbhin or Miscellanies Christian and
Judaicall, and Others. London, printed by G. Miller for Robert
Swayne and William Adderton, 1629. 8vo, cont. sheep, later label,
hinges rubbed, monogram on title and notes on last leaf, decent copy.
First edition. Ravenstree 97-45 1983 $273

LIGHTWOOD, JAMES T.   Charles Dickens and Music. 1912.
First edition. Half title, front. Orig. green cloth, t.e.g. With
marginal notes; relevant cuttings attached to prelims. and inserted
loosely into an envelope. Jarndyce 30-210 1983 £24

LIGNELL, LOIS   Three Japanese Mice and Their Wiskers.
NY: Farrar & Rinehart (1934). Oblong octavo. Illus. Edges
slightly darkened, else very fine in pictorial boards and lightly
chipped matching dust wrapper. Bromer 25-363 1983 $45

LILBURNE, JOHN   The hunting of the foxes from New-
Market... (London): printed in a corner of freedome..., 1649.
First edition. Small 4to. Disbound. Slight stains on title,
otherwise a very good copy. Ximenes 63-102 1983 $90

LILFORD, LORD   Lord Lilford on Birds. 1903. 13 plates
by Thorburn, cr. 4to, cloth, binding slightly-worn, frontispiece
waterstained. Wheldon 160-793 1983 £15

LILFORD, LORD   Notes on the Birds of Northamptonshire.
1880-83. 8vo, cloth, very scarce. Wheldon 160-792 1983 £32

LILIENFELD, KARL   Arent de Gelder. Haag: Martinus
Nijhoff, 1914. 25 illus. hors texte. 4to. Wrappers. From the
library of Jakob Rosenberg. Ars Libri 32-252 1983 $125

LILLEY, A. E. V.   A Book of Studies in Plant Form.
Chapman & Hall, 1916. With 247 illus., 8vo, orig. cloth, casing working
loose, otherwise a very good copy. Fenning 60-252 1983 £21.50

LILLJEBORG, W.   Cladocera Sueciae. (Uppsala, 1900).
Facsimile Reprint, Stockholm, 1982. 87 plates of 1378 figures, 3
parts in 1 vol., 4to, cloth. Wheldon 160-1315 1983 £58

LILLO, GEORGE   The London Merchant. London: printed
for J. Gray and sold by J. Roberts, 1731. 8vo, 2nd ed., title a little
spotted, wrappers. Pickering & Chatto 19-35 1983 $150

LIMA, E. DA CRUZ   Mammals of Amazonia, Vol. 1, General
Introduction and Primates. Rio de Janeiro, 1945. 42 coloured plates
by the author, cr. folio, original wrappers. Scarce. English
language edition limited to 975 copies. Wheldon 160-574 1983 £65

LIMPRICHT, HEINRICH FRANZ PETER   Grundriss der Organischen
Chemie. Braunschweig: C.A. Schwetschke & Sohn, 1855. 8vo.
Modern buckram. Acid staining, some holes. Repairs title pages
and margins with loss of a few characters. Zeitlin 264-262 1983
$110

LINCOLN, ABRAHAM   His Autobiographical Writings. Kingsport,
Tn., (1947). Color port., facs. letters. Privately printed, ltd.
edition on rag paper. Argosy 716-239 1983 $22.50

LINCOLN, ABRAHAM   The Life and Public Service of General
Zachary Taylor. Boston, 1922. Ed. limited to 435 copies and the
1st printing in book form. 12mo, orig. marbled boards, cloth back,
paper label, partly broken box, fine. Morrill 288-628 1983 $27.50

LINCOLN, ABRAHAM   Political Debates... Columbus: Follett,
Foster and Company, 1860. 8vo, 23-1/2 cm. Orig. brown blind-stamped
cloth, worn at extremities; margins dampstained. First edition,
the later issue with the letter from Stephen A. Douglas objecting to
the publishers' alterations of his words. Grunder 7-49 1983 $40

LINCOLN, ABRAHAM   Political Debates Between Hon. Abraham
Lincoln and Hon. Stephen A. Douglas... Columbus, 1860. First
edition (not first state). Ex-Library, foxed, slightly stained,
spine ends frayed. King 46-66 1983 $35

LINCOLN, CHARLES HENRY   A Calendar of John Paul Jones Manuscripts in the Library of Congress. Washington: GPO, 1903. Frontis.,
cloth, a little wear, front cover creased. Dawson 470-190 1983 $40

LINCOLN, CHARLES HENRY   Naval Records of the American Revolution. Washington, 1906. 1st ed. Prepared from the originals in
Library of Congress. 4to, ex-library. Morrill 288-237 1983 $30

LINCOLN, RUFUS   The Papers of Captain Rufus Lincoln
of Wareham, Mass. N.P., Privately Printed, 1904. 1st ed. Fac.
Tall 8vo. Some light dampstains on covers. Morrill 286-250 1983
$37.50

LIND, JAMES   An Essay on Diseases Incidental to
Europeans in Hot Climates. For T. Becket and P.A. de Hondt, London,
1768. First edition. Quaritch NS 5-66 1983 $950

LIND, JAMES   Versuch ueber die Krankheiten denen
Europaer in Heisen Climaten unterworfen sind. Riga & Leipzig: J.F.
Hartnoch, 1773. First edition in German. 8vo, cont. calf, worn;
a few stains. Argosy 713-339 1983 $250

LINDAHL, ERIK   Penningpolitikens Medel. Malmo, 1930.
1st ed., large 8vo, uncut in original printed wrappers, edges frayed.
Pickering & Chatto 21-65 1983 $100

LINDAU, G.   Kryptogamenflora fur Anfanger, Vol. 2,
Pt. 2. Berlin, 1922. 520 text-figures, 8vo, cloth (ex-library copy).
Wheldon 160-1854 1983 £15

LINDBERGH, ANNE MORROW   North to the Orient. New York, 1935.
8vo. Cloth. Fine in intact dj which has some tears. In Our Time
156-508 1983 $35

LINDBERG, CHARLES   Spirit of St. Louis. N.Y., Scribner,
1953. First edition. Maroon cloth, acetate jacket. Fine. Ltd.,
presentation edition, signed by Lindberg. Houle 21-571 1983 $425

LINDBERGH, CHARLES   We - Pilot & Plane. London, 1927. First
edition. Frontis. 14 plates. Sm. 8vo. Spine faded. Good. Edwards
1042-600 1983 £25

LINDEMANN, FREDERICK ALEXANDER   The Physical Significance of the
Quantum Theory. Oxford: Clarendon, 1932. First edition. 8vo.
Orig. cloth. A little rubbed. Very good copy. Zeitlin 264-263
1983 $35

LINDGREN, O.   The Trials of a Planter. Kalimpong, 1933.
Plates. 8vo. Orig. cloth. Inscribed by author on front endpaper.
Good. Edwards 1044-436 1983 £20

LINDGREN, WALDEMAR   The Gold and Silver Veins of Silver
City. Washington, 1897. Folding elevations. Half leather, joints
and spine rubbed, top of backstrip torn. Ex. lib. Reese 19-327
1983 $125

LINDLEY, J.   An Introduction to Botany. 1839.
Third edition, 6 plates and numerous text-figures, 8vo, original
cloth, used. Wheldon 160-1543 1983 £15

LINDLEY, J.   Rosarum Monographia: or, a botanical
history of Roses. 1820. 8vo, modern half morocco, in a slip case,
plain and hand-coloured plates. Fine copy. The Last leaf of text
has the margin very neatly repaired. Wheldon 160-61 1983 £575

LINDLEY, J.   Sertum Orchidaceum: a wreath of the most
beautiful Orchidaceous flowers. (1837-) 1838 (-1842). Imp. folio,
half green morocco, gilt, coloured frontis. and 49 coloured plates.
The joints are a trifle rubbed and the head of the spine a trifle
worn. Some foxing of the plates and text, plate 1 being the most
seriously affected. Wheldon 160-62 1983 £5,000

LINDLEY, J.   Sertum Orchidaceum. (1837- , 1838-42),
Facsimile Reprint, 1974. Imp. folio, cloth, 50 coloured plates. A
full size reproduction. Wheldon 160-63 1983 £195

LINDLEY, J   Sertum Orchidaceum. NY: Johnson
Reprint Corp. (n.d. ca 1973). Tall folio, facs. reprint of the
orig. edition published in 1838. With frontis. + 49 full-page color
botanical plates. Edition ltd. to 1,000 numbered copies. Green gilt-
stamped cloth. Fine. Karmiole 76-25 1983 $250

LINDLEY, J   The theory of horticulture. London:
Longman, etc., 1840. First edition. 8vo. Orig. grey-green cloth.
Many illus. Bookplate removed. A little rubbed. Ximenes 63-180
1983 $75

LINDMAN, C. A. M.   Nordens Flora. Stockholm, 1974-75.
New edition, 663 coloured plates and 16 distribution maps, 10 vols.,
8vo, boards. Wheldon 160-1736 1983 £53

LINDSAY, JACK   Dionysos: Nietzsche Contra Nietzsche.
London, Fanfrolico Press (1928). 4to, with 12 plates by Norman Lindsay and others. Blue cloth, t.e.g., uncut. One of 500, signed by
the author. Houle 21-572 1983 $65

LINDSAY, JACK   Men of Forty-Eight. London, 1948.
First edition. Dust wrapper. Fine. Rota 230-359 1983 £12

LINDSAY, JACK   Theocritus. Fanfrolico Press, n.d.
4to. Frontis. 18 woodcut plates. Small flaw in title. Green parchment, gilt, top joint tender. Edition limited to 500 copies, No. 165.
Greer 40-98 1983 £35

LINDSAY, VACHEL   The Chinese Nightingale and Other Poems.
New York, 1916. 1st ed. Review copy with publisher's perforated
notice on title page. Decorated yellow cloth. Rare. Bradley 63-88
1983 $50

LINDSAY, VACHEL   The Chinese Nightingale and Other Poems.
New York, 1916. First edition. Review copy, with publisher's perforated notice on title page. Decorated yellow cloth. Bradley 65-117
1983 $45

LINDSAY, VACHEL   Collected Poems. N.Y., 1923. First
edition. Argosy 714-471 1983 $35

LINDSAY, VACHEL   General William Booth Enters into
Heaven and Other Poems. New York, 1921. Red cloth. An unusual
association (and presentation) copy jointly inscribed by poet and
his brother-in-law Paul Wakefield to a friend. Lindsay wrote the
main presentation on first free end paper, December 31, 1923. Very
good copy. Bradley 65-118 1983 $65

LINDSAY, VACHEL   Going-to-the-Stars. N.Y., 1926.
First edition. Illus. Owner's bookplate. Argosy 714-472 1983
$20

LINDSAY, VACHEL   The Golden Whales of California. NY,
1920. Light interior foxing, else very good in stained, lightly
chipped dustwrapper, owner's name. Quill & Brush 54-809 1983 $75

LINDSAY, VACHEL   The Golden Whales of California. N.Y.,
1920. First edition. Argosy 714-473 1983 $40

LINDSLEY, PHILIP   Speech in Behalf of the University of
Nashville. Nashville: S. Nye, 1837. Later cloth, morocco label.
Signed in ink by James Hamilton, a professor. Jenkins 152-206 1983
$65

LINEBARGER, PAUL M. A.   Psychological Warfare. Washington (1948).
First ed. Illus., cloth, corner chipped else good in frayed dw.
King 46-480 1983 $20

LINFORD, MADELINE   Bread and Honey. Kingswood, Surrey:
William Heinemann Ltd. at The Windmill Press, 1928. First edition.
Frontis. illus. Orig. cloth. Limited to 250 copies for private
circulation. Spine darkened. Good. MacManus 279-3296 1983 $25

LINGARD, JOHN   A History of England. Philadelphia:
Eugene Cummiskey, 1827. First American edition. 14 vols. Orig.
cloth-backed boards. Paper labels. Foxed throughout. Annotated on
the flyleaves by a former owner. MacManus 279-3297 1983 $150

LINGAY, JOSEPH   Histoire du Cabinet des Tuileries.
Paris, chez Chanson, 1815. First edition, including the half-title,
8vo, wrapper. A little light foxing at beginning and end, but a
nice copy. Fenning 61-255 1983 £10.50

LINGEL, R. J. C.   A Bibliographical Checklist of the Writings... Metuchen: Americana Collector, 1926. First edition. 1 of
151 copies. Orig. boards, dj. Mint copy, with ink presentation from
Lingel. Jenkins 155-783 1983 $25

LINGENFELTER, RICHARD E.   Presses of the Pacific Islands 1817-
1867. Los Angeles, 1967. Woodcuts by Edgar Dorsey Taylor. 8vo,
cloth, paper label, vignette in gilt on front cover. One of 500
copies. A fine copy Perata 27-151 1983 $75

LINLEY, THOMAS (1732-1795)   The Duenna. Constable, 1925. 12 colour
plates, 14 collotype illus. & facs. of first edition. Grey decor.
cloth (d/w soiled & discolored with wear on top). Very good copy.
Hodgkins 27-493 1983 £25

LINLEY, WILLIAM   The adventures of Ralph Reybridge.
London: Phillips, 1809. First edition. 4 vols. 12mo. Cont.
dark blue half morocco, spines gilt. Fine copy. Rare. Ximenes
63-127 1983 $475

LINLEY, WILLIAM   The Adventures of Ralph Reybridge.
Richard Phillips, 1809. First edition, 4 vols., half title vol. III.
Some foxing, half red roan, a little rubbed and sl. chipped. Jarndyce
30-455 1983 £150

LINN, WILLIAM   The Blessings of America. N.Y.: Thomas
Greenleaf, 1791. First edition, 8vo, sewed. With half title. At
end, 3pp patriotic Ode by Wm. Pitt Smith. Argosy 716-463 1983 $30

LINN, WILLIAM   Serious Considerations on the Election
of a President. Trenton: Sherman, Mershon & Thomas, 1800. 3/4
morocco. Very good. Felcone 19-27 1983 $85

LINNAEUS, CAROLUS
Please turn to
LINNE, CARL VON (1707-1778)

LINNE, CARL VON   Amoenitates Academicae. Stockholm
and Leipzig, 1749. 8vo, contemporary boards (rebacked), title
vignette and engraved plates. 2nd issue. Wheldon 160-173 1983
£100

LINNE, CARL VON   Critica Botanica. Ray Society, 1938.
8vo, cloth. Wheldon 160-1548 1983 £20

LINNE, CARL VON   Entomologia Faunae Suecicae. Lyons,
1789. 4 vols., 8vo, new cloth. Rare. Without the atlas of 12
plates and lacking pp. lxv-ccxiii of Synopsis in Vol. 4. Wheldon
160-1115 1983 £60

LINNE, CARL VON   Flora Lapponica. Amsterdam, 1737.
8vo, contemporary boards, new calf, back. Rare first edition.
Lacks the frontispiece and 12 plates. Some foxing, but generally
in good condition. Wheldon 160-1737 1983 £80

LINNE, CARL VON   Genera Plantarum. Frankfort am Main,
1789-91. Editio octava post Reichardianam secunda. 2 vols. in 1,
8vo, diced calf, m.e. Crest of E. Rudge on spine. Wheldon 160-1545
1983 £75

LINNE, CARL VON   Hortus Cliffortianus. Amsterdam, 1737.
Engraved allegorical frontis. and 36 engraved plates, folio, new half
calf. Some very slight dust-soiling and foxing, else a good copy.
Wheldon 160-64 1983 £1,950

LINNE, CARL VON   Lachesis Lapponica, or a Tour in Lapland.
1811. 55 illustrations, 2 vols., royal 8vo, original boards (neatly
rebacked), uncut. A good copy. Wheldon 160-403 1983 £250

LINNE, CARL VON   Museum S:ae R:ae M:tis Ludovicae Ulricae
Reginae Svecorum. Stockholm, 1764. 8vo, new half calf (antique style).
Rare. Wheldon 160-178 1983 £475

LINNE, CARL VON   Museum Tessinianum. Stockholm, 1753.
Folio, contemporary calf-backed boards spine worn, plates. Plate 2 is
duplicate and plate 3 is missing. Wheldon 160-177 1983 £250

LINNE, CARL VON   Natuurlyke Historie of Uitvoerige
Beschryving der Dieren, Planten en Mineraalen. Amsterdam, 1761-62.
28 plates, 3 vols., 8vo, original calf-backed boards (worn, some
covers detached). Wheldon 160-575 1983 £60

LINNE, CARL VON   Natuurlyke Historie of Uitvoerige
Beschryving der Dieren, Planten en Mineraalen. Amsterdam, 1762-63.
21 engraved plates, 2 vols., 8vo, original calf-backed boards (worn).
Wheldon 160-794 1983 £50

LINNE, CARL VON   Natuurlyke Historie of Uitvoerige
Beschryving der Dieren, Planten en Mineraalen. Amsterdam, 1764.
7 plates, 8vo, original calf-backed boards (worn). Vol. 1, Stuk 6.
Wheldon 160-980 1983 £30

LINNE, CARL VON   Natuurlyke Historie of Uitvoerige
Beschryving der Dieren, Planten en Mineraalen. Amsterdam, 1764.
Stuk 7, De Visschen. 6 engraved plates, 8vo, original calf-backed
boards, front cover detached, worn. Wheldon 160-981 1983 £30

LINNE, CARL VON   Philosophia Botanica. Vienna, 1770.
11 plates, 8vo, contemporary calf, rebacked. Reprint of the first
edition. Wheldon 160-1544 1983 £40

LINNE, CARL VON   Systema Naturae... Leyden: Jo.
Wilhelm de Groot for Theodorus Haak, 1735. First edition. Folio.
19th-century leather-backed boards, by J. Edmond of Aberdeen. With
engraved exlibris of Sir Charles W. Thomson. In cloth case. Some
damp and dust discoloration. Rare. Kraus 164-148 1983 $48,500

LINNE, CARL VON   Systema Naturae per regna tria naturae.
Stockholm, 1758-59. Editio decima, 2 vols., 8vo, modern full calf.
Some foxing but a good copy. Wheldon 160-174 1983 £1,350

LINNE, CARL VON   Systema Vegetabilium. Gottingen, 1825-
27. 16th edition, 4 vols. (of 5), 8vo, contemporary half calf,
worn. The 2 parts of vol. 4 are bound together. Wheldon 160-1546
1983 £60

LINTON, E. LYNN   Under which Lord? London: Chatto &
Windus, 1879. First edition. 12 illus. by A. Hopkins. 3 vols.
Orig. decorated cloth. Bookplates on front endpapers. Very good.
MacManus 279-3298 1983 $235

LINTON, E. LYNN   Witch Stories. London: Chapman & Hall,
1861. First edition. Orig. brown cloth. Spine and covers faded and
worn. Preliminary pages foxed. Good. MacManus 279-3299 1983 $125

LINTON, E. LYNN   Witch Stories. London: Chapman & Hall,
1861. First edition. Orig. green cloth. Former owner's name stamped
on title-page and endpapers. A bit soiled and worn. Very good.
MacManus 279-3300 1983 $125

LINTON, RALPH   Arts of the South Seas. New York:
Museum of Modern Art, 1946. Color illustrations by Miguel Covarrubias. Prof. illus. 4to. Cloth. Ars Libri 34-830 1983 $30

LIPPARD, GEORGE   The Quaker City; or, The Monks of Monk-
Hall. Phila.: Publ. by the author, (1845) 2 vols, new wrs, worn,
continuously paged. Argosy 710-160 1983 $75

LIPPERHEIDE, FRANZ JOSEPH VON   Katalog der Freiherrlich von
Lipperheide'schen Kostumbibliothek. New York: Hacker Art Books,
1963. 2 vols., hundreds of illus., cloth. Reprint of the 1896-1905
ed. Dawson 470-192 1983 $75

LIPPITT, FRANCIS J.   A Treatise on Intrenchments. N.Y.,
1866. Many diagrams, one folding. Orig. stipple cloth. Argosy
716-297 1983 $22.50

LIPPMANN, E. O.   Von Enstehung und Ausbreitung der
Alchemie mit einem Anhange zur alteren Geschichte der Metalle.
Berlin, 1919. 8vo. Cloth. Gurney JJ-235 1983 £25

LIPPMANN, F.   Les gravures sur bois du Maitre I.B.
a l'Oiseau. Paris, 1894. 11 facsimile plates. 1 text illus.
Large folio. Boards. Printed on fine laid paper. Uncut. Ars
Libri 32-434 1983 $100

LIPPMANN, F.   Zeichnungen von Sandro Botticelli
zu Dantes Gottlicher Komodie. Berlin: G. Grote, 1896. 99 collotype plates. 20 text illus. Small folio. Cloth. Ars Libri 33-
47 1983 $175

LIPS, JULIUS E.   The Savage Hits Back. New Haven:
Yale University Press, 1937. 213 illus. by Bronislaw Malinowski.
4to. Cloth. Ars Libri 34-28 1983 $65

LIPSIUS, JUSTUS   A Brief Outline of the History of
Libraries. Chicago: A.C. McClurg, 1907. 12mo. Cloth spine,
marbled paper over boards, leather spine label. One of 250 copies.
Printed at The Merrymount Press. The spine label is chipped.
Oak Knoll 49-270 1983 $25

LISSITZKY-KUPPERS, SOPHIE   El Lissitzky: Life, Letters, Texts.
Greenwich: New York Graphic Society, 1968. 278 plates (110 color).
Large 4to. Cloth. Dust jacket. Ars Libri 32-409 1983 $225

LIST, FREIDRICH   Systeme National D'Economie Politique.
Paris, Capelle, 1851. 1st ed. in French, 8vo, occasional light
spotting, pencilled marginalia here and there, cont. morocco backed
marbled boards, spine elaborately gilt. A very good copy. Pickering
& Chatto 21-66 1983 $450

LIST of Books by Women, Natives or Residents of the State of New
York. N.p., 1893. 8vo, quarter morocco, orig. wraps. bound with.
Interleaved. Ownership inscription of Sarah M Sage/Menands/Albany/
1894. Rostenberg 88-93 1983 $125

LISTER, CHARLES   The College Chums. London: T.C. Newby,
1845. First edition. 2 vols. Orig. cloth. Spines faded and slightly
worn at the ends. Piece missing from the free endpaper of vol. two.
Good. MacManus 279-3302 1983 $250

LISTER, HERBERT   Hamilton, Canada. Hamilton & London,
(1913). 22 1/2cm. Numerous illus. Blue cloth, some soiling else
a very good copy. McGahern 53-99 1983 $45

LISTER, JOSEPH   Chirurgie Antiseptique et Theorie
des Germes. Brussels, 1882. 8vo. Wrappers. Half-title and title
dustsoiled. Half title mounted. A few tears at beginning of vol.
roughly repaired. Gurney JJ-236 1983 £25

LISTER, JOSEPH   Collected Papers. Oxford: Clarendon
Press, 1909. Thick large 4to, buckram. First edition. Argosy 713-340
1983 $60

LISTER, JOSEPH   Contributions to Psysiology and Pathology... London: Printed by Taylor and Francis, 1859. Orig. offprint,
4to, title with 2 engr. plates, 1 coloured. Inscribed on title "Dr.
Bullock with the author's kind regards", pencil annotations in a few
margins, title a little dust soiled, orig. paper wrappers, spine repaired. Rare. Pickering & Chatto 22-61 1983 $225

LISTER, JOSEPH   On the Coagulation of the Blood.
London: Printed by Taylor and Francis, 1863. Orig. offprint, 8vo,
6 illus. in text, inscribed on the title "With the author's kind
regards", marbled wrappers. Pickering & Chatto 22-60 1983 $700

LISTER, MARTIN   De Frontibus Medicatis Angliae. London,
1684. Second edition, 2 parts in one vol., folding plate, a small
patch of worm in the upper margin, early calf, rebacked. K Books 307-
119 1983 £112

LISTER, RAYMOND   For Love of Leda. (Linton, Eng.):
Windmill House Press, 1976. Octavo. Printed from calligraphy by
Jacqueline J. Richardson with color illus. by Lister tipped onto every
page. Limited to 14 copies signed by author/illustrator with an orig.
drawing for one of the illus. in this book tipped-in. Near mint in
full vellum and slip-case covered with decorated paper. Bromer 25-
249 1983 $265

LISTER, RAYMOND   Gabha. Cambridge: The Golden Head Press,
1964. Sm. 8vo. Pictorial title. 6pp of illus. 2pp of text printed
in dark red on vellum. Edition limited to 26 copies. Inscribed by
Lister to D.R. Cammell. Greer 40-132 1983 £45

LISTER, RAYMOND   The Song of Theodosius. Cambridge:
The Golden Head Press, 1963. Sm. 8vo. 3 text illus. printed in dark
green on vellum. Cream cloth, gilt. Edition limited to 41 copies,
15 on vellum. Also presentation inscription. Greer 40-133 1983 £45

LISTER, THOMAS HENRY   Granby, A Novel. Henry Colburn, 1826.
3 vols, 12mo, half blue calf, gilt backs; a very good and tall
copy; half-titles in vols. I and III only. First edition. Hill
165-70 1983 £75

LISTER, THOMAS HENRY   Granby. Henry Colburn, 1833. 3 vols.,
half calf, red labels, v.g. Jarndyce 30-456 1983 £38

LISTER, THOMAS HENRY   Herbert Lacy. London: Colburn, 1828.
First edition. 3 vols. Orig. boards, paper labels. Front hinge
cracked (cords sound) on vol. one. In a cloth slipcase. Fine.
MacManus 279-3303 1983 $375

LISTON, ROBERT   Memoir on the Formation and Connexions
of the Crural Arch. Edinburgh: Printed for Peter Hill and Co., 1819.
1st ed., 8vo, 3 engraved plates; disbound. Pickering & Chatto 22-62
1983 $185

LITCHFIELD, FREDERICK   Pottery and Porcelain. Truslove,
Hanson & Comba, 1900. First edition, with 40 plates (7 coloured) and
numberous other illus., roy. 8vo, orig. cloth, gilt, t.e.g., two small
sections working loose, but still a very good copy. Fenning 60-253
1983 £18.50

LITCHFIELD, R. B.   Tom Wedgwood, the First Photographer.
London, 1903. First edition. Illustrated. 8vo. Morrill 290-234
1983 $50

THE LITERARY and Artistic Properties of the Late Evert Jansen Wendell
Other Than That Taken by Harvard University... New York, 1919.
Catalog in 6 parts. 8vo, orig. wrappers. Morrill 286-506 1983
$27.50

LITERARY leisure, or the recreations of Solomon Saunter, Esq.
London: William Miller, 1802. First collected edition. 2 vols.
8vo. Contemporary diced calf, spines gilt. A few leaves foxed,
but a fine copy. Scarce. Ximenes 63-247 1983 $225

THE LITERARY Miscellany. Cambridge, William Hilliard, 1805.
Vol. 1. 8vo, contemporary calf, leather label. Only 2 vols. pub.
Morrill 286-254 1983 $25

LITTLE, DAVID F.   The Wanderer, and Other Poems. Los
Angeles: Mirror Printing and Binding House, 1880. Jenkins 153-97
1983 $50

LITTLE, ELIZABETH M.   Persephone, and Other Poems. Dublin:
William McGee, 1884. First edition, 8vo, orig. cloth, gilt. Fore-edge
of boards lightly discoloured otherwise a nice copy. Fenning 60-
254 1983 £21.50

LITTLE, W. J.   On Spinal Weakness & Spinal Curvatures.
London, 1868. Small 8vo, cloth; ex-lib. First edition. Argosy 713-
341 1983 $90

LITTLE Gem Brand Book. Kansas City, 1900. First edition. Illus.
Printed calf over boards. Back and front boards chipped, secured at
spine with tape; first end paper and title leaf detached but present.
A very rare book in any condition. Bradley 65-42 1983 $750

A LITTLE Girl's Visit to a Country Garden. Routledge, nd (ca. 1850).
1st edn. Decor. title page & 7 full page illus. printed in colours by
Edmund Evans. Green boards with page illus. repeated on fr.
cvr., pub's adverts on rear cvr. (re-backed with new bkstrip, edges
of cvrs. discol'd with some wear, re-cased), rare, fine. Hodgkins 27-
380 1983 £50

LITTLE Goody Two-Shoes. NY: McLoughlin Bros., (ca. 1855-60). Octavo.
12 hand-colored engravings. Printed self-wrappers soiled, else very
nice. Bromer 25-364 1983 $30

THE LITTLE Warbler. Edinburgh: Oliver & Boyd, (ca. 1820). 3 vols. in
1, with 3 frontispieces. All have both engraved and printed title-
pages. Red morocco binding rebacked. Some foxing throughout, still a
nice, thick volume. (2 13/16 x 1 3/4; 72x45mm). Bromer 25-449 1983
$150

LITTLEJOHN, DAVID   Dr. Johnson and Noah Webster. San
Francisco: The Book Club of California, 1971. Small folio, illus.
1st ed., 1 of 500 copies printed by Grabhorn-Hoyem. Orig. cloth-
backed gilt boards, leather spine label. At the end are inserted
two fine matching leaves from Johnson's Dictionary and Webster's
1828 dictionary. Mint copy. Jenkins 155-489 1983 $200

LITTLEJOHN, DAVID   Dr. Johnson and Noah Webster, Two Men
& Their Dictionaries. San Francisco: The Book Club of California,
1971. Limited to 500 copies printed by Grabhorn-Hoyem. Tall 4to.
Cloth-backed boards. Illus. with two matched leaves from the
dictionaries of Johnson and Webster. Fine. Oak Knoll 49-265 1983
$200

LITTLEJOHN, DAVID   Dr. Johnson and Noah Webster: Two Men
and their Dictionaries. S.F.: 1971. Illus. with a matched pair of
orig. leaves from A Dictionary of the English by Samuel Johnson, A. M.
(1755) and An American Dictionary of the English Language by Noah
Webster, L.L.D. (1828). Lg. 4to, 1/2 over decorated boards, gilt,
leather label. One of 500 copies. Perata 28-66 1983 $150

LITTLETON, THOMAS   Little-Tons Tenvres in Englishe.
(Colophon: London, Rychard Tottel, 1581). 8vo, late 19th century
sheep, rubbed, 2 early names on title, one being that of Robert South.
Outer blank edge of title reinforced, lower blank edge of several
signatures wormed, some usual minor smudges and stains. Ravenstree
97-47 1983 $540

LITTLETON, THOMAS   Littleton's Tenures in English. London,
1627. Folios, 8vo. Lightish dampstaining to last several leaves,
title page dusty, small paper repair to it & to next leaf, just affecting 3 letters of latter, top margin cut close, affecting very few head-
notes, bound in full contemp. calf, quite worn, covers blind-dec.,
sometime neatly rebacked, spine double blind-ruled & gilt-lettered.
Clean, crisp copy. Boswell 7-114 1983 $350

LIVEING, GEORGE DOWNING   Chemical Equilibrium. Cambridge:
Deighton Bell, 1885. First edition. 8vo. Orig. cloth. 1 double-
page graph, 1 plate. Spine darkened. Very good copy. Zeitlin
264-265 1983 $40

LIVERMORE, MARY A.   My Story of the War. Hartford, 1889.
Steel engravings. Blind-stamped cloth with fancy gilt-decorated spine.
Very nice. King 45-576 1983 $20

LIVERMORE, THOMAS L.   Days and Events, 1860-1866. Boston,
1920. 1st ed. Illus. Large 8vo, orig. boards, cloth back.
Morrill 288-631 1983 $30

LIVERPOOL, CHARLES JENKINSON, EARL OF   A Treatise on the Coins of
the Realm. Oxford, at the University Press, for Cadell and Davies,
1805. 1st ed., 4to, slight spotting of title-page and early leaves,
cont. half calf, neatly rebacked preserving original black morocco
label. Pickering & Chatto 21-67 1983 $650

THE LIVING Talmud. NY: Spiral Press, 1960. Quarto. Illus. with
drawings by Ben-Zion. Limited to 1500 copies signed by the illustrator.
Extremely fine in quarter-leather and boards and faintly rubbed slipcase. Bromer 25-246 1983 $165

LIVINGSTON, B. E.   The Distribution of Vegetation in the
United States. Washington, 1921. Maps, royal 8vo, half cloth,
good ex-library. Wheldon 160-1738 1983 £18

LIVINGSTON, EDWARD   A Faithful Picture of the Political
Situation of New Orleans... Boston, 1808. Cloth, leather label,
discreet library stamp on title-page, else fine. Reese 18-309 1983
$750

LIVINGSTON, FLORA   Bibliography of the Works of Rudyard
Kipling. N.Y., 1927. Thick 8vo, cloth backed boards. Ltd. edition.
Fine. One of only 55 large paper copies, designed by Bruce Rogers.
This copy is signed, with a quotation from Kipling, by Flora
Livingston. Argosy 714-448 1983 $175

LIVINGSTON, JOHN   Livingston's Law Register. New York,
1851. 1st issue. 12mo. Binding and text partly dampstained, some
rubbing, lacks front fly-leaf. Morrill 287-191 1983 $20

LIVINGSTON, JOHN H.   A Dissertation on the Marriage of a
Man with His Sister in Law. New Brunswick (N.J.), 1816. 1st ed.
8vo, contemporary calf. Lacks label. Scarce. Morrill 286-252
1983 $100

LIVINGSTON, LUTHER   Franklin and his Press at Passy.
New York: The Grolier Club, 1914. 8vo, marbled board sides, cloth
back, paper label. Frontis. in color after mezzotint by S. Arlent
Edwards, facs. reproductions etc. One of 300 copies printed by the
Riverside Press. Slight wear to the backstrip, bookplate by
Rockwell Kent. Orig. prospectus laid in. Duschnes 240-190 1983
$125

LIVINGSTON, LUTHER   Franklin and His Press at Passy. New
York: Grolier Club, 1914. Frontis., plates, facsims. 1st ed.,
limited to 300 copies designed by Bruce Rogers. Orig. cloth-backed
marbled boards, uncut. Fine copy with four page prospectus laid in.
Jenkins 155-441 1983 $100

LIVINGSTON, ROBERT R.   Essay on Sheep. N.H., 1813. Title
vignette. 12mo, orig. mottled calf (worn; some foxing). Argosy
716-144 1983 $100

LIVINGSTON, WILLIAM   A Letter to the Right Reverend Father in
God, John, Lord Bishop of Landaff... New York: Garrat Noel, 1768.
First edition. Modern cloth. Very good. Felcone 20-90 1983 $175

LIVINGSTONE, DAVID   Dr. Livingstone's 17 Years' Explorations and Adventures in the Wilds of Africa. Philadelphia, 1857. 1st
American ed. Folding map (partly torn) and illustrations. Small
8vo. Binding partly faded. Morrill 286-253 1983 $35

LIVINGSTONE, DAVID   The last journals of David Livingstone.
London: John Murray, 1874. 2 vols. 8vo. 2 folding maps. 21
plates. Orig. pictorial cloth in very good condition. Adelson
Africa-101 1983 $300

LIVINGSTONE, DAVID   Missionary travels and researches in
South Africa. London: John Murray, 1857. First edition, first
issue. 8vo. 2 folding maps. 25 plates (3 tinted). Orig. brown
embossed cloth. Rubbed, some minor foxing and stains. Adelson
Africa-99 1983 $300

LIVINGSTONE, DAVID   Missionary Travels and Researches in
South Africa. London, 1857. First edition, folding tinted lithograph
frontis., 2 other tinted lithograph plates, portrait, 2 folding maps,
folding diagram, woodcuts, roy. 8vo, old style half calf. Special
issue with lithograph plates. K Books 301-114 1983 £110

LIVINGSTONE, DAVID   Missionary Travels and Researches in
South Africa. New York, 1858. First American edition. 8vo. Orig.
binding. Folding maps and plates. Fye H-3-344 1983 $100

LIVINGSTONE, DAVID   Missionary Travels and Researches in
South Africa. New York, 1858. 8vo. Rebound in library buckram.
Fye H-3-345 1983 $60

LIVINGSTONE, DAVID   Missionary Travels and Researches in
South Africa. NY 1858. Illus, 1/2 calf, marbled boards, folding
maps, covers detached. King 46-750 1983 $25

LIVINGSTONE, DAVID   Narrative of an expedition to the
Zambesi and its tributaries. London: John Murray, 1865. First
edition. 8vo. Folding map. 12 plates. Orig. decorated cloth.
Rubbed, spine slightly faded and starting to chip. Adelson Africa-
100 1983 $275

LIVINGSTONE, DAVID   Narrative of an Expedition to the
Sambesi. NY, 1866. Folding maps, edges rubbed and slightly sunned,
front hinge starting, name stamp in two places, minor tear to fore
edge, else very good. Quill & Brush 54-1695 1983 $60

LIVINGSTONE, DAVID STANLEY   Full and By. New York, (1936). Cloth
spine has a snag, else vg-fine. In Our Time 156-556 1983 $20

LIVINGSTONE, PATRICK   Selections from the Writings of...
Charles Gilpin, 1847. First edition, large 12mo, orig. cloth, a
very good copy. Fenning 60-255 1983 £14.50

LIVINGSTONE, R. W.   The Greek Genius and its Meaning to Us.
Oxford, 1915. 2nd edition. 8vo, cloth. Salloch 387-30 1983 $25

LIZARS, JOHN   A System of Anatomical Plates. W. H.
Lizars, Edinburgh, 1822-26. First edition, first issue of the plates.
Folio and 8vo, with engraved titles and 101 hand coloured engraved
plates; minor marginal tears in plate 9, occasional light foxing;
cont. half calf, text volume rebacked. A good copy. Quaritch NS 5-
67 1983 $1,750

LJUNGSTEDT, ANDREW   An Historical Sketch of the
Portuguese Settlements in China. Boston: James Munroe, 1836. With a
folding plate, and 2 folding maps, complete in spite of pagination
jump, roy. 8vo, orig. cloth, title dusty, a large and good to very good
copy. This copy does not have a frontis. view, which was present in
the last copy sold at auction. Fenning 60-256 1983 £65

LLEWELLYN, RICHARD   How Green was my Valley. London: Michael
Joseph Ltd., (1939). First edition. Orig. cream buckram with red
leather label on spine. In publisher's slipcase (some splitting at
hinges, with tape-repair on top). One of 200 signed copies, of which
100 were for sale. Slipcase somewhat damaged. Fine. MacManus 279-
3307 1983 $250

LLEWELLYN, RICHARD   How Green Was My Valley. London, 1939.
First edition. Dustwrapper. Fine. Gekoski 2-122 1983 £25

LLEWELLYN, RICHARD   None But The Lonely Heart. London:
Michael Joseph Ltd., (1943). First edition. Orig. cream buckram with
leather label on spine. One of 250 copies printed on handmade paper &
signed by author. Fine. MacManus 279-3308 1983 $125

LLEWELLYN, RICHARD   None But The Lonely Heart. N.Y.: The
Macmillan Co., 1943. First American edition. Orig. cloth. Dust
jacket (slightly worn at edges). Very good. MacManus 279-3309 1983
$25

LLOYD, DAVID   Economy of Agriculture. Germantown,
Pa., 1832. Ex-library, rebacked; some foxing. First edition.
Felcone 22-124 1983 $25

LLOYD, JAMES   Mr. Lloyd's Speech, in the Senate...
(Washington, 1808). Dsb. Slight loss to text at the bottom of the
first leaf, not affecting the sense. Reese 18-308 1983 $20

LLOYD, JAMES T.   Lloyd's Steamboat Directory, and
Disasters on the Western Waters... Cincinnati, 1852. Cloth, worn
at top, else good. Reese 19-328 1983 $400

LLOYD, JOHN   Sketch Map Of The Three Fishery Districts. Stanfords Geographical Establishment, 1867. Double page
coloured lithograph map, folio, laid down on linen, limp calf, title
in gilt on upper board, some slight worming to binding, not affecting
the map. Deighton 3-208 1983 £145

LLOYD, LODOWICK   Stratagems of Jerusalem. London,
printed by Thomas Creede, 1602. 4to, 19th century calf gilt, gilt
supralibros on cover, title bit soiled with corner frayed and lower and
upper edge amateurishly repaired, minor tears, article on the Cecil
family (to whom the work is dedicated) from Burke's on verso of title.
First edition. Ravenstree 97-48 1983 $250

LLOYD, ROBERT   The Actor. A poetical epistle to Bonnell
Thornton, Esq. London: printed for R. and J. Dodsley, 1760. 4to,
quarter morocco, first edition. Half-title present. Ximenes 64-
356 1983 $225

LLOYD, ROBERT   The Actor. Addressed to Bonnell Thornton, Esq. London: printed for G. Kearsly, 1764. 4to, wrappers,
4th edition. Half-title present (quite dust-soiled); last page
dusty. Uncut copy. Ximenes 64-357 1983 $75

LLOYD, ROBERT   Poems. London: printed for the author,
by Dryden Leach; sold by T. Davies, 1762. 4to, old half calf (some
wear). 1st edition. Half-title present. Ximenes 64-358 1983 $125

LLOYD, THOMAS   The Trials of William S. Smith and
Samuel G. Ogden. NY, 1807. Inscription and bookplate of Thomas A.
Emmet, 3/4 leather, some interior foxing, very good or better. Quill
& Brush 54-1620 1983 $90

LLOYD, WILLIAM　　　　　　Considerations Touching the True Way
to Suppress Popery in this Kingdom. Printed for Henry Brome, 1677.
First edition, 4to, page numerals on the last four pages touched,
but otherwise a nice copy. Fenning 62-210 1983 £24.50

LLOYD, WILLIAM　　　　　　The Difference Between the Church and
Court of Rome. Printed by Andrew Clark for Henry Brome, 1674. First
edition, 4to, wrapper, title dusty and with some spotting but a
good to very good copy. Fenning 61-256 1983 £12.50

LLOYD, WILLIAM　　　　　　A Sermon at the Funeral of Sr. Edmund-Bury
Godfray... Printed by Tho. Newcomb, for Henry Brome, 1678. Imprimatur
leaf, 4to. Fenning 62-211 1983 £21.50

LLOYD Family Papers, ... of the Manor of Queens Village. NY, 1926-7.
2 vols, thick 8vo. Argosy 710-175 1983 $45

LLOYD-JONES, W.　　　　　　K.A.R. London, 1926. First edition.
Frontis. 35 plates, 1 folding coloured map. Slightly worn and soiled.
Some slight, mostly marginal foxing. Good. Edwards 1042-567 1983
£55

LOBB, THEOPHILUS　　　　　　A Treatise of the Small Pox. London,
1731. First edition. Thick 4to, cont. panelled calf, (ex-lib).
Argosy 713-342 1983 $125

LOBO, JEROME　　　　　　A Voyage to Abyssinia. London, A.
Bettesworth and C. Hitch, 1735. 8vo, cont. sheep rebacked, later
end-papers, hinges rubbed, few stains, minor soiling, good, and one
of few copies printed on thick paper. Thick paper issue of the first
edition. Ravenstree 97-49 1983 $750

LOBO, JEROME　　　　　　A Voyage to Abyssinia. London & Edinburgh, 1789. Ad. leaf, heavily foxed throughout, blank upper margin
of title cut away not affecting text, new half calf. K Books 307-120
1983 £160

THE LOCAL History of Andover, Vermont. Perth Amboy, 1922. 3 ports.,
1 view, cloth-backed boards, tall 8vo. Argosy 710-548 1983 $40

LOCATELLI, PASINO　　　　　　I dipinti di Lorenzo Lotto nell-
Oratorio Suardi in Trescoro Balneario. Bergamo: Bolis, 1891.
8 plates. Folio. Full vellum. Edition limited to 300 copies.
Ars Libri 33-204 1983 $150

LOCKE, D. R.　　　　　　The Morals of Abou Ben Adhem. Boston,
1875. First edition. Cloth, bookplate, inner hinges cracked, end
papers cloudy, spine ends slightly frayed. King 46-307 1983 $25

LOCKE, JOHN　　　　　　De l'Education des Enfans. Amsterdam:
Antoile Schelte, 1695. First edition of the first translation into
any language. 12mo, cont. calf, spine gilt. A very uncommon title.
Lacking front endpaper, hinges worn, else a very good copy. Trebizond
18-204 1983 $450

LOCKE, JOHN　　　　　　An Essay Concerning Humane Understanding. London: for Thomas Basset, 1690. First edition, second
issue with cancel title. Folio. 18th century calf, neatly rebacked,
binder's ticket of T. Goodere, Swansea. Traylen 94-530 1983
£2,200

LOCKE, JOHN　　　　　　An Essay Concerning Human Understanding.
London: Printed for Edmund Parker, 1731 (1690). Tenth edition. Two
vols. Frontis. portrait, ad leaf. Contemporary calf, front joint
to Vol. I very weak. Gach 95-327 1983 $125

LOCKE, JOHN　　　　　　An Essay Concerning Human Understanding.
Printed for Edmund Parker, 1735. 2 vols., 8vo, portrait in vol. 1,
cont. calf, morocco labels. Joints cracked, but binding firm.
Upper corner neatly cut from both front flies to remove an inscription.
Bickersteth 77-40 1983 £48

LOCKE, JOHN　　　　　　Mr. Locke's reply to the Right Reverend
the Lord Bishop of Worcester's answer to his letter... London:
printed by H. Clark, etc., 1697. First edition. Small 8vo. Cont.
panelled calf, gilt, spine gilt. Complete with half-title and two
final leaves of ads. Very slight wear to foot of spine. Fine
copy. Ximenes 63-348 1983 $250

LOCKE, JOHN　　　　　　Some Familiar Letters Between Mr.
Locke, and Several of his Friends. London, A. and J. Churchill, 1708.
8vo, cont. calf newly rebacked period style, minor tears to end, not
affecting text to E1, P1, minor worming from page 373 to end,
mainly in upper inner blank margin. First edition. Ravenstree 97-
50 1983 $275

LOCKE, JOHN　　　　　　Some Thoughts Concerning Education.
London, printed for A. and J. Churchill, 1699. 8vo, orig. calf.
Ravenstree 97-51 1983 $215

LOCKE, JOHN　　　　　　Two Treatises of Government. London:
printed 1689, reprinted for the 7th time, 1772. 8vo, cont. tree calf,
spine gilt, green morocco label, joints cracking but sound, bookplate.
Pickering & Chatto 21-68 1983 $125

LOCKE, JOHN　　　　　　The Works. London: printed for D.
Browne, 1759. 6th ed., 3 vols., folio, cont. diced calf, wide
filigre gilt borders, marbled endpapers and edges, spine elaborately
gilt, green and black morocco labels, bookplate. A fine large paper
copy. Pickering & Chatto 21-69 1983 $600

LOCKE, RICHARD ADAMS　　　　　　The Moon Hoax. New York, William
Gowans, 1859. First book edition. Illustrated. 8vo, original wrappers. Lacks backstrip; top blank margin of front cover torn off;
front wrapper partly frayed. Morrill 290-235 1983 $85

LOCKE, WILLIAM J.　　　　　　A Christmas Mystery. London: John Lane,
The Bodley Head, 1922. First edition. Illus. by W.W. Lendon. Orig.
cloth. Fine. MacManus 279-3310 1983 $20

LOCKE, WILLIAM J.　　　　　　The Coming of Amos. London: Bodley
Head, (1924). First edition. Orig. cloth. Signed by author. Covers
slightly spotted. MacManus 279-3311 1983 $20

LOCKE, WILLIAM J.　　　　　　Septimus. N.Y.: John Lane Co., 1909.
First American edition. Orig. cloth. Pictorial dust jacket (a little
worn & foxed). Fine. MacManus 279-3313 1983 $50

LOCKER-LAMPSON, FREDERICK　　　　　　Lyra Elegantiarum. London: Ward, Lock,
& Co., 1891. Revised and Enlarged edition. Small thick 4to. Orig.
parchment-backed cloth. Limited to 250 copies signed by editor. From
the library of Edith Mary Webb, with her bookplate and ownership
signature. Spine somewhat darkened. Very good. MacManus 279-3317
1983 $65

LOCKER-LAMPSON, FREDERICK　　　　　　Lyra Elegantiarum. London: Ward, Lock,
& Co., 1891. Revised and enlarged edition. Frontis. port. Orig.
cloth. Covers rubbed and darkened. MacManus 279-3318 1983 $20

LOCKETT, W. G.　　　　　　Robert Louis Stevenson at Davos.
Hurst & Blackett, n.d. (c. 1930). First edition, half title, front.
illus. 8 pp ads. Orig. blue cloth. Jarndyce 30-1144 1983 £10.50

LOCKHART, JOHN GIBSON　　　　　　Ancient Spanish Ballads, Historical
and Romantic. London, 1823. 1st ed. 4to, contemporary marbled
boards with red roan backstrip, pictorial title-page, title foxed,
slightly rubbed. Morrill 288-240 1983 $50

LOCKHART, JOHN GIBSON　　　　　　The History of Matthew Wald. Edinburgh:
William Blackwood, 1824. First edition. Orig. cloth-backed boards
with paper spine label (slightly chipped & darkened). Spine and covers
slightly worn. Very good. MacManus 279-3319 1983 $250

LOCKHART, JOHN GIBSON　　　　　　The Life of Sir Walter Scott. Edinburgh, 1902-03. 10 vols. 8vo. Orig. blue buckram, gilt, t.e.g.,
others uncut. Frontis. to each vol. and numerous plates. Limited
edition of 1,040 sets, numbered and signed by the publisher. Traylen
94-712 1983 £38

LOCKHART, JOHN GIBSON　　　　　　Peter's Letters to his Kinsfolk.
Edinburgh: Blackwood; London: Cadell & Davis; Glasgow: John
Smith, 1819. 1st ed., 8vo, 3 vols., original boards and paper
labels. Uncut copy with all half-titles. 4 vignettes, 13 portraits.
An exceptionally fine copy, very rare in this condition. Trebizond
18-60 1983 $225

LOCKHART, JOHN GIBSON　　　　　　Reginald Dalton. Edinburgh, William
Blackwood, etc, 1823. First edition, 3 vols, 8vo, lacks half-titles
and advertisement leaves in vol. III. Cont. half calf. Hannas 69-125
1983 £60

LOCKHART, JOHN GIBSON   Some Passages in the Life of Mr. Adam Blair. Edinburgh, William Blackwood, etc, 1822. First edition. 8vo, lacks half-title and ad. leaves. Cont. half calf. Hannas 69-126 1983 £35

LOCKHART, JOHN GIBSON   Valerius; A Roman Story. Edinburgh, Blackwood; London, Cadell, 1821. 3 vols., 8vo, orig. quarter cloth, boards, trifle shaken, slightly worn without first half-title, later end-papers, a good set. First edition. Ravenstree 96-72 1983 $195

LOCKHART, JOHN GIBSON   Valerius; a Roman Story. Edinburgh, for William Blackwood, etc, 1821. First edition. 3 vols, 12mo, half-titles. Cont. half calf. Hannas 69-127 1983 £50

LOCKRIDGE, FRANCES   Murder within Murder. Philadelphia: J.B. Lippincott, (1946). First edition. 8vo. Cloth. Dust jacket. Piece missing out of jacket, else very good. Oak Knoll 49-153 1983 $20

LOCKRIDGE, RICHARD   A Matter of Taste. Phila., Lippincott, (1949). First edition. Dust jacket (sm chips, light soiling), else very good. Houle 21-573 1983 $30

LOCKWOOD, FRANK C.   Arizona Characters. Los Angeles: Times-Mirror Press, 1928. Plates. Cloth in taped dust wrapper. Dawson 471-179 1983 $85

LOCKWOOD, FRANK C.   Life. Chicago, 1929. Illus., gilt top, slip case. Clark 741-52 1983 $35

LOCKWOOD, FRANK C.   Life in Old Tucson, 1854-1864. Los Angeles: Ward Ritchie Press, 1943. First edition. Illus. Blue cloth. Very good in dust jacket. Bradley 66-458 1983 $45

LOCKWOOD, FRANK C.   Life in Old Tucson 1854-1864. Los Angeles: Ward Ritchie Press, 1943. Plates. Cloth. Dawson 471-180 1983 $35

LOCKWOOD, FRANK C.   The Life of Edward E. Ayer. Chicago: A.C. McClurg & Company, 1929. Frontis. and plates. Original cloth, fine copy. Jenkins 153-21 1983 £45

LOCKWOOD, FRANK C.   The Life of Edward E. Ayer. Chicago: A.C. McClurg & Co., 1929. First edition. 8vo. Cloth. Oak Knoll 48-253 1983 $25

LOCKWOOD, FRANK C.   Pioneer Days in Arizona. New York, 1932. Illustrations and maps. First edition. Jenkins 153-9 1983 $65

LOCKWOOD, FRANK C.   Pioneer Days In Arizona From the Spanish Occupation to Statehood. New York, 1932. Photos, cloth, some cover wear. First edition. King 46-8 1983 $35

LOCKWOOD, GEORGE B.   The New Harmony Communities. Marion, Indiana, 1902. 1st ed. T.e.g. Illus. Library stamps on title page. Covers a bit speckled only. Very scarce. Jenkins 153-330 1983 $40

LOCKWOOD, HENRY H.   Exercises in Small-Arms. Phila., 1852. First edition. 8vo. Orig. cloth. 104 engraved plates, errata leaf. Some slight foxing. Good. Edwards 1042-123 1983 £140

LOCKYER, CHARLES   An account of the trade in India. London: printed for the author, and sold by Samuel Crouch, 1711. First edition. 8vo. Cont. panelled calf, rebacked. The author's own copy, on thick paper, with manuscript corrections throughout. Calf a bit worn. Ximenes 63-211 1983 $1,500

LOCKYER, NORMAN   The Meteoritic Hypothesis... London: Macmillan, 1890. First edition. 8vo. Modern half calf old style. Numerous text figures, diagrams and tables, 7 photographic plates (including frontis.). Many full page text figures. Uncut. Zeitlin 264-267 1983 $60

LOCKYER, NORMAN   Stonehenge and Other British Stone Monuments Astronomically Considered. 1906. 65 illus., orig. cloth. K Books 307-209 1983 £25

LOCQUIN, M. F.   Flore Mycologique, Vols. 3 and 4. 1977. 75 coloured and 75 plain outline plates, 2 vols., 8vo, cloth. Wheldon 160-1855 1983 £46

LOCRE, ELIZA DE   I See The Earth. Poems. Scholartis Press, 1928. 1st ed., slim roy. 8vo, uncut in quarter green linen gilt over paper boards, slight wear to one corner, otherwise very good unopened copy in chipped dustwrappers. Pen and ink tail-pieces by Meadows. 525 numbered copies on hand-made paper and signed by author. Deighton 3-209 1983 £18

LODGE, EDMUND   Portraits of Illustrious Personages of Great Britain. William Smith, circa, 1840. With 241 engraved portraits, with the half-titles in all but the final volume, 8vol., cr. 8vo, cont. half brown morocco, t.e.g., other edges uncut, a fine library set. Fenning 61-258 1983 £65

LODGE, GEORGE EDWARD   George Edward Lodge: Unpublished Bird Paintings. 1983. Roy 4to, boards, cloth back, 89 fine coloured plates. Wheldon 160-65 1983 £79

LODGE, HENRY CABOT   Life and Letters of George Cabot. Boston, 1877. 8vo. 1st ed. Morrill 287-192 1983 $25

LODGE, OLIVER   Atoms and Rays... London: Benn, 1924. First edition. 8vo. Orig. cloth. 1 photographic plate, text figures. A very good copy. Zeitlin 264-269 1983 $40

LODGE, THOMAS   Rosalynde, or Euphues golden legacie. Elston Press, 1902. 8vo, printed throughout in red and black, original black cloth gilt, t.e.g., others uncut, fine. Scarce, 160 copies only. Deighton 3-210 1983 £58

LOEB, JACQUES (1859-1924)   Die Chemische Entwicklungserregung des Tierischen Eies. Berlin, 1909. 56 text-figures, 8vo, cloth, good ex-library. Wheldon 160-501 1983 £15

LOEB, JACQUES (1859-1924)   Forced Movements, Tropisms, and Animal Conduct. Philadelphia: 1918. First edition. Spine tips slightly rubbed. Gach 94-47 1983 $45

LOEB, JACQUES (1859-1924)   Forced Movements, Tropisms, and Animal Conduct. 1918. Wheldon 160-503 1983 £15

LOEB, JACQUES (1859-1924)   Comparative Physiology of the Brain and Comparative Psychology. London: John Murray, 1905 (1901). Spine faded. Gach 94-598 1983 $35

LOEB, JACQUES (1859-1924)   The Mechanistic Conception of Life. Chicago: 1912. Second impression (same year as first). Spine tips rubbed, occasional marginalia. Gach 94-599 1983 $25

LOEB, JACQUES (1859-1924)   The Organism as a Whole. From a Physio-chemical Viewpoint. NY: Putnam's, 1916. First edition. Rear hinges cracked. Gach 94-49 1983 $35

LOEB, JACQUES (1859-1924)   The Organism as a Whole. New York, 1916. 20 tables and 51 text-figures, 8vo, cloth, ex-library, joints loose. Wheldon 160-502 1983 £15

LOEB, JACQUES (1859-1924)   Regeneration. From a Physio-Chemical Viewpoint. NY: McGraw-Hill, 1924. First edition, second impression. Hinges cracked, library bookplate and stamp, very good copy in orig. beige cloth. Gach 94-50 1983 $35

LOEB, JACQUES (1859-1924)   Vorlesungen uber die Dynamik der Lebenserscheinungen. Leipzig, 1906. 8vo. Orig. cloth. Illus. in text. First German edition. Library stamp on title and dedication leaf. Gurney JJ-238 1983 £15

LOFTIE, W. J.   Lessons in the Art of Illuminating... London: Blacke & Son, n.d. (ca. 1880). Small 4to. Orig. cloth. Gilt decorated. Contains 9 tipped-in chromolithographic plates of Illuminations. Some foxing. Oak Knoll 49-129 1983 $85

LOFTING, HUGH   Doctor Dolittle in the Moon. (New York), Frederick A. Stokes, (1928). 8vo, orig. cloth, pictorial cover, complete with the 72 plates by the author, including two in color. First edition. Ravenstree 96-76 1983 $29.50

LOFTING, HUGH   Doctor Dolittle's Circus. New York,
Frederick Stokes, (1924). 8vo, orig. pictorial cloth, spine ends
trifle worn, else very good in orig. dust jacket (soiled and a bit
chipped). First edition. Ravenstree 96-77 1983 $37.50

LOFTING, HUGH   Doctor Dollittle's Garden. New York,
F.A. Stokes, (1927). 8vo, orig. pictorial cloth, bit worn, few small
marks on cover, inner hinges cracked, note on verso of frontis. Fairly
decent copy of the first edition. Ravenstree 96-78 1983 $25

LOFTING, HUGH   The Story of Doctor Dolittle. New
York, Frederick Stokes, 1920. 8vo, orig. pictorial cloth, somewhat
worn, with small girl's ownership inscription on fly title, plate at
p. 142 has tear from upper center out to margin with slight loss of
surface; generally a better-than average copy. First edition.
Ravenstree 96-80 1983 $85

LOFTING, HUGH   The Story of Doctor Doolittle. New
York, 1920. 1st ed. Illus. by author. 8vo, pictorial front cover.
Morrill 286-622 1983 $50

LOGA, VALERIAN VON   Francisco De Goya. Leipzig: Klinkhardt & Biermann, n.d. Second edition. 72 collotype plates. 4to.
Cloth. Ars Libri 32-271 1983 $60

LOGA, VALERIAN VON   Francisco De Goya. Zweite, vermehrte
Auflage. Berlin: G. Grote, 1921. 97 plates with 144 illus. 1
facsimile in text. Large stout 4to. Boards, 1/4 cloth. From the
library of Jakob Rosenberg. Ars Libri 32-270 1983 $100

LOGAN, JOHN   Poems. London: Printed for T. Cadell...
MDCCLXXXI. 8vo, uncut copy with half-title and blanks, orig.
blue-grey wraps. buff spine, lettered in ink; in a cloth folding
case. First edition. Quaritch NS 7-74 1983 $450

LOGAN, JOHN   Poems by the Rev. Mr. Logan... London:
for T. Cadell, 1781. First edition. 8vo. Half title. Cont.
polished calf, rebacked. Good copy. Heath 48-351 1983 £165

LOGAN, OLIVE   Apropos of Women and Theatres. New
York: Carleton; London: S. Low, 1869. First edition, orig. purple
cloth, bevelled boards, v.g. Jarndyce 31-383 1983 £65

LOGAN, RAYFORD W.   The Diplomatic Relations of the United
States with Haiti 1776-1891. Chapel Hill, 1941. D.w. Argosy 710-
612 1983 $25

LOGUE, ROSCOE   Tumbleweeds and Barb Wire Fences.
Amarillo, 1936. Illus. Orig. pictorial stiff wrappers. Minor chipping. Signed by author. Fine copy. Jenkins 153-331 1983 $75

LOHMEYER, KARL   Johannes Seiz. Kurtrierischer Hof-
architekt... Heidelberg: Carl Winter, 1914. 10 plates. 78 text
illus. Large 4to. Wrappers. Ars Libri 32-629 1983 $85

LOMAX, JOHN A.   Adventures of a Ballad Hunter. New
York, 1947. Cloth, very good in worn dust jacket. Reese 19-329
1983 $35

LOMAX, JOHN A.   American Ballads and Folk Songs. New
York: Macmillan, 1934. Large quarto. Cloth. First edition. One
of 500 numbered copies, specially printed on fine paper, and signed
by the author. The white backstrip is tanned, otherwise about fine.
Reese 19-331 1983 $200

LOMAX, JOHN A.   Cowboy Songs and Other Frontier Ballads.
NY, 1938. Rev. & enlgd. Thick 8vo, d.w. Argosy 710-590 1983
$25

LOMAX, JOHN A.   Songs of the Cattle Trail and Cowboy
Camp. New York: Macmillan, 1919. Pictorial orange cloth. Pub.'s
perforated stamp: "Advance Copy for Review. Not for Sale" on the
title-page. Printed pictorial dust jacket, which is lightly chipped
at the head and toe of the spine, but otherwise fresh and crisp.
Reese 19-330 1983 $200

LOMAX, JOHN A.   Songs of the Cattle Trail and Cow Camp.
New York: Macmillan, 1919. First edition. 12mo. Orig. orange pic-
torial cloth. Cont. owner's presentation poem on endpaper. Fine.
Jenkins 152-690 1983 $45

LOMAX, JOHN A.   Sour Singing Country. New York, 1941.
Orig. cloth. Signed by Lomax. Light waterstain. Jenkins 153-332
1983 $45

LOMBROSE, CESARE   The Female Offender. NY: Appleton,
1895. Publisher's brown cloth, some spotting to rear board. First
American edition. Generally very good copy. Gach 95-329 1983 $50

LOMBROSE, CESARE   The Female Offender. New York, 1898.
Illus. K Books 301-116 1983 £25

LOMBROSE, CESARE   The Man of Genius. London, 1891.
First edition in English. 8vo. Orig. cloth. Map and plates.
Gurney JJ-240 1983 £20

LOMMUS, JODOCUS   The Medicinal Observations. London:
W. Owen, 1747. 12mo, cont. 1/2 calf, (inner front hinge strengthened).
First edition in English. Argosy 713-343 1983 $150

LONDON, CHARMIAN   The Book of Jack London. NY: The
Century Co., 1921. In two vols. With 34 photographic plates. Green
cloth. Bookplates. Karmiole 73-63 1983 $60

LONDON, JACK   Before Adam. N.Y., MacMillian, 1907.
First edition. Tan buckram with design stamped in brown, red, and
white (spine somewhat darkened) else very good. Illus. with color
frontis., 7 color plates, numerous drawings in text, and one map by
Charles Livingston Bull. Zane Grey's copy with his library blind
stamp on front free endpaper. Houle 22-605 1983 $150

LONDON, JACK   Before Adam. NY, 1907. Cover slightly
rubbed, pastedown and front and rear endpapers offset, else very good,
illus. Quill & Brush 54-811 1983 $60

LONDON, JACK   Before Adam. NY: 1907. Illus. with
8 color plates by Charles Livingston Bull. Spine faded, else fine
copy. First edition. Bromer 25-64 1983 $50

LONDON, JACK   Before Adam. New York: MacMillan,
1907. Frontis., illus. 1st ed. Orig. tan pictorial cloth. Some
offsetting from the orig. dj (not present) else a fine copy. Jenkins
155-827 1983 $50

LONDON, JACK   Burning Daylight. N.Y., Macmillan,
1910. First edition. Illus. Pictorial blue cloth (light soiling
and rubbing), else very good. Houle 21-576 1983 $95

LONDON, JACK   Burning Daylight. Toronto: Henry
Frowde, 1911. 1st Canadian ed. Orig. reddish brown cloth, stamped
in black and gilt, lower edges uncut. But for a minute touch of
fraying at crown a fine copy. Jenkins 155-828 1983 $150

LONDON, JACK   The Call of the Wild. N.Y., 1903.
First edition. Illus. First issue, with vertical ribbed cloth.
Argosy 714-878 1983 $125

LONDON, JACK   Call of the Wild. London: Heinmann,
1903. Illus., frontis. 1st English ed. Stamped from same brass as
the American ed. but in different arrangement. Scarcer than the
American 1st ed. of the same year. Orig. blue pictorial cloth.
Rear hinge cracked, else bright copy. Jenkins 155-829 1983 $125

LONDON, JACK   The Call of the Wild. NY: 1903.
Slight stain at edge of front and rear covers, light rubbing to
extremities. T.e.g. First edition. Bromer 25-65 1983 $85

LONDON, JACK   The Call of the Wild. New York:
Limited Editions Club, 1960. 1st ed., 1 of 1500 copies signed by
the illustrator, Henry Varnum Poor. Printed by the Ward Ritchie
Press. Orig. plaid cloth, leather label, plaid box. Mint copy.
Jenkins 155-830 1983 $85

LONDON, JACK   A Daughter of the Snows. Philadelphia:
Lippincott, 1902. Frontis., plates. 1st ed. Orig. red pictorial
cloth. White lettering effaced from spine (with faint traces) else
very good copy with some soiling of cover. Scarce. Jenkins 155-1412
1983 $60

LONDON, JACK   A Daughter of the Snows. London:
Isbister, 1904. 1st English ed. Orig. red cloth, gilt, uncut. A
scarce ed. Was printed from American sheets, with the list of illus.
(and the illus.) deleted, and replaced with an English title-page that
also deletes the illus. note. Ad leaf at end is replaced with a
single ad leaf for two of London's English eds. Bookplate of German
collector, else fine copy. Jenkins 155-831 1983 $125

LONDON, JACK   The Game. New York: MacMillan, 1905.
Frontis., plates. 1st ed., state A of rubber-stamp (no sequence).
Orig. grey-green pictorial cloth, gilt. Bookplate, else nearly fine.
Jenkins 155-833 1983 $50

LONDON, JACK   The Game. NY, 1905. Color and b&w
illus., front signature loose, edges of blue-grey cover rubbed, good
plus, owner's name. Quill & Brush 54-813 1983 $30

LONDON, JACK   Iron Heel. N.Y., Macmillan, 1908.
First edition. Gilt stamped dark blue pictorial cloth. Very good-
fine. Houle 21-577 1983 $200

LONDON, JACK   Little Lady of the Big House. N.Y.,
Macmillan, 1916. First edition. Color frontis. Pictorial blue
cloth. Very good. Houle 21-578 1983 $115

LONDON, JACK   The Little Lady of the Big House. New
York: MacMillan, 1916. Frontis. 1st ed. Orig. pictorial blue cloth,
gilt. Near fine copy. Jenkins 153-832 1983 $100

LONDON, JACK   Martin Eden. New York, 1909. First
edition. Frontis. by the Kinneys. Foot of title-page torn at hinge.
Very nice. Rota 231-386 1983 £50

LONDON, JACK   The Sea-Wolf N.Y., MacMillian, 1904.
First edition (second state of binding, with spine lettered in
white). Frontis. with five plates by W.J. Alyward. Blue cloth
stamped in red, white, and blue, t.e.g. Very good. Houle 22-607
1983 $150

LONDON, JACK   The Sea-Wolf. NY, 1904. Edges rubbed,
cover slightly soiled, spine lettering rubbed, else near very good.
Quill & Brush 54-814 1983 $50

LONDON, JACK   The Sea-Wolf. New York: MacMillan,
1904. Frontis., plates. 1st ed., second state binding. Orig. blue
pictorial cloth, lettered entirely in white, t.e.g. Bright copy
with traces of rubbing, and clipping. Jenkins 155-836 1983 $50

LONDON, JACK   The Sea-Wolf. NY, 1904. Hinges cracked,
cover worn and soiled, good. Quill & Brush 54-815 1983 $30

LONDON, JACK   Smoke Bellew. NY, 1912. Hinges starting, cover edges rubbed and soiled, good, owner's name. Quill & Brush
54-812 1983 $35

LONDON, JACK   White Fang. New York: MacMillan,
1906. Frontis., plates. 1st ed., with title-page cancel on laid
paper. Orig. gray pictorial cloth, gilt. Very good unworn copy.
Jenkins 155-839 1983 $45

LONDON, JACK   White Fang. NY, 1906. Second issue
with tipped-in title page, hinges cracked, edges worn, good. Quill
& Brush 54-816 1983 $50

LONDON Almanac for the Year 1789. London: for the Company of
Stationers, (1788). Venetian mosiac binding in red morocco with
cream and green onlays richly gilt, arranged in a double herringbone design with a frame of ornamental fillets, gilt edges, in
matching slip-case. Engraved throughout. Folding plate of Carleton
House. Slipcase slightly worn at top, almanack very fine. Traylen
94-582 1983 £120

THE LONDON Group - Retrospective Exhibition 1914-1928 - Catalogue.
London, 1928. Wrappers. Cover design by Duncan Grant. Covers nicked.
Very good. Jolliffe 26-196 1983 £85

THE LONDON Medical Review and Magazine. London, Printed for the
Society, 1799-1800. 3 vols. 8vo. Contemporary boards, calf backs
and corners, leather labels. Two covers loose; two hinges cracked.
Scarce. Morrill 289-134 1983 $75

THE LONDON Stage, A Collection of the Most Reputed Tragedies, Comedies,
Operas, Melo-Dramas, Farces and Interludes. London, n.d. (ca. 1825-
27). Vols. 2, 3 & 4. Eng. frontispieces, woodcuts, lea. backed
marbled boards, double-col. pp. worn, hinges loose. Affixed to
inside covers are 4 holograph letters by Barney Williams, Joseph
Jefferson, John Edmond Owen, and John Brougham. King 46-410 1983
$100

THE LONDON Stage: a collection of the most reputed Tragedies,
Comedies, Operas... London, 1825-27. 4 vols. 8vo. Binder's
cloth. 21 engraved portraits on 3 plates, title-page to each
vol. printed in blue and black, and engraved vignette at the head
of each play. Traylen 94-532 1983 £40

LONDONDERRY, THE MARCHIONESS OF   Narrative of a Visit to the
Courts of Vienna... London, 1844. 1st ed. Portrait. 8vo, half
morocco, marbled sides, raised bands. Bookplate removed. Very
nice. Morrill 286-255 1983 $25

LONE, E. MIRIAM   Some Noteworthy Firsts in Europe during
the Fifteenth Century. NY: 1930. Sm 8vo, wrap-around buckram bds.
Illustrated. One of 425 copies signed by the author. Perata 28-103
1983 $65

LONG, CHARLES, BARON FARNBOROUGH   Short remarks and suggestions,
upon improvments now carrying on... London: Hatchard, 1826. First
edition. 8vo. Disbound. Ximenes 63-264 1983 $45

LONG, FRANK B   The Hounds of Tindalos. Sauk City:
Arkham House, 1946. First edition. Black cloth. Laid in is Arkham
House postcard signed by August Derleth. Fine in dust jacket.
Bradley 66-128 1983 $125

LONG, FRANK B.   On Reading Arthur Machen. Pengrove,
Dog & Duck Press, 1949. First edition. One of 20 privately printed
copies. Fine. Houle 21-593 1983 $85

LONG, HANIEL   Malinche (Dona Marina). Santa Fe:
Writers' Editions, (1939). Cloth. First edition. Printed at the
Rydal Press. Fine in dust jacket. Reese 20-847 1983 $65

LONG, HANIEL   Pittsburgh Memoranda. Santa Fe: (Rydal
Press, 1935). Limited to 1000 copies signed by Long. Very fine.
First edition. Bromer 25-66 1983 $75

LONG, HANIEL   Pittsburgh Memoranda. Santa Fe:
Writers' Editions, 1935. Cloth. First edition. One of 1000
numbered copies, printed at the Rydal Press, and signed by the author.
Ink sentiment, and offset from paperclip, else just short of fine in
dust jacket. Reese 20-846 1983 $40

LONG, JOHN D.   The New American Navy. London, 1904.
8vo. Orig. cloth. Frontis., numerous plates, 4 folding coloured maps.
2 vols. Slightly worn and soiled. Faint ink stamps on verso of maps.
Signet Library copy. Good. Edwards 1042-124 1983 £30

LONG, STEPHEN H.   Voyage in a Six-Oared Skiff to the Falls
of Saint Anthony in 1817. Phila., 1860. Map. First edition. Orig.
gold stamp cloth. Ginsberg 46-411 1983 $175

LONG, STEPHEN H.   Voyage in a Six-Oared Skiff to the
Falls of Saint Anthony in 1817. Philadelphia, 1860. Map. Wraps.
Very good. Reese 19-332 1983 $150

LONG, WILLIAM J.   William J. Long and His Books, A
Pamphlet Consisting Chiefly of Typical Letters and Reviews in Reply
to Mr. Burroughs' Unwarranted Attack on Mr. Long. Boston: Ginn,
(1903). 1st ed. Orig. wrappers, with printed letter of transmittal
laid in. Fine. Jenkins 155-160 1983 $20

LONGAKER, MARK   Ernest Dowson. Philadelphia: Univ.
of Pennsylvania Press, 1944. First edition. 8vo. Cloth. Dust
jacket. Oak Knoll 49-162 1983 $20

LONGET, FRANCOIS   Achille. Paris, 1860-61. 2 vols. in 3,
8vo, orig. 1/2 cloth. Argosy 713-344 1983 $50

LONGFELLOW, HENRY WADSWORTH The Courtship of Miles Standish. B,
1858. First edition, first issue, spine ends a little soft, otherwise very good to fine. Quill & Brush 54-818 1983 $225

LONGFELLOW, HENRY WADSWORTH The Courtship of Miles Standish. B,
1858. First edition, first issue, rear blank endpaper missing, spine
edges rubbed and lightly frayed, otherwise very good. Quill & Brush
54-819 1983 $75

LONGFELLOW, HENRY WADSWORTH The Courtship of Miles Standish, and
Other Poems. W. Kent, 1858. First English edition, half title, front.
40 pp ads. Orig. pink cloth, spine gilt, v.g. Jarndyce 31-793 1983
£20

LONGFELLOW, HENRY WADSWORTH The Courtship of Miles Standish.
Routledge, etc., 1859. Frontis. & 24 illus. by John Gilbert engr'd
by Bros. Dalziel. Green morocco grain decor. cloth gilt, a.e.g.
Bkstrip sl. soiled, contemp. insc. fr. ep., vg. Hodgkins 27-301 1983
£16

LONGFELLOW, HENRY WADSWORTH The Courtship of Miles Standish. Indianapolis, (1903). Decorated cloth. Ink inscription. Shaken. Covers
moderately soiled. 8 full page color plates plus other drawings by
H.C. Christy. King 45-386 1983 $20

LONGFELLOW, HENRY WADSWORTH Elements of French Grammar. Boston,
Gray and Bowen, 1831. 8vo, orig. quarter muslin, boards, now worn,
some scribbled on end-papers and underlinings and notations through
text, name on end-paper, one signature loose. Second edition,
first title-page to carry Longfellow's name. Ravenstree 97-54 1983
$250

LONGFELLOW, HENRY WADSWORTH The Golden Legend. Hodder & Stoughton,
n.d. 4to. Mounted colour frontis. Title decorated in gold. 24
mounted colour plates (1 small crease). Full white vellum decorated,
gilt, light wear. Lacks ties. Edition limited to 250 copies, No. 83.
Signed by Meteyard. Greer 40-139 1983 £110

LONGFELLOW, HENRY WADSWORTH Hyperion. New York, Samuel Colman,
1839. 2 vols., 8vo, orig. boards rebacked, with orig. printed paper
labels, now rubbed and chipped, brown endpapers, title of first
vol. in first state, that of 2nd vol. in 2nd state. Other than a note
on the front blank endpaper of each vol., nice copies of the first
edition. Ravenstree 97-56 1983 $150

LONGFELLOW, HENRY WADSWORTH Hyperion. New York, Samuel Colman,
1839. 2 vols., 8vo, orig. boards, name on endpaper, soiled, orig.
printed paper spine labels gone; untrimmed copy. Of two slight
variants in the titles, this is Blanck's "A" variant, and with the
white wove endpapers. First edition. Ravenstree 97-57 1983 $125

LONGFELLOW, HENRY WADSWORTH Hyperion. A.W. Bennett, 1868. Re-issue,
mounted frontis. & 11 mounted photo illus., decor. initial letters,
head & tail pieces, etc. Green sand grain cloth gilt (designed by
John Leighton), bevelled boards, a.e.g. (cvrs. sl. dust soiled &
gilt sl. dull, some foxing to mounts, top/bottom bkstrip sl. wear),
v.g. Hodgkins 27-349 1983 £75

LONGFELLOW, HENRY WADSWORTH Keramos and other Poems. Boston:
Houghton, Osgood, 1878. 1st ed., first issue of the binding. 8vo,
original terracotta cloth gilt, spine gilt. Advertisement leaf.
A very tight, clean copy. Trebizond 18-61 1983 $55

LONGFELLOW, HENRY WADSWORTH The Leap of the Roushan Beg. N.Y., 1931.
8vo, gilt-decorated cloth. A complete facsimile. Covers lightly
sunned. One of 500 copies. Perata 28-218 1983 $20

LONGFELLOW, HENRY WADSWORTH Manuel de Proverbes Dramatiques.
Portland, Samuel Colman, Griffin's Press: Brunswick, 1830. 8vo,
modern blue half morocco gilt extra, t.e.g., faint pencilling throughout. First edition. Ravenstree 97-59 1983 $250

LONGFELLOW, HENRY WADSWORTH Manuel de Proverbes Dramatiques.
Boston, Gray et Bowen, 1832. 8vo, orig. quarter muslin, orig. printed
paper label on spine, joints splitting, boards bit worn and stained,
spine faded and label little worn, name on endleaf, light pencilling
throughout; a better than average copy. Ravenstree 97-60 1983 $125

LONGFELLOW, HENRY WADSWORTH The New-England Tragedies. Boston:
Ticknor & Fields, 1868. 1st ed., first printing. Original green
cloth, gilt, spine gilt. A very good copy. Trebizond 18-62 1983
$50

LONGFELLOW, HENRY WADSWORTH Poems on Slavery. Cambridge, 1842.
Second edition. Glazed off-white wrappers. Pencil-and-ink inscription on front wrapper. Lower edge of front wrapper chipped and with
small crease. Contained in tan half-morocco folding case. Bradley
66-234 1983 $45

LONGFELLOW, HENRY WADSWORTH Poetical Works. Routledge, 1857. New
edn. Illus. by J. Gilbert & engr'd by Bros. Dalziel. Dark blue sand
grain cloth gilt (designed by John Seligh), a.e.g. Binder's ticket of
Bone & Son. Foxing first & last pp. & occasionally in contents, nice.
Hodgkins 27-300 1983 £35

LONGFELLOW, HENRY WADSWORTH Poetical Works. Routledge, etc., 1865.
149 illus. by John Gilbert engr'd by Bros. Dalziel. New edn.
Frontis. portrait. Black morocco gilt, gilt dentelles, a.e.g. Bookpl. fr. ep.,
contents foxed, cvrs. sl. rubbed. Inscribed to Dr. Robert Ramsay...
"from his Sincere Friend Haddington" PALACE OF HOLYROOD 5/6/1867.
Hodgkins 27-303 1983 £30

LONGFELLOW, HENRY WADSWORTH The Poetical Works. Routledge, etc.,
1865. 149 illus. by John Gilbert engr'd by Bros. Dalziel. New edn.
Frontis. portrait. Green pebble grain cloth gilt (designed by John
Sleigh), a.e.g., fr. ep. broken at hinge, occasional foxing, 2 sec.
sl. sprung, vg. Hodgkins 27-304 1983 £30

LONGFELLOW, HENRY WADSWORTH The Poets and Poetry of Europe.
Philadelphia: Carey & Hart, 1845. Frontis., engraved title. 1st
ed., 2nd printing. Orig. full tan sheep, black morocco label, gilt.
A few spots to binding, but fine copy. Jenkins 155-848 1983 $65

LONGFELLOW, HENRY WADSWORTH The Seaside and the Fireside. B, 1850.
December 1849 ads tipped-in at front. Cover rubbed and moderately
worn, top edge of spine chipped. Good. Quill & Brush 54-821 1983
$75

LONGFELLOW, HENRY WADSWORTH The Song of Hiawatha. David Bogue,
1855. First edition, 24pp ads. Orig. light blue cloth, spine gilt.
V.g. First issue. Jarndyce 31-792 1983 £200

LONGFELLOW, HENRY WADSWORTH The Song of Hiawatha. Boston: Ticknor
& Fields, 1855. Plus ads. 1st ed., 1st printing, 1st state with
missing "n" on p. 279. Orig. brown cloth, gilt. Fine copy. Jenkins
155-849 1983 $150

LONGFELLOW, HENRY WADSWORTH The Song of Hiawatha. Boston: Ticknor
& Fields, 1855. 1st ed., 2nd printing. Orig. brown cloth, gilt.
Fine copy. Jenkins 153-334 1983 $40

LONGFELLOW, HENRY WADSWORTH The Song of Hiawatha. Boston: Ticknor
& Fields, 1855. 1st ed., 3rd printing. Orig. brown cloth, gilt.
Waterstain to front end paper and flyleaf, else a near fine copy with
few signs of wear. Jenkins 153-335 1983 $25

LONGFELLOW, HENRY WADSWORTH The Song of Hiawatha. W. Kent, 1860.
Illus. by George H. Thomas, 24 wood engrs. engr'd by W. Thomas & H.
Harral. Brick red mor. grain cloth gilt, with white & gilt onlay
cvrs. a.e.g. Binder's ticket of Leighton, Son & Hodge. Cvrs. sl.
soiled, contemp. insc. ep. fr. ep. broken at hinge, occasional foxing,
vg. Hodgkins 27-302 1983 £20

LONGFELLOW, HENRY WADSWORTH The Song of Hiawatha. Chicago, (1911).
Player's edition. Full leather., a.e.g. Top of spine slightly
chipped. Covers rubbed. King 45-112 1983 $35

LONGFELLOW, HENRY WADSWORTH The Song of Hiawatha. London, (1912).
8vo, cloth with mounted illus. in color by Maxfield Parrish on
front cover. Color frontis. by N.C. Wyeth. Printed on jap vellum.
Duschnes 240-134 1983 $150

LONGFELLOW, HENRY WADSWORTH   Sonnets. Bruce Rogers, Riverside Press, 1907. Slim 8vo, decorative title-page printed in red and black, uncut in original blue paper boards, printed paper label with spare, an extremely fine unopened copy in damaged slip-case. Large paper issue, 275 numbered copies only. Deighton 3-211 1983 £38

LONGFELLOW, HENRY WADSWORTH   Tales of A Wayside Inn. B, 1863. Second state, edges worn, spine edges frayed, spine sunned, front pastedown stained, good. Quill & Brush 54-817 1983 $50

LONGFELLOW, HENRY WADSWORTH   Tales of a Wayside Inn. Boston: Ticknor & Field, 1863. 1st ed., 1st printing, 2nd state of catalogue. Orig. rich brown pebbled cloth, gilt, t.e.g. Fine copy in seldom seen color and cloth type. Jenkins 155-852 1983 $50

LONGFELLOW, WILLIAM P.   Cyclopaedia of Works of Architecture in Italy, Greece, and the Levant. New York, 1895. Edition limited to 500 copies. Plates and text illustrations. Large heavy 4to, original vellum boards, red morocco back. Boards dust-soiled; backstrip slightly rubbed; sound. Morrill 290-237 1983 $50

LONGFIELD, ADA K.   Anglo-Irish Trade in the Sixteenth Century. George Routledge, 1929. First edition, folding map and plate, 8vo, orig. cloth, a very good copy. Fenning 61-259 1983 £21.50

LONGHI, ROBERT   Il Caravaggio. Milano: Aldo Martello, 1952. 50 tipped-in color plates. 36 text illus. Small folio. Cloth. Ars Libri 33-71 1983 $125

LONGHI, ROBERT   Carlo Braccesco. Milano: Castello Sforzesco, 1942. 42 plates. Frontis. in color. Folio. Wrappers. Edition limited to 1000 copies. Ars Libri 33-49 1983 $65

LONGRIDGE, C. N.   The "Cutty Sark". London, 1933. First edition. 8vo. Orig. cloth. 5 folding plans in end pockets, numerous illus., some full page. 2 vols. Good. Edwards 1042-126 1983 £20

LONGSTREET, AUGUSTUS BALDWIN   Georgia Scenes, Characters, Incidents, etc. in the First Half Century of the Republic. (Quitman), 1894. Privately printed. Small 12mo., illus. Argosy 710-201 1983 $45

LONGSTREET, JAMES   From Manassas to Appomattox. Dallas, The Dallas Publishing Company, 1896. Gilt stamped cloth, slight bubbling, but overall a fine copy. Reese 19-333 1983 $300

LONGUEVILLE, PETER   The Hermit. Westminster, J. Cluer and A. Campbell, 1717. 8vo, full panelled polished calf gilt antique style, edges gilt, by Pratt; washed, with one plate repaired in blank edge. Rare first edition. Ravenstree 96-82 1983 $950

LONGUEVILLE, PETER   The Hermit: Or, The Unparallel'd Sufferings and Surprising Adventures of Mr. Philip Quarll. Printed for J. Wren, S. Crowder, H. Woodgate, J. Fuller, and J. Warcus, 1768. 4th edition. 12mo, 19th-cent. calf. Frontispiece and map. Hill 165-71 1983 £60

LONGUS   Les Amours Pastorales de Daphnis et Chloe. London: the Ashendene Press, 1933-(34). 4to. Half vellum, preserved in the orig. boards slip-case. Woodcuts by Gwendolen Raverat, and initial letters in Graily Hewitt. Limited edition of 290 copies. Traylen 94-534 1983 £495

LONGUS   Daphnis & Chloe. London: Geoffrey Bles, 1925. Translated out of the Greek of Longus by George Thornley in 1657. Decorations by John Austen. 4to. Orig. cloth. Dust jacket (torn). First edition. Bookplate. Fine copy. MacManus 277-131 1983 $45

LONGUS   Daphnis & Chloe. N.Y.: Privately Printed for Rarity Press, 1931. Translated out of the Greek of Longus by George Thornley in 1657. With decorations by John Austen. Orig. decorated cloth. Dust jacket (trifle worn). First edition. Near-fine copy. MacManus 277-134 1983 $25

LONGUS   Daphnis and Chloe. London, 1982. Large 4to. Bound by Susan Allix in full beige-brown Oasis Niger over modelled boards, blind-tooled and painted in brown, blue and yellow, enclosed in a quarter leather box. With 20 etched plates in colour by Susan Allix. Printed on Velin Arches, with text hand-set and printed letter press. Traylen 94-533 1983 £500

LONGWORTH, MARIA THERESA   Zanita. NY: Hurd and Houghton, 1872. Orig. green cloth, gilt-stamped spine. Fine copy. This copy inscribed by C. Hart Merriam. Karmiole 75-82 1983 $100

LONSDALE, MARGARET   George Eliot. Thoughts upon her life, her books, and herself. London: Kegan Paul, 1886. First edition. Slim 8vo. Orig. pale green cloth. A trifle soiled. Ximenes 63-652 1983 $40

LOOSLI, C. A.   Aus der Werkstatt Ferdinand Holders. Basel: Birkhauser, 1938. 1 tipped-in illus. 4to. Wrappers. No. 18 of a limited edition of 100 copies only, printed on Butten and signed in the colophon by the author. Ars Libri 32-309 1983 $100

LOPEZ, MATHIAS   Acting American Theatre. Phila.: A.R. Poole, (1826). Lopez & Wemyss' edition. 5 vols. in one. Each with engraved portrait (the first ragged). Half calf, worn, soiled & foxed. Dawson 471-328 1983 $100

LORANT, STEFAN   The New World, the First Pictures of America Made by John White & J. LeMoyne and Engr. by Theodore De Bry. NY, (1946). 1st ed. Illus, large 4to, dw. Argosy 710-133 1983 $27.50

LORANT, STEFAN   The New World. New York, (1946). 1st ed. The First Pictures of America made by John White and Jacques LeMoyne and engraved by Theodore DeBry. Illus., several in color. 4to. Dust wrapper. Morrill 289-394 1983 $25

LORCA, FEDERICO GARCIA   Selected Poems. London, 1943. First edition of this translation. Dust wrapper. Fine. Rota 231-581 1983 £15

LORD, DANIEL   Opinion on the Validity and Sufficiency in Law of the First Mortgage Bonds of the Union Pacific Railroad Company. (N.Y., 1866). Dbd. First edition. Ginsberg 47-892 1983 $35

LORD, ELIOT   Comstock Mining and Miners. Washington, 1883. Illus. and map. Later cloth with morocco label. Ex-library. Jenkins 152-283 1983 $250

LORD, JOHN   Frontier Dust. Hartford: Edwin Valentine Mitchell, 1926. Dust jacket. 1st ed. Scarce. Fine copy. Jenkins 153-336 1983 $35

LORD, JOSEPH L.   A Defence of Dr. Charles T. Jackson's Claims to the Discovery of Etherization. Boston, 1848. 1st ed. Tall 8vo. Orig. wrappers. Torn along backstrip. Morrill 289-136 1983 $60

LORENTZ, HENDRIK   Clerk Maxwell's Electromagnetic Theory... Cambridge: University Press, 1923. First edition. 8vo. Orig. printed papers wrappers. A very good copy. Zeitlin 264-270 1983 $30

LORENZETTI, GIULIO   Il quaderno dei Tiepolo al Museo Correr di Venezia. Venezia: Daria Guarnati, 1946. 173 color facsimile plates. Folio. Boards. Ars Libri 33-356 1983 $165

LORENZINI, CARLO   Pinocchio. Racine, Whitman (1917). First edition thus. Illus. by Alice Carsey with eight color and 32 line drawings. Red cloth with large color pictorial label. Very good. Houle 21-230 1983 $75

LORENZINI, CARLO   Pinocchio. Phila.: Lipp., 1920. First edition. 4to. Tan cloth. Pictorial paste-on. Gift edition with color illus. by M. Kirk plus page decorations in green on all pages. Near fine. Aleph-bet 8-62 1983 $36

LORENZINI, CARLO   Pinocchio. Phila.: Winston, n.d. (ca.1920). 8vo. Orange cloth. Pictorial paste-on. Frayed dust wrapper. 8 color plates by F. Richardson. Many full-page and smaller black and whites by C. Folkard. Fine. Aleph-bet 8-64 1983 $30

LORING, CHARLES   Correspondence on the Present Relations Between Great Britain and the United States. Boston, 1862. Wrs., unopened, (first flyleaves dampstained). Wrs., unopened. Argosy 716-80 1983 $25

LORING, F. H.   The Chemical Elements. London:
Methuen, 1923. First edition. 8vo. Orig. cloth. Various
tables and diagrams. Spine chipped. Very good copy. Zeitlin
264-272 1983 $40

LORIOUS, FELIX   Contes de Perrault. Hachette, Paris,
1927. Pictorial title. 28 colour plates & 4 text illus. Colour
pictorial boards, rebacked. Greer 39-80 1983 £28

LORMIAN, HENRI   L'art malgache. Paris: E. De
Boccard, (1934). 16 plates. 4to. Cloth. Orig. wrappers bound
in. Ars Libri 34-685 1983 $45

LOS ANGELES COUNTY MUSEUM OF ART   Pre-Columbian Art. March-April,
1940. Los Angeles, 1940. 12 plates. 4to. Wrappers. Ars Libri
34-346 1983 $20

LOS ANGELES DEPARTMENT OF PUBLIC SERVICE   Complete Report on Construction of the Los Angeles Aqueduct. Los Angeles: Department of
Public Service, 1916. Index, 24 folding maps or diagrams laid in at
back. Cloth, a little used. Dawson 471-182 1983 $75

LOS ANGELES DEPARTMENT OF PUBLIC WORKS   First Annual Report of the
Bureau of Los Angeles Aqueduct Power. Los Angeles: Dept. of Public
Works, 1910. Folding map, illus. Wrappers. Dawson 471-183 1983
$25

LOSKIEL, GEORGE HENRY   History of the Mission of the United
Brethren Among the Indians in North America. London, 1794. First
English edition. 3 parts in 1. Fine folding map. Later 1/4 mor.
marbled boards, a.e.g. Argosy 716-218 1983 $300

LOSKIEL, GEORGE HENRY   History of the Mission of the United
Brethren Among the Indians in North America. London, 1794. First
edition in English. Lacks the map. 8vo, original boards, paper
label. All edges untrimmed, slightly rubbed. Morrill 290-239 1983
$75

LOSSING, BENSON J.   Our Country. N.Y., 1875-80. Engrs.,
plus 500 additional illus., 1/2 mor., g.e. 3 vols. Argosy 716-193
1983 $50

LOSSING, BENSON J.   The Pictorial Field-Book of the Revolution. New York, 1851-52. First edition. 2 vols. Modern mocca
brown 3/4 morocco by Stikeman of New York City. Maps and illus.
throughout. Jenkins 152-778 1983 $150

THE LOST Inheritance. Colburn & Co., 1852. First edition, 3 vols.,
half titles vols. I & II, 2 pp ads. vol. I; 8 pp ads. vol. II. Orig.
fine ripple-grained green cloth, blocked in blind, sl. rubbed. Very
good. Inscribed presentation copy from the author. Jarndyce 30-278
1983 £90

LOTHROP, SAMUEL KIRKLAND   Cocle. An archaeological study of
Central Panama. Part II: Pottery of the Sitio Conte... Cambridge,
1942. 3 color plates. 491 illus. Folio. Cloth. Ars Libri 34-
349 1983 $125

LOTHROP, SAMUEL KIRKLAND   Essays in Pre-Columbian Art and
Archaeology. Cambridge: Harvard University Press, 1961. Prof.
illus. Small 4to. Cloth. Presentation copy, inscribed by F.J.
Dockstader, who contributed to the book. Ars Libri 34-352 1983
$125

LOTHROP, SAMUEL KIRKLAND   Inca Treasure As Depicted by Spanish
Historians. Los Angeles: Southwest Museum, 1938. 4 plates. 10
text illus. Small 4to. Wrappers. Ars Libri 34-350 1983 $35

LOTHROP, SAMUEL KIRKLAND   Treasures of Ancient America. Geneva:
Skira, 1964. 145 plates (85 tipped-in color). Folio. Cloth. Dust-
jacket. Ars Libri 34-351 1983 $85

LOTT, EMMELINE   The Mohaddetyn in the Palace. London:
Chapman & Hall, 1867. First edition. 2 vols. Orig. cloth. Inner
hinges cracked. Spines slightly torn. Institutional bookplates.
MacManus 279-3320 1983 $65

LOUBERE, DE LA   A New Historical Relation of the Kingdom
of Siam. London, 1693. Title printed in red and black. 2 maps, 9
plates. 2 vols. bound in 1. Folio. Slight worming to margins of last
5 leaves. Calf, rebacked with spine laid down, recornered. 8vo.
Edwards 1044-440 1983 £365

LOUDON, J   Arboretum Et Fruticetum Britannicum.
London: Henry Bohn, 1854. 2d ed. 8 vols in 6. Some foxing in
text, little light wear to the extremities of the spines, mainly
fine. In Our Time 156-510 1983 $400

LOUDON, J.   The Green-House Companion. London,
1825. 8vo. Old diced calf, rebacked with orig. spine. Hand-coloured
lithograph by Hullmandel, and a few woodcuts in text. Gurney 90-74
1983 £50

LOUIS SIEGBERT & BROTHERS   Crown Bindings. New York: Louis
Siegbert & Bro., 1922. 8vo. Cloth. Oak Knoll 48-46 1983 $95

LOUISIANA. SUPREME COURT   In the Supreme Court of the State of
Louisiana. Policy Jury of Concordia, Versus Geo. M. Davis, Peter Young
et als. Vidalia, La., 1878. Orig. printed wrappers. Jenkins 153-795
1983 $65

LOUISVILLE; A Guide to the Falls City. New York, 1940. 1st ed.
Maps, illus. Backstrip faded. Clark 741-4 1983 $45

LOUNSBURY, RALPH G.   The British Fishery at Newfoundland,
1634-1763. New Haven, 1934. Cloth, very good. Reese 19-336 1983
$30

LOUVET DE COUVRAY, JEAN B.   Interesting History of the Baron de
Lovzinski. New York, 1807. 2nd ed. 16mo, orig. boards, leather
back, part of paper covering worn off, lacks front blank leaf, sound.
Morrill 288-243 1983 $35

LOUYS, P   The Collected Tales of... Ch., 1930.
Illus. by John Austen. Color and b&w illus., edges slightly bumped
with minor scuffing to cover, very good. Quill & Brush 54-823 1983
$35

LOUYS, P   Satyrs and Women. N.Y., 1930. Limited
to 1250 numbered copies (this one unnumbered). Cloth. Each page
ruled and decorated. Spine darkened and rubbed. Defective slipcase.
15 tipped-in nude plates in color by Majeska. King 45-411 1983 $25

LOVECRAFT, HOWARD PHILLIPS   The Shuttered Room and Other Pieces.
Sauk City: Arkham House, 1959. First edition. Frontis and 4 other
full-page plates. Cloth. Very fine in dust jacket. Bradley 66-129
1983 $100

LOVECRAFT, HOWARD PHILLIPS   Something About Cats and Other Pieces.
Sauk City: Arkham House, 1949. First edition. Portrait. Black
cloth. Very fine in dj. Bradley 65-119 1983 $125

LOVEDAY, R.   Loveday's Letters, Domestick and
Foreign. Printed by J. Rawlins for Obadiah Blagrave, 1684. 8vo,
engraved portrait, pub.'s book list, waterstaining at foot of
central margin towards end of the book with wormhole, not touching the
text, orig. calf, worn at top of spine, rubbed. Bickersteth 75-49
1983 £48

LOVEGROVE, EDWIN J.   Attrition Tests of Road-Making Stones.
St. Bride's Press, (1906). First edition, with 79 illus., 4to, orig.
cloth, a very good copy. Fenning 60-260 1983 £18.50

LOVELING, BENJAMIN   Latin and English Poems. London:
1738. 1st edition, a fair copy in marbled boards. Pickering &
Chatto 19-36 1983 $250

LOVELL, JAMES   An Oration Delivered April 2nd, 1771.
Boston: Edes and Gill, 1771. Half-title present. Later 3/4
morocco (worn). Margins of most pages damaged and professionally
restored; loss of a few words of text on last leaf. With the
Anson Phelps Stokes and Justin G. Turner bookplates. Felcone 21-67
1983 $350

LOVER, SAMUEL   Handy Andy. London: Lover & Groombridge, 1842. First edition. Illus. by author. 8vo. Orig. cloth. Plates somewhat foxed. Few paint flecks on front cover. A. Edward Newton's copy, with his bookplate. Fine. MacManus 279-3321 1983 $225

LOVER, SAMUEL   Handy Andy; a Tale of Irish Life. London, Frederick Lover, 1842. 8vo, orig. cloth gilt, worn, blank endpaper loose, bookplates, frontis. foxed. First edition. Ravenstree 96-83 1983 $125

LOVER, SAMUEL   Handy Andy; a Tale of Irish Life. New York, Appleton, 1843. 8vo, orig. cloth gilt, spine ends worn, little shaken, some foxing and minor soiling, decent copy. First American edition. Ravenstree 96-85 1983 $45

LOVER, SAMUEL   Legends and Stories of Ireland. London: Baldwin & Cradock, 1837. Second edition. Illus. Orig. embossed green cloth. Presentation copy, inscribed on the front free endpaper "In remembrance of a pleasant day with Willm. Napier by Samuel Lover, Edinburgh Apr 19/49." Inner hinges cracked, covers darkened. Protective cloth wrapper. Good. MacManus 279-3322 1983 $65

LOVER, SAMUEL   Rory O'More. London, Richard Bentley, 1839. 8vo, orig. cloth gilt, little worn, faded and shaken, else good, with series title, engraved frontis. and both engraved and printed titles. Ravenstree 96-86 1983 $25

LOVER, SAMUEL   Songs and Ballads. Chapman & Hall, 1839. First edition. Half title, half maroon morocco, v.g. Jarndyce 30-777 1983 £20

LOVER, SAMUEL   The White Horse of the Peppers. N.Y.: & London: Samuel French, n.d. French's Minor Drama edition. Orig. wrappers. Very fine. MacManus 279-3323 1983 $35

A LOVER'S Progress. London: the Golden Cockerel Press, 1938. 4to. Quarter white morocco with yellow buckram boards, t.e.g., others uncut. Limited edition of 215 numbered copies, printed in red and black, title-page blocked in gold. A little soiled throughout. Traylen 94-535 1983 £50

LOVE'S Invention. London: Printed for W. Cook...1746. 8vo, title and final page slightly dust-soiled; modern brown wraps. First printing. Quaritch NS 7-75 1983 $375

THE LOVES of Mirtil, Son of Adonis. London, 1770. 8vo, engraved title page with vignette, and 6 other plates after Gravelot, cont. English red morocco gilt, spine tooled in compartments with floral ornaments, and broad border of floral ornaments in each cover, a.e.g. Spine a little faded, but a fine copy. Bickersteth 77-41 1983 £135

THE LOVES of Mirtil, Son of Adonis. London, no printer, 1770. First English edition. Small 8vo, engraved title and 6 plates by J. Caldwall after Gravelot. Cont. red morocco, gilt, wallet-type binding (flap worn). Hannas 69-128 1983 £85

LOVETT, A. C.   The Armies of India. London, 1911. 72 coloured plates, text illus. Orig. decorative cloth, slight wear. 8vo. Good. Edwards 1044-442 1983 £90

LOW, CHARLES RATHBONE   Battles of the British Army. London, 1908. Illustrated by R. Caton Woodville. 8vo, full polished calf, all edges marbled. Slightly rubbed, front hinge slightly started. Bookplate. Morrill 286-258 1983 $35

LOW, CHARLES RATHBONE   Her Majesty's Navy. London, (ca.1892). 4to. Orig. cloth. 3 vols. Chromolithograph frontis. and extra titles. 40 chromolithograph plates. Publishers half blue morocco, gilt. Marbled edges, marbled endpapers. Good. Edwards 1042-128 1983 £300

LOW, CHARLES RATHBONE   History of the Indian Navy (1613-1863). London, 1877. First edition. 2 vols. Spines very slightly soiled. 8vo. Orig. cloth. Fine. Edwards 1044-443 1983 £250

LOW, CHARLES RATHBONE   Maritime Discovery. London, 1881. First edition. 8vo. Orig. cloth. Half-titles. 2 vols. Very slightly soiled. Neatly rebacked with orig. spines laid down. Good. Edwards 1042-129 1983 £95

LOW, D. M.   London is London. London, 1949. First edition. Numerous full-page black and white drawings by Edward Bawden. Dustwrapper by Bawden. Fine. Jolliffe 26-44 1983 £28

LOW, FRANCES H.   Queen Victoria's Dolls. Newnes, 1894. 1st ed. Illus. by Alan Wright. Frontis. & 39 colour plates printed by Marcus Ward & b&w title page & 4 b&w shoulder decor. (unpaginated). Green decor. cloth, bevelled boards, col. patterned eps. (cvrs. worn, contents some thumbing), good copy. Hodgkins 27-381 1983 £30

LOW, SAMPSON   The Charities of London in 1861. Sampson Low, Son & Co., 1862. First edition, engraved title by Leighton, charity ads. Orig. maroon cloth, gilt, with flap-over edges. Very good. Jarndyce 31-272 1983 £45

LOW Down: Wayside Thoughts in Ballad, and Other Verse. George Redway, Covent Garden, 1886. 6 pp ads. Orig. brown wraps. a little worn. Printed on 7 different coloured papers. Jarndyce 30-618 1983 £16

LOWE, PERCIVAL   Five Years a Dragoon '49 to '54. Kansas City, 1906. Cloth, fine. Reese 19-337 1983 $100

LOWE, PETER   A Discourse of the Whole Art of Chyrurgerie. London: Thomas Purfott, 1634. Two parts in one. 12 leaves. Final leaf of second part wanting. Large woodcut arms on verso of title; numerous woodcut illus. of medical instruments. Nineteenth century calf (very shabby and broken). Save very minor defects to a few margins. With the signature of Thomas Addis Emmet on title. Felcone 21-68 1983 $500

LOWE, R. T.   A History of the Fishes of Madeira. 1843-60. Roy. 8vo, half roan (head of spine neatly repaired), 28 plates. The work was issued in five parts and never completed. Wheldon 160-66 1983 £350

LOWE, RALPH P.   Biennial Message of Gov...Delivered to the Eighth General Assembly of the State of Iowa. Des Moines, 1859. Orig. printed wraps. First edition. Ginsberg 47-371 1983 $75

LOWELL, AMY   John Keats. Boston: Houghton Mifflin, (1925). 2 vols. Illus. Orig. cloth. MacManus 279-3033 1983 $25

LOWELL, AMY   Men, Women and Ghosts. Boston, (1922). 8vo, cloth backed boards. Reprint edition. Inscribed by the author: "Cross-ribboned shoes; a muslin gown." Argosy 714-475 1983 $20

LOWELL, AMY   Tendencies in Modern American Poetry. NY: The Macmillan Co., 1917. Numerous photographic plates. Presentation copy, signed by Lowell to Katharine D. White, Dec. 25th, 1917. Green cloth. Fine copy. Karmiole 73-64 1983 $150

LOWELL, AMY   Tendencies in Modern American Poetry. N.Y., MacMillian, 1917. First edition. Inscribed and signed by Lowell, Dec. 25, 1917. Illus. with 6 plates. Gilt stamped bluish cloth. Houle 22-608 1983 $225

LOWELL, CHARLES   A Discourse Delivered March 16, 1817, the Sabbath After the Execution of Henry Phillips Stonehewer Davis... Boston, 1817. 1st ed. Small 8vo, orig. wrappers. Bound into stiff wrapper binder. Morrill 289-623 1983 $20

LOWELL, JAMES RUSSELL   Among My Books: Second Series. Boston: Osgood, 1876. 1st ed., 1st issue with error on title-page (Belles-Letters). Orig. mauve cloth, gilt. Rare. Very good copy. Jenkins 155-856 1983 $35

LOWELL, JAMES RUSSELL   The Biglow Papers. Cambridge: Nichols, 1848. 1st ed., single imprint. Orig. grey boards, rebacked. Only a small number of the 1500 copies printed were put into boards. Fine copy in the scarcest binding. Jenkins 155-862 1983 $65

LOWELL, JAMES RUSSELL   The Bigelow Papers. London: Hotten, 1859. 1st Cruikshank ed. Orig. purple cloth, gilt. Frontispiece by Cruikshank. Near fine copy of a book always found dull and worn. Jenkins 153-344 1983 $35

LOWELL, JAMES RUSSELL   The Biglow Papers. London: Hotten, 1859. 1st Cruikshank ed. Orig. purple cloth, gilt. Frontispiece by Cruikshank. Near fine copy. Jenkins 155-857 1983 $35

LOWELL, JAMES RUSSELL   The Bigelow Papers. London: Hotten, 1859. 2nd ed., and the first to have Cruikshank's frontispiece hand-colored. Orig. purple cloth, gilt. Very fine. Jenkins 153-346 1983 $25

LOWELL, JAMES RUSSELL   The Biglow Papers. London: Hotten, 1859. 2nd ed., and the first to have Cruikshank's frontispiece and hand-colored. Very fine. Jenkins 155-859 1983 $25

LOWELL, JAMES RUSSELL   Poems. Boston: Ticknor, Reed & Fields, 1849. 8vo., cloth. 2 vols. Presentation inscription by Lowell on the flyleaf of vol. 1, blank flyleaf has been excised from vol. 2. Brown cloth with embossed seal on front and rear covers, unstamped. Some rubbing to ends of spines, else a fine set. In Our Time 156-512 1983 $250

LOWELL, JAMES RUSSELL   Poems. Boston: Ticknor, Reed & Fields, 1849. 2nd ed., revised, with the addition of 19 previously un-collected poems. 8vo, 2 vols., original cloth, spine gilt, half-titles, bookplates. Extremities of spines worn, but a very good set; each volume is in an individual slipcase. Trebizond 18-63 1983 $90

LOWELL, JAMES RUSSELL   Poems. Cambridge: John Owen, 1844. 8vo. One of a few copies issued large paper. This copy in a gift binding of the period and bears a presentation inscription from an early owner. With bookplate. Some light scuffing to leather, else a fine copy. In Our Time 156-511 1983 $150

LOWELL, JAMES RUSSELL   Poems. Cambridge, 1848. Orig. glazed yellow boards, paper spine label. Backstrip a bit damaged and label slightly rubbed, glue stain on endsheet. In a morocco-backed slipcase. First edition. Presentation copy from the author, inscribed on the front endsheet "To L.L. Thaxter with J.R.L.'s love." With an autograph correction in Lowell's hand on page 34, line 6. Felcone 21-69 1983 $225

LOWELL, JAMES RUSSELL   The Power of Sound, A Rhymed Lecture. New York: Privately printed, 1896. First edition. Small 8vo. Three-quarter cloth over marbled paper covered boards. Limited to 75 numbered copies and printed by the Gillis Press. Inscribed by DeWitt Miller, a former owner. With an article on Lowell tipped to the first few pages and a note from Edwin B. Holden on Grolier Club stationery to Miller. Covers are rubbed. Scarce. Oak Knoll 49-271 1983 $75

LOWELL, JAMES RUSSELL   Works. Boston, Houghton, Mifflin (1899-1901). Standard library ed. 13 vols., 8vo, nice. Morrill 287-599 1983 $45

LOWELL, JAMES RUSSELL   A Year's Life. Boston: Little, Brown, 1841. 1st ed., in a variant binding of tan boards, with the label at crown of spine. Without the errata. Chip at top of spine with some loss of label. Half morocco slipcase. Crisp tight copy. Jenkins 153-

LOWELL, JAMES RUSSELL   A Year's Life. Boston: Little, Brown, 1841. 1st ed., in a variant binding of tan boards, with the label at crown of spine rather than one-third way down. An early copy, without the errata that was inserted in later copies. Half morocco slipcase. Chip at top of spine with some loss of label, else a crisp tight copy. Jenkins 155-861 1983 $100

LOWELL, JOHN   Analysis of the Late Correspondence Between our Administration and Great Britain & France. Boston: Russell and Cutler, (1809). Stitched. Felcone 22-128 1983 $25

LOWELL, JOHN   Analysis of the Late Corespondence Between Our Administration and Great Britain & France. Boston (1809). Dsb., good. Reese 18-326 1983 $35

LOWELL, JOHN   An Appeal to the People, on the Causes and Consequences of a War with Great Britain. Boston: T.B. Wait & Co., 1811. Dbd. A fine, untrimmed copy. Reese 18-348 1983 $40

LOWELL, JOHN   Peace without Dishonour-War without Hope. Boston, 1807. Dsb., good. Reese 18-295 1983 $40

LOWELL, JOHN   Supplement to the Late Analysis of the Public Correspondence Between Our Cabinet and Those of France and Great Britain. (Boston, 1809?). Dsb., very good. Reese 18-327 1983 $35

LOWELL, JOHN   Thoughts Upon the Conduct of Our Administration... Boston: Printed at the Repertory Office, 1808. Dbd. A very good copy. Reese 18-311 1983 $35

LOWELL, JOHN   Thoughts upon the Conduct of Our Administration, in Relation Both to Great Britain and France... Boston: Printed at the Repertory Office, 1808. Small 4to, 21 cm. Fine; disbound. First edition. Grunder 7-50 1983 $20

LOWELL, PERCIVAL   Mars and its Canals. NY: Macmillan, 1906. First edition, with numerous plates (some color) and text illus. Index. Green cloth, a few rubber stamp marks of previous owner. Karmiole 75-85 1983 $75

LOWELL, PERCIVAL   Mars as The Abode of Life. NY: The Macmillan Co., 1908. First edition, with 8 plates (one color) and numerous text illus. Index. Red cloth. Karmiole 75-86 1983 $75

LOWELL, ROBERT   4 by Robert Lowell. Cambridge, Mass., 1969. One of 100 copies signed by Lowell; with a suite of four separate broadsides of the poems, limited to 100 and signed by the illustrator and printer Laurence Scott. Fine. Gekoski 2-126 1983 £200

LOWELL, ROBERT   Land of Unlikeness. Cummington Press, 1944. First edition. One of 250 copies. Except for a tiny blemish to front boards, a mint copy. In special collector's case. Gekoski 2-124 1983 £1,750

LOWELL, ROBERT   Land of Unlikeness. (Cummington): The Cummington Press, 1944. Blue printed boards. First edition. One of 250 copies. Woodcut by Gustav Wolf. Very slight traces of rubbing at the edges, otherwise a fine copy, sans the unprinted glassine dust jacket. Reese 20-626 1983 $2,700

LOWELL, ROBERT   Lord Weary's Castle. New York: Harcourt, Brace and Company, (1946). First edition. 8vo. Orig. cloth. Dust jacket. Very fine copy. Jaffe 1-230 1983 $225

LOWELL, ROBERT   The Mills of the Kavanaughs. New York, (1951). Black cloth. First edition. A few pencil marks in text. Former owner's name on end paper. Very good in jacket. Bradley 65-120 1983 $75

LOWELL, ROBERT   The Mills of the Kavanaughs. New York: (1951). First edition. Black cloth. Former owner's name on end paper, few light pencil marks in text, but nice in dust jacket with a few breaks. Laid in is ticket for a poetry reading by Lowell and Isabella Gardner at the Oriental Theater in Chicago on February 14, 1960. Bradley 66-236 1983 $75

LOWELL, ROBERT   The Mills of the Kavanaughs. New York, 1951. First American edition. Title-page drawing by Francis Parker. Top corners slightly bumped. Nicked dustwrapper with a few small tears and slightly faded at the spine. Fine. Jolliffe 26-329 1983 £75

LOWELL, ROBERT   The Old Glory. New York, (1965). 8vo. Cloth. Inscribed by Lowell on the half title page. A fine copy in dj. In Our Time 156-513 1983 $250

LOWELL, ROBERT   Poems 1938-1949. London, 1950. First edition. Bookplate, in damaged and internally strengthened dustwrapper, otherwise fine. Gekoski 2-125 1983 £30

LOWER, A. R. M.   The North American Assault on the Canadian Forest. Toronto: Ryerson; New Haven: Yale Un. Press; London: Oxford Un. Press, 1938. 24 1/2cm. 5 maps, 11 diagrams. Mapped endpapers. Blue cloth. Very good. McGahern 53-101 1983 $150

LOWER, MARK A.   The Curiosities of Heraldry. John Russell Smith, 1845. First and apparently only edition, with an additional litho title in gold and colours by Hanhart and many text woodcuts. 8vo, recent boards, cancelled library stamps on printed title, but a good copy. Fenning 62-213 1983 £18.50

LOWNDES, MARIE BELLOC   Letty Lynton. London: William Heinemann, (1931). First edition. Orig. blue cloth. Presentation copy
inscribed: "Mrs. Louis Duey (?) with happy memories...,Marie Belloc
Lowndes." Good. MacManus 279-3326 1983 $65

LOWNDES, MARIE BELLOC   Letty Lynton. London: William Heinemann, (1931). First edition. Orig. cloth. Presentation copy
inscribed: "Martha Dillon-Jones, with great love from her old friend,
the writer, Marie Belloc Lowndes." Corners bumped. Head and foot of
spine slightly rubbed. Very good. MacManus 279-3327 1983 $65

LOWNDES, MARIE BELLOC   Letty Lynton. Lon., (1931). Signed
inscription from author, edges rubbed, minor interior foxing, else
near very good. Quill & Brush 54-824 1983 $60

LOWNDES, WILLIAM   A Report Containing an Essay for
the Amendment of the Silver Coins. London: Charles Bill, 1695.
First edition. Disbound. Felcone 31-70 1983 $175

LOWNDES, WILLIAM T.   The bibliographer's manual of English
literature. Pickering, 1834. First edition, 4 vols. in 2, thick
8vo, printed on ribbed paper, publisher's half roan gilt, marbled
paper boards, edges and endpapers, rubbed at extremities, otherwise
a good copy. Deighton 3-212 1983 £120

LOWNDES, WILLIAM T   The Bibliographer's Manual of English
Literature... London: Henry G. Bohn, 1864. New ed., revised,
corrected and enlarged. 4 vols., library cloth, paper a bit brittle,
the first 3 leaves in Vol. II out (half-title, title, and Notice to
the Fourth Part). Dawson 470-196 1983 $150

LOWNE, BENJAMIN THOMPSON   The Anatomy, Physiology, morphology,
and development of the Blow-Fly. 1890-95. 52 plates, 2 vols.,
8vo, cloth (trifle used). Wheldon 160-1116 1983 £60

LOWNE, BENJAMIN THOMPSON   The Anatomy & Physiology of the Blow-Fly.
London 1870. 10 colored plates, cloth, frontis loose, ink inscription
on title, spine frayed and torn, some pp loose. King 46-519 1983
$75.

LOWREY, LAWSON G.   Orthopsychiatry 1923-1948. American
Orthopsychiatric Assn., 1948. Very good ex-library copy. Gach 94-231
1983 $35

LOWRY, MALCOLM   Dark as the Grave Wherein My Friend
Is Laid. New York, (1968). Tall 8vo. Wraps. Advance uncorrected
proof copy. Some tanning and spotting to the wrappers, else a vg-
fine copy. In Our Time 156-519 1983 $275

LOWRY, MALCOLM   Lunar Caustic. London, (1968). First
edition in English. Stiff white wrappers. Scarce in this immaculate
condition. Mint in first issue (Cape Editions) dj. Bradley 65-122
1983 $85

LOWRY, MALCOLM   Ultramarine. London, 1933. First
edition. With original review slip from Jonathan Cape laid in,
announcing publication date of June 12. Very slightly nicked dustwrapper. Fine. Very scarce. Gekoski 2-128 1983 $3,000

LOWRY, MALCOLM   Ultramarine. New York, 1962. 8vo, cloth.
First American edition. Presentation inscription on front flyleaf by
Marjorie Lowry dated October 1962. A very good-fine copy in dust
jacket. In Our Time 156-518 1983 $150

LOWRY, MALCOLM   Ultramarine. Phila., (1962). 12mo,
cloth, d.w. (chipped). First American edition. Argosy 714-483 1983
$45

LOWRY, MALCOLM   Under the Volcano. N.Y., (1947).
First edition. Fine, in a dust jacket which is ragged at the edges.
Argosy 714-404 1983 $200

LOWRY, MALCOLM   Under the Volcano. New York: Reynal
& Hitchcock, (1947). First edition. 8vo. Orig. cloth. Dust
jacket. Very fine copy. Jaffe 1-231 1983 $575

LOWRY, ROBERT   Bad Girl Marie. (Cinn, Little Man
Press, 1942). First edition, sm 8vo, illus. by James Flora. Stiff
printed jacket, very good-fine. One of 100 copies. With a checklist
of the press laid in loose. Houle 21-584 1983 $75

LOWRY, ROBERT   Casualty. (New York): New Directions,
(1946). First edition. Gray cloth. Inscribed by the author and
signed: "For Harry / Good Guy / Bob Lowry / New York / 7 May 48."
Very good in dj. Bradley 65-123 1983 $35

LOWRY, ROBERT   Casualty. New York: New Directions,
(1946). Cloth. First edition. Fine in dust jacket. Reese 20-629
1983 $35

LOWTH, ROBERT   A Short Introduction to English Grammar.
J. Dodsley & T. Cadell, 1769. A new edition, calf, v.g. Jarndyce
31-46 1983 £32

LOWTH, ROBERT   A Short Introduction to English Grammar.
J. Dodsley & T. Cadell, 1776. 1 p ads. Cont. red morocco, gilt
borders and spine, label, a.e.g. A new edition. Jarndyce 31-47
1983 £45

LOWTHER, CHARLES C.   Dodge City, Kansas. Phila., 1940.
First edition. Drawings. Fine. Jenkins 152-181 1983 $30

THE LOYAL man in the moon. London: C. Chapple, etc., 1820. First
edition. 8vo. Disbound. 13 woodcuts in the Cruikshank manner.
Scarce. Ximenes 63-501 1983 $60

LOZOYA, JUAN CONTRERAS Y LOPEZ DE AYALA, MARQUES DE   Vicente
Lopez, 1772-1850. Barcelona, 1943. 61 plates. Frontis. Large
4to. Cloth, 1/2 leather. Orig. wrappers bound in. Edition limited
to 1200 numbered copies. Ars Libri 32-411 1983 $125

LUARD, J   A History of the Dress of the British
Soldier. London, 1852. Roy. 8vo. Orig. cloth. Mounted frontis. and
49 mounted plates of uniform. Slightly worn and soiled. Some foxing
throughout. Bookplate. Presentation inscription from author on title.
Good. Edwards 1042-401 1983 £40

LUARD, J.   Views in India. London, (1830). Title
and 60 lithograph plates on India paper. Folio. Half calf, spine gilt.
Some slight rubbing to hinges. 8vo. Good. Edwards 1044-444 1983
£365

LUBBOCK, BASIL   Adventures by Sea. London, 1925.
Limited edition. 4to. Orig. blue buckram gilt. 115 plates and illus.
of which 22 are coloured. Orig. dust jacket. Mint. Edwards 1042-130
1983 £120

LUBBOCK, BASIL   Adventures by Sea. London, 1925.
Limited edition. 4to. Orig. blue buckram gilt. Spine slightly
faded. Very fine. Edwards 1042-131 1983 £100

LUBBOCK, BASIL   The China Clippers. Lauriat, (1914).
1st American ed. Illus. and plans. 8vo. Morrill 286-259 1983
$30

LUBBOCK, BASIL   The China Clippers. Glasgow: James
Brown, 1925. With plages and illus., 8vo, orig. cloth. Fenning
62-214 1983 £18.50

LUBBOCK, BASIL   The Opium Clippers. Glasgow, 1933.
First edition. Thick imperial 8vo. Green cloth presentation binding
of the Society of Master Mariners (South Africa), with their presentation bookplate. Frontis., 1 coloured and 1 folding plate, 45 other
plates, 2 folding and 4 other maps. Good. Edwards 1042-132 1983 £40

LUBBOCK, PERCY   Mary Cholmondeley: A Sketch from Memory.
London: Jonathan Cape, (1928). First edition. Orig. cloth. Dust
jacket (soiled and frayed). Edges slightly worn and faded. Slightly
browned at the endpapers. Good. MacManus 277-965 1983 $35

LUBBOCK, PERCY   The Region Cloud. London: Jonathan
Cape, (1925). First edition. Orig. cloth-backed boards. Good. Mac-
Manus 279-3329 1983 $20

LUCANUS, MARCUS ANNAEUS   Pharsalia Cum Notis Hugonis Grotii et
Richardi Bentleii. Strawberry-Hill, 1760. 4to, orig. calf gilt,
hinges cracked, bookplate, bit worn about hinges and spine ends, a
large, clean and crisp copy; the rare second issue. 500 copies were
printed about 400 of which it is surmised were of the first issue.
Ravenstree 95-71 1983 $385

LUCAS, A. H. S.   The Birds of Australia. Melbourne, 1911. Coloured frontispiece, numerous illus. (some coloured). 8vo, original cloth (trifle used), first edition. Scarce. Wheldon 160-798 1983 £25

LUCAS, EDWARD VERRALL   All of a Piece. London: Methuen & Co. Ltd., (1937). First edition. Frontis. Orig. cloth. Dust jacket. Fine. MacManus 279-3330 1983 $35

LUCAS, EDWARD VERRALL   "--And Such Small Deer." London: Methuen & Co. Ltd., (1930). First edition. Frontis. Orig. cloth-backed boards with paper label on spine. Dust jacket (slightly dust-soiled). Very good. MacManus 279-3331 1983 $25

LUCAS, EDWARD VERRALL   At "The Pines." (London: Privately Printed by Clement Shorter, 1916.). First separate edition. Orig. wrappers. One of only 25 copies signed by publisher. Fine. Mac-Manus 279-3332 1983 $125

LUCAS, EDWARD VERRALL   At the Shrine of St. Charles. N.Y.: E.P. Dutton & Co., Inc., (1934). First American edition. 4 illus. Orig. cloth. With a new preface. Fine. MacManus 279-3333 1983 $20

LUCAS, EDWARD VERRALL   The Barber's Clock. London: Methuen & Co., (1931). First edition. Frontis. Orig. cloth-backed boards with paper labesl. Dust jacket (slightly dust-soiled). Fine. MacManus 279-3335 1983 $20

LUCAS, EDWARD VERRALL   The British School. London: Methuen & Co. Ltd., (1913). First edition. 16 illus. Orig. cloth. Dust jacket (a little darkened & worn). Very good. MacManus 279-3337 1983 $45

LUCAS, EDWARD VERRALL   Charles Lamb and The Lloyds. London: Smith, Elder, & Co., 1898. First edition. Port. Orig. cloth. Very good. MacManus 279-3338 1983 $35

LUCAS, EDWARD VERRALL   The Colvins & Their Friends. London: Methuen & Co., Ltd., (1928). First edition. Frontispiece in photo-gravure and 25 other illus. Orig. cloth with paper label on spine. Dust jacket. Very good. MacManus 277-1051 1983 $30

LUCAS, EDWARD VERRALL   The Colvins and Their friends. London: Methuen & Co. Ltd., (1928). First edition. With a frontispiece in photogravure and 25 illus. Orig. cloth with paper label on spine. Very good. MacManus 279-3340 1983 $20

LUCAS, EDWARD VERRALL   Down the Sky. London: Methuen & Co. Ltd., (1930). First edition. Orig. cloth. Dust jacket (creased). Very good. MacManus 279-3341 1983 $35

LUCAS, EDWARD VERRALL   The Friendly Town. London: Methuen & Co., (1905). First edition. Orig. cloth. Shaken. Good. MacManus 279-3345 1983 $20

LUCAS, EDWARD VERRALL   God and the Typist. N.p.: Printed for Private Circulation, n.d. 12mo. First edition. Orig. wrappers. Fine. MacManus 279-3348 1983 $150

LUCAS, EDWARD VERRALL   Good Company. London: Methuen & Co., (1909). First edition. Orig. cloth. Dust jacket. Fine. MacManus 279-3349 1983 $50

LUCAS, EDWARD VERRALL   A Group of Londoners. Minneapolis: Privately printed, 1913. First edition. Orig. cloth-backed boards. A bit worn. MacManus 279-3350 1983 $30

LUCAS, EDWARD VERRALL   Guillaumism. (London: Privately Printed by Clement Shorter, 1914). First separate edition. Orig. wrappers. One of 25 copies printed and signed by publisher. This copy is also inscribed "Written during the war. E.V. Lucas" by the author. Very good. MacManus 279-3351 1983 $125

LUCAS, EDWARD VERRALL   Harvest Home. London: Methuen & Co. Ltd., (1913). First edition. Orig. cloth. Dust jacket. Spine slightly stained. Fine. MacManus 279-3353 1983 $50

LUCAS, EDWARD VERRALL   If. A nightmare in the Conditional Mood. (London): Sir Isaac Pitnam & Sons, Ltd., (1908). First edition. Illus. by Geo. Morrow. Orig. wrappers. Spine of wrappers a little worn. Near-fine. MacManus 279-3354 1983 $125

LUCAS, EDWARD VERRALL   The Ladies' Pageant. N.p.: The Mac-millan Co., (1908). First edition. Small 8vo. Orig. cloth. Dust jacket (defective). Inscription on flyleaf. Very good. MacManus 279-3355 1983 $25

LUCAS, EDWARD VERRALL   Lemon Verbena and Other Essays. London: Methuen & Co. Ltd., (1932). First edition. Frontis. Orig. cloth. Dust jacket (spine a little darkened). Fine. MacManus 279-3356 1983 $35

LUCAS, EDWARD VERRALL   Life and Work of Edwin Austin Abbey. New York & London, 1921. 8vo. Cloth, paper labels. 2 vols. A fine set. In Our Time 156-2 1983 $150

LUCAS, EDWARD VERRALL   The Life of Charles Lamb. London: Metheun & Co., (1905). First edition. 2 vols. Extra-illus. Full green morocco, gilt, a.e.g., marbled endpapers. Fine. MacManus 279-3112 1983 $250

LUCAS, EDWARD VERRALL   The Open Road. London: Richards, 1899. First edition. 12mo. Orig. limp leather. Rubbed. MacManus 279-3363 1983 $35

LUCAS, EDWARD VERRALL   Out of a Clear Sky. London: Methuen & Co. Ltd., (1928). First edition. Frontis. Orig. cloth-backed boards with paper label on spine. Dust jacket. Fine. MacManus 279-3364 1983 $35

LUCAS, EDWARD VERRALL   Outposts of Mercy. London: Methuen & Co. Ltd., (1917). First edition. 16 illus. Orig. wrappers. Very good. MacManus 279-3365 1983 $50

LUCAS, EDWARD VERRALL   Pleasure Trove. London: Methuen & Co. Ltd., (1935). First edition. Frontis. Orig. cloth. Dust jacket. Fine. MacManus 279-3366 1983 $35

LUCAS, EDWARD VERRALL   Remember Louvain! London: Methuen & Co. Ltd., (1914). First edition. Orig. wrappers. Very good. Mac-Manus 279-3368 1983 $35

LUCAS, EDWARD VERRALL   The Same Star. London: Methuen & Co. Ltd., (1924). First edition. Orig. boards with paper label. Dust jacket (spine darkened). Very good. MacManus 279-3369 1983 $35

LUCAS, EDWARD VERRALL   Sparks from a Flint. London: Howe & Co., (1890). First edition. Orig. red cloth. Extremities of spine a trifle rubbed. Front inner hinges strained. Very good. MacManus 279-3370 1983 $200

LUCAS, EDWARD VERRALL   Specially Selected. London: Methuen & Co. Ltd., (1920). First edition. Orig. cloth. Dust jacket (creased). MacManus 279-3371 1983 $35

LUCAS, EDWARD VERRALL   Turning Things Over. London: Methuen & Co. Ltd., (1929). First edition. Frontis. Orig. cloth. Dust jacket (creased). Very good. MacManus 279-3372 1983 $25

LUCAS, EDWARD VERRALL   Variety Lane. London: Methuen & Co. Ltd., (1916). First edition. Orig. cloth. Dust jacket. Fine. MacManus 279-3373 1983 $50

LUCAS, EDWARD VERRALL   The Vermilion Box. London: Methuen & Co. Ltd., (1916). First edition. Orig. cloth. Dust jacket (tape repaired near top of spine, torn). Fine. MacManus 279-3374 1983 $50

LUCAS, EDWARD VERRALL   Windfall's Eve. London: Methuen & Co. Ltd., (1929). First edition. Orig. cloth. Dust jacket (creased, spine darkened & rubbed). Very good. MacManus 279-3378 1983 $20

LUCAS, F. L.   Gilgamesh: King of Erech. London, 1948. Tall 8vo, cloth-backed pict. boards, gilt, t.e.g. One of 500 copies with engr. by Dorothea Brady. A fine copy. Perata 28-33 1983 $75

LUCAS, F. L.   The River Flows. London: The Hogarth Press, 1926. First edition. Orig. green cloth. Fine. MacManus 279-3382 1983 $25

LUCAS, ROBERT   Message. Gentlemen of the Senate and of the House of Representatives. Columbus, Ohio, 1833. First edition. Ginsberg 46-577 1983 $125

LUCAS, UNA   A Phantasie in Honour of Virgil 70 B.C.-1930 A.D. Greenwich, Conn., 1931. 8vo, cloth-backed boards, t.e.g., (soiled) slipcase. Signed presentation from the author. Perata 28-156 1983 $125

LUCAS, W. J.   British Dragonflies (Odonata). 1900. 27 coloured plates and 57 text-figures, 8vo, original buckram. Front inner joint loose, otherwise a good ex-library copy. Wheldon 160-1118 1983 £38

LUCAS, W. J.   A Monograph of the British Orthoptera. Ray Society, 1920. 6 coloured and 19 plain plates, 8vo, cloth. Wheldon 160-1119 1983 £30

LUCCESE, ROMEO   Brancaccio. Roma: De Luca, 1972. 359 illus. (numerous color). Large square 4to. Cloth. Ars Libri 33-418 1983 $75

LUCE, EDWARD S.   Keogh, Comanche and Custer. N.p., (1939). Illus. Orig. cloth. First edition. Ginsberg 46-215 1983 $300

LUCIAN   The Works of Lucian, from the Greek. London, T. Cadell, 1780. 2 vols., 4to, cont. calf (joints broken, title and first few leaves of volume 1 damaged in blank inner margin, bookplate, few minor spots or stains, partly unopened) with list of subscribers. First edition. Ravenstree 95-72 1983 $145

LUCKENBACH, A.   Forty-Six Select Scripture Narratives from the Old Testament. Embellished with Engravings, for the Use of Indian Youth. Translated Into Delaware Indian... New York: Fanshaw, 1838. About 80 woodcut illus. Orig. full sheep, green leather label. Light binding wear and occasional light foxing. 1st and only ed. Well-preserved copy. Jenkins 155-864 1983 $600

LUCKOMBE, P.   A Concise History of the Origin and Progress of Printing... London: W. Adlard and J. Browne, 1770. First edition. 8vo. Modern half leather over cloth. Frontis. repaired, else fine. Oak Knoll 48-256 1983 $350

LUCKOMBE, P.   The History and Art of Printing. London: J. Johnson, 1771. Second printing. 8vo. Modern half leather over cloth, leather spine label. Frontis. Wood-engraving of Gutenberg as a frontis. Illus. Some faint foxing. From the library of Allen Hazen with his memorial bookplate. Oak Knoll 49-272 1983 $350

LUCRETIUS   Titi Lucretii Cari de Rerum Natura Libri Sex. Cantabrigiae, Joann. Hayes, 1675. Large 12mo, cont. calf, spine ends worn, front cover detached. First edition to be printed in England. Ravenstree 95-73 1983 $95

LUCRETIUS   De Rerum Natura. Paris, Bude, 1924. 2 vols. 8vo, cloth. Salloch 385-614 1983 $25

LUCRETIUS   De Rerum Natura. Madison, 1942. Thick 4to, cl., lettering on spine faded. Cloth. Salloch 385-613 1983 $40

LUCY, HENRY W.   A Diary of the Home Rule Parliament, 1892-95. Cassell, 1896. First edition, front. of Randolph Churchill, 16pp ads. Orig. green cloth. Jarndyce 31-199 1983 £12.50

LUCY, HENRY W.   A Diary of the Salisbury Parliament, 1886-1892. Cassell, 1892. Illus. by Harry Furniss. Half title, 16 pp ads. Orig. maroon cloth. Jarndyce 31-309 1983 £14.50

LUCY, HENRY W.   East by West. London: Bentley, 1885. First edition. 2 vols. Orig. cloth (covers soiled). Covers worn. Shaken. MacManus 279-3383 1983 $75

LUDLOW, EDMUND   Memoirs. Vivay, Switzerland, 1698-99. 3 vols. 8vo. 3 inserted portraits. Half red morocco & marbled boards, gilt backs. 1st ed. Fine. O'Neal 50-36 1983 $125

LUDWIG, EMIL   Bismark. N.Y., Putnam, 1921. 16 plates, 3/4 red morocco. Spine with gilt stamped military devices, t.e.g., very good. Houle 21-587 1983 $65

LUDWIG, H.   Asteroidea of "Albatross" Expedition to Tropical Pacific 1899-1900. Cambridge, Mass., 1905. 35 plates, 4to, new cloth. Wheldon 160-1319 1983 £20

LUFF, JOHN N.   The Postage Stamps of the United States. N.P. (ca. 1940). Reprint. Illus. 4to, buckram. Morrill 288-244 1983 $25

LUHAN, MABEL DODGE   Edge of Taos Desert. N.Y., Harcourt, (1937). First edition. Illus., including a photo by Ansel Adams. Dust jacket (chipped, worn, dampstaining to lower corners of text), good. Houle 21-538 1983 $20

LUHAN, MABEL DODGE   European Experiences. N.Y., Harcourt, (1935). First edition. Illus. Blue cloth, good-very good. Houle 21-832 1983 $45

LUHAN, MABEL DODGE   Intimate Memories: Background. N.Y., Harcourt (1933). First edition. Illus. Dust jacket. Very good-fine. Houle 21-588 1983 $50

LUHAN, MABEL DODGE   Winter in Taos. Denver, Sage, (1935). Second edition. Dust jacket. Signed by the author on the title page. Houle 21-589 1983 $60

LUMLEY, L. R.   History of the Eleventh Hussars. London, 1936. Portrait frontis. 22 plates, 12 folding maps, 26 full page maps, 1 text map. Thick imperial 8vo. Orig. cloth. Good. Edwards 1042-526 1983 £35

LUMMIS, CHARLES F.   Birch Bark Poems. (Chillocothe, Ohio): 1882. Extremely fine. (3 x 2 1/2; 75x62mm). Bromer 25-451A 1983 $75

LUMMIS, CHARLES F.   Birch Bark Poems. (Chillocothe, Ohio): 1883. Vol. I. Fine. (3 x 2 1/2; 75x62mm). Bromer 25-451B 1983 $60

LUMMIS, CHARLES F.   Birch Bark Poems. (Chillocothe, Ohio): 1883. Vol. II. Fine. (3 x 2 1/2; 75x62mm). Bromer 25-415C 1983 $60

LUNDBORG, EINAR   The Artic Rescue. NY, 1929. Photos, card signed by author laid-in, corners slightly rubbed, else fine in slightly chipped, very good dustwrapper. Quill & Brush 54-1645 1983 $50

LUNDY'S LANE HISTORICAL SOCIETY   The Centenary Celebration of the Battle of Lundy's Lane... Niagara Falls: L.L.H.S., 1919. 23cm. 28 illus. Printed wrappers. Fine. McGahern 53-102 1983 $25

LUNGE, GEORGE   A Theoretical and Practical Treatise on the Manufacture of Sulphuric Acid... London: Van Voorst, 1879. First edition. 3 vols. 8vo. Orig. maroon cloth. 11 folding plates and tables. Numerous text figures, many full page. Partially unopened. A little worn. Zeitlin 264-274 1983 $120

LUNGE, GEORGE   A Treatise on the Distillation of Coal-Tar and Ammoniacal Liquor... London: Van Voorst, 1882. First English edition. 8vo. Orig. cloth. Numerous text figures. Ads. Rubbed, inside front cover partially detached. Zeitlin 264-275 1983 $40

LUNT, CARROLL   Breaks in the Clouds. (Prairie City): The Decker Press, (1948). Cloth. First edition. Inscribed by the author on the dedication page. Fine in dust jacket which is chipped at the head and toe of the spine. Reese 20-308 1983 $25

LUNT, ROSETTA   Mabel Clare. Chicago, ca. 1864. Folio sheet music. Ginsberg 46-331 1983 $25

LUPTON, DONALD　　　　The Glory of their Times. London, I.
Okes, 1640. 4to, orig. calf, joints breaking, tear to outer edge
of title causing no loss. A large copy. First and only edition.
Ravenstree 97-64　1983　$225

LUPTON, THOMAS　　　　A Thousand Notable Things, on various
Subjects; disclosed from the Secrets of Nature and Art. London: G.
& T. Wilkie; Salisbury: E. Easton, 1785. Cont. calf, spine gilt,
morocco label. A fine copy. Trebizond 18-205　1983　$165

LUSSAN, RAVENEAU DE　　　　Les Filibustiers de la Mer du Sud.
Paris, (1926). Orig. pr. wraps., (some pp. unopened). Ltd.,
numbered edition. Argosy 716-632　1983　$30

LUST, HERBERT C.　　　　Giacometti: The Complete Graphics
and 15 drawings. New York: Tudor, 1970. 368 illus. Large 4to.
Cloth. Dust jacket. Ars Libri 32-256　1983　$85

LUTCHER, HENRY J.　　　　A Stronger and More Permanent Union.
Orange, Texas, 1896. Orig. dark blue printed wrappers. Library stamp
on title only. Jenkins 152-213　1983　$35

LUTHER, MARTIN　　　　A Commentarie of M. Doctor Martin
Lvther Vpon the Epistle of S. Paule to the Galathians... (London)
Thomas Vautroullier, 1588. 4to, old quarter sheep, boards, title
frayed about edges with early mend at top; a well-used copy with
minor age and waterstains, top of 12 gone but with no text lost.
Ravenstree 97-65　1983　$195

LUTHER DE GARBENFELD, JOSEPH　Dissertatio medica inauguralis de Tabaci
usu et abusu... Strassburg: Wilhelm Schmuck, 1744. Small 4to.
Boards. First edition. Kraus 164-235　1983　$280

LUTHGEN, EUGEN　　　　Romanische Plastik in Deutschland. Bonn/
Leipzig, 1923. Lg. 4to, 145 plates, boards, 3/4 leather. Ars Libri
SB 26-130　1983　$150

LUTHI, WALTER　　　　Urs Graf und die Kunst der alten
Schweizer. Zurich/Leipzig: Orell Fussli, 1928. 100 illus. hors
texte. 5 figs. Large 4to. Cloth. Dust jacket. From the library
of Jakob Rosenberg. Ars Libri 32-279　1983　$75

LUTKEN, C. F.　　　　Dijmphna-Togets Zoologisk-botaniske
Udbytte. Copenhagen, 1887. Map and 41 plates, royal 8vo. Wheldon
160-405　1983　£15

LUYS, JULES　　　　The Brain & Its Functions. N.Y., 1893.
Fine. Argosy 713-346　1983　$50

LYALL, ARTHUR　　　　The Rise and Expansion of the British
Dominion in India. London, 1914. 5 coloured folding maps. Uncut.
8vo. Orig. cloth. Good. Edwards 1044-445　1983　£12

LYDEKKER, JOHN WOLFE　　　　The Faithful Mohawks. Cambridge:
at the University Press, 1938. 22cm. First edition. 15 plates
and rear folding map. Very good. McGahern 53-103　1983　$25

LYDEKKER, R.　　　　A Geographical History of Mammals.
Cambridge, 1896. Map and text-figures, 8vo, cloth. Wheldon 160-577
1983　£30

LYDEKKER, R　　　　A Hand-Book to the Carnivora.
London 1896. 32 color plates, 1/2 lea, some pencil scribbles,
covers rubbed, 1 plate torn. King 46-520　1983　$35

LYDEKKER, R.　　　　A Hand-Book to the Marsupialia and
Monotremata. 1896. 38 coloured plates, sm. 8vo, cloth (spine faded,
repaired). Wheldon 160-578　1983　£35

LYDEKKER, R.　　　　Reptiles, Amphibia, Fishes and lower
chordates. 1912. 35 plates (4 coloured), map and text-figures, 8vo,
cloth (trifle used). Wheldon 160-983　1983　£15

LYDON, A. F.　　　　Fairy Mary's Dream. Groombridge, 1870.
Sm. 4to. Colour printed frontis. & pictorial title (stained).
6 colour printed plates & 9 text illus. Edges worn. Brown decorated
cloth, rebacked & worn. Greer 40-79　1983　£25

LYELL, CHARLES　　　　Travels in North America... New York,
1845. 2 vols. Folding map in color, 6 plates. Contemp. calf. Fine
set. Jenkins 153-348　1983　$400

LYELL, CHARLES　　　　Principles of Geology. (1830-33).
Reprint, 1970. First edition, 11 plates and maps, 3 vols., 8vo,
cloth. Wheldon 160-1439　1983　£67

LYLE, JAMES A.　　　　Handbook for Receivers. Dublin: King,
1878. First edition, 8vo, orig. limp cloth, gilt. Fenning 62-215
1983　£18.50

LYLE, MARIUS　　　　The Virgin. A Tale of Woe. Boar's Head
Press, 1932. 1st ed., 8vo, wood engraved frontis. by Lettice Sandford,
Cockerell marbled cloth lettered in gilt, t.e.g., others uncut,
cloth a little chafed at extremities, bookplate, good. 200 numbered
copies. Deighton 3-213　1983　£45

LYMAN, ALBERT　　　　Journal of a Voyage to California, and
Life in the Gold Diggings. And Also a Voyage from California to
the Sandwich Islands. Hartford, 1852. 2 full-page woodcut views,
numerous woodcut text-illus. Original blind-stamped cloth, spine
restored. First edition. Jenkins 151-196　1983　$125

LYMAN, GEORGE　　　　John Marsh, Pioneer. The Life Story of
a Trail-Blazer on Six Frontiers. New York: Charles Scribner's
Sons, 1930. Frontis and illus. One of twenty presentation copies
signed by the author. T.e.g. Boxed. Very fine copy. Jenkins 151-
205　1983　$150

LYMAN, GEORGE　　　　John Marsh, Pioneer. N.Y., Scribner,
1930. First edition. Illus. Dust jacket. Very good. Houle 22-
1128　1983　$45

LYMAN, GEORGE　　　　The Saga of the Comstock Lode. N.Y.,
Scribner, 1934. First edition. Illus. Dust jacket. Signed and
inscribed by the author. Very good - fine. Houle 22-1129　1983
$45

LYMAN, GEORGE　　　　Ralston's Ring California Plunders the
Comstock Lode. New York, 1937. Plates. Fine copy of the first
edition. Scarce. Jenkins 151-197　1983　$40

LYMINGTON, LORD　　　　Spring Song of Iscariot. Paris: The
Black Sun Press, 1929. Printed wraps. First edition. One of 100
numbered copies printed on Holland Van Gelder Zonen, of 150 (25 on
Japan, 25 H.C.). Slight chipping of orig. glassine, else fine in gilt
slipcase (top and bottom panels broken). Reese 20-131　1983　$100

LYNAM, C. C.　　　　To Norway and the North Cape in 'Blue
Dragon II'. Sidgwick & Jackson, 1913. First edition. 7 maps, 62
plates, some other illus. Roy. 8vo, orig. cloth, gilt, t.e.g. Very
good. Fenning 61-262　1983　£24.50

LYNCH, BOHUN　　　　A History of Caricature. London, 1926.
First edition. Frontis., 20 black and white plates, and 12 illus.
in the text. Bookplate. Prelims and endpapers spotted and browned.
Very good. Jolliffe 26-79　1983　£32

LYNCH, JEREMIAH　　　　Three Years In The Klondike.
London, 1904. Photos, drawings, cloth, f.e.p. lacking, spine torn
at both outer edges, worn. First edition. King 46-5　1983　$20

LYND, ROBERT　　　　The Pleasures of Ignorance. London:
Grant Richards Ltd., 1921. First edition. Orig. cloth. Dust jacket.
Fine. MacManus 279-3392　1983　$20

LYND, ROBERT　　　　The Sporting Life and Other Trifles.
London: Grant Richards Ltd., 1922. First edition. Orig. cloth.
Dust jacket. Fine. MacManus 279-3393　1983　$22.50

LYNDE, FRANCIS　　　　The Taming of Red Butte Western. N.Y.,
Scribner, 1910. First edition. Frontis. and three full page
plates by Maynard Dixon. Pictorial blue cloth stamped in black,
orange, and white with a design of railroad tracks and a locomotive
approaching. Very good - fine. Houle 22-1130　1983　$95

LYON, E. WILSON   The Man Who Sold Louisiana. Norman, 1942. First edition in dust jacket. Frontis portrait. Illus. Some fading to spine. Jenkins 152-118 1983 $30

LYON, GEORGE FRANCIS   A narrative of travels in northern Africa... London: John Murray, 1821. 4to. Folding map, 17 hand-colored plates. Modern 1/2 brown calf, marbled boards. Adelson Africa-102 1983 $450

LYON, IRVING WHITALL   Colonial Furniture of New England. Boston, 1891. 1st ed. Illus. 4to, leaf of errata. Dampstain bottom of spine extending into several adjoining leaves, front and back. Morrill 287-601 1983 $35

LYON, JOHN   The Harp of Zion. Liverpool: S.W. Richards,...London: T.C. Armstrong, 1853. First edition. Orig. embossed cloth. Very fine. MacManus 279-3394 1983 $50

LYON, T. M.   In Kilt and Khaki. Kilmarnock, 1915. Sm. 8vo. Orig. tan half cloth. Portrait frontis. Grey boards. Spine faded. Good. Edwards 1042-403 1983 £12

LYON Memorial, Massachusetts Families... Detroit, 1905. 1st ed. 8vo. Dust wrapper. Inner side of d/w repaired. Morrill 289-425 1983 $25

LYONS, ALBERT S.   Medicine: An Illustrated History. Abrams, 1978. 1020 illus., including 266 plates in full color. Thick folio, cloth, d.w. Argosy 713-347 1983 $75

LYONS, EUGENE   The Red Decade. Indianapolis, Bobbs-Merrill, (1941). First edition. Dust jacket (small nicks) else, very good. With the bookplate of Cecil B. DeMille. Houle 22-609 1983 $20

LYRA Americana. Relig. Tract Soc., 1865. Decor. initial letters printed in black & red, 8pp illus. adverts. Green sand grain cloth, gilt, a.e.g., corners sl. bumped, insc. ep., vg. Hodgkins 27-305 1983 £10.50

LYRA Germanica. Longman, etc., 1861 (1st series). Illus. & engr'd under supervision of John Leighton. Numerous illus. by Armitage, Flaxman, Lawless, Keene, Marks, Leighton. Green mor. grain decor. cloth gilt. Contemp. insc. half title sl. wear top/bottom bkstrip & corners, fine copy. Hodgkins 27-306 1983 £35

LYRA Germanica. Longmans, etc., 1868 (2nd series). Illus. by Leighton, Armitage, F. Madox Brown. Pub's brown morocco decor. binding, vg. Hodgkins 27-307 1983 £35

LYRA Graeca. London, 1924-1928. 3 vols. 8vo, cloth. Salloch 385-621 1983 $30

LYSER, ALICE I.   Spain and Spanish America in the Libraries of the University of California: A Catalogue of Books. Berkeley: (Univ. of California), 1930. Vol. II. Cloth, fine. Dawson 470-199 1983 $25

LYSER, ALICE I.   Spain and Spanish America in the Libraries of the University of California. New York: Burt Franklin, (1969). 2 vols., cloth. Reprint of the 1928-30 ed. Dawson 470-198 1983 $75

LYSONS, DANIEL   Magna Britannia. 1808. First edition, double page county map, an engraved plan of Cambridge, 11 double-page and 20 full page engraved plates (including one coloured), half calf, 4to, slightly rubbed. K Books 307-123 1983 £75

LYSONS, DANIEL   Magna Britannia... 1810. 4to, 33 + 35 plates, including the county maps, orig. half calf, rubbed, lower joint cracked, contents clean. Bickersteth 75-154 1983 £40

LYTE, H. C. MAXWELL   A History of Eton College. 1911. 8vo, folding map, 10 plates, numerous text figures, maroon calf, spine rubbed. Bickersteth 75-157 1983 £12

LYTLE, HORACE   Point: A Book About Bird Dogs. NY, (1941). Limited to 950 copies, signed inscription from Lytle, cover slightly faded, tape stains on flys, still very good or better. Quill & Brush 54-826 1983 $100

LYTTLETON, GEORGE   Dialogues of the Dead. London: Printed for W. Sandby, 1760. First edition. 8vo. Orig. calf-backed marbled boards with red morocco label. Fine. MacManus 279-3396 1983 $350

LYTTLETON, GEORGE   Dialogues of the Dead. London: W. Sandby, 1760. First ed., 8vo., contemporary calf, spine gilt, lacking mor. label. Binding worn, front cover loose; internally fine. Trebizond 18-64 1983 $275

LYTTELTON, GEORGE   Dialogues of the Dead. Printed for W. Sandby, 1760. 8vo, errata leaf, cont. calf, crack in top of upper joint. Tear in the title neatly repaired. Bickersteth 75-51 1983 £24

LYTTELTON, GEORGE   Letters from a Persian in England to his friend in Ispahan. Printed for J. Millan, 1735. 12mo, 2 ad. leaves, orig. calf, rubbed. Bickersteth 77-42 1983 £22

LYTTLETON, GEORGE   The Poetical Works...with Life of the Author. London, 1826. Frontis. 1st illus. ed. Contemporary leather, elaborately gilt. Fine copy. Unusual. Jenkins 155-426 1983 $350

LYTTLETON, GEORGE   The Poetical Works. London: by C. Whittingham, for Cadell and Davies, etc., 1801. 8vo. Cont. straight-grained red morocco, gilt, gilt borders, gilt panelled spine, edges gilt. Vignette title-page and 4 engraved plates. Traylen 94-539 1983 £30

LYTTON, EDWARD GEORGE EARLE LYTTON BULWER-LYTTON, 1st BARON (1803-1873) The Caxtons. A Family Picture. Edinburgh: Blackwood, 1849. First edition. 3 vols. Orig. cloth. Shaky, backstrips damaged and hastily repaired. MacManus 277-772 1983 $35

LYTTON, EDWARD GEORGE EARLE LYTTON BULWER-LYTTON, 1ST BARON (1803-1873) Devereux; A Tale. London, Henry Colburn, 1829. 3 vols., 8vo, bound without half titles in cont. half calf, joints rather worn and weak, top of spine of vol. 2 defective, name on title; with errata slips in each volume and with advertisement leaf in vol. 2. First edition. Ravenstree 96-89 1983 $125

LYTTON, EDWARD GEORGE EARLE LYTTON BULWER-LYTTON, 1ST BARON (1803-1873) Devereux. London, Henry Colburn, 1833. 3 vols., 8vo, orig. cloth, spots of mildew throughout. Ravenstree 96-90 1983 $63

LYTTON, EDWARD GEORGE EARLE LYTTON BULWER-LYTTON, 1ST BARON (1803-1873) The Disowned. Henry Colburn, 1829. 3 vols. Large 12mo, half calf, gilt (a little rubbed), bookplate of George Thomas Wyndham. Small tear in margin of one leaf, not touching text. Hannas 69-16 1983 £15

LYTTON, EDWARD GEORGE EARLE LYTTON BULWER-LYTTON, 1ST BARON (1803-1873) Eugene Aram. Henry Colburn and Richard Bentley, 1832. 3 vols., 12mo, orig. boards uncut, some wear to backstrips, a hinge of vol. II partly cracked, lending lists removed from inside covers. With all half-titles. First edition. Hill 165-72 1983 £60

LYTTON, EDWARD GEORGE EARLE LYTTON BULWER-LYTTON, 1ST BARON (1803-1873) Eugene Aram. Stockholm, L.J. Hjerta, 1834. First Swedish edition. 12mo. Cont. half calf. Hannas 69-18 1983 £10

LYTTON, EDWARD GEORGE EARLE LYTTON BULWER-LYTTON, 1ST BARON (1803-1873) Falkland. London, Henry Colburn, 1827. 8vo, later half calf, worn, covers detached, spine ends chipped, mend across F6, clean and not affecting legibility, occasional foxing, but generally a decent copy. Bookstamp of Lady Alice Peel. First edition. Ravenstree 96-91 1983 $295

LYTTON, EDWARD GEORGE EARLE LYTTON BULWER-LYTTON, 1ST BARON (1803-1873) Kenelm Chillingly His Adventures and Opinions. Edinburgh and London, Blackwood, 1873. 3 vols., 8vo, without half titles in cont. quarter red roan gilt, bit worn. First edition. Ravenstree 96-92 1983 $65

LYTTON, EDWARD GEORGE EARLE LYTTON BULWER-LYTTON, 1ST BARON (1803-1873)
The Last Days of Pompeii. London, Bentley, 1834. 3 vols., 8vo,
bound without ads and errata slips in orig. quarter linen, boards
(Carter's "C" variant, with no priority given "A" or "B"), with half
titles as called for, name torn from upper corner of half title to
vol. 3, binding and orig. printed paper spine labels worn, minor
stain to pp. 258-9 of vol. 3. First edition. Ravenstree 96-93 1983
$185

LYTTON, EDWARD GEORGE EARLE LYTTON BULWER-LYTTON, 1ST BARON (1803-1873)
The Last Days of Pompeii. London: Richard Bentley, 1834. First edition. 3 vols. 12mo. Half dark blue morocco, gilt, t.e.g., others
uncut. Half-titles in vols. 2 and 3 (none called for in vol. 1), with
12 pp. of ads. in vol. 3 and errata slip in each vol. Traylen 94-540
1983 £75

LYTTON, EDWARD GEORGE EARLE LYTTON BULWER-LYTTON, 1ST BARON (1803-1873)
The Last Days of Pompeii. New York, Harper, 1835. 2 vols. in 1,
8vo, orig. muslin, printed paper label on spine, now faded and lightly
worn, slight foxing throughout. Ravenstree 96-94 1983 $50

LYTTON, EDWARD GEORGE EARLE LYTTON BULWAR-LYTTON, 1ST BARON (1803-1873)
The Last Days of Pompeii. Verona: 1956. Octavo. Illus. with wood
engr. by Kurt Craemer. Limited to 1500 copies printed for the Limited
Editions Club, signed by the printer, Giovanni Marderstein, and the
illustrator. One corner lightly bumped, else extremely fine with
slightly rubbed plain dust wrapper and slip-case. Publisher's announcement and monthly newsletter laid-in. Bromer 25-269 1983 $85

LYTTON, EDWARD GEORGE EARLE LYTTON BULWER-LYTTON, 1st BARON (1803-1873)
The Last of the Barons. London: Saunders & Otley, 1843. First
edition. 3 vols. Boards backed with cont. cloth. Paper spine labels.
Front cover of Vol. 1 soiled. Head of one spine nicked. One paper
label slightly chipped. Near-fine. MacManus 277-775 1983 $250

LYTTON, EDWARD GEORGE EARLE LYTTON BULWER-LYTTON, 1ST BARON (1803-1873)
The Last of the Barons. London, Saunders & Otley, 1843. 3 vols.
8vo, bound without half titles in cont. quarter red roan gilt, bit
worn, and with the rare errata slip. First edition. Ravenstree 96-95
1983 $95

LYTTON, EDWARD GEORGE EARLE LYTTON BULWER-LYTTON, 1ST BARON (1803-1873)
The Lost Tales of Miletus. London, John Murray, 1866. 8vo, orig.
cloth gilt, little soiled and worn, bookplate, hinges weak. First
edition. Ravenstree 96-96 1983 $35

LYTTON, EDWARD GEORGE EARLE LYTTON BULWER-LYTTON, 1ST BARON (1803-1873).
The New Timon. A romance of London. London: Colburn, 1846. First
book edition. 8vo. Cont. half calf, gilt, spine gilt. Some rubbing.
Scarce. Ximenes 63-440 1983 $60

LYTTON, EDWARD GEORGE EARLE LYTTON BULWER-LYTTON, 1ST BARON (1803-1873)
Pelham; or, The Adventures of a Gentleman. London, Henry Colburn,
1828. 3 vols., 8vo, orig. boards, worn, spines quite chipped, covers
detached, minor age and dust soiling, with all proper cancels as in
Sadleir except Q in vol. I uncanceled and in orig. state, name on
end-papers, uncut and with all half titles and ads. First edition.
Ravenstree 96-98 1983 $295

LYTTON, EDWARD GEORGE EARLE LYTTON BULWER-LYTTON, 1ST BARON (1803-1873)
Pelham; or, the Adventures of a Gentleman. London: Henry Colburn,
1828. First edition. 3 vols. 8vo. Orig. blue-grey boards, paper
spines (neatly repaired), printed paper labels, uncut. Half-titles and
2 pp. ads. at end of vol. 3. Traylen 94-541 1983 £95

LYTTON, EDWARD GEORGE EARLE LYTTON BULWER-LYTTON, 1ST BARON (1803-1873)
Pelham; or, The Adventures of a Gentleman. New York, printed by J. &
J. Harper, 1829. 2 vols., 8vo, orig. quarter muslin, boards, worn,
somewhat soiled, faded, orig. printed paper spine labels bit age-
darkened and chipped, some foxing. Ravenstree 96-99 1983 $35

LYTTON, EDWARD GEORGE EARLE LYTTON BULWER-LYTTON, 1ST BARON (1803-1873)
The Pilgrims of the Rhine. New York, Harper & Brothers, 1834. 8vo,
orig. muslin, somewhat faded, soiled name on end-paper, orig. printed
paper spine label chipped, untrimmed copy, with slight foxing. The
first American edition. Ravenstree 96-100 1983 $37.50

LYTTON, EDWARD GEORGE EARLE LYTTON BULWER-LYTTON, 1ST BARON (1803-1873)
Rienzi, the Last of the Tribunes. London, Saunders & Otley, 1835.
3 vols., 8vo, orig. boards, uncut, much soiled and worn, covers detached
spines defective, bookplate, few spots of foxing; with half titles
and ads. First edition. Ravenstree 96-101 1983 $120

LYTTON, EDWARD GEORGE EARLE LYTTON BULWER-LYTTON, 1ST BARON (1803-1873)
A Strange Story. London: Sampson Low, 1863. New edition, 8vo, orig.
cloth gilt, spine ends worn, bit shaken, inner hinges cracking, bookplate, good copy. This edition carries the revisions as well as a
sepia photographic frontis. of author. Scarce. Ravenstree 96-103
1983 $65

LYTTON, EDWARD GEORGE EARLE LYTTON BULWER-LYTTON, 1ST BARON (1803-1873)
Tannhauser; or, the Battle of the Bards. Mobile (Alabama), S.H.
Goetzel, 1863. 8vo, orig. printed stiff paper covers, little worn,
paper age-browned, paper spine perished, but a respectable copy.
First and only Confederate edition. Ravenstree 97-67 1983 $125

LYTTON, EDWARD GEORGE EARLE LYTTON BULWER-LYTTON, 1ST BARON
1803-1873 What will he do with it? Edinburgh and London: by
Pisistratus Caxton. Blackwood & Sons, 1859. First edition, 8vo,
4 vols., original scarlet decorated cloth, spines gilt, half-titles,
advertisements, bookplate. Trebizond 18-12 1983 $210

LYTTON, ROBERT BULWER LYTTON, 1ST EARL OF (1831-1891) Fables in
Song. Edinburgh: Blackwood, 1874. First edition, 2 vols., full dec.
morocco. Gilt, a.e.g. Special presentation binding inscribed to C.
B. Saunders from author. MacManus 279-3395 1983 $125

M

M'ADAM, JOHN L.   Remarks on the Present System of Road-making... Bristol: by J.M. Gutch..., 1819. Second edition, carefully revised. 8vo. Wrappers. Heath 48-515 1983 £65

MC AFEE, ROBERT B.   History of the Late War in the Western Country. Lexington, 1816. Cont. calf, slight cracking and rubbing, overall very good. Reese 18-499 1983 $850

MAC ALISTER, ROBERT A. S.   Ancient Ireland. Methuen, 1935. First edition, folding map, plates, illus., 8vo, orig. cloth, gilt, a very good copy in the dust wrapper. Fenning 61-265 £10.50

MC ALLISTER, GILBERT   Town and Country Planning. Faber & Faber, 1941. First edition, with 11 plates, 8vo, orig. cloth. Fenning 60-262 1983 £18.50

MC ALMON, ROBERT   Post-Adolescence. (Paris): Contact, (1923). Printed wraps. First edition. Reese 20-635 1983 $350

MC ALMON, ROBERT   Post-Adolescence. n.d. (Dijon). Contact Press. 8vo. Wrappers. Little rubbing to spine, mainly a fine copy. In Our Time 156-552 1983 $300

MC ALPINE'S Wayne County Farm Atlas. Birmingham, 1925. 17 folding color maps, in leather binder. Some maps broken at folders. Former owner's rubber stamps. Covers detached and well frayed. King 46-167 1983 $45

MC ARTHUR, ALDERMAN   A British Protectorate in Fiji. 1873. First edition. Disbound. Jarndyce 31-111 1983 £24

MAC BRIDE, E. W.   Text Book of Embryology. 1914-19. 722 text-figures, 2 vols., 8vo, cloth. Binding of vol. 1 worn. Wheldon 160-504 1983 £32

MAC BETH, R. G.   Sir Augustus Nanton. Toronto: Mac-Millan, 1931. 22cm. Frontis. portrait and 14 illus. Blue cloth. Very good. McGahern 54-118 1983 $25

MAC BRIDE, DAVID   A Methodical Introduction to the Theory and Practice of Physic. Printed for W. Straham; T. Cadell; A. Kincaid and W. Creech; and J. Balfour, 1772. 4to, orig. calf, rebacked, preserving the orig. label. Old labels of the North Staffordshire Infirmary Library inside the front cover, and pale library stamp on title. First edition. Bickersteth 75-251 1983 £75

MC CABE, JAMES DABNEY   Life and Campaigns of General Robert E. Lee. Philadelphia, (1870). Portrait and maps. 8vo. Morrill 286-630 1983 $25

MC CABE, JAMES DABNEY   Pathways of the Holy Land. Phil., (1875). 1st ed. Illus. Thick 8vo. Morrill 286-261 1983 $25

M'CALL, HUGH   The History of Georgia. Savannah: Seymour & Williams, 1811. 8vo, full levant, raised bands, gilt dentelles, a.e.g., (lib. stamp on titles). Argosy 716-203 1983 $500

MAC CALLAN, A. F.   Trachoma & Its Complications in Egypt. Cambridge, 1913. First edition. 1/2 st. grain mor.; ex-lib. Argosy 713-349 1983 $40

MC CALLEN, ROBERT SETH   "Palaces of Sin" or "The Devil in Society." St. Louis: National Book Concern, (c. 1902). 21 cm. 16 illus. Orig. green decorated cloth, rubbed. The wood pulp paper darkened but good. Grunder 6-47 1983 $30

MAC CALLUM, WILLIAM G.   William Stewart Halsted, Surgeon. Baltimore, 1930. First edition. 8vo. Orig. binding. Scarce. Fye H-3-765 1983 $60

MAC CALLUM, WILLIAM G.   William Stewart Halsted, Surgeon. Baltimore, 1931. Second printing. 8vo. Orig. binding. Fye H-3-766 1983 $60

MC CANN, IRVING GOFF   With the National Guard on the Border. St. Louis, 1917. Illus. Orig. cloth. First edition. Ginsberg 47-488 1983 $75

MC CARTHY, DON   Language of the Mosshorn. Billings: The Gazette Printing Co., 1936. Orig. pictorial stiff wrappers. Illus. by Will James and Dale Petit. 1st ed. Scarce. Fine copy. Jenkins 153-350 1983 $50

MAC CARTHY, JOHN H.   Leading Cases in Land Purchase Law. Dublin: John Falconer, 1892. First edition, roy. 8vo, orig. cloth, gilt. Fenning 62-217 1983 £18.50

MC CARTHY, JUSTIN HUNTLY   If I Were King. N.Y.: B.H. Russell, 1901. First edition. Illus. Orig. pictorial cloth. Former owner's signature on flyleaf. Fine. MacManus 279-3398 1983 $25

MC CARTHY, JUSTIN HUNTLY   The Lady of Loyalty House. N.Y.: Harper & Brothers, 1904. First American edition. Orig. decorated cloth. Fine. MacManus 279-3399 1983 $20

MC CARTHY, JUSTIN HUNTLY   Miss Misanthrope. N.Y.: Sheldon & Co., 1877. First edition. Orig. cloth. Covers a bit rubbed. Very good. MacManus 279-3400 1983 $25

MC CARTHY, JUSTIN MCCARTHY   Songs for Cecilia. New York: Lotus Press, 1895. First edition. 12mo. Orig. grey printed wrappers. One of 100 copies, numbered and initialled by the author. Presentation copy, inscribed by McCarthy to Clement Shorter. Ximenes 53-451 1983 $40

MAC CARTHY, MARY   Fighting Fitzgerald, and Other Papers. 1930. First edition, with 6 plates, 8vo, orig. cloth, small library label on upper cover. Fenning 61-267 1983 £12.50

MC CARTHY, MARY   The Oasis. London: February, 1949. Wrappers. Lightly soiled covers. Bradley 66-241 1983 $37.50

MC CARTY, JOHN L.   Maverick Town: the story of Old Tascosa. Norman, 1946. 1st ed. Illus. Argosy 710-528 1983 $25

MC CLELLAN, GEORGE B.   Report on the Organization and Campaigns of the Army of the Potomac. New York, 1864. Folding map and several smaller maps. Cloth (slightly chipped at extremities). First edition. Felcone 22-129 1983 $20

M'CLINTOCK, FRANCIS LEOPOLD   The Voyage of the 'Fox' in the Arctic Seas. John Murray, 1859. First edition, with 14 plates, 3 folding maps (1 in pocket, neatly repaired without loss), and a folding facs. 8vo, orig. cloth, gilt. Inside joints neatly repaired. A very good copy. Fenning 61-268 1983 £65

M'CLINTOCK, FRANCIS LEOPOLD   The Voyage of the "Fox" in the Arctic Seas. Boston, 1860. First American edition. Maps and illus. 8vo. Slightly rubbed; few signatures slightly pulled. Morrill 290-244 1983 $30

MC CLINTOCK, JOHN N.   History of New Hampshire. Colony, Province, State, 1623-1888. Boston: B.B. Russell, 1889. Large 8vo, profusely illus., including 33 steel engravings. Brown dec. cloth. Karmiole 72-66 1983 $45

MC CLINTOCK, WALTER   The Old North Trail. London, 1910. First edition. Color frontis., many photo. plates, folding map. Gilt vignette stamped on front, g.t. Argosy 716-219 1983 $45

MC CLUNG, C. E.   Handbook of Microscopical Technique. 1937. 2nd ed. Wheldon 160-179 1983 £20

M'CLUNG, JOHN A.   Sketches of Western Adventure. Dayton, 1852. Ads. 2 plates. Cloth. Foxing. Very good. Felcone 20-93 1983 $25

MC CLUNG, NELLIE L.   The Next of Kin. Toronto: Thomas Allen & Boston & New York: Houghton Mifflin, 1917. 18 1/2cm. First edition. Red cloth. Fine. McGahern 53-104 1983 $20

MC CLUNG, NELLIE L.   Three Times and Out. Toronto: Allen; Boston & New York: Houghton Mifflin, 1918. 18 1/2cm. First edition. 14 illus. Blue cloth. Very good. McGahern 53-105 1983 $20

MC CONVILLE, BERNARD   The Gentleman on Horseback. New York, 1935. Clark 741-132 1983 $22

MC CORD, DAVID   Floodgate. Cambridge, Washburn & Thomas, 1927. First edition. 12mo. With a fine 10-line inscrip. by McCord dated 1931. Morrill 290-245 1983 $35

MC CORKLE, SAMUEL   Incident on the Bark Columbia. Cummington, Mass., (1941). Small 8vo, edition ltd. to 300 numbered copies, printed by hand by Harry Duncan, et al. Linen, soiled along bottom edge. Karmiole 73-35 1983 $150

MC CORMICK, CYRUS HALL   The Century of the Reaper. Boston, 1931. First edition. Illustrated. 8vo. Morrill 290-249 1983 $20

MC CORMICK, JAY   Nightshade. New York, 1948. First edition. Presentation copy from the author, inscribed to Theodore Roethke. Corners bumped. Torn and creased, internally repaired dustwrapper. Very good. Jolliffe 26-447 1983 £16

MC CORMICK, RICHARD C.   Arizona: Its Resources and Prospects. New York: 1865. First edition. Large folding map. Printed wrappers. Fine. Bradley 66-459 1983 $150

MC CORMICK, RICHARD C.   Arizona: Its Resources and Prospects. N.Y., 1865. Folded map inside front wrapper. Orig. wraps. First edition. Ginsberg 46-29 1983 $75

MC CORMICK, RICHARD C.   A Visit to the Camp before Sevastopol. New York, 1855. First edition. 8vo, orig. cloth. Folding sepia lithograph frontis. 8 sepia lithograph plates (2 double-page), 4 pages ads. Spine slightly worn at head and tail. Gilt lettering and design (of a cannon) faded. Ink inscriptions on endpapers. Good Edwards 1042-404 1983 £50

MC COY, EDWARD   Miscellanous Poems. Dublin: J.F. Fowler, 1869. First edition of these translations, in Irish and English. Errata leaf, small 8vo, orig. stiff printed paper wrappers, wraps. a little dusty, otherwise a very good copy. Fenning 61-269 1983 £35

MC COY, ISAAC   History of the Baptist Indian Missions. Wash., 1840. Cloth backed boards with leather label. First edition. Ginsberg 46-426 1983 $175

MC COY, JAMES C.   Jesuit Relations of Canada 1632-1673. Paris: Arthur Rau, 1937. Frontispiece. Cloth, frontispiece off-setting faintly on title. 1 of 350 numbered copies. Dawson 470-204 1983 $40

MC COY, JOSEPH G.   Historic Sketches of the Cattle Trade of the West and Southwest. Kansas City: Ramsey, Millett & Hudson, 1874. Ads, frontispiece portrait, numerous illus., many full-page. Orig. brown cloth, spine gilt (expertly rebacked). Few minor stains on upper cover. 1st ed. Very fine. Jenkins 153-351 1983 $1000

MC CRACKEN, HAROLD   The Charles M. Russell Book The Life and Work of the Cowboy Artist. New York, 1957. Illustrated. Special edition in genuine leather binding. Boxed. Mint copy. Jenkins 151-300 1983 $200

MC CRACKEN, HAROLD   The Frank Tenney Johnson Book. A Master Painter of the Old West. New York, 1974. Full morocco. A.e.g. Boxed. Limited to 350 copies signed by the author. Many illus. Jenkins 151-199 1983 $350

MC CRACKEN, HAROLD   Frederic Remington. Philadelphia, 1947. 43 plates. Cloth, very good in dust jacket. Presentation from the author on the front flyleaf. Reese 19-339 1983 $100

MC CRACKEN, HAROLD   George Catlin and the Old Frontier. N.Y., 1959. Ltd. to 250 numbered, autographed, morocco-bound copies. Ginsberg 47-214 1983 $285

MC CRACKEN, HAROLD   Portrait of the Old West. New York, 1952. Cloth, very good in dust jacket. A signed presentation copy from the author. Reese 19-340 1983 $75

MC CRACKIN, JOSEPHIN CLIFFORD The Woman Who Lost Him and Tales of the Army Frontier. Pasadena, Cal.: James, 1913. Photo illus. 1st ed. Orig. mottled lavender boards, lettered in black. Bierce wrote the intro. Fine fresh copy but for light aging of spine. Jenkins 155-88 1983 $50

MC CRAE, JOHN   In Flanders Fields. N.Y., 1921. Thin 8vo, gilt boards, ltd. edition. One of 265 copies printed by Wm. Edwin Rudge. Argosy 714-488 1983 $30

MC CREADY, T. L.   Mr. Stubbs. NY: Ariel Books, (1956). Octavo. First edition. Generously illus. by Tasha Tudor. Very fine copy signed by both McCready and Tudor. Pictorial dust wrapper very slightly chipped. Bromer 25-401 1983 $110

MC CREERY, JOHN   The press, a poem, in two parts. London: Pickering, 1828. Second edition. 8vo. Orig. brown boards, black cloth spine, printed paper label. A bit worn. Ximenes 63-417 1983 $75

M'CRIE, THOMAS   Life of John Knox. Edinburgh, T. Cadell, London, 1831. 2 vols., 8vo, 2 portraits, cont. half calf, rubbed, chip at top of spine of vol. 1. Bickersteth 77-145 1983 £22

MC CULLERS, CARSON   Reflections in a Golden Eye. Cambridge, MA: 1941. Covers slightly soiled, else fine copy. Dust wrapper with acetate window creased in few places. First edition. Bromer 25-68 1983 $135

MC CULLEY, JOHNSTON   The Black Star. NY, (1921). Top page edge soiled, edges slightly rubbed, else very good in wearing and torn, frayed and chipped dustwrapper. Quill & Brush 54-880 1983 $50

MC CULLOCH, JOHN RAMSEY (1789-1864)   The Literature of Political Economy. Longman, Brown, 1845. First ed., half title, 32 pp. ads. Largely unopened. Orig. dark green cloth, hinges rubbed, repaired. Jarndyce 31-312 1983 £160

MC CULLOCH, JOHN RAMSEY (1789-1864)   A Statistical Account of the British Empre. London: Charles Knight, 1837. Two vols., 3/4 leather, edges worn, hinges starting, else good or better. Quill & Brush 54-1675 1983 $200

MC CULLOCH, JOHN RAMSEY (1789-1864)   A Treatise on the Succession to Property Vacant by Death. Longman, Brown, 1848. First edition, 8vo., orig. cloth, very good. Fenning 60-263 1983 £55

MC CULLOUGH, TOM L.   Memories of the Hills of Home and County Side... Dallas, 1939. Orig. printed blue wrappers. 1st ed. Fine copy. Jenkins 153-602 1983 $25

MC CURDY, E. A. M.   Views of the Neilgherries. London, (1830). Title vignette and 4 finely handcoloured plates, 1 leaf of text, waterstain in upper margin. Oblong 4to. Cloth portfolio, leather title label. Good. Edwards 1044-457 1983 £350

MAC CURDY, JOHN T.   Problems in Dynamic Psychology. Cambridge: 1923. First edition. Library gift bookplate and stamp on titlepage, else very good. Gach 94-172 1983 $25

MAC CURDY, JOHN T.   The Psychology of Emotion. New York,
Harcourt, 1925. First American ed., cloth scratched. Gach 95-332
1983 $25

MC CURDY, MICHAEL   Genesis. (Boston: Hillside Press,
1965-66). Folio. Frenchfold. Illus. with wood engravings throughout.
Limited to 20 copies. Near mint in quarter-leather and boards signed
by McCurdy in 1981. Slightly chipped glassine. Bromer 25-252 1983
$200

MC CURDY, MICHAEL   Noah. (Boston, 1963). Oblong small
quarto. Wood engravings by McCurdy throughout. Of an edition of
6 copies, 1/2 copies bound by McCurdy and signed by him. Extremely
fine. Bromer 25-253 1983 $250

MC CUTCHEON, GEORGE BARR   Brewster's Millions. Chicago: Herbert
Stone, 1903. 1st., 2nd issue, 2nd binding. Orig. red cloth, gilt,
t.e.g., uncut. Very fine copy. Jenkins 155-867 1983 $25

MC DANIEL, RUEL   Vinegarroon. (Kingsport), (1936).
Pictorial cloth. Very fine copy, in very slightly chipped pictorial
dust jacket. Reese 19-341 1983 $75

MAC DERMOT, H. E.   History of the Montreal General Hospital.
Montreal: Montreal General Hospital, 1950. 23cm. Frontis and 14
illus. Fine in dust jacket. McGahern 54-119 1983 $45

MAC DERMOT, H. E.   A History of the Montreal General
Hospital. Montreal, 1950. 8vo. Orig. binding. First edition.
Fye H-3-350 1983 $30

MC DERMOT, MARTIN   A philosophical inquiry into the source
of the pleasures derived from tragic representations. London: printed
for Sherwood, Jones, and Co., 1824. 8vo, original quarter cloth and
boards, printed paper label (quite worn, front cover detached).
1st edition. A very good copy internally. Ximenes 64-360 1983 $40

MAC DIARMID, HUGH, PSEUD.
Please turn to
GRIEVE, CHRISTOPHER MURRAY

MAC DONAGH, THOMAS   The Poetical Works of Thomas MacDonagh.
Dublin: Talbot Press, 1916. First edition. Head of spine rubbed.
Nice. Rota 231-400 1983 £18

MAC DONALD, AENEAS   Whisky. Garden City: Henry & Longwell,
1930. First edition. Thin 8vo, half calf. One of 307 copies
signed by author, publishers and Christopher Morley. Argosy 714-535
1983 $30

MAC DONALD, ARTHUR   Education and Psycho-Analysis.
Inscribed to Adolf Meyer. Gach 95-333 1983 $20

MAC DONALD, D.   Illustrated Atlas of the Dominion of
Canada... Toronto: Belden & Co., 1881. Folio. 114p. of maps and
views. Crudely rebacked and hinged. Internally a very good copy.
McGahern 53-114 1983 $200

MC DONALD, EDWARD D.   A Bibliography of the Writings of D. H.
Lawrence. Philadelphia: The Centaur Bookshop, 1925. 8vo, cloth,
decorated boards. Total edition was 500 copies, of which this is 1 of
100 copies on large-paper signed by Lawrence and McDonald. Some light
bumping at the corners, mainly fine. In Our Time 156-493 1983 $600

MC DONALD, EDWARD D.   A Bibliography of the Writings of
D.H. Lawrence. Philadelphia: The Centaur Book Shop, 1925. First
edition. 4to. Frontis. Orig. cloth-backed boards with paper
label. One of 100 copies on large-paper signed by Lawrence and
McDonald. Fine copy. Jaffe 1-225 1983 $285

MC DONALD, EDWARD D.   A Bibliography of the Writings of D.H.
Lawrence. Phila.: The Centaur Book Shop, 1925. First edition.
Frontis. port. Orig. holland-backed boards with paper label on spine.
One of 100 large-paper copies signed by both Lawrence and McDonald.
Bookplate removed from front endsheet. Spine label a bit dusty. Edges
of boards slightly rubbed. Very good. MacManus 279-3169 1983 $275

MC DONALD, EDWARD D.   The Writings of D.H. Lawrence, 1925-
1930. Philadelphia: The Centaur Book Shop, 1931. First edition.
4to. Frontis. Orig. cloth-backed boards with paper label. Glassine
dust jacket. One of 60 large-paper copies signed by the author.
Very fine copy. Jaffe 1-227 1983 $75

MAC DONALD, FLORA   Mary Melville The Psychic. Toronto:
The Austin Publishing Co. Limited, 1900. First edition. Orig. wraps.
Wrapper detached but whole. Fine. MacManus 279-3435 1983 $35

MAC DONALD, GEORGE   At the Back of the North Wind. Phila.:
MaKay, 1919. First edition. 4to. Tan cloth. Pictorial paste-on.
Gilt spine. T.e.g. Pictorial title page. Endpapers plus 8 color
plates. Fine. Aleph-bet 8-237 1983 $60

MAC DONALD, GEORGE   A Book of Strife in the form of The
Diary of an Old Soul. London, 1880. First edition. Thin 8vo. Orig.
cloth with paper label on spine. Presentation copy, inscribed on the
title-page to "Robert R. Glover with kindest regards from George Mac-
Donald." Covers worn & soiled, with new endpapers. MacManus 279-3436
1983 $125

MAC DONALD, GEORGE   A book of strife in the form of the
diary of an old soul. London: printed for the author..., 1880.
First edition. 8vo. Orig. red cloth. Printed paper label. Slightly
rubbed and soiled. Ximenes 63-452 1983 $50

MAC DONALD, GEORGE   David Elginbrod. Hurst and Blackett,
1863. 3 vols., 8vo, half titles in each volume, orig. reddish-brown
pebble cloth lettered in gilt on the spine. Spines a little soiled,
short slit in the cloth in the upper joint of final volume, and
paper peeling on the same inner joint, a little spotting on a few
pages, no ownership inscriptions. First edition. Generally a very
good copy. Bickersteth 75-158 1983 £110

MAC DONALD, GEORGE   David Elginbrod. Hurst & Blackett,
1863. First edition, 3 vols., half title, cont. green cloth, gilt
spine lettering, v.g. Jarndyce 30-459 1983 £85

MAC DONALD, GEORGE   Dealings with the Fairies. Alexander
Strahan, 1867. First edition, with 12 plates engraved on wood by the
Dalziel brothers after drawings by Arthur Hughes, ads. dated December
1866. Small square 8vo, orig. green cloth, gilt, edges gilt, the
binding a little rubbed but sound, the casing a little weak and with
a few light finger marks, but otherwise a very good copy. Fenning
62-219 1983 £165

MAC DONALD, GEORGE   The Marquis of Lossie. Philadelphia:
Lippincott, 1878. The "Author's Edition" and most likely the first
American edition. Orig. cloth. MacManus 279-3437 1983 $25

MAC DONALD, GEORGE   The Poetical Works. London: Chatto &
Windus, 1893. First edition. 2 vols. Orig. cloth. Covers partially
faded. Spines worn. MacManus 279-3438 1983 $85

MAC DONALD, GEORGE   Ranald Bannerman's Boyhood. Blackie,
1911. Sq. 8vo. Colour frontis. 11 colour plates by M. V. Wheelhouse.
36 text illus. by A. Hughes. Blue decorated cloth gilt. Onlaid colour
plates. Greer 39-135 1983 £22.50

MAC DONALD, GEORGE   St. George and St. Michael. Hurst &
Blackett, 1863. Half calf, spines a little rubbed, black labels.
First edition, 3 vols. Jarndyce 30-461 1983 £58

MAC DONALD, GEORGE   A Threefold Cord: Poems By Three Friends.
London: Mr. W. Hughes, (1883). First edition, privately printed.
Orig. red cloth with paper label on spine. With a tipped-in slip
announcing to obtain the volume from Chatto & Windus. Covers soiled
and rubbed at edges. Endpapers browned. Good. MacManus 279-3439
1983 $150

MAC DONALD, GEORGE   Within and Without. Longman, etc.
1857. 2nd edition, 24 pp ads. Orig. brown cloth, sl. rubbed.
Jarndyce 30-784 1983 £10.50

MAC DONALD, GEORGE   Works of Fancy & Imagination. London:
Strahan & Co., 1871. First edition. 10 vols. 12mo. Orig. green
cloth. Spines and & covers elaborately gilt-tooled, a.e.g., with
ribbon markers. The largest collected edition of MacDonald's works.
MacManus 279-3440 1983 $650

MAC DONALD, GOLDEN   The Littel Island. N.Y.: Doubleday,
1946. Oblong 8vo. Later dust wrapper. Color illus. Fine. Aleph-bet
8-261 1983 $25

MACDONALD, GREVILLE   George Macdonald and His Wife. George
Allen & Unwin, 1924. First edition, half title, 28 illus. Orig. blue
cloth, very good. Jarndyce 30-1059 1983 £36

MAC DONALD, GREVILLE   The Magic Crook or the Stolen Baby. Vineyard Press, 1911. Frontis. Title vignette. 1 full-page & 57 text
illus. Light green cloth, decorated. Greer 40-115 1983 £25

MAC DONALD, HUGH   John Dryden, a Bibliography... Oxford:
at the Clarendon Press, 1939. First edition. Roy. 8vo. Orig.
cloth, gilt. Portrait. Traylen 94-295 1983 £50

MAC DONALD, JAMES M.   A Sketch of the History of the Presbyterian Church in Jamaica, LI. NY, 1847. Thin 12mo, lightly foxed,
ex library, pres. copy, signed by the author. Argosy 710-359
1983 $35

MAC DONALD, JAMES RONALD LESLIE   Soldiering and surveying in
British East Africa. London: Edward Arnold, 1897. 8vo. 8 maps.
13 plates. Orig. red cloth. Rubbed. Adelson Africa-103 1983
$100

MAC DONALD, JOHN   Diary of the Parnell Commission.
T. Fisher Unwin, 1890. First edition, half title, 24 pp ads. Orig.
green cloth. Jarndyce 31-200 1983 £16.50

MAC DONALD, JOHN   The Moving Target. NY, 1949. Cover
slightly soiled, book slightly bowed, else very good. Quill & Brush
54-829 1983 $60

MAC DONALD, NORMAN   The Barton Lodge. Toronto: Ryerson
Press, 1945. 21 1/2cm. 12 illus. Blue cloth. Very good. Scarce.
McGahern 54-120 1983 $35

MAC DONALD, NORMAN   Canada, 1763-1841. Immigration and
Settlement. London/New York/Toronto: Longmans, Green & Co., 1939.
22cm. First edition. Folding map. Tired dust jacket. Fine.
Scarce. McGahern 53-106 1983 $85

MAC DONALD, ROSS   A Collection of Reviews. CA, 1979.
Limited to 50 numbered and signed, specially bound deluxe copies,
corners slightly rubbed, fine. Quill & Brush 54-830 1983 $100

MAC DONALD, ROSS   A Collection of Reviews. Northridge,
1979. Half blue cloth. One of 50 copies, signed by the author.
Houle 21-594 1983 $75

MAC DONALD, ROSS   The Galton Case. NY, 1959. Edges
slightly discolored, else very good or better in lightly frayed and
soiled dustwrapper. Quill & Brush 54-832 1983 $225

MAC DONALD, ROSS   The Instant Enemy. NY, 1968. Near
fine in slightly soiled, near fine dustwrapper. Quill & Brush 54-833
1983 $100

MC DONALD, ROSS   The Zebra-Striped Hearse. N.Y., Knopf,
1962. First edition. Dust jacket (a trifle soiled). Very good.
Houle 22-611 1983 $75

MAC DONELL, A. G.   England Their England. London, 1933.
First English edition. Covers patchily faded. Chipped, nicked and
slightly rubbed dustwrapper. Very good. Jolliffe 26-333 1983 £20

MAC DONNELL, ALEXANDER   Rum and British Spirit Duties.
Effingham Wilson, 1830. First edition, 8vo, wrapper. Fenning 61-
272 1983 £65

MC DONNELL, RANDAL WILLIAM   When Cromwell Came to Drogheda.
Dublin: Gill, 1906. First edition, with 2 folding maps, cr. 8vo,
orig. cloth, gilt, a very good copy. Fenning 61-274 1983 £14.50

MAC DONOGH, FELIX   The Hermit Abroad. For Henry Colburn
and Co, 1823. First edition, 4 vols. 12mo, advert. leaf in vol. II,
possibly lacking in vol. I. Cont. half calf (joints cracking).
Hannas 69-130 1983 £30

MAC DONOGH, FELIX   The Hermit in Edinburgh. London: Printed
for Sherwood, Jones & Co., 1824. First edition. 3 vols. Orig. cloth-
backed boards with paper spine labels. Spines and covers slightly
soiled and worn. Spine labels chipped. Endpapers slightly browned.
Very good to near-fine. MacManus 279-3403 1983 $225

MAC DONOGH, FELIX   The Highlanders. London: Henry
Colburn, 1834. First edition. 3 vols. 12mo. Orig. boards,
printed paper labels, uncut edges. Spines a little defective.
Traylen 94-544 1983 £60

MC DONOGH, JOHN   The Last Will and Testament of...
Late of MacDonoghville, State of Louisiana. New Orleans, 1851.
Dbd. First edition. Ginsberg 47-466 1983 $125

MC DONOUGH, MARY LOU   Poet Physicians. Springfield, 1945.
First edition, second printing. 8vo. Orig. binding. Fye H-3-351
1983 $40

M'DOUALL, CHARLES   A Discourse of the Study of Oriental
Languages and Literature. Edinburgh, 1849. Calf-backed marbled boards.
8vo. Good. Edwards 1044-459 1983 £30

MACDOUGALL, ALEXANDER WILLIAM   The Maybrick Case. London: 1891.
First edition. Frontis. portrait. Green cloth. Nice copy, name in
ink on title page. Bradley 66-412 1983 $30

MC DOUGALL, JOHN   Pathfinding on Plain and Prairie.
Toronto, Briggs, 1898. Illus. Orig. cloth. First edition. Ginsberg
46-147 1983 $65

MC DOUGALL, WILLIAM (1871-1938)   The Group Mind. Cambridge,
England: At the Univ. Press, 1920. First edition. Ad leaf. Orig.
beige cloth, library bookplate and stamp, else very good. Gach 95-
334 1983 $30

MC DOUGALL, WILLIAM (1871-1938)   Introduction to Social Psychology.
London: Methuen, (1912). Sixth edition. Ads. Orig. red cloth,
crown shelfworn. Adolf Meyer's copy, signed on titlepage and
flyleaf. Gach 95-335 1983 $25

MC DOUGALL, WILLIAM (1871-1938)   Janus: The Conquest of War. NY:
Dutton, (1927). 16mo. First edition. Fine in dusty dust jacket.
Gach 95-336 1983 $27.50

MC DOUGALL, WILLIAM (1871-1938)   Modern Materialism and Emergent
Evolution. NY: D. Van Nostrand Co., 1929. First edition. Spine
rubbed, else very good. Gach 95-337 1983 $27.50

MC DOUGALL, WILLIAM (1871-1938)   Psycho-Analysis and Social
Psychology. London, Methuen, (1936). First edition. Gach 95-341
1983 $27.50

MC DOUGALL, WILLIAM (1871-1938)   Religion and the Science of Life.
Durham, N. C.: Duke Univ. Press, n.d. First edition. Fine in
chipped dust jacket. Gach 95-339 1983 $25

MC DOUGALL, WILLIAM (1871-1938)   The Riddle of Life. London:
Methuen, (1938). First edition. Fine in dust jacket (chipped).
Gach 95-340 1983 $27.50

MAC DOWELL, MAEVE CAVANAGH   A Voice of Insurgency. (Dublin:)
Printed for the author, 1916. First edition, 8vo, orig. printed
paper wraps., v.g. Fenning 61-275 1983 £18.50

MC ELRATH, THOMSON P.   A Press Club Outing. New York: International League of Press Clubs, 1893. Frontis. portrait and plates.
Orig. cloth. Fine. Jenkins 152-219 1983 $200

MAC ENERY, J.   Cavern researches... London: Simpkin,
Marshall, and Co., 1859. First edition. 8vo. Orig. purple cloth,
rubbed and faded. Ximenes 63-6 1983 $95

MC EVOY, J. P.   The Bam Bam Clock. N.Y.: Algonquin;
London: John Lane, (1920,1936). Sq. 8vo. Pictorial boards. Light
fading. Color illus. throughout. Fine. Aleph-bet 8-126 1983 $20

MAC FALL, HALDANE   Aubrey Beardsley: The Clown, the
Harlequin, the Pierrot of His Age. New York: Simon and Schuster,
1927. 54 plates. 4to. Cloth. No. 151 of a edition limited to
300 copies, signed by the author. Ars Libri 32-24 1983 $85

MAC FALL, HALDANE   Aubrey Beardsley. New York, Simon &
Schuster, 1927. 1st edn., limited to 300 signed & numbered copies.
Mounted frontis. & 8 mounted plates & 45 other illus. Black cloth,
t.e.g. (bkstrip some rubbing), v.g. Hodgkins 27-571 1983 £35

MAC FALL, HALDANE   The Book of Lovat. London, J. M. Dent &
Sons, 1923. First edition, large paper. Illus. by C. L. Fraser. Orig.
cloth-backed decorated boards. Dust jacket (quite faded, worn and
soiled; spine ends chipped). One of 150 copies printed on hand-made
paper, signed by Haldane MacFall. Spine ends worn, paper spine label
slightly faded and chipped. Covers slightly faded and a trifle soiled.
Very good. MacManus 278-2994 1983 $350

MAC FALL, HALDANE   The Book of Lovat Claud Fraser. London:
J. M. Dent & Sons, 1923. First edition. Illus., orig. pictorial
cloth-backed boards. Spine label slightly chipped, covers slightly
foxed and soiled. Bookplate. Very good. MacManus 278-2005 1983
$125

MAC FALL, HALDANE   A History of Painting. 1911. 8 vols.,
4to, coloured plates, orig. cloth with coloured reproduction on upper
covers. A fine set. Bickersteth 77-225 1983 £56

MAC FALL, HALDANE   A History of Painting. Boston: D.D.
Nickerson & Co., n.d. Milan edition. 8 vols. Illus. with 200
plates in color. 4to. Full morocco with colored inlays, moire
free endpapers, t.e.g., by Harcourt Bindery. Limited to 100 numbered
sets. Very fine. MacManus 279-3442 1983 $750

MAC FALL, HALDANE   Ibsen. London: Richards, 1907. First
edition. Illus. by J. Simpson. 12mo. Orig. cloth-backed boards.
Presentation copy, inscribed, "To Frank Brangwyn from his friend
Haldane Macfall. Feb. 1907." Very good. MacManus 279-3443 1983
$55

MAC FALL, HALDANE   The Spendid Wayfaring. London, 1913.
First edition. 4to. Orig. decorated cloth. Frontis. by Gordon
Craig and illus. in the text by Lovat Fraser, etc. Traylen 94-545
1983 £25

MAC FALL, HALDANE   The Wooings of Jezebel Pettyfer. London:
Simpkin, Marshall, Hamilton, Kent & Co. Ltd., (1913). Second edition.
Tipped-in frontispiece by author. Orig. decorated cloth. With an ALS,
2 pages, 8vo, 1 Perham Crescent, West Kensington, London, 17 November
1923, from MacFall to Christopher Millard. Former owner's inscription
on half-title. Inner hinges weak. Good. MacManus 279-3444 1983
$150

MAC FALL, HALDANE   The Wooings of Jezebel Pettyfer. London:
Simpkin, Marshall, Hamilton, Kent & Co., (1913). A re-issue of the
1898 edition. Orig. decorated cloth. Spine slightly faded. Edges
slightly worn, little foxing. Good. MacManus 279-3445 1983 $20

MAC FARLAN, J. F.   Remarks on the Scotch Banking System.
Adam & Charles Black, 1845. First edition, disbound. Inscribed
presentation from the author to the Royal Medical Society, Edinburgh,
with its stamp on title. Jarndyce 31-311 1983 £25

MAC FARLANE, C.   Constantinople in 1828. London, 1829.
5 plates, including 3 coloured, one in sepia and a double paged view
of Constantinople. 4to. Cont. calf, rebacked with orig. label.
Leather library label on upper cover of Margaret Poulett wife of the
5th Earl. Good. Edwards 1044-450 1983 £250

MAC FARLANE, C.   A History of British India. London,
1852. Sm. thick 8vo. From the Elphinstone Carberry Tower Library.
Orig. cloth. Good. Edwards 1044-448 1983 £25

MAC FARLANE, C.   Kismet; or the Doom of Turkey. London,
1853. Sm.8vo. Orig. cloth. Inscribed on front endpaper with author's
best respects dedicated to Mountstuart Elphinstone with the Carberry
Tower Library bookplate. Good. Edwards 1044-449 1983 £35

MC FEE, WILLIAM   Born To Be Hanged. Gaylordsville:
The Slide Mountain Press, 1930. First edition. 8vo. Cloth-
backed boards, paper spine label. Limited to 91 numbered and
signed copies. Label chipped; edges of covers worn. Oak Knoll
49-274 1983 $45

MC FEE, WILLIAM   Casuals of the Sea. London, 1916. First
edition. Spine a little faded. Name on flyleaf. Very good. Rota
230-375 1983 £12.50

MC FEE, WILLIAM   The Harbour Master. NY, 1932. Fine in
like dustwrapper with special printed glassine wrapper indicating advance copy. Quill & Brush 54-884 1983 $35

MC FEE, WILLIAM   Letters from an Ocean Tramp. London:
Cassell & Co., Limited, 1908. First edition. Orig. cloth. Inscribed
on the half-title "To M.S. Slocum Esq. with the warm regards of the
author, William McFee." Spine faded. In a half-morocco slipcase.
Fine. MacManus 279-3408 1983 $250

MC FEE, WILLIAM   North of Suez. Garden City: Doubleday,
1930. First edition. Orig. cloth-backed boards. Publisher's box.
One of 350 signed copies. Fine. MacManus 279-3411 1983 $25

MC FEE, WILLIAM   Pilgrims of Adversity. N.Y., Doubleday,
1928. First edition. Dust jacket. Inscribed and signed by the
author in 1959 with a 1 1/2 page inscription. Fine copy. Houle
22-612 1983 $150

MC FEE, WILLIAM   Sailor's Wisdom. London: Jonathan
Cape, (1935). First edition. 8vo. Orig. cloth. Dust jacket.
Fine copy. Jaffe 1-232 1983 $45

MC FEE, WILLIAM   A Six-Hour Shift. GC, 1920. No. 299 of
375 numbered and signed copies, top edge of spine neatly worn and
spine slightly discolored, near fine. Quill & Brush 54-883 1983 $35

MC FEE, WILLIAM   Spenlove in Arcady. New York, (1941).
8vo. Cloth. A fine copy in dj. In Our Time 156-554 1983 $35

MAC GEORGE, G. W.   Ways and Works in India. London, 1894.
5 folding maps. Plates, some slight wear. 8vo. Orig. cloth. Good.
Edwards 1044-451 1983 £28

MAC GILL, PATRICK   The Brown Brethren. London: Herbert
Jenkins Limited, 1917. First edition. Orig. cloth. Former owner's
signature on free endpaper. Covers buckling. Very good. MacManus
279-3446 1983 $25

MAC GILLIVRAY, W.   Lives of Eminent Zoologists... Edinburgh: Oliver & Boyd, 1834. 12mo. Second edition. 12mo. Old
half-roan. Portrait. Ownership stamp on title. Binding slightly
worn. Gurney 90-75 1983 £25

MAC GILLIVRAY, W.   The Naturalist's Library. Mammalia.
British Quadruped. 1866. Portrait, vignette, and 34 coloured plates.
Sm. 8vo, original red cloth. Wheldon 160-580 1983 £25

MC GILLYCUDDY, JULIA B.   McGillycuddy: Agent. Stanford, (1941).
First edition. Portrait frontis., numerous other illus. Tan cloth.
Fine copy in chipped dust jacket. Bradley 66-583 1983 $60

MC GILLYCUDDY, JULIA B.   McGillycuddy Agent. Stanford Univ.,
1941. Frontis. and illus. 1st ed. Jenkins 153-353 1983 $55

MC GILLYCUDDY, JULIA B.   McGillycuddy, Agent. Stanford, Ca.,
(1941). 1st ed. Ports., plates. Clark 741-314 1983 $51.50

MC GIVERN, ED   Ed McGivern's Book on Fast and Fancy
Revolver Shooting and Police Training. Springfield, Mass., 1938.
1st ed. Illus. 8vo. Morrill 288-113 1983 $50

MC GLASHAN, CHARLES FAYETTE   History of the Donner Party. San Francisco: A. L. Bancroft, 1880. Second edition. Illus. Brown cloth,
covers worn, top and bottom edges reinforced with cloth. Penciled
name on end paper. Bradley 66-484 1983 $235

MC GLASHAN, CHARLES FAYETTE   History of the Donner Party, A Tragedy of the Sierra. Stanford, 1940. Dust jacket, fine copy. Jenkins 153-354 1983 $30

MC GOWAN, EDWARD   Narrative of Edward McGowan. Oakland: Gillick Press, 1946. Reissue of the 1857 original. Limited to 675 copies. Illus. Jenkins 153-99 1983 $30

MC GREEVY, THOMAS   T. S. Eliot. Lon., 1931. Cover slightly soiled, near very good in price clipped, slightly darkened dustwrapper. Quill & Brush 54-419 1983 $50

MC GREEVY, THOMAS   Thomas Stearns Eliot. London: Chatto & Windus, 1931. Pictorial boards. First edition. Fine in dust jacket. Reese 20-642 1983 $45

MC GREEVY, THOMAS   T. S. Eliot. Lon., 1931. Edges slightly worn, good in slightly frayed and age darkened dustwrapper. Quill & Brush 54-418 1983 $40

MAC GREGOR, BARRINGTON   King Longbeard. John Lane, 1898. Sq. 8vo. Pictorial half-title. Map-frontis. Pictorial title. 11 plates & 100 text illus. Blue decorated cloth gilt, worn. Presentation copy from author, dated Christmas, 1897. Greer 39-104 1983 £75

MAC GREGOR, DUNCAN   A Narrative of the Loss of the Kent East Indiaman, by Fire. Edinburgh: Waugh and Innes, 1825. First edition. Boards, paper label on spine, worn. 8vo. Good. Edwards 1044-452 1983 £80

MAC GREGOR, DUNCAN   A Narrative of the Loss of the Kent East Indiaman, by Fire, in the Bay of Biscay, on the 1st March, 1825. 12mo, uncut, orig. boards, spine defective. First edition. Bickersteth 77-226 1983 £18

MAC GREGOR, J.   Gardens of Celebrities. (1919). 20 coloured and 6 plain plates, 4to, cloth (trifle used). Wheldon 160-1981 1983 £15

MC GRIGOR, JAMES   The Autobiography of Sir James McGrigor Bart. London, 1861. 8vo. Old red-morocco, gilt. T.e.g. Upper cover rubbed. Gurney JJ-246 1983 £25

MC GUFFEY, WILLIAM H.   McGuffey's New Eclectic Readers. 1939 facs. reprints by Henry Ford. Cloth backed printed boards, top edges of first two vols. water stained, marbled edges, else O.K. 3 vols. King 46-453 1983 $20

MC GUFFEY, WILLIAM H.   McGuffey's Newly Revised Eclectic Fourth Reader. Cincinnati, (1853). 1/4 leather, stipple cloth. Argosy 716-497 1983 $30

MC HENRY, DEAN E.   The Third Force in Canada. Berkeley & Los Angeles: Un. California Press & Toronto: Oxford Un. Press, 1950. 21 1/2cm. Dust jacket. Very good. McGahern 54-121 1983 $25

M'HENRY, JAMES   Waltham: An American Revolutionary Tale. New York: E. Bliss & E. White..., 1823. Orig. printed wrappers (spine covering chipped). Very good. Felcone 20-94 1983 $35

MC HENRY, ROY C.   Smith & Wesson Hand Guns. Huntington, W. Va., 1945. 1st ed. Illus. 4to. Morrill 288-114 1983 $35

MC HENRY, ROY C.   Smith & Wesson Hand Guns. Huntington, W. Va., 1945. Illus, cloth, very good in chipped dw. King 46-613 1983 $35

MAC ILWAIN, GEORGE   Memoirs of John Abernethy, F.R.S. New York, 1853. 8vo. Orig. binding. First American edition. Hinges torn, binding worn, rear endpapers torn. Fye H-3-653 1983 $25

MC ILWRAITH, THOMAS   The Birds of Ontario. Toronto: William Briggs, 1894. 21 1/2cm. Second edition. Many line-drawn illus., gilt decorated blue cloth, fade spots on the bottom outer half of the binding, else very good. McGahern 53-109 1983 $45

MAC INNES, COLIN   To the Victors the Spoils. London, 1950. First edition. Slightly torn and chipped, internally repaired dustwrapper. Very good. Jolliffe 26-335 1983 £36

MAC INNES, TOM   Chinook Days. Vancouver: Sun Pub. Co., 1926. 15cm. Limited to 1000 signed copies, this being number 773. 9 drawings by Howard Smith and 2 by John Innes. Limp blue cloth. Very good. McGahern 53-110 1983 $20

MC INTOSH, C.   The Flower Garden. 1838. Coloured title vignette, 10 coloured and 8 plain plates and text-figures, post 8vo, half green morocco, gilt. Very scarce. A nice copy. Wheldon 160-1982 1983 £70

MC INTOSH, C.   The New and Improved Practical Gardener and Modern Horticulturist. 1859. Portrait, text-figures and 20 hand-coloured plates, 8vo, cloth. Portrait foxed. Wheldon 160-1983 1983 £40

MAC INTOSH, DONALD   A Collection of Gaelic Proverbs... Edinburgh: for the Author, 1785. First edition. 8vo. Uncut in orig. grey wrappers, one loose. Heath 48-352 1983 £55

MC INTOSH, WALTER H.   Allen and Rachel. Caldwell, Idaho: The Caxton Printers, 1938. With 8 plates. Gilt-stamped purple cloth, spine faded. Karmiole 72-4 1983 $40

M'INTYRE, ALEXANDER   A Letter to His Excellency Daniel D. Tompkins, Late Governor of the State of New-York. Albany: Jeremiah Tryon, 1819. Disbound. Old library stamp on title. Felcone 22-164 1983 $20

MAC INTYRE, CARLYLE   The Brimming Cup and Potsherds. Pasadena, Harry Ward Ritchie, 1930. Wrappers, a little chipped. Dawson 471-189 1983 $100

MC INTYRE, CHARLES   The Percentage of College-Bred Men in the Medical Profession. Philadelphia, 1883. 8vo. Wrappers. Fye H-3-353 1983 $25

MAC IVOR, RALPH W. EMERSON   The Chemistry of Agriculture... Melbourne: Stilwell, 1879. 8vo. Orig. cloth. Errata and ad. leaves. Zeitlin 264-276 1983 $50

MAC KALL, LAWTON   Poodle-Oodle of Doodle Farm. N.Y.: Stokes, 1929. First edition. Oblong 8vo. Cloth. Pictorial paste-on. Corners rubbed. Full-page color and black & whites. Very good. Aleph-bet 8-263 1983 $25

MACKANESS, GEORGE   The Life of Vice-Admiral William Bligh. New York, n.d. (ca. 1931). First American edition. Illustrated with contemporary charts and engravings. 2 vols. in 1, 8vo. Binding faded. Morrill 290-250 1983 $20

MAC KAY, ANDREW   The Complete Navigator. London, 1810. Plates. Half calf. Front cover detached, heavily worn and soiled. 2nd ed., improved. King 45-529 1983 $50

MAC KAY, CHARLES   History of the Mormons. Auburn, 1852. First American edition? Lightly dampstained. Illus. Orig. stamped cloth. Argosy 716-562 1983 $75

MAC KAY, CHARLES   The Lump of Gold. G. Routledge, 1856. First edition, orig. green cloth, recased. Jarndyce 31-864 1983 £15

MAC KAY, CHARLES   The Salamandrine. Ingram, Cooke, 1853. 46 illus. by J. Gilbert, engr'd by Bros. Dalziel. Pale green wavy grain cloth gilt, bevelled edges, a.e.g., cvrs. some soiling & fading, corners sl. worn & bruised, prelims. foxed. Signed presentation from John Gilbert dd. 1853. Very good. Hodgkins 27-308 1983 £35

MC KAY, CLAUDE   Spring in New Hampshire. L, 1920. Paper-wraps, cover label very slightly chipped, minor cover wear, interior lightly foxed, many pages unopened. Quill & Brush 54-886 1983 $400

MAC KAY, DOUGLAS   The Honourable Company: a History of the Hudson's Bay Company. Indianapolis, 1936. 1st ed. Many illus. & maps. Dw. Argosy 710-51 1983 $35

MC KAY, GEORGE L.   American Book Auction Catalogues
1713-1934. New York: The New York Public Library, 1937. First
edition. 8vo. Thick, paper wrappers. 8 page supplement loosely
inserted. Oak Knoll 49-463 1983 $85

MC KAY, GEORGE L.   A Bibliography of Robert Bridges.
New York: Columbia Univ. Press, 1933. 8vo. Three-quarter cloth
over marbled boards, t.e.g. Limited to 550 numbered copies, this
copy has "canceled" written in the blank left for the number.
Fine. Book label of George Sims. Oak Knoll 49-420 1983 $65

MAC KAY, JOHN   The Rape of Ireland. Dublin: Talbot,
1940. First edition, with 8 plates, 8vo, orig. cloth. In a
frayed dust wrapper. Fenning 61-276 1983 £24.50

MAC KAY, K.   Across Papua. London, 1909. Folding
map, plates, spine faded. 8vo. Orig. cloth. Good. Edwards 1044-
453 1983 £30

MC KAY, WILLIAM   John Hoppner, R. A. Colnaghi and G. Bell,
1909. First edition. 62 plates, inserted addendum slip, folio, orig.
cloth, gilt, t.e.g., very light stain on the extreme lower outer corners of the boards, but otherwise a nice copy. Fenning 61-209 1983
£65

MC KEAN, JOSEPH   Sermon. Boston, 1808. Dbd. Near fine.
Reese 18-312 1983 $30

MC KEEN, SILAS   Heroic Patriotism. Windsor, 1860.
Orig. printed wraps. First edition. Ginsberg 46-764 1983 $25

MAC KELLAR, THOMAS   The American Printer: A Manual of
Typography... Philadelphia: MacKellar, Smiths & Jordan, 1868.
Fourth edition. 8vo. Orig. cloth with spine laid down on new
cloth and tips repaired with new cloth. With a two page advertisement of the Johnson Type and Stereotype Foundry at end. Except
for the cover repair (professionally done), a fine copy. Oak
Knoll 49-275 1983 $100

MAC KELLAR, THOMAS   The American Printer: A Manual of
Typography... Philadelphia: MacKellar, Smiths & Jordan, 1876. Tenth
edition. 8vo. Orig. cloth. With one page of ads. for printers'
text books, two of type and one of printing ink. Small spot on
front cover and black ink spot on front upper hinge, else very good.
Oak Knoll 49-276 1983 $65

MAC KELLAR, THOMAS   The American Printer: A Manual of
Typography... Philadelphia: MacKellar, Smiths & Jordan, 1876.
Eighteenth edition, revised and enlarged. 8vo. Orig. cloth. Frontis.
The spine is labelled "Enlarged Edition." Covers faded, paper cracked
on inside hinge. Oak Knoll 49-277 1983 $60

MC KELVEY, SUSAN DELANO   Botanical Exploration of the Trans-
Mississippi West, 1790-1850. Jamaica Plain, Mass., 1955. Folded
maps in pocket. Orig. thick cloth. First edition. Ginsberg 47-
491 1983 $85

MC KENDRICK, JOHN   Hermann Ludwig Ferdinand von Helmholtz.
New York, 1899. First American edition. 8vo. Orig. binding. Fye
H-3-780 1983 $40

MC KENNA, JAMES A.   Black Range Tales. New York, 1936.
Cloth, fine in dust jacket. One of 500 signed copies. Reese 19-342
1983 $75

MC KENNA, JAMES A.   Black Range Tales. New York: Wilson-
Erickson, Inc., 1936. Frontis. and illus. First edition in dust
jacket. Fine copy. Jenkins 151-201 1983 $45

MC KENNA, STEPHEN   Beyond Hell. London: Chapman & Hall,
1931. First edition. Orig. cloth. Dust jacket. Very fine. Mac-
Manus 279-3415 1983 $25

MAC KENNA, STEPHEN   Off Parade. London: Hurst & Blackett,
1872. First edition. 3 vols. Orig. cloth. Covers soiled and worn.
MacManus 279-3459 1983 $125

MC KENNA, STEPHEN   The Oldest God. Boston: Little, Brown
and Co., 1926. First American edition. Orig. cloth. Presentation
copy inscribed: "For E.J. Dickie, with every good wish for Christmas
and the New Year. From Stephen McKenna. 23 December, 43." Edges
rather worn and faded. Spine faded and slightly stained. MacManus
279-3418 1983 $25

MC KENNA, STEPHEN   The Oldest God. London: Thornton
Butterworth Ltd., (1926). First edition. Orig. cloth. Very good.
MacManus 279-3417 1983 $20

MC KENNA, STEPHEN   Tales Of Intrigue And Revenge. Boston:
Little, Brown & Co., 1925. First American edition. Orig. cloth.
Presentation copy inscribed: "For E.J. Dickie...from Stephen McKenna."
Spine and cover ends and edges worn. Good. MacManus 279-3419 1983
$25

MC KENNA, THEOBALD   Political Essays. Printed for J.
Debrett, 1794. First collected edition, 8vo, calf-backed marbled
boards, some neat cont. marginal notes, but still a nice copy.
Fenning 61-277 1983 £75

M'KENNEY, THOMAS L.   Memoirs, Official and Personal.
New York, 1846. 2 vols. in one. Cloth, skillfully rebacked, very
good. Reese 19-383 1983 $375

M'KENNEY, THOMAS L.   Reply to Kosciusko Armstrong's
Assault upon Col. M'Kenney's Narrative on the Causes that Lead to
General Armstrong's Resignation of the Office of Secretary of War
in 1814. New York, 1847. Wraps., fine. Presentation copy from
the author. Reese 19-384 1983 $125

MC KENNY, MARGARET   Birds in the Garden, and How To
Attract Them. New York, (1939). 1st ed. 16 illus. in color, and 32
pages in halftone. Tall 8vo. Morrill 289-625 1983 $20

MAC KENZIE, ALEXANDER   History of the Frasers of Lovat. Inverness, 1896. Rebound cloth, index. Covers spotted and heavily rubbed,
few loose pp. King 45-59 1983 $35

MAC KENZIE, ALEXANDER   The Life and Speeches of Hon. George
Brown. Toronto: Globe Printing Co., 1882. 21 1/2cm. Frontis.
portrait. Orig. cloth. Very good. McGahern 54-124 1983 $25

MAC KENZIE, ALEXANDER   Voyages from Montreal on the River St.
Laurence... London: Printed for T. Cadell..., 1801. 4to. First
edition. Frontis. portrait and three folding maps. Full cont. tree
calf, rebacked with new red morocco label. Small repairs to a few
folds. Some offsetting and foxing, wanting the half title as usual,
small blank repair to the title page. A very good copy. McGahern
53-111 1983 $2,000

MAC KENZIE, ALEXANDER   Voyages from Montreal, on the River St.
Laurence through the Continent of North America, to the Frozen and
Pacific Ocean...1789-1793. London: Cadell, 1801. Fine engraved
portrait. 3 large maps with protective backing. Later half calf.
A fine copy. First edition. Jenkins 151-202 1983 $1,750

MAC KENZIE, ALEXANDER   Voyages from Montreal, on the River St.
Laurence...in the Years 1789 and 1793. New York: G.F. Hopkins, 1802.
Large folding map. Orig. mottled calf, expertly rebacked in
sprinkled calf, gilt morocco label. Early ownership signatures,
otherwise a fine, clean copy, without any of the staining or browning.
Reese 18-248 1983 $1,000

MAC KENZIE, ALEXANDER   Voyages from Montreal, on the St.
Laurence... New York: Evert Duyckinck, 1803. Folding map. Orig.
tree calf with red morocco label. Some browning to text. 3rd ed. is
quite scarce. Jenkins 153-355 1983 $450

MAC KENZIE, ALEXANDER   Voyages from Montreal through the
Continent of America to the Frozen and Pacific Oceans. N.Y., 1902.
2 maps, port. Thick 8vo, cloth-backed boards, spine labels faded,
one of 210 numbered copies of Howes M-133. Argosy 716-48 1983
$100

MC KENZIE, CHARLES H.   The Religious Sentiments of Charles
Dickens. 1884. First edition. Orig. maroon dec. cloth, v.g.
Jarndyce 30-212 1983 £20

MAC KENZIE, COLIN   One Thousand Experiments in Chemistry...
London: Phillips and Co., 1822. New edition. 8vo. Cont. half
calf. Folding color frontis., 20 plates. Hinges split. Very good.
Zeitlin 264-277 1983 $100

MAC KENZIE, COMPTON   First Athenian Memories. Lon., (1931).
Small tear to top edge of rear spine gutter, edges slightly worn, else
very good in slightly frayed and chipped, very good dustwrapper. Quill
& Brush 54-840 1983 $35

MAC KENZIE, COMPTON   Guy and Pauline. London, 1915. First
edition. Argosy 714-491 1983 $20

MAC KENZIE, COMPTON   Marathon and Salamis. Peter Davis,
1934. 3 plates, 8vo, orig. cloth in dustwrapper. Signed by the
author on the fly, with the date "May 25. 38". First edition.
Bickersteth 75-159 1983 £20

MAC KENZIE, COMPTON   Poems. Oxford: B.H. Blackwell, 1907.
First edition. Orig. wrappers (a little frayed). In a cloth folding
box. Very good. MacManus 279-3462 1983 $85

MC KENZIE, DAN   The Infancy of Medicine. London, 1927.
First edition. 8vo. Cloth. Gurney JJ-247 1983 £15

MAC KENZIE, DONALD   The Flooding of the Sahara. 1877.
Col'd folding map. K Books 301-119 1983 £54

MAC KENZIE, GEORGE   The Tryal and Process of High-Treason
and Doom of Forfaulture Against Mr. Robert Baillie of Jerviswood
Traitor. Edinburgh: Heir of Andrew Anderson and Reprinted at London
by Tho. Newcomb, 1685. Folio, 30 x 19 cm. Disbound with a few
leaves detached. Grunder 7-51 1983 $35

MAC KENZIE, HENRY   Julia de Roubigne. London, Strahan and
Cadell, 1787. 2 vols., 8vo, new tan half morocco gilt, t.e.g., name
on titles, faint watermarking. Ravenstree 96-107 1983 $95

MAC KENZIE, HENRY   Julia de Roubigne, a Tale. A. Strahan,
T. Cadell, 1787. Fourth edition, 2 vols. 12mo, half titles, 1 p
ads. vol. II. Tree calf labels. Jarndyce 31-49 1983 £42

MAC KENZIE, HENRY   The Man of Feeling. T. Cadell, 1771.
Calf, spine gilt, red label, hinges sl. weakening. 12mo. Jarndyce
31-48 1983 £85

MAC KENZIE, HENRY   The Man of the World. London, A.
Strahan and T. Cadell, 1787. 2 vols., 8vo, new tan half morocco gilt,
t.e.g., name on titles, faint watermarking. Ravenstree 96-108 1983
$95

MAC KENZIE, HENRY   A Man of the World. London, 1787.
Fourth edition. 2 vols. 12mo. Cont. tree calf, gilt panelled
spines with swan ornaments, morocco labels, gilt. Half-titles.
Traylen 94-547 1983 £24

MAC KENZIE, HENRY   The Man of the World. Dublin: Printed
for T. Heery, 1787. 2 vols. in one, 12mo, cont. tree calf; slight
wear to upper hinge. Hill 165-73 1983 £45

MAC KENZIE, HENRY   The Man of Feeling. London, 1794.
A New edition. 12mo. Cont. tree calf, gilt panelled spine with
swan decorations, morocco label, gilt. Engraved frontis. Traylen
94-546 1983 £15

MAC KENZIE, HENRY   The Mirror, a Periodical Paper. London:
Strahan & Cadell; Edinburgh: W. Creech, 1783. Fifth edition, corrected. 3 vols., 8vo, cont. calf, spines gilt, morocco labels.
Corner of one spine chipped, otherwise a fine copy. Trebizond 18-78
1983 $150

MAC KENZIE, JAMES   The Study of the Pulse, Arterial,
Venous, and Hepatic and of the Movements of the Heart. Edinburgh:
Y.J., Pentland, 1902. First edition, with 335 text illus., 8vo,
orig. cloth, t.e.g., a tiny nick in the headband. Inscribed by
the publisher. Fenning 62-221 1983 £95

MAC KENZIE, JAMES   The Study of the Pulse. Edinburgh:
Y. J. Pentland, 1902. First edition, with 335 text illus., 8vo,
orig. cloth, t.e.g., a tiny nick in the headband, but otherwise a
nice copy. Fenning 62-220 1983 £45

MAC KENZIE, JAMES   Symptoms and Their Interpretation.
8vo, cloth. First edition. Argosy 713-350 1983 $50

MAC KENZIE, JAMES D.   The Castles of England. London, 1897.
4to. Orig. cloth. Half titles, titles in red and black. 2 vols.
Frontis. 38 plates, 158 illus. and 70 plans. T.e.g. Slightly worn
and soiled. R.U.S.I. bookplates on front endpapers. Small library
stamps on endpapers and titles and library labels on spine. Good.
Edwards 1042-406 1983 £70

MAC KENZIE, JOHN   Ten years north of the Orange River.
Edinburgh: Edmonston and Douglas, 1871. 12mo. Folding map. 8
plates. Orig. green cloth, a.e.g. Lightly rubbed. Adelson Africa-
104 1983 $165

MAC KENZIE, JOHN   Ten Years of the Orange River. Edinburgh,
1871. Folding map (very slightly torn without loss), 8 lithograph
plates, 6 woodcuts, covers dull and very slightly stained. K Books
301-121 1983 £55

MAC KENZIE, MARY JANE   Geraldine. T. Cadell & W. Blackwood,
1821. In three vols. 2nd edition, half calf, a little rubbed.
Jarndyce 30-463 1983 £44

MAC KENZIE, MARY JANE   Private Life. T. Cadell, 1829.
First edition, 2 vols., half green calf, brown labels, v.g. Jarndyce
30-464 1983 £62

MAC KENZIE, MORELL   Essays. London, 1893. 8vo. Orig.
cloth. Gurney JJ-249 1983 £12

MAC KENZIE, MORELL   The Fatal Illness of Frederick the
Noble. Sampson Low, 1888. First edition, with 22 illus., 8vo,
orig. cloth. Fenning 61-278 1983 £18.50

MAC KENZIE, MORELL   A Manual of Diseases of the Throat
and Nose... London, 1880-84. First edition. 8vo. Orig. cloth,
stained, with library label on cover of vol. 2. Ex-library copy
with stamps here and there, and a few leaves loosening. Gurney
JJ-250 1983 £40

MAC KENZIE, RONALD   Musical Chairs. London: Victor Gollancz
Ltd., 1932. First edition. Orig. wrappers, with wrap-around band.
Very good. MacManus 279-3464 1983 $20

MC KERRELL, JOHN   A grammar of the Carnataca language.
Madras: printed at the College Press, 1820. First edition. 4to.
Half morocco. Very small hole in title, affecting one letter,
otherwise a very good copy. Rare. Ximenes 63-212 1983 $425

MC KINLEY, WILLIAM   Opening of Kiowa, Comanche, Apache and,
Wichita Indian Lands in the Territory of Oklahoma. (Washington, D.C.),
1901. Caption title. Later cloth with morocco label. Jenkins 152-
729 1983 $150

MC KINNEY, ROLAND   Thomas Eakins. New York: Crown, 1942.
83 plates (8 color). 4to. Cloth. Dust jacket. Ars Libri 32-200
1983 $50

MACKINTOSH, JAMES   Memoirs of the Life of... Moxon, 1836.
Second ed., 2 vols. Straight-grained morocco, hinges weak, spines a
little chipped, black labels. Jarmdyce 30-1060 1983 £12.50

M'KNIGHT, JOHN   The Divine Goodness to the United States
of America... New York, 1795. 2 leaves of subscribers names.
Later wraps., very good. Reese 18-203 1983 $35

MC LAIN, J. S.   Alaska and the Klondike. New York, 1905.
Illus. Orig. cloth. Fine copy of the first edition. Folding map.
Jenkins 151-2 1983 $45

MC LANE, DAVID   The Trial of David McLane for High
Treason, at the City of Quebec. Quebec, 1797. Plain wraps., frayed
on backstrip, very good. Reese 18-224 1983 $850

MC LAREN, MORAY   The Capital of Scotland. Edinburgh: Douglas & Foulis, 1950. Illus. in color. Orig. decorated cloth. First edition. Max Beerbohm's copy, inscribed in pencil by him: "Max Beerbohm, Rapallo, ex dono auctoris." Very good. MacManus 277-280 1983 $75

MC LAREN, WALTER S. B.   Report to the Worshipful Cloth-Workers' Company of London on the Weaving and Other Technical Schools of the Continent. 1877. First edition, 8vo, orig. cloth, gilt. Fenning 60-264 1983 £14.50

MAC LAREN-ROSS, JULIAN   Bitten By The Tarantula. London: Allan Wingate, (1945). First edition. 8vo. Orig. cloth. Dust jacket. Fine copy. Jaffe 1-233 1983 $75

MAC LAREN-ROSS, JULIAN   The Nine Men of Soho. London: Allan Wingate, (1946). First edition. 8vo. Orig. cloth. Dust jacket. Fine copy. Jaffe 1-234 1983 $75

MC LAURIN, C. C.   Pioneering in Western Canada. Calgary: Published by the Author. London, 1939. 22cm. Frontis. and 112 illus. Red cloth. Very good to fine. McGahern 54-125 1983 $45

MAC LAURIN, COLIN   An Account of Sir Isaac Newton's Philosophical Discoveries, in Four Books. Printed for the author's children, 1748. 4to, 6 folding plates, orig. calf rebacked and repaired, rubbed and a little scratched, new end papers. Stamp of the Medical Chirurgical Society of Aberdeen at the beginning and end of the main text, and hand-written inscription at top of the title. First edition, with 19 page list of subscribers. Bickersteth 77-292 1983 £90

MC LEAN, JOHN   John McLean's Notes of a Twenty-Five Years Service in the Hudson's Bay Territory. Toronto: Champlain Society, 1932. Tall 8vo, with a large folding map. Index. Edition ltd. to 550 copies (this copy not numbered). Red gilt-stamped cloth. Karmiole 75-33 1983 $85

MAC LEAN, JOHN PATTERSON   The Mound Builders. Cincinnati, 1879. First edition. Map and illustrations. Small 8vo. Slightly rubbed. Morrill 290-387 1983 $25

MAC LEISH, ARCHIBALD   The Fall of the City. New York & Toronto: Farrar & Rinehart, (1937). Printed boards. First edition. Light offset on endsheets from glassine wrapper, in slightly chipped orig. glassine. Reese 20-653 1983 $25

MAC LEISH, ARCHIBALD   The Happy Marriage and Other Poems. Boston: Riverside Press, 1924. First edition. Sq. 16mo, boards. Argosy 714-492 1983 $45

MAC LEISH, ARCHIBALD   The Happy Marriage and Other Poems. B, 1924. Spine faded, cover lightly worn, else good or better. Quill & Brush 54-835 1983 $30

MAC LEISH, ARCHIBALD   The Human Season: Selected Poems, 1926-1972. Boston: Houghton, Mifflin, 1972. 1st ed., 1 of 500 numbered and signed copies. Orig. full leatherette, gilt, plain box, a.e.g. Mint copy with orig. glassine. Jenkins 155-880 1983 $75

MAC LEISH, ARCHIBALD   Land of the Free. N.Y.: Harcourt, Brace & Co., (1938). Cloth with dust wrapper. 88 photographs, 33 were taken by D. Lange. Dawson 471-190 1983 $100

MAC LEISH, ARCHIBALD   The Pot of Earth. B, 1925. Paper covered gold board slightly rubbed, very good or better. Quill & Brush 54-836 1983 $50

MAC LEISH, ARCHIBALD   The Pot of Earth. Boston, 1925. "Special Limited edition of 100 copies." Cloth back. Pictorial boards. Ink inscription, rubbed. King 45-215 1983 $25

M'LEOD, ALEXANDER   A Scriptural View of the Character, Causes and Ends of the Present War... New York, 1815. Bound in three quarter black morocco, raised bands, gilt, t.e.g. Some scattered foxing, but a very nice copy. Reese 18-483 1983 $60

MC LEOD, DONALD   History of Wiskonsan, from Its First Discovery to the Present Period. Buffalo, 1846. 1st ed. 4 plates and folding map, partly in color. 12mo. Binding partly faded, few minor scotch tape repairs on verso of map, signature slightly pulled. Morrill 288-542 1983 $250

M'LEOD, JOHN   Voyage of His Majesty's Ship 'Alceste,' along the Coast of Corea, to the Island of Lewchew, with an Account of her subsequent Shipwreck. London: John Murray, 1818. 2nd ed., 8vo, modern calf antique, spine gilt, engraved frontis. portrait, five hand-colored aquatints. A very good copy. Trebizond 18-153 1983 $250

MAC LEOD, NORMAN   Eastward. London, 1866. Folding frontis. Numerous maps and illus. Decorated cloth frayed. 8vo. Good. Edwards 1044-447 1983 £25

MAC LEOD, NORMAN   Eastward. London, Strahan, 1866. First edition, 70 illustrations from photographs, engraved by Joseph Swain. 8vo., all edges gilt, nice. Morrill 290-254 1983 $25

MAC LEOD, NORMAN   The Old Lieutenant and His Son. London: Alexander Strahan & Co., 1862. First edition. 2 vols. Orig. cloth. Edges slightly worn. Cloth on covers slightly bubbled by damp. Very good. MacManus 279-3468 1983 $100

MC LEOD, ROBERT R.   Markland or Nova Scotia. (Toronto), 1903. Map and illustrations. Large 8vo. Rubbed and partly stained; lacks back fly-leaf. Morrill 290-645 1983 $27.50

MC MECHEN, EDGAR CARLISLE   The Moffat Tunnel of Colorado. (Denver, Colorado: Wahlgreen Pub. Co. 1927). The de luxe edition. 4to, profusely illus. with steel engravings, photos and maps. No. 597 of an unspecified number of the de luxe edition. Signed by the author. Bound in full black calf; gilt-stamped spines. Fine set. Karmiole 72-34 1983 $150

MC MECHEN, EDGAR CARLISLE   The Moffat Tunnel of Colorado an Epic of Empire. Denver, 1927. 2 vols., plates and maps. De Luxe Edition numbered and signed by the author. Minor wear. Jenkins 151-38 1983 $125

MAC MICHAEL, WILLIAM   The Gold-Headed Cane. New York, 1915. 8vo. Orig. binding. Ex-library. Fye H-3-432 1983 $40

MAC MICHAEL, WILLIAM   The Gold-Headed Cane. New York, 1915. 8vo. 1/2 vellum. Water-stain affecting outer margin of most leaves, backstrip soiled. Fye H-3-431 1983 $40

MAC MICHAEL, WILLIAM   The Gold-Headed Cane. London, 1923. 8vo. Orig. binding. Fye H-3-358 1983 $45

MAC MICHAEL, WILLIAM   The Gold-Headed Cane. New York, 1926. 8vo. Orig. binding. Fye H-3-359 1983 $45

MAC MILLAN, C.   The Metaspermae of the Minnesota Valley. Minneapolis, 1892. Maps, royal 8vo, quarter morocco, trifle worn. Wheldon 160-1739 1983 £20

MAC MILLAN, FREDERICK   The Net Book Agreement 1899... Glasgow: Robert MacLehose & Co., Ltd., 1924. First edition. 8vo. Boards. Oak Knoll 49-283 1983 $25

MAC MILLAN, HAROLD   The Price of Peace. October, 1938. 8vo. Bickersteth 77-227 1983 £12

MAC MINN, EDWIN   On the Frontier with Colonel Antes. Camden, N.J., 1900. Numerous plates. Cloth. A fine copy. First edition. Felcone 22-132 1983 $45

MC MULLEN, THOMAS   Hand-Book of Wines, Practical, Theoretical, and Historical: With a Description of Foreign Spirits and Liquers. New York: Appleton, 1852. 1st ed. Orig. publisher's full tan morocco, fully gilt, raised bands, gilt, a.e.g. Few stains, but a fine copy. Jenkins 155-1330 1983 $250

MAC MUNN, GEORGE   The Armies of India. A. & C. Black, 1911. First edition, with 72 coloured plates and 19 other illus., roy. 8vo, orig. cloth, gilt, t.e.g. Fenning 61-279 1983 £24.50

MAC MUNN, GEORGE   The Romance of the Indian Frontiers. London, 1931. 5 maps, 1 folding, 26 plates, fine. 8vo. Orig. cloth. Edwards 1044-456 1983 £25

MC MURRICH, J. PLAYFAIR   Leonardo da Vinci: The Anatomist, 1452-1519. Baltimore, (c. 1930). First edition. 4to, decor. cloth. Argosy 713-332 1983 $125

MC MURRICH, J. PLAYFAIR   Leonardo Da Vinci, The Anatomist. Baltimore, 1930. 4to. First edition. Orig. wraps. Fye H-3-726 1983 $100

MC MURRICH, J. PLAYFAIR   Leonardo da Vinci the Anatomist. London, 1930. Large 8vo. Cloth. Frontis. and numerous plates. Slightly dampstained. Gurney JJ-228 1983 £20

MC MURTRIE, DOUGLAS C.   A Bibliography of Morristown Imprints, 1798-1820. Newark, 1936. Pr. wrs. One of 200 privately printed copies reprinted from NJ Hist. Soc. Argosy 710-337 1983 $45

MC MURTRIE, DOUGLAS C.   The Book: The Story of Printing and Bookmaking. New York: Covici Friede, 1937. Illus. 1st ed. Orig. cloth, dj. Fine copy in lightly rubbed dj of McMurtrie magnum opus. Jenkins 155-102 1983 $60

MC MURTRIE, DOUGLAS C.   Early Printing in New Orleans 1764-1810. New Orleans: 1929. 4to, cloth-backed decorated boards. Illustrated. Signed presentation from the author. One of 410 copies. Perata 28-104 1983 $100

MC MURTRIE, DOUGLAS C.   Early Printing in New Orleans 1764-1810. New Orleans: Searcy & Pfaff, 1929. Boards, cloth spine, front hinge cracked and repaired, boards worn. 1 of 410 numbered copies. Dawson 470-205 1983 $25

MC MURTRIE, DOUGLAS C.   Early Printing in Tennessee. Chicago, 1933. Several facs. title-pages. One of 900 copies. Argosy 710-522 1983 $60

MC MURTRIE, DOUGLAS C.   The First Printing in Jamaica. Evanston: Privately Printed, 1942. Folio. Orig. tan printed wrappers. First edition. Very fine. Jenkins 152-220 1983 $35

MAC MURTRIE, DOUGLAS C.   The Golden Book. Chicago: Pascal Covici, 1927. First edition. Thick 4to. Blue moire covers. Extensive gilt decoration on spine & covers. Gilt dentelles. Limited to 2000 copies. Illus. throughout in black & whites. Index, notes. Fine. Aleph-bet 8-169 1983 $60

MC MURTRIE, DOUGLAS C.   The Golden Book. Chicago: Pascal Covici, 1927. Second edition. Illus. Gilt decorated blue cloth, top edges gilt. Very good copy. Bradley 66-244 1983 $35

MC MURTRIE, DOUGLAS C.   The Gutenberg Documents. New York: Oxford, 1941. Cloth and boards. First edition. One of 900 copies, designed by McMurtrie. Very fine copy in dust jacket, but for a light pencil signature. Reese 20-643 1983 $45

MC MURTRIE, DOUGLAS C.   Modern Typography & Layout. Chicago: Eyncourt Press, 1929. First edition. Large 4to. Cloth. Limited to 2000 copies. Well illus. Covers faded, shaken. Oak Knoll 48-261 1983 $30

MC MURTRIE, DOUGLAS C.   Printer's Marks and Their Significance. Chicago, 1930. 12mo, black cloth, gilt, illus. One of 250 copies. Very nice. Perata 27-132 1983 $65

MC MURTRIE, DOUGLAS C.   Wings for Works, The Story of Johann Gutenberg... New York: Rand McNally & Co., 1940. First edition. Small 4to. Cloth. Dust jacket, light wear. Oak Knoll 49-281 1983 $35

M'MURTRIE, HENRY   Sketches of Louisville and its Environs. Louisville, 1819. Later cloth, ex. lib. Title-page clipped at top, not affecting text. Lacks the map, otherwise good. Reese 13-532 1983 $525

MC MURTRIE, WILLIAM   Report on the Culture of the Sugar Beet and the Manufacture of Sugar Therefrom in France and the United States. Wash.: Gov't Printing Office, 1880. First edition. 4 large folding maps, some color, 32 full-page plates, 5 folding, text illus. & many tables. Half morocco. Argosy 716-145 19 3 $45

MC MURTRY, LARRY   Cadillac Jack. New York: Simon & Schuster, (1982). Printed wraps. Uncorrected proofs of the first edition. Fine. Reese 20-1013 1983 $125

MC MURTRY, LARRY   Cadillac Jack. New York: Simon & Schuster, (1982). 1st ed., 1 of 250 numbered and signed copies. Orig. cloth, gilt, boxed. Mint copy. Jenkins 155-870 1983 $100

MC MURTRY, LARRY   Cadillac Jack. New York: Simon & Schuster, (1982). Cloth. First edition. One of 250 numbered copies, specially bound and signed by the author. Mint as issued. Slipcased. Reese 20-1014 1983 $85

MC MURTRY, LARRY   Daughter of the Tejas. Greenwich: New York Graphic Society, (1965). 1st ed., presumed 1st state of dj. Orig. cloth, dj. Mint. Jenkins 155-875 1983 $85

MC MURTRY, LARRY   The Desert Rose. New York: Simon & Schuster, 1983. 1st ed., advance uncorrected proofs. Orig. yellow printed wrappers. Mint copy. Jenkins 155-871 1983 $110

MC MURTRY, LARRY   Horseman, Pass By. NY, (1961). Minor cover wear, erasure front fly, else near fine in price clipped, lightly frayed and chipped, very good dustwrapper. Quill & Brush 54-891 1983 $400

MC MURTRY, LARRY   In a Narrow Grave. Austin: The Encino Press, 1968. Cloth. First edition, first printing. Inscribed and signed by the author. Very fine in preliminary dust jacket. Reese 20-644 1983 $950

MC MURTRY, LARRY   In a Narrow Grave: Essays on Texas. Austin: Encino Press, 1968. 1st ed., 1 of 250 numbered and signed copies. Orig. half suede and printed boards, uncut, boxed. Some soiling to box; book mint. Jenkins 155-872 1983 $275

MC MURTRY, LARRY   In a Narrow Grave. Austin: The Encino Press, 1968. Cloth, paper label. First published edition. Inscribed and signed by the author. Fine in dust jacket. Reese 20-1012 1983 $175

MC MURTRY, LARRY   In a Narrow Grave. Austin: The Encino Press, 1968. Cloth, paper label. First edition, second printing. Fine copy in dust jacket. Reese 19-343 1983 $100

MC MURTRY, LARRY   In a Narrow Grave. Austin: Encino Press. 1st trade ed. Orig. cloth, dj. Mint copy. Jenkins 155-873 1983 $100

MC MURTRY, LARRY   It's Always We Rambled. NY, 1974. Limited to 300 numbered and signed copies, fine. Quill & Brush 54-892 1983 $125

MC MURTRY, LARRY   The Last Picture Show. N.Y., Dial, 1966. First edition. Dust jacket. Fine copy. Houle 22-1214 1983 $95

MC MURTRY, LARRY   The Last Picture Show. New York: Dial Press, 1966. Cloth. First edition. Fine in slightly soiled dust jacket. Reese 20-1011 1983 $75

MC MURTRY, LARRY   Leaving Cheyenne. NY, (1963). Very minor cover foxing, fine in fine dustwrapper with slightly soiled rear panel and remnants of price-sticker over orig. price. Quill & Brush 54-893 1983 $300

MC MURTRY, LARRY   Leaving Cheyenne. NY, (1963). Light erasure front fly, else fine in lightly frayed and soiled, near fine dustwrapper, owner's name. Quill & Brush 54-894 1983 $275

MC NAB, WILLIAM   Hints on the Planting and general treatment of hardy evergreens... Edinburgh: Thomas Clark, 1830. First edition. 8vo. Sewn, as issued. A fine unopened copy. Ximenes 63-181 1983 $50

MC NABB, VINCENT   Geoffrey Chaucer. Sussex: St.
Dominic's Press, 1934. Small woodcut illus. on title-page. Edition
ltd. to 300 numbered copies, printed on handmade paper. Bound in
half blue cloth over green boards. Karmiole 76-95 1983 $50

MAC NAMARA, DANIEL GEORGE   The History of the Ninth Regiment
Massachusetts Volunteer Infantry... Boston, 1899. 1st ed. 8vo.
Morrill 287-239 1983 $35

M'NEEL-CAIRD, ALEXANDER   Mary Stuart, Her Guilt or Innocence.
Edinburgh, Adam and Charles Black, 1866. 8vo, light pencil notes and
some underlining in the text, cont. half calf, rebacked, preserving
orig. rather worn spine. Bickersteth 77-149 1983 £24

MC NEER, M.   The Story of Califronia. N.Y.: Harpers,
1944. Stated first edition. Large sq. 4to. Cloth backed pictorial
boards. Dust wrapper. Fine. Aleph-bet 8-86 1983 $30

MC NEER, M   Tales from the Crescent Moon. N.Y.:
Farr. Rine, (1930). First edition. 4to. Cloth. Dust wrapper.
Color plates, many black & whites. Fine. Aleph-bet 8-170 1983 $30

MAC NEICE, LOUIS   Autumn Journal. London, 1939. Browned
dustwrapper missing three small chips. Fine. Gekoski 2-214 1983
£30

MAC NEICE, LOUIS   The Last Ditch. Dublin: Cuala Press,
1940. First edition. One of 450 copies. Corners a little rubbed.
Very nice. Rota 231-403 1983 £60

MAC NEICE, LOUIS   Modern Poetry. London, 1938. First
edition. Spine a little faded and covers marked. Very good. Rota
230-382 1983 £30

MAC NEICE, LOUIS   Poems. London, 1935. First edition.
Covers a little soiled. Very good. Rota 231-402 1983 £20

MAC NEICE, LOUIS   Poems. NY, (1937). Flys offset, cover
slightly dulled, else very good is soiled and slightly frayed good
dustwrapper. Quill & Brush 54-838 1983 $45

MAC NEICE, LOUIS   Poems. Springboard, 1941-1944. New
York: Random House, (1945). 1st ed. Orig. cloth, dj. Very fine
with publicity photo laid in. Jenkins 155-884 1983 $25

MAC NEICE, LOUIS   The Poetry of W. B. Yeats. New York,
1941. First American edition. Spine a little faded. Name on flyleaf.
Nice. Rota 230-383 1983 £21

MAC NEICE, LOUIS   Selected Poems. London, 1940. First
edition of this selection. Advance proof copy. Wrappers. Very nice.
Rota 231-404 1983 £20

MAC NEILL, HECTOR   The Links O'Forth. Edinburgh: Printed
for Archibald Constable...1799. 8vo, with half-title. Uncut copy in
orig. plain blue wraps., spine slightly worn. First edition. Quaritch
NS 7-76 1983 $200

MAC NEILL, JOHN G. SWIFT   The Constitutional and Parliamentary
History of Ireland till the Union. Dublin: Talbot, 1917. First
edition, 8vo, orig. cloth, a very good copy. Fenning 61-280 1983
£18.50

MC NEILL-MOSS, G.   The Epic of the Alcazar. London, 1937.
First edition. 8vo. Orig. cloth. Frontis. map. 36 plates, 2 folding
plans. Very slightly soiled. Good. Edwards 1042-405 1983 £15

MC NEMAR, RICHARD   A Revision and Confirmation of the
Social Compact of the United Society Called Shakers, at Pleasant
Hill, Kentucky. Harrodsburg, Kentucky, 1830. Stitched, a fine copy.
Reese 18-650 1983 $300

M' NICOLL, DAVID   A rational enquiry concerning the operation of the stage on the morals of society. Newcastle upon Tyne:
printed by Edward Walker; and sold by Messrs. Charnley, Finlay, Horn,
etc., 1832. 8vo, disbound. Title a bit soiled. First edition.
Scarce. Ximenes 64-364 1983 $75

MAC ORLAN, PIERRE   Felicien Rops. Paris: Marcel Seheur,
1928. 116 plates (5 color). Numerous text illus. 4to. Wrappers.
Dust jacket. Ars Libri 32-588 1983 $75

MAC ORLAN, PIERRE   Port d'Eaux-Mortes. Paris: Au Sans
Pareil, 1926. With 8 orig. full-page lithos. by Groxz. One of 1,000
numbered copies on velin Lafuma (total edition 1260). In orig.
printed wraps. and glassine. Karmiole 75-62 1983 $250

MC PARLIN, THOMAS A.   Notes on the History and Climate of
New Mexico. Wash., GPO, 1877. Orig. printed wraps. X-1. Ginsberg
47-676 1983 $75

MC PEAK, J. A. S.   Catullus in Strange and Distant Britain.
Cambridge, 1939. 8vo, cloth. Salloch 385-39 1983 $22

MC PHEE, JOHN   Road Kills: A Collection of Prose
and Poetry. The Cheloniidae Press, 1981. With etchings and wood
engravings by Alan James Robinson. Folio, cloth, boards. Deluxe
ed. 1 of 50 copies signed by McPhee, et al. The deluxe ed. is
accompanied by a separate folder containing the etchings of
Robinson, each signed by same. A fine copy in clamshell box. In
Our Time 156-662 1983 $600

MAC PHERSON, H. A.   A Vertebrate Fauna of Lakeland. 1892.
Map and 8 plates (2 coloured), 8vo, cloth (faded). The 2 coloured
plates are by Keulemans. Wheldon 160-406 1983 £45

MAC PHERSON, H. B.   The Home-Life of a Golden Eagle. 1910.
Second edition, 32 photographic plates, royal 8vo, half morocco
(trifle worn). Wheldon 160-804 1983 £15

MAC PHERSON, JAMES   The Poems of Ossian. London: Printed
for A. Strahan & T. Cadell, 1796. New Edition. 2 vols. Later half-
calf and marbled boards. Ownership signatures on title-pages. Covers
somewhat worn. Bookplates. Some foxing. Good. MacManus 279-3469
1983 $45

MAC PHERSON, JOHN   Critical Dissertations on the Origin,
Antiquities, Language, Government, Manners, and Religion of the
ancient Caledonians... London: for T. Becket and P.A. De Hondt,
and J. Balfour, Edinburgh, 1768. First edition. 4to. Cont. calf,
spine gilt extra, red morocco label, gilt. 2 pp. of ads. Very fine
copy. Traylen 94-549 1983 £110

MAC QUOID, KATHERINE S.   Appledore Farm. London: Ward & Downey,
1894. First edition. 3 vols. Orig. cloth with floral endpapers.
Heads and feet of spines worn, corners slightly bumped. Covers a
little soiled. Former owner's signature and blind-stamp on each half-
title. Good. MacManus 279-3470 1983 $160

MAC RITCHIE, DAVID   Ancient and Modern Britons. 1884.
2 vols., 8vo. K Books 301-87 1983 £38

MAC RITCHIE, DAVID   Scottish Gypsies Under the Stewarts.
Edinburgh, 1894. 8vo. K Books 301-88 1983 £34

MAC TAGGART, JOHN   Three Years in Canada. London: Henry
Colburn, 1829. 20cm. 2 vols. Orig. boards, rebacked with paper
labels. Very good. McGahern 53-113 1983 $300

MAC VICAR, JOHN GIBSON   The First Lines of Science Simplified...
Edinburgh: Sutherland & Knox, 1860. 8vo. Orig. cloth. 1 folding
plate of crystal forms. Boards buckles with damp. Good internally.
Zeitlin 264-278 1983 $35

MAC WHORTER, ALEXANDER   A Funeral Sermon. Newark: Jacob Halsey,
1800. Disbound. Very good. Felcone 19-28 1983 $65

MC WILLIAM, G. M.   The Birds of the Firth of Clyde. 1936.
10 plates and a map, 8vo, cloth. Binding a trifle used. Wheldon
160-805 1983 £25

MAASKAMP, EVERT   Representations of Dresses, Morals and
Customs in the Kingdom of Holland. Amsterdam: 1808(?). Small folio.
Illus. with allegorical frontis. and 20 full-page, hand-colored engravings. The 2 printed leaves have small marginal damp stain at top,
date rubbed out on title-page. Plates very clean. Bound in full dark
green, straight-grain morocco, gilt rules with corner ornaments, spine
gilt, inner dentelles gilt. T.e.g. Fine copy. Bromer 25-251 1983
$850

MABLY, GABRIEL BONNOT DE   Doutes Proposes Aux Philosophes
Economistes Sur L'Ordre Naturel Et Essentiel Des Societes Politiques.
Paris, Chez Nyonet Veuve Durand, 1768. 1st ed., 12mo, cont. mottled
calf, spine gilt, red morocco label, a very good copy of this rare
work. Pickering & Chatto 21-70 1983 $500

MABLY, GABRIEL BONNOT DE   Remarks Concerning the Government and
the Laws of the United States of America. Dublin, 1785. Calf.
K Books 301-118 1983 £35

MACARTNEY-BARROW, JOHN   Some Account of the Public Life and a
Selection from the Unpublished Writings of the Earl of Macartney. London, 1807. Engraved portrait frontis. 2 vols. 4to. Cont. diced calf,
rebacked. Good. Edwards 1044-446 1983 £125

MACAULAY, FANNIE CALDWELL   The Lady of the Decoration. New York:
Century, 1906. 1st ed. Orig. cloth, gilt. Fine copy. Jenkins
155-877 1983 $20

MACAULAY, ROSE   Staying with Relations. London, 1930.
First edition. Mark on upper cover. Inscribed by author, dated January 1934. Nice. Rota 230-369 1983 £25

MACAULAY, ROSE   The Towers of Trebizond. London:
Collins, 1956. Corrected Proofs. Orig. wrappers with paper label.
With numerous minor corrections in the author's hand and a few signif-
icant revisions. Laid in are: a brief ANS from the author to her publisher; and the author's typed blurb for the nvoel, 1 page, 8vo, with
several holograph corrections. Wrappers a bit worn. Very good.
MacManus 279-3429 1983 $350

MACAULAY, ROSE   The Two Blind Countries. London, 1914.
First edition. Corners a little bruised and spine a little faded.
Very nice. Rota 231-389 1983 £25

MACAULAY, ROSE   The Writings of E. M. Forster. New York,
(1938). 8vo, cloth. A fine copy in just jacket. In Our Time 156-520
1983 $50

MACAULAY, ROSE   The Writings of E. M. Forster. Hogarth
Press, 1938. First edition. Spine darkened and covers a little
marked. Very good. Rota 230-370 1983 £21

MACAULAY, THOMAS BABINGTON   The History of England from the Accession
of James the Second. London: Macmillan & Co., 1913-1915. First
edition. Orig. cloth. 6 vols. Edges slightly worn. Cvoers a trifle
soiled. Very good. MacManus 279-3431 1983 $125

MACAULAY, THOMAS BABINGTON   Life of Frederick the Great. N.Y.:
American Book Exchange, 1880. Orig. yellow wrapper. Fine. MacManus
279-3432 1983 $20

MACAULAY, THOMAS BABINGTON   The Works. London, 1866. 8 vols.
8vo. Full polished calf, gilt, gilt panelled spines with crimson
and green morocco labels, gilt. Engraved portrait. A little
rubbed. Traylen 94-542 1983 £60

MACAULAY, THOMAS BABINGTON   The Complete Works. London, 1898.
Albany edition. 12 vols. 8vo. Half dark brown morocco, gilt,
panelled spines, gilt, t.e.g. Engraved portrait printed on Japanese
vellum. Spines lightly faded. Traylen 94-543 1983 £160

MACAULAY, THOMAS BABINGTON   Works. New York, Sproul, 1908. Limited
ed. Illus. 20 vols., 8vo. Morrill 287-603 1983 $65

MACENDIE, FRANCOIS   Elementary Treatise on Human Physiology.
N.Y., 1855. Enlarged & illus. by John Revere. Old sheep (worn,
joints mended). Ex-lib. Argosy 713-351 1983 $100

MACH, ERNST   Contributions to the Analysis of the
Sensations. Chicago: Open Court, 1897. First English edition.
Gach 95-343 1983 $50

MACH, ERNST   Erkenntnis Und Irrtum. Skizzen zur
Psychologie der Forschung. Leipzig: Johann A. Barth, 1926. Fifth
edition. Bookplate removed, stamp on rear pastedown. Gach 94-601
1983 $30

MACH, ERNST   The Science of Mechanics. Chicago:
Open Court Pub. Co., 1902. Second edition in English, revised and
enlarged. Thick 12mo. Publisher's green cloth. Library bookplate
and stamp on rear paste-down, else very good. Gach 94-602 1983
$27.50

MACHADO, ANTONIO   Cantiones. West Branch, Iowa: The
Toothpaste Press, 1980. First edition in English. One of 150 copies
numbered and signed by the translator, Robert Bly. Fine. Jolliffe
26-60 1983 £40

MACHEN, ARTHUR   The Anatomy of Tobacco. (London): Geo.
Redway, 1884. First edition. Orig. full parchment. Covers worn,
several pages soiled. Poor. MacManus 279-3447 1983 $185

MACHEN, ARTHUR   The Bowmen and Other Legends of the War.
London: Simpkin, 1915. First edition. 12mo. Orig. printed boards.
MacManus 279-3448 1983 $20

MACHEN, ARTHUR   Bridles & Spurs. Cleveland: 1951. 4to,
1/2 natural cloth over boards, paper label, decorated slipcase. Port.
frontis., symbolic devices in gold by Mallette Dean. One of 178
copies. Signed, presentation from Ed Grabhorn. Minor spotting to backstrip. Perata 28-60 1983 $175

MACHEN, ARTHUR   Bridles & Spurs. Cleveland: 1951.
Preface by Nathan van Patten. 4to, cloth-backed bds., paper label,
slipcase. Portrait frontis, symbolic devices in gold by Mallette
Dean. Perata 27-72 1983 $145

MACHEN, ARTHUR   The Canning Wonder. London: Chatto &
Windus, 1925. First edition. Illus. Orig. parchment-backed boards.
Limited to 130 copies signed by author. A bit dust-soiled. Very good.
MacManus 279-3450 1983 $40

MACHEN, ARTHUR   The Canning Wonder. London, 1925.
First edition. Spine faded and some foxing of foreedges. Nice.
Rota 231-408 1983 £12

MACHEN, ARTHUR   The Chronicle of Clemendy. Carbonnek:
Privately printed, 1923. Orig. parchment-packed boards. One of 1050
copies signed by author. Spine a bit worn. MacManus 279-3451 1983
$25

MACHEN, ARTHUR   Dog and Duck. London: Cape, (1924).
First edition. Orig. cloth-backed boards. Limited to 150 copies
signed by Machen. Ends of spine chipped. MacManus 279-3452 1983
$35

MACHEN, ARTHUR   Far Off Things. London: Martin
Secker, (1922). First edition. 8vo. Boards. Paper spine label.
One of 100 large paper copies numbered and signed by the author.
Fine copy. Oak Knoll 48-263 1983 $45

MACHEN, ARTHUR   The Gray's Inn Coffee House. Stanford,
Nathan Van Patten, 1949. One of 50 copies printed at the Greenwood
Press. Very good. Houle 22-614 1983 $75

MACHEN, ARTHUR   Hill of Dreams. London, Secker (1922).
Dust jacket (sm. nicks). Very good. One of 150 copies, signed by
the author. Large paper edition on blue paper. Houle 21-592 1983
$150

MACHEN, ARTHUR   The House of Souls. London, 1906.
First edition, first binding. Frontis. by S.H. Sime. Endpapers a
little foxed. Very nice. Rota 231-407 1983 £45

MACHEN, ARTHUR   The London Adventure or the Art of
Wandering. London: Martin Secker, (1924). First edition. Orig.
boards with paper label on spine. One of 200 large-paper copies
signed by Machen. Top of spine rubbed, a little stained. Former
owner's signature. Very good. MacManus 279-3454 1983 $40

MACHEN, ARTHUR   Precious Balms. London: Spurr & Swift,
1924. First edition. Orig. cloth. One of 265 copies signed by
author. Very good. MacManus 279-3455 1983 $45

MACHEN, ARTHUR   Strange Roads. London: The Classic
Press, 1923. First edition. 12mo. Illus. Orig. cloth. Tissue
dust jacket. Fine. MacManus 279-3456 1983 $22.50

MACHEN, ARTHUR   The Terror: A Fantasy. London,
(1927). 12mo. Boards. Name on fly, paper browned from aging,
otherwise fine in lightly nicked dj. In Our Time 156-521 1983
$45

MACHEN, ARTHUR   Things Near and Far. London: Secker,
(1923). Cloth. First trade edition, preceding the ltd. edition by
two months. Traces of foxing at foredge. Dust jacket. Reese 20-
650 1983 $50

MACHEN, ARTHUR   The Three Imposters or the Transmutations.
London: John Lane, 1895. Pictorial cloth after Aubrey Beardsley.
First edition. Traces of shelfrubbing at edges. Reese 20-649 1983
$150

MACHIAVELLI, NICCOLO   The Art of War, in Seven Books...
Albany: Printed by Henry C. Southwick, 1815. Orig. boards, edges
untrimmed, partially unopened, unpressed. Folding tables. Cuts.
Spine slightly chipped, and scattered foxing, but a near fine copy.
Reese 18-481 1983 $500

MACHIAVELLI, NICCOLO   The Florentine Historie. London,
T(homas). C(reede). for W(illiam). P(onsonby)., 1595. Folio, orig.
calf, joints cracked, later endpapers, title and last leaf bit
soiled, age-darkened, last few leaves bit frayed at blank edges,
early names on verso of title, armorial bookplate. Ravenstree 97-
71 1983 $960

MACHIAVELLI, NICCOLO   Machiavel's Discourses upon the First
Decade of T. Libius. London, Chas. Harper & John Amery, 1674. 8vo,
cont. calf, worn, front cover detached. Fine frontis. by White of
Machiavelli appended, but not listed on the title page. Slight
worming in extreme lower margin of preliminaries, some light waterstaining. Ravenstree 97-70 1983 $75

MACHIAVELLI, NICCOLO   Le Prince de Machiavel. Amsterdam:
Henri Wetstein, 1686. 12mo, engraved frontis. portrait. Old
calf, badly chipped on spine and front outer hinge; old underlining &
a few annotations in text; some water staining. Karmiole 73-66 1983
$85

MACHMINN, GEORGE R.   The Theater of the Golden Era of
California. Caldwell, Caxton, 1941. First edition. Illus. Dust
jacket (small chips at edges). Very good. Houle 22-1131 1983 $55

MACKWORTH, DIGBY   Diary of a Tour through Southern India...
London, 1823. First edition. 2 folding maps, 2 plates. Half morocco,
spine gilt, marbled boards. 8vo. Good. Edwards 1044-454 1983 £200

MACKWORTH-PRAED, C. W.   African Handbook of Birds. 1952-73.
Series 1 to 3, 265 coloured plates, black and white photographic
illus. and numerous marginal distribution maps and drawings, 6 vols.,
8vo, cloth. First editions. Wheldon 160-801 1983 £180

MACKWORTH-PRAED, C. W.   African Handbook of Birds. 1962-63.
Series 2, Birds of the Southern Third of Africa. Coloured plates and
numerous illus., 2 vols., 8vo, cloth. Wheldon 160-802 1983 £75

MACLAY, EDGAR S.   A History of American Privateers. New
York: D. Appleton & Co., 1899. First edition. Frontis. and plates.
Orig. pictorial cloth. Jenkins 152-221 1983 $75

MACLAY, EDGAR S.   A History of American Privateers. New
York, 1899. 1st ed. Illus. 8vo. Dampstain on front cover.
Morrill 287-605 1983 $25

MACLAY, SAMUEL   Journal While Surveying the West Branch
of the Susquehanna... Williamsport, John F. Meginness, 1887. 1st
ed. Presentation copy from publisher. Pasted in is an 8vo broadside,
signed by Meginness; also small stamp pasted on title. 8vo, half
leather, lacks half of backstrip, front hinge cracked. Morrill 288-
402 1983 $45

MACOMB, ALEXANDER   A Treatise on Martial Law, and Courts-
Martial. Charleston, 1809. Old leather, some wear, and boards. Light
foxing, overall good. Reese 18-328 1983 $300

MACOUN, JOHN   Catalogue of Canadian Birds. Ottawa,
1900-04. 3 parts, in 1 volume, royal 8vo, cloth. Wheldon 160-803
1983 £25

MACOUN, JOHN   Catalogue of Canadian Birds. Ottawa:
Dept. of Mines, 1909. 24cm. Orig. brown pebbled cloth. A fine
copy. McGahern 53-115 1983 $45

MACRAY, WILLIAM DUNN   A manual of British historians to
A.D. 1600. London: William Pickering, 1845. First edition. 8vo.
A rig. "Roxburghe-style" quarter morocco. Book label of A.N.L.
Numby. Fine copy. Ximenes 63-7 1983 $95

MACREADY, WILLIAM   Fact versus Fallacy; or, the true state
of the case between John Prosser Edwin, comedian, late of the Theatre-
royal, Newcastle, and William M'Cready. Newcastle on Tyne: printed
by J. Mitchell, 1807. First edition. 8vo, disbound. Very rare.
Ximenes 64-365 1983 $175

MACREIGHT, D. C.   Manual of British Botany. 1837.
Post 8vo, cloth. Wheldon 160-1616 1983 £18

MACURA, P.   Elsevier's Dictionary of Botany. Vol.
1 Plant names. 1979. 8vo, cloth. Wheldon 160-1510 1983 £58

MACY, OBED   The History of Nantucket... Boston,
1835. First edition. Ads. 2 plates (by W.S. Pendleton). Morocco-
backed boards (worn, hinges broken). Felcone 20-95 1983 $85

MADACS, PETER   Theoria Affinitatum Chemicarum. Nagy-
Szombath, 1774. 8vo. Old floral wrappers. Rare. Gurney 90-76
1983 £30

MADAME Jovial. (London: Dean & Sons, ca. 1860's). Octavo. Printed
on one side only. A "Hole-Book" with clay head of Madame Jovial on
inside rear cover coming through hole cut-out of each page and front
cover. Well-preserved, both "bead" eyes present. French text, color-
printed illus. Light offsetting to blank versos, slight rubbing to
cloth-backed pictorial boards. Bromer 25-365 1983 $285

MADAN, FALCONER   The Lewis Carroll Centenary in London
1932. Bumpus, 1932. Edition limited to 400 copies. Port. frontis. &
5 plates. White cloth, gilt, dust wrappers. Loosely inserted 8pp
list of additional exhibits & corrigenda list. Very good. Greer 39-8
1983 £45

MADARIAGA, SALVADOR DE   Shelley & Calderon. N.Y.: E.P. Dutton
& Co., n.d. (1920). First edition. Bound in 3/4 green morocco & cloth.
Fine. MacManus 280-4729 1983 $50

MADDEN, DODGSON H.   The Diary of Master William Silence.
Longmans, Green, 1897. First edition, 8vo, orig. cloth, gilt, t.e.g.
Fenning 62-222 1983 £18.50

MADDEN, DODGSON H.   The Law and Practive of the High Court
of Justice in Ireland. Dublin: E. Ponsonby, 1879. 8vo, cont. half
calf, rubbed but thoroughly sound and a very good copy. Fenning 62-223
1983 £21.50

MADISON, JAMES   The Journal of the Debates in the
Convention Which Framed the Constitution of the United States May-
Sept., 1787. NY, 1903. 2 vols. Illus. Argosy 710-122 1983 $35

THE MADRESFIELD Hours. A Fourteenth Century Manuscript... Oxford:
the Roxburghe club, 1975. Limited edition. Folio. Orig. quarter
morocco. 4 coloured plates and 46 full-page facsimiles. Printed
for members only. Sir Owen Morshead's copy. Traylen 94-550 1983
£130

MAETERLINCK, MAURICE   The Blue Bird. Methuen, 1912. 4to.
Mounted colour frontis. 24 colour plates (several creased). Decorated
endpapers. Blue pictorial cloth gilt. Greer 39-106 1983 £35

MAETERLINCK, MAURICE   The Buried Temple. N.Y.: Dodd, Mead &
Co., 1902. First American edition. Orig. embossed cloth. Dust jacket
(slightly worn). Fine. MacManus 279-3472 1983 $25

MAETERLINCK, MAURICE   The Intelligence of Flowers. NY: Dodd,
Mead, 1907. Frontis. and three other photographic illus. by Alvin
Langdon Coburn. Page decorations by William Edgar Fisher. Cloth
over boards; with label on front cover. Karmiole 74-76 1983 $125

MAETERLINCK, MAURICE   L'Ornement des Noces Spirituelles. Brussels, 1891. First edition. Rebound in full brown levant morocco. Inscribed by author. From the library of E. Meynell, bearing his book-plate. Nice. Rota 230-385 1983 £30

MAETERLINCK, MAURICE   The Plays of... Chicago: Stone & Kimball, 1896. First edition, second series. Covers a bit soiled and worn. MacManus 279-3476 1983 $20

MAETERLINCK, MAURICE   Wisdom and Destiny. London: George Allen, Ruskin House, 1898. First English edition. Orig. decorated cloth. Spine and covers slightly faded and worn. Some offsetting to the endpapers. Good. MacManus 279-3478 1983 $25

MAGDA, JOICEY   Cook-Book Note-Book. London, 1946. Numerous full-page drawings by Edward Bawden. Very slightly torn dustwrapper by Bawden. Fine. Jolliffe 26-39 1983 £25

MAGGS BROS. LTD.   Canada, Newfoundland, Labrador and the Canadian Arctic. London: Maggs Bros., 1939. 24cm. 44 plates. Printed wrappers. Very good. McGahern 54-126 1983 $35

THE MAGIC lantern; or, green bag plot laid open... London: S.W. Fores, 1820. First edition. With 6 woodcut illus. Ximenes 63-502 1983 $45

MAGINN, WILLIAM   The Odoherty Papers. N.Y.: Redfield, 1855. First edition. 2 vols. Orig. cloth. MacManus 279-3479 1983 $85

MAGNAT, G.- E.   Poesie de l'Ecriture. Geneve: H. Sack, (1944). First edition. Small 4to. Paper wrappers. 38 foldout plates. Limited to 1000 numbered copies. Some yellowing of covers. Unopened. Oak Knoll 48-266 1983 $20

MAGNE, EMILE   Nicolas Poussin, premier peintre du roi, 1594-1665. Bruxelles/Paris: G. Van Oest, 1914. Ca. 150 plates. Stout folio. Marbled boards, 3/4 leather. No. 306 of a limited edition of 500 copies. Printed on fine laid paper. Uncut. Very fine. Rare. Ars Libri 32-537 1983 $450

MAGNER, D.   Magner's ABC Guide to Sensible Horse-shoeing. Akron: Werner, 1899. First edition. Over 200 illus., including 17 colored plates. 4to. Orig. green pictorial cloth. Very fine. Jenkins 152-222 1983 $75

THE MAGNET Stories... Groombridge, nd (ca. 1870). Vols. 1, 2, 3 & 5. Wood engrs. by D.H. Friston (57 full page illus. & 70 text illus); engr'd by W. Whimper. Pub's green sand grain decor. cloth, binding designed by Harry Rogers & signed. Occasional foxing & thumbing, vg. Hodgkins 27-144 1983 4 vols. £25

MAGNIFICENZA di Roma, nelle vedute di Giovanni Battista Piranesi. Milano: Edizioni II Polifilo, 1977. 28 double-page plates. Folio. Boards. Ars Libri 33-280 1983 $85

MAGNINUS MEDIOLANENSIS
Please turn to
MAYNO DE MAYNERI

MAGNUS, HUGO   Superstition in Medicine. New York, 1905. First English translation. 8vo. Orig. binding. Fye H-3-365 1983 $40

MAGUIRE, JOHN F.   The Irish in America. Longmans, Green, 1868. First edition, 8vo, orig. cloth, neatly repaired, a few leaves carelessly opened, but a very good copy. Fenning 61-512 1983 £38.50

MAHAFFY, J. P.   Social Life in Greece. London, 1875. 1883. 8vo, cloth. Sallcoh 385-247 1983 $30

MAHAN, ALFRED THAYER   The Influence of Sea Power. London, 1890. First edition. 8vo. Orig. cloth. 4 maps (1 folding), 18 battle maps. Full cont. tree calf, gilt. Joints slightly worn, marbled edges, marbled endpapers, ink inscription on front endpaper. Good. Edwards 1042-133 1983 £35

MAHAN, ALFRED THAYER   The Influence of Sea Power upon History. Boston, 1890. Half morocco, gilt. First edition. Jenkins 151-203 1983 $200

MAHAN, ALFRED THAYER   The Life of Nelson. London, 1897. First edition. 8vo. Orig. cloth. 2 photogravure frontis., 17 photogravure portraits and plates, 21 maps (2 folding). 2 vols. Gilt. T.e.g. Spines very slightly worn and faded. Good. Edwards 1042-144 1983 £35

MAHAN, ALFRED THAYER   The Navy in the Civil War. London, 1898. Sm. 8vo. Orig. cloth. Engraved portrait frontis. 3 folding, 4 full page and 1 other map. Cont. half dark blue morocco, marbled boards. Gilt, by Azehnsdorf. T.e.g. Very slightly worn and soiled. Some slight offsetting on half title and title. Fine. Edwards 1042-230 1983 £35

MAHON, DENIS   Poussiniana. Afterthoughts arising from the exhibition. Paris/New York: Gazette des Beaux-Arts, 1962. 58 illus. Large 4to. Wrappers. Backstrip chipped at head. Ars Libri 32-538 1983 $80

MAHON, P. A. O.   Oeuvres Posthumes. Paris & Rouen, 1804. 8vo. Old half-calf, vellum corners. "Table des Auteurs" neatly written in cont. ms. on endpapers. Some foxing. Gurney 90-77 1983 £50

MAHON, R. H.   Life of General, The Hon. James Murray. London: John Murray, 1921. 22cm. 4 plates and 4 maps, red cloth. A fine copy. Rare. McGahern 54-127 1983 $125

MAHONY, FRANCIS   The Reliques of Father Prout, Late P.P. of Watergrasshill, in the County of Cork, Ireland. Bell & Daldy, 1868. Illus. by Alfred Croruis, Esq. (D. Maclise). New edition, folding front. engr. title. Ads. Orig. green cloth, spine browned, v.g. Jarndyce 31-801 '983 £12.50

MAIDMENT, JAMES   Fragmenta Scoto-dramatica. 1715-1758. Edinburgh: 1835. 12mo, cont. half calf (spine defective). First edition. Rare. Ximenes 64-366 1983 $125

MAIGNE, M.   The Private Journal of Madame Campan. London, 1825. 8vo. Orig. cloth. Half title. Contemporary half blue morocco gilt. T.e.g. Some slight foxing. Good. Edwards 1042-294 1983 £25

MAILER, NORMAN   Barbary Shore. NY, (1951). Advance copy in black and red paperwraps, edges rubbed, very good or better. Quill & Brush 54-842 1983 $350

MAILER, NORMAN   Barbary Shore. NY, (1951). Signed inscription from author on title, edges slightly worn, front pastedown slightly soiled, else very good in worn dustwrapper rubbed on edges. Quill & Brush 54-841 1983 $150

MAILER, NORMAN   Barbary Shore. NY: (1951). Ends of spine faintly rubbed, else fine in slightly rubbed dust wrapper. First edition. Together with first English edition (1952). Fine in dust wrapper, and first paperback edition (1953). Some cover rubbing and browning to pages. Bromer 25-69 1983 $85

MAILER, NORMAN   The Deer Park. NY, (1955). Signed, dated inscription from author, minor cover soiling, else very good in worn and chipped dustwrapper. Quill & Brush 54-846 1983 $150

MAILER, NORMAN   Gargoyle, Guignol, False Closet. D, 1964. One page folded, limited to 100 copies, fine. Quill & Brush 54-843 1983 $175

MAILER, NORMAN   Marilyn. (NY: Grosset & Dunlap, (1973) First printing. 4to, profusely illus. with full-page photos (many in color). The "limited, signed edition", (number of copies not specified) signed by Mailer and by Lawrnece Schiller (on behalf of the photographers). Bound in white padded cloth; laid inside folding box. Top edge of box with small bump. Karmiole 73-68 1983 $100

MAILER, NORMAN   Marilyn: A Biography. (N.Y., 1973). First edition. Illus., in black & white and color by the world's foremost photographers. Sq. 4to, d.w. Presentation copy. Argosy 714-496 1983 $85

MAILER, NORMAN   The Naked and the Dead. New York,
(1948). 8vo. Orig. printed wrappers. Advance copy, bound in the
published dj. Jacket has some light wear at the base of spine, else
about fine. In Our Time 156-527 1983 $900

MAILER, NORMAN   The Naked and the Dead. NY, (1948).
Bottom edges rubbed, else very good in price clipped, internally mended, frayed dustwrapper. Quill & Brush 54-847 1983 $100

MAILER, NORMAN   The Naked and the Dead. NY: (1948).
Extremities lightly rubbed, else very fine in slightly chipped dust
wrapper. Owner's signature. First edition. Bromer 25-70 1983
$100

MAILER, NORMAN   Of a Small and Modest Malignancy,
Wicked and Bristling with Dots. CA, 1980. Limited to 300 numbered
and signed copies, as new in slipcase. Quill & Brush 54-845 1983
$75

MAIER, NORMAN R. F.   Frustration. The Study of Behavior
Without a Goal. NY: McGraw-Hill, 1949. First edition. Name
stamped on top edge of paste-down, else very good. Gach 94-603
$25

MAIER, NORMAN R. F.   Studies of Abnormal Behavior in the Rat.
NY: Harper & Brothers, (1939). First edition. Illus. with 16 black
and white figures. Gach 94-57 1983 $25

MAINE DE BIRAN, (MARIE FRANCOIS PIERRE GOUTHIER, 1766-1824).   The
Influence of Habit on the Faculty of Thinking. Baltimore: 1929.
First English edition. Fine copy in publisher's blue cloth. Gach
95-344 1983 $50

MAIR, JOHN   Book-Keeping Methodiz'd. Edinburgh:
W. Sands, A. Kincaid & J. Bell, and A. Donaldson, 1763. 2 pp ads.
Calf, repairs to head and tail of spine, new end papers. Jarndyce 31-
50 1983 £62

MAIRAN, JEAN JACQUES DORTOUS DE   Traite Physique et Historique de
l'Aurore Boreale...Suite des Memoires de l'Academie Royale des
Sciences. Imprimerie Royale, Paris, 1733. 4to, with 15 folding
engraved plates; cont. mottled calf, gilt spine, rubbed. First
edition. Quaritch NS 5-71 1983 $650

MAISSIN, EUGENE   The French in Mexico and Texas (1838-
1839). Salado: Anson Jones Press, 1961. First edition in English;
limited edition (No.98 of 500 copies signed by editor-translator
Shepherd). Numerous illus. Map of the Republic of Texas. 4to. Orig.
turquoise cloth. Very fine. Jenkins 152-223 1983 $85

MAITLAND, JULIA C.   The Doll and Her Friends. Grant &
Griffith, 1852. 4 illus. by H.K. Browne. Dark blue morocco grain
blind stamp decor. cloth, rear cvr. sl. marked, contemp. insc. fr. ep.,
sl. sprung, vg. Hodgkins 27-145 1983 £20

MAJOR, EMIL   Urs Graf. Basel: Holbein-Verlag, n.d.
112 plates with 151 illus. Frontis. Large 4to. Cloth. Dust jacket.
Ars Libri 32-280 1983 $65

MAJOR, RALPH H.   Classic Description of Disease with
Biographical Sketches of the Authors. Springfield, 1932. First
edition. 8vo. Orig. binding. Fye H-3-368 1983 $60

MAJOR, RALPH H.   Classic Descriptions of Disease.
Springfield, (1939). 4to, d.w. Mint. Argosy 713-353 1983 $85

MAJOR, RALPH H.   Classic Descriptions of Disease.
Springfield, 1939. Second edition. 8vo. Orig. binding. Fye H-3-
369 1983 $50

MAKOWER, STANLEY   The Mirror of Music. London: John Lane,
1895. First edition. Orig. decorated cloth. Fine. MacManus 279-
3482 1983 $45

MAKOWER, WALTER   Practical Measurements in Radio-
Activity. London: Longmans, 1912. First edition. 8vo. Orig.
blue cloth. A little rubbed. Zeitlin 264-280 1983 $50

MAKOWER, WALTER   The Radioactive Substances, their
properties and behaviour... London: Kegan Paul, etc., 1908.
First edition. 8vo. Orig. red stamped cloth. Ads. 23 full
page graphs and photographic plates. A very good copy. Zeitlin
264-281 1983 $40

MALAMUD, BERNARD   Dubin's Lives. New York, (1979). 8vo.
Cloth. 1 of 750 copies specially bound (red cloth). One corner
lightly bumped, else fine. In Our Time 156-528 1983 $85

MALAMUD, BERNARD   God's Grace. New York: Farrar, (1982).
Cloth. First edition. One of 300 numbered copies, specially bound,
and signed by the author. Mint as issued, in cloth slipcase. Reese
20-656 1983 $75

MALATESTA, ENZIO   Armi Ed Armaioli D'Italia. Roma 1946.
Photos, boards, front inner hinge detached, slight staining to
covers. King 46-617 1983 $45

MALCOLM, JOHN   The Government of India. London, 1833.
Half calf, hinges and corners rubbed and chipped. 8vo. Good.
Edwards 1044-463 1983 £850

MALCOLM, JOHN   The History of Persia. London, 1815.
First edition. Large thick paper copy. Folding map, 22 plates.
2 vols. Uncut. Unopened. Orig. boards rebacked with orig. spines
laid down. Good. Edwards 1044-462 1983 £850

MALCOLM, JOHN   A Memoir of Central India. London, 1823.
2 folding maps. Cont. half tan calf, red labels. With the Marquis of
Tweeddale's bookplate. 8vo. Good. Edwards 1044-468 1983 £100

MALCOLM, JOHN   A Memoir of Central India. London, 1823.
Folding map, folding coloured geological sketch. 2 vols. Straight-
grain calf, labels. 8vo. Good. Edwards 1044-465 1983 £75

MALCOLM, JOHN   The Political History of India. London,
1826. 2 Vols. Diced calf, morocco labels. 8vo. Good. Edwards 1044-
466 1983 £75

MALCOLM, JOHN   Sketch of the Political History of India.
London, 1811. Calf, label. The Signet Library copy with their crest
on boards. 8vo. Good. edwards 1044-464 1983 £50

MALCOLM, JOHN   Sketches of Persia. London, 1827.
2 vols. Sm.8vo. Half calf, by J. Marshall of Alloa, with his ticket.
Hinges rubbed. From the Alva House library with its bookplate. Good.
Edwards 1044-467 1983 £95

MALCOLM, JOHN   Sketches in Persia... London:
Murray, 1827. First edition. 2 vols. 8vo. Cont. half calf,
spine gilt. A fine copy. Ximenes 63-607 1983 $150

MALCOLM, JOHN   Sketches of Persia. London, 1828.
New edition. 2 vols. Quarter calf. 8vo. Good. Edwards 1044-469
1983 £80

MALESCI, GIOVANNI   Catalogazione illustrata della pittura
a olio di Giovanni Fattori. Novara: Istituto Geografico De Agostini,
1961. 804 illus. Large 4to. Cloth. Dust jacket. Ars Libri
33-462 1983 $125

MALET, H.   The Historical Memoirs of the XVIIIth
Hussars. Winchester, 1907. Portrait frontis. 7 coloured uniform
plates, 16 other plates, illus. T.e.g. Good. Edwards 1042-529
1983 £90

MALET, LUCAS, PSEUD.
Please turn to
HARRISON, MARY ST. LEGER KINGSLEY

MALGAIGNE, JOSEPH FRANCIS   Concours Pour La Chaire De Medecine
Operatoire Et Appareils. Paris, Imprimerie Administrative de Paul
Dupont, 1850. 1st ed., 8vo, stamp on title, some light spotting,
recent quarter green morocco, marbled boards, orig. plain paper upper
wrapper preserved with signed presentation inscription from author.
Pickering & Chatto 22-63 1983 $185

MALINOWSKI, BRONISLAW   A Scientific Theory of Culture. Chapel Hill, N. C.: Univ. of North Carolina Press, 1944. First edition. Dust jacket. Gach 95-346 1983 $20

MALLE, LUIGI   Il Sacro Monte di Orta. Trieste, 1963. 32, (8)pp., 25 color plates. 12 text illus. (2 tipped-in color). Folio. Boards. D.j. Ars Libri SB 26-131 1983 $75

MALLE, LUIGI   Incontri con Gaudenzio. Torino: Tipografia Impronta, 1969. 281 plates (partly in color). Stout 4to. Cloth. Ars Libri 33-136 1983 $100

MALLESON, G. B.   The Decisive Battles of India. London, 1914. Fourth edition with corrected index. Portrait frontis. Folding map, 3 plans, 1 folding. 8vo. Orig. cloth. Good. Edwards 1044-472 1983 £15

MALLESON, G. B.   History of Afghanistan. London, 1878. Folding map. 8vo. Orig. cloth. Presentation copy from publisher: "Joseph Hatton Esq With the Publisher's Compts." Good. Edwards 1044-474 1983 £40

MALLESON, G. B.   History of the French in India. London, 1868. 3 maps, 1 folding. Morocco, gilt dentelles. 8vo. The Marquis of Sligo's Crest at head of spine. Good. Edwards 1044-473 1983 £45

MALLESON, G. B.   The Indian Mutiny of 1857. London, 1891. 3 plans, 4 portraits. Sm.8vo. Lacks front free endpaper, a few pages marked, worn. Good. Edwards 1044-475 1983 £20

MALLET, CHARLES EDWARD   A History of the University of Oxford (13th-18th centuries). N.Y.: Longmans, Green & Co., 1924. First American edition (?). 2 vols. Illus. Orig. decorated cloth. Dust jackets (slightly faded and worn; spine ends a trifle frayed). A bit dusty. Near-fine. MacManus 279-3498 1983 $35

MALLET, DAVID   Amyntor and Theodora, or The Hermit. London: printed for Paul Vaillant, 1747. 1st ed., a nice copy in wrappers. Pickering & Chatto 19-37 1983 $200

MALLET, DAVID   Eurydice. A tragedy. London: printed for A. Millar, 1731. 8vo, disbound, 1st edition. Stain on title-page. Ximenes 64-367 1983 $60

MALLOCH, ARCHIBALD   Finch and Baines. Cambridge U. Press, 1917. Illus. Tall 4to, presentation card from Lady Osler. Front cover waterstained. Argosy 713-354 1983 $85

MALLOCK, WILLIAM H.   The Heart of Life. London: Chapman & Hall, 1895. First edition. 3 vols. Orig. cloth. With the bookplates of Maurice Baring. Edges very slightly worn. Endpapers browned, previous owner's stamp. Front cover of Vol. two slightly soiled. Small newspaper clipping pasted to front endpaper of Vol. one. Good. MacManus 279-3499 1983 $400

MALLOCK, WILLIAM H.   In an Enchanted Island; or, a Winter's Retreat in Cyprus. London: Richard Bentley & Son, 1892. Third edition. Orig. pictorial cloth. Edges slightly worn. Previous owner's signature on front free endpaper. Bookseller's stamp on front pastedown endpaper. Little browning of the rear free endpaper. Good. MacManus 279-3500 1983 $25

MALLOCK, WILLIAM H.   Memoirs of Life and Literature. Chapman & Hall, 1920. First edition, half title. Orig. blue cloth. Jarndyce 31-803 1983 £30

MALLOCK, WILLIAM H.   Memoirs Of Life And Literature. London: Chapman & Hall, 1920. First edition. Orig. blue cloth. Spine and covers worn and slightly faded. Bookplate. Good. MacManus 279-3501 1983 $35

MALLOCK, WILLIAM H.   The Old Order Changes. Richard Bentley & Son, 1886. First edition, including half-titles, 3 vols., 8vo, orig. cloth, very light discolouration of the boards of one volume, but still a very good copy. Fenning 60-265 1983 £45

MALLOCK, WILLIAM H.   A Romance Of The Nineteenth Century. London: Chatto & Windus, 1881. Second edition with new preface. 2 vols. Orig. grey decorated cloth. Spines and covers slightly worn at the edges and ends. Former owner's signature. Very good. MacManus 279-3502 1983 $250

MALLOCK, WILLIAM H.   A Romance of the Nineteenth Century. Chatto & Windus, 1881. Half titles, half calf, red and green labels, marbled boards faded. First edition, 2 vols. Jarndyce 30-468 1983 £32

MALLOCK, WILLIAM H.   A Romance of the Nineteenth Century. London: Chatto & Windus, 1892. New edition, revised. Orig. cloth. Very fine. MacManus 279-3503 1983 $20

MALLOCK, WILLIAM H.   Studies Of Contemporary Superstition. London: Ward & Downey, 1895. First edition. Orig. green cloth. Spine ends a trifle rubbed. Cover corners slightly bent. Former owner's signature. Very good. MacManus 279-3504 1983 $50

MALO, CHARLES   La Corbeille de Fruits. Paris: Janet, (1819). First edition. 12mo. Illus. with hand-colored plates. Cont. quarter-calf (rebacked) with marbled boards. Slightly foxing. Near-fine. MacManus 279-3505 1983 $250

MALONE, EDMOND   Historical account of the rise and progress of the English stage. Basil: printed and sold by J. J. Tourneisen, 1800. 8vo, 19th-century half morocco (some wear). Scarce. 4 large folding tables. A very good copy. Ximenes 64-368 1983 $75

MALONE, EDMOND   An Inquiry into the Authenticity of Certain Miscellaneous Papers and Legal Instruments. Printed by H. Baldwin for T. Cadell, jun. and W. Davies, 1796. 8vo, 3 folding plates of facs., orig. calf, rebacked with new morocco label. First edition. Bickersteth 75-54 1983 £65

MALORY, THOMAS   Lancelot & Elaine. (London): Hague & Gill, 1948. First of this edition. Engravings by Joan Hassall. Orig. decorated boards with printed label. One of 200 copies printed. Spine slightly faded. Bookplates. Near-fine. MacManus 279-3507 1983 $150

MALORY, THOMAS   La Mort D'Arthur. London: R. Wilks, 1816. 3 vols. 12mo. Engraved frontispieces & one folding frontis. Cont. 3/4 calf & marbled boards, marbled endpapers. Offsetting, occasional pencil marks in text. Bookplates. Very good. MacManus 279-3506 1983 $45

MALORY, THOMAS   The Romance of King Arthur and his Knights of the Round Table. London, 1917. 4to. Orig. white vellum, gilt, t.e.g. 16 mounted coloured plates and 7 other illus. by Arthur Rackham. Limited edition of 500 copies on large paper, numbered and signed by Arthur Rackham. Traylen 94-551 1983 £280

MALOUIN, PAUL JACQUES   Chimie Medicinale... Paris: D'Houry, 1755. 2 vols. 12mo. Cont. mottled calf, gilt compartmented spine. Some worm-holing, lightly rubbed. Library stamp title-page. Otherwise a very good set. Zeitlin 264-282 1983 $100

MALPIGHI, MARCELLO   Consultationum Medicinalium Centuria Prima... Padua, 1713. First edition. 4to. Old vellum, torn. Gurney 90-78 1983 £70

MALRAUX, ANDRE   Dessins de Goya au Musee du Prado. Geneve: Albert Skira, 1947. 195 plates. Large 4to. Wrappers. Dust jacket. Ars Libri 32-272 1983 $40

MALTBY, FRANCES GOGGIN   The Dimity Sweetheart, O. Henry's Own Love Story. Richmond, Va.: Dietz, 1930. 1st ed., limited to 855 copies. Orig. half morocco & "dimity" cloth sides, gilt, label. Some relevant clippings laid in. Some wear to cloth, else fine copy. Very scarce. Jenkins 155-1030 1983 $85

MALTHUS, THOMAS ROBERT   An Essay on the Principle of Population. London: John Murray, 1817. 5th edition, with important additions. 3 vols., 8vo, cont. calf, blind stamped borders, spine gilt, red morocco labels, upper joint of volume beginning to split, but a very good set. Pickering & Chatto 21-71 1983 $600

MALTHUS, THOMAS ROBERT Essai Sur Le Principe De Population. Paris, Guillaumin, 1845. 8vo, engraved portrait, some light foxing, cont. morocco backed boards, spine gilt, raised bands. Pickering & Chatto 21-72 1983 $250

MALTHUS, THOMAS ROBERT Principles of Political Economy. London: John Murray, 1820. First edition, 8vo, publisher's advertisements, later half calf, maroon hard grain cloth sides, rebacked, occasional light blue pencil marginalia, internally a fine copy. Pickering & Chatto 21-73 1983 $1,250

MALTHUS, THOMAS ROBERT Principles of Political Economy. London: William Pickering, 1836. 2nd. ed., 8vo, full polished calf, gilt borders, spine gilt, raised bands, black morocco labels rubbed, internally a fine copy, bookplate. Rare 2nd ed. bound in the distinctive style of H.M. Treasury Library. Pickering & Chatto 21-74 1983 $600

MALVASIA, CARLO CESARE Il Claustro di S. Michele in Bosco di Bologna, dipinto dal famoso Lodovico Carracci... Bologna: Eredi d'Antonio Pisarri, 1694. 20 full-page copperplate engravings (4 folding). Culs-de-lampe, lettrines. Small folio. Old speckled heavy-paper wrappers. The frescoes engraved by Giacopo Giovannini are almost totally obliterated. Rare. Ars Libri 33-96 1983 $1,250

MALVAUX, ABBE J. DE Les Moyens De Detruire La Mendicite En France. Chalons -sur-Marne, Chez Seneuze, 1779. 1st ed., 8vo, errata and privilege, cont. speckled calf, spine with raised bands, red morocco label. A very good, crisp copy. Pickering & Chatto 21-75 1983 $750

MALVEZZI, VIRGILIO Considerations Upon the Lives of Alcibiades and Corialanus... London, printed by William Wilson for Hunphrey Mosely, 1650. 12mo, orig. sheep, inner cords breaking, bit worn, name on title. First and only edition. Ravenstree 97-72 1983 $180

MALVEZZI, VIRGILIO Romulus and Tarquin. London: J. Haviland for John Benson, 1638. Second edition. Small 8vo. Orig. calf. Engraved title-page by William Marshall. Slight marginal browning on first 3 leaves, but a crisp copy. Traylen 94-552 1983 £70

MAMMY Tittleback and Her Family. David Bogue, n.d. (ca.1880). Sq. 8vo. Frontis. Title vignette & 7 plates by Al (Lydon?). Red decorated cloth. Recased & worn. Small onlaid plate. Greer 39-57 1983 £15

MAN, HENRY Mr. Bentley; Or, The Rural Philosopher. A Tale. Dublin; Printed for W. Whitestone, 1777. 2 vols. in one, 12mo, cont. calf, a trifle rubbed. Hill 165-74 1983 £60

MANAZZALE, ANDRE Itineraire instructif de Rome et de ses Environs. Rome: Francois Bourlie, 1816. 3rd ed., 12mo, 2 vols, orig. boards and paper labels. Engraved views on plates, imprimatur leaves. Hinges of one cover tender, else a fine copy. Trebizond 18-144 1983 $125

MANCHESTER, HERBERT Four Centuries of Sport in America, 1490-1890. NY: Derrydale Press, 1931. Illus. from orig. sources. With 100 illus. (many full-page). Edition ltd. to 850 copies. Brown gilt-stamped cloth. Karmiole 76-36 1983 $175

MANCHESTER, IRVING E. The History of Colebrook... (Winsted), 1935. Ed. limited to 750 copies. Illus. 8vo. Morrill 288-589 1983 $25

MANCHINI, MARIA The Apology: or the Genuine Memoirs of Madam Maria Manchini. London: J. Magnes & R. Bentley, 1679. First (only) edition in English. 8vo, cont. panelled calf, license leaf, 1 page advertisements, orig. initial and final blanks present. Minor wear to hinges, but a very good copy. Very rare. Trebizond 18-108 1983 $375

MANCIGOTTI, MARIO Simone Cantarini il Pesarese. Pesaro: Banca Popolare Pesarese, 1975. 30 color plates. 187 illus. Small folio. Cloth. Slipcase. Ars Libri 33-66 1983 $150

MANCO-CAPAC, PSEUD.
Please turn to
MAURY, MATTHEW FONTAINE

MANDER, SAMUEL S. Our Opium Trade with China. Simpkin, Marshall; Wolferhampton: J. McD. Roebuck, 1877. Disbound, retaining front. printed wrapper. First edition. Jarndyce 31-110 1983 £22

MANDERSON, CHARLES F. The Twin Seven-Shooters. NY (1902). Illus., tall 8vo, gilt-pict. cloth, rubbed. Argosy 710-89 1983 $25

MANDEVILLE, JOHN Tractato de le piu maravegliose cosse e piu notabile che se trovano in le parte del mondo... Milan: Petrus de Corneno, July 31, 1480. First Italian edition. 4to, vellum. 9 ff. supplied in facs. on old paper. Title mounted, with lower blank part cut off. Some stains and wormholes. Kraus 164-152 1983 $4,800

MANET, EDOUARD Manet raconte par lui-meme. Paris: Henri Laurens, 1926. 2 vols. 353 heliogravure plates with tissue guards. Large 4to. Marbled boards, 3/4 leather. Orig. wrappers bound in. Edition limited to 700 copies. Printed on Arches. Ars Libri 32-420 1983 $850

MANFREDI, GIROLAMO Opera nova intitulata il Perche utlis-sima ad intendere le cagioni de molte cose. Venice: Benedetto de Bendoni, 13 September 1532. Woodcut on title. Small 8vo. Modern flexible boards. Ms. title on spine. Title stained and with library stamps. Marginal worming, some of it repaired. Kraus 164-154 1983 $350

MANFREDI, GIROLAMO Prognosticatio 1481/82. Bologna: Henricus de Colonia, 1481. 4to. Half vellum. From the Giuseppe Martini Library. Only known copy. Kraus 164-153 1983 $4,200

MANGAM, WILLIAM DANIEL The Clarks of Montana. (New York: Silver Bow Press), 1939. First edition. Portrait, plates, folding facsimile. Stiff brown wrappers. Fine. Bradley 65-133 1983 $325

MANGILI, RENZO Filippo Comerio. Bergamo: Edizioni "Monumenta Bergomensia", 1978. 310 illus. Large 4to. Cloth. Dust jacket. Slipcase. Ars Libri 33-114 1983 $100

MANGILI, RENZO Vincenzo Bonomini. Bergamo: Edizioni "Monumenta Bergomensia", 1975. 287 illus. Small folio. Cloth. Dust jacket. Ars Libri 33-41 1983 $85

MANGIN, NICOLE S. L'oeuvre de Georges Braque. Peintures. Paris: Maeght Editeur, 1959-1973. 6 vols. Most prof. illus. in heliogravure and color. Large square 4to. Decorated cloth ring-binders, embossed in color with a design by Braque. Ars Libri 32-64 1983 $1,250

MANHOOD, HAROLD A. Apples By Night. London: Jonathan Cape, (1932). First edition. 8vo. Orig. cloth. Dust jacket. Fine copy. Jaffe 1-239 1983 $65

MANHOOD, HAROLD A. Bread and Vinegar. London: The White Owl Press, 1931. First edition. Orig. vellum. One of 20 copies on iridescent Japam vellum signed by author. With a leaf from the orig. manuscript tipped in, and a publisher's ad. for the book laid in. Covers slightly spotted and warped. A trifle foxed. Very good. MacManus 279-3508 1983 $150

MANHOOD, HAROLD A. Bread and Vinegar. London: The White Owl Press, 1931. First edition. 8vo. Frontis. by Royland Hilder. Orig. cloth. Limited to 205 copies signed by the author. Covers somewhat darkened, but a fine copy. Jaffe 1-237 1983 $75

MANHOOD, HAROLD A. Bread and Vinegar. The White Owl Press, 1931. With a frontis. by Rowland Hilder, 8vo, orig. cloth. Fine copy. Ltd. edition of 205 copies numbered and signed by the author. Fenning 62-227 1983 £16.50

MANHOOD, HAROLD A. Crack of Whips. London: Jonathan Cape, (1934). First edition. 8vo. Orig. cloth. Dust jacket. Very slightly dust-soiled jacket. Fine copy. Jaffe 1-241 1983 $65

MANHOOD, HAROLD A. Gay Agony. London: Jonathan Cape, (1930). First edition. 8vo. Orig. cloth. Dust jacket. Limited to 2000 numbered copies. Fine copy. Jaffe 1-236 1983 $65

MANHOOD, HAROLD A.   Little Peter The Great. London:
William Jackson (Books) Ltd., 1931. First edition. 4to. Orig.
cloth. Transparent dust jacket. Limited to 550 copies signed
by the author. Joiner & Steele, Ltd. slip tipped-in over the
imprint. Fine copy. Jaffe 1-238 1983 $50

MANHOOD, HAROLD A.   Little Peter the Great. William
Jackson, 1931. Ltd. edition of 550 numbered copies, signed by the
author, roy. 8vo, orig. buckram, gilt, t.e.g. A fine copy. Fenning
62-228 1983 £18.50

MANHOOD, HAROLD A.   Maiden's Fury. London: Grayson &
Grayson, 1935. First edition. 8vo. Orig. decorated cloth. Dust
jacket. Very slightly dust-soiled jacket. Fine copy. Jaffe 1-242
1983 $75

MANHOOD, HAROLD A.   Maiden's Fury. Grayson & Grayson, 1935.
Ltd. edition of 285 numbered copies, signed by the author, 8vo,
orig. cloth, gilt. In dust wrapper. Fenning 62-229 1983 £16.50

MANHOOD, HAROLD A.   Nightseed. London: Jonathan Cape,
(1928). First edition. 8vo. Orig. cloth. Dust jacket. Signed
by the author. Slightly chipped jacket. Fine copy. Jaffe 1-235
1983 $75

MANHOOD, HAROLD A.   Three Nails. London: The White
Owl Press, 1933. First edition. 8vo. Orig. boards. Dust jacket.
Slightly torn jacket, but fine copy. Jaffe 1-240 1983 $45

MANHOOD, HAROLD A.   Three Nails. The White Owl Press,
1933. Ltd. edition of 125 numbered copies, signed by the author,
8vo, orig. cloth, gilt. A fine copy. Fenning 62-230 1983 £16.50

MANIFOLD, JOHN   Selected Verse. New York, (1947).
8vo. Cloth. A copy for review with slip laid in. Review pasted
on inside endboard else fine in dj. In Our Time 156-532 1983
$35

MANKOWITZ, WOLF   Wedgwood. London, Batsford, 1953.
Large 4to, orig. dust jacket somewhat worn, but good copy in the
orig. cloth. First edition. Ravenstree 97-73 1983 $75

MANLEY, MARY DE LA RIVIERE   L'Atlantis de Madame Manley, contenant
les Intrigues politiques et amoureuses de la Noblesse d'Angleterre.
(The Hague and Amsterdam, 1713-4). Two volumes in one. First
edition in French of the second, second French edition of the first
volume. 12mo, cont. vellum, engraved frontis., vignette title
pages, bookplate of the royal library of Leichtenstein. Label excised,
hole in spine, otherwise a fine copy. Trebizond 18-65 1983 $125

MANLIUS DE BOSCO, J. J.   Das Luminare majus 1536 ubersetzt und
mit Anmerkungen versehen von B. Schumacher. Mittenwald, (1936).
Large 8vo. Half-morocco. Gurney JJ-255 1983 £25

MANLY, G. B.   Aviation From the Ground Up.
Chicago (1929). Illus, cloth, bookplates, ink inscription, covers
soiled. King 46-724 1983 $25

MANLY, WILLIAM L.   Death Valley in '49 an Important Chapter
of California Pioneer History. New York: Wallace Hebberd, 1929.
Illus. Orig. cloth. Fine copy. Jenkins 153-357 1983 $35

MANN, HERMAN   The Material Creation. Dedham (Mass.),
1818. First edition. 12mo, contemporary calf, leather label. Ex-
library. Morrill 290-267 1983 $30

MANN, JAMES   Medical Sketches of the Campaigns of
1812, 13, 14. Dedham, 1816. First edition. 8vo. Recent 1/4
leather. A fine copy. Scarce. Fye H-3-373 1983 $275

MANN, LUDOVIC MACLELLAN   Mary Queen of Scots at Langside, 1568.
1918. Small 4to, 7 plates, boards, worn at head and foot of spine.
Bickersteth 77-153 1983 £10

MANN, THOMAS   The Beloved Returns. NY, 1940. Limited
to 395 numbered and signed copies, t.e.g., fine, bright copy in
slightly soiled and torn, very good dustwrapper in slightly soiled and
wearing, good slipcase. Quill & Brush 54-855 1983 $225

MANN, THOMAS   Buddenbrooks. NY, 1924. First American
edition, two vols., minor cover soiling, very good or better in lightly
worn and chipped dustwrappers. Quill & Brush 54-852 1983 $125

MANN, THOMAS   Doctor Faustus. NY, 1948. Bright, very
good in chipped and wearing dustwrapper. Quill & Brush 54-854 1983
$50

MANN, THOMAS   An Exchange of Letters. Stamford,
Connecticut: The Overbrook Press, 1938. Small 8vo, printed in red
and black. Edition ltd. to 350 copies. Red wraps., paper cover
label. Karmiole 72-110 1983 $30

MANN, THOMAS   Listen Germany. N.Y., Knopf, 1943.
First edition. Dust jacket (sm nicks). Very good. Houle 21-599
1983 $45

MANN, THOMAS   Thomas Mann Presents the Living Thoughts
of Schopenhauer. New York: Longmans, 1939. Cloth. First edition.
Fine in lightly used dust jacket. Reese 20-662 1983 $20

MANN, THOMAS   The Transposed Heads. Lon., 1941. Edges
sunned, minor cover stains, near very good in soiled and darkened,
near very good dustwrapper. Quill & Brush 54-857 1983 $30

MANN, WILLIAM B.   Trial, Life and Execution of Anton
Probst. Philadelphia: T.B. Peterson & Brothers, 1866. Orig. printed
wrappers. Uncut and unopened. Minor chipping. Jenkins 153-358 1983
$55

MANNERS, CATHERINE REBECCA   Poems. John Bell, 1793. 1st ed., tall
8vo, final blank leaf, uncut in original green paper boards, pink
paper spine, printed paper label, corners slightly worn, very good
clear and crisp large paper copy. Deighton 3-214 1983 £74

MANNERS, CATHERINE REBECCA   Poems. John Booth, G. G. & J. Robinson
and B. &. J. White, 1794. 2nd ed., 8vo, preliminary blank and half-
title, uncut and unopened in drab paper boards, excellent copy.
Deighton 3-215 1983 £54

MANNERS, CATHARINE REBECCA   Review of Poetry, Ancient and Modern.
London: Printed for J. Booth...1799. 4to, complete with half-title,
uncut copy, stitched as issued. A fine copy. First edition.
Quaritch NS 7-77 1983 $200

MANNERS, CATHERINE REBECCA   Review of Poetry, Ancient and Modern.
Printed for J. Booth, 1799. 4to, half title, title, 30 pages uncut,
sewn as issued, fine. Bickersteth 77-43 1983 £75

MANNERS, JOHN   England's trust, and other poems.
London: Rivington, 1841. First edition. 8vo. Orig. rose cloth.
Spine faded. Very good. Ximenes 63-453 1983 $45

MANNERS, VICTORIA   Angelica Kauffmann: Her Life and
Works. London: John Lane The Bodley Head, 1924. 58 plates (10
color) with 79 illus. Large 4to. Boards, 1/4 cloth. Ars Libri
32-358 1983 $150

THE MANNERS and Customs of the Jews. Hartford, 1833. First American
edition. Illus. by 120 engravings, binder's cloth, heavily foxed,
ink name, 1/2 of spine lacking. King 46-476 1983 $20

MANNHARDT, J. W.   Der Faschismus. Munich 1925. Cloth,
slight underlining else very good. King 46-766 1983 $25

MANNING, ANNE   The Duchess of Trajetto. London: Arthur
Hall & Co., 1863. First edition. Orig. cloth (publisher's presenta-
tion binding). Presentation copy, inscribed: "Beatrice Batty, from
her affectionate friend Anne Manning. Christmas, 1862." Spine faded.
One or two signatures coming loose. Edges very slightly worn. Good.
MacManus 279-3509 1983 $185

MANNING, ANNE   Family Pictures, Etc. Etc. London:
Arthur Hall, Virtue & Co., 1861. First edition. Orig. cloth. Spine
darkened. Spine ends worn. Cont. owner's signature. Good. MacManus
279-3510 1983 $65

MANNING, FREDERIC   Eidola. London: John Murray, 1917.
First edition. Orig. cloth. Dust jacket (a little torn). MacManus
279-3511 1983 $50

MANNING, FREDERIC   The Middle Parts of Fortune. The Piazza Press: Issued to Subscribers by Peter Davies, 1929. First edition. 2 vols. Orig. cloth with marbled endpapers. One of 520 copies printed on handmade paper. Bookplate. Fine. MacManus 279-3512 1983 $350

MANNING, FREDERIC   The Middle Parts of Fortune. London: The Piazza Press, issued to subscribers by Peter Davies, 1929. 2 vols. 8vo. Orig. buckram with marbled endpapers. T.e.g. First unexpurgated edition. Limited to 520 copies printed on hand-made paper. Fine copy. Jaffe 1-243 1983 $275

MANNING, FREDERIC   Scenes & Portraits. London: Peter Davies, 1930. First of this revised and enlarged edition. Orig. cloth. In publisher's box. One of 250 copies signed by author. Fine. MacManus 279-3514 1983 $150

MANNING, FREDERIC   Scenes & Portraits. London: Peter Davies, 1930. New edition, revised and enlarged. Orig. cloth. Dust jacket (spine and covers faded and worn). Slight offsetting to the free endpapers. Near-fine. MacManus 279-3513 1983 $45

MANNING, OLIVIA   The Remarkable Exhibition... London, 1947. First English edition. Frayed and slightly torn, internally repaired, price-clipped dustwrapper. Very good. Jolliffe 26-341 1983 £16

MANNING, SAMUEL   Italian Pictures Drawn with Pen and Pencil. New edition. Many additional illus. 8 ads., small folio, orig. cloth, gilt, edges gilt, a very good copy. Fenning 62-231 1983 £10.50

MANNING, WILLIAM R.   Diplomatic Correspondance of the United States. Washington: Carnegie Endowment for International Peace, 1940. 24 1/2cm. 3 vols. Some folding facsimiles, call no. on spine else very good. Very scarce. McGahern 54-128 1983 $200

MANNINGHAM, THOMAS   A Sermon at the Funeral of Sir John Norton, Bart. Lately Deceased. Printed for William Crooke, 1687. First edition, 4to, wraps. Fenning 62-232 1983 £18.50

MANNINGHAM, THOMAS   A Sermon Preach'd Before...Sir Robert Clayton Lord Mayor of London...December 7.1679. Printed for William Crooke, 1680. 4to. Fenning 62-233 1983 £18.50

MANNIX, J. BERNARD   Mines and Their Story. Philadelphia & London, 1913. Colored frontispiece, illus. Tall 8vo. Morrill 288-256 1983 $27.50

MANSEL, ROBERT   Propositions on the Direct Motion of Steam Vessels... Glasgow: Printed by William Munro, 1876. 1st ed., 8vo, printed table and folding plate; inscribed "from the author" on title, and stamp of the Glasgow Philosophical Society; disbound. Pickering & Chatto 22-65 1983 $50

MANSEL-PLEYDELL, J. C.   The Mollusca of Dorsetshire. Dorchester, 1898. Map, 8vo, cloth. Wheldon 160-1217 1983 £15

MANSFIELD, CHARLES BLACHFORD   A theory of salts. London: Macmillan, 1865. First edition. 8vo. Orig. orange-brown cloth. 2 folding tables. Entirely unopened. Very fine copy. Ximenes 63-530 1983 $200

MANSFIELD, EDWARD D.   The Means of Perpetuating Civil Liberty. Cincinnati, 1835. First edition. Dbd. Ginsberg 46-579 1983 $50

MANSFIELD, KATHERINE   The Aloe. N.Y., 1930. First American edition. Boards. Extremities moderately rubbed. Spine paper label chipped. Limited to 975 numbered copies. King 45-217 1983 $25

MANSFIELD, KATHERINE   The Aloe. London: Constable & Co., 1930. First edition. Orig. cloth. Limited to 750 copies. Endpapers foxed. Very good. MacManus 279-3515 1983 $20

MANSFIELD, KATHERINE   The Doves' Nest and Other Stories. (1923). 8vo, bookplate on fly, orig. cloth. First edition. Bickersteth 75-161 1983 £18

MANSFIELD, KATHERINE   The Doves' Nest and Other Stories. London: Constable & Co., (1923). First edition, second issue. Orig. cloth. Fine. MacManus 279-3516 1983 $20

MANSFIELD, KATHERINE   Journal of Katherine Mansfield. London, 1927. First edition. Covers used. Inscription on endpaper. Very good. Rota 231-409 1983 £15

MANSFIELD, KATHERINE   Journal. Paris: Stock, 1932. Printed wraps. First French edition. One of 2551 numbered copies on alfa. Fine. Reese 20-665 1983 $22

MANSFIELD, KATHERINE   The Letters of Katherine Mansfield. London, 1928. First edition. 2 vols. Spines a little darkened. Nice. Rota 231-410 1983 £20

MANSFIELD, KATHERINE   Novels and Novelists. London: Constable, 1930. 1st ed. Orig. printed boards, dj. Very fine. Jenkins 155-886 1983 $50

MANSFIELD, KATHERINE   Poems. London, 1923. First edition. T.e.g. Free endpapers browned. Nicked and slightly torn and foxed dustwrapper. Near fine. Jolliffe 26-345 1983 £75

MANSFIELD, KATHERINE   Something Childish and Other Stories. London: Constable & Co. Ltd., (1924). First edition. Orig. cloth. Dust jacket (a trifle worn & soiled). Fine. MacManus 279-3517 1983 $75

MANSFIELD, KATHERINE   Something Childish. London, 1924. First edition. Bookplate. Nice. Rota 230-386 1983 £20

MANSON, MARSDEN   The Yellow Peril in Action. San F. 1907. Illus., folded map. Orig. printed wraps. First edition. Ginsberg 47-130 1983 $35

MANTELL, G.   The Fossils of the South Downs; or Illustrations of the Geology of Sussex. 1822-27. Frontispiece, folding geological map with sections and 21 plates, 2 vols. in 1, 4to, contemporary calf (rebacked, preserving part of original spine). Very scarce. Some foxing and offsetting and a few plates shaved by the binder. Nice copies. Of the second only 150 copies were produced. Wheldon 160-1443 1983 £250

MANTZ, PAUL   Francois Boucher, Lemoyne et Natoire. Paris: A. Quantin, 1880. 32 heliogravure and other plates. 58 illus. Folio. Cloth. Soiled. Ars Libri 32-56 1983 $100

MANUAL of the Arts, for Young People. Boston: James French and Co., 1857. Small 8vo, litho. title & printed title. Profusely illus., with wood engravings (some full-page). Orig. purple cloth. Karmiole 73-26 1983 $50

MANUEL, H. T.   The Education of Mexican and Spanish-Speaking Children in Texas. Austin: UT, 1930. First edition. Illus. Maps. Orig. blue cloth (worn). Jenkins 152-224 1983 $37.50

MANWARING, CHARLES WILLIAM   A Digest of the Early Connecticut Probate Records. Hartford, 1904-1906. Limited ed. 3 vols., tall 8vo, uncut and partly unopened, nice. Morrill 287-75 1983 $35

MANWARING, G. E.   My Friend the Admiral. London, 1931. 8vo. Orig. cloth. Frontis., 11 plates. Very slightly worn and soiled. Bookplate. With a presentation inscription from the author to H.R.H. Vaughan on endpaper. Good. Edwards 1042-134 1983 £15

MANWARING, H. M.   A treatise on the cultivation and growth of hops... London: Whittaker and Co., 1855. First edition. Slim 8vo. Orig. green cloth. Wood-engraved frontis., several tables. Issued in a numbered edition (this copy is no. 58). Binding a little rubbed. Rare. Ximenes 63-2 1983 $150

MANWOOD, JOHN   A Treatise and Discovrse of the Lawes of the Forrest. First edition. Ravenstree 97-75 1983 $1,500

MANZITTI, CAMILLO   Valerio Castello. Genova: Sagep, 1972. 20 color plates. 208 illus. 4to. Cloth. Dust jacket. Ars Libri 33-99 1983 $85

MANZONI, ALESSANDRO   I Promessi Sposi. Officina Bodoni, Verona, for The Limited Editions Club, 1951. Illus. with the designs of Francesco Gronin engraved by Bruno Bramanti. 8vo, 51 fine wood engravings, t.e. tinted, qtr. cloth, grey label gilt, russet patterned paper boards, spine very slightly darkened and label slightly rubbed, lacking slip-case, fine otherwise. Edition limited to 1,500 numbered copies signed by Giovanni Mardersteig, the printer, and Bruno Bramanti. Deighton 3-216 1983 £75

MAPLESON, T. W. GWILT   Pearls of American Poetry. New York: Wiley and Putman, n.d. (ca. 1853). First edition. Square 8vo. Beveled black morocco publisher's binding, a.e.g., metal band around cover edges. 53 plates on 28 leaves. Cover slightly rubbed and there is foxing to the tissue guards and endpapers only throughout the book. Small stain at top of pages. Metal clasps missing. Oak Knoll 49-131 1983 $325

MARANGONI, MATTEO   Il Caravaggio. Firenze: Luigi Battistelli, 1922. 46 plates. Small 4to. Leather. Edition limited to 1000 copies. Binding worn at spine. Ars Libri 33-73 1983 $50

MARANGONI, MATTEO   I Carloni. Firenze: Alinari, 1925. 88 plates. 4to. Wrappers. Ars Libri 33-85 1983 $75

MARANGONI, MATTEO   Giotto: La Cappella degli Scrovegni. Bergamo: Istituto Italiano d'Arti Grafiche, 1938. 46 plates (6 tipped-in color). Large 4to. Cloth. Dust jacket. Ars Libri 33-171 1983 $22.50

MARBECKE, JOHN   A Booke of Notes and Common Places... London, Thomas East, 1581. 4to, modern half calf gilt, antique style, complete with the preliminary leaf, blank except for woodcut device and signature "A" (title trifle soiled, few leaves mended, with one mend obscuring a word, minor worming to outer blank edge of last several leaves, faint watermarking) large copy with several uncut edges. Very rare first edition. Ravenstree 97-76 1983 $420

MARBECKE, JOHN   The Lyvves of Holy Sainctes, Prophetes, Patriarches, and Others. London, (H. Denham and R. Watkins), 1574. 4to, 18th century calf gilt, bookplate, hinges cracked, gilt crest on covers, minor soiling. First edition. Ravenstree 97-77 1983 $850

MARC, ANDRE   Psychologie Reflexive. Brussels: L'Edition Universelle/Paris: Desclee De Brouwer, 1949. Two vols. First edition. Orig. printed wrappers. Gach 95-347 1983 $35

MARC, CHARLES CHRETIEN HENRI De la Folie. Paris, 1840. 2 vols. 8vo, cloth. First edition. Argosy 713-358 1983 $200

MARC, ELIZABETH   Doris and David All Alone. Hutchinson, n.d. Sm. 4to. Colour frontis. Pictorial title, foxed. 3 colour plates & 53 text illus. Decorated endpapers. Red pictorial cloth, gilt. Greer 40-190 1983 £30

MARC, FRANZ   Briefe, Aufzeichnungen und Aphorismen. Berlin: Paul Cassirer, 1920. 2 vols. 1 double-page color collotype plate. 35 plates. Small 4to. Cloth. Ars Libri 32-425 1983 $125

MARCELLINA   Ireland's True Daughter. London: Remington & Co., 1881. First edition. 3 vols. Orig. decorated cloth. Edges slightly worn. Covers, endpapers and spines soiled. Good. MacManus 279-3519 1983 $125

MARCET, JANE   Conversations on Chemistry... London: Longmans, 1809. 2 vols. 12mo. 21 engraved plates. Cont. quarter red morocco. Lightly rubbed. Zeitlin 264-284 1983 $130

MARCET, JANE   Conversations on Chemistry... New Haven: Sidney's Press, 1813. 8vo. Cont. calf. Ads. Engraved frontis. and 11 plates. Worn, front cover detached. Zeitlin 264-285 1983 $80

MARCET, JANE   Conversations on Political Economy. Longman, Rees, 1827. Orig. drab boards, defective at head and tail of spine, otherwise v.g. Jarndyce 31-313 1983 £22

MARCET, JANE   John Hopkins's Notions on Political Economy by the Auther of "Conversations on Chemistry... 1833. Full green morocco, gilt dec. spine, very good. K Books 307-126 1983 £35

MARCH, DANIEL   The Story of Massachusetts. New York, (1938). Illus. 4 vols., 4 to, orig. buckram, nice. Morrill 286-295 1983 $40

MARCH, JOSEPH MONCURE   Fifteen Lyrics. New York: The Fountain Press, 1929. First edition. Cloth. 1/417 signed. Very fine. Bradley 66-248 1983 $22.50

MARCHAND, PROSPER   Histoire de l'Origine et des Premiers Progres de l'Imprimerie. La Haye: La Veuve le Vier, et Pierre Paupie, 1740. First edition. 4to. Cont. full calf, gilt stamping on spine, a.e. stained red. Frontis. Covers rubbed with front hinge partially cracked but solid. Some foxing of preliminary leaves. Oak Knoll 49-284 1983 $375

MARCHETTI, PIETRO DI   Recueil d'Observations Rares de Medecine et de Chirurgie. Paris, 1858. 8vo. Disbound. Signed presentation copy. Gurney JJ-257 1983 £12

MARCHI, MARGHERITA   Michelangelo Grigoletti. Venezia: "Le Tre Venezie", 1941. Second edition. 37 plates. 4to. Cloth. Ars Libri 33-489 1983 $50

MARCHIAFAVA, E.   On Summer-Autumn Malarial Fevers. London: New Sydenham Soc., 1894. Illus. Argosy 713-359 1983 $85

MARCHMONT, ARTHUR W.   The Man Who Was Dead. NY, (1908). Cover slightly soiled and rubbed, else very good. Quill & Brush 54-859 1983 $30

MARCONI, PAOLO   La Roma del Borromini. Roma: Capitolium-Rivista di Roma, 1968. 142 plates (partly folding). Small folio. Cloth. Dust jacket. Ars Libri 33-42 1983 $100

MARCOU, JULES   American Geological Classification and Nomenclature. Cambridge, printed for the author, 1888. Orig. printed wraps. First edition. Ginsberg 46-430 1983 $50

MARCOU, JULES   American Geology. Letter on Some Points of the Geology of Texas, New Mexico, Kansas, and Nebraska; Addressed to Messrs. F.B. Meek and F.V. Hayden. Zurich, 1858. First edition. Dbd. Ginsberg 47-493 1983 $125

MARCOU, JULES   La Dyas au Nebraska. Paris, 1867. Illus., folded plan. Dbd. Ginsberg 47-635 1983 $60

MARCOU, JULES   The Geological Map of the United States and the United States Geological Survey. Cambridge, printed for the author, 1892. Orig. printed wraps. First edition. Ginsberg 46-431 1983 $50

MARCOU, JULES   On the Use of the Name Taconic. (Boston, 1887). Sewn. Inscribed presentation copy from the "author." Ginsberg 46-433 1983 $50

MARCOU, JULES   Reply to the Criticisms of James D. Dana ...Including Dana's Two Articles with a Letter of Louis Agassiz. Zurich, printed for the author by Zurcher & Furrer, 1859. Orig. 8vo, printed wraps. First edition. Ginsberg 46-434 1983 $150

MARCOU, JULES   The Taconic of Georgia and the Report on the Geology of Vermont. Boston, 1888. Illus., plate. Orig. printed wraps. Ginsberg 46-437 1983 $25

MARCOU, JULES   The Taconic System and Its Position in Stratigraphic Geology. (Boston, 1885). New boards, leather label. Ginsberg 46-438 1983 $30

MARCY, RANDOLPH BARNES   Exploration of the Red River of Louisiana. (Washington, 1853). Map portfolio only. Two folding maps, the first torn in folds and some scotch tape damage. The second in fine condition. In orig. cloth covers. Dawson 471-345 1983 $40

MARCY, RANDOLPH BARNES   The Prairie Traveler. A Hand-Book for Overland Expeditions. New York: Harper & Brothers, 1859. Frontis. and illustrations. Folding map. Original black cloth, blind embossed sides, title stamped in gilt on backstrip. Spine neatly repaired. Wear to corners, else a very good copy. Scarce. Bookplate. Jenkins 151-204 1983 $300

MARCY, RANDOLPH BARNES   The Prairie Traveler. N.Y.: Harper & Brothers, 1859. With maps, illus. Folding map, cloth, some wear. Spine with small piece missing and stabilized with plastic coating. Red pencil marks in text. First edition. Dawson 471-192 1983 $60

MARDEN, PHILIP S.   Greece and the Aegean Islands. Boston & NY, 1907. 47 plates, map. 8vo, cloth. Salloch 385-372 1983 $22

MARDERSTEIG, GIOVANNI   The Officina Bodoni; The Works of a Hand Press. Verona: Officina Bodoni, 1980. First edition. 4to. Cloth. One of 500 copies for America. Oak Knoll 48-457 1983 $120

MARDERSTEIG, GIOVANNI   The Remarkable Story of a Book Made in Padua in 1477. London: Mattali & Maurice, (1967). First edition. Illus. Orig. boards. Covers a bit worn, soiled, and slightly foxed. Bookplates. Very good. MacManus 279-3520 1983 $75

MARESCHAL, M.-A.-A.   Les Faiences Anciennes & Modernes... Paris: Eugene Delaroque, 1873. Second edition, revised and enlarged. Small 4to. Orig. boards. The illustrations are done in Chromolithography by Mareschal. Both ends of spine have paper cover chipped away. Oak Knoll 49-285 1983 $100

MARETZEK, MAX   Crotchets and Quavers. New York, S. French, 1855. 1st ed. 8vo. Morrill 288-257 1983 $25

MARGARETE OF NAVARRE
Please turn to
MARGUERITE D'ANGOULEME

MARGRY, PIERRE   Les Navigations Francaises et la Revolution Maritime du XIV au XVI Siecle. Paris, Tross, 1867. 2 plates. 8vo, original wrappers, uncut and unopened. Fine copy of the first edition. Morrill 290-269 1983 $37.50

MARGUERITE D'ANGOULEME   Heptameron. New York: Alfred A. Knopf, 1924. First ed., orig. dec. cloth, one of 2000 copies, edges very sl. worn. Near fine. MacManus 279-3458 1983 $20

MARHERR, PH. AMB.   Dissertatio Chemica de Affinitate Corporum... Vienna: J. Kurzbock, 1762. First edition. 8vo. Old limp boards. 4 plates. Gurney 90-79 1983 £90

MARIACHER, GIOVANNI   Bronzetti veneti del Rinascimento. (Saggi e Studi di Storia dell'Arte. Vol. 13.) Vicenza, 1971. Lg. 4to, cloth. 189 plates. Dust jacket. Ars Libri SB 26-134 1983 $150

MARIANA, JOANNES   De ponderibus et mensuris. Toledo: Tomas Guzman, 1599. First edition. Title woodcut of arms of the Society of Jesus, woodcut diagram of measures, woodcut initials. 4to. 18th-century crimson morocco with wide gilt-borders. From the Pembroke Library. Small chip at top of spine. Kraus 164-155 1983 $750

MARIANI, VALERIO   Arnolfo di Cambio. Roma: Tumminelli, 1943. 56 plates. 10 text illus. 4to. Wrappers. Ars Libri 33-13 1983 $22.50

MARIANI, VALERIO   Michelangelo e la facciata di San Pietro. Roma: Fratelli Palombi, 1943. 30 plates. 4to. Boards. Ars Libri 33-243 1983 $45

MARIANI, VALERIO   Michelangelo pittore. Milano: Ricordi, 1964. 86 color plates. 20 text illus. (1 folding). Small folio. Boards. Dust jacket. Slipcase. Issued on the fourth centenary of the artist's death. Ars Libri 33-244 1983 $100

MARIANI, VALERIO   Studiando Piranesi. Roma: Fratelli Palombi, 1938. 16 plates. 4to. Boards. Ars Libri 33-279 1983 $37.50

MARIE, ARISTIDE   Alfred et Tony Johannot, peintres, graveurs et vignettistes. Paris: H. Floury, 1925. Prof. illus. 4to. Wrappers. Dust jacket. Uncut. Ars Libri 32-344 1983 $85

MARIE, ARISTIDE   Celestin Nanteuil, peintre, aquafortiste et lithographe, 1813-1873. Paris: H. Floury, 1924. Heliogravure plates hors texte. Numerous illus. 4to. Wrappers. Ars Libri 32-489 1983 $85

MARIE, ARISTIDE   Henry Monnier (1799-1877). Paris: Floury, 1931. 22 pochoir and heliogravure plates. Most prof. illus. 4to. Wrappers. Backstrip chipped. Ars Libri 32-469 1983 $100

MARIE, PIERRE   Lectures on Diseases of the Spinal Cord. London: New Suydenham Soc., 1895. First edition in English. 284 illus. Argosy 713-360 1983 $75

MARINELLI, GIOVANNI   Gli Ornamenti delle donne. In Venetia, appresso Francesco de'Franceschi Senese, 1562. First edition, device on title, woodcut initials, 8vo, light old brown stain in corner of some leaves, but otherwise a very good copy in old vellum, wanting ties. Fenning 60-267 1983 £385

MARIOTTE, EDME   Seconde Lettre...a M. Pecquet pour montrer que la Choroide est le principal organe de la veue. Paris: Jean Cusson, 1671. Only separate edition. 4to. Half calf. Kraus 164-156 1983 $675

MARISON, FISCAR   O'er Oceans and Continents with the Setting Sun. Chicago: Calument Pub. Co., 1904. Orig. cloth with pictorial paper label. Illus. Fine copy. Jenkins 153-359 1983 $40

MARIVAUX, PIERRE CARLET DE CHAMBLAIN DE   Pharsamond: Or, The New Knight-Errant. Printed for C. Davis and L. Davis, 1750. 1st. edition in English. 2 vols, 12mo, contemporary calf, lacks labels otherwise a fine copy. 4 pages of advertisements in vol. II. Hill 165-75 1983 £275

MARJORIBANKS, ALEXANDER   Travels in South and North America. London, 1853. Frontis. Argosy 710-538 1983 $40

MARKHAM, C. L.   A History of the Abyssinian Expedition. London, 1869. 4 folding maps, 1 plan. Quarter morocco, raised bands. 8vo. Good. Edwards 1044-477 1983 £135

MARKHAM, C. R.   A Memoir of the Indian Surveys. London, 1878. Second edition. 5 folding maps, some occasional spotting. Roy.8vo. Orig. printed boards, morocco spine. Good. Edwards 1044-476 1983 £75

MARKHAM, EDWIN   California the Wonderful. New York: Hearst, (1914). Frontis., plates. First edition. Original pictorial rust cloth, gilt. Inscribed by author on front end papers "Edwin Markham, West New Brighton, N.Y., Jan., 1917." Fine bright copy. Jenkins 153-100 1983 $50

MARKHAM, EDWIN   The Man with the Hoe and Other Poems. Toronto: William Briggs, 1898. First Canadian edition. Sepia frontispiece print of Millet's painting. Green cloth, gilt. Seldom seen edition. Very good. Bradley 64-108 1983 $20

MARKHAM, EDWIN   The Man with the Hoe and Other Poems. NY: Doubleday & McClure Co., 1900. First edition with the Pyle illus. 4to, with 2 plates (one in sepia tones) and dozens of vignette illus. by Pyle. This is a presentation copy, inscribed by Edward DeWitt Taylor, brown gilt-stamped cloth. Karmiole 76-91 1983 $150

MARKHAM, EDWIN   Man with the Hoe. S.F., Book Club of California, 1916. 4to, portrait and decorations by Ray Coyle. Half cloth, paper label. One of 300 printed by John Henry Nash. Printed letter laid in loose. Very good-fine. Houle 21-601 1983 $65

MARKHAM, GERVASE   The Inrichment of the Weald of Kent. London: printed by Anne Griffin for John Harison, 1636. 2nd separate edition, small 4to, woodcut device on the title-page, small wormhole in the lower margins not affecting text. Modern half calf. A good crisp copy. Pickering & Chatto 21-76 1983 $250

MARKOWSKI, JOZEF   Entwicklung der Sinus durae matris und der Hirnvenen des Menschen. Cracove, 1922. First edition. Tall 8vo, library buckram; orig. wrs. bound in. 15 color plates, some folding; text illus. Argosy 713-362 1983 $75

MARKS, LILLIAN   Saul Marks and the Plantin Press.
Plantin Press, 1980. Tall 8vo, illus., qtr. cloth gilt over marbled
paper boards, fine in slip-case. 350 numbered copies. Signed by
Lillian Marks. Deighton 3-242 1983 £45

MARLBOROUGH, JAMES LEY, 1ST DUKE OF   A Learned Treatise
Concerning Wards and Liveries. Printed by G. Bishop, and R. White,
for Henry Shepheard, and Henry Twyford, 1642. First edition, including
the initial leaf A1 blank, 12mo, cont. unlettered calf. Fenning
61-253 1983 £125

MARLIANUS, BART   Urbis Romae Topographia. Venice, 1588.
Cont. vellum, 87 woodcuts. 8vo, cloth. Salloch 385-390 1983 $600

MARLOWE, CHRISTOPHER   Edward the Second. Kensington, Aquila
Press, 1929. First edition thus, 4to, illus. with heraldic designs
by Alexina Ogilvie. Full vellum, with leather inlay of Edward's coat
of arms on upper cover, t.e.g., uncut. One of 450 copies. Light
soiling. Very good. Houle 21-602 1983 $55

MARLOWE, CHRISTOPHER   Tamburlaine the Great. Hesperides Press,
1930. 4to. 15 plates & several text illus. Black cloth, gilt.
Edition limited to 400 copies, No. 1. Greer 40-205 1983 £38

MARLY, ROBERT   Fifteen Year Old Mistresses.
N.p. (French), 1937. Limited to 500 numbered copies. Wraps, very
loose, spine torn. King 46-464 1983 $22.50

MARMELZAT, WILLARD   Musical Sons of Aesculapius. New York,
1946. 16 pages of plates, orig. cloth, lettered in gilt, with orig.
dustwrapper. Inscribed on the front fly by the author to Dr Elmer Belt
with the date Xmas 1952, and with Belt's personal bookplate showing
rolling hills, massive white cloud and a eucalyptus tree, inside
front cover. Bickersteth 75-252 1983 £88

MARMELSZAT, WILLARD   Musical Sons of Aesculapius. NY:
Froben Press, 1946. First edition. 16 plates. Lacking front flyleaf, else very good in dust jacket. Gach 95-348 1983 $20

MARMERY, J. VILLIN   Wit, Wisdom and Folly. London:
Digby Long and Co., (1896). 8vo. Half red morocco, gilt, gilt
panelled spines, edges gilt, by Bayntun. 100 illus. by Alfred
Touchemolin. Traylen 94-555 1283 £25

MARMONTEL, JEAN FRANCOIS   Belisarius. London: P. Vaillant, etc.,
1767. First edition in English. 8vo. Cont. calf, gilt, spine gilt.
Minor wear. Ximenes 63-128 1983 $125

MARMONTEL, JEAN FRANCOIS   Belisaire. A Paris, chez Merlin, 1767.
First edition. 8vo, large paper copy. Frontis. and 3 plates before
letters. Cont. wraps. (backstrip defective), uncut. Title dust-
soiled and a little frayed. Hannas 69-131 1983 £45

MARMONTEL, JEAN FRANCOIS   Belisarius. London, P. Vaillant, 1767.
8vo, orig. calf, joints cracked, blank endpaper loose; decent copy.
The first edition in English. Ravenstree 97-78 1983 $85

MARMONTEL, JEAN FRANCOIS   The Incas. Printed for J. Nourse, P.
Elmsly, and E. Lyde; and G. Kearsly, 1777. 2 vols., 12mo, cont. calf.
First edition in English. Bickersteth 75-55 1983 £65

MARMONTEL, JEAN FRANCOIS   The Incas; Or the Destruction of the
Empire of Peru. Dublin: Printed for Messrs. Price, Whitestone
(etc), 1777. 2 vols, 12mo, contemporary tree calf, gilt. Hill
165-76 1983 £45

MARNIX, PHILIP VON   The Bee Hiue of the Romische Church.
(London, Thomas Dawson), 1580. 8vo, full tan crushed levant gilt
extra, a.e.g., very slight wear. Complete with all woodcuts.
Ravenstree 97-79 1983 $395

MARQUAND, JOHN P.   Lord Timothy Dexter of Newburyport Mass.
NY, 1925. Very good, owner's name. Quill & Brush 54-860 1983 $30

MARQUAND, JOHN P.   So Little Time. B, 1943. Signed on
front fly, very good in very good dustwrapper that is worn at edge.
Quill & Brush 54-861 1983 $35

MARQUINA, IGNACIO   Arquitectura prehispanica. Mexico,
1964. Second edition. 16 color plates. 863 illus. Small stout
folio. Cloth. Ars Libri 34-355 1983 $150

MARQUIS, DON   Carter and Other People. N.Y., 1921.
First edition. Argosy 714-501 1983 $25

MARQUIS, DON   The Revolt of the Oyster. Garden City,
1922. Pic. boards, linen back. The author's copy, with his rubber
stamp on the flyleaf. Argosy 714-502 1983 $30

MARQUIS, DON   Sonnets to a Red-Haired Lady, and
Famous Love Affairs. N.Y., 1922. First edition. 8vo, d.w. Drawings
by Stuart Hay. 8vo, d.w. Argosy 714-503 1983 $40

THE MARRIAGE Mart; Or, Society In India By An Indian Officer. London:
Henry Colburn, 1841. 2 vols. Original cloth-backed boards with
paper spine labels (worn; darkened). First edition. Front inner
hinges repaired. Spines and covers rather worn. Bookplate. Good.
MacManus 277-84 1983 $75

MARRIOTT, JOHN   A Short Account of Marriott, including
extracts from some of his letters . Doncaster, D. Boys, 1803. 1st
ed., sm. 8vo, errata leaf, neatly rebound in modern qtr. calf over
paper boards. Very good copy. Deighton 3-217 1983 £24

MARROT, H. V.   William Buler. Thomas Bensley, A Study
in Transition. London: The Fleuron Limited, 1930. First edition.
Small 4to. Cloth. T.e.g. Dust jacket. Limited to 300 copies,
printed by the Curwen Press. With a number of reproductions in the
text. Some foxing to endpapers, bookplate, dust jacket lightly soiled.
Oak Knoll 49-286 1983 $135

MARRYAT, FLORENCE   Her Father's Name. London: Tinsley
Brothers, 1876. First edition in the remainder binding. 3 vols. in
one. Orig. dark green cloth. Spine and covers worn. Inner hinges
weak. Former owner's signature. Good. MacManus 279-3522 1983 $125

MARRYAT, FLORENCE   No Intentions. London: Richard Bentley
& Son, 1874. First edition. 3 vols. Orig. brown decorated cloth.
Spine and covers worn and slightly spotted. Good. MacManus 279-
3524 1983 $250

MARRYAT, FRANCIS S.   Mountains and Molehills or Recollections
of a Burnt Journal. New York: Harper & Brothers, 1855. Illus. by
the author. Orig. red cloth, stamped in blind. Front fly-leaf
excised, and a noted bookseller's stamp, otherwise a near fine copy.
Reese 19-347 1983 $325

MARRYAT, FREDERICK   Diary in America, with Remarks on
Its Institutions. London, 1839. 6 vols. Lacks half-titles but
with two maps. Rebound in leather, boards. Bookplate. A fine set.
In Our Time 156-536 1983 $200

MARRYAT, FREDERICK   A Diary in America. London, Longman,
1839. 3 vols., 8vo, cont. blue half calf gilt, worn. First edition.
Ravenstree 97-81 1983 $135

MARRYAT, FREDERICK   A Diary in America. Philadelphia,
Carey & Hart, 1839. 2 vols., 8vo, orig. quarter cloth, boards,
library stamp on endpaper and title, note on titles, somewhat foxed,
title to vol. 2 bit wrinkled, leaf 5☆ in vol. 1 loose. First
American edition. Ravenstree 97-83 1983 $65

MARRYAT, FREDERICK   Jacob Faithful. Saunders and Otley,
1834. 3 vols, large 12mo, lacking advert. leaf in vol. II. Cont.
grey calf, blind-tooled and gilt, red labels. Some brown stains.
Hannas 69-133 1983 £25

MARRYAT, FREDERICK   Jacob Faithful. Saunders & Otley, 1834.
3 vols., 2nd edition. Orig. half calf, marbled boards, red and brown
labels, v.g. Jarndyce 30-469 1983 £25

MARRYAT, FREDERICK   Japhet, In Search of a Father. London:
Saunders & Otley, 1836. First edition. 3 vols. Orig. boards, paper
labels. Front cover detached along the outer hinge of vol. one.
Slightly chipped. The ads at the end of vol. three are not present.
Fine. MacManus 279-3525 1983 $135

MARRYAT, FREDERICK   The Little Savage, in Two Parts.
H. Hurst & Co., 1849. 3 illus. and half titles in both vols. 2 pp
ads. preceding half title vol. II, 4 pp ads. vol. I. Dark green
cloth, blocked in gilt, Westleys label, v.g. Jarndyce 30-474 1983
£24

MARRYAT, FREDERICK   Masterman Ready. Longman, 1841/42.
First edition, small 8vo, 3 vols. Front. full calf by Riviere &
Son, gilt borders, spines and dentelles, labels, t.e.g., v.g.
Jarndyce 30- 472 1983 £80

MARRYAT, FREDERICK   Masterman Ready. London, 1841-45.
First edition. 3 vols. Cr. 8vo. Orig. decorated cloth. Frontis.
and other illus. by the author. 32 pp. of ads. in vol. 1 and 2.
Spine of vol. 1 worn. Traylen 94-557 1983 £60

MARRYAT, FREDERICK   Narrative of the Travels and Adventures
of Monsieur Violet. London: Longman, Brown, Green, & Longmans, 1843.
3 vols. Folding map. Cloth, waterstains on cover of first volume.
Dawson 471-346 1983 $100

MARRYAT, FREDERICK   Newton Forster: or, The Merchant Service.
London: James Cochrane, 1832. First edition. 3 vols. Orig. boards,
paper labels. Uncut. Geo. Cruikshank's copy with his signature on
the title page in vol. I. Binding and flyleaf loose on the first
vol. With the Herschel V. Jones bookplate. In a cloth slipcase.
Very fine. MacManus 279-3526 1983 $450

MARRYAT, FREDERICK   Newton Forster: Or the Merchant
Service. London, 1832. 3 vols. Rebound in 19th century leather,
boards. With half-titles. Some light scuffing to spines, else
fine. In Our Time 156-535 1983 $100

MARRYATT, FREDERICK   Newton Forster; or the Merchant
Service. Philadelphia: Godey, 1836. Early one-vol. ed. Orig.
muslin-backed printed boards. Published as part six of the fifth
uniform ed. Very good. Uncommon. Jenkins 155-891 1983 $25

MARRYAT, FREDERICK   The Pacha of Many Tales. Saunders and
Otley, 1835. First edition. 3 vols. Large 12mo, half-titles in
all vols. and 2 advert. leaves in vol. I. Binder's half cloth.
Slight traces of use throughout. Hannas 69-135 1983 £25

MARRYATT, FREDERICK   The Pacha of Many Tales. Philadelphia:
Godey, 1836. Early one-vol. ed. Orig. muslin-backed printed boards.
Published as part 7 of the 5th uniform ed. Very good. Uncommon.
Jenkins 155-888 1983 $25

MARRYATT, FREDERICK   Peter Simple; or, the Adventures of
a Midshipman. Philadelphia: Godey, 1836. Early one-vol. ed.
Orig. muslin-backed printed boards. Published as part one of the
fifth uniform ed. Very good. Uncommon. Jenkins 155-889 1983
$25

MARRYATT, FREDERICK   The Pirate. Philadelphia: Godey,
1836. Early one-vol. ed. Orig. muslin-backed printed boards. Pub.
as part three of the fifth uniform ed. Very good copy. Uncommon.
Jenkins 155-890 1983 $25

MARRYAT, FREDERICK   The Pirate and the Three Cutters.
London: Henry Bohn, 1851. Illus. with 20 engraved plates by Clarkson
Stanfield. Orig. cloth. Spine and covers worn. Good. MacManus
279-3527 1983 $35

MARRYAT, FREDERICK   Poor Jack. Longman, Orme, etc, 1840.
First edition. 8vo, 36 plates, illus. in text. Cont. half calf
(rebacked). Hannas 69-136 1983 £40

MARRYAT, FREDERICK   Poor Jack. London: Longmans, 1840.
First edition. Illus. by C. Stanfield. Old 3/4 morocco, a.e.g.
MacManus 279-3528 1983 $35

MARRYAT, FREDERICK   The Privateer's-Man. London: Longman,
Brown, Green & Longmans, 1846. First edition. 2 vols. 12mo. Orig.
cloth. Back inner hinge cracked on vol. one. In a half morocco
folding box. MacManus 279-3529 1983 $125

MARRYAT, FREDERICK   The Settlers in Canada. Longman, 1844.
First edition, 2 vols., small 8vo, front. 32 pp ads. vol. I. Full
calf by Riviere & Son, gilt borders, spines and dentelles, labels,
t.e.g., v.g. Jarndyce 30-473 1983 £72

MARRYAT, FREDERICK   The Settlers in Canada. London, 1844.
First edition. 3 vols. Cr. 8vo. Orig. brown embossed cloth, gilt.
Frontis. A little soiled and joints worn. Traylen 94-558 1983
£50

MARRYAT, FREDERICK   Snarleyvow. Henry Colburn, 1837.
2nd edition, 3 vols. Half titles, some sl. browning, half blue
calf, brown labels, v.g. Jarndyce 30-471 1983 £34

MARRYAT, FREDERICK   Snarleyyow. Henry Colburn, 1853.
3 vols. in one. Large 12mo, orig. red blind-stamped cloth (slightly
worn), uncut and largely unopened. The sheets of the first edition
of 1837, with cancel titles. Hannas 69-139 1983 £20

MARRYAT, FREDERICK   The Travels and Romantic Adventures
of Monsieur Violet... London, 1843. 3 vols., folding map, cloth,
slight wear to headbands, but overall very good. Reese 19-348 1933
$250

MARRYAT, JOSEPH   Collections Towards a History of Pottery
& Porcelain... Murray, 1850. 1st edn. Illus. with 11 mounted col.
plates & b&w woodcuts on India paper. Large paper copy. Half red
morocco, blue 'moire' cloth with gilt vignette cvrs., t.e.g. others
uncut (contents foxed, leather worn top/bottom bkstrip & rubbed at
extremities, bookpl.fr.ep.), scarce, v.g. Hodgkins 27-382 1983 £80

MARRYAT, JOSEPH   A History of Pottery & Porcelain.
Murray, 1857. 2nd edn., revised & augmented with 6 col. plates, many
b&w woodcuts, 12pp. adverts. Beige morocco grain cloth with gilt
vignette, uncut (binding poor, occasional foxing of contents), v.g.
Hodgkins 27-383 1983 £18

MARRYAT, JOSEPH   A History of Pottery & Porcelain.
Murray, 1868. 3rd edn. revised & augmented, col. frontis. & 5 col.
plates printed by Clowes & Son, numerous b&w woodcuts. Green blind
stamped cloth, gilt vignette fr. cvr. (lower corners worn, top/bottom
bkstrip worn, eps. broken at hinges), contents v.g. Hodgkins 27-384
1983 £30

MARSDEN, THOMAS   The Poet's Orchard. Dolgelley for
the author, by Richard Jones, 1848. Half title, subscribers' list
(with three additional names in ms.). Orig. blue cloth, fine.
Jarndyce 30-786 1983 £12.50

MARSDEN, WILLIAM   The History of Sumatra. London, 1784.
Second edition. Folding map. 4to. Half calf, rebacked. With the
bookplate of A.S. Cumming. Good. Edwards 1044-478 1983 £180

MARSDEN, WILLIAM   The History of Sumatra. London, 1811.
Third edition, revised and enlarged. Large folding map, 28 plates,
some slight browning. 4to. Morocco spine. Good. Edwards 1044-
479 1983 £240

MARSH, ANNE   Aubrey. London: Hurst & Blackett,
1854. First edition. 3 vols. Orig. cloth. Spines and covers worn
and faded. Inner hinges weak. Good. MacManus 279-3530 1983 $275

MARSH, ANNE   Castle Avon. London: Colburn & Co.,
1852. First edition. 3 vols. Orig. cloth-backed boards with paper
spine labels. Labels defective. Hinges cracking. All edges a little
worn. Covers a bit soiled. Armorial bookplates. Good. MacManus 279-
3531 1983 $135

MARSH, ANNE   Cronicles of Dartmoor. London: Hurst &
Blackett, 1866. First edition. 3 vols. Rebound in cont. 3/4 calf &
marbled boards. Bookplates. Rubbed. Good. MacManus 279-3532 1983
$175

MARSH, ANNE   Father Darcy. London: Chapman & Hall,
1846. First edition. 2 vols. Cont. cloth-backed marbled boards with
leather spine labels. Lacks the ads and half-titles. Covers a bit
worn. Bookplates. Very good. MacManus 279-3533 1983 $125

MARSH, ANNE   Mordaunt Hall. Henry Colburn, 1849.
First edition, 3 vols. Half calf, a little rubbed, maroon and green
labels, v.g. Jarndyce 30-475 1983 £58

MARSH, ANNE   Mount Sorel. Chapman & Hall, 1845.
First edition, 2 vols. Half calf, spines gilt, red and green labels.
Very good. Jarndyce 30-476 1983 £54

MARSH, ANNE   Norman's Bridge; Or, The Modern Midas.
London: Richard Bentley, 1847. First edition. 3 vols. Cont. green
cloth with marbled boards. Covers slightly worn. Bookplate. Good.
MacManus 279-3534 1983 $185

MARSH, ANNE   Norman's Bridge. Bentley, 1850.
A new edition, half title. Orig. green cloth, a little mottled spine
gilt. Jarndyce 31-804 1983 £10.50

MARSH, BARTON W.   The Uncompahgre Valley and the
Gunnison Tunnel. Montrose, Colo., 1905. Illus., many fine plates.
Orig. pictorial cloth. First edition. Ginsberg 47-244 1983 $50

MARSH, CHARLES   Review of Some Important Passages in
the Late Administration of Sir G.H. Barlow, Art. of Madras. Black,
Parry & Co., 1813. 8vo, orig. boards, uncut, with printed paper
label, spine worn. Second edition. Fenning 62-235 1983 £18.50

MARSH, J. B. T.   The story of the Jubilee Singers.
London: Hodder and Stoughton, 1876. Third edition. 8vo. Orig.
green cloth. Mounted photographic frontis. Presentation copy,
inscribed by one of the singers. Fine. Ximenes 63-332 1983
$60

MARSH, JAMES B.   Four Years in the Rockies... New Castle:
Privately Printed, 1884. Portrait. Original cloth. Some wear.
Scarce. Jenkins 153-214 1983 $400

MARSH, JAMES B.   Four Years in the Rockies. Newcastle,
Pa., 1884. Orig. pictorial cloth. Illus. First edition. Ginsberg
46-440 1983 $350

MARSH, JOHN   The Great Sin and Danger of Striving with
God. A Sermon Preached...at the Funeral of Mrs. Lydia Beadle, Wife
of the Later William Beadle... Hartford: Hudson and Goodwin, (1783).
Disbound. A fine copy, complete with half-title. Reese 18-142 1983
$275

MARSH, LAMBERT H. G. C.   The Tot and Tim ABC. Collins n.d.
(ca.1930). 4to. Colour title vignette & 23 colour plates. Colour
pictorial cream boards. Dust wrapper torn. Greer 39-4 1983 £65

MARSH, LAMBERT H. G. C.   The Tot and Tim ABC. Collins, n.d.
(ca.1930). 4to. Colour title vignette & 23 colour plates. Colour
pictorial cream boards. Dust wrapper, torn. Greer 40-18 1983 £45

MARSH, NGAIO   Final Curtain. Lon., (1947). Edges
slightly sunned, clipping tipped-in at rear, else near fine in
slightly chipped, lightly soiled dustwrapper, "first edition" neatly
written in ink on front pastedown. Quill & Brush 54-862 1983 $40

MARSH, RICHARD   A Metamorphosis. London, 1903. Edges
slightly worn, spine slightly frayed, minor interior foxing. Small
tear to paper covering rear hinge, bookplate. Good or better. Quill
& Brush 54-864 1983 $60

MARSH, SIDNEY H.   An Inaugural Discourse. Burlington,
Free Press, 1856. Dbd. First edition. Ginsberg 46-604 1983 $75

MARSHALL, ARTHUR   Explosives. L, 1917. Second edition,
3 vols. Quill & Brush 54-1643 1983 $50

MARSHALL, ARTHUR HAMMOND   Anthony Dare. London: W. Collins Sons
& Co. Ltd., (1923, 1924, 1925). First editions. 3 vols. Orig. cloth.
Dust jackets (lightly used, a bit soiled). Very good. MacManus 279-
3535 1983 $100

MARSHALL, ARTHUR HAMMOND   The Eldest Son. London: Methuen & Co.,
(1911). First edition. Orig. cloth. Signature on front flyleaf.
MacManus 279-3536 1983 $20

MARSHALL, ARTHUR HAMMOND   The House of Merrilees. London: Alston
Rivers, 1905. First edition. Frontis. Orig. pictorial cloth. Good.
MacManus 279-3537 1983 $85

MARSHALL, ARTHUR HAMMOND   Richard Baldock. N.Y., 1918. First
American edition. Argosy 714-504 1983 $45

MARSHALL, ARTHUR HAMMOND   Watermeads. London: Stanley Paul & Co.,
n.d. (1916). First edition. Orig. decorated cloth. Dust jacket
(chipped, darkened). Very good. MacManus 279-3538 1983 $45

MARSHALL, CHARLES   An introduction to the knowledge and
practice of gardening. London: printed for the author, by John
Rider, etc., 1796. First edition. 12mo. Cont. calf. 4-page list
of subscribers. Joints a bit cracked, but firm. Ximenes 63-182
1983 $175

MARSHALL, EDWARD CHAUNCEY   The Ancestry of General Grant, and
Their Contemporaries. New York, 1869. First edition. Small 8vo.
Morrill 290-272 1983 $37.50

MARSHALL, EMMA   Cross Purposes: or The Deanes of Dean's
Croft. London: Griffith, Farran, Browne & Co. Ltd., (1899). First
edition. Illus. by A.A. Dixon. Orig. cloth. Endpapers browned.
Former owner's signatures. Very good. MacManus 279-3539 1983 $45

MARSHALL, EMMA   Lizette and Her Mission. London: James
Nisbet & Co., 1895. First edition. Illus. by W. Lance. Orig. pictorial brown cloth. Former owner's signature on front endsheet. Covers
a bit rubbed. Good. MacManus 279-3540 1983 $35

MARSHALL, JIM   Swinging Doors. Seattle, (1949). First
edition. Illustrated. Pictorial cloth. Lightly worn. Scarce.
Bradley 65-134 1983 $25

MARSHALL, JIM   Swinging Doors. Seattle: Frank McCaf-
frey, Publishers, (1949). First edition. Illus. Pictorial cloth.
Bookplate. Covers lightly worn. Bradley 66-584 1983 $22.50

MARSHALL, JOHN   A History of the Colonies Planted
by the English on the Continent of North America. Phila., 1824.
First edition. Argosy 716-97 1983 $60

MARSHALL, JOHN   The Life of George Washington. London
1804-7. 2nd London ed. accompanied by the fine & scarce atlas.
5 vols., colored maps, 10 maps, 5 plates, 8vo, full tree-calf,
shows some wear. Argosy 710-566 1983 $200

MARSHALL, JOHN   The Life of George Washington. New York,
1925. 5 vols. Orig. tan buckram, contrasting red & black spine labels,
gilt; with 40 illus. Nice. Boswell 7-120 1983 $75

MARSHALL, JOHN   The Life of George Washington,
Commander in Chief of the American Forces, First President of the
U. S. NY, 1925. 5 vols., engrs., buckram, leather labels (2 chipped),
Fredericksburg ed. Argosy 710-567 1983 $75

MARSHALL, JULIAN   The Life and Letters of Mary Wollstonecraft. Richard Bentley, 1889. First edition, 2 vols. Half titles,
fronts. 2 pp ads. in both vols; facs. letter vol. II. Orig. half
mustard cloth, worn. Ex-library copy with stamps on titles and
margins. Jarndyce 30-1181 1983 £34

MARSHALL, ORSAMUS H.   The First Visit of De La Salle to the
Senecas, Made in 1669. (Buffalo, 1874). Privately printed for author.
First edition. Orig. printed wrappers. Unopened. Minor chipping to
spine. Marshall's calling card laid in. Fine. Jenkins 152-403 1983
$75

MARSHALL, THOMAS MAITLAND   Early Records of Gilpin County,
Colorado, 1859-1861. Boulder, 1920. Folded map. Orig. cloth,
some discoloration. Ginsberg 47-245 1983 $25

MARSHALL, WILLIAM I.   Acquisition of Oregon, and the Long
Suppressed Evidence About Marcus Whitman. Seattle: Lowman & Hanford
Co., 1911. 2 vols. Illus. 1st ed., with page of orig. typed manu-
script, with corrections laid in. Fine set unopened in orig. binding.
Jenkins 153-412 1983 $175

MARSHMAN, J. C.   Memoirs of Major-General Sir Henry
Havelock. London, 1861. Portrait frontis, worn. 8vo. Orig. cloth.
Good. Edwards 1044-328 1983 £30

MARSTON, EDWARD   Frank's Ranche, or My Holiday in the
Rockies. London: 1886. First edition. Illus. Orig. brown cloth.
Worn at extremities but sound. Bradley 66-585 1983 $185

MARSTON, EDWARD   Frank's Ranche. Boston: Houghton, Mifflin and Company, 1886. Frontis. and illus. Orig. cloth. 1st ed. Fine copy. Jenkins 153-362 1983 $125

MARTELLI, UGOLINI   De anni integra in integrum restitutione. Lyons: Francois Conrard, 1582. First edition. With woodcut printer's device on both titles. Cont. limp vellum. Kraus 164-157 1983 $350

MARTIIS, L. C. DE   Gli Oligocheti della Regione Neotropicale. (Turin), 1905. 3 plates, 2 parts in 1 vol., 4to, wrappers. Wheldon 160-1322 1983 £15

MARTIN, ANDRE   Le Livre Illustre en France au Sve Siecle. Paris: Librairie Felix Alcan, 1931. Small 4to, 32 leaves of plates. Orig. wraps. Karmiole 73-69 1983 $60

MARTIN, BENJAMIN   Bibliotheca Technologica. Printed for James Hodges, 1740. Without the half-titles, 8vo. Library stamp on one leaf and with some light browning, but a good to very good copy in calf-backed marbled boards. Fenning 62-236 1983 £75

MARTIN, BENJAMIN   Bibliotecha Technologica. James Hodges, 1740. Calf, a little rubbed, label. Jarndyce 31-52 1983 £58

MARTIN, BENJAMIN   The Description and Use of a New, Portable, Table Air-Pump and Condensing Engine. London: Printed and Sold by the Author, 1766. 8vo. Wrappers. 38 copper-engravings cut out from the original 2 plates and pasted in the margin at the appropriate places. There is a ms. note at foot of p. 33, probably in Martin's hand. First edition. Gurney 90-80 1983 £115

MARTIN, BENJAMIN   The young trigonometer's compleat guide. London: J. Noon, 1736. First edition. 2 vols. 8vo. Cont. calf. 11 folding engraved plates (one with movable flaps), 3 engraved illus. on folding leaves of text, one folding paste-on engraved illus., and hundreds of woodcut diagrams in the text. Old library stamps on titles. Rubbed, spine a little worn. Very scarce. Ximenes 63-531 1983 $300

MARTIN, CHARLES F.   Proceedings of the National Stock Growers' Convention. Denver: News Job Printing Company, 1898. Frontis. and illus. Orig. cloth. Light wear. Scarce. Jenkins 153-363 1983 $200

MARTIN, CHARLES W   The History and Description of Leeds Castle, Kent. Westminster, England: Nichols and Sons, 1869. Illus. with 8 large orig. mounted photographs of the castle; 4 charts (one double-page), a double-page facs., a color map and 9 wood-engraved text illus. Orig. maroon gilt-stamped cloth; spine extremities and corners frayed. Karmiole 75-104 1983 $250

MARTIN, CHARLES W.   The History & Description of Leeds Castle. Kent, Nichols & Sons, 1869. 1st edn., limited to 500 copies, with mounted frontis. & 7 mounted photographs by J. Cruttenden. Red pebble grain blind stamped cloth, bevelled boards, uncut (fore-edge foxed, eps. cracked at hinges, corners bruised & worn, prelims. & some mounts foxed, re-backed with orig. bkstrip), scarce, v.g. Hodgkins 27-350 1983 £100

MARTIN, EDUARD   Atlas of Gynaecology and Obstetrics. Cincinnati: A.E. Wilde, (1881). Over 500 figures, some in color, and 60 fine lithographed plates. Atlas folio, 1/2 mor., (broken; plates stamped on versos; ex-lib). Argosy 713-364 1983 $100

MARTIN, EDUARD   Der Haftapparat der Weiblichen Genitalien. Berlin, 1911. 40 plates, some in color. 2 vols. Folio, printed boards, cloth backs. Ex-lib. Argosy 713-363 1983 $75

MARTIN, EDWARD WINSLOW, PSEUD.
Please turn to
MC CABE, JAMES DABNEY

MARTIN, FRED   A Travel Book. San Francosco: Arion Press, 1976. Oblong quarto. Numerous photo-engraved line drawings colored using linoleum blocks. Limited to 200 copies signed by both Martin and the printer, Andrew Hoyem. Near Mint with orange plexi-glass slip-case. Bromer 25-134 1983 $350

MARTIN, FREDERICK   The Life of John Clare. London: Macmillan & Co., 1865. First edition. Half-morocco and marbled boards, with marbled endpapers. Edges rather rubbed. Front cover a bit warped. Bookplate. MacManus 277-976 1983 $35

MARTIN, GEORGE   The First Two Years in Kansas. Topeka, 1907. Orig. printed wrappers. Jenkins 153-300 1983 $75

MARTIN, HERBERT, MRS.   Suit And Service. London: Hurst & Blackett, 1894. First edition. 2 vols. Orig. blue-green decorated cloth. Spines and covers faded and worn. Good. MacManus 279-3542 1983 $135

MARTIN, MRS. HERBERT   Suit and Service. London, Hurst and Blackett, 1894. 2 vols., 8vo, orig. cloth gilt, quite worn, shaken spines worn, end-papers little chipped, a well-read copy. Author's autograph presentation copy to her daughter, with her note on half title. First edition. Ravenstree 96-110 1983 $85

MARTIN, MRS. HERBERT   An Unlessoned Girl. Marcus Ward and Co., and Royal Ulster Works, Belfast, 1881. First edition, 2 vols. Half titles, orig. dec. turquoise cloth. Mint. Jarndyce 30-477 1983 £95

MARTIN, JOHN   The Dance. N.Y., (1946). Numerous old photos. Cloth. Blind-stamped name on both endpapers. Defective dust wrapper. Very good. King 45-330 1983 $20

MARTIN, JOHN H.   A manual of microscopic mounting with notes on the collection and examination of objects. London: Churchill, 1872. First edition. 8vo. Orig. dark green cloth. 10 lithographed plates and numerous drawings. Fine copy. Ximenes 63-532 1983 $120

MARTIN, JOSEPH G.   Martin's Boston Stock Market. Boston, Author, 1886. 1st ed. 8vo. Some rubbing. Morrill 286-296 1983 $25

MARTIN, MARIA   History of the Captivity and Sufferings of. Phila.: J. Rakestraw, 1809. 16mo, orig. boards, (worn, rebacked). Argosy 716-256 1983 $40

MARTIN, MARY JANE   Ethel Mildmay's Follies. London: Chapman & Hall, 1872. First edition. 3 vols. Orig. decorated brown cloth. Minor traces of tape stains on endpapers, covers rubbed at edges. Good. MacManus 279-3543 1983 $175

MARTIN, MONTGOMERY   The Indian Empire. London, (1859). 2 maps, 120 steel-engraved plates, imperial 8vo, some occasional foxing throughout, one plate torn without loss, calf. 3 vols., engraved and printed titles. K Books 301-123 1983 £95

MARTIN, ROBERT   Thanksgiving Proclamation... Guthrie, November 18, 1891. Small folio sheet. Rare. Jenkins 153-408 1983 $275

MARTIN, W. C.   A Flora of New Mexico. 1980-81. 1300 maps and 463 figures, 2 vols., royal 8vo, buckram. Wheldon 160-1742 1983 £100

MARTINDALE, E. W.   A Bibliography of the Works of Rudyard Kipling (1811-1921). New York: 1922. First edition. Frontis, 9 other illus. Black cloth. 1/450 signed copies. Pencil checks, otherwise fine. Bradley 66-47 1983 $85

MARTINDALE, THOMAS   With Gun and Guide. Philadelphia, (1910). 1st ed. Illus. from photographs. 8vo. Pictorial front cover. Morrill 289-407 1983 $25

MARTINDELL, E. W.   A Bibliography of Rudyard Kipling (1881-1923). London, 1923. A New Edition Much Enlarged. Roy. 8vo. Orig. white buckram, gilt, t.e.g., others uncut. 52 plates. Limited edition of 50 copies on large paper, numbered and signed by the author. Traylen 94-494 1983 £50

MARTINE, CHARLES   Ingres. Paris: Helleu et Sergent, 1926. 65 collotype facsimile plates tipped-in on grey wove mounts. Folio. Portfolio. Cloth over boards, linen ties. Contents loose, as issued. No. 239 of an unspecified limitation. Ars Libri 32-338 1983 $300

MARTINEAU, HARRIET   Berkeley the Banker. London: Charles Fox, 1833. First edition. Parts I & II, in 2 vols. Orig. printed wrappers. Parisian bookseller's label on front wrappers. Short tear at bottom of Part II along outer hinge. Very good. MacManus 279-3544 1983 $135

MARTINEAU, HARRIET   Dawn Island. Manchester: J. Gadsby, 1845. First edition. Orig. decorated cloth. Fine. MacManus 279-3545 1983 $150

MARTINEAU, HARRIET   Dawn Island. Manchester: J. Gadsby, 1845. First edition, front. engr. title. Orig. green cloth blocked in blind and gilt, a.e.g. Fine copy. Jarndyce 31-808 1983 £48

MARTINEAU, HARRIET   Deerbrook. Edward Moxon, 1839. First edition, 3 vols. Half calf, a little rubbed, maroon labels. Jarndyce 30-478 1983 £58

MARTINEAU, HARRIET   French Wines and Politics. London: Charles Fox, 1833. First edition. 12mo. Orig. printed wrappers. Parisian bookseller's label on front wrapper. Very fine. MacManus 279-3546 1983 $75

MARTINEAU, HARRIET   Letters on the laws of man's nature and development. London: Chapman, 1851. First edition. A fine copy, mostly unopened. Ximenes 63-349 1983 $475

MARTINEAU, HARRIET   The Positive Philosophy of Auguste Comte, 1853. First edition, 2 vols. Half titles, 36 pp ads. vol. I, 2 pp ads. Orig. brown cloth, sl. rubbing, v.g. Jarndyce 31-314 1983 £48

MARTINEAU, HARRIET   Retrospect of Western Travel. (1942) 2 vols. Facsimile reprint of 1838 edition. Cloth. Very good in dws with sunned spines and in broken box. King 46-131 1983 $25

MARTINEZ Y SALAFRANCA, MIGUEL   Respuesta de la Dama Curiosa... (Madrid, 1727). Small 4to. Disbound. From the library of Sir Thomas Phillipps. Kraus 164-42 1983 $250

MARTINI, PIETRO   Il Correggio. Studi. Parma: Pietro Grazioli, 1871. Second edition. Small 4to. Boards. Paper somewhat browned. Ars Libri 33-118 1983 $65

MARTINOTTI, SILVIA   P.F. Guala. Torino: La Cartostampa, 1976. 26 tipped-in color plates. 139 illus. Small folio. Cloth. Dust jacket. Ars Libri 33-180 1983 $100

MARTIUS, C. F. P. VON   Flora Brasiliensis. (Munich 1840-1906) Reprint, 1965-67. 15 vols. in 40, royal 8vo and 4to, cloth, some vols. a trifle shelf-worn, 1 or 2 not uniform. A slightly reduced facsimile. Wheldon 160-1743 1983 £1,800

MARTIUS, C. F. P. VON   Hortus Botanicus R. Academiae Monacensis. Munich, 1825. 2 folding plates, cr. 4to, wrappers (title-page dust-soiled). Wheldon 160-1985 1983 £25

MARTIUS, C. F. P. VON   Nova Genera et Species Plantarum, quas in itinere per Brasiliam annis 1817-20. Munich, (1823-) 1824-29 (-1832). Imp. 4to, half calf, 3 pictorial titles, 291 hand-coloured and 9 plain plates, 3 vols. Excessively rare. Binding neatly repaired. Wheldon 160-67 1983 £5,500

MARTUIS, T. G.   The King's Wish. Toronto: Ryerson, 1924. 21cm. Clip cut decorations by L. Hummel. Very good. McGahern 54-130 1983 $20

MARTORELLI, G.   Gli Uccelli d'Italia. Milan, 1960. Third edition, 24 coloured plates and 408 other illustrations, 4to, cloth. Wheldon 160-806 1983 £45

MARTYN, BENJAMIN   An Impartial Enquiry into the State and Utility of the Province of Georgia. London, 1741. Half calf and boards. Library deaccession stamp on title, else very good. Reese 18-53 1983 $450

MARVEL, IK, PSEUD.
Please turn to
MITCHELL, DONALD GRANT

MARX, KARL   Capital. New York: Appleton, 1889. 1st American ed. Orig. yellow cloth, gilt. Very good copy with light fraying of spine tips, and crack in front inner hinge. Jenkins 155-892 1983 $450

MARX, KARL   Salaires Prix, Profits. Paris, 1899. 8vo, orig. printed wraps. (spine chipped). Rostenberg 88-135 1983 $40

MARX, KARL   The Story of the Life of Lord Palmerston. Swan Sonnenchein, 1899. First edition, half title, orig. brown printed wraps., sl. chipping to edges and spine. Jarndyce 31-315 1983 £30

MARY, The Blessed Virgin. London: Richard Fawkes, 1530. Black Letter. Folio. 19th century panelled calf, joints repaired. Woodcut title-page with a large woodcut on verso, one full-page and other woodcuts in the text, and full-page printer's device at end of second part, woodcut initials. Some marginal staining and some lower blank margins repaired. Bookplate of Daniel Canon Rock, with a letter signed from James Danelle to Sir N.W. Throckmorton. From the library of Throckmorton. Very rare. Traylen 94-559 1983 £3,000

MARYLAND; A Guide to the Old Line State. New York, (1941). 2nd ed. Map, illus. Clark 741-7 1983 $35

MARYLAND. LAWS.   Laws of, to Which Are Prefixed the Original Charter. Annapolis: Frederick Green, 1799-1800. 2 vols. Thick 4to, (lightly dampstained) lea. wrapped in cont. coarse cloth. Signed several times by Thomas Buchanan. Argosy 716-258 1983 $150

MASEFIELD, JOHN   Ballads. London: Elkin Mathews, 1903. First edition. Orig. wrappers. With an ALS, 2 pages, 8vo, Hill Crest, Boar's Hill, Oxford, Dec. 12, no year, to the publisher Grant Richards. With orig. envelope. Some fading to wrappers. In a half-morocco slipcase. Fine. MacManus 279-3547 1983 $250

MASEFIELD, JOHN   Basilissa. N.Y.: The Macmillan Co., 1940. First American edition. Orig. cloth. Dust jacket. Fine. MacManus 279-3548 1983 $25

MASEFIELD, JOHN   Berenice London: William Heinemann, 1922. First edition. Orig. boards. Tissue jacket. Fine. MacManus 279-3549 1983 $25

MASEFIELD, JOHN   The Dream. N.Y.: Macmillan Co., 1922. First American edition. Orig. cloth-backed boards. Dust jacket (defective). One of 750 copies signed by author and illustrator. Very good. MacManus 279-3554 1983 $25

MASEFIELD, JOHN   End and Beginning. 1933. 8vo, t.e.g., other edges uncut, orig. buckram, slightly discoloured. No. 134 of a ltd. edition of 275 copies, signed by the author. First edition. Bickersteth 77-156 1983 £35

MASEFIELD, JOHN   Enslaved and Other Poems. London: William Heinemann, 1920. First edition. Orig. boards. Bookplate. In a half-morocco folding case. Very good. MacManus 279-3556 1983 $25

MASEFIELD, JOHN   Enslaved and Other Poems. London: William Heinemann, 1920. First edition. Orig. boards. Dust jacket (spine darkened). Very good. MacManus 279-3557 1983 $20

MASEFIELD, JOHN   The Faithful. London: William Heinemann, (1915). First edition, first issue. Orig. cloth. Dust jacket (spine darkened). Very good. MacManus 279-3558 1983 $20

MASEFIELD, JOHN   Gautama the Enlightened and other verse. London: William Heinemann Ltd, (1941). First edition. Orig. cloth. Dust jacket. Presentation copy, inscribed "For N. de Garis Davies, from John Masefield Novr 17, 1941." With a TLS from Masefield to Mrs. Davies presenting the book laid in. Fine. MacManus 279-3560 1983 $100

MASEFIELD, JOHN   Good Friday, a Play in Verse. Letchworth: Garden City Press Limited, 1916. First editions. 4 vols. Orig. printed wrappers (very slightly frayed at the edges). Limited to 200 copies each. In a slightly rubbed half-morocco case. Very good. MacManus 279-3562 1983 $150

MASEFIELD, JOHN   Good Friday. Letchworth: Garden City Press Limited, 1916. First edition. Orig. wrappers. Limited to 200 copies. Wrappers worn at edges. MacManus 279-3561 1983 $25

MASEFIELD, JOHN   The Hawbucks. London: William Heinemann Ltd., (1929). First edition. Orig. cloth. Presentation copy to the Galsworthys, inscribed on the flyleaf "For A(da) & J(ohn) from C(on) & J(ohn), Oct. 1929." Very good. MacManus 279-3564 1983 $100

MASEFIELD, JOHN   The Hawbucks. London: William Heinemann Ltd., 1929. First edition. Orig. vellum-backed boards. Dust jacket. One of 275 copies signed by author. Small bookplate. Fine. MacManus 279-3563 1983 $20

MASEFIELD, JOHN   John M. Synge: A Few Personal Recollections. Dundrum: The Cuala Press, 1915. First edition. Orig. cloth-backed boards. Publisher's cloth dust jacket (spine slightly faded; some foxing to the covers). One of 350 copies. Near-fine. MacManus 280-5073 1983 $125

MASEFIELD, JOHN   King Cole. London, 1921. 8vo. Boards parchment spine, t.e.g. Limited edition fo 750 copies, numbered and signed by the author. Spine soiled. Traylen 94-560 1983 £12

MASEFIELD, JOHN   Land Workers. London: William Heinemann Ltd, (1942). First edition. Orig. wrappers. Presentation copy, inscribed on the half-title "For Nina de Garis Davies, from Constance and John Masefield, Christmas, 1942." With an ALS from Masefield presenting the book to Mrs. Davis laid in. Fine. MacManus 279-3568 1983 $100

MASEFIELD, JOHN   The Locked Chest. Letchworth: Garden City Press Limited, 1916. First edition. Orig. wrappers. Limited to 200 copies. Very good. MacManus 279-3570 1983 $25

MASEFIELD, JOHN   Lollingdon Downs and Other Poems. London: William Heinemann, (1917). First edition. Orig. cloth. Dust jacket. Very good. MacManus 279-3571 1983 $20

MASEFIELD, JOHN   Lost Endeavour. London: Thomas Nelson & Sons, (1910). First edition. Illus. Orig. cloth. Dust jacket (torn). Bookplate. Half morocco case (a bit rubbed). Very good. MacManus 279-3573 1983 $25

MASEFIELD, JOHN   Martin Hyde. London: Wells Gardner, Darton & Co., Ltd., (1910). First edition. Illus. by T.C. Dugdale. Orig. pictorial cloth. Dust jacket (torn). Fine. MacManus 279-3574 1983 $35

MASEFIELD, JOHN   Martin Hyde. London: Wells Gardner, Darton & Co., (1910). First edition. Illus. by T.C. Dugdale. Orig. pictorial cloth. Small bookplate. Fine. MacManus 279-3575 1983 $20

MASEFIELD, JOHN   Melloney Holtspur or the Pangs of Love. N.Y.: Macmillan Co., 1922. First edition. Orig. cloth-backed boards. Dust jacket (spine darkened). One of 1000 copies signed by author. Very good. MacManus 279-3577 1983 $25

MASEFIELD, JOHN   The Midnight Folk. N.Y.: The Macmillan Co., 1927. First edition. Orig. cloth-backed boards. Publisher's slipcase (quite worn, damaged). One of 250 copies signed by author. Spine slightly spotted. Bookplate. Near-fine. MacManus 279-3578 1983 $50

MASEFIELD, JOHN   Multitude and Solitude. London: Grant Richards, 1909. First edition. Orig. cloth. Very good. MacManus 279-3581 1983 $25

MASEFIELD, JOHN   The Old Front Line, or The Beginning of the Battle of the Somme. London: William Heinemann, 1917. First edition. 12mo. Illus. with photographs. Orig. cloth. Dust jacket (chipped at spine). MacManus 279-3585 1983 $35

MASEFIELD, JOHN   Philip the King and other poems. London: William Heinemann, (1914). First edition. Orig. cloth. Dust jacket (rubbed, dusty, a few tape repairs). With an address slip to Miss Dorothy Hewlett in Masefield's hand tipped to the front flyleaf. Very good. MacManus 279-3586 1983 $30

MASEFIELD, JOHN   A Poem and Two Plays. London: William Heinemann, (1919). First edition. Orig. cloth. Dust jacket (faded, a bit worn). Very good. MacManus 279-3588 1983 $20

MASEFIELD, JOHN   Reynard the Fox or the Ghost Heath Run. L, 1921. Illus. in color and b&w by G. D. Armour, dark blue leather, t.e.g., corners slightly rubbed, endpapers slightly foxed, else near fine. Quill & Brush 54-865 1983 $60

MASEFIELD, JOHN   Right Royal. London, 1920. Roy. 8vo. Boards vellum spine, gilt, t.e.g. Limited edition of 500 copies, numbered and signed by the author. Printed on hand-made paper. Traylen 94-562 1983 £18

MASEFIELD, JOHN   Right Royal. London: William Heinemann, 1920. First English edition. 12mo. Orig. boards. Dust jacket (slightly worn). Fine. MacManus 279-3589 1983 $20

MASEFIELD, JOHN   St. George and the Dragon. London: William Heinemann, (1919). First edition. Orig. cloth. Dust jacket (a little darkened at edges). Bookplate. In a half-morocco folding box. Fine. MacManus 279-3591 1983 $35

MASEFIELD, JOHN   Salt Water Ballads. London, 1902. 12mo. Blue buckram, t.e.g. 1st issue. In slipcase box. Some very light soiling on the rear endboard, but overall a fine bright copy. In Our Time 156-537 1983 $375

MASEFIELD, JOHN   Selected Poems. London: William Heinemann, 1922. First edition. Orig. cloth. Presentation copy to Harley Granville-Barker inscribed: "H.G.B. from Jan. Nov. 30. 1922." Very good. MacManus 279-3593 1983 $110

MASEFIELD, JOHN   Some Memories of W. B. Yeats. Dublin: The Cuala Press, 1940. First edition. Frontis. Orig. cloth-backed boards with hand-numbered tissue jacket (a bit nicked at top of spine). Limited to 370 copies. Very fine. MacManus 280-5688 1983 $125

MASEFIELD, JOHN   The Taking of the Gry. London: William Heinemann Ltd., (1934). Proof copy of the first edition. Orig. wrappers. A bit worn. Fine. MacManus 279-3597 1983 $65

MASEFIELD, JOHN   The Trial of Jesus. London: William Heinemann Ltd., 1925. First edition. Orig. vellum-backed boards. Dust jacket (frayed). One of 530 copies signed by author. Very good. MacManus 279-3598 1983 $20

MASEFIELD, JOHN   William Shakespeare. London: Williams & Norgate, (1911). First edition. 12mo. Orig. cloth. Bookplate. In half-morocco folding case. Fine. MacManus 279-3600 1983 $25

MASEFIELD, JOHN   Wonderings (Between One and Six Tears). London: William Heinemann Ltd., (1943). First edition. Orig. cloth. Dust jacket. Presentation copy, inscribed "For N. de Garis Davies, from Constance & John Masefield, Christmas, 1943." With an ALS from Masefield to Mrs. Davies presenting the book laid in. Very fine. MacManus 279-3602 1983 $100

MASON, ALFRED EDWARD WOODLEY   The Dean's Elbow. Hodder & Stoughton, 1930. First edition. Orig. cloth. Dust jacket (a little worn). Fine. MacManus 279-3605 1983 $25

MASON, ALFRED EDWARD WOODLEY   Fire Over England. London: Hodder & Stoughton Limited, 1936. First edition. Orig. cloth. Dust jacket. Very fine. MacManus 279-3606 1983 $75

MASON, ALFRED EDWARD WOODLEY   The House in Lordship Lane. London, (1946). Edges sl. rubbed, else very good in sl. frayed and chipped, soiled d.w. Quill & Brush 54-867 1983 $35

MASON, ALFRED EDWARD WOODLEY   The Life of Francis Drake. London, 1941. First edition. 8vo. Orig. cloth. Portrait frontis. Double-page map. Folding facsimile. Spine very slightly faded. Good. Edwards 1042-52 1983 £15

MASON, ALFRED EDWARD WOODLEY   Musk and Amber. London, (1942). Edges rubbed, front fly sl. chipped, front endpapers yellowed, good or better, chipped and waring d.w. Quill & Brush 54-866 1983 $30

MASON, ALFRED EDWARD WOODLEY   The Prisoner in the Opal. London, (n.d.). Flys sl. offset, edges sl. rubbed, else very good in chipped and waring d.j. Quill & Brush 54-868 1983 $75

MASON, ALFRED EDWARD WOODLEY   The Sapphire. London, 1933. Edges very sl. rubbed, else fine, sl. frayed and soiled, very good d.j. Bookplate. Quill & Brush 54-869 1983 $100

MASON, ARTHUR   The Flying Bo'Sun. New York, 1922. 8vo. Cloth. Presentation inscription by the author on the front flyleaf. About fine copy in dj which is lightly chipped. In Our Time 156-538 1983 $45

MASON, EUGENE   Old World Love Stories. J.M. Dent, 1913. Mounted colour frontis. Decorated title. 7 mounted colour plates. Several text illus. Beige ornately gilt cloth. Greer 40-124 1983 £38

MASON, F. VAN WYCK   Stars on the Sea. Ph., (1940). Signed, dated inscription on half-title, fine in bright, near fine dustwrapper with light wear to edges and few short tears. Quill & Brush 54-870 1983 $40

MASON, FINCH   The Tame Fox and Other Sketches. London: Hurst & Blackett, n.d. First edition. Illus. Orig. decorated cloth. Covers somewhat worn and soiled. MacManus 279-3610 1983 $35

MASON, FRANCIS   On the Surgery of the Face. London, 1878. First edition in book form. 8vo. Orig. cloth. Numerous illus. Library stamp on title. Gurney JJ-257 1983 £15

MASON, GEORGE   A Supplement to Johnson's English Dictionary. New-York, H. Caritat, 1803. 8vo, orig. tree sheep, joints breaking, name on title, some age-browning and foxing, minor spotting, large copy of the first American edition. Ravenstree 97-84 1983 $265

MASON, GEORGE C.   Newport Illustrated in a Series of Pen & Pencil Sketches. Newport: C.E. Hammett, Jr., (1854). Illus., plates. Printed wraps. First edition. Felcone 22-212 1983 $20

MASON, J. ALDEN   Costa Rican Stonework. New York, 1945. 49 plates. 44 text illus. 4to. Wrappers. Ars Libri 34-356 1983 $30

MASON, JAMES   The Anatomie of Sorcerie. London: printed by John Legatte, sold by Simon Waterson, 1612. First edition. Small 4to. Cont. calf, rebacked at an early date. Printer's device on title-page. A few margins age-stained. Traylen 94-565 1983 £600

MASON, JOHN   Select Remains of Connecticut. Bridgeport: S. Backus & Co., 1809. Calf, lea. label, 18mo. Argosy 710-117 1983 $75

MASON, JOHN   Self-Knowledge. Wilm: Bonsal & Niles, 1801. 2nd American from 12th London edition. Cont. calf, lea. label. Argosy 716-134 1983 $40

MASON, KENNETH A.   An Anthology of Animal Poetry. Harmondsworth: Penguin Books Limited, (1940). First edition, very rare in this binding. Contains poems by W.H. Davies, T.S. Eliot, R. Brooke, W. de la Mare, and others. Rebound by "Everybody's rebound." Spine and covers slightly worn. Very good. MacManus 278-1294 1983 $65

MASON, MONCK   Account of the Late Aeronautical Expedition from London to Weilburg. New York, 1837. Jenkins 152-780 1983 $175

MASON, RICHARD L.   Narrative of...in the Pioneer West, 1819. New York: Charles F. Heartman, (1915). 1st ed. Limited to 150 copies. Jenkins 153-365 1983 $75

MASON, ROBERT LINDSAY   The Lure of the Great Smokies. Boston, 1927. First edition. Maps and illustrations. 8vo. Morrill 290-279 1983 $20

MASON, THEODORE L.   Inebrity a Disease. N.Y., 1878. 8vo, orig. pr. wrs. Argosy 713-365 1983 $35

MASON, VIRGINIA   The Public Life and Diplomatic Correspondence of James M. Mason... New York & Washington, Neale, 1906. Second thousand. Portrait. 8vo, half-leather, marbled sides. Ex-library. Morrill 286-642 1983 $50

MASON, WILLIAM   The dean and the squire: a political eclogue. London: J. Debrett, 1782. First edition. 4to. Disbound. Ximenes 63-372 1983 $125

MASON, WILLIAM   Elfrida, a dramatic poem, written on the model of the ancient Greek tragedy. London: printed for J. and P. Knapton, 1752. 1st ed., 4to, a little spotting with some light waterstaining at the end, wrappers. Pickering & Chatto 19-38 1983 $125

MASON, WILLIAM   The English Garden: a Poem. Book I. London, 1772. Book II. York, Ward, 1777. 1st ed., 2 works in 1, small 4to, advt. leaf, modern qtr. cloth, marbled boards, excellent clean and large copy. Deighton 3-220 1983 £34

MASON, WILLIAM   The English Garden. Printed by A. Ward: and sold by J. Dodsley; T. Cadell; and R. Faulder; and J. Todd, in York. 1783. 8vo, orig. calf, spine gilt. Damp stain in inner margin of title and front fly wear at head and foot of spine, upper joint cracked. First collected edition. Bickersteth 75-57 1983 £65

MASON, WILLIAM   An Epistle to Dr. Shebbeare. London: Printed for J. Almon...MDCCLXXVII. 4to, new wraps. First edition. A fine copy. Quaritch NS 7-78 1983 $175

MASON, WILLIAM   An Heroic Postscript to the Public. London: Printed for J. Almon...MDCCLXXIV. 4to, complete with half-title and final leaf of ads.; new wraps. Seventh edition. Quaritch NS 7-79 1983 $75

MASON, WILLIAM   An Heroic Epistle to Sir William Chambers, Knight... London: for J. Almon, 1773. Eleventh edition. 4to. Wrappers. Heath 48-361 1983 £25

MASON, WILLIAM   Ode to Mr. Pinchbeck. London: Printed for J. Almon...MDCCLXXVI. 4to, new wraps. First edition. A fine copy. Quaritch NS 7-80 1983 $200

MASON, WILLIAM   Poems. A new edition. York, Ward, 1771. 2nd edition, first York edition, sm. 8vo, contents leaf, cont. calf, morocco label, upper joint cracking but secure, a very good clean copy. Deighton 3-221 1983 £55

MASON, WILLIAM   Poems. York: Ward, 1770. 5th ed. Old half calf and marbled boards. Fine copy. Jenkins 155-899 1983 $30

MASON, WILLIAM   Poems. Glasgow: by Robert and Andrew Foulis, 1774. 2 vols. 16mo. Cont. calf, russia, some wear at spine. Heath 48-362 1983 £45

MASON, WILLIAM   Poems. York, 1779. 8vo, orig. calf, slight wear at head and foot of spine. Bickersteth 75-58 1983 £24

MASON, WILLIAM   The Works. London: for T. Cadell and W. Davies, 1811. First collected edition. 4 vols. 8vo. Cont. diced calf, gilt, fully gilt panelled spines with morocco labels, gilt. Engraved portrait. Traylen 94-566 1983 £38

MASPERO, GASTON   Egyptian Art. NY: D. Appleton & Co., 1913. Tall 8vo, index. Decorative blue cloth. Karmiole 75-47 1983 $100

THE MASQUERADE. A poem. London: printed for, and sold by J. Roberts, 1724. Folio, disbound, first edition. A very rare poem. Ximenes 64-369 1983 $600

MASSACHUSETTS. CONSTITUTION. The Constitution, or Frame of Government for the Commonwealth of Massachusetts. Worcester, Isaiah Thomas, 1787. 18mo, cont. calf, (light dampstain on few pp.). Argosy 716-266 1983 $100

MASSACHUSETTS. LAWS.   Acts and Laws, Passed by the General
Court of Massachusetts... (Boston, Young & Minns, 1797). Small
folio, sewn. Morrill 290-280 1983 $35

MASSARIA, ALESSANDRO   The Womans Counsellour: or, The
Feminine Physitian... London: J. Streater for M. Brooks, 1664.
12mo. Modern calf. Some light soiling or staining, marginal tear
in title repaired. Kraus 164-158 1983 $1,800

MASSE, GERTRUDE C. E.   A Bibliography of First Editions of Books
Illustrated by Walter Crane. London: 1923. First edition. Very
slightly bumped at top and bottom of spine, else fine with chipped
dust wrapper. Bromer 25-335 1983 $60

MASSEE, G.   British Fungus-Flora. 1892-95. Text-
figures, 4 vols., 8vo, cloth. Wheldon 160-1859 1983 £30

MASSEY, GERALD   The Ballad of Babe Christabel. David
Bogue, 1855. 5th edition, revised and enlarged, half title. Orig.
green cloth, spine gilt. 6 pp 'opinions of the press'. Jarndyce
30-789 1983 £16.50

MASSINGER, PHILIP   The Maid of Honour. London: I.B.
for Robert Allot, 1632. First edition. Small 4to. Half green calf,
slightly cropped. Traylen 94-568 1983 £425

MASSINGER, PHILIP   Plays. London, 1813. Second edition.
4 vols. 8vo. Cont. diced calf, rebacked with orig. worn spines
preserved. Traylen 94-567 1983 £20

MASSINGER, PHILIP   The Unnaturall Combat. London: E.G.
for John Waterson, 1639. First edition. Small 4to. Modern red
morocco, gilt, gilt edges, a little rubbed, by Riviere. Traylen
94-569 1983 £350

MASSON, CHARLES   Narrative of Various Journeys in Baloch-
istan... London, 1842. 6 tinted lithograph plates, including 1 folding panorama. Numerous woodcuts in text, small library stamp on verso
of titles. 3 vols. Spines and upper corner of 1 vol., sunned. Good.
Edwards 1044-480 1983 £265

MASSON, CHARLES   Narrative of Various Journeys in Baloch-
istan... London, 1844. Large folding map, 6 tinted lithograph plates
including 1 folding panorama. Numerous woodcuts in text. 4 vols.
Cont. half calf gilt, slight wear. Second edition with the 4th vol.
8vo. Good. Edwards 1044-481 1983 £325

MASSON, FREDERICK   Cavaliers de Napoleon. Paris,
Boussod, Valadon, 1895. First edition. Small folio, full color
engraved frontis. and 31 fine steel engravings, by Edouard Detaille
(20 are full page). 3/4 red morocco by Durand, marbled boards, t.e.g.
Very good. Houle 21-656 1983 $325

MASTERMAN, J.   Worth Waiting for. C. Kegan Paul,
1878. First edition, 3 vols. bound as one. Orig. blue cloth.
Jarndyce 30-479 1983 £24

MASTERS, D. C.   The Rise of Toronto, 1850-1890.
Toronto: University of Toronto Press, 1947. 23cm. First edition.
Very good. McGahern 53-116 1983 $20

MASTERS, EDGAR LEE   Across Spoon River. New York, (1936).
8vo. Cloth. A fine copy in lightly worn dj. In Our Time 156-540
1983 $45

MASTERS, EDGAR LEE   Across Spoon River. N.Y., (1936).
First edition. Illus. d.w. Review copy. Argosy 714-505 1983 $40

MASTERS, EDGAR LEE   Godbey. NY, 1931. Signed, limited to
347 numbered copies, this being no. 201, fine, owner's name. Quill &
Brush 54-871 1983 $40

MASTERS, EDGAR LEE   Invisible Landscapes. New York:
MacMillan, 1935. 1st ed. Orig. cloth, dj. Very fine copy.
Jenkins 155-900 1983 $22.50

MASTERS, EDGAR LEE   Lincoln the Man. N.Y., 1931. Illus.
Tall 8vo, parchment-backed buckram. One of 150 numbered copies,
signed by the author. Argosy 714-506 1983 $125

MASTERS, EDGAR LEE   Mitch Miller. NY: Grosset & Dunlap,
(1920). Inscribed and signed by the author. Illus. by John Sloan,
cloth, covers heavily soiled. King 46-311 1983 $20

MASTERS, EDGAR LEE   Mitch Miller. New York: MacMillan,
1920. 1st ed. Orig. blue cloth, gilt. Fine copy. Jenkins 155-
901 1983 $20

MASTERS, EDGAR LEE   Skeeters Kirby, a Novel. New York:
MacMillan, 1923. 1st ed. Orig. blue cloth, gilt. Fine copy with
signed presentation inscription from Masters, Oct. 10, 1927.
Jenkins 155-903 1983 $45

MASTERS, EDGAR LEE   Spoon River Anthology. NY: 1942. Small
quarto. Numerous full-page b&w illus. by Boardman Robinson. Limited
to 1500 copies signed by the author and the illustrator. Spine
slightly sunned, else extremely fine. Slip-case rubbed and splitting
at edges. Bromer 25-248 1983 $75

MASTERS, EDGAR LEE   Toward the Gulf. NY, 1918. Blue cloth
covers rubbed and bumped, good plus. Quill & Brush 54-872 1983 $25

MATHER, COTTON   Ecclesiastes. Massachuset; Printed by
B. Green and J. Allen, in Boston, 1697. 8vo, cont. calf over boards,
some stains, little fraying of blank edges; with the four pages of
poetry and the five lines of errata at the end, name on last blank
leaf with accounts in ink. First edition. Ravenstree 97-85 1983
$2,750

MATHER, COTTON   A Good Man Making a Good End. Boston in
N.E., B. Greene, 1698. 12mo, orig. sheep, worn, endleaves frayed,
note on endpaper. Other than some time soiling and wear, and a
waterstain, this is a respectable copy. Ravenstree 97-86 1983 $3,200

MATHER, COTTON   Magnalia Christi American. Hartford,
Silas Andrus, 1820. 2 vols., tall 8vo, orig. tree sheep, lightly
worn, joints trifle cracked, minor foxing, exceptionally fine set.
First American edition. Ravenstree 97-88 1983 $310

MATHER, COTTON   Magnalia Christi America... Hartford,
1855. 2 vols. Illus. Half-leather, good. Reese 19-349 1983
$125

MATHER, COTTON   Psalterium Americanum. Boston, 1718.
Blindstamped cont. calf, rebacked. A fine copy, laid in a folding
half morocco box. Reese 18-40 1983 $1,750

MATHER, INCREASE   A Discourse Concerning the Grace of
Courage... Boston, 1710. Old three-quarter leather, somewhat worn,
rather foxed, but good. Reese 18-36 1983 $1,500

MATHER, INCREASE   The First Principles of New-England,
Concerning the Subject of Baptism & Communion of Churches... Cambridge,
1675. Stitched. A large copy, somewhat stained, but overall very
good. Laid in a slipcase. Reese 18-28 1983 $4,500

MATHER, INCREASE   A Letter from Some Aged Nonconforming
Ministers, to their Christian Friends... Boston: Samuel Gerrish,
1712. Nineteenth century calf. The leaf of publisher's ads at the end
is not present in this copy. Very good. Felcone 20-101 1983 $100

MATHER, INCREASE   A Sermon Shewing, that the Present
Dispensations of Providence Declare, that Wonderful Revolutions in
the World are Near at Hand. Edinburgh: John Reid, 1713. Later
plain boards. Felcone 22-141 1983 $85

MATHER, RICHARD   A Platform of Church-Discipline.
Boston, 1731. Trimmed, slightly affecting text on some pages. Bottom
corner of title missing. Calf, new endpapers. Good. Reese 18-48
1983 $350

MATHER, SAMUEL   All Men will not be Saved Forever.
Boston, Benjamin Edes & Sons, 1782. 8vo, bound without half title
in new quarter morocco, boards, some age-browning and foxing,
minor spotting. First edition. Ravenstree 97-89 1983 $185

MATHER, SAMUEL   An Apology for the Liberties of the
Churches in New England. Boston, T. Fleet for Daniel Henchman,
1739. 8vo, orig. quarter sheep, marbled boards, joints broken,
first portion waterstained, title age-browned, large copy complete
with errata leaf. First and only edition. Ravenstree 97-90 1983
$120

MATHER, SAMUEL   A Dissertion Concerning the Most
Venerable Name of Jehovah. Boston, Edes and Gill, 1760. 8vo in
fours, unbound, uncut, stitched as issued, complete with the two
unsigned leaves at end. First edition. Ravenstree 97-91 1983 $185

MATHER, SAMUEL   The Fall of the Mighty Lamented. Boston,
J. Draper, 1738. 8vo, half morocco gilt, lower half of text stained
throughout, a large copy. First and only edition. Ravenstree 97-92
1983 $75

MATHER, SAMUEL   Life of Cotton Mather. Small 8vo, cont.
paneled calf, (hinges mended). First edition. Foxing throughout;
half-title rehinged. Argosy 713-366 1983 $300

MATHERS, E. POWYS   Red Wise. Waltham Saint Lawrence,
1926. 8vo, cloth-backed bds. Wood-engravings by Robert Gibbings.
A fine copy. Perata 27-47 1983 $135

MATHERS, HELEN   Comin' Thro' the Rye. London: Richard
Bentley & Son, 1875. First edition. 3 vols. Orig. cloth. All edges
and corners a bit worn. Covers and endpapers a little soiled. One
or two hinges cracking. Good. MacManus 279-3612 1983 $225

MATHESON, J.   England to Delhi. London, 1870. Map,
numerous plates, name cut from half-title. 4to. Spine faded. Orig.
cloth. Good. Edwards 1044-482 1983 £30

MATHEWS, ANNE   Memoirs of Charles Mathews, comedian.
London: Richard Bentley, 1839. 4 vols, 8vo, original purple cloth.
2nd edition of vols. I and II, first edition of vols. III and IV.
The text of the first two volumes has been reset and corrected, and
some material added to Vol. II. Frontis. in each volume and 13 other
plates; 5 are double-page tinted lithographs. Some plates a bit
foxed, but a fine copy in original condition. Ximenes 64-370 1983
$250

MATHEWS, ANNE   Tea-table talk, ennobled actresses,
and other miscellanies. London: Thomas Cautley Newby, 1857. 2 vols.,
8vo, original grey cloth, spines decorated in gilt. 1st edition.
A fine copy. Scarce. Ximenes 64-371 1983 $125

MATHEWS, CHARLES JAMES   The life of Charles James Mathews.
London: Macmillan and Co., 1879. 2 vols., 8vo, original dark green
cloth. First edition. Frontis. in each volume, and 3 other plates.
A fine set. Ximenes 64-374 1983 $75

MATHEWS, G. M.   Systema Avium Australasianarum. 1927-30.
2 vols., 8vo, half cloth. Wheldon 160-807 1983 £28

MATHEWS, M. M.   Ten Years in Nevada. Buffalo: 1880.
First edition. Frontis., 2 ports. Orig. brown cloth. Bradley 66-586
1983 $250

MATHIAS, ROLAND   Break in Harvest and Other Poems.
London: Routledge, (1946). Cloth. First edition. Pencil note,
else fine in slightly soiled dust jacket. Reese 20-671 1983 $30

MATHIAS, THOMAS JAMES   The Grove. A satire. London: printed
for the author; and sold by R. H. Westley, n.d. (1798?). 4to,
disbound, 2nd edition. Half-title present. Rather waterstained,
especially at the beginning and end; stitching loose. Ximenes 64-
375 1983 $90

MATHIAS, THOMAS JAMES   The imperial epistle from Kien Long...
London: R. White, n.d. (1795). First edition. 4to. Disbound.
Ximenes 63-373 1983 $75

MATHIAS, THOMAS JAMES   The Pursuits of Literature. London:
Printed for T. Becket...1797. 8vo, with half-title, an uncut copy
in orig. boards, white paper backstrip worn away at spine. First
complete edition. In addition to a general half-title and title,
each part has its own separate half-title and title and is separately
paginated. First two parts have pub.'s ads. on the final leaf.
Quaritch NS 7-81 1983 $125

MATHIAS, THOMAS JAMES   Pursuits of Literature. Phila.: Printed
by H. Maxwell, for J. Nancrede, Boston; & A. Dickins, & J. Ormrod,
Phila., 1800. First American, from the seventh London, edition, revised. 8vo. Full cont. calf with red morocco label on spine. Some
foxing. Corners of several leaves wrinkled. Top of spine slightly
chipped. Fine. MacManus 279-3613 1983 $50

MATHIAS, THOMAS JAMES   Runic Odes. London: Payne, 1781.
First edition. 4to. New cloth. Fine. MacManus 279-3614 1983 $100

MATHIEU, PIERRE-LOUIS   Gustave Moreau. Oxford: Phaidon, 1977.
486 illus. (40 color). Large 4to. Cloth. Dust jacket. Boxed.
Ars Libri 32-475 1983 $125

MATON, WILLIAM GEORGE   Observations relative chiefly to the
natural history, picturesque scenery, and antiquities, of the western
counties of England... Salisbury: J. Easton, etc., 1797. First
edition. 2 vols. 8vo. 19th-century polished calf, spines gilt.
Folding map and 16 aquatints. Occasional spotting. Ximenes 63-629
1983 $225

MATTHEW OF PARIS
Please turn to
PARIS, MATTHEW

MATTHEWS, HENRY   The Diary of an Invalid. John Murray,
1820. Second edition. 8vo, some light signs of use, but a good
copy in recent boards. Fenning 60-268 1983 £32.50

MATTHEWS, LEONARD   A Long Life in Review. Privately
printed, 1928. Illus. Orig. cloth. First edition. Ginsberg 46-448
1983 $100

MATTHEWS, NOEL H.   Challenge and Other Poems. Wellington,
N.Z.: A.H. & A.W. Reed, (n.d.). Boards. First edition. Signed
and dated by the author. Very fine in dust jacket. Reese 20-673
1983 $25

MATTHEWS, V. D.   Studies on the genus Pythium. Chapel
Hill, 1931. 29 plates, royal 8vo, cloth. Wheldon 160-1860 1983 £15

MATTHEWS, WILLIAM   Canadian Diaries and Autobiographies.
Berkely & Los Angeles: University California Press, 1950. 23 1/2cm.
Dust jacket. A fine copy. McGahern 54-132 1983 $25

MATTHEWS, WILLIAM E.   Gems of the Isle. Ryde: By Henry
Wayland, I.o.W. Times Office. Orig. turquoise cloth, v.g. 1884.
Jarndyce 30-756 1983 £12.50

MATTHIAE, GUGLIELMO   Andrea Delitio nel Duomo di Atri.
Torino: Cassa di Risparmio di Torino, 1965. 24 color plates.
13 illus. (2 tipped-in color). Folio. Boards. Dust jacket.
Ars Libri 33-128 1983 $85

MATTHIAE, GUGLIELMO   Pietro Cavallini. Roma: De Lucca,
1972. 106 plates. 91 illus. hors texte. Large square 4to. Cloth.
Dust jacket. Ars Libri 33-101 1983 $75

MATTHIOLI, PIETRO ANDREA   Opera Omnia. Frankfurt, Nicolai
Bassaei, 1598. Folio. Engraved title. Profusely illus. throughout
with woodcuts of plants, flowers, fish, shels, etc., by Arnold
Nicolai. Full early tan calf (rebacked), with the gilt initials
"R.B." on both covers, enclosed in a cloth slipcase. Bound in
at the end is Matthioli's "Apologia," 1598. Extra illustrated with
woodcut plates from an English herbal. Houle 21-606 1983 $3,975

MATTISON, J. B.   The Mattison Method in Morphinism. NY:
E. B. Treat & Co., 1902. First edition. Publisher's red cloth,
somewhat soiled, front hinge cracked, rear hinge detaching. Gach
95-349 1983 $35

MATURIN, CHARLES ROBERT Melmoth the Wanderer. Edinburgh, 1820. First edition, with engraved portrait, half-titles. 4 vols. 12mo. Cont. half morocco. Lacks ad. leaf in vol. 4. Traylen 94-570 1983 £330

MATURIN, CHARLES ROBERT Melmoth the wanderer. London: Bentley, 1892. New edition. 8vo. 3 vols. Orig. dark green cloth. Portrait. Fine copy. Ximenes 63-129 1983 $225

MATZ, B. W. Dickensian Inns and Taverns. Cecil Palmer, 1923. 2nd edition, half title, front. & illus. Orig. dark blue cloth. Jarndyce 31-613 1983 £12.50

MATZ, B. W. The Life of John Forster. Chapman and Hall, 1911. 500 portraits, facs. and other illus. Half titles, untrimmed, orig. blue cloth, gilt, t.e.g. 2 vols. Jarndyce 30-188 1983 £45

MAUCO, GEORGES Education. Paris: Editions Familiales de France, (1948). First edition. Inscribed to Rudolph Loewenstein. Orig. printed wrappers. Gach 95-350 1983 $20

MAUDE, THOMAS Verbeia. Printed at York, by W. Blanchard...1782. 4to, title-page slightly stained but otherwise a fine copy in new wraps. First edition. Quaritch NS 7-82 1983 $165

MAUDE, THOMAS Viator, a Poem. Published by B. White... and the Booksellers in York. MDCCLXXXII. 4to, new wraps. First edition. A fine copy. Quaritch NS 7-83 1983 $185

MAUDLIN, BILL A Sort of Saga. N.Y., Sloane, (1949). First edition. Dust jacket. Illus. by the author. Fine copy. Houle 21-611 1983 $45

MAUDSLEY, HENRY The Physiology and Pathology of the Mind. NY: D. Appleton, 1867. Orig. mauve cloth, rebacked with paper label. First American edition. Gach 95-351 1983 $125

MAUDSLEY, HENRY The Physiology and Pathology of the Mind. NY: Appleton, 1890 (1872). Publisher's brown cloth. Gach 94-394 1983 $30

MAUGE, GILBERT The Unknown Quantity. L, (n.d.). Limited to 845 copies, this being no. 231, on English hand-made paper, fine in very good dustwrapper in fine slipcase. Quill & Brush 54-795 1983 $50

MAUGE, GILBERT The Unknown Quantity. L, (n.d.). Limited to 845 copies, this being no. 265, on English hand-made paper, fine. Quill & Brush 54-794 1983 $35

MAUGHAM, WILLIAM SOMERSET Ah King. London, Heinemann, 1933. Tan cloth, leather label, t.e.g., uncut. Pub.'s slipcase (cracked). One of 175 deluxe numbered copies, signed by Maugham. Fine copy. Houle 21-607 1983 $295

MAUGHAM, WILLIAM SOMERSET Ah King. London, (1933). 8vo. Wraps. Proof copy. A vg-fine copy. In Our Time 156-546 1983 $200

MAUGHAM, WILLIAM SOMERSET Ah King. New York: Doubleday, 1933. 1st American ed. Orig. cloth, dj. Fine copy in mildly chipped dj. Jenkins 155-906 1983 $45

MAUGHAM, WILLIAM SOMERSET Ah King. London: William Heinemann Ltd., (1933). First edition. Orig. cloth. MacManus 279-3619 1983 $20

MAUGHAM, WILLIAM SOMERSET Andalusia. N.Y.: Alfred A. Knopf, 1920. Second American edition, first edition with this title and first edition printed in the United States. Orig. cloth-backed boards with paper label. Good. MacManus 279-3620 1983 $45

MAUGHAM, WILLIAM SOMERSET Ashenden. London. Later printing. 8vo. Cloth. Inscribed by Maugham on front flyleaf. This copy contains a short ALS from Maugham. With envelope. Some wear to edge of spine, else vg. In Our Time 156-547 1983 $150

MAUGHAM, WILLIAM SOMERSET The Book-Bag. Florence: G. Orioli, 1932. First separate edition. Frontis. port. Orig. cloth-backed boards. Dust jacket (a little darkened). Limited to 725 copies signed by author. Bookplate. Very good. MacManus 279-3621 1983 $250

MAUGHAM, WILLIAM SOMERSET The Book-Bag. Flo., 1932. Limited to 725 numbered copies with a signed frontis., handmade paper, cover corners chipped, spine edges rubbed and slightly frayed, cover sunned, good. Quill & Brush 54-875 1983 $75

MAUGHAM, WILLIAM SOMERSET Cakes and Ale. London, n.d. (1954). Birthday edition. One of 1000 copies signed by the author and illustrator. Orig. lithograph printed at The Curwen Press and several black and white decorations by Graham Sutherland. 4 facsimile reproductions of the first and last pages of the orig. manuscript. T.e.g. Head and tail of spine slightly rubbed. Fine. Jolliffe 26-350 1983 £75

MAUGHAM, WILLIAM SOMERSET Cakes and Ale. London, 1930. First edition. Bookplate. Slightly torn dustwrapper slightly darkened at the spine. Very good. Jolliffe 26-349 1983 £35

MAUGHAM, WILLIAM SOMERSET The Casuarina Tree. New York: Doran, (1926). 1st American ed. Orig. tan cloth. Fine bright copy. Jenkins 155-907 1983 $40

MAUGHAM, WILLIAM SOMERSET The Casuarina Tree. London: William Heinemann Ltd., 1926. First edition. Orig. cloth. A little rubbed. Good. MacManus 279-3622 1983 $25

MAUGHAM, WILLIAM SOMERSET Catalina. London: William Heinemann Ltd., (1948). First edition, variant binding with sliver blocking. Orig. cloth. Dust jacket. Fine. MacManus 279-3623 1983 $50

MAUGHAM, WILLIAM SOMERSET Catalina, Roman. Paris: Plon, (1950). Printed wraps. First French edition. One of 11 hors commerce copies, from an edition of 111 on alfa. Fine, unopened. Reese 20-676 1983 $45

MAUGHAM, WILLIAM SOMERSET Christmas Holiday. London, (1939). First edition. Spine a little creased and faded. Torn dust wrapper. Very nice. Rota 230-396 1983 £12

MAUGHAM, WILLIAM SOMERSET Cosmopolitans. London: William Heinemann Ltd., (1936). First edition, third issue. Orig. cloth. Dust jacket (a bit worn). Inscribed on the half-title "For Lawrence R. Thomsen, New York, 3 May 1946." Fine. MacManus 279-3625 1983 $250

MAUGHAM, WILLIAM SOMERSET Cosmopolitans. London, 1936. 8vo. Orig. red buckram, t.e.g., others uncut, in the orig. slip-case. Limited edition of 173 copies, numbered and signed by the author. Traylen 94-571 1983 £85

MAUGHAM, WILLIAM SOMERSET Cosmopolitans. London: William Heinemann Ltd., (1936). First edition, third issue. Orig. cloth. Dust jacket (spine slightly darkened). Fine. MacManus 279-3624 1983 $35

MAUGHAM, WILLIAM SOMERSET Don Fernando. London: William Heinemann Ltd., 1935. First edition. Orig. cloth with leather label on spine. Limited to 175 copies signed by author. Bookplate. Very good. MacManus 279-3626 1983 $225

MAUGHAM, WILLIAM SOMERSET Don Fernando or Variations on Some Spanish Themes. London: William Heinemann Ltd., (1935). Reprint. Orig. cloth. Inscribed on the title-page "for Petronella Armstrong, Thanking her for asking me to write my name in this book, 18 Sept. 1938, W. Somerset Maugham." Fine. MacManus 279-3627 1983 $125

MAUGHAM, WILLIAM SOMERSET The Explorer. N.Y.: The Baker & Taylor Company, 1909. First American edition. Orig. cloth. Presentation copy to "E. Ording" inscribed; "For E. Ording a very early novel by W. Somerset Maugham Edgetown." Good. MacManus 279-3628 1983 $250

MAUGHAM, WILLIAM SOMERSET First Person Singular. New York: Doubleday, 1931. 1st American ed. Orig. cloth, dj. Some inner strengthening of dj, else nice copy. Jenkins 155-908 1983 $30

MAUGHAM, WILLIAM SOMERSET   For Services Rendered: A Play in Three Acts. London, 1932. 8vo. Wraps. A proof copy. Pencilled note on front wrapper that notes that only 15 copies were run off for the members of the orig. cast. A fine copy. In Our Time 156-545 1983 $250

MAUGHAM, WILLIAM SOMERSET   For Services Rendered. London: William Heinemann Ltd., 1932. First edition. 8vo. Orig. cloth. Dust jacket. Slightly darkened jacket. Fine copy. Jaffe 1-249 1983 $45

MAUGHAM, WILLIAM SOMERSET   Gentleman in the Parlour. London, Heinemann, (1930). First edition. A fine copy in a fine dust jacket. Houle 21-608 1983 $185

MAUGHAM, WILLIAM SOMERSET   Jack Straw. London: William Heinemann, 1912. First edition. 8vo. Orig. cloth. H.L. Mencken's copy, with his bookplate on the front endsheet. Very good copy. Jaffe 1-246 1983 $85

MAUGHAM, WILLIAM SOMERSET   The Judgement Seat. London: The Centaur Press. 1934. First edition. Frontis. by Ulrica Hyde. Thin 8vo. Orig. cloth. Tissue jacket. One of 150 copies signed by the author and artist. Very fine copy. Jaffe 1-251 1983 $285

MAUGHAM, WILLIAM SOMERSET   The Letter - a Play in Three Acts. New York, 1925. Wrappers. A souvenir of the New York premiere, given away by the producer and publisher on the opening night. A leaf listing the cast tipped in. Covers slightly soiled and nicked, Very good. Jolliffe 26-348 1983 £75

MAUGHAM, WILLIAM SOMERSET   The Letters of William Somerset Maugham to Lady Juliet Duff. Pacific Palisades, Cal.: Rasselas Press, 1982. First edition. One of 26 lettered copies printed on Ragston paper. Signed by editor and printer. Rota 231-415 1983 £65

MAUGHAM, WILLIAM SOMERSET   Lisa of Lambeth. London, 1897. 8vo. Cloth. 1st ed. Inscribed by Maugham on front flyleaf. Laid into this copy is a two page ALS written by Maugham. With envelope. Vg-fine copy in slipcase box. In Our Time 156-541 1983 $2500

MAUGHAM, WILLIAM SOMERSET   Liza of Lambeth. London, Heinemann, 1947. Jubilee edition. Half vellum, leather label, t.e.g., uncut. Dust jacket. Endpapers a bit foxed, one of 1,000 copies, signed by Maugham. Very good. Houle 21-610 1983 $175

MAUGHAM, WILLIAM SOMERSET   The Making of A Saint. Boston: L.C. Page and Compny, 1898. First edition. Illus. by Gilbert James. 8vo. Orig. pictorial cloth. Variant binding ii, with lettering on spine in both gilt and black. Fine copy. Jaffe 1-245 1983 $450

MAUGHAM, WILLIAM SOMERSET   Mrs. Craddock. New York: Doubleday, Doran, (1928). 1st American ed. Orig. maroon cloth, gilt. Very good copy, lacking dj. Jenkins 155-911 1983 $20

MAUGHAM, WILLIAM SOMERSET   The Moon and Sixpence. London, 1919. 8vo. Cloth. 1st issue with inserted ads in rear. From the library of Michael Sadleir with his bookplate. Laid into book is a short TLS from Maugham to a later owner of the book. With envelope. In Our Time 156-543 1983 $300

MAUGHAM, WILLIAM SOMERSET   The Moon and Sixpence. London: Heinemann, 1919. 1st ed., 3rd issue. Orig. pale green cloth, stamped in black. Printed on war time paper of inferior quality, and although brittle, quite sound and unchipped internally, and covers showing only slightest signs of use. Jenkins 155-910 1983 $100

MAUGHAM, WILLIAM SOMERSET   The Moon and Sixpence. London, 1919. First edition, first issue. Pages browned. Name on flyleaf. Nice. Rota 231-412 1983 £30

MAUGHAM, WILLIAM SOMERSET   The Moon and Sixpence. N.Y.: Doran, (1919). First American edition. Orig. cloth. Fine. MacManus 279-3629 1983 $25

MAUGHAM, WILLIAM SOMERSET   The Narrow Corner. London: William Heinemann Ltd., 1932. First edition. 8vo, orig. cloth, dust jacket. Fine. Jaffe 1-248 1983 $50

MAUGHAM, WILLIAM SOMERSET   Of Human Bondage. N.Y., Doran, (1915). First edition, first issue. Thick 8vo, gilt stamped green cloth. Very good. Houle 22-1216 1983 $450

MAUGHAM, WILLIAM SOMERSET   Of Human Bondage. N.Y.: Doubleday, Doran & Co., 1936. First illustrated edition. Illus. by R. Schwabe. Orig. decorated cloth. Dust jacket (slightly worn). Publisher's slipcase. One of 751 copies signed by Maugham and R. Schwabe. Slightly cracked slipcase. Fine. MacManus 279-3630 1983 $275

MAUGHAM, WILLIAM SOMERSET   Of Human Bondage. Garden City, Doubleday, 1936. First edition illustrated. 4to, with 24 full page plates by Randolph Schwabe. One of 751 copies signed by Maugham and Schwabe. Dust jacket. Pub.'s slipcase (a bit rubbed). Fine. Houle 22-623 1983 $225

MAUGHAM, WILLIAM SOMERSET   On a Chinese Screen. N.Y., Doran, (1922). First edition. Dust jacket (small stains and 3 chips) inner back hinge starting. 2,000 copies printed. Good - very good. Houle 22-624 1983 $85

MAUGHAM, WILLIAM SOMERSET   Orientations. London, 1899. 8vo. Cloth. Presentation inscription by Maugham on the half-title page. Signed in full by Maugham. The front flyleaf is tanned and has some light wear, overall a vg-fine copy. In Our Time 156-542 1983 $750

MAUGHAM, WILLIAM SOMERSET   Our Betters. London: William Heinemann, 1923. First edition. Orig. wrappers (a little soiled or faded, and slightly worn, at the edges). Good. MacManus 279-3631 1983 $50

MAUGHAM, WILLIAM SOMERSET   The Painted Veil. NY, (1925). One of 250 numbered and signed copies, spine darkened and lightly worn, spine label chipped, cover slightly discolored and soiled with light wear, near very good, bookplate. Quill & Brush 54-874 1983 $60

MAUGHAM, WILLIAM SOMERSET   The Painted Veil. N.Y.: George H. Doran Co., (1925). First trade edition. Orig. cloth. Good. MacManus 279-3632 1983 $25

MAUGHAM, WILLIAM SOMERSET   La Passe Dangerfeuse. Paris: Les Editions de France, 1926. 8vo. Orig. wrappers bound in a three-quarter leather binding. 1st French ed. 1 of 40 copies on velin signed by Maugham. Fine. In Our Time 156-544 1983 $350

MAUGHAM, WILLIAM SOMERSET   Sheppey. London: William Heinemann Ltd., 1933. First edition. 8vo. Orig. cloth. Dust jacket. Slightly darkened jacket. Fine copy. Jaffe 1-250 1983 $45

MAUGHAM, WILLIAM SOMERSET   Six Stories Written In The First Person Singular. London: William Heinemann Ltd., (1931). First English edition. Orig. cloth. Dust jacket (a bit worn). Presentation copy, inscribed on the front flyleaf "For Lawrence Thomsen, W. Somerset Maugham." Fine. MacManus 279-3633 1983 $300

MAUGHAM, WILLIAM SOMERSET   Smith. London: William Heinemann, 1913. First edition, wrappered issue. Orig. wrappers, paper label on front cover noting temporary rise in price. Presentation copy, inscribed on the half-title "For Fred from his friend W. Somerset Maugham." Book-plate of Albert Parsons Sachs on half-title, spine of wrappers a bit darkened and worn. Very good. MacManus 279-3634 1983 $250

MAUGHAM, WILLIAM SOMERSET   Strictly Personal. London: William Heinemann Ltd., (1942). First English edition. Frontis. by G. P. Lynes. Orig. cloth, dust jacket. Inscribed on the front flyleaf "For Lawrence Thomsen, W. Somerset Maugham." Endsheets browned. Covers rubbed. Very good. MacManus 279-3635 1983 $250

MAUGHAM, WILLIAM SOMERSET   The Summing Up. London: William Heinemann Ltd., (1938). First edition. 8vo, orig. cloth, dust jacket. Fine. Jaffe 1-252 1983 $75

MAUGHAM, WILLIAM SOMERSET   Theatre. London: William Heinemann Ltd., (1937). Uncorrected Proof copy of the first English edition. Orig. proof wrappers. Bookplate on front inner wrapper. In a cloth slipcase. Fine. MacManus 279-3636 1983 $350

MAUGHAM, WILLIAM SOMERSET   Then and Now. Garden City, N.Y.:
Doubleday & Co., Inc., 1946. First American edition. Orig. cloth.
Dust jacket. Presentation copy, inscribed "For Rosemary Thomsen, W.
Somerset Maugham, on her wedding anniversary, New York, 1946." Fine.
MacManus 279-3637 1983 $225

MAUGHAM, WILLIAM SOMERSET   Then and Now. London: William Heinemann
Ltd., (1946). First edition. Orig. cloth. Dust jacket (slightly
chipped). Very good. MacManus 279-3638 1983 $20

MAUGHAM, WILLIAM SOMERSET   The Trembling of a Leaf. London: William Heinemann, 1921. First edition, first issue. Orig. cloth. Presentation copy inscribed: "For E.J. Bernheimer, W. Somerset Maugham,
New York, 29 September 1924." Some offsetting and foxing to the
endpapers and preliminary pages. In a cloth slipcase. Very good.
MacManus 279-3639 1983 $225

MAUGHAM, WIILLIAM SOMERSET   The Trembling of a Leaf. London: William Heinemann Ltd., 1921. First English edition, second issue. Orig.
cloth. Cloth a little bubbled. Good. MacManus 279-3640 1983 $25

MAUGHAM, WILLIAM SOMERSET   The Unattainable. London: William
Heinemann, 1923. First edition. Orig. wrappers (wrappers a little
frayed and worn at the edges). 2-inch tear in front wrapper where it
meets the foot of the spine. Good. MacManus 279-3641 1983 $50

MAUGHAM, WILLIAM SOMERSET   The Unconquered. N.Y.: House of Books,
Ltd., 1944. First edition. Orig. blue cloth. Plain tissue jacket
(edges worn). One of 300 copies signed by author. Very fine. Mac-
Manus 279-3642 1983 $175

MAUGHAM, WILLIAM SOMERSET   The Unconquered. New York, 1944. 1st
ed., 1 of 300 numbered and signed copies. Orig. blue cloth, gilt.
Near fine copy. Jenkins 155-913 1983 $125

MAUGHAM, WILLIAM SOMERSET   Up at the Villa. London: William Heinemann Ltd., (1941). First English edition. Orig. cloth. Dust jacket
(reinforced with tape). Very good. MacManus 279-3643 1983 $40

MAUNDER, SAMUEL   The Treasury of History. New York,
1850. Large folding frontispiece plate. Illus. by J.H. Colton.
2 vols. 8vo. Engraved plates. Small tear repaired on verso.
Morrill 289-434 1983 $25

MAUPASSANT, GUY DE   A Woman's Life. New York: (The Marchbanks Press, for) The Limited Editions Club, 1952. Royal 8vo, 16
hand coloured illustrations, quarter cream leather with brown label
gilt, marbled paper boards, similar slip-case with printed paper
label, fine. Edition limited to 1,500 numbered copies. Deighton 3-223
1983 £42

MAUQUEST DE LA MOTTE, GUILLAUME   Traite des Accouchements naturels,
non Naturels, et contre Nature. A la Haye: Pierre Gosse, 1726.
4to (rebound). Title printed in red and black. Argosy 713-368 1983
$250

MAURICE, FREDERICK   Robert E. Lee, the Soldier. London,
1925. First edition. Maps and illustrations. 8vo. Few light
cover stains. Morrill 290-305 1983 $20

MAURICE, FREDERICK DENISON   The Life of...Chiefly Told in His Own
Letters. Macmillan, 1884. First edition, 2 vols. Half title vol. 1.
Front. ports. 2 pp. ads. vol. II. Orig. blue cloth. Jarndyce 30-1070
1983 £32

MAURICE, HENRY   Doubts Concerning the Roman Infallibility.
Printed for James Adamson, 1688. First edition, including imprimatur
leaf, 4to, wrapper, a very good copy. Fenning 61-289 1983 £14.50

MAURICE, T.   Indian Antiquities. London, 1806. Fold-
ing map, 26 plates, 24 folding. Occasional slight foxing. 7 vols.
Half calf, slight wear at corners, inner hinges cracked. 8vo. Good.
Edwards 1044-483 1983 £220

MAURICEAU, FRANCOIS   Traite des Maladies des Femmes Grosses,
et de celles qui Sont Accouchees. Paris, 1721. Numerous full-page
and smaller copperplates. 2 vols. Large 4to, cont. mottled calf,
spine with raised bands and gilt with fleurons, (some foxing); ex-
lib. Argosy 713-369 1983 $350

MAUROIS, ANDRE   Byron. Paris: Grasset/Les Cahiers
Verts, (1930). Two vols. Quarto. Printed wraps. First edition.
Copy no. 1 of 44 numbered copies printed on Montval, in quarto
format. A very fine set, enclosed in the orig. slipcase (slightly
rubbed). Reese 20-680 1983 $75

MAUROIS, ANDRE   Chelsea Way. L, 1930. Limited to 500
numbered and signed copies, offset on endpapers, otherwise very good
in slightly chipped dustwrapper. Quill & Brush 54-877 1983 $50

MAUROIS, ANDRE   Tragedy in France. N.Y., Harper, (1940).
Later printing. Signed and inscribed by the author in French.
Dust jacket (slight rubbing and nicking) else good - very good.
Houle 22-626 1983 $20

MAUROIS, ANDRE   A Voyage to the Island of the Articoles.
L, (1928). Wood engravings by E. Carrick, near fine with slightly
faded spine, bookplate. Quill & Brush 54-876 1983 $35

MAURONER, FABIO   Luca Carlevarijs. Padova: "Le Tre
Venezie", 1945. 101 plates. Small 4to. Wrappers. Dust jacket.
Ars Libri 33-83 1983 $50

MAURY, ANN   Memoirs of a Hugenot Family. New
York, 1853. Portrait, cloth, fine. Reese 19-350 1983 $150

MAURY, JEAN SIFFREIN   The Principles of Eloquence. Albany:
Loring Andrews & Co., for Thomas, Andrews & Penniman, 1797. Full
calf, elaborately tooled spine. Signature "Oliver P. Sargeant's
1799." Felcone 22-142 1983 $30

MAURY, MATTHEW FONTAINE   The Physical Geography of the Sea.
N.Y., 1855. Illus., 4 woodcuts in text, folded pilot sheet, 7
folded maps and charts. Orig. cloth. Small rubber library stamp on
title page, endpaper and flyleaves. First edition. Ginsberg 46-449
1983 $300

MAURY, MATTHEW FONTAINE   The Physical Geography of the Sea.
New York, 1856. Sixth edition. 13 plates, including 9 large folding
plates. Original cloth. Top of spine worn, but a sound and very good
copy. Bradley 65-136 1983 $75

MAURY, MATTHEW FONTAINE   The Physical Geography of the Sea.
T. Nelson, 1861. With 13, mostly folding, charts, orig. cloth,
gilt. A very good copy. Fenning 62-239 1983 £21.50

MAVOR, WILLIAM   The English Spelling-Book. London: Geo.
Routledge & Sons, 1885. First edition. Illus. by Kate Greenaway.
Engraved and printed by Edmund Evans. Orig. pictorial boards (some-
what worn). Very good. MacManus 278-2370 1983 $125

MAWE, T.   Every Man his own Gardener. 1813.
20th edition, new cloth. Wheldon 160-1987 1983 £15

MAX-MUELLER, FREDRICH   Chips from a German Workshop. London:
Longmans, Green, 1867, 1870, 1875. 4 vols., marginal pencilling,
titlepage to vol. 3 repaired. Vols. 1-3 in contemporary half polished purple calf with brightly gilt spines, vol. 4 in orig. cloth (front
hinge broken). First editions. Gach 95-352 1983 $100

MAXIMILIAN, PRINCE OF WIED-NEUWIED   Travels in Brazil, in the Years
1815-17. London: Colburn, 1820. First English edition. 6 lithographed plates of jungle scenes and Indians. Folding map of Brazil
outlined in color. Cont. marbled boards skillfully rebacked. Very fine
Exeter duplicate. Jenkins 152-26 1983 $750

MAXIMILIEN, LOUIS   Le Vodou Haitien. Port-Au-Prince,
Haiti, (1945). Illus. Pr. wraps. Argosy 716-633 1983 $25

MAXWELL, CONSTANTIA   Irish History from Contemporary Sources.
Allen & Unwin, 1923. First edition, 8vo, orig. cloth, nice copy in
d.w. Fenning 61-290 1983 £16.50

MAXWELL, DONALD   The Log of the Griffin. John Lane,
1905. First edition, with 16 coloured plates and 99 other plates and
illus., 8vo, orig. cloth, gilt, t.e.g. Fenning 62-240 1983 £14.50

MAXWELL, GILBERT   Look to the Lightning. New York,
1933. 8vo. Inscribed by poet. A vg-fine copy. No jacket. In
Our Time 156-548 1983 $35

MAXWELL, HERBERT   The Art of Love; Or, New Lessons In Old
Lore. Edinburgh: David Douglas, 1889. First edition. 3 vols. Orig.
blue decorated cloth. Spine ends and covers slightly worn. Very good.
MacManus 279-3645 1983 $350

MAXWELL, HERBERT   Flowers: a garden notebook. 1923.
12 coloured plates, 4to, cloth. Wheldon 160-1988 1983 £15

MAXWELL, JAMES CLERK   Matter and Motion. London: Society
for Promoting Christian Knowledge, 1894. 8vo. Orig. red cloth.
Some minor flaws, but a very good copy internally. Zeitlin 264-
286 1983 $50

MAXWELL, JAMES CLERK   On Reciprocal Figures, Frames, and
Diagrams of Forces... Edinburgh: Printed for the Society by Neill
and Company, 1870. Orig. offprint, 4to, title page, 3 plates, minor
staining the lower margin but a good copy in the orig. plain paper
wrapper. Pickering & Chatto 22-68 1983 $300

MAXWELL, JAMES CLERK   On Stresses in Rarified Gases... Part I.
1879. Orig. offprint, 4to, title page; orig. printed paper wrapper,
early owner's stamp in upper margin of wrapper. Pickering & Chatto
22-70 1983 $300

MAXWELL, MARY ELIZABETH BRADDON   Birds of Prey. London: Ward, Lock
& Tyler, 1868. First one-volume edition. Orig. cloth. Somewhat worn.
MacManus 277-640 1983 $85

MAXWELL, MARY ELIZABETH BRADDON   Birds of Prey, a Novel. Ward, Lock
& Tyler, 1868. Engr. frontis. & title. 2 pp. ads. Lacking leading
free end paper. Orig. blue cloth, a little rubbed. First one-volume
edition. Jarndyce 31-440 1983 £20

MAXWELL, MARY ELIZABETH BRADDON   The Christmas Hirelings. London:
Simpkin, Marshall, Hamilton, Kent & Co., 1894. First edition. Illus.
by F. H. Townsend. Orig. cloth-backed pictorial boards. Dust jacket
(repaired at head of spine). Rarely found in dust jacket. Fine.
MacManus 277-641 1983 $350

MAXWELL, MARY ELIZABETH BRADDON   The Christmas Hirelings. London:
Simpkin, Marshall, Hamilton, Kent & Co., 1894. First edition. Illus.
by F. H. Townsend. Orig. cloth-backed pictorial boards. With a holograph presentation slip tipped in, reading: "With the author's love."
Edges and corners worn. Covers a bit soiled. Endpapers a little
browned. Good. MacManus 277-642 1983 $150

MAXWELL, MARY ELIZABETH BRADDON   The Day Will Come. London: Simp-
kin, Marshall, & Co., (1892). First edition. 3 vols. Orig. cloth.
Former owner's signatures on half-titles and title-pages. Very fine.
MacManus 277-643 1983 $500

MAXWELL, MARY ELIZABETH BRADDON   The Day Will Come. Simpkin, Marshall, (1892). Half titles. Orig. dark green cloth. End papers laid
down in vol. 1. First edition. 3 vols. Jarndyce 30-309 1983 £54

MAXWELL, MARY ELIZABETH BRADDON   Eleanor's Victory. London: Tinsley Bros., 1863. First edition. 3 vols. Orig. cloth (covers worn;
quite stained). Inner hinges cracked. MacManus 277-644 1983 $85

MAXWELL, MARY ELIZABETH BRADDON   Gerard or the World, the Flesh, and
The Devil. London: Simpkin, Marshall, Hamilton, Kent & Co., 1891.
First edition. 3 vols. Orig. cloth. Presentation copy to Joseph
Hatton inscribed: "To the author of the Queen of Bohemia, with an old
friend's kindest regards, M. E. Braddon..., August 6, '92." Spines
slightly worn and darkened, spine edges slightly frayed. Inner hinges
cracking, volumes 1 and 2 recased. In a half-morocco case. Good set.
MacManus 277-645 1983 $450

MAXWELL, MARY ELIZABETH BRADDON   The Golden Calf. London: John &
Robert Maxwell, 1883. First edition. 3 vols. Orig. cloth. Badly
worn at extremities. Inner hinges cracked. Pages dusty & smudged.
Several signatures sprung. Very scarce. MacManus 277-646 1983 $75

MAXWELL, MARY ELIZABETH BRADDON   Hostages to Fortune. London: John
Maxwell & Co., 1875. First edition. 3 vols. Orig. cloth. Extremities
worn. Covers a bit soiled. Inner hinges cracked (front cover of vol. 1
almost detached). MacManus 277-648 1983 $185

MAXWELL, MARY ELIZABETH BRADDON   In High Places. London: Hutchison
& Co., 1898. First edition. Orig. red decorated cloth. Covers a
little rubbed and soiled. Good. MacManus 277-647 1983 $100

MAXWELL, MARY ELIZABETH BRADDON   Lady Audley's Secret. London:
Tinsley Brothers, 1862. Vol 1 & 2, fourth edition, vol. 3, fifth edition. A rather dilapidated set with spines and covers rubbed, soiled
and worn, inner hinges weak & cracking, with a subscription library
plate on the paste-down endpaper of vol. 1. Orig. cloth. MacManus
277-649 1983 $185

MAXWELL, MARY ELIZABETH BRADDON   Lady Audley's Secret. London:
Tinsley, 1862. Seventh edition, revised. 3 vols. Orig. cloth. Rather
shaken, covers darkened and rubbed. One of the earliest available editions of this classic Victorian rarity. Good. MacManus 277-650 1983
$350

MAXWELL, MARY ELIZABETH BRADDON   London Pride; or When the World Was
Younger. (London: Simpkin, Marshall, 1896). First edition. Orig.
decorated ribbed cloth. With a 2 pp. ALS from the author tipped in and
long note by a previous owner, W. H. Barnes, on the endpaper describing a meeting with Mary Braddon in London on Oct. 20 & 21, 1896.
Covers considerably worn and soiled. Part of front endpaper torn away. Mac-
Manus 277-652 1983 $85

MAXWELL, MARY ELIZABETH BRADDON   London Pride; or When the World Was
Younger. London: Simpkin, Marshall, (1896). First edition. Orig.
cloth. In the smooth dark green cloth binding. Inner hinges cracked.
Good. MacManus 277-653 1983 $50

MAXWELL, MARY ELIZABETH BRADDON   London Pride; or When the World Was
Younger. London: Simpkin, Marshall, Hamilton, Kent & Co., (1896).
First edition. Orig. decorated cloth. Inner hinges cracked. In the
vertical-ribbed cloth. Good. MacManus 277-651 1983 $45

MAXWELL, MARY ELIZABETH BRADDON   Only A Clod. London: John Maxwell
& Co., 1865. Fifth edition. 3 vols. Orig. cloth. Fine. MacManus
277-654 1983 $150

MAXWELL, MARY ELIZABETH BRADDON   Ralph the Bailiff, and Other Tales.
London: Ward, Lock & Tyler, (1867). First edition. Frontis. Orig.
cloth. Spine and covers worn. Bookplate. MacManus 277-655 1983
$135

MAXWELL, MARY ELIZABETH BRADDON   The Trail of the Serpent. 1861.
Revised and retitled edition. Half calf, boards a little rubbed. Red
labels. Very scarce. Jarndyce 31-429 1983 £120

MAXWELL, MARY ELIZABETH BRADDON   The Venetians. London: Simpkin,
Marshall, Hamilton, Kent & Co., 1892. First edition. 3 vols. Orig.
green cloth. Covers on vol. 2 soiled. Library labels removed from
two volumes. Good. MacManus 277-658 1983 $250

MAXWELL, MONTGOMERY   My Adventures. Henry Colburn, 1845.
First edition, 2 vols. Front. ports. Half titles, 24 pp ads. vol. II.
Orig. blue cloth. Jarndyce 30-1071 1983 £18.50

MAXWELL, ROBERT   The Practical Husbandman. Edinburgh,
1757. First edition. Old calf. Index. Bookplate of Earl of Rose-
berry. Hinges loose, slight staining, ink inscription. Covers very
worn and heavily spotted. One reverse of title page, "This Book is
entered in Stationers Hall; and further to prevent pirating, I have
signed each genuine Copy on the Back of the Title-page". Signed by
author. King 45-219 1983 $95

MAXWELL, WILLIAM   They Came Like Swallows. New York,
1937. 8vo. Cloth, paper label on spine. Lacks dj. Bookplate.
Else vg-fine copy. In Our Time 156-550 1983 $25

MAXWELL, WILLIAM AUDLEY   Crossing the Plains: Days of '57. (San
Francisco: 1915). First edition. Illus. Pictoiral brown wrappers
stamped in gold. Front wrappers chipped at corners but very good copy.
Bradley 66-588 1983 $55

MAXWELL, WILLIAM HAMILTON   The Fortunes Of Hector O'Halloran. London: Richard Bentley, (1842-1843). First edition. Illus. by J. Leech & R. Doyle. Orig. 13 parts in white decorated wrappers (backstrips repaired). Spines and covers slightly worn and soiled. In a quarter-morocco slipcase. Very good. MacManus 279-3646 1983 $350

MAXWELL, WILLIAM HAMILTON   The Fortunes of Hector O'Halloran, and his Man Mark Antony O'Toole. London: Richard Bentley, (1842-43). First edition, with an orig. illustrated wrapper from the edition in parts inserted before the title-page. Illus. by J. Leech. Orig. cloth. Spine lightly faded. With the bookplates of John Byram and Douglas C. Ewing. Fine. MacManus 279-3647 1983 $250

MAY, J. B.   The Hawks of North America. New York, 1935. 4 plain plates and 37 coloured plates, royal 8vo, original cloth. Wheldon 160-808 1983 £40

MAY, PHIL   Songs and Their Singers from "Punch." Bradbury, Agnes, 1898. 1st edn. 15 mounted proof on Jap. paper laid down on card. Printed title page & contents. Brick red cloth folder (lacks ties). Inscribed signed presentation copy "with our united fond love & wishes for a very happy Christmas to you all. Phil May" Hodgkins 27-475 1983 £45

MAY, RALPH   Early Portsmouth History. Boston, 1926. 1st ed. Presentation copy. Illus. 8vo. Morrill 288-334 1983 $30

MAYDON, H. C.   Simen Its Heights. London, 1925. 3 maps, 3 plans, plates. Thick 8vo. Orig. cloth. Good. Edwards 1044-484 1983 £45

MAYER, ALEXANDER   Die Genreplastik an Peter Vischers Sebaldusgrab. Leipzig: Insel, 1911. 31 collotype plates. 42 text illus. Folio. Boards, 1/4 cloth. Edition limited to 1000 copies. Ars Libri 32-689 1983 $85

MAYER, ALFRED M.   Sport with Gun and Rod in American Woods and Waters. New York, (1883). 1st ed., 4to, corners worn, former owner's writing on half-title, lacks front fly-leaf. Morrill 289-435 1983 $37.50

MAYER, AUGUST L.   Francisco De Goya. Munchen: F. Bruckmann, 1923. 261 plates with 434 illus. Large 4to. Cloth. Ars Libri 32-274 1983 $85

MAYER, AUGUST L.   Mittelalterliche Plastik in Italien. Munchen, 1923. Lg. 4to, 40 collotype plates. Cloth. Ars Libri SB 26-135 1983 $60

MAYER, AUGUST L.   Murillo. Des Meisters Gemalde. Stuttgart: Deutsche Verlags-Anstalt, 1923. 292 illus. 4to. Boards, 1/4 cloth. Ars Libri 32-487 1983 $65

MAYER, BRANTZ   Mexico, Central America and West Indies. Chicago, (1910). Illus. Thick 8vo, orig. blue mor., g.t. Some pp. unopened. Argosy 716-291 1983 $40

MAYER, BRANTZ   Tah-Gah-Jute. Albany, Joel Munsell, 1867. Presentation inscription by Munsell. Enlarged and most complete ed. 8vo, half morocco, raised bands, marbled board sides, errata slip. Fine copy in fine binding. Morrill 288-306 1983 $100

MAYER, JOHN   The Sportsman's Directory; or, Park and Gamekeeper's Companion. London: Baldwin, Cradock, & Joy; et al, 1823. Fourth edition. Frontis. engraving. Orig. printed boards. Covers detached. Boards rubbed. Preserved in a full morocco pull-off case. MacManus 278-1972 1983 $125

MAYER, MORITZ   Electricity in its Relations to Practical Medicine. NY: D. Appleton & Co., 1869. Ads. Library label on spine. Publisher's mauve cloth, joints taped. First American edition. Gach 95-188 1983 $30

MAYFIELD, JOHN S.   Mark Twain vs. the Street Railway Co. (New York): Privately printed, 1926. Photos, facsim. 1st ed. Orig. printed buff wrappers. A fine fresh copy. Jenkins 155-227 1983 $75

MAYFIELD, JOHN S.   Mark Twain Vs. The Street Railway Company. (N.p.): Privately printed, 1926. Printed wraps. One corner nicked, else fine. Inscribed presentation copy from the author to C. C. Peters, Jr. Reese 19-352 1983 $20

MAYHEW, AUGUSTUS   Faces For Fortunes. London: Tinsley Brothers, 1865. First edition. 3 vols. Orig. cloth. Spines faded. Front cover of Vol. three partially stained. Fine. MacManus 279-3649 1983 $350

MAYHEW, EDWARD   The Illustrated Horse Management... Philadelphia, 1864. More than 400 engravings from original designs made expressly for this work. 8vo. Rubbed; ends of spine worn. Morrill 290-306 1983 $25

MAYHEW, EXPERIENCE   Grace Defended, in a Modest Plea for an Important Truth. Boston, 1744. Cont. calf, rebacked. Internally a crisp, clean copy. Reese 18-59 1983 $375

MAYHEW, HENRY   The Criminal Prisons of London, and Scenes of Prison Life. London: Griffin, Bohn, 1862. Folding frontis. Numerous illus. and plates. 1st ed. Orig. lavender embossed cloth, gilt. Some expert and almost invisible strengthening of the joints, else a very good copy with the usual spine fading. Jenkins 155-915 1983 $225

MAYHEW, HENRY   1851. Bogue, nd (1851). 8 illus. Frontis. pull-out & title vignette. Blue moire blind stamped cloth gilt decor. bkstrip. Eps. broken at hinges & top/bottom of bkstrip. worn & soiled, corners some wear, plates foxed, name plate & insc. fr. ep., good copy. Hodgkins 27-310 1983 £40

MAYHEW, HENRY   London Labour and the London Poor. London, 1861-2. 4 vols. numerous plates. 1st complete ed. Orig. lavender cloth, gilt. Very good set with some fading of spines. Scarce in complete form. Jenkins 155-916 1983 $650

MAYNE, JOHN   The Siller Gun. Thomas Cadell, Wm. Blackwood, 1836. First complete edition, orig. blue cloth, dulled and a little rubbed. Jarndyce 30-790 1983 £18.50

MAYNE, LEGER D.   What Shall We Do Tonight? New York, (1873). 1st ed. Illus. Small 8vo. Morrill 286-127 1983 $25

MAYNO DE MAYNERI, SUPPOSED AUTHOR   Regimen Sanitatis Please turn to REGIMEN SANITATIS SALERNITANUM

MAYO, ELIZABETH   Lessons on Objects, as Given in a Pestozzian School, at Cheam, Surrey. Published by R.B. Seeley and W. Burnside; and sold by L.B. Seeley and Sons, 1831. Large 12mo, uncut, orig. boards and cloth spine, joints slit at the foot. Very good copy. Bickersteth 77-229 1983 £35

MAYO, JOSEPH A.   Guide to Magistrates. Richmond, 1850. 1st ed. 8vo, contemporary calf, leather label. Ink stain on back cover. Morrill 289-567 1983 $20

MAYR, E.   Birds of the Southwest Pacific. New York, 1945. Text-figures and 3 coloured plates, cr. 8vo, cloth. The very scarce original issue, third printing. Wheldon 160-809 1983 £18

MAZRO, SOPHIA   Turkish Barbarity. Providence, (1828). Folding frontispiece. 12mo, orig. wrappers, partly torn. Morrill 287-273 1983 $50

MAZURE, M. A.   Illustrations. Paris, Lehuby, n.d. (former owner's inscription of 1857). Small 8vo, all edges gilt. Some foxing, some rubbing of corners. Morrill 287-274 1983 $40

MAZZANOVICH, ANTON   Trailing Geronimo. Los Angeles: Privately printed, 1931. Rev. ed. Colored frontis and other illus. Argosy 710-14 1983 $30

MAZZEI, FILIPPO   Recherches Historiques et Politiques sur Les Etats-Unis. Paris, 1788. 4 vols. New spines, orig. boards. Nice clean set. Jenkins 153-796 1983 $200

MAZZINI, JOSEPH   Royalty and Republicanism in Italy.
London: Gilpin, 1850. 8vo, with ads. at beginning & 24 page
list at end. Blind-stamped cloth. First edition. Rostenberg 88-118
1983 $95

MAZZUCHELLI, SAMUEL   Memoirs Historical and Edifying of
a Missionary Apostolic of the Order of the Saint Dominic Among Various
Indian Tribes... Chicago, 1915. Illus., 2 maps and 2 plates. Title
page mended. Old cloth. First English translation, with
additions. Ginsberg 47-497 1983 $35

MAZZUCHELLI, GIAMMARIA   La Vita di Pietro Aretino. Padova:
Giuseppe Comino, 1741. 1st ed., 8vo, original stiff wrappers, sewn
as issued. Engraved frontis. portrait, six engraved plates, vignette
title page. Approbation leaf, advertisements, uncut copy. A very
fine copy. Trebizond 18-117 1983 $250

MEACHAM, ALFRED G.   Wigwam and War-Path. Boston, 1875.
Plates. 3/4 morocco (rubbed at extremities). Second edition.
Felcone 22-143 1983 $35

MEAD, KATE CAMPBELL HURD   A History of Women in Medicine...
Haddam, 1938. First edition. 8vo. Orig. binding. Fye H-3-381
1983 $90

MEAD, RICHARD   A Discourse on the Plague. Printed for
A. Millar; and J. Brindley, 1744. 8vo, strip cut from top of title
to remove inscription, other old inscriptions on the title, old
library stamp on two other pages, old half calf, upper joint cracked,
but binding firm. Bickersteth 77-300 1983 £45

MEAD, RICHARD   A Discourse on the Plague. 1744. 8vo,
large paper, printed on thick paper, small ink stain on 2 pages, old
ink inscription on title, bound in modern buckram with morocco label and
new end papers. Bickersteth 77-301 1983 £30

MEAD, RICHARD   A Discourse on the Small Pox and Measles.
Printed for J. Brindley, 1755. 8vo, orig. calf, rebacked. Old book
label on the Norwich and Norfolk Medical Book Society inside the
front cover, and their circular stamp on the title page. Bickersteth
77-302 1983 £65

MEAD, RICHARD   A Mechanical Account of Poisons in
Several Essays. Printed by M.J. for Ralph Smith, 1708. 8vo, folding
engraved plate, cont. calf gilt, monogram in gilt with cornet in the
centre of each cover, upper joint cracked, light brown stains on
four pages, but a crisp copy, binding sound. Bickersteth 77-298
1983 £150

MEAD, RICHARD   A Mechanical Account of Poisons in
Several Essays. Printed for J.R. by Ralph South. 1702. 8vo,
folding engraved plate, all uncut, modern calf antique with the orig.
grey wraps. bound in. A fine copy. First edition. Bickersteth 77-
295 1983 £150

MEAD, RICHARD   A Mechanical Account of Poisons in
Several Essays. Printed by M.R. for Ralph South, 1702. Bound in
speckled calf, spine gilt, lacking the label, and with, bound at the
end, two leaves of Books printed for J. Millan, dated 1741. Bickersteth 77-296 1983 £120

MEAD, RICHARD   Medica Sacra. Londini, Prostant apud
Joannem Brindley, 1749. 8vo, old calf, rebacked. First edition.
Bickersteth 77-303 1983 £60

MEAD, RICHARD   The Medical Works. Edinburgh, 1775.
8vo, 5 folding plates (side margin of one plate frayed), lacks front
fly, old ink inscription on title, outer edge of margin of title
browned, old calf, rebacked. Bickersteth 77-294 1983 £75

MEAD, RICHARD   The Medical Works. London, 1762.
Thick 4to, old calf (inner hinges repaired). Mezzotint port. Several
plates. Argosy 713-370 1983 $250

MEAD, RICHARD   Monita et Praecepta Medica. Londini,
Prostant apud Joannem Brindley, 1751. 8vo, old calf, rebacked.
Half title and title a little spotted and dusty, old ink inscription
on title. First edition. Bickersteth 77-304 1983 £55

MEAD, RICHARD   A Short Discourse Concerning Pestilential
Contagion... London, Sam. Buckley and Ralph Smith, 1720. 8vo,
disbound, title a bit dust-soiled, otherwise a large, clean copy with
some uncut lower edges. Ravenstree 97-97 1983 $350

MEAD, RICHARD   A Short Discourse Concerning Pestilential
Contagion... London, Buckley, 1722. Tall 8vo, orig. red morocco
gilt extra, a.e.g., rebacked period style with cipher and coronet of
Duke of Devonshire in upper panel, and with his Chatsworth bookplate.
Ravenstree 97-98 1983 $250

MEAD, RICHARD   A Treatise Concerning the Influence
of the Sun and Moon upon Human Bodies. Printed for J. Brindley, 1748.
8vo, title soiled, with ink inscription of the Medical Chirurgical
Society of Aberdeen on the title, and the library's stamp on the
following and on the final leaves, final page also dusty, and lacking
lower outer corner, but printed surface not affected, old half calf
with marbled boards, rebacked. Bickersteth 77-299 1983 £55

MEAD, WILLIAM EDWARD   The Grand Tour in the Eighteenth
Century. Boston, Houghton Mifflin, 1914. 1st ed. Presentation
from G. H. Mifflin, the publisher. Illustrated from contemporary
prints. 8vo. Morrill 286-319 1983 $20

MEADE, L. T.   A Band of Mirth. W. & R. Chambers, n.d.
(ca.1928). Colour frontis. & 3 colour plates. Light blue pictorial
cloth. Greer 40-36 1983 £10.50

MEADE, L. T.   The Honourable Miss. London: Methuen
& Co., 1891. First edition. 2 vols. Orig. dark-green cloth. Spines
and covers slightly worn and soiled. Bookplate. Good. MacManus 279-
3650 1983 $150

MEADLEY, GEORGE WILSON   Memoirs of Algernon Sydney. London:
Printed by Thomas Davison, 1813. First edition. Frontis. port. 8vo.
Cont. calf & marbled boards. Spine chipped. Hinges weak. MacManus
280-5025 1983 $35

MEAKIN, JAMES E. BUDGETT   The Land of the Moors. Swan
Sonnenschein, 1901. First edition, with a folding map and 83-full-
page and other illus., preliminaries seem complete in spite of the
pagination jump, 8vo, cont. cloth, a very good copy. Fenning 61-
294 1983 £18.50

MEANS, JAMES   Manflight. Boston, 1891. First ed.
Printed blue wrappers. Very fine. Bradley 65-21 1983 $100

MEANS, PHILIP AINSWORTH   Ancient Civilizations of the Andes.
New York/London: Charles Scribner's Sons, 1931. 223 illus. Small
4to. Cloth. Ars Libri 34-359 1983 $30

MEASE, JAMES   Geological Account of the U.S.
Phila., 1807. First edition. Thick 16mo, cont. lea. 4 copperplate
views. Lacking 2 leaves. Argosy 716-195 1983 $35

MECHI, JOHN J.   An Appeal on Behalf of the Royal
Agricultural Benevolent College. (May, 1859). Small 8vo, unbound,
sewn as issued, fine. Loosely inserted are two copies of a
subscription form and a 2-page facs. letter from the author dated
January, 9th, 1860. Fenning 62-246 1983 £14.50

MECHNIKOV, IL'IA IL'ICH   The Founders of Modern Medicine Pasteur,
Koch, Lister. New York, 1939. First ed., 8vo., orig. binding. Fye
H-3-392 1983 $20

MECKEL VON HEMSBACH, H.   Mikrogeologie. Berlin, 1845. First
edition. 8vo. Boards. Gurney JJ-264 1983 £30

MECKLENBERG, GEORGE   The Last of the Old West. Washington:
(1927). First edition. Illus. Green cloth. Signed by author. Pencil notes in text, but good copy. Bradley 66-602 1983 $40

MEDBERY, R. B.   Memoir of William G. Crocker... Boston:
Gould & Lincoln, 1860. 12mo. Portrait. Orig. brown cloth. Rubbed,
staining. Adelson Africa-205 1983 $30

MEDDEN, DODGSON H.   The Law and Practice of the High Court of
Justice in Ireland. Dublin: E. Ponsonby, 1889. 8vo, orig. cloth.
Very good copy. Third edition. Fenning 62-224 1983 £28.50

MEDER, JOSEPH   Durer-Katalog. Ein Handbuch uber
Albrecht Durers Stiche, Radierungen, Hozschnitte... Wien: Gilhofer
& Ranschburg, 1932. 52 plates with more than 350 watermarks. 190
illus. 4to. Marbled boards, 3/4 cloth. Dust jacket. Ars Libri
32-183 1983 $325

THE MEDICAL & Agricultural Registter for 1806-7. Boston: Manning &
Loring, (1807). 8vo, old boards, crude linen back; (ex-library,
dampstained). Argosy 713-371 1983 $150

THE MEDICAL Intelligencer. Boston, May 18, 1824-May 9, 1826. 2 vols.
4to. Orig. boards, calf backs. Rubbed; some dampstains. Scarce.
Morrill 289-156 1983 $75

MEDICAL SOCIETY OF THE STATE OF NEW YORK   Transactions of the
Medical Society of the State of New York... Albany, 1868. First
edition. 8vo. Orig. binding. Very fine. Scarce. Fye H-3-414
1983 $60

MEDITATIONS and Reflections for Every Day in the Year, from the
Diary and Journal of an Exile. (Inverness, Scotland?, ca. 1875).
Hand-drawn frontispiece. Contemporary full red morocco, gilt,
a.e.g. Bit rubbed. Jenkins 155-427 1983 $275

MEDWIN, THOMAS   Conversations with Lord Byron... London:
Colburn, 1824. Second edition. 8vo, cont. half red morocco, spine
gilt. With a folding facs. frontis. (offset). Binding rubbed.
Ximenes 63-55 1983 $150

MEDWIN, THOMAS   The Life of Percy Bysshe Shelley.
London: Thomas Cautley Newby, 1847. First edition. 2 vols. Facs.
frontis. Rebound in 3/4 morocco & marbled boards. Fine. MacManus
280-4730 1983 $150

MEEHAN, JEANNETTE PORTER   The Lady of the Limberlost, The Life
and Letters of Gene Stratton-Porter. Garden City, 1928. First ed.,
photos, cloth, ink inscription, sm. snag in front cover, heavily
rubbed. King 46-337 1983 $50

MEEK, A. B.   Songs and Poems of the South. Mobile:
1857. 282pp. Original cobalt blue cloth. Designated second
edition. A scarce imprint in very nice condition. Jenkins 151-1
1983 $100

MEEK, F. B.   Palaeontology of the Upper Missouri:
Invertebrates Pt. 1. Philadelphia, 1864. 5 plates, 4to, wrappers
(trifle dustsoiled). Wheldon 160-1445 1983 £12

MEEK, GEORGE   George Meek, Bath Chair-man. London:
Constable & Co., Ltd., 1910. First edition. Orig. cloth. In a half-
morocco slipcase. Good. MacManus 280-5505 1983 $45

MEEK, THOMAS   A small tribute to the memory of
Ossian... Edinburgh: printed by Robert Menzies, etc., 1809.
8vo. Disbound. First edition. Title and last leaf dusty, uncut
copy. Ximenes 63-245 1983 $85

MEEKER, EZRA   Ventures and Adventures of Ezra Meeker
or Sixty Years of Frontier Life. Seattle: Rainer Printing Co.,
1909. Illus., original cloth with pictorial paper label. Presentation copy from the author. Jenkins 151-206 1983 $45

MEEKER, EZRA   Washington Territory West of the
Cascade Mountains. Olympia, 1870. Orig. printed wraps. First
edition. Ginsberg 47-937 1983 $1,000

MEERSCH, MAXENCE VAN DER   Pecheurs d'Hommes. Paris: Albin Michel,
(1940). 21 cm. Orig. printed wraps., glassine dust jacket. Nearly
fine, top edge dusty. Uncut. First edition. No. "K" of 20 copies
after the copy on Japon in a larger total edition. On Holland paper.
Grunder 7-58 1983 $35

MEGGENDORFER, LOTHAR   Neue Thierbilder. Munchen: Braun &
Schneider, n.d. 4to, 8 handcoloured moveable plates, carefully repaired. Colour pictorial boards, spine defective. Greer 40-138 1983
£195

MEIBOM, HEINRICH   Disputatio Medica de Hydrophobia.
Helmstedt: Henning Mueller, 1659. 4to. Sewn. Modern boards.
Kraus 164-159 1983 $75

MEIER, NELLIE SIMMONS   Lions' Paws. NY: Barrows Mussey,
(c. 1937). 24 cm. Orig. cloth faded. Numerous illus. Grunder 7-
62 1983 $35

MEIER-GRAEFE, JULIUS   Cezanne. London: Ernest Benn Ltd.,
1927. 4to, 105 plates with captions and a frontis. Edition ltd. to
650 numbered copies. Tan cloth. Karmiole 72-103 1983 $65

MEIER-GRAEFE, JULIUS   Courbet. Neue Auflage. Munchen:
R. Piper, 1921. 118 plates. 8 collotype plates with tissue guards.
Large 4to. Boards, 1/4 cloth. Worn. Inside front hinge broken.
Ars Libri 32-125 1983 $45

MEIER-GRAEFE, JULIUS   Degas. Ein Beitrag zur Entwicklungs-
geschichte der modernen Malerei. Munchen: R. Piper, 1920. 104
collotype plates. Large 4to. Boards, 1/2 leather. Edition limited
to 1200 numbered copies. Binding rubbed. Ars Libri 32-154 1983
$100

MEIER-GRAEFE, JULIUS   Vincent Van Gogh. London/Boston: The
Medici Society, 1926. 2 vols. 102 collotype plates. Tissue guards.
Large 4to. Boards, 1/4 cloth. Ars Libri 32-260 1983 $85

MEIGS, JOHN   The Cowboy in American Prints. Chicago,
1972. Illus. Special edition of 300 copies numbered and signed by
the editor, including a lithograph especially executed for this
book by Peter Hurd. Three quarter morocco. Boxed. Jenkins 151-
207 1983 $175

MEIGS, JOHN F.   Practical Treatise on Diseases of
Children. Phila., 1848. Cont. sheep, leather label; ex-lib. First
edition. Argosy 713-372 1983 $45

MEINERTZHAGEN, R.   Birds of Arabia. 1954. Coloured folding
map, coloured and plain plates, roy. 8vo, original cloth. Scarce
original edition. Nice copy with dust jacket. Wheldon 160-59 1983
£320

MEINHOLD, WILLIAM   Mary Schweidler, the Amber Witch.
John Murray, 1861. New edition, 8vo, original cloth. Hill 165-84
1983 £20

MEINHOLD, WILLIAM   Sidonia the Sorceress. London: Reeves
& Turner, 1894. First English edition in this format. 2 vols. Orig.
cloth. Spines a little soiled and worn. Good. MacManus 280-5562
1983 $65

MEINHOLD, WILLIAM   Sidonia the Sorceress. 1894. 2 vols.,
half titles, orig. olive cloth, dulled. First edition. Jarndyce
30-480 1983 £20

MELA, POMPONIUS   Cosmographia sive de situ orbis. Venice:
Erhard Ratdolt, 18 July 1482. First edition. With full-page woodcut
map (supplied from another copy), 2 large and 11 smaller floral woodcut
initials. Small 4to. Modern brown calf, blind ruled. Old ms. exlibris "Citta dell S: Francisci" and shelf mark. Bookplate of Jose M.
Rodriquez. Corners of 4 leaves lightly waterstained. Kraus 164-160
1983 $6,500

MELA, POMPONIUS   Cosmographia sive de situ orbis.
Venice: Gristophorus de Pensis, de Mandello, (after 1493?). Many
ornamental woodcut initials. Small 4to. Wrappers. From the library
of Harrison D. Horblit. Portions waterstained. Contemporary marginalia. Some edges uncut. Kraus 164-161 1983 $2,750

MELDRUM, ANDREW NORMAN   Avogadro and Dalton: The Standing in
Chemistry of their Hypotheses. Edinburgh: James Thin, 1906. 8vo.
Orig. cloth. Very good copy. Zeitlin 264-290 1983 $70

MELDRUM, ANDREW NORMAN　　　The Development of the Atomic Theory.
London: Humphrey Milford, Oxford University Press, 1920. First
edition. 8vo. Orig. printed paper wrappers. Stamped "publisher's
compliments" on title page. Edges frayed, covers detached. Zeitlin
264-291　1983　$30

MELI, FILIPPO　　　Giacomo Serpotta. Vita ed opere.
Palermo: Privately Printed, 1934. 71 plates with 108 illus. 4to.
Wrappers. Numbered copy of an unsepcified limitation. Ars Libri
33-338　1983　$150

MELI, FILIPPO　　　Matteo Carnilivari e l'architettura
del Quattro e Cinquecento in Palermo. Roma: Fratelli Palombi,
1958. 92 plates. 4to. Boards. Dust jacket. Ars Libri 33-88
1983　$125

MELINE, JAMES F.　　　Two Thousand Miles on Horseback.
New York, 1867. Map lacking. First edition. Felcone 22-148　1983
$45

MELISH, JOHN　　　A Military and Topographical Atlas of
the United States. Philadelphia, 1813. Cont. calf and boards.
A very good copy. Reese 18-416　1983　$150

MELISH, JOHN　　　The North American Tourist. New York,
(1839, i.e., 1840). Maps and views. 12mo, new cloth. Morrill 290-
308　1983　$60

MELLEN, PETER　　　Jean Clouet. London: Phaidon, 1971.
193 plates (4 color). Large 4to. Cloth. Dust jacket. Ars Libri
32-115　1983　$100

MELLER, SIMON　　　Peter Vischer der Altere und seine
Werkstatt. Leipzig: Insel, 1925. 145 illus. 4to. Cloth. Ars
Libri 32-690　1983　$75

MELLING, M.　　　Voyage Pittoresque de Constantinople,
et des Rives du Bosphore. Paris: Treuttel & Wurtz, 1829. 3 double
page maps, portrait, 48 double page plates, guarded, some occasional
foxing. 2 vols. in one. Thick folio, diced leather. Heavily gilt
arabesques on covers and spine, spine faded. The Furstenburg Copy,
with stamp on title. Good. Edwards 1044-486　1983　£9,500

MELLON, HARRIOT　　　Secret memoirs of Harriott Pumpkin,
or the birth, parentage, and education of an actress. London: printed
and published by J. Cahuac, n.d. (1823). 8vo, wrappers, first ed.
Ximenes 64-378　1983　$225

MELTON, ELSTON J.　　　Towboat Pilot. Caldwell, Idaho: The
Caxton Printers, ltd., 1948. 24 cm. Pictorial endpapers. Orig.
green cloth. Very good in chipped dust wrapper. Unopened. First
printing; no. 679 of 1,000 copies signed by the author, this copy
further inscribed by the author in 1965. Colored

MELTZER, DAVID　　　Poems. (San Francisco): Privately
printed, (1957). Printed wraps. First edition. Fine. One of 470
copies (of 500). Reese 20-686　1983　$600

MELVILLE, HERMAN　　　Battle-Pieces and Aspects of the War.
NY, 1866. First issue with "hnndred" in copyright notice, ex-lib.,
endpapers skinned, edges frayed, hinges starting, good. Quill & Brush
54-901　1983　$600

MELVILLE, HERMAN　　　Benito Cereno. London: Nonesuch Press,
1926. Folio. Cloth. Illus. by E. McKnight Kauffer. First
edition thus, one of 1650 copies. Bookplate, else a near fine copy.
Reese 20-728　1983　$45

MELVILLE, HERMAN　　　Benito Cereno. London, Nonesuch Press,
1926. Edition limited to 1650 copies. Illustrated by E. McKnight
Kauffer. 4to. Spine and part of covers faded; back cover slightly
bent; bookplate removed. Morrill 290-309　1983　$25

MELVILLE, HERMAN　　　Billy Budd. London: Lehmann, 1946.
First separate edition. Orig. cloth, gilt, d.j. D.j. is price clipped
and covers very faintly mottled from chemical instability of the cloth
just jacket used, else fine copy. Jenkins 155-918　1983　$50

MELVILLE, HERMAN　　　The Confidence-Man. NY, 1857. First
issue without half-title, rebacked, ex-lib., cover worn, corner of
rear fly missing, good. Quill & Brush 54-904　1983　$350

MELVILLE, HERMAN　　　Israel Potter. N.Y., 1855. First edition, second state, with the imperfect type on p. 113. Brown cloth.
Binding worn and stained, front flyleaf missing. Argosy 714-509　1983
$400

MELVILLE, HERMAN　　　Journal of a Visit to London and the
Continent, 1849-1950. Cambridge: Harvard Univ. Press, 1948. 1st
ed. Orig. cloth, dj with one scuff. Fine copy. Jenkins 155-919
1983　$25

MELVILLE, HERMAN　　　Journal up the Straits, October 11,
1856-May 5, 1857. NY: The Colophon, 1935. Photogravure frontis.
One facs. plate, bound-in. Edition ltd. to 650 copies, printed by
the Pynson Printers from plans of Bruce Rogers. Marbled cloth,
leather spine label. Karmiole 75-89　1983　$75

MELVILLE, HERMAN　　　Journal Up the Straits. NY, 1935.
Limited to 650 copies, with facsimile inserted. Many pages uncut,
front hinge starting at title, spine label missing, marbled muslin-
covered boards rubbed and worn at edges, pages edges slightly stained,
good or better. Quill & Brush 54-902　1983　$50

MELVILLE, HERMAN　　　Mardi: And a Voyage Thither. New York,
1849. 2 vols. First American edition. Rebound in three-quarter morocco, gilt stampings on spines and upper edges. From the library of
L. A. Godey and signed by same in both vols. on the title page. A copy
for review. Inscription by Melville in vol. 1. In the rebinding of
the volume the leaf with the inscription has been set into a blank new
endpaper. Enclosed is a short TLS from the Newberry Library. A fine
clean copy. In Our Time 156-560　1983　$7,500

MELVILLE, HERMAN　　　Mardi, and a Voyage Thither. New York,
Harpers, 1849. 2 vols., octavos, orig. cloth, blank lower half of
last leaf of first volume restored, with new back end-papers, small
puncture to hinge of first volume, bindings lightly worn, spine ends
with usual wear, name on title, an offset onto blank fly-leaf, light
foxing. Preserved in cloth slip-case with folding protective inner
wrapper. First American edition. Ravenstree 96-112　1983　$650

MELVILLE, HERMAN　　　Mardi, and a Voyage Thither. New York,
Harpers, 1849. 2 vols., 8vo, orig. cloth, blank lower half of last
leaf of first volume restored with new back end-papers lightly worn,
spine ends with usual wear, name on title, offset onto blank leaf,
minor foxing. Preserved in folding cloth slip-case with protective
inner wraps. First American edition. Ravenstree 97-101　1983　$590

MELVILLE, HERMAN　　　Moby Dick. N.Y., Random, 1930.
First edition thus. Thick 8vo, illus. by Rockwell Kent. Bound in
fine 3/4 navy blue morocco by Bayntun, spine w/gilt nautical devices,
t.e.g., marbled endpapers; original cloth bound in. Fine. Houle
22-630　1983　$250

MELVILLE, HERMAN　　　Moby Dick Or The Whale. N.Y., 1930.
Silver stamped pictorial black cloth. Front inner hinge broken.
Somewhat worn. Numerous woodcuts by R. Kent. King 45-409　1983　$25

MELVILLE, HERMAN　　　Moby-Dick; or The Whale. San Francisco:
Arion Press, 1979. Folio. Limited to 265 copies. Illus. with wood
engravings of Barry Moser. Bound in full blue morocco with numerous
onlays. Extremely fine in morocco-backed, cloth-covered clamshell box.
Bromer 25-153　1983　$4500

MELVILLE, HERMAN　　　Narrative of a Four Month's Residence
Among the Natives of a Valley of the Marquesas Islands. London, 1846.
First issue, very minor foxing on preliminary pages, otherwise very
good internally with hinges strengthened with tape. Front and rear
panels have some wear on corners and front edges, book has been rebacked
and orig. spine missing top third. "Colonial and Home Library" stamped
on new spine, balance of lettering on orig. spine present and laid down
on new backing. Good. Quill & Brush 54-903　1983　$1000

MELVILLE, HERMAN　　　Pierre, or the Ambiguities. New York:
Harper, 1852. 1st ed. Modern quarter brown morocco & marbled
boards. Fine copy of this scarce title. Jenkins 155-920　1983
$300

MELVILLE, HERMAN　　　Typee. NY, 1935. 8vo, decorated paper
over boards, slipcase. Color illus. by Miguel Covarrubias. One of
1500 copies signed by the artist. Very nice. Perata 27-123　1983　$75

MELVILLE, HERMAN   Typee. New York, Limited Editions
Club, 1935. 1 of 1500 copies signed by artist. Illus. in color
by Miguel Covarrubias. 8vo, orig. boards, boxed. Bookplate removed, otherwise very nice. Morrill 287-276 1983 $40

MELVILLE, HERMAN   White Jacket. N.Y., 1850. First
edition. Foxed throughout, backstrip wormed & chipped, old library
label on flyleaf. Argody 714-510 1983 $400

MELVILLE, LEWIS   The Life of William Makepeace Thackeray.
Chicago: Herbert S. Stone & Co., 1899. First edition. With port. &
illus. 2 vols. Orig. cloth with leather labels on spines. Heads of
spines slightly worn. Bookplate. Good. MacManus 280-5141 1983 $25

MEMOIR and theatrical career of Ira Aldridge, the African Roscius.
London: published by Onwhyn; and printed by Frederic Ledger, n.d.
(1848?). 8vo, original pink printed wrappers (a bit dusty, slightly
dog-eared, tears in back wrapper). 1st ed. Inscribed by Aldridge
to Mrs. H. Hughes. With a wood engraved portrait. Very scarce.
Ximenes 64-8 1983 $225

MEMOIRS of Junius Brutus Booth, from his birth to the present time.
London: printed by E. Thomas; published by Chapple; Miller; Rowden;
and E. Wilson, 1817. 8vo, sewn, 1st ed. Title-page and final leaf of
errata both chipped and dusty (title loose). An uncut copy; very
scarce. Ximenes 64-57 1983 $100

MEMOIRS of Sylvester Daggerwood, comedian, etc. deceased. London:
printed and published by M. Allen, 1807. 2 vols., 12mo, original
light blue boards, drab paper backstrips (spines worn, hinges tender).
First edition. Rare. An uncut copy. Ximenes 64-379 1983 $400

MEMOIRS of the Life of Lord Lovat. Printed for M. Cooper, 1746.
8vo, speckled calf gilt, rebacked, preserving the orig. spine. First
edition. Bickersteth 77-48 1983 £28

MEMOIRS of the life of Robert Wilks, Esq., containing an account of
his transactions before his coming to England...and other memorable
circumstances of his life. London: printed by W. Rayner, 1732.
8vo, modern half calf. 2nd edition. With a fine frontis. portrait.
Rare. A fine copy. Ximenes 64-578 1983 $425

MEMOIRS of the Lord Viscount Dundee... London: for Jonas Brown,
1714. First edition. 8vo. Modern vellum. Heath 48-135 1983
£65

A MEMORIAL and Biographical History of the Counties of Fresno, Tulare,
and Kern, California. Chicago: Lewis Pub. Co., n.d. (ca.1912).
Plates. Publisher's leather. A.e.g. Some wear. Dawson 471-193
1983 $100

A MEMORIAL of Brevet Brigadier General Lewis Benedict. Albany,
Munsell, 1866. 200 copies printed. Portrait. Tall 8vo. Ends of
spine worn. Orig. poem by Alfred B. Street, remarks, messages, etc.
Morrill 286-663 1983 $50

MEMORIAL of Joseph Henry. Washington, 1881. First edition. 8vo.
Wrappers. Portrait lacking, library stamp on front wrapper, else
fine. Fye H-3-781 1983 $20

MEMORIAL of Sundry Citizens of Missouri Praying that Further
Provision be Made for the Confirmation of Land Titles Derived
from the French and Spanish Governments... Wash., 1828. Dbd. First
edition. Ginsberg 47-468 1983 $25

MEMORIAL of the Citizens of St. Louis, Missouri, to the Congress
of the United States... St. Louis, 1844. Double columns. Orig.
printed wraps. First edition. Ginsberg 47-534 1983 $100

MEMORIAL of the People of California Against Refunding Pacific
Railroad Debt. (San F., 1896). Orig. printed wrappers. First
edition. Small embossed library stamp. Ginsberg 46-620 1983
$25

A MEMORIAL Of William Sever Lincoln... (Worcester? ca. 1889). 1st
ed. 8vo. Morrill 286-297 1983 $27.50

MEN and Ghosts of Gough Square. N.P.: privately printed, 1930.
First edition. Small square 8vo. Blue paper wrappers. Frontis.
Fine. Scarce. Oak Knoll 48-301 1983 $20

MEN of the Pacific Coast. San Francisco: The Pacific Art Co.,
1903. With photo portraits. Black calf, a bit rubbed. Karmiole
72-24 1983 $35

MENCKEN, HENRY LOUIS   The American Language. N.Y., 1945,
1948. First edition. Tall 8vo, cloth, d.w. Fine. Argosy 714-512
1983 $25

MENCKEN, HENRY LOUIS   Bookmen's Holiday. N.Y., 1943. First
edition. Illus. Cloth. One of 1,000 copies. Very good. Houle 21-
617 1983 $65

MENCKEN, HENRY LOUIS   Christmas Story. N.Y., Knopf, 1946.
First edition. Sm square 8vo, illus. by Bill Crawford. Dust jacket
(a few nicks). Very good. Houle 21-612 1983 $35

MENCKEN, HENRY LOUIS   Criticism in America: It's Function
and Status. N.Y., Harcourt, Brace, (1924). First edition. Dust
jacket (spine slightly faded). Very good. Houle 22-639 1983 $45

MENCKEN, HENRY LOUIS   Europe After 8:15. N.Y., Lane, 1914.
First edition. Illus. by Thomas Hart Benton. Dust jacket (a few
nicks). Inscribed and signed by HLM. Very good-fine. Houle 21-613
1983 $250

MENCKEN, HENRY LOUIS   Happy Days, 1880-1892. N.Y., Knopf,
1940. First edition. Dust jacket (rubbed, small stains), else very
good. Signed by HLM on front free endpaper. Houle 21-614 1983
$85

MENCKEN, HENRY LOUIS   Menckeniana: A Schimpflexikon. NY,
1928. Limited to 230 numbered and signed copies, cover slightly
soiled, else fine. Quill & Brush 54-906 1983 $135

MENCKEN, HENRY LOUIS   Newspaper Days 1899-1900. NY, 1941.
Advance sample copy, paperwraps, cover slightly soiled and book slightly cocked, very good or better. Quill & Brush 54-908 1983 $100

MENCKEN, HENRY LOUIS   The Philisophy of Friedrich Nietzsche.
London, 1908. First English edition. Portrait. T.e.g. Ink name,
moderately rubbed. King 45-222 1983 $45

MENCKEN, HENRY LOUIS   Prejudices: Fifth Series. NY, (1926).
No. 3 of 200 signed and numbered copies, front hinge starting but
tight, spine and lable faded, else very good, extra label tipped-in,
in wearing slipcase. Quill & Brush 54-909 1983 $175

MENCKEN, HENRY LOUIS   Prejudices: Sixth Series. N.Y.,
Knopf, 1940. First edition. Dust jacket (rubbed, small stains), signed
by HLM on front free endpaper. Very good. Houle 21-614 1983 $85

MENCKEN, HENRY LOUIS   Supplement Two: The American Language.
New York: Knopf, 1948. 1st ed. Orig. cloth, dj. Small tears at
two edges of dj, else very fine copy. Jenkins 155-1415 1983 $25

MENCKEN, HENRY LOUIS   Treatise on the Gods. NY, L, 1930.
Limited to 375 numbered and signed copies, Goldstones copy, boards
rubbed at edges, else very good in worn dustwrapper frayed on edges
and in wearing slipcase. Quill & Brush 54-911 1983 $175

MENDELEEFF, DIMITRI IVANOVICH   An Attempt Towards a Chemical
Conception of the Ether... London: Longmans, 1904. First
English edition. 8vo. Orig. soft cloth. Ads. Light wear.
Zeitlin 264-292 1983 $90

MENDELEEFF, DIMITRI IVANOVICH   The Principles of Chemistry...
London: Longmans, 1905. Third English edition. 2 vols. 8vo.
Frontis., text figures. Spine sunned, defect to upper spine vol.
II; edges a little worn. Zeitlin 264-294 1983 $90

MENDELSSOHN-BARTHOLDY, FELIX The Music to Racine's Athalie. London,
Ewer, n.d. (c. 1845). Engraved music, tall folio, cloth-backed orig.
printed boards (a little shaky in binding). Salloch 387-120 1983 $75

MENDELSSOHN-BARTHOLDY, FELIX Paulus. Bonn, Simrock, n.d. (1837). Full score, engraved music. With lithograph portrait and lithograph title. Uncut, folio, 1/2 calf, orig. printed boards bound in. First edition. Fine copy. Salloch 387-121 1983 $300

MENEN, AUBREY The Prevalence of Witches. L, 1947. Good or better in slightly worn dustwrapper by Edward Bawden, dustwrapper slightly chipped at top of spine, owner's name. Quill & Brush 54-912 1983 $30

MENGE, H. Griechische-Deutsches Schulwoertertuch. Berlin, 1903. 4to, cloth. Salloch 385-94 1983 $35

MENKEN, ADAH ISAACS Infelicia. London: 1868. First edition. Orig. cloth. 16mo. Dedicated to Charles Dickens. Covers a bit rubbed. Very good. MacManus 279-3651 1983 $50

MENKEN, JAMES Biography of Adah Isaacs Menken. New York, (1881). 8vo, with frontis., 2 full-page & 1 half-page plate. Orig. printed pictorial wraps. (portrait of Menken on front cover, theatrical ads on back). Rostenberg 88-68 1983 $45

MENNINGER, KARL Love Against Hate. NY: Harcourt, (1942). First edition. Cloth, good copy with some cover wear. Presentation from Jean and Karl Menninger to the Bartemeirs. Gach 95-353 1983 $30

MENOTTI, GIAN CARLO The Saint of Bleecker Street. (N.Y., Circle Blue Print Co., 1954). Folio. 25 leaves. With notations of changes in red ink in the hand of Fedele d'Amico. Pencil corrections throughout by Menotti. Together with a TLS from Francis Rizzo, Menotti's former private secretary. Italian text. Houle 22-642 1983 $1,950

MENPES, MORTIMER Gainsborough. London: Adam and Charles Black, 1909. 15 tipped-in color plates. Folio. Cloth. Inside front hinge cracked. Ars Libri 32-236 1983 $85

MENPES, MORTIMER World Pictures. Black, 1902. 1st edn. Col'd frontis. & 99 col'd & two-tone illus., & numerous b&w illus. Red decor. cloth, bevelled boards, t.e.g. others uncut. Hodgkins 27-476 1983 £40

MENSCHUTKIN, NICOLAI ALEKSANDROVICH Analytical Chemistry... London: Macmillan, 1895. First English edition. 8vo. Orig. green cloth. Text table. Stamped presentation copy on title page. Text table. Ads. Very good copy. Zeitlin 264-295 1983 $30

MENSI, ARTURO Giovanni Migliara. Alessandria, 1937. 28 plates (2 tipped-in). Small 4to. Wrappers. Ars Libri 33-525 1983 $25

MENZELIUS, PH. Theses, de Methodo Therapeutica... Ingolstadt: A. Vueissenhorn, 1569. 8vo. Wrappers. Gurney JJ-269 1983 £20

MENZIES, LOUISA L. J. Legendary Tales of The Ancient Britons. London: John Russell Smith, 1864. First edition. Orig. blue cloth. Cont. inscription on front free endpaper. Ink stamping on endsheet. Fine. MacManus 279-3652 1983 $25

MENZIES, ROBERT A Dissertation on Respiration. Edinburgh, 1796. 8vo. Old half-leather. Errata leaf. Plate. Small library and cancellation stamp on title; title creased. Binding worn. Gurney 90-81 1983 £125

THE MERCANTILE Agency Reference Book. San Francisco: R.G. Dun & Co., September 1903. Limp leather, worn. Labels pasted on flyleaf. Dawson 471-194 1983 $60

MERCER, ASA SHINN The Banditti of the Plains. SF, 1935. 8vo, cloth-backed boards, paper label. Illus. by Arvilla Parker. Perata 27-63 1983 $65

MERCER, ASA SHINN Washington Territory: The Great Northwest, Her Material Resources, and Claims to Emigration... Seattle: The Dogwood Press, 1939. Limited to 350 copies. Illus. The scarce reissue of the rare orig. ed. of 1865. Mint as issued. Jenkins 153-672 1983 $50

MERCER, F. A. Modern Publicity, Commercial Art Annual 1932. London. Illustrated, cloth, covers rubbed and soiled. King 46-380 1983 $25

MERCER, HENRY C. Ancient Carpenter's Tools. Doylestown, Pa., 1929. 1st ed. Illus. 8vo, some light cover spots. Morrill 288-307 1983 $45

MERCER, HENRY C. The Bible in Iron or the Pictured Stoves and Stove Plates of the Pennsylvania Germans. Doylestown, 1914. Profusely illus., sq. 8vo, stiff pr. wraps. (spine somewhat worn). Argosy 716-401 1983 $40

MERCER, HENRY C. The Hill-Caves of Yucatan. Phila.: Lippincott, 1896. First edition. Map. Over 70 illus. Orig. beige pictorial cloth. Some binding wear. With ownership signature of Mesoamericanist Robert Wauchope. Internally fine. Jenkins 152-241 1983 $85

MERCER, THOMAS The Sentimental Sailor. Edinburgh: Printed for A. Kincaid and W. Creech and Sold by E. & C. Dilly, London. MDCCLXXII. 4to, complete with half-title, engraved title-page with striking vignette, disbound. First and only edition. Quaritch NS 7-84 1983 $125

MERCIER, CHARLES Criminal Responsibility. Oxford, 1905. 8vo. 1st ed. Some light cover stains. Morrill 289-157 1983 $25

MERCIER, LOUIS SEBASTIEN Memoirs of the Year Two Thousand Five Hundred. Philadelphia: Dobson, 1795. 8vo, orig. tree calf. Bookplate of portsmouth Athenaeum. First American edition. Rostenberg 88-74 1983 $375

MERCK'S 1896 Index. An Encyclopedia for the Physician and the Pharmacist. New York, 1896. 8vo. Orig. binding. Numerous woodcut Illustrations. Fye H-3-391 1983 $45

MEREDITH, GEORGE The Adventures of Harry Richmond. London: Smith, Elder & Co., 1871. First edition. 3 vols. Rebound in full calf with morocco labels on spines. Orig. cloth bindings preserved at the back. Fine. MacManus 279-3653 1983 $250

MEREDITH, GEORGE The Amazing Marriage. Archibald Constable, and Co., 1895. First edition. 2 vols. 8vo, half-titles and 3 blank leaves. Orig. green cloth (spines darkened), uncut. A fine unnused set. Hannas 69-142 1983 £45

MEREDITH, GEORGE The Amazing Marriage. Westminster: Archibald Constable & Co., 1895. First edition, first impression. 2 vols. Rebound in full calf with morocco labels. Orig. cloth covers bound in at the back of each vol., by Riviere. Top of spine of vol. two a bit worn. Fine. MacManus 279-3654 1983 $75

MEREDITH, GEORGE The Amazing Marriage. Westminster: Constable, 1895. First edition. 2 vols. Orig. cloth. First impression. Soiled and worn. MacManus 279-3655 1983 $30

MEREDITH, GEORGE Ballads and Poems of Tragic Life. London: Macmillan & Co., 1887. First edition. Rebound in full polished calf with morocco labels on spines. Orig. cloth bound in. Fine. MacManus 279-3656 1983 $75

MEREDITH, GEORGE Ballads and Poems of Tragic Life. Lon., 1887. Spine edges bumped and franed. Good plus. Quill & Brush 54-913 1983 $35

MEREDITH, GEORGE Beauchamp's Career. London: Chapman and Hall, 1876. First edition, half-titles. 3 vols. 8vo. Half blue morocco, gilt, gilt panelled spines, t.e.g., the orig. green cloth spines bound at the end of each vol. Traylen 94-573 1983 £85

MEREDITH, GEORGE Beauchamp's Career. London: Chapman & Hall, 1876. First edition. 3 vols. Orig. cloth. Worn; shaken; some inner hinges cracked. Labels removed from front covers. MacManus 279-3658 1983 $135

MEREDITH, GEORGE Bibliography and Various Readings. London: Constable & Co. Ltd., 1911. Memorial edition. Frontis. Orig. cloth. Fine. MacManus 279-3659 1983 $35

MEREDITH, GEORGE   A Catalogue of the Astschul Collection of George Meredith in the Yale University Library. N.P.: privately printed, cloth-backed marbled boards, paper spine label, t.e.g. First edition, limited to 500 copies printed by D.B. Updike at the Merrymount Press. A very fine copy. Unopened. Oak Knoll 49-470 1983 $65

MEREDITH, GEORGE   "Chillianwallah." (Jamaica, Queensborough, New York: The Marion Press, 1909). First separate edition. Small 4to. Blue 3/4 morocco & marbled boards. Orig. blue paper wraps. bound in. One of 112 copies printed. Bookplate of Willis Vickery on front endsheet. Fine. MacManus 279-3660 1983 $75

MEREDITH, GEORGE   Correspondence from the Seat of War in Italy. For Private Circulation, (1912). First edition. Ex-staff College Library copy. Label on front endpaper. Rota 231-416 1983 £50

MEREDITH, GEORGE   Diana of the Crossways. London: Chapman & Hall, 1885. First edition. 3 vols. Handsomely rebound in full calf with morocco labels on spines. Orig. cloth bindings bound in. Fine. MacManus 279-3661 1983 $250

MEREDITH, GEORGE   Diana of the Crossways. London: Chapman & Hall Limited, 1885. First edition. 3 vols. Orig. cloth. Recased with new endpapers. Covers worn. In a half-morocco slipcase. Good. MacManus 279-3662 1983 $150

MEREDITH, GEORGE   Diana of the Crossways. Chapman & Hall, vols. I & III. First edition. Vol. II, 2nd edition, half titles, orig. brown cloth, a little rubbed, otherwise very good. Jarndyce 30-482 1983 £36

MEREDITH, GEORGE   The Egoist. London: C. Kegan Paul & Co., 1879. First edition. 3 vols. Rebound in full calf with morocco labels on spines. Orig. cloth bindings bound in. Fine. MacManus 279-3664 1983 $250

MEREDITH, GEORGE   The Egoist. London: Kegan Paul, 1879. First edition. 3 vols. Orig. cloth. Library labels neatly removed from front endsheet. Binding faded and worn. A few inner hinges cracked. MacManus 279-3663 1983 $225

MEREDITH, GEORGE   Emilia in England. London: Chapman & Hall, 1864. First edition. 3 vols. Rebound in full calf with morocco labels. Orig. cloth binding bound in at the backs, by Riviere. Fine. MacManus 279-3665 1983 $125

MEREDITH, GEORGE   Evan Harrington. London: Bradbury & Evans, 1861. First edition. 3 vols. Rebound in full calf with morocco labels on spines. Orig. cloth bindings bound in. Fine. MacManus 279-3667 1983 $250

MEREDITH, GEORGE   Jump to Glory Jane. London: Swan, Sonnenschein & Co., 1892. First edition. With 44 designs invented, drawn, and written by L. Housman. Orig. decorated boards. Small bookplate. Covers darkened and a bit worn. Good. MacManus 279-2797 1983 $50

MEREDITH, GEORGE   Last Poems. Constable, 1909. First edition, half title. Orig. brown calico cloth, v.g. Jarndyce 31-810 1983 £15

MEREDITH, GEORGE   Last Poems. L, 1909. Cover rubbed and lightly worn, good. Quill & Brush 54-914 1983 $30

MEREDITH, GEORGE   Letters. London: Constable & Co., 1912. Second edition. 2 vols. Illus. Orig. cloth. Spines faded. Signatures on flyleaves. Very good. MacManus 279-3668 1983 $22.50

MEREDITH, GEORGE   Lord Ormont and His Aminta. London, 1894. 8vo. Cloth. 3 vols. Newspaper clipping about Meredith glued to front and back endboards of vol. 1, otherwise a very nice copy. In Our Time 156-561 1983 $150

MEREDITH, GEORGE   Lord Ormont and His Aminta. London, Chapman & Hall, 1894. 3 vols., 8vo, orig. cloth gilt, a bit worn, hinges bit rubbed with one small snag, but a rather good, tight set. First edition. Ravenstree 96-113 1983 $115

MEREDITH, GEORGE   Lord Ormont and His Aminta. London, 1894. 8vo, cloth, hinges cracking, else fine. In Our Time 156-562 1983 $85

MEREDITH, GEORGE   Modern Love and Poems of the English Roadside. London, 1862. First edition. Carter's "C" binding. Corners slightly rubbed. Very nice. Rota 230-399 1983 £85

MEREDITH, GEORGE   Modern Love and Poems of the English Roadside with Poems and Ballads. Chapman & Hall, 1862. First edition, orig. dark green cloth, v.g. Jarndyce 31-809 1983 £48

MEREDITH, GEORGE   Modern Love; a Reprint, to which is added "The Sage enamoured and the honest Lady." London and New York: Macmillan, 1892. 1st ed., 8vo, orig. cloth, spine gilt, bookplate. Title slightly soiled, but a fine copy in a slipcase. Trebizond 18-66 1983 $40

MEREDITH, GEORGE   Modern Love. (Stamford, Conn.): Overbrook Press, 1934. 12mo, ltd. to 150 copies, printed on handmade paper. Gilt-stamped black cloth. Orig. slipcase. T.e.g. Karmiole 73-80 1983 $50

MEREDITH, GEORGE   Modern Love. Stamford, Conn.: The Overbrook Press, 1934. One of only 150 copies. Argosy 714-514 1983 $25

MEREDITH, GEORGE   Odes In Contribution to the Song of French History. Westminster: Archibald Constable & Co., 1898. First edition. Rebound in full polished calf with morocco labels on spine. Orig. cloth bound in. Fine. MacManus 279-3669 1983 $75

MEREDITH, GEORGE   One of Our Conquerors. London: Chapman & Hall, 1891. First edition. 3 vols. Rebound in full calf with morocco labels on spines. Orig. cloth bindings bound in. Fine. MacManus 279-3670 1983 $125

MEREDITH, GEORGE   One of Our Conquerors. Chapman and Hall, 1891. First edition, 3 vols., 8vo, orig. royal-blue cloth, a rather nice copy. With ad. panel on the verso of each front flyleaf. Fenning 61-296 1983 £65

MEREDITH, GEORGE   One of Our Conquerors. London, Chapman & Hall, 1891. 3 vols., 8vo, orig. cloth, light wear but good copy. First edition. Ravenstree 96-115 1983 $85

MEREDITH, GEORGE   One of Our Conquerors. Chapman & Hall, 1891. First edition, 3 vols. Orig. blue cloth, sl. rubbed, otherwise good. Jarndyce 30-483 1983 £35

MEREDITH, GEORGE   One of Our Conquerors. London: Chapman & Hall, 1891. First edition. 3 vols. Orig. cloth. Slightly worn. Front inner hinge cracked in vol. one. Good. MacManus 279-3671 1983 $50

MEREDITH, GEORGE   The Ordeal of Richard Feverel. London: Chapman & Hall, 1859. First edition. 3 vols. Rebound in full calf with morocco labels on spines. Orig. cloth bindings bound in. Fine. MacManus 279-3672 1983 $250

MEREDITH, GEORGE   The Ordeal of Richard Feverel. London: Chapman & Hall, 1859. First edition, secondary binding. 3 vols. Orig. chocolate-colored cloth. Covers worn. Inner hinges cracked, Small institutional stamp in gutters of contents pages. MacManus 279-3673 1983 $150

MEREDITH, GEORGE   Poems. London: Macmillan & Co., 1892. First edition. Orig. cloth. Very good. MacManus 279-3674 1983 $25

MEREDITH, GEORGE   Poems and Lyrics of The Joy of Earth. London: Macmillan & Co., 1883. First edition. Rebound in full polished calf with morocco labels on spine. Orig. binding bound in. Fine. MacManus 279-3675 1983 $75

MEREDITH, GEORGE   Poems and Lyrics of the Joy of Earth. Macmillan and Co., 1883. First edition, 8vo, orig. cloth. Fenning 61-297 1983 £24.50

MEREDITH, GEORGE　　　　A Reading of Earth. London: Macmillan & Co., 1888. First edition. Rebound in full polished calf with morocco labels on spine. Orig. cloth binding bound in. Fine. MacManus 279-3676　1983　$75

MEREDITH, GEORGE　　　　A Reading of Earth. London and New York: Macmillan, 1888. 1st ed., 8vo, original cloth, spine gilt, half-title, bookplate. Bound without advertisement slip glued into later issues of the first edition. Auction slip pasted on flyleaf, but a very good copy in a foldout slipcase. Trebizond 18-67　1983　$45

MEREDITH, GEORGE　　　　The Shaving of Shagpat. London: Chapman & Hall, 1856. First edition. Orig. cloth. Edges a little worn. Front endpapers slightly soiled. Very good. MacManus 279-3677　1983　$275

MEREDITH, GEORGE　　　　The Shaving of Shagpat. London, Chapman & Hall, 1856. 8vo, orig. cloth (rehinged, preserving orig. spine, bit worn, trifle soiled, bookplate) decent copy in Carter's "A" binding. A decent copy of the first binding of the first edition. Ravenstree 96-116　1983　$165

MEREDITH, GEORGE　　　　The Tale of Chloe and Other Stories. London: Ward, Lock & Bowden, 1894. First collected edition. Orig. parchment-backed boards. One of 250 large paper copies. Covers soiled. Very good. MacManus 279-3678　1983　$75

MEREDITH, GEORGE　　　　The Tale of Chloe--The House on the Beach--The Case of General Ople and Lady Camper. London: Warde, Lock & Bowden, 1894. First English (small paper) edition. Rebound in full calf with morocco labels. Orig. cloth binding bound in at the back, by Riviere. Very good. MacManus 279-3680　1983　$50

MEREDITH, GEORGE　　　　The Tale of Chloe--The House of the Beach--The Case of General Ople and Lady Camper. London: Ward, Lock & Bowden, Limited, 1894. First edition. Rebound in full polished calf with morocco labels on spine. Fine. MacManus 279-3679　1983　$50

MEREDITH, GEORGE　　　　The Tale of Chloe--The House on the Beach--The Case of General Ople and Lady Camper. London: Ward, Lock & Bowden, 1894. First English (small paper) edition. MacManus 279-3681　1983　$25

MEREDITH, GEORGE　　　　The Tragic Comedians. London: Chapman & Hall, 1880. First edition. 2 vols. Orig. cloth. Labels removed from front covers. Very good. MacManus 279-3682　1983　$135

MEREDITH, GEORGE　　　　The Tragic Comedians. London: Chapman & Hall, 1880. First edition. 2 vols. Rebound in full calf with morocco labels on spines. Orig. cloth bindings bound in. Fine. MacManus 279-3683　1983　$125

MEREDITH, GEORGE　　　　The Tragic Comedians. Chapman & Hall, 1880. First edition, 2 vols., half titles, 28 pp ads. vol. II. Orig. dark sage-green cloth, sl. rubbed. Mudie's labels on upper covers. Jarndyce 30-481　1983　£40

MEREDITH, GEORGE　　　　The Works. London, 1896-1911. 36 vols. 8vo. Half crimson levant morocco, gilt, fully gilt panelled spines with ornaments, t.e.g., by Birdsall, the orig. pink cloth covers bound in at end of each vol. Frontis. to each vol. Limited edition of 1025 sets, numbered and signed by the publisher. Traylen 94-572　1983　£650

MEREDITH, GEORGE　　　　The Works. London: Constable & Co., 1909. Memorial edition. Illus. 27 vols. Bound in 3/4 blue morocco & marbled boards by Zaehnsdorf. Bookplates. Spines darkened. Very good. MacManus 279-3684　1983　$650

MEREDITH, GEORGE　　　　The Works. London, 1912. Surrey edition. 24 vols. 8vo. Orig. blue cloth with gilt emblems, t.e.g. Frontis. to each vol. Traylen 94-923　1983　£60

MEREDITH, OWEN PSEUD.
Please turn to
LYTTON, EDWARD ROBERT BULWER-LYTTON, 1ST EARL OF 1831-1891

MEREDITH, WILLIAM　　　　Ships and Other Figures. Princeton U.P. 1948. 8vo. Cloth. Fine in near perfect dj. In Our Time 156-564　1983　$125

MEREUX, AMEDEE　　　　Les Clavecinistes de 1637-1790. Paris, Heugot, 1867. With 4 lithographed title pages in different colors, and 16 lithographed, tinted portraits by Lemaire, a woodcut plate illustrating keyboard instruments, and musical examples. Tall folio, green buckram with label, orig. wraps. bound in; uncut. Special edition, in "formate Pantheon," printed for the Exposition Universelle, the World's Fair, of 1867. Salloch 387-122　1983　$225

MEREWEATHER, F. H. S.　　　　A Tour Through the Famine District of India. London, 1898. Folding map, plates, recased. 8vo. Good. Edwards 1044-489　1983　£30

MERIMEE, PROSPER　　　　Carmen and Letters from Spain. Paris, Harrison of Paris, 1931. Illus. by Maurice Barraud. One of 595 copies on Rives paper. Houle 21-620　1983　$30

MERIVALE, HERMAN　　　　Lectures on Colonization and Colonies. London: Longman, Green, Longman, and Roberts, 1861. Thick 8vo, index. Orig. cloth, skillfully rebacked, with orig. spine laid down. With an embossed stamp on title: "Presented by the Publishers". Karmiole 75-90　1983　$50

MERRICK, GEORGE B.　　　　Old Times on the Upper Mississippi. Cleveland: The Arthur H. Clark Co., 1909. Illus. and maps. T.e.g. Orig. cloth. Some wear. Very good. Jenkins 152-244　1983　$55

MERRICK, JOHN　　　　Heliocrene, a poem in Latin and English on the chalybeate well at Sunning-Hill in Windsor Forest. Reading, printed and sold by J. Newbery and C. Micklewright, 1744. 2nd ed., first to contain the appendix. 4to, some staining with a small hole in the title page not affecting the text, stab-sewn in the original blue wrappers, rather worn. Rare. Pickering & Chatto 19-39　1983　$100

MERRICK, LEONARD　　　　A Chair On The Boulevard. London: Hodder & Stoughton, (1919). First edition. Orig. cloth. Spine and covers slightly worn and soiled. In a half-morocco slipcase. Good. MacManus 279-3687　1983　$65

MERRICK, LEONARD　　　　Conrad in Quest of His Youth. London: Grant Richards, 1903. First edition. Orig. decorated cloth. Covers rubbed. MacManus 279-3688　1983　$25

MERRICK, LEONARD　　　　Cynthia. A Daughter of the Philistines. London: Chatto & Windus, 1896. First edition. 2 vols. Orig. cloth. Hinges cracked. Front flyleaf loose in Vol. II. Library labels removed from covers of both volumes. MacManus 279-3691　1983　$75

MERRICK, LEONARD　　　　Four Stories. London: (The Bookman's Journal), 1925. First edition. Orig. full vellum. One of 200 copies signed by Merrick. Covers a little soiled and warped. Bookplate. MacManus 279-3691　1983　$50

MERRICK, LEONARD　　　　The House of Lynch. London: Hodder & Stoughton, 1907. First edition. Orig. cloth. Inner hinges cracked. In a half morocco slipcase. Good. MacManus 279-3693　1983　$65

MERRICK, LEONARD　　　　The House of Lynch. London: Hodder & Stoughton, n.d. (1919). Intro. by G.K. Chesterton. Front inner hinge weak. Orig. cloth. Good. MacManus 279-3694　1983　$20

MERRICK, LEONARD　　　　The Little Dog Laughed. London: Hodder & Stoughton Limited, n.d. (1930). First edition. Orig. cloth. Dust jacket (chipped, torn at folds). Fine. MacManus 279-3695　1983　$35

MERRICK, LEONARD　　　　The Man Who Understood Women and Other Stories. London: Nahs, 1908. First edition. Orig. cloth. Spine stained. Good. MacManus 279-3697　1983　$22.50

MERRICK, LEONARD　　　　The Man Who Understood Women. London: Hodder & Stoughton, n.d. First edition. Intro. by W.J. Locke. Orig. cloth. Dustjacket (somewhat worn). Very good. MacManus 279-3696　1983　$20

MERRICK, LEONARD　　　　The Man Who Was Good. London: Chatto & Windus, 1892. First edition. 2 vols. Orig. blindstamped decorated cloth. Covers a bit worn. Inner hinges cracked. MacManus 279-3698　1983　$250

MERRICK, LEONARD   Mr. Bazalgette's Agent. London: George
Routledge & Sons, 1888. First edition. Orig. wrappers. Spine and
covers slightly faded and worn. In a quarter-morocco slipcase. Near-
fine. MacManus 279-3699 1983 $750

MERRICK, LEONARD   One Man's View. London: Grant Richards,
1897. First edition. Orig. decorated buckram. Loosely laid in is a
"TLS" from the then president, Henry Clapp Smith, of Duttons Publishing
Co. in New York, 1 page, December 5, 1929. Spine a trifle faded. Near
fine. MacManus 279-3700 1983 $225

MERRICK, LEONARD   The Quaint Companions. London: Grant
Richards, 1903. First edition. Orig. decorated cloth. Inscribed on
the half-title page: "Signed for Mrs. Langdon Thorne, Leonard Merrick."
Spine edges a trifle rubbed. Former owner's signature neatly removed
from the front free endpaper. In a quarter'morocco slipcase. London
book dealer's small blindstamp on front free endpaper. Near-fine.
MacManus 279-3702 1983 $135

MERRICK, LEONARD   This Stage of Fools. London: Chatto &
Windus, Piccadilly, 1896. First edition. Orig. decorate; cloth.
Presentation copy inscribed: "To Sir Henry and Lady Isaacs, with sincerest regard, from the Author, Leonard Merrick, June '96." Spine
margins, cover edges and corners slightly worn and rubbed. In a
quarter-morocco slipcase. Very good. MacManus 279-3703 1983 $185

MERRICK, LEONARD   This Stage of Fools. London: Chatto &
Windus, 1896. First edition. Orig. cloth. Spine and covers very
faded. Good, sound copy. MacManus 279-3704 1983 $25

MERRICK, LEONARD   To Tell You the Truth. London: Hodder &
Stoughton, (1922). First edition. Orig. cloth. Dust jacket (spine
and covers a trifle faded and worn). Slight offsetting to the free
endpapers. In a quarter-morocco slipcase. Fine. MacManus 279-3705
1983 $165

MERRICK, LEONARD   To Tell You the Truth. London: Hodder &
Stoughton, n.d. (1911). First edition. Orig. cloth. Bookseller's
stamp on title-page. Good. MacManus 279-3706 1983 $20

MERRICK, LEONARD   While Paris Laughed. London: Hodder &
Stoughton, (1918). Orig. cloth. Half morocco slipcase. Very good.
MacManus 279-3707 1983 $65

MERRICK, LEONARD   Whispers About Women. London: Nash,
1906. First edition. Orig. cloth (very faded, extremities frayed).
Presentation copy, inscribed "To Comyns Braumont with the kindest
regards of his contributor Leonard Merrick. June '06." MacManus
279-3708 1983 $35

MERRICK, LEONARD   The Worldlings. London: Murray, 1900.
First edition. Orig. decorated cloth. Covers a bit soiled. With an
ALS, one page, Paris, March 18, 1933, to John Macrae laid in. Good.
In a half-morocco slipcase. MacManus 279-3709 1983 $125

MERRILD, KNUT   A Poet and Two Painters. N.Y., Viking,
1939. First American edition, from English sheets. 10 illus. Blue
cloth. Very good. Houle 21-540 1983 $65

MERRILL, JAMES   First Poems. NY, 1951. Limited to 950
numbered copies, paperclip impression on limitation page, near fine in
price clipped, very good dustwrapper that is lightly worn on edges.
Quill & Brush 54-915 1983 $125

MERRITT, JOSEPH FOSTER   Old Time Anecdotes of the North River
and the South Shore. Rockland, 1928. 1st ed. Illus. 8vo. Morrill
288-286 1983 $22.50

MERRIWELL, MARK   My Own Annual. A Gift Book for Boys &
Girls. John Sands, Sydney, n.d. (ca.1840). Handcoloured frontis.
Handcoloured pictorial title & some 100 engravings. Green pictorial
cloth gilt. Verg good. Greer 39-131 1983 £25

MERRY Alphabet. N.Y.: McLoughlin, 1888. 4to. Stiff colored pictorial
wrappers. Light spine wear. Corner creased. Many bright chromoliths.
Printed on linen. Very good. Aleph-bet 8-3 1983 $33

MERRY Children's Nursery Rhymes. Nister, nd (1890). Mounted col.
frontis., b&w illus. title & numerous text illus., 3 pp. adverts.
Blue cloth backed colour pictorial bds., corners sl. bruised & worn,
insc. fr. ep., vg. Hodgkins 27-148 1983 £15

MERSENNE, MARIN   Les Questions Theologiques, Physiques,
Morales, et Mathematiques. Paris: Henri Guenon, 1634. First
edition. Small 8vo. Vellum. Kraus 164-92 1983 $3,000

MERSHON, STEPHEN L.   The Power of the Crown in the Valley of
the Hudson. Montclair, N.J., 1925. 1st ed. Maps, illus., facs.
8vo. Morrill 288-348 1983 $30

MERSHON, WILLIAM B.   Recollections of my Fifty Years Hunting
and Fishing. Boston 1923. Photos, cloth, spine sunned, covers
soiled. King 46-620 1983 $35

MERTON, AMBROSE   The Old Story Books of England. Cundall,
1845. Colour printed frontis. & 11 colour printed plates (light stains)
by J. Franklin, J. Absolon & F. Tayler. Coloured borders & initials
throughout. Full brown morocco, top boards loose, spine worn. Bound
in also is Gammer Gurton's Garland with extra colour plate. Greer 40-
83 1983 £35

MERTON, THOMAS   A Man in the Divided Sea. (Norfolk:
New Directions, 1946). Cloth, stamped in gilt. The correct first
edition. A fine copy in slightly used dust jacket, with some slight
chips at the edges. Reese 20-690 1983 $50

MERTON, THOMAS   Thirty Poems. Norfolk: New Directions,
(1944). Printed wraps. First edition, wrapper issue. A very fine
copy. Reese 20-689 1983 $50

MERTON, THOMAS   Waters of Silence. London, 1950.
First English edition. Top edge partially faded. Slightly rubbed
and chipped dustwrapper. Fine. Jolliffe 26-353 1983 £12

MERWIN, RAYMOND E.   The Ruins of Holmul, Guatemala.
Cambridge, 1932. 36 plates. 30 text illus. Folio. Buckram,
3/4 leather. Slightly worn. Orig. wrappers bound in. Presentation
copy, inscribed by the authors. Ars Libri 34-362 1983 $75

MERYMAN, RICHARD   Andrew Wyeth. Boston, 1969. Limited to
300 numbered copies, signed by Andrew Wyeth. With 132 very fine collotype illus. chiefly in color, including a color pictorial title and 10
pages. Slipcase. Thick paper, blue quarter suede, linen sides, a.e.g.
Blue buckram folding-case lettered 'AW', slightly rubbed case. King
45-438 1983 $2,500

MERYMAN, RICHARD   Andrew Wyeth. Boston, 1968. First
edition. Fine color plates. Two-tone cloth. Frayed and torn dust
wrapper. Very good. King 45-612 1983 $250

MESMER, FRANZ ANTON   Dissertatio physico-medica de plane-
tarum influxu. Vienna: Typis Chelenianis, 1766. Woodcut initials,
headpiece and tailpiece. 8vo. Half calf. Very rare. Kraus 164-
162 1983 $1,500

MESPOULET, M.   Creators of Wonderland. N.Y.: Arrow,
(1934). 4to. Red cloth. Number 86 of unknown quantity. Illus. in
black & white, color frontis. Fine. Aleph-bet 8-219 1983 $55

MESSER, ASA   An Oration, Delivered before the
Providence Association of Mechanics and Manufacturers. Providence:
John Carter, (1803). Sewed, uncut & unopened. Argosy 710-470
1983 $25

METCALF, M. M.   The Opalinid Ciliate Infusorians.
U.S. Nat. Mus. Bull., 1923. 258 text-figures, maps, 8vo, wrappers
(neatly rebacked). Wheldon 160-1324 1983 £15

METCALFE, JOHN   The Feasting Dead. Sauk City: Arkham
House, 1954. First edition. Cloth. Fine in perfect dust jacket.
1242 printed. Bradley 66-136 1983 $80

METCALFE, RICHARD   Sanitas Sanitatum et Omnia Sanitas.
London, 1877. Large folding litho-plates, volume 1 only. Argosy 713-
373 1983 $75

METCALFE, SAMUEL LYTLER   Caloric: Mechanical, Chemical and
Vital Agencies... Philadelphia: Lippincott, 1859. 2 vols. 8vo.
Orig. cloth. Worn. Zeitlin 264-297 1983 $20

METCHNIKOFF, ELIAS
Please turn to
MECHNIKOV, IL'IA IL'ICH

METHLEY, NOEL T.   The Life-Boat and its Story. Phila.
1912. Photos, cloth, t.e.g., bookplate, else a nice copy. King
46-746 1983 $20

THE METHODIST and Mimick. A tale, in Hudibrastick verse. London:
printed for C. Moran, 1766. 4to, wrappers, 1st edition. A fine copy,
complete with the final leaf of ads. Very rare. Ximenes 64-5 1983
$450

THE METRICAL miscellany: consisting chiefly of poems hitherto
unpublished. London: printed, at the Oriental Press, by Wilson
and Co., for Cadell and Davies, 1802. First edition. 8vo. Cont.
half calf, spine gilt. Hinges cracked. Some spotting; lacks a
half-title. Ximenes 63-421 1983 $75

METROPOLITAN Grievances. Sherwood, Neely and Jones, 1812. First
edition, 12mo, hand-col. front. by George Cruikshank. Title sl.
trimmed and with small library stamp. Rebound in green cloth,
maroon label. Jarndyce 31-227 1983 £38

METTLER, FRED A.   Neuroanatomy. St. Louis, 1942. First
edition. 337 illus., including 30 in color. Argosy 713-374 1983
$40

METZLER, NORBERT   Illustrated Halifax. Montreal:
Published by John McConniff, 1891. Oblong 14 1/2 x 22 1/2cm.
64 illus. from photographs. Cloth backed illus. boards. Shaken,
else very good. McGahern 54-133B 1983 $60

MEURSIUS, JOANNES   Fortuna Attica. Leyden, 1622. 4to,
cont. calf, spine gilt. Salloch 385-248 1983 $225

MEW, CHARLOTTE   The Farmer's Bride. London: The Poetry
Bookshop, 1921. New edition, with eleven new poems. Orig. pictorial
boards. Dust jacket (extremities of spine slightly worn). With 3
ALSs, 6 pages, 8vo, May 31 and June 27, 1923, Dec. 8, 1924, Hogarth
Studios, 64 Charlotte Street, Fitzroy Square, W. 1, London, in their
original stamped envelopes, to Louis Untermeyer. With Untermeyer's
bookplate on front flyleaf. Few penciled notes in his hand. Fine.
MacManus 279-3734 1983 $1,250

MEW, CHARLOTTE   The Farmer's Bride. London: The Poetry
Bookshop, 1929. Third edition. Orig. pictorial boards. Pasted to
the front free endpaper is a copy of New's poem "Song" which appears
on page 51 of this book, copied out and illustrated in the margin in
wash by Siegfried Sassoon, whose monogram is in the lower right hand
corner. Bookplate of Luis van Rooten on the front endsheet. Boards
faded at edges. Good. MacManus 279-3735 1983 $350

MEW, CHARLOTTE   The Farmer's Bride. London: The Poetry
Bookshop, 1916. "Second Edition." Orig. pictorial wrappers. Presentation copy from Cockerell, inscribed on the front wrapper: "M.M.S.
from S.C.C. 17 April 1930"; with an ALS from Cockerell to "My dear
Margaret," also dated 17 April 1930 (one page). Wrappers frayed and
soiled. Text lightly foxed. Good. MacManus 279-3731 1983 $90

MEW, CHARLOTTE   The Farmer's Bride. London: Poetry
Bookshop, 1916. Second edition. Orig. pictorial wrappers. MacManus
279-3732 1983 $25

MEW, CHARLOTTE   The Rambling Sailor. London: The Poetry
Bookshop, 1929. First edition. 8vo. Orig. boards. Dust jacket.
Fine. MacManus 279-3736 1983 $27.50

MEW, CHARLOTTE   Saturday Market. NY, 1921. Cover
slightly soiled, else very good, owner's name and date. Quill & Brush
54-920 1983 $35

MEW, CHARLOTTE   Shorter Lyrics of the Twentieth Century,
1900-1922. London: The Poetry Bookshop, (1922). First edition. Orig.
printed lavender boards. Presentation copy, inscribed on the front
free endpaper "For Louis & Jean Starr Untermeyer with cordial greetings
from Charlotte Mew, Nov. 3, 1922." Spine faded. Fine. MacManus 279-
3737 1983 $350

MEXICAN Typical View Album. Laredo: Thos. J. Cockrell, 1889. Title
plus 12 albertype photoplates of life and scenery along the border.
Orig. red gilt decorated cloth with orig. string ties. Fine. Jenkins
152-330 1983 $65

MEYER, ADOLF   Birth Control. Baltimore: Williams
& Wilkins, 1925. Ads. 12mo. Publisher's green cloth. Very good
ex-library copy. Gach 95-355 1983 $40

MEYER, ADOLF   Collected Papers of. Baltimore: Johns
Hopkins Press, 1950; 1951. Numerous illus., including 1 folding litho.
plate. 2 vols. Buckram; ex-lib. Argosy 713-375 1983 $35

MEYER, ADOLF   The Commonsense Psychiatry of... NY:
McGraw-Hill, 1948. First trade edition. Gach 94-398 1983 $25

MEYER, ARTHUR   Die Grundlagen und die Methoden fur die
mikroskopische Untersuchung von Pflanzenpulvern. Jena, 1901. 8
plates and text-figures, 8vo, boards, cloth back (small stain on
title). Wheldon 160-2176 1983 £12

MEYER, CARL   Prospectus to Form a Society for
Emigration to California... Claremont, Ca., Sunders, 1938. Orig.
boards. One of 440 numbered copies. Ginsberg 47-136 1983 $35

MEYER, E. H. F.   Geschichte der Botanik. (Konigsberg,
1854-57), Facsimile reprint, Amsterdam, 1965. 4 vols, 8vo, cloth.
Wheldon 160-253 1983 £76

MEYER, FRANX S.   A Handbook of Ornament. Batsford,
1896. Third English edition, 8vo, orig. cloth, t.e.g. Fenning 62-247
1983 £10.50

MEYER, FRANZ   Marc Chagall. New York: Abrams, (1961).
More than 1250 illus. (53 tipped-in color). Small folio, cloth, dust
jacket. Ars Libri 32-99 1983 $85

MEYER, FRANZ   Marc Chagall. New York: (1963). First
American edition. Thick quarto, cloth. Illus. Fine in jacket.
Bradley 66-399 1983 $85

MEYER, FRANZ   Marc Chagall: New York: Abrams,
1957. 4 color plates (2 double-page). 147 illus. 4to. Cloth.
Dust jacket. Ars Libri 32-100 1983 $75

MEYER, H. L.   Illustrations of British Birds. (1835-
41). 318 hand-coloured plates, 4 vols., imp. 4to, full red morocco,
gilt (neatly rebacked). A good copy. 1st ed. The reverse of one of
the plates in vol. 2 is stained and a very small marginal tear in
the same plate neatly repaired, else a very clean copy. Wheldon
160-68 1983 £3,500

MEYER, OSKAR EMIL   The Kinetic Theory of Gases...
London: Longmans, 1899. First English edition. 8vo. Orig.
cloth. Ads. Shook and rubbed, internally a very good copy.
Zeitlin 264-302 1983 $75

MEYER, RICHARD EMIL   Victor Meyer: Leben und Wirken
eines deutschen Chemikers und Naturforschers 1848-1897. Leipzig:
Akademische Verlags., 1917. First edition. 8vo. Orig. cloth.
Frontis. portrait, facsimile, 79 text photographs and an appendix.
Very good copy. Zeitlin 264-303 1983 $50

MEYER, RUDOLF   Sterbensspiegel. Auerich, Bodmer, 1650.
Engraved frontis., 60 engraved plates. 4to, very fine English binding
by Charles Hering (London, c. 1790), black morocco, tooled with cross-
bones and skulls, spine with 5 raised bands, with binder's ticket.
First edition. Salloch 387-123 1983 $2,500

MEYLERT, ASA P.   Notes on the Opium Habit. NY: Putnam's
Sons, 1885 (1884). Fourth edition. Wrappers. Gach 94-803 1983
$25

MEYNELL, ALICE   The Children. London: John Lane: The
Bodley Head, 1897. First American edition. Orig. decorated cloth.
First book designed by Will Bradley at The Wayside Press. Covers a
little dull. Very good. MacManus 277-660 1983 $65

MEYNELL, ALICE   The Children. London, 1897. First edition. Title-page and gilt cover designs by C. Robinson. Upper cover a little stained. Nice. Rota 230-401 1983 £20

MEYNELL, ALICE   Collected Poems. Burns & Oates, 1913. New edition. Spine and edges of covers darkened. Preliminaries and several leaves of text foxed. Author's autograph presentation inscription. Very good. Rota 231-419 1983 £20

MEYNELL, ALICE   Poems. London: John Lane; Boston: Copeland & Day, 1896. Fourth edition. 12mo. Orig. cloth. Covers a bit soiled. MacManus 279-3738 1983 $20

MEYNELL, ALICE   The Poems. London: Burns Oates & Washbourne Ltd., 1923. First edition. Frontis. port. by E. Walker after J.S. Sargent. Orig. cloth. One of 250 large-paper copies. Spine a little worn and faded. Very good. MacManus 279-3739 1983 $40

MEYNELL, ALICE   Preludes. London, 1975. First edition. Illus., orig. green cloth, with the errata slip correcting three errors in the text, but itself containing five misprints. Covers marked. Ex-library copy. Good. Rota 231-418 1983 £95

MEYNELL, ALICE   The Spirit of Place. London: Lane, 1923. Second edition. Orig. cloth. Signed by author on the flyleaf. Near-fine. MacManus 279-3740 1983 $20

MEYNELL, VIOLA   A Girl Adoring. London: Edward Arnold & Co., (1927). First edition. Orig. cloth. With an ALs by Forster to the publisher, thanking him for sending the book. Very good. MacManus 279-3741 1983 $175

MEYNEN, EMIL   Bibliography on German Settlements in Colonial North America... Leipzig: Otto Harrassowitz, 1937. Cloth, bumped. Dawson 470-206 1983 $50

MEYRICK, FREDERICK   What is the Working of the Church of Spain? Oxford, John Henry Parker, 1851. 8vo, disbound. Bickersteth 77-230 1983 £15

MICHAEL, A. D.   British Tyroglyphidae. Ray Society, 1901-03. 42 plates (28 coloured), 2 vols., 8vo, cloth. No more than 500 copies were produced. Wheldon 160-1325 1983 £20

MICHAEL SCOTUS
Please turn to
SCOTT, MICHAEL

MICHALSKI, ERNST   Joseph Christian. Ein Beitrag zum Begriff des deutschen Rokokos. Berlin: R. Jacosthal, n.d. 80 plates with 114 illus. 4to. Cloth. Ars Libri 32-107 1983 $75

MICHEL, ALBIN   Petition of...in Behalf of the Heirs of Madame de Lusser. Wash., 1840. First edition. Dbd. Ginsberg 46-4 1983 $25

MICHEL, NICHOLAS   Ruins of Many Lands. William Tegg, 1849. First edition, with a portrait and 5 plates, 8vo, cont. half calf, a very good copy. Fenning 61-298 1983 £35

MICHELANGELO
Please turn to
BUONARROTI, MICHEL ANGELO

MICHELI, MARIO DE   Evidenza di Picasso. Milano: Seda, 1962. 26 color plates in passepartouts (1 inserted loose, as issued). 2 plates in text (1 tipped-in original photograph). Boards, 1/4 leather. No. 253 of a limited edition of 1000 copies on Fabriano and Ventura papers. Ars Libri 32-523 1983 $175

MICHELI, MARIO DE   Guttuso. Milano: SEDA, 1963. 30 tipped-in color plates. Frontis. portrait (orig. tipped-in photograph). Folio. Boards, 1/4 leather. Edition limited to 500 numbered copies. Ars Libri 33-493 1983 $150

MICHELI, PIER ANTONIO   Nova Plantarium Genera. Florence, 1729. Folio, rebacked in leather, boards. Some foxing in text, otherwise a nice copy, with the plates clean and in fine condition. In Our Time 156-568 1983 $750

MICHELL, LEWIS   The life and times of the Right Honourable Cecil John Rhodes, 1853-1902. New York: Mitchell Kennerley, 1910. 2 vols. 8vo. 5 plates. Orig. red cloth. Adelson Africa-206 1983 $30

MICHENER, JAMES A.   Chesapeake. NY, (1978). Limited to 500 specially bound, numbered and signed copies, very fine in fine slipcase. Quill & Brush 54-922 1983 $100

MICHENER, JAMES A.   Facing East. NY/Paris: Maecenas Press, 1970. Elephant folio. Two parts in sep. folders laid-in a clam shell box with lettering on box and leather clasp. Orig. woodcuts and lithos. by Levine. Limited to 2500 copies signed by both author and artist, Jack Levine. Lithos. on Rives paper, text on Kawanaka Jap. vellum. 54 watercolors, gouaches and drawings printed by phototype and pochoir processes on Ingres paper. 2 to 40 colors hand-brushed on each. Mint. Quill & Brush 54-921 1983 $425

MICHENER, JAMES A.   The Fires of Spring. New York: Random House, (1949). First edition. 8vo. Orig. cloth. Dust jacket. Very fine copy. Jaffe 1-254 1983 $100

MICHENER, JAMES A.   The Fires of Spring. NY, (1949). Presentation edition, not signed, fine. Quill & Brush 54-924 1983 $30

MICHENER, JAMES A.   The Floating World. N.Y., Random, (1954). First edition, first printing. Dust jacket (a few small chips), else very good. With 40 color plates and 26 b/w plates. Houle 22-646 1983 $150

MICHENER, JAMES A.   Floating World. N.Y., Random (1954). First edition, third printing. Dust jacket. Very good. 40 color and 26 b/w. Houle 21-621 1983 $95

MICHENER, JAMES A.   The Hokusai Sketch-Books. Rutland (Vt.), Tuttle, (1958). First edition, first printing. Small 4to, profusely illus. in color by Katsushika Hokusai. Dust jacket (minor rubbing). Very good. Houle 22-645 1983 $125

MICHENER, JAMES A.   South Pacific. New York: Random House, (1949). 1st ed. Orig. cloth, dj. Fine copy. Jenkins 155-927 1983 $40

MICHENER, JAMES A.   Space. NY, (1982). Limited to 500 specially bound, numbered and signed copies, very fine in fine slipcase. Quill & Brush 54-923 1983 $100

MICHENER, JAMES A.   The Spell of the Pacific: An Anthology of Its Literature. New York, 1949. 8vo. Cloth. Bookplate of a private library on inside endboard, else a fine copy in colorful dj which has some light wear. In Our Time 156-569 1983 $40

MICHENER, JAMES A.   Tales of the South Pacific. New York: MacMillan, 1947. 1st ed. Orig. tan cloth. No dj, but close to fine copy. Scarce. Jenkins 155-928 1983 $75

MICHENER, JAMES A.   Tales of the South Pacific. NY, 1947. First edition. Cloth, ink inscription else very good in badly chipped and soiled dustwrapper. King 46-312 1983 $25

MICHIELS, ALFRED   Rubens et l'ecole de l'Anvers. Paris: Adolphe Delahays, 1854. 4to. Boards, 3/4 leather. Ars Libri 32-601 1983 $150

THE MICHIGAN Almanac for the Year 1869. Detroit, 1869. Orig. printed wraps. Ginsberg 46-461 1983 $50

MICHIGAN. LAWS.   Acts of the Legislature of the State of Michigan. Detroit, 1841. Cloth backed boards. Very rough copy. King 46-135 1983 $20

MICHIGAN. LAWS. Acts of the Legislature of the State of Michigan. Detroit, 1844. Cloth backed boards, some staining, well worn, spine label mostly gone. King 46-136 1983 $20

MICHIGAN Log Marks, Their function and use during the great Michigan pine harvest. East Lansing, 1942. Illus., pict. wrs. Argosy 710-622 1983 $25

MICHIGAN PIONEER AND HISTORICAL SOCIETY Historical Collections. Lansing, Mich., 1905. 23cm. Illus. Spine faded, else very good. McGahern 53-118 1983 $25

MICHIGAN SOUTHERN AND NORTHERN INDIANA RAILROAD Rules and Regulations for Operating the Michigan Southern & Northern Indiana Railroad. Adrian: Jermain's Steam Press, 1855. Orig. cloth worn. Some staining. Jenkins 152-252 1983 $40

MICHIGAN SOUTHERN RAILROAD Circular Statement of the Condition and Prospects of the Michigan Southern Railroad. New York: Van Norden & Amerman, Printers, 1849. Orig. printed wrappers. Two folding maps. Small piece missing from back wrapper and last page but not affecting text. Jenkins 152-251 1983 $100

MICHON, JEAN-HIPPOLYTE Histoire de Napoleon. Paris: Flammarion, 1879. First edition. Orig. printed wrappers. Library bookplate, spine taped. Gach 95-362 1983 $35

MICHON, L. M. Memoire et Observations sur quelques cas d'Autoplastie de la Face. Paris, n.d. (ca. mid 19th c.). 8vo. Wrappers. Offprint. Gurney JJ-270 1983 £15

MICKS, WILLIAM LAWSON An Account of the Constitution, Administration and Dissolution of the Congested Districts Board for Ireland, from 1891 to 1923. First edition, with 18 plates, errata slip, 8vo, orig. cloth, a nice copy in the dust wrapper. With a signed inscription by the author. Fenning 61-299 1983 £48.50

MIDANA, ARTURO L'Arte Del Legno In Piemonte Nel Set E Nel Settecento. Torino, n.d. (1930's?). Profusely illus. Cloth. Disbound, some pp transposed. King 45-352 1983 $35

MIDDLE East Science, a survey of subjects other than agriculture. 1946. Royal 8vo, cloth, 5 maps (2 coloured) and 16 plates. Wheldon 160-288 1983 £15

MIDDLEMASS, JEAN Nelly Jocelyn (Widow). London: F. V. White, 1887. First edition. 3 vols. Orig. cloth. Covers slightly soiled and waterstained. Edges slightly worn. The red coloring of the covers has bled onto the floral endpapers in a few minor spots. Previous owner's signatures. Very good. MacManus 279-3742 1983 $225

MIDDLEMASS, JEAN Poisoned Arrows. London: White, 1884. First edition. 3 vols. Orig. cloth. Slight fading of the spines. Fine. MacManus 279-3743 1983 $175

MIDDLEMISS, H. S. Narcotic Education. Edited Report of the Proceedings of the First World Conference on Narcotic Education, Philadelphia, July 5-9, 1926. Cloth, covers bear a few spots. Gach 94-804 1983 $25

MIDDLETON, CONYERS A Free Inquiry into the Miraculous Powers which are supposed to have Subsisted in the Christian Church. Printed for R. Manby and S. Cox, 1749. Small 4to, half title, cont. calf, rebacked. First edition. Bickersteth 75-59 1983 £30

MIDDLETON, CONYERS The History of the Life of Marcus Tullius Cicero. London, for the author, 1741. 2 vols., large, stout 4tos, cont. diced Russia gilt, joints cracked. Large paper copy. Ravenstree 95-77 1983 $175

MIDDLETON, CONYERS The History of the Life of Marcus Tullius Cicero. London: printed for the author, 1741. 1st ed., large paper copy, 4to, 2 vols., cont. calf, spines gilt, two engraved portrait title pages, 27 large engraved head- and tail-pieces. Subscribers' list. Binding worn, hinges cracked, lacking labels on spines; internally a very clean copy. Trebizond 18-118 1983 $175

MIDDLETON, CONYERS A Letter from Rome, Shewing an Exact Conformity between Popery and Paganism. London, printed for W. Innys, 1729. 4to, unbound, uncut, stitched as issued, now dust-soiled, uncut edges worn, small piece torn from top blank tip of title, some minor turning under of corners. First edition. Ravenstree 97-103 1983 $95

MIDDLETON, EDGAR The Great War in the Air. Lon., 1920. 4 vols., illus. and photos, minor interior foxing, very good in remnants of dustwrappers. Quill & Brush 54-1660 1983 $75

MIDDLETON, J. General view of the Agriculture of Middlesex. 1807. Second edition, coloured folding map, 8vo, new cloth. Half-title mounted. Wheldon 160-2129 1983 £30

MIDDLETON, R. HUNTER Chicago Letter Founding. Chicago, 1937. 12mo, cloth-backed bds., gilt. One of 750 copies. A very nice copy. Perata 27-16 1983 $35

MIDDLETON, R. HUNTER Chicago Letter Founding. Chicago, 1937. 12mo, cloth-backed boards, gilt. One of 750 copies. Very nice. Perata 28-201 1983 $35

MIDDLETON, RICHARD The Day Before Yesterday. London: T. Fisher Unwin, 1912. First edition. Orig. cloth. Dust jacket (spine faded). Fine. MacManus 279-3744 1983 $40

MIDDLETON, RICHARD Poems and Songs. Second Series. London: T. Fisher Unwin, 1912. First edition. Orig. cloth. Dust jacket (quite faded and slightly worn). Some offsetting to the endpapers. Spine cracking although cords and webbing intact. Very good. MacManus 279-3745 1983 $40

MIDDLETON, RICHARD Queen Melanie and the Wood-Boy. S.F., 1931. 4to, gold cloth-backed boards. Illus. by Lawrence A. Patterson. Presswork and binding by Lawton & Freda Kennedy. One of 110 copies. Perata 28-77 1983 $75

MIEGE, GUY A Relation of Three Embassies from His Sacred Majestie Charles II to the Great Duke of Muscovie, the King of Sweden, and the King of Denmark. London: John Starkey, 1669. 1st ed., 8vo, cont. panelled calf, morocco label, original initial blank leaf present. Bookplate, frontis. engraved portrait; folding engraved portrait. Errata/license page. A fine copy. Trebizond 18-162 1983 $600

MIERS, J. A Collection of 11 papers. Trans. Linn. Soc., 1847-66. 14 plates, 4to, wrappers. Wheldon 160-1747 1983 £20

MIERS, J. Contributions to Botany. 1864-71. Vol. 3, 67 plates by the author, 4to, cloth. Rare. Wheldon 160-1749 1983 £30

MIERS, J. Illustrations of South American Plants, Vol. 2. 1849-57. 53 plates, 4to, cloth. Very rare. Only two volumes were published. Wheldon 160-1748 1983 £35

MIGNET, F. A. The History of Mary Queen of Scots. Richard Bentley, 1851. 2 vols., 8vo, portrait, orig. cloth, blocked in blind, worn at top of spines, cloth slit on lower joint of vol. 1 and upper joint of vol. 2. First edition in English. Bickersteth 77-157 1983 £28

MILAN, LUYS Libro de Musica de Vihuela de Mano. Leipzig, 1927. Oblong folio, cl. Facs. edition. Salloch 387-124 1983 $150

MILBERT, JACQUES G. Itineraire Pittoresque du Fleuve Hudson. Paris, 1828. First edition. Large folio, modern 1/2 calf. 2 vols. in 1. Atlas vol. lacking. Argosy 716-358 1983 $200

MILCHSACK, CONRAD REINHARD Disputatio botanica de Tabaco Toback... Marburg: Johann Heinrich Stocken, 1682. First edition. Small 4to. Orig. paper backstrip. Kraus 164-236 1983 $280

MILDRED, FELIX Leonilda. John Mitchell, 1857. First edition. Half title. Orig. red cloth. Jarndyce 30-791 1983 £12.50

MILES, ALFRED H.   Fifty-Two Excelsior Stories for Boys.
London: Hutchinson & Co., (1907). First edition. Illus. Orig.
pictorial cloth. Good. MacManus 279-3746 1983 $20

MILES, ALFRED H.   Fifty-Two More Stories for Boys. London:
Hutchingosn & Co., (1890). First edition. Illus. Orig. pictorial
cloth. Good. MacManus 279-3747 1983 $20

MILES, ALFRED H.   Natural History. New York, (1895).
1st ed. 20 colored plates, each with several illus. 8vo. Morrill
286-322 1983 $20

MILES, ALFRED H.   The Poets and the Poetry of the Century.
London, 1898. 10 vols. Thick cr. 8vo. Orig. blue cloth, decorated
gilt, t.e.g., others uncut. Portraits. Traylen 94-575 1983 £95

MILES, CHARLES   Indian and Eskimo Artifacts of North
America. New York: Bonanza Books, n.d. Prof. illus. 4to. Cloth.
Dust jacket. Ars Libri 34-367 1983 $30

MILES, NELSON A.   Oration... Portland, Ore., July 4th,
1883. Orig. printed wraps. First edition. Ginsberg 46-467 1983
$75

MILES, NELSON A.   Personal Recollections and Observations.
Chicago, 1896. Illus. by F. Remington. Orig. pictorial cloth.
First edition. Ginsberg 47-502 1983 $125

MILES, NELSON A.   Report of Brig. -Gen. Vancouver
Barracks, W.T., 1884. Orig. printed wraps. First edition. Ginsberg
47-938 1983 $150

MILES, WILLIAM   Journal of the Sufferings and Hardships
of Capt. Parker H. French's Overland Expedition to California Which
Left N.Y. City, May 13th, 1850. (N.Y., 1916). Orig. printed wraps.
Facs. reprint of the Chambersburg, Pa., 1851 orig. One of 250
copies printed. Ginsberg 46-468 1983 $25

MILES, WILLIAM   Journal of the Sufferings & Hardships of
Capt. Parker H. French. Chambersburg, 1851; reprinted, New York:
Cadmus Book shop, 1916. Wrappers. Few marginal pen marks by Noel
Loomis. Dawson 471-195 1983 $25

MILES, WILLIAM AUGUSTUS   A Description of the Deverel Barrow,
Opened A.D. 1825. Nichols & Son (Frome printed), 1826. First
edition, with 2 additional engraved title-pages and 8 engraved plates,
roy. 8vo, a large copy on thick paper, recent boards, very light
marginal worming in the corner of seven leaves otherwise a very
good copy. Includes a 4-page letter to Sir Richard Colt Hoare, to
whom the volume is dedicated. Fenning 60-281 1983 £35

MILFORD, Massachusetts, 1880-1930. N.P., 1930. 1st ed. Illus. 8vo.
Corners rubbed. Morrill 287-618 1983 $20

MILHAM, WILLIS I.   Time & Timekeepers... New York:
The Macmillan Company, 1923. First edition. Thick 8vo. Cloth.
339 illus. Presentation copy. Covers rubbed. Oak Knoll 48-283
1983 $85

MILHAM, WILLIS I.   Time & Timekeepers. New York, 1923.
1st ed. Illus., 8vo. Morrill 287-624 1983 $35

MILITARY and Other Poems upon several occasions, and to several persons.
London: printed for the author, and sold by J. Browne, 1716. First
edition, 8vo, waterstaining throughout, small portion of the lower
outside corner of the title frayed, catchword on one leaf shaved, half
russia by T. & H. Lancaster of Bristol, spine chipped at head and
foot, rubbed and joints cracked. Pickering & Chatto 19-76 1983 $850

MILITARY Enterprise. London: Frederick Warne & Co., n.d. First edition. 12 color-plate illus. Spine slightly worn. Some offsetting to
free endpapers. Former owner's inscription with the date 1875 on front
paste-down endpaper. Near-fine. MacManus 279-3748 1983 $75

MILIZIA, FRANCESCO   Trattato Completo, Formale & Materiale
del Teatro. Venice, 1794. With 6 engraved folding plates, 4to, calf-
backed boards, with label. Salloch 387-125 1983 $275

MILL, JAMES   Elements of Political Economy. Henry G.
Bohn, 1844. Orig. brown cloth. Third edition. Very good. Jarndyce
31-319 1983 £75.

MILL, JOHN STUART   Autobiography. Longmans, Green, 1873.
First edition, half title, 2 pp ads. Orig. dark green cloth, sl.
rubbed, v.g. Jarndyce 31-322 1983 £45

MILL, JOHN STUART   Autobiography. Longmans, Green, 1873.
First edition. Half title, 2 pp ads. Orig. green cloth. Jarndyce
30-1079 1983 £40

MILL, JOHN STUART   Autobiography. NY: Henry Holt, n.d.
(ca. 1895). Spine lightly rubbed. Gach 94-241 1983 $20

MILL, JOHN STUART   Le Gouvernement Representatif. Paris,
Guillaumin, 1864. 1st ed. in French, small 8vo, morocco backed
marbled boards, a very good copy. Pickering & Chatto 21-77 1983 $125

MILL, JOHN STUART   Le Gouvernment Representative. Paris:
Guillaumin, 1865. 2nd ed., 8vo, occasional light spotting, else a
very good copy uncut in the original printed wrappers. Pickering &
Chatto 21-78 1983 $85

MILL, JOHN STUART   Principles of Political Economy With
Some of their Applications to Social Philosophy. London, John W.
Parker, 1848. 1st ed., 2 vols., 8vo, advertisements, a few marginal
pencil notes in Vol. II, original green cloth, slightly faded, head of
spines repaired, paper labels chipped but internally a fine copy.
Contemporary ownership inscription on the titles. Pickering & Chatto
21-79 1983 $1,250

MILL, JOHN STUART   Principes D'Economie Politique.
Paris, Guillaumin, 1854. 1st ed. in French, 2 vols., 8vo, uncut in
original printed wrappers, a very good copy. Pickering & Chatto 21-
80 1983 $350

MILL, JOHN STUART   The Subjection of Women. London: Longmans, Green, Reader & Dyer, 1869. First edition. Orig. light brown
cloth. Presentation copy from the publisher with his small blind
stamp on both the half-title and title pages. Spine slightly darkened.
Spine and covers slightly rubbed. Very good. MacManus 279-3749 1983
$450

MILL, JOHN STUART   The Subjection of Women. New York:
Appleton, 1869. 8vo, orig. cloth. Raymond bookplate & ownership
inscription of Nettie A. Raymond. First American edition.
Rostenberg 88-95 1983 $200

MILL, JOHN STUART   The Subjection of Women. Longmans,
Green, Reader, and Dyer, 1869. Half title, orig. mustard cloth,
sl. rubbed. One or two pages carelessly opened. First edition.
Jarndyce 31-321 1983 £140

MILL, JOHN STUART   L'Utilitarisme. Paris: Librarie Germer
Bailliere, 1883. 8vo, occasional light spotting, original green
printed wrappers. Pickering & Chatto 21-81 1983 $50

MILL River Disaster. Springfield, 1874. Illus. Pr. wraps.
Argosy 716-273 1983 $35

MILLAIS, JOHN EVERETT   Millais's Illustrations. Strahan, 1866.
80 plates. Royal blue sand grain decor. cloth, bevelled boards, a.e.g.
Binder's ticket Burn & Co. Corners sl. bruised & bkstrip. sl. rubbed,
award label fr. free ep. with news cutting of the Award (1874), nice.
Hodgkins 27-311 1983 £50

MILLAIS, JOHN GUILLE   The Life and Letters of Sir John
Everett Millais. London: Methuen, 1899. 2 vols. 319 illus.
(9 photogravure). 4to. Cloth. Extremities of spine worn. Ars
Libri 32-453 1983 $125

MILLAIS, JOHN GUILLE   Life of Frederick Courtenay Selous,
D.S.O. Capt... New York: Longmans, Green, 1919. 8vo. 16 plates.
Orig. blue cloth. Second impression. Adelson Africa-207 1983
$100

MILLAIS, JOHN GUILLE　　Magnolias. 1927. 34 plates from drawings and photos, royal 8vo, cloth. Very scarce. Ex-library copy with small tear in upper joint. Wheldon 160-2094 1983 £25

MILLAIS, JOHN GUILLE　　The Natural History of the British Surface-Feeding Ducks. 1902. 6 photogravures, colored plates and illus., roy. 4to, original cloth. Edition limited to 600 copies, all on large paper. Some very slight foxing and binding a trifle used, but generally a good clean copy. Wheldon 160-70 1983 £400

MILLAIS, JOHN GUILLE　　Newfoundland and its Untrodden Ways. London: Longmans, Green & Co., 1907. 4to. 6 photogravure and 6 colour plates and 73 line and half-tone illus. 2 maps. Orig. wine cloth. Gilt titles and gilt decorations on the upper cover. T.e.g. Spine slightly dulled else a very good copy. McGahern 53-123 1983 $75

MILLAR, GEORGE　　Horned Pigeon. Garden City, Doubleday, 1946. First edition. Pictorial dust jacket (few small nicks) else, very good. Houle 22-648 1983 $20

MILLAR, H. R.　　The Strand Fairy Book. George Newnes, n.d. (ca.1910). Sq. 8vo. 2 full-page & 67 text illus. Blue blind decorated cloth. Greer 39-87 1983 £12.50

MILLAR, JAMES　　Elements of Chemistry... Edinburgh: Tait, 1820. First edition. 8vo. Orig. cloth backed boards. 3 folding plates. Misbound. Boards worn. In protective cloth box. Zeitlin 264-305 1983 $120

MILLAR, JOHN　　Observations on the Asthma... London, 1769. First edition. 8vo. Half-calf. Gurney 90-82 1983 £175

MILLARD, F. W.　　Game and Foxes. London: Horace Cox, 1906. First edition. Orig. cloth. Covers slightly soiled & rubbed. In a half-morocco slipcase. Very good. MacManus 278-1973 1983 $125

MILLAY, EDNA ST. VINCENT　　The Ballad of the Harp-Weaver. New York: Shay, 1927. First edition. Woodcut frontis. Pict. orange wrappers (light foxing, mostly at edges). 500 copies printed. Very good. Houle 22-650 1983 $175

MILLAY, EDNA ST. VINCENT　　Conversation at Midnight. N.Y., 1937. First edition. Cloth backed obards. Rubbed, soiled and slightly frayed dust wrapper. Very good. King 45-225 1983 $20

MILLAY, EDNA ST. VINCENT　　The King's Henchman. NY, 1927. One of 500 numbered and signed copies, facsimile page from operatic score signed by composer, Deems Taylor and three proof etchings of Joseph Urban's sets. Minor cover stains, else fine in worn slipcase. Quill & Brush 54-929 1983 $150

MILLAY, EDNA ST. VINCENT　　The Kings Henchman. N.Y., Harper, 1927. First edition. Frontis. illus. by Cimino, title page in red and black. Dust jacket. Very good - fine. Houle 22-651 1983 $50

MILLAY, EDNA ST. VINCENT　　The Lamp and the Bell. N.Y., Shay, 1921. First edition. Green wraps. stamped in black (faded on spine, light foxing at edges). First issue in green wraps. Very good. Houle 22-652 1983 $125

MILLAY, EDNA ST. VINCENT　　The Lamp and the Bell. N.Y., Shay, 1921. First edition. Stiff orange wraps. (a bit faded, a few small chips) else very good. Second state color of binding. Houle 22-653 1983 $80

MILLAY, EDNA ST. VINCENT　　Renascence. NY, 1917. Second edition, very good, initials on front endpaper. Quill & Brush 54-926 1983 $60

MILLAY, EDNA ST. VINCENT　　Renascence. NY, 1917. Second edition, spine and corners worn, otherwise good. Quill & Brush 54-927 1983 $35

MILLAY, EDNA ST. VINCENT　　Second April. NY, 1921. Bliss Carman's copy with "B. C./Twilight Park/July, 1921" on fly, light cover soiling and wear, very good. Quill & Brush 54-928 1983 $75

MILLAY, EDNA ST. VINCENT　　Two Slatterns and a King. Cincinnatti, Kidd (1921). First edition. Stiff white wraps. (Slight foxing to parts of text), else very good-fine. Houle 21-630 1983 $125

MILLAY, EDNA ST. VINCENT　　Wine from These Grapes. N.Y., 1934. First edition. Half cloth. Ink name and date. Tape repaired and spotted dust wrapper. Very good. King 45-226 1983 $25

MILLER, ARTHUR　　After the Fall. NY, (1964). Limited to 500 signed copies, very fine in fine slipcase. Quill & Brush 54-930 1983 $100

MILLER, ARTHUR　　Death of a Salesman. New York: The Viking Press, 1949. First edition. 8vo. Orig. cloth. Pictorial endpapers. Dust jacket. Very fine copy. Jaffe 1-255 1983 $150

MILLER, ARTHUR　　Death of a Salesman. NY, 1949. Corners slightly worn, else very good in very good dustwrapper with three tiny chips. Quill & Brush 54-932 1983 $100

MILLER, ARTHUR　　Death of a Salesman. NY, 1949. Edges very slightly faded, else very good or better in frayed and slightly worn, price clipped dustwrapper. Quill & Brush 54-931 1983 $75

MILLER, ARTHUR　　First Impressions of Greece. Santa Barbara: Capra Press, 1973. 1st ed., 1 of 250 numbered and signed copies, with photo of Miller tipped in at rear. Orig. cloth, gilt. Mint. Jenkins 155-933 1983 $75

MILLER, ARTHUR　　Focus. N.Y., Reynal & Hitchcock, (1945). First edition. Dust jacket (several chips, rubbing) else good - very good. Houle 22-657 1983 $45

MILLER, ARTHUR　　Focus. London, 1949. First English edition. Argosy 714-519 1983 $20

MILLER, BARNETTE　　Leigh Hunt's Relations with Byron, Shelley and Keats. (New York), 1910. First edition. Red cloth, top edges gilt. Fine. Bradley 64-77 1983 $20

MILLER, CINCINNATUS HINER　　'49 the Gold Seeker of the Sierras. New York: Funk & Wagnalls, 1884. 2 ads, 10 ads. 8vo, original decorated buff wrappers. Fragile wrappers with minor chipping. First edition, the paper issue. Very fine. Jenkins 153-101 1983 $100

MILLER, CINCINNATUS HINER　　Ship in the Desert. Boston, Roberts, 1875. First edition. Green cloth, stamped in gilt (hinges rubbed, small stain in margin of few pages), else very good. Presentation copy. Inscribed and signed by Miller, Wellesley, Sept., '84. Houle 21-1108 1983 $150

MILLER, F. T.　　Byrd's Great Adventure. Phila., 1930. Coloured frontis. 81 plates, coloured endpaper maps. Orig. decorated cloth with mounted pictorial illus. Spine faded. Good. Edwards 1042-602 1983 £20

MILLER, G. S.　　List of N. American Recent Mammals. U.S. Nat. Mus., 1924. 8vo, wrappers. Wheldon 160-583 1983 £12

MILLER, GENEVIEVE　　Wm. Beaumont's Formative Years - Two Early Notebooks 1811-1821. New York, 1947. First edition. 8vo. Orig. binding. Scarce. Fye H-3-671 1983 $45

MILLER, HENRY　　Air Conditioned Nightmare. N.Y., New Directions, (1945). First edition. Tall 8vo, half cloth. Good. Houle 21-632 1983 $95

MILLER, HENRY　　The Air-Conditioned Nightmare. (NY, 1945). First issue, front hinge starting at title, else very good in interior mended, slightly frayed very good dustwrapper. Quill & Brush 54-939 1983 $75

MILLER, HENRY　　Aller Retour New York. N.p., 1945. 8vo, cloth, one of 500 numbered copies printed for private circulation. With bookplate from Institute for Sex Research. Duschnes 240-152 1983 $150

MILLER, HENRY   Aller Retour New York. London, 1945.
First edition. One of 500 copies for private circulation. Presen-
tation copy from the author, inscribed. Spine faded. Very good.
Jolliffe 26-356 1983 £65

MILLER, HENRY   Aller Retour New York. N.p., 1945.
Privately printed, limited to 500 copies, this copy unnumbered, cover
very slightly soiled, else near fine. Quill & Brush 54-933 1983
$100

MILLER, HENRY   Black Spring. P, (1938). Second printing, very worn, fragile copy. Quill & Brush 54-934 1983 $75

MILLER, HENRY   The Colossus of Marouyssi. San Francisco,
1941. 8vo, cloth. Salloch 385-375 1983 $25

MILLER, HENRY   The Cosmological Eye. CT, (1939).
First issue with eye on cover, very fine, dustwrapper is from 1943
edition and is chipped. Quill & Brush 54-940 1983 $50

MILLER, HENRY   Happy Rock. (Berkeley, Packard Press,
1945). First edition. Tall 8vo, half cloth. Good. Houle 21-633
1983 $25

MILLER, HENRY   Into the Night Life. Berkeley:
Privately printed, (1947). Folio. Pictorial cloth. Printed entirely
in silkscreen and serigraph. Miller's holograph text and Schatz's
illus. One of 800 numbered copies, signed by Miller and Schatz, of
which some 300 copies were reported destroyed by vermin in storage.
A fine copy in pub.'s slipcase. Reese 20-695 1983 $850

MILLER, HENRY   Joseph Delteil: Essays in Tribute.
(L), 1962. No. 12 of 150 numbered copies signed by Miller and Delteil, fine. Quill & Brush 54-935 1983 $75

MILLER, HENRY   Letters to Anais Nin. New York, (1965).
8vo, cloth, dust-jacket. With ten-line presentation by the author
dated 8/18/67. First edition. Duschnes 240-154 1983 $200

MILLER, HENRY   Maurizius Forever. S.F.: 1946. 8vo,
green boards, lettering in white, plain d/w. The illus. are from orig.
drawing and water colors by the author. One of 500 copies. Perata
28-57 1983 $135

MILLER, HENRY   Money and How It Gets that Way.
Paris: Booster Publications (1938). Sq. 12mo, black wraps. printed
in gold. The signature of Benjamin G. Benno is on the half title
and the inscription by Miller is dated 11/38 to Benno. Wrappers
are intact on this fragile booklet. Duschnes 240-151 1983 $450

MILLER, HENRY   My Life and Times. New York: Gemini
Smith, n.d. Quarto, cloth, dust-jacket. The endpapers include a
chronology of Henry Miller's life from birth to age 80. With
numerous photos., reproductions of Henry Miller's art work and
facs. pages and manuscripts. Signed and dated presentation by the
author. First edition. Duschnes 240-156 1983 $50

MILLER, HENRY   Obscenity and the Law of Reflection.
Yonkers: Alicat Book Shop, 1945. 8vo, pr. wrs. No. one of the
"Outcast" series of chapbooks. Argosy 714-520 1983 $35

MILLER, HENRY   The Paintings of Henry Miller, with
Collected Essays by Henry Miller. Santa Barbara: Capra Press,
(1982). First edition. Oblong 4to. Cloth. Slipcase. Limited
to 250 numbered copies. Signed by Laurence Durrell, the author of
the foreword. Oak Knoll 49-288 1983 $100

MILLER, HENRY   The Paintings of Henry Miller.
Santa Barbara: Capra Press, (1982). Oblong 4to, profusely illus.
with color plates. This copy is part of a special numbered edition
ltd. to 250 copies, signed by Lawrence Durrell. Blue cloth.
Illus. Slipcase. Karmiole 71-71 1983 $100

MILLER, HENRY   The Paintings of Henry Miller. Santa
Barbara: Capra Press, (1982). Oblong quarto. Cloth. First edition.
One of 250 numbered copies, signed by Lawrence Durrell, who wrote
the forward. One of 250 numbered copies, signed by Durrell. Mint
as issued, in cloth slipcase. Reese 20-700 1983 $150

MILLER, HENRY   Plexus. Paris: Olympia Press, 1953.
First edition. One of 2000 numbered copies, printed for private
circulation. 2 vols. Wrappers. Very nice. Rota 230-404 1983 £50

MILLER, HENRY   The Plight of the Creative Artist in
the United States of America. N.p., n.d. Fragile in paperwraps,
cover slightly soiled, book separated from cover, else very good.
Quill & Brush 54-941 1983 $100

MILLER, HENRY   Remember to Remember. (NY, 1947). Cover
slightly soiled, very good in chipped and wearing dustwrapper. Quill
& Brush 54-937 1983 $50

MILLER, HENRY   Scenario. Paris: The Obelisk Press,
1937. Orig. printed wraps., unbound signatures laid in. Folding
frontis. by Abraham Rattner. First edition. One of only 200
numbered copies, signed by Miller. Light fraying of overlap edges
at top, and discoloration of lower portion of spine due to damp,
internally a fine copy. Reese 20-693 1983 $750

MILLER, HENRY   Smile at the Foot of the Ladder. N.Y.,
Duell, (1948). First edition. Tall 8vo, illus. Dust jacket (faded,
nicked), else very good. Designed by Merle Armitage. Houle 21-631
1983 $95

MILLER, HENRY   Sunday after the War. Norfolk: New
Directions, (1944). 1st ed. Orig. cream cloth, no dj. Fine.
Jenkins 155-937 1983 $20

MILLER, HENRY   To Remember. (NY, 1947). Very good.
Quill & Brush 54-944 1983 $30

MILLER, HENRY   Tropique du Cancer. Paris: Editions
Denoel, (1945). Printed wraps. First French edition. One of 1,000
numbered copies printed on verge creme Jahonnet. Very fine in tissue
jacket. Reese 20-694 1983 $125

MILLER, HENRY   What Are You Going to do About Alf? (P,
1938). Paperwraps, near fine. Quill & Brush 54-945 1983 $150

MILLER, HENRY   The Wisdom of the Heart. CT, (1941).
Offset from dustwrapper on endpapers, else near fine in slightly chipped and darkened dustwrapper, very good. Quill & Brush 54-943 1983
$40

MILLER, HUGH   The Cruise of the Betsey. Edinburgh: T.
Constable, 1858. First collected edition, 8vo, orig. cloth, very
good. Fenning 60-282 1983 £28.50

MILLER, HUGH   The Dream of Mr. H-The Herbalist. Edinburgh & London: William Blackwood & Sons, 1896. First edition. Photogravure frontispiece. Orig. red cloth. Spine faded. Fine. MacManus
279-3750 1983 $135

MILLER, HUGH   My Schools and Schoolmasters. Edinburgh:
W.P. Nimmo, 1907. First edition. Illus. Orig. cloth. Fine. Mac-
Manus 279-3751 1983 $20

MILLER, JAMES   The Great Man's Answer to Are These
Things So? London: Printed for T. Cooper...MDCCXL. Folio, a large
copy complete with half-title; disbound. First edition. Quaritch
NS 7-85 1983 $225

MILLER, JAMES   Harlequin Horace: or the Art of
Modern Poetry. London: for Lawton Gilliver, 1731. First edition.
8vo. Modern quarter morocco. Engraved frontis. very slightly
shaved. Heath 48-363 1983 £125

MILLER, JAMES   The Mother-in-Law: or, The Doctor the
Disease. London: Watts, 1734. First edition. 3/4 morocco (spine
rubbed). MacManus 279-3752 1983 $50

MILLER, JAMES   Of Politeness. London: Printed for L.
Gilliver and J. Clark...1738. Folio, first edition. Disbound. A
good copy. Quaritch NS 7-86 1983 $185

MILLER, JAMES G.   Unconsciousness. NY: Wiley, 1942.
First edition. Inscribed ex-library copy. Gach 95-364 1983 $25

MILLER, JAMES MARTIN   The Amazing Story of Henry Ford.
Chicago, (1922). Photos. Cloth with oval portrait. Salesman's
sample book with order sheets at end and with sample pages & photos.
throughout this thin book. King 45-650 1983 $35

MILLER, JOAQUIN
Please turn to
MILLER, CINCINNATUS HINER

MILLER, JOHN ANDERSON   Fares Please! N.Y., Appleton-Century,
1941. First edition. 120 illus. Dust jacket (trifle rubbed) very
good - fine. Houle 22-1134 1983 $25

MILLER, LEWIS B.   Saddles and Lariats. Boston, (1912).
Illus. Orig. pictorial cloth. First edition. Ginsberg 47-503 1983
$125

MILLER, MAX   The Beginning of a Mortal. N.Y.,
Dutton, 1933. First edition. Illus. with 20 plates by John Sloan.
Halftone frontis. Dust jacket printed in yellow, blue, & black
(back faded, a few nicks) else, very good. Houle 22-660 1983 $45

MILLER, MAX   It Must be the Climate. N.Y., McBride,
(1941). First edition. Dust jacket. Very good. With tipped-in
leaf, signed by Miller. Houle 21-1109 1983 $27.50

MILLER, MORRIS S.   Speech of the Hon..., of New York, on
the Army Bills. Georgetown, 1814. Dsb., very good. Chancellor
Kent's copy. Reese 18-448 1983 $45

MILLER, MORRIS S.   Speech of the Hon...on the Army
Bill. Georgetown, 1814. Dsb. Good. Reese 18-447 1983 $25

MILLER, PHILIP   The Abridgement of the Gardeners
Dictionary. 1763. 5th edition, with engraved frontispiece and 12
plates, 4to, boards, calf back (worn, backstrip defective). A few
leaves slightly dampstained. Wheldon 160-1990 1983 £45

MILLER, PHILIP   The Gardeners Dictionary. London:
Printed for the author and sold by John and James Rivington. 1752.
Printed in double columns. Complete with engraved frontis. 9 plates.
Index. Bound in cont. calf, rebacked, with orig. spine label
laid down. Binding a bit rubbed. Bookplate. Karmiole 76-45 1983
$350

MILLER, PHILIP   The Gardeners Dictionary. 1754. 4th
edition, abridged from the last folio edition, with frontispiece
and 3 plates, 3 vols., 8vo, new half calf. Wheldon 160-1989 1983
£120

MILLER, SAMUEL   A Discourse- Delivered April 12, 1797.
New York: T. and J. Swords, 1797. Disbound. Felcone 22-227 1983
$65

MILLER, THOMAS   Picturesque Sketches of London Past and
Present. (1852). First edition, front. engr. title & numerous
illus. 2 pp ads. Orig. dark green blind-stamped cloth, gilt spine.
A fine copy. Jarndyce 31-277 1983 £20

MILLER, WARREN H.   Red Mesa. New York & London, 1923.
Frontis. Pictorial cloth. Ink name, else a near fine copy in dust
jacket, which lacks a segment at the lower edge. Reese 19-361 1983
$20

MILLER, WILLIAM   The Dickens Student and Collector. Chapman & Hall, 1946. Half title, lib. stamp on title, orig. blue cloth,
first English edition. Jarndyce 30-213 1983 £16

MILLER, WILLIAM   Evidence from Scripture and History of
the Second Coming of Christ... Boston, 1840. 4th ed. 12mo, few
signatures slightly pulled, otherwise nice. Scarce. Morrill 288-314
1983 $50

MILLER, WILLIAM ALLEN   Elements of Chemistry: Theoretical
and Practical. London: J.W. Parker, 1855-7. First edition. 3
vols. 8vo. Orig. cloth. Many text figures and colored plates.
Rebacked, with backstrips laid down. Zeitlin 264-306 1983 $75

MILLER, WILLIAM J.   Celebration of the 200th Anniversary of
the Settlement of the Town of Bristol, R.I. (Providence, 1880). Orig.
stipple cloth. Illus. of badges. Argosy 716-486 1983 $27.50

MILLER, WILLIAM R.   The Practice of the Queen's Bench Division
(Probate) and of the County Courts in Ireland. Dublin: John Falconer,
1900. Roy. 8vo, orig. cloth, very good copy. Fenning 62-248 1983
£18.50

MILLET, JOSHUA   A Brief History of the Baptists in
Maine. Portland, 1845. First edition. Small 8vo, contemporary
calf, leather label. Front hinge slightly cracked. Morrill 290-262
1983 $22.50

MILLIKAN, ROBERT ANDREWS   The Electron. Chicago: University
of Chicago, 1918. 8vo. Orig. cloth. 4 photographic plates,
numerous text illus. and diagrams. Ads. Spine sunned. Zeitlin
264-307 1983 $30

MILLIKAN, ROBERT ANDREWS   Science and Life. Boston: Pilgrim
Press, 1924. 8vo. Orig. cloth. Frontis. portrait. Zeitlin 264-308
1983 $40

MILLIN, SARAH GERTRUDE   General Smuts. Boston, 1936. 1st
ed. Illus. 2 vols., 8vo, dust wrappers. Morrill 287-280 1983 $20

MILLNER, EDITH   Life in Oberammergau. York (England),
1910. 1st ed. Sketches by Lucia Lang. 50 colored plates. 4to.
Morrill 287-281 1983 $32.50

MILLS, A. J. M.   Report on the Province of Assam.
Calcutta, 1854. 4to, half morocco, worn. Inscription on title-page.
Wheldon 160-407 1983 £55

MILLS, ENOS   The Spell of the Rockies. London: 1912.
First English edition. Illus. Pictorial green cloth. Fine book.
Bradley 66-518 1983 $30

MILLS, ENOS   Your National Parks. Boston, 1917.
Orig. pict. cloth. Argosy 716-544 1983 $20

MILLS, GEORGE   The Beggar's Benison. Cassell, Petter
and Galpin, 1866. First edition, 2 vols. Half titles, illus. 'by
upwards of 300 amateur pen and ink sketches'. Inner hinges cracked.
Orig. blue cloth a little rubbed. Jarndyce 31-502 1983 £54

MILLS, GEORGE   Meredith and Co. OUP, 1933. Colour
frontis. Attractive colour pictorial boards & dust wrappers. Greer
40-57 1983 £12.50

MILLS, HIRAM FRANCIS   Natural Resources and Their Development.
Augusta, 1867. 1st ed. Partly colored folding map. 8vo, orig.
wrappers. Lacks back wrapper. Morrill 286-323 1983 $22.50

MILLS, J. P.   The Ao Nagas. London, 1926. 2 maps,
1 folding. Numerous plates. 8vo. Orig. cloth. Good. Edwards
1044-492 1983 £35

MILLS, J. P.   The Lhota Nagas. London, 1922. 3 folding maps, coloured frontis, plates. Pictorial cloth gilt. 8vo. Good.
Edwards 1044-493 1983 £40

MILLS, J. P.   The Rengma Nagas. London, 1937.
Plates, pictorial cloth gilt. 8vo. Good. Edwards 1044-491 1983
£40

MILLS, J. S.   Africa and mission work in Sierra Leone.
Dayton, Ohio: United Brethren, 1898. 12mo. 3 maps. 18 plates.
Orig. green cloth. Rubbed. Adelson Africa-208 1983 $20

MILLS, JOHN   The Flyers of the Hunt. "The Field"
Office, 1859. Illus. by John Leech. First edition, with 6 plates,
8vo, orig. red cloth, gilt. Inside joints neatly repaired, with
some very light fingering, but a very good copy. Fenning 62-249
1983 £18.50

MILLS, JOHN   On The Spur of the Moment. London:
Hurst & Blackett, 1884. First edition. 3 vols. Orig. cloth.
Library labels neatly removed from front covers. Very good. Mac-
Manus 279-3753 1983 $300

MILLS, JOHN   Our County. Henry Colburn, 1852.
First edition, 3 vols. Small repair to title vol. I. Half calf.
Jarndyce 30-486 1983 £48

MILLS, JOHN   Stable Secrets; or, Puffy Doddles.
London: Ward & Lock, 1863. First edition. Orig. blue pictorial
cloth. Illus. Presentation copy, inscribed on the recto of the
frontispiece to "H. Bailey Esq. with the compliments of John Mills
March 4th, 1863." Covers somewhat soiled and worn. Preserved in a
half-morocco slipcase. Good. MacManus 279-3754 1983 $135

MILLS, JOHN   Stable Secrets; or, Puffy Doddles.
London: Ward & Lock, 1863. First edition. Frontis. Orig. decorated
cloth. Former owner's signature on front flyleaf. Fine. MacManus
279-3755 1983 $125

MILLS, ROBERT   Atlas of the State of South Carolina...
Baltimore: F. Lucas Jr., (1826). Folio, 29 maps. Orig. boards,
rebacked in brown calf. Modern end papers. Maps printed on
brittle paper. Title-page somewhat browned on verso, has minor
chipping to lower margin, and a couple of repairs. Reese 18-602
1983 $5,500

MILLS, W. J.   The Girl I Left Behind Me. N.Y.: Dodd,
1910. First edition. 4to. Half cloth. Edges rubbed, covers slightly
darkened. 10 color plates by Rae. Very good. Aleph-bet 8-216 1983
$45

MILLS, WESLEY   The Nature and Development of Animal
Intelligence. London: T. Fisher Unwin, 1898. First edition,
inscribed. Publisher's crimson cloth, gilt. Gach 95-366 1983 $50

MILLSPAUGH, C. F.   Flora of the Island of St. Croix.
Chicago, Field Mus., 1902. Map, 8vo, cloth. Wheldon 160-1750 1983
£12

MILNE, ALAN ALEXANDER   By Way of Introduction. NY, (1929).
Endpapers slightly foxed and offset, tiny skinned circle on front board,
very good in chipped and wearing, good dustwrapper. Quill & Brush 54-
947 1983 $50

MILNE, ALAN ALEXANDER   The Christopher Robin Story Book. New
York, Dutton, 1929. Dec. by E.H. Shepard. 1st edn. thus, large paper
copy limited to 350 numbered & signed copies by artist & author.
Printed on Japanese vellum. Half lime green cloth, fawn bds., with
decor. & titling in black on fr. cvr., paper title label bkstrip,
green eps., uncut, tear across p.57 repaired, affecting one line of
text, sl. wear top/bottom bkstrip, scarce, vg copy. Hodgkins 27-151
1983 £200

MILNE, ALAN ALEXANDER   Fourteen Songs from "When We Were Very
Young." Methuen, 1924. Decorations by E.H. Shepard. Title vignette
& numerous b&w vignettes throughout. Pub's bds., fr. cvr. marked at
top, sl. foxing eps. & corners & edges sl. worn, good. Hodgkins 27-
149 1983 £12.50

MILNE, ALAN ALEXANDER   Gallery of Children. Stanley Paul, 1925.
Large 4to. Colour pictorial title, 12 colour plates. White pictorial
cloth, gilt. Light wear to head of spine. Edition limited to 500
copies, No. 109. Signed by A. A. Milne. Greer 40-129 1983 £125

MILNE, ALAN ALEXANDER   The House at Pooh Corner. London,
1927. 4to. Orig. cloth backed boards with printed paper label,
uncut edges, in the orig. dustwrapper. Numerous full-page and
other illus. by E.H. Shepherd. Limited edition of 350 numbered
copies, signed by the author and artist, finely printed on hand-
made paper. Traylen 94-577 1983 £400

MILNE, ALAN ALEXANDER   The House at Pooh Corner. N.Y.: E.P.
Dutton & Co., (1928). First American edition. With decorations by
E.H. Shepard. 4to. Orig. cloth-backed pictorial boards. In publisher's box. One of 250 copies printed on large paper and signed by
author. Fine. MacManus 279-3759 1983 $750

MILNE, ALAN ALEXANDER   The House at Pooh Corner. N.Y.: E.P.
Dutton & Co., (1928). First American edition. Orig. cloth. Dust
jacket (slightly torn). One of 250 copies signed by Milne and
Shepard. Near-fine. MacManus 279-3760 1983 $450

MILNE, ALAN ALEXANDER   The House at Pooh Corner. London,
Methuen, (1928). Decorations by Ernest H. Shepard. 12mo. Illus.
Rose cloth, gilt, gt., dj. 1st ed. Jacket slightly chipped at top
corners & top of spine. Very fine copy. O'Neal 50-115 1983 $150

MILNE, ALAN ALEXANDER   The House at Pooh Corner. London:
Methuen & Co., Ltd., (1928). First edition, with "First Published in
1929" on verso of title page. Pictorial pink cloth, gilt, t.e.g.
Small gouge in cloth near base of spine, very light fading near cover
edges, otherwise nice copy in worn and soiled jacket. Bradley 66-258
1983 $125

MILNE, ALAN ALEXANDER   The House at Pooh Corner. Methuen,
1928. With decorations by Ernest H. Shepard. First edition, 8vo,
orig. pink cloth, gilt, t.e.g. Dust wrapper. Fenning 62-250
1983 £65

MILNE, ALAN ALEXANDER   The House at Pooh Corner. London:
Methuen & Co. Ltd., (1928). First edition. With decorations by E.H.
Shepard. Orig. cloth. Spine a bit worn. Good. MacManus 279-3761
1983 $30

MILNE, ALAN ALEXANDER   Michael & Mary. London: Chatto &
Windus, 1930. First edition. Orig. cloth. Dust jacket (a bit worn,
inner tape repairs). Presentation copy, inscribed on the title-page
by the author. Very good. MacManus 279-3764 1983 $135

MILNE, ALAN ALEXANDER   Michael and Mary. London: Chatto &
Windus, 1930. First edition. Orig. cloth with paper label. Dust
jacket. Bookplate. Fine. MacManus 279-3763 1983 $25

MILNE, ALAN ALEXANDER   Not That It Matters. London: Methuen &
Co., (1919). First edition. Orig. cloth. Presentation copy, inscribed "To Arthur Rogers from A.A. Milne, August 1921." With Rogers'
bookplate on the front pastedown. In an improvised dust jacket and
box. Fine. MacManus 279-3754 1983 $250

MILNE, ALAN ALEXANDER   Now We are Six. London: Methuen, 1927.
Gilt cloth. Illus. by E.H. Shepherd. First edition. A fine copy,
in slightly soiled dust jacket, with some minor mends at edges.
Reese 20-702 1983 $125

MILNE, ALAN ALEXANDER   Now We are Six. London, (1927). First
edition. Decorations by E.H. Shepard. 12mo, pictorial olive leather.
Argosy 714-523 1983 $100

MILNE, ALAN ALEXANDER   Songs from "Now We Are Six." Methuen,
1927. Decor. by E.H. Shepard. Title vignette & numerous vignettes
throughout. Pub's bds., vg. Hodgkins 27-150 1983 £15

MILNE, ALAN ALEXANDER   The Secret and Other Stories. New
York: The Fountain Press, London, Methuen, 1929. First edition,
8vo, orig. cloth, with printed paper label, a fine copy. Ltd. edition
of 742 numbered copies, signed by the author. Fenning 62-251 1983
£28.50

MILNE, ALAN ALEXANDER   Two People. N.Y.: E.P. Dutton & Co.,
1931. First American edition. Orig. cloth. Dust jacket (spine and
covers slightly faded and worn). Very good. MacManus 279-3766 1983
$45

MILNE, ALAN ALEXANDER   Two People. London: Methuen & Co Ltd.,
(1931). First edition. Orig. cloth. Worn dust jacket. Very good.
MacManus 279-3767 1983 $25

MILNE, ALAN ALEXANDER   War With Honour. London: Macmillan &
Co. Ltd., 1940. First edition. Orig. wrappers. Fine. MacManus 279-
3768 1983 $20

MILNE, ALAN ALEXANDER   When I Was Very Young. N.Y., Fountain
Press, (1930). Pictorial pink cloth. Enclosed in a half leather
slipcase. One of 842 copies, signed by Milne. Fine copy. Houle 21-
639 1983 $425

MILNE, ALAN ALEXANDER   When I was Very Young. New York, The
Fountain Press, London, Methuen, 1930. First edition, 8vo, orig.
patterned cloth, with printed paper label. A fine copy. Ltd.
edition of 842 numbered copies, signed by the author. Fenning 62-
252 1983 £35

MILNE, ALAN ALEXANDER   When We Were Very Young. London:
Methuen & Co., (1924). First edition. Decorations by E. Shepard.
Orig. pictorial cloth. Endpapers a bit browned. Edges slightly
worn. In a cloth box. Very good. MacManus 279-3769 1983 $125

MILNE, ALAN ALEXANDER   Winnie-the-Pooh. London, 1926. 4to.
Orig. cloth backed boards with printed paper label, uncut edges,
in the orig. dustwrapper. Numerous full-page and other illus. by
E.H. Shepherd. Limited edition of 350 numbered copies, signed by
the author and artist. A Presentation copy, finely printed on hand-
made paper. Traylen 94-578 1983 £450

MILNE, ALAN ALEXANDER   Winnie the Pooh. London, Methuen (1926).
First edition. Decorations by E.H. Shepard. Endpaper maps. Pictorial
dust jacket (slight soiling and rubbing) t.e.g., else very good.
Houle 22-1217 1983 $275

MILNE, ALAN ALEXANDER   Winnie-the-Pooh. London: Methuen Children's Books (1976). 12mo, handbound in full leather by Zaehnsdorf,
gilt, a.e.g., pictorial endpapers. Illus. by Ernest H. Shepard. One
of 300 copies signed by Christopher Milne and published on the 50th
anniversary. Duschnes 240-157 1983 $300

MILNE, C.   A Botanical Dictionary. 1770. 2 folding
tables, 8vo, contemporary calf, worn. Wheldon 160-1553 1983 £18

MILNE, JOSHUA   A Treatise on the Valuation of Annuities
and Assurances on Lives and Survivorships. London: Longman, Hurst,
Rees, Orme and Brown, 1815. 1st ed., 2 vols., 8vo, slightly browned,
cont. calf, a little rubbed, rebacked, corners repaired, later paper
labels, bookplate. Pickering & Chatto 21-82 1983 $600

MILNE, L.   The Home of an Eastern Clan. Oxford,
1924. Numerous plates, some slight wear. 8vo. Orig. cloth. Good.
Edwards 1044-495 1983 £40

MILNE, L.   Shans at Home. London, 1910. Map,
numerous plates. Thick 8vo. Spine faded and slightly worn, back cover
marked. Good. Edwards 1044-494 1983 £22

MILNE EDWARDS, A.   Observations sur deux Orang-Outans
adultes morts a Paris. Paris, Nouv. Arch. Mus., 1895. 2 coloured and
3 plain plates, 4to, wrappers. Some marginal waterstaining. Wheldon
160-585 1983 £25

MILNE EDWARDS, A.   Recherches sur la Famille des Chevrotains.
Paris, 1864. 11 plates (2 coloured), 4to, qtr. calf. Wheldon 160-
584 1983 £20

MILNE-EDWARDS, H.   Cours Elementaire d'Histoire Naturelle:
Zoologie. Paris, 1852. 6th edition, 466 figures and a map (repaired),
8vo, contemporary half calf. Two leaves somewhat stained.
Wheldon 160-506 1983 £12

MILNER, JOHN   A Collection of the Church-History of
Palestine. Printed for Thomas Dring, 1688. First edition, 4to,
wrapper, first and final page dust soiled, but a good to very good
copy. Fenning 61-300 1983 £24.50

MILNES, RICHARD MONCKTON   Life, Letters and Literary Remains of
John Keats. Edward Moxon, 1848. First edition, 2 vols., half
titles, frontis., one page of ads in vol. 2. Orig. brown cloth,
very good. Jarndyce 30-1038 1983 £78

MILTON, JOHN   L'Allegro & Il Penseroso. Glen Head,
Long Island, 1932. 2 vols., 12mo, boards, gilt. One of 400 copies
with title-page woodcuts by Rudolph Ruzicka (printed from the original
wood blocks). Fine set in lightly rubbed slipcase. Perata 27-199
1983 $75

MILTON, JOHN   The Complete Poetical Works of Milton.
Ph., 1895. Limited to 60 numbered sets of 4 vols., 50 photogravures,
limp leather, a.e.g., leather edges worn, interior fine. Quill &
Brush 54-948 1983 $250

MILTON, JOHN   Comus: A Mask. Montgomeryshire,
1931. Sm 4to, linen-backed bds., gilt-lettering. One of 250
copies on Japon vellum, containing a frontis and 6 wood-engravings
by Blair Hughes-Stanton. Perata 27-84 1983 $450

MILTON, JOHN   A defence of the people of England, in
answer to Salmasius's Defence of the King. 1692. 1st English ed.,
sm. 8vo, advts, cont. calf rebacked, morocco label, corners little
worn, a good copy with armorial bookplate. Deighton 3-227 1983
£185

MILTON, JOHN   A Defence of the People of England.
(Amsterdam?): Printed in the year 1692. Full paneled calf, gilt,
by Ramage. Hinges broken and crudely taped. Bookplates. First
edition in English. Felcone 21-75 1983 $150

MILTON, JOHN   Eikonoklastes, an Answer to a Book
initul'd 'Eikon Basiliki' the Portraiture of his Sacred Majesty in
his Solitudes and Sufferings. London: printed by Matthew Simmons,
1649. 1st ed., 4to, later vellum, spine gilt, a.e.g. Title in
red and black. A fine copy. Trebizond 18-68 1983 $900

MILTON, JOHN   The History of Britain. Printed by R.E.
for R. Scot, R. Chiswell, R. Bently, G. Sawbridge, 1695. Panelled
calf, a little rubbed. Jarndyce 31-5 1983 £85

MILTON, JOHN   Ode on the Morning of Christ's Nativity.
Sewanee, Tennessee: University Press, n.d. (ca.1904). 12mo. Orig.
cloth-backed blue gray paper boards. Limited to 250 copies printed on
Strathmore paper. Fine. MacManus 279-3773 1983 $35

MILTON, JOHN   On the Morning of Christ's Nativity.
Cambridge, 1923. A note by Geoffrey Keynes with hitherto unpublished
drawings by William Blake. 4to, vellum-backed cloth gilt,
t.e.g., others uncut, d/w. De-Luxe Edition limited to 150 copies.
Bookplate. A fine copy with endpapers heightened in gold. Perata
27-205 1983 $300

MILTON, JOHN   Paradise Lost. Printed for J. and R.
Tonson and S. Draper, 1749. 2 vols., 4to, 2 portraits and 12
plates, cont. calf. Wormhole in central margin in a few pages in
the middle of each volume, binding rubbed, and small defective spot on
the upper cover of second volume. Bickersteth 75-61 1983 £86

MILTON, JOHN   Paradise Lost. Glasgow: R. & A.
Foulis, 1770. Folio. 19th century green morocco, blind tooled
panels on sides, inner gilt dentelles, edges gilt. Vignette
portrait on title-page. Traylen 94-579 1983 £160

MILTON, JOHN   Paradise Lost. Philadelphia, 1791.
3rd American ed. 12mo, contemporary calf, leather label, hinges
slightly cracked, former owner's inscriptions on title. Morrill
289-441 1983 $25

MILTON, JOHN   Paradise Lost, with the Life of the
Author. Printed by C. Whittingham, for T. Heptinstall, 1799. 8vo,
subscriber's list, portrait, engraved title with vignette and 12
plates, orig. tree calf gilt, rebacked preserving orig. label.
Bickersteth 75-62 1983 £18

MILTON, JOHN   Paradise Lost. The Doves Press
Hammersmith, 1902. 8vo. Vellum. 1 of 300 copies. A fine copy
in slipcase box. In Our Time 156-215 1983 $600

MILTON, JOHN   Paradise Lost. Hammersmith, 1902.
8vo, vellum, printed in red and black. One of 300 copies. Duschnes
240-74 1983 $500

MILTON, JOHN   Paradise Lost. G. Routledge, 1905.
Frontis. Pictorial title & 10 plates. Light brown cloth, gilt.
Greer 40-213 1983 £18

MILTON, JOHN   Paradise Lost. N.Y.: Heritage, (1940).
4to. Tan cloth. Full-page illus. printed in color. Fine. Aleph-bet
8-40 1983 $20

MILTON, JOHN   Paradise Regain'd. Printed for John
Starkey, 1680. 8vo, 4 pages bookseller's ads. A.e.g., polished
mottled calf gilt by Riviere. A fine copy. Bickersteth 75-60 1983
£190

MILTON, JOHN   Paradise Regained. The Fleuron, 1924.
1st ed., sm. 4to, illus., uncut in qtr. black linen over green
paper boards, a fine copy. 350 numbered copies on hand-made paper.
Deighton 3-224 1983 £36

MILTON, JOHN   Paradise Regained. London: The
Flueron, 1924. 1st ed. with illustrations by Thomas Lowinsky, 1
of 350 numbered copies. Orig. cloth-backed boards, gilt, uncut.
Finely printed on handmade paper, with extra suite of illus. on
Japan paper in pocket at rear. Fine copy. Jenkins 155-942 1983
$35

MILTON, JOHN   The Poems. London: the Florence
Press, 1925. 2 vols. 8vo. Orig. black buckram, gilt, t.e.g.,
others uncut. Traylen 94-580 1983 £22

MILTON, JOHN   Poems in English. London: the Nonesuch Press, 1926. 2 vols. Roy. 8vo. Orig. parchment backed boards,
uncut and unopened. 53 illus. by William Blake. Limited edition
of 1,450 copies numbered on Van Gelder rag paper. Traylen 94-581
1983 £120

MILTON, JOHN   Poems in English. London: Nonesuch
Press, 1926. Two octavo vols. Illus. Limited to 1450 copies.
Slight rubbing to extremities of vellum-backed decorated boards,
otherwise a very fine set. Bromer 25-266 1983 $150

MILTON, JOHN   The Poetical Works. William Pickering,
1832. With portrait, 3 vols., small 8vo, cont. morocco, gilt, e.g.
Very good. Signed presentation inscription from Isaac Butt to
Lady Hayes (?) dated December 25th, 1833. Fenning 61-301 1983
£32.50

MILTON, JOHN   Poetical Works. London, Macrone, 1835.
First edition thus. Small 8vo. 12 engravings by J.M.W. Turner.
Fine 3/4 red morocco over marbled boards, each spine with four small
inlaid green leather flowers, spine decorated in gilt, covers ruled
in gilt, t.e.g., marbled endpapers. 6 vols. Fine. Houle 22-665
1983 $375

MILTON, JOHN   The Portraits, Prints and Writings of...
Cambridge: 1908. Numerous full-page plates. Printed gray wrappers.
Covers chipped, a little light staining and dust soiling on a few
leaves. Bradley 66-52 1983 $55

MILTON, JOHN   Pro populo Anglicano defensio. Londini,
Typis du Gardianis, 1652. Early edition, 12mo, title with Commonwealth
arms, cont. calf neatly rebacked in calf, morocco label, very good.
Bookplate. Deighton 3-226 1983 £36

MILTON, JOHN   The Prose Works. Hansard for Johnson:
Nichols...and Mathews and Leigh, 1806. 1st ed., 7 vols, roy. 8vo,
cont. polished calf gilt and blind-stamped, double morocco labels,
marbled edges and endpapers, 5 vols. cracked along joints. Very clean
set. Deighton 3-228 1983 £90

MILTON, JOHN   Sampson Agonistes. NY, Elston Press,
1904. Printed in red and black, first page within woodcut border,
woodcut decorations by H.M.O'Kane. Ltd. edition of 120 copies only,
8vo, cl., uncut. Salloch 387-126 1983 $150

MILWARD, M.   Artist in Unknown India. London, 1948.
Plates, text illus. 8vo. Orig. cloth. Good. Edwards 1044-496
1983 £15

THE MIMIAMBS of Herondas. London: Fanfrolico Press, ca. 1926.
Quarto, Illus. throughout by Alan Ode. Limited to 375 copies. Extremely fine in cloth-backed decorated boards. Slip-case starting to
split at edges. Bromer 25-202 1983 $265

MINER, THOMAS   Typhus Syncopalis, Sinking Typhus.
Middletown, 1825. 1st ed. 8vo. Lacks wrappers. Morrill 289-159
1983 $37.50

MINET, PIERRE   Circoncision du Coeur. Paris: Edward
Titus, 1928. Printed wraps.   First edition. One of 300 numbered
copies, initialled by Titus.   Slight traces of soiling and foxing at
edges, otherwise about fine.   Reese 20-126 1983 $50

MINOR, DEMOCRITUS   The Anatomy of Melancholy...Sixth
Edition. Corrected, and Enriched by Translations of the Numerous...
Philadelphia, 1854. 8vo. Binding rubbed and partly spotted; inner
hinges cracked. Morrill 289-32 1983 $20

MINOT, GEORGE RICHARDS   Continuation of the History of the
Province of Massachusetts Bay, from the Year 1748. Boston, 1798 and
1803. Two vols. Full leather, paper labels. Slight foxing. Very
good. Reese 18-228 1983 $155

MINOT, GEORGE RICHARDS   The History of the Insurrections in Massachusetts, in the Year MDCCLXXXVI, and the Rebellion Consequent Thereon. Worcester, 1788. Leather, expertly rebacked. Very good. Printed
by Isaiah Thomas. Reese 18-161 1983 $225

MINTO, JOHN   Speeches of Presentation and
Acceptance of the Oil Painting of Dr. John McLoughlin, Delivered
by Hon. John Minto, and His Excellency, Sylvester Pennoyer...1889.
Salem, 1889. Orig. printed wraps. First edition. Ginsberg 47-741
1983 $50

MINTO, WALTER   An Inaugural Oration, on the Progress and
Importance of the Mathematical Sciences. Trenton: Isaac Collins, 1788.
Modern cloth. Very good. Felcone 19-29 1983 $200

MIRA, GIUSEPPE M.   Bibliografia Siciliana... New York:
Burt Franklin, n.d. 3 vols., including the additions and corrections.
Cloth. Reprint of the 1875-81 ed. Dawson 470-209 1983 $75

MIRABEAU, HONORE GABRIEL RIQUETTE, COMTE DE   Memoire sur l'Agriculture. Avignon, 1761. 8vo., calf, rare. Wheldon 160-2131 1983 £28

MIRABEAU, HONORE GABRIEL RIQUETTE, COMTE DE   Reflections on the
Observations on the Importance of the American Revolution, and the
Means of Making it Benefit the World. Philadelphia, 1786. Rebound
in cloth. Very good. Reese 18-156 1983 $150

MIRAEUS, AUBERTUS
Please turn to
LE MIRE, AUBERT

MIRO, JOAN   Joan Miro Lithographe. II: 1953-
1963. Paris: Maeght, 1975. 215 color illus., 11 orig. color
lithographs by Miro, printed by Mourlot. Large 4to. Cloth. Dust
jacket. Ars Libri 32-457 1983 $250

MIRO, JOAN   Joan Miro Lithographs. III: 1964-
1969. Paris: Maeght, 1977. 247 color illus., 5 orig. color lithographs by Miro, printed by Mourlot. Large 4to. Cloth. Dust jacket.
Ars Libri 32-458 1983 $175

MIRO, JOAN   Oiseau Solaire, Oiseau Lunaire, Etin-
celles. New York: Pierre Matisse Gallery, 1967. Colored repro.,
sandpaper prints, black and white illus. Folio, orig. paper wrappers
with decorations by artist. Limited eds. (1200 copies). Very fine.
Jenkins 155-943 1983 $250

THE MIRROR of the Graces. Printed for B. and R. Crosby, circa 1812.
With 4 engraved plates (lightly browned), including half-title,
12mo, orig. printed paper boards, uncut. Boards rubbed but thoroughly
sound and otherwise a nice copy in orig. state. Fenning 61-302 1983
£85

THE MIRROR of the graces. Edinburgh: Adam Black, etc., 1830.
12mo. Cont. half calf. A little rubbed. Ximenes 63-112 1983
$75

MISCELLANEOUS Poems by several hands. London: published by D. Lewis,
printed by J. Watts, 1726 (and 1730). 1st editions, 2 vols., 8vo,
cont. mottled calf gilt, but not uniform and very rubbed, upper
upper joints cracked but holding, cont. armorial bookplate in the
second volume, and a later bookplate. Pickering & Chatto 19-54
1983 $850

A MISCELLANY of Poetry, 1920-1922. N.Y.: Seltzer, 1924. First
American edition, 8vo, cloth backed boards. Argosy 714-22 1983 $20

MISCELLANY Poems. London, Tonson, 1684. Leaf of pub.'s ads. Cont.
calf. First edition. 8vo. Salloch 387-12 1983 $400

MISCH, GEORG   Der Weg in Die Philosophie. Leipzig/
Berlin: B. G. Teubner, 1926. First edition. Gach 95-369 1983 $25

MISSOURI. CONSTITUTION.   Constitution of the State of Missouri.
St. Louis, 1854. Illus., large folded map, orig. printed wraps.
First edition. Ginsberg 46-488 1983 $100

MISSOURI Dental Journals. Vols. XI-XV. Kansas City, 1879-1883.
5 vols., 8vo, 1/2 calf (rubbed, joints mended); ex-lib. Argosy 713-
378 1983 $100

MISSOURI. LAWS.   Laws of the State of Missouri. St.
Louis, 1825. 2 vols. Full orig. calf. First edition. Ginsberg 47-
531 1983 $275

MISSOURI. LAWS.   Laws of the State of Missouri, Passed at
the First Session of the Ninth General Assembly. St.Louis: Chambers
& Knapp, 1841. Orig. full calf with morocco label. Jenkins 152-259
1983 $150

MISSOURI. LAWS.   Laws of the State of Missouri Passed
at the First Session of the Twelfth General Assembly. Jefferson
City, Hammond, 1843. Orig. boards, calf spine. First edition.
Ginsberg 47-530 1983 $150

MISSOURI. LAWS.   The Revised Statutes of the State of
Missouri Revised and Digested by the Eighth General Assembly. St.
Louis: Chambers & Knapp, 1841. Index. Orig. calf with morocco label.
Normal wear for this type of book. Third edition. Jenkins 152-260
1983 $125

MR. Henry Irving and Miss Ellen Terry in America. Opinions of the
press. Chicago: John Morris, printers, 1884. 8vo, original printed
parchment wrappers (soiled). 1st edition. Ximenes 64-306 1983 $35

MITCHELL, DAVID M.   Cri du Coeur. London: Elkin Mathews
& Marrot, 1931. First edition. Preface by W.H. Davies. Orig. printed
boards. Signed by author on the title-page. Spine and covers slightly
faded and worn, with some offsetting to the endpapers. Good. MacManus
278-1313 1983 $30

MITCHELL, DONALD GRANT   Fresh Gleanings. New York, Harpers, 1847.
8vo, orig. tan cloth gilt, worn, spine ends chipped. This copy is in
a close variant of Blanck's "A" binding with the same spine and
cover decoration and lettering; the sheets are untrimmed as in the
"A" binding. First edition. Ravenstree 97-108 1983 $35

MITCHELL, DONALD W.   History of the Modern American Navy.
London, 1947. 8vo. Orig. cloth. Signet Library copy. Frontis., 5
maps, numerous photographic illus. Good. Edwards 1042-135 1983 £12

MITCHELL, HORACE   Raising Game Birds. Phila. (1936)
Illus, cloth, spine very worn. Richard E. Bishop's copy,
with his signature. King 46-621 1983 $35

MITCHELL, JOHN   The Contest in America between Great
Britain and France with its Consequences and Importance...by an
Impartial Hand. London: Printed for A. Millar, 1757. Old three
quarter calf and boards, one board reattached. Internally fine.
Reese 18-69 1983 $400

MITCHELL, JOHN   The Fall of Napoleon. London, 1846.
Second edition. 3 vols in one. Thick sm. 8vo. Cont. full blue calf,
gilt. Half titles, maps in text. Spine gilt in compartments, red
morocco label. Very slightly worn and faded. Marbled edges, marbled
endpapers. Ink inscription on endpaper. Good. Edwards 1042-431
1983 £60

MITCHELL, JOHN   The Life of Wallenstein. London, 1840.
Second edition. Engraved portrait frontis. 1 leaf ads. at end.
Sm. 8vo. Orig. cloth. Spine slightly worn and faded. Blind library
stamps on title and frontis. Bookplate. Good. Edwards 1042-502
1983 £30

MITCHELL, JOHN H.   The Pacific Railroad Indebtedness.
(Wash.), 1889. Sewn. First edition. Ginsberg 47-781 1983 $25

MITCHELL, JOHN K.   Indecision, a Tale of the Far West.
Phila.: E.L. Carey & A. Hart, 1839. First edition. Ads. Cloth.
Very good. Felcone 20-107 1983 $20

MITCHELL, JONATHAN   Nehemiah on the Wall in Troublesom
Times... Cambridge (Mass.) printed by S.G. and M.J., 1671. 4to,
recent half morocco gilt, inscribed presentation copy with "John
Whiting ex dono S.G. printer" on the title, without final blank
leaf, running headline on last leaf of text damaged with loss of three
letters not touching text, minor watermarking, but a fine large copy.
First edition. Ravenstree 97-109 1983 $4,500

MITCHELL, MARGARET   Gone with the Wind. N.Y., MacMillian,
1936. First edition, first state, May. Orig. grey cloth. Zane
Grey's copy. Cloth slipcase. A fine copy. Houle 22-667 1983 $450

MITCHELL, MARGARET   Gone with the Wind. N.Y., 1939. Small
4to, green cloth; edges rubbed. Illus. Motion Picture edition.
Cheap edition, printed in double columns, with color scenes from the
motion picture. Argosy 714-524 1983 $45

MITCHELL, PETER CHALMERS (1864-1912)   The Childhood of Animals.
NY: Frederick A. Stokes Co., (1912). First American edition. 12
color plates and numerous text illus. Gach 95-370 1983 $30

MITCHELL, S. AUGUSTUS   Traveller's Guide through the United
States. Phila., 1834. Large folded table inside front cover. Ginsberg 47-554 1983 $175

MITCHELL, SILAS WEIR   Hugh Wynne Free Quaker Sometime Brevet
Lieutenant-Colonel on the Staff of His Excellency General Washington.
New York: The Century Co., 1897. Two vols., large quarto. Parch-
ment and boards. One of 60 numbered copies. Printed on large paper,
specially bound, and signed by the author, for the author's use.
Two leaves carelessly opened, with no loss, otherwise a fine set.
In the orig. slipcase (joints taped). Reese 19-332 1983 $175

MITCHELL, SILAS WEIR   Hugh Wynne, Free Quaker, Sometime
Brevet Lieutenant-Colonel on the Staff of His Excellency General
Washington. New York, Century Co., 1897. 2 vols., 8vo, orig. cloth,
trifle soiled. First edition. Ravenstree 97-110 1983 $28

MITCHELL, SILAS WEIR   In War Time. Boston, Houghton, Mifflin,
1885. 8vo, orig. cloth, bit bubbled and age-darkened with ends of spine
frayed, name on end-paper. Complete with pub.'s catalogue. The
first edition. Ravenstree 96-118 1983 $35

MITCHELL, SILAS WEIR   Researches upon the Venom of the
Rattlesnake. (Washington), July, 1860. 1st ed. Presentation copy.
4to. Text illus. Contemporary boards, leather back and corners.
Rubbed; backstrip partly chipped; covers loose. Very scarce.
Morrill 289-160 1983 $275

MITCHELL, SILAS WEIR   Some Recently Discovered Letters of
William Harvey with Other Miscellanea. Phila., 1912. 2 illus.,
stiff wrs., paper label. Argosy 713-380 1983 $30

MITCHELL, SILAS WEIR   The Wager and Other Poems. N.Y.,
1900. First edition. Thin 8vo, cloth. Presentation copy. Argosy
714-525 1983 $50

MITCHELL, SILAS WEIR   The War Time. Boston, Houghton-Mifflin,
1885. 8vo, orig. cloth, bit bubbled, worn, name on end-paper. First
edition. Ravenstree 97-111 1983 $35

MITCHELL, SILAS WEIR   Works. New York, Century, 1915. Illus.
16 vols., 8vo, ex-library. Morrill 288-318 1983 $45

MITCHELL, SILAS WEIR   The Youth of Washington, Told in the
Form of an Autobiography. NY: The Century Co., 1904. Printed at
the DeVinne Press. Limited ed. of 100 copies, 1/4 vellum, 4to,
uncut & unopened. Argosy 710-568 1983 $60

MITCHELL, WILLIAM   Skyways, A Book on Modern Aeronautics.
Phila. 1930. 1st ed., illus, cloth, in slightly chipped. dw.
King 46-725 1983 $25

MITCHISON, NAOMI   Beyond This Limit. London: Jonathan
Cape, (1935). First edition. Pictures by W. Lewis. 4to. Orig. cloth
& foil. Dust jacket designed by Lewis (dust-soiled & badly chipped).
Extremities of spine a trifle rubbed. Fine. MacManus 279-3275 1983
$85

MITCHISON, NAOMI   The Price of Freedom. London: Jonathan
Cape, (1931). First edition. Orig. cloth. Dust jacket. Presentation
copy, inscribed on the front free endpaper to "Maurice Bowra from
Naomi Mitchison, Easter 1931." Unopened. Fine. MacManus 279-3775
1983 $75

MITFORD, G. N.   The Chronicles of a Traveller. London,
1840. Paper covered boards. 8vo. Orig. cloth. Presentation copy
from author to the dedicatee, Thomas Newnham. Good. Edwards 1044-
498 1983 £65

MITFORD, JOHN   My Cousin in the Army. London: Printed
for J. Johnston, 1822. First edition. Full polished calf, gilt, with
morocco labels on spines, by Morrell. Some marginal soiling and foxing
to a few plates. Very good. MacManus 279-3776 1983 $500

MITFORD, JOHN   A peep into W-----r Castle, after the
lost mutton. London: J. Johnston, 1820. Third edition. 8vo. Disbound. Hand-colored frontis. Ximenes 63-503 1983 $90

MITFORD, MARY RUSSELL   Atherton, and Other Tales. Hurst &
Blackett, 1854. First edition, 3 vols. Front. vols. I & III. Ex-
library, but a clean copy rebound in blue cloth. Jarndyce 30-487
1983 £32

MITFORD, MARY RUSSELL   The Carpenter's Daughter. London,
Smith, Elder, 1834. 8vo, orig. embossed morocco gilt, scuffed and
worn, upper half of spine gone, front cover detached, back hinge
cracked, inscription on engraved title, a.e.g. First edition.
Ravenstree 96-119 1983 $25

MITFORD, MARY RUSSELL   Our Village. London: Macmillan & Co.,
1893. First edition with Thomson's illus. Intro. by A.T. Ritchie.
100 illus. by H. Thomson. Full olive green morocco. Elaborately gilt,
with green, brown, purple and yellow inlays, silk endpapers, a.e.g.,
by Sangorski & Sutcliffe. Head of spine rubbed. Outer hinges cracking
at top and bottom of spine. MacManus 280-5229 1983 $350

MITFORD, MARY RUSSELL   Our Village. London: Macmillan & Co.,
1893. First edition containing the Thomson illustrations. 100 illus.
Orig. gilt-decorated cloth. Edges very slightly worn. Near-fine.
MacManus 279-3777 1983 $35

MITFORD, MARY RUSSELL   Recollections of a Literary Life.
London, Richard Bentley, 1852. 3 vols., 8vo, later maroon half
morocco gilt, t.e.g., joints trifle worn, with half titles in vols. I
and III. First edition. Ravenstree 97-112 1983 $173

MITFORD, MARY RUSSELL   Recollections of a Literary Life.
London: Richard Bentley, 1852. First edition. 3 vols. 8vo.
Orig. bright blue cloth, gilt. Half-titles in vols. 1 and 3,
2 pp. of ads. Slightly worn. Traylen 94-586 1983 £35

MITFORD, WILLIAM   The History of Greece. London: for
T. Cadell, 1795. Third edition. 6 vols. 8vo. Cont. calf, gilt
spines with crimson morocco labels, gilt. Traylen 94-587 1983
£85

MITFORD, WILLIAM   The History of Greece. London: T.
Cadell, 1838. 8 vols. 8vo. Full tan calf, red and green morocco
labels, gilt, arms of Trinity College on the covers of each vol.
Portrait. Traylen 94-588 1983 £110

MIVART, ST. GEORGE J.   The Cat. New York, 1881. 200 illus.,
roy. 8vo, neatly recased in the orig. cloth. K Books 307-128 1983
£34

MIVART, ST. GEORGE J.   On the Genesis of Species. 1871. Second
edition, frontis, vignette, and illus. 8vo, cloth, trifle used.
Wheldon 160-181 1983 £25

MIVART, SAINT GEORGE J.   Types of Animal Life. Osgood,
McIlvaine, 1894. With 103 illus., 8vo, orig. cloth, very good.
Unchanged reissue of the first edition. Fenning 61-304 1983 £10.50

MOBERLY, A.   Lady Valeria. Richard Bentley, 1886.
First edition. 3 vols. Lacking following free end paper, vol. I & II.
Orig. brown cloth. A good copy. Jarndyce 31-814 1983 £42

MODE, PETER G.   Source Book and Bibliographical Guide
for American Church History. Menasha: George Banta Publishing
Company, 1921. First edition. Thick 8vo. Cloth. Covers lightly
spotted. Oak Knoll 49-473 1983 $75

MODERN Architectural Sculpture. London, 1930. 160 plates. Folio.
Cloth (slightly shaken). xvi pp. Ars Libri SB 26-3 1983 $100

MODERN Poster Annual, A Collection of the Year's Best Specimens of
Modern Colored Advertising Designs. NY, 1928-29. Vol. 5 Loose in
folder, very soiled, worn. King 46-402, 1983 $50

THE MODERN practice of the London hospitals. London: for J. Coote,
etc., 1764. First edition. 12mo. Cont. calf. Slight wear. Ximenes
63-284 1983 $200

THE MODERN Traveller. London: Duncan, 1825. 16mo, complete with folding map and three engr. views. Full calf, spine decorated in gilt,
red and blue leather spine labels, covers ruled in gilt and stamped in
blind, marbled edges and endpapers (slightly chipped at top of spine),
else very good. Houle 22-28 1983 $85

MOELLER, J.   Mikroskopie der Nahrungs- und Genuss-
mittel aus dem Pflanzenreiche. Berlin, 1905. Second edition.
599 text-figures, 8vo, wrappers (with cloth binding case). Wheldon
160-2132 1983 £18

MOENKEMOELLER, DR.   Geisteskrankheit Und Geistesschwaeche
in Satire, Sprichwort Und Homor. Halle: Carl Marhold, 1906. First
edition. Orig. printed boards. Very good ex-library copy. Gach
94-404 1983 $27.50

MOERLEIN, GEORGE   A Trip Around the World. Cincinnati:
M. & R. Burgheim, 1886. First edition. 110 chromolithographed illus.
after photographs. Map. Large 4to. Orig. red gilt-decorated cloth.
A.e.g. Unusually fine. Jenkins 152-261 1983 $225

MOFFAT, J. M.   The Protestant's Prayer-Book. Bristol:
for Arthur Browne..., 1785. First edition. 8vo. Half calf, backstrip worn. Some light damping. Heath 48-556 1983 £45

MOFFAT, ROBERT   Missionary labours and scenes in
southern Africa. London: John Snow, 1842. 8vo. Color frontis.
Folding map. 6 plates. New 1/2 brown morocco. Red label. Marbled
boards. Adelson Africa-105 1983 $185

MOGOLLONG Gold and Copper Co. Operating in Mogollon Mountains, Cooney
Mining District, Socorro County, New Mexico. New York, ca. 1904.
Frontis. and illus. Folding map. Fine. Jenkins 153-390 1983 $60

MOGRIDGE, EDWARD CHARLES   Poems. Hudd & Glass, 1858. First
edition, half title, 16 pp ads. Orig. green cloth, spine browned,
v.g. Jarndyce 30-795 1983 £14.50

MOGRIDGE, GEORGE   Serjeant Bell and his Raree Show.
London: Thomas Tegg, 1839. 1st ed., 4to, full red morocco gilt,
spine gilt by Riviere. Frontis. designed by George Cruikshank, as
well as the vignette title and some of the woodcuts. Front hinges
very tender, proof lightly foxed, otherwise a fine copy. Trebizond
18-23 1983 $275

MOHLE, HANS   Die Zeichnungen Adam Elsheimers.
Berlin: Deutscher Verlag fur Kunstwissenschaft, 1966. 133 plates.
Large 4to. Cloth. Ars Libri 32-203 1983 $150

MOHOLY-NAGY, SIBYL   Moholy-Nagy. Experiment in totality.
New York: Harper & Brothers, 1950. 81 illus. Small 4to. Cloth.
First edition. Ars Libri 32-464 1983 $75

MOHR, FRANCIS   Practical Pharmacy. London, 1849.
First edition. 8vo. Half-leather. Numerous illus. in text.
Slightly rubbed. Gurney JJ-271 1983 $25

MOHUN, CHARLES LORD   The tryal of Charles Lord Mohum, before the House of Peers in Parliament, for the murder of William Mountford. London: printed by Edward Jones in the Savoy; and published by Him and Randal Taylor, 1694. Folio, wrappers, 1st edition. Short tear in the foot of the title-page, but a good copy, complete with the preliminary license leaf. Ximenes 64-547 1983 $275

MOIR, D. M.   Domestic Verses by Delta. Blackwood, 1843. First edition, half title, 2 pp ads. Lacks leading free end paper. Orig. blue cloth, fine. Jarndyce 30-796 1983 £16

MOISSAN, HENRI   Classification des Corps Simples. Paris: Masson & Cie., 1904. First edition. 8vo. Orig. printed paper wrappers. An uncut presentation copy. Somewhat frayed. Zeitlin 264-316 1983 $100

MOISSAN, HENRI   The Electric Furnace. London: Arnold, 1904. First English edition. 8vo. Orig. cloth. Ads. Zeitlin 264-317 1983 $90

MOISSAN, HENRI   The Electric Furnace. London, 1904. First English edition. 8vo. Orig. cloth, slightly stained. Ex-library copy, but internally clean. Gurney JJ-272 1983 £20

MOISSAN, HENRI   Le Four Electrique. Paris: Steinheil, 1897. First edition. 8vo. Cont. half morocco. 42 text figures. A fine copy. Zeitlin 264-319 1983 $120

MOISSAN, HENRI   Le Fluor et ses Composes. Paris: Steinheil, 1900. First edition. 8vo. Cont. half calf. Frontis. portrait, text illustrations (2 full-page). Rebacked old style with orig. label laid down. Good copy. Zeitlin 264-318 1983 $90

MOISSAN, HENRI   Recherches sur les Differentes Varietes de Carbone. Paris: Gauthier-Villars, 1896. First edition. 8vo. Orig. printed paper wrappers. Worn, front cover detached. Zeitlin 264-321 1983 $60

MOISSAN, HENRI   Recherches sur l'isolement du fluor. Paris: Gauthier-Villars, 1887. 8vo. Cont. half calf. 4 offprints, separately paginated. Zeitlin 264-322 1983 $85

MOISSAN, HENRI   These...Serie du Cyanogene... Paris: A. Parent, 1882. First edition. 4to. Orig. wrappers. Inscribed presentation copy. Wrappers frayed, small tear extending into margin. Internally very good. Zeitlin 264-320 1983 $140

MOKLER, ALFRED J.   History of Natrona County, Wyoming... Chicago: 1923. Plates. 1st ed. Rare. Privately printed in a small ed. and very scarce. Fine copy. Jenkins 153-370 1983 $175

MOLIERE, JEAN-BAPTISTE   Tartuffe: or the French Puritan. London: for James Magnus, 1670. 1st English ed. Contemporary plain wrappers. Lacking pp. 57-64, but the very rare 1st ed. in English. Cloth slipcase. Jenkins 155-945 1983 $75

MOLINIER, EMILE   Les bronzes de la renaissance: les plaquettes. Paris, 1886. Catalogue raisonne. (Bibliotheque Internationale de l'Art.) 2 vols. Orig. wraps. bound in. Edition limited to 500 copies. Ars Libri SB 26-142 1983 $150

MOLINIER, EMILE   Les ivoires. Paris, n.d. Large folio. 24 superb collotype plates, numerous text illus. Orig. wraps. From the library of Vittorio Emanuele III, King of Italy. Ars Libri SB 26-143 1983 $475

MOLL, HERMAN   The Complete Geographer... London, 1709. Third edition. 2 parts in 1 vol. Engraved frontis. 44 engraved text maps. Folio. Modern black calf, blind-stamped, spine gilt. Small tears on a few corners, few pages browned, mostly in index. Kraus 164-165 1983 $2,500

MOLLER, F. PECKEL   Cod-liver Oil and Chemistry. London: Christiania, Peter Moller, 1895. 8vo. Orig. blue pictorial cloth. Map of Sweden and Norway in color, 2 folding tables, diagrams, and frontis. Publisher's presentation inscription on title. Cloth shaken, small cut on backstrip. Zeitlin 264-324 1983 $97.50

MOLLIEN, GASPARD THEODORE   Travels in Africa, to the sources of the Senegal and Gambia, in 1818. London: Sir Richard Phillips, 1820. 8vo. Folding map. 4 plates. Modern red buckram. Uncut. Adelson Africa-106 1983 $150

MOLLOY, CHARLES   De Jure Maritimo et Navali. London, 1688. 4th ed. Engraved frontispiece; engraved title page. 8vo. Some embrowning & spotting throughout, occasional lightish dampstaining, few annotations in two hands, bound in full, contemp. calf, quite worn, sometime rebacked, spine double blind-ruled, with orig. red morocco label, gilt-ruled & dec. & lettered, preserved, the title page in wood-ruled border. Boswell 7-124 1983 $350

MOLLOY, LEO T.   Tercentenary Pictorial and History of the Lower Naugatuck Valley. Ansonia, 1935. Illus, 4to, orig. pr. wrs. Argosy 710-118 1983 $40

MOLMENTI, POMPEO   G.B. Tiepolo. Milano: Ulrico Hoepli, n.d. 80 plates. 350 illus. Large stout 4to. Vellum. Ars Libri 33-357 1983 $200

MOLMENTI, POMPEO   Vittore Carpaccio e la Confrerie de Sainte Ursule a Venise. Firenze: Bemporad, 1903. 54 illus. Folio. Wrappers. From the library of Vittore Emanuele III, King of Italy. Ars Libri 33-91 1983 $85

MOLTKE, J. W. VON   Govaert Flinck, 1615-1660. Amsterdam: Menno Hertzberger, 1965. 70 plates. Large 4to. Cloth. Ars Libri 32-223 1983 $175

MONAGHAN, FRANK   French Travellers in the United States, 1765-1932. New York Public Library, 1933. 1st ed. Presentation copy. Illus. 8vo, orig. wrappers. Morrill 286-329 1983 $20

MONAGHAN, JAY   Lincoln Bibliography 1839-1939. Springfield, 1943. 2 vols. Orig. cloth. First edition. Ginsberg 46-410 1983 $50

MONAGHAN, JAY   The Overland Trail. Indianapolis, 1947. Illus. and maps. 1st ed. in dust jacket. Jenkins 151-225 1983 $35

MONARDES, NICOLAS   De simplicibus medicamentis ex occidentali India delatis... Antwerp: Chrisopher Plantin, 1574. 10 text woodcuts. 8vo. 17th-century half vellum. With the ms. exlibris of Albrecht von Haller, dated 1725, and of Dr. Giller (19th c.), plus a 16th-century dedication inscription. Ms. additions on front endpaper and last leaf. Kraus 164-166 1983 $2,200

MONDAINI, GENNARO   La Questione dei Negri nella Storia e nella Societa Nord-Americana. Torino, 1898. 1st ed., 12mo, 1/2 cloth, title-leaf torn, ex-library. Inscribed. Argosy 710-25 1983 $35

MONDEVILLE, HENRI DE   Die Anatomie... Berlin, Druck and Verlag von Georg Reimer, 1889. Editio Princeps, 8vo, uncut and un-opened in the orig. printed paper wrapper. Pickering & Chatto 22-71 1983 $200

MONDINO DEI LUZZI   Anatomia Corporis Humani. Venice: Bernardinus Venetus, de Vitalibus, for Hieronymus de Durantibus, 20 Feb. 1494 (1495). 4to. Boards. With ms. exlibris (17th cent.) of Jo. Ant. Balbani. Some minor staining. Kraus 164-169 1983 $7,500

MONET, A.- L.   Machines Typographiques et Procedes d'Impression. Paris: Gauthier-Villars et Fils, 1898. Third edition, entirely rewritten. Tall 8vo. Orig. paper wrappers. 99 illus. Minor chipping of covers. Oak Knoll 48-287 1983 $85

MONEY, J. W. B.   Java: or, How to Manage a Colony. London, 1861. 2 folding tables. 2 vols. Spines faded. 8vo. Orig. cloth. Good. Edwards 1044-487 1983 £125

MONGAN, ELIZABETH   The First Century of Printmaking, 1400-1500. Chicago: Art Institute of Chicago, 1941. Printed at Lakeside Press. 135 plates and illus. Stiff tan wrappers. Fine copy. Bradley 66-402 1983 $27.50

MONIZ, EGAS   Tentatives Operatoires Dans le
Traitement de Certaines Psychoses. Paris: Masson et Cie, 1936.
Tall 8vo., orig. printed stiff grey wrappers. Library stamp on half-
title, small chip to upper front wrappers, else a fine unopened copy.
First edition. Gach 95-104 1983 $125

MONKHOUSE, ALLAN   Books and Plays. London: Elkin Mathews
& John Lane, 1894. First edition. Orig. decorated cloth. Limited to
400 copies. Spine darkened and slightly rubbed. Very good. MacManus
279-3779 1983 $35

MONKHOUSE, ALLAN   Sons & Fathers. London: Ernest Benn
Limited, 1925. First edition. Orig. wrappers. Ellen Terry's copy,
with her bookplate designed by Gordon Craig on the verso of the front
free endpaper. Fine. MacManus 279-3780 1983 $45

MONKHOUSE, COSMO   The Christ upon the Hill. London:
Smith, Elder & Co., 1895. Folio. Illus. with 9 orig. proof
etchings (including title page), signed by Strang and tipped inside
a mat. This is one of 50 special proof copies, signed by the
artist. Printed at the Chiswick Press on rag paper. Bound in
1/4 calf over gilt-stamped cloth. Spine rubbed; cloth somewhat
soiled. Internally fine. Karmiole 71-87 1983 $350

MONNET, ANTOINE GRIMOALD   Traite de eaux minerales... Paris:
Didot, 1768. 8vo. Cont. mottled calf. Table, errata leaf. Front
hinge split, a little wear, otherwise a very good copy. Zeitlin
264-325 1983 $110

MONNET, JEAN   Supplement au 'Roman Comique,' ou
Memoires pour servir a la View de Jean Monnet. London, 1772. 1st
ed., 8vo, 2 vols. in one, cont. calf, spine gilt, morocco label,
engraved frontis. portrait, half-titles, bookplate. Hinges rubbed,
but a fine copy of an uncommon title. Trebizond 18-119 1983 $325

MONRO, D. B.   A Grammar of the Homeric Dialect.
Oxford, 1891. 8vo, cloth. 2nd edition. Salloch 385-570 1983
$75

MONRO, EDWARD   Basil, The Schoolboy; Or, The Heir of
Arundel. Joseph Masters, 1854. First edition. 8vo, half roan,
gilt back, marbled sides. Hill 165-86 1983 £65

MONRO, EDWARD   Leonard and Dennis; or, the Soldier's
Life. London: J. Masters, 1855. First edition. Thick cr. 8vo.
Cont. half calf, gilt spine with crimson morocco label, gilt. Title
within a lithograph border. Traylen 94-589 1983 £20

MONRO, HAROLD   Before Dawn. London: Constable & Co.
Ltd., 1911. First edition. Orig. cloth. Former owner's signature
on flyleaf. Near-fine. MacManus 279-3781 1983 $65

MONRO, HAROLD   Children of Love. London: The Poetry
Bookshop, 1914. First edition. Full calf, with orig. pictorial
wrappers bound in. Presentation copy, inscribed by author to his
second wife: "A(lida). K(lementaski). from H.M. March 1915." In a
handsome presentation binding. A trifle rubbed at edges. MacManus
279-3785 1983 $225

MONRO, HAROLD   The Collected Poems. London, 1933.
First edition. Covers a little dust-marked. Nice. Rota 231-426
1983 £12

MONRO, HAROLD   The Earth for Sale. London: Chatto &
Windus, 1928. First edition. Orig. cloth. Dust jacket (dust-soiled).
One of 50 copies signed by author. Fine. MacManus 279-3786 1983 $85

MONRO, HAROLD   Real Property. London: The Poetry Bookshop, 1922. First edition. Orig. decorated wrappers. Backstrip and
edges a little worn. MacManus 279-3788 1983 $20

MONRO, HAROLD   The Silent Pool And Other Poems. London:
Faber & Faber, (1942). First edition. Orig. orange printed wrappers.
Dust jacket (worn at the edges). Very good. MacManus 279-3790 1983
$25

MONRO, HAROLD   Strange Meetings. London: Poetry Bookshop, 1917. First edition. Orig. pictorial wrappers. Near-fine.
MacManus 279-3791 1983 $35

MONRO, HAROLD   Trees. Poetry Bookshop, 1916. First
edition. One of 400 copies. Unopened. Very nice. Rota 231-425
1983 £18

MONRO, HENRY   Remarks on Insanity: Its Nature and
Treatment. London, 1851. 1st ed. Presentation copy. 8vo. Some
cover stains. Morrill 289-161 1983 $25

MONROE, JAMES   Documents Accompanying the Message of the
President of the U.S. Washington: Gales & Seaton, 1822. Numerous
folding tables. Later black cloth. Jenkins 152-262 1983 $225

MONROE, JAMES   Documents from the Department of State,
Intended to Accompany the President's Message to Congress. Washington:
Gales & Seaton, 1825. Later black cloth. Jenkins 152-263 1983 $175

MONROE, JAMES   Message from the President of the U.S.
Washington: De Krafft, 1818. Folding statistical tables. Wrappers.
With cont. ink notations. Very fine. Jenkins 152-264 1983 $75

MONROE, JAMES   Message from the President...in
Relation to the Various Tribes of Indians within the United States.
Washington, 1825. Disbound. Felcone 22-94 1983 $25

MONROE, JAMES   Message from...Transmitting a Report
from the Secretary of War (John C. Calhoun)...Rules and Regulations
Adopted for the Government of the Military Academy at West Point.
Wash., 1819. 9 folded tables of statistics. Dbd. First edition.
Ginsberg 46-804 1983 $75

MONROE, JAMES   Message from...Transmitting Information
in Relation to the War with the Seminoles. Washington, 1818. Later
wrappers. Jenkins 153-502 1983 $65

MONROE, JAMES   Message from...Transmitting...the
Correspondences with the Government of France... Wash., 1825.
Half morocco. First edition. Ginsberg 47-470 1983 $75

MONROE, JAMES   Message of...Transmitting...Information
in Relation to Our Affairs with Spain, as, in His Opinion, is Not In-
consistent with the Public Interest to Divulge. Wash., 1819. Uncut.
Sewn as issued, laid in a cloth slipcase. First edition. Ginsberg
46-260 1983 $100

MONROE, JAMES   A Narrative of a Tour of Observation,
Made During the Summer of 1817... Philadelphia, 1818. Orig. printed
boards, untrimmed. Spine chipped, some scattered foxing, else a
generally fine copy. Reese 18-525 1983 $250

MONROE, JAMES   A View of the Conduct of the Executive,
in the Foreign Affairs of the United States, Connected with the
Mission to the French Republic, during the Years 1794, 5, & 6.
Philadelphia: Benj. Franklin Bache, 1797. Orig. paper-backed
boards, uncut. Spine crudely repaired with glue and a typewritten
label. Bookplate. Timothy Pickering's copy, with his signature
on front pastedown. Felcone 21-76 1983 $250

MONSARRAT, NICHOLAS   N. M. Corvette. London, 1942. First
edition. Photographs. Wrappers just a little marked and worn. Very
nice. Rota 231-427 1983 £12

MONSELL, J. R.   Polichinelle, Old Nursery Rhymes of
France. H. Milford, 1928. Oblong Sm. 4to. Pictorial title. 55 pic-
torially decorated pages with music, in various colours. Little loose.
Orange pictorial boards. Greer 40-143 1983 £15

MONTAGNANI, PIETRO PAOLO   Illustrazione storico-pittorico con
incisioni a contorni delle pitture di Raffaello Sanzio da Urbino...
Roma: Domenico Ercole, 1834. 30 engraved plates. 4to. Boards.
Ars Libri 33-299 1983 $125

MONTAGNANI, PIETRO PAOLO   Illustrazione storico-pittorica con
incisioni a contorni dei dipinti della gran sala... Roma: Domenica
Ercole, 1834. 25 engraved plates (mostly folding). 4to. Boards.
Ars Libri 33-298 1983 $125

MONTAGU, EDWARD WORTLEY   Reflections on the Rise and Fall of the Antient Republicks. London, A. Millar, 1759. 8vo, cont. calf gilt, front joint cracked; tear to leaf E4, text rubbed on verso; a good, large copy. First edition. Ravenstree 97-113 1983 $55

MONTAGU, ELIZABETH   An Essay on the Writings and Genius of Shakespear, compared with the Greek and French Dramatic Poets. London: J. Dodsley, 1769. 1st ed., 8vo, cont. calf and morocco label. Half-title not called for. A fine copy. Trebizond 18-70 1983 $200

MONTAGU, ELIZABETH   An Essay on the Writings and Genius of Shakespear, compared with the Greek and French Dramatic Poets. Dublin: Printed for H. Saunders, J. Potts, W. Sleater, D. Chamberlaine, and J. Williams, 1769. 12mo, wormhole at foot of inner margin in first quarter of the book, nowhere near the text, orig. calf, rubbed. First Dublin edition. Bickersteth 77-52 1983 £38

MONTAGU, ELIZABETH   An Essay on the Writings and Genius of Shakespeare. Printed by H. Hughs, for Edward and Charles Dilly, 1772. 8vo, orig. calf, rebacked, preserving the orig. label. Bickersteth 75-64 1983 £38

MONTAGU, H. W.   Monsieur Mallet: Or My Daughter's Letter. London: Griffiths, 1830. 1st ed. Orig. salmon printed wrappers. Six plates by Cruikshank, with extra suite of same plates bound in facing the first set, hand-colored. Bound in full crimson polished calf by Riviere (spine labels lacking). Very good. Jenkins 155-267 1983 $50

MONTAGU, MARY WORTLEY   Letters of the Right Honourable Lady Mary Wortley Montague, Written During her Travels... Phila.: William Duane, 1801. Full calf. Signature "An. Dn. Woodruff 1802" on title and full page of holograph notes on endsheet. Nice. Felcone 20-108 1983 $25

MONTAGU, MARY WORTLEY   Letters... London: for T. Becket and P.A. De Hondt, 1763. First edition. 3 vols. in 1. 12mo. Cont. calf, preserved in a brown morocco slip-case. This copy is from the library of Arthur A. Houghton, Jr., with his morocco book-label. Joints cracked and label defective. Traylen 94-590 1983 £195

MONTAGU, RICHARD   Appello Caesarem... London, 1625. 4to. A variant of 1st ed. 1st & last leaves chipped & dusty, embrowning throughout, rebound in 3/4 calf over marbled boards, spine blind-dec. & gilt-ruled, with brown morocco label, gilt-lettered, sound & clean copy. Boswell 7-125 1983 $250

MONTAGU, WALTER   Miscellanea spiritualia, or devout essayes. London: for William Lee, Daniel Pakman and Gabriell Bedell, 1648 & 1654. 1st ed., 2 vol. in 1, 4to, engraved title-page, printed title cut away from upper margin, repaired, verso with imprimatur, cont. mottled calf with gilt insignia, neat 19th century rebacking in calf, morocco label, marbled edges, a good copy. First and second series. Deighton 3-230 1983 £68

MONTAGUE, CHARLES   Works and Life. E. Curll, J. Pemberton and J. Hooke, 1715. 1st ed, 8vo, engraved portrait by Van der Gucht, cont. blind-panelled calf, spine gilt and with morocco label, joints just cracking but sound. A very good copy. Deighton 3-229 1983 £60

MONTAGUE, CHARLES EDWARD   Action and Other Stories. London: Chatto & Windus, 1928. First edition. Orig. cloth with paper label. Dust jacket (darkened). Very good. MacManus 279-3792 1983 $25

MONTAGUE, CHARLES EDWARD   Fiery Particles. London: Chatto & Windus, 1923. First edition. Orig. cloth with paper label. Dust jacket (darkened, a little rubbed). Very good. MacManus 279-3794 1983 $35

MONTAGUE, CHARLES EDWARD   Fiery Particles. London: Chatto & Windus, 1923. First edition. Orig. cloth. Inscribed by author. Very good. MacManus 279-3793 1983 $25

MONTAGUE, CHARLES EDWARD   A Hind Let Loose. London: Methuen & Co., (1910). First edition. 8vo. Orig. green cloth. Spine faded. Front inner hinge cracked. (Sir) Michael Ernest Sadler's copy with his bookplate and signature and 1-2/3 page ALS from Montague to Sadler laid in. MacManus 279-3795 1983 $45

MONTAGUE, CHARLES EDWARD   A Hind Let Loose. London: Methuen & Co., (1910). First edition. Orig. cloth. Spine darkened. Very good. MacManus 279-3796 1983 $35

MONTAGUE, CHARLES EDWARD   The Morning's War. London: Methuen & Co., (1913). First edition. Orig. decorated cloth. Dust jacket (somewhat faded and worn; spine margins slightly worn through). Edges foxed. With a color-printed publisher's advertisement slip loosely laid in. Bookplate of Dennis Wheatley. Near-fine. MacManus 279-3797 1983 $40

MONTAGUE, CHARLES EDWARD   Right Off the Map. London: Chatto & Windus, 1927. First edition. Orig. cloth. One of 260 copies signed by author. Bookplates. Spine faded. Endpapers lightly foxed. Good. MacManus 279-3798 1983 $45

MONTAGUE, CHARLES EDWARD   Right Off the Map. London, 1927. First edition. One of 260 numbered copies on large paper, signed by author. Full blue buckram. Spine a little faded. Bookplate. Very nice. Rota 230-409 1983 £25

MONTAGUE, CHARLES EDWARD   Right Off the Map. London: Chatto & Windus, 1927. First edition. Orig. cloth. Dust jacket. Small bookplate. MacManus 279-3799 1983 $25

MONTAGUE, CHARLES EDWARD   Rough Justice. London: Chatto & Windus, 1926. First edition. Orig. cloth. Dust jacket (chipped, tape-repaired). Bookplate. Good. MacManus 279-3801 1983 $25

MONTAGUE, CHARLES EDWARD   A Writer's Notes on His Trade. London: Chatto & Windus, 1930. First edition. Orig. cloth-backed patterned boards. Dust jacket (a little soiled). Limited to 750 copies signed by Tomlinson. Very good. MacManus 279-3802 1983 $50

MONTAGUE, CHARLES EDWARD   A Writer's Notes on His Trade. London, 1930. First edition. Intro. essay by H.M. Tomlinson. Of 750 signed by Tomlinson, this is one of 50 "complimentary" copies. Dust wrapper. Very good. Rota 230-410 1983 £20

MONTAGUE, EDWARD   The Legends of a Nunnery. J.F. Hughes, 1807. First edition, 4 vols., half green morocco, v.g. Jarndyce 30-488 1983 £250

MONTAGUE, EDWARD   Modern Characters. 1808. Half titles, half calf, labels. Fine. Jarndyce 30-489 1983 £160

MONTAGUE, EDWARD P.   Narrative of the Late Expedition to the Dead Sea. Philadelphia, 1849. 1st ed. Colored folding map. 8vo. Morrill 288-319 1983 $30

MONTAGUE, EDWARD P.   Narrative of the Late Expedition to the Dead Sea. Philadelphia, 1849. 1st ed. Colored folding map. 8vo. Binding rubbed and faded, text lightly dampstained, ex-library. Morrill 286-331 1983 $25

MONTAIGNE, MICHEL DE   Essays written in French by Michael Lord of Montaigne... London: Melch. Bradwood for Edward Blount and William Barret, 1613. Second edition in English. 18th century panelled calf, neatly rebacked, gilt, black morocco label, gilt. Engraved portrait of Florio by William Hole. Complete with the final blank leaf. With the bookplate of Edward Conyers. A fine copy. Traylen 94-591 1983 £500

MONTAIGNE, MICHEL DE   Essays. London: Privately Printed for the Navarre Society, 1923. 5 vols. 4to. Full white vellum, gilt, with decorations, t.e.g., others uncut. Large-paper edition de luxe limited to 150 numbered sets, printed on Arnold's hand-made paper, with numerous portraits from orig. engravings in the British Museum. Traylen 94-593 1983 £190

MONTAIGNE, MICHEL DE   Essays. London: M. Gillyflower and W. Hensman, 1700. Third edition, with additions. 3 vols. 8vo, cont. calf, gilt. 2 engr. portraits. Binding a little worn and joints cracked. Traylen 94-592 1983 £48

MONTAIGNE, MICHEL DE   The Essays of Montaigne. Cambridge: Harvard Univ. Press, 1925. 4 vols. 1st ed. thus. Orig. cloth, gilt. Very fine set. Jenkins 155-1416 1983 $50

MONTANA. CONSTITUTION.   Constitution of the State of Montana
as Adopted by the Constitutional Convention Held at Helena, Montana,
July 4, A.D. 1889. Printed wraps. A mint copy. Reese 19-386
1983 $150

MONTANA. CONSTITUTION.   Constitution of the State of. Helena,
(1889). 12mo, orig. pr. wraps., (back lacking). Argosy 716-313
1983 $50

MONTANA. CONSTITUTION   Constitution of the State of Montana.
Helena, (1889). First edition. Printed on salmon-colored wrappers.
Front cover detached, spine chipped, edges of few leaves of newsprint
text chipped. Bradley 66-598 1983 $20

MONTANA TERRITORY. LAWS.   Laws, Memorials and Resolutions of the
Territory of Montana Passed at the Sixth Session of the Legislative
Assembly...1869... Helena, 1869. Half morocco. First edition.
Ginsberg 47-575 1983 $75

MONTANUS, JOANNES BAPTISTA   Consultationum Medicarum.
(Basel, 1565). 1024 numbered (double) columns. Folio, cont. calf
(worn, corners chipped, back-strip lacking; small marginal wormholing
in first and last 50 leaves, without loss of text). Argosy 713-382
1983 $300

MONTBARD, GEORGES   Among the Moors. New York: Chas.
Scribner's, 1894. 8vo. 24 plates. Orig. cloth. Spine ends
starting. Adelson Africa-209 1983 $30

MONTEITH, W.   Kars and Erzeroum. London, 1856. Folding coloured map, 2 tinted lithograph plates. Cont. calf, some wear.
8vo. Good. Edwards 1044-499 1983 $95

MONTELL, GOSTA   Dress and Ornaments in Ancient Peru.
Goteborg: Elanders, 1929. 3 plates. 99 text illus. Small 4to.
Wrappers. Ars Libri 34-372 1983 $50

MONTENEGRO, ROBERTO   Mascaras Mexicanas. (Mexico City, Los
Talleres Graticos de la Nacion, 1926). First edition. 4to, illus.
endpapers. 50 b/w plates, 1 in color. Title page signed and inscribed
by the author. One of 2000 copies. Good. Houle 22-1132 1983 $45

MONTESSORI, MARIA (1870-1952)   Pedagogical Anthropology. NY:
Frederick A. Stokes Co., 1913. First English edition. Small stain
to rear board, else fine in orig. blue linen. Gach 95-372 1983 $75

MONTEVAL, MARION   The Klan Inside Out. Claremore, Okla.:
1924. First edition. Illus. Printed brown wrappers. Wrappers soiled
and chipped. Bradley 66-577 1983 $45

MONTGOMERY, A.   The Story of the Fourth Army. London,
1919. 4to. Orig. red decorated cloth. gilt. Map volume neatly rebacked in red morocco with orig. cloth spine laid down. Very slightly
worn and faded. Small ink library stamps. Bookplates. 2 vols.
Portrait frontis. 100 plates, 10 sketch plates (8 folding), 4 diagrammatic plates (2 folding), 9 folding panoramic plates, 19 folding
coloured maps in separate case. Good. Edwards 1042-418 1983 £40

MONTGOMERY, ALEXANDER   The Cherry and the Slae, with other
Poems. Glasgow, printed and sold by Robert and Andrew Foulis, 1751.
Small 8vo, 19th century half calf, upper joint cracked. Bickersteth
77-53 1983 £28

MONTGOMERY, FLORENCE   Behind the Scenes in the Schoolroom.
London: Macmillan & Co., Limited, 1913. First edition. Orig. cloth.
Cont. owner's signature on front flyleaf. Very good. MacManus 279-
3804 1983 $25

MONTGOMERY, JAMES   A poet's portfolio. London: Longman,
etc., 1835. First edition. 12mo. Orig. grey boards, printed paper
label. Spine a bit rubbed. A fine copy. Ximenes 63-418 1983 $75

MONTGOMERY, JAMES   Satan. Samuel Maunder, 1830. First
edition, half title, errata slip. Rebound in moire-patterned cloth,
label. Jarndyce 30-800 1983 £15

MONTGOMERY, JAMES   Songs of Zion. Longman, Hurst, 1822.
First edition, half calf, sl. rubbed. Jarndyce 30-797 1983 £20

MONTGOMERY, JAMES   Verses to the memory of the Late Richard
Reynolds, of Bristol. London, Longman, etc., 1815. 8vo, disbound.
Light stain on half-title, last page of ads dusty. Ximenes 63-419
1983 $95

MONTHERLANT, H.   Le Chant des Amazones. Paris, 1931.
4to. Colour frontis. 7 other lithographs. Silver & green wrappers.
Spine little worn. Edition limited to 165 copies, No. 44. Greer 40-
135 1983 £85

THE MONTHLY Miscellany of Western India. Bombay: Printed and published by H. A. Cannon, St. Andrew's Library, at the "Bombay Gazette
Press." 1850, Vol. 1, no. 1 - Vol 1, no. 7. 8vo, rebound in modern
leather, old label. Waterstaining to plates and minor patching with
scotch-tape, mainly a very good-fine copy. Folding chart, 3 maps and
elevations of Bombay churches engr. by H. O. Flower, and frontis.
Pasted on the verso of the frontis. is a note. In Our Time 156-573
1983 $250

THE MONTHS Illustrated by Pen and Pencil. Religious Tract Society,
(1864). 8vo, numerous text illus., some full page, orig. green cloth
with bevelled edges, richly gilt, a.e.g. Covers a little faded.
Bickersteth 77-232 1983 £15

MONTI, RAFFAELE   Andrea del Sarto. Milano: Edizioni
di Comunita, 1965. 14 tipped-in color plates, 374 catalogue illus.
Square 4to. Cloth. Ars Libri 33-325 1983 $100

MONTMORT, LE COMTE DE   Antoine Charles Du Houx. Baltimore:
The Johns Hopkins Press, 1935. Sm. 8vo. Orig. cloth backed blue
printed boards. Very slightly soiled. Portrait frontis., 1 plate.
Endpaper maps. Good. Edwards 1042-419 1983 £12

MONTOLIEU, ELISABETH JEANNE ISABELLE PAULINE DE   Caroline of
Lichtfield Printed for G.G.J. and J. Robinson, 1786. First English
edition, 3 vols, 12mo, contemporary mottled calf; with all half-
titles; two advertisement leaves in vol. III. Hill 165-87 1983
£195

MONTORGUEIL, GEORGES   Les Trois Couleurs. Paris, n.d. (ca.
early 20th century). Illus. in color by Job. Tall 4to, pictorial
front cover, 76 unnumbered pages, ex-library, nice. Morrill 288-644
1983 $25

MONYPENNY, W. F.   The Life of Benjamin Disraeli. London,
1910-20. 6 vols. 8vo. Orig. blue cloth. Numerous portrait and
other illus. Traylen 94-276 1983 £30

MOODIE, SUSANNA   Roughing It In The Bush. New York:
G.P. Putnam & Co., 1852. 18 1/2cm. First American edition. Orig.
blind stamped cloth. Rubbed and faded. Good. Rare. McGahern
53-119 1983 $100

MOODY, SOPHY   The Palm Tree. T. Nelson, 1864.
First edition, with 6 coloured plates, small 8vo, orig. cloth, gilt,
edges gilt, a very good copy. Fenning 61-307 1983 £21.50

MOODY, WILLIAM VAUGHN   The Masque of Judgment. Boston: 1900.
First edition. Blue cloth. Very good with slight wear. Bradley 66-
259 1983 $45

MOON in the Steeple. Texas, (1937). 8vo, cloth. Very good copy. In
Our Time 156-480 1983 $35

MOOR, E.   Plates Illustrating the Hindu Pantheon.
London, 1861. 104 plates. 4to. Orig. decorated cloth, slight wear.
Good. Edwards 1044-783 1983 £125

MOORE, ALAN   Sailing Ships of War, 1800-1860. Halton
& Truscott Smith, 1926. First edition, 90 plates, including 12
mounted coloured plates, large 4to, orig. half pigskin over patterned
boards, gilt, t.e.g., a fine copy in orig. slip-case. Ltd. edition
of 100 numbered copies on hand-made paper. Fenning 62-255 1983
£145

MOORE, CHARLES   History of Michigan. Chicago, 1915.
4 vols. Illus, 1/2 leather, t.e.g., a very nice set which is
usually found falling apart. King 46-181 1983 $100

MOORE, CHARLES   The Improvement of the Park System of
the District of Columbia. Wash., 1902. Illus., many folded maps,
plates, diagrams, etc. Orig. cloth, recased. First edition.
Ginsberg 46-234 1983 $75

MOORE, CLARENCE B.   Aboriginal Sites on Tennessee River.
Phila., 1915. Folio, full mor., (slight chip on front edge), a.e.g.
Argosy 716-3 1983 $100

MOORE, CLARENCE B.   Certain Mounds of Arkansas and of
Mississippi. Phila., 1908. Thin folio, full mor., a.e.g. Many
illus., some color plates. Argosy 716-5 1983 $85

MOORE, CLEMENT C.   Observations Upon Certain Passages
in Mr. Jefferson's Notes on Virginia, Which Appear to Have a Tendency
to Subvert Religion, and Establish a False Philosophy. N.Y., 1804.
Orig. wraps. First edition. Ginsberg 46-782 1983 $100

MOORE, COLLEEN   The Enchanted Castle. New York, 1935.
Special ed. (of the 1st ed.) printed for R.H. Macy. Illus. by
Marie A. Lawson. 4to, orig. boards, cloth back. Morrill 286-334
1983 $30

MOORE, EDMUND J.   The Law of Charities in Ireland.
Dublin: E. Ponsonby, 1906. First edition, 8vo, orig. cloth. Fenning
62-256 1983 £14.50

MOORE, EDWARD   The Foundling. London: printed for
R. Francklin, 1748. 1st ed., 8vo, 19th century half calf. Pickering
& Chatto 19-40 1983 $300

MOORE, EDWARD   Poems, Fables, and Plays. London:
J. Hughs, for R. and J. Dodsley, 1756. First collected edition.
4to. Cont. calf, morocco label, gilt. Printed on thick paper.
8 pp. list of subscribers. A little worn. Traylen 94-595 1983
£110

MOORE, EDWARD A.   The Story of a Cannoneer Under Stonewall
Jackson. New York & Washington, Neale, 1907. 1st ed. Portraits.
8vo. Morrill 288-320 1983 $57.50

MOORE, F.   The Lepidoptera of Ceylon. London 1880-
87. 215 finely handcoloured lithograph plates. 4to. Spines faded.
Orig. cloth. Fine set. Edwards 1044-501 1983 £1,400

MOORE, FORRIS JEWELL   A History of Chemistry. New York:
McGraw-Hill, 1918. First edition. 8vo. Modern buckram. Frontis.
portrait, numerous plates, 2 tables. Zeitlin 264-326 1983 $30

MOORE, FRANK   Rebel Rhymes and Rhapsodies. New York:
1864. First edition. Orig. half morocco. Jenkins 152-712 1983 $65

MOORE, FRANK FRANKFORT   The Fatal Gift. London: Hutchinson &
Co., 1898. First edition. Covers slightly rubbed & dull. Very good.
MacManus 279-3806 1983 $35

MOORE, FRANK FRANKFORT   The Life of Oliver Goldsmith. N.Y.:
E.P. Dutton & Co., 1911. First American edition. Orig. decorated
cloth. Bottom of spine a trifle chipped. Front hinge weak. Very
fine. MacManus 278-2292 1983 $20

MOORE, FRANK FRANKFORT   Mate of the Jessica. London: Marcus
Ward & Co., Belfast and Philadelphia, 1879. First edition. 2 vols.
Half titles, 2pp ads in both vols. Orig. brown cloth, dec. in
black, spine lettered in gilt. Mint. Jarndyce 30-491 1983 £95

MOORE, FRANK FRANKFORT   Sir Roger's Heir. London: Hodder &
Stoughton, (1904). First edition. Orig. pictorial cloth. Presentation copy from the author. MacManus 279-3808 1983 $25

MOORE, GEORGE   An Anthology of Pure Poetry. N.Y.:
Boni & Liveright, 1924. First American edition. Orig. parchment-
backed boards. Limited to 1000 copies signed by the editor. Spine
darkened, a bit worn. Very good. MacManus 279-3809 1983 $25

MOORE, GEORGE   Aphrodite in Aulis. L/NY, (1930).
Limited to 1825 numbered and signed copies, many pages uncut, paper
vellum boards slightly rubbed and lightly soiled, else very good.
Quill & Brush 54-950 1983 $40

MOORE, GEORGE   Aphrodite in Aulis. London: William
Heinemann Ltd., (1930). First edition. Orig. full vellum. Limited
to 1825 copies signed by the author. Louis Untermeyer's Rockwell
Kent bookplate on endsheet. Vellum covers discolored. Very good.
MacManus 279-3810 1983 $35

MOORE, GEORGE   The Apostle. London, 1923. Boards,
vellum spine, in the orig. dustwrapper. Limited edition of 1030 copies,
numbered and signed by the author. Traylen 94-596 1983 £16

MOORE, GEORGE   The Apostle. London: William Heinemann
Ltd., 1923. First edition. Orig. parchment-backed boards. Dust
jacket (slightly worn at edges). Limited to 1030 copies signed by
author. Fine. MacManus 279-3811 1983 $35

MOORE, GEORGE   Avowals. Privately Printed for Subscribers only, 1919. First edition. One of 1000 numbered copies,
signed by author. Half parchment. Covers a little marked. Nice.
Rota 231-429 1983 £21

MOORE, GEORGE   Avowals. London: Privately Printed
for Subscribers Only, 1919. Roy. 8vo. Boards, vellum spine, in the
orig. dustwrapper. Limited edition of 1,000 numbered copies, signed
by the author. Traylen 94-597 1983 £20

MOORE, GEORGE   Avowals London: Privately Printed for
Subscribers Only, 1919. First edition. Orig. parchment-backed boards.
Limited to 1000 copies signed by author. Very good. MacManus 279-3813
1983 $25

MOORE, GEORGE   The Brook Kerith. Edinburgh: Printed
for T. Werner Laurie, ltd., 1916. Cont. three quarter morocco,
gilt extra. First edition. A.l.s. from the author bound in, with
envelope addressed in his hand. Fine. Reese 20-708 1983 $175

MOORE, GEORGE   The Brook Kerith. Edinburgh: Printed
for T. Werner Laurie Ltd. By the Dunedin Press Ltd., 1921. Fifth
impression, with new preface by author. Orig. cloth-backed marbled
boards with paper label on spine. Dust jacket (darkened). Presentation copy, inscribed to John Freeman and dated July 5th, 1922. An
ALS & a TLS, 2-2/3 pages, 121 Ebury Street, London, 1920 & 1932, from
Moore to John Freeman. Fine. MacManus 279-3814 1983 $400

MOORE, GEORGE   The Brook Kerith, a Syrian Story.
NY: 1929. Sm 4to, parchment-backed bds., gilt, t.e.g. With 12
engravings by Stephen Gooden. One of 500 copies signed by the
artist & author. A fine copy in lightly worn slipcase. Perata 27-
220 1983 $90

MOORE, GEORGE   Celibates. London: Scott, 1895. First
edition. Orig. cloth. MacManus 279-3816 1983 $25

MOORE, GEORGE   Celibates. London, 1895. First edition.
Spine a little faded and marked. Nice. Rota 230-411 1983 £12.50

MOORE, GEORGE   The Coming of Gabrielle. A Comedy.
London: Privately Printed for Subscribers only, 1920. 1st ed.
with this title. Limited to 1000 copies signed by author. Original
parchment spine, paper-covered boards, minor soiling to boards;
a very good copy. Trebizond 18-71 1983 $50

MOORE, GEORGE   The Coming of Gabrielle. London: Privately Printed for Subscribers Only, 1920. First edition. Orig.
parchment-backed boards with paper label on spine. Dust jacket, a
little torn. Limited to 1000 copies signed by author. Fine. Mac-
Manus 279-3817 1983 $30

MOORE, GEORGE   The Coming of Gabrielle. London:
Privately Printed for Subscribers Only, 1920. 8vo. Boards, vellum
spine, in the orig. dustwrapper. Limited edition of 1,000 numbered
copies, signed by the author. Traylen 94-598 1983 £20

MOORE, GEORGE   A Communication to my friends. London:
the Nonesuch Press, 1933. 8vo. Boards, calf spine, gilt, in the
orig. dustwrapper. Limited edition of 1,000 numbered copies. Traylen
94-599 1983 £12

MOORE, GEORGE   Conversations in Ebury Street. London,
1924. Tall 8vo, ltd. first edition. Ltd. signed edition. Argosy
714-529 1983 $40

MOORE, GEORGE   Conversations in Ebury Street. London,
1924. First edition. One of 1030 numbered copies, signed by author.
Half parchment. Frayed dust wrapper. Very nice. Rota 231-431 1983
£21

MOORE, GEORGE   A Drama in Muslin. Vizetelly, 1886.
First edition. Frontis. from a drawing by J.E. Blanche. Bookplate.
Very nice. Rota 231-428 1983 £30

MOORE, GEORGE   Esther Waters. London: Walter Scott,
Ltd., 1894. First edition, second impression. Orig. cloth. Minor
soiling and wear. In a half-morocco slipcase. MacManus 279-3819
1983 $85

MOORE, GEORGE   Esther Waters. London: Walter Scott,
1894. Ads. at rear. First edition, first issue (binding), bound in
plain green cloth. Karmiole 72-71 1983 $75

MOORE, GEORGE   Esther Waters. London: Privately
Printed for Subscribers only, 1920. New edition. One of 750 numbered
copies, signed by author. Half parchment. Dust wrapper. Very nice.
Rota 230-413 1983 £15

MOORE, GEORGE   Evelyn Innes. London: T. Fisher Unwin,
1898. First edition. Orig. cloth. Very good. MacManus 279-3821
1983 $60

MOORE, GEORGE   Evelyn Innes. London: T. Fisher Unwin,
(1908). Fifth printing, with the new preface not found in any other
edition. Orig. decorated cloth. Presentation copy inscribed: "To
Betty Webb from me, George Moore. Dec. 1908." Covers slightly soiled.
Endpapers lightly browned. Very good. MacManus 279-3822 1983 $125

MOORE, GEORGE   Fragments From Heloise and Abelard.
London: Privately printed, 1921. First separate edition. 8vo. Orig.
wrappers, cord ties as issued. Wrappers partially faded. Very good.
MacManus 279-3823 1983 $20

MOORE, GEORGE   Hail and Farewell! London: William
Heinemann, 1911, 1912, (1914). First editions; second issue (with
advertisement leaf) of "Ave." First issue of "Salve." Second issue
(with corrected half-title) of "Vale." 3 vols. Orig. cloth. Fine.
MacManus 279-3825 1983 $75

MOORE, GEORGE   Hail and Farewell. London: Heinemann,
(1914). First edition, second state. Orig. cloth. Near-fine. Mac-
Manus 279-3824 1983 $25

MOORE, GEORGE   Hail and Farewell. London, 1925.
2 vols. Roy. 8vo. Boards, vellum spines, in the orig. dustwrappers.
Limited edition of 780 sets, numbered and signed by the author.
Traylen 94-600 1983 £28

MOORE, GEORGE   Hail and Farewell! London, 1925. New
edition, revised. One of 780 numbered copies, signed by author.
2 vols. Parchment spines just a little foxed. Dust wrappers. Very
nice. Rota 230-416 1983 £25

MOORE, GEORGE   Heloise and Abelard. Privately Printed
for Subscribers Only, 1921. First edition. One of 1500 numbered
copies, signed by author. 2 vols. Half parchment. Dust wrappers.
Fine. Rota 231-430 1983 £30

MOORE, GEORGE   Heloise and Abelard. London: Privately
Printed for Subscribers Only, 1921. 2 vols. Roy. 8vo. Boards,
parchment spines, in the orig. dustwrappers. Limited edition of
1,500 numbered copies, signed by the author. Traylen 94-601 1983
£26

MOORE, GEORGE   Impressions and Opinions. London: David
Nutt, 1891. First edition, first state. Orig. cloth. Extremities
of spine a trifle rubbed. Fine. MacManus 279-3826 1983 $35

MOORE, GEORGE   In Single Strictness. N.Y.: Printed
Privately for Subscribers only by Boni & Liveright, 1922. First
American edition. Orig. parchment-backed boards. Dust jacket (a
little worn). Limited to 1000 copies signed by author. Fine. Mac-
Manus 279-3827 1983 $25

MOORE, GEORGE   In Single Strictness. London, 1922.
First edition. One of 1030 numbered copies, signed by author. Half
parchment. Spine a little foxed. Dust wrapper. Very nice. Rota
230-415 1983 £15

MOORE, GEORGE   The Lake. London: William Heinemann,
1905. First edition. Orig. cloth. With the leaf of publisher's ads
before half-title (uncommon). Spine a little faded. Very good. Mac-
Manus 279-3828 1983 $125

MOORE, GEORGE   The Making of an Immortal. N.Y.: The
Bowling Green Press, 1927. First edition. Orig. boards with leather
label on spine. Limited to 1250 copies signed by author. Fine.
MacManus 279-3829 1983 $25

MOORE, GEORGE   Memoirs of My Dead Life. London:
William Heinemann, 1906. First edition. Orig. cloth. Bookplate.
Spine a little faded and worn. In a half-morocco slipcase. Good.
MacManus 279-3830 1983 $60

MOORE, GEORGE   Memoirs of My Dead Life. London, 1921.
"Moore Hall" edition. One of 1030 numbered copies, signed by author.
Half parchment. Dust wrapper. Nice. Rota 230-414 1983 £15

MOORE, GEORGE   Memoirs of My Dead Life. London:
William Heinemann Ltd., 1928. Fourth edition (uniform), revised.
Orig. cloth-backed marbled boards. Dust jacket (foxed). Presentation
copy, inscribed on the half-title "To The Duchess of Marlborough with
many thanks for some beautiful flowers, roses and peonies--peonies
fancier than roses almost as wonderful as tulips. June 1st 1928, George
Moore." Fine. MacManus 279-3832 1983 $125

MOORE, GEORGE   The Pastoral Loves of Daphnis and Chloe.
London, 1924. First edition of this translation. One of 1250 numbered
copies, signed by Moore. Bookplates. Very nice. Rota 230-417 1983
£20

MOORE, GEORGE   The Pastoral Loves of Daphnis and Chloe.
London, 1924. Roy. 8vo. Boards, buckram spine, gilt. Limited
edition of 1,280 numbered copies, signed by the author. Traylen
94-602 1983 £16

MOORE, GEORGE   Peronnik the Fool. New York: William
Edwin Rudge, 1926. Limited edition of 785 copies, designed by
Bruce Rogers. Traylen 94-603 1983 £20

MOORE, GEORGE   Salve. London: William Heinemann,
1912. First edition, first issue. Orig. cloth. Good. MacManus
279-3835 1983 $35

MOORE, GEORGE   Sister Teresa. London: T. Fisher
Unwin, 1901. First edition. 8vo. Frontis. Orig. cloth. Dust
jacket (rare). Fine copy. Jaffe 1-256 1983 $165

MOORE, GEORGE   Spring Days. London: Vizetelly & Co.,
1888. First edition, later impression, without publisher's advertisements at the back. Orig. green cloth. MacManus 279-3836 1983 $75

MOORE, GEORGE   Spring Days. Vizetelly & Co., 1888.
First edition, 32 pp ads. Orig. brown cloth, v.g. Jarndyce 31-817
1983 £15

MOORE, GEORGE   A Story-Teller's Holiday. N.Y.: Pri-
vately printed for Subscribers Only, 1918. First American edition.
Orig. cloth with leather label on spine. Limited to 1250 copies.
Louis Untermeyer's copy, with his signature and bookplate. 2 TLS,
2 pages, 8vo, Great Hill Road, Newtown, Conn., Oct. 30 & Nov. 1, 1955.
Very good. MacManus 279-3837 1983 $50

MOORE, GEORGE   A Story-Teller's Holiday. N.Y.: Horace
Liveright, 1928. 2 vols. Orig. cloth. Limited to 1250 sets signed
by author. Some foxing. Good. MacManus 279-3838 1983 $20

MOORE, GEORGE   Ulick and Soracha. London: The Nonesuch Press, 1926. 8vo, uncut edges, cloth. Dustwrapper designed by
Marion V. Dorn. Copper-plate engr. designed by Stephen Gooden.
Limited edition of 1,250 copies, numbered and signed by the author,
finely printed on Japanese vellum. Traylen 94-604 1983 £30

MOORE, GEORGE   Vain Fortune. London: Henry & Co.,
(1891). First edition. Illus. by M. Greiffenhagen. Covers a bit
worn. Orig. cloth. Contents somewhat shaken. Former owner's signature. Good. MacManus 279-3840 1983 $125

MOORE, GEORGE EDWARD (1873-1958)   Principia Ethica. Cambridge:
At the University Press, 1903. Publisher's olive cloth. First
edition. Good copy, some shelfwear and finger smudging. Few marginal pencilnotes. Gach 95-373 1983 $250

MOORE, HAMILTON   Nautical Sketches. London: William
Edward Painter, 1840. First edition. Illus. Orig. pictorial cloth.
Pictorial design on spine a little worn. Covers bumped. Inscription
on front free endpaper. Good. MacManus 279-3844 1983 $135

MOORE, HARRY THORNTON   John Steinbeck and His Novels: An
Appreciation. London: Heinemann, 1939. First English edition.
Wrappers, with Steinbeck portrait on inside of front wrapper. Signed
by Moore in 1973. Fine copy. Bradley 66-316 1983 $75

MOORE, HENRY   Henry Moore. Sculpture and drawings.
New York: Curt Valentin, 1946. Second edition. 229 plates (partly
tipped-in color). Large 4to. Cloth. Dust jacket. Ars Libri 32-
473 1983 $75

MOORE, HUGH   A Dictionary of Quotations from Various
Authors in Ancient and Modern Languages with English Translations.
Whittaker, Treacher, 1831. First edition, 12 pp inserted cata. Orig.
blue boards, well respined, retaining orig. label, v.g. Jarndyce 31-
663 1983 £38

MOORE, HUGH   Memoir of Col. Ethan Allen: Containing
the Most Interesting Incidents Connected with His Private and Public
Career. Plattsburgh: O. R. Cook, 1834. 1st ed, 16mo, paper label,
front flyleaf lacking, front hinge reinforced, foxed. Argosy 710-
454 1983 $35

MOORE, JAMES   History of the Cooper Shop Volunteer
Refreshment Saloon. Philadelphia, Jas. B. Rodgers, 1866. 1st ed.
Frontispiece. Small 8vo. Morrill 287-351 1983 $40

MOORE, JOHN   The Cotswolds. London, 1937. First
edition. Illustrations by Barrington-Browne. Torn and frayed dustwrapper. Very good. Jolliffe 26-360 1983 £16

MOORE, JOHN   Edward; Various Views of Human Nature,
Taken from Life and Manners, Chiefly in England. London, A. Strahan,
1796. 2 vols., 8vo, cont. calf gilt, somewhat worn, bumped, rebacked
to match. Bookplate, manuscript Moore family tree and signature on
front flyleaves of vol. 1, few minor stains, decent, sound copy.
First edition. Ravenstree 96-122 1983 $185

MOORE, JOHN   Edward. Various Views of Human Nature.
Printed for A. Strahan and T. Cadell jun. and W. Davies, 1796.
1st ed., 2 vols, lge. 8vo, cont. calf; half-titles; fragment torn
from blank corner of one title-page, but a fine copy. Hill 165-77
1983 £60

MOORE, JOHN   Edward. For A. Strahan, T. Cadell jun.
and W. Davies, 1796. First edition, 2 vols., 8vo, both half-titles
(glue-stained), errata leaf and advert. leaf at end of vol. II.
Cont. tree calf, gilt spines (a little rubbed, lacking one label,
another torn). Occasional slight foxing. Hannas 69-144 1983 £55

MOORE, JOHN   Mordaunt. London, G.G.J. Robinson,
1800. 3 vols., cont. quarter calf, new labels, bookplate. The first
edition. Ravenstree 96-123 1983 $165

MOORE, JOHN   A Sermon Preach'd before the Lord
Mayor, and the Court of Aldermen, at Guild-Hall Chappel, on the 28th of
May, 1682. Printed for Walter Kettilby, 1682. First edition, 4to.
Fenning 62-257 1983 £14.50

MOORE, JOHN   Works. Edinburgh, 1820. First
collected edition. Port. 7 vols. Tall 8vo, worn 1 page repaired.
Argosy 713-383 1983 $150

MOORE, JOHN   Zeluco. London, Strahan and Cadell,
1789. 2 vols., 8vo, orig. red morocco gilt extra, green morocco gilt
lettering pieces. Very fine, and possibly an Irish binding. Gilt
cipher on cover and bookplate of Robert Handcock. First edition,
complete with half titles. Ravenstree 96-124 1983 $575

MOORE, JOHN   Zeluco. Various Views of Human Nature,
taken from Life and Manners, foreign and domestic. London: A
Strahan and T. Cadell, 1789. First edition, 8vo, 2 vols., cont.
calf, spines gilt, morocco labels, half-titles, errata leaves, bookplate. A fine copy. Trebizond 18-72 1983 $275

MOORE, JOHN   Zeluco. Various Views of Human Nature.
Dubling: Printed for Messrs. L. White (etc), 1789. 2nd edition.
2 vols, 12mo, contemporary sheep; covers slightly rubbed. Hill 165-
78 1983 £40

MOORE, JOHN M.   The West. (Wichita Falls): Wichita
Printing Co., 1935. Frontis. and plates. Fine copy in dust jacket.
First edition. Scarce. Jenkins 151-228 1983 $85

MOORE, JONAS   Modern fortification: or, elements of
military architecture. London: W. Godbid, for Nathaniel Brooke,
1673. First edition. 8vo. Cont. black morocco, gilt, a.e.g. Engraved frontis. and 10 plates at the end. Presentation binding, with the signature of Richard Towneley on the title-page,
and his inscription "The gift of ye Authour" at the top; Towneley's
bookplate on verso, dated 1702. Slight wear to hinges and head of
spine. Fine. Rare. Ximenes 63-318 1983 $1,350

MOORE, JOSEPH SHERIDAN   The Ethics of the Irish under the
Pentarchy and Other Essays. Sydney, E.F. Flanagan, 1872. First
edition, errata slip, 8vo, half calf. Fenning 62-258 1983 £28.50

MOORE, JULIA A.   The Sweet Singer of Michigan.
Chicago, 1928. First collected edition. Portrait, cloth backed
patterned boards, slight wear and cover discolored. Top corners
bumped. Some related newsp. clippings present. King 46-182
1983 $20

MOORE, MARIANNE   Eight Poems. New York: Museum of
Modern Art, 1962. Cloth and boards. First edition. Illus. with
handcolored drawings by Robert Andrew Parker. One of 195 numbered
copies, signed by the author and artist. A very fine copy in
slipcase, with the "Addendum" slip laid in. Reese 20-711 1983
$600

MOORE, MARIANNE   Marriage. New York: Monroe Wheeler,
(1924). Pictorial wraps. First edition. Laid in front, as issued,
is the 4pp. leaflet by Glenway Wescott entitled, "Miss Moore's
Observations." The spine is very slightly sunned; essentially a
fine copy. Reese 20-710 1983 $450

MOORE, MARIANNE   Nevertheless. N.Y., (1944). First
edition. Thin 16mo. Argosy 714-533 1983 $25

MOORE, MARIANNE   Selected Poems. London: Faber and
Faber Limited, (1935). Uncorrected proof copy of the first edition,
with the printer's stamp on the front free endpaper dated 30 Nov,
1934. 8vo. Orig. wrappers rebound in cloth. Endpapers foxed,
otherwise a very good copy. Jaffe 1-258 1983 $250

MOORE, MARIANNE   Selected Poems. London, 1935. First
English edition. Intro. by T.S. Eliot. Endpapers slightly foxed.
Dust wrapper. Very nice. Rota 230-419 1983 £50

MOORE, MARIANNE   What Are Years. New York: MacMillan,
1941. 1st ed. Orig. cloth, gilt, dj. Fine copy. Jenkins 155-946
1983 $50

MOORE, MAURICE   British Plunder and Irish Blunder.
Budlin: The Gaelic Press, circa 1927. First edition, cr. 8vo,
orig. printed wrapper. Fenning 61-308 1983 £10.50

MOORE, MERRILL   M: One Thousand Autobiographical Sonnets. New York, (1938). 8vo. Cloth. This copy from the library of Moore's good friend Louis Untermeyer. Inscribed by Moore on front flyleaf to Untermeyer dated 1938. With a one page TLS dated Dec. 19, 1938 to Untermeyer. With various clippings and reviews laid in by Untermeyer for possible quotations in reviews. A vg-fine copy. In Our Time 156-576 1983 $150

MOORE, MERRILL   Poems of American Life. New York, (1958). 8vo. Cloth. One of several copies of the book from the Untermeyer library. This copy contains several finalized corrections in the introductory note by Untermeyer. It has a short note from Mrs. Moore to Louis and also a short note from Moore's son. With review laid in. Fine copy in rubbed dj. In Our Time 156-577 1983 $100

MOORE, MILES C.   Report of the Governor of Washington Territory to the Secretary of the Interior. 1889. Wash., GPO, 1889. Large folded colored map. Orig. printed wraps. First edition. Ginsberg 47-939 1983 $50

MOORE, NICHOLAS   A Book for Priscilla. Cambridge, 1941. First edition. Wrappers a little marked. Nice. Rota 230-420 1983 £12

MOORE, PHIL H.   With Gun and Rod in Canada. Boston, 1922. 1st American ed. Autographed. Illus. 8vo, paper label, torn piece from pp. 63-64 put back with scotch tape. Morrill 288-321 1983 $22.50

MOORE, R.   The Universal Assistant, and Complete Mechanic... New York, 1880. Over 500 engravings. Small 8vo. Morrill 289-442 1983 $22.50

MOORE, THOMAS   The Epicurean. A Tale. Printed for Longman, Rees (etc), 1827. First edition. 12mo, contemporary half calf gilt, marbled sides; with squirrel crest at head of spine. Hill 165-79 1983 £48

MOORE, THOMAS   Fables for the Holy Alliance... London: Longmans, etc., 1823. First edition. 8vo. Orig. drab boards. Somewhat rubbed and soiled, label chipped. Ximenes 63-420 1983 $45

MOORE, THOMAS   Moore's Irish Melodies. Longman, Brown, 1846. First edition thus, with an additional engraved title-page, frontis. and pages iv, 280, engraved throughout. 4to, full green morocco, gilt extra, edges gilt, by Suttaby. Fenning 61-519 1983 £75

MOORE, THOMAS   Lalla Rookh, An Oriental Romance. London, 1817. First edition. 4to. Occasional light foxing. Calf by A. Milne of Forres. Gilt. Good. Edwards 1044-503 1983 £65

MOORE, THOMAS   Lalla Rookh. London: Printed for Longman, Hurst, Rees, Orme, and Brown, 1818. Ninth edition. Cont. green morocco, gilt. With a fore-edge painting of a scene from the poem. Cont. owners' inscriptions on front endsheet. Inner hinges cracked. Covers slightly faded and rubbed. In a cloth slipcase. MacManus 278-1939 1983 $450

MOORE, THOMAS   Lalla Rookh. Longman, Green, 1861. Sm. 4to. First edition. Colour printed ornamental page & 4 other ornamental pp. 69 illus. by Tenniel. Blue decorated cloth, gilt, bumped. Greer 40-221 1983 £35

MOORE, THOMAS   Lalla Rookh. Longmans, 1880. New edn. with 5 ornamental title pages (one illumin.) in col. & gold designs by T. Sulman, Jr. & 69 illus. by John Tenniel. Red decor. cloth gilt, bevelled boards, a.e.g. (contemp. insc. half title, sl. shaken), v.g. Hodgkins 27-386 1983 £15

MOORE, THOMAS   Memoirs of the Life of the Right Honorable Richard Brinsley Sheridan. London: Longman, Hurst, 1825. 1st ed., large 4to, modern half morocco gilt, marbled boards. Engraved frontis. and another plate. Half-title; errata slip tipped in. A very fine copy. Trebizond 18-73 1983 $140

MOORE, THOMAS   The Poetical Works of Thomas Moore. London, 1843. Eng. portrait, extra title. Fine full green morocco with gilt-dec. spine, Inner dentelles, a. e. g. Rubbed along outer hinges, portrait foxed else a handsome book. King 46-431 1983 $350

MOORE, THOMAS   The Poetical Works... London, 1856. Frontis. Contemporary full morocco, fully gilt, a.e.g. Near fine copy. Jenkins 155-428 1983 $300

MOORE, THOMAS   A Selection of Irish Melodies. London, J. Power (1807-1821). 5 engraved plates and one facs. Bound in three vols. Folio, 3/4 leather, backstrips repaired. First edition. Salloch 387-134 1983 $150

MOORE, THOMAS   Travels of an Irish Gentleman in Search of a Religion. London: for Longman, etc., 1833. First edition. Small 8vo. Cont. half blue calf, gilt, morocco labels, gilt. Traylen 94-605 1983 £30

MOORE, THOMAS (1821-1887)   British Ferns and Their Allies. Routledge, 1861. 1st edn, thus, with 12 plates printed in colour by Edmund Evans; illus. by W.S. Coleman. Blue bead grain blind stamped cloth, gilt decor. bkstrip (top/bottom of bkstrip worn, insc. fr. ep.), v.g. Hodgkins 27-385 1983 £15

MOORE, THOMAS GEORGE   The Bachelor. Henry Colburn, 1809. In three vols. First edition. Half titles, 4 pp ads. end vol. II. Half tan calf, gilt spines, drab boards. Jarndyce 31-818 1983 £180

MOORE, THOMAS STURGE   The Vinedresser and Other Poems. London: At the sign of the Unicorn, 1899. First edition. 16mo. Orig. cloth. Very good. MacManus 279-3845 1983 $100

MOORE, THOMAS STURGE   The Vinedresser. London, 1899. First edition, first issue, gilt rules on covers, one leaf little soiled, name or rear free endpaper, very good. Rota 231-434 1983 £35

MOOREHEAD, FREDERICK B.   Pathology of the Mouth. Phila. & London, 1925. First edition. 8vo, cloth. Illus. Argosy 713-384 1983 $50

MOOREHEAD, WARREN   A Report of the Susquehanna River Expedition. Andover: Andover Press, 1938. Frontis., text illus., 37 plates. Argosy 716-6 1983 $25

MOORMAN, J. J.   Mineral Springs of North America. Philadelphia: J.B. Lippincott & Co., 1873. Small 8vo, with 2 folding maps (1 color) + 5 lithograph plates. Brown gilt-stamped cloth. Top of spine a little frayed. Karmiole 73-75 1983 $45

MOORMAN, MADISON BERRYMAN   Journal of Madison Berryman Moorman, 1850-1851. San Francisco, 1948. Portrait, fldg. map. Edges untrimmed. Clark 741-387 1983 $31.50

MOQUIN-TANDON, A.   Le Monde de la Mer. Paris, 1865. Royal 8vo, half morocco, 21 attractive coloured plates and 200 text-figures. The last 3 plates are misnumbered. Wheldon 160-312 1983 £40

MORA, A Fragment of a Tale. Saunders & Otley, 1840. First edition, half title, orig. brown wraps., worn. Paper label on upper cover. Jarndyce 30-619 1983 £20

MORAES, FRANCISCO DE   Palmerin of England. Longon: Longmans etc., 1807. 4 vols. fcap. 8vo. Cont. half red morocco, gilt, the cross patte and cinquefoil in the compartment of the spine, gilt edges. With a page of pencil notes by Beckford in which he comments "The original of Vathek is still unpublished." Traylen 94-606 1983 £225

MORAIS, HENRY SAMUEL   The Jews of Philadelphia. Philadelphia, 1894. Cloth, inner hinges loose, covers soiled, spine ends frayed. King 46-119 1983 $75

THE MORAL legacy; or, simple narratives. London: William Miller, 1801. First edition. 8vo. Orig. blue-grey boards, white paper spine, printed paper label. Some wear. Rare. Ximenes 63-130 1983 $125

MORAN, J. BELL   The Moran Family, 200 Years in Detroit. Detroit, 1949. Numbered edition, signed by the author. Portraits, cloth. Very good in frayed dust wrapper. King 46-183 1983 $20

MORAN, JAMES   Heraldic Influence on Early Printers'
Devices. (Leeds): The Elmete Press, 1978. Small 4to. Decorated
cloth. Large letter spine label, t.e.g. One of 475 numbered
copies. Printed in two colors throughout. Fine. Oak Knoll 48-288
1983 $110

MORAND, J. S.   Le Magnetisme Animal. Paris, 1889.
First edition. 12mo, 1/2 cloth; (foxed). Argosy 713-385 1983 $50

MORAND, PAUL   Closed All Night. L, 1924. Number 61
of 275 numbered and signed copies, near fine. Quill & Brush 54-954
1983 $35

MORANT, G. M.   A Bibliography of Statistical and
Other Writings of Karl Pearson. Cambridge, 1939. First edition.
8vo. Orig. binding. Fye H-3-1069 1983 $45

MORASSI, ANTONIO   Tiziano. Milano: Silvana, 1964.
40 tipped-in color plates. 32 text illus. Folio. Boards, 1/4
cloth. Dust jacket. Ars Libri 33-369 1983 $85

MORAVIAN Journals Relating to Central New York 1745-66. Syracuse,
N.Y., 1916. Orig. wraps. First edition. Ginsberg 46-532 1983 $30

MORE, CRESACRE   The Life of Sir Thomas More, Kt...
London, James Woodman and David Lyon, 1720. 8vo, cont. deep red
crimson straight-grained morocco, a.e.g.; this is the bibliographer
of Bacon's copy, R.W. Gibson with his book-label and his note on
the fly-leaf. Ravenstree 97-116 1983 $165

MORE, HANNAH   Coelebs in Search of a Wife. London,
Cadell and Davies, 1808. 2 vols., 8vo, cont. calf newly rebacked to
match, gilt labels, large and fine set. First edition. Ravenstree 96-
125 1983 $350

MORE, HANNAH   Florio: A Tale, for Fine Gentlemen and
Fine Ladies: and, The Bas Bleu; or, Conversation. Printed for T.
Cadell, 1786. 4to, ad. leaf, orig. half calf, rebacked. First
edition. Bickersteth 77-58 1983 £85

MORE, HANNAH   A Memoir of Mrs. Hannah More. H. Risher,
R. Fisher & P. Jackson, 1834. Rebound in half calf. Small stamps
on title and front, otherwise v.g. First edition, 12mo. Jarndyce
30-1086 1983 £20

MORE, HANNAH   Thoughts on the Importance of the
Manners of the Great to General Society. Wilmington: Joseph Jones,
1805. 12th Amer. ed., sq. 24mo, cont. calf., ex-library. Argosy
710-129 1983 $35

MORE, HANNAH   The Works of Hannah More. Dublin:
Printed by and for D. Graisberry, 1803. First Irish collected edition,
4 vols., 8vo. cont. half calf, the endpapers recently renewed and
with some light internal staining, but not serious, a very good copy.
Fenning 60-285 1983 £35

MORE, HENRY   A Collection of Several Philosophical
Writings. Printed by James Flesher, for William Morden, 1662. Folio,
slight waterstaining at the foot of the page at the end of the
volume, lower outer corner of final leaf repaired, not affecting the
text, orig. calf, rebacked, new end papers, rubbed. Bickersteth 77-
59 1983 £240

MORE, HENRY   Divine Dialogues. Printed and sold by
Joseph Downing, 1713. With 2 folding engraved plates, 8vo, cont.
panelled calf, a very good copy. Fenning 60-286 1983 £75

MORE, JOHN   A Table from the Beginning of the World
to this Day. (Cambridge) printed by Iohn Legate, 1593. 12mo, orig.
limp vellum, worn, spine chipped and defective, name on title,
complete with orig. initial blank, signed "A" and with the Christie
Miller, Britwell Court shelf mark on the blank end-paper facing the
orig. blank. First and only edition. Ravenstree 97-118 1983 $510

MORE, THOMAS   A Dyaloge... 1530 (Colophon dated
May 1531). Second edition. Folio. Modern red morocco, gilt,
by Sangorski and Sutcliffe. Errata leaf at end, woodcut initials,
title-page and first leaf of table repaired, slightly affecting
the text. Traylen 94-607 1983 £1,500

MORE, THOMAS   Letters and Journals of Lord Byron.
London, John Murray, 1830. 2 vols., large 4tos, old quarter calf
very worn, badly rubbed, minor age-spotting and light soil, faint
watermarking, occasional pencil marks, the frontis. has the lower
line of imprint cropped. First edition. Ravenstree 97-115 1983
$150

MORE, THOMAS   Utopia. London, Richard Chiswell, 1684.
8vo, cont. calf rebacked, signature of Vere Adams dated 1687 on flyleaf, a very nice copy. First Gilbert Burnet translation into English.
First edition, first issue. Ravenstree 96-126 1983 $450

MORE, THOMAS   Utopia. London: printed by William
Bulmer at the Shakespeare Head Press for William Miller, 1808. New
edition. Large 4to, fine cont. morocco binding bordered in gilt,
a.e.g., inner dentelles gilt. Large and thick paper copy. Frontis.
portrait engraved, plates, some foxing. Trebizond 18-26 1983 $650

MORE, THOMAS   Utopia. London, William Bulmer at the
Shakespeare Press, 1808. 2 vols., 8vo, orig. boards (bit worn, rubbed,
hinges cracked, spines chipped, lightly age-browned, frontis. little
stained) good uncut set. Ravenstree 96-127 1983 $165

MORE, THOMAS   Utopia. NY: Limited Editions Club,
1934. Octavo. Limited to 1500 copies printed at the Rudge Press
under supervision of Bruce Rogers and signed by him. Extremely fine
in vellum-backed pastepaper over boards with chipped glassine and
slip-case, which is split at one edge. Bromer 25-290 1983 $100

MORE Broad Grins. John Lowndes, 1819. First edition, dulled purple
binders' cloth, v.g. Jarndyce 30-620 1983 £16

MOREAU, E.   Manuel d'Ichtyologie Francaise.
Paris, 1892. 3 plates, 8vo, wrappers (repaired). Wheldon 160-
988 1983 £15

MOREAU, F. J.   Practical Treatise on Midwifery. Phila.,
1844. First American edition. 80 fine hand-colored lithographic
plates by Duval. Small folio, orig. cloth, (spine repaired). Phila.,
1844. First American edition. Argosy 713-386 1983 $175

MOREAU, P. G.   L'Hypnotisme. Paris, 1891. First
edition. 12mo, 1/2 cloth. Argosy 713-387 1983 $50

MOREAU, VICTOR   The Life and Campaigns of Victor
Moreau. New York, Printed for David Bliss, 1806. 1st American ed.
Portrait by Scoles, 12mo, contemporary calf, leather label, hinges
cracked. Morrill 289-444 1983 $22.50

MOREAU-NELATON, ETIENNE   Jongkind raconte par lui-meme.
Paris: Henri Laurens, 1918. 173 fine heliogravure plates with
tissue guards. Large 4to. Orig. wrappers. Dust jacket. No.
116 of a limited edition of 600 copies. Ars Libri 32-345 1983
$500

MORELAND, ARTHUR   Dickens Landmarks in London. 1931.
First edition. 4to, half title. Orig. pink printed boards, sl.
faded, otherwise very good. Jarndyce 30-214 1983 £10.50

MORENO, J. L.   Plan and Technique of Developing a
Prison Into a Socialized Community. NY: National Committee on
Prisons and Prison Labor, 1932. First edition. Library buckram,
retaining original green wrappers. Gach 95-374 1983 $20

MORENO, J. L.   The Words of the Father. NY: Beacon
House, (1941). First English edition. Inscribed copy. Library
bookplate, else very good. Gach 95-379 1983 $35

MORERY, LEWIS   The Great Historical Geographical and
Poetical Dictionary. Printed for Henry Rhodes, Luke Meredith, John
Harris, and Thomas Newborough, 1694. 2 vols. in 1, folio, titles
in red and black, wormhole at top of first six leaves, touching the
ruled border of the title and subscriber's list, orig. calf, spine
gilt, joints cracked and calf peeling a little along the joints,
but binding firm, most of the label missing. First edition in English.
Bickersteth 75-65 1983 £115

MORES, EDWARD ROWE   A Dissertation upon English Typographical Founders and Foundries. New York: The Grolier Club,
1924. First edition, thus. 8vo. Decorated cloth, paper spine label.
Illus. with specimens. Limited to 250 copies printed by Updike
at the Merrymount Press. Fine. Scarce. Oak Knoll 48-289 1983
$125

MOREWOOD, SAMUEL   An Essay on the Inventions and Customs of both Ancients and Moderns... London: Longmans, 1824. First edition. 8vo. Cont. half green calf. Somewhat worn, internally a good copy. Zeitlin 264-327 1983 $125

MORFIT, CAMPBELL   Chemical and Pharmaceutical Manipulations... Philadelphia: Lindsay and Blakiston, 1857. 8vo. Cont. sheep. 2 plates, frontis., numerous text illus. Ads. Worn. Zeitlin 264-328 1983 $55

MORFORD, HENRY   John Jasper's Secret. 1872. First edition bound from the parts. 12 illus. Half green calf, spine rubbed, red label. Pencilled on e.p. 'Montague Summers' Copy' Jarndyce 30-171 1983 £72

MORGAGNI, GIAMBATTISTA   Adversaria Anatomica Omnia. Venetiis, 1762. 11 fine copperplates. Tall folio, cont. calf (expertly rebacked). Fine copy. Argosy 713-388 1983 $475

MORGAGNI, GIAMBATTISTA   Consulti Medici. Bologna, 1935. 4 facs. Small folio, boards (repaired). Edition ltd. to 500 numbered copies. Argosy 713-389 1983 $85

MORGAN, ABEL   Anti-Paedo Rantism. Philadelphia: B. Franklin, 1747. Later 3/4 calf (front hinge repaired). Errata leaf not present. Felcone 21-41 1983 $400

MORGAN, CHARLES   Epitaph on George Moore. London: Macmillan & Co. Ltd., 1935. First edition. Frontis. port. Orig. linen-backed marbled boards. MacManus 279-3847 1983 $20

MORGAN, CHARLES   The Flashing Stream. London, 1938. First edition. 8vo. Orig. cloth, gilt. Signed by the author on the title-page, June, 1944. Traylen 94-609 1983 £12

MORGAN, CHARLES   The Gunroom. London, 1919. First edition. Spine just a little faded. Very nice. Rota 230-422 1983 £50

MORGAN, CHARLES   My Name is Legion. London: William Heinemann, Ltd., (1925). First edition. Orig. cloth. Dust jacket. Fine. MacManus 279-3850 1983 $35

MORGAN, CHARLES   Reflections in a Mirror. London: Macmillan & Co., 1944-46. First editions. 2 vols. Orig. cloth. Dust jackets, (spines darkened, with small tear). Very good. MacManus 279-3851 1983 $35

MORGAN, CHARLES   The River Line. London: Macmillan & Co., 1949. First edition. Orig. cloth. Dust jacket (spine darkened). Very good. MacManus 279-3852 1983 $20

MORGAN, CHARLES   Sparkenbroke. London: Macmillan & Co., 1936. First edition. Orig. cloth. Dust jacket (spine darkened). MacManus 279-3855 1983 $75

MORGAN, CHARLES   Sparkenbroke. N.Y., 1936. First American edition. Mint. Argosy 714-534 1983 $25

MORGAN, CONWAY LLOYD   Animal Sketches. London: Edward Arnold, (1891). Ads. Cloth-backed pictorial boards. 53 photo-engravings. Hinges cracked, small stamp on title. Good copy of the first edition. Gach 94-58 1983 $25

MORGAN, CONWAY LLOYD   Habit and Instinct. London: Edward Arnold, 1896. First edition. With publisher's catalog dated March 1898. Publisher's blue cloth, minor wear, library bookplate. Light foxing to preliminary leaves. Gach 94-59 1983 $50

MORGAN, CONWAY LLOYD   An Introduction to Comparative Psychology. London: Walter Scott, 1894. Lacking front end-paper, library stamps on titlepage, else a fine, tight copy of the first edition. Gach 94-60 1983 $50

MORGAN, CONWAY LLOYD   Mind at the Crossways. NY: Holt, 1930. First American edition. Gach 94-61 1983 $25

MORGAN, DALE   Overland in 1846. Georgetown: The Talisman Press, 1963. 2 vols. Maps. Cloth and boards. Dust wrappers. Dawson 471-200 1983 $100

MORGAN, DALE   Overland in 1846 Diaries and Letters of the California-Oregon Trail. Georgetown, 1963. 2 volumes. Illus. and maps. Limited to 1000 copies and now scarce. Jenkins 151-227 1983 $85

MORGAN, EVAN   The Eel, and other poems. London, 1926. First edition. 8vo. Black cloth, gilt, in the orig. dustwrapper. Presentation copy with author's signature on the title-page and presentation inscription on the half-title. Traylen 94-610 1983 £20

MORGAN, FORREST   Connecticut as a Colony and as a State. Hartford, 1904. 4 vols., plates, g.t., ex-library. Argosy 710-119 1983 $85

MORGAN, JOHN   Reminiscences of the Founding of a Christian Mission on the Gambia. London, 1864. Small 8vo. K Books 301-126 1983 £38

MORGAN, JOHN HILL   The Life Portraits of Washington and their Replicas. Philadelphia, printed for the subscribers, (1831). Many illus. Folio, cloth, fine. Orig. dust wrapper. Reese 19-579 1983 $300

MORGAN, LEWIS H.   The American Beaver and His Works. Phila., 1868. Many plates, maps & illus. Buckram, (prefatory pp. loose) ex lib. Argosy 716-303 1983 $30

MORGAN, R. W.   Raymond de Monthault, The Lord Marcher. London: Richard Bentley, 1853. First edition. 3 vols. Orig. boards with paper labels on spines. Spines of first two volumes partially defective. Good. MacManus 279-3858 1983 $150

MORGAN, SYDNEY OWENSEN   The Missionary. An Indian Tale. Printed for J.J. Stockdale, 1811. 2nd ed., 3 vols. in one, 12mo, 19th-century half calf. Portrait (slightly foxed). No half-titles, but a good copy. Hill 165-80 1983 £52

MORGAN, SYDNEY OWENSON   O'Donnel. London: Colburn, 1814. First edition. 12mo. 3 vols. Later 3/4 calf. Lacking the half-titles in vols. 2 & 3. Very good. MacManus 279-3857 1983 $90

MORGAN, THOMAS   Col. Morgan Governor of Glocester's Letter to the Honoble William Lenthal Esq... London: for Edw. Husband, March 24, 1645. 4to. Modern boards, leather label. Heath 48-142 1983 £85

MORGAN, THOMAS HUNT   Die Entwickelung des Froscheies. Leipzig, 1904. 8vo, boards with buckram spine. First edition in German. Bickersteth 75-253 1983 £12

MORGAN, THOMAS HUNT   Some possible Bearings of Genetics on Pathology. Lancaster, Pa., 1922. 8vo. Orig. wrappers. Illus. in text. Signed presentation inscription on wrapper. Gurney 90-83 1983 £32

MORGAN, THOMAS J.   A Glance at Texas...History, Government, Population, Climate. Columbus, Ohio, 1844. 1st ed., half morocco. Inscribed by the author in pencil on title-page. Jenkins 151-229 1983 $1,500

MORGAN, WILLIAM   The American College of Physicians... Philadelphia, 1940. First edition. 8vo. Orig. binding. Fye H-3-408 1983 $40

MORGENLANDISCHE Motive. Plauen (Germany), Christian Stoll, n.d. (ca. 1900). 20 colored plates. Folio, orig. half board portfolio, ribbon ties. Ex-library. Fine. Morrill 289-479 1983 $37.50

MORGENSTERN, SOPHIE   La Pensee Magique Chez L'Enfant. Paris: Les Editions Denoel et Steele, 1934. First edition. Orig. printed orange wrappers. Gach 95-380 1983 $25

MORGENSTERN, SOPHIE   La Psychanalyse Infantile. Paris: Les Editions Psychalytiques, 1931. First edition. Orig. printed orange wrappers. Gach 95-381 1983 $25

MORGENSTERN, SOPHIE   Psychanalyse Infantile. Paris: Editions Denoel, (1937). First edition. Orig. printed wrappers, spine broken. 77 illus. Gach 95-382 1983 $20

MORGENSTERN, SOPHIE   La Structure de la Personnalite. Paris: Les Editions Denoel, 1939. First edition. Orig. printed green wrappers, edges faded. Gach 95-383 1983 $20

MORICE, CHARLES   Paul Gauguin. Paris: H. Floury, 1920. New edition. 33 plates. Illus. 4to. New boards, 1/4 leather. Orig. wrappers bound in. Half-title mended. Ars Libri 32-249 1983 $120

MORICE, CHARLES   Paul Gauguin. Paris: H. Floury, 1919. 4to, profusely illus. (most full-page, some color). Rebound in blue buckram; orig. wraps. bound in. Karmiole 76-6 1983 $60

MORIER, DAVID R.   Photo The Suliote: A Tale of Modern Greece. London: L. Booth, 1857. First edition. 3 vols. Full calf. Presentation copy inscribed: "To Vice Admiral Morier from his affectionate Brother, The Author. Eastbourne, 21 September 1863, for the 24th." Spines and covers slightly worn and scratched. Preliminary pages foxed. Good. MacManus 279-3859 1983 $350

MORIER, JAMES JUSTINIAN   Abel Allnutt. London: Richard Bentley, 1837. First edition. 3 vols. Orig. drab boards with paper labels. Spines worn and partially defective. Some foxing. Preserved in separate cloth folding boxes. With the Esher bookplates. One of the lesser-known titles by the author. Very good. MacManus 279-3860 1983 $250

MORIER, JAMES JUSTINIAN   Abel Allnutt. London, Richard Bentley, 1837. 3 vols., 8vo, cont. half calf newly rebacked period style, corners bit rubbed and bumped. The first edition. Ravenstree 96-128 1983 $195

MORIER, JAMES JUSTINIAN   The Adventures of Hajji Baba of Ispahan. John Murray, 1824. 3 vols. Small 8vo, colophon leaf in vol. III, but lacking half-title in vol. II. Cont. calf, gilt. Hannas 69-145 1983 $25

MORIER, JAMES JUSTINIAN   The Adventures of Hajji Baba, of Ispahan, In England. London: John Murray, 1828. First edition. 2 vols. Orig. cloth-backed boards with paper labels on spines. Spines and corners worn. Bookplates. Very good. MacManus 279-3862 1983 $250

MORIER, JAMES JUSTINIAN   The Adventures of Hajji Baba, of Ispahan. London, John Murray, 1828. 2 vols., bound without half title to volume II in modern quarter calf, boards. First edition. Ravenstree 96-129 1983 $115

MORIER, JAMES JUSTINIAN   The Adventures of Hajji Baba, of Ispahan, In England. John Murray, 1828. First edition, 2 vols, 12mo, contemporary half calf. Hill 165-81 1983 $50

MORIER, JAMES JUSTINIAN   The Adventures of Hajji Baba, of Ispahna, In England. London: Murray, 1828. First edition. 2 vols. 12mo. Cont. 3/4 morocco (somewhat rubbed). Complete with the half-title in volume two. MacManus 279-3863 1983 $85

MORIER, JAMES JUSTINIAN   The Mirza. London: Richard Bentley, 1841. First edition. 3 vols. Orig. cloth-backed boards with paper spine labels. Spines faded. Labels rubbed. Internally perfect. Near-fine. MacManus 279-3864 1983 $450

MORIER, JAMES JUSTINIAN   The Adventures of Hajji Baba of Ispahan. Chicago: Stone & Kimball, 1895. First Stone & Kimball edition. 2 vols. Orig. cloth. Fine. MacManus 279-3861 1983 $50

MORIER, JAMES JUSTINIAN   The Adventure of Hajji Baba of Ispahan. New York: The Limited Editions Club, 1947. 2 vols. Quarto. Half calf. Illustrated by Honore Guilbeau. 1 of 1500 numbered copies, printed The Aldus Printers after a design by Dwiggins, and signed by the illustrator. Slipcased. A fine set. Jenkins 155-817 1983 $45

MORIER, JAMES JUSTINIAN   Ayesha, the Maid of Kars. London: Richard Bentley, 1834. First edition. 3 vols. 8vo. Cont half calf, gilt panelled spines, green morocco labels, gilt. Traylen 94-611 1983 £45

MORIER, JAMES JUSTINIAN   Ayesha, the Maid of Kars. London: Richard Bentley, 1934. First edition. 3 vols. 8vo. Cont. diced calf, morocco labels, gilt. Slightly rubbed. Traylen 94-612 1983 £38

MORIER, JAMES JUSTINIAN   Zohrab the Hostage. London, Richard Bentley, 1832. 3 vols., 8vo, orig. boards, joints breaking, spines worn, ends chipped, bookplate, uncut set. First edition. Ravenstree 96-130 1983 $225

MORIER, JAMES JUSTINIAN   Zohrab the Hostage. London, 1832. First edition. 3 vols., without the ad. leaf in vol. 1 and the half-titles in vols. 2 & 3. Half calf, labels, gilt. Vol. 2 spine repaired, others rubbed at hinges. 8vo. Good. Edwards 1044-502 1983 £85

MORIER, JAMES JUSTINIAN   Zohrab the Hostage. Richard Bentley, 1832. First edition. 3 vols, 12mo, cont. half russia gilt, marbled sides; bound without half-titles; a very fine copy. Hill 165-82 1983 £50

MORIER, JAMES JUSTINIAN   Zohrab the Hostage. Richard Bentley, 1833. Third edition, revised and corrected. 3 vols., half green calf, brown labels, v.g. Jarndyce 30-495 1983 £35

MORIER, JAMES JUSTINIAN   Zohrab, the Hostage. London: Richard Bentley, 1932. Second edition, revised and corrected. Cont. half calf, gilt panelled spines, green morocco labels, gilt. Traylen 94-613 1983 £18

MORIN, ANDRE SATURNIN   Du Magnetisme et des Sciences Occultes. Paris, 1860. Large 8vo, early 1/2 cloth with orig. cover label; uncut; ex-lib. First edition. Argosy 713-390 1983 $100

MORIN, LOUIS   French Illustrators in Five Parts. N.Y., 1893. Portfolio, heavily rubbed. Spine splitting. Limited to 1030 numbered copies, with 11 (of 15) plates, each with lettered tissue-guards and other illus., each of the five parts with color ill. cover & 2 India proofs. King 45-412 1983 $95

MORISANI, OTTAVIO   Saggi sulla scultura napoletana del Cinquecento. Mapoli, 1941. 105, (3)pp., 24 plates. Sm. 4to. Wraps. (covers taped). Ars Libri SB 26-144 1983 $37.50

MORISANI, OTTAVIO   La scultura napoletana del Cinquecento. Napoli, n.d. (Storia di napoli, Vol. V. Estratto.) (60)pp. 37 illus. hors. texte. 4to. Wraps. Ars Libri SB 26-145 1983 $30

MORISON, J. COTTER   Gibbon. London, 1878. Inscribed by author to George Meredith. Some light wear to inside front endboard, else fine in slipcase. In Our Time 156-563 1983 $45

MORISON, M. C.   A Lonely Summer in Kashmir. London, 1904. Numerous plates. Sm.4to. Orig. cloth. Good. Edwards 1044-500 1983 £15

MORISON, R.   Plantarum historiae universalis Oxoniensis. Oxford, 1680-99. 2 vols., folio, new half calf (antique style), portrait and plates. First edition. Some missing plates. Several of the plates are somewhat browned and there is some dust-soiling. Wheldon 160-71 1983 £360

MORISON, SAMUEL ELIOT   Builders of the Bay Colony. Boston, 1930. Illus. Argosy 710-104 1983 $35

MORISON, SAMUEL ELIOT   The Development of Harvard University Since the Inauguration of President Eliot 1869-1929. Cambridge, 1930. Illus. Argosy 710-291 1983 $35

MORISON, SAMUEL ELIOT   The Founding of Harvard College. Cambridge: Harvard U. Press, 1935. Illus., 8vo, cloth, d.w. (torn), g.t. Argosy 710-292 1983 $30

MORISON, SAMUEL ELIOT   Harvard College in the Seventeenth
Century. Cambridge, 1936. Illus. & maps. 2 vols., dw, g.t.
Argosy 710-293 1983 $50

MORISON, SAMUEL ELIOT   Harvard College in the Seventeenth
Century. Cambridge, 1936. 1st ed. Illus. 2 vols., 8vo, very
fine in orig. tissue dust wrappers. Morrill 287-585 1983 $35

MORISON, SAMUEL ELIOT   The Maritime History of Massachusetts,
1783-1860. Boston, 1921. Illus. 8vo. 1st ed. Former owner's
embossed stamp on title. Morrill 287-243 1983 $35

MORISON, SAMUEL ELIOT   Three Centuries of Harvard 1636-1936.
Cambridge, 1936. Cloth-backed boards, d.w. Argosy 710-294 1983
$35

MORISON, STANLEY   A Brief Survey of Printing, History and
Practice. London: At the Office of the Fleuron, 1923. First edition.
8vo. Three-quarter cloth over boards, paper spine label. Fine copy.
Oak Knoll 48-290 1983 $30

MORISON, STANLEY   The Fleuron, A Journal of Typography.
Cambridge: University Press, 1928. First edition. Thick 4to.
cloth. Dust jacket. One of the 160 copies printed on handmade
paper. With many fine illus., some of which are in color. Cloth
on front cover is slightly wrinkled, jacket is chipped. Oak Knoll
49-182 1983 $150

MORISON, STANLEY   Handbuch der Druckerkunst. Berlin,
1925. 8vo, cloth, dust-jacket. Duschnes 240-159 1983 $65

MORLEY, CHRISTOPHER   Blythe Mountain, Vermont. Brattleboro,
(ca. 1930). 1st ed., frontis., 4to. One of 500 copies. Argosy
710-550 1983 $25

MORLEY, CHRISTOPHER   The Haunted Bookshop. Garden City:
Doubleday, Page & Co., 1919. First edition, state three. 8vo.
Cloth. Covers rubbed, back inside hinge cracked. Oak Knoll 48-134
1983 $30

MORLEY, CHRISTOPHER   "It's a kind of a Memorabilia".
Privately Printed, (New York), 1937. First edition. Wrappers. Very
nice. Rota 231-436 1983 £15

MORLEY, CHRISTOPHER   The Palette Knife. (N.Y. Chocorua Press,
1928). Four proof copies of illus. used in the book; together with a
signature of pages, which is signed by Morley. Also an ALS in pencil,
1 page, narrow 8vo, undated, but 1927 or 1928, from Morley to the
publisher. Houle 21-645 1983 $150

MORLEY, CHRISTOPHER   Parnassus on Wheels. Garden City:
Doubleday, Page & Co., 1917. First edition, second issue. Small
8vo. Cloth-backed boards. Signed by Morley on title page. Spine
darkened a bit by age; other cover soiling. Oak Knoll 48-291 1983
$85

MORLEY, CHRISTOPHER   Seacoast of Bohemia. GC, 1929. Fine
in slightly darkened and chipped, very good dustwrapper. Quill &
Brush 54-956 1983 $25

MORLEY, CHRISTOPHER   Swiss Family Manhattan. GC, 1932. Special advance edition, limited to 250 copies, gold and green paper
covered boards, near fine in orig. glassine. Quill & Brush 54-955
1983 $50

MORLEY, CHRISTOPHER   Thunder on the Left. London, 1926.
First English edition. Spine dull and covers a little marked. Bookplate. Very good. Rota 230-424 1983 £12

MORLEY, CHRISTOPHER   The Trojan Horse. (Phila.), 1937.
Signed, endpapers slightly soiled, else very good in very good dustwrapper. Quill & Brush 54-957 1983 $30

MORLEY, EDWARD W.   On the Densities of Oxygen and
Hydrogen... Washington: Smithsonian, 1895. Large 4to. Orig.
printed paper wrappers. Unopened. A little worn, small tear
front hinge. Zeitlin 264-329 1983 $75

MORLEY, JOHN   The Life of Richard Cobden. London:
Chapman & Hall, 1881. First edition. 2 vols. Frontis. port. Orig.
cloth. Bookplates. Very good. MacManus 277-1008 1983 $25

MORLEY, JOHN   The Struggle for Natural Education.
Chapman & Hall, 1873. First edition, half title, orig. brown cloth
a little rubbed. Library stamp on verso of title. Jarndyce 31-157
1983 £14.50

MORLEY, SYLVANUS G.   The Ancient Maya. Stanford (1946).
1st ed. Illus, thick 8vo, mod. buckram, ex-library. Argosy 710-62
1983 $30

MORLEY, THOMAS   A Plain and Easy Introduction to Practical
Music. London, Wm. Randall, 1771. Engraved music, engraved title
page, with a vignette of angel musicians. 4to, cont. 1/2 calf. With
list of subscribers. Salloch 387-136 1983 $500

MORMON, Book of
Please turn to
BOOK OF MORMON

MORMONE, RAFFAELE   La scultura napoletana del Settecento.
Napoli, n.d. (Storia di Napoli. Vol. VIII. Estratto.) (56)pp.
36 illus. hors texte. 4to. Wraps. Ars Libri SB 26-146 1983 $30

MORNAY, PHILLIPPE DE   A Treatise of the Chvrch, in which are
Handled all the Principall Questions that have beene Mooued in Our
Time Concerning that Matter. London, Christopher Barker, 1581.
12mo, cont. calf rebacked period style, bookplate, minor waterstaining,
two small holes in title with slight loss, marginal glosses in cont.
half, upper inner blank corner of last several leaves restored.
Ravenstree 97-127 1983 $350

MORNAY, PHILLIPPE DE   A Woorke Concerning the Trewness of
the Christian Religion, written in French. Imprinted at London for
Thomas Cademan, 1587. 4to, cont. sheep newly rebacked period style,
very minor waterstains. First edition. Ravenstree 97-126 1983
$1,650

MORRELL, BENJAMIN   A Narrative of Four Voyages to the
South Sea, North and South Pacific Ocean. N.Y., 1832. Illus.,
port. Full calf. First edition. Ginsberg 46-508 1983 $300

MORRELL, L. A.   The American Shepherd. New York, 1851.
Illustrated with portraits. 8vo. Some foxing. Morrill 290-325
1983 $32.50

MORRILL, V. E.   Men of Today in the Eastern Townships.
Sherbrooke, Que.: Sherbrooke Record Co., 1917. 22cm. Numerous
illus. and portraits. Half leather binding. A fine copy. Scarce.
McGahern 53-120 1983 $75

MORRIS, D.   The Colony of British Honduras, its
Resources and Prospects. London: Edward Stanford, 1883. Frontis.
is color folding map. Ornately gilt-stamped green cloth. Karmiole
73-59 1983 $50

MORRIS, EARL H.   The Temple of the Warriors. New York/
London: Charles Scribner's Sons, 1931. 61 plates. Small 4to.
Cloth. Ars Libri 34-374 1983 $30

MORRIS, FRANCIS ORPEN   Bible Natural History. 1852. Sm. 4to,
half blue calf, gilt, plates and decorated hand-coloured frontis.
Wheldon 160-255 1983 £60

MORRIS, FRANCIS ORPEN   A History of British Birds. 1870. 2nd
ed., 365 hand-coloured plates, 6 vols., roy. 8vo, original cloth,
gilt. Some slight foxing, mostly confined to the beginning of each
volume, except for 2 plates rather badly foxed in vol. 5. Wheldon
160-72 1983 £450

MORRIS, FRANK THOMPSON   Birds of the Australian Swamps, Vols.
and 2. Melbourne, 1978-82. 2 vols., folio, half leather, coloured
plates. Wheldon 160-73 1983 £565

MORRIS, FRANK THOMPSON   Folio of Finches. Melbourne, 1976.
Folio, quarter calf, 18 coloured plates. Edition limited to 360
copies only and now out of print. Wheldon 160-74 1983 £150

MORRIS, FRANK THOMPSON   Robins and Wrens of Australia, a selection. Melbourne, 1979. Folio, half leather, 19 coloured plates. Edition limited to 500 numbered and signed copies. Wheldon 160-75 1983 £125

MORRIS, GOUVERNEUR   A Diary of the French Revolution. Boston: 1939. 2 vols. First edition. Boxed. Frontis. and illus. Jenkins 271 1983 $75

MORRIS, GWLADYS EVAN   Tales from Bernard Shaw. London, 1929. Drawings in colour and black-and-white by P.A. Trery. First edition. Frayed dust wrapper. Fine. Rota 231-541 1983 £15

MORRIS, HENRY   Bird & Bull Pepper Pot. North Hills: Bird & Bull Press, 1977. Quarto. Limited to 250 copies. Mint in quarter-leather and paste-paper over boards. Pospectus laid-in. Bromer 25-144 1983 $175

MORRIS, HENRY   Japonica; The Study and Appreciation of the Art of Japanese Paper. North Hills, Pennsylvania: Bird & Bull Press, 1981. 8vo. Leather spine with leather label, Japanese paper over boards. One of 250 numbered copies. With samples. Oak Knoll 39-41 1983 $350

MORRIS, HENRY   A Short List of Handy Phrases in the Dutch Language... North Hills, Pa.: Henry Morris at the Bird & Bull Press, 1972. Small 4to. Limited to 70 copies. Fine. Oak Knoll 48-25 1983 $100

MORRIS, JANE KESNER   Women Inc. N.Y., Holt, (1946). First edition. Signed and inscribed by the author. Pictorial dust jacket (slight rubbing). Very good. Houle 22-669 1983 $45

MORRIS, LERONA R.   Oklahoma Yesterday-Today-Tomorrow. Guthrie, 1930. Signed by author. Jenkins 153-409 1983 $55

MORRIS, MAURICE   Rambles in the Rocky Mountains. London: Smith, Elder and Co.; 1864. Original cloth. Very fine copy. Unopened. Jenkins 151-230 1983 $500

MORRIS, MAURICE O'CONNOR   Hibernia Venatica. London: Chapman & Hall, 1878. First edition. Illus. with mounted photographs. Full green morocco. Fine. MacManus 278-1974 1983 $250

MORRIS, MAURICE O'CONNOR   Triviata or Crossroad Chronicles of Passages in Irish Hunting History during the Season of 1875-76. Chapman and Hall, 1877. First edition, with an actual photograph of the mounted author (Woodbury type), additional pictorial title and 7 plates by Walter Sculthorpe and Adrian Jones, 8vo, orig. cloth, gilt, neatly repaired, a sound and very good copy. Fenning 60-287 1983 £18.50

MORRIS, MAY   William Morris. Oxford: Basil Blackwell, 1936. 8vo, holland boards with cloth backs, illus. Printed at the Shakespeare Head Press in an edition of 750 copies. Two vols., unopened. First edition. Duschnes 240-164 1983 $500

MORRIS, R. O.   Contrapuntal Technique in the Sixteenth Century. Oxford, 1922. Tall 8vo, cl., binding spotty. Salloch 387-353 1983 $25

MORRIS, RALPH   The Life and Astonishing Adventures of John Daniel. Lon., 1926. Reprint of 1751 edition with 4 orig. illus. Deluxe edition with vellum spine, lacks limitation page, good to very good. Quill & Brush 54-958 1983 $50

MORRIS, THOMAS   Smoke, London Fogs, and Steps taken to Prevent the Former. Warrington, (1881). First edition, orig. light blue printed wraps. Jarndyce 31-278 1983 £12.50

MORRIS, WILLIAM   Address Delivered Before the Society of California Volunteers...April 25th, 1866. San F., 1866. Half morocco. First edition. Ginsberg 47-140 1983 $85

MORRIS, WILLIAM   Art and the Beauty of the Earth. (London: Chiswick Press, 1898). 8vo, boards and linen back. Duschnes 240-162 1983 $40

MORRIS, WILLIAM   A Book of Verse. The Scolar Press, London, (1980). 1st and only ed. 1 of 238 copies quarter bound. (Total ed. 325.) A fine copy with orig. prospectus and intro. notes by Roy Strong and Joyce Irene Whalley issued separately. Enclosed in clamshell slipcase box. List. In Our Time 156-582 1983 $440

MORRIS, WILLIAM   Child Christopher and Goldilind the Fair. (Hammersmith: Kelmscott Press, 1895). First edition, complete with erratum slip. 2 vols. 12mo. Orig. holland-backed boards with paper labels on spines. Presentation copy, inscribed on the front flyleaf "to Algernon Ch. Swinburne from William Morris, Sept. 25, 1895." Fleece-lined cloth folding box. MacManus 279-3038 1983 $2,500

MORRIS, WILLIAM   The Collected Works. London: Longmans Green, 1910-15. 24 octavo vols. Numerous illus. including several photographic portraits of Morris. Limited to 1050 copies. Hinges slightly started in vols. 1, 17 and 23 with some occasional light foxing to exteriors, otherwise a fine set in cloth-backed boards. Bromer 25-255 1983 $1250

MORRIS, WILLIAM   The Decorative Arts. London: Ellis & White, (1878). First edition. Orig. printed wrappers. Spine very slightly faded. One very small tear to front cover. Fine. MacManus 279-3865 1983 $150

MORRIS, WILLIAM   The Doom of King Acrisius. NY: R.H. Russell, 1902. With 12 full-page Burne-Jones plates + 4 additional tipped-in text illus. Decorative initials. Karmiole 71-72 1983 $50

MORRIS, WILLIAM   A Dream of John Ball and A King's Lesson. London: Reeves & Turner, 1888. First edition. Full green morocco, gilt, with elaborate floral decorations, by L. Underwood 1904. Corners slightly worn. In a binding in the style of the Doves Bindery. Fine. MacManus 279-3866 1983 $250

MORRIS, WILLIAM   Five Arthurian Poems. Elston Press, 1902. Tall slim 8vo, printed throughout in red and black, large decorative woodcut initials by O'Kane, original dark green cloth lettered in gilt, t.e.g., others uncut, very slight internal crack, fine. 178 copies only. Deighton 3-234 1983 £80

MORRIS, WILLIAM   Gothic Architecture. (Hammersmith, 1893). 1500 copies printed. With the misspelling on p.45. 16mo, orig. boards, cloth back, ex-library, very slightly rubbed, slight discoloration & evidence of removal of small tab from front cover, otherwise very clean & sound. Morrill 288-221 1983 $85

MORRIS, WILLIAM   Guenevere. London: The Fanfrolico Press, 1930. First edition. One of 450 numbered copies. 8 reproductions of drawings by D.G. Rossetti. T.e.g. Tail of spine slightly bumped. Very good. Jolliffe 26-179 1983 £45

MORRIS, WILLIAM   How I Became a Socialist. London: Twentieth Century Press, (1896). First separate edition. Orig. pictorial wrappers. Edges slightly browned by age. Very good. MacManus 279-3867 1983 $85

MORRIS, WILLIAM   The Life and Death of Jason. F.S. Ellis, 1869. Half title, red morocco, gilt borders, dentelles, spine; sl. rubbing, otherwise a very good copy, a.e.g. Jarndyce 31-820 1983 £12.50

MORRIS, WILLIAM   Love is Enough. London, 1873. Orig. paper-backed boards. Paper covering spine a bit chipped along hinge and slightly darkened, else a very nice copy. One of 25 large-paper copies printed for private circulation. Presentation copy, inscribed "Charles F. Murray from his friend William Morris." Felcone 21-77 1983 $600

MORRIS, WILLIAM   Monopoly, Or How Labour Is Robbed. London: Office of the "Freedom," n.d. (1893). Third edition. Orig. printed wrappers. Slightly stained by rust at the staple. Very good. MacManus 279-3868 1983 $85

MORRIS, WILLIAM   Poems by the Way. Hammersmith: 1891. Octavo. Woodcut border and numerous ornamental initials. Limited to 300 copies. Very fine in full vellum with ribbon ties. Bromer 25-236 1983 $625

MORRIS, WILLIAM   Poems by the Way. (Hammersmith, 1891).
8vo, bound in vellum over boards, gilt, with ties. Printed in red
and black in Golden type. With woodcut border and initials. Duschnes
240-123 1983 $550

MORRIS, WILLIAM   Poems By The Way. Boston: Roberts
Brothers, 1896. First American edition. Orig. cloth. Extremities of
spine a trifle rubbed. Very good. MacManus 279-3869 1983 $35

MORRIS, WILLIAM   Pre-Raphaelite Ballads. NY: A.
Wessels Co., 1900. With 5 plates, several illus. initials and
dec. text borders. Printed in orange and black on Japan vellum.
This is one of 250 numbered large paper copies on Imperial Japanese
paper (total edition 750). Parchment cover boards, gilt-stamped.
Karmiole 73-113 1983 $85

MORRIS, WILLIAM   The Sundering Flood. Hammersmith,
(1898). 8vo, boards with linen back. Chaucer type in black and
red; map paste-down by H. Cribb, woodcut border by Morris. One of
300 copies, paper label chipped. Enclosed in half leather slipcase
with inner wrapper. Duschnes 240-126 1983 $500

MORRIS, WILLIAM   Textile Fabrics. London, 1884. Orig.
pr. wrs. Argosy 716-152 1983 $20

MORRIS, WILLIAM   Two Poems of...: The Defence of Guenevere and King Arthur's Tomb. London: Fanfrolico Press, 1930.
Octavo. Illus. with 8 collographs of drawings by Dante Gabriel
Rossetti. Limited to 450 copies. Near mint in quarter-cloth and
boards. Bookplate. Bromer 25-203 1983 $165

MORRIS, WILLIAM   Useful Work versus Useless Toil. London:
Office of "Freedom," n.d. (1893). Second edition. Orig. printed
wrappers. Edges slightly worn. Rust staining from staple. Very good.
MacManus 279-3870 1983 $85

MORRIS, WILLIAM   The Water of the Wondrous Isles.
Hammersmith, 1897. Large quarto, limp vellum woodcut borders,
Chaucer type in black and red. One of 250 copies; one of the last
compositions of William Morris. Vellum soiled. Duschnes 240-125
1983 $950

MORRIS, WILLIAM   The Water of the Wondrous. Longmans,
Green, and Co., (printed at Cambridge, Mass.), 1897. First trade
edition. 8vo, orig. cloth (label rubbed), uncut. Hannas 69-148
1983 £15

MORRIS, WILLIAM   The Wood Beyond the Wood. Lawrence &
Bullen (Chiswick Press), 1895. First edition, half title, orig.
maroon calico cloth, spine faded. Jarndyce 31-821 1983 £28

MORRIS, WILLIAM O'CONNOR   The Land System of Ireland. Dublin,
1888. Cr. 8vo, orig. cloth, v.g. Fenning 61-309 1983 £21.50

MORRISON, A.   The Collection of Autograph Letters.
Printed for private circulation, 1893-6. 3 vols. Imperial 8vo. Orig.
cloth backed blue boards. Paper labels on spines, Very slightly soiled
and faded. Uncut. Partially unopened. Good. Edwards 1042-137 1983
£75

MORRISON, ARTHUR   Cunning Murrell. NY, 1900. Dec. cloth
cover soiled, front hinge starting, good, owner's name. Quill & Brush
54-961 1983 $35

MORRISON, ARTHUR   Fiddle O'Dreams, And More. London:
Hutchinson & Co., (1933). First edition. Orig. cloth. Dust jacket
(worn and slightly soiled, with a few small tears to the spine edges).
Presentation copy inscribed: "Charles Lyale Mason from Arthur Morrison,
High Barn, Chalfont Saint Peter, Bucks, February 4th, 1940..." Edges
slightly foxed. Near-fine. MacManus 279-3874 1983 $85

MORRISON, ARTHUR   The Hole in the Wall. Methuen, 1902.
First edition, half title, 40 pp ads. Orig. dark green cloth, sl.
rubbed. Jarndyce 31-822 1983 £38

MORRISON, ARTHUR   The Hole in the Wall. London, 1902.
First edition. Some light foxing. Name of flyleaf. Bookplate. Nice.
Rota 230-425 1983 £25

MORRISON, ARTHUR   The Painters of Japan. London: T.C. &
E.C. Jack, 1911. Folio. 57 leaves of plates; some of the plates are
mounted color illus.; all have printed tissue guards. The edition
de luxe, ltd. to 150 numbered copies, signed by the pub.'s. A fine
set in lightly chipped and soiled dust jackets. Karmiole 74-64 1983
$400

MORROW, G. F.   The Art of Aquatint. New York:
G.P. Putnam's Sons, 1935. First edition. Small 4to. Cloth.
43 illus. Covers faded. Oak Knoll 48-293 1983 $25

MORROW, WILLIAM   Morrow's Almanack for 1928. William
Morrow, (1927). 8vo, cloth, decorated boards. About fine in the
scarce dust jacket which is internally spotted and lightly chipped.
In Our Time 156-754 1983 $100

MORSE, HORACE J.   Catalogue of Connecticut Volunteer
Organizations, with Additional Enlistments & Casualties to July, 1864.
Hartford, 1864. 1/4 leather, waterstained, worn. Argosy 710-90
1983 $40

MORSE, JEDEDIAH   The American Gazetteer. Boston: At the
Presses of S. Hall & Thomas & Andrews, 1797. Seven folding maps (some
offsetting). Errata. Calf. Front fly out. Endpapers browned.
Dawson 471-202 1983 $300

MORSE, JEDIDIAH   Annals of the American Revolution.
Hartford, 1824. 6 engraved plates (1 folding). Later 3/4 calf.
Spine label wanting. Very good. Felcone 20-110 1983 $35

MORSE, JEDIDIAH   A Compendious History of New-England.
Charlestown, 1820. 3rd edition, full calf, leather label. 16mo.
Argosy 716-324 1983 $60

MORSE, JEDIDIAH   Geography Made Easy. Boston: Samuel
Hall, 1791. Errata slip. 7 maps. Cont. calf (worn, front hinge
broken). Signature "Abraham Clarks/Book Bought/1793". Felcone
22-154 1983 $60

MORSE, JEDIDIAH   A Report to the Secretary of War...on
Indian Affairs. New Haven: Davis & Force (etc.), 1822. Errata
slip. Port., colored folding map (mended on verso). Uncut. Later
cloth. Frontis. and title foxed. First edition. Felcone 21-78
1983 $200

MORSE, JEDIDIAH   A Sermon...in Consequence of a
Declaration of War with Great Britain. Charlestown, 1812. Dsb.,
good. Reese 18-387 1983 $20

MORSE, JOHN FREDERICK   The First History of Sacramento City,
written in 1853. Sacramento Book Collectors Club, 1945. Cloth.
Dawson 471-203 1983 $85

MORSE, JOHN T.   Life and Letters of Oliver Wendell
Holmes. Boston, 1896. 2 vols. First edition. 8vo. Orig. binding.
Fye H-3-787 1983 $49

MORSE, SAMUEL   The Present Attempt to Dissolve the American Union. N.Y., 1862. Orig. pr. wrappers. Privately printed.
Argosy 716-83 1983 $20

MORSE, SAMUEL F. B.   Examination of the Telegraphic Appartus
and the Process in Telegraphy. Wash., 1869. Illus. Charts. Printed
wrappers. Uncut and untrimmed. 1st ed. Very rare. Jenkins 153-554
1983 $125

MORTARI, LUISA   Bernardo Strozzi. Roma: De Lucca,
1966. 8 tipped-in color plates. 475 illus. Large square 4to.
Cloth. Dust jacket. Ars Libri 33-350 1983 $225

MORTENSEN, T.   Handbook of the Echinoderms of the
British Isles. 1927. 269 text-figures, 8vo, cloth (stained, contents
good). Wheldon 160-1329 1983 £22

MORTENSEN, WILLIAM   Monsters & Madonnas. S.F., Camera
Craft (1936). First edition, second printing. 4to, with 20 full
page gravures. Stiff wraps., spiral bound. Very good. Houle 21-
647 1983 $125

MORTON, ARTHUR S.   A History of The Canadian West To
1870-71. London, Toronto, New York: Thomas Nelson & Sons Ltd.,
(1939). 23cm. 12 maps (mostly folding). Errata slip. Green cloth.
Signed by the author on the title-page of the scarce first edition
in good dust jacket. Very good. McGahern 54-137 1983 $275

MORTON, H. V.   In the Steps of Saint Paul. London,
(1936). 4to. Half tan morocco, morocco label, gilt, t.e.g.,
others uncut. In the orig. slip-case. Limited edition of 75
copies, numbered and signed by the author, with 48 plates by Mary
and H.V. Morton. Traylen 94-616 1983 £50

MORTON, J. B.   The Bastille Falls and other studies
of the French Revolution. London, 1936. First edition. 8 portraits.
8vo. Half red morocco, gilt. From the library of A.J.A. Symons,
with his book-label. Traylen 94-617 1983 £20

MORTON, J. B.   Brumaire. The Rise of Bonaparte.
London, 1948. 8vo. Half red morocco, gilt. Traylen 94-618 1983
£20

MORTON, JOHN W.   The Artillery of Nathan Bedford Forrest's
Cavalry. Nashville, 1909. First edition. T.e.g. Jenkins 152-629
1983 $150

MORTON, LESLIE   A Medical Bibliography. Philadelphia,
Lippincott, (1970). Third revised edition. Thick 8vo, dust jacket,
very good. Houle 22-628 1983 $125

MORTON, LOUIS   Robert Carter of Nomini Hall, a Virginia
Tobacco Planter of the 18th century. Williamsburg, 1941. Illus.,
d.w. Argosy 710-557 1983 $25

MORTON, NATHANIEL   The New-Englands Memorial... Plymouth,
1826. Old leather, hinges weak. Reese 18-603 1983 $65

MORTON, RICHARD   Pyretologia seu Evercitationes de Morbis
Universalibus Acutis. London: Samuel Smith, 1692. First edition.
Small 8vo, later 1/2 calf. Argosy 713-391 1983 $300

MORTON, SAMUEL GEORGE   Illustrations of Pulmonary Consumption.
Philadelphia, 1834. With 12 plates, drawn and coloured from nature.
8vo, orig. calf. First edition. Fine. Argosy 713-392 1983 $250

MORTON, THOMAS   A Cure for the Heart-Ache, a Comedy.
Dublin: Printed by P. Wogan, 1797. First Irish edition 12mo, small
flaw in final leaf affecting a few letters. A fine copy. Fenning
62-259 1983 $12.50

MORTON, THOMAS   The History of the Pennsylvania Hospital
1751-1895. Philadelphia, 1895. First edition. 8vo. Orig. binding.
First four leaves loose in binding, else fine. Fye H-3-409 1983
$75

MORTON, WILLIAM T.G.   Proceedings in Behalf of the Morton
Testimonial. Boston, 1861. 8vo. 1st ed. Orig. wrappers. Morrill
289-163 1983 $50

MORWOOD, VERNON S.   Our Gipsies in City, Tent and Van.
Sampson Low, 1885. First edition, tall 8vo, 17 illus. 32 pp ads.
Free end papers replaced with matching paper. Dec. blue cloth, v.g.
Jarndyce 31-172 1983 £42

MOSCHETTI, ANDREA   La Cappella degli Scrovegni e gli
affreschi di Giotto in essa dipinti. Firenze: Alinari, 1904.
Prof. illus. Small 4to. Vellum. Ars Libri 33-172 1983 $50

MOSCHINI, VITTORIO   Giambellino. Bergamo: Istituto
Italiano d'Arti Grafiche, 1943. 153 plates. 1 tipped-in color.
Square 4to. Cloth. Slightly shaken. Ars Libri 33-159 1983
$75

MOSCHINI, VITTORIO   Vivarini. Milano: Amilcare Pizzi,
1948. 29 plates (partly tipped-in color). Folio. Boards, 1/4
cloth. Ars Libri 33-390 1983 $37.50

MOSELEY, SYDNEY A.   Television To-Day and To-morrow.
London, Sir Isaac Pitman, 1930. Numerous plates and illus. K Books
301-130 1983 £34

MOSER, CHARLES   Reminiscences of the West Coast of
Vancouver Island. Victoria, B.C., (1926). Illus. Orig. printed
wraps. First edition. Ginsberg 46-509 1983 $60

MOSER, JAMES H.   Remarkable Collection of 12 Original
Sketch-books. 1870's-80's. 8vo and 12mo, original boards. The
collection. Argosy 710-492 1983 $1,500

MOSER, WOLFGANG HEINRICH   Dissertatio medica de ortu dentium...
Tubingen: typis Fuesianis, 1770. Woodcut initial and head-piece.
Small 4to. Cont. backstrip. Kraus 164-56 1983 $150

MOSHEIM, JOHN L.   The Ecclesiastical History, Antient
and Modern... London: for T. Cadell, 1782. Traylen 94-619 1983
£65

MOSHEIM, JOHN L.   The Ecclesiastical History, Antient
and Modern... London, 1826. 6 vols. 8vo. Cont. calf, blind-
tooled and gilt panels, green morocco labels, gilt. Traylen 94-
620 1983 £40

MOSORIAK, ROY   The Curious History of Music Boxes.
Chicago, 1943. First edition. 40 plates plus text illustrations.
4to. Very slightly dampstained. Morrill 290-328 1983 $20

MOSS, C. E.   Vegetation of the Peak District.
Cambridge, 1913. 2 coloured folding maps in pocket and 36 figures,
8vo, cloth. Wheldon 160-1617 1983 £35

MOSS, GEOFFREY   Defeat. London: Constable & Co., 1924.
First edition. Orig. cloth. Dust jacket (very slightly foxed and
rubbed, with a few small tears to the spine and covers). Presentation
copy inscribed: "To Owen in remembrance of many happy days, From the
Author, Geoffrey." Spine faded. Edges foxed, with some offsetting to
the endpapers. Good. MacManus 279-3875 1983 $35

MOSSMAN, THOMAS WIMBERLEY   Mr. Gray and His Neighbours. John
Hodges, 1876. First edition, 2 vols., bound as one. 4 pp ads vol. II.
Orig. green remainder cloth. Cutting loosely inserted. Jarndyce
30-496 1983 £42

MOSSO, ANGELO   La Paura. Milan, 1884. First edition.
8vo. Cloth. Gurney JJ-275 1983 £30

THE MOST DELECTABLE History of Reynard the Fox. Macmillan, 1895.
First edition. Done into pictures by W. Frank Calderon, dark green
cloth, gilt, a.e.g. Occasional foxing, very nice, 4pp. ads.
Hodgkins 27-461 1983 £18

MOSZEIK, OTTO   Die Malereien der Buschmanner in
Sudafrika. Berlin: Dietrich Reimer, 1910. 3 color plates. 173
text illus. 4to. Cloth. Ars Libri 34-693 1983 $85

MOTHER GOOSE   Mother Goose's Nursery Rhymes. N.p.:
n.d. (ca. 1890). 4to. Red pictorial cloth. Covers dusty. Edges
slightly bumped. Printed on heavy paper. Color lithographs. Full-
page and small, plus 2 color illus. and silhouettes. Very Good.
Aleph-bet 8-176 1983 $30

MOTHER GOOSE   Mother Goose Nursery Tales. J. Coker,
n.d. 4to, colour frontis., 15 colour plates and 100 text illus.
Colour pictorial boards, repaired colour pictorial dust wrapper.
Greer 40-218 1093 £25

MOTHER GOOSE   The Old Mother Goose Nursery Rhyme Book.
T.C. & E.C. Jack, n.d. Colour frontis. Title vignette. 29 colour
plates. 89 text illus (12 colour). Light green pictorial cloth.
Very good. Greer 39-14 1983 £75

MOTHER GOOSE   Mother Goose Rhymes. G.G. Harrap, 1920.
4to. Colour frontis. & 11 colour plates by S.B. Pearse. Pictorial
title & 113 text illus. by W.M. Ackroyd. Colour pictorial boards, edges
worn. Greer 39-94 1983 £45

MOTHER GOOSE   Mother Goose Rhymes. G.G. Harrap, 1920. 4to. Colour frontis. 11 colour plates by S.B. Pearse. Pictorial title & 113 text illus. by W.M. Ackroyd. Colour pictorial boards, edges worn. Greer 40-165 1983 £38

MOTHER GOOSE   Mother Goose. Hodder & Stoughton, 1938. 4to. Colour frontis. Title vignette. 11 colour plates (1 short tear). Text illus to every page. Grey decorated cloth. Greer 39-117 1983 £60

MOTHER GOOSE   Real Children in Mother Goose. Whit., (1935). 4to. Pictorial boards. Frayed dust wrapper. Fine. Aleph-bet 8-173 1983 $27

THE MOTHER'S Song Book. Wells, Gardner Darton, n.d. (ca. 1898). Illus. by Charles Robinson. Frontis. decor. title, 26 full page illus. and numerous dec. throughout. Blue vertical ribbed cloth, gilt, t.e.g., others uncut, gilt rubbed away on backstrip, covers slightly soiled, occasional foxing. Very good. Hodgkins 27-155 1983 £25

MOTLEY, JOHN LOTHROP   Complete Historical Works. London, 1869-75. 9 vols. Cr. 8vo. Cont. full pink calf, two-line gilt borders on sides, fully gilt panelled spines with green morocco labels, gilt. Portraits and maps. Traylen 94-621 1983 £105

MOTLEY, JOHN LOTHROP   Merry-Mount; a Romance of the Massachusetts Colony. Boston & Cambridge: James Munroe, 1849. 2 vols. bound in one. 1st Ed. Orig. claret cloth. Corner portion of front free endpaper wanting, else a very good copy. Jenkins 155-955 1983 $45

MOTLEY, WILLARD   Knock on any Door. New York & London: Appleton, (1947). 1st ed., later printing. Orig. cloth, dj lightly frayed. Fine. Jenkins 155-956 1983 $30

MOTT, FRANK LUTHER   A History of American Magazines, 1741-1930. Cambridge: The Belknap Press of Harvard University Press, 1957-1968. 5 vols. Illus. Cloth. Dust wrapper. Complete set with cumulative index to the five volumes. Dawson 471-204 1983 $125

MOTT, VALENTINE   Eulogy of the Late John W. Francis, M.D. N.Y., 1861. 2 ports. 8vo, wraps. Inscribed, on slip mounted on free endpaper--"To Chas. King, LL.D., President of Columbia College, with the regards of V. Mott." Argosy 713-393 1983 $75

MOTT, VALENTINE   Eulogy on the Late John W. Francis, M.D. N.Y., 1865. 8vo, cloth-backed bds.; ex-lib. Frontis. Ports. Argosy 713-394 1983 $30

MOTTELAY, APUL F.   The Soldier in Our Civil War. New York & Atlanta, 1893. At top of title: Frank Leslie's Illustrations. 2 vols., folio, rebound in new cloth, very nice. Morrill 290-330 1983 $55

MOTTEUX, PETER ANTHONY   Beauty in distress. A tragedy. London: printed for Daniel Brown; and Rich. Parker, 1698. Sm. 4to, disbound, 1st edition. A fine copy, complete with the leaf of ads at the end. Ximenes 64-387 1983 $325

MOTTLEY, JOHN   Joe Miller's Jests. Whittaker & Co., 1836. Half title, orig. dull purple patterned cloth, black label, v.g. Jarndyce 31-823 1983 £18

MOTTRAM, RALPH HALE   Another Window Seat. London: Hutchinson & Co., (1954). First edition. Orig. boards. Dust jacket (faded, worn and tape-repaired at the spine-ends). Presentation copy inscribed on the title-page: "E.J.F. from R.H.M., 3 June 1957." Near-fine. MacManus 279-3876 1983 $50

MOTTRAM, RALPH HALE   The Apple Disdained. London: Elkin Mathews, 1928. First edition. Orig. boards. Dust jacket. One of 530 copies signed by author. Fine. MacManus 279-3877 1983 $25

MOTTRAM, RALPH HALE   At the Sign of The Lame Dog. Boston: Houghton Mifflin Co., 1933. First American edition. Orig. cloth. Dust jacket. Fine. MacManus 279-3878 1983 $25

MOTTRAM, RALPH HALE   The Boroughmonger. London: Chatto & Windus, 1929. First edition. Orig. cloth. Dust jacket (slightly worn and soiled, with a tiny nick on the front cover). Presentation copy "For Dennis Wheatley 'Who made this dirty bargain,' page 334. R.H. Mottram." With Wheatley's bookplate. With two of the publisher's prospectai describing other Mottram books, loosely laid in. Near-fine. MacManus 279-3879 1983 $65

MOTTRAM, RALPH HALE   Bowler Hat. London: Hutchinson & Co., (1940). First edition. Illus. Orig. cloth. Signed by author on the title-page. Spine and covers slightly faded, worn and rubbed. Good. MacManus 279-3881 1983 $40

MOTTRAM, RALPH HALE   Castle Island. London: Chatto & Windus, 1931. First edition. Orig. cloth-backed patterned boards. One of 160 copies signed by author. Spine faded, boards darkened at edges. MacManus 279-3883 1983 $35

MOTTRAM, RALPH HALE   Europa's Beast. London: Chatto & Windus, 1930. First edition. Orig. cloth-backed boards. One of 350 copies signed by author. Very good. MacManus 279-3892 1983 $35

MOTTRAM, RALPH HALE   Europa's Beast. London: Chatto & Windus, 1930. First edition. Orig. cloth. Inscribed by the author on the title page: "Ralph H. Mottram, 11 June 1930." Spine and covers slightly spotted. Very good. MacManus 279-3891 1983 $20

MOTTRAM, RALPH HALE   The Golden Calf. London: June, 1925. First edition. Orig. printed wrappers. Contains an illustrated cartoon by Max Beerbohm. Covers faded and slightly worn. Very good. MacManus 279-3897 1983 $25

MOTTRAM, RALPH HALE   A Good Old Fashioned Christmas. London: The Lindsey Press, (1933). First edition. Orig. wrappers. Spine and covers slightly faded. Near-fine. MacManus 279-3898 1983 $40

MOTTRAM, RALPH HALE   The Headless Hound and other Stories. London: Chatto & Windus, 1931. First edition. Orig. cloth. Dust jacket, (torn; tape-repaired). Very good. MacManus 279-3901 1983 $25

MOTTRAM, RALPH HALE   A History of Financial Speculation. London: Chatto & Windus, 1929. First edition. Illus. Orig. cloth. Dust jacket (somewhat faded, worn, and soiled; slightly chipped with a few tears). Presentation copy "To Dennis Wheatley, 'Credit is suspicion asleep,' page 100, R. H. Mottram." Edges a trifle foxed. Wheatley's bookplate. Near-fine. MacManus 279-3902 1983 $65

MOTTRAM, RALPH HALE   A History of Financial Speculation. London: Chatto & Windus, 1929. First edition. Illus. Orig. cloth. Spine and covers slightly faded, worn, and spotted. Good. MacManus 279-3903 1983 $20

MOTTRAM, RALPH HALE   John Crome Of Norwich. London: John Lane, The Bodley Head, (1931). First edition. Illus. Orig. cloth. Presentation copy to the Galsworthys inscribed: "A. & J.G. from Ralph, 30 November 1931." Spine darkened. Slightly foxed. Good. MacManus 279-3905 1983 $85

MOTTRAM, RALPH HALE   The Lost Christmas Presents. London: The Lindsey Press, (1931). First edition. Orig. printed wrappers. Presentation copy "For Dennis Wheatley 'Behold the wasted gifts,' page 13, R.H. Mottram." Covers a trifle worn, endpapers slightly foxed. With Wheatley's bookplate. Near-fine. MacManus 279-3907 1983 $65

MOTTRAM, RALPH HALE   The Lost Christmas Presents. London: The Lindsey Press, (1931). First edition. Orig. green printed wraps. Fine. MacManus 279-3908 1983 $40

MOTTRAM, RALPH HALE   Miss Lavington. London: Hutchinson & Co., (1939). First edition. Orig. cloth. Dust jacket (somewhat faded, soiled, and worn at the spine ends and margins). Presentation copy inscribed: "E. Forrest from R.H. Mottram, Christmas 1939." Very good. MacManus 279-3912 1983 $45

MOTTRAM, RALPH HALE   The New Providence. London: Chatto & Windus, 1930. First edition. Orig. decorated boards. Dust jacket (spine and covers slightly faded and worn). Presentation to Dennis Wheatley. With an ALS from Mottram to Wheatley, 2 pages, Poplar Ave., Eaton, Norwich. 1 Jan 1934. With Wheatley's bookplate. Very good. MacManus 279-3915 1983 $100

MOTTRAM, RALPH HALE   The New Providence. London: Chatto &
Windus, 1930. First edition. Orig. cloth-backed boards. One of 210
copies signed by author. Presentation copy to Juliet Standing, the
publisher of Mottram's "Twelve Poems." Fine. MacManus 279-3916
1983 $40

MOTTRAM, RALPH HALE   Noah. London: Rich & Cowan Ltd.,
(1937). First edition. Orig. cloth. Dust jacket (a bit rubbed).
Fine. MacManus 279-3919 1983 $40

MOTTRAM, RALPH HALE   The Old Man of the Stones. London: The
Lindsey Press, (1930). First edition. Orig. printed wrappers. Presentation copy "For Dennis Wheatley 'However shallow be their thoughts,'
page 17, R. H. Mottram." Covers faded and slightly worn. Endpapers a
trifle foxed. Wheatley's bookplate. Very good. MacManus 279-2931
1983 $65

MOTTRAM, RALPH HALE   The Old Man Of The Stones. London: The
Lindsey Press, (1930). First edition. Orig. printed wrappers.
Slightly foxed. Near-fine. MacManus 279-3922 1983 $40

MOTTRAM, RALPH HALE   Poems New and Old. London: Duckworth,
1930. First edition. Orig. cloth. Buff dust jacket. One of 215
copies signed by Mottram. Fine. MacManus 279-3926 1983 $50

MOTTRAM, RALPH HALE   Poems New and Old. London: Duckworth,
1930. First edition. Orig. cloth. Dust jacket (a trifle worn and
torn). MacManus 279-3925 1983 $25

MOTTRAM, RALPH HALE   The Spanish Farm. London: Chatto &
Windus, (1930). First Phoenix Library edition. Orig. cloth. Signed
by Mottram on the title-page. Fine. MacManus 279-3932 1983 $25

MOTTRAM, RALPH HALE   Strawberry Time, and, The Banquet.
London: Golden Cockerel Press, Ten Staple Inn, 1934. First edition.
Illus. with engravings by G. Hermes. Orig. quarter-morocco. One of
250 copies signed by author. Spine and covers slightly faded. Very
good. MacManus 279-3935 1983 $25

MOTTRAM, RALPH HALE   Time To Be Going. London: Hutchinson
& Co., (1937). First edition. Orig. cloth. Dust jacket (spine edges
rubbed, covers slightly worn, with a few small tears). Presentation
copy to Dennis Wheatley, dated 28 April 1937. With Wheatley's bookplate. Preliminary pages and edges slightly foxed. Very good. Mac-
Manus 279-3938 1983 $65

MOTTRAM, RALPH HALE   The World Turns Slowly Round. London:
Hutchinson & Co., (1942). First edition. Orig. cloth. Spine and
covers slightly worn. Good. MacManus 279-3946 1983 $20

MOTTRAM, WILLIAM   The True Story of George Eliot in
Relation to "Adam Bede". T. Fisher Unwin, 1905. First edition,
front. port. & illus. Half title, orig. olive green cloth, t.e.g
Jarndyce 30-986 1983 £15

MOULTON, CHARLES   A Biographical Cyclopedia of Medical
History. New York, 1905. 8vo. Orig. binding. First edition.
Fye H-3-410 1983 $50

MOULTON, JOSEPH W.   An Address Delivered at St. Paul's Church,
Buffalo. Buffalo, N.Y.: D.M. Day and H.A. Salisbury, 1821. Wrappers.
Very good. Felcone 20-127 1983 $35

MOULTRIE, JOHN   Poems. Wm. Pickering, 1837. First
edition, half red morocco, a little rubbed. Jarndyce 30-803 1983
£10.50

MOUNT Desert Souvenir. (West Gardner, Mass.), 1884. 20 fine
heliotype plates. Large oblong 8vo. Morrill 290-263 1983 $25

MT. LOWE, 6100 Feet Altitude (cover title). (Los Angeles): (Baumgardt
Print, published by Pacific Electric, n.d.) (ca.1906). Wrappers.
Library stamp on front cover. Dawson 471-205 1983 $50

MT. Tom & Mt. Tom Railroad, Views on and About. Holyoke, (ca. 1900).
Photos, oblong 8vo, pr. pict. wrs. Argosy 710-295 1983 $35

MOUREAU, ADRIEN   Les Moreau. Paris: G. Pierson, 1893.
105 illus. (2 hors texte). 4to. Wrappers. Ars Libri 32-476 1983
$40

MOUREAU, ADRIEN   Les Saint-Aubin. Paris: Librairie
de l'Art, 1894. 121 illus. (3 hors texte). 4to. Wrappers. Ars
Libri 32-613 1983 $50

MOURLOT, FERNAND   Chagall Lithographe, 1957-1962.
Monte Carlo: Andre Sauret, 1963. 11 orig. lithographs (6 color).
185 illus. Large 4to. Cloth. Dust jacket with orig. lithograph.
Vol. II of the catalogue raisonne. Ars Libri 32-93 1983 $1,000

MOURLOT, FERNAND   Picasso Lithographs. Boston: Boston
Book and Art, 1970. 407 illus. (numerous color). Large square 4to.
Cloth. Dust jacket. Ars Libri 32-524 1983 $100

MOURLOT, FERNAND   Souvenirs Et Portraits D'Artistes.
Paris, (1972). Limited to 800 numbered copies. 25 lithos (most in
color). Loose (as issued) in folding box. Two edges of box slightly
tearing. Very good. King 45-614 1983 $600

THE MOUSE'S Wedding. (Tokyo: Hasegawa, ca. 1898). 12mo. Frenchfold.
Crepe-paper book. Illus. Fine in colored pictorial self-wrappers
bound Japanese style. Bromer 25-356 1983 $60

MOUTIN, LUCIEN   Le Nouvel Hypnotism. Paris, 1887.
12mo, new front wr. First edition. Argosy 713-395 1983 $60

MOWAT, GRACE HELEN   The Diverting History of a Loyalist
Town. St. Andrews, 1937. 2nd ed. 8vo, dw. Morrill 288-327 1983
$20

MOXON, EDWARD   The Prospect, and Other Poems. Longman,
Rees, Orme, Brown, and Green, 1826. Small 8vo, orig. boards, paper
spine, worn at head and foot. First edition. Bickersteth 77-231
1983 £38

MOXON, JAMES   Mechanick-Powers. For the authors
and sold by Ven. Mandey, London, 1696. 4to, with 17 folding engraved
plates; 1 plate cropped; a good copy in cont. panelled calf, upper
joint cracked but sound. First edition, first issue. Quaritch NS
5-73 1983 $2,000

MOYLE, SETH   My Friend O. Henry. New York:
Privately Printed--Not for Sale, 1914. 1st ed. Orig. printed
brown wrappers. Scarce. Jenkins 155-1023 1983 $20

MOYNIHAN, BERKELEY   American Addresses. Phila., 1917.
First edition. Thin 8vo, cloth (ex-lib). Argosy 713-396 1983 $25

MOZART, WOLFGANG AMADEUS   Ah Perdona al Primo Affetto. Liverpool,
H. Himes, n.d. Engraved title and music. Folio, unbound. Salloch 387-
139 1983 $40

MOZART, WOLFGANG AMADEUS   Arien und Gesaenge Aus Don Juan. Berlin,
n.d. (c. 1830). Small 8vo, marbled wrs. Salloch 387-141 1983 $35

MOZART, WOLFGANG AMADEUS   Arien und Gesaenge zu dem Singspiel.
Berlin, n.d. (c. 1830). Small 4to, marbled wrs. Salloch 387-145
1983 $30

MOZART, WOLFGANG AMADEUS   Ave Verum Corpus. Vienna, 1790. Cont.
manuscript copy. 4 leaves, oblong folio. Ink inscription on the
title gives 1790 as the date. Salloch 387-138 1983 $225

MOZART, WOLFGANG AMADEUS   Don Juan. Leipzig, Breitkopf & Haertel,
n.d. (1818). 2 engraved and one printed title, engraved music.
Oblong folio, orig. grey wrs. The printed title, in German, is on
the outer cover. The first of the engraved titles has a large vignette
by Fr. Bolt. Second engraved title is in German again, with the
addition: "Nebst einem Anhang von spaeter eingelegten Stuecken".
Salloch 387-140 1983 $500

MOZART, WOLFGANG AMADEUS   Misericordias Domini. Bonn & Coeln,
Dimrock, n.d. (1823). Engraved music. Plate #2076. Oblong folio.
Salloch 387-146 1983 $150

MOZART, WOLFGANG AMADEUS   Le Nozze di Figaro. Bonna & Colonia, Simrock, n.d. (1819). Engraved title, table of contents, engraved music, full score with German and Italian text. Folio, full green calf, gilt decorated with scrollwork and flowers, blind-tooled centerpiece, a.e.g. Plate mark 1603. Mendelssohn's signature on front fly leaf. Corner's slightly rubbed, otherwise splendid copy. Salloch 387-144 1983 $4,000

MOZART, WOLFGANG AMADEUS   Oeuvres, Cahier V. Leipzig, Breitkopf & Haertel, n.d. (1799). With engraved title vignette by Boehm after Kininger. Oblong folio, orig. printed green wrs. (binding showing traces of use and age). Salloch 387-150 1983 $300

MOZART, WOLFGANG AMADEUS   Sancta Maria. Offenbach, Andre (c. 1815). Oblong folio, orig. wrs., engraved music. Salloch 387-149 1983 $200

MOZEEN, THOMAS   Young Scarron. London: printed and sold by T. Trye, and W. Reeve, 1752. 8vo, cont. half calf (slight worming at foot of spine). First edition. A fine copy, complete with half-title. Ximenes 64-388 1983 $600

MOZLEY, HARRIET   The Lost Brooch, Or, The History of Another Month. A Tale for Young People. James Burns..., 1841. First edition. 2 vols, 12mo, original purple cloth, spines slightly faded, uncut; frontispieces; a very nice copy. Hill 165-83 1983 £55

MUDD, HARVEY   The Plain of Smokes. Santa Barbara: Black Sparrow Press, 1982. Cloth and pictorial boards. First edition. Illus. by Ken Price. One of only 26 lettered copies, specially bound, signed by the author, and accompanied by a separate, matted, orig. serigraph, also ltd. to 26 numbered copies, signed by Price. Mint as issued. Reese 20-715 1983 $150

MUDD, HARVEY   The Plain of Smokes. Black Sparrow Press, 1982. Illustrated by Ken Price. 8vo. Cloth, boards. 1 of 26 copies lettered and signed by the poet. Each of the lettered copies contain an orig. serigraph by Ken Price issued separately, lettered and signed by the artist. In Our Time 156-583 1983 $125

MUDD, JOSEPH A.   With Porter in North Missouri. Wash., 1909. Illus. Orig. cloth. First edition. Ginsberg 47-537 1983 $75

MUDDIMAN, BERNARD   The Men of the Nineties. London: Daniel-son, 1920. First edition. 12mo. Orig. boards. Worn. MacManus 279-3948 1983 $25

MUDFORD, WILLIAM   A critical examination of the writings of Richard Cumberland, Esq. London: printed by Charles Squire, for Sherwood, Neely, and Jones; and J. Asperne, 1812. Two vols., 8vo, cont. half calf, spines gilt. First published edition. Half-titles present; with a portrait. Some foxing and light browning, else a fine copy. Ximenes 64-398 1983 $175

MUDIE, ROBERT   Man, as a Moral and Accountable Being. Wm. S. Orr, 1840. First edition, with coloured frontis. and additional tinted vignette title-page, both by Baxter. Large 12mo, orig. green cloth. Fenning 60-288 1983 £14.50

MUDIE, ROBERT   Man, in His Relation to Society. Wm. S. Orr, 1840. First edition, hand-coloured front. Orig. green cloth, v.g. Jarndyce 31-326 1983 £18.50

MUDIE, ROBERT   Mental philosophy. London: Orr, 1838. First edition. 8vo. Orig. purple-brown cloth. Rubbed. Spine faded. Ximenes 63-299 1983 $100

MUDIE, ROBERT   The Picture of India. London, n.d. (c.1833). Third edition. 2 folding maps, vignettes in text. 2 vols. bound in one. Thick 12mo. Orig. cloth. Good. Edwards 1044-505 1983 £45

MUELLER, HANS ALEXANDER   The Booklover. NY: Philip C. Duschnes, n.d. (ca. 1942). Folio. Five orig. signed color wood engravings, each placed inside a thin paper mat. Engravings laid inside stiff paper portfolio with color cover label with wood-engraving on it. Karmiole 71-74 1983 $125

MUELLER, HANS ALEXANDER   Woodcuts & Wood Engravings: How I Make Them. N.Y., 1939. First edition. Limited to 3000 copies, by the Pynson Printers, profusely illus. Blind-stamped names & rubber stamped. Heavily chipped dust wrapper. King 45-437 1983 $100

MUENSTER, SEBASTIAN   Mappa Europa... Frankfurt am Main: Christian Egenolph, 1536. First edition. Full-page woodcut map of Heidelberg, and separate folding maps of Europe and the Upper Rhine. Woodcut on title and first text page (slightly touched with color) and 22 small wodcuts of city views in the text. 4to. Modern vellum. Light marginal dampstain. Kraus 164-167 1983 $6,800

MUENSTERBERG, HUGO (1863-1916)   Grundzuege der Psychologie. Leipzig: Verlag von Johann A. Barth, 1900. Contemporary cloth-backed marbled boards. First edition. Gach 95-384 1983 $50

MUHLESTEIN, HANS   Ferdinand Hodler. Ein Deutungsversuch. Weimar: Gustav Kiepenheuer, 1914. 2 vols. 87 collotype plates on move mounts (loose, as issued in clamshell case). Large stout 4to. Boards, 1/2 leather. T.e.g. No. 11 of 100 copies on handmade van Gelder. Ars Libri 32-310 1983 $475

MUIR, ALAN   Tumbledown Farm. Spencer Blackett, 1889. First edition, 3 vols. Half title vol. I. Orig. light green cloth, a little dulled on spines. Jarndyce 31-824 1983 £38

MUIR, EDWIN   John Knox: Portrait of a Calvinist. Jonarhan Cape, 1930. 8vo, 4 plates, cloth. Bickersteth 77-158 1983 £12

MUIR, EDWIN   Latitudes. New York, 1924. First edition. Head of spine a little darkened. Torn dust wrapper. Very nice. Rota 230-428 1983 £45

MUIR, EDWIN   The Present Age from 1914. London: Cresset Press, 1939. Inscribed by the author to Van Wyck Brooks. Spine faded and slightly creased, otherwise a very good copy. Gekoski 2-133 1983 £40

MUIR, EDWIN   The Present Age from 1914. London, 1939. First edition. Spine darkened. Name of flyleaf. Nice. Rota 230-432 1983 £20

MUIR, EDWIN   Scottish Journey. London, 1935. First edition. Inscription on front endpaper. Nice. Rota 230-431 1983 £25

MUIR, EDWIN   Scottish Journey. London, 1935. Proof copy in slightly soiled wrappers, inscribed in pencil on half-title "Read 14 Sept. 1935. To be published in October." A very good copy. Gekoski 2-132 1983 £20

MUIR, EDWIN   The Structure of the Novel. Hogarth Lectures, 1928. First edition. Spine dull. Name on flyleaf. Very good. Rota 230-429 1983 £15

MUIR, EDWIN   The Three Brothers. London, 1931. First edition. Spine a little creased. Nice. Rota 230-430 1983 £40

MUIR, EDWIN   We Moderns. NY, 1920. First American edition, cover slightly faded, edges rubbed, small tape stain on front end paper, good to very good. Quill & Brush 54-963 1983 $30

MUIR, JOHN   Original Sanskrit Texts ... London, 1872-1874. 4 vols. Uniformily bound in cont. half red morocco, raised bands, gilt. Slight wear on corners. 8vo. Good. Edwards 1044-506 1983 £110

MUIR, JOHN   A Thousand-Mile Walk to the Gulf. Boston, 1916. 1st ed. Illus. 8vo. Lettering on backstrip partly effaced. Morrill 287-291 1983 $27.50

MUIR, PERCY   Bibliographies of the First Editions of Books by Aldous Huxley and by T.F. Powys. London: Dulau & Co. Ltd, 1927. First edition. 8vo. Orig. black cloth. Gilt. One of only 50 copies printed on Japan vellum and signed by both Huxley and Powys. Very fine copy. Jaffe 1-192 1983 $250

MUIR, P. H.   Book-Collecting, More Letters to
Everyman. London: Cassell and Co., (1949). First edition. Small
8vo. Two-toned cloth, dust jacket. Presentation "For C.E. Kenney,
these foundation stones, hoping that no bricks have been dropped.
P.H. Muir." From the library of Adrian Goldstone with his bookplate.
Oak Knoll 49-297 1983 $60

MUIR, PERCY   Catnachery. San Francisco: Book Club
of California, 1955. Octavo. Numerous reproductions of orig. woodcuts, 5 fold-out facsimiles of broadsides bound-in. Limited to 325
copies printed at Greenwood Press. Near mint in cloth-backed illus.
boards with orig. plain dust wrapper, slightly soiled and chipped.
Bromer 25-368 1983 $65

MUIR, PERCY   English Children's Books, 1600-1900.
London: B.T. Batsford Ltd., (1954). First edition. 4to. Cloth,
dust jacket. Over 100 illus. including some in color. Jacket
slightly chipped. Oak Knoll 49-118 1983 $125

MUIR, PERCY   English Children's Books, 1600-1900.
London, (1954). 8vo, cloth, with more than 100 illus., many in
color. First edition. Duschnes 240-168 1983 $100

MUIR, PERCY   Points 1874-1930, being extracts from
a Bibliographer's Note-book. London: Constable & Co., 1931. First
edition. 8vo. Parchment-backed marbled boards. Limited to 500
numbered copies. 4 plates and 6 facsimiles. Barton Currie's copy
with his bookplate. Covers rubbed. Oak Knoll 49-478 1983 $160

MUIR, PERCY   Points, 1874-1930, being Extracts from
a Bibliographer's Note-book. London: Constable & Co., 1931. First
edition. 8vo. Parchment-backed marbled boards. Limited to 500
copies. Some cover wear and age yellowing of parchment. Scarce.
Bookplate. Oak Knoll 48-465 1983 $160

MUIR, R. CUTHBERTSON   The Early Political and Military History
of Burford. Quebec, 1913. 22 1/2cm. 33 plates and illus. Errata
leaf. Orig. red cloth. Fine. McGahern 53-121 1983 $85

MUKINS, ISAAC   The History of Charlotte Villars: A
Narrative Founded on Truth, Interspersed with Variety of Incidents
Instructive and Entertaining. Printed for S. Crowder and H.
Woodgate, 1756. 12mo, contemporary calf; covers somewhat rubbed,
slight wear to hinges; a very fair copy. A rare novel. Hill 165-
88 1983 £350

MULFORD, PRENTICE   Prentice Mulford's Story. N.Y., 1889.
Orig. cloth. First edition. Ginsberg 47-608 1983 $35

MULGRAVE, JOHN SHEFFIELD, 3RD EARL OF
Please turn to
BUCKINGHAM, JOHN SHEFFIELD, DUKE OF

MULLALLA, JAMES   An Essay on Polite Literature. Dublin:
Printed by Wm. McKenzie, 1792. First edition, large 12mo, wrapper.
Fenning 60-289 1983 £28.50

MULLCARDT, LOUIS CHRISTIAN   The Architecture and Landscape Gardening
of the Exposition. San Francisco, Paul Elder, (1915). 2nd edition,
revised. Illus. with tipped-in plates. Marbled endpapers. Tan
cloth stamped in gilt. Very good. Houle 22-1146 1983 $20

MULLEN, SAMUEL   The Pilgrim of Beauty, and Other Poems.
Clark, 1839. Second edition, tall 8vo, lacking leading free end papers.
Orig. black cloth. Jarndyce 30-804 1983 £10.50

MULLER, FREDERIK   Catalogue of Books, Maps, Plates on
America... Amsterdam, 1872. Plates. Half leather, worn, orig.
wrappers bound in (the latter blind-stamped); ex-library. Dawson
470-216 1983 $25

MULLER, HEINRICH   Die Spate Graphik von Lovis Corinth.
Hamburg: Lichtwarkstiftung, 1960. 465 illus. hors texte. Large
4to. Cloth. Edition limited to 600 numbered copies. Ars Libri
32-121 1983 $400

MULLIN, ROBERT N.   The Strange Story of Wayne Brazel. N.p.,
(1969). Illustrations by J. Cisneros plus photo illustrations. 50
copies bound. Bound in light tan cloth. Signed by J. Evetts Haley
and manuscript notation on free flyleaf. Jenkins 153-238 1983 $100

MULOCK, DINAH MARIA
Please turn to
CRAIK, DINAH MARIA MULOCK

MULSANT, E.   Lettres a Julie sur l'Ornithologie.
Paris (1868). Imp. 8vo, half red morocco, 16 fine hand-coloured
plates. Occasional foxing, but a nice copy. Wheldon 160-76 1983
£280

MULVANY, C. PELHAM   Toronto: Past and Present. Toronto:
W.E. Caiger, 1884. 20cm. Numerous plates and illus. from engravings.
Orig. brown cloth, gilt and black stamped titles and decorations.
Some moderate Wear else a very good copy. McGahern 53-122 1983
$65

MUMBY, FRANK A.   Elizabeth and Mary Stuart: a Narrative
in Contemporary Letters. 8vo, 9 plates, cloth. Bickersteth 77-159
1983 £18

MUMEY, NOLIE   The Art and Activities of John Dare
Howland Painter, Soldier, Indian Trader and Pioneer. Boulder, 1973.
Frontis and illus. Many in color. Limited to 350 copies and signed
by the author. Boxed. Jenkins 151-232 1983 $85

MUMEY, NOLIE   John Williams Gunnison (1812-1853) The
Last of the Western Explorers. Denver: Artcraft Press, 1955. Limited
to 500 copies numbered and signed by author. Frontis. Illus. Folding
map. Jenkins 152-139 1983 $75

MUMEY, NOLIE   March of the First Dragoons to the Rocky
Mountains in 1835. Denver, 1957. Index. Folding map, frontis., and
illus. Orig. cloth, folio. Limited to 350 copies signed by Mumey.
Jenkins 152-276 1983 $100

MUMEY, NOLIE   Old Forts and Trading Posts of the West.
Denver, 1956. Colored frontis., maps and illus. Limited and signed
edition. Nice copy. Jenkins 151-95 1983 $125

MUMEY, NOLIE   Old Forts and Trading Posts of the
West. Denver, Artcraft, (1956). Thick 8vo, illus. with 36 halftones.
One of 500 copies, signed by the author. Dust jacket. Fine. Houle
21-1119 1983 $25

MUMEY, NOLIE   Poker Alice. Denver, 1951. Orig. pic.
stiff wrappers. Folding map. Limited to 500 numbered and signed
copies. Fine copy. Jenkins 153-377 1983 $75

MUMFORD, JAMES   Surgical Memoirs and other Addresses.
New York, 1906. First edition. 8vo. Orig. binding. Fye H-3-411
1983 $30

MUMFORD, JOHN KIMBERLY   Oriental Rugs. New York: Scribner's,
1900. 24 plates of carpets (16 in full color), 8 photo-plates.
Large 4to. Orig. decorated maroon buckram. First edition. Very fine.
Jenkins 152-713 1983 $100

MUNARI, BRUNO   Mai Contenti. (Verona): Mondadori,
(1945). Quarto. First edition. Illus. Very fine in pictorial
self-wrappers with chipped glassine. Bromer 25-370 1983 $65

MUNARI, BRUNO   Il Prestigiatore Verde. (Verona):
Mondadori, (1945). Quarto. First edition. Two full-sized leaves
with attached smaller pages to be unfolded. Fine in cloth-backed
pictorial boards. Chipped glassine torn in few places. Bromer 25-
369 1983 $55

MUNARI, BRUNO   Storie de tre Uccellini. (Verona):
Mondadori, (1945). Quarto. First edition. Colored illus. throughout.
Fine in cloth-backed pictorial boards with defective glassine. Bromer
25-371 1983 $55

MUNCHAUSEN, BARON   Travels and Surprising Adventures.
N.Y.: American Book Exchange, 1880. Orig. wrappers. Fine. Mac-
Manus 279-3957 1983 $20

MUNDELL, F.   Stories of the Victoria Cross. London,
Ca. 1897. 2 vols. in one. Thick sm. 8vo, orig. green decorated cloth.
T.e.g., edges slightly foxed. Presentation bookplate. Frontis. 20
full page and 13 other illus. Good. Edwards 1042-422 1983 £12

MUNDEN, THOMAS SHEPHERD   Memoirs of Joseph Shepherd Munden, comedian. London: Richard Bentley, 1844. 8vo, original purple cloth (spine slightly faded). First edition. With a portrait (some foxing). A fine copy of a scarce biography. Ximenes 64-390 1983 $200

MUNDY, FRANCIS NOEL CLARKE   Poems. Oxford: Printed by W. Jackson. MDCCLXVIII. 4to, cont. sprinkled calf, gilt, red morocco label, joints cracking slightly, errata slip attached to rear pastedown. First edition, privately printed on thick paper. Presentation copy to author's brother-in-law, Mr. Ware, who has inscribed on the front flyleaf a lengthy key to the anonymous addresses, et al. Cont. manuscript of Christopher Anstey's elegy laid in. Quaritch NS 7-89 1983 $350

MUNDY, TALBOT   The Winds of the World. Ind., (1917). Illus. by Joseph C. Coll, small paper remnants on pastedowns, pastedowns and flys slightly skinned, minor cover wear, else very good. Quill & Brush 54-964 1983 $60

MUNK, JOSEPH A.   Activities of a Lifetime. Los Angeles: The Times-Minor Press, 1924. Frontis. and plates. 1st ed. Orig. cloth with presentation from Munk. Jenkins 153-379 1983 $50

MUNK, JOSEPH A.   Arizona Sketches. New York: The Grafton Press, 1905. First edition. Frontis. Illus. Orig. pictorial cloth. Slight staining to several pages. Presentation copy from author. Jenkins 152-13 1983 £50

MUNK, JOSEPH A.   Arizona Sketches. N.Y.: Grafton Press, (1905). Plates. Cloth. Signed presentation from author. Dawson 471-208 1983 $75

MUNK, JOSEPH A.   Southwest Sketches. N.Y. & London: G.P. Putnam's Sons, 1920. Plates. Cloth. With an inscription, "Everything in Califronia is love and sunshine", signed by author. Dawson 471-209 1983 $75

MUNRO, H. A. J.   Criticsms and Elucidations of Catullus VIII. NY, 1938. 8vo, cloth. Salloch 385-502 1983 $25

MUNRO, HECTOR HUGH   The Background. (Chicago: The Art Institute of Chicago, June 1930.) First separate edition. Illus. with woodcuts by Kam Young Wong. 4to. Orig. cloth-backed boards with paper label. Very fine. MacManus 280-4484 1983 $100

MUNRO, HECTOR HUGH   The Westminster Alice. (London): Reprinted from the Westminster Gazette, (1902). First edition. Illus. by F.C. Gould. Orig. pictorial wrappers. Inscription in an unknown hand on front wrapper, which is foxed, faded and worn along spine. MacManus 279-3958 1983 $50

MUNRO, NEIL   Fancy Farm. Edinburgh and London, 1910. First edition. Very good. Rota 230-435 1983 £12

MUNRO, NEIL   The Shoes of Fortune. London: Isbister & Co., 1901. First edition. Illus. by A.S. Boyd. Orig. cloth. Inscribed to a friend. With an inscription by a later owner beneath. Ink stamping on edges. Front inner hinge strained. MacManus 279-3959 1983 $35

MUNRO, WILFRED   The History of Bristol, R.I. Providence, 1880. Illus., engr. Plates, (2 ports. marginally damp-stained). 8vo, 1/2 red mor., gilt edging. Argosy 716-487 1983 $125

MUNRO, WILFRED   Tales of an Old Sea Port. Princeton, 1917. Argosy 716-488 1983 $40

MUNSELL, FRANK   A Genealogy of the Munsell Family. Albany, 1884. Illus., 8vo, stipple cloth, backstrip top chipped. With tipped-in manuscript on Hezekiah Munsell & descendants. Argosy 710-176 1983 $30

MUNSON, GORHAM B.   Waldo Frank. New York: Boni & Liveright, (1923). Cloth and boards, paper labels. First edition. One of 500 numbered copies. With an orig. print of Stieglitz's portrait of Frank tipped in as the frontis. This copy is inscribed by Munson. Title has offset a trifle on the photograph, otherwise an about fine copy, sans dust jacket. Reese 20-944 1983 $250

MUNSTER, SEBASTIAN   Cosmographei. Mappa Evropae... Frankfurt am Main: Christian Egenolph, 1537. Second edition. Full-page woodcut map of Heidelberg, and 24 small woodcuts on the title-page and in the text. Small 4to. Old vellum. Kraus 164-168 1983 $3,500

MUNSTER, SEBASTIAN
Please turn to
MUENSTER, SEBASTIAN

MUNZ, LUDWIG   Bruegel. The Drawings. London: Phaidon, 1961. Complete edition. 240 illus. Large 4to. Cloth. Dust jacket. Ars Libri 32-70 1983 $75

MUNZ, LUDWIG   Die kunst Rembrandts und Goethes Sehen. Leipzig: Heinrich Keller, 1934. 23 plates with 72 illus. 4to. Wrappers. From the library of Jakob Rosenberg. Ars Libri 32-561 1983 $40

MURARO, MICHELANGELO   Victor Carpaccio alla Scuola di San Giorgio degli Schiavoni in Venezia. Roma: Edizioni Mediterranee, 1956. 36 color plates (mostly double page or folding). Folio. Cloth. Dust jacket. Edition limited to 1050 numbered copies. Ars Libri 33-92 1983 $85

MURCHISON, R. I.   Siluria. 1854. 8vo, original cloth, text-figures, 37 plates of fossils. First edition. Wheldon 160-1449 1983 £80

MURDOCH, DAVID   The Dutch Dominie of the Catskills. N.Y., 1861. First edition. Ex lib. Argosy 716-359 1983 $25

MURDOCH, IRIS   The Flight from the Enchanter. London, 1956. First edition. Slightly nicked dustwrapper missing one miniscule chip. Fine. Gekoski 2-135 1983 £100

MURDOCH, IRIS   Henry and Cato. London: Chatto & Windus, 1976. First edition, advance proofs. Orig. printed wrappers. Spine slightly faded. Very good. MacManus 279-3960 1983 $85

MURDOCH, IRIS   Nuns and Soldiers. London: Chatto & Windus, 1980. First edition, advance proofs. Orig. printed wrappers. Covers and spine very slightly worn. Near-fine. MacManus 279-3961 1983 $85

MURDOCH, IRIS   Nuns and Soldiers. New York, n.d. 8vo. Wraps. Uncorrected proof copy. A fine copy. In Our Time 156-586 1983 $50

MURDOCH, IRIS   The Sandcastle. London, 1957. Uncorrected proof copy. Grey wrappers. Fine. Gekoski 2-215 1983 £120

MURDOCH, IRIS   The Sandcastle. London, 1957. First edition. Dustwrapper showing the very slightest signs of use. Fine. Gekoski 2-136 1983 £85

MURDOCH, IRIS   Sartre. Cambridge, 1953. First edition. Dustwrapper with one tiny chip at the foot of the spine. Fine. Gekoski 2-134 1983 £70

MURDOCH, IRIS   Under the Net. London, 1954. First English edition. Chipped, frayed, and slightly torn dustwrapper. Fine. Jolliffe 26-369 1983 £135

MURDOCH, IRIS   A Word Child. London: Chatto & Windus, 1974. First edition, advance proofs. Orig. printed wrappers. Covers and spine very slightly worn. Very good. MacManus 279-3962 1983 $85

MURDOCH, IRIS   A Year of Birds. Tisbury: The Compton Press, 1978. First edition. One of 350 numbered copies signed by the author and artist. 12 wood engravings by Reynolds Stone. T.e.g. Zerkall mould made paper. Mint. Jolliffe 26-372 1983 £75

MURDOCH, IRIS   A Year of Birds. (Wiltshire): Compton Press, 1978. Ltd. first edition. Thin 8vo, cloth backed marbled boards. One of 350 numbered copies, signed by the author & the artist. Argosy 714-536 1983 $100

MURDOCH, W.G. BURN
Please turn to
BURN-MURDOCH, WILLIAM GORDON

MURDOCK, JOYCE EMERSON PRESTON   The Shadow of Evil. London: Everett & Co., 1907. First edition, orig. cloth, spine nicked, other edges slightly worn, rear hinges cracking, good. MacManus 278-1601 1983 $50

MURGER, HENRI   The Bohemians of the Latin Quarter. London: Vizetelly & Co., 1888. Green cloth. Back inner hinge starting, otherwise very good. Bradley 66-260 1983 $65

MURIE, J.   On the Anatomy of the Lemuroidea. Trans. Zoo. Soc., 1869. 6 plates, 4to, wrappers. Wheldon 160-586 1983 £20

MURPHY, ARTHUR   The Apprentice. London: printed for Paul Vaillant, 1756. 1st ed., 8vo, title and last leaf rather stained, in wrappers. Pickering & Chatto 19-41 1983 $250

MURPHY, ARTHUR   The Citizen. P. Vaillant, T. Caslon, 1770. Rebound in blue boards. 3rd edition. Jarndyce 31-63 1983 £15

MURPHY, ARTHUR   An Essay on the Life and Genius of Samuel Johnson, LL.D. London, 1792. First edition. 8vo. Cont. grey boards, backstrip neatly repaired, uncut edges. Half-title. Traylen 94-472 1983 £70

MURPHY, ARTHUR   The life of David Garrick. London: printed for J. Wright, by J. F. Foot, 1801. 2 vols., 8vo, cont. calf, spines gilt (some rubbing). First edition. Half-titles present. With a portrait. A very good set. Ximenes 64-391 1983 $100

MURPHY, ARTHUR   The life of David Garrick, Esq. Dublin: printed by Brett Smith, for Messrs. Wogan, etc., 1801. 8vo, original blue boards, drab paper backstrips (spines worn). First Dublin edition. Stain on upper corners near the end, else an excellent uncut copy, largely unopened. Ximenes 64-392 1983 $60

MURPHY, GWENDOLEN   Bibliography of English character-books, 1608-1700. Oxford University Press for the Bibliographical Society, 1925. First edition, sm. 4to, uncut in dusty wrappers, very good. Author's presentation copy inscribed: "Dorothy Ellis with love from Gwendolen Murphy." Deighton 3-235 1983 £25

MURPHY, JAMES   The Inside Passenger. Dublin: James Duffy, (1913). First edition. Double columns. Roy. 8vo. Orig. printed wrappers, a very good copy. Fenning 60-290 1983 £24.50

MURPHY, JAMES CAVANAH   The Arabian Antiquities of Spain. London: Cadell & Davies, 1815. Oversize folio, 22pp of text consisting of engraved title, etc. 102 engraved plates, each with title. Cont. half red calf, gilt; extremities rubbed. A.e.g. Plates are clean with only minor foxing. Karmiole 71-75 1983 $850

MURRAY, ALEXANDER   Account of the life and writings of James Bruce of Kinnaird... Edinburgh: Archibald Constable, etc., 1808. 4to. 2 folding maps. 20 plates. 1/2 calf. Gilt. Marbled boards, rebacked. Adelson Africa-107 1983 $200

MURRAY, ALEXANDER   Journal Du Yukon, 1847-48. Ottawa, 1910. French ed. Fldg. map, illus. Orig. wrps. bnd. in. Clark 741-1 1983 $28

MURRAY, CHARLES A.   The Prairie-Bird. London, 1844. 3 vols. Orig. boards, some chipping, but overall fine, with orig. paper labels wholly intact. Reese 19-393 1983 $325

MURRAY, CHARLES A   The Prairie-Bird. Richard Bentley, 1844. First edition, 3 vols., full rebound in half red morocco, marbled boards. Jarndyce 30-497 1983 £38

MURRAY, DAVID CHRISTIE   John Vale's Guardian. London: Macmillan, 1890. First edition. 3 vols. Orig. cloth. Slightly shaken and soiled. Very good. MacManus 279-3963 1983 $200

MURRAY, DAVID CHRISTIE   My Contemporaries in Fiction. London: Chatto & Windus, 1897. First edition. Orig. cloth. Endpapers foxed. Covers somewhat rubbed. MacManus 279-3964 1983 $35

MURRAY, ELSIE   Azilum, French Refuge Colony of 1793. Athens, Pa.: Tioga Point Museum, 1940. Illus, aqua cloth. Argosy 710-148 1983 $20

MURRAY, GILBERT   The Foreign Policy of Sir Edward Grey, 1906-1915. Oxford: At the Clarendon Press, 1915. First edition. Orig. wrappers. Dust-soiled. Very good. MacManus 279-3966 1983 $25

MURRAY, GILBERT   Great Britain's Sea Policy. London: T. Fisher Unwin, Ltd., 1917. First edition. Orig. wrappers. Fine. MacManus 279-3967 1983 $35

MURRAY, GILBERT   The United States and The War. London: W. Speaight & Sons, 1916. First edition. Orig. wrappers (dust-soiled). Good. MacManus 279-3970 1983 $25

MURRAY, HENRY   A Man of Genius. London: Ward & Downey, 1895. First edition. 2 vols. Orig. cloth. Covers slightly soiled. Spines very slightly soiled. Very good. MacManus 279-3971 1983 $185

MURRAY, HUGH   Historical account of discoveries and travels in Africa... Edinburgh: Archibald Constable, etc., 1818. Second edition. 2 vols. 8vo. 7 maps. Modern 1/2 black calf, gilt, green labels, marbled boards, some foxing. Adelson Africa-108 1983 $285

MURRAY, HUGH   History of British India. London, 1863. Folding map, frontis. 8vo. Orig. cloth. Good. Edwards 1044-511 1983 £18

MURRAY, J. A.   The Avifauna of the Island of Ceylon. 1890. 2 coloured plates, royal 8vo, original cloth. Very scarce. Wheldon 160-816 1983 £45

MURRAY, J. A.   Opuscula. Gottingen, 1785-86. 2 vols., 8vo, old half calf, plates. Rare. Some slight foxing. Wheldon 160-182 1983 £30

MURRAY, JAMES   Letters of... Boston, 1901. Privately printed. Illus., facs. G.t., unopened. Argosy 716-466 1983 $40

MURRAY, JOHN   A Manual of Experiments illustrative of Chemical Science systematically arranged. London, 1833. Third edition. 12mo. Orig. boards, uncut. 1 plate and woodcuts in text. Gurney JJ-278 1983 $20

MURRAY, JOHN   A Publisher and His Friends. John Murray, 1891. 2nd edition, 2 vols. Fronts. and one other port. 32 pp ads. vol. I. Orig. blue cloth, v.g. Jarndyce 30-1088 1983 £42

MURRAY, JOHN   A Supplement to the First Edition of a System of Chemistry... Philadelphia: E. Parker, 1811. 8vo. Orig. blue boards. Unopened and uncut. Backstrip off. Zeitlin 264-332 1983 $75

MURRAY, JOHN   A System of Chemistry... Edinburgh: F. Pillans, 1819. 4 vols. 8vo. Modern library buckram. 6 extending plates (foxed). Preliminary leaves vols. 1 & 2 foxed. Zeitlin 264-331 1983 $125

MURRAY, JOHN   A System of Materia Medica and Pharmacy. New York, 1821. 2 vols. 8vo. Contemporary calf, leather labels. Text of Vol. 1 lightly dampstained. Morrill 289-165 1983 $25

MURRAY, JOHN FISHER   A Picturesque Tour of the River Thames in its Western Course. 1862. 4 maps, 5 steel-engraved plates, over 100 wood-engravings, roy 8vo, pictorial gilt cloth, gilt edges. K Books 307-131 1983 £35

MURRAY, JOHN FISHER   The World of London. Thomas Tegg, 1844. Half title, orig. red cloth, rebacked. Jarndyce 31-279 1983 £28

MURRAY, LINDLEY   Abridgement of Murray's English Grammar
with an Appendix. Bennington, Vt.: Smead & Haswell, 1811. Maps,
illus. Prs. wraps. Argosy 716-499 1983 $150

MURRAY, LINDLEY   Exercises, adapted to Murray's English
Grammar. Phila.: A. Dickins, 1800. 12mo, cont. mottled calf, leather
label. First edition. Some leaves wrinkled, some early penciling.
With the half title. Argosy 710-480 1983 $45

MURRAY, LINDLEY   The Power of Religion on the Mind.
London, printed; New Brunswick: Re-printed by Abraham Blauvelt, 1795.
Calf-backed wooden boards (very worn). Endsheets lacking. Very good.
Felcone 19-30 1983 $85

MURRAY, LINDLEY   The Power of Religion on the Mind.
Trenton: Isaac Collins, 1795. Later cloth-backed boards. Signature
"Richard S Hallett ... 1797" on title. Very nice. Felcone 19-31
1983 $45

MURRAY, LINDLEY   Sequel to the New English Reader.
New York, 1806. Calf, good. Reese 13-283 1983 $35

MURRAY, MAELIA M.   Letters from the United States, Cuba,
and Canada. London, John W. Parker, 1856. 2 vols., 8vo, orig.
cloth gilt, canceled library bookplate inside front cover of each
vol., joints cracked, spine ends worn, internally good. First edition.
Ravenstree 97-129 1983 $65

MURRAY, MARISCHAL   Ships and South Africa. Oxford, 1933.
First edition. Imperial 8vo. Orig. cloth. Frontis., 84 plates.
Slightly worn and soiled, very slight staining and foxing of prelimin-
aries. Good. Edwards 1042-140 1983 £95

MURRAY, NICHOLAS   Notes, Historical and Biographical, Concerning Elizabeth Town... Elizabeth Town, 1844. Engraved frontis.
(view). Calf-backed boards. Very good. Felcone 20-123 1983 $85

MURRAY, WILLIAM HENRY HARRISON   Adventures in the Wilderness: or,
Camp Life in the Adirondacks. Boston: Fields, Osgood, & Co.,
1869. Frontis. and illus. Original pictorial cloth gilt, Some
wear to the extremities of the spine. Ads. Jenkins 151-233 1983
$85

MURRY, JOHN MIDDLETON   Cinnamon & Angelica. (Edinburgh):
Richard Cobden-Sanderson, 1920. First edition. Orig. blue wrappers
with paper label. Fine. MacManus 279-3972 1983 $20

MURRY, JOHN MIDDLETON   D. H. Lawrence. Cambridge: Minority
Press, 1930. First edition. Wrappers. Nice. Rota 230-348 1983
£12.50

MURRY, JOHN MIDDLETON   Reminiscences of D.H. Lawrence. N.Y.,
Holt (1933). First American edition, reset and printed in the USA.
8vo, green cloth, good-very good. Houle 21-546 1983 $30

MUSARD, PHILIPPE   Les Chasseurs au Bal. Paris, E.
Troupenas & Co., n.d. (mid-19th century). Engraved title and music.
Plate #T. 406. Pub.'s rubberstamp (faded) on title. Oblong folio,
unbound. Slightly foxed. Salloch 387-154 1983 $30

MUSARD, PHILIPPE   Deux Quadrilles de Contredanses. Paris,
Delahante, n.d. (early 19th century). Lithograph title in decorative
frame, with two dancers. Oblong folio, pate mark #1298. Pub.'s
signature in rubber stamp on title. Salloch 387-153 1983 $40

MUSARUM Anglicanorum Analecta. Tonson and Watts, 1721. 4th edition,
2 vols, 12mo, engraved head and tail pieces, full cont. calf panelled
in blind, slightly differing morocco labels, slight wear. Bookplates.
Small early library labels on spines. An excellent crisp copy.
Deighton 3-244 1983 £48

MUSCHLER, R.   A Manual Flora of Egypt. Berlin, 1912.
2 vols. in 1, 8vo, binder's cloth. Two leaves repaired without
loss of text, paper slightly browned and a few pencil annotations,
but a sound copy of this rare work. Wheldon 160-1752 1983 £40

MUSEO NACIONAL DE ANTROPOLOGIA   El arte indigena de Norte America.
Mexico, 1945. 92 illus. Large 4to. Wrappers. Ars Libri 34-363 1983
$35

MUSEO NACIONAL DE ANTROPOLOGIA   Catalogo de la coleccion de codices.
Mexico, 1964. 139 plates. 4to. Cloth. Ars Libri 34-364 1983 $150

THE MUSES Mercury: or monthly miscellany. London, printed by J.
H. for Andrew Bell, 1707. 4to, somewhat waterstained, uncut in old
wrappers. Pickering & Chatto 19-47 1983 $450

MUSGRAVE, MRS.   Illusions. London: Richard Bentley &
Sons, 1887. First edition. 3 vols. Orig. cloth. Covers a bit stained
and soiled. Inner hinge of vol. one cracked. Very good. MacManus
279-3973 1983 $185

MUSGRAVE, RICHARD   Memoirs of the Different Rebellions
in Ireland. Dublin: Printed by Robert Marchband, for John Milliken,
1801. With the engraved plate and the 9 folding engraved maps,
with the half-title, 4to, cont. rebacked calf. With the Springwood
Park, Kelso label. Fenning 62-260 1983 £85

MUSGRAVE, THOMAS   Castaway on the Auckland Isles.
London: Lockwood & Co., 1866. First edition. 8vo. Cont. half
green calf gilt. Portrait. Vignette, folding map. Slight wear.
Heath 48-586 1983 £75

MUSHET, ROBERT   An Attempt to Explain from Facts the
Effects of the Issues of The Bank of England. London: Baldwin,
Cradock, and Joy, 1826. 1st ed., 8vo, a very good copy. Disbound.
Pickering & Chatto 21-85 1983 $150

THE MUSICAL World. London, 1839. Vols. 11 and 12. Two vols. 8vo,
cl., ex-library, with bookplate and release. Salloch 387-356 1983
$40

LA MUSIQUE des Origines a Nos Jours. Paris, 1946. 800 illus., 7 color
plates, folio, profusely illus. Salloch 387-311 1983 $80

MUSSCHENBROEK, PIETER VAN   Essai de Physique... Samuel
Luchtmans, Leyden, 1739. 2 vols. bound as 1, 4to, with 35 folding
engraved plates; stamp partially erased from first title and cont.
signatures of F. v. Heespen on both titles; cont. calf, gilt
spines, head and foot of spine slightly defective. First edition in
French. Quaritch NS 5-76 1983 $900

MUSSET, ALFRED DE   Ses Plus Beaux Vers. Paris: Editions
Nilsson, n.d. (ca. 1920's). Wraps, slightly worn. With tipped-in
aquarelles printed on tissue and colored by hand, drawn by Robert
Polack. King 46-432 1983 $25

MUSSEY, REUBEN D.   An Oration, Together with an Address to
the Ipswich Light Infantry. Salem: Joshua Cushing, 1807. Stitched.
Uncut. Stain on title. Very good. Felcone 20-121 1983 $20

MY FIRST PUBLICATION. (San Francisco): Book Club of California,
1961. 1st ed., 1 of 475 copies. Orig. linen-backed pictorial
boards, uncut. Portraits of each author by David Martin. Authors
include Dana, Twain... Mint copy. Jenkins 155-1373 1983 $100

MY Lady's Cabinet. Sampson Low, 1873. First edition, containing
81 actual mounted photos. of drawings by Turner, Stanfield, Birket
Foster, Creswick, and others. 4to, orig. blue cloth, gilt, edges
gilt, by Burn & Co., with their ticket, in need of recasing but
a very good copy. The preface signed "J.C." and dated from
Bournemouth. Fenning 61-310 1983 £18.50

MY Lord Bag-O'-Rice. (Tokyo: Hasegawa, 1898). 12mo. Frenchfold.
Crepe-paper book. Colored illus. Fine in pictorial self-wrappers,
Japanese-bound. Bromer 25-357 1983 $60

MYERS, DENYS PETER   Manual of Collections of Treaties...
New York: Burt Franklin, n.d. Cloth. Reprint of the 1922 ed.
Dawson 470-218 1983 $40

MYERS, FRANK   Soldiering in Dakota. Pierre, S.D.,
1936. Orig. printed wraps. Ginsberg 47-289 1983 $25

MYERS, SAMUEL D.   The Permian Basis: Petroleum Empire of
the Southwest. El Paso, 1977. 1st ed., autographed. Slipcased. Mint
in dj. Jenkins 153-573 1983 $100

MYERS, WILLIAM S.   The Story of New Jersey. NY, 1945.
5 vols. Illus. Thick 4to, buckram. Argosy 716-335 1983 $100

MYLAR, ISAAC   Early Days at the Mission San Juan
Bautista. Watsonville (1929). Illus. One of 300 copies. Dust jacket
(a few tape mends), signed by author and compiler. Very good.
Houle 21-1121 1983 $60

MYRDAL, GUNNAR   Finanspolitikens Ekonomiska Verkningar.
Stockholm, Nordstedt & Soner, 1934. 1st ed., 8vo, original orange
printed wrappers. Pickering & Chatto 21-86 1983 $100

MYRDAL, GUNNAR   Konjunktur Och Offentlig Hushallning.
Stockholm, Kooperativa forbundets bokforlag, 1933. 8vo, original
printed wrappers. Pickering & Chatto 21-87 1983 $45

MYRDAL, GUNNAR   Prisbildningsproblemet Och Forander-
Ligheten. Uppsala and Stockholm, Almquist & Wiksells, 1927. 1st ed.,
8vo, uncut in original printed wrappers, edges frayed. Pickering &
Chatto 21-88 1983 $65

MYRDAL, GUNNAR   Vetenskap Och Politik I Nationalekonomien.
Stockholm, Norstedt & Soners, 1930. 1st ed., 8vo, uncut and largely
unopened, original printed wrappers, small library stamps. Pickering
& Chatto 21-89 1983 $100

MYRICK, HERBERT   Cache La Poudre; The Romance of a
Tenderfoot in the Days of Custer. New York: Chicago, Orange Judd
Company, 1905. Bound in fringed, smoked buckskin. Limited to 500
copies. Illustrated by Charles Schreyvogel, Edward W. Deming, and
Henry Fangel. A splendid copy. Rare. Jenkins 151-234 1983 $500

THE MYSTIC Cottager of Chamouny. Philadelphia: Printed by W. W.
Woodward, 1795. 8vo. Full cont. calf. First American edition. Top
of spine slightly chipped. Some dampstaining. Small hole in last few
leaves. Good copy. MacManus 277-85 1983 $50

N

NABOKOV, VLADIMIR   Bend Sinister. NY, (1947). Endpapers lightly offset, edges rubbed, else very good in slightly rubbed and soiled, very good dustwrapper. Quill & Brush 54-966 1983 $100

NABOKOV, VLADIMIR   Laughter in the Dark. Indianapolis: Bobbs-Merrill, (1938). 1st American ed. Orig. cloth, dj. Cloth is lightly spotted and a two-inch piece is wanting from upper spine of dj. Jenkins 155-1417 1983 $65

NABOKOV, VLADIMIR   Lectures on Ulysses. Bloomfield Hills, Michigan: Bruccoli Clark, 1980. Quarto. 1st ed., limited to 500 numbered copies. Orig. cloth, gilt, tissue dj. Mint, as issued. Jenkins 155-1401 1983 $75

NABOKOV, VLADIMIR   Lolita. Paris: The Olympia Press, (1955). 2 vols. 1st ed., 1st issue with 900 franc price on covers. Orig. green printed wrappers. Fine set. Jenkins 155-960 1983 $350

NABOKOV, VLADIMIR   Lolita. Paris: Olympia Press, 1955. 8vo. Wraps. 2 vols. Slight crease on front wrapper of vol. 2, else a vg-fine set. In Our Time 156-587 1983 $350

NABOKOV, VLADIMIR   The Real Life of Sebastian Knight. L, (1945). Fore edges stained, free end papers slightly offset, else very good in stained, chipped, fragile dustwrapper. Quill & Brush 54-972 1983 $60

NABOKOV, VLADIMIR   Rodnaia Zemlia, Sbornik Pervyi. New York, 1920. 1st ed. Orig. printed grey wrappers, uncut. Very fine. Jenkins 155-961 1983 $350

NACOGDOCHES Texas Centennial, 1716-1936. Nacogdoches, Redlands Herald, 1935. Orig. pictorial wrappers. 1st ed. Fine copy. Jenkins 153-618 1983 $25

NADI, ALDO   On Fencing. NY (1943). Photos, cloth, minor wear. King 46-626 1983 $20

NAGEL, CHARLES   A Boy's Civil War Story. St. Louis: Privately printed, 1934. First edition. Jenkins 152-279 1983 $125

NAGEL, CHARLES   Charles Nagel, Speeches and Writings. NY: Putnam's, 1931. 2 vols. Photogravure frontis. in both vols. "Author's Autograph Edition", limited and signed by Nagel. Blue cloth. Fine set. Karmiole 73-61 1983 $30

NAIPAUL, VIDIADHAR SURAJPRASAD   Miguel Street. London, 1959. First edition. Very slightly worn dustwrapper. Very good copy. Gekoski 2-148 1983 £85

NAIRNE, ALEXANDER K.   The Konkan. Bombay, 1875. Half morocco. 8vo. Inscribed "My dear Wife with Alxdr's love. Oct. 1875". Good. Edwards 1044-513 1983 £40

NANCE, R. MORTON   Sailing-Ship Models. London, 1924. Limited edition. 4to. Coloured frontis. and 124 plates (some photogravures), illus. Orig. blue cloth gilt. Slightly worn and soiled. Good. Edwards 1042-141 1983 £140

NANDOR, H. S.   Tibet and Nepal. London, 1905. Map, 75 coloured plates, decorative cloth. 8vo. Good. Edwards 1044-514 1983 £35

NANSEN, FRIDTJOF   Eskimo Life. London, 1893. First edition in English. 8vo. Ex-library; foxed. Scarce. Morrill 290-332 1983 $60

NANSEN, FRIDTJOF   Farthest North. New York, 1897. 1st American ed. With an appendix by Otto Sverdrup. Maps and illus. 2 vols., 8vo, ex-library, lacks front endleaves. Morrill 289-449 1983 $40

NANSEN, FRIDTJOF   In Northern Mists, Arctic Exploration in Early Times. NY 1911. Vol. 2 (of 2). Illus, dec. cloth, blind-stamped name on f.e.p., few sm. snags in front cover, some wear, stamped name on bottom edge. King 46-752 1983 $25

NANSEN, FRIDTJOF   Russia & Peace. London, 1923. First edition. Covers a little sprung. Author's signed autograph presentation inscription to Lord Robert Cecil. Nice. Rota 231-443 1983 £18

NANTUA, SIMON   Histoire d'Albert. Paris, 1862. Oblong 4to. Pictorial title. Notice about Topffer & 40 plates. Red pictorial cloth, gilt. Greer 40-225 1983 £35

NAPHEYS, GEORGE H.   The Transmission of Life. Philadelphia: N.C. Watts, 1880. "New Edition." 19-1/2 cm. Frontis. portrait. Orig. decorated cloth. Very good. With the bookseller's stamp of Barkalow Bros., Cheyenne, W. (yoming) T. (erritory), and the private library stamp of Andrew Jenson. Grunder 6-55 1983 $22.50

NAPIER, C. J.   Defects, Civil and Military, of the Indian Government. London, 1853. Second edition. Half calf by Geton & Mackenzie. Ownership signature of R.A. Trotter. 8vo. Good. Edwards 1044-515 1983 £60

NAPIER, FRANCIS   Notes on Modern Painting at Naples. London: John W. Parker & Son, 1855. 16mo, orig. cloth. Karmiole 76-7 1983 $50

NAPIER, GEORGE G.   The Homes and Haunts of Alfred Lord Tennyson. N.Y.: Macmillan & Co., 1892. First American edition. Orig. decorated cloth. Limited to 75 copies (out of 300 printed). Covers darkened. Fine. MacManus 280-5110 1983 $50

NAPIER, ROBERT W.   John Thomson of Duddingston, Landscape Painter. Oliver and Boyd, 1919. First edition, with 31 plates, 4to, orig. cloth, t.e.g., the headbands rubbed and with some very light marginal foxing, but still a very good copy with the orig. prospectus for the work tipped in. Fenning 61-450 1983 £65

NARES, EDWARD   Think's-I-to-Myself. London, Law and Gilbert, 1811. 2 vols., 8vo, new cloth. First edition. Ravenstree 96-134 1983 $150

NARRATIVE of Mr. John Dodge During His Captivity at Detroit. Cedar Rapids: The Torch Press, 1909. Cloth backed boards. Very good in worn slipcase. Limited to 63 copies. King 46-184 1983 $65

NARRATIVE of Privations and Sufferings of U.S. Officers and Soldiers while Prisoners of War in the Hands of Rebel Authorities. Phila., 1864. Illus., front. pr. wrap. Argosy 716-84 1983 $25

NASATIR, ABRAHAM P.   French Activities in California... Palo Alto, 1945. Orig. cloth in dj. 1st ed. Jenkins 153-380 1983 $55

NASH, C. W.   Vertebrates of Ontario. Toronto, 1908. 8vo, 32 plates and text figures, cloth (trifle used). Wheldon 160-412 1983 £15

NASH, GEORGE   The drama, a treatise on poetry and verse, dramatic composition, dramatic authors, and the effects of dramatic amusements. London: Saunders and Otley, 1839. 8vo, later wrappers, 1st edition. Title-page a bit soiled; small piece torn from the blank inner margin. Rare. Ximenes 64-393 1983 $45

NASH, JOHN   English Garden Flowers. London, 1948. First edition. 12 full-page color plates by Nash. Inscription erased. Top corners bumped. Very good indeed. Jolliffe 26-384 1983 £25

NASH, JOHN   English Garden Flowers. 1948. 12
coloured plates by the author, 4to, boards. Wheldon 160-1991 1983
£12

NASH, JOHN HENRY   The Kasidah. San Francisco: Book
Club of California, 1919. Quarto, marbled boards with vellum back.
Printed by John Henry Nash in an edition of 500 copies. Duschnes
240-169 1983 $75

NASH, JOSEPH   The Mansions of England in Olden Times.
London, 1869. First, Second, Third & Fourth Series. 4 vols. in 2.
Folio. Morocco (rebacked). A.E.G. With 104 chromolithographs carefully reproduced by Samuel Stanseby. Some scuffing to the bindings,
mainly a fine set. In Our Time 156-588 1983 $850

NASH, OGDEN   The Bad Parents' Garden of Verse. NY,
1936. Illus. by Reginal Birch, cover slightly soiled, else very good
in lightly chipped and stained, very good dustwrapper. Quill & Brush
54-975 1983 $50

NASH, OGDEN   Free Wheeling. N.Y., Simon & Schuster,
1931. First edition. Illus. by O'Soglow. Dust jacket (small chips
and rubbing). Good. Houle 22-690 1983 $60

NASH, OGDEN   Happy Days. N.Y., Simon & Schuster,
1933. First edition. Illus. by O. Soglow. Dust jacket (one chip on
spine), else very good. Houle 22-691 1983 $45

NASH, PAUL   Dorset. London, n.d. Wrappers. 4
watercolours by the author reproduced. 12 of the photographs were
taken by the author. Covers slightly creased and worn. A corner of
one page spotted. Very good. Jolliffe 26-387 1983 £35

NASH, WALLIS   Two Years in Oregon. New York, 1892.
Orig. cloth. Illus. O. O. Winter's copy, bearing his signature.
Lacking front free endpaper and flyleaf. Jenkins 153-413 1983 $35

NASHE, THOMAS   Songs from the Dramatists. Norwich,
Kinder at the Walpole Press, 1929. Slim 8vo, woodcut illus., uncut
in parchment boards, some light spotting and original green dustwrappers faded, good. 250 numbered copies. Deighton 3-236 1983 £15

NASMYTH, ALEXANDER   Three Memoirs on the Development and
Structure of the Teeth and Epithelium... London, 1841. 8vo. Orig.
cloth. 9 plates (6 coloured). Second edition. Gurney 90-85 1983
£115

NASMYTH, JAMES   The Moon. John Murray, London, 1874.
4to, with 24 plates, mostly mounted Woodburytypes, and several
woodcut text illus.; inscribed "Thomas Webster...with the best wishes
of J.W.B. Herschel on his 74th Birthday, March 1874" on half title;
orig. cloth gilt, a good copy. Quaritch NS 5-77 1983 $500

NASON, ELIAS   Chapin's Hand-Book of St. Augustine.
St. Augustine, Chapin, 1884. Illus., folded map, woodcuts. Orig.
printed pictorial wraps. First edition. Ginsberg 46-261 1983
$75

NASON, ELIAS   Sir Charles Henry Frankland, Baronet.
Albany, Munsell, 1865. 1st ed., 300 copies printed. 8vo. Fine.
Morrill 286-299 1983 $50

NASSE, HERMANN   Jacques Callot. Leipzig: Klinkhardt
& Biermann, 1919. Second edition. 50 collotype plates with 104
illus. Large 4to. Cloth. Ars Libri 32-76 1983 $65

NATHAN, GEORGE JEAN   Materia Critica. N.Y., Knopf, 1924.
First edition. Dust jacket (a little faded). A fine copy.
Advertising sheet for the American Mercury Monthly. Houle 22-693 1983
$45

NATHAN, MANFRED   The Voortrekkers of South Africa.
(Johannesburg), South Africa: Central News Agency, Ltd., 1937.
With 28 plates. Index. Dust jacket. Karmiole 71-5 1983 $35

NATHAN, ROBERT   There is Another Heaven. Ind., (1929).
Spine slightly faded, else very good in faded and slightly chipped,
good dustwrapper. Quill & Brush 54-978 1983 $35

NATHAN, ROBERT   Winter in April. NY, 1938. Advance
review copy in paperwraps, cover split at gutters and frayed on spine
edges, good, interior very good. Quill & Brush 54-979 1983 $35

NATHAN, ROBERT   The Woodcutters House. Ind., (1927).
Very good in soiled, slightly frayed and chipped, very good dustwrapper. Quill & Brush 54-977 1983 $35

NATIONAL GALLERY OF CANADA.   Jacob Jordaens, 1593-1678. Ottawa,
1968. 5 color plates. 315 illus. Square 4to. Wrappers. Dust
jacket. Ars Libri 32-347 1983 $75

THE NATIONAL Melodies of Scotland. London & NY, J. & F. Tallis,
1849. Folio, cont. cloth, spine repaired. Salloch 387-156 1983
$85

THE NATIONAL Portrait Gallery of Distinguished Americans. Phil.,
1865. 146 steel engraved portraits. 4 vols., 4to, half leather,
ex-library but with no external or internal marks, some rubbing.
Morrill 289-450 1983 $50

A NATION'S Benefactor: Gen'l John A. Sutter. Memorial of His Life
and Public Services... New York: Barnes, 1880. Orig. blue printed
wrappers. 1st ed. Scarce. Fine copy. Jenkins 153-543 1983 $75

NATURAL History of Quadrupeds and Cetaceous Animals. Bungay, 1811.
117 hand-coloured plates, 2 vols., 8vo, modern half leather. Lacks
plates 87, 88, and 120. A few plates slightly soiled and a marginal
tear in plate 30 neatly repaired. Wheldon 160-587 1983 £75

NAU, CLAUDE   The History of Mary Stewart from the
Murder of Riccio until her Flight into England. Edinburgh, 1883.
8vo, orig. cloth gilt, a little soiled. Bickersteth 77-161 1983
£24

NAUBERT, CHRISTIANE BENEDICTE EUGENIE   Herman of Unna: a Series
of Adventures of the Fifteenth Century. Dublin: Printed by
William Porter, 1794. 2 vols, 12mo, contemporary sheep; hinges
cracking, spines chipped. First Dublin edition. Hill 165-89 1983
£60

NAUDE, GABRIEL   News From France or a Description of
the Library of Cardinal Mazarin... Chicago: A.C. McClurg & Co.,
1907. First edition thus. Cloth-backed boards, leather
spine label. Limited to 275 copies printed by Updike at the Merrymount Press. Label chipped. Oak Knoll 49-298 1983 $25

NAUMANN, EMIL   The History of Music. London, (1886).
Five vols. Illus. and facs. Etches portrait plates, frontis. in
color, 8vo, orig. gilt-decorated pictorial cloth, a.e.g. Salloch 387-
361 1983 $80

NAUMANN, J. A.   Naturgeschichte der Vogel Mitteleuropas.
Gera, (1897-1905). Vol. 7, 20 coloured plates, folio, half morocco.
Wheldon 160-819 1983 £70

NAUMANN, J. A.   Naturgeschichte der Vogel Mitteleuropas.
Gera, (1897-1905). Vol. 9, 34 coloured plates, folio, half morocco,
lower corners slightly defective. Wheldon 160-820 1983 £100

NAUMANN, J. A.   Naturgeschichte der Vogel Mitteleuropas.
Gera, (1897-1905). Vol. 10, 29 coloured plates, folio, half morocco
(used). Wheldon 160-821 1983 £100

NAUMANN, J. A.   Naturgeschichte der Vogel Mitteleuropas.
Gera, (1897-1905). Vol. 12, 27 coloured and 3 plain plates, folio,
cloth. Wheldon 160-822 1983 £80

NAUMBURG, E. M. B.   The Birds of Matto Grosso, Brazil.
New York, 1930. 43 text-figures, 17 plates (5 coloured) and 5 maps,
8vo, cloth. Wheldon 160-823 1983 £35

NAVAL Battles of the United States in the Different Wars with
Foreign Nations, from the Commencement of the Revolution to the
Present Time. Boston, 1857. 1st ed. 20 engravings. 8vo. Rubbed.
Morrill 289-451 1983 $30

NAVAL Documents Related to the Quasi-War Between the United States and France. Washington, 1935-1938. Maps and illus. 7 vols., 8vo. Bookplates. In vol. 1, title-page and pp. iv-v, viii-x, xii-xiv are blank. Very fine set. Morrill 289-452 1983 $75

NAYLOR, ISAAC   The Stars and Stripes of America Insulted and the Union Jack of Britain Dragged in the Dust. Phila., 1894. Orig. pictorial printed wraps. First edition. Ginsberg 46-511 1983 $25

NAYLOR, ROBERT   From John o' Groat's to Land's End. Caxton, 1916. First edition, with 27 plates and very many other illus., 4to, orig. cloth, gilt, a very good copy. Label to that effect on front endpaper. Fenning 61-312 1983 £10.50

NEAL, AVON   Early American Stone Sculpture Found in the Burying Grounds of New England. NY: Sweetwater Editions, (1981). Oblong quarto. Illus. Limited to 175 copies. Gilt-stamped calf with blind-embossed gravestone design on front cover. With one matted signed orig. rubbing and two mounted signed orig. photographs. Signed by Neal and Ann Parker. All housed in clamshell box. Bromer 25-261A 1983 $650

NEAL, AVON   Early American Stone Sculpture Found in Burying Grounds of New England. NY: Sweetwater Editions, (1981). Oblong quarto. Illus. Limited to 300 copies. Quarter-calf and pictorially printed boards. With matted signed orig. rubbing. Signed by Neal and Ann Parker. In clamshell box. Bromer 25-261B 1983 $395

NEAL, E.   The Badger. New Naturalist Monograph, 1948. 30 photographs (1 coloured). Wheldon 160-588 1983 £12

NEAL, JOHN   The Battle of Niagara. Baltimore: N.G. Maxwell, 1819. Extra engr. vignette title. 24mo, later leather-backed marbled boards, (last pp. dampstained). Argosy 716-421 1983 $35

NEALE, FREDERICK ARTHUR   Evenings at Antioch. Lon., 1854. Cover edges rubbed and moderately worn, some cover staining, minor interior foxing, good. Quill & Brush 54-1679 1983 $75

NEALE, H. ST. JOHN   Chirurgical Institutes... London: printed by T. Jones, 1804. First edition. 8vo. Cont. red straight-grained morocco, g.e., slightly rubbed. Gurney 90-86 1983 £145

NEALE, J   Good King Wenceslas. Hingham: Village Press, 1904. 12mo. Illus. Limited to 185 copies, of which approx. destroyed in Barker Building fire. Boards slightly rubbed, else fine. Bromer 25-307 1983 $250

NEALE, J.   Seatonian Poems. J. Masters, (1864). Half title. First edition. Orig. dark purple cloth. Jarndyce 30-807 1983 £10.50

NEALE, SAMUEL   Some Account of the Life and Religious Exercises of Mary Neale. Dublin: Printed by John Gough, 1795. 12mo, cont. calf. Fenning 62-262 1983 £24.50

NEALE, SAMUEL   Some Account of the Life and Religious Labours of Samuel Neale. Dublin: Printed by Robert Napper for John Gough, 1805. First edition, 12mo, cont. calf, a fine copy. Fenning 60-294 1983 £24.50

NEALE, W. JOHNSON   The Port Admiral. London: Cochrane & M'Crone, 1833. First edition. 3 vols. Cont. 3/4 morocco & marbled boards, marbled endpapers. Prelims foxed. Good. MacManus 279-3975 1983 $225

NEALE, WALTER   The Sovereignty of the States. Neale, 1910. Orig. cloth. First edition. Ginsberg 46-512 1983 $20

NEANDER, JOHANN A. W.   General History of the Christian Religion and Church. H. G. Bohn, 1853-58. 9 vols. in 10, cr. 8vo, orig. cloth, a very good set. Fenning 60-295 1983 £28.50

NEANDER, MICHAEL   Synopsis. Basle: Johann Operinus, 1555. First edition. Woodcut initials. 4to. Eighteenth century calf, gilt back. From the Pembroke Library. Kraus 164-170 1983 $600

NEATE, CHARLES   Considerations on the Punishment of Death. James Ridgway, 1857. First edition, orig. dull purple cloth. Jarndyce 31-327 1983 £20

NEAVES, CHARLES   Songs and Verses. Blackwood, 1869. 3rd edition, enlarged, 'Extracts from Reviews', half title, 16 pp ads. Orig. dark purple cloth rubbed at head of spine. Jarndyce 30-808 1983 £10.50

NEBELTHAU, JESSIE H.   The Diary of a Circuit Rider. Minneapolis, 1933. First edition in dust jacket. Limited to 500 copies. Frontis. portrait. Jenkins 152-529 1983 $35

NEBRASKA. N.p., (1875). Illus. Orig. printed wraps., back wrapper, worn. First edition. Ginsberg 47-636 1983 $50

NEDHAM, MARCHAMONT   Christianissimus Christianadus. London, Henry Hills for Jonathan Edwin, 1678. 4to, disbound, title and last leaf little soiled. First edition. Ravenstree 97-132 1983 $39

NEDHAM, MARCHAMONT   A Pacquet of Advices and Animadversions sent from London to the Men of Shaftesbury. London, printed in the year 1676. 4to, disbound, title and last page little soiled. First edition. Ravenstree 97-133 1983 $45

NEDZUMI No Yome-Iri. Kobuntha, Tokyo, nd. No. 5. 10 coloured illus. (some double page), each page text within col'd decor. border, col'd pictorial cvrs., bound Japanese style with silk cords on bkstrip, vg. Hodgkins 27-109 1983 £20

NEEDELL, J. H., MRS.   The Story of Philip Methuen. London: William Blackwood & Sons, 1886. First edition. 3 vols. Orig. light-brown decorated cloth. Presentation copy from the publisher with his small blind stamp on the title-page of the first volume. Spines and covers worn, soiled and darkened. Good. MacManus 279-3976 1983 $150

NEELE, HENRY   The Romance of History. 1828. First edition, 3 vols., for Edward Bull. Half dark olive calf, labels, sl. rubbing, otherwise v.g. Jarndyce 30-499 1983 £30

NEESE, GEORGE M.   Three Years in the Confederate Horse Artillery. NY: Neale, 1911. First edition. Spine slightly darkened, covers rubbed. King 46-69 1983 $250

NEHRLING, H.   Die Nordamerikanische Vogelwelt. Milwaukee, 1891. 36 coloured lithographic plates of numerous figures, 4to, cloth. 8 pp. of text are inserted loose. Wheldon 160-824 1983 £75

NEHRU, JAWAHARLAL   Points of View. New York: The John Day Company, (January 1, 1941). First edition. One of 1,000. Advance publication. No copies were offered for sale. Title page printed in red and black. 14 unnumbered pages, tan boards, gilt. Fine in chipped glassine dj. Rare. Bradley 65-141 1983 $85

NEIHARDT, JOHN G.   A Bundle of Myrrh. New York: Outing Publishing Company, 1907. First commercial edition. Decorated boards and cloth. Nice copy. Bradley 66-265 1983 $75

NEIHARDT, JOHN G.   The Lonesome Trail. New York: John Lane Co., 1907. Frontis. by F.E. Schoonover. Orig. pictorial cloth. Light wear. Jenkins 152-281 1983 $45

NEIHARDT, JOHN G.   The Song of the Indian Wars. New York: MacMillan, 1925. First edition. One of 500 signed by the poet. Illustrated in color by Allen True. Pictorial tan boards, blue cloth spine, decorated in blue, yellow, and gold, top edges blue, others uncut. Very fine in publisher's glassine jacket and slipcase. Bradley 65-143 1983 $185

NEIHARDT, JOHN G.   The Song of the Indian Wars. New York, 1925. Cloth-backed pictorial boards, pictorial endpapers. 1st edition. Nice copy. Limited to 500 copies signed by the author. Also a signed presentation by the illustrated, Allen True. Quite scarce. Jenkins 151-238 1983 $125

NEIHARDT, JOHN G.   The Song of the Indian Wars. New York, 1925. Illus. 1st edition. Fine copy. Laid in a typed letter signed by the author. Scarce. Jenkins 151-239 1983 $55

NEIHARDT, JOHN G.   The Song of the Messiah. New York,
1935. 1st edition in dust jacket. Scarce. Jenkins 151-240 1983
$50

NEIL, HENRY   Thrilling Personal Adventures in Mexico.
Chicago, 1914. Profusely illus. with photo-plates and cartoons. Orig.
red gilt pictorial cloth. First edition. Fine. Jenkins 152-282 1983
$55

NEILL, EDWARD D.   The Founders of Maryland as Portrayed
in Manuscripts... Albany, Munsell, 1876. 1st ed. 8vo. Light
dampstains along edges of text. Morrill 287-210 1983 $35

NEILL, J. M. B.   Recollections of Four Years' Service in
the East. Lithograph portrait on India Paper. Half green calf, spine
faded. 8vo. Inscribed on title by Lt. Col. R.A. Trotter. Good.
Edwards 1044-518 1983 £85

NEILL, P   The Fruit, Flower, and Kitchen Garden.
Edinburgh: A. and C. Black, 1838. First separate edition, with
illus., 8vo, orig. cloth, neat repair to inside joints. Fenning
61-313 1983 £21.50

NEILL, P.   Journal of a horticultural tour through
some parts of Flanders, Holland and the north of France. Edinburgh,
1823. 7 plates, 8vo, buckram. Rare. Marginal waterstaining of
plates. Wheldon 160-1992 1983 £55

NELSON, E.   Monographie und Ikonographie der
Orchidaceen-Gattungen Serapias, Aceras, Loroglossum, Barlia. Chernin-
Montreaux, 1968. Atlas of 8 maps, 6 plain and 30 coloured plates,
2 vols., 4to and imp. 4to. Wheldon 160-2049 1983 £94

NELSON, HORATIO   Memoirs of the Life of the Late Lord
Horatio Nelson... Pittsburg, 1813. Foxed, title somewhat worn,
but good. Reese 18-417 1983 $150

NELSON, J. B.   The Sulidae: Gannets and Boobies.
1978. 14 coloured and 18 plain plates, 404 text-figures, 4to, finely
rebound in half morocco. Wheldon 160-825 1983 £50

NELSON, JAMES   An Essay on the Government of Children.
Printed for R. and J. Dodsley: And sold by M. Cooper. 1756. 12mo,
errata leaf, orig. calf, rubbed, worn at top and bottom of spines and
at edges of the covers. Bickersteth 75-66 1983 £55

NELSON, WILLIAM   Check-List of the Issues of the Press of
New Jersey. Paterson, 1899. 100 copies printed. Later cloth. Very
good. Felcone 19-68 1983 $65

NELSON, WILLIAM   Records of the Paterson Fire Association,
1821-1854 With the Laws Relating to the Association. Paterson, 1894.
Illus. Cloth with leather label. First edition. Only 100 copies
were printed. Ginsberg 46-519 1983 $75

NELSON, WILLIAM   Some New Jersey Printers and Printing in
the Eighteenth Century. Worcester, 1911. Printed wrappers. Offprint
from Proceedings of the American Antiquarian Society. Very good.
Felcone 19-69 1983 $50

NELSON, WILLIAM   Some New Jersey Printers and Printing
in the 18th Century. Worcester: Amer. Antiquarian Soc., 1911.
8vo, mod. buckram, pr. wrs. bound in. Argosy 710-338 1983 $25

NELVILLE, ALEXANDER   Alexandri Nevilli Kettvs... Londoni,
Henrici Binnemani, 1582. 8vo, orig. vellum gilt, lightly dust soiled.
Ravenstree 97-134 1983 $185

NEMBHARD, MABEL   Fantasies. George Allen, 1896. 17 full-
page & 11 text illus. Light internal wear. Yellow cloth, worn.
Greer 39-34 1983 £12.75

NEMBHARD, MABEL   Fantasies. George Allen, 1896. First
edition. Illus. by Maud Linley Sambourne, etc. Orig. blue cloth
blocked in gilt and black. T.e.g. Very good. Jarndyce 31-827 1983
£10.50

NEMEROV, HOWARD   The Image and the Law. (NY, 1947).
Good or better in slightly soiled dustwrapper with half inch chip at
top of spine edge. Quill & Brush 54-980 1983 $75

NEMEROV, HOWARD   The Melodramatists. NY, (1949). Signed
on title, near fine in chipped and worn dustwrapper. Quill & Brush 54-
981 1983 $75

NEPOS, CORNELIUS   Excellentium Imperatorum Vitae. Londini,
Ex Officina Jacobi Tonson & Johannis Watts, 1715. 12mo, orig. calf,
joints cracked, foxed, early owner's signature on endleaves.
The first Mattaire edition. Ravenstree 95-78 1983 $33

NEPOS, CORNELIUS   Excellentium Imperatorum Vitae. Glasguae,
Excudebat Andreas Foulis, 1777. 8vo, cont. calf, worn, covers
detached, bookplate. Ravenstree 95-78 1983 $33

NEPOS, CORNELIUS   Excellentium Imperatorum Vitae. Editio
Tertia. Glasquae, Excudebat Andreas Foulis, 1777. 8vo, cont. calf,
worn, covers detached, bookplate. Ravenstree 95-79 1983 $45

NEPOS, CORNELIUS   Excellentium Imperatorum Vitae. Editio
Prima Americana. Novi Eboraci, Gul. A. Davis, E. Duyckinck, 1809.
12mo, orig. sheep, bit worn, front hinge cracked, name on fly, very
early American bookseller's ticket on endpaper. Ravenstree 95-80
1983 $20

NERNST, WALTHER   Experimental and Theoretical Appli-
cations of Thermodynamics to Chemistry. New Haven: Yale University
Press, 1913. 8vo. Orig. blue cloth. Text figures and tables.
A little rubbed, otherwise a very good copy. Zeitlin 264-337 1983
$40

NERVAL, GERARD DE
Please turn to
GERARD DE NERVAL

NESBIT, EDITH   The Hurdy Gurdy. E. Nister, 1895. 4to.
Colour frontis. Pictorial title. 12 colour plates & other illus.
Colour pictorial boards, corners bumped. Greer 39-89 1983 £28

NESBIT, EDITH   The Phoenix and the Carpet. Geo. Newnes,
n.d. (1904). First edition. Colour frontis. 7 full-page & 61 text
illus. Blue decorated cloth, gilt. Greer 39-86 1983 £45

NESBIT, EDITH   The Rainbow And The Rose. London:
Longmans, Green & Co., 1905. First edition. Orig. decorated cloth.
Presentation copy inscribed "To Harold Monro from E. Nesbit who wrote
these verses, November 1913." Spine ends slightly frayed. Covers worn
with a tear to the top front margin. Former owner's inscription.
Good. MacManus 279-3978 1983 $45

NESBIT, JOHN COLLIS   On Agriculture Chemistry and the
Nature and Properties of Peruvian Guano. London: Longmans, (1856).
First edition. 8vo. Orig. stamped cloth. With tail-piece
vignettes. Ads. Small defect to top of spine. Zeitlin 264-341
1983 $40

NESS, ZENOBIA B.   Iowa Artists of the First Hundred
Years. N.p., 1939. Illus. Orig. cloth. First edition. Ginsberg
47-375 1983 $25

NESSEL, MATHIAS   A Treatise concerning the Medicinal
Spaw Waters. London, 1714. Second edition. 8vo. Disbound. Title
lightly dustsoiled. Light dampstains. Small copy. Gurney 90-84
1983 £25

NETTLESHIP, RICHARD L.   Lectures on the Republic of Plato.
London, 1920. 8vo, cloth. Salloch 385-688 1983 $30

NEU MAYR, ANTONIO   Vita ed opere di Alberto Durer. N.P.,
n.d.: Venezia, 1823. 4to. Decorated boards with leather labels.
Ex libris Heinrich Rottinger. Ars Libri 32-184 1983 $125

NEUBER, HANS   Ludwig Juppe von Marburg. Marburg:
N.G. Elwertsche Verlagsbuchhandlung, 1915. 20 plates with 44
illus. 4to. Wrappers. Ars Libri 32-349 1983 $85

NEUBURGER, MAX   Geschichte der Medizin. Stuttgart 1906,
1908, 1911. Two volumes. Volume 1 and volume 2, part 1 bound together.
Volume 2, part 2 in original printed wrappers. Two inch by one-half
inch piece torn from title page and dedication leaf of volume 1,
else very good. Fye H-3-412 1983 $150

NEUHAUS, EUGEN   The Art of the Exposition. San
Francisco, (1915). Illus, mounted photo. plates, 8vo, stamped
boards. 2nd ed., rev. Argosy 710-152 1983 $35

NEUHAUS, EUGEN   The Art of the Exposition.
San Francisco (1915). Tipped-in plates, boards. 2nd edition
revised. Very good. King 46-93 1983 $20

NEUKOMM, SIGISMOND   David. Boston, Handel & Haydn Society,
1835. Oblong 4to, 1/2 cloth with paper label. Salloch 387-157 1983
$110

NEUMANN, C. G.   Pathologische Untersuchungen als
Regulative des Heilverfahrens. Berlin, 1841-2. First edition. 8vo.
2 vols. in one. Old boards. With numerous library stamps. Gurney
JJ-279 1983 £15

NEUMANN, CARL   Aus der Werkstatt Rembrandts. Heidelberg: Carl Winter, 1918. 1 folding plate. 57 text illus. 4to.
Boards. Ars Libri 32-563 1983 $85

NEVADA. LAWS.   Statutes of the State of Nevada Passed
at the Fourth Session of the Legislature, 1869. Carson City, 1869.
Full calf. First edition. Ginsberg 47-658 1983 $100

NEVADA (TERRITORY) LAWS.   Laws of the Territory of Nevada Passed
at the First Regular Session of the Legislative Assembly... November,
1861. San Francisco, 1862. Later boards, very good. Reese 19-398
1983 $375

NEVADA (TERRITORY) LAWS.   Laws of the Territory of Nevada Passed
at the First Regular Session of the Legislative Assembly Begun the
First of October and Ended on the Twenty Ninth Day of November, 1861,
at Carson City. San Francisco, 1862. Half morocco. First ed. Ginsberg 47-649 1983 $175

NEVILE, THOMAS   Imitations of Horace. London: for
W. Thurlbourn, etc., 1758. First edition. 8vo. Cont. calf. Minor
rubbing. A fine copy. Ximenes 63-374 1983 $125

NEVILL, RALPH   Old French Line Engravings. London:
1924. First edition. Illus. Blue cloth. 1/1250. Fine in tissue
jacket. Boxed. Bradley 66-403 1983 $135

NEVISON, HENRY W.   Neighbours of Ours. Bristol: (1895).
First edition. Dark plum cloth, cockney sketches. End papers browned,
inner hinges started, otherwise very good. Bradley 66-267 1983 $25

NEW Bedford and Vicinity, 1938. New Bedford: Reynolds Printing,
(1938). Oblong 12mo, pr. wrs. Argosy 710-296 1983 $30

A NEW Discovery of Hidden Secrets... London: for John Wright,
1645. Large 4to. Half cloth, marbled sides. Each leaf has been
neatly repaired at margins and laminated. Heath 48-144 1983 £95

THE NEW Hampshire Directory and Gazetteer for 1892. Boston, 1892.
1st issue. 8vo, orig. boards, cloth back. Morrill 288-335 1983
$22.50

NEW JERSEY. LAWS.   Acts of the General Assembly of the State
of New Jersey, from the Establishment of the Present Government, and
Declaration of Independence, to ... December, 1783. Trenton: Isaac
Collins, 1784. Calf-backed boards (worn, hinges broken). Contains
the scarce variant titlepage. Very good. Felcone 19-35 1983 $325

NEW JERSEY. LAWS.   Laws of the State of New Jersey, Revised
and Published under the Authority of the Legislature. New Brunswick:
Abraham Blauvelt, 1800. Large folio. Full calf. Woodcut of the
state seal on titlepage is by Peter Rushton Maverick. Very good.
Felcone 19-36 1983 $200

NEW JERSEY. LAWS.   Laws of the State of New Jersey; Revised
and Published, under the Authority of the Legislature. Newark:
Matthias Day, 1800. Quarto. Full calf. Very good. Felcone 19-37
1983 $200

NEW JERSEY. LAWS.   Acts of the Twenty-Fifth General Assembly
of the State of New Jersey. Trenton: Sherman, Mershon & Thomas, 1800.
Stitched. Small tape repair to last leaf. Uncut. Very good. Felcone
19-38 1983 $40

NEW MEXICO (TERRITORY) LAWS.   Laws of the Territory of New Mexico
Passed by the Legislative Assembly. Santa Fe: Santa Fe Weekly
Gazette Office, 1858. First ed., text in English and Spanish on
alternate pages. Later brown cloth. Pennsylvania State Library
duplicate, with their identification stamps on second title. Fine.
Jenkins 152-290 1983 $350

NEW MEXICO (TERRITORY) LAWS.   Laws of the Territory of New
Mexico. Santa Fe, 1862. Later buckram, very good. Reese 19-400 1983
$450

NEW ORLEANS BOARD OF PORT COMMISSIONERS   Facts about the Port of
New Orleans...Compiled by the Board of Port Commissioners. New
Orleans, (1912). 1st ed. Pict. wrapper. 20 page photograph
section. Jenkins 151-188 1983 $65

NEW Orleans City Guide. Boston, 1938. 1st ed. Fldg. and end maps,
illus., backstrip faded. Very scarce. Clark 741-6 1983 $28.50

THE NEW Pilgrim's Progress. London: W. Wright, 1820. First
edition. 8vo. Disbound. 15 woodcut illus. Scarce. Ximenes 63-
505 1983 $45

THE NEW Pilgrim's Progress. W. Wright, 1820. First edition, woodcuts, some browning, rebound in marbled boards. Jarndyce 30-621
1983 £15

NEW Puss in Boots. Dean & Son, nd (ca. 1850s). Transforming pic.
6 coloured pages with transforming flaps, 3pp adverts. rear. Beige
col. pictorial bds., rebacked, hinges of text strengthened & carefully
repaired, scarce, vg. Hodgkins 27-204 1983 £110

THE NEW-YORK Business Directory for 1844 & 1845. New York, (1844).
Leather-backed printed boards. Hinges breaking. Felcone 22-165
1983 $100

NEW YORK HISTORICAL SOCIETY. Muster and Pay Rolls of the War of the
Revolution. 1775-1783. NY, 1914-1915. 2 vols. Lower left corner
dampstained, vol. 1 unopened pp. Argosy 710-455 1983 $50

NEW Zealand Ferns. New Zealand, n.d. (ca. 1900). Half morocco.
Binding rubbed. Morrill 288-363 1983 $42.50

NEWBERRY, JOHN   The Newtonian System of Philosophy.
Philadelphia, 1808. 2nd American ed. Illus. with copper plates and
cuts. 12mo, contemporary calf, leather label. Front hinge slightly
cracked. Morrill 286-665 1983 $100

NEWBIGGING, T.   The Scottish Jacobites. London, 1899.
Frontis. map, 5 photogravure plates, 3 maps. Sm. 8vo. Orig. cloth.
Very slightly worn and soiled. T.e.g., other uncut. Inscription on
endpaper. Good. Edwards 1042-440 1983 £12

NEWBOLT, FRANCIS   The Enchanted Wood. London: Philip
Allan & Co., 1925. First edition. Orig. decorated, cloth-backed
boards. Presentation copy to Anthony Hope, dated March, 1928. Bookplate of a later owner. All edges worn and faded. Spine label chipped.
MacManus 279-2753 1983 $45

NEWBOLT, HENRY   Aladore. Edinburgh and London, 1914.
First edition. Head of spine creased and corners worn. Presentation
copy to C.L. Fraser, dated April, 1918. Very good. Rota 230-444
1983 £15

NEWBOLT, HENRY   A Fair Death. London: Simpkin, (ca.
1881). First edition. 12mo. Orig. wrappers. Mint. MacManus 279-
3979 1983 $100

NEWBOLT, HENRY   The Idea of an English Association.
(London): The English Association, 1928. First edition. Orig. printed
wrappers. In a cloth folder with the Esher bookplate. Fine. MacManus
279-3980 1983 $35

NEWBOLT, HENRY   The Island Race. London: Elkin Mathews,
1898. First edition. Orig. cloth-backed boards. On of 65 large paper
copies. Covers a bit stained. MacManus 279-3981 1983 $50

NEWBOLT, HENRY   The Linnet's Nest. N.Y.: William Edwin
Rudge, 1927. First American edition, copyright issue. Orig. wrappers.
Limited to 27 copies printed. Mint. MacManus 279-3982 1983 $125

NEWBY, P. H.   The Snow Pasture. London, 1949. First
edition. Chipped and slightly torn dustwrapper. Very good. Jolliffe
26-388 1983 £18

NEWCOMB, HERVEY   The Wyandot Chief. Boston: Massachusetts
Sabbath School Society, 1835. Frontis. Ex-library. Orig. cloth worn.
Jenkins 152-535 1983 $45

NEWCOMB, MARY A.   Four Years of Personal Reminiscences
of the War. Chicago: H.S. Mills & Co., 1893. First edition.
Portrait frontispiece, pictorial brown cloth. Very good. Bradley
64-40 1983 $25

NEWCOMB, PEARSON   The Alamo City. San Antonio, 1926.
Illus. 1st ed. Jenkins 153-591 1983 $35

NEWCOMB, THOMAS   The Woman of Taste. London: Printed
for J. Batley...MDCCXXXIII. Folio, last leaf slightly worn and with
a tear, though no loss of text, disbound. First edition. Quaritch
NS 7-90 1983 $175

NEWCOMB, THOMAS   The Woman of Taste... Dublin: reprinted
by James Hoey, 1733. First Dublin edition. 12mo. Modern quarter
calf. Heath 48-374 1983 £75

NEWELL, FREDERICK HAYNES   Irrigation in the United States. N.Y.:
Thomas Y. Crowell, (1902). 62 plates. Page of ads. Cloth, a little
wear. Dawson 471-211 1983 $20

NEWELL, PETER   The Rocket Book. New York, (October,
1912). 1st ed. Colored illus. by author. Square 8vo, orig. pic.
front cover. Morrill 288-365 1983 $65

NEWELL, R. H.   Versatilities. Boston & New York, 1871.
First edition. Orig. cloth, gilt. Bookplate removed but a very good
copy. Jenkins 155-966 1983 $20

NEWHALL, JOHN B.   Sketches of Iowa. N.Y., 1841. Illus.,
folded map. Orig. cloth. First edition. Ginsberg 47-376 1983
$300

NEWHALL, JOHN B.   Sketches of Iowa, or the Emigrant's
Guide... New York, 1841. Folding map, separated at one fold,
otherwise sound. Cloth, very good. Reese 19-401 1983 $300

NEWLANDS, JOHN ALEXANDER REINA   On the Discovery of the Periodic
Law... London: E. & F.N. Spon, 1884. 8vo. Orig. cloth. 2 folding
tables, ads. Presentation copy from the author. Portion of backstrip detached. Zeitlin 264-342 1983 $160

NEWLANDS, JOHN ALEXANDER REINA   On the Discovery of the Periodic
Law... London, 1884. First edition. 8vo. Orig. cloth. 2 folding
tables, 15 pages of adv. Library stamps (crossed out) and shelf mark
on title. Gurney 90-87 1983 £65

NEWMAN, EDWARD   An Illustrated Natural History of
British Moths. London: W. Tweedie, 1869. 730 wood-engraved illus.,
imperial 8vo, half green morocco gilt, gilt edges. K Books 307-133
1983 £37

NEWMAN, HENRY S.   Days of Grace in India. Lon., (n.d.).
Signed and dated (1882) by author, illus., fold-out map, spine edges
frayed and slightly torn along spine gutter, very good, inscription.
Quill & Brush 54-1678 1983 $35

NEWMAN, JOHN B.   Texas and Mexico in 1846. New York: J.K.
Wellman, 1846. First edition. Folding lithographed map, with Texas
outlined in color and a large red, white and blue American flag extending from the Red River to Point Isabel. Orig. yellow printed wrappers,
sewn. Tall, untrimmed copy. Very fine. Jenkins 152-298 1983 $1,000

NEWMAN, JOHN HENRY   Apologia Pro Vita Sua. London: Longmans,
1864. First edition. Orig. cloth. Covers a little faded and worn.
With John Lowe bookplate. In a half morocco folding box. MacManus
279-3984 1983 $450

NEWMAN, JOHN HENRY   Apologia Pro Vita Sua. London, Longman
et al., 1864. 8vo, orig. cloth recased and spine ends restored with
new end-papers. Name and number on title, few gatherings little
sprung and slightly frayed, but passable copy of the first edition
complete with the Appendix, Notes and Postscriptum. Ravenstree 96-
135 1983 $189

NEWMAN, JOHN HENRY   Apologia Pro Vita Sua. London: Longman,
Green, Longman, Roberts, & Green, 1864. First edition. Orig. cloth.
Spine chipped at extremities. Rubbed along hinges. Front inner hinge
cracked. Good. MacManus 279-3986 1983 $75

NEWMAN, JOHN HENRY   The Arians of the Fourth Century. London
& Oxford, 1843 & 1844. First editions. 10 vols. Uniformly bound in
full cont. calf, gilt spines, marbled endpapers. Bookplates. Some
marginal dampstaining. MacManus 279-3987 1983 $500

NEWMAN, JOHN HENRY   Discussions and Arguments on Various
Subjects. London, Basil Montagu Pickering, 1872. 8vo, orig. cloth,
slightly worn, faded corners scraped, name on end-paper. First
edition. Ravenstree 97-137 1983 $45

NEWMAN, JOHN HENRY   An Essay on the Development of Christian
Doctrine. London: James Toovey, 1845. First edition. Rebound in
3/4 morocco & cloth. Extensive marginal annotations in a cont. hand.
Some foxing. MacManus 279-3988 1983 $75

NEWMAN, JOHN HENRY   A Letter Addressed to...the Duke of
Norfolk on Occasion of Mr. Gladstone's recent Expostulation. B.M.
Pickering, 1875. First edition, 8vo, wrapper. Fenning 60-296 1983
£28.50

NEWMAN, JOHN HENRY   A Letter Addressed to His Grace The Duke
of Norfolk. London: B.M. Pickering, 1875. First edition. Orig.
printed wrappers, (spine and top edge taped). Unopened. MacManus
279-3989 1983 $35

NEWMAN, JOHN HENRY   Loss and Gain. London, Burns, 1848.
8vo, bound without ad leaf at end in cont. half calf, neat
ownership inscription on title, blank flyleaf with a note neatly
attached. First edition. Very rare. Ravenstree 96-135 1983 $290

NEWMAN, JOHN HENRY   Loss and Gain. James Burns, 1848.
First edition. 8vo, lacks final advert. leaf. Cont. half morocco.
Occasional slight foxing. Hannas 69-150 1983 £75

NEWMAN, JOHN HENRY   Miscellanies from the Oxford sermons
and other writings. London: Strahan, 1870. First edition. 8vo.
Orig. dark green cloth. Covers a bit soiled. Ximenes 63-583
1983 $45

NEWMAN, JOHN HENRY   Mr. Kingsley and Dr. Newman. London:
Longman, Green, Longman, Roberts, & Green, 1864. First edition. Cont.
white calf & marbled boards. Morocco labels on spine. Bookplates of
Edward C. Lowe, D.D. and E. Hubert Lichfield on front endpapers. A few
pencil annotations in margins. Covers dust-soiled. MacManus 279-3990
1083 $75

NEWMAN, JOHN HENRY   Selection from the First Four Volumes of
Parochial Sermons. London, printed for J.G.F. & J. Rivington, 1841.
8vo, orig. cloth worn, joints and spine ends frayed, orig. printed
paper spine label very age darkened and chipped. First edition.
Ravenstree 97-139 1983 $22.50

NEWMAN, JOHN HENRY   Sermons Preached on Various Occasions.
London, Burns and Lambert, 1857. 8vo, orig. cloth, bit faded and
worn, cancel title mounted on orig. stub, presentation copy inscribed
"From the author" on fly-leaf. First edition. Ravenstree 97-140
1983 $52.50

NEWMAN, JOHN HENRY   Verses on Various Occasions. Burnes, Oates, & Co., 1868. 8vo, orig. cloth, inner joints a little weak. First edition. Bickersteth 77-233 1983 £36

NEWMAN, JOHN HENRY   Verses on Various Occasions. London: Burns, Oates, & Co., 1868. Orig. cloth. First edition, second issue, paginated at 368pp. Cloth very slightly soiled. Reese 20-718 1983 $25

NEWMAN, JOHN HENRY   Verses on Various Occasions. Burns, Oates & Co., 1868. First edition, half title. Leading inner hinge poorly repaired. Orig. brown cloth, a little rubbed. Inscribed presentation copy from the author, Sept. 2, 1869. Jarndyce 30-809 1983 £15

NEWMAN, JOHN HENRY   Verses on various occasions. London: Burns, Oates, 1868. Second edition. 8vo. Orig. green cloth. Fine copy. Ximenes 63-454 1983 $50

NEWMAN, JOHN P.   The Thrones and Palaces of Babylon and Nineveh. N.Y., 1876. Numerous illus. Gilt-decorated cloth. Ink inscription. Covers heavily worn and slightly stained. King 45-547 1983 $45

NEWMAN, TOM   Advanced Billiards. London, 1924. Photos. Charts. Cloth. Index. Minor spotting on rear cover. Some soil. Good. King 45-495 1983 $35

NEWPORT, MAURICE   Seneniss. Londini. Typis Neucomianis, 1669. 8vo, wormhole at edge of lower margin of four leaves in the middle of the book, cont. calf. Bickersteth 75-68 1983 £65

NEWSHOLME, ARTHUR   Evolution of Preventive Medicine. Baltimore, 1927. First edition. 6 ports. Argosy 713-400 1983 $35

NEWSON, T. M.   Pen Pictures of St. Paul, Minnesota... St. Paul, Minn., privately published by author, 1886. Vol. 1 (all pub.). Frontispiece portrait. Clark 741-349 1983 $27.50

NEWSON, T. M.   Thrilling Scenes Among the Indians. Chicago, (1890). Illus. Orig. cloth. Clark 741-214 1983 $35

NEWSON, WILLIAM MONYPENY   Whitetailed Deer. New York, 1926. First edition. Illustrated from photographs and drawings. 8vo. Morrill 290-377 1983 $20

NEWTON, ALFRED   A Dictionary of Birds. London 1896. First ed. Cloth, uncut, bookplate, hinges loose, covers scuffed. King 46-523 1983 $65

NEWTON, ALFRED EDWARD   Christmas Greetings from Mr. and Mrs. A. Edward Newton. N.p., privately printed, 1937. First edition. Two pages with a quote from Charles Lamb and a b/w drawing by C.E. Brock. Stiff printed blue wraps. Fine. Houle 21-660 1983 $25

NEWTON, ALFRED EDWARD   Derby Day and Other Adventures. B, 1934. Limited to 1129 numbered and signed copies, fine in chipped glassine in near fine slipcase, with facsimile of Charlotte Bronte's story. Quill & Brush 54-985 1983 $100

NEWTON, ALFRED EDWARD   Derby Days and Other Adventures. Boston, 1934. 8vo, cloth-backed boards, slipcase. Illus., including facs. of the unpublished novelette, "A Leaf from an Unopened Volume", by Charlotte Bronte. Bookplate, news-clipping pasted in. One of 1129 copies signed by the author. Fine. Perata 28-115 1983 $75

NEWTON, ALFRED EDWARD   Derby Day and Other Adventures. B, 1934. Limited to 1129 numbered and signed copies, spine very lightly soiled, else fine in splitting slipcase, with facsimile of Charlotte Brontes' story. Quill & Brush 54-986 1983 $75

NEWTON, ALFRED EDWARD   Doctor Johnson A Play. Boston, Atlantic Monthly Press (but actually Daniel Berkeley Updike, the Merrymount Press), 1923. Large 8vo, orig. quarter cloth, boards, bookplate, fine partly unopened copy. First edition. Ravenstree 97-143 1983 $21

NEWTON, ALFRED EDWARD   Doctor Johnson: A Play. B, 1923. One of 585 numbered, signed copies on hand-made paper, edges slightly rubbed, else fine. Quill & Brush 54-982 1983 $75

NEWTON, ALFRED EDWARD   End Papers. B, 1933. Limited to 1351 numbered and signed copies, facsimile of Lamb's "Dream Children" in rear pocket, spine slightly soiled, else fine in sightly soiled, slightly split slipcase. Quill & Brush 54-984 1983 $80

NEWTON, ALFRED EDWARD   End Papers. B, 1933. Limited, signed edition, missing facsimile in rear pocket, else fine in splitting slipcase, bookplate. Quill & Brush 54-983 1983 $60

NEWTON, ALFRED EDWARD   George Dyer. Privately printed, "Oak Knoll," 1938. First edition. Port. pr. blue wrs. Laid in: printed enclosure on orange paper concerning Mr. Newton's condition, and his wishes for the year 1939. Fine. Argosy 714-540 1983 $20

NEWTON, ALFRED EDWARD   The Greatest Book in the World. London, (1926). Numerous photos. Index. Half calf. Marbled boards and endpapers, raised bands, leather labels. T.e.g., by Sangorski & Sutcliffe, London. Minor cover staining and wear. King 45-293 1983 $35

NEWTON, ALFRED EDWARD   I Want! I want! N.p., printed for the friends of A.E.N. Christmas, 1932. First edition. Presentation copy. Fine. Argosy 714-541 1983 $25

NEWTON, ALFRED EDWARD   John Mytton. Privately Printed for friends of the Author, (Daylesford, Pa.), Christmas, 1924. First edition. Wrappers. Author's initialled autograph presentation inscription to F.V. Morley. Very nice. Rota 231-445 1983 £25

NEWTON, ALFRED EDWARD   A Johnson Bookplate. (Daylesford), 1909. First edition. With Newton's Johnson bookplate on Japan vellum. Stiff printed blue wraps., stitched. Very good. A nine page booklet on the origins of the Newton "Johnson" bookplate. With the orig. mailing envelope. Houle 21-661 1983 $75

NEWTON, ALFRED EDWARD   A Magnificent Farce and Other Diversions of a Book Collector. Boston, 1922. First edition, fourth impression. Illus. 3/4 green morocco, t.e.g. Very good. Houle 21-662 1983 $45

NEWTON, ALFRED EDWARD   Mr. Strahan's Dinner Party. San Francisco: Printed for the Book club of California by John Henry Nash, 1930. First edition. Folio. Cloth-backed boards, paper spine label. Limited to 350 numbered and signed copies. Loosely inserted is a letter of inquiry to Nash, and a T.l.s. letter from Nash in response. With paper dust jacket. Oak Knoll 48-304 1983 $250

NEWTON, ALFRED EDWARD   Pope, Poetry and Portrait. Oak Knoll: Privately printed, 1936. 12mo, pr. blue wrs. First edition. Argosy 714-543 1983 $20

NEWTON, ALFRED EDWARD   This Book-Collecting Game. Boston: 1928. First edition. Frontis. in color, numerous illus. Decorated boards. Fine in orig. slipcase. 1/990 large paper copies signed by Newton. Bradley 66-50 1983 $75

NEWTON, ALFRED EDWARD   Thomas Hardy. (Phila.) Privately printed, 1929. Illus. Thin 4to, ltd. first edition. One of 950 copies. With a four-line presentation. Fine. Argosy 714-881 1983 $75

NEWTON, ALFRED EDWARD   A Thomas Hardy Memorial. Oak Knoll, privately printed, 1931. First edition. 12mo, blue wrs. Presentation copy. Argosy 714-544 1983 $30

NEWTON, ALFRED EDWARD   The Trollope Society. Phila., 1934. First edition. 16mo, pr. wrs. Fine, in orig. mailing envelope. Argosy 714-545 1983 $20

NEWTON, C. T.   Travels and Discoveries in the Levant. L, 1865. 2 vols., 14 plates and maps, front fly removed from vol. 1, edges rubbed, very good, owner's name. Quill & Brush 54-1690 1983 $175

NEWTON, EPHRAIM H.   The History of the Town of Marlborough, Windham County, Vermont. Montpelier, 1930. Ed. limited to 500 copies. Illus. 8vo. Morrill 286-494 1983 $25

NEWTON, ISAAC   Chronology of Ancient Kingdoms
Amended. London: Printed for J. Tonson, 1728. Large 8vo. Rebound
in leather, boards. 1st ed. With 3 folding plates. A fine copy.
In Our Time 156-594 1983 $350

NEWTON, ISAAC   The Chronology of Ancient Kingdoms
Amended. London: J. Tonson, 1728. Three folding plates. Cont.
calf (rebacked, hinges cracking). Armorial bookplate. First
edition. Felcone 21-84 1983 $150

NEWTON, ISAAC   Opticks. For Sam. Smith and Benj.
Walford, London, 1704. First edition, first issue. 4to, title
printed in red and black, with 19 folding engraved plates; light
stain in upper inner margins of first 10 leaves, cont. panelled
calf, rebacked and corners repaired. A good clean copy. Quaritch
NS 5-79 1983 $9000

NEWTON, ISAAC   Optices Libri Tres: accedunt ejusdem
Lectiones Opticae... Padua: Seminarii, 1749. 4to. Folding
engraved plates, half title. Cont. calf. Small repair at foot
of spine, small library stamps, but very clean. Heath 48-518
1983 £250

NEWTON, ISAAC   Philosophiae Naturalis Principia Mathe-
matica. Cambridge, 1713. Second edition. 4to. Old calf, rebacked
and retooled. Folding plate. Some slight foxing including title;
plate and 3 leaves of text very foxed. Good copy. Gurney 90-88
1983 £800

NEWTON, ISAAC   A Treatise of the System of the World.
For F. Fayram, London, 1728. 8vo, with 2 engraved plates; cont.
panelled calf, rebacked. First edition in English. Quaritch NS 5-
81 1983 $1,500

NEWTON, JOHN   The Art of Natural Arithmetick...
London: printed by E.T. and R.H. and are to be sold by Rob. Walton,
(1671). First edition. 8vo. Modern red morocco, inner dentelles,
g.e. Kraus 164-171 1983 $950

NEWTON, JOHN   An Authentic Narrative of Some Remarke-
able and Interesting Particulars in the Life of... London: for J.
Johnson, 1799. 9th edition, 12mo, cont. calf. K Books 301-128 1983
£30

NEWTON, JOHN   Olney Poems. Burlington: Isaac Neale,
1795. 3 books. Paper-covered boards (worn, spine glue-covered).
Endsheets lacking. Very good. Felcone 19-41 1983 $45

NEWTON, R. B.   Systematic List of the F. E. Edwards
Collection of British Oligocene and Eocene Mollusca. British
Museum, 1891. 8vo, cloth (trifle worn). Wheldon 160-1451 1983 £18

NEWTON, THOMAS   Dissertations on the Prophecies. Elizabeth Town: Shepard Kollock for Robert Hodge, 1787. 2 vols. Full
calf. One spine numeral label wanting. Very good. Felcone 19-42
1983 $65

THE NEWTON Kansan Fiftieth Anniversary Number. Newton, 1922. Illus.
Orig. pictorial wrappers. Some chipping. Folio. Jenkins 153-301
1983 $40

NEWTON-ROBINSON, CHARLES   The Viol of Love and Other Poems. London:
John Lane, 1895. First edition. Orig. decorated cloth. Covers and
ornaments designed by Housman. Presentation copy. Spine a bit rubbed.
Very good. MacManus 279-2796 1983 $65

NEWTON-ROBINSON, CHARLES   The Viol of Love. John Lane, 1895. Decorated title in red. 2 text decorations. Green decorated cloth, gilt.
Edition limited to 350 copies. Greer 40-113 1983 £25

NIBLEY, PRESTON   Brigham Young. Salt Lake City, 1937.
Portrait. Ink inscription, else a very good to fine copy. Reese
19-388 1983 $35

NICCO, GUISTA   Jacopo della Quercia. Firenze:
Bemporad, 1934. 47 plates with 64 illus. Small 4to. Wrappers.
Slightly worn. Slight marginal waterstaining of plates. Ars
Libri 33-294 1983 $45

NICCOLO Marini, or, The Mystery Solved. Parker Son & Bourn, 1862.
First edition, 2 vols. Half title, 8 pp ads. Orig. maroon cloth,
sl. marking. Jarndyce 31-412 1983 £85

NICHOLAS, FRANCIS C.   Around the Carribbean and Across
Panama. Boston, Caldwell, (1903). First edition. Frontis. and 39
plates and maps. Fine trade cloth binding, the upper 1/3 red cloth,
the lower 2/3 grey cloth, the red stamped in gilt, the grey stamped
in blue, brown, yellow, and gilt with decorative symbols and designs,
t.e.g., uncut. Very good - fine. Houle 22-695 1983 $85

NICHOLLS, FRANK   Compendium Anatomico-Oeconomicum ea
omnia complectens... London: John Clarke, 1736. Third edition.
4to. Cont. calf. Interleaved copy, the first twelve leaves having
pressed flowers mounted, with descriptions in an old hand. Gurney
90-89 1983 £90

NICHOLLS, WILLIAM   A Conference with a Theist. Printed by
T.W., 1698. With a folding engraved plate, including the preliminary
leaf A1 blank, 2 parts in 1 vol., 8vo, cont. unlettered panelled calf,
spine worn but sound, a very good copy. Fenning 60-297 1983 £45

NICHOLLS, WILLIAM J.   The Story of American Coals.
Philadelphia, 1904. Cloth, fine. Reese 19-151 1983 $50

NICHOLS, BEVERLEY   Are they the Same at Home. N.Y.,
Doran, (1927). First edition. Dust jacket, a little sunned, but a
fresh copy with the paper labels bright. Houle 21-103 1983 $45

NICHOLS, BEVERLEY   A Book of Old Ballads. Hutchinson, 1934.
1st edn. 16 colour plates & many b&w head & tail pieces, illus. by
H.M. Brock. Lt. brown cloth, uncut (corners bruised, gilt dull, insc.
fr. ep. & some of head & tail pieces nicely coloured in by hand), v.g.
Hodgkins 27-478 1983 £15

NICHOLS, JEANETTE P.   Alaska a History of Its Administration,
Exploitation, and Industrial Development During Its First Half Century
Under the Rule of the United States. Cleveland: Arthur H. Clark,
1924. Maps and portraits. Jenkins 153-3 1983 $75

NICHOLS, JOHN   Biographical Anecdotes of William
Hogarth... London: by and for J. Nichols, 1782. Second edition,
enlarged and corrected. 8vo. Early 19th Century half calf.
Engraved half title (in duplicate). Slight wear. Very scarce.
Heath 48-596 1983 £125

NICHOLS, ROBERT   Aurelia and Other Poems. London:
Chatto & Windus, 1920. Cloth and boards. First edition. Engraved
frontis. after "The Colossus" by Goya. One of 110 numbered copies
(100 for sale), signed by the author. Slight soiling to boards, and
offset from frontis., otherwise a very good copy. Reese 20-724
1983 $25

NICHOLS, ROBERT   The Budded Branch. (London) 1918.
12mo, decorated boards with vellum back. With decorations hand-
colored by Anne Estelle Rice. One of 30 copies printed by hand on
Japanese vellum signed by the author and artist. Duschnes 240-7 1983
$150

NICHOLS, ROBERT   Fantastica. N.Y., MacMillian, 1923.
First American edition (reset and printed in USA). Dust jacket
(slight nicking at edges, small stain) else very good. Signed and
inscribed by the author. Houle 22-696 1983 $45

NICHOLS, ROBERT   Fisbo or The Looking-Glass Loaned.
London: William Heinemann, 1934. First edition. Orig. cloth. Dust
jacket. Limited to 1000 copies signed by author. Very fine. MacManus
279-3991 1983 $40

NICHOLS, ROBERT   Invocation & Peace Celebration. London:
Hendersons, 1919. First edition. Orig. printed wrappers. Fine.
MacManus 279-3992 1983 $65

NICHOLS, ROBERT   Invocation: War Poems & Others. London:
Elkin Mathews, 1915. First edition. Orig. blue wrappers. Spine torn.
MacManus 279-3993 1983 $35

NICHOLS, ROBERT   The Smile of the Sphinx. Westminster:
Beaumont Press, 1920. Octavo. Woodcut decorations by Ethelbert
White. Limited to 295 copies. Very fine in cloth-backed decorated
paper over boards. Bromer 25-141 1983 $85

NICHOLS, ROBERT   Winter Berries 1924. Hollywood: Youth-
land Press, 1924. First edition. Orig. wrappers with paper label on
front cover. One of 15 copies in Japanese paper wrappers, each copy
signed by authors. Presentation copy to Siegfried Sassoon, dated
Christmas 1924 and signed by both Robert & Norah Nichols. Wrappers
a bit worn and sunned. Good. MacManus 279-3994 1983 $350

NICHOLS, THOMAS LOW   Forty Years of American Life, 1821-1861.
NY, (1937). Dw. Argosy 710-332 1983 $30

NICHOLS, WALTER H.   A Morgan Rifleman. N.Y., Century,
(1928). First edition, first printing (so stated). Frontis. and
three plates by W.P. Couse. Presentation copy inscribed by the
author: "Professor...Hoping you'll not find over 10,000 historical
mistakes herein..." Fine. Houle 22-1143 1983 $50

NICHOLS, WILLIAM FORD   Days of My Age. San Francisco, priv.
prntd., 1923. Illus. Bookplate removed from front endpaper. Clark
741-143 1983 $27.50

NICHOLSON, CHARLES   A School for the Flute. Published
for the author, by Cramer, Addison & Beale, (1836). First edition,
with 2 litho plates, folio, small puncture in last six leaves neatly
repaired without serious loss, a very good copy in recent cloth.
Fenning 60-298 1983 £125

NICHOLSON, H. A.   A Manual of Palaeontology. 1899.
Third (last) edition, 1,419 text-figures, 2 vols., 8vo, cloth.
Vol. 1 neatly repaired. Wheldon 160-1454 1983 £30

NICHOLSON, H. A.   A Monograph of the Silurian Fossils
of the Girvan District in Ayrshire. 1878-79. Fasc. 1 and 2,
folding table and 15 plates, 2 parts, royal 8vo, boards (trifle
soiled). Only 3 fasc., with a total of 24 plates, were published.
Wheldon 160-1453 1983 £18

NICHOLSON, H. A.   On the Structure and Affinities of the
Genus Monticulipora and its sub-genera. 1881. 6 plates and 50
figures, royal 8vo, cloth. Wheldon 160-1452 1983 £20

NICHOLSON, H. WHALLEY   From Sword to Share. London, 1881.
Folding map. 9 mounted Woodbury-type photos. Three-quarter leather,
slightly cracking, internally fine. Reese 19-404 1983 $425

NICHOLSON, JOHN   The Operative Mechanic, and British
Machinist. Philadelphia: H.C. Carey & I. Lea, 1826. 2 vols. in
1. Over 100 engraved plates, many folding. Orig. vellum-backed
boards. Uncut. Spine label worn. First American edition.
Felcone 21-85 1983 $150

NICHOLSON, JOHN   Paetus and Arria, a tragedy; in five
acts. Cambridge: printed by Francis Hodson, for Lackington, Allen,
and Co.; and J. Nicholson and Son, 1809. 8vo, wrappers. First
edition. Ximenes 64-394 1983 $50

NICHOLSON, JOHN GAMBRIL   A Chaplet of Southernwood. Moray
Press, Derby, 1896. Front. of naked boy, orig. wraps. First edition.
Inscribed presentation copy from the publisher. Jarndyce 30-810 1983
£10.50

NICHOLSON, MARJORIE   Voyages to the Moon. New York, 1948.
First edition. Illustrated. Red cloth. Fine in dj. Bradley 64-22
1983 $40

NICHOLSON, NORMAN   The Fire of the Lord. London, 1944.
First edition. Frayed dust wrapper. Inscription on flyleaf. Nice.
Rota 230-446 1983 £17.50

NICHOLSON, NORMAN   Rock Face. London, 1948. First
edition. Very slightly torn dustwrapper. Fine. Jolliffe 26-390
1983 £35

NICHOLSON, WATSON   The Historical Sources of Defoe's
Journal of the Plague Year. Boston, 1919. First edition. 8vo.
Orig. binding. Fye H-3-415 1983 $45

NICHOLSON, WILLIAM   The First Principles of Chemistry...
London: Robinson, 1796. Third edition. 8vo. Modern half calf
with the orig. label laid down. Folding plate of apparatus,
numerous text tables. A good copy. Zeitlin 264-343 1983 $95

NICHOLSON, WILLIAM   A Journal of Natural Philosophy,
Chemistry, and the Arts. For G.G. Robinson and J. Robinson, 1797-
1802. 5 vols., 4to, with 113 engraved plates, several folding;
no half-title in volume IV; a fine set in cont. tree calf, red
morocco lettering pieces, two joints cracked but sound, bookplates
of Desmond Geoghegan. Quaritch NS 5-83 1983 $1,200

NICHOLSON, WILLIAM   London Types. N.Y., 1898. First
American edition. 12 full page colored plates (plus cover). Cloth
backed pictorial boards. Covers soiled, worn and a bit chipped.
Quatorzains by W.E. Henley. King 45-415 1983 $200

NICODEMI, GIORGIO   Antonio Calderara. Milano: "Ariel",
1947. 22 tipped-in color plates. 4 text illus. 4to. Boards.
Edition limited to 1000 numbered copies. Ars Libri 33-420 1983
$25

NICODEMI, GIORGIO   Francesco Hayez. Milano: Ceschina,
1962. 2 vols. 24 plates. 331 plates (partly in color). 4to.
Cloth. Dust jacket. Slipcase. Ars Libri 33-494 1983 $85

NICODEMI, GIORGIO   I Calegari. Brescia: Ateneo Bresciano
di Scienze, Lettere ed Arte, 1924. 31 tipped-in plates. Large 4to.
Boards. Edition limited to 150 copies. Heads of spine slightly
chipped. Ars Libri 33-57 1983 $185

NICODEMI, GIORGIO   Piazzetta. 17 disegni inediti.
Milano: G.G. Gorlich, 1945. 17 plates. Small folio. Wrappers.
Edition limited to 300 numbered copies. Ars Libri 33-269 1983
$37.50

NICOL, DAVID   The Political Life of Our Time.
Chapman & Hall, 1889. First edition, 2 vols. 40 pp ads. vol. II.
Orig. blue cloth, v.g. Jarndyce 31-328 1983 £18.50

NICOLAS, HARRIS   History of the Battle of Agincourt. 1833.
Frontis., maps (some coloured), coloured plate, calf, spine slightly
rubbed, good ex-library copy with blind stamps. K Books 307-135
1983 £38

NICOLAS, N. H.   The Dispatches and Letters of Vice
Admiral Lord Viscount Nelson. London, 1844-6. 8vo. Orig. cloth.
Engraved portrait frontis., 4 folding engraved facsimiles, 3 folding
battle plans (2 coloured) and 1 other battle plan. 7 vols. Blue
buckram. Labels on spines. Red speckled edges, small occasional
library stamps. Good. Edwards 1042-145 1983 £200

NICOLAY, CHARLES G.   The Oregon Territory... London:
Charles Knight & Co., 1846. Frontis. and folding map. Half morocco.
Scarce in wrappers. Jenkins 153-397 1983 $250

NICOLL, ALLARDYCE   A History of Late Eighteenth Century
Drama 1750-1800. Cambridge, University Press, 1927. 8vo, orig.
quarter cloth, boards, name on endpaper, but a good copy. Ravenstree
97-144 1983 $65

NICOLL, M.   Nicoll's Birds of Egypt. 1930. Portrait,
31 coloured plates, photogravures, maps and text-figures. 2 vols.,
4to, original cloth (neatly refixed, with new endpapers). A few
small wormholes, some marginal foxing of some plates and facing text
margins. Wheldon 160-77 1983 £190

NICOLL, MAURICE (1884-1953) Dream Psychology. London: Oxford
Univ. Press, 1917. First edition. 12mo. Smith Ely Jelliffe's copy,
signed on titlepage and paste-down. Gach 95-387 1983 $35

NICOLL, W. ROBERTSON   The Problem of Edwin Drood. London,
n.d. First edition. 8vo, cloth. Owner's bookplate. Argosy 714-231
1983 $25

NICOLL, W. ROBERTSON   The Problem of 'Edwin Drood', a Study
in the Methods of Dickens. Hodder & Stoughton, 1913. 2nd edition,
half title, front. Orig. brown calico cloth. Jarndyce 31-570 1983
£10.50

NICOLSON, HAROLD   Curzon: The Last Phase 1919-1925. B,
1934. Illus., cover slightly soiled, very good in frayed and chipped
dustwrapper. Quill & Brush 54-987 1983 $30

NICOLSON, HAROLD   Dwight Morrow. London, 1935. First
edition. Author's autograph signature. Very nice. Rota 231-446
1983 £12.50

NICOLSON, HAROLD   Helen's Tower. London, (1937). First
edition. Illus. 8vo, cloth. Argosy 714-549 1983 $35

NIEBUHR, CARSTEN   Travels through Arabia... Edinburgh:
G. Mudie etc., 1792. First English edition. 2 vols. 8vo. 10
plates. 3 folding maps. New 1/2 tan polished calf, raised bands,
red and green labels, lacks 1/2 title in vol. 1. Stains on titles
and repairs to two leaves with no loss of text. Adelson Africa-109
1983 $375

NIELSEN, KAY   East of the Sun and West of the Moon.
London, (1913). First edition. 4to. Orig. dark blue decorated
cloth, gilt, illustrated endpapers. 25 mounted coloured plates, and
illus. in the text, from drawings by Kay Nielsen. Traylen 94-636
1983 £350

NIELSON, J. M.   Agnosia, Apraxia, Aphasia. Los Angeles,
(1936). Illus. Argosy 713-402 1983 $35

NIEMANN, AUGUST   Der Weltkrieg, Deutsche Traume.
Berlin-Leipzig (1904). Cloth with original wraps bound in,
covers a bit rubbed and spotted. King 46-314 1983 $35

NIETHAMMER, J.   Handbuch der Saugetiere Europas.
Wiesbaden, 1978. 85 text-figures and 105 tables, 8vo, art. leather.
To be completed in 5 volumes. Wheldon 160-590 1983 £91

NIETZKI, RUDOLF HUGO   Chemistry of the Organic Dyestuffs.
London: Gurney & Jackson, 1892. First English edition. 8vo.
Orig. red cloth. Numerous text illus., partially unopened.
Ads. Rubbed, chipped, defects to back cover. Zeitlin 264-345
1983 $45

NIETZSCHE, FRIEDRICH   Ainsi Parlait Zarathoustra. Paris:
Cres et Cie, 1919. Orig. printed wraps. Ltd. numbered edition on
Rives. Wraps. slightly soiled, but near fine. Reese 20-720 1983
$30

NIETZSCHE, FRIEDRICH   Dionysos Dithyramben. Munich:
Verlag der Nietzsche-Gesellschaft, 1923. 4to, edition ltd. to 440
copies. Orig. boards, plain paper dust jacket. A fine copy.
Karmiole 72-75 1983 $75

NIEUWENHUIS, A. W.   Die Veranlagung der Malaiischen Volker
des Ost-Indischen Archipels... Leiden: E.J. Brill, 1913. 31 plates
(partly in color). Text figures. Large 4to. Buckram. Orig. wrappers
bound in. Ars Libri 34-845 1983 $100

NIGGLI, P.   Lehrbuch der Mineralogie. Berlin, 1920.
560 text-figures, royal 8vo, boards. Wheldon 160-1455 1983 £15

NIGHTINGALE, FLORENCE   Florence Nightingale to her Nurses.
Macmillan and Co., 1914. 8vo, portrait and facs. plates, orig. cloth.
First edition. Bickersteth 75-256 1983 £24

NIGHTINGALE, FLORENCE   Notes on Nursing: What It Is, and
What It Is Not. New York: Appleton, 1860. 1st American ed. Orig.
pebbled brown cloth, gilt. Spine ends frayed but very good copy.
Jenkins 155-968 1983 $100

NIGHTINGALE, FLORENCE   Notes on Nursing. (1860). 8vo, ads.
printed on the end papers, and "(the Right of Translation is
reserved.)" underneath the imprint on the title, orig. limp cloth,
rebacked. First edition. Bickersteth 77-306 1983 £55

NIGHTINGALE, FLORENCE   Notes on Nursing. New York, 1860.
Ads. Cloth. Flyleaves foxed, early circulating library label on
pastedown, covers very slightly soiled. First American edition.
Felcone 22-169 1983 $35

NIGHTINGALE, FLORENCE   Notes on Nursing. New York, 1860. 1st
American ed. Small 8vo. Some foxing. Morrill 289-173 1983 $27.50

NIGHTINGALE, FLORENCE   Organization of Nursing. Liverpool:
London: 1865. 8vo, 2 plates, a.e.g., full cont. calf, ruled gilt, a
little rubbed. Inscribed on the fly "E.L. Rathbone, 1867".
Bickersteth 75-254 1983 £85

THE NIGHTS of Straparola. London: Lawrence & Bullen, 1894. 2
vols. 4to. three-quarter red morocco, gilt panelled spines, t.e.g.
20 engraved plates by E.R. Hughes. Limited edition of 210 numbered
copies, printed on Japanese vellum. Traylen 94-787 1983 £36

NIHELL, JAMES   Novae Raraeque Observationes circa
Variarum Crisium Praedictionen ex Pulsu Nullo Habito Respectu ad
Signa Critica Antiquorum. Benetiis, 1748. Cont. vellum. Argosy 713-
402 1983 $175

NIHIMA Ayamie-Mazinahigna. Moniang: Fabre-Endatch, 1830. Sm. 16mo.
Sheep, newly rebacked. A fine copy. In Our Time 156-15 1983 $450

NIJINSKY, VASLAV   Diary. London, 1937. First English
edition. Spine faded. Edges spotted. Chipped and slightly torn
dustwrapper browned at the spine. Very good. Jolliffe 25-391 1983
£25

NILES, JOHN M.   The Life of Oliver Hazard Perry.
Hartford, 1820. Orig. calf, spine gilt extra. One (of three)
plates, otherwise a very good copy. Reese 18-545 1983 $40

NILES, JOHN M.   Post Office Fines and Deductions. Wash.,
1841. First edition. Dbd. Ginsberg 46-648 1983 $20

NILES, NATHANIEL   The Perfection of God the Fountain of
Good. Norwich, printed; Elizabeth Town: re-printed by S. Kollock,
1791. Modern cloth, closely trimmed. Minor damage to corners of title-
page and final page, with loss of a few words. Very good. Felcone
19-43 1983 $45

NILSSON, S.   Skandinavisk Fauna. Lund, 1847.
2nd ed., text-figures, 8vo, new cloth. Small stamp on title-page and
tear in pp. i-ii neatly repaired. Wheldon 160-591 1983 £20

NILSSON, T. A.   The Pleistocene. 1982. 8vo, cloth.
Wheldon 160-1456 1983 £66

NIMMO, A.   Songs and ballads of Clydesdale.
Edinburgh: Menzies, 1882. First edition. 8vo. Orig. dark brown
cloth. Trifle rubbed. Very good copy. Ximenes 63-455 1983
$30

NIMMO, JOSEPH   The Insurrection of June and July 1894.
Washington, 1894. Orig. printed wrappers. Jenkins 152-300 1983 $35

NIMMO, JOSEPH   Report on the Internal Commerce of the
United States. Wash., pt. 3, 1885. Five folding maps, tables. Full
calf. Slipcased. Jenkins 153-398 1983 $1750

"NIMROD", PSEUD.
Please turn to
APPERLY, CHARLES JAMES

NIMS, JOHN FREDERICK   The Iron Pastoral. New York, (1947).
8vo. Cloth. A review copy with slip laid in. Endpapers browned
else fine in worn dj. In Our Time 156-597 1983 $45

NIN, ANAIS   The Four Chambered Heart. London,
(1959). 8vo. Cloth. This copy bears a full page presentation
inscription by Nin on the front flyleaf. A very fine copy in dj.
In Our Time 156-598 1983 $150

NIN, ANAIS   The Four-Chambered Heart. NY, (1950).
Edges very slightly rubbed, else fine in slightly frayed and rubbed,
very good dustwrapper, owner's name. Quill & Brush 54-991 1983
$100

NIN, ANAIS House of Incest. Gemor Press, n.d. First American edition. Autographed by the author. 8vo, orange cloth. Argosy 714-882 1983 $75

NIN, ANAIS Ladders to Fire. N.Y., Dutton, 1946. First edition. Illus. by Ian Hugo. Signed and inscribed by Nin. Black cloth (dull). Good. Houle 22-1218 1983 $55

NIN, ANAIS Twice a Year, No. 1. N.Y., 1938. First edition. Illus. Printed stiff wraps. Very good - fine. Houle 22-697 1983 $75

NIN, ANAIS Under a Glass Bell. (N.Y.: Gemor Press, 1944). 8vo, pict. boards. Second edition, ltd. to 800 copies. Argosy 714-551 1983 $50

NINE O'Clock Stories. London: G. Bell & Sons Ltd., 1934. First edition. 8vo. Orig. cloth. Dust jacket. Slightly darkened jacket. Fine. Very scarce. Jaffe 1-13 1983 $250

THE NINETIES in America & England. (Boston, 1934). Illus. Pictorial wrappers. Owned by Matthew J. Bruccoli and bears his small holographic "MJB" printed pook label inside front cover. Bradley 66-51 1983 $35

NISBET, HUGH Experiences of a Jungle Wallah. London, (c.1930). Plates, leather, soft boards. 8vo. Good. Edwards 1044-521 1983 £18

NISBET, HUME 'Bail Up.' Chatto & Windus, 1890. First edition, half title, front. 32 pp ads. Orig. pic. dec. light blue cloth, spine a little browned. Jarndyce 31-831 1983 £10.50

NISBET, JOHN Our Forests and Woodlands. London: J.M. Dent & Co., 1900. First edition. Illus. with photogravures. With decorations, including covers and endpapers, by A. Rackham. Orig. pictorial cloth. With Rackham's orig. pen-and-ink drawing for the head-piece to Chapter III tipped in at the appropriate place. Drawing is signed and dated by the artist. Bookplate. Extremities of spine worn. Good. MacManus 280-4312 1983 $750

NISBET, JOHN Our Forests and Woodlands. London: J. M. Dent & Co., 1900. First edition. Illus. Orig. decorated vellum. One of 150 copies printed on hand-made paper. Rackham designed the end-papers and head and tail pieces. Vellum slightly soiled. Fine. MacManus 280-4310 1983 $300

NISBET, JOHN Our Forests and Woodlands. London: J.M. Dent & Co., 1900. First edition. Illus. Orig. decorated cloth. Rackman designed the endpapers and contributed vignettes throughout. Covers a bit rubbed. Slight foxing. Very good. MacManus 280-4311 1983 $85

NISSEN, C. Die Ornithologische Illustration. Vienna, 1935. 6 parts, 8vo, wrappers, numerous illus. Wheldon 160-260 1983 £20

NIVEN, ARCHIBALD C. The Centennial Memorial. N.Y., 1859. Fine. Argosy 716-362 1983 $25

NIX, EVETT D. Oklahombres. (St. Louis, 1929). 1st ed. Illus. Inner hinges taped. Clark 741-397 1983 $61.50

NIX, EVETT D. Oklahombres. St. Louis, 1929. First edition. Illus. Orig. pictorial cloth. Fine. Jenkins 152-313 1983 $45

NIXON, RICHARD MILLHOUSE Setting the Course, The First Year. NY, (1970). Signed Presidential plate on front fly (may be secretarial), near fine in lightly frayed, very good dustwrapper. Quill & Brush 54-992 1983 $75

NIXON, RICHARD MILHOUSE Six Crises. Garden City, 1962. Cloth, bookplate, else fine in dust jacket. Special pub.'s presentation issue, with the extra leaf inserted before the half-title, signed by the author. Reese 19-433 1983 $175

NIXON, RICHARD MILHOUSE Six Crises. N.Y., Doubleday, 1962. First edition, dust jacket. Inscribed and signed: - "Best to... from Dick Nixon." The autopen signature appears on another page. Very good-fine. Houle 21-672 1983 $150

NOAD, HENRY M. Lectures on Chemistry. London: Simpkin, Marshall, and Co., 1843. 8vo. Orig. cloth. Large folding table, numerous text illus. and diagrams. Errata leaf. Somewhat faded. Zeitlin 264-346 1983 $80

NOBILITY Run Mad. Minerva Press, for Lane and Newman, 1802. First edition, 4 vols. Half titles, half green morocco, v.g. Jarndyce 30-279 1983 £360

NOBLE, MARK Memoirs of the Protectoral House of Cromwell. Birmingham, Pearson and Rollason, 1787. 2 vols., 8vo, orig. French calf, quite rubbed and worn, joints breaking. Internally fine, with all plates present and intact. Ravenstree 97-145 1983 $42.50

NODIER, CHARLES The Luck of the Bean-Rows. London: Daniel O'Connor, (December, 1921). First edition, first issue. Illus. by C.L. Fraser. Orig. cloth-backed decorated boards. Publisher's glassine jacket (badly chipped and worn). Cover margins a trifle worn. Near-fine. MacManus 278-2010 1983 $75

NODIER, CHARLES The Luck of the Bean-Rows. London: Daniel O'Connor, (n.d.). First edition, third issue. Orig. cloth-backed decorated boards. Illus. by C.L. Fraser. Spine and covers slightly faded and worn. Very good. MacManus 278-2011 1983 $40

NODIER, CHARLES The Woodcutter's Dog. London: Daniel O'Connor, (1921). First edition. Illus. by C.L. Fraser. Orig. boards with yellow printed label. Spine faded and a trifle worn at the edges. Back cover slightly spotted. Near-fine. MacManus 278-2014 1983 $65

NODIER, CHARLES The Woodcutter's Dog. London: Daniel O'Connor, 1921. First edition, first issue with the de la More Press imprint. Illus. by. C.L. Fraser. Orig. boards with paper cover label (slightly worn). Spine and covers faded, worn and chipped at the margins. Good. MacManus 278-2013 1983 $35

NOEHLES, KARL La Chiesa dei SS. Luca e Martina nell' opera di Pietro da Cortona. Roma: Banco di Santo Spirito, 1969. 18 tipped-in color plates. 278 illus. Large square 4to. Cloth. Dust jacket. Ars Libri 33-274 1983 $140

NOEL, AUGUSTA Owen Gwynne's Great Work. London: Macmillan & Co., 1875. First edition. 2 vols. Orig. presentation binding of cont. vellum gilt. Presentation copy inscribed on the title page of vol. one: "S. Albermarle from the author." Covers and spines slightly rubbed. Near-fine. MacManus 279-3996 1983 $350

NOEL, J. B. L. Through Tibet to Everest. London, 1927. First edition, second issue. Frontis., 25 illus. 8vo. Orig. cloth. Good. Edwards 1044-522 1983 £35

NOFERI, G. B. The Opera Dances for 1779. London, John Welcker, n.d. (1779). Engraved music, oblong 8vo, marbled boards. Salloch 387-158 1983 $135

NOGUCHI, NONE Hiroshige and Japanese Landscapes. Tokyo: 1936. Second edition. 3 color plates, numerous illus. Wrappers, with color print on front cover. Fine in tissue jacket. Bradley 66-423 1983 $20

NOGUERA, EDUARDO La ceramica arqueologica de Meso-america. Mexico, 1965. 159 plates. Small stout 4to. Cloth. Dust jacket. Ars Libri 34-401 1983 $100

NOLAN, FRANCIS The Statutes Relating to the Law of Landlord and Tenant and Land Purchase in Ireland, from 1860 to 1896. Dublin: E. Ponsonby, 1898. Fifth edition, 8vo, orig. cloth, inside joints weak, very good copy. Fenning 62-264 1983 £28.50

NOLAN, L. E. Cavalry. London, 1853. First edition. Fine coloured lithograph frontis. and 4 coloured lithograph plates. 2 other plates (1 folding) and 1 illus. Orig. red roan-backed blue cloth. 8vo. Spine slightly worn, some slight mostly marginal foxing. Bookplate. Good. Edwards 1042-444 1983 £75

NOLHAC, PIERRE DE　　　　　Hubert Robert, 1733-1808. Paris: Goupil & Cie, 1910. 61 illus. mostly hors texte (4 tipped-in color facsimiles) printed on chine blanc with captioned tissue-guards printed on papier teinte. Small stout folio. Orig. wrappers. Uncut. No. 342 of a limited edition of 500 copies. Rare. Ars Libri 32-583　1983　$400

NOLTE, VINCENT　　　　　Fifty Years in Both Hemispheres...Life of a Former Merchant. N.Y., 1854. 1st ed. Nice copy. Jenkins 151-251　1983　$100

NOLTE, VINCENT　　　　　Fifty Years in Both Hemipsheres or, Reminiscences of the Life of a Former Merchant. NY, 1854. 12mo, later buckram, adv. pp, 1st ed. in English. Argosy 710-539　1983　$50

THE NON mi ricordo song book... London: J. Bailey, n.d. (1820). First edition. 8vo. Disbound. Hand-colored frontis. Ximenes 63-503　1983　$90

NORDAU, MAX　　　　　Degeneration. N.Y.: D. Appleton & Co., 1895. First American edition. Orig. decorated cloth. Fine. Mac-Manus 279-3997　1983　$20

NORDEN, H　　　　　Fresh Tracks in the Belgian Congo. Boston: Small, Maynard & Co., n.d. (ca. 1930). Two folding maps. Green cloth. Karmiole 74-2　1983　$40

NORDEN, H.　　　　　Under Persian Skies. London, 1928. Folding coloured map. Frontis. and numerous plates. 8vo. Orig. cloth. Good. Edwards 1044-523　1983　£55

NORDENSKIOLD, A. E.　　　　　Voyage de la "Vega" Autour de l'Asie et de l'Europe. (Paris, 1882-3). Numerous wood-engravings, small folio, wrs. Complete extract from Le Tour du Monde. Argosy 710-10　1983　$40

NORDHOFF, CHARLES　　　　　California: For Health, Pleasure and Residence... New York: Harper & Brothers, 1873. Map, illus. Orig. blue gilt cloth. Fine copy. Jenkins 153-399　1983　$100

NORDHOFF, CHARLES　　　　　The Communistic Societies of the United States from Personal Visit and Observation. New York: Harper, 1375. Gilt cloth, frontis. First edition. Very slight shelfwear, ownership stamp, otherwise a nice, bright copy. Reese 19-405　1933　$150

NORDHOFF, CHARLES　　　　　The Cotton States in the Spring and Summer of 1875. N.Y., 1876. 1st ed. Orig. printed wrappers. Near-mint copy. Jenkins 153-455　1983　$175

NORDHOFF, CHARLES　　　　　The Hurricane. N.Y., Blue Ribbon, (1937). Motion picture edition. Dust jacket. Very good. Houle 21-682　1983　$150

NORDHOFF, CHARLES　　　　　Men Without Country. Boston: Little, Brown, 1942. 1st ed. Orig. cloth, dj. Fine copy in near fine dj. Jenkins 155-969　1983　$25

NORDHOFF, CHARLES　　　　　Mutiny on the Bounty. Boston, Little, Brown, 1932. First edition. Dust jacket (sm nick), else very good-fine. Houle 21-682　1983　$150

NORDSIECK, F.　　　　　Die Europaischen Meeres-Gehauseschnecken. Stuttgart, 1982. Second revised and enlarged edition, 2018 figures on 106 partly coloured plates, royal 8vo, cloth. Wheldon 160-1222　1983　£62

NORDYKE, LEWIS　　　　　Cattle Empire. New York, 1949. First edition in dust jacket. Signed by author. Plates. Jenkins 152-302　1983　$35

NORFLEET, J. FRANK　　　　　Norfleet, the Amazing Experiences of an Intrepid Texas Rancher with an International Swindling Ring. Sugar Land, Texas: Imperial Press, (1927). 21 cm. Orig. decorated orange cloth. Shaken with wear to extremities. Signed by Norfleet. Frontis. illus. of the author astride "Hornet," and the 23 plates. Grunder 7-89　1983　$25

NORMAN, A. M.　　　　　Crustacea Isopoda. Trans. Zoo. Soc., 1886-1913. 15 plates (upper corners waterstained), 2 parts, 4to, unbound. Wheldon 160-1330　1983　£12

NORMAN, B. M.　　　　　Rambles in Yucatan. New York: Langley, 1843. First edition. Lithographed title, map, 24 lithographed plates (several on tinted grounds) of archaeological remains. Text illus. Orig. purple gilt pictorial cloth. Spine slightly faded. Very fine. Jenkins 152-305　1983　$250

NORMAN, C. B.　　　　　Battle Honours of the British Army. London, 1911. First edition. Frontis. 8vo. Orig. cloth. 7 plates, 4 maps (2 folding). Very slightly worn. Good. Edwards 1042-445　1983　£25

NORMAN, DOROTHY　　　　　Dualities. New York: Privately printed for an American Place, 1933. Large octavo. Parchment and boards. First edition. One of 400 numbered copies on laid paper. Very slight rubbing, else a fine, partially unopened copy. Residue of tipped-in bookplate. Reese 20-730　1983　$150

NORMANBY, CONSTANTINE HENRY PHIPPS, MARQUIS OF　　　　　The Contrast. London: Colburn & Bentley, 1832. 3 vols. 12mo. Later russet half morocco, spines gilt. First edition. Presentation copy, inscribed on half-title to "Lord Dover, from his affectionate friend the Author." Half-titles present. Fine. Ximenes 63-131　1983　$175

NORMANBY, CONSTANTINE HENRY PHIPPS, MARQUIS OF　　　　　Historiettes, or Tales of Continental Life. London: Saunders & Otley, 1827. First edition. 3 vols. Orig. cloth-backed boards with paper spine labels (darkened & worn). Library labels removed. Spines faded and slightly worn. Good. MacManus 279-3998　1983　$250

NORMANBY, CONSTANTINE HENRY PHIPPS, MARQUIS OF　　　　　Matilda. A Tale of the Day. Henry Colburn, 1825. First edition. Large 12mo, lacks half title and advert. leaves. Cont. half calf. Hannas 69-152　1983　£60

NORMANBY, CONSTANTIN HENRY PHIPPS, MARQUIS OF　　　　　Yes and No. London, Colburn, 1828. First edition, 2 vols., old three quarter calf, possibly lacking half titles. Very good. MacManus 280-4223　1983　$50

NORRIS, CHARLES　　　　　Eastern Upland Shooting. Philadelphia, (1946). 1st ed. Illus. 8vo. Morrill 286-372　1983　$20

NORRIS, CHARLES　　　　　Pig Iron. New York: Dutton, (1926). 1st ed., 1 of 750 numbered and signed copies. Orig. cloth-backed boards, labels. Edge wear, but a very good copy. Jenkins 155-970　1983　$25

NORRIS, FRANK　　　　　Blix. New York: Doubleday, 1899. 1st ed., 1st printing. Orig. pictorial cream cloth, stamped in orange and black. Indecipherable signature on front end paper with date "Sept. 19, 1899". Spine very slightly aged, else fine copy. Jenkins 155-971　1983　$75

NORRIS, FRANK　　　　　A Deal in Wheat. NY, 1903. Front hinge starting before frontis., endpapers and frontis. soiled, cover edges worn and pitted, good. Quill & Brush 54-994　1983　$40

NORRIS, FRANK　　　　　McTeague: A Story of San Francisco. SF, 1941. Introduction by Charles Norris. Illustrations by Otis Oldfield. 4to, cloth-backed decorated bds., paper label. A very nice copy in variant bliding. One of 500 copies. Perata 27-27　1983　$75

NORRIS, FRANK　　　　　The Pit. NY, 1903. Special presentation edition (to Bliss Carman), edges slightly worn and top edge of spine chipped, good or better. Quill & Brush 54-995　1983　$75

NORRIS, FRANK　　　　　The Pit. NY, 1903. Cover slightly soiled, spine edges slightly frayed, good or better. Quill & Brush 54-996　1983　$35

NORRIS, FRANK　　　　　The Responsibilities of the Novelists. New York: Doubleday, 1903. Frontis. 1st ed. 1st binding. Orig. slate green cloth, gilt, t.e.g., others uncut. Near fine copy. Jenkins 155-972　1983　$45

NORRIS, FRANK   Works. N.Y., Doubleday, 1928. 10 vols. 8vo. Frontis. of Norris by Arnold Genthe. Full folio page of the manuscript in Norris' hand. White parchment, orange paper corners & side-strips, gilt lettering, teg. Vol. 10 is 1st printing of prev. uncollected material. 245 sets only. Rare set in fragile orig. binding, & complete with manuscript. O'Neal 50-38 1983 $1,000

NORRIS, GEORGE WILLIAM   Studies in Cardiac Pathology. Phila. & London, 1911. Tall 8vo, 85 photo illus. First edition. Argosy 713-404 1983 $50

NORRIS, JOHN   Hierocles upon the Golden Verses of the Pythagoreans. London: M. Flesher for Thomas Fickus, 1682. 1st ed. of this translation, 8vo, later calf gilt, spine gilt, morocco label. Hinges rubbed, but a fine copy. Trebizond 18-120 1983 $250

NORRIS, WILLIAM EDWARD   Adrain Vidal. London: Smith, Elder, & Co., 1885. First edition. 3 vols. Half calf and marbled cloth with leather labels on spines. Heads of spines a bit rubbed. Some light foxing. Vol. three scored in pencil on several pages. Armorial bookplate in each volume. MacManus 279-3999 1983 $85

NORRIS, WILLIAM EDWARD   A Bachelor's Blunder. London: Richard Bentley & Son, 1886. First edition. 3 vols. Half calf and marbled cloth with leather labels on spines. Head and foot of each spine slightly rubbed. Some light foxing. Armorial bookplate in each vol. MacManus 279-4000 1983 $85

NORRIS, WILLIAM EDWARD   Billy Bellew. London: Chatto & Windus, 1895. First edition. 2 vols. Orig. decorated cloth. Former subscription copy, spines and covers rather rubbed and worn at the margins. Spotted. Inner hinges weak. Subscription labels partly removed. Fair. MacManus 279-4001 1983 $125

NORRIS, WILLIAM EDWARD   Chris. London: Macmillan, 1888. First edition. 2 vols. Half calf and marbled cloth with leather labels on spines. Edges slightly rubbed. Armorial bookplate in each volume. MacManus 279-4002 1983 $85

NORRIS, WILLIAM EDWARD   A Deplorable Affair. London: Methuen & Co., 1893. First edition. Illus. Orig. decorated cloth. Spine and covers faded, worn and rubbed at the margins. Former owner's signature in pencil on the front free endpaper. Good. MacManus 279-4003 1983 $45

NORRIS, WILLIAM EDWARD   Lone Marie. London: Macmillan, 1905. First edition. Orig. cloth. Small stamp on flyleaf. Blind-stamped presentation copy. Fine. MacManus 279-4004 1983 $25

NORRIS, WILLIAM EDWARD   Major and Minor. London: Richard Bentley & Son, 1887. First edition. 3 vols. Half calf and marbled cloth with leather labels on spines. Spines a bit worn. Armorial bookplate in each volume. MacManus 279-4005 1983 $85

NORRIS, WILLIAM EDWARD   Marcia. London: John Murray, 1891. Third edition. 3 vols. Half calf and marbled cloth with leather labels on spines. Heads of spines a bit rubbed. Armorial bookplate in each volume. MacManus 279-4006 1983 $50

NORRIS, WILLIAM EDWARD   Misadventure. London: Spencer Blackett, 1890. First edition. 3 vols. Half calf and marbled cloth with leather labels on spines. Heads of spines a bit worn. Armorial bookplate in each volume. MacManus 279-4007 1983 $85

NORRIS, WILLIAM EDWARD   Miss Shafto. London: Richard Bentley & Son, 1889. First edition. 3 vols. Half calf and marbled cloth with leather labels on spines. Edges slightly rubbed. Armorial bookplate in each volume. MacManus 279-4008 1983 $85

NORRIS, WILLIAM EDWARD   My Friend Jim. London: Macmillan, 1886. First edition. 2 vols. Half calf and marbled cloth with leather labels on spines. Edges very slightly rubbed. Armorial bookplate in each volume. MacManus 279-4009 1983 $85

NORRIS, WILLIAM EDWARD   Not Guilty. London: Constable & Co. Ltd, 1910. First edition. Orig. cloth. Bookplate. Spine and corners worn. MacManus 279-4010 1983 $60

NORRIS, WILLIAM EDWARD   The Rogue. London: Richard Bentley & Son, 1888. First edition. 3 vols. Half calf and marbled cloth with leather labels on spines. Heads of two spines a bit worn. Armorial bookplate in each volume. MacManus 279-4011 1983 $85

NORRIS, WILLIAM EDWARD   The Rogue. London: Richard Bentley & Son, 1889. First American edition. Orig. cloth. Edges of spine rubbed. Inner hinges starting. Bookplate. Good. MacManus 279-4012 1983 $75

NORTH, F. J.   Snowdonia, the National Park of North Wales. New Naturalist, 1949. 72 plates (40 coloured), 8vo, cloth. First edition in torn dust jacket. Wheldon 160-415 1983 £18

NORTH Australian Exploring Expedition. Melbourne, 1855. Folio, disbound, but a fine copy. Fenning 61-315 1983 £55

NORTH CAROLINA. LAWS.   Public Laws of the State of North Carolina. Raleigh: William E. Pell, 1866. Sheep, (scuffed, hinges weak). Argosy 716-388 1983 $125

NORTH Dakota History. Bismarck, N.d., 1926-80. Vols. 1-47. Orig. printed wraps. Ginsberg 47-290 1983 $650

NORTHEY, W. B.   The Ghurkas Their Manners. London, 1928. Folding map, plates. 8vo. Orig. cloth. Good. Edwards 1044-525 1983 £55

NORTON, A. TIFFANY   History of Sullivan's Campaign Against the Iroquois. Lima, New York, 1879. 1st ed. Illus. and folding map. 8vo. Bookplate removed, some pencil marks in text. Morrill 289-467 1983 $30

NORTON, ANTHONY BANNING   The Great Revolution of 1840. Mount Vernon, O., and Dallas, 1888. Frontis. Cloth. First edition. Felcone 22-171 1983 $25

NORTON, CAROLINE   The Undying One, and Other Poems. Henry Colburn and Richard Bentley, 1830. First edition. Half dark blue calf, maroon label, v.g. Jarndyce 30-811 1983 £28

NORTON, CHARLES ELIOT   Considerations on Some Recent Social Theories. Boston: Little, Brown, 1853. Brown cloth, paper label. First edition. Signed by the author on the title-page at a later date. Label slightly rubbed, else a near fine copy. Reese 20-733 1983 $125

NORTON, CHARLES ELIOT   A Leaf of Grass from Shady Hill. (Cambridge, 1928). First edition. Port. Small folio, uncut. Argosy 714-808 1983 $50

NORTON, HARRY H.   A Bird's-Eye View of the Black Hills Gold Mining Region. N.Y., 1879. Orig. printed wraps., fine. Half morocco slipcase. First edition. Ginsberg 47-699 1983 $1,000

NORVELL, CLAUDIA   Texas. Dallas: Southwest Press, (1933). Map. Author's edition. Jenkins 152-306 1983 $35

NORWOOD, HENRY   A Voyage to Virginia. (1649). N.p., (ca. 1750's). 12mo, pr. wrs. Argosy 710-558 1983 $75

NORWOOD, RICHARD   Trigonometrie. Printed by W. Godbid, for Benj. Hurlock, 1672. Small 4to, numerous diagrams in the text, half calf antique with marbled boards and new end papers. Bickersteth 77-307 1983 £220

NOSHPITZ, JOSEPH   Basic Book of Child Psychiatry. NY: Basic Books (1979). Four vols. Gach 940409 1983 $145

NOTES of a trip to the west coast of New Zealand. Timaru (N.Z.): printed at the "Timaru Herald" Printing Office, 1878. First edition. Small 4to. Orig. lilac printed wrappers. A folding map. A bit worn. Very good copy. Ximenes 63-605 1983 $225

NOTES of Naples and its Environs. James Bohn, (1838). First edition, errata slip, 8vo, orig. cloth, inside front joint neatly repaired, otherwise a nice copy. Fenning 60-292 1983 £38.50

NOTES on Niagara. Chicago, 1883. Large quarto. Profusely illus., including maps and numerous wood engravings. Black cloth. Very good. Bradley 66-623 1983 $25

NOTT, CHARLES C.   Sketches of the War. N.Y., 1865. Fourth edition. Argosy 716-85 1983 $25

NOTT, SAMUEL   An Appeal to the Temperate. Albany, 1828. First edition. Orig. cloth-backed boards, (faintly foxed). Ex lib. With lengthy inscription by A. Henry Dumont. Argosy 716-531 1983 $30

NOTT, STANLEY CHARLES   A Catalogue of Rare Chinese Jade Carvings. Palm Beach, FL: The House of Jade, 1940. Folio. From a ltd. numbered edition (total number of copies not specified). With the card of Stanely Charles Nott mounted on front pastedown end-paper. Orig. green cloth. Bookplate removed. Karmiole 75-98 1983 $150

NOTTEBOHM, GUSTAV   Zweite Beethoveniana. Leipzig, J. Rieter-Biedermann, 1887. Pub.'s ads. 8vo, cont. 1/2 leather, rubbed at hinges and edges. First edition. Salloch 387-19 1983 $90

NOTTINGHAM, JOHN   Diseases of the Ear. London, 1857. First edition. 8vo. Orig. cloth. Frontis. Gurney JJ-282 1983 £20

NOURSE, W. E. C.   On the Organs of the Senses and the Cerebral Faculties Connected with Them. Brighton, England: 1860. Wrappers, new covers. Gach 94-739 1983 $20

NOVOTNY, FRITZ   Romanische Bauplastik in Osterreich. Wien, 1930. (Arbeiten des I. Kunsthistorischen Instituts der Universitat Wien. Vol. 26.) 118, (2)pp., 54 plates. 4to. Cloth. Ars Libri SB 26-161 1983 $45

NOW That You Belong. Boston: New England Telephone and Telegraph Company, (1937). First edition. 8vo. Paper wrappers. Hand-lettered by Dwiggins throughout. Paper yellowed on second page from old catalogue description of this item which has been loosely inserted. Oak Knoll 49-169 1983 $30

NOWOTNY, KARL A.   Codex Borbonicus. Bibliotheque de l'Assemblee Nationale, Paris (Y 120). Graz: Akademische Druck-und Verlagsanstalt, 1974. Text: 4 plates. Wrappers. Facsimile: Folding color facsimile plate on special heavy coated stock. Square folio. Clamshell box. Boards 1/4 leather. Ars Libri 34-406 1983 $375

NOWOTNY, KARL A.   Codex Borgia. Biblioteca Apostolica Vaticana (Messicano Riserva 28). Graz: Academisch Druck- und Ver-lagsanstalt, 1976. Text: Folding plate. 3 text illus. Wrappers. Facsimile: Folding color facsimile plate. Clamshell box. Boards. 1/4 pigskin. Large square 4to. German text, with English-language summary. Ars Libri 34-404 1983 $375

NOWOTNY, KARL A.   Codex Cospi. Calendario Messinaco 4093, Biblioteca Universitaria Bologna. Graz: Akademische Druck-und Verlagsanstalt, 1968. Text: Folding chart. Wrappers. Fac-simile: Folding color facsimile plate. Mounted at each end on boards. 4to. Clamshell box. Boards. 1/4 pigskin. German text, with English language summary. Ars Libri 34-405 1983 $150

NOWOTNY, KARL A.   Codices Becker I/II. Museum fur Volke-kunde, Wien, Inv. Nr. 60306 and 60307. Graz: Akademische Druck-und Verlagsanstalt, 1961. Text: 3 illus. Wrappers. Facsimile I: Folding color plate, linen-backed, printed on two separate panels. Oblong 4to. Facsimile II: folding color plate, linen-backed. Large square 4to. Folding portfolio. Cloth. 1/4 leather. Ars Libri 34-404 1983 $85

NOYE, WILLIAM   The Principal Grounds and Maxims, with an Analysis of the Laws of England. Richmond: Thomas W. White, 1824. Full calf. Felcone 22-251 1983 $35

NOYES, AL J.   In the Land of Chinook. Helena, (1917). Orig. cloth, 24 plates. 1st ed. Fine copy. Jenkins 153-402 1983 $100

NOYES, ALFRED   Ballads and Poems. Edinburgh: William Blackwood & Sons Ltd., 1928. First edition. Orig. cloth. Publisher's prospectus tipped to front free endpaper. Front inner hinge cracking. Very good. MacManus 279-4014 1983 $15

NOYES, ALFRED   Collected Poems. Edinburgh: William Blackwood & Sons, 1910-1927. First edition. 4 vols. Orig. cloth. Vol. III, fourth impression. Presentation copies, inscribed by the author to John Drinkwater in Vols. I, III, and IV, the last inscription dated 1929. With Drinkwater's bookplates. Covers dull. Very good. MacManus 279-4016 1983 $85

NOYES, ALFRED   Collected Poems. N.Y.: Frederick A. Stokes Co., (1913). First American edition. Frontis. port. 2 vols. Orig. cloth. Dust jackets (lightly worn). Contents differ from the English edition. Very good. MacManus 279-4015 1983 $35

NOYES, ALFRED   Drake, An English Epic. Edinburgh: William Blackwood & Sons, 1906-1908. First edition. Frontis. 2 vols. Orig. cloth. MacManus 279-4017 1983 $35

NOYES, ALFRED   The Enchanted Island And Other Poems. Edinburgh; William Blackwood & Sons, 1909. First edition. Orig. cloth. Prelims lightly foxed. Fine. MacManus 279-4018 1983 $25

NOYES, ALFRED   The Enchanted Island and Other Poems. Edinburgh: William Blackwood & Sons, 1909. First edition. Orig. cloth. Very good. MacManus 279-4019 1983 $20

NOYES, ALFRED   The Flower of Old Japan. London: Grant Richards, 1903. First edition. Orig. parchment-backed boards. Slightly soiled. Very good. MacManus 279-4020 1983 $25

NOYES, ALFRED   The Forest of Wild Thyme. Edinburgh: Blackwood & Sons, 1905. First edition. Orig. cloth. MacManus 279-4021 1983 $20

NOYES, ALFRED   Forty Singing Seamen And Other Poems. Edinburgh: William Blackwood & Sons, 1907. First edition. Orig. cloth. Fine. MacManus 279-4022 1983 $25

NOYES, ALFRED   The Loom of Years. London: Richards, 1902. First edition. 12mo. Orig. vellum-backed boards. Very good. MacManus 279-4023 1983 $50

NOYES, ALFRED   Poems. Edinburgh: William Blackwood & Sons, 1904. First edition. Orig. cloth. Near mint. MacManus 279-4025 1983 $35

NOYES, ALFRED   Poems of the New World. New York, (1942). 8vo. Cloth. Fine copy in dj. In Our Time 156-600 1983 $25

NOYES, ALFRED   Rada. A Belgian Christmas Eve. London: Methuen & Co. Ltd., (1915). First edition. 4 illus. after Goya. Orig. cloth. Dust jacket (worn and badly chipped). Fine. MacManus 279-4026 1983 $35

NOYES, ALFRED   The Return of the Scare-Crow. London: Cassell & Co., (1929). First edition. Orig. cloth. Dust jacket (extremities of spine worn). Very good. MacManus 279-4027 1983 $35

NOYES, ALFRED   Robin Hood. Edinburgh: William Black-wood & Sons Ltd., 1926. First edition. Orig. cloth. Dust packet (dust-soiled, spine dampstained). Very good. MacManus 279-4028 1983 $35

NOYES, ALFRED   Songs of Shadow-of-a-Leaf. London, 1924. First edition. Author's signed autograph presentation inscription to A. St. John Adcock. Very good. Rota 230-449 1983 £12.50

NOYES, ALFRED   A Tale of Old Japan. Edinburgh: William Blackwood & Sons, 1914. First separate edition. Illus. by K. Riches. Orig. pictorial wrappers. Presentation copy, inscribed by author in 1919 on the front flyleaf. Very good. MacManus 279-4030 1983 $45

NOYES, ALFRED   The Torch-Bearers. Edinburgh: William Blackwood & Sons, 1913. First editions. 3 vols. Orig. cloth. Pre-sentation copies, inscribed on the front endpapers of Vols. one & two "For John Drinkwater with very best wishes from Alfred Noyes," in-scriptions dated May and Oct. 1925. With Drinkwater's small leather bookplate in the first two volumes and his stamp in the third. Very good. MacManus 279-4032 1983 $75

NOYES, ALFRED   Walking Shadows. London: Cassell & Co.,
Ltd., (1918). First edition. Orig. cloth. Covers dull. Good. Mac-
Manus 279-4033 1983 $35

NOYES, ETHEL J.R.C.   The Women of the Mayflower and Women of
Plymouth Colony. Plymouth, 1921. 1st ed. Illus. 8vo. Morrill 289-
426 1983 $20

NOYES, JOHN HUMPHREY   History of American Socialisms. Phila.,
1870. Orig. cloth. 1st ed. Fine copy. Jenkins 153-403 1983 $125

NOYES, WILLIAM C.   The Argument of... NY, 1840. Orig.
pr. wraps., (lightly foxed). Argosy 716-363 1983 $20

NOYES, WILLIAM C.   Argument of, on the Trial of
Frederick A. Tallmadge. NY, 1858. Orig. pr. wraps. Argosy 716-381
1983 $20

NUCK, ANTONI   Sialographia et Ductuum Aquosorum
Anatome Nova... Leiden: J. Luchtmans, 1695. Second edition. 8vo.
Cont. calf. Black leaf at end. Engraved frontis. 6 folding plates.
Back worn. Browned. Gurney 90-91 1983 £120

NUCKEL, OTTO   Destiny: A Novel in Pictures. NY:
1930. Sq 8vo, red cloth, vignette on front cover. First American
edition. A very nice copy. Perata 27-141 1983 $65

NUGENT, CHRISTOPHER   An Essay on the Hydrophobia. Printed
for James Leake and William Frederic, Booksellers in Bath; and sold
by M. Cooper, 1753. 8vo, cont. calf, a crisp copy. First edition.
Bickersteth 77-308 1983 £120

NUGENT, MARIA   A Journal for the Year 1811 till the
Year 1815. London, 1839. Portrait frontis., 2 vols. Half calf, gilt,
rubbed, gilt edges. Two tipped-in autograph letters: One from Sir
George Nugent to Mr. Boone. The second from Mr. Boone to Mr. Eyton.
Mr. Eyton's elaborate bookplate in each volume. Good. Edwards 1044-
526 1983 £95

NUGENT, MEREDITH   New Games and Amusements. New York,
1905. 1st ed. Illus. 8vo. Morrill 288-368 1983 $22.50

NUGENT, THOMAS   The Grand Tour. J. Rivington, B. Law,
T. Caston, 1778. Half title vol. I. Lacks leading free end paper,
vol. IV. Calf, sl. local rubbing to leading boards vol. IV, otherwise
v.g. Labels. Jarndyce 31-54 1983 £180

NUMERUS et Tituli Cardinalium, Archiepiscoporum, & Episcoporum
Christianorum. Paris, 1625. 16mo, marbled boards, morocco back,
raised bands. Bookplate removed. Morrill 289-474 1983 $25

NUNN, ANCEL E.   And Where Goes the Parade. Palestine,
Texas: The Foundary, 1977. Brightly illus. by Nunn's art. Signed
by artist and most likely a limited ed. Jenkins 153-404 1983 $85

NURSERY Nonsense. N.Y.: Hurd & Hought. 12mo. Yellow pictorial
wrappers. Bottom of spine re-stitched. Corner of front wrapper ripped
(and 1st leaf). Illus. with 6 half-page color engravings & 2 full-page
color illus. Very good. Aleph-bet 8-189 1983 $25

NURSERY Rhymes Alphabet. Ward Lock, n.d. (ca.1870). 4to. 4 colour
pages with 26 images. Colour pictorial wrappers, small defect top
wrapper. Greer 40-14 1983 £18.50

NUTTALL, THOMAS   An Introduction to Systematic and
Physiological Botany. Boston, 1827. Old boards, new cloth spine.
Some foxing throughout, good. 12 plates. Reese 18-615 1983 $150

NUTTALL, THOMAS   A Journal of Travels into the
Arkansas Territory, During the Year 1819. Philadelphia: Thos. H.
Palmer. 1821. Folding map and five plates. Orig. paper over boards,
paper label. Slight chipping at edges and at base of spine, usual
slight browning, but a very good to fine copy, untrimmed and unpressed.
Rare in the orig. boards. Preserved in half morocco case. Reese
18-556 1983 $900

NYE, ELWOOD L.   Marching with Custer. Glendale: The
Arthur H. Clark Co., 1964. Including the orig. manuscript of the
Equestrian Custer by Carroll Friswold. Nice archive laid in cloth
folding case. Jenkins 152-800 1983 $300

NYE, GORHAM H.   Testimony of...in Regard to the Title
of the Island of Zerba Buena. N.Y., 1868. Orig. printed wraps.
First edition. Ginsberg 46-109 1983 $50

NYLANDER, W.   Synopsis Methodica Lichenum. Paris,
(1858-60). Reprint c. 1900. Vol. 1 and Vol. 2 part 1. 9 coloured
plates, 8vo, new cloth. Wheldon 160-1868 1983 £25

O

OATEN, E. F.   A Sketch of Anglo-Indian Literature.
London, 1908. 8vo. Orig. cloth. Good. Edwards 1044-527 1983 £16

OATES, JOYCE CAROL   All the Good People I've Left Behind.
Black Sparrow Press, 1979. 8vo. Cloth, boards. 1 of 50 copies
numbered and signed by Oates. A fine copy in acetate jacket and box.
In Our Time 156-603 1983 $100

OATES, JOYCE CAROL   Angel of Light. New York, (1981). 8vo.
Wraps. Uncorrected proof copy. A fine copy. In Our Time 156-608
1983 $85

OATES, JOYCE CAROL   The Assassins: A Book of Poems. New
York, (1975). Tall 8vo. Wraps. Uncorrected proof copy. Some
light spotting to the wraps, light wear along the spine, otherwise
a vg-fine copy. In Our Time 156-605 1983 $125

OATES, JOYCE CAROL   By the North Gate. New York:
Vanguard, (1963). 1st ed. Orig. cloth, dj. Fine copy. Jenkins
155-974 1983 $100

OATES, JOYCE CAROL   By the North Gate. NY, (1963). Fine
in dustwrapper with bookplated signed by Oates laid in. Quill & Brush
54-1038 1983 $100

OATES, JOYCE CAROL   Contraries: Essays. New York, 1981.
8vo. Wraps. Uncorrected proof copy. A fine copy. In Our Time
156-609 1983 $85

OATES, JOYCE CAROL   Cupid and Psyche. NY, 1970. Copy "x"
of 26 letter copies signed by Oates, fine in paperwraps and dustwrapper. Quill & Brush 54-1039 1983 $125

OATES, JOYCE CAROL   Cybele. Black Sparrow Press, 1979.
8vo. Cloth, boards. 1 of 50 copies signed by Oates. A fine copy
in acetate jacket and slipcase box. In Our Time 156-604 1983 $100

OATES, JOYCE CAROL   The Lamb of Abyssalia. Mass.
Pomegranate Press, 1979. 8vo. Cloth, boards. Design and graphics
by Karyl Klopp. 1 of 50 deluxe copies signed by Oates and Klopp.
Each of the deluxe copies contain a set of plates tipped in. A
fine copy in acetate jacket. In Our Time 156-602 1983 $150

OATES, JOYCE CAROL   Season of Peril. Black Sparrow Press,
1977. 8vo. Cloth, boards. 1 of 60 copies signed by Oates. With an
orig. drawing by same. Fine in acetate jacket. In Our Time 156-607
1983 $125

OATES, JOYCE CAROL   Sentimental Education. Los Angeles:
Sylvester & Orphanos, 1978. Cloth, leather label. First edition.
One of 300 numbered copies, printed at the Plantin Press, and signed
by the author. Mint as issued, in acetate dust jacket, at pub.'s
price. Reese 20-738 1983 $75

OATES, JOYCE CAROL   A Sentimental Education: Stories.
New York, (1981). 8vo. Wraps. Uncorrected proof copy. Fine. In
Our Time 156-610 1983 $85

OATES, JOYCE CAROL   The Step-Father. CA, 1978. Limited to
26 lettered and signed copies, mint. Quill & Brush 54-1041 1983
$90

OATES, JOYCE CAROL   Triumph of the Spider Monkey. Black
Sparrow Press, 1976. 8vo. Cloth, boards. 1 of 50 copies numbered
and signed by Oates. A fine copy in acetate jacket and slipcase box.
In Our Time 156-606 1983 $100

OATES, JOYCE CAROL   Women in Love and Other Poems. NY, 1968.
Limited to 176 numbered and signed copies, this copy again signed on
front fly, paperwraps, flys slightly offset from wrapper, bottom edge
of rear wrapper slightly chipped. Quill & Brush 54-1043 1983 $75

OBER, FREDERICK A.   Travels in Mexico and Life Among the
Mexicans. San Francisco: J. Dewing and Co., 1884. Tall thick 8vo,
with 190 illus. The deluxe pub.'s binding of half black calf.
Karmiole 73-72 1983 $50

OBERHAMMER, VINZENZ   Die Bronzestatuen am Grabmal
Maximilian I. Innsbruck/Wien, 1947. 128pp. 155 plates. 4to.
Boards, 1/4 cloth, D.j. Ars Libri SB 26-163 1983 $45

OBERHOLSER, H. C.   The Bird Life of Texas. Austin, Texas,
1974. 2 coloured frontispieces, 2 maps, 2 portraits, 34 coloured
plates of birds, 36 black and while illus. of birds and 38 illus. of
habitats. 2 vols., 4to, cloth. Wheldon 160-830 1983 £72

OBERHOLTZER, ELLIS P.   Jay Cooke, Financier of the Civil
War. Phila., 1907. 2 volumes, with the extremely scarce dust
jackets. t.e.g. Illus. First edition. Many facsimiles. A
very handsome set. Jenkins 151-44 1983 $100

OBERNDORF, CLARENCE   The Psychiatric Novels of Oliver Wendell
Holmes. New York, 1944. First edition. 8vo, orig. binding. Dust
wrapper. Fye H-3-788 1983 $20

OBLER, ARCH   Obler Omnibus. N.Y., (1945). Dust
wrapper. Argosy 714-555 1983 $25

OBOOKIAH, HENRY   Memoirs of Henry Obookiah, a Native of
Owhyhee, and a Member of the Foreign Mission School...1881. New
Haven, 1818. Old leather, worn. Reese 18-526 1983 $85

O'BRIEN, D. H.   My Adventures During the Late War.
London, 1902. New edition. Photogravure frontis. portrait. 3 photo-
gravure plates, 1 full page map. 8vo. Orig. cloth. Spine faded.
Some very slight foxing. Good. Edwards 1042-446 1983 £40

O'BRIEN, EDWARD   The Dance of the Machines. New York,
1929. 8vo. Cloth. A fine copy in a highly colorful dj designed by
Louis Lozowwick. Jacket has a chip at top edge of spine. In Our
Time 156-611 1983 $50

O'BRIEN, FLANN   At Swim-Two-Birds. (NY, 1951). First
thus, bottom edges very slightly worn, else near fine in slightly
soiled, very slightly chipped and frayed, very good dustwrapper,
owner's name. Quill & Brush 54-997 1983 $125

O'BRIEN, FLANN   The Hard Life. London, 1961. First
English edition. Slightly chipped and dusty dustwrapper. Near fine.
Jolliffe 25-394 1983 £85

O'BRIEN, J. P.   Will Rogers Ambassador of Good Will.
Chicago, 1935. Frontis. portrait. Illus. Orig. pictorial cloth.
Jenkins 152-362 1983 $25

O'BRIEN, KATE   Farewell Spain. London, 1937. Advance
Proof copy. Drawings by Mary O'Neill. Wrappers. Very good. Rota
230-450 1983 £12

O'BRIEN, MICHAEL J.   Pioneer Irish in New England. New York,
(1937). 8vo, paper label, inner back hinge cracked. 1st ed. Morrill
288-371 1983 $25

O'BRIEN, WILLIAM   The Downfall of Parliamentarianism.
Dublin: Maunsel, 1918. First edition, 8vo, orig. printed paper
wraps., a very good copy. Fenning 62-265 1983 £12.50

O'BRYEN, DENIS   A view of the Treaty of Commerce with
France: signed at Versailles, September 20, 1786. London: J.
Debrett, etc., 1787. First edition. 8vo. Disbound. Ximenes 63-
599 1983 $50

OBSERVATIONS Anatomicae Selectiores Amstelodamensium 1667-1673.
Reading: University of Reading, 1938. 12mo. Orig. quarter-
morocco, t.e.g. Portrait and plates. Reprint of 1667 edition.
Gurney JJ-281 1983 £15

OBSERVATIONS on Lord Castlereagh's speech of the 19th of July, 1804. London: J. Budd, 1805. 8vo. Disbound. First edition. Ximenes 63-214 1983 $40

O'BYRNE, CATHAL   Ashes on the Hearth. Dublin: Three Candles, 1948. First collected edition, woodcuts by Karl Uhlemann, 8vo, orig. printed boards. Fenning 61-521 1983 £12.50

O'CASEY, SEAN   The Flying Wasp. London: Macmillan & Co. Ltd., 1937. First edition. 8vo. Orig. cloth. Dust jacket, darkened. Fine copy. Jaffe 1-262 1983 $50

O'CASEY, SEAN   Inishfallen Fare Thee Well. New York: 1949. First American edition, first printing. Frontis. Gray cloth. Advance copy for review, with dated slip, photo and publisher's release laid in. Very fine in dust jacket. Bradley 66-274 1983 $25

O'CASEY, SEAN   The Plough And The Stars. London: Macmillan And Co., Limited, 1926. First edition. 8vo. Orig. cloth-backed boards with paper labels. Dust jacket, slightly worn and soiled. Fine copy. Jaffe 1-260 1983 $65

O'CASEY, SEAN   The Plough and the Stars. L, 1926. Near fine in slightly frayed, chipped dustwrapper. Quill & Brush 54-1001 1983 $60

O'CASEY, SEAN   The Plough and the Stars. L, 1926. Offset on half-title, very good in chipped dustwrapper, bookplate. Quill & Brush 54-1000 1983 $40

O'CASEY, SEAN   The Plough and the Stars. London: Macmillan & Co., 1935. A printer's proof, with corrections in pencil for the Caravan Library edition of 1937. Port. of author by A. John. Orig. wrappers. With a stamp on the half-title and title-page reading: "R. & R. Clark Limited, Edinburgh. Office Copy. 16 May 1935." Wrappers worn and soiled. Some pages soiled in margins. MacManus 279-4037 1983 $250

O'CASEY, SEAN   Purple Dust. London, 1940. First edition. Dust wrapper. Fine. Rota 231-450 1983 £30

O'CASEY, SEAN   Purple Dust. London: Macmillan & Co. Ltd., 1940. First edition. 8vo. Orig. cloth. Dust jacket. Price clipped from inner flap of jacket, otherwise a fine copy. Jaffe 1-263 1983 $50

O'CASEY, SEAN   The Silver Tassie. London: Macmillan And Co., Limited, 1926. First edition. 8vo. Orig. cloth-backed boards with paper labels. Slightly worn and soiled dust jacket. Fine copy. Jaffe 1-261 1983 $60

O'CASEY, SEAN   The Star Turns Red. London: Macmillan & Co. Ltd., 1940. First edition. 8vo. Orig. cloth. Dust jacket. Very fine copy. Jaffe 1-264 1983 $50

O'CASEY, SEAN   The Story of the Irish Citizen Army. Dublin and London, 1919. First edition. Original grey wrappers. Very good. Gekoski 2-149 1983 £75

O'CASEY, SEAN   The Story of the Irish Citizen Army. Dublin and London: Maunsel & Co., Ltd., 1919. First edition. 8vo. Orig. wrappers. Wrappers slightly worn at spine, but a very good copy. Jaffe 1-259 1983 $85

OCCOM, SAMSON   Sermon at the Execution of Moses Paul, an Indian, Who has Been Guilty of Murder... London, 1788. Cald and boards, fine. Reese 18-162 1983 $300

OCEAN Steamships. New York, 1891. 1st ed. Illus. 8vo, pictorial front cover. Morrill 288-56 1983 $30

OCHSE, J. J.   Fruits and Fruitculture in the Dutch East Indies. Batavia, 1931. 57 coloured plates, royal 8vo, cloth. Good ex-library copy. Wheldon 160-2133 1983 £35

OCHSE, J. J.   Vegetables of the Dutch East Indies. Amsterdam, 1980. New edition, 463 text-figures, royal 8vo, cloth. Wheldon 160-2134 1983 £46.50

OCKLAND, CHRISTOPHER   Anglorvm Praelia ab anno Domini 1327. Londini, Radulphm Nuberie, 1582. 8vo, 18th century calf, hinges restored, small wormhole at lower blank tip of several leaves; fine, sound copy. Ravenstree 97-146 1983 $225

O'CONAIRE, PADRAIC   Field and Fair. Dublin: Talbot Press, 1929. First edition thus, with portrait and 13 illus. by Michael Mac Liammoir, 8vo, orig. cloth, with printed paper labels, a nice copy in a slightly worn dust wrapper. Fenning 60-300 1983 £12.50

O'CONNELL, DANIEL   A Letter...to His Grace, the Duke of Wellington. John Limbird, 1835. 8 pp pamphlet, modern blue boards, v.g. Jarndyce 31-201 1983 £20

O'CONNELL, DANIEL   O'Connell on Socialism. Glasgow: Hugh Margey, 1843. Modern blue boards, v.g. Jarndyce 31-202 1983 £20

O'CONNELL, J. J.   Catholicity in the Carolinas and Georgia. New York, (1879). First edition. Portrait. Ex-library. Some wear. Jenkins 152-307 1983 $65

O'CONNELL, JEPHSON B.   The Financial Administration of Saorstat Eireann. Dublin, (1934). First edition, 8vo, orig. cloth. In dust wrapper. Fenning 61-323 1983 £18.50

O'CONNOR, FLANNERY   Everything That Rises Must Converge. NY, (1965). Fine in nice clean dustwrapper with very slight wear on edges. Quill & Brush 54-1002 1983 $90

O'CONNOR, FLANNERY   The Violent Bear it Away. N.Y., (1960). First edition. Fine, in a slightly rubbed dust wrapper. Argosy 714-558 1983 $100

O'CONNOR, FRANK   The Big Fellow. A Life of Michael Collins. London: Thomas Nelson & Sons Limited, (1937). First edition. Frontis. from the bust by F. Doyle-James. 8vo. Orig. cloth. Dust jacket, slightly worn. A fine copy. Jaffe 1-265 1983 $125

O'CONNOR, FRANK   Guests of the Nation. NY, 1931. First American edition, very good plus in remnants of dustwrapper. Quill & Brush 54-1005 1983 $40

O'CONNOR, FRANK   A Picture Book. Dublin: Cuala Press, 1943. First edition. Illus. by E. Rivers. One of 480 numbered copies. Unopened. Fine. Rota 230-452 1983 £60

O'CONNOR, FRANK   The Road to Stratford. London, 1948. First edition. Frayed dust wrapper. Neat rubber-stamp on title-page. Nice. Rota 230-453 1983 £12.50

O'CONNOR, FRANK   Towards An Appreciation Of Literature. Dublin: Metropolitan Publishing Co. Ltd., 1945. First edition. 8vo. Orig. boards. Dust jacket. Fine copy. Jaffe 1-266 1983 $50

O'CONNOR, THOMAS   An Impartial and Correct History of the War Between the United States of America, and Great Britain... New York, 1816. Engraved frontis. plate. Cont. calf, expertly rebacked. A very good copy. Reese 18-503 1983 &75

O'CONNOR, V. C. SCOTT   The Silken East. London, 1904. Folding maps, 22 colour plates. Numerous illus. including several full-page. 2 vols. Decorative cloth, gilt. 8vo. Good. Edwards 1044-529 1983 £75

O'CONNOR, WINNIE   Jockeys, Crooks and Kings. N.Y.: Jonathan Cape & Harrison Smith, (1930). First edition, complete with errata slip. Frontis. port. Woodcuts by L. Ward. Orig. cloth-backed pictorial boards. Very good. MacManus 279-4040 1983 $25

O'DAY, NELL   A Catalogue of Books Printed by John Henry Nash. San Francisco: 1937. Octavo. First edition. Frontis. portrait. Limited to 500 copies printed by Nash. Covers slightly faded, else fine. Bromer 25-257 1983 $150

ODDI, MUTIO   De Gli Horologi Solari Nelle Svperficie Piane trattato Di Mutio Oddi Da Vrbino. In Milano, Per Giacomo Lantoni M.DC.XIV, (1614). 4to, bound in full modern pigskin. Title stamped in gold on spine. New endpapers. Waterstaining in lower margins of a few leaves. First edition. Very good. Arkway 22-69 1983 $700

ODETS, CLIFFORD   Golden Boy. New York: Random House, (1937). Cloth. Photos. First edition. A fine copy in dust jacket, which shows the lightest signs of use. Reese 20-746 1983 $65

ODINGSELLS, GABRIEL   The Capricious Lovers. A comedy. London: printed for Jonah Bowyer, and J. Walthoe; and sold by J. Roberts, 1726. 8vo, disbound. A variant issue of the first edition, with the six leaves of signature A reprinted on slightly coarser paper, and with somewhat cruder ornaments. Ximenes 64-396 1983 $175

ODINGSELLS, GABRIEL   The Capricious Lovers. A comedy. London: printed for Jonah Bowyer, and J. Walthoe; and sold by J. Roberts, 1726. 8vo, disbound. First edition. Rare. Ximenes 64-395 1983 $150

O'DONOGHUE, EDWARD G.   The Story of Bethlehem Hospital From Its Foundation in 1247. London: T. Fisher Unwin, (1914). First edition. Library discard stamp on titlepage, else very good in modern blue buckram. Illustrated. Gach 94-250 1983 $50

O'DONOVAN, EDMOND   The Merv Oasis. London, 1882. Large folding map in endpocket, portrait and numerous other plates and folding facsimiles. Some very slight spotting. 2 vols. Thick 8vo. Good. Edwards 1044-530 1983 £225

O'DONOVAN, EDMOND   Merv. Smith, Elder, 1883. First edition of this abridgment, with a portrait, 8vo, orig. cloth. Fenning 60-301 1983 £14.50

O'DOWD, JAMES C.   Practical Hints to Courts Martial upon Many Matters Usually Coming Under their Notice. William Clowes and Sons, 1882. First edition, small 8vo, orig. red cloth, gilt. The binding lightly stained but sound and otherwise a very good copy. Fenning 62-266 1983 £10.50

O'DWYER, M.   India as I Knew It. London, 1925. 2 folding maps. 8vo. Orig. cloth. Good. Edwards 1044-531 1983 £15

OEHLER, GOTTLIEB F.   Description of a Journey and Visit to the Pawnee Indians on Platte River, 1851. New York, 1914. Wrps. Scarce. Clark 741-318 1983 $39.50

O'FAOLAIN, SEAN   The Born Genius. Detroit, 1936. Covers (esp. spine) darkened. Limited to 250 numbered copies, signed by author. Very good. Rota 45-232 1983 $35

O'FAOLAIN, SEAN   Constance Markievicz or The Average Revolutionary. London: Jonathan Cape, (1934). First edition. 8vo. Illus. Orig. cloth. Dust jacket. Fine copy. Jaffe 1-269 1983 $85

O'FAOLAIN, SEAN   The Life Story of Eamon De Valera. Dublin and Cork: The Talbot Press Limited, (1933). First edition. Small 8vo. Frontis. Orig. cloth. Dust jacket, slightly chipped. Fine copy. Jaffe 1-268 1983 $45

O'FAOLAIN, SEAN   A Nest of Simple Folk. London: Jonathan Cape, (1933). First edition. 8vo. Orig. cloth. Dust jacket. Jacket slightly soiled and chipped at head of spine, otherwise a very good copy. Jaffe 1-267 1983 $85

O'FAOLAIN, SEAN   There's A Birdie In The Cage. London: Grayson & Grayson, 1935. First edition. 8vo. Orig. cloth. Dust jacket. One of 285 copies signed by the author. Fine copy. Jaffe 1-270 1983 $75

OFF to Story Land. Nister, nd (ca. 1900). Mounted colour frontis. & 2 b&w illus. by Louis Wain & numerous illus. by other artists. Unpag. Brown cloth backed pictorial bds., corners v. sl. worn, nice copy. Hodgkins 27-156 1983 £12.50

O'FLAHERTY, LIAM   The Assassin. London: Jonathan Cape, (1928). First edition. 8vo. Orig. cloth. Dust jacket. Small book-label removed from front endsheet, otherwise a fine copy. Jaffe 1-276 1983 $50

O'FLAHERTY, LIAM   The Assassin. London: Jonathan Cape, (1928). First edition. Orig. cloth. Dust jacket (chipped at head of spine). Review Copy, so stamped on the dust jacket. Bookplate. Very good. MacManus 279-4042 1983 $35

O'FLAHERTY, LIAM   The Black Soul. London: Jonathan Cape, (1924). First edition. Orig. cloth with paper label on spine. Dust jacket (a little worn and soiled). Inscribed to Jack Lyne by author. Good. MacManus 279-4043 1983 $150

O'FLAHERTY, LIAM   The Child of God. London: 1926. First edition. Limited to 100 copies signed by author. Printed marbled wrappers, bound into decorated cloth over boards, paper spine label. Scot Cunningham's copy, with his bookplate. Very good. Bradley 66-276 1983 $125

O'FLAHERTY, LIAM   Civil War. London: E. Archer, November, 1925. First edition. 4to. Orig. marbled wrappers. Limited to 100 copies signed by O'Flaherty. Very fine. MacManus 279-4044 1983 $150

O'FLAHERTY, LIAM   Darkness. London: E. Archer, May, 1926. First edition. 4to. Frontis. port. by W. Roberts. Unbound. Unopened signatures as issued. One of 12 copies printed simultaneously with the edition of 100 copies, with cast of preformance produced in the Studio of William Roberts. Signed by author, on front page. A trifle dusty. Very fine. MacManus 279-4045 1983 $350

O'FLAHERTY, LIAM   The Fairy Goose And Two Other Stories. N.Y.: Crosby Gaige, 1927. First edition. Orig. cloth-backed boards. Paper label on spine. Dust jacket. One of 12 copies printed on blue hand-made paper, as inscribed by the author on the colophon page. Very fine. MacManus 279-4046 1983 $350

O'FLAHERTY, LIAM   The Fairy Goose and Two Other Stories. N.Y.: Gaige, 1927. First edition. Orig. cloth-backed boards. Limited and signed by the author. Bookplate of B. George Ulizio. Fine. MacManus 279-4047 1983 $40

O'FLAHERTY, LIAM   Famine. London: Victor Gollancz Ltd., 1937. First edition. 8vo. Orig. cloth. Dust jacket, slightly torn. Fine copy. Jaffe 1-285 1983 $50

O'FLAHERTY, LIAM   Hollywood Cemetery. London, 1935. First edition. Covers marked and worn and edges bruised. Name of flyleaf. Very good. Rota 230-458 1983 £18

O'FLAHERTY, LIAM   The House of Gold. London, (1929). 8vo. Cloth. Presentation copy, inscribed the year of publication dated September 27, 1929. In Our Time 156-613 1983 $200

O'FLAHERTY, LIAM   The House of Gold. London, (1929). 8vo. Cloth. Fine in dj. This copy signed by author on front flyleaf. In Our Time 156-612 1983 $150

O'FLAHERTY, LIAM   The House of Gold. London: Jonathan Cape, (1929). First edition. 8vo. Orig. cloth. Dust jacket. Bookplate removed from front endsheet, otherwise a fine copy. Jaffe 1-278 1983 $35

O'FLAHERTY, LIAM   The House of Gold. L, (1929). Minor cover stains, else very good in frayed and lightly chipped dustwrapper. Quill & Brush 54-1012 1983 $35

O'FLAHERTY, LIAM   The House of Gold. London, 1929. First edition. Inscription on flyleaf. Good. Rota 230-456 1983 £15

O'FLAHERTY, LIAM   The Informer. London: Jonathan Cape Ltd., (1925). First edition. 8vo. Orig. cloth. Dust jacket, lightly dust-soiled and nicked. Fine copy. Jaffe 1-273 1983 $275

O'FLAHERTY, LIAM   Insurrection. London: Victor Gollancz Ltd., 1950. Uncorrected Proof copy of the first edition. Orig. wrappers. Very good. MacManus 279-4048 1983 $125

O'FLAHERTY, LIAM   I Went to Russia. London, 1931. First edition. Some foxing of Preliminaries. Repaired dust wrapper. Author's signed autograph presentation inscription to E. Goldston. Very nice. Rota 231-454 1983 £60

O'FLAHERTY, LIAM   I Went To Russia. London: Jonathan Cape, (1931). First edition. 8vo. Frontis. Orig. cloth. Dust jacket, slightly torn and dusty. Fine copy. Jaffe 1-281 1983 $45

O'FLAHERTY, LIAM   Joseph Conrad. An Appreciation. London: E. Lahr, (n.d.). First edition. Orig. printed wrappers (a bit faded). Very good. MacManus 277-1113 1983 $25

O'FLAHERTY, LIAM   Land. Lon., 1946. Fine in soiled and faded slightly frayed and chipped, very good dustwrapper. Quill & Brush 54-1008 1983 $60

O'FLAHERTY, LIAM   The Life of Tim Healy. London: Jonathan Cape, (1927). First edition. Frontis. 8vo. Orig. cloth. Very good copy. Jaffe 1-275 1983 $25

O'FLAHERTY, LIAM   The Life of Tim Healy. London: Jonathan Cape, (1927). First edition. Orig. cloth. Fine. MacManus 279-4049 1983 $25

O'FLAHERTY, LIAM   The Martyr. London: Gollancz, 1933. Cloth. First edition. Presentation copy from the author, inscribed on the front free end sheet to "Teddy" Goldston. Small nick in foredge of one board, else fine in dust jacket. Reese 20-745 1983 $200

O'FLAHERTY, LIAM   Mr. Gilhooley. London, (1926). First edition. 8vo, cloth. Fine. Argosy 714-566 1983 $40

O'FLAHERTY, LIAM   The Mountain Tavern. London, 1929. First edition. Spine and covers faded. Author's autograph signature. Nice. Rota 231-452 1983 £40

O'FLAHERTY, LIAM   The Mountain Tavern and Other Stories. London: Jonathan Cape, 1929. First edition. 8vo. Orig. cloth. Dust jacket, slightly chipped. Fine copy. Jaffe 1-279 1983 $45

O'FLAHERTY, LIAM   The Puritan. Lon., (1932). Top page edges slightly soiled, else near fine in lightly chipped and soiled, very good dustwrapper with few short tears. Quill & Brush 54-1013 1983 $125

O'FLAHERTY, LIAM   The Puritan. London: Jonathan Cape, (1932). First edition. 8vo. Orig. cloth. Dust jacket, chipped. Fine copy. Jaffe 1-282 1983 $45

O'FLAHERTY, LIAM   Red Barbara and Other Stories. N.Y.: Crosby Gaige, 1928. First edition. Illus. by Cecil Salkeld. Orig. cloth-backed boards. One of 600 copies signed by author. Covers somewhat faded. Bookplate partially removed. MacManus 279-4050 1983 $45

O'FLAHERTY, LIAM   The Return of the Brute. London: Mandrake Press, 1929. First edition. Orig. cloth. Dust jacket (chipped; soiled). Presentation copy inscribed, "To Jack Lyne with best wishes from Liam O'Flaherty." MacManus 279-4051 1983 $125

O'FLAHERTY, LIAM   Return of the Brute. L, 1929. Minor interior foxing, flys slightly offset, else very good in lightly chipped, very good dustwrapper, bookplate. Quill & Brush 54-1009 1983 $75

O'FLAHERTY, LIAM   Return of the Brute. NY, 1930. Near fine in slightly dulled very good dustwrapper, slightly frayed at edges. Quill & Brush 54-1010 1983 $60

O'FLAHERTY, LIAM   Return of the Brute. London: The Mandrake Press, 1929. First edition. 8vo. Orig. cloth. Dust jacket. Frayed jacket. Fine copy. Jaffe 1-277 1983 $45

O'FLAHERTY, LIAM   Shame The Devil. London: Grayson & Grayson, (1934). First edition. 8vo. Frontis. Orig. cloth with paper label. Glassine jacket with printed flaps. Jacket torn, otherwise a very good copy. Jaffe 1-284 1983 $75

O'FLAHERTY, LIAM   Shame the Devil. London, 1934. First edition. Covers a little marked. Nice. Rota 231-455 1983 £12

O'FLAHERTY, LIAM   Skerrett. London: Gollancz, 1932. Cloth. First edition. Presentation copy from the author, inscribed on the front free endsheet to "Teddy". Traces of foxing at edges, else fine in dust jacket. Reese 20-744 1983 $200

O'FLAHERTY, LIAM   Skerrett. NY, 1932. Bottom corner of rear board slightly bumped, edges lightly rubbed, spine edges show light wear, else very good in lightly chipped and frayed, very good dustwrapper. Quill & Brush 54-1011 1983 $75

O'FLAHERTY, LIAM   Skerrett. London: Victor Gollancz, 1932. First edition. 8vo. Orig. cloth. Dust jacket, slightly faded. Fine copy. Jaffe 1-283 1983 $50

O'FLAHERTY, LIAM   Spring Sowing. London, 1924. First edition. Boards just a little marked. Nice. Rota 230-455 1983 £25

O'FLAHERTY, LIAM   Spring Sowing. London: Jonathan Cape, (1924). First edition. 8vo. Orig. cloth. Dust jacket, lightly torn and soiled. Fine copy. Jaffe 1-272 1983 $45

O'FLAHERTY, LIAM   The Tent. London: Jonathan Cape, (1926). First edition. Orig. cloth with paper label on spine. Dust jacket (a trifle worn). Signed by author on flyleaf. Fine. MacManus 279-4052 1983 $75

O'FLAHERTY, LIAM   The Tent. London: Jonathan Cape, (1926). First edition. 8vo. Orig. cloth. Dust jacket. Bookplate removed from front endsheet, otherwise a very good copy. Jaffe 1-274 1983 $35

O'FLAHERTY, LIAM   The Terrorist. London: E. Archer, February, 1926. First edition. Orig. wrappers. One of 100 copies privately printed and signed by author. Very good. MacManus 279-4053 1983 $150

O'FLAHERTY, LIAM   Thy Neighbour's Wife. London: Jonathan Cape, (1923). First edition. 8vo. Orig. cloth. Dust jacket. Head of spine a trifle nicked, otherwise a very good copy. Jaffe 1-271 1983 $75

O'FLAHERTY, LIAM   A Tourist's Guide to Ireland. Mandrake Press, (1929). First edition. 12mo. Dust wrapper. Author's autograph presentation inscription to E. Goldston, owner of Mandrake Press. Fine. Rota 231-453 1983 £45

O'FLAHERTY, LIAM   Two Lovely Beasts and Other Stories. London, 1948. First edition. Argosy 714-567 1983 $30

O'FLAHERTY, LIAM   Two Years. London: Jonathan Cape, (1930). First edition. 8vo. Frontis. Orig. cloth. Dust jacket, slightly dust-soiled and torn. Fine copy. Jaffe 1-280 1983 $45

O'FLAHERTY, LIAM   The Wild Swan, and Other Stories. London, 1932. Ltd. first edition. Buckram, one of 550 signed copies. Argosy 714-568 1983 $40

O'FLYNN, JOHN   "Provincialisms" and "Dialects" in Modern Spoken Irish. Dublin: Gill, 1910. First edition, cr. 8vo, orig. printed wrapper, v.g. copy. Fenning 61-325 1983 £18.50

OGDEN, JOHN C.   An Excursion into Bethleham & Nazareth, in Pennsylvania, in the Year 1799. Philadelphia: Charles Cist, 1800. Calf-backed boards. Top half-inch of spine defective, few signatures pulled, else a very nice copy. With the cont. signatures of Josiah and Enoch Eithian. First edition. Felcone 22-172 1983 $175

OGDEN, UZAL   Antidote to Deism. Newark: John Woods, 1795. 12mo, later cloth-backed boards. Ex-library. Ink blot on t.p. & fly leaf. Argosy 710-73 1983 $50

OGILBY, J.　　Asia, the First Part... London, 1673.
Engraved title, 4 double page maps, 25 plates including nine double
page, text illus. Folio. Cont. calf, rebacked. 8vo. Fine. Edwards
1044-534　1983　£900

OGILVIE-GRANT, W. R.　　A hand-book to the Gamebirds. 1896-97.
48 coloured plates, 2 vols., cr. 8vo, cloth. Wheldon 160-831　1983
£30

OGILVY, GAVIS, PSEUD.
Please turn to
BARRIE, JAMES MATTHEW

OGLE, JOHN J.　　The Free Library, its History and
Present Condition. George Allen, 1897. First edition. Orig. green
cloth, sl. rubbed. Jarndyce 31-223　1983　£10.50

OGLESBY, CATHERINE　　Modern Primitive Arts of Mexico...
New York/London: Whittlesey House, 1939. 12 plates. Text figures.
Small 4to. Cloth. Ars Libri 34-407　1983　$30

O'GRADY, STANDISH　　Finn and His Companions. nd Illus.
by Jack B. Yeats. Frontis. & 1 illus, 8pp adverts. Bkstrip, discol'd,
sl. mark fr. cvr. & sl. foxing, vg. Hodgkins 27-44　1983　£15

O'HANLON, JOHN　　History of the Queen's County. Dublin,
1907-14, reprinted Kilkenny, 1981. With maps, plates and other illus.
2 vols., 8vo, orig. cloth, new in matching slip-case. Ltd. edition
of 1,000 numbered copies. Fenning 60-302　1983　£50

O'HANLON, JOHN　　Life and Scenery in Missouri. Dublin:
James Duffy, 1890. First edition, 12mo, orig. cloth, gilt. Inside
joints just a little weak, but still a nice copy. Fenning 62-268
1983　£35

O'HARA, FRANK　　Collected Poems. N.Y., 1971. First
edition. Small 4to, d.w. In the first issue dust wrapper with the
nude drawing by Larry Rivers. Fine. Argosy 714-883　1983　$100

O'HARA, FRANK　　In Memory of My Feelings. NY, (1967).
Illus. by Lichtenstein, Motherwell, et al., limited to 2500 numbered
copies, slightly soiled, else fine in fine slipcase. Quill & Brush
54-1014　1983　$125

O'HARA, JOHN　　Appointment in Samarra. New York:
Harcourt, Brace and Company, (1934). First edition, first issue.
8vo. Orig. cloth. Dust jacket. Very fine copy. Jaffe 1-286
1983　$850

O'HARA, JOHN　　Appointment in Samarra. New York:
Harcourt, Brace, (1934). 1st ed., with inserted slip present.
Orig. cloth. Spine gilt dull, but very good copy. Scarce.
Jenkins 155-978　1983　$25

O'HARA, JOHN　　Five Plays. (L, 1962). Fine in dustwrapper with color rubbed and very minor wear to edges, very good or
better. Quill & Brush 54-1016　1983　$100

O'HARA, JOHN　　Hellbox. NY, (1947). Bright with
slightly offset endpapers in bright dustwrapper, slightly frayed and
chipped at spine edges, bookplate. Quill & Brush 54-1017　1983　$30

O'HARA, JOHN　　Here's O'Hara: Three Novels and Twenty
Short Stories. NY, (1946). Very good in slightly frayed, slightly
aged dustwrapper, owner's name. Quill & Brush 54-1018　1983　$35

O'HARA, JOHN　　Hope of Heaven. New York: Harcourt,
Brace, (1938). 1st ed. Orig. cloth. Gilt dulled, but very good.
Jenkins 155-980　1983　$20

O'HARA, JOHN　　The Instrument. NY, (1967). Limited to
300 numbered and signed, specially bound copies, fine in slightly
nicked, near fine slipcase. Quill & Brush 54-1022　1983　$150

O'HARA, JOHN　　The Lockwood Concern. NY, (1965). One
of 300 numbered and signed, specially bound copies, fine in very good
slipcase. Quill & Brush 54-1023　1983　$150

O'HARA, JOHN　　Lovely Childs. NY, (1969). No. 31 of
200 specially bound and signed copies, very fine in slipcase. Quill
& Brush 54-1019　1983　$125

O'HARA, JOHN　　Pal Joey. N.Y., Duell, (1940). First
edition. Dust jacket (rubbed, few nicks). Very good. Houle 22-1219
1983　$85

O'HARA, JOHN　　A Rage to Live. NY, (1949). Very good
in slightly nicked dustwrapper. Quill & Brush 54-1015　1983　$35

O'HARA, JOHN　　Sermons and Soda-Water. NY: (1906).
Three vols. Limited edition, signed by O'Hara, with autograph
announcement card from The First Edition Circle laid-in. Fine set
in slip-case. Bromer 25-80　1983　$85

O'HARA, JOHN　　Waiting For Winter. NY, (1966). Limited
to 300 numbered and signed, specially bound copies, fine in red cloth
in slightly nicked else fine slipcase. Quill & Brush 54-1024　1983
$125

O'HICKEY, MICHAEL P.　　Language and Nationality. Waterford,
1918. First collected edition, with a portrait, 8vo, orig. cloth.
Fenning 61-327　1983　£28.50

OHIO. CONSTITUTION.　　The Constitutions of Ohio. Cleveland,
1912. Facs. Illus. Uncut. Cloth, very good. Reese 19-407　1983
$60

OHIO. LAWS.　　Acts of the State of Ohio, Passed and
Revised. Chillicothe, 1805. Orig. calf, worn. Internally good.
Reese 18-274　1983　$600

O-JIB-UE SPELLING Book, Designed for the Use of Native Learners.
Boston, 1835. 107pp. Illustrated. Second edition. Corrected
and Englarged. Original paper boards and cloth backing. Fine
copy. Jenkins 151-36　1983　$175

OKE, RICHARD　　The Boy From Apulia. London: Arthur
Barker Ltd., (1936). First edition. 8vo. Frontis. Orig. cloth.
Dust jacket, slightly dust-soiled. Fine copy. Jaffe 1-290　1983
$35

OKE, RICHARD　　Frolic Wind. London: Victor Gollancz
Ltd., 1929. First edition. 8vo. Orig. cloth. Dust jacket. One of
a number of copies signed by him, with a label on the spine of the
jacket advertising this fact. Fine copy. Jaffe 1-287　1983　$45

OKE, RICHARD　　India's Coral Strand. (London):
Faber And Faber, (1934). First edition. 8vo. Orig. cloth. Dust
jacket, slightly chipped and dust-soiled. Very good copy. Jaffe
1-289　1983　$25

OKE, RICHARD　　Wanton Boys. London: Victor Gollancz
Ltd., 1932. First edition. 8vo. Orig. cloth. Dust jacket, darkened
and chipped. Very good copy. Jaffe 1-288　1983　$25

O'KEEFFE, JOHN　　Recollections of the life of John O'
Keeffe, written by himself. London: Henry Colburn, 1826. 2 vols.,
8vo, original grey boards, printed paper labels (spines a bit worn,
corners bumped). First edition. Laid into this copy is a one-page
manuscript labelled "for the next edition,"... No further editions
were printed. With a portrait. Stain in inner margins towards the
end of the 2nd volume, else a very good copy in original condition.
Ximenes 64-397　1983　$175

O'KEEFFE, ROBERT　　Ultramontanism Versus Civil and
Religious Liberty. Dublin: Hodges, Foster, 1875. First edition,
8vo, orig. cloth, gilt. Fenning 62-269　1983　£26.50

OKES, THOMAS VERNEY　　An Account of the Providential
Presentation of Eliz. Woodcock. Cambridge, n.d. (1799). Third
edition, 16mo, boards, vellum spine. Jarndyce 31-55　1983　£36

OKIE, HOWARD PITCHER　　Old Silver and Old Sheffield Plate.
New York, 1928. 1st ed. Illus. 4to. Morrill 287-633　1983　$25

OKLAHOMA. LAWS.   Laws Relating to the Five Civilized
Tribes in Oklahoma 1890-1914. Washington, 1915. Orig. cloth. Slight
insect damage to covers. Jenkins 152-728 1983 $35

OLBRECHTS, FRANS M.   Bijdrage tot de Kennis van de Chrono-
logie der afrikaansche Plastiek. Bruxelles, 1941. 10 plates. 8
text illus. Small 4to. Wrappers. Ars Libri 34-713 1983 $65

THE OLD Ballad of the Boy and the Mantle. (Bedford Park: Cardoc
Press, 1900). 12mo. Orig. cloth-backed paper covered boards,
paper cover label. Limited to 300 copies. Covers lightly soiled.
Oak Knoll 48-95 1983 $35

OLD Ballads, Historical and Narrative, with Some of Modern Date...
London, T. Evans, 1777. 2 vols., 8vo, cont. calf gilt, labels
lacking, bookplate partly scraped away, hinges a little worn, with
half titles in both vols. First edition. Ravenstree 94-76 1983
$53

THE OLD black cock and his dunghill advisers in jeopardy. London:
Effingham Wilson, 1820. First edition. 8vo. Disbound. With 12
woodcut illus. Ximenes 63-506 1983 $45

OLD English, Scotch and Irish Songs with Music. NY: Frederick A.
Stokes, (ca. 1900). American edition. 24 sketches by A. S. Boyd.
Wine leather wrappers lightly bent, still near fine. (1 1/4 x 3/4;
27x19mm). Bromer 25-458 1983 $185

OLD-TIME Ships of Salem. Salem, Essex Institute, 1925. Third Ed.
Colored plates; also black and white illustrations. 4to, original
wrappers, paper label. Few stains on front cover. Morrill 290-389
1983 $25

OLDENBOURG, RUDOLF   P.P. Rubens. Des Meisters Gemalde.
Stuttgart: Deutsche Verlags-Anstalt, (1921). 538 illus. 4to.
Cloth. Ars Libri 32-602 1983 $125

OLDER, FREMONT   The Life of George Hearst, California
Pioneer. San Francisco: Printed for William R. Earst by John Henry
Nash, 1933. Folio. Full gilt vellum. Frontis portrait. Vignette
chapter openings. Limited to 1000 copies. Fine copy. Jenkins 153-
801 1983 $450

OLDER, FREMONT   My Own Story. N.Y., Macmillan, 1926.
First edition. Blue cloth. Very good. Houle 21-1122 1983 $20

OLDFIELD, CLAUDE HOUGHTON   Christina. London: William Heinemann
Ltd., (1936). First edition. 8vo. Orig. cloth. Dust jacket.
Very fine copy. Jaffe 1-154 1983 $25

OLDFIELD, CLAUDE HOUGHTON   A Hair Divides. London: Thornton
Butterworth Limited, (1930). First edition. 8vo. Orig. cloth.
Dust jacket. Signed by the author. Two-inch tear to front of
jacket, otherwise a fine copy. Jaffe 1-149 1983 $45

OLDFIELD, CLAUDE HOUGHTON   Judas. London: C.W. Daniel, Ltd.,
1922. First edition. 8vo. Orig. orange boards with paper labels.
Dust jacket. Signed by the author. Fine copy. Jaffe 1-148 1983
$50

OLDFIELD, CLAUDE HOUGHTON   Julian Grant Loses His Way. London:
William Heinemann, 1933. First edition. Orig. cloth. Dust jacket
(spine and covers a bit worn and chipped, with a piece missing from
the upper ocrner of the back cover). Contains an ALS, 2 pages, 8vo.,
Savage Club, Adelphi, W.C.2., 26 April 1933, to H.W. Fennell. Slight
foxing. Front inner hinge cracking. Very good. MacManus 279-2769
1983 $45

OLDFIELD, CLAUDE HOUGHTON   Julian Grant Loses His Way. London:
William Heinemann, 1933. First edition. Orig. cloth. Presentation
copy inscribed: "Gratefully, to Louise Morgan Claude Houghton, Savage
Club W.C.2." Covers and spine slightly faded and worn. Good. Mac-
Manus 279-2770 1983 $35

OLDFIELD, CLAUDE HOUGHTON   Julian Grant Loses His Way. London:
William Heinemann Ltd., (1933). First edition. 8vo. Orig. cloth.
Dust jacket. Signed by the author. Fine copy. Jaffe 1-151 1983
$35

OLDFIELD, CLAUDE HOUGHTON   The Passing of the Third Floor Back.
London: The Queensway Press, n.d. First edition. 8vo. Orig. cloth.
Dust jacket. Very fine copy. Jaffe 1-150 1983 $50

OLDFIELD, CLAUDE HOUGHTON   The Phantom Host and Other Verses.
London: Elkin Mathews, 1917. First edition. 12mo. Orig. wrappers.
Fine. Signed by author. MacManus 279-2771 1983 $45

OLDFIELD, CLAUDE HOUGHTON   Strangers. London: Collins Publishers,
(1938). First edition. 8vo. Orig. cloth. Dust jacket. Fine copy.
Jaffe 1-155 1983 $25

OLDFIELD, CLAUDE HOUGHTON   This Was Ivor Trent. London: William
Heinemann Ltd., (1935). First edition. 8vo. Orig. cloth. Dust
jacket. With the orig. Book Society wraparound band. Fine copy.
Jaffe 1-153 1983 $45

OLDFIELD, CLAUDE HOUGHTON   This Was Ivor Trent. London: William
Heinemann, 1935. First edition. Orig. cloth. Dust jacket (quite
faded and worn, with some chipping to the spine). Presentation copy
inscribed: "Inscribed to S.J. Feldman, Claude Houghton." Good. Mac-
Manus 279-2772 1983 $35

OLDFIELD, CLAUDE HOUGHTON   Three fantastic tales. New York:
Chiswick Press for Frederick C. Joiner, 1934. First edition, tall
8vo, frontis., yellow cloth gilt, t.e.g., others uncut, very fine.
250 numbered copies signed by author. Deighton 3-177 1983 £32

OLDFIELD, CLAUDE HOUGHTON   Three Fantastic Tales. (London):
Frederick C. Joiner, 1934. First edition. Frontis. by John Farleigh.
4to. Orig. yellow cloth. One of 275 copies signed by the author.
Fine copy. Jaffe 1-152 1983 $35

OLDHAM, JOHN   Works. London: for Dan. Brown, etc.,
1703. Sixth edition, corrected. Thick 8vo. Cont. panelled calf,
gilt, morocco label, gilt. Engraved portrait after Van der Gucht.
A little worn. Traylen 94-637 1983 £40

OLDMIXON, JOHN   Gleanings from Piccadilly to Pera. Lon-
don, 1854. Coloured frontis. 3 coloured plates, engraved title.
Decorated cloth, spine frayed at head and tail, all edges gilt. 8vo.
Good. Edwards 1044-533 1983 £50

OLDMIXON, JOHN   Reflections on the stage, and Mr.
Collyer's Defence of the Short View. In four dialogues. London:
printed for R. Parker, and P. Buck, 1699. 8vo, cont. mottled calf
(spine and corners a bit worn). 1st edition. Wanting fly-leaves,
contemporary scribbling on the pastedowns; one small printing flaw,
affecting several words. A very good copy of a very scarce title.
Ximenes 64-400 1983 $600

OLDROYD, OSBORN H.   The Assassination of Abraham Lincoln.
Wash., 1901. 1st ed. Illus. & ports, ex lib. Argosy 710-262 $35

OLDROYD, OSBORN H.   The Assassination of Abraham Lincoln.
Washington, Author, 1901. 1st ed. Illus. 8vo. Ends of spine
slightly frayed. Morrill 286-376 1983 $30

OLDROYD, OSBORN H.   The Assassination of Abraham Lincoln.
Washington, Author, 1917. Illus. Small 8vo. Inscribed by author.
Morrill 289-476 1983 $20

OLDSCHOOL, OLIVER   Brief Outline of the Life of Henry Clay.
Washington: John T. Towers, (1944). Sewn as issued. Light stain to
upper right corner. Jenkins 152-51a 1983 $45

O'LEARY, JOHN   Recollections of Fenians and Fenianism.
Downey & Co., 1896. First edition, with 5 portraits, 2 vols., 8vo,
orig. cloth, a very good copy. Fenning 61-328 1983 £48.50

OLIPHANT, JAMES   A Sacramental Catachism, Designed for
Communicants Old and Young. Philadelphia: W. Young, 1788. 24mo,
calf-backed boards, early amateur calf rebacking. Felcone 22-173
1983 $60

OLIPHANT, LAURENCE   Altiora Peto. Edinburgh: William Blackwood, 1915. First edition. Four parts bound into 2 full-morocco vols.
Orig. pictorial wrappers retained. With the title-pages for the 2
volumes book-form edition bound in. Edges a bit rubbed. With marbled
endpapers and all edges gilt. Former owner's signature in both vols.
Near-fine. MacManus 279-4056 1983 $185

OLIPHANT, LAURENCE   Altiora Peto. Blackwood, 1883. First edition, 2 vols., wood engr. front. Pic. title (painted in buff ochre and brown), and 1 full-page plate in each vol. Half maroon morocco, v.g. Jarndyce 30-502 1983 £40

OLIPHANT, LAURENCE   Altiora Petro. London: William Blackwood & Sons, 1883. "Third edition." 2 vols. Frontispiece. Orig. cloth. Spines and covers worn. Inner hinges weak. Labels removed from front covers. Good. MacManus 279-4057 1983 $25

OLIPHANT, LAURENCE   Masollam: A Problem of the Period. Edinburgh: Blackwood, 1886. First edition. 3 vols. Orig. decorated cloth. Covers slightly darkened. MacManus 279-4058 1983 $350

OLIPHANT, LAURENCE   Minnesota and the Far West. Edinburgh, 1855. Plates, folding map. Cloth, covers worn, interior a bit smudged; a solid copy. Felcone 21-88 1983 $100

OLIPHANT, LAURENCE   Narrative of the Earl of Elgin's Mission to China and Japan in the Years 1857, '58, '59. 1860. Second edition, 2 vols., 20 coloured and tinted lithographs, 5 folding maps, text illus., orig. blue cloth gilt, spines a bit rubbed and udst stained, 1860. K Books 307-138 1983 £90

OLIPHANT, LAURENCE   Narrative of the Earl of Elgins' Mission. London, 1859. 5 folding maps, 20 coloured and tinted lithograph plates. Illus. 2 vols. 8vo. Some slight wear. Orig. cloth. Good. Edwards 1044-535 1983 £140

OLIPHANT, LAURENCE   Narrative of the Earl of Elgin's Mission. London, 1859. 5 folding maps, 20 coloured lithographs, wood engravings in text. 2 vols. Plates and endpapers spotted, large folding map in vol. 1 repaired. Ex-library, half calf, rubbed. 8vo. Good. Edwards 1044-532 1983 £75

OLIPHANT, LAURENCE   Piccadilly. Edinburgh: William Blackwood & Sons, 1870. First edition. 8 illus. by R. Doyle. Orig. cloth. Covers worn and soiled. Inner hinges cracked. MacManus 279-4059 1983 $75

OLIPHANT, MARGARET OLIPHANT (WILSON) (1828-1897)   Caleb Field. Colburn & Co., 1851. First edition. 24 pp. ads. Orig. blue cloth, sl. rubbed. Very good. Jarndyce 31-833 1983 £42

OLIPHANT, MARGARET OLIPHANT (WILSON) (1828-1897)   A Country Gentleman and His Family. London: Macmillan & Co., 1886. First edition. 3 vols. Orig. cloth. Presentation copy from the publisher to an unknown recipient stamped "With the Publisher's compliments" on the title-page of each volume. Spines faded and slightly worn. Preliminary pages and edges a trifle foxed. Near-fine. MacManus 279-4060 1983 $450

OLIPHANT, MARGARET OLIPHANT (WILSON) (1828-1897)   Dress. London: Macmillan & Co., 1878. First edition. Illus. Orig. cloth. Worn. MacManus 279-4061 1983 $65

OLIPHANT, MARGARET OLIPHANT (WILSON) (1828-1897)   The Duke's Daughter and The Fugitives. Edinburgh: Blackwood, 1890. First edition. 3 vols. Orig. cloth. In a variant (remainder?) binding of red cloth, issued without the publisher's catalogue in vol. 2. Spines slightly faded. Very good. MacManus 279-4062 1983 $500

OLIPHANT, MARGARET OLIPHANT (WILSON) (1828-1897)   Lady William. Macmillan, 1893. First edition. 3 vols. Inner hinges weak. Ex-library copy. Orig. green cloth, rubbed. Half titles. Jarndyce 30-504 1983 £28

OLIPHANT, MARGARET OLIPHANT (WILSON) (1828-1897)   The Land of Darkness. London: Macmillan & Co., 1888. First edition. Orig. cloth. Endpapers slightly foxed. Fine. MacManus 279-4063 1983 $150

OLIPHANT, MARGARET OLIPHANT (WILSON) (1828-1897)   The Literary History of England in the End of the Eighteenth and Beginning of the Nineteenth Century. London: Macmillan, 1882. First edition. 3 vols. Orig. cloth. Covers a bit worn and marked. MacManus 279-4064 1983 $65

OLIPHANT, MARGARET OLIPHANT (WILSON) (1828-1897)   Magdalen Hepburn. London: Macmillan, 1882. First edition. 3 vols. Orig. cloth. Spines faded. Tipped-in labels neatly removed from front endpapers. Near-fine. MacManus 279-4064 1983 $650

OLIPHANT, MARGARET OLIPHANT (WILSON) (1828-1897)   May. London: Hurst & Blackett, 1873. First edition. 3 vols. Library labels on front endsheets. Covers rubbed and faded. Several inner hinges cracked. Front flyleaf in vol. 1 pasted to front endsheet. MacManus 279-4066 1983 $350

OLIPHANT, MARGARET OLIPHANT (WILSON) (1828-1897)   Merkland. Henry Colburn, 1851. First edition. 3 vols. Half calf, green labels. Very good. Jarndyce 30-503 1983 £65

OLIPHANT, MARGARET OLIPHANT (WILSON) (1828-1897)   Merkland. Henry Colburn, 1851. First edition. 3 vols. Endpapers laid down. Orig. boards, green cloth spines, paper labels. Worn but sound. Jarndyce 31-834 1983 £20

OLIPHANT, MARGARET OLIPHANT (WILSON) (1828-1897)   Neighbours on the Green. Macmillan, 1889. First edition. 3 vols. Half titles, 6 pp. ads. vol. III. Inner hinges weak, ex-library copy. Orig. green cloth, rubbed. Jarndyce 30-505 1983 £30

OLIPHANT, MARGARET OLIPHANT (WILSON) (1828-1897)   Queen Victoria. London: Cassell & Co., Ltd.. 1900. First edition. Illus. 4to. Orig. cloth. Fine. MacManus 279-4067 1983 $65

OLIPHANT, MARGARET OLIPHANT (WILSON) (1828-1897)   A Rose in June. London: Hurst & Blackett, 1874. First edition. 2 vols. Orig. cloth. Spines and covers worn and soiled. Spine edges fraying. Cont. owner's signature. Good. MacManus 279-4068 1983 $375

OLIPHANT, MARGARET OLIPHANT (WILSON) (1828-1897)   Royal Edinburgh. London: Macmillan & Co., 1890. First edition. Illus. by George Reid. Orig. cloth. Covers a little worn, fore-edge of back cover nicked, inner hinges weak. Inscription on half-title. Good. MacManus 279-4069 1983 $50

OLIPHANT, MARGARET OLIPHANT (WILSON) (1828-1897)   The Second Son. London: Macmillan & Co., 1888. First edition. 3 vols. Orig. cloth. Spine ends and edges worn. Inner hinges to vol. 3 weak. Cont. owner's signature partially removed from vol. 3. Former owner's signature in vol. 1. MacManus 279-4070 1983 $250

OLIPHANT, MARGARET OLIPHANT (WILSON) (1828-1897)   Sheridan. London: Macmillan & Co., 1883. First edition. Orig. cloth with paper label on spine. Soiled. Good. MacManus 279-4073 1983 $35

OLIPHANT, MARGARET OLIPHANT (WILSON) (1828-1897)   Sons and Daughters. William Blackwood, 1891. Second edition. Half title. Orig. green cloth. Very good. Jarndyce 31-838 1983 £24

OLIPHANT, MARGARET OLIPHANT (WILSON) (1828-1897)   William Blackwood and His Sons. Edinburgh: William Blackwood & Sons, 1897. 2 vols. Tall 8vo. 4 etched plates, orig. blue gilt-stamped cloth. Labels removed from upper section of front covers, resulting in slight discoloration. Karmiole 76-21 1983 $30

OLIPHANT, MARGARET OLIPHANT (WILSON) (1828-1897)   Zaidee. Edinburgh: William Blackwood & Sons, 1856. First edition. 3 vols. Orig. cloth. Inscription on front endsheets. Inner hinges cracked, front cover loose on vol. 3. Some fading and wear to covers. MacManus 279-4071 1983 $350

OLIPHANT, THOMAS   La Musa Madrigalesca. 1837. 8vo, half calf, rubbed. Bickersteth 75-164 1983 £14

OLIVER, D.   Flora of Tropical Africa. 1868-1902. Vols. 1 to 8 in 10 vols., 8vo, cloth. Complete except for the section on Gramineae. Wheldon 160-1753 1983 £75

OLIVER, D.   Illustrations of the Principal Natural Orders of the Vegetable Kingdom. 1893. Second edition, 109 coloured plates, large 8vo, cloth, trifle used. Wheldon 160-1555 1983 £25

OLIVER, JAMES   A Voice from the People. N.p., ca. 1878. Orig. printed wraps. First edition. Ginsberg 46-756 1983 $25

OLIVIER, G.   Monographie des Pies-Grieches du genre Lanius. Rouen, 1944. 14 plates (some coloured), 8vo, half cloth. Wheldon 160-832 1983 £30

OLIVIER, JOSEPH   Traite de Magnetisme. Toulouse, 1849. 8vo, pr. wrs. (torn); uncut & unopened. First edition. Argosy 713-406 1983 $75

OLLIFFE, CHARLES   Scenes Americaines, Dix-Huit Mois Dans le Nouveau Monde. Brussels, 1853. 2 plates, printed boards, rebacked with kraft paper. Reprint of the second edition. Felcone 22-174 1983 $75

OLLIVANT, ALFRED   Bob, Son of Battle. New York: Doubleday, 1898. 1st ed. Orig. cloth, gilt. Fine copy. Scarce. Jenkins 155-981 1983 $85

OLMSTED, FREDERICK LAW   A Journey In The Back Country. NY, 1860. Cloth, shaken, spine sunned and slightly frayed. First edition. King 46-14 1983 $40

OLMSTED, FREDERICK LAW   A Journey In The Seaboard Slave States, With Remarks on Their Economy. NY, 1859. Cloth, spine ends frayed. King 46-15 1983 $20

OLMSTED, FREDERICK LAW   A Journey Through Texas; or, A Winter of Saddle and Camp Life. London, 1857. First published English edition, printed in New York by Dix, Edwards & Co. Original three-quarter calf. Fld. map, linen backed. Library stamp on spine. A good copy. Jenkins 151-259 1983 $100

OLMSTEAD, FREDERICK LAW   A Journey Through Texas. NY, 1860. Cloth, worn and badly shaken. King 46-236 1983 $20

OLMSTED, J. M. D.   Claude Bernard Physiologist. New York, 1938. First edition. 8vo. Orig. binding. Philip Bard's copy with his autograph. Fye H-3-680 1983 $35

OLSCHKI, LEO S.   Choix de livres anciens rare et curieux... Florence, 1940. 8vo. Cloth. With plates and illus. in text. Gurney JJ-283 1983 £16

OLSON, CHARLES   Call Me Ishmael. NY, (1947). Bright, very good or better in lightly chipped and worn, very good dustwrapper. Quill & Brush 54-1044 1983 $100

OLSON, CHARLES   Charles Olson & Robert Creeley: The Complete Correspondence. Black Sparrow Press, 1980-82. 4 vols. 1 of 26 sets signed by Robert Creeley and George Butterick. Fine copies in acetate jackets. In Our Time 156-614 1983 $250

OLSON, CHARLES   Charles Olson & Robert Creely: The Complete Correspondence...Volume 5. Santa Barbara: Black Sparrow Press, 1983. Deluxe ed. 1 of 26 lettered copies, signed. Orig. cloth-backed boards. Mint copy at published price. Jenkins 155-983 1983 $75

OLSON, CHARLES   The Complete Correspondence. Santa Barbara: Black Sparrow Press, 1980-83. Five vols. Cloth and boards. First editions. Each volume is one of 250 numbered copies, specially bound and signed by Creeley. Mint as issued. Reese 20-748 1983 $150

OLSON, ELDER   Thing of Sorrow: Poems. New York, 1934. 8vo. Cloth. A fine copy in dj which has some light wear. In Our Time 156-616 1983 $35

O'MALLEY, AUSTIN   The Ethics of Medical Homicide and Mutilation. New York, 1919. First edition. 8vo, orig. binding. Fye H-3-419 1983 $20

O'MALLEY, L. S. S.   The Indian Civil Service 1601-1930. London, 1931. First edition. 8vo. Orig. cloth. Good. Edwards 1044-536 1983 £20

OMAN, CHARLES   A History of England. London, 1911-34. 8 vols. 8vo. Cloth. Traylen 94-638 1983 £12

OMAN, CHARLES   A History of the Peninsular War. New York, 1980. 8vo. Orig. cloth. Frontis. portraits (5 photogravure), plates, portraits and numerous maps (mostly folding and coloured). 7 vols. Slightly worn and faded. Some bookplates and ownership inscriptions. Oxford, 1902-1922, Vol. 7 reprint. Good. Edwards 1042-449 1983 £500

OMAR KHAYYAM   Rubaiyat of Omar Khayyam. London: Bernard Quaritch, 1872. Orig. quarter roan and cloth. Ink name, and spine slightly rubbed, otherwise a fine copy. Reese 20-408 1983 $175

OMAR KHAYYAM   Rubaiyat of Omar Khayyam. Boston: Houghton Mifflin, 1884. Large folio, 57 leaves of plates with illus. and decorative borders, printed on Japanese paper and mounted on stiff sheets; sheets mounted on linen guards. Edition ltd. to 100 numbered copies, signed by Vedder. Printed at the Riverside Press and bound at their bindery. Full calf, with gilt-stamped cover and spine, inner dentelles and silk endpapers, designed by Vedder. A.e.g. Karmiole 76-107 1983 $500

OMAR KHAYYAM   Rubiayat of Omar Khayyam... New York: Published for Will Bradley by R. H. Russell, (1887). First edition thus. Translated by Fitzgerald. Orig. decorated boards, label uncut. A few clippings removed with slight traces. Very good copy printed by Bradley at the Wayside Press, August, 1897. Jenkins 155-117 1983 $65

OMAR KHAYYAM   Rubaiyat of Omar Khayyam. London: Grant Richards, 1897. First edition. Paraphrase of several literal translations by Richard LeGallienne. Orig. vellum-covered boards. One of 30 copies on Japan vellum signed by author. With the bookplate of Francis Kettaneh. Covers a bit soiled and faded. Half-levant green slipcase. Very good. MacManus 279-3239 1983 $450

OMAR KHAYYAM   The Rub'iyat. N.S. Nichols, 1898. Second edition. With frontis., additional decorative title-page, 41 plates of facs., and other illus., roy. 8vo, orig. cloth, gilt, top edges gilt, upper joint cracked but holding. Ltd. edition of 1,000 copies. Fenning 60-303 1983 £32

OMAR KHAYYAM   Rubaiyat of Omar Khayyam. London: Siegle, Hill, n.d. (ca. 1900). 4to. White cloth. Elaborate gilt design. Rear cover smudged. Calligraphic text with decorative initials. Full-page color illus. (some with slight discoloration in margin). Very good. Aleph-bet 8-232 1983 $125

OMAR KHAYYAM   Rubaiyat of Omar Khayyam. The Riverside Press, 1900. Marginal guides in red. Tall 8vo, buckram backed boards (slightly rubbed); uncut. Ltd. edition. One of 300 copies. Argosy 714-640 1983 $60

OMAR KHAYYAM   Rubaiyat. New York, Dodge, (1905). Photogravure plates on thin paper by Adelaide Hanscom. Large 8vo, lettering and decorations on front cover in color. Few light fingerprints on back cover, otherwise fine. Morrill 287-329 1983 $50

OMAR KHAYYAM   Rubaiyat of... N.p.: Carolon Press, 1908. Octavo. Partly unopened. Limited to 300 copies. Bottom corners slightly bumped, else fine in cloth-backed boards with decorated paper label. Bromer 25-178 1983 $65

OMAR KHAYYAM   Rubaiyat of Omar Khayyam. Methuen, 1913. 4to, colour frontis., 75 plates. Red decorated cloth, gilt. Greer 40-215 1983 £38

OMAR KHAYYAM   Rubaiyat of... Methuen, 1913. 1st edn. Col'd frontis. & 75 b&w illus. by Edmund J. Sullivan, unpaginated, plates. Red cloth gilt designed by Sullivan, t.e.g. others uncut (bkstrip sl. faded with damage to top part thereof, occasional sl. foxing), good copy. Hodgkins 27-465 1983 £20

OMAR KHAYYAM   Rubaiyat of Omar Khayyam. London, Hodder and Stoughton, (ca. 1915). Illus. in color by Edmund Dulac. 4to, orig. buckram, binding dust-soiled, interior nice. Morrill 288-92 1983 $22.50

OMAR KHAYYAM   Rubaiyat of Omar Khayyam, NY: n,d, (ca. 1920). First American edition. 4to, green cloth, pictorial paste label, gilt. With 38 tipped-in plates (some in color) plus numerous drawings by Balfour. A fine copy. Scarce in this condition. Perata 27-7 1983 $225

OMAR KHAYYAM   Rubaiyat of Omar Khayyam. N.Y., Doran,
ca. 1920. Large 8vo, color frontis. & eleven color plates by
Edmund Dulac. Green cloth, good-very good. Houle 21-343 1983
$50

OMAR KHAYYAM   Rubiayat of... London: Harrap, (1930).
Small 4to, mostly printed on one side of leaf. 12 tipped-in colored
plates, more than 40 tipped-in vignettes in black and gold, numerous
borders, etc. by Pogany. Full green polished calf, by Sangorski and
Sutcliffe, sides with triple rule gold border with arabesques in corners and title on upper cover. Spine elab. gilt, a.e.g., brightly
patterned endpapers. Matching slipcase. First of this edition, handsomely bound. Fine. O'Neal 50-41 1983 $150

OMAR KHAYYAM   Rubaiyat of Omar Khayyam. Philadelphia:
David McKay, (c. 1942). 25 cm. 20 black & white gravure illus. with
additional border and page decorations. Orig. maroon gilt-decorated
cloth; some wear to extremities. Very good. Grunder 6-72 1983
$37.50

OMAR KHAYYAM   Rubiayat of Omar Khayyam. N.Y.: Heri-
tage, (1946). 4to. Cloth backed decorated boards. Light edgewear.
Full-page color illus. by Szyk. Calligraphic text, double pages.
Very good. Aleph-bet 8-247 1983 $35

OMAR KHAYYAM   Rubaiyat of Omar Khayyam. Hodder &
Stoughton, n.d. 4to. Mounted colour frontis. Decorated title, 9
mounted colour plates, 19 mounted colour text illus. & over 50 text
illus. Brown pictorial cloth blue & gilt. Rubbed. Greer 40-74 1983
£55

OMBREDANE, ANDRE   Etudes de Psychologie Medicale. Rio de
Janeiro: Atlantica Editora, (1944). First edition. Orig. printed
wrappers. Gach 95-389 1983 $30

O'MEARA, BARRY E.   Napoleon in Exile. London, 1822. Fourth
edition. 8vo, 2 engr. frontis. portraits, 2 engr. plates. 2 vols.
Orig. grey boards, slightly worn and soiled. Orig. paper labels on
spines. Uncut. Some very slight foxing and offsetting. Good.
Edwards 1042-432 1983 £70

OMWAKE, JOHN   The Conestoga Six-Horse Bell Teams of
Eastern Pennsylvania. Cincinnati, 1930. Illus., 4to. Argosy 710-
403 1983 $75

ONDERDONK, HENRY   Queens County in Olden Times. Jamaica,
1865. 1st ed. 4to, orig. cloth, leather back. Spine rubbed and
bottom third lacking. Morrill 286-366 1983 $40

ONE Hundred Influential American Books Printed Before 1900... New
York: The Grolier Club, 1947. First edition. 8vo. Cloth. With
a number of full page plates. Limited to 600 copies. Oak Knoll
48-433 1983 $115

ONE Hundred Years of American Psychiatry. NY: Columbia Univ. Press,
1944. Large 8vo, ex-library, spine rubbed, hinges loose. Gach 94-196
1983 $35

ONE Hundred Years of Publishing 1837-1937. Bos., (1937). Illus.,
rear endpapers offset from publisher's laid-in blurbs, fine in slightly
rubbed and soiled, lightly scratched, very good dustwrapper with few
ink marks. Quill & Brush 54-1626 1983 $35

O'NEALE, LILA M.   Textile Periods in Ancient Peru.
Berkeley: University of California Press, 1930. 48 plates.
13 text illus. Small 4to. Wrappers. Ars Libri 34-409 1983
$25

O'NEIL, GEORGE   The White Rooster: Poems. New York:
Boni & Liveright, 1927. 8vo. Cloth. From the library of Alexander
Laing with his signature on the fly. Label on spine has some wear
and is faded, else vg-fine. In Our Time 156-617 1983 $25

O'NEIL, JAMES B.   They Die But Once. New York, 1935.
1st ed. Clark 741-398 1983 $35

O'NEIL, JOHN   The Official Report of the Trial of...
Boston, 1901. 1st ed. 8vo, contemporary calf, leather label.
Morrill 288-651 1983 $20

O'NEILL, EUGENE   Anna Christie. New York, 1930. Illus.
by Alexander King. Limited signed edition, being 1 of 775 copies
signed by author. A very fine copy in just jacket. Orig. box has some
slight scuffing. In Our Time 156-619 1983 $350

O'NEILL, EUGENE   Beyond the Horizon. New York: Boni
& Liveright, (1920). 1st ed., 1st state binding, 1st printing.
Orig. cloth-backed printed boards. Good copy. Jenkins 155-984
1983 $22.50

O'NEILL, EUGENE   Days Without End. New York: Random
House, (1934). First edition. 8vo. Orig. cloth. Dust jacket,
slightly torn. Very fine copy. Jaffe 1-292 1983 $65

O'NEILL, EUGENE   Days Without End. NY, (1934). Very
good in torn and soiled dustwrapper. Quill & Brush 54-1026 1983 $30

O'NEILL, EUGENE   Dynamo. NY, 1929. Limited to 775 numbered and signed copies, covers bowed and badly dampstained, interior
very good. Quill & Brush 54-1027 1983 $50

O'NEILL, EUGENE   The Emperor Jones. OH, (1921). Paperwraps, slightly soiled, good. Quill & Brush 54-1032 1983 $100

O'NEILL, EUGENE   Gold. NY, (1920). Edges slightly
rubbed, good or better, name stamp on endpapers. Quill & Brush 54-
1028 1983 $25

O'NEILL, EUGENE   The Hairy Ape. NY: 1929. First
separate edition. 9 tipped-in color illus. Limited to 775 copies
signed by O'Neill. Extremely fine in cloth-backed batiked boards.
Slightly chipped dust wrapper and slip-case which lacks pieces from
top and bottom surfaces. Bookplate. Bromer 25-81 1983 $165

O'NEILL, EUGENE   The Iceman Cometh. New York: Random
House, (1946). First edition. 8vo. Orig. cloth. Dust jacket.
Very fine copy. Jaffe 1-293 1983 $100

O'NEILL, EUGENE   The Iceman Cometh. N.Y.: Limited
Editions Club, 1982. Illus. and an orig. lithograph by Leonard
Baskin. Narrow 4to, boards, paper label; boxed. Signed by the artist.
Argosy 714-574 1983 $125

O'NEILL, EUGENE   Lazarus Laughed. New York: Boni &
Liveright, 1927. 1st ed., limited to 775 numbered and signed copies.
Orig. vellum-backed decorated boards, label, uncut, slightly used
box. Very fine copy. Jenkins 155-986 1983 $150

O'NEILL, EUGENE   Lazarus Laughed. NY, 1927. One of 775
numbered and signed copies, hinges cracked, else very good, bookplate.
Quill & Brush 54-1029 1983 $75

O'NEILL, EUGENE   Marco Millions. NY, 1927. No. 279 of
450 numbered and signed copies, some top edges uncut, spine very
lightly soiled, else fine. Quill & Brush 54-1031 1983 $100

O'NEILL, EUGENE   Marco Millions. NY, 1927. Very good
in chipped dustwrapper. Quill & Brush 54-1030 1983 $30

O'NEILL, EUGENE   The Moon of the Caribbees. New York:
Boni & Liveright, 1919. 1st ed., 1st state (bulks 7/8" across
covers). 1 of 1200 copies printed. Orig. cloth-backed boards,
stamped in black. Fine copy, sans dj. Jenkins 155-986-A 1983 $80

O'NEILL, EUGENE   Mourning Becomes Electra. New York,
1931. 8vo. Cloth. A fine copy in dj. In Our Time 156-620 1983
$150

O'NEILL, EUGENE   Mourning Becomes Electra. New York:
Horace Liveright, Inc., 1931. First edition. 8vo. Orig. cloth.
Dust jacket. Fine copy. Jaffe 1-291 1983 $75

O'NEILL, EUGENE   The Provincetown Plays: First Series:
Bound East for Cardiff. New York: Frank Shay, 1916. 1st ed.
Later plain wrappers, uncut. Only 1200 copies printed, and uncommon.
Fine copy. Jenkins 155-987 1983 $75

O'NEILL, EUGENE   Strange Interlude. New York: Boni
& Liveright, 1928. 8vo. Cloth. Fine copy in perfect dj. In Our
Time 156-618 1983 $150

O'NEILL, EUGENE   Thirst and Other One Act Plays. B,
(1914). Minor cover wear on edge, very good. Quill & Brush 54-1033
1983 $250

O'NEILL, EUGENE   Complete Works. N.Y., Boni & Liveright,
1924. First edition. Copy number 1 of 1,200 copies signed by O'Neill.
Half blue cloth over grey boards, stamped in gilt with facs. signature
(trifle rubbed) else very good. 2 vols. Houle 22-701 1983 $350

O'NEILL, ROSE   The Goblin Woman. N.Y., 1930. First
edition. Illus. by the author. Mint copy, in pictorial dust
wrapper designed by the author, of Kewpie book fame. Argosy 714-
576 1983 $50

ONIONS, OLIVER   A Crooked Mile. London: Methuen &
Co., (1914). First edition. Orig. cloth. Dust jacket (faded; margins
& edges worn and slightly frayed). Covers a trifle spotted. Edges
foxed. Near-fine. MacManus 279-4076 1983 $75

ONIONS, OLIVER   The Odd-Job Man. London, 1903. First
edition. Covers a little marked and worn. Internally nice. Rota
231-457 1983 £12.50

ONIONS, OLIVER   Tales from a Far Riding. London, 1902.
First edition. Some light foxing of preliminaries and endleaves.
Bookplate. Very nice. Rota 231-456 1983 £12.50

OOSTER, W. A.   Protozoe Helvetica. Basel, 1869-70.
32 plates and a map, 2 vols. in 1, 4to, quarter morocco. Foxed, else
a nice copy. Wheldon 160-1456 1983 £30

THE OPERA: a poem. By the author of the Coach Drivers. London:
printed for the author; and sold by W. Flexney; C. Bathurst; G.
Kearsly; and M. Hingeston, 1767. 4to, disbound, first edition.
Half-title present; nice copy; rare. Ximenes 64-402 1983 $375

OPIE, AMELIA   Adeline Mowbray. Longman, 1805. Half
title and 2 pp ads. vol. I. Tree calf, spines rubbed, black labels.
In three vols. Jarndyce 30-506 1983 £48

OPIE, AMELIA   Illustrations of Lying, in All its
Branches. Longman, Hurst, etc, 1825. First edition, 2 vols., 12mo,
calf, gilt borders and spines, black labels. Very good. Jarndyce
30-510 1983 £48

OPIE, AMELIA   Poems. New York: Inskeep & Bradford,
1808. 12mo. Calf, leather label on spine. Bookplate of a public
library on front endboard with "Withdrawn" on the plate, else a
very good-fine copy. This copy bears a presentation inscription
by Cooper on the table of contents page. In Our Time 156-165 1983
$1500

OPIE, AMELIA   Tales of Real Life. Longman, Hurst,
etc., 1813. 2nd edition, 3 vols. 12mo, calf, gilt borders and
spines, v.g. Jarndyce 30-508 1983 £32

OPIE, AMELIA   Tales of the Heart. Printed for Longman,
Hurst (etc), 1820. First edition. 4 vols, 12mo, contemporary half
calf, gilt backs with monogram and boar crest; a nice copy. Hill
165-90 1983 £75

OPIE, AMELIA   Temper, or, Domestic Scenes. New York,
James Eastburn, 1812. 2 vols., 8vo, cont. quarter sheep, bit worn,
spine ends chipped foxed, few short minor tears, decent set. First
American edition. Ravenstree 96-138 1983 $97.50

OPIE, AMELIA   Temper. Longman, Hurst, etc., 1812.
First edition, 12mo, half black calf, a little rubbed, red labels.
Jarndyce 30-507 1983 £58

OPIE, AMELIA   Valentine's Eve. Longman, Hurst,
etc., 1816. 2nd edition, 3 vols. 12mo, calf, gilt borders and
spines, black labels, v.g. Jarndyce 30-509 1983 £40

THE O-POEIAD, a satire. By a mad bull. London: printed for the
author, and sold by James Cawthorn, 1810. 8vo, disbound, 1st edition.
Rare. Ximenes 64-403 1983 $90

OPPE, A. P.   The Drawings of Paul and Thomas Sandby
in the Collection of His Majesty the King at Windsor Castle. London/
Oxford: Phaidon, 1947. 158 plates (2 tipped-in color). Large 4to.
Cloth. Ars Libri 32-614 1983 $85

OPPE, A. P.   Thomas Rowlandson. His drawings and
water-colors. London: The Studio, 1923. 96 plates (numerous
tipped-in color). Large 4to. Gold-embossed boards, 1/4 vellum.
Partly unopened. T.e.g. Ex-libris Abby Aldrich Rockefeller. Rare.
Ars Libri 32-596 1983 $200

OPPENHEIM, E. PHILLIPS   A Pulpit in the Grill Room. Lon., (1938).
Light interior staining, else very good in internally mended soiled,
chipped and frayed, good dustwrapper. Quill & Brush 54-1047 1983
$40

OPPENHEIM, H.   Der Fall N. Ein weiterer Beitrag zur
Lehre von den traumatischen Neurosen... Berlin, 1896. 8vo. Orig.
wrappers. Tear through bottom margin repaired. Gurney JJ-285 1983
£15

OPPENHEIM, H.   Text-Book of Nervous Diseases for
Physicians and Students. Edinburgh: Otto Schulze, New York, G. E.
Stechert, 1911. 2 vols., first English ed., 432 illus., 8 plates,
publisher's green cloth, joints and edges rubbed, ex-lib. Good copy.
Gach 95-390 1983 $125

OPPENHEIM, JAMES   The Mystic Warrior. New York: Knopf,
1921. Quarto. Cloth and paper over boards, paper label. First
edition. One of 535 numbered copies. Corners bumped, but a very
good copy. Laid in is a pub.'s publicity photo of the author.
Reese 20-753 1983 $20

OPPENHEIMER, JANE   New Aspects of John and William
Hunter. New York, 1946. First edition. 8vo. Orig. cloth. Fye
H-3-799 1983 $20

OPPERT, FRANZ   Visceral and hereditary syphilis...
London: Churchill, 1868. First edition. Slim 8vo. Orig. brown
cloth. Head of spine a trifle chipped. Very good copy. Ximenes
63-286 1983 $20

O'RAHILLY, THOMAS F.   Early Irish History and Mythology.
Dublin: D.I.A.S., 1946. First edition, 8vo, orig. cloth. Fenning
62-271 1983 £24.50

O'RAHILLY, THOMAS F.   Irish Dialects Past and Present. Dublin,
1932. First edition, errata slip, 8vo, orig. printed paper, a very
good to nice copy. Fenning 61-330 1983 £21.50

ORATIONS, Delivered at the Request of the Inhabitants of the town of
Boston... Boston, 1807. Second edition. Contributions by Joseph
Warren, John Hancock, et al. 12mo, contemp. calf. Lacks part of
label, hinges cracked and weak. Morrill 287-43 1983 $35

ORCUTT, WILLIAM DANA   The Book Collectors. N.Y., Harper,
1928. Folio. 96 b/w and three color plates. Half blue cloth.
Very good-fine. One of 750 copies. Bookplate of Adrian Goldstone.
Houle 21-140 1983 $85

ORCUTT, WILLIAM DANA   The Book in Italy During the Fifteenth
and Sixteenth Centuries. N.Y., Harper, 1928. Folio. 96 b/w and
three color plates. One of 750 copies. With the bookplate of Adrian
Goldstone. Very good - fine. Houle 22-122 1983 $85

ORCUTT, WILLIAM DANA   The Book in Italy. NY: Harper &
Brothers, 1928. Folio. With 128 plates, including 3 tipped-in color
plates. Edition ltd. to 750 numbered copies. Black cloth over
boards, paper cover label. Outer edges of boards sl. discolored.
Karmiole 73-25 1983 $75

ORCUTT, WILLIAM DANA   Burrows of Michigan and the Republican
Party. New York, 1917. 1st ed. Illus. 2 vols., 8vo. Morrill 287-
331 1983 $30

ORCUTT, WILLIAM DANA   In Quest of the Perfect Book. Boston,
1926. 8vo, decorated cloth, illus. Bookplate. Duschnes 240-180
1983 $30

ORCUTT, WILLIAM DANA   In Quest of the Perfect Book.
Boston: Little, Brown, & Co., (1926). First edition. Cloth.
Dust jacket. Prof. illus. Fine condition, in slightly chipped
dust jacket. Oak Knoll 48-207 1983 $25

ORCUTT, WILLIAM DANA   The Kingdom of Books. Boston, 1927.
8vo, decorated cloth, gilt, illus. Duschnes 240-181 1983 $30

ORCUTT, WILLIAM DANA   The Magic of the Book. Boston, (1930).
8vo, decorated cloth, illus. Duschnes 240-183 1983 $30

ORCUTT, WILLIAM DANA   Master Makers of the Book. New York,
1928. 12mo, cloth, frontis. Duschnes 240-182 1983 $27.50

ORCZY, EMMUSKA   Blue Eyes and Grey. London: Hodder &
Stoughton, (1928). First edition. Orig. cloth. Dust jacket (a bit
nicked). Fine. MacManus 279-4078 1983 $30

ORCZY, EMMUSKA   I Will Repay. London: Greening, 1906.
First edition. Orig. cloth. Covers worn. MacManus 279-4079 1983
$20

ORCZY, EMMUSKA   A Spy of Napoleon. London: Hodder &
Stoughton, (1934). First edition. Orig. cloth. Dust jacket (a trifle
worn). Fine. MacManus 279-4080 1983 $75

ORCZY, EMMUSKA   The Uncrowned King. London: Hodder &
Stoughton, (1935). First edition. Orig. cloth. Dust jacket. Fine.
MacManus 279-4081 1983 $60

ORD, JAMES   Memoirs of...of Ord Rancho, California.
Altoona, Pa., 1920. Illus. Orig. printed wraps. First edition.
Ginsberg 47-143 1983 $75

AN ORDINANCE of the Lords and Commons assembled in Parliament...
London: for Edward Husbands, July 6, 1644. 4to. Full polished
calf, gilt by Riviere. Fine copy. Heath 48-99 1983 £90

ORDWAY, ADAM   The Description and Use of the Double-
Horizontal-Dial... London: William Godbid, 1662. First edition.
Small 8vo. Calf. From the library of the Earls of Kinnoul, Dupplin
Castle. The first line of the title and a few page-numbers have
been shaved by the binder. Kraus 164-173 1983 $1,580

OREGON. Wash., (1845). Double columns, dbd. First edition.
Ginsberg 47-744 1983 $75

OREGON. The Cost, and the Consequences. Phila., 1846. Half
morocco. First edition. Ginsberg 47-747 1983 $100

O'REILLY, HARRINGTON   Fifty Years on the Trail... London:
Chatto & Windus, Piccadilly, 1889. Illus. Pictorial cloth. 1st ed.
Jenkins 153-414 1983 $125

O'REILLY, MILES   The Life and Adventures, Songs, Services,
and Speeches of Private Miles O'Reilly. New York, 1864. 1st ed.
With comic illus. by Mullen. 12mo. Fine copy. Morrill 287-138
1983 $20

ORIGINAL Manuscript on the Estate of Thos. Robertson, Public Sale.
Baton Rouge, 14 January 1830. Folio. Sewn. Jenkins 153-814 1983
$400

AN ORIGINAL Wager. London, Frederick Warne & Co., 1895. First ed.,
illus., orig. pictorial cloth. Presentation copy from author to
Conan Doyle. With Doyle's signature on title-page, armorial bookplate
on front paste-down. Spine and covers rather worn, with a large tear
to the spine. Endpapers quite foxed, spine cracking. MacManus 278-
1630 1983 $185

ORIOLI, G.   Adventures of a Bookseller. New York:
Robert M. McBride & Co., 1938. First US edition. 8vo. Cloth,
dust jacket. Foxing throughout, jacket chipped. Oak Knoll 48-308
1983 $40

ORLICH, LEOPOLD VON   Reise in Ostindien. Leipzig, 1845.
First edition. 2 plans, 10 chromolithograph and 11 plain plates.
Some occasional spotting. 4to. Cont. half morocco, spine sunned.
Presentation inscription on front free endpaper to Lord Altamont,
dated December 12, 1844. Good. Edwards 1044-542 1983 £235

ORLICH, LEOPOLD VON   Travels in India. London, 1845. First
Edglish edition. 2 coloured frontis. 8 plates, plan, 2 folding tables
and numerous text illus. 2 vols. Orig. blind stamped cloth, spines
sunned. 3vo. Earl of Ellenborough's copy with his stamp and bookplate.
Good. Edwards 1044-543 1983 £175

ORLOFF, GREFOIRE   Essai sur l'Histoire de la Musique en
Italie. Paris, 1822. Two vols. in one. Second volume has no title
page. Thick 8vo, bound together, in library buckram. The Lowell
Mason copy, with bookplate, and release. Salloch 387-366 1983 $35

ORME, ROBERT   A History of the Military Transactions of
the British Nation in Indostan. London, 1775. Second edition, corrected, with alterations, additions, and an index. 4 folding maps, 6
plans, 4 folding. 4to. Calf, hinges rubbed. With ownership inscription on title of John Jamieson, dated 1828, and in the same hand a note
on the previous leaf "This book belonged to Dr. Jamieson Author of the
Scotch Dictionary". Good. Edwards 1044-538 1983 £85

ORME, ROBERT   A History of Military Transactions of the
British Nation in Indostan. London, 1803. Fourth edition, revised by
author. 8 folding maps, 28 plans, 19 folding, 2 folding plates.
2 vols. bound in 3. 4to. Cont. tree calf rebacked, some wear to
corners. With the bookplate of Lt.Gen. Sir Thomas Hislop. Good.
Edwards 1044-539 1983 £150

ORMSBY, ANNE   Memoirs of a Family in Swisserland.
Strahan for T.N. Longman, 1802. First edition, 4 vols. Half green
calf, v.g. Jarndyce 30-511 1983 £180

ORMSBY, R. MCKINLEY   A History of the Whig Party. Boston,
1859. 1st ed. 8vo. Backstrip faded. Morrill 289-480 1983 $25

ORNSTEIN, MARTHA   The Role of Scientific Societies in the
Seventeenth Century. Chicago: University of Chicago Press, (1928).
First edition. 8vo. Cloth-backed boards. Ex-library copy with
corresponding markings. Oak Knoll 49-304 1983 $20

ORR, ALEX B.   King Longbeard. John Lane, 1898. Sq.
8vo. Pictorial half-title, map-frontis. Pictorial title. 11 plates
& 100 text illus. Blue decorated cloth, gilt, worn. Presentation
copy from author. Greer 40-189 1983 £60

ORRERY, JOHN BOYLE, 5TH EARL OF
Please turn to
CORK AND ORRERY, JOHN BOYLE, 5TH EARL OF

ORTEGA, LUIS B.   California Stock Horse. Sacramento:
Privately Printed, 1949. Numerous illus, plates, portraits. Orig.
gilt pictorial brown cloth. First edition. Very fine. Jenkins 152-
731 1983 $100

ORTEGA Y GASSET, JOSE   Invertebrate Spain. London: George
Allen & Unwin, (1937). First English edition. Gach 95-392 1983 $20

ORTEGA Y GASSET, JOSE   Mison de la Universidad. Madrid, 1930.
First edition. 16mo, pr. wrs. Argosy 714-577 1983 $35

ORTON, HELEN FULLER   The Little Lost Pigs. W. & R. Chambers,
n.d. Oblong 8vo. Colour frontis. 10 plates (4 colour). 7 text illus.
Pictorial endpapers, lacks flyleaf. Dark green cloth. Onlaid colour
plate. Greer 39-99 1983 £12.75

ORUETA, RICARDO DE   Berruguete y su obra. Madrid:
Editorial "Saturnino Calleja", n.d. 166 illus. hors texte. Cloth.
Orig. wrappers bound in. Ars Libri 32-33 1983 $75

ORWELL, GEORGE   Animal Farm. New York: Harcourt,
Brace and Company, (1946). Advance Copy of the first American
edition, with label on front wrapper giving date of publication.
8vo. Orig. printed wrappers. Fine copy. Jaffe 1-294 1983 $450

ORWELL, GEORGE   Animal Farm. New York, (1946). First
American edition. Black cloth. Corners of 3 leaves creased, otherwise very fine in dj. Bradley 65-151 1983 $85

ORWELL, GEORGE   Animal Farm. N.Y., (1946). First
American edition. Thin 16mo, cloth, d.w. Argosy 714-578 1983
$35

ORWELL, GEORGE   British Pamphleteers. London, 1947-
1951. 1st ed. Illus. 2 vols., 8vo. Morrill 286-379 1983 $35

ORWELL, GEORGE   Burmese Days. London, 1935. First
edition. Half-title spotted and with signs of the removal of a
gummed label on the top inch, otherwise a good copy. Gekoski 2-150
1983 £130

ORWELL, GEORGE   Dickens, Dali and Others. NY, (1946).
Slightly offset on front fly and pages 108-113, else very good or better in slightly frayed and nicked, very good dustwrapper with slight
fraying. Quill & Brush 54-1048 1983 $100

ORWELL, GEORGE   England Your England and Other Essays.
L, 1953. Spine edges faded, minor foxing to pastedown, else very good
in slightly stained, very good dustwrapper with chipped top spine edge.
Quill & Brush 54-1049 1983 $150

ORWELL, GEORGE   The English People. London: Collins,
1947. First edition. 8 plates in color & 17 illus. in black & white.
Orig. decorated boards. Dust jacket. Fine. MacManus 279-4085 1983
$65

ORWELL, GEORGE   The English People. L, 1947. Edges
slightly rubbed, flys very slightly offset, very good or better in nice
dustwrapper slightly rubbed at edges. Quill & Brush 54-1053 1983
$40

ORWELL, GEORGE   The English People. L, 1947. Flys offset from dustwrapper, light wear to edges, else near fine in very good
dustwrapper with only slightly rubbed edges, owner's name. Quill &
Brush 54-1052 1983 $35

ORWELL, GEORGE   The English People. London, 1947.
Slight offsetting to endpaper. Dustwrapper. Fine. Gekoski 2-216
1983 £25

ORWELL, GEORGE   Homage to Catalonia. London: Secker
& Warburg, (1938). First edition. Orig. cloth. Covers somewhat
soiled and rubbed. MacManus 279-4087 1983 £125

ORWELL, GEORGE   Homage to Catalonia. London, 1938.
First edition. One of 1500 copies. Spine slightly faded and lower
cover a little marked. Some foxing of preliminaries. Very good.
Rota 231-458 1983 £65

ORWELL, GEORGE   Nineteen Eighty-Four. New York:
Harcourt, Brace and Company, (1949). Advance Review copy of the
first American edition. 8vo. Orig. printed wrappers. Spine
darkened, with a few small nicks, otherwise a very good copy.
Jaffe 1-295 1983 $350

ORWELL, GEORGE   Nineteen Eighty-Four. New York: (1949).
Gray cloth. First American edition. Fine in lightly worn first issue
(red) dust jacket. Bradley 66-279 1983 $125

ORWELL, GEORGE   Nineteen Eighty-Four. Toronto:
Saunders, (1949). 1st Canadian ed. Orig. grey cloth, red dj. Dj
carries the Canadian publisher's imprint. Fine copy, less common
than the American ed. Jenkins 155-989 1983 $100

ORWELL, GEORGE   Nineteen Eighty-Four. N.Y., Harcourt,
(1949). First American edition. Dust jacket (second state, blue),
a trifle nicked at edges. Very good-fine. Houle 21-698 1983 $95

ORWELL, GEORGE   The Road to Wigan Pier. London: Victor
Gollancz Ltd., 1937. First edition. Illus. from photographs. Orig.
wrappers, a bit soiled and worn. Good. MacManus 279-4089 1983 $75

ORWELL, GEORGE   The Road to Wigan Pier. London: Victor
Gollancz Ltd., 1937. First trade edition, second impression. Illus.
Orig. blue cloth. Dust jacket (head of spine badly chipped, reinforced
with heavy tape). Very good. MacManus 279-4088 1983 $65

ORWELL, GEORGE   The Road to Wigan Pier. Left Book Club,
1937. First edition. Limp cloth. Photographs. Very nice. Rota
230-460 1983 £20

ORWELL, GEORGE   Shooting an Elephant and other Essays.
London: Secker & Warburg, 1950. 1st ed., 8vo, original cloth, in
the original dust-jacket. Small tear in edge of dust-jacket, but a
very good copy. Trebizond 18-75 1983 $75

ORY, WILLIAM JOHNSON   Ionica. London: Smith, Elder & Co.,
1858. First edition. Orig. green cloth. (With:) Ionica II. (Cambridge: At the University Press,) 1877. Orig. blue gray paper wrappers. Minor wear. Bookplates. Fine. Extremely rare. MacManus
277-1153 1983 $550

OSBALDESTON, GEORGE   Squire Osbaldeston. John Lane, 1926.
First edition, with 16 coloured plates, 60 other plates and a folding
map, 4to, orig. cloth, light marginal foxing in a few plates,
but still a very good copy. Fenning 60-305 1983 £28.50

OSBORN, ARTHUR W.   The Superphysical. London: Ivor
Nicholson & Watson, 1937. First edition. Dust jacket worn. Gach
94-614 1983 $20

OSBORN, CHASE S.   Schoolcraft--Longfellow-Hiawatha.
Lancaster, Pa., 1942. Advance copy of 1st ed. Illus. Thick 8vo,
orig. wrappers. Morrill 287-333 1983 $27.50

OSBORN, FRANCIS   A Miscellany of Sundry Essayes...Together
with Politicall Deductions from the History of the Earl of Essex...
Printed by John Grismond, 1659. 12mo, title and early leaves lightly
waterstained, old calf, rebacked. First edition. Bickersteth 77-60
1983 £60

OSBORN, HENRY FAIRFIELD (1859-1935)   Evolution and Religion in
Education. NY: Charles Scribner's Sons, 1926. First edition.
Inscribed copy. Gach 95-393 1983 $30

OSBORN, HENRY FAIRFIELD (1859-1935)   Men of the Old Stone Age. New
York, 1921. Third edition. Wheldon 160-1458 1983 £15

OSBORN, PAUL   A Bell for Adano. New York: Knopf,
1945. Cloth. First edition. Fine in very slightly used dust
jacket. Reese 20-516 1983 $25

OSBORN, R. D.   Islam under the Khalifs of Bagdad.
London, 1878. Orig. cloth. 8vo. Good. Edwards 1044-540 1983 £40

OSBORN, SHERARD   Stray Leaves from an Arctic Journal.
New York, 1852. 1st American ed. Illus. Small 8vo. Spine faded,
some cover spots. Morrill 289-481 1983 $30

OSBORNE, E. ALLEN   The Facts about a Christmas Carol.
Ptd. for the author by The Bradley Press, 1937. First edition.
Orig. printed wraps., v.g. 1000 copies printed. Folding table of
textual variations of the early editions. Jarndyce 31-543 1983
£18.50

OSBORNE, LUCY EUGENIA   The Chapin Library, Williams College.
Portland, Me., 1939. Ed. limited to 500 copies. Portrait. Large
8vo. Morrill 289-634 1983 $50

OSBORNE, W. G.   The Court and Camp of Runjeet Sing.
London, 1840. 16 plates, 1 loose, foxed, pictorial cloth, chipped
at head and tail of spine. From the Duke of Ellenborough's library
with his bookplate. 8vo. Good. Edwards 1044-541 1983 £125

OSBOURNE, KATHERINE D.   Robert Louis Stevenson in California.
Ch., 1911. Illus., minor cover soiling, spine slightly darkened,
very good. Quill & Brush 54-1309 1983 $50

OSBOURNE, LLOYD   The Grierson Mystery. Lon., (1928).
Edges slightly rubbed and cover slightly soiled and rolled, else very
good in soiled and slightly frayed dustwrapper with two chips out of
spine. Quill & Brush 54-1056 1983 $75

OSGOOD, DAVID   A Solemn Protest Against the Late Declaration of War... Exeter, 1812. Printed self-wrappers, sewn. Historical society stamp, otherwise a very good copy. Reese 18-390 1983
$25

OSGOOD, ERNEST S.   The Day of the Cattleman.
Minneapolis, 1929. Illus., frontis. by Borein, 14 maps and plates.
Orig. cloth. First edition. Ginsberg 47-764 1983 $100

OSGOOD, HERBERT L.   The American Colonies in the 18th Century. NY (1930, '24, '25). 4 vols., cloth. Vol. 1 light water stains.
Vol. 3 ex lib. Argosy 710-105 1983 $100

OSKAMP, T. L.   Disquisito Chemico-Medica de Calcina-
tione Mettallorum per Aquae Analysin... Marburg, 1791. 8vo. Orig.
wrappers. Gurney 90-93 1983 £60

OSKINSON, JOHN M.   Brothers Three. New York: Macmillan,
1935. Cloth. First edition. Reese 20-747 1983 $25

OSLER, WILLIAM   An Address on the Hospital Unit in
University Work, delivered before the Northumberland & Durham Medical
Society, n.p., 1911. 8vo, sewed. Reprinted from the Lancet, Jan. 28,
1911. Argosy 713-408 1983 $50

OSLER, WILLIAM   Aequanimitas and other Addresses.
Philadelphia, 1904. First edition. 8vo. Orig. binding. Wear
to head and tail of spine. Scarce. Fye H-3-421 1983 $125

OSLER, WILLIAM   Aequanimitas, with other Addresses to
Medical Students, Nurses & Practitioners of Medicine. N.Y., 1904.
8vo, orig. cloth (top of backstrip chewed). First edition. Argosy
713-407 1983 $85

OSLER, WILLIAM   Aequanimitas and other Addresses.
London, 1906. Second edition. 8vo. Orig. binding. One half by
one half inch tear in top of backstrip which is faded, contents
fine. Fye H-3-422 1983 $75

OSLER, WILLIAM   An Alabama Student and other Biographical Addresses. New York, 1909. First edition, second printing.
8vo. Orig. binding. Scarce. Fye H-3-424 1983 $60

OSLER, WILLIAM   The Army Surgeon. 1894. Offprint.
Wrappers. 8vo. Fye H-3-425 1983 $30

OSLER, WILLIAM   Bibliotheca Osleriana. Montreal, 1969.
Facsimile of the 1929 edition. 8vo. Orig. binding. New. Fye H-3-
1014 1983 $90

OSLER, WILLIAM   British Medicine in Greater Britain.
1897. Offprint. Wrappers. 8vo. Fye H-3-426 1983 $60

OSLER, WILLIAM   Contributions to Medical and Biological
Research, dedicated to Osler in Honour of his 70th Birthday. N.Y.,
1919. 2 vols. Illus. Ltd., numbered edition. Argosy 713-410 1983
$125

OSLER, WILLIAM   The Evolution of Modern Medicine. New
Haven, Yale, 1921. 1st ed. Illus. 4to. Morrill 289-177 1983
$135

OSLER, WILLIAM   The Evolution of Modern Medicine.
New Haven, 1922. First edition, second printing. 8vo. Orig.
binding. Fye H-3-428 1983 $150

OSLER, WILLIAM   Intensive Work in Science at the
Public Schools... 1916. Offprint. Wrappers. 8vo. Library
stamp on title, else very fine. Fye H-3-430 1983 $22

OSLER, WILLIAM   Man's Redemption of Man. New York, 1913.
First American edition. 8vo. Orig. binding. Very fine. Fye H-3-436
1983 $50

OSLER, WILLIAM   Science and Immortality. Boston,
1904. 12mo. Orig. binding. First printing. Fye H-3-439 1983
$45

OSLER, WILLIAM   The Student Life and other Essays.
Boston, 1931. First American edition. 8vo. Orig. binding. Fye
H-3-442 1983 $40

OSLER, WILLIAM   Teacher and Student. 1893. Offprint.
Wrappers. 8vo. Fye H-3-443 1983 $60

OSLER, WILLIAM   A Way of Life. Baltimore, 1932.
8vo. Orig. binding. Dust wrapper. Fye H-3-445 1983 $20

OSLER, WILLIAM   A Way of Life. New York, 1937. 12mo.
Marbled paper-covered boards. Hand-set at the Golden Hind Press.
Fye H-3-446 1983 $25

OSPOVAT, HENRY   The Work of... St. Catherine Press,
1911. 1st edn. Mounted col. frontis. portrait & 2 mounted col.
plates & 50 b&w plates. Full vellum, bevelled boards, a.e.g. (faint
sml. red stain top fr. cover, gilt rubbed on bkstrip & bkstrip some
spotting, lower corner of frontis. creased), nice copy. Hodgkins 27-
572 1983 £40

OSTHAUS, KARL ERNST   Van de Velde. Leben und Schaffen des
Kunstlers. Hagen i.W.: Folkwang-Verlag, 1920. 156 illus. 4to.
Boards, 1/4 cloth. Rare. Ars Libri 32-685 1983 $200

OSTRANDER, ISABEL   The Mathematics of Guilt. NY, 1926.
Very good in internally mended, price clipped dustwrapper with chip
out of top spine edge. Quill & Brush 54-1057 1983 $40

OSTWALD, WILHELM   Leitlinien Der Chemie. Leipzig, 1906.
First edition. Cloth, bookplate, stamped name, spine sunned.
King 46-524 1983 $25

OSTWALD, WILHELM   Manual of Physico-Chemical Measure-
ments... London: Macmillan, 1894. First English edition. 8vo.
Orig. green cloth. Text tables and diagrams. Slight rubbing.
Zeitlin 264-354 1983 $40

OSTWALD, WILHELM   Outlines of General Chemistry...
London: Macmillan, 1890. First English edition. 8vo. Orig.
cloth. Text figures and diagrams. Ownership inscription title-
page. Small cut in lower margin of center section. Zeitlin 264-
355 1983 $65

OSTWALD, WILHELM   The Principles of Inorganic Chemistry...
London: Macmillan, 1904. Second edition. 8vo. Orig. cloth.
126 text figures and diagrams. Shook, spine chipped with small
defect at top. Zeitlin 264-356 1983 $40

OSTWALD, WILHELM   The Scientific Foundations of
Analytical Chemistry... London: Macmillan, 1900. Second English
edition. 8vo. Orig. green cloth. Slightly rubbed, shook. A
good copy. Zeitlin 264-357 1983 $40

OSTWALD, WILHELM   Solutions... London: Longmans, 1891.
Second edition. 8vo. Full calf prize binding. Numerous text
illus. and tables. A very good copy. Zeitlin 264-358 1983 $45

O'SULLIVAN, DONAL   The Irish Free State and Its Senate.
Faber & Faber, 1940. First edition, 8vo, orig. cloth. In dust
wrapper. Fenning 62-272 1983 £32.50

O'SULLIVAN, MARY D.   Old Galway. Cambridge: Heffer, 1942.
First edition, folding map and 8 plates, 8vo, orig. cloth, dust
wrapper. Fenning 62-273 1983 £35

O'SULLIVAN, SEAMAS, PSEUD.
Please turn to
STARKEY, JAMES SULLIVAN

O'SULLIVAN, VINCENT   A Book of Bargains. London: Leonard
Smithers, 1896. Frontispiece by A. Beardsley. Orig. cloth. First
edition. Edges slightly worn. Spine a bit faded. A good copy.
MacManus 277-238 1983 $85

OSWALD, JOHN CLYDE   Benjamin Franklin Printer. N.P.:
Doubleday, Page & Co., 1917. First edition. 8vo. Cloth. Oak
Knoll 48-309 1983 $25

OSWALD, JOHN CLYDE   Printing in the Americas. N.Y., 1937.
First edition, thick 8vo, green buckram, blind-stamped design on front
of cover and spine, gilt. Illus. throughout. A fine copy. Scarce.
Perata 29-129 1983 $90

OTERO, MIGUEL A.   The Real Billy the Kid with New Light
on the Lincoln County War. New York, 1936. Illus. 1st ed. in
dust jacket. Fairly nice copy. Jenkins 151-166 1983 $75

OTEY, JAMES H.   The Duty of Ministers of the Gospel,
to Their People. Nashville, 1837. First edition. Dbd. Ginsberg
46-728 1983 $50

OTIS, ELIZA HENDERSON BORDMAN (1796-1873)   The Barclays of Boston.
Boston: Ticknor, Reed & Fields, 1854. First edition. Orig. cloth,
gilt. Very good copy. Jenkins 155-990 1983 $25

OTIS, MRS. HARRISON GRAY
Please turn to
OTIS, ELIZA HENDERSON BORDMAN (1796-1873)

OTTANI CAVINA, ANNA   Carlo Saraceni. Milano: Mario
Spagnol, 1968. 165 plates (10 color). 4to. Cloth. Dust jacket.
Ars Libri 33-322 1983 $125

OTTER, WILLIAM   The Life and Remains of the Rev.
Edward Daniel Clarke... London: for George Cowie, 1824. First
edition. 4to. Cont. polished calf, Russia, gilt, full gilt spine.
Portrait. Some offsetting, else fine copy. Heath 48-592 1983
£65

OTTER, WILLIAM   The Life and Remains of Edward Daniel
Clarke, Professor of Mineralogy in the University of Cambridge, 1825.
2 vols., 8vo, portrait, cont. calf. Upper inner joint of vol. 2
weak. Bickersteth 77-234 1983 £14

OTWAY, THOMAS   The Atheist. London: Printed for R.
Bentley, and J. Tonson, 1684. First edition. 4to. Later 3/4 calf
& cloth. Spine and corners slightly rubbed. Bookplate. Very good.
MacManus 279-4098 1983 $250

OTWAY, THOMAS   The Works of Mr. Thomas Otway. London,
printed for C. Bathurst, et al., 1768. 3 vols., orig. calf gilt,
hinges cracked, spine ends chipped, numbering labels gone. Ravenstree
97-149 1983 $87.50

OUDEMANS, A. C.   Kritisch-historish overzicht der Acar-
ologie, III, 1805-1850. Leiden, 1936-37. 7 parts in 6 vols., 8vo,
sewed. Numerous illustrations. Wheldon 160-1331 1983 £85

OUIDA, PSEUD.
Please turn to
DE LA RAMEE, LOUISE

OUR Exagmination Round His Factification for Incamination of Work in
Progress. Paris: Shakespeare and Company, 1929. Limited to 96
copies. Fine, unopened copy. Faintly chipped printed wrappers.
First edition. Bromer 25-60 1983 $1250

OUR Exagmination Round His Factification for Incamination of Work in
Progress. Paris: Shakespeare & Company, 1929. 8vo. Some light wear
and chipping to outer extremities of wraps, otherwise a fine copy.
In Our Time 156-60 1983 $300

OUR Generals. N.Y.: Leavitt & Allen, (1862). CDV-size engr. portraits
(most full-length) of 24 outstanding Union generals. Bound in full
brown morocco, expertly rebacked. Orig. ornate brass clasps present.
A.e.g. Jenkins 152-732 1983 $175

OURSLER, WILL   The Trial of Vincent Doon. NY, 1941.
Advance reading copy with printed wrapper, spine slightly worn, else
fine. Quill & Brush 54-1058 1983 $65

OUSELEY, JOHN THOMAS   A Vision of Death's Destruction,
Miscellaneous Poems. J.G. Brown, Leicester, 1837. (2nd edition).
Straight-grained maroon morocco, gilt, a.e.g. Inscribed presentation
copy from the author. Jarndyce 30-813 1983 £32

AN OUTLINE of the Life and Works of Col. Paul Revere. Newburyport,
Mass., Towle Mfg. Co., Silversmiths, (1901). Illus. Tall 8vo,
orig. wrappers. Wrappers bit dust-soiled. Morrill 286-413 1983
$22.50

OVER the Plains to Colorado. New York: Harper's New Monthly Magazine,
June, 1867. Illustrations. Later wrappers. Maps. Jenkins 153-136
1983 $45

OVERBURY, THOMAS   Sir Thomas Overbury His Wife. London,
Iohn Haviland for a Crooke, 1638. 8vo, old calf, hinges broken and
spine loose. Fair copy. Ravenstree 96-139 1983 $330

OVERS, JOHN   Evenings of a Working Man. T.C. Newby,
1844. First edition, half title, 3 pp ads. Orig. pink cloth, a little
wear to hinges. Jarndyce 30-66 1983 £82

OVERS, JOHN   Evenings of a Working Man. T.C. Newby,
1844. Half title. Calf by Morrell. First edition. Gilt borders &
spine, labels, t.e.g. Very good. Jarndyce 30-67 1983 £72

OVERTON, RICHARD C.   Burlington West: A Colonization History
of the Burlington Railroad. Cambridge, 1941. Illus. 1st ed.
Extremely fine. Jenkins 153-418 1983 $40

OVIDIUS NASO, PUBLIUS   Metamorphoses. Vernon, 1958. Octavo.
Illus. with etchings by Hans Erni. Limited to 1500 copies for members
of the Limited Editions Club, signed by Erni and Giovanni Mardersteig,
the printer. Near Mint in cloth-backed patterned boards and slipcase. Bromer 25-270 1983 $125

OVIDIUS NASO, PUBLIUS   The Metamorphoses. London: the
Golden Cockerel Press, 1968. Folio. Buckram, gilt, morocco spine,
t.e.g., others uncut, in the orig. slip-case. 14 drawings by
J. Yunge Bateman. Limited edition of 200 numbered copies. Traylen
94-641 1983 £220

OVIDIUS NASO, PUBLIUS   Opera Tribus Tomis Comprehensa.
Londini, Ex Officina Jacobi Tonson & Johannis Watts, 1715. 3 vols.,
12mo, cont. calf newly rebacked period style, some waterstaining.
Ravenstree 95-83 1983 $84

OWEN, DAVID DALE   Report of a Geological Exploration of
Part of Iowa, Wisconsin, and Illinois... (Washington), 1844. 25
plates (including colored folding maps, charts and sections).
Disbound. One plate halved by trimming. Felcone 22-177 1983 $100

OWEN, DAVID DALE   Report of a Geological Survey of
Wisconsin, Iowa, and Minnesota... Philadelphia: Lippincott, 1852.
1st ed. Folio. Contemp. half morocco, decorative gilt extra. Illus.
27 plates. Sev. large folding color maps. Jenkins 153-701 1983
$275

OWEN, MARY ALICIA   Voodoo Tales as Told Among the Negroes
of the Southwest. N.Y., 1893. 1st ed. Orig. pictorial cloth. Illus.
Extremely scarce. Fine copy. Jenkins 153-803 1983 $150

OWEN, RICHARD   Palaeontology or a Systematic Summary
of Extinct Animals and their Geological Relations. Edinburgh, 1861.
Numerous text figures, orig. cloth. Slit in cloth at top of lower
joint, library notice of Gloucester Public Library on upper cover,
and library label inside front cover, and a few light library stamps.
Bickersteth 75-259 1983 £20

OWEN, ROBERT (1771-1858)   A New View of Society: Or, Essays on
the Formation of the Human Character... Cincinnati: Published by
Luman Watson, 1825. Dbd. Light scattered foxing, else a nice,
crisp copy. The first American edition. Reese 18-591 1983 $525

OWEN, ROBERT DALE   Footfalls on the Boundary of Another
World. Philadelphia, 1860. Orig. cloth. Endsheets show scattered
foxing, light fraying of head and toe of spine, and one signature
starting, otherwise a near fine copy. Reese 19-413 1983 $275

OWEN, ROBERT DALE   Threading My Way. New York, 1874. 1st
ed. 12mo. Backstrip faded, slightly rubbed. Morrill 289-483 1983
$22.50

OWEN, WILFRED   Poems. London: Chatto & Windus, 1920.
First edition. Intro. by S. Sassoon. Orig. boards. Paper label
(darkened; rubbed). Covers badly stained. Sound copy. MacManus 279-
4113 1983 $150

OWEN, WILFRED   Poems. N.Y.: B.S. Huebsch, Inc., (1921).
First American edition. Intro. by Siegfried Sassoon. Frontis. port.
Orig. boards. Fine. MacManus 279-4112 1983 $250

OWEN, WILLIAM FITZWILLIAM   Narrative of voyages to explore the
shores of Africa... London: Richard Bentley, 1833. 2 vols. 8vo.
4 folding maps. 10 plates. 1/4 red morocco. Rubbed. Some foxing
to plates. Adelson Africa-110 1983 $350

OWENS COLLEGE   Studies from the Biological Laboratories.
Owens College, Manchester, 1886-99. Vols. 1 to 4, 8vo, wrappers.
Wheldon 160-508 1983 £18

THE OWL. Chico: Published by the Owl Club, 1882. Ads. Wrappers,
weakening at spine and folded. Christmas number. Dawson 471-221
1983 $45

OXBERRY, WILLIAM   The actor's budget; consisting of
monologues, prologues, epilogues, and tales, serious and comic: together with a rare and genuine collection of theatrical anecdotes and
comic songs. London: published by W. Simpkin and R. Marshall, 1820.
12mo, original boards (spine defective, covers loose, remains of
printed paper label). Scarce. Ximenes 64-405 1983 $75

OXBERRY, WILLIAM   Oxberry's anecdotes of the stage.
London: printed by C. Baynes; published by G. Virtue, 1827. 12mo,
old half red morocco (scuffed). First edition. Frontis. portrait.
An uncut copy. Rare. Ximenes 64-406 1983 $150

THE OXFORD Annual for Children. H. Milford, n.d. 4to., colour
frontis., colour plate and 3 text illus. by C.E. Brock. Many other
illus. Colour pictorial boards & dust wrappers. Very good. Greer
40-53 1983 £25

THE OXFORD Annual for Children. H. Milford, n.d. Colour frontis.
Colour plate and 3 text illus. by C.E. Brock. Orange cloth. Greer
40-54 1983 £18

THE OXFORD Book of Greek Verse. Oxford, 1938. 8vo, cloth. Salloch
385-640 1983 $25

OXFORD Poetry 1922. Oxford: Basil Blackwell, 1922. 8vo. Orig.
parchment-backed boards with paper labels. Orig. tissue dust
jacket. Unopened copy. First edition. Very fine. Jaffe 1-5
1983 $45

OXFORD Poetry 1924. Oxford: Basil Blackwell, 1924. First edition.
8vo. Orig. wrappers with paper labels. Wrappers slightly split at
base of spine. Unopened. Fine. Jaffe 1-6 1983 $150

OXFORD Poetry 1925. Oxford: Basil Blackwell, 1925. First edition.
8vo. Orig. parchment-backed boards with paper labels. Spine a bit
worn, but a very good copy. Jaffe 1-7 1983 $100

THE OXFORD Sausage: Or, Select Poetical Pieces. Printed for J.
Fletcher and Co., 1764. 8vo, woodcut plate, and 22 large woodcuts
in the text, additional poem in cont. hand tipped in at page 108,
final page laid down, 19th century polished calf, tooled in blind.
First edition. Bickersteth 75-69 1983 £85

P

PAATZ, WALTER   Bernt Notke und sein Kreis. Berlin: Deutscher Verlag fur Kunstwissenschaft, 1939. 2 vols. 212 plates. Small folio. Cloth. Scarce. Ars Libri 32-495 1983 $275

PACIFIC MAIL STEAMSHIP COMPANY   Information for Emigrants to New South Wales, New Zealand, Sandwich Islands, British Columbia, Queensland, and Other British Provinces of Australia. N.Y., ca. 1876. First edition. Dbd. Ginsberg 46-614 1983 $100

PACINI, PIERO   Gino Severini. Firenze: La Nuova Italia, 1977. 64 fine color plates (several folding). Folio. Cloth. Ars Libri 33-587 1983 $125

PACKARD, FRANCIS R.   Ambroise Pare Life and Times (1510-1590). 1921. First edition. 2 folding maps, 27 plates. 22 text illus. Tall 8vo, cloth (back faded). Argosy 713-417 1983 $37.50

PACKARD, FRANCIS R.   Life and Times of Ambroise Pare (1510-1590)... London: Oxford University Press, 1922. 8vo. Cloth. With numerous plates and illus. Inner hinge broken. Gurney JJ-291 1983 £25

PACKARD, FRANCIS R.   Guy Patin; and the Medical Profession in Paris in the 17th Century. Illus., uncut. One of 1059 copies. Argosy 713-421 1983 $40

PACKARD, FRANCIS R.   Guy Patin and the Medical Profession in the XVIIIth Century. New York, 1925. 8vo. Cloth. With 10 plates and illus. in text. Gurney JJ-296 1983 £12

PACKARD, JOHN H.   Sea-Air & Sea-Bathing. Phila., 1885. Several text woodcuts. Thin 16mo. Argosy 713-413 1983 $27.50

PACKARD, WINTHROP   Florida Trails as Seen from Jacksonville to Key West... Boston, (1910). 1st ed. Illus. from photos by author and others. 8vo. Morrill 288-124 1983 $25

PACKMAN, ANA BEGUE   Early California Hospitality. Glendale: Arthur H. Clark, Co., 1938. 3 illus., 8vo. Argosy 716-40 1983 $45

PADEN, IRENE D.   The Wake of the Prairie Schooner. New York, 1943. First edition, first printing. Maps, illustrations by author. Red cloth. Fine. Bradley 65-153 1983 $30

PADOVANI, GIOVANNI   Ioannis Padvanii Veronensis Opvs de Compositione et Vsv multiformium Horologiorum Solarium pro Diuersis mundi regionibus, idq ubique locorum... Venetiis, MDLXX, Apud Franciscum Franciscium Senensem, (1570). 4to, bound in full early vellum. Ink stained in upper margin of several leaves, little text affected. Front joint beginning to split. Very good. Arkway 22-67 1983 $900

PADUANIUS, JOANNES
Please turn to
PADOVANI, GIOVANNI

PAETOW, LOUIS JOHN   A Guide to the Study of Medieval History. New York: F.S. Crofts, 1931. Revised ed. Cloth. Dawson 470-221 1983 $35

PAGE, DAVID (1814-1878)   Advanced text-book on Geology. 1876. 6th edition, numerous text-figures, 8vo, modern half calf. Wheldon 160-1459 1983 £12

PAGE, THOMAS NELSON   Old Gentleman of the Black Stock. N.Y., Scribner, 1901. First edition. Eight color plates by Howard Chandler Christy. Fine decorated cloth binding by Margaret Armstrong. Houle 21-699 1983 $30

PAGE, THOMAS NELSON   Santa Claus' Partner. N.Y., Scribner, 1899. Eight plates by W. Glackens. Printed by D.B. Updike at the Merrymount Press. Good. Houle 21-700 1983 $35

PAGET, J. OTHO   Hunting. London: J.M. Dent & Co., 1900. First edition. Illus. Orig. decorated cloth. Rackham designed the endpapers and head and tail pieces. Some foxing. Covers a bit rubbed. Very good. MacManus 280-4313 1983 $85

PAGET, JAMES   Clinical Lectures and Essays. N.Y., 1875. 8vo, modern buckram; ex-lib. First American edition. Extensive pub.'s catalogue at end. Argosy 713-414 1983 $85

PAGET, VIOLET   Baldwin: Being Dialogues on Views and Aspirations. London: T. Fisher Unwin, 1886. First edition. Orig. cloth. Spine slightly rubbed. Inner hinge cracked. MacManus 279-3187 1983 $75

PAGET, VIOLET   The Beautiful. Cambridge: At the University Press, 1913. First edition, in a variant binding (red). Orig. cloth. Fine. MacManus 279-3188 1983 $25

PAGET, VIOLET   Beauty and Ugliness. London: John Lane, 1912. First edition. Orig. cloth. Covers a bit faded. Waterstain on front cover. Good. MacManus 279-3189 1983 $35

PAGET, VIOLET   Genius Loci. London: Grant Richards, 1899. First edition. Orig. cloth. Fine. MacManus 279-3190 1983 $30

PAGET, VIOLET   The Golden Keys. London, John Lane, The Bodley Head, (1925). First edition. Orig. cloth. Edges a bit worn. Endpapers slightly browned. Good. MacManus 279-3191 1983 $45

PAGET, VIOLET   Louis Norbert. London: John Lane, The Bodley Head, etc., 1914. First edition. Orig. cloth. Former owner's stamp on endsheet. Pencil inscription on free endpaper. Good. MacManus 279-3192 1983 $45

PAGET, VIOLET   Miss Brown. Blackwood, 1884. First edition, 3 vols. Half titles, orig. light brown cloth, blocked in dark brown, spines gilt lettered, v.g. Jarndyce 30-513 1983 £72

PAGET, VIOLET   Proteus or The Future of Intelligence. London: Kegan Paul, Trench, Trubner & Co., Ltd., 1925. First edition. 16mo. Orig. boards with paper labels. Dust jacket (soiled, a little torn). Good. MacManus 279-3193 1983 $25

PAGET, VIOLET   The Sentimental Traveller. London: John Lane, The Bodley Head,...1908. First edition. Orig. cloth. Presentation copy, inscribed at a later date on the front free endpaper. Covers a little soiled and rubbed. Good. MacManus 279-3195 1983 $65

PAGET, VIOLET   The Sentimental Traveller. London: John Lane, 1908. First edition. Orig. cloth. Bookplate of W. MacDonald MacKay on endsheet. Very good. MacManus 279-3194 1983 $25

PAGET, VIOLET   Sister Benvenuta and The Christ Child. N.Y.: Mitchell Kennerley, n.d. (1906). First American edition. 12mo. Orig. cloth. Bound from the English sheets with cancel title-page. Inscription on front free endpaper. Cloth lightly faded. Very good. MacManus 279-3196 1983 $27.50

PAHER, STANLEY W.   Nevada: An Annotated Bibliography... Las Vegas: Nevada Publications, (1980). Cloth. Dawson 470-222 1983 $95

PAILLOUX, XAVIER   Le Magnetisme, le Spiritisme, et la Possession. Paris, 1863. 12mo, pr. wrs. First edition. Argosy 713-416 1983 $60

PAIN, BARRY   The Luck of Norman Dale. London:
Eveleigh Nash, 1908. First edition. Orig. cloth. Good. MacManus
280-4121 1983 $20

PAIN, BARRY   The One Before. London, 1902. First
edition. Cover design and 87 illus. by T. Browne. Hinges weak.
Very nice. Rota 230-461 1983 £15

PAIN, BARRY   Playthings and Parodies. London: Cassell
& Co., 1892. First edition. Orig. cloth. Front and back inside hinges
cracked. Cover stained. Owner's inscription on half-title page.
Bookplate of Adrain Homer Goldstone. MacManus 280-4123 1983 $35

PAINE, ALBERT BIGELOW   The Lure of the Mediterranean. NY, 1921.
Profusely illus. from drawings by Th. Fogarty & photos. 8vo, cloth.
Salloch 385-377 1983 $45

PAINE, MARTIN   Letters on the Cholera Asphyxia...
New York: by Collins & Hannay, 1832. Tall 8vo. Large copy.
Uncut in orig. cloth backed boards. Half title. Presentation
copy to "Andrew Dunlop". Slight wear. Heath 48-523 1983 £45

PAINE, ROBERT T.   The Works in Verse and Prose, of the
Late... Boston: J. Belcher, 1812. Later cloth. Morocco label,
first edition. Title and two leaves a bit soiled, else a very good
copy, untrimmed. Reese 18-391 1983 $30

PAINE, THOMAS   The American Crisis, and a Letter to Sir
Gray Carleton, on the Murder of Captain Huddy... London: Daniel
Isaac Eaton, (1796?) Disbound. Early library blindstamp on title
and bookplate on last leaf. Second issue. Felcone 22-178 1983
$75

PAINE, THOMAS   Common Sense. Albany: Charles R. and
George Webster, 1791. 3/4 morocco. A fine copy. Felcone 22-179
1983 $75

PAINE, THOMAS   Common Sense. NY: Rimington & Hooper,
1828. Frontis. Edition ltd. to 376 numbered copies. Printed
by W.A. Kittredge, at the Lakeside Press, Chicago. Black cloth.
Slipcase. Fine. Karmiole 76-65 1983 $75

PAINE, THOMAS   Letter Addressed to the Abbe Raynal
on the Affairs of North-America. Philadelphia: Melchior Steiner
for Robert Aitken, 1782. Disbound. First edition. Felcone 21-89
1983 $175

PAINE, THOMAS   Letter Addressed to the Abbe Raynal,
on the Affairs of North-America. Albany: Charles R. & George
Webster, (1792). Disbound. Half-title wanting. Felcone 22-180
1983 $45

PAINE, THOMAS   Letter to George Washington... Phila.:
Benj. Franklin Bache, 1796. First edition. 3/4 calf, by Riviere.
Half-title lacking. Very good. Felcone 20-139 1983 $150

PAINE, THOMAS   Letters, by the Author of Common Sense.
Albany: Printed by Charles R. & George Webster, 1792. Disbound. Very
good. Reese 18-181 1983 $100

PAINE, THOMAS   The Theological Works of Thomas Paine...
New York: Blanchard, (1860). 1st ed., bound, as issued. Orig.
cloth. Spine ends chipped, and heavily used and marked by Field,
who has signed his name in ink and pencil 5 times, lined numerous
passages, quoted Paine on front end paper, and affixed two of his
bookplates. Jenkins 155-400 1983 $50

PAINE, THOMAS   The Works of... London, 1796.
Full tree calf, leather label. Bound with 2 pamphlets on the English
System of Finance. Argosy 716-443 1983 $100

PAINTER, WILLIAM   The Palace of Pleasure. London:
The Cresset Press, 1929. 4 vols. Folio. Orig. decorated boards
with canvas spines. Coloured frontis., and other illus. Limited
edition of 500 numbered sets. Traylen 94-644 1983 £105

PAIRPOINT, A. J.   Rambles in America. Boston, 1891.
Portrait, illus. Presentation copy, inscribed by author. 8vo, orig.
cloth. Good. Edwards 1044-544 1983 £15

PAIS, ETTORE   Ancient Legends of Roman History. NY,
1905. 8vo, cloth. Salloch 385-252 1983 $25

PAJES BERRIMAN, MIRA   Giuseppe Maria Crespi. Milano:
Rizzoli, 1980. 16 color plates. 544 illus. Large 4to. Cloth.
Dust jacket. Edition limited to 2000 numbered copies. Ars Libri
33-123 1983 $100

PALAFOX Y MENDOZA, JUAN DE Histoire de la Conqueste de la Chine
par les Tartares. A Paris, A. Bertier, 1670. Old quarter parchment
and boards. K Books 307-140 1983 £275

PALEY, WILLIAM   The Principles of Moral and Political
Philosophy. Philadelphia: Printed by Thomas Dobson, 1794. 2 pages
of pub. ads. Orig. calf, front hinge starting. Some text paper
browning. Karmiole 73-81 1983 $150

PALFREY, JOHN GORHAM   History of New England. Boston, 1859-
1892. Maps. 5 vols., 8vo. Ex-library, hinges of vol. 1 cracked,
front hinge of vol. 3 partly cracked, rubbed. Morrill 289-490 1983
$40

PALFREY, JOHN GORHAM   History of New England During the
Stuart Dynasty. Boston, 1859-64. 3 vols., maps, full cont. calf,
gilt dec. spines, (few top edges dampstained). Argosy 716-325 1983
$75

PALGRAVE, FRANCIS   The Five Days Entertainments at
Wentworth Grange. Macmillan, 1868. First edition, half title, 2pp
ads. Designs by Arthur Hughes. Orig. blue cloth a little rubbed,
and sl. marked on following board. Jarndyce 31-841 1983 £14.50

PALGRAVE, FRANCIS   The Golden Treasury of the Best Songs
& Lyrical Poems in the English Language. Cambridge, 1861. 1st ed.,
2nd issue, uncut in original green cloth gilt, gilt lettering on
spine slightly faded, upper inner hinge cracking, otherwise a very
good copy. Second issue of 1,200 copies. Deighton 3-238 1983 £60

PALGRAVE, FRANCIS   Palgrave's Golden Treasury... Dent,
1927. Re-issue. Illus. in colour by Robert Anning Bell, 24 color
plates and many b&w head and tail pieces. Pale green cloth gilt,
t.e.g., good copy. Hodgkins 27-479 1983 £10.50

PALGRAVE, FRANCIS   The Rise and Progress of the English
commonwealth. London, 1832. First edition. 2 vols. 4to. Cont.
polished calf, gilt panelled spines with crimson and blue morocco
labels, gilt. Traylen 94-645 1983 £38

PALGRAVE, REGINALD F. D.   The House of Commons. Macmillan, 1869.
First edition, half title, 50 pp ads. Orig. red cloth a little
rubbed. Jarndyce 31-331 1983 £10.50

PALGRAVE, WILLIAM GIFFORD   Hermann Agha: An Eastern Narrative.
London: Henry S. King, 1874. Probably the first edition sheets, with
new title-page. 2 vols. in one. Orig. publisher's remainder binding.
Worn. MacManus 280-4124 1983 $25

PALGRAVE, WILLIAM GIFFORD   Narrative of a Year's Journey through
Central and Eastern Arabia (1862-62). London & Cambridge: Macmillan,
1865. 1st ed., 8vo, 2 vols., cont. half morocco gilt, marbled bds.
Engraved frontis. portrait, folding map colored in outline, half-
title. Pencilled annotations by earlier owner on rear flyleaves; but
a very good copy, with maps and plates in fine condition. Trebizond
18-156 1983 $325

PALGRAVE, WILLIAM GIFFORD   Narrative of a Year's Journey through
Central and Eastern Arabia. London, 1865. Folding map mounted on
linen, 4 folding plans, frontis. 2 vols. Half calf, back boards
slightly marked and slight rubbing. 8vo. Good. Edwards 1044-545
1983 £125

PALINURUS
Please turn to
CONNOLLY, CYRIL

PALLADINO, LAWRENCE B.   May Blossoms from the Rocky Mountains in Honor of the B. Mother of God. St. Ignatius' Print, Montana, 1886. Uncut and dbd. in sheets. First edition. Ginsberg 47-579 1983 $50

PALLAS, PETER SIMON   Travels through the Southern Provinces of the Russian Empire in the years 1793 and 1794. 1812. 2nd ed., maps, plates, vignettes, 2 vols., roy 4to, contemporary straight-grained morocco, gilt, g.e. Bindings trifle rubbed, upper joint of Vol. 2 cracking; tear at plate mark of plate 4 in vol. 2 neatly repaired, this plate being a trifle waterstained. Generally a good copy in a fine binding. Wheldon 160-78 1983 £400

PALLISER, JOHN   Solitary Rambles and Adventures of a Hunter in the Prairies. London: John Murray, 1853. 8 illus., ads, pictorial title-page. Original pictorial cloth, neatly rebacked. Nice copy. Jenkins 151-264 1983 $250

PALLISER, JOHN   Solitary Rambles and Adventures of a Hunter in the Prairies. London: John Murray, 1853. 19cm. First edition. 8 illus. Orig. cloth, gilt titles and decoration. Worn and faded, section jumped, else good to very good. Rare. McGahern 53-124 1983 $150

PALLISER, JOHN   Solitary Rambles and Adventures of a Hunter in the Prairies. London, 1853. Illus., frontis. and 6 plates. Half morocco. X-1. First edition. Ginsberg 47-799 1983 $125

PALLUCCHINI, RODOLFO   Giovanni Battista Piazzetta. Roma: Tumminelli, 1943. 56 plates. Text illus. 4to. Wrappers. Dust jacket. Worn. Ars Libri 33-270 1983 $27.50

PALLUCCHINI, RODOLFO   Gli affreschi di Giambattista e Giandomenico Tiepolo alla Villa Valmarana di Vicenza. Bergamo: Istituto Italiano d'Arti Grafiche, 1945. 134 plates. Frontis. in color. Text illus. Folio. Boards, 1/4 cloth. Covers partly detached. Ars Libri 33-359 1983 $85

PALLUCCHINI, RODOLFO   Il polittico del Greco della R. Galleria Estense e la formazione dell'artista. Roma: Istituto Poligrafico dello Stato, 1937. 10 plates loose in portfolio as issued. 17 text illus. Large folio. Wrappers. Ars Libri 32-284 1983 $100

PALMATARY, HELEN CONSTANCE   The Pottery of Marajo Island, Brazil. Philadelphia, 1950. 112 plates. Large 4to. Wrappers. Ars Libri 34-413 1983 $30

PALMER, BENJAMIN MORGAN   The South: Her Peril, and Her Duty. New Orleans, True Witness and Sentinel, 1860. Orig. printed wraps. mounted on cardboard. Half cloth. First edition. Ginsberg 47-472 1983 $100

PALMER, E. H.   The Desert of the Exodus. Cambridge, 1871. 5 folding maps, coloured frontis. 15 plates, and several illus. 2 vols. Pictorial cloth gilt. 8vo. Good. Edwards 1044-547 1983 £125

PALMER, E. W.   A Course in Bookbinding for Vocational Training. New York: Employing Bookbinders of America, 1927. 8vo. Cloth. Some rubbing. Oak Knoll 49-77 1983 $50

PALMER, EVE   Trees of South Africa. Cape Town, 1972-73. Second enlarged edition with 24 coloured plates, many photographs and line drawings, 3 vols., 4to, cloth. Wheldon 160-2096 1983 £145

PALMER, FRIEND   Early Days In Detroit. Detroit, (1906). Portrait, two-tone cloth, t.e.g., front hinge slightly eroded. Slight soiling. King 46-185 1983 $45

PALMER, H. M.   Donald Duck Sees South America. Boston: D.C. Heath, 1945. Sq. 8vo. Colour title vignette. 9 colour plates. 47 colour text illus. & 58 vignettes. Decorated endpapers. Internal wear. Blue pictorial cloth, rubbed. Greer 40-89 1983 £18

PALMER, HERBERT   The Judgement of Francois Villon. London, 1927. One of 400 copies, this being unsiged and designated "Out of Series." Half parchment, patterned boards. Slight discoloration of parchment on upper cover. Dust wrapper. Very nice. Rota 230-292 1983 $30

PALMER, HERBERT   Season and Festival. London: Faber, (1943). Cloth and boards. First edition. Pencil note, else fine in dust jacket. Reese 20-755 1983 $20

PALMER, JOHN W.   The New and the Old; or, California and India in Romantic Aspects. NY, 1859. 1st ed. illus, 2 plates, cloth stained. Argosy 710-38 1983 $40

PALMER, LEWIS   A Genealogical Record of the Descendants of John and Mary Palmer. Chester (Now Delaware) Co., Pa... Phila., 1875. Woodcuts. Cloth. Covers detached. Fair. King 45-60 1983 $30

PALMER, M. G.   Fauna and Flora of the Ilfracombe District of North Devon. Exeter, 1946. Map and 7 plates, 8vo, cloth. Wheldon 160-419 1983 £15

PALMER, R. S.   Handbook of North American Birds. 1962-76. 3 vols., royal 8vo, cloth. Wheldon 160-836 1983 £60

PALMER, SAMUEL   St. Pancros. Samuel Palmer and Field & Tuer, 1870. First edition, 8 pp. ads. Orig. dull purple cloth, small repair to head of spine with no loss. Jarndyce 31-280 1983 £40

PALMER, THOMAS   The Dental Adviser. Fitchburg, Mass., 1853. 1st ed. Illus. 16mo. Fine copy. Morrill 189-179 1983 $30

PALOU, FRAY FRANCISCO   Historical Memoirs of New California. Berkeley, University of California Press, 1926. First edition in English. Thick 8vo, 30 illus., maps. Gilt stamped blue cloth. Signed and inscribed by the editor in vol. I. One of 750 sets. Four vols. Fine. Houle 22-1144 1983 $395

PALTOCK, ROBERT   The Life and Adventures of Peter Wilkins; Containing an Account of His Visit to the Flying Islander... Boston: Bedlington, 1847. Orig. printed pictorial tan boards. Fragile binding, a fine copy. Jenkins 155-991 1983 $85

PALUDAN-MULLER, FREDERIK   The Fountain of Youth. Macmillan and Co., 1867. First English edition. 8vo, ten plates. Orig. cloth. Hannas 69-154 1983 £15

PALUDETTI, GIOVANNI   Giovanni de Min, 1786-1859. Udine: Del Bianco, 1959. 56 plates (2 color). 4to. Wrappers. Dust jacket. Ars Libri 33-528 1983 $100

PANCKRIDGE, H. R.   A Short History of the Bengal Club. Calcutta, 1927. 4 plates. 8vo. Orig. cloth. Good. Edwards 1044-548 1983 £16

PANCOAST, CHALMERS LOWELL   Trail Blazers of Advertising. New York, Frederick H. Hitchcock, 1926. 1st ed. Presentation copy. Drawings by Ray Highet. 8vo. Morrill 289-491 1983 $35

PANCOAST, HENRY SPACKMAN   Impressions of the Sioux Tribes in 1882 with Some First Principles in the Indian Question. Phila., 1883. Orig. printed wraps. First edition. Ginsberg 47-800 1983 $75

PANE, ROBERTO   Andrea Palladio. Torino: Giulio Einaudi, 1961. Second edition. 363 illus. Large stout 4to. Cloth. Dust jacket. Ars Libri 33-261 1983 $100

PANIKKAR, K. M.   His Highness the Maharajah of Bikanner. London, 1937. Plates. 8vo. Orig. cloth. Good. Edwards 1044-549 1983 £18

PANOFSKY, ERWIN   Albrecht Durer. Princeton: Princeton University Press, 1948. 2 vols. 325 collotype illus. hors texte. Large 4to. Cloth. Ars Libri 32-185 1983 $175

PANOFSKY, ERWIN   Die deutsche Plastik kes elften bis driezehnten Jahrhunderts. Firenze/Munchen, 1924. 2 vols. 11 collotype plates with captioned tissue guards. Sm. folio, cloth. Ars Libri SB 26-166 1983 $175

PANOFSKY, ERWIN   Durers Stellung zur Antike. Wien: Eduard Holzer, 1922. 34 illus. 4to. Boards. Ars Libri 32-186 1983 $35

PANOFSKY, ERWIN   Tomb Sculpture. New York, 1964. Sq. 4to, cloth, 446 illus. Ars Libri SB 26-167 1983 $125

THE PANORAMIC Automobile Road Map & Tourist Guide of Southern California, Season 1914-15. Los Angeles: Cadmus Press, 1914. Folding map. Cloth. Compass inset into front cover, some use. Dawson 471-223 1983 $100

THE PANTHEON or The Age of Black. N.Y.: Rollo, 1860. Later cloth, morocco label. Orig. printed wrappers bound in. Jenkins 152-734 1983 $45

PAOLETTI, PIETRO   L'architecture et la sculpture de la renaissance a Venise. Venezia: Ferd. Ongania, 1897-1898. 2 vols. 4to. Wraps. Ars Libri 30-432 1983 $150

PAPAGEIEN und Grosssittich-Zucht. Bomlitz, (1981). Numerous coloured photos., 3 vols., sq. 8vo, boards. Wheldon 160-837 1983 £38

PAPAL Negotiations with Mary Queen of Scots during her Reign in Scotland, 1561-1567. Edinburgh (Publications of the Scottish Historical Society, vol. 37). 1901. 8vo, orig. cloth gilt. Bickersteth 77-162 1983 £24

PAPAZZONI, FLAMINIO   Considerazioni sopra il Discorso del Sig(nor) Galileo Galilei Intorno alle cose... Pisa: Boschetti e Fontani, 1612. First edition. Small 4to. Vellum. Exlibris of Lorenzo de Vecchis (Florence). Corner of title slightly eroded without loss, small inkspot on pp. 1-2 affecting a few letters. Kraus 164-93 1983 $2,500

PAPIN, DENIS   Nouvelle Maniere pour lever leau par la force du feu. Kassel: Jacob Estienne, 1707. One folding plate. Small 8vo. Cont. calf, spine and sides gilt. First edition. 2-line label pasted on title, correcting a printer's error. Browned. Kraus 164-175 1983 $2,200

PAPINI, ROBERTO   Fra Giovanni Angelico. Bologna: Casa Editrice Apollo, 1925. 60 heliotype plates. Large 4to. Cloth. Edition limited to 425 numbered copies. Presentation copy, inscribed by the author. Ars Libri 33-7 1983 $100

PAPWORTH, JOHN BUONAROTTI   Rural Residences, Consisting of a Series of Designs... London: Ackermann, 1832. Second edition. 27 colored lithographic plates. Royal 8vo, half grey morocco over marbled boards. Black morocco label. Occasional light marginal staining. Cont. ownership inscription of British explorer John Wilkinson. In half grey morocco slipcase. Fine. Jenkins 152-735 1983 $525

THE PAPYRUS Ebers. The Greatest Egyptian Medical Document. Copenhagen, 1937. 8vo. Wrappers. Gurney JJ-107 1983 £15

PARDEE, JEAN   The Yale Man up to Date. New Haven, 1894. Illus. Frontis. Pictorial cloth. Fine. Reese 19-608 1983 $20

PARDOE, JULIA   The Beauties of the Bosphorus. Virtue and Co., circa, 1839. With additional engraved title-page, 2 engraved portrait, an engraved map and 83 engraved plates, 4to, cont. dark blue morocco gilt, gilt panelled sides, gilt spine, inside gilt borders, edges gilt, a little rubbed but thoroughly sound and a very good copy. Fenning 61-332 1983 £165

PARDOE, JULIA   The Beauties of the Bosphorus. James S. Virtue, circa, 1839. With additional engraved title-page, 2 portraits, a map and 84 engraved plates, 4to, cont. half red calf, gilt, very good copy. Wanting pages 139-142 of text and with a light stain in the outer corner of seven plates, the other plates are all in clean and fresh state. Fenning 60-313 1983 £85

PARDON, GEORGE FREDERICK   The Faces in the Fire. London: Willoughby, n.d. (1849). First edition. Orig. decorated cloth. Illus. Bound and illustrated in the style of Dickens' Christmas books. Ends of spine slightly frayed. MacManus 280-4126 1983 $65

PARFITT, IRIS G. J.   Jailbird Jottings. (Kuala Lumpur, 1947). First edition, with numerous illus. by the author, some coloured, 4to, orig. printed paper wrappers, a fine copy. Fenning 60-306 1983 £14.50

PARGETER, EDITH   The Face of Wax. Good Housekeeping, December, 1936. 4to. 4 illus. by W.H. Robinson. 4pp of colour illus. by C. Robinson. Colour pictorial wrappers. Greer 39-111 1983 £15

PARIS, MATTHEW   Flores Historiarvm per Mattaeum Westmonasteriensem. Londoni, Ex Officina Thomae Marsh, 1570. Folio, cont. calf, joints cracked, few headlines shaved, light waterspots, some minor age-spotting. On verso title is the Chippendale bookplate of Thomas Ward of Great Silbraham. Ravenstree 97-93 1983 $640

PARISET, FRANCOIS-GEORGES   Georges de la Tour. Paris: Henri Laurens, 1948. 48 plates. 5 text illus. Large square 4to. Wrappers. Dust jacket. Presentation copy, inscribed by the author to Andre Lhote. Ars Libri 32-392 1983 $125

PARISH, ELIJAH   Sacred Geography. Boston, 1813. 1st ed. Folding map. 8vo, contemporary calf, leather label. Some rubbing, title signature slightly torn with no loss of text. Morrill 286-383 1983 $20

PARK, EDWIN AVERY   New Backgrounds for a New Age. New York, (1927). 1st ed. Illus. with line drawings & photographs. 8vo, inner front hinge slightly cracked. Morrill 288-395 1983 $20

PARK, J.   Napoleon in Captivity. London, 1928. 8vo. Orig. cloth. 8 plates, 2 facsimiles (1 folding, 1 double page). Spine faded. Paper label slightly worn. Good. Edwards 1042-433 1983 £15

PARK, LAWRENCE   Gilbert Stuart. An illustrated descriptive list of his works. New York: William Edwin Rudge, 1926. 4 vols. 610 plates (4 photogravure). 8 text illus. Small folio. T.e.g. Slipcase. Fine copy. Rare. Ars Libri 32-654 1983 $1,000

PARK, MUNGO   The journal of a mission to the interior of Africa, in the year 1805. London: John Murray, 1815. First edition. 4to. Folding map. Full brown calf, red label, transfer to title. Adelson Africa-112 1983 $375

PARK, MUNGO   Travels in the interior districts of Africa. London: G. & W. Nicol, 1799. Third edition. 4to. 3 folding maps, 6 plates. Orig. marbled boards, rebacked in brown calf, orig. black label. Some light spotting. Adelson Africa-113 1983 $225

PARK, MUNGO   Travels in the Interior of Africa in the Years 1795, 1796, 1797. London and Huddersfield, 1800. Frontis., second edition, corrected, half calf. K Books 301-137 1983 £48

PARK, ROSWELL   An Epitome of the History of Medicine. Philadelphia, 1899. Second edition. 8vo. Orig. binding. Fye H-3-451 1983 $25

PARK, ROSWELL   An Epitome of the History of Medicine. Philadelphia, 1899. Second edition. 8vo. Orig. binding. Ex-library. Fye H-3-452 1983 $20

PARKER, B.   Arctic Orphans. Edinburgh: M'lagan & Cumming, n.d. Oblong 4to. 12 colour plates & 64 text illus. Colour pictorial boards. Very good. Greer 40-161 1983 £60

PARKER, B.   Larder Lodge. W. & R. Chambers, n.d. (ca.1915). Oblong 4to. Colour title vignette. 14 colour plates & many text illus. Pictorial endpapers. Grey green colour pictorial boards. Greer 40-162 1983 £45

PARKER, B.   Out in the Wood. W. & R. Chambers, n.d. Oblong 4to, colour title vignette, colour pictorial contents page. 14 colour plates, 71 text illus. Pictorial endpapers. Brown colour pictorial boards. Greer 40-163 1983 £45

PARKER, CHARLES S.   Town of Arlington Past and Present.
Arlington, Author, 1907. 1st ed. Illus. 8vo, rubbed. Morrill 288-
289 1983 $25

PARKER, CLEMENT C.   Compendium of Works on Archery.
Phila.: George S. MacManus Co., 1950. 8vo. Cloth. Limited to
300 copies. Oak Knoll 49-411 1983 $25

PARKER, DOROTHY   Not so Deep as a Well. NY, 1936. Illus.
by Valenti Angelo. Limited to 485 numbered and signed copies, edges
and front cover slightly worn, illus. have offset onto facing pages,
else very good. Quill & Brush 54-1059 1983 $75

PARKER, ERIC   Promise of Arden. London: Smith, Elder,
1912. First edition. Orig. cloth. Presentation copy, inscribed,
"To Florence Beerbohm from Eric Parker, Dec. 4, 1912." Fine. Mac-
Manus 280-4128 1983 $25

PARKER, FRANK   Anatomy of the San Francisco Cable
Car. Stanford, Delkin (1946). First edition. Illus. Dust jacket.
Fine. Houle 21-1126 1983 $25

PARKER, GEORGE HOWARD (1864-1955)   The Elementary Nervous System.
Philadelphia, 1919. 8vo. Cloth. Illus. in text. First edition.
Gurney JJ-292 1983 £25

PARKER, GILBERT   An Adventurer of the North. N.Y.: Stone
& Kimball, 1896. First edition. Orig. cloth. MacManus 280-4129
1983 $35

PARKER, GILBERT   Donovan Pasha, and Some People of Egypt.
London: William Heinemann, 1902. First edition. Orig. cloth. Binding very slightly worn and soiled. Previous owner's stamp on front
free endpaper. Very good. MacManus 280-4130 1983 $25

PARKER, GILBERT   A Lover's Diary. Cambridge and Chicago:
Stone & Kimball, 1894. First edition. Orig. boards and paper spine
label. One of 60 large-paper copies. With frontispiece and cover
designs by W.H. Low. Head and foot of spine chipped. Covers a bit
soiled. MacManus 280-4134 1983 $135

PARKER, GILBERT   Mrs. Falchion. London: Methuen & Co.,
1893. First edition. 2 vols. Orig. cloth. Bindings very slightly
worn and soiled. A few leaves very lightly foxed. Previous owner's
signatures. Near-fine. MacManus 280-4136 1983 $250

PARKER, GILBERT   Northern Lights. London: Methuen & Co.,
(1909). First edition. Orig. cloth. With ads at the back dated May,
1909. Spine a little faded. Corners bumped. Covers slightly soiled.
Endpapers a bit browned. Good. MacManus 280-4137 1983 $35

PARKER, GILBERT   Old Quebec. London, 1903. First edition.
Engraved portrait frontis. 8vo. Orig. cloth. 24 engraved plates.
22 full page and numerous other illus. Slightly worn and soiled.
Slight foxing throughout. Bookplate. Good. Edwards 1042-451 1983
£20

PARKER, GILBERT   The Right of Way. London: William Heinemann, 1906. Fourth impression. Orig. cloth. Inscribed by the author
to Arnold Furst, with an ALS from Parker to Furst tipped in. Bookplate.
Rubbed. Good. MacManus 280-4139 1983 $20

PARKER, GILBERT   The Trail of the Sword. London: Methuen
& Co., 1895. First edition. Orig. cloth. Edges and corners slightly
worn. Endpapers a trifle browned. Very good. MacManus 280-4141 1983
$40

PARKER, GILBERT   The Translation of a Savage. London:
Methuen & Co., 1894. First edition. Orig. cloth. Edges very slightly
worn. A little light foxing. Ads at back dated March, 1897. Very
good. MacManus 280-4142 1983 $45

PARKER, GILBERT   The Weavers. N.Y.: Harper & Brothers,
1907. First edition. Orig. boards with paper label on front cover.
Advance copy for private distribution and not for sale, according to
the paper label. With the following inscription on the front free endpaper: "Compliments of Harper & Brothers." All edges a bit worn.
Covers a bit soiled. Good. MacManus 280-4143a $65

PARKER, GILBERT   When Valmond Came to Pontiac. Toronto:
The Copp, Clark Company, Limited, (1898). First Canadian edition.
Orig. cloth. Inscribed by author on the front flyleaf with a full-page
letter addressed to C.S. Applegate Esq., dated 19th Aug. 1926. Fine.
MacManus 280-4144 1983 $45

PARKER, K. T.   The Drawings of Hans Holbein in the
Collection of His Majesty the King at Windsor Castle. London:
Phaidon, 1945. 85 plates. Frontis. tipped-in color. 4to. Cloth.
Ars Libri 32-324 1983 $60

PARKER, K. T.   The Drawings of Watteau. London:
B.T. Batsford, 1931. 117 plates (1 color). Large 4to. Cloth.
Edition limited to 1000 copies. Ars Libri 32-696 1983 $125

PARKER, SAMUEL   A Demonstration of the Divine Authority
of the Law of Nature. Printed by M. Flesher, for R. Royston...and
R. Chiswell, 1681. First edition, 4to, cont. mottled calf, gilt
spine, a nice copy. Fenning 61-333 1983 £35

PARKER, SAMUEL   Journal of an Exploring Tour Beyond
the Rocky Mountains...Performed in the Years 1835, '36, and '37.
Ithaca, N.Y.: The author, 1838. Plate. Folding map. Orig. cloth,
paper spine label. Covers somewhat worn; inner hinges and two
tears in map professionally restored. First edition. Felcone
22-181 1983 $300

PARKER, THOMAS JEFFERY (1850-1897)   A Textbook of Zoology. 1947.
Sixth edition. 1389 text-figures. 2 vols. Royal 8vo. Cloth. Wheldon
160-510 1983 £20

PARKES, HENRY   Fifty Years in the Making of Australian
History. Lon., 1892. Two vols., edges worn, minor interior foxing,
else good or better. Quill & Brush 54-1680 1983 $150

PARKES, JOSEPH   The plagiary "warned," A vindication of
the drama, the stage, and public morals, from the plagiarisms and com-
pilations of the Revd. John Angell James. Birmingham: published by
J. Drake; and Bladwin, Cradock and Joy (London), 1824. 8vo, wrappers.
First edition. Presentation copy, inscribed by the author to Rev.
Higginson. Title-page dust-soiled; uncut copy. Ximenes 64-409 1983
$50

PARKES, SAMUEL   A Chymical Catechism. Ph., 1807. Rebound, interior foxed, very good. Quill & Brush 54-1631 1983 $45

PARKES, SAMUEL   The Chemical Catechism... London:
Baldwin, Cradock and Joy, 1819. 8vo. Cont. half calf. Ads.
2 engraved plates (1 folding). Some minor offsetting, calf a little
rubbed. A good copy. Zeitlin 264-360 1983 $75

PARKES, SAMUEL   The Chemical Catechism. London:
by the Author, 1826. 12th edition. 8vo. Cont. half calf.
Frontis. portrait, 2 plates (1 folding). Ads. Lightly rubbed.
Zeitlin 264-361 1983 $55

PARKES, SAMUEL   Thoughts on the laws relating to salt.
London: for the author; Baldwin, Cradock and Joy, 1817. First
edition. 8vo. Orig. drab boards, printed paper label. Presentation
copy, inscribed by the author to the Philadelphia naturalist George
Ord. Some rubbing. Fine copy. Ximenes 63-574 1983 $150

PARKMAN, FRANCIS   The California and Oregon Trail: Being
Sketches of Prairie and Rocky Mountain Life. New York, 1849.
Handsome three quarter tan morocco, gilt. T.e.g. First edition,
second issue. Jenkins 151-265 1983 $250

PARKMAN, FRANCIS   The Conspiracy of Pontiac and the
Indian War after The Conquest of Canada. Boston: Little, Brown &
Co., 1878. 20 1/2cm. 8th edition. 2 vols. 4 maps (2 double-page)
rebound in brown fabrikoid. Fine. McGahern 53-125 1983 $25

PARKMAN, FRANCIS   A Half-Century of Conflict. Boston 1892.
1st ed. 2 vols. 3 maps. Argosy 710-53 1983 $50

PARKMAN, FRANCIS   History of the Conspiracy of Pontiac.
Boston: 1851. First edition. Cloth. 4 maps. Very good copy.
Bradley 66-642 1983 $165

PARKMAN, FRANCIS   The Journals of... New York, 1947. 2
vols. 1st eds. in dust jackets. Maps and illus. Fine set. Jenkins
153-422 1983 $75

PARKMAN, FRANCIS   The Journals of Francis Parkman.
New York & London: Harper & Bros., 1947. 24cm. 2 vols. First
edition. 16 plates and 9 drawings by Parkman. 1 map, mapped
endpapers. Fine. McGahern 54-143 1983 $50

PARKMAN, FRANCIS   Journals. New York, 1947. 1st ed.
Illus. 2 vols., 8vo, dust wrappers, boxed, virtually as new.
Morrill 287-340 1983 $30

PARKMAN, FRANCIS   Montcalm and Wolfe. Macmillan, 1884.
First U.K. edition, with 2 portraits and 9 maps, without the half-
titles, 2 vols., 8vo, cont. half calf, gilt, t.e.g., a very good
copy. Fenning 61-334 1983 £32.50

PARKMAN, FRANCIS   The Old Regime in Canda. Boston:
Little, Brown, 1874. 21cm. Double-page engraved map, brown
pebbled cloth. First edition. Very good. McGahern 54-144 1983
$35

PARKMAN, FRANCIS   The Oregon Trail: Sketches of Prairie
and Rocky-Mountain Life. Boston: Little, Brown, and Co., 1925.
Illustrated by N.C. Wyeth and Frederick Remington. Limited to 950
numbered copies. Orig. pictorial cloth, t.e.g. Several pages
carelessly opened. Part unopened. Fairly nice copy. Jenkins
155-996 1983 $300

PARKMAN, FRANCIS   The Oregon Trail. Boston, 1892.
Frontis. Plates. Illus. Gilt pictorial cloth, a.e.g. Spine very
slightly darkend, otherwise a fine copy. First illus. edition.
Reese 19-462 1983 $250

PARKMAN, FRANCIS   Pioneers of France in the New World.
Boston, 1865. Cloth, inner hinges cracking, otherwise very good.
Reese 19-416 1983 $30

PARKMAN, FRANCIS   The Works of Francis Parkman. Boston:
Little, Brown and Co., 1897. 20 vols. Deluxe ed. limited to 300
sets. Three quarter morocco. T.e.g. Raised bands with gilt dec.
Jenkins 155-997 1983 $750

PARKMAN, FRANCIS   Works. Boston, Little, Brown, 1909. 13
vols. 8vo. Frontispieces & other plates. 3/4 dark green levant
morocco & marbled boards & endpapers, backs gilt, raised bands, aeg.
Fine. O'Neal 50-116 1983 $300

PARKMAN, FRANCIS   Works. London: Macmillan and Co.,
1899-1908. Complete set. 12 vols. 8vo. Orig. light green cloth,
gilt, t.e.g. Frontis. Traylen 94-646 1983 £55

THE PARLEMENT of the Thre Ages... London: the Roxburghe Club,
1897. Limited edition, printed for Members only. 4to. Orig.
quarter brown morocco, gilt, t.e.g., others uncut. The Earl of
Cawdor's copy. Traylen 94-647 1983 £35

PARLMAN, MOSHE   The Army of Israel. New York,
Philosophical Library, 1950. First edition, maps, plates, etc. 8vo,
orig. cloth. Fenning 60-314 1983 £10.50

PARMELIN, HELENE   Picasso: Women. Paris & Amsterdam,
(ca. 1964). Ed. in English. Illus. in color and black and white by
Picasso. Square 4to. Dust wrapper, nice. Morrill 286-385 1983
$75

PARMENTIER, A. A.   Experiences et Reflexions relatives a
L'Analyse du Bled et des Farines. Paris: Monory, 1776. First
edition. 8vo. Quarter-calf. Gurney 90-94 1983 £65

PARMLY, ELEAZAR   Dentologia: A Poem on the Diseases of
the Teeth, and Their Proper Remedies. With Notes, Practical... by
Eleazar Parmly, Dentist. New York, 1833. 1st ed. 8vo. Binding
faded; few pencil marks in text. Morrill 289-22 1983 $47.50

PARNELL, EDWARD A.   Elements of Chemical Analysis, Qualitative
and Quantitative. Taylor and Walton, 1845. With 55 illus., 8vo,
orig. cloth, fine. Fenning 60-307 1983 £14.50

PARNELL, HENRY   De La Reforme Financiere En Angleterre.
Paris: Delaunay, etc., 1832. 1st ed. in French, 8vo, uncut and
unopened, occasional light spotting, original printed wrappers,
edges slightly frayed. Pickering & Chatto 21-93 1983 $80

PARNELL, HENRY   Observations on the Paper Money, Banking,
and Overtrading. London: James Ridgway, 1838. 2nd ed., 8vo,
advertisements, uncut in original grey boards, occasional pencilled
marginalia, original paper label, spine slightly chipped but sound.
A very nice copy. Pickering & Chatto 21-92 1983 $250

PARNELL, HENRY   A Treatise On Roads. London: Longman,
1833. 1st ed., 8vo, advertisements, half-title, 7 folding engraved
plates, some slight spotting, original green diced cloth, uncut and
unopened, original printed paper label, upper joint just beginning
to split at the head but a very good copy. Pickering & Chatto 21-94
1983 $385

PARNELL, THOMAS   Poems on Several Occasions. London:
Printed for B. Lintot...1722. 8vo, title in red and black in mid-
eighteenth-century binding of dark blue polished sheep, richly gilt,
red morocco spine-label, light blue marbled endleaves, g.e. Slipcase.
First edition. With the bookplate of Harry Buxton Forman. Quaritch
NS 7-95 1983 $1,500

PARNELL, THOMAS   Poems on Several Occasions. London:
printed for B. Lintot, 1722. 1st ed., 8vo, errata and index, cont.
calf, joints split at head and foot, spine and corners worn, bookplate. A nice copy. Pickering & Chatto 19-42 1983 $650

PARNELL, THOMAS   Poems on Several Occasions. London:
Printed for B. Lintot...1722. 8vo, cont. calf, slight wear to
hinges and corners, but sound, with blind borders. First edition.
Some internal foxing or staining, C2 torn in lower blank margin,
not affecting text. Quaritch NS 7-96 1983 $135

PARNELL, THOMAS   The Poetical Works. London, 1866.
Cr. 8vo. Dark blue calf, two-line gilt borders with corner ornaments,
gilt panelled spine, morocco label, gilt. Portraits, vignette title-
page. Traylen 94-648 1983 £16

PARQUIN, C.   Napoleon's Victories. Chicago, Werner,
1893. 20 full-page colored plates, 4 of which are double-page; many
in balck and white, by F. de Myrbach, H. Dupray, J.A. Walker, L.
Sergent and Marius Roy. Small folio, some rubbing. Orig. cloth.
Morrill 290-393 1983 $30

PARR, HARRIET   Basil Godfrey's Caprice. Smith, Elder,
1868. First edition, 3 vols. Half brown morocco, v.g. Jarndyce
30-452 1983 £42

PARR, OLIVE KATHARINE   Back Slum Idyls. R. & T. Washbourne,
1907. Illus. by E.J. Wheeler, half title, 1 p ads. Orig. blue
cloth, sl. rubbed, pic. blocked. Jarndyce 31-281 1983 £14.50

PARRISH, RANDALL   The Great Plains. Chicago: A.C. McClurg
& Co., 1907. Frontis. and illus. Orig. pictorial cloth. 1st ed.
Jenkins 153-423 1983 $40

PARRISH, RANDALL   Great Plains. Chicago, 1907. Illus.,
edges untrimmed. Clark 741-280 1983 $24.50

PARRISH, THOMAS C.   Colorado Springs. Colorado Springs,
1889. Orig. printed wraps. Illus. First edition. Ginsberg 47-247
1983 $75

PARRONI, GIUSEPPE   Un caposcuola fiorentino del verismo:
Raffaello Paglaccetti. Milano: "Esperia", 1927. 64 plates. Small
4to. Boards. Shaken. Ars Libri 33-555 1983 $40

PARROT, E.   Journey to Ararat. London, n.d. (c.1850).
First edition. Folding map, woodcuts in text. Calf, spine gilt,
raised bands. 8vo. Good. Edwards 1044-552 1983 £85

PARROT, JOHANN J. F. W. VON   Journay to Ararat (in 1829-30). Longman,
Brown, (1845). First edition in English, with a folding map and some
woodcut illus., 8vo, a very good copy in recent morocco-backed marbled
boards, with label. Fenning 60-309 1983 £75

PARRY, EDWARD   The Persecution of Mary Stewart.
(1931). 8vo, 8 plates, cloth. Bickersteth 77-163 1983 £12

PARRY, EDWARD ABBOTT   Butterscotia. Nutt, 1896. Illus. by
Archie MacGregor. Frontis., illus. title & 6 full page illus., 28
text illus. & folding map. Pub's adverts. Beige decor. cloth, eps.
sl. foxed & occasional fox mark, nice copy. Hodgkins 27-158 1983
£17.50

PARRY, EDWARD ABBOTT   Charles Macklin. Kegan Paul, 1891.
First edition, half title, orig. boards, grey cloth spine, v.g.
Jarndyce 30-1062 1983 £10.50

PARRY, EDWARD ABBOTT   Katawampus. Nutt, 1895. Illus. by
Archie MacGregor. 7 full page b&w illus. & numerous text illus. &
decor. initial letters. Pale green decor. cloth, uncut, bkstrip v.
sl. faded, contents some foxing, nice. copy. Hodgkins 27-157 1983
£16.50

PARRY, N. E.   The Lakhers. London, 1932. Folding map,
3 coloured plates. Numerous others. Thick 8vo. Pictorial cloth gilt.
Good. Edwards 1044-554 1983 £45

PARRY, WILLIAM   The Last Days of Lord Byron.
Philadelphia, H.C. Carey et al., 1825. 8vo, orig. drab boards, worn,
soiled, name on title, another name cut from blank portion of title,
quite age-browned and foxed, uncut. First American edition.
Ravenstree 96-152 1983 $75

PARSONS, ARTHUR JEFFREY   Catalog of the Gardiner Greene Hubbard
Collection... Washington: GPO, 1905. Thick 4to. Orig. half calf
over boards. 2707 engr. described, 12 illus. Covers stained and
rubbed. Oak Knoll 49-314 1983 $45

PARSONS, GEORGE F.   The Life and Adventures of James W.
Marshall... Sacramento: James W. Marshall and W. Burke, 1870.
Frontis. portrait. Orig. cloth with fading to cloth. Good copy.
Jenkins 153-424 1983 $125

PARSONS, GEORGE F.   The Life and Adventures of James W.
Marshall. San Francisco, 1935. Orig. boards, paper label. Reprint
edition. Ltd. to 500 copies. Ginsberg 47-144 1983 $60

PARSONS, JAMES   Philosophical Observations on the Analogy
between the Propagation of Animals and that of Vegetables. Printed
for C. Davis, 1752. First edition, with a folding engraved plate,
8vo, cont. unlettered gilt-ruled calf, the bindings a little worn
but sound and otherwise a very good copy. Fenning 62-276 1983
£125

PARSONS, JOHN HERBERT   An Introduction to the Theory of
Perception. NY: Macmillan, 1927. First American edition. Gach
94-741 1983 $27.50

PARSONS, ROBERT   A Sermon Preached at the Funeral of the
Rt. Honorable John Earl of Rochester. Oxford, printed at the
Theater for Richard Davies and Tho: Bowman, 1680. 4to, disbound.
First edition. Ravenstree 97-153 1983 $21

PARSONS, USHER   The Life of Sir William Pepperrell...
Boston, 1856. 2nd ed. Map and portrait. 8vo. Rubbed at corners
and some edges, bookplate. Morrill 287-342 1983 $27.50

PARSONS, W. F.   Guide to Penmanship and Letter
Writing... Battle Creek: J.E. White, 1883. First edition. 8vo.
Orig. cloth-backed boards. With Library of Congress Copyright
stamp on titlepage. Covers soiled and rubbed along edges. Oak
Knoll 48-83 1983 $45

PARTRIDGE, C. S.   Stereotyping, a Practical Treatise of
All Known Methods of Stereotyping... Chicago: Inland Printer Co.,
1909. Second edition, revised. 8vo. Cloth. Covers rubbed. Hole
in endpaper. Oak Knoll 49-315 1983 $30

PARUTA, PAOLO   Discorsi Politici..., ne i quali si
considerano diversi Fatti illustri e Memorabili di Prencipi. Venetia:
Tomaso Baglioni, 1629. 4to, cont. calf, spine gilt, morocco label.
Vignette title page. Extremities of spine chipped, a few wormholes
not affecting text, but a good copy. Trebizond 18-208 1983 $80

PARVIN, T. S.   Who Made Iowa? Davenport, Iowa: Egbert,
Fidlar, & Chambers, 1896. Orig. printed wrappers. Frontis. and illus.
Jenkins 152-172 1983 $40

PASCAL, ANDRE   Documents sur la vie et l'oeuvre de
Chardin, reunis et annotes. Paris: Editions de la Galerie Pigalle,
1931. 19 heliogravure plates. Large 4to. New cloth. Orig. wrappers
bound in. Ars Libri 32-104 1983 $150

PASCAL, BLAISE   Pascal's Pensees. London, 1931.
Slightly dusty dustwrapper. First edition. Scarce. Fine.
Gekoski 2-43 1983 £30

PASCAL, BLAISE   Les Provinciales. London, Printed for
J.G. for R. Royston, 1657. 12mo. Cont. calf, bit rubbed. 1st ed.
in English. Clean & crisp. O'Neal 50-40 1983 $400

PASCAL, BLAISE   Les Provinciales or, The Mystery of
Jesuitisme. London, Richard Royston, 1658. Large 12mo, half calf,
boards, front cover loose, frontis. mounted. A large copy, complete
with the 147 page appendix at end. Second edition in English.
Ravenstree 97-154 1983 $115

PASCHALL, JOHN   Mr. Paschall's Letter to a Friend in
the Country. Printed for A. Bell, 1701. First edition, folio,
wrapper, edges uncut, a fine copy. Fenning 62-277 1983 £24.50

PASLEY, THOMAS   Private Sea Journals. J.M. Dent, 1931.
First edition, maps & plates, 8vo, orig. cloth, gilt, v.g. Fenning 61-
335 1983 £14.50

PASQUIN, ANTHONY, PSEUD.
Please turn to
WILLIAMS, JOHN (1761-1818)

PASS, CRISPIN DE   Hortus Floridus. Contayning a very
lively and true description of the flowers of the Springe, Summer,
Autumn and Winter. Cresset Press, 1928-29. Facsimile reproductions,
2 vols., oblong 4to, original half leather. Limited to 500 copies.
Wheldon 160-79 1983 £100

PASSAMANI, BRUNO   La scultura romanica del trentino.
Trento, 1963. 210, (2)pp. 86 plates. 4to. Cloth. D.j. Ars Libri
SB 26-180 1983 $100

PASSAVANT, GUNTER   Verrocchio. Sculture, pitture e
disegni. Venezia: Alfieri, n.d. 4 color plates. 216 illus.
Large 4to. Cloth. Dust jacket. Ars Libri 33-386 1983 $75

PATCHEN, KENNETH   Before the Brave. NY, (1936). Cover
lightly stained, spine faded, pencil notes, good or better. Quill &
Brush 54-1060 1983 $35

PATCHEN, KENNETH   The Dark Kingdom. N.Y., (1942). 8vo,
wraps., backstrip frayed & chipped. Ltd. first edition. One of
only 75 signed copies, with original cover decorations painted by the
author. Argosy 714-584 1983 $250

PATCHEN, KENNETH   The Journal of Albion Moonlight. (Mount
Vernon: 1941). First edition. Limited to 295 copies. Slight worming
to rear inner hinge, some facing to covers, else fine copy. Bromer
25-83 1983 $85

PATCHEN, KENNETH   The Journal of Albion Moonlight. NY,
1944. Limited to 3000 copies, front hinge tender, flys offset from
dustwrapper, stain on front pastedown, edges rubbed, good in price
clipped, lightly chipped dustwrapper. Quill & Brush 54-1062 1983
$30

PATCHEN, KENNETH   The Journal of Albion Moonlight. NY,
1944. Limited to 3000 copies, edges worn, very good in worn and rubbed
dustwrapper. Quill & Brush 54-1063 1983 $30

PATCHEN, KENNETH   See You in the Morning. N.Y., (1947).
First edition. D.w. Argosy 714-585 1983 $45

PATCHEN, KENNETH   Sleepers Awake. (NY, 1946). Signed by
author, edges rubbed, else very good in lightly frayed and chipped,
moderately worn, good dustwrapper. Quill & Brush 54-1061 1983 $60

PATCHEN, KENNETH   They Keep Riding Down all the Time.
(New York: Padell, 1946). Pictorial wrapper over stiff wraps.
First edition. Trace of paperclip, else about fine. Reese 20-758
1983 $35

PATER, WALTER   Gaston de Latour. London: Macmillan &
Co., 1896. First edition. Orig. cloth. Very good. MacManus 280-4145
1983 $35

PATER, WALTER   Marius the Epicurean. London: Macmillan
& Co., 1885. First edition. 2 vols. Orig. cloth. Front inner hinges
cracking. Very good. MacManus 280-4147 1983 $100

PATERSON, JAMES   The contemporaries of Burns... Edinburgh: Hugh Paton, 1840. First edition. 8vo. Orig. brown cloth,
printed paper label. Frontis. and six plates. Rubbed. Ximenes
63-246 1983 $60

PATERSON, ROBERT   Memorials of the Life of James Syme.
Edinburgh, 1874. First edition. Ex-lib. Ports. (joints mended).
Argosy 713-523 1983 $45

A PATHFINDER in the Southwest: The Itinerary of Amiel Weeks Whipple.
Norman, 1941. Plates and folding map, first edition, dust jacket.
Jenkins 153-198 1983 $35

PATMORE, COVENTRY   The Angel in the House: Volume I.
The Bethrothal. Volume II. The Espousals. John W. Parker, 1854/56.
4 pp ads. vol. I, half title vol. II. Orig. brown cloth, paper
labels rubbed, otherwise v.g. First editions. Jarndyce 30-816 1983
£18.50

PATMORE, COVENTRY   The Angel in the House. London, 1854 &
1856. First edition, first issue, in 2 vols. Orig. cloth, paper
labels on spines. Cloth somewhat worn on spine of Vol. II. Very
good. Inscription on flyleaf of Vol. I. The second volume bears the
inscription: "From the Author". Rota 231-462 1983 £100

PATMORE, COVENTRY   The Angel in the House; The Espousals;
The Betrothal. Boston, 1856. First American editions. 2 vols.,
8vo, brown cloth; extremes of backstrips chipped. Argosy 714-884
1983 $125

PATON, G.   Historical Records of the 24th Regiment.
Devonport, 1892. 8vo. Photogravure frontis. 4 photogravure and 6
coloured plates, 11 illus. Orig. green calf backed red cloth boards.
Neatly repaired. Slightly soiled. Marbled endpapers, frontis.
slightly soiled. Good. Edwards 1042-540 1983 £65

PATON, JAMES   John G. Paton, D.D., Missionary to the
New Hebrides. 1894. Fifth edition. With a portrait and a map, 8vo,
ads., orig. cloth, gilt. A very good copy. Fenning 60-311 1983
£12.50

PATON, JOSEPH NOEL   Poems by A Painter. Edinburgh: William
Blackwood & Sons, 1861. First edition. Orig. cloth. Soiled, front
endpaper rubbed. MacManus 280-4149 1983 $40

PATRICK, JOHN   The Virgin Mary Misrepresented by the
Roman Church. Printed for Richard Chiswell, 1688. First edition,
all published, 4to, wrapper, small hole in blank portion of half-
title, otherwise nice. Fenning 61-337 1983 £16.50

PATRICK, SYMON   A Discourse about Tradition. Printed
for T. Basset...and Abel Swalle, 1685. Second edition. 4to.
Fenning 62-278 1983 £14.50

PATRICK, SYMON   The Parable of the Pilgrim. London,
Robert White, for Francis Tyton, 1668. 4to, old calf rebacked in
sheep, joints broken and covers detached. Ravenstree 96-141 1983
$250

PATRICK, SYMON   A Sermon Preached at S. Paul Covent-
Garden. Printed by R.E. for J. Magnes and R. Bentley, 1678.
First edition, 4to. Fenning 62-279 1983 £12.50

PATRICK, SYMON   A Sermon Preached upon St. Peter's Day.
Printed for Ric. Cheswell, 1687. First edition, including imprimatur
leaf. Fenning 61-338 1983 £14.50

THE PATRIOT DAUGHTERS OF LANCASTER   Hospital Scenes After the Battle
of Gettysburg, July. 1863. Philadelphia: Henry B. Ashmead. 1864.
First edition. 16mo. Orig. cloth wrappers. Morrill 289-367 1983
$40

PATRIOTIC Songs. New York, (1840's?) Disbound. Preliminary leaf
is an added title, "New Whig Songs, for Clay Glee Clubs." Felcone
22-182 1983 $25

PATRIZI, FRANCESCO   A Moral Methode of Ciuile Policie
Contayninge a Learned and Fruictful Discourse o (sic) the
Institution, State and Gouernment of a Common Weale... London,
Thomas Marsh, 1576. 4to, 19th century straight-grain green morocco,
bit rubbed, joints breaking, minor waterstaining, few headlines cut
close. Sole Tudor edition. First edition. Ravenstree 97-155 1983
$750

PATRIZI, PATRIZIO   Il Giambologna. Milano: L.F. Cogliati,
1905. Prof. illus. 4to. Cloth, 3/4 leather. Orig. wrappers bound
in. Worn. Ars Libri 33-160 1983 $100

PASTON, GEORGE, PSEUD.
Please turn to
SYMONDS, EMILY MORSE

PATTEN, NATHAN VAN   The Lost Bookplate of Arthur Machen.
San Francisco, Privately Printed, 1949. First edition. With facs.
of Machen's bookplate. One of 50 copies printed at the Greenwood
Press. Very good. Houle 22-615 1983 $85

PATTERSON, A. B.   The Collected Verse of A.B. Patterson.
Australia: Angus & Robertson, 1921. First edition. Frontispiece
portrait. Orig. cloth. Presentation copy from the publishers to
Arthur Conan Doyle inscribed: "Sir Arthur Conan Doyle, with Compliments,
Angus & Robertson." Good. MacManus 278-1639 1983 $135

PATTERSON, FLOYD   Victory Over Myself. (N.Y.), Bernard
Geis Associates, (1962). Second printing. Illus. with 16 halftone
prints. Dust jacket (soiled) else very good. Houle 22-131 1983 $75

PATTERSON, J. H.   In the Grip of the Nyika. New York:
Macmillan, 1909. 8vo. Map. Numerous photographs. Orig. blue cloth.
Slightly rubbed. Adelson Africa-211 1983 $50

PATTERSON, J. H.   The Man-eaters of Tsavo and other
East African Adventures. London: Macmillan & Co., 1907. 8vo.
Map. Numerous text illus. 1/2 green crushed levant by Bayntun.
T.e.g. Spine faded to brown. Adelson Africa-114 1983 $100

PATTERSON, LOUIS HARMAN   The Pageant of Newark-on-Trent in
Nottinghamshire. Newark, Carteret Book Club of Newark, New Jersey,
1927. Ed. limited to 200 copies. Illus. Tall 8vo, orig. boards,
buckram back, uncut and unopened, very nice. Morrill 287-345 1983
$20

PATTERSON, ROBERT   A Narrative of the Campaign in the
Valley of the Shenandoah, in 1861. Philadelphia, 1865. Presentation
from author. Map. 8vo. Rubbed, lacks half of backstrip. Morrill
287-346 1983 $27.50

PATTERSON, ROBERT   Who Wrote the Book of Mormon? Phila.:
L.H. Everts & Co., 1882. Orig. printed wrappers. Jenkins 153-374
1983 $45

PATTIE, JAMES OHIO   The Personal Narrative of James O.
Pattie, of Kentucky. Chicago, 1930. Illus., 16mo, g.t. Argosy
710-520 1983 $30

PATTISON, EMILIA FRANCIS   French Architects and Sculptors of
the XVIIIth Century. London, 1900. xvii, (1), 217pp., 52 plates.
4to. Buckram. Ex-library. Ars Libri SB 26-181 1983 $65

PATTISON, ROBERT E.   Extracts from the Report of the U.S.
Pacific Railway Commision, 1888. (Wash.), 1888. Orig. printed
wraps. Ginsberg 47-784 1983 $35

PATTON, HENRY E.   Fifty Years of Disestablishment. Dublin:
A.P.C.K., 1922. First edition, with 41 plates, cr. 8vo, orig.
cloth, a nice copy. Fenning 60-312 1983 £10.50

PAUL, C. KEGAN   Memories. Kegan Paul, Trench, Trubner, 1899. First edition, half title. Orig. brown cloth, t.e.g. Jarndyce 30-1098 1983 £12.50

PAUL, ELLIOT   Springtime in Paris. New York: Random House, (1942). Cloth. First edition. Neat pencil inscription, else fine in slightly used dust jacket. Reese 20-759 1983 $30

PAUL, ELLIOT   Springtime in Paris. New York: Random House, (1950). Cloth. First edition. Fine in near fine dust jacket. Reese 20-760 1983 $30

PAUL, WILLIAM   Remarks on the Speeches of William Paul, Clerk, and John Hall of Otterburn, Esq. Printed for J. Baker and T. Warner, 1716. 8vo, final blank leaf, modern plain boards. Bickersteth 75-70 1983 £18

PAUL OF AEGINA   The Seven Books... London, 1844-47. 3 vols. First English translation. 1/2 leather with marbled boards. 8vo. Ex-library but a fine set. Fye H-3-455 1983 $250

PAULDING, JAMES K.   Letters from the South, written during an Excursion in the Summer of 1816. NY, 1817. First edition, 2 vols., 12mo, later linen-backed boards. Occasional foxing, margin corner dampstained first few pp, ex-library. Argosy 710-559 1983 $50

PAULDING, JAMES K.   Letters from the South. NY, 1835. New edition. 2 vols., orig. designed cloth, (back-strips faded, tops chipped). Argosy 716-503 1983 $30

PAULDING, JAMES K.   Westward Ho! NY, 1832. Two vols. Front endpaper in vol. 1 and rear endpaper in vol. 2 missing, top half-inch of title page in vol. 1 torn off, some foxing and staining throughout, good, orig. cloth covers faded and show only minor wear on spine ends and corners. Quill & Brush 54-1067 1983 $150

PAULHAN, FREDERICK (1856-1931)   La Fonction de la Memoire et le Souvenir Affectif. Paris: Felix Alcan, 1904. Ads. 12mo. Orig. printed green wrappers. First edition. Library bookplate, else fine, unopened copy. Gach 95-394 1983 $20

PAULI, GUSTAV   Paula Modersohn-Becker. Berlin: Kurt Wolff, 1919. Third edition. 59 plates (1 color). 4to. Cloth. Presentation copy, inscribed by the author to Arthur Burkhard. Ars Libri 32-463 1983 $75

PAULLIN, CHARLES O.   Atlas of the Historical Geography of the United States. Wash., Carnegie Inst., 1932. 166 plates and maps in color. Orig. 4to, cloth, front cover creased. First edition. Ginsberg 46-623 1983 $150

PAULLIN, CHARLES O   Commodore John Rodgers. Cleveland: Arthur H. Clark Co., 1910. Tall 8vo, illus. with 9 plates. Blue cloth. Karmiole 73-82 1983 $40

PAULSON, RONALD   Hogarth's Graphic Works. New Haven: Yale University Press, 1965. First complete edition. 2 vols. 346 illus. Large oblong 4to. Cloth. Dust jacket. Ars Libri 32-315 1983 $250

PAULY, JOACHIM   Der Sexuelle Fetischismue. Hamburg: Lassen, (1957). First edition. Illus. 4to, cloth. Privately printed numbered edition. Argosy 713-423 1983 $85

PAUSCH, GEORG   Journal of Captain Pausch Chief of the Hanau Artillery During the Burgoyne Campaign. Albany: Joel Munsell's Sons, 1886. Plates. Original cloth. First printing. Jenkins 151-267 1983 $85

PAVLOV, IVAN PETROVITCH   Conditioned Reflexes: An Investigation of the Physiological Activity of the Cerebral Cortex. (London): Oxford University Press, 1928. 1 plate. Large 8vo. Publisher's cloth. Ownership entry of Hugh Thompson on first free endpaper. First edition. Kraus 164-186 1983 $240

PAVLOV, IVAN PETROVITCH   Conditioned Reflexes. Oxford: Oxford Univ. Press, 1927. Fine in worn dust jacket. Gach 95-395 1983 $185

PAVLOV, IVAN PETROVICH   Lectures on Conditioned Reflexes. N.Y., (1928). 9 text illus. First edition of vol. 1. Argosy 713-424 1983 $125

PAVLOV, IVAN PETROVICH   Lectures on Conditioned Reflexes. (Twenty-five Years of Objective Study of the Higher Nervous Activity (behavior of Animals)). NY: 1936 (1928). Dust jacket a bit worn. Gach 94-618 1983 $25

PAVLOV, IVAN PETROVICH   Lectures on Conditioned Reflexes. Vol. Two: Conditoned Reflexes and Psychiatry. NY: International Publishers, (1941). First edition in English. Publisher's black cloth. Very good in defective dust jacket. Gach 94-619 1983 $45

PAVLOV, IVAN PETROVICH   Die Physiologie der Hoechsten Nervantaetigkeit. Tivoli: Arti Grafiche Aldo Chicca, 1932. Orig. printed brown wrappers. First edition. Gach 95-396 1983 $150

PAVLOV, IVAN PETROVICH   Le Travail des Glandes Digestives. Paris: Masson & Cie, 1901. First French edition. Large 8vo. Half-cloth. Some pencil underlining. Kraus 164-184 1983 $250

PAXSON, FREDERIC L.   History of the American Frontier 1763-1893. Boston, 1924. First edition. Maps. Orig. cloth. Fine. Jenkins 152-319 1983 $45

PAXTON, JOSEPH   Paxton's Flower Garden. London, 1850-53. 314 wood-engravings in the text, 4to, 108 hand-coloured lithograph plates. Cont. half roan, gilt spines, gilt edges. First edition. K Books 301-138 1983 £600

PAYN, JAMES   The Burnt Million. London: Chatto & Windus, 1890. First edition. 3 vols. Orig. cloth with floral endpapers. Edges and corners a bit worn. Covers a little soiled. Good. MacManus 280-4150 1983 $285

PAYN, JAMES   The Heir of the Ages. London: Smith, Elder, & Co., 1886. First edition. 3 vols. Orig. cloth. Extremities of spines a little rubbed. Covers of vol. two darkened. Good. MacManus 280-4151 1983 $250

PAYN, JAMES   Leaves From Lakeland. London: Hamilton, Adams & Co., (1858). First edition. Orig. green decorated cloth. Top spine end slightly repaired. Very good. MacManus 280-4152 1983 $85

PAYN, JAMES   Lost Sir Massingberd. Sampson Low, 1864. First edition, half titles, lacking following free end papers vol. I. Cont. fine-grained blue cloth by Birdsall, brown leather labels, yellow edges, v.g. Jarndyce 30-515 1983 £40

PAYN, JAMES   Maxims, by a Man of the World. Tinsley Bros., 1869. First edition, half title, 6 pp ads. Orig. blue cloth, spine sl. marked. Jarndyce 31-845 1983 £12.50

PAYN, JAMES   A Modern Dick Whittington. Cassell & Co., 1892. First edition, 2 vols., half titles, 16 pp ads. in both vols. Ex-library copy, orig. brown cloth, rubbed. Jarndyce 30-516 1983 £24

PAYN, JAMES   A Stumble on the Threshold. London: Horace Cox, 1892. First edition. 2 vols. Orig. cloth. Recased, with new endpapers. Very good. MacManus 280-4153 1983 $40

PAYNE, ARTHUR H.   Payne's Royal Dresden Gallery. Dresden, Leipzig & London, ca. 1850. With 136 engr. plates, including the additional engr. title-pages, 2 vols. 4to, bound in 1. Cont. dark blue morocco, gilt, gilt bordered sides, gilt spine, inside gilt borders, edges gilt. Fenning 61-339 1983 £245

PAYNE, E. GEORGE   The Menace of Narcotic Drugs. A Discussion of Narcotics and Education. NY: Prentice-Hall, 1931. First edition. Inscribed copy. Gach 94-812 1983 $25

PAYNE, EDGAR   Composition of Outdoor Painting. Hollywood: Seward Publishing Co., (1946). Illus. cloth. Second printing. Two plates not in first printing. Dawson 471-225 1983 $50

PAYNE, HUMFRY   Archaic Marble Sculpture from the
Acropolis. N.Y., Morrow, (1950). Second edition. 4to, illus.
with 470 photos. Dust jacket (some nicks, 2 inch chip on front).
Very good. Houle 22-779 1983 $75

PAYNE, JOHN H   Accusation or the Family of D'Anglade.
Boston, 1818. 8vo. Wraps. Disbound. Very good-fine copy. In Our
Time 156-626 1983 $35

PAYNE, JOHN H.   Indian Justice. A Cherokee Murder Trial
at Tahlequah in 1840. Oklahoma City: Harlow Publishing, 1935.
Frontis. 1st ed. in dust jacket. Minor spotting, and wear. Nice
copy. Jenkins 151-268 1983 $85

PAYNE, WILLIAM   A Discourse Concerning the Adoration of
the Host. Printed for Brabazon Aylmer, 1685. First edition, 4to,
wrapper, a very good copy. Fenning 61-340 1983 £16.50

PAYNE, WILLIAM   A Discourse of the Sacrifice of the
Mass. Printed for Brabazon Aylmer, 1688. First edition, 4to,
wrapper, a very good copy. Fenning 61-341 1983 £14.50

PAYNE, WILLIAM   An Introduction to the Game of Draughts.
London: for the Author, 1756. First edition. Small 4to, cont. calf,
neatly rebacked with morocco label, gilt. Traylen 94-473 1983 £240

PAYNE, WYNDHAM   Town & Country. London: C.W. Beaumont.
N.d. (circa 1928). 4to, illus. with 44 mounted plates (wood or
linoleum cuts), each hand-colored. 1 of 250 numbered copies on antique
paper. Linen spine over batik boards. Karmiole 75-21 1983 $150

PEACOCK, EDWARD   Ralf Skirlaugh, The Lincolnshire Squire.
London: Chapman & Hall, 1870. First edition. 3 vols. Orig. brown
cloth (library labels on vols. 2 & 3). Presentation copy to his wife
inscribed on the half-title page of the first volume: "Lucy Peacock
from the author, All S(oul's Day), 1870, more faithful than fortunate."
Loosely laid in is a photograph of the author as an old man. Front
inner hinge to vol. one cracked. Spines and covers rather worn. Fair.
MacManus 280-4154 1983 $250

PEACOCK, EDWARD   Ralf Skirlaugh. Chapman & Hall, 1870.
First edition, 3 vols. Half titles. Orig. brown cloth, a little
mottled. Jarndyce 30-517 1983 £80

PEACOCK, THOMAS LOVE   Crotchet Castle. Published by T. Hookham, 1831. First edition. Small 8vo, advert. leaf bound in after
title. Modern half morocco, uncut. Small marginal tear in one leaf
repaired. Hannas 69-155 1983 £110

PEACOCK, THOMAS LOVE   The Misfortunes of Elphin. Published
by Thomas Hookham, 1829. First edition, 12mo, original boards,
uncut; wear to backstrip, hinges and label, endpapers and half-
title foxed and minor foxing of a few other leaves, but a good,
unpressed copy. Hill 165-91 1983 £145

PEACOCK, THOMAS LOVE   The Plays... David Nutt, 1910. Half
title, untrimmed, orig. pink cloth, t.e.g. First edition. Jarndyce
31-846 1983 £20

PEAKE, MERVYN   Captain Slaughterboard Drops Anchor.
London, 1945. 4to. Cloth. First published ed. Profusely illustrated by author. Two corners bumped, else a fine copy in uncommon
dj. In Our Time 156-627 1983 $250

PEAKE, MERVYN   The Glassblowers. London, 1950. First
English edition. Free endpapers very slightly browned. Nicked and
slightly rubbed dustwrapper by the author. Very good. Jolliffe 26-
628 1983 £45

PEAKE, MERVYN   Gormenghast. London, 1950. First
edition. Covers a little faded. Somewhat worn dust wrapper. Very
nice. Rota 231-465 1983 £40

PEAKE, MERVYN   Letters from a Lost Uncle. London, 1948.
First edition. Illus. by author. Name on endpaper. Very nice.
Rota 231-464 1983 £60

PEAKE, MERVYN   Rhymes without Reason. London, 1944.
First edition. Coloured illus. by author. Covers a little marked.
Erasure from flyleaf. Nice. Rota 231-463 1983 £30

PEAKE, MERVYN   Titus Groan. N.Y.: Reynal & Hitchcock,
(1946). First American edition. Orig. cloth. Dust jacket (chipped).
MacManus 280-4159 1983 $45

PEAKE, MERVYN   Titus Groan. NY, (1946). Edges slightly
darkened, else very good in moderately worn and chipped dustwrapper.
Quill & Brush 54-1070 1983 $40

PEAKE, ORA BROOKS   The Colorado Range Cattle Industry.
Glendale: 1937. First edition. Portrait frontis. Folding maps.
Blue cloth, t.e.g. Bookplate and an inscription. Fine copy. Bradley
66-495 1983 $85

PEALE, REMBRANDT   Account of the Skeleton of the Mammoth,
a Nondescript Carnivorous Animal of Immense Size Found in America.
London, 1802. Stitched, very good. Reese 18-249 1983 $350

PEARCE, NATHANIEL   The Life and Adventures... London, 1831.
2 vols. Half calf, corners and hinges rubbed. 8vo. Cont. bookplates
of the Castle-Douglas Library and its name stamped on spines. Good.
Edwards 1044-556 1983 £90

PEARCE, WALTER   Painting and Decorating. 1898. First
edition, half title, colour front. 3 other colour plates and numerous
b. & w. illus. Orig. maroon cloth, v.g. Jarndyce 31-333 1983 £35

PEARD, FRANCES MARY   The Swing Of Teh Pendulum. London:
Richard Bentley & Son, 1893. First edition. 2 vols. Orig. brown
decorated cloth. Spines and covers slightly worn and a trifle soiled.
Former owner's inscription. Near-fine. MacManus 280-4161 1983 $300

PEARSE, JAMES   A Narrative of the Life of James
Pearse, in Two Parts. Rutland, Vt., 1825. Orig. leather backed
boards, very good. Reese 18-592 1983 $400

PEARSE, JOHN B.   A Concise History of the Iron
Manufacture of the American Colonies, up to the Revolution, and
of Pennsylvania Until the Present Time. Phila., 1876. Illus.,
frontis., large folded map. Orig. cloth. First edition. Ginsberg
46-624 1983 $85

PEARSE, P. H.   The Separatist Idea. Dublin: Tracts
for the Times No. 11, 1916. First edition. Some rust marks from
staple. Wrappers. Very good. Rota 231-471 1983 £25

PEARSE, P. H.   The Sovereign People. Dublin, Tracts
for the Times No. 13, 1916. First edition. Wrappers. Some rust
marks from staple and wrappers loose. Very good. Rota 231-472 1983
£25

PEARSON, EDMUND   Books in Black or Red. N.Y.,
Macmillan, 1923. First edition. Illus. Half cloth, paper labels.
Bookplate of Adrian Goldstone. Very good. Houle 21-141 1983 $22.50

PEARSON, EDMUND   Dime Novels. Boston, Little, Brown,
1929. First edition. Sixteen plates and facs. Cloth. Bookplate
of Adrian Goldstone. Very good. Houle 21-142 1983 $30

PEARSON, EDMUND   Queer Books. Garden City, Doubleday,
1928. First edition. Illus. Red cloth, inner hinge starting,
spine dull, else very good. Bookplate of Adrian Goldstone. Houle
21-143 1983 $22.50

PEARSON, EDMUND   Trial of Lizzie Borden. New York, 1937.
1st ed. Illus. 8vo. Ex-library, no external marks. Morrill 286-
393 1983 $20

PEARSON, EDWIN   Banbury Chap Books and Nursery Toy Book
Literature... London: Arthur Reader, 1890. First edition. Thick
tall 4to. Orig. half leather over boards. Several hundred woodcut
blocks by T. J. Bewick, Blake, Cruikshank, etc. Covers soiled and
rubbed. Oak Knoll 49-317 1983 $175

PEARSON, EMILY C.   Gutenberg and the Art of Printing.
Boston: Noyes, Holmes & Co., 1871. 8vo, title within gilt frame,
frontis. & several full-page plates. Gilt-stamped cloth depicting on
front cover old & modern presses. Bookplate of Horace Bacon.
Rostenberg 88-35 1983 $115

PEARSON, EMILY C.   Ruth's Sacrifice. Boston, 1864. Plates.
Covers drab, a few signatures pulled. Felcone 22-249 1983 $20

PEARSON, H.   Memoirs of the Life and Correspondence
of the Reverend Christian Frederick Swartz. London, 1835. Second
edition. Map, portrait. 2 vols. Half calf. 8vo. Good. Edwards
1044-681 1983 £65

PEARSON, HENRY J.   Three Summers Among the Birds of
Russian Lapland. R.H. Porter, 1904. First edition, with a folding
map and 68 plates, roy. 8vo, orig. cloth, gilt, t.e.g. Fenning 62-
281 1983 £45

PEARSON, JOSEPH   Speech of the Hon...the Act for the
More Perfect Organization of the Army of the United States...
Georgetown, 1813. Stitched, fine. Reese 18-420 1983 $50

PEARSON, THOMAS GILBERT   Birds of America. New York, 1936.
1st ed. Plates in color by Louis Agassiz. Other illus. 4to.
Morrill 288-399 1983 $22.50

PEARY, JOSEPHINE MARIE   Children of the Arctic. N.Y.: Stokes,
(1903, 3nd ed.). 4to. Cloth. Spine extremities chipped, light wear.
Inscribed on the half-title page by each of the Pearys. Illus. throughout with photos of Arctic life. Very good. Aleph-bet 8-194 1983 $95

PEARY, JOSEPHINE MARIE   The Snow Baby. N.Y.: Stokes, (1901).
Sixth edition. 4to. Blue cloth. Photo paste-on. Very good.
Aleph-bet 8-196 1983 $30

PEARY, ROBERT EDWIN   Nearest the Pole. A Narrative of the
Polar Expedition of the Peary Artic Club in the S. S. Roosevelt,
1905-1906. New York, 1907. Maps and numerous photo-illus. Original
green cloth with gilt decorations. Fine. 1st edition. Jenkins
151-269 1983 $100

PEARY, ROBERT EDWIN   Nearest the Pole. New York, 1907. First
edition. Map and illustrations. 4to. Morrill 290-398 1983 $50

PEARY, ROBERT EDWIN   The North Pole...With an Introduction
by Theodore Roosevelt. London, 1910. Folding map, numerous photo-
illustrations. Original green cloth, front cover embossed with
gold medallion of Peary. Fine. First English edition. Jenkins
151-270 1983 $125

PEARY, ROBERT EDWIN   The North Pole. New York, 1910. 1st
ed. 8 colored illus., 100 illus. from photographs, and folding map.
8vo. Some light cover stains. Morrill 289-492 1983 $35

PEATTIE, DONALD C.   A Book of Hours. N.Y., Putnam, 1937.
First edition. Illus. with woodcuts by Lynd Ward. Silver stamped
blue cloth, one of 26 lettered copies (of 550) signed by the author.
Fine. Houle 22-934 1983 $95

PEATTIE, DONALD C.   Sons of the Martian. New York, 1932.
First edition. Beige cloth. Scarce. Very good in fine jacket.
Bradley 65-154 1983 $20

PECHEL, SAMUEL   An historical account of the settlement
and possession of Bombay... London: printed by W. Richardson, for
J. Robson, 1781. First edition. 8vo. Cont. half calf, spine gilt.
Slight worming in the inner margin towards the end, some light
browning, but a fine copy. Very rare. Ximenes 63-215 1983 $800

PECK, FRANCIS   Academia tertia Anglicana. Printed for
the Author, by James Bettenham, 1727. Folio, with altogether 33
plates, including a fine folding Prospect of the Town as frontis.
5 text engravings, orig. calf, spine gilt. Lacks label and joints
cracked, but binding sound. Bickersteth 75-71 1983 £85

PECK, JESSE T.   The History of the Great Republic
Considered from a Christian Stand-Point. New York: Broughton and
Wyman, 1868. Frontis. and 34 steel plate portraits. Orig. brown
cloth. Minor spine wear. 1st ed. Fine copy. Jenkins 153-426 1983
$35

PECK, JOHN   A Gazetteer of Illinois, in 3 Parts.
Phila., 1837. 2nd ed., rev. & enlgd., 16mo orig. cloth, slightly
spotted, paper label, chipped, lacks front flyleaf. Argosy 710-213
1983 $60

PECK, JOHN   An Historical Sketch of the Baptist
Missionary Convention of the State of New York. Utica, 1837. Orig.
cloth. First edition. X-1 stamps. Ginsberg 46-538 1983 $50

PECK, THOMAS BELLOWS   William Slade of Windsor, Conn. Keene,
N. H.: 1910. First edition. Illus., including portraits, maps,
plans and facsimiles. Blue cloth. Nice copy. Bradley 66-667 1983
$65

PECKHAM, HOWARD H.   Guide to the Manuscript Collections in
the William L. Clements Library. Ann Arbor: Univ. of Michigan Press,
1942. Cloth, some water-bleaching to covers. Dawson 470-235 1983
$30

PECKHAM, HOWARD H.   Guide to the Manuscript Collections in
the William L. Clements Library. Ann Arbor, 1942. Port., 4to, cloth,
spine faded. Argosy 710-21 1983 $30

PEDDIE, ROBERT   The Dungeon Harp. Edinburgh: Printed
for the author, 1844. Orig. cloth. K Books 307-145 1983 £55

PEDRINI, AUGUSTO   Portoni e porte maestre dei secoli
XVII e XVIII in Piemonte. Torino, 1955. xxi, (3)pp., 96 plates
with 131 illus. Sm. folio. Boards. D.j. Ars Libri SB 26-182
1983 $100

PEEK, HEDLEY   Nema & Other Stories. Chapman & Hall.
Illus. by C.E. Brock: 6 photogravures & 20 full page illus. & 9 text
illus. Full vellum, gilt vignette fr. cvr., a.e.g. (top of bkstrip
has 2 sml. snags, vellum spotted & bkstrip discol'd, free eps. sl.
discol'd), scarce, v.g. Hodgkins 27-480 1983 £20

PEEL, EDMUND   An Appeal to Europe on Behalf of Greece.
I.o.W. for the Author, by J. Hall, Newport, 1829. Orig. dull green
silk cloth, leather label. Inscribed presentation copy from the
author to Joseph Peel. Jarndyce 30-758 1983 £38

PEEL, EDMUND   Echoes from Horeb, and Other Poems.
Macmillan, 1877. First edition, orig. brown cloth. Signed
presentation copy from the author, Aug. 1877. Jarndyce 30-762 1983
£15

PEEL, EDMUND   The Fair Islands. F. & J. Rivington,
1851. First edition, orig. green cloth, v.g. Jarndyce 30-760
1983 £14.50

PEEL, EDMUND   Judas Maccabaeus. London and Cambridge:
Macmillan, 1864. First edition. Half title, orig. green cloth,
signed presentation copy from the author, 1872. Jarndyce 30-761
1983 £16.50

PEEL, EDMUND   Judge Not. C. & J. Rivington, 1834.
First edition, orig. purple cloth, paper label, v.g. Jarndyce 30-759
1983 £24

PEEL, ROBERT   Sir Robert Peel, from his Private Papers.
John Murray, 1891/99. First edition. 3 vols. Half titles, front.
Leading end papers replaced, orig. dark blue cloth. Jarndyce 31-334
1983 £24

A PEEP at the P*v***n; or, broiled mutton with caper sauce... London:
E. Wilson, 1820. First edition. 8vo. Disbound. Woodcut on title
page by Robert Cruikshank. Ximenes 63-507 1983 $45

A PEEP into the Holy Land... London: John Duncombe, n.d. (1835).
Small 8vo, orig. blue-grey boards, very neatly rebacked, cloth slipcase. With a hand-colored frontis., printed on the verso of the half-
titles. This is ascribed in a pencilled note to Robert Cruikshank.
Very good. Ximenes 63-265 1983 $150

PEET, STEPHEN   The Ashtabula Disaster. Chicago, 1877.
1st edition. Illus. Jenkins 151-257 1983 $45

PEET, STEPHEN   History of the Presbyterian and Congregational Churches and Ministers in Wisconsin. Milwaukee: Silas
Chapman, 1851. Original cloth, nice copy, 1st ed. Jenkins 151-378
1983 $75

PEETERS, LEON   Salubrite Publique. Guerison Radicale de la Maladie des Pommes de Terre... Namur: D. Gerard, 1855. First edition. 12mo. orig. yellow printed wrappers. Large folding engraved plate. Ms. writing on half title. Heath 48-25 1983 £45

PEGGE, SAMUEL   Anonymiana; or, Ten Centuries of Observations on Various Authors and Subjects. John Nichols, 1809. First edition. Half red morocco, spine gilt. Very good. Jarndyce 31-847 1983 £30

PEGGS, JAMES   Capital Punishment. Thomas Ward, (1839). First edition, half title, ads. Orig. blue cloth, v.g. Jarndyce 31-335 1983 £15

PEILE, W. O.   West of Swardham. Hurst and Blackett, 1885. First edition, 3 vols. Half titles, 8 pp. ads. vol. III. Orig. brown cloth, lib. labels on end papers. Jarndyce 30-518 1983 £62

PEISSE, LOUIS   La Medecine et les Medecins. Paris: Bailliere, 1857. 12mo. 2 vols. in one. Half-cloth, worn. Some foxing. Gurney JJ-300 1983 £12

PELLHAM, EDWARD   Gods Power and Providence. London: Printed by R.Y. for John Partridge. 1631. Large folding map. Small quarto. Full 17th century polished calf, with gold ducal monogram stamped on covers. Short tears in A3 and A4 repaired neatly, with no losses, light uniform stain, title cropped at foot, with loss of last line of imprint, otherwise a very good copy. Reese 18-19 1983 $3,750

PELLOW, THOMAS   The History of the Long Captivity and Adventures of Thomas Pellow. Printed for R. Goadby, (1740). 12mo, ad. leaf before title, orig. calf, small hole in spine, rubbed. Bickersteth 77-61 1983 £120

PELLY, L.   The Miracle Play of Hasan & Husain. London, 1879. 2 vols. Roy.8vo. White cloth, bevelled boards, cloth soiled. Presentation copy to "Mr. William Mackinnon with Lady Pelly's very kind regards". Good. Edwards 1044-558 1983 £85

PELSENEER, P.   A Treatise on Zoology, Part V. Mollusca. 1906. Text-illustrations, 8vo, cloth. Wheldon 160-1215 1983 £18

PELTIER, H.   Des accidents consecutifs a l'emploi de l'Atropine. Paris, 1877. 8vo, wrappers. Wheldon 160-2179 1983 £12

PELTIER, JEAN G.   The Late Pictures of Paris. London: J. Owen, 1792-93. First edition. 2 vols. 8vo. Cont. speckled calf, gilt spines with crimson morocco labels, gilt. Traylen 94-649 1983 £55

PELTON, JOHN COTTER   Life's Sunbeams and Shadows. San Francisco: Bancroft, 1893. Frontis. Orig. cloth, 2 plates, vol. 1 only one published. Jenkins 153-427 1983 $125

PELTON, JOHN COTTER   Life's Sunbeams and Shadows. San F., 1893. Orig. cloth. Illus. First edition. Long autograph presentation inscription from Pelton to J.N. Mitchell on front endpaper. Ginsberg 47-145 1983 $75

PELZER, LOUIS   The Cattlemen's Frontier. Glendale, 1936. Cloth, very good. Reese 19-418 1983 $90

PELZER, LOUIS   Marches of the Dragoons in the Mississippi Valley. Iowa City, 1917. Orig. cloth. First edition. Ginsberg 47-802 1983 $100

PEMBERTON, ISRAEL   An Address to the Inhabitants of Pennsylvania, by Those Freeman, of the City of Philadelphia... Philadelphia, 1777. Half leather and boards, very good. Reese 18-119 1983 $900

PEMBERTON, MAX   The House Under the Sea. London: George Newnes, 1902. First edition. Illus. Orig. pictorial cloth. Lending library label inside front cover. Soiled. MacManus 280-4163 1983 $20

PEMBERTON, MAX   My Sword For Lafayette. London: Hodder & Stoughton, 1906. First edition. Orig. pictorial cloth. Fine. MacManus 280-4165 1983 $20

PEMBERTON, RALPH   Arthritis and Rheumatoid Conditions. Phila., 1929. First edition. 42 illus. & 1 colored plate. 4to, cloth. Argosy 713-425 1983 $40

PEMBERTON, T. EDGAR   A Very Old Question. London: Samuel Tinsley, 1877. First edition. 3 vols. 8vo. Orig. embossed purple cloth, gilt, spines faded and a little worn. Traylen 94-650 1983 £18

PEMBROKE, ANNE CLIFFORD, COUNTESS OF (1590-1676)   The Diary of Lady Anne Clifford. London, 1923. First edition, pres. copy from Iolo Williams. Edges sl. spotted, chipped and nicked d.w. browned at the spine and edges. Jolliffe 26-456 1983 £36

PEMBROKE, ANNE CLIFFORD, COUNTESS OF (1590-1676)   The Diary of Lady Anne Clifford. London, 1923. First ed., 8vo., cloth. Argosy 714-651 1983 $20

PENCIL, MARK   The White Sulphur Papers. New York, Samuel Colman, 1839. 1st ed. Small 8vo, paper label; rubbed and faded, some foxing, portion of pp. 97-98 torn out affecting small amount of text on each page. Morrill 288-505 1983 $20

PENDERED, MARY L.   Musk of Roses. London: Cassell, 1903. First edition. Orig. pictorial cloth. Inscribed by author. Fine. MacManus 280-4168 1983 $25

PENDLEBURY, HENRY   A Plain Representation of Transubstantiation, as it is Received in the Church of Rome. Printed for J. Johnson, 1687. First edition, 4to, wrapper, light old stain in lower margins, but still a very good copy. Fenning 61-343 1983 £16.50

PENFIELD, WILDER   Epilepsy and the Functional Anatomy of the Human Brain. Boston: Little, Brown & Co., (1954). First edition. Fine in lightly worn dust jacket. Gach 95-398 1983 $75

PENINGTON, ISAAC   The Works of the Long-Mournfull and Sorely-Distressed Isaac Penington. Printed, and sold by Benjamin Clark, 1680-81. First collected edition, pagination erratic in places, but complete, in 1 vol., folio, cont. unlettered panelled calf, little wear at the headbands, but sound, brown stain on title, 2 clean tears without loss, three small paper faults, a very good copy. Fenning 60-315 1983 £65

PENINGTON, JOHN   An Examination of Beachamp Plantagenet's Description of the Province of New Albion. Phila., 1840. Argosy 716-98 1983 $35

PENINGTON, MARY   A Brief Account of My Exercises from my Childhood. Phila., 1848. First edition. Privately printed. 1/4 mor., marbled boards. With inscription by Henry Penington tipped in. Argosy 716-400 1983 $75

PENN, WILLIAM   An Address to Protestants of All Perswasions. London: T. Sowle, 1692. Disbound. Enlarged second edition. Felcone 22-183 1983 $75

PENN, WILLIAM   A Brief Account of the Rise and Progress of the People Called Quakers. Dublin: re-printed for Robert Jackson, 1776. Large 12mo, cont. unlettered sheep. Little wear to spine, but a very good copy. This copy inscribed to Mary Leadbeater by Ann Grubb. Fenning 62-283 1983 £21.50

PENN, WILLIAM   Fruits of a Father's Love: the Advice of Penn to his Children. Phila.: B. Johnson, 1792. 8th ed., 12mo, disbound, stained, with some tears. Argosy 710-404 1983 $40

PENN, WILLIAM   No Cross, No Crown. London: T. Sowle, 1702. Calf (worn, amateur cloth rebacking). Library bookplate. Felcone 22-184 1983 $50

PENN, WILLIAM   No Cross, No Crown. London: Luke Hinde, 1750. Ninth edition. Full calf (worn, hinges broken). Signature of Caleb James, 1762, and bookseller's label (slightly damaged) of David Hall, Franklin's Philadelphia partner. Very good. Felcone 20-143 1983 $40

PENN, WILLIAM   No Cross, no Crown. Dublin: Printed by John Gough, 1797. The fourteenth edition. 2 vols. in 1, 8vo, recent boards. Fenning 60-316 1983 £16.50

PENN, WILLIAM   No Cross, No Crown. Phila.: Kimber, Conrad & Co., 1807. Later cloth, ex lib. In 2 parts. Argosy 716-66 1983 $50

PENN, WILLIAM   Primitive Christianity Revived in the Faith and Practice of the People Called Quakers. Dublin: Printed in the Year, 1702. First Irish edition, 12mo, some page numerals just touched and with some signs of use, but a good copy in the 19th century half calf. Fenning 62-284 1983 £45

PENN, WILLIAM   Send-Brieff an die Burgermeister und Raht der Stadt Danzig. Ambsterdam: Christoff Cunraden, 1675. Later 3/4 calf. First edition. Felcone 22-186 1983 $150

PENN, WILLIAM   Some Free Reflections Upon Occasion of Public Discourse About Liberty of Conscience. Printed and sold by Andrew Sowle, 1687. First edition, 4to, wrapper, a very good copy. Fenning 61-344 1983 £75

PENNANT, THOMAS (1726-1798) British Zoology. 1776-77. 4th edition, with 3 engraved titles, a folding plates of music and 280 engraved plates, 4 vols., 8vo, contemporary calf. Front joints of vols. 1 and 2 broken. Wheldon 160-42 1983 £100

PENNANT, THOMAS (1726-1798) British Zoology. London, Printed for Wilkie and Robinson, et al., 1812. 4 vols. 8vo. Extra engraved titlepages in each vol. 281 engraved plates (several folded). Cont. 3/4 green calf, gilt backs, marbled boards. New Ed., and the last ed. of this illus. work. Mod. rubbed, some off-setting from plates, else nice set. O'Neal 50-117 1983 $200

PENNANT, THOMAS (1726-1798) History of Quadrupeds. 1781. 2 engraved title pages, 52 plates, 2 vols., 4to, cont. calf, gilt (trifle rubbed, joints cracking). 2nd edition, with new title, of the Synopsis of Quadrupeds, 1771. A few margins slightly stained and marginal wormhole in last few leaves of vol. 1, else an unusually clean copy. Wheldon 160-593 1983 £85

PENNANT, THOMAS (1726-1798) The literary life of the late Thomas Pennant, Esq. London: sold by Benjamin and John White, and Robert Faulder, 1793. First edition. 4to. Cont. calf, spine gilt. Bookplate of John Waldie. Slight cracking of upper hinge. Ximenes 63-33 1983 $150

PENNECUIE, ALEXANDER   An Historical Account of the Blue Blanket... Edinburgh: by John Mosman, 1722. First edition. Small 8vo. Half red morocco. Edge of title frayed, generally dusty, very slightly cropped in a few places. Very scarce. Heath 48-212 1983 £225

PENNECUIE, ALEXANDER   An Historical Account of the Blue Blanket... Edinburgh: by Alexander Robertson, 1780. Second edition, enlarged. Small 8vo. Cont. half calf. 14 woodcut illus. Slight wear. Heath 48-213 1983 £100

PENNECUIE, ALEXANDER   An History of the Blue Blanket... Edinburgh: by Thomas Turnbull, 1832. Third edition. Small 8vo. Woodcuts. Cont. straight grain morocco, gilt. Heath 48-214 1983 £55

PENNELL, ELIZABETH R.   The Life of James McNeill Whistler. London/Philadelphia: William Heinemann/J.B. Lippincott, 1908. 2 vols. 161 photogravure and halftone illus. hors texte. 5 text illus. 4to. Cloth, 3/4 leather. T.e.g. Ars Libri 32-705 1983 $85

PENNELL, ELIZABETH R.   The Life of James McNeill Whistler. L, 1908. Illus. by Whistler. Edges worn, hinges starting, minor interior foxing, good or better, bookplate. Quill & Brush 54-1517 1983 $75

PENNELL, ELIZABETH R   Mary Wollenscraft Godwin. London: Allen, 1885. First English edition. 8vo. Orig. green cloth. Slightly rubbed. Ximenes 63-654 1983 $45

PENNELL, H. CHOLMONDELEY   Pegasus Re-Saddled. London, 1878. Second edition. Small 4to. Orig. green cloth, gilt. 10 plates by Du Maurier. Traylen 94-651 1983 £12

PENNELL, JOSEPH   The Adventures of an Illustrator. Unwin, 1925. 1st edn. Coloured frontis. portrait & 216 b&w illus. Scarlet buckram, uncut, d/w, nice copy. Hodgkins 27-573 1983 £30

PENNELL, JOSEPH   Aubrey Beardsley and Other Men of the Nineties. Phila.: Privately Printed for the Pennell Club, 1924. 4to. Illus. with a hitherto unpublished drawing by Beardsley. Orig. yellow cloth. First edition. Limited to only 100 copies. Covers dust soiled. Title-page & frontis. partially browned. MacManus 277-239 1983 $125

PENNELL, JOSEPH   The Graphic Arts. Chicago, 1920. 4to, illus. Cloth over vellum, t.e.g., uncut. Very good. One of 150 numbered copies on Japan vellum, signed by Pennell. Bookplates of E.L. Doheny & Family. Very good. Houle 22-715 1983 $195

PENNELL, JOSEPH   The Jew at Home. NY, 1892. Illus. also by Pennell, cover slightly soiled, else very good or better. Quill & Brush 54-1073 1983 $30

PENNELL, JOSEPH   A London Reverie. London: Mac., 1928. 4to. Cloth. 56 full-page drawing. Very good. Aleph-bet 8-197 1983 $28

PENNINGTON, A. S.   British Zoophytes. 1885. 24 plates, 8vo, cloth. Wheldon 160-1332 1983 £15

PENNINGTON, SARAH   An Unfortunate Mother's Advice to her Absent Daughters... Dublin: for Peter Wilson, 1761. First Dublin edition. 12mo. Cont. calf. Some wear. Heath 48-397 1983 £55

PENNSYLVANIA. LAWS   Laws of the Commonwealth. Phila., 1803. 8vo, cont. sheep, lea. labels (very slightly rubbed). Vols. 1, 4, 5 & 6. Argosy 716-406 1983 $100

PENNY, F. E.   On the Coromandel Coast. London, 1908. Endpapers slightly foxed. 8vo. Orig. cloth. Good. Edwards 1044-560 1983 £20

PENNY, H. E.   Southern India. London, 1914. Folding map, 50 coloured plats by Lady Lawley. Decorative cloth. 8vo. Edwards 1044-559 1983 £18

PENZER, NORMAN M.   An Annotated Bibliography of Sir Richard Francis Burton. London: A. M. Philpot Ltd., 1923. Royal 8vo, 24 plates. Limited edition of 500. Orig. brown buckram, on hand-made paper, uncut, lightly rubbed. Adelson Africa-64 1983 $200

PEOPLE's Pacific Railroad Company.   Boston: Alfred Mudge & Son, 1860. First edition. Marbled boards and leather. Fine. Bradley 66-639 1983 $175

PEPPER, JOHN HENRY   The Playbook of Metals. 1861. Nearly 300 wood-engravings, cr 8vo. K Books 301-139 1983 £32

A PEPPER-Pod. New York, 1947. 8vo, cloth. Fine copy in rubbed just jacket. In Our Time 156-285 1983 $25

PEPPER Pot. Ingredients: Choice bits of uncommon papermaking, publishing and printing history... Prepared with a zestful variety of type faces and served by Henry Morris. North Hills, Pa., 1977. 4to, morocco-backed decorated bds., gilt. Illustrated (including 2 paper samples). Approximately 250 copies were printed. Fine as issued. Perata 27-13 1983 $250

PEPYS, SAMUEL   The Diary of Samuel Pepys. London: George Bell & Sons, 1893-1899. Complete in 10 vols. Set has many illustrations throughout, including mounted India proof plates, photogravures, folding genealogical charts, etc. The large paper edition, ltd. to 250 numbered sets, printed on handmade paper. Bound in 1/4 vellum over cloth; gilt-stamped spines. Some slight discoloration to a few of the spines. Otherwise, a fine set. Karmiole 76-86 1983 $300

PEPYS, SAMUEL   The Diary of Samuel Pepys. Boston:
Francis A. Niccolls & Co., (1893-99). The Sheatley edition. Complete
in 18 vols. Numerous illus., including a handcolored frontis.
in some vols. Edition ltd. to 1,000 numbered sets. In red cloth;
paper spine labels. Karmiole 75-99 1983 $125

PEPYS, SAMUEL   Diary and Correspondence of Samuel Pepys,
F.R.S. Secretary to the Admiralty in the Reign of Charles II and
James II. New York: Bigelow, Brown, 1920. 4 vols. Orig. cloth.
Large 8vo. Spines a bit age-darkened and printed paper labels somewhat
soiled and chipped, but a decent set of the Edition de Luxe. Ravens-
tree 97-158 1983 $53

PEPYS, SAMUEL   Memoirs of Samuel Pepys, Esq. F.R.S.
Secretary to the Admiralty in the Reigns of Charles II, and James II.
London, Henry Colburn, 1825. 2 vols., large 4tos, later half green
morocco gilt, top edge gilt, light wear, minor spotting. First
edition. Ravenstree 97-157 1983 $375

PERCIVAL, JAMES G.   Poem Delivered Before the Connecticut
Alpha of the Phi Beta Kappa, September 13, 1825. Boston:
Richardson & Lord, 1826. Disbound. First edition. Very good.
Reese 18-606 1983 $25

PERCY, JOHN   Prize Thesis: ...Concerning the Presence
of Olcohol in the Ventricles of the Brain. London, 1839. First
edition. 1 illus. Thin 8vo, cloth-backed bds. Argosy 713-426 1983
$75

PERCY, THOMAS   Reliques of Ancient English Poetry.
London: Printed for J. Dodsley in Pall-Mall, 1765. First edition.
Illus. with engraved frontispiece. Title-page vignettes, tail-pieces
& sheet-music. 3 vols. Full cont. calf with red morocco labels
on spines. Cont. bookplates & signatures of Paul Panton, later bookplates of Gulielmi Hamilton, on endpapers. Extremities of spines a
little worn. Front outer hinge of Vol. 3 strained. Fine. MacManus
280-4173 1983 $450

PERCY, THOMAS   Reliques of Ancient English. Ptd. for
J. Dodsley, 1767. Half titles, front. Vol. I, page of music Vol. II,
2 pp ads. vol. III. Calf, hinges a little weak, rubbed and lacking
title labels. A good copy. Jarndyce 31-57 1983 £38

PERCY, THOMAS   Reliques of English Poetry. London:
for J. Dodsley, 1765. First edition. 3 vols. Cr. 8vo. Cont.
calf, neatly rebacked with morocco labels, gilt. Vignette to
title-page to each vol., frontis. to vol. 1, half-titles to vols.
2 and 3, the leaf of music in vol. 2, and 14 pp. of Additions and
Corrections at the end of vol. 3. Traylen 94-654 1983 £160

PERCY, WALKER   Bourbon. Winston-Salem (1979). First
edition. Wraps., stitched, paper label. One of 230 copies, signed
by the author. Fine. Houle 21-706 1983 $75

PERCY, WALKER   The Last Gentleman. New York:
Farrar, Straus and Giroux, (1966). First edition. 8vo. Orig.
cloth-backed boards, dust jacket. Mint copy. Jaffe 1-296 1983
$150

PERCY, WALKER   Questions They Never Asked Me. CA, 1979.
Limited to 50 numbered and signed deluxe copies bound in full blue
leather. Quill & Brush 54-1076 1983 $150

PERCY, WALKER   Questions They Never Asked Me. CA, 1979.
Limited to 300 numbered and signed copies, as new. Quill & Brush 54-
1077 1983 $90

PERCY, WALKER   The Second Coming. NY, (1980). Limited
to 450 specially bound, numbered and signed copies, very fine in fine
slipcase. Quill & Brush 54-1080 1983 $125

PERCY, WALKER   The Second Coming. New York, (1980).
8vo. Cloth. This copy signed by Percy on the title page. In addition, this copy bears an early presentation inscription by same on
front flyleaf: "For Sid with thanks as always-Walker, Jan. 30, 1980
Covington". A fine copy in dj. In Our Time 156-631 1983 $100

PERCY, WALKER   The Second Coming. New York: Farrar
Straus Giroux, (1980). First edition. 8vo. Orig. cloth. In
publisher's slipcase. One of 450 copies signed by Percy. Mint copy.
Jaffe 1-301 1983 $100

PERCYVALL, RICHARD   A dictionarie in Spanish and English.
London: Ed. Bollifants, 1599. First edition. Folio. Cont. calf,
gilt ornament on covers. Traylen 94-655 1983 £350

PEREIRA, I. RICE   Crystal of the Rose. N.Y., I.R.
Pereira, The Nordness Gallery, (1959). Narrow 8vo. 2 orig. signed
watercolors on paper by the author-artist laid in. Cloth-backed
marbled boards. 1st ed. 300 numbered copies, 99 were numbered and
signed and contained an orig. watercolor. Fine. O'Neal 50-77 1983
$400

PEREZ, J. V.   A Selection of Botanical and Other
Papers. 1925. 8vo, cloth, writing on endpapers. Wheldon 160-1754
1983 £12

PEREZ CANTO, JULIO   Chile. An Account of its Wealth and
Progress. Chicago & New York, 1912. First edition. 2 folding colored
maps. Orig. red cloth. Fine. Jenkins 152-324 1983 $30

PEREZ DE BARRADAS, JOSE   Arqueologia agustiniana. Bogota:
Imprenta Nacional, 1943. 189 plates. 179 text illus. Small
folio. Boards, 1/4 cloth. Ars Libri 34-420 1983 $125

PEREZ DE BARRADAS, JOSE   Orfebreria prehispanica de Colombia.
Madrid: Talleres Graficos "Jura", 1954-58. 4 vols. I: Estilo
Calima. 2 vols. 20 color plates. 201 text illus. 300 plates.
II: Estilo Tolima y Muisca. 2 vols. 10 color plates. 147 text
illus. 287 plates. Folio. Cloth. Dust jacket. Ars Libri 34-421
1983 $500

PEREZ GALDOS, BENITO   Gloria: a Novel. New York: William
Gottsberger, 1882. First American edition, 4to, 2 vols., orig.
cloth decorated in gilt, spines gilt. An uncommon title. Slightly
shaken; one rear cover waterstained. Trebizond 18-122 1983 $85

PERI, JACOPO   Le Musiche Sopra Euridice. Rome, 1934.
Facs. edition. Salloch 387-177 1983 $95

PERION, JOACHIM   Conciones et Orationes Ex Historicis
Latinis. Oxonii, Typis W. Hall, 1667. 12mo, orig. calf, ends of
spine chipped. Ravenstree 97-160 1983 $47.50

PERKINS, DEXTER   The Monroe Doctrine 1826-1867.
Baltimore, 1937. DW. Argosy 710-189 1983 $35

PERKINS, FREDERICK B.   Devil-Puzzlers and Other Studies.
NY, 1877. First edition. Cloth, bookplate, spine ends slightly
frayed. King 46-319 1983 $25

PERKINS, MRS. GEORGE A.
Please turn to
PERKINS, JULIA ANNA (SHEPARD)

PERKINS, J. R.   Trails, Rails and War. Indianapolis,
(1929). 1st ed. Endpaper and other photos, portraits. Untrimmed,
edges worn, covers lightly soiled. Clark 741-343 1983 $30

PERKINS, JAMES H.   Annals of the West: Embracing a Concise
Account of Principal Events, which Have Occurred in the West States
& Territories. St. Louis, 1851. 2d ed., rev. & enlarged. Modern
buckram. Argosy 710-397 1983 $40

PERKINS, JANE GREY   The Life of Mrs. Norton. London: John
Murray, 1909. First edition. With portraits. Orig. cloth. Spine
faded. Bookplate. Remains of what appears to be a bookseller's
ticket pasted to rear endpaper. Good. MacManus 279-4013 1983 $20

PERKINS, JOHN   A Profitable Booke...Treating of the
Lawes of Englande. (London): Richard Tottell, (1565). Contemp.
full calf, ruled and stamped in blind with shield at center of
covers. Binding fine and tight. Jenkins 155-1001 1983 $850

PERKINS, JOHN   A Profitable Booke... London, 1609.
Folios, 12mo. 2nd 17th century ed. Title page dusty, small hole in
margin of leaf A4 not affecting text, extensive marginal annotations.
Bound in full, 19th century mottled calf, bit rubbed, sometime rebacked,
spine laid down, marbled endpapers, covers gilt-decorated & spine gilt-
decorated & ruled, with black leather label gilt-ruled, decorated &
lettered. Clean and very tall copy from Farnborough Abbey. Boswell
7-131 1983 $450

PERKINS, JULIA ANNA (SHEPARD)   Early Times on the Susquehanna. Binghamton, 1840. First edition. Sm. 8vo. Ex-library with no external marks, corners slightly rubbed, lacks front endleaf. Morrill 288-406 1983 $27.50

PERKINS, MARY E.   Old Houses of the Ancient Town of Norwich, 1660-1800. Norwich: 1895. First edition. Quarto. Large folding color pictorial map. Profusely illus. Decorated cloth. Very good copy, some soiling and dampstaining to light gray cloth covers. Library blind stamp on preliminary page and a discard slip laid in. Bradley 66-520 1983 $45

PERLS, KLAUS G.   Jean Fouquet. London: The Hyperion Press, 1940. 16 color plates. 289 illus. Square 4to. Wrappers. Dust jacket. Ars Libri 32-224 1983 $90

PERNKOPF, EDUARD   Atlas of Topographical & Applied Human Anatomy. Phila. & London, 1963. First edition in English. 2 vols. 4to, cloth. Hundreds of illus. & color plates. Argosy 713-428 1983 $85

PEROCCO, GUIDO   Arturo Martini. Treviso: Neri Pozza, 1966. 631 illus. hors texte. Large 4to. Cloth. Dust jacket. Edition limited to 1200 copies. Ars Libri 33-518 1983 $100

PEROLD, A. I.   A Treatise on Viticulture. 1927. 108 figures, 8vo, cloth. Very scarce. Wheldon 160-2135 1983 £30

PEROTTI, AURELIA   I pittori Campi da Cremona. Milano: Privately Printed, n.d. 60 illus. 4to. Wrappers. Ars Libri 33-61 1983 $100

PERRAULT, CHARLES   La Belle au Bois Dormant & Le Petit Chaperon Rouge. Deux Contes de ma Mere Loye. N.p.: The Eragny Press, 1899. Sm. 8vo. patterned board sides and plain boards back, gilt. The elaborate double-page frontis., printed in two colors and gold, the illus., the borders and capital letters were all drawn by the Printer, Lucien Pissaro, and cut on wood by him and his wife. Minor wear and light soiling to covers. Limited to 224 copies. Perata 28-204 1983 $400

PERRAULT, CHARLES   Les Contes de Perrault. Paris: 1880. Octavo. 1/58 copies on China paper initialled by publisher. Illus. with portrait frontis. and 12 other etchings. Printed within red borders. Rebound by Carayon in full blue morocco, gilt-tooled ruled borders, spine gilt. Some very faint wear to extremities, else very fine copy with orig. covers bound-in. Bromer 25-378 1983 $250

PERRAULT, CHARLES   Fairy Tales of Perrault. Paris: Sporck, 1910. English version. 8vo. Cloth backed pictorial boards. Some shelfwear. Few margin rips. Illus. by G. DeLaw, in color. Very good. Aleph-bet 8-198 1983 $25

PERRAULT, CHARLES   Tales of Passed Times Written for Children. Adelphi: (1922). Octavo. Numerous colored and b&w illus. by John Austen. Very fine in boards with pictorial paper label. In slightly soiled dust wrapper. Bromer 25-136 1983 $110

PERRET, ROBERT   La Geographie de Terre-Neuve. Paris: Librairie Orientale & Americaine, 1913. 22cm. Many illus. and maps (some in colour). New buckram binding. Fine. McGahern 54-145 1983 $50

PERRIER, R.   La Faune de la France en Tableaux Synoptiques. Paris, 1923-40. 10 vols. (1a, 1b, 2, 3, 5 to 10), numerous text-figures, 8vo, original boards. Wheldon 160-421 1983 £25

PERROTT, C. L. E.   A Selection of British Birds. 1979. Roy. folio, 5 coloured plates, half brown morocco in a half morocco slip case. Limited to 250 numbered copies. Wheldon 160-80 1983 £240

PERRY, BLISS   The Broughton House. New York: Charles Scribner, 1890. 1st ed., 12mo. Original decorated cloth, spine gilt, inscribed the the author, front cover slightly soiled, otherwise a very good copy. Trebizond 18-79 1983 $30

PERRY, BLISS   Park-Street Papers. Boston, 1908. 8vo, brown boards paper label. First edition. Fine. Argosy 714-638 1983 $45

PERRY, CHARLES   A View of the Levant. London, 1743. Map and 32 engravings on 20 plates. Folio. Some slight spotting, half calf. 8vo. Good. Edwards 1044-561 1983 £250

PERRY, GEORGE SESSIONS   Hold Autumn in Your Hand. New York: Viking, 1941. First edition. Author's signed presentation note. Dust jacket. Fine. Jenkins 152-325 1983 $85

PERRY, GEORGE SESSIONS   Roundup Time. New York, 1943. First edition in dust jacket. Presentation copy from Paul Horgan. Jenkins 152-326 1983 $45

PERRY, WALTER COPLAND   Sancta Paula. London: Swan Sonnenschein, 1902. First edition. Illus. Orig. cloth. Presentation inscription from the author on the flyleaf. Covers soiled and worn. MacManus 280-4175 1983 $20

PERRY, WILLIAM   The standard French and English pronouncing dictionary. London: printed for Murray, etc., 1795. First edition. Square 12mo. Cont. mottled calf, spine gilt. Ximenes 63-226 1983 $65

PERSEUS and Adromeda. With the rape of Colombine: or, the flying lovers. In five interludes; three serious, and two comic. ... As it is perform'd at the Theatre-Royal in Drury-Lane. London: printed for W. Trott, 1728. First edition. Very rare. Half-title present. Ximenes 64-408 1983 $650

PERSHING, JOHN J.   My Experiences in the World War. NY 1931. 2 vols. 1st ed. Photos, cloth, very good in chipped dws. King 46-798 1983 $20

PERSIUS, CHARLES   Rouge Et Noir. London: Lawler & Quick & Stephen Couchman, 1823. First edition. Hand-colored frontispiece. Full calf. Spine slightly faded. Slight foxing to the preliminary pages. Very good. MacManus 280-4176 1983 $125

PERSIUS FLACCUS, AULUS   Aulus Flaccus Persius Cum glassis Scipionis ferrarii Georgii filii de monte ferrato... (S.l., s.d., but Venice, probably Bernardinus Venetus, probably after January 30, 1501). 4to, old calf rebacked preserving orig. backstrip, minor soiling, few light stains, excellent copy from the Earl of Hopetoun Collection, with the Hopetoun bookplate. Ravenstree 95-84 1983 $785

PERTWEE, GUY   Scenes from Dickens for Drawing-Room and Platform Acting. N.d. (c. 1910). Half title, 48 costume-plates by E. Handley Read. Half title. Orig. green cloth. First edition. Jarndyce 30-216 1983 £10.50

PETER Parley's Annual for 1864. Kent, 1864. Colour frontis. & title page, 6 coloured illus. & numerous b&w illus. Red morocco grain cloth gilt, a.e.g., cvrs. sl. dull & rubbed & sl. marked, vg. Hodgkins 27-161 1983 £20

PETER Parley's Annual for 1886. George, 1886. 16 col'd plates, 8pp adverts. Red fine ribbed decor. cloth, a.e.g., eps. cracking at hinges, some thumbing, corners sl. worn & sl. shaken, insc. fr. ep., vg. Hodgkins 27-162 1983 £15

PETER Wilkins or, The Flying Islanders. New York: Samuel French, (n.d.). Orig. printed wraps. A fine copy. Reese 20-390 1983 $75

PETERDI, GABOR   Gabor Peterdi: Graphics, 1934-1969. New York: Touchstone Publishers, 1970. 282 illus. (24 color). Folio. Cloth. With an original three-color etching by the artist loosely inserted, as issued. Ars Libri 32-510 1983 $125

PETERKIN, GEORGE W.   A History and Record of the Protestant Episcopal Church in the Diocese of West Virginia, and, Before the Formation of the Diocese in 1878. Charleston, 1902. Illus., map, orig. cloth. First edition. Ginsberg 46-814 1983 $50

PETERKIN, JULIA   Black April. Ind., (1927). Minor cover staining, else very good in lightly chipped and frayed dustwrapper. Quill & Brush 54-1082 1983 $50

PETERKIN, JULIA   Bright Skin. Indianapolis: Bobbs-
Merrill, (1932). Cloth, t.e.g. First edition. One of 250 numbered
copies, specially bound, and signed by the author. Very fine,
unopened copy, in orig. glassine, and slightly rubbed slipcase.
Reese 20-768 1983 $65

PETERS, CARL   The Eldorado of the Ancients. London:
Pearson, 1902. 8vo. Folding maps. 97 illus. Orig. red cloth.
Very fine copy. Adelson Africa-212 1983 $90

PETERS, CHARLES   The Autobiography, in 1915. Sacramento,
ca., 1915. Illus. 12mo, pr. wraps. Argosy 716-563 1983 $45

PETERS, DEWITT C.   The Life and Adventures of Kit Carson.
New York, 1859. Illus. Cloth, rehinged. Internally good. Reese
19-419 1983 $150

PETERS, DEWITT C.   Pioneer Life and Frontier Adventures.
Boston 1883. Numerous wood-cuts, dec. cloth, ink name, inner
hinges loose, spine ends frayed. King 46-238 1983 $35

PETERS, FRANCISCUS JULIUS   Dissertatio medica inauguralis de
Odontalgia... Jena: Samuel Krebs, 1669. Woodcut initial and
head-piece. Small 4to. Cont. paper backstrip. Kraus 164-57
1983 $150

PETERS, H.   Aus der Geschichte der Pflanzenwelt
in Wort und Bild. Mittenwald, (1928). 8vo. Half-morocco. Illus.
Gurney JJ-302 1983 £20

PETERS, J. L.   Checklist of Birds of the World.
Cambridge, Mass., 1931-79. 14 vols., 8vo, original cloth. A
complete set of the original printing. Wheldon 160-840 1983 £150

PETERS, JOHN R.   Miscellaneous Remarks Upon the Government, History, Religions, Literature, Agriculture, Arts, Trades, Manners... New York, 1849. Disbound, very good. Reese 19-420 1983
$125

PETERSEN, WILLIAM F.   The Patient and the Weather. Ann Arbor,
1934-38. First edition. 5 vols., 4to, cloth; ex-lib. Lacks vols. I,
part II and vol. II. Argosy 713-429 1983 $175

PETERSEN, WILLIAM J.   Steamboating on the Upper Mississippi.
Iowa City: 1937. First edition. Green cloth. Fine copy. Bradley
66-568 1983 $57.50

PETERSHAM, MAUD   An American ABC. N.Y.: Mac., 1946.
4to. Blue cloth, light wear. Signed by Maud & Miska Petersham on
front flyleaf. 6th printing. Illus. in color. Very good. Aleph-bet
8-201 1983 $30

PETERSHAM, MAUD   Auntie and Celia Jane and Miki. N.Y.:
Doubleday, 1932. Stated first edition. Cloth backed pictorial
boards. Torn dust wrapper. 4to. Color illus. throughout. (large
format) Fine. Aleph-bet 8-200 1983 $35

PETERSHAM, MAUD   Miki and Mary. N.Y.: Vik., 1934. First
edition. 4to. Cloth backed pictorial boards. Light edge rub. Color
illus. throughout. Fine. Aleph-bet 8-199 1983 $35

PETERSON, FREDERICK   Medical Notes in Egypt. NY: M. J.
Rooney, 1893. Orig. printed wrappers. Library stamp on cover,
edges chipped. Gach 95-399 1983 $25

PETHERICK, JOHN   Egypt, the Soudan and Central Africa.
Edinburgh: William Blackwood, 1861. 8vo. Folding map. New 1/2
calf. Red label, marbled boards, repairs to map. Adelson Africa-
115 1983 $225

PETIT, JEAN-LOUIS   Oeuvres Completes. (Paris), 1837.
8vo. Old quarter calf. Name on title. Gurney JJ-304 1983 £25

PETO, GLADYS   Jolly Times. John F. Shaw, n.d. 4to
Colour frontis. Pictorial title. 3 colour plates & many illus.
Colour pictorial boards, rubbed, spine snagged. Greer 40-168 1983
£18

PETO, GLADYS   Told in the Gloaming. John F. Shaw, n.d.
(ca.1930). 4to. Colour frontis. 7 colour plates, 21 other plates.
168 text illus. Colour pictorial boards. Greer 40-169 1983 £22.50

PETRARCA, FRANCESCO   Opera de Rimedi de l'Vna et l'Altra
Fortvna. Venice: Giolito, 1549. Thick 8vo, printer's device on
title-page, repeated at end. Gilt calf, dentelle. With bookplate
(at end) of A.L. McLaughlin. First Italian edition. Fine copy.
Rostenberg 88-107 1983 $250

PETRE, F. LORAINE   Napoleon's Last Campaign in Germany.
London, 1912. 8vo. Orig. cloth. Half title. 4 folding sheets of
maps and at end. Uncut. Largely unopened. Good. Edwards 1042-434
1983 £18

PETRIE, GRAHAM   Tunis, Kairouan & Carthage. Heinemann,
1908. First edition, with 48 coloured plates, 4to, recent morocco
backed cloth, gilt, t.e.g., with label. Fenning 61-346 1983 £12.50

PETRONIUS ARBITER, TITUS   Satyricon. Londini, Impensis E. Curll,
1711. 12mo, disbound, fairly good copy with the frontis. slightly
dust soiled. Re-issue, with new title-page. First edition with the
illus. Ravenstree 95-85 1983 $87.50

PETRY, ANN   The Street. B, 1946. Edges very slightly
faded, else near fine in lightly worn, very good dustwrapper. Quill &
Brush 54-1083 1983 $75

PETTENKOFER, MAX V.   Boden und Grundwasser in ihren
Beizichungen zu Cholera und Typhus. Muenchen, 1869. Thin 8vo, orig.
pr. wrs. worn. First separate edition. Argosy 713-430 1983 $100

PETTIGREW, JAMES B.   Animal Locomotion. 1891. 4th edition,
130 wood-engravings, 8vo, cloth. Wheldon 160-511 1983 £15

PETTIGREW, T. J.   Medical Portrait Gallery. Vols. I and
II. London, (1838). Large 8vo. 2 vols. Quarter-morocco. T.e.g.
35 portraits. Lacking vols. 3 and 4. Gurney JJ-305 1983 £25

PETTIGREW, THOMAS   Edward Jenner, M.D. 1838. 8vo.
Orig. binding. Extract. Fye H-3-812 1983 $20

PETTIGREW, THOMAS LETTSON   Lucien Grenville. London, Saunders &
Ottley, 1833. 3 vols., 8vo, old quarter dark blue-green roan, spines
faded, to brown rehinged, quite worn, later end-papers chipped away,
a well-read set, cage darkened and lightly soiled, partly uncut set.
First edition. Ravenstree 96-144 1983 $195

PETTIS, GEORGE H.   Kit Carson's Fight with the Comanche
and Kiowa Indians, at the Adobe Walls, on the Canadian River, November
25, 1864. Providence: Sidney S. Rider, 1878. Original printed
wrappers. Original edition. Jenkins 151-273 1983 $250

PETTIS, GEORGE H.   Personal Narratives of the Battles
of the Rebellion. Santa Fe, N.M., 1908. Illus. Orig. printed wraps.
First edition. Ginsberg 47-212 1983 $125

PETTIT, JOHN   Address Before the Wabash County
Agricultural Society at Its Fifth Annual Fair. Wabash, Ind., 1857.
Dbd. First edition. Ginsberg 46-347 1983 $50

PETTY, WILLIAM   Several Essays in Political Arithmetick.
London: printed for D. Browne, J. Shuckburgh, and J. Whiston and
B. White, 1755. 8vo, 4th ed. corrected. Publisher's advertisement,
very occasional spotting, nineteenth century half morocco, marbled
boards and endpapers, slightly rubbed. Pickering & Chatto 21-96
1983 $275

PETULENGRO, GIPSY   Romany Remedies and Recipes. New York,
Dutton, 1936. 1st ed. Small 8vo. Morrill 289-185 1983 $20

THE PEYOTE Ritual. San Francisco: Grabhorn Press, 1957. Quarto.
14 full-page color reproductions of paintings by Tsa Toke. Limited to
325 copies. One corner slightly bumped, else an extremely fine copy
in cloth-backed decorated boards. Laid-in are prospectus and order
form for this book plus ALS from Herman Cohen, proprietor of the Chiswick Book Ship, and TLS from Jane Grabhorn. Bromer 25-223 1983 $425

PFEIFFER, IDA   A Lady's Visit to California, 1853. Oakland, 1950. Illus. Orig. cloth. One of 500 copies. Ginsberg 47-803 1983 $25

PFEIFFER, IDA   Visit to Iceland and the Scandinavian north. London: Ingram, Cooke, 1852. First edition. 8vo. Orig. green cloth, neatly recased. Engraved title and seven tinted plates. Ximenes 63-631 1983 $75

PFEIFFER, IDA   A Visit to the Holy Land. London, 1852. 8 tinted lithographs. Occasional browning. 8vo. Orig. cloth. Good. Edwards 1044-564 1983 £30

PFEIFFER, J. P.   De Houtsoorten van Suriname. Amsterdam, 1926-27. 42 plates of 201 figures and 66 text-figures, 2 vols. in 4, 8vo, wrappers. Wheldon 160-2097 1983 £25

PFISTER, OSKAR (1873-1956) Psychoanalyse Und Weltanschauung. Leipzig 1928. Cloth, ex-library, inner hinges cracked, worn. First combined ed. King 46-525 1983 $20

PFUHL, ERNST   Meisterwerke Griechischer Zeichnung & Malerei. Munich, 1924. 160 plates, some in color. Folio, cloth. Salloch 385-302 1983 $80

PHAIR, CHARLES   Atlantic Salmon Fishing. NY: Derrydale Press, (1937). Illus. from photos, drawings, and maps. T.e.g., gilt-stamped cloth, extremities worn, corners slightly bumped else very good. Limited to 950 copies. King 46-563 1983 $400

PHANTASIES. Dent, nd (1905). New edn. with 33 illus. by Arthur Hughes. 1st edn. thus. Blue cloth, gilt titling, t.e.g., others uncut, bkstrip sl. soiled & gilt dull. Association copy. Pres. from W.L. Troup dd. 1920. Very good. Hodgkins 27-141 1983 £25

PHARMACOPOEIA Augustana. Madison: State Historical Society of Wisconsin, 1927. Facsimile of 1564 first edition. Folio. Half-cloth. Torn at top and bottom of spine. Gurney JJ-307 1983 £25

PHARMACOPOEIA Collegii Medicorum Edinburgensis. London, 1732. Second edition (pirated). 12mo. Cont. calf. Gurney JJ-309 1983 £35

PHARMACOPOEIA Collegii Medicorum Edinburgensis. Edinburgh, 1756. 12mo. Cont. calf, rebacked. Fifth edition. A few old scorings and ms. notes. Gurney JJ-310 1983 £40

PHARMACOPOEIA Collegii Medicorum Edinburgensis. Edinburgh, 1817. Tenth edition. 8vo. Half-morocco. Gurney JJ-312 1983 £25

PHARMACOPOEIA Collegii Regalis Medicorum Londenensis. Paris, 1788. 8vo. Cont. calf. Ownership stamp on title. Fine copy. Gurney JJ-313 1983 £35

PHARMACOPOEIA Collegii Regalis Medicorum Londinensis M.DCCC.XXIV. London, 1824. 12mo. Old calf, rubbed. Gurney JJ-314 1983 £15

PHARMACOPOEIA Collegii Regalis Medicorum Londinensis. London, 1836. First edition of the ninth pharmacopoeia. 8vo. Half-morocco. Name on title. Gurney JJ-316 1983 £30

PHARMACOPOEIA Edinburgensis. Additamentis aucta ab Ern. Godofr. Baldinger. Bremen, 1776. 12mo. Cont. French calf. A few leaves wormed and some light foxing. Gurney JJ-311 1983 £20

THE PHARMACOPOEIA of the King and Queen's College of Physicians in Ireland. Dublin, 1850. 8vo. Orig. cloth. Slightly torn at joints, 2 leaves at end torn without loss of surface through careless opening. Gurney JJ-319 1983 £12

PHELAN, CHARLOTTE ELIZABETH Izram, a Mexican tale; and other poems. London: James Nisbet, 1826. First edition. 8vo. Cont. glazed boards. Soiled, spine worn, upper hinge weak. Ximenes 63-396 1983 $40

PHELPS, JOHN S.   Inaugural Address of Governor...to the Twenty-Ninth General Assembly of the State of Missouri. Jefferson City, 1877. Orig. printed wraps. First edition. Ginsberg 47-539 1983 $30

PHELPS, S. L.   Review of the Proposed Tehuantepec Ship-Railway. Washington, 1881. First edition. Folding map. Orig. light grey printed wrappers. Backstrip of fragile wraps reinforced. Ink note at top of wrappers. Fine. Jenkins 152-736 1983 $75

PHELPS, WILLIAM D.   Fore and Aft... Boston: Nichols & Hall, 1871. Later half morocco. Littell's copy with his bookplate. Jenkins 153-430 1983 $275

PHENIX, RICHARD   On My Way Home. N.Y., (1947). First edition. D.w. Presentation copy, with an ALS to Lewis Gannett, who "helped...with the book." Argosy 714-587 1983 $40

PHILBY, HARRY ST. J. B.   Arabian Days. Robert Hale, 1948. First edition, 8vo, orig. cloth, very good copy in a frayed d.w. Fenning 60-318 1983 £24.50

PHILBY, HARRY ST. J. B.   Arabian Highlands. Cornell University Press, Ithaca, 1952. First edition, map in pocket & other maps & plates, thick 8vo, orig. cloth, gilt. Fenning 60-319 1983 £85

PHILBY, HARRY ST. J. B.   The Empty Quarter. London, 1933. 8vo. 2 folding maps, plan, plates. Orig. cloth. Good. Edwards 1044-565 1983 £50

PHILBY, HARRY ST. J. B.   Harun al Rashid. Peter Davies, 1933. First edition, frontis., cr. 8vo, orig. cloth, very good copy. Fenning 60-322 1983 £21.50

PHILBY, HARRY ST. J. B.   The Heart of Arabia. Constable, 1922. First edition, maps, plates, 2 vols., 8vo, orig. cloth. Very neat repair to spines, otherwise a nice copy. Fenning 60-323 1983 £185

PHILBY, HARRY ST. J. B.   The Heart of Arabia. New York: Putnam's, 1923. First American edition, maps, plates, 2 vols., 8vo, orig. cloth, a very neat repair to the spines, otherwise a nice copy. Fenning 60-324 1983 £135

PHILBY, HARRY ST. J. B.   A Pilgrim in Arabia. Robert Hale, 1946. Second edition, plates, 8vo, orig. cloth, gilt, a very good copy. Fenning 60-325 1983 £24.50

PHILIP, ALEXANDER PHILIPS WILSON A Treatise on Febrile Diseases, Including Intermitting, Remitting, and Continued Fevers... Hartford, 1809. 1st American ed. 2 vols. 8vo. Plate. Contemporary calf, leather labels. Bookplates removed; Vol. 1 lacks blank leaves before title. Morrill 289-186 1983 $35

PHILIPPART, JOHN   The East India Military Calendar. London, 1823-24. Folding plan. 2 vols. 4to. Half calf. Good. Edwards 1044-566 1983 £95

PHILIPPS, JOHN   Titles and Honours conferred by his late Majesty King Geprge I... London: for R. Gosling, 1728. First edition. 8vo. Half title. Uncut in orig. grey wrappers. Some light waterstains, little frayed and stitched as issued. Heath 48-146 1983 £45

PHILIPS, AMBROSE   Humfrey, Duke of Gloucester. A tragedy. London: printed, and sold by J. Roberts, 1723. 8vo, disbound, 1st edition. Half-title present. Ximenes 64-425 1983 $90

PHILIPS, AMBROSE   The life of John Williams... Cambridge: printed at the University Press, for A. Bosvile, 1700. First edition. 8vo. Cont. panelled calf, later label. Portrait. Slight wear. Ximenes 63-34 1983 $100

PHILIPS, GEORGE   Travels in North America. London: C. J. G. & F. Rivington, 1831. First London edition, 12mo, cont. cloth, spine gilt. Five illus. plates; vignette title page. A fine copy. Trebizond 18-158 1983 $95

PHILIPS, GEORGE   Travels in North America. London,
1831. Plates. Tipped-in list of plates. Calf-backed boards
(hinges glued). Felcone 22-194 1983 $35

PHILIPS, JOHN   Bleinheim, a poem... London: Tho.
Bennet, 1705. First edition. Folio. Disbound. Presentation copy,
inscribed on the title-page. Rather foxed; trimmed a bit close at
the top, shaving a couple of page numbers. Ximenes 63-375 1983
$125

PHILIPS, JOHN   Cyder. London: Printed for Jacob
Tonson...1708. 8vo, engraved frontis. by Vander Gucht, a fine large-
paper copy in orig. panelled calf, spine gilt, m.e. First edition.
Quaritch NS 7-98 1983 $950

PHILIPS, JOHN   Cyder. A Poem. In Two Books. London:
Jacob Tonson, 1708. 1st ed., 8vo, large and thick paper copy. Cont.
unlettered calf, panelled covers tooled in blind; rebacked. Frontis.
engraving. A very good copy. Trebizond 18-80 1983 $325

PHILIPS, JOHN   Cyder. Printed for Jacob Tonson, 1708.
8vo, engraved frontis., orig. mottled calf, worn at the foot of the
spine, three small holes in the calf on both upper and lower covers,
but a good copy. First edition. Bickersteth 75-72 1983 £85

PHILIPS, JOHN   Poems by Mr. John Philips late of
Christ Church, Oxon... London: (by E. Curll), 1715. First
collected edition. 12mo. Cont. panelled calf. Engraved portrait.
Fine copy. Heath 48-401 1983 £85

PHILIPS, JOHN F.   Speeches of...Prosecuting Attorney, in
the Trial of Frank James for Murder... N.p., (1898). Printed wrappers.
Portraits. Rare. Jenkins 153-282 1983 $85

PHILIPS, WILLIAM   Hibernia Freed. A Tragedy. London:
printed for Jonah Bowyer, 1722. 1st ed., 8vo, half-title, advertisements, uncut, two holes in the title-page, one repaired on the
verso, disbound, and unstitched, in new brown wrappers, detached.
Rare. Pickering & Chatto 19-43 1983 $250

PHILLIPPS, EVELYN MARCH   Pintoricchio. London: George Bell
& Sons, 1901. 41 plates. Small 4to. Cloth. Ars Libri 33-275 1983
$30

PHILLIPS, A. M.   Los Angeles: A Guide Book. Los Angeles,
1907. Map and plates. Orig. cloth. Jenkins 152-583 1983 $35

PHILLIPS, CATHERINE COFFIN   Cornelius Cole: California Pioneer and
United States Senator. San Francisco: John Henry Nash, 1929. First
edition. Frontis. with illus. Unopened. Fine. Jenkins 152-327
1983 $70

PHILLIPS, CATHERINE COFFIN   Memoirs of the Life of Catherine
Phillips. Printed and sold by James Phillips and Son, 1797. First
edition, 8vo, nineteenth century half calf, neat repair to foot of
spine, a very good copy. Fenning 60-328 1983 £38.50

PHILLIPS, CATHERINE COFFIN   Portsmouth Plaza. San Francisco: John
Henry Nash, 1932. Frontis. Vellum-backed marbled boards, slipcase.
Signed presentation date March 25, 1933. One page ALS. The frontis.
is signed in the plate "Wilke" many of the other illus. are signed
with the initial "W." Jenkins 152-328 1983 $100

PHILLIPS, CATHERINE COFFIN   Portsmouth Plaza. San F., Nash, 1932.
Illus. Orig. boards, vellum spine. First edition. Orig. prospectus
laid in. Ginsberg 47-146 1983 $100

PHILLIPS, CATHERINE COFFIN   Portsmouth Plaza. San Francisco: John
Henry Nash, 1932. Errata slip, marbled boards, Vellum spine, slight
wear. In slipcase. Dawson 471-231 1983 $50

PHILLIPS, CHARLES   Recollections of Curran. For W. Simpkin
and R. Marshall, 1822. 8vo, orig. cloth-backed boards, with printed
paper label, a very good copy. Fenning 61-347 1983 £10.50

PHILLIPS, CLAIRE   Manila Espionage. Portland, Binfords &
Mort, (1947). First edition. Illus. Pictorial dust jacket (slight
nicking & rubbing). Signed and inscribed by Claire Phillips and
the coauthor, Myron B. Goldsmith. Houle 22-1206 1983 $45

PHILLIPS, EDWARD   The New World of Words... London:
W.R. for Obadiah Blagrave, 1678. Fourth edition. Folio. Cont.
calf, joints neatly repaired. With engraved title-page, and ad.
leaves at end. Traylen 94-656 1983 £160

PHILLIPS, EDWARD   The stage-mutineers: or, a play-house
to be lett. London: printed for Richard Wellington, 1733. 8vo,
wrappers, first edition. An excellent copy. Ximenes 64-426 1983
$450

PHILLIPS, GEORGE   The Elements of Syriac Grammar.
Cambridge: at the University Press..., 1837. First edition.
8vo. Complete with publisher's adverts., partly unopened, partly
untrimmed, in orig. blue grained cloth, gilt label. Very fine
copy. Heath 48-587 1983 £65

PHILLIPS, H.   The Companion for the Orchard. 1831.
3 plates, 8vo, buckram, uncut. Wheldon 160-1995 1983 £20

PHILLIPS, JOHN (1800-1874)   Illustrations of the Geology of
Yorkshire... 1835-1836. 2 parts in 1 volume. 2 coloured maps, 47
plates (including hand coloured lithographed plates, half calf
rebacked, 4to, a clean bright copy. K Books 307-148 1983 £145

PHILLIPS, JOHN (1800-1874)   Manual of Geology. 1885. 2 coloured
frontispieces, 36 plates, tables and text-figures, 2 vols., royal
8vo, cloth. Sound ex-library copy. Wheldon 160-1461 1983 £25

PHILLIPS, JOHN CHARLES (1876-1938)   Classics of the American Shoot-
ing Field. Boston, 1930. First trade edition. 2 copies. Frontis by
Frank W. Benson, other illus. Cloth, foxed, heavily rubbed, loose.
King 46-639 1983 $25

PHILLIPS, JOHN CHARLES (1876-1938)   Wenham Great Pond. Salem, 1938.
Limited to 500 copies. Illustrated, cloth, t.e.g., covers a bit
stained. King 46-133 1983 $20

PHILLIPS, MORRIS   Abroad and at Home. New York, (1892).
Illus. 12mo. Hotel ads. Inscription to Mildred Levine. Morrill
289-500 1983 $20

PHILLIPS, P. LEE   The Beginnings of Washington as
Described in Book Maps and Views. Wash., privately printed, 1917.
Illus. Orig. 4to, cloth. First edition. Ginsberg 46-234 1983
$75

PHILLIPS, PAUL C.   Medicine in the Making of Montana.
Missoula: Montana State University Press, 1962. Special edition
limited to 300 copies and handbound in buckskin. Plates. Frontis.
portraits. Fine. Jenkins 152-267 1983 $75

PHILLIPS, PHEBE   The Woman of the Town. Printed for
Ann Lemoine...sold by T. Hurst, 1799. With an engraved frontis., 12mo,
Fenning 62-286 1983 £55

PHILLIPS, RICHARD   A Grammar of Natural and Experimental
Philosophy. Hartford, S.G. Goodrich, 1822. One hundred engravings
of wood. Small 8vo, orig. tree sheep, bit worn age-browned and
foxed. Ravenstree 97-161 1983 $28

PHILLIPS, RICHARD   Memoirs of the Public and Private
Life of Sir Richard Phillips... London: J. Dean, 1808. Small
8vo. Cont. blue straight-grained half morocco, gilt, gilt decorated
spine, edges gilt. With 2 pp. of pencil notes by Beckford and some
enghusiastic comments in the margins by Lord Rosebery. Traylen
94-657 1983 £200

PHILLIPS, SAMUEL   Crystal Palace. 1855. 4th edition,
folding plates. Ads., orig. pink printed wraps, v.g. Jarndyce 31-
282 1983 £32

PHILLIPS, SHINE   Big Spring, The Casual Biography of a
Prairie Town. New York, 1942. Illus. 1st ed. in dj. Presentation
from the author. Jenkins 153-607 1983 $40

PHILLIPS, STEPHEN   Christ in Hades. London: John Lane,
The Bodley Head; N.Y.: John Lane Co., 1917. First illustrated edition.
Orig. pictorial cloth. Contains Hind's 67-page introduction. Very
fine. MacManus 280-4178 1983 $35

PHILLIPS, STEPHEN   Endymion. London: Privately printed, (n.d.). Full crimson crushed levant, gilt extra, by Stikeman. First edition. One of only 30 numbered copies, of which this is copy no. 1. Reese 20-769 1983 $100

PHILLIPS, STEPHEN   New Poems. London: John Lane, 1908. First edition. Orig. cloth. Dust jacket. Fine. MacManus 280-4183 1983 $35

PHILLIPS, STEPHEN   Ulysses. N.Y.: The Macmillan Co., 1902. First American edition. Orig. parchment. One of 100 copies printed on Japanese vellum. Parchment wrappers soiled along spine. Very good. MacManus 280-4187 1983 $50

PHILLIPS, THOMAS   Bibliotheca Phillippica. London, Nov. 30, 1965-Nov. 28, 1973. Parts 1-8 (of 11). 28 colored and 267 monochrome plates. 8 vols., 4to, original boards, 617 items, with the printed price lists. Morrill 290-405 1983 $75

PHILLIPS, W.   A Manual of the British Discomycetes. 1893. Second edition. Wheldon 160-1871 1983 £18

PHILLIPS, W. J.   Colour in the Canadian Rockies. Toronto: Thomas Nelson, 1937. 24cm. First edition. 32 colour plates and many line-drawn text illus. Some foxing. Chipped and tired dustjacket. Very good copy. McGahern 53-126 1983 $75

PHILLIPS, WENDELL   Arguments before the Comm. on Federal Relations. Boston, 1855. Outer pp. somewhat dust-smudged. Argosy 716-20 1983 $20

PHILLIPS, WILLIAM   The Conquest of Kansas by Missouri and her Allies. Boston: Phillips, Sampson and Company, 1856. Original black cloth. Some chipping to the spine and corners. Fairly nice copy. 1st ed. Jenkins 151-154 1983 $55

PHILLIPS, WILLIAM   The Conquest of Kansas, by Missouri and Her Allies. Boston, Phillips, Sampson & Co., 1856. 8vo, orig. cloth gilt, ex-library with bookplate, date stamp on endpaper, slight wear and light age-browning. First edition. Ravenstree 97-162 1983 $30

PHILLIPS, WILLIAM B.   North Carolina Phosphates. Wilmington, 1883. Orig. printed wraps. First edition. Rubber library stamp. Ginsberg 46-554 1983 $35

PHILLIPSON, CAROLINE GIFFORD Mental Flights. Chapman & Hall, 1871. Half title. Orig. red cloth. Jarndyce 30-818 1983 £10.50

PHILLPOTTS, EDEN   The American Prisoner. London: Methuen & Co., 1904. First edition. Frontis. Orig. cloth. Bookplate. MacManus 280-4188 1983 $20

PHILLPOTTS, EDEN   Arachne. London: Faber & Gwyer, (1927). First edition. Orig. cloth. Dust jacket. Fine. MacManus 280-4189 1983 $35

PHILLPOTTS, EDEN   Becoming. (London): Ernest Benn, 1932. First edition. Orig. parchment-backed cloth boards. One of 110 copies printed on Navigator mould made paper and signed by author. Spine ends very slightly worn. Covers a trifle dusty. Very good. MacManus 280-4190 1983 $45

PHILLPOTTS, EDEN   Bred in the Bone. London: Hutchinson & Co. Ltd., (1932). First edition. Orig. cloth. Dust jacket. Fine. MacManus 280-4191 1983 $65

PHILLPOTTS, EDEN   The Captain's Curio. N.Y.: The Macmillan Co., 1933. First American edition. Orig. cloth. Dust jacket (slightly worn and soiled). Near-fine. MacManus 280-4192 1983 $45

PHILLPOTTS, EDEN   "Cheat-the-Boys." London: William Heinemann Ltd., (1924). First edition. Orig. cloth. Dust jacket (chipped & dust-soiled). Very good. MacManus 280-4193 1983 $45

PHILLPOTTS, EDEN   Children of the Mist. A Novel. London: A. D. Innes, 1898. 1st ed., first printing. 4to. Original cloth gilt, spine gilt. Uncut copy. Frontis. Half-title. Advertisements. A fine copy. Trebizond 18-81 1983 $125

PHILLPOTTS, EDEN   Children of the Mist. London, Innes, 1898. First edition. Frontis. Gilt stamped blue cloth, uncut and partly unopened. Very good. Houle 21-713 1983 $55

PHILLPOTTS, EDEN   Children of the Mist. London: Innes, 1898. First edition. Orig. cloth. Very good. MacManus 280-4194 1983 $45

PHILLPOTTS, EDEN   The Contrast. London: Henry Colburn & Richard Bentley, 1832. First edition. 3 vols. Cont. cloth with marbled boards. Spines faded, spine-ends worn. Covers rubbed and slightly worn at the edges. Slightly foxed. Good. MacManus 280-4222 1983 $125

PHILLPOTTS, EDEN   The Dartmoor Novels. London, 1927. The Widecombe edition. 12 vols. 8vo. Half vellum, gilt. Frontis. to each vol. Limited edition of 1,500 sets, signed by Eden Phillpotts. Traylen 94-658 1983 £180

PHILLPOTTS, EDEN   Devonshire Cream. London: Duckworth, (1925). First edition. Orig. cloth. Presentation copy, inscribed on the front flyleaf "To Stringer Davis--a memento of 'Devonshire Cream'-- with the author's grateful thanks from Phillpotts March 1925." Very good. MacManus 280-4196 1983 $45

PHILLPOTTS, EDEN   Devonshire Cream. London: Duckworth, (1925). First edition. Orig. wrappers. Very good. MacManus 280-4197 1983 $25

PHILLPOTTS, EDEN   Flowers of the Gods. N.Y.: The Macmillan Co., 1943. First American edition. Orig. cloth. Dust jacket (worn at the edges). Near-fine. MacManus 280-4198 1983 $37.50

PHILLPOTTS, EDEN   Folly and Fresh Air. London, Trischler, 1891. 8vo, orig. cloth, name on title, bit worn. First issue in the primary binding. First edition. Ravenstree 96-145 1983 $75

PHILLPOTTS, EDEN   The Good Red Earth. N.Y.: Doubleday, 1901. First American edition. Orig. decorated cloth. Presentation copy, inscribed, "To Albert H. Whitin Esq. with hearty regard, Eden Phillpoitts, Sep: 1901." Fine. MacManus 280-4200 1983 $25

PHILLPOTTS, EDEN   Goodwill. London: Watts & Co., (1928). First edition. Orig. cloth. Dust jacket. Fine. MacManus 280-4201 1983 $35

PHILLPOTTS, EDEN   Grey Room. N.Y., Macmillan, 1921. First American edition, reset and printed in USA. Brown cloth, very good. Houle 21-714 1983 $22.50

PHILLPOTTS, EDEN   The Human Boy Again. London: Chapman & Hall, 1908. First edition. Illus. Orig. cloth. MacManus 280-4202 1983 $20

PHILLPOTTS, EDEN   A Human Boy's Diary. London: William Heinemann Ltd., 1924. First edition. Frontis. Orig. cloth. Dust jacket (somewhat worn at edges, reinforced with tape at top of spine). Blind-stamped presentation copy. Very good. MacManus 280-4203 1983 $35

PHILLPOTTS, EDEN   A Hundred Lyrics. (London): Ernest Benn Ltd., 1930. First edition. Orig. vellum-backed cloth. One of 160 copies signed by author. Fine. MacManus 280-4204 1983 $85

PHILLPOTTS, EDEN   A Hundred Lyrics. (L), 1930. One of 160 numbered and signed copies, boards bowed, name embossed in several places, flys offset, good. Quill & Brush 54-1084 1983 $35

PHILLPOTTS, EDEN   The Jury. N.Y.: The Macmillan Co., 1927. First American edition. Orig. cloth. Dust jacket (slightly faded, worn and soiled; price neatly clipped from the front inside leaf). Spine and covers slightly worn and a trifle soiled. Good. MacManus 280-4206 1983 $45

PHILLPOTTS, EDEN   My Devon Year. NY, 1903. Front hinge starting, minor cover wear, very good. Quill & Brush 54-1085 1983 $30

PHILLPOTTS, EDEN   The Secret Woman. London: Methuen & Co., (1905). First edition. Frontis. Orig. cloth. MacManus 280-4210 1983 $20

PHILLPOTTS, EDEN   A Shadow Passes. London: Cecil Palmer & Hayward, (1918). First edition. Orig. cloth. Spine and covers a bit worn and soiled. Good. MacManus 280-4211 1983 $35

PHILLPOTTS, EDEN   There Was An Old Woman. London: Hutchinson & Co., (1947). First edition. Orig. cloth. Dust jacket (faded, worn and soiled). Presentation copy inscribed: "Inscribed for L'dorie A. Foiles by Eden Phillpotts, 22nd March 1955." Spine ends slightly faded and worn. Very good. MacManus 280-4212 1983 $50

PHILLPOTTS, EDEN   They Were Seven (A Mystery). London: Hutchingosn & Co., (1944). First edition. Orig. cloth. Dust jacket (quite torn). Bookplate of Adrian Homer Goldstone. MacManus 280-4214 1983 $25

PHILLPOTTS, EDEN   They Were Seven, A Mystery. N.Y.: The Macmillan Co., 1945. First American edition. Orig. cloth. Dust jacket (soiled; chipped slightly at the edges). Spine ends slightly faded and worn. Good. MacManus 280-4213 1983 $35

PHILLPOTTS, EDEN   Thoughts In Prose and Verse. London: Watts & Co., 1924. First edition. Orig. cloth. Dust jacket (slightly darkened & worn). Very good. MacManus 280-4216 1983 $45

PHILLPOTTS, EDEN   The Torch and Other Tales. Lon., (1929). Mixed state, edges lightly rubbed, else near fine in darkened, rubbed, slightly frayed, very good dustwrapper. Quill & Brush 54-1086 1983 $30

PHILLPOTTS, EDEN   The Treasures of Typhon. London: Grant Richards Ltd., 1924. First edition. Orig. cloth. Dust jacket (a bit worn & dust-soiled). Very good. MacManus 280-4219 1983 $45

PHILLPOTTS, EDEN   Up-along & Down-along. Methuen, 1905. 4to, orig. lithograph frontis., 7 orig. lithograph plates. Blue boards, gilt. Dust wrapper. Pencil note says "Claude Shepperson's copy." Edition limited to 500 copies, signed by Phillpotts. Greer 40-204 1983 £35

PHILLPOTTS, EDEN   A Voice From The Dark. N.Y.: Macmillan, 1925. First American edition. Orig. cloth. Bookplate of Adrian Homer Goldstone. MacManus 280-4218 1983 $20

PHILLPOTTS, EDEN   Wood Nymph. N.Y.: E.P. Dutton & Co., (1937). First American edition. Orig. cloth. Dust jacket (a little frayed, torn). Head of spine slightly worn. MacManus 280-4221 1983 $25

PHILLPOTTS, EDEN   A Year with Bisshe-Bantam. London: Blackie & Son Ltd., (1934). First edition. Orig. cloth. Dust jacket (a bit chipped). Fine. MacManus 280-4220 1983 $35

PHILOSOPHICAL Classics for English Readers. London, 1880-88. 9 works in 5 vols. Cr. 8vo. Half green morocco, gilt, t.e.g. 9 portraits. Traylen 94-659 1983 £38

PHIPPEN, GEORGE   The Life of a Cowboy Told Through the Drawings, Paintings, and Bronzes of George Phippen. Tucson: The University of Arizona Press, 1969. Full morocco. Limited to 100 copies. Signed by Louise Phippen, wife of George Phippen. Finely illustrated, many in color. Jenkins 151-274 1983 $175

PHIPPS, CONSTANTIN HENRY, MARQUIS OF NORMANBY Please turn to NORMANBY, CONSTANTIN HENRY PHIPPS, MARQUIS OF

PHIPPS, JOSEPH   The Original, and Present State of Man. Philadelphia, 1783. Cont. calf, front board, detached. Somewhat foxed. First American edition. Reese 18-145 1983 $30

PHIPPS, JOSEPH   The Original and Present State of Man, Briefly Considered...by the People Called Quakers... New York, 1788. Calf, slightly rubbed. Internally very good. Reese 18-163 1983 $90

PHIPPS, JOSEPH   The Original and Present State of Man. Trenton: Isaac Collins, 1793. Full calf (worn, spine damaged). Very good. Felcone 19-45 1983 $40

PHIPPS, MARY   All About Patsy. N.Y.: Doubleday, 1930. First edition. 8vo. Cloth. Full-page color plates. Full-page and smaller black & whites. Very good. Aleph-bet 8-184 1983 $25

PHOTOGRAPHIC portrait and memoir of Mr. Henry Irving. London: 1878. 8vo, original grey printed wrappers. First edition. Fine copy. Ximenes 64-309 1983 $35

PHYSICIANS of the Mayo Clinic and the Mayo Foundation. Minneapolis, 1937. 8vo. Orig. binding. Fye H-3-380 1983 $50

PHYSICIANS of the Mayto Clinic and the Mayo Foundation. Minneapolis, 1937. 8vo, orig. cloth. Bickersteth 77-310 1983 £12

PHYSIOGNOMY. London, (n.d.). Illus., some interior foxing, page 247 torn where misprinted, good or better in wearing leather binding, owner's bookplate. Quill & Brush 54-1651 1983 $40

PHYSIOLOGUS, The Very Ancient Book of Beasts, Plants and Stones. San Francisco: 1953. Quarto. Limited to 325 copies printed by Mallette Dean for the Book Club of California. Illus. with 54 linoleum blocks engraved and hand-colored by Dean. Numerous hand-colored initials throughout. Some light browning to covers, else fine copy in patterned vellum boards. Bromer 25-190 1983 $150

THE PIC Nic Papers. London: Henry Colburn, 1841. First edition. Illus. by G. Cruikshank, Phiz, &co. 3 vols. Orig. green cloth. Some occasional foxing, spines faded. Edges of spine of Vol. 1 a bit torn. Covers a little soiled. Good. MacManus 278-1544 1983 $450

THE PIC Nic Papers. London: Henry Colburn, 1861. First edition, first issue. Illus. by G. Cruikshank, Phiz, etc. 3 vols. Orig. cloth. Spine faded and slightly worn at the corners, cover to Vo. 1 slightly bent at top with a small tear to the hinge. A bit of foxing. MacManus 278-1543 1983 $650

PICAZO, MIGUEL   Lyrio Coronado en el Religioso Reyno: Sermon Panegyrico. Mexico: Imprenta Real, 1739. 4to, wrs. Argosy 710-306 1983 $50

PICCINNI, NICOLA   Didon. Paris, n.d. (19th century). 4to, 1/2 calf. With lithographed wrs. bound in, and frontis. Salloch 387-179 1983 $75

PICCOLOMINI, ALESSANDRO   La Prima Parte Dele Theoriche Overo Speculationi dei Pianeti. Venice: Giovanni Varisco & Compagni, 1558. Small 4to, with printer's device on title, woodcut portrait, and many woodcut diagrams throughout the text. Bound in cont. vellum, soiled and with a few stains. Front free endpaper lacking. Karmiole 76-97 1983 $750

PICENI, ENRICO   Zandomeneghi. Milano: Bramante, 1967. 83 color plates. 751 catalogue illus. Stout folio. Full leather. Slipcase. Edition limited to 1000 numbered copies. Ars Libri 33-606 1983 $175

PICHON, LEON   The New Book-Illustration in France. London: The Studio Ltd., 1924. Folio. With 112 illus. (25 in color). Green gilt-stamped cloth. Karmiole 76-22 1983 $75

PICKARD, MADGE   The Midwest Pioneer - His Ills, Cures, & Doctors. New York, 1946. First edition. 8vo. Orig. binding. Dust wrapper. Fye H-3-460 1983 $30

PICKERING, CHARLES   The Races of Man. London, 1854. New Edition. Map and plates. Small 8vo, contemporary calf, lacks label. Morrill 290-406 1983 $25

PICKERING, TIMOTHY   Declaration of the County of Essex... But Its Delegates...at Ipswich, on Tuesday the 21st of July, 1812. Salem: Thomas C. Cushing, 1812. First printing. Signed in type by Timothy Pickering. Stitched, uncut. Rare. Bradley 64-113 1983 $40

PICKERING, TIMOTHY   Mr. Pickering's Speech in the House of
Representatives. Georgetown, 1814. Modern cloth. Light foxing, else
fine, with errata leaf bound in. Reese 18-452 1983 $85

PICKERING, TIMOTHY   Mr. Pickering's Speech in the Senate.
(Hanover, 1808). Dsb. Good. Chancellor Kent's copy. Reese 18-316
1983 $30

PICKERING, WILLIAM   Annual Message of the Governor of the
Territory of Washington, Delivered December 17, 1862. Olympia, Poe,
1862. Sewn as issued. Ginsberg 47-942 1983 $100

PICKERING, WILLIAM   Thoughts and Opinions of a Statesman.
London: William Pickering, 1849. 16mo, this copy with the bookplate
of Arthur Hoe, noted collector. Orig. green cloth, paper spine
and cover labels. Karmiole 76-89 1983 $30

PICKERING & CHATTO   Catalogue of Old and Rare Books. 1900.
Orig. olive brown cloth, paper label, v.g. Jarndyce 31-95 1983
£30

PICKETT, LASALLE CORBELL   What Happened to Me. New York, 1917.
First edition. 8vo. Orig. cloth. Portrait frontis. 6 plates.
Very slightly soiled. T.e.g. Inscription on endpaper. Good. Edwards
1042-241 1983 £12

PICKFORD, MARY   Demi-Widow. Indianapolis, Bobbs-Merrill
(1935). First edition. Dust jacket. Boldly signed by Pickford.
Very good. Houle 21-715 1983 $65

PICKWELL, GAYLE   Deserts. N.Y., (1939). First edition,
4to, cloth. Argosy 716-9 1983 $45

PICOT, EMILE   Catalogue des Livres Composant la
Bibliotheque... New York: Burt Franklin, n.d. 5 vols., cloth.
Reprint of the 1884-1920 ed. Dawson 470-240 1983 $75

THE PICTORIAL ABC. New York: Gates & Stedman, n.d. 4to, colored
plates & orig. blue printed decorative wrappers. With ad. of
publications on back cover. Rostenberg 88-36 1983 $90

PICTORIAL Pickwickiana.   Chapman & Hall, 1899. In 2 vols., 350
drawings & engravings by Robert Seymour, Buss, Phiz, Leech, Crowquill,
Onwhyn, Sibson, Heath, John Gilbert, etc. Bottle green vertical
ribbed cloth with gilt vignette front covers, t.e.g. Bookplate.
Fine. Hodgkins 27-313 1983 £45

PICTURE Palace in Story Town. London: Nister; N.Y.: Dutton.
Folio. Cloth backed pictorial boards. Illus. throughout with chromolithographs. Very good. Aleph-bet 8-203 1983 $75

THE PICTURE Scrap Book. Relig. Tract Soc., nd (ca. 1860). 2 parts
in 1 vol. Frontis. & decor. title page, b&w illus. Dark blue bead
grain cloth gilt, a.e.g. Corners rubbed, sml. tear pp. 5&6 also
bottom p. 25, occasional foxing, vg. Hodgkins 27-315 1983 £15

THE PICTURE Scrap Book... Relig. Tract Soc., nd (ca. 1860). New
series. Colour frontis. & 136 pages of b&w illus. Dark green bead
grain blind stamped cloth, a.e.g. Cvrs. some rubbing, lt. stain
centre of title page, vg. Hodgkins 27-314 1983 £12.50

PICTURES of Comical People. Bos., 1862. Illus., cover slightly
rubbed, else very good, owner's name and address. Quill & Brush 54-
1652 1983 $25

PICTURESQUE Berkshire. Northampton, (1893). 2 vols. 1200 illus.
Thin folio, later linen-backed boards, ex lib. Argosy 716-277 1983
$50

PICTURESQUE Hampden. Northampton, 1891. 2 vols., 1500 illus., thin
folios, pict. cloth, ex library. Date 1892 stamped on cloth. Argosy
710-298 1983 $50

PICTURESQUE Hampshire, a Supplement to the Quarter Centennial Journal.
Northampton, Nov. 1890. Illus., folio, pict. cloth, ex library.
Argosy 710-299 1983 $30

PIDGIN, CHARLES FELTON   The Chronicles of Quincy Adams Sawyer
Detective. Bos., 1912. "Ellery Queen" and "Barnaby Ross" written on
half-title in Frederick Danay's hand, pic. cover slightly rubbed and
soiled, bottom edge of pages 211 to 214 slightly torn in margins, near
very good, bookplate. Quill & Brush 54-1087 1983 $175

THE PIED Printer's Primrose Path. Stamford, Conn., 1940. 12mo, gold
cloth, gilt, dec. d/w. With illus. printed in many colors. One of 250
copies. Fine. Perata 28-121 1983 $115

PIERCE, FRANKLIN   Indian Hostilities in Oregon and
Washington. Wash., 1856. Dbd. First edition. Ginsberg 47-769
1983 $45

PIERCE, FRANKLIN   Indian Hostilities in Oregon and
Washington. Wash., 1856. First edition. Dbd. Ginsberg 46-637
1983 $35

PIERCE, FRANKLIN   Indian Hostilities in Oregon and
Washington Territories. Wash., 1856. Dbd. First edition.
Ginsberg 47-770 1983 $30

PIERCE, FRANKLIN   Message from...Communicating the Report
of an Investigation of the Charges of Fraud and Misconduct in Office,
Alleged Against Alexander Ramsey, Supt. of Indian Affairs in Minnesota.
Wash., 1854. Half morocco. First edition. Ginsberg 46-479 1983
$125

PIERCE, FRANKLIN   Message of...Communicating...Copies
of the Papers Relating to the Proclamation of Martial Law in
Washington Territory. Wash., 1856. Sewn and uncut. First edition.
Ginsberg 47-945 1983 $40

PIERCE, GEORGE F.   Incidents of Western Travel...
Nashville, 1859. Cloth, spine very worn and chipped, edges also
worn, a fair copy only. Reese 19-427 1983 $125

PIERCE, HENRY H.   Report of an Expedition from Fort
Colville to Puget Sound, Washington Territory. Wash., 1882. Orig.
blue printed wraps. Folded map. Ginsberg 46-638 1983 $450

PIERCE, JOHN   A Discourse Delivered at Brookline...
Cambridge, 1806. Disbound, very good. Reese 18-285 1983 $25

PIERCE, LORNE   A Catalogue of Canadian Manuscripts.
Toronto: Ryerson, 1946. 23cm. Blue cloth. Fine. McGahern 54-
146 1983 $20

PIERCE, THOMAS   A Decade of Caveats to the People of
England. London, Davis, 1679. 8vo, old cont. calf (worn, lower
corner of title lacking), else good-very good. Houle 21-716 1983
$95

PIERPONT, JOHN   Airs of Palestine. Boston: Wells &
Lilly, 1817. Half title, engraved title, uncut, orig. brown boards,
spine worn. Jarndyce 30-819 1983 £10.50

PIERPONT, JOHN   The Portrait. Boston: Bradford and
Read, 1812. Disbound. First edition. About fine. Reese 18-392
1983 $30

PIERS, CHARLES P.   Sport and Life in British Columbia.
London: Heath Cranton Ltd., (1923). 22cm. 8 plates. Orange cloth.
Fine. McGahern 53-127 1983 $45

PIGAFETTA, ANTONIO   Magellan's Voyage. New Haven: Yale
University Press, 1969. 2 vols. Complete, numerous illus., including
a full color facsimile of the Yale manuscript. Folio, orig. white
cloth. Mint set in publisher's box. Jenkins 152-331 1983 $250

PIGMAN, WALTER GRIFFITH   The Journal of... Mexico, Missouri,
1942. Illus. Maps. Orig. paper boards with printed paper label
on front cover. Limited to 200 copies. Jenkins 153-431 1983 $85

PIGNATTI, TERISIO   Il quaderno di disegni del Canaletto
alle Gallerie di Venezia. Milano: Daria Guarnati, 1958. 2 vols.
54 text illus. Facsimile. 4to. Boards, 1/4 calf. Slipcase. Ars
Libri 33-63 1983 $150

PIKE, GODFREY HOLDEN   Byeways of Two Cities. Hodder &
Stoughton, 1873. First edition. Half title, front. Inner hinges
sl. weak, orig. blue cloth. Jarndyce 31-283 1983 £20

PIKE, JOSEPH   An Apistle to the National Meeting
of Friends in Dublin... Wilmington, Del., 1783. Dsb. Good.
Reese 18-146 1983 $50

PIKE, MARY H.   Ida May; A Story of Things Actual and
Possible. Boston & New York, 1854. 1st ed. Orig. cloth, gilt.
Very good copy. Jenkins 155-1005 1983 $25

PIKE, NICHOLAS   A New and Complete System of Arithmetic.
Newbury-Port, John Mycall, 1788. 4to, orig. sheep, some foxing,
lacks blank leaves before title, bookplate removed, blank foredge
of pp. 19-22 trimmed touching a few letters but not affecting
legibility. This copy is the first edition. Ravenstree 97-165
1983 $125

PIKE, ZEBULON MONTGOMERY   Exploratory Travels Through the Western
Territories of North America... London, 1811. Large quarto. 1st
English ed. Tall untrimmed copy in orig. boards with paper label.
Spine and extremities are lightly scuffed. Fine. Jenkins 153-434
1983 $2500

PILCHER, GEORGE   A Treatise on the Structure, Economy,
and Diseases of the Ear. Philadelphia, 1843. 1st American ed. 16
lithograph plates, 8vo. Orig. stiff wrappers. Most of paper label
lacking. Morrill 289-188 1983 $25

PILES, ROGER DE   Receuil de divers ouvrages sur la
peinture et le coloris. Paris: chez Ch. Ant. Jombert, 1755. First
edition. 12mo. Cont. mottled calf, gilt, spine gilt. Lacks label.
Ximenes 63-17 1983 $40

PILKINGTON, MARY HOPKINS   Tales of the Hermitage. London: Printed
by J. D. Dewick for Vernor and Wood, and sold by E. Newberry, 1800.
12mo. Engraved frontis. Fine copy, except for torn front endpaper.
Orig. vellum-backed marbled boards, rubbed. Early owner's signature.
Bromer 25-379 1983 $100

PILLING, JAMES CONSTANTINE   Bibliography of the Algonquian Languages.
Washington: GPO, 1891. Numerous plates, wrappers. In a protective
envelope of cloth-covered boards. Overall rather chipped and worn
but still integral and internally fine. Dawson 470-241 1983 $35

PILLING, JAMES CONSTANTINE   Bibliography of the Iroquoian Languages.
Washington: GPO, 1888. Cloth, slight wear and soiling. Dawson 470-
242 1983 $25

PILO, GIUSEPPE MARIA   Giulio Carpioni. Tutta la pittura.
Venezia: Alfieri, 1961. 209 plates (5 color). Small 4to. Cloth.
Dust jacket. Ars Libri 33-95 1983 $85

PILON, EDMOND   Watteau et son ecole. Bruxelles/
Paris: G. Van Oest, 1912. 50 plates. 4to. Wrappers. Chipped.
Ars Libri 32-697 1983 $50

PILON, FREDERICK   The drama, a poem. London: printed by
J. Chapman and sold by J. Williams, 1775. 4to, sewn, as issued.
First edition. Somewhat dog-eared, but entirely uncut; last few leaves
stained. Half-title present. Ximenes 64-427 1983 $200

THE PIN basket. To the children of Thespis. A satire. London:
printed for the author; and sold by J. S. Jordan, 1796. 4to, disbound.
1st edition. Half-title present. Fine copy. Scarce. Ximenes 64-
586 1983 $300

PINCKEY, CHARLES   Three Letters, Written, and Originally
Published, Under the Signature of a South Carolina Planter.
Phila., Aurora-Office, 1799. 1st ed., 8vo, sewed, uncut & unopened.
T.p. loose. Argosy 710-516 1983 $100

PINDAR, PETER, PSEUD.
Please turn to
WOLCOT, JOHN (1738-1819)

PINDAR, WILLIAM   A Sermon Preached before the Right
Honourable the Lord Mayor, and Alderman of London. London, printed
for Henry Brome, 1677. 4to, disbound, very fine copy of the first
and only edition. Ravenstree 97-166 1983 $27.50

PINDARUS   Carmina. Lg. 1900. Folding plate,
pencil marked by Prof. James Hutton. 8vo, cloth. Salloch 385-655
1983 $30

PINDARUS   Pythian Odes. L, 1928. No. 374 of 1050
copies, spine slightly soiled, endpapers offset, else fine in sightly
worn and split slipcase, bookplate. Quill & Brush 54-1088 1983 $50

PINDARUS   Works in Greek. Glasgow: R. & A.
Foulis, 1754-1758. 4 vols. in 3. Four title-pages. Printed in
Greek. Contemporary calf with three raised bands on spine and red
leather labels. Some browning to preliminary and final leaves, else
fine set with provenance of Arthur A. Houghton as former owner.
AHA bookplate on each vol. (3 1/8 x 2 1/8; 79x53mm). Bromer 25-
460 1983 $550

PINDER, WILHELM   Die deutsche Plastik des vierezehnten
Jahrhunderts. Munchen, 1925. Lg. stout 4to, 104 plates with titled
tissue guards, cloth. From the library of Jakob Rosenberg. Ars Libri
SC 26-186 1983 $100

PINDER, WILHELM   Die deutsche Plastik vom ausgehenden
Mittelalter bis zum Ende der Renaissance. Berlin-Neubabelsberg, 1929.
4to, 2 vols. 21 tipped-in plates, prof. illus. Boards, 3/4 cloth.
From the library of Georg Swarzenski. Ars Libri SB 26-187 1983
$37.50

PINELLI, ANTONIO   Genga architetto. Roma: Bulzoni,
1971. 160 plates. Small 4to. Cloth. Ars Libri 33-155 1983
$85

PINERO, ARTHUR W.   The Gay Lord Quex. London: Heinemann,
1900. First edition. Orig. cloth-backed boards. One of 200 large
paper copies. Slightly soiled and worn. Very good. MacManus 280-
4226 1983 $27.50

PINKERTON, ALAN   The Spy of the Rebellion. New York,
(Sold only by Subscription), 1885. Third edition. Thick roy. 8vo.
Orig. cloth. Frontis. 23 plates. Very slightly worn and soiled.
Good. Edwards 1042-242 1983 £65

PINKERTON, JOHN   The Literary Correspondence. Henry
Colburn and Richard Bentley, 1830. First edition, 2 vols. Half title
and front. vol. 1. Recently rebound in half calf. Jarndyce 30-1104
1983 £32

PINTER, HAROLD   The Caretaker. London: Encore Publishing Co., (1960). First edition. Orig. printed wrappers. Spine and
covers slightly faded, worn and soiled. Very good. MacManus 280-
4227 1983 $225

PINWELL, G. J.   Dalziel's Illustrated Goldsmith. Ward
Lock, n.d. (ca.1870). 4to. Frontis. & 99 illus. Green decorated cloth
gilt. Tight, good copy. Greer 39-95 1983 £35

PIOZZI, HESTER LYNCH   Anecdotes of the Late Samuel
Johnson. Printed for T. Cadell, 1786. First edition, without the
half-title. 8vo., in a later half calf. Fenning 62-287 1983
£135

PIOZZI, HESTHER LYNCH   Mrs. Piozzi and Isaac Watts. Grafton &
Co., 1934. Grey boards, cream cloth spine, paper label, v.g.
Jarndyce 31-997 1983 £10.50

PIOZZI, HESTER LYNCH   Retrospection. London: John Stockdale, 1801. First edition. 2 vols. 4to. Cont. tree calf, gilt
panelled spines with morocco labels, gilt. Engraved portrait by
M. Bovi, 2 half-titles, 1 pp. of publisher's ads., 3 pp. of subscribers. Traylen 94-660 1983 £160

PIOZZI, HESTER LYNCH   Thraliana. Oxford. Clarendon Press,
1942. First edition. 2 vols. Orig. cloth. Spines a bit faded.
Covers slightly scratched. Good. MacManus 280-4228a 1983 $35

PIPER, THOMAS W.   The Official Report of the Trial of...
Boston, 1887. 1st ed. 8vo, contemporary calf, leather labels.
Morrill 288-652 1983 $20

PIRCHAN, EMIL   Gustav Klimt. Wien: Berland Verlag,
1956. 162 plates (12 color). Tall 4to. Cloth. Dust jacket.
Ars Libri 32-372 1983 $75

PISTRE, MARCEL   Histoire Toulousaine du metier d'Apo-
thicaire. Toulouse, 1943. 8vo. Wrappers. Map and illus. Gurney
JJ-320 1983 £15

PITEZEL, JOHN H.   Lights and Shades of Missionary Life.
Cincinnati: printed at the Western Book Concern, 1859. Frontis. and
illustrations. Original cloth. Jenkins 151-275 1983 $65

PITKIN, ALBERT HASTINGS   Early American Folk Pottery. Hartford,
1918. Edition limited to 260 copies. Illustrated. 8vo, original
boards. Morrill 290-409 1983 $100

PITKIN, J. B.   A Discourse, Embracing Several Important
Objections... Richmond: Samuel Shepherd & Co., 1834. Printed wraps.
Small piece missing from lower blank margin of title. Felcone 20-181
1983 $20

PITKIN, WALTER B.   On My Own. N.Y., Scribner, 1944.
First edition. Dust jacket (some rubbing and small nicks, spine
faded) else very good. Inscribed by the author Dec. 25, 1944: "In
memory of Santa Barbara days..." Houle 22-721 1983 $45

PITKINS, TIMOTHY   A Political and Civil History of the
United States of America 1763-1797. New Haven, 1828. 2 vols.,
port., thick 8vo, 19th century mottled calf, lea. labels, some
foxing. 1st ed. Argosy 710-191 1983 $75

PITMAN, ISAAC   A plea for spelling reform. London:
Fred, Pitman, etc., 1878. Small 8vo. Orig. maroon cloth. Fine
copy. Ximenes 63-227 1983 $45

PITTIS, WILLIAM   Some memoirs of the life of John
Radcliffe, M.D. London: printed for E. Curll, 1715. First edition.
Small 8vo. Old cloth. Faded. One tear repaired, affecting a few
letters, a few page numberes shaved. Ximenes 63-35 1983 $125

PITTMAN, PHILIP   The Present State of the European
Settlements on the Mississippi. London, 1770. 5 folding maps, three
plans (two folding). A tall uncut copy, never bound, with the back
wrapper present. Slight tear in half-title, in every other way a fine,
crisp copy, with the plates in perfect condition. Laid in a folding
cloth case. Reese 18-94 1983 $3,750

PITTSBURGH Directory for 1815: with an Appendix. Pittsburgh:
Printed for James Riddle, comp. & ed., 1815. Small 16mo, disbound,
adv. leaf at end, lacking blank flyleaves, water stained title.
Argosy 710-407 1983 $100

THE PLACE-BILL, a Ballad. London: Printed for John Cooper...1740.
Folio, disbound. First edition. Quaritch NS 7-99 1983 $275

PLAIN Facts About Dakota. Milwaukee, 1888. Illus. Orig. printed
wraps. First edition. Ginsberg 47-292 1983 $75

PLANCHE, JAMES ROBINSON   An Old Fairy Tale Told Anew. Routledge,
1865. Sm. 4to. Frontis. Title vignette. 5 full-page and 13 text
illus. Foxed. Green cloth, gilt, rubbed. Greer 40-90 1983 £25

PLANCHE, JAMES ROBINSON   Twelve designs for the costume of
Shakespeare's Richard the Third, by C. F. Tomkins. London: Colnaghi
and Son, 1830. Folio, in sheets, as printed. First edition, with 12
hand-colored costume plates, an additional title-page with an attractive border, colored and gilt. Some wear along the spine (the first
title and last leaf of text are conjugate, and form a wrap-around
sheet), but a very good unopened copy. Scarce. Ximenes 64-429 1983
$325

PLANISCIG, LEO   Die Bronzeplastiken. Wien, 1924.
Statuetten, Reliefs, Gerate und Plaketten. Katalog mit den
Abbildungen samtlicher Stucke. (Wien. Kunsthistorisches Museum.
Publikationen aus den Sammlungen fur Plastik und Kunstgewerbe.
Vol. IV.) viii, 278pp. 495 illus. Sm. folio. Boards, 1/4 cloth.
Ars Libri SB 26-189 1983 $425

PLANISCIG, LEO   Piccoli bronzi italiana del rinaschi-
mento. Milano, 1930. Sm. folio, cloth. 226 plates. Ars Libri
SB 26-190 1983 $550

PLANISCIG, LEO   Venezianische Bildhauer der Renaissance.
Wein, 1921. Lg. stout 4to, 711 illus. Cloth (very slightly shaken).
Ars Libri SB 26-191 1983 $750

PLATE, L.   Vererbungslehre. Jena, 1932-38. 2nd
edition, 2 plates and 331 test-figures, 3 vols., royal 8vo, wrappers.
Wheldon 160-185 1983 £15

PLATEARIUS   Le Livre des simples medicins. Paris,
1913. 8vo. Quarter morocco. Gurney JJ-322 1983 £20

PLATH, SYLVIA   The Colossus. London, 1960. First
edition. One of 600 copies. Slightly faded spine. Fine. Very
scarce. Gekoski 2-153 1983 £60

PLATH, SYLVIA   Crystal Gazer. Rainbow Press, 1971.
First edition. One of 400 numbered copies. 3to. Half black buckram
with Japanese patterned paper sides. Slipcase. 23 uncollected poems,
finely printed at the Daedalus Press in hand-set Centaur types on
Barcham Green's handmade paper. Fine. Rota 231-473 1983 £50

PLATH, SYLVIA   Lyonnesse. London: Rainbow Press,
1971. Half calf and patterned boards. First edition. One of 300
copies, of 400, printed at the Rampant Lions Press. Fine in slipcase.
Reese 20-815 1983 $125

PLATH, SYLVIA   Winter Trees. London: Faber and Faber,
(1971). Uncorrected Proof of the first edition. Unbound signatures
loose in preliminary dust jacket not used on the published edition.
8vo. Wrappers a little dust-soiled, otherwise a fine copy. Jaffe
1-303 1983 $175

PLATNER, JOHANN ZACHARIAS   Institutiones Chirurgiae Rationalis,
tum Medicae tum Manualis. Lipsiae, 1758. 6 folding copperplates,
thick small 8vo, old bds.; ex-lib. Argosy 713-432 1983 $125

PLATNER, SAMUEL B.   The Topography and Monuments of Ancient
Rome. Boston, 1911. Maps. 8vo, cloth. Salloch 385-303 1983
$25

PLATO   The Banquet of Plato. (Boston:
Houghton Mifflin.) 1908. Small 8vo, ltd. to 440 copies. Boards;
paper spine label. Fine copy. Karmiole 74-82 1983 $100

PLATO   The Dialogues. Oxford, 1924. 5 vols.
8vo, cloth. Salloch 385-660 1983 $50

PLATO   The Dialogues. NY, 1937. 2 vols.,
8vo, cloth. Salloch 385-661 1983 $45

PLATO   Opera Omnia. Lg & London, 1873.
Folio, double columns, vellum bilt, with label. Handwritten inscription
by the Rector. Salloch 385-658 1983 $110

PLATO   Opera Omnia. Zuerich, 1846. 18 vols.,
bound together in 3 vols. 8vo, full wine-red levant morocco, gilt
tooled, a.e.g. The set lacks Republic and Sophistes; otherwise
complete. Salloch 385-662 1983 $65

PLATO   Phaedon: Or Dialogue on the
Immortality of the Soul. New York: Gowan, 1833. 1st American ed.
Orig. muslin-backed boards, label. Very good copy. Jenkins 155-1006
1983 $300

PLATO   Phaedrus, Ion, Gorgias, Symposium. NY,
1948. 4to, cloth. Salloch 385-668 1983 $25

PLATO   The Republic of Plato, in Ten Books.
Glasgow: Robert and Andrew Foulis, 1763. Plus ads. 1st English
ed. Contemporary calf, gilt. Hinges just cracking; still a fine
copy. Jenkins 155-1007 1983 $400

PLATO   The Republic. NY: The Limited
Editions Club, 1944. 2 vols. Edition ltd. to 1,200 numbered copies
printed by William E. Rudge's Sons and signed by Bruce Rogers
and by Fritz Kredel. Black calf spine over boards. In a lightly
chipped box. Karmiole 71-83 1983 $60

PLATO   ...Symposium or Supper. London:
Fortune Press, ca. 1930. Octavo. Limited to 175 copies signed by
translator, Shane Leslie. Some very light foxing to fore-edge and
rear cover, otherwise fine in gilt-stamped full vellum. T.e.g.
Bromer 25-209 1983 $55

PLATO   The works of Plato abridg'd... London:
A. Bell, etc., 1719-20. Second edition. 2 vols. 12mo. Cont. calf.
Frontis. in each volume. Binding slightly rubbed. Fine copy. Xime-
nes 63-68 1983 $250

PLAUT, FELIX   The Wasserman Sero-Diagnosis of Syphillis
in its Application to Psychiatry. NY: J.N.M. Pub. Co., 1911. Sound
ex-library copy. Gach 94-416 1983 $20

PLAUT, JAMES S.   Oskar Kokoschka. New York: Chanticleer Press, (1948). 2 orig. lithographs by Kokoschka, 8 color
plates. 48 photogravure plates. 4to. Cloth. Dust jacket. Ars
Libri 32-375a 1983 $100

PLAUTUS, TITUS MACCIUS   Dionysius Lambini Monstroliensis
emendatus. (Geneva) Apud haeredes Eustathij Jivnon, 1595. 4to, orig.
vellum, worn, title soiled, light stains. V5-6 reversed in binding.
Some early marginalia. Ravenstree 95-87 1983 $115

PLAUTUS, TITUS MACCIUS   Ex Plavti Comoediis. XX. (Colophon:
Venic, in Aedibus Aldi et Andrae Asulani Soceri, 1522). Large 8vo,
early 19th century red straight-grained morocco gilt, gilt edges,
light age-browning, but a very fine copy. Ravenstree 95-86 1983 $745

PLAUTUS, TITUS MACCIUS   Marci Accii Plauti Comoediae Quae
Supersunt. Parisiis, Typis Jos. Barbou, 1759. 3 vols., 12mo, orig.
french calf gilt, few wormholes to spines, hinges little chafed, spine
ends bit chipped, few quite minor spots, spines gilt extra, a.e.g.
Ravenstree 95-89 1983 $185

PLAUTUS, TITUS MACCIUS   Plautus's Comedies, Amphitryon,
Epidicus, and Rudens, Made English. London, Abel Swalle and T. Child,
1694. 8vo, later speckled calf, little worn, recently rebacked to
match, signature on flyleaf, few pencil marks, tiny hole in b4
removed only part of 2 letters. Good, sound copy. Ravenstree 95-90
1983 $275

THE PLAYERS: a satire. London: printed for W. Mears, 1733. 8vo,
original light blue wrappers (some wear to spine). First edition.
Some light foxing, but a very fine copy in original condition,
entirely uncut and partly unopened. Ximenes 64-434 1983 $900

PLAYFAIR, G. M. H.   The Cities and Towns of China. Shanghai,
1910. Binder's cloth, recased. 8vo. Good. Edwards 1044-570 1983
£40

PLAYFAIR, R. L.   The Scourge of Christendom. London, 1884.
First edition. Orig. brown decorated cloth. 8vo. Folding sepia
frontis. plan, 3 folding sepia maps and facsimiles, 3 sepia plates.
Gilt. Spine faded. Slightly foxed throughout. Good. Edwards 1042-
152 1983 £35

PLAYFORD, JOHN   The Musical Companion. London,
printed by W. Godbid for John Playford...1663. Engraved vignette on
title. Oblong 4to, new calf, spine with four raised bands label.
One page with marginal repair, otherwise fine copy. Salloch 387-181
1983 $2,000

THE PLAYHOUSE pocket-companion, or, theatrical vade-mecum. London:
printed and sold by Messrs. Richardson and Urquhart; J. Wenman; and
J. Southern, 1779. 12mo, disbound, first edition. Scarce. Title-
page dusty; some waterstains throughout. Ximenes 64-435 1983 $175

PLAYS. N.Y.: David Longworth, 1808-1814. A group of eleven plays
bound in three volumes, quite worn. Dawson 471-331 1983 $100

PLAZ, ANTON WILHELM   De tabaco sternutatorio vulgo...
Leipzig, 1727. First edition. Small 4to. Modern boards. Kraus
164-237 1983 $180

A PLEA for Authors and the Rights of Literary Property. New York:
Adlard & Saunders, 1838. 1st ed. Old wrappers. A contemporary
ink inscription at the top of the title reading "From the Author"
resembles Irving's hand. Scarce. Fine copy. Jenkins 155-666 1983
$100

PLEGER, JOHN J.   Paper Ruling. Chicago, Inland Printer
Co., 1925. Illus. 8vo. Morrill 289-502 1983 $35

PLENN, J. H.   Saddle in the Sky. Indianapolis, 1940.
First edition in dust jacket. Map on endpapers. Presentation copy
from author. Jenkins 152-334 1983 $45

PLESCH, ARPAD   The Magnificent Botanical Library of
the Stiftung fur Botanik... London, 1975-76. Complete. Colored
plates and other illustrations. 3 vols., 4to, original boards, very
nice. Morrill 290-42 1983 $75

PLEYNET, MARCELIN   "Derriere le Miroir." Miro. Paris:
Maeght, 1978. 12 plates, 51 reference illus. 2 double-page orig.
color lithographs by Miro (including covers). Small folio. Wrappers,
loose under boards, as issued. Slipcase. One of 150 numbered copies
on uncut velin d'Arches comprising the edition de tete. Ars Libri
32-459 1983 $175

PLIETZSCH, EDUARD   Vermeet van Delft. Leipzig: Karl
W. Hiersemann, 1911. 35 plates. 4to. Cloth. From the library
of Jakob Rosenberg. Ars Libri 32-686 1983 $50

PLIMPTON, GEORGE A.   The Hornbook and Its Use in America.
Worcester: American Antiquarian Society, 1916. Octavo. 19 b&w
illus. Some light offsetting of plates, else fine in printed wrappers.
Bromer 25-351 1983 $30

PLIMPTON, GEORGE A.   Marks of Merit Together with an Article
on Hornbooks and Their use In America. N.p.: Ginn and Co., n.d.
Octavo. Illus. Fine in slightly rubbed half-leather with cloth-
covered boards. Engraved bookplate of George A. Plimpton with hornbook motif. Owner's signature. Bromer 25-352 1983 $65

PLINIUS SECUNDUS, GAIUS   Epistulae. Lg, 1903. 8vo, cloth.
Salloch 385-703 1983 $20

PLINIUS SECUNDUS, GAIUS   Historia Naturale. Venice: Bartho-
lomaeus de Zanis, 12 September 1489. 8-line illuminated initial.
Capital spaces with guide letters. Small folio. Orig., presumably
Venetian, dark morocco (joints repaired), blind-ruled panel design,
center panel with blind-stamped Landino arms, smaller later armorial
stamps, 2 brass catches (no clasps). From the library of Cristoforo
Landino, the translator. A few light stains. First blank not present.
Kraus 164-193 1983 $12,000

PLINIUS SECUNDUS, GAIUS   The Letters of Pliny the Younger...
London: James Bettenham, for Paul Vaillant, 1751. 2 vols. 8vo.
First edition of this translation. Cont. polished calf, two-line
gilt borders, fully gilt panelled spines with crimson morocco
labels, gilt. Half-titles, vignette title-pages, engraved head-
and tail-pieces. Traylen 94-662 1983 £28

PLINIUS SECUNDUS, GAIUS   Naturalis Historia. Rome: Conradus
Sweynheym and Arnoldus Pannarts, 7 May 1473. Thick folio. Late
18th-century English red morocco, gilt-ruled borders, gilt inside
dentelles, back richly gilt, g.e.; by Richard Wier. Including the
last blank, but lacking the first blank. Capital spaces, with some
initials supplied in the first half of the second book, in red, blue
and gold. Headings of books 1 and 2 in gold. Bookplate, ms. notes
on flyleaf. Kraus 164-191 1983 $30,000

PLINIUS SECUNDUS, GAIUS   Naturalis Historia. Venice: Renaldus de Novimagio, 6 June 1483. Incl. first blank. Capital spaces, mostly with guide letters. Folio. Vellum. From the library of Harrison D. Horblit. Portions of a few leaves very lightly waterstained, minor worming towards end. Kraus 164-192 1983 $4,500

PLINIUS SECUNDUS, GAIUS   Naturalis Historia. Lg, 1897-1909. 5 vols. 8vo, cloth. Salloch 385-702 1983 $125

PLINY THE ELDER
Please turn to
PLINIUS SECUNDUS, GAIUS

PLOMER, HENRY R.   A Short History of English Printing 1476-1898. London, 1900. 8vo, cloth, g.t. Frontis., text illus. Backstrip darkened. Duschnes 240-186 1983 $50

PLOMER, WILLIAM   The Case is Altered. Hogarth Press, 1932. First edition. Covers somewhat used. Very good. Rota 230-470 1983 £15

PLOMER, WILLIAM   The Case is Altered. Hogarth Press, 1935. "Cheap edition" from first edition sheets. Inscribed by author to John Morris, dated Christmas 1943. Very nice. Rota 231-478 1983 £40

PLOMER, WILLIAM   Cecil Rhodes. London, 1933. First edition. Fine. Rota 231-477 1983 £18

PLOUCQUET, WILHELM GOTTFRIED Rosz-Arzt oder Unterricht die Krankheiten der Pferde zu Erkennen und zu Curizen. Tubingen, 1792. 12mo. Old boards. Morrill 289-189 1983 $25

PLOWDEN, FRANCES   Virginia, an opera, in three acts. London: printed and published by J. Barker, 1800. 8vo, wrappers, 1st edition. Ximenes 64-436 1983 $40

PLUCHE, NOEL ANTOINE   Spectacle de la Nature. London: J. Pemberton, et al. 1733. First English edition. Thick 8vo, 2 parts bound in one volume. With frontis. + 20 plates (many folding), containing illus. of insects, plants, birds, etc. Index. Bound in cont. panelled calf, rebacked. Karmiole 75-38 1983 $200

PLUECKER, L.   Ueber die Constitution der elektrischen Spectra der verschiedenen Gase und Dampfe. (Berlin, 1859). Offprint. 8vo. Boards. Gurney 90-136 1983 £150

PLUES, MARGARET   British Grasses. (1867). 16 coloured plates, cr. 8vo, cloth. Wheldon 160-1621 1983 £20

PLUES, MARGARET   British Grasses. Reeve, 1867. 1st edn. Col. frontis. & 15 plates, 16pp adverts. Dark green decor. cloth (rear ep. cracked at hinge, corners sl. bumped), v.g. Hodgkins 27-389 1983 £15

PLUES, MARGARET   Rambles in Search of Flowerless Plants. London, 1864. 1st ed. Colored plates. 8vo, spine slightly torn along front hinge. Morrill 288-412 1983 $50

PLUES, MARGARET   Rambles in search of wild flowers. 1864. 18 hand-coloured plates, 8vo, quarter morocco, joints slightly rubbed. Wheldon 160-1620 1983 £18

PLUMBE, JOHN   Memorial Against Mr. Asa Whitney's Railroad Scheme. (Washington: Buell & Blanchard, Printers, 1851). Half morocco. Rare. Jenkins 153-419 1983 $200

PLUMER, WILLIAM   William Plumer's Memorandum of Proceedings in the United States Senate, 1803-1807. New York, 1923. 1st ed. 8vo. Morrill 289-503 1983 $20

PLUMMER, CHARLES GRIFFIN   Gun-Grabbing Johnny. Pasadena: Radiant Life Press, 1923. Intro. by G.W. James. Plated. Cloth. Dawson 471-160 1983 $20

PLUMPTRE, ANNE   Antoinette, A Novel. Printed for William Lane, at the Minerva Press, 1796. 2 vols, 12mo, contemporary qtr. calf, marbled sides. Imperfect, lacking 1 2 and 1 11 of Vol. 11; but a rare Minerva. Hill 165-93 1983 £30

PLUMPTRE, C. E.   Giordano Bruno. London: Chapman & Hall, 1884. First edition. 2 vols. Orig. brown decorated cloth. Spine and covers slightly worn and soiled. Very good. MacManus 280-4231 1983 $185

PLUMPTRE, JAMES   Four discourses on subjects relating to the amusement of the stage. Cambridge: printed by Francis Hodson, for Messrs. F. C. and J. Rivington, etc., 1809. 8vo, original blue boards, drab paper spine. First edition. A very fine copy in original condition. Ximenes 64-437 1983 $125

PLUNKETT, ELIZABETH GUNNING The Gipsy Countess: A Novel. Dublin, Printed for G. Burnet (etc), 1799. 2 vols., 12mo., contemporary tree sheep, slightly rubbed, hinges worn, very fair copy, first Dublin edition. Hill 165-50 1983 £50

PLUNKETT, GRACE   Twelve Nights at the Avvey Theatre. Dublin: Printed for the Subscribers by Colm O. Locklainn. 1929. Oblong 4to, with 12 black and white plates, each with descriptive text on facing page. Edition ltd. to 200 numbered copies, signed by Plunkett. 1/4 white cloth, lightly soiled, over boards. Paper cover label. Karmiole 74-90 1983 $125

PLUNKETT, JOSEPH MARY   The Poems of Joseph Mary Plunkett. London, 1916. First edition. Spine darkened. Nice. Rota 231-481 1983 £12.50

PLUTARCHUS   Lives of Illustrious Men. Boston, 1889. Double columns. 4to, dec. cloth. Salloch 385-709 1983 $30

PLUTARCHUS   The Lives of the noble Grecians and Romans... Cambridge: by John Hayes for George Sawbridge, 1676. Thick folio. 19th century boards half morocco spine, gilt, morocco label, gilt. Engraved title-page, title-page printed in red and black, engraved chapter-headings and woodcut initial letters. Worn. Traylen 94-663 1983 £65

PLUTARCHUS   Lives. London: for J. Tonson, 1727. 8 vols. 8vo. Cont. black morocco, gilt. Two-line gilt borders with corner ornaments, fully gilt panelled spines with crimson morocco labels, gilt, edges gilt. 58 engr. plates by Giles King and G. van der Gucht from drawings by Louis Cheron. Title-pages printed in red and black. Traylen 94-664 1983 £65

PLUTARCHUS   Plutarch's Lives. New York, 1924. 5 vols., illus., 8vo., paper labels. Morrill 287-636 1983 $30

PLUTARCHUS   Lives of the Noble Grecians and Romans. London: the Nonesuch Press, 1929-30. 5 vols. Folio. Orig. buckram with printed paper labels. 54 full-page plates by T.L. Poulton. Limited edition of 1,050 numbered sets. Traylen 94-665 1983 £65

PLUTARCHUS   Vitae Parallelae. Lg, 1908. 5 vols., 8vo, cloth. Salloch 385-708 1983 $150

A POCKET Companion for Oxford. London, 1756. 12mo, 5 engraved plates, orig. grey wraps., outer corners of the first 30 pages creased, wraps. defective on the spine. Bickersteth 75-73 1983 £24

POCOCK, DORIS A.   The Elves of the Alphabet. Chambers, n.d. (ca.1920). Sm. 4to. Colour frontis. 26 plates. 62 text illus. (some amateur colouring). Internal wear. Alphabet endpapers. Red pictorial cloth, worn. Greer 40-16 1983 £15

POCOCK, R. I.   Fauna of British India, Mammalia. 1939-41. Second edition, folding map, 43 plates and 221 text-figures, 2 vols., 8vo, cloth (trifle faded). Very scarce. A good ex-library copy. Wheldon 160-555 1983 £45

PODSON, T. C.   The Naga Tribes. London, 1911. Folding map, coloured frontis. Other plates. Pictorial cloth gilt, slightly soiled. 8vo. Good. Edwards 1044-571 1983 £35

POE, EDGAR ALLAN   Anastatic Printing. Gehenna Press, 1972
(published 1975). Slim 8vo, title-page printed in red and black,
with mounted portrait of Poe by Baskin, 2 wood-cuts, uncut in mustard
cloth gilt, fine in marbled paper slip-case. Deighton 3-243 1983
£55

POE, EDGAR ALLAN   Doings of Gotham...Pottsville:
Spannuth, 1929. 1st ed., 1 of 749 copies. Orig. cloth-backed
boards. Ex library with markings, but otherwise a fine copy of a
scarce volume. Jenkins 155-1009 1983 $30

POE, EDGAR ALLAN   Edgar Allan Poe Letters Till Now Unpublished. Phila., 1925. First edition. Limited to 1550 numbered copies.
Cloth backed. Gilt-patterned boards. Uncut. Corners worn. Very
good. King 45-233 1983 $45

POE, EDGAR ALLAN   Eureka. Paris: Michel Levy Freres,
1864. Orig. printed wraps. First edition in French. Spine
cracked, some scattered foxing and staining, but a good copy.
Reese 20-777 1983 $375

POE, EDGAR ALLAN   The Fall of the House of Usher. Paris:
Editions Narcisse, 1928. Quarto. Illus. by Alastair. Cont.
patterned boards, leather label, orig. wraps. bound in. First edition
thus, one of 300 numbered copies on Holland Van Gelder Zonen. With
the bookplate of Carl Van Vechten. A couple of nicks in joint, otherwise fine. Reese 20-132 1983 $300

POE, EDGAR ALLAN   The Gift...for 1842. Philadelphia:
Carey & Hart, (1841). Frontis., plates. 1st ed., 1st printing.
Orig. cream calf, heavily gilt, a.e.g. Some aging of calf at spine,
but an attractive worn copy. Jenkins 155-1010 1983 $75

POE, EDGAR ALLAN   The Gift...for 1842. Philadelphia:
Carey & Hart, (1841). Frontis., plates. 1st ed., 1st printing.
Black morocco, heavily gilt, a.e.g. Front free end paper lacking
and hinge-cracks as usual. Good only. Jenkins 155-1011 1983
$30

POE, EDGAR ALLAN   The Journal of Julius Rodman. San
Francisco, 1947. Boards, fine. Printed by the Grabhorn Press for
the Colt Press in an edition of 500 copies. Reese 19-428 1983
$100

POE, EDGAR ALLAN   The Journal of Julius Rodman. San
Francisco: Colt Press, 1947. Cloth and patterned boards. Woodcut.
1 of 500 copies printed by the Grabhorns for the Colt Press. Fine.
Jenkins 155-490 1983 $85

POE, EDGAR ALLAN   The Journal of Julius Rodman. San Francisco: The Colt Press, 1947. Quarto. 1/500. Pictorial title page
in color. Illus. with colored wood engravings by Mallette Dean.
Decorated orange, blue and Gray boards with white cloth spine and
paper label. Very fine in plain brown dust jacket. Bradley 66-286
1983 $75

POE, EDGAR ALLAN   The Journal of Julius Rodman. SF:
1947. 4to, cloth-backed decorated bds., paper label. With color
wood-engravings by Mallette Dean. Perata 27-71 1983 $75

POE, EDGAR ALLAN   Mystery and Imagination. Illus. London
News, Christmas, 1935. 4 colour plates. 4to. 6 colour illus. by
Lionel Edwards & many other illus. Colour pictorial wrappers. Greer
40-202 1983 £18

POE, EDGAR ALLAN   The Narrative of Arthur Gordon Pym.
Lg 4to, parchment-back bds., slipcase. Illustrated by Rene Clark.
One of 1500 copies signed by the artist. A fine copy. Perata 27-
122 1983 $50

POE, EDGAR ALLAN   Poems. London, 1881. 16mo, vellum
boards. 16mo. Argosy 714-591 1983 $30

POE, EDGAR ALLAN   Poesies Completes. Paris: Mercure de
France, 1910. Orig. printed wraps. Portrait. First edition thus.
A fine copy. Reese 20-778 1983 $50

POE, EDGAR ALLAN   The Poetical Works. Charles Griffin,
circa, 1863. With 8 plates and 19 other illus., small 8vo, orig.
cloth, gilt. Fenning 60-331 1983 £16.50

POE, EDGAR ALLAN   The Raven. New York, 1884. Illus. by
Gustave Dore. Folio, pictorial front cover. Some rubbing, back
cover lightly stained, dampstain on blank fore-edge margin of last
9 plates. Morrill 287-354 1983 $45

POE, EDGAR ALLAN   The Raven and the Philosophy of Composition. San Francisco: Paul Elder, (1907). Octavo. Quarto Photogravure Edition. 13 photogravures. Limited to 1000 copies. Few
pages lightly foxed, else extremely fine in quarter-suede and
decoratively stamped boards. Printed dust wrapper very slightly
chipped. Slip-case lacks spine. Bromer 25-260 1983 $175

POE, EDGAR ALLAN   The Raven. Mass., 1980. Folio,
pictorial rag paper over boards. With five orig. etchings printed
by the artist, Alan James Robinson, text handset and printed by
Harold McGrath in 24 pt. Centaur type designed by Bruce Rogers.
Printed on Arches paper in an edition of 125 copies signed and
numbered by the artist. Two signed proofs of wood engravings used
on title page and colophon are laid in the book. Enclosed in half
leather folding box. Duschnes 240-45 1983 $450

POE, EDGAR ALLAN   Tales of Mystery and Imagination. N.Y.,
1936. Black cloth with paper cover label. Spine worn and discolored.
Removal marks from rear endpapers. Slightly loose covers. 32 drawings
(incl. 8 tipped-in full page color plates) by H. Clarke. King 45-
387 1983 $85

POE, EDGAR ALLAN   Works. N.Y., Armstrong, 1895. Fordham
edition. Illus. with etchings and facs. plates. Red cloth, t.e.g., 6
vols. Very good. Houle 22-723 1983 $125

POE, EDGAR ALLAN   Complete Works. N.Y., Putnam, (1902).
Arnheim edition. Illus. with steel engravings and b/w drawings by
Frederick Simpson Coburn. Half vellum stamped in gilt over grey
boards stamped in gilt with a picture of the raven, t.e.g., one of
500 numbered sets. 10 vols. Fine. Houle 22-722 1983 $750

POE, JOHN W.   The Death of Billy the Kid. Boston,
1933. Frontis. and illus. First of this ed. Dust jacket. Jenkins
153-437 1983 $55

POE, JOHN W.   The Death of Billy the Kid. Boston,
1933. 1st ed. Illus. 12mo. Clark 741-61 1983 $40

POEHLS, MENO   A Compend of German Grammar.
Cambridge (Mass).: Printed at the University Press by Hilliard &
Metcalf, 1817. 12mo, later wrs. Argosy 710-205 1983 $40

POEMS of the Dance. NY, 1921. 16 plates, 8vo, 1/2 cl. Pictorial
photographs by Edward R. Dickson. Salloch 387-307 1983 $25

POEMS, Supposed To Have Been Written at Bristol, by Thomas Rowley
and Others in the Fifteenth Century... London: Printed for T. Payne,
1777. 1st ed., with leaf C4 a cancel. Orig. half calf and marbled
boards, gilt label. Very good copy. Jenkins 155-201 1983 $350

POESIE di Montale. Milan, 1960. Wrappers. One of 550 copies.
Frontis. by Giorgio Morandi. English text by Robert Lowell. Fine.
Jolliffe 26-331 1983 £45

POET Lore, Vol. 16, No. 1. Boston, Spring 1905. Boards, covers
well rubbed. Probably first U.S. appearance as book was not
published till 1911 here. King 46-304 1983 $25

THE POETIC Epistles of Edmund: with notes, illustrations, and reflections. London: printed for the editor; published and sold by
Effingham Wilson, 1825. 8vo, sewn, as issued. First ed. Title a
bit dusty, but a very good copy of a very rare poem. Ximenes 64-328
1983 $175

THE POETICAL Entertainer. London: Printed and sold by J. Woodward...
and J. Morphew...MDCCXIII. 8vo, uncut, disbound. First edition.
Quaritch NS 7-103 1983 $250

THE POETICAL Entertainer. London: Printed and Sold by J. Morphew...
MDCCXII. 8vo, signed in fours, some very light foxing, a large copy.
Disbound. First edition. Quaritch NS 7-100 1983 $200

THE POETICAL Entertainer. London: Printed and Sold by J. Woodward... and J. Morphew...MDCCXII. 8vo, disbound. First edition, with MS entries of price and date of acquisition by Narcissus Luttrell. Quaritch NS 7-101 1983 $150

POETICAL Miscellanies, the fifth part. London: printed for Jacob Tonson, 1704. 1st ed., 8vo, engraved frontis., worming affecting the text in several places, cont. calf, skilfully rebacked with red morocco label lettered in gilt, gilt monogram in the centre of each cover. Pickering & Chatto 19-48 1983 $350

THE POETRY of Flowers. James Williams, 1845. First edition. Colour front. Orig. blue paper wraps., a little worn, a.e.g. Jarndyce 30-624 1983 £12

THE POETRY of South Africa. London: Sampson Low, etc., 1887. First edition. 8vo. Orig. bright blue cloth. Spine a trifle dull. Fine copy. Ximenes 63-432 1983 $50

POETRY of the Anti-Jacobin. 1890. Six illus. and a folio plate by James Gillray. 4to, 7 plates reproducing Gillray caricatures, one being a large folding one in pocket in back cover, t.e.g., other edges uncut, orig. cloth with paper label on the spine, no. 59 of the 250 large paper copies. Bickersteth 75-166 1983 £15

POETRY of the Orient. New York, 1928. 8vo., cloth boards, from the library of Alexander Laing, signed by same on front endpaper, very good to fine. In Our Time 156-797 1983 $20

POETS of Australia. Sydney, 1946. First edition. Frayed and slightly torn dustwrapper. Fine. Jolliffe 26-593 1983 £30

POHL, JOHANN CHRISTOPH   Ordinis medicorum in Academia Lipsiensi... Leipzig: Langenheim, 1776. Woodcut initial, head- and tail-piece. Small 4to. Boards. Kraus 164-58 1983 $180

POINCARE, LEON   Prophylaxie et Geographie Medicale des Principales Maladies tributaires de l'Hygiene. Paris, 1884. 8vo, mod. bds., orig. pr. wrs. bound in. First edition. 24 colored maps. Argosy 713-433 1983 $125

POINSETT, JOEL R.   Defences-Frontiers. Letter from...Trans- mitting Information in Relation to the State of Defences of the Atlantic Seaboard and Gulf of Mexico, and On the Northern and Eastern Frontier. Wash., 1838. Dbd. First edition. Ginsberg 47-324 1983 $25

POINSETT, JOEL R.   Discourse on the Objects and Importance of the National Institution for the Promotion of Science. Washington, 1841. Printed wraps. Good. Reese 19-429 1983 $50

POINSETT, JOEL R.   Military Road, Western Frontier... Wash., 1838. Sewn as issued. Uncut. Fine copy. Jenkins 153-438 1983 $50

POINSETT, JOEL R.   Report from...In Relation to the Mode of Furnishing Supplies of Goods or Merchandise to the Indian Department. Wash., 1839. First edition. Dbd. Ginsberg 46-357 1983 $25

POINTER, JOHN   A rational account of the weather, shewing the signs of its several changes... Oxford: printed by L.L. for I. Wilmot, etc., 1723. First edition. 8vo. Half calf, scuffed. Ximenes 63-306 1983 $150

POINTER, JOHN   A Rational Account of the Weather. Oxford, 1723. 8vo, disbound. First edition. Bickersteth 75-74 1983 £45

POISONERS and Propagandists. London: Charles Westerton, 1856. Orig. cloth. First edition. Presentation copy, inscribed: "To Jas. Whitton, Esq., with the author's kind regards." With Whitton's signa- ture in two places, and a note in the hand of the minor author Rev. George Gilfillan. Edges & corners a bit worn. Bindings soiled. A good set. MacManus 277-86 1983 $150

POISSON DE GOMEZ, MEDELEINE ANGELIQUE   La Belle Assemblee. Printed for D. Browne, J. Brotherton, W. Meadows, R. Ware, H. Linotot, T. Cox, T. Astley, S. Austen, J. Hodges, and E. Comins. 1743. 4 vols., 12mo, frontis. in each volume, 16 other plates, orig. calf, all vols. rebacked. Bickersteth 77-62 1983 £120

POLACK, W. G.   Bringing Christ to the Ojibways in Michigan. N.Y., n.d. (1920's?). Photos. Drawings. Cloth backed pictorial boards. Corners bumped, covers slightly rubbed and soiled. King 45-116 1983 $22.50

POLE, THOMAS   The Anatomical Instructor. London, 1790. 10 copperplates, some folding. Thick 8vo, orig. bds. (back defective); uncut. First edition. One plate stained. Argosy 713- 434 1983 $185

POLEJAEFF, N.   Report on the Calcarea. 1883. 4to, 9 plates, new wrappers. Wheldon 160-297 1983 £12

POLHILL, R. M.   Crotalaria in Africa and Madagascar. Rotterdam, 1982. Coloured frontispiece and numerous figures and maps in the text, royal 8vo, cloth. Wheldon 160-1756 1983 £45

THE POLICY of Extending Government Aid to Additional Railroads to the Pacific.   Washington: 1869. Printed wrappers. Light dampstains, otherwise good. Bradley 66-651 1983 $55

POLICY of Great Britain, Considered with Relation to Her American Pro- vinces, and West India Possessions. Phila.: M. Carey, 1816. First American edition. 12mo, later half calf, leather label, very lightly foxed. Argosy 710-100 1983 $100

POLIDORI, JOHN   The Vampyre. London, Sherwood, Neely, and Jones, 1819. Tall 8vo, modern half calf gilt, half title bit grubby, last leaf a little dust-soiled. Ravenstree 96-147 1983 $420

POLITI, LEO   Little Pancho. N.Y., Viking, 1938. First edition. Small 8vo, seventeen full page illus. by the author; decorations in text. With a bold inscription and orig. ink drawing of "Pancho." Very good. Houle 22-726 1983 $150

POLITI, LEO   Pedro, the Angel of Alvera Street. NY: Charles Scribners Sons, (1946). Small 8vo, profusely illus. with color plates. Presentation copy, with watercolor drawing of a singing bird, signed by Politi. Dust jacket. Karmiole 72-30 1983 $65

POLITIANUS, ANGELUS
Please turn to
POLIZIANO, ANGELO

POLITICAL Debates between Hon. Abraham Lincoln and Hon. Stephen A. Douglas. Columbus: Follett, Foster and Company, 1860. Third edition, state 5. Cloth. Spine ends frayed and a break of about an inch in cloth along spine, some sun-fading and spots on covers. Former owner's name in pencil on title page, as well as on front end papers. Dull-looking copy but sound and complete. Bradley 64-103 1983 $20

POLITICAL dialogues between the celebrated statues of Pasquin and Marforio at Rome. London: T. Boreman, 1736. First edition. 8vo. Disbound. Title a bit dusty. Ximenes 63-467 1983 $45

THE POLITICAL History of England. London, 1906-10. 12 vols. 8vo. Orig. cloth, gilt. Numerous coloured maps. Traylen 94-666 1983 £38

POLITZER, ADAM   A Text-Book of the Diseases of the Ear for Students and Practitioners. London, 1902. Fourth edition. 8vo. Cloth. 346 orig. illus. Library stamp and cancellation on title. Gurney JJ-327 1983 £20

POLIZIANO, ANGELO   Illvstrivm Virorum Epistolae. (Paris): Gaudoul, 1520. vvo. Fine printer's device on title-page, woodcut initials. Quarter morocco. 16th century ownership inscr. on title- page including that of Johannes Dugonnier. Small wormholes, marginal dampstain at end. Rostenberg 88-108 1983 $475

POLK, JAMES K.   Executive Proceedings, Correspondence,
and Documents, Relating to Oregon. Wash., 1846. First edition.
Dbd. Ginsberg 46-606 1983 $25

POLK, JAMES K.   Message from the President of the
United States Communicating...Papers in Relation to the Seizure of
the American Ship Admittance. Wash., 1848. First edition. Dbd.
Ginsberg 46-455 1983 $25

POLK, JAMES K.   New Mexico and California. Wash., 1848.
Dbd. First edition. Ginsberg 47-806 1983 $25

POLK, JOHN M.   The North and South American Review.
Austin, Tx., (1914). Illus., 2 folded maps, illus. in text. Orig.
printed wraps. Ginsberg 46-737 1983 $75

POLLARD, ALFRED W.   Fine Books. Putnam, 1912. First
American edition. 4to, frontis. engraving and numerous plates.
Green cloth stamped in gilt and blind, uncut. Very good copy.
Houle 21-144 1983 $75

POLLARD, ALFRED W.   The Romance of King Arthur. N.Y., 1917.
First American edition. Gilt-pictorial cloth. Inner hinges broken.
Covers show wear. 16 full page color plates & other drawing by A.
Rackham. King 45-620 1983 $95

POLLARD, ALFRED W.   A Select Bibliography of the Writings
of Aldred W. Pollard. Oxford, 1938. First edition. Frontis. gravure
portrait, half blue cloth. Very good. One of 260 copies. Houle
21-145 1983 $55

POLLARD, ALFRED W   Shakes Folios and Quartos... London:
Methuen and Company, 1909. Folio. Orig. boards, linen spine with
printed paper label, uncut edges. With 37 plates of facsimile
title-pages. Traylen 94-733 1983 £38

POLLARD, ALFRED W.   A Short-Title Catalogue of Books Printed
in England, Scotland, & Ireland... London: Bibliographical Society,
1926. Boards, holland spine, foxing, tape marks on endpapers, covers
rather worn and repaired, but tight. Dawson 470-243 1983 $60

POLLARD, EDWARD A.   Black Diamonds Gathered in the Darkey
Homes of the South. NY, 1859. Cover worn, spine badly chipped, front
fly missing, some interior staining, good. Quill & Brush 54-1611 1983
$35

POLLARD, EDWARD A.   La Cause Perdue, Historie De La Guerre
Des Confederes... Nouvelle-Orleans: Publiee par la Renaissance
Louisianise, 1867. 4to. First edition in French. 34 separate parts,
bound together in half morocco. 8 engraved portraits and three maps,
each apparently issued loose, and placed in a pocket at rear. Varying
color and quality of paper used for the printed wrappers. Paper goes
from a light green to a wheat color rather coarse in appearance, then
to a light blue and finally to white. Jenkins 152-211 1983 $950

POLLARD, HUGH B. C.   The Secret Societies of Ireland. Philip
Allan, 1922. First and apparently only edition, 8vo, orig. cloth.
Fenning 61-350 1983 £18.50

POLLOCK, EMMA   Volume of Ms. Verse. 1832-49. Orig.
green cloth, v.g. Jarndyce 30-820 1983 £25

POLLOCK, MRS. JULIUS   Eunice. Tinsley Bros., 1876. First
edition, 3 vols. Half titles laid onto leading free end papers, with
names cut from corners vol. I & II; half title and leading free end
paper removed vol. III. Orig. grey-brown cloth. Jarndyce 31-872
1983 £24

POLLOCK, ROBERT   The Course of Time. Blackwood, 1857.
Illus. by Birket Foster, J. Tenniel, J.R. Clayton, engr'd by Bros.
Dalziel, Edmund Evans & H.N. Woods. Blue pebble grain cloth gilt
(designed by John Sleigh), bevelled boards, a.e.g. Contemp. insc. fr.
ep., prelim. foxed & occasional foxing contents, top corners bumped
& cvrs. some fading, nice copy. Hodgkins 27-321 1983 £25

POLLOCK, WALTER HERRIES   Impressions of Henry Irving. London:
Longmans, Green, and Co., 1908. 12mo, original light blue printed
boards, linen spine, printed paper label. First edition. Inscribed
by the author. A fine copy. Ximenes 64-310 1983 $20

POLUNIN, O.   Flowers of Greece and the Balkans.
1980. Colour photographs, line drawings and maps, 8vo, cloth.
Wheldon 160-1757 1983 £41.50

POLYBIUS   The history of Polybius the Megalopolitan. The five first bookes entire... London: printed by
N. Okes for Cornelius Bee, 1634. First edition. Folio. Cont.
calf, spine gilt. With a woodcut title-page. Lacks label. Very
fine. Ximenes 63-69 1983 $275

POLYBIUS   The History of Polybius the
Megalopolitan. London, Samuel Briscoe, 1693. 2 vols., 8vo, orig.
calf, blank endeaves of vol. 1 excised, worn and joints breaking,
fine early bookplates of William Dummer dated 1706; with the fine
engraved folding map of Sicily in vol. 1 and the folding engraved
map of "Antient Greece: and its Territories" in vol. 2. First
edition of Sheeres' translation. Ravenstree 95-93 1983 $225

POMEROY, ALBERT A.   History and Genealogy of the Pomeroy
Family... Detroit, 1922. Illus., maps, color coats-of-arms, 3
parts bound in 2 vols. Thick 4to, 3/4 mor., g.t. Numbered copies,
vol. 1 ltd. to 400. Argosy 716-181 1983 $150

POMEROY, BRICK, PSEUD.
Please turn to
POMEROY, MARCUS

POMEROY, MARCUS   Nonesense, or Hits and Criticisms on
the Follies of the Day. New York: Carleton, 1868. 1st ed. Orig.
green cloth, gilt. Near fine copy. Jenkins 155-1012 1983 $25

POMEROY, MARCUS   Sense, or Saturday-Night Musings and
Thoughtful Papers. New York: Carleton, 1868. Illus. 1st ed.
Orig. lavender cloth, gilt. Fine copy. Jenkins 155-1013 1983
$30

POMEROY, R.   History of the Royal Scots Greys.
London, (1932). 8vo. Orig. cloth. Very slightly soiled. Good.
Edwards 1042-524 1983 £25

POMET, PIERRE   Histoire Generale des Drougues. Paris,
1735. Frontis. & 161 figures. 4to, old calf (hinges repaired); ex-
lib. Argosy 713-435 1983 $125

POMPONAZZI, PIETRO   Tractatvs de Immortalitate Animae.
N.p. (18th Century). 12mo, title within delicate arabesque border.
Calf. Ownership entry: "Gobets 1762 achete a Paris." With
ownership entry of Denis Gobets, noted 18th-century bibliographer and
collector. Rostenberg 88-109 1983 $150

POMPONIUS, MELA   Pomponii Melae de Situ Orbis, Libri
Tres. In Aedibus Academicis Excudebant Robertus et Andreas Foulis,
1752. 8vo, 19th century polished half calf gilt, gilt supralibros on
covers, bookplate, except for slight foxing a very nice copy.
Ravenstree 95-94 1983 $97.50

PONCE DE LEON, NESTOR   The Columbus Gallery. NY, 1893.
Illus., 4to. Argosy 710-426 1983 $75

PONCETTON, F.   Les arts sauvages: Oceanie. Paris:
Albert Morance, ca. 1936. 50 superb photogravure plates loose in
portfolio as published. Folio. Boards. Ties. Rare. Ars Libri
34-848 1983 $250

PONSONBY, ARTHUR   English Dairies. London, 1923.
Second edition. 8vo. Boards, cloth spine. Traylen 94-667 1983
£12

PONSONBY. John Richardson, 1817. First edition, 2 vols. Half blue
calf, maroon labels, sl. rubbed. Jarndyce 30-280 1983 £110

POOL, EUGENE   Surgery at the New York Hospital
One Hundred Years Ago. New York, 1930. First edition. 8vo.
Orig. binding. Fye H-3-461 1983 $30

POOLE, JOHN   Little Pedlington and the Pedlingtonians.
Henry Colburn, 1839. First edition, 2 vols. 2 vols. bound as one.
Half calf, spine gilt, red label. Very good. Jarndyce 30-520 1983
£28

POOLE, JOHN   Married and Single. A comedy. In three acts. London: printed for John Miller, 1824. 8vo, old half calf (rubbed). First edition. Ximenes 64-438 1983 $40

POOLE, JOSHUA   The English Parnassus: or a help to English Poesie. London: for H. Brome, T. Basset and J. Wright, 1677. 2nd edition, thick 8vo, engraved frontis. verso blank, cont. calf, corners worn, neatly rebacked and with double morocco labels, a fine clean and crisp copy. Deighton 3-245 1983 £110

POOLE, WILLIAM F.   Anti-Slavery Opinions Before the Year 1800. Cincinnati: Robert Clarke, 1873. First edition. Later cloth, morocco label. Orig. printed wrappers bound in. Jenkins 152-336 1983 $45

POOR Covent Garden! Or, a scene rehearsed: an occasional prelude, intended for the opening of the New Theatre Royal, Covent-Garden, this season. London: printed by T. Wilkins, 1792. 8vo, disbound, 1st edition. Scarce; very good copy. Ximenes 64-439 1983 $175

POOR Will's Almanack for the Year of Our Lord, 1779. Philadelphia, 1778. Stitched, very good. Reese 18-121 1983 $1,000

POPE, ALEXANDER   Additions to the works... London: H. Baldwin, etc., 1776. 2 vols. 8vo. Cont. calf, contrasting morocco labels. A bit worn. Scarce. Ximenes 63-377 1983 $175

POPE, ALEXANDER   Eloisa to Abelard...the second edition. London: printed for Bernard Lintot, 1720 (1719). First separate edition, 8vo, engraved frontis., modern wrappers. Pickering & Chatto 19-49 1983 $650

POPE, ALEXANDER   An Epistle from Mr. Pope, to Dr. Arbuthnot. London: Printed by J. Wright for Lawton Gilliver... 1734. Folio, last page trifle dust-soiled, disbound. First edition. Quaritch NS 7-105 1983 $375

POPE, ALEXANDER   An essay on man. London: J. and P. Knapton, 1755. 12mo. Cont. sheep. Engraved frontis. Rubbed. Ximenes 63-378 1983 $60

POPE, ALEXANDER   An Essay on Man, in Four Epistles. Newbury: Printed by John Mycall, for N. Coverly of Boston, 1780. Sewn. Cont. wraps. Title torn, with no losses, some marginal fraying, else a very good copy. Reese 18-132 1983 $85

POPE, ALEXANDER   An Essay on Man. Lexington, Ky., 1804. Later half morocco. Some foxing and staining. Very good. Reese 18-263 1983 $5,000

POPE, ALEXANDER   Poems, a Chosen Collection. Printed and sold by the Booksellers of London and Edinburgh (Edinburgh 1735 or 1736). 8vo, calf, rehinged. One of two surviving copies. Lacks two leaves. Advertisement. Pickering & Chatto 19-51 1983 $3,500

POPE, ALEXANDER   The Poetical Works. London: for F.J. Du Roveray, by T. Bensley, 1804. Large paper copy. 6 vols. in 2. Roy. 8vo. Cont. straight-grained red morocco, gilt, two-line gilt borders, gilt spines, edges gilt. 16 engraved plates after drawings by Fuseli, etc. Traylen 94-668 1983 £95

POPE, ALEXANDER   The Poetical Works. London, 1866. 3 vols. Cr. 8vo. Dark blue calf, two-line gilt borders with corner ornaments, gilt panelled spines, morocco labels, gilt. Portrait, vignette title-pages. Traylen 94-669 1983 £45

POPE, ALEXANDER   The Rape of the Lock. London: Leonard Smithers, 1897. Embroidered with 11 drawings by A. Beardsley. Orig. cloth. Second edition. This edition has a new cover design by Beardsley. Spine slightly faded. Bookseller's stamp on inside of front cover. A good copy. MacManus 277-240 1983 $125

POPE, ALEXANDER   The Rape of the Lock. London: Smithers, 1897. Gilt cloth, a.e.g. Illus. with plates by Beardsley, and with a cover design after him. One of 1,000 copies, with a new cover design, and plates reproducing that of the 1896 edition. Endsheets slightly foxed, else fine. Reese 20-74 1983 $85

POPE, ALEXANDER   The Second Epistle of the Second Book of Horace Imitated. London: printed for R. Dodsley, 1737. 1st ed., "B" issue, second state, footnote corrected to '15' on p. 12. Folio, a fine copy in marbled wrappers. Pickering & Chatto 19-52 1983 $250

POPE, ALEXANDER   The Works. London: by W. Bowyer for Bernard Lintot, and, by J. Wright for Lawton Gilliver, 1717-35. First issue of the first collected folio edition. 2 vols. Folio. Cont. speckled calf, neatly rebacked with crimson morocco labels, gilt. A folding engraved portrait by Vertue, half-title in each vol. Traylen 94-670 1983 £190

POPE, ALEXANDER   The Works of Mr. Alexander Pope. Printed by J. Wright for Lawton Gilliver. 1735. 2 vols., 4to, folding portrait in vol. 1, lower inner corner torn off, with loss of the left-hand end of architectural tablet with Pope's name on it below the actual portrait. Both vols. uniformly bound in speckled calf. Fine head and tail-pieces throughout both vols. First edition. Bickersteth 75-75 1983 £180

POPE, ALEXANDER   Works of.... London: Richard Priestley, High Holborn, 1822. Third edition. 9 vols. Illus. Full tooled calf. Covers and spines slightly rubbed. Some spotting to the covers. Occasional foxing. Bookplate. Cont. binding. Very good. MacManus 280-4234 1983 $500

POPE, ALEXANDER   The Works. London, 1871-86. New edition. 10 vols. 8vo. Three-quarters olive morocco, gilt, gilt panelled spines, t.e.g. Portraits and other illus. Traylen 94-671 1983 £395

POPE, CHARLES HENRY   The Pioneers of Massachusetts. Boston, Author, 1900. 1st ed. 4to, orig. half leather. Corners rubbed, otherwise nice. Morrill 287-248 1983 $35

POPE, JOSEPH   Memoirs of the Right Honourable Sir John Alexander Macdonald. Toronto: Musson, n.d. 22cm. Illus'd. black cloth. Good to very good copy. McGahern 53-128 1983 $25

POPE, THOMAS   A Treatise on Bridge Architecture. New York, 1811. Illus. Boards, chipped leather spine. Some foxing, but good. Reese 18-356 1983 $400

POPE, WILLIAM F.   Early Days in Arkansas. Little Rock, Ark., 1895. Illus. Orig. cloth, x-1. First edition. Ginsberg 36-40 1983 $100

POPE, WILLIAM F.   Early Days in Arkansas... Little Rock, 1895. First edition. Later cloth. Illus. Jenkins 153-19 1983 $100

POPE-HENNESSY, JOHN   An Introduction to Italian Sculpture. London, 1955-63. 3 vols. in 5 parts. 4to, 168 plates, cloth. Ex-Library. Ars Libri SB 26-193 1983 $350

POPE-HENNESSY, JOHN   Italian Gothic Sculpture. London, 1955. Lg. 4to, 108 plates, 101 illus. hors texte. Cloth. Ars Libri SB 26-194 1983 $125

POPE'S Own Miscellany. London, 1935. 8vo, green buckram, gilt, t.e.g. Dustwrappers, one of 750 copies. Perata 28-117 1983 $65

POPIANA. Memoirs of the Society of Grub-Street. London: printed for J. Wilford, 1737. First collected edition, 2 vols., 12mo, errata and index, cont. calf, rather rubbed, joints split and spines a little chipped, morocco labels. A nice copy. Pickering & Chatto 19-55 1983 $850

POPKIN, MARTIN E.   Organization, Management and Technology in the Manufacture of Mens' Clothing. Sir I. Pitman, 1929. First edition, with 15 folding plates and tables and many full-page and other illus. 8vo, orig. cloth, gilt. Very good copy. Fenning 62-288 1983 £10.50

PORNY, MARK ANTHONY   The Elements of Heraldry. London: J. Newbery, 1765. 1st ed., 8vo, cont. calf, spine gilt. Frontis. and 23 engraved plates, half-title. A very good copy. Trebizond 18-194 1983 $200

PORPHYRIUS, POMPONIUS   Commentarii in Horatium. Lg, 1874.
1/2 calf. 8vo. Salloch 385-713 1983 $40

PORSILD, A. E.   Vascular Plants of Continental North-
west Territories of Canada. Ottawa, 1980. 1155 maps and 976 figures,
8vo, cloth. Wheldon 160-1758 1983 £70

PORSON, PROFESSOR   The Devil's Walk. London, 1830. 12mo.
Illus. by Robert Cruikshank. Very good copy in lightly worn slipcase
box. In Our Time 156-181 1983 $35

PORT Arthur. Houston, 1940. Illus. 1st ed. Orig. pictorial cloth,
fine. Jenkins 153-610 1983 $30

PORTA, GIOVANNI BATTISTA DELLA   De Humana Physiognomonia libri iiii.
Vico Equense, Giuseppe Cacchi, 1586. Folio, engraved portrait of
the author within an elaborate architectural border on the title-
page; engraved portrait of the dedicatee, Cardinal Luigi d'Este within
a scrollwork border and 81 engravings by repetition of 54 copperplates
printed in the text; the engraving on 2B2r is a pasted-on cancel.
Occasional very light browning; crimson morocco, gilt edges. Bookplates. First edition. Good copy. Quaritch NS 5-86 1983 $3,850

PORTAL, ANTOINE   Observations sur les Effets des Vapeurs
Mephitiques dans l'Homme. Paris, Imprimerie Royale, 1787. 8vo, old
calf, (crudely rebacked in cloth; first few leaves dampstained); ex-
lib. Argosy 713-436 1983 $100

PORTAL, PAUL   La Pratique des Accouchemens soutenue
d'un grand nombre d'observations. Paris: Gabriel Martin, 1685.
First edition. Frontis. engraved portrait of author and 8 engraved
plates. 8vo. Cont. calf. Ms. exlibris of one Eschard, surgeon,
dated An 4, le 10 Vendemiaire (Sept. 1795), on inside back cover.
Portion of a ms. letter laid in at back of book. Kraus 164-109
1983 $1,450

PORTALIS, ROGER   Charles-Etienne Gaucher, Graveur. Paris:
Damascene Morgand et Charles Fatout, 1879. Engr. frontis., present in
2 states. 4to, wrappers, unopened. Printed in chine, obviously in a
small edition. Ars Libri 32-239 1983 $85

PORTALIS, ROGER   Henri-Pierre Danloux, peintre de
portraits... Paris: Edouard Rahir, 1910. 46 heliogravure and
phototype plates. 185 illus. Folio. Marbled boards, 3/4 morocco,
gilt. Raised bands. T.e.g. One of 250 copies on uncut Arches,
of a limited edition of 280 copies, printed for the Societe des
Bibliophiles Francais. Ars Libri 32-137 1983 $325

PORTE, R. T.   Letters to a Printer's Devil. Salt
Lake City: Porte Publishing Co., (1924). First book appearance.
8vo. Stamped cloth. Oak Knoll 49-327 1983 $20

PORTEOUS, JOHN   The Trail of Capt. John Porteous.
Printed for T. Cooper, 1736. 8vo, final blank, 19th century half
morocco, upper margin trimmed close. Bickersteth 75-77 1983 £18

PORTER, A. KINGSLEY   Spanish Romanesque Sculpture. New York,
n.d. 2 vols, 160 collotype plates with titled tissue guards. Small
stout folio. Cloth. Ars Libri SB 26-197 1983 $200

PORTER, ALAN   The Signature of Pain and Other Poems.
London: Cobden-Sanderson, 1930. Cloth, paper label. First edition.
Pencil erasure, else a very fine copy in slightly darkened and lightly
worn dust jacket. Reese 20-780 1983 $25

PORTER, ANNA MARIA   Don Sebastian. Longman, Hurst, 1809.
First edition. 4 vols. Half calf, boards a little rubbed, red
labels. Very good. Jarndyce 30-521 1983 £95

PORTER, ANNA MARIA   The Fast of St. Magdalen. For Longman,
Hurst, etc, 1819. 3 vols., 12mo, 3 advert. leaves, but lacking
half-titles. Cont. half calf (slightly worn). Hannas 69-156 1983
£25

PORTER, ANNA MARIA   The Recluse of Norway. Longman, Hurst,
etc, 1814. First edition. 4 vols. 12mo, half-titles in vols. II-IV,
not called for in I. Errata leaf in II, label leaf for all vols.
combined with errata for vol. III found at end of vol. IV. Cont.
half morocco (slightly rubbed). Some foxing, occasionally rather
heavy. Hannas 69-157 1983 £85

PORTER, ARTHUR KINGSLEY   Lombard Architecture. New Haven: Yale
University Press, 1915. Folio. 244 photo plates, many containing
multiple illus. Edition ltd. to 750 copies. Cloth portfolio.
Karmiole 72-7 1983 $125

PORTER, ELEANOR H.   Pollyanna Grows Up. Bos., 1915. Spine
sunned and worn at edges, hinges cracked, else good or better, inscription. Quill & Brush 54-1091 1983 $25

PORTER, EUGENE O.   San Elizario: a History. Austin:
Jenkins Publishing Co., 1973. Special edition limited to 50 numbered
copies (this is seven), bound in half morocco with vellum boards and
slipcased. Jenkins 151-276 1983 $200

PORTER, GEORGE B.   The Trail of Robert W. Houston, Versus
General John Dicks, and Others, Members of a Court Marial...
Philadelphia, 1817. Modern cloth, leather label. A very good copy.
Reese 18-515 1983 $75

PORTER, JACOB   Topographical Description and
Historical Sketch of Plainfield. Greenfield, 1834. Mod. wraps.
Argosy 716-274 1983 $25

PORTER, JANE   The Scottish Chiefs. London: Longman,
Hurst, Rees, and Orme, 1810. First edition. 5 vols. Cont. 3/4 morocco
and marbled boards with marbled endpapers. Spines slightly rubbed.
Edges a little worn. Small tear in Vol. five, and a previous owner's
signature on each title-page. MacManus 280-4237 1983 $450

PORTER, JANE   The Scottish Chiefs. For Longman,
Hurst, etc, 1810. First edition, 5 vols., 12mo, half-titles, errata
leaf in vol. I, final blank in vol. IV. Cont. half morocco (slightly
worn). Some brown stains, particularly in vol. I. Minor marginal
tears, just touching text in one leaf. Hannas 69-160 1983 £75

PORTER, JANE   The Scottish Chiefs. N.Y.: Baldwin,
1826. 5 vols. in two. Orig. boards. Fine. MacManus 280-4238 1983
$75

PORTER, JANE   The Scottish Chiefs. Ca. 1840. 2
vols., revised, corrected, and illustrated. Engravings, half
morocco. K Books 301-148 1983 £30

PORTER, JANE   Sir Edward Seaward's Narrative of His
Shipwreck. Longman, Rees, etc, 1831. First edition. 3 vols. 8vo,
half-title in vol. I. 8 plates inserted from a later edition. Red
half morocco, gilt, t.e.g., others uncut. Hannas 69-158 1983 £65

PORTER, JANE   Sir Edward Seaward's Narrative of His
Shipwreck. Longmans, Rees, etc, 1831. First edition. 3 vols. Lacks
half-title. Cont. half roan (very worn). Internally a good copy.
Hannas 69-159 1983 £15

PORTER, JANE   Thaddeus of Warsaw. Printed by A.
Strahan, 1804. Half-titles, 4 vols., large 12mo, orig. boards,
uncut, the spines a trifle worn but the cords strong. In orig.
state. Fenning 61-352 1983 £125

PORTER, JOSIAS LESLIE   The Giant Cities of Bashan; and Syria's
Holy Places. T. Nelson, 1874. With additional vignette title and 7
tinted litho plates, 8vo, orig. cloth, gilt, a very good copy.
Fenning 60-332 1983 £12.50

PORTER, KATHERINE ANNE   A Christmas Story. NY: (1967). Illus.
by Ben Shahn. 1/500 copies signed by both Shahn and Porter. Very
fine in cloth slip-case. Bromer 25-84 1983 $85

PORTER, KATHERINE ANNE   The Collected Essays and Occasional
Writings of... NY, (1970). Limited to 250 numbered and signed, specially bound copies, gilt-stamped green leather spine with marbled
boards, very fine in very fine slipcase. Quill & Brush 54-1096 1983
$150

PORTER, KATHERINE ANNE   The Collected Essays and Occasional
Writings. New York: Delacorte Press, (1970). 1st ed., 1 of 250
numbered and signed copies. Orig. half morocco & marbled boards,
boxed. Mint copy. Jenkins 155-1014 1983 $100

PORTER, KATHERINE ANNE   The Days Before. NY: (1952). First
edition. Inscribed by author. Edges of covers faded, else fine
with very slightly chipped and soiled dust wrapper. Bromer 25-85
1983 $95

PORTER, KATHERINE ANNE   French Song Book. P, (1933). One of
595 numbered and signed copies on Van Gelden rag paper, fine in lightly
soiled and chipped, very good dustwrapper. Quill & Brush 54-1092
1983 $250

PORTER, KATHERINE ANNE   Hacienda. P, (1934). Limited to 895
copies, fine in remnants of slipcase. Quill & Brush 54-1093 1984 $125

PORTER, KATHERINE ANNE   The Leaning Tower. New York: Harcourt,
Brace, (1944). 1st ed. Orig. cloth, dj. A few light spots of
foxing, but fresh copy in fine dj with two very tiny chips. Jenkins
155-1015 1983 $45

PORTER, KATHERINE ANNE   The Leaning Tower. NY, (1944). Very
good in lightly frayed and chipped, very good dustwrapper. Quill &
Brush 54-1097 1983 $35

PORTER, KATHERINE ANNE   The Leaning Tower. N.Y., (1944).
First edition. D.w. Fine copy, except that 2 pp have been creased.
Argosy 714-595 1983 $30

PORTER, KATHERINE ANNE   My Chinese Marriage, by M.T.F. New
York: Duffield, 1921. 1st ed. Orig. cloth-backed boards, gilt,
label. Lightly rubbed copy. Very scarce. Jenkins 155-1017 1983
$200

PORTER, KATHERINE ANNE   My Chinese Marriage. NY, 1921. Cover
lightly soiled, edges bumped and slightly frayed, foxing on pastedowns,
good. Quill & Brush 54-1095 1983 $75

PORTER, KATHERINE ANNE   My Chinese Marriage. NY, 1922. Later
printing, edges slightly worn and cover soiled, else good or better,
bookplate, owner's name. Quill & Brush 54-1094 1983 $40

PORTER, KENNETH   No Rain from These Clouds: Poems
1927-1945. New York, (1946). 8vo. Cloth. Review clipping pasted
on inside endboard, price clipped, else a fine copy in dj. In Our
Time 156-634 1983 $30

PORTER, MURIEL NOE   Pipas precortesianas. Mexico: Escuela
Nacional de Antropologia e Historia, 1948. 28 plates. 3 folding
maps. Small 4to. Wrappers. Ars Libri 34-428 1983 $30

PORTER, RUFUS   Aerial Navigation. SF, 1935. 8vo,
cloth-backed pictorial bds. Illustrated with 3 colored lithographs
issued as burlesques in 1849 by N. Currier & A. Donnelly.
Perata 27-98 1983 $60

PORTER, THOMAS   The Villain. London: for H.
Herringman, 1670. Second edition. 4to. 19th Century cloth.
Title lightly discoloured, and inner margin reinforced. Heath
48-399 1983 £55

PORTER, WILLIAM SYDNEY   Cabbages and Kings. New York: McClure,
Phillips & Co., 1904. Pictorial cloth. First edition. Primary
binding. There is a neat ink name, and a modicum of light cover
wear. Reese 20-1028 1983 $125

PORTER, WILLIAM SYDNEY   Cabbages and Kings. New York:
McClure, Phillips, 1904. 1st ed., 1st binding. Orig. pictorial
black cloth. Inner hinges strained, but a bright unworn copy, with
all of the green orange stamping intact on spine and cover. Jenkins
155-1019 1983 $100

PORTER, WILLIAM SYDNEY   The Complete Writings of O. Henry.
Garden City: Doubleday, Page, 1917. Fourteen vols. Three quarter
parchment and boards. Illus. by Gordon Grant. One of 1075
numbered sets, signed by the publishers and the artist in the first
volume. Normal offsetting from dust jacket flaps, else a fine set. In
the orig. blue linen dust jackets. Reese 20-1029 1873 $450

PORTER, WILLIAM SYDNEY   The Gentle Grafter. New York:
McClure, 1908. 1st ed., 1st printing, 1st binding. Orig. red
cloth, gilt. Very good. Jenkins 155-1022 1983 $25

PORTER, WILLIAM SYDNEY   Heart of the West by O'Henry. New York:
McClure, 1907. First edition. Orig. brown pictorial cloth. Spine
flecked. Very good. Jenkins 152-337 1983 $125

PORTER, WILLIAM SYDNEY   Options. New York & London: Harper,
1909. Frontis. 1st ed. Orig. green cloth, gilt. Fine copy.
Jenkins 155-1024 1983 $20

PORTER, WILLIAM SYDNEY   Roads of Destiny. New York:
Doubleday, 1909. 1st ed., 1st state with missing "h". Orig. red
cloth, gilt. Fine copy. Jenkins 155-1026 1983 $30

PORTER, WILLIAM SYDNEY   Sixes and Sevens. New York:
Doubleday, 1911. 1st ed. Orig. red cloth, gilt. Very good.
Jenkins 155-1027 1983 $20

PORTER, WILLIAM SYDNEY   Strictly Business. New York:
Doubleday, 1910. 1st ed. Orig. red cloth, gilt. Fine copy.
Jenkins 155-1028 1983 $30

PORTER, WILLIAM SYDNEY   Strictly Business. N.Y., Doubleday,
1910. First edition. Gilt stamped red cloth. Very good. Houle 22-
469 1983 $20

PORTER, WILLIAM SYDNEY   The Trimmed Lamp. N.Y., 1907. First
edition. Cloth. Ink inscription, spine sunned. Covers moderately
soiled. King 45-198 1983 $25

PORTER, WILLIAM SYDNEY   The Trimmed Lamp. N.Y., McClure,
Phillips, 1912. First edition. Gilt stamped red cloth. Very good.
Houle 22-470 1983 $25

PORTER, WILLIAM SIDNEY   The Voice of the City and Other Stories.
NY: Limited Editions Club, 1935. Octavo. Numerous full-page color
illus. by George Grosz. Limited to 1500 copies signed by artist.
Covers slightly rubbed, else very fine with slip-case. Bromer 25-226
1983 $225

PORTER, WILLIAM SYDNEY   Whirligigs. New York: Doubleday,
1910. 1st ed. Orig. red cloth, gilt. Very good. Jenkins 155-1029
1983 $25

PORTER, WILLIAM SYDNEY   Whirligigs. N.Y.: Doubleday, 1910.
First edition. Red gilt stamped cloth. Very good. Houle 22-471 1983
$20

PORTEUS, BEILBY   Sir Ewain. Bell & Daldy. Carlisle:
Charles Thurnhan; Penrith: W. Atkinson, 1860. First edition. Half
title. Orig. green cloth, dulled & browned. Jarndyce 30-822 1983
£10.50

PORTIER, A.   Les arts sauvages: Afrique. Paris:
Albert Morance, ca. 1936. 50 superb collotype plates loose in
portfolio as issued. Folio. Boards, 1/4 cloth. Ties. Rare.
Ars Libri 34-728 1983 $250

PORTLOCK, JOSEPH ELLISON   Report on the Geology of the County of
Londonderry. Dublin, 1843. Folding coloured geological map, 7
plates of sections (5 coloured), 2 plates of views, 45 plates of
fossils and 26 woodcuts, 8vo, original cloth (neatly repaired).
Wheldon 160-1462 1983 £40

PORTLOCK, NATHANIEL   Der Kapitaine Portlock's und Dixon's
Reise um die Welt Besonders nach der Nordwestlichen Kuste von
Amerika wahrend der Jahre 1785 bis 1788 in den Schiffen King George
und Queen Charlotte. Berlin, 1790. 13 plates (several folding),
folding map. Cont. vellum-backed boards. First German edition.
Felcone 21-93 1983 $650

PORTMAN, LIONEL   Hugh Rendal. London: Alston Rivers,
1904. First edition. Orig. cloth. Dust jacket (slightly torn). Fine.
MacManus 280-4239 1983 $30

PORTOGHESI, PAOLO   Borromini. Architettura come linguaggio.
Milano/Roma: Electa/Ugo Bozzi, 1967. Prof. illus. Large square
4to. Cloth. Ars Libri 33-44 1983 $150

PORTOGHESI, PAOLO   The Rome of Borrowmini. NY, 1968.
Folio, slip case. 401 illus. & plates. 8vo, cloth. Salloch 385-381
1983 $75

PORTRAIT and Biographical Album of Lenawee County, Mich.... Chicago, 1888. Portraits and views. Thick large 4to, full orig. morocco, rubbed at corners. Morrill 288-311 1983 $50

PORTRAIT and Biographical Record of Portland and Vicinity Oregon. Chicago: Chapman Publishing Co., 1903. Profusely illustrated, full morocco, gilt. Minor rubbing, else a nice copy. Jenkins 151-263 1983 $200

A PORTRAIT Bust of Harvey Cushing - Ceremonies at the Unveiling. 1949. Wrappers. 8vo. With photographic illustration of the bust. Fye H-3-721 1983 $20

THE PORTS, Harbours, Water-Places, and Coast Scenery of Great Britain. London: George Virtue, 1842. 2 vols, 4to, engraved vignette and printed title-pages, engraved plates. Engraved vignette title pages heavily spotted, some light spotting to remaining plates, library stamps on printed title pages, polished half calf, marbled endpapers, all edges gilt. Deighton 3-130 1983 £310

PORY, JOHN   Lost Description of Plymouth Colony in the Earliest Days of the Pilgrim Fathers. Boston, 1918. Illus. Folding map, small 4to, paper label, ex lib. Argosy 716-100 1983 $35

POSADA, JOSE GUADALUPE   50 Grabados de Jose Guadalupe Posada. Mexico: Instituto Nacional de Bellas Artes, n.d. 50 plates loose in portfolio, as issued. Large 4to. Cloth. Ties. Ars Libri 32-530 1983 $125

POSADA, JOSE GUADALUPE   Primicias litograficas del grabador Jose Guadalupe Posada. Aguascalientes: Privately Printed, 1952. 90 plates with 134 illus., loose in portfolio, as issued. 4to. Orig. wrappers. Edition limited to 600 copies. Ars Libri 32-529 1983 $75

POSNANSKY, ARTHUR   Tihuanacu. The cradle of American man. New York: J.J. Augustin, 1945. 2 vols. in 1. 64 plates. 180 illus. hors texte. 9 folding maps and charts loose in rear pocket. Small folio. Cloth. Text in Spanish and English. Ars Libri 34-430 1983 $150

POSSE, HANS   Der romanische Maler Andrea Sacchi. Leipzig: E.A. Seemann, 1925. 24 plates. 4to. Marbled boards, 3/4 leather. Ars Libri 33-317 1983 $200

POST, CHANDLER RATHFON   A History of European and American Sculpture from the Early Christian Period to the Present Day. Cambridge, 1921. 2 vols., 4to, boards, 1/4 cloth. Ars Libri SB 26-198 1983 $65

POST, MELVILLE DAVISSON   Dwellers in the Hills. New York, 1901. First edition. Pictorial cloth. Fine. Rota 230-475 1983 £20

POSTANS, T.   Personal Observations on Sindh. London, 1843. Coloured frontis. Folding map (slightly spotted), vignettes and illus. Orig. decorated cloth, recased, slight marked and faded. 8vo. Good. Edwards 1044-784 1983 £125

POSTL, KARL   The Americans as they are; Described in a Tour Through the Valley of the Mississippi. London: Hurst, Chance, and Co., 1828. Original cloth with morocco label. Fine copy. Very scarce. First English edition. Jenkins 151-277 1983 $200

POSTLETHWAYT, MALACHY   Great-Britain's Commercial Interest Explained and Improved. W. Owen, 1759. 2 vols: Ad. leaf preceding both titles. Calf, heads of spine sl. worn, labels. Very Good. Jarndyce 31-66 1983 £160

POTONIE, R.   Die Sporae dispersae des Ruhrkarbons. Stuttgart, 1981. 22 plates, 88 figures and 4 tables, 3 parts in 1 vol., 4to, reprint. Wheldon 160-1463 1983 £115

POTTER, BEATRIX   The Fairy Caravan. Phila., McKay, 1929. 6 colour plates, b&w illus. by author. Dark green ribbed cloth with mounted colour pictorial title label fr. cvr. Pub. expressly for America only & only issued in this country in a private numbered ed. Very nice copy. Hodgkins 27-166 1983 £65

POTTER, BEATRIX   Ginger & Pickles. London, 1909. First edition. Illus. by author. Spine restored. Inscription on half-title page. Good. Rota 231-482 1983 £50

POTTER, BEATRIX   Ginger and Pickles. London: Frederick Warne and Co., 1909. First edition. Small 4to. Orig. coloured picture boards. 10 coloured plates and other illus. Spine slightly worn and small stain on upper cover. Traylen 94-673 1983 £30

POTTER, BEATRIX   The Pie and the Patty-Pan. Warne, nd (ca. 1908). Early issue, col'd frontis., 9 col. plates, b&w illus. Dark brown bds. with circular col'd plate, white titling, 2 colour dec. eps., sl. wear top/bottom bkstrip & corners, 1 plate & page creased across bottom, good copy. Hodgkins 27-165 1983 £16

POTTER, BEATRIX   The Roly-Poly Pudding. Warne, 1908. Col. frontis. & title page vignette & 17 col. illus., 35 b&w illus. Maroon cloth with mounted col. illus. fr. cvr., blue titling, col'd pictorial eps., contemp. insc. fr. free ep., lower edges of eps. & last 7 pages lower corner stained red from dye of cvrs., plates have sl. water stain lower edge, sl. thumbing, good copy. Hodgkins 27-164 1983 £30

POTTER, BEATRIX   The Tale of Mrs. Tiggy-Winkle. Warne, 1905. Col. frontis, b&w title vignette, 26 colour plates, printed on one side only. Brown bds. with mounted col. plate fr. cvr., white titling., col'd pictorial eps., sml. piece repaired bottom of bkstrip, contemp. insc. half title & rubber name stamp verso fr. free ep., vg copy. Hodgkins 27-163 1933 £45

POTTER, BEATRIX   The Tale of Mr. Tod. London: Warne, 1912. 12mo. First edition. 15 color plates, many b&w drawings. Fine in printed boards, rubbed at extremities. Color pictorial label. Owner's inscription on blank verso of frontis. Bromer 25-383 1983 $195

POTTER, BEATRIX   The Tale of the Flopsy Bunnies. London: Warne, 1909. 12mo. First edition. Printed on one side only. Color illus. throughout. In printed boards with color pictorial label, slightly rubbed at extremities. Else fine. Bromer 25-382 1983 $195

POTTER, BEATRIX   Wag-by-Wall. Boston, Horn Book Co., 1944. Decorations by J.J. Lankes. Mounted frontis. portrait, title vignette & 4 b&w text illus. Unpaginated. Grey buckram with mounted b&w illus. fr. cvr., red titling, d/w worn top edge with sml. piece missing, vg copy. Hodgkins 27-167 1983 £45

POTTER, JOHN (1674-1747)   Archaeologia Graeca. 1722. 2 vols. 8vo, with altogether 31 plates, many folding, titles in red and black, orig. calf, vol. 2 rebacked. Bickersteth 75-78 1983 £24

POTTER, STEPHEN   D.H. Lawrence: A First Study. London, (1930). First edition. Portrait frontispiece. Black cloth. Fine in chipped and soiled dj. Bradley 64-98 1983 $35

POTTER, STEPHEN   D.H. Lawrence. London: Jonathan Cape, (1930). First edition. 8vo. Illus. Orig. cloth. Fine copy. Jaffe 1-226 1983 $25

POTTER, STEPHEN   D.H. Lawrence - a First Study. London, 1930. First English edition. With the ownership signature of Theodore Roethke. Chipped and rubbed, internally repaired dustwrapper. Very good. Jolliffe 26-449 1983 £25

POTTLE, FREDERICK A.   Boswell and the Girl from Botany Bay. New York: The Viking Press, 1937. First edition. Tall 8vo. Cloth-backed decorated boards, t.e.g., slipcase. Limited to 500 numbered copies. Fine. Oak Knoll 48-67 1983 $65

POTTLE, FREDERICK A.   Boswell and the Girl from Botany Bay. N.Y.: Viking Press, 1937. First edition. Orig. cloth-backed decorated boards. One of 500 copies. Previous owner's inscription on front free endpaper. Endpapers lightly browned. Slightly soiled publisher's box. Very good. MacManus 277-624 1983 $45

POULIOT, J. CAMILLE   Historical Reminder. Quebec and The Isle of Orleans. Quebec, n.p., 1927. 24 1/2cm. Many drawn and photo. illustrations. Printed wrappers. Very good. McGahern 54-147 1983 $20

POULTER, JOHN   The Discoveries of John Poulter...
(Sherbourne): for R. Goadby..., 1753. Seventh edition, with
additions. 8vo. Marbled wrappers. Heath 48-147 1983 £75

POULTON, E. B.   Essays on evolution, 1889-1907. 1908.
8vo, cloth. Wheldon 160-186 1983 £15

POUND, ARTHUR   The Turning Wheel, The Story of General
Motors. Garden City 1934. 1st ed., signed by author and then
president of GM, Alfred P. Sloan. Drawings, cloth, slightly mildewed.
King 46-740 1983 $25

POUND, EZRA   ABC of Reading. London, 1934. First
edition. Covers a little marked. Nice. Rota 230-476 1983 £20

POUND, EZRA   Antheil. Ch., 1927. Edges slightly
rubbed, else very good, bookplate, owner's name. Quill & Brush 54-
1101 1983 $60

POUND, EZRA   Cantos LII-LXXI. London, 1940. First
edition. Fine. Dust wrapper. Rota 230-477 1983 £30

POUND, EZRA   Cathay. London: Elkin Mathews. 1915.
8vo. Wraps. A fine copy. In Our Time 156-635 1983 $375

POUND, EZRA   Cathay. London, 1915. First edition.
Wrappers. Fine. Rota 231-484 1983 £160

POUND, EZRA   The Catholic Anthology. London, 1915.
Corners bumped. Spine darkened and with a half-inch tear, but a very
good copy. Gekoski 2-217 1983 £300

POUND, EZRA   Cavalcanti Poems. (Verona): A New
Directions Book, (1966). First edition. 4to. Orig. vellum-backed
boards. Glassine dust jacket. In publisher's slipcase with paper
label. One of 190 copies designed by Giovanni Mardersteig and
printed in Dante type on the hand-press of the Officina Bodoni.
Signed by Pound. Mint copy. Jaffe 1-305 1983 $775

POUND, EZRA   Eleven New Cantos: XXXI-XLI. New York,
(1934). First edition, first issue, with the F & R emblem on copyright page. Black cloth. In a specially made red cloth folding box
with printed white spine label. Fine in dj. Bradley 64-139 1983
$85

POUND, EZRA   Eleven New Cantos XXXI-XLI. NY, (1934).
One of 1000 copies, first issue, cover slightly dulled and spine let-
tering very lightly rubbed, else near fine, owner's name. Quill &
Brush 54-1103 1983 $40

POUND, EZRA   Gaudier-Brzeska: A Memoir. London:
1916. First binding. Numerous b&w photographic reproductions of
Gaudier-Brzeska's work. 450 copies published. Blind-embossed covers
slightly rubbed at extremities, faintly soiled. Owner's signature.
Bromer 25-86 1983 $200

POUND, EZRA   Jefferson and/or Mussolini. NY, (1936).
Cover slightly stained, corners slightly worn, else near very good in
worn and frayed dustwrapper torn along panel creases, bookplate.
Quill & Brush 54-1104 1983 $75

POUND, EZRA   Letters, 1907-1941. N.Y., (1950).
First edition. Argosy 714-598 1983 $25

POUND, EZRA   "Noh" or Accomplishment. Lon, 1916.
Edges very slightly rubbed, else very good in frayed and slightly
chipped dustwrapper, owner's name. Quill & Brush 54-1099 1983 $300

POUND, EZRA   Personae. London, Elkins Mathews,
1909. First edition. Drab brown boards; uncut; backstrip rubbed.
16mo. Argosy 714-599 1983 $300

POUND, EZRA   Personae. London: 1909. Second binding. Edges of spine slightly rubbed, else fine in boards. Bromer
25-87 1983 $200

POUND, EZRA   Personae, The Collected Poems. NY: 1926.
First edition. Ends of spine slightly rubbed, else about fine. Bromer
25-88 1983 $50

POUND, EZRA   Poems 1918-1921. New York: Boni &
Liveright, (1921). Parchment and boards. First edition. The crown
of the spine is slightly bumped, with a short snag, otherwise a near
fine copy, wanting the scarce dust jacket. Reese 20-785 1983 $85

POUND, EZRA   Poems 1918-21. NY, (1921). Spine darkened and worn (lower edge chipped), corners slightly bumped and worn,
light interior foxing, top edge of boards dented with slight damage to
paper covering, good. Quill & Brush 54-1105 1983 $75

POUND, EZRA   Polite Essays. NY, (n.d.). Cover spotted
along spine, interior has some staining, good, owner's name. Quill &
Brush 54-1106 1983 $35

POUND, EZRA   Quia Pauper Amavi. The Egoist, (1919).
First edition. One of 500 copies. Skilfully rebound to pattern
(orig. green buckram spine with new green paper sides) incorporating
origl paper label. Some foxing throughout. Very nice. Rota 231-485
1983 £100

POUND, EZRA   Sonnets and Ballate of Guido Cavalcanti.
London: Stephen Swift & Co., 1912. First English edition. 8vo,
cloth, A previous owner has written in several alternative translations from the 1931 edition. Argosy 714-600 1983 $65

POWDERMAKE, HORTENSE   Life in Lesu. NY: W. W. Norton, (1933).
Dust jacket. First edition. Gach 95-400 1983 $30

POWEL, GABRIEL   A refutation of an Epistle Apologeti-
call written by a Puritan-Papist... London: printed by Arnold
Hatfield, for Thomas Man Jr., 1605. First edition. Small 4to.
Sewn. A fine copy. Ximenes 63-586 1983 $175

POWELL, ANNE   Clifton, Caractacus, Boadicea, and
other Pieces... Bristol: Albion Press, 1821. First edition. 8vo.
Uncut in orig. quarter blue cloth. Heath 48-400 1983 £30

POWELL, ANTHONY   The Acceptance World. London, 1955.
First English edition. Chipped and strengthened dustwrapper defective
at the head of the spine. Very good. Jolliffe 26-414 1983 £55

POWELL, ANTHONY   From a View to a Death. London,
1948. New revised edition. Edges slightly spotted. In Dustwrapper
with a minute tear. Fine. Jolliffe 26-412 1983 £12.50

POWELL, ANTHONY   The Military Philosophers. London, 1968.
First edition. Dust wrapper. Author's autograph signature on the
title-page and his inscription on the flyleaf. Fine. Rota 231-490
1983 £40

POWELL, ANTHONY   A question of Upbringing. London,
1951. First edition. Slightly soiled dustwrapper, with a couple of
short tears and some creasing at the top of the spine. Gekoski
2-155 1983 £185

POWELL, ANTHONY   A Question of Upbringing. London,
1951. First English edition. Spine slightly rubbed and faded.
Very good. Jolliffe 26-413 1983 £45

POWELL, ANTHONY   The Soldiers Art. London, (1966).
First edition, d.w. This copy was used by Jean Stafford as a review
copy for the American edition. A label from little, Brown reading
"Uncorrected Advance Proof" is pasted on the dust jacket. Inside is
a N.Y. Herald Tribune request for a review. Offset marks from paper
clip on first few pages. Argosy 714-601 1983 $75

POWELL, ANTHONY   The Valley of Bones. London, 1964.
First English edition. Dustwrapper. Very fine. Jolliffe 26-415
1983 £45

POWELL, ENOCH   Casting Off and other poems. London,
1939. First edition. Wrappers torn and marked. Author's initialled
autograph presentation inscription. Nice. Rota 231-491 1983 £30

POWELL, GEORGE D.   The Practice of Medical Electricity.
Dublin: Fannin, 1869. First edition, with 20 illus., large 12mo,
orig. cloth, gilt, a very good copy. With a signed inscription by
the author, dated 1869. Fenning 60-333 1983 £28.50

POWELL, JOHN W.   First Annual Report of the Bureau of
Ethnology 1879-80. Wash., 1881. Thick 4to, orig. cloth, backstrip
ends frayed, shaken. Illus. Color plates, folding (torn but extant.)
Illus. Argosy 716-220 1983 $60

POWELL, LAWRENCE CLARK   The Manuscripts of D.H. Lawrence.
Los Angeles: Los Angeles Public Library, 1937. First edition.
8vo. Stiff paper wrappers. Limited to 750 copies printed at
the Ward Ritchie Press. Covers slightly yellowed. Oak Knoll 48-453
1983 $25

POWELL, LAWRENCE CLARK   Philosopher Pickett. Berkeley, U.
Calif., 1942. First edition, frontis. Dust jacket. Fine. Houle
21-1129 1982 $35

POWELL, LAWRENCE CLARK   To Remember Gregg Anderson. (Los
Angeles), Privately Printed, 1949. First edition. Illus. with 6
halftone plates. Gilt stamped black cloth. Very good. Houle 22-
1155 1983 $80

POWELL, PETER JOHN   People of the Northern Cheyenne Chiefs
and Warrior Societies 1830-1879 with an Epilogue 1969-1974. San
Francisco, 1981. 2 volumes. First edition, boxed. Profusely
illustrated with Indian art in color with excellent text.
Jenkins 151-35 1983 $145

POWELL, PETER JOHN   People of the Sacred Mountain. San
Francisco, (1981). 1st ed. Illus. in color, photographs. 2 vols.,
buckram, in slip case. Clark 741-321 1983 $150, set

POWELL, RICHARD   The Pharmacopoeia of the Royal College
of Physicians of London M.DCCC.IX. London, 1809. 8vo. Old calf.
Top of spine slightly torn. Gurney JJ-349 1983 £25

POWER, D'ARCY   British Masters of Medicine. London,
1936. 8vo. First edition. Orig. binding. Fye H-3-462 1983
$45

POWER, JOHN   A Hand-Book about Books... London:
John Wilson, 1870. First edition. 8vo. Cloth-backed decorated
boards. Illus. Covers rubbed. Oak Knoll 48-326 1983 $85

POWER, MARGUERITE COUNTESS OF BLESSINGTON
Please turn to
BLESSINGTON, MARGUERITE POWER FARMER GARDINER, COUNTESS OF

POWERS, STEPHEN   Afoot and Alone; a Walk from Sea to
Sea by the Southern Route. Hartford, Ct., 1872. First edition.
Illus. A good copy. Jenkins 151-278 1983 $250

POWERS, STEPHEN   Afoot and Alone; A Walk from Sea to Sea
by the Southern Route. Hartford: Columbian Book Co., 1886. Plates.
Ads. Cloth. Signatures. Few gatherings loosening. Later printing.
Dawson 471-234 1983 $30

POWNEY, RICHARD   The Stag Chace in Windsor Forest.
London: Printed for J. Shuckburgh. MDCCXXXIX. Folio, disbound.
First edition. Quaritch NS 7-111 1983 $350

POWYS, JOHN COWPER   The Art of Happiness. London: John Lane,
The Bodley Head, (1935). First English edition. Orig. cloth. Dust
jacket. Very fine. MacManus 280-4243 1983 $85

POWYS, JOHN COWPER   Autobiography. N.Y.: Simon & Schuster,
1934. First edition. Illus. Orig. cloth. Very good. MacManus 280-
4244 1983 $25

POWYS, JOHN COWPER   Dostoievsky. London, 1946. First
English edition. Front free endpaper very slightly spotted. Dustwrapper with a single nick. Fine. Jolliffe 26-416 1983 £15

POWYS, JOHN COWPER   Ducdame. London, 1925. First English
edition. Spine darkened and marked. Good. Rota 230-484 1983 £17.50

POWYS, JOHN COWPER   The English House. Benn's Sixpenny
Library, 1929. First edition. Wrappers. Head and foot of backstrip
worn. Very good. Rota 231-492 1983 £12

POWYS, JOHN COWPER   Enjoyment of Literature. N.Y.: Simon &
Schuster, 1938. First edition. Orig. cloth. Dust jacket (slightly
worn, darkened, price clipped). Former owner's inscription on front
free endpaper. Good. MacManus 280-4246 1983 $20

POWYS, JOHN COWPER   Jobber Skald. London, 1935. First
English edition, revised. Covers marked and faded. Label on flyleaf.
Good. Rota 230-485 1983 £15

POWYS, JOHN COWPER   Lucifer. London: Macdonald, (1956).
First edition. With wood engravings by A. M. Parker. Orig. half
morocco & cloth. Acetate dust jacket. Limited to 560 copies signed
by Powys. Small bookplate on front endsheet. Very fine. MacManus
280-4247 1983 $85

POWYS, JOHN COWPER   Mandragora. New York, 1917. First
edition. Edges of covers a little faded. Bookplate. Very nice.
Rota 230-483 1983 £100

POWYS, JOHN COWPER   Mandragora: Poems. N.Y., 1917.
12mo, cloth; slightly rubbed. First edition. Argosy 714-602 1983
$45

POWYS, JOHN COWPER   The Meaning of Culture. London: Jonathan Cape, (1930). First English edition. Orig. cloth. Dust jacket
(very slightly rubbed). Bookplate of Sybil Waller on front endsheet.
Fine. MacManus 280-4248 1983 $65

POWYS, JOHN COWPER   Owen Glendower. N.Y.: Simon & Schuster,
1940. First edition. 2 vols. Orig. cloth, in publisher's box (lacks
its cellophane window and is somewhat dusty and worn). Fine. Mac-
Manus 280-4249 1983 $85

POWYS, JOHN COWPER   Poems. London: William Rider & Son,
1899. First edition. Orig. decorated cloth. Presentation copy
inscribed: "From J.C.P. June 1900." Covers slightly soiled, corners
slightly worn. Very good. MacManus 280-4250 1983 $750

POWYS, JOHN COWPER   Visions and Revisions. London: William
Rider & Son, Ltd., 1915. First edition. Orig. cloth-backed boards.
Covers lightly soiled. Former owner's signature on free endpaper.
Good. MacManus 280-4251 1983 $35

POWYS, JOHN COWPER   The War and Culture. N.Y.: G. Arnold
Shaw, 1914. First edition. Small 8vo. Orig. cloth. Extremities of
spine & edges a bit chewed. Good. MacManus 280-4252 1983 $25

POWYS, JOHN COWPER   Weymouth Sands. New York, 1934. 8vo.
Cloth. A collector's copy, as new in dj. In Our Time 156-638 1983
$150

POWYS, JOHN COWPER   Wolf Solent. New York, 1929. 2 vols.
8vo. Cloth. This set is specially signed by Powys. A fine set,
lacking the jackets. In Our Time 156-637 1983 $100

POWYS, JOHN COWPER   Wood and Stone. N.Y.: G. Arnold Shaw,
1915. First edition. Orig. cloth. Head and foot of spine a bit worn.
Good. MacManus 280-4252a 1983 $85

POWYS, JOHN COWPER   Wood and Stone. New York, 1915. 8vo.
Cloth. A vg-fine copy. In Our Time 156-636 1983 $50

POWYS, LAURENCE   Winter Again. N.p., (1931). Small 4to,
full page illus. One of 100 copies numbered and signed. Colophon
title: "Blue Moon Poem for Christmas, 1931." Fine. Houle 22-728
1983 $95

POWYS, LLEWELYN   Black Laughter. London, 1925. First
English edition. Spine and edges of covers a little darkened. Bookplate. Nice. Rota 230-486 1983 £20

POWYS, LLEWELYN   Glory of Life. London: the Golden
Cockerel Press, 1934. Folio. Quarter white vellum, cloth, sides,
t.e.g., others uncut. 15 wood-engravings by Robert Gibbings, printed
in red and black. Limited edition of 277 numbered copies. Traylen
94-674 1983 £290

POWYS, LLEWELYN   Skin For Skin. L, 1926. One of 900 numbered copies, spine edges slightly rubbed, minor interior foxing, else very good. Quill & Brush 54-1115 1983 $40

POWYS, LLEWELYN   Skin for Skin. London, 1926. First English edition. One of 900 numbered copies. Head and foot of spine a little rubbed. Very nice. Rota 231-494 1983 £15

POWYS, LLEWELYN   The Verdict of Bridlegoose. New York, 1926. First edition. Spine a little creased. Nice. Rota 231-495 1983 £15

POWYS, THEODORE FRANCIS   Black Bryony. London: Chatto & Windus, 1923. First edition. Five woodcuts by R.A. Garnett. 8vo. Orig. cloth with paper label. Fine copy. Jaffe 1-308 1983 $75

POWYS, THEODORE FRANCIS   Captain Patch. Twenty-One Stories. London: Chatto & Windus, 1935. First edition. 8vo. Orig. cloth. Dust jacket. A fine copy. Jaffe 1-326 1983 $75

POWYS, THEDORE FRANCIS   Christ in the Cupboard. London: E. Lahr, 1930. First edition. 8vo. Frontis. Orig. wrappers. Limited to 500 copies signed by the author. Very fine copy. Jaffe 1-317 1983 $75

POWYS, THEODORE FRANCIS   The Dewpond. London: Elkin Mathews & Marrot, 1928. First edition. 8vo. Orig. decorated boards. Dust jacket. One of 530 copies signed by the author. Very fine copy. Jaffe 1-314 1983 $75

POWYS, THEODORE FRANCIS   Fables. London: Chatto & Windus, 1929. First edition. Four drawings by Gilbert Spences. Tall 8vo, orig. cloth with leather label. Dust jacket. Limited to 750 copies signed by the author. Slightly dust-soiled jacket. Fine copy. Jaffe 1-315 1983 $125

POWYS, THEODORE FRANCIS   Fables. Chatto & Windus, 1929. First edition, 8vo, orig. green buckram, t.e.g., leather spine label, a fine copy in the dust wrapper. Ltd. edition of 75- numbered copies on large paper signed by the author. Fenning 62-290 1983 £38.50

POWYS, THEODORE FRANCIS   Innocent Birds. London: Chatto & Windus, 1926. First edition. 8vo. Orig. cloth. Dust jacket slightly soiled and nicked, but a very good copy. Jaffe 1-312 1983 $60

POWYS, THEODORE FRANCIS   An Interpretation of Genesis. London: Chatto & Windus, 1929. First edition. 4to. Orig. cloth-backed decorated boards. Slightly chipped dust jacket. Fine copy. Jaffe 1-316 1983 $125

POWYS, THEODORE FRANCIS   An Interpretation of Genesis. Chatto and Windus, 1929. First edition, roy. 8vo, orig. buckram-backed patterned boards, t.e.g. A fine copy in the dust wrapper. Ltd. edition of 490 copies, numbered and signed by the author. Fenning 62-291 1983 £45

POWYS, THEODORE FRANCIS   The Key Of The Field. London: William Jackson (Books) Ltd, 1930. First edition. Woodcut by R.A. Garnett. 4to. Orig. cloth. Limited to 550 copies signed by the author. Fine copy. Jaffe 1-319 1983 $60

POWYS, THEODORE FRANCIS   Kindness in a Corner. London: Chatto & Windus, 1930. First edition. 8vo. Orig. cloth. Dust jacket, slightly soiled and chipped, front free endpaper browned, otherwise a very good copy. Jaffe 1-320 1983 $45

POWYS, THEODORE FRANCIS   The Left Leg. London: Chatto & Windus, 1923. First edition. 8vo. Orig. cloth with paper label. Dust jacket with darkened spine, otherwise a fine copy. Jaffe 1-309 1983 $75

POWYS, THEODORE FRANCIS   Mark Only. London: Chatto & Windus, 1924. First edition. 8vo. Orig. cloth with paper label. Dust jacket. Fine copy. Jaffe 1-310 1983 $75

POWYS, THEODORE FRANCIS   Mr. Tasker's Gods. London: Chatto & Windus, 1925. First edition. Orig. cloth. Dust jacket. In a half-morocco slipcase. Fine. MacManus 280-4253a 1983 $100

POWYS, THEODORE FRANCIS   Mr. Tasker's Gods. London, 1925. First edition. Spine a little faded. Dust wrapper. Author's signed autograph presentation inscription. Very nice. Rota 230-487 1983 £45

POWYS, THEODORE FRANCIS   Mr. Weston's Good Wine. London: Chatto & Windus, 1927. First edition. With drawings by George Charlton. Tall 8vo. Orig. black cloth. One of 660 copies signed by the author. Fine copy. Jaffe 1-313 1983 $125

POWYS, THEODORE FRANCIS   Mr. Weston's Good Wine. L, 1927. No. 311 of 660 numbered and signed copies, illus. by George Charlton, slight wear and soiling to cover, else very good. Quill & Brush 54-1116 1983 $60

POWYS, THEODORE FRANCIS   Mockery Gap. London: Chatto & Windus, 1925. First edition. 8vo. Orig. cloth with paper label. Dust jacket a trifle nicked at base of spine, otherwise a fine copy. Jaffe 1-311 1983 $65

POWYS, THEODORE FRANCIS   The Only Penitent. London, 1931. First edition. Frayed dust wrapper. Very nice. Rota 230-488 1983 £12.50

POWYS, THEODORE FRANCIS   The Soliloquy of A Hermit. New York: G. Arnold Shaw, 1916. First edition. 8vo. Frontis. portrait. Orig. cloth. Presentation copy from the author's brother, J.C. Powys, inscribed on the front flyleaf. Spine dulled, but a fine copy. Jaffe 1-306 1983 $500

POWYS, THEODORE FRANCIS   Soliloquies Of A Hermit. London: Andrew Melrose Ltd., 1918. First English edition, first issue. 8vo. Orig. cloth-backed pale blue boards. Dust jacket (rare), lightly dust-soiled and chipped, otherwise a fine copy. Jaffe 1-307 1983 $450

POWYS, THEODORE FRANCIS   Soliloquies of a Hermit. London: Andrew Melrose Ltd., 1918. First English edition, first issue. Orig. cloth-backed boards, in a later (1926) dust jacket. Fine. MacManus 280-4254 1983 $100

POWYS, THEODORE FRANCIS   Soliloquies of a Hermit. London, 1918. First English edition of "The Soliloquy of a Hermit". Frayed dust wrapper. Very good. Rota 231-496 1983 £45

POWYS, THEODORE FRANCIS   The Two Thieves. London: Chatto & Windus, 1932. First edition. 8vo. Orig. cloth. Dust jacket, with short tear, otherwise a fine copy. Jaffe 1-325 1983 $60

POWYS, THEODORE FRANCIS   Unclay. Chatto & Windus, 1931. First edition, 8vo, orig. buckram-backed marbled boards, t.e.g. A fine copy. Ltd. edition of 160 copies, numbered and signed by the author. Fenning 62-292 1983 £55

POWYS, THEODORE FRANCIS   Unclay. London: Chatto & Windus, 1931. First edition. 8vo. Orig. cloth. Dust jacket. Very fine copy. Jaffe 1-324 1983 $75

POWYS, THEODORE FRANCIS   Uncle Dottery. Bristol: Douglas Cleverdon, 1930. First edition. 2 wood-engravings by Eric Gill. Thin 8vo. Orig. cloth-backed boards. Limited to 350 copies signed by Powys. Very fine copy. Jaffe 1-322 1983 $185

POWYS, THEODORE FRANCIS   Uriah on the Hill. Cambridge: The Minority Press, 1930. First edition. 8vo. Orig. wrappers. With the publisher's prospectus laid in. Fine copy. Jaffe 1-318 1983 $35

POWYS, THEODORE FRANCIS   When Thou Wast Naked. Reading, Berks.: The Golden Cockerel Press, 1931. First edition. Engravings by John Nash. 4to. Orig. half-morocco and decorated boards. Tissue jacket. Limited to 500 copies signed by the author. Very fine copy. Jaffe 1-323 1983 $175

POWYS, THEODORE FRANCIS   The White Paternoster And Other Stories. London: Chatto & Windus, 1930. First edition. 8vo. Orig. cloth. Dust jacket. Fine copy. Jaffe 1-321 1983 $75

POZZO, AGOSTINO   Puteo, A Gnominices Biformis, Geometricae, scilicet, & Arithmetical Synopsis, In quatour partes diuisa. Venetiis, Typis Antonij Bosij, M.DCLXXIX (1679). 4to, some light waterstaining, lightly toned throughout. Bound in full vellum. Title in MS on spine. First edition. Good. Arkway 22-71 1983 $625

PRACTICAL economy; or, the application of modern discoveries to the purposes of domestic life. London: Colburn, 1821. First edition. Large 12mo. Orig. blue boards, drab paper backstrip, printed paper label. Spine worn and partly split. Ximenes 63-87 1983 $85

PRAETORIUS, HIERONYMUS   Cantiones Sacrae de Praecipuis Festis Totius Anni. Hamburg, Philipp de Ohr, 1599. Music type-set, with large woodcut initials. Title within wide woodcut border. 4to, 1/2 calf. Salloch 387-182 1983 $225

PRAMPOLINI, GIACOMO   Franco Lombardi. Milano: Amilcare Pizzi, 1950. 51 gravure plates. 4to. Wrappers. Edition limited to 1000 numbered copies. Ars Libri 33-503 1983 $20

PRANG, LOUIS   Prang's Standard Alphabets. Boston: L. Prang & Co., 1886. Revised edition. Oblong 8vo. Orig. cloth. 39 leafs of which 36 are full page plates. Includes an illum. title page, tinted specimens of alphabets, five illuminated plates and two plates of colored maps. Minor cover wear and an early ink inscription on the front free endpaper. Oak Knoll 48-111 1983 $275

PRASSE, LEONA E.   Lyonel Feininger. Das graphische Werk. Berlin/Cleveland: Gebr. Mann/Cleveland Museum of Art, 1971. Prof. illus. Large 4to. Cloth. Ars Libri 32-217 1983 $100

PRATT, A. E.   Two Years Among the New Guinea Cannibles. London, 1906. Second edition. Folding map, plates, some wear. 8vo. Presentation inscription on the half title from the co-author. Good. Edwards 1044-573 1983 £30

PRATT, ANNE (1806-1893)   The Flowering Plants, Grasses, Sedges and Ferns of Great Britain. 1899-1905. New edition, revised, 5 plain and 319 coloured plates, 4 vols. in original 12 parts, royal 8vo, original decorated wrappers (spines worn). Two leaves of contents of vol. 4 carelessly opened, else a good copy. Best edition of this standard work. Wheldon 160-1624 1983 £100

PRATT, ANNE (1806-1893)   Poisonous, noxious, and suspected plants of our fields and woods. S.P.C.K., (1857). 44 coloured plates, 12mo, original cloth, trifle worn and loose. Very scarce. Wheldon 160-2183 1983 £20

PRATT, JOSEPH   A Year with Osler 1896-1897... Baltimore, 1949. First edition. 8vo. Orig. binding. Fye H-3-892 1983 $40

PRATT, JULIUS H.   Reminiscences, Personal and Otherwise. N.p., 1910. Frontis. and plates. Orig. cloth. 1st ed. Privately printed. Presentation copy from author. Scarce. Fine copy. Jenkins 153-443 1983 $85

PRATT, JULIUS H.   Reminiscences, Personal and Otherwise. N.p., 1910. Orig. cloth. Illus. Ginsberg 47-808 1983 $75

PRATT, ORSON   Divine Authenticity of the Book of Mormon. (Liverpool, 1851). Complete in 6 parts. Cloth. Ginsberg 47-601 1983 $60

PRATT, ORSON   Remarkable Visions. (Liverpool, 1848). Dbd. Ginsberg 47-602 1983 $35

PRATT, SAMUEL JACKSON   Emma Corbett. London: for R. Baldwin, 1783. Seventh edition. 2 vols. Small 8vo. Cont. calf. Engraved frontis. to each vol. Heath 48-380 1983 £45

PRATT, SAMUEL JACKSON   The Tutor of Truth. Richard and Urquhart, 1779. In two vols. 12mo, half titles, wormed in bottom margin vol. II. Calf, spines gilt, red and green labels. First edition. Jarndyce 31-67 1983 £240

PRATT, TINSLEY   Wordsworth at Rydal. John Heywood, Manchester, 1897. First edition, half title, orig. blue boards, cream spine, sl. chipped, v.g. Jarndyce 31-865 1983 £20

PRAVAZ, C.-G.   Considerations sur quelques Anomalies de la Vision. Paris, n.d. (ca. 1825). 8vo. Cloth. Gurney JJ-329 1983 £10.50

PRAZ, MARIO   The Romantic Agony. London, 1933. First English edition. Frayed dust wrapper. Fine. Rota 230-489 1983 £15

PRAZ, MARIO   Studies in Seventeenth Century Imagery. Rome: Edizioni di Storia e Letteratura. 1964. Tall 8vo, illus. Cloth; dust jacket. Second edition. Karmiole 73-19 1983 $75

PREBLE, GEORGE HENRY   A Chronological History of the Origin and Development of Steam Navigation. Philadelphia, 1883. 1st ed. 8vo. Ex-library, rubbed. Morrill 289-508 1983 $47.50

PRECERUTTI GARBERI, MERCEDES Giambattista Tiepolo: gli affreschi. Torino: ERI. Edizioni RAI. Radiotelevisione Italiana, 1970. 40 color plates under passepartouts and 54 monochrome illus. in text. Small folio. Cloth, 1/4 calf. Slipcase. Edition limited to 600 copies, printed for the Amici della Sipra. Ars Libri 33-360 1983 $150

PREETORIUS, EMIL   Emil Preetorius. Das szenische Werk. Berlin/Wien: Albert Limbach, 1941. 86 plates (13 color hors texte). 4to. Cloth. Ars Libri 32-539 1983 $75

PREGL, FRITZ   Quantitative Organic Microanalysis. London, 1924. First English edition. 8vo. Cloth. Gurney JJ-330 1983 £20

PRENTICE, ARCHIBALD   History of the Anti-Corn-Law League. W. & F. G. Cash, 1853. First edition, half calf, label, v.g. Jarndyce 31-338 1983 £72

PRENTISS, CHARLES   The Life of the Late Gen. William Eaton. Brookfield: E. Merriam & Co., 1813. First edition. Full calf, (lacks port., one corner darkened). Argosy 716-545 1983 $50

PRENTISS, JOHN   A Sermon, Preached at Holliston... Cambridge, 1812. Stitched, very good. Reese 18-393 1983 $20

PREPARATORY studies for political reformers. London: Baldwin, 1810. 8vo. Orig. drab boards, blue printed paper label. First edition. Spine and corners a bit worn. Ximenes 63-468 1983 $75

PRESBYTERIAN Church in the U. S. Elizabethtown: Mervin Hale, 1821. Calf, lea. label. Argosy 710-75 1983 $40

PRESCOTT, WILLIAM HICKLING (1796-1859)   History of the Conquest of Mexico. London: Bentley, 1843. 3 vols. Complete, titles printed in red and black. 3 portraits, 2 folding maps, 1 plate. Cont. 3/4 green calf over marbled boards. Spines gilt with raised bands. First English edition. Jenkins 152-741 1983 $375

PRESCOTT, WILLIAM HICKLING (1798-1859)   History of the Conquest of Mexico. New York: Harper, 1843. First edition, first printing with early readings in first two vols. and errata in vol. 3. 3 vols. 3 portraits, 2 double-page maps, plate. Orig. blue-green H cloth, gilt. Extremely bright fresh set. Jenkins 155-1033 1983 $400

PRESCOTT, WILLIAM HICKLING (1796-1859)   History of the Conquest of Mexico. London: Bentley, 1847. Third edition. Half titles. Frontis. Full tan calf by Tout, spines decorated in gilt, contrasting red and green leather spine labels, covers ruled in gilt, gilt inner dentelles, t.e.g., marbled endpapers. 3 vols. Very good. Houle 22-1158 1983 $295

PRESCOTT, WILLIAM HICKLING (1798-1859)   History of the Conquest of Mexico. Philadelphia, (1873). 3 vols. Illus. 12mo. Clark 741-341 1983 $26.50

PRESCOTT, WILLIAM HICKLING (1798-1859)   History of the Conquest of Mexico. Phila.: (ca. 1890). 3 vols. 3 portraits, 2 maps, facs. signature. 12mo. Cont. half calf, leather labels (one partly eradicated), g.t. Argosy 710-307 1983 $35

PRESCOTT, WILLIAM HICKLING (1798-1859)   History of the Conquest of Peru. Phila.: 1864. 2 vols. Frontis. 8vo. Straight-grained morocco, g.t. Argosy 710-511 1983 $50

PRESCOTT, WILLIAM HICKLING (1796-1859)   History of the Reign of
Charles the Fifth. London: Routledge, 1851. First edition. Half
titles in volume 2. Frontis. Full tan calf by Tout. Spines richly
decorated in gilt, contrasting red and green leather spine labels,
covers ruled in gilt, gilt inner dentelles, t.e.g., marbled endpapers.
2 vols. Very good. Houle 22-730 1983 $195

PRESCOTT, WILLIAM HICKLING (1796-1859)   History of the Reign of
Ferdinand and Isabella. London: Bentley, 1838. First edition. Half
titles. Frontis. Full polished tan calf by Tout, spines richly decorated in gilt, contrasting red and green leather spine labels, covers
ruled in gilt, gilt inner dentelles, t.e.g., marbled endpapers. 3 vols.
Very good. Houle 22-731 1983 $275

PRESCOTT, WILLIAM HICKLING (1796-1859)   History of the Reign of
Philip the Second, King of Spain. London: Bentley, 1855-59. First
English edition. 2 half titles. Frontis., folding facs. Full tan
calf by Tout, spines richly decorated in gilt, contrasting red and
green leather spine labels, covers ruled in gilt, gilt inner dentelles,
t.e.g., marbled endpapers (small nick). 3 vols. Very good. Houle 22-
732 1983 $185

PRESCOTT, WILLIAM HICKLING (1796-1859)   Works. Phila.: Lippincott,
(1904). Montezuma edition. Illus. with steel engr., black & white
drawings, and maps. Blue cloth, paper labels, t.e.g., uncut. 22 vols,
complete. One of 1,000 sets. Very good. Houle 22-1159 1983 $375

PRESCOTT, WILLIAM HICKLING (1796-1859)   Works. London, 1857-62.
15 vols. Cr. 8vo. Cont. half blue calf, gilt, gilt panelled spines
with red and brown morocco labels, gilt. Engr. portraits. Traylen
94-675 1983 £140

THE PRESCRIBER'S Pharmacopoeia... London, 1864. Fifth edition.
12mo. Orig. cloth, back slightly torn. Gurney JJ-331 1983 £10.50

THE PRESENT Alteration in Religion in France. Printed for Rich. Janeway, 1682. First edition, 4to, wrapper, lightly dampstained in the
outer margins, which are a little frayed in the lower outer corner,
a good sound copy. Fenning 61-356 1983 £14.50

PRESENT-DAY American Stories. New York, 1929. 8vo. Cloth. Few
pages near the end carelessly opened, else fine in dj. In Our Time
156-14 1983 $45

A PRESENT for a Husband or Wife. Springfield (Mass.), G. & C.
Merriam, 1833. Orig. roan. Prob. 1st ed. Morrill 286-404 1983
$25

THE PRESENT state of the stage in Great-Britain and Ireland. And the
theatrical characters of the principal performers, in both kingdoms,
impartially considered. London: printed for Paul Vaillant; and M.
Cooper, 1753. 8vo, wrappers, first edition. A fine large copy.
Ximenes 64-441 1983 $450

PRESENT Times and Modern Manners; or, Tale of a Rector's Family.
London: Appleyards, 1810. First (only) edition, 12mo, 4 vols.,
cont. qtr. calf gilt, boards. A very uncommon title. A fine copy.
Trebizond 18-47 1983 $350

THE PRESIDENTS of the United States 1789-1898. NY, (1898). Illus.,
plates, 8vo, 3/4 mor., g.t. Argosy 710-420 1983 $30

PRESTON, CHLOE   Somebody's Darlings. Raphael Tuck, n.d.
4to. Colour frontis. Colour title vignette. 12 colour plates,
printed on thick board. Colour pictorial boards, extra designs on both
boards, edges bumped. Greer 39-98 1983 £45

PRESTON, GEORGE H.   Hawkeye, A Sequel to the Deerslayer.
Cincinnati: Razall, 1897. Frontis., illus. 1st ed. Orig. pictorial cloth, gilt. Very good copy of this scarce novel. Jenkins
155-249 1983 $35

PRESTON, HAYTER   The House of Vanities. London: John
Lane, The Bodley Head, 1922. First edition. Illus. by C.L. Fraser.
Orig. decorated stiff wrappers with pink advertisement label on front
cover (label slightly faded and chipped). Spine darkened, worn and
cracking. Covers a trifle soiled, with slight foxing to the endpapers.
Good. MacManus 278-2018 1983 $85

PRESTON, WILLIAM   Journal in Mexico. (Paris): Privately
printed, (1937). 4to, designed by Jack Kahane. Bound in maroon
morocco, ruled in black and gilt, with additional onlays in red,
gold and green. Binding sl. rubbed in a few places. T.e.g.
Bookplates mounted inside front cover and on front blanks. With a
tipped-in letter from Galignani's bookstore in Paris, signed by
Galignani, indicating that this is a specially bound copy. Karmiole
76-90 1983 $300

PRETTY Tales for the Nursery. London: Religious Tract Society, n.d.
(ca.1840). 8vo. Blind stamped red cloth. Gilt decoration. A.e.g.
Light wear. Illus. with 4 color plates by Kronheim. Very good.
Aleph-bet 8-209 1983 $50

PREUSS, JULIUS   Biblisch-Talmudische Medizin. Berlin,
1921. 4to, cloth. Argosy 713-438 1983 $175

PREVERT, JACQUES   Miro. Paris: Maeght, 1956. 8 orig.
color lithographs (4 folding). Prof. illus. Square 4to. Wrappers.
Lithographs printed by Mourlot. Soiled. Ars Libri 32-462 1983
$135

PREVIATI, GAETANO   Lettere al fratello. Milano: Ulrico
Hoepli, 1946. 28 plates. Wrappers. Dust jacket. Ars Libri 33-
566 1983 $20

PREVOST D'EXILES, ANTOINE FRANCOIS   The History of a Fair Greek...
London, J. Roberts, 1741. 2 vols., 12mo, orig. calf gilt, hinges
worn, one joint broken, bookplates. First edition in English.
Ravenstree 96-149 1983 $215

PREYER, W.   Die Entdeckung des Hypnotismus. Berlin:
Paetel, 1881. First edition. 8vo. Quarter-cloth. Inner margin of
title slightly torn. Gurney 90-24 1983 £70

PREYER, W   Mental Development in the Child. NY:
D. Appleton & Co., 1897 (1893). 12mo. Ads at front and back.
Publisher's decorative green cloth. Gach 94-623 1983 $20

PRIBRAM, ALFRED   Der Acute Gelenkrheumatismus. Wien,
1899. Thick tall 8vo, cloth. Illus. Argosy 713-439 1983 $75

PRICE, D.   Chronological Retrospect. London, 1811.
First edition. 3 vols. in 4. 4to. Occasional spotting. Half morocco
by Riviere. Spines ornately gilt in compartments. Good. Edwards 1044-
574 1983 £750

PRICE, ELEANOR C.   Red Towers. London: Richard Bentley &
Son, 1889. First edition. 3 vols. Orig. cloth. Signed by author on
the verso of the front free endpaper of Vol one. dated Dec. 15, 1888,
(signed same place in vol. two). Spines faded. Fine. MacManus 280-
4256 1983 $200

PRICE, FREDERICK NEWLIN   The Etchings and Lithographs of
Arthur B. Davies. New York/London: Mitchell Kennerly/Morley &
Mitchell Kennerly, 1929. 205 plates. Frontis. Large 4to. Cloth.
T.e.g. Ars Libri 32-148 1983 $225

PRICE, LIAM   The Place-Names of Co. Wicklow.
Dublin, 1945-46-49-53. Nos. 1-4. 8vo, cloth, the orig. upper printed
paper wraps. preserved. Fenning 61-357 1983 £21.50

PRICE, MARGARET EVANS   A Child's Book of Myths. Chicago: Rand.,
(1924, ed. of 1929). 4to. Cloth. Pictorial paste-on. Color plates
and text color illus. Fine. Aleph-bet 8-210 1983 $40

PRICE, MARGARET EVANS   Once Upon a Time. Chicago: Rand.,
(1921). First edition. Folio. Blue cloth. Pictorial paste-on
(small rip). Color illus. throughout. Very good to fine. Aleph-bet
8-211 1983 $40

PRICE, REYNOLDS   Nine Mysteries. (Winston-Salem):
Palaemon Press, (1979). Cloth. First edition. One of 309 numbered
copies, signed by the author. Mint as issued. Reese 20-795 1983
$75

PRICE, RICHARD   Observations on the Nature of Civil
Liberty, the Principles of Government, and the Justice and Policy
of the War with America. London, 1776. 3rd edition of 13 printed
that year in London. Disbound. Argosy 710-458 1983 $50

PRICE, RICHARD   Observations on the Importance of the American Revolution. Trenton: Isaac Collins, 1785. Later half morocco. Printed on paper manufactured in Trenton at the Potts & Reynolds mill, with the watermark clearly visible on several pages. Fine. Felcone 19-46 1983 $175

PRICHARD, JAMES C.   The Natural History of Man. H. Bailliere, 1848. With 55 engraved plates, including 50 coloured plates, and with some 100 text illus., 8vo, recent half calf, gilt. Fenning 60-335 1983 £95

PRIDEAUX, HUMPHREY   The True Nature of Imposture fully Displayed in the Life of Mahomet. Printed for William Rogers, 1697. Cont. calf, rebacked. A good copy. First edition. Bickersteth 77-63 1983 £70

PRIDEAUX, HUMPHREY   The True Nature of Imposture Fully Display'd in the Life of Mahomet. London, Printed for William Rogers, 1697. 8vo, cont. calf, front cover loose, worn. Ravenstree 97-169 1983 $41

PRIDEAUX, HUMPHREY   The True Nature of Imposture Fully Display'd in the Life of Mahomet. London: William Rogers, 1698. 8vo, 2 parts in 1. Cont. calf; minor rubbing. Karmiole 73-84 1983 $175

PRIDEAUX, HUMPHREY   The Validity of the Orders of the Church of England. Printed by John Richardson for Brabazon Aylmer, 1688. First edition, 4to, wrapper, a very good copy. Fenning 61-358 1983 £14.50

PRIDEAUX, S. T.   Bookbinders and Their Craft. NY: Scribner's, 1903. Octavo. First American edition. Limited to 500 copies. Fine in slightly darkened boards with dust wrapper lacking about one third of spine. Bromer 25-149 1983 $325

PRIDEAUX, S. T.   Bookbinders and their Craft. New York: Charles Scribner's Sons, 1903. First edition. Tall 8vo. Parchment-backed boards, t.e.g, others uncut, dust jacket, slipcase. Limited to 500 numbered copies. Numerous photographs. Partially broken slipcase. Fine. Oak Knoll 48-36 1983 $250

PRIDEAUX, WILLIAM FRANCIS (1840-1914)   Notes for a Bibliography of Edward Fitzgerald. London: Frank Hollings, 1901. First edition. 12mo. Cloth. From the library of Thomas Mosher with Prideaux's card tipped in presenting this book to Mosher. Bookplate. Extremities worn, cover soiled. Oak Knoll 49-442 1983 $65

PRIEST, JOSIAH   American Antiquities and Discoveries in the West. Albany, 1835. Illus., two folding plates. Full calf (rear hinge neatly glued). Felcone 22-195 1983 $35

PRIEST, JOSIAH   A View of the Expected Christian Millennium... Albany: Published for Subscribers, 1828. Very large folding engraved frontis. Old calf, a bit dry. A very good copy. Reese 18-625 1983 $40

PRIEST, WILLIAM   Travels in the United States of America, 1793-1797. London: J. Johnson, 1802. First edition. Frontis. in color. Half calf, morocco label. Foxed. Jenkins 152-744 1983 $350

PRIEST, WILLIAM   Travels in the United States of America. London: J. Johnson, 1802. Colored frontis. Orig. boards (rubbed), rebacked in cloth. First edition. Felcone 22-196 1983 $100

PRIESTLEY, JOHN BOYNTON   Albert Goes Through. London: William Heinemann Ltd., (1933). Proof copy of the first edition. Illus. by E. Blampied. Orig. wrappers (faded and a bit chipped). Good. MacManus 280-4257 1983 $35

PRIESTLEY, JOHN BOYNTON   Brief Diversions. Cambridge: Bowes & Bowes, 1922. First edition. Orig. cloth-backed boards with paper label. Very good. MacManus 280-4260 1983 $50

PRIESTLEY, JOHN BOYNTON   Faraway. London, (1932). First edition. One of 25 copies with a special title-page by K. Hobson. Specially bound in full green levant morocco with onlaid design in blue, brown and black morocco on upper cover by H.T. Wood Ltd. Front endpapers a little soiled. Very nice. Rota 230-490 1983 £75

PRIESTLEY, JOHN BOYNTON   Midnight on the Desert. New York, 1937. Second edition. Dark blue cloth. Nice copy in jacket. Bradley 65-12 1983 $20

PRIESTLEY, JOHN BOYNTON   Paper From Lilliput. Cambridge: Bowes & Bowes, 1922. First edition. Orig. cloth-backed boards with paper spine label. Dust jacket (worn and faded). Near-fine. MacManus 280-4266 1983 $65

PRIESTLEY, JOHN BOYNTON   The Town Major of Miraucourt. London: William Heinemann, 1930. First edition. Orig. full vellum. In publisher's box. One of 525 copies signed by author. Small bookplate. Fine. MacManus 280-4269 1983 $25

PRIESTLY, JOSEPH   Discourses on Various Subjects. Northumberland (PA): John Binns, 1805. 8vo, disbound, ex-library. Argosy 710-76 1983 $35

PRIESTLEY, JOSEPH   A free address to Protestant dissenters, on the subject of the Lord's Supper. London: J. Johnson, 1768. First edition. 8vo. Disbound. Scarce. Ximenes 63-587 1983 $75

PRIESTLEY, JOSEPH   Experiments and Observations on Different Kinds of Air, and Other Branches of Natural Philosophy, Connected with the Subject. By Thomas Pearson, Birmingham, 1790. 3 vols., 8vo, with 9 folding engraved plates; foxed; cont. half russia, spines chipped, joints cracked. Quaritch NS 5-87 1983 $365

PRIESTLEY, JOSEPH   The History of the Present State of Discoveries relating to Vision, Light, and Colours. Printed for J. Johnson, 1772. 4to, 6 page subscriber's list, errata leaf, ads., folding engraved biographical chart as frontis., and 24 folding plates, cont. half calf with marbled boards, boards rather rubbed, rebacked, with new morocco label. Waterstaining on about 100 pages in the middle of the book. First edition. Bickersteth 77-311 1983 £450

PRIESTLEY, JOSEPH   Lectures on History and General Policy. Dublin: Printed by Luke White, 1788. First Irish edition, with two folding engraved tables, cont. calf, 8vo, neatly rebacked, retaining orig. label, v.g. copy. Fenning 60-336 1983 £55

PRIESTLEY, R. E.   Breaking the Hindenburg Line. London, 1919. Orig. cloth, 8vo. Frontis., 15 plates, 2 folding coloured maps, spine faded. Slightly worn. Bookplate. Good. Edwards 1042-577 1983 £12

PRIESTMAN, AUSTIN   Songs and Sonnets 1906-1936. Edinburgh & London: Oliver and Boyd, 1937. First edition. With the author's full-page inscription to The Rt. Hon. Ernest Brown (Minister of Heath). A fine copy, in slightly soiled unprinted dust jacket. Reese 20-800 1983 $35

PRIETO, GREGORIO   The Crafty Farmer. London, 1938. First edition. 4to. Covers marked. Inscription on flyleaf. Illus. by G. Prieto. Nice. Rota 230-491 1983 £12

PRIME, FREDERICK   Second Geological Survey of Pennsylvania. Har., 1878. 5 map-sheet, 5 plates, signed by author, sheets fine, spine torn, cover rubbed, interior clean. Quill & Brush 54-1654 1983 $40

PRIME, WILLIAM C.   The Old House by the River. London: Chapman & Hall, 1853. First edition (English). Orig. cloth. Spine and extremities darkened. Inner hinges weak. Good. MacManus 280-4270 1983 $45

PRIME, WILLIAM C.   The Old House by the River. New York: Harper, 1853. 1st ed. Orig. cloth. Lightly wear, but very good copy. Jenkins 155-1034 1983 $20

PRIME, WILLIAM C.   Pottery and Porcelain of All Times and Nations. New York, 1878. Illus. Thick 8vo. Occasional rubbing, few binding stains. Morrill 286-405 1983 $45

PRIMROSE, JAMES   De Vulgi Erroribus in Medicina, Libri IV. Roterodami: A. Leers, 1658. Thick 16mo, later 1/2 calf, (mended). Title in red & black, with vignette. Old library stamp on title. Argosy 713-440 1983 $200

PRINCE, F. T.   Poems. London, 1938. First edition.
Signature of previous owner on free end-paper. Dustwrapper with a
sunned spine and small tear at head of spine. A fine copy. Gekoski
2-157 1983 £18

PRINCE, F. T.   Poems. London, 1939. First edition.
Presentation copy from the author in 1938. Nicked and slightly
torn, internally repaired dustwrapper slightly browned at the spine.
Very good. Jolliffe 26-417 1983 £30

PRINCE, L. BRADFORD   Spanish Mission Churches of New Mexico.
Cedar Rapids: Torch Press, 1915. Illus. Cloth. Front hinge repaired.
Dawson 471-235 1983 $60

PRINCE, THOMAS   A Chronological History of New England,
in the Form of Annals. Boston, 1736. Half calf and cloth, title
page repaired, otherwise very good. Reese 18-51 1983 $375

PRINCE, THOMAS   A Chronological History of New-England,
in the form of Annals: from 1602-1730. Boston: Cummings, Hilliard,
and Co., 1826. 2 vols. in 1. Orig. boards, paper label, uncut, spine
mended. First complete edition. Argosy 710-106 1983 $75

PRINCE, THOMAS   The Natural and Moral Government and
Agency of God In Causing Droughts and Rains. Reese 18-64 1983
$175

PRINCE, THOMAS   Precious in the Sight of the Lord is the
Death of His Saints. Boston: S. Kneeland & T. Green, 1735. 8vo,
wrs., mod. bd. folder (lib. blindstamp on t.p.). Argosy 716-102
1983 $100

PRINCE, THOMAS   The Salvations of God in 1746. Boston
printed, London reprinted: T. Longman, 1747. 1st Eng. ed. Jenkins
153-444 1983 $65

PRINCE, THOMAS   A Sermon...The Day of Thanksgiving for
the Great Deliverance of the British Nations... Boston printed,
London reprinted: John Lewis, 1747. 1st Eng. ed. Jenkins 153-445
1983 $85

THE PRINCESS and Curdie. Blackie, nd (1900). 1st edn. thus. Frontis.
& 30 illus. by Helen Stratton. Adverts. rear. Binding designed by
Laurence Housman. Traces of label fr. ep., sl. mark fr. cr. & circ.
gilt prize stamp centre rear cvr., vg. Hodgkins 27-139 1983 £15

PRINCESS Mary's Gift Book. London: Hodder & Stoughton, n.d. First
edition. 4to. Illus. with tipped-in colored plates. Orig. cream
cloth. Dust jacket. In soiled and partly defective jacket. Very
good. MacManus 278-1664 1983 $75

PRINGLE, JAMES R.   History of the Town and City of
Gloucester, Cape Ann, Massachusetts. Gloucester, Author, 1892. 1st
ed. Illus. 8vo. Ads. Morrill 287-249 1983 $25

PRINGLE, JOHN (1707-1782)   Observations on the Diseases of the
Army. London, 1774. 8vo. Cont. calf, rebacked. Gurney 90-95
1983 £50

PRINGLE, JOHN (1707-1782)   Observations on the Diseases of the Army.
Phila., 1812. 8vo. Modern boards, leather label. Argosy 713-441
1983 $200

PRINGLE, JOHN JAMES   An Atlas of Skin Diseases. (1904).
Small folio, 50 large coloured plates with names at the foot, no text,
orig. cloth, discoloured, with title on upper cover. Bickersteth 77-
312 1983 £45

PRINSEP, H. T.   History of the Political and Military
Transactions in India... London, 1825. Second enlarged edition.
Frontis. 5 folding maps, 2 folding tables. 2 vols. Half calf.
Good. 8vo. Edwards 1044-575 1983 £90

PRINSEP, H. T.   A Narrative of the Political and Military
Transactions of British India. London, 1820. Portrait, large folding
map. 17 views and plans on 9 plates. 4to. Calf rebacked. From the
library of the 4th Earl of Minto, with a few marginal notes in his hand.
Good. Edwards 1044-576 1983 £155

PRINSEP, H. T.   Origin of the Sikh Power. Calcutta, 1834.
Folding map, plan, frontis., rebacked. 8vo, orig. cloth. Good.
Edwards 1044-577 1983 £95

PRINSEP, J.   History of the Punjab. London, 1846.
2 vols. Half blue morocco, raised bands. Gilt in compartments. 8vo.
Good. Edwards 1044-578 1983 £75

PRINSEP, J   Useful Tables. Calcutta Printed at
the Baptist Mission Press, 1836. 2 engraved plates only of 3, lacking
the map of Calcutta, and 2 text engravings, orig. plain calf, upper
joint cracked. Bickersteth 75-167 1983 £20

PRIOR, MATTHEW   Miscellaneous Works. Printed for the
editor, 1740. 8vo, engraved portrait, cont. calf, label defective.
Published by Joseph Bancks, who signs the dedication. Bickersteth
77-64 1983 £26

PRIOR, MATTHEW   A New Collection of Poems on Several
Occasions... London: for Tho. Osborne, 1725. First edition. 12mo.
Cont. calf. Engraved portrait, plates. Some light waterstains.
Heath 48-404 1983 £45

PRIOR, MATTHEW   An Ode in Imitation of the Second Ode
of the Third Book of Horace. London: for Jacob Tonson, 1692.
First edition. Folio. Wrappers. Heath 48-406 1983 £125

PRIOR, MATTHEW   An Ode, humbly inscrib'd to the Queen.
London: for Jacob Tonson, 1706. First edition. Folio. Wrappers.
Without the Half title. Heath 48-405 1983 £85

PRIOR, MATTHEW   Poems on Several Occassions. For
Jacob Tonson, 1717. 12mo, frontis., a new title label inset on red
morocco, cont. calf. K Books 307-151 1983 £35

PRIOR, MATTHEW   Poems on Several Occasions. Printed
for J. and R. Tonson and S. Draper, and H. Lintot, 1754. 12mo,
portrait, cont. calf. Bickersteth 77-65 1983 £16

PRIOR, MATTHEW   The Poetical Works of Matthew Prior.
London: Printed for W. Strahan, T. Payne, J. Rivington & Sons, et al,
1779. First collected edition. Bookplates. 2 vols. Engraved frontis.
Full cont. calf with red & green morocco labels. Offsetting from
frontispiece. MacManus 280-4272 1983 $150

PRIOR, MATTHEW   The Poetical Works. London, 1866.
Cr. 8vo. Dark blue calf, two-line gilt borders with corner ornaments,
gilt panelled spines, morocco labels, gilt. Traylen 94-676 1983
£30

PRITCHARD, ALAN   Alchemy; A Bibliography of English-
Language Writings. London: Routledge & Kegan Paul, (1980). First
edition. 8vo. Cloth. Dust jacket. Fine. Oak Knoll 48-389 1983
$75

PRITCHARD, JAMES COWLES   Natural History of Man. L, 1855. 62
colored plates, 100 wood engravings, 2 vols., bound in 3/4 leather,
slight foxing, else very good. Quill & Brush 54-1649 1983 $225

PRITZEL, G. A.   Iconum Botanicarum Index. Berlin, 1866.
2nd ed., 2 parts in 1 vol., 4to, cloth. Some foxing. Wheldon
160-261 1983 £55

PROBST, ANTOINE   The Life, Confession, and Atrocious
Crimes of Antoine Probst. Phila., (1866). Many crude woodcut
illus., orig. pict. wraps. Argosy 716-130 1983 $65

PROCEEDINGS at the Ceremonies in Commemoration of the One Hundred and
Fiftieth Anniversary of the First Meeting of the Supreme Court...
Washington, 1940. Stapled self-wraps, 1 fold, little bit of wear.
Justice Brandeis's copy, with full signature in ink on front wrap.
Good condition. Boswell 7-29 1983 $250

PROCEEDINGS of the Association for Promoting the Discovery of the
Interior Parts of Africa. London: The Association, 1790. 4to.
Folding map. New 1/2 claf. Marbled boards. Adelson Africa-116
1983 $400

PROCEEDINGS of the Friends of a Rail-Road to San Francisco. Boston: Dutton & Westworth, 1849. First edition. Orig. yellow printed wraps. Trifle dust-soiled. Fine. Jenkins 152-341 1983 $175

PROCEEDINGS of the General Court of Assizes, Held in the City of New York, October 6, 1680 to October 6, 1682. New York, 1913. Orig. pebbled buckram, gilt, uncut, very nice. Boswell 7-129 1983 $45

PROCEEDINGS of the M. Ill. Grand Council of Royal and Select Masters of Indian Territory... Dension, Texas: Herald Pub. Co., 1899. Orig. printed wrappers. Jenkins 153-410 1983 $75

PROCTER, ADELAIDE ANNE   Legends and Lyrics. Bell & Daldy, 1866. 4to, front. prt. and illus. by Dobson, Palmer, Tenniel, etc., half title. Small waterstain on upper inner corner of front. and a few plates. Red morocco a little rubbed, a.e.g. Jarndyce 30-121 1983 £120

PROCTER, ADELAIDE ANNE   Legends and Lyrics. Bell & Daldy, 1866. 4to, half title, front. port. and illus. by Samuel Palmer, John Tenniel, W.H. Millais, etc. Brown, heavily embossed, morocco, bevelled boards, rubbed, a.e.g. Jarndyce 31-561 1983 £82

PROCTER, BRYAN WALLER   Charles Lamb: A Memoir. London, Edward Moxon, 1866. 8vo, orig. cloth gilt, little wear, inner joints weak, frontis. trifle foxed, good large copy. First edition. Ravenstree 97-170 1983 $87.50

PROCTER, BRYAN WALLER   The Life of Edmund Kean. London: Edward Moxon, 1835. 2 vols., 12mo, cont. half calf, spines gilt (just a trifle rubbed). 1st edition. With a portrait (foxed), bound without half-titles, but a very good copy. Ximenes 64-442 1983 $125

PROCTER, GEORGE H.   The Fishermen's Memorial and Record Book. Gloucester, Procter Brothers, 1873. 1st ed. Illus. 8vo. Ads. Binding rubbed and some light stains. Morrill 287-250 1983 $32.50

PROCTER, RICHARD WRIGHT   Memorials of Manchester (England) Streets. Manchester, 1874. 1st ed. Plates. 4to. Morrill 288-414 1983 $25

PROCTOR, FRANK   Fox Hunting in Canada and Some Men Who Made It. Toronto: Macmillan, 1929. 22 1/2cm. 106 full-page illus. (incl. one colour plate). Blue cloth. Very good to fine. McGahern 54-149 1983 $25

PROCTOR, RICHARD ANTHONY (1837-1888)   Saturn and its system. London: Longman, 1865. First edition. 8vo. Orig. bright blue cloth, spine gilt-stamped. Folding frontis. and 13 plates. Fine. Ximenes 63-533 1983 $175

PROKOSCH, FREDERIC   The Asiatics. New York and London: Harper & Brothers, 1935. First edition. 8vo. Orig. cloth. Dust jacket (pictorial foil). Near mint. Jaffe 1-327 1983 $225

PROKOSCH, FREDERIC   The Assassins. London: Chatto & Windus, 1936. First edition. 8vo. Orig. cloth-backed boards. Dust jacket. Unopened. Very fine. Jaffe 1-328 1983 $45

PROKOSCH, FREDERIC   Banquet Song. Barcelona, 1953. 12mo. Marbled paper, paper label. Of an edition limited to 44 copies, this is 1 of 10 copies on Cordoba. This copy inscribed by the author and signed Fritz P. Christmas 1953. A fine copy. In Our Time 156-641 1983 $200

PROKOSCH, FREDERIC   The Carnival. London: Chatto & Windus, 1938. First edition. 8vo. Orig. cloth-backed boards. Dust jacket. Fine copy. Jaffe 1-330 1983 $45

PROKOSCH, FREDERIC   The Conspirators. NY, 1943. Small faint spot on rear board, else fine in slightly soiled, fine dustwrapper. Quill & Brush 54-1121 1983 $35

PROKOSCH, FREDERIC   The Seven Who Fled. New York and London: Harper & Brothers Publishers, 1937. First edition. 8vo. Orig. cloth. Dust jacket. Fine copy. Jaffe 1-329 1983 $45

PROKSCH, J. K.   Die Geschichte der Venerischen Krankheiten. Bonn, 1895. 8vo, 2 vols. 1/2 cloth. Argosy 713-442 1983 $150

PROLOGUE to "Britons' Rights," or "What Do You Want?" a tragi-comedy, as performed by His Majesty's liege subjects. London: printed by J. Dean; for R. Ryan, 1809. 8vo, disbound. First edition. Very good copy. Ximenes 64-443 1983 $125

PROMETHEUS. Poem and Woodcuts by Gillian Haven. N.p. 1980. 8vo, leather-backed decorated bds., gilt, clamshell slipcase with leather label. Signed by the poet-artist. Perata 27-91 1983 $135

PROMINENT People of the Maritime Provinces. St. John, N.B., McMillan, 1922. Orig. gold stamped leather. Illus. First edition. Ginsberg 46-150 1983 $125

PROSCH, CHARLES   Reminiscences of Washington Territory. Seattle. 1904. Cloth, very good. This copy is inscribed from the author. Reese 19-442 1983 $100

PROSCH, CHARLES   Reminiscences of Washington Territory. Seattle, Wash., 1904. Illus. Orig. cloth. Autograph presentation copy from Charles Prosch. Ginsberg 46-796 1983 $75

PROSE Quartos. New York: Random House, 1930. 6 vols., boxed. 1st eds., limited to 875 copies. Orig. wrappers, in orig. box, with label. Jenkins 155-16 1983 $100

PROUDETT, ALEXANDER   Ministerial Labour and Support: a Sermon Preached at Middlebury. Salem: Dodd & Rumsey, 1810 8vo, uncut, sewed, foxed, ex lib. Argosy 710-551 1983 $35

PROUDHON, PIERRE-JOSEPH   Theorie De L'Impot. Paris: Dentu, 1861. 1st ed., small 8vo, cont. marbled boards. Pickering & Chatto 21-99 1983 $200

PROUST, MARCEL   Correspondance avec sa Mere. Paris: Librairie Plon, 1953. First edition. One of 175 numbered copies on Lafuma paper. Wrappers. Fine. Rota 231-497 1983 £45

PROUST, MARCEL   Quelque Lettres de Marcel Proust precedes de Remarques sur les derniers Mois de sa Vie. Paris: E. Flammarion, 1928. 1st ed., 4to, 1 of 525 copies on Marais paper. Later cloth, one corner lightly dampstained; original wrappers bound in. A very good copy. Trebizond 18-123 1983 $60

PROUST DE LA GIRONIERE, PAUL Twenty Years in the Philippines. Longman, Brown, 1853. First edition of this translation, small 8vo, wrapper. Fenning 60-338 1983 £10.50

PROUT, HENRY G.   A Life of George Westinghouse. London, 1922. 8vo. Cloth. Portrait and 7 plates. Gurney JJ-422 1983 £15

PROUTY, LORENZO   Fish: Their Habits and Haunts and the Methods of Catching Them. Boston: Cupples, Upham and Co., 1883. Pub.'s catalog. Illus. with a glossy photo of the author. Red cloth, with a gilt fish on the corner. Karmiole 71-77 1983 $35

PRUDHOMME, SULLY   Testament Poetique. Paris, 1901. First edition. Wrappers worn and sewing loose. Inscribed. Flyleaf bears Grenier's critical notes on the book and the text bears several of his marginal pencilled comments. Preserved in a cloth folder and slipcase. Good, Rota 230-495 1983 £20

PRYNNE, WILLIAM   A new Magna Carta. N.p. (london): printed in the yeere 1648. First edition. Small 4to. Disbound. Title-page a bit soiled. Ximenes 63-103 1983 $65

PRYNNE, WILLIAM   The Perpetvitie of a Regenerate Mans Estate. London, William Iones, 1626. 4to, 19th century calf gilt, front cover detached, else fine large copy. First edition. Ravenstree 97-171 1983 $250

PRYNNE, WILLIAM   A True and Full Relation of the
Prosecution, Arraignment, Tryall, and Condemnation of Nathaniel
Fiennes... London: for Michael Sparks senior, 1644. First
edition. 4to. Full 19th Century polished calf, full gilt spine.
Small hole in title, repaired, and leaf backed, short tear in next
3 leaves repaired. Heath 48-149 1983 £150

PRYNNE, WILLIAM   The unlovelinesse of love-lockes.
London, 1628. First edition. Small 4to. Full dark green morocco,
gilt, a.e.g. Ximenes 63-113 1983 $225

PRYOR, MRS. ROGER A.
Please turn to
PRYOR, SARA AGNES (RICE)

PRYOR, SARA AGNES (RICE)   Reminiscences of Peace and War. New
York, 1905. 8vo. Orig. cloth. Portrait frontis., 12 plates, 1 double-
page map. Spine faded. T.e.g. Good. Edwards 1042-243 1983 £12

PSYCHOLOGY: A Study of a Science. NY: McGraw Hill, 1859-1863. Six
vols. Publisher's green cloth. Sound secondhand set. Gach 94-582
1983 $125

PUCCINI, VINCENTIO   The Life of St. Mary Magdalene of Pazzi.
At Paris, for Sebastian Cramoisy, 1670. Comprising title-leaf. 1
blank page, pages 39-138, pages 133-138 wanting and provided in a
neat cont. hand, 4to, wrapper, little dusty in places, but very good.
Fenning 61-360 1983 $16

PUCKLER-LIMPURG, SIEGFRIED   Nie Nurnberger Bildnerkunst um die Wenda
des 14. und 15. Strassburg, 1904. Sm. 4to. 7 plates, 5 text illus.
Cloth. Ars Libri SB 26-199 1983 $37.50

PUDNEY, JOHN   Almanack of Hope. London, 1944. First
edition. Drawings by J. Nash. One of 50 numbered copies, signed by
author. Covers a little marked. Very good. Rota 230-496 1983 £18

PUDNEY, JOHN   Flight Above Cloud: Poems. New York,
(1944). 8vo. Clothboards. From the library of another poet with
his autograph and comment on front flyleaf. Very good-fine in
chipped dj. In Our Time 156-643 1983 $25

PUERARI, ALFREDO   Boccaccino. Milano: Ceschina, 1957.
150 plates with 175 illus. (8 color). 4to. Cloth. Dust jacket.
Ars Libri 33-35 1983 $100

PUFFENDORF, SAMUEL   An Introduction to the History of the
Principal Kingdoms and States of Europe. Printed for Tho. Newborough;
and Dan. Midwinter, 1706. 8vo, portrait, orig. panelled calf,
rebacked. First edition in English. Bickersteth 77-66 1983 £48

PUGIN, AUGUSTUS CHARLES   Specimens of the Architecture of Normandy.
1874. New edition, with engr. and printed titles, 78 plates, 4to. A
little foxed but good in half calf, a bit chafed. K Books 307-152
1983 £55

PUJOL, JOHANNES   Opera Omnia. Barcelona, 1926-1932. Two
vols., 4to, buckram. Ex-library copies, with bookplate and release.
Salloch 387-186 1983 $150

PULLEIN, SAMUEL   The Culture of Silk. In Four Parts.
1755. 8vo, 2 engraved plates, orig. calf, rebacked, new morocco
label, new end papers. Title page and facing plate dusty. Dark
stain in the upper margin of all pages in final third of book.
Bickersteth 75-81 1983 £145

PULTENEY, WILLIAM EARL OF BATH
Please turn to
BATH, WILLIAM PULTENEY, EARL OF

PUNCH'S Almanack 1848. London: Published at the Punch Office, Fleet
Street, 1848. First edition. Illus. by John Leech. Full morocco with
marbled endpapers. Folio. Orig. wrappers bound in. Contains 6 full-
page hand colored plates drawn by Leech and R. Doyle. With two orig.
preparatory pencil sketch drawings by Leech, neatly mounted to size,
and bound in alongside the finished plate. Spine & covers somewhat
worn, spine a bit chipped. Some foxing. Very good. Bookplate.
MacManus 279-3201 1983 $350

PURCELL, HENRY   Dioclesian. London, 1961. Folio, wrs.
Salloch 387-187 1983 $110

PURCELL, HENRY   Harmonia Sacra. London, I. Walsh, n.d.
(c. 1730). Engraved music. Folio, wrs. Salloch 387-188 1983 $200

PURCELL, HENRY   Orpheus Britannicus. London, 1698-
1722. Two vols. Folio, 1/2 calf over marbled boards. Music type-set.
Lacks portrait; otherwise fine set. First edition, the second volume
in second edition with additions. Salloch 387-189 1983 $1,100

PURCELL, HENRY   Sacred Harmony. London, Henry Thorowgood,
n.d. (ca. 1760-1765). Folio, unbound. Engraved title and 25 pp.
engraved music. Salloch 387-190 1983 $150

PURCELL, HENRY   Saul and the Witch of Endor. London:
printed by Clementi, Banger, Hyde, Collard & Davis, n.d. (early 19th
century between 1802-1806). 4 leaves, engr. music, folio, unbound.
Salloch 387-191 1983 $90

PURCELL, HENRY   Te Deum et Jubilate. London, Walsh,
n.d. (ca. 1730). Folio, wrs. Engraved title and 18 pp. engraved
music. Salloch 387-192 1983 $150

PURCELL, JOHN   A treatise of vapours, or, hysterick
fits. London: Edward Place, 1707. Second edition. 8vo. Cont.
calf. Somewhat worn, upper hinge weak. Ximenes 63-288 1983 $175

PURDY, JAMES   Lessons and Complaints. (NY, n.d.).
Limited to 174 numbered and signed copies, fine. Quill & Brush 54-
1123 1983 $40

PURDY, JAMES   Mr. Evening. Black Sparrow Press,
1968. 8vo. Cloth, boards. Printed by the Plantin Press. 1 of
75 copies bound, signed by author with an orig. drawing by same.
Fine in acetate jacket. In Our Time 156-645 1983 $100

PURDY, JAMES   Mr. Evening. Black Sparrow Press,
1968. 8vo. Cloth, boards. Printed by the Plantin Press. 1 of
300 in wrappers signed by Purdy. In Our Time 156-646 1983 $75

PURDY, JAMES   On the Rebound. Black Sparrow Press,
1970. 8vo. Cloth, boards. 1 of 26 copies lettered and signed by
Purdy. Fine in acetate jacket. In Our Time 156-647 1983 $125

PURDY, JAMES   An Oyster Is a Wealthy Beast. Black
Sparrow Press, 1967. 8vo. Oblong boards. Wrapper ed. being 1 of
200 copies signed by author. Fine. In Our Time 156-644 1983 $100

PURDY, JAMES   Proud Flesh. CA, 1980. Limited to 50
numbered and signed deluxe copies, as new. Quill & Brush 54-1124
1983 $75

PURDY, VICTORY   Poetical Miscellanies. Bristol: John
Wansburgh, 1825. Front. facs. Errata slip, list of subscribers.
Half dark blue calf, brown labels, t.e.g. Bookplate of Lord Battersea.
Fine. Jarndyce 30-825 1983 £38

PURRY, JEAN PIERRE   Memorial...Upon the Present Condition
of Carolina, and the Means of Its Amelioration. Augusta, Ga., 1880.
Sq. 8vo, orig. pr. wraps., (fore-edges stained), unopened. One of
250 privately printed, numbered copies, initialed by the editor,
Charles C. Jones, Jr. Argosy 716-523 1983 $85

PURSUIT after happiness: a poem. To which is added, An ode to Mr.
Garrick, on his quitting the stage. Also, an elegy on the death of
Mr. Barry. London: printed for the author; published by G. Kearsly;
and sold by J. Ridley; S. Hooper; and T. Sewell, 1777. 4to, wrappers.
First edition. A fine uncut copy. Very scarce. Ximenes 64-445
1983 $275

PURVIANCE, ROBERT   A Narrative of Events which Occurred
in Baltimore Town During the Revolutionary War. Baltimore, 1949.
First edition. 12mo, orig. cloth, paper label (chipped, slight
foxing). Inscribed "To W.M. Burwell from the author." Argosy 716-
467 1983 $100

PUSEY, WILLIAM   The History and Epidemiology of Syphilis. Springfield, 1933. First edition. 8vo. Orig. cloth. Dust wrapper. Fye H-3-466 1983 $40

PUSEY, WILLIAM   The History of Dermatology. Springfield, 1933. First edition. 8vo. Orig. cloth. Fye H-3-467 1983 $45

PUSHKIN, ALEXANDER   The Golden Cockerel. NY: Limited Editions Club, (1950). Small quarto. Full-color illus. and decorations by Edmund Dulac. Limited to 1500 copies signed by Dulac. Bound in cloth with onlaid gold-colored metal cockerel. Orig. glassine and double slip-case, faded at spine and slightly rubbed at extremities; otherwise very fine with monthly newsletter laid-in. Bromer 25-192 1983 $175

PUTNAM, CHARLES E.   Elephant Pipes in the Museum of the Academy of Natural Sciences, Davenport, Iowa. Davenport, 1885. Wraps., fine. Reese 19-296 1983 $50

PUTNAM, CLAUDE GEORGE   Log Book, Harbors & Islands, California Coast. Los Angeles & Chicago: Rambeau, (1941). Illus., plus guest and trip logs. Cloth, wraped and somewhat used. Dawson 471-237 1983 $30

PUTNAM, GEORGE HAVEN   The Question of Copyright... New York: G. P. Putnam's Sons, 1891. First edition. 8vo. Orig. cloth. Oak Knoll 38-331 1983 $50

PUTNAM, ISRAEL   The Two Putnams, Israel and Rufus in the Havana Expedition... Hartford, 1931. 1st ed. Illus. 8vo, orig. boards, cloth back. Morrill 287-367 1983 $27.50

PUTTI e stucchi di Giacomo Serpotta, 1656-1732. Milano: Bestetti & Tumminelli, n.d. Title-page. 50 heliotype plates loose in portfolio as issued. Small folio. Cloth. Ars Libri 33-336 1983 $75

PUYVELDE, LEO VAN   Jordaens. Paris/Bruxelles: Elsevier, 1953. 101 plates (5 color). Large 4to. Cloth. Dust jacket. Ars Libri 32-348 1983 $100

PUYVELDE, LEO VAN   Rubens. Paris: Elsevier, 1952. 62 plates (10 tipped-in color). Large 4to. Cloth. Ars Libri 32-603 1983 $85

PUYVELDE, LEO VAN   The Sketches of Rubens. New York: Beechhurst Press, 1951. 104 plates. Large 4to. Cloth. Ars Libri 32-604 1983 $75

PYCRAFT, W. P.   The British Museum of Natural History. (1910). 6 plates and 38 text figures, 8vo, cloth. Wheldon 160-187 1983 £12

PYE, JOHN   Patronage of British art... London: Longman, etc., 1845. First edition. 8vo. Orig. green cloth. Ximenes 63-19 1983 $125

PYLE, KATHERINE   Fairy Tales from India. Philadelphia, 1926. 1st ed. Illustrated in color by editor. 8vo, dust wrapper, almost fine. Morrill 286-408 1983 $25

PYM, JOHN   The Heads of a Conference Delivered by Mr. Pym. Printed in the Year 1641. First edition, woodcut device on title, 4to, wrapper, a nice copy. Fenning 60-340 1983 £45

PYM, JOHN   The Heads of a Conference delivered by Mr. Pymm... (London), 1641. First edition. 4to. Modern boards. Heath 48-150 1983 £45

PYM, JOHN   A Speech Delivered by Mr. Pym, at a Conference of Both Houses. Printed for John Bull, June 15, 1642. First edition, 4to, wrapper. Fenning 60-341 1983 £24.50

PYM, JOHN   The Speech or Declaration of John Pym, Esq. &c. (London, 1641). First edition, drop-title, 4to, wrapper, a nice copy. Fenning 60-342 1983 £26.50

PYNCHON, THOMAS   The Crying of Lot 49. Philadelphia (&) New York: J.B. Lippincott Company, (1966). First edition. 8vo. Orig. cloth-backed boards. Dust jacket. Mint copy. Jaffe 1-332 1983 $175

PYNCHON, THOMAS   The Crying of Lot 49. Phila., (1966). First edition. 12mo, fine. Argosy 714-609 1983 $50

PYNCHON, THOMAS   Gravity's Rainbow. New York: The Viking Press, (1973). First edition. Thick 8vo. Orig. cloth. Dust jacket. Mint copy. Jaffe 1-333 1983 $125

PYNCHON, THOMAS   Gravity's Rainbow. New York, (1973). 8vo. Cloth. A fine copy in dj. In Our Time 156-648 1983 $125

PYNCHON, THOMAS   Rainbow. (Paris): Plon, (1975). First French edition. Tall 8vo. Orig. pictorial wrappers. Orange wraparound band. Mint copy. Jaffe 1-334 1983 $100

PYNCHON, THOMAS   V. A Novel. Philadelphia and New York: J.B. Lippincott Company, (1963). First edition. 8vo. Orig. cloth. Dust jacket. A few half-inch hair-line tears at bottom of back panel of jacket, otherwise a very fine copy. Jaffe 1-331 1983 $500

PYNCHON, THOMAS   V, A Novel. Philadelphia & New York: Lippincott, (1963). 1st ed. Orig. lavender cloth, dj. Minute edge-fading, and light wear to dj, but a very nice copy. Scarce. Jenkins 155-1046 1983 $200

PYNE, WILLIAM HENRY   The History Of The Royal Residences Of Windsor Castle... London, printed for A. Dry, 1819. 1st ed., 3 vols, large 4to, half-titles, 100 fine coloured aquatint plates, coloured vignette tail-piece, dark blue half morocco, gilt, matching cloth boards, t.e.g., other edges uncut. Deighton 3-246 1983 £950

PYNE, WILLIAM HENRY   The Twenty-Ninth of May. London: Knight & Lacy, 1825. First edition. 2 vols. Orig. boards with paper spine labels (rather worn; chipped). Spines and covers worn and chipped. Slight foxing to the edges of the text. Former owner's signature. Very good. MacManus 280-4280 1983 $185

PYNE, WILLIAM HENRY   The Twenty-Ninth of May. Knight & Lacey, 1825. First edition, half titles, half red morocco, t.e.g. Very good. Jarndyce 30-524 1983 £44

Q

"Q", PSEUD.
Please turn to
QUILLER-COUCH, ARTHUR

QUAD, M.   Field, Fort and Fleet... Detroit, 1885.
Engs; woodcuts, 1/2 lea., hinge cracked. Top of spine badly
chipped. Scuffed. King 46-74 1983 $20

QUADRI, LODOVICO   Tavole Gnomoniche per delineare
orologj a sole Che Mostrino l'ore conforme a quelle degli Orologj.
In Bologna Nella Stamperia di: e;op dalla Volpe. MDCCXXXIII. (1733).
4to, six folding plates. In quarter vellum, paper covered boards,
slightly stained and rubbed at corners. Title stamped in gold on
spine. Occasional light waterstaining in lower centerfold margin.
First edition. Arkway 22-72 1983 $775

QUADRILLER, Valsar och Anglaiser. (Stockholm, 1827). Folio, unbound.
Salloch 387-238 1983 $65

QUAIFE, MILO M   The Bark Covered House. Chicago:
The Lakeside Press, 1937. Cloth, t.e.g., extremities worn. Ink
inscription (to William Scripps). King 46-186 1983 $20

QUAIFE, MILO M.   Chicago and the Old Northwest, 1673-
1835. Chicago, 1913. Cloth, fine. Reese 19-444 1983 $75

QUAIFE, MILO M.   Chicago's Highways Old and New.
Chicago, 1923. 1st ed. Maps and illus. 8vo. Morrill 287-163 1983
$30

QUAIFE, MILO M.   Chicago's Highways Old and New.
Chicago, 1923. Illustrated, cloth, corners bumped, some wear.
King 46-106 1983 $25

QUAIFE, MILO M.   The Development of Chicago, 1674-1914.
Chicago, 1914. Half vellum and boards. Illus. Overall very good.
Reese 19-445 1933 $85

QUAIFE, MILO M.   The Development of Chicago 1674-1914.
Chicago: The Caxton Club, 1916. Frontis., illus., half vellum
and paper boards. Fine copy. Boxed. Limited to 175 copies. Uncut
and unopened. Jenkins 151-143 1983 $150

QUAIFE, MILO M.   Lake Michigan. Indianapolis, 1944.
Illustrations. Maps. First edition. Fine copy. Signed by the
author. Jenkins 151-279 1983 $35

QUAIFE, MILO M.   Pictures of Gold Rush California. Chicago, 1949. Map & illus. 16mo, g.t. Argosy 710-37 1983 $20

QUAIN, JONES   The Viscera of the Human Body. London,
1837. Hand-colored lithographic plates. Atlas folio, gilt-lettered
cloth, rebacked in buckram. First edition. Argosy 713-445 1983 $250

QUARIN, JOSEPH   Animadersiones Practicae in Diversos
Morbos. Ticini, apud Balthassarem Comini, 1792. 8vo, cont. calf,
small snag in spine, but quite sound and otherwise a fine copy. Fenning 61-361 1983 £24.50

QUARLES, FRANCIS   Emblems, Divine and Moral. London:
for John Clarke, 1736. Engraved frontis. and 195 engravings in the
text, 12mo, generally a little thumbed and used, cont. calf, neatly
rebacked. K Books 307-153 1983 £85

QUATREFAGES, J. L. A. DE   Histoire naturelle des Anneles marins
et d'eau douce, Vols. 1 and 2. Paris, 1865. 8vo, half leather.
The 20 plates are not included. Wheldon 160-1333 1983 £20

QUAYLE, ANTHONY   On Such a Night. London: Heinemann,
(1947). Sm. 8vo, original cream cloth. 1st ed. Presentation copy,
inscribed by author "To Alec, with great affection, from Tony, on the
first night of Richard II. 23 April 1947." Ximenes 64-252 1983 $35

QUEEN, ELLERY   The Red Chipmunk Mystery. Ph., (1946).
Top edge of boards slightly gnawed, else very good in internally
mended, chipped and soiled dustwrapper. Quill & Brush 54-1127 1983
$40

THE QUEEN'S budget opened... London: T. Dolby, etc., 1820. First
edition. 8vo. Distbound. 8 humorous wood-engravings. Ximenes
63-508 1983 $45

QUEKETT, JOHN   Lectures on Histology Delivered at the
Royal College of Surgeons of England in the Session 1850-51. 1852-
54. 2 vols. in one, well illus., orig. cloth. K Books 307-154 1983
£30

QUENNELL, M.   Everyday Things in Homeric Greece.
London, 1929. 8vo, cloth. Illus. Salloch 385-572 1983 $20

QUENNELL, PETER   Poems. New York: Cape and Smith, (n.d.).
Quarto. Cloth, stamped in blind. First edition. One of 500 copies
printed by Thieme of Holland for Cape and Smith. Inscribed by the
author on the front free endsheet: "For Cyril from Peter Quennel."
Spine very slightly sunned, else fine. Reese 20-809 1983 $100

QUENTIN, PATRICK   Puzzle for Wantons. N.Y., Simon &
Schuster, 1945. First edition. Dust jacket (small tears). Very
good - fine. Houle 22-736 1983 $30

QUEVEDO PESSANHA, CARMEN DE   Vita artistica de Mariano Benlliure.
Madrid: Espasa-Calpe, 1947. Prof. illus. Stout 4to. Cloth.
Ars Libri 32-31 1983 $150

QUICK, HERBERT   Mississippi Steamboatin', a History of
Steamboating on the Mississippi and Its Tributaries. NY, (1926).
Illus. Argosy 710-272 1983 $35

THE QUICKSILVER MINING COMPANY.   Charter and By-Laws. N.Y., 1864.
Orig. printed wraps. First edition. Ginsberg 46-113 1983 $125

QUILLER-COUCH, ARTHUR   The Astonishing History of Troy Town,
By Q. London, Cassell, 1888. 8vo, orig. pictorial cloth, worn and
rubbed, the Welbeck Abbey (Duke of Portland) copy with bookplate.
Ravenstree 96-152 1983 $43

QUILLER-COUCH, ARTHUR   Dead Man's Rock. London: Cassell & Co.,
1887. First edition. Orig. pictorial cloth. Michael Sadlier's copy
with his bookplate. Spine bumped. Very fine. MacManus 280-4281
1983 $125

QUILLER-COUCH, ARTHUR   Green Bays. London: Methuen, 1893.
First edition. Orig. buckram. One of 50 large paper copies signed
by publisher. Very fine. MacManus 280-4283 1983 $75

QUILLER-COUCH, ARTHUR   Hocken and Hunken. Edinburgh: William
Blackwood & Sons, 1912. First edition. Orig. cloth. Some foxing.
Former owner's signature on flyleaf. Very good. MacManus 280-4284
1983 $25

QUILLER-COUCH, ARTHUR   Lady Good-for-Nothing. N.Y.: Charles
Scribner's Sons, 1910. First American edition. Orig. cloth. Presen-
tation copy to "Bevil Quiller-Couch from his father Arthur Quiller-
Couch." Head and foot of spine rather worn. Corners slightly bumped.
A trifle foxed. MacManus 280-4285 1983 $65

QUILLER-COUCH, ARTHUR   The Sleeping Beauty & Other Fairy Tales.
Hodder & Stoughton, n.d. 4to. First edition. Mounted colour frontis.
Decorated title. 29 colour plates. Several text illus. Brown decor-
ated cloth, gilt. Greer 40-95 1983 £60

QUILLER-COUCH, ARTHUR "Virgil, An Address to the boys of Sevenoaks School. Cambridge: The University Press, 1930. First edition. Orig. printed wrappers. One of 250 copies signed by author and printed for private circulation only. Spine and covers a trifle worn and foxed. Near-fine. MacManus 280-4287 1983 $45

QUIN, TARELLA Before the Lamps are Lit. Melbourne: Robertson, n.d. Oblong large 8vo, frontis. Title vignette, 26 (ex 27) plates & 20 text illus (3 amateur coloured). Green pictorial cloth, worn. Some drawings singed by Rentoul & some Outhwaite. Scarce. Greer 40-153 1983 £45

QUINBY, HENRY COLE Richard Harding Davis, A Bibliography. NY: Dutton, (1924). Large 8vo, with numerous photographic illus. and facs. Edition ltd. to 1,000 copies. Karmiole 74-80 1983 $50

QUINCE, PETER A Parnassian Shop... Boston, 1801. 1st ed. Small 8vo, orig. boards, all edges untrimmed. Covers rubbed and partly stained, backstrip lightly cracked, lacks label. Morrill 286-459 1983 $100

QUINCY, JOHN Pharmacopoeia Officinalis et Extemporanea. London, 1782. Fifteenth Edition. 8vo. Cont. calf. Gurney JJ-333 1983 £20

QUINCY, JOSIAH History of Harvard University. Cambridge, 1840. Thick 8vo, (neatly rebacked, one orig. backstrip). First edition. Pencilled signature of Ezra Stiles Gannett. Argosy 716-275 1983 $65

QUINCY, JOSIAH The History of the Boston Athenaeum... Cambridge, 1851. First edition. 8vo, some rubbing at corners. Morrill 290-653 1983 $32.50

QUINCY, JOSIAH The Memory of the late James Grahame, the Historian of the United States. Boston: Crosby & Nichols, 1846. 1st ed., 8vo, original wrappers. One leaf torn in center and a few corners dampstained, else a very good copy. Trebizond 18-210 1983 $20

QUINLAN, JAMES ELDRIDGE History of Sullivan County. Liberty, 1873. Mod. buckram. With illus. ads & addenda slip. Argosy 716-364 1983 $125

QUINTAVALLE, ARMANDO OTTAVIANO Antelami scultore. Milano: Istituto Editoriale Italiano, 1947. 40 plates. Large 4to. Boards, 1/4 cloth. Ars Libri 33-9 1983 $40

QUIZ, ROLAND King Pippin. James Henderson, n.d. (ca.1860). 4to. 22 plates, some spotting. Dark green cloth, rubbed. Greer 40-174 1983 £25

R

RABAGLIATI, A.   Aphorisms, Definitions, Reflections, and Paradoxes. London, 1901. Tall 8vo, cloth; ex-lib. Argosy 713-446 1983 $30

RABAUD, ETIENNE   La Teratogenese. Paris, 1914. 12mo. Orig. cloth. 97 illus. Gurney JJ-335 1983 £15

RABELAIS, FRANCOIS   All the Extant Works. N.Y.: Covici-Friede, 1929. 3 vols. Illus. by Jean de Bosschere. Folio. Orig. cloth-backed boards with leather labels on spines. Limited to 1300 copies. Spines faded, extremities a bit rubbed. Bookplates. Very good. MacManus 278-1438 1983 $100

RABELAIS, FRANCOIS   Gargantua and Pantagruel. NY, (n.d.). Illus. by Joseph Hemard, cover slightly soiled and tears on spine edges, else near very good in torn dustwrapper. Quill & Brush 54-1130 1983 $30

RABELAIS, FRANCOIS   Works. London: H.G. Bohn, 1849. New edition, revised with notes. 2 vols. 8vo. Half maroon morocco, gilt, gilt panelled spines, t.e.g., by Bayntun. Spines slightly faded. Traylen 94-678 1983 £25

RABENHORST, L.   Flora Europaea Algarum Aquae Dulcis et Submarinae. Leipzig, 1865. 73 illustrations, 8vo, boards. Section 2. Wheldon 160-1878 1983 £15

RACHEL: A Tale. For Taylor and Hessey, 1821. 12mo, frontis., half-title. Cont. maroon morocco, blind-tooled and gilt, a.e.g. Hannas 69-164 1983 £15

RACKHAM, ARTHUR   Friends at the Farm. Blackie, n.d. 4to. Colour frontis. One colour plate by A.Rackham. 3 other colour plates & other illus. Colour pictorial boards. Greer 40-176 1983 £45

RACKHAM, ARTHUR   Queen Mab's Fairy Realm. G. Newnes, 1901. Sm. 4to. Splendid double-page colour title spread by Savage. 27 full-page & 40 text illus. Blue pictorial cloth, gilt. Base of spine damaged. Greer 40-177 1983 £25

RADCLIFF, THOMAS   A Report on the Agriculture of Eastern and Western Flanders. Printed for John Harding, 1819. First edition, with a folding coloured engraved map and 22 engraved plates, 8vo, calf-backed marbled boards, gilt, with label, a very good copy. Fenning 60-347 1983 £75

RADCLIFFE, ANN   Ellena: A Romance. Cincinnati: U.P. James, (ca. 1850). Early American ed. Orig. wrappers, stitched as issued. Nice copy. Jenkins 155-1049 1983 $45

RADCLIFFE, ANN   The Italian. London, Cadell & Davis, 1797. 3 vols., bound without half titles in cont. maroon roan gilt, hinges little rubbed. First edition. Ravenstree 96-153 1983 $360

RADCLIFFE, ANN   The Italian or the Confessional of the Black Penitents. London: for T. Cadell, jun & W. Davies, 1797. First edition. 3 vols. 8vo. Half calf, marbled sides, respined. Heath 48-381 1983 £425

RADCLIFFE, ANN   The Italian. Dublin, Printed for P. Wogan (etc), 1797. First Dublin edition, 2 vols, 12mo, contemporary tree calf; hinges cracking. Hill 165-96 1983 £45

RADCLIFFE, ANN   A journey made in the summer of 1794... London: Robinson, 1794. First edition. 4to. Cont. half calf. A trifle worn. Some foxing, last leaf ink-spotted. With the Rosebery bookplate. Ximenes 63-632 1983 $325

RADCLIFFE, ANN   A Journey made in the Summer of 1794... London: for G.G. and J. Robinson, 1795. First edition. Half-title. 4to. Cont. half calf, gilt, morocco label, gilt, marbled boards. From the library of Lord Leigh, of Stoneleigh Abbey, with his book-plate. Traylen 94-680 1983 £160

RADCLIFFE, ANN   The Mysteries of Udolpho. London: G.G. & J. Robinson, 1794. Four vols. 12mo, cont. mottled calf, expertly rebacked, orig. gilt backstrips and labels preserved. First edition. Small tear in C6 of first volume expertly repaired, otherwise a fine, clean set, bound complete with the half-titles. Reese 20-811 1983 $850

RADCLIFFE, ANN   The Mysteries of Udolpho. Dublin: Printed by Hillary and Barlow, for Messrs. P. Wogan, W. Jones, and H. Colbert, 1794. 3 vols, 12mo, contemporary calf, red and green labels. First Dublin edition. Hill 165-97 1983 £65

RADCLIFFE, ANN   The Mysteries of Udolpho. Longman, 1806. 6th edition, illus. with copperplates, 4 vols. Tree calf, spines a little rubbed, black labels. Jarndyce 30-527 1983 £38

RADCLIFFE, ANN   The Romance of the Forest. London, T. Hookham and J. Carpenter, 1791. 3 vols., 8vo, cont. half calf, paper flaw mended in leaf N9 of vol. 2 not affecting legibility of text. First edition. Ravenstree 96-154 1983 $395

RADCLIFFE, ANN   The Romance of the Forest: Interspersed with some Pieces of Poetry. Dublin: Printed for Messrs. P. Wogan (etc), 1792. 2 vols, 12mo, contemporary tree calf; a short crack in upper hinge of vol. I, otherwise a fine copy. First Dublin edition. Hill 165-98 1983 £75

RADCLIFFE, ANN   The Romance of the Forest. Longman, 1806. 7th edition, 3 vols. Tree calf, heads of spines rubbed, black labels. Jarndyce 30-525 1983 £30

RADCLIFFE, ANN   The Romance of the Forest. Longman, etc., 1816. 8th edition, 3 vols. Orig. half brown calf, gilt spines. Jarndyce 30-526 1983 £30

RADCLIFFE, ANN   A Sicilian Romance. Dublin: Published by Brett Smith, for the Proprietors, 1796. 12mo, contemporary tree calf; a nice copy. Hill 165-99 1983 £50

RADCLIFFE, WINIFRED   The Saint's Garden. SPCK., 1927. Illus. by Charles Robinson. Frontis. & 10 illus. Pub's cloth. Few sl. marks cvrs., nice copy. Hodgkins 27-133 1983 £12.50

RADEMACHER, FRANZ   Der Thronende Christus der Chorschranken aus Gustorf. Koln/Graz, 1964. 4to, cloth, 124 illus. Ars Libri SB 26-200 1983 $75

RADER, JESSE L.   South of Forty... Norman: Univ. of Oklahoma Press, 1947. Cloth, ownership signature. Dawson 470-248 1983 $60

RADFORD, WILLIAM   History "Of Plimoth Plantation." Boston, 1899. Thick 8vo, (backstrip edge slightly worn). Ex lib. Numerous plates, (rubber-stamped). Argosy 716-94 1983 $30

THE RADICAL harmonist. London: W. Wright, 1820. First edition. 8vo. Disbound. With an etched frontis. Ximenes 63-509 1983 $50

THE RADICAL-HOUSE which Jack would build. Exeter: S. Hedgeland, etc., n.d. (1820). Third edition. 8vo. Disbound. 10 unusual etched illus. (slightly shaved in the outer margin). Ximenes 63-510 1983 $50

RADIN, PAUL   African Folktales and Sculpture. New York: Pantheon Books, 1952. 165 plates. Large 4to. Cloth. Photographs by Walker Evans. Ars Libri 34-731 1983 $100

RAEVSKII, S.   Plakat A. Strakhova/Le placard de A.
Strakhov. Khar'kov: Gosudarstvennoe Izdatel'stvo "Mistetstvo", 1936.
20 plates (1 color), 4to. Cloth. Published in an edition of 1000
copies. Ars Libri 32-650 1983 $75

RAFINESQUE, CONSTANTINE S.   Ancient History. Frankfort, Ky., 1824.
1st ed. Half morocco. Jenkins 153-313 1983 $150

RAGATZ, LOWELL   A Guide for the Study of British
Caribbean History, 1763-1834. Wash., GPO, 1932. Cloth, loose at
joint, internally very good. Reese 19-70 1983 $85

RAGG, THOMAS   Heber. Longman, 1840. First edition,
maroon morocco, gilt, sl. rubbed, a.e.g. Very good. Jarndyce 30-826
1983 £20

RAGGHIANTI, CARLO L.   Carlo Levi. Firenze: Edizioni U,
1948. 55 plates (7 tipped-in color). Text illus. Large 4to.
Boards, 1/4 cloth. Ars Libri 33-501 1983 $20

RAIKES, CHARLES   Notes on the Revolt in the North-Western
Provinces of India. London, 1858. Folding table, pebbled cloth.
Marquis of Tweeddales' bookplate. 8vo. Good. Edwards 1044-581 1983
£65

RAIKES, THOMAS   Private Correspondence...with the
Duke of Wellington. Bentley, 1861. First edition. Orig. brown
cloth, v.g. Jarndyce 30-1108 1983 £16

RAINE, KATHLEEN   Fifteen Short Poems. London: Privately
printed at the Tragara Press, 1978. First edition. One of 30
numbered copies signed by the author. Very fine. Jolliffe 26-421
1983 £45

RAINE, KATHLEEN   The Pythoness and other poems. London,
1949. First edition. Slightly torn dust wrapper. Very nice. Rota
231-499 1983 £21

RAINE, WILLIAM MAC LEOD   Cattle. New York, 1930. Illus. Light
wear to spine. 1st ed. Scarce in the 1st ed. Jenkins 153-449 1983
$50

RAINE, WILLIAM MAC LEOD   Cattle. Garden City: Doubleday, Doran,
1930. First edition. Illus. Orig. tan pictorial cloth.Some wear.
Fine. Jenkins 152-343 1983 $50

RAINE, WILLIAM MAC LEOD   Famous Sheriffs & Western Outlaws. New
York, 1929. First edition. Orig. cloth. Fairly nice. Jenkins 152-
342 1983 $45

RAINE, WILLIAM MAC LEOD   Famous Sheriffs and Western Outlaws.
Garden City, 1929. 1st ed. Clark 741-399 1983 $29.50

RAINFORTH, S. I.   The Stereoptic Skin Clinic. N.Y.,
(c. 1910). 127 separate color photos. Complete with stereopticon
viewer. Boxed. Argosy 713-447 1983 $250

RALEIGH, WALTER   Brevis & admiranda descriptio Regni
giuanae... Nuremberg: Lavinus Hulsius, 1599. Folding map by
Hondius and 6 folding engravings. Small 4to. Vellum. A fine copy.
Kraus 164-198 1983 $3,500

RALEIGH, WALTER   An Introduction to a Breviary of the
History of England with the Reign of King William the I. 1693.
8vo, 3 pages ads., engraved frontis. portrait, cont. calf. Inner
margin of frontis. torn in places, upper joint of cover cracked.
First edition. Bickersteth 77-67 1983 £46

RALEIGH, WALTER   Judicious and Select Essayes and
Observations... London: by T.W. for Humphrey Moseley, 1650.
First collected edition. 12mo. Engraved portrait, each part
with separate title, 19th century calf Russia. Joints cracked.
Heath 48-152 1983 £350

RALEIGH, WALTER   The Last Fight of the Revenge. Toronto,
Musson Book Co., nd. 1st Canadian edn. Illus by Frank Brangwyn:
6 colour plates & many b&w text illus. Grey decor. buckram, t.e.g.
others uncut, v.g. Hodgkins 27-482 1983 £20

RALEIGH, WALTER   Remains of Sir Walter Raleigh. London,
1661. Portrait. 12mo. 2nd ed. Title page & few leaves dusty,
occasional spotting, bound in early panelled calf, quite worn, early
marbled endpapers preserved, covers in double gilt-ruled borders,
newly rebacked, spine blind-decorated & gilt-ruled, with brown morocco
label, gilt-lettered, clean copy. Boswell 7-134 1983 $250

RALEY, LOKER   Salute to the New-Born. New York,
1941. 8vo. Cloth. Review copy with slip laid in. Fine in dj.
In Our Time 156-649 1983 $20

RALPH, GEORGE M.   Something about Sugar. San Francisco:
John J. Newbegin, 1917. 4to, profusely illus. Tan cloth. Karmiole
73-88 1983 $65

RALPH, JAMES   The case of authors by profession or
trade, stated. With regard to booksellers, the stage, and the public.
No matter by whom. London: printed for R. Griffiths, 1758. 8vo,
disbound, first edition. Very good copy. Ximenes 64-449 1983 $475

RALPH, JAMES   The case of our present theatrical disputes, fairly stated. London: printed for Jacob Robinson, 1743.
8vo, wrappers, first edition. Excellent copy; uncommon. Ximenes 64-
450 1983 $375

RALPH, JAMES   The Fall of the Earl of Essex. London:
printed for W. Meadows and S. Billingsley, 1731. 1st ed. of this
version, 8vo, recent orange half morocco, originally bound for John
Philip Kemble in his characteristic fashion with each leaf inlaid,
and with his initials, mark of collation and date 1798 in the margin
of the title page. A fine copy. Pickering & Chatto 19-57 1983
$450

RALPH, JAMES   The touch-stone: or, historical,
critical, political, philosophical, and theological essays on the
reigning diversions of the town. London: printed and sold by the
booksellers, 1728. 12mo, cont. panelled calf, spine gilt (spine
rubbed). First edition. A very good copy, complete with half-title.
Ximenes 64-451 1983 $800

RALPH, JAMES   Zeuma: or the love of liberty. A
Poem. London: printed by C. Ackers, for S. Billingsley, 1729.
1st ed., 8vo, 3 books, leaf R1 misbound, author's name cropped at the
end of the dedication, four catch-words shaved or cropped at the
beginning, title and last leaf a little dust-soiled, modern wrappers.
Pickering & Chatto 19-56 1983 $250

RALPH, JULIAN   On Canada's Frontier. New York:
Harper & Bros., 1892. 22cm. First edition. 70 illus. and plates
from paintings and drawings by Frederick Remington. Brown decorated
cloth, spine ends frayed, internal lib. stamps else very good.
Scarce. McGahern 54-151 1983 $45

RALPH, JULIAN   Our Great West... New York: Harper &
Brothers, 1893. Ads. Illus. Frontis. by Frederick Remmington. Orig.
pictorial cloth. Some light foxing to covers. Jenkins 152-344 1983
$75

RAMAZZINI, BERNARDINO   Essai sur les maladies des artisans.
Paris: chez Moutard, etc., 1777. First edition in French. 12mo.
Cont. mottled calf, spine gilt. A bit rubbed. Very good copy.
Ximenes 63-289 1983 $275

RAMCKE, BERNHARD   Vom Schiffsjungen Zum Fall-Schirmjager-
general. Berlin, 1943. First edition. 39 illus. on 36 plates. Sq.
roy. 8vo. Orig. cloth backed decorated boards. Slightly worn and
soiled. Good. Edwards 1042-456 1983 £20

RAMEAU, JEAN PHILIPPE   Les Fetes d'Hebe ou les Talents
Liriques. Paris, chez l'Auteur, la Veuve Boivin, M. le Clair, (1739).
Engraved music, bound in-between. Oblong folio, cont. calf, spine
gilt, with five raised bands. Salloch 387-193 1983 $1,500

RAMEE, LOUISE DE LA
Please turn to
DE LA RAMEE, LOUISE

RAMEY, EARL   The Beginnings of Marysville. SF:
1936. Special Publication No. 12. 8vo, cloth-backed bds., paper
labels. Illustrated, folding map. Corners bumped. Perata 28-79
1983 $65

RAMON Y CAJAL, SANTIAGO (1852-1934)   Recollections of my Life.
Mass.: M.I.T. Press, (n.d., first published in 1937 by the American
Philosophical Society). Dust jacket. Gach 94-259 1983 $35

RAMON Y CAJAL, SANTIAGO (1852-1934)   Studies on the Cerebral Cortex.
Chicago: The Year Book Publishers, Inc., 1955. First edition in
English. Gach 95-408 1983 $75

RAMON Y CAJAL, SANTIAGO (1852-1934)   Studies on Vertebrate Neuro-
genesis. Springfield: Charles C. Thomas, (1960). First American
edition. Gach 95-409 1983 $75

RAMSAY, ALEX   Report of Survey of Buffalo, Bayou,
Texas. Wash., 1881. Jenkins 153-577 1983 $30

RAMSAY, ALLAN   An essay on ridicule. London: printed
for A. Millar, 1753. First edition. 8vo. Disbound. Very good
copy. Ximenes 63-248 1983 $125

RAMSAY, ALLAN   The Gentle Shepherd. Ptd. for the
author by T. Bensley, 1790. Calf, sl. rubbed, red label, v.g.
Jarndyce 31-68 1983 £25

RAMSAY, ALLAN   The Gentle Shepherd. Edinburgh:
Abernathy & Walker, 1808. 2 vols. 1st ed. Orig. boards, labels,
uncut. Spine wear, but nice set for this kind of binding with
bindings sound and tight and labels fully intact. Jenkins 155-1050
1983 $35

RAMSAY, ALLAN   Poems. London: Printed for J. Clarke,
A. Millar, F. Cogan (etc.), 1731. First London edition. Illus. with
frontis port. by Smibert. 2 vols. 8vo. Full cont. calf with gilt
armorial stamps. Labels worn away. Fine. MacManus 280-4335 1983
$200

RAMSAY, ALLAN   Poems by Allan Ramsay. Dublin:
printed by S. Powell, for George Risk, 1733. 1st Dublin edition,
8vo, frontis. portrait, portrait and title a little browned, but
generally a clean copy in cont. calf, rubbed and rebacked. A very
rare early edition. Pickering & Chatto 19-58 1983 $650

RAMSAY, ALLAN   Poems by Allan Ramsay with New
Additions and Notes... Dublin: by S. Powell for George Risk, 1733.
First Dublin edition. Small 8vo. Engraved portrait. Cont. calf.
Heath 48-407 1983 £80

RAMSAY, ANDREW M.   The Travels of Cyrus. Burlington:
Isaac Neale, Oct. 1, 1793. Full calf (very worn, covers detached).
Very good. Felcone 19-47 1983 $45

RAMSAY, DAVID   The History of the American Revolution.
Philadelphia; R. Aitken & Son, 1789. 2 vols. Orig. paper-backed
boards, uncut. Some boards detached, much of paper covering spine
worn away. First edition. Felcone 22-205 1983 $200

RAMSAY, DAVID   The History of the Revolution of South
Carolina, from a British Province to an Independent State. Trenton:
Isaac Collins, 1785. 2 vols. Five large engraved folding maps. Both
half-titles present. Extra-illus. with engraved portraits of Ramsay
and John Rutledge. 3/4 morocco (extremities a bit rubbed). First book
to be granted a copyright by Congress. Very good. Felcone 19-48
1983 $750

RAMSAY, DAVID   The Life of George Washington.
Boston: D. Mallory and Co. (S. Etheridge, Jr., pr.), 1811. Frontis.
(Engraved port. of Washington by Anderson). Full calf. Felcone
22-206 1983 $50

RAMSAY, DAVID   Memoirs of the Life of Martha Laurens
Ramsay... Lexington: Thomas T. Skillman, 1813. Orig. calf, light
occasional staining, tiny hole in last three leaves, affecting a
couple of letters, else fine. Reese 18-424 1983 $350

RAMSAY, GEORGE   An enquiry into the principles of
human happiness... London: Pickering, 1843. 8vo. Orig. rose cloth.
Printed paper label. First edition. Spine faded, label rubbed.
Uncommon. Ximenes 63-351 1983 $125

RAMSDEN, CHARLES   London Bookbinders 1780-1840. London:
B.T. Batsford Ltd. (1956). 40 plates, small bookplate. Fine copy in
dust jacket. Karmiole 72-19 1983 $125

RAMSDEN, GUENDOLEN   A Smile Within a Tear. London: Hutchinson, 1897. First edition. Illus. Orig. pictorial cloth. Very fine.
MacManus 280-4336 1983 $20

RAMSEY, ALEX   Annual Message of Governor...to the
Senate and House of Representatives of the State of Minnesota. St.
Paul, Marshall, 1861. Orig. printed wraps. Ginsberg 46-480 1983
$65

RAMSEY, JAMES G. M.   The Annals of Tennessee... Charleston,
1853. 1st ed. Map and plan. 8vo, new boards, cloth back and
corners, plates. Foxed. Morrill 287-456 1983 $75

RAND, AYN   Atlas Shrugged. N.Y., Random (1957).
First edition. Dust jacket (short tear). Very good-fine. Houle
21-746 1983 $125

RAND, BENJAMIN   Modern Classical Philosophers. Boston:
Houghton Mifflin, 1908. First edition. Gach 94-259 1983 $25

RAND, EDWARD   The Building of Eternal Rome. Cambridge,
1943. Frontis. 8vo, cloth. Salloch 385-382 1983 $25

RAND, EDWARD   In Quest of Virgil's Birthplace.
Cambridge, Harvard, 1930. First edition. Illus., folding maps.
Cloth. Very good. Zane Grey's copy, with his library stamp.
Houle 21-899 1983 $20

RAND, PAUL   Thoughts on Design. (N.Y., 1947).
First edition. Illus. Cloth. Endpapers blind-stamped. In chipped
dust wrapper. Very good. King 45-316 1983 $40

RAND, SILAS TERTIUS   Legends of the Micmacs. New York, 1894.
First edition. Portrait. 8vo, ex-library. Morrill 290-416 1983
$45

RANDALL, M. J.   The Adventures of a Captain's Wife.
N.Y., 1877. Wrappers. Back-strip repaired. Signed on title by
Charles F. Lummis, 1902. Dawson 471-238 1983 $300

RANDOLPH, EDMUND   Address on the History of California
from the Discovery of the Country to the Year 1849. N.p., 1860.
Orig. printed wraps. Ginsberg 46-115 1983 $50

RANDOLPH, EDMUND   Mostly Fools. Sampson Low, 1886.
First edition, 8vo, orig. cloth, inside joints neatly repaired, a
very good copy. Fenning 61-362 1983 £48.50

RANDOLPH, EDMUND   Speech of...Delivered at Musical
Hall, San Francisco, August 5th, 1859. San F., 1859. Double
columns. Dbd. First edition. Ginsberg 47-151 1983 $75

RANDOLPH, EDMUND   Titles to Land in the City of San
Francisco. Sacramento, 1860. Orig. printed wraps. First edition.
Ginsberg 47-152 1983 $125

RANDOLPH, EDMUND   A Vindication of Mr. Randolph's
Resignation. Phila., 1795. Errata leaf, half cloth, first edition.
Ginsberg 46-653 1982 $75

RANDOLPH, GEORGE   An Enquiry into the Medicinal Virtues
of Bristol Water... London: for R. Baldwin, 1750, First edition.
8vo. Cont. half calf, marbled sides. Heath 48-525 1983 £125

RANDOLPH, MARY   The Virginia Housewife. Baltimore,
1838. Calf. Felcone 22-42 1983 $90

RANDOLPH, SARAH N.   The Life of Gen. Thomas J. Jackson.
Phila., 1876. 8vo. Orig. cloth. Portrait frontis. 8 plates. Very
slightly worn and soiled. Good. Edwards 1042-252 1983 £55

RANDOLPH, THOMAS   Poems, with the muses looking-glasse.
Oxford: printed by Leonard Lichfield, for Francis Bowman, 1638.
First edition. Small 4to. Full blue crushed levant, gilt, spine
gilt, a.e.g., by Riviere. A few small restorations, but a clean
copy, with good margins. Ximenes 63-379 1983 $850

RANDOLPH, VANCE   From Anozark Holler, Stories of Ozark
Mountain Folk. NY (1933). Illus. by Richard A. Loederer. Pict.
cloth, very good. King 46-324 1983 $25

RANDOM DE BERENGER, CHARLES, BARON DE BEAUFAIN
Please turn to
BERENGER, CHARLES RANDOM DE, BARON DE BEAUFAIN

RANELAGH: A Poem. London: Printed for J. Almon...1777. Second
edition. 4to, new wraps. Quaritch NS 7-113 1983 $95

RANGER's Progress. London: Printed for the author...MDCCLX. 8vo.
Cont. calf gilt, spine gilt, lower hinge cracked but cords quite sound,
red label. First and only edition. Fine. Quaritch NS-7-114 1983
$425

RANK, OTTO   Das Inzest-Motiv in Dichtung Und Sage.
Leipzig/Wien: Deuticke, 1912. First edition. Contemporary cloth-
backed boards, some fraying to front joint and label, very good copy.
Gach 95-410 1983 $225

RANK, OTTO   The Practical Bearing of Psychoanalysis.
NY: Nat'l. Committee for Mental Hygiene, 1927. Wrappers. Gach 94-
421 1983 $20

RANK, OTTO   Das Trauma Der Geburt und Seine Bedeutung
Fuer Die Psychoanalyse. Leipzig/Vienna/Zurich: IPV, 1924. First
edition. Publisher's 1/2 cloth. Fine copy. Gach 95-411 1983 $175

RANK, OTTO   Will Therapy and Truth and Realty.
NY: Knopf, 1945. First printing of combined edition. Gach 94-422
1983 $20

RANKE, LEOPOLD   The Ecclesiastical and Political
History of the Popes of Rome. London, Murray, 1841. Second edition.
3/4 brown morocco over marbled boards, spine decorated in gilt,
covers ruled in gilt, t.e.g, marbled endpapers. 3 vols. Very good.
Houle 22-739 1983 $150

RANKIN, MELINDA   Twenty Years Among the Mexicans. Cincinnati: Chase & Hall, 1875. First edition. Brown cloth. Very fine
copy. Bradley 66-679 1983 $100

RANNIT, ALEKSIS   Signum et Verbum. The Elizabeth
Press, 1981. 8vo. Cloth. Vellum spine. Total ed. is 32 copies
designed and printed by Martino Mardersteig. 1 of 26 copies
lettered and signed by Mardersteig. A fine copy in slipcase box.
Box has some light wear at the base. In Our Time 156-533 1983

RANSOM, JOHN CROWE   Chills and Fever. NY, 1924. Paper-
covered boards, cloth spine, corners worn, still very good in chipped
and worn dustwrapper, owner's name. Quill & Brush 54-1135 1983 $250

RANSOM, JOHN CROWE   Chills and Fever. New York: Knopf,
1924. 1st ed., 1st binding. Orig. cloth-backed Batik boards, paper
label. Very fine copy in near perfect dj, and scarce thus. Jenkins
155-1051 1983 $225

RANSOM, JOHN CROWE   Grace After Meat. London: Printed &
published by Leonard & Virginia Woolf at the Hogarth Press, 1924.
First edition. Orig. decorated boards, label. Uncut. From the
library of Lyman Butterfield, with his pencil signature and date on
front endpaper. One of 400 copies printed. Fine. Jenkins 152-746
1983 $325

RANSOM, JOHN CROWE   Grace After Meat. London: The Hogarth
Press, 1924. First edition. Decorated boards, printed front cover
label. 1/400. Spine darkened, extremities worn. Laid in a ticket
for a poetry reading by Ransom at the Prudential Plaza in Chicago on
November 17, 1957. Bradley 66-295 1983 $285

RANSOM, JOHN CROWE   Grace After Meat. London: The Hogarth
Press, 1924. 1st ed. 400 copies printed. Decorated boards, printed
front cover label. Spine darkened by age, extremities worn, very
good copy. Bradley 63-108 1983 $300

RANSOM, JOHN CROWE   Selected Poems. New York, 1945.
D.w. First edition. Thin tall 8vo. Fine. Argosy 714-612 1983
$65

RANSOM, JOHN CROWE   The World's Body. New York: 1938.
First edition. Cloth. Worn, some pencil marks, but sound copy.
Bradley 66-296 1983 $40

RANSOME, ARTHUR   Foul Air and Lung Diseases. Manchester &
Salford Sanitary Association; G. Renshaw, (1877). Disbound. Jarndyce
31-347 1983 £15

RANSOME, ARTHUR   Peter Duck. London, 1932. First
edition. Advance proof copy in green wrappers. Very good. Gekoski
2-159 1983 £25

RANSOME, ARTHUR   Pigeon Post. London, 1936. First
edition. Advance proof copy in green wrappers. Torn at foot of
spine, otherwise very good. Gekoski 2-160 1983 £25

RANSON, STEPHEN W.   Anatomy of the Nervous System from the
Standpoint of Development and Function. Phila., 1927. Many illus.,
4to, cloth, rubbed. Argosy 713-448 1983 $35

RAPER, ELIZABETH   The Receipt Book. The Nonesuch Press,
1924. Orig. blue cloth, a little faded. Jarndyce 31-998 1983 £28

RAPHAELSON, SAMSON   The Human Nature of Playwriting. New
York: 1949. First edition, first printing. Sewed but unbound signatures. Reviewer's copy with publication date rubber-stamped at head
of title page. Advance copy laid into dust jacket for finished work.
Bradley 66-297 1983 $20

A RAPID Tour Around the World... Amherst, 1846. Numerous full-page
woodcuts. Cloth. Very nice. Felcone 20-78 1983 $35

RAPPORT du Comite Central de Vaccine... Paris, 1803. First edition.
8vo. Cont. calf. Browned. Gurney 90-96 1983 £50

RAREY, JOHN S.   The Art of Taming Horses. George
Routledge, 1838. With 8 plates and 14 other illus., small 8vo,
orig. roan-backed cloth. Fenning 62-293 1983 £28.50

RASCOE, BURTON   Titans of Literature. N.Y., Putnam,
1932. First edition, illus. with twelve portraits, 3/4 blue morocco,
t.e.g. Very good. Houle 21-294 1983 $55

RASPE, RUDOLPH ERICH   An Account of Some German Volcanos.
1776. 2 folding plates, 8vo, boards. Wheldon 160-1466 1983 £75

RASPE, RUDOLPH ERICH   Account of the Present Stock and
Arrangement of Mr. James Tassie's Collection of Pastes and
Impressions from Ancient and Modern Gems. London, 1786. 8vo, boards.
Intaglio pastes the size of seals and rings. Rostenberg 88-52 1983
$600

RASTELL, JOHN   Les Termes de la Ley. Printed by
Samuel Roycroft and James Rawlins, 1708. Pagination erratic but
complete, 8vo, cont. unlettered calf, trifle worn but sound; a very
good copy. Fenning 60-348 1983 £45

RATCLIFFE, D. U.   Swallow of the Sea. London, 1937.
Imperial 8vo. Orig. blue decorated cloth. Coloured frontis. Gilt.
Good. Edwards 1042-155 1983 £20

RATCLIFFE, HENRY   Observations On The Rate Of Mortality &
Sickness Existing Amongst Friendly Societies. Colchester, printed for
the Order by Edward Benham, 1862. 4to, margins slightly browned,
original brown cloth, a good copy. Pickering & Chatto 21-100 1983
$75

RATHBONE, EDGAR P.   On Copper Mining in the Lake
Superior District. London, 1887. Illus., 8 plates. Orig. printed
wraps. First edition. Ginsberg 46-654 1983 $35

RATHBORNE, A. B.   Camping and Tramping in Malaya. London,
1898. Folding map, 19 plates. Pictorial cloth. 8vo. Good. Edwards
1044-582 1983 £68

RATHBUN, JONATHAN   Narrative of, with Accurate Accounts
of the Capture of Groton Fort. (New London, 1840). 12mo, 1/2 red
mor., g.t., (very light foxing). First edition. Argosy 716-469 1983
$50

RATHER, ETHEL Z.   Recognition of the Republic of Texas
by the United States. Austin, 1911. Orig. printed wraps. First
edition. Ginsberg 46-738 1983 $75

RATTIGAN, TERENCE   Collected Plays. London, Hamish
Hamilton (1960-64). First edition (volume III only, vols. I & II are
later printings). Dust jackets. 3 vols. Fine. Each volume inscribed
by Rattigan to Andre and Dory (Previn); with each inscription being
slightly different. Houle 22-740 1983 $95

RAU, THEODOR AUGUST   Dissertatio inauguralis medica sistens
pathemata infantum ex difficili dentione... Basel: Friedrich Ludi,
1719. Uncut. Woodcut initial, head- and tail-piece. Small 4to.
Wrappers. Kraus 164-59 1983 $220

RAUCH, FREDERICK AUGUSTUS (1806-1841)   Psychology. NY: M. W. Dodd,
1841. Orig. embossed cloth, joints and edges chipped, foxed. Second
edition. Gach 95-414 1983 $75

RAUM, JOHN O.   The History of New Jersey, from Its
Earliest Settlement to the Present Time. Phila., (1877). First
edition. 2 vols. Thick 8vo, ex lib. Argosy 716-336 1983 $60

RAUNKIAER, C.   The Life Forms of Plants. Oxford, 1934.
189 photos and figures, royal 8vo, cloth. Wheldon 160-1560 1983 £25

RAUSHENBUSH, STEPHEN   Men Atwhiles Are Sober. New York:
Boni & Liveright, 1928. 8vo. Cloth, boards. A fine copy in almost
flawless dj. In Our Time 156-651 1983 $35

RAVA, ALDO   Pietro Longhi. Bergamo: Istituto
Italiano d'Arti Grafiche, 1909. 8 plates. 156 illus. 4to. Boards,
1/2 cloth. Ars Libri 33-197 1983 $40

RAVAL, MARCEL   Claude Nicolas Ledoux 1736-1806.
Paris: Arts et Metiers Graphiques, 1945. 406 illus. 4to. Wrappers.
Glue stains on flyleaf. Very scarce. Ars Libri 32-393 1983 $200

RAVELL, CHARLES H.   Sixty Years of Banking in Michigan.
Battle Creek, 1910. Cloth. First edition. Jenkins 151-215 1983
$45

RAVITCH, MICHAEL L.   Romance of Russian Medicine. N.Y.,
(c. 1937). First edition, dust wrapper. Argosy 713-449 1983 $75

RAWLINSON, H. G.   British Beginnings in Western India.
Oxford, 1920. 10 plates. 8vo. Orig. cloth. Good. Edwards 1044-
584 1983 £15

RAWLINSON, H. G.   The History of the 2/6th Rajputana Rifles.
Oxford, 1936. Maps, plates. 8vo. Orig. cloth. Good. Edwards 1044-
583 1983 £15

RAWLINSON, RICHARD   Somnouthshire. A Small Specimen of the
Many Mistakes in Sir William Dugdale's Baronage... Monmouth: by
Charles Heath, 1801. 8vo. Specially bound for Sir Thomas Phillipps
in quarter green calf, Middle Hill boards. Presentation copy with a
long inscription from the editor, Charles Heath, and Phillipp's notes
requesting the binder to preserve the two end papers. Fine copy.
Heath 48-288 1983 £225

RAWLINSON, W. G.   Catalogue of Mr. W.G. Rawlinson's
Collection of Turner's Liber Studiorum. London: Privately Printed,
1912. Large 4to. Boards. Presentation copy, inscribed by the
author to Francis Bullard. Ars Libri 32-679 1983 $60

RAWSON, EDWARD   The Revolution in New-England
Justified, and the People there Vindicated from the Aspersions Cast
Upon them by Mr. John Palmer. Boston, 1773. Boards, very good.
Reese 18-98 1983 $250

RAWSON, MARION   Candleday Art. N.Y., Dutton, 1938.
First edition. 4to, many illus. by the author. Pictorial endpapers.
Pictorial dust jacket (slight rubbing). Fine copy. Houle 22-742
1983 $37.50

RAWSON, MARION   The Old House Picture Book. New York,
1941. 1st ed. Illus. by author. Royal 8vo. Clark 741-224 1983
$23.50

RAY, JAMES   A Compleat History of the Rebellion...
Bristol: by S. Farley, 1752. 8vo. Engraved portrait. Uncut
in orig. boards, respined. Very rare. Heath 48-176 1983 £65

RAY, JIM   The Inside Story of the Flying Fortress.
New York, 1943. First edition. Illustrations by the author in color
and black and white. Oblong 4to, original colored pictorial boards.
Morrill 290-624 1983 $20

RAY, JOHN   Miscellaneous Discourses Concerning the
Dissolution and Changes of the World. Printed for Samuel Smith, 1692.
8vo, license leaf facing title, one page of ad. at the end, small
rust hole in S2 affecting one letter, old calf, rebacked. First
edition. Bickersteth 77-313 1983 £190

RAY, JOHN   Synopsis Methodica Animalium Quadru-
pedum et Serpentini Generis. London: S. Smith & B. Walford, 1693.
First edition. 8vo. Cont. calf. Portrait. Lightly browned.
Gurney 90-97 1983 £160

RAY, JOHN   Synopsis Methodica Avium et Piscium.
1713. 4 engraved plates, 8vo, cont. panelled calf, neatly rebacked.
Wheldon 160-513 1983 £140

RAY, JOHN   Synopsis Methodica Stirpium Britannicarum. Londini: Impensis Gulielmi & Joannis Innys, in area occidentali
D. Pauli, & S. Tooke & B. Motte, ad Medii Templi Portam, Fleetstreet,
1724. 24 plates, 2 vols., 8vo, cont. calf, neatly rebacked. The
second issue comprising copies of the first issue divided into two
volumes and with new title pages. Wheldon 160-1625 1983 £120

RAY, JOHN   Synopsis Methodica Stirpium Britannicarum.
Impensis Gulielmi & Joannis Innys, 1724. 8vo, 2 vols., 24 engraved
plates, some folding, orig. calf, rubbed, upper joint of vol. 2
cracked, but firm. Bickersteth 77-314 1983 £90

RAY, JOHN F.   Travels through the Low-Countries,
Germany, Italy and France. London: J. Walthoe, 1738. 2nd ed.,
corrected and improved. 8vo, 2 vols., cont. calf gilt, morocco
labels. Half-titles. Three engraved plates. Bound into this copy
is Ray's Catalogus Stirpium In Exteris Regionibus (London, 1738),
not found in all copies of the "Travels." Bindings worn, hinges of
one volume tender, but a good copy. Trebizond 18-159 1983 $250

RAY, WILLIAM   Poems, on Various Subjects, Religious,
Moral, Sentimental and Humorous. Auburn, N.Y.: U.F. Doubleday,
1821. Orig. boards, uncut. First edition. Covers quite worn,
disbound. Felcone 22-207 1983 $60

RAY, WORTH S.   Austin Colony Pioneers. Austin, 1949.
Illus. 1st ed. Scarce. Jenkins 153-452 1983 $50

RAY, WORTH S.   Down in the Cross Timbers. Austin, Texas,
1947. Illus. Limited to 500 copies. Dust jacket. Fine. Jenkins
152-337a 1983 $45

RAYMER, ROBERT G.   Raymer's Dictionary of Spokane.
Spokane, 1908. Illus., folded map laid in. Illus. throughout text.
Orig. printed 12mo, wraps. First edition. Ginsberg 46-870 1983
$35

RAYMOND, CHARLES W.   Report of a Reconnaissance of the Yukon
River... Washington, 1871. Later cloth with morocco label. Jenkins
153-453 1983 $85

RAYMOND, DANIEL   Thoughts on Political Economy.
Baltimore: Fielding Lucas, Jr., 1820. 1st ed., neatly rebacked
later boards, ex lib. Argosy 710-144 1983 $250

RAYMOND, GEORGE   The life and enterprises of Robert
William Elliston, comedian. London: G. Routledge and Co., 1857.
Sm. 8vo, original yellow pictorial cloth (slightly rubbed). First one-
volume edition. With a portrait, 3 plates by George Cruikshank,
and two plates by "Phiz". Nice copy. Ximenes 64-453 1983 $75

RAYMOND, THOMAS L.   Stephen Crane. Newark, NJ: The Carteret
Book Club, 1923. Wood engr. of Crane by Rudolf Ruzicka. Edition ltd.
to 250 numbered copies, printed by D. B. Updike at the Merrymount
Press. Red cloth over boards, paper spine label. Bookplate. Karmiole
71-78 1983 $60

RAYNOLDS, WILLIAM F.   Report on the Exploration of the
Yellowstone & the Country Drained by that River. Wash., 1868.
Lacks maps. Argosy 716-644 1983 $40

RAYNSFORD, JOHN   The young souldier. London: printed
by J.R. for Joseph Hunscott, 1642. First edition. Small 4to. Disbound. Very rare. Ximenes 63-319 1983 $650

A RAZOR for the Whig... Bristol: by Gutch & Martin, 1832. First
edition. Tall 8vo. Uncut in quarter blue morocco. Lightly rubbed.
Heath 48-153 1983 £40

REA, J.   Flora: seu de Florum cultura. 1676.
Second edition, engraved frontispiece, 3 engraved headpieces by F. H.
van Hove and 8 engraved plates, folio, new half calf antique style.
Title-page in red and black. Some slight browning and the margins
of the first two leaves a trifle frayed. Wheldon 160-1999 1983 £225

READ, CHARLES HERCULES   Catalogue of the Works of Art
Bequeathed to the British Museum by Baron Ferdinand Rothschild, M.P.,
1898. London: The Trustees of the British Museum, 1902. 4to,
55 leaves of photogravure plates, printed on Japan vellum, in
addition, there is a frontis. + 42 text illus. Index. Green cloth,
gilt-stamped spine. Karmiole 76-8 1983 $100

READ, D. B.   The Life and Times of Gen. John Graves
Simcoe... Toronto: George Virtue, 1890. 21 1/2cm. 10 illus. and
portraits (including steel engraved portraits of Simcoe and Joseph
Brant). Orig. brown cloth. Minor wear at the edges. Hinges repaired
else very good copy. McGahern 53-129 1983 $30

READ, DANIEL   Address of... Indianapolis, 1869.
Orig. printed wraps. First edition. Ginsberg 46-655 1983 $35

READ, DANIEL   Address on the Means of Promoting
Common School Education... Indianapolis, 1852. First edition. Dbd.
Ginsberg 46-348 1983 $30

READ, HERBERT   Art Now. London: Faber and Faber
Limited, (1933). First edition. 8vo. Illus. Orig. decorated
cloth. Dust jacket, rubbed and chipped jacket. Jaffe 1-337 1983
$35

READ, HERBERT   Art Now. London, 1933. First edition.
Cover design by E.M. Kauffer. Spine a little creased. Very nice.
Rota 230-509 1983 £15

READ, HERBERT   The Education of Free Men. Freedom Press,
1944. First edition. Wrappers faded. Author's signed autograph
presentation inscription. Nice. Rota 230-510 1983 £18

READ, HERBERT   The End of a War. (London): Faber
and Faber, (1933). First edition. 8vo. Orig. boards. Dust jacket,
slightly torn, but a fine copy. Jaffe 1-338 1983 $85

READ, HERBERT   The End of the War. (London): Faber,
(1933). Boards. First edition. Inscribed by the author to another
writer. Some soiling, but a very good copy in worn dust jacket.
Reese 20-817 1983 $20

READ, HERBERT   The Green Child. London: William
Heinemann Ltd., (1935). First edition. 8vo. Orig. cloth. Dust
jacket. Fine copy. Jaffe 1-339 1983 $185

READ, HERBERT   The Philosophy of Anarchism. London,
1940. First edition. Wrappers a little darkened and creases at
edges. Author's initialled autograph presentation inscription to
F. Morley. Very nice. Rota 231-510 1983 £30

READ, HERBERT   Reason and Romanticism. (London):
Faber and Gwyer, (1926). First edition. 8vo. Orig. cloth. Dust
jacket. Fine copy. Jaffe 1-335 1983 $45

READ, HERBERT   The Sense of Glory. Cambridge: At
The University Press, 1929. First edition. 8vo. Orig. cloth.
Dust jacket, chipped. Fine. Jaffe 1-336 1983 $35

READ, HERBERT   The Sense of Glory. London, 1929. First
edition. Spine and covers faded. Author's initialled autograph presentation inscription to F. Morley. Nice. Rota 231-507 1983 £30

READ, HERBERT   Unit 1. The Modern Movement in English
Architecture, Painting and Sculpture. London: Cassell and Company
Ltd, (1934). First edition. 4to. Illus. Orig. decorated cloth.
Dust jacket. Brown paint flaking on front cover, otherwise a fine
copy. Jaffe 1-340 1983 $225

READ, HERBERT   Wordsworth: The Clark Lectures 1929-
1930. London, 1930. First edition. One corner bruised. Worn dust
wrapper. Author's initialled autograph presentation inscription to
F. Morley. With an autograph postcard, initialled, from E. Blunden.
Very nice. Rota 231-508 1983 £45

READ, HERBERT   A World Within a War. The Hampden Press,
1943. First edition. Printed in red and black, with woodcut decorations, small folio, orig. unlettered cloth-backed paper boards, uncut.
A fine copy. Ltd. edition of 50 numbered copies. Signed by the author
and also by the typographer and designer John R. Biggs. Fenning 61-365
1983 £38.50

READ, JAMES A.   Journey to the Gold Diggings...
Burlingame: Wreden, 1950. Color reproductions of the 113 orig. Read
illus. Oblong 12mo, orig. yellow plaid boards, orange cloth back with
paper label, blue dj. Limited ed. (390 copies printed at the Grabhorn
Press). Very fine. Jenkins 153-454 1983 $75

READ, JOHN M.   Speech of Hon...at the Democratic
Town Meeting in Favor of the Union and California, Held in the
Hall of the Chinese Museum...1850. Phila., 1850. Double columns.
Orig. printed self wraps. First edition. Ginsberg 47-153 1983
$65

READ, OPIE   An Arkansas Planter. Chicago: Rand-
McN., (1896). First edition. 8vo. Green pictorial cloth. 2 small
red spots on edge of cover. Cover, half-tone frontis. plus text.
Illus. by Denslow, others by I. Morgan. T.e.g. Very good. Aleph-bet
8-83 1983 $30

READ, THOMAS BUCHANAN   The Wagoner of the Alleghanies.
Philadelphia, 1863. Full blind-tooled morocco. Felcone 22-190
1983 $25

READ, WILLIAM A.   Louisiana-French. Baton Rouge: LSU
Press, 1931. First edition. Orig. printed wrappers. Illus. Maps.
Jenkins 152-851 1983 $45

READE, CHARLES   Christie Johnstone. London, Richard
Bentley, 1853. 8vo, cont. red half calf worn, joints cracked,
bookplate, well-read copy. Ravenstree 96-155 1983 $125

READE, CHARLES   The Cloister and the Hearth. New York,
Rudd & Charleton, 1861. Tall 8vo, orig. patterned cloth, faded,
spine ends worn, decent copy. Ravenstree 96-156 1983 $115

READE, CHARLES   The Cloister and the Hearth. NY, 1932.
Illus. by Lynd Ward. Limited Editions Club. One of 1500 copies numbered and signed by Ward, 2 vols., fine in chipped and torn dustwrappers with faded spines, slipcase slightly faded, bookplate. Quill &
Brush 54-1138 1983 $60

READE, CHARLES   The Course of True Love Never Did Run
Smooth. London, Richard Bentley, 1857. 8vo, orig. printed pink
boards, now quite worn and soiled, spine rebacked with later paper,
minor interior dust-soiling. First edition, in the rare first issue
binding. Ravenstree 96-157 1983 $40

READE, CHARLES   Foul Play. London: Bradbury, Evans &
Co., 1868. First edition. 3 vols. Orig. red cloth. Spines and
covers rather worn. Inner hinges cracked. Bookplates. Fair.
MacManus 280-4337 1983 $200

READE, CHARLES   Foul Play, A Novel. Boston: Ticknor
& Fields, 1868. Plates. 1st American ed. Illustrated by George
Du Maurier. Orig. pink printed wrappers. Some chipping, but a
very good copy. Jenkins 155-1053 1983 $85

READE, CHARLES   Griffith Gaunt; or, a Jealousy.
Boston: Fields, Osgood, 1869. Plates. 1st American ed. Orig.
pink printed wrappers. A couple of minor nicks, but very tight copy.
Jenkins 155-1054 1983 $85

READE, CHARLES   Hard Cash. Sampson, Low, Son & Marston,
1863. First edition, 3 vols. Jarndyce 30-533 1983 £42

READE, CHARLES   Hard Cash. Sampson Low, Son & Marston,
1864. 2nd edition, inserted ad. slip at front vol. II. Orig.
green cloth, v.g. Jarndyce 30-531 1983 £36

READE, CHARLES   "It is Never too Late to Mend." London,
Richard Bentley, 1856. 3 vols., 8vo, orig. cloth, rather worn,
bumped, faded and bit shaken, soiled. First edition. Ravenstree 96-
158 1983 $285

READE, CHARLES   The King's Rival. Richard Bentley,
1854. First edition, half title. Rebound in maroon cloth, v.g.
Jarndyce 31-852 1983 £16.50

READE, CHARLES   "Love Me Little, Love Me Long." London:
Trubner & Co., 1859. First edition. 2 vols. Orig. blue cloth.
MacManus 280-4338 1983 $185

READE, CHARLES   "Love me Little, Love me Long." New
York, Harpers, 1859. 8vo, orig. cloth gilt, spine ends frayed,
bookplate, name on flyleaf. First American edition. Ravenstree 96-
159 1983 $115

READE, CHARLES   "Love me Little, Love me Long".
Trubner & Co., 1859. First edition, 2 vols. Half titles, orig. blue
pebble-grained cloth, borders in blind, gilt spine lettering. V.g.
Jarndyce 30-530 1983 £58

READE, CHARLES   Masks and Faces. Richard Bentley, 1854.
First edition, rebound in maroon cloth, v.g. Jarndyce 31-850 1983
£16.50

READE, CHARLES   Peg Woffington. Boston, Tichnor and
Fields, 1855. 8vo, orig. cloth gilt, slight wear, very fine copy.
First American edition. Ravenstree 96-160 1983 $135

READE, CHARLES   Peg Woffington. George Allen, 1899.
1st edn. Illus. by Hugh Thomson. Frontis. & illus. title p. & many
text illus. Dark green cloth gilt designed by Thomson, a.e.g. (sl.
foxing prelims. & some pages), nice copy. Hodgkins 27-483 1983 £14

READE, CHARLES   A Simpleton. Chapman & Hall, 1873.
First edition, 3 vols. Half titles. Jarndyce 30-535 1983 £40

READE, CHARLES   A Terrible Temptation. London, Chapman &
Hall, 1871. 3 vols., 8vo, somewhat worn, faded, joints worn and
splitting, bookplate, spine ends chipped. First English edition.
Ravenstree 96-162 1983 $215

READE, CHARLES   A Terrible Temptation. Chapman & Hall,
1871. First edition, 3 vols. Half titles. Jarndyce 30-534 1983 £42

READE, CHARLES   A Terrible Temptation. B, 1871. Illus.,
spine sunned, spine edges frayed, corners worn, good. Quill & Brush
54-1137 1983 $35

READE, CHARLES   Two Loves and a Life. Richard Bentley,
1854. First edition, half title. Rebound in maroon cloth, v.g.
Jarndyce 31-851 1983 £16.50

READE, CHARLES   White Lies. Trubner, 1857. First
edition, 3 vols. Half calf, spines gilt, v.g. Jarndyce 30-529 1983
£48

READE, CHARLES   White Lies. Trubner & Co., 1857.
First edition, 3 vols. Jarndyce 30-532 1983 £42

READE, CHARLES   A Woman-Hater. Edinburgh and London,
Blackwood, 1877. 3 vols., 8vo, orig. cloth, very worn and faded,
inner hinges breaking, labels removed from upper covers. First
English edition. Ravenstree 96-163 1983 $95

READE, CHARLES   A Woman-Hater. Wm. Blackwood, 1877.
First edition, 3 vols. Half titles. Jarndyce 30-536 1983 £38

READE, CLARA   The Old English Baron. (London) Wood &
Co., 1813. 12mo, orig. calf, worn, blank endleaf gone, names on
endpapers and back of title, a well used copy. Ravenstree 96-168
1983 $35

READE, JOHN EDMUND   The Drama of a Life. Saunders & Otley,
1840. First edition, tall 8vo, dark blue roan, rubbed. Inscribed
presentation copy from the author. Jarndyce 30-828 1983 £12.50

READE, JOHN EDMUND   Man in Paradise. Longman, 1856.
First edition. Half title, 24 pp ads. Orig. orange cloth. Jarndyce
30-829 1983 £12.50

READING, JOSEPH H.   The Ogowe Band. Phila.: Reading & Co.,
1890. 8vo. Numerous plates and maps. Orig. pictorial cloth. Rubbed.
Adelson Africa-213 1983 $30

THE REAL or Constitutional House that Jack Built. London: Sams,
1819. 8vo, title vignette & 12 illus. Wraps. Rostenberg 88-5 1983
$75

THE REAL or constitutional house that Jack built. London: printed
for J. Asperne, etc., 1819. First edition. 8vo. Disbound. 12
woodcuts. Ximenes 63-512 1983 $45

REALE ACCADEMIA D'ITALIA   105 opere di Antonio Mancini. Roma,
1940. 30 plates. Small 4to. Boards. Ars Libri 33-508 1983
$35

LA REALE Medicide. Florence, 1778. 4to, 1/2 calf, uncut. Paper
slightly foxed in some spots. Salloch 387-161 1983 $650

REASON versus passion; or, an impartial review of the dispute between
the public and the proprietors of Covent Garden Theatre. London:
printed by W. Lewis; for Wilson, n.d. (1809). 8vo, disbound, first
edition. Very good copy. Ximenes 64-454 1983 $125

REASONS for giving encouragement to the sea-faring people of Great-
Britain... London: J. Millan, 1739. First edition. 8vo. Disbound. Title dusty. Ximenes 63-341 1983 $75

REAU, LOUIS   Les Lemoyne. Une dynastie de sculpteurs
au XVIIIe siecle. Paris: Les Beaux-Arts, 1927. 80 heliogravure
plates with 136 illus. Small folio. Buckram. Ars Libri 32-399
1983 $150

REAVEY, GEORGE   Quixotic Perquisitions. London: Europa
Press, (1939). Cloth. Frontis. by John Buckland-Wright. First
edition. One of 300 numbered copies. Inscribed by the author "To
William Troy and Naomi Adams. Good neighbors in our Joycean
Peregrinations..." Near fine in lightly used dust jacket. Reese 20-
818 1983 $60

THE REBELLION; or, all in the wrong. A serio-comic hurly burly, in
scenes, as it was performed for two months at the New Theatre Royal,
Covent-Garden. London: printed for Vernor, Hood, and Sharoe; Taylor
and Hessey; Sharp and Hailes; and J. Booker, 1809. 8vo, disbound.
First edition. With a portrait. Ximenes 64-455 1983 $125

RECENT Election in Louisiana: Testimony Taken by the Select Committee on the Recent Election... Wash., 1877. 3 vols. All 6 parts included. Later cloth, orig. morocco labels. Very good set. Jenkins 153-340 1983 $125

RECHINGER, K. H.   Flora of Lowland Iraq. 1964. Royal 8vo, cloth. Wheldon 160-1760 1983 £39

RECK, FRANK   The Romance of American Transportation. N.Y., Crowell, (1938). First edition. Illus. with many halftones, maps and diagrams. Dust jacket. Fine. Houle 22-1160 1983 $20

RECORD, S. J.   Timbers of the New World. New Haven (1943), 1947. 58 plates (including 22 photomicrographs) and 8 maps, royal 8vo, cloth. Spine trifle faded. Wheldon 160-2099 1983 £25

RECORD, First Michigan Engineers and Mechanics, Civil War 1861-1865. Lansing, n.d. (1900's). A used copy. Vol. 43 in the Brown Book Series. King 46-75 1983 $35

RECORD of Connecticut Men in the War of the Revolution... Hartford, 1889. 1st ed. 4to, new buckram. Morrill 287-76 1983 $40

RECORDS of the Massachusetts Volunteer Militia Called Out by the Governor...To Suppress a Threatened Invasion During the War of 1812-14. Boston, 1913. First edition. 4to, very nice. Morrill 290-654 1983 $22.50

REDDALL, HENRY FREDERIC   Fact, Fancy, and Fable: A New Handbook for Ready Reference on Subjects Commonly Omitted from Cyclopaedias. Chicago, 1889. 1st ed. 8vo, half orig. leather. Top of backstrip chipped. Morrill 286-670 1983 $20

REDDING, CYRUS   Memoirs of Remarkable Misers. London: Charles J. Skeet, 1863. First edition. 2 vols. Orig. cloth. From the collection of Hugh Walpole, with his Brackenburn bookplates. Covers a little rubbed. Cont. owner's initials on front endsheets. Very good. MacManus 280-4341 1983 $150

REDE, LEMAN THOMAS   Bibliotheca Americana... London: J. Debrett, 1789. 4to. Early paper covered boards with modern leather back, uncut. Oak Knoll 49-338 1983 $750

REDFIELD, ISAAC F.   A Practical Treatise Upon the Law of Railroads. Boston, 1858. Second edition. Full calf (dry and shabby; needs rebinding). Felcone 22-203 1983 $60

REDGROVE, PETER   Work in Progress. London, 1969. First English edition. One of 26 lettered copies signed by Peter Redgrove. Very fine. Jolliffe 26-511 1983 £60

REDI, FRANCESCO   Esperienze intorno alla Generazione degl'Insetti... Florence: all'Insegna della Stella, 1668. First edition. 4to. Orig. pasteboards, repaired, in a drop-box. 28 plates and 10 engravings in text. Bookplate of the Nordkirchen library. Gurney 90-99 1983 £650

REDI, FRANCESCO   Osservazioni...intorno agli animali viventi... Florence: Piero Matini, 1684. First edition. 26 engraved copperplates, including 2 folding, and engraved portrait opposite half title. 4to. 18th-century boards with calf back and corners. Slight rubbing on corner tips. With a note on the half title in the hand of Geminiano Montanari that it was given to him by the author, 1684. A very fine copy. Rare. Kraus 164-200 1983 $3,400

REDI, FRANCESCO   Osservazioni intorno alle Vipere... Florence, 1664. First edition. Small 4to. Old half-vellum, 2 leaves (including errata leaf and imprimatur leaf at end) with device of Academy at end of text. Top of spine worn. Lacks half-title. Gurney 90-100 1983 £250

REDIG DE CAMPOS, D.   Raffaello nelle Stanze. Milano: Aldo Martello, 1965. 76 color plates. Folio. Cloth. Dust jacket. Slipcase. Ars Libri 33-300 1983 $100

REDPATH, JAMES   Hand-Book to Kansas Territory and the Rocky Mountains' Gold Region. New York: J. H. Colton, 1859. 3 maps, ads. Original blind-embossed brown cloth, title in gilt on front cover. Neatly rebacked. Jenkins 151-281 1983 $650

REDWAY, LAURANCE   History of the Medical Society of the County of Westchester 1797-1947. New York, 1947. First edition. 8vo. Orig. cloth. Fye H-3-470 1983 $25

REECE, BYRON HERBERT   Ballad of the Bones and Other Poems. New York, 1945. 8vo, cloth. With blurbs on the jacket by Alfred Kreymborg, et al. Clipping about the book pasted on inside endboard (under jacket) else fine in lightly worn dust jacket. In Our Time 156-652 1983 $50

REED, ALFRED ZANTZINGER   The Territorial Basis of Government Under the State Constitutions Local Divisions and Rules for Legislative Apportionment. N.Y., 1911. Orig. printed wraps. First edition. Ginsberg 46-659 1983 $20

REED, ALMA   Jose Clemente Orozco. New York: Delphic Studios, 1932. 248 plates. 4to. Cloth. Frontis. after a photograph by Arnold Genthe. Ars Libri 32-498 1983 $125

REED, ANDREW   No Fiction: A Narrative, founded on recent and interesting Facts. Printed for Francis Westley (etc), 1820. Third edition, corrected. 2 vols, 8vo, contemporary blind- and gilt-stamped calf. Hill 165-100 1983 £20

REED, EDWARD TENNYSON   Mr. Punch's Book of Arms. London, (1899). 1st ed. Illus. by author. 4to, orig. vellum. Binding soiled. Morrill 289-513 1983 $30

REED, JOHN   The Day in Bohemia or Life Among the Artists. New York: Printed for the author, 1913. Printed wraps. First edition. One of 500 copies. This copy bears the bookplate of Carl Van Vechten. Another bookplate has been neatly removed from the rear, and the binding reglued after the first signature. A very good copy, sans slipcase. Reese 20-819 1983 $125

REED, JOSEPH   Madrigal and Truletta. A mock-tragedy. London: printed for W. Reeve, 1758. 8vo, wrappers, first edition. Very good copy. Rare. Ximenes 64-456 1983 $175

REED, MYRTLE   The Book of Clever Beasts. N.Y.: Put., 1904. 8vo. Red cloth. Illus. with 9 full-page plates by Newell. Very good. Aleph-bet 8-187 1983 $31

REED, PARKER MC COBB   History of the Lower Kennebec, 1602-1889. Bath, 1889. Orig. printed wraps. Illus. First edition. Ginsberg 46-862 1983 $35

REEDY, MARION   The Law of Love... East Aurora: The Roycrofters, 1905. Half suede over boards, leather spine label, t.e.g., others uncut. With decorative title page printed in three colors, colored initial letters and a decorative colophon. Name in ink on endpaper, else a very fine copy. Oak Knoll 49-351 1983 $30

REES, J. D.   The Duke of Clarence. London, 1891. Map, portraits and illus. Roy.8vo. Good. Edwards 1044-585 1983 £46

REES, L. E. R.   A Personal Narrative of the Siege of Lucknow. London, 1858. Folding plan, portrait. 8vo, orig. cloth. Marquis of Tweeddale's copy with his bookplate. Good. Edwards 1044-586 1983 £55

REESE, DAVID M.   Humbugs of New York. N.Y., 1838. First edition. Argosy 713-451 1983 $35

REESE, DAVID M   Observations on the Epidemic of 1819. Baltimore: The Author, 1819. First edition. Small 12mo, orig. mottled calf, (joints repaired); ex-lib. Argosy 713-452 1983 $150

REESE, DAVID M.   Phrenology Known by Its Fruits. New York, Howe and Bates, 1836. 12mo., orig. patterned brown cloth, remains of label on spine, first ed. Gach 95-416 1983 $40

REEVE, ARTHUR B.   Craig Kennedy Listens in. N.Y., Harper (1923). First edition, "H-X." Fresh pictorial cloth. Dust jacket (short tears, nicks). Houle 21-751 1983 $65

REEVE, CLARA   The Old English Baron; A Gothic Story.
Printed for J. Mawman (etc), 1807. 12mo, contemporary sprinkled
calf. 7 engraving plates. Hill 165-101 1983 £25

REEVE, H.   An Essay on the Torpidity of Animals.
1809. 8vo, original boards, roughly rebacked, uncut. Rare. A hole
in the lower blank margin of pp. 41/42. Wheldon 160-514 1983 £20

REEVE, L.   Elements of Conchology; an introduction
to the natural history of shells and the animals which form them.
1860. 2 vols., roy. 8vo, recently bound in half green morocco, m.e.,
62 hand-coloured plates. Very scarce. Small blind stamps on title-
pages, half-titles and last plate of each volume. Library accession
stamps on reverse of each title-page. Slight foxing on a few plates
in vol. 2. Wheldon 160-83 1983 £450

REEVES, CHARLES EVANS   Diseases of the Spinal Cord & Its
Membranes. London, 1858. 8vo, orig. blind-stamped cloth. First
edition. Two private ex-libris stamps on title. Argosy 713-453 1983
$85

REFERENCE Catalogue of British Topography and Family History Offered
for Sale by Henry Gray, Antiquarian and Topographical Bookseller...
London, 1887. Orig. dark green blind-stamped cloth, gilt-lettered
spine. Fine; ownership stamps on title. Grunder 6-8 1983 $40

REFORMED Dutch Church in the United States of America, Constitution.
NY: William Durell, 1793. 12mo, disbound, ex-library. Argosy 710-
77 1983 $35

THE REFUGE. Philadelphia: Lorenzo Press, 1804. 12mo. Cont. calf.
First American edition. Hinges partly cracked. Covers worn. Good.
MacManus 277-87 1983 $45

REGAN, C. T.   Biologia Centrali-Americana: Pisces.
1906-08. 26 plates and 2 maps, 4to, binder's cloth. Wheldon 160-
929 1983 £220

REGAN, C. T.   Natural History. (1936). 16 coloured
plates and numerous photographs. Royal 8vo, cloth. Wheldon 160-515
1983 £15

REGIMEN SANITATIS SALERNITANUM   Regimen Sanitatis. Paris: Ulrich
Gering, 5 March 1483-84. First blank. Initials and paragraph marks
in red and blue. Small 4to., modern vellum. Inscription on first
blank leaf attesting to this copy being a gift from the painter
Alexander Paul Joseph Veron, called Bellecourt. A leaf with 19th
century bibliographical notes on this work tipped-in at front. Lower
margins stained in varying degree, some worm punctures, few neat
marginalia. Kraus 164-151 1983 $5,800

THE REGISTER of Folly... London: by F. Newbery..., 1773. First
edition. 8vo. Uncut in modern boards. Errata leaf. Heath 48-408
1983 £65

THE REGISTER of Folly... to which is added a Trip to Bristol Vauxhall... Bath: for S. Hazard..., 1779. Fourth edition. 8vo.
Cont. calf, rebacked. Engraved frontis. Heath 48-409 1983 £45

REGIUS, J. M. F.   Essai sur l'histoire naturelle des
Vertebres de la Provence. Bull. Soc. Sci. Draguignan, 1880-81.
Text figures, 8vo, wrappers, rebacked. Wheldon 160-427 1983 £15

REGULATIONS respecting deserters. London: printed by March and
Teape, for HMSO, n.d. (1801). Only edition. Small 8vo. Orig.
marbled wrappers, printed paper side-label. Ximenes 63-320 1983
$35

REICH, SHELDON   John Marin. A stylistic analysis and
catalogue raisonne. Tucson: University of Arizona Press, 1970.
2 vols. 209 illus.; 1975 catalogue illus. 4to. Cloth. Dust
jacket. Slipcase. Ars Libri 32-429 1983 $150

REICH, WILHELM (1897-1957)   Character-Analysis. NY: Orgone
Institute Press, 1945. First English edition. Spine lightly soiled,
else very good. Gach 95-417 1983 $35

REICH, WILHELM (1897-1957)   Contact With Space: Oranur. NY: Core
Pilot Press, 1957. Fine in dust jacket. Gach 95-418 1983 $475

REICH, WILHELM (1897-1957)   Der Einbruch der Secualmoral. Berlin:
Verlag von Sexualpolitik, (1932). First edition. Fine in worn dust
jacket. Gach 95-419 1983 $175

REICH, WILHELM (1897-1957)   Der Genitale und der Neurotische
Charakter. Orig. printed wrappers, spine worn, unopened. Gach 95-
420 1983 $25

REICH, WILHELM (1897-1957)   Orgonomic Diagnosis of Cancer Biopathy.
Orgonon, Rangeley, Maine: The Wilhelm Reich Foundation, (1952).
Orig. printed stiff wrappers. First separate edition. Gach 95-421
1983 $75

REICH, WILHELM (1897-1957)   The Sexual Revolution. NY: Orgone
Institute Press, 1945. First edition in English. Owner's signature,
else a very good copy. Gach 95-422 1983 $37.50

REICH, WILHELM (1897-1957)   Wilhelm Reich Biographical Material.
Orgonon, Rangeley, Maine: Orgone Institute Press, 1955. Orig.
printed self-wrappers. Gach 95-423 1983 $75

REICH, WILHELM (1897-1957)   Wilhelm Reich Biographical Material.
Orgonon, Rangeley, Maine: Orgone Institute Press, 1953. Orig.
printed wrappers. First separate edition. Gach 95-424 1983 $75

REICHARD, GLADYS A.   Navajo Shepherd and Weaver. New
York: J.J. Augustin, 1936. 15 plates. Text figures. Small 4to.
Cloth. Ars Libri 34-438 1983 $75

REICHEL, WILLIAM C.   A History of the Rise, Progress, and
Present Condition of the Moravian Seminary for Young Ladies at
Bethlehem. Phila., 1874. Orig. gilt-stamped cloth, g.t. 2nd
edition. Argosy 716-69 1983 $40

REICHENBACH, KARL VON   Researches on magnetism, electricity,
heat, light, crystallization, and chemical attraction... London:
Taylor, etc., 1850. First edition. 3 plates. Fine copy. Ximenes
63-535 1983 $150

REID, C. LESTOCK   Commerce and Conquest. London, 1947.
9 plates and 2 full-page illus. Bookplate of Lt. Col. M.E.S. Lows.
8vo. Orig. cloth. Good. Edwards 1044-587 1983 £15

REID, CHARLES   Record Of The Services In The Field.
London: Henry S. King & Co., (n.d.). First edition (?). Orig. red
stiff wrappers (detached). Presentation copy inscribed: "John
Galsworthy from Charles Reid." MacManus 278-2142 1983 $25

REID, D. A.   Fungorum Rariorum Icones Coloratae.
1966-81. 96 coloured plates, 8vo, sewed. Parts I to XII. Wheldon
160-1828 1983 £100

REID, EDITH   The Great Physician - A Short Life
of Sir William Osler. Oxford, 1931. First edition. 8vo. Orig.
binding. Fye H-3-893 1983 $35

REID, EDITH   The Life and Convictions of William
Sydney Thayer Physician. New York, 1936. First edition. 8vo.
Orig. binding. Dust wrapper. Fye H-3-975 1983 $20

REID, FORREST   Brian Westby. London: Faber & Faber
Limited, (1934). First edition. 8vo. Orig. cloth. Dust jacket.
Fine copy. Jaffe 1-343 1983 $50

REID, FORREST   Illustrators of the Sixties. London:
Faber & Gwyer Ltd. (1928). 4to, with frontis. + 90 plates. Index.
Dust jacket. Karmiole 71-80 1983 $150

REID, FORREST   Illustrators of the Sixties. Faber,
1928. 1st edn. Frontis. & 90 b&w illus. Green cloth, t.e.g. others
uncut (covers worn & faded), some splits to joints), contents v.g.
Hodgkins 27-574 1983 £65

REID, FORREST   Notes and Impressions. (Ulster), 1942.
Stiff paper boards, edges slightly faded, else very good in slightly
chipped and sunned, very good dustwrapper with price clipped. Quill &
Brush 54-1139 1983 $35

REID, FORREST   Pirates of the Spring. Dublin: The
Talbot Press Ltd.; London: T. Fisher Unwin Ltd., 1919. First
edition. 8vo. Orig. cloth. Dust jacket, chipped. Fine copy.
Jaffe 1-341 1983 $150

REID, FORREST   Uncle Stephen. London: Faber & Faber
Limited, (1931). First edition. 8vo. Orig. cloth. Slightly
soiled and worn dust jacket. Fine copy. Jaffe 1-342 1983 $65

REID, HIRAM A.   History of Pasadena. Pasadena: Pasadena
History Co., 1895. 5 plates and 2 folding maps. Errata slip. Half
leather, rebacked in fabricoid with old leather panels laid down.
Dawson 471-240 1983 $200

REID, JOHN COLEMAN   Reid's Tramp; or a Journal of the
Incidents of Ten Months Travel through Texas, New Mexico, Arizona,
Sonora, and California. Selma, Alabama: Hardy, 1858. 8vo, original
plum cloth, spine gilt, sides blind embossed. Slight fading of
cloth, else a very fine, tight copy, with gilt-lettered morocco
book-label of noted collector Frank C. Deering and remains of another.
An exceptionally clean copy. Preserved in a half rose gilt calf
case. First edition. Jenkins 151-282 1983 $12,500

REID, MAYNE   The Bandolero. London: Bentley, 1866.
First edition. Illus. Orig. pictorial cloth. Somewhat worn. Very
good. MacManus 280-4342 1983 $175

REID, MAYNE   The Flag Of Distress. London: Tinsley
Brothers, 1876. First edition. 3 vols. Orig. light-blue decorated
cloth. Spines and covers slightly worn and soiled. Bookplate. Good.
MacManus 280-4343 1983 $450

REID, MAYNE   The Giraffe Hunters. London: Hurst &
Blackett, 1867. First edition. 3 vols. Orig. cloth. Library labels
removed from front upper covers. Covers slightly soiled and rubbed.
Former owner's inscriptions on flyleaves. Front inner hinge of Vol. I
cracked. MacManus 280-4344 1983 $350

REID, MAYNE   The Headless Horseman, a Strange Tale
of Texas. London: Chapman & Hall, (1866). 20 parts. 1st ed.
Orig. salmon printed wrappers, uncut, as issued. Half morocco folding
case. Wrapper to part 14 supplied, and 1st part trimmed down, else
very good set with ALS from author laid in. Jenkins 155-1055
1983 $350

REID, MAYNE   The Hunters' Feast... New York, Robert
M. DeWitt, n.d. Ads, illus. Orig. pictorial cloth, gilt. Fine copy
overall. Jenkins 153-460 1983 $125

REID, MAYNE   No Quarter! London: Swan Sonnenschein,
Lowery & Co., 1888. First edition. 3 vols. Orig. dark-blue cloth.
Spine ends and edges a trifle rubbed. Fine. MacManus 280-4345 1983
$450

REID, MAYNE   The Quadroon. London: Hyde, 1856.
First edition. 3 vols. Orig. cloth. Paper labels. Covers stained.
Somewhat worn. Good, sound copy. MacManus 280-4346 1983 $300

REID, MAYNE   The Wood-Rangers. London: Hurst &
Blackett, 1860. First edition. 3 vols. Orig. cloth. Spines slightly
faded. Small inkspot on spine of Vol. II and on front cover of Vol.
III. Previous owner's signature on each title-page. A little light
foxing. Very good. MacManus 280-4348 1983 $400

REID, MAYNE   The Young Voyageurs. London: David
Bogue, 1854. First edition. 12 illus. Small 8vo. Orig. decorated
cloth. Former owner's signatures on front flyleaf. Inner hinges
cracked. MacManus 280-4349 1983 $250

REID, THOMAS MAYNE
Please turn to
REID, MAYNE

REID, THOMAS WEMYSS
Please turn to
REID, WEMYSS

REID, W. MAX   The Mohawk Valley. New York: G.P. Putnam's Sons, 1901. Frontis. Later cloth. Illus. Jenkins 152-341a
1983 $35

REID, WEMYSS   Charlotte Bronte. A Monograph. N.Y.:
Schribner, Armstrong & Co., 1877. Probably the first American edition.
Orig. decorated cloth. Spine edges slightly worn. Covers slightly
soiled. Good. MacManus 277-691 1983 $25

REIK, THEODOR   From Thirty Years with Freud.
London: The Hogarth Press and the Institute of Psycho-Analysis.
1942. First English edition. Karmiole 72-82 1983 $25

REIN, DAVID   Vardis Fisher: Challenge to Evasion.
Chicago: Normandie House, 1938. 1st ed., limited to 400 copies.
Orig. red cloth, gilt, glassine dj. Very fine copy with Fisher
autograph at conclusion of introduction. Jenkins 155-408 1983
$75

REINEGGS, JACOB   Systematis Chemici ex Demonstrationibus
Tyrnaviensibus Pars Naturalis et Experimentalis Theoretica. Nagy-
Szombath: Tyrnau, 1773. 8vo. Old floral wrappers. Gurney 90-101
1983 £50

REINHARDT, KARL   Poseidonios. Munich, 1921. 4to, cloth.
Salloch 385-715 1983 $55

REINHEIMER, SOPHIE   Im Blumenhimmel. Oldenburg: Stalling,
1929. 4to, colour title, 16 colour illus. pages. Colour pictorial
boards. Very good. Greer 40-238 1983 £25

RELACION verdadera, y copia de Carta...de Venecia... (Madrid, 1695).
Title woodcut showing the Habsburg eagles. Folio. Unbound. From
the library of Sir Thomas Phillipps. Kraus 164-41 1983 $250

RELACION y carta, escrita, y emblada a esta Corte, por un Corres-
pondiente, desde la Ciudad de Sevilla... (Madrid), ca. 1689. Title
woodcut of scimitar-shaped comet, ornamental initial, large botanical
tailpiece. Folio. Sewn. From the library of Sir Thomas Phillipps.
Kraus 164-40 1983 $150

REMAK, ROBERT   Galvanotherapie. Paris, 1860. First
edition in French. 8vo, orig. pr. wrs., spine split; uncut &
Unopened. Argosy 713-455 1983 $125

REMARKS Occasioned by the Late Conduct of Mr. Washington, as
President of the United States. Philadelphia: Benjamin Franklin
Bache, 1797. Later boards. Felcone 22-210 1983 $75

REMARKS on the Conduct and Probable Designs of Russia. James Ridgeway,
1832. 8vo, disbound. Bickersteth 77-237 1983 £12

REMARKS on the Oude question. London: printed for W.I. and I.
Richardson, 1806. First edition. 8vo. Disbound. Scarce.
Ximenes 63-216 1983 $60

REMARKS upon a Jacobite Pamphlet privately handed about...
London: by J. Roberts., (1715). Sole edition. 8vo. Uncut in
modern quarter morocco. Heath 48-177 1983 £75

REMARKS upon Mr. Webber's Scheme and the Drapers Pamphlet. London:
by J. Roberts, 1741. First edition. 8vo. Marbled boards. Heath
48-202 1983 £45

REMINGTON, FREDERIC   Crooked Trails. New York: Harper &
Brothers Publishers, 1899. Illustrated by the author. Original
pictorial cloth. Some wear to the head and heal of the spine, else
a fairly nice copy. 2nd edition. Jenkins 151-283 1983 $75

REMINGTON, FREDERIC   Drawings. New York, 1897. 60 plates,
cloth and pictorial boards, very good copy. Laid in a folding cloth
box. Reese 19-461 1983 $1,250

REMINGTON, FREDERIC   Frederic Remington's Own West. N.Y.,
Dial Press, 1960. 4to, profusely illus. by Remington in color and
b/w. Full brown leather stamped in gilt, t.e.g. One of 167 deluxe
copies signed by the editor. Pub.'s slipcase. Houle 22-1161 1983
$275

REMINGTON, FREDERIC   John Ermine of the Yellowstone. New
York: The Macmillan Co., 1902. Original brown pictorial cloth. Ads.
Illustrated by the author. Fine copy of the first edition. Author
name misspelled on spine. Jenkins 151-284 1983 $75

REMINGTON, FREDERIC   Men With the Bark On. New York: Harper
& Brothers, 1900. First edition. Illus. by author. Some wear to
extremities. Orig. cloth. Jenkins 152-344a 1983 $100

REMINGTON, FREDERIC   Men With The Bark On. New York:
Harper & Brothers Publishers, 1900. Original pictorial cloth.
Some wear. Light ex-library. First edition. Illustrated by the
author. Jenkins 151-285 1983 $75

REMINGTON, FREDERIC   Men with the Bark on. New York, 1900.
1st issue. Illus. by author. Small 8vo, pictorial front cover.
Backstrip very lightly time-darkened and with 2 minute tears at top;
otherwise nice. Morrill 286-672 1983 $65

REMINGTON, FREDERIC   Pony Tracks. New York: Harper and
Brothers, 1895. Illus. by the author. Original pictorial cloth,
1st ed. Fine copy. Jenkins 151-286 1983 $350

REMINGTON, FREDERIC   Stories of Peace and War. New York &
London, 1899. Frontis. Gilt cloth (as always, the author's name
is mistakenly spelled 'Frederick' on the covers). A fine copy.
Reese 19-463 1983 $45

REMINGTON, FREDERIC   Sundown Leflare. New York and London:
Harper & Brothers, 1899. Original pictorial cloth, ads. Fine copy
of the 1st ed. Illus. by the author. Jenkins 151-287 1983 $85

REMINGTON, FREDERIC   Toro, Toro! NY, 1890. Hand-colored.
Argosy 716-621 1983 $125

REMINISCENCES of an Eastern Tour, 1869. Dublin, 1870. First and
apparently only edition, with 31 orig. mounted photographs, 8vo,
orig. blue cloth, gilt, edges gilt, a little rubbed at corners and with
some light marginal foxing, but a very good copy. Fenning 61-370
1983 £145

REMMELIN, JOHANN   Cataoptrum Miscrocosmicum... Davidis
Francki, Augsburg, 1619. Folio, engraved title with architectural
border engraving of the author on verso, and 3 engraved plates with
numerous overlays; title and several other leaves a little dust
soiled and frayed, tear in 1 text leaf repaired, other minor tears
in a few blank margins of text and 1 plate repaired; bound in 2
vellum bifolia,. First authorised edition. Drawings made by
Remmelin and engraved by Lucas Kilian. Quaritch NS 5-89 1983 $5,500

REMMELIN, JOHANN   Dissertatio Medica Inauguralis De
Palpitatione Cordis. Tubingen: Martin Rommey, 1681. 4to. Modern
boards. Marginalia. Kraus 164-32 1983 $100

REMMELIN, JOHANN   Historia Anatomico-Medica Thymi.
Tubingen: Officina Reisiana, 1679. 4to. Paper backstrip. Kraus
164-201 1983 $150

REMONDINO, PETER CHARLES   History of Circumcision from the
Earliest Times to the Present. Phila., 1891. 8vo, orig. cloth; ex-
lib. First edition. Argosy 713-456 1983 $40

REMY, JULES   A Journey to Great-Salt-Lake City.
London, W. Jeffs, 1861. 2 vols., 8vo, orig. cloth, worn shaken,
joints split, covers bumped and spines faded. First edition in
English. Ravenstree 97-122 1983 $150

RENAN, ERNEST   The Song of Songs. London: Wm. M.
Thomas, n.d. First English edition. Orig. cloth. Inscribed on the
verso of the flyleaf to "Lucian R.F. Oldershaw from G.K. Chesterton.
Covers slightly rubbed. MacManus 277-960 1983 $200

RENDERS, EMILE   Jean Van Eyck et le Polyptyque.
Bruxelles: Librairie Generale, 1950. 2 vols. 37 plates, 5 plates
mounted on boards, loose in portfolio. Folio. Wrappers. Edition
limited to 2000 copies. Ars Libri 32-213 1983 $225

RENFROW, WILLIAM C.   Report of the Governor of Oklahoma
Territory... Wash., 1893. Orig. printed wraps. First edition.
Ginsberg 47-706 1983 $25

RENN, LUDWIG   War. London, 1929. First English
edition. Spine slightly darkened. Dustwrapper darkened at the
spine. Very good. Jolliffe 26-367 1983 £16

RENNELL, JAMES   Memoir of a Map of Hindoostan. London,
1788. First edition. 3 folding maps, plan. 4to. Mottled calf, rebacked, wear at corners and hinges. Slight worming in boards and last
few leaves. Good. Edwards 1044-589 1983 £95

RENNELL, JAMES   Memoir of a Map of Hindoostan. London,
1792. Second edition, with considerable additions and corrections.
4 folding maps, plan. 4to. Half calf, diced on spine. Good. Edwards
1044-590 1983 £125

RENNOLDS, EDWIN H.   A History of the Henry County (Tennessee)
Commands Who Served in the Confederate States Army...with Portraits.
Jacksonville, Fla., 1904. 1st ed. Illus. Slight fading to spine.
Rare. Fine copy. Jenkins 153-555 1983 $450

RENOIR, AUGUSTE   Dix aquarelles, sanguines et pastels
de Auguste Renoir. Paris/Geneve: Georg, 1921. Text: 4to.
Wrappers. Printed on uncut van Gelder. Unopened. Plates: 10
color facsimile plates, printed by Clot and Jacomet, within passepartouts (loose, as issued). Folio. Portfolio. No. 184 of a
limited edition of 200 copies only. Backstrip defective. Ars
Libri 32-572 1983 $200

RENOIR, AUGUSTE   Renoir, peintre de nu. Paris: Bernheim-Jeune, 1923. 40 plates (several tipped-in color). Folio.
Orig. wrappers, imprinted with original etching by Renoir. One
of 150 copies on Arches, of a limited edition of 200 copies, printed
by Jacomet and (for the etching) Louis Fort. Ars Libri 32-573
1983 $475

RENOUARD, P. V.   History of Medicine, from Its Origin
to the Nineteenth Century, with an Appendix... Cincinnati, 1856.
1st American ed. 8vo. Contemporary calf, leather label. Presentation from the translator, Cornelius G. Comegys, M.D., to William H.
Rockwell, M.D. Morrill 289-194 1983 $40

RENTOUL, J. N.   Growing Orchids. Beaverton, Or., 1981-
82. Many coloured and plain illus., 3 vols., royal 8vo, hard cover.
Wheldon 160-2053 1983 £57.50

REPORT of the D'Hauteville Case. Philadelphia: Printed by William
S. Martin, 1840. Orig. printed wrappers, detached. Gach 95-426 1983
$35

REPORT of the Dinner Given to Charles Dickens in Boston, Feb. 1, 1842.
Boston: Wm. Crosby & Co., 1842. First edition, title foxed, full
dark blue calf, borders in blind, spine gilt. Very good. Jarndyce
30-47 1983 £100

REPORT of the Evidence & Arguments of Counsel at the Trial of Levi
and Laban Kenniston...Boston, 1817. 1st ed. 8vo, sewn. Morrill
289-629 1983 $20

REPORT of the Select Committee, on Petitions for the Draining of
Tonawanda Swamp. Albany, 1855. Folding map in color. 8vo, orig.
wrappers. Ex-library, back wrapper and map loose, small part of
blank fore-edge of front wrapper and text gnawed. Morrill 289-469
1983 $20

REPORT of the Special Committee of the City Council of Chicago on the
Street Railway Franchises...Chicago, 1898. Maps & tables. Tall 8vo,
ex-library, lettering on backstrip effaced. Morrill 288-195 1983
$22.50

REPORT On Shipping and Ship-Building...of San Francisco. San
Francisco, 1885. Wraps. Felcone 22-25 1983 $30

REPORT on the Collections of the British Ornithologists Union and Wollaston Expeditions in Dutch New Guinea 1910-13.   1914-16. 2 maps, 13 coloured and 28 plain plates, 21 parts, royal 4to, 1 part half calf, rest in wrappers. Wheldon 160-350 1983 £160

REPORT of the Trial of John Wade... Dedham, H. Mann, 1835. 8vo, sewn. Morrill 287-253 1983 $20

REPORT of the Trial of Leavitt Alley.   Boston: 1875. First edition. Brown cloth. Bradley 66-526 1983 $35

REPORT of the Trial of Prof. John W. Webster.   Boston: 1850. First edition. Illus. Black morocco and boards, uncut. Light stains and marks on few pages, otherwise fine. Bradley 66-525 1983 $65

REPORT of the Trial of Uriel H. Crocker. (Cambridge, 1851). Presentation from Coolidge, counsel for government, to his wife. 8vo, orig. wrappers, double columns. Morrill 287-254 1983 $25

REPORT of the Committee Appointed by the Philomathean Society of the University of Pennsylvania To Translate the Inscription on the Rosetta Stone. Philadelphia, 1858. Ed. limited to 400 copies. Presentation copy from Charles R. Hale, one of the authors, to Mrs. Mary Welles, Christmas, 1858. Text and illus. were produced by lithography with the aid of Max Rosenthal. Illus. with colored plates, decorations and borders, etc. 8vo, rebound in laber buckram, orig. brown wrappers, bound in, nice. Morrill 287-399 1983 $135

REPORTS on Penobscot and Snowdrift Mine and Belmont Mine, Montana, (N.Y., 1880). Illus. Orig. printed wraps. First edition. Ginsberg 47-584 1983 $125

REPTON, H.   Observations on the Theory and Practice of Landscape Gardening. Printed by T. Bensey, for J. Taylor, 1803. 4to, portrait, 12 coloured aquatint plates, 9 of them with overlays, 15 uncoloured aquatint plates, 3 of them with overlays, 11 uncoloured aquatint text figures, 3 of them with overlays. 15 woodcut text figures, one of them coloured. cont. red morocco gilt, rebacked preserving the orig. spine, a.e.g. In cont. binding. Bickersteth 75-169 1983 £1,650

REPTON, H.   Observations on the theory and practice of Landscape Gardening. 1980. Roy. 4to, quarter calf, with raised bands, in a buckram slip case. 14 coloured plates. A facsimile of the first edition, limited to 445 copies. Wheldon 160-84 1983 £225

THE REPUBLIC of the ants; a poem. London: Simpkin and Marshall, 1822. First edition. Small 8vo. Orig. quarter roan and grey boards, printed paper side-label. Engraved title-page. Very good copy. Ximenes 63-422 1983 $75

RERESBY, JOHN   The Travels and Memoirs. 1813. 8vo, t.e.g., other edges uncut, 40 engraved plate as issued with 11 of them hand coloured, and one inserted portrait, cont. smooth morocco, ruled gilt, slightly rubbed, faded at the top of upper cover. Bickersteth 75-170 1983 £38

THE RESCUED Nun. New York: Burgess & Stringer, 1843. Orig. printed wraps., untrimmed. Wraps. printed "Second Edition...Price one Shilling." Rear wrap detached, some foxing, but a very good copy. Reese 20-33 1983 $30

RESIMONT, CHARLES DE   Le Magnetisme Animal Considere Comme Moyen Therapeutique. Paris & Londres, 1843. 8vo, cont. calf-backed bds. First edition. Argosy 713-457 1983 $75

RESOURCES of Dakota...Containing Descriptive Statements and General Information Relating to the Soil, Climate, Productions... Sioux Falls, Dakota, 1887. Illus. Orig. cloth. First edition. Ginsberg 47-275 1983 $100

THE RESOURCES of the State of Oregon: A Book of Statistical Information on Oregon as a Whole and by Counties. Salem, 1899. Printed wraps. Ginsberg 46-609 1983 $45

RETANA, W. E.   Apartado Bibliografico de la historia general de las Filipinas... Manila: Pedro B. Ayuda, 1964. 3 vols., imitation alligator skin, tape marks on endpapers. Reprint of the 1906 ed. Dawson 470-251 1983 $250

RETBERG, R. V.   Durers Kupferstiche und Holzschnitte. Munchen: Theodor Ackermann, 1871. 2 plates. 4to. New wrappers, mounted with orig. cover. Ars Libri 32-187 1983 $100

REUILLY, JEAN DE   Voyage en Crimee et sur les Bords de la Mer Noire, pendant l'Annee 1803. Paris: Bossange, 1806. First (only complete) edition, 8vo, modern panelled calf antique, spine gilt, morocco label. Uncut copy, two folding maps (lightly foxed); 3 folding plates; 3 folding tables; 6 text vignettes. A very scarce title. Old library stamp neatly placed on title and half-title, but a fine and otherwise pristine copy. Trebizond 18-160 1983 $675

REUTER, FRITZ   An Old Story of my Farming Days. London, n.d. 8vo. Cloth. Copyright ed. 3 vols. Little reinforcing on inside endboard of vol. 1, else vg-fine set. In Our Time 156-657 1983 $150

REVENTLOW, ERNEST ZU   The Vampire of the Continent. N.Y., 1916. First American Edition. Review Copy. Pictorial cloth. Covers very worn and soiled. King 45-562 1983 $20

REVERDY, PIERRE   Selected Poems. (NY): New Directions, (1969). Limited to 150 copies signed by translater Rexroth. Mint in slip-case. First edition. Bromer 25-94 1983 $75

REVERE, JOSEPH WARREN   A Tour of Duty in California. Oakland: Biobooks, 1947. Illus. Map. Fine color plates of Revere's 6 orig. sketches and his map of San Francisco harbor. Jenkins 153-466 1983 $30

REVERE, JOSEPH WARREN   A Tour of Duty in California. New York: 1849. First edition. Illus., including folding map. Orig. cloth. Some cover wear, top of spine repaired. Bradley 66-656 1983 $250

REVERE, JOSEPH WARREN   A Tour of Duty in California. NY 1849. 1st ed. Folding map and 6 lithographic plates. Short tear on map neatly repaired with paper strip on verso. 12mo, later 1/2 calf, gilt, somewhat foxed, new endpapers. Argosy 710-39 1983 $175

REVESZ, GEZA (1878-1955)   The Psychology of a Musical Prodigy. London: Kegan Paul, 1925. Ads. First edition. Gach 95-427 1983 $40

REVIEW in verse, of the performers from the Theatre Royal, Norwich, during the season at Lynn, of 1802. Lynn: printed and sold by T. Hunt..., n.d. (1802). 8vo, sewn (stitching loose). 2nd edition. Ximenes 64-458 1983 $325

REVOIL, G.   Faune et Flore des Pays Comalis. Paris, 1882. 5 parts (of 10) and 3 odd plates, in 1 vol., royal 8vo, wrappers. Extremely scarce. Wheldon 160-426 1983 £30

REWALD, JOHN   Maillol. London/New York/Paris: Hyperion, 1939. 127 gravure and color plates. Large 4to. Cloth. Ars Libri 32-416 1983 $75

REXROTH, KENNETH   Between Two Wars. (Athens, OH & San Francisco, CA): Labyrinth Editions & The Iris Press, 1982. Folio. 5 color illus. by Daniel Goldstein tipped-in. Designed and printed by Richard Bigus. Signed by Bigus, Rexroth and Goldstein. As new in quarter-vellum with decorative paper over boards. Deluxe edition. Limited to 50 copies with accompanying portfolio of 4 folded broadsides with illus. Double tray linen box. Separate signed woodblock by Goldstein. Bromer 25-89A 1983 $550

REXROTH, KENNETH   Between Two Wars. (Athens, OH & San Francisco, CA): Labyrinth Editions & The Iris Press, 1982. Folio. 5 color illus. by Daniel Goldstein tipped-in. Designed and printed by Richard Bigus. Signed by Bigus, Rexroth and Goldstein. As new in quarter-vellum with decorative paper over boards. Regular edition. Limited to 80 copies. Bromer 25-89B 1983 $350

REXROTH, KENNETH   The Heart's Garden, the Garden's Heart. Cambridge: Pym-Randall Press, (1967). Of 300 clothbound copies, 1/75 signed by Rexroth. Near mint in dust wrapper. First edition. Bromer 25-90 1983 $85

REXROTH, KENNETH   In What Hour. NY: 1940. Spine and rear cover faded. First edition. Bromer 25-91 1983 $60

REXROTH, KENNETH   In What Hour. NY, 1940. Edges faded,
light cover stains, top spine edge torn, good in price clipped, chipped
and wearing dustwrapper. Quill & Brush 54-1144 1983 $60

REXROTH, KENNETH   The Phoenix and the Tortoise. Norfolk:
New Directions, (1944). Cloth. First edition. Fine copy in lightly
soiled dust jacket. Reese 20-822 1983 $100

REXROTH, KENNETH   The Signature of All Things. (NY):
New Directions, (1949). Limited to 1500 copies designed by Hans
Madersteig and printed at the Stamperia Valdonega. Very fine in
cloth-backed boards and dust wrapper. First edition. Bromer 25-
92 1983 $75

REY, H. A.   Tit for Tat. N.Y.: Harp., (1942).
Stated first edition. 4to. Worn dust wrapper. Color illus. on each
page. Fine. Aleph-bet 8-224 1983 $25

REYMOND, MARCEL   La sculpture florentine. Firenze, 1897-
1900. 4 vols. in 2, prof. illus. Folio, marbled boards, 3/4 leather.
Ars Libri SB 26-204 1983 $350

REYMOND, MARCEL   La sculpture florentine. Firenze, 1897.
Folio, prof. illus., boards, 1/4 cloth. Ars Libri SB 26-203 1983
$75

REYNARDSON, FRANCIS   The Stage: a poem. London: printed
for E. Curll, 1713. 8vo, modern marbled wrappers, first edition.
Very good copy; very scarce. Ximenes 64-459 1983 $750

REYNOLDS, FREDERICK   The Rage: a comedy. London: printed
for T. N. Longman, 1795. 8vo, cont. calf (worn, spine defective).
First edition. Ximenes 64-460 1983 $40

REYNOLDS, GEORGE   The State of the Greatest King...
Bristol: by J. Penn, 1721. Sole edition. 8vo. Early sheep.
Heath 48-527 1983 £125

REYNOLDS, GEORGE WILLIAM M. Pickwick Abroad, or, The Tour in France.
Crowquill & Phillips, and Bonner, n.d. (c. 1845). 2nd edition, 8 pp
ads. Orig. pink cloth. Jarndyce 30-156 1983 £32

REYNOLDS, GEORGE WILLIAM M. Works. London, privately printed,
n.d., ca. 1915. Illus., some plates on Japan vellum. 3/4 red
morocco (some rubbing and small chips), else very good. 20 vols.
One of 1,000 sets. Houle 21-753 1983 $100

REYNOLDS, HORACE   A Providence Episode in the Irish
Literary Renaissance. Providence: The Study Hill Club, 1929. First
edition. Limited to 300 copies. Signed by Reynolds on end-leaf.
Cloth-backed boards rubbed at edges. Owner's signature. Bromer 25-
95 1983 $50

REYNOLDS, J. J.   Footprints of Emmet. Dublin: M.H. Gill,
1903. First edition, with mostly full-page illus., roy. 8vo, cloth
(orig.), gilt, a very good copy. Fenning 61-129 1983 £14.50

REYNOLDS, J. N.   Pacific and Indian Oceans. New York,
1841. 8vo. Label chipped off, text partly foxed and stained,
binding partly faded. Morrill 286-673 1983 $20

REYNOLDS, JOHN   The Svmme of the Conference Betwene
Iohn Rainolds and Iohn Hart. Londini, Impensis Iohn Vvolfe for
George Bishop, 1584. 4to, old calf rebacked,title shaved touching
top line, backed, soiled, six smallish holes of which one removes
most of the imprint date, two others remove portions of four
letters not affecting legibility, many running titles shaved, upper
blank tip of most leaves wormed sometimes slightly affecting side-
notes. First edition. Ravenstree 97-176 1983 $320

REYNOLDS, JOHN (1788-1865) My Own Times, Embracing Also the History
of My Life. Belleville, Ill., 1855. Orig. cloth. First edition.
400 copies printed. Ginsberg 46-505 1983 $450

REYNOLDS, JOHN (1788-1865) The Pioneer History of Illinois...
Belleville, Ill., 1852. Cloth. Very good. Reese 19-465 1983 $375

REYNOLDS, JOHN M.   The Twin Hells: a Thrilling Narrative
of Life in Kansas and Missouri Penitentiaries. Chicago: Donohue,
(ca. 1902). Illus. Woodpulp paper, binding spotted. Argosy 710-249
1983 $27.50

REYNOLDS, JOSEPH WILLIAM   The Supernatural in Nature. C. Kegan
Paul, 1878. First edition, 87 plates and illus., 8vo, orig. cloth,
t.e.g., a very good copy. Fenning 60-351 1983 £18.50

REYNOLDS, JOSHUA   English Children as Painted by Sir
Joshua Reynolds. London, 1867. 1st ed. Illus. by A. and E. Seeley-
15 mounted photographs. 4to, half morocco. 1st ed. Slightly rubbed,
small ink stain on back cover. Morrill 289-516 1983 $37.50

REYNOLDS, JOSHUA   Seven Discourses Delivered in the
Royal Academy by the President. London, T. Cadell, 1778. 8vo,
orig. tree calf, joints cracking, ends of spine chipped. A large
copy, with half title and leaf of ads. First edition. Ravenstree
97-178 1983 $210

REYNOLDS, SAMUEL   A History of the City of Williamsburgh.
Williamsburgh, 1852. Bound with Reynolds' Williamsburgh City Directory
and Business Advertiser and The Illustrated Phrenological Almanac for
1852. Calf-backed printed boards. Usual spine wear. Very good.
Felcone 20-128 1983 $85

REYNOLDS-BALL, EUSTACE   Outfit & Equipment for the Traveller...
London, Reynolds-Ball's Guides, 1912. First edition. 6 full-page
illustrations. 8vo. Morrill 290-423 1983 $35

REZANOV, NIKOLAI PETROVICH   The Rezanov Voyage to Nueva
California in 1806. San F., Russell, 1926. Illus. Orig. boards,
paper label on spine. One of 260 numbered copies, this being an
unnumbered review copy. Ginsberg 47-159 1983 $125

REZNICEK, E. K. J.   Die Zeichnungen von Hendrik Goltzius.
Utrecht: Haentjens Dekker & Gumbert, 1961. 2 vols. 38 plates. 461
illus. 4to. Cloth. Dust jacket. Ars Libri 32-262 1983 $185

REZNIKOFF, CHARLES   By the Waters of Manhattan. New York:
Bonu Paper Books, 1930. 8vo. Wraps. Cover design by Rockwell
Kent. A fine copy. In Our Time 156-660 1983 $25

REZNIKOFF, CHARLES   Nine Plays. New York, (1927). 8vo.
Cloth. Total ed. is 400 copies. Fine copy in dj. In Our Time
156-659 1983 $100

RHEAD, LOUIS   Fisherman's Lures and Game-Fish Food.
N.Y., Scribner, 1920. First edition. Illus. with color and b/w
plates by the author. Blue pictorial cloth stamped in light blue
and black. Very good. Houle 22-1057 1983 $75

RHEES, WILLIAM   The Smithsonian Institution Documents
Relative to its Origin and History. Washington, 1901. 2 vols.
First edition. Full leather. 8vo. Part of label of one volume
missing, else fine. Fye H-3-473 1983 $100

RHIND, A. H.   Thebes Its Tombs and Their Tenants...
London, 1862. 8 tinted lithograph plates, text illus. Large 8vo.
Ex-library. Orig. cloth. Good. Edwards 1044-591 1983 £32

RHINE, J. B.   Extra-Sensory Perception. London:
Faber and Faber, (1935). First British edition. Gach 95-428 1983
$25

THE RHINE: From Rotterdam to Constance. Leipzig, Baedeker, 1906.
Small 8vo., profusely illus. with maps, most in color and some
folding, marbled edges, dust jacket, very good. Houle 22-63 1983
$45

RHOADES, W.   A Houseful of Rebels. A. Constable, 1897.
Frontis. 9 plates, printed in sepia, some pages poorly opened. Green
cloth decorated, gilt. Greer 40-242 1983 £25

RHOADS, ASA   An American Spelling-Book. Stanford (NY):
Daniel Lawrence, 1802. 2nd ed., 16mo, cloth-backed boards.
Argosy 710-481 1983 $35

RHODE, JOHN   The Venner Crime. L, (1933). Good in slightly chipped, slightly worn dustwrapper internally mended, good or better. Quill & Brush 54-1145 1983 $35

RHODE Island Imprints, 1727-1800. New York: The Bibliographical Society of America by R.R. Bowker Co., 1949. First edition. 8vo. Cloth. Minor cover rubbing. Oak Knoll 49-486 1983 $75

RHODE ISLAND. LAWS.   The Public Laws of the State of Rhode Island and Providence Plantations...Jan. 1793. Providence; by Carter & Wilkinson, 1798. 8vo. cont. calf, lea. label, usual rubbing, slight foxing on few pp. Argosy 710-472 1983 $150

RHODES, EUGENE MANLOVE   The Best Novels and Stories. Boston: Houghton, Mifflin, 1949. 1st ed. Orig. cloth, dj, with a few small chips at crown of spine. With Bernard DeVoto's name cancelled and Dobie's name overprinted below on inside front flap. Fine copy. Uncommon. Jenkins 155-1058 1983 $75

RHODES, EUGENE MANLOVE   Beyond the Desert. Boston, 1934. 1st ed. Orig. cloth. Some fading to spine, otherwise very good copy. Jenkins 153-467 1983 $25

RHODES, EUGENE MANLOVE   Copper Streak Trail. Boston, 1922. Orig. cloth. Nice copy. Jenkins 153-468 1983 $30

RHODES, EUGENE MANLOVE   The Desire of the Moth. New York, 1916. Ads, frontis. and 1 illus. by H.T. Dunn. 1st ed. Orig. pic. cloth. Jenkins 153-469 1983 $150

RHODES, EUGENE MANLOVE   Good Men and True. New York, 1910. Ads. 1st ed. Orig. pictorial cloth. Frontis. and 1 illus. by Harvey Dunn. Fine copy. Jenkins 153-470 1983 $300

RHODES, EUGENE MANLOVE   The Little World Waddies. Chico: Printed by Carl Hertzog for William Hutchinson, (1946). Cloth in faded dust wrapper. With an intro. by J.F. Dobie. Dawson 471-241 1983 $100

RHODES, EUGENE MANLOVE   Once in the Saddle and Paso Por Aqui. Boston, 1927. 1st ed. in orig. cloth. Fine. Jenkins 153-471 1983 $45

RHODES, EUGENE MANLOVE   Say Now Shibboleth. Chicago: Bookfellows, 1921. 1st ed., 1 of 400 copies printed at the Torch Press. Orig. cloth-backed boards, labels, uncut. Fine copy with signed inscription by Rhodes on front end paper. Jenkins 155-1060 1983 $175

RHODES, EUGENE MANLOVE   Stepsons of Light. Boston, 1921. Orig. pictorial cloth. Nice copy. Jenkins 153-473 1983 $25

RHODES, EUGENE MANLOVE   The Trusty Knaves. Boston, 1933. 1st ed. in dj. Very fine copy. Jenkins 153-474 1983 $50

RHODES, EUGENE MANLOVE   West Is West. New York, 1917. Orig. pictorial cloth. 1st ed. Frontis. by Harvey Dunn. A very good copy with some wear. Jenkins 153-475 1983 $40

RHODES, JOSEPH   The English-Esperanto Dictionary. New York, Fleming H. Revell, (1908). First American edition. 8vo. Morrill 290-425 1983 $40

RHODES, MAY DAVISON   The Hired Man on Horseback. Boston, 1938. First edition. Frontis. portrait. Some fading to spine. Jenkins 152-349 1983 $45

RHODION, EUCHARIUS
Please turn to
ROESLIN, EUCHARIUS

RHYS, ERNEST   The English Fairy Book. Fisher Unwin, 1912. Colour frontis. Title vignette. 25 full-page & 55 text illus. Red decorated initials throughout. Pictorial endpapers. Green decorated cloth, gilt, spine faded. Greer 40-243 1983 £24

RHYS, ERNEST   The Fiddler of Carne. Edinburgh: Patrick Geddes & Colleagues, 1896. First edition. Orig. cloth. Dust jacket. Very fine. MacManus 280-4353 1983 $75

RHYS, HORTON   A Theatrical Trip for a Wager! Through Canada and the United States. London: Published for the Author by Charles Dudley, 1861. First (only) edition, 8vo, cont. half calf gilt, marbled boards. Engraved portraits, 3 colored plates. A very good copy. Trebizond 18-133 1983 $185

RIBES, JOSE   Modo de hacer la operacion cesarea... Buenos Aires: Imprenta de Ninos Expositos, 1805. First edition. Folio. Morocco-backed boards. From the library of Oscar E. Carbone. Kraus 164-110 1983 $2,500

RIBEYROLLES, CHARLES   The prisons of Africa, Guina, and Cayenne. Melton Mowbray: W. Darley, Printer, 1857. 12mo. Orig. cloth. Lightly rubbed. Adelson Africa-117 1983 $100

RIBOT, THEODULE   Diseases of Memory. An Essay in the Positive Psychology. London: Kegan Paul, Trench & Co., 1883 (1882). Second edition. Red decorative cloth, spine worn. Gach 94-626

RIBOT, THEODULE   The Diseases of Personality. Chicago, 1891. First edition, review copy. Argosy 713-458 1983 $85

RIBOT, THEODULE   Essay on the Creative Imagination. Chicago: Open Court, 1906. First English edition. Blue cloth, fine copy. Gach 95-430 1983 $50

RIBOT, THEODULE   The Evolution of General Ideas. Chicago: Open Court, 1899. First English edition. Ads. Very good copy in orig. brown cloth, occasional pencilling. Gach 95-431 1983 $37.50

RIBOT, THEODULE   La Psychologie Allemande Contemporaine. Paris: Librarie Germer Bailliere, 1879. Half-title, titlepage. Ads. Modern green cloth, retaining orig. green printed wrappers (repaired). First edition. Inscribed copy. Gach 95-432 1983 $135

RIBOT, THEODULE   Psychology of Attention. No. 112 from the Hunboldt Library of Science. NY: 1889. First edition in English. Wrappers. Gach 94-632 1983 $25

RIBOT, THEODULE   The Psychology of the Emotions. NY: Scirbner's, 1902. Gach 94-633 1983 $20

RICARDO, DAVID   The Works. John Murray, 1846. First edition. Half title, 16 pp ads. Orig. dull purple cloth, spine faded to brown, a very good copy. Jarndyce 31-356 1983 £200

RICCALTOUN, ROBERT   A sober enquiry into the grounds of the present difference in the Church of Scotland. N.p.: printed in the year 1723. First edition. 12mo. Cont. calf. On the end-paper of this copy is a long inscription from Cornelius Brem, dated Rotterdam, April 1800 to John Newton. Binding worn, rebacked. Ximenes 63-584 1983 $125

RICCI, CORRADO   Gli affreschi del Correggio nella cupola del Duomo di Parma. Torino/Roma: Itala Ars, ca. 1910. 123 plates. 26 text illus. Large 4to. Cloth. Ars Libri 33-119 1983 $125

RICCI, CORRADO   I Bibiena. Architetti teatrali. Milano: Alfieri & Lacroix, 1915. 83 tipped-in plates. 10 text illus. (partly tipped-in). Small folio. Marbled boards, 1/4 cloth. Intermittent foxing. Ars Libri 33-33 1983 $175

RICCI, CORRADO   Leon Battista Alberti. Torino: E. Celanza, 1917. 50 plates. 4to. Wrappers. Ars Libri 33-4 1983 $65

RICCI, CORRADO   Melozzo da Forli. Roma: D. Anderson, 1911. 61 superb photogravure plates loose in portfolio as issued. Large folio. Cloth. Ties. Ars Libri 33-233 1983 $300

RICCI, CORRADO   Raffello. Milano: Treves, 1926. 90 illus. Large 4to. Cloth. Ars Libri 33-301 1983 $60

RICCI, JAMES   The Cystocele in America. Philadelphia, 1950. First edition. 8vo. Orig. binding. Ex-library.
Binding worn. Fye H-3-474 1983 $45

RICCI, SEYMOUR DE   Louis XVI Furniture. London: William
Heinemann, (1913). Folio. Photographic plates. Red cloth, spine
extremities rubbed. Karmiole 74-47 1983 $75

RICCOBONI, LEWIS   A general history of the stage, from
its origin. London: printed for W. Owen, and Lockyer Davis, 1754.
8vo, old calf (crudely repaired, worn). 2nd ed. in English. Ximenes
64-462 1983 $150

RICCOBONI, LEWIS   An historical and critical account of
the theatres in Europe. ...Together with two celebrated essays.
London: printed for T. Waller; and R. Dodsley, 1741. 8vo, cont.
calf (spine worn, front hinge weak). First edition in English.
Half-title present; some marginal waterstains near the end, else a very
good copy. Ximenes 64-461 1983 $225

RICCOBONI, MARIE JEANNE   Letters from Elizabeth Sophia de
Valiere to her Friend Louisa Hortensia de Canteleu. Printed for
T. Becket; and P.A. De Hondt, 1772. 12mo, 2 vols, contemporary calf,
gilt' half-titles; errata and advertisements in vol. II. First edition
in English. A fine copy. Hill 165-102 1983 £195

RICE, HOWARD C.   Barthelemi Tardiveau: A French Trader in
the West. Baltimore: John Hopkins Press, 1938. Biographical sketch,
including letters from B. Tardiveau to St. John de Crevecoeur (1788-
1789). 4to, cloth-backed boards, paper label, glassine d/w. Illus.
Folding map. Perata 28-146 1983 $85

RICE, HOWARD C.   Barthelemi Tardiveau: A French Trader
in the West... Baltimore, 1938. 1st ed. Illus. A handsome book.
Jenkins 153-551 1983 $30

RICE, MARTIN   Rural Rhymes, and Talks and Tales
of Olden Times. Kansas City, 1893. Port. Cloth. Third edition.
With a lengthy presentation inscription by the author, signed
at Lone Jack, Missouri. Felcone 22-213 1983 $45

RICE, S. P.   Occasional Essays on Native South Indian
Life. London, 1901. Edges foxed. 8vo. Orig. cloth. Good. Edwards
1044-592 1983 £25

RICE, WILLIAM   Tiger-shooting in India. London:
Smith, Elder & Co., 1857. Royal 8vo. 12 tinted plates. 1/2 new
brown calf, green label. Light waterstaining to plates. Adelson
Africa-118 1983 $225

RICH, C. J.   Narrative of a Jounrey to the Site of
Babylon in 1811. London, 1839. 26 plates. Half morocco. 8vo. Good.
Edwards 1044-593 1983 £180

RICH, JOHN   A Dramatick Entertainment, Call'd the
Necromancer: or, Harlequin, Doctor Faustus. London: printed and
sold by T. Wood, 1724. 6th ed., 8vo, disbound in wrappers. Pickering
& Chatto 19-59 1983 $150

RICH, JOHN   Mr. Rich's answer to the many falsities
and calumnies advanced by Mr. John Hill, apothecary. London: printed
for J. Roberts, 1739. 8vo, wrappers. First edition. Half-title
present. Fine copy of a very rare title. Ximenes 64-465 1983 $600

RICH, O.   Bibliotheca Americana Nova... New York:
Burt Franklin, n.d. 2 vols., cloth. Reprint of the 1835-46 ed.
Dawson 470-253 1983 $29.50

RICH, SHEBNAH   Truro--Cape Cod. Boston, 1884. 2nd
ed. Revised and corrected. Illus. 8vo. Morrill 286-306 1983
$37.50

RICHARD, J.   L'Oceanographie. Paris, 1907. 4to,
wrappers, 339 illustrations. Wheldon 160-328 1983 £15

RICHARD DE BURY
Please turn to
AUNGERVILLE, RICHARD

RICHARDS, ANNA M.   A New Alice in the Old Wonderland.
Phila., Lippincott, 1895. 67 illus. by author. Scarlet cloth with
small circular gilt vignette fr. cvr., t.e.g., occasional fox mark,
bkstrip sl. faded & mottled, vg copy. Hodgkins 27-185 1983 £25

RICHARDS, CHARLES   Hearken, O Ye People! Printed for the
Author, 1805. 1st ed. Only 1 copy can be located. 12mo, orig.
boards, calf back. Morrill 288-424 1983 $65

RICHARDS, ELLEN H.   The Chemistry of Cooking and Cleaning.
Boston: Estes & Lauriat, 1882. Square 8vo, orig. gilt-stamped
cloth. Waldo Lincoln bookplate. Richards, 1842-1911. Rostenberg 88-
85 1983 $40

RICHARDS, EUGENIE   Dolly's ABC. Apsley Colour, Nottingham,
n.d. (ca.1919). 8 full-page colour & 12 colour text illus., loose.
Red pictorial wrappers, edges worn. Greer 40-19 1983 £22.50

RICHARDS, FRANK   Old Soldier Sahib. London, 1936.
First edition. Edges and prelims slightly spotted. Covers
slightly rubbed. Head of spine slightly creased. Very good.
Jolliffe 26-434 1983 £35

RICHARDS, GRANT   Caviare. Boston: Houghton Mifflin Co.,
1912. First American edition. Frontis. Orig. cloth. Fine. Mac-
Manus 280-4354 1983 $20

RICHARDS, GRANT   Valentine. Boston: Houghton Mifflin Co.,
1913. First American edition. Orig. cloth. Covers a little soiled.
Good. MacManus 280-4355 1983 $20

RICHARDS, LAURA   Julia Ward Howe 1819-1910. Boston,
1915. 2 vols. Cloth, leather labels on spines. The manuscript ed.,
1 of 450 numbered sets, eact set containing a page of Miss Howe's
manuscript bound in. Little rubbing to spines, else fine. In Our
Time 156-411 1983 $150

RICHARDS, ROBERT   The California Crusoe. London, Parker;
York, Stanford and Swords, 1854. 8vo, orig. cloth; faded, joints
torn, bookplate. First edition. Ravenstree 97-124 1983 $250

RICHARDS, WILLIAM CAREY   Harry's Vacation. New York: Evans
& Dickerson, 1854. Frontis. 1st ed. Orig. cloth, pictorially
gilt. Copyright notice inserted on singleton after title. Very
fine copy. Jenkins 155-1061 1983 $45

RICHARDSON, BENJAMIN WARD   Diseases of Modern Life. N.Y., 1876.
Ex-lib. Argosy 713-459 1983 $50

RICHARDSON, CHARLES   A New Dictionary of the English Language.
Wm. Pickering, 1844. First edition, 2 vols. 4to, orig. dull green
cloth. Paper labels a little worn, otherwise v.g. Jarndyce 31-664
1983 £65

RICHARDSON, CHARLES   A New Dictionary of the English Language.
1849. 24 pp ads. Well rebound in blue cloth, brown leather label.
3rd edition. Jarndyce 31-665 1983 £25

RICHARDSON, DOROTHY M.   Clear Horizon. London, 1935. First
edition. Spine darkened. Nice. Rota 231-521 1983 £18

RICHARDSON, DOROTHY M.   Dawn's Left Hand. London, 1931. First
edition. Spine faded. Very good. Rota 231-520 1983 £15

RICHARDSON, DOROTHY M.   Deadlock. London: Duckworth & Co.,
(1921). First edition. Orig. cloth. Pictorial dust jacket (very
slightly worn). Very fine. MacManus 280-4356 1983 $225

RICHARDSON, DOROTHY M.   Honeycomb. London: Duckworth & Co.,
(1917). First edition. Orig. cloth. Dust jacket (a few internal
tape-repairs). Fine. MacManus 280-4357 1983 $150

RICHARDSON, DOROTHY M.   Honeycomb. London, 1917. First edition.
Spine darkened. Nice. Rota 231-516 1983 £25

RICHARDSON, DOROTHY M.   Interim. London: Duckworth, (1919).
First edition. Orig. cloth. Dust jacket (worn and soiled). With a
holograph note by W.H. Hudson. In a cloth slipcase. Very good. Mac-
Manus 280-4359 1983 $250

RICHARDSON, DOROTHY M.   Interim. London: Duckworth & Co.,
(1919). First edition. Orig. cloth. Dust jacket (creased). Fine.
MacManus 280-4358 1983 $150

RICHARDSON, DOROTHY M.   Interim. London, 1919. First edition.
Spine a little faded. Very nice. Rota 231-517 1983 £25

RICHARDSON, DOROTHY M.   John Austen. London: William Jackson,
1930. First edition. Foreword & decorations by J. Austen. 8vo. Orig.
cream buckram. Acetate dust jacket. One of 125 copies printed on
hand-made paper, specially bound, and signed by the author and illus.
Lacking the orig. signed woodcut called for. Fine. MacManus 280-4360
1983 $75

RICHARDSON, DOROTHY M.   John Austen and the Inseparables. London,
1930. First edition. Foreward and decorations by J. Austen. Very
nice. Rota 230-516 1983 £15

RICHARDSON, DOROTHY M.   Revolving Lights. London, 1923. First
edition. Very nice. Rota 230-515 1983 £25

RICHARDSON, DOROTHY M.   The Trap. London, 1925. First edition.
Some foxing of the preliminaries. Nice. Rota 231-519 1983 £20

RICHARDSON, DOROTHY M.   The Tunnel. London, 1919. First edition.
Inscription on flyleaf. Very nice. Rota 231-518 1983 £25

RICHARDSON, GEORGE BURR   Report of a Reconnaissance in Trans-
Pecos Texas North of the Texas and Pacific Railway. Austin, 1904.
Illus. Stapled. Very good. Reese 19-466 1983 $60

RICHARDSON, H. N. B.   A Dictionary of Napoleon. London, 1920.
First edition. Thick roy. 8vo. Orig. cloth. 25 text maps. Slightly
worn and faded. Good. Edwards 1042-435 1983 £15

RICHARDSON, HENRY HANDEL   Ultima Thule. London, 1929. First
edition. Fine. Argosy 714-620 1983 $35

RICHARDSON, J. D.   A Compilation of Messages and Papers of
the Confederacy. Nashville, 1906. 8vo. Orig. cloth. 2 frontis.
6 portraits plates. 2 vols. Very slightly soiled. Good. Edwards
1042-244 1983 £35

RICHARDSON, JAMES   Narrative of a mission to central
Africa performed in the years 1850-51. London: Chapman and Hall,
1853. 2 vols. 8vo. Folding map. Orig. cloth. Rebacked, ex-
library, library stamps on verso of titles. Adelson Africa-120
1983 $200

RICHARDSON, JAMES   Travels in the Great Desert of
Sahara... London: Richard Bentley, 1848. 2 vols. 8vo. Folding
map. 3 plates. Orig. green cloth. Spines slightly faded. A
fine copy. Adelson Africa-119 1983 $300

RICHARDSON, JOHN   Hardscrabble, or the Fall of Chicago.
Chicago, 1812. NY: Pollard & Moss, 1888. 12mo, dec. cloth, woodpulp paper. Argosy 716-211 1983 $40

RICHARDSON, JONATHAN   The works of Mr. Jonathan Richardson.
London: printed for T. Davies, 1773. First collected edition.
8vo. Cont. calf, gilt, spine gilt. Spine a bit rubbed, lacks
label. Ximenes 63-20 1983 $150

RICHARDSON, JONATHAN   The Works of... Sold by B. White,
1792. With 12 plates on paper coated with sienna-tinted china clay,
including the half-title, 4to, recent calf-backed marbled boards, with
label. The issue with "Printed at Strawberry Hill" above the
title-page vignette and with B. White in the imprint. Fenning
61-371 1983 £85

RICHARDSON, JOSEPH   The Fugitive: a Comedy. J. Debrett,
1792. Second/third edition, slim 8vo, half-title, rebound in quarter
red morocco gilt, red clothsides, marbled edges, 1 leaf torn without
loss, a fine copy. Deighton 3-248 1983 £22

RICHARDSON, MOSES AARON   A Collection of Armorial Bearings,
Inscriptions, etc. Newcastle: Edward Walker, 1820. 2 vols. 84pp
of text, 102 numbered plates (mostly 2 coats-of-arms per plate), many
hand-colored. Text woodcuts and 2 other plates. Late 19th century
half calf, gilt spines; shelfworn, but sound. Karmiole 73-48 1983
$150

RICHARDSON, R. H.   Wickedness in High Places. Chicago:
S.C. Griggs and Co., 1851. Half morocco. Presentation copy from
George C. Walker. Jenkins 152-841 1983 $175

RICHARDSON, ROBERT   Travels along the Mediterranean...
London: T. Cadell, 1822. 2 vols. 8vo. 8 plates (1 hand-
colored). Cont. tree calf, rebacked, orig. red and black labels.
Adelson Africa-121 1983 $175

RICHARDSON, SAMUEL   An answer to the London ministers
letter... London: printed by I.C. for Hanah Alin, 1649. First
edition. Small 4to. Disbound. Last leaf a bit torn and soiled
(without loss); "Finis" cropped from the end of the text. Ximenes
63-104 1983 $45

RICHARDSON, SAMUEL   Clarissa. London, printed for S.
Richardson, sold by A. Millar et al., 1748. 7 vols., 8vo, later calf
gilt, few spines chipped, joints rubbed, several vols. rebacked
preserving orig. spines, bookplates, name on end-papers. First
edition. Ravenstree 96-169 1983 $685

RICHARDSON, SAMUEL   Clarissa, a Novel. Tinsley Brothers,
1868. 3 vols., half titles, 2pp ads. vol. III. Orig. green cloth,
spines a little dulled. Jarndyce 31-875 1983 £20

RICHARDSON, SAMUEL   The History of Pamela. New York, W.C.
Borradaile, 1830. 12mo, orig. quarter sheep, boards, spine
defective, frontis. loose, other plates and the frontis. hand-colored.
Ravenstree 96-170 1983 $35

RICHARDSON, SAMUEL   The History of Sir Charles Grandison.
London, S. Richardson, 1754. 7 vols., 12mo, orig. calf, now worn
with some joints cracked, spine ends chipped. First edition.
Ravenstree 96-171 1983 $750

RICHARDSON, SAMUEL   The History of Sir Charles Grandison.
For S. Richardson; sold by C. Hitch, L. Hawes, etc, 1754. First
edition, issue with misprinted catchword "my" on p. 279. 7 vols.,
12mo, final advert. leaf in vol. IV. Early 19th century half calf
(corners a little rubbed). Small tear in two leaves, removing a few
letters only. Some occasional slight foxing. Hannas 69-167 1983
£200

RICHARDSON, SAMUEL   The Novels. London, 1902. 19 vols.
8vo. Orig. blue cloth, fully gilt decorated spines, t.e.g. Limited
edition of 375 numbered sets with numerous fine plates by Burney,
Stothard, and others. Traylen 94-924 1983 £220

RICHARDSON, SAMUEL   Pamela, ou la Vertu Recompensee.
Amsterdam, 1743. 4 vols. in 2, 8vo, orig. calf gilt, little worn,
but good copy. Ravenstree 96-174 1983 $150

RICHARDSON, SAMUEL   Pamela; or, Virtue Rewarded. London,
Rivington and Osborn, 1741. 2 vols., 8vo, orig. calf, worn, joints
cracked and chipped. Ravenstree 96-173 1983 $110

RICHARDSON, WILLIAM   A Catalogue of 7385 Stars...prepared
from Observations made in the Years 1822, 1823, 1824, 1825, and 1826,
at the Observatory at Paramatta, New South Wales. William Clowes and
Sons, London, 1835. 4to, engraved frontis.; offset from frontis.
onto title; cont. half russia, joints weak. First edition. Quaritch
NS 5-90 1983 $1,500

RICHARDSON, WILLIAM   Essay on the improvement of healthy
and peaty mountains... Belfast: printed by Francis D. Finlay,
1818. First edition. 8vo. Disbound. Very rare. Ximenes 63-3
1983 $100

RICHARDSON, WILLIAM   Essays on Shakespeare's dramatic characters of Macbeth, Hamlet, Jaques, and Imogen. London: printed for J. Murray, 1786. Sm. 8vo, disbound, 4th edition. Ximenes 64-466 1983 $40

RICHARDSON, WILLIAM   Essays on Some of Shakespeare's Dramatic Characters... London, 1797. 8vo. Cont. half calf, marbled boards, morocco label, gilt. Traylen 94-734 1983 £24

RICHARDSON, WILLIAM H.   Journal of...A Private Soldier in the Campaign of New and Old Mexico, Under the Command of Colonel Doniphan of Missouri. N.Y., 1850. Illus., 3 plates., etc. Orig. printed pictorial wraps., rebacked in cloth slipcase. Third edition. Ginsberg 47-813 1983 $550

RICHARDSON, WILLIAM M.   The New-Hampshire Town Officer. Concord, 1829. Leather. Foxed, else very good. Reese 18-641 1983 $25

RICHET, CHARLES   Thirty Years of Psychical Research. NY: Macmillan, 1923. First American edition. Gach 95-433 1983 $30

RICHMAN, IRVING B.   The Spanish Conquerors. New Haven, 1921. Plates. Gilt cloth. Fine. Reese 19-467 1933 $20

RICHMOND, WILLIAM B.   Assisi. Macmillan, 1919. 1st edn. Illus. in colour from orig. paintings & sketches by author, 38 colour plates. Canvas backed grey bds., uncut (lacks ties at front, occas. thumb mark & cvrs. marked at edges). Inscription at front "Margaret Dalziel, Priors Field, 1923." V.g. Hodgkins 27-485 1983 £12.50

RICHTER, CONRAD   Brothers of No Kin. New York: Hinds, Hayden & Eldredge, (1924). 8vo. Cloth. Newspaper photo of author pasted on the inside endboard. This copy inscribed: "To Elizabeth Dunham . . ." A fine copy. In Our Time 156-661 1983 $250

RICHTER, CONRAD   Early Americana and Other Stories. New York: Alfred A. Knopf, 1936. First edition. 8vo. Orig. cloth. Dust jacket. Fine copy. Jaffe 1-344 1983 $150

RICHTER, CONRAD   The Sea Of Grass. New York: Alfred A. Knopf, 1937. First edition. 8vo. Orig. cloth. Dust jacket. Foxing, otherwise a fine copy. Jaffe 1-345 1983 $65

RICHTER, GISELA M.   Archaic Greek Art Against its Historical Background. NY, 1949. 337 illus. on plates, endpaper maps. 8vo, cloth. Salloch 385-306 1983 $45

RICHTER, HANS   Hans Richter by Hans Richter. New York: Holt, Rinehart and Winston, 1971. 141 plates (16 color). Large square 4to. Cloth. Dust jacket. Ars Libri 32-579 1983 $100

RICKARDS, R.   India. London, 1832. 3 folding tables. 2 vols. Half crushed blue morocco by Sangorski & Sutcliffe. 8vo. Good. Edwards 1044-594 1983 £80

RICKELL, RICHARD   The Green Box of Monsieur de Sartine. Sold by A. Becket, and R. Faulder, 1779. First edition. 8vo, incl. half-title. Modern wraps. A few slight stains. Hannas 69-215 1983 £45

RICKETSON, SHADRACH   Means of Preserving Health, and Preventing Diseases... New York: Collins, Perkins, and Co., 1806. Full calf. Covers broken and shabby and in need of rebinding. Contains the leaf of recommendations. Internally, very good. Felcone 20-103 1983 $35

RICKETTS, BENJAMIN MERRILL   Surgery of the Heart and Lungs. N.Y., 1904. First edition. Illus. Thick 4to, ex-lib. Argosy 713-460 1983 $50

RICKETTS, CHARLES   Unrecorded Histories. Martin Secker, 1933. 1st edn. limited to 950 copies. 6 designs by author. Beige cloth with design in red on both covers by Ricketts, gilt titling on bkstrip (secondary binding), t.e.g. others uncut, d/w with design repeated thereon, fine. Hodgkins 27-486 1983 £45

RICKWORD, EDGELL   A Handbook of Freedom. London, 1939. Advance Proof copy. Wrappers a little creased. Nice. Rota 230-517 1983 £15

RICKWORD, EDGELL   Invocations to Angels. London: Wishart & Co., 1928. First edition. Orig. cloth-backed decorated boards. Dust jacket (dust-soiled). Presentation copy, inscribed by the author on the front flyleaf: "Just for Joy from Edgell." Fine. MacManus 280-4361 1983 $45

RICKWORD, EDGELL   Invocations to Angels. Wishart, 1928. First edition. Paterned boards. Corners a little rubbed. Dust wrapper. Bookplate. Very nice. Rota 231-523 1983 £15

RIDDELL, JOHN   Meaning No Offense being Some of the Life, Adventures and Opinions of Trader Riddell. NY (1928). Cloth back pict. boards, front hinge cracked, spine lettering rubbed off, extremities heavily worn. First edition, with 8 full page plates by Covarrubias. King 46-427 1983 $35

RIDDLE, GEORGE W.   History of Early Days in Oregon. Riddle, Oregon, 1920. Orig. blue printed wrappers. Portrait and plat. Jenkins 153-476 1983 $75

RIDDLE, GEORGE W.   History of Early Days in Oregon. Riddle, Ore., 1920. Illus. Orig. printed wraps. First edition. Ginsberg 46-610 1983 $40

RIDEAL, SAMUEL   Water and its Purification. Crosby Lockwood, 1897. First edition, with a folding table, a folding plate and 64 other illus. 16 ads. 8vo, orig. cloth. Fenning 62-298 1983 £12.50

RIDER, SIDNEY S.   Bibliographical Memoirs of Three Rhode Island Authors: Joseph K. Angell, Frances H. (Whipple) McDougall, and Catherine R. Williams. Providence, 1880. Orig. printed wraps. First edition. One of 250 sets. Ginsberg 46-661 1983 $25

RIDER, SIDNEY S.   An Inquiry Concerning the Origin of the Clause in the Laws of Rhode Island (1719-1783). Providence, 1889. Orig. printed wraps. First edition. One of 250 copies. Ginsberg 46-662 1983 $25

RIDER, SIDNEY S.   Soul Liberty. Providence, 1897. Orig. printed wraps. First edition. One of 250 copies. Ginsberg 46-663 1983 $25

RIDGE, JOHN R.   Poems. San F., 1868. Photo frontis. Orig. cloth. First edition. Inscribed presentation copy from E.A. Ridge to Miss Harriet Godfrey. Ginsberg 47-160 1983 $175

RIDGE, JOHN R.   Trumpet of Our Own. S.F., 1981. First edition. Illus. Half cloth. Plain jacket. One of 650 copies, by the Blackstone Press. Houle 21-1134 1983 $80

RIDGELY, MABEL LLOYD   The Ridgelys of Delaware & Their Circle. Portland, Maine, 1949. 1st ed. Illus. Large 8vo, dust wrapper. Morrill 287-88 1983 $25

RIDGWAY, CHARLES   Through the Golden Gate. Yokohama, 1923. Orig. printed wraps. Ginsberg 46-665 1983 $100

RIDGWAY, R.   A Nomenclature of Colors for Naturalists. Boston, 1886. 8vo, cloth, colour and plain plates. Rare. Original edition. Wheldon 160-189 1983 £75

RIDGWAY, THOMAS S.   Geological Report Upon the Iron Ore. N.Y., 1872. Orig. back wrapper. First edition. Ginsberg 46-666 1983 $50

RIDING, LAURA   The Close Chaplet. N.Y.: Adelphi Co., n.d. (1926). First American edition. Orig. pale blue boards with paper label on upper cover. Plain tissue jacket (torn). Extremities of spine a trifle scuffed. Corner of flyleaf very slightly torn. Unopened. Fine. MacManus 280-4362 1983 $500

RIDING, LAURA   Contemporaries and Snobs. N.Y., 1928.
First American edition. Name eradicated from front flyleaf.
Pub.'s rubber stamp on title page. Argosy 714-622 1983 $35

RIDING, LAURA   Poet: A Lying Word. London, 1933.
First edition. Covers a little marked. Very nice. Rota 230-518
1983 £45

RIDING, LAURA   A Trojan Ending. New York: Random
House, (1937). 1st American ed. Orig. cloth, dj. Few nicks to
jacket but a very nice copy. Jenkins 155-1063 1983 $100

RIDING, LAURA   A Trojan Ending. London, 1937. First
edition. Lower cover and hinges a little marked. Very nice.
Rota 231-526 1983 £40

RIDING, LAURA   Twenty Poems Less. Paris: Hours Press,
1930. First edition. Photographic cover by Len Lye. One of 200
numbered copies, signed by author. 4to. Quarter morocco. Corners
bruised and worn. Nice. Rota 231-525 1983 £95

RIDINGS, SAM   The Chisholm Trail. Guthrie: Co-
operative Pub. Co., 1935. First edition. Frontis. portrait. Illus.
Folding map. Orig. black pictorial cloth. Dust jacket. Fine.
Jenkins 152-350 1983 $125

RIDLER, ANNE   A Dream Observed. Poetry London, (1941).
Wrappers. Author's signed autograph presentation inscription. Very
nice. Rota 230-519 1983 £15

RIDLEY, H. N.   Materials for a Flora of the Malay
Peninsula. Singapore, 1907. 3 parts, 8vo, wrappers. Front wrappers
and a few leaves of part 1 torn, and a little foxing, but a good
set. Rare. Wheldon 160-1763 1983 £30

RIDLEY, JAMES   The Tales of the Genii. For James
Wallis, by Thomas Divison, 1805. 2 vols. 8vo, frontis. and 12
plates after W.M. Craig. 8 additional plates after R. Westall
inserted. Cont. richly gilt, purple morocco, a.e.g. A fine set.
Hannas 69-168 1983 £45

RIDPATH, GEORGE   The stage condemn'd, and the encouragement given to the immoralities and profaneness of the theatre, by the
English schools, universities and pulpits, censur'd. London:
printed for John Salusbury, 1698. 8vo, cont. calf (top of spine a
bit rubbed). First edition. A fine copy. Ximenes 64-467 1983 $400

RIDPATH, JOHN CLARK   The Life and Trial of Guiteau the
Assassin... Cincinnati, Philadelphia, etc., 1882. 1st ed. Illus.
8vo. Morrill 288-425 1983 $37.50

RIEGEL, ROBERT E.   Young America 1830-1840. Norman, 1949.
1st ed. in dj. Jenkins 153-477 1983 $25

RIEMANN, HUGO   Geschichte der Musiktheorie. Berlin,
1920. 8vo, 1/2 cl. Salloch 387-377 1983 $25

RIES, FERDINAND   The Morning: A Cantate. Boston, Kidder
& Wright, 1838. Oblong folio, orig. printed wrs. Wrappers torn, some
light foxing. First American edition. Salloch 387-195 1983 $75

RIESENBERG, FELIX   The Story of Cape Horn. NY, 1940.
Color frontis. by Gordon Grant, illus., 4to, pict. buckram, ex lib.
Argosy 710-513 1983 $35

RIESMAN, DAVID   Thomas Sydenham. New York, 1926.
First edition. 8vo. Orig. binding. Fye H-3-971 1983 $20

RIETDORF, ALFRED   Gilly. Wiedergeburt der Architektur.
Berlin: Hans von Hugo, 1940. 170 illus. 4to. Cloth. Ars Libri
32-258 1983 $65

RIGBY, WALLIS   Rigby's Easy-to-Build Models of Naval
Craft. New York, 1944. Large oblong 4to, orig. wrappers. Fine, unused copy, with all pieces intact. Morrill 288-426 1983 $45

RIGGS, STEPHEN R.   Model First Reader. Chicago, (1873).
Orig. pictorial printed boards. First edition. Ginsberg 46-667
1983 $125

RIGNANO, EUGENIO   Psychologie due Raisonnement. Paris:
Felix Alcan, 1920. First edition in French, same year as the Italian.
Unopened copy. Wrappers browned, chipped at head and foot of spine,
front wrapper detached. Gach 94-636 1983 $25

RIGNANO, EUGENIO   The Psychology of Reasoning. London:
Kegan Paul, Trench, Trubner & Co., 1923. First edition in English.
Gach 94-637 1983 $25

RIHANI, AMEEN   Ibn Sa'oud of Arabia. London, 1928.
First edition. 2 maps, numerous plates. 8vo. Orig. cloth. Good.
Edwards 1044-595 1983 £15

RIJKS ETHNOGRAPHISCH MUSEUM   Catalogus van 's Rijks Ethnographisch
Museum. Leiden: E.J. Brill, 1909. 4to. New cloth. A few pages
repaired with tape. Ars Libri 31-818 1983 $100

RIJKS ETHNOGRAPHISCH MUSEUM   Catalogus van 's Rijks Ethnographisch
Museum. Deel IV: De Eilanden om Sumatra. Leiden: E.J. Brill, 1909.
11 plates (partly in color). Text illus. 4to. New cloth. Marginal
waterstaining throughout. Ars Libri 31-819 1983 $100

RIJKS ETHNOGRAPHISCH MUSEUM   Catalogus van 's Rijks Ethnographisch
Museum. Deel V: Javaansche Oudheden. Leiden: E.J. Brill, 1909.
15 plates. Text illus. 4to. New cloth. Marginal waterstaining
of first few pages. Ars Libri 31-820 1983 $100

RIJKS ETHNOGRAPHISCH MUSEUM   Catalogus van 's Rijks Ethnographisch
Museum. Deel VII: Bali em Lombok. Leiden: E.J. Brill, 1912.
16 plates. 4to. New cloth. Ars Libri 31-821 1983 $125

RIJKS ETHNOGRAPHISCH MUSEUM   Catalogus van 's Rijks Ethnographisch
Museum. Deel IX: Java. Leiden: E.J. Brill, 1914. 15 plates.
Text illus. 4to. New cloth. Ars Libri 34-823 1983 $125

RIJKS ETHNOGRAPHISCH MUSEUM. Catalogus van 's Rijks Ethnographisch
Museum. Deel X: Midden-Sumatra. Leiden: E.J. Brill, 1916. 12
plates. Text illus. 4to. New cloth. Ars Libri 34-824 1983
$125

RIJKS ETHNOGRAPHISCH MUSEUM   Catalogus van 's Rijks Ethnographisch
Museum. Deel XI: Java. Leiden: E.J. Brill, 1916. 12 plates.
Text illus. 4to. New cloth. Ars Libri 34-825 1983 $125

RIJKS ETHNOGRAPHISCH MUSEUM   Catalogus van's Rijks Ethnographisch
Museum. Band XII: Sud-Sumatra. Leiden: E.J. Brill, 1918. 16
plates. Frontis., text illus. 4to. New cloth. First few pages
with faint marginal waterstain. Ars Libri 34-826 1983 $125

RIJKS ETHNOGRAPHISCH MUSEUM   Catalogus van 's Rijks Ethnographisch
Museum. Deel XVI: Celebes. I. Zuid-Celebes. Leiden: E.J. Brill,
1922. 10 plates. 4to. New cloth. Ars Libri 34-827 1983 $125

RIJKS ETHNOGRAPHISCH MUSEUM   Catalogus van 's Rijks Ethnographisch
Museum. Deel XVII: De Oostelijke Kleine Soenda-Eilanden. Leiden:
E.J. Brill, 1922. 10 plates. Text illus. 4to. New cloth. Lower
right corner of first 34 pages chewed off, not affecting text. Ars
Libri 34-828 1983 $85

RIKER, JAMES   Revised History of Harlem. New York,
1905. 8vo. Maps and illus. Ends of spine frayed. Morrill 289-
632 1983 $50

RILEY, ATHELSTAN   Athos, or the Mountain of the Monks.
London, 1887. 8 plates, 20 illus. Gilt-decorated cloth. 8vo.
Salloch 385-384 1983 $75

RILEY, CHARLES V.   The Locust Plague in the United States.
Chicago, 1877. 1st book ed. Illus. Small 8vo, binding partly worn.
Morrill 288-427 1983 $27.50

RILEY, HENRY H.   The Puddleford Papers. New York, 1857.
Plates. Cloth. One signature pulled. First edition. Felcone 22-214
1983 $35

RILEY, I. WOODBRIDGE   American Philosophy. New York, 1907.
First edition. 8vo. Morrill 290-426 1983 $20

RILEY, JAMES   An authentic narrative of the loss of
the American Brig Commerce... Hartford: S. Andrus, (1844). 8vo.
7 plates. Orig. cloth. Spine slightly faded. Adelson Africa-214
1983 $40

RILEY, JAMES   Loss of the American Brig Commerce.
1817. Large folding map neatly repaired, new half old style calf,
a little thumbed. K Books 301-160 1983 £95

RILEY, JAMES WHITCOMB   Armazindy. Indianapolis: Bowen-
Merrill, 1894. 1st ed., state 2, in the more elaborate "Holliday"
binding. Orig. red cloth, gilt, t.e.g., others uncut. Inscribed
at front by Riley: "For--Mrs. Ammorsette Lindley...James Whitcomb
Riley. Indianapolis, Ind., Nov. 10, 1894..." Fine copy. Jenkins
155-1064 1983 $135

RILEY, JAMES WHITCOMB   Armazindy. Indianapolis: Bowen-
Merrill, 1894. 1st ed., 1st printing. Orig. two-tone green cloth,
gilt, t.e.g. Fine. Jenkins 155-1065 1983 $20

RILEY, JAMES WHITCOMB   Character Sketches. The Boss Girl.
Indianapolis: Bowen-Merrill, 1886. 1st ed., 2nd printing, binding
E. Orig. mustard pictorial cloth. The binding has the statement
"Third Edition" on spine. Uncommon. Fine copy with inscription by
Riley on flyleaf: "To--Robert Burns Wilson, With warm regards.
James Whitcomb Riley." Jenkins 155-1067 1983 $150

RILEY, JAMES WHITCOMB   A Child-World. Indianapolis & Kansas
City: Bowen-Merrill; London: Longmans, 1897. Frontis. 1st ed.,
state 2 (no priority). Orig. red cloth, gilt, t.e.g., others uncut.
Very fine copy inscribed at front by Riley: "With all best greetings--
James Whitcomb Riley. Indianapolis, Mh 18, 1897." Jenkins 155-1068
1983 $125

RILEY, JAMES WHITCOMB   The Flying Islands of the Night.
Indianapolis: 1913. Sm 4to, cloth-backed bds., lettering &
design in gilt. First edition thus. With 16 tipped-in color
plates plus decorative borders & endpapers by Booth. Large
scratch on front cover, else a very nice copy. Perata 27-19
1983 $75

RILEY, JAMES WHITCOMB   Green Fields and Running Brooks.
Indianapolis: Bowen-Merrill, 1893. 1st ed., 1st state. Orig.
two-tone cloth, gilt, t.e.g. Pasted to the front pastedown is the
orig. manuscript to a poem that appears in this book, in pencil,
signed, with Riley's request for criticism appended below poem. The
poem appears on p. 70, with minor revisions. Fine copy with presen.
slip inserted at front inscribed by Riley. Jenkins 155-1070 1983
$225

RILEY, JAMES WHITCOMB   Green Fields and Running Brooks.
Indianapolis, 1895. A later edition, covers worn. Green cloth.
With the book's concluding poem written out in the poet's hand on
the verso of the dedication page, and signed in full. Newspaper
clippings on end pages. Bradley 65-162 1983 $55

RILEY, JAMES WHITCOMB   James Whitcomb Riley's Letter from
Boston. St. Louis, Privately printed, 1922. First edition. Thin 8vo,
title page woodcut by Rudolph Rusicka. 4 pages of facs. manuscript.
Printed blue boards. One of 500 copies printed by D.B. Updike at
the Merrymount Press. Very good. Houle 22-744 1983 $35

RILEY, JAMES WHITCOMB   Morning. Indianapolis: Bobbs-Merrill,
(1907). 1st ed., 1st state, trial binding, which was used on a small
number of copies. Orig. smooth green cloth, gilt, t.e.g. Fine copy
inscribed by Riley on front end papers: "To--Dr. Franklin W. Hays...
James Whitcomb Riley, Oct. 10, 1907. Jenkins 155-1071 1983 $90

RILEY, JAMES WHITCOMB   An Old Sweetheart of Mine. Indianapolis,
Bobbs-Merrill, (1902). Maroon cloth stamped in pink, orange, and
gilt. Decorated endpapers, oval pictorial paper label by Christy on
upper cover (a bit rubbed) else very good. With 19 full page
illus. and vignettes by Howard Chandler Christy. Houle 22-745 1983
$25

RILEY, JAMES WHITCOMB   Pipes O'Pan at Zekesbury. Indianapolis:
1889 (actually 1888). First edition, first binding, first state.
Pictorial cocoa-colored cloth. Plain end papers, printer's slug on
copyright page. Very nice copy, cover edges lightly worn. Bradley
66-298 1983 $25

RILEY, JAMES WHITCOMB   The Raggedy Man. Indianapolis: Bobbs
Merrill, (c. 1907). 29-1/2 cm. Eight full-page color illus. Orig.
green cloth. Very good. First edition, state 2, with the large
pictorial onlay on front cover. Grunder 7-66 1983 $50

RILEY, JOSIAH   Reports of...on the Purchase and
Properties of the Steptoe Silver Mining Co. of Nevada. N.Y.. 1865.
Folded map. Orig. wraps. Ginsberg 47-654 1983 $85

RILEY, PATRICK   Memories of a Blue-Jacket. Sampson
Low, (1927). First edition, with 24 plates, roy. 8vo, orig. cloth.
Fenning 62-299 1983 £14.50

RILING, RAYMOND   Guns and Shooting. New York, 1951.
Limited edition of 1500 copies. Frontis. 11 plates (1 double page).
8vo. Orig. cloth. Orig. dust jacket. Inscription on front endpaper
"20 February 1951 High regards and best wishes to Archer L. Jackson,
from the auhtor, Raymond Riling", with Jackson's bookplate. Good.
Edwards 1042-457 1983 £120

RILKE, RAINER MARIA   Das Buch der Bilder. (Darmstadt:
Ernst Ludwig Presse, 1913). Edition ltd. to 300 copies. Bound in
orig. half calf over marbled boards. T.e.g. Karmiole 72-43 1983
$85

RILKE, RAINER MARIA   Duino Elegies. New York, 1939. First
American edition. With the ownership signature of Theodore Roethke.
Corners bumped. Head and tail of spine rubbed. Chipped, torn, and
creased dustwrapper. Very good. Jolliffe 26-450 1983 £30

RILKE, RAINER MARIA   The Lay of Love and Death of Cornet
Christopher Rilke. London: Lindsay Drummond, 1948. First English
edition. Orig. cloth. Dust jacket (faded and slightly worn). Near-
fine. MacManus 280-4363 1983 $35

RILKE, RAINER MARIA   The Lay of Love and Death of Coronet
Christopher Rilke. London: Lindsay Drummond, 1948. Cloth. First
edition. Fine in slightly tanned dust jacket. Reese 20-827 1983 $25

RILKE, RAINER MARIA   Poems. NY, 1943. "Review copy" stamped
on front fly, endpapers slightly foxed, else very good in slightly
chipped and soiled, aging dustwrapper. Quill & Brush 54-1148 1983
$40

RILKE, RAINER MARIA   Requiem and other poems. Hogarth Press,
1935. First edition. Intro. by J.B. Leishman. Spine dull. Nice.
Rota 230-523 1983 £12

RILKE, RAINER MARIA   Selections from Letters to a Young Poet.
Wisconsin: Penstemon Press, 1975. Tall, slim 8vo, 10 full-page
lithographs uncut in thick textured hand-made paper wrappers lettered
in black, fine. 25 numbered copies only. Deighton 3-249 1983 £55

RILKE, RAINER MARIA   Sonnets to Orpheus. N.Y., (1942).
First edition. Fine, in a sunned dust wrapper. Argosy 714-626 1983
$20

RILKE, RAINER MARIA   The Tale of the Love and Death of
Cornet Christopher Rilke. N.Y., (1932). First edition. Thin 8vo.
Argosy 714-627 1983 $20

RIMBAUD, ARTHUR   A Season in Hell. N, (1939). Limited
to 750 copies, minor interior foxing, else very good, owner's name
and date. Quill & Brush 54-1207 1983 $35

RINALDIS, ALDO DE   Simone Martini. Roma: Palombi,
(1936). 80 plates. 4to. Cloth. Slightly shaken. Ars Libri
33-224 1983 $125

RINDER, FRANK　　　　　D. Y. Cameron, An Illustrated Catalogue of his Etched Work. Glasgow, 1912. Limited to 700 numbered copies, this copy is one of the first 200 which has proofs of all the illus. on Japanese vellum and an orig. signed etching. 434 illus. Vellum backed cloth boards. Index. One hinge starting to split. A bit rubbed, corners frayed. Vellum slightly soiled. King 45-329 1983 $185

RINDER, FRANK　　　　　Old World Japan. Allen, 1895. Illus. by T.H. Robinson: 34 b&w illus. (some full page). 1st edn. Scarlet pictorial cloth gilt, t.e.g. others uncut, decor. eps. (bkstrip sl. faded), vg. Hodgkins 27-487 1983 £25

RINEHART, FRANK A.　　　　　The Face of Courage The Indian Photographs of Frank Rinehart. Fort Collins, Colorado: Old Army Press, 1972. Limited edition of 100 copies, bound in leather, with three original Rinehart photos. Boxed. Profusely illus. Portraits. Jenkins 151-289 1983 $150

RINEHART, MARY ROBERTS　　　　　The Red Lamp. NY, (1925). Signed, dated and numbered (18) inscription from Rinehart on front fly, bound in 3/4 leather, rear hinge cracked, good. Quill & Brush 54-1151 1983 $40

RINEHART, MARY ROBERTS　　　　　This Strange Adventure. N.Y., 1929. First edition. Mint copy, in a pictorial dust wrapper. Argosy 714-628 1983 $75

RINEHART, MARY ROBERTS　　　　　Twenty-Three and a Half Hour's Leave. N.Y., Doran, (1918). First edition (probably second printing) lacking pub.'s initials on copyright page. With frontis and one plate by May Wilson Preston. Dust jacket (minor chips, slight spotting), else, very good. Houle 22-746 1983 $45

RINGELBERG, JOACHIM STERCK VAN　　　　　Cosmographia. Paris: Pierre Gromors, 1529. First edition. Cont. marginalia. Small 4to. Antique blind-ruled calf. Rare. Kraus 164-203 1983 $6,500

RIORDAN, JOSEPH W.　　　　　The First Half Century of St. Ignatius Church & College. San Francisco: (H.S. Crocker Co.), 1905. Plates. Cloth. Ex-library with slips removed. Stamps. Call number effaced from spine. Dawson 471-242 1983 $65

RIPLEY, GEORGE　　　　　The Condensed American Cyclopaedia. New York, Appleton, 1877. Maps and text illus. 4 vols., 4to, full contemporary calf. Ends of few spines chipped. Morrill 287-392 1983 $25

RIPLEY, MARY CHURCHILL　　　　　The Oriental Rug Book. New York: Stokes, 1904. First edition. Profusely illus., including color plates. Orig. maroon and blue decorated cloth. Bookplate. Fine. Jenkins 152-351 1983 $35

RIPLEY, MARY CHURCHILL　　　　　The Oriental Rug Book. New York, (1904). 1st ed. Illus., a few in color. 8vo. Spine faded. Morrill 287-393 1983 $25

RIPLEY, THOMAS　　　　　They Died with their Boots on. N.Y., Doubleday, 1935. First edition. Illus. Dust jacket. Very good. With a tls from the author tipped in. Houle 21-1135 1983 $85

RIQUER, ALEXANDRE DE　　　　　Ex-Libris. (Barcelona: J. Thomas). 1903. 4to, frontis. and 63 orig. mounted bookplates, each on the recto of a sheet, some color printed. Karmiole 71-31 1983 $150

RISLEY, H. H.　　　　　The People of India. London, 1908. Folding map, 24 photographic plates. Thick 8vo. Pictorial cloth a little soiled and worn. Good. Edwards 1044-596 1983 £35

RISSO, A.　　　　　Histoire Naturelle de l'Europe Meridionale. Paris, 1826. Vol. 2, 8 plates by Turpin and Pretre, 8vo, half calf. Contains Articles 3-8; articles 1 and 2 were contained in vol. 1, which is not present. Wheldon 160-1764 1983 £20

RIST, JOHN　　　　　Depositio Cornuti Typographici... New York: The Grolier Club, 1911. First edition thus. 8vo. Cloth-backed boards. One of 250 copies printed by D.B. Updike at the Merrymount Press. Private bookplates stamped "withdrawn". Oak Knoll 38-337 1983 $35

RITCHIE, ANNE ISABELLA THACKERAY　　　　　Blackstick Papers. London: Smith, Elder, & Co., 1908. First edition. With portraits. Orig. cloth. Front cover scraped in two places. Endpapers foxed. Publisher's slip tipped in. Good. MacManus 280-4372 1983 $50

RITCHIE, ANNE ISABELLA THACKERAY　　　　　Blackstick Papers. Smith, Elder, 1908. First edition. Half title, 3 ports. Orig. blue cloth. Jarndyce 31-876 1983 £14.50

RITCHIE, ANNE ISABELLA THACKERAY　　　　　Old Kensington. London: Smith, Elder, 1873. First edition. 2 vols. Orig. cloth. Spines torn; shabby. Lacking title page in vol. two. MacManus 280-5114 1983 $20

RITCHIE, ANNE ISABELLA THACKERAY　　　　　Records of Tennyson, Ruskin and Browning. Macmillan, 1892. First edition, half title, 2 pages of ads, orig. dark blue cloth, v.g. Jarndyce 31-938 1983 £12.50

RITCHIE, ANNE ISABELLA THACKERAY　　　　　The Story of Elizabeth. London: Smith, Elder & Co., 1863. First edition. Orig. cloth. Head and foot of spine a bit worn. Bookplate. Good. MacManus 280-5113 1983 $225

RITCHIE, ANNE ISABELLA THACKERAY　　　　　The Works of Miss Thackeray. London: Smith, Elder & Co., 1875. 8 vols. 3/4 morocco with marbled boards and endpapers. Spines and covers slightly faded and a trifle worn. Bound. Very good. MacManus 280-5115 1983 $350

RITCHIE, DAVID G.　　　　　Philosophical Studies. London: Macmillan & Co., 1905. First edition. Spine tips frayed. Gach 95-435 1983 $27.50

RITCHIE, J. EWING　　　　　Here and There in London. W. Tweedie, 1859. First edition. Half title, 4 pp ads. Orig. dull purple cloth, v.g. Jarndyce 31-287 1983 £20

RITCHIE, J. EWING　　　　　The Night Side of London. Tinsley Bros., 1869. 1 page ads. Half title, orig. green cloth, bevelled boards. Very good. Signed by Charles Collins. Jarndyce 31-286 1983 £25

RITCHIE, LEITCH　　　　　The British World in the East. London, 1847. 2 vols. Half calf. 8vo. Good. Edwards 1044-597 1983 £95

RITCHIE, LEITCH　　　　　Travelling Sketches in the North of Italy, the Tyrol, and on the Rhine. Longman, Rees, 1832. First edition, with additional engr. vignette title-page, frontis. and 24 engr. plates of views after drawings by Clarkson Stanfield, errata slip. 8vo, orig. pub.'s red morocco, gilt, edges gilt, by F. Westley, with his ticket. Fenning 62-301 1983 £65

RITCHIE, LEITCH　　　　　Travelling Sketches on the Rine, and in Belgium and Holland. Longman, Rees, 1833. First edition, with additional engraved vignette title-page, frontis. and 24 engraved plates of views after Clarkson Stanfield. 8vo, orig. pub.'s red morocco, gilt, edges gilt, by F. Westley, with his ticket. Fenning 62-303 1983 £55

RITCHIE, LEITCH　　　　　Travelling Sketches on the Sea-Coasts of France. 1834. Finished engravings from drawings by Clarkson Stanfield. Cloth a little rubbed. K Books 301-161 1983 £35

RITCHIE, LEITCH　　　　　Wanderings by the Seine, from Rouen to the Source. 1835. With additional engraved vignette title-page and 18 engraved plates of views after Turner, 8vo, orig. pub.'s morocco, edges gilt. A very good copy. Fenning 62-304 1983 £35

RITCHIE, WARD　　　　　Job Printing in California. L.A., 1955. Tan cloth. One of 200 copies. Printed by Will Cheney. With four orig. examples of early California printing tipped-in. Fine. Houle 21-1136 1983 $95

RITCHIE, WARD　　　　　John Gutenberg 1440-1940. Los Angeles, Ward Ritchie Press, 1940. First edition. Decorations by Fletcher Martin. One of 300 copies. Printed note from the publisher laid in loose. Very good. Houle 22-1163 1983 $35

RITSON, JOSEPH　　　　　Letters from Joseph Ritson, Esq. to Mr. George Paton. Edinburgh: printed for John Stevenson, 1829. First edition. 8vo. Orig. quarter cloth and boards. One of only 100 copies printed. A fine unopened copy. Ximenes 63-259 1983 $125

RITSON, JOSEPH   Letters to Mr. George Paton. Edinburgh: John Stevenson, 1829. First (only) edition, 8vo, original cloth-backed boards, paper label. Uncut and unopened copy with the half-title. Edition of only one hundred copies. Some wear to spine, else a fine copy. Trebizond 18-82 1983 $120

RITTER, FRANCOIS   Francois Viete Inventeur de l'Algebre Moderne. Paris, 1895. 8vo. Orig. wrappers, rebacked. With presentation inscription, and a.l.s. tipped in from the author's son. Gurney 90-117 1983 £30

RITTER, WILLIAM EMERSON   The California Woodpecker and I. Berkeley: Univ. of California Press, 1938. First edition. 8vo, buckram, d/w. Illus., color frontis. Perata 28-148 1983 $35

RIVA PALACIO, VICENTE   Mexico A Traves De Los Siglos... Barcelona: Espacia y Co., (1883-1890). First edition. 5 vols. Complete, 72 plates and maps, hundred of wood-engravings. Folio. Orig. cobalt blue cloth and brown calf. Spines gilt-decorated. Occasional light foxing. (Full color chromolithographs, some highlighted with gilt; sepia tone plates; a few photogravures). Fine. Jenkins 152-748 1983 $1,250

RIVERA, DIEGO   The Frescoes of Diego Rivera. New York: Harcourt, Brace and Co., 1929. 89 plates. Large 4to. Cloth. Ars Libri 32-581 1983 $100

RIVERA, DIEGO   Portrait of Mexico. NY: Covici Friede, (1937). Tall 8vo, 249 plates. A presentation copy, signed by Rivera in March of 1937. In a chipped dust jacket. Karmiole 71-81 1983 $150

RIVERS, THOMAS   Filterable Viruses. Baltimore, 1928. First edition. 4to. Argosy 713-462 1983 $37.50

RIVES, AMELIE   The Quick or the Dead? Phila., (1888). Tall 8vo, cloth-backed marbled boards uncut. Argosy 714-629 1983 $50

RIVES, WILLIAM C.   Letter from the...to a Friend, on the Important Questions of the Day. Richmond, 1860. Sewn as issued. First edition. Ginsberg 46-785 1983 $75

RIVETT, EDITH CAROLINE   Bats in the Belfry. London, 1937. First edition. Chipped and slightly torn dustwrapper. Near fine. Jolliffe 26-151 1983 £75

RIVIERE, GEORGES   Le maitre Paul Cezanne. Paris: H. Floury, 1923. 37 heliogravure plates. 56 illus. 4to. Cloth. Orig. wrappers bound in. Ars Libri 32-89 1983 $175

RIVINGTONS & COCHRAN   A Catalogue of Books in various Languages... London: by R. Gilbert..., 1824. Large thick 8vo. Quarter dark blue morocco. Lightly rubbed. Heath 48-410 1983 £55

RIZZI, ALDO   Antonio Carneo. Udine: Doretti, 1960. 133 plates. 4 tipped-in color. 4to. Cloth. Dust jacket. Slipcase. Ars Libri 33-87 1983 $75

RIZZI, ALDO   L'opera grafica dei Tiepolo: Le acqueforti. Milano: Electa, n.d. 252 illus. Large square 4to. Full leather. Slipcase. No. 5 of a special edition for the Raffineria di Roma. Milano: Electa, n.d. Ars Libri 33-361 1983 $150

RIZZO, TANIA   Bibliotheca de Re Metallica. Claremont: Libraries of the Caremont Colleges, 1980. One of 500 copies printed at the Arion Press. Frontis., plates. Cloth in dustwrapper. Dawson 470-255 1983 $125

ROBACK, A.   A Dictionary of International Slurs. Cambridge, Mass., (1944). 1st ed., 1000 copies printed. 8vo, dw, very nice. Morrill 288-662 1983 $25

ROBACK, A   I. L. Peretz. Psychologist of Literature. Cambridge, Mass.: Sci-Art Publishers, 1935. First edition. Publisher's catalog. Gach 94-263 1983 $27.50

ROBB, DOUGLAS   Medicine and Health in New Zealand. Auckland, 1940. First edition. 8vo. Orig. binding. Fye H-3-479 1983 $40

ROBB, JOHN S.   Streaks of Squatter Life, and Far-West Scenes. Phila.: T. B. Peterson, ca. 1848. Original color pictorial wrappers. Nice copy. Illus. by Darley. Jenkins 151-290 1983 $100

ROBBINS, ARCHIBALD   Robbins' Journal. Greenwich, Conn.: Conde Nast, 1931. 8vo. Numerous illus. No. 85 out of 355 copies. Signed by the illustrator Earle Winslow. Blind stamped full calf. A.e.g. Mint in box. Adelson Africa-215 1983 $85

ROBBINS, CHANDLER   A History of the Second Church, or Old North in Boston. Boston, 1852. Engrs. Argosy 710-300 1983 $27.50

ROBBINS, CHANDLER   A Sermon Preached at Plymouth, December 22, 1793. Boston, 1794. Disbound. Reese 13-188 1983 $40

ROBBINS, HAROLD   The Dream Merchants. N.Y., Knopf, 1949. First edition. Dust jacket (slight soiling on spine) else very good - fine. Houle 22-749 1983 $30

ROBBINS, WARREN M.   African Art in American Collections. New York: Praeger, 1966. 347 illus. Large 4to. Cloth. Dust jacket. Ars Libri 34-735 1983 $175

ROBERSON, HAMMOND   Liversedge bells; or a little sober thinking on the use and abuse of church bells. Dewsbury: Bailey, printed, n.d. (1829). First edition. 8vo. Disbound. Some soiling. Ximenes 63-334 1984 $20

ROBERT, L. J. M.   Recherches et Considerations Critiques sur le Magnetisme Animal. Paris, 1824. 8vo, orig. wrs., label on spine; uncut & unopened. Fine copy. Argosy 713-464 1983 $85

ROBERT the Devyll. A Metrical Romance, from an ancient Illuminated Manuscript. London: Egerton, 1798. 1st ed. with an intro. by the editor, J. Herbert. 8vo, later half calf gilt, marbled boards. Vignette on title-page; frontis. and 13 other plates. Uncut copy. Bookplate. Foxing throughout, but a good copy of this uncommon volume. Trebizond 18-83 1983 $185

ROBERTON, WILLIAM   The Kipling Guide Book. Birmingham, the Holland Co., 1899. Half title, front. Orig. light blue printed cloth. Jarndyce 31-769 1983 £12.50

ROBERTS, A.   The Mammals of South Africa. Cape Town, 1951. 24 coloured and 54 plain plates, 4to, original half green calf (trifle rubbed). Subscribers' Edition limited to 500 copies. MS. note pasted on reverse of frontispiece. Wheldon 160-595 1983 £75

ROBERTS, CHARLES G. D.   The Book of the Rose. Boston: L. C. Page, 1903. 8vo, cloth. First edition preceding Canadian edition. This copy inscribed by author. Some light flaking to cloth on front endboard, else fine copy. In Our Time 156-663 1983 $45

ROBERTS, CHARLES G. D.   They That Walk In The Wild. London & Toronto: J.M. Dent, 1924. 20 1/2cm. First edition. Frontis. and 4 plates. Frayed dust jacket. Very good. McGahern 53-133 1983 $20

ROBERTS, ELIZABETH MADOX   A Buried Treasure. N.Y., 1931. First edition. Limited to 200 numbered copies, signed by author. Cloth. T.e.g. Spine sunned. Very good. King 45-238 1983 $25

ROBERTS, ELIZABETH MADOX   A Flying Fighter. NY, (1918). Flys offset and title slightly foxed, else very good in slightly chipped and worn, good dustwrapper. Quill & Brush 54-1632 1983 $30

ROBERTS, EMMA   The East India Voyage. London, 1839. Folding table, calf rebacked with spine laid down. 8vo. Good. Edwards 1044-598 1983 $50

ROBERTS, F. M.   Memoir Major-General Sir Henry Tombs. Woolwich: At the Royal Artillery Institution, 1913. 5 plates, gilt-stamped calf, spine rubbed. 8vo. Good. Edwards 1044-599 1983 £32

ROBERTS, JANE　　　　　　Lowenstein, King of the Forests. Printed for Whittaker and Co, 1836. 2 vols, 12mo, contemporary half calf gilt. Hill 165-103　1983　£40

ROBERTS, JOHN　　　　　The compleat canonier: or, the gunners guide. London: E. Okes, sold by Benjamin Hurlock, 1672. Fourth edition. Small 4to. Disbound. Woodcut frontis. Rare. Ximenes 63-321　1983　$750

ROBERTS, KENNETH L.　　　　Black Magic. Indianapolis, (1924). 1st ed. Frontispiece. 8vo. Morrill 286-675　1983　$27.50

ROBERTS, KENNETH L.　　　Concentrated New England. A Sketch of Calvin Coolidge. Indianapolis: The Bobbs-Merrill Company, (1924). First edition. 8vo. Orig. cloth. Covers soiled, but a good copy. Jaffe 1-346　1983　$35

ROBERTS, KENNETH L.　　　I Wanted to Write. GC, 1949. Very good in worn and lightly chipped, internally mended dustwrapper. Quill & Brush 54-1155　1983　$35

ROBERTS, KENNETH L.　　　I Wanted to Write. N.Y., 1949. First edition. D.w. Review copy. Dust wrapper ragged at edges. Argosy 714-630　1983　$25

ROBERTS, KENNETH L.　　　Lydia Bailey. New York, 1947. 8vo. Cloth. The limited signed ed., being 1 of 1050 copies signed by Roberts, each copy containing a corrected page of the orig. typescript for the book. A fine copy. Orig. box has some light wear. In Our Time 156-664　1983　$175

ROBERTS, KENNETH L.　　　Lydia Bailey. Garden City: Doubleday & Company, Inc., 1947. First edition. Large 8vo. Colored frontis. Orig. cloth. Glassine dust jacket. In publisher's slipcase. Limited to 1050 copies containing a page of the original manuscript and signed by the author. Very fine copy. Jaffe 1-349　1983　$125

ROBERTS, KENNETH L.　　　March To Quebec. New York: Doubleday, 1938. 20cm. Reprinted with addenda. Frontis. portrait, mapped endpapers. Very good copy. McGahern 53-134　1983　$25

ROBERTS, KENNETH L.　　　Northwest Passage. Garden City, 1937. Special first ed., limited to 1050 numbered copies, signed by the author. Cloth, t.e.g., very good in chipped dust wrappers, in worn and stained box. King 46-326　1983　$125

ROBERTS, KENNETH L.　　　Northwest Passage. Garden City: Doubleday, Doran & Compnay, Inc., 1937. First edition. Large 8vo. Orig. cloth. Dust jacket. Limited to 1050 copies signed by the author. Chipped jackets. Fine set. Jaffe 1-347　1983　$100

ROBERTS, KENNETH L.　　　Oliver Wiswell. Barden City, Doubleday, 1940. First edition. Large 8vo, brown cloth, spines stamped in gilt, t.e.g., fore edges uncut, illus. endpapers. One of 1050 numbered copies, signed by Roberts. Acetate wraps. 2 vols. Slipcase. Very good - fine. Houle 22-748　1983　$150

ROBERTS, KENNETH L.　　　Oliver Wiswell. New York: Doubleday, Doran & Company, Inc., 1940. First edition. 2 vols. 8vo. Colored frontis. by Grant Wood. Orig. cloth. Glassine dust jackets. In publisher's slipcase. Jackets torn, but a very fine set. Jaffe 1-348　1983　$125

ROBERTS, KENNETH L.　　　Trending into Maine...with Illustrations by N.C. Wyeth. Boston: Little, Brown, 1938. Color frontis., color illus. 1st ed., 1 of 1,075 numbered copies, signed by both Roberts and Wyeth. Roberts' bookplate laid in. Fine copy in box, with the rare extra suite of illus. in separate envelope present in fine condition. Jenkins 155-1077　1983　$275

ROBERTS, KENNETH L.　　　Trending into Maine. Boston, 1938. First edition. 14 color plates by N.C. Wyeth. Dust jacket. Very good. Houle 21-970　1983　$85

ROBERTS, KENNETH L.　　　Trending into Maine. Boston, 1938. First edition. 8vo, cloth. Illus. by N.C. Wyeth. Argosy 714-631　1983　$50

ROBERTS, KENNETH L.　　　Water Unlimited. New York, (1957). 8vo. Cloth. Laid into this copy is a short TLS from Roberts dated Maine, 1951, Water Unlimited, Inc. to a client in Michigan. Signed, with envelope. A fine copy in near perfect dj. In Our Time 156-665　1983　$85

ROBERTS, MARY　　　　　The Annals of My Village. J. Hatchard & Son, 1831. First edition, front. & plates (foxed), vignettes, half vellum, spine gilt, black label, v.g. Jarndyce 31-877　1983　£42

ROBERTS, MORLEY　　　　Captain Balaam of The 'Cormorant'. London: Eveleigh Nash, 1905. FIrst edition. Orig. cloth. Former owner's stamp on prelims. Top edges somewhat dampstained. Good. MacManus 280-4375　1983　$35

ROBERTS, MORLEY　　　　The Flying Cloud. London: Hurst & Blackett, 1907. First edition. Orig. cloth. Former owner's inscription on verso of flyleaf. Spine faded. Good. MacManus 280-4377　1983　$45

ROBERTS, MORLEY　　　　On the Old Trail. London: Eveleigh Nash & Grayson, Ltd., 1927. First edition. Former owner's signature on flyleaf. Very good. MacManus 280-4380　1983　$50

ROBERTS, MORLEY　　　　Painted Rock. London: Eveleigh Nash, 1907. First American edition. Orig. cloth. Slightly worn. MacManus 280-4381　1983　$45

ROBERTS, MORLEY　　　　Short Stories of To-Day and Yesterday. London: George C. Harrap & Co. Ltd., (1928). First edition. Orig. cloth. Dust jacket. Former owner's signature on front flyleaf. Fine. MacManus 280-4384　1983　$45

ROBERTS, MORLEY　　　　Songs of Energy. London: Lawrence & Bullen, 1891. First edition. 8vo. Orig. cloth. Shelf number on front endsheet. Former owner's signature and newspaper clipping on flyleaf. Newspaper photograph of author on final endsheet. Very good. MacManus 280-4385　1983　$55

ROBERTS, MORLEY　　　　Tales of Changing Seas. London: Eveleigh Nash & Grayson, 1927. First edition. Orig. cloth. Very fine. MacManus 280-4386　1983　$50

ROBERTS, MORLEY　　　　W. H. Hudson, A Portrait. London: Eveleigh Nash & Grayson, (1924). First edition. Frontis. Illus. Orig. cloth. Dust jacket. Fine. MacManus 279-2875　1983　$35

ROBERTS, MORLEY　　　　W. H. Hudson, A Portrait. London: Nash, 1924. First edition. Illus. Orig. cloth. MacManus 279-2876　1983　$25

ROBERTS, MORLEY　　　　The Western Avernus or Toil and Travel in Further North America. London: Smith, Elder, 1887. First edition. Orig. cloth. Folding map. Covers slightly worn. Former owner's signature on half-title. Very good. MacManus 280-4387　1983　$150

ROBERTS, NED H.　　　　The Muzzle-Loading Cap Lock Rifle. Manchester, N.H., 1944. 2nd ed. Photos, drawings, cloth, slight cover discolor and wear. Revised and enlarged. King 46-648　1983　$35

ROBERTS, ORAN M.　　　　A Description of Texas... St. Louis, 1881. First edition. 9 attractive color plates, 5 double-spread maps in color. Orig. decorated brown cloth. Covers worn but a nice copy otherwise. Bradley 65-181　1983　$185

ROBERTS, ORLANDO W.　　　Narrative of Voyages and Excursions on the East Coast and In the Interior of Central America. Edinburgh: Constable & Co., 1827. 12mo, engraved frontis. + folding map. Bound in full calf, gilt; an 1840's "gift" binding. A.e.g. Extremities lightly rubbed. No engraved title but an engraved frontis. Karmiole 76-67　1983　$200

ROBERTS, ROBERT　　　　The House Servant's Directory... New York, 1827. Early boards, rebacked in fabric. Blank upper margin of title clipped, otherwise a very good, untrimmed copy. Reese 18-609　1983　$100

ROBERTS, SARAH ELIZABETH   Jose Toribio Medina... New York: W. H. Wilson, 1941. Cloth, light water-stains to covers. Dawson 470-256 1983 $25

ROBERTS, W.   The Book-Hunter in London... London: Elliot Stock, 1895. First edition, a large paper copy. 4to. Orig. half leather over cloth, t.e.g., others uncut. Prof. illus. Presentation from author. Some cover rubbing, light foxing throughout. This copy scarce. Oak Knoll 49-343 1983 $150

ROBERTS, W. J.   The Tragedy of a Blue Stocking. Andrew Melrose, 1913. First edition. Front. and illus. Half title. Orig. dark blue cloth a little rubbed, t.e.g. Inscribed presentation copy from the author. Jarndyce 30-1084 1983 £16.50

ROBERTS, W. MILNOR   Engineering Facts and Reasons for Locating the Northern Pacific Railroad Upon the Line Selected West of the Rocky Mountains. N.Y., 1877. Cloth with morocco label. Ginsberg 46-565 1983 $125

ROBERTS, WILLIAM ISAAC   Poems and Letters by the late William Isaac Roberts of Bristol... London: for Longman, Hurst..., 1811. First edition. 8vo. Uncut in orig. boards. Engraved frontis. Fine copy. Heath 48-412 1983 £35

ROBERTSHAW, J.   Meditative Hours and Other Poems. Arthur Hall, Virtue, Keighley: R. Aked, 1856. First edition. Orig. red cloth, dulled, a.e.g. Jarndyce 30-831 1983 £12.50

ROBERTSON, ALEC   In the Little Things. Worcester: Stanbrook Abbey Press, 1969. 12mo. Frenchfold. Of 300 copies, 1/25 bound in full vellum. Mint with slip-case and prospectus laid-in. Bromer 25-303 1983 $300

ROBERTSON, DAVID   Reports of the Trials of Colonel Aaron Burr... Phila.: Hopkins & Earle, 1808. 2 vols. 8vo, orig. boards, paper labels, untrimmed. First edition. Fine. O'Neal 50-8 1983 $150

ROBERTSON, DAVID   Reports of the Trials of Colonel Aaron Burr. Phila.: Published by Hopkins & Earle; Fry & Kammerer Printers, 1808. 2 vols. Calf. Vol. I weak at front hinge. Dawson 471-243 1983 $150

ROBERTSON, GEORGE   Scrap Book on Law and Politics, Men and Times. Lexington, Ky: A.W. Elder, 1855. Jenkins 152-188 1983 $100

ROBERTSON, JAMES ALEXANDER   Louisiana Under the Rule of Spain, France, and the United States 1785-1807. Cleveland, 1911. 2 vols., maps. Illus. Cloth, slightly rubbed, very good, uncut. Reese 19-469 1983 $750

ROBERTSON, JAMES ALEXANDER   Louisiana Under the Rule of Spain, France, and the United States, 1785-1807. Cleveland, Clark, 1911. 2 vols., illus. Orig. cloth. First edition. Ginsberg 47-479 1983 $175

ROBERTSON, JOHN   Edgar A. Poe: A Study. S.F., 1921. Large thick 8vo, color frontis.; numerous plates. Dust jacket, t.e.g., uncut and unopened. Privately printed, 1td. edition. Bookplate of Adrian Goldstone. Fine. Houle 21-719 1983 $85

ROBERTSON, JOHN PARISH   Solomon Seesaw. London: Saunders and Otley, 1839. First edition. 3 vols. 12mo. Orig. purple cloth. 8 plates by "Phiz." A fine copy. Ximenes 63-160 1983 $225

ROBERTSON, JOHN W.   Francis Drake and Other Early Explorers along the Pacific Coase. SF, 1927. Tall 8vo, vellum-backed bds., gilt. With 28 maps, illustrations by Valenti Angelo. Perata 27-58 1983 $150

ROBERTSON, JOSEPH   An Essay on Punctuation. Phila.; Joseph James, 1789. 18mo, calf, lacks rear flyleaf. Argosy 710-482 1983 $45

ROBERTSON, JOSEPH CLINTON   London: or, interesting memorials of its rise, progress, and present state. London: Thomas Boys, 1824. 3 vols. 12mo. Orig. grey printed boards. Engraved title-pages, five plates (one loose), and a large folding map. Ximenes 63-266 1983 $100

ROBERTSON, JOSEPH CLINTON   The Percy Anecdotes. London: T. Voys, (1821)-1823. First collected edition. 12mo. 40 vols. bound in 20. Each vol. with engr. frontis. and engr. title-page. Uniformly bound in 19th century half green calf, with ornately gilt spines. Minor rubbing. Karmiole 72-79 1983 $200

ROBERTSON, WILLIAM   An Historical Disquisition concerning the Knowledge which the Ancients had of India. London: W. Strahan & T. Cadell; Edinburgh: E. Balfour, 1791. 1st ed., 4to, cont. calf, spine gilt, morocco label. 2 folding maps (somewhat foxed), half-title, early bookplate. Binding and hinges rubbed, but a good copy. Trebizond 18-161 1983 $120

ROBERTSON, WILLIAM   The Historical Works of... Edinburgh, 1813. 6 vols., 8vo, cont. calf, gilt bordered sides, gilt spines with double lettering pieces. Fenning 60-353 1983 £58.50

ROBERTSON, WILLIAM   The History of America. London, 1792. 3 vols., 6th edition, fine engr. folding maps. Bound 8vo in full mottled calf, raised cords, leather labels. Argosy 710-192 1983 $350

ROBERTSON, WILLIAM   The History of Scotland During the Reigns of Queen Mary and of King James VI. London 1776. 2 vols. Old calf, lacks some flys & end papers, very worn-age mellowed set. A new edition. King 46-769 1983 $50

ROBERTSON, WILLIAM   The History of Scotland during the Reigns of Queen Mary and King James VI till his Accession to the Crown of England. Printed for A. Millar. 1759. 2 vols., 4to, cont. tree calf, rubbed at the edges, joints cracked, but covers held firmly by the cords. Bickersteth 77-68 1983 £24

ROBERTSON, WILLIAM S.   The Life of Miranda. Chapel Hill, 1929. 2 vols., 38 illus. Argosy 710-509 1983 $75

ROBESON, ESLANDA GOODE   Paul Robeson, Negro. New York, 1930. Illustrated. 8vo, original boards, cloth back, slightly rubbed. Morrill 290-427 1983 $20

ROBIN, JEAN   Histoire des Plantes nouvellement trouvees en l'isle Virgine & autres lieux... Paris: Guillaume Mace, 1620. First edition. 14 fine botanical woodcuts, and a woodcut title border. 12mo. Binding by Devauchelle of dark green morocco, with double gilt line borders, back delicately gilt-tooled in six compartments, inner gilt dentelles. Rare. Kraus 164-204 1983 $6,500

ROBINEAU-DESVOIDY, J. B.   Recherches sur l'organisation vertebrale. Paris, 1828. Original wrappers, scarce, some foxing, wrapper and half-title repaired. Wheldon 160-1334 1983 £20

ROBINS, WILLIAM   Paddington: Past and Present. For the author, 1853. First edition. Front. Orig. brown cloth, fine. Jarndyce 31-288 1983 £20

ROBINSON, AGNES MARY F.   Emily Bronte. London: Allen, 1883. 8vo. Orig. green cloth. Slightly rubbed. Ximenes 63-655 1983 $37.50

ROBINSON, ALAN JAMES   An Odd Bestiary. (Easthampton, Mass.): Cheloniidae Press, 1982. Folio, 78 leaves. 26 animals included, each with a page of description and a linecut followed by a full-page wood-engraved plate. Printed throughout in red and black with 26 large calligraphic letters supplied in red. Bound in 1/4 red morocco with gilt-stamped spine over beige cloth. With a suite of the 26 orig. wood-engraved plates, each numbered and signed by Robinson. Karmiole 75-108 1983 $695

ROBINSON, ALFRED   Life in California. Oakland: Biobooks, 1947. Illus. Fine copy of this ed. Jenkins 153-479 1983 $30

ROBINSON, C. W.　　　　　　　Wellington's Campaigns. London, 1914-27.
3 vols. Mixed editions. 8vo. Orig. cloth. 2 folding frontis maps.
34 folding maps, 2 page facsimile. Slightly worn and faded. Library
ink stamps and bookplates on endpapers. Good. Edwards 1042-459
1983 £40

ROBINSON, CHARLES　　　　　The Mother's Book of Song. Wells,
Gardner, Darton, n.d. (ca.1915). Frontis. Title bordered in red.
20 plates & 118 text illus. Little loose. Blue decorated cloth
gilt, worn & light stain. Greer 39-103 1983 £16

ROBINSON, DON　　　　　　News of The 45th. Oklahoma City, 1944.
Cloth. Frayed and torn dust wrapper. "Complimentary copy, not for
sale". Very good. King 45-564 1983 $20

ROBINSON, DUNCAN W.　　　　Judge Robert McAlpin Williamson.
Austin, 1948. First edition. Inscribed by author. Illus. Covers a
bit spotted. Jenkins 152-775 1983 $40

ROBINSON, EDWARD C.　　　　In an Unknown Land. Elliot Stock,
1909. First edition, 8 plates, cr. 8vo, orig. cloth. Very good.
Fenning 62-306 1983 £18.50

ROBINSON, EDWIN ARLINGTON　　Amaranth. New York, 1934. 8vo.
Cloth. Lacks jacket. Specially signed and dated by Robinson.
A fine copy. In Our Time 156-668 1983 $45

ROBINSON, EDWIN ARLINGTON　　Avon's Harvest. New York: MacMillan,
1921. First edition. Orig. cloth-backed boards, label, gilt, dj.
Very fine in dj, and uncommon thus. Jenkins 155-1079 1983 $25

ROBINSON, EDWIN ARLINGTON　　Collected Poems. New York, 1927.
12mo. Cloth. 5 vols. 1st trade ed. In a variant binding not
cited by Hogan. The binding on this set is blue cloth stamped
in black lettering. Name on flyleaves, else a fine set in the
uncommon dust jackets which have some minimal wear. In Our Time
156-666 1983 $200

ROBINSON, EDWIN ARLINGTON　　Matthias at the Door. New York:
MacMillan, 1931. 1st ed. Orig. cloth, dj. Mint copy with review
slip pasted in. Jenkins 155-1083 1983 $20

ROBINSON, EDWIN ARLINGTON　　Nicodemus. New York, 1932. 8vo.
Cloth. This copy specially signed by Robinson on front flyleaf
and dated July 28, 1933. No jacket. A fine copy. In Our Time
156-667 1983 $45

ROBINSON, EDWIN ARLINGTON　　Nicodemus, a Book of Poems. New York:
MacMillan, 1932. 1st ed., 1 of 253 numbered and signed copies. Orig.
red cloth, gilt, t.e.g., untrimmed. Fine. Jenkins 155-1085 1983
$35

ROBINSON, EDWIN ARLINGTON　　The Porcupine: A Drama in Three Acts.
NY, 1915. Corner slightly rubbed, else fine in slightly rubbed, lightly
chipped dustwrapper. Quill & Brush 54-1161 1983 $30

ROBINSON, EDWIN ARLINGTON　　Roman Bartholow. NY, 1923. Limited to
750 numbered and signed copies, t.e.g., spine soiled, else near fine
in remnants of slipcase. Quill & Brush 54-1160 1983 $35

ROBINSON, EDWIN ARLINGTON　　Sonnets, 1889-1927. New York: Crosby
Gaige, 1928. 1st ed., 1 of 500 numbered and signed copies. Orig.
cloth-backed decorated boards. Fine copy of this limited ed.
Jenkins 155-1087 1983 $40

ROBINSON, EDWIN ARLINGTON　　Sonnets 1889-1927. New York, 1928.
First edition. One of 561 numbered copies, signed by author. Edges
of covers soiled. Nice. Rota 230-525 1983 £18

ROBINSON, EDWIN ARLINGTON　　The Three Taverns. New York: MacMillan,
1920. 1st ed., 1st binding with four dots on spine. Orig. cloth,
gilt. Very fine. Jenkins 155-1088 1983 $25

ROBINSON, EDWIN ARLINGTON　　Torrent and the Night Before.
(Gardiner, Maine), printed for the author, 1896. First edition, 12mo,
printed wraps., spine split. Enclosed in a blue silk chemise and
enclosed in a cloth slipcase. Signed and inscribed, 12 December
1896. Houle 21-756 1983 $1,350

ROBINSON, EDWIN ARLINGTON　　Tristam. New York: MacMillan, 1927.
1st ed. Orig. cloth, gilt, dj which is tattered. Very fine.
Jenkins 155-1089 1983 $20

ROBINSON, EMMA　　　　　　Caesar Borgia. Henry Colburn, 1846.
First edition. 3 vols. 12mo, lacks final advertisement leaf in vols.
II and III. Cont. green morocco, gilt, by Wiseman (slightly rubbed).
Hannas 69-169 1983 £75

ROBINSON, EMMA　　　　　　Christmas at Old Court. Richard
Bentley, 1864. First edition, 8vo, orig. cloth, binding dull and
stained but internally a nice copy. Fenning 62-307 1983 £18.50

ROBINSON, FAYETTE　　　　California and Its Gold Regions, with a
Geographical and Topographical View of the Country... New York,
1849. Orig. printed wraps., slightly chipped, but overall fine,
with the large folding map in fine condition. In a quarter black
morocco slipcase. Reese 19-471 1983 $800

ROBINSON, HEATH　　　　　How To Make a Garden Grow. Hutchinson,
nd (ca. 1927). Numerous text illus. by Heath Robinson. Pub's cloth.
Occasional foxing, vg. Hodgkins 27-136 1983 £10.50

ROBINSON, JOHN　　　　　An Account of Sueden. Printed for Tim.
Goodwin, 1694. 8vo, cont. speckled calf with old paper label at top
of the spine. First edition. Bickersteth 77-69 1983 £80

ROBINSON, JOHN　　　　　A justification of separation from
the Church of England... (Amsterdam): printed in the yeere 1639.
Second edition. Small 4to. Cont. calf. Woodcut device on the
title page. Some wear to spine. Very good copy. Ximenes 63-588
1983 $275

ROBINSON, JUDITH　　　　　Tom Cullen of Baltimore. New York,
1949. First edition. 8vo. Orig. binding. Inscribed and autographed
by Cullen. Fye H-3-714 1983 $40

ROBINSON, JUDITH　　　　　Tom Cullen of Baltimore. New York,
1949. First edition. 8vo. Orig. binding. Fye H-3-715 1983 $20

ROBINSON, LENNOX　　　　　The Far-Off Hills. N.Y.: The Macmillan
Co., 1932. First American edition. Orig. cloth with paper label on
spine. Presentation copy, inscribed on the half-title by the author.
With a TLS laid in. Good. MacManus 280-4390 1983 $35

ROBINSON, LENNOX　　　　　A Golden Treasury of Irish Verse. N.Y.:
The Macmillan Co., 1925. First American edition. Orig. cloth. Dust
jacket (darkened, chipped). Inscribed on the half-title by the author,
"The best book I ever wrote!" With a TNS laid in. Very good. Mac-
Manus 280-4397 1983 $30

ROBINSON, MARY　　　　　Angelina: A Novel. Dublin, Printed by
N. Kelly, for P. Wogan (etc), 1796. 2 vols, 12mo, contemporary calf;
slight wear to hinges and covers; a little waterstaining. First
Dublin edition. Hill 165-104 1983 £45

ROBINSON, ROBERT　　　　Researches in Organic Chemistry.
London, Cambridge, &c., 1909-1938. 8vo. Bound in 8 vols. in buck-
ram. Vols. 1 and 5 with signed presentation inscriptions to Richard
Kuhn. Gurney 90-103 1983 £350

ROBINSON, ROWLAND　　　　Works. Rutland, (1933). Centennial
ed., 7 vols., many illus., tall 8vo, cloth, d.w. Argosy 710-328
1983 $125

ROBINSON, SAMUEL　　　　A Course of Fifteen Lectures, on
Medical Botany. Columbus (O): Printed for the proprietor,
1830. Calf-backed boards. Felcone 22-146 1983 $50

ROBINSON, SAMUEL　　　　A Course of Fifteen Lectures, on Medical
Botany, Denominated Thomson's Theory of Medical Practice...
Columbus, 1832. Worn cont. calf, some inked notes and stains, good.
Reese 19-472 1983 $100

ROBINSON, SARAH JANE　　　The Official Report of the Trial of...
Boston, 1888. 1st ed. 8vo, contemporary calf, leather labels.
Morrill 288-653 1983 $20

ROBINSON, SOLON   How To Live: Saving and Wasting. New
York, Fowler & Wells, 1860. 1st ed. Small 8vo. Binding partly
faded. Scarce. Morrill 289-522 1983 $20

ROBINSON, THOMAS   An Essay towards a Natural History
of Westmorland and Cumberland... London: by J.L. for W. Freeman,
1709. First edition. 8vo. Cont. panelled calf. Stain at lower
inner margin fading out after 20 or so pages. Heath 48-571 1983
£125

ROBINSON, THOMAS   The Last Days of Bishop Heber. London,
1830. Endpapers foxed. Half calf. 8vo. Bookplate of Algernon George,
Duke of Northumberland. Good. Edwards 1044-600 1983 £35

ROBINSON, THOMAS ROMNEY   Juvenile Poems. Belfast: Printed by
J. Smyth & D. Lyons, 1806. 8vo, engraved portrait of the author.
Ad. leaf, including list of subscribers, all uncut, orig. boards with
paper spine and label. Spine cracked, but a fine copy. Bickersteth
77-238 1983 £65

ROBINSON, THOMAS ROMNEY   Juvenile Poems. J. Johnson, 1807.
First London edition, half title, front. Subscribers' list. Uncut,
orig. pink boards water stained. Orig. label. Jarndyce 30-832
1983 £22

ROBINSON, THOMAS ROMNEY   Poems, written between the Age of 7 &
13. Brooklyn: T. Kirk for Inskeep & Bradford, 1808. Wood-engr.
port. of the author. 12mo, cont. tree calf (scuffed). 1st American
ed. Argosy 710-372 1983 $125

ROBINSON, VICTOR   An Essay on Hasheesh. New York, (1930).
Cr. 8vo, 2nd edition. K Books 301-162 1983 £30

ROBINSON, WILLIAM   The English Flower Garden. 1933. 15th
edition, 17 plates and numerous other illustrations, royal 8vo, cloth
(faded). Wheldon 160-2002 1983 £15

ROBINSON, WILLIAM   Flora and Sylva. Printed and published
for W. Robinson, 1903-04-05. With 66 fine coloured plates and
numerous full-page and other illus., 3 vols. Large 4to, orig. half
vellum, t.e.g. Fenning 62-308 1983 £145

ROBINSON, WILLIAM   Flora and Sylva. 1903-05. 66 coloured
plates, numerous engravings, 3 vols., 4to, original cloth, uncut.
A good copy. A few of the plates are foxed, but the majority are
clean. Slight marginal waterstaining at the end of vol. 2. Wheldon
160-30 1983 £110

ROBINSON, WILLIAM   The Garden Beautiful. 1906. 8vo,
original cloth-backed boards, trifle used, uncut. Scarce first ed.
Wheldon 160-2001 1983 £20

ROBINSON, WILLIAM   Home Landscapes. John Murray, Chiswick
Press, 1914. First edition, with 32 fine plates from photographs
by George Champion, large 4to, orig. half vellum, t.e.g. A fine copy.
Fenning 62-309 1983 £65

ROBINSON, WILLIAM   The Parks and Gardens of Paris
Considered in Relation to the Wants of Other Cities and of Public
and Private Gardens. Macmillan, 1878. With over 500 full-page and
other illus., 8vo, orig. cloth, gilt, t.e.g., by Burn & Co., with their
ticket, the inside joints neatly repaired, otherwise a nice copy. With
a signed and dated inscription by the author who has also amended
title-page to read "...being notes made in Paris gardens". Fenning
60-354 1983 £45

ROBINSON, WILLIAM DAVIS   Northwest Coast. Baltimore, March 10,
1821. Cloth with leather label. Ginsberg 47-816 1983 $75

ROBINSON, WILLIAM H.   Absurdities. Hutchinson & Co., (1934).
First edition, 90 full-page illus., large 4to, orig. printed paper
boards, in a frayed dust wrapper. Fenning 60-355 1983 £24.50

ROBINSON, WILLIAM H.   A Selection of extremely Rare and Important Books and Ancient Manuscripts. London, 1948. Original boards,
many facsimile illus., boards sun-darkened on edges, a very good
copy. Trebizond 18-14 1983 $50

ROBINSON, WILLIAM M.   Justice in Grey. Cambridge, 1941. First
edition. Dust jacket. Map. Jenkins 152-749 1983 $100

ROBSON, ALBERT H.   A.Y. Jackson. Toronto: Ryerson, 1938.
First edition. 15 1/2cm. Frontis. portrait and 10 colour plates,
grey cloth. Dust worn and faded, else very good. Signed. McGahern
53-27 1983 $100

ROBSON, ALBERT H.   A.Y. Jackson. Toronto: Ryerson, 1938.
First edition. 15 1/2cm. Frontis. portrait and 10 colour plates.
Illustrated wrappers. Upper cover from a drawing by Jackson. Dust
worn else very good. McGahern 53-28 1983 $50

ROBSON, ALBERT H.   J.E.H. MacDonald. Toronto: Ryerson,
1937. 15 1/2cm. First edition. Frontis. portrait and 10 colour
plates. Illustrated wrappers. Foxed else very good. McGahern 53-
29 1983 $25

ROBSON, ALBERT H.   Paul Kane. Toronto: Ryerson, 1938.
First edition. 15 1/2cm. Frontis. portrait and 8 colour plates.
Yellow cloth. Soiled. Internally very good. McGahern 53-30 1983
$20

ROBSON, ALBERT H.   Tom Thomson. Toronto: Ryerson, 1937.
15 1/2cm. Frontis. portrait and 10 colour plates. Illustrated
wrappers. Wanting one page of text (29-30). First edition. Very
good. McGahern 53-31 1983 $25

ROBSON, F.   The Life of Hyder Ally. London, 1786.
Some spotting. Calf-backed marbled boards. 8vo. Good. Edwards
1044-786 1983 £125

ROCCA, M. DE   Memoirs of the War of the French in Spain.
London, 1816. Second edition. Orig. brown paper backed blue boards.
8vo. Slightly worn. Orig. printed paper label on spine. Edges uncut.
Some very slight foxing. Preserved in blue cloth slipcase. Good.
Edwards 1042-460 1983 £40

ROCCO, GIOVANNI   Pellegrino pellegrini. Milano:
Ulrico Hoepli, 1939. 96 illus. (1 tipped-in color). Large 4to.
Wrappers. Ars Libri 33-265 1983 $125

ROCCOMINI, EUGENIO   Ordine e vaghezza. Bologna, 1972. Large
4to, 367 illus. (partly in color). Cloth, dust jacket. Ars Libri
SB 26-205 1983 $95

ROCHE, JAMES J.   The Story of the Filibusters. NY, 1891.
Signed presentation by "the author", hinges cracked, offset front end
paper, spine edges bumped and wearing, good. Quill & Brush 54-1666
1983 $60

ROCHE, REGINA MARIA   The Discarded Son; Or, Haunt of the
Banditti. Printed at the Minerva Press, for Lane, Newman, and Co.,
1807. First edition. 5 vols, 12mo, contemporary qtr. sheep, marbled
sides, uncut; five half-titles, advertisements, some trivial wear
to spines. Hill 165-105 1983 £235

ROCHEBLAVE, S.   Charles-Nicolas Cochin. Paris/
Bruxelles: G. Van Oest, 1927. 72 heliotype plates. Large 4to.
Wrappers. Ars Libri 32-116 1983 $150

ROCHESTER, JOHN   Poems &c. on Several Occasions with
Valentinian. London: for Jacob Tonson, 1696. Fourth edition.
8vo. Modern quarter morocco. Heath 48-411 1983 £125

ROCKWELL, JOHN A.   California and New Mexico. Wash.,
1849. Orig. printed wraps. First edition. Ginsberg 46-119 1983
$45

ROCKWELL, JOHN A.   Canal or Railroad Between the Atlantic
and Pacific Oceans. Washington, 1849. Orig. cloth neatly rebacked.
Folding maps and charts. Jenkins 153-480 1983 $200

ROCKY Mountain Song Book. Providence: Du Dah & Co., 1856. 8vo.,
orig. blue printed wrappers, sewn. Small piece missing from upper
wrapper. First edition. Rare. Very fine. Jenkins 153-205 1983
$175

A ROD for the Back of the Binder. Chicago: Lakeside Press, 1928. Quarto. 16 full-page plates plus text illus. Decorated cloth, printed front cover label. Bradley 66-53 1983 $35

A ROD for the Back of the Binder. Chicago, 1929. Some Considerations of Book Binding with Reference to the Ideals of the Lakeside Press. 4to, decorated cloth, leather label. First edition. Illus. throughout. Top of front board lightly sunned. Fine. Perata 27-120 1983 $50

RODDIS, LOUIS   William Withering - The Introduction of Digitalis into Medical Practice. New York, 1936. First edition. 8vo. Orig. binding. Fye H-3-1002 1983 $20

RODGERS, H. J.   Twenty-Three Years Under a Skylight, or Life and Experiences of a Photographer. Hartford, 1872. Errata leaf. Numerous illus. Cloth, spine a bit faded. First edition. Laid in is a cabinet photo of a young man taken by Rodgers in Hartford. Felcone 21-91 1983 $150

RODKER, JOHN   Poems. London: Privately Printed, (1914). First edition. Orig. decorated wrappers. Presentation copy to "E. O. Hoppe, John Rodker." Spine and covers rather chipped, worn and soiled. Good. MacManus 280-440 1983 $350

RODOCANACCHI, E.   The Roman Capitol in Ancient and Modern Times. NY, 1906. 49 illus., map. 8vo, cloth. Salloch 385-385 1983 $30

RODWAY, J.   In the Guiana Forest. 1897. 3rd edition, 16 plates, 8vo, cloth, trifle used. Wheldon 160-428 1983 £20

ROE, ALFRED S.   An Angel of the Shenandoah. Worcester, Mass., 1913. Orig. printed wrappers. Illus. Jenkins 152-492 1983 $65

ROE, ALFRED S.   Monocacy: A Sketch of the Battle of Monocacy, MD. Worcester, Mass., 1894. First edition. Printed wraps. Jenkins 152-357 1983 $25

ROE, FRED   A History of Oak Furniture. London, 1920. First edition. Illustrated with drawings by the author and from photographs. 4to, plates. Morrill 290-428 1983 $25

ROE, NORMAN   Sonnets of Old Things and Other Verses. Liverpool: Daily Post Printers, 1919. First edition. Orig. cloth. Presentation copy to Arthur Conan Doyle inscribed: "Sir Arthur Conan Doyle, with the author's compliments. ix.iv.xix." Spine very slightly faded, with some offsetting to the free endpapers. Very good. MacManus 278-1640 1983 $135

ROENIGK, ADOLPH   Pioneer History of Kansas. (Denver) 1933. Photos, cloth, bookplate, dw blurb taped to f.e.p. (tape stains), extremities rubbed, couple corners bumped. King 46-125 1983 $40

ROESSLIN, EUCHARIUS   The birth of mankinde, otherwise named The Womans Booke. London: Thomas Adams, (1604). Title within woodcut border. 9 pages of woodcuts. Small 4to. Modern calf. Kraus 164-115 1983 $2,800

ROESSLIN, EUCHARIUS   Kreutterbuch vonn aller Kreuter, Baum, Gesteud und Frucht... Frankfurt am Main: Christian Egenolff, 1546. Woodcut title. Woodcuts throughout text. Folio. Cont. blindstamped pigskin over wooden boards with incised metal clasps, dated 1549. Exlibris dated 1598 of Petrus Myllerus a Millhaus, and of the Convent of the Barefoot Carmelites. From the libraries of Alistair Livingston Gunn and Alfred M. Hellman with their bookplates. Some rubbing. Kraus 164-116 1983 $15,000

ROESSLIN, EUCHARIUS   De partu hominis, et quae circa ipsum accidunt. Frankfurt: Christian Egenolph, 1532. First Latin edition. Several marginalia in two early hands, one in black ink, one in faded red. With 21 woodcuts of which 2 are repeats. 8vo. Modern grey boards. From the libraries of Alistair Livingston Gunn and Alfred H. Hellman. Kraus 164-114 1983 $5,200

ROESSLIN, EUCHARIUS   Der Schwanngeren Frawen und Hebammen Rosegarten. Augsburg: Heinrich Steiner, 1528. 22 woodcuts of which 2 are repeats. 4to. Modern vellum. From the libraries of Alistair Livingston Gunn and Alfred M. Hellman, with their bookplates. Kraus 164-112 1983 $9,200

ROESSLIN, EUCHARIUS   Der Swangern Frauwen und hebamen Rosegarten. Strassburg: Martin Flach, 1513. First edition. 24 woodcuts of which 4 are repeats. Title with woodcut border. 4to. Eighteenth-century boards with calf back and corners. From the libraries of Ernst, Duke of Gotha, with his exlibris stamped in gold on front cover and Gotha library stamp on verso of title overlaid by another unidentifiable stamp; Alistair Livingston Gunn and Alfred M. Hellman, with bookplates. Kraus 164-111 1983 $65,000

ROETHEL, HANS KONRAD   Kandinsky: Das graphische Werk. Koln: M. DuMont Schauberg, 1970. More than 200 plates (70 color). 109 illus. Large 4to. Cloth. Dust jacket. Slipcase. No. 643 of a limited edition of 1500 copies. Ars Libri 32-354 1983 $850

ROETHKE, THEODORE   The Lost Son. L, (1949). Spine lettering lightly rubbed, else near fine in lightly chipped, price clipped, very good dustwrapper. Quill & Brush 54-1168 1983 $60

ROETHKE, THEODORE   Sequence, Sometimes Metaphysical. The Stone Wall Press, 1963. With wood engravings by John Roy. Tall 8vo. Cloth. 1 of 330 copies. A fine copy in slipcase box. In Our Time 156-675 1983 $400

ROETHKE, THEODORE   Words for the Wind. London: Secker & Warburg, 1957. 8vo. Orig. boards. Dust jacket. First edition. Very fine copy. Jaffe 1-350 1983 $125

ROETHKE, THEODORE   Words for the Wind. New York, 1958. 8vo. Cloth. From the library of poet Cid Corman. Pencilled notations in text covering more than a third of the poems. In some cases Corman has written lengthy interpretations. Some browning on endpapers from newspaper clippings having been laid in, else a vg-fine copy in dj. In Our Time 156-674 1983 $150

ROETHKE, THEODORE   Words for the Wind. New York, (1958). 8vo. Cloth. A fine copy in dj which has some very tight tanning at top edge of rear flap. In Our Time 156-673 1983 $150

ROETHLISBERGER, MARCEL   Claude Lorrain: The Paintings. New Haven: Yale University Press, 1961. 2 vols. 437 illus. 4to. Cloth. Ars Libri 32-114 1983 $275

ROETHLISBERGER, MARCEL   Claude Lorrain: The Drawings. Berkeley/Los Angeles: University of California Press, 1968. 2 vols. 1244 illus. Large 4to. Cloth. Dust jacket. Ars Libri 32-113 1983 $175

ROFFENI, GIOVANNI ANTONIO   Discorso Astrologico... Bologna: Heredi di Gio. Rossi, 1611. First edition. Small 4to. Boards. From the library of Piero Ginori Conti, with his bookplate. Kraus 164-94 1983 $4,200

ROGER-MARX, CLAUDE   Bonnard lithographe. Monte Carlo: Andre Sauret, 1952. 98 color plates. Folio. Wrappers. Dust jacket. Slipcase. Printed by Mourlot on grand velin Renage. Ars Libri 32-47 1983 $325

ROGER-MARX, CLAUDE   Eva Gonzales. Paris: Editions de Neuilly, 1950. 16 plates. Small 4to. Wrappers. Unopened. Ars Libri 32-263 1983 $30

ROGER-MARX, CLAUDE   Les lithographies de Renoir. Monte-Carlo: Andre Sauret, 1951. 34 illus. (6 color). 4to. Wrappers. Dust jacket. One of 3000 numbered copies on grand velin Renage, printed by Mourlot. Ars Libri 32-574 1983 $200

ROGERS, AMMI   Memoirs of the Rev. Ammi Roger, A.M... Schenectady, 1826. Old leather, hinges cracking, internally water-stained. Reese 18-607 1983 $75

ROGERS, BRUCE   Epicurus. NY, 1947. Limited Editions Club. Limited to 1500 numbered copies, signed by Rogers, fine in slightly worn, near fine slipcase, bookplate. Quill & Brush 54-1169 1983 $60

ROGERS, CHARLES — Ottawa Past and Present. Ottawa: Printed for the proprietors by the Times Printing & Publishing Co., 1871. 21 1/2cm. 23 pages of illus'd. ads. Bound in new quarter brown moro-co and marbled boards. Benj. Slute's copy with his name on the title-page, wanting the upper wrapper. Rare. McGahern 53-135 1983 $200

ROGERS, EDWARD H. — Reminiscences of Military Service in the Forty-Third Regiment, Massachusetts Infantry, During the Great Civil War, 1862-63. Boston, 1883. 1st ed. 8vo. 4 heliotype plates. Morrill 286-307 1983 $40

ROGERS, HENRY — The Protestant Church Existent. Printed by Richard Badger, 1638. First edition, 4to, wrapper, a very few running headlines just touched, but otherwise a nice copy. Fenning 61-373 1983 £135

ROGERS, HENRY D. — Address Delivered at the Meeting of the Association of American Geologists and Naturalists. N.Y., 1844. Orig. front printed wrapper. First edition. Ginsberg 46-669 1983

ROGERS, J. HENRY — The California Hundred. San Francisco: Bancroft, 1865. 1st ed. Orig. flexible black cloth, gilt. This copy inscribed by Moses S. Prince, San Francisco, July, 1865, with an orig. three stanza poem in his hand on rear end paper. Few small chips to spine but a nice copy. Scarce. Jenkins 155-1093 1983 $130

ROGERS, JOHN RANKIN — The Inalienable Rights of Man. Olympia, 1900. First edition. Dbd. Complimentary rubber stamped slip from Rogers attached. Ginsberg 47-946 1983 $30

ROGERS, JOHN WILLIAM — Finding Literature on the Texas Plains. Dallas: The Southwest Press, 1931. First edition. Frontis. photo. Boards and cloth. 1/300 presentation copies. Presentation inscribed with name of Mrs. Kenneth Horan. Very good. Bradley 66-537 1983 $125

ROGERS, MARY ELIZA — Domestic Life in Palestine. Bell & Daldy, 1862. First edition, without half-title, small 8vo, cont. calf, edges gilt, a very good copy. Fenning 61-374 1983 £18.50

ROGERS, MEYRIC R. — Carl Milles. An interpretation of his work. New Haven: Yale University Press, 1940. 164 plates. Folio. Cloth. Edition limited to 2000 copies. Ars Libri 32-455 1983 $100

ROGERS, ROBERT — A Concise Account of North America. London, 1765. Orig. calf, rehinged, slight offsetting from endsheets to title, else a very good copy. Reese 18-81 1983 $1,350

ROGERS, ROBERT — Journals of Major Robert Rogers. Dublin: Printed by R. Acheson, at Horace's-Hbad (sic), 1769. Late nineteenth century three quarter morocco, t.e.g. Neat Marginal repair in K4, otherwise a fine copy. First Dublin edition. Reese 18-90 1983 $675

ROGERS, SAMUEL — Italy, A Poem. London: T. Cadell, 1830. First illustrated edition. Vellum. Finely and profusely illus. Spine and covers slightly worn. Some foxing throughout. Near-fine. Bookplate. MacManus 280-4402 1983 $60

ROGERS, SAMUEL — Italy, a Poem. T. Cadell; Jennings and Chaplin, and E. Moxon, 1830. Vignette illus. by Stothard & Turner. Orig. drab board, paper label, v.g. With the loosely inserted slip apologising for the increase in price. Jarndyce 31-879 1983 £32

ROGERS, SAMUEL — Poems. T. Caldell & W. Davies, by T. Bensley, 1812. First edition, woodcut vignettes. Straight-grained tan morocco, elaborate gilt borders and spine; purple silk end papers, a.e.g. Signed presentation inscription: 'To Psyche from her sincere friend The Author'. Jarndyce 31-878 1983 £120

ROGERS, SAMUEL — Recollections of the Table-Talk of Samuel Rogers. London, Edward Moxon, 1846. 8vo, orig. cloth gilt, faded, bit worn and trifle shaken. First edition. Ravenstree 97-182 1983 $57.50

ROGERS, THOMAS — Of the Imitation of Christ. The Essex House Press, 1903. 4to. Total ed. is 110 copies. Newly rebound in leather, paneling on the front endboard. A fine copy. In Our Time 156-253 1983 $250

ROGERS, THOMAS — The Royal Pattern. London: Printed for J. Roberts...(1741). Folio, uncut, disbound. First edition. Quaritch NS 7-117 1983 $425

ROGERS, WILL — The Autobiography of... Boston, 1949. Frontis. portrait. Dust jacket. Jenkins 152-361 1983 $20

ROGERS, WILL — Tom Masson's Annual for 1924. N.Y., Doubleday, 1924. First edition. Illus. by Reginald Birch, H.T. Webster and others. Dust jacket. Some light foxing at edges, else fine. Houle 21-1139 1983 $65

ROGERS, WOODES — A Cruising Voyage Round the World. London: Printed for A. Bell & B. Lintot. 1712. Large folding map of the world by H. Moll, and four others. Full orig. panelled calf, morocco label. A fine copy. Reese 18-37 1983 $1,900

ROGERSON, JOHN BOLTON — Rhyme, Romance and Revery. Wm. Pickering, 1840. First edition. Front. engr. title. Orig. purple cloth, rebacked retaining orig. spine. Jarndyce 30-833 1983 £18.50

ROGERSON, S. — Both Sides of the Road. 1949. Illus. by C. Tunnicliffe, 23 coloured plates and many figures, 4to, cloth. Good, with slightly soiled dust jacket. Wheldon 160-2137 1983 £25

ROGET, JOHN L. — A History of the 'Old Water-Colour" Society. Longmans, Green, 1891. First edition, 2 vols., roy. 8vo, orig. cloth, t.e.g., a nice copy. Fenning 61-375 1983 £85

ROGET, PETER MARK — Roget's Thesaurus. Longman, Brown, 1852. First edition, orig. brown cloth, sl. damaged on spine. Jarndyce 31-880 1983 £48

ROHAULT, JACQUES — A Treatise of Mechanicks. London: Edward Symon, 1719. First English edition. 4 engraved folding tables. 8vo. Cont. panelled calf, back repaired. With the book-plate of John Peyto Verney, Lord Willoughby de Broke. Kraus 164-205 1983 $275

ROHMER, SAX — Daughter of Fu Manchu. N.Y., Doubleday, 1931. First edition. Yellow cloth stamped in black. Very good. Houle 22-751 1983 $30

ROHMER, SAX — Tales of Secret Egypt. NY, 1919. Front fly stamped "sample copy", edges rubbed and lightly frayed at spine, good or better. Quill & Brush 54-1170 1983 $30

ROLAND, JOSEPH — The Amateur of Fencing. London 1809. Bound in later 1/2 morocco lea. Rather stained but useable copy with worn but not stained binding. King 46-650 1983 $65

ROLAND, WALPOLE — Algoma West. Toronto: Warwick & Sons, 1887. 21 1/2cm. 23 pages of illus'd. ads. 3 full-page litho. views and many text illus. Orig. blue cloth. Gilt and black stamped titles and decorations. Bottom cover worn, spotted else very good. Scarce. McGahern 53-136 1983 $75

ROLAND, WALPOLE — Algoma West. Toronto, 1887. Folding map. Illus. Decorated cloth. Local ads. Bookseller's stamp on front endpaper. Some wear. Nice. King 45-11 1983 $35

ROLFE, FREDERICK WILLIAM — Chronicles of the House of Borgia. N.Y.: E.P. Dutton & Co., 1901. First edition, America issue. 4to. Illus. Orig. red decorated cloth. Of the edition of 1250 copies, 520 were sent to America and issued with the Dutton title-page and binding. Covers a little rubbed. Hinges weak. MacManus 277-1147 1983 $150

ROLFE, FREDERICK WILLIAM — Chronicles of the House of Borgia. Grant Richards, 1901. First edition, with 10 plates, roy. 8vo, orig. red cloth, gilt, t.e.g. Binding dull but sound, label removed from upper cover, but a good copy. Fenning 62-311 1983 £35

ROLFE, FREDERICK WILLIAM — The Desire and Pursuit of the Whole. London: Cassell and Company, Limited, (1934). First edition, first impression. 8vo. Orig. cloth. Dust jacket. A few small worm-holes in front outer hinge, in a slightly soiled dust jacket, otherwise a fine copy. Jaffe 1-71 1983 $125

ROLFE, FREDERICK WILLIAM   Hubert's Arthur. London, 1935. First edition, first state. Edges slightly spotted. Tail of spine slightly bumped. Dustwrapper browned at the spine. Fine. Jolliffe 26-107 1983 £75

ROLFE, FREDERICK WILLIAM   In His Own Image. London: John Lane, The Bodley Head, 1901. First edition. Orig. slate grey cloth. Inner hinges weak. Small bookplate. Half-morocco slipcase. Very good. MacManus 277-1148 1983 $150

ROLFE, FREDERICK WILLIAM   In His Own Image. NY, 1901. White lettering, t.e.g., spine faded and edges frayed, cover soiled and lettering rubbed, review tipped-in, poor. Quill & Brush 54-317 1983 $40

ROLFE, FREDERICK WILLIAM   Letters to Harry Bainbridge. London, 1977. 8vo. Cloth. 1 of 45 copies on Basingwek parchment. Fine copy in acetate jacket. In Our Time 156-168 1983 $100

ROLFE, FREDERICK WILLIAM   Nicholas Crabbe. Chatto & Windus, 1958. First edition, 8vo, orig. cloth. Fine in dust wrapper. Fenning 62-313 1983 £35

ROLFE, FREDERICK WILLIAM   Nicholas Crabbe, or the one and the Many. Chatto & Windus, 1960. Ltd. edition of 215 numbered copies, 8vo, orig. buckram, t.e.g. Fine in orig. slip-case. Fenning 62-314 1983 £28

ROLFE, FREDERICK WILLIAM   The Quest for Corvo. NY, 1934. Minor cover stains, else very good in internally mended, frayed and lightly chipped, slightly soiled, still presentable dustwrapper, owner's name. Quill & Brush 54-319 1983 $60

ROLFE, FREDERICK WILLIAM   Stories Toto Told Me. London: John Lane. The Bodley Head, 1898. Printed wraps. First edition. Presentation inscription from Henry and Aline Harland to Thomas and Catherine Janvier. Bookplate removed from edge of gutter, slight wear, otherwise a near fine copy, in a folding cloth case. Reese 20-833 1983 $400

ROLFE, FREDERICK WILLIAM   Stories Toto Told Me. Lon., 1898. Marbled boards with leather spine, front cover bound in and cropped on outer edge affecting last letter in title, else fine. Quill & Brush 54-318 1983 $175

ROLFE, FREDERICK WILLIAM   Tarcissus: The Boy Martyr of Rome. (Saffron Walden, Essex: Boardman, 1880). First edition. 16mo. Orig. printed paper boards. Mint. MacManus 277-1149 1983 $3,500

ROLFE, FREDERICK WILLIAM   The Weird of The Wanderer... London: William Rider & Son, Limited, 1912. First edition. Thick 8vo. Orig. cloth. Rare but fragmentary and tape-repaired dust jacket. Very fine copy. Jaffe 1-72 1983 $500

ROLFINCK, WERNER   Chimia in Artis Formam redacta... Jena, 1662. 4to. Quarter-calf. Double-page table. Gurney 90-104 1983 £75

ROLFINCK, WERNER   Dissertationes Chimicae Sex de Tartaro, Sulphure, Margaritis, Perfectis Metallis duobus Auro et Argento... Jena: Krebs, 1679. In six parts, each with separate title 1660, apart from general and last sub-title dated 1679. Gurney 90-105 1983 £65

ROLFS, WILHELM   Die Grunewald-Legende. Kritische Beitrage zur Grunewald-Forschung. Leipzig: Karl W. Hiersemann, 1923. 24 collotype plates with 29 illus. Large 4to. Cloth. Ars Libri 32-295 1983 $100

ROLI, RENATO   Donato Creti. Milano: Mario Spagnol, 1967. 9 color plates. 129 illus. 4to. Cloth. Dust jacket. Ars Libri 33-124 1983 $85

ROLLE, SAMUEL   A sober answer to the friendly debate, betwixt a conformist and a nonconformist. London: printed in the year 1669. 8vo, cont. sheep (spine and corners rather rubbed). First edition. Irregularly paginated; there is a change of printer after p. 156. Ximenes 64-469 1983 $75

ROLLESTON, T. W.   The Tale of Lohengrin. Harrap, 1913. 4to. 8 mounted colour plates. 192 profusely illus. grey pages. Brown cloth pictorial, gilt. Very good. Greer 40-171 1983 £65

ROLLI, PAOLO   Riccardo I. Re d'Inghilterra. Londra, 1727. 1st ed., text in Italian and English, damp staining throughout, title page is soiled and a tear in it (now repaired on verso) has affected the word 'Accademia', in modern wrappers. Pickering & Chatto 19-60 1983 $200

ROLLIN, C.   The Method of Teaching and Studying the Belles Lettres... Edinburgh: by R. Fleming, 1759. Fifth edition. 4 vols. 12mo. Cont. calf, gilt spines. With the book-label of John Rutherford of Edgerston, and his signature on the title-page. Lacking labels. Traylen 94-691 1983 £18

ROLLINAT, R.   La Vie des Reptiles de la France Centrale. Paris, 1934. Second edition, 11 coloured and 24 plain plates, royal 8vo, wrappers (trifle worn). Wheldon 160-992 1983 £30

ROLLINS, PHILIP ASHTON   The Cowboy. New York, 1922. Cloth, fine in dust jacket. Reese 19-473 1983 $125

ROLLINS, PHILIP ASHTON   The Cowboy: His Characteristics, His Equipment, and His Part in the Development of the West. N.Y., 1922. Illus. Orig. cloth, faded. First edition. Autograph presentation inscription from Rollins with a quotation from Badger Clark added. Ginsberg 46-670 1983 $50

ROLLINS, PHILIP ASHTON   The Cowboy, His Characteristics, His Equipment, and His Part in the Development of the West. New York, 1922. Frontis. by Charles Russell, illus. 1st ed. Fairly nice copy with fading to spine. Jenkins 153-482 1983 $50

ROLLINS, PHILIP ASHTON   Gone Haywire, Two Tenderfoots on the Montana Cattle Range in 1886. New York, 1939. Illus. by Peter Hurd. 1st ed. Light soiling but very good copy. Jenkins 153-483 1983 $35

ROLLINS, PHILIP ASHTON   Jinglebob, a True Story of a Real Cowboy. New York, 1927. Cloth, very good. Reese 19-474 1983 $125

ROLLINSON, JOHN K.   Hoofprints of a Cowboy and U. S. Ranger; Pony Trails in Wyoming. Caldwell: Caxton Printers, 1941. Illus., 1st ed. in dust jacket. Scarce. Jenkins 151-385 1983 $50

ROLLINSON, JOHN K.   Pony Trails in Wyoming. Caldwell, Idaho: Caston Printers, 1941. First edition. Illus. Tan cloth. Very good copy. Bradley 66-703 1983 $42.50

ROLLINSON, JOHN K.   Wyoming Cattle Trails. Caldwell, Idaho, 1948. Cloth, very fine in dust jacket. One of 1,000 copies signed by the author. Reese 19-475 1983 $125

ROLLINSON, JOHN K.   Wyoming Cattle Trails. Caldwell: Caxton, 1948. First edition. Limited edition, No.746 of 1000 signed by author. Color frontis. Maps, photographic plates. Dust jacket. Mint. Jenkins 152-363 1983 $100

ROLT, J.   On Moral Command. London, 1842. 12mo. Cont. morocco, slight wear. Inscribed by author to the Right Honble Lord Ellenborough, dated July 14, 1843. Good. Edwards 1044-603 1983 £50

ROMAINE, WILLIAM   Works. London: for T. Chapman, 1796. First collected edition. 8vo. 8 vols. Cont. tree calf, gilt panelled spines with red and green morocco labels and tulip ornaments, gilt. Traylen 94-692 1983 £45

ROMAINS, JULES   Le Fauconnier. Paris: Marcel Seheur, 1927. 86 plates (1 color). 4to. New cloth. Orig. wrappers bound in. Ars Libri 32-394 1983 $85

THE ROMAN HISTORY, in a Series of Letters, from a Nobleman to his Son. Printed for R. Snagg, (1774). 2 vols., 12mo, cont. polished calf, spines gilt with red and green labels, a little rubbed. Bickersteth 77-70 1983 £32

ROMANES, GEORGE JOHN (1848-1894)   Animal Intelligence. London:
Kegan Paul, 1883. Third edition. Orig. red cloth (worn), crown quite
chipped. Gach 94-69 1983 $25

ROMANES, GEORGE JOHN (1848-1894)   An Examination of Weismannism.
London: Longmans, Green and Co., 1893. Slight rubbing to spine.
First edition. Inscribed. Gach 95-436 1983 $75

ROMANES, GEORGE JOHN (1848-1894)   Mental Evolution in Animals. NY:
D. Appleton, 1884. Front endpaper excised, tips lightly frayed, else
very good copy. Ads. First American edition. Gach 95-437 1983 $50

ROMANES, GEORGE JOHN (1848-1894)   Mental Evolution in Man. NY:
Appleton, 1-89. First American edition. Publisher's red cloth, spine
faded, else fine. Gach 94-70 1983 $50

ROMANES, GEORGE JOHN (1848-1894)   Thoughts on Religion. Chicago:
Open Court, 1895. Second edition. Gach 95-438 1983 $30

ROMANIS, J. MANNERS   The Great Western Mystery. London:
White, 1886. First edition. 3 vols. Orig. cloth. Labels removed
from front covers. Bindings quite stained. Sound. MacManus 280-
4404 1983 $125

ROMANOV, PATHELEMION   Without Cherry Blossom. New York:
Scribner, 1932. Cloth. First American edition. Near fine in
slightly chipped dust jacket. Reese 20-836 1983 $25

ROMBERG, ANDREAS   Schiller's Lay of the Bell. London:
Sacred Music Warehouse Novello & Co., n.d. Tall 8vo, 3/4 leather.
Salloch 387-198 1983 $50

ROMEI, ANNIBALE   The Courtiers Academie. (London)
Valentine Sims (1598). 4to, old calf, bit worn and rubbed, minor
marginal worming, light soiling. First edition in English. Ravenstree
97-186 1983 $1,650

ROMERO, MATIAS   Coffee and India-Rubber Culture in
Mexico. N.Y., 1898. Few illus. Cloth. Index. Covers stained,
moderately worn. King 45-101 1983 $35

ROMERO, MATIAS   Dinner to Senor Matias Romero. New York,
1866. First separate edition in English. Title printed in red and
green, with actual invitation headed with gilt Mexican eagle and the
special Delmonico menue on royal blue paper with gold printing. Orig.
green paper wrappers with gold lettering. Matias Romero's own copy,
with his stamp. Fine. Jenkins 152-235 1983 $350

ROMERS, H.   J. de Beijer Oeuvre-Catalogus. The
Hague: Kruseman, 1969. 92 plates. Large 4to. Cloth. No. 235
of an unspecified limitation. Ars Libri 32-36 1983 $140

ROMILLY, H. H.   From My Verandah in New Guinea. London,
1889. Large folding map. Front boards affected by damp. 8vo. Good.
Edwards 1044-604 1983 £70

ROMILLY, SAMUEL   Memoirs of the Life of... John Murray,
1840. Second edition, 3 vols. Half title vol. III, 16 pp. inserted
ads and front. port. vol. 1. Orig. boards, cloth spines, paper labels.
Some wear to board edges, otherwise very good. Jarndyce 30-1115 1983
£30

RONALDS, ALFRED   The Fly-Fisher's Entomology. Longmans,
Green, 1877. With 20 coloured plates, 8vo, orig. cloth, gilt, the
spine neatly repaired, a very good copy. Fenning 60-358 1983 £65

RONDOT, NATALIS   Jacques Gauvain. Orfevre, graveur et
medailleur a Lyon... Lyon: Pitrat Aine, 1887. 5 heliogravure
plates. Engraved armorial frontis. 4to. Wrappers. No. 125 of
a limited edition of 200 copies, printed on fine laid paper. Ars
Libri 32-251 1983 $100

RONSARD, PIERRE DE   La Fleur des Musiciens de Ronsard.
Paris, la Cite des Livres, 1923. Small folio, 3/4 red morocco, gilt
top, spine with 5 raised bands and gilt lettering. Frontis. woodcut
portrait of Orlando de Lasso. Very fine copy. Salloch 387-199 1983
$120

ROOD, ROLAND   Color and Light in Painting. NY:
Columbia Univ. Press, 1941. First edition. Front flyleaf excised,
else very good. Gach 95-439 1983 $25

ROOK, CLARENCE   London Side-Lights. Edward Arnold,
1908. First edition, half title front. 8pp ads. Orig. red dec.
spine a little dulled. Jarndyce 31-289 1983 £15

ROOKIE Rhymes. New York, 1919. 8vo. Orig. boards. Vg-fine. In
Our Time 156-80 1983 $35

ROONEY, WILLIAM   Prose Writings. Dublin and Waterford:
J.H. Gill, (1909). First collected edition, with a portrait, small
8vo, orig. cloth, gilt, a very good copy. Fenning 61-376 1983 £12.50

ROOSES, MAX   Antoine Van Dyck. Cinquante chefs-
d'oeuvre publiees sous le patronage de la commission... Paris:
Hachette, 1912. 50 heliogravure plates with titled tissue guards.
Folio. Cloth. Ars Libri 32-197 1983 $175

ROOSES, MAX   Rubens. London: Duckworth & Co.,
1904. 2 vols. 70 heliogravure and facsimile plates. Over 250
text illus. Small folio. Cloth, 3/4 morocco. Ars Libri 32-605
1983 $400

ROOSEVELT, ELLIOTT   Hunting Big Game in the Eighties. New
York, 1933. First edition. Portrait. 8vo, dust wrapper. Top blank
portion of front panel of d/w partly torn off, otherwise very nice.
Morrill 290-431 1983 $22.50

ROOSEVELT, FRANKLIN DELANO   The Democratic National Convention,
1936. Philadelphia, 1936. Folio, original leather-backed suede,
gilt, t.e.g., watered silk end papers. Limited edition signed by
author on colophon page beneath water-color etching of the White
House. Jenkins 151-293 1983 $400

ROOSEVELT, FRANKLIN DELANO   Program of the Ceremonies Attending
the Inauguration of the President and the Vice President of the United
States. Washington, 1933. 13 leaves. Wraps., stitched, fine.
Reese 19-436 1983 $35

ROOSEVELT, ROBERT BARNWELL   Fish Hatching and Fish Catching.
Rochester 1879. Illus, cloth, covers soiled and rubbed. King 46-652
1982 $65

ROOSEVELT, ROBERT BARNWELL   Florida and the Game Water-Birds of the
Atlantic Coast. NY 1884. 1st ed. Illus, cloth, very worn and
shaken copy. King 46-651 1983 $20

ROOSEVELT, THEODORE (1858-1919)   African Game Trails. N.Y., 1910.
Pictorial cloth, fine copy, first edition, inscribed and signed by
author. Jenkins 151-294 1983 $485

ROOSEVELT, THEODORE (1858-1919)   African Game Trails. New York:
Chas. Scribners, 1910. First edition. 8vo. Map, 9 photogravures,
text illus. Orig. cloth, spine slightly faded. Adelson Africa-216
1983 $45

ROOSEVELT, THEODORE (1858-1919)   African Game Trails. New York,
1910. First edition in the B binding. Illus. from photographs by
Kermit Roosevelt and others. 8vo. Pictorial front cover. Few light,
small stains on covers, mostly edges. Morrill 286-420 1983 $32.50

ROOSEVELT, THEODORE (1858-1919)   Big Game Hunting in the Rockies and
on the Great Plains. N.Y.: Putnam, 1899. Large, thick quarto, 3/4
orig. pebbled grain morocco. Spine evenly faded to brown. Photogravure
frontis. portrait. Illus. Very light rubbing at extremities, small
scrape on rear board, otherwise a fine copy. One of 1,000 numbered
copies, signed by Roosevelt on the frontis. Illus. by Remington,
Beard, Frost, et al. First edition. Reese 19-476 1983 $750

ROOSEVELT, THEODORE (1858-1919)   Hunting Trips of a Ranchman. N.Y.,
1886. Illus. by A. B. Front, etc. Cloth. Spine ends frayed, covers
darkened and rubbed. Cut signature of Roosevelt mounted to inside
front cover. King 45-496 1983 $100

ROOSEVELT, THEODORE (1858-1919)   The Naval War of 1812...To Which
is Appended an Account of The Battle of New Orleans. N.Y.: Putnam's,
1902. The "Allegheny" edition. T.e.g., illus. Jenkins 151-358
1983 $55

ROOSEVELT, THEODORE (1858-1919)　　Oliver Cromwell, N.Y.: Scribner, 1900. First edition. Illus. Green cloth (spine faded), t.e.g., uncut. Very good. Houle 21-1144 1983 $30

ROOSEVELT, THEODORE (1858-1919)　　Outdoor Pastimes of an American Hunter. N.Y., 1905. First edition. Photos, gilt-dec. cloth, t.e.g. Frint inner hinge glued, spine slightly sunned, some wear. Bookplate. King 46-653 1983 $25

ROOSEVELT, THEODORE (1858-1919)　　The Winning of the West. New York, 1889-1896. First edition. Four vols. Cloth. Signature of James Platt White in one volume; bookplates. Laid in is a three-page Roosevelt autograph letter signed, Washington, 4 February 1891, to James White. Fine set. Felcone 22-215 1983 $650

ROOSEVELT, THEODORE (1858-1919)　　The Winning of the West. N.Y.: Putnam's, 1899. 4 vols. Fine set. Illus. Jenkins 151-295 1983 $100

ROOSEVELT, THEODORE (1858-1919)　　Works of..., Hunting Trips of a Ranchman. New York, (1885). Presidential edition, illustrated. Clark 741-440 1983 $23.50

ROOSEVELT, THEODORE (1887-1944)　　The Works of... N.Y.: Scribner's, 1926 The national edition. Green cloth, paper labels on spines, t.e.g. Uncut and partially unopened. Dust jackets. Complete in 20 vols. Vol. I illus. with frontis. portrait of Theodore Roosevelt. Fine. Houle 22-752 1983 $275

ROOT, CHARLES　　The Feast of Lamps. Chicago: Whit., 1938. First edition. 8vo. Dust wrapper. Colorful pictures. Fine. Aleph-bet 8-101 1983 $25

ROOT, EDWARD W.　　Philip Hooker. New York: Charles Scribner's Sons, 1929. 100 plates. Large 4to. Cloth. No. 6 of a limited edition of 750 copies. Binding slightly shaken. Ars Libri 32-330 1983 $125

ROOT, FRANK　　The Overland Stage to California. Topeka, privately printed by authors, 1901. 1st ed. Illus., fldg. route map. Author's autographed copy. Clark 741-392 1983 $185

ROOT, GEORGE F.　　Just Before the Battle, Mother. Chicago, 1863. Folio sheet music. Ginsberg 46-337 1983 $75

ROOT, HENRY　　Personal History and Reminiscences. San Francisco: Printed for private circulation, 1921. Frontispiece. 1st ed. No more than 100 copies were printed. Jenkins 153-484 1983 $100

ROOT, SIDNEY　　Primary Bible Questions for Young Children. Atlanta, 1864. Orig. printed stiff wraps. Third edition. Ginsberg 46-201 1983 $75

ROPARTZ, J. GUY　　Oeuvres Vocales. Strasbourg, 1929. Tall thin 4to, wrs. Autographed presentation copy, inscribed: "Mr. Paul Fleche en cordial souvenir de mon dernier concert a Strasbourg auquel il a participe. Strasbourg 24 Avril 1929, J. Guy Ropartz". Salloch 387-200 1983 $40

ROPES, J. C.　　The Campaign of Waterloo. London, 1895. Third edition. 8vo. 2 folding maps (both linen backed). Library blue buckram. Spines slightly faded. Title slightly dampstained in outer margin. Bookplates. Good. Edwards 1042-461 1983 £20

ROQUETTE-PINTO, E.　　Rondonia. Anthropologia-ethnographia. Rio de Janeiro: Imprensa Nacional, 1917. 72 plates. 32 text illus. Large 4to. Marbled boards. 3/4 leather. Ars Libri 34-452 1983 $50

RORTY, JAMES　　What Michael Said to the Census-Taker. S.F., 1922. 12mo, blue boards, lettering & design in silver. Title page illus. One of 150 copies. Fine. Perata 28-38 1983 $50

ROS, JOHN FREDERICK FITZGERALD DE
Please turn to
DE ROS, JOHN FREDERICK FITZGERALD (1804-1861)

ROSA, THOMAS　　Idaea sive de Jacobi Magnae Britanniae... Londini, Excudebat Iohannes Norton, 1608. 8vo, woodcut of Royal arms on verso of title, orig. vellum, lacking ties, coming away at inner upper joint, cancelled 18th century bookplate of Magdalene College Cambridge. First edition. Bickersteth 77-71 1983 £48

ROSA in London, and other Tales. London: H. Colburn, 1809. First edition. 4 vols. Half-titles in vols. 1-3, not called for in vol. 4. 12mo. Cont. half calf. Some browning throughout. Traylen 94-18 1983 £330

ROSAHN, BEATRICE GREENFIELD　　Housing Management, Principles & Practices. New York, (1937). First edition. Illustrated. 8vo, dust wrapper. Morrill 290-466 1983 $20

ROSALES, VICENTE PEREZ　　California Adventure. SF: 1947. Introduction by Edwin S. Morby and Arturo Torres-Rioseco. 8vo, decorated cloth, gilt. With decorations by Albert J. Camille. One of 250 copies. Bookplate. A fine copy. Perata 27-169 1983 $110

ROSCIUS in London. London: printed by J. Swan, for B. Crosby and Co., 1805. 8vo, wrappers, 1st edition under this title. With a portrait (foxed). Signature clipped from the title-page. Rare. Ximenes 64-45 1983 $100

ROSCIUS in London. London: printed by J. Swann, for B. Crosby, 1805. 8vo, early boards, crudely rebacked. 2nd edition. A very good uncut copy, with a portrait. Ximenes 64-46 1983 $75

ROSCOE, EDWARD STANLEY　　Rambles with a fishing-rod. Edinburgh: Blackwood, 1883. First edition. 8vo. Orig. green cloth. Fine copy. Ximenes 63-560 1983 $45

ROSCOE, H. E.　　John Dalton and the Rise of Modern Chemistry. London: Cassell, 1895. First edition. 8vo. Orig. green cloth. Frontis. portrait and 2 folding facsimiles. Ads. Zeitlin 264-104 1983 $60

ROSCOE, THOMAS　　The Book of the Grand Junction Railway. London, 1839. 8vo, with coloured folding map, 3 plans and 16 engraved plates; orig. pub.'s cloth, gilt spine and lettering. First edition. Quaritch NS 5-91 1983 $650

ROSCOE, THOMAS　　The German Novelists. London: Henry Colburn, 1826. First edition. 4 vols. Orig. cloth-backed boards. Paper spine labels. Joints cracked on top volumes. Very good. MacManus 280-4406 1983 $100

ROSCOE, THOMAS　　The Tourist in Italy. For the Proprietors, by Robert Jennings and William Chaplin, 1831. First edition, with additional engraved vignette title-page, frontis. and 24 engraved plates of views after drawings by Samuel Prout. 8vo, orig. pub.'s green morocco, edges gilt, by F. Westley, with his ticket, a very good copy. Fenning 62-317 1983 £65

ROSCOE, THOMAS　　The Tourist in Italy. London: Jennings & Chaplin, 1831. First edition. Illus. from drawings by S. Prout, Esq. Orig. full morocco. Covers and spine a bit worn. Front hinge cracked. Some foxing. Good. MacManus 280-4407 1983 $40

ROSCOE, THOMAS　　The Tourist in Italy. Jennings & Chaplin, 1832. First edition, with additional engraved vignette title-page, frontis. and 24 engraved plates of views after drawings by J.D. Harding, 8vo, orig. pub.'s green morocco, edges gilt, by F. Westley, with his ticket. Fenning 62-318 1983 £45

ROSCOE, THOMAS　　The Tourist in Spain and Morocco. London: Robert Jennings and Co., 1838. With 21 engraved plates, including frontis. and engraved titel-page. Orig. green calf, gilt-stamped spine. Bookplates. A.e.g. Karmiole 72-112 1983 $125

ROSCOE, THOMAS　　The Tourist in Switzerland and Italy. London, Robert Jennings, 1830. 8vo, orig. pub.'s morocco gilt, spine ends chipped and joints breaking, name on end-paper, light foxing, complete with all 26 fine steel engravings including the half title which bears the note that this is the Landscape Annual for 1830. First issue of the Landscape Annual. Ravenstree 97-189 1983 $165

ROSCOE, THOMAS   Wanderings and Excursions in South Wales.
C. Tilt, and Simpkin and Co., (1837). With the full series of 48 engr.
plates and illus. Half-title, roy. 8vo, cont. half morocco, t.e.g.
Fenning 61-377 1983 £75

ROSE, BILLY   Wine, Women & Words. Reinhardt, 1949.
First English edition. Frontis. Title vignette. 15 plates in pink &
black headpieces. Red cloth, torn pictorial dust wrappers. Greer 40-
85 1983 £25

ROSE, FRANCIS   The Shadowy Pine Tree. SPCK, 1946.
8 illus. Orig. colour pictorial wrappers. Orig. drawing & inscription on title by Rose. Greer 40-199 1983 £45

ROSE, J. HOLLAND   The Mediterranean in the Ancient World.
Cambridge, 1933. 8vo, cloth. Salloch 385-393 1983 $20

ROSE, M.   Faune de France 26 Copepodes Pelagiques.
Paris, 1933. 19 plates and 456 text-figures, royal 8vo, cloth,
tape marks on endpapers. Wheldon 160-1277 1983 £15

ROSE, WILLIAM S   Letters from the north of Italy.
London: Murray, 1819. First edition. 2 vols. 8vo. Cont. half
calf. Fine copy. Ximenes 63-633 1983 $100

ROSE, WILLIAM S   Letters from the North of Italy Addressed
to Henry Hallam, Esq. John Murray, 1819. 2 vols., 8vo, cont. half
calf, rubbed. Bickersteth 75-171 1983 £34

ROSEN, GEORGE   The History of Miner's Diseases.
New York, 1943. First edition. 8vo. Orig. binding. Dust wrapper.
Fye H-3-484 1983 $55

ROSEN, PETER   Memorial Service at Fort Ridgley,
Minnesota, May 30, 1894. St. Paul, Pioneer Press, 1894. Orig.
printed wraps., some chipping. Ginsberg 46-481 1983 $45

ROSEN, PETER   Pa-Ha-Sa-Pah. St. Louis: Nixon-Jones,
1895. Orig. pictorial cloth. Minor repair to spine. 1st ed.
Jenkins 153-152 1983 $175

ROSENBACH, ABRAHAM SIMON WOLF   A Book Hunter's Holiday... Boston:
Houghton Mifflin Co., 1936. First trade edition. 8vo. Cloth, dust
jacket (chipped with some spotting of spine). Oak Knoll 49-344 1983
$45

ROSENBACH, ABRAHAM SIMON WOLF   Books and Bidders. The Adventures
of a Bibliophile. London: George Allen & Unwin Ltd., (1928). Orig.
cloth. First English edition. Arnold Bennett's copy with his bookplate on the front endsheet. Shaken. A good copy. MacManus 277-292
1983 $85

ROSENBACH, ABRAHAM SIMON WOLF   A Book Hunter's Holiday. Boston,
1936. 8vo, cloth, leather label. Illus. and facs. One of 760
copies signed by the author. Duschnes 240-197 1983 $175

ROSENBACH, ABRAHAM SIMON WOLF   An Introduction to Herman Melville's
"Moby Dick." New York: Mitchell Kennerley, 1924. First edition. 8vo.
Boards, paper spine label. Limited to 250 numbered copies. Slight
fading to spine, else a fine copy. Scarce. Oak Knoll 49-345 1983
$145

ROSENBACH, ABRAHAM SIMON WOLF   An Introduction to Herman Mellville's
"Moby Dick." N.Y.: Mitchell Kennerley, 1924. Boards. One of 250
copies, printed by John Henry Nash of San Francisco. Argosy 714-511
1983 $25

ROSENBACH, ABRAHAM SIMON WOLF   The Unpublishable Memoirs. London:
John Castle, (1924). First English edition. 8vo. Cloth, dust jacket.
Spine of jacket spotted. Scarce in jacket. Oak Knoll 49-346 1983
$50

ROSENBERG, ADOLF   Rubensbriefe. Leipzig: E.A. Seeman,
1881. 4to. Marbled boards, 3/4 leather. From the library of
Jakob Rosenberg, also with the Lanna bookplate. Rubbed. Ars Libri
32-606 1983 $85

ROSENBERG, ISAAC   Moses. London: Paragon Printing Works,
1916. First edition. Orig. yellow wrappers. Presentation copy inscribed in pencil: "I. Rosenberg to L. Aaronson, September 1917."
With the publisher's corrections written in hand in the text. Spine
and covers quite worn and somewhat soiled. A very small number of
Rosenberg presentation copies are known. Good. MacManus 280-4408
1983 $2,500

ROSENBERG, JAKOB   Die Zeichnungen Lucas Cranachs D.A.
Berlin: Deutscher Verein fur kunstwissenschaft, 1960. 103 plates.
Large 4to. Cloth. Ars Libri 32-133 1983 $65

ROSENBERG, JAKOB   Rembrandt. Cambridge: Harvard
University Press, 1948. 2 vols. 281 plates. 4to. Cloth. Ars
Libri 32-565 1983 $100

ROSENBERG, JIM   Notes for the Foundations of a Theory
of Meter. San Francisco, Grabhorn-Hoyem, 1970. First edition.
Small 8vo, half cloth over printed boards, spine label, uncut. One
of 100 copies on handmade paper. Signed by the author. Houle 22-
442 1983 $75

ROSENBERG, MARC   Jamnitzer. Alle erhaltenen Gold-
schmiedearbeiten, verlorene Werke, Handzeichnungen. Frankfurt:
Joseph Baer, 1920. 86 tipped-in plates. Folio. Wrappers. Dust
jacket. Uncut. From the library of Georg Swarzenski. Ars Libri
32-343 1983 $275

ROSENDAHL, C. E.   What About the Airship? NY 1938.
1st ed. Photos, cloth, front hinge loose else very good in worn dw.
King 46-727 1983 $25

ROSENGARTEN, ALBERT   A Handbook of Architectural Styles.
Chatto & Windus, circa, 1880. With 639 full-page and other illus.,
ads. dated April 1880, 8vo, orig. cloth, gilt, a very good copy.
Fenning 60-360 1983 £16.50

ROSENTHAL, LEONARD   The Kingdom of the Pearl. London: Nisbet & Co., (1920). First edition. Illus. by Edmund Dulac. Orig.
cloth-backed decorated boards. Dust jacket (a bit worn and faded).
Bookplates. Near-fine. MacManus 278-1723 1983 $300

ROSS, A. H. D.   Ottawa, Past and Present. Toronto:
Musson, 1927. 24cm. First edition. 18 plates. Limited edition
to 150 signed and numered copies, this being no. 23. Red cloth with
red leather label, fine. McGahern 54-152 1983 $75

ROSS, ALAN   Time Was Away. London, 1948. First
edition. Colour and black-and-white illus. by J. Minton. Late
binding. Torn and repaired dust wrapper. Fine. Rota 231-423 1983
£20

ROSS, CHARLES H.   A London Romance. London: Tinsley
Brothers, 1869. First edition. 3 vols. Orig. brown cloth. Spines
faded and a trifle rubbed at ends and edges. Former owner's signature.
Very good. MacManus 280-4410 1983 $225

ROSS, CHARLES H.   "Stage Whispers," and "Shouts Without."
London: "Judy" Office, n.d. (1881). 8vo, original colored pictorial
wrappers (dusty, spine defective). First edition. Profusely illus.
with cartoons, caricatures, etc. Included are 8 color-printed costume
plates by Archibald Chasemore. Aside from the spine, a very good
copy. Scarce. Ximenes 64-470 1983 $75

ROSS, FREDERICK   The Ruined Abbeys of Britain. Mackenzie,
nd (1882) in 2 vols. 1st edn. Illus. with colored plates & wood
engrs. from drawings by A.F. Lydon, 12 colour plates printed by Benjamin Fawcett, numerous b&w text illus. Dark green morocco grain
decor. cloth, bevelled boards, a.e.g. (corners sl. worn, lower edge
of fr. cvr. worn, some foxing contents), v.g. Hodgkins 27-390 1983
£65

ROSS, GEORGE W.   Getting into Parliament and After.
Toronto: Briggs, 1913. 22cm. 2 portraits. Wine cloth. Unopened.
A fine copy. McGahern 54-153 1983 $30

ROSS, ISHBELL   Through the Lich-Gate. NY, 1931.
Folio, full vellum, gilt vignette, g.t. 16 illus. Grand de Luxe
edition, ltd. to 175 copies, signed by Otis Skinner, the Rector, &
the Vestry. Argosy 716-383 1983 $75

ROSS, JOHN   Narrative of a Second Voyage in Search
of a North-West Passage...During the Years 1829, 1830, 1831, 1832,
1833. London, 1835. Folding maps. Illus. Cloth, very good.
Waterstain in lower left corner. A large paper copy. Reese 19-478
1983 $500

ROSS, JOHN   Narrative of a Second Voyage in Search
of a North-West Passage... Philadelphia: E.L. Carey & A. Hart, 1835.
Folding map. Half calf and marbled boards. Repairs to spine. 1st
American ed. Fairly nice copy. Jenkins 153-805 1983 $150

ROSS, JOHN   Narrative of a Second Voyage in Search
of a North-West Passage. Phila., 1835. Half morocco. First
American edition. Ginsberg 46-22 1983 $125

ROSS, JOHN   A Voyage of Discovery, in H.M.S. Isabella
and Alexander. 1819. Second edition, 2 vols., 8vo, original boards,
spines worn, uncut. Includes appendices on geology, zoology, and
botany. Wheldon 160-429 1983 £40

ROSS, PETER   A History of Long Island From Its
Earliest Settlement to the Present Time. NY, 1903. 2 vols., many
photos. Plates & text illus., sq. 1/2 leather, g.t., ex library.
Vol. lacking 1/2 backstrip, chipped & scuffed. Argosy 710-367
1983 $45

ROSS, PHILIP D.   Retrospects of a Newspaper Person.
Toronto: Oxford Un. Press, 1931. 22cm. Frontis. portrait.
Author's signed presentation copy. Blue cloth. Very good copy.
McGahern 53-138 1983 $20

ROSS, ROBERT   Aubrey Beardsley. London: John Lane,
1909. 16 full-page illus. and a revised iconography by A. Vallance.
Orig. decorated cloth. First edition. Bookplate; signature. Slightly
soiled. Very good copy. MacManus 277-241 1983 $45

ROSS, ROBERT   Masques and Phases. London, 1909.
First edition. Spine a little darkened and rubbed. Nice. Rota
231-527 1983 £12

ROSSBACH, E. EDMUND   Making Marionettes. N.Y., (1938).
First edition. Photos. Drawings. Pictorial cloth. Moderately rubbed.
King 45-443 1983 $22.50

ROSSETTI, CHRINTINA GEORGINA (1830-1894)   Goblin Market. London:
Macmillan & Co., 1893. First of this edition. Illus. by L. Housman.
Orig. decorated cloth. Spine slightly worn, with some offsetting to
the free endpapers. Bookplate. Former owner's signature. Near-fine.
MacManus 280-4412 1983 $250

ROSSETTI, CHRISTINA GEORGINA (1830-1894)   Goblin Market. Phila.:
J. B. Lippincott Co., (1933). First American edition. Illus. by A.
Rackham. Orig. cloth with pictorial label. Dust jacket (rather torn).
Fine. MacManus 280-4331 1983 $100

ROSSETTI, CHRISTINA GEORGINA (1830-1894)   Goblin Market. G. G. Harrap, 1933. First edition. Colour frontis. Title vignette. 3 colour
plates, 20 text illus. Decorated endpapers. Colour pictorial wrappers.
Greer 40-183 1983 £35

ROSSETTI, CHRISTINA GEORGINA (1830-1894)   Goblin Market. Phila.,
(1933). First American edition. Small 4to. Illus. boards with the
orig. coloured dustwrapper. 4 coloured plates and 19 other illus. from
drawings by A. Rackham. Dustwrapper torn. Traylen 94-694 1983 £35

ROSSETTI, CHRISTINA GEORGINA (1830-1894)   Goblin Market. London:
George G. Harrap & Co., Ltd., (1939). Later edition. Illus. by A.
Rackham. Orig. dec. wrappers (somewhat worn & split along spine).
Very good. MacManus 280-4315 1983 $45

ROSSETTI, CHRISTINA GEORGINA (1830-1894)   A Pageant, and Other Poems.
Macmillan, 1881. First edition, half title, orig. dark green cloth,
gilt. Jarndyce 31-883 1983 £32

ROSSETTI, CHRISTINA GEORGINA (1830-1894)   A Pageant and Other Poems.
London: Macmillan & Co., 1881. First edition. Orig. cloth. Front
hinge weak, front cover a little soiled. Good. MacManus 280-4412
1983 $50

ROSSETTI, CHRISTINA GEORGINA (1830-1894)   Poems. Boston: Roberts
Brothers, 1866. First American edition. Frontis. Orig. green cloth,
gilt, t.e.g. Very fine. Jenkins 155-1095 1983 $85

ROSSETTI, CHRISTINA GEORGINA (1830-1894)   Poems. Boston: Roberts
Brothers, 1866. Frontis. First American edition. Spine tips rubbed,
in unfaded purple cloth. Very fine. Jenkins 155-1096 1983 $65

ROSSETTI, CHRISTINA GEORGINA (1830-1894)   Poems. Blackie, n.d. (ca.
1910). Mounted colour frontis. Pictorial title. 35 mounted colour
plates (1 crease) & 150 text illus. White pictorial gilt cloth. Excellent. Greer 40-108 1983 £65

ROSSETTI, DANTE GABRIEL   Ballads and Sonnets. London, 1881.
1st ed. Orig. dark blue cloth, heavily gilt. A very fine copy in
the orig. binding gilt-stamped from designs by the author. Jenkins
155-1097 1983 $100

ROSSETTI, DANTE GABRIEL   Ballads and sonnets. London: Ellis
and White, 1881. First edition. 8vo. Orig. dark blue-green cloth,
decorated in gilt after a design by the author. Ximenes 63-457
1983 $80

ROSSETTI, DANTE GABRIEL   The Ballad of Jan Van Hunks. London,
(1942). Small 4to. Orig. vellum, gilt. 2 plates and other illus.
by Monro S. Orr. Limited edition of 620 numbered copies. Traylen
94-695 1983 £25

ROSSETTI, DANTE GABRIEL   The Blessed Damozel. London: Duckworth
& Co., 1898. Sq. 8vo, frontis. Each page of text within unique
ornate decorative border. Beige cloth over boards. Karmiole
71-84 1983 $35

ROSSETTI, DANTE GABRIEL   Dante and His Circle. London: Ellis &
White, 1874. First of this edition. Orig. cloth. Ellen Terry's
copy, with her signature in pencil on the front free endpaper. Inner
hinges cracked. Bookplate. Covers dull. Good. MacManus 280-4415
1983 $85

ROSSETTI, DANTE GABRIEL   Henry the Leper (Der Arme Heinrich)
Paraphrased. Boston: Bibliophile Soc., 1905. 2 vols. Half vellum.
Limited to 467 copies on Italian handmade paper. A fine set in a
work orig. board case. Jenkins 155-1098 1983 $125

ROSSETTI, DANTE GABRIEL   The House of Life... (Boston: Copeland
& Day, 1893). First edition. Orig. paper-covered boards. Limited to
500 copies with designs by B. Grosvenor Goodhue. Spine slightly worn.
Very good. MacManus 280-4416 1983 $125

ROSSETTI, DANTE GABRIEL   Poems. London: F.S. Ellis, 1870. First
edition, first issue. Orig. gilt-decorated cloth. Binding, endpapers
& layout designed by author. Former owner's signatures on half-title.
Fine. MacManus 280-4417 1983 $225

ROSSETTI, LUCY MADOX   Mrs. Shelley. London: W.H. Allen & Co.,
1890. First edition. Orig. cloth. Publisher's presentation copy,
stamped on the title-page. Top of spine worn. Inner hinges cracking.
Good. MacManus 280-4709 1983 $20

ROSSETTI, WILLIAM MICHAEL   Life of John Keats. London: Scott,
1887. Frontis. 1st ed. Orig. blue cloth, gilt, uncut. Tiny nick
at head of spine but very fine copy. Jenkins 155-1099 1983 $35

ROSSI, PAUL A.   The Art of the Old West from the Collection of the Gilcrease Institute. New York, 1973. Illus., many
in color. Specially bound deluxe edition limited to 450 copies,
signed by the authors. Handsome. Boxed. Jenkins 151-297 1983 $200

ROSSI-PAGNONI, P.   Quelques Essais de Mediumite Hypotique.
Paris, 1889. 8vo, pr. wrs. (frayed). Uncut & unopened. Argosy 713-
463 1983 $45

ROSSKAM, EDWIN   Towboat River. New York, (1948). First
edition. Quarto, red cloth. Photographs. First free end paper
wrinkled. Chipped dj. Bradley 64-142 1983 $22.50

ROSTINIO, PIETRO   Compendio di tutta la Cirugia.
Heredi Jacomo Simbeni, Venice, 1588. 8vo, with woodcut illus. on
8 leaves, slight damp-staining and worm-holes affecting one or two
letters, title-page torn and with library stamp and some early
annotations; cont. vellum. Worn. Reprint of the first edition.
Quaritch NS 5-92 1983 $550

ROSTOVTZEFF, M.   A History of the Ancient World. Oxford,
1926/7. 2 vols., 4to, cloth. Salloch 385-255 1983 $40

"ROTALDE." The shade of Riego. London: Richard Taylor, 1827.
First edition. 8vo. Orig. plain wrappers. Lithograph frontis.
Fine copy. Ximenes 63-133 1983 $85

ROTH, PHILIP   Goodbye, Columbus and Five Short Stories.
B, 1959. Edges slightly rubbed, cover slightly dulled, very good in
lightly frayed and chipped, slightly worn dustwrapper, owner's name.
Quill & Brush 54-1173 1983 $125

ROTH, PHILIP   Goodbye, Columbus. London, 1959.
First edition. Two small chips in dustwrapper, and very slightly
worn. Very good. Gekoski 2-165 1983 £40

ROTH, PHILIP   Portnoy's Complaint. New York, 1969.
8vo. Cloth. 1 of 600 copies signed by Roth. Fine in dj. Boxed.
In Our Time 156-679 1983 $100

ROTH, PHILIP   Portnoy's Complaint. NY: (1969).
Limited to 600 copies signed by Roth. Mint in dust wrapper and
slip-case. First edition. Bromer 25-98 1983 $85

ROTH, PHILIP   Portnoy's Complaint. NY, (1969). No.
68 of 600 numbered and signed copies, fine in slightly soiled, else
fine slipcase. Quill & Brush 54-1174 1983 $75

ROTH, SAMUEL   Lady Chatterly's Husbands. N.Y., Farr,
1931. First edition. Illus. Blue cloth, edges untrimmed (spine
dull), else very good. Houle 21-547 1983 $55

ROTHENBERGER-KLEIN, CHRISTIAN   Ceschichte und Kritik des
Schwurgerichts-Verfahrens in der Schweiz. (n.p.): (no publisher),
1903. Orig. printed green wrappers, worn. Rear wrapper has brief
note by Adolf Meyer. Gach 95-361 1983 $25

ROTHERT, OTTO A.   The Outlaws of Cave-In-Rock. Cleveland:
The Arthur H. Clark Co., 1924. Original cloth. Fairly nice copy.
Frontis. and plates. Scarce. Jenkins 151-298 1983 $75

ROTHFELD, O.   With Pen and Rifle in Kishtwar. Bombay,
1918. First edition. 6 plates, cloth. Slight wear. 8vo. Good.
Edwards 1044-608 1983 £25

ROTHWELL, RICHARD P.   Report on the Stormont Silver Mining
Company's Property, Silver Reef, Utah. N.p., 1879. Illus. 22
maps and plates, many folded. Orig. 4to, printed wraps. First
edition. Ginsberg 47-909 1983 $125

ROTHWELL, SELIM   Scraps from an Artist's Sketchbook.
Bolton, The Dily Chronicle, 1877. 1st edn. Illus. from the author's
orig. sketches. Frontis. photo portrait & 12 mounted photo illus.
Brown blind stamped cloth, bevelled bds., a.e.g. (eps. broken at
hinges, top/bottom bkstrip sl. wear, some foxing & dust soilding of
contents), v.g. Hodgkins 27-351 1983 £40

ROTHWELL, WILLIAM THOMAS   Bimetallism. Manchester: Samuel
Blomeley, 1890. First edition, orig. pink cloth, v.g. Inscribed
presentation copy from the author. Jarndyce 31-360 1983 £15

ROTILI, MARIO   Salvator Rosa incisore. Napoli:
Societa Editrice Napoletana, 1974. 152 plates. Large 4to. Cloth.
Dust jacket. Ars Libri 33-313 1983 $85

ROUART, DENIS   Edouard Manet. Catalogue raisonne.
Lausanne/Paris: La Bibliotheque des Arts, 1975. 2 vols. Vol. 1:
430 illus. Vol. 2: 697 illus. Folio. Cloth. Dust jacket.
Binding slightly worn at extremities. Ars Libri 32-421 1983 $375

ROUECHE, BERTON   The Greener Grass. N.Y., (1948).
First edition. D.w. Argosy 714-646 1983 $45

ROUGH-Hewer: Devoted to the Support of the Democratic Principles of
Jefferson. Albany; Thomas M. Burt, Feb.-Dec. 1840. Nos. 1-39,
complete. 4to, 1/4 calf. Argosy 710-427 1983 $300

A ROUGH Shaking. Blackie, nd (1900). 1st edn. thus. 12 illus. by
W. Parkinson. 16 pp adverts rear. Binding designed by Laurence
Housman. Bookpl. fr. ep., gilt prize stamp centre rear cvr. vg.
Hodgkins 27-140 1983 £15

ROUGHEAD, WILLIAM   Trial of Mary Blandy. Edinburgh: (1914).
First edition. Illus. Red cloth. Henry Kitchell Webster's name
rubber-stamped on front pastedown. Except for snags on spine, very
good copy. Bradley 66-414 1983 $50

ROULE, L.   Les Poissons et le monde vivant des
eaux. Paris, 1926. Volume 1. 16 coloured plates, royal 8vo,
wrappers. Wheldon 160-994 1983 £10

ROULE, L.   Les Poissons et le monde vivant des
eaux. Paris, 1934. Vol. 7, 16 coloured plates and 83 text-figures,
royal 8vo, wrappers (trifle soiled). Wheldon 160-995 1983 £15

ROULLIER, AUGUSTE   Exposition Physiologue des Phenomenes
du Magnetisme Animal et du Somnambulisme. Paris, 1817. 8vo, orig.
wrs. label on spine; uncut. First edition. Argosy 713-465 1983 $125

ROUNTREE, HARRY   Wee Willie Winkie. London: Nelson,
n.d. (ca.1916). 4to. Stiff linen wrappers. Light wear. Full-page
color illus. Black & whites on text-pages. Very good. Aleph-bet
8-229 1983 $30

ROURKE, CONSTANCE   Charles Sheeler. Artist in the
American tradition. New York: Harcourt, Brace and Co., 1938.
48 plates. 4to. Cloth. Ars Libri 32-632 1983 $75

ROUSSEAU, JEAN JACQUES   The Confessions. London: the Nonesuch Press, 1938. 2 vols. 8vo. Orig. niger morocco, brown leather
lettering pieces, gilt, t.e.g., in the orig. slip-case. Wood-
engravings by Reynolds Stone. Limited edition of 800 numbered
copies, printed in black and brown. Traylen 94-695 1983 £75

ROUSSEAU, JEAN JACQUES   The Confessions of... New York, 1823.
2 vols. Very good-fine. In Our Time 156-891 1983 $45

ROUSSEAU, JEAN-JACQUES   Discours Sur L'Origine et les
Fondemens de l'Inegalite Parmi les Hommes. Amsterdam: Rey, 1755.
8vo, title in red & black. Frontis. signed by Eisen, with title-page
of "Liberte" engraved by Fokke & arms of the city of Geneva on
first page of Dedication. Calf, rebacked. First edition.
Rostenberg 88-119 1983 $750

ROUSSEAU, JEAN JACQUES   Eloisa. For R. Griffiths, T. Becket, and
P.A. De Hondt, 1761. First English edition. 4 vols. 12mo, has 3
of 4 half-titles. Cont. calf (rubbed, one label defective). A few
small repairs, tears and holes, without loss of text. Some foxing.
Hannas 69-170 1983 £180

ROUSSEAU, JEAN-JACQUES   Eloisa: Or, a Series of Original Letters.
London: R. Griffiths, T. Becket and P. A. De Hondt, 1761. 2nd ed.,
4 vols., 12mo, lacking half-titles, cont. speckled calf, raised bands,
bookplate, a very good set. Pickering & Chatto 21-101 1983 $200

ROUSSEAU, JEAN-JACQUES   Emile, Ou De L'Education. La Haye,
Chez Jean Neaulme, 1762. 4 vols., 8vo, titles in red and black,
5 engraved plates by Eisen, cont. mottled calf, spine elaborately
gilt, blue and black morocco labels, corners slightly rubbed, else a
very good copy. Pickering & Chatto 21-103 1983 $650

ROUSSEAU, JEAN-JACQUES   Emile, Ou De L'Education. Amsterdam,
Chez Jean Neaulme, 1762. 1st ed., 4 vols., 12mo, titles in red and
black, 5 engraved plates by Eisen, cont. mottled calf, spine elaborately
gilt in compartments, red morocco labels, corners a little worn but
a very good set. Pickering & Chatto 21-102 1983 $800

ROUSSEAU, JEAN-JACQUES   Emilius and Sophia: Or a New System of Education. London, H. Baldwin, 1783. 12mo, 4 vols., frontis. portrait, 5 engraved plates, cont. tree calf, rebacked, red and black morocco labels. Pickering & Chatto 21-104 1983 $250

ROUSSEAU, JEAN JACQUES   Julia: or the New Eloisa. Edinburgh: for John Donaldson, 1774. 3 vols. Small 8vo. Half titles. Cont. polished calf. Very rare. Heath 48-382 1983 £150

ROUSSEAU, JEAN-JACQUES   Julia: or, the New Eloisa. A Series of Original Letters. Edinburgh: W. Coke, 1773. 4th ed. in English, but the first bearing this title, and the first edition published in Scotland. 12mo, 3 vols., cont. gilt-bordered calf, carefully rebacked in antique style. A fine copy. Trebizond 18-124 1983 $175

ROUSSEAU, JEAN JACQUES   Letters of an Italian Nun and an English Gentleman. J. Bew, 1784. Second edition, half title, 1 p. ads. Calf, maroon label, v.g. Jarndyce 31-69 1983 £45

ROUSSEAU, JEAN JACQUES   The Miscellaneous Works. London, Becket and DeHondt, 1767. 5 vols., small 8vo, 19th century tan hard grain half morocco gilt, joints cracking, spine ends worn. Ravenstree 97-193 1983 $345

ROUSSEAU, JEAN-JACQUES   Les Pensees De J. J. Rousseau. Paris: Chez Prault, 1766. 2nd ed., 2 vols., 12mo, cont. speckled calf, spine elaborately gilt, red and green morocco labels, head of spines chipped but a very attractive set. Pickering & Chatto 21-105 1983 $200

ROUSSEAU DE LA VALETTE, MICHEL   The Life of Count Ulfeld. Printed in the Year 1695. First English edition. 8vo, cont. mottled calf, gilt spine. Ink smear on one page. Hannas 69-172 1983 £160

ROUSSELET, L.   India and Its Native Princes. London, 1882. Large folding map, numerous illus. Thick roy.8vo. Decorative cloth gilt. A.e.g. Good. Edwards 1044-609 1983 £55

ROUSSIER, L'ABBE   Traite des Accords et de Leur Successions selon le Systeme de la Basse-Fondamentale. Paris, 1764. 4 engraved plates, 8vo, old marble wrs., uncut. One leaf missing and replaced by a copy, title stains. Salloch 387-201 1983 $75

ROWAN, RICHARD W.   The Pinkertons. Boston, 1931. First edition. Frontis. and illus. Jenkins 152-367 1983 $45

ROWBOTHAM, FRANCIS JAMESON   A Trip to Prairie-Land Being a Glance at the Shady Side of Emigration. London, 1885. Orig. cloth. First edition. Ginsberg 47-294 1983 $125

ROWCROFT, CHARLES   Tales of the Colonies; or, the Adventures of an Emigrant. London: Saunders & Otley, 1843. 2nd ed., 12mo, 3 vols., cont. half calf gilt, marbled boards. Wanting half-titles. Library labels inside front covers. Binding rubbed, but a very good copy. Trebizond 18-84 1983 $175

ROWE, G. R.   Practical Observations on Nervous Diseases... London, 1842. Fourth edition. 8vo. Orig. quarter-cloth. Gurney JJ-346 1983 £15

ROWE, JOHN   Letters and Diary of... Boston, 1903. Illus. 8vo. Morrill 286-678 1983 $35

ROWE, JOHN   Tragi-comoedia. Being a brief relation of the strange, and wonderful hand of God discovered at Witny. Oxford: printed by L. Lichfield, for Henry Cripps, 1653. Sm. 4to, half olive morocco, a.e.g., by Bedford. First edition. Illustrated with a woodcut diagram. An excellent copy of a very rare pamphlet. Ximenes 64-471 1983 $2,000

ROWE, NICHOLAS   The Biter. A Comedy. London: printed for Jacob Tonson, 1705. 1st ed., 4to, half-title, browned throughout, in modern cloth. Pickering & Chatto 19-61 1983 $350

ROWECK, H.   Die Gefasspflanzen von Schwedisch-Lappland. Vaduz, 1981. Map, 8vo, boards. Wheldon 160-1767 1983 £52

ROWEL, M.   Letters from Hell. Richard Bentley, 1866. First edition, 2 vols. Half dark green calf, a little rubbed, brown labels. Jarndyce 31-885 1983 £48

ROWELL, A. S.   The Silver Bullett. Greenville, 1897. 1st ed. Illus. 8vo. Covers stained. Morrill 286-447 1983 $30

ROWELL, GEORGE AUGUSTUS   An essay on the cause of rain... Oxford: published and sold by the author, 1859. First edition. 8vo. Orig. brown cloth. Folding frontis. Four pages of subscribers. Ximenes 63-307 1983 $90

ROWELL, HOPKINS   The Great Resources, and Superior Advantages of the City of Joliet, Illinois. Joliet, 1871. 2 maps. Orig. printed wraps. First edition. Ginsberg 46-338 1983 $85

ROWLAND, DUNBAR   History of Mississippi: Heart of the South. Chicago: 1925. First edition. 2 vols. Illus. Green cloth. Bookplates, ex-library but very nice set. Bradley 66-593 1983 $25

ROWLAND, DUNBAR   The Official and Statistical Register of the State of Mississippi, 1908. Nashville, 1908. 1st ed., illus., many folding maps. Jenkins 151-223 1983 $50

ROWLAND, E.   Varina Howell. New York, 1927-31. First edition. 8vo. Orig. cloth. Portrait frontis. 7 portraits and 1 other plate. 2 vols. Very slightly faded. Good. Edwards 1042-245 1983 £20

ROWLANDSON, THOMAS   The Watercolor Drawings. New York, 1947. 1st ed. From the Albert H. Wiggin Collection in the Boston Public Library. 52 plates. 4to. Morrill 289-526 1983 $27.50

ROWLEY, O. R.   The Anglican Episcopate of Canada and Newfoundland. Milwaukee & London: Morehouse Pub. co., 1928. 23cm. Numerous portraits. Printed stiff purple wrappers. Very good. McGahern 53-139 1983 $20

ROWLEY, WILLIAM   A Treatise on the Regular, Irregular, Atonic, and Flying Gout. Printed for J. Wingrave; E. Newbery; and T. Hookham, 1792. 8vo, old marbled boards, worn at the edges, with recent calf spine and new label. First edition. Bickersteth 77-315 1983 £80

ROWNTREE, JOHN S.   Quakerism, Past and Present. Smith, Elder, 1859. First edition, 24 ads., 8vo, orig. cloth. Fenning 62-319 1983 £18.50

ROWSE, A. L.   West-Country Stories. London: Macmillan & Co. Ltd., 1945. First edition. Orig. cloth. Dust jacket (top of spine chipped, a bit dusty). Very good. MacManus 280-4423 1983 $20

ROWSON, SUSANNA   Charlotte Temple. Phila.: Mathew Carey (J. Robinson, pr., Baltimore), 1812. Ninth American edition. Full calf. A rather smudged and worn copy internally, but complete, lacking front endsheet. Felcone 20-43 1983 $25

ROWSON, SUSANNA   Charlotte Temple: a Tale of Truth. Hartford: Silas Andrus, 1825. 18mo, paper-covered wood boards, leather back, foxed. Argosy 710-162 1983 $35

ROWSON, SUSANNA   Charlotte Temple, a Tale of Truth. Hartford, 1833. Woodcut frontis. 18mo, cont. marbled boards, roan back, (some dampstains). Argosy 716-161 1983 $30

ROXBURGHE CLUB   Quatuor Sermones. London, Nichols & Sons, 1883. 4to, orig. quarter leather gilt, boards; covers trifle worn. Ravenstree 97-195 1983 $145

ROY, P. G.   Les Judges de la Province de Quebec. Quebec, 1933. 4to. Ca. 300 portraits. Original printed wrappers. Expertly rebacked. A fine copy. McGahern 53-187 1983 $45

ROY, P. G.   L'Ile D'Orleans. Quebec: Published
by the Historic Monuments Commission of the Province of Quebec, 1928.
4to. 14 colour and ca. 450 black and white full-page plates. Illus'd.
stiff wrappers. Very good copy. McGahern 54-154 1983 $75

ROY, P. G.   L'Ile D'Orleans. Quebec: Historic Monuments Commission of the Privince of Quebec, 1928. 4to, 14 colour and
about 450 black and white full-page plates, illus. stiff wrappers.
Wrappers frayed, spine cap chipped, else very good. McGahern 54-155
1983 $50

ROY, P. G.   Old Manors Old Houses. Quebec:
Historic Monuments Commission, 1927. 4to. 6 colour and 269 full
page plates, in orig. printed wrappers. Frayed at the edges else
very good. McGahern 54-156 1983 $75

ROY, P. G.   Les Vieilles Eglises de la Province
de Quebec, 1647-1800. Quebec: Commission des Monuments Historiques,
1925. 4to. 27cm. Colour frontis. and 214 plates. Orig. printed
wrappers, frayed, else good to very good copy. McGahern 54-157
1983 $60

ROYAL COLLEGE OF PHYSICIANS OF EDINBURGH   Pharmacopoeia Collegii
Regii Medicorum Edinburgensis. Edinburgh: Bell & Bradfute, 1792. 8vo.
Cont. tree calf with gilt. Ads. Slight wear. Fine. Zeitlin 264-131
1983 $130

ROYAL COLLEGE OF PHYSICIANS OF EDINBURGH   Pharmacopoeia Colegii
Regii Medicorum Edinburgensis. Edinburgh: Bell & Bradfute, 1792. 8vo.
Cont. tree calf with gilt. Ads. Zeitlin 264-132 1983 $130

THE ROYAL house that Jack built; or, 1820. London: W. Wright,
1820. First edition. 8vo. Disbound. 14 woodcut illus. Ximenes
63-513 1983 $45

THE ROYAL letter-bag. London: T. Dolby, etc., 1820. First edition.
8vo. Disbound. Ximenes 63-515 1983 $30

A ROYAL Record. Kansas. First in Corn, First in Wheat, First in the
Hearts of the Stock Raisers... (Chicago: Poole Bros., ca 1884). 24
printed panels. 2 maps. Cover title. Fine copy. Jenkins 153-302
1983 $175

THE ROYAL SOCIETY EMPIRE SCIENTIFIC CONFERENCE   Report. London,
1948. 8vo. 2 vols. Cloth. Gurney JJ-342 1983 £15

ROYCE, JOSIAH   Outlines of Psychology. NY: Macmillan,
1903. Second printing (same year as first). Gach 94-639 1983 $20

ROYCE, WILLIAM HOBART   A Balzac Bibliography. Chicago:
Chicago Univ. Press, 1929-30. 2 vols. 1st ed. Orig. cloth-backed
boards, djs. Fine set. Jenkins 155-1354 1983 $50

ROYDE-SMITH, NAOMI   Incredible Tale. London: Ernest Benn
Limited, (1932). First edition. Orig. printed wrappers. Very good.
MacManus 280-4425 1983 $20

ROZIER, FIRMIN A.   Rozier's History of the Early Settlement
of the Mississippi Valley. St. Louis, 1890. First edition. Illus.
Slight chipping to spine, repaired. Jenkins 152-368 1983 $85

ROZIER, FIRMIN A.   Rozier's History of the Early Settlement
of the Mississippi Valley. St. Louis, 1890. Illus. Orig. cloth.
First edition. Ginsberg 46-486 1983 $50

RUBENS, PETER PAUL   Die Landschaften von Peter Paul Rubens.
Wien: Anton Schroll, 1940. 44 tipped-in plates (34 color). 18
text illus. Oblong 4to. Cloth. Light wear at extremities. Ars
Libri 32-597 1983 $125

RUBIN DE LA BORBOLLA, DANIEL F.   Mexico: Monumentos historicos
y arqueologicos. Mexico, 1953. 475 illus. Small folio. Cloth.
Ars Libri 34-456 1983 $85

RUCKER, MAUDE A.   West Virginia. New York, Walter
Neale, 1930. First edition. Illustrated. 8vo. Morrill 290-591
1983 $20

RUDDOCK, MARGOT   The Lemon Tree. London: Dent, (1937).
Boards. First edition. Pencil note, else very fine in dust jacket.
Reese 20-840 1983 $45

RUDGE, WILLIAM E.   Elijah. NY, 1930. Illustrative
Drawings by Bertram Brooker. Folio, pictorial bds., matching d/w.
One of 500 copies with 10 full-page drawings. A fine copy.
Perata 27-161 1983 $100

RUDING, WALT   An Evil Motherhood. London, Matthews,
1896. First edition. Frontis. by Aubrey Beardsley. Illus.
Pictorial blue cloth stamped in grey and gilt with spiderweb design,
uncut. Very good. Houle 22-84 1983 $85

RUDING, WALT   An Evil Motherhood. Elkin Mathews,
1896. First edition, front. by Aubrey Beardsley. Half title, 20pp
ads. Untrimmed. Orig. dec. blue cloth, a little marked. Jarndyce
31-886 1983 £22

RUDING, WALT   An Evil Motherhood. London: Elkin
Mathews, 1896. First edition. Orig. pictorial cloth. Frontis. by
A. Beardsley. Very good. MacManus 280-4426 1983 $40

RUEFF, JACOB   De conceptu et generatione hominis...
Zurich: Christopher Froschauer, 1554. First Latin edition. 68
woodcuts. 4to. Cont. vellum, in dark blue morocco-backed box. From
the libraries of Alistair Livingston Gunn and Alfred M. Hellman.
Inscription in a contemporary hand at bottom of last leaf. Kraus
164-117 1983 $6,200

RUEFF, JACOB   De conceptu et generatione hominis...
Frankfurt am Main: Sigismund Feyerabend for Georg Cornvivus, 1580.
Second edition. 76 woodcuts (incl. 2 repeats) by Jost Amman, and
including woodcut coat of arms of Leonhard Thurneisser zum Thurn,
to whom the work is dedicated. 4to. Cont. vellum in dark blue
morocco-backed box. Ms. exlibris of Adam Werner. Kraus 164-118
1983 $5,200

RUEFF, JACOB   De Conceptu, et Generatione Hominis...
Frankfurt am Main: Sigismund Feyerabend for Peter Fabricius, 1587.
With 70 woodcuts by Jost Amman of which 3 are repeats, title in
black and red. 4to. Modern vellum. From the library of Alistair
Livingston Gunn with his bookplate. Some minor staining in second
half of book and occasional browning. Kraus 164-119 1983 $1,800

RUEFF, JACOB   Hebammen Buch, daraus man alle Heim-
ligkeit desz weiblichen Geschlects erlehrnen... Frankfurt am Main:
Sigismund Feyerabend, 1588. With 73 woodcuts of which 3 are repeats.
Title in black and red. 4to. Cont. blindstamped calf over wooden
boards. Cont. ms. inscription on title noting the volume was a gift.
From the libraries of Piero Gall, Alistair Livingston Gunn and Alfred
Hellman, with their bookplates. Occasional spotting on woodcuts.
Front hinge worn, no clasps. Kraus 164-120 1983 $4,800

RUESS, STELLA KNIGHT   Los Angeles in Block Print. (Hollywood,
Ca: Bryant Press, 1932). 4to, 22 leaves. With 25 prints, printed in
brown and an orig. woodcut, printed in blue and green, tipped-in. This
copy signed by Ruess. Illus. yellow wraps. Karmiole 74-31 1983 $60

RUFFHEAD, OWEN   The life of Alexander Pope. London:
C. Bathurst, etc., 1769. First edition. 8vo. Cont. calf. Portrait.
Slightly rubbed. A fine copy. Ximenes 63-36 1983 $225

RUFUS King in the Development of Cincinnati During the last Fifty
Years. Cincinnati: Robert Clarke & Co., 1891. Frontis. portrait.
A.e.g. Privately printed and distributed. Fine copy in original
cloth. Jenkins 151-168 1983 $50

RUGELEY, ROWLAND   Miscellaneous poems and translations
from La Fontaine and others. Cambridge: Fletcher and Hodson, etc.,
1763. First edition. Small 8vo. Cont. calf. Slight wear. Ximenes
63-380 1983 $500

RUGGERI, UGO   Gian Giacomo Barbelli. Bergamo:
Edizioni "Monumenta Bergomensia", 1974. 224 illus. Large 4to.
Boards. Dust jacket. Slipcase. Ars Libri 33-17 1983 $100

RUGGERI, UGO   Dipinti e disegni di Giulia Lama.
Bergamo: Edizioni "Monumenta Bergomensia", 1973. 212 illus. Large
4to. Wrappers. Dust jacket. Ars Libri 33-190 1983 $75

RUGGIERO, GUIDO DE   Modern Philosophy. London: George
Allen & Unwin, (1921). First English edition. Gach 95-440 1983
$25

RUGGLE, GEORGE   Ignoramus. Comedia. London, 1630.
12mo, finely engraved frontis. Calf (rubbed). 2nd edition, stained.
Rostenberg 88-69 1983 $150

RUGGLES, J.   Recollections of a Lucknow Veteran.
London, 1906. Portrait frontis. Cloth worn and marked. Good. 8vo.
Edwards 1044-602 1983 £30

RUGGLES, THOMAS   The Barrister. Dublin: Printed for
Messrs. E. Lynch, 1792. First Irish collected edition, large 12mo,
a very good copy in a later unlettered quarter calf. Fenning 62-320
1983 £48.50

RUHRAH, JOHN   Pediatrics of the Past. New York,
1925. First edition. 8vo. 1/4 leather with marbled boards. Scarce.
Fye H-3-490 1983 $125

RUKEYSET, MURIEL   The Centaur Press, San Francisco,
1949. 8vo. Wraps. With an illustration by Picasso. 1 of 500
copies. A review copy with slip laid in (from the publisher).
Name of a reviewer on second free endpaper, else very good-fine
copy. In Our Time 156-680 1983 $100

RULE, W. H.   Oriental Records. London, 1877.
2 folding plans, 5 plates including 2 folding. 2 vols. Cr.8vo.
Orig. cloth. Good. Edwards 1044-610 1983 £30

RUMBAUGH, JACOB   Reminiscences of... N.p., 1910. Illus.
Orig. pictorial cloth, gilt. First edition. Ginsberg 46-674 1983
$25

RUMBOLD, GILBERT   The Wayside Book. London, 1934. First
English edition. Illus. by the author. Dustwrapper with a small tear
and slightly darkened at the spine. Fine. Jolliffe 26-454 1983
£18

RUMFORD, SIR BENJAMIN THOMPSON, COUNT   Complete Works. Boston,
Estes & Lauriat for the American Academy of Arts and Sciences, (1870-
75). 5 vols., 8vo., plates, text illus., orig. green cloth, first
complete collected ed., very scarce set, very good. O'Neal 50-51
1983 $200

RUNCIMAN, THOMAS   Songs, Sonnets & Miscellaneous Poems.
Temple Sheen Press, March, 1922. 4to. Boards, uncut edges. Limited
edition of 150 copies. Traylen 94-697 1983 £21

RUNDELL, MARIA ELIZA   A New System of Domestic Cookery...
London, Murray, 1837. 16th edition, reexpanded with many new
recipies. Small 8vo, engraved frontis. and 9 full page plates.
Cont. boards (rebacked). Very good. Houle 22-250 1983 $135

RUNGE, C.   Ueber die Strahlung des Quecksilbers
im magnetischen Felde. Berlin, 1902. 4to. Orig. boards. 6
plates. Offprint. Gurney 90-137 1983 £20

RUPP, I. DANIEL   He Pasa Ekklesia. Philadelphia, 1844.
8vo, full blue calf. 1st ed. Morrill 287-402 1983 $60

RUPPELL, E.   Neue Wirbelthiere zu der Fauna von
Abyssinien gehorig - Vogel. Frankfurt, 1835. Folio, new qtr.
morocco, 42 hand-coloured plates. Rare. Marginal browning and waterstaining of the text. Slight foxing on some plates with more general
browning of the last 4. Wheldon 160-84 1983 £225

RUPPRICH, HANS   Wilibald Pirckheimer und die erste Reise
Durers nach Italien. Vienna, 1930. First edition, with 14 plates,
roy. 8vo, orig. cloth, gilt. A fine copy in the dust wrapper.
Fenning 62-321 1983 £21.50

RURAL Mail Directory. Smith Falls... Perth Ont.: Rural Mail
Directory Co., (1927). 21cm. Printed wrappers. Rare. McGahern
53-140 1983 $75

RUSCHENBERGER, WILLIAM S. W. Narrative of a Voyage Round the World
During...1835, 36 and 37. Richard Bentley, 1838. First English
edition, with 4 tinted litho plates, 2 vols., 8vo, light off-setting
on the plates, but otherwise a very good copy in calf-backed marbled
boards, gilt. With an autograph letter signed by the author, dated
Oct. 29th, 1837 from aboard the USS Peacock, loosely tipped in.
Fenning 60-365 1983 £215

RUSH, BENJAMIN   An Account of the Bilious Remitting
Yellow Fever. Thomas Dobson, Philadelphia, 1794. 8vo, small hole
in title with loss of first letter and a signature partially
erased; cont. sheep, slightly worn. First edition. A good copy.
Quaritch NS 5-93 1983 $750

RUSH, BENJAMIN   Medical Inquiries and Observations,
upon the Diseases of the Mind. Phila., Kimber & Richardson, 1812.
First edition. Cont. sheep (mended). Rare second issue, with signature
"H," pp. 57-64, reset. Argosy 713-468 1983 $850

RUSH, BENJAMIN   The Selected Writings of Benjamin
Rush. New York, 1947. First edition. 8vo. Orig. cloth. Fye
H-3-492 1983 $40

RUSH, RICHARD   Memoranda of a Residence at the Court of
London. Phila., 1833. 2nd edition. Full calf, foxed. Argosy 716-396
1983 $45

RUSH, RICHARD   Report of...Showing the Money in Hands
of Thomas A. Smith, Receiver of Public Moneys, at Franklin,
Missouri; and Amounts of Deposites and Instructions Given to Him...
Wash., 1828. Dbd. First edition. Ginsberg 47-545 1983 $30

RUSH, WILLIAM   Introductory Lecture Delivered Before
the Class of the Philadelphia School of Medicine. Phila., 1833.
Presentation on front wrapper, "Dr. Helmuth- with the respects
of Dr. Rush." Title defaced with numerous crude pencil sketches.
8vo, orig. pr. wrs. Argosy 713-467 1983 $35

RUSHDIE, SALMAN   Grimus. London, 1975. First English
edition. Dustwrapper with a single nick at the head of the spine.
Fine. Jolliffe 26-453 1983 £45

RUSHWORTH, JOHN   Historical Collections of Private
Passages of State. London, Tho. Newcomb for George Thomason, 1659.
Folio, orig. calf gilt, joints breaking, bookplate. With the four
page dedication to Richard Cromwell. Large paper copy, with "Ex Dono
Avthoris" stamped in gilt on the upper cover. First edition.
Ravenstree 97-200 1983 $350

RUSK, RALPH LESLIE   The Literature of the Middle Western
Frontier. New York, 1926. 2 volumes. Jenkins 153-46 1983 $75

RUSK, RALPH LESLIE   The Literature of the Middle Western
Frontier. New York: Columbia University Press, 1926. 2 vols.
8vo. Cloth. Gilt partially worn off spines. Oak Knoll 49-353
1983 $45

RUSKIN, JOHN   Arrows of the Chase. Sunnyside,
Orpington, Kent: George Allen, 1880. First edition. 2 vols. Orig.
paper covered boards. Paper labels (a trifle worn). Spines somewhat
worn. Very good. MacManus 280-4427a 1983 $45

RUSKIN, JOHN   The Elements of Perspective. L, 1859.
Minor interior foxing, cover slightly rubbed, else near fine. Quill
& Brush 54-1179 1983 $100

RUSKIN, JOHN   Friendship's Offering of Sentiment and
Mirth. London: Smith, Elder, 1844. Frontis., plates. 1st ed.
Orig. tan cloth, fully gilt, a.e.g. Presentation copy inscribed by
Ruskin to Miss Mills, in ink on front end paper: "To Miss Mills,
with every good wish from her sincere friend, J.R., 1st January
1844." Some light chipping of spine tips, but a very good copy.
Jenkins 155-1101 1983 $225

RUSKIN, JOHN   The King of the Golden River. Smith,
Elder, 1851. Second edition. Sq. 8vo. Frontis. Pictorial title.
20 illus. Some internal wear. Yellow cloth decorated, gilt. Rare
orig. trumpet-nose on frontispiece. Greer 40-91 1983 £45

RUSKIN, JOHN   The King of the Golden River. N.Y.:
William Edwin Rudge, 1930. Intro. by E.A. Noble. Illus. by F.H.
Horvath (frontis. signed in pencil). Fine full black calf in half
red leather solander case. T.e.g. Case, (slightly darkened). Limited
to 50 copies, each with a signed holograph letter (one letter is called
for, 2 are present). Fine. King 45-248 1983 $450

RUSKIN, JOHN   The King of the Golden River.
London: 1930. Introduction by Eugene A. Noble. 8vo, two-
tone cloth, gilt, d/w. Illustrated by Ferdinand Huszti Horvath.
One of 1500 copies. A fine, unopened copy. Perata 27-162 1983
$85

RUSKIN, JOHN   Lectures on Architecture and Painting.
NY, 1854. 15 plates, tiny tear top spine edge, corners slightly worn,
small tear on blank endpaper, near very good, bookplate and inscription.
Quill & Brush 54-1178 1983 $75

RUSKIN, JOHN   Letters Upon Subjects of General Interest.
London: Privately Printed, (Not For Sale), 1892. First edition.
8vo. Full green morocco, gilt floral decorations, t.e.g., by De Sauty.
One of 7 copies printed on vellum for private circulation by Thomas
James Wise. Fine. MacManus 280-4428 1983 $1,250

RUSKIN, JOHN   Love's Meinie. Kent: G. Allen, 1873-81.
First edition. 3 vols. Orig. printed wrappers. Upper corners slightly
creased. In cloth folding box with leather spine label. Fine.
MacManus 280-4429 1983 $350

RUSKIN, JOHN   Modern Painters. London, 1846-1860.
Tall 8vo. 5 vols. Full gold stamped calf. The first vol. is the
3rd ed. revised, & vol. 2 through 5 are all 1st eds. Some light
foxing and former owner's bookplate, otherwise a fine copy. In
Our Time 156-682 1983 $450

RUSKIN, JOHN   Modern Painters. London, Allen (1904).
Illus. with 87 plates (including two colored lithographs) design in
the text. 3/4 gilt stamped blue calf, t.e.g. Fine set enclosed in
a cloth slipcase. 6 vols. Houle 22-765 1983 $295

RUSKIN, JOHN   Of Kings' Treasuries. (London: George
Allen, 1902). Three octavo vols. Elaborate woodcut borders, initials
and printing in two colors on handmade papers. Uniformly bound in full
vellum with ties and gilt lettering to spines. Each vol. in fine condition and with bookplate of D. G. Bridgson. Bromer 25-295 1983
$450

RUSKIN, JOHN   On the Old Road. Sunnyside, Orpington,
Kent: George Allen, 1885. First edition. 3 vols. Orig. paper
covered boards, paper labels. Spines a trifle worn. Outer hinges
cracked affecting the paper covers only. 1000 copies were printed.
Very good, sound. MacManus 280-4430 1983 $85

RUSKIN, JOHN   "Our Fathers Have Told Us." Kent: Geo.
Allen, 1880-1885. First edition in the orig. parts. Illus. with
engraved plates drawn by Ruskin. 5 vols. Orig. printed wrappers.
A few backstrips slightly torn. In a half-morocco case. Fine.
MacManus 280-4431 1983 $750

RUSKIN, JOHN   The Political Economy of Art. Smith,
Elder & Co., 1857. Small 8vo, title dusty, orig. olive green cloth,
discoloured. First edition. Bickersteth 77-239 1983 £18

RUSKIN, JOHN   The Seven Lamps of Architecture.
London, 1849. Tall 8vo. With illustrations by the author. Bound
in leather, top edge gilt decorations on the spine. This copy has
tipped in a one page ALS from Ruskin to Mr. Dickinson. Letter is
undated and on poor blue paper. Signed in full, John Ruskin. A
little light wear to the top edge of the spine, else a fine copy
of the 1st ed. In Our Time 156-681 1983 $450

RUSKIN, JOHN   The Seven Lamps of Architecture. New
York: Wiley, 1849. Double-page plates. 1st American ed. Orig.
green cloth, gilt. Very fine copy. Jenkins 155-1103 1983 $150

RUSKIN, JOHN   Stones of Venice. London, Allen,
(1908). Illus. with 53 plates (some colored, including 6 lithographs).
3/4 blue calf, t.e.g., 3 vols. Fine set enclosed in a cloth slipcase.
Houle 22-766 1983 $185

RUSKIN, JOHN   The Storm Cloud of the Nineteenth
Century. Kent: George Allen, 1884. First edition. 2 vols. Orig.
wrappers (slightly soiled and frayed). In a cloth folding box with
leather spine label. Very good. MacManus 280-4432 1983 $250

RUSKIN, JOHN   "Unto This Last." London: Smith, Elder
& Co., 1862. First edition. Orig. green cloth. Bookplate. Very good.
MacManus 280-4433 1983 $75

RUSKIN, JOHN   Unto This Last: Four Essays on the
First Principles of Political Economy. The Doves Press: Hammersmith,
1907. 8vo. Vellum. Inscribed on inner flyleaf. Fine copy in slipcase box. In Our Time 156-214 1983 $850

RUSKIN, JOHN   The Works of John Ruskin. London,
1903-12. Library edition. 39 vols. Roy. 8vo. Orig. maroon
cloth, gilt, uncut edges. Numerous plates, some of which are
coloured, facsimiles and other illus. Limited edition of 2,062
sets. Traylen 94-698 1983 £800

RUSLING, J. F.   Men and Things I saw in Civil War Days.
New York, 1899. 8vo. Orig. cloth. Portrait frontis. 12 portrait
plates. Cont. half calf, joints worn. Good. Edwards 1042-247 1983
£15

RUSSELL, BERTRAND, 3RD EARL OF (1872-1970)   The Analysis of Mind.
London: George Allen & Unwin, Ltd., (1921). Spine faded, else very
good copy. First edition. Gach 95-441 1983 $60

RUSSELL, BERTRAND, 3RD EARL OF (1872-1970)   Bolshevism. NY: Harcourt, Brace & Rowe, 1920. First American edition. Fine in lightly
worn dust jacket. Gach 95-442 1983 $25

RUSSELL, BERTRAND, 3RD EARL OF (1872-1970)   Philosophy and Politics.
London: National Book League, 1947. First edition. Orig. cloth.
Dust jacket (dust-soiled). Inscr. on front flyleaf. Near-fine. Mac-
Manus 280-4437 1983 $25

RUSSELL, BERTRAND, 3RD EARL OF (1872-1970)   The Problem of China.
London: George Allen & Unwin, (1922). Cloth. First edition. Edges
a trifle dusty, otherwise about fine. Russell's inscr. on the front
fly,"Elizabeth from Bertie." Reese 20-842 1983 $125

RUSSELL, CHARLES   The Parnell Commission. Macmillan,
1889. First edition, half title, orig. blue cloth, v.g. Jarndyce
31-204 1983 £30

RUSSELL, CHARLES E.   The Greatest Trust in the World. New
York: Ridgeway-Thayer Company, 1905. Illus. Pictorial cloth. Some
fading to cloth. Jenkins 153-489 1983 $85

RUSSELL, CHARLES J. F.   A horn of chase. Woburn: Fisher,
1886. First edition, privately printed in an edition of 36 copies.
Square 12mo. Orig. red cloth. Slightly faded. Ximenes 63-561
1983 $175

RUSSELL, CHARLES M.   A-Rafting of the Mississip'. New York,
1928. First edition. Frontis. and plates. Map endpapers. Fine.
Jenkins 152-373 1983 $35

RUSSELL, CHARLES M.   Back Trailing on the Old Frontiers.
Great Falls, 1922. Orig. printed wraps., in the first state of red on
green. 10 plates by Russell. A fine copy. First edition. Reese 19-
480 1983 $500

RUSSELL, CHARLES M.   The Charles M. Russell Book. Seattle,
Salisbury Press, (1970). First edition. Folio. 32 color plates,
31 b/w illus. Full tan leather stamped in gilt. One of 250
deluxe copies. As new. Houle 22-1169 1983 $150

RUSSELL, CHARLES M.   Good Medicine. Garden City: Doubleday,
1930. First trade edition. Almost every page with Russell illus.,
most in color. Folio. Orig. beige pictorial cloth. Initialled by
Russell on half title. Fine. Jenkins 152-370 1983 $200

RUSSELL, CHARLES M.   More Rawhides. Great Falls, Montana, 1952. First edition. Illus. by Russell, Orig. dark green pictorial wraps. Fragile wraps chipped. From the library of Frederic G. Renner, with his bookplate designed by Russell. Very fine. Jenkins 152-371 1983 $275

RUSSELL, CHARLES M.   Pen Sketches by...the Cowboy Artist. Great Falls, Montana, (1899). 12 plates, with interleaved text. Oblong quarto. Gilt pictorial pebbled morocco. Extremities a bit chipped, but a very good copy. Reese 19-482 1983 $400

RUSSELL, CHARLES M.   Seven Drawings by... El Paso: Carl Hertzog (for C.R. Smith). (1950). Eight plates, contained in stiff paper folder. Slight chipping at corners of folder, else fine. One of 675 copies. Reese 19-484 1983 $500

RUSSELL, CHARLES M.   Trails Plowed Under. Garden City, Doubleday, 1927. First edition. 4to, brown cloth wrapper, spine stamped in gilt. 5 double page color plates, 5 full page halftone plates, 46 illus. in text. Inscribed on front free endpaper by Will Rogers: "O henry (sic.) left, then Charlie Russell left, and there was nobody left to tell a good short story. Will Rogers." Houle 22-1170 1983 $900

RUSSELL, DON   One Hundred and Three Fights and Scrimmages. Washington: U. S. Cavalry Association, 1936. First edition. Profusely illus. Printed stiff wrappers. Line 17 as 15th line on p. 163. Fine presentation copy. Bradley 66-564 1983 $135

RUSSELL, EDWARD R.   Irving as Hamlet. London: Henry S. King and Co., 1875. 8vo, original grey printed wrappers (light wear). First edition. Very good copy; very scarce. Ximenes 64-311 1983 $65

RUSSELL, GEORGE WILLIAM   Dark Weeping. Ariel Poems, 1929. First edition. One of 400 numbered copies on large paper, signed by author. Edges of covers darkened. Designs by P. Nash. Nice. Rota 230-7 1983 £25

RUSSELL, GEORGE WILLIAM   Deirdre. Dublin: Maunsel & Co. Ltd., 1907. First edition. Orig. decorated wrappers. Signed by author on half-title. Preserved in a green half-morocco slipcase. Very fine. MacManus 280-4438 1983 $250

RUSSELL, GEORGE WILLIAM   Enchantment and Other Poems. N.Y.: The Fountain Press, 1930. First edition. Orig. cloth-backed decorated boards. Limited to 542 copies signed by author. Very fine. MacManus 280-4439 1983 $50

RUSSELL, GEORGE WILLIAM   The Inner and the Outer Ireland. Dublin: Talbot Press, 1932. First edition. 16-page pamphlet, wire-stitched. Very nice. Rota 230-6 1983 £18

RUSSELL, GEORGE WILLIAM   National Being. London, MacMillian, 1925. Gilt stamped blue cloth (soiled); stamps on endpapers. With an orig. ink and red pencil drawing, on title page, of a seacoast, signed "George Russell - AE". Good. Houle 22-767 1983 $56

RUSSELL, GEORGE WILLIAM   The Renewal of Youth. (N.p.): Orpheus Press, 1911. Printed wraps., sewn. First edition. Signed on the title-page as both Russell and A.E. Overlap edges slightly used, but a fine copy. Reese 20-843 1983 $45

RUSSELL, GEORGE WILLIAM   Some Passages from the Letters of AE to W. B. Yeats. Dublin: Cuala Press, 1936. First edition. One of 300 copies. Covers a little soiled and some marks on flyleaf. Very good. Rota 231-2 1983 £40

RUSSELL, JOHN   Essays and Sketches of Life and Character. By a Gentleman who has left his Lodgings. London: Longman, 1820. 1st ed., 8vo, cont. half calf, morocco label, boards. Some foxing of outer leaves, but a fine copy. Trebizond 18-85 1983 $60

RUSSELL, JOHN   Max Ernst. New York: Abrams, (1967). 475 illus. (49 tipped-in color plates). Large 4to. Cloth. Dust jacket. Ars Libri 32-210 1983 $100

RUSSELL, MARGARITA   Jan Van de Cappelle, 1624/6-1679. Leigh-on-Sea: F. Lewis, 1975. 96 illus. hors texte. 4to. Cloth. Edition limited to 600 copies. Ars Libri 32-81 1983 $100

RUSSELL, OSBORNE   Journal of a Trapper. Boise, 1921. Original cloth, fine copy. 2nd edition. Limited to 100 copies. Jenkins 151-96 1983 $150

RUSSELL, OSBORNE   Journal of a Trapper. Boise: Syms-York Co., 1921. Cloth. Bumped. Back strip faded. Dawson 471-250 1983 $85

RUSSELL, PERCY   Sir Henry Irving. London: S. Champness and Co., n.d. (1895). 8vo, original white printed wrappers. First edition. Fine copy. Ximenes 64-312 1983 $20

RUSSELL, RICHARD   The Junto. London: Printed in the year MDCCXII... 8vo, with half title; modern brown wraps. A re-issue of the 1712 London edition. Quaritch NS 7-118 1983 $300

RUSSELL, ROBERT   North America. Edinburgh, 1857. 1st ed. Maps. 8vo, new buckram, new endpapers, nice. Morrill 286-422 1983 $75

RUSSELL, THOMAS O'N.   An Bhoramha Laighean, or the Lienster Tribute. Dublin: M.H. Gill, 1901. First thus, 8vo, orig. cloth. Fenning 61-380 1983 £12.50

RUSSELL, WILLIAM   Eccentric personages. London: John Maxwell, 1864. First edition. 2 vols. 8vo. Orig. blue cloth. A bit rubbed. Very good copy. Ximenes 63-37 1983 $100

RUSSELL, WILLIAM (1741-1793) The History of Modern Europe. G. Routledge, 1856. 4 vols. 8vo. Cont. half pale blue calf, richly gilt spines, with red labels. Fenning 61-382 1983 £65

RUSSELL, WILLIAM (1741-1793) The History of Modern Europe. London, 1850. 4 vols. 8vo. Cont. tree calf, gilt, gilt panelled spines with red and green morocco labels, gilt. Traylen 94-699 1983 £60

RUSSELL, WILLIAM CLARK   Abandoned. London: Methuen & Co., 1904. First edition. Orig. cloth. Spine and covers slightly worn. Some foxing to the edges and preliminary pages. Very good. MacManus 280-4441 1983 $165

RUSSELL, WILLIAM CLARK   A Book for the Hammock. London: Chatto & Windus, 1887. First edition. Orig. pictorial cloth. Fine. MacManus 280-4442 1983 $125

RUSSELL, WILLIAM CLARK   The Good Ship "Mohock." London: Chatto & Windus, 1894. First edition. 2 vols. Orig. embossed cloth. Extremities a little rubbed. Inner hinges cracked. Very good. MacManus 280-4443 1983 $275

RUSSELL, WILLIAM CLARK   Heart of Oak. London: Chatto & Windus, 1895. First edition. 3 vols. Orig. cloth (patterned with an oak-grain design). Slightly worn and shaken. One outer hinge with minor fraying. Unusual 19th century publisher's binding. Very good. MacManus 280-4444 1983 $150

RUSSELL, WILLIAM CLARK   The Honour of the Flag and Other Stories. London: Unwin, 1896. First edition. Orig. decorated cloth. Published in a 'nineties binding. Fine. MacManus 280-4445 1983 $125

RUSSELL, WILLIAM CLARK   Horatio Nelson and the Naval Supremacy of England. N.Y.: Putnams, 1890. First American edition. Orig. cloth. Paper label. One of 250 large paper copies. Institutional bookplate on front pastedown. MacManus 280-4446 1983 $20

RUSSELL, WILLIAM CLARK   John Holdsworth: Chief Mate. London: Sampson Low, Marston, Low, & Searle, 1875. First edition. 3 vols. Orig. cloth. Extremities of spines worn. Hinges cracked. Some dampstaining to top edges, shaken. Library labels removed from front covers. MacManus 280-4447 1983 $85

RUSSELL, WILLIAM CLARK   The "Lady Maud": Schooner Yacht. London: Sampson Low, Marston, Searle & Rivington, 1882. First edition. 3 vols. Orig. cloth. Spine slightly darkened. Edges worn with a few small tears. Bookplates. Very good. MacManus 280-4448 1983 $450

RUSSELL, WILLIAM CLARK   The Last Entry. London: Chatto & Windus, 1897. First edition. Orig. cloth. Inner hinges starting. Very good. MacManus 280-4449 1983 $65

RUSSELL, WILLIAM CLARK   List, Ye Landsmen! London: Cassell & Co., 1893. First edition. 3 vols. Orig. cloth. Inner hinges cracked, covers rubbed. Labels removed from front covers. Vol. 1 badly shaken. MacManus 280-4450 1983 $100

RUSSELL, WILLIAM CLARK   List, Ye Landmen. Cassell, 1893. First edition, 3 vols., half title and 16 pp ads. in each vol. Orig. dull turquoise cloth, a little rubbed on spines. Jarndyce 30-537 1983 £52

RUSSELL, WILLIAM CLARK   My Shipmate Louise. London: Chatto & Windus, 1890. First edition. 3 vols. Orig. decorated navy cloth. Top portion of front cover of Vol. I dust-soiled. Spine of Vol. II nicked and dampstained. Very good. MacManus 280-4451 1983 $235

RUSSELL, WILLIAM CLARK   The Mystery of the "Ocean Star". London: Chatto & Windus, 1888. First edition. Orig. pictorial cloth. Cont. inscription on verso of free endpaper. Covers a little rubbed. Very good. MacManus 280-4452 1983 $85

RUSSELL, WILLIAM CLARK   An Ocean Free-Lance. London: Richard Bentley, 1881. First edition. 3 vols. Orig. cloth. Extremities rubbed. Covers faded and soiled. Former owner's stamp and signature on flyleaves. Inner hinges weak. MacManus 280-4454 1983 $150

RUSSELL, WILLIAM CLARK   On the Fo'k'sle Head. London: Chatto & Windus, 1884. First edition. Orig. pictorial cloth. Bookplate. Covers worn, slightly soiled. Inner hinge cracked. MacManus 280-4455 1983 $65

RUSSELL, WILLIAM CLARK   Overdue. London: Chatto & Windus, 1903. First edition. Orig. pictorial cloth. Foxing. Fine. MacManus 280-4456 1983 $75

RUSSELL, WILLIAM CLARK   The Romance of a Midshipman. London: Unwin, 1898. First edition. Orig. cloth. Near-fine. MacManus 280-4458 1983 $85

RUSSELL, WILLIAM CLARK   Round the Galley Fire. London: Chatto & Windus, 1883. First edition. Orig. pictorial cloth. Edges slightly worn. Front endpapers a bit soiled. Former owner's signature on title-page. Covers slightly wrinkled by damp. Good. MacManus 280-4459 1983 $85

RUSSELL, WILLIAM CLARK   A Sea Queen. London: Sampson Low, 1883. "Second edition," published in the same year and format as the first. 3 vols. Orig. cloth. Covers a bit soiled and worn. MacManus 280-4460 1983 $60

RUSSELL, WILLIAM CLARK   The Tale of the Ten. London: Chatto & Windus, 1896. First edition. 3 vols. Orig. cloth. Edges very slightly worn. Former owner's stamp on a few leaves. Near-fine. MacManus 280-4461 1983 $350

RUSSELL, WILLIAM CLARK   The Turnpike Sailor or Rhymes of the Road. London: Skeffington & Son, 1907. First edition. Orig. pictorial cloth. Head of spine very slightly worn. Lettering on spine worn off. Good. MacManus 280-4463 1983 $50

RUSSELL, WILLIAM CLARK   The Two Captains. London: Sampson Low, Marston & Co., 1897. First edition. Illus. by B.J. Rosenmeyer. Inner hinges weak. Very good. MacManus 280-4464 1983 $85

RUSSELL, WILLIAM CLARK   What Cheer! London: Cassell & Co., 1896. First edition. Orig. decorated cloth. Nice. MacManus 280-4465 1983 $85

RUSSELL, WILLIAM CLARK   Wrong Side Out. London: Cassell & Co., 1896. First edition. Orig. pictorial cloth. Very good. MacManus 280-4466 1983 $75

RUSSELL, WILLIAM H.   The Atlantic Telegraph. Day and Son, London, (1866). Folio, with hand-coloured lithographed title and 24 hand-coloured lithographed plates and a chart all mounted with gilt titling and line borders; 6 plate mounts repaired in the margins and several others slightly foxed or stained but the plates themselves clean; orig. purple cloth with an inlay of green cloth blocked in gilt. Quaritch NS 5-94 1983 $2,750

RUSSELL, WILLIAM H   A Diary in the East. London, 1869. 6 tinted lithographs, illus. in text. Half morocco, rubbed. 8vo. Good. Edwards 1044-611 1983 £50

RUSSELL, WILLIAM H   A Diary in the East. Routledge, 1869. First edition, half title, 6 colour plates, and vignette text illus. 6 pp ads. Orig. red cloth, fine. Jarndyce 31-363 1983 £64

RUSSELL, WILLIAM H   My Diary North and South. Boston, 1863. Minor wear, ink inscription, lacks page before title. King 46-79 1983 $20

RUSSELL, WILLIAM S.   Guide to Plymouth... Boston, Pub. for the Author, 1846. First edition. Folding map; also plates. 12mo. Morrill 290-295 1983 $27.50

RUSSELL, WILLIAM S.   Pilgrim Memorials, and Guide to Plymouth. Boston: Crosby Nichols and Co., 1855. Small 8vo, includes a folding map. Purple cloth, spine faded. Karmiole 72-85 1983 $25

RUSSELL, WILLIS   Quebec: As It Was, and As It Is. Quebec: P. Lamourex, 1857. First edition. Ad leaf. Printed green wrappers (lower wrapping lacking). Front wrapper spotted and chipped at lower right corner. Bradley 66-490 1983 $40

RUSSELL, WILLIS   Quebec: As It Was, and As It Is. Quebec: P. Lamourex, 1857. First edition. Ad leaf, printed green wrappers, lower wrapper lacking. Front wrapper is spotted and chipped at lower right corner. Scarce. Bradley 64-34 1983 $25

RUSSIAN Ballet. London: 1939. Camera Studies by Gordon Anthony. Introduction by Arnold Haskett. First edition, Lg 4to, two-tone cloth, gilt. With 96 tipped-in plates. Backstrip lightly foxed. A very nice copy. Perata 27-8 1983 $125

RUSSO, ANTHONY J.   A Bibliography of James Whitcomb Riley. Indianapolis: Indiana Historical Society, 1944. First edition. 8vo. Cloth. Printed by the Lakeside Press. Oak Knoll 48-473 1983 $45

RUSSO, PASQUALE   Ku Klux Klan: Church and Labor. Chicago, (1923). 1st ed., pict. wrp., illus. Jenkins 151-172 1983 $35

RUSSOW, K. E.   Bruno Liljefors, an appreciation. Stockholm, 1929. 4to, cloth, 24 coloured plates and numerous illus. Edition limited to 1000 copies. Wheldon 160-247 1983 £55

RUTGERS, LISPENARD   On and Off the Saddle. N.Y., 1894. Illus. Orig. cloth. First edition. Ginsberg 46-700 1983 $75

RUTH, BABE   The Babe Ruth Story, as Told to Bob Considine. N.Y., Dutton, 1948. First edition. Illus. with 49 photos. Red cloth (slight fraying at hinge). Signed and inscribed by Ruth. Very good. Houle 21-759 1983 $225

RUTLEDGE, NANCY   Blood on the Cat. N.Y., Farrar & Rinehart, (1945). First edition. Dust jacket (trifle rubbed, small tears). Very good. Houle 22-768 1983 $35

RUTTER, OWEN   Anne Alone. London: Michael Joseph, (1938). First edition. Orig. cloth. Dust jacket (slightly faded and worn). Presentation copy to Joan & Dennis Wheatley, dated Sept. 1938. Edges foxed. Bookplate of Dennis Wheatley. Near-fine. MacManus 280-4473 1983 $40

RUTTNBER, EDWARD M.   History of the Town of New Windsor. Orange County, NY, 1911. Plates, map. Argosy 716-366 1983 $40

RUTTY, JOHN   An Account of Some New Experiments and Observations on Joanna Stephens's Medicine for the Stone. Printed for R. Manby, 1742. 8vo, modern calf antique, new end papers, lettered gilt on the spine. First edition. Bickersteth 77-316 1983 £50

RUXTON, GEORGE F.   Adventures in Mexico and the Rocky Mountains. London: John Murray, 1847. Half calf. Weak at hinges. Dawson 471-252 1983 $65

RUXTON, GEORGE F.   Adventures in Mexico and the Rocky Moun-
tians. New York: Harper & Bros., 1848. First American edition.
Orig. blue gilt cloth. Lower cover lightly stained. Cont. ownership
inscription of L.H. Scott. Fine. Jenkins 152-374 1983 $125

RUXTON, GEORGE F.   Adventures in Mexico and the Rocky
Mountains. New York, 1848. Later 3/4 morocco (some wear, front
hinge cracking). First American edition. Felcone 22-216 1983 $60

RUXTON, GEORGE F.   Adventures in Mexico. London, 1849.
Half calf. Ginsberg 47-820 1983 $85

RUXTON, GEORGE F   Life in the Far West. Edinburgh,
1849. Orig. cloth, top of backstrip chipped. First edition.
Ginsberg 47-821 1983 $150

RUXTON, GEORGE F.   Life in the Far West. N.Y.: Harper &
Brothers, 1849. 4 pages of ads. Cloth, some foxing. Dawson 471-253
1983 $125

RUYSCH, HENDRIK   Disputatio Medica Inauguralis De
Peripneumonia. Franeker: Johann Gyzelaar, 1696. 4to. Modern
boards. Kraus 164-208 1983 $150

RYAN, FREDERICK   House of the Temple. London, Burns,
1939. First edition. Thick 8vo, 42 illus. Dust jacket. Very
good. Houle 21-760 1983 $25

RYAN, MARAH ELLIS   The Flute of the Gods. New York, (1909).
24 full-page plates after photographs by Curtis. Pictorial cloth.
Edges slightly shelf-rubbed, still a very good copy. First state of
the first edition, with the full complement of plates. Reese 19-496
1983 $150

RYAN, MARAH ELLIS   For the Soul of Rafael. Chicago, 1906.
Mounted photo. illus. by H. Taylor, 8vo, pict. cloth, dec. designs.
2nd ed. Argosy 710-309 1983 $25

RYAN, RICHARD   Dramatic table talk; or scenes, situa-
tions, and adventures, serious and comic, in theatrical history and
biography. London: John Knight and Henry Lacey, 1825. 3 vols.,
sm. 8vo, original boards, green cloth spines, printed paper labels.
First edition. With an engraved frontis. and title-page in each
volume, and 18 other plates, portraits, charts and facsimile letters
(many folding). In very fine original condition, and rare thus.
Ximenes 64-476 1983 $275

RYAN, WILLIAM P.   The Irish Labour Movements, from the
'Twenties to our own Day. Dublin: The Talbot Press, Modern Ireland
in the Making, 1919. First edition, 8vo, orig. cloth, a very good
copy. Fenning 60-366 1983 £12.50

RYAN, WILLIAM R.   Personal Adventures in Upper and Lower
California in 1848-9... London: Shoberl, 1850. 2 vols., complete,
3 tinted lithographic plates and 20 engraved plates. Original red
pictorial gilt cloth (rebacked), with ownership markings and some signs
of wear. First edition. Jenkins 153-104 1983 $250

RYCAUT, PAUL   The History of the Present State of the
Ottoman Empire. London, 1675. 12 plates, 16 full-page engravings in
text. Illus. Sm.8vo. Calf rebacked for John Starkey & Henry Brome.
Good. Edwards 1044-613 1983 £120

RYCAUT, PAUL   The History of the Turkish Empire.
London, 1680. 2 portraits and 3 full-page illus. including "A Turkish
Pageant" cropped. Folio. Calf, slightly worn, corner of title slight-
ly frayed. 8vo. Good. Edwards 1044-612 1983 £260

RYCE, JOHN   The Rector of Amesty. London: Sampson
Low, Marston & Co., 1891. First edition. 3 vols. Orig. cloth with
floral endpapers. Covers slightly soiled. Edges and corners very
slightly worn. Former owner's signature on each title-page. Very
good. MacManus 280-4474 1983 $225

RYDBERG, J. R.   Recherches sur la Constitution des
Spectres d'Emission des Elements Chimiques. Stockholm, 1890. Large
4to. Buckram, wrappers bound in. 4 plates. Gurney 90-138 1983
£175

RYDEN, STIG   Archaeological Researches in the Highlands of Bolivia. Goteborg, 1947. 2 color plates. 245 illus. 75
maps. Small 4to. Wrappers. Ars Libri 34-458 1983 $75

RYDEN, STIG   Contributions to the Archaeology of the
Rio Loa Region. Goteborg, 1944. 5 color plates. 132 illus. Large
8vo. Wrappers. Ars Libri 34-459 1983 $40

RYDER, DAVID W.   Memories of the Mendocino Coast. San
Francisco, 1948. Privately printed. 1st ed. Decorations by Dan
Adair, plates, map. Boards, cloth back. Clark 741-152 1983 $50

RYDER, DAVID W.   Memories of the Mendocino Coast. San
Francisco, 1948. Privately printed. 1st ed. Decorations by Dan
Adair, plates, map. Boards, cloth back, heavy paper. Clark 741-153
1983 $45

RYDER-TAYLOR, HENRY   History of the Alamo and of the Local
Franciscan Missions. San Antonio, (1907). Illus. Orig. pictorial
wrappers. Scarce. Jenkins 153-592 1983 $50

RYE, EDGAR   The Quirt and the Spur; Vanishing
Shadows of the Texas Frontier. Chicago: W. B. Conkey Co., Publishers,
1909. Frontispiece, illus., nice copy in original pictorial cloth.
Rare. Jenkins 151-302 1983 $175

RYE, WALTER   Records and Record Searching. Elliot
Stock, 1888. 8vo, cloth. First edition. Bickersteth 75-172 1983
£15

RYFF, WALTHER HERMANN   Des aller furtrefflichsten hochsten
und adelichsten gschopffs... Strassburg: Balthassar Beck, 1541.
First edition. 30 woodcuts of which 6 are repeats. Elaborate woodcut initials. Folio. Old vellum, in green morocco-backed box. Ms.
note on flyleaf dated 1747. From the libraries of Alistair Livingston
Gunn and Alfred M. Hellman. Kraus 164-121 1983 $12,500

RYFF, WALTHER HERMANN   Frawen Rosengarten. Frankfurt am Main:
Christian Egenolff, 1545. First edition. Title with large woodcut
printed in black and red and numerous small woodcuts scattered through-
out the text. Folio. Modern vellum. From the libraries of Alistair
Livingston Gunn and Alfred M. Hellman. In maroon morocco-backed box.
Kraus 164-122 1983 $14,500

RYLAND, JOHN WILLIAM   Records of Wroxall Abbey and Manor,
Warwickshire. London, 1903. Limited edition of 100 numbered copies,
folio, title-page in red and black, 31 photogravure and other plates,
original half calf, green boards, top edges gilt, others uncut,
marbled endpapers. Deighton 3-254 1983 £165

RYMAN, JAMES   Illustrations of Oxford. Oxford: Published by James Ryman, 1839. First edition, all published, with engr.
vignette title-page and 40 fine engr. plates. India proofs, after
Prout, Nash, Voys, Buckler, Hollar, Ince, and others. Large folio.
Cont. (orig.?) morocco, gilt, edges gilt, a little scratching of the
sides, but thoroughly sound and otherwise a very good copy. Fenning
60-367 1983 £225

RYMER, JAMES MALCOLM   The Unspeakable. London: Charles H.
Clarke, 1856 (1855). 12mo. Publisher's embossed blue cloth, joints
and edges frayed. Gach 95-444 1983 $50

RYMER, THOMAS   A short view of tragedy; it's original,
excellency, and corruption. London: printed and are to be sold by
Richard Baldwin, 1693. 8vo, cont. panelled calf (slight wear to
hinges). First edition. Wanting a flyleaf at the front, but the
preliminary blank is present, as is the final leaf of ads. Ximenes
64-478 1983 $450

RYMER, THOMAS   A Short View of Tragedy. London:
by Richard Baldwin, 1693. First edition. Cr. 8vo. Calf, rebacked,
small hole in title-page which has the outer margin cut. Traylen
94-700 1983 £220

RYMER, THOMAS   The tragedies of the last age consider'd
and examin'd by the practice of the ancients, and by the common sense
of all ages. London: printed for Richard Tonson, 1678. 8vo, old
panelled calf, gilt, spine gilt. First edition. An excellent copy,
complete with the preliminary license leaf. Ximenes 64-479 1983
$475

S

S., M.   The Adamic Race. New York, Russell
Bros., 1868. First edition. Small 8vo, original wrapper. Lacks
backstrip and back cover. Morrill 290-468 1983 $35

SABATIER, J. C.   D'Orleans. Paris, 1832. 8vo, printed
wrappers, first leaf crudely mended, some gutter stains. First edition.
At end is Bailliere's 32pp. priced catalogue of medical publications.
Argosy 713-469 1983 $75

SABATINI, RAFAEL   The Writings of... Boston, 1924-26.
Autograph edition. Limited to 750 numbered sets, signed by author.
Vols. 1-20 (of 34). Frontis. Cloth backed boards. Paper labels.
Spines a bit darkened. Couple labels slightly frayed. King 45-249
1983 $150

SABATINI, RAFAEL   The Writings of Rafael Sabatini. Boston:
Houghton Mifflin Co., 1924-1931. The Definitive edition. 29 vols.
Orig. cloth. Good. MacManus 280-4475 1983 $150

SABBATH Bells Chimed by the Poets. (Publisher & date omitted from
title page.) New edn., frontis., title vignette & 14 woodcuts
printed & engr'd in colour by Edmund Evans; illus. by Birket Foster.
Magenta morocco grain blind embossed cloth, bevelled boards, a.e.g.
(bkstrip faded, occas. foxing), v. nice copy. Hodgkins 27-391 1983
£40

SABBE, MAURITS   Christopher Plantin. Antwerp: J.-E.
Buschmann, 1923. Thin 8vo. Boards, dust jacket. Illus. by Joseph
Pennell. Fine. Oak Knoll 49-354 1983 $35

SABIN, EDWIN L.   Building the Pacific Railway.
Philadelphia, Lippincott, 1919. First edition. With 22 illus.;
folding map. Dust jacket (short tear). Very good. Houle 22-1171
1983 $60

SABIN, EDWIN L.   Kit Carson Days Adventures in the Path
of Empire. New York, 1935. 2 vols., illus., fine copy. Revised
edition. Jenkins 151-97 1983 $75

SABIN, ELIJAH R.   Life and Reflections of Charles
Observator. Boston: Printed by Rowe & Hooper, 1816. Orig. full
calf. First edition. Calf a bit dry and scattered foxing, else a very
good copy. Reese 18-505 1983 $75

SABIN, FLORENCE   Franklin Paine Mall - Anatomist.
Baltimore, 1934. 8vo. Orig. binding. Scarce. Fye H-3-848 1983
$30

SABIN, JOSEPH   Catalogue of the Library of Andrew
Wight, of Philadelphia. New York: J.E. Cooley, 1864. Small 4to.
Cont. three-quarter leather over marbled paper covered boards, t.e.g.,
others uncut. The copy is priced in ink and has the buyers' names
also written in ink. Covers rubbed. Oak Knoll 49-515 1983 $225

SABIN, JOSEPH   A Dictionary of Books Relating to
America from Its Discovery to the Present Time. New York: Kraus,
n.d. 29 vols., in 2. New, orig. cloth. Miniprint facsimile of the
1928 ed. Jenkins 153-744 1983 $200

SACCARDO, P. A.   Sylloge Fungorum Vol. 2 Pyrenomycetae
II: Sphaeriaceae. (Patavii, 1883) Reprint c. 1900. 8vo, half
morocco. Wheldon 160-1885 1983 £16

SACCARDO, P. A.   Sylloge Fungorum Vol. 12 Supplementum
Universale Pars VI. Patavii, 1905. Half morocco. Wheldon 160-1886
1983 £25

SACCARDO, P. A.   Sylloge Fungorum Vol. 23 Supplementum
Universale Pars X. Abellini, 1925. Half morocco. Wheldon 160-1887
1983 £20

SACHEVERELL, HENRY   The Reasons of those Lords that
Enter'd their Protest... London, 1710. First edition. 8vo. Half
title. Modern quarter cloth. Heath 48-160 1983 £50

SACHS, HANNS   Freud. Master and Friend. London:
Imago, (1945). First British edition. Fine in dust jacket. Gach
94-176 1983 $20

SACHSE, JULIUS F.   The Music of the Ephrate Cloister.
Lancaster, 1903. Cloth, very good. Reese 19-499 1983 $25

SACHSSE, ROBERT   Die Chemie und Physiologie der Farbstoffe.
Leipzig, 1877. 8vo, text figures, orig. cloth. Bickersteth 77-317
1983 £16

SACKVILLE-WEST, VICTORIA   Aphra Behn: The Incomparable Astrea.
L, (1927). Edges slightly rubbed, else very good or better. Quill &
Brush 54-1508 1983 $30

SACKVILLE-WEST, VICTORIA   Country Notes. London, 1939. First
edition. 4to. Cloth. 83 photographs by Bryan and Norman Westwood.
Traylen 94-701 1983 £15

SACKVILLE-WEST, VICTORIA   The Dark Island. London, Hogarth
Press, 1934. First edition. Map on front endpaper. Dust jacket,
designed by Ben Nicolson (a few small nicks). Very good. Houle 22-
769 1983 $95

SACKVILLE-WEST, VICTORIA   The Dark Island. L, 1934. Spine edges
frayed and cover faded, else very good in chipped dustwrapper. Quill
& Brush 54-1511 1983 $35

SACKVILLE-WEST, VICTORIA   The Garden. L, (1946). One of 750 numbered and signed copies, printed on handmade paper, t.e.g., fine, some
pages uncut. Quill & Brush 54-1512 1983 $150

SACKVILLE-WEST, VICTORIA   The Garden. London, 1946. First edition.
One of 750 numbered copies, signed by author. Very nice. Rota 231-
529 1983 £55

SACKVILLE-WEST, VICTORIA   Heritage. London, 1919. First edition.
Free endpapers browned. Spine slightly rubbed and faded. Very good.
Jolliffe 26-455 1983 £30

SACKVILLE-WEST, VICTORIA   The Land. London, William Heinmann,
1926. First edition. Pictorial dust jacket designed by George
Plank. Very good - fine. Houle 22-770 1983 $125

SACKVILLE-WEST, VICTORIA   Nursery Rhymes. London: The Dropmore
Press, 1947. First edition. Orig. decorated cloth. Dust jacket
(spine slightly faded and worn, with a few small pencil marks to the
cover). One of 550 copies. Bookplate. Near-fine. MacManus 280-
4476 1983 $65

SACKVILLE-WEST, VICTORIA   Orchard and Vineyard. L, 1921. Some
pages uncut, flys offset, very good in chipped and faded dustwrapper.
Quill & Brush 54-1509 1983 $90

SACKVILLE-WEST, VICTORIA   Poems of West and East. L, 1917. Flys
offset, edges slightly bumped and cover has some staining, spine paper
label slightly chipped, good. Quill & Brush 54-1510 1983 $60

SACKVILLE-WEST, VICTORIA   Saint Joan of Arc. London, 1936.
First edition. Boards slightly soiled and some browning on the
spine. Previous owner's name neatly stamped on endpaper. One of
100 copies signed by the author. A very good copy. Gekoski 2-166
1983 £100

SACKVILLE-WEST, VICTORIA   Saint Joan of Arc. London: Cobden-
Sanderson, (1936). First edition. Illus. Orig. white buckram. One
of 120 copies, this being number 8 of 100 for sale, signed by author.
Spine darkened. Covers a little dust-soiled. Prelims foxed. Very
good. MacManus 280-4477 1983 $150

SACKVILLE-WEST, VICTORIA   Sissinghurst. London: Hogarth Press, 1931. Thin square 8vo, printed boards. One of 500 copies signed by the author. Fine, except that the top corners are slightly bent. Argosy 714-649 1983 $75

SACKVILLE-WEST, VICTORIA   Twelve Days. London: Hogarth Press, 1928. Tall 8vo, first edition. Argosy 714-650 1983 $50

SACKVILLE-WEST, VICTORIA   Twelve Days. London: Hogarth Press, 1928. 8vo, cloth, photographs. First edition. Bookplate. Duschnes 240-199 1983 $50

SACKVILLE-WEST, VICTORIA   Twelve Days. London: The Hogarth Press, 1928. First edition. Orig. decorated cloth. 2025 copies printed. Lacking jacket. Endpapers foxed. Good. MacManus 280-4478 1983 $40

THE SACRED Treasury. Procter, nd (ca. 1845). 1st edn. Illuminated drawings, large paper with hand-col'd frontis. & 14 hand col'd engrs. Mauve net grain decor. cloth, gilt decor. bkstrip, a.e.g. (bkstrip & cvrs. faded), v.g. Hodgkins 27-392 1983 £45

SADGER, J.   Sleep Walking and Moon Walking. N.Y., 1920. Tall 8vo, pr. wrs.; uncut. Argosy 713-470 1983 $37.50

SADLEIR, MICHAEL   Desolate Splendour. London, 1923. First edition. Covers a little marked. Name on flyleaf. Very nice. Rota 230-527 1983 £15

SADLIER, MICHAEL   Excursions in Victorian Bibliography. London, Chaundy & Cox, 1922. First edition. Dust jacket. With errata slip. Fine. Houle 21-762 1983 $135

SADLEIR, MICHAEL   Forlorn Sunset. London: Constable, (1947). First edition. Illus. with colored frontis. & jacket designed by J. Piper. Maps. Orig. cloth. Dust jacket (worn). Good. MacManus 280-4479 1983 $25

SADLEIR, MICHAEL   XIX Century Fiction. Cambridge, 1951. 2 vols. 4to. Cloth. Orig. dustwrappers. 48 full-page plates. Limited edition of 1,025 copies. Traylen 94-702 1983 £180

SADLEIR, MICHAEL   Trollope, a Bibliography. 8vo. Orig. buckram, gilt. Portrait, 7 plates and illus. in the text. Limited edition of 500 copies. Traylen 94-835 1983 £50

SADLER, MICHAEL E.   Arts of West Africa (Excluding Music). London: International Institute of African Languages and Cultures, 1935. 32 plates. 4to. Boards, 1/4 cloth. Ars Libri 34-738 1983 $85

SAERCHINGER, CESAR   Hello America! Boston, 1938. First edition. Presentation from author. Illustrated. 8vo, dust wrapper, nice, in a cloth folding case. Morrill 290-469 1983 $25

SAFFELL, WILLIAM   Records of the Revolutionary War. NY, 1858. First edition. Orig. cloth, (backstrip somewhat faded). Argosy 716-471 1983 $50

SAFFORD, WILLIAM H.   The Life of Harman Blennerhassett. Chillicothe, 1850. 1st ed. Lithograph frontispiece. Small 8vo. Morrill 288-435 1983 $40

SAGE, LEE   The Last Rustler, The Autobiography of... Illus. 1st ed. Jenkins 153-492 1983 $45

SAGE, RUFUS B.   Scenes in the Rocky Mountains, and in Oregon, California, New Mexico... Philadelphia, 1846. Large folding map. Full calf, fine. Reese 19-502 1983 $1,750

SAGGIO, CARLO   25 pastelli del 1911 di Arturo Tosi. Milano: Edizioni del Milione, 1946. 25 color plates. Folio. Boards, 1/4 cloth. Dust jacket. Ars Libri 33-599 1983 $35

SAHAGUN, BERNARDINO DE   Historia General De Las Cosas De Nueva Espana... Mexico: Valdes, 1829-30. 3 vols. First printing. Text complete, but lacking folding plate that did not appear in all copies. Cont. dark brown French morocco over marbled boards. Spines gilt raised bands. Very fine. Jenkins 152-376 1983 $1,500

SAID, R.   The Geological Evolution of the River Nile. New York, 1981. 73 text-figures, 4 folding geological maps, 8vo, boards. Wheldon 160-1468 1983 £43

THE SAILOR Boy, and Other Tales. Phila.: Henry F. Anners, 1847. Frontis. Illus. rear wrapper; front wrapper and endsheet lacking. Lightly soiled. Frontis. signed "W. Stott lith." Very good. Felcone 20-79 1983 $30

SAIN, CHARLES M.   Trip to Hawaii. Honolulu, Paradise of the Pacific Print. 1910. Small 8vo, illus. with 23 halftones plates. Text written in verse. Pictorial wraps., stitched with large thick fibre cords (cords a bit worn) else very good. Houle 22-1103 1983 $60

SAINT-AMANT, PIERRE CHARLES FOUNIER DE   Voyages En Californie Et Dans L'Oregon. Paris: Libraririre L. Maison, 1854. 2 maps. Illus. Orig. printed blue wrappers bound in later cloth with morocco label. Signed presentation copy from author. Jenkins 152-380 1383 $250

SAINT-ANGE, G. J. M.   Etude de l'appareil reproducteur. (Paris, 1856). 4to, wrappers, 17 plates (1 coloured), corner of first few leaves dampstained. Wheldon 160-518 1983 £15

SAINT-EVREMONT, C. M. DE SAINT DENIS   Miscellaneous Essays. London: J. Everingham, 1692. First English edition. 8vo. Orig. calf. A few leaves a little foxed. Traylen 94-703 1983 £90

SAINT-GAUDENS, HOMER   The American Artist. N.Y., 1941. First edition. 65 illus. Cloth. Index. Ink inscription rubbed out. Newspaper clipping attached to front endpaper. Chipped and frayed dust wrapper. Very good. King 45-362 1983 $20

SAINT GERMAN, CHRISTOPHER   The Dialogve in Englishe, Betweene a Doctor of Diuinitie, and a Student in the Lawes of England. London, printed by Thomas Wight, and Bonham Norton, 1598. 8vo, cont. calf, spine ends chipped. Ravenstree 97-202 1983 $265

SAINT-GUILHEM, P. D.   Theorie nouvelle de l'equilibre et du mouvement des corps. Toulouse: J.-B. Paya, 1837. First edition. 8vo. Cont. green quarter morocco. Folding plate. Spine a bit worn. Ximenes 63-536 1983 $50

SAINT JOHN, BAYLE   The Memoirs of the Duke of Saint Simon. London, Chapman & Hall, 1857. First edition. Frontis. Full green calf by Tout, spines decorated in gilt with floral and pointille designs, contrasting red and orange leather spine labels, covers ruled in gilt, gilt inner dentelles, t.e.g., marbled endpapers. 4 vols. A fine set. Houle 22-771 1983 $375

SAINT JOHN, BAYLE   Two Years' Residence in a Levantine Family. Chapman and Hall, 1850. Ad. leaf, 8vo, recent boards. Fenning 60-368 1983 £35

SAINT JOHN, HENRY, VISCOUNT BOLINGBROKE
Please turn to
BOLINGBROKE, HENRY ST. JOHN 1678-1751

ST JOHN, JAMES AUGUSTUS   Weighed in the Balance. Tinsley Bros., 1864. First edition, 3 vols., half titles. Orig. red cloth, spines darkened and rubbed. Jarndyce 30-538 1983 £28

ST. JOHN, OLIVER   An Argument of Law Concerning the Bill of Attainder of High-Treason of Thomas Earle of Strafford. Printed for Iohn Stafford and Francis Eaglesfield, 1641. First edition, 4to, wrapper, signatures or cathwords touched on 6 pages, otherwise a nice copy. Fenning 60-369 1983 £35

ST. LEGER, FRANCIS BARRY BOYLE   Tales of Passion. Henry Colburn, 1829. First edition. 3 vols. Large 12mo, lacks half-titles and two final advert. leaves in vol. III. Cont. half calf, gilt, with George Thomas Wyndham's book-plate. Hannas 69-173 1983 £45

SAINT-PIERRE, JACQUES HENRI BERNARDIN DE (1737-1814)   Paul & Virginia. Boston: Spotswood and Nancrede, 1796. 32mo. 3 copperplates by Samuel Hill (one folding, partly split & frayed). Orig. sheep leather rebacked. Foxed. Rostenbery 88-63 1983 $465

SAINT-PIERRE, JACQUES HENRI BERNARDIN DE (1737-1814)   Paul & Virginia. New York: Duyckinck, 1805. 8vo. 13 woodcuts by Anderson (some full-page). Orig. calf, ownership entry of Catharine Mary Adams. Rostenberg 88-62 1983 $225

SAINT-PIERRE, JACQUES HENRI BERNARDIN DE   Paul and Virginia. Printed for John Sharpe, Longman, (etc), 1819. 12mo. Orig. pink boards, uncut. Half-title, printed and engr. titles, and four other plates. A fine copy. Hill 165-107 1983 £48

SAINT-PIERRE, JACQUES HENRI BARNARDIN DE   Paul et Virginie. Paris: Chez Marcilly, (ca. 1835). Title-page with vignette plus 5 full-page plates, engr. Gilt-stamped full brown morocco with 4 raised bands at spine and richly gilt dentelles. Some very light occasional foxing to text pages only, otherwise extremely fine internally with binding pristine. Arthur A. Houghton bookplate. A.e.g. Vertical fore-edge painting. 2 3/4 x 2; 69x50mm. Bromer 25-466 1983 $950

SAINT-PIERRE, JACQUES HENRI BERNARDIN DE (1737-1814)   Paul et Virginia & La Chaumiere Indienne. Paris: L. Curmer, 1838. 4to. Hand-coloured map of the Isle de France. 7 steel engr. port. & 29 woodengr. plates. All mounted on China paper. Some 500 text engr. Full blue morocco gilt by Chambolle-Duru. ribbed. Presentation copy from the people of Mauritius to Sir John Pope-Hennessky. Greer 40-122 1983 £75

SAINT-PIERRE, JACQUES HENRI BERNARDIN DE (1737-1814)   Paul and Virginia. London: George Routledge & Sons, 1879. Orig. memoir of the author. 316 illus. Later 3/4 green morocco & cloth, with a fore-edge painting. MacManus 280-4480 1983 $150

SAINT PIERRE, JACQUES-HENRI BERNARDIN DE   Studies of Nature. Worcester (Mass.): J. Nancrede, 1797. First American edition. 3 vols. 8vo. Orig. tree sheep, rubbed, worn, mend to tear in leaf 202 of vol. 2. Light pencilling on titles and throughout text, blank fly-leaf gone from vol. 3. Minor spotting, few slight tears with no text lost. Bookplates removed. One of the folding engr. plates torn along fold, all others in fine condition. Ravenstree 94-28 1983 $290

SAINT-PIERRE, JACQUES HENRI BERNARDIN DE (1737-1814)   The Works. Albion Press Printed: Published by James Cundee, 1807. Additional engr. title-page and 18 engr. plates. 4 vols. 8vo. Cont. diced calf, gilt bordered sides, gilt spines with double lettering pieces. Fenning 60-370 1983 £65

SAINT SIMON, DUC DE   The Memoirs of the Duke of Saint Simon. London: Chapman & Hall, 1857. 4 vols. Later 3/4 purple morocco & marbled boards, gilt, t.e.g. with marbled endpapers, by Zaehnsdorf. Spines darkened. Ownership signatures of J.A. St. John in each vol. Fine. MacManus 280-4483 1983 $125

SAINT-SIMON, DUC DE   Memoirs of... London, 1899. 4 vols. Roy. 8vo. Half green morocco, gilt, gilt panelled spines, t.e.g. 24 plates on japanese vellum. Traylen 94-704 1983 £60

SAINT-YVES, CHARLES DE   Nouveau Traite des Maladies des Qeux... Amsterdam & Leipzik, 1767. 12mo, cont. green boards. Argosy 713-472 1983 $250

SAINTENOY, PAUL   Jehan Money. Le statuaire Jan Mone, maitre artiste de Charles-Quint. Bruxelles/Paris: Librairie Nationale d'Art et d'Histoire, 1931. 29 plates. Large 4to. Wrappers. Ars Libri 32-468 1983 $60

SAINTSBURY, GEORGE   A Last Scrap Book. London: Macmillan, 1924. First edition. Orig. half-buckram & parchment. One of 250 large paper copies signed by author. Parchment slightly discolored. Bookplate dust soiled. Fine. MacManus 280-4481 1983 $35

SAKI, PSEUD.
Please turn to
MUNRO, HECTOR HUGH

SALA, GEORGE AUGUSTUS   Accepted Addresses. London: Tinsley Brothers, 1862. First edition. Orig. dark green decorated cloth. Inner hinges cracked, webbing intact. Spine ends and edges worn. Former owner's signature. Good. MacManus 280-4486 1983 $65

SALA, GEORGE AUGUSTUS   The Baddington Peerage. London: Charles J. Skeet, 1860. First edition. 3 vols. Orig. cloth. Spines faded, a few corners bumped. Very good. MacManus 280-4487 1983 $450

SALA, GEORGE AUGUSTUS   Charles Dickens. George Routledge, (1870). First edition. Ads. Orig. yellow printed wrapps., spine a little worn. Jarndyce 31-619 1983 £24

SALA, GEORGE AUGUSTUS   Charles Dickens. George Routledge, (1870). Orig. yellow wraps. (a little worn) bound in. Half green calf. 2 pp ads. Jarndyce 30-224 1983 £20

SALA, GEORGE AUGUSTUS   Dutch Pictures. London: Tinsley Brothers, 1861. First edition. Some sketches in the Flemish manner. 12mo. Orig. cloth. Spine faded. Some light wear along edges of spine. Very good. MacManus 280-4488 1983 $35

SALA, GEORGE AUGUSTUS   Echoes of the Year Eighteen Hundred and Eighty-Three. Remington & Co., 1884. First edition, front. port. Orig. red cloth, dec. in black and gilt, bevelled boards. Very good. Jarndyce 31-891 1983 £24

SALA, GEORGE AUGUSTUS   A Journey Due North. London: Richard Bentley, 1858. First edition. Orig. brown cloth. Spine and covers worn and slightly spotted. Inner hinges weak. Very slight damp-staining at the bottom of the first preliminary pages. Cont. owner's signature. Good. MacManus 280-4489 1983 $125

SALA, GEORGE AUGUSTUS   Lady Chesterfield's Letters to Her Daughter. London: Houlston & Wright, 1860. First edition. Orig. decorated cloth. Spine and covers slightly worn and faded. Illus. with several drawings. Very good. MacManus 280-4490 1983 $65

SALA, GEORGE AUGUSTUS   Lady Chesterfield's Letters to Her Daughter. London: Houlston & Wright, 1860. First edition. Illus. Orig. cloth. Bookplates removed from endpapers. Spine a little faded and worn. Very good. MacManus 280-4491 1983 $55

SALA, GEORGE AUGUSTUS   The Life and Adventures of George Augustus Sala. N.Y.: Charles Scribner's Sons, 1895. First American edition. 2 vols. With portrait. Orig. cloth. Very good. MacManus 280-4492 1983 $20

SALA, GEORGE AUGUSTUS   Looking at Life. London: Routledge, 1860. First edition. Orig. cloth. Worn. MacManus 280-4493 1983 $20

SALA, GEORGE AUGUSTUS   Papers Humorous and Pathetic. London: Tinsley Brothers, 1872. First edition. Orig. decorated cloth. Former owner's inscription on front flyleaf. Spine faded. Very good. MacManus 280-4494 1983 $65

SALA, GEORGE AUGUSTUS   Papers Humorous and Pathetic. Tinsley Brothers, 1872. First edition, half title, preface, 36 pp ads. Orig. green cloth, new end papers. Jarndyce 31-888 1983 £16.50

SALA, GEORGE AUGUSTUS   Robson: A Sketch. London: John Camden Hotten, 1864. First edition. Orig. pictorial wrappers (slightly soiled, with a few short marginal tears). Spine partly chipped away. Good. MacManus 280-4495 1983 $125

SALA, GEORGE AUGUSTUS   The Seven Sons of Mammon. London: Tinsley Brothers, 1862. First edition. 3 vols. Orig. cloth. Covers rubbed. Inner hinges cracking. Good. MacManus 280-4496 1983 $200

SALA, GEORGE AUGUSTUS   The seven sons of Mammon: a story. London: Tinsley, 1862. First edition. 3 vols. in one. 8vo. Cont. half calf. Ximenes 63-161 1983 $80

SALA, GEORGE AUGUSTUS   Things I Have Seen and People I Have Known. London: Cassell and Co., 1894. First edition. 2 vols. Orig. cloth. Presentation copy, inscribed on the title-page of each vol.: "To my dear sister Louis, from George Augustus Sala. Brighton, June, 1894." With the bookplates of the artist Adele Herbert. Bindings a bit worn and soiled. Endpapers soiled. Good. MacManus 280-4497 1983 $175

SALA, GEORGE AUGUSTUS   Things I Have Seen, and People I have Known. Cassell & Co., 1894. Front. port. vol. I; half title vol. II; 16 pp ads. in both vols. Orig. blue cloth, v.g. Inscribed presentation copy from the publishers, Christmas 1894. Jarndyce 30-1125 1983 £36

SALA, GEORGE AUGUSTUS   Twice Round the Clock. Houlston & Wright, (1878). Front. port. and illus. on wood, from drawings by Wm. M'Connell. Half green morocco, a little rubbed. Jarndyce 31-291 1983 £38

SALA, GEORGE AUGUSTUS   The Two Prima Donnas. London: Tinsley Bros., 1862. First edition. Orig. cloth. Front inner hinges cracked. Tear in front cover near head of spine, edges and corners a bit worn. Small spot on front cover. Bookseller's ticket. Library blind-stamp. Former owner's signature on endpapers. MacManus 280-4498 1983 $75

SALA, GEORGE AUGUSTUS   The Two Prima Donnas, and the Poor Dumb Door Porter. Tinsley Brothers, 1862. First edition. 2pp ads., orig. green cloth slightly rubbed. Jarndyce 31-889 1983 £28

SALA, GEORGE AUGUSTUS   Windsor Castle at Chicago. Port Sunlight, Near Birkenhead: Lever Brothers, Limited, n.d. (1893). First edition. 12mo. Orig. wrappers. Fine. MacManus 280-4499 1983 $45

SALDEN, DOUGLAS   Sicily, the New Winter Resort. London, 1905. 234 illus., map. 8vo, cloth. Salloch 385-395 1983 $30

SALE, EDITH TUNIS   Old Time Belles and Cavaliers. Phila., 1912. First ed. 61 illustrations. 8vo, ex-library. Morrill 290-566 1983 $25

SALE, F.   A Journal of the Disasters in Affghanistan, 1841-2. London, 1843. Map, folding plan. Decorated cloth, some wear. 8vo. Good. Edwards 1044-614 1983 £55

SALINGER, JEROME DAVID   The Catcher in the Rye. B, 1951. Very minor cover and interior stains, else near fine in internally reinforced, moderately worn and chipped dustwrapper with price clipped. Quill & Brush 54-1187 1983 $300

SALINGER, JEROME DAVID   For Esme-With Love and Squalor. L, (1953). Spine very slightly soiled in very good dustwrapper with small closed tear on front panel and small chip at top of hinge flap. Quill & Brush 54-1183 1983 $275

SALINGER, JEROME DAVID   The Kit Book for Soldiers, Sailors and Marines. Ch., 1943. Paper covered boards worn on corners and edges, good. Quill & Brush 54-1182 1983 $50

SALINGER, JEROME DAVID   Nine Stories. Boston, Little, Brown (1953). First edition. Black cloth (spine with gilt a bit dull), else very good. Houle 21-764 1983 $125

SALISBURY, ALBERT   Here Rolled the Covered Wagons. Seattle, (1948). 1st ed. End maps, illus. Royal 8vo, buckram, dj. Clark 741-393 1983 $23.50

SALISBURY, E. A.   The Sea Gypsy. New York, 1924. First edition. 8vo, orig. cloth. Frontis., 30 plates, inscription on endpaper "to Mrs. Mary Y. Moore with best wishes from the Author E. A. Salisbury", with Moore bookplate. Small ink library stamps. Good. Edwards 1042-158 1983 £18

SALKELD, JOHN   The Pilgrim's Progress, and Other Rhymes. Penrith: Thomas Hodgson, 1879. First edition, orig. dull blue cloth, sl. mottled by damp. Jarndyce 30-836 1983 £12.50

SALLUSTIUS CRISPUS, GAIUS   Crispi Sallustii Opera Quae Supersunt, Omnia. Andreas Foulis, 1751. 8vo, cont. red morocco gilt spine, hinges cracked, bookplate, name on end-paper. Ravenstree 95-95 1983 $110

SALLUSTIUS CRISPUS, GAIUS   Quae Extant. Londini, F. & C. Rivington, 1793. 8vo, orig. sheep, worn, front cover detached, name on flyleaf, bit age-soiled. Ravenstree 95-96 1983 $21

SALMASIUS, CLAUDIUS   De re Militari Remanorum Liber. 1657. 4to, a few woodcut diagrams of military defense formations. Cont. vellum, with later endpapers. Karmiole 75-51 1983 $175

SALMI, MARIO   Piero della Francesca: Gli affreschi di San Francesco in Arezzo. Bergamo: Istituto Italiano d'Arti Grafiche, 1944. 40 gravure plates. Large 4to. Wrappers. Backstrip slightly worn. Ars Libri 33-272 1983 $35

SALMI, MARIO   Romanesque Sculpture in Tuscany. Firenze, 1928. Large 4to, 80 plates with 248 illus., cloth. Ars Libri SB 26-209 1983 $225

SALMON, ANDRE   Modigliani. Paris: Quatre Chemins, 1926. 50 heliogravure plates. 4to. Wrappers. Backstrip defective. Ars Libri 33-542 1983 $75

SALMON, JAMES   Ten Years' Growth of the City of London. 1891. First edition. Large folding col. map. Orig. blue cloth, bevelled boards, v.g. Presentation label to Cripplegate Institute from the Corporation of the City of London; pin-prick stamps of Cripplegate Free Libraries. Jarndyce 31-292 1983 £34

SALMON, N.   A New Survey of England wherein the Defects of Camden are supplied... London: for J. Walthoe, 1731. First edition. 2 vols. 8vo. Full cont. polished calf, gilt borders, fully gilt spine, tan labels. Large folding engraved map. Slight wear at foot of one spine. Very fine copy. Heath 48-572 1983 £165

SALMON, THOMAS   The Chronological Historian. Printed for W. Mears, 1733. 8vo, cont. calf. Bickersteth 75-84 1983 £26

SALMON, WILLIAM   Praxis Medica. Printed for J. Knapton, and W. Innys, 1716. 8vo, old ink notes on front fly, recent calf antique. Bickersteth 77-318 1983 £85

SALMONS, C. H.   The Burlington Strike. Aurora, Ill., 1889. 1st ed. Illus. 8vo, all edges gilt, corners rubbed. Morrill 288-438 1983 $25

SALOMON, JACQUES   E. Vuillard: Cahier de dessins. Paris: Quatre Chemins-Editart, 1950. Text fascicle and facsimile of 50 leaves, stitched as issued. 4to. Portfolio. Marbled boards, 1/4 cloth. No. 274 of a limited edition of 550 copies only. Ars Libri 32-692 1983 $125

SALOMONSEN, F.   The Birds of Greenland. Copenhagen, 1950-51. Folio, original boards, neatly rebacked with morocco, 52 coloured plates, map. Wheldon 160-86 1983 £220

SALT, HENRY   A voyage to Abyssinia... London: F.C. & J. Rivington, 1814. First edition. Large 4to. 7 maps (5 folding, 4 colored), 27 plates. Modern 1/2 tan morocco. A very fine copy. Adelson Africa-122 1983 $850

SALT, HENRY   A voyage to Abyssinia... Phila.: M. Carey, 1816. 8vo. Folding map. 1/2 black morocco. Rubbed. Adelson Africa-217 1983 $75

SALT, HENRY S.   Life of Henry D. Thoreau. London: Scott, 1896. Revised ed. Orig. maroon cloth, gilt. Nice copy. Jenkins 155-1213 1983 $20

SALT, HENRY S.   The Logic of Vegetarianism. London: The Ideal Publishing Union, Limited, 1899. First edition. Orig. cloth. Review copy, with publisher's slip tipped in. Covers a bit dustsoiled. Fine. MacManus 280-4500 1983 $20

SALTMARSH, JOHN   Holy Discoveries and Flames. London, printed by R.Y. for P. Nevill, 1640. 12mo, new calf antique style, contents little age-browned, few light watermarks, complete with engraved title. First edition. Ravenstree 97-205 1983 $225

SALTUS, EDGAR   Purple and Fine Women. Chicago, Pascal Covici, 1925. First edition. Pictorial dust jacket (a few small nicks, trifle rubbed) else, very good. Houle 22-772 1983 $45

SALVERSON, LAURA GOODMAN   Confessions of an Immigrant's Daughter. London: Faber & Faber, 1939. 20 1/2cm. First edition. Brown cloth. Very good to fine copy. McGahern 53-142 1983 $35

SALVIATI, ANTONIO   On mosaics... London: Wertheimer, 1865. First edition. 8vo. Orig. buff printed wrappers. Soiled. Ximenes 63-21 1983 £50

SALVINI, ROBERTO   Giotto bibliografia. Roma: Fratelli
Palombi, 1938. 4to. Wrappers. 845 entries. Ars Libri 33-173
1983 $135

SALWEY, REGINALD E.   Ventured in Vain. London: Hurst and
Blackett, 1894. First edition. 2 vols. Orig. cloth. Signed on the
half-title of Vol. I: "Herbert A. Salwey, Sept. 7th, 1894." Spine
and covers slightly faded and worn. Good. MacManus 280-4501 1983
$200

SALZMANN, MAXIMILIAN   Anatomy and Histology of the Human
Eyeball in the Normal State. Chicago, 1912. First English edition.
Tall 4to, buckram. 5 text illus. Argosy 713-474 1983 $50

SAMBRICIO, VALENTIN DE   Tapices de Goya. Madrid: Archivo
General de Palacio, 1946. 193 gravure plates. Small stout folio.
Wrappers. Uncut. Unopened. Edition limited to 1000 numbered
copies on laid paper. Ars Libri 32-275 1983 $350

SAMEK, LUDOVICI, SERGIO   Miniature di Belbello Da Pavia...
Milano: Aldo Martello, 1954. 36 tipped-in color plates with
commentary opposite. 4to. Cloth. Dust jacket. Printed at the
Stamperia Valdonega. Ars Libri 33-24 1983 $125

SAMPFORD, H.   A Coppie of a Letter read in the
House of Commons... London: for Tho. Bankes & W. Ley, 1642.
Second impression. 4to. Wrappers. Heath 48-164 1983 £75

SAMPSON, ARTHUR W.   Range and Pasture Management. New
York: John Wiley & Sons, 1923. Colored frontis. Plates. Scarce.
Jenkins 153-493 1983 $175

SAMPSON, ARTHUR W.   Range and Pasture Management. N.Y.,
1923. Illus. Orig. cloth. First edition. Ginsberg 47-822 1983
$25

SAMPSON, WILLIAM   Sampson Against the Philistines...
Philadelphia, 1805. Dsb., good. Reese 18-275 1983 $40

SAMS, CONWAY WHITTLE   The Conquest of Virginia. New York,
1916. 1st ed. Illus. 8vo. Morrill 287-482 1983 $22.50

SAMSON, C. R.   Fights and Flights. London, 1930. First
edition. Frontis. 23 plates, 3 maps. Roy. 8vo. Orig. cloth. Spine
faded. Good. Edwards 1042-603 1983 £40

SAMUEL Beckett: an exhibition held at Reading University Library, May
to July 1971. (London): Turret Books, 1971. Illus. Orig. cloth.
First edition. One of 100 copies signed by Beckett. Fine copy.
MacManus 277-255 1983 $150

SAMUELS, EDWARD A.   The Birds of New England and Adjacent
States. Boston 1870. Illus., cloth, shaken, covers very worn.
5th ed., revised & enlarged.

SAN ALBERTO, J. A.   Carta...A Los Indio Infieles Chiriguanos.
Buenos Aires, 1927. Limited edition. Portrait of San Alberto and
complete photofacsimile of the Carta printed in Madrid ca. 1790. Orig.
printed wrappers. Very fine. Jenkins 152-381 1983 $100

SAN DIEGO, "Our Italy." San Diego: Gould, Hutton & Co., printers,
1895. Wrappers. Part of back cover lacking. Dawson 471-255 1983
$50

THE SAN FRANCISCO Earth Quake and Fire of April 18, 1906. Wash.,
GPO, 1907. Illus., 54 plates, folded plate and folded map. Orig.
wraps., worn, in cloth. Ginsberg 47-92 1983 $35

SAN LAZZARO, G. DI   Paul Cezanne. Paris: Chroniques du
Jour, 1936. 59 gravure plates (3 color). 3 text illus. 4to.
Wrappers. Uncut. Presentation copy, inscribed by the author.
Ars Libri 32-90 1983 $85

SANBORN, FRANK   Recollections of Seventy Years. Boston:
Gorham Press, 1909. 2 vols. 1st ed. Orig. green cloth, gilt, t.e.g.
Very good set with pencil notes in text. Jenkins 155-1214 1983 $30

SANCHEZ CANTON, F. J.   Los Dibujos de Goya. Madrid: Museo
del Prado, 1954. 2 vols. 466 plates (many color). 7 tipped-in
facsimiled hors texte. Folio. Boards, 1/4 cloth. Ars Libri 32-
276 1983 $275

SANCROFT, WILLIAM   A Sermon Preach'd to the House of Peers,
Novemb. 13th, 1678. In the Savoy: Printed by Tho. Newcomb, for
Robert Beaumont, 1678. First edition, 4to, wraps. Fenning 62-322
1983 £14.50

SAND, GEORGE   Winter in Majorca. London, (1955). 8vo,
wraps. Proof copy of the book. Light wear to the bottom edge of the
spine, mainly a fine copy. In Our Time 156-331 1983 $200

SANDARS, JOSEPH   A Letter on the Subject of the Projected
Rail Road between Liverpool and Manchester. Liverpool, (1824). 8vo.
Recent calf backed boards. Quaritch NS 5-95 1983 $175

SANDBERG-VAVALA, EVELYN   La croce dipinta italiana e l'
iconografia della Passione. Roma, 1980. xiii, (1), 943, (3)pp.,
4 plates. 585 text illus. Stout folio. Cloth. D.j. Reprint,
limited to 300 numbered copies, of the 1929 edition. Ars Libri
SB 26-212 1983 $175

SANDBURG, CARL   Always the Young Strangers. New York:
Harcourt, Brace, (1953). 1st ed., 1 of 600 numbered and signed
copies printed on all rag paper. Orig. blue cloth, paper label,
uncut, box with label. Mint copy in near fine box. Jenkins 155-1114
1983 $100

SANDBURG, CARL   Breathing Tokens. New York: (1977).
First edition. Printed blue wrappers. Advance uncorrected proofs.
Bradley 66-302 1983 $85

SANDBURG, CARL   Carl Sandburg's 'Remembrance Rock.'
(New York, 1949). First edition. Promotion booklet issued by
Sandburg's publishers for his novel. Pictorial wrappers. Cover illus.
is a montage of Sandburg portraits by Steichen. Bradley 65-165 1983
$35

SANDBURG, CARL   The People, Yes. N.Y., (1936). Later
printing, but a presentation copy. Argosy 714-653 1983 $20

SANDBURG, CARL   The Photographs of Abraham Lincoln.
New York, (1944). First edition of the text. Text only, 2 signatures, in plain paper binder. Advance copy for reviewers. Pasted
to inside of back wrapper is printed notice from the publishers, also
a typed note. Rare. Bradley 64-146 1983 $40

SANDBURG, CARL   Remembrance Rock. NY: (1948). Two
vols. Limited to 1000 copies signed by Sandburg. Mint in slightly
rubbed slip-case. First edition. Bromer 25-99 1983 $100

SANDBURG, CARL   Remembrance Rock. N.Y., Harcourt,
(1948). First edition. Thick 8vo, dust jacket. Very good. Houle 21-
766 1983 $20

SANDEMAN, CHRISTOPHER   Thyme and Bergamot. London, 1947.
4to, 1/2 mottled vellum over cloth bds., gilt extra. Wood-engravings
by John O'Connor. One of 25 copies specially bound & signed by the
author. Perata 28-24 1983 $175

SANDER, MAX   Die Illustrierten Franzosischen
Bucher des 18 Jahrhunderts. Stuttgart, (1926). Vol. 3 of Taschen-
bibliographien fur Buchersammler. Small 8vo. Spine faded. Morrill
287-410 1983 $50

SANDER, MAX   Les Livres Illustres Francais du Dix-
Neuvieme Siecle. Stuttgart, (1924). Vol. 1 of the Taschenbiblio-
graphie series. 8 plates. Small 8vo. Spine faded. Morrill 287-409
1983 $75

SANDERS, ALVIN H.   At the Sign of the Stock Yard Inn.
Chicago: Breeder's Gazette Print, 1915. First edition. Illus. 3/4
morocco. Jenkins 152-751 1983 $45

SANDERS, ALVIN H.   Shorthorn Cattle. Chicago: Sander Publishing Co., 1918. Frontis. and illus. 3/4 morocco. Some fading to spine. Fine. Jenkins 152-383 1983 $85

SANDERS, ALVIN H.   Shorthorn Cattle. Chicago, 1918. Illus. Orig. cloth. Ginsberg 47-823 1983 $25

SANDERS, B. H.   Emily Murphy. Toronto: Macmillan, 1945. 22cm. Frontis. and 34 illus. Green cloth. Dustjacket. Fine. McGahern 54-158 1983 $20

SANDERS, CHARLES W.   Murder Trail. London, Collins (1929). First edition. Dust jacket. Very good-fine. Houle 21-767 1983 $37.50

SANDERS, DANIEL C.   A History of the Indian Wars with the First Settlers of the United States. Vt.: Wright & Sibley, 1812. Trimmed rather closely. Bound by Riviere in full levant morocco, spine gilt in panels, inner dentelles gilt, a.e.g.; enclosed in a full levant molded solander case by Riviere. In fine condition. First edition. Felcone 21-94 1983 $450

SANDERS, JOHN   Memoirs on the Military Resources of the Valley of the Ohio... Pittsburgh, 1845. Half morocco. Jenkins 153-494 1983 $175

SANDERS, PRINCE   Maytian Papers. Boston: Hingham, 1818. 8vo, orig. printed boards. Bingham's ad on back cover. Rostenberg 88-11 1983 $240

SANDERS, WILLIAM PERRY   Days that are Done. L.A., 1918. Illus. Orig. pictorial printed wraps. First edition. Ginsberg 46-676 1983 $60

SANDERS' Orchid Guide. St. Albans, 1927. Revised edition, frontispiece (portrait), royal 8vo, cloth (trifle used). Scarce original printing. Wheldon 160-2056 1983 £25

SANDERSON, G. P.   Thirteen Years Among the Wild Beasts of India. Edinburgh, 1912. 3 maps, 21 plates. Thick sq.8vo. Edges slightly spotted. Pictorial cloth. Good. Edwards 1044-615 1983 £35

SANDERSON, I. T.   Animal Treasure. 1937. 32 illus., 8vo, cloth. Wheldon 160-431 1983 £15

SANDES, E. W. C.   The Indian Sappers and Miners. Chatham, 1948. First edition. Portrait frontis. 30 plates, 3 folding coloured maps, numerous other maps, many folding. Roy. 8vo. Spine slightly worn and faded. Good. Edwards 1042-572 1983 £20

SANDES, E. W. C.   In Kut and Captivity. London, 1919. First edition. Frontis. 6 folding maps, 4 plans, 3 folding. 13 plates. Worn. 8vo. Orig. cloth. Good. Edwards 1044-616 1983 £25

SANDFORD, D. A.   Leaves from the Journal of a Subaltern. London, 1849. Binding dampstained, frayed at head and tail of spine. Joints cracked. Tipped-in ALS from Elizabeth Sandford to Lady Queensberry. With Lady Queensberry's ownership inscription. 8vo. Good. Edwards 1044-617 1983 £50

SANDFORD, ELIZABETH POOLE   Thomas Poole and His Friends. Macmillan, 1888. First edition. 2 vols. Half titles, front. port. vol. I. 2 pp ads. vol. II. Orig. black cloth, v.g. Jarndyce 30-1106 1983 £30

SANDFORD, MRS. JOHN
Please turn to
SANDFORD, ELIZABETH (POOLE)

SANDHAM, ALFRED   Ville-Marie, or, Sketches of Montreal... Montreal: George Bishop & Co., 1870. 21 1/2cm. Orig. green pebbled cloth. Very good copy. McGahern 53-143 1983 $75

SANDOZ, MARI   The Beaver Men. NY, (1964). Limited to 185 numbered and signed, specially bound copies, boxed together with signed map, tipped-in are signed manuscript leaves, review of later book and notice from bookseller, laid-in is invitation for publication party for book and color photo of Ms. Sandoz at this reception, handwritten note, very fine in slipcase. Quill & Brush 54-1617 1983 $225

SANDOZ, MARI   Capital City. Boston, 1939. Orig. cloth, dust jacket. First edition. Ginsberg 46-677 1983 $25

SANDOZ, MARI   The Cattleman from the Rio Grande Across the Far Marias. New York, 1958. Illus., boxed and limited to 199 copies. Signed by the author. Jenkins 151-303 1983 $150

SANDOZ, MARI   Crazy Horse The Strange Man of the Oglalas. New York, 1942. Folding map, 1st ed. in dust jacket. A scarce title. Jenkings 151-56 1983 $45

SANDOZ, MARI   Crazy Horse, The Strange Man of the Oglalas. NY, 1942. Cloth, slight tear at top of spine. Outer hinges stained else good in frayed and soiled dust wrappers. First edition. King 46-114 1983 $40

SANDOZ, MARI   Old Jules. Boston, 1935. Illus. Orig. cloth, dust jacket, worn. First edition. Autograph presentation copy signed by Sandoz. Ginsberg 46-678 1983 $25

SANDOZ, MAURICE   Fantastic Memories. GC, 1944. Illus. by Salvador Dali. Dampstained at bottom left affecting last ten or so pages, otherwise good in very good, lightly soiled dustwrapper. Quill & Brush 54-346 1983 $75

SANDOZ, MAURICE   The Maze. New York, 1945. First edition. Illus. by Salvador Dali. Covers a little marked. Torn dust wrapper. Author's signed autograph presentation inscription. Nice. Rota 230-149 1983 £15

SANDOZ, MAURICE   On the Verge. New York: Doubleday, 1950. First edition. Plates. Illus. by Salvador Dali who also designed the dust jacket. Orig. cloth. Dust jacket chipped. Fine. Jenkins 152-752 1983 $75

SANDRAS, GATIEN DE COURTILZ, SIEUR DE
Please turn to
COURTILZ, GATIEN DE, SIEUR DE SANDRAS

SANDS, JAMES   Count di Novini; Or, The Confederate Carthusians. A Neapolitan Tale. Printed for G.G. and J. Robinson, 1799. 3 vols, 12mo, contemporary qtr. sheep, marbled sides; with three half-titles; a fine copy. Hill 165-106 1983 $235

SANDYS, CHARLES   Consuetudines Kanciae. London: John Russell Smith, 1851. First edition. 8vo. Orig. black cloth. Folding frontis. and two folding plates, and a large folding genealogy printed on oilcloth. 6-page list of subscribers. Scarce. Ximenes 63-8 1983 $90

SANDYS, EDWIN   Sermons of the Most Reuerend Father in God, Edwin, Arch-bishop of Yorke... London, Iohn Beale, 1616. 4to, orig. calf, hinges broken, worn, spine defective, age-stained and browned, title and first leaves loose, some marginalia cropped Ravenstree 97-207 1983 $150

SANDYS, EDWYN   Upland Game Birds. NY 1902. 1st ed. Illus, gilt-pict. cloth, t.e.g., front hinge loose, spine dull, covers rubbed. King 46-656 1983 $25

SANDYS, RUTH   Numerous Names Nimbly Narrated. H. Milford, 1930. 4to. Colour pictorial title & 26 colour plates, very stylized. Yellow pictorial boards. Greer 40-20 1983 £25

SANDYS, WILLIAM   Transactions of the Loggerville Literary Society. John Russell Smith, 1867. Printed for Private Circulation. Frontis., title vignette & some text illus. Maroon bead grain cloth, a.e.g., bkstrip faded with sl. wear top/bottom, corners bruised, scarce, vg. Hodgkins 27-187 1983 £25

SANFORD, JOHN   Old Man's Place. N.Y., Boni, (1935). First edition. Dust jacket. Fine copy. Houle 21-768 1983 $50

SANFORD, JOHN   Seventy Times Seven. NY, 1939. Minor stains to bottom and fore edge, very good in soiled, very good dust-wrapper with light chipping and wear to edges. Quill & Brush 54-1191 1983 $30

SANGER, ZEDEKIAH   The Meridian Harmony. Dedham: H. Mann, for the author, 1808. Calf-backed wooden boards (quite worn, much of paper covering gone). Very good. Felcone 20-120 1983 $30

SANGSTON, LAWRENCE   The Bastiles of the North. Baltimore, 1863. Orig. printed wraps. First edition. Ginsberg 46-679 1983 $50

SANSOM, JOSEPH   Sketches of Lower Canada, Historical and Descriptive... New York, 1817. Later cloth spine, marbled boards. Ex-lib., with stamp and call number on title, otherwise a clean copy. Reese 18-516 1983 $250

SANSOM, KATHARINE   Living in Tokyo. New York, 1937. 1st American ed. Illustrated in color and black and white by Marjorie Nishiwaki. Tall 8vo. Binding partly faded. Morrill 287-411 1983 $20

SANSON, N.   The Present State of Persia. London, 1695. First English edition. 6 plates, 2 folding. 12mo. Cont. calf, lacking label, rubbed at hinges and corners, from the Signet Library with their emblem gilt-stamped on boards, for M. Gilliflower. Good. Edwards 1044-618 1983 £265

SANTA ANNA, ANTONIO LOPEZ DE Biografia Del... Mexico: Torres, 1849. First edition. 12mo. Orig. yellow printed wrappers, sewn. Wraps with one neat repair. Very fine. Jenkins 152-391 1983 $275

SANTAYANA, GEORGE   A Hermit of Carmel And Other Poems. London: R. Brimley Johnson, 1902. First English edition. Orig. cloth. Inscribed on the front free endpaper "To E.S.P. H(aynes) from Edward Thomas 1902." Spine faded. Good. MacManus 280-5199 1983 $350

SANTAYANA, GEORGE   Sonnets and Other Verses. New York: Stone & Kimball, 1896. Green cloth. Second edition. Very good. Bradley 66-304 1983 $45

SANTEE, ROSS   Apache Land. New York: 1947. First edition. Illus. Gray cloth. Very good. Bradley 66-462 1983 $30

SANTEE, ROSS   Men and Horses. New York & London: Century, 1926. First edition. Orig. drawings by author. Numerous illus. Orig. blue cloth over orange pictorial cloth. Backstrip slightly faded. Fine. Jenkins 152-394 1983 $100

SANTINI, PIER CARLO   Rozai. Firenze: Vallecchi, 1972. Second edition. 210 plates. 168 vignettes hors texte. 50 tipped-in color plates in text. Small folio. Cloth. Dust jacket. Ars Libri 33-575 1983 $100

SANTLEBEN, AUGUST   A Texas Pioneer... N.Y., Neals, 1910. 1st ed. Unusually fine copy. Jenkins 153-496 1983 $300

SAPPEY, M. P. C.   Etudes sur l'appareil mucipare et sur le systeme lymphatique des Poissons. Paris, 1880. 12 double page lithograph plates, folio, new cloth. Rare. Some slight marginal dust-soiling. A tear in plate 2 neatly repaired. Wheldon 160-997 1983 £35

SAPPINGTON, JOHN   The Theory and Treatment of Fevers. Arrow Rock, (Missouri): Published by the author, 1844. 8vo, calf, worn, (crudely rebacked; light foxing). First edition. Argosy 713-475 1983 $250

SARDA, H. B.   Ajmer: Historical and Descriptive. Ajmer, 1911. Large folding map/plan. 29 plates, some slight wear. 8vo. Good. Edwards 1044-620 1983 £20

SARFATTI, MARGHERITA G.   Daniele Ranzoni. Roma: Reale Accademia d'Italia, 1935. Prof. illus. 4to. Boards. Ars Libri 33-569 1983 $45

SARGANT, JANE ALICE   An address to the peers of England. London: W. Wright, 1820. First edition. 8vo. Disbound. Ximenes 63-515 1983 $30

SARGANT, WILLIAM LUCAS   Robert Owen, and His Social Philosophy. Smith, Elder, 1860. First edition, orig. green cloth, sl. rubbed. Jarndyce 30-1093 1983 £40

SARGENT, C. S.   Trees and Shrubs. Boston and New York, (1902) - 1905. Vol. 1 (of 2). 100 plates from drawings by C. E. Faxon, sm. folio, original half buckram. Rare. Wheldon 160-2103 1983 £70

SARGENT, EPES   Peculiar: A Tale of the Great Transition. Hurst & Blackett, 1864. First English edition. 3 vols. Half titles, 8 pp. ads. vol. III. Vol. I a little loose. Orig. orange cloth, dulled. A good copy. Jarndyce 31-892 1983 £58

SARGENT, EPES   The Scientific Basis of Spiritualism. Boston: Colby and Rich, 1881. Hinges severely cracked, spine tips worn. Gach 95-456 1983 $25

SARGENT, GEORGE A.   A Busted Bibliophile and His Books. Boston: 1928. Octavo. First edition. Limited to 600 copies. This copy inscribed by Sargent and Edward A. Newton. Fine in marbled boards with cloth spine. Bromer 25-262 1983 $100

SARGENT, GEORGE B.   Lecture on the "West;" Delivered by Special Request at the Tremont Temple, Boston, Mass., Feb. 24, 1858. Davenport, 1858. Dbd. First edition. Ginsberg 47-383 1983 $125

SARGENT, M. P.   Pioneer Sketches. Pa., 1891. Illus., edges rubbed and slightly worn, front hinge starting at preface, else good. Quill & Brush 54-1615 1983 $60

SARGEANT, P.W.
Please turn to
SERGEANT, PHILIP W

SARGENT, WINTHROP   Boston: a Poem. Boston: J. Nancrede, 1803. 8vo, sewed. 1st ed. Argosy 710-31 1983 $75

SARJANT, JANE ALICE   The Broken Arm. SPCK., 1847. Frontis. & one illus., text illus. engr'd by Whymper. Dark purple ribbed cloth. Binder's label of S. Curtis. Hodgkins 27-188 1983 £20

SAROYAN, WILLIAM   An Act or Two of Foolish Kindness. Lincoln, Neb., Penmaen Press, 1977. Illus. by Helen Siegl. Orig. gilt stamped half blue cloth, over decorated boards. One of 300 copies, signed by the author and illustrator. Fine. Houle 22-774 1983 $75

SAROYAN, WILLIAM   Adventures of Wesley Jackson. N.Y., Harcourt (1946). First edition. Dust jacket (chipped). Very good. Houle 21-770 1983 $20

SAROYAN, WILLIAM   The Daring Young Man on the Flying Trapeze and other stories. New York: Random House, 1934. First edition. Tall 8vo. Orig. two-tone cloth with foil band. Dust jacket, slightly darkened and soiled, but a fine copy. Jaffe 1-352 1983 $85

SAROYAN, WILLIAM   The Daring Young Man on the Flying Trapeze. New York: Random House, 1934. 1st ed., 2nd printing. Orig. cloth, wrap-around label. Fine copy. Jenkins 155-1116 1983 $20

SAROYAN, WILLIAM   The Fiscal Hoboes. New York: Press of Valenti Angelo, 1949. First edition. 8vo. Paper wrappers. Limited to 250 numbered copies signed by Saroyand and the illustrator-printer, Valenti Angelo. Title page and colophon decorations cut in linoleum by Angelo, typography and printing by Angelo. Oak Knoll 49-14 1983 $115

SAROYAN, WILLIAM   Get Away Old Man. N.Y., Harcourt, (1944). First edition. Dust jacket. Very good. Houle 21-771 1983 $55

SAROYAN, WILLIAM   Get Away Old Man. N.Y., Harcourt (1944).
First edition. Dust jacket (stained, short tear), else very good.
Houle 21-772 1983 $32.50

SAROYAN, WILLIAM   Human Comedy. N.Y., Harcourt (1943).
First edition. Dust jacket (a bit faded and chipped), else very
good. Illus. by Don Freeman. Houle 21-773 1983 $100

SAROYAN, WILLIAM   Inhale & Exhale. New York: Random
House, (1936). First edition. 8vo. Orig. cloth. Dust jacket,
torn and slightly nicked. A fine copy. Jaffe 1-353 1983 $65

SAROYAN, WILLIAM   Inhale et Exhale. NY, (1936). Cover
soiled, good or better in worn dustwrapper. Quill & Brush 54-1193
1983 $35

SAROYAN, WILLIAM   L'Audacieux Jeune Homme au Trapeze
Volant. Paris, (1946). Ltd. edition. 8vo, pr. wraps. One of 125
copies, uncut & unopened. Argosy 714-892 1983 $25

SAROYAN, WILLIAM   Love Here is My Hat. N.Y., Modern
Age (1938). First edition, illus. by John Groth. Pictorial wraps.
Very good. Houle 21-776 1983 $40

SAROYAN, WILLIAM   My Heart's In the Highlands. New
York: Harcourt, (1939). Cloth. First edition. Inscribed by the
author on the front endsheet: "For Walter Winchell, sincerely,
William Saroyan, NY June 1939." A fine copy, but without dust jacket.
Reese 20-857 1983 $65

SAROYAN, WILLIAM   My Name is Aram. New York: Harcourt,
(1940). Cloth. First edition. Fine in dust jacket, missing some
chips from the head and toe of spine. Reese 20-859 1983 $30

SAROYAN, WILLIAM   The Saroyan Special. NY, (1934). Illus.
by Don Freeman, rear cover slightly stained, else very good in very
good dustwrapper with chipped edges, owner's inscription. Quill &
Brush 54-1195 1983 $35

SAROYAN, WILLIAM   Three Plays. N.Y., Harcourt, (1940).
First edition. Dust jacket (back faded, a few nicks), else very good.
Boldly signed and inscribed by Saroyan. Houle 21-784 1983 $125

SAROYAN, WILLIAM   Three Times Three. (L.A.), Conference
Press, 1936. First edition. Title page in red and black. One of 750
copies. Very good. Houle 21-786 1983 $75

SARPI, PAOLO   The History of the Inquisition.
London: J. Oakes for Humphrey Moseley, 1639. 1st ed. in English,
4to, 18th century qtr. calf, marbled boards, imprimatur leaf. Lower
margin of one leaf shaved, excising part of one line; a fine copy.
Trebizond 18-197 1983 $275

SARRETT, LEW   The Uncollected Poems of Lew Sarett.
N.Y., Holt, 1941. First edition. Brown cloth stamped in gilt (trifle
rubbed at corners) else very good. Signed by the author. Houle 22-
773 1983 $37.50

SARS, G. O.   An Account of the Crustacea of Norway,
Vol. 5, Copepoda, Harpacticoida. Bergen, 1911. 284 plates, 4 vols.,
4to. Wheldon 160-1335 1983 £25

SARS, M.   Memoires pour servir a la connaissance
des Crinoides vivants. Christiania, 1868. 6 plates, 4to, wrappers,
some dustsoiling. Wheldon 160-1336 1983 £15

SARTRE, JEAN PAUL   The Age of Reason, a Novel. New York:
Knopf, 1947. 1st American ed. Orig. cloth, dj. Fine. Jenkins
155-1118 1983 $30

SARTRE, JEAN-PAUL   Le Mur. Paris, 1939. Orig. wraps.,
wraps. a little soiled and detached. Author's signed inscription
on free end-paper "A mon petit camerade Rene Mahen...et pour la
diffusion en Angleterre...J.P. Sartre". K Books 307-162 1983 £240

SARTON, MAY   The Leaves of the Tree. Mount Vernon,
Iowa, 1950. Pr. wrs. One of 300 copies. Argosy 714-659 1983 $25

SARTORIS, ADELAIDE   A Week in a French Country-House. London:
Smith, Elder & Co., 1867. First edition. Orig. gilt-decorated cloth.
Spine and upper edges of covers faded. Corners slightly worn. Signature and small stain on front free endpaper. Good. MacManus 280-
4503 1983 $75

SARU-KANI Kassen. Kobunsha, Tokyo, nd. No. 3. 10 coloured illus.,
col'd pictorial cvrs., silk cords bkstrip. Hodgkins 27-110 1983 £18

SASS, ELSE KAI   Thorvaldsens Portraetbuster. Kobenhavn: G.E.C. Gads Forlag, 1963-1965. 3 vols. Prof. illus. Small
folio. Boards, 1/4 calf. Slight rippling of pages at edges. Ars
Libri 32-661 1983 $225

SASSOON, SIEGFRIED   Collected Poems. London: Faber & Faber
Limited, (1947). First edition. Orig. cloth. Dust jacket. Very fine.
MacManus 280-4511 1983 $50

SASSOON, SIEGFRIED   The Complete Memoirs of George Sherston.
London: Faber & Faber, (1937). First edition. Orig. red cloth.
Dust jacket (slightly faded and worn, with a few small tears to the
cover edges). Sassoon's copy with a number of holograph corrections
both in the text and listed separately on a sheet loosely laid in.
Fine. MacManus 280-4512 1983 $1,500

SASSOON, SIEGFRIED   Counter-Attack and Other Poems. London:
William Heinemann, 1918. First edition. Orig. printed wrappers
(front cover and half-title missing). From the library of Sassoon
with five one-word revisions and two corrections in pencil in his hand.
MacManus 280-4513 1983 $450

SASSOON, SIEGFRIED   Counter-Attack & Other Poems. London:
William Heinemann, 1918. First edition. Orig. wrappers. Spine and
cover edges slightly worn. In a quarter-morocco slipcase. Near-fine.
MacManus 280-4514 1983 $275

SASSOON, SIEFGRIED   Discoveries. (London: Printed for
Siegfried Sassoon, April 1915). First edition. Orig. printed light
green wrappers. One of 50 copies. From the library of Sassoon.
Right side slightly trimmed. Near-fine. MacManus 280-4515 1983
$500

SASSOON, SIEGFRIED   Four Poems. Cambridge, 1918. First
separate edition. Reprinted from The Cambridge Magazine. Inscribed
on the front page "To E.M. Forster from Siegfried Sassoon. May 1st
1918." One fold in centre, slight browning, but a very good copy.
Scarce. Gekoski 2-167 1983 £325

SASSOON, SIEGFRIED   The Heart's Journey. N.Y.: Crosby
Gaige, 1927. First edition. Orig. cloth-backed boards. Limited to
590 copies signed by author. Fine. MacManus 280-4519 1983 $85

SASSOON, SIEGFRIED   In Sicily. London: Faber & Faber Ltd.,
1930. First edition. Drawing by S. Tennant. Orig. boards. One of
400 copies signed by Sassoon. Backstrip torn. Good. MacManus 280-
4521 1983 $20

SASSOON, SIEGFRIED   Memoirs of a Fox-Hunting Man. N.Y.:
Coward-McCann, (1929). First American illus. edition. Illus. by Wm.
Nicholson. Orig. pictorial cloth. Dust jacket (slightly faded and
worn; spine ends a trifle frayed). Printed at the Chiswick Press,
London. Near-fine. MacManus 280-4524 1983 $150

SASSOON, SIEGFRIED   Memoirs Of An Infantry Officer. London:
Faber & Faber, (1930). First edition. Orig. blue cloth. Presentation
copy to Dame Nellie Burton inscribed on the half-title page. Spine
faded. Very good. MacManus 280-4526 1983 $2,000

SASSOON, SIEGFRIED   Memoirs of An Infantry Officer. London:
Faber & Faber, 1930. First edition. Orig. blue buckram. One of 750
copies printed on English hand-made paper and signed by author. Fine.
MacManus 280-4528 1983 $150

SASSOON, SIEGFRIED   Memoirs of an Infantry Officer. London,
(1930). D.w. First edition. Argosy 714-664 1983 $40

SASSOON, SIEGFRIED   Meredith. London: Constable, (1948).
First edition. Frontis. port. Orig. boards. Dust jacket (slightly
faded and rubbed, with a few small tears to the covers). Near-fine.
MacManus 280-4531 1983 $35

SASSOON, SIEGFRIED   Nativity. N.Y.: William Edwin Rudge, 1927. First American edition, copyright issue. Orig. wrappers. Limited to 27 copies, of which twelve were for sale. Mint. MacManus 280-4534 1983 $450

SASSOON, SIEGFRIED   Nativity. (London: Faber & Gwyer, 1927). Proof copy of the first edition. Orig. decorated yellow wrappers instead of the purple ones as issued. Designs by Paul Nash. Fine. MacManus 280-4532 1983 $225

SASSOON, SIEGFRIED   Nativity. New York, 1927. First edition. One of 27 copies, of which only 12 were for sale. Mint. Gekoski 2-168 1983 £145

SASSOON, SIEGFRIED   An Octave. London, 1966. First edition. Set of uncorrected galley proofs for this privately printed edition of 350 copies. Rota 231-532 1983 £50

SASSOON, SIEGFRIED   An Ode For Music. (Privately printed for Sassoon at The Chiswick Press, Took Court, Chancery Lane, London, 1912). First edition. Orig. light brown printed wrappers with a small floral decoration on the front cover. One of 60 copies written by Sassoon on the limitation page. Signed by Sassoon. From Sassoon's library. Very fine. MacManus 280-4505 1983 $650

SASSON, SIEGFRIED   The Old Century and Seven More Years. NY, 1939. Ink notation on half-title and rear fly, spine gutters slightly stained, else very good in lightly chipped and frayed, very good dustwrapper. Quill & Brush 54-1199 1983 $30

SASSOON, SIEGFRIED   The Path to Peace. Worcester: Stanbrook Abbey Press, 1940. Octavo. First edition. Limited to 500 copies. Corners slightly bumped, else very fine in quarter-vellum and decorated paper over boards. Separate small broadside poem by Sassoon with calligraphed initial laid-in. Bromer 25-304 1983 $325

SASSOON, SIEGFRIED   Poems. (London): Duckworth, 1931. Boards. First edition. One of 1000 copies printed. Slightest traces of foxing, else a fine copy in slightly chipped glassine jacket. Reese 20-864 1983 $75

SASSOON, SIEGFRIED   Poems Newly Selected, 1916-1935. London: Faber & Faber, (1940). First edition. Orig. printed boards. Dust jacket. Fine. MacManus 280-4537 1983 $50

SASSOON, SIEGFRIED   Prehistoric Burial. (N.Y.: Printed by the Pynson Press for Alfred Knopf, 1932). First edition. Illus. by W. Gordon. Orig. decorated wrappers. Publisher's envelope (slightly faded and worn). Near-fine. MacManus 280-4538 1983 $75

SASSOON, SIEGFRIED   Recreations. (London): Printed for the Author, (1923). First edition. Orig. boards. One of 75 copies signed by Sassoon in monogram, this copy inscribed to Eddie Marsh. Covers very slightly worn and soiled. Very good. MacManus 280-4540 1983 $750

SASSOON, SIEGFRIED   The Redeemer. Cambridge: W. Heffer & Son, May 1916. First separate publication. 4-page, unnumbered, folded leaf, reprinted from the Cambridge Magazine for April 29, 1916. Number 2. One of 200 copies. Fine. MacManus 280-4541 1983 $275

SASSOON, SIEGFRIED   Rhymed Ruminations. London: Faber & Faber, (1940). First trade edition. Orig. cloth. Dust jacket (faded and worn at the edges). Covers soiled. MacManus 280-4542 1983 $27.50

SASSOON, SIEGFRIED   Rhymed Ruminations. London, 1940. First Trade edition. Covers sprung. Dust wrapper. Very nice. Rota 231-531 1983 £12

SASSOON, SIEGFRIED   The Road to Ruin. London: Faber & Faber, (1933). First edition. Orig. red boards. Dust jacket (chipped, faded, with tears to the cover edges). Backstrip chipped. Covers soiled. MacManus 280-4543 1983 $27.50

SASSOON, SIEGFRIED   Sherston's Progress. London: Faber & Faber, (1936). First edition. Orig. cloth. Presentation copy to his mother inscribed: "Dearest Ash, with love from Sig." Spine and cover edges slightly rubbed. Good. MacManus 280-4547 1983 $350

SASSOON, SIEGFRIED   Sherston's Progress. London, 1936. First edition. One of 300 numbered copies, signed by author. Fine. Rota 231-530 1983 £60

SASSOON, SIEGFRIED   Sherston's Progress. Leipzig: Bernard Tauchnitz, (1937). First Tauchnitz edition. Orig. 3/4 morocco with marbled boards. Specially bound and presented to the authro by the publisher (with the latter's printed Presentation Slip loosely laid in. In the publisher's box. Near-fine. MacManus 280-4548 1983 $1,250

SASSON, SIEGFRIED   Siegfried's Journey. Lon., (1945). Edges rubbed, light cover soiling, minor interior foxing, else very good in badly chipped dustwrapper, gift inscription. Quill & Brush 54-1198 1983 $30

SASSOON, SIEGFRIED   Something About Myself. (Worcester: Stanbrook Abbey Press, September 1966). First edition. Illus. by M. Adams. Orig. decorated wrappers. One of 250 copies reproduced from line blocks made by Siviter Smith, printed on hand-made paper. Near-fine. MacManus 280-4550 1983 $150

SASSOON, SIEGFRIED   Sonnets. (N.p.): Privately Printed, 1909. First edition. Orig. cloth-backed blue-grey boards. Sassoon's copy with numerous corrections and revisions throughout the text in pencil and ink. One of probably 50 copies. Spine slightly soiled. Cover corner slightly worn. Very good. MacManus 280-4552 1983 $1,750

SASSOON, SIEGFRIED   A Suppressed Poem. (N.p.): The Known Press, 1919. First edition. 4-page folded leaf. Printed self-wraps. One of 50 numbered copies with a port. of the author on the front cover. Water stain to lower right side. With a small tear to the bottom fold. Very good. MacManus 280-4553 1983 $375

SASSOON, SIEGFRIED   To My Mother. (London: Faber & Gwyer, 1928). Proof copy of the first edition. Illus. by S. Tennant. Orig. blue wrappers. Contains numerous corrections (none in the text of the poem itself) by an editor from Faber. Spine and covers foxed and faded. Good. MacManus 280-4555 1983 $375

SASSOON, SIEGFRIED   To My Mother. London: Faber & Gwyer, 1928. First edition. Illus. by S. Tennant. Orig. boards. One of 500 large-paper copies signed by author. Very good. MacManus 280-4556 1983 $50

SASSOON, SIEGFRIED   To the Red Rose. London, 1931. First edition. One of 400 numbered copies signed by the author. Illus. by Stephen Tennant. Head and tail of spine nicked, otherwise fine. Jolliffe 26-458 1983 £30

SASSOON, SIEGFRIED   Twelve Sonnets. (London: Privately Printed, 1911). First edition. Orig. blue wrappers. One of 35 copies. "To J.B. Wirgman" is inscribed in pencil on the title-page. Covers stained, with a small piece missing from the last page. From the library of Sassoon. Very good. MacManus 280-4558 1983 $500

SASSOON, SIEGFRIED   Vigils. (N.p.: Privately Printed), 1934. First edition. Title-page designed and engraved by S. Gooden. Entire book engraved on copper. Orig. pigskin with gilt spine lettering (rubbed away). Inscribed to mother-in-law by author: "For Hester's Mother, with love." One of 272 ordinary copies signed by Sassoon, which contains Gooden's signature on the title-page. Very good. MacManus 280-4561 1983 $450

SASSOON, SIEGFRIED   Vigils. London: William Heinemann, 1935. First edition. Orig. cloth. Signed in monogram and dated "i.xi. 35" by Sassoon on the front endpaper. Laid in is an "Autograph Manuscript", 1 page, 8vo., fair copy, by Sassoon of the poem "Memorandum." Spine slightly faded. Very good. MacManus 280-4562 1983 $750

SASSOON, SIEGFRIED   Vigils. London: William Heinemann, 1935. First English ordinary edition. Orig. blue buckram. Dust jacket (slightly faded, worn and soiled, with a few small tears). Contains 35 poems, 13 of which have been added from the limited first edition. Near-fine. MacManus 280-4563 1983 $45

SASSOON, SIEGFRIED   War Poems. London, 1919. First English edition. Bookplate. Upper cover creased. Very good. Jolliffe 26-457 1983 £30

SASSOON, SIEGFRIED   The Weald of Youth. London: Faber & Faber, (1942). First edition. Orig. cloth. Dust jacket (slightly faded, worn and soiled). Fine. MacManus 280-4564 1983 $40

SATIRES in India. Calcutta: printed for the author, by P. Crichton, 1819. First edition. 12mo. Cont. half calf. Spine and corners worn, hinges weak. Rare. Ximenes 63-217 1983 $225

SATO, SHOZO   Art of Arranging Flowers. N.Y., Abrams (1965). Folio. Illus. with tipped in color plates and numerous b/w photographs. Gilt stamped green cloth. Fine. Houle 22-375 1983 $95

SAUERLANDT, MAX   Die deutsche Plastik des achtzehnten Jahrhunderts. Firenze/Munchen, 1926. Large 4to. 108 hinged collo-type plates. Cloth. Ars Libri SB 26-213 1983 $100

SAUERLANDT, MAX   Emil Nolde. Munchen: Kurt Wolff, 1921. 91 plates (2 tipped-in color). 9 text illus. 4to. Cloth. Ars Libri 32-493 1983 $125

SAUERMANN, ERNST   Die mittelalterlichen Taufsteine der Provinz Schleswig Holstein. Lubeck, 1904. 72pp., 1map. 52 illus. 4to. Wraps. Ars Libri SB 26-215 1983 $37.50

SAULCY, F. DE   Narrative of a Journey Round the Dead Sea. London, 1854. Folding map, folding plan. 2 vols., slight wear, inner hinges weak. 8vo. Orig. cloth. Good. Edwards 1044-621 1983 £75

SAUMAISE, CHAUDE DE   De Re Militari Romanorum. Leyden, 1657. First edition. Roy. 8vo. Cont. vellum, blank flyleaf repaired. Some slight stains. Bookplates. Orig. cloth. Good. Edwards 1042-468 1983 £60

SAUNDERS, CHARLES   Capistrano Nights. N.Y., McBride, 1930. First edition. Illus. by Charles P. Austin. From the library of Zane Grey. Houle 21-1155 1983 $35

SAUNDERS, EDITH   Fanny Penquite. London, 1932. First English edition. Profusely illus. in colour by the author. Very slightly frayed dustwrapper by Lynton Lamb. Very good. Jolliffe 26-461 1983 £35

SAUNDERS, H. ST. G.   Valiant Voyaging. London, 1948. Endpaper map, plates. Library stamp on front endpaper. 8vo. Orig. cloth. Good. Edwards 1044-622 1983 £20

SAUNDERS, JAMES EDMONDS   Early Settlers of Alabama. New Orleans: 1899. First edition. Illus. Quarto, red cloth. Covers worn, front hinge cracked, clippings pasted to front end paper. Bradley 66-444 1983 $100

SAUNDERS, JOHN   Bound to the Wheel. London: Hurst & Blackett, 1866. First edition. 3 vols. Orig. decorated cloth. Covers and spines slightly worn and spotted. Back free endpaper missing from vol. II. Inner hinges weak. Contents shaken. Former owner's signature. Good. MacManus 280-4567 1983 $225

SAUNDERS, JOHN B.   Andreas Vesalius Bruzellensis. N.Y., ca. 1948. Ex-lib. Argosy 713-553 1983 $35

SAUNDERS, JOHN B.   Vesalius - The Illustrations from his Works. New York, 1850. First edition. 4to. Orig. binding. Dust wrapper. Fine. Fye H-3-580 1983 $50

SAUNDERS, JOHN CUNNINGHAM   The Anatomy of the Human Ear, Illustrated by a Series of Engravings, of the Natural Size; with a Treatise... With Notes and Additions... Philadelphia, 1821. 1st American ed. 4 folding engraved plates in color. 8vo. Contemporary calf, leather label. Morrill 289-202 1983 $60

SAUNDERS, L.   The Knave of Hearts. Racine: Art & Writ. Gld., n.d. (ca.1925). 4to. Spiralbound. Owner stamp neatly removed from front cover and blank margin of 2 plates. Color plates throughout. Near fine. Aleph-bet 8-190 1983 $275

SAUNDERS, MARSHALL   Beautiful Joe. Ph., 1894. Second issue with Charles Banes imprint, title loosened, cover edges worn to boards in some places, good. Quill & Brush 54-1200 1983 $30

SAUNDERS, MONTAGU   The Mystery in the Drood Family. Cambridge: The University Press, 1914. First edition. Orig. cloth. Some offsetting to the endpapers. Former owner's signature. Good. MacManus 278-1563 1983 $35

SAUNDERS, MONTAGU   The Mystery in the Drood Family. Cambridge at the University Press, 1914. Half title, orig. light olive cloth, paper label, very good. Jarndyce 30-178 £12.50

SAUNDERS, RICHARD WEST   Skallagrim. Privately printed, 1925. First edition. Thin 8vo, boards. One of 500 copies printed by William Rudge. Presentation copy signed by the author to actress Bebe Daniels. Good - very good. Houle 22-777 1983 $45

SAUNDERS, WILLIAM   A Treatise on the Structure, Economy, and Diseases of the Liver... Boston, 1797. 1st American ed. 12mo. New cloth. Morrill 289-203 1983 $75

SAUNDERS, WILLIAM   A Treatise on the Structure, Economy, and Diseases of the Liver. Walpole, New Hampshire, 1810. 12mo, cont. calf (foxed). Saunders name on flyleaf. Argosy 713-476 1983 $150

SAUNDERSON, NICHOLAS   The Elements of Algebra. Cambridge: University Press, 1740. 2 vols. 4to, bound in cont. full panelled calf, rubbed; gilt-stamped spines (lacking labels). Outer hinges cracking in a few places. Some faded water-staining in text. Karmiole 75-87 1983 $175

SAVAGE, EDWARD H.   Police Records and Recollections. Boston, 1873. 1st ed. Lithographs by Bufford. 8vo. Morrill 286-647 1983 $20

SAVAGE, JAMES W.   The Discovery of Nebraska and a Visit to Nebraska in 1662. Wash., 1893. Orig. front wrapper, dbd. First edition. Ginsberg 47-639 1983 $35

SAVAGE, JOHN   Horace to Scaeva. London: Printed for John Brindly...MDCCXXX. 8vo, wanting half-title, with fine engraved horse in red-brown ink on title, Richard Farmer's copy with note in his hand on title, an uncut copy in later wraps. First edition. Quaritch NS 7-119 1983 $175

SAVAGE, JOHN   Horace to Scaeva. Epistle XVII, Book I. London: John Brindly, 1730. 1st ed., 8vo, modern qtr. morocco gilt, boards. Vignette title page in red ink, half-title. Limited printing of only 750 copies. A very fine copy. Trebizond 18-86 1983 $160

SAVAGE, JOHN   Horace to Scaeva. Epist. XVII, Book I imitated. London: printed for John Brindley, 1730. 1st ed., 8vo, fine engraved vignette, modern wrappers. Pickering & Chatto 19-62 1983 $125

SAVERY, THOMAS   The Miner's Friend. For S. Crouch, London, 1702. 8vo, with a folding engraved plate; signature of William Alexander in upper margin of title and British Museum stamp, cancelled, on verso; small tear in plate just affecting the engraved surface; nineteenth century panelled calf. First edition. A good copy. Quaritch NS 5-97 1983 $3,500

SAVI, G.   Istituzioni Botaniche. Florence, 1833. 8vo, half roan, small stain in outer blank margin of pages 247-274. Wheldon 160-1563 1983 £15

SAVILE, B.   How India was Won by England. London, 1881. Folding coloured map, plates. Cr. 8vo. Pictorial cloth. Good. Edwards 1044-623 1983 £20

SAVILE, B   Man; or, The Old and New Philosophy. London: Hust and Blackett, 1863. Orig. blue cloth, a bit spotted. Ads. Karmiole 76-96 1983 $50

SAVILE, GEORGE, MARQUIS OF HALIFAX
Please turn to
HALIFAX, GEORGE SAVILE, MARQUIS OF

THE SAVOY. London: Leonard Smithers, 1896. No. 1 to No. 8 complete in three quarto vols. of blue cloth with design in gold by Aubrey Beardsley on the three covers. Tipped in is the scarce large size Christmas card designed by Beardsley. 3 vols. with wear to top and bottom of backstrips. Duschnes 240-6 1983 $350

SAWYER, CHARLES J.   English Books, 1475-1900. London: Charles J. Sawyer, n.d. (1922). 2 vols. Edition ltd. to 2,000 sets. Fine. Karmiole 74-26 1983 $85

SAWYER, EUGENE T.   The Life and Career of Tiburcio Vasquez: The California Stage Robber. Oakland: 1944. Sm 4to, cloth-backed decorated bds., paper label. Forward by Joseph A. Sullivan. Illustrated. Perata 27-69 1983 $65

SAWYER, JAMES   Points of Practice in Maladies of the Heart. Birmingham, 1908. First edition. 12mo, orig. cloth. Argosy 713-477 1983 $30

SAWYER, JAMES A.   Wagon Road from Niobrara to Virginia City... Wash., 1866. Dbd. First edition. Ginsberg 47-824 1983 $35

SAWYER, JOSEPH DILLAWAY   The Romantic and Fascinating Story of the Pilgrims and Puritans. New York, (1925). 1st ed. Illus. by 1700 engravings. 3 vols., tall 8vo, half leatherette. Ends of spines partly frayed, few inches of fore-edge of back cover of vol. 3 worn. Morrill 287-256 1983 $40

SAWYER, LORENZO   Opinion of the Circuit Court of the United States for the Northern District of California in the Matter of David Neagle Upon Habeas Corpus. Wash., 1889. Orig. printed wraps. First edition. Ginsberg 47-163 1983 $50

SAWYER, LORENZO   Way Sketches. N.Y., Eberstadt, 1926. Illua. Orig. vellum-backed boards. One of 35 numbered large paper copies. Ginsberg 47-825 1983 $125

SAWYER, LORENZO   Way Sketches, Containing Incidents of Travel Across the Plains. New York, 1926. Limited to 385 copies. Fine copy. Jenkins 153-498 1983 $55

SAXON, LYLE   Gumbo Ya-Ya. Boston, (1945). 2nd printing. Illus. Clark 741-5 1983 $24

THE SAXON and The Gael; Or, The Northern Metropolis. Printed for Thomas Tegg, 111, Cheapside, (by Aikman, Edinburgh), 1814. 4 vols, 12mo, contemporary half calf, gilt backs, marbled sides; a fine copy. Hill 165-108 1983 £235

SAY, HORACE   Rapport Sur Le Commerce Entre La France Et L'Angleterre. Paris, La Librarie du Commerce, 1835. 1st ed., 8vo, a fine copy in modern green boards, original printed wrappers bound in. Pickering & Chatto 21-106 1983 $60

SAY, JEAN-BAPTISTE   Cours Complet D'Economie Politique Pratique. Paris, Guillaumin, 1840. 2nd ed., large 8vo, 2 vols., red morocco backed marbled boards, spine gilt, slightly rubbed, but internally a very good copy. Pickering & Chatto 21-107 1983 $300

SAY, JEAN-BAPTISTE   Petit Volume Contenant Quelques Apercus des Hommes et de la Societe. Paris, Guillaumin, 1839. 12mo, publisher's advertisement, uncut in original printed wrappers. A very good copy. Extremely scarce. Pickering & Chatto 21-109 1983 $400

SAY, JEAN-BAPTISTE   Traite D'Economie Politique. Paris, Antoine-Augustin Renouard, 1814. 2nd ed., 2 vols., 8vo, uncut and the second volume entirely unopened, in original blue wrappers. Very rare in this condition: an exceptional copy. Pickering & Chatto 21-108 1983 $1,000

SAY, LEON   Le Socialisme D'Etat. Paris, Calmann Levy, 1884. 1st ed., 8vo, light spotting, original yellow printed wrappers. Pickering & Chatto 21-110 1983 $50

SAY, T.   American Entomology. Philadelphia, 1824-28. 3 vols. in 1, roy. 8vo, new half morocco, engraved title-page, coloured plates. Some isolated slight foxing. Wheldon 160-88 1983 £1,000

SAYCE, R. U.   Primitive Arts and Crafts. Cambridge: Cambridge University Press, 1933. 57 illus. Large 8vo. Cloth. Ars Libri 34-69 1983 $30

SAYER, GEORGE S.   Southern Institutes. Phila., 1858. First edition, orig. blind-stamped cloth, (slightly stained, backstrip top chipped). Argosy 716-21 1983 $75

SAYERS, DOROTHY LEIGH   Catholic Tales & Christian Songs. (Oxford: Basil Blackwell, 1918). First edition. Orig. pictorial wrappers. Dust-soiled, with signature on front cover. Good. MacManus 280-4570 1983 $125

SAYERS, DOROTHY LEIGH   Creed or Chaos? London: Hodder & Stoughton, (1947). First edition. Orig. wrappers. Slightly worn. MacManus 280-4571 1983 $20

SAYERS, DOROTHY LEIGH   Creed or Chaos? London: Methuen & Co. Ltd., (1947). First edition. Orig. cloth. Nice. MacManus 280-4572 1983 $20

SAYERS, DOROTHY LEIGH   Four Sacred Plays. L, 1948. Front hinge starting at title, endpapers lightly stained, good or better in remnants of dustwrapper. Quill & Brush 54-1201 1983 $30

SAYERS, DOROTHY LEIGH   The Man Born to Be King. London: Gollancz, 1943. First edition. Orig. cloth. Former owner's inscription on flyleaf. Very good. MacManus 280-4575 1983 $20

SAYERS, DOROTHY LEIGH   The Story of Easter. London: Hamish Hamilton, n.d. (1955). First edition. Orig. pictorial wrappers. The picture painted by B. Biro. Wrappers very slightly worn and soiled. Good. MacManus 280-4577 1983 $250

SAYERS, DOROTHY LEIGH   Unpopular Opinions. London: Gollancz, 1946. First edition. Orig. cloth. Dust jacket. Includes 5 essays on detective fiction, three of which are on Sherlock Holmes and Dr. Watson. Very fine. MacManus 280-4579 1983 $100

SAYERS, EDWARD   The American Flower Garden Companion. Boston, Joseph Breck, 1838. 1st ed. 12mo, ads. Partly faded and rubbed. Morrill 288-666 1983 $20

SAYERS, FRANK   Poems, containing dramatic sketches on northern mythology, etc. Norwich: printed by Stevenson and Matchett, for Cadell and Davies (London), 1807. Fourth edition. 8vo. Orig. blue boards, white paper backstrip, pink printed paper label. Presentation copy, inscribed on the half-title. A fine copy. Ximenes 63-423 1983 $100

SAYRE, ELEANOR A.   The Changing Image: Prints by Francisco Goya. Boston: New York Graphic Society, 1974. 268 illus. Large 4to. Cloth. Dust jacket. Slightly worn. Ars Libri 32-277 1983 $75

SAYRE, LEWIS A.   The Alleged Malpractice Suit of Walsh vs. Sayre. New York, Geo. H. Shaw, 1870. 1st ed. Orig. wrappers. Small portion of back wrapper lacking. Presentation copy from Dr. Sayre. Morrill 289-204 1983 $45

SAYWELL, WILLIAM   The Reformation of the Church of England Justified. Cambridge: Printed by John Hayes...for Edward Hall, 1688. 4to, wrapper, a very good copy. Fenning 61-390 1983 £21.50

SCACCHI, A.   Contribuzioni Mineralogiche. Naples, 1872-73. 7 plates with 6 plates, 4to, leather-backed boards. Wheldon 160-1469 1983 £18

SCALIA, NATALE   Antonella da Messina e la pittura in Sicilia. Milano: Alfieri & Lacroix, 1914. 46 plates. 4to. Wrappers. Ars Libri 33-12 1983 $40

SCANNELL, FLORENCE   Christmas in Many Lands. Griffith Farran n.d. (1888). 4 vols. in one. Sq. 8vo. 4 frontis. & title vignettes. 4 full-page & 56 text illus. Blue decorated cloth gilt. Greer 39-113 1983 £12.75

SCARBOROUGH, DOROTHY   The Supernatural in Modern English Fiction. New York and London: Putnam's, 1917. Green cloth. First edition. Gilt lettering on spine slightly patinated, otherwise a fine copy in dust jacket, with very slight chipping at the top edge. Reese 20-1036 1983 $185

SCARDOVI, LUDVIG   Dissertatio inauguralis medica de dentibus anatomice ac physiologice consideratis... Erfurt: litteris Nonnianis, 1785. Woodcut initial and head-piece. Small 4to. Cont. paper backstrip. Kraus 164-60 1983 $180

SCARGILL, ARTHUR PITT   Truckleborough Hall. Henry Colburn, 1827. First edition, 3 vols., bound as two. Without title to vol. III. Half blue calf, spines gilt, labels. Very good. Jarndyce 30-540 1983 £45

SCARGILL, ARTHUR PITT   Truth. Hunt & Clarke, 1826. First edition, 3 vols. bound as two. Without title to vol. III. Half red calf, spines gilt, labels, v.g. Jarndyce 30-539 1983 £42

SCARGILL, WILLIAM PITT   Rank and Talent. Henry Colburn, 1829. First edition. 3 vols. Large 12mo, cont. half calf (slightly rubbed), gilt. Hannas 69-174 1983 £55

SCARGILL, WILLIAM PITT   Tales of My Time. Colburn & Bentley, 1829. First edition, 3 vols. Half red roan, rubbed at heads of spines, black labels. Jarndyce 31-893 1983 £48

SCARLATTI, DOMENICO   Opere Complete per Clavicembalo. Milan, 1947-1953. Eleven vols. Folio, wrs. Salloch 387-204 1983 $250

SCARPA, ANTONIO (1747?-1832) Oratio de promovendis anatomicarum administrationum rationibus. Leipzig, 1785. Woodcut title vignette. 8vo. Orig. paper backstrip. Water damage in lower inner margin affecting 1 letter of imprint only. Kraus 164-210 1983 $250

SCARPA, ANTONIO (1747?-1832) Traite des Maldies des Yeux. Paris, Montpellier, 1821. 4 folding plates, 2 vols. 8vo. Green half calf. Fine copy, with the half-title. Argosy 713-478 1983 $225

SCARPA, ANTONIO (1747?-1832) Traite Pratique des Hernies, ou Memoires Anatomiques et. Chirurgicaux sur Ces Maladies. Paris, Gabon, 1812. 1st ed. in French. 21 full-page engraved plates. Folio, old boards, leather back and corners. Ex-library; rubbed. Morrill 289-205 1983 $125

SCARPA, ANTONIO (1747?-1832) Traite Pratique des Maladiese des Yeux on Experiences et Observations sur les Maladies qui Affectent ces Organes. Paris, 1855. 526 double col. pages, 8vo. Morocco-backed boards. Argosy 713-479 1983 $100

SCARRON, PAUL   The Whole Comical Works of Monsr. Scarron. London, S. and J. Sprint et al., 1700. 8vo, modern half calf gilt, name on title, bookplates, fine. First edition in English. Ravenstree 96-183 1983 $375

SCARRON, PAUL   The Whole Comical Works of Monsieur Scarron. London: S. & J. Sprint, 1703. 2nd ed., revised and corrected, of this first collected edition. 8vo, modern buckram, engraved and printed title pages, engraved frontis. and another engraved plate. Two contents leaves bound in from another work, engraved title repaired, else a very good copy. Trebizond 18-125 1983 $200

SCENES and Characters from the Works of Charles Dickens. Chapman & Hall, 1908. Half title. Orig. red cloth. Printed from the orig. woodblocks, engr. for the "Household Edition". Jarndyce 30-144 1983 £38

SCENES and Sketches of English Life. Reynolds & Son, n.d. (c. 1840). First edition, 3 vols. Fronts. of Bulwer Lytton, Miss Mitford and Washington Irving. Orig. purple cloth, sl. rubbed. Jarndyce 30-261 1983 £58

SCENES in the Bad Lands, North Dakota. (N.p., ca. 1835). Photograph album of 24 mounted sepai photographs. Mounts chipped, cloth covers worn, images bright and fine. Reese 19-406 1983 $850

SCENIC America. (Binghampton, N.Y., 1942). All photos. Pictorial spiral wraps. Covers at extremities heavily worn. King 45-367 1983 $25

SCHABACKER, PETER H.   Petrus Christus. Utrecht: Haentjens Dekker & Gumber, 1974. 55 plates. 4to. Cloth. Ars Libri 32-108 1983 $100

SCHACT, MARSHALL   Fingerboard. New York, (1949). 8vo. Cloth. This copy inscribed by the author to Alexander Laing. No jacket. Fine copy. In Our Time 156-685 1983 $20

SCHACHT, ROLAND   Alexander Archipenko. Berlin: Der Sturm, (1923). 25 illus. 4to. Boards, 1/4 cloth. Covers somewhat soiled. Ars Libri 32-11 1983 $125

SCHAEDER, HANS HEINRICH   Ein Weg Zu TS Eliot. Verlag, 1948. 8vo. Cloth, boards. This copy has laid in a short TLS from T.S. Eliot dated 8th Jan. 1948. Signed "TS Eliot". Fine copy in dj. In Our Time 156-246 1983 $125

SCHAEFFER, EMIL   Sandro Botticelli. Ein Profil. Berlin: Julius Bard, 1921. 88 plates. Text illus. Small folio. Vellum. From the library of Helena, Queen of Italy. Ars Libri 33-48 1983 $95

SCHAEFFER, J.   Russula-Monographie. (Bad Heilbrunn, 1952) Reprint, (1970). 22 plates (20 coloured double plates), 2 vols. in 1, 8vo, cloth. Wheldon 160-1889 1983 £52

SCHAEFFER, SAMUEL BERNARD   Pose Please. N.Y., (1936). Photos of nudes. Pictorial spiral wraps. Blind-stamped names. Worn. King 45-378 1983 $40

SCHALDACH, WILLIAM J.   Currents & Eddies. N.Y., (1944). First edition. Limited to 5000 copies. Illus. Cloth. Minor cover soil and wear. King 45-499 1983 $25

SCHARDT, ALOIS J.   Franz Marc. Berlin: Rembrandt-Verlag, 1936. 5 color plates. 115 illus. 4to. Orig. wrappers with vignette. Rare. Ars Libri 32-427 1983 $150

SCHARFF, R. F.   European Animals: their geological history and geographical distribution. 1907. 70 illustrations, 8vo, cloth. Wheldon 160-432 1983 £15

SCHARLING, CARL HEINRIK   Noddebo Parsonage. Richard Bentley, 1867. First edition of this translation, 2 vols., 8vo, some light fingermarks, but a very good uncut copy in recent boards. Fenning 61-391 1983 £48.50

SCHAUFFLER, ROBERT HAVEN   Florestan. NY, 1945. 19 plates, 8vo, cl. Salloch 387-394 1983 $45

SCHAUINGER, HERMAN   A Bibliography of Trovillion Private Press... Herrin, Ill: Trovillion Private Press, 1943. 8vo. Cloth. Limited to 277 signed and numbered copies. Fine copy. Oak Knoll 49-508 1983 $35

SCHECH, PH.   Diseases of the Mouth, Throat, Nose. Edinburgh, 1886. 8vo. Orig. cloth. Illus. in text. Upper cover torn. Gurney JJ-59 1983 £15

SCHEIWILLER, F.   Modigliani. Paris: Editions des Chroniques du Jour, 1928. 25 plates (1 color). Wrappers. Edition limited to 1000 copies. Wrappers worn. Ars Libri 33-543 1983 $20

SCHELLEY, JOE   Life and Adventures of Mexican Joe in the Western Wilds of America. Manchester: Frank Nodal & Co., printers, ca. 1900. 8vo, orig. coloured pictorial printed paper wrappers. Very good copy. Fenning 61-400 1983 £18.50

SCHELLING, FELIX   Elizabethan Drama 1558-1642. Boston: Houghton Mifflin Co., (1911). Second edition. 2 vols. Orig. cloth. Fine. MacManus 280-4580 1983 $35

SCHELTEMA, J. F.   Monumental Java. London, 1912. 8vo. Orig. cloth. 40 plates. Good. Edwards 1044-624 1983 £50

SCHERING, ARNOLD   Geschichte der Musik in Beispielen. NY, 1950. Folio, new cloth with leather label. Salloch 387-385 1983 $75

SCHERPF, GEORGE A.   Entstehungsgeschichte und Gegenwartiger Zustand des Neuen Unabhaengigen Amerikanischen States Texas. Augsburg: M. Rieger, 1841. Orig. printed wrappers, entirely uncut and unopened, with both large folding maps. 1st and only ed. of one of the rarest Texas books. Very fine copy. Jenkins 153-578 1983 $4500

SCHETKY, JOHN C.   Illustrations of W. Scott's Lay of the Last Minstrel. Printed for Longman, Hurst, 1810. Engraved by J. Heath, from designs taken on the spot by J.C. Schetky. With 12 engraved plates, half-title, 8vo, cont. mottled calf, gilt. A very little offsetting on to the text. Fenning 62-324 1983 £32.50

SCHETTINI, ALFREDO   Gemito. Milano: Edizioni dell' Esame, 1944. 148 illus. Small folio. Boards, 1/4 cloth. Ars Libri 33-479 1983 $50

SCHEVILL, F.   The Great Elector. Chicago U.P., 1947. 8vo. Orig. cloth. Portrait frontis. 5 plates, folding coloured map. Slightly soiled and faded. Good. Edwards 1042-344 1983 £15

SCHIAVO, ARMANDO   La donna nella scultura italiana dal XII al XVIII secolo. Roma, 1950 471pp. 369 plates. Folio. Cloth. Ars Libri SB 26-217 1983 $75

SCHIAVO, ARMANDO   La Fontana di Trevi e le altre opere di Nicola Salvi. Roma: Istituto Poligrafico dello Stato, 1956. 179 illus. Large 4to. Cloth. Ars Libri 33-319 1983 $125

SCHIAVO, ARMANDO   Michelangelo architetto. Roma: Libreria dello stato, 1949. 168 plates. Small folio. Cloth. Ars Libri 33-248 1983 $75

SCHIAVO, ARMANDO   La vita e le opere architettoniche di Michelangelo. Roma: Libreria dello Stato, 1953. 62 illus. 4to. Cloth. Ars Libri 33-249 1983 $100

SCHICK, LOUIS   Chicago and Its Environs. Chicago, 1891. 1st ed. Maps & illus., some heliotypes. Small 8vo, orig. red cloth, ads. Morrill 288-196 1983 $25

SCHIERN, FREDERIK   Life of James Hepburn Earl of Bothwell. Edinburgh: David Douglas, 1880. 8vo, cloth. Bickersteth 77-166 1983 £16

SCHIFF, SYDNEY   Celeste. London, 1930. First English edition. One of 700 copies numbered. 6 wood engravings by John Nash. Bookplate. Fine. Jolliffe 26-382 1983 £36

SCHIFF, SYDNEY   Myrtle. London: Constable & Co., 1925. First edition. Orig. cloth. Dust jacket (slightly faded, worn and soiled, with a few very small tears). Presentation copy inscribed: "For S.S. Koteliansky ('Kot') with my love whether he wants it or not, Stephen Hudson (Sydney), March 28. '25." Endpapers and edges slightly foxed. Dennis Wheatley's bookplate. Near-fine. MacManus 279-2802 1983 $85

SCHIFF, SYDNEY   Myrtle. London: Constable & Co. Ltd., 1925. First edition. 8vo. Orig. cloth. Chipped and dusty dust jacket. Fine copy. Jaffe 1-160 1983 $45

SCHIFF, SYDNEY   Prince Hempseed. London: Martin Secker, (1923). First edition. Orig. cloth. Dust jacket (faded, worn, and slight soiled). Presentation copy inscribed: "S. S. Koteliansky from Stephen Hudson. March 16, '23." Spine and cover faded and slightly worn. Slight offsetting to the endpapers. Dennis Wheatley's bookplate. Good. MacManus 279-2804 1983 $85

SCHIFF, SYDNEY   Tony. London: Constable & Co. Ltd., 1924. First edition. 8vo. Orig. cloth. Dust jacket. Slightly darkened and dust-soiled jacket. Fine copy. Jaffe 1-159 1983 $50

SCHILLER, FRIEDRICH   Mary Stuart, a Tragedy. London: by G. Auld, 1805. First English edition. Half-title. 8vo. Orig. boards, uncut edges. A trifled soiled. Traylen 94-706 1983 £16

SCHILLER, FRIEDRICH   The Piccolomini. London: Printed for J.N. Longman & O. Rees, 1800. First editions. Illus. Cont. marbled boards with label on spine. Boards rather worn along spine and at extremities. Bookplate. MacManus 277-1018 1983 $150

SCHILLER, FRIEDRICH   Works. London, 1903. 10 vols. 8vo. Orig. buckram with crimson morocco labels, gilt, t.e.g. 63 plates and 7 facsimiles. Slightly worn. Traylen 94-705 1983 £75

SCHILLINGS, C. G.   Flashlights in the Jungle. New York: Doubleday, Page, (1906). 8vo. 302 photographs. Orig. cloth. Lacks front fly, damage to some blank pp. edges. Adelson Africa-218 1983 $20

SCHILLINGS, C. G.   In Wildest Africa. New York: Harper, 1907. 8vo. Numerous illus. Orig. green cloth. Rubbed. Adelson Africa-219 1983 $40

SCHILTBERGER, JOHANN   The bondage and travels of Johann Schiltberger... London: Hakluyt Soc., 1879. 8vo. Folding map. Orig. cloth. Spine darkened and chipped, ex-lib. Adelson Africa-220 1983 $35

SCHINDLER, ANTON FELIX   The life of Beethoven... London: Colburn, 1841. First edition in English. 2 vols. 8vo. Orig. blue cloth. Portrait, and 2 folding facsimiles. Spines evenly faded. Ximenes 63-335 1983 $150

SCHLAGINTWEIT, ROBERT VON   Californie en Zijne Bevolking. Deventer, 1872. Illus., Orig. front wrapper bound in boards. First edition in Dutch. Ginsberg 47-164 1983 $150

SCHLECHTER, R.   Beitrage zur Orchideenkunde von Zentral-amerika. (Berlin, 1922-23) reprint Koenigstein, 1980. 2 parts in 1 vol., 8vo, cloth. Wheldon 160-2058 1983 £39

SCHLEGEL, H.   De Vogels van Nederlandsch Indie. Leyden and Amsterdam, (1863-66). 3 parts in 1 vol., roy. 4to, original cloth, 50 hand-coloured plates. Rare. Wheldon 160-90 1983 £300

SCHLEGEL, H.   Traite de Fauconnerie. (Leyden and Dusseldorf, 1844-53), Paris, 1980. Folio, decorated cloth, pictorial title-page, 14 coloured plates. Facsimile; limited edition of 500 copies. Wheldon 160-91 1983 £87

SCHLEGEL, JOHANN F. W.   Neutral Rights. Philadelphia, 1801. Dsb. Fine. Reese 18-245 1983 $50

SCHLEGL, ISTVAN   Samuel Hofmann (um 1595-1649). Stafa-Zurich/Munchen: (Th. Gut/Prestel), 1980. Prof. illus. Large 4to. Cloth. Dust jacket. Ars Libri 32-312 1983 $100

SCHLEIDEN, M. J.   The Plant. 1853. Second edition, 7 plates (5 coloured), 8vo, cloth. Some light foxing and binding a trifle used, but a good copy. Wheldon 160-1564 1983 £20

SCHLESINGER, ARTHUR M.   Orestes A. Brownson. B, 1939. Very good in dustwrapper slightly worn on spine and reinforced on bottom of spine with couple of chips, very good. Quill & Brush 54-1203 1983 $50

SCHLESINGER, ARTHUR M.   Robert Kennedy and his Times. Boston: 1978. Special edition, limited to 500 numbered, autographed copies, bound in half morocco, slipcased. Near mint. Jenkins 151-160 1983 $85

SCHLESINGER, ARTHUR M.   A Thousand Days: John F. Kennedy in the White House. B, 1965. One of 1000 numbered, specially bound in full leather and signed by author. Fine in fine slipcase. Quill & Brush 54-1202 1983 $90

SCHLESINGER, ARTHUR M.   A Thousand Days: John F. Kennedy in the White House. Boston, 1965. Limited, numbered, autographed edition, bound in full calf, slipcased. Near mint. Jenkins 151-158 1983 $85

SCHLESINGER, HERMAN   Die Syringomvelie. Leipzig: Franz
Deuticke, 1902. 8vo, cont. cloth-backed bds.; ex-lib. Argosy 713-
484 1983 $100

SCHLESINGER, MAX   Saunterings in and About London.
Nathaniel Cooke, 1853. Dark maroon calf, front. engr. title and illus.
First edition. Jarndyce 31-293 1983 £20

SCHLESINGER, MAX   Saunterings in and about London.
Nathaniel Cooke, 1853. First edition, front. engr. title and illus.
Dark maroon calf. Jarndyce 31-292 1983 £34

SCHLIEMANN, H.   Mycenae. London, 1878. Numerous maps,
plans, plates and illus. Occasional foxing. Thick 8vo. Pictorial
cloth, some wear, front inner joint cracked. Good. Edwards 1044-625
1983 £125

SCHLOSSER, LEONARD B.   A Pair on Paper. North Hills: Bird &
Bull Press, 1976. Octavo. Limited to 220 copies. Mint in leather-
backed boards. Bromer 25-145 1983 $200

SCHLOSS'S English Bijou Almanac for 1839. London: published by
the Proprietors, (1839). Orig. gilt paper covers, gilt edges,
enclosed in a blue velvet case, lined with red and cream velvet,
and with the magnifying glass. Portraits. Rare. Traylen 94-583
1983 £120

SCHMALENBACH, WERNER   Kurt Schwitters. New York: Abrams,
(1970). 420 illus. (54 tipped-in color). Large 4to. Cloth. Dust
jacket. Ars Libri 32-623 1983 $85

SCHMELTZ, J. D. E.   Sudsee-Reliquien. Leiden, 1888. 2
color plates. Text illus. Large 4to. Wrappers. Disbound. Presentation copy, inscribed by the author. Ars Libri 34-855 1983 $27.50

SCHMID, HEINRICH ALFRED   Hans Holbein der Jungere. Basel:
Holbein-Verlag, 1945-1948. 3 vols. 140 illus. 120 plates. Large
4to. Cloth. Dust jacket. Ars Libri 32-326 1983 $200

SCHMIDLIN, JOHANNES   Singendes und Spielendes Vergnuegen
Reiner Andacht. Zuerich, Buergkli, 1777. Music in diamond-shaped
notes, typeset. With engraved frontis. Thick tall 8vo, cont. calf.
4th edition. Salloch 387-205 1983 $300

SCHMIDT, ALFRED   Die Koelner Apotheken, von den aeltesten
Zeit bis zum Ende reichsstaedtischen Veerfassung. Mittenwald, 1930.
Tall thin 8vo, pr. wrs. 27 illus. Argosy 713-481 1983 $35

SCHMIDT, PAUL FERDINAND   Philip Otto Runge. Leipzig: Insel,
1923. 80 plates. 4to. Boards. A little foxed. Ars Libri 32-
608 1983 $65

SCHMIDT-DEGENER, F.   Jan Steen. A critical study. London:
John Lane, 1927. 40 hinged photogravure plates with titled tissue
guards. Large 4to. Cloth. Dust jacket. Ars Libri 32-644 1983
$100

SCHMIDT-DEGENER, F.   Rembrandt und der hollandische Barock.
Leipzig: B.G. Teubner, 1928. 16 collotype plates with 23 illus.
4to. Wrappers. Ars Libri 32-566 1983 $75

SCHMIED, WIELAND   Alfred Kubin. New York/Washington:
Praeger, 1969. 188 plates. 12 text illus. Square 4to. Cloth.
Dust jacket. Ars Libri 32-379 1983 $100

SCHMITT, MARTIN F.   Fighting Indians of the West. N.Y.,
1948. First edition. Numerous illus. Cloth. Blind-stamped names.
Covers rubbed, soiled. King 45-85 1983 $35

SCHMITZ, CARL A.   Oceanic Art. New York: Abrams, (1971).
337 plates (50 tipped-in color). Small oblong folio. Cloth. Dust
jacket. Ars Libri 34-856 1983 $150

SCHNABL, LEOPOLD   Buenos-Aryes. Stuttgart: Levy & Muller,
1886. First edition. Orig. brown gilt cloth. Light foxing on first
and last leaves. Very fine. Jenkins 152-396 1983 $65

SCHNEIDER, ISIDOR   Comrade: Mister. NY, 1934. Illus. by
Gyula Zilzer. Minor interior foxing, paper boards, very good or bet-
ter in chipped and slightly foxed dustwrapper, owner's name. Quill &
Brush 54-1204 1983 $50

SCHNEIDER, OTTY   Sonderbare Kauze, Graphische Phantasien.
N.p.: 1921. Octavo portfolio. Orig. tissues present. Illustrated
wrappers rubbed. Bromer 25-384 1983 $75

SCHNIEWIND, CARL O.   Paul Cezanne: Sketchbook Owned by
The Art Institute of Chicago. New York: Curt Valentin, 1951.
2 vols. Vol. 1: Boards. Vol. 2: 50 gravure plates, with facsimile
endpapers and flyleaves. Cloth. Small oblong 4to. Slipcase.
Edition limited to 1500 copies. Ars Libri 32-91 1983 $125

SCHNIEWIND, CARL O.   A Sketch Book by Toulouse-Lautrec
Owned by The Art Institute of Chicago. New York: Curt Valentin,
1952. Wrappers, stitched as issued, for the text fascicle.
Facsimile: 92 gravure plates (incl. color), with facsimile endpapers and flyleaves. Cloth. Small oblong 4to. Slipcase.
Edition limited to 1200 copies, printed by Jacomet. Ars Libri
32-675 1983 $175

SCHNITZLER, ARTHUR   Casanova's Homecoming. London n.d.
(1922). Limited to 250 copies on hand made paper. Cloth backed
boards, spine label rubbed, covers soiled. King 46-330 1983 $25

SCHNITZLER, ARTHUR   Hands Around. NY: Privately printed
for members of the Schnitzler Society, 1929. Limited to 1475
numbered copies. Cloth backed boards, ink name, white spine
darkened, covers bumped. King 46-331 1983 $20

SCHOBERLIN, MELVIN   From Candles to Footlights. Denver: Old
West Publishing Co., 1941. First edition in dust jacket. Frontis. and
plates. Jenkins 152-397 1983 $50

SCHOBERLIN, MELVIN   From Candles to Footlights. Denver:
Fred A. Rosenstock, The Old West Publishing Co., 1941. Illus. Cloth.
Dawson 471-333 1983 $25

SCHOENBERG, ARNOLD   Gurre-Lieder. Vienna, 1940. Folio,
wrs. Salloch 387-207 1983 $125

SCHOENBERG, ARNOLD   Saemtliche Werke. Mainz, 1973. Six
vols. in folio and three vols. in 4to. Together in 9 vols. Cloth.
Salloch 387-206 1983 $285

SCHOENBERGER, GUIDO   The Drawings of Mathis Gothart Nithart,
Called Grunewald. New York: H. Bittner, 1948. 44 plates. Large
4to. Cloth. Ars Libri 32-296 1983 $45

SCHOENER, JOHANN   Globi Stelliferi sive Sphaerae stellarum
fixarum usus et explicationes. Nuremberg: (Johannes Petreius), after
5 June 1533. First edition. 1 full-page woodcut globe on verso of
title, 1 woodcut initial, 1 diagram. 4to. Modern morocco, gilt-
stamped title on spine, g.e. Kraus 164-211 1983 $3,800

SCHOENRICH, OTTO   Santo Domingo, a Country With a Future.
NY, 1918. Illus. Argosy 710-615 1983 $35

SCHONBERG, ERICH VON   Travels in India and Kashmir. London:
Hurst & Blackett, 1853. 2 vols. 8vo. 2 plates. New 1/4 black
calf, small library stamps on titles. Adelson Africa-124 1983
$180

THE SCHOOL for Mothers. For G. and W. B. Whittaker, 1823. First
edition. 3 vols. 12mo, half-titles, Orig. boards, cloth spines
(faded), printed labels, uncut. One leaf torn across. Hannas 69-175
1983 £220

THE SCHOOL of Fashion. Henry Colburn, 1829. First edition. 3 vols.
Half calf, labels, v.g. Jarndyce 30-284 1983 £82

SCHOOLCRAFT, HENRY R.   Narrative Journal of Travels, Through
the Northwestern Regions of the United States. Albany, 1821. Errata
slip, plates, folding map. Engraved title-page, original calf,
somewhat worn and foxed. Jenkins 151-304 1983 $150

SCHOOLCRAFT, HENRY R.   Summary Narrative of An Exploratory Expedition to the Sources of the Mississippi River, in 1820. Phila.: Lippincott, Grambo, & Co., 1855. Frontis. map. Maps and illus. One folding map. Orig. cloth. Wear at the extremities of the spine. Nice. Jenkins 152-398 1983 $125

SCHOONOVER, THOMAS J.   Life and Times of General John A. Sutter. Sacramento, Bullock-Carpenter, 1907. Enlarged printing of the 1895 edition. Illus. Errata slip. Tan cloth. Very good. Houle 21-1156 1983 $50

SCHOPENHAURER, ARTHUR   Religion: A Dialogue. London, Sonnenschein, 1893. Portrait. 3/4 red morocco (ends rubbed), t.e.g. Very good. Houle 21-790 1983 $22.50

SCHOTTMULLER, FRIDA   Furniture and Interior Decoration of the Italian Renaissance. N.Y., 1921. "With 590 illus." Cloth backed boards. Blind-stamped names. Ink inscription. Minor spine soil. Tattered dust wrapper. Very good. King 45-363 1983 $35

SCHRADE, LEO   Monteberdi, Creator of Modern Music. NY, 1950. 10 plates, 8vo, cl. First edition. Salloch 387-351 1983 $24

SCHREINER, OLIVE   Dreams. London. T. Fisher Unwin, 1891. First edition. Orig. decorated cloth. Review copy from "The Academy," with a card stating the journal's needs, and signed by a Mr. J.S. Cotton, January 2, 1890, pasted to the front paste-down endpaper. Spine and covers faded, worn and soiled. With a few penciled notes in the text. Good. MacManus 280-4582 1983 $125

SCHREINER, OLIVE   Dream Life and Real Life. London, 1893. First edition. Orig. wrappers. Backstrip defective. Good reading copy. Rota 231-533 1983 £12

SCHREINER, OLIVE   Dreams. London: T. Fisher Unwin, 1891. First edition. Frontis. port. of the author. Orig. decorated cloth. Spine and covers slightly faded, worn and soiled. Good. MacManus 280-4581 1983 $100

SCHREINER, OLIVE   From Man to Man or Perhaps Only... London: T. Fisher Unwin Ltd., (1926). First edition. Frontis. port. Orig. cloth. Covers very slightly rubbed and spotted. Very good. MacManus 280-4584 1983 $35

SCHREINER, OLIVE   Stories, Dreams and Allegories. N.Y.: Stokes, 1923. Orig. cloth. Former owner's signature on title page. Fine. MacManus 280-4585 1983 $35

SCHREINER, OLIVE   The Story of An African Farm. London: Chapman & Hall, Limited, 1889. New edition. Orig. boards (rubbed at spine & corners). Inner hinges cracked. Cont. owner's signature of free endpaper. MacManus 280-4586 1983 $35

SCHREINER, OLIVE   Trooper Peter Halket of Mashonaland. London: Unwin, 1897. First edition. Orig. cloth. Very good. MacManus 280-4588 1983 $85

SCHREINER, OLIVE   Trooper Peter Halket of Mashonaland. Boston: Roberts, 1897. First American edition. Frontis. Orig. cloth. Spine darkened. Very good. MacManus 280-4587 1983 $45

SCHREINER, OLIVE   Trooper Peter Halket of Mashonaland. L, 1897. Cover stained and edges rubbed, hinges tender, endpaper slightly stained, remnants of bookplate on front pastedown, good, name sticker. Quill & Brush 54-1205 1983 $40

SCHREINER, OLIVE   Trooper Peter Halket of Mashonaland. Boston, 1897. First edition. Photo. of 3 lynched people, 8x5". Cloth. Ink inscription. Front cover and spine with some staining. Good. King 45-7 1983 $25

SCHREINER, OLIVE   Trooper Peter Halket of Mashonaland. London, 1897. First edition, first issue, with the suppressed frontis. Covers a little marked. Bookplate. Very nice. Rota 231-534 1983 £20

SCHREINER, OLIVE   Undine. London: Benn, (1929). First edition. Orig. cloth. Dust jacket (chipped at extremities). Fine. MacManus 280-4589 1983 $65

SCHREINER, OLIVER   Woman and Labour. London: T. Fisher Unwin, 1911. First edition. Orig. cloth. Presentation copy from Mrs. Bernard Shaw to the Sesame Club, inscribed on the flyleaf. Bookplate neatly removed from front endsheet. Fine. MacManus 280-4590 1983 $65

SCHRETLEN, M. J.   , Dutch and Flemish Woodcuts of the Fifteenth Century. Boston, 1925. Plates. 4to, nice. Morrill 288-442 1983 $65

SCHROCKIO, LUCA   Historia Moschi, Ad Norman Academiae Naturae Curiosorum. Augustae Vindelicorum, 1682. 1st ed., 4to, engraved frontis., 2 engraved plates and 1 engraved folding plate, decorative woodcut initials, light staining throughout, cont. calf, worn, corners and part of backstrip missing, joints weak. Deighton 3-257 1983 £150

SCHROETER, J. S.   Ueber den innern Bau der See- und Einiger Auslandischen Erd- und Fluss-schnecken. Frankfort, 1783. 5 plates, 4to, half-calf (worn). Some light waterstaining. Bookplate. Wheldon 160-1226 1983 £35

SCHUBERT, FRANZ   Duo (en La) pour Piano et Violon. Vienna, Diabelli, (1851). First edition. Engraved title, engraved music. Salloch 387-209 1983 $75

SCHUBERT, FRANZ   Das Meer Erglaenzte Weit Hinaus. Vienna, Tobias Haslinger, n.d. Engraved title and music. 3 leaves, folio, new wraps. Salloch 387-214 1983 $30

SCHUBERT, FRANZ   Rondeau Brillant pour Pianoforte et Violon. Vienna, Artaria, (1827). First edition. Engraved title and 18 pp. engraved music. Salloch 387-211 1983 $20

SCHUBERT, FRANZ   Die Schoene Muellerin. Vienna, Diabelli, (ca. 1850). Each part with lithograph title in two colors. Contents tables bound in behind parts III and IV. Folio, new wrs. Some pages foxed. Salloch 387-215 1983 $90

SCHUBERT, G. H. VON   Naturgeschichte des Pflanzenreichs. Esslingen, 1876. Third edition, 53 double-page coloured plates containing 601 figures, small folio, original decorated boards. Trifle loose, else a good copy. Wheldon 160-1567 1983 £100

SCHUBRING, PAUL   Die italienische Plastik des Quattrocenta. Berlin-Neubabelsberg, 1915. 4to, boards, 1/4 cloth, 11 tipped-in color plates, 370 text illus. Ars Libri SB 26-219 1983 $25

SCHUCK, H.   Medieval Stories. Sands & Co., 1902. Frontis., decorated title, 9 plates, vignettes & pictorial endpapers. Bull pictorial cloth. Nice. Greer 40-197 1983 £25

SCHULL, JOSEPH   The Far Distant Ships. Ottawa: National Defence. King's Printer, 1950. 22cm. 30 illus. and 35 maps and diagrams (some in colour). Blue cloth. Fine. McGahern 53-188 1983 $50

SCHULLIAN, DOROTHY   Music and Medicine. New York, 1948. First edition. 8vo. Orig. binding. Fye H-3-499 1983 $25

SCHULT, FRIEDRICH   Ernst Barlach: Das plastische Werk. Hamburg: Hauswedell, 1960. 400 illus. 4to. Cloth. Edition limited to 600 copies. Ars Libri 32-20 1983 $500

SCHULTE, J. F. VON   Die Geschichte der Quellen und Literatur des Canonischen Rechts von Gratian bis auf die Gegenwart. Graz, Austria, 1956. 3 vols. bound in 2. Boswell 7-37 1983 $125

SCHULTZ, C. H.   Sur la circulation et sur les vaisseaux laticiferes dans les plantes. Paris, 1839. 23 plates, 4to, cloth, a little foxing. Wheldon 160-1568 1983 £12

SCHULZE, F. E.   Account of the Indian Triaxonia. Calcutta, 1902. 23 plates, 4to, wrappers (trifle dustsoiled). Wheldon 160-1338 1983 £20

SCHULZE, JOHANN GOTTFRIED   Dissertatio inauguralis medica. De masticatione foliorum tabaci... Halle, 1744. First edition. Small 4to. Boards. Kraus 164-238 1983 $540

SCHUMANN, ROBERT   Drei Gedichte von Emanuel Geibel. Berlin, Bote & Bock, n.d. (1841). First edition. Engraved title in decorative frame. Folio, unbound. Salloch 387-221 1983 $90

SCHUMANN, ROBERT   Lieder und Gesaenge. Leipzig, F. Whistling, (before 1844). Engraved music, lithographed title in two colors. Folio, unbound. Salloch 387-222 1983 $60

SCHUMANN, ROBERT   The life of Robert Schumann told in his letters. London: Bentley, 1890. First edition in English. 2 vols. 8vo. Orig. olive green cloth. Spines just a trifle dull. Very good set. Ximenes 63-336 1983 $35

SCHUMANN, ROBERT   Myrthen. Leipzig, Kistner, 1840. First edition. Engraved music, plate #1290. Lithographed title page with green decorative frame. Separate dedication plate "Seiner geliebten Braut". First edition. Salloch 387-216 1983 $200

SCHUMANN, ROBERT   Sechs Gedichte. Hamburg & Leipzig, Schuberth, (1842). Folio, engraved music. Unbound. First issue. Salloch 387-219 1983 $45

SCHUMANN, ROBERT   Zwoelf Gedichte von Justinus Kerner. Leipzig, C.A. Kelmm, n.d. (after 1841). Early edition, printed from the orig. plates. Folio, lithographed title pages with brown decorative frame. Salloch 387-220 1983 $90

SCHUMANN, VICTOR   Ueber ein neues Verfahren Zur Herstellung ultraviolettempfindlicher Platten. Vienna, 1893. Offprint. 8vo. Boards. Wrappers. With presentation inscription on wrapper. Gurney 90-139 1983 £50

SCHURER, F. L.   Historia Praecipuorum Experimentorum circa Analysis Chemicam Aeris Atmosphaerici... Strasburg: J.H. Heitz, 1789. 4to. Boards. Gurney 90-107 1983 £70

SCHURMEYER, WALTER   Hieronymus Bosch. Munchen: R. Piper, 1923. 57 hinged collotype plates. Large 4to. Boards, 1/4 cloth. Ars Libri 32-53 1983 $50

SCHURZ, CARL   The New South. N.Y., 1885. First edition. Orig. wrap. Argosy 716-504 1983 $35

SCHUSTER, R. M.   The Hepaticae and Anthocerotae of North America. New York, 1966-80. Vols. 1-4, royal 8vo, cloth. Wheldon 160-1891 1983 £214

SCHWAB, GEORGE   Tribes of the Liberian Hinterland. Cambridge: Peabody Museum, 1947. 111 plates. Folding map in rear pocket. 4to. Wrappers. Slightly worn. Ars Libri 34-740 1983 $125

SCHWARTZ, DELMORE   The World is a Wedding. Norfolk, Conn., 1948. First edition. Very nice. Rota 230-529 1983 £30

SCHWARTZ, HARRY W.   This Book Collecting Racket. Chicago: Normandie House, 1937. First collected edition, revised. 8vo. Cloth. Oak Knoll 48-346 1983 $40

SCHWARTZ, J. VAN DER POORTEN   God's Fool. London: Richard Bentley & Son, 1892. First edition. 3 vols. Orig. cloth. Edges slightly worn. Covers of Vol. two rather soiled. Good. MacManus 279-3419 1983 $185

SCHWARTZ, J. VAN DER POORTEN   God''s Fool. Richard Bentley, 1892. First edition. 3 vols. Half titles, 4pp. ads. vol. III. Orig. dark blue cloth, slight damage to lower outer corner of front board vol. I, otherwise very good. Patterned edges. Jarndyce 31-806 1983 £54

SCHWARTZ, J. VAN DER POORTEN   The Greater Glory. London: Bentley, 1894. First edition. 3 vols. Orig. decorated cloth. A shabby ex-library copy (labels removed from front covers; darkened, spines torn) of one of the few examples of an art nouveau binding design on a three-decker. MacManus 279-3421 1983 $135

SCHWARTZ, J. VAN DER POORTEN   The Greater Glory. Richard Bentley, 1894. First edition. 3 vols. Half title, 4pp. ads. vol. III. Orig. black cloth, blocked with a butterfly design in bronze. Edges patterned with the same design. Very slight wear to heads of spines. Very good. Jarndyce 31-807 1983 £68

SCHWARTZ, J. VAN DER POORTEN   The Healers. London: Archibald Constable & Co., Ltd., 1906. First edition. Orig. cloth. With an ALS, 4 pages, 8vo, De Zonheuvel, Doorn, no year, from author to an unnamed gentleman, tipped in at the front. Small spot on front cover. Fine. MacManus 279-3422 1983 $85

SCHWARTZ, J. VAN DER POORTEN   Joost Avelingh. N.Y.: D. Appleton & Co., 1894. First American edition. Orig. decorated cloth. Edges and corners slightly worn. Covers a trifle soiled. Signature (in pencil) on front free endpaper. Bookseller's stamp. Good. MacManus 279-3423 1983 $25

SCHWARTZ, J. VAN DER POORTEN   My Lady Nobody. London: Richard Bentley & Son, 1895. First edition. Orig. embossed cloth. Fine. MacManus 279-3424 1983 $85

SCHWARTZ, J. VAN DER POORTEN   An Old Maid's Love. London: Richard Bentley and Son, 1891. First edition. 3 vols. Orig. decorated cloth. Edges a bit worn. Endpapers a little soiled. Bookplates and signatures of a previous owner. Very good. MacManus 279-3425 1983 $250

SCHWARTZ, J. VAN DER POORTEN   An Old Maid's Love. Richard Bentley, 1892. First edition. 3 vols. 2pp. ads. vol. III. Orig. dark blue cloth, slightly rubbed, blocked with petal pattern in light green. Some inner hinges cracked. A good set. Jarndyce 31-805 1983 £48

SCHWARTZ, J. VAN DER POORTEN   The Sin of Joost Avelingh. London: Remington & Co., 1889. First edition. 2 vols. Orig. decorated cloth. Endpapers browned. Fine. MacManus 279-3426 1983 $365

SCHWARTZ, J. VAN DER POORTEN   Some Women I Have Known. London: William Heinemann, 1901. First edition. Orig. cloth. Blind-stamped presentation copy. Spine slightly faded. Endpapers foxed. Very good. MacManus 279-3427 1983 $50

SCHWARZ, ARTURO   The Complete Works of Marcel Duchamp. New York: Abrams, n.d. 765 illus. (75 color). Small folio. Cloth. Dust jacket. Ars Libri 32-171 1983 $200

SCHWARZ, IGNAZ   Geschichte der Apotheken und des Apothekerwesens in Wien. Wien, 1917-1930. Numerous plates & text illus. 3 vols. Tall 8vo, 1/2 cloth. Argosy 713-486 1983 $150

SCHWEEGER-HEFEL, ANNEMARIE   Afrikanische Bronzen. Wien: Wolfram, 1948. 48 plates. Large 8vo. Boards. Dust jacket. Ars Libri 34-741 1983 $20

SCHWEINFURTH, GEORG   The Heart of Africa. London: Sampson Low, Marston, etc. Third edition. 2 vols. 8vo. Folding map. 16 plates. Orig. red pictorial cloth. Spines slightly faded. Adelson Africa-125 1983 $80

SCHWEINFURTH, GEORG   Im Herzen von Afrika. Leipzig: Brockhaus, 1922. Fourth edition. Illus. Large 4to. Boards, 1/4 cloth. Paper browned. Ars Libri 34-742 1983 $50

SCHWIMMER, ROSIKA   Tisza Tales. N.Y.: Doubleday, (1928). Stated first edition. 4to. Dust wrapper. 8 full-page color plates. Full-page and smaller black & whites. Fine. Aleph-bet 8-205 1983 $60

SCLATER, EDWARD   Consensus Veterum. Printed by Henry Hills...for Him and Matt. Turner, 1686. First edition, 4to, wrapper, a very good copy. Fenning 61-393 1983 £16.50

SCLATER, P. L.   Challenger Voyage. Report on the Birds. 1881. 4to, cloth, good ex-library copy with a few stamps. Text only. Wheldon 160-572 1983 £25

SCOBEE, BARRY   The Story of Fort Davis, Jeff Davis County and the Davis Mountains. N.p., 1936. Orig. pictorial wrappers. Some wear. 1st ed. Quite scarce. Jenkins 153-608 1983 $45

SCOBLE, JOHN   The rise and fall of Krugerism.
New York: Frederick Stokes, 1900. 8vo. Orig. cloth. Rubbed.
Adelson Africa-221 1983 $20

SCOT, REGINALD   The Discovery of Witchcraft. London:
Printed for Andrew Clark, 1665. Folio. Cont. sheep, repaired.
Woodcuts in text. Lacks leaf before title. Gurney 90-108 1983
£350

SCOTT, CLEMENT   From "The Bells" to "King Arthur." A
critical record of the first-night productions at the Lyceum Theatre
from 1871 to 1895. London: John Macqueen, 1897. 8vo, original
light blue buckram cloth. First edition. With a mounted frontis.
photograph and numerous other illus. This was the author's own copy,
and has his bookplates; he has inserted a number of further illus.
A nice copy. Ximenes 64-481 1983 $40

SCOTT, EMMETT J.   Scott's Official History of the American
Negro in the World War... N.P., (1919). 1st ed. Illus. 8vo. Lacks
part of back endleaf. Morrill 288-554 1983 $22.50

SCOTT, EVELYN   A Calendar of Sin. New York: Cape,
(1931). 2 vols. 1st ed. Orig. cloth, gilt, dj. Fine set in
lightly used dj and uncommon thus. Jenkins 155-1120 1983 $30

SCOTT, FRANKLIN WILLIAM   Newspapers and Periodicals of Illinois
1814-1879. Springfield, IL: Illinois State Historical Library, 1910.
Illus., cloth, stamped name, spine sunned, couple corners bumped.
Bibliographical series, Vol. 1. Collections of the Ill. St. Hist.
Lib. Vol. 6. Revised and enlarged edition. King 46-107 1983 $35

SCOTT, H.   In the High Yemen. London, 1942.
Maps and numerous plates, some folding. 8vo. Orig. cloth. Good.
Edwards 1044-630 1983 £22

SCOTT, HUGH STOWELL   Barlasch of the Guard. London: Smith,
Elder & Co., 1903. First edition. Orig. cloth. Edges very slightly
worn. Spine a trifle faded. Bookplate. Very good. MacManus 279-
3711 1983 $50

SCOTT, HUGH STOWELL   Dross. Chicago: Stone, 1899. First
edition. Orig. decorated cloth. MacManus 279-3713 1983 $40

SCOTT, HUGH STOWELL   Flotsam. London: Longmans, 1896. First
edition. Illus. Orig. cloth. Fine. MacManus 279-3714 1983 $35

SCOTT, HUGH STOWELL   From One Generation to Another. London:
Smith, Elder, 1892. First edition. 2 vols. Orig. green cloth.
Covers slightly soiled. MacManus 279-3715 1983 $125

SCOTT, HUGH STOWELL   From Wisdom Court. London: William
Heinemann, 1893. First edition. 30 illus. by E. Courboin. Orig.
pictorial cloth. Spine and covers soiled. Corners bumped. Bookseller's stamp. Endpapers a little browned. Good. MacManus 279-
3716 1983 $35

SCOTT, HUGH STOWELL   In Kedar's Tents. London: Smith, Elder,
1897. First edition. Orig. cloth. Inner hinges cracked. Extremities
of spine very slightly rubbed. Very good. MacManus 279-3717 1983
$45

SCOTT, HUGH STOWELL   In Kedar's Tents. Smith, Elder, 1897.
First edition. Half title, 4 pp. ads. Orig. blue cloth. Very good.
Jarndyce 31-812 1983 £24

SCOTT, HUGH STOWELL   The Last Hope. London: Smith, Elder,
1904. First edition. Orig. cloth. MacManus 279-3720 1983 $20

SCOTT, HUGH STOWELL   The Money-Spinner. London, Smith, Elder
and Co., 1896. First ed., 12 illus. by Arthur Rackham, orig. cloth,
spine quite worn and spotted, rear hinge cracked, bookplate, good.
MacManus 280-4309 1983 $85

SCOTT, HUGH STOWELL   The Phantom Future. London: Bentley,
1888. First edition. 2 vols. Orig. cloth. Front inner hinge
cracked in vol. one. Slightly shaken and worn. With Hugh Walpole's
Brackenburn bookplate. Very good. MacManus 279-3722 1983 $125

SCOTT, HUGH STOWELL   Prisoners and Captives. Richard Bentley,
1891. First edition. 3 vols. Half titles, orig. light blue cloth,
slightly rubbed. Jarndyce 31-811 1983 £56

SCOTT, HUGH STOWELL   The Slave of the Lamp. London: Smith,
Elder, 1892. First edition. 2 vols. Orig. cloth. Very good. Mac-
Manus 279-3723 1983 $250

SCOTT, HUGH STOWELL   Suspense. London: Richard Bentley &
Son, 1890. First edition. 3 vols. Orig. decorated cloth. Former
owner's signature on title-page of first volume. Very good. Mac-
Manus 279-3725 1983 $225

SCOTT, HUGH STOWELL   The Velvet Glove. London, Smith,
Elder, 1901. 8vo, orig. cloth gilt, bookplate; fine. First edition.
Ravenstree 96-185 1983 $75

SCOTT, HUGH STOWELL   The Velvet Glove. London: Smith, Elder
& Co., 1901. First edition. Orig. blue cloth. Spine and covers
slightly worn. Rear inner hinge cracking. Good. MacManus 279-
3728 1983 $45

SCOTT, HUGH STOWELL   With Edged Tools. London: Smith, Elder,
1894. First edition. 3 vols. Orig. cloth. Covers a bit worn.
MacManus 279-3729 1983 $125

SCOTT, JAMES   A History of the Life and Death of
John, Warl of Gowrie. Edinburgh, 1818. Large 8vo, uncut, orig.
pebble cloth, paper label. Bickersteth 77-167 1983 £25

SCOTT, JAMES   Recollections of a Naval Life.
Richard Bentley, 1834. First edition, 3 vols. Half blue calf,
lacking one label. Jarndyce 30-1128 1983 £36

SCOTT, JAMES GEORGE   Burma As It Was... London, 1886.
Sm.8vo. Orig. cloth. Good. Edwards 1044-628 1983 £15

SCOTT, JAMES GEORGE   The Burman: His Life and Notions.
Macmillan and Co., 1882. First edition. 2 vols. Orig. cloth. Hinges
cracked. Covers a little scratched. Previous owner's signature on
front free endpapers. Good. MacManus 280-5689 1983 $50

SCOTT, JOB   Journal of the Life, Travels and Gospel
Labours of... New York: Isaac Collins, 1797. First edition. Full
calf (hinges broken). Very good. Felcone 20-158 1983 $30

SCOTT, JOB   Journal of the Life, Travels and Gospel
Labours of That Faithful Servant and Minister of Christ, Job Scott.
New York, 1797. 1st ed. Small 8vo, contemporary calf, leather
label. Rubbed, hinges cracked, lacks front blank endleaves. Morrill
286-429 1983 $25

SCOTT, JOB   Journal of the Life, Travels and
Gospel Labours of...Job Scott. New-York: Isaac Collins, 1797.
Full calf (hinges broken). First edition. Felcone 22-218 1983
$30

SCOTT, JOB   Journal of the Life and Travels of...
New-York printed, and Dublin reprinted by John Gough, 1798. First
Irish edition, large 12mo, recent boards, v.g. Fenning 60-372 1983
£18.50

SCOTT, JOHN   Critical essays on some of the poems,
of several English poets. London: Phillips, 1785. First edition.
8vo. Cont. tree calf, spine gilt. Upper cover detached. Lacks a
half-title. Ximenes 63-249 1983 $225

SCOTT, JOHN   The Indiana Gazetteer, or Topographical
Dictionary... Centreville, 1826. Stitched. Laid in a blue cloth
box. Very good. Reese 18-599 1983 $1,100

SCOTT, JOHN   The Indiana Gazetteer, or Topographical
Dictionary. Indianapolis: Douglass and Maguire, 1833. Orig. cloth,
leather label. Label slightly chipped, and short worm trail in rear
hinge. Reese 19-504 1983 $275

SCOTT, JOHN   A Sermon Preached before...the Lord
Mayor, and Court of Alermen, and the Guild-Hall Chappel, the 16th
of December, 1683. Printed by Ralph Holt, for Robert Horn and Walter
Kettilby, 1684. First edition, 4to, wrapper. Fenning 62-325 1983
£24.50

SCOTT, JOHN   The staggering state of the Scots
statesmen... Edinburgh: Ruddiman, etc., 1754. First edition.
12mo. Cont. sheep. Worn. Some marginal worming and stains at
the beginning. Ximenes 63-545 1983 $100

SCOTT, JOHN   A visit to Paris in 1814. (With:)
Paris revisited, in 1815... London: Longman, etc., 1816. Fourth
edition for the first title, second edition for the second title.
2 vols. 8vo. Cont. half calf, silt, spines gilt. Ximenes 63-634
1983 $50

SCOTT, LYDIA   A Marriage In High Life. London: Henry
Colburn, 1828. First edition. 2 vols. Cont. half-calf with marbled
boards and endpapers. Spine ends and cover edges worn. Bookplate.
Very good. MacManus 280-4591 1983 $225

SCOTT, MICHAEL   The Cruise of the Midge. Edinburgh:
Blackwood, 1836. First edition. 2 vols. 12mo. Orig. cloth. Binding
"B." Michael Sadleir's copy with his bookplate and the bookplate of
Ralph Sanders. Wear at the ends of each spine. Very good. MacManus
280-4592 1983 $125

SCOTT, MICHAEL   The Cruise of the Midge. In Two Volumes.
Edinburgh: Blackwood; London: Cadell, 1836. 1st ed., 8vo, original
decorated cloth, spines gilt. Uncut copy. Wear to upper edges
of spines, but a very clean copy. Trebizond 18-87 1983 $125

SCOTT, MICHAEL   The Cruise of the Midge. Blackwood and
T. Cadell, 1836. First edition, 2 vols. Half titles. Orig. dark
green cloth, gilt spine. Sl. rubbing, v.g. Jarndyce 30-542 1983
£48

SCOTT, MICHAEL   Exposito super auctorum spherae.
Bologna: Justinianus de Ruberia, 16 September 1495. Large woodcut
printer's device at end and one woodcut initials, both with cont.
hand-coloring. Small 4to. Modern limp vellum. First edition.
From the library of Harrison D. Horblit. Kraus 164-163 1983 $4,500

SCOTT, MICHAEL   Tom Cringle's Log. Edinburgh: Blackwood
& Cadell, 1833. First edition. 2 vols. Orig. boards (backstrips
missing or repaired). Inner hinges cracked although cords still intact. Bookplate. In a cloth case. Good. MacManus 280-4594 1983
$85

SCOTT, MICHAEL   Tom Cringle's Log. Edinburgh: William
Blackwood, 1833. First edition, first binding. 2 vols. Orig. cloth.
Signatures on front flyleaves. Parsons-Ewing copy. In a half-morocco
slipcase. Very fine. MacManus 280-4593 1983 $250

SCOTT, MICHAEL   Tom Cringle's Log. Blackwood and T.
Cadell, 1833. First edition. 2 vols. Half green calf, lacking one
label. Jarndyce 30-541 1983 £25

SCOTT, NATALIE   Old Plantation Houses in Louisiana.
New York, 1927. First edition. Illustrated from drawings by
William P. Spratling. Large 8vo. Morrill 290-240 1983 $27.50

SCOTT, ROBERT K.   Special Message of His Excellency.
Columbia, 1872. Dbd. First edition. Ginsberg 46-705 1983 $75

SCOTT, TEMPLE   Book Sales of 1896 & 1897. George
Bell, 1897-8. Half titles, 2 pp ads. vol. I. Untrimmed. Orig. blue
cloth, t.e.g., v.g. Jarndyce 31-97 1983 £12.50

SCOTT, TEMPLE   Lord Chesterfield and his Letters to
His Sons. Indianapolis: Meridian Bookshop, 1929. 8vo. Tall 8vo.
Cloth-backed boards. Limited to 200 numbered and signed copies.
Oak Knoll 48-347 1983 $20

SCOTT, TEMPLE   Oliver Goldsmith, Bibliographically
and Biographically considered... New York: The Bowling Green
Press, 1928. First edition. 4to. Black cloth with gilt cover
design, t.e.g., others uncut. Colored frontis. and 84 other illus.
Limited to 1000 numbered copies. Oak Knoll 48-302 1983 $90

SCOTT, TEMPLE   Oliver Goldsmith Bibliographically
and Biographically considered. New York, Bowling Green Press, 1928.
4to, orig. cloth gilt, now bit worn, shaken. One of 750 copies for
sale; with presentation inscription from W.M. Elkins. The first
edition. Ravenstree 94-144 1983 $87.50

SCOTT, WALTER   The Abbot. Edinburgh, Longman et al..
London and Constable. Edinburgh, 1820. 3 vols., 8vo, cont. quarter
vellum, label worn and chipped, minor spotting, genuine first issue
titles with five-line imprint. First edition. Ravenstree 96-187
1983 $75

SCOTT, WALTER   The Abbot. Edinburgh, 1820. First
edition, with the half-titles in the second and third vols. only,
3 vols., large 12mo, half brown calf, gilt spines, with green labels,
t.e.g. Fenning 60-373 1983 £25

SCOTT, WALTER   Anne of Geierstein. Edinburgh, Cadell,
1829. 3 vols., 8vo, cont. quarter vellum, bit worn and chipped,
few minor tears, clear tear to leaf H8 volume 3 with no text lost,
small mend not touching text. First edition. Ravenstree 96-188 1983
$72.50

SCOTT, WALTER   Anne of Geierstein. Edinburgh, for
Cadell and Co, etc, 1829. First edition. 3 vols. Large 12mo, half-
titles, final advert. leaf in vol. III. Orig. boards (new cloth
spines), uncut. Small tear in two leaves. Hannas 69-176 1983 £25

SCOTT, WALTER   The Antiquary. Edinburgh, Ballantyne et
al., 1816. 3 vols., 8vo, cont. half vellum gilt, bit worn, spine
labels rubbed, few signatures loose in second volume, minor spotting,
decent set. First edition. Ravenstree 96-189 1983 $135

SCOTT, WALTER   The Antiquary. Edinburgh: by James
Ballantyne and Co., for Archibald Constable, etc, 1816. First
edition. 3 vols. Large 12mo, three half- and fly-titles. Cont.
straight grained blue morocco, blind-tooled, gilt spine. Occasional
slight stains. Hannas 69-178 1983 £65

SCOTT, WALTER   The Antiquary. Phila.: T.B. Peterson
& Brothers, n.d. Peterson's Cheap edition. 8vo. Orig. pictorial
yellow wrappers. A little dust-soiled. Very good. MacManus 280-
4595 1983 $20

SCOTT, WALTER   Autobiography. Phila.: Cary & Lea, 1831.
First American edition. Frontis. port. Orig. cloth with paper label
on spine. Covers worn. Foxing throughout. Good. MacManus 280-4596
1983 $50

SCOTT, WALTER   Chronicles of The Canongate. Edinburgh:
Printed for Cadell & Co., 1827. First edition. 2 vols. Orig. boards
with paper labels. Vol. I, pp. 203-204 with cancelled reading; Vol.
II, pp.63-64 uncancelled; pp. 65-66 cancelled, with second reading.
Spines worn. Very good. MacManus 280-4597 1983 $200

SCOTT, WALTER   Chronicles of the Canongate. Edinburgh,
for Cadell and Co, etc, 1827-28. First editions. 5 vols. 8vo,
first series in later paper boards, second series in orig. boards,
all with printed labels, uncut. Hannas 69-178 1983 £65

SCOTT, WALTER   Chronicles of the Canongate. Edinburgh,
Cadell et al., 1827. 2 vols., 8vo, cont. quarter vellum gilt, labels
bit rubbed, minor spotting. First edition. Ravenstree 96-190 1983
$75

SCOTT, WALTER   Chronicles of the Canongate. Edinburgh:
Printed for Cadell & Co., 1828. First edition. Second Series. 3 vols.
Orig. boards with paper spine labels. Back cover of Vol. I detached.
All spines and labels worn and chipped. Covers soiled. With the
armorial bookplates of George Sowerby. In a slightly soiled cloth box.
Good. MacManus 280-4598 1983 $125

SCOTT, WALTER   Chronicles of the Canongate. Edinburgh,
Cadell et al., 1828. 3 vols., 8vo, cont. quarter vellum gilt, spine
labels rubbed, few signatures sprung, some leaves loose, minor
spotting, fair set. First edition. Ravenstree 96-191 1983 $75

SCOTT, WALTER   Count Robert of Paris. Phila.: T.B.
Peterson & Brothers, n.d. Peterson's Cheap edition. Orig. pictorial
wrappers (a bit frayed). Fine. MacManus 280-4599 1983 $20

SCOTT, WALTER   Familiar Letters. Edinburgh: David Douglas, 1894. First edition. 2 vols. Illus. Orig. cloth. Fine. MacManus 280-4600 1983 $45

SCOTT, WALTER   Familiar Letters. Edinburgh: David Douglas. 1894. Half title, front. and folding map vol. I; 20 pp ads. vol. II. Orig. brown cloth, v.g. Jarndyce 30-1130 1983 £20

SCOTT, WALTER   The Fortunes of Nigel. Edinburgh: Printed for Archibald Constable and Co., 1822. First edition. 3 vols. Orig. cloth-backed boards with paper spine labels. Spines slightly faded, labels a bit chipped and worn. Covers a little worn. Spines a bit worn and torn. In a rather worn imitation leather box with paper label. Very good. MacManus 280-4601 1983 $150

SCOTT, WALTER   The Fortunes of Nigel. Edinburgh, Constable et al., 1822. 3 vols., 8vo, cont. half vellum gilt, spine labels rubbed, few leaves loose, minor spotting but decent set. First edition. Ravenstree 96-192 1983 $83

SCOTT, WALTER   Fortunes of Nigel. Phila.: T.B. Peterson & Brothers, n.d. Peterson's Cheap edition. Orig. pictorial wrappers (a little dusty and slightly torn). Very good. MacManus 280-4602 1983 $20

SCOTT, WALTER   Guy Mannering. Phila.: T.B. Peterson & Brothers, n.d. Peterson's Cheap edition. Orig. pictorial wrappers (a bit frayed at edges). Very good. MacManus 280-4603 1983 $20

SCOTT, WALTER   The Highland Widow. Phila.: T.B. Peterson & Brothers, n.d. Peterson's Cheap edition. Orig. pictorial wraps. (a little dust-soiled & worn). Very good. MacManus 280-4605 1983 $20

SCOTT, WALTER   Halidon Hall. Edinburgh: Archibald Constable & Co., 1822. First edition. Cont. 3/4 calf & marbled bds. Bookplate. Very good. MacManus 280-4604 1983 $85

SCOTT, WALTER   Halidon Hill; a Dramatic Sketch, from Scottish History. Edinburgh: A. Constable and Co., 1822. First edition. 8vo. Orig. grey wrappers, uncut. With 4 pp. (of 4) at beginning and 6 pp. (of 8) at end, of publishers ads. Spine a little defective. Traylen 94-708 1983 £20

SCOTT, WALTER   Harold the Dauntless. Edinburgh: 1817. First edition, uncut. Orig. drab boards, paper spine, label, sl. rubbed. Very good. Jarndyce 31-894 1983 £42

SCOTT, WALTER   Ivanhoe. Edinburgh: Constable, 1820. 3 vols. 1st ed., 2nd state of 1st vol. as usual. Orig. paper-backed paper-covered boards, labels, uncut. Recased with new end papers, spine paper of first two vols. partially restored, orig. labels remounted on two vols.; one label replaced. Internally a clean set complete with all three half-titles, and very scarce uncut. Jenkins 155-1121 1983 $300

SCOTT, WALTER   Ivanhoe. Edinburgh, Constable, 1820. 3 vols., 8vo, cont. quarter vellum, boards, rubbed, few signatures sprung, complete with half titles. First edition, first state. Ravenstree 96-194 1983 $125

SCOTT, WALTER   Ivanhoe. New York: The Limited Editions Club, 1940. 2 vols. Chain mail finish cloth. 1 of 1500 numbered copies, printed at the Marchbanks Press, and signed by the illustrator, Allen Lewis. A fine set. Jenkins 155-818 1983 $35

SCOTT, WALTER   The Journal...from the Original ms. at Abbotsford. Edinburgh: David Douglas, 1890. First edition, half titles, front. port. vol. I. 20 pp ads. vol. I. Orig. brown cloth. Jarndyce 30-1129 1983 £22

SCOTT, WALTER   Kenilworth. Edinburgh, Constable et al., 1821. 3 vols., 8vo, without half titles or ads in new boards, little rubbed; text is second state of the first edition. First edition. Ravenstree 96-195 1983 $95

SCOTT, WALTER   The Lay of the Last Minstrel. 1805. First 8vo edition, cont., complete in spite of pagination jump, 8vo, later half calf, inscirption on half title, fine otherwise. Fenning 60-374 1983 £10.50

SCOTT, WALTER   Letters on Demonology and Witchcraft, Addressed to J.G. Lockhart, Esq. London, 1830. Engraved frontis. Full polished calf, spine and dentelles gilt. Bookplate removed. Hinges slightly rubbed. First edition, extra-illus. with twelve hand-colored Cruikshank plates. A fine copy. Felcone 21-27 1983 $150

SCOTT, WALTER   Lives of the Novelists. Paris, Galignani, 1825. First collected edition, 2 vols. 2 vols. bound as one. Half calf, maroon label, v.g. Jarndyce 31-895 1983 £32

SCOTT, WALTER   The Lord of the Isles. Edinburgh, Black, 1862. Re-issue. Illus. by numerous engrs. by Birket Foster & John Gilbert engr'd by Edmund Evans & J.W. Whymper. Blue morocco grain cloth gilt, a.e.g. Extremities sl. rubbed, bkstrip faded with sl. wear top/bottom, vg. Hodgkins 27-322 1983 £15

SCOTT, WALTER   Marmion: A Tale of Flodden Field. Edinburgh: J. Ballantyne & Co., 1808. First edition. Half-title. 4to. Cont. calf, gilt border, neatly rebacked with orig. spine preserved. Traylen 94-710 1983 £25

SCOTT, WALTER   Marmion; A Tale of Flodden Field. London: Printed by J. M'Creery,...For Archibald Constable & Co., 1810. Fifth edition. Cont. 3/4 calf & marbled boards. Bookplates. Covers a bit rubbed. Slight foxing. Very good. MacManus 280-4607 1983 $45

SCOTT, WALTER   The Monastery. Edinburgh: Printed for Longman, Hurst, Rees, Orme & Brown, 1820. First edition. 3 vols. Orig. boards with paper labels on spines. Former owner's signature on front covers. Spines a little worn. Very good. MacManus 280-4608 1983 $200

SCOTT, WALTER   The Monastery. Edinburgh, Longmans et al., 1820. 3 vols., 8vo, cont. quarter vellum, boards, front hinge of first volume splitting, bit rubbed and worn, complete with all half titles. First edition. Ravenstree 96-196 1983 $65

SCOTT, WALTER   The Monastery. Phila.: T.B. Peterson & Brothers, n.d. Peterson's Cheap edition. Orig. pictorial wrappers. A bit dusty. Fine. MacManus 280-4609 1983 $20

SCOTT, WALTER   Peveril of the Peak. Edinburgh: Archibald Constable & Co., 1822. First edition. 4 vols. Cont. 3/4 calf & marbled boards. Bookplates. Covers a bit rubbed. Very good. MacManus 280-4610 1983 $185

SCOTT, WALTER   Peveril of the Peak. Edinburgh, for Archibald Constable and Co, etc, 1822. First edition. 4 vols. 8vo, errata slip in vol. III. Orig. boards, printed labels, in cloth box. Hannas 69-179 1983 £75

SCOTT, WALTER   Peveril of the Peak. Edinburgh, Constable, 1822. 4 vols., 8vo, later half calf gilt, boards, little worn, joints rubbed, but good set. First edition, first state, and complete with all half titles. Ravenstree 96-197 1983 $90

SCOTT, WALTER   Peveril of the Peak. Edinburgh, 1822. First edition, 4 vols., calf, rebacked. K Books 301-165 1983 £30

SCOTT, WALTER   Peveril of the Peak. Edinburgh, for Archibald Constable and Co, etc, 1822. Half-titles, errata slip, cont. calf, (lacks one label). A very good set. Hannas 69-180 1983 £20

SCOTT, WALTER   Peveril of the Peak. Phila.: T.B. Peterson & Brothers, n.d. Peterson's Cheap edition. Orig. pictorial wrappers. Spine of wrappers slightly torn. Near-fine. MacManus 280-4615 1983 $20

SCOTT, WALTER   The Pirate. Edinburgh, Constable, 1822. 3 vols., 8vo, cont. quarter vellum, boards, bit rubbed, spine labels reversed on second and third vols., page 17 of second volume in second state, decent set. First edition. Ravenstree 96-198 1983 $55

SCOTT, WALTER   Quentin Durward. Edinburgh, Constable, 1823. 3 vols., 8vo, cont. quarter vellum, boards, bit rubbed, complete with half titles. First edition. Ravenstree 96-199 1983 $87.50

SCOTT, WALTER   Quentin Durward. Edinburgh: Archibald
Constable & Co., 1823. First edition. 3 vols. Full blue calf, gilt,
marbled endpapers. Spines a bit rubbed. Bookplates. With the ticket
of Ingalton, Bookseller & Stationer, Eton, inside the front cover of
Vol. I. MacManus 280-4612 1983 $150

SCOTT, WALTER   Quentin Durward. Phila.: T.B. Peterson
& Brothers, n.d. Peterson's Cheap edition. Orig pictorial yellow
wrappers. Fine. MacManus 280-4614 1983 $20

SCOTT, WALTER   Redgauntlet. Edinburgh, 1824. 12mo.
Boards, leather spine, leather labels. 3 vols. With all half-titles
present. Little rubbing to the bindings, mainly a fine set. In Our
Time 156-688 1983 $100

SCOTT, WALTER   Redgauntlet, a Tale of the Eighteenth
Century. Edinburgh: Constable, 1824. 3 vols. 1st ed. Orig.
paper-backed paper-covered boards, uncut, no labels. Neatly rebacked,
else a fine set, complete with half-titles. Jenkins 155-1122 1983
$85

SCOTT, WALTER   Redgauntlet, a Tale of the Eighteenth
Century. Edinburgh, Constable, 1824. 3 vols., later half calf gilt,
boards, a little worn. First edition, first state, complete with all
half titles. Ravenstree 96-200 1983 $75

SCOTT, WALTER   Rob Roy. Edinburgh, Ballantyne, 1818.
3 vols., 8vo, cont. quarter vellum, boards, bit rubbed and worn,
blank edge of one leaf in second volume torn from careless opening.
Page 193 of second volume in uncorrected state. First edition.
Ravenstree 96-201 1983 $115

SCOTT, WALTER   Rob Roy. Edinburgh, by James Ballantyne
and Co, 1818. First edition, first state, with inverted commas in
vol. II. 3 vols. Large 12mo, final blank leaf in vol. I, and all
half-titles. Modern olive morocco, gilt lettering, by Douglas
Cockerell with his bill from 1971 loosely inserted. A fine set.
An orig. end-paper kept in vol. I, with Henry Jardine's
signature. His book-plates have also been transferred to the new
binding in each volume. Hannas 69-181 1983 £60

SCOTT, WALTER   Rokeby; a Poem. Edinburgh: Ballantyne,
1813. 1st ed. Quarto. Contemporary full tan calf, extra gilt.
Fine. Jenkins 155-1123 1983 $200

SCOTT, WALTER   Rokeby; a Poem. Edinburgh: J. Ballantyne & Co., 1813. First edition. 4to. Cont. calf, gilt border,
neatly rebacked with orig. spine preserved. 8 pp. publisher's catalogue bound at end. Traylen 94-711 1983 £25

SCOTT, WALTER   St. Ronan's Well. Edinburgh, Constable,
1824. 3 vols., 8vo, cont. quarter vellum, boards, without ads, bit
worn, decent set. First edition. Ravenstree 96-202 1983 $47.50

SCOTT, WALTER   St. Ronan's Well. Edinburgh, 1824.
In three vols. First edition, wanting half-titles, 3 vols. 8vo,
cont. half calf. Fenning 6-2327 1983 £24

SCOTT, WALTER   Surgeon's Daughter. Phila.: T.B. Peterson & Brothers, n.d. Peterson's Cheap edition. Orig. pictorial
wrappers. Fine. MacManus 280-4617 1983 $20

SCOTT, WALTER   Tales of a Grandfather. Phila.: T.B.
Peterson & Brothers, n.d. Peterson's Cheap edition. First Series.
Orig. wrappers (a bit soiled and nicked). Good. MacManus 280-4618
1983 $35

SCOTT, WALTER   Tales of My Landlord. Edinburgh,
Blackwood; London, Murray, 1816. 4 vols., 8vo, cont. quarter calf
gilt (lightly rubbed, joints slightly cracked, bookplate). This has
pate 46 with the corrected numeral, signifying the second state;
the reading on page 234 also of volume 1, is in the first state.
Ravenstree 96-203 1983 $75

SCOTT, WALTER   Tales of My Landlord. Edinburgh, for
Archibald Constable and Company, 1818. First edition, first state of
vol. I. 4 vols. Large 12mo, final blank leaf in vol. II. Six
advert. leaves dated June 1818 inserted at end of vol. IV. Orig.
boards (joints cracked), printed labels, uncut, each volume in a
fleece-lined, blue, gilt, half calf book-box. Hannas 69-182 1983
£85

SCOTT, WALTER   Tales of My Landlord. Edinburgh: Blackwood, 1817. Second edition. 4 vols. Orig. boards. Paper labels.
Soiled; several covers edtached. MacManus 280-4623 1983 $35

SCOTT, WALTER   Tales of My Landlord. Edinburgh, for
Archibald Constable and Company, 1818. Lacks half-title in vol. I.
Cont. binder's cloth, printed labels. Slight marginal worming in one
gathering, another foxed. Hannas 69-183 1983 £20

SCOTT, WALTER   Tales of My Landlord. Edinburgh,
Constable, 1819. 4 vols., bound without ads in cont. quarter vellum,
boards, bit rubbed, decent set complete with all half titles.
First edition. Ravenstree 96-206 1983 $77.50

SCOTT, WALTER   Tales of My Landlord. London: Cadell,
1832. First edition. Fourth and Last Series. 4 vols. Orig. boards.
Paper labels. Spines torn. Hinges cracked. In a cloth folding box.
Very good. MacManus 280-4620 1983 $250

SCOTT, WALTER   Tales of My Landlord. Edinburgh,
Cadell, 1832. 4 vols., 8vo, cont. quarter vellum, boards, bit
rubbed, complete with all half titles and errata leaf, and with the
extra set of fly titles. First edition. Ravenstree 96-207 1983
$53.50

SCOTT, WALTER   Tales of the Crusaders. Edinburgh:
Archibald Constable; London: Hurst, Robinson, 1825. 4 vol., half-
titles, lacking the advertisements. Some hinges repaired, but a
very good copy. Trebizond 18-88 1983 $75

SCOTT, WALTER   Tales of the Crusaders. Edinburgh,
Constable, 1825. 4 vols., 8vo, cont. quarter vellum, boards,
bit rubbed, few signatures sprung and some minor pencilling in vol. 4,
complete with half titles and ads. First edition. Ravenstree 96-208
1983 $45

SCOTT, WALTER   The Vision of Don Roderick. New York:
Ezra Sargeant, 1811. 1st American ed. Orig. printed boards, uncut.
Very good copy. Jenkins 155-1124 1983 $30

SCOTT, WALTER   The Vision of Don Roderick. Edinburgh:
Printed by James Ballantyne and Co., 1811. 4to, leaf of advertisements,
t.e.g., other edges uncut, modern plain calf with marbled end papers.
First edition. Bickersteth 75-175 1983 £20

SCOTT, WALTER   Waverley. Phila.: T.B. Peterson &
Brothers, n.d. Peterson's Cheap edition. Orig. pictorial wrappers
(a bit worn & dusty). Very good. MacManus 280-4624 1983 $20

SCOTT, WALTER   The Waverley Novels. Edinburgh, 1814-
1832. 4 vols., sm. 8vo, a few of the novels in various cont. bindings,
but the majority in full modern tawny calf gilt, uncut and complete
with all half titles, fly titles and ads, and all virtually being first
state throughout. Ravenstree 96-186 1983 $1,950

SCOTT, WALTER   The Waverley Novels. N.Y.: D. Appleton
& Co., n.d. (c.1842). The Abbotsford edition. 12 vols. Large 8vo.
Profusely illus. with engravings. Orig. gilt-decorated green cloth.
Printed in England. Bookplates. Some offsetting onto free endpapers.
Some inner hinges cracking. Fine. MacManus 280-4624 1983 $350

SCOTT, WALTER   The Waverly Novels. Edinburgh, Adam
and Charles Black, n.d. 8vo. Leather, boards. 25 vols. Illus.
with over 400 photographs. Little fading to edges of the spines,
mainly a fine set. In Our Time 156-689 1983 $350

SCOTT, WALTER   The Waverley Novels. Edinburgh, 1842.
Abbotsford edition. 12 vols. Roy. 8vo. Cont. straight-grained
green morocco, 4 line gilt borders on sides, fully gilt panelled
spines with coats-of-arms, etc., inner gilt borders, edges gilt.
Engraved frontis. and vignette titles to each vol. 46 steel-engraved
plates and many hundreds of wood-engravings in the text. Traylen
94-707 1983 £180

SCOTT, WALTER   Waverley; or, 'Tis Sixty Years Since.
Edinburgh: Archibald Constable & Co., 1814. First edition. 3 vols.
Cont. 3/4 calf with leather labels. Rubbed. Hinges broken. In a
half morocco slipcase. Sound copy. MacManus 280-4625 1983 $185

SCOTT, WALTER   Woodstock; or, the Cavalier.
Edinburgh, Constable, 1826. 3 vols., 8vo, cont. quarter vellum,
boards, little foxing, minor wear, decent set complete with all
half titles. First state of the first edition. Ravenstree 96-212
1983 $77.50

SCOTT, WALTER   The Works. London: Adam & Charles Black,
1897. Victoria edition. 25 vols. 8vo. Illus. Cont. 3/4 calf &
marbled boards, marbled endpapers. Several covers slightly rubbed.
A few pages torn at top margin. Very good. MacManus 280-4628 1983
$350

SCOTT, WILLIAM BELL   Autobiographical Notes of the Life of...
N.Y.: Harper & Brothers, 1892. First American edition. 2 vols.
Illus. Spines slightly faded and worn with a few very small tears
to the edges. Front free endpaper to vol. I loose. Front inner hinge
to Vol. II weak. Bookplates. Very good. MacManus 280-4629 1983
$125

SCOTT, WILLIAM BELL   A Poet's Harvest Home. London: Elliot
Stock, Paternoster Row, 1882. First edition. Orig. vellum. Presentation copy inscribed: 'Rafe Leycester with kindest regards of the
author." Spine slightly faded. Endpapers slightly foxed. With one
small tear to the front inner hinge. Good. MacManus 280-4630 1983
$135

SCOTT, WINFIELD TOWNLEY   Biography For Traman. NY, (1937).
Signed by author, mint in dustwrapper. Quill & Brush 54-1208 1983
$50

SCOTT, WINFIELD TOWNLEY   To Marry Strangers. New York, 1945.
8vo. Cloth. This copy inscribed by poet to another poet dated
1945. Vg-fine. In Our Time 156-691 1983 $35

SCOTT, WINFIELD TOWNLEY   Wind The Clock. The Dicker Press,
Illinois, 1941. 8vo. Cloth (faded). With short inscription to
another poet by Scott on front fly dated 1942. Vg-fine copy. In
Our Time 156-690 1983 $35

SCOTT-MONCRIEFF, GEORGE   A Book of Uncommon Prayer. London,
1937. Numerous woodcuts by Robert Gibbings. Spine slightly
rubbed. Fine. Jolliffe 26-204 1983 £45

THE SCOTTISH Mist Dispel'd... London: by M.S. for Henry Overton,
1648. 4to. Quarter morocco. Heath 48-179 1983 £30

SCOTUS, MICHAEL
Please turn to
SCOTT, MICHAEL

THE SCOURGE: or Monthly Expositor. London: Printed by W. N. Jones,
for M. Jones, 1811-16. First editions of the complete first Series.
11 vols., 8vo., illus. with folding colored plates by G. Cruikshank.
Modern three quarter red mor. and cloth by the Atelier Bindery.
Some foxing, some plates reinforced. Fine. MacManus 277-1228 1983
$1500

SCOUTETTEN, H.   Memoir on the Radical Cure of Club-Foot.
Phila., 1840. First edition in English. 6 folding litho. plates. 8vo,
orig. cloth (crudely rebacked); uncut; ex-lib. Argosy 713-487 1983
$150

SCRATCHLEY, ARTHUR   Industrial Investment and Emigration...
London, 1851. Many ad. leaves. Cloth, label chipped, slight wear to
headbands, overall good. Reese 19-505 1983 $125

SCRIBE, AUGUSTE EUGENE   Piquille Alliaga: Or, The Moors under
Philip the Third of Spain. George Peirce, 1846. 8vo, 19th-century
half calf. Woodcut illustrations. Hill 165-111 1983 £21

SCRIPTURE Natural History. S.P.C.K., 1848. First edition, with 103
illus., small 8vo, orig. cloth. Preface signed "M.F.M." Fenning
61-394 1983 £9.50

SCROPE, G. P.   The Geology and Extinct Volcanos of
Central France. 1858. 2 coloured maps and 17 plates (some coloured),
8vo, cloth (neatly refixed). Wheldon 160-1471 1983 £40

SCUDDER, HORACE   The Game of Croquet. New York, 1867.
Frontis. Illus. Pictorial cloth. Slightly dampstained, but quite
good. Reese 19-506 1983 $100

SCUDDER, HORACE   James Russell Lowell, A Bibliography.
Cambridge: Riverside Press, 1901. 1st ed., 1 of 350 copies of
the large paper ed. 2 vols. Orig. linen-backed boards, labels,
wholly uncut. Fine set. Jenkins 155-1414 1983 $25

SEABURY, SAMUEL   An Alarm to the Legislature of the
Province of New York. New York: James Rivington, 1775. 3/4
morocco. Felcone 21-95 1983 $225

SEABURY, SAMUEL   Captain Henry Martin Beare (1760-1828),
His Life, Ancestry, and Descendants. NY, 1936. Pr. paper covers,
sewed. Privately printed. Argosy 716-182 1983 $35

SEABURY, SAMUEL   275 Years of East Hampton, Long
Island, NY, 1926. Illus., 4to, linen-backed boards. Argosy 716-367
1983 $27.50

SEAGER, H. W.   Natural History in Shakespeare's Time.
1896. Cloth (used). Wheldon 160-266 1983 £15

SEALE, A.   Sea Products of Mindanao and Sulu.
Philippine Jnl. of Science, 1909-16. 2 maps and 20 plates, 5 parts
in 4, royal 8vo, wrappers. Wheldon 160-333 1983 £12

SEALY, T. H.   The Porcelain Tower. London, 1841.
Frontis. 2 plates, illus. Half morocco, by J.W. Horn of Stirling with
his label. Illus. by John Leech. 8vo. Good. Edwards 1044-631 1983
£75

SEAMAN, EZRA   Essays on the Progress of Nations...
Detroit: M. Geiger & Co., Printers, 1846. Orig. full calf, worn.
Internally nice. Jenkins 152-250 1983 $50

SEARIGHT, THOMAS B.   The Old Pike. Uniontown, Pa.: Published
by the Author, 1894. First edition. Illus. Orig. cloth. Fine.
Jenkins 152-401 1983 $50

SEARS, CLARA ENDICOTT   Days of Delusion. Boston, 1924. 1st
ed. Illus. 8vo. Morrill 289-532 1983 $20

SEARS, ROBERT   Pictorial History of the American
Revolution. NY: Robert Sears, 1845. Engr. illus., maps, extra
engr. title, 8vo, 1/2 lea., usual light foxing. Argosy 710-461
1983 $25

SEASHORE, CARL E.   Elementary Experiments in Psychology.
NY: Holt, (1908), early printing. With separate envelope of Milton
Bradley's color sheets. Gach 94-643 1983 $20

SEASON of 1886-7. The Southern Pacific Company Atlantic System...
Chicago: Poole Bros., (1886). 16 printed panels with map. Colorful,
printed in at least 6 colors. Jenkins 153-105 1983 $75

THE SEASONS of the Year. Nelson, 1858. Mounted frontis., title page
vignette & 4 mounted engrs. printed in mauve each engr. within a floral
border printed in gold. Green sand grain cloth gilt, a.e.g. Some
thumbing & stains on a few pp., occasional sl. foxing, vg. Hodgkins
27-323 1983 £15

SEAVER, JAMES E.   Life of Mary Jemison. Buffalo, 1877.
Plates. Cloth. Fifth edition. A nearly fine copy. Felcone 22-219
1983 $40

SEBASTIANI, CLAUDIO   Bellum Musicale. Strasbourg, Paulus
Machaeropoeus, 1563. Printer's device on title, five full-page
woodcuts, musical examples throughout. 4to, bound in old flowered
calico. A few faded old waterstains, but a fine copy. Salloch 387-223
1983 $4,500

SEBITZ, MELCHIOR   Discursus medico-philosophicus de casu
adolescentis cuiuadam Argentoratensis mirabili. Strassburg: Anton
Bertram for Paul Ledertz, 1617. First edition. Small 4to. 18th-
century boards. 2 engraved plates and 14 text engravings. Dampstained towards end. Kraus 164-217 1983 $350

SECKER, THOMAS   An Answer to Dr. Mayhew's Observations
on the Charter and Conduct of the Society for the Propagation of the
Gospel in Foreign Parts. Boston, 1764. Dbd. Some marginal
staining throughout, but a very good copy. Reese 18-77 1983 $125

SECKER, THOMAS   A Sermon Preached Before the Incorporated
Society for the Propagation of the Gospel in Foreign Parts. London,
1741. Later wraps, a fine copy. Reese 18-54 1983 $150

THE SECOND American Caravan. New York: Macaulay, 1928. 1st ed.
Orig. cloth, gilt. Spine lightly aged, else fine copy. Jenkins
155-34 1983 $30

A SECOND Appeal to the People of Pennsylvania on the Subject of an
Asylum for the Insane Poor of the Commonwealth. Philadelphia, 1840.
Disbound. Early library stamp. Felcone 22-149 1983 $30

THE SECOND Book of the Author's Club: Liber Scriptorum. New York:
Published by the Author's Club, 1921. 4to. Cloth. 1st and only
ed. Total ed. is 251 copies. Inside endboard has some light repair,
mainly a vg-fine copy. Signed by most of the contributors. Those
signing include: George Barr McCutcheon, Irving Bacheller, et al.
In Our Time 156-692 1983 $350

THE SECOND Mercury Story Book. London: Longmans, Green, 1931. 1st
ed. Orig. cloth, dj. But for small strip of residue from subscription card that was issued pasted to front panel of dj, a fine copy.
Jenkins 155-66 1983 $30

THE SECRET History of the Calves-Head Clubb. London: Printed, and
sold by the Booksellers of London and Westminster, 1703. 8vo, new
wraps. First edition. Quaritch NS 7-120 1983 $375

THE SECRET history of the Green-Room: containing authentic and
entertaining memoirs of the actors and actresses in the three Theatres
Royal. London: printed for J. Owen, 1795. 2 vols., 12mo, cont. tree
calf, spines gilt (bit rubbed, Vol. II lacks labels). 4th and most
complete edition. Half-titles present; very good copy. Ximenes
64-483 1983 $250

SECRET memoirs of the late Mr. Duncan Campbel... London: J. Millan,
etc., 1732. First edition. 8vo. Cont. mottled calf, gilt, neatly
rebacked, spine gilt. Engraved portrait and a list of subscribers.
Fine copy. Ximenes 63-135 1983 $200

SECRET Springs of Dublin Song. Dublin: The Talbot Press, 1918.
Edition ltd. to 500 numbered copies, printed on handmade paper.
Orig. brown cloth, laid-in is a listing of authors included.
Karmiole 76-57 1983 $75

SECRETA Monita Societatis Jesu. The Secret Instructions of the
Jesuits. London: John Walthoe, jun., 1723. 1st English ed., 12mo,
cont. panelled calf, decorated in gilt, rehinged. A very good copy.
Trebizond 18-199 1983 $65

SECUNDUS, DICK HUMELBERGUIS   Apician Morsels. London: Whittaker,
1834. 12mo. Orig. cloth-backed oboards. Spine broken. Good, sound
copy. MacManus 280-4634 1983 $35

SECUNDUS, JOANNES   Kisses. Printed for J. Nunn, 1803.
Large 12mo, engraved portrait, title with engraved vignette, all uncut,
orig. boards with paper spine and printed paper label. Bickersteth
77-241 1983 £28

SECUNDUS, JOHANNES   Kisses, being the Basia of Johannes
Secundus rendered into English Verse. London: the Nonesuch Press,
1933. 4to. Decorated boards, printed paper label. Limited edition
of 725 numbered copies. Traylen 94-713 1983 £18

SEDGWICK, A.   On the Phenomena Connected with some
Trap Dykes in Yorkshire and Durham. Cambridge Phil. Soc., 1823.
4to, wrappers. Wheldon 160-1472 1983 £10

SEDGWICK, A.   A Student's Text-Book of Zoology.
1927, 1905, 1927. 3 vols., 8vo, cloth. Edges of Vols. 1 and 3 worn.
Wheldon 160-519 1983 £25

SEDGWICK, A.   A Synopsis of the Classification of
the British Palaeozoic Rocks. (1851-) 1855. Atlas only, 25 plates
of many figures, 4to, contemporary cloth. Worn. Wheldon 160-1473
1983 £25

SEDGWICK, CATHERINE   Hope Leslie. New York, Harper &
Brothers, 1842. 2 vols., 8vo, orig. cloth, faded, bit worn, orig.
printed paper spine labels chipped and worn. Ravenstree 96-214 1983
$45

SEDGWICK, CATHARINE   The Linwoods. London: Edward Churton,
1835. First English edition. 3 vols. Cont. 3/4 green calf with
marbled boards. Spines a bit rubbed at edges. Very good. MacManus
280-4635 1983 $150

SEDGWICK, CATHARINE   The Linwoods; or, "Sixty Years Since", in
America. William Smith, 1840. Double columns, roy. 8vo, orig.
printed paper wraps., a very good copy. Fenning 60-375 1983 £10.50

SEDGWICK, JOHN   Correspondence of John Sedgwick, Major-
Genera. (N.Y.: DeVinne Press), 1902-03. 2 vols., 1st ed. Limited
to 300 copies. Privately printed, t.e.g., original cloth, slipcased.
Illus. Very scarce. Jenkins 151-307 1983 $400

SEDGWICK, JOHN   Correspondence. (NY), 1902. Ltd.
edition of 300 copies, privately printed at the DeVinne Press on
hand-made paper. 2 vols., 2 engr. Frontis. Blue cloth with
embossed medallion profile of Sedgwick inlaid on front. Argosy 716-
86 1983 $175

SEDLMAYR, HANS   Johann Bernhard Fischer Von Erlach.
Wien/Munchen: Herold, 1956. 337 illus. hors texte. Large stout
4to. Cloth. Ars Libri 32-221 1983 $150

SEEBOHM, H   The Birds of Siberia. John Murray,
1901. First collected edition, with a folding map and many illus.,
8vo, orig. cloth, gilt, t.e.g. Just a little wear at the corners,
but thoroughly sound. Fenning 62-329 1983 £45

SEEBOHM, H.   Siberia in Asia. London, 1882. Folding
map, numerous illus., in binding uniform with the above. 8vo. Good.
Edwards 1044-633 1983 £40

SEEBOHM, H.   Siberia in Europe. London, 1880.
Folding map, numerous illus. Half morocco, raised bands, gilt. 8vo.
Good. Edwards 1044-632 1983 £40

SEEGER, ALAN   Letters and Diary. L, 1917. Offset on
front end paper, cover shows minor wear, good to very good. Quill &
Brush 54-1209 1983 $20

SEEK and You Shall Find. Printed by Henry Hills, 1686. 4to, wrapper,
a very good copy. Fenning 61-395 1983 £18.50

SEELEY, H. G.   The Fresh-water Fishes of Europe.
1886. 214 illustrations, royal 8vo, original cloth. A little foxing,
small hole at foot of spine, else a good copy. Wheldon 160-999
1983 £35

SEELEY, H. G.   Dragons of the Air. 1901. 80 illus.,
8vo, cloth. Wheldon 160-1474 1983 £15

SEELEY, MABEL   The Chuckling Fingers. Garden City,
Doubleday, 1941. First edition. Signed by the author? Dust jacket
(rubbing and small chips), else very good. Houle 22-782 1983 $30

SEELEY, MABEL   Eleven Came Back. Garden City,
Doubleday, 1943. First edition. Signed by the author? Dust jacket
(small chips), else very good. Houle 22-782 1983 $30

SEELEY, THADDEUS D.   History of Oakland County, Michigan.
Chicago, 1912. 2 vols. Illus., 1/2 leather, t.e.g. Slightly
rubbed else a nice set. King 46-193 1983 $125

SEELY, HOWARD   A Lone Star Bo-Peep, and Other Tales of
Texan Ranch Life. New York: Mershon & Co., 1885. Gilt cloth. First
edition. A very fine, bright copy. Reese 19-54 1983 $75

SEGARD, ACHILLE   Giov.-Antonio Bazzi detto Sodoma...
Paris: Henri Floury, 1910. 21 plates. Large 8vo. Wrappers.
Worn. Ars Libri 33-344 1983 $37.50

SEGARD, ACHILLE   Mary Cassatt. Un peintre des enfants
et des meres. Paris: Paul Ollendorff, 1913. Second edition. 37
plates. Wrappers. Worn. Backstrip renewed. Ars Libri 32-85 1983
$60

SEGER, HERMANN AUGUST   Collected Writings of... Easton, Pa.,
Chemical Pub. Co., 1902. 1st American ed. 2 vols., 8vo, ex-library,
bindings and blank margins of text waterstained. Morrill 288-670
1983 $25

SEGUR, COMTESSE DE   Old French Fairy Tales. Phila.: Penn,
(1920). 4to. Cloth, pictorial paste-on. Light wear. Illus. with 8
color plates with tissue guards plus many half-page and smaller black
& whites by V. Sterrett. Very good. Aleph-bet 8-244 1983 $110

SEGY, LADISLAS   African Sculpture Speaks. NY (1952).
First edition, presentation copy, inscribed & signed by the author.
Illus, cloth, very good in chipped dw. King 46-405 1983 $37.50

SEIDENADEL, CARL WILHELM   The First Grammar of the Language
Spoken by the Bontoc Igorot. Chicago: Open Court Pub. Co., 1909.
Large 4to, frontis. 12 photographic plates. Red gilt-stamped cloth.
Karmiole 72-64 1983 $150

SEIDLITZ, WOLDEMAR VON   Die Radierungen Rembrandts. Leipzig:
E.A. Seemann, 1922. 375 collotype vignettes hors texte. Square 4to.
Boards, 3/4 leather. From the library of Jakob Rosenberg. Ars Libri
32-567 1983 $125

SEIGNE, JOHN W.   Irish Bogs. Longmans, 1928. First
edition, 8vo, orig. cloth, very good copy. Fenning 61-396 1983
£21.50

SEILHAMER, GEORGE O.   History of the American Theatre. Phila.:
Globe Printing House, 1888-1891. Cloth, somewhat used and bumped.
Dawson 471-334 1983 $125

SEIPP, HEINRICH   Wahres und Unwahres in Architektur und
Plastic. Strassburg, 1929. Sm. 4to, 18 plates. Wraps. Ars Libri
SB 26-220 1983 $35

SEITZ, DON C.   Paul Jones. New York: E.P. Dutton,
1917. Frontispiece, cloth, presentation inscription. Dawson 470-267
1983 $30

SEITZ, DON C.   Writings By and About James Abbott
McNeill Whistler, A Bibliography. Edinburgh, 1910. Large paper
copy, limited to 350 copies, inscribed by author to local Detroit
artist Roy Gamble. Cloth, t.e.g., covers stained and soiled.
King 46-414 1983 $40

SELDEN, CATHARINE   The English Nun. NY: J. Swaine, 1806.
12mo, calf, lea. label. First American edition. Argosy 716-162
1983 $30

SELDEN, JOHN   Tituli Honorum. Francofurti, impensis
Jeremia Schrey, 1696. First edition in Latin. 6 engr. plates and
many ext woodcuts, some full-page. 4to, some light browning in places,
headband chipped and some unimportant worming in the lower margin, but
otherwise a very good copy in cont. calf. Fenning 61-397 1983 £45

A SELECT Bibliography of the Writings of Alfred W. Pollard. Oxford:
Printed for the subscribers, 1938. Prontis., boards, cloth spine,
2 corners repaired, very light foxing. 1 of 260 copies. Dawson 470-
268 1983 $30

SELECT Biography. Newcastle-upon-Tyne, (1812). 2 vols., 8vo, 25
portraits, cont. calf, lacking label with the title on vol. 1, a little
rubbed. Bickersteth 77-243 1983 £36

A SELECT Collection of Poems... London: J. Hughs for R. and J.
Dodsley, 1758. First complete edition. 6 vols. Cr. 8vo. Cont.
calf, gilt spines with morocco labels, gilt. Vignette title-page
to each vol., and engraved plate and 9 other illus. Traylen 94-278
1983 £60

SELECT Essays from the Batchelor... Dublin: by James Hoey, 1772.
First edition. 8vo. Cont. calf. 2 folding engraved plates. Some
general light usage. Heath 48-339 1983 £125

A SELECTION of the Most Favourite Scots Songs. London, printed for
William Napier, n.d. (1772-1779). Engraved title, engraved music,
with printed text accompanying each song. Tall folio, cont. calf,
skilfully rebacked, spine gilt, with tooling and black label.
With formers owner's bookplate and library release. Salloch 387-224
1983 $175

A SELECTION of the Patriotic Addresses, to the President of the
United States, Together with the President's Answers. Boston,: John
W. Folsom, 1798. Calf, hinges neatly glued. Ex-library. Signature
of George S. Boutwell on the front endsheet. Felcone 22-220 1983
$35

SELECTIONS from Godwin's "Caleb Williams," giving the history in
brief of Sir Edward Mortimer's revenge. London: Darling and Son,
1879. 8vo, original light brown printed wrappers, 1st edition.
Fine copy. Ximenes 64-315 1983 $25

SELECTIONS from the fine private Library of Mr. Theodore L. De Vinne.
of New York City. New York: Scott & O'Shaughnessy, 1919. 8vo.
Orig. paper wrappers. Wrappers chipped. Oak Knoll 49-157 1983
$20

SELECTIONS from the Poetical Literature of the West. Cincinnati,
1841. Half morocco. Fine ed. Contributions by Gallagher, Hanney,
et al. Jenkins 155-457 1983 $75

SELFE, ISAAC   A Catalogue of Chemicals, Drugs, &c.
(Bristol): by R. Edwards, 1800. 16mo. Orig. grey wrappers.
Slight waterstains, but very good copy. Heath 48-530 1983 £65

SELIGMAN, GERMAIN   The Drawings of Georges Seurat. New
York: Curt Valentin, 1947. 46 plates. Large 4to. Boards, 1/4
cloth. Ars Libri 32-630 1983 $100

SELIGMANN, C. G.   The Veddas. Cambridge, 1911. Folding
map in end-pocket. Numerous plates. Thick 8vo. Some browning,
recased, a working copy. Good. Edwards 1044-638 1983 £15

SELIGMANN, HERBERT J.   D. H. Lawrence: An American Interpretation. New York: Thomas Seltzer, 1924. First edition. White wrappers. Rare in wrappers. Bradley 65-113 1983 $75

SELIGMANN, HERBERT J.   D. H. Lawrence. N.Y.: Seltzer, 1924.
First edition. Orig. cloth. Paper labels on spine & upper cover.
Fine. MacManus 279-3171 1983 $25

SELLAR, ROBERT   The Tragedy of Quebec. Huntingdon,
Que., 1907. 1st ed. 8vo. Morrill 287-416 1983 $40

SELLERS, EDWIN JAQUETT   Allied Familes of Delaware. Phila.,
1901. Edition limited to 200 copies. 8vo. Morrill 290-93 1983
$30

SELOUS, FREDERICK COURTENEY   Sunshine and storm in Rhodesia.
London: Rowland Ward, 1896. Second edition. 8vo. Folding map.
10 plates. Orig. cloth. Rubbed, spine darkened. Adelson Africa-
222 1983 $80

SELOUS, FREDERICK COURTENEY   Travel and adventure in south-east
Africa. London: Rowland Ward, 1893. First edition. 8vo. Folding
map. 23 plates. Orig. orange cloth. Lightly rubbed. Adelson
Africa-126 1983 $225

SELWYN-BROWN, ARTHUR   The Physician throughout the Ages.
N.Y., 1928. First edition. 2 vols., thick large 4to, orig. embossed
cloth, (inner front hinge vol. mended). Argosy 713-489 1983 $125

SELWYN-BROWN, ARTHUR   The Physician Throughout the Ages.
New York, 1928. 1st ed. Illus. 2 vols. 4to. Morrill 289-208
1983 $30

SEMENZATO, CAMILLO   La scultura veneta del Seicento e del
Settecento. Venezia, 1966. Large sq. 4to, cloth, 258 illus. hors
texte. Dust jacket. Ars Libri SB 26-222 1983 $100

SEN, D. N.   Contributions to the Ecology of Halo-
phytes. The Hague, 1982. 8vo, cloth. Wheldon 160-1569 1983 £42

SENDAK, MAURICE   Zehn Kleine Kerlchen. (Zurich):
Diogenes, (1977). Pictorial wrappers slightly darkened, spine lightly
rubbed, otherwise extremely fine. (2 7/8 x 2 3/8; 72x60mm). Bromer
25-468 1983 $85

SENECA, LUCIUS ANNAEUS   Scenecae (sic) Tragoediae. (Venice),
Aldvs, (1517). 8vo, early 19th century red straight-grain morocco
gilt, a.e.g., gilt Aldine device on covers, by Ridge and Storr of
Grantham, and with the Syston Park bookplate of Sir John Thorold
(1773-1831). Aside from a smudge on the title and last leaf, an
exceptionally clean and well preserved copy from the collection of
Aldines. Ravenstree 95-100 1983 $820

SENECA, LUCIUS ANNAEUS   Tragoediae Septem. Lvdgvni, Seb.
Gryphivm, 1541. 8vo, 18th century calf, joints broken, worn, ex-
library with 2 withdrawn stamps on endpapers, names on endpapers.
Ravenstree 95-102 1983 $115

SENECA, LUCIUS ANNAEUS   The Tragedies of L. Annaeus Seneca.
London: printed for J. Smith and B. Walford, 1702. First edition
of this translation by Sir Edward Sherburne, in the issue with
title dated 1702. 8vo, advertisements, engraved frontis. portrait,
5 plates, cont. mottled calf, rather rubbed and worn, upper joint
cracked, but generally a good copy in a sound binding. Pickering &
Chatto 19-64 1983 $200

SENECA, LUCIUS ANNAEIUS   The Tragedies. Chicago, 1907. 8vo,
cloth. Salloch 385-739 1983 $20

SENECA, LUCIUS ANNAEIUS   The Tragedies. London, 1904. 8vo,
cloth. Salloch 385-738 1983 $20

SENECA, LUCIUS ANNAEIUS   The Works, Both Morall and Naturall...
London, William Stansby, 1614. Folio, orig. calf, very worn, joints
breaking, peeling outer blank edges of first few leaves frayed, both
engraved and printed titles lightly dust-soiled. Internally a very
large, fine, clean copy of the first edition. Ravenstree 95-101 1983
$450

SENECA'S Morals, by Way of Abstract. Boston, 1800. 3rd American ed.
4 engraved plates. Small 8vo, contemporary calf, leather label.
Ex-library. Morrill 286-433 1983 $20

SENEFELDER, ALOIS   The Invention of Lithography. NY:
The Fuches & Lang Manufacturing Co., 1911. First English language
edition, tipped-in front. + 1 plate. Red cloth. Karmiole 76-98 1983
$75

SENN, EDWARD L.   "Wild Bill" Hickok, "Prince of
Pistoleers." Deadwood, S.D., 1939. Cover title. Scarce. Fine.
Jenkins 153-692 1983 $35

SENN, NICHOLAS   Surgical Bacteriology. Phila., 1891.
13 plates, some in color. Argosy 713-491 1983 $35

SENNERT, DANIEL   Disputationem hanc De Arthritide.
Wittenberg: Johann Gormann, 1615. 4to. Paper backstrip. Kraus
164-212 1983 $150

SERAFINI, GIANCARLO   Ommagio a Campigli. Roma: Carlo
Bestetti, 1972. 170 plates (51 color). Large square 4to. Cloth.
Dust jacket. Ars Libri 33-423 1983 $85

SERAPION THE YOUNGER   Liber Serapionis aggregatus in medi-
cinus simplicibus. Venice: Reynaldus de Novimagio, 8 June, 1479.
With many decorative initials in red and blue penwork. Numerous
smaller ones in red and blue. Folio. 19th-century half calf. With
ms. exlibris of John Lawson. Donated by him to Sion College, 1705,
with their stamped, printed and engraved exlibris. Second edition.
Kraus 164-214 1983 $3,850

SERGEANT, ADELINE   In the Wilderness. London: Melrose,
n.d. (1896). First edition. Orig. cloth. Front inner hinge cracked.
MacManus 280-4637 1983 $20

SERGEANT, ADELINE   A Rise in the World. N.Y.: F.M. Buckles
& Co., 1900. First American edition. Orig. cloth. Review Copy. With
slip pasted to front endsheet. Covers a little faded and soiled. Good.
MacManus 280-4636 1983 $20

SERGEANT, ADELINE   Seventy Times Seven. Edinburgh:
Oliphant, Anderson & Ferrier, 1888. First edition. 3 vols. Orig.
dark green cloth. Spines and covers slightly worn at the ends and
edges. Cont. owner's signature. Very good. MacManus 280-4638 1983
$250

SERGEANT, ADELINE   The Surrender of Margaret Bellarmine.
London: William Heinemann, 1894. First edition. 2 vols. Orig. cloth.
Lacking front flyleaves, front inner hinges cracked. Spines faded and
a little rubbed. MacManus 280-4639 1983 $85

SERGEANT, ADELINE   The Work of Oliver Byrd. London: James
Nisbet, 1902. First edition. Orig. green cloth. Spine and covers
slightly worn and spotted. Some foxing. Former owner's initials.
Good. MacManus 280-4640 1983 $25

SERGEANT, JOHN   Select Speeches. Philadelphia, 1832.
First edition. 8vo, original boards, cloth back, paper label. Top
right corner of front cover torn off. Morrill 290-485 1983 $25

SERGEANT, PHILIP W.   Witches and Warlocks. London, 1936.
First edition. Preface by A. Machen. Frayed dust wrapper. Nice.
Rota 230-378 1983 £18

SERMONS by Artists. London: Golden Cockerel Press, 1934. Octavo.
Very fine in leather-backed decorated paper over boards. Bromer
25-220 1983 $285

SERRA, JUNIPERO   Letter of Captain Don Pedro Pages and The
Rev. President Fr. Junipero Serra... San Francisco: Grabhorn Press,
1936. Limited edition, 110 copies printed. Including facs. of letters, title printed in red and black. Tall folio, orig. printed
wrappers. Presentation copy inscribed by Henry R. Wagner to Charles L.
Camp. Fine. Jenkins 152-404 1983 $175

SERRA, LUIGI   Alessandro Vittoria. Roma: Alfieri
& Lacroix, n.d. 36 plates. 4to. Boards, 1/2 cloth. Ars Libri
33-389 1983 $85

SERRA, LUIGI   Domenico Zampieri detto il Domenichino.
Roma: "Bollettino d'Arte", 1909. 17 plates. 56 illus. 4to.
Wrappers. Foot of spine torn. Ars Libri 33-130 1983 $100

SERRES, ANTOINE ETIENNE REYMAUD AUGUSTIN (1786-1868)   Anatomie
Comparee du Cerveau. Paris: Chez Gabon et Compagnie, 1824. Two
vols. First editions. Orig. drab brown wrappers, detached and worn.
Without atlas. Housed in modern cloth slipcase. Gach 95-447 1983
$350

SERULLAZ, MAURICE   Eugene Delacroix: dessins, aquarelles
et lavis, Musee du Louvre. Paris: Albert Morance, n.d. 48 fine
collotyped plates with 81 illus. (4 color). Loose in portfolio as
issued. Small 4to. Boards, 1/4 cloth. Ars Libri 32-158 1983 $65

SERVICE, ROBERT W.   Ploughman of the Moon. N.Y., Dodd,
1945. Page proofs, printed on one side of the page. Stiff printed
wraps. According to an inscription by the author: "The only bound
copy of the page proofs, for...Robert W. Service." With author's
corrections on pages 408-423; with a further fine line inscription by
Service facing p. 331. Houle 21-793 1983 $850

SERVICE, ROBERT W.   Ploughman of the Moon. N.Y., Dodd,
Mead, 1945. Page proofs, printed on one side of the page only. Stiff
printed wraps. Inscribed by Service on front cover for Earle
Bernheimer. With the author's corrections on pages 408-23; and with
a further five line inscription facing page 331. Houle 22-785a 1983
$600

SERVICE, ROBERT W.   Rhymes of a Red Cross Man. N.Y., Brace
& Hopkins, (1916). Illus. with 8 color plates by Charles Wrenn. Red
cloth, ornately decorated with battlefield design in gilt, black,
green, white and purple, t.e.g. Very good. Houle 22-786 1983 $37.50

SERVICE, ROBERT W.   Rhymes of a Red Cross Man. Toronto,
1916. 1st ed. Small 8vo, dust wrapper. Light dampstain on part of
front cover and endleaf; d/w partly torn and lacks top inch of backstrip. Morrill 287-418 1983 $20

SERVICE, ROBERT W.   Rhymes of a Rolling Stone. Toronto,
1912. 1st ed. Illus. 8vo. Fine copy. Morrill 287-417 1983 $30

SETH-SMITH, D.   Parrakeets. 1926. Revised edition,
roy. 8vo, original cloth, coloured plates. Wheldon 160-92 1983 £220

SETON, ANYA   Dragonwyck. Boston, 1944. 8vo.
Cloth. Fine copy in lightly worn dj. In Our Time 156-693 1983
$35

SETON, ERNEST THOMPSON   Animal Heroes. NY, 1905. Illus, spine
sunned, front hinge cracked but tight, very good, owner's name and
address. Quill & Brush 54-1211 1983 $30

SETON, ERNEST THOMPSON   Bannertail. N.Y., Scribner, 1922.
First edition. With 100 illus. by the author. Gilt stamped brown
cloth (spine dull). Very good. Houle 22-787a 1983 $45

SETON, ERNEST THOMPSON   The Biography of a Grizzly. N.Y.,
Century, 1900. First edition. Illus. with 75 drawings by the author.
Orig. red cloth stamped in black and orange with grizzly and natural
designs. Signed and inscribed by the author, with a TLS from the
author. Very good. Houle 22-788 1983 $200

SETON, ERNEST THOMPSON   Bird Portraits. Boston: Ginn & Co.,
1901. 4to. 30cm. 20 full-page plates from painting by Seton.
Decorated green cloth, some wear at the edges else a very good copy.
Scarce. McGahern 53-144 1983 $75

SETON, ERNEST THOMPSON   Lives of the Hunted. NY, 1901. Spine
slightly sunned and soiled with edges very slightly frayed, else very
good. Quill & Brush 54-121 1983 $60

SETON, ERNEST THOMPSON   Monarch, The Big Bear of Tallac.
NY 1904. First edition. Cloth, minor wear else a nice copy.
King 46-455 1983 $35

SETON, ERNEST THOMPSON   Rolf in the Woods. Garden City, Doubleday, 1911. First edition. Over 200 illus. by the author. Dust
jacket (scarce in dust jacket, slight nicks) else very good. Houle
22-789 1983 $75

SETON, ERNEST THOMPSON   Two Little Savages. N.Y., Doubleday,
1903. First edition. Illus. by the author. Light green cloth
stamped in gilt and dark green. A fine copy. Houle 22-790 1983
$85

SETON, ERNEST THOMPSON   Woodsmith & Fable. N.Y., Doubleday,
1905. First edition. Illus. by the author. Gilt stamped red cloth.
Very good. Houle 22-791 1983 $85

SETON-THOMPSON, ERNEST
Please turn to
SETON, ERNEST THOMPSON (1860-1946)

SETTLE, ELKANAH   A farther defence of dramatick poetry:
being the second part of the review of Mr. Collier's View of the
Immorality and Profaneness of the Stage. London: printed for Eliz.
Whitlock, 1698. 8vo, disbound, 1st edition. Half-title present;
title-page dusty. Very uncommon. Ximenes 64-484 1983 $300

SETTLE, ELKANAH   Notes and observations on the Empress
of Morocco revised. London: printed for William Cademan, 1674.
Sm. 4to, disbound, 1st edition. Title and last page of errata dusty;
a couple of tears in the inner margin, not affecting the text, else
a sound copy of a rare Restoration theater tract. Ximenes 64-485
1983 $700

SEUPHOR, MICHEL   Piet Mondrian. Life and work. New
York: Harry N. Abrams, (1956). More than 600 illus. (34 tipped-
in color). Large 4to. Cloth. Dust jacket. Ars Libri 32-466 1983
$85

SEVERALL Letters containing a Message from the States Provinciall
of Holland sent by an Ambassador... London: for J.C., 1650.
Sole edition. 4to. Wrappers. Heath 48-185 1983 £85

SEVERANCE, FRANK H.   An Old Frontier of France, the Niagara
Region and Adjacent Lakes under French Control. NY, 1917. 2 vols.
Illus. Argosy 710-107 1983 $75

SEVERIN, MARK F.   Making a Bookplate. London: The
Studio Publications, (1949). First edition. 8vo. Cloth. Dust
jacket. Many illus. Dust jacket chipped and soiled. Oak Knoll
48-63 1983 $20

SEVERN, JOHN PERCY   The Adventures of Ariston. By an Eton
Boy. Printed for T. Cadell, 1830. 12mo, contemporary black calf,
gilt borders and spine panels of foliage and tendrils; lacking label,
endpapers damp-spotted; author's signed presentation copy to "T.S.
Carter (whose bookplate is present). The gift of the Author...
July 1830". Hill 165-112 1983 £65

SEVERN, WALTER   The Order for Morning & Evening Prayer.
Longman, etc., 1874. Title page printed in gold & text within floral
borders printed in gold & colours. Dark green sand grain decor. cloth.
Explanatory Notes, etc., have been tipped in before title page - these
sheets were generally supplied loose & lower edge of 2 sheets have 1/2"
tears and some creases (sl. wear top bkstrip, bookpl.). 3 photos
inserted by previous owner. V.g. Hodgkins 27-393 1983 £42

SEVERSKY, A. P. DE   Victory Through Air Power. New York,
1942. First edition. Portrait frontis. 11 plates, 3 text maps, 2
full page diagrams. 8vo. Orig. cloth. Spine faded. Covers dampstained. Good. Edwards 1042-604 1983 £15

SEWALL, ALICE ARCHER   The Ballad of the Prince. N.Y.:
Russell, 1900. 4to. Cloth backed pictorial boards. Light edgewear
and rub. 3/4 page illus. Very good. Aleph-bet 8-233 1983 $30

SEWALL, JOSEPH   Nineveh's Repentance and Deliverance.
Boston: J. Draper for D. Henchman, 1740. Stitched. Small holes
in last leaf. Felcone 22-221 1983 $30

SEWALL, JOSEPH   When the Godly Cease. Boston: S.
Kneeland & T. Green for D. Henchman,1737. Stitched. Margins of
titlepage damaged. Cont signature of Elizabeth Leonard. Felcone
22-222 1983 $30

SEWALL, SAMUEL   The History of Woburn, Middlesex
County, Mass... Boston, 1868. 1st ed. With a memorial sketch of
author by Charles C. Sewall. 8vo. Small tear on backstrip. Morrill
287-257 1983 $35

SEWALL, THOMAS   Memoir of Dr. Godman. New York,
1832. 8vo. Wrappers. Corner of wrappers and first leaf chewed,
foxed. Scarce. Fye H-3-750 1983 $25

SEWARD, ANNA   Memoirs of the Life of Dr. Darwin.
London: Johnson, 1804. 1st ed., with errata. Contemp. 3/4 green
morocco, gilt. Very good copy in binding of the period. Jenkins
155-285 1983 $150

SEWARD, WILLIAM   Anecdotes of Distinguished Persons.
Printed for T. Cadell jun. and W. Davies, 1798. 4 vols., 8vo, 14
engraved pages of music, 12 plates, cont. tree calf, spines with
red labels. Bickersteth 77-73 1983 £38

SEWARD, WILLIAM HENRY (1801-1872)   Correspondence. Mr. Seward to
Mr. Adams... (Washington), 1861. Disbound, first edition. Ginsberg
46-745 1983 $25

SEWARD, WILLIAM HENRY (1801-1872)   Life and Public Services of
John Quincy Adams... Auburn, 1849. First ed., portrait, 8vo., half
leather. Corners lightly rubbed, front hinge sl. cracked. Morrill
290-486 1983 $20

SEWARD, WILLIAM HENRY (1801-1872)   Oration at Plymouth, Dec. 21,
1855. Albany, 1856. Paper wrappers, cover·stained and wearing. Good.
Quill & Brush 54-1215 1983 $35

SEWARD, WILLIAM HENRY (1801-1872)   Speech of...on the Admission of California Delivered in the Senate of the United States. Washington, 1850. Orig. printed wraps. First edition. Ginsberg 47-166 1983 $50

SEWEL, WILLEM
Please turn to
SEWEL, WILLIAM (1653-1720)

SEWEL, WILLIAM (1653-1720)   The History of the Rise, Increase and Progress, of the Christian People Called Quakers. Burlington: Isaac Collins, 1774. Folio. Modern cloth. Signature "Francis Chase's Book 1775." Very good. Felcone 19-49 1983 $175

SEWEL, WILLIAM (1653-1720)   The History of the Rise, Increase, and Progress of the Christian People Called Quakers. Printed and Sold by the Assigns of J. Sowle, 1722. First edition in English, complete in spite of pagination jump. Folio. A very good copy in recent calf-backed marbled boards, with label. Fenning 62-331 1983 £75

SEWELL, ANNA   Black Beauty. London, Jarrold, (ca. 1920). Illus. by G. Vernon Stokes and Alan Wright. Pictorial light green cloth stamped with yellow, black and white with rural scene. Very good. Houle 22-792 1983 $45

SEWELL, ELIZABETH MISSING   Amy Herbert. Printed for Longman, Brown, (etc), 1844. First edition. 2 vols, 12mo, original cloth, gilt spines; half-title in vol. II; a fine copy. Hill 165-113 1983 £48

SEWELL, ELIZABETH MISSING   The Earl's Daughter. Longman, Brown, 1850. Third edition. 2 vols, 12mo, original light blue embossed cloth, gilt. Hill 165-114 1983 £30

SEWELL, ELIZABETH MISSING   Ivors. London: Longman, Brown, Green, Longmans, & Roberts, 1856. First edition. Orig. cloth. 2 vols. Covers a little rubbed and soiled. Bookplates on endsheets. Former owner's signature on half-titles. Good. MacManus 280-4643 1983 $325

SEWELL, ELIZABETH MISSING   Ivors. Longman, Brown, (etc), 1856. First edition, 2 vols, 12mo, original light green cloth; vol. I a trifle loose in binding, but a very fair copy. With both half-titles. Hill 165-115 1983 £50

SEWELL, ELIZABETH MISSING   Laneton Parsonage; a Tale for Children. Longman, Brown (etc), 1846. First edition, 2 vols, 12mo, original cloth, gilt-titled spines; half-titles not called for; a fine copy. Hill 165-116 1983 £48

SEWELL, ELIZABETH MISSING   Margaret Percival. London: Printed for Longman, Brown, Green, & Longmans, 1847. First edition. 2 vols. Orig. cloth. Spines sligtly faded. Foot of one spine very slightly nicked. Former owner's signature on title-pages. Near-fine. Mac-Manus 280-4641 1983 $225

SEWELL, ELIZABETH MISSING   Ursula. London: Longman, Green, Long-mans & Roberts, 1858. First edition. 2 vols. Orig. cloth. Spines and covers a trifle worn and spotted. Binder's ticket. Nice. MacManus 280-4642 1983 $275

SEWELL, GEORGE   Observations upon Cato, a tragedy. London: printed for A. Baldwin, 1713. 4to, wrappers. First edition. A very good copy. Ximenes 64-486 1983 $500

SEWELL, W.   Christian Politics. James Burns. 1844. Half title, 16 pp ads. Orig. blue cloth, v.g. Jarndyce 31-367 1983 £14

SEXTON, ANNE   The Book of Folly. B, 1972. Special edition limited to 500 signed copies, very fine in near fine slipcase. Quill & Brush 54-1216 1983 $75

SEYMOUR, CHARLES   How the World Votes. Springfield, Mass., 1918. 1st ed. Illus. 2 vols., 8vo. Morrill 287-419 1983 $22.50

SEYMOUR, CHARLES   Masterpieces of Sculpture from the National Gallery of Art. N.Y., Coward-McCann, (1949). First edition. 4to, illus. with 142 pages of gravures. Dust jacket (trifle rubbed). Very good - fine. Houle 22-781 1983 $35

SEYMOUR, ERNEST ROBERT   Mignonette, A Sketch. London: Henry & Parker, 1858. First edition. 2 vols. 12mo. Orig. cloth. Shaken and worn. Inner hinges cracked. MacManus 280-4644 1983 $35

SEYMOUR, GEORGE DUDLEY   Captain Nathan Hale. New Haven; privately printed, 1933. Limited ed. Illus. Argosy 710-462 1983 $30

SEYMOUR, HENRY D.   Russia on the Black Sea and Sea of Azof. John Murray, 1855. First edition, with 3 folding maps and 3 plates, 8vo, orig. cloth, the spine neatly repaired, a very good copy. Fenning 60-377 1983 £55

SEYMOUR, RALPH FLETCHER   Across the Gulf. (Chicago): The Alderbrink Press, (1928). 4to, with illus. title-page, folding map, dec. initials and 20 other large woodcut illus. by Seymour. Edition ltd. to 425 numbered copies, signed by Seymour. Fine copy in half beige cloth over illus. boards, paper spine. Karmiole 76-79 1983 $65

SEYMOUR, SILAS   Incidents of a Trip Through the Great Platte Valley. New York: D. Van Nostrand, 1867. Frontis. portrait. Orig. cloth. 2nd ed. Jenkins 153-504 1983 $145

SEZNEC, JEAN   La Survivance des Dieux Antiques. London, (Warburg Institute), 1940. 8vo, cloth. Salloch 385-47 1983 $60

SHADRACH. London: George Bell and Sons, 1879. 3 vols. Orig. cloth. First edition. Spines a bit soiled. Corners bumped, verso of each free endpaper a little browned. Very good set. MacManus 277-88 1983 $185

SHAFER, HUGH B.   A Stockman's Poems. San Antonio, Tex., 1903. Orig. printed wrappers. Jenkins 153-506 1983 $45

SHAFFER, NEWTON M.   Pott's Disease. New York, 1879. 1st ed. Few text illus. Small 8vo. Presentation copy. Morrill 289-209 1983 $22.50

SHAHN, BEN   The Alphabet of Creation. New York, 1954. First edition. One of 500 copies signed by Shahn. Slightly bumped and rubbed slipcase. Fine. Gekoski 2-169 1983 £100

SHAHN, BEN   The Alphabet of Creation. NY: Pantheon. (1954). Tall 8vo, each page illus. with a drawing by Shahn, printed in brown. Edition ltd. to 500 numbered copies, signed by Shahn, and printed at the Spiral Press. This copy unnumbered but marked "Review Copy." Beige cloth. A fine copy in a slipcase. Karmiole 71-113 1983 $150

SHAIRP, JOHN CAMPBELL   Glen Desseray and Other Poems Lyrical and Elegiac. Macmillan and Co., 1888. 8vo, orig. cloth. First edition. Bickersteth 77-245 1983 £12

SHAKESPEARE, WILLIAM   The Tragedie of Anthony and Cleopatra. (Hammersmith, Doves Press, 1912). 4to, printed in red and black. Full vellum stamped in gilt. One of 200 copies. Slipcase. Fine. Houle 22-314 1983 $750

SHAKESPEARE, WILLIAM   As You Like It. William Jackson, 1930. Large 4to. Mounted colour frontis. Title vignette. 5 mounted colour plates. 8 full-page & 10 text illus. Blue cloth gilt, faded. Edition limited to 115 copies, No. 94, signed by Austen. Greer 40-38 1983 £55

SHAKESPEARE, WILLIAM   Comedies, Histories & Tragedies... Oxford: at the Clarendon Press, 1902. With a supplement to the Reproduction of the Facsimile. 2 vols. Folio. Orig. reversed calf with ties, crimson morocco labels, gilt. 3 portraits and 2 plates. Limited edition of 1,000 copies, numbered and signed by Sidney Lee. From the library of Charles Tennant, an orig. subscriber. Traylen 94-727 1983 £180

SHAKESPEARE, WILLIAM   Coriolanus. Oxford: Clarendon Press, 1886. 12mo, original orange-brown printed boards, linen spine. In very good condition. Ximenes 64-523 1983 $50

SHAKESPEARE, WILLIAM   The Tragedy of Coriolanus. (Hammersmith: The Doves Press, 1914). 8vo, full lavender morocco classic
binding by Rene Keiffer with his label. One of 200 copies printed
in black and red, leather-tipped matching slipcase. Duschnes 240-12
1983 $475

SHAKESPEARE, WILLIAM   The Double Falshood; or, the distrest
lovers. London: printed by J. Watts, 1728. First edition. Revised
and adapted to the stage by Lewis Theobald. 8vo, half-title with
privilege on verso, some offsetting of the text, modern morocco-
backed boards, spine lettered in gilt. Pickering & Chatto 19-63
1983 $165

SHAKESPEARE, WILLIAM   The First Part of Henry the Fourth.
San Francisco, 1961. Folio, decorated boards with cloth back.
Illus. with colored blocks by Mary Grabhorn. One of 180 copies.
Duschnes 240-103 1983 $325

SHAKESPEARE, WILLIAM   Guide to the Mss. & Printed Books Exhibited in Celebration of the Tercentenary of the First Folio Shakespeare.
(London): 1923. 8 plates, 1 folding. Printed gray wrappers. Covers
soiled. Bradley 66-54 1983 $40

SHAKESPEARE, WILLIAM   Hamlet, Prince of Denmark. Selwyn &
Blount, 1922. 4to. Decorated title. 12 plates & 134 text illus.
Decorated endpapers. Black boards, green & gilt decorated, some wear.
Greer 40-39 1983 £75

SHAKESPEARE, WILLIAM   Hamlet. Cambridge University Press:
1936. Sm. 8vo, original brown cloth. Signed by Alec Guinness on
the front flyleaf (Dec. 1939). In fine condition. Ximenes 64-253
1983 $125

SHAKESPEARE, WILLIAM   The Tragedy of Hamlet. (1951). Seven
page proof signatures for the Peter Pauper Press edition, including
the double-page illustrated title, and three full page linoleum cuts.
Houle 21-20 1983 $275

SHAKESPEARE, WILLIAM   Kalender fur das Jahr 1910. Vienna: M.
Munk, 1909. 4to, 12 excellent colour plates & 12 text decorations.
Grey pictorial wrappers, light wear, spine worn. Greer 40-173 1983
£25

SHAKESPEARE, WILLIAM   The Tragedie of King Lear. 1927.
Illus. by Paul Nash. Minor cover staining and discoloration, else
very good in remnants of soiled dustwrapper. Quill & Brush 54-1218
1983 $40

SHAKESPEARE, WILLIAM   King Lear. SF: 1930. Introduction
by G. K. Chesterton. Folio, buckram, gilt, t.e.g. With 10 full-
page illustrations in b/w by Yunge. One of 240 copies. A very
nice copy. Perata 27-35 1983 $175

SHAKESPEARE, WILLIAM   The London Shakespeare. London, 1958.
6 vols. 8vo. Orig. green buckram gilt. Traylen 94-728 1983 £40

SHAKESPEARE, WILLIAM   The Merchant of Venice. Venice: S.
Rosen, 1906. Frontis. portrait and 3 full-page b&w drawings. Last
text page and rear endpapers very slightly foxed, otherwise fine in
printed boards with rawhide ties. (2 3/4 x 2 1/8; 70x52mm). Bromer
25-469 1983 $75

SHAKESPEARE, WILLIAM   A Midsummer Nights Dreame. B. Quaritch,
1892. Folio. Frontis. Pictorial title. 13 plates & 60 text illus.
Blue cloth, gilt. Edition limited to 275 copies, No. 146, signed by
J.M. Smith. Greer 40-206 1983 £48

SHAKESPEARE, WILLIAM   Miscellaneous papers and legal instruments under the hand and seal of William Shakespeare. Cooper &
Graham for Egerton, White, and Sael, 1796. 2nd ed., first 8vo ed.,
half-title and folding engraved portrait, contemporary half green
calf rebacked in modern green calf, marbled boards, 19th century
marbled endpapers corners a little rubbed, some light foxing, good.
Bookplate. Deighton 3-259 1983 £85

SHAKESPEARE, WILLIAM   The Plays of William Shakespeare...
London: for C. Bathurst, etc., 1773. Second edition edited by
Samuel Johnson. 10 vols. 8vo. Cont. calf, gilt spines with
orange and green morocco labels, gilt. Portrait. With bookplate
of Honble. Windham Quin. Slightly worn and some marginal worming
not affecting the text. Traylen 94-715 1983 £150

SHAKESPEARE, WILLIAM   The Plays of William Shakespeare...
London, 1785. Third edition. 10 vols. 8vo. Full crimson morocco,
gilt, gilt panelled spines, edges gilt. 5 plates, one of which is
folding. Traylen 94-716 1983 £220

SHAKESPEARE, WILLIAM   The Plays of William Shakespeare...
London, 1785. 10 vols. 8vo. Cont. calf, gilt spines with crimson
morocco labels, and inset numerals, a little worn. Traylen 94-717
1983 £195

SHAKESPEARE, WILLIAM   The Plays, in Twenty-One volumes...
London, 1803. 21 vols. 8vo. Cont. straight-grained red morocco,
wide gilt borders with decorations, fully gilt panelled spines
with floral decoration, inner gilt dentelles, edges gilt. Portrait
of Shakespeare, engraved by Neagle, facsimile handwriting plate,
and 20 other engraved plates. Traylen 94-718 1983 £900

SHAKESPEARE, WILLIAM   The Plays, in Twenty-One Volumes...
London, 1803. Fifth edition. 21 vols. 8vo. Cont. straight-
grained red morocco, wide gilt borders with floral decorations,
gilt panelled spines, inside gilt borders, edges gilt. Traylen
94-719 1983 £550

SHAKESPEARE, WILLIAM   The Plays. London: by T. Davidson,
1807. 8 vols. 8vo. Cont. blue morocco, three-line gilt borders
on sides with corner ornaments, gilt panelled spines, inner gilt
dentelles, edges gilt. With woodcut vignette title-pages and
numerous woodcuts by J. Thruston and Nesbit. Traylen 94-720 1983
£180

SHAKESPEARE, WILLIAM   The Plays... London, 1847. Engraved
portrait. 8 vols. 8vo. Cont. tree-calf, neatly rebacked with fully
gilt spines, crimson and blue morocco labels, gilt. Traylen 94-721
1983 £110

SHAKESPEARE, WILLIAM   The Plays of... Routledge, 1858/61. 3
vols. Illus. by John Gilbert, engr'd by Bros. Dalziel. Frontis.
portrait vol. 1 & numerous text & full page engrs. Bound in full
crimson calf, gilt tooled bkstrip with raised bands & 2 dark green
lea. title labels each vol., marbled eps. & edges. Sl. wear top
bkstrip of vol. 3, lea. rubbed at joints & some marks to covers,
corners some bruising, occasional foxing, vg set. Hodgkins 27-325
1983 £55

SHAKESPEARE, WILLIAM   The Poems. London, 1866. Cr. 8vo.
Dark blue calf, two-line gilt borders with corner ornaments, gilt
panelled spine, morocco label, gilt. Portrait, vignette title-
page. Traylen 94-730 1983 £18

SHAKESPEARE, WILLIAM   The Poems of William Shakespeare
Printed after the Original Copies. (Hammersmith), (1893). Full
vellum, silk ties. One of 500 copies printed on paper. An unsoiled
copy, with the silk ties intact. Reese 20-572 1983 $850

SHAKESPEARE, WILLIAM   The Poems of... NY: Limited Editions
Club, 1941. Two quarto vols. Limited to 1500 copies signed by Bruce
Rogers. Fine set in cloth-backed decorated boards with chipped
glassines. Bromer 25-289 1983 $100

SHAKESPEARE, WILLIAM   The Rape of Lucrece. (Hammersmith):
Doves Press, (1915). Small quarto. Full red morocco, elaborately
gilt, by Cobden-Sanderson, signed in the rear. From a total edition
of 185 copies, this is one of only ten printed in black and red on
pure vellum. Preserved in a half morocco folding slipcase. Reese 20-
330 1983 $7,000

SHAKESPEARE, WILLIAM   The Rape of Lucrece. (Hammersmith,
Doves Press, 1915). 4to, initials printed in red. Full vellum
stamped in gilt (partially removed bookplate on front free endpaper).
Slipcase. One of 175 copies. Very good - fine. Houle 22-313 1983
$700

SHAKESPEARE, WILLIAM   Romeo Et Juliette. Paris: Editions
Nilsson, n.d. (ca. 1920's). Wraps, slightly worn and chipped. With
6 tipped-in aquarelles printed on tissue and colored by hand, drawn
by Maurice Berty. King 46-433 1983 $25

SHAKESPEARE, WILLIAM   The Shakespeare Songs. N.Y.: William
Morrow & Co., (1929). First edition. Orig. two-tone cloth with paper
label on spine. In publisher's slipcase. Limited to 365 copies. Top
of spine slightly soiled. Bookplate. Very fine. MacManus 280-4649
1983 $45

SHAKESPEARE, WILLIAM   Sonnets, being a Reproduction in Fac-simile of the First Edition, 1609... Oxford: at the Clarendon Press, 1905. 5 vols. 4to. Full vellum, gilt panelled sides, uncut edges. Traylen 94-731 1983 £90

SHAKESPEARE, WILLIAM   Shakspere's Sonnets. L, 1881. One of 50 numbered, large paper presentation copies, a.e.g., vellum boards and interior slightly stained, cover bowed, else very good. Quill & Brush 54-1220 1983 $35

SHAKESPEARE, WILLIAM   The Tempest. San Francisco, 1951. 7 illus. by Mary Grabhorn, printed in red and black throughout, dec. in red. Tall folio, orig. natural linen over green decorated boards, red leather label stamped in gold. Limited ed. (160 copies printed). Very fine. Jenkins 155-491 1983 $350

SHAKESPEARE, WILLIAM   Twelfth Night, or, What You Will. Waltham Saint Lawrence, 1932. Folio, dec. cloth boards with leather spine and tips. 29 wood-engr. by Eric Ravilious. Covers lightly shelfworn; a very good copy. One of 275 copies. Perata 28-205 1983 $275

SHAKESPEARE, WILLIAM   Venus and Adonis. Ducros and Colas for Harrison of Paris, 1930. Tall 8vo, headlines and pagination printed in blue, qtr. black paper lettered in silver, silvered paper boards patterned in black, silvered endpapers, t.e. silvered, others uncut, a fine copy in black paper slip-case with silver paper label. 440 numbered copies on Arches vellum. Deighton 3-258 1983 £78

SHAKESPEARE, WILLIAM   Venus and Adonis. Harrow Weald, Middlesex, 1931. Wood engr. by Horace Walter Bray. Folio, dec. cloth, leather label, raven in gilt on upper cover, t.e.g., others uncut, matching slipcase. Printed by Robert Ashwin Maynard and Horace Walter Bray. One of 275 copies signed by Maynard. Perata 28-143 1983 $375

SHAKESPEARE, WILLIAM   Works. Vol. VIII. London: Wm. S. Orr, 1851. 16mo, original blue cloth. Ximenes 64-296 1983 $30

SHAKESPEARE, WILLIAM   The Works. London, 1875-76. Portrait. 9 vols. 8vo. Half dark red morocco, gilt, gilt panelled spines, t.e.g. Traylen 94-722 1983 £295

SHAKESPEARE, WILLIAM   Works. Philadelphia, Barrie, ca. 1890. Interlinear edition. 8vo, with 171 steel engravings after Boydell and 64 photogravures. 3/4 gilt stamped yellow calf, contrasting red and purple leather labels, t.e.g., uncut, by Brian Frost. Spines a little faded, else a fine set. 16 vols. complete. One of 500 sets printed on Japan vellum. Houle 22-794 1983 $1,500

SHAKESPEARE, WILLIAM   The Works. London, 1898. 8 vols. 4to. Half crimson morocco, gilt panelled spines, edges gilt. Engraved portrait and numerous illus. by Gordon Browne. Traylen 94-723 1983 £135

SHAKESPEARE, WILLIAM   The Works. Edinburgh: for Grant Richards, 1901-04. 10 vols. Folio. Half red morocco, gilt, gilt panelled spines, marbled boards with vellum corners. Portrait frontis. to each vol., and title-pages printed in red and black, each with a vignette. Limited edition of 1,000 numbered copies, signed by the printer. Traylen 94-724 1983 £700

SHAKESPEARE, WILLIAM   The Works. Edingurgh: for Grant Richards, 1901-04. 40 orig. parts. Folio. Printed grey boards. Portrait frontis. and title-pages printed in red and black, each with a vignette. The Edinburgh Folio edition, limited to 1,000 numbered copies, signed by the printer. Traylen 94-725 1983 £105

SHAKESPEARE, WILLIAM   Works. Glasgow, David Bryce & Son, (1904). Frontis. Full red suede stamped in gilt and blind, a.e.g. (some light rubbing, a few nicks), else very good. 36 vols. Contained in a cont. inlaid mahogany revolving "barrister" type bookcase, 6 X 4 inches. Houle 22-666 1983 $375

SHAKESPEARE, WILLIAM   The Works. London, 1906. The Henry Irving edition. 14 vols. 4to. Orig. green cloth. With a coloured frontis. to each vol., portrait, and many hundreds of illus. in the text. Traylen 94-726 1983 £28

SHAKESPEARE, WILLIAM   The Works. London, 1929-1933. 8vo. Full niger morocco, t.e.g. as issued. One of 1,600 sets printed by the Cambridge University Press. 7 vols. Duschnes 240-174 1983 $850

SHAKESPEARE, WILLIAM   Works. London: the Nonesuch Press, 1929-30. 7 vols. Roy. 8vo. Orig. full niger morocco, gilt, t.e.g., others uncut. Limited edition of 1,600 sets. Traylen 94-927 1983 £495

SHAKESPEARE'S England: An Account of the Life and Manners of his Age. Oxford, 1916. First edition. 2 vols. Roy. 8vo. Orig. blue cloth, gilt. 195 illus. after early engravings, facsimiles, etc. Traylen 94-735 1983 £35

SHALER, NATHANIEL S.   The United States of America, a Study of the American Commonwealth. NY, 1898. 3 vols., maps, illus. (many photographic), 8vo, 1/2 mor., g.t. Argosy 710-193 1983 $60

SHALER, WILLIAM   Journal of a Voyage Between China and the North-Western Coast of America Made in 1804. Claremont, Saunder Press, 1935. First book edition. Small 4to, folding map, 2 pages of facs. Illus. by Ruth Saunders. Dust jacket (a little darkened) else fine. One of 700 copies. Houle 22-1174 1983 $85

SHALLENBERGER, ELIZA JANE (HALL)   Stark County and Its Pioneers. Cambridge, B.W. Seaton, 1876. 1st ed. 8vo, half orig. leather, some rubbing. Morrill 288-197 1983 $55

SHAMBAUGH, BENJAMIN F.   Constitution and Records of the Claim Association of Johnson County Iowa. Iowa City, Iowa: State Historical Society, 1894. Orig. printed front wrapper. Light ex-library. Uncut & unopened. Jenkins 152-174 1983 $40

SHAND, ALEXANDER INNES   Fortune's Wheel. London: William Blackwood & Sons, 1886. First edition. 3 vols. Orig. brown cloth. Spines and covers worn. Library check-out labels. Bookplate. Good. MacManus 280-4656 1983 $150

SHANE, SUSANNAH   Lady in Lilac. NY, 1941. Paperwraps, advance reading copy, edges slightly worn, spine faded, minor cover stains, else very good. Quill & Brush 54-1221 1983 $30

SHANKS, DAVID C.   As They Passed Through the Port. Washington, Cary Pub. Co. (1927). 1st ed. Presentation from author. Illus. 8vo. Few pencil marks erased from portrait. Morrill 288-555 1983 $22.50

SHANKS, EDWARD   Images from the Progress of the Seasons. London: Dropmore Press, 1947. Sm. 8vo, full crushed green morocco, gilt. Decorations by Charles Berry. One of 50 copies specially bound and signed by the author and artist. Bookplate. Perata 28-23 1983 $150

SHANKS, EDWARD   Images from the Progress of the Seasons. Dropmore Press, 1947. 1st ed., 8vo, decorative title and colophon, uncut in qtr. green morocco gilt, green cloth boards, fine partially unopened copy in dustwrappers. 400 numbered copies hand-set and printed on hand-made paper. Deighton 3-263 1983 £24

SHANKS, EDWARD   The Island of Youth: A Poem. N.P. (London), 1921. No. 17 of 50 copies, signed. Privately printed for the poet. Light yellow buckram, printed front cover label. Covers lightly soiled. Bradley 65-166 1983 $30

SHANKS, EDWARD   The Universal War and the Universal State. London, 1946. 4to, blue cloth, gilt extra, d/w. One of 550 copies. A very fine copy. Perata 28-22 1983 $50

SHANKS, EDWARD   The Universal War and the Universal State. London: the Dropmore Press, 1946. Thin 4to. Orig. cloth. Title printed in red and black. Limited edition of 550 numbered copies. Traylen 94-736 1983 £12

SHANKS, JOHN P. C.   Vindication of Major General John C. Fremont Against the Attacks of the Slave Power and Its Allies. Washington: Scammel, 1862. 8vo, original pale blue printed wrappers. First edition. Few foxmarks. Very fine. Jenkins 153-206 1983 $100

SHANKS, WILLIAM F. G.   Personal Recollections of Distinguished Generals. N.Y., 1866. First edition. Bookplate and signature of Gen. Winfield Scott Hancock. Orig. cloth, illus. Fine copy. Jenkins 151-309 1983 $200

SHAPIRO, KARL   Trial of a Poet. NY, (1947). Limited to 250 numbered and signed copies, front pastedown and free endpaper offset, cover slightly soiled, else near fine in lightly sunned slip-case with minor wear. Quill & Brush 54-1223 1983 $50

SHAPIRO, KARL   Trial of a Poet and Other Poems. New York: Reynal & Hitchcock, (1947). Gray cloth. First edition. Review by Robert Fitzgerald laid in. Very good in dust jacket. Bradley 66-306 1983 $30

SHAPIRO, KARL   V-Letter and Other Poems. New York: (1944). First edition. Cloth. Very good in worn and mended dust jacket. Bradley 66-307 1983 $20

SHARP, ABRAHAM   Life and Correspondence of Abraham Sharp. Samson Low etc., London, 1889. 4to, with a frontis., 5 plates, 2 folding tables and several text illus. and reproductions; uncut, orig. half vellum. Only edition. Quaritch NS 5-99 1983 $175

SHARP, CUTHBERT   The Bishoprick garland, or a collection of legends, songs, ballads, etc... London: Nicholas, etc., 1834. First edition. Slim 8vo. Orig. blue cloth. Presentation copy, inscribed by Sharp to J.H. Fletcher. Privately printed in Sunderland, in an edition of 150 copies. With 2 plates, 2 engraved leaves of music, and a number of wood-engraved illustrations in the text. A bit rubbed and dull. Very good copy. Ximenes 63-260 1983 $45

SHARP, EVELYN   The Story of the Weathercock. Blackie, n.d. Sm. 4to. Colour frontis. Decorated title. 15 colour plates & 154 text illus. Pictorial endpapers, some wear. Red pictorial cloth, worn. Greer 40-191 1983 £35

SHARP, GRANVILLE   The Law of Liberty. London, 1776. 1st ed. Orig. paper boards, expertly rebacked. Library stamps on title-page. Jenkins 153-517 1983 $75

SHARP, JOHN   Mount Lowe and its Wonderful Railway. Mount Lowe: Echo Publishing Co., 1896. Second edition, enlarged. Folding view. Wrappers. Very good. Dawson 471-258 1983 $85

SHARP, JOHN   A Sermon Preached on the Day of the Public Fast, April the 11th. Walter Kettilby, 1679. First edition, including the initial blank leaf, 4to. Fenning 62-332 1983 £12.50

SHARP, JOHN   Scenic Mount Lowe and it Wonderful Railway. Los Angeles: Pacific Electric Railway, 1904. Fourth edition. Taped and marked. Half title pasted down to front wrapper. Dawson 471-259 1983 $75

SHARP, LUKE, PSEUD.
Please turn to
BARR, ROBERT

SHARP, WILLIAM   The Dominion of Dreams. Westminster: Archibald Constable & Co., 1899. First edition. Orig. cloth. Very good. MacManus 280-4657 1983 $35

SHARP, WILLIAM   Green Fire. Westminster: Archibald Constable & Co., 1896. First English edition. Orig. cloth. Fine. MacManus 280-4658 1983 $50

SHARP, WILLIAM   Life of Percy Bysshe Shelley. London: Walter Scott, 1887. First edition. Rebound in 3/4 navy morocco & cloth. Ex-library copy, with perforation and marks on title-page and copyright page. Fine. MacManus 280-4732 1983 $35

SHARP, WILLIAM   Madge o' the Pool, The Gypsy Christ and Other Tales. London: Archibald Constable & Co., 1896. First edition. Orig. pictorial cloth. Edges a little worn. Covers slightly worn. Very good. MacManus 280-4660 1983 $65

SHARP, WILLIAM   The Sin-Eater and Other Tales. Edinburgh: Geddes, (1895). First edition. Orig. cloth. Fine. MacManus 280-4662 1983 $45

SHARP, WILLIAM   The Washer of the Ford. New York: Stone & Kimball, 1896. 1st ed. Orig. blue cloth, t.e.g., others uncut. Not quite fine. Jenkins 155-869 1983 $30

SHARP, WILLIAM   Where the Forest Murmers. London: Country Life, 1906. First edition. Orig. cloth. MacManus 280-4664 1983 $35

SHARP, WILLIAM   The Winged Destiny. London: Chapman $ Hall, 1904. First edition. Orig. cloth. MacManus 280-4665 1983 $35

SHARPE, PHILIP B.   Complete Guide to Handloading. New York, (1942). 2nd ed., completely revised and enlarged with supp. Illus. 4to. Morrill 288-118 1983 $30

SHARPE, PHILIP B.   The Rifle in America. NY, 1938. Signed inscription from Sharpe, edges rubbed, else fine. Quill & Brush 54-1664 1983 $90

SHARPE, PHILIP B.   The Rifle in America. NY, (1947). Second edition, revised and enlarged, edges slightly rubbed, else fine. Quill & Brush 54-1665 1983 $35

SHARPE, R. B.   British Museum Catalogue of Birds. British Museum, 1875-98. 387 coloured plates, 27 vols., 8vo, rebound in black cloth. Extremely scarce. Vols. 1-11 have either one or both title-pages in xerox facsimile. The title page to vol. 3 is defective and restored. Plate 1 in Vol. 2 has frayed margins. Vols. 16, 17, 19, 20 and 21-27 have some (mostly slight) waterstaining of the plates, else the set is in good condition. Wheldon 160-11 1983 £2,000

SHARPE, R. B.   A Monograph of the Hirundinidae, or family of the Swallows. 2 vols., 4to, new half red morocco, gilt. Very scarce. A fine clean copy. Wheldon 160-94 1983 £2,200

SHARPE, R. B.   Monograph of the Paradiseidae, or Birds of Paradise, and Ptilonorhynchidae, or Bower-Birds. 1891-98. 2 vols., folio, half red morocco, gilt, 79 hand-coloured plates by Gould and Hart. A very fine copy. Wheldon 160-93 1983 £10,000

SHAW, ALBERT   A Cartoon History of Roosevelt's Career. N.Y., (1910). Illus. Orig. cloth. First edition. Ginsberg 46-672 1983 $25

SHAW, ALEXANDER   An Account of Sir Charles Bell's Discoveries in the Nervous System. London, 1860. 16mo, flexible cloth. "With the Author's Compts", on fly-leaf. Argosy 713-43 1983 $60

SHAW, BARNABAS   Memoirs of South Africa. London, J. Mason; Hamilton, Adams & Co., (York: J. Coultas, Printer), 1840. Orig. cloth a little stained and frayed. K Books 301-167 1983 £55

SHAW, BYAM   Old King Cole's Book of Nursery Rhymes. MacMillan, n.d. (ca.1900). 4to. Colour pictorial title & 24 colour plates, superbly printed by E. Evans. Colour pictorial glazed boards, corners bumped. Greer 40-203 1983 £65

SHAW, CHARLES G.   New York - Oddly Enough. NY, (1938). Illus., d.w. Argosy 710-382 1983 $25

SHAW, CHARLES P.   *Argument of...Esq. Before the Judiciary Committee of the House of Representatives in the Matter of the Application of William McGarrahan, for the Rancho Panoche Grande, California. Washington City, 1870. Half morocco. First edition. Ginsberg 47-167 1983 $65

SHAW, DONALD A.   Eldorado or California as Seen by a Pioneer. Los Angeles, Cal.: B.R. Baumgardt & Co., 1900. Frontis. Illustrations. First edition in original cloth. Jenkins 153-106 1983 $75

SHAW, G   Cimelia Physica. Figures of rare and
curious quadrupeds, birds, etc., together with several of the most
elegant plants. 1796. Imp. folio, cont. full dark blue straight-
grained morocco, g.e., hand-coloured plates. A fine and rare work.
Lacks plate 2. Some dampstains in the lower margins at the beginning
and end. Small tears repaired in lower margins of 2 leaves of text and
2 plates. Slight staining of upper margins of 2 leaves of text and
2 plates. A good copy. Wheldon 160-95 1983 £1,000

SHAW, GEORGE BERNARD   The Adventures of the Black Girl in her
Search for God. London: Constable & Co., 1932. First edition. Illus.
with wood-engravings by J. Farleigh. Orig. pictorial boards. Fine.
MacManus 280-4666 1983 $20

SHAW, GEORGE BERNARD   Androcles and the Lion, Overruled,
Pygmalion. London: Constable & Co., 1916. First edition. Orig.
cloth. Covers soiled. MacManus 280-4667 1983 $20

SHAW, GEORGE BERNARD   The Apple Cart: A Political Extrava-
ganza. L, 1920. Fine in slightly frayed dustwrapper, very good or
better. Quill & Brush 54-1224 1983 $30

SHAW, GEORGE BERNARD   The Apple Cart. London: Constable,
1930. 1st ed. Orig. cloth, dj. Very fine in near fine dj. Jenkins
155-1128 1983 $20

SHAW, GEORGE BERNARD   Back to Methuselah. London: Constable
& Co. Ltd., 1921. First edition. Orig. cloth. Presentation copy to
Max Beerbohm, inscribed on the half-title, dated June 16th, 1921.
Beerbohm's signature. Rebacked with orig. spine laid down. Numerous
pages dog-eared throughout text. Covers a little darkened. In a
fleece-lined folding box. A fine association. MacManus 280-4669
1983 $650

SHAW, GEORGE BERNARD   Back to Methuselah. London: Constable,
1921. Green cloth. First edition. A fine copy in dust jacket,
wanting one chip from top edge. Inscribed by Shaw to H.S. Salt.
Enclosed in half morocco slipcase. Reese 20-881 1983 $375

SHAW, GEORGE BERNARD   Back to Methuselah. London, 1921.
First edition. Slightly torn dust wrapper. Fine. Rota 230-537
1983 £25

SHAW, GEORGE BERNARD   Buoyant Billions. London, 1949.
4to. Illus. buckram, vellum spine. Decorative title-page and 19
plates from drawings by Clare Winsten. Limited edition of 1,025
copies. Traylen 94-739 1983 £18

SHAW, GEORGE BERNARD   Buoyant Billions. London, 1949. First
edition. Drawings by C. Winsten. One of 1025 numbered copies. 4to.
Half parchment. Very nice. Rota 230-539 1983 £12.50

SHAW, GEORGE BERNARD   Cashel Byron's Profession. Chicago:
Herbert S. Stone & Co., 1901. First American authorized edition.
Orig. pictorial cloth. With the signed bookplate of Archibald
Henderson, Shaw's official biographer, on the front pastedown. Extrem-
ities of spine a trifle worn. Covers faded. Very good. MacManus 280-
4670 1983 $50

SHAW, GEORGE BERNARD   The Collected Works. New York: Wise &
Company, 1930-1932. Thirty vols. Linen and boards, paper labels,
t.e.g. The Ayot St. Lawrence edition, limited to 1,790 numbered sets.
Photogravure frontis. A couple of labels very slightly rubbed, else a
fine set, partially unopened. Reese 20-879 1983 $500

SHAW, GEORGE BERNARD   The Collected Works. New York, 1930-
32. The Ayot St. Lawrence edition. 30 vols. 8vo. Orig. blue
boards, linen spines with paper labels, gilt, t.e.g., others uncut.
Portrait in each vol. Limited to 1,750 numbered sets. Traylen
94-738 1983 £180

SHAW, GEORGE BERNARD   The Common Sense of Municipal Trading.
London, 1904. First edition. 8vo, fine. Argosy 714-893 1983
$50

SHAW, GEORGE BERNARD   The Common Sense of Municipal Trading.
Westminster: Archibald Constable & Co., 1904. First edition. Orig.
cloth. Bookplate. Covers slightly soiled. In half morocco slipcase.
Good. MacManus 280-4672 1983 $25

SHAW, GEORGE BERNARD   The Doctor's Dilemma. London: Constable
& Co., Ltd., 1911. First edition. Orig. cloth. Spine a little
darkened. Very good. MacManus 280-4673 1983 $20

SHAW, GEORGE BERNARD   Dramatic Opinions and Essays. London:
Archibald Constable & Co., 1907. First English edition. 2 vols. Orig.
cloth. Dust jackets. Spine of dust jacket on Vol. I chipped. Very
fine. MacManus 280-4675 1983 $100

SHAW, GEORGE BERNARD   Ellen Terry & Bernard Shaw. N.Y.,
Fountain Press, 1931. First American edition. Orig. gilt stamped
green cloth (spine sunned), t.e.g., uncut and unopened. Title
printed in red and black. Pub.'s box (worn). Review from the
"London Times" laid in. One of 3,000 copies printed by D.B. Updike
at the Merrymount Press. Fine. Houle 22-796 1983 $75

SHAW, GEORGE BERNARD   Fabian Tracts, Nos. 1 to 139. London:
The Fabian Society, n.d. Thick 8vo, buckram. Argosy 714-670 1983
$100

SHAW, GEORGE BERNARD   Heartbreak House. London: Constable,
1919. First edition. Orig. cloth. Top edges slightly soiled. In
the orig. dust jacket (worn). Very nice. MacManus 280-4676 1983
$25

SHAW, GEORGE BERNARD   The Intelligent Woman's Guide To Social-
ism and Capitalism. London: Constable & Co., 1928. First edition.
Orig. decorated cloth. Presentation copy to Maurice Baring inscribed
on the half-title page. Spine and covers slightly faded and worn.
In a quarter-morocco slipcase. Bookplate of Maurice Baring. Near-fine.
MacManus 280-4678 1983 $500

SHAW, GEORGE BERNARD   The Intelligent Woman's Guide to
Socialism and Capitalism. London, 1928. Tall 8vo, dec. cloth, d.w.
First edition. Fine. Argosy 714-667 1983 $45

SHAW, GEORGE BERNARD   The Intelligent Woman's Guide to Socialism and Capitalism. London: Constable & Co., 1928. First English
edition. Orig. cloth. Dust jacket (defective). MacManus 280-4677
1983 $35

SHAW, GEORGE BERNARD   The Irrational Knot. London: Constable,
1905. First edition. Orig. cloth. Half morocco case. Very good.
MacManus 280-4679 1983 $50

SHAW, GEORGE BERNARD   The Irrational Knot. London, 1905.
First English edition. 8vo, cloth. Argosy 714-666 1983 $25

SHAW, GEORGE BERNARD   Love Among the Artists. Chicago, 1900.
First edition. Neatly tipped-in on the front endpaper is Shaw's
printed postcard refusing to sign copies of his books for collectors.
In a half dark blue morocco slipcase and matching cloth folder. Fine.
Rota 231-538 1983 £125

SHAW, GEORGE BERNARD   Love Among the Artists. Chicago: Stone,
1900. First edition. Orig. decorated cloth. Spine darkened. Half
morocco slipcase (a little rubbed). Good. MacManus 280-4681 1983
$75

SHAW, GEORGE BERNARD   Love Among the Artists. London, 1924.
First edition. Cr. 8vo. Cloth. Orig. coloured illus. dustwrapper
by Horosho. Traylen 94-740 1983 £20

SHAW, GEORGE BERNARD   Misalliance, The Dark Lady of the Sonnets.
London: Constable & Co., 1914. First edition. Orig. cloth. Dust
jacket. Fine. MacManus 280-4682 1983 $60

SHAW, GEORGE BERNARD   Misalliance, The Dark Lady of the Sonnets.
London, 1914. First edition. Dust wrapper. Very nice. Rota 230-
535 1983 £25

SHAW, GEORGE BERNARD   Mrs. Warren's Profession. London: Grant
Richards, 1902. First separate edition. Illus. after photographs.
Orig. printed pale green wrappers. Prelims and edges foxed. In a
green half morocco slipcase. Unusually fine. MacManus 280-4685
1983 $125

SHAW, GEORGE BERNARD   Peace Conference Hints. London: Constable & Co., 1919. First edition. Orig. printed wrappers. Half morocco slipcase. Fine. MacManus 280-4686 1983 $25

SHAW, GEORGE BERNARD   The Perfect Wagnerite. Chicago: Herbert S. Stone & Co., 1899. First American edition. Orig. cloth with paper spine label. Edges and corners slightly worn. Spine label slightly soiled and chipped. Previous owner's signature on front free endpaper. Good. MacManus 280-4683 1983 $35

SHAW, GEORGE BERNARD   Plays: Pleasant and Unpleasant. London: Grant Richards, 1898. First edition. 2 vols. Frontis. port. Spines darkened and worn; a bit soiled. A few clippings and photos tipped in. In two half morocco cases. MacManus 280-4687 1983 $125

SHAW, GEORGE BERNARD   Prefaces. London, 1934. First edition. 4to. Title-page design by J. Farleigh. Very nice. Rota 231-539 1983 £12.50

SHAW, GEORGE BERNARD   The Quintessence of Ibsenism. London: Walter Scott, 1891. First edition. Orig. cloth. Very good. MacManus 280-4690 1983 $65

SHAW, GEORGE BERNARD   The Quintessence of Ibsenism. London: Constable & Co. Ltd., 1913. First revised edition. Orig. cloth. Dust jacket (spine faded). Fine. MacManus 280-4691 1983 $50

SHAW, GEORGE BERNARD   Rhyming Picture Guide to Ayot Saint Lawrence. London, 1950. First edition. Illus. Thin 12mo, cloth, d.w. Argosy 714-668 1983 $30

SHAW, GEORGE BERNARD   The Simpleton, The Six and The Millionairess. London: Constable & Co., (1936). First of this edition. Orig. cloth. Presentation copy to the photographer F.H. Evans, inscribed on the half-title page, dated April 30th, 1936. Bookplate of Frederick H. Evans. Near-fine. MacManus 280-4684 1983 $250

SHAW, GEORGE BERNARD   Three Plays for Puritans. London, 1901. First edition. 8vo, cloth, somewhat soiled & rubbed. Argosy 714-669 1983 $60

SHAW, GEORGE BERNARD   Translations and Tomfooleries. London: Constable & Co., 1926. First edition. Orig. cloth. Dust jacket (sl. chipped). Fine. MacManus 280-4697 1983 $25

SHAW, GEORGE BERNARD   The Unprotected Child and the Law. London: Six Point Group, (n.d.). 1st ed. Orig. wrappers. Uncommon. Jenkins 155-1136 1983 $45

SHAW, HENRY   Details of Elizabethan Architecture. London: William Pickering, (1834)-1839. 4to, a few hand-colored. Orig. calf over cloth. Lower spine extremity slightly chipped. Some foxing. Karmiole 75-7 1983 $150

SHAW, IRWIN   The Gentle People. NY, (1939). Very good in worn dustwrapper. Quill & Brush 54-1227 1983 $30

SHAW, IRWIN   Sons and Soldiers. NY, (1944). Review copy with slip laid in, near fine in near fine dustwrapper. Quill & Brush 54-1226 1983 $50

SHAW, IRWIN   Sons and Soldiers. NY, (1944). Fine in very good dustwrapper. Quill & Brush 54-1225 1983 $35

SHAW, JOSEPH   Parish Law. In the Savoy: Henry Lintot...for F. Cogan and J. Nourse, 1743. Fifth edition. Calf, leading hinge a trifle weak. Jarndyce 31-45 1983 £54

SHAW, NAPIER   The Smoke Problem of Great Cities. Constable, 1925. First edition, half title, front. illus. Ex-library stamp on title. Orig. blue cloth. Jarndyce 31-337 1983 £10.50

SHAW, ROBERT K.   A Biography of Samuel Swett Green. Chicago: American Library Association, 1926. First edition. Small 8vo. Cloth-backed boards, paper spine label. Printed by D.B. Updike at the Merrymount Press. Oak Knoll 49-208 1983 $25

SHAW, S.   A Tour to the West of England in 1788. London: for Robson and Clarke..., 1789. First edition. Thick 8vo. Cont. polished calf, gilt. Very slight foxing. Heath 48-573 1983 £100

SHAW, T.   Travels, or Observations Relating to Several Parts of Barbary and the Levant. London, 1757. Second edition. 10 maps, 7 folding, folding Peutinger Table, full-page rabbinical map. 3 plans, 1 folding, 22 plates, 2 folding. Full page illus. of music, engraved headpieces including 3 maps. Engraved initials. 4to. Preface mis-bound but complete. Half calf. Good. Edwards 1044-787 1983 £180

SHAW, WILLIAM   Golden Dreams and Waking Realities. London: Smith, Elder and Co., 1851. Ads. Orig. cloth with minor repair. Light staining to text, otherwise a nice copy. Jenkins 153-507 1983 $150

SHAW, WILLIAM   The Story of My Mission in South-Eastern Africa. 1860. Folding map and 4 plates, orig. cloth, blocked in blind. Small library stamp on title, spine faded. Bickersteth 77-246 1983 £22

SHAW, WILLIAM A.   The Knights of England. Sherratt and Hughes, 1906. First edition, 2 vols., 4to, orig. cloth, t.e.g. The sides a little discoloured, otherwise nice. Fenning 60-378 1983 £45

SHEA, JOHN GILMARY   A History of the Catholic Church in the United States... New York, 1886-1892. First edition. Illus. 4 vols., 8vo, rebound in buckram, ex-library, nice. Morrill 290-488 1983 $60

SHEE, MARTIN ARCHER   Alasco: a tragedy, in five acts. London: Sherwood, Jones, and Co.; Shackell and Arrowsmith, printers, 1824. 8vo, cont. qtr. cloth and boards. First ed. Half-title present. Ximenes 64-487 1983 $50

THE SHEEPSHANKS Gallery. Bell & Daldy, 1870. 20 mounted plates repro. by Cundall & Fleming, printed at the Chiswick Press). Green fine bead grain on cloth gilt (designed by W. Harry Rogers), bevelled boards, a.e.g. 1" split top rear joint & sl. wear top/bottom bkstrip, insc. fr. ep., vg. Hodgkins 27-326 1983 £38

SHEETS, E. W.   The Beef Calf: Its Growth and Development. Wash., 1920. Pictorial wrappers. Illus. Jenkins 152-595 1983 $35

SHEFFIELD, JOHN, DUKE OF BUCKINGHAM AND NORMANBY
Please turn to
BUCKINGHAM, JOHN SHEFFIELD, DUKE OF

SHEFFIELD, T.   The Story of the Settlement with a Sketch of Grahamstown as it was and Grahamstown as it is. Grahamstown, 1884. 22 engravings, second edition, new cloth. K Books 301-168 1983 £48

SHELDON, HAROLD P.   Tranquility. NY: Derrydale Press, (1936). With 5 plates. Edition ltd. to 950 numbered copies. Red gilt-stamped cloth. Bookplate. Illus. by Ralph L. Boyer. Karmiole 75-44 1983 $125

SHELDON, HAROLD P.   Tranquility Regained. NY (1945). 1st ed., limited to 5000 copies. Illus, cloth, very good in discolored dw. King 46-649 1983 $25

SHELDON, J. M. ARMS   Concretions from the Champlain Clays of the Connecticut Valley. 1st ed. Illus. by Katharine Peirson Ramsay and others on 14 heliograph plates. 4to. Morrill 286-437 1983 $20

SHELLEY, HARRIET   Letters to Catherine Nugent. London: Printed for Private Circulation, 1889. Orig. printed wrappers. Limited to 250 copies. Specially made cloth slipcase. Fine. MacManus 280-4704 1983 $250

SHELLEY, MARY WOLLSTONECRAFT GODWIN   Frankenstein: or, the Modern Prometheus. London: Richard Bentley, 1831. New edition. 12mo. Cont. half calf. Frontis. Binding rather rubbed and worn, lacks label. Lacks a half-title. Ximenes 63-136 1983 $85

SHELLEY, MARY WOLLSTONECRAFT GODWIN   Frankenstein, or the Modern Prometheus. N.Y.: Grosset & Dunlap, n.d. Orig. cloth. Spine a bit faded. Very good. MacManus 280-4705 1983 $50

SHELLEY, MARY WOLLSTONECRAFT GODWIN   The Last. Henry Colburn, 1826. First edition. 3 vols. Large 12mo, lacks the initial blank leaves in vols. II and III (no half-titles called for), and final blank leaf in vol. I. Cont. cloth. Hannas 69-187 1983 £300

SHELLEY, MARY WOLLSTONECRAFT GODWIN   Tales and Stories. London: William Paterson & Co., 1891. First edition. Intro. by R. Garnett. Frontis. port. Orig. decorated cloth. Good. MacManus 280-4707 1983 $150

SHELLEY, MARY WOLLSTONECRAFT GODWIN   A Vindication of the Rights of Woman. Boston: Edes for Thomas and Andrews, 1792. 8vo. Woodcut of Faust's statue. Orig. calf (rubbed). Andrew J. Chase, Ebenezer Weston & other ownership inscr. Half-title. Bearing inscr. indicating copy was owned by the mate of the ship "Rose" in Baltimore, by someone aboard sloop "Elisabeth" in Bermuda in 1811...and by Ebenezer Weston of Bangor, Maine. Rostenberg 88-97 1983 $500

SHELLEY, PERCY BYSSHE   An Address to the Irish People. London: Published for the Shelley Society by Reeves & Turner, 1890. Orig. printed borads. Limited to 200 copies. Fine. MacManus 280-4710 1983 $50

SHELLEY, PERCY BYSSHE   The Cenci, a Tragedy in Five Acts. Reeves & Turner, 1886. Frontis. 4 pp. ads. Orig. blue printed boards. Unopened. Fine. Jarndyce 31-904 1983 £24

SHELLEY, PERCY BYSSHE   The English Replicas. N.Y.: Payson & Clarke Ltd., 1927. 4to. Facs. of the first edition of Adonais printed at Pisa. Orig. full vellum. Limited to 100 copies printed on handmade rag paper bound in vellum. Fine. MacManus 280-4711 1983 $85

SHELLEY, PERCY BYSSHE   Essays, Letters From Abroad. London: Moxon, 1840. First edition. 2 vols. Orig. cloth. Covers considerably worn. Inner hinges cracked. MacManus 280-4712 1983 $85

SHELLEY, PERCY BYSSHE   Harriet & Mary, being the relations between Percy Bysshe Shelley, Harriet Shelley, Mary Shelley, and Thomas Jefferson Hogg... London: the Golden Cockerel Press, 1944. 4to. Cloth. Orange morocco spine, gilt, t.e.g., others uncut. Portrait. Limited edition of 500 numbered copies. Traylen 94-742 1983 £48

SHELLEY, PERCY BYSSHE   The Letters of Percy Bysshe Shelley. London, 1909. First edition. Portrait frontispieces and other illus. 2 vols., dark blue cloth, gilt top edges, others uncut. Very nice set. Bradley 65-167 1983 $85

SHELLEY, PERCY BYSSHE   Letters...To J. H. Leigh Hunt. London: Privately Printed, 1894. First Wise edition. 2 vols. 8vo. Rebound in 3/4 green morocco & cloth. Limited to 30 copies. Bookplate. Very fine. MacManus 280-4713 1983 $250

SHELLEY, PERCY BYSSHE   The Narrative Poems. London, 1927. 2 vols. Small 4to. Black buckram, gilt, uncut edges, in the orig. slip-case. Traylen 94-743 1983 £22

SHELLEY, PERCY BYSSHE   Note Books. Boston, Bibliophile Soc., 1911. 3 vols. Large 8vo. Frontis. portrait & 9 facsimile plates (mostly drawings). Gilt-stamped parchment. 1st ed. 465 copies only. Fine. O'Neal 50-45 1983 $125

SHELLEY, PERCY BYSSHE   The Poems of Percy Bysshe Shelley. (London: The Vale Press, 1901). 3 vols. With several decorative wooduct page borders and initials by Charles Ricketts. In beige cloth, with gilt-stamped spines. Binding sl. soiled. With 4 page prospectus of the press laid in. Karmiole 76-106 1983 $250

SHELLEY, PERCY BYSSHE   The Poetical Works. London: Edward Moxon, Dover Stree, 1839. First edition. 4 vols. Frontis. port. in vol. I. Orig. blind-stamped red cloth. Spines and covers slightly faded and rubbed. Endpapers slightly glue-stained from former owner's bookplates. Very good, tight copy. MacManus 280-4715 1983 $450

SHELLEY, PERCY BYSSHE   The Poetical Works of... London: Moxon, 1839. First edition. 4 vols. Orig. cloth. Heads of spines worn. Very good. MacManus 280-4716 1983 $250

SHELLEY, PERCY BYSSHE   The Poetical Works. Edward Moxon, 1839. First collected edition. 4 vols. Half titles, frontis. port. vol. I. Maroon morocco, gilt, spines and hinges slightly rubbed, a.e.g. Jarndyce 31-899 1983 £140

SHELLEY, PERCY BYSSHE   The Poetical Works. The Prose Works. London, 1878-80. 8 vols. 8vo. Half maroon morocco, gilt, gilt panelled spines, t.e.g. Portraits and other illus. Traylen 94-741 1983 £220

SHELLEY, PERCY BYSSHE   The Poetical Works of Percy Bysshe Shelley. 1894-1895. 8vo, vellum. Printed in Golden Type. Woodcut titles and borders. A fine double-page opening, the first recto p. entirely in capitals. 3 vols. One of 250 copies. Some discoloration to yap edges of vellum on vols. I and III. Duschnes 240-124 1983 $1,000

SHELLEY, PERCY BYSSHE   Posthumous Fragments of Margaret Nicholson... Oxford: by J. Munday, (reprint ca. 1880). 4to. half title. Orig. boards. Scarce. Heath 48-417 1983 £65

SHELLEY, PERCY BYSSHE   Posthumous Poems. London: 1824. Octavo. First edition. In superb signed Zaehnsdorf binding of full wine-colored morocco with elaborate gilt-stamped and white inlaid decoration. Gilt-decorated spine with five raised bands. Wide dentelles with gilt ornamental border, burgundy silk endpapers. A.e.g. Protective oilcloth dust wrapper. Near mint. Gilt-stamped leather bookplate. Bromer 25-154 1983 $1500

SHELLEY, PERCY BYSSHE   Prometheus Unbound. (Campden, Glocs., Essex House Press, 1904). Large 4to, orig. vellum, orig. cloth ties, printed in red and black, uncut copy. One of only 200 copies. Ravenstree 94-73 1983 $295

SHELLEY, PERCY BYSSHE   Relics of Shelley. Edward Moxon, 1862. First edition. 8 pp. inserted ads. Half title, 2 pp. ads. Orig. purple cloth, slightly rubbed at head of spine. Jarndyce 31-901 1983 £42

SHELLEY, PERCY BYSSHE   Rosalind and Helen, A Modern Eclogue; With Other Poems. London: 1819. Half-title and ads. Fine, uncut copy, quarter-leather and marbled boards, rubbed at extremities and slightly sunned at spine. Bookplate. First edition. Bromer 25-100 1983 $650

SHELLEY, PERCY BYSSHE   St. Irvyne; or, the Rosicrucian. London: printed for J.J. Stockdale, 1822. First edition, second issue. 12mo. 19th-century half roan (rather rubbed). Some soiling and signs of use throughout. Scarce. Ximenes 63-137 1983 $900

SHELLEY, PERCY BYSSHE   Shelley's Lost Letters to Harriet. Lon., 1930. Limited to 950 numbered and signed copies by Leslie Hotson, endpapers lightly offset, minor cover soiling, else very good in worn, split slipcase. Quill & Brush 54-1230 1983 $40

SHELLEY, PERCY BYSSHE   Zastrossi. London, 1955. Quarto, full black niger morocco, gilt, g.t. by Sangorski & Sutcliffe. With eight engravings by Cecil Keeling. One of 60 copies specially bound, with an extra set of the engravings. Slipcase. Duschnes 240-94 1983 $200

SHELLEY, PERCY BYSSHE   Zastrossi. London, 1955. Half leather with marbled boards. One of 140 copies. Duschnes 240-95 1983 $100

SHELLEY, PERCY BYSSHE   Zastrozzi. London, 1955. 8vo, black morocco-backed decorated bds., t.e.g., slipcase. One of 200 copies with engravings by Cecil Keeling. A fine copy. Perata 27-53 1983 $100

SHELLEY and His Circle... London, 1961-70. 4 vols. 4to. Cloth, in the orig. dustwrapper. 68 facsimiles, portrait, maps, etc. Traylen 94-744 1983 £85

SHELTON, LOUIS   Beautiful Gardens in America. NY: Charles Scribner's Sons, 1924. 4to, with 195 photo plates. Color frontis. Green cloth. Karmiole 72-87 1983 $35

SHELTON, WILLIAM HENRY   The Salmagundi Club... Boston:
Houghton Mifflin Company, 1918. Tall 8vo, illus. Index. Edition
ltd. to 500 copies. Cloth over boards; paper spine label. Karmiole
72-88 1983 $30

SHENSTONE, WILLIAM   Men & Manners. Waltham Saint Laurence,
1927. Sm. 8vo, leather-backed boards, gilt, t.e.g. One of 500 copies.
Perata 28-29 1983 $60

SHENSTONE, WILLIAM   Songs. Chelsea, Swan Press, 1930.
Slim 8vo, decorative typographical head lines, uncut in original
qtr. cream buckram over red and white paper boards, paper label,
slight wear, very good unopened copy. 100 copies on hand-made paper.
Deighton 3-265 1983 £18

SHENSTONE, WILLIAM   The Works in Verse and Prose. Edinburgh,
for Donaldson, 1765. 1st Edinburgh edition, 2 vols, tall 12mo,
engraved portrait and title to each vol., cont. calf decorated in
gilt with red and green morocco labels, slight wear. Excellent
set. Deighton 3-266 1983 £68

SHENTON, EDWARD   The Gray Beginning. Philadelphia:
Penn Publ., 1924. 1st ed. Orig. cloth. Inscribed by author who
describes this copy as the first one sold. Jenkins 155-1139 1983
$20

SHEPARD, GEORGE   Urania: A Treatise on Transits. N.p.:
1834. Square small quarto. One hand-drawn chart. Hand-written
manuscript. Three-quarters black calf and cloth. Covers worn, contents fine. Bradley 66-404 1983 $250

SHEPARD, ISAAC F.   Memorial Day. May 30, 1870. St.
Louis, 1870. Orig. printed wraps. Embossed library stamp. First
edition. Ginsberg 46-498 1983 $30

SHEPHARD, ESTHER   Paul Bunyan. NY, (1924). Illus. by
Rockwell Kent. Spine edges lightly frayed, otherwise very good.
Quill & Brush 54-1231 1983 $40

SHEPHERD, DANIEL   Saratoga, a Story of 1877. NY, (1856).
1st ed., adv. pp., orig. designed cloth, few pp. tops stained.
Argosy 710-363 1983 $35

SHEPHERD, WILLIAM   Prairie Experiences in Handling Cattle
and Sheep. London: Chapman & Hall, 1884. First edition. Illus.
from sketches by author. Folding map, 8 plates. Orig. green gilt
cloth. Very fine. Jenkins 152-408 1983 $275

SHEPHERD, WILLIAM   Prairie Experience in Handling
Cattle and Sheep. N.Y., 1885. Illus. Orig. gold stamped cloth.
First American edition. Ginsberg 47-829 1983 $85

SHEPHERD, WILLIAM   Prairie Experiences in Handling Cattle
and Sheep. New York: O. Judd Co., 1885. Frontis. and illus.
Original pictorial cloth. Wear to covers. First American edition.
Presentation copy from the publishers. Jenkins 151-311 1983 $75

SHEPPARD, ELIZABETH SARA   Charles Auchester. London: Hurst &
Blackett, 1853. First edition. 3 vols. Orig. cloth. Fine, tight
copy. MacManus 280-4741 1983 $450

SHEPPARD, ELIZABETH SARA   Charles Auchester. Hurst & Blackett,
1853. First edition, 3 vols. Titles foxed, half blue calf, labels.
Jarndyce 30-544 1983 £40

SHEPPERD, TAD   Pack and Paddock. NY, 1938.
12mo, 3/4 red cloth over bds., leather label, t.e.g. Illustrated by
Paul Brown. One of 950 copies. Perata 28-21 1983 $100

SHERBORN, C. D.   An Index to the Genera and Species of
Foraminifera. Washington, Smiths. Misc. Coll., 1893-96. 2 parts,
8vo, original wrappers, back wrapper to part 2 missing. Wheldon 160-
1340 1983 £20

SHERBURNE, ANDREW   Memoirs of... Utica, 1828. First ed.
12mo, contemporary calf, leather label, ex-library. Morrill 290-490
1983 $50

SHERER, JOSEPH MOYLE
Please turn to
SHERER, MOYLE

SHERER, MOYLE   Scenes and impressions in Egypt and in
Italy. London: printed for Longman, etc., 1824. First edition.
8vo. Cont. tree calf, spine gilt. Upper hinge partly cracked, but
firm. Ximenes 63-608 1983 $125

SHERER, MOYLE   The story of a life. London: Longman,
etc., 1825. First edition. 2 vols. 8vo. Cont. half calf, spines
gilt. Half-titles present. Very good copy. Ximenes 63-138 1983
$150

SHERER, MOYLE   The Story of a Life. Longman, Hurst,
etc., 1825. 3rd edition, 2 vols. Half calf, a little rubbed.
Jarndyce 30-545 1983 £20

SHERIDAN, FRANCES   The Discovery, A Comedy in Five Acts.
London: Chatto & Windus, 1924. 1st ed., limited to 210 numbered
(no. 13) copies. Orig. cloth-backed decorated boards, paper label,
uncut, spare label at end. Signed by Huxley on an inserted leaf
that appears to be orig. with the book. Very fine and unopened.
Jenkins 155-655 1983 $125

SHERIDAN, P. H.   Personal Memoirs of... New York, 1888.
8vo. Orig. green decorated cloth. 2 vols. Pirtrait frontis. 15 full
page illus., 11 folding maps, 14 full page and 2 other maps. Gilt.
Upper cover vol. 1 slightly soiled. Very slightly worn. Good.
Edwards 1042-249 1983 $60

SHERIDAN, RICHARD BRINSLEY   The Critic; or, A Tragedy Rehearsed.
Phila.: Thomas H. Palmer, 1822. Stitched. Title very slightly dust
soiled. Very good. Flecone 20-35 1983 $50

SHERIDAN, RICHARD BRINSLEY   The Duenna.
Please turn to
LINLEY, THOMAS (1751-1816)

SHERIDAN, RICHARD BRINSLEY   The Filipino Martyrs. London, 1900.
Folding map. 3 plates. 8vo. Orig. cloth. Good. Edwards 1044-640
1983 £18

SHERIDAN, RICHARD BRINSLEY   The Plays. London: George Routledge
& Sons, 1886. First of this edition. Orig. cloth. Covers and spine
worn and soiled. Paper label on spine chipped. In a half-morocco
slipcase. Good. MacManus 280-4742 1983 $35

SHERIDAN, RICHARD BRINSLEY   The School for Scandal. London, (1891).
Large 4to. Orig. blue cloth decorated with 16 coloured miniatures.
With 19 illus, of which 17 are chromolithographs. Traylen 94-747
1983 £16

SHERIDAN, RICHARD BRINSLEY   The School for Scandal & the Rivals.
Macmillan, 1896. 1st edn. Illus. by E.J. Sullivan. Late issue with
60 b&w illus., 6pp adverts. Dark green decor. cloth gilt, a.e.g.
(contemp. insc. fr. ep.), fine copy. Hodgkins 27-491 1983 £16.50

SHERIDAN, RICHARD BRINSLEY   The School for Scandal. Hodder, nd
(ca. 1920). 1st edn. Illus. by Hugh Thomson: mounted colour frontis,
& 24 mounted col. plates & numerous b&w illus. Mauve decor. cloth
gilt (bkstrip faded, corners sl. bumped), v.g. copy. Hodgkins 27-492
1983 £30

SHERIDAN, RICHARD BRINSLEY   A Trip to Scarborough. London: for G.
Wilkie, 1781. First edition. Half-title, 8vo, full light blue crushed
morocco, gilt, inner gilt dentelles, edges gilt, by Riviere. Traylen
94-748 1983 £105

SHERIDAN, RICHARD BRINSLEY   Verses to the Memory of Garrick.
London: T. Evans, 1779. 4th ed., 4to, disbound, half-title, engraved plate by A. Albanesi. A very fine copy. Trebizond 18-89
1983 $75

SHERIDAN, THOMAS   A humble appeal to the publick, together
with some considerations on the present critical and dangerous state
of the stage in Ireland. Dublin: printed for G. Faulkner, 1758. 8vo,
original pale blue wrappers (spine defective). First edition.
Portion of the title-page abraded, leaving a few small holes but not
affecting the legibility of the text; else a fine uncut copy. Rare.
Ximenes 64-489 1983 $400

SHERIDAN, THOMAS   Remarks on two letters signed Theatricus
and Hibernicus, and published in the Dublin Journal of the 12th and
23rd of February, 1754. Dublin: 1754. 8vo, disbound, first ed.
Trimmed a bit close at the top, but a good copy of a very rare pamphlet.
Ximenes 64-491 1983 $500

SHERIDAN, THOMAS   Mr. Sheridan's speech addressed to a
number of gentlemen assembled with a view of considering the best means
to establish one good theatre in this city. Dublin: printed by and
for George Faulkner, 1772. 8vo, disbound, first edition. Extremely
rare. Ximenes 64-490 1983 $500

SHERLEY, THOMAS   A philosophical essay: declaring the
probable causes, whence stones are produced in the greater world.
London: Cademan, 1672. First edition. 8vo. Cont. sheep. Trifle
worn. Some worming in the blank upper corners of the first dozen
leaves, otherwise a fine crisp copy. Ximenes 63-290 1983 $375

SHERLOCK, THOMAS   A letter from the Lord Bishop of
London... London: Whiston, 1750. First edition. 8vo. Disbound.
Ximenes 63-91 1983 $25

SHERLOCK, WILLIAM   An Answer to a Discourse Intituled, Papists Protesting Against Protestant-Popery. Printed for John Amery and
William Rogers, 1686. First edition. Imprimatur leaf, complete in
spine of pagination jump, 4to, wrapper. Fenning 61-401 1983 £14.50

SHERLOCK, WILLIAM   An Answer to the Amicable Accomodation of
the Differences Between the Representer and the Answerer. Printed for
John Amery and William Rogers, 1686. First edition. 4to, wrapper,
a very good copy. Fenning 61-402 1983 £12.50

SHERLOCK, WILLIAM   A Papist not Misrepresented by
Protestants. Printed for Ric. Chiswell, 1686. First edition, 4to,
wrapper, a very good copy. Fenning 61-403 1983 £14.50

SHERLOCK, WILLIAM   A Practical Discourse concerning
Death. London: for R. Ware, etc., 1749. 8vo. Cont. speckled
calf, gilt, gilt spine with crimson morocco label, gilt. Vignette
title-page, ad. leaf. Traylen 94-749 1983 £18

SHERLOCK, WILLIAM   A Preservative Against Popery. Printed
for William Rogers, 1688. First editions, two parts, all published,
4to, wrapper, a very good copy. Fenning 61-404 1983 £24.50

SHERLOCK, WILLIAM   A Protestant of the Church of England.
Printed for T. Basset, 1686. First edition, 4to, wrapper, a little
dusty but a v.g. copy. Fenning 61-405 1983 £16.50

SHERLOCK, WILLIAM   A Sermon Preached at the Funeral of the
Rev. Benj. Calamy D.D. Printed for John Amery and William Rogers,
1686. First edition, wanting half-title, 4to, wrapper, v.g.
Fenning 62-335 1983 £18.50

SHERLOCK, WILLIAM   A Short Summary of the Principal
Controversies Between the Church of England, and the Church of Rome.
Printed for Richard Chiswell, 1687. First edition, including
imprimatur leaf, 4to, wrapper. Fenning 61-407 1983 £16.50

SHERLOCK, WILLIAM   A Vindication of Both Parts of the
Preservative Against Popery. Printed for William Rogers, 1688.
First edition, 4to, wrapper. Fenning 61-409 1983 £16.50

SHERMAN, CLIFFORD LEON   The Great Dot Mystery. Boston: HM,
1916. First edition. 4to. Green pictorial cloth. Light wear to
extremities. Very good. Aleph-bet 8-234 1983 $20

SHERMAN, DEWITT   Semi-Centennial Volume of the American
Pediatric Society. Menasha, 1938. First edition. 8vo. Orig.
binding. Fye H-3-506 1983 $40

SHERMAN, FREDERIC FAIRCHILD Albert Pinkham Ryder. New York:
Privately Printed, 1920. 33 gravure illus. hors texte (1 color).
Titled tissue guards. 4to. Boards, 1/4 cloth. T.e.g. Uncut.
Edition limited to 225 copies only, printed on Dutch handmade
paper. Rare. Ars Libri 32-609 1983 $200

SHERMAN, JOHN H.   A General Account of Miranda's Expedition.
New York: M'Farlane and Long, 1808. Lacking title and contents leaf.
Uncut. Orig. drab blue upper wrapper with cont. ms notations. First
edition. Jenkins 152-258 1983 $75

SHERMAN, WILLIAM T.   Memoirs. New York, 1875. 1st ed.
2 vols., 8vo, few rubbed spots. Morrill 288-448 1983 $25

SHERMAN, WILLIAM T.   Personal Memoirs of General W. T.
Sherman. NY, 1890. 2 vols. Third edition, revised and corrected.
Moderately rubbed. King 46-80 1983 $37.50

SHERO, RONALD   Underdogs of War. L.A., Wetzel,
(1948). First edition. Illus. with halftones. Cloth. Good-very
good. Houle 21-801 1983 $20

SHERRINGTON, C. S.   The Integrative Action of the Nervous
System. Cambridge, (1947). New edition, portrait and 85 text-figures,
8vo, cloth. Wheldon 160-521 1983 £15

SHERRINGTON, CHARLES   The Endeavor of Jean Fernel. Cambridge,
1946. First edition. 8vo. Orig. binding. Dust wrapper. Fye
H-3-737 1983 $60

SHERSTON, PETER   The Months, commencing with Early
Spring. Bath: for the Benefit of the General Hospital by W.
Meyler..., 1809. First edition. 8vo. Modern quarter cloth.
Engraved plates. Slight foxing. Heath 48-419 1983 £40

SHERWELL, ARTHUR   Life in West London. Methuen, 1897.
2nd edition, revised. Half title, 40 pp ads. Orig. red cloth.
Jarndyce 31-294 1983 £16.50

SHERWOOD, ROBERT E.   Roosevelt and Hopkins. New York: (1948).
First edition. Illus. Portrait frontis. Dark blue cloth. Fine in
jacket. Bradley 66-658 1983 $35

SHETLER, S. G.   Variation and evolution of the Nearctic
Harebells. Phan. Mon., XI, 1982. 50 figures, 8vo, cloth. Wheldon 160-
1571 1983 £52

SHICKELL, EDWARD HAMPTON   Bookplates for Libraries. N.p.: Roger
Beacham, (1968). Oblong 8vo, 39 leaves of plates. With a total of
77 illus. of college bookplates, most printed in two colors. Cloth-
backed boards; paper labels. Karmiole 75-27 1983 $25

SHIELDS, G. O.   Crusings in the Cascades... Chicago &
N.Y.: Rand, McNally, 1889. Ads. Cloth. Dawson 471-260 1983 $30

SHILAND, ANDREW   From Ocean to Ocean with Notes and
Observations on the Way. New York: For Sale by American Tract Soc.,
1892. Orig. cloth, gilt. Some chipping to endsheet. Very scarce.
Very fine copy. Jenkins 153-509 1983 $100

SHIMER, FLORENCE   Twelve Poems. (Hingham: Press of the
Little Red Hen, 1950). First edition. Square 8vo. Boards, wraparound paper cover label, orig. mailing box with a mailing label
designed by Dwiggins. Title page designed by W.A. Dwiggins and printed
in two colors. Loosely inserted is a cancelled check signed on the
back by Dwiggins and a one-page T.L.s. from Dorothy Abbe concerning
this book and enclosing a bill. Very fine copy. Scarce. Oak Knoll
49-170 1983 $225

SHINN, CHARLES HOWARD   Mining Camps. New York: 1885. First
edition. Orig. cloth. Extremities frayed, library sticker on spine,
front inner hinge cracked, some brittle fore-edges jammed without
affecting type. Bradley 66-665 1983 $35

SHINN, CHARLES HOWARD   Mining Camps. New York, 1948. 1st
Borzoi edn. Clark 741-254 1983 $29.50

SHIPLEY, JONATHAN   A Speech Intended to Have Been Spoken
on the Bill for Altering the Charters of the Colony of Massachusett's
Bay. London, 1774. Leather and cloth, spine cracked, internally
very good. Reese 18-106 1983 $150

SHIPLEY, MARY   Cousin Deborah's Whim. London: Samuel Tinsley & Co., 1878. First edition. 3 vols. Orig. cloth. Spines and covers rather faded and slightly spotted. Former owner's signature. Good. MacManus 280-4745 1983 $150

SHIPPEN, WILLIAM   Faction Display'd. London: 1704. 4to, offsetting onto title, last line of the preface shaved by the binder, in wrappers. Pickering & Chatto 19-65 1983 $200

SHIPPEN, WILLIAM   Moderation Display'd. London: 1704. 1st ed., 4to, old blue wrappers, lower margins uncut. A nice copy. Pickering & Chatto 19-66 1983 $250

THE SHIPWRECK, or The Desert Island. Phila., 1840. 6 engraved plates, colored. Cloth. Light cover wear. Very clean. Felcone 20-80 1983 $35

SHIRK, DAVID   The Cattle Drives of David Shirk from Texas to the Idaho Mines. Portland: Champoeg Press, 1956. First edition. Limited to 750 copies. Frontis. Tipped in portrait. Orig. pictorial cloth. Orig. glassine jacket. Mint. Jenkins 152-411 1983 $100

SHIRLEY, WILLIAM   Correspondence of William Shirley. New York, 1912. 1st ed. Illus. 2 vols. 8vo. Dust wrappers, boxed (part of d/w of vol. 1 lacking; box worn and torn. Morrill 289-431 1983 $40

SHIRLEY, WILLIAM   The parricide: or, innocence in distress. A tragedy. London: printed for J. Watts, 1739. 8vo, wrappers, first edition. Half-title present. Ximenes 64-492 1983 $75

SHOBERL, FREDERICK   The World in Miniature; Africa. London: R. Ackermann, 1821. 4 vols. 16mo. 45 hand-colored plates. 2 maps. Cont. 1/2 red calf, gilt, rubbed, some plate transfer. Adelson Africa-127 1983 $600

SHOEMAKER, ALFRED L.   A Check List of Imprints of the German Press of Northampton County, Pennsylvania, 1766-1905. Easton: Northampton County Historical and Genealogical Society, 1943. 4 plates, cloth. 1 of 200 copies. Dawson 470-269 1983 $25

SHOEMAKER, HENRY W. BLACK   Forest Souvenirs Collected in Northern Pennsylvania. Reading, 1914. Frontis., many photo plates. (Light stains on lower front). With "Compliments of the author" slip. Argosy 716-408 1983 $35

SHOFIELD, JOHN M.   Forty Six Years in the Army. N.Y., 1897. Illus. Orig. cloth. First edition. Ginsberg 47-827 1983 $75

SHOPPELL'S Modern Houses. New York, (1903). Drawings and floor plans. Small folio, orig. wrappers. Backstrip torn and chipped. Morrill 287-422 1983 $22.50

SHORE, C.   With British Snipers to the Reich. Georgetown, S.C. (1948). Photos, cloth, very good in worn dust wrapper. King 46-801 1983 $75

SHORE, HENRY N. BARON TEIGNMOUTH
Please turn to
TEIGNMOUTH, HENRY N. SHORE BARON

SHORT, THOMAS   A Rational Discourse of the Inward Uses of Water. Printed for Samuel Chandler, 1725. 8vo, modern buckram, first edition. Bickersteth 77-320 1983 £38

A SHORT Account of the Naval Actions of the Last War. London: J. Murray, 1788. Folding chart. Calf-backed boards (outer hinges cracking but sound). Felcone 21-96 1983 $150

A SHORT History of the Conduct of the Present Ministry with Regard to the American Stamp Act. London: J. Almon, 1766. Later wraps. Final leaf of ads. lacking. Felcone 21-97 1983 $175

SHORT System of Polite Learning: an Epitome of the Arts & Sciences for the Use of Schools. Phila., 1820. Frontis.; plate. Small 12mo, old calf, heavily foxed and stained. Argosy 710-483 1983 $60

SHORTER, CLEMENT K.   Highways and Byways in Buckinghamshire. London: Macmillan & Co., 1910. First edition. Illus. by F.L. Griggs. Orig. cloth. Very good. MacManus 280-4746 1983 $35

SHORTER, CLEMENT K.   Immortal Memories. London: Hodder & Stoughton, 1907. First edition. Orig. cloth. Rear inner hinge weak. Fine. MacManus 280-4747 1983 $45

SHORTER, CLEMENT K.   Immortal Memories. Hodder and Stoughton, 1907. 1st ed., 8vo, uncut in oatmeal cloth lettered in black and red, very good. Deighton 3-268 1983 £18

SHORTER, CLEMENT K.   Napoleon. London, 1910. First edition. Photogravure frontis. and photogravure plate, 3 plates, roy. 8vo. Spine slightly worn and soiled. Small library label. Good. Edwards 1042-436 1983 £18

SHORTHOUSE, JOHN   John Inglesant. Macmillan, 1882. 2 vols. Half calf, spines gilt, black and green labels, v.g. Jarndyce 30-547 1983 £18

SHORTHOUSE, JOSEPH HENRY   Blanche, Lady Falaise. London: Macmillan, 1891. First edition. Orig. cloth. With Hugh Walpole's bookplate. Front inner hinge cracked. MacManus 280-4749 1983 $25

SHORTHOUSE, JOSEPH HENRY   John Inglesant. London, MacMillan, 1881. 2 vols., tall 8vo, modern 3/4 tan crushed levant gilt, t.e.g., others untrimmed, joints little worn, bookplate removed. First edition. Ravenstree 96-217 1983 $55

SHORTHOUSE, JOSEPH HENRY   The Little Schoolmaster Mark. London: Macmillan, 1883. First edition. 12mo. Orig. cloth, Presentation copy from the author's wife. MacManus 280-4750 1983 $30

SHORTHOUSE, JOSEPH HENRY   Sir Percival. London, MacMillan, 1886. 8vo, orig. cloth gilt, light soiling and minor wear, note on end-paper and with author's autograph presentation inscription to the Dean of Norwich, signed and dated October 30, 1886 on half-title. First edition. Ravenstree 96-218 1983 $53

SHORTHOUSE, JOSEPH HENRY   A Teacher of the Violin & Other Tales. London: Macmillan & Co., 1888. First edition. Orig. decorated blue cloth. A trifle rubbed. Very good. MacManus 280-4752 1983 $25

SHORTRIDGE, G. C.   The Mammals of South-West Africa. 1934. Numerous illustrations and maps, 2 vols., royal 8vo, cloth. Wheldon 160-604 1983 £75

SHORTT, ADAM   Documents relating to Canadian Currency... Ottawa: Archives, 1925-16. 25cm. 2 vols. 8 plates. Bottom wrapper on vol. 2 chipped without loss of text. Printed wrappers. Very good to fine. McGahern 54-159 1983 $75

SHOUP, GEORGE L.   Idaho. (Boise, 1889). Orig. printed wraps. First edition. Ginsberg 46-324 1983 $25

SHRADY, JOHN   The College of Physicians and Surgeons... New York, (ca. 1903). 2 vols. First edition. 1/2 leather. 8vo. Outer front hinges cracked, top of spine of volume 1 torn, contents fine. Scarce. Fye H-3-507 1983 $150

SHREWSBURY, EARL OF   Letter to Ambrose Phillips. London, 1842. Second edition. 8vo. Orig. boards, rebacked, uncut. A few leaves rather roughly opened. Gurney JJ-371 1983 £15

SHRIMPTON, CHARLES   The Black Phantom, or Woman's Endurance. New York: Published by James Miller, 1867. 19cm. Orig. cloth. Good. McGahern 53-147 1983 $45

SHRYOCK, RICHARD   American Medical Research Past and Present. New York, 1947. First edition. 8vo. Orig. binding. Fye H-3-508 1983 $40

SHUCK, OSCAR T.   History of the Bench and Bar of California. Los Angeles: Commmercial Printing House, 1901. Large thick 8vo, illus. Index. Orig. brown cloth. Karmiole 76-70 1983 $100

SHUCK, OSCAR T.   Representative and Leading Men of the Pacific being Original Sketches. San Francisco, 1870. Title page with ex. lib. perforation, wear to top and bottom of spine. Reese 19-509 1983 $65

SHUFELDT, GEORGE A.   History of the Chicago Artesian Well. Chicago, 1866. Orig. printed wraps. First edition. Ginsberg 46-339 1983 $125

SHUMARD, BENJAMIN F.   Report on the Chouteau League Tract. St. Louis, 1873. Errata. 2 plates and 2 maps. Orig. front printed wrapper. First edition. Ginsberg 47-546 1983 $100

SHUMWAY, A. L.   Oberliniana. Cleveland, 1883. 1st ed. Illus. Small 8vo, orig. boards, cloth back, rubbed. Morrill 288-374 1983 $25

SHURTLEFF, NATHANIEL B.   A Topographical and Historical Description of Boston. Boston, 1871. 1st ed. 2 maps. 4to. Backstrip faded and frayed at ends. Morrill 287-620 1983 $35

SHURTLEFF, ROSWELL   A Discourse Delivered at the Funeral of Mrs. Mary Woodward. Hanover: Moses Davis, 1807. Disbound. Foxed and worn. Felcone 22-160 1983 $20

SHUTE, NEVIL   On the Beach. London, (1957). 8vo. Cloth. About fine copy in dj. Jacket has some light wear at the extremities of spine. In Our Time 156-695 1983 $100

SHUTE, NEVIL   On the Beach. London, 1957. First edition. D.w. A very good copy, the dust wrapper slightly worn at the head of the spine. Argosy 714-672 1983 $25

SHUTE, NEVIL   Vineland the Good. (NY), 1946. Corners slightly worn, else very good or better in slightly frayed, good dust-wrapper. Quill & Brush 54-1232 1983 $35

SIBBALD, R.   Scotia Illustrata. Edinburgh, 1684. Plate of arms and 22 engraved plates on 20 leaves, folio, contemporary calf. Very scarce. Some copies have a portrait which is not here present. Contains a catalogue of plants in the medical garden at Edinburgh. Some slight marginal waterstaining and worming, one plate stained, but generally a good clean copy in a well-preserved binding. Wheldon 160-434 1983 £225

SIBLEY, HENRY H.   Governor's Message to the Senate and House of Representatives of the State of Minnesota, 1859. St. Paul, Goodrich, 1859. Orig. printed wraps. Ginsberg 46-482 1983 $75

SIBLY, EBENEEZER   Celestial Science of Astrology. London, Nichol, 1784-1788. First edition. Four parts in one. With four title pages. 4to, engraved frontis. and 30 copper plates (three of which are handcolored). Hundreds of diagrams in the text, many full page; one folding. Full old calf (joints crudely repaired), else good-very good. Houle 21-803 1983 $950

SIBLY, MANOAH   The Trial of Mr. Thomas Hardy. Dublin, 1794. Rebound, interior foxed and edges slightly chipped, very good in new, fine cover. Quill & Brush 54-1668 1983 $100

SIBORNE, W.   The Waterloo Campaign 1815. London, 1895. Fourth edition. 13 full page portraits. 15 full page battle maps. Thick sm. 8vo. Cont. blue morocco. Spine faded and very slightly worn. A.e.g. Bookplate. Good. Edwards 1042-471 1983 £35

SIBREE, J.   Madagascar and its Poeple. London, n.d. (1872). Map, plates. Occasional spotting. Thick cr.8vo. Spine faded, slight wear. Good. Edwards 1044-642 1983 £40

SIBSON, FRANCIS   Collected Works. London, 1881. First edition. 4 vols., tall 8vo, uncut & unopened. Argosy 713-494 1983 $150

SICARD, A.   Monographie de la Canne a Sucre. Marseille, 1856. Hand-coloured chart, 8vo, wrappers. Wheldon 160-2138 1983 £12

SICARD, J. A.   The Use of Lipiodol in Diagnosis and Treatment. Oxford: Oxford University Press, 1932. First English edition. 8vo. Cloth. Numerous illus. Gurney JJ-372 1983 £20

SICCAMA, W. HORA   Louis Bernard Coclers et son oeuvre. Amsterdam: Frederick Muller & Cie., 1895. 3 very fine facsimile plates. Small 4to. Wrappers. Edition limited to 100 numbered copies. Catalogue Raisonne. Ars Libri 32-117 1983 $135

SICHEL, JULES   Traite de l'Ophthalmie, la Cataracte, et l'Amaurose. Paris, 1837. Thick large 8vo, old-calf backed bds. (worn). Argosy 713-495 1983 $75

SICKLES, DANIEL E.   Trial of the Hon. Daniel E. Sickles... New York, R.M. De Witt, (1859). First edition. Illustrated. 8vo, double columns, bound into a stiff wrapper binder. Morrill 290-492 1983 $50

SIDDONS, HENRY   Practical Illustrations of Rhetorical Gesture and Action. London, Richard Philip, 1807. Errata and ads. With 66 engraved plates, 8vo, 3/4 calf with label, rebacked. First edition. Salloch 387-225 1983 $450

SIDDONS, HENRY   Practical illustrations of rhetorical gesture and action. London: printed for Richard Phillips, 1807. 8vo, 19th-cent. half calf (very worn). First ed. Slightly grubby at the beginning, but a complete copy, with the list of plates and final leaf of ads. Ximenes 64-493 1983 $50

SIDDONS, HENRY   Practical illustrations of rhetorical gesture and action. London: printed for Sherwood, Neely, and Jones, 1822. 8vo, later 19th-cent. half green morocco, spine gilt (some rubbing, but sound). Second edition, improved. 66 plates. Some foxing but a very good copy, complete with half-title. Ximenes 64-494 1983 $100

SIDEBOTTOM, H.   Recent Foraminifera. Manchester, 1904-09. 19 plates and text-figures, 6 parts in 1 vol., 8vo, boards. Wheldon 160-1341 1983 £15

SIDNEY, EDWARD WILLIAM   The Partisan Leader: a Tale of the Future. (Wash.), 1856. 2 vols. in one, 12mo, later boards, cloth rebacked, ex lib. Printed by James Caxton. Argosy 710-92 1983 $200

SIDNEY, PHILIP   Astrophel and Stella. N.p., 1931. Edited by Mona Wilson. Tall 8vo, decorated paper over bds., paper labels, slipcase. One of 1210 copies printed by the Kynoch Press. A fine copy. Perata 27-140 1983 $50

SIDNEY, PHILIP   Defence of Poesie. Cambridge, University Press, 1904. Small 4to, half vellum, uncut. One of 250 copies. Reprint of the 1594 edition. Light foxing to ends, else fine. Houle 21-804 1983 $45

SIEBERT, KARL   Verzeichnis der Werke des Malers Georg Cornicelius. Stranssburg: J.H. Ed. Heitz, 1914. 12 plates. 4to. Wrappers. Loose. Ars Libri 32-133 1983 $55

SIEGEL, MORRIS   The Mackenzie Collection. Menasha, Wisconsin: American Anthropological Association, 1940. Numerous text illus. Small 4to. Wrappers. Ars Libri 34-748 1983 $37.50

SIEVERS, JOHANNES   Pieter Aertsen. Ein Beitrag zur Geschichte der niederlandischen Kunst im XVI. Jahrhundert. Leipzig: Karl W. Hiersemann, 1908. 32 collotype plates with 35 illus. 4to. Cloth. From the library of Jakob Rosenberg. Ars Libri 32-2 1983 $300

SIGERIST, HENRY   Amerika Und Die Medizin. Leipzig: Georg Thieme, 1933. First edition. Folding map. Inscribed to Adolf Meyer. Fine in chipped dust jacket. Gach 95-448 1983 $75

SIGERIST, HENRY   The Great Doctors. New York, 1933. First English translation. 8vo. Orig. binding. Fye H-3-514 1983 $50

SIGERIST, HENRY   Grosse Aerzte. Munich: J. F. Lehmanns, 1932 (1931). Orig. printed wrappers. Library stamp on wrapper and titlepage, taped at head and foot of spine. Gach 94-279 1983 $25

SIGERIST, HENRY   Medicine and Health in the Soviet
Union. New York, 1947. 8vo. Orig. binding. Autographed by
Sigerist. Ex-library. Fye H-3-519 1983 $40

SIGERIST, HENRY   Medicine and Health in the Soviet
Union. New York, 1947. First edition. 8vo. Orig. binding.
Ex-library. Fye H-3-520 1983 $20

SIGERIST, HENRY   The University at the Cross Roads.
New York, 1946. First edition. 8vo. Orig. binding. Fye H-3-532
1983 $25

SIGERSON, GEORGE   Political Prisoners at Home and Abroad.
Kegan Paul, 1890. First edition, 8vo, orig. cloth. Fenning 62-336
1983 £32.50

SIGORGNE, PIERRE   Institutions Newtoniennes ou
Introduction a la Philosophie de M. Newton. A Paris: chez
Jacques Francois Quillau, 1747. First edition. 2 vols. in 1.
8vo. Cont. mottled calf, full gilt spine. Heath 48-521 1983
£150

SILIUS ITALICUS, TIBERIUS CATIUS   Silii Italici de Bello Pvnico
Secvndo XVII Libri Nvper Diligentissime Castigati. (Colophon:
Venetiis in Aedibvs Aldi, et Andrae Asvlani Soceri, Mense Ivlio 1523).
8vo, later vellum, slightly worn, joints starting to crack, minor
staining, title bit soiled and spotted, complete with colophon leaf
plus the next leaf following, blank save for the Aldine device.
Ravenstree 95-106 1983 $565

SILL, EDWARD ROWLAND   The Hermitage and Other Poems. San
Francisco: Bancroft, 1868. 1st ed., with the rarer imprint. Orig.
maroon cloth, gilt, t.e.g. Near fine copy with the four pages of
ads at end excised. Jenkins 155-1142 1983 $150

SILL, EDWARD ROWLAND   Poems. Cambridge: Riverside Press,
1902. Tall 8vo, buckram backed boards; uncut. Ltd. edition. One of
500 copies. Argosy 714-642 1983 $45

SILLAR, DAVID   Poems... Kilmarnock: Printed by John
Wilson...MDCCLXXXIX. 8vo, half tan polished calf, gilt, by Bayntun.
First edition. Quaritch NS 7-121 1983 $350

SILLARD, ROBERT M.   Barry Sullivan and His Contemporaries.
London: T. Fisher Unwin, 1901. First edition. 2 vols. Illus. Orig.
cloth. Spines very slightly worn. In a half-morocco slipcase. Very
good. MacManus 280-4955 1983 $65

SILLIMAN, BENJAMIN   Report on the United Reese River
Silver Mining Co., Situated in Austin, Lander County. N.Y., 1865.
Dbd. Printed for private distribution. Ginsberg 47-656 1983 $100

SILLITOE, ALAN   Israel. (London: Steam Press, 1981).
Small 4to, black cloth, in a double binding; boxed. One of only 98
copies, signed by the poet and the illustrator, Ralph Steadman.
Argosy 714-673 1983 $250

SILLITOE, ALAN   The Loneliness of the Long-distance
Runner. London: W.H. Allen, 1959. First edition. 8vo. Orig.
cloth. Dust jacket with Book Society wraparound band. Very fine
copy. Jaffe 1-354 1983 $185

SILLITOE, ALAN   The Loneliness of the Long-distance
Runner. London: W.H. Allen, 1959. First edition. Orig. cloth.
Dust jacket (one minor internal tape-repair). Fine. MacManus 280-
4753 1983 $125

SILTZER, FRANK   The Story of British Sporting Prints.
N.Y., 1925. 20 illus. (4 in color). Cloth. Index. Some pencil
notations. Front inner hinge cracked. Spine slightly sunned and
worn. Good. King 45-500 1983 $125

SILVA LEITE, ANTONIO DE   Rezumo de Todas as Regras e Preceitos
da Cantoria, da Musica Metrica, como de Canto Chao. Porto, Antonio
Alvarez Ribeiro, 1787. 4 leaves, with 2 engraved plates (one folding &
one full-page) of musical samples. 4to, cont. marbled calf, spine
gilt, loose in binding. Salloch 387-226 1983 $75

SIMCOX, A. H. A.   A Memoir of the Khandesh Bhil Corps.
London, 1912. Large folding map in end-pocket. 5 plates. Roy.8vo.
Orig. cloth. Good. Edwards 1044-644 1983 £60

SIMENON, GEORGES   On the Danger Line. N.Y., Harcourt,
(1944). First American edition. Dust jacket (small nicks). Very
good. Houle 22-801 1983 $37.50

SIMES, THOMAS   A Military Course For The Government
and Conduct of a Battalion. London: printed for the author, 1777.
2nd ed., 8vo, hand-coloured engraved frontis., 20 hand-coloured
engraved plans on 17 plates, subscribers list, cont. calf, gilt,
crimson morocco label, text dampstained, mainly in margins, but
affecting the first five lines of text. Deighton 3-269 1983 £105

SIMMONDS, P. L.   Sir John Franklin and the Arctic
Regions. Buffalo 1852. Illus, cloth, bookplate, lacks f.e.p.,
spine ends very worn, spine sunned. King 46-753 1983 $20

SIMMONS, ALBERT DIXON   Wing Shots. New York: Derrydale
Press, (1936). 83 photographic plates. Spine lettering just the
slightest bit chipped, one of 950 numbered copies. Felcone 21-33
1983 $75

SIMMONS, CHARLES H.   A Bibliography of John Masefield.
New York: Columbia Univ. Press, 1930. First edition, limited
to 750 numbered copies. 8vo. 3/4 cloth over marbled boards, t.e.g.
With addenda and errata sheet inserted in the rear. Fine. Oak
Knoll 49-466 1983 $50

SIMMS, GEORGE A.   Notable Men of New Orleans, 1905.
New Orleans, (1905). 1st ed. Full morocco. Photographs. Jenkins
151-191 1983 $85

SIMMS, HENRY H.   Life of John Taylor. Richmond, Va.,
1932. Illus. Orig. cloth. First edition. Ginsberg 46-788 1983
$25

SIMMS, WILLIAM GILMORE   Views and Reviews in American Literature,
History and Fiction. N.Y., Wiley and Putnam, 1845. First series.
12mo. Orig. printed wrappers. 1st ed. Rare in wrappers. Fine.
O'Neal 50-118 1983 $85

SIMON, HOWARD   500 Years of Art & Illustration.
Cleveland, (1942). Cloth. Index. Blind-stamped names and rubber
stamped names. Defective dust wrapper. Good. King 45-433 1983
$25

SIMON, OLIVER   Printing of Today. London & New York,
1928. Folio. Cloth. First edition. Plates. Facs. Ltd. to 300
numbered copies, printed on handmade paper. A fine copy in (later?)
plain dust wrapper. Reese 20-541 1983 $150

SIMON, OLIVER   Printing of To-Day, an Illustrated
Survey of Post-War Typography in Europe and the United States. With
a General Introduction by Aldous Huxley. London: Peter Davies.
New York: Harper, 1928. Small folio, 122 illus. 1st ed. Orig.
cloth-backed decorated boards. Some rubbing to corners, else a nice
copy. Jenkins 155-656 1983 $85

SIMON, P. MAX   Le Monde des Reves. Paris, 1882. 12mo,
orig. pr. wrs. (spine mended); uncut & unopened. First edition.
Argosy 713-497 1983 $45

SIMONSEN, R.   The Diatom Plankton of the Indian Ocean
Expedition of R. V. "Meteor", 1964-65. Berlin and Stuttgart, 1974.
41 plates, royal 8vo, wrappers. Wheldon 160-1893 1983 £38

SIMONSON, LEE   Untended Grove. New York, 1946. 8vo.
Cloth. Review copy with laid in. Fine in dj. In Our Time 156-697
1983 $25

THE SIMPLE Plan. London: Sherratt and Hughes, 1906. Orig. cloth.
First edition. Presentation copy from the author inscribed: "To
Brother Charles from the author, December 1906." Spine and covers
worn. Front inner hinge cracking, with some foxing to the endpapers
and preliminary pages. Good copy. MacManus 277-89 1983 $35

SIMPSON, BERTRAM L.　　　　The Re-Shaping of the Far East. Macmillan, 1905. First edition, with a large folding map and 62 plates, 2 vols. 8vo, orig. cloth, v.g. Fenning 62-337　1983　£18.50

SIMPSON, CLARENCE O.　　　　The Technic of Oral Radiography. St. Louis, 1928. 8vo, cloth. 165 illus., mostly from x-rays. Argosy 713-498　1983　$45

SIMPSON, G. G.　　　　A catalogue of the Mesozoic Mammalia. British Museum, 1928. 12 plates and 56 text-figures, 4to, cloth. Wheldon 160-1475　1983　£20

SIMPSON, HAROLD　　　　Old Not-too-Bright and Lillywhite. Ward Lock, n.d. (ca.1915). 12mo. Colour frontis. 27 colour plates, light wear. Pictorial endpapers. Brown boards, rebacked. Onlaid colour plate. Greer 39-114　1983　£18.50

SIMPSON, HELEN　　　　Boomerang. London, 1932. First English edition. Nicked and strengthened dustwrapper by Rex Whistler, slightly spotted internally. Very good. Jolliffe 26-592　1983　£18

SIMPSON, HENRY I.　　　　The Emigrant's Guide to the Gold Mines. Haverford, Pa.: Headframe Publishing Co., 1978. 8vo. Leather spine, marbled paper over boards. Fold-out map. One of 250 numbered copies. Designed and printed by Henry Morris at the Bird & Bull Press, and bound by G. Parrot. Oak Knoll 39-38　1983　$100

SIMPSON, JAMES H.　　　　Report of Explorations Across the Great Basin of...Utah for a Direct Wagon Route... Wash., 1876. Illus., 25 maps and plates. Orig. quarto cloth. First edition. Ginsberg 47-835　1983　$150

SIMPSON, JAMES YOUNG　　　　Remarks on the Superinduction of Anaesthesia in Natural and Morbid Parturition...With an Appendix. Boston, 1848. 1st American ed. 8vo. Orig. wrappers. Presen. from the publisher, William Little. Morrill 289-210　1983　$175

SIMPSON, JOHN PALGRAVE　　　　Second Love and Other Tales from the Notebook of A Traveller. London: Richard Bentley, 1846. First edition. 3 vols. Half-morocco with marbled boards and endpapers. Cover edges worn at the edges. Very good, tight set. MacManus 280-4754　1983　$185

SIMPSON, LESLEY B.　　　　The Econmienda in New Spain, Forced Native Labor in the Spanish Colonies. Berkeley, 1929. Argosy 716-515　1983　$25

SIMPSON, STEPHEN　　　　Biography of Stephen Girard, with his Will Affixed. Phila., 1832. 12mo, engr. port, calf, neatly rebacked, leather label. Argosy 710-145　1983　$40

SIMPSON, THOMAS　　　　Essays on several curious and useful subjects... London: H. Woodfall, for J. Nourse, 1740. 4to. First edition. Cont. half calf, spine gilt. Some foxing, but a fine copy. Ximenes 63-537　1983　$250

SIMPSON, THOMAS　　　　Select exercises for young proficients in the mathematicks. London: J. Nourse, 1752. First edition. 8vo. Cont. calf. Slightly rubbed. Generally a little browned, and with some worming at the end affecting a few letters. Ximenes 63-538　1983　$125

SIMPSON, THOMAS　　　　Select Exercises for Young Proficients in the Mathematicks. Lon., 1792. Rebound in full leather in fine condition, text stained. Quill & Brush 54-1655　1983　$50

SIMPSON, VIOLET A.　　　　Occasion's Forelock. London: Edward Arnold, 1906. First edition. Orig. cloth. Some foxing throughout. Corners slightly bent, with a few scratches to the spine. Former owner's signature. Good. MacManus 280-4755　1983　$25

SIMPSON, W. DOUGLAS　　　　The Historical Saint Columba. Aberdeen: Milne & Hutchison, 1927. 25 cm. Frontis. Orig. cloth-backed boards. Very good; pub.'s review slip laid in. Grunder 6-12　1983　$35

SIMS, ALAN　　　　Phoinix. Boston, 1929. 8vo, cloth. Salloch 385-181　1983　$22

SIMS, GEORGE R.　　　　Ballads and Poems. London: John P. Fuller, (1883). First edition. Illus. with a photographic frontis. by A.E. Fradelle. Orig. cloth. Extremities of spine worn. Inner hinges weak. Good. MacManus 280-4758　1983　$35

SIMS, GEORGE R.　　　　Dagonet Abroad. London: Chatto & Windus, 1895. First edition. Orig. decorated cloth (spine slightly faded). Very fine. MacManus 280-4760　1983　$50

SIMS, J. MARION　　　　Clinical Notes on Uterine Surgery. New York, William Wood, 1866. 1st American ed. 8vo. Illus. Morrill 289-211　1983　$200

SIMS, RICHARD　　　　A Manual for the Genealogist, Topographer, Antiquary, and Legal Professor. Edward Avery, 1888. 8vo, frontis., t.e.g., other edges uncut, quarter morocco. Bickersteth 75-177　1983　£15

SINCLAIR, CATHERINE　　　　Modern Flirtations. Edinburgh: William Whyte & Co., 1841. First edition. 3 vols. Orig. cloth-backed boards with paper labels on spines. Back of Vol. I dampstained. Former owner's signature on front endsheet of Vol. II. Front flyleaf of Vol. III clipped. Very good. MacManus 280-4762　1983　$350

SINCLAIR, CATHERINE　　　　Modern Flirtations. Edinburgh: William Whyte, etc., n.d. (c. 1841). In three vols. Half titles, orig. purple/brown cloth, blocked in blind. A fine copy. Jarndyce 30-548　1983　£40

SINCLAIR, CATHERINE　　　　Sir Edward Graham; Or, Railway Speculators. Printed for Longman, Brown (etc), 1839. First edition, 3 vols, 12mo, original cloth-backed boards, uncut; recased; labels defective; half-titles in vols. II and III. Hill 165-117　1983　£45

SINCLAIR, GEORGE　　　　Hortus Gramineus Woburnensis. 1825. 60 coloured plates, royal 8vo, original boards (rebacked with cloth). Uncut. One plate foxed, very slight foxing elsewhere. Boards a trifle worn. Wheldon 160-2139　1983　£50

SINCLAIR, GEORGE　　　　The hydrostaticks; or, the weight, force, and pressure of fluid bodies... Edinburgh: George Swintoun, etc., 1672. First edition. Small 4to. Cont. mottled calf. Engraved frontis., a large folding coat of arms (loose), and seven folding plates. A fine crisp copy. Ximenes 63-539　1983　$750

SINCLAIR, JAMES　　　　The Beauties of Nature. Houlston & Stoneman, 1852. First edition, orig. brown cloth, v.g. Colour 'Baxter' front. Jarndyce 30-840　1983　£40

SINCLAIR, JOHN　　　　The Code of Agriculture. London: for Sherwood, Gilbert & Piper, 1832. Fifth edition. Roy. 8vo. Portrait, plates, some manuscript notes, orig. cloth backed boards. Heath 48-9　1983　£40

SINCLAIR, JOHN　　　　Observations on the Scottish dialect. London: W. Strahan, etc., 1782. First edition. 8vo. Cont. half russia, spine gilt. Presentation copy, inscribed on the verso of the title from the author to Archibald McDonald Esq. Ximenes 63-228　1983　$275

SINCLAIR, MAY　　　　The Divine Fire. London: Constable, 1904. First edition. Orig. cloth. Spine faded. News-clippings tipped in. MacManus 280-4763　1983　$45

SINCLAIR, MAY　　　　Fame. London: Elkin Mathews & Marrot, 1929. First edition. Orig. decorated boards. Dust jacket. Number 13 of The Woburn Books. Limited to 530 copies signed by author. Fine. MacManus 280-4764　1983　$25

SINCLAIR, MAY　　　　Far End. N.Y.: Macmillan Co., 1926. First American edition. Orig. cloth. Dust jacket (slightly worn). Fine. MacManus 280-4765　1983　$20

SINCLAIR, MAY   The Rector of Wyck. London: Hutchinson & Co., (1925). First edition. Orig. cloth. Fine. MacManus 280-4766 1983 $20

SINCLAIR, MAY   Mr. Waddington of Wyck. London, (1921). First edition. Argosy 714-675 1983 $20

SINCLAIR, ROBERT   An Island Story. London: Lamley, 1894. First edition. Orig. cloth. MacManus 280-4767 1983 $20

SINCLAIR, UPTON   Between Two Worlds. New York & California, (1941). 8vo. Cloth. Fine in dj. In Our Time 156-703 1983 $25

SINCLAIR, UPTON   Bill Porter: A Drama of O'Henry in Prison. Pasadena, The Author, 1925. First edition. Dust jacket, uncommon in jacket (a few short tears and small chips). Very good. Houle 22-803 1983 $55

SINCLAIR, UPTON   The Cry for Justice: An Anthology of Social Protest. Philadelphia, (1915). 8vo. Cloth. Vg copy. In Our Time 156-700 1983 $20

SINCLAIR, UPTON   Dragon Harvest. London, (1945). 12mo. Cloth. 1st English ed. Vg-fine. In Our Time 156-707 1983 $20

SINCLAIR, UPTON   Dragon Harvest. California, (1945). 8vo. Cloth. Fine in dj which is rubbed. In Our Time 156-706 1983 $20

SINCLAIR, UPTON   The Goose Step. Pasadena: Published by the author, (1923). Pictorial cloth. First edition. About fine. Reese 20-889 1983 $20

SINCLAIR, UPTON   The Goslings, a Study of the American Schools. Pasadena: Sinclair, (1924). 1st ed. Orig. printed wrappers. Nice copy, 1 of 5,000 copies so issued. Jenkins 155-1146 1983 $20

SINCLAIR, UPTON   Hell: A Verse Drama and Photo Play. Pasadena, California, 1923. First edition. Orig. wrappers. Scarce. Very fine. Gekoski 2-170 1983 £35

SINCLAIR, UPTON   The Jungle. N.Y.: The Jungle Publishing Co., (1906). First edition. 3 pages of ads. Green decorative cloth. Slip pasted inside front cover reading "Sustainers' Edition.... About five thousand copies were ordered, of which this is one. The Author." Dawson 471-262 1983 $85

SINCLAIR, UPTON   Little Steel. New York and Pasadena, 1938. Inscribed "To V.R. Krymov with sincere esteem Upton Sinclair". Dustwrapper browned at the spine. Fine. First edition. Gekoski 2-172 1983 £30

SINCLAIR, UPTON   Love's Pilgrimage. New York, 1911. 8vo. Cloth. Name on fly, a vg-fine copy. In Our Time 156-698 1983 $40

SINCLAIR, UPTON   Manassas. New York & London: Macmillan, 1904. Gilt pictorial cloth. First edition. Neat ink name, tiny nick in one board, otherwise a fine, bright copy. Reese 20-888 1983 $30

SINCLAIR, UPTON   Our Lady. Pasadena, 1938. Inscribed - upside down on rear end-paper - "To V. Krymov with sincere regards Upton Sinclair". Very slightly used dustwrapper. First edition. Very good. Gekoski 2-171 1983 £25

SINCLAIR, UPTON   Presidential Agent. London, (1944). 12mo. Cloth. 1st English ed. Fine. In Our Time 156-705 1983 $20

SINCLAIR, UPTON   Presidential Mission. London, (1948). 12mo. Cloth. 1st English ed. Fine. In Our Time 156-709 1983 $20

SINCLAIR, UPTON   Samuel the Seeker. (Racine: Western Publishing, 1910). 1st ed. Orig. yellow cloth. Fine copy. Scarce. Jenkins 155-1149 1983 $30

SINCLAIR, UPTON   Sylvia's Marriage. California, (1914). 8vo. Cloth. Fine. In Our Time 156-699 1983 $20

SINCLAIR, UPTON   Upton Sinclair Presents William Fox. Los Angeles, Privately printed, (1933). First edition. Orange cloth stamped in black (trifle rubbed) else, very good. Signed by Sinclair on front free endpaper. Jacket remnants laid in loose. Houle 22-806 1983 $45

SINCLAIR, UPTON   A World To Win. Monrovia: the Author, (1946). 1st ed., advance copy in wrappers marked "Gift copy-Not for sale". Lower corner of front wrapper torn, else a nice copy. Uncommon. Jenkins 155-1150 1983 $25

SINCLAIR-COWAN, BERTHA   Casey Ryan. Boston: Little, Brown, and Company, 1921. Ads, frontispiece by Frank Tenney Johnson. First ed. with August, 1921 printed on copyright page. Fine pictorial cloth. Jenkins 153-284 1983 $30

SINCLAIR-COWAN, BERTHA   Chip of the Flying U. New York: G.W. Dillingham, 1904. Illus. by Charles Russell. Orig. pictorial cloth. Nice copy. Jenkins 153-490 1983 $30

SINCLAIR-COWAN, BERTHA   The Lure of the Dim Trails. New York: G.W. Dillingham, 1907. Illus. by Charles M. Russell. 1st ed. in worn dj. Very good copy. Jenkins 153-491 1983 $30

SINCLAIR-COWAN, BERTHA   The Trail of the White Mule. Boston: Little, Brown, and Company, 1922. Ads, frontispiece by Frank Tenney Johnson. First edition with September, 1922 printed on copyright page. Fine copy in pictorial cloth. Jenkins 153-285 1983 $30

SINDONA, ENIO   Pisanello. Paris: Bibliotheque des Arts, 1962. 173 plates (29 tipped-in color). Text illus. Large 4to. Cloth. Dust jacket. Ars Libri 33-282 1983 $125

SINEL, JOSEPH   A Book of American Trade-Marks & Devices. New York: Alfred A. Knopf, 1924. 4to. cloth-backed boards. Pages French-folded. Limited to 2050 numbered copies. Plates by Beck Engraving, Paper by Japan Paper Company and printing by the Pynson Printers. Some cover soiling. Oak Knoll 49-361 1983 $55

SINGER, CAROLINE   White Africans and Black. NY, (1929). Illus. by C. L. Baldridge. Limited to 500 numbered and signed copies, profusely illus., very fine in slipcase. Quill & Brush 54-1240 1983 $100

SINGER, CHARLES   From Magic to Science. London: Ernest Benn, 1928. 8vo. Cloth. 14 coloured plates and numerous plates and illustrations. Gurney JJ-376 1983 £25

SINGER, CHARLES   Greek Biology and Greek Medicine. Oxford: The Clarendon Press, 1922. 12mo. First edition. Gach 95-450 1983 $25

SINGER, CHARLES   Short History of Medicine. N.Y., 1928. First American edition. Illus. Rebound in library buckram; ex-lib. Argosy 713-499 1983 $45

SINGER, CHARLES   A Short History of Medicine. New York, 1928. First edition. 8vo. Orig. binding. Fye H-3-541 1983 $25

SINGER, CHARLES   A Short History of Science to the Nineteenth Century. (1941), 1943. Wheldon 160-268 £12

SINGER, HANS W   Versuch einer Durer Bibliographie. Strassburg: J.H. Ed. Heitz, 1903. Small 4to. Marbled boards, 1/4 cloth. Orig. wrappers bound in. Ars Libri 32-188 1983 $50

SINGER, HANS W.   Zeichnungen von Albert Besnard.
Leipzig: A. Schumann, 1912. 52 collotype plates. Large 4to.
Cloth. Ars Libri 32-35 1983 $60

SINGER, HANS W.   Zeichnungen von Max Klinger. Leipzig:
Glass & Tuscher, 1912. 52 collotype plates. Large 4to. Cloth.
Ars Libri 32-373 1983 $85

SINGER, HANS W.   Zeichnungen von William Strang. Leipzig:
A. Schumann, 1912. 50 collotype plates. Large 4to. Cloth. Very
slightly shaken. Ars Libri 32-652 1983 $60

SINGER, ISAAC B.   The Collected Stories of... New York:
Farrar, (1982). Cloth. A special edition, ltd. to 1048 numbered
copies, specially printed and bound, and signed by the author, of which
1,000 copies were offered for sale to members of the Book-of-the-
Month Club. This is copy 1039. Reese 20-890 1983 $75

SINGER, ISAAC B.   The Gentleman From Cracow and The
Mirror. NY, 1979. Illus. by Raphael Soyer. 2000 copies signed by
both Singer and Soyer, fine in glassine wrapper in fine slipcase.
Quill & Brush 54-1243 1983 $75

SINGER, ISAAC B   One Day of Happiness. NY: Red Ozier
Press, 1982. Octavo. First separate edition. Illus. with three
color lithographs by Richard Callner, all signed by the artist.
Protective tissues for prints bound-in. Limited to 155 copies signed
by Singer. As new in quarter-leather and paste-paper over boards.
With cloth-covered slip-case. Bromer 25-284 1983 $400

SINGER, R.   The Agaricales in modern Taxonomy.
1975. Third edition, 84 plates (3 coloured), 8vo, cloth. A completely
revised edition. Wheldon 160-1895 1983 £65

SINGLETON, ESTHER   The Golden Fairy Book. N.Y.: Dodd,
(1903). First edition. 8vo. Blue gilt & pictorial cloth. Illus.
with color illus, by Falls. Decorated border on all pages. Very good
to fine. Aleph-bet 8-107 1983 $75

SINGLETON, JOHN   A General Description of the West-Indian
Islands. Barbados, printed by George Esmand and William Walker, for
the author, (1762). Orig. boards, leather spine, hinges cracked,
rubbed, internally a fine copy. Reese 19-36 1983 $1,850

SINGTON, DERRICK   The Goebbels Experiment. New Haven, 1943.
Portraits. Cloth. Index. Very good. King 45-566 1983 $25

SINJOHN, JOHN, PSEUD.
Please turn to
GALSWORTHY, JOHN

SINNETT, A. P.   Karma. London: Chapman & Hall, 1885.
First edition. 2 vols. Orig. cloth. Bookplates. Very good. Mac-
Manus 280-4768 1983 $115

SINNETT, MRS. PERCY   Byeways of History, from the Twelfth to
the Sixteenth Century. London: Richard Bentley, 1854. Second edition.
Orig. calf-backed marbled boards. With an armorial bookplate of Arthur
Conan Doyle on the front paste-down endpaper. Covers and spine rubbed
and worn. Spine cracked with cords intact. Former owner's signature
partially removed. Good. MacManus 278-1622 1983 $75

SINTON, PETER   Childhood Memories of Summers at
Lake Tahoe. San Francisco: Privately Printed (by the Grabhorn
Press). 1962. 4to, illus. with a mounted glossy photo. Edition
ltd. to 30 copies "printed for Florence S. Walter, her children
and grandchildren". Bound in white paper boards over patterned
cloth. Paper spine labels. Very fine copy in plain paper dust
jacket. Karmiole 72-107 1983 $175

SIOUX Falls, Dakota. Chicago, R.R. Donnelley & Sons, ca. 1886.
Pictorial pink wraps. Cover title. Folded map of Dakota Territory.
Ginsberg 46-224 1983 $200

SIPES, WILLIAM B.   The Pennsylvania Railroad. Phila.,
1875. Illus., plates. Cloth. Worn. First edition. Profusely
illus. from drawings by Moran, Darley and others. Felcone 22-202
1983 $60

SIPLEY, LOUIS WALTON   A Half Century of Color. NY: Macmillan,
(c. 1951). 26 cm. Numerous black & white illus. and the 28 color
inserts, including "an actual 1950 Printon color print" in the
glassine envelope bound in. Fine in somewhat worn dust wrapper. First
edition. Grunder 7-63 1983 $40

SIR William Osler, Bart. Brief Tributes... Baltimore, 1920. Orig.
olive cloth. 8vo. First edition. Fye H-3-901 1093 $75

SIR William Osler, Bart. Brief Tributes... Baltimore, 1920. Orig.
olive cloth. 8vo. Ex-library. Fye H-3-902 1983 $50

SIRINGO, CHARLES A.   A History of "Billy The Kid." Santa Fe,
N.M.: The Author, 1920. Orig. stiff pictorial wrappers. Light
scruffing to wrappers. Laid in half morocco case. Fine. Jenkins 152-
414 1983 $750

SIRINGO, CHARLES A.   History of "Billy the Kid." (Santa Fe:
Privately published, 1920). Wrappers, worn. Front hinge repaired.
Dawson 471-263 1983 $60

SIRINGO, CHARLES A.   A Lone Star Cowboy. Santa Fe, 1919.
Cloth, very good. A presentation copy from Siringo to the publisher of
the Saturday Evening Post, J.W. Murphy. Reese 19-512 1983 $175

SIRINGO, CHARLES A.   A Lone Star Cowboy. Santa Fe, 1919.
1st ed. Illus. Pictorial dark red cloth. Very good. Bradley 63-
114 1983 $85

SIRINGO, CHARLES A.   A Lone Star Cowboy. Santa Fe, 1919.
Illus. Orig. cloth. Jenkins 153-515 1983 $85

SIRINGO, CHARLES A.   Riata and Spurs. Boston, 1927. Cloth,
a fine copy in a torn dust jacket. First edition, first issue. Reese
19-513 1983 $225

SIRINGO, CHARLES A.   Rita and Spurs. New York: Houghton
Mifflin, 1927. Illus., original cloth, fine copy of the first
edition. Very scarce. Jenkins 151-312 1983 $150

SIRINGO, CHARLES A.   Riata and Spurs. Boston & N.Y.: Houghton Mifflin, 1927. First edition. Intro. by G. Pinchot. Plates.
Fine condition (newspaper clipping pasted inside front cover) in
tattered dust wrapper. Dawson 471-264 1983 $100

SIRINGO, CHARLES A.   Riata and Spurs. Boston & N.Y.: Houghton Mifflin, 1927. First edition. Intro by G. Pinchot. Plates.
A couple of leaves roughly opened, a bit of wear. Inscriptions. No
dust wrapper. Dawson 471-265 1983 $65

SIRINGO, CHARLES A.   A Texas Cow Boy. Chicago & N.Y.: Rand,
McNally, (1886). Ads. Wrappers, quite chipped. First page pasted
to front cover. Paper browned and brittle. Inscribed and signed by
Siringo, dated Altadena, 1927. Dawson 471-267 1983 $200

SIRINGO, CHARLES A.   Two Evil Isms. Chicago, 1915. First
edition. Stiff printed colored pictorial wraps. (light soiling, a
few small spots). Very good. Houle 22-1176 1983 $650

SITWELL, CONSTANCE   Flowers and Elephants. New York, n.d.
8vo. Cloth. First American ed. with English sheets. A fine copy.
Jacket has some light chipping around top edges of the jacket. In
Our Time 156-295 1983 $45

SITWELL, EDITH   Alexander Pope. London: Faber & Faber
Limited, (1930). First edition. Illus. Orig. yellow buckram, with
both pictorial & glassine dust jackets, in orig. publisher's slipcase
(a little worn). One of 220 copies printed on English hand-made
paper and signed by author. Very fine. MacManus 280-4769 1983 $200

SITWELL, EDITH   Aspects of Modern Poetry. London,
1934. First edition. Spine darkened and covers a little marked.
Inscription on flyleaf. Internally a nice copy. Rota 231-551 1983
£12

SITWELL, EDITH   Bucolic Comedies. London, 1923. First
edition. Spine just a little darkened and worn. Very nice. Rota
231-545 1983 £30

SITWELL, EDITH   The Canticle of the Rose. N.Y.: The
Vanguard Press, (1949). First American edition. Orig. cloth. Dust
jacket (spine ends and cover edges slightly chipped; darkened).
Presentation copy inscribed: "For my dear Miss Sally Galleshaw,
with all best wishes from Edith Sitwell." Near-fine. MacManus 280-
4771 1983 $65

SITWELL, EDITH   The Canticle of the Rose. N.Y., (1949).
First American edition. Presentation copy. Argosy 714-894 1983
$45

SITWELL, EDITH   Collected Poems. London, 1930. First
edition. Edge of lower cover very slightly dampstained. Torn dust
wrapper. Bookplate. Author's signed autograph presentation inscription. Very nice. Rota 231-549 1983 £40

SITWELL, EDITH   The English Eccentrics. London: Faber
& Faber, (1933). First edition. Illus. Orig. cloth. Dust jacket
(head of spine slightly worn). 2748 copies printed. Fine. MacManus
280-4772 1983 $85

SITWELL, EDITH   Epithalamium. (London), 1931. Small
quarto. Cloth. First edition. One of 100 numbered copies, printed
on handmade paper, and signed by the author. A very fine copy in
orig. glassine wrapper. Reese 20-893 1983 $165

SITWELL, EDITH   Five Variations on a Theme. London,
1933. First edition. Endpapers a little discoloured. Very nice.
Rota 231-550 1983 £12

SITWELL, EDITH   Gold Coast Customs. London, 1929.
First edition. Frayed dust wrapper. Very nice. Rota 231-548
1983 £18

SITWELL, EDITH   Green Song & Other Poems. London: Macmillan & Co., 1944. First edition. Orig. cloth. Dust jacket (lightly
used). Fine. MacManus 280-4774 1983 $25

SITWELL, EDITH   Green Song and Other Poems. New York,
(1946). 8vo. Cloth. Frontispiece by Pavel Tchelitchev. A review
copy with slip from publisher laid in. Name of a reviewer on front
fly, else vg-fine copy in dj. In Our Time 156-718 1983 $40

SITWELL, EDITH   Look! The Sun. London: Victor Gollancz
Ltd., 1941. First edition. Orig. cloth. Dust jacket (slightly
soiled). Very good. 3500 copies. MacManus 280-4775 1983 $25

SITWELL, EDITH   Look! The Sun. London, 1941. First
edition. Spine faded. Frayed dust wrapper. Very nice. Rota 230-
547 1983 $15

SITWELL, EDITH   Poetry & Criticism. London: Hogarth
Press, 1925. Pictorial wraps., after a design by Vanessa Bell.
First edition. Spine a trifle used, else a near fine copy. Reese
20-892 1983 $45

SITWELL, EDITH   Poetry and Criticism. Hogarth Press,
1925. Wrappers. Backstrip defective and wrappers badly marked. Good.
Rota 231-547 1983 £17.50

SITWELL, EDITH   Popular Song. London: 1928. Drawings
by Edward Bawden. Limited to 500 large-paper copies signed by Sitwell.
First edition. About fine in orange boards. Bromer 25-102 1983 $50

SITWELL, EDITH   Selected Poems. London: Duckworth,
1936. First edition. Orig. cloth. Author's copy with many corrections and instructions to the printer in her hand. Binding rather
worn and soiled. Good. MacManus 280-4776 1983 $450

SITWELL, EDITH   The Song of the Cold. London: Macmillan & Co., 1945. First edition. Orig. cloth. Dust jacket (a
few small tears). Very good. MacManus 280-4778 1983 $25

SITWELL, EDITH   A Song of the Cold. London, 1945.
First edition. 8vo. Orig. printed wrappers. A presentation copy
with Edith Sitwell's signature on the front cover. Traylen 94-751
1983 £12

SITWELL, GEORGE RERESBY   Tales of My Native Village Being Studies
of Medieval Life, Manners, Art, Minstrelsy, and Religion... Oxford
University Press, 1933. Illus., 4to, dust stained but good. K Books
301-169 1983 £38

SITWELL, OSBERT   All at Sea. London, 1927. First
edition. Spine darkened. Nice. Rota 230-553 1983 £15

SITWELL, OSBERT   Argonaut and Juggernaut. London: Chatto
& Windus, 1919. First edition. Orig. cloth with paper label on spine.
Dust jacket (darkened and chipped at bottom of spine and corners).
1000 copies printed. Fine. MacManus 280-4782 1983 $85

SITWELL, OSBERT   The Collected Satires and Poems. London:
Duckworth, 1931. First edition. Orig. cloth. Dust jacket (slightly
rubbed). Signed by author on title-page. Fine. MacManus 280-4784
1983 $65

SITWELL, OSBERT   Collected Satires and Poems. London,
1931. First edition. Covers spotted and some foxing throughout.
With an ALS to R. Church. Loosely inserted is a carbon typescript
of Church's review of this book. Very good. Rota 231-556 1983 £30

SITWELL, OSBERT   Discursions on Travel, Art and Life.
London, 1925. First edition. Illus. Dust wrapper. Fine. Rota 231-
555 1983 £35

SITWELL, OSBERT   Dumb Animal. London, Duckworth, 1930.
First edition. Dust jacket. Presentation copy, inscribed by the
author to Rex Whistler, 1930. With Rex Whistler's signature on
title page. Very good. Houle 22-810 1983 $195

SITWELL, OSBERT   England Reclaimed. NY, 1928. 500 to
520 copies, fine in very good dustwrapper. Quill & Brush 54-1246
1983 $35

SITWELL, OSBERT   Escape with Me. London, 1939. First
English edition. Wrappers. Advance proof copy. Covers slightly
dusty. Very good. Jolliffe 26-629 1983 £30

SITWELL, OSBERT   Great Morning. London, 1948. First
English and First Illus. edition. Spine and covers a little dampstained. Torn dust wrapper. Author's signed autograph presentation
inscription to N. Pearn. Nice. Rota 231-558 1983 £30

SITWELL, OSBERT   Laughter in the Next Room. London, 1949.
First English and First Illus. edition. Spine and covers a little
dampstained. Torn dust wrapper. Author's signed autograph presentation inscription to N. Pearn. Nice. Rota 231-559 1983 £30

SITWELL, OSBERT   A Letter to My Son. (London): Home &
Van thal Ltd., 1944. First edition. Orig. cloth. Dust jacket.
Fine. MacManus 280-4786 1983 $35

SITWELL, OSBERT   The Man Who Lost Himself. London: Duck-
worth, 1929. First edition. Orig. cloth-backed decorated boards.
Dust jacket (slightly worn). 5000 copies printed. Very good. Mac-
Manus 280-4787 1983 $25

SITWELL, OSBERT   Out of the Flame. London: Grant
Richards, 1923. 1st ed., original cloth and spine label. A fine copy.
Trebizond 18-90 1983 $65

SITWELL, OSBERT   The Scarlet Tree. London, 1946. First
English and First Illus. edition. Covers a little dampstained and top
edge of some leaves stained from running of the dye used to colour the
edges. Torn dust wrapper. Author's signed autograph presentation
inscription to N. Pearn. Nice. Rota 231-557 1983 £25

SITWELL, OSBERT   Triple Fugue. London, Grant Richards,
n.d. (1924). 8vo, orig. quarter linen, boards (boards and spine
ends worn), orig. printed paper spine label chipped, decent copy,
from the collection of C.D. Broad, with his ownership inscription on
endpaper. First edition. Ravenstree 96-228 1983 $30

SITWELL, OSBERT　　　　Who Killed Cock-Robin? London:
Daniel, 1921. 1st ed. Orig. printed wrappers over boards. Fine.
Jenkins 155-1153 1983 $45

SITWELL, SACHEVERELL　　　Beckford and Beckfordism. London,
1930. First edition. One of 265 numbered copies signed by the
author. Free endpapers browned. Very good. Jolliffe 26-465 1983
£35

SITWELL, SACHEVERELL　　　British Architects and Craftsmen.
London, 1945. First edition. Torn dust wrapper. Name on flyleaf.
Very nice. Rota 230-556 1983 £12

SITWELL, SACHEVERELL　　　Doctor Donne & Gargantua. London:
Gerald Duckworth & Co., 1930. First edition. Frontis. by R. Whistler.
Orgi. cloth-backed paterned boards. One of 215 copies signed by author.
Slightly worn at edges. Very good. MacManus 280-4792 1983 $50

SITWELL, SACHEVERELL　　　Fine Bird Books, 1700-1900. 1953.
Folio, half buckram, coloured and collotype plates. Plates 13 and 22
are slightly foxed, and plate 28 is neatly repaired at the fold.
Wheldon 160-97 1983 £300

SITWELL, SACHEVERELL　　　The Gothick North. London: Duckworth,
1929-1930. First editions. 3 vols. Illus. Orig. cloth. Dust
jacket (faded, somewhat worn). 2500 copies of each vol. printed.
Bookplates removed from front endsheets. Good. MacManus 280-4793
1983 $75

SITWELL, SACHEVERELL　　　Great Flower Books, 1700-1900. London:
Collins, 1956. Deluxe edition, limited to 295 numbered copies on
amstel special mould made paper, and signed by the authors, large
folio, 36 large plates, green half morocco, gilt, marbled boards, original marbled paper slip-case. A fine copy. Deighton 3-270 1983
£400

SITWELL, SACHEVERELL　　　Great Flower Books, 1700-1900. 1956.
Roy. folio, original half cloth, coloured and plain plates. Wheldon
160-96 1983 £350

SITWELL, SACHEVERELL　　　Narrative Pictures. London, 1937. First
edition. Profusely illus. 4to. Spine string-marked. Very good.
Rota 230-555 1983 £25

SITWELL, SACHEVERELL　　　Old Garden Roses. 1955-57. 16 fine
coloured plates by Charles Raymond, 2 vols., folio, boards. Edition
limited to 2000 numbered copies and now scarce. A fine copy in
pictorial dust-jackets. Wheldon 160-2009 1983 £50

SITWELL, SACHEVERELL　　　Sacred and Profane Love. London, 1940.
First edition. Illus. Frayed dust wrapper. Nice. Rota 231-564
1983 £15

SITWELL, SACHEVERELL　　　The Thirteenth Caesar and Other Poems.
London: Grant Richards Ltd., 1924. First edition. Orig. cloth with
paper label on spine. Presentation copy inscribed on the copyright
page: "for darling Edith with Sachie's very best love 8.X.24." Annotations throughout book, probably in Edith Sitwell's hand. Label
rubbed. Very good. MacManus 280-4795 1983 $500

SITWELL, SACHEVERELL　　　Touching the Orient. London, 1934.
First edition. Endpapers foxed. Small label removed from rear endpaper. Nice. Rota 230-554 1983 £12.50

SITWELL, SACHEVERELL　　　Two Poems, Ten Songs. London, 1929.
First edition. One of 250 numbered copies signed by the author.
Head and tail of spine slightly rubbed. Very good. Jolliffe 26-
464 1983 £45

SITWELL, W. H.　　　　Visitors Book belonging to Colonel Sitwell.
London, 1913-14. Imp.8vo. Green straight grained morocco, gilt.
A.e.g. Marbled endpapers, slightly worn. Good. Edwards 1044-645
1983 £20

SIXTEEN Humerous Designs, to illustrate Virgil, Horace and Livy.
For Private Circulation only, (circa 1850). 16 lithographed plates.
Oblong 8vo. Orig. wrappers, printed paper label. Plates slightly
stained, wrappers worn. Traylen 94-753 1983 £15

SIZER, THEODORE　　　The Works of Colonel John Trumbull,
Artist of the American Revolution. New Haven: Yale University
Press, 1950. 46 plates. Text illus. 4to. Cloth. Edition
limited to 750 copies. Ars Libri 32-677 1983 $85

SIZZI, FRANCESCO　　　Dianoia (Graece) Astronomica...
Venice: Pietro Maria Bertano, 1611. First edition. 4to. Vellum.
Kraus 164-95 1983 $3,000

SKAGGS, WILLIAM H.　　　The Southern Oligarchy. N.Y., 1924.
First edition. Argosy 716-22 1983 $35

SKELTON, ISABEL　　　The Life of Thomas D'Arcy McGee.
Gardenvale: Garden City Press, 1925. 22cm. 16 illus. and portraits.
Wanting the front free fly, a few marginal notes else a very good to
fine copy. Scarce. McGahern 54-160 1983 $75

SKELTON, JOHN　　　The Impeachment of Mary Stuart sometime
Queen of Scots. William Blackwood and Sons, 1876. 8vo, orig. cloth.
Bickersteth 77-170 1983 £22

SKELTON, JOHN　　　Maitland of Lethington and the Scotland
of Mary Stuart. 1887-1888. 2 vols., 8vo, orig. cloth, and papers
peeling at the inner joints of vols. 1, but sound. Bickersteth 77-
171 1983 £20

SKELTON, JOHN　　　Poems. London, 1924. First edition.
One of 780 numbered copies. Foot of spine just a little faded. Torn
dust wrapper. Unopened. Nice. Rota 230-304 1983 £18

SKELTON, OSCAR DOUGLAS　　　Life and Letters of Sir Wilfrid
Laurier. Toronto: S.B. Gundy & Oxford Un. Press, 1921. 22 1/2cm.
2 vols. 37 portraits and illus. Wine cloth. Small ink mark on
vol. one else a very good set. McGahern 54-161 1983 $45

SKELTON, OSCAR DOUGLAS　　　The Life and Times of Sir Alexander
Tilloch Galt. Toronto: Oxford University Press, 1920. 23 1/2cm.
Errata slip. 16 illus. and portraits. Wine cloth. Minor damp-
stain through the bottom margin, still a very good copy. Scarce.
McGahern 53-145 1983 $85

SKELTON, OSCAR DOUGLAS　　　Life and Times of Sir Alexander Tilloch
Galt. Toronto: Oxford University Press, 1920. 23cm. 16 illus.
Damp-stain on the bottom interior margin, wine cloth. Very good.
Scarce. McGahern 54-162 1983 $45

SKELTON, OSCAR DOUGLAS　　　Socialism. A Critical Analysis.
Boston & New York: Houghton Mifflin Co., 1911. 20 1/2cm. First
edition. Wine cloth. Pencil underlining else fine. McGahern
53-146 1983 $50

SKENE, ALEXANDER　　　Memorialls for the Government of the
Royalburghs in Scotland. Aberdeen: John Forbes, 1685. Small
8vo, each part with separate title-page. Dec. headpieces and
initials. Cont. calf, sl. rubbed; rebacked, with red leather spine
label. Karmiole 72-86 1983 $200

SKENE, F.　　　A Strange Inheritance. Wm. Blackwood,
1886. First edition, 3 vols. Half titles; some foxing, orig. maroon
cloth. One or two sl. marks to boards, otherwise v.g. Jarndyce 30-
549 1983 £58

SKENE, F　　　Wayfaring Sketches Among the Greeks and
Turks. London, 1847. First edition. Half calf, with the bookplate
and ownership inscription of the 7th Earl of Kintore. 8vo. Good.
Edwards 1044-646 1983 £48

SKENE, JAMES HENRY　　　The Frontier Lands of the Christian and
the Turk. London, 1853. Second edition. Folding map. Frontis.,
foxed. 2 vols. Spines faded and frayed. 8vo. Good. Edwards 1044-
647 1983 £85

A SKETCH of the life of the late Lieut.-Colonel Champion, of the
95th Regiment. N.p.: for private circulation only, n.d. (1855).
First edition. 12mo. Orig. purple cloth. Spine slightly faded.
Fine copy. Ximenes 63-310 1983 $60

SKETCHES of character, or specimens of real life. London: Longman, etc., 1808. First edition. 3 vols. 12mo. Later quarter cloth. Uncut copy, complete with half-titles. A few marginal tears. Ximenes 63-139 1983 $200

SKETCHES of Rush County, Indiana. Rushville, Ind., 1915. Illus. Orig. cloth. First edition. Ginsberg 46-344 1983 $25

SKETCHES of Successful New Hampshire Men. Manchester: John B. Clarke, 1882. Large 8vo, profusely illus. with 88 steel engr. plates. A.e.g. Karmiole 72-102 1983 $30

SKETCHLEY, ARTHUR   Mrs. Brown and Disraeli. London: George Routledge & Sons, n.d. First edition. Orig. pictorial wrappers. Boards a little rubbed. Lacking front free endpaper. Very good. MacManus 280-4796 1983 $50

SKETCHLEY, ARTHUR   Mrs. Brown at the International Exhibition. London: George Routledge & Sons, n.d. First edition. Orig. pictorial boards. Bootom of spine slightly rubbed. Fine. MacManus 280-4797 1983 $50

SKETCHLEY, ARTHUR   Mrs. Brown at the Paris Exhibition. London: George Routledge & Sons, 1878. First edition. Orig. pictorial boards (a bit rubbed and soiled). Very good. MacManus 280-4798 1983 $50

SKETCHLEY, ARTHUR   Mrs. Brown on Spelling Bees. London: George Routledge & Sons, n.d. First edition. Orig. pictorial boards. Edges rubbed. Very good. MacManus 280-4799 1983 $50

SKETCHLEY, ARTHUR   Mrs. Brown up the Nile. London: George Routledge & Sons, n.d. First edition. Orig. pictorial boards (a bit rubbed). Contents shaken. Very good. MacManus 280-4803 1983 $50

SKETCHLEY, ARTHUR   Mrs. Brown's Christmas Box. London: George Routledge & Sons, n.d. Orig. pictorial boards (a little rubbed). Near-fine. MacManus 280-4800 1983 $50

SKETCHLEY, ARTHUR   Mrs. Brown's " 'Olliday Outins." London: George Routledge & Sons, n.d. First edition. Orig. pictorial boards. Spine rubbed at edges. Short split across lower spine. Very good. MacManus 280-4801 1983 $50

SKETCHLEY, ARTHUR   Mrs. Brown's Visits to Paris. London: George Routledge & Sons, n.d. First edition. Orig. pictorial boards. Fine. MacManus 280-4802 1083 $50

SKINNER, CONSTANCE L.   Adventurers of Oregon. New Haven, 1921. Cloth, fine. Reese 19-514 1983 $20

SKINNER, STEPHEN   Etymologicon Linguae Anglicanae. T. Roycroft, 1671. Folio, calf, marked a little on boards, rebacked. Jarndyce 31-2 1983 £130

SKINNER, THOMAS   The Life of General Monk: Late Duke of Albemarle... Dublin: for Patrick Dugan, 1724. First Dublin edition. 8vo. Portrait. Calf, slight ink stain. Heath 48-141 1983 £55

SKIPPER, MERVYN   The Meeting-Pool. Mathews & Marrot, 1929. Illus. by R.W. Coulter. Many b&w illus. Pub's pictorial cloth. Fine. Hodgkins 27-191 1983 £10.50

SKOTTSBERG, C.   The Wilds of Patagonia. 1911. 3 maps and 53 illustrations, 8vo, cloth. Wheldon 160-436 1983 £35

SKRINE, F. H.   Fontenoy. London, 1906. First edition. Portrait frontis. 2 coloured plates, 4 other plates, 2 folding maps (1 coloured). Gilt library stamp on cover and ink stamp on endpaper and title. Fine. Edwards 1042-473 1983 £30

SKRINE, HENRY   A general account of all the rivers of note in Great Britain. London: printed by T. Bensley, for P. Elmsly, 1801. First edition. 8vo. Cont. calf, neatly rebacked. Presentation copy, inscribed "From the Author." Double-page aquatint frontis. and 17 engraved maps. Ximenes 63-635 1983 $300

SLACK, LINA M.   Rock Engravings from Driekops Eiland and other Sites... London: Centaur Press, 1962. 104 illus. Small folio. Cloth. Dust jacket. Ars Libri 34-750 1983 $75

SLACUM, WILLIAM A.   Memorial...Praying Compensation for His Services in Obtaining Information in Relation to the Settlements on the Oregon River. Wash., 1837. Dbd. First edition. Ginsberg 47-756 1983 $25

SLADE, LOFTUS   Paddington. For the author, 1877, 24 pp of local ads. Orig. green cloth. Jarndyce 31-295 1983 £24

SLAFTER, EDMUND F.   The Copper Coinage of the Earl of Stirling, 1632. Boston: Privately printed, 1874. Small 4to, illus. Ltd. to 100 copies, signed by "Carlos Slafter." Orig. cloth, sl. soiled, t.e.g. Karmiole 72-76 1983 $60

SLATER, JOHN HERBERT   Book Collecting. Swan Sonnenschein, 1892. First edition. Orig. dark blue cloth, gilt. T.e.g., v.g. No. 450 of 500 large paper copies. Jarndyce 31-100 1983 £20

SLATER, JOHN HERBERT   Book Plates and Their Value. London, 1898. First edition. Small 8vo, English and American Plates. Morrill 290-494 1983 $25

SLATER, JOHN HERBERT   The Library Manual. L. Upcott Gill, 1883. First edition, 16 pp ads. Orig. lilac cloth, spine browned. Jarndyce 31-98 1983 £20

SLATER, JOHN HERBERT   The Romance of Book-Collecting. Elliot Stock, 1898. First edition, half title, front. Orig. dec. mustard cloth, v.g. Jarndyce 31-101 1983 £15

SLATER, JOHN HERBERT   Round and About the Book-Stalls. L. Upcott Gill, 1891. Orig. dark olive-green cloth, half title, 14 pp ads. First edition. Jarndyce 31-99 1983 £10.50

SLATIN PASHA, RUDOLF CARL   Fire and Sword in the Sudan. London: Edward Arnold, 1896. 8vo. 22 plates. 2 folding map. Orig. green pictorial cloth. T,e,g, Very good. Adelson Africa-129 1983 $120

SLAUGHTER, PHILIP   A History of St. Mark's Parish, Culpeper County, Virginia. (Richmond: Author). 1877. 12mo, with large folding map + 2 other maps in text. Errata tipped-in at back. Orig. purple gilt-stamped cloth; spine faded. Karmiole 76-108 1983 $50

SLEEMAN, W. H.   A Journey Through the Kingdom of Oude. London, 1858. Folding map, 2 vols. Orig. decorative cloth. 8vo. Good. Edwards 1044-650 1983 £145

SLEEMAN, W. H.   Ramaseeasa. London, 1836. 2 vols. 3 folding plates of Thug Family Trees. Half brown morocco by Sangorski & Sutcliffe. Author's own copy with many annotations in ink possibly for a subsequent edition. This copy also has the title page to the second volume which is not found in the copy in the India Office Library. 8vo. Good. Edwards 1044-648 1983 £1,700

SLEEMAN, W. H.   Rambles and Recollections of an Indian Official. London, 1844. First edition. 32 coloured plates. 2 vols. Roy.8vo. Orig. cloth gilt, rebacked with spines laid down. Good. Edwards 1044-649 1983 £175

SLEIDANUS, JOHN   An Historical Account of the Four Chief Monarchies. London, 1695. First English edition. Sm.8vo. Cont. calf, slight wear, re-backed. Good. Edwards 1044-65i 1983 £85

SLEIGH, BERNARD   A Handbook of Elementary Design. Pitman, 1934. 1st edn. Colour frontis. & 5 col. plates, & 23 b&w illus. Canvas backed boards (cvrs. sl. marked, corners sl. bruised, insc. fr. ep), vg copy. Hodgkins 27-489 1983 £12.50

SLESINGER, TESS   Time: the Present; a Book of Short Stories. N.Y., Simon and Schuster, (1935). First edition. Colored story heading pages. Dust jacket (slight rubbing). Signed and inscribed by the author to editor Frank Crowninshield, 1935. Very good. Houle 22-811 1983 $65

SLEVOGT, MAX   Die Zauberfloete. Berlin, 1924. Folio,
1/2 cl. Salloch 387-143 1983 $165

SLICK, JONATHAN   High Life in New York. Jeremiah How,
1844. First English edition. half titles, half calf, maroon labels,
very good. Jarndyce 30-555 1983 £48

SLIGO, MRS. SMITH   Thistledown. Williams & Norgate, 1865.
Orig. green cloth, first edition. Very good. Signed presentation
copy from the authoress. Jarndyce 30-842 1983 £15

SLIVE, SEYMOUR   Frans Hals. London: Phaidon, 1970-
1974. 3 vols. Vol 1: 8 color plates. 221 text illus. Vol. 2:
360 plates (8 color). Vol. 3: 205 illus. hors texte. Large 4to.
Cloth. Dust jacket. Ars Libri 32-300 1983 $325

SLOAN, JOHN   Gist of Art. New York, American Artists
Group, (1939). Illus. 8vo. 1st ed. Autographed by the author
and artist. Morrill 286-443 1983 $65

SLOAN, RICHARD E.   Memories of an Arizona Judge. Stanford
University, 1932. First edition in d.j. Scarce. Jenkins 153-14
1983 £50

SLOANE, H.   A Voyage to the Islands Madera, Barbados,
Nieves, S. Christophers and Jamaica. 1707-25. 2 vols., folio, cont.
calf (not uniform), large folding map, double-page plates. A nice
clean copy with the text and plates on guards throughout. Wheldon
160-98 1983 £1,900

SLOANE, WILLIAM M.   The Treaty of Ghent. New York, 1914.
Chipped wraps., very good. Reese 19-516 1983 $20

SLOCUM, HENRY WARNER   In Memoriam 1826-1894. Albany: NY
Monument Comm., 1904. 4 maps, engr. frontis, photo illus, 4to,
mod. fabricoid, ex-library. Argosy 710-91 1983 $40

SLOCUM, JOHN J.   A Bibliography of James Joyce (1882-
1941). New Haven: Yale University Press, 1953. First edition.
8vo. Cloth. Dust jacket. Fine in slightly yellowed wrapper. Oak
Knoll 49-457 1983 $85

SLOP'S shave at a broken Hone. London: W. Wright, 1820. First
edition. 8vo. Disbound. Ximenes 63-516 1983 $60

SLUYTERMAN, K.   Alte Innenraume in Holland. The Hague,
1908. 100 full-page plates from photographs by L. Van Leer of
Amsterdam. Small folio, comprising title. Plates, all loose as
issued in the orig. buckram portfolio, ribbon ties. Ex-library,
partly dust-soiled, few margins of plates partly torn. Morrill 289-
536 1983 $37.50

SMALL, HUGH   Oregon and Her Resources, from
Personal Observation and Investigation. San Francisco, 1872.
Errata slip. Folded map. Orig. printed front wrapper. First
edition. Ginsberg 46-611 1983 $100

SMALLEY, JANET   Rice to Rice Pudding. N.Y., Morrow,
(1928). First edition. Illus. by the author. Half cloth. Very good.
Houle 21-822 1983 $37.50

SMALRIDGE, GEORGE   Reflections on the Historical Part of
Church-government, Part V. Oxford: Printed at the Theater, 1687.
First edition, 4to, wrapper, a very few catchwords just touched,
but otherwise a very good copy. Fenning 61-413 1983 £14.50

SMART, ALEXANDER   Rambling Rhymes. Edinburgh: A. & C.
Black. 1834. First edition. Half green roan, rubbed on corners,
spine gilt. Jarndyce 30-843 1983 £18

SMART, CHRISTOPHER   Poems on several occasions. London:
printed for the author, by W. Strahan..., 1752. First edition.
4to. Cont. calf, neatly rebacked. With two plates, and a 10-page
list of subscribers. Some light spotting. Ximenes 63-381 1983
$600

SMART, CHRISTOPHER   A Song to David with other poems. London:
1924. First edition. Label on spine a little faded. G. Finzi's
copy, with his autograph signature, beneath what the editor has inscribed. Very nice. Rota 230-85 1983 £25

SMART, HAWLEY   Cecil; Or, Modern Idolaters. London:
Richard Bentley, 1871. First edition. 3 vols. Orig. blue cloth.
Spines and covers slightly worn and soiled. Former owner's signature.
Good. MacManus 280-4804 1983 $225

SMART, HAWLEY   Cecile; Or, Modern Idolaters. London:
Bentley & Son, 1871. First edition. 3 vols. Orig. brown cloth.
Spines and covers badly worn. Inner hinges weak. Former owner's
signature. Fair. MacManus 280-4805 1983 $50

SMART, HAWLEY   From Post to Finish. London: Chapman
& Hall, 1884. First edition. 3 vols. Orig. red decorated cloth.
Spines and covers worn at ends and edges. Slightly spotted and soiled.
Good. MacManus 280-4806 1983 $350

SMART, HAWLEY   Sunshine and Snow. London: Chapman &
Hall, 1878. First edition. 3 vols. Orig. grass green decorated
cloth. Spine and covers slightly worn. Inner hinge to vol. III
cracking. Former owner's small rubber blind-stamp. Good. MacManus
280-4807 1983 $300

SMART, JANE   A Letter from a Lady at Madras. London:
For H. Piers, 1743. Engraved head and tail pieces. Cloth-backed paper
covered boards. 8vo. Good. Edwards 1044-652 1983 £70

SMEDLEY, FRANK EDWARD   The Fortunes of The Colville Family.
London: George Hoby, 1853. First edition. Illus. by "Phiz." Orig.
gilt-decorated red cloth. Engraved frontis. Title partially dampstained. Former owner's inscription on flyleaf. Covers darkened.
Very good. MacManus 280-4808 1983 $85

SMEDLEY, FRANK EDWARD   The Fortunes of the Colville Family.
London: G. Hoby, 1853. First edition. Cr. 8vo. Orig. decorated
red cloth, gilt. Title-page and frontis. by H.K. Browne. Traylen
94-754 1983 £15

SMEDLEY, FRANK EDWARD   Frank Farleigh: or Scenes from the
Life of a Private Pupil. London, n.d. 8vo. Full polished calf,
three-line gilt border, gilt panelled spine with green morocco
label, t.e.g., by Zaehnsdorf. 30 engraved plates by George Cruikshank. Traylen 94-755 1983 £20

SMEDLEY, FRANK EDWARD   Harry Coverdale's Courtship...
London: Routledge, n.d. 8vo. Half green morocco, gilt, t.e.g.,
by Riviere. With coloured frontis. and vignette title-page and
28 plates by "Phiz" (H.K. Browne). Traylen 94-756 1983 £25

SMEDLEY, FRANK EDWARD   Lewis Arundel or the Railroad of Life.
London: Routledge, n.d. 8vo. Half green morocco, gilt, t.e.g.
by Riviere. With coloured frontis. and vignette title-page and
40 plates by "Phiz" (H.K. Browne). Traylen 94-757 1983 £28

SMEDLEY, R. C.   History of the Underground Railroad
in Chester & the Neighboring Counties of Pennsylvania. Lancaster,
1883. Illus. Argosy 716-23 1983 $40

SMEDLEY, WILLIAM   Across the Plains in '62. (Denver,
1916). Cloth and boards, frontis. portrait. Fine copy. Privately
printed in a small edition. First edition. Presentation copy from
the author. Very scarce. Jenkins 151-318 1983 $300

SMEE, ALFRED   Instinct and Reason. Reeve, Benham and
Reeve, 1850. First edition, half title, front. & 9 other plates (7
col. 2 printed in red), vignettes. Half green calf, maroon label.
Fine. Jarndyce 31-370 1983 £82

SMELLIE, WILLIAM   A Treatise on the Theory and Practice
of Midwifery. London, 1752. Second edition. 8vo. Cont. calf,
rebacked. Gurney JJ-379 1983 £50

SMILES, SAMUEL   The Life of George Stephenson, Railway
Engineer. John Murray, 1857. 2nd edition, tall 8vo, front. port.
foxed. Orig. maroon cloth, sl. rubbed on hinges. Jarnduce 30-1141
1983 £18

SMIRKE, ROBERT   Review of a Battalion of Infantry,
Including the Eighteen Manoeuvers... New York, 1811. 24 plates, new
cloth and boards, leather label, very good. Second American edition.
Reese 18-351 1983 $175

SMITH, A. JACKSON   The Three Mysteries. London: Arthur
H. Stockwell, n.d. First edition (?). Orig. cloth. Spine and covers
slightly faded and worn. Good. MacManus 280-4809 1983 $20

SMITH, ADAM   An Inquiry into the Nature and Causes
of the Wealth of Nations. Philadelphia: Dobson, 1789. 3 vols. 8vo,
gilt calf, rebacked. First American edition. Rostenberg 88-139
1983 $1,250

SMITH, ADAM   An Inquiry Into The Nature And Causes
Of The Wealth Of Nations. London: A. Strahan and T. Cadell, 1791.
6th edition, 3 vols., 8vo, slight spotting of the preliminary gatherings in each volume, cont. tree calf, spines elaborately gilt, green
morocco labels, slight cracking to two joints, but otherwise a fine,
crisp set. Pickering & Chatto 21-114 1983 $550

SMITH, ADAM   An Inquiry Into The Nature And Causes
Of The Wealth Of Nations. Edinburgh, Adam and Charles Black, 1863.
New edition, revised corrected and improved. 8vo, frontis. 'medallion'
portrait, another standing portrait, woodcut, full polished calf by
Bedford, spine elaborately gilt, gilt fillets and dentelles, red
morocco label, marbled edges and endpapers. A fine copy. Pickering
& Chatto 21-115 1983 $250

SMITH, ADAM   An Inquiry into the Nature and Causes
of the Wealth of Nations. Edinburgh: A. & C. Black, 1863. New
edition. Front. Orig. brown cloth, v.g. Jarndyce 31-371 1983 £35

SMITH, ADAM   An Inquiry Into The Nature And Causes
Of The Wealth Of Nations. Oxford, at the Clarendon Press, 1869.
8vo, 2 vols., 24 publisher's advertisements, frontis. 'medallion'
portrait, original brown cloth, minor repairs to spines. Pickering
& Chatto 21-117 1983 $275

SMITH, ADAM   An Inquiry Into The Nature And Causes
Of The Wealth Of Nations. London: W. Strahan, T. Cadell, 1776.
(Reprinted Yushodo Booksellers Ltd., 1976). Facsimile reprint of
the first edition, limited to 1,000 copies, 2 vols., 4to, advertise-
ments, full maroon imitation morocco, contained in a blue slipcase.
An excellent reprint on fine paper. Pickering & Chatto 21-116 1983
$250

SMITH, ADAM   Lectures on Justice, Police, Revenue
and Arms. Oxford, at the Clarendon Press, 1896. First edition,
half title, 8 pp ads. Ex-library copy, but v.g. in orig. maroon
cloth. Jarndyce 31-372 1983 £46

SMITH, ADAM   Recherches Sur La Nature Et Les Causes
De La Richesse Des Nations. Paris: Chez Mme. veuve Agasse, 1822.
2nd ed., 6 vols., 8vo, advertisements, lacking frontis. portrait to
Vol. I, calf backed marbled boards, spines gilt, very slightly
rubbed, spines uniformly faded, but a very good set. Scarce.
Pickering & Chatto 21-118 1983 $850

SMITH, ADAM   The Theory of Moral Sentiments. London:
A. Strahan and T. Cadell, 1790. 6th ed., 2 vols., 8vo, cont. speckled
calf, gilt borders, spines elaborately gilt, red and black morocco
labels, joints cracking but sound, bookplate. Pickering & Chatto
21-119 1983 $500

SMITH, ALBERT   The Adventures of Mr. Ledbury and His
Friend Jack Johnson. Richard Bentley, 1844. First edition, 3 vols.
Front. & Illus. by John Leech. Bound by Riviere & Son in calf,
gilt borders and spines, brown labels, t.e.g. Fine. Jarndyce 30-550
1983 £58

SMITH, ALBERT   The Adventures of Mr. Ledbury. London:
G. Routledge & Co., 1856. New edition, with a new preface. Frontis.
Orig. cloth. Frontis. partially dampstained. Near-fine. MacManus
280-4810 1983 $20

SMITH, ALBERT   A Month in Constantinople. London:
David Bogue, 1850. 1st ed., 8vo, orig. cloth gilt, spine gilt.
Colored frontis. Hinges worn, some signatures sprung but firm; a
good copy. Trebizond 18-155 1983 $95

SMITH, ALBERT   The Pottleton Legacy. London: David
Bogue, 1849. First edition. Illus. by H.K. Browne. Orig. gilt-decorated cloth. Fine. MacManus 280-4811 1983 $150

SMITH, ALBERT   The Pottleton Legacy. David Bogue,
1859. First edition, bound from the parts, illus. by Hablot K.
Browne (Phiz). Half green calf, a little rubbed, maroon label.
Jarndyce 31-906 1983 £16.50

SMITH, ALBERT   The Struggles and Adventures of Christopher Tadpole. London: Richard Bentley, 1846-1848. First edition.
Illus. by Leech. 16 orig. parts in pictorial wrappers (spines renewed).
Some wrappers rather soiled and a bit frayed. 3/4 morocco solander
case (slightly rubbed and soiled). Very good. MacManus 280-4813
1983 $450

SMITH, ALBERT   The Struggles and Adventures of Christopher Tadpole at Home and Abroad. London: Richard Bentley, 1848.
First edition. Illus. by Leech. 16 orig. parts bound as one in full
gilt morocco with dentelles. Orig. pictorial wrappers and ads together at the back. Armorial bookplate of James Allen Young. A few
wrappers slightly frayed and soiled. In a handsome binding. Near-
fine. MacManus 280-4812 1983 $150

SMITH, ALEXANDER   Dreamthorp. London, Strahan, 1863.
Orig. green cloth gilt, first edition. Ravenstree 96-232 1983 $45

SMITH, ALEXANDER   Dreamthorp. Boston, J.E. Tilton, 1864.
8vo, orig. cloth gilt, bit faded, trifle worn, inner joints cracked,
bookplate of Moncure Biddle. First American edition. Ravenstree 96-
233 1983 $420

SMITH, ALICE R. HUGER   A Carolina Rice Plantation of the Fifties.
N.Y., 1936. Illus. in water-color (30), 4to. Argosy 716-524 1983
$35

SMITH, ARTHUR D.   Old Fuss and Feathers. New York: Grey-
stone Press, 1937. First edition. Frontis. and illus. Orig. cloth.
Fading to spine and some wear. Good. Jenkins 152-400 1983 $30

SMITH, BRADLEY   The Horse in the West. New York & Cleveland, 1969. First edition, first printing. Limited to 500 copies
signed by author. In special binding, with parchment insert, gold
leaf endpapers, etc. Copy No.180. Numerous color illus., map. Folio.
Orig. bent split cowhide. Hinges cracked from the heavy boards. In
publisher's box. Very fine. Jenkins 152-420a 1983 $150

SMITH, BUCKINGHAM   An Inquiry into the Authenticity of
Documents Concerning a Discovery in North American Claimed to Have
Been Made by Verrazzano. N.Y., 1864. Uncut. Illus., folded map,
orig. printed wraps. First edition. Ltd. to 250 copies. Ginsberg
46-698 1983 $85

SMITH, CALEB B.   Fort Ridgely and South Pass Wagon Road.
Wash., 1862. Dbd. First edition. Ginsberg 46-699 1983 $45

SMITH, CECIL   The Birds of Somersetshire. 1869.
Cr. 8vo, cloth. Wheldon 160-888 1983 £35

SMITH, CHARLES EDWARD   The Jazz Record Book. NY 1942.
Cloth, ink inscription, good in soiled and chipped dw. King 46-398
1983 $22.50

SMITH, CHARLES MANBY   The Little World of London. Arthur Hall,
Virtue, 1857. First edition, 24 pp ads. Orig. pink cloth, recased.
Jarndyce 31-296 1983 £22

SMITH, CHARLES W.   Journal of a Trip to California. New
York, n.d. Orig. cloth. Jenkins 153-518 1983 $50

SMITH, CHARLES W.   Oriental Ornithology. Behar Lithographic Press, 1827-29. Illuminated title and hand-coloured plates,
oblong folio, half morocco. Extremely rare. The plates have been
trimmed without affecting the figures. Wheldon 160-99 1983 £500

SMITH, CHARLES W.   Pacific Northwest Americana... Portland: Oregon Historical Society, 1950. Third edition, revised
and extended. Small 4to. Cloth. Bruise at spine head. Oak
Knoll 49-496 1983 $65

SMITH, CHARLOTTE   Celestina. London, T. Cadell, 1791.
4 vols., small 8vo, cont. half calf recently rebacked preserving
orig. morocco gilt labels, some foxing, bookplate, with half titles
as called for, decent set. First edition. Ravenstree 96-234 1983
$420

SMITH, CHARLOTTE   Celestina. A Novel. Printed for T.
Cadell, 1791. First edition, 4 vols, 12mo, contemporary calf, gilt
backs; slight foxing. Hill 165-118 1983 £265

SMITH, CHARLOTTE   Celestina. London: for T. Cadell,
1791. First edition. 4 vols. 12mo. Cont. panelled calf, gilt,
morocco labels, gilt, (four neatly renewed). From the library at
Ragley Hall, with bookplates. Calf worn. Traylen 94-758 1983
£105

SMITH, CHARLOTTE   Celestina. Dublin: Printed for R.
Cross, P. Wogan (etc), 1791. 3 vols, 12mo, contemporary mottled
calf, red and green labels. First Dublin edition. Hill 165-119
1983 £40

SMITH, CHARLOTTE   Conversations Introducing Poetry.
London, J. Johnson, 1804. 2 vols., 12mo, cont. green straight-grain
morocco gilt, a.e.g. First edition. Ravenstree 96-235 1983 $185

SMITH, CHARLOTTE   Desmond. A Novel. Printed for G.G.J.
and J. Robinson, 1792. First edition. 3 vols, 12mo, original
boards, uncut; backstrips renewed; with all half-titles, errata in
vol. I, two advertisement leaves in vol. III; signature N in vol. I
misbound but complete. Rare in this condition. Hill 165-120 1983
£325

SMITH, CHARLOTTE   Emmelina. London, printed at the
Minerva Press for A.K. Newman, 1816. 4 vols., cont. green
quarter morocco, bookplate, little foxing. Ravenstree 96-236 1983
$265

SMITH, CHARLOTTE   Ethelinde, or the Decluse of the Lake.
London, T. Cadell, 1789. 5 vols., 12mo, later cloth (now soiled,
little bubbled, few blank tips chipped, little pinhole worming to
several blank tips, several leaves with blank tip wormed, few minor
tears, last few leaves in final volume damp-stained, several inner
hinges broken). First edition. Ravenstree 96-237 1983 $320

SMITH, CHARLOTTE   Marchmont. London, Smapson Low,
1796. 4 vols., orig. boards (spines defective, covers worn), uncut
set complete with half titles. First edition. Ravenstree 96-238
1983 $475

SMITH, CHARLOTTE   The Old Manor House. London, J. Bell,
1793. 4 vols., 8vos, modern half calf gilt antique style, a fine
set and complete with all half titles. First edition. Ravenstree
96-239 1983 $395

SMITH, CLARK ASHTON   Genius Loci and Other Tales. Sauk City:
Arkham House, 1947. Cloth, first edition. One of ca. 3,000 copies.
Fine in dust jacket. Reese 20-895 1983 $75

SMITH, CLARK ASHTON   Nero and Other Poems. Lakeport, CA:
Futile Press, 1937. 12mo, cloth over boards. Karmiole 74-84 1983
$85

SMITH, CLARK ASHTON   Poems in Prose. Sauk City: Arkham
House, 1964. First edition. Illus. Cloth. 1000 copies printed.
Fine in perfect jacket. Bradley 66-142 1983 $125

SMITH, CLARK ASHTON   The Star-Treader and Other Poems. San
Francisco: A.M. Robertson, 1912. Gilt boards. First edition.
Book ticket of John Howell-Books. A very fine copy in the scarce dust
jacket. Reese 20-894 1983 $200

SMITH, CLINTON L.   The Boy Captives. (Bandera, Tex., 1927).
Frontis. Rumpled wraps., hole in wrapper going through several leaves
without textual loss. Good. Reese 19-517 1983 $125

SMITH, DAVID   David Smith by David Smith. New York:
Holt, Rinehart and Winston, 1968. Prof. illus. (7 color). Square
4to. Cloth. Dust jacket. Ars Libri 32-639 1983 $85

SMITH, DAVIE EUGENE   Rara Arithmetica, A Catalogue of the
Arithmetics Written before the year MDCI... Boston: Ginn & Company,
1908. First edition. Full vellum stamped in gold, t.e.g., others
uncut. Limited to 151 numbered and signed copies. Printed on hand-
made paper. Some cover soiling and foxing of endpapers. Very scarce.
Oak Knoll 49-497 1983 $350

SMITH, DODIE   Call it a Day. N.Y., French, 1936.
First edition. Dust jacket. Very good-fine. Houle 21-823 1983
$37.50

SMITH, DOUGLAS   American Guerilla. Indianapolis,
(1943). 1st ed. Illus. 8vo, dust wrapper. Morrill 288-568 1983
$22.50

SMITH, E. BOYD   The Story of Pocahontas and Captain John
Smith. Boston: HM, (Nov.,1906). Oblong 4to. Cloth backed pictorial
boards. Edges rubbed, light soil. Full-page color illus. opposite
each page of text. Good to very good. Aleph-bet 8-235 1983 $45

SMITH, EDMOND REUEL   The Araucanians. NY: Harper &
Bros., 1855. With 17 engraved illus., many full-page. Orig. green
cloth. Ex-library copy with paper spine label, bookplate and small
rubber stamp on title-page. Karmiole 76-68 1983 $75

SMITH, EDMUND   The Works of Mr. Edmund Smith. London:
printed for Bernard Lintot, 1719. 8vo, engraved frontispiece, modern
half morocco gilt. Pickering & Chatto 19-67 1983 $350

SMITH, EDWARD   You Can Escape. N.Y., MacMillian, 1929.
First edition. Dust jacket (slight rubbing) else very good - fine.
Houle 22-1179 1983 $45

SMITH, EDWIN W.   The Ila-Speaking Peoples of North
Rhodesia. Macmillan, 1920. First edition, with a folding map and
186 full-page and other illus., 2 vols., 8vo, orig. cloth. The
inside joints neatly strengthened and the covers a little spotted.
Fenning 61-414 1983 £65

SMITH, ELBERT H.   Ma-Ka-Me-She-Kia-Kiak. N.Y., Kearny,
1848. First edition. Lithographed frontis. and title page. Finely
bound in 3/4 black morocco, the spine with gilt Indian motifs,
t.e.g. Some light foxing in text, else a fine copy. Houle 21-1160
1983 $150

SMITH, ELBERT H.   Ma-Ka-Tai-Me-She-Kia-Kiak. New York:
Edward Kearny, 1848. Lithographed frontis. and fore-title. Orig.
decorated cloth, signed in the border by the binder, Samuel Middle-
brook. Endsheets foxed. First edition. Felcone 22-232 1983 $50

SMITH, ELEANOR   Flamenco. Ind., (1931). Advance reading
copy, three vols, stiff paperboards, spine edges slightly frayed and
boards slightly creased, else very good in splitting slipcase. Quill
& Brush 54-1247 1983 $30

SMITH, ELEANOR   Flamenco. Ind., (n.d.). 3 vols., stiff
paper boards, advance reading copy, spine edges slightly frayed and
boards slightly creased, else very good in splitting slipcase. Quill
& Brush 54-1248 1983 $30

SMITH, ELEANOR   Song Devices & Jingles. G.G. Harrap,
1926. 4to. Colour frontis. Title vignette. 7 colour plates & 11
text illus. Buff boards. Onlaid colour plate. Orig. dust wrapper.
Greer 40-249 1983 £15

SMITH, ELIAS   The American Physician & Family Assistant.
Boston, 1832. Small 12mo, old calf, (joints mended), red leather
label. Argosy 713-501 1983 $75

SMITH, ELIZA   The Compleat Housewife. London, J.&H.
Pemberton, 1741. 8vo. Engraved frontis. & 6 engraved plates. Recent
three-quarter cloth & marbled boards. 10th ed., with very large
additions. O'Neal 50-12 1983 $200

SMITH, ELIZABETH OAKES   The Western Captive; or, The Times of
Tecumseh. New York: October, 1842. Fine copy, preserved in worn
cloth case. Bradley 66-309 1983 $125

SMITH, EMILY A.   Life and Letters of Nathan Smith.
Yale Univ. Press, 1914. First edition. Only 1,000 copies. Many
plates, roan-backed boards, (mended). Argosy 713-502 1983 $35

SMITH, ERNEST BRAMAH   Kai Lung's Golden Hours. London: Grant
Richards Ltd., 1922. First edition. Preface by Hilaire Belloc. Orig.
cloth, dust jacket (rare). Cloth wraparound jacket with leather label.
Very fine. MacManus 277-662 1983 $350

SMITH, ERNEST BRAMAH   Kai Lung's Golden Hours. N.Y.: George
H. Doran Co., (1923). First American edition. Preface by Hilaire
Belloc. Orig. cloth-backed pictorial boards. Former owner's neat
signature on free endpaper. Covers a bit rubbed. Good. MacManus 277-
663 1983 $35

SMITH, ERNEST BRAMAH   The Return of Kai Lung. NY, (1937).
Minor interior soiling, edges slightly rubbed, still very good in
slightly frayed and worn, good dustwrapper. Name front endpaper.
Quill & Brush 54-175 1983 $40

SMITH, EUGENE W.   Trans-Atlantic Passenger Ships Past and
Present. Boston, George H. Dean, (1947). First edition. Autographed.
Illustrated. 12mo. Morrill 290-497 1983 $25

SMITH, F.   The Canary. 1872. Third edition,
12 coloured plates, 8vo, cloth, somewhat worn. Wheldon 160-889
1983 £18

SMITH, FRANCIS HOPKINSON   Charcoals of Old New York. Garden City,
1912. Illus. with mounted plates, 4to, ex library. Argosy 710-384
1983 $40

SMITH, FRANCIS HOPKINSON   Colonel Carter of Cartersville. Boston:
1891. First edition, first state. Illus. Green cloth. Bookplate,
inner hinges split, covers worn and spotted. In green linen jacket
with leather spine label. Bradley 66-310 1983 $45

SMITH, FRANCIS HOPKINSON   In Dicken's London. N.Y.: Charles
Scribner's Sons, 1916. A reprint of the 1914 first edition. Illus.
with charcoal drawings by author. Edges slightly worn. Very good.
MacManus 278-1564 1983 $20

SMITH, FRANK   A History of Dedham, Massachusetts.
Dedham, 1936. First edition. Illustrated. 8vo. Morrill 290-298
1983 $25

SMITH, FRANK E.   Yazoo River. NY, (1942). Illus.
Argosy 710-523 1983 $30

SMITH, FREDERICK RICHARD   Bookbinding. London: Isaac Pitman
& Sons, 1937. Small 8vo. Cloth-backed boards, dust jacket. With
a full color frontis. Slightly chipped jacket. Fine. Oak Knoll
48-37 1983 $25

SMITH, FREDERICK RICHARD   Bookbinding. New York: Pitman
Publishing Co., n.d. (ca. 1940). Small 8vo. Cloth. Dust jacket.
Oak Knoll 48-38 1983 $25

SMITH, GEORGE   Assyrian Discoveries. 1875. First edition. Illus., orig. gilt dec. cloth. Bright crisp copy. K Books
307-167 1983 £30

SMITH, GEORGE   A Collection of Armorial Bookbindings
of the Tudor, Stuart and Hanoverian Periods. London: Ellis, 1927.
First edition. Small 4to. Three-quarter cloth over printed fabric.
With a frontis. and five full page plates. Covers rubbed. Oak
Knoll 49-76 1983 $55

SMITH, GEORGE   The Life of William Carey. London, 1885.
Plan, 10 plates, illus. in text. 8vo. Orig. cloth. Good. Edwards
1044-654 1983 £30

SMITH, GEORGE   A Narrative of an Exploratory Visit to
Each of the Consular Cities of China. London: Seeley, Burnside and
Seely, 1847. First edition. Illus. with 12 plates (4 tinted
lithographs and 8 mounted India proof lithos.) + a double-page
color map. Orig. purple gilt-stamped cloth, soiled; with some
chipping to lower spine extremity and back outer hinge. Karmiole
75-40 1983 $125

SMITH, GEORGE   A narrative of an exploratory visit to
each of the consular cities in China... New York: Harper, 1847.
First American edition. Large 12mo. Later 19th-century half red
morocco, gilt, spine gilt, t.e.g. With a frontis., folding map,
and 11 wood-engraved plates. Slight rubbing. Some foxing, otherwise a very good copy. Ximenes 63-609 1983 $125

SMITH, GEORGE   An Universal Military Dictionary.
J. Millan, 1779. First edition. Engraved title, small engraving on
dedication leaf. 4 leaf list of Subscribers, 16 engraved plates (4
folding) and 1 folding engraved table. 3 pp. publisher's ads. 4to.
Cont. half calf. Very slightly worn and soiled. Marbled edges.
Bookplate. Good. Edward 1042-472 1983 £200

SMITH, GEORGE A.   The Rise, Progress and Travels of the
Church of Jesus Christ of Latter-Day Saints. SLC, 1872. 2nd edition,
orig. pr. wraps. Argosy 716-572 1983 $85

SMITH, GEORGE G.   Spencer Kellogg Brown: His Life in
Kansas and His Death as a Spy. New York, 1903. First edition. Illus.
Jenkins 152-574 1983 $35

SMITH, GEORGE W.   A Defence of the System of Solitary
Confinement of Prisoners Adopted by the State of Pennsylvania.
Philadelphia, 1833. Disbound. Scattered foxing and light soiling
of first and last leaves. Felcone 22-198 1983 $35

SMITH, GUSTAVUS W.   Report on the Affairs of the Dubuque
and Pacific R.W. N.Y., Roe & Co., 1865. Cloth. Ginsberg 46-238
1983 $175

SMITH, H. ALLEN   Lo, the Former Egyptian. NY: 1947.
Drawings by Leo Hershfield. Very fine in faintly chipped dust
wrapper. Two-page TLS from Smith to Louis Untermeyer laid-in. Fine
condition in orig. addressed envelope. Bromer 25-103 1983 $200

SMITH, H. M.   Handbook of Lizards. New York, 1946.
Numerous illus., 8vo, cloth (trifle used). Wheldon 160-1001 1983
£18

SMITH, HAL H.   The Story of Lac Ste. Claire. Detroit:
Privately printed by the Press of the Round Circle, (1939). Limited,
Numbered edition. Illus. Folding maps (in facsimile). Limp cloth.
Ex-library. A bit worn, couple maps with minor tears. King 45-119
1983 $20

SMITH, HAROLD CLIFFORD   Sulgrave Manor and the Washingtons.
London, (1933). First edition. Illustrated. 4to, ex-library; nice.
Morrill 290-583 1983 $22.50

SMITH, HARRY B.   A Sentimental Library... N.P.:
privately printed, 1914. First and only edition. 4to. Vellum
backed cloth, t.e.g., others uncut, dust jacket, slipcase. Presentation copy "To Mrs. Haskell with compliments and regards Harry
B. Smith. Slipcase partially cracked. Fine copy. Oak Knoll 48-
350 1983 $350

SMITH, HARRY J.   Romance of the Hoboken Ferry. NY, 1931
Illus. 1/4 mor., expertly rebacked in cloth. Argosy 710-340 1983
$45

SMITH, HARRY WORCESTER   Life and Sport in Aiken. NY: Derrydale
Press, (1935). Tall 8vo, with 45 plates. Edition ltd. to 950
copies. Green gilt-stamped cloth. Spine sl. faded. Karmiole 75-
45 1983 $125

SMITH, HORACE   Barmbletye House, or Cavaliers and
Roundheads. London: Colburn, 1826. First edition. 3 vols. Orig.
boards. Paper labels. A few hinges partly cracked. Labels slightly
chipped. Fine. MacManus 280-4814 1983 $175

SMITH, HORACE   Gaieties and Gravities: a Series of
Essays, Comic Tales and Fugitive Vagaries. London: Henry Colburn,
1825. 1st ed. in book form, 12mo, cont. half calf gilt, marbled
boards. Half-title in vol. I, lacking advertisement leaf in Vol 3.
Trebizond 18-91 1983 $120

SMITH, HORACE　　　　Gale Middleton. Richard Bentley, 1833.
First edition. 3 vols. Large 12mo, all half-titles, but lacks final
leaf of vol. I. Cont. cloth, with the label of S. Roberts, Oswestry.
Hannas 69-189 1983 £40

SMITH, HORACE　　　　Horace in London; consisting of
Imitations of the first two Books of the Odes of Horace. London:
John Miller; Edinburgh: John Ballantyne, 1813. 2nd ed., 8vo, orig.
boards, paper label. Uncut copy with the half-title. Advertisements.
Spine and label slightly chipped, but a fine copy. Trebizond 18-92
1983 $50

SMITH, HORACE　　　　The New Forest. Henry Colburn, 1834.
3 vols. Half calf, dark green labels. Very good. Jarndyce 30-552
1983 £32

SMITH, HORACE　　　　Reuben Apsley. Henry Colburn, 1827.
3 vols, 12mo, half calf; backs slightly rubbed, no half-titles present,
but a good copy. First edition. Hill 165-121 1983 £30

SMITH, HORACE　　　　Tales of the Early Ages. London:
Colburn and Bentley, 1832. Three vols. bound in one. Pub.'s
remainder cloth, bound complete with the half-title for each volume.
A fine copy. Reese 20-896 1983 $100

SMITH, HORACE　　　　The Tor Hill. London, Colburn, 1826.
3 vols. 8vo. Cont. half calf gilt, without the errata slip and ads.
First edition. Ravenstree 96-240 1983 $135

SMITH, HORACE　　　　The Tor Hill. Henry Colburn, 1826. First
edition. 3 vols. Large 12mo, lacks two final advert. leaves in
vol. III. Cont. half calf, gilt, book-plates of George Thomas Wyndham.
One corner each of two leaves torn off, not affecting text. Occasional
small stains. Hannas 69-190 1983 £45

SMITH, HORACE　　　　The Tor Hill. Henry Colburn, 1826.
3 vols, 12mo, half calf; backs slightly rubbed, no half-titles; a
fair copy. First edition. Hill 165-122 1983 £30

SMITH, HORACE　　　　The Tor Hill. Henry Colburn, 1826.
First edition, 3 vols. Half calf, black labels. Jarndyce 30-551 1983
£30

SMITH, HUMPHRY　　　　A Collection of the Several Writings
and Faithful Testimonies of...who Dyed a Prisoner...in Winchester
common-goal...1663. Printed and sold by Andrew Sowle, 1683.
First collected edition, 4to, nineteenth century half calf, a very
good copy. Fenning 62-340 1983 £65

SMITH, J.　　　　Sketches in Indian Ink. Calcutta, 1880.
Some slight soiling. 8vo. Orig. cloth. Good. Edwards 1044-655
1983 £15

SMITH, JAMES　　　　Memoirs, letters and comic miscellanies
in prose and verse. London: Colburn, 1840. First edition. 2 vols.
12mo, orig. brown cloth. With a portrait. Ximenes 63-38 1983 $75

SMITH, JAMES　　　　Memoirs, Letters and Comic Miscellanies,
in Prose and Verse, of the Late James Smith. Henry Colburn, 1840.
First edition, 2 vols. Front. vol. I, and numerous other port.
extra-illustrations. Half titles. Half red morocco by Rimell, v.g.
Jarndyce 30-1136 1983 £56

SMITH, JAMES EDWARD　　　　The English Flora. 1828-30. Second
edition, 4 vols., 8vo, cont. full calf, gilt, slightly rubbed and
joints cracking, spines faded, one label defective, g.e. Small stain
on a few outer margins in vol. III, but a nice clean copy. Wheldon
160-1629 1983 £30

SMITH, JAMES EDWARD　　　　A Grammar of Botany. Printed for
Longman, Hurst, Rees, Orme, and Brown, 1821. 8vo, entirely uncut,
21 hand-coloured plates, orig. pink boards, spine slightly
defective at the top, and paper label partly defective. First
edition. Bickersteth 77-321 1983 £85

SMITH, JAMES EDWARD　　　　A Grammar of Botany... London:
Hurst..., 1821. First edition. 8vo. 21 pages of hand-coloured
plates, uncut in orig. pink boards, respined. Slight foxing.
Heath 48-10 1983 £65

SMITH, JAMES EDWARD　　　　An Introduction to Physiological and
Systematical Botany. 1819. Fourth edition, 15 hand-coloured plates
of many figures, 8vo, contemporary calf, rebacked. Wheldon 160-1573
1983 £30

SMITH, JAMES REUEL　　　　Springs and Wells of Manhattan and the
Bronx... New York, 1938. First edition. 154 illustrations from
photographs taken by author. Tall 8vo. Morrill 290-372 1983 $37.50

SMITH, JEROME V. C.　　　　Turkey and the Turks. Boston: James
French; New York: Appleton; Philadelphia: Lippincott, 1854. 1st ed.,
12mo, original decorated cloth, spine gilt. Frontis. Light foxing,
but a fine copy. Trebizond 18-163 1983 $80

SMITH, JESSIE WILCOX　　　　The Jessie Wilcox Smith Mother Goose.
N.Y.: Dodd, (1914). Oblong 4to. Black cloth. Pictorial paste-on.
White spine lettering. Orig. paper wrapper. Orig. pictorial box.
Illus. with 12 large color plates, 5 full-page black & whites, many
text drawings. DeLuxe Edition. Wrapper frayed, box repaired. Mint.
Aleph-bet 8-236 1983 $200

SMITH, JESSIE WILCOX　　　　Have You a Red Cross Service Flag. Boston: Forbes, 1918. Folio, 28 x 21 inches. Orig. full color poster,
designed for the Red Cross. Signed in the plate. Two short marginal
tears, else fine. Houle 22-812 1983 $150

SMITH, JOHN　　　　The art of painting in oyl. London:
printed for Samuel Crouch, 1705. Fourth edition. Small 8vo. Cont.
sheep. Some wear to hinges. Some foxing. Ximenes 63-22 1983
$300

SMITH, JOHN (1580-1631)　　　　Advertisements for the Unexperienced
Planters of New England, or Anywhere; or, the Pathway to Erect a
Plantation. Boston: William Veazie, 1865. Fine folding map.
Edition limited to 250 copies. Jenkins 151-319 1983 $75

SMITH, JOHN CALVIN　　　　The Western Tourist or Emigrant's
Guide... New York, J.H. Colton, 1847. Folding map. 12mo, corners
rubbed. Morrill 290-499 1983 $47.50

SMITH, JOHN J.　　　　American Historical & Literary
Curiosities. Phila., W. Brotherhead, 1861. Folio, dec. cloth,
neatly rebacked. Argosy 710-194 1983 $60

SMITH, JOHN RUSSELL　　　　Bibliotheca Americana... London: Alfred
Russell Smith, 1871. Cloth, good. Dawson 470-272 1983 $40

SMITH, JOHN RUSSELL　　　　A Catalogue of 25,000 volumes of Choice,
Useful, and Curious Books. Printed by F. Pickton, 1860. Half brown
morocco, rubbed, end papers, dusted. Jarndyce 31-102 1983 £28

SMITH, JOSEPH　　　　Book of Mormon.
Please turn to
BOOK OF MORMON

SMITH, JOSEPH　　　　The Pearl of Great Price. Liverpool,
1851. First edition, 2 text woodcuts, disbound. Folding plate,
1/2 lacking. Argosy 716-574 1983 $175

SMITH, JOSEPH　　　　The Pearl of Great Price. SLC, 1878.
2 text plates, mod. wraps. First American edition. Argosy 716-575
1983 $100

SMITH, JOSEPH　　　　Western Reserve Chronicle. Warren,
Ohio: Hapgood & Pease, complete orig. issue for Dec. 9, 1830.
Jenkins 153-520 1983 $35

SMITH, JOSEPHINE　　　　Perth-On-The-Tay. Ottawa, 1901. 18cm.
Errata leaf. Blue cloth with mounted illus. paper cover on the upper
boards. Very good. McGahern 53-148 1983 $45

SMITH, JOSEPHINE　　　　Perth-On-The-Tay. Ottawa, 1901. 18cm.
Errata leaf. Stiff wrappers. Fine. McGahern 53-149 1983 $25

SMITH, JOSHUA H.   An Authentic Narrative of the Causes which Led to the Death of Major Andre, Adjutant General of His Majesty's Forces in North America. London, 1808. Illus. Morocco spine, boards, fine. Reese 18-317 1983 $125

SMITH, JOSHUA H.   An Authentic Narrative of the Causes Which Led to the Death of Major Andre. London: Printed for Mathews and Leigh, 1809. Two plates. One folding map of North America. Orig. paper boards with printed paper label. Some chipping to spine. Jenkins 152-7 1983 $200

SMITH, JUSTIN H.   Our Struggle For The Fourteenth Colony. New York & London: Putnam's, 1907. 22cm. 2 vols. 315 illus. and 23 maps. Orig. green cloth. A fine set. McGahern 53-150 1983 $65

SMITH, JUSTIN H.   The Troubadours at Home. New York, 1899. 1st ed. Illus. 2 vols., 8vo. Some light stains on front cover of vol. 2, otherwise nice. Morrill 287-425 1983 $37.50

SMITH, LAWRENCE B.   American Game Preserve Shooting. NY (1933). Photos, cloth, spine very worn. King 46-665 1983 $25

SMITH, LAWRENCE B.   Dude Ranches and Ponies. New York: Coward-McCann, 1936. Illus. 1st ed. Jenkins 153-521 1983 $45

SMITH, LAWRENCE B.   Fur or Feather, Days with Dog and Gun. NY 1946. 1st ed., presentation copy, inscribed & signed by author. Cloth, slightly spotted cover else very good in poor dw. King 46-666 1983 $30

SMITH, LILLIAN   Killers of the Dream. New York, (1949). 8vo. Cloth. A fine copy in dj which has some very light rubbing at the corners. This copy contains a short TLS from Smith to a book reviewer in Ohio. The letter is dated Nov. 15, 1949. Signed Lillian Smith. With orig. envelope posted from Georgia. In Our Time 156-722 1983 $75

SMITH, LILLIAN   Killers of the Dream. N.Y., (1949). First edition. D.w. Argosy 714-679 1983 $25

SMITH, LOGAN PEARSALL   The Life and Letters of Sir Henry Woton. Oxford: At the University Press, 1907. First edition. 2 vols. Illus. Orig. cloth. Presentation copy, inscribed by the author in each volume. Endpapers foxed. Very good. MacManus 280-5662 $125

SMITH, LOGAN PEARSALL   The Prospects of Literature. London: The Hogarth Press, 1927. First edition. Orig. decorated wrappers, designed by Vanessa Bell. Rear cover torn. Good. MacManus 280-4816 1983 $25

SMITH, LUCY   Biographical Sketches of Joseph Smith, the Prophet, and his Progenitors for Many Generations. Plano, Illinois: published by the Reorginanized Church of Jesus Christ of Latter Day Saints, 1880. Original cloth, some wear. Original edition. Jenkins 151-320 1983 $65

SMITH, MICHAEL   A Geographical View of the Province of Upper Canada. Trenton: Moore and Lake..., November 1813. Frontis. Later 3/4 morocco. Minor foxing, margin of plate chipped slightly, else a nice copy. Third edition. Felcone 22-233 1983 $150

SMITH, MOSES   History of the Adventures and Sufferings of Moses Smith, During Five Years of His Life. Albany, 1814. Worn calf. Good. Reese 18-461 1983 $125

SMITH, NATHAN   The Life and Letters of Nathan Smith, M.D. New Haven, 1914. 1st ed., 1000 copies printed. 8vo. Orig. boards, leather back. Illus. Ex-library; spine partly torn and chipped. Morrill 289-212 1983 $22.50

SMITH, NORA ARCHIBALD   Boys and Girls of Bookland. Phila., (1923). Cloth with color pictorial label. Spine lacking. Covers soiled. Foredge slightly stained. One plate with marginal tear. 11 full-page color plates by J.W. Smith. King 45-434 1983 $35

SMITH, PAUL JORDAN   A Key fo the Ulysses of James Joyce. New York: Covici Friede, (1934). Third printing. 8vo. Cloth, dust jacket. Fine. Oak Knoll 49-253 1983 $20

SMITH, PERCY   Sixteen Drypoints and Etchings. London: The Soncino Press, 1930. First edition. Small folio. Orig. gilt-decorated cloth. Limited to 167 copies, of which this is one of 145 copies printed on Dutch mould-made paper. Prospectus pages from The Soncino Press pasted to front flyleaf. Covers somewhat rubbed at edges. Very good. MacManus 280-5278 1983 $150

SMITH, PHILIP   The Book: Art & Object. Merstham: (Philip Smith), 1982. First edition. 4to. Cloth. Dust jacket. One of the 230 numbered and signed copies bound in cloth. 115 illus., most in color. Oak Knoll 49-72 1983 $85

SMITH, PHILIP E.   The Induction of Precocious Sexual Maturity by Pituitary Homeotransplants. March, 1927. Thin 4to, pr. wrs., stapled. First separate edition. Argosy 713-503 1983 $50

SMITH, R. BAIRD   The Cauvery, Kistnah, and Godavery. London, 1856. 21 folding maps and plans mounted on linen in orig. cloth case bound in with text. 8vo. Good. Edwards 1044-656 1983 £480

SMITH, REGINALD BOSWORTH   Life of Lord Lawrence. Smith, Elder, 1883. With 2 portraits and 2 folding maps, 2 vols., 8vo, cont. half calf, a very good copy. Fenning 62-341 1983 £28.50

SMITH, REGINALD BOSWORTH   Life of Lord Lawrence. London, 1885. Sixth edition, revised. Folding map, folding plan. Portrait frontis. Endpapers foxed. 2 vols. Half morocco, gilt, spine sunned. 8vo. Good. Edwards 1044-657 1983 £48

SMITH, RICHARD   First English Settler of the Narragansett Country. Boston: Merrymount Press, 1937. Argosy 716-490 1983 $25

SMITH, RICHARD   A Tour of Four Great Rivers. New York, 1906. Plates, and 33 skillfully executed drawings and water-colors in extra-illus. by Cronin. Library withdrawal stamp, but a good sound copy in orig. boards. Reese 19-169 1983 $1,000

SMITH, ROBERT   Robert Smith's Address to the People of the United States. (n.p., 1811). Dsb., tear to the first leaf, mended, a fair copy. Reese 18-358 1983 $75

SMITH, ROBERT ANGUS   Memoir of John Dalton, and History of the Atomic Theory up to His Time. London: H. Bailliere, 1856. First edition. Frontis. Index. Orig. cloth, faded, spine extremities a bit frayed. Karmiole 72-26 1983 $75

SMITH, ROBERT PAUL   The Man with the Gold-Headed Cane. N.Y., Hart, (1943). First edition. Stiff decorated wraps., paper label on front cover. One of 300 copies, with a TLS by the author laid in loose. Very good. Houle 22-813 1983 $30

SMITH, ROSWELL C.   Smith's First Book in Geography. NY, 1856. 126 engrs., 20 maps, 29th ed., rev. Sq. 16mo, mod. wrs. Argosy 710-484 1983 $27.50

SMITH, SAMUEL   The Nationalisation of the Land. Kegan Paul, 1884. First separate edition, 8vo, disbound, with the upper orig. printed paper wrapper. Fenning 62-342 1983 £18.50

SMITH, SAMUEL STANHOPE   An Essay On The Causes of the Variety of Complexion and Figure in the Human Species. Philadelphia, printed; London, reprinted: For John Stockdale, 1789. First London edition, 8vo, cont. half calf, marbled boards, spine gilt, joints cracked but sound, slightly rubbed, internally a fine copy. Pickering & Chatto 21-120 1983 $100

SMITH, SAMUEL STANHOPE   Sermons. Newark: Jacob Halsey & Co., 1799. Full calf (worn, early rebacking). Old library markings. Contains the list of subscribers, not present in all copies. Very good. Felcone 19-51 1983 $45

SMITH, SAMUEL STANHOPE   Sermons. Newark: Jacob Halsey & Co.,
1799. Full calf (worn). Front endsheet lacking. Very good. Felcone
19-50 1983 $40

SMITH, SOLOMON   Theatrical Management in the West and
South for Thirty Years. New York, 1868. Cloth, slight nick in spine,
otherwise very good. Waller Barrett duplicate, with his bookplate.
Reese 19-518 1983 $200

SMITH, SOUTHWOOD   A Treatise on Fever. Boston, 1831.
Orig. boards. Two works in one volume. Argosy 713-505 1983 $125

SMITH, STEVIE   The Holiday Book. Glasgow, 1946. First
edition. Spine and covers just a little faded and marked. Torn dust
wrapper. Very nice. Rota 231-568 1983 £20

SMITH, SUSAN   Tranquilina's Paradise. N.Y.: Milt.
Balch, (1930). Large 4to. Cloth backed boards. Pictorial paste-on.
Slight edgewear. Color pictorial endpapers. Line drawings on each
page by Handforth. Very good. Aleph-bet 8-135 1983 $25

SMITH, TEVIS C.   Frontier's Generation. Brownwood, Texas,
1931. First edition. Orig. printed wrappers. Illus. Fine. Jenkins
152-459 1983 $50

SMITH, THOMAS   Voiage and Entertainment in Rushia.
London: Nathanyell Butter, 1605. First edition. Printer's woodcut
device. Small 4to. Light brown morocco by Riviere, triple gilt
rules on sides, ornaments in the angles, back elaborately gilt,
gilt dentelles, g.e. Lower outer corner of title clipped diagonally
not affecting text. Kraus 164-216 1983 $5,800

SMITH, THOMAS (1790-1878)   Extracts from the Diary of a Huntsman.
London: Whittaker & Co., 1838. First edition. Illus. by author.
8vo. Orig. cloth. Spine darkened and worn. Some light marginal
dampstaining. Bookplates. In a folding cloth box. Very nice.
MacManus 280-4819 1983 $250

SMITH, THOMAS (1790-1878)   The Life of a Fox. London: Whittaker &
Co., 1843. First edition. Illus. by T. Smith, Esq. Orig. pictorial
cloth. Unusual early pictorial binding, which reproduces the frontis.
lithographically on both covers. Covers lightly soiled. In a folding
cloth box. Very nice. MacManus 280-4820 1983 $250

SMITH, THORNE   The Passionate Witch. GC, 1941. Minor
rubbing to edges, else bright copy in lightly frayed, bright dustwrapper. Quill & Brush 54-1250 1983 $150

SMITH, THORNE   The Stray Lamb. NY, 1929. Cover rubbed
and edges slightly frayed, good, store stamp front fly. Quill & Brush
54-1251 1983 $25

SMITH, W. C. S.   A Journey to California in 1849. (Napa
City, 1925?). Wrappers. Catalogue description pasted inside back
wrapper. Dawson 471-272 1983 $40

SMITH, WALLACE   Garden of the Sun. Los Angeles, 1939.
Illustrations and maps. First edition in dust jacket. Jenkins 153-107
1983 $75

SMITH, WALTER C.   North Country Folk-Poems. Glasgow:
James Maclehose, 1883. Half title, 16 pp ads. Orig. blue cloth.
Jarndyce 30-845 1983 £10.50

SMITH, WALTER GIFFORD   The Story of San Diego. San Diego:
City Printing Co., 1892. New wrappers with orig. front and back
wrappers laid down. Three leaves taped. Dawson 471-273 1983 $20

SMITH, WALTER H. B.   Mannlicher Rifles and Pistols.
Harrisburg, PA (1947). Drawings, cloth, very good in frayed dw.
King 46-668 1983 $30

SMITH, WALTER H. B.   Pistols & Revolvers. Rifles. Harrisburg, PA (1948). 2 vols. Vol. 1 is 2nd corrected printing. Illus.
Cloth, minor wear. King 46-670 1983 $35

SMITH, WALTER H. B.   Small Arms of the World. Harrisburg,
PA (1949). 4th ed., revised and enlarged. Illus, cloth, good.
King 46-671 1983 $20

SMITH, WALTER H. B.   Walther Pistols. Washington, DC (1946)
Photos, cloth, very good in chipped dw. King 46-672 1983 $25

SMITH, WALTER R.   Brief History of the Louisiana Territory.
St. Louis, 1904. First edition. Jenkins 152-853 1983 $20

SMITH, WILLIAM   The History of the Late Province of New
York... New York, 1829. First edition to contain the orig. work of
1757. 2 vols. Orig. paper-backed boards, paper labels. Uncut. Early
library stamps inside, paper hinges cracking. Felcone 20-129 1983
$60

SMITH, WILLIAM   The History of the Province of New
York, from the First Discovery to the Year 1732. London: Thomas
Wilcox, 1757. First edition. 4to, cont. boards, leather back.
Argosy 716-368 1983 $850

SMITH, WILLIAM A.   Lectures on the Philosophy and Practice
of Slavery. Nashville, 1857. 8vo. Rubbed, lacks blank leaves before title. Morrill 287-427 1983 $35

SMITH, WILLIAM GARDNER   Last of the Conquerors. New York,
1948. 8vo. Cloth. A fine copy in dj which has some light wear.
In Our Time 156-723 1983 $75

SMITH, WILLIAM H.   Smith's Canadian Gazetteer. Toronto,
1846. Orig. cloth, slight wear, but a fine copy. Reese 19-123
1983 $300

SMITH, WILLIAM R.   Discourse Delivered Before the State
Historical Society of Wisconsin. Madison, 1850. Orig. printed
wraps. Ginsberg 46-832 1983 $100

SMITH, WILLIAM R.   The History of Wisconsin. Madison:
Beriah Brown, Printer, 1854. 2 vols. (vol. 1 & 3). Orig. pictorial
cloth, gilt. Jenkins 153-702 1983 $150

SMITH, WILLOUGHBY   The Rise and Extension of Submarine
Telegraphy. First ed. Orig. publishers green morocco backed cloth.
Frontis., 3 coloured and 4 other plates (1 folding), numerous illus.
and tables (some full-page). Very slightly worn. Ink signature on
half title. Roy. 8vo. Fine. Edwards 1042-161 1983 £65

SMITH & WINCHESTER   Illustrated Catalogue of Steel...
Boston, 1890. Numerous illustrations. 4to, rubbed, some cover
stains, arithmetical computations on blank endleaves. Fine catalog.
Morrill 290-503 1983 $25

SMITHSONIAN INSTITUTION   Contributions to Knowledge. Wash., 1876-
86. Vols. 21-25. Maps & plates, some stamped on verso. 5 vols, thick
large 4to, cloth, ex lib. Argosy 710-488 1983 $200

SMITHERS, LEONARD   Memoirs of Paul de Kock. Smithers, 1899.
First edition. Nice. Rota 230-557 1983 £35

SMOLLETT, TOBIAS   The Adventures of Peregrine Pickle.
London: printed for the author, 1751. 4 vols, 1st ed., 12mo, cont.
gilt-bordered calf, spines gilt, morocco labels, bookplate. Small
holes in one leaf affecting some letters, otherwise a very fine copy.
Trebizond 18-93 1983 $800

SMOLLETT, TOBIAS   The Adventures of Peregrine Pickle.
London, for the author, 1751. 4 vols., 8vo, orig. calf joints
cracked, little chipped, bookplate, name on endpaper; in orig.
condition. First edition. Ravenstree 96-242 1983 $650

SMOLLETT, TOBIAS   The Adventures of Peregrine Pickle.
London: for the Author, 1751. First edition. 4 vols. 12mo. Full
sprinkled calf, gilt, three-line gilt borders, gilt panelled spines,
red and green morocco labels, gilt, edges gilt, by Riviere. Traylen
94-763 1983 £335

SMOLLETT, TOBIAS   The Adventures of Peregrine Pickle.
For the author, sold by D. Wilson, 1751. First edition. 4 vols.
12mo, lacks final blank leaves in vols. II & III. In vol. III,
leaf L12 is a cancel. Cont. calf (very worn). Faint water stains
in vol. IV. Hannas 69-191 1983 £150

SMOLLETT, TOBIAS   The Adventures of Peregrine Pickle.
Dublin: Printed by Henry Saunders and James Potts, 1768-9. 3rd
edition, revised, corrected, and altered by the author. 4 vols. in 2,
12mo, contemporary mottled calf; minor defects and scuffing to covers,
slight dampstaining at foot of leaves of first volume. Hill 165-123
1983 £50

SMOLLETT, TOBIAS   The Adventures of Peregrine Pickle.
London: James Cochrane & Co., 1831. First edition. Illus. by
Cruikshank. 2 vols. Full light-blue morocco with marbled endpapers
by Azehnsdorf. Spines a trifle darkened. Fine. MacManus 277-1235
1983 $250

SMOLLETT, TOBIAS   The Adventures of Roderick Random.
London, J. Osborn, 1748. 2 vols., 12mo, orig. calf (slightly worn,
joints tender, spine ends bit chipped, fine early bookplate). First
edition. Ravenstree 96-243 1983 $1,250

SMOLLETT, TOBIAS   The Adventures of Roderick Random.
Edinburgh; Printed by W. Darling and Son, 1791. 2 vols, 12mo,
contemporary tree calf. Frontispiece in each volume. Hill 165-
124 1983 £40

SMOLLETT, TOBIAS   The Adventures of Roderick Random.
London: Cochrane & Co., 1831. First edition. Illus. by Cruikshank.
Full morocco with marbled endpapers. Near-fine. MacManus 277-1236
1983 $125

SMOLLETT, TOBIAS   The Adventures of Sir Lancelot Greaves.
Edinbrugh: for Bell & Bradfute, 1808. Tall 8vo. Engraved frontis.
Orig. cloth. Heath 48-420 1983 £40

SMOLLETT, TOBIAS   The Adventures of Telemachus. London,
S. Crowder et al., 1776. 2 vols., 8vo, orig. sheep, worn, joints
breaking and spines chipped, internally nice and complete with
half-titles. First edition of Smollett's translation. Ravenstree
96-246 1983 $250

SMOLLETT, TOBIAS   The Expedition of Humphry Clinker.
London, W. Johnston, and B. Collins, 1671 (i.e. 1771). 3 vols., 8vo,
cont. calf newly rebacked, some age-stains; minor soiling, name torn
from upper blank edge of titles, note on half title of vol. 3,
complete with half titles. First edition. Ravenstree 96-244 1983
$950

SMOLLETT, TOBIAS   The Expedition of Humphrey Clinker.
London: W. Johnston, 1771. First edition, first issue. 3 vols.
12mo. Cont. calf, a little worn, a few ink deletions on 2 pp.,
joints weak. Traylen 94-764 1983 £280

SMOLLETT, TOBIAS   The Expedition of Humphrey Clinker.
Dublin; Printed for A. Leathley, J. Exshaw (etc), 1771. First Dublin
edition. 2 vols, 12mo, contemporary calf, gilt backs; a neat copy.
Bookplates of Marcus McCausland. Hill 165-125 1983 £50

SMOLLETT, TOBIAS   The Expedition of Humphry Clinker.
For W. Johnston, and B. Collins, 1771. 3 vols. 12mo, half-titles.
Lacks two final blank leaves. Cont. calf (rebacked) with slight
traces of use throughout. Hannas 69-193 1983 £45

SMOLLETT, TOBIAS   A Journal of the Expedition of
Carthagena, with Notes. London, 1744. Half calf, very good.
Reese 18-60 1983 $850

SMOLLETT, TOBIAS   The Miscellaneous Works... Edinburgh,
David Ramsay, 1790. 6 vols., large 8vos, cont. calf rebacked
period style, a.e.g., minor wear and thumbing, light age-soiling,
name on titles, few cont. mss. identification of characters, the
frontis. by Rowlandson have lower blank edge restored, and one has
inner blank edge mended. Set has been extra-illus. with cont.
engravings. Ravenstree 96-245 1983 $430

SMOLLETT, TOBIAS   The Miscellaneous Works... London,
1796. 6 vols. 8vo. Cont. tree calf, gilt, with red morocco
spines, decorated gilt. Traylen 94-760 1983 £80

SMOLLETT, TOBIAS   The Miscellaneous Works of... Edinburgh,
for Silvester Doug & Andrew Stirling, etc, 1811. 6 vols., 8vo,
portrait. Cont. half calf (a little worn). Some foxing at beginning
and end of each volume. Hannas 69-194 1983 £45

SMOLLETT, TOBIAS   The Novels. Boston & N.Y.: Houghton
Mifflin Co., (1925-1926). First of this edition. 11 vols. Frontis.
illus. Orig. 3/4 morocco. Printed at the Shakespeare Head Press.
Fine. MacManus 280-4822 1983 $750

SMOLLETT, TOBIAS   The Regicide: or, James the first, of
Scotland. London: printed for J. Osborn and A. Millar, 1749.
First published edition, 8vo, a good copy in modern red quarter morocco,
spine lettered in gilt. Pickering & Chatto 19-68 1983 $300

SMOLLETT, TOBIAS   The Regicide. 1749. Half speckled calf
by Bayntun, brown spine label, t.e.g., v.g. Jarndyce 31-70 1983
£180

SMOLLETT, TOBIAS   Works. London: B. Law, etc., 1797.
Engraved portrait. 8 vols. 8vo. Cont. calf, red and green lettering
pieces. Traylen 94-761 1983 £160

SMOLLETT, TOBIAS   Works. London, Bickers & Son, 1872. A
New Edition. Illus. 8vols., 8vo, orig. cloth, leather backs, some
rubbing on backstrips. Morrill 287-643 1983 $50

SMOLLETT, TOBIAS   The Works. London, 1899-1901. 12
vols. 8vo. Half calf, gilt spines with morocco labels, gilt.
Portrait and other illus. Traylen 94-762 1983 £250

SMOLLETT, TOBIAS   Works. London, Navarre Society, n.d.
Illus. 12 vols, 12mo, gilt tops, untrimmed, ex-library but nice.
Morrill 288-673 1983 $27.50

SMUCKER, SAMUEL M.   Life of John C. Fremont & His Narrative
of Exploration and Adventure in Kansas, Nebraska, Oregon and
California. NY, 1856. 1st ed., illus., cloth somewhat faded.
Argosy 710-597 1983 $30

SMYTH, ALEXANDER   Regulations for the Field Exercises...
of the Infantry of the United States. Philadelphia, Anthony Finley,
1812. First edition. Folding plates. 8vo, contemporary calf.
Lacks label, rubbed, bottom of spine chipped, bookplate removed.
Morrill 290-504 1983 $85

SMYTH, B.   History of the XX Regiment. London, 1889.
2 portrait frontis. 11 coloured plates, 5 folding maps, spine slightly
soiled and worn. 8vo. Orig. cloth. Good. Edwards 1042-538 1983
£60

SMYTH, HENRY DEWOLF   Atomic Energy for Military Purposes.
N.J., 1945. Photos, edges slightly rubbed, else near fine in lightly
frayed and soiled, slightly rubbed, very good dustwrapper, inscription. Quill & Brush 54-1638 1983 $150

SMYTH, HENRY DEWOLF   Atomic Energy for Military Purposes.
N.J., 1945. Paperwraps, photos, minor cover soiling, else very good
or better. Quill & Brush 54-1637 1983 $125

SMYTH, HENRY DEWOLF   A General Account of the Development of
the Methods of Using Atomic Energy for Military Purposes. Washington:
August, 1945. First edition. Orig. printed tan wrappers. Fine copy.
Bradley 66-465 1983 $485

SMYTH, JOHN F. D.   A Tour in the United States of America.
London: G. Robinson, 1784. 2 vols., modern cloth. Both errata
present. One leaf of text in volume one and the half-title in
vol. two neatly supplied in facs., else perfect. First edition.
Felcone 21-98 1983 $450

SMYTH, W. H.   Sidereal Chromatics. London, 1864.
8vo. Orig. cloth. Coloured plate. Presentation copy with Admiral
Smyth's bookplate. Binding loosening. Gurney JJ-380 1983 £16

SMYTHE, FRANK S.   Climbs in the Canadian Rockies. London:
Hodder & Stoughton, 1950. 22 1/2cm. First edition. 40 illus. (2
in colour) and 2 maps. Tired dust jacket. Good to very good.
McGahern 53-151 1983 $35

SMYTHE, JOHN   Certain Discourses... London:
by Richard Johnes, 1 Maii 1590. First edition. Small 4to.
Modern quarter cloth. Title and last leaf dusty, blank margin
of title frayed, two clean cross tears. Rare. Heath 48-186
1983 £250

SMYTHE, WILLIAM E.   The Conquest of Arid America. N.Y.:
Macmillan, 1905. New and revised edition. Plates. Cloth, a little
worn. Front hinge repaired. Dawson 471-274 1983 $20

SMYTHIES, B. E.   The Birds of Borneo. 1960. Coloured
frontispiece, 51 coloured and 47 plain plates and a map, royal 8vo,
cloth. Very scarce original edition. Wheldon 160-891 1983 £120

SNEAD, THOMAS L.   The Fight for Missouri: From the
Election of Lincoln to the Death of Lyon. NY, 1886. 2 maps,
1 folding. Argosy 710-323 1983 $35

SNELL, W. H.   The Boleti of Northeastern North
America. 1970. 84 plates (72 coloured), 4to, cloth. A clean second
hand copy. Wheldon 160-1899 1983 £40

SNELL, WILLEBRORD   Tiphys Batavus. Ex Officina Elzevir,
Leiden, 1624. First edition. Sm. 4to. Engraved frontis. and engraved
plate of bi-remes and tri-remes, engraved illus. of points of compass.
Woodcut device on title and numerous diagrams and tables, errata leaf
at end. Cont. calf, worn, rebacked, some soiling to title and prelimi-
aries. Some slight marginal staining and foxing. Ink ownership
inscriptions on upper margin and verso of title. Good. Edwards 1042-
163 1983 £600

SNELLEN VAN VOLLENHOVEN, S. C.   De Dieren van Nederland. Haarlem,
1859. 35 plates, 8vo, half morocco. Wheldon 160-1165 1983 £30

SNELLING, THOMAS   A View of the Coins at this Time
Current throughout Europe. London: Snelling, 1766. 8vo, with 25
engraved plates of coins. Orig. wraps. Gaisford bookticket
at end. Illus. averaging 12 per plate. Rostenberg 88-140 1983
$185

SNEYD, WALTER   Portraits of the Spruggins Family.
N.p., no printer (privately printed), 1829. First edition, 4to,
44 lithographed plates, plus 2 plates of "facsimiles", coloured
frontis. inserted. Title, 37 letter-press leaves. Cont. half morocco
gilt spine. Hannas 69-195 1983 £70

SNIDER, C. H. J.   The Glorious "Shannon's" Old Blue Duster
and other Faded Flags of Fadeless Fame. Toronto: M&S, 1923. Frontis.
and 80 illus. (including 5 in colors). 22 1/2cm. Blue cloth. Gilt
decorated. Fine. McGahern 54-165 1983 $45

SNIDOW, GORDON   Gordon Snidow Chronicler of the Contemporary West. Flagstaff, 1973. 1st edition, limited and boxed
with an original drawing by Snidow. Limited to 100 copies. Numerous
plates in color. Jenkins 151-321 1983 $300

SNODGRASS, J. J.   Narrative of the Burmese War. London,
1827. Folding map. Frontis. Calf, rebacked. Large paper copy.
From the library of the Earl of Ellenbrough with his bookplate & stamp.
8vo. Good. Edwards 1044-660 1983 £90

SNODGRASS, R. E.   Principles of Insect Morphology.
New York, (1935). 319 text-illus., 8vo, cloth. Wheldon 160-1166
1983 £18

SNODGRASS, W. D.   After Experience, Poems and Translations.
NY: (1968). Inscribed by Snodgrass. Very fine in faintly rubbed
dust wrapper. First edition. Bromer 25-104 1983 $175

SNODGRASS, W. D.   Heart's Needle. N.Y., 1959. First
edition, consisting of 1500 copies. Cloth. Bookplate. In worn and
soiled dust wrapper. Very good. King 45-256 1983 $85

SNOW, CHARLES WILBERT   Songs of the Neukluk. Council,
Alaska, 1912. 8vo. Orig. cloth. The only ed. One of the earliest
literary vols. to be produced in Alaska. Little rubbing to back endboard, else a fine copy. In Our Time 156-727 1983 $275

SNOW, ELLIOT   The Sea, The Ship and The Sailor.
Salem, Mass.: Marine Research Society, 1925. Roy. 8vo. Orig. cloth.
Frontis. and 31 plates. Slightly worn. Illus. endpapers, occasional
slight browning. Good. Edwards 1042-164 1983 £30

SNOW, JOHN   Snow on Cholera being a reprint of
two papers... New York, 1936. First edition. 8vo. Orig. binding.
Fye H-3-547 1983 $50

SNOW, LORENZO   The Italian Mission. London, 1851.
Sewed. Argosy 716-576 1983 $100

SNOWDEN, RICHARD   The History of North and South America.
Phila.: Johnson & Warner (Alexander & Phillips, Carlisle, Pa., pr.),
1809. Full calf (worn, spine broken). Very good. Felcone 20-171
1983 $20

SNOWMAN, KENNETH   The Art of Carl Faberge. Boston:
Boston Book & Art Shop, n.d. 84 color plates. 407 illus. hors
texte. 4to. Cloth. Dust jacket. Second edition, enlarged. Ars
Libri 32-215 1983 $75

SNYDER, GARY   Three Worlds, Three Realms, Six Roads.
Marlboro, VT: Griffin Press (1966). 100 copies printed. Small
stain to top front cover, else fine. First edition. Bromer 25-106
1983 $110

SOANE, GEORGE   New Curiosities of Literature and
Book of the Months. E. Churton, 1847. 2 vols., 12mo, orig. maroon
cloth, blocked in blind, spine faded. First edition. Bickersteth
75-179 1983 £12

SOANS, R. G.   John Gilbert, Yeoman. London: Warne,
n.d. (1897). First edition. Illus. Orig. cloth. MacManus 280-4823
1983 $20

SOBOTTA, JOHANNES   Atlas & Text-Book of Human Anatomy.
Phila., 1909-11. 3 vols. Illus., mostly in color. 4to, buckram.
Most of the plates are on coated stock or light-weight cardboard
stock. Argosy 713-506 1983 $125

SOBY, JAMES THRALL   The Early Chirico. New York: Dodd,
Mean & Co., 1941. 69 plates. 4to. Cloth. Slightly worn. Ars
Libri 33-443 1983 $75

SOBY, JAMES THRALL   The Prints of Paul Klee. New York:
Curt Valentin, 1945. 40 gravure plates (8 color pochoir). Large
4to. Portfolio. Edition limited to 1000 copies. Text fascicle and
loose plates, as issued. Ars Libri 32-367 1983 $125

SOCIEDAD DE ARTE MODERNO   Mascaras mexicanas. Mexico, 1945.
2 color plates. 80 illus. 4to. Wrappers. Ars Libri 34-366 1983
$30

SOCIETY FOR THE PROTECTION OF GERMAN EMIGRANTS TO TEXAS   Gesammelte
Aktenstucke Des Vereins Zum Schutze Deutscher Einwanderer in Texas.
Mainza: Victor von Zabern, 1845. First edition. Fine in cont. marbled wrappers. Laid in half morocco slipcase. Map an excellent facsimile. Jenkins 152-857 1983 $2,750

SOEMMERRING, S. T.   Iconologie de l'Organe de l'Ouie.
Paris: Crevot, 1825. 4to. Old quarter-calf. 16 plates. 8vo.
Bottom margin of 5 plates torn, nowhere affecting the engravings.
Gurney 90-110 1983 £75

SOLANO DE LUQUE, FRANCISCO   Observaciones sobre el Pulso.
Madrid, 1787. Small 4to, cont. mottled calf, gilt back. First
edition. Argosy 713-507 1983 $200

LE SOLDAT Magicien. Amsterdam, Hupkes, 1761. Woodcut vignette on
cover. Salloch 387-169 1983 $30

THE SOLDIERS' and Sailors' Half-Dime Tales: of the Late Rebellion (Volume 1). N.Y., 1868. 1st ed., original three-quarter morocco. Illus. Scarce. Jenkins 151-322 1983 $175

THE SOLDIER'S companion, or martial recorder... London: printed for the editor by Edward Cock, 1824. First edition. 8vo. Orig. boards, printed paper label. Top of spine chipped. Ximenes 63-322 1983 $30

SOLE, W.   Menthae Britannicae: being a New Botanical Arrangement... Bath: by R. Cruttwell, 1798. First edition. Large paper copy. Uncut in orig. boards. 24 full page engraved plates, half title. Backstrip worn and loose. Copy of William Withering, with his signature and a Mss list of contents. Heath 48-532 1983 £325

SOLER, PADRE ANTONIO   Sonatas par Instrumentos de Tecla. Madrid, n.d. 4 vols. Folio, wrs. Salloch 387-227 1983 $75

SOLIER, W. DU   Ancient Mexican Costume. Mexico: Ediciones Mexicanas, 1950. 32 color plates. Large 4to. Cloth. Dust jacket. Ars Libri 34-478 1983 $50

SOLIS, ANTONIO DE   The History of the Conquest of Mexico by the Spaniards. London, 1724. Folding maps and plates. Frontis. portrait present but misbound. Old calf, rebacked, internally very good, except for slight tears to one folding plate. Library stamps on the title page, but no other markings. Overall a good copy. First English edition. Reese 18-43 1983 $350

SOLLY, EDWARD   Rural Chemistry. 1843. First edition, full green morocco, gilt dec. spine, with the bookplate of the Somerhill Library. Very good. K Books 1983 £30

SOLOMON Logwood. London: W. Wright, 1820. First edition. 8vo. Disbound. Etched frontis. signed J.H. (some foxing). Ximenes 63-517 1983 $45

SOMARE, ENRICO   Masaccio. Milano: L'Esame, 1924. 57 plates. Large 4to. Wrappers. Worn. Ars Libri 33-227 1983 $40

SOMARE, ENRICO   Masaccio. Milano: Bottega di Poesia, 1925. 56 plates. Large 4to. Cloth. Text in French. Slightly shaken. Ars Libri 33-226 1983 $85

SOMARE, ENRICO   L'opera di Egisto Ferroni. Milano: Rizzoli, 1939. 50 plates (partly in color). Large 4to. Boards, 1/4 cloth. Loose. Ars Libri 33-464 1983 $45

SOMARE, ENRICO   Uccello. Milano: Edizioni dell' Esame, 1946. 84 plates. Small folio. Wrappers. Paper slightly browned. Ars Libri 33-375 1983 $35

SOME remarks on Shakespeare before the Roxburghe Club of San Francisco, by Oscar Sutro on the Evening of September 18, 1933. S.F., 1933. 8vo, linen-backed boards, paper label. One of 50 copies. Inscribed by the author. Fine. Scarce. Perata 28-44 1983 $135

SOMERS, ROBERT   The Martyr of Glencree. Sampson Low, 1878. First edition, 3 vols. 3 vols. bound as one. Half title vol. I, orig. green cloth, inner hinges repaired and spine wrinkled. Jarndyce 30-554 1983 £18.50

SOMERSET, EDWARD   A century of the Names and Scantlings of such Inventions... London: J. Grismond, 1663. Woodcut of English royal arms. 12mo. Cont. diced calf. Rebacked, corners and edges worn. Ms. exlibris. From the Dendy Marshall Railway Library. First edition. Kraus 164-219 1983 $2,400

SOMERSET, WILLIAM SEYMOUR   The Lord Marquesse of Hertford... London: for Joseph Hunscott and John Wright, 1642. 4to. Modern marbled boards, leather label. Heath 48-188 1983 £65

SOMERVILLE, EDITH ANNE OENONE   All on the Irish Shore. London: Longmans, 1903. First edition. Illus. by E. OE. Somerville. Orig. pictorial cloth. Covers a bit soiled & worn. MacManus 280-4825 1983 $75

SOMERVILLE, EDITH ANNE OENONE   Beggars on Horseback. Edinburgh: Blackwood & Sons, 1895. First edition, secondary binding (with smooth, slightly glazed linen-grain cloth and grey-green endpapers). Orig. cloth. Spine faded. edges a little worn. Good. MacManus 280-4826 1983 $165

SOMERVILLE, EDITH ANNE OENONE,   Dan Russell The Fox. London: Methuen, (1911). First edition. Orig. pictorial cloth. Covers soiled; foxed. MacManus 280-4827 1983 $30

SOMERVILLE, EDITH ANNE OENONE   An Enthusiast. London: Longmans, Green, & Co., 1921. First edition. Orig. cloth. Bookplate. Spine faded and worn. MacManus 280-4828 1983 $20

SOMERVILLE, EDITH ANNE OENONE   In Mr. Knox's Country. London: Longmans, Green & Co., 1915. First edition. 8 illus. by E. OE. Somerville. Orig. cloth. Very good. MacManus 280-4829 1983 $35

SOMERVILLE, EDITH ANNE OENONE   In Mr. Knox's Country. London, 1915. First edition. Illus. Spine faded and small nick in cloth at head of spine repaired. Very good. Rota 231-572 1983 £12

SOMERVILLE, EDITH ANNE OENONE   Mount Music. London: Longmans, 1919. First edition. Illus. by E. OE. Somerville. Orig. cloth. Spine faded. MacManus 280-4830 1983 $25

SOMERVILLE, EDITH ANNE OENONE   Notions in Garrison. London: Methuen & Co., Ltd., (1941). First edition. Illus. by E. OE. S. Small 4to. Orig. cloth. Dust jacket (a bit dusty). Fine. MacManus 280-4831 1983 $85

SOMERVILLE, EDITH ANNE OENONE   Slipper's ABC of Fox Hunting. London: Longmans, 1903. First edition. Folio. Orig. pictorial cloth. Covers a bit soiled. Very good. MacManus 280-4832 1983 $400

SOMERVILLE, EDITH ANNE OENONE   Stray-Aways. London, 1920. First edition, first issue. Title lettered in white on the upper cover. Lower corners a little bruised. Nice. Rota 230-559 1983 £15

SOMERVILLE, EDITH ANNE OENONE   Stray-Aways. London: Longmans, Green & Co., 1920. First edition. Illus. by Somerville. Orig. cloth. Dust jacket (torn). A bit shaken and worn. MacManus 280-4833 1983 $35

SOMERVILE, WILLIAM   The Chace. London: Printed for G. Hawkins...MDCCXXXV. 4to, engraved frontis. by Scotin after Gravelot; cont. calf, gilt, spine gilt, red morocco label. First edition. Quaritch NS 7-124 1983 $275

SOMERVILLE, WILLIAM   The Chace. London: for G. Hawkins and sold by T. Cooper, 1735. First edition. 4to. Cont. calf, gilt spine with morocco label. Engraved frontis. after Gravelot, mounted, and errata leaf. Traylen 94-765 1983 £48

SOMERVILLE, WILLIAM   The Chase; A Poem. London: Printed by W. Bulmer & Co., Shakespeare Printing Office, Cleveland-Row, 1802. First edition. Illus. with engravings by Bewick. 8vo. Full cont. calf, rebacked & recornered. Cont. owner's signature on title-page. Bookplate of S. Weir Mitchell on the front endsheet. Some soiling to leaves. MacManus 277-771 1983 $125

SOMERVILLE, WILLIAM   The Chase; a Poem. London: for T. Cadell, 1804. 4to. Cont. Spanish calf, gilt panelled sides with lozenge centre-panel, neatly rebacked, morocco label. With vignette title-page, 4 plates and 8 vignettes by Thomas Bewick. A little worn. Traylen 94-767 1983 £28

SOMERVILLE, WILLIAM   Hobbinol, or the rural games. London: printed for J. Stagg, 1740. 3rd ed., 8vo, a pristine copy in the original blue paper wrappers, uncut. Pickering & Chatto 19-69 1983 $150

SOMERVILLE, WILLIAM   Occasional Poems. London: for Bernard Lintot, 1727. First collected edition. 8vo. Cont. calf, gilt, gilt panelled spine with morocco label, gilt. Vignette title-page, engraved head- and tail-pieces. From the library of John Osborn of Christ Church college, with his book-plate. A very fine copy. Traylen 94-768 1983 £220

SOMETHING Concerning Nobody, Edited By Somebody. London: Robert Scholey, 1814. Illus. with 14 etchings. Full calf. First edition. Spine edges slightly rubbed. Very good, clean copy. MacManus 277-90 1983 $75

SOMMER, HEINRICK OSKAR   The Vulgate Version of the Arthurian Romances. Washington: The Carnegie Institution of Washington, 1909-1913. First edition. 7 vols. and an index. Illus. Orig. printed wrappers. Very fine. MacManus 280-4834 1983 $350

THE SONG of Roland. (Cambridge, Mass.): The Riverside Press, 1906. Tall folio. With 7 hand-illuminated color illus. and 3 hand-illuminated initials. Printed in "black letter," inked in red, black, and gold on handmade paper. Edition ltd. to 220 numbered copies. Bound in vellum spine over fleur-de-lis patterned boards, sl. soiled. Karmiole 76-94 1983 $600

SONGS and Carols. London, printed for the Percy Society, Oct. 1847. Uncut. 8vo, orig. printed wrs., cloth-backed. Salloch 387-228 1983 $40

SONGS of Shakespeare. Day & Son, nd (ca. 1865). Illum. title p. & 12 plates printed on card in colours & heightened in gold by H.C. Hoskyns Abrahall. Lt. red sand grain decor. cloth, bevelled boards, a.e.g. (bkstrip. repr'd at bottom & sl. worn at top, occasional lt. foxing contents, title p. has sml. repair to foredge, sl. wear rear joint), v.g. Hodgkins 27-394 1983 £50

SONGS of Shakespeare. Day & Son, nd (ca. 1865). Illum. title p. & 12 plates printed on card in colours & heightened in gold by H.C. Hoskyns Abrahall. Dark green sand grain decor. cloth, bevelled edges, a.e.g. (lt. foxing throughout & sml. waterstain of foredge not affect. illumination, 1st 8 pp. sl. worn at edges), v.g. Hodgkins 27-395 1983 £50

SONNECK, O. G.   Bibliography of Early Secular American Music. Washington, 1905. Tall 8vo, cloth (chipped at corners). Ltd., numbered edition of 200 copies, with author's autograph inscription for W.R. Whittlesay. Salloch 387-398 1983 $110

SONNERAT, M.   Voyage Aux Indes Orientales et a la Chine. London, 1782. First edition. 140 engraved plates, many folding. 2 vols. 4to. Half calf, rebacked, boards worn, gilt edges. Good. Edwards 1044-661 1983 £800

SONNICHSEN, CHARLES L.   Law West of the Pecos. New York, 1943. 1st prntg. Illus. Clark 741-374 1983 $32.50

SONNICHSEN, CHARLES L.   Roy Bean. N.Y., Macmillan, 1943. First edition. Illus. Dust jacket, very good-fine. Houle 21-1161 1983 $75

SONNTAG, AUGUST   Professor Sonntag's Thrilling Narrative Of The Grinnell Exploring Expedition. Phila. (1857). Nearly 100 engravings, cloth, f.e.p. lacking large piece of corner, covers spotted and worn. King 46-754 1983 $25

SOP in the Pan for Peter Pindar, Esq. G.G.J. and J. Robinson, 1788. First edition. 4to, rebound in hand-marbled boards, paper label, v.g. Jarndyce 31-10 1983 £65

SOPHOCLES   Ajax of Sophocles. London: Bernard Lintott, 1714. First edition. 12mo. Disbound. Frontis. Scarce. Ximenes 63-70 1983 $60

SOPHOCLES   The Plays and Fragments. Cambridge, 1889-1908. 7 vols. 8vo, cloth. Salloch 385-747 1983 $90

SOPHOCLES   Sophoclis Tagoediae Septem. (Geneva,) Henricus Stephanus, 1568. 4to, 18th century red morocco gilt, covers detached, considerable wear, bit age-darkened, some minor staining, bookplate, a.e.g. This copy has the rare second volume. The first Stephanus (Estienne) edition. Ravenstree 95-107 1983 $195

SOPHOCLES   Tragoediae. Lg, 1901. 3/4 calf. Salloch 385-745 1983 $20

SOREL, CHARLES   The Extravagant Shepherd. London, T. Newcomb for Thomas Heath, 1654. Folio, cont. calf rebacked, frontis. tipped on stub and hand-colored. 2 other engraved plates hand-colored, near-cont. watercolors. Ravenstree 96-247 1983 $420

SOREL, CHARLES   The Extravagant Shepherd. For Thomas Bassett, 1660. Folio, frontis. (just shaved), and 3 plates (one folding), by Jan Baptist Jaspers. Cont. calf (worn). Title cut short. Hannas 69-196 1983 £250

SORENSEN, THEODORE C.   Kennedy. N.Y., 1965. Limited, numbered, authographed copy, specially bound and slipcased. Jenkings 151-159 1983 $100

SORENSON, ALFRED   History of Omaha from the Pioneer Days to the Present Time. Omaha, 1889. Orig. cloth. Second edition. Ginsberg 46-513 1983 $50

SORLIER, CHARLES   Chagall Lithographe, 1969-1973. Monte Carlo: Andre Sauret, 1974. 1 orig. color lithograph. 148 illus. Large 4to, cloth, dust jacket with orig. lithograph. Vol. IV of the catalogue raisonne. Ars Libri 32-95 1983 $375

SORRENTINO, GILBERT   Corrosive Sublimate. Black Sparrow Press, 1971. 8vo. Cloth, boards. 8 of 26 lettered and signed by the poet. Fine in acetate jacket. In Our Time 156-729 1983 $100

SORRENTINO, GILBERT   Flawless Play Restored. Black Sparrow Press, 1974. 8vo. Cloth, boards. 1 of 26 copies lettered and signed by the author. Fine in acetate jacket. In Our Time 156-730 1983 $100

SORRENTINO, GILBERT   White Sail. Black Sparrow Press, 1977. 8vo. Cloth, boards. 1 of 26 copies lettered and signed by the author. Fine in acetate jacket. In Our Time 156-732 1983 $100

SORTAIN, JOSEPH   Count Arensberg, or The days of Luther. Brighton: R. Folthorp, 1853. First edition. 2 vols. Orig. cloth. All edges and corners a bit worn. Covers slightly soiled. Bookplates. Very good. MacManus 280-4835 1983 $135

SOTHEBY, SAMUEL LEIGH   Ramblings in the Elucidation of the Autograph of Milton. London, printed for the author by Thomas Richards, 1861. Large folio, orig. half morocco gilt, covers worn, detached; sunken panels in covers depicting scenes from Paradise Lost. Two frontis. are early photographs. First and only edition. Printed in a very ltd. edition. This copy is one of very few with the author's presentation stamp on the verso of the title page. Ravenstree 97-164 1983 $165

SOTHEBY, SAMUEL LEIGH   Ramblings in the Elucidation of the Autograph of Milton. London: Printed for the Author by Thomas Richards, 1861. First edition. Small folio. Frontis., portraits. Facsimiles. Cont. green morocco, gilt, by J. Wright, with inset panels portraying Paradise Lost & Paradise Regained by Tupper. Presentation copy, inscribed on the verso of the title-page to the editor of The Illustrated Times, dated August 13th, 1861. Rubbed. MacManus 279-3774 1983 $150

SOULIE, MAURICE   The Wolf Cub. Indianapolis, 1927. Cloth, fine. Reese 19-459 1983 $60

SOULSBY, B.   A Catalogue of the Works of Linnaeus. British Museum, 1933-36. 2 vols., 4to, cloth and wrappers. Wheldon 160-248 1983 £16

SOUPAULT, PHILIPPE   Jean Lurcat. Paris: Editions "Cahiers d'Art", 1928. 24 gravure plates. Large 4to. Wrappers. Edition limited to 500 copies on velin de Torpes. Ars Libri 32-413 1983 $85

SOUTH, COLON   Out West. London: Wyman & Sons, 1884. Orig. cloth. 1st ed. Jenkins 153-523 1983 $85

SOUTH, R.   The Moths of the British Isles. (1907-09). 318 plates, 2 vols., 8vo, original cloth (spines faded). Wheldon 160-1169 1983 £20

SOUTH Dakota Guide. (Pierre), 1938. 1st ed. Fldg. and other maps, illus. Small neat patch on spine; otherwise fine. Clark 741-9 1983 $85

A SOUTH Dakota Guide. Pierre, 1938. Illus. 1st ed. Scarce. Jenkins 153-154 1983 $45

SOUTHALL, ELIZA   Portions of the Diary, Letters and Other Remains of... Birmingham: Printed by White and Pike, 1855. First edition, small 8vo, orig. cloth. Fenning 60-386 1983 £18.50

SOUTHERN, A. C.   Elizabeth Recusant Prose, 1582-1599. London, (1950). 8vo. Orig. buckram. Traylen 94-770 1983 £38

A SOUTHERN Vanguard. NY, (1947). Very good in slightly sunned, lightly chipped, very good dustwrapper. Quill & Brush 54-1334 1983 $35

SOUTHESK, THE EARL OF   Saskatchewan and the Rocky Mountains. Edinburgh: Edmonston & Douglas, 1875. 22cm. First edition. Errata. 7 full-page wood-engraved plates. 22 text illus. 2 facsimiles. 2 folding maps. Orig. blue cloth, gilt titles and borders on the spine and upper cover, expertly restored. A fine copy. McGahern 53-152 1983 $175

SOUTHEY, ROBERT   Letters from England. London, Longmans et al., 1808. 3 vols., bound in cont. quarter calf gilt, joints cracked, bookplates, fly leaf of first volume torn out. Ravenstree 96-248 1983 $150

SOUTHEY, ROBERT   The life of Nelson. London: Murray, 1813. First edition. 2 vols. 8vo. Cont. calf, spines gilt. With a portrait, and a plate of facsimile signatures. Bound without half-titles. A bit worn. Ximenes 63-39 1983 $125

SOUTHEY, ROBERT   The Life of Wesley, and Rise and Progress of Methodism. Longman, 1846. 2 vols., fronts. Some foxing to prelims. Half calf, gilt spines, labels, v.g. Jarndyce 30-1175 1983 £18

SOUTHEY, ROBERT   Omniana, or Horae Otiosiores. London, Longman et al., 1812. 2 vols., 12mo, cont. diced russia now very worn and covers detached, bookplate no half-title to volume 1. First edition. Ravenstree 96-249 1983 $185

SOUTHEY, ROBERT   Omniana, or Horae Otiosiores. London, 1812. 12mo. 2 vols. Calf, boards, no half-title in vol. 1. Name on title, mainly a fine set of the 1st ed. In Our Time 156-735 1983 $175

SOUTHEY, ROBERT   Poems. Bristol: printed by N. Biggs, for Joseph Cottle, etc., 1797. Second edition, with revisions. Small 8vo. Cont. tree calf, spine gilt. With the final ad leaf. Rubbed, joints worn. Ximenes 63-425 1983 $150

SOUTHEY, ROBERT   Poems. Simpkin, Marshall, 1872. Mounted photo within blue & brown ornamental border frontis. Red morocco backed wooden boards with engraved portrait & title fr. cvr., gilt titling bkstrip, raised bands & simple gilt decor. bkstrip, a.e.g., green eps. gilt dentelles. Occasional sl. foxing mainly at prelims, nice copy. Hodgkins 27-328 1983 £20

SOUTHEY, ROBERT   Wat Tyler; a dramatic poem. London: Benbow, 1822. 12mo. Orig. plain blue wrappers. A fine copy. Ximenes 63-426 1983 $75

SOUTHWEST Louisiana Up To Date. (Omaha, Neb., 1899). Ads. Special full morocco presentation binding, rebacked, illustrated. Jenkins 153-341 1983 $125

SOUTHWOLD, STEPHEN   Life Comes to Seathorpe. London: Eyre & Spottiswoode, (1946). Orig. cloth. Dust jacket (slightly faded and worn). First edition. Near-fine. MacManus 277-284 1983 $35

SOUTHWORTH, ALVAN S.   Four thousand miles of African travel. New York: Baker, Pratt & Co., 1875. 8vo. 2 maps, 22 plates. Orig. green pictorial cloth. Rubbed, spine ends worn. Adelson Africa-130 1983 $100

SOUTHWORTH, MAY E.   A Certain Young Man of Assisi. San Francisco, 1934. Ed. limited to 650 copies printed by John Henry Nash. Illus. by Will Wilke. 4to, orig. marbled boards, buckram back, paper label, 2 corners very slightly rubbed, otherwise very nice. Morrill 288-452 1983 $35

SOUTHWORTH, MAY E.   A Certain Young Man of Assisi. SF, 1934. Folio, cloth-backed boards, paper label. Name stamp on copyright page. Very good. Perata 27-136 1983 $20

SOWELL, ANDREW J.   Early Settlers and Indian Fighters of Southwest Texas. Austin: 1900. First edition. Illus. Orig. decorated red cloth. Covers worn and hinges cracked. Bradley 66-680 1983 $350

SOWERBY, A. DE C.   A Naturalist's Holiday by the Sea. 1923. 42 illustrations, 8vo, cloth, trifle used. Wheldon 160-334 1983 £15

SOWERBY, G. B.   The Conchological Illustrations. (1832-41). 200 hand-coloured plates of 1568 figures, 8vo, full levant morocco, gilt, buckram slip case. An almost complete copy (lacking only title-page and 1 leaf of text) of this very rare work. Attractive binding. Wrongly dated 1870 on spine. Wheldon 160-1230 1983 £700

SOWERBY, G. B.   A Conchological Manual. 1842. Second edition, 27 plain plates of 564 figures, 2 folding tables and many figures, 8vo, original cloth (neatly repaired). Wheldon 160-1229 1983 £28

SOWERBY, G. B.   6 Catalogues of Shells. 1906-27. Royal 8vo, wrappers. Wheldon 160-1231 1983 £15

SOWERBY, GITHA   The Dainty Book. H. Milford, n.d. Sq. 8vo. Decorated title. 12 colour plates & 12 text illus. Some offsetting. Colour pictorial repousse boards, wear. Colour dust wrapper. Greer 40-208 1983 £27.50

SOWERBY, GITHA   The Wise Book. J.M. Dent, 1906. Sm. sq. 8vo. Colour frontis. 12 colour plates & 12 text illus. Cream pictorial boards. Greer 40-209 1983 £18

SOWERBY, J.   English Botany. 1790-1863 (-1866). With Supplement, 41 vols. 8vo, half green morocco. A complete set. Some foxing, but overall a nice set. Wheldon 160-100 1983 £3,300

SPADAFORA, GIACOMO   Icona gaginesca nel Duomo di Marsala. Palermo: G.B. Palumbo, 1942. 24 plates. Wrappers. Ars Libri 33-150 1983 $30

SPALDING, JAMES   Maine Physicians of 1820. Lewiston, 1928. First edition. 8vo. Orig. binding. Ex-library. Fye H-3-550 1983 $30

SPALDING, ROBERT   A practical treatise on the adjustment of the theodolite... Rochester: J. Hickmutt, 1831. First edition. 8vo. Orig. violet printed wrappers. Numerous tables and wood-engraved diagrams. Small stain affecting some lower margins. Wrappers a little faded. Rare. Ximenes 63-565 1983 $125

SPANTON, ERNEST F.   In German Gaols. 1917. 16 illus., pictorial cloth. K Books 301-171 1983 £20

SPARK, MURIEL   Child of Light. Hadleigh, Sussex: Tower Bridge Publications Limited, (1951). First edition. Frontis. port. Orig. cloth. Dust jacket. Very fine. MacManus 280-4839 1983 $250

SPARK, MURIEL   Child of Light: A Reassessment of Mary Wollstonecraft Shelley. Tower Bridge Publications Ltd., 1951. Hadleigh, England. 8vo. Cloth. A fine copy in dj. In Our Time 156-736 1983 $175

SPARKE, WILLIAM   Vis Naturae et Virtus Vitae explicatae... London: Richard Field, 1612. First edition. Small 8vo. Cont limp vellum. Device on title-page and penultimate leaf. Traylen 94-772 1983 £180

SPARKS, JARED   A Sermon, Preached in the Hall of the
House of Representatives in Congress...March 3, 1822. Washington,
1822. Stitched, good. Reese 18-564 1983 $35

SPARKS, WILLIAM   The Apache Kid. L.A., 1926. Illus.
Orig. cloth. First edition. Ginsberg 46-711 1983 $75

SPARKS, WILLIAM   The Apache Kid, and other True Stories
of the Old West. Los Angeles: Skelton Publishing Co., 1926. 4 plates.
Fabricoid, a little wear. Clipping pasted inside front cover. Dawson
471-276 1983 $25

SPARRMAN, ANDERS   A voyage to the Cape of Good Hope.
Longon: G.G.J. & J. Robinson, 1785. First edition. 2 vols.
4to. Folding map. 10 plates. New 1/2 tan calf, marbled boards,
red labels. Adelson Africa-131 1983 $800

SPARRY, C.   The Illustrated Christian Martyrology.
Philadelphia: Leary & Gets, 1858. Tall 8vo. Orig. full red leather
ornately stamped in gilt, a.e.g. With 24 handcoloured plates. Covers
worn around the edges. Oak Knoll 48-109 1983 $45

SPAULDING, THOMAS M.   Early Military Books in the University
of Michigan Libraries. Ann Arbor: University of Michigan Press,
1941. First edition. 4to. Cloth. 37 full page plates over 100
titles page facsimiles. Oak Knoll 49-472 1983 $100

SPEARMAN, CHARLES (1863-1945)   The Abilities of Man. NY: Macmillan, 1927. First American edition. Pencil marginalia throughout.
Gach 95-452 1983 $20

SPEARMAN, CHARLES (1863-1945)   Creative Mind. London: Nisbet &
Co., (1930). First edition. Very good in worn dust jacket. Gach
95-453 1983 $25

SPECIMENS: A Stevens-Nelson Paper Catalogue. (NY: ca. 1950).
Quarto. Corners very lightly rubbed, else extremely fine in quarter-
leather and marbled boards and slip-case. Price list laid-in. Bromer
25-275 1983 $300

SPECIMENS. (New York: Stevens-Nelson, 1951). Small folio. 1st ed.
Orig. half morocco, gilt, past-paper boards, uncut. Contributions by
Bruce Rogers, Anthoensen Press, Goudy, et al. But for a book-label
stain on the calligraphic presentation slip (an insert), a mint copy.
Jenkins 155-1419 1983 $300

SPECKTER, OTTO   Picture Fables. Routledge, 1858.
Frontis., decor. title, printed title & 100 b&w illus. engr'd on wood
by Bros. Dalziel. Blue morocco grained blind stamped cloth, gilt
vignette fr. cvr., a.e.g., pink eps. Binder's ticket of Westley's &
Co., sl. wear top/bottom bkstrip, some thumbing of contents, vg.
Hodgkins 27-192 1983 £16.50

THE SPECTATOR. J & R Tonson and S. Draper, n.d. (1747). 8vols., tall
12mo, engr. frontis. by Grignon after Hayman, engr. vignette titles,
full contemp. calf gilt, morocco labels, some spines chipped at head
and foot, otherwise a good set with cancelled armorial bookplates.
Deighton 3-2 1983 £36

SPECTOR, BENJAMIN   History of Tufts College Medical School.
(Boston, c. 1943). Illus. Ex-lib. Presentation copy. Argosy 713-
508 1983 $45

SPECTOR, BENJAMIN   A History of Tufts College Medical
School. Boston, 1943. First edition. 8vo. Orig. binding. Fye
H-3-551 1983 $40

SPEECHLY, WILLIAM   A Treatise on the Culture of the Pine-
apple and the Mangement of the Hot-House... York for the Author...,
1796. Second edition. 8vo. Engraved plates, early calf, rebacked.
Heath 48-11 1983 £65

SPEED, JOHN   Batt upon Batt. London: Samuel
Crouch, 1680. First edition. Small 4to. Half calf. From the
Britwell Library. Ximenes 63-382 1983 $350

SPEER, JOHN   Life of General James H. Lane, the
Liberator of Kansas. Garden City, 1896. Portrait and plates. Orig.
cloth. Outer wear only. Jenkins 153-303 1983 $65

SPEER, W.   The Oldest and Newest Empire. Hartford,
1870. Frontis., and 40 plates, some slight spotting. Thick 8vo.
Good. Edwards 1044-663 1983 £90

SPEKE, JOHN HANNING   Journal of the discovery of the source
of the Nile. Edinburgh & London: Wm. Blackwood & Sons, 1863.
First edition. 1 vol. 8vo. Folding map. 25 plates. Orig.
brown cloth. Rubbed & Worn. Internally very good. Adelson Africa-
132 1983 $225

SPEKE, JOHN HANNING   Journal of the Discovery of the
Source of the Nile. Edinburgh & London, 1863. First edition, portrait
frontis., folding map, one other map, numerous full page and other
illus., roy. 8vo, old style half calf, good ex-library, unobtrusive
blind stamps. K Books 307-169 1983 £100

SPEKE, JOHN HANNING   Journal of the Discovery of the Source of
the Nile. Edinburgh: Blackwood, 1863. First edition, with 2
portraits, a large folding map (neatly repaired without loss), another
map, 24 plates and many text illus., cont. half calf, a very good
copy. Fenning 60-387 1983 £95

SPEKE, JOHN HANNING   Journal of the discovery of the source
of the Nile. New York: Harper, 1864. First American edition.
8vo. 2 maps. 24 plates. Orig. cloth. Spine faded. Adelson Africa-
223 1983 $80

SPEKE, JOHN HANNING   Journal of the discovery of the source
of the Nile. Edinburgh & London: Wm. Blackwood, 1864. Second
edition. 8vo. Folding map. 25 plates. Orig. green pictorial
cloth. Slightly rubbed, library stamp on title. Adelson Africa-
133 1983 $175

SPELDING, JAMES   An Account of the Life and Times of
Francis Bacon. London, Trubner, 1878. 2 vols. 12mo. Extra-illus.
with 85 portraits, many hand-colored. Full maroon morocco, sides
gilt-tooled with rules & corner ornaments, spines gilt-extra, gilt
inner dentelles & silk endpapers, aeg. Fine binding by Root. O'Neal
50-46 1983 $250

SPENCE, ELIZABETH ISABELLA   Summer excursions through parts of
Oxfordshire, Gloucestershire, Warwickshire... London: Longman, etc.,
1809. First edition. 2 vols. 12mo. Cont. calf, spine gilt.
Frontis. in each vol. Ximenes 63-636 1983 $225

SPENCE, JAMES   The American Union. London, 1861.
Cloth, ink name. College library bookplate. Minor stain. Good. King
45-45 1983 $25

SPENCE, JOSEPH   Anecdotes, Observations, and Characters,
of Books and Men. Published by W.H. Carpenter and Archibald
Constable and Co., 1820. 8vo, portrait, uncut, orig. boards with
paper label, upper joint cracked and paper defective at head and foot
of the spine. First edition. Bickersteth 75-180 1983 £45

SPENCE, JOSEPH   Anecdotes, Observations, and Characters,
of Books and Men. London: W.H. Carpenter, 1820. First edition.
8vo. Cont. full calf, a.e.m. Some rubbing of hinges, number stamped
on front cover, frontis. foxed. Oak Knoll 48-353 1983 $40

SPENCE, LEWIS   Myths & Legends of Ancient Egypt.
London (1922). Color plates, illus, cloth, slightly rubbed and
loose. King 46-758 1983 $25

SPENCE, THOMAS   The Prairie Lands of Canada. Montreal,
1879. Orig. printed wraps. First edition. Ginsberg 46-712 1983
$75

SPENCER, BERNARD   Aegean Islands. London: Poetry London,
1946. First edition. Extremities worn as commonly. Dustwrapper
very slightly nicked and darkened at the spine. Near fine. Jolliffe
26-471 1983 £25

SPENCER, CLAIRE   Gallow's Orchard. New York: Cape &
Smith, (1930). Cloth. First edition. The spine is slightly dull,
otherwise a fine copy in a dust jacket. Reese 20-909 1983 $30

SPENCER, GEORGE   Traduzione di una lettera dell'. Malta:
Francesco Cumbo, 1839. Large 12mo, fore and lower edges uncut.
Fenning 61-418 1983 £32.50

SPENCER, HERBERT   An Autobiography. Williams and Norgate.
First edition, 2 vols. Half titles, front. ports. 1 p ads. vol. II.
Orig. brown cloth, v.g. Jarndyce 30-1138 1983 £32

SPENCER, HERBERT   Social Statics. John Chapman, 1851.
First edition, 1 p inserted 'opinions of the Press'. Half title,
20 pp ads. Orig. brown cloth, sl. rubbed at head and tail of spine.
Jarndyce 31-373 1983 £48

SPENCER, J. B.   The Maple Sugar Industry in Canada.
Ottawa: Dept. of Agriculture, 1923. 25cm. Third edition. 29
illus. Lib. stamps. Printed wrappers. Very good. McGahern 53-
154 1983 $20

SPENCER, JOHN W.   The Early Days of Rock Island and
Davenport. Chicago, Lakeside Press, 1942. 1st ed. Ports. 12mo,
gilt top. Clark 741-287 1983 $22.50

SPENCER, ORSON   The Prussian Mission of the Church
of Jesus Christ of Latter Day Saints. Liverpool, 1853. Dbd.
First edition. Ginsberg 47-604 1983 $50

SPENCER, PLATT R.   Spencerian Key to Practical Penmanship...
New York: Ivison, Blakeman, Taylor & Co., 1871. 8vo. Orig. cloth.
10 plates and many illus. in the text. Some staining of endpaper,
else very good. Oak Knoll 49-363 1983 $30

SPENCER, THEODRE   An Acre in the Seed. Harvard U.P.,
1949. 8vo. Cloth. Review copy with slip and name of reviewer on
front flyleaf, a fine copy in dj. In Our Time 156-743 1983 $20

SPENDER, STEPHEN   The Burning Cactus. London: Faber
And Faber Limited, (1936). First edition. 8vo. Orig. cloth.
Dust jacket, partially soiled and chipped. Very good copy. Jaffe
1-360 1983 $25

SPENDER, STEPHEN   The Destructive Element. London:
Jonathan Cape, (1935). First edition. 8vo. Orig. cloth. Dust
jacket. Fine copy. Jaffe 1-359 1983 $150

SPENDER, STEPHEN   The Edge of Being. New York, 1949.
First American edition. Chipped dust wrapper. Nice. Rota 230-
561 1983 £15

SPENDER, STEPHEN   Forward From Liberalism. London: Victor
Gollancz Ltd., 1937. First edition. Orig. orange wrappers. Fine.
MacManus 280-4841 1983 $35

SPENDER, STEPHEN   Letters to Christopher. Black Sparrow
Press, 1980. 1 of 50 copies signed by Spender. A fine copy in
acetate jacket and slipcase box. In Our Time 156-744 1983 $100

SPENDER, STEPHEN   The New Realism. London: The Hogarth
Press, 1939. First edition. Orig. wrappers. Fine. MacManus 280-
4844 1983 $25

SPENDER, STEPHEN   Poems. London: Faber & Faber, (1933).
First edition. 8vo. Orig. cloth. Dust jacket, slightly dust-soiled.
Unopened. Very fine. Jaffe 1-357 1983 $175

SPENDER, STEPHEN   Poems of Dedication. NY: (1947).
First American edition. Signed on half-title by Spender. Extremely
fine in cloth-backed boards, lightly rubbed dust wrapper. Bromer
25-108 1983 $40

SPENDER, STEPHEN   Returning to Vienna, 1947. N.p., (1947).
Paperwraps, limited to 500 numbered and signed copies, few short tears
to front cover, minor cover wear, inner folding flap missing, else
very good. Quill & Brush 54-1262 1983 $75

SPENDER, STEPHEN   The Still Centre. London: Faber & Faber,
(1939). First edition. Orig. cloth. Dust jacket. Unopened. Very
fine. MacManus 280-4846 1983 $65

SPENDER, STEPHEN   The Still Centre. London, 1939. First
edition. Dust wrapper. Fine. Rota 231-578 1983 £18

SPENDER, STEPHEN   Trial of a Judge. London: Faber & Faber,
(1938). First edition. Orig. cloth. Dust jacket. With a flyer for
the Group Theatre laid in. Near-mint. MacManus 280-4847 1983 $65

SPENDER, STEPHEN   Trial of a Judge. London, 1938. First
edition. Foot of spine rubbed and worn. Slightly frayed dust wrapper.
Name on flyleaf. With the programme of the Group Theatre production
at the Unity Theatre, London, March 1938, folded and loosely inserted.
Also the 4-page leaflet publicising "The Aim of the Group Theatre".
Very nice. Rota 231-577 1983 £17.50

SPENDER, STEPHEN   Twenty Poems. Oxford, (1930). First
edition. Of 135 copies, this is one of 75 numbered copies, signed by
author. Wrappers soiled. Nice. Rota 231-576 1983 £350

SPENDER, STEPHEN   Vienna. London: Faber And Faber,
(1934). First edition. 8vo. Orig. cloth. Dust jacket. Mint
copy. Jaffe 1-358 1983 $75

SPENSER, EDMUND   Colin Clouts Come Home Again. London:
(Thomas Creed) for William Ponsonbie, 1595. First edition. Small
4to. Full green morocco with lozenge ornament on sides, by Riviere.
Title with ornamental border, device on title. Bookplate of Edgar
F. Leo. A very fine copy. Traylen 94-773 1983 £1,500

SPENSER, EDMUND   Epithalamion. (New York: Fleming &
Carnick, 1898). Printed on rectos only. Hand-colored title-page
border decorations. Initial letters on each page printed in orange,
with gold applied by hand. Printed on handmade paper. Bound in full
blue morocco, gilt Epithalamion on front cover. Leather dentelles,
silk doublures and silk free endpapers. Karmiole 72-90 1983 $100

SPENSER, EDMUND   The Faerie Queene. London: William
Ponsonbie, 1590-96. First edition, first issue. 2 vols. Small 4to.
Full red morocco, wide gilt borders on sides, fully gilt panelled
sides, inner gilt dentelles, edges gilt, by Riviere. Belonged
to the poet Samuel Rogers, and given to him by William Jackson,
whose signature appears on title-page. An A.L.S. from Rogers and
related documents are tipped in at the beginning of Vol. 1 A fine
copy. Very rare. Traylen 94-774 1983 £4,800

SPENSER, EDMUND   The Faerie Queen; The Shepheards
Calendar... London: H.L. for Mathew Lownes, 1617. Folio. Cont.
calf gilt, double-saw-tooth border, in the centre of the sides the
large device of the Prince of Wales, flanked by the initials C.P.,
joints neatly repaired with the orig. spine and morocco lettering
piece, new end-papers. General title with woodcut border, woodcuts
in the text. Traylen 94-775 1983 £750

SPENSER, EDMUND   The Poetical Works. London, 1866.
5 vols. Cr. 8vo. Dark blue calf, two-line gilt borders with corner
ornaments, gilt panelled spines, morocco labels, gilt. Portrait,
vignette title-pages. Traylen 94-776 1983 £70

SPENSER, EDMUND   Prothalamion. Boston: Houghton
Mifflin, 1902. Folio. With 2 large tinted lithographs, mounted.
Ltd. to 419 numbered copies, designed by Bruce Rogers and printed at
the Riverside Press. Boards, soiled. Extremities a little rubbed.
Karmiole 73-87 1983 $60

SPENSER, EDMUND   Prothalamion: Epithalamion.
Riverside Press, 1902. Quarto, three-quarter leather with marbled
boards, decorations and illustrations in sepia. One of 400 copies,
bookplate. Duschnes 240-188 1983 $125

SPENSER, EDMUND   The Faerie Queene. Printed by William
Faden, 1758. 4 vols., 8vo, cont. calf. Outer margin of each title
lightly browned, four pages in the centre of volume 3 loose, slight
wear at tops of spines. Bickersteth 77-75 1983 £50

SPERRY, A. F.   History of the 33D Iowa Infantry Volunteer
Regiment. Des Moines, 1866. First edition. Covers a bit worn. Jenkins 152-428 1983 $250

SPIELMANN, M　　　　　　　The Child of the Air. Duckworth, 1910.
Colour frontis. 4to. (small). Pictorial title. 5 colour plates & 20
text illus. Blue pictorial cloth, gilt, rubbed. Greer 40-241 1983
£15

SPIELMAN, M.　　　　　　　Henriette Ronner. London, Cassell, 1891.
First edition. Folio. Frontis. portrait and 12 full page mounted
photogravures of drawings and paintings of cats. Numerous illus.
in the text. Gilt stamped white cloth, pictorial portrait of a
cat on cover, a.e.g. Good - very good. Houle 22-179 1983 $250

SPILLANE, MICKEY　　　　　I, the Jury. New York: Dutton, 1947.
Cloth. First edition. Fine in slightly used dust jacket. Reese
20-912 1983 $200

SPILSBURY, FRANCIS B.　　　Account of a voyage to the western
coast of Africa. London: Richard Phillips, 1807. 8vo. 9 plates
(3 folding). Modern 1/2 calf. Marbled boards. Adelson Africa-134
1983 $175

SPINOZA, BENEDICTUS DE　　　Tractatus Theologico-Politicus, Cui
Adjunctus est Philosophia S. Scripturae Interpres. N.p., 1674.
2 works in one. 8vo, calf (front hinge weak). 2nd edition.
Rostenberg 88-120 1983 $1,250

A SPINSTER'S Tour in France, the States of Genoa, &c.. Longman, Rees,
1828. First edition, 12mo, 12 pp inserted ads. Orig. drab boards,
paper label. Slight rubbing. Fine. Jarndyce 31-84 1983 £30

SPIRTUAL Conceits. Griffin & Farran, 1862. Illus. by W. Harry Rogers.
Title page printed in black & red. Brown morocco grain cloth gilt
(designed by Rogers), bevelled boards, a.e.g. Cvrs. faded, light
foxing 2 pp., 1 section sl. sprung, corners sl. bruised, vg. Hodgkins
27-329 1983 £15

SPLENDID Shackles. London: John and Robert Maxwell, n.d.
3 vols. Orig. cloth. First edition. Shabby copy. Inner hinges
cracking. Extremities rubbed. Covers stained. MacManus 277-91
1983 $85

SPOHR, LOUIS　　　　　　　Duetto fuer Pianoforte und Violine. Bonn,
Simrock, n.d. Lithographic title in two colors, with garlands of ivy, and
an eagle carrying a lyre in its claws. Engraved music. Folio,
unbound. Salloch 387-229 1983 $35

SPOHR, LOUIS　　　　　　　Septieme Concerto Pour le Violon.
Leipzig, Peters. Engraved music. Folio, unbound, inner margins
damaged and repaired. A few water stains. Salloch 387-230 1983
$50

SPONTINI, GASPARD　　　　　La Vestale. Paris, chez Mlles Erard,
n.d. (1807). First edition. Two vols. Engraved title, with a large
engraving of an Imperial eagle in front of a sunburst. Engraved
dedication leaf. Engraved music. Plate mark 700. Folio, new
boards with leather label. With the pub.'s rubber stamp on the title,
certifying the edition. Salloch 387-231 1983 $400

The SPORTSMAN'S Companion or an Essay on Shooting. Burlington (N.J.):
Isaac Neale, 1791. Nineteenth century calf, spine label wanting.
Very minor soiling at one corner of title, else a very nice copy.
Cont. signatures "Joseph Leas" and "Joseph Lea Jr's." Felcone
21-99 1983 $3,500

SPRAGUE, MRS. FRANK JULIAN　　A List of Manuscripts, Books, Portraits..
Washington: LC, 1939. 1st ed. Orig. wrappers. Pasted at rear is a
short note from Sprague to Ann Harned. Fine copy. Jenkins 155-1313
1983 $35

SPRAGUE, WILLIAM B.　　　　A Sermon Addressed to the Second
Presbyterina Congregation, Albany...on the Completion of the
Atlantic Telegraph. Albany, 1858. Disbound. Felcone 21-7 1983
$20

SPRAT, THOMAS　　　　　　The Bishop of Rochester's Second Letter
to...In the Savoy: Printed by Edward Jones, 1689. First edition,
4to, wrapper, some light old damp stains, but a good sound copy.
Fenning 61-420 1983 £10.50

SPRAT, THOMAS　　　　　　A Letter from the Bishop of Rochester.
In the Savoy: Printed by Edward Jones, 1688. First edition, 4to,
wrapper, a very good copy. Fenning 61-419 1983 £16.50

SPRAT, THOMAS　　　　　　A Sermon Preached before the...Commons
at St. Margaret Westminster, January 30th, 1677. Printed by T.N.
for Henry Brome, 1678. First edition, 4to. Fenning 62-344 1983
£18.50

SPRATLING, WILLIAM　　　　Little Mexico. New York, (1932). 8vo.
Cloth. With portraits and decorations by the author and a foreword
by Diego Rivera. Inscription on fly. Dj has a small chip at the
top of the spine. A fine copy. In Our Time 156-745 1983 $40

SPRATT, GEORGE　　　　　Obstetric Tables. John Churchill for
the author, London, 1835. 2 vols., 4to, with 19 lithographed plates,
mostly handcoloured and with many moveable coloured overslips
showing the anatomical parts; some slight foxing; cont. cloth,
printed labels on upper covers. Second edition. Quaritch NS 5-102
1983 $950

SPRATT, GEORGE　　　　　Obstetric Tables. London: The Author,
1845. 4th edition. 21 lith. plates, most colored, most overfolding
movable flaps. 4to, orig. cloth. Argosy 713-509 1983 $600

SPRATT, THOMAS ABEL BRIMAGE　On the evidence of the rapid silting
in progress at Port Said... London: Taylor and Francis, 1870.
First edition. 8vo. Disbound. With 2 large folding plans (hand-
colored), and a very large folding map with neat manuscript annotations. A bit dusty; a few short marginal tears; library blindstamps. Ximenes 63-610 1983 $60

SPRING, AGNES WRIGHT　　　Caspar Collins: The Life and Exploits of
an Indian Fighter of the Sixties. New York: 1927. First edition.
Frontis., numerous other illus. Brown cloth. Very good in worn
jacket. Bradley 66-704 1983 $40

SPRINGER, JOHN S.　　　　Forest Life and Forest Trees. New
York: Harper & Bros., 1851. 19cm. 20 plates from engravings.
Orig. blue pebbled cloth, with gilt titles and decorations on the
spine and upper cover, blind stamped decoration on the bottom cover.
A fine copy. Scarce. McGahern 53-155 1983 $125

SPRINZ, HEINER　　　　　Die Bildwerke der Furstlich Hohen-
zollernschen Sammlung Sigmaringen. Stuttgart/Zurich, 1925. xiv,
46pp., 66 plates. 55 text illus. Lrg. 4to. Cloth. Ars Libri SB
26-227 1983 $125

SPROUT, HAROLD　　　　　The Rise of American Naval Power 1776-
1918. Princeton U.P., 1939. First edition. 8vo. Frontis. 10 plates.
Orig. blue buckram, very slightly soiled. Orig. dust jacket. Fine.
Edwards 1042-165 1983 £30

SPRY, W.　　　　　　　　The British Coleoptera Delineated.
1840. 94 engraved plates, 8vo, cloth (slightly faded and soiled).
A few of the plates are slightly browned or soiled, but generally
a good copy of this scarce work. Wheldon 160-1172 1983 £20

SPURLING, FANNIE SMITH　　　Postmarked Vermont and California 1862-
1864. Rutland (Vt.), Tuttle, (1940). First edition. Illus. by
Rollin Ayers. Dust jacket (trifle nicked at edges). Very good - fine.
Houle 22-1180 1983 $20

SPURZHEIM, JOHANN GASPAR　　Observations on the Deranged Manifesta-
tions of the Mind, or Insanity. London, 1817. 1st ed. 4 copper
plates. 8vo. Half contemporary calf, marbled board sides. Some
rubbing; front hinge cracked. Morrill 289-214 1983 $75

SPURZHEIM, JOHANN GASPAR　　Phrenology. Boston, 1833. 2nd Am.
ed. Engraved plates. 2 vols. 8vo. Paper labels. Bindings faded;
backstrip of vol. 1 partly torn. Morrill 289-215 1983 $25

SPYRI, JOHANNA　　　　　Heidi. Chicago: Rand McN., (1921).
First edition. 4to. Blue cloth. Pictorial paste-on. Illus. by
M.W. Enright with 8 color plates. Pictorial endpapers. Aleph-bet
8-242 1983 $30

SPYRI, JOHANNA   Heidi. Phila.: McKay, 1922. First
edition. 4to. Blue cloth. Pictorial paste-on. Top edge red. Light
wear, spine slightly faded. Second issue. Illus. with pictorial
title page. Pictorial endpapers. 10 color plates, many full-page
line drawings. Very good. Aleph-bet 8-241 1983 $55

SPYRI, JOHANNA   Heidi. Phila.: McKay, (1923). 8vo.
Green cloth. Pictorial paste-on. Title and verso of frontis. slightly
foxed. In frayed pictorial dust wrapper. Illus. by. A. Anderson with
8 color plates plus over and dust wrapper. Very good. Aleph-bet 8-
243 1983 $25

SQUIRE, J. C.   The Grub Street Nights Entertainments.
London: Hodder and Stoughton Ltd., n.d. 8vo. Cloth. Paper spine
label. Very good copy. Oak Knoll 49-364 1983 $20

SQUIRE, J. C.   The Survival of the Fittest and Other
Poems. London: George Allen & Unwin Ltd., (1916). First edition.
Orig. wrappers. Presentation copy from author. Cover detached.
MacManus 280-4850 1983 $37.50

SQUIRE, JOHN   Cheddar Gorge. New York, 1938. 1st
American ed. Illustrated by Ernest H. Shepard. Tall 8vo. Morrill
286-451 1983 $20

STABLES, GORDON   For Life and Liberty. London: Blackie
& Son, Limited, 1896. First edition. 8 illus. by S. Paget and a map.
Orig. pictorial cloth. Paget's copy, with his signature and address
on the front free endpaper. Covers a bit rubbed. Contents somewhat
shaken. Good. MacManus 280-4851 1983 $35

STACEY, C.   Canada and The British Army, 1846-1871.
London: Longmans, 1936. 22cm. Ex-lib. else very good. Scarce.
McGahern 53-156 1983 $35

STACEY, C.   The Canadian Army, 1939-1945. Ottawa:
National Defence. King's Printer, 1948. 24 1/2cm. Colour illus.
from painting by Canadian war artists and 18 maps (15 folding). Very
good. McGahern 54-168 1983 $25

STACEY, C   Records of the Nile Voyageurs 1884-85.
Toronto: The Champlain Society, 1959. 8vo. 2 maps, 9 plates.
Orig. red cloth. T.e.g. No. 258 out of 600 copies. Adelson
Africa-135 1983 $100

STACEY, C   Records of the Nile Voyageurs, 1884-
1885. Toronto: The Champlain Society, 1959. 24cm. Frontis. 8
plates and 2 maps. Limited to 550 copies, this being no. 181. Red
cloth. T.e.g. Unopened. Fine. McGahern 53-157 1983 $100

STACPOOLE, HENRY DE VERE   Pierrette. John Lane, 1900. Illus. by
Charles Robinson. Fenning 62-345 1983 £10.50

STACY, NATHANIEL   Memoirs of the Life of Nathaniel
Stacy. Columbus, Pa., 1850. Frontis. Full calf. Hinges broken,
spine label mostly gone. Felcone 22-234 1983 $35

STAEL-HOLSTEIN, ANNE LOUISE GERMAINE NECKER, BARONNE DE   Margaret of
Strafford, an Historical Romance. Printed by R. Exton, for J.F. Hughes,
1803. 5 vols. 12mo. Contemp. quarter calf, marbled sides, uncut.
With 5 half-titles. A very good copy. First edition in English.
Scarce. Hill 165-127 1983 £185

STAFFORD, JEAN   Boston Adventure. NY, (1944). Two
inch stain on back board, else very good in chipped and mended, worn
dustwrapper. Quill & Brush 54-1266 1983 $30

STAFFORD, THOMAS   Pacata Hibernia. Dublin: reprinted by
the Hibernia Press Company, 1820. With 2 engraved portraits and the
full series of 18 large folding engraved maps, 2 vols. Roy. 8vo,
orig. boards, uncut, neatly rebacked, a very good large uncut copy.
Fenning 62-346 1983 £85

STAFFORD, WILLIAM   Things That Happen Where There Aren't
Any People. Brockport, New York, 1980. First edition. One of 26
lettered and specially bound copies signed by the author. Loosely
inserted is an advertisement for this book. Very fine. Jolliffe
26-487 1983 $55

THE STAGE Acquitted. Being a full answer to Mr. Collier, and the
other enemies of the drama. London: printed for John Barnes, and
sold by D. Brown, and R. Parker, 1699. 8vo, cont. mottled calf
(slightly rubbed). 1st edition. Light waterstains at the beginning
and end, else a fine large copy. Early armorial bookplates. Ximenes
64-119 1983 $400

THE STAGE in 1816. A satirical poem, in three parts. With notes
and illustrations. Part the first. London: printed and published
for the author by Hughes and Baynes, 1816. 8vo, disbound, 1st ed.
Extremely rare. Ximenes 64-499 1983 $275

STAGG, AMOS ALONZO   Touchdown! N.Y., 1927. First edition.
Photos. Cloth. Good. King 45-502 1983 $20

STAHL, GEORG   Opusculum Chymico-Physico-Medicum...
Halle, 1715. 4to. Old vellum, with clasps. Small tear in head of
spine. Lacks portrait. Gurney 90-109 1983 £65

STAHL, GEORG   Specimen Beccherianum sistens Funda-
menta, Documenta, Experimenta... Leipzig: J.L. Gleditsch, 1703.
8vo. Decorative boards. Foxed. Kraus 164-220 1983 $180

STAHL, JOHN M.   The Battle of Plattsburg. N.p.: Privately printed for author, 1918. First edition. Signed presentation
copy from author. Jenkins 152-500 1983 $35

STAHL, JOHN M.   Growing with the West. London: Longmans, Green and Co., 1930. First edition. Frontis. and illus. Long
presentation from author. Jenkins 152-430 1983 $35

STALINGRAD. Moscow, Foreign Languages Publishing House, 1943. 1st
ed. Portraits and illus. 8vo, orig. stiff wrappers, scarce.
Morrill 288-569 1983 $25

STALLENGE, WILLIAM   Instructions for the increasing of
Mulberie Trees... London: by E.A. for Eleazar Edgar, 1609. First
edition. 4to. Woodcut emblem on title, 3 full page woodcut plates.
Modern half green morocco. Moderately browned throughout, one headline cropped. Heath 48-12 1983 £300

THE STANDARD Blue Book of Texas, 1912-14... Dallas, 1914. Jenkins
153-599 1983 $60

STANDING, P. C.   Guerilla Leaders. London, 1912. First
edition. Frontis. 15 plates. Orig. green cloth, gilt. 8vo. Very
slightly foxed throughout. Good. Edwards 1042-477 1983 £12

STANDISH, FRANK HALL   The Life of Voltaire. Printed for John
Andrews, 1821. First and apparently only edition. Without the
half-title, 8vo, a small neat stamp on the titel-page, but otherwise
a nice copy in cont. half calf. Fenning 60-389 1983 £21.50

STANDLEY, P. C.   Studies of American Plants, 1-11.
Chicago, 1929-40. 10 parts, 8vo, wrappers. Wheldon 160-1768 1983
£20

STANDLEY, P. C.   Trees and Shrubs of Mexico. (Washington,
1920-26) Reprint, 1982. 5 parts in 1 vol., 8vo, cloth. Wheldon
160-2106 1983 £63

STANESBURY, SAMUEL   Aphorisms of the Wise and Good.
Griffith & Farran, nd (ca. 1865). 1st edn. Mounted photo of John
Milton on gilt & illuminated page & 30 illumin. pp. printed on thin
card, each with tissue guard. Pale green morocco grain col'd decor.
cloth, bevelled boards, a.e.g. (some foxing prelims. bkstrip faded,
insc. fr. ep.), scarce, v.g. Hodgkins 27-396 1983 £50

STANESBURY, SAMUEL   The Floral Gift. Griffith & Farran, nd
(ca. 1865). 32 pages printed in colours & gold by Thomas Bessent on
card, interleaved. 1st edn. Green fine ribbed cloth with inset
central panel & hinges embossed with leaf & flower decor. in gilt,
central panel contains titling on both cvrs. gilt decor. bkstrip,
bevelled boards, a.e.g. (foxing of interleaves & some pp.), scarce,
fine copy. Hodgkins 27-366 1983 £70

STANHOPE, PHILIP DORMER
Please turn to
CHESTERFIELD, PHILIP DORMER STANHOPE

STANLEY, EDWARD   Elmira, a dramatick poem; with thoughts
on tragedy. Norwich: printed by Crouse and Stevenson; and sold by
the booksellers in Norwich, Yarmouth...and Colchester, 1790.
8vo, original light blue wrappers (spine worn). 1st ed., a fine
uncut copy, complete with half-title and a 10-page list of subscribers.
Scarce. Ximenes 64-500 1983 $250

STANLEY, F.   Fort Union. (Canadian, Texas, 1953).
Illus. Clark 741-472 1983 $85

STANLEY, F.   One Half Mile from Heaven. Denver, 1959.
Orig. printed stiff wrappers. Fine. Jenkins 152-294 1983 $150

STANLEY, HENRY MORTON   Autobiography. Boston: Houghton
Mifflin, 1909. 8vo. Folding map. 16 plates. Orig. red cloth.
Rubbed. Adelson Africa-226 1983 $35

STANLEY, HENRY MORTON   The Congo and the founding of its
Free State. New York: Harper & Bros., 1885. 2 vols. 8vo. 5 maps.
44 plates. Orig. pictorial cloth. Rubbed, ex-lib. Adelson Africa-
224 1983 $60

STANLEY, HENRY MORTON   Coomassie and Magdala: the story of
two British campaigns in Africa. New York: Harper & Bros., 1874.
8vo. 2 folding maps, 17 plates. Orig. green cloth. Rubbed, ex-
library. Adelson Africa-137 1983 $100

STANLEY, HENRY MORTON   Coomassie. London, 1896. 15 plates.
2 maps, 11 text illus., together 2 vols. Sm. 8vo. Orig. and binders
cloth. Library stamps and bookplates. Good. Edwards 1042-478 1983
£20

STANLEY, HENRY MORTON   In Darkest Africa. New York: Charles
Scribner's Sons, 1890. First edition. 2 vols. Thick 4to. 3 folding
maps, 48 plates. Copy no. 106 of limited edition of 250, signed by
Stanley. 1/2 brown morocco, vellum boards. Adelson Africa-138 1983
$600

STANLEY, HENRY MORTON   In Darkest Africa. N.Y., Scribner's,
1890. 2 vols. 8vo. 2 steel-engraved portraits, 43 other plates,
map, 3 large folded maps in pocket at back, 100 text illus. Dec.
green cloth, gilt. 1st American ed. Fine. O'Neal 50-47 1983 $130

STANLEY, HENRY MORTON   In Darkest Africa. New York: Scribners,
1890. 2 vols. 8vo. 3 folding maps. 46 plates. Orig. green pict.
cloth. Rubbed. Adelson Africa-225 1983 $80

STANLEY, HENRY MORTON   In Darkest Africa. New York, 1890.
1st American ed. 2 steel engravings, illus., maps. 2 vols., 8vo.
Very nice. Morrill 287-433 1983 $50

STANLEY, HENRY MORTON   In Darkest Africa. New York, 1890.
First American edition. Maps and illustrations. 2 vols., 8vo.
Light binding stains, some rubbing. Morrill 290-508 1983 $30

STANLEY, HENRY MORTON   Through the Dark Continent. New York:
Harper & Bros., 1878. 2 vols. 8vo. 10 maps, 34 plates. Orig.
green pictorial cloth. Very good. Adelson Africa-136 1983 $120

STANLEY, HENRY MORTON   Through the Dark Continent. New York,
ca 1878. 2 vols., maps in pocket, other maps, numerous illus., roy.
8vo, some tears in folds of maps, orig. pictorial cloth, a slightly
used ex-library set. K Books 307-170 1983 £45

STANLEY, MARY   Hospitals and Sisterhoods. John Murray,
1855. 2nd edition, some occasional underlining. Orig. light
blue limp cloth wraps. Jarndyce 31-375 1983 £24

STANLEY, THOMAS   The History of Philosophy. London, 1743.
4to, calf. Spine chipped. Salloch 385-187 1983 $150

STANLEY, THOMAS BLAINE   The Technique of Advertising Production.
N.Y., 1941. Illus. Index. Couple blind-stamps. In chipped dust
wrapper. 2nd printing. Very good. King 45-317 1983 $20

STANLEY, WILLIAM   The Rejected Addresses; or, the triumph
of the ale-king: a farce. London: printed by T. Harper, for John
Cawthorn, n.d. (1812). 8vo, wrappers, first edition. Half-title
present. Very uncommon. Ximenes 64-501 1983 $75

STANNARD, HENRIETTA ELIZA VAUGHAN   A Blameless Woman. London: F.
V. White & Co., 1896. Fourth edition. Orig. cloth. Presentation copy
inscribed to J. Grant Reid. Front endpapers browned. Spine a bit
faded, edges slightly worn. Good. MacManus 280-5583 1983 $50

STANNARD, HENRIETTA ELIZA VAUGHAN   Cavalry Life. London: Chatto
& Windus, 1881. First edition. 2 vols. Orig. pictorial red cloth.
Lacking front flyleaf in Vol. I. Covers somewhat dust-soiled. Very
good. MacManus 280-5584 1983 $150

STANNARD, HENRIETTA ELIZA VAUGHAN   Garrison Gossip Gathered in
Blankhampton. London: F. V. White & Co., 1887. First one-volume
edition. Orig. red cloth. Very fine. MacManus 280-5585 1983 $35

STANNARD, HENRIETTA ELIZA VAUGHAN   The Luck of the Napiers. London:
F. V. White & Co., 1911. First edition. Orig. cloth. Presentation
copy inscribed to Molly New. Spine faded, torn at the head. Endpapers very slightly foxed. Good. MacManus 280-5587 1983 $60

STANNARD, HENRIETTA ELIZA VAUGHAN   A Self-Made Countess. London:
George Bell & Sons, 1900. First edition. Orig. cloth. Cover soiled.
Endpapers slightly foxed. Armorial bookplate. Bookseller's stamp on
front pastedown endpaper. Good. MacManus 280-5589 1983 $35

STANSBERY, LON R.   The Passing of the 3D Ranch. (Tulsa:
ca. 1930). First edition. Illus. Pictorial green cloth. Small
split in cloth along spine, lettering imperfectly registered in the
printing of the cloth cover. Bradley 66-628 1983 $250

STANSBERY, LON R.   The Passing of 3D Ranch. N.p. (Tulsa,
Oklahoma), n.d. (ca. 1930). Orig. pictorial cloth. 1st ed., printed
for author. Very fine copy. Jenkins 153-528 1983 $250

STANSBURY, CHARLES FREDERICK The Lake of the Great Dismal. New York,
1925. First edition. Folding map; also illustrations. 8vo. Backstrip, half of back cover and small portion of front cover dampstained. Morrill 290-568 1983 $20

STANSBURY, HOWARD   Exploration and Survey of the Valley of
the Great Salt Lake of Utah... Philadelphia, 1852. Plus separate
atlas volume. Orig. cloth. Illus. with 57 lithographed plates, some
folding. Scattered foxing. Reese 19-521 1983 $400

STANSBURY, HOWARD   Exploration and Survey of the Valley of
Great Salt Lake. Phila., 1852. Complete with all 34 plates and 23
scientific plates, the 2 huge fldg. maps in 2nd vol. 2 vols., top
edge of spine worn, otherwise fine. Clark 741-480 1983 $325

STANTON, EDWIN M.   Protections Across the Frontier. Wash.,
1866. Dbd. First edition. Ginsberg 47-843 1983 $50

STANYAN, TEMPLE   The Grecian History, from the Origin
of Greece... London: J. & R. Tonson, 1739. Second edition, revised
and enlarged. 2 vols. 8vo. Cont. polished calf, gilt, gilt
panelled spines with morocco labels, gilt. Engraved frontis. after
Van de Gucht, title-pages printed in red and black. Traylen 94-777
1983 £38

STAPLEDON, OLAF
Please turn to
STAPLEDON, WILLIAM OLAF

STAPLEDON, WILLIAM OLAF   Last and First Men. London, 1930. First
edition. Erasure from flyleaf. Nice. Rota 230-566 1983 £40

STAPLEDON, WILLIAM OLAF   Star Maker. London, 1937. First edition.
Covers a little marked. Nice. Rota 230-567 1983 £25

STAPLES, WILLIAM R.   Rhode Island in the Continental Congress.
Providence, 1870. Limited to 500 copies. Orig. green, pebbled buckram, gilt, extremely nice. Boswell 7-135 1983 $75

STARK, FRANCIS R.   The Abolition of Privateering and the
Declaration of Paris. NY, 1897. Fine, bookplate. Quill & Brush 54-
1657 1983 $35

STARK, FREYA   Seen in the Hadhramaut. John Murray,
1938. First edition, map & plates, 8vo, orig. cloth, v.g. copy in
frayed d.w. Fenning 60-396 1983 £10.50

STARK, JAMES   Antique Views of Ye Towne of Boston.
Boston, Photo-Electrotype Engraving Co., (1882). Plates, illus. and
maps, some folding. 4to. Orig. front cover and backstrip in cloth,
back cover of boards with illus. and printing. Ends of spine frayed;
corners bit rubbed. Morrill 289-432 1983 $45

STARK, JAMES   The Loyalists of Massachusetts and the
Other Side of the American Revolution. New York, 1910. 1st ed.
Map. 8vo, nice. Morrill 288-296 1983 $25

STARK, JAMES   Stark's Illustrated Bermuda Guide.
Boston, (1890). Maps, engravings and 16 photo-prints. Small 8vo.
Morrill 290-510 1983 $20

STARK, R. M.   A Popular History of British Mosses.
1854. 20 coloured plates, 8vo, cloth. Wheldon 160-1900 1983 £25

STARKEY, DIGBY PILOT   Ireland. Dublin: Hodges and Smith,
1849. First collected edition, 8vo, cont. half calf, little
rubbed but thoroughly sound, very good. Fenning 61-422 1983 £55

STARKEY, JAMES   Common Adventures. Dublin: Orwell Press,
1926. First edition. Orig. wrappers. One of 200 copies. Presentation
copy from the author to the printer James Guthrie, inscribed: "To
James Guthrie with kind regards from Seumas O'Sullivan November 1926."
Wrappers rather frayed and a bit soiled. Good. MacManus 279-4097
1983 $100

STARKEY, JAMES   The Rose & the Bottle and Other Essays.
Dublin, Talbot Press, (1946). First edition. Tan cloth over black.
Signed by the author. Very good. Houle 22-708 1983 $30

STARKEY, MARION L.   The Cherokee Nation. NY, 1946.
First edition. Cloth, spine lettering wearing. Good. King 46-115
1983 $25

STARR, M. ALLEN   Synopsis of Lectures upon Diseases of the
Nervous System. N.Y., 1894. 8vo, 24 text illus. Some hand-written
notes and illus. by a former owner on several blank leaves. Argosy
713-510 1983 $40

STARRETT, VINCENT   All About Mother Goose. N.p.: 1930.
12mo, cloth-backed decorated boards, paper label. One of 275 copies
signed by the author. Printed at the Merrymount Press. Backstrip
lightly sunned; a very nice copy. Perata 28-161 1983 $75

STARRETT, VINCENT   Autolycus in Limbo. New York, 1943.
8vo. Cloth. From the library of Alexander Laing with note on fly
that the author sent him this book. Vg-fine copy. In Our Time
156-749 1983 $20

STARRETT, VINCENT   Banners in the Dawn: Sixty-Four
Sonnets. Chicago: Walter Hill, 1923. 8vo. Cloth, boards. Total
ed. is 250 copies. This copy bears a presentation inscription by
Starrett dated 1928 to Alexander Laing. A vg-fine copy. In Our
Time 156-747 1983 $65

STARRETT, VINCENT   Buried Caesars. Chicago, 1923. 8vo.
Cloth. From the library of Alexander Laing with a humorous comment
by same on front flyleaf. A vg-fine copy. In Our Time 156-748
1983 $35

STARRETT, VINCENT   Dead Man Inside. N.Y., Doubleday, (1931).
First edition. Black cloth. Very good-fine. Houle 21-826 1983
$30

STARRETT, VINCENT   Ebony Flame. Chicago, (1922). 8vo.
Cloth, boards. 1 of 350 copies signed by author. From the library
of Alexander Laing with his autograph and comment on inside blank
flyleaf. Paper label on spine chipped else vg-fine copy. In Our
Time 156-746 1983 $45

STARRET, VINCENT   An Essay on Limited Editions. Chicago:
The Black Cat Press, 1939. First edition. 8vo. Paper wrappers,
cord tied. Limited to 250 copies. Printed in Electra type designed
by Dwiggins. Fine, unopened copy. Oak Knoll 48-355 1983 $65

STARRETT, VINCENT   Flame and Dust. Chicago, Covici, 1924.
Sm 4to, dust jacket (small nicks). Else very good. One of 450
copies. Printed by the Renshaw Press. Houle 21-827 1983 $30

STARRETT, VINCENT   Fourteen Great Detective Stories.
New York: The Modern Library, (1928). Small 8vo. Cloth. Dust
jacket. Signed and dated by Starrett on title page. Pencil note
at end indicates that this is the author's copy. Oak Knoll 49-365
1983 $45

STARRETT, VINCENT   The Great Hotel Murder. N.Y., Sun Dial
Press, (1935, 1937). Dust jacket. Fine copy. Houle 22-817 1983
$22.50

STARRETT, VINCENT   Penny Wise and Book Foolish. New
York: Covici Friede, 1929. First edition. 8vo. Green cloth,
dust jacket. Wrapper is quite worn with a piece missing from spine.
Cloth cover is faded where wrapper part is missing. Oak Knoll 48-
356 1983 $35

STARRETT, VINCENT   Persons From Porlock. Chicago: The
Bookfellows, 1923. First edition. Gray wrappers, stitched. One
corner reinforced internally. Bradley 66-312 1983 $125

THE STATE of Rome Under Nero and Domitian. London (i.e. Edinburgh):
Printed for C. Corbett, 1739. 8vo, wraps. Edinburgh piracy of
the London edition. Quaritch NS 7-125 1983 $300

STATENS ETNOGRAFISKA MUSEUM & GOTEBORG   Primitive kinst. Stockholm:
Aktiebolaget Bokverk, 1947. 424 illus. Large 4to. Boards. 3/4 leather. Ars Libri 34-71 1983 $100

STATIA, W. E.   Statia's Hotel List Guide. Portland (Me),
B. Thurston, 1875. 12mo. Binding partly rubbed and faded, lacks blank
endleaves. Illus. Morrill 287-435 1983 $30

STATIUS, PUBLIUS PAPINUS   Sylvarvm Libri Qvinqve Thebaidos Libri
Dvodecim Achilleidos Dvo. (Venetiis, in Aedibus Aldi, 1502). 8vo,
later vellum-backed boards trifle worn, minor spotting, fine with the
missing 80 page "Orthographia" at end, followed by the leaf bearing
the Aldine anchor. First Aldine anchor. Ravenstree 95-108 1983
$750

STATON, FRANCIS M.   A Bibliography of Canadiana. Toronto:
The Public Library, 1934. 25cm. First edition. Facsimiles. Wine
cloth. Green title label. A fine copy. McGahern 53-158 1983 $300

STATON, FRANCES M.   A Bibliography of Canadiana. Toronto,
1934. First edition. Illustrated, including 28 facsimiles. Red
cloth, leather spine label. Very good copy in dj. Bradley 65-34
1983 $245

STATON, FRANCES M.   A Bibliography of Canadiana. Toronto:
1934. First edition. Illus. Orig. red cloth, leather spine label.
In dust jacket. Bradley 66-56 1983 $235

STAUNTON, G. L.   Authentic Account of an Embassy from the
King of Great Britain... London, 1798. Portraits. 2 vols. 4to.
Tree calf, rebacked. Folio Atlas of 44 plates, boards, rebacked, to-
gether 3 vols. Good. Edwards 1044-665 1983 £1,350

STAWELL, MRS. RODOLPH   My Days with the Fairies. London,
Hodder & Stoughton, (1913). 8 colored plates by Edmund Dulac, each
with tissue-guards with descriptive letterpress. 8vo. Pictorial
front cover. Evidence of a page lacking between title-page and
Dedication. Morrill 289-544 1983 $40

STEAD, CHRISTINA   The Beauties and Furies. New York:
D. Appleton-Century Company, 1936. First American edition. 8vo.
Orig. cloth with paper labels. Dust jacket, somewhat worn. Fine
copy. Jaffe 1-361 1983 $35

STEAD, WILLIAM FORCE　　　　The House of the World and Other Poems. London: Dobden-Sanderson, 1930. Printed wraps. First edition. Inscribed on the half-title: "To Humbert Wolfe with the sincere regards of the author. May 1930." Pencil note, and overlap edges a trifle used, but a near fine copy. Reese 20-919　1983　$50

STEAD, WILLIAM T　　　　Borderland. London, 1894-95. Illus. 2 vols., large 8vo, vol. 1 in cloth, vol. 2 in half roan. Bindings faded, rubbed and partly chipped. Scarce. Morrill 286-457　1983 $37.50

STEAD, WILLIAM T.　　　　If Christ Came to Chicago! N.p., 1894. First English edition. Half title, folding plate showing brothels, pawnbrokers, saloons and lodging houses. Frontis., 4 pp. ads. Orig. maroon cloth. Very good. Jarndyce 31-376　1983　£18.50

STEAD, WILLIAM T.　　　　Josephine Butler. London: Morgan & Scott, n.d. (1888). First edition. Orig. cloth. Presentation copy to Grant Richards. Spine soiled. Very good. MacManus 280-4853 1983　$40

STEAD, WILLIAM T.　　　　Truth about Russia. London: Cassell & Co., 1888. First edition. Orig. cloth. Presentation copy, inscribed to Grant Richards. Soiled. MacManus 280-4854　1983　$40

STEARNS, LYMAN MARSHALL　　　　The Draughts Marvel and Twentieth Century Checker Compendium. Manchester, N.H., Draughts Marvel Pub. Co., (1909). Copy No. 263 of a limited edition. Portraits and checker diagrams. 4to, inner hinges cracked; stain on backstrip. Morrill 290-512　1983　$25

STEARNS, OLIVER　　　　The Duty of Moral Reflection with Particular Reference to the Texas Question. Hingham, Mass.: Jedidiah Farmer, 1845. 1st ed. Fine copy. Jenkins 153-580　1983 $250

STEBBINS, HORATIO　　　　The President, the People and the War. San F., 1864. Dbd. First edition. Ginsberg 47-173　1983　$60

STEBBINS, N. L.　　　　The Illustrated Coast Pilot. Boston, N.L. Stebbins, 1891. First edition. Numerous illustrations. Oblong 4to, original limp buckram (or canvas). Morrill 290-513　1983　$50

STEBBINS, N. L.　　　　The Yachtsman's Album. Boston, Stebbins, 1896. First edition. Reproduced from Photographs by Stebbins with a Descriptive Index. Oblong 8vo, 60 plates, 4 illustrations per plate. Morrill 290-514　1983　$125

STECK, FRANCIS BORGIA　　　　A Tentative Guide to Historical Materials on the Spanish Borderlands. Philadelphia, 1943. 1st ed. 8vo, double columns. Morrill 287-437　1983　$22.50

STEDMAN, EDMUND CLARENCE　　　　Elizabeth Barrett Browning. Boston: James R. Osgood & Co., 1877. First edition. 12mo. Frontis. port. Orig. decorated cloth. Spine and covers slightly worn and soiled. Good. MacManus 277-722　1983　$35

STEDMAN, EDMUND CLARENCE　　　　The Prince's Ball. N.Y., 1860. First edition. Illus. Thin 8vo, orig. cloth. Argosy 714-689　1983 $35

STEEL, FLORA ANNIE　　　　Inidan Scene. N.Y.: Longmans, Green & Co., 1934. First American edition. Orig. cloth. Dust jacket. Very fine. MacManus 280-4856　1983　$45

STEEL, FLORA ANNIE　　　　In the Permanent Way. London: Heine- mann, 1898. First edition. Orig. pictorial cloth. MacManus 280- 4857　1983　$40

STEEL, FLORA ANNIE　　　　Marmaduke. N.Y.: Frederick A. Stokes Co., 1917. First American edition. Orig. cloth. Dust jacket (rare). Very fine. MacManus 280-4858　1983　$50

STEEL, FLORA ANNIE　　　　The Potter's Thumb. London: William Heinemann, 1894. First edition. 3 vols. Orig. dark red cloth. Presentation copy, inscribed on the title-page; "R.G. Hardy from F.A.S." Spines faded, rubbed at edges. A little soiled. A few inner hinges weak. Good. MacManus 280-4860　1983　$350

STEEL, FLORA ANNIE　　　　A Sovereign Remedy. London: William Heinemann, 1906. First edition. Orig. decorated apple-green cloth. Presentation copy, inscribed on the title-page: "R.G. Hardy...F.A. Steel." Near-fine. MacManus 280-4861　1983　$85

STEEL, FLORA ANNIE　　　　Tales of the Punjab. London: Macmillan & Co., 1894. First edition. Illus. by J. Lockwood Kipling. Orig. pictorial cloth. Head of spine nicked. Other edges a little worn. Trifle foxed. Good. MacManus 280-4862　1983　$35

STEEL, FLORA ANNIE　　　　Voices in the Night. London: Heinemann, 1900. First edition. Orig. pictorial cloth. Near fine. MacManus 280-4863　1983　$50

STEELE, ELIZABETH　　　　The memoirs of Mrs. Sophia Baddeley. Late of Drury-Lane Theatre. Dublin: printed for Messrs. Colles, Moncrieffe, etc., 1787. 3 vols., 12mo, cont. green calf, spines gilt (trifle rubbed, covers of one volume a little stained). 1st Irish ed. Half-titles present, and an errata leaf at the end of Vol. III. A few light waterstains. Ximenes 64-502　1983　$250

STEELE, JOHN　　　　Across the Plains in 1850. Chicago: Printed for the Caxton Club, 1930. Illus. Limited to 350 copies. Jenkins 153-530　1983　$85

STEELE, MATTHEW FORNEY　　　　American Campaigns. Wash., 1943. 2 vols., 8vo, cloth, vinyl. Argosy 710-316　1983　$60

STEELE, OLIVER G.　　　　Steele's Book of Niagara Falls. Buffalo: 1840. Seventh edition. 16mo. Folding frontis. map. Full leather, gilt. Covers worn and spotted, contents fine. Bradley 66-624　1983 $35

STEELE, RICHARD　　　　The Christian Hero. For S. Vanderbergh, 1775. 12mo, verso blank, attractively rebound in modern calf gilt, morocco label, fine. Deighton 3-273　1983　£18

STEELE, RICHARD　　　　The Conscious Lovers. Gli Amanti Interni, Commedia Inglese. Londra, 1724. 1st ed. of this translation, 12mo, cont. gilt-bordered morocco, spine gilt. Engraved frontis., vignette title. A very fine copy, in a slightly rubbed contemporary binding. Trebizond 18-94　1983　$125

STEELE, RICHARD　　　　The Correspondence of Richard Steele. Oxford University Press, 1941. First edition, 6 illus, fine. Deighton 3-275　1983　£12

STEELE, RICHARD　　　　The Epistolary Correspondence. London: 1787. Two vols. Engraved portrait of Steele in Vol. 1. Fine set bound in half-green morocco with marbled boards. First edition. Bromer 25-109　1983　$50

STEELE, RICHARD　　　　The Lover and the Reader. Printed for J. Tonson, 1723. 12mo, cont. calf. Bickersteth 77-76　1983　£48

STEELE, RICHARD　　　　Poetical Miscellanies. London: Printed for Jacob Tonson...MDDCXIV (sic, i.e. 1714). 8vo, frontis., M5 neatly repaired; new polished sheep antique with red morocco label. First edition. Quaritch NS 7-126　1983　$350

STEELE, RICHARD　　　　Poetical Miscellanies, consisting of original poems and translations. J. Tonson, 1727. 2nd ed., 12mo, engraved frontis. and head and tail pieces, cont. calf gilt, very neatly rebacked, a very good clean and crisp copy. Deighton 3-274 1983　£65

STEELE, RICHARD　　　　The Romish Ecclesiastical History of Late Years. London: printed for J. Roberts, 1714. First edition, first issue. 8vo, engraved frontis., cont. sheep, single gilt fillet border, skilfully rebacked. Pickering & Chatto 19-70　1983　$150

STEELE, RICHARD　　　　The state of the case between the Lord Chamberlain of His Majesty's Household, and the Governor of the Royal Company of Comedians. London: printed for W. Chetwood; J. Roberts; J. Graves; and Charles Lillie, 1720. 8vo, half calf, spine gilt. First edition. Title slightly dusty, but a very good copy. Ximenes 64-503　1983　$350

STEELE, RICHARD   The state of the case between the Lord Chamberlain of His Majesty's Household, and the Governor of the Royal Company of Comedians. London: printed for W. Chetwood; J. Roberts; J. Graves; and Charles Lillie, 1720. 8vo, disbound, 2nd ed. Outer margins uncut; very good copy. Scarce. Ximenes 64-504 1983 $175

STEELE, RICHARD   The Theatre, by Richard Steele; to which are added, The Anti-Theatre; The Character of Sir John Edgar; Steele's case with the Lord Cahmberlain; The Crisis of Property, with the sequel, two pasquins, etc. London: printed by and for the editor; and sold by G. G. and J. Robinson, etc., 1791. 8vo, old half calf, spine gilt (some rubbing). 1 volume. Half-title present, with an engraved vignette portrait of the author. Ximenes 64-505 1983 $250

STEELE, ROBERT   The Story of Alexander. D. Nutt, 1894. 1st edn., large paper copy limited to 50 copies signed by publisher. Title p. illus. & 6 full page illus. & head/tail pieces by Fred Mason. Mustard decor. cloth, uncut (eps. foxed, name fr. ep., sl. rubbing edges of cvrs.), v.g. Hodgkins 27-495 1983 £45

STEELE, ROBERT   The Story of Alexander. David Nutt, 1894. Sm. 4to. Title in red & black. 18 text illus. & 6 plates. Few pages roughly opened. Red cloth, gilt. Edition limited to 50 copies, No. 45. Greer 40-137 1983 £45

STEELE, ROBERT   The Story of Alexander. D. Nutt, 1894. 1st trade edn. Title p. illus. & 6 full page illus. & head/tail pieces by Fred Mason. Mustard decor. cloth, uncut (free eps. foxed, foredge sl. dust soiled), v.g. copy. Hodgkins 27-496 1983 £12.50

STEELE, RUFUS   Mustangs of the Mesas, A Saga of the Wild Horse. Hollywood: Press of Murray & Genn, 1941. Frontis. and illus. 1st ed. Scarce. Fine copy. Jenkins 153-531 1983 $50

STEENSTRUP, J. J. S.   On the Alternation of Generations. London: printed for the Ray Society, 1845. 8vo. Orig. cloth. T.e.g. 3 folding plates. First English edition. Back slightly torn. Gurney 90-111 1983 £28

STEEVENS, G. W.   With Kitchener to Khartum. New York: Dodd, Mead, 1898. 12mo. 7 maps and plans. Orig. cloth. Spine faded and stained, ex-lib. Adelson Africa-227 1983 $20

STEFANSSON, VILHJALMUR   The Friendly Arctic. NY 1939. Photos, cloth, map in pocket, blind-stamped name, rubbed. King 46-755 1983 $25

STEGNER, WALLACE   On a Darkling Plain. NY, (1940). Minor internal foxing, else very good in soiled and wearing, good dustwrapper. Quill & Brush 54-1267 1983 $40

STEGNER, WALLACE   Remembering Laughter. B, 1937. Cover slightly spotted, else very good in lightly chipped, good dustwrapper. Quill & Brush 54-1268 1983 $75

STEICHEN, EDWARD   Power in the Pacific. (New York, 1945). 1st ed. Illus. 4to, dust wrapper. Morrill 289-586 1983 $50

STEIG, WILLIAM   All Embarrassed. N.Y., (1944). First edition. Illus., small 8vo. Presentation copy, signed "Bill". Argosy 714-690 1983 $30

STEIGER, HUGO   Euripides. Lg (Das Erbe der Alten), 1912. Vellum. 8vo, cloth. Salloch 385-533 1983 $30

STEIN, AARON MARC   Only the Guilty. N.Y., Doubleday, 1942. First edition. Dust jacket (small nicks and tape on verso) else very good. Houle 22-818 1983 $45

STEIN, ALBERT   Letter to Samuel J. Peters, Esq. Phila., 1841. Folded map. Orig. printed wraps. Ginsberg 47-509 1983 $75

STEIN, AUREL   On Ancient Central-Asian Tracks. London, 1933. Folding map, colour plates, folding panoramas and numerous other illus. Thick 8vo. Some slight wear. Orig. cloth. Edwards 1044-666 1983 £200

STEIN, GERTRUDE   An Acquaintance with Description. London: Seizen Press, 1929. Ltd. first edition. Thin 8vo, white cloth. One of 225 signed copies, with the limitation label pasted in. Offset marks from scotch tape on flyleaves. Argosy 714-895 1983 $400

STEIN, GERTRUDE   Blood on the Dining Room Floor. N.p., (1948). Limited to 626 numbered copies, edges very slightly rubbed, else fine in lightly rubbed, good slipcase that is skinned at spine, discreet owner's name. Quill & Brush 54-1273 1983 $250

STEIN, GERTRUDE   Blood on the Dining Room Floor. (Pawlet): The Banyan Press, (1948). Quarto. Cloth and marbled boards. First edition. One of 600 numbered copies (of 626), this being copy no. 20. A fine copy in orig. glassine and slipcase. Reese 20-924 1983 $175

STEIN, GERTRUDE   An Elucidation. Paris, 1927. 8vo. Wraps. A fine copy. In Our Time 156-751 1983 $150

STEIN, GERTRUDE   Everybody's Autobiography. N.Y., (1937). First edition. Photo illus., 8vo, linen. Argosy 714-691 1983 $45

STEIN, GERTRUDE   First Reader & Three Plays. Boston: Riverside Press, 1948. Dec. by Francis Rose. Thin 8vo, pict. cloth. First edition. Fine. Dust wrapper torn. Argosy 714-692 1983 $50

STEIN, GERTRUDE   Four in America. New Haven, 1947. First edition. Dust wrapper dampstained. Argosy 714-693 1983 $100

STEIN, GERTRUDE   Four Saints in Three Acts. (N.Y.), 1934. First edition thus. 4to, illus. with halftone portraits and scenes from the play. Stiff wraps. Very good. Houle 22-819 1983 $60

STEIN, GERTRUDE   Four Saints in Three Acts. NY, 1934. Very good in price clipped, chipped, good dustwrapper. Quill & Brush 54-1274 1983 $40

STEIN, GERTRUDE   Four Saints in Three Acts. N.Y., 1934. First edition. Thin 8vo, black cloth. Argosy 714-694 1983 $35

STEIN, GERTRUDE   The Geographical History of America. Random House, n.p. (1936). Sq. 8vo, black & white cloth, d.w. (chipped). First edition. Argosy 714-695 1983 $300

STEIN, GERTRUDE   Geography and Plays. Boston: Four Seas Co., (1922). First edition. 8vo, boards, cloth back. First issue binding, mottled gray boards, with lettering on front cover. Slightly rubbed; spine label chipped. Argosy 714-696 1983 $125

STEIN, GERTRUDE   Geography and Plays. Boston: Four Seas Co., (1922). 8vo. Cloth, boards. 1st ed., third state of the binding. Dj has some light wear. Very fine copy. In Our Time 156-750 1983 $125

STEIN, GERTRUDE   Have they Attacked Mary. (New York), (1917). Small quarto. Printed wraps. First edition. One of 200 numbered copies. One corner slightly creased, and some light soiling, otherwise an about fine copy. Reese 20-921 1983 $25

STEIN, GERTRUDE   Ida. NY, (1941). Cover lightly stained, page edges slightly foxed, else very good in lightly chipped, price clipped, very good dustwrapper. Quill & Brush 54-1275 1983 $100

STEIN, GERTRUDE   Lectures in America. New York, 1935. First edition. Late binding, omitting the frontis. From the library of David Gascoyne, with his autograph signature on the flyleaf and his pencilled list of other books by Stein on the rear endpapers. Good. Rota 230-569 1983 £35

STEIN, GERTRUDE   Lucy Church Amiably. Paris: 1930. 1000 copies printed. Edges slightly rubbed, else fine in blue "neon" boards with glassine. First edition. Bromer 25-111 1983 $200

STEIN, GERTRUDE   Lucy Church Amiably. Paris, 1930. First edition. One of 1000 copies. Blue paper boards severely worn. Internally good reading copy. Rota 230-568 1983 £30

STEIN, GERTRUDE   Lucy Church Amiably. Paris, 1930. First edition. 8vo, blue boards; backstrip very worn & stained, with 1 inch piece missing. Argosy 714-697 1983 $50

STEIN, GERTRUDE   The Making of Americans. (Paris: Three Mountains Press, 1925). First edition. Rebound in buckram; orig. printed wrs. bound in. Argosy 714-698 1983 $600

STEIN, GERTRUDE   The Making of Americans. Paris: Three Mountains Press, (1925). Sq. 8vo, full leather binding by Bayntun, black lettering pieces, orig. wraps. bound in. Issued in an edition of 500 unnumbered copies. First edition. Duschnes 240-202 1983 $300

STEIN, GERTRUDE   Money. Black Sparrow Press, 1973. 8vo. Boards. 1 of 100 numbered copies. Fine in acetate jacket. In Our Time 156-753 1983 $100

STEIN, GERTRUDE   Operas and Plays. Paris: Plain Edition, (1932). Stiff wraps. First edition. Bookplate neatly removed, short crack in one joint, otherwise a fine copy, in the slightly soiled slipcase. Reese 20-922 1983 $175

STEIN, GERTRUDE   Portraits and Prayers. NY, (1934). Cover slightly discolored, very good. Quill & Brush 54-1276 1983 $75

STEIN, GERTRUDE   A Primer for the Gradual Understanding of Gertrude Stein. Black Sparrow Press, 1971. 8vo. Cloth, boards. 1 of 60 copies signed by Miss Stein and issued posthumously. Enclosed in slipcase box. In Our Time 156-752 1983 $150

STEIN, GERTRUDE   Selected Writings of... NY, (1946). Near fine in chipped, slightly frayed dustwrapper. Quill & Brush 54-1278 1983 $40

STEIN, GERTRUDE   Three Lives. Pushkin Press, 1945. New edition. Dust wrapper designed by E. Marx. Name of flyleaf. Nice. Rota 230-571 1983 £15

STEIN, GERTRUDE   Useful Knowledge. New York: Payson & Clarke, Ltd., 1928. 8vo. cloth lettered in red, worn dust-jacket. First edition. Duschenes 240-203 1983 $150

STEIN, GERTRUDE   Useful Knowledge. N.Y., (1928). First edition. Tall 8vo, cloth; extremes of backstrip chipped. Argosy 714-700 1983 $85

STEIN, GERTRUDE   Wars I Have Seen. N.Y., (1945). First edition. D.w.; (rubbed). Argosy 714-701 1983 $20

STEIN, GERTRUDE   What Are Masterpieces. Los Angeles, Conference Press, (1940). First edition. Frontis. portrait and 1 plate by Francis Picabia. Dust jacket (small chips). One of 50 numbered copies signed by Gertrude Stein, printed by the Ward Ritchie Press. This copy is marked "Editorial Copy." Very good. Houle 22-820 1983 $600

STEIN, GERTRUDE   What are Masterpieces. Los Angeles; the Conference Press, (1940). First edition. Fine in a lightly chipped dust wrapper. Argosy 714-702 1983 $100

STEIN, GERTRUDE   What Are Masterpieces. Los Angeles, 1940. First edition. Dust wrapper. Nice. Rota 230-570 1983 £30

STEIN, WILHELM   Holbein. Berlin: Julius Bard, 1929. 135 illus. 4to. Cloth. Ars Libri 32-327 1983 $65

STEINACH, AUGEN   Verjuengung durch Experimentelle Neubelung der Alternden Pubertaetsdruese. Berlin, 1920. 10 plates, some in color. Tall 8vo, pr. wrs. First edition. Argosy 713-511 1983 $85

STEINBART, KURT   Johann Liss. Der Maler aus Holstein. Berlin: Deutscher Verein fur Kunstwissenschaft, 1940. 56 plates. Frontis. in color, 75 text illus. Large 4to. Cloth. Ars Libri 32-408 1983 $150

STEINBECK, JOHN   Burning Bright. N.Y., Viking, 1950. First edition. Grey cloth stamped in red, t.e. orange. Dust jacket. Very good - fine. Houle 22-824 1983 $110

STEINBECK, JOHN   Burning Bright. NY, 1950. Bright, fine copy in bright, very good dustwrapper showing only light wear. Quill & Brush 54-1280 1983 $75

STEINBECK, JOHN   Cannery Row. New York: The Viking Press, 1945. First edition, second binding. Small 8vo. Orig. yellow cloth. Dust jacket. Very fine copy. Jaffe 1-367 1983 $150

STEINBECK, JOHN   Cup of Gold. NY: Covici, Friede (1936 c. 1929). 2nd edition. Fine copy in bright dust jacket, very slightly soiled. Karmiole 74-87 1983 $125

STEINBECK, JOHN   Cup of Gold. NY, (1936). Bright, near fine copy in bright, very good or better dustwrapper with very slight wear. Quill & Brush 54-1281 1983 $125

STEINBECK, JOHN   Cup of Gold. NY, (1936). Second edition, cover slightly stained, else very good in chipped and worn reprint dustwrapper. Quill & Brush 54-1282 1983 $20

STEINBECK, JOHN   East of Eden. NY, 1952. Limited to 1500 signed copies, some ink underlinings and margin notations, minor cover and page stains, good plus, owner's inscription. Quill & Brush 54-1284 1983 $200

STEINBECK, JOHN   East of Eden. N.Y., Viking, 1952. First edition, third printing (October). Green cloth stamped in dark green and orange (covers a bit soiled and stained, tiny tear at top of spine). Inscribed by Steinbeck on front free endpaper, "...from John Steinbeck." Good - very good. Houle 22-825 1983 $275

STEINBECK, JOHN   The Grapes of Wrath. N.Y., Viking, (1939). First edition. Pictorial dust jacket. A fine copy. Houle 22-827 1983 $425

STEINBECK, JOHN   The Grapes of Wrath. New York: The Viking Press, (1939). First edition. 8vo. Orig. pictorial cloth. Dust jacket, slightly worn. Fine copy. Jaffe 1-365 1983 $225

STEINBECK, JOHN   The Grapes of Wrath. NY, (1939). Front hinge starting at half-title, top page edge very lightly bruised, spine slightly darkened, ink mark front end paper, good to very good in worn and chipped, good dustwrapper. Quill & Brush 54-1291 1983 $125

STEINBECK, JOHN   The Grapes of Wrath. London, 1939. Boards very slightly bowed and bumped, dustwrapper frayed at corners, head and tail of spine, otherwise excellent. Gekoski 2-176 1983 £55

STEINBECK, JOHN   The Grapes of Wrath. New York, 1940. Thick 8vo, bound by Bayntun in full blue crushed levant, fillet borders. In the center of front and back cover is a pictorial shield by Benton. A.e.g. With two-color lithographs, numerous full-page and head-pieces by Thomas Hart Benton. Four pictorial endleaves. Signed by the artist. One of 1146 copies signed. Presentation from the artist and a small pen and ink sketch. Duschnes 240-14 1983 $650

STEINBECK, JOHN   In Dubious Battle. New York: Covici-Friede, (1936). First edition. 8vo. Orig. cloth. Dust jacket, a trifle rubbed at head of spine, but still a very fine copy. Jaffe 1-363 1983 $500

STEINBECK, JOHN   In Dubious Battle. NY, (1936). Ex-lib., flap from dustwrapper pasted on front fly, cover soiled, good. Quill & Brush 54-1285 1983 $50

STEINBECK, JOHN   The Moon Is Down. New York: The
Viking Press, 1942. First edition, first issue. 8vo. Orig. cloth.
Dust jacket. Very fine copy. Jaffe 1-366 1983 $150

STEINBECK, JOHN   The Moon is Down. NY, 1942. Maroon
binding, spine lettering slightly rubbed, very good in slightly
frayed and rubbed dustwrapper, owner's name. Quill & Brush 54-1293
1983 $40

STEINBECK, JOHN   The Moon is Down. L, (1942). Very good
in lightly chipped and frayed, good dustwrapper, owner's name. Quill
& Brush 54-1294 1983 $75

STEINBECK, JOHN   The Moon is Down. London. 1942.
First English edition. Covers very slightly faded by the spine.
Dustwrapper frayed at the head of the spine. Very good. Jolliffe
26-490 1983 $20

STEINBECK, JOHN   Of Mice And Men. New York: Covici
Friede, (1937). First edition, first issue. 8vo. Orig. cloth.
Dust jacket. Very fine copy. Jaffe 1-364 1983 $400

STEINBECK, JOHN   Of Mice and Men. New York: Covici-
Friede, (1937). 1st ed., 2nd state. Orig. cloth. Fine copy lacking
dj. Jenkins 155-1161 1983 $50

STEINBECK, JOHN   Of Mice and Men. NY, (1937). Second
issue, book slightly rolled and has red mark on bottom book edge, else
very good in chipped and wearing dustwrapper. Quill & Brush 54-1288
1983 $30

STEINBECK, JOHN   The Pastures of Heaven. NY, 1932.
Spine slightly faded, good or better copy that is slightly cocked.
Quill & Brush 54-1295 1983 $200

STEINBECK, JOHN   The Pearl. New York, 1947. First
edition. Drawings by J.C. Orozco. Small stain on upper cover.
Slightly frayed dust wrapper. Bookplate. Very nice. Rota 230-
572 1983 £35

STEINBECK, JOHN   The Red Pony. N.Y., 1933. 8vo, pr.
wraps. Argosy 714-704 1983 $45

STEINBECK, JOHN   A Russian Journal. New York, 1948.
First edition. Photographs by R. Capa. Corners a little rubbed.
Covers a trifle marked. Nice. Rota 230-573 1983 £25

STEINBECK, JOHN   Sea of Cortez. New York: Viking, (1941).
Cloth. Illus. First edition. A fine copy. Dust jacket lightly
chipped at extremities. Reese 19-523 1983 $300

STEINBECK, JOHN   Sea of Cortez. New York: The Viking
Press, 1941. First edition. Review copy, with publisher's slip laid
in giving details of publication. Large 8vo. Illus., orig. cloth.
Dust jacket, chipped. Jaffe 1-369 1983 $275

STEINBECK, JOHN   Sea of Cortez. N.Y., Viking, 1941.
First edition. Thick 8vo, illus. Orig. cloth. Good - very good.
Houle 22-829 1983 $85

STEINBECK, JOHN   Sweet Thursday. New York: The Viking
Press, 1943. First edition. 8vo. Orig. cloth. Dust jacket.
Fine copy. Jaffe 1-368 1983 $75

STEINBECK, JOHN   To A God Unknown. New York: Covici-
Friede Publishers, (1933). First edition, second issue. 8vo.
Orig. cloth. Dust jacket. Very fine. Jaffe 1-362 1983 $400

STEINBECK, JOHN   The Winter of Our Discontent. New
York, 1961. 8vo. Cloth. An advance copy, being 1 of 500 copies
specially bound, sent out to friends of the author and his publisher.
A fine copy. In Our Time 156-755 1983 $300

STEINBRUCKER, CHARLOTTE   Briefe Daniel Chodowieckis an die
Grafin Christiane von Solms-Laubach. Strassburg: J.H. Ed. Heitz,
1927. 3 plates. 4to. Wrappers. Ars Libri 32-106 1983 $60

STEINHEIL, ADOLPH   Applied Optics. London, 1918. 1st
English ed. 2 vols., 8vo. Morrill 288-464 1983 $27.50

STEINMANN, ERNST   Das Grabmal Pauls III. in St. Peter
zu Rom. Leipzig, 1912. (4), 32, (2)pp., 14 collotype plates with
tissue guards. Lrg 4to. Wraps. Edition limited to 300 copies.
Ars Libri SB 26-228 1983 $85

STEINMANN, ERNST   Die Portraitdarstellungen des Michelangelo. Leipzig: Klinkhardt & Biermann, 1913. 107 superb collotype plates. 15 tipped-in text illus. Stout folio. Cloth. Lower
right corner of text portion waterstained. No. 1 of a limited
edition of 300 copies. From the library of Helena, Queen of Italy.
Ars Libri 33-250 1983 $550

STEJNEGER, LEONARD   Georg Wilhelm Steller, the Pioneer of
Alaskan Natural History. Cambridge: Harvard Univ., 1936. Plates,
folding map, colored frontis., dust wrapper. Argosy 710-7 1983 $35

STELLUTI, FRANCESCO   Persio Tradotto in verso schiolto
e dichiarato. Rome: G. Mascardi, 1630. With engraved title and
portrait of Persius, 1 full-page and 5 text engravings. Small 4to.
19th cent. red morocco, gilt- and blind-tooled, new endleaves.
First edition. Kraus 164-221 1983 $2,500

STELMASIAK, MIERCZYSLAW   Anatomical Atlas of the Human Brain and
Spinal Cord. Warsaw, 1956. 242 illus., cloth, folio. Argosy 713-
512 1983 $85

STENELAUS And Amylda. London: Griffith & Farran, 1858. First ed.,
illus. by G. Cruikshank, orig. wrappers bound in, three quarter mor.
with marbled endpapers. Loosely laid in is Cruikshank's autograph
taken from another source. Cloth case. MacManus 277-1218 1983 $85

STEP, E.   Shell Life. 1901. 32 plates and
numerous figures, cr. 8vo, cloth. A few annotations. Wheldon 160-
1232 1983 £12

STEP, E.   Wild Flowers. 1906. 342 illus. (2
coloured) from the author's photos, 2 vols., 8vo, original decorated
cloth. Wheldon 160-1630 1983 £15

STEPHANUS, HENRICUS   Caesarvm Vitae Post Svetonivm Tranqvillum
Conscriptae. Lvgd. Apvd Seb. Gryphivm, 1551. 2 vols. in 1, 12mo,
18th century half calf gilt, spine little rubbed, bookplate; good
copy. Ravenstree 95-111 1983 $95

STEPHANUS, HENRICUS   Histoire des Empereur S. Romains, Avec
Levrs Portraits en Taille-Douce... Paris, Nicolas le Graw, 1699.
Small 8vo, cont. calf, gilt, little worn, spine ends worn. Ravenstree
95-113 1983 $30

STEPHANUS, HENRICUS   Parodiae morales H. Stephani, in
Poetarum vet. (Geneva,) Excudebat Henricus Stephanus, 1575. 8vo,
modern boards, title soiled with small hole in blank portion, blank
upper tip torn away, some minor foxing. First edition. Ravenstree 95-
110 1983 $175

STEPHANUS, HENRICUS   Le Vite de Dodoci Caesari de Galo
Sventonio Tranqvillo Tradottee... Venetia, Balda-sare Cosantini (1554).
Small 8vo, 18th century calf gilt, spine little rubbed, label missing,
bookplate, upper margin cut close but nice, clean copy. Ravenstree
95-114 1983 $65

STEPHEN, HENRY JOHN   A Treatise on the Principles of Pleading
in Civil Actions. Philadelphia, 1837. 3rd American ed. Rebound in
1/4 sheep and linen sides, orig. label preserved, lightish spotting &
marginal dampstaining, very clean. Boswell 7-142 1983 $150

STEPHEN, JAMES FITZJAMES   A Digest of the Criminal Law. Macmillan,
1894. Half title. 5th edition. Orig. brown cloth. Mint. Jarndyce
31-219 1983 £15

STEPHEN, JOHN   The Dangers of the Country. London,
1807. New cloth and boards, leather label, very good. Reese 18-297
1983 $150

STEPHEN, LESLIE   English Literature and Society in the Eighteenth Century. London, 1904. First edition. Endpapers foxed. Bookplate. Nice. Rota 230-574 1983 £15

STEPHEN, LESLIE   Hours in a Library. London: Smith, Elder, & Co., 1874. First edition. Orig. cloth. Spine faded. Endsheets stained. Inner hinges cracked. MacManus 280-4865 1983 $20

STEPHEN, LESLIE   Hours in a Library. London: Smith, Elder, & Co., 1892. First revised edition. 3 vols. Orig. cloth. Former owner's signatures on flyleaves. Outer hinge of Vol. I a bit rubbed. Inner hinges weak. Very good. MacManus 280-4866 1983 $50

STEPHEN, LESLIE   The Life and Letters of Leslie Stephen. Duckworth & Co., 1910. Half title, front. port. Orig. olive cloth, v.g. Jarndyce 31-910 1983 £18.50

STEPHEN, LESLIE   Some Early Impressions. Hogarth Press, 1924. First edition. Bookplate. Signed autograph presentation inscription of A. Birrell. Very good. Rota 231-320 1983 £30

STEPHEN, LESLIE   Studies of A Biographer. London: Duckworth & Co., 1898. First edition. 2 vols. Orig. cloth. Very good. MacManus 280-4867 1983 $65

STEPHENS, ALEXANDER H.   A Constitutional View of the Late War Between the States... Philadelphia, (1868-1870). First edition. Illustrated. 2 vols., 8vo. Back cover of Vol. 2 stained and top of back hinge with half-inch tear. Morrill 290-516 1983 $40

STEPHENS, ALEXANDER H.   Recollections of Alexander H. Stephens. NY, 1910. First edition. Inner hinges broken, covers heavily rubbed and soiled. King 46-39 1983 $35

STEPHENS, HENRY   The Book of the Farm. NY, 1851. 450 illus., including engr. plates. 2 vols. 8vo, orig. stamped cloth, gilt-stamped spine. Argosy 716-1 1983 $150

STEPHENS, J. F.   Illustrations of British Entomology: Haustellata Vol. II. 1829. 12 hand-coloured plates, 8vo, cloth (trifle worn). Title-page rather soiled, a few marginal waterstains and a small nail-hole through pp. 1-26. A sound copy. Wheldon 160-1173 1983 £20

STEPHENS, JAMES   The Crock of Gold. London: Macmillan, 1912. First edition. Orig. cloth (rubbed). Worn. Covers stained. MacManus 280-4868 1983 $75

STEPHENS, JAMES   The Crock of Gold. London: Macmillan, 1912. First edition. 8vo. Green cloth, with the orig. dustwrapper. Spine torn. Traylen 94-780 1983 £40

STEPHENS, JAMES   The Crock of Gold. London, 1926. 4to. Boards, vellum spine, gilt, uncut edges, in the orig. dustwrapper. 12 mounted coloured illus. and decorative head- and tailpieces by Thomas Mackenzie. Limited edition of 525 copies, signed by the author. Traylen 94-781 1983 £135

STEPHENS, JAMES   Etched in Moonlight. New York, 1928. 8vo, boards and cloth, slipcase. One of 750 copies printed by William E. Rudge and signed by the author. First edition. Unopened. Duschnes 240-204 1983 $50

STEPHENS, JAMES   Five New Poems. London: A.T. Stevens for Flying Fame, 1913. First edition. Illus. by C.L. Fraser. Orig. pictorial wrappers. Large paper issue. Wrappers slightly worn and soiled. In a half-morocco slipcase (slightly rubbed). Good. MacManus 280-4870 1983 $100

STEPHENS, JAMES   Here Are Ladies. London: Macmillan & Co., 1913. First edition. Orig. cloth. Dust jacket (defective). Signed by author on the free endpaper. Bookplate of Geo. Ulizio on front endsheet. In a green half-morocco slipcase. Fine. MacManus 280-4871 1983 $125

STEPHENS, JAMES   Insurrections. Dublin: 1909. First edition. Tan boards and cloth. Corners bumped. Bradley 66-318 1983 $50

STEPHENS, JAMES   The Insurrection in Dublin. NY, 1916. Cover stained, edges bumped, else very good, owner's name. Quill & Brush 54-1301 1983 $35

STEPHENS, JAMES   Little Things. Freelands, Privately printed, 1924. Grey stiff wraps printed in black. With tipped in etching by Power O'Malley, signed in pencil. One of 200 copies. Very good. Houle 22-830 1983 $75

STEPHENS, JAMES   On Prose and Verse. New York: Bowling Green Press, 1928. Boards, paper lablel. First edition. From an edition of 1,000 copies printed by Rudge, this is one of a number of lettered copies in addition to the 51 signed copies. This is copy "A" and is inscribed: "To G.W. Sturgis with the compliments of James Stephens." Fine in lightly chipped glassine wrapper. Reese 20-931 1983 $175

STEPHENS, JAMES   Optimist. Gaylordsville, Slide Mountain Press, 1929. Decorated tan boards over sand cloth. One of 83 copies, signed by the author. Very good. Houle 22-831 1983 $185

STEPHENS, JAMES   Reincarnations. N.Y.: The Macmillan Co., 1918. First American edition. Orig. cloth-backed boards. Dust jacket (chipped). Very good. MacManus 280-4874 1983 $20

STEPHENS, JAMES   Strict Joy. N.Y.: The Macmillan Co., 1931. First American edition. Orig. cloth. Signed by Stephens on the front free endpaper. Spine very slightly faded. Very good. MacManus 280-4876 1983 $85

STEPHENS, JAMES   Theme and Variations. N.Y.: The Fountain Press, 1930. First edition. Orig. cloth. Limited to 892 copies signed by author. Fine. MacManus 280-4877 1983 $40

STEPHENS, WALTER   Blackfriars; or, the Monks of Old. London: Longman, 1864. First edition. 3 vols. Orig. cloth. Presentation copy, inscribed, "Thos. Wrigley Esq. with the compliments of The Author. July, 1864." Spines slightly darkened. Fine. MacManus 280-4879 1983 $250

STEPHENS, WALTER   Westminster Abbey. London: John Mortimer, 1854. First edition. 3 vols. Orig. cloth. All edges and corners a bit worn. Covers a bit soiled (library labels removed from front covers). Hinges cracked. Bookplates. Shelf numbers, and bookseller's tickets. MacManus 280-4880 1983 $85

STEPHENSEN, PERCY R.   Policeman of the Lord. The Sophistocles Press, (1929). With 7 full-page illus., 4to, orig. white parchment. A fine copy. Fenning 62-347 1983 £28.50

STEPHENSON, GRAHAM   Ida Milton. Tinsley Brothers, 1877. First edition, 3 vols. Half titles, 6 pp ads. vol. III. 3 vols. bound as one. Orig. pink cloth, spine faded, otherwise fine. Jarndyce 30-556 1983 £30

STEPHENSON, JOHN   Medical Zoology, and Mineralogy. London, 1838. First edition. 44 colored litho. plates, 4to, cloth (inner front hinge mended); ex-lib. Argosy 713-513 1983 $250

STEPHENSON, JOHN   Medical Zoology and Mineralogy. 1838. Roy. 8vo, new half morocco, hand-coloured and plain plates. Second issue. Some slight signs of use internally. Half-title discarded by the binder. Wheldon 160-102 1983 £150

STEPHENSON, JOHN   Medical Zoology, and Mineralogy. John Churchill, 1838. 8vo, 44 coloured and 2 uncoloured plates, orig. half calf, joints cracked, but covers held firmly. Bickersteth 75-263 1983 £110

STERBA, RICHARD   Introduction to the Psychoanalytic Theory of the Libido. NY 1942. Boards, extremities worn and starting to fray. King 46-528 1983 $20

STERBEECK, F. VAN   Theatrum Fungorum oft het tooneel der Campernoelien. Antwerp, 1675. Frontispiece, portrait and 36 engraved plates of figures (some folding), 4to, cont. half calf (joints cracking). A nice, clean copy. The very rare first edition. Wheldon 160-1901 1983 £900

STERBEECK, F. VAN   Theatrum Fungorum oft het tooneel der
Campernoelien. Antwerp, 1712. Second edition, frontispiece, portrait
and 36 plates of figures (some folding), 4to, cont. calf, gilt (trifle
worn). Half-title and frontispiece supplied in xerox, else contents
are original, complete and in good condition. Wheldon 160-1902 1983
£360

STERLAND, W. J.   The Birds of Sherwood Forest. London,
Reeve, 1869. 1st ed. 3 colored plates and a black and white lithograph. Small 8vo. Morrill 287-438 1983 $30

STERLING, GEORGE   The Binding of the Beast and Other
War Verse. San Francisco, 1917. First edition. 12mo, red cloth.
Argosy 714-706 1983 $50

STERLING, GEORGE   Lilith. N.Y., MacMillian, 1926.
First edition thus. Dust jacket (a little soiled) else very good -
fine. Houle 22-832 1983 $35

STERLING, GEORGE   Ode on the Opening of the Panama-
Pacific International Exposition. San Francisco; A.M. Robertson,
1915. Ltd. edition. One of 525 copies. Later inscription (1952)
from the San Francisco bookseller, John Howell. Argosy 714-707
1983 $75

STERLING, GEORGE   Ode on the Opening of the Panama-Pacific
International Exposition. S.F.: A. M. Robertson, 1915. Sq. 8vo,
linen-backed boards. First edition. One of 525 copies. Very nice.
Perata 28-168 1983 $50

STERLING, GEORGE   Sails Mirage and Other Poems. San
Francisco, 1921. 8vo. Cloth. From the library of Alexander Laing
with his autograph on front flyleaf. A vg-fine copy. In Our Time
156-756 1983 $25

STERLING, GEORGE   Sonnets to Craig. Long Beach, Upton
Sinclair, (1928). First edition. Frontis. portrait. Red cloth
stamped in black and gilt (spine trifle sunned) else, very good.
Houle 22-833 1983 $45

STERLING, GEORGE   Yosemite: An Ode. San Francisco,
1916. First edition. Illus. after photographs by W.E. Dassonville,
8vo, wraps. over boards. Inscribed by San Francisco bookseller
John Howell. Argosy 714-708 1983 $75

STERLING, JAMES   The Loves of Hero and Leander from the
Greek of Masaeus. Dublin: Printed by Andrew Crooke, 1728. First
edition, including the 8-page subscriber list, 12mo, wrapper, cut
close without serious loss and with some light old pencil marks on
some leaves towards end, a good sound copy. Fenning 60-398 1983
£35

STERLING, JOHN   Fitzgeorge. Eddingham Wilson, 1832.
First edition, 3 vols. Half titles, orig. boards, green cloth spines,
paper labels a little chipped. Jarndyce 30-557 1983 £90

STERLING, JOHN   Strafford. Moxon, 1843. First edition,
orig. brown cloth, v.g. Signed by Katy Susan Sterling, 'South
Place April 7th, 1851'. Jarndyce 31-912 1983 £26

STERLING, ROBERT W.   The Burial of Sophocles. Oxford:
Blackwell, 1914. Small quarto. Printed wraps. First edition.
Bookplate, and slight chipping of overlap edges, else about fine.
Reese 20-932 1983 $25

STERLING, STEWART   Alarm in the Night. N.Y., Dutton, 1949.
First edition. Dust jacket (light rubbing). Very good. Houle 22-
834 1983 $30

STERN, H. A.   Wanderings Among the Falashas. London,
1862. Folding map mounted on linen. 8 chromoxylographic plates,
numerous illus. Quarter calf, 1862. 8vo. Good. Edwards 1044-669
1983 £140

STERN, JOHN A.   To Hudson's Bay by Paddle and Portage.
(Chicago), privately printed, 1934. Illus. from photos by Kirkland
and Barber. Orig. boards. First edition. Ginsberg 46-153 1983
$50

STERNBERG, MAXIMILIAN   Die Akromegalie. Vienna, 1897. Illus.
Argosy 713-514 1983 $40

STERNE, LAURENCE   A Fragment in the Manner of Rabelais and
the Memoirs. Los Angeles, 1932. First edition. Sm. 8vo, black cloth,
hand-colored paper label. One of 125 copies. A very nice copy with
hand-colored decorations throughout. Perata 28-163 1983 $90

STERNE, LAURENCE   A Fragment in the Manner of Rabelais.
L.A., Stricker, 1932. Hand colored text decorations. Black cloth,
paper label, uncut. One of 125 copies. Printed by J.W. Robinson.
Houle 21-836 1983 $45

STERNE, LAURENCE   Letters from Yorick to Eliza. Printed by
G. Kearsley, and T. Evans, 1775. Small 8vo, lacking the half title,
orig. marbled boards with calf spine, joints cracked, label chipped.
Bickerseth 77-77 1983 £22

STERNE, LAURENCE   The Life and Opinions of Tristam
Shandy. London, 1760-67. 9 vols. bound in 8. 1st eds. of the last
7 vols.; 1st London ed. of the first 2 vols. orig. printed in York.
Contemporary calf, labels. Very good set, with the half-titles in
vols. 4, 5, 6, and 9 and signed by Sterne on the first page of text
in vols. 5, 7, and 9. Jenkins 155-1422 1983 $1,200

STERNE, LAURENCE   A Sentimental Journey through France and
Italy. London: Printed for T. Becket and P.A. De Hondt, in the
Strand, 1768. First edition. 2 vols. Small 8vo. Rebound in full
blue morocco. Spines heavily gilt, marbled endpapers, by Bedford.
Lacking the rare laid-in adv. slip. MacManus 280-4882 1983 $650

STERNE, LAURENCE   A Sentimental Journey through France and
Italy. London: Printed for T. Becket & P.A. De Hondt, in the Strand,
1768. New (Second) edition. 2 vols. 12mo. Orig. blue paper wrappers
with manuscript labels on spines. Wrappers stained. Inner hinges
reinforced with silk tape. Front wrapper of Vol. I almost detached.
Entirely uncut. In a folding cloth box. Unusually fine. MacManus
280-4883 1983 $450

STERNE, LAURENCE   A Sentimental Journey through France and
Italy. For T. Becket and P.A. De Hondt, 1768. First edition, 8vo,
2 vols. bound in one. List of subscribers. Lacks half-titles.
Early 19th century half calf, gilt (rubbed). Some slight stains.
Hannas 69-197 1983 £190

STERNE, LAURENCE   A Sentimental Journey Through France
and Italy, by Mr. Yorick. London: printed for T. Caddel, 1780.
Four parts in one volume, 12mo, bookplate, cont. tree calf gilt,
morocco label. Pickering & Chatto 19-71 1983 $250

STERNE, LAURENCE   A Sentimental Journey. B, (n.d.).
Illus. by T. H. Robinson. Pic. covers, spine wearing, very good.
Quill & Brush 54-1302 1983 $35

STERNE, LAURENCE   Voyage Sentimental. Lund, de l'imprimerie
du Prof. J. Lundblad, 1800. 8vo, list of subscribers. Cont.
marbled paper boards (rubbed). Hannas 69-198 1983 £25

STERNHEIM, CARL   Gauguin und van Gogh. Berlin: Die
Schmiede, 1924. Large 4to. Boards, 1/4 morocco. Raised bands.
T.e.g. Edition limited to 150 copies. Rare. Ars Libri 32-250
1983 $250

STERRETT, R. R. SITLINGTON   An Epigraphical Journey in Asia Minor.
Boston, 1888. 8vo, cloth. Salloch 385-188 1983 $60

STEUART, HENRY   The Planter's Guide. Edinburgh: John
Murray, London, 1828. 8vo, ad. slip at the end. 4 page publisher's
catalogue at the front, and another similar at the end, 6 fine
engraved plates, four of them after designs by W.M. Turner, orig.
boards, all uncut, new paper spine preserving the orig. printed label.
Bickersteth 77-242 1983 £75

STEUART, HENRY   The Planter's Guide. Edinburgh, 1828.
6 plates, full embossed calf, second edition. A very good copy.
K Books 307-210 1983 £54

STEUART, JAMES   Recherche Des Principes de L'Economie Politique. Paris, Didot L'Aine, 1789-90. First ed. in French, 5 vols., 8vo, cont. mottled calf, spines gilt, black morocco labels, worn, but internally a very good copy. This French edition is very rare. Pickering & Chatto 21-123 1983 $850

STEUART, JOHN A.   The Cap of Youth. Phila. & London: J.B. Lippincott Co., 1927. First edition. Orig. cloth. Publisher's slipcase (somewhat worn & soiled). One of 385 copies signed by Steuart. Bookplate. Near-fine. MacManus 280-4890 1983 $40

STEUART, THOMAS RUDDIMAN   The Reminiscences of... Privately Printed, 1900. Portrait. 8vo. Orig. cloth. Good. Edwards 1044-670 1983 £30

STEUER, ROBERT   Aetiological Principle of Pyaemia in Ancient Egyptian Medicine. 1848. 8vo. Wrappers. Fye H-3-557 1983 $20

STEVANS, CHARLES MC CLELLAN
Please turn to
STEVENS, CHARLES MC CLELLAN

STEVEN, WILLIAM   Memoir of George Heriot... Edinburgh, 1845. Small 8vo. Orig. calf, with Heriot's arms in gilt. 3 plates. Slightly rubbed. Gurney JJ-171 1983 £25

STEVENS, CHARLES MC CLELLAN   Lucy Ten Bar of Paradise Valley. Chicago, 1900. Illus. Pict. cloth. Photographs are by H.S. LeMay. Minor repair to title page. Scarce. Fairly nice copy. Jenkins 153-532 1983 $100

STEVENS, EDWARD F.   Thomas Bird Mosher of Portland, Maine. Portland: Southworth-Anthoensen Press, 1941. First edition. 12mo. Parchment-backed decorated boards. Limited to 350 copies. Karl Kup's copy. Some yellowing of spine. Oak Knoll 48-294 1983 $30

STEVENS, FRANK E.   The Black Hawk War. Chicago: by the author, 1903. Tall 8vo, cloth, paper label, g.t. Illus. with over 300 ports. & views. Argosy 716-221 1983 $45

STEVENS, GEORGE ALEXANDER   Distress upon Distress: or, tragedy in true taste. London: reprinted from the Dublin edition, for R. Griffiths, 1752. 8vo, wrappers, 1st London edition. Uncommon. Very good copy. Ximenes 64-506 1983 $175

STEVENS, GEORGE ALEXANDER   The dramatic history of Master Edward, Miss Ann, and others, the extraordinaries of these times. London: printed for J. Murray, 1785. 8vo, old half calf (some wear). 1st ed., 2nd issue. Frontis. and 13 satirical plates (one folding), some signed T. White. Also present is the rare leaf captioned "Zaphaniel's Exhortation to his Fellows in the Faith,", with an engraved vignette and letterpress text. Very scarce. Some foxing, but an excellent uncut copy. Ximenes 64-507 1983 $400

STEVENS, HAZARD   The Life of Isaac Ingalls Stevens. Boston and New York, 1900. First edition. 8vo. Orig. cloth. Portrait frontis. 38 plates, double-page facsimile, 14 maps (1 folding, 2 double page) and 4 text maps. 2 vols. Cont. green half calf gilt. T.e.g. Very slightly faded and stained. Bookplates. Fine. Edwards 1042-250 1983 £70

STEVENS, HENRY   Historical Nuggets. London, 1862. 2 vols. Blue cloth, fine. Reese 19-524 1983 $250

STEVENS, HENRY   Rare Americana... London: Stevens, ca. 1927. Plates, wrappers, slight soiling, splitting at hinges. Dawson 470-280 1983 $25

STEVENS, HENRY   Recollections of Mr. James Lenox of New York...London, 1886. First edition. Portraits. 12mo, orig. marbled boards, cloth back and corners, leather label, uncut, very nice. Morrill 290-517 1983 $75

STEVENS, HENRY N.   Lewis Evans: His Map of the Middle British Colonies in America: A Comparative Account... London: Henry Stevens, Son, and Stiles, 1905. 8vo. Red cloth stamped in gilt, t.e.g. Printed at the Chiswick Press. Oak Knoll 49-465 1983 $35

STEVENS, HENRY N.   Lewis Evans: His Map of the Middle British Colonies in America. London, 1905. Orig. printed wraps. First edition. Ginsberg 46-249 1983 $25

STEVENS, ISAAC I.   Address on the Northwest, Before the American Geographical and Statistical Society. Washington: G.S. Gideon, Printer, 1858. Orig. yellow printed wrappers. Presentation copy from author. Jenkins 153-533 1983 $300

STEVENS, ISAAC I.   Address on the Northwest. Wash., 1858. Orig. printed wraps. First edition. On title page "with the respect of the author." Ginsberg 47-845 1983 $225

STEVENS, ISAAC I.   Campaigns of the Rio Grande and of Mexico. N.Y., 1851. Half morocco. Ginsberg 47-501 1983 $450

STEVENS, ISAAC I.   Remarks of...of Washington, on the War Expenses of Washington and Oregon Territories Made Before the Committee of Military Affairs... Wash., 1860. Orig. printed wraps. First edition. Ginsberg 47-846 1983 $50

STEVENS, ISAAC I.   Speech of...of Washington, on the War Expenses of Washington and Oregon Territories Made Before the Committee of Military Affairs... Wash., 1860. Orig. printed wraps. First edition. Ginsberg 47-846 1983 $50

STEVENS, JOHN   The Royal Treasury of England. Printed for T. Tebb and J. Wilcox, 1725. 8vo, cont. panelled calf, spine gilt, lacking label, both joints cracked, but covers held firmly by the cords. First edition. Bickersteth 75-85 1983 £55

STEVENS, JOHN AUSTIN   Yorktown Centennial Handbook. N.Y., 1881. Illus. & maps, (scuffed). Ltd. edition without ads. Argosy 716-476 1983 $20

STEVENS, THADDEUS   Speech...in Favor of the Bill to Establish a School of Arts in the City of Philadelphia... Harrisburg, 1838. Disbound. Foxing. Felcone 22-191 1983 $20

STEVENS, THOMAS WOOD   The Morning Road. Chicago: Blue Sky Press, 1902. Slim octavo. Limited to 200 copies. Unbound copy in sheets. Mint. Bromer 25-147 1983 $30

STEVENS, WALLACE   The Auroras of Autumn. New York: Knopf, 1950. Cloth. First edition, one of 3,000 copies. A very fine copy in dust jacket. Reese 20-943 1983 $150

STEVENS, WALLACE   The Auroras of Autumn. New York: Knopf, 1950. 1st ed. Orig. purple cloth, dj. Mild sunning to spine of jacket only, else a mint copy. Jenkins 155-1165 1983 $125

STEVENS, WALLACE   The Auroras of Autumn. New York, 1950. Slightly nicked dustwrapper missing a tiny chip at tail of spine. First edition. Very good. Gekoski 2-180 1983 £35

STEVENS, WALLACE   The Collected Poems of Wallace Stevens. New York: Alfred A. Knopf, 1954. First edition. Large 8vo. Portrait. Orig. cloth. Dust jacket. One of 2500 numbered copies. Mint copy. Jaffe 1-370 1983 $350

STEVENS, WALLACE   The Collected Poems. New York, 1954. First edition. One of 2,500 printed, of which this is no. 15. Dustwrapper. Fine. Gekoski 2-182 1983 £85

STEVENS, WALLACE   The Collected Poems of... NY, 1954. Limited to 2500 copies, fine in very good dustwrapper with slight wear to edges. Quill & Brush 54-1304 1983 $125

STEVENS, WALLACE   Esthetique De Mal. Cummington, Mass.: Cummington Press, 1945. First edition. One of 300 numbered copies, unsigned. Orig. black morocco over green Natsume straw paper-covered boards, gilt. Uncut. Pen and ink drawings by Wightman Williams. Little foxing at inner joints. Fine. Jenkins 152-436 1983 $325

STEVENS, WALLACE   Harmonium. New York: Knopf, 1923.
Cloth and boards, first edition. Of the total printing of 1,500
copies, 500 were bound in the first binding, 215 in this binding, and
715 in a remainder binding. Paper label a bit rubbed, else a very
good, internally fine copy. Reese 20-936 1983 $250

STEVENS, WALLACE   Harmonium. NY, 1923. First issue binding, edges slightly worn, spine label darkened and stained, good or
better. Quill & Brush 54-1303 1983 $200

STEVENS, WALLACE   Harmonium. New York: Alfred A. Knopf,
1923. 8vo, blue cloth, paper label. Only 1500 copies were printed
of the first edition. In remainder binding of blue V cloth. Worn
at top and bottom of backstrip. First edition. Duschnes 240-205 1983
$75

STEVENS, WALLACE   Ideas of Order. New York: Knopf,
1936. Yellow boards, paper label. First this edition, third binding.
A very fine copy in dust jacket. 1,000 copies printed, 250 bound
thus. Reese 20-937 1983 $250

STEVENS, WALLACE   Ideas of Order. New York, 1936. Signature on free end-paper. First trade edition, in the striped binding.
Slightly chipped and soiled dustwrapper. Fine copy. Gekoski 2-178
1983 £100

STEVENS, WALLACE   The Man with the Blue Guitar and
Other Poems. New York, 1937. 8vo. Cloth. The dj is the second
jacket noted by Edelstein, with the word "conjunctions". A fine
copy. In Our Time 156-757 1983 $350

STEVENS, WALLACE   The Man with the Blue Guitar & Other
Poems. New York: Knopf, 1937. Yellow cloth. First edition, one
of 1,000 copies printed. Slight tanning of joints, else a fine
copy in the second state of the dust jacket; the spine of the jacket
is very slightly darkened. Reese 20-938 1983 $200

STEVENS, WALLACE   The Man with the Blue Guitar & Other
Poems. New York, 1937. 8vo, cloth. First edition. Only 1,000
copies printed. Duschnes 240-206 1983 $75

STEVENS, WALLACE   The Necessary Angel. N.Y., Knopf, 1951.
First edition. Dust jacket (small nicks) very good. Houle 22-835
1983 $125

STEVENS, WALLACE   The Necessary Angel. New York, 1951.
First edition. Fine in nicked dustwrapper browned at the top of the
lower panel. Jolliffe 26-492 1983 £75

STEVENS, WALLACE   Notes Toward a Supreme Fiction.
Cummington: The Cummington Press, (1943). Cloth and boards.
Second edition, one of 330 copies. A very fine copy, sans the
unprinted dust jacket. Reese 20-940 1983 $150

STEVENS, WALLACE   Opus Posthumous. New York: Alfred
A. Knopf, 1957. First edition. Large 8vo. Orig. cloth. Dust
jacket. Mint copy. Jaffe 1-371 1983 $85

STEVENS, WALLACE   Parts of a World. New York: Knopf,
1942. Cloth. First edition, one of 1000 copies. Dust jacket very
slightly tanned, else a fine copy.   Reese 20-939 1983 $200

STEVENS, WALLACE   Parts of a World. New York, 1942. First
edition. One of 1000 copies. Upper corners just a little bruised.
Repaired and partially defective dust wrapper. Very nice. Rota 230-
576 1983 £65

STEVENS, WALLACE   Parts of a World. New York: 1942.
First edition, first printing, first binding. Blue cloth. 1000 copies
only. Almost fine copy. Bradley 66-319 1983 $85

STEVENS, WALLACE   Three Academic Pieces. Cummington
Press, 1947. 1st ed., 1 of 102 numbered copies on Worthy Dacian
paper. Orig. Japanese style binding of plain tan wrappers inserted
around French-folded end papers of different stock than text, end-
over-end open sewing in black thread, black cloth wrap-around tie,
top and fore-edges uncut. Smyth-sewn with end papers of same stock as
text, etc. Very fine copy. Jenkins 155-1166 1983 $1200

STEVENS, WALLACE   Transport to Summer. New York: Knopf,
1947. Cloth and boards, paper label. First edition. About fine in
dust jacket. Inscribed by the author. Reese 20-942 1983 $1,500

STEVENS, WALLACE   Transport to Summer. New York, 1947.
Slight browning to inside hinges, dustwrapper sunned on the spine
and slightly frayed. Very good copy. Gekoski 2-179 1983 £40

STEVENS, WILLIAM   Memoirs of... 1812. First edition.
Printed by the Philanthropic Society. Uncut, orig. boards. Inscribed
Presentation copy from the author. Jarndyce 30-1142 1983 £10.50

STEVENS, WILLIAM   The Unjust Judge. Mansfield, Ohio,
1854. Orig. cloth. First edition. Ginsberg 46-586 1983 $50

STEVENS, WILLIAM OLIVER   Pistols at Ten Paces. Boston, 1940.
Illus, cloth, very good in slightly frayed dw. King 46-676 1983 $25

STEVENS-NELSON PAPER CO.   Specimens: A Stevens-Nelson Paper
Catalogue. (N.Y., 1953). 4to. Illus., in many colors. 8-page price
list & supplemental index & errata laid in. Morocco-backed marbled
boards, boxed. Fine. O'Neal 50-39 1983 $275

STEVENSON, ALAN   Account of the Skerryvore Lighthouse.
Edinburgh: By Order of the Commissioners of Northern Lighthouses,
1848. 1st ed., 4to, 34 folding and other plates of diagrams, charts,
maps, etc. Some water-staining, original cloth, gilt vignette on
upper board, gilt back, worn. Deighton 3-276 1985 £240

STEVENSON, JOHN   The Maid of Marlivale. Liverpool,
Hime & Son, & sold by Clementi, London, n.d. (mid-nineteenth century).
Engraved title. Folio, unbound. Small marginal repair on title.
Salloch 387-232 1983 $45

STEVENSON, JOHN HALL   Makarony Fables. London: Printed for
Circulation Amongst Private Subscribers Only, 1897. Orig. cloth.
Limited to 300 copies printed on hand-made paper. Bookplate. Fine.
MacManus 280-4888 1983 $25

STEVENSON, R. SCOTT   A History of Oto-Laryngology. Edinburgh, 1949. 8vo. Cloth. Dust wrapper. Gurney JJ-384 1983 £15

STEVENSON, ROBERT LOUIS   Across the Plains. (Hillsborough,
Calif., The L-D Allen Press, 1950). Tall 8vo, decorated cloth. With
illus. by Mallette Dean. One of 200 copies, handset on all rag
paper. Designed, printed and bound by Lewis and Dorothy Allen. Orig.
prospectus laid in. Duschnes 240-1 1983 $250

STEVENSON, ROBERT LOUIS   Across the Plains. (Hillsborough, Ca.):
The L-D Allen Press, (1950). With 8 illus. by Mallette Deane.
Editions ltd. to 200 copies, printed on all-rag oxbow paper. In
boards. Orig. prospectus laid in. Karmiole 72-3 1983 $250

STEVENSON, ROBERT LOUIS   Admiral Guinea. London, 1897. First
Separately Published edition. Of 1000 copies, this in one of 200 in
cloth. Extremities a little rubbed. Nice. Rota 231-589 1983 £20

STEVENSON, ROBERT LOUIS   Aes Triplex. (Boston): Printed for the
American Subscribers to The Stevenson Memorial, 1898. First separate
edition. Orig. parchment. Frontis. One of 160 copies printed by
the De Vinne Press for individual subscribers, this copy for Samuel P.
Avery, signed by the publisher Charles Fairchild. Foreedge of front
cover split. In a blue half-morocco slipcase. Fine. MacManus 280-
4889 1983 $185

STEVENSON, ROBERT LOUIS   An Apology for Idlers. Oakland, 1931.
First edition. No. 1 of 110 numbered copies. Illus. Very nice.
Rota 231-592 1983 £25

STEVENSON, ROBERT LOUIS   The Beach of Falesa. Los Angeles, Limited
Editions Club, 1956. First edition thus. 4to, illus. by Millard
Sheets. Half brown cloth over beige boards, printed in browns and
gilt, fore edge uncut, slipcase (a bit sunned) else fine. One of
1500 printed by the Ward Ritchie Press. Signed by the illustrator.
Houle 22-1193 1983 $75

STEVENSON, ROBERT LOUIS   The Best Thing in Edinburgh. SF, 1923. 4to, linen-backed boards, paper label. One of 250 (of 265) copies printed by the Kennedy-ten Bosch Co., under the direction of Haywood H. Hunt. Very nice. Perata 27-165 1983 $60

STEVENSON, ROBERT LOUIS   The Black Arrow. NY, 1883. Cover soiled and edges worn, good. Quill & Brush 54-1305 1983 $50

STEVENSON, ROBERT LOUIS   The Black Arrow. Cassell, 1923. 4to. Colour pictorial title. 14 colour plates. Pictorial endpapers. Green cloth, gilt. Spotted. Onlaid colour plate. Greer 40-247 1983 £25

STEVENSON, ROBERT LOUIS   The Castaways of Soledad. Buffalo, Privately printed, 1928. First edition. Illus. with 2 gravure plates and folding manuscript facs. Japan vellum over boards, uncut. Very good - fine. One of 75 copies. Presentation copy from the publisher, Thomas B. Lockwood. Typography by Frederick Ward. Printed by William E. Rudge. Houle 22-836 1983 $225

STEVENSON, ROBERT LOUIS   Catriona. L, 1893. First edition with 18 pages of ads, front hinge cracked, otherwise tight, near very good, inscription front end paper. Quill & Brush 54-1306 1983 $75

STEVENSON, ROBERT LOUIS   Catriona. London: Cassell, 1893. First edition. Orig. blue buckram (a little rubbed). Inner hinges cracked. Covers a little worn. MacManus 280-4891 1983 $30

STEVENSON, ROBERT LOUIS   A Child's Garden of Verses. London: Longmans, Green & Co., 1885. First edition. Orig. cloth. Corners a bit worn. Covers slightly soiled. A little browning to the endpapers. Previous owner's stamp on front free endpaper. In a half-morocco slipcase. Good. MacManus 280-4892 1983 $450

STEVENSON, ROBERT LOUIS   A Child's Garden of Verses. John Lane, 1896. First edition. Pictorial title. 19 plates & 140 text illus. Green cloth ornate gilt, head of spine tender. 16pp of ads. Greer 40-192 1983 £35

STEVENSON, ROBERT LOUIS   A Child's Garden of Verses. N.Y., Dodge, ca. 1910. Title page in red and black. Small 8vo, black cloth stamped in an art nouveau style. Very good. Houle 21-837 1983 $30

STEVENSON, ROBERT LOUIS   A Child's Garden of Verses. N.Y.: Garden City Pub., 1942. 4to. Cloth backed pictorial boards, dust wrap. Full-page color illus. by Joane plus color text illus. Fine. Aleph-bet 8-88 1983 $20

STEVENSON, ROBERT LOUIS   A Child's Garden of Verses. N.Y.: Heritage, 1944. 4to. Red cloth. Dust wrapper. Full-page color illus. Fine. Aleph-bet 8-100 1983 $25

STEVENSON, ROBERT LOUIS   A Child's Garland of Songs. Longmans, 1892. Many illus. Scarlet pictorial cloth gilt titling, a.e.g., fine. Hodgkins 27-194 1983 £25

STEVENSON, ROBERT LOUIS   A Christmas Sermon. New York, Charles Scribner's Sons, 1900. 8vo, orig. boards with cloth spine. First edition thus, printed by D.B. Updike at the Merrymount Press. Bickersteth 77-249 1983 £12

STEVENSON, ROBERT LOUIS   A Christmas Sermon. (S.F.): 1954. Sm. 4to, parchment boards, gilt. Printed in red & black with initial in blue, vignette in gold. One of 50 copies printed for Jane and Robert Grabhorn. Scarce. Perata 28-62 1983 $125

STEVENSON, ROBERT LOUIS   David Balfour, Being Memoirs of His Adventures at Home and Abroad. Charles Scribner's Sons, 1893. First American edition, half title, 4pp ads. Orig. mustard cloth blocked and lettered in maroon, silver & gilt. Very good. Jarndyce 31-914 1983 £20

STEVENSON, ROBERT LOUIS   David Balfour. New York, 1893. First American edition of "Catriona". Inscription (part of which has been untidily erased) on front endpaper. Bookplate. Very good. Rota 231-586 1983 £15

STEVENSON, ROBERT LOUIS   Diogenes in London. San Francisco: John Howell, 1920. Tall 8vo, dec. title-page border. Printed in red and black. Edition ltd. to 150 numbered copies, printed on handmade paper by Edwin and Robert Grabhorn. Orig. parchment-backed marbled boards. Fine. Karmiole 76-53 1983 $150

STEVENSON, ROBERT LOUIS   The Dynamiter. New York: Scribners, 1889. 1st American ed. Orig. red cloth, gilt. Very nice copy. Jenkins 155-1169 1983 $30

STEVENSON, ROBERT LOUIS   The Ebb-Tide. Chicago: Stone & Kimball, 1894. First edition. 12mo. Orig. dark green decorated cloth. Spine a bit dark. Very good. MacManus 280-4895 1983 $65

STEVENSON, ROBERT LOUIS   The Ebb Tide. L, 1894. First issue with 20 pages of ads, very slight interior foxing, gold cover rubbed, else very good. Quill & Brush 54-1311 1983 $60

STEVENSON, ROBERT LOUIS   The Ebb-Tide. London: William Heinemann, 1894. First English edition. Orig. pictorial cloth. Spine and covers a bit dark. MacManus 280-4898 1983 $50

STEVENSON, ROBERT LOUIS   The Ebb Tide. Ch., 1894. Rear cover slightly spotted, otherwise very good. Quill & Brush 54-1312 1983 $50

STEVENSON, ROBERT LOUIS   The Ebb-Tide. London, 1894. First English edition. 12mo, pict. cloth, uncut. With 20pp ads. dated August, 1894, at end. Argosy 714-710 1983 $20

STEVENSON, ROBERT LOUIS   Essays in the Art of Writing. Chatto & Windus, 1905. First edition, half title. Orig. dark blue cloth, t.e.g. Jarndyce 31-916 1983 £12.50

STEVENSON, ROBERT LOUIS   Father Damien. B, 1900. First American edition, hinges cracked, otherwise very good. Quill & Brush 54-1307 1983 $50

STEVENSON, ROBERT LOUIS   A Footnote to History. London: Cassell, 1892. First edition. Orig. cloth. Endpapers foxed. The McCutcheon copy. In a half morocco case. Very good. MacManus 280-4899 1983 $200

STEVENSON, ROBERT LOUIS   A Footnote to History. London, Cassell, 1892. First edition. Frontis. map. Gilt stamped green cloth. Very good. Houle 22-837 1983 $85

STEVENSON, ROBERT LOUIS   A Footnote to History: Eight Years of Trouble in Samoa. London: Cassell, 1892. 1st ed., with ads dated 5B.5.92. Orig. green cloth, gilt. Fine copy with a few unopened leaves. Jenkins 155-1170 1983 $25

STEVENSON, ROBERT LOUIS   History of Moses. Daylesford, Newton, 1919. Illus. with four facs. of Stevenson drawings, etc. Stiff printed blue wraps., stitched. Very good. Inscribed by A.E. Newton: "This is a first edition of R.L.S......" Houle 21-668 1983 $75

STEVENSON, ROBERT LOUIS   The History of Moses. Pennsylvania, 1919. 12mo, blue printed wraps., with illus. and page manuscript in facs. First edition. Duschnes 240-209 1983 $50

STEVENSON, ROBERT LOUIS   The History of Moses. Daylesford, Pa., A. Edward Newton, 1919. 1st ed., privately printed, in a limited quantity. Autographed by Newton. Tipped in is a newspaper offprint from the London Times by Edmund Gosse. Facsimiles. 12mo, orig. wrappers, fine. Scarce. Morrill 287-440 1983 $30

STEVENSON, ROBERT LOUIS   In the South Seas. London, 1900. 12mo, black buckram. First separately published English edition. Argosy 714-711 1983 $35

STEVENSON, ROBERT LOUIS   An Inland Voyage. London, C. Kegan Paul, 1878. 8vo, orig. cloth gilt, (a bit worn, old visiting card pasted to front end-paper, name stamped on fly-leaf, and former owner's name erased from half-title, inner hinges cracking), decent copy. One of but 750 copies only of the first edition. Ravenstree 96-250 1983 $185

STEVENSON, ROBERT LOUIS   An Inland Voyage. Boston, Roberts Brothers, 1888. 8vo, orig. cloth gilt (bit worn, little spotting, covers and spine age-darkened, name on end-paper, some pencil marks throughout and one note), decent copy of the first American edition. Ravenstree 96-251 1983 $95

STEVENSON, ROBERT LOUIS   Island Nights' Entertainments. London, Cassell, 1893. First English edition, first issue. Colored map and 27 plates by Gordon Browne and W. Hatherell. Pictorial blue cloth (minor rubbing and slight darkening), else good-very good. Houle 21-838 1983 $145

STEVENSON, ROBERT LOUIS   Island Night's Entertainments. London: Cassell & Co., 1893. Illus. 1st ed., 1st issue with ink correction in ads at front. Orig. pictorial blue cloth, gilt. Fine copy. Jenkins 155-1171 1983 $90

STEVENSON, ROBERT LOUIS   Island Nights Entertainment. London: Cassell & Co., 1893. First edition. 8vo. Orig. cloth. In a half-morocco folding box. Good. MacManus 280-4902 1983 $50

STEVENSON, ROBERT LOUIS   Island Nights' Entertainments. London: Cassell & Co., 1893. First English edition, first issue. Illus. Orig. decorated cloth. Spine darkened. Spine ends rubbed. Inner hinges weak. Good. MacManus 280-4900 1983 $40

STEVENSON, ROBERT LOUIS   Island Night's Entertainments. London, 1893. First edition, second issue, with the ads. dated 7G-3.93. Spine a little darkened. Bookplate. Very nice. Rota 231-587 1983 £20

STEVENSON, ROBERT LOUIS   Kidnapped. (London): Cassell, 1886. Folding map. 1st ed., 1st issue. Orig. red cloth, gilt. Light spotting of covers, else an unrubbed copy. Jenkins 155-1172 1983 $175

STEVENSON, ROBERT LOUIS   Kidnapped. L, 1886. First issue point but not cloth, map, edges slightly rubbed, spine slightly stained, some minor interior foxing, near very good. Quill & Brush 54-1308 1983 $150

STEVENSON, ROBERT LOUIS   Kidnapped. London, 1886. First edition, first issue, with the uncorrected text on pp.40,64 &101. Eight leaves of ads. dated "5G.4.86". Covers rather bruised and the map has been repaired at the folds. Bookplate. Good. Rota 231-584 1983 £25

STEVENSON, ROBERT LOUIS   Kidnapped. London, Cassell, 1887. First illus. edition, 8vo, color frontis. map and 16 plates. Dark green cloth (lacking rear endpaper). 3/4 morocco slipcase. Very good. Bret Harte's copy. With his signature, dated London, August, 1889. Houle 21-839 1983 $350

STEVENSON, ROBERT LOUIS   Kidnapped. N.Y., MacMillian, 1925. First edition. Illus. with 2 gravure plates and folding manuscript facs. Japan vellum over boards, uncut. One of 75 copies. Presentation copy from the publisher, Thomas B. Lockwood. Typography by Frederick Ward. Printed by William E. Rudge. Very good - fine. Houle 22-836 1983 $225

STEVENSON, ROBERT LOUIS   Lay Morals & Other Papers. London, 1911. First edition. Argosy 714-712 1983 $20

STEVENSON, ROBERT LOUIS   A Lodging for the Night. East Aurora, Roycroft Press, 1902. Frontis. portrait. Hand colored designs in text. 3/4 red morocco, gilt decorated and stamped spine, t.e.g., uncut (one corner bruised). One of 100 copies on Japan vellum, signed by Hubbard and the illuminator, Josephine Droyer. Very good. Houle 22-839 1983 $175

STEVENSON, ROBERT LOUIS   The Manuscripts of Robert Louis Stevenson's Records of a Family of Engineers. Chicago: Walter Hill, 1929. Quarto, facsimiles. 1st ed., 1 of 300 copies printed by the Torch Press. Orig. cloth-backed marbled boards, uncut. Fine copy, nearly as new. Jenkins 155-1174 1983 $20

STEVENSON, ROBERT LOUIS   The Master of Ballantra. London: Cassell, 1889. 1st ed. Orig. red cloth, gilt. Very good copy. Jenkins 155-1175 1983 $35

STEVENSON, ROBERT LOUIS   The Master of Ballantrae. Lon., 1889. Cover soiled and spine edges frayed, good or better, owner's name, gift inscription, bookplate. Quill & Brush 54-1313 1983 $75

STEVENSON, ROBERT LOUIS   Memories and Portraits. London: Chatto & Windus, 1887. First edition. 12mo. Orig. cloth. Inner hinges cracked. Foxed. MacManus 280-4906 1983 $25

STEVENSON, ROBERT LOUIS   Memories and Portraits. London, 1887. First edition. Fine. Argosy 714-713 1983 $25

STEVENSON, ROBERT LOUIS   The Merry Men and Other Tales and Fables. L, 1887. First edition with 32 pages of ads dated Sept., shaken, covers very rubbed, rear hinge cracked, good. Quill & Brush 54-1314 1983 $50

STEVENSON, ROBERT LOUIS   The Merry Men. London, 1887. First edition, first issue, with the ads. dated September, 1886. Spine a little creased. Bookplate. Nice. Rota 231-585 1983 £30

STEVENSON, ROBERT LOUIS   The Merry Men, and Other Tales and Fables. Chatto & Windus, 1887. First edition, half title, 32 pp ads. Orig. blue dec. cloth sl. rubbed and dulled. Jarndyce 31-913 1983 £24

STEVENSON, ROBERT LOUIS   Moral Emblems. London: S.L. Osbourne & Co., (1882). First edition. Illus. Orig. printed, self-wrappers. Covers slightly soiled. With one small tear at the fold. Very good. MacManus 280-4907 1983 $850

STEVENSON, ROBERT LOUIS   Moral Emblems & Other Poems. London, 1921. First collected edition. 19 woodcuts by the author. Argosy 714-714 1983 $24

STEVENSON, ROBERT LOUIS   More New Arabian Nights: The Dynamiter. London, 1885. First edition. Wrappers. Backstrip a little rubbed and worn. Very good. Rota 231-583 1983 £45

STEVENSON, ROBERT LOUIS   More New Arabian Nights. London: Longmans, 1885. First edition. Orig. cloth. Outer hinge partly torn. In a wooden slipcase. MacManus 280-4908 1983 $50

STEVENSON, ROBERT LOUIS   An Object of Pity. N.Y.: Dodd, Mead & Co., 1900. First American edition. Orig. boards. Limited to 110 copies. Spine worn. MacManus 280-4909 1983 $20

STEVENSON, ROBERT LOUIS   The Old Pacific Capital: Story of Monterey. SF, 1944. 12mo, cloth-backed decorated bds., paper label. Illustrated. One of 500 copies. A very good copy. Perata 27-28 1983 $35

STEVENSON, ROBERT LOUIS   Poems. (Boston) Privately printed for Edmund Brooks, 1917. First edition thus. Small 4to, one of 20 copies. Presentation copy from the author. Half cloth. Very good. Houle 22-1220 1983 $85

STEVENSON, ROBERT LOUIS   Prince Otto. London: Chatto & Windus, 1885. First edition. Orig. decorated cloth. With the ads dated "January 1885." Spine darkened. Half morocco case. Good. MacManus 280-4910 1983 $125

STEVENSON, ROBERT LOUIS   St. Ives. NY, 1897. First edition, spine darkened, name with inscription, otherwise very good. Quill & Brush 54-1310 1983 $60

STEVENSON, ROBERT LOUIS   St. Ives Being the Adventures of a French Prisoner in England. London: Heinemann, 1898. First English edition. 8vo. Orig. cloth. Spine a trifle rubbed. Very good. MacManus 280-4912 1983 $20

STEVENSON, ROBERT LOUIS   The Silverado Squatters. N.Y.: Scribners, 1923. Folio. Orig. cloth, slipcase. One of 380 copies printed by John Henry Nash. Woodcuts by Howard W. Willard. Head of spine slightly torn. Fine. MacManus 280-4911 1983 $145

STEVENSON, ROBERT LOUIS   Some Letters. N.Y.: Ingalls Kimball, 1902. First edition. Frontis. port. Orig. decorated boards. One of 50 copies. Contains five letters from Stevenson to A. T. Haddon. Spine and covers a bit faded and worn. Former owner's signature. Very good. MacManus 280-4913   1983 $85

STEVENSON, ROBERT LOUIS   Songs with Music from a Child's Garden of Verses. T. C. & E. C. Jack, n.d. (ca. 1915). 4to, colour frontis. Colour title vignette. 12 colour text illus. Colour pictorial cream boards, rubbed. Orig. dust wrapper. Greer 40-219   1983   £24

STEVENSON, ROBERT LOUIS   Strange Case of Dr. Jekyll and Mr. Hyde. London: Longmans, Green and Co., 1886. First edition. 8vo. Orig. pink decorated cloth. The Alfred Sutro copy with his bookplate. Slightly rubbed. Heath 48-423   1983   £150

STEVENSON, ROBERT LOUIS   Dr. Jekyll and Mr. Hyde. London, 1948. First edition with these illus. (by M. Peake). Lettering on spine a little faded. Torn dust wrapper. Very nice. Rota 231-470   1983   £15

STEVENSON, ROBERT LOUIS   Tales and Fantasies. Chatto & Windus, 1905. First edition, half title. Orig. dark blue cloth, t.e.g. Jarndyce 31-915   1983   £12.50

STEVENSON, ROBERT LOUIS   Three Plays. London, 1892. First edition. 8vo, cloth, uncut; backstrip faded. First edition. Argosy 714-715   1983 $20

STEVENSON, ROBERT LOUIS   Treasure Island. London, Cassell, 1883. First edition. Frontis. map. Ads dated 5 G-783. Full red crushed levant morocco, gilt stamped ship device on spine, watered silk endpapers, edges extra gilt (original cloth bound in). Cloth slip case. With a detailed colored leather inlay on upper cover of Long John Silver. Houle 22-840   1983 $875

STEVENSON, ROBERT LOUIS   Treasure Island. London, 1883. First edition. Spine darkened and covers marked and some slight foxing throughout. Nice. Rota 231-582   1983   £250

STEVENSON, ROBERT LOUIS   Treasure Island. Phila.: The Anderson Books, 1930. First of this edition. Orig. light-brown decorated cloth. Illus. with one fold-out, two page color plate. Worn publisher's glassine jacket. Fine. MacManus 280-4917   1983 $150

STEVENSON, ROBERT LOUIS   Treasure Island. London, 1949. Numerous black and white drawings, many of which are full-page, by Mervyn Peake. Chipped and slightly torn dustwrapper. Very good. Jolliffe 26-403   1983   £65

STEVENSON, ROBERT LOUIS   Treasure Island. NY: n.d. First American edition. Sq 8vo, green cloth, blind-stamped design on front cover, gilt. With 12 tipped-in color plates plus drawings in b/w by Dulac. Inscription on fly; a very nice copy. Perata 27-41   1983 $75

STEVENSON, ROBERT LOUIS   Underwoods. London: Chatto & Windus, 1887. First edition. Orig. unbound sheets. One of 50 large paper copies numbered and signed by R. and R. Clark and printed on hand-made paper. First and last sheet rather soiled. First few leaves slightly waterstained. Good. MacManus 280-4918   1983 $175

STEVENSON, ROBERT LOUIS   Vailima Letters. London: Methuen & Co., 1895. Large paper edition. Illus. Orig. buckram with paper label. Presentation copy from W.E. Henley inscribed: "To T.W.G. W.E.H. 31.1.'96." One of 125 copies printed on wove paper with watermark "Unbleached Arnold." Spine slightly faded and a trifle worn. Good. MacManus 280-4919   1983 $175

STEVENSON, ROBERT LOUIS   Vailima Letters. London, 1895. Tall 8vo, buckram; uncut, (backstrip rubbed). Ltd. first edition. Large paper edition ltd. to 125 numbered copies. With the Mildred & Robert Woods Bliss ex-libris. Argosy 714-716   1983 $50

STEVENSON, ROBERT LOUIS   Virginibus Puerisque and Other Papers. London: C. Kegan Paul & Co., 1881. First edition. Orig. decorated cloth. Covers slightly soiled. Corners and edges very slightly worn. In a half-morocco slipcase. Very good. MacManus 280-4921   1983 $250

STEVENSON, ROBERT LOUIS   Virginibus Puerisque and Other Papers. London, C. Kegan Paul, 1881. 8vo, orig. cloth gilt, bit faded and lightly soiled, but a decent copy. First issue of the first edition. Ravenstree 96-252   1983 $140

STEVENSON, ROBERT LOUIS   Voluntaries For an East London Hospital. London: Stott, 1887. First edition, with the subscription slip. Orig. cloth. Covers a bit soiled. MacManus 280-4922   1983 $25

STEVENSON, ROBERT LOUIS   Weir of Hermiston. London: 1896. First edition, first issue. Ads dated March. Dark blue cloth. Bookplate. Covers worn, edges dusty. Bradley 66-320   1983 $35

STEVENSON, ROBERT LOUIS   When the Devil Was Well. Boston: Bibliophile Society, 1921. Ports. & facs. Tall 8vo, 1/2 vellum. Ltd. edition. Fine. Argosy 714-717   1983 $40

STEVENSON, ROBERT LOUIS   The Works. London, 1906-07. Pentland edition. 20 vols. 8vo. Buckram, t.e.g., others uncut. Limited to 1,550 numbered sets, with a frontis. to each vol. Traylen 94-783   1983   £130

STEVENSON, ROBERT LOUIS   Works. N.Y., Scribner, 1921-23. Valima edition. Frontis. and facs. Blue cloth, paper labels, uncut and mostly unopened. All in pub.'s slipcases, most in glassine dust jackets. One of 1030 sets. 26 vols. complete. This set initialled by Lloyd Osbourne, who wrote the introduction. Fine. Houle 22-841   1983 $525

STEVENSON, ROBERT LOUIS   The Works. London, 1922. The Vailima edition. 26 vols. Roy. 8vo. Dark blue buckram, gilt, t.e.g., others uncut. Numerous portraits and facsimiles. Limited to 1,060 numbered sets printed on hand-made paper. Traylen 94-784   1983   £180

STEVENSON, SINCLAIR, MRS.   Bridget's Fairies. R.T.S., n.d. (1919). Colour frontis. Title vignette & 22 text illus. Blue cloth, gilt, mounted colour plate. Greer 40-193   1983   £25

STEVENSON-HAMILTON, J.   Our South African National Parks. (Cape Town, 1940). Coloured frontispiece and 100 coloured cigarette cards, 4to, boards. Wheldon 160-440   1983   £12

STEWARD, J. A.   The Myths of Plato. New buckram with label. 8vo, cloth. Salloch 385-693   1983 $45

STEWART, ALVAN A.   Legal Argument Before the Supreme Court of N.H. NY, 1845. Orig. pr. wraps. Argosy 716-24   1983 $20

STEWART, C.   The History of Bengal. London, 1813. Folding map. 4to. Last few leaves repaired at spine, foxing in three gatherings. New half morocco. Good. Edwards 1044-672   1983   £85

STEWART, CECIL   Topiary. London, (1954). 8vo, 1/2 orange cloth over decorated boards. Color-engr. by Peter Barker-Mill. Fine. Perata 27-52   1983 $85

STEWART, DUGALD   Elements of the Philosophy of the Human Mind. Philadelphia, 1793. 8vo. Contemporary calf. 1st Am. ed. Lacks label; front hinge slightly cracked; top blank portion of title torn off. Morrill 289-218   1983 $27.50

STEWART, DUGALD   The Works. Cambridge, 1829. First collected edition. 7 vols. 8vo. Cont. full maroon morocco, gilt, elaborately gilt panelled sides, gilt panelled spines, edges gilt. Traylen 94-786   1983   £240

STEWART, FRANCES ANNE, MARCHIONESS OF LONDONDERRY   A journal of a three months' tour in Portugal... London, 1843. First edition. 8vo. Orig. pink cloth. Frontis. and three plates. A trifle rubbed and soiled. Ximenes 63-637   1983 $80

STEWART, GEORGE R.   Bret Harte. Boston, Houghton, 1931. First edition. Illus. Signed and inscribed by the author. Dust jacket (small nicks), very good. Houle 71-1164   1983 $45

STEWART, JAMES DOUGLAS   Open Access Libraries, their Planning, Equipment and Organisation. Grafton & Co., 1915. First edition, illus. Half title, orig. olive cloth. Jarndyce 31-224 1983 £10.50

STEWART, JOSEPH B.   The Bastile: Testimony Before a "Select Committee" 18 and 29 of January 1873... Washington: Gibson Brothers, 1873. Half calf with morocco label. Nice. Jenkins 153-650 1983 $150

STEWART, MRS. PHILO PENFIELD A Worker, and Workers' Friend. New York, Author, 1873. 1st ed. Portrait. 12mo, spine faded and frayed at top. Morrill 288-468 1983 $20

STEWART, PURVES   Nerve Injuries & Their Treatment. London, 1916. First edition. 97 illus. Argosy 713-516 1983 $35

STEWART, WILLIAM M.   Bondholders' Conspiracy to Demonetize Silver. San Francisco, 1885. Orig. printed wraps. First edition. Ginsberg 47-662 1983 $50

STEWART, WILLIAM M.   Reminiscences of ... Of Nevada. New York: Neale, 1908. First edition. Portrait. T.e.g. Original cloth, gilt. Light ex-library else a fine copy. Jenkins 151-241 1983 $85

STEWART, WILLIAM M.   Reminiscences. New York, 1908. 1st ed. Portrait. Clark 741-366 1983 $46.50

STIEBEN, E.   La Pampa. Rio de Janeiro, 1946. Map and numerous illustrations, royal 8vo, boards. Wheldon 160-441 1983 £15

STIEDA, LUDWIG   Untersuchungen uber die Entwickelung der Glandula Thymus... Leipzig, 1881. 4to. Old quarter-cloth, wrappers bound in. With 2 plates. Gurney JJ-385 1983 £10.50

STIEHL, HENRY S.   The Life of a Frontier Builder: Autobiography of... Salt Lake City, 1941. Frontis. and illus. Orig. cloth. Fine copy of the 1st ed. Jenkins 153-536 1983 $50

STILES, EZRA   A History of Three of the Judges of King Charles I... Hartford: Printed by Elisha Babcock, 1794. 19th century full pebbled morocco, gilt-extra, by Matthews. Portrait. Two folding maps. Plates. A fine copy, complete with the ad. leaf. Reese 18-198 1983 $325

STILES, HENRY R   Bundling; Its Origin, Progress and Decline in America. Albany: 1871. Cloth. Bradley 66-670 1983 $20

STILES, HENRY R.   The Civil, Political, Professional and Ecclesiastical History and Commercial and Industrial Record of the County of Kings and the City of Brooklyn. N.Y., New York, (1882). 2 vols. Plates. Very thick quarto, 3/4 morocco. Orig. binding. Felcone 21-80 1983 $175

STILES, JOSEPH C.   Modern Reform Examined; or, The Union of North and South on the Subject of Slavery. Philadelphia, 1857. Argosy 710-26 1983 $35

STILES, ROBERT   Four Years Under Marse Robert. N.Y.: Neale, 1903. 1st ed. Pictorial cover. Frontis. Covers slightly faded. Good copy. Jenkins 153-800 1983 $125

STILES, WILLIAM H.   An Address Delivered Before the Georgia Democratic State Convention, Assembled at Milledgeville, July 4th, 1856. Atlanta, 1856. Orig. printed wraps. First edition. Ginsberg 46-278 1983 $35

STILL, JAMES   River of Earth. New York: 1940. First edition. Pictorial beige linen. Chipped dust jacket. Bradley 66-321 1983 $40

STILL, JOHN   The Jungle Tide. Edinburgh: 1930. First edition. Frontis. Red cloth. Coffee stains on fore-edges, white dust jacket soiled, otherwise nice. Bradley 66-433 1983 $25

STILLE, CHARLES J.   Northern Interests and Southern Independence. Philadelphia: William S. & Alfred Martien, 1863. Orig. printed wraps., a bit chipped. Karmiole 71-38 1983 $25

STILLINGFLEET, BENJAMIN   An Essay on Conversation. London: Printed for L. Gilliver and J. Clarke... Folio, disbound. First edition. A good copy. Quaritch NS 7-127 1983 $200

STILLINGFLEET, EDWARD   An answer to some papers lately printed, concerning the authority of the Catholick Church... London: printed for Ric. Chiswel, 1686. First edition. Small 4to. Disbound. Ximenes 63-590 1983 $30

STILLINGFLEET, EDWARD   An Answer to Some Papers (by Charles II). Printed for Ric. Chiswell, 1686. Complete in spite of pagination jump, with the imprimatur leaf, 4to, wrapper, a very good copy. Fenning 61-425 1983 £16.50

STILLINGFLEET, EDWARD   The Council of Trent Examin'd and Disprov'd by Catholick Tradition. Printed for H. Mortlock, 1688. All published, 4to, wrapper, a very good copy. Fenning 61-426 1983 £16.50

STILLINGFLEET, EDWARD   A Discourse Concerning the Nature and Grounds of the Certainty of Faith, in Answer to J.S. his Catholick Letters. Printed for Henry Mortlock, 1688. First edition, 4to, wrapper, a very good copy. Fenning 61-427 1983 £14.50

STILLINGFLEET, EDWARD   The Mischief of Separation. Printed for Henry Mortlock, 1680. Third edition. 4to. Fenning 62-349 1983 £18.50

STILLINGFLEET, EDWARD   Protestant Charity. Printed by M. Flesher, for Henry Mortlock, 1861. 4to. Fenning 62-350 1983 £14.50

STILLINGFLEET, EDWARD   A Sermon Preached Before the King at White-Hall, March 7.1678.9. Printed for Henry Mortlock, 1679. 4to. Fenning 62-353 1983 £12.50

STILLINGFLEET, EDWARD   A Sermon Preached on the Fast-Day, November, 13. Printed by Margaret White, for Henry Motlock, 1679. Fifth edition. 4to. Fenning 62-352 1983 £18.50

STIMPSON'S Boston Directory. Boston, 1845. Cloth-backed printed boards (a bit worn). Felcone 22-138 1983 $50

STINE, THOMAS OSTENSON   Scandinavians on the Pacific, Puget Sound. (Seattle, Denny-Coryell), 1900. Illus. Orig. cloth. First edition. Ginsberg 47-848 1983 $85

STIRLING, PATRICK JAMES   The Australian and Californian Gold Discoveries, and Their Proble Consequences. Edinburgh, 1853. Folded graph. Orig. cloth, top of spine chipped. First edition. Ginsberg 47-849 1983 $150

STISSER, JOHANN ANDREAS   De Machinis Fumiductoriis Curiosis... Hamburg: Gottfried Liebezeit, 1686. First edition. 4 copper engravings. Small 4to. Modern boards. Kraus 164-239 1983 $320

STISTED, GEORGIANA M.   The true life of Capt. Sir Richard F. Burton. London: H.S. Nichols, 1896. 8vo. Portrait. Orig. blue cloth. Slightly rubbed. Adelson Africa-174 1983 $50

STIX, ALFRED   H.F. Fuger. Wien: Manz, 1925. 60 hinged collotype plates (19 tipped-in color). Title tissue guards. Large 4to. Boards, 3/4 leather. T.e.g. Edition limited to 1225 numbered copies. Ars Libri 32-229 1983 $325

STOBART, J. C.   The Glory that was Greece. NY, 1935. 97 plates, many text illus., 8vo, cloth. Salloch 385-398 1983 $25

STOBART, J. C.   The Grandeur that was Rome. London, 1912. Illus. 4to, gilt-decorated cloth. Salloch 385-399 1983 $30

STOCKDALE, JOHN   The Whole Proceedings of the Trial of...
for a Libel on the House of Commons...December, 1789. Printed for
John Stockdale, 1790. First edition, 8vo, wrapper, a very good copy.
Fenning 62-354 1983 £24.50

STOCKER, RICHARD   Pharmacopoeia Officinalis Britannica.
London, 1810. New edition. 8vo. Half-morocco. Some foxing.
Gurney JJ-386 1983 £30

STOCKLEY, V.   Bungalow Ballads. Published by Mrs. V.
Stockley at the 16th Bengal Lancers' Press, January, 1901. Sm.8vo.
Decorated boards. Presentation copy, "To my dear 'devoted' with love
from her friend Joan Stockley, 9.XII.03". Good. Edwards 1044-673
1983 £15

STOCKTON, FRANK R.   The Bee-Man of Orn and Other Fanciful
Tales. New York: Scribners, 1887. 1st ed., early state on laid
paper. Orig. green cloth, gilt. Tiny snag at crown, else a fine
copy. Jenkins 155-1179 1983 $25

STOCKTON, FRANK R.   The Captain's Toll-Gate. NY, 1903. No.
37 of 160 deluxe copies, signed by wife, artist and a clip signature
of author, bibliography included, fine. Quill & Brush 54-1316 1983
$100

STOCKTON, FRANK R.   Girl at Cobhurst. N.Y., Scribner, 1898.
First edition. Pictorial cloth binding by Margaret Armstrong. Fine.
Houle 21-846 1983 $45

STOCKTON, FRANK R.   The Late Mrs. Null. New York:
Scribners, 1886. 1st ed., 1st issue. Orig. pictorial cloth. Fine
copy. Jenkins 155-1180 1983 $20

STOCKTON, FRANK R.   A Story-Teller's Pack. New York, 1897.
1st ed. Orig. decorated cloth, gilt. Nice copy. Jenkins 155-1183
1983 $22.50

STOCKTON, RICHARD   Speech of the Hon. Richard Stockton,
Delivered in the House of Representatives... Georgetown, 1814.
Dsb., very good. Reese 18-462 1983 $35

STODDARD, CHARLES WARREN   In the Footprints of the Padres.
San Francisco: A.M. Robertson, 1912. New and enlarged edition.
Intro. by C. Phillips. Plates. Cloth and boards. Dawson 471-
279 1983 $20

STODDARD, CHARLES WARREN   Poems. San Francisco, 1867. First ed.
Tall 8vo, green cloth. Very fine. Argosy 714-718 1983 $50

STODDARD, HERBERT L.   The Bobwhite Quail. NY 1931. 1st ed.
Illus, cloth, letter affixed to f.e.p., covers a bit dull. King 46-
677 1983 $80

STODDART, JANE T.   The Girlhood of Mary Queen of Scots
from her Landing in France in August 1548 to her Departure from France
in August 1961. (1908). 8vo, 6 plates, cloth. Bickersteth 77-174
1983 £18

STOKELEY, EDITH K.   Pantaloon. N.Y.: Doran, (1927). 4to.
Orange cloth. Some cover soil. Illus. by G.A. Kay. Full-page color
plates and black & whites. Very good. Aleph-bet 8-146 1983 $27

STOKER, BRAM   Dracula. New York, Doubleday & McClure,
1899. 8vo, orig. pictorial cloth gilt (bit age-darkened, spine
ends chipped, name on end-leaf) uncut copy. Rare first American
edition. Ravenstree 96-255 1983 $425

STOKER, BRAM   Personal reminiscences of Henry Irving.
New York: Macmillan, 1906. 2 vols., 8vo, original magenta cloth
(trifle rubbed, spines a little faded). 1st American edition.
Numerous plates. Ximenes 64-313 1983 $30

STOKES, ANSON PHELPS   Memorials of Eminent Yale Men. New
Haven, 1914. 2 vols., thick, large 4to, cloth, g.t. Ltd. edition.
Argosy 716-126 1983 $75

STOKES, LESLIE   Oscar Wilde. N.Y., Random (1938).
First edition, dust jacket. Very good. Houle 21-940 1983 $30

STOKES, MARGARET   Early Christian Art in Ireland. Chapman
& Hall, 1887. First edition. Folding table and 106 full-page and
other illus. 8vo. Orig. cloth. Fenning 60-399 1983 £10.50

STOKES, WHITLEY   The Old-Irish Glosses at Wurzburg and
Carlsruhe. For the Philological Societies of London and Cambridge,
1887. 8vo, recent boards. Fenning 60-400 1983 £28.50

STOKES, WILL   The Vaulting Master: Or, The Art Of
Vaulting. Oxon, printed for Richard Davis, 1652. 2nd ed., small
oblong 4to, engraved frontis. by Glover, 15 finely engraved plates,
calf-backed marble boards, some staining. Deighton 3-278 1983 £450

STOKES, WILL E.   Episodes of Early Days in Central and
Western Kansas. Great Bend, 1926. Illus. 1st ed. Vol. 1 only one
published. Jenkins 153-538 1983 $35

STOKES, WILLIAM   On Supra-Candyloid Amputation of the
Thigh. London, 1870. First edition. 8vo, sewn. Argosy 713-517
1983 $175

STOLBERG, FREDERIC LEOPOLD   Travels through Germany, Switzerland,
Italy and Sicily. London, 1802. 4 vols., folding map and 18 folding
plates, cont. tree calf, gilt spines, a little browned throughout and
bindings a little worn. Second edition. K Books 301-173 1983 £140

STOLL, WILLIAM T.   Silver Strike. Boston, 1932. Cloth,
good. Reese 19-526 1983 $50

STONE, A. R.
Please turn to
STONE, REYNOLDS

STONE, DORIS   Archaeology of the North Coast of
Honduras. Cambridge, 1941. 99 illus. Folio. Wrappers. Worn.
Ars Libri 34-484 1983 $75

STONE, DORIS   Archaeology of the North Coast of
Honduras. Cambridge, 1941. Many illus, map. Folio, pr. wrs.
Inscribed by the author. First 8 pp edges water damaged, and few
crudely taped. Argosy 710-63 1983 $35

STONE, EDMUND   Some Reflections on the Uncertainty of
Many Astronomical and Geographical Positions... For J. Marks,
London, 1766. 8vo, cont. green calf, joints cracked but sound, from
the library of the Earl of Bute with engraved bookplate and gilt
arms on sides. Only edition. A fine copy. Quaritch NS 5-103 1983
$550

STONE, ELIAB   A Discourse Delivered at Reading...
Salem, 1811. Disbound. Reese 18-359 1983 $20

STONE, IRVING   Sailor on Horseback. Cambridge:
Houghton, Mifflin, 1938. Illus. 1st ed. Orig. cloth. Fine copy
signed by Stone. No dj, but uncommon in the 1st ed. Jenkins 155-
843 1983 $30

STONE, JACOBLEON   A Reply to Bishop Colenso's Attack
Upon the Pentateuch. San F., 1863. Orig. cloth, first edition.
Ginsberg 47-174 1983 $75

STONE, JAMES S.   Woods and Dales of Derbyshire. Phila.,
Jacobs, 1894. Edition limited to 400 copies. Illustrated. 4to,
ex-library. Morrill 290-519 1983 $20

STONE, REYNOLDS   A Book of Lettering. London, 1935.
First English edition. Covers slightly spotted. Soiled, foxed,
chipped, and torn dustwrapper. Very good. Jolliffe 26-494 1983 £45

STONE, ROBERT   A Flag for Sunrise. New York, 1981.
8vo. Wraps. Uncorrected proof copy. Fine. In Our Time 156-759
1983 $100

STONE, ROBERT   A Hall of Mirrors. Boston, 1967. 8vo. Cloth. Dust jacket has a few small tears. Some light rubbing to bottoms edge of the cloth, price clipped, else a fine copy. In Our Time 156-758 1983 $125

STONE, RUFUS BARRETT   McKean, the Governor's County. New York, 1926. 1st ed. Presentation from author with 2 pasted snapshots. Illus. 8vo. Morrill 289-498 1983 $27.50

STONE, WILLIAM L.   Life of Joseph Brant-Thayendanegea. NY, 1838. First edition. 2 vols. Illus., engr. plates, extra engr. titles (lacks 2 maps). 8vo, designed cloth (lightly spotted, usual foxing). Argosy 716-222 1983 $50

STONE, WILLIAM L.   Reminiscences of Saratoga and Ballston. NY, 1875. 1st ed., 12mo, illus., dec. cloth, ex-library. Argosy 710-365 1983 $30

STONE, WILLIAM L.   Tales and Sketches, Such as They Are. New York, 1834. 2 vols. Orig. cloth, paper spine labels (labels rubbed). First edition. Felcone 22-236 1983 $35

STONEBACK, H. R.   Cartographers of the Deus Loci: The Mill House. North Hills: Bird & Bull Press, 1982. 1st ed., limited to 240 copies. Orig. vellum-backed pictorial paste-paper boards, uncut, plain dj, as issued. Mint copy printed by Henry Morris on paper made by Dard Hunter. Jenkins 155-993 1983 $135

STONEBACK, H. R.   Cartographers of the Deus Loci: The Mill House. North Hills: Bird & Bull Press, 1982. First edition. 8vo. Calf vellum spine and Morris' paste-paper sides. Printed on a limited supply of Dard Hunter's own paper. Limited to 240 numbered copies. Loosely inserted is a "note to standing order customers." With illus. by William Osborne. Oak Knoll 49·36 1983 $90

STONEHOUSE, J. H.   Green Leaves. 1931. In orig. 5 parts, orig. blue printed wraps. Very good. Jarndyce 30-228 1983 £28

STONEMAN, VERNON C.   John and Thomas Seymour, Cabinetmakers in Boston, 1794-1816. Boston: Special Publications, 1959-1965. More than 290 illus. (numerous color). 4to. Cloth. With a supplement containing more than 75 illus. Ars Libri 32-631 1983 $225

STONG, PHIL   Horses and Americans. N.Y., Stokes, 1939. First edition. 4to, 103 illus. Endpapers and chapter headings by Kurt Weise. Pictorial dust jacket with a reproduction of a Frederic Remington painting (short tears, creases). Very good - fine. Houle 22-1182 1983 $60

STONG, PHIL   Horses and Americans. New York, 1939. 1st ed. Frontispiece in color & illus. from old prints and photos. 4to. Morrill 288-469 1983 $20

STOPES, C.   The Bacon-Shakespeare Question Answered. London: Turbner & Co., 1889. Second edition. Orig. cloth. Corrected and enlarged. Very good. MacManus 280-4654 1983 $25

STOPES, MARIE CARMICHAEL   Contraception (Birth Control): Its Theory, History, and Practice. London: John Bale, Sons & Danielsson, 1923. First edition. 4 full-page plates. Green cloth. Very good. Bradley 66-434 1983 $125

STOPES, MARIE CARMICHAEL   Contraception (Birth Control). John Bale, 1923. First edition, with 4 plates, 8vo, orig. cloth, gilt. Fenning 60-401 1983 £45

STOPFORD, EDWARD A.   A Hand-book of Ecclesiastical Law and Duty, for the Use of the Irish Clergy. Dublin: Hodges, Smith, 1861. First edition. Fenning 62-355 1983 £21.50

STOPFORD, JOHN S. B.   Sensation and the Sensory Pathway. London: Longmans, Green and Co., 1930. First edition. Gach 94-754 1983 $20

STOPPARD, TOM   Lord Malquist & Mr. Moon. (London): Anthony Blond, (1966). 1st ed. Red boards. Fine in lightly worn dj. Bradley 63-120 1983 $85

STORBEL, ABNER J.   The Old Plantations and Their Owners of Brazoria County. Houston, 1930. First edition. Orig. printed wraps. Jenkins 152-847 1983 $35

STORER, J.   The Wild White Cattle of Great Britain. (1880). New edition, 12 illustrations in the text, 8vo, original cloth. Wheldon 160-609 1983 £40

STOREY, DAVID   This Sporting Life. London, 1960. First English edition. Nicked dustwrapper. Near fine. Jolliffe 26-496 1983 £45

STORIES of the American Revolution. Phila., 1852. Sq. 18mo, numerous engr., frontis. hand-colored. A.e.g., (minor brown spots). Argosy 716-477 1983 $35

STORM, COLTON   Fifty Texas Rarities. Ann Arbor: The William L. Clements Library, 1946. Plates. Orig. printed wrappers. One of fifty copies printed for Mr. Everett D. Graff. Fine. Jenkins 152-563 1983 $75

STORM, COLTON   Invitation to Book Collecting. New York: R.R. Bowker Co., 1947. First edition. 8vo. Cloth, dust jacket. Spot on back of jacket. Oak Knoll 49-369 1983 $35

STORM, COLTON   Invitation to Book Collecting. N.Y., Bowker, 1947. First edition. Illus. Dust jacket. Pub.'s prospectus laid in loose. Fine. Houle 21-148 1983 $25

STORM, HANS OTTO   Of Good Family. New York: Swallow & Morrow, 1948. Cloth. First edition. Fine in slightly used dust jacket. Reese 20-945 1983 $25

STORM, MARIAN   Hoofways into Hot Country. Mexico, 1939. 2 folding maps, 8vo, pr. wrs., illus. by Silvanio Rodriguez. Inscribed. Argosy 710-310 1983 $30

STORRIE, J.   The Flora of Cardiff. Cardiff, 1886. 8vo, cloth, title page a trifle foxed. Wheldon 160-1631 1983 £20

STORY, ALFRED T.   Fifine. London: George Redway, 1887. First edition. 2 vols. Decorated cloth. Inscr. on the title-page to Vol. I: "Presented by the Publisher." With the stamp of The Daily Chronicle on each title-page. Spines slightly darkened or soiled. All edges very slightly worn. A little light foxing. Very good. MacManus 280-4933 1983 $135

STORY, JOSEPH   Commentaries on Equity Jurisprudence. Boston, 1849. 2 vols. 5th ed. Bound in 1/4 leather, covers & spines double gilt-ruled, with matching red morocco labels, gilt-ruled & lettered. Very attractive set. Boswell 7-143 1983 $150

STORY, JOSEPH   Discourse...in Commemoration of the First Settlement of Salem. Boston, 1828. Orig. pr. wraps., (loose). Argosy 716-283 1983 $35

STORY, JOSEPH   The Miscellaneous Writings of Joseph Story. Boston: Charles C. Little and James Brown, 1852. Large 8vo, orig. green cloth, rubbed. Karmiole 71-66 1983 $45

STORY, JOSEPH   The Power of Solitude. Salem: Barnard B. Macaulty, 1804. Cont. calf. A fine copy. Reese 18-265 1983 $75

STORY, ROBERT   Love and literature; being the reminiscences, literary opinions, and fugitive pieces of a poet... London: Longman, 1842. First edition. 8vo. Orig. purple-brown cloth. Ximenes 63-250 1983 $80

STORY, ROBERT   The Magic Fountain, with Other Poems. W. Crofts, 1829. First edition, later half maroon calf, v.g. Jarndyce 31-868 1983 £25

STORY, THOMAS   A Journal of the Life of Thomas Story.
Newcastle upon Tyne: Printed by Isaac Thompson and Company, 1747.
Folio. Cont. calf, expertly rebacked. A fine copy. First edition,
the publisher's issue. Reese 18-63 1983 $325

STORY, THOMAS   A Journal of the Life of Thomas Story.
Newcastle upon Tyne: Printed by Isaac Thompson and Company, 1747.
Folio, old calf, worn, joints cracked, but binding sound. First
edition. Bickersteth 77-79 1983 £36

STORY, WILLIAM W.   Castle St. Angelo and The Evil Eye.
London: Chapman & Hall, 1877. First edition. Illus. Orig. red cloth.
Covers darkened at edges. Extremities a little rubbed. Very good.
MacManus 280-4934 1983 $50

THE STORY of the Stubby Dub. W. Westall, n.d. 4to. Title vignette.
7 colour plates (1 double) & 17 other illus., loose. Light internal
wear. Colour pictorial boards, worn. Greer 40-175 1983 £18

THE STORY of the tragedy of Agis. London: printed for M. Cooper,
1758. 8vo, wrappers, 1st edition. Very rare. Ximenes 64-282 1983
$500

STOUGHTON, JOHN   Notices of Windsor in the Olden Time.
Bogue, 1844. 1st edn. Frontis. within elab. decor. border printed
in red, 2nd frontis. by W. Evans, engr'd by E. Findon, red & black
decor. title page, each page text set within 'rustic' border. Brown
wavy grain blind stamped cloth, mostly unopened & uncut. Bkstrip
faded with sl. wear at top, frontis foxed, vg copy. Hodgkins 27-330
1983 £16.50

STOUT, BENJAMIN   Narrative of the Loss of the Ship
Hercules...London, Printed: Hudson, Re-Printed...1800. 24mo, old
limp leather wrappers. Small piece lacking from last leaf, affecting
a few words each page; few other tears. Morrill 290-520 1983 $75

STOUT, REX   Broken Vase. N.Y., Farrar, (1941).
First edition. Orange cloth. Very good. Houle 21-848 1983 $75

STOUT, REX   The Silent Speaker. New York: Viking,
1946. 1st ed. Orig. cloth, dj. Fine in near fine dj. Jenkins 155-
1184 1983 $35

STOVER, JOHANN   Disputatio physica de quaestione illa:
Utrum ventriculum chylo nutriatur... Herborn: Christopher Corvin,
1593. Woodcut vignette on title. 4to. Boards. Ms. inscription on
title. Kraus 164-223 1983 $250

STOW, SARAH D. L.   History of Mount Holyoke Seminary,
S. Hadley, Mass. South Hadley: by the Seminary, 1887. Many illus.
Gilt-dec. cloth. G.t., (lib. bookplate). Argosy 716-284 1983
$25

STOWE, HARRIET BEECHER   Earthly Care, a Heavenly Discipline.
Boston & Cleveland: Jewett, 1853. 1st ed. thus. Orig. green
printed wrappers, a.e.g. Fine copy of this very scarce printing.
Jenkins 155-1185 1983 $85

STOWE, HARRIET BEECHER   The Key to Uncle Tom's Cabin: Presenting the Original Facts and Documents Upon Which the Story is Founded...
London: Clarke, Beenton, (1853). 1st English ed. Orig. green
cloth, gilt. End paper heavily printed in blue with ads for other
works, and an inserted leaf at front for a companion vol. Very good
copy of an uncommon ed. Jenkins 155-1186 1983 $35

STOWE, HARRIET BEECHER   A Key to Uncle Tom's Cabin. B, 1853.
Newly bound in black cloth, interior foxed, bottom corner of first few
pages chipped. Quill & Brush 54-1318. 1983 $30

STOWE, HARRIET BEECHER   A Key to Uncle Tom's Cabin. Boston,
1853. First edition. Tall 8vo, (faded, scuffed, few pp. torn & foxed,
but extant). Argosy 716-25 1983 $25

STOWE, HARRIET BEECHER   A Key to Uncle Tom's Cabin. Boston,
1853. Ads. Cloth. Very good. Felcone 20-176 1983 $25

STOWE, HARRIET BEECHER   The Mayflower. New York, Harper, 1844.
12mo, orig. cloth quite worn, soiled, endpapers foxed from pressing
leaves. Ravenstree 96-256 1983 $35

STOWE, HARRIET BEECHER   Men of Our Times. Hartford, 1868.
First edition. Thick 8vo, orig. cloth. Fine. 18 steel engraved
portraits. Fine. Argosy 714-720 1983 $45

STOWE, HARRIET BEECHER   My Wife and I. New York: J.B. Ford
& Co., 1872. First edition, front. & illus. 8pp ads. Orig. brown
cloth, v.g. Jarndyce 31-919 1983 £36

STOWE, HARRIET BEECHER   The Pearl of Orr's Island. Sampson
Low, 1862. First English edition, half title, front. Orig. purple
cloth, spine faded, v.g. Jarndyce 31-918 1983 £35

STOWE, HARRIET BEECHER   Poganuc People. N.Y., (1878). First
edition. Illus. Argosy 716-163 1983 $25

STOWE, HARRIET BEECHER   Sunny Memories of Foreign Lands. B,
1854. 2 vols., covers chipped, some signatures loose, minor interior
staining, good, bookplate. Quill & Brush 54-1319 1983 $25

STOWE, HARRIET BEECHER   Uncle Tom's Cabin. Boston: Jewett,
1852. 2 vols. 1st ed., 1st issue. Orig. light brown cloth, gilt.
Spine ends lightly rubbed, but a fine copy with a non-authorial
owner's inscription in the 2nd vol. Jenkins 155-1187 1983 $1500

STOWE, HARRIET BEECHER   Uncle Tom's Cabin. Boston: John P.
Jewett & Company, and Cleveland: Jewett, Proctor & Worthington, 1852.
Two vols. Gilt cloth. First edition in clothbound form. There is
some slight chipping at the toe of each spine, with a neat repair in
the bottom of the rear joint of volume two, and some spotting from some
liquid on the cover of volume one. Two bookplates have been neatly
removed. Reese 20-946 1983 $1,250

STOWE, HARRIET BEECHER   Uncle Tom's Cabin; or Life Among the
Lowly. Boston: 1852. Two vols. First issue with "Hobart &
Robbins" slug on copyright page. Rebacked with orig. spines laid-
down, endpapers renewed. Some wear to edges, else nice tight copy.
Bookplates of John Taylor Bottomley. First edition. Bromer 25-
112 1983 $450

STOWE, HARRIET BEECHER   Uncle Tom's Cabin. Boston: Jewett,
1852. 2 vols. 1st ed., later issue, later binding. Orig. black
cloth, gilt. Very good rubbed set. Jenkins 155-1188 1983 $100

STOWE, HARRIET BEECHER   Uncle Tom's Cabin. London: Clarke &
Co., 1852. Heavily gilt pictorial cloth. Engraved vignette title-
page. Frontis. A trifle shaken and some slight shelf-rubbing, but
a very good copy. Illus. after Cruikshank. Reese 20-947 1983 $75

STOWE, HARRIET BEECHER   Uncle Tom's Cabin: or, Life Among the
Lowly. Boston, 1852 2 vols, illus, pict. cloth, spine edges
chipped. Argosy 710-163 1983 $30

STRABO   Geographia. (Venice): Vindelinus de
Spira, 1472. Final blank not present. Large and small initials
supplied in red. Cont. lemmata in red ink. Large folio. Cont.
binding of wooden boards with blind-stamped leather back, 2 clasps.
From the library of Harrison D. Horblit. 4 leaves and corners of
last 4 leaves repaired, 2 leaves stained in margins. Kraus 164-224
1983 $35,000

STRACHAN, JAMES MORGAN   Juggernaut: its present state...
London: Hatchard, 1843. First edition. 8vo. Sewn, as issued.
Presentaiton copy, inscribed on the title from the author to the
Rev. Dr. Jarvis. Title dusty. Very good copy. Ximenes 63-218
1983 $80

STRACHAN, WALTER   Poems. Skelton Press, 1976. 8vo,
2 copper-engraved illus., uncut in quarter canvas, matching slip-case,
blue Ingres paper boards, fine. 160 numbered copies signed by author
and artist (Charles Marq, engraver). Deighton 3-279 1983 £100

STRACHEY, LYTTON   Books and Characters, French and
English. 1922. First edition, half title, front. Orig. green cloth,
paper label. Jarndyce 31-999 1983 £12.50

STRACHEY, LYTTON   Characters And Commentaries. London:
Chatto & Windus, 1933. First edition. 8vo. Frontis. Orig. cloth.
Dust jacket. Very fine copy. Jaffe 1-374 1983 $45

STRACHEY, LYTTON   Elizabeth and Essex. N.Y.: Gaige, 1928.
First edition. Orig. cloth-backed boards. Limited to 1000 copies
signed by author. Good. MacManus 280-4936 1983 $50

STRACHEY, LYTTON   Elizabeth And Essex. London: Chatto
& Windus, 1928. First edition. 8vo. Illus. Orig. cloth. Dust
jacket, slightly chipped. Fine copy. Jaffe 1-373 1983 $35

STRACHEY, LYTTON   Elizabeth and Essex. London: Chatto &
Windus, 1928. First edition. Illus. Orig. brown buckram. Front
inner hinge strained. Fine. MacManus 280-4935 1983 $30

STRACHEY, LYTTON   Pope. Cambridge at the University
Press, 1925. First edition, half title. Orig. paper wraps., label,
sl. chipped, v.g. Jarndyce 31-1000 1983 £10.50

STRACHEY, LYTTON   Portraits in Miniature. London: Chatto
& Windus, 1931. First edition. Orig. cloth. Dust jacket. Fine.
MacManus 280-4937 1983 $35

STRACHEY, LYTTON   Portraits in Miniature, and Other
Essays. London, 1931. First edition. Argosy 714-721 1983 $20

STRAHAN, EDWARD   The Highways and Byways of American
Travel. Philadelphia, 1878. First edition. 8vo, minute gash on
back hinge. Many fine illustrations. Morrill 290-521 1983 $27.50

STRAHAN, KAY CLEAVER   Footprints. GC, 1929. Minor cover
soiling, else bright, near fine in lightly frayed and chipped, very
good dustwrapper with wraparound blurb still present. Quill & Brush
54-1320 1983 $35

STRAHORN, ROBERT E.   The Resources and Attractions of Idaho
Territory. Boise City (printed at Omaha): 1881. First edition.
Illus., including large folding map. Pictorial and printed wrappers.
Covers worn but sound copy. Bradley 66-555 1983 $185

STRANAHAN, C. H.   A History of French Painting from Its
Earliest to Its Latest Practice. New York, 1888. 1st ed. Repro.
of 16 representative paintings. 8vo. Inner hinges slightly cracked.
Morrill 289-547 1983 $20

STRAND, PAUL   Time in New England. New York, 1950.
Large 8vo. Cloth. With 106 photographs by Paul Strand. Fine copy
in slightly worn dj. In Our Time 156-760 1983 $100

STRANG, H. MRS.   The Rose Fairy Book. H. Frowde, n.d.
4to. Colour frontis. 11 colour plates & many other illus. White
decorated cloth. Onlaid round colour plate. Very attractive.
Greer 39-71 1983 £45

STRANG, WILLIAM   The Earth Fiend. London: Elkin
Mathews and John Lane, 1892. Folio. 11 orig. etchings, each
mounted and within a paper mat, and with a tissue guard sheet.
Each etched plate is signed by Strang and Frederick Goulding,
engraver. Edition ltd. to 55 numbered copies, signed by Strang &
Goulding. Orig. calf-backed cloth; spine rubbed and cloth soiled.
Karmiole 71-86 1983 $500

STRANGMAN, T.   Indian Courts and Characters. London,
1931. 8 plates. 8vo. Orig. cloth. Good. Edwards 1044-674 1983
£16

STRASBURGER, E.   Rambles on the Riviera. 1906. 87
coloured illustrations, royal 8vo, cloth, small tears in spine.
Wheldon 160-443 1983 £15

STRATFORD, NICHOLAS   A Discourse of the Pope's Supremacy.
Printed for Richard Chiswell, 1688. First edition, all published,
4to, wrapper. Fenning 61-430 1983 £14.50

STRATFORD, NICHOLAS   The Lay-Christian's Obligation to Read
the Holy Scriptures. Printed for Richard Chiswell, 1687. First
edition, 4to, wrapper, a nice copy. Fenning 61-431 1983 £10.50

STRATFORD, NICHOLAS   The People's Right to Read the Holy
Scripture Asserted. Printed for Richard Chiswell, 1687. First
edition, 4to, wrapper, the imprimatur leaf a little dusty, but
otherwise a nice copy. Fenning 61-432 1983 £12.50

STRATTON, MARY CHASE   Ceramic Processes. (Detroit), 1941.
Presentation copy, inscribed and signed by author. Drawings. Cloth.
Covers slightly darkened. King 45-364 1983 $35

STRAUB, PETER   Ishmael. Turret Books, (1972). 8vo.
Wraps. 1st and only ed. 1 of 100 copies signed by author. A fine
copy. In Our Time 156-761 1983 $200

STRAUS, RALPH   Dickens: A Portrait in Pencil. Victor
Gollancz, 1928. First edition, half title, front. illus. Half calf
by Riviere & Son, spine gilt, green label, t.e.g. Fine. Jarndyce
31-620 1983 £20

STRAUS, RALPH   John Baskerville, a Memoir. Cambridge:
University Press for Chatto and Windus, 1907. First edition. 4to.
Red buckram. 14 full page plates. Limited to 350 copies. Covers
faded, foxed. Part of cloth at head of spine missing. Oak Knoll
48-17 1983 $145

STRAUS, RALPH   A Whip for the Woman. London: Chapman
& Hall, 1931. First edition. Orig. cloth. Dust jacket (spine and
covers a trifle faded). Presentation copy to Dennis Wheatley inscribed:
"To Dennis Wheatley....Ralph Straus, 16 Dec. 1935." Covers slightly
spotted. Edges a trifle foxed. Very good. MacManus 280-4941 1983
$65

STRAUSS, JOHANN   Philomenen-Walzer. Vienna, Tobias
Haslinger, 1835. First edition. Plate #6894. Dated in the pub.'s
postscript on the last page. Engraved title with vignette of crown
and heraldry over a star, engraved music. Oblong folio, unbound.
Salloch 387-234 1983 $80

STREATER, JOHN   The continuation of this session of
Parliament justified. London, 1659. First edition. Disbound.
8vo. Ximenes 63-105 1983 $35

STREET, GEORGE G.   Che! Wah! Wah! or the Modern
Montezumas in Mexico. Rochester, N.Y., 1883. Illus. with wood
engravings (frontis. tinted) and 33 mounted albumen photographs on
printed mounts by R.D. Cleveland. Folding map. Orig. gilt-illus.
pebble grain morocco. First and only edition. A fine copy.
Felcone 21-101 1983 $450

STREET, GEORGE G.   Che! Wah! Wah! Rochester, 1883.
Rebound in orig. stamped pict. cloth, (few pp. misplaced). Argosy
716-293 1983 $400

STREETER, FLOYD BENJAMIN   The Kaw the Heart of a Nation. New
York, 1941. Illus. 1st ed. Jenkins 153-540 1983 $30

STREETER, FLOYD BENJAMIN   Michigan Bibliography. Lansing, 1921.
2 vols. Cloth. Index. Ex-library. Hinges broken, spines frayed.
Standard reference in dire need of bringing up to date. King 45-120
1983 $150

STREETER, FLOYD BENJAMIN   Michigan Bibliography. Lansing: Mich.
Historical Commission, 1921. 2 vols., cloth, medium wear, 1 hinge
cracked and repaired. Dawson 470-284 1983 $65

STREETER, FLOYD BENJAMIN   Prairie Trails & Cow Towns. Boston:
Chapman & Grimes, 1936. First edition. Illus. Brown cloth. Some
pages roughly opened, tear on page 26 with no loss of text. Very good
copy. Bradley 66-572 1983 $175

STREETER, JOHN W.   The Fat of the Land, the Story of an
American Farm. New York: MacMillan, 1904. 1st ed. Orig. pic.
cloth, gilt. Fine copy. Jenkins 155-1189 1983 $20

STREETER, THOMAS W.   Bibliography of Texas 1795-1845.
Cambridge: Harvard Univ. Press, 1955-60. 5 vols., cloth in dws, the
latter rather used but the vols. fine. Dawson 470-283 1983 $600

STREETER, THOMAS W.   The Celebrated Collection of Americana.
N.Y., 1966-69. 7 vols. Illus., some in color. Tall 8vo, cloth,
first edition. Ginsberg 47-852 1983 $450

STREETT, WILLIAM B.   Gentlemen Up. NY: The Derrydale
Press, 1930. 4to, 30 leaves of plates. Edition ltd. to 850 copies.
Green dec. cloth, sl. soiled at extremities. Karmiole 76-37 1983
$85

STRICKLAND, AGNES   Lives of the Queens of England...
London, 1841. First edition. 12 vols. 8vo. Orig. embossed pink
cloth, gilt. Portrait and vignette title-page to each vol. Traylen
94-789 1983 £48

STRICKLAND, AGNES   Lives of the Queens of England...
London, 1844-48. 12 vols. 8vo. Orig. blue embossed cloth, gilt.
Portrait and vignette title-page to each vol. Traylen 94-790
1983 £68

STRICKLAND, AGNES   Lives of the Queens of England. London,
Colburn, 1852. New edition. Profusely illustrated. Full tan
calf, spines richly decorated in gilt with floral and scrolling
designs, contrasting red and blue leather spine labels, covers ruled
in gilt, gilt inner dentelles, t.e.g., marbled endpapers (a few nicks,
one volume cracked), else very good. 8 vols. Houle 22-847 1983
$300

STRICKLAND, W.   Catholic Missions to Southern India.
London, 1865. First edition. 8vo. Orig. cloth. Presentation copy.
Good. Edwards 1044-675 1983 £40

STRICTURES, in verse, on the performances at the Theatre-Royal, Norwich, toward the close of the season of 1799. Norwich: printed and
sold by Bacon;...n.d. (1799). Small 4to, sewn (stitching loose).
First edition. Very rare. Outer margins trimmed a bit close, half-
title present. Ximenes 64-508 1983 $400

STRID, A.   Wild Flowers of Mount Olympus. Kifissia,
1980. 2 coloured maps and 109 coloured plates of 465 illus. from
photos, 4to, cloth. Wheldon 160-1770 1983 £55

STRINDBERG, AUGUST   There Are Crimes and Crimes. British
Broadcasting Corp., 1929. First edition. Illus. Orig. wrappers.
Fine. MacManus 279-3856 1983 $25

STROBEL, ABNER J.   The Old Plantations and Their Owners.
Houston, 1930. Revised ed. Scarce. Jenkins 153-593 1983 $35

STROMBECK, FREDERICK CHARLES DE   Histoire de la Guerison d'une
Jeune Personne, par le Magnetisme Animal. Paris, 1814. 8vo, old
worn wrs.; uncut. First edition. Argosy 713-518 1983 $100

STRONG, CALEB   Patriotism and Piety. Newburyport,
Edmund M. Blunt, 1808. First edition. Portrait. 8vo, original
boards, paper label, all edges untrimmed. Lacks small portion of
label and part of backstrip. Morrill 290-299 1983 $20

STRONG, CHARLES J.   L. S. Strong's Book of Designs.
Chicago, Frederick J. Drake, 1917. New and enlarged edition. Large
oblong 8vo, 90 plates, all pictorial, no text. One plate partly torn
with no loss of content. Very fine. Morrill 290-523 1983 $85

STRONG, LEONARD ALFRED GEORGE   A Defence of Ignorance. New York:
House of Books Ltd., 1932. First edition. 8vo. Orig. cloth. Tissue
dust jacket. One of 200 copies signed by author. Very fine. Jaffe
1-387 1983 $45

STRONG, LEONARD ALFRED GEORGE   A Defence of Ignorance. N.Y.: House
of Books, 1932. First edition. Orig. cloth. One of 200 copies signed
by author. Spine slightly faded. Near-fine. MacManus 280-4943 1983
$35

STRONG, LEONARD ALFRED GEORGE   The Garden. London: Victor Gollancz,
1929. Fourth impression. Orig. cloth. Presentation copy, inscribed
to "John Galsworthy with the admiration & gratitude of L.A.G. Strong,
March 24th, 1932." Spine faded and slightly worn. Covers spotted.
Bookplate of Viola & Rudolph Sauter. Good. MacManus 280-4945 1983
$45

STRONG, LEONARD ALFRED GEORGE   Light Above the Lake. London:
Methuen & Co., (1958). First edition. Orig. cloth. Dust jacket.
Endpapers slightly browned. Near-fine. MacManus 280-4946 1983 $20

STRONG, N.   An Astronomical Ephemeris, Calendar, or
Almanack, for ... 1786. Hartford: Hudson & Goodwin, (1785). Stitched.
Very good. Felcone 20-1 1983 $35

STRONG, T. W.   Strong's Cabinet of Conjurations! New
York, T. W. Strong, n.d. (ca. 1850s-1860s). Frontispiece. 24 mo,
orig. cloth. Morrill 286-462 1983 $25

STRONG, WILLIAM DUNCAN   The Uhle Pottery Collections from
Ancon. Berkeley: University of California Press, 1925. 9 plates.
11 text illus. Small 4to. Wrappers. Ars Libri 34-487 1983
$25

STROUD, T. B.   The Elements of Botany, Physiological
and Systematical... Greenwich: for the Author by Eliz. Delahoy,
1821. First edition. 8vo. Uncut in orig. boards, respined. Scarce.
Heath 48-13 1983 £75

STRUTT, BENJAMIN   The History and Description of
Colchester. Colchester: Printed and sold by W. Keymer, 1803. First
edition, with 6 engraved plates and one text engraving, wanting half-
titles, 2 vols., 8vo, full polished calf, gilt, gilt spines, with
red and green labels, by Riviere. Fenning 60-403 1983 £110

STRUTT, ELIZABETH   Drelincourt & Rodalvi. For A.K. Newman
and Co, 1819. 3 vols. 12mo, cont. half calf. Second edition.
Hannas 69-200 1983 £65

STRUTT, JOSEPH   The bumpkin's disaster... London:
printed for Appleyards, etc., 1808. First edition. 4to. Later
wrappers. Slight browning. Ximenes 63-427 1983 $80

STRUTT, JOSEPH   Queenhoo-Hall, a Romance. Edinburgh,
James Ballantyne, 1808. 4 vols., 12mo, modern burgundy half calf
gilt, minor wear and light soiling, good set. First edition.
Ravenstree 96-258 1983 $270

STRUTT, JOSEPH   The Regal and Ecclesiastical Antiques
of England. Published for the author, by J. Thane, 1772. 4to, 60
sepia plates on india paper, proof copies, bound in full straight
grained red morocco, with gilt filets and arms in gilt in the centre
of each cover, gilt dentelles. Beckford's copy. First edition.
Bickersteth 75-86 1983 £65

STRYKER, WILLIAM S.   The Battles of Trenton and Princeton.
Boston, 1898. 1st ed., ports., illus., & maps, 1 folding. G.t.,
ex library. Argosy 710-463 1983 $40

STRYPE, JOHN   The Works. Oxford: at the Clarendon
Press, 1822. 5 portraits. 14 vols. 8vo. Cont. calf, gilt, gilt
panelled spines with morocco labels, gilt. Traylen 94-792 1983
£105

STUART, A. FRANCIS   Trial of Mary Queen of Scots. William
Hodge & Company Limited. 1923. 8vo, pub.'s catalogue, 7 plates,
cloth. Bickersteth 77-173 1983 £15

STUART, GRANVILLE   Forty Years on the Frontier. Cleveland,
1925. Illus. from original sketches by the author, port. 2 vols.,
gilt tops. Nice set, very scarce. Clark 741-255 1983 $200

STUART, JAMES F.   To the Honorable Secretary of the
Interior...Petition of Settlers on Government Lands Fraudulently
Included in Patent to Rancho Milpitas. (San F., 1876). Folded map.
Orig. printed wraps. First edition. Ginsberg 47-175 1983 $100

STUART, JAMES F.   To the Honorable Secretary of the
Interior. Petition of Settlers to Have Lands, Illegally Withdrawn,
Restored to Pre-Emption and Homestead Settlement. San F., ca. 1873.
Orig. printed wraps. First edition. Ginsberg 47-176 1983 $75

STUART, JESSE   Foretaste of Glory. New York: 1946.
First edition. Red cloth. Inscribed and signed by the author in 1977.
Very good in chipped dust jacket. Bradley 66-325 1983 $65

STUART, JESSE   Hie to the Hunters. N.Y., McGraw-Hill,
(1950). First edition. Signed and inscribed by the author to
Vernon King, April 1950. Pictorial dust jacket (light nicking) else
very good. Houle 22-848 1983 $65

STUART, JESSE   The Thread that Runs so True. N.Y.,
Scribner, 1949. First edition. Dust jacket (small nicks), very good.
Houle 21-851 1983 $45

STUART, JESSE   Tree of Heaven. New York, 1940. 8vo.
Cloth. Price clipped at bottom of inside flap of jacket, else a
fine copy in intact dj which has very minimal wear. In Our Time
156-762 1983 $100

STUART, JESSE   Trees of Heaven. NY, 1940. Very good
in bright dustwrapper with only minimal wear. Quill & Brush 54-1323
1983 $100

STUART, JOHN   A Lost Chapter in the History of Mary
Queen of Scots Recovered. Edinburgh, 1874. Small 4to, portrait and
folding facs., cloth gilt, rubbed at edges, small holes in cloth of
upper joint. Bickersteth 77-175 1983 £24

STUART, MARY   The Psychology of Time. NY: Harcourt,
1925. First American edition. Publisher's green cloth. Gach 95-460
1983 $25

STUART, ROBERT   The Discovery of the Oregon Trail.
NY, 1935. Illus., 6 maps, sq. 8vo, buckram, lea. spine label.
Argosy 710-598 1983 $85

STUART, ROBERT   The Discovery of The Oregon Trail. New
York: Edward Eberstadt & Sons, (1935). First edition. Portrait
frontis., plates, maps. Dark red cloth. Very fine. Bradley 66-634
1983 $55

STUART, RUTH MC ENERY   Napoleon Jackson, the Gentleman of the
Plush Rocker. NY, 1902. Illus. Printed at the DeVinne Press.
Argosy 716-164 1983 $20

STUBBE, HENRY   A letter to an officer of the army
concerning a select senate... London: printed, and are to be
sold by T.B., 1659. First edition. Small 4to. Disbound. Slight
flaws in the lower margins towards the end. Ximenes 63-106 1983
$100

STUBBS, WILLIAM C.   Irish Forms and Precedents. Butterworth,
1910. Fenning 62-357 1983 £21.50

STUDIES in the History and Method of Science. Vol. II. Oxford:
Clarendon Press, 1921. Large 8vo. Cloth. 55 plates. Gurney JJ-377
1983 £20

STUHLMANN, FRANZ   Handwerk und Industrie in Ostafrika.
Hamburg: L. Friedrichsen, 1910. 2 maps. 77 text illus. Large 4to.
Cloth. Ars Libri 34-753 1983 $100

STUMPF, CARL (1848-1936)   Tonpsychologie. Leipzig: Verlan von
S. Hirzel, 1883, 1890. Two vols. Contemporary marbled boards, 1/4
leather (worn and dry). First editions. Gach 95-459 1983 $385

STURGE, JOSEPH   A Visit to the United States in 1841.
London, 1842. Cloth (somewhat worn, top of spine damaged). Early
stamp on endsheets. Felcone 22-237 1983 $40

STURGE-MOORE, THOMAS
Please turn to
MOORE, THOMAS STURGE

STURGIS, CYRULS   Desiccated Stomach in the Treatment
of Pernicious Anemia. Chicago, 1929. 12mo, pr. wrs. Argosy 713-
519 1983 $75

STURGIS, JULIAN   John Maidment. London: Longmans, Green,
& Co., 1885. First editiin. 2 vols. Orig. cloth. Covers a little
worn and soiled. Spines darkened. Very good. MacManus 280-4948
1983 $125

STURGIS, WILLIAM   The Oregon Question. Boston, 1845.
Illus., folded map. Orig. printed wraps. First edition. Ginsberg
47-759 1983 $75

STURMY, SAMUEL   The Mariners Magazine. London: E.
Cotes for G. Hurlock, W. Fisher, E. Thomas and D. Page, 1669.
Engraved portrait of the author by A. Hertochs. Fine engraved title
by Thomas Cross. 7 folding engraved plates and 3 engraved plates
with volvelles. Also folding woodcut table, and numerous text woodcuts and engravings, several of which are full-page. Folio. Cont.
calf (rubbed). First edition. Kraus 164-225 1983 $3,400

STYLES, JOHN   An essay on the character and influence
of the stage on morals and happiness. London: printed for Messrs.
Williams and Smith; R. Tilling, printer (Isle of Wight), 1807. 12mo,
original light blue boards, cream paper backstrip, rose printed paper
label. 2nd edition; a fine copy. Ximenes 64-510 1983 $125

STYLES, JOHN   An essay on the character, immoral, and
anti-Christian tendency of the stage. Newport, Isle of Wight:
printed for the author, at the Medina Press, by R. Tilling; sold by
Williams and Smith (London), 1806. 12mo, original boards (soiled,
spine defective). 1st edition. Half-title removed; several relevant
clippings from Victorian periodicals tipped in. A scarce Isle of
Wight imprint. Ximenes 64-509 1983 $150

STYRON, WILLIAM   Admiral Robert Penn Warren. Palaemon
Press, (1981). 1st ed., limited to 150 copies, of which 100 were for
sale, each signed by both Styron and Warren. Orig. linen-backed
decorated boards, label, and printed on handmade paper. Mint.
Jenkins 155-1190 1983 $80

STYRON, WILLIAM   Lie Down in Darkness. Ind., (1951).
Good copy in dustwrapper worn on edges and internally reinforced,
still good or better. Quill & Brush 54-1325 1983 $75

STYRON, WILLIAM   Sophie's Choice. New York: (1979).
First edition. Printed red wrappers. Advance uncorrected proofs.
Publisher's dated slip taped to front wrapper. Bradley 66-328 1983
$125

A SUCCINCT account of the dispute which occurred at the Charleston
Theatre, America, on the evening of the 12th of March, 1817, with the
addresses to the public by Mr. Holman, the manager, and Mr. Caldwell.
Manchester: printed by M. Wilson, 1817. 12mo, disbound, 1st English
edition. A very rare pamphlet. Ximenes 64-511 1983 $225

SUCKLING, JOHN   A Coppy of a Letter found in the
Privy Lodgeings at Whitehall. (London?), 1641. Sole edition.
4to. Wrappers. Heath 48-191 1983 £55

SUCKOW, GEORGE ADOLPH   Anfangsgrunde der Mineralogie nach den
neusten Entdeckungen. Leipzig, 1803. Second edition, enlarged to
2 vols. 8vo. 2 vols. Cont. half-calf, with morocco gilt labels.
Some light browning. Gurney JJ-386 1983 £30

SUE, EUGENE   The Mysteries of Paris. Chapman & Hall,
1845-46. 3 vols., tall 8vo. Half titles. With the vignette illus.
by Valentin throughout. Orig. chocolate brown pebble-grained cloth,
blocked in blind gilt spine lettering. Fine. Jarndyce 30-560 1983
£38

SUE, EUGENE   The Wandering Jew. London: Chapman &
Hall, 1844-1845. First English book edition. 3 vols. Orig. cloth, in
a secondary green cloth binding. Minor wear. Bookplates. Very good.
MacManus 280-4949 1983 $75

SUE, EUGENE   The Wandering Jew. London & N.Y.: Geo.
Routledge & Sons, 1889. 182 illus from designs by A. Ferdinandus.
3 vols. 4to. Orig. green cloth with paper labels on spines. Labels
a little worn. Very good. MacManus 280-4950 1983 $75

SUE, EUGENE   The Works of Eugene Sue. Boston:
Francis A. Niccolls & Co., (n.d.). Edition de Luxe. 20 vols. Illus.
with etchings. Orig. cloth with paper label. Paper spine labels
slightly soiled. Near-fine. MacManus 280-4951 1983 $150

SUETONIUS TRANQUILLUS, CAIUS Opera Quae Exstant. Basilae: (typis
Genathianis), 1675. First edition thus, with engraved frontis.,
engraved vignette title-page, a plate, a folding table and many
engravings in the text of coins and medals, complete with the colophon
leaf with device, 4to, old calf, gilt, neatly and recently rebacked,
very good copy. First edition. Fenning 62-358 1983 £48.50

SUEVERN, JOHANN W.   Two Essays on "The Clouds". John
Murray, 1836. First edition of this translation. Orig. cloth, by
Hering, with printed paper label. Fenning 60-404 1983 £32.50

SUFFOLK County's Ten Great Townships of Long Island. N.P. (ca. 1946).
Illus. 4to, full leatherette. Morrill 286-367 1983 $22.50

SUFFOLK Deeds. Boston, 1880-1906. 14 vols., 8vo, vol. 1 in orig.
wrappers, other 13 in cloth. Vol. 1 partly broken along backstrip;
ex-library with no external marks; nice set. Morrill 286-309 1983
$75

SULIVAN, R. J. F.   One Hundred Years of Bombay. Bombay,
1936. 2 maps, 1 folding. Plates. Roy.8vo. Leather. Good. Edwards
1044-678 1983 £30

SULLIVAN, A. M.   Elbows of the Wind. New York, 1932. 8vo,
cloth, boards. This copy inscribed by the poet to Alexander Laing.
Fine. In Our Time 156-763 1983 $25

SULLIVAN, ARABELLA JANE   Recollections of a Chaperon. Richard
Bentley, 1833. First edition. 3 vols. 12mo, lacks half-titles.
Half morocco (slightly rubbed). Occasional stains. Hannas 69-201
1983 £45

SULLIVAN, ARABELLA JANE   Recollections of a Chaperon. Richard
Bentley, 1833. First edition, 3 vols. Orig. half calf, marbled
boards. Jarndyce 30-563 1983 £38

SULLIVAN, ARABELLA JANE   Recollections of a Chaperon. Richard
Bentley, 1833. First edition, 3 vols. Two quires sl. sprung.
Half green calf, maroon labels, v.g. Jarndyce 30-564 1983 £24

SULLIVAN, ARABELLA JANE   Tales of the Peerage and the Peasantry.
London: Richard Bentley, 1835. First edition. 3 vols. 3/4 morocco
with marbled boards and marbled edges and leather spine labels. Edges
slightly rubbed. Bookseller's tickets on endpapers. Signature of
former owner. Very good. MacManus 280-4952 1983 $250

SULLIVAN, ARABELLA JANE   Tales of the Peerage and the Peasantry.
Richard Bentley, 1835. First edition, 3 vols. Half green calf,
brown labels, v.g. Jarndyce 30-561 1983 £48

SULLIVAN, ARABELLA JANE   Tales of the Peerage and the Peasantry.
Richard Bentley, 1835. 2nd edition, 3 vols. Half maroon calf,
gilt spines, v.g. Cancel titles. Jarndyce 30-562 1983 £32

SULLIVAN, EDWARD   The Book of Kells. London: "The
Studio", 1933. Fourth edition. 4to. Cloth, dust jacket. 24
colored plates. A fine copy. Oak Knoll 49-242 1983 $55

SULLIVAN, GEORGE   Speech of the Hon. George Sullivan...
Exeter, 1812. Dsb., stained and somewhat chipped, good. Reese 18-
395 1983 $20

SULLIVAN, HARRY STACK (1892-1949)   Conceptions of Modern Psychiatry.
Orig. yellow wrappers. Near fine copy. Gach 95-462 1983 $50

SULLIVAN, HARRY STACK (1892-1949)   The Collected Works of... NY:
Norton, (ca. 1966). Five vols. in two. Thick 8vo's. Gach 95-461
1983 $50

SULLIVAN, HARRY STACK (1892-1949)   Peculiarity of Thought in
Schizophrenia. Orig. printed brown wrappers, right edge chipped.
Inscribed to Adolf Meyer. Gach 95-465 1983 $185

SULLIVAN, HARRY STACK (1892-1949)   Schizophrenia: Its Conservative
and Malignant Features. Orig. printed brown wrappers. Inscribed to
Th. Robinson. Gach 95-468 1983 $250

SULLIVAN, JAMES   History of New York State, 1523-1927.
NY, (1927). 5 vols., many plates, thick 4to, blue leatherette.
Argosy 710-366 1983 $100

SULLIVAN, JOHN   Letters and Papers. Concord, 1930-1939.
First edition. Frontispieces. 3 vols., 8vo. Morrill 290-340 1983
$60

SULLIVAN, JAMES   One Hundred Years of Progress. Boston
& Portland, 1895. 1st ed. Illus. 4to. Morrill 288-297 1983 $40

SULLIVAN, MARK   Our Times 1900-1925. N.Y., (1935).
Avondale edition. Hundreds of portraits, caricatures, etc. Two-tone
cloth. Paper labels, t.e.g. Some darkening to white spines. Defective slipcases. 6 vols. Limited to 770 numbered sets, signed by
Sullivan. Very good. King 45-135 1983 $95

SULLIVAN, MARK   Our Times. N.Y., Scribner, 1927-1935.
First editions (except vol. I). Large 8vo, illus. All vols. with
dust jackets (small nicks and light wear). TLS from the author laid
in loose. 6 vols. complete. Very good. Houle 22-851 1983 $85

SULLIVAN, MAURICE S.   The Travels of Jedediah Smith. Santa
Ana: The Fine Arts Press, 1934. Maps and illus. First edition.
A fairly nice copy. Jenkins 151-98 1983 $225

SULLY, HENRY   Observations on, and plain directions
for, all classes to people... Taunton: printed for the author,
by J. Marriott, etc., 1828. First edition. 8vo. Cont. half calf.
Presentation copy, inscribed by the author to William Ayshford Sanford. With a lithographed plate. Slightly rubbed. Rare. Ximenes
63-291 1983 $100

SULLY, JAMES   The Human Mind. A Text-Book of
Psychology. London: Longmans, Green, 1892. Two vols. Publisher's
brown cloth. Spine labels removed, joints rubbed. Very good set of
the first edition. Gach 94-652 1983 $100

SULLY, JAMES   Outlines of Psychology with Special
Reference to the Theory of Education. NY: Appleton & Co., 1892.
Publisher's pebble-grained cloth. Good copy, edges rubbed. First
American printing of revised edition. Gach 94-653 1983 $25

SULLY, JAMES   Studies of Childhood. NY: Appleton,
1898. Worn copy lacking front flyleaf. Gach 94-654 1983 $25

SULLY, JAMES   The Teacher's Handbook of Psychology.
NY: Appleton, 1887 (1886). Gach 94-655 1983 $20

SUMMARY View of the Millennial Church or United Society of Believers,
Commonly Called Shakers. Albany, 1848. 8vo, calf, (minor edge stains).
Second edition. Argosy 716-64 1983 $85

THE SUMMER Miscellany: or, a present for the country. London:
printed for T. Cooper, 1742. First ed., 8vo, title a little spotted
but a good copy in modern quarter morocco. Pickering & Chatto 19-79
1983 $650

SUMMERHAYES, MARTHA   Vanished Arizona. Philadelphia, 1908.
Cloth, fine. Reese 19-527 1983 $85

SUMMERHAYES, MARTHA   Vanished Arizona. Salem: Salem Press
Co., (1911). Plates. Cloth, light wear. Tape marks on endpapers.
Signed presentation from author dated 1913. Dawson 471-280 1983
$100

SUMMERHAYES, MARTHA   Vanished Arizona. Salem, Mass.: (1911).
Second edition, enlarged and augmented with pictures. 28 plates.
Blue cloth. Fine copy. Bradley 66-463 1983 $65

SUMMERHAYES, MARTHA   Vanished Arizona...Salem, (1911). Illus.
Top edges of spine worn. Clark 741-36 1983 $60

SUMMERS, MONTAGUE   Compenium Maleficarium. London,
Rodker, 1929. 4to, with 45 woodcuts in the text. Black cloth over
boards, uncut. Very good-fine. One of 1275 copies. Houle 21-852
1983 $55

SUMMERS, MONTAGUE   Demoniality by Ludovico Maria Sinistrari.
London: The Fortune Press, (1927). First edition. Orig. black buckram. Limited to 1200 copies on hand-made paper. Covers a little
rubbed. Good. MacManus 280-4956 1983 $35

SUMMERS, MONTAGUE   Essays in Petto. London, Fortune,
(1928). First edition. Frontis. portrait. Grey cloth over boards,
spine stamped in gilt, uncut and partly unopened. Very good. Houle
22-853 1983 $40

SUMMERS, MONTAGUE   The Geography of Witchcraft. NY: Alfred
A. Knopf, 1927. First American edition. Rear hinge cracked, spine
tips slightly worn, else very good. Gach 95-469 1983 $35

SUMMERS, MONTAGUE   Grimoire and Other Supernatural Stories.
London, Fortune Press, (1936). First edition, frontis. Gilt
stamped black cloth (ink name on top edge), else good-very good.
Houle 21-854 1983 $27.50

SUMMERS, MONTAGUE   Vampire: His Kith and Kin. London,
Kegan, 1928. First edition. Eight plates. Red cloth (a bit faded),
else very good. Bookplate of Adrian Goldstone. Houle 21-857 1983
$95

SUMMERS, MONTAGUE   The Vampire. London: Kegan Paul,
Trench, Trubner & Co., 1928. First edition. Gach 95-471 1983 $50

SUMNER, CHARLES   Speech of Hon. Charles Sumner, of
Massachusetts, for Welcome to Louis Kossuth. Washington: Buell &
Blanchard, 1851. 22 cm. self-wraps. Disbound & creased. With
clipped signature "C. Sumner" on a slip of paper 3 x 7 cm. and
Kossuth's black-bordered card with a holograph note in the third
person, 1893. Grunder 6-81 1983 $45

SUMNER, CHARLES   Then and Now. San Francisco, (1876).
Orig. printed wraps. Ginsberg 46-124 1983 $75

THE SUNLIGHT of Song. Routledge, 1875. 1st edn. Illus. by designs
engr'd by Bros. Dalziel, 8pp adverts. Blue sand grain decor. cloth,
bevelled boards, a.e.g. (bkstrip faded with wear top/bottom, corners
sl. bruised & worn, insc. half title, rear ep. broken at hinge, occas.
foxing), vg. Hodgkins 27-331 1983 £17.50

A SURGICAL Pilgrim's Progress Reminiscences of Lewis Stephen Pilcher.
Philadelphia, 1925. First edition. 8vo. Orig. binding. Fye H-3-919
1983 $40

SURPRISING Comical Characters (and) More Comical Characters. Dean &
Son, n.d. (ca. 1850s). 2 vols. Each capable of over 500 metamorphoses.
6pp colour transforming flaps in each vol. Beige pictorial bds., both
vols. carefully rebacked, scarce, vg. Hodgkins 27-205 1983 £220

THE SURPRISING Life of Richard Turpin. London: Dean & Murray, n.d.
First edition, frontis. by R. Cruikshank, 12mo., disbound, orig.
watercolour drawing for the frontis. accompanies book. MacManus 277-
1244 1983 $350

SURR, T. S.   A Winter in London. Newman & Co., 1824.
3 vols. '13th Edition', half calf, black labels. Jarndyce 30-566
1983 £35

SURREY, HENRY HOWARD   The Poems. London, 1857. Cr. 8vo.
Dark blue calf, two-line gilt borders with corner ornaments, gilt
panelled spine, morocco label, gilt. Traylen 94-793 1983 £16

SURTEES, ROBERT SMITH   "Ask Mamma". London, n.d. (ca.1920's).
Fancy decorated cloth. Uncut. Ink inscription. Spine sunned and a
bit worn. Numerous wood-engravings and 13 colored steel engravings
by J. Leech. Very good. King 45-410 1983 $35

SURTEES, ROBERT SMITH   Handley Cross; or, The Spa Hunt. London:
Colburn, 1843. First edition. 3 vols. Orig. cloth-backed boards,
paper labels (slightly rubbed). Inner hinges cracked in vol. one.
With the bookplate of H.C. Taylor in each vol. In a cloth slipcase.
Very good. MacManus 280-4958 1983 $250

SURTEES, ROBERT SMITH   Hillingdon Hall Or The Cockney Squire.
London: John Nimmo, 1888. First illus. edition. Illus. with 12 hand-
colored plates. Orig. red decorated cloth. Front inner hinge cracking. First preliminary pages loose. Spine faded and slightly rubbed
at the ends and edges. In a half-morocco case. Good. MacManus 280-
4959 1983 $350

SURTEES, ROBERT SMITH   Robert Smith Surtees. N.Y.: Charles
Scribner's Sons, 1924. First American edition. Illus. Orig. cloth.
Endpapers foxed. Fine. MacManus 280-4960 1983 $20

SURTEES, ROBERT SMITH   Sporting Novels. London, 1888, etc.
A set of first and early editions, profusely illus. with numerous
coloured plates and drawings by John Leech. 7 vols. 8vo. Half
blue calf, fully gilt panelled spines with red morocco labels, gilt.
Traylen 94-794 1983 £240

SURTEES, ROBERT SMITH   Young Tom Hall. Edinburgh, 1926. Illus.
by G.D. Armour. Nicely decorated cloth. T.e.g. Spine slightly
sunned. Nice. King 45-503 1983 $35

SUTCLIFF, ROBERT   Travels in some Parts of North America,
in the Years 1804, 1805 and 1806. York: C. Peacock for W. Alexander,
1811. 1st ed., 12mo, cont. calf and morocco label, rebacked. 6
engraved plates. Bookplate. A fine copy. Trebizond 18-164 1983
$300

SUTCLIFF, ROBERT   Travels in Some Parts of North America.
York: Peacock for Alexander, 1811. 8vo, with engraved frontis. &
5 full-page plates. Calf, rebacked. First edition. Rostenberg 88-13
1983 $250

SUTCLIFFE, THOMAS   Crusoniana. Manchester, (Eng.), P.
Grant for the author, 1843. 8vo. Engraved frontis., extra engraved
title, map & 6 engraved plates. Orig. cloth, gilt, aeg. In cloth,
lettered protective jacket. 1st & only ed. Fine. O'Neal 50-49
1983 $150

SUTCLIFFE, THOMAS   The earthquake of Juan Fernandez...
Manchester: printed at the "Advertiser" Office, 1839. First
edition. 8vo. Orig. tan printed wrappers. Half morocco folding case.
Four lithographed plates (three tinted) and one map. Binding bit
chipped, spine worn. In very good condition. Rare. Ximenes 63-92
1983 $375

SUTHERLAND, DAVID   A Tour up the Straits. Printed for
the author; and sold by J. Johnson, 1790. 8vo, light waterstaining on
title and subsequent few leaves, orig. calf, rubbed, lacking label.
First edition. Bickersteth 75-87 1873 £35

SUTOR, ALEXANDER   An essay on the stage: in which the
arguments in its behalf, and those against it, are considered.
Aberdeen: printed by D. Chalmers and Co., 1820. 12mo, original
boards, printed paper label (spine worn). First edition. A scarce
work. A very good copy in original condition. Ximenes 64-512 1983
$125

SUTRO, ADOLPH   The Bank of California Against the
Sutro Tunnel. (Wash., 1874). Sewn. First edition. Ginsberg 47-178
1983 $35

SUTRO, ADOLPH   The Sutro Tunnel and Railway to the
Comstock Lode in the State of Nevada. London, 1873. Illus. 3
large folded colored maps. Orig. printed wraps. First edition.
Ginsberg 47-665 1983 $125

SUTRO, ADOLPH   Why Does the Bank of California Oppose
the Sutro Tunnel? Wash., D.C., 1873. Sewn. First edition. Ginsberg
47-179 1983 $50

SUTTER, JOHN A.   New Helvetia Diary. San F., Grabhorn
Press, 1939. Folio. Cloth backed paper over boards, ltd. edition
of 950 copies. Ginsberg 47-181 1983 $125

SUTTON, ERNEST V.   A Life Worth Living. Pasadena, 1948.
Frontis. and portraits. 1st ed. Fine copy uncut and unopened.
Jenkins 153-545 1983 $35

SUTTON, M. J.   Permanent and temporary pastures. 1902.
23 coloured plates, royal 8vo, morocco. Inscribed by the Author to
his wife. Wheldon 160-2141 1983 £15

SUTTON, PETER C.   Pieter der Hooch. Oxford/Ithaca:
Phaidon/Cornell University Press, 1980. Complete edition. 16
color plates. 260 illus. hors texte. 4to. Cloth. Dust jacket.
Ars Libri 32-328 1983 $95

SUTTON, THOMAS   Tracts on Delirium Tremens, on Peritonitis, and on Some Other Internal Inflammatory Affections, and on the Gout. London, 1813. 1st ed. 8vo. New cloth. Library stamp on title; tear on title-page repaired. Morrill 289-221 1983 $75

SUYS, F. T.   Palais Massimi a Rome. New York, Architectural Book Pub. Co., n.d. (ca. early 1900s). 40 full-page plates of different portions. Folio, original boards, cloth back and corners, ribbon ties, all loose as issued. Backstrip torn and front hinge partly broken. Morrill 290-526 1983 $25

SWADOS, HARVEY   A Radical at Large. Lon., 1967. Appears to be advance reading copy, paperwraps, very good. Quill & Brush 54-1326 1983 $75

SWAIN, CHARLES   Letters of Laura d'Auverne. London: Longman, etc., 1853. First edition. Small 8vo. Orig. blue cloth. Presentation copy, inscribed by the author on the title-page to Robert Leech. Ximenes 63-458 1983 $90

SWAIN, ROBERT B.   Address Before the First Unitarian Society of San Francisco in Memory of Their Late Pastor, Rev. Thomas Starr King... San F., 1864. Orig. printed wraps. First edition. Ginsberg 47-183 1983 $50

SWAINSON, W   Exotic Conchology... London: for William Wood and J. & A. Arch, 1821. First edition. 4to. 32 hand coloured Aquatint plates. Half green morocco. Some few light foxing markes, else fine copy. Heath 48-14 1983 £950

SWAINSON, W   Exotic Conchology or Drawings and Descriptions of Rare, Beautiful or Undescribed Shells. (Princeton, 1968). Limited ed. of 2,000 copies. Repro. of 1834 title page of Swainson's plate book. Repro. of the 1841 title page, text, and 48 colored plates. Red cloth. Very fine. Bradley 63-122 1983 $85

SWAINSON, W   Exotic Conchology or Drawings and Descriptions of Rare, Beautiful or Undescribed Shells. (Princeton: 1968). Limited edition (2,000 copies). 48 color plates. Red cloth. Very fine. Bradley 66-435 1983 $75

SWAINSON, W.   The Natural History of Fishes, Amphibians and Reptiles or Monocardian Animals. 1838-39. 2 engraved title-vignettes and 235 text-figures, 2 vols., post 8vo, original cloth. Spines faded, vignette title to Vol. 2 slightly frayed in margin. Wheldon 160-1007 1983 £25

SWAINSON, W.   On the Natural History and Classification of Quadrupeds. 1835. Engraved title-page and 176 text-figures, sm. 8vo, modern full calf, gilt. Engraved title trifle foxed but a fine copy. Wheldon 160-610 1983 £25

SWAINSON, W.   A Treatise on the Geography and Classification of Animals. 1835. Engraved title-page and figures in the text, sm. 8vo, modern full calf, gilt. Engraved title a trifle foxed but a fine copy. Wheldon 160-525 1983 £25

SWALLOW, GEORGE CLINTON   Geological Report of the Country Along the Pacific Railroad, State of Missouri. St. Louis: Printed by George Knapp & Co., 1859. Orig. cloth. Folding map. Jenkins 153-546 1983 $225

SWAMMERDAM, JAN   Histoire Generale des Insectes. Utrecht: Jean Ribbius, 1685. Folding table, 13 plates (most folding). Cont. calf (spotted). Later front endsheet. Felcone 21-103 1983 $375

SWAN, ALONZO M.   Canton: Its Pioneers and History. Canton, 1871. Orig. cloth, spine slightly chipped. First edition. Ginsberg 46-340 1983 $100

SWAN, OLIVER   Frontier Days. Philadelphia. 1928. Pictorial cloth. Illus. in color. 1st ed. Scarce. Fine copy. Jenkins 153-547 1983 $45

SWANN, A. J.   Fighting the Slave-Hunters in Central Africa. London, 1910. Folding map, numerous plates. Thick 8vo. Occasional spotting, pictorial cloth, slightly marked. Good. Edwards 1044-680 1983 £35

SWANN, H. K.   A Monograph of the Birds of Prey: Accipitres. 1924-25. 2 vols., 4to, half red morocco, coloured and photogravure plates. Limited edition of 412 copies. Wheldon 160-104 1983 £380

SWANTON, E. W.   British Plant-galls. 1912. 32 plates (16 coloured), 8vo, contemporary calf, rebacked. Wheldon 160-1574 1983 £15

SWARTH, H. S.   The Avifauna of the Galapagos Islands. Occ. Papers Calif. Acad. Sci., 1931. Folding map, royal 8vo, cloth. Wheldon 160-896 1983 £25

SWAYNE, F.   A Woman's Pleasure Trip in Somaliland. Bristol, 1907. Map, frontis. 61 vignette photographs by author. Sm.8vo. Slight wear. Good. Edwards 1044-682 1983 £30

SWEDENBORG, EMANUEL   The Economy of the Animal Kingdom. 1846. 2 vols., 8vo, cloth. Wheldon 160-526 1983 £20

SWEDENBORG, EMANUEL   A Treatise Concerning Heaven and Hell... London: James Phillips, 1778. 1st ed. in English. Contemporary black morocco, inner dentilles gilt, label. Very fine. Jenkins 155-1423 1983 $250

SWEENEY, JAMES   African Negro Art. New York: Museum of Modern Art, 1935. 81 plates with 100 illus. 4to. Boards, 1/4 cloth. Dust jacket. Slightly worn. Ars Libri 34-755 1983 $85

SWEENEY, JAMES   Stuart Davis. N.Y., Moma, (1945). First edition. 4to, three color and 28 halftone plates. Dust jacket. Very good. One of 3,000 copies. Houle 21-280 1983 $30

SWEET, ALEXANDER EDWIN   On a Mexican Mustang Through Texas from the Gulf to the Rio Grande. Hartford: Scranton, 1883. Hundreds of woodcut illus. (many full-page). Orig. tan gilt pictorial cloth. 1st ed. Fine copy. Jenkins 153-548 1983 $85

SWEET, R.   Geraniaceae. The Natural Order of Gerania. 1820-28. 4 vols., roy. 8vo, half morocco, 400 hand-coloured plates. Rare. Light stain on title-page of vol. 1. Wheldon 160-105 1983 £2,100

SWEETSER, M. F.   Kings Handbook of Boston Harbor. Cambridge, Moses King, (1882). Over 200 original illustrations. 8vo, ads. Bookplate removed. Morrill 290-300 1983 $35

SWEETSER, M. F.   White Mountain Scenery. Portland, Me., Chisholm Brothers, n.d. (ca. 1880s). 8vo, view book, 16 plates, foldout. Morrill 290-341 1983 $20

SWEETSER, WILLIAM   Treatise on Digestion, and the Disorders Incident to it. Boston, 1837. First edition. Orig. cloth. Argosy 713-521 1983 $50

SWEM, EARL G.   A Bibliography of Virginia. Richmond, 1916-17. 2 vols. Library cloth, hinges weak. Dawson 470-285 1983 $35

SWETTENHAM, FRANK   British Malaya. London, 1920. Fourth edition. Folding map. Frontis., and numerous illus. 8vo. Orig. cloth. Good. Edwards 1044-683 1983 £16

SWIFT, DEANE   An Essay upon the Life, Writings, and Character, of Dr. Jonathan Swift... London: Printed, Dublin: Reprinted, 1755. Cont. calf, one board reattached. First Dublin edition, issued in the same year as the first London edition. Slight foxing of first two leaves. Reese 20-955 1983 $85

SWIFT, JONATHAN   A Complete Collection of Genteel and Ingenious Conversation. Printed for B. Motte, and C. Bathurst, 1738. 8vo, ad. leaf, title, cont. calf, short slits just beginning at top of each joint, old hand written paper label at top of spine. First London edition. Bickersteth 75-90 1983 £170

SWIFT, JONATHAN   A Complete Collection of Genteel and
Ingenious Conversation. London: for B. Motte, and C. Bathurst,
1738. First edition. 8vo. Cont. calf, neatly rebacked. Ad. leaf
before the title-page and "Neptune" ornament heading the Introduction.
Traylen 94-795 1983 £135

SWIFT, JONATHAN   Good Queen Anne vindicated... London:
W. Owen, 1748. Second edition. 8vo. Disbound. Half-title dusty.
Ximenes 63-469 1983 $75

SWIFT, JONATHAN   Gulliver's Travels. Macmillan, 1894.
First edition. 103 illus. by Charles E. Brock. 4pp. ads. Green dark
blue decor cloth, a.e.g. Late issue. Very good. Hodgkins 27-497
1983 £15

SWIFT, JOHNATHAN   Gulliver's Travels. N.Y.: Mac., 1923.
8vo. Cloth. Illus. by C.E. Brock with color frontis. and nearly
100 intricate black & whites both full-page and smaller. Fine.
Aleph-bet 8-246 1983 $30

SWIFT, JONATHAN   Gulliver's Travels. Garden City: Doubleday & Doran, 1945. First of this edition. Illus. with black-and-white
drawings and color plates. Orig. red decorated cloth. Publisher's
box (slightly worn at the edges). Illus. by Jon Corbino. Spine a
trifle faded. Near-fine. MacManus 280-4963 1983 $25

SWIFT, JONATHAN   Gullivers Travels. Wells, Gardner,
Darton, n.d. Sq. 8vo. Frontis. 4 maps. Portraits. 15 full-page
& 16 text illus. Brown pictorial cloth gilt. Spine darkened. Presentation copy from editor to Vernon Knowles. Greer 39-53 1983 £25

SWIFT, JONATHAN   Gulliver's Travels Into Several Remote
Nations of the World. London: J.M. Dent & Co., 1900. First edition.
Illus. by A. Rackham. Orig. calf. Spine faded. Covers worn. Book-
plate. Very good. MacManus 280-4317 1983 $85

SWIFT, JONATHAN   Gulliver's Travels into Several Remote
Nations of the World. London, 1909. 4to. White buckram, gilt,
t.e.g., others uncut, new silk ties. 13 mounted coloured plates,
and other illus. by Arthur Rackham. Limited edition of 750 copies,
numbered and signed by Arthur Rackham. Traylen 94-796 1983 £225

SWIFT, JONATHAN   Gulliver's Travels into Several Remote
Nations of the World. London: J.M. Dent & Co.; E.P. Dutton & Co.,
1909. First edition. Illus. by A. Rackham. 4to. Orig. cream buckram,
t.e.g. One of 750 copies printed on large paper and signed by Rackham.
Bookplate. Cloth ties lacking. Fine. MacManus 280-4333 1983 $650

SWIFT, JONATHAN   Gulliver's Travels into Several Remote
Nations of the World. London: The Temple Press, (1937). First of
this edition. Illus. by A. Rackham. Orig. cloth. Dust jacket (spine
darkened, a little chipped). Fine. MacManus 280-4332 1983 $150

SWIFT, JONATHAN   Gulliver's Voyages to Lilliput and Brob-
dingnag. London: The Folio Society, 1948. First edition. 12 full-
page colour lithographs by Edward Bawden. Nicked, price-clipped dustwrapper by Bawden. Very good. Jolliffe 26-41 1983 £28

SWIFT, JONATHAN   The History of the Four Last Years of the
Queen. London: A. Millar, 1758. First edition. Cont. calf,
a bit rubbed; top of spine with a small chip. Karmiole 72-92 1983
$150

SWIFT, JONATHAN   The Life and Genuine Character of
Doctor Swift. Written by Himself. London: for J. Roberts, 1733.
First edition. Folio. Modern quarter morocco. Half title. Joint
repaired. Heath 48-428 1983 £225

SWIFT, JONATHAN   Miscellaneous Poems of Jonathan Swift.
London: the Golden Cockerel Press, 1928. 4to. Marbled boards,
vellum spine, in the orig. printed dustwrapper. Wood-engravings
by Robert Gibbings. Limited edition of 375 numbered copies (of
which this is a Traveller's Copy). Dustwrapper torn. Traylen 94-
797 1983 £50

SWIFT, JOHATHAN   Miscellanies in Prose and Verse. London,
John Morphew, 1711. 8vo, new calf. This copy has pages 91-94
replaced with the revised text. Ravenstree 96-262 1983 $330

SWIFT, JONATHAN   The Poetical Works of Dr. Jonathan
Swift... London: by A. Manson, R. Dilton..., (ca. 1760-70). 8vo.
2 vols. Cont. calf gilt. New labels. Engraved portrait. Slight
wear. Heath 48-426 1983 £125

SWIFT, JONATHAN   The Poetical Works. London, 1866.
3 vols. Cr. 8vo. Dark blue calf, two-line gilt borders with corner
ornaments, gilt panelled spines, morocco labels, gilt. Portrait,
vignette title-pages. Traylen 94-798 1983 £45

SWIFT, JONATHAN   Political Tracts. London: for C.
Davis, 1738. First London edition. 2 vols. 8vo. Half green
morocco, gilt, t.e.g. Spines faded. Traylen 94-799 1983 £130

SWIFT, JONATHAN   Selected Essays. London: the Golden
Cockerel Press, 1925. 4to. Green boards, vellum spine. 14 wood-
engravings by John Farleigh. Limited edition of 450 numbered
copies (of which only 190 were issued). Traylen 94-800 1983 £65

SWIFT, JONATHAN   Some Remarks on the Barrier Treaty
between Her Majesty and the States-General. Printed for John Morphew,
1712. 8vo, uncut, recent marbled boards with morocco spine lettered
in gilt, new end papers. First edition. Bickersteth 75-88 1983
£120

SWIFT, JONATHAN   A Tale of a Tub. London, John Nutt,
1704. 8vo, full brown morocco gilt extra, a.e.g., by Riviere,
washed, pinhole worming to blank tip of last portion. Ad. leaf and the
blank space for "Uterinus" on p. 320. First edition. Ravenstree 96-
259 1983 $1,250

SWIFT, JONATHAN   A Tale of a Tub. London: for John
Nutt, 1704. First edition. 8vo. Cont. calf. Ad. leaf. Worn,
some scoring and light marginal staining (not affecting the text).
Traylen 94-801 1983 £385

SWIFT, JONATHAN   A Tale of a Tub. For John Nutt, 1704.
8vo, initial advert. leaf, final blank leaf. Cont. calf (worn,
rebacked, new end-papers). Hannas 69-202 1983 £65

SWIFT, JONATHAN   A Tale of a Tub... London: for John
Nutt, 1710. Fifth edition. 8vo. Modern boards. Engraved frontis.,
plates. Very minor marginal worming of a few leaves. Heath 48-427
1983 £65

SWIFT, JONATHAN   A Tale of a Tub. 1711. 12mo, contemporary panelled calf, a little rubbed but a very nice copy. Without
the blanks after the _Battle_ and at the end. Pickering & Chatto 19-72
1983 $350

SWIFT, JONATHAN   A Tale of a Tub. N.p.: Anno 1711. 12mo.
Cont.. calf. Front cover detached, covers rubbed. Good. MacManus
280-4967 1983 $50

SWIFT, JONATHAN   A tale of a tub. London: Charles
Bathurst, 1747. "Eleventh" edition, issued as part of a 1747
collected edition, but sold separately. Small 8vo. Cont. calf.
Frontis. and seven plates. Some wear. Ximenes 63-477 1983 $25

SWIFT, JONATHAN   A Tale of a Tub... London, Thomas Tegg,
1811. 8vo. 7 (including frontis.) hand-colored etched plates by
Rhodes after Thurston. Full rose polished calf, gilt back, by
Zaehnsdorf, gt. Very slightly rubbed, but fine. O'Neal 50-119 1983
$85

SWIFT, JOHATHAN   Travels into Several Remote Nations of
the World... London, for Benj. Motte, 1726. 2 vols., 8vo, modern
polished speckled calf gilt extra, top edge gilt, lightly washed, fine
red and green morocco gilt lettering pieces. Preserved in slipcase.
First edition. Ravenstree 96-263 1983 $4,200

SWIFT, JONATHAN   Travels into Several Remote Nations
of the Works. London: for Bej. Motte, 1726. First edition. 2
vols. 8vo. Cont. panelled calf. Frontis. portrait of Gulliver
(second state, with vertical chainlines), and 2 maps in vol. 1,
3 maps and an illus. in vol. 2. With the bookplates of William
Constable. A very fine copy. Traylen 94-802 1983 £450

SWIFTIANA. Letters, Poems and Tales. London: printed for E. Curll
1718. First edition, advertisement, modern quarter morocco. Pickering
& Chatto 19-73 1983 $1,850

SWINBURNE, ALGERNON CHARLES   The Age of Shakespeare. London: Chatto & Windus, 1908. First edition. Large 8vo. Orig. cloth. One of 110 large-paper copies. Front cover a little spotted. Very good. Mac-Manus 280-4969 1983 $100

SWINBURNE, ALGERNON CHARLES   The Age of Shakespeare. London: Chatto & Windus, 1908. First edition. Orig. cloth. Front cover a little spotted. Very good. MacManus 280-4968 1983 $20

SWINBURNE, ALGERNON CHARLES   Astrophel and Other Poems. London, 1894. 8vo. Cloth. Bookplate. Inscribed by Swinburne on half-title page: "To W.H. Davenport Adams from A.C. Swinburne". One textual correction in ink on p. 118. Some foxing to front flyleaf, else fine copy. In Our Time 156-773 1983 $750

SWINBURNE, ALGERNON CHARLES   Atalanta in Calydon. London: John Camden Hotten, Piccadilly, 1866. Third edition. Full green morocco with marbled endpapers. Presentation copy to James Lorimer Graham, inscribed. Tiny nick from top spine end. Swinburne's calling card tipped to the second preliminary page. Bookplate of J.L. Graham. Very good. MacManus 280-4970 1983 $350

SWINBURNE, ALGERNON CHARLES   Atalanta In Calydon. London: The Medici Society, 1923. Orig. cloth-backed patterned boards. Limited to 1025 copies printed on hand-made paper. Bookplate. Fine. MacManus 280-4971 1983 $35

SWINBURNE, ALGERNON CHARLES   Atalanta In Calydon. London: Oxford University Press, 1930. First of this edition. Orig. white buckram. Limited to 500 copies. Bookplate. Fine. MacManus 280-4972 1983 $35

SWINBURNE, ALGERNON CHARLES   A Century of Roundels. London: Chatto & Windus, 1883. First edition. Orig. cloth. 1000 copies printed. Maurice Baring's copy, with his bookplate and one other on the front endpapers. Good. MacManis 280-4974 1983 $50

SWINBURNE, ALGERNON CHARLES   A Century of Roundels. London: Chatto & Windus, 1883. First edition. Orig. cloth. E.C. Stedman's copy, with his bookplate and one other on the front endpapers. Good. MacManus 280-4973 1983 $50

SWINBURNE, ALGERNON CHARLES   A Channel Passage and other poems. London: Chatto & Windus, 1904. First edition. Orig. cloth. 1500 copies printed. Endpapers foxed. Unopened. Fine. MacManus 280-4975 1983 $25

SWINBURNE, ALGERNON CHARLES   Charles Dickens. London: Chatto & Windus, 1913. First edition. Orig. cloth. Fine. MacManus 280-4977 1983 $25

SWINBURNE, ALGERNON CHARLES   Charles Dickens. Chatto & Windus, 1913. Half title, orig. dark green cloth, lettering and borders in gilt. Fine. Jarndyce 30-230 1983 £16.50

SWINBURNE, ALGERNON CHARLES   Chastlelard: A Tragedy. L, 1865. Hinges starting, edges rubbed and lightly worn, some page edges lightly chipped where carelessly opened, good. Quill & Brush 54-1327 1983 $35

SWINBURNE, ALGERNON CHARLES   Chastelard; A Tragedy. London: Edward Moxon & Co., 1865. First edition. Orig. cloth. 1000 copies printed. 16 pages of Moxon's ads at the front. Library bookplate removed from front cover. Very good. MacManus 280-4979 1983 $35

SWINBURNE, ALGERNON CHARLES   Chastelard; A Tragedy. London: John Camden Hotten, Piccadilly, 1866. First Hotten edition. Full green morocco with marbled endpapers. Presentation copy to James Lorimer Graham inscribed on the second preliminary page. Graham's bookplate. Fine. MacManus 280-4978 1983 $350

SWINBURNE, ALGERNON CHARLES   The collected Poetical Works. London, 1917-20. 6 vols. 8vo. Orig. cloth, gilt. Traylen 94-803 1983 £12

SWINBURNE, ALGERNON CHARLES   Complete Poetical Works. N.Y., Williams (1887). Thick 8vo, half green morocco over marbled boards, all edges gilt. Fine. Houle 21-859 1983 $85

SWINBURNE, ALGERNON CHARLES   Dead Love. London: John W. Parker & Son, 1864. Orig. orange paper wrappers. The orig. Wise forgery, not the facsimile done 'about 1904.' Wrappers a bit chipped. In a worn half-morocco slipcase. Fine. MacManus 280-4980 1983 $350

SWINBURNE, ALGERNON CHARLES   The Duke of Gandia. London: Chatto & Windus, 1908. First edition. 12mo. Orig. cloth. Very good. MacManus 280-4982 1983 $25

SWINBURNE, ALGERNON CHARLES   Erechtheus: A Tragedy. London: Chatto & Windus, 1876. Second edition. Orig. cloth. Inscribed by the author's mother on the half-title, dated July 1883. Fine. MacManus 280-4983 1983 $75

SWINBURNE, ALGERNON CHARLES   Essays and Studies. London: Chatto & Windus, 1875. First edition. Orig. cloth. 1000 copies printed. Theo. Wratislaw's copy, with his signature on flyleaf. Bookplates Spine worn. MacManus 280-4984 1983 $25

SWINBURNE, ALGERNON CHARLES   The Heptalogia. Portland, Maine: Thomas B. Mosher, 1898. First American (unauthorized) edition. Orig. blue boards with paper label on spine. Dust jacket (lightly soiled). Limited to 450 copies printed on Van Gelder hand-made paper. Fine. MacManus 280-4985 1983 $50

SWINBURNE, ALGERNON CHARLES   Locrine. A Tragedy. London: Chatto & Windus, 1887. First edition. Orig. cloth. With 32 pages of ads at the back dated "October 1887." Presentation copy inscribed to Edward Burne Jones, dated New Year's Eve, 1887. With Burne Jones's bookplate on the front pastedown endpapers foxed. In a half morocco, soft-lined folding case by Sangorski & Sutcliffe. Very good. MacManus 280-4986 1983 $1,000

SWINBURNE, ALGERNON CHARLES   Locrine. A Tragedy. London: Chatto & Windus, 1887. First edition. Orig. cloth. MacManus 280-4987 1983 $25

SWINBURNE, ALGERNON CHARLES   Love's Cross-Currents. London: Chatto & Windus, 1905. First edition. Orig. cloth. Bookplate. Spine faded. Endpapers lightly foxed. Good. MacManus 280-4988 1983 $20

SWINBURNE, ALGERNON CHARLES   Marino Faliero. London: Chatto & Windus, 1885. First edition. Orig. cloth. With 32 pages of ads dated "January 1885." Presentation copy inscribed to Edward Burne Jones on the half-title. Burne Jones's bookplate on the front pastedown endpaper. Slightly worn, with light foxing to the endpapers. In a half morocco, soft-lined, folding case by Sangorski & Sutcliffe. Very good. Mac-Manus 280-4989 1983 $1,000

SWINBURNE, ALGERNON CHARLES   Marino Faliero. London: Chatto & Windus, 1885. First edition. Orig. cloth. MacManus 280-4990 1983 $25

SWINBURNE, ALGERNON CHARLES   Mary Stuart. London: Chatto & Windus, 1885. First edition. Orig. cloth. With 32 pages of ads inserted at the back dated "November 1881." Presentation copy inscribed to Edward Burne Jones on the half-title. With Burne Jones's bookplate on the front paste-down endpaper. Preliminaries slightly browned. Covers slightly bubbled. In a half morocco folding, soft-lined case by Sangorski & Sutcliffe. Very good. MacManus 280-4991 1983 $1,000

SWINBURNE, ALGERNON CHARLES   A Midsummer Holiday. London: Chatto & Windus, 1884. First edition. Orig. cloth. MacManus 280-4993 1983 $25

SWINBURNE, ALGERNON CHARLES   Miscellanies. London: Chatto & Windus, 1886. First edition. Orig. cloth. Very good. MacManus 280-4994 1983 $25

SWINBURNE, ALGERNON CHARLES   A Note on Charlotte Bronte. Chatto & Windus, 1877. First edition (3rd issue). Half title, inserted dedication leaf and 32 pp ads. Orig. dark blue cloth, gilt border and spine, v.g. Jarndyce 30-911 1983 £24

SWINBURNE, ALGERNON CHARLES   Notes of An English Republican on the Muscovite Crusade. London: Chatto & Windus, 1876. First edition. Orig. grey paper wrappers (a bit dustly and worn). Bookplate of Robert Hoe. Very good. MacManus 280-4995 1983 $75

SWINBURNE, ALGERNON CHARLES   Notes on Poems and Reviews. London:
John Camden Hotten, 1866. First edition. Stitched as issued. 1000
copies printed. First few leaves torn, one leaf tape-repaired.
MacManus 280-4996 1983 $75

SWINBURNE, ALGERNON CHARLES   Poems and Ballads. John Camden Hotten,
1866. First edition, second issue. Half title. Orig. green cloth,
bevelled boards. Tipped-in Hotten title, but in the orig. Moxon binding: 'London Moxon' at base of spine. Jarncyde 31-922 1983 £22

SWINBURNE, ALGERNON CHARLES   Poems and Ballads. London: Hotten, 1866.
First Hotten edition. 12mo. Orig. cloth. Inner hinges repaired.
Good, sound copy. MacManus 280-4999 1983 $25

SWINBURNE, ALGERNON CHARLES   Poems and Ballads. London: Chatto &
Windus, 1878. First edition. Second Series. Orig. dark green cloth.
Fine. MacManus 280-5000 1983 $35

SWINBURNE, ALGERNON CHARLES   Poems and Ballads. John Camden Hotten,
1878. First edition, 1p ads., half title. Orig. dark green cloth,
bevelled boards, spine lettered in gilt, v.g. The foolscrap 8vo
issue uniform with the first series. Jarndyce 31-926 1983 £20

SWINBURNE, ALGERNON CHARLES   Poems and Ballads. N.Y.: Worthington
Co., 1889. First American edition. Third Series. Orig. cloth.
Former owner's signature on the title page. MacManus 280-4998 1983
$35

SWINBURNE, ALGERNON CHARLES   Posthumous Poems. London: William Heinemann, 1917. First edition. Orig. cloth. Fine. MacManus 280-5001
1983 $25

SWINBURNE, ALGERNON CHARLES   Shakespeare. London: Henry Frowde,
1909. First edition. Red cloth. Fine. Bradley 66-331 1983 $22.50

SWINBURNE, ALGERNON CHARLES   Shakespeare. Oxford: Henry Frowde,
Oxford University Press, 1909. First edition. Orig. cloth. Fine.
MacManus 280-5003 1983 $25

SWINBURNE, ALGERNON CHARLES   The Sisters. London: Chatto & Windus,
1892. First edition. Orig. cloth. Slight pencil scoring in text.
Near-fine. MacManus 280-5004 1983 $25

SWINBURNE, ALGERNON CHARLES   The Sisters. London: Chatto & Windus,
1892. First edition. Orig. cloth. 1250 copies were printed. Very
good. MacManus 280-5008 1983 $25

SWINBURNE, ALGERNON CHARLES   A Song of Italy. London, 1867. 12mo.
Blue cloth. The advertisements appear in each of the seven known
binding variants. Georgiana Burne-Jones copy, with her signature
dated 1910 on (A1) recto. Former owner's bookplate and light rubbing,
but basically a fine copy. In Our Time 156-771 1983 $150

SWINBURNE, ALGERNON CHARLES   A Song of Italy. London: 1867. First
edition. Orig. royal blue cloth. Roger Senhouse's copy with his
bookplate on front pastedown. Extremities worn, front cover spotted,
otherwise very good. Bradley 66-332 1983 $60

SWINBURNE, ALGERNON CHARLES   A Song of Italy. London: John Camden
Hotten, 1867. First edition, first issue. Orig. green cloth. Covers
a little worn, shaken. Good. MacManus 280-5005 1983 $45

SWINBURNE, ALGERNON CHARLES   A Song of Italy. London: John Camden
Hotten, 1867. First edition, remainder binding. Orig. bright blue
cloth. With 8 pages of ads at the front, and 16 pages of ads at the
back. Fine. MacManus 280-5006 1983 $30

SWINBURNE, ALGERNON CHARLES   Songs Before Sunrise. L, 1871. Green
and gold pic. cover slightly spotted, minor interior foxing, front
hinge starting, spine slightly rubbed and worn, good. Quill & Brush
54-1328 1983 $60

SWINBURNE, ALGERNON CHARLES   Songs before Sunrise. London: the
Florence Press, 1909. 4to. Parchment boards, vellum spine, gilt,
t.e.g. Limited edition of 650 numbered copies, printed on hand-
made paper with initial letters in red. Traylen 94-805 1983 £38

SWINBURNE, ALGERNON CHARLES   Songs Before Sunrise. London & N.Y.:
The Florence Press, 1909. 4to, cloth backed boards; dust soiled.
Fine. One of 650 copies. Argosy 714-722 1983 $40

SWINBURNE, ALGERNON CHARLES   Songs of Springtides. Chatto & Windus,
1880. First edition. 8vo. Orig. cloth, gilt. 1,500 copies printed.
Fenning 61-438 1983 £14.50

SWINBURNE, ALGERNON CHARLES   Songs of the Springtides. London:
Chatto & Windus, 1880. First edition. Orig. cloth. 1500 copies
printed. Good. MacManus 280-5007 1983 $25

SWINBURNE, ALGERNON CHARLES   Songs of Two Nations. London: Chatto
& Windus, 1875. First edition. Orig. cloth. 1000 copies printed.
E.C. Stedman's copy, with his signature on the title-page and his
bookplate on the front paste-down. Very good. MacManus 280-5010
1983 $40

SWINBURNE, ALGERNON CHARLES   The Springtide of Life. Poems of
Childhood...Illustrated by Arthur Rackham. London: Heinemann,
(1918). Frontis., color plates. 1st ed. Orig. green cloth, gilt,
dj. 3/4 inch piece lacking from crown of dj, else fine copy,
uncommon in dj. Jenkins 155-1047 1983 $100

SWINBURNE, ALGERNON CHARLES   The Springtide of Life. London, 1918.
4to. Orig. green cloth, gilt. 60 illus., including 8 coloured
plates, from drawings by Arthur Rackham. Traylen 94-806 1983 £35

SWINBURNE, ALGERNON CHARLES   Studies in Prose and Poetry. London:
Chatto & Windus, 1894. First edition. Orig. cloth. 1250 copies
printed. Bookplate. Very good. MacManus 280-5011 1983 $25

SWINBURNE, ALGERNON CHARLES   Studies in Song. London, 1880. 8vo.
Cloth. This copy bears a lengthy (for Swinburne) presentation
inscription by the author on inner flyleaf: "To William Smith, Esq.
with the best regards of A. Swinburne Nov. 16, 1981". Small clipping
pasted to front endboard, tiny nick at spinal extremity, otherwise a
fine copy. In Our Time 156-772 1983 $850

SWINBURNE, ALGERNON CHARLES   Studies in Song. London: Chatto & Windus, 1880. First edition. Orig. cloth. Bookplate. Very good.
MacManus 280-5012 1983 $25

SWINBURNE, ALGERNON CHARLES   A Study of Shakespeare. London: Chatto
& Windus, 1880. First edition. Orig. cloth. 1000 copies printed.
Former owner's signature on half-title. Covers partially dampstained.
Good. MacManus 280-5013 1983 $25

SWINBURNE, ALGERNON CHARLES   The Tale of Balen. London: Chatto &
Windus, 1896. First edition. Orig. cloth. Foxed. MacManus 280-
5014 1983 $25

SWINBURNE, ALGERNON CHARLES   Theophile. London: Printed for Private
Circulation, 1915. First edition. 8vo. Orig. gray paper wrappers.
Limited to only 20 copies. Unopened. Very fine. MacManus 280-5015
1983 $200

SWINBURNE, ALGERNON CHARLES   Tristram of Lyonesse and Other Poems.
Portland: Mosher, 1904. Ltd. edition. Thick 8vo, boards. One of
450 copies. Fine. Argosy 714-723 1983 $50

SWINBURNE, ALGERNON CHARLES   Under the Microscope. Portland, Maine:
Thomas B. Mosher, 1899. First American (unauthorized) edition. Orig.
blue boards with paper label on spine. Limited to 450 copies printed
on Van Gelder hand-made paper. Fine. MacManus 280-5016 1983 $40

SWINBURNE, ALGERNON CHARLES   Wearieswa'. London: Printed for Private
Circulation, 1917. First edition. 8vo. Orig. printed wrappers.
Limited to 30 copies. With a brief intro. note by Edmund Gosse. Very
fine. MacManus 280-5018 1983 $175

SWINBURNE, ALGERNON CHARLES   William Blake. London: John Camden
Hotten, 1868. 9 superb facsimile plates (7 hand-colored). on special
facsimile paper. 4to. Cloth. With the publisher's prospectus
ticket for other Blake facsimiles tipped onto front flyleaf. Binding
a little shaken and worn. Ars Libri 32-42 1983 $150

SWINBURNE, ALGERNON CHARLES   William Blake. John Camden Hotten, 1868. 2nd edition, with illus. from Blake's designs in facs., coloured and plain, 16pp ads. Orig. blue cloth, very sl. rubbed, v.g. Jarndyce 31-923 1983 £72

SWINBURNE, ALGERNON CHARLES   A Year's Letters. Portland, Maine: Thomas B. Mosher, 1901. First book edition. Orig. parchment-backed boards with paper label on spine. Dust jacket, in publisher's box (a little worn). Limited to 450 copies printed on Van Gelder paper. Very fine. MacManus 280-5019 1983 $50

SWINNERTON, FRANK   George Gissing, a Critical Study. 1912. 2pp ads. Half title, front. port. Orig. blue cloth, t.e.g. Jarndyce 31-714 1983 £20

SWINNERTON, FRANK   George Gissing. A Critical Study. N.Y.: George H. Doran, (1923). First American edition. Orig. cloth. Dust jacket. Very good. MacManus 278-2237 1983 $20

SWINTON, A. H.   Insect Variety. (1881). 8 plates (some coloured), 8vo, original cloth. Wheldon 160-1174 1983 £15

SWINTON, JOHN   A Momentous Question, The Respective Attitudes of Labor and Capital. Phila., 1895. Illustrated, cloth, first few pp. heavily stained. Sm. piece of spine gone. Covers worn. King 46-129 1983 $35

SWYNNERTON, C.   Romantic Tales from the Panjab with Indian Nights' Entertainment. London, 1908. One. vol. edition. 8vo. Orig. cloth. Decorative cloth. Good. Edwards 1044-684 1983 £12

SYDENHAM, THOMAS   Tractatus de Podagra et Hydrope. Typis R.N. Impensis Gualt. Kettilby, 1683. First edition, 8vo, cont. calf, neatly rebacked, a very good copy. Fenning 60-405 1983 £550

SYDENHAM, THOMAS   The Works of Thomas Sydenham MD. Sydenham Society, London, 1848-50. 2 vols., 8vo, orig. cloth, t.e.g., a little rubbed. Quaritch NS 5-104 1983 $200

SYDENHAM, THOMAS   Works. London, Printed for the Sydenham Society, 1848-1850. 2 vols. 8vo. Binding of vol. 2 faded and with a few stains. Morrill 289-223 1983 $85

SYDNEY, SAMUEL   The History of Australia. New York, Hurst & Co., ca. 1876. Illus., cr 8vo, orig. cloth. Shoddy auto-destruct production but in good cond. K Books 301-174 1983 £50

SYDOW, ECKART VON   Afrikanische Plastik. Aus dem Nachlass heraus-gegeben von Gerdt Kutscher. Berlin: Gebr. Mann, 1954. 144 plates. Small folio. Boards, 1/4 cloth. Ars Libri 34-756 1983 $150

SYDOW, ECKART VON   Kunst der Naturvolker. Berlin: Bruno Cassirer, 1932. Prof. illus. Large 4to. Wrappers. Dust jacket. Ars Libri 34-74 1983 $100

SYDOW, ECKART VON   Die Kunst der Naturvolker und der Vorzeit. Berlin: Propylaen-Verlag, 1923. 24 tipped-in plates. Over 1000 illus. 4to. Boards, 3/4 leather. First edition. Ars Libri 34-75 1983 $100

SYDOW, ECKART VON   Die Kunst der Naturvolker und der Vorzeit. Berlin: Propylaen-Verlag, n.d. 24 tipped-in plates. Over 1000 illus. 4to. Boards. 3/4 leather. Ars Libri 34-76 1983 $100

SYDOW, ECKART VON   Kunst und Religion der Naturvolker. Oldenburg: Gerhard Stalling, 1926. 3 tipped-in color plates. 83 monochrome plates. 55 text illus. Large 4to. Boards, 1/4 cloth. Ars Libri 34-77 1983 $100

SYKES, E.   Digesta Malacologica, Nos. 1-2. 1901-03. 8vo, wrappers. Wheldon 160-1235 1983 £15

SYKES, E.   Through Deserts and Oases of Central Asia. London, 1920. 2 maps, 1 folding in pocket. Numerous plates. 8vo. Orig. cloth. Good. Edwards 1044-685 1983 £50

SYKES, PERCY   A History of Afghanistan. 1940. 2 vols., 8 maps, illus., d/w. Inscribed "To the Most Honorable the Marquis of Zetland...Sir Percy Sykes, September 1940". K Books 307-172 1983 £38

A SYLLABUS of a Course of Chemical Lectures Read at Guy's Hospital. Printed by William Phillips, 1816. With an engraved frontis. of the chemical theatre at Guy's. Interleaved throughout with unused blank leaves. 8vo, small library stamp in three or four places, but otherwise a very good to nice copy in calf-backed marbled boards. Fenning 62-14 1983 £95

SYLVESTER, HERBERT MILTON   Romance of the Maine Coast. Boston, 1909. Author's edition, each is limited to 1000 numbered copies. Illus. Vols. 1, 3, 4 & 5 (of 5). T.e.g. Ex-library. Very worn. Vol. 4, spine damaged. King 45-97 1983 $25

SYLVESTER, NATHANIEL BARTLETT   Historical Sketches of Northern New York and the Adirondack Wilderness. Troy, 1877. First edition. Portraits. 8vo. Binding slightly rubbed and faded; stains on back cover; backstrip with several tears, 3 small blank pieces lacking; text nice. Morrill 290-373 1983 $30

SYLVESTER, TIPPING   Original Poems and Translations. London: Printed for J. Wilford...1733. 8vo, without the errata slip included in "some copies"; new quarter morocco. First edition. Quaritch NS 7-122 1983 $425

SYMES, M.   Gesandschaftsreise Nach Dem Konigreiche Ava im Jahre 1795. Hamburg, 1800. Folding map, 8 plates, 3 folding. Half calf. 8vo. Good. Edwards 1044-686 1983 £90

SYMINGTON, C. F.   Foresters' Manual of Dipterocarps. Kuala Lumpur, 1941. 114 figures, royal 8vo, wrappers. Issued during the war in 500 copies. Wheldon 160-2107 1983 £15

SYMINGTON, JOHNSON   An Atlas Illustrating the Topographical Anatomy of the Head, Neck and Trunk. Belfast, (Nov. 1917). Ex-lib. Complete set of 34 oblong folio plates of glossy cardboard, enclosed in orig. cloth portfolio with ties. Argosy 713-524 1983 $75

SYMINGTON, JOHNSON   An Atlas of Skiagrams Illustrating the Development of the Teeth, with Explanatory Text. London, 1908. 5 text illus., 4to, cloth. First edition. Argosy 713-525 1983 $65

SYMINGTON, NOEL HOWARD   The Night Climbers of Cambridge. Chatto and Windus, 1937. 8vo, 55 pages of photographs, orig. cloth, spotted, slightly frayed at top of spine. First edition. Bickersteth 77-251 1983 £18

SYMOND, ARTHUR   London Nights. London: Leonard C. Smithers, 1895. First edition. Orig. cloth. One of 50 large paper copies. Presentation copy to Vincent O'Sullivan, inscribed and dated June 14, 1895. Spine and covers water-stained. Good. MacManus 280-5040 1983 $165

SYMONDS, JOHN   Remarks upon an Essay, Intituled, the History of the Colonization of the Free States of Antiquity... London, 1778. Later wraps., a large, untrimmed copy. Reese 18-123 1983 $275

SYMONDS, JOHN ADDINGTON   Animi Figura. London: Smith, Elder, & Co., 1882. First edition. Orig. cloth. Covers slightly rubbed, foxed. Former owner's signature on verso of front free endpaper. Very good. MacManus 280-5027 1983 $35

SYMONDS, JOHN ADDINGTON   In the Key of Blue, and Other Prose Essays. Elkin Mathews, 1893. First edition, half title, 15pp ads. Untrimmed. Orig. light brown cloth, gilt, t.e.g. Jarndyce 31-927 1983 £15

SYMONDS, JOHN ADDINGTON   Our Life in The Swiss Highlands. London & Edinburgh: Adam & Charles Black, 1892. First edition. Orig. cloth. Plain buff dust jacket printed on spine (hinges torn, dust-soiled). Inner hinges weak. Flyleaf torn. MacManus 280-5028 1983 $25

SYMONDS, JOHN ADDINGTON   A Problem in Modern Ethics. London:
Privately printed, 1896. Orig. cloth. Limited to 100 copies. Mac-
Manus 280-5029 1983 $45

SYMONDS, JOHN ADDINGTON   Renaissance in Italy... New York:
Henry Holt, 1881-3. 5 vols. 1st ed. Orig. blue cloth, gilt. Fine
set. Jenkins 155-1194 1983 $75

SYMONDS, JOHN ADDINGTON   Shelley. London: Macmillan & Co., 1884.
Eleventh Thousand; originally published in 1878. Rebound in 3/4
brown morocco & cloth. Fine. MacManus 280-4736 1983 $45

SYMONDS, JOHN ADDINGTON   A Short History of the Renaissance in
Italy. N.Y.: Henry Holt & Co., (c.1893). Possibly the first American
edition. Orig. decorated cloth. Near-fine. MacManus 280-5030 1983
$20

SYMONS, ALPHONSE JAMES ALBERT   The Nonesuch Century. London: Nonesuch Press, 1936. Quarto. Illus. Limited to 750 copies. Covers
slightly faded, else very fine. Bookplate. Bromer 25-267 1983 $750

SYMONS, ALPHONSE JAMES ALBERT   The Quest For Corvo. London: Cassell
& Co., (1931). First edition. Orig. cloth. Dust jacket (worn, soiled,
with a few small tears). Author's copy with his bookplate on the front
pastedown endpaper. Near-fine. MacManus 277-1150 1983 $135

SYMONS, ALPHONSE JAMES ALBERT   The Quest for Corvo. London: The
Curwen Press, 1934. First edition. 8vo. Orig. black cloth, gilt.
Presentation copy, inscr. on fly-leaf "Vincent Ranger with the cordial
& grateful salutations of his friend the author." A little dull.
Traylen 94-690 1983 £30

SYMONS, ALPHONSE JAMES ALBERT   The Quest for Corvo. New York: Macmillan Co., 1934. First U.S. edition. 8vo. Cloth. Dust jacket.
Fine. Oak Knoll 48-113 1983 $20

SYMONS, ALPHONSE JAMES ALBERT   Tradition and Experiment in Present-
Day Literature. N.Y.: Oxford University Press, 1929. First edition.
Orig. cloth. Spine edges a bit worn. A.J.A. Symons's copy with his
bookplate. Good. MacManus 280-5033 1983 $50

SYMONS, ARTHUR   Aubrey Beardsley. London, 1948.
16 plates. Dust jacket. Very good. Houle 21-79 1983 $20

SYMONS, ARTHUR   Charles Baudelaire, a Study.
London: Elkin Mathews, 1920. First edition. 8vo. Half-parchment
over boards, t.e.g., others uncut. One of 100 copies printed on
handmade paper and with the author's signed and numbered paragraph
on limitation. Covers lightly soiled; tape marks on front and
back endpapers. Oak Knoll 48-18 1983 $35

SYMONS, ARTHUR   The Collected Works of Arthur Symons.
London: Martin Secker, 1924. First edition. 9 vols. Orig. cloth.
One of 100 sets signed by author. Some covers and endpapers a bit
spotted. Very good. MacManus 280-5046 1983 $350

SYMONS, ARTHUR   Confessions, A Study in Pathology.
NY 1930. First edition, limited to 542 numbered copies, signed
by the author. Gilt-dec. cloth, t.e.g., minor wear. King 46-339
1983 $60

SYMONS, ARTHUR   Great Acting in English. (London):
Privately Printed, 1907. First edition. Orig. wrappers. Very fine.
MacManus 280-5038 1983 $50

SYMONS, ARTHUR   Images of Good and Evil. London: William Heinemann, 1899. First edition. Orig. buckram. Spine and covers
a trifle worn. Very good. MacManus 280-5036 1983 $65

SYMONS, ARTHUR   An Introduction to the Study of Browning.
London: Cassell & Co., 1886. First edition. Orig. cloth. From the
library of A.J.A. Symons, with his bookplate on the front paste-down
endpaper. Corners a bit rubbed. Front endpaper cracked along inner
hinge. Very good. MacManus 280-5039 1983 $100

SYMONS, ARTHUR   An Introduction to the Study of Browning.
London: Cassell & Co., 1886. First edition. Orig. cloth. Signature
on title-page. Extremities of spine worn. Bookplate. Good. MacManus
280-5037 1983 $45

SYMONS, ARTHUR   Knave of Hearts. NY/Lon., 1913. Edges
lightly worn, minor soiling to cover and endpapers, else very good,
owner's name, date. Quill & Brush 54-1329 1983 $30

SYMONS, ARTHUR   Notes on Joseph Conrad. London: 1925.
First edition. Boards. Fine in dust jacket. Advance promotional
flyer for book laid in. Bradley 66-77 1983 $40

SYMONS, ARTHUR   Notes on Joseph Conrad. London, 1926.
First edition. One of 250 numbered copies signed by the author.
T.e.g. Hand made paper. Spare title label. Dustwrapper slightly
stained at the spine. Near fine. Jolliffe 26-103 1983 £45

SYMONS, ARTHUR   Studies in Two Literatures. London:
Leonard Smithers, 1897. First edition. 8vo. Orig. polished
buckram. Limited to 400 copies. Small tear in back hinge, some
material pasted in. Shaken. Oak Knoll 48-357 1983 $20

SYMONS, ARTHUR   Tragedies. London: William Heinemann,
1916. First edition. Orig. cloth with paper spine label. Dust jacket
(spine faded; margins rubbed). Spine a trifle faded. Some offsetting
to the endpapers. Uncut. Near-fine. MacManus 280-5044 1983 $65

SYMONS, ARTHUR   Tristan and Iseult. London: William
Heinemann, 1917. First edition. Orig. cloth with paper spine label.
Dust jacket (spine and covers slightly faded and worn). Uncut. Near-
fine. MacManus 280-5045 1983 $65

SYMONS, ARTHUR   William Blake. London, 1907. First
edition. 8vo. Orig. buckram, gilt. Traylen 94-83 1983 £20

SYMONS, J.   Synopsis Plantarum Insulis Britannicis
Indigenarum... London: apud J. White, 1798. First edition. 12mo.
Half calf, light wear. Heath 48-15 1983 £35

SYMONS, THOMAS W.   Information...Respecting the Navigable
Waters of the Upper Columbia River and Its Tributaries, and of the
Country Adjacent Thereto. Wash., 1882. 7 plates, map in 25 sheets.
Orig. printed wraps. First edition. Ginsberg 46-619 1983 $65

SYMONS, THOMAS W.   Report of an Examination of the Upper
Columbia River and the Territory in its Vicinity in September and
October 1881. Washington, 1882. 25 plates of sectional map. Folding
map. Illus. Printed wraps. Very fine. Reese 19-580 1983 $135

SYMPOSIUM Lincolniana, Patriotic Speeches by Abraham Lincoln and Poems
by Victor Hugo. New York: Cog d'Or Press, (1942). Specimens of Denby
Type. 4to. Cloth. Limited to 400 numbered copies and signed by
Denby. Illus. Oak Knoll 48-374 1983 $25

SYNGE, JOHN MILLINGTON   Dierdre of the Sorrows. Churchtown: The
Cuala Press, 1910. First edition. Orig. cloth-backed boards. One of
250 copies. Some offsetting to covers and free endpapers, spine a bit
darkened. Good. MacManus 280-5049 1983 $135

SYNGE, JOHN MILLINGTON   Dierdre of the Sorrows. Boston: John
W. Luce & Co., 1911. First American trade edition. Orig. parchment-
backed boards. Spine lightly soiled. MacManus 280-5050 1983 $25

SYNGE, JOHN MILLINGTON   The Playboy of the Western World. Dublin:
Maunsel & Co., 1907. First theatre edition. Orig. pictorial wrappers.
Spine a bit faded and slightly chipped, with several small tears to
the overlapping edges of the covers. Contents in very good condition.
MacManus 280-5054 1983 $125

SYNGE, JOHN MILLINGTON   The Playboy of the Western World. Dublin:
Maunsel & Co., 1907. First edition. Frontis. port. Orig. cloth.
Spine and covers a bit worn. Some offsetting to the free endpapers.
Bookplate. Very good. MacManus 280-5053 1983 $85

SYNGE, JOHN MILLINGTON   Poems and Translations. Dundrum: Cuala
Press, 1909. First edition. Orig. cloth-backed boards. Spine slightly
faded and worn. One of 250 copies. Near-fine. MacManus 280-5057
1983 $150

SYNGE, JOHN MILLINGTON   Poems and Translations. Dublin: Maunsel
& Company, 1911. First Dublin edition. Orig. cloth. Covers slightly
spotted. Endpapers a trifle foxed. Former owner's signature. Very
good. MacManus 280-5056 1983 $85

SYNGE, JOHN MILLINGTON   The Tinker's Wedding. Dublin: Maunsel,
1907. First edition. Orig. cloth-backed boards. Bookplate. Good.
MacManus 280-5058 1983 $85

SYNGE, JOHN MILLINGTON   The Tinker's Wedding. Dublin, 1907.
First edition. Flyleaf lightly foxed. Nice. Rota 230-583 1983 £20

SYNGE, JOHN MILLINGTON   The Well of the Saints. N.Y.: Privately
Printed, 1905. First American edition. Orig. printed wrappers. One
of 50 copies, privately printed for John Quinn, and numbered and
initialed by him. Near-fine. MacManus 280-5061 1983 $450

SYNGE, JOHN MILLINGTON   The Well of the Saints. Dublin: The
Abbey Theatre, 1905. First theatre edition. Orig. pictorial wrappers.
Spine faded and worn. A few small tears to the overlapping edge of
the covers. Contents in very good condition. MacManus 280-5062 1983
$125

SYNGE, JOHN MILLINGTON   The Works of John M. Synge. Dublin:
Maunsel & Co., 1910. First edition. 4 vols. Orig. brown buckram,
dust jackets (somewhat worn, one defective). Slight foxing to the
endpapers. Near-fine. MacManus 280-5065 1983 $850

SYNGE, JOHN MILLINGTON   Works. Dublin, Manusel, 1910. First
collected edition. Frontis. portraits. Gilt stamped brown cloth,
t.e.g., uncut. Bookplates. 4 vols. Very good. Houle 22-858 1983
$250

SYNGE, JOHN MILLINGTON   The Works of John M. Synge. Boston:
John W. Luce & Co., 1912. First American edition. 4 vols. Illus.
Orig. cloth with leather labels. Spines very slightly rubbed. Former
owner's signature. Near-fine. MacManus 280-5063 1983 $250

SYNGE, SAMUEL   Letters to My Daughter. Dublin: The
Talbot Press, (n.d.). Orig. boards. Dust jacket. Illus. Fine.
MacManus 280-5080 1983 $35

SYPHER, J. R.   School History of Pennsylvania. Phila.:
J.B. Lippincott & Co., 1869. Ads. Illus. Orig. cloth. Some wear at
extremities of spine. Presentation copy from author. Jenkins 152-323
1983 $45

SYSTEM of Exercise and Instruction of Field Artillery...Boston, 1829.
First edition. 56 engraved plates. Small 8vo, contemporary calf.
Very nice copy. Morrill 290-528 1983 $75

SZUKALSKI, STANISLAW   Projects in Design. Chicago:
University of Chicago Press, (1929). Large 4to, plates. This is
one of 150 numbered copies with an orig. woodblock frontis. designed,
printed and signed by Szukalski. The plate is printed on rice
paper and mounted and is both titled and signed by the artist.
Fine copy in gilt-stamped cloth. Karmiole 74-17 1983 $250

SZYK, ARTHUR   The Book of Ruth. (NY): Limited
Editions Club, 1947. 4to, with 8 mounted color plates. Initials
in gold. Ltd. to 1950 copies, signed by Szyk, and printed at the
Aldus Printers. Bound in half white leather over gilt-stamped
boards. Te.g. Slipcase. Very fine copy. Karmiole 71-88 1983
$135

T

TABARANT, A.   Manet et ses oeuvres. Paris: Galli-mard, 1947. 678 reference illus. Stout 4to. Buckram. Ars Libri 32-422 1983 $50

TABARANT, A   Utrillo. Paris: Bernheim-Jeune, 1926. Prof. illus. Large 4to. Wrappers. Flyleaf clipped. Ars Libri 32-682 1983 $100

TABARES, DON DIEGO   Defensa De Don Diego Tabares. (Madrid, 1764). First edition. Folio. Cont. marbled wrappers. Fine. Jenkins 152-441 1983 $300

TABLES of Distances and Iteneraries of Routes in the Department of Texas. San Antonio: Headquarters Department of Texas, Engineer Off., Oct. 1, 1893. Orig. printed wrappers. Sewn as issued. Jenkins 153-623 1983 $150

TABOR, ELIZA   Dimplethorpe. Hurst & Blackett, 1880. First edition, 3 vols. Half titles, 16 pp ads. vol. III. Orig. light blue cloth, a little rubbed and spines faded. W.H. Smith labels on inside covers. A good copy. Jarndyce 30-567 1983 £36

TABOR, ELIZA   Hester's Sacrifice. London: Hurst & Blackett, 1866. First edition. 3 vols. Orig. brown cloth. Spines and covers worn and slightly soiled. Good. MacManus 280-5082 1983 $135

TACHE, ALEXANDRE ANTONIN   Sketch of the North-West of America. Montreal: Lovell, 1870. 22 1/2cm. Printed wrappers. First English edition. Fine. Scarce. McGahern 54-172 1983 $125

TACHE, J. C.   Canada at the Universal Exhibition of 1855. Toronto: Printed by John Lovell, 1856. 24 1/2cm. Frontis., 2 full-page plans, folding map. Smooth cloth with paper label, a variant. Frayed at the head band, label chipped else very good. McGahern 53-159 1983 $45

TACITUS, GAIUS CORNELIUS   The Annals. London, 1884. 8vo, cloth. Salloch 385-763 1983 $22

TACITUS, GAIUS CORNELIUS   The Annals. London, 1904. 2 vols., 8vo. Salloch 385-762 1983 $30

TACITUS, GAIUS CORNELIUS   Opera Quae Supersunt. Zuerich, 1859 & 1877. 2 vols., 4to, wrs. Cloth. Salloch 385-758 1983 $45

TACITUS, GAUIS CORNELIUS   De Vita et Moribus Iulii Agricolae Liber. London: the Doves Press, 1900. Small 4to. Orig. vellum, gilt. Limited edition of 225 copies. Traylen 94-808 1983 £165

TACOMA and Vicinity. (Tacoma), 1888. Illus., 32 tinted plates of scenery, etc. Orig. pictorial cloth. First edition. Ginsberg 46-798 1983 $75

TACONET, TOUSSAINT-GASPARD   Les Ecosseuses de la Halle, Ambigu-Poissard. Paris, 1767. 8vo, wrs. Salloch 387-170 1983 $60

TAEVERNIER, AUGUST   James Ensor. Gent: N.V. Erasmus Ledeberg, 1973. Ca. 150 illus. Large 4to. Cloth. Dust jacket. Catalogue raisonne. Ars Libri 32-207 1983 $225

TAFT, LORADO   Modern Tendencies in Sculpture. Chicago, 1921. Sm. 4to, 429 illus. hors texte, cloth. Ars Libri SB 26-231 1983 $30

TAGGARD, GENEVIEVE   For Eager Lovers. NY, 1922. Signed inscription from author, edges wearing and spine edges lightly chipped, paper covering front gutter torn, spine label chipped, interior very good. Quill & Brush 54-1330 1983 $75

TAGGARD, GENEVIEVE   The Life and Mind of Emily Dickinson. N.Y., 1930. First edition. Illus. 8vo, cloth. D.w. Argosy 714-236 1983 $30

TAGGARD, GENEVIEVE   Long View: Poems. New York, 1942. 8vo. Cloth. Small review clipping on inside of endboard, else fine in dj. In Our Time 156-775 1983 $25

TAGGARD, GENEVIEVE   Not Mine to Finish. NY, 1934. Signed inscription to her parents, tiny tear to paper on front hinge, edges slightly bumped, near fine in slightly soiled, lightly chipped, very good dustwrapper. Quill & Brush 54-1331 1983 $100

TAGGARD, GENEVIEVE   A Part of Vermont. Vermont, 1945. 8vo. Wraps. Inscribed by Taggard to Alexander Laing. A fine copy. In Our Time 156-776 1983 $35

TAGGARD, GENEVIEVE   Slow Music. New York, 1946. 8vo. Cloth. Inscribed by the poet to Alexander Laing. Some fading to spine, else fine copy. In Our Time 156-777 1983 $25

TAGGARD, GENEVIEVE   Travelling Standing Still. NY, 1928. Limited to 110 numbered and signed copies, edges very slightly rubbed, else bright fine copy in chipped glassine wrapper in slightly soiled, very good slipcase. Quill & Brush 54-1332 1983 $125

TAGGART, SAMUEL   Mr. Taggart's Address to his Constituents. (Washington, 1813). Dsb. Good. Reese 18-426 1983 $30

TAGORE, SOURINDRO MOHUN   Six Principal Ragas. Calcutta, 1876. With lithograph frontis. and six lithograph plates. Folio, dec. cloth. Salloch 387-240 1983 $225

TAINE, HIPPOLYTE   Reise in Italien. Jena, 1910. 2 vols. 8vo, cloth. Salloch 385-400 1983 $24

TAINSH, EDWARD CAMPRELL   A Study of the Works of Alfred Tennyson. Chapman & Hall, 1868. First edition. Half title. Orig. green cloth, a little rubbed, bevelled boards. Jarndyce 31-937 1983 £10.50

TALBOT, EDWARD ALLEN   Five Years' Residence in the Canadas. London: Longman, Hurst, Rees, Orme, Brown, 1824. 23cm. First edition. Preliminary 16p. ads. 2 lithographic frontis. views. 2p. plan. Orig. boards, with paper labels. A fine set. Rare thus. McGahern 54-173 1983 $450

TALBOT, J. S.   Foxes at Home. London: Horace Cox, 1906. First edition. Illus. with photographs. Orig. cloth. Presentation copy, inscribed on the front flyleaf "With the Author's respectful compliments, 1906." Bookplates. Edges of spine a bit rubbed. In a half-morocco slipcase. Fine. MacManus 278-1976 1983 $135

TALBOT, THEODORE   The Journals of...1843 and 1849-52. Portland, Ore., 1931. Orig. cloth. First edition. Ginsberg 47-853 1983 $45

TALBOT, THEODORE   The Journals of Theodore Talbot... Portland, 1931. Fine copy. Jenkins 153-549 1983 $35

TALBOT, THOMAS   The Granvilles. London: Sampson, Low, Marston, Searle, & Rivington, 1882. First edition. 3 vols. Orig. cloth. Extremities rubbed. Good. MacManus 280-5085 1983 $125

TALBOT, WILLIAM   The Bishop of Oxford's Charge to the Clergy of His Diocese. Printed for Jonah Bowyer, 1712. First edition, 4to, wrapper. Very good copy. Fenning 62-360 1983 £12.50

THE TALE Of Gamelyn. (New Rochelle): Elston Press, (1901). 12mo. Cloth-backed boards, paper spine label. Limited to 200 copies. Printed at the private press of Clarke Conwell in black letter with red heading. Minor cover soiling, else a fine copy. Oak Knoll 49-177 1983 $75

TALES of Frontier Life as Told by Those who Remember the Days of the Territory and Early Statehood of Washington. N.p., (1937-38). 3 vols. Orig. pictorial cloth. First edition. Ginsberg 47-963 1983 $75

TALFOURD, THOMAS NOON   The Castilian. London: Edward Moxon, 1853. First edition, privately printed. Orig. cloth. Presentation copy inscribed on the half-title to Horace Waddington Esq., dated February 1854. With the words "not published" on the half-title and title-page, and several corrections, in the author's hand. Extremities of spine rubber. Inner hinges weak. Good. MacManus 280-5086 1983 $75

TALFOURD, THOMAS NOON   Ion; a tragedy, in five acts. To which are added a few sonnets. London: printed by A. J. Valpy, for private circulation. Not published, n.d. (1835). 8vo, cont. dark green morocco (slightly scuffed). 2nd edition. An association copy, inscribed on the title-page by the author. Bound in are several relevant newspaper clippings, portions of playbills, for the opening night and subsequent performances, a one-page ALS of thanks, and a letter. In very good condition. Ximenes 64-513 1983 $200

TALFOURD, THOMAS NOON   The Letters...With A Sketch of his Life. London: Edward Moxon, 1837. First edition. 2 vols. Frontis. Orig. cloth. Presentation copy, inscribed on the half-title to "John Jackson Blandy Esq. From the Editor." Spines and edges faded. Hinges splitting near heads of spines. The Borowitz copy. In a cloth slipcase. Very good. MacManus 279-3107 1983 $150

TALFOURD, THOMAS NOON   The Letters of Charles Lamb, with a Sketch of his Life. London: Moxon, 1837. First edition. 2 vols. Orig. cloth (spines faded). With the half-titles. In a half-morocco slipcase. Fine. MacManus 279-3108 1983 $110

TALLEYRAND, CHARLES M.   Memoir Concerning the Commercial Relations of the United States with Great Britain. (London? 1806). Stitched, good. Reese 13-287 1983 $50

TALLMADGE, SAMUEL   Orderly Books of the Fourth N. Y. Regiment, 1778-1780. Albany, 1932. Plates, tall, thick 8vo. Argosy 710-464 1983 $35

TANGUAY, CYPRIEN   Dictionnaire Genealogique des Familles Canadiennes... Quebec: Eusebe Senecal, 1871-1890. 25cm. 7 vols. Folding map. Bound in wine pebbled cloth, gilt and black stamped titles and decorations, spine and bottom boards damp-stained on vol. 4. Some hinges shaken else good to very good set. Scarce. McGahern 54-174 1983 $350

TANGUAY, CYPRIEN   Dictionnaire Genealogique des Familles Canadiennes. Vol. 1, 1608-1700. Quebec, 1871. Port., 8vo, straight-grained morocco (edges rubbed). Argosy 710-180 1983 $65

TANNER, HEATHER   Woodland Plants. London, 1981. First English edition. One of 950 numbered copies. Numerous black and white drawings by Robin Tanner. T.e.g. Fine in dustwrapper. Jolliffe 26-500 1983 $55

TANNER, HENRY S.   An Alphabetical Index to the Four Sheet Map of the United States. Philadelphia, (1848,). Cloth, chipped at head of spine, otherwise good. Reese 19-531 1983 $50

TANNER, HENRY S.   Memoir on the Recent Surveys, Observations, and Internal Improvements, in the United States... Philadelphia: The author, 1830. Orig. 3/4 morocco, gilt dec. spine. Scattered foxing. Felcone 22-239 1983 $125

TANNER, JOHN   The hidden treasures of the art of physick... London: George Sawbridge, 1659. First edition. Thick 12mo. Cont. sheep. A few headlines trimmed close, some slight marginal worming, but generally an excellent copy. Ximenes 63-292 1983 $750

TANSILL, CHARLES C.   Documents Illustrative of the Formation of the Union of the American States. Washington, GPO, 1927. 1st ed. Small folio. Inner hinges repaired. Morrill 286-465 1983 $25

TANSILL, CHARLES C.   The United States & Santo Domingo, 1798-1873, a Chapter in Caribbean Diplomacy. Baltimore, 1838. D.w. Argosy 710-616 1983 $30

TANSLEY, A. G.   Aims and Methods in the Study of Vegetation. 1926. Wheldon 160-1575 1983 £15

TANS'UR, WILLIAM   Heaven on Earth; or, the Beauty of Holiness. Printed by A. Pearson, for S. Birt. Also sold by the author. 1738. 8vo, woodcut frontis., old calf, rebacked, preserving the label. First edition. Bickersteth 77-80 1983 £95

TANSWELL, JOHN   The History and Antiquities of Lambeth. Fredk. Pickton, 1858. First edition, front. and illus. Well rebound in maroon cloth, gilt spine lettering. Jarndyce 31-298 1983 £36

THE TAPESTRIES of the Vienna Imperial Court. Vienna: Krystallverlag. 1922. 4to, 44 leaves of plates (20 in color) each with printed tissue guard. Green cloth spine over boards; paper spine label. Karmiole 74-88 1983 $75

TAPLEY, HARRIET SILVESTER   Salem Imprints 1768-1825. Salem: Essex Institute, 1927. Plates, cloth. Dawson 470-287 1983 $45

TAPPE, JACOB   Oratio de Tabaco ejusque hodierno abusu. Helmstedt: Georg-Wolfgang Hamm, 1689. Small 4to. Modern boards. Kraus 164-240 1983 $250

TAPPER, J. W. E.   Songs, Poems and Prose. Printed for Private Circulation, and sold only by the author. 1897. First edition, front. Orig. olive cloth, a.e.g. Signed presentation copy to his cousins by the author, Jan 18 1898. Fine. Jarndyce 30-853 1983 £12.50

TAPRELL DORLING, H.   Ribbons and Medals. London, 1946. Enlarged and revised edition. 17 coloured plates, numerous illus. Sm. 8vo. Orig. dust jacket. Fine. Edwards 1042-482 1983 £12

TARAVAL, SIGISMUNDO   The Indian Uprising in Lower California, 1734-1737. Los Angeles: The Quivira Society, 1931. Illus. Boards with vellum spine. 1 of 35 copies. Signed by the editor Marguerite Eyer Wilbur. Jenkins 153-550 1983 $125

TARCHANOFF, JEAN DE   Hypnotisme, Suggestion et Lecture des Pensees Trad. par Ernest Jaubert. Paris, 1891. Small 8vo, pr. wrs.; uncut & unopened. First edition. Argosy 713-526 1983 $45

TARDIEU, AMBROISE   Etude Medico-Legale sur la Folie. Paris, 1872. First edition. 8vo, cont. boards crudely rebacked. Argosy 713-527 1983 $100

TARDUCCI, FRANCISCO   The Life of Christopher Columbus. Detroit, 1890. 1st American ed. Illus. 2 vols., 8vo. Morrill 286-467 1983 $25

TARG, WILLIAM   The Book-Hunter's Guide. Chicago: The Black Archer Press, 1935. First edition. Stiff tan wrappers. Signed on front pastedown. Inscribed. Nice copy. Bradley 66-393 1983 $35

TARG, WILLIAM   Carousel for Bibliophiles. N.Y., Duschnes, 1947. First edition. 4to, illus. Dust jacket. Fine copy. Prospectus laid in loose. Printed by the Southworth-Anthoesen Press. Houle 21-618 1983 $45

TARKINGTON, BOOTH   Beauty and the Jacobin. NY, 1912. Signed inscription from Tarkington. Hinge starting at title, corners rubbed, else very good. Bookplate. Quill & Brush 54-1333 1983 $50

TARKINGTON, BOOTH   Christmas This Year. (Los Angeles, Ward Ritchie Press, 1945). First and only edition. Folio. Stiff blue printed wraps., stitched. One of 52 copies, signed by the publisher, Earle Bernheimer. Fine. Houle 22-860 1983 $300

TARKINGTON, BOOTH   The Gentleman from Indiana. N.Y., 1899. First edition, mixed state. Decorated cloth. Ink inscription, hinges loose. A bit rubbed. Good. King 45-263 1983 $25

TARKINGTON, BOOTH   The Man from Home. N.Y., 1908.
First edition with this title. Illus. with scenes from the play.
8vo, pict. cloth. Argosy 714-724 1983 $35

TARKINGTON, BOOTH   Mary's Neck. N.Y., Doubleday, 1932.
First edition. Color frontis. by Wallace Morgan. Dust jacket
(2 in. chip at lower back), else very good. Houle 21-864 1983
$35

TARKINGTON, BOOTH   Monsieur Beaucaire. N.Y., McClure,
Phillips, 1900. First edition. With frontis. and 5 plates by C.D.
Williams. Red cloth stamped in gilt, t.e.g. (minor fraying at spine
tips, some foxing to text, a few short tears at margins) else good.
Red cloth slipcase. Signed and inscribed by the author "...with
grateful affection of his old classmate. Booth Tarkington. New
York, April 25, 1901." Houle 22-861 1983 $85

TARKINGTON, BOOTH   An Overwhelming Saturday. N.Y.,
International Magazine (1913). First edition. Small 8vo, wrappers
lacking. Good. Houle 21-863 1983 $22.50

TARKINGTON, BOOTH   The Spring Concert. New York: Ridgway
Co., (1916). 1st ed. Orig. green printed wrappers. Fine copy of
this very scarce printing. Jenkins 155-1199 1983 $20

TARKINGTON, BOOTH   The Works of Booth Tarkington. New
York, 1918-19. 8vo. Cloth, boards. 16 vols. 1 of 565 copies
signed by Tarkington. A few bookplates in several vols., else a
fine set. In Our Time 156-778 1983 $350

TARUFFI, CESARE (1821-1902) Hermaphrodismus und Zeigungsfaehigkeit.
Berlin: Hermann Bersdorff, 1908. Second edition. 40 plates, orig.
printed wrappers, edges worn. Gach 95-472 1983 $40

TASISTRO, LOUIS F.   Random Shots and Southern Breezes.
New York, 1842. Two vols. Orig. cloth. Some slight soiling and
foxing, but a good set. Reese 19-532 1983 $250

TASKER, WILLIAM   An elegy on the death of David Garrick,
Esq. London: for the author, printed at Laidler's office; and sold
by Dodsley; Bew; etc., 1779. 4to, wrappers, 1st ed. Half-title
present; a very good copy. Rare. Ximenes 64-514 1983 $275

TASKER, WILLIAM   An elegy on the death of David Garrick,
Esq. London: for the author, printed at Laidler's office; sold by
Dodsley, Bew, etc., 1779. 4to, sewn (stitching loose). 2nd ed.
Very uncommon. Ximenes 64-515 1983 $175

TASMAN, ABEL J.   Journal of His Discovery of Van Dieman's
Land and New Zealand in 1642. L.A., 1965. Illus., charts, maps,
etc. in pocket. Orig. folio cloth, dust jacket. One of 225 copies.
Ginsberg 46-723 1983 $250

TASSI, ROBERTO   La cupola del Correggio nel Duomo
di Parma. Milano: Silvana, 1968. 77 gravure and color plates
in text. Small folio. Boards. Ars Libri 33-121 1983 $75

TASSO, TORQUATO   Jerusalem Delivered; an Heroic Poem.
London: printed by T. Bensley, 1803. Eighth edition, with engraved
portrait and 14 engraved plates by Fittler and others from drawings
by S. Shelley. 2 vols. 4to. Cont. tree calf, gilt decorated
spines with red and blue morocco labels, gilt. Traylen 94-810
1983 £50

TATE, ALLEN   Fragment of a Meditation. The
Cummington Press, 1947. 8vo. Wraps. Printed in a small ed. and
sent out by the poet as a Christmas gift from Allen and Caroline
Tate. Some fading to wrappers, vg-fine copy. In Our Time 156-779
1983 $150

TATE, ALLEN   The Golden Mean and Other Poems.
Palaemon Press, (n.d.). Facsimile of the rare 1st ed. of 1923,
limited to 200 numbered copies. Orig. printed wrappers. Mint copy.
Jenkins 155-1202 1983 $30

TATE, ALLEN   On the Limits of Poetry. N.Y., 1948.
First edition. D.w. Argosy 714-725 1983 $45

TATE, ALLEN   On the Limits of Poetry. NY, 1948.
Very good, owner's name, date. Quill & Brush 54-1335 1983 $30

TATE, ALLEN   Poems 1920-1945. London, 1947. First
edition. Offsetting to endpaper, head of spine slightly bumped, in
dustwrapper with a small nick to head of slightly sunned spine, otherwise a very good copy. Gekoski 2-183 1983 £15

TATE, ALLEN   Poems 1922-1947. NY, 1948. Cloth,
edges slightly soiled else a very good copy. First edition. In
soiled and worn (minor tear) dust wrapper. King 46-340 1983 $25

TATE, ALLEN   Reactionary Essays on Poetry and Ideas.
NY, 1936. Signed, dated inscription from Tate on title, spine faded,
spine label aged and lightly chipped, good, owner's name. Quill &
Brush 54-1336 1983 $60

TATE, ALLEN   Two Conceits for the Eye to Sing,
If Possible. (N.p.): The Cummington Press, 1950. Plain wraps.,
sewn. First edition. One of 300 copies. Reese 20-960 1983 $50

TATE, ALLEN   Who Owns America? Boston & New York,
1936. First edition. Spine and edges of covers a little faded.
Tate's autograph signature. Nice. Rota 230-586 1983 £40

TATE, NAHUM   A duke and no duke. London: printed
for Henry Bonwicke, 1693. Sm. 4to, disbound. Second edition.
Title dusty, a few headlines slightly shaved, else a very good copy.
Uncommon. Ximenes 64-516 1983 $250

TATE, NAHUM   Poems Written on Several Occasions.
London: B. Tooke, 1684. Second edition. Full calf, blind-tooled.
Front hinge cracked and tender, some wear to extremities. Small hole
in last three leaves, affecting several letters, else nice. Beverly
Chew's copy with his engraved bookplate. Bromer 25-113 1983 $150

TATHAM, EDWARD H. R.   Francesco Petrarca. London: The Sheldon
Press, 1925-1926. First edition. Frontis. 2 vols. Large 8vo. Orig.
cloth. Fine. MacManus 280-4177 1983 $25

TATHAM, GEORGE N.   An Exposition of the Character and Management of the New Jersey Joint Monopolies. Philadelphia: 1852.
Gray wrappers. Bradley 66-611 1983 $30

TAUBERT, SIGFRED   Bibliopola: Pictures and Texts About
the Book Trade. Hamburg: Hauswedell, (1966). Two quarto vols. Text
in English, French and German. Near mint set with slip-case. Bookplate. Bromer 25-163 1983 $100

TAVERNER, P. A.   Birds of Canada. 1938. 87 coloured
plates, text-figures, royal 8vo, cloth, spine faded. Wheldon 160-
899 1983 £30

TAVERNER, P. A.   Birds of Eastern Canada. Ottawa, 1919.
50 coloured plates and 68 text-figures, 8vo, cloth. Wheldon 160-898
1983 £20

TAVERNIER, J. B.   The Six Voyages...Through Turkey into
Persia. London: For R.L. & M.P., 1678 &1677. 24 plates, 7 folding,
engravings in text. Folio. Very slight marginal staining and worming.
Cont. panelled calf rebacked, some wear. 8vo. Good. Edwards 1044-
688 1983 £550

TAYLOR, A. E.   Plato. The Man and His Work. 4to,
cloth. Salloch 385-694 1983 $25

TAYLOR, ALBERT PIERCE   Under Hawaiian Skies. Honolulu, 1922.
Photos. Pictorial cloth. Ink inscription. Covers slightly worn and
soiled. King 45-64 1983 $20

TAYLOR, ANN   Original Poems. Routledge, 1868. 1st
edn. thus with illus. by R. Barnes, A.W. Bayes, E.M. Wimperis, J.
Lawson, A.T. Elwes, T. Green, J. Jellicoe, R. Moore, et al. 2pp ads.
Blue sand grain gilt decor. cloth, bevelled edges, a.e.g., top/bottom
of skstrip worn away, bookpl. fr. ep., light foxing contents, good
copy. Hodgkins 27-197 1983 £15

TAYLOR, BAYARD   A Journey to Central Africa. New York:
G.P. Putnam, 1854. 12mo. Folding map. 5 plates. Orig. pictorial
cloth. Rubbed. Adelson Africa-228 1983 $50

TAYLOR, BAYARD   The National Ode. Boston, 1877. Illus.
by T. Moran & others. 8vo, gilt pict. cloth; extremes of spine
rubbed. First edition. Argosy 714-727 1983 $20

TAYLOR, BENJAMIN F.   Summer-Savory, Gleaned from Rural Nooks
in Pleasant Weather. Chicago, S.C. Griggs and Company, 1897. Orig.
green cloth, gilt. 1st ed. Jenkins 153-552 1983 $85

TAYLOR, BERT LESTON   Motley Measures. New York, 1927. 8vo.
Cloth. Bookstore stamp on front fly, spine faded, else a very good
copy. In Our Time 156-484 1983 $20

TAYLOR, EDWARD ROBENSON   Chants with the Soul. San Francisco,
privately printed by Taylor & Taylor, 1920. First edition. Half
orange board over patterned boards, uncut. One of 200 copies. With
a signed presentation from the author. Very good. Houle 22-1185
1983 $60

TAYLOR, ELIZABETH   Nibbles and Me. N.Y., (1946). Thin
8vo, cloth. Illus. by the author. Library edition, with 8p of
photographs of Miss Taylor. Presentation copy. Argosy 714-728
1983 $50

TAYLOR, ELIZABETH   A View of the Harbour. London, 1947.
First English edition. Chipped and slightly spotted dustwrapper.
Fine. Jolliffe 26-501 1983 £25

TAYLOR, ELIZABETH   A Wreath of Roses. London, 1949. First
English edition. Very slightly torn dustwrapper frayed at the head
of the spine. Very good. Jolliffe 26-502 1983 £25

TAYLOR, FENNINGS   Portraits of British North Americans by
W. Notman, Photographer to Her Majesty. Montreal, Lovel, 1865-68.
3 vols. bound in 6. Half morocco. Illus. with 84 mounted orig.
photographs by W. Notman. Ginsberg 46-154 1983 $850

TAYLOR, FRED G.   A Saga of Sugar. (Salt Lake), 1944.
Signed. Illus. Argosy 716-577 1983 $40

TAYLOR, FREDERICK   Recollections of a horse dealer.
London: Ward and Lock, 1861. First edition. Small 8vo. Orig.
yellow printed boards. Slight rubbing. Fine copy. Ximenes 63-186
1983 $40

TAYLOR, GEORGE   Maps Of The Roads Of Ireland. Originally
Published for the Authors as The Act Directs, 1778. Sold by T. Longman
1783. 2nd ed., tall 8vo, engraved vignette title-page, large folding
engraved map, torn, without loss, cont. calf, neatly rebacked, gilt.
Deighton 3-281 1983 £260

TAYLOR, GEORGE H.   Massage. New York, Fowler & Wells,
1884. 1st ed. Small 8vo. Morrill 289-225 1983 $20

TAYLOR, HENRY   Edwin the Fair. John Murray, 1842.
First edition, half title, 2 pp. ads. Orig. brown cloth, paper
label. Jarndyce 30-855 1983 £10.50

TAYLOR, IDA ASHWORTH   Venus' Doves. London: Hurst and
Blackett, 1884. First edition. 3 vols. Orig. decorated cloth.
Spines darkened and worn. Other edges rather worn as well. Covers
slightly soiled. Bookplates. Former owner's signature in all three
volumes. MacManus 280-5088 1983 $85

TAYLOR, ISAAC   Natural History of Enthusiasm. London,
1830. Third edition. Full calf, gilt. K Books 301-177 1983 £25

TAYLOR, ISAAC   The Ship. John Harris, 1835. 4th edn.
with additional illus. Hand-col'd frontis. & 3 other hand-col'd
plates & 16 engrs., 16pp adverts. dd. 1837. Scarlet roan backed
cvrs. sl. discol'd, vg. Hodgkins 27-198 1983 £20

TAYLOR, ISAAC   The World of Mind. An Elementary Book.
NY: 1858. Worn, slight staining to text. Gach 94-657 1983 $25

TAYLOR, J. ORVILLE   The Farmers' School Book. Albany, Pub.
at the Common School Depository, 1837. First edition. 16mo, orig.
printed boards, calf back. Rubbed, some lettering on covers effaced,
light dampstain in text. Morrill 290-530 1983 $35

TAYLOR, JAMES   A Letter to the Misrepresenter of
Papists. Printed by J.D. for J. Robinson...and Thomas Newborough,
1687. First edition, 4to, wrapper, a very good copy. Fenning 61-443
1983 £14.50

TAYLOR, JANE   Little Ann and Other Poems. London,
Routledge, (1883). 1st ed. Illus. by Kate Greenaway. Printed in
Colours by Edmund Evans. 8vo, orig. pictorial boards, cloth back &
corners. Morrill 287-582 1983 $60

TAYLOR, JANE   Meddlesome Matty. London, 1925. First
edition. Intro. by E. Sitwell. Coloured illus. by W. Payne.
Patterned boards. Spine darkened and corners a little worn. Nice.
Rota 230-548 1983 £12

TAYLOR, JANE   Rhymes for the Nursery. Printed for
Darton & Harvey, 1834. 26th edn., frontis. engr. by Moses, 4pp
adverts. rear. Orig. green roan bkstrip, marbled bds., gilt titling,
bkstrip sl. wear & splitting, contents thumbed & foxed, extremities
of cvrs. worn, good. Hodgkins 27-196 1983 £12.50

TAYLOR, JEREMY   XXVIII Sermons preached at Golden
Grove. London: R.N. for R. Royston, 1651. First edition.
Folio. Old calf, rebacked. Engraved vignette on title, which
is ruled in red. Traylen 94-811 1983 £55

TAYLOR, JOHN (1580-1653)   The Water Poet. London: Printed for J.
T(rundle) & H. G(losson), 1621. First edition. 12mo. 19th century
half straight grained morocco and cloth sides (engraved title-page
supplied in a fairly adept pen-and-ink facsimile. Some typographical
ornaments shaved at head of leaves. Several sidenotes cut into, general light browning). Good. MacManus 280-5089 1983 $400

TAYLOR, JOHN (1580-1653)   "The Water Poet". All the Workes
of the John Taylor the Water-Poet. London: J.B. for James Boler,
1630. First collected edition. Folio. Red levant morocco, two-
line gilt borders with inner gilt panel, gilt panelled spine, edges
gilt, by Riviere, preserved in a quarter morocco case. With
curious engraved title-page by T. Cockson introducing a small oval
portrait of the author (re-margined), woodcuts of the Kings in the
text, etc. Front joints worn. Traylen 94-812 1983 £525

TAYLOR, JOHN (1781-1864)   The Identity of Junius with a Distinguished Living Character (Sir Philip Francis) Established. New
York, 1818. 1st American ed. Facsimiles of handwriting, illus.
Portrait. 8vo, orig. boards, paper label. Pasted on front cover is
bookplate of David Hoffman. Ex-library, lacks part of spine,
hinges cracked. Morrill 289-549 1983 $20

TAYLOR, JOSEPH   Apparitions. Lackington, Allen, 1814.
First edition, front. orig. pink boards, rubbed, rebacked with brown
cloth, retaining label. Jarndyce 31-379 1983 £35

TAYLOR, JOSEPH HENRY   Beavers Their Ways and Other Sketches.
Washburn, N. Da., 1904. Original boards with cloth spine, fine copy.
20 plates. A scarce title. Jenkins 151-330 1983 $200

TAYLOR, JOSEPH HENRY   Beavers, Their Ways; and Other Sketches.
Washburn, N.Dak.: Printed and Published by the Author, 1904. Plates.
Cloth, somewhat worn. Rear fly out and last two blanks a little torn.
Dawson 471-281 1983 $75

TAYLOR, JOSHUA C.   William Page, The American Titian.
Chicago: University of Chicago Press, 1956. 57 illus. 4to.
Cloth. Ars Libri 32-503 1983 $85

TAYLOR, KATHERINE AMES   Lights and Shadows of Yosemite, Being
a Collection of Favorite Views. San Francisco: H.S. Crocker, (1926).
Cloth band batik boards. First edition. Illus. with full page plates.
A fine copy. Reese 19-4 1983 $150

TAYLOR, LANDON   The Battle Field Reviewed. Chicago,
1888. Illus. Orig. cloth. First edition. Ginsberg 47-855 1983
$125

TAYLOR, LILLIE J.   Life History of Thomas Orr, Jr. N.p.,
1930. Orig. printed wrappers. Portrait and plates. Jenkins 153-553
1983 $45

TAYLOR, MARSHALL W.   The Fastest Bicycle Rider In The World...
Worcester, Mass. (1928). Photos, cloth, library stamps on inside
front cover, spine slightly frayed and worn, else a good copy.
King 46-16 1983 $35

TAYLOR, MEADOWS   Confessions of a Thug. London: Richard
Bentley, 1839. First edition. 3 vols. Orig. cloth-backed boards
later covered with cloth. Paper spine labels. Covers somewhat faded.
Labels a bit worn. Some foxing. Each volume a little shaken. Good.
MacManus 280-5090 1983 $350

TAYLOR, MEADOWS   Ralph Darnell. Edinburgh: Blackwood,
1865. First edition. 3 vols. Orig. decorated cloth. Fine.
MacManus 280-5091 1983 $250

TAYLOR, MEADOWS   Tara. Edinburgh: William Blackwood &
Sons, 1863. First edition. 3 vols. Orig. cloth. Extremities of
spines slightly worn. First inner hinge weak. Some light foxing.
With 19 pages of ads. Bookplates of D.C. Ewing. Very good. MacManus
280-5092 1983 $185

TAYLOR, NORMAN   Cinchona in Java: the Story of Quinine.
N.Y., (c. 1945). D.w. Illus. Argosy 713-529 1983 $75

TAYLOR, RICHARD   Destruction and Reconstruction. New
York, 1879. First edition. 8vo. Bookplate removed, otherwise very
nice. Morrill 290-531 1983 $55

TAYLOR, SILVANUS   Common-good: or, the improvement of
commons, forrests, and chases, by inclosure. London: Francis Tyton,
1652. First edition. Small 4to. Modern wrappers. Some foxing;
trimmed a bit close at the top, affecting some page numbers. Scarce.
Ximenes 63-183 1983 $175

TAYLOR, THOMAS E.   Running the Blockade. London, 1896.
First edition. 8vo. Orig. cloth. Frontis., 4 plates, 1 folding
coloured map, 1 text map. Orig. blue buckram. T.e.g. Slightly soiled,
faded. Bookplate. Good. Edwards 1042-169 1983 £12

TAYLOR, TOM   Birket Foster's Pictures of English
Landscape. Boston, J.E. Tilton, n.d. (ca. 1863). American ed.
Engraved by the Brothers Dalziel. Plates, 4to. Ends of spine
chipped and frayed, foxed. Morrill 289-550 1983 $35

TAYLOR, TOM   Masks and faces; or, before and behind
the curtain. A comedy in two acts. London: Richard Bentley, 1854.
Sm. 8vo, cont. half roan (spine rubbed). First edition. Scarce.
Tipped in is a clipped signature of Charles Reade, an autograph note
signed by Tom Taylor, an ALS, and 2 photographs of scenes in the
play. Ximenes 64-519 1983 $60

TAYLOR, TOM   Pictures of English Landscape. Routledge
1864. 4to. 30 plates engraved by Brothers Dalziel. Heavy foxing.
Loose. Green ornately gilt cloth. Greer 40-48 1983 £45

TAYLOR, UNA   Knight Asrael and Other Stories. London:
Swan Sonnenschein & Co., 1889. First edition. Orig. gilt-decorated
cloth. Presentation copy, inscribed to Anna, dated April 27 (no year).
Very good. MacManus 280-5087 1983 $65

TAYLOR, UNA   Nets for the Wind. London: John Lane,
1896. First edition. Orig. pict. cloth. Cover and title page designed
by A. Beardsley. Spine slightly soiled. Good. MacManus 280-5093
1983 $45

TAYLOR, W. THOMAS   Twenty-One Years of Bird & Bull, A
Bibliography, 1958-1979. Bird & Bull Press, 1980. 1st ed., 1 of
170 special copies with portfolio containing wide variety of ephemera,
text-pages, and prospectuses. Quarter oasis, gilt, patterned cloth
sides, incut, the book and portfolio housed in a cloth folding case,
leather label. Mint copy. Jenkins 155-91 1983 $485

TAYLOR, WALTER H.   Four Years with General Lee...
NY, 1877. First edition. Eng. portrait, ink names, spine top
frayed, inner hinges cracked. King 46-82 1983 $50

TAYLOR, WILLIAM   Scenes and Adventures in Afghanistan.
London, 1842. Recased, spine worn. 8vo, orig. cloth. Initials scored
through dedication leaf not affecting text. Good. Edwards 1042-483
1983 £50

TAYLOR, WILLIAM   Seven Years' Street Preaching In San
Francisco, California. NY (1856). Portrait, cloth, ink inscription,
spine sunned. 22 thou. King 46-29 $25

TAYLOR, GARNETT, EVANS & CO.   Printing Old & New. Manchester:
Taylor, Garnett, Evans & Co., n.d. (ca. 1900). 4to. Stiff paper
wrappers. Tipped-in plates. Covers soiled. Oak Knoll 48-359 1983
$20

TEAKLE, THOMAS   The Spirit Lake Massacre. Iowa City,
Iowa, 1918. 1st ed. Deckle edges. Fine copy. Clark 741-328 1983
$60

TEALE, T. PRIDGIN   Dangers to Health. London, 1883.
8vo. Orig. cloth. 70 partially coloured plates. Gurney JJ-393
1983 £12

TEASDALE, SARA   The Collected Poems of Sara Teasdale.
New York, 1937. 8vo. Cloth. Reviewer's name on front flyleaf,
else about fine in dj. In Our Time 156-781 1983 $35

TEASDALE, SARA   A Country House. (New York: 1932).
First edition. Cover drawing and one plate by Herbert F. Roese. Very
fine in orig. gray envelope, as issued. Bradley 66-333 1983 $25

TEASDALE, SARA   Dark of the Moon. NY, (1926). One of
250 numbered and signed copies, fine in slightly worn, very good slipcase. Quill & Brush 54-1338 1983 $150

TEASDALE, SARA   Stars Tonight. N.Y.: Mac., 1930.
First edition. 8vo. Cloth. Frontis. and title-page lightly foxed,
in margins. Color frontis, many black & whites (full-page). Aleph-bet
8-157 1983 $38

TECHNICAL ASSOCIATION OF THE PULP AND PAPER INDUSTRY   Paper Testing
Methods... New York: Technical Association of the Pulp and Paper
Industry, (1929). First edition. 8vo. Cloth. Library stamps in ink,
else very good. Oak Knoll 49-313 1983 $45

TEERINK, HERMAN   A Bibliography of the Writings of
Jonathan Swift. Philadelphia: Univ. of Pennsylvania Press, (1963).
2nd ed., revised & corrected. Frontispiece. Cloth in dw. Dawson
470-288 1983 $150

TEICHMAN, ERIC   Travels of a Consular Officer. Cambridge,
1921. First edition. 4 maps, 2 folding in pocket. 58 plate, slightly
worn. 8vo. Orig. cloth. Edwards 1044-690 1983 £25

TEICHMEYER, HERMANN FRIEDRICH   Institutiones Medicinae Legalis
vel Forensis. Jeane, 1762. 4to, cont. blue boards. Argosy 713-530
1983 $100

TEIGNMOUTH, HENRY N. SHORE, BARON   Charles Dickens and His Friends.
1909. Second impression, illus., orig. blue cloth, gilt, very good.
Jarndyce 30-226 1983 £10.50

TELLIER, ANDRE   Vagabond April. Madison, N.J., 1936.
Sq 8vo, limp cloth bds., gilt. Drawings by Clinton Balmer.
Limited, autographed edition. A very good copy. Perata 27-55
1983 $35

TELLO, JULIO C.   Origen y desarollo de las civilizaciones
prehistoricas andinas. Lima, 1942. 23 plates. Small 4to. Cloth.
Presentation copy, inscribed by the author. Ars Libri 34-494 1983
$30

TELLUCCINI, AUGUSTO   L'arte dell'architetto Filippo Juvara
in Piemonte. Torino: C. Crudo, 1926. 77 plates. Numerous text
illus. 4to. Cloth. Shaken. Ars Libri 33-188 1983 $125

TEMPLE, R.   A Bird's Eye View of Picturesque India.
London, 1898. Map, 32 plates. Cr.8vo. Orig. cloth. Good. Edwards
1044-691 1983 £15

TEMPLE, WILLIAM   The Works of Sir William Temple.
London: for Benj. Motte, and J. Round, J. Tonson, J. Clarke, B.
Motte, S. Wotton, S. Birt, and T. Osborne, 1731. 2 vols. Folio.
Cont. polished calf, fully gilt panelled spines with crimson
morocco labels, gilt. Engraved portrait by Vertue. Traylen 94-
813 1983 £130

TEMPLEMAN, DANIEL   The Secret History of the Late Directors of the South-Sea Company. London: printed for the author, 1735. 1st ed., 8vo, uncut and stitched in the original blue wrappers as issued, contained in a blue cloth slipcase. A very good copy. Pickering & Chatto 21-122 1983 $200

TEMPLETON, WILLIAM   The Millwright and Engineer's Companion. Egerton Smith and Co., London, 1832. First edition. 12mo. in 6's with engraved frontis. and 1 plate; 1 leaf torn and crudely repaired; orig. cloth with orig. paper label on side. Quaritch NS 5-105 1983 $150

TEMPSKY, F. G. VON   Mitla. A Narrative of Incidents and Personal Adventures... Longman, et al., 1858. First edition. Colored folding map, 5 colored lithographic plates, 9 full-page woodcut plates, 2 textcuts. Orig. gilt decorated cloth. Fine. Jenkins 152-444 1983 $850

TENDE, GASPAR DE   An Account of Poland. Printed for T. Goodman, and H. Newman, 1698. 8vo, cont. speckled calf, rebacked. Bickersteth 77-81 1983 £110

TENISON, THOMAS   A Discourse Concerning a Guide in Matters of Faith. Printed for Ben. Tooke...and F. Gardiner, 1683. First edition, initial ad. leaf, 4to, wrapper. One signature misbound, otherwise a very good copy. Fenning 61-444 1983 £14.50

TENISON, THOMAS   Mr. Pulton Consider'd in His Sincerity, Reasonings, Authorities. Printed for Richard Chiswell, 1687. First edition, including the imprimatur leaf and the ads., 4to, wrapper, a very good copy. Fenning 61-445 1983 £14.50

TENNANT, CHARLES   A tour through parts of the Netherlands, Holland, Germany... London: Longman, etc., 1824. 2 vols. 8vo. Orig. drab boards, printed paper labels. Minor wear. Ximenes 63-638 1983 $175

TENNANT, E.   The Royal Deccan Horse. Aldershot, 1939. Coloured frontis. of colours. 2 coloured uniform plates, 5 folding maps. Imp. 8vo. Good. Edwards 1042-573 1983 £30

TENNANT, J. E.   In The Clouds Above Baghdad. London, 1920. First edition. Frontis. 10 maps (1 folding), 17 plates. Signet Library copy. Good. Edwards 1042-608 1983 £35

TENNANT, PAMELA   Windlestraw. London, 1905. Printed at the Chiswick Press. First edition. Author's signed autograph presentation inscription. Very good. Rota 230-587 1983 £15

TENNANT, W.   Indian Recreations. London, 1804. Second edition, enlarged and corrected. Portrait, 5 plates. 3 vols. Half calf. 8vo. Good. Edwards 1044-692 1983 £95

TENNENT, GILBERT   Sermons on Important Subjects. Philadelphia: James Chattin, 1758. Modern boards (author's name misspelled on spine). Pages browned and first and last few leaves chipped around margins, else a tight copy. Felcone 22-240 1983 $85

TENNEY, JACK B.   Red Fascism Boring from Within... Los Angeles (1947). Cloth, bookplate, ink name, covers slightly discolored and worn. King 46-24 1983 $45

TENNYSON, ALFRED TENNYSON, 1ST BARON (1809-1892)   Ballads and Other Poems. London: C. Kegan Paul & Co., 1880. First edition. Orig. cloth. Spine and covers worn and slightly soiled. Good. MacManus 280-4094 1983 $20

TENNYSON, ALFRED TENNYSON, 1ST BARON (1809-1892)   The Death of Oenone and Other Poems. London: Macmillan & Co., 1892. First edition. 12mo. Orig. cloth, bookplate. Near-fine. MacManus 280-5096 1983 $20

TENNYSON, ALFRED TENNYSON, 1ST BARON (1809-1892)   The Death of Oenone, Akbar's Dream, and other Poems. London, 1892. 4to. White buckram, gilt, uncut edges. 5 engr. portraits. Limited edition of 500 numbered copies on large paper. Traylen 94-818 1983 £10

TENNYSON, ALFRED TENNYSON, 1ST BARON (1809-1892)   Demeter and Other Poems. London: Macmillan & Co., 1889. First edition. Orig. cloth. Presentation copy, inscribed on half-title, with a further inscription of six lines headed "Errata" written out in Tennyson's hand and on the same page. Covers a little worn. Some foxing. Bookplate of G. Harmsworth, F.S.A. Good. MacManus 280-5097 1983 $1,250

TENNYSON, ALFRED TENNYSON, 1ST BARON (1809-1892)   The Devil and the Lady. Macmillan, 1930. First edition, tall 8vo, 2 facs., uncut in qtr. parchment gilt over batik paper boards. Very good in torn dust-wrappers. 1,500 copies printed. Deighton 3-282 1983 £22

TENNYSON, ALFRED TENNYSON, 1ST BARON (1809-1892)   The Devil and The Lady. N.Y.: The Macmillan Co., 1930. First American edition. Illus. with facsimilies. Large 8vo. Orig. cloth-backed boards with paper label. Dust jacket. Limited to 500 copies. Bookplate. Fine. MacManus 280-5098 1983 $35

TENNYSON, ALFRED TENNYSON, 1ST BARON (1809-1892)   Enoch Arden. B, 1864. Spine sunned and edges frayed, else very good. Bookplate. Quill & Brush 54-1339 1983 $50

TENNYSON, AFRED TENNYSON, 1ST BARON (1809-1892)   Enoch Arden. London: Moxon, 1864. First edition. 12mo. Orig. cloth. Spine faded. Extremities worn. MacManus 280-5100 1983 $45

TENNYSON, ALFRED TENNYSON, 1ST BARON (1809-1892)   Enoch Arden. London: Edward Moxon, 1864. First edition, first binding. Sept. 1864 ads inserted at front. Orig. green cloth, gilt. Spine lightly sunned, else fine copy. Jenkins 155-1205 1983 $40

TENNYSON, ALFRED TENNYSON, 1ST BARON (1809-1892)   Enoch Arden. London: Edward Moxon & Co., 1864. First edition. Full morocco by Riviere, with dentelles and buff-colored endpapers. Offsetting to endpapers. Bookplate. Previous owner's initials on flyleaf. All edges a bit rubbed. Good. MacManus 280-5099 1983 $25

TENNYSON, ALFRED TENNYSON, 1ST BARON (1809-1892)   Enoch Arden, etc. London, 1865. First edition. Sm. 8vo. Cont. full green morocco, gilt, edges gilt. Traylen 94-819 1983 £18

TENNYSON, ALFRED TENNYSON, 1ST BARON (1809-1892)   Enoch Arden. London, 1866. 8vo. Cloth (recased). Illus. by Arthur Hughes. Gold stamped cloth. First illustrated edition. Inscr. on title page: "Julia Margaret Cameron from Tennyson". A fine copy in cloth protective dust jacket. In Our Time 156-783 1983 $1,000

TENNYSON, ALFRED TENNYSON, 1ST BARON (1809-1892)   Enoch Arden. Moxon, 1866. First illustrated edition. Illus. by Arthur Hughes. 26 engr. & frontis. from medallion by T. Woolner. Publisher's blue morocco, gilt vignette front cover, raised bands, gilt dentelles, a.e.g. Leather discolored, front endpapers broken at hinge, one section slightly spring. Very good. Hodgkins 27-333 1983 £30

TENNYSON, ALFRED TENNYSON, 1ST BARON (1809-1892)   Enoch Arden, etc. London: Moxon, n.d. Octavo. Bright fore-edge painting. Full dark green leather, blind-ruled with gilt ornaments in each corner. Five raised bands to spine, gilt-decorated dentelles. Slight rubbing to extremities, else about fine. Owner's signature. Bookplate of George L. Lincoln. Bromer 25-205 1983 $275

TENNYSON, ALFRED TENNYSON, 1ST BARON (1809-1892)   The Foresters: Robin Hood and Maid Marian. NY, 1892. Spine edges lightly worn, else very good. Bookplate, owner's name. Quill & Brush 54-1341 1983 $50

TENNYSON, ALFRED TENNYSON, 1ST BARON (1809-1892)   Idylls of the King. London, 1859. 8vo. Cloth. Inscr. on half-title page: "To D. Hassall from his friend Julia Margaret Cameron, July 19, 1859". Bookplate and inscr. by former owner, else a very good copy. In Our Time 156-782 1983 $400

TENNYSON, ALFRED TENNYSON, 1ST BARON (1809-1892)   Idylls of the King. London: Edward Moxon & Co., 1859. First edition. Spine and covers a trifle faded and rubbed. Near-fine. MacManus 280-5102 1983 $125

TENNYSON, ALFRED TENNYSON, 1ST BARON (1809-1892)   Idylls of the King. London: Edward Moxon, 1861. Early edition. Contemp. full green polished calf, double gilt fillets, inner dentelles blindtooled, raised banks, gilt compart. incorporating fluerons on a field of gilt dots, scarlet morocco label, a.e.g. Binding signed J. & C. Treacher of Brighton. Inscr. in ink on front flyleaf dated June 3, 1862. Fine. Jenkins 155-429 1983 $425

TENNYSON, ALFRED TENNYSON, 1ST BARON (1809-1892)   Idylls of the King. Hodder & Stoughton, n.d. 4to. Mounted colour frontis. and 20 mounted colour plates. Full white vellum decorated gilt, lacks ties. Edition limited to 350 copies. No. 244, signed by Brickdale. Greer 40-52 1983 £150

TENNYSON, ALFRED TENNYSON, 1ST BARON (1809-1892)   In Memoriam. NY/ London, 1900. 8vo. Full crushed blue morocco, raised bands, gilt extra, t.e.g. by Sotheran & Co. Rubricated initials from designs by Blanche McManus. One of 100 copies (of 500) reserved for Great Britain. Orig. cloth covers bound in. Bookplate. Fine. Perate 27-9 1983 $150

TENNYSON, ALFRED TENNYSON, 1ST BARON (1809-1892)   In Memoriam. London, 1933. 4to, black paper over boards, one of 2,000 copies, printed by Ernest Ingham at the Fanfare Press. Designed by Francis Meynell. Very good. Houle 21-681 1983 $45

TENNYSON, ALFRED TENNYSON, 1ST BARON (1809-1892)   The Lady of Shalot. N.Y., (1881). Decorated by Howard Pyle. Sq. 8vo. Gilt pict. cloth. Rubbed. Expertly rebacked. First Pyle edition. Argosy 714-608 1983 $50

TENNYSON, ALFRED TENNYSON, 1ST BARON (1809-1892)   The Life and Works. London, 1898. Edition-de-Luxe. 12 vols. Roy. 8vo. Orig. green satin cloth, gilt decorated spines, uncut edges. Limited to 1,050 sets, with four frontis. and eight portraits. Traylen 94-817 1983 £85

TENNYSON, ALFRED TENNYSON, 1ST BARON (1809-1892)   The Lover's Tale. London: C. Kegan Paul & Co., 1879. First edition. Orig. cloth. Presentation copy, inscribed "Mary Trotherton from A. Tennyson" on the half-title. Few pencil markings in text. Covers a bit worn. Bookplate of G. Harmsworth F.S.A. Very good. MacManus 280-5108 1983 $850

TENNYSON, ALFRED TENNYSON, 1ST BARON (1809-1892)   Maud, and Other Poems. B, 1855. First edition but without ads. Spine edges chipped, lightly foxed, edges worn, bookplate. Good plus. Quill & Brush 54-1340 1983 $35

TENNYSON, ALFRED TENNYSON, 1ST BARON (1809-1892)   Maud. Macmillan, 1922. Illus. by Edmond J. Sullivan. 8 colour illus., 12 b&w illus. & 26 b&w head pieces. First edition. White decor. cloth silver, uncut. Slight discoloration front endpapers, foxing fore-edge, backstrip & edges of covers discolored. Very good. Hodgkins 27-487 1983 £16.50

TENNYSON, ALFRED TENNYSON, 1ST BARON (1809-1892)   The May Queen. George Berridge, ca. 1872. First edition thus, illuminated title-page and leaves chromo-tinted with flat and hatched tints in colours and gold, silver and black. 4to, orig. cloth, gilt, edges gilt, the headbands chipped and the casing just a little weak, but still a nice clean and fresh copy. Fenning 60-407 1983 £75

TENNYSON, ALFRED TENNYSON, 1ST BARON (1809-1892)   Ode on the Death of Wellington. London: Moxon, 1852. First edition. Orig. blue printed wrappers. Fine copy. Scarce. Jenkins 155-1424 1983 $150

TENNYSON, ALFRED TENNYSON, 1ST BARON (1809-1892)   Poems, Chiefly Lyrical. Effingham Wilson, 1830. First edition, second state, with p. 91 misprinted 19, and carcanet correctly spelled p. 72. 2 pps. ads. Some marking. Finely rebound in crushed green morocco, gilt borders, dentelles and spine. Jarndyce 31-929 1983 £150

TENNYSON, ALFRED TENNYSON, 1ST BARON (1809-1892)   Poems. London, Edward Moxon, Dover Street, 1842. First edition. 2 vols. Orig. boards with printed spine labels. Outer joints cracked. One-inch portion of backstrip of vol. I neatly restored. Bookplate. Former owner's signature. Very good. MacManus 280-5105 1983 $500

TENNYSON, ALFRED TENNYSON, 1ST BARON (1809-1892)   The Princess: A Medley. Moxon, 1850. Third ed., half title, 1 p. ads. Orig. green cloth, dulled, head of spine worn but intact, inner hinges weak. A good copy. Signed presentation inscription on a slip affixed to inner cover: 'Lewis Fytche from his affectionate cousin A. Tennyson'; followed by an inscription in the hand of Lewis Fytche: 'Margaret Turner fr. L.F. while on a pleasant visit at Pengethley May 27, 1850'. Jarndyce 31-930 1983 £280

TENNYSON, ALFRED TENNYSON, 1ST BARON (1809-1892)   The Princess. Moxon, 1866. Re-issue. 26 illus. by Daniel Maclise & engr. by Dalziel. Green sand grain cloth gilt, bevelled boards, a.e.g. Bookplate and traces of bookplate front endpapers. Foxing prelims and some pages. Very good. Hodgkins 27-332 1983 £16

TENNYSON, ALFRED TENNYSON, 1ST BARON (1809-1892)   Vivien. N.;., n.d. (ca. 1880). Nine photos mounted on stiff boards. Laid in loose in folding green case. Karmiole 72-39 1983 $25

TENNYSON, ALFRED TENNYSON, 1ST BARON (1809-1892)   A Welcome. London, 1863. Self-wrappers. First edition, first issue. J. Christian Bay's copy with his printed bookplate, tipped into an orange-colored pamphlet folder. Bradley 66-334 1983 $85

TENNYSON, ALFRED TENNYSON, 1ST BARON (1809-1892)   A Welcome. London: Moxon, 1863. First edition. 4to, sheet folded to form four pages. Printed by Bradbury and Evans. Very good-fine. Houle 22-866 1983 $60

TENNYSON, ALFRED TENNYSON, 1ST BARON (1809-1892)   The Works. London, 1888-93. 9 vols. Cr. 8vo. Cont. full brown morocco, arms in gilt on sides, gilt panelled spines, edges gilt. Frontis. Traylen 94-816 1983 £105

TENNYSON, ALFRED TENNYSON, 1ST BARON (1809-1892)   Works. Boston: Estes, (1895). Illus. with etchings, gravures and views. Full green cloth, paper spine labels, t.e.g., uncut. 12 vols. One of 1,000 numbered copies. Very good. Houle 22-867 1983 $250

TENNYSON, ALFRED TENNYSON, 1ST BARON (1809-1892)   Works. N.Y.: MacMillan, 1896. Sm. 8vo, 3/4 green morocco over marbled boards, spines ruled and stamped in gilt with small floral designs in compartments, covers ruled in gilt, t.e.g., marbled endpapers, uncut and mostly unopened. Cloth slipcase. 6 vols. Fine. Houle 22-868 1983 $375

THE TERCENTENARY Celebration of the Discovery of Lake Champlain and Vermont. (Montpelier), 1910. 1st ed. Illus. 4to, orig. limp buckram. Stain on back cover. Morrill 286-495 1983 $22.50

TERENCE
Please turn to
TERENTIUS AFER, PUBLIUS

TERENTIUS AFER, PUBLIUS   P. Terentii Comoediae sex, tum ex Donati comentariis... Parisiis, Roberti Stephani, 1541. 4to, 17th century calf gilt, top corner of title slightly frayed from erasure, light smudge, blank endpaper nearly loose, but an exceptionally fine and large copy. With the Evelyn family library shelf-number and bookplate. Ravenstree 95-121 1983 $250

TERENTIUS AFER, PUBLIUS   Publii Terentii Comoediae Sex, Quibus accedunt Notae Marginales John. Min-ellii. Cantabrigiae, Ex Officina Joannis Hayes et al., 1676. Stout 12mo, older half calf, boards, fine early bookplate, signature of William Riggall dated 1684. Ravenstree 95-123 1983 $85

TERENTIUS AFER, PUBLIUS   Publii Terentii afri Comoediae Sex: Ex Editione Weaterhoviana Recensita ad Fidem duodecim amplius MSstorum Codicum... Glaguae, Cura & impensis Robertus Foulis, Typis Roberti Urie et al., 1742. Tall 8vo, cont. vellum, little worn and soiled, two names on end-paper, minor stains, little dust soiling, a very large, wide-margined copy and most likely one of the forty copies only printed on "Grand Royal Paper," or large paper. Ravenstree 95-124 1983 $225

TERENTIUS AFER, PUBLIUS   The Comedies of Terence. London, T. Becket and P.A. De Hondt and R. Baldwin, 1768. 2 vols., 8vo, orig. calf, worn, joints cracked, bookplates, name on endpaper, with the fine folding engraved plates, and the Merchant of Plautus at end. Ravenstree 95-127 1983 $45

TERENTIUS AFER, PUBLIUS   Publi Terentii Afri Comoediae. Birminghamiae, Typis Johannis Baskerville, 1772. 12mo, old half morocco, joints broken and covers detached, minor waterstain to lower half of pates, without the unsightly foxing usually found in this edition, large wide-margined copy of Gaskell Baskerville. Ravenstree 95-126 1983 $95

TERENTIUS AFER, PUBLIUS   Comodiae. Oxford, 1902. India paper ed., red cloth, gilt edges. Salloch 385-771 1983 $24

TERHUNE, ALBERT PAYSON   My Friend the Dog. New York, 1926. 1st ed. 8 colored plates by Marguerite Kirmse. 8vo, colored illus. on front cover. Few light cover spots. Morrill 286-471 1983 $20

TERRASSON, JEAN   Sethos, Histoire ou Vie Tiree Des Monu-
mens Anecdotes de L'Ancienne Egypte. Paris: Guerin, 1731. 3 vols.
8vo, titles in red & black. With 2 folding maps. Gilt calf. Armorial
bookticket "A. R." in each vol. First edition. Pristine Beckford
copy. Rostenberg 88-75 1983 $250

TERRASSON, JEAN   The Life of Sethos. Printed for J.
Walthoe, 1732. 2 vols, 8vo, contemporary calf gilt; some wear to
hinges, 2 folding maps. Hill 165-130 1983 £250

TERRY, DANIEL   British theatrical gallery, a collection
of whole length portraits, with biographical notices. London:
published by H. Berthoud, 1825. Folio, full red morocco, gilt,
spine and inner dentelles gilt, t.e.g., by Riviere. 1st ed, with
20 hand colored plates. Bound in at the end is the printed label from
the original binding. Occasional minor foxing. Ximenes 64-520 1983
$650

TERRY, MARIAN DICKINSON   Old Inns of Connecticut. Hartford,
Conn.: The Prospect Press, 1937. Tall 8vo, profusely illus. with
photogravures of the inns, architectural drawings and other
sketches. Index. Edition ltd. to 1,000 copies, printed at the
sign of the Stone Book. 1/4 blue morocco, gilt-stamped, over
cloth. Karmiole 71-89 1983 $100

TESORONE, GIOVANNI   L'antico pavimento delle Logge di
Raffaello in Vaticano. Napoli: Reale Accademia delle Scienze,
1891. 2 double-page chromolithographic plates. 4to. Vellum
wrappers. Printed on fine laid paper. Uncut. Ars Libri 33-303
1983 $55

TESTE, ALPHONSE   Le Magnetisme Animal Explique. Paris,
1845. First edition. 8vo, unbound; orig. pr. wrs. Argosy 713-531
1983 $75

THE TESTIMONY of truth to exalted merit: or, a biographical sketch
of the Right Honourable the Countess of Derby. London: printed and
published by George Cawthorn, 1797. 4to, disbound, 1st ed. With a
portrait. Half-title present. Very good copy of a very rare title.
Ximenes 64-199 1983 $275

TEXAS, A Guide to the Lone Star State. New York, WPA, 1940. Plates.
1st ed. Jenkins 153-583 1983 $45

THE TEXAS Almanac for 1859. (Galveston: W. & D. Richardson). 1858.
Orig. printed wraps. Neat library withdrawal stamp, slight marginal
staining to a few leaves. Reese 19-546 1983 $600

TEXAS. LAWS.   Laws of the Republic of Texas. Houston,
1841. Errata, attestation leaf, verso blank; lacks last leaf, supplied
in facs. Stitched, self-wraps. Foxed throughout. Good. Reese 19-541
1983 $250

TEXAS. LAWS.   General Laws of the State of Texas.
Austin, 1873. Printed wraps., fine. Reese 19-536 1983 $100

TEXIER, CHARLES   Byzantine Architecture. Day & Son, 1864.
1st edn. Col'd illum. title page, printed title, 13 colour printed
plates (some heightened in gold) & 56 tinted plates & 27 wood engrs. in
text. Maroon sand grain decor. cloth gilt, a.e.g. (cvrs. worn, shaken
in binding & some plates have sl. thumbing & one or two have sml. tear
at foredge), scarce, v.g. Hodgkins 27-397 1983 £115

THACHER, JAMES   A Military Journal during the American
Revolutionary War, 1775-1783. Boston, 1823. 1st ed., orig. bds.,
pp. uncut, spine cracked. Presentation copy to Ezra Stiles Gannett
by the author. Argosy 710-465 1983 $200

THACHER, JOHN BOYD   Christopher Columbus. New York, 1903.
Three vols. Large, thick quarto. Half gilt vellum and gilt linen,
t.e.g., others untrimmed. Frontis. Plates (some folding). Facs.
Illus. Portraits. Spine of volume one shows slight rubbing, otherwise
a fine set. Deluxe issue, specially bound. Reese 19-551 1983 $275

THACHER, THOMAS   The Principles and Maxims on which the
Security and Happiness of a Republic Depend: A Sermon... Boston,
1811. Disbound, good. Reese 18-360 1983 $25

THACKERAY, ANNE ISABELLA
Please turn to
RITCHIE, ANNE ISABELLA THACKERAY

THACKERAY, WILLIAM MAKEPEACE The Adventures of Philip. London: Smith,
Elder, 1862. First edition. 3 vols. Orig. brown cloth. Faint traces
of labels removed from paste-downs. Covers a little soiled. Very good.
MacManus 280-5117 1983 $200

THACKERAY, WILLIAM MAKEPEACE The Adventures of Philip on His Way
through the World. London, 1862. 3 vols. Full red levant, spines
gilt in panels. Orig. cloth spines mounted to pastedowns. Just
the slightest bit of wear at extremities, else a fine set. Bookplates. First edition, first issue, with the half-title in the
first volume and the missing numeral on page 9 in third volume.
Felcone 21-104 1983 $150

THACKERAY, WILLIAM MAKEPEACE Ballads. London: Bradbury & Evans, 1855.
First edition. Full brown morocco, with orig. wrappers bound in, by
Bickers & Son, Leicester. Former owner's inscr. on front wrapper.
Bookplate. Fine. MacManus 280-5118 1983 $125

THACKERAY, WILLIAM MAKEPEACE Ballads & Songs. Cassell, 1896. 1st
edn. Illus. by H.M. Brock: frontis. & 110 b&w illus., 16pp adverts.
Maroon decor. cloth gilt, a.e.g. (occasional light foxing, bkstrip
faded with v. sl. wear to bottom), v.g. copy. Hodgkins 27-500 1983
£12.50

THACKERAY, WILLIAM MAKEPEACE A Book of Drawings. Phila.: The Pennell Club, 1925. First edition. Orig. marbled boards. One of 110
copies signed by Repplier and Pennell. Spine very slightly faded. In
soiled publisher's box. Very good. MacManus 280-5116 1983 $175

THACKERAY, WILLIAM MAKEPEACE Catalogue of an Exhibition of the
Works... Philadelphia: Privately Printed, 1940. 1st ed. Orig.
cloth-backed wrappers. 1 of 250 copies printed. Jenkins 155-1208
1983 $22.50

THACKERAY, WILLIAM MAKEPEACE The English Humourists of the
Eighteenth Century. London, 1853. First edition. 12mo, 1/2 red
morocco, gilt spine. Fine. Argosy 714-729 1983 $100

THACKERAY, WILLIAM MAKEPEACE English Humourists of the Eighteenth
Century. London: Smith, Elder, 1853. First published edition. Orig.
cloth. Covers a little worn. Bookplates. Very good. MacManus 280-
5122 1983 $85

THACKERAY, WILLIAM MAKEPEACE The English humourists of the eighteenth
century. London: Smith, Elder, 1853. Second edition. 8vo. Orig.
dark blue marbled cloth. Ximenes 63-251 1983 $30

THACKERAY, WILLIAM MAKEPEACE Etchings by the late William Makepeace
Thackeray while at Cambridge, illustrative of University Life, etc.
(London: H. Sotheran, 1878). Only edition, 8vo, orig. cloth-backed
printed boards. Bookplate of the Order of the Garter. Upper margin
of front cover chipped, else a very good copy. Trebizond 18-213 1983
$110

THACKERAY, WILLIAM MAKEPEACE The History of Henry Esmond, Esq. London,
Smith, Elder, 1852. 3 vols., 8vo, orig. cloth, somewhat chafed, orig.
printed paper spine labels worn, bookplate, name on endpaper. First
edition. Ravenstree 96-265 1983 $185

THACKERAY, WILLIAM MAKEPEACE The History of Henry Esmond. Smith,
Elder, 1853. 3rd edition, 3 vols. Half titles, orig. purple cloth,
v.g. Jarndyce 30-570 1983 £30

THACKERAY, WILLIAM MAKEPEACE The History of Henry Esmond. Allen,
1896. Illus. by T.H. Robinson: frontis. & b&w text illus. 1st edn.
Dark green pictorial cloth gilt, a.e.g., v. nice copy. Hodgkins 27-
499 1983 £14

THACKERAY, WILLIAM MAKEPEACE The History of Pendennis. London: 1848-
50. Illus. with steel and wood engravings by Thackeray. 24 parts in
23. Ads and slips lacking in part 22. Some wear and occasional chipping to spines, else very nice. Preserved in 2 morocco-backed, cloth
solander boxes. Leather bookplates of Stephen M. Dreyfoos. Bromer
25-114 1983 $500

THACKERAY, WILLIAM MAKEPEACE The History of Pendennis. NY, 1850.
First American edition, two vols., illus. by author, discreet ex-lib.
marking on title pages, minor interior foxing, edges slightly worn,
very good. Quill & Brush 54-1342 1983 $125

THACKERAY, WILLIAM MAKEPEACE The History of Samuel Titmarsh & the Great Hogarty Diamond. Wells Gardner, 1902. Re-issue. Illus. by Hugh Thomson: Frontis., title p. illus. & 16 b&w illus. Blue decor. cloth, t.e.g. (insc. half title, sl. foxing prelims. & foredge, sml. tear lower margin p. xv, bkstrip sl. faded), v.g. Hodgkins 27-501 1983 £12

THACKERAY, WILLIAM MAKEPEACE The Memiors of Mr. Charles J. Yellow-plush. London: Bradbury & Evans, 1856. Full green morocco, gilt, with orig. wrappers bound in at back, by Riviere & Son. Van Duzer's copy, with his bookplate, along with one other, on the front endpaper. Spine faded to brown. Fine. MacManus 280-5126 1983 $150

THACKERAY, WILLIAM MAKEPEACE Miscellanies. London, Bradbury & Evans, 1855-57. 4 vols., 8vo, orig. cloth (bit worn, spines and hinges repaired, name erased from blank fly-leaves in each volume), a sound set. Ravenstree 96-266 1983 $135

THACKERAY, WILLIAM MAKEPEACE The Newcomes. London: Bradbury & Evans, 1853-1855. First edition in the orig. parts. 24 parts in 23. Illus. by R. Doyle. Orig. printed wrappers, a bit soiled and worn. Back-strips expertly repaired, In two full red morocco solander cases. Bookplates. Very good. MacManus 280-5128 1983 $500

THACKERAY, WILLIAM MAKEPEACE The Newcomes, Memoirs of a Most Respectable Family. London, 1853-55. Illus. on steel and wood by Richard Doyle. 24 parts in 23. 8vo. Orig. printed wrappers (one spinal wrapper worn, rest vg-fine condition). Lacks all the ads. In Our Time 156-785 1983 $400

THACKERAY, WILLIAM MAKEPEACE The Newcomes. Bradbury and Evans, 1855. First edition, 2 vols. Illus. on steel and wood by Richard Doyle. Half titles. Ads. printed on leading end papers. Orig. blue cloth. One gathering vol. II a little loose, otherwise v.g. Jarndyce 31-942 1983 £52

THACKERAY, WILLIAM MAKEPEACE Notes of a Journey from Cornhill to Grand Cairo. Smith, Elder, 1865. 3rd edition, front. & 16 vignette illus. Orig. pink cloth, sl. rubbed at head and tail of spine, otherwise v.g. First edition with the vignette illus. and with Thackeray's name on the title. Jarndyce 31-940 1983 £15

THACKERAY, WILLIAM MAKEPEACE The Orphan of Pimlico. London: Smith, Elder, & Co., 1876. First edition. Folio. Illus. Orig. blue cloth. Two pages of initials drawn by Thackeray pasted to the back endsheet. Lower right corner of front cover chewed. Bookplate. Fine. MacManus 280-5129 1983 $200

THACKERAY, WILLIAM MAKEPEACE Reading a Poem. London: The Chiswick Press, 1891. First edition. 24mo, full brown crushed levant, bound by Riviere, uncut. One of 321 numbered copies. Etched frontis. by W.D. Almond. Argosy 714-730 1983 $60

THACKERAY, WILLIAM MAKEPEACE   Rebecca and Rowena. Chapman & Hall, 1850. Small 4to., frontis., title vignette, 7 plates and 2 text illus. Quarter green calf, rubbed. Greer 40-92 1983 £18

THACKERAY, WILLIAM MAKEPEACE The Rose and the Ring. New York, Harper & Brothers, 1855. Square 8vo, orig. pictorial cloth gilt, bit worn, trifle shaken, decent copy. First American edition. Ravenstree 96-268 1983 $49.50

THACKERAY, WILLIAM MAKEPEACE Roundabout Papers. London: Smith, Elder, & Co., 1863. First edition. Illus. Orig. cloth. Spine slightly dull. Bookplate. Very good. MacManus 280-5132 1983 $100

THACKERAY, WILLIAM MAKEPEACE The Student's Quarterly. London: Hotten, (n.d.). 5 hand-colored plates. 1st ed. Orig. blue cloth, gilt. Hinges cracked, but a good copy of this uncommon work. Jenkins 155-1206 1983 $45

THACKERAY, WILLIAM MAKEPEACE The Tremendous Adventures of Major Gaha-gan. London: Bradbury & Evans, 1855. First separate edition. Orig. yellow printed wrappers, somewhat dust-soiled. Spine a little worn. Former owner's signature on title-page. Good. MacManus 280-5135 1983 $75

THACKERAY, WILLIAM MAKEPEACE Vanity Fair. London: Published at the Punch Office, January 1847-July 1848. First edition in the orig. monthly parts. Illus. Orig. pictorial yellow wrappers, repaired in places with some soiling. 20 parts in 19. First issue with the head-ing on page one in rustic type. Woodcut of the Marquis of Steyne on page 336. Very good. MacManus 280-5136 1983 $1,500

THACKERAY, WILLIAM MAKEPEACE Vanity Fair. London: Bradbury and Evans, 1848. First book edition, first issue. Engraved and printed title pages, numerous illus. Full brown morocco by Zaehnsdorf. Two letters in author's name obscured on engraved title, otherwise very fine. Bradbury & Evans announcement leave bound in. Bradley 66-335 1983 $475

THACKERAY, WILLIAM MAKEPEACE Vanity Fair: A Novel Without a Hero. London: Bradbury and Evans, 1848. Full contemporary polished calf, rebacked. 1st ed. in book form, 1st issue, with the heading on page 1 in rustic type, the woodcut of the Marquis of Steyne on p. 336, and "Mr. Pitt" for "Sir Pitt" on p. 453. Top edge of engraved title a bit mussed, still very good. Jenkins 155-1207 1983 $250

THACKERAY, WILLIAM MAKEPEACE Vanity Fair. Bradbury & Evans, 1848. First edition, 2nd issue, ad. leaf, front. engr. title, plates & vignettes. Some browning of plates. Orig. blue-green cloth a little rubbed at extremities. Jarndyce 31-941 1983 £68

THACKERAY, WILLIAM MAKEPEACE Vanity Fair. Bradbury and Evans, 1848. 8vo, contemporary half red calf (hinges rubbed, short split in upper), marbled sides. Frontispiece, additional engraved title, plates, and wood engravings in text, by the author. Later issue of the First Edition. Hill 165-131 1983 £48

THACKERAY, WILLIAM MAKEPEACE Vanity Fair. London, 1849. 8vo. Orig. cloth. Illus. by author. Enclosed in clamshell slipcase box. Some light wear along spine, but overall a vg-fine copy.

THACKERAY, WILLIAM MAKEPEACE The Virginians. London, 1857-59. 8vo. Wraps. 24 parts. In slipcase box. Some wear to a few spines, overall a nice set. In Our Time 156-786 1983 $400

THACKERAY, WILLIAM MAKEPEACE The Virginians. London, Bradbury and Evans, 1857-59. 24 orig. parts, orig. printed paper wraps. now dust-soiled, trifle stained, some minor wear, few backstrips quite worn. Uncut, as issued. First editions of all the orig. parts, complete. Ravenstree 96-269 1983 $225

THACKERAY, WILLIAM MAKEPEACE The Virginians. London, Bradbury & Evans, 1858-59. 2 vols. 8vo. 48 engraved plates after illus. by Thackeray & numerous wood-engraved vignettes. Full polished calf, gilt-extra backs, gilt tules on sides, red & green morocco labels, gilt board edges & inner dentelles, aeg. 1st ed. Without half-title in vol. I. Finely bound by Riviere. Very fine. O'Neal 50-50 1983 $200

THACKERAY, WILLIAM MAKEPEACE The Virginians. A Tale of the Last Century. Bradbury and Evans, 1858-59. First book edition. 2 vols. 8vo. 48 engr. plates, numerous wood engr. vignettes, uncut in the orig. glue cloth gilt. Vol. I with half-title, none required by Vol. II. Spines slightly and uniformly faded and one with small nick at head, inner joints cracking, plates foxed, bookplates, nevertheless a good copy. Deighton 3-283 1983 £75

THACKERAY, WILLIAM MAKEPEACE   Works. London, Smith, Elder, 1869. Illus. with full page engravings and text drawings. Three quarter black morocco over marbled boards, spines decorated in gilt, covers ruled in gilt, t.e.g., marbled endpapers, 18 vols., very good. Houle 22-872 1983 $425

THACKERAY, WILLIAM MAKEPEACE Works. London: Smith, Elder, 1869. Illus. 22 vols., 8vo, marbled sides, red leather back and corners, raised bands. Some occasional light rubbing, but nice set. Morrill 286-689 1983 $85

THACKERAY, WILLIAM MAKEPEACE The Works. London: Smith, Elder & Co., 1869-86. 24 vols. 8vo. Half dark blue calf, gilt, fully gilt panelled spines, t.e.g. Numerous illus. by the author and Richard Doyle. Traylen 94-820 1983 £475

THACKERAY, WILLIAM MAKEPEACE The Works. London: Smith, Elder & Co., 1879. 24 vols. Cr. 8vo. Half brown morocco, gilt, gilt panelled spines. Numerous illus. by the author and others. A little rubbed. Traylen 94-821 1983 £135

THACKERAY, WILLIAM MAKEPEACE Works. London, Smith, Elder, 1883-1886. Large 8vo, illus. by the author and others. 3/4 dark green morocco, t.e.g., uncut. 26 vols. complete. A fine set. Houle 21-868 1983 $975

THACKERAY, WILLIAM MAKEPEACE The Works. London, 1885-87. 13 vols. Small 8vo. Half crimson morocco, gilt panelled spines, marbled edges. Frontis. Traylen 94-822 1983 £95

THACKWELL, E. J. Narrative of the Second Seikh War. London, 1851. Ink annotations on title. Red morocco. 8vo. Good. Edwards 1044-693 1983 £55

THANET, OCTAVE, PSEUD.
Please turn to
FRENCH, ALICE

THAYER, ELI The New England Emigrant Aid Company and Its Influence through the Kansas Contest, upon National History. Worcester, Mass., 1887. Wraps., chipped. Very good. Reese 19-552 1983 $65

THAYER, ELI The New England Emigrant Aid Company and Its Influence. Worcester, Mass.: Franklin P. Rice, 1887. 25 cm. Orig. printed wraps. chipped, with pencil scribblings. Several short tears without loss; old stamp on title. Grunder 7-71 1983 $22.50

THAYER, EMMA HOMAN Wild Flowers of Colorado. NY: Cassell & Co., ltd. (1885). Folio. 24 leaves of chromolithograph plates, each with tissue guard. Elaborately dec. blue cloth. Spine extremities and corners slightly frayed. Bookplate. A.e.g. Karmiole 74-35 1983 $150

THAYER, JOHN M. Botschaft Von...Vouverneur an Die Legislatur Von Nebraska. Lincoln, 1889. Orig. printed wraps. Ginsberg 47-641 1983 $45

THAYER, W. S. Lectures on the Malarial Fevers. N.Y., 1897. First edition. 3 color plates, charts. Argosy 713-532 1983 $40

THE THEATRE-Royal turn'd into a mountebank's stage. London: printed for John Morphew, 1718. 8vo, wrappers, 1st ed. Ximenes 64-98 1983 $425

THE THEATRIC count, a tragic comedy, in five acts. London: printed by J. G. Barnard; published by Sherwood, Neely, and Jones, 1809. 8vo, disbound, 1st edition. Rare. Half-title present. Ximenes 64- 526 1983 $150

THE THEATRICAL Banquet, or, Actors Chum. London: Duncombe, (ca. 1825). 12mo. Illus. Occasional browning and foxing to text, else fine in gilt-stamped full calf, rubbed at extremities. Bookplate. Bromer 25-306 1983 $150

THE THEATRICAL Bouquet: containing an Alphabetical Arrangement of the Prologues and Epilogues... London: for T. Lowndes, 1780. First edition. 8vo. Calf, rebacked. Engraved frontis. Heath 48-430 1983 £95

THEATRICAL correspondence in death. An epistle from Mrs. Oldfield. London: printed for Jacob Robinson, 1743. 8vo, wrappers, 1st edition. An exceptional pamphlet, complete with half-title, in fine condition, rare. Ximenes 64-525 1983 $600

THE THEATRICAL examiner: an enquiry into the merits and demerits of the present English performers in general. London: printed for J. Doughty, 1757. 8vo, wrappers, 1st edition. Fine copy of a rare pamphlet. Ximenes 64-257 1983 $450

THE THEATRICAL house that Jack built. London: printed by and for Joseph Grove, 1819. 8vo, disbound. First edition. With 13 woodcut illus. Very uncommon. Ximenes 64-528 1983 $150

THE THEATRICAL monopoly. London: printed by Woodfall and Kinder, 1865. 8vo, wrappers. First edition. Edges of title dusty. Rare. Ximenes 64-529 1983 $50

THEATRICAL portraits, epigrammatically delineated. London: printed for J. Bew, n.d. (1774). 4to, sewn, as issued. First edition. Half-title present; last page a bit dusty, else an excellent uncut copy of a rare pamphlet. Ximenes 64-530 1983 $350

THEATRICAL records: or, an account of English dramatic author, and their works. London: printed for R. and J. Dodsley, 1756. 12mo, cont. calf (trifle rubbed). 1st ed. With a leaf of ads at the end. A fine copy, with the Constable bookplate. Ximenes 64-531 1983 $350

THE THEATRICAL remembrancer, containing a complete list of all the dramatic performances in the English language. London: printed for T. and J. Egerton, 1788. 12mo, original light blue boards, white paper backstrip. First edition. A splendid copy, entirely uncut, in the original binding. Ximenes 64-532 1983 $450

THEATRICAL taxation; which embraces reflections on the state of property in the Theatre-Royal, Covent-Garden, and the engagement of Madame Catalani. London: printed, by J. Dean, for G. Hughes, n.d. (1809). 8vo, disbound, first edition. Very scarce. Ximenes 64- 533 1983 $125

THEBESIUS, GEORG DANIEL Deutliche und ausfuhrliche Nachricht vom Rauch-und Schnupf-Taback... Halle: Johann Christian Hendel, 1751. Second edition. Woodcut head- and tailpieces. Small 4to. Modern boards. Kraus 164-241 1983 $280

THEOBALD, F. V. The Insect and other Allied Pests of Orchard, Bush and Hothouse Fruits and their Prevention and Treatment. 1909. Privately printed. 328 original illus., royal 8vo, cloth. Front joint loose. Scarce. Wheldon 160-1175 1983 £20

THEOBALD, LEWIS The life and character of Marcus Portius Cato Uticensis. London: printed for Bernard Lintott, 1713. 4to, disbound, 2nd edition. Margins trmmed close, affecting some headlines. Ximenes 64-535 1983 $100

THEOBALD, LEWIS The vocal parts of an entertainment, call'd, Merlin. London: printed for John Watts, 1734. 7vo, disbound, first edition. Half-title present. Very good copy. Ximenes 64-536 1983 $500

THEOCRITUS The Idylls. London, 1919. 8vo, cloth. Salloch 385-772 1983 $36

THEOCRITUS The Idylls of Theocritus. London, Riccardi Press, 1922. First edition, 4to., 20 tipped-in color plates by W. Russell Flint. Cloth backed boards, paper labels, t.e.g., uncut, bookplates. One of 500 numbered copies, bookplates, very good to fine, 2 vols. Houle 22-372 1983 $350

THEOCRITUS Sixe Idillia. Stanley Morison at the Cloister Press for Duckworth, 1922. Slim 4to, numerous wood-engraved illus., uncut in original qtr. linen gilt over paper boards, upper board with short strip slightly rubbed, free endpapers, slightly discoloured, bookplate, very good. Illus. by Viven Gribble. 350 copies signed by Gribble. Deighton 3-284 1983 £55

THEOCRITUS Theocritus (Opera) Quae Extant Cum Graecis Scholiis. Oxoniae, E Theatro Sheldoniano, Impensis Sam. Smith & Benj. Walford, 1699. 8vo, orig. panelled calf, joints cracked, tiny duplicate stamp inside back cover, fine folding engraved frontis. Fine edition. Ravenstree 95-129 1983 $87.50

THEORIAE Electro-Dynamicae Symopsis. Rome, 1825. 8vo. Old wrappers. Gurney 90-113 1983 £30

THEORY and Practice of Bookbinding. Washington: GPO, 1950. 8vo. Cloth. Fine. Oak Knoll 48-54 1983 $30

THEROUX, PAUL The Old Patagonian Express. Boston, 1979. 8vo. Wraps. Uncorrected proof copy. A fine copy. In Our Time 156-788 1983 $125

THE THESPIAD. London: printed for Stockdale, Junior, 1809. 8vo, disbound, first edition. Uncommon. Ximenes 64-537 1983 $150

THE THESPIAN dictionary; or, dramatic biography of the eighteenth century. London: printed by J. Cundee, for T. Hurst; W. Porter, and J. Archer (Dublin); and C. Chappell, 1802. 12mo, original pale blue boards, light green printed paper backstrip (some wear to ends of spine). First edition. With a frontis. and six plates, all colored stipple-engravings, including portraits. Almost entirely unopened; very uncommon in original binding. Ximenes 64-538 1983 $300

THE THESPIAN Preceptor; or, A full Display of the Scenic Art. Boston: Printed by Joshua Belcher, and for sale by Elam Bliss, 1810. Foxed. Boards and leather, worn. Dawson 471-336 1983 $60

THIAN, RAPHAEL P. Legislative History of the General Staff of the Army of the United States from 1775 to 1901. Wash., 1901. Orig. cloth. First edition. Ginsberg 47-886 1983 $50

THIEBAULT, DIEUDONNE Original Anecdotes of Frederic the Second, King of Prussia. Printed for J. Johnson, 1805. First edition in English, including half-titles, 2 vols., 8vo, cont. calf, gilt, one label chipped, a sound and very good copy. Fenning 60-408 1983 £24.50

THIERENS, A. E. The General Book of the Tarot. Philadelphia: McKay Co., (n.d.). Gach 95-525 1983 $27.50

THIERS, LOUIS ADOLPHE The History of the French Revolution. London: Richard Bentley, 1838. 5 vols. 8vo. Half crimson calf, gilt. 41 engraved plates. Traylen 94-823 1983 £48

THIERS, LOUIS ADOLPHE De La Propriete. Paris, Paulin, L et Cie., 1848. Small 8vo, modern blue morocco backed marbled boards, original printed wrappers bound in. A very good copy. Pickering & Chatto 21-124 1983 $75

THIERY, MAURICE Bougainville Goldier and Sailor. London: 1932. First edition. 8vo. Orig. cloth. Portrait frontis. 6 plates. 3 maps. Spine very slightly faded. Good. Edwards 1042-10 1983 £25

THIES, LOUIS Catalogue of the Collection of Engravings Bequeathed to Harvard College by Francis Calley Gray... Cambridge, 1869. 1st ed. Portrait, 4to. Ex-library. Morrill 286-473 1983 $25

THIMM, CARL A. A Complete Bibliography of the Art of Fence. Franz Thimm & Co., (1891). First edition. Sm. 8vo. Orig. red cloth backed decorated boards. Very slightly worn. T.e.g., others uncut. Partially unopened. Good. Edwards 1042-485 1983 £55

THINGS by Their Right Names. George Robinson, 1812. First edition, 2 vols. Half calf, labels, very good. Jarndyce 30-281 1983 £140

THIRION, H. Les Adam et Clodion. Paris: A. Quantin, 1885. 15 heliogravure plates. Numerous illus. Buckram. A trifle stained. Ex-library. Ars Libri 32-1 1983 $200

THIRKELL, ANGELA The Brandons. N.Y., Knopf, 1939. First American edition. Dust jacket (spine sunned, slight nicking) else very good. Houle 22-877 1983 $30

THIRKELL, ANGELA Love Among the Ruins. N.Y., Knopf, 1948. First American edition. Endpaper map. Dust jacket. Very good. Houle 22-882 1983 $22.50

THIRKELL, ANGELA Marling Hall. N.Y., Knopf, 1942. First American edition. Dust jacket. Very good. Houle 22-883 1983 $30

THIRKELL, ANGELA Private Enterprise. N.Y., Knopf, 1948. First American edition. Endpaper map. Dust jacket. Very good. Houle 22-884 1983 $22.50

THIRTY Old-Time Nursery Songs. Jack, nd. Illus. by Paul Woodroffe. 35pp have coloured pictures. White linen backed col'd bds. lower corners some wear, cvrs. sl. dust soiled, some thumbing contents, vg. Hodgkins 27-199 1983 £35

THIRTY Two Scenic Views of Western Canada. (N.p. ca. 1920). Oblong 8vo, pr wrs. tied. Full-page photos. Argosy 710-54 1983 $30

THIS is the House That Jack Built. London: Dean & Son, (ca. 1860's). Octavo. Hand-colored wood engravings throughout. Printed self-wrappers slightly chipped at spine, else fine. Bromer 25-394 1983 $37.50

THIS Was California. N.Y.: G. P. Putnam's Sons, 1938. A collection of woodcuts & engravings. Cloth. Signed by compiler, A. S. Pennoyer. Dawson 471-227 1983 $100

THISELTON-DYER, T. F. Great Men at Play. London: Remington, 1889. First edition. 2 vols. Orig. cloth. Very good. MacManus 280-5144 1983 $30

THISELTON-DYER, T. F. The Loves and Marriages of some Eminent Persons. London: Ward & Downey, 1890. 2 vols. in 1. 8vo. Half dark blue morocco, gilt, gilt panelled spine, edges gilt, by Bayntun. Traylen 94-824 1983 £25

THOM, ADAM The Claims to the Oregon Territory Considered. London, 1844. Sewn as issued. First edition. Ginsberg 47-761 1983 $125

THOM, ALEXANDER An inquiry into the nature and causes of storms in the Indian Ocean... London: Smith, Elder, 1845. First edition. 8vo. Orig. green cloth. With 8 charts. Some cont. annotations, but a fine copy. Ximenes 63-308 1983 $225

THOMA, KURT H. Clinical Pathology of the Jaws, with a Histologic & Roentgen Study of Practical Cases. Springfield, (1834). Profusely illus., many plates from orig. x-rays. Tall 8vo, cloth. First edition. Argosy 713-533 1983 $50

THOMA, KURT H. Oral Abscesses. Boston, 1916. Illus., 8vo, cloth. First edition. Argosy 713-534 1983 $65

THOMA, KURT H. Oral Roentgenology. Boston, 1917. 1st ed. Tall 8vo. Corners rubbed. Morrill 289-228 1983 $25

THOMAS, ANDRE Le Cervelet: Etude Anatomique, Clinique et Physiologique. Paris, 1897. Large 8vo, buckram; orig. pr. wrs., bound in. First edition. Large 8vo, buckram. Argosy 713-535 1983 $75

THOMAS, ANTOINE LEONARD Essai sur le Caractere, les Moeurs et l'Esprit des Femmes dans les differens Siecles. Amsterdam: Harrevelt, 1772. 8vo, with pub.'s announcement. Wraps. Rostenberg 88-96 1983 $130

THOMAS, B. Arabia Felix: across the empty quarter of Arabia. (1932). Maps and many illustrations, royal 8vo, cloth, second impression. Wheldon 160-444 1983 £25

THOMAS, B. F. The Improvement of Rivers. New York, 1913. 2nd ed., rewritten and enlarged. Illus. 2 vols., 4to. Morrill 286-474 1983 $37.50

THOMAS, MRS. C. B. A Primary Geography; in Sgau Karen. Rangoon, American Mission Press, 1865. 12mo. Extra woodcut title, 200 woodcut illus, maps & diagrams. Full red leather, rubbed. 1st ed. - 2,000 copies. Fine. O'Neal 50-42 1983 $125

THOMAS, DAVID The Life And Labours Of Hablot Knight Browne. London: Chapman & Hall, 1884. First edition. 130 illus. 3/4 morocco with marbled boards and endpapers (the orig. cloth wrappers have been bound in). One of 200 copies. Presentation copy to the publisher inscribed on the limitation page: "Mr. Chapman's presentation copy, with the author's compliments and thanks, August 15th, 1884." With a signed, engraved frontispiece portrait of Browne. Fine. MacManus 280-4225 1983 $350

THOMAS, DAVID Travels Through the Western Country in 1816. Auburn, N.Y.,: printed by David Rumsey, 1819. Original calf with morocco label. Folding map. 1st edition. Some wear and staining else a nice copy. Jenkins 151-335 1983 $300

THOMAS, DAVID Travels through the Western Country in the Summer of 1816. Auburn, N.Y., 1819. Leaf of errata present but clipped and laid down. Only one half of the map present. Worn calf. Reese 18-536 1983 $175

THOMAS, DONALD MICHAEL The Flute-Player. London, 1979. First English edition. Signed by the author. Dustwrapper. Very fine. Jolliffe 26-518 1983 £45

THOMAS, DONALD MICHAEL   The Rock. Knotting: The Sceptre Press, 1975. First edition. Wrappers. One of 150 numbered copies signed by the author. Mint. Jolliffe 26-515 1983 £45

THOMAS, DYLAN   Adventures in the Skin Trade. L, (1955). Very good in lightly foxed and chipped dustwrapper. Quill & Brush 54-1346 1983 $75

THOMAS, DYLAN   A Child's Christmas in Wales. Norfolk: New Directions, (1954). Boards. First separate edition. Very fine in dust jacket. Reese 20-1054 1983 $100

THOMAS, DYLAN   Collected Poems. (Norfolk, 1953). First American edition. Port., d.w. First issue. Argosy 714-735 1983 $125

THOMAS, DYLAN   Deaths and Entrances. L, (1946). Orange cloth cover slightly rubbed at edges, very good in slightly frayed, slightly soiled dustwrapper, owner's name. Quill & Brush 54-1348 1983 $150

THOMAS, DYLAN   In Country Sleep. (NY, 1952). Signed by Thomas on front fly, front endpapers offset, paper covering spine slightly chipped, else very good in slightly darkened, very good dustwrapper. Quill & Brush 54-1349 1983 $300

THOMAS, DYLAN   In Country Sleep. New York, 1952. Advance Review Copy, with Poetry magazine review slip laid in, and Theodore Roethke's signature and the date "1st April 52" on front endpaper. Stamp of Poetry on endpaper. Slightly worn dustwrapper. Fine. Gekoski 2-184 1983 £190

THOMAS, DYLAN   In Country Sleep. New Directions, (1952). 8vo. Boards. Inscribed by Alexander Laing to his son. Fine copy in dj which has tiny nick at base of spine. In Our Time 156-789 1983 $125

THOMAS, DYLAN   In Country Sleep. New Directions, (1952). 8vo. Boards. A fine copy in dj. In Our Time 156-790 1983 $125

THOMAS, DYLAN   The Map of Love. London: (1939). First binding. Fine in dust wrapper, with very few small tears. Bromer 25-115 1983 $300

THOMAS, DYLAN   The Map of Love. London, 1939. First edition, fourth issue. Lettered in blue and with top edge unstained. Dust wrapper. Fine. Rota 231-599 1983 £50

THOMAS, DYLAN   The Map of Love: Verse and Prose. L, (1939). Very good. Quill & Brush 54-1354 1983 $75

THOMAS, DYLAN   Seven Poems. Camberwell: Art School Press, 1974. Quarto. Limited edition. Texts cut from linoleum by Keith Holmes in calligraphic style, printed in brown and olive green. Limited to 75 copies signed by Holmes. Near mint in full limp vellum with olive green ribbon ties and matching hinged box. Bromer 25-118 1983 $275

THOMAS, DYLAN   Twenty-Six Poems. London, (1949). Tall 8vo, decorated boards and cloth. One of 140 copies printed on Fabriano handmade paper at the Officina Bodoni in Verona signed by the author. Slipcase broken. Duschnes 240-176 1983 $1,550

THOMAS, EDWARD   Algernon Charles Swinburne. London: Martin Secker, 1912. First edition. Frontis. Orig. cloth. Covers a little worn. Frontis. detached. Good. MacManus 280-5148 1983 $35

THOMAS, EDWARD   Beautiful Wales. London: A. & C. Black, 1905. First edition. Orig. decorated cloth. Presentation copy, inscribed on the front free endpaper to E.S.P. Haynes. Endpapers foxed. Very good. MacManus 280-5149 1983 $1,250

THOMAS, EDWARD   Beautiful Wales. London: A. & C. Black, 1905. First edition. Large 8vo. Illus. in color. Rebound in full morocco, t.e.g., with orig. cloth covers used as front endsheet. Decorated spine, by Jones & Evans. Spine faded and rubbed at hinges. MacManus 280-5150 1983 $50

THOMAS, EDWARD   The Chessplayer. Andoversford: Whittington Press, 1981. First edition. One 375 numbered copies, this is one of 25 on Arches Creme paper, specially bound in full vellum, signed by the artist. Slipcase. Fine. Rota 230-594 1983 £70

THOMAS, EDWARD   The Childhood of Edward Thomas. London: Faber & Faber, (1938). First edition. Orig. cloth. Dust jacket (a bit rubbed, spine faded). With an ALS, 2 pages, 19, Adelaide Road, Surbiton, 4.iv.38, from Thomas' younger brother to E.S.P. Haynes laid in. MacManus 280-5151 1983 $350

THOMAS, EDWARD   Chosen Essays. The Gregynog Press, 1926. Orig. cloth. Limited to 350 copies printed. Spine faded. Some foxing. Very good. MacManus 280-5152 1983 $250

THOMAS, EDWARD   Cloud Castle and Other Papers. London: Duckworth, (1922). First edition. Orig. cloth. Frail dust jacket is present, though defective. Fine. MacManus 280-5153 1983 $65

THOMAS, EDWARD   Cloud Castle and other papers. London, 1922. First edition. Leonard Clark's copy, with his bookplate. Nice. Rota 230-592 1983 £25

THOMAS, EDWARD   Collected Poems. London: Selwyn & Blount, Ltd, 1920. First edition. Frontis. port. Orig. cloth with paper label on spine. Presentation copy from Thomas' brother to E.S.P. Haynes, inscribed on the front free endpaper, dated 28.ix.20. An ALS, 2 pages, 8vo, 13 Rusham Road, S.W. 12, 29.ix.20 also from Julian Thomas (Thomas' younger brother) to Haynes. Association copy. Very good. MacManus 280-5154 1983 $350

THOMAS, EDWARD   The Diary of Edward Thomas - 1 January - 8 April, 1917. Andoversford: The Whittington Press, 1977. First edition. One of 525 numbered copies signed by Myfanwy Thomas. 8 wood engravings by Hellmuth Weissenborn. T.e.g. Slipcase. Mint. Jolliffe 26-530 1983 £55

THOMAS, EDWARD   Feminine Influence on the Poets. London: Martin Secker, 1910. First edition, first issue. Illus. Orig. cloth. Laid in is an ALS, 1 page, 8vo, Wick Green, Peterfield, 20 September 1910, from Thomas to C.F. Casenove. With a carbon copy of Casenove's reply. Fine. MacManus 280-5156 1983 $1,000

THOMAS, EDWARD   George Borrow. London: Chapman & Hall, Ltd., 1912. First edition. With ports. and illus. Orig. cloth. Dedication copy, inscribed on the half-title "E.S.P. Haynes from Edward Thomas 1912." With an ALS, 1 page, 8vo, Wick Green, Peterfield, 18.ix.12, laid in. Haynes' bookplate on the front endsheet. Spine a bit faded. Fine. MacManus 280-5158 1983 $2,500

THOMAS, EDWARD   The Happy-Go-Lucky Morgans. London: Duckworth & Co., 1913. First edition. Frontis. Orig. cloth. Presentation copy "To Walter de la Mare 9 XI 12." Spine slightly faded. Covers a bit worn. Very good. MacManus 280-5159 1983 $650

THOMAS, EDWARD   Horae Solitariae. London: Duckworth & Co., 1902. First edition. Orig. cloth. Presentation copy, inscribed to "William H. Davies from Edward Thomas Seven Oaks 19 viii 1912." Spine a bit faded and slightly worn. Bookplate. Very good. MacManus 280-5160 1983 $1,000

THOMAS, EDWARD   Horae Solitariae. London, 1902. First edition. Covers just a little rubbed ar hinges. Endpapers lightly foxed. Leonard Clark's copy, with his bookplate. Very nice. Rota 230-590 1983 £60

THOMAS, EDWARD   The Icknield Way. London: Constable & Co. Ltd., 1913. First edition. Illus. by A.L. Collins. Orig. cloth. Very good. MacManus 280-5161 1983 $50

THOMAS, EDWARD   The Icknield Way. London: Constable & Co. Ltd., 1916. Second edition. Illus. by A.L. Collins. Orig. cloth-backed boards. Holograph note in pencil on back endsheet. Good. MacManus 280-5162 1983 $35

THOMAS, EDWARD   In Pursuit of Spring. London: Thomas Nelson & Sons, (1914). First edition, second issue. Illus. with tipped-in plates by Haslehurst. 8vo. Orig. cloth. Dust jacket (a little worn). With an ALS, 3 pages, 8vo, 8.3.21, from Julian Thomas to E.S.P. Haynes. Cloth a bit bubbled. Fine. MacManus 280-5165 1983 $350

THOMAS, EDWARD   Keats. London: T.C. & E.C. Jack, (1914).
First edition. Orig. wrappers. Good. MacManus 280-5166 1983 $50

THOMAS, EDWARD   Lafcadio Hearn. London: Constable &
Co., 1911. First edition, publisher's advance copy. Orig. unprinted
wrappers. Presentation copy to Walter de la Mare inscribed. With
several corrections in the text in Thomas's hand. Spine slightly
darkened. Covers a trifle worn. Some foxing to the endpapers. Very
good. MacManus 280-5167 1983 $1,500

THOMAS, EDWARD   Lafcadio Hearn. London: Constable &
Co., 1912. First English edition, second issue with tipped-in ad.
Frontis. port. Orig. cloth. MacManus 280-5168 1983 $50

THOMAS, EDWARD   Lafcadio Hearn. London: Constable &
Co., 1912. First English edition, first issue. Frontis. port. Orig.
cloth. Fine. MacManus 280-5169 1983 $50

THOMAS, EDWARD   Last Poems. London: Selwyn & Blount,
1918. First edition. Orig. boards with paper label. Dust jacket
(covers and spine a bit darkened and worn, with a few small tears to
the covers). Slightly foxed. Some offsetting to the endpapers. Bookplates. Near-fine. MacManus 280-5170 1983 $350

THOMAS, EDWARD   Last Poems. London: Selwyn and Blount,
1918. First edition. Orig. boards with paper label. From the library
of Walter de la Mare, containing his abbreviated signature: "de la M."
Spine and covers faded and worn. Some offsetting to the free endpapers.
Good. MacManus 280-5171 1983 $150

THOMAS, EDWARD   Last Poems. London: Selwyn & Blount,
1918. First edition. Orig. buff boards with paper label on spine.
Cont. owner's signature on front flyleaf. Boards rubbed. Good.
MacManus 280-5172 1983 $85

THOMAS, EDWARD   The Last Sheaf. London, 1928. First
English edition. Top edge slightly spotted. Nicked dustwrapper
frayed at the head of the spine. Very good. Jolliffe 26-529 1983
£65

THOMAS, EDWARD   The Life of the Duke of Marlborough.
London: Chapman & Hall, Ltd, 1915. First edition. Illus. Orig.
cloth. Dust jacket (a bit worn). First issue. Fine. MacManus 280-
5173 1983 $150

THOMAS, EDWARD   Light and Twilight. London: Duckworth
& Co., 1911. First edition, first issue. Orig. cloth. Dedication
copy, inscribed on the half-title "Arthur Yorke Hardy from Edward
Thomas." The dedication page reads simply "To A.Y.H. 1891-1911."
Inner hinges cracked. Spine torn and internally repaired. Good.
MacManus 280-5174 1983 $1,500

THOMAS, EDWARD   A Literary Pilgrim in England. London:
Methuen & Co. Ltd., (1917). First edition. 8 illus. in colour and
12 in monotone. Orig. cloth. Dust jacket (a bit soiled). Fine.
MacManus 280-5176 1983 $150

THOMAS, EDWARD   A Literary Pilgrim in England. N.Y.:
Dodd, Mead & Co., 1917. First American edition. 8 illus. in colour
and 12 in monotone. Orig. cloth. Dust jacket (a little faded & rubbed
at margins). Bookplate. Fine. MacManus 280-5175 1983 $45

THOMAS, EDWARD   Maurice Maeterlinck. London: Methuen
& Co. Ltd., 1911. First edition. 8 illus. Orig. cloth. Presentation
copy, inscribed on the front flyleaf "E.S.P.H. from E.T. 1911." Fine.
MacManus 280-5177 1983 $1,250

THOMAS, EDWARD   Maurice Maeterlinck. London: Methuen
& Co. Ltd., (1911). First edition, first issue. 8 illus. Orig. cloth.
Extremities of spine a trifle rubbed. Good. MacManus 280-5178 1983
$45

THOMAS, EDWARD   Norse Tales. Oxford: At the Clarendon
Press, 1912. First edition. Orig. cloth. Very good. MacManus 280-
5179 1983 $125

THOMAS, EDWARD   Oxford. London: A. & C. Black, (1903).
First edition. Painted by John Fulleylove. Illus. Orig. cloth.
Endpapers browned. Covers a bit worn. MacManus 280-5180 1983 $25

THOMAS, EDWARD   Poems. London: Selwyn & Brount, 1917.
First edition. With a port. from a photo. by Duncan Williams. Orig.
boards with paper label on spine. One of 525 copies of the English
issue. Extremities of spine worn. Boards darkened. MacManus 280-
5181 1983 $150

THOMAS, EDWARD   Rest and Unrest. London: Duckworth &
Co., 1910. First edition. Orig. cloth. Presentation copy, inscribed
on the front free endpaper "E.S.P. Haynes from Edward Thomas 1910."
Fine. MacManus 280-5183 1983 $1,250

THOMAS, EDWARD   Rest and Unrest. London, 1910. First
issue. Very nice. Rota 230-591 1983 £30

THOMAS, EDWARD   Richard Jefferies. His Life and Work.
Boston: Little Brown & Co., 1909. First American edition, second
state. Illus. Orig. cloth. Dust jacket (somewhat faded and slightly
chipped). Offsetting from dust jacket on endpapers. Very good.
MacManus 280-5182 1983 $125

THOMAS, EDWARD   Richard Jefferies. His Life and Work.
London: Hutchinson & Co., (n.d.). Second edition. Orig. cloth.
Presentation copy, inscribed "Walter de la Mare from E.T. 1911."
With notes and several caricatures drawn in pencil by de la Mare on
the back endpapers. Spine slightly faded. Some foxing to the end-
papers and frontis. Very good. MacManus 280-5184 1983 $600

THOMAS, EDWARD   Richard Jefferies. His Life and Work.
London: Hutchinson & Co., n.d. Second edition. Frontis. port. Orig.
cloth. Presentation copy, inscribed on the front free endpaper to
"Jesse Berridge D.D. Edward Thomas--1914." Spine faded. Very good.
MacManus 280-5185 1983 $500

THOMAS, EDWARD   Richard Jefferies. His Life and Work.
London: Hutchinson & Co., (1911). Second edition. Orig. cloth.
Dust jacket (worn). Very good. MacManus 279-2973 1983 $65

THOMAS, EDWARD   Rose Acre Papers. London: Printed by
the Lanthorn Press, and Published in London by S.C. Brown Langham &
Co., Ltd, 1904. First edition. Small 8vo. Orig. cloth-backed boards
with paper label on spine. Presentation copy, inscribed on the front
flyleaf "to E.S.P. Haynes from P(hilip) E(dward) T(homas)." Very good.
MacManus 280-5186 1983 $1,750

THOMAS, EDWARD   The South Country. London: J.M. Dent
& Co., 1909. First edition. Orig. pictorial cloth. Rack inner hinge
strengthened. Good. MacManus 280-5188 1983 $85

THOMAS, EDWARD   The Tenth Muse. London: Martin Secker,
n.d. (1917). First edition, third issue. Orig. cloth with paper label
on spine. Very good. MacManus 280-5189 1983 $60

THOMAS, EDWARD   Twenty-four poems. London: Ernest Benn,
Ltd., (1926). First edition of this selection. Orig. wrappers (soiled
and worn). MacManus 280-5193 1983 $25

THOMAS, EDWARD   The Woodland Life. London & Edinburgh:
William Blackwood and Sons, 1897. First edition. Frontis. Orig.
decorated green cloth. Near-fine. MacManus 280-5194 1983 $750

THOMAS, ELIZABETH   The Metamorphoses of the Town. London:
Printed for J. Wilford...1731. 8vo, light foxing, new wraps. Third
edition. A good copy. Quaritch NS 7-130 1983 $125

THOMAS, ELIZABETH PATTERSON   Old Kentucky Homes and Gardens.
Louisville: Standard Printing Co. (1939). 4to, double column
text. Profusely illus. with photographic plates. Edition ltd. to
250 numbered copies, signed by the author. Karmiole 72-8 1983
$75

THOMAS, G. P.   Views of Simla. London, 1846. Map,
23 tinted lithograph plates. Folio, elaborately gilt cont. morocco.
Upper joint cracked. 8vo. Good. Edwards 1044-696 1983 £425

THOMAS, GEORGE C.   Golf Architecture in America. Los Angelus: Times-Mirror Press, 1927. Tall 8vo, profusely illus., including
folding plate at rear. Signed by the author. Karmiole 75-60 1983
$75

THOMAS, HELEN   World Without End. London: William Heinemann Ltd., 1931. First edition. Orig. cloth. Dust jacket (soiled & slightly worn at edges). E.S.P. Haynes' copy, with an ALS from Helen Thomas to him, laid in; accompanied by a copy of Haynes' review. Haynes' holograph pencil notes in text. Very good. MacManus 280-5198 1983 $65

THOMAS, ISAIAH   The History of Printing in America. Barre: Imprint Society, 1970. Thick large octavo. Cloth. One of 1950 numbered copies, printed at the Stinehour Press, signed by the editor, and with a leaf from the orig. edition inserted. This is copy no. 138; signed. Very fine in slipcase. Reese 20-1055 1983 $75

THOMAS, JOSEPH   Randigal Rhymes and a Glossary of Cornish Words. Penzance: F. Rodda, 1895. Front. port. List of subscribers. Orig. blue cloth, very good. Jarndyce 30-856 1983 £15

THOMAS, JOSEPH B.   Hounds and Hunting Through the Ages. New York: Derrydale Press, 1928. Plates (some in color). Cloth. One of 750 copies. Felcone 21-34 1983 $275

THOMAS, JOSEPH B.   Observations On Borzoi. Boston 1912. 1st ed. Photos, boards, ink inscription, covers chipped. King 46-684 1983 $30

THOMAS, KATHERINE ELWES   The Real Personages of Mother Goose. Boston, (1930). 1st ed. Illus. 8vo. Morrill 287-459 1983 $20

THOMAS, LOWELL   Count Luckner, the Sea Devil. New York, n.d. (after 1927). Later printing. Inscribed "By Joe never say die and carry on. To Max Rickert...Felix Count Luckner, July 27, 31." Illus. 8vo, rubbed. Morrill 288-556 1983 $25

THOMAS, LOWELL   European Skyways. London, 1928. First edition. Frontis. 31 plates. Endpaper maps. Spine faded. Edges slightly foxed. Good. Edwards 1042-609 1983 £15

THOMAS, LOWELL   The First World Flight. London, 1926. Frontis. 39 plates. Endpaper maps. Roy. 8vo. Slightly soiled and faded. Some very slight foxing. Good. Edwards 1042-610 1983 £35

THOMAS, LOWELL   Woodfill of the Regulars. London, 1930. First edition. Portrait frontis. 15 plages, 3 facsimiles in text. 8vo. Orig. cloth. Bookplate. Fine. Edwards 1042-486 1983 £15

THOMAS, LLOYD   Travellers' Verse. London, 1946. First English edition. 15 full-page colour lithographs by Edward Bawden. Very slight worn dust wrapper by Bawden. Very good. Jolliffe 26-40 1983 £16

THOMAS, NATHANIEL S.   Building an Indian Village, St. Michael's Mission, Ethete, Wyoming. (n.p., ca. 1920's) Orig. pictorial wrappers. Fine copy. Jenkins 153-714 1983 $30

THOMAS, NATHANIEL S.   St. Michael's Mission Project. Ethete, Wy., (1920). Orig. printed wraps. First edition. Ginsberg 47-1001 1983 $30

THOMAS, NATHANIEL S.   St. Michael's Mission Project, Ethete, Wyoming. N.p., ca. 1920's. Orig. printed wrappers. Jenkins 153-715 1983 $20

THOMAS, NATHANIEL S.   Sherwood Hall Cathedral School for Boys, Laramie. (Laramie, 1925). Stiff printed wrappers. Jenkins 153-716 1983 $20

THOMAS, NATHANIEL S.   This Is a Strange Land... N.p., ca. 1926. Cover title. Illus. Jenkins 153-717 1983 $30

THOMAS, R. C. MUIRHEAD   Assam Valley Beliefs and Customs of the Assamese Hindus. London, 1948. Plates. 8vo. Orig. cloth. Good. Edwards 1044-701 1983 £18

THOMAS, ROBERT   Modern Practice of Physic. N.Y.: Collins, 1820. Thick 8vo, wrs. Argosy 713-536 1983 $50

THOMAS, ROBERT   The Modern Practice of Physic, Exhibiting the Characters, Causes, Symptoms, Prognostic Morbid Appearances,... With an Appendix... Austin, 1892. 4th American ed. 8vo. Contemp. calf, leather label. Morrill 289-229 1983 $27.50

THOMAS, T. GAILLARD   Practical Treatise on the Diseases of Women. Phila., 1872. Tall 8vo, cloth (faded; ex-lib.). 46 illus. Argosy 713-537 1983 $100

THOMAS, WILLIAM   Curll Papers. Stray Notes and the Life and Publications of Edmund Curll... (London): Reprinted for Private Circulation, 1879. 12mo. Half title. Orig. grey printed wrappers. Heath 48-268 1983 £45

THE THOMAS LAUGHLIN CO.   Catalogue No. 80. Portland, (1920). Illus. Tall 8vo. Morrill 287-209 1983 $40

THOMASON, JOHN W.   Jeb Stuart. N.Y., 1943. In dj, slight chipping. Jenkins 153-630 1983 $25

THOMASSY, RAYMOND   Geologie Pratique de la Louisiane. New Orleans, 1860. 1st ed. Orig. cloth, recased. Illus. 6 plates, including 5 maps. Jenkins 153-342 1983 $300

THOME, JAMES A.   Emancipation in the West Indies. New York: American Anti-Slavery Society, 1838. First edition. Engraved folding map of West Indies. Orig. brown cloth. Binding worn. Jenkins 152-463 1983 $125

THOME, JAMES A.   Emancipation in the West Indies. New York, 1838. Folding map frontispiece. Green printed boards and cloth. First edition. Foxed throughout, covers worn and soiled. Bradley 64-154 1983 $40

THOMEE, IOANNES HENRICUS   Historia Insanorum apud Graecos. Bonn: (Thomanni) 1835. Contemporary 1/4 leather. Gach 94-285 1983 $75

THOMPSON, ALBERT W.   They Were Open Range Days. Denver, 1946. First edition in dust jacket. Limited to 500 copies. Jenkins 152-464 1983 $100

THOMPSON, ALBERT W.   They were Open Range Days. Denver: World Press, 1946. 22 cm. 24 illus. including a photo of a hanging. Orig. maroon cloth. Shelf number on spine & stamp on verso of the ittle, but a very good copy. Grunder 7-72 1983 $35

THOMPSON, SIR BENJAMIN, COUNT RUMFORD
Please turn to
RUMFORD, SIR BENJAMIN THOMPSON, COUNT

THOMPSON, C.   Travels through Turkey in Asia... Glasgow, 1798. Folding map, 3 folding plates. Half calf. 8vo. Good. Edwards 1044-697 1983 £95

THOMPSON, DUSTAN   Lament for the Sleepwalker. New York, 1947. 8vo. Cloth. Review copy with slip laid in. Fine in dj. In Our Time 156-793 1983 $20

THOMPSON, E.   The Making of Indian Princes. Oxford, 1843. 8vo. Orig. cloth. Good. Edwards 1044-698 1983 £22

THOMPSON, E.   Rise and Fullfilment of British Rule in India. London, 1934. Numerous folding maps. 8vo. Orig. cloth. Good. Edwards 1044-699 1983 £20

THOMPSON, EDWARD   The Collected Poems. London: Ernest Benn Limited, 1930. First edition. Orig. cloth. Dust jacket (a little chipped, darkened along spine). Fine. MacManus 280-5201 1983 $25

THOMPSON, EDWARD   Poems, 1902-1925. London: Selwyn & Blount, Ltd., (1926). First edition. Orig. boards. Paper label on spine. Presentation copy, inscribed on the front free endpaper "Viola Garvin ex dono auctoris, 25.1.29." With an ALS, 2 pages, 8vo, no place, no date, from Thompson to an unnamed individual. Boards a bit rubbed. Good. MacManus 280-5203 1983 $40

THOMPSON, EDWARD   Trinculo's trip to the Jubilee. London:
printed for C. Moran; W. Flexney; and R. Riddley, 1769. 4to, wrappers,
first edition. Half-title present. An excellent copy of a rare
poem. Ximenes 640539 1983 $375

THOMPSON, EDWARD H.   The Chultunes of Lagna, Yucatan.
Cambridge, 1897. 13 plates. 13 text illus. Folio. Wrappers.
Ars Libri 34-495 1983 $75

THOMPSON, ERNEST SETON
Please turn to
SETON, ERNEST THOMPSON (1860-1946)

THOMPSON, FRANCIS   The Collected Poetry of Francis
Thompson. London: Hodder & Stoughton, 1913. Thick quarto. Full
brown crushed levant, gilt extra, t.e.g. by Riviere. Etched
portrait frontis. after Raeburn. One of 500 numbered copies, signed
by the publisher and the printer. Joints show slightest traces of
rubbing, else a fine copy. Inset into two extra binder's prelims
is an original autograph letter, signed, from Francis Thompson to
Everard Meynell. Reese 20-1057 1983 $450

THOMPSON, FRANCIS   Health & Holiness. London: Burns &
Oates, Ltd., 1905. First edition, first issue. Orig. wrappers. With-
out the imprimatur on the verso of the title-page. Very good. Mac-
Manus 280-5208 1983 $50

THOMPSON, FRANCIS   Health & Holiness. London: Burns &
Oates, Ltd., 1905. First edition. Orig. wrappers. Second issue.
Cancel title-page bearing the imprimatur on the verso. Very good.
MacManus 280-5206 1983 $40

THOMPSON, FRANCIS   Health & Holiness. London: Burns &
Oates, Ltd., 1905. First edition, second issue. Orig. cloth. Cancel
title-page bearing the imprimatur on the verso. Very good. Mac-
Manus 280-5207 1983 $35

THOMPSON, FRANCIS   New Poems. Westminster: Archibald Constable & Co., 1897. First edition. Orig. decorated cloth. Endpapers
foxed. Fine. MacManus 280-5210 1983 $85

THOMPSON, FRANCIS   New Poems. Boston: Copeland & Day, 1897.
First American edition. Orig. decorated cloth. 500 copies were
printed. Fine. MacManus 280-5209 1983 $50

THOMPSON, FRANCIS   Poems. Elkin Matthews & John Lane, 1893.
First edition. Sm. 4to. Frontis. Title vignette. Grey boards, gilt,
worn. 14pp of ads. Edition limited to 500 copies. Greer 40-114
1983 £35

THOMPSON, FRANCIS   Poems. London: Elkin Mathews and John
Lane, Boxton: Copeland & Day, 1894. Second edition. Orig. boards.
Cover and frontis. by Laurence Housman. One of 500 copies printed.
Covers a bit worn. MacManus 280-5211 1983 $25

THOMPSON, FRANCIS   A Renegade Poet and Other Essays. Boston:
The Ball Publishing Co., 1910. First edition. Orig. cloth. Very good.
MacManus 280-5214 1983 $50

THOMPSON, FRANCIS   A Renegade Poet and Other Essays.
Boston, 1910. First edition. Argosy 714-738 1983 $25

THOMPSON, FRANCIS   Saint Ignatius Loyola. London: Burns &
Oates, 1909. First edition. Illus. Orig. cloth. Faint traces of
tape on endpapers. Fine. MacManus 280-5215 1983 $85

THOMPSON, FRANCIS   Shelley. London: Burns & Oates, 1909.
First edition. 8vo. Orig. boards. Dust jacket (slightly browned and
torn). Large paper copy. Endpapers a little browned. Head of spine
bumped. Near-fine. MacManus 280-5217 1983 $50

THOMPSON, FRANCIS   Shelley. London: Burns & Oates, 1909.
First edition. Spine faded. Intro. by Geo. Wyndlam. Orig. cloth.
MacManus 280-5218 1983 $25

THOMPSON, FRANCIS   Sir Leslie Stephen As A Biographer. N.p.:
(Clement Shorter), n.d. (1915). First edition, privately printed. 4to.
Orig. wrappers. One of 20 copies numbered and initialed by Clement
Shorter. In a half-morocco slipcase. Mint. MacManus 280-5219 1983
$300

THOMPSON, FRANCIS   Sister Songs, An Offering to Two Sisters.
London & N.Y.: John Lane & Copeland & Day, 1895. First edition.
Frontis. Orig. decorated buckram with front cover design by L. Housman.
Spine and covers faded and slightly worn at the spine ends. Endpapers
foxed. Bookplate. Good. MacManus 280-5221 1983 $65

THOMPSON, FRANCIS   .Sister Songs. London: John Lane, 1895.
First edition. Frontis. by L. Housman. Orig. decorated cloth. Bookplates. Very good. MacManus 280-5220 1983 $50

THOMPSON, FRANCIS   Sister Songs. London, 1895. First edition. Frontis. and cover design by L. Housman. Nice. Rota 230-596
1983 £25

THOMPSON, FRANCIS   Sister-Songs. London, 1895. First
edition. 8vo, gilt buckram; darkened. Fine. Argosy 714-739 1983
$25

THOMPSON, FRANCIS   Uncollected Verses. London: Privately
Printed by Clement Shorter, July 1917. First edition. 4to. Orig.
wrappers. One of 25 copies printed and signed by Shorter. In a cloth
slipcase. Very fine. MacManus 280-5222 1983 $350

THOMPSON, FRANCIS   The Works. London: Burns & Oates Ltd.,
(1913). "Fourteenth Thousand." Illus. with photogravures. Bound in
blue 3/4 morocco & cloth. Fine. MacManus 280-5223 1983 $150

THOMPSON, GEORGE   Prison Life and Reflections. Oberlin:
Printed by James M. Fitch, 1847. Ads. Orig. cloth rebacked. Some
staining. 1st ed. Jenkins 153-633 1983 $50

THOMPSON, GEORGE G.   Bat Masterson: The Dodge City Years.
Topeka, 1943. Printed wrappers. Fine copy. Jenkins 153-632 1983
$35

THOMPSON, GEORGE W.   The Charter and Ordinances of the
City of Chicago...Together with Acts of the General Assembly Relating
to the City... Chicago, 1856. Full gold tooled presentation
morocco. First edition. Ginsberg 46-341 1983 $125

THOMPSON, HAROLD STUART   Alpine Plants of Europe Together with
Cultural Hints. London, (1911). 64 colored plates, folding map.
8vo. Morrill 289-552 1983 $30

THOMPSON, HENRY   "All But." London: Kegan Paul, Trench
& Co., 1886. First edition. Orig. cloth. 20 illus. by author. All
edges a bit worn. One corner badly bumped. Former owner's inscription
on half-title. A little light foxing. Good. MacManus 279-4074
1983 $45

THOMPSON, HUNTER S.   Fear and Loathing in Las Vegas. NY,
(1971). Remainder stamp bottom page edge, else near fine in slightly
soiled, very good dustwrapper. Quill & Brush 54-1356 1983 $75

THOMPSON, HUNTER S.   Hell's Angels. New York, (1967). 8vo.
Cloth. Review copy with slip laid in from publisher. Fine copy in
dj. In Our Time 156-794 1983 $125

THOMPSON, JOHN LEWIS   Historical Sketches of the Late War,
Between the United States and Great Britain, Blended with Anecdotes.
Philadelphia, 1816. Plates. Large folding plates browned and torn on
some folds. Calf and boards, hinges cracked. Reese 18-506 1983
$175

THOMPSON, LESSLIE R.   The Canadian National Railway Problem.
Toronto: Macmillan, 1938. 25 1/2cm. Numerous charts and maps.
Orig. blue cloth. A fine copy. McGahern 53-192 1983 $65

THOMPSON, MAURICE   Alice of Old Vincennes. Ind., (1900).
Illus. by Yohn, first issue without "acknowledgements" at end, cover
worn, rear hinge cracked, good. Quill & Brush 54-1359 1983 $40

THOMPSON, ROBERT FARRIS   Black Gods and Kings. Los Angeles,
1971. Prof. illus. 4to. Wrappers. First edition. Ars Libri
34-760 1983 $125 1

THOMPSON, THOMAS   An Account of Two Missionary Voyages...
London: Beni, Ddo, 1758. Old half calf. 1st ed. Jenkins 153-635
1983 $200

THOMPSON, THOMAS   Researches into the History of Welton and its Neighbourhood with a few remarks chiefly on an Antiquarian Nature. Kingston-Upon-Hull, 1869. 2 litho plates, some foxing. K Books 301-178 1983 £40

THOMSON, DAVID CROAL   The Life and Works of Thomas Bewick. London, The Art Journal, 1882. 5 plates, 100 illus., large 4to., cloth, no. 69 of a limited edition of 250 copies. Ars Libri 32-38 1983 $300

THOMSON, EDWARD   The adventures of a carpet bag. London: Piper, 1853. First edition. 8vo. Orig. decorated wrappers. Illus. by Robert Cruikshank, and lithographed wrappers designed by Percy Cruikshank. Bookplate of Albert M. Cohn. Slight wear, a bit soiled. Scarce. Ximenes 63-162 1983 $60

THOMSON, ELIZABETH   Harvey Cushing Surgeon, Author, Artist. New York, 1950. First edition. 8vo. Orig. binding. Dust wrapper. Fye H-3-719 1983 $30

THOMSON, H. C.   The Chitral Campaign. London, 1895. First edition. Frontis. 4 full page maps and plans, 32 full page and 25 other illus. Endpaper ads. Spine faded. Very slightly worn preliminaries. 8vo. Orig. cloth. Very slightly foxed. Good. Edwards 1042-487 1983 £18

THOMSON, H. C   The Story of the Middlesex Hospital Medical School. (1935). 8vo, 20 plates, library stamp on verso of title and inside front cover, lacks front fly, orig. cloth. Bickersteth 77-323 1983 £12

THOMSON, JAMES (1700-1748)   Autumn. London: printed by N. Blandford for J. Millan, 1730. First separate edition, second issue. 8vo, engraved frontis., some light waterstaining in the outer margins, marbled wrappers. Pagination corrected for pp. 42-3. Pickering & Chatto 19-74 1983 $300

THOMSON, JAMES (1700-1748)   The Castle of Indolence. Holloway, 1845. 1st edn. Illus. by William Rimmer. Frontis. & 11 illus. Dark green fine ribbed cloth gilt, a.e.g. (cvrs. faded & some marks top/bottom bkstrip. sl. wear, some foxing contents), v.g. Hodgkins 27-334 1983 £25

THOMSON, JAMES (1700-1748)   Edward and Eleonora. Dublin: Printed by S. Powell, for G. Faulkner, 1739. First Irish edition. 12mo, wrapper. Very good copy. Fenning 60-409 1983 £24.50

THOMSON, JAMES (1700-1748)   A Poem to the Memory of the Right Honourable the Lord Talbot... London: Printed for A. Millar... MDCCXXXVII. 4to, with half-title bound after title and pub.'s ads. on final leaf; a partly uncut copy in polished calf, rebacked. First edition. Quaritch NS 7-131 1983 $275

THOMSON, JAMES (1700-1748)   The Seasons... Phila.: John Bioren, for Benjamin and Jacob Johnson, 1801. Added titlepage, engraved (dated 1802). Full calf. Binding quite worn, front endpaper lacking. Felcone 20-179 1983 $25

THOMSON, JAMES (1700-1748)   The Seasons. London: by T. Bensley, 1807. 4to. Full red levant morocco, gilt, inside gilt borders, edges gilt, by Maclehose, Glasgow. Illus. with engravings by F. Bartolozzi & P.W. Tomkins, from orig. pictures painted for the work by William Hamilton. Traylen 94-827 1983 £130

THOMSON, JAMES (1700-1748)   Spring. London: A. Millar, 1728. 1st ed., 8vo, later calf gilt, morocco label, a.e.g. With the rare half-title. A very fine copy. Trebizond 18-96 1983 $200

THOMSON, JAMES (1700-1748)   The tragedy of Sophonisba. London: printed for A. Millar, 1739. 8vo, disbound, 1st edition. Title a bit dusty. Ximenes 64-540 1983 $75

THOMSON, JAMES (1700-1748)   The Works of Mr. James Thomson, with His Last Corrections and Improvements. For R. Baldwin, 1803-02. With engraved portrait and 10 engraved plates by Medland, Neagle, Anker Smith, Grignion and others after Metz, Burney and Stothard. 3 vols., tall 8vo, cont. tree calf, gilt spines, with double lettering pieces. Fenning 62-362 1983 £38.50

THOMSON, JAMES (1834-1882)   The City of Dreadful Night. London: Bertram Dobell, 1899. First edition. Orig. cloth. Fine. MacManus 280-5238 1983 $65

THOMSON, JAMES (1834-1882)   The City of Dreadful Night. London: Bertram Dobell, 1899. An early edition. Orig. cloth. Spine and covers very slightly worn. Bookplate. Near-fine. MacManus 280-5239 1983 $25

THOMSON, JAMES (1834-1882)   The City of Dreadful Night, and Other Poems. Reeves & Turner, 1880. First edition, half title, orig. dark green cloth, dulled, otherwise v.g. One of 40 large-paper copies. Pencil note indicating purchase from Dobell in September 1886. Jarndyce 31-944 1983 £60

THOMSON, JAMES (1834-1882)   The City of Dreadful Night. London: Reeves & Turner, 1880. First edition. Orig. cloth. Trade issue. 1000 copies printed. With errata leaf. Covers somewhat worn, inner hinges weak. Inscription on half title. In a half-morocco pull-off case. MacManus 280-5240 1983 $75

THOMSON, JAMES (1834-1882)   The Poetical Works. London, 1862. 2 vols. Cr. 8vo. Dark blue calf, two-line gilt borders with corner ornaments, gilt panelled spines, morocco labels, gilt. Portrait, vignette title-pages, facsimile. Traylen 94-826 1983 £30

THOMSON, JAMES (1834-1882)   Vane's Story, Weddah and Om-el-Bonain, and Other Poems. Reeves & Turner, 1881. First edition, half title, 8 pp 'Opinions of the Press'. Orig. dark green cloth, dulled, otherwise v.g. One of 40 large-paper copies. Jarndyce 31-945 1983 £52

THOMSON, JAMES (1834-1882)   Vane's Story, Weddah and Om-El-Bonain. London: Reeves & Turner, 1881. First edition. Orig. cloth. Good. MacManus 280-5242 1983 $65

THOMSON, JAMES (1834-1882)   A Voice from the Nile. London: Reeves & Turner, 1884. First edition. Photogravure frontis. Orig. cloth. Former owner's signature on title-page. Very good. MacManus 280-5243 1983 $75

THOMSON, JAMES (1834-1882)   A Voice from the Nile, and Other Poems. Reeves & Turner, 1884. First edition, half title, front. port. 4pp 'Opinions of the Press'. Orig. light blue cloth, dulled and spine faded. One of 40 large-paper copies. Jarndyce 31-946 1983 £42

THOMSON, JOHN   The Letters of Curtius... Richmond, 1804. Bound in half leather and boards, front board detached. Very good. Reese 18-266 1983 $300

THOMSON, JOSEPH   Through Masai Land. Boston: Houghton, Mifflin, 1885. 8vo. 2 folding maps. 15 plates. Orig. pictorial cloth. Rubbed. Ex-lib. Adelson Africa-229 1983 $50

THOMSON, JOSEPH   To the central African lakes and back. London: Sampson Low, etc., 1881. Third edition. 2 vols. 12mo. 2 folding maps, 2 mounted photographs. Orig. brown pictorial cloth. Rubbed. Adelson Africa-139 1983 $275

THOMSON, JOSEPH   Ulu. An African Romance. Sampson Low, Marston, 1888. First edition, 2 vols. Front. map vol. I. Half title and 32 pp cata. (April 1888) vol. II. Orig. dark green cloth, gilt, v.g. Jarndyce 30-571 1983 £120

THOMSON, M.   The Story of Cawnpore. London, 1859. Folding plan, 3 plates, stamp removed from frontis. Half morocco. 8vo. Good. Edwards 1044-700 1983 £65

THOMSON, PETER G.   A Bibliography of the State of Ohio... Cincinnati: Pub. by author, 1880. Chromolithographed title. Half leather, worn but still tight, some water damage to endpapers but not to text. Dawson 470-290 1983 $75

THOMSON, WILLIAM   Orpheus Caledonius: or, a Collection of Scots Songs set to Musick. London: printed for the Author, 1733. 1st complete edition (second printing of Vol. I, first edition of vol. 2). Tall 8vo, 2 volumes, later half calf gilt, morocco labels, marbled boards. Vignette title pages; privilege leaf; subscribers' list. In the present copy, the music is not present. A fine copy. Trebizond 18-97 1983 $375

THOMSON, WILLIAM MC CLURE   The Land and the Book. New York, 1859. 2 vols., 8vo. Maps & illus. Nice. Morrill 288-484 1983 $27.50

THOMSON, WILLIAM MC CLURE   The Land and the Book. T. Nelson, 1867. Map, 12 coloured plates and many other illus. Cr. 8vo. Very good in cont. divinity style calf, edges gilt. Fenning 60-410 1983 £28.50

THONNER, F.   The Flowering Plants of Africa. (1916) 1962. Map and 150 plates, royal 8vo, cloth. Wheldon 160-1771 1983 £47

THORBURN, GRANT   Forty Years' Residence in America. Boston, 1834. 1st ed. 12mo, better than average copy. Morrill 286-476 1983 $27.50

THOREAU, HENRY DAVID   Cape Cod. B, 1865. Cover and spine edges moderately worn and stained, light internal stains still good or better. Quill & Brush 54-1363 1983 $450

THOREAU, HENRY DAVID   Cape Cod. Boston, 1865. First edition. Small 8vo. Ex-library but with no external marks; backstrip faded and worn at ends; corners slightly rubbed; name on title. Morrill 290-534 1983 $75

THOREAU, HENRY DAVID   Cape Cod. B, 1965. Spine sunned, spine edges rubbed and frayed, rear hinge cracked but intact, bookseller's catalog description tipped-in. Quill & Brush 54-1362 1983 $400

THOREAU, HENRY DAVID   A collection of early editions of the works. Boston, 1865-80. 6 vols. Cr. 8vo. Orig. pebble-grained cloth, gilt. Traylen 94-828 1983 £75

THOREAU, HENRY DAVID   The First and Last Journeys of Thoreau... Boston: Bibliophile Soc., 1905. 2 vols. 8vo, 2 engr. certs. of issue, portrait, 3 facs. (1 folded). 3/4 maroon calf, gilt, uncut and un-opened. First edition. 489 copies only. Orig. slipcases and boxes, with paper label. Fine. O'Neal 50-52 1983 $90

THOREAU, HENRY DAVID   Homes of American Authors... New York: Putnam, 1853. First edition. Frontis., engraved title. 14 color printed wood engravings, 19 steel engravings, 16 manuscript facsimiles. Orig. green cloth, gilt. Very fine. Jenkins 152-466 1983 $250

THOREAU, HENRY DAVID   The Transmigration of the Seven Brahmans. New York, Rudge, 1932. 1st ed., 1200 copies printed. 4to, orig. boards, cloth back. Ex-library but very nice with no external marks. Morrill 289-553 1983 $30

THOREAU, HENRY DAVID   Walden. Boston, Tickner and Fields, 1854. 8vo. Map. Orig. cloth. 1st ed. Expertly restored by light mending of extremities of spine, recasing to tighten. Fine. O'Neal 50-53 1983 $800

THOREAU, HENRY DAVID   Walden: or, Life in the Woods. Boston: Ticknor and Fields, 1854. With April ads. Top and bottom of spine rubbed, covers slightly faded, else fine. Owner's signature. With protective stiff dust wrapper and quarter-leather slip-case. Bromer 25-119 1983 $750

THOREAU, HENRY DAVID   Walden; or, Life in the Woods. Boston: Ticknor & Fields, 1854. Map. 1st ed., 1st state of binding. Orig. brown cloth, gilt. Recased with the orig. spine laid down rather sloppily, and therefore priced at 1/5 the cost of a fine copy. The ads, dated May, are of no importance in establishing the priority of copies of this book which consisted of a single printing of 2,000 copies. A good copy. Jenkins 155-1209 1983 $375

THOREAU, HENRY DAVID   Walden. London: Walter Scott, 1886. 1st ed., 1st printing of the 1st ed. printed in England. Orig. blue cloth, paper label, wholly uncut. Fine copy. Jenkins 155-1210 1983 $450

THOREAU, HENRY DAVID   Walden. London, Chapman & Hall, 1927. First edition thus. 16 tipped-in woodcuts by Eric Fitch Daglish. Full black morocco, a.e.g., marbled endpapers; gilt stamped trees on spine. A fresh copy. Houle 22-889 1983 $325

THOREAU, HENRY DAVID   Walden. Boston: Limited Editions Club, 1936. Illus. with photographs by Edward Steichen. Cloth-backed boards, tall 8vo, boxed. Signed by Steichen. Argosy 714-742 1983 $350

THOREAU, HENRY DAVID   A Week on the Concord & Merrimack Rivers. Boston: Ticknor & Fields, 1868. 2nd ed., only 1,330 copies were printed. Orig. cloth, gilt. Chipped spine, else a good copy. Jenkins 155-1211 1983 $50

THOREAU, HENRY DAVID   Writings. Cambridge, Riverside Press, 1894. Cambridge edition. Frontis. Half white cloth over blue boards, paper labels, uncut and mostly unopened. One of 150 numbered sets on large paper. 22 vols. complete. Houle 21-873 1983 $395

THOREAU, HENRY DAVID   The Writings... Boston: 1906. 20 oc-tavo vols. Limited "Manuscript Edition", containing a fragment of manuscript by Thoreau bound into Vol. I. Numerous illus. Limited to 600 copies signed by the publisher. Fine in gilt-stamped half-leather with gilt-stamped floral decorations to spine which has 5 raised bands and marbled boards. Small vertical stain to rear cover of Vol. 1, else fine set. T.e.g. Bookplate removed from Vol. I. Bromer 25-120 1983 $2500

THOREAU, HENRY DAVID   The Writing of... Boston & New York: Houghton, Mifflin, 1906. First edition. Limited to 600 numbered sets signed by publisher, with a leaf of Thoreau manuscript inserted in the first volume. 20 vols. Photo illus. Frontis. Orig. cloth, labels. Uncut. Choice leaf of orig. manuscript reflecting Thoreau's deep interest in Hindu thought. Very good. Jenkins 152-465 1983 $1,650

THOREAU, HENRY DAVID   A Yankee in Canada. B, 1866. Hinges cracked but intact, spine edges frayed, lettering bright, covers good despite mentioned fraying. Quill & Brush 54-1361 1983 $350

THORN, W.   Memoir of the War in India. London, 1818. Folding engraved map, 8 handcoloured plans, some offsetting of the map onto the title. Uncut. 4to. Half red crushed levant morocco. Good. Edwards 1044-702 1983 £155

THORN, W   Voyage dans l'Inde britannique. Paris: Gide Fills, 1818. 1st ed. in French, 8vo, cont. qtr. calf gilt, morocco label, boards. Half-title. A fine copy, despite rubbed boards and somewhat discolored endpapers. Trebizond 18-146 1983 $75

THORNBURY, GEORGE WALTER   The monarchs of the main. London: Hurst and Blackett, 1855. First edition. 8vo. 3 vols. Cont. half morocco, gilt. Very good set. Ximenes 63-353 1983 $353

THORNBURY, WALTER   Haunted London. Chatto & Windus, 1880. Illus. F.W. Fairhold. Half title, 32 pp ads. Orig. dark blue cloth, dec. in green and gilt. Jarndyce 31-300 1983 £28

THORNDIKE, HERBERT   Just Weights and Measures. Printed by S. Roycroft for J. Martyn, 1680. 4to. Fenning 62-363 1983 £24.50

THORNDIKE, LYNN   A History of Magic and Experimental Science. New York & London: Columbia Univ. Press, (1964-66). 8 vols., cloth, just about new in the glassine wrappers. Dawson 470-291 1983 $200

THORNDIKE, RUSSELL   Doctor Syn. London, 1915. First edition. Spine faded and covers marked. Nice. Rota 230-597 1983 £21

THORN-DRURY, GEORGE   Catalogue of the Library of English Poetry, Drama & other Literature, principally of the XVII and early XVIII Centuries. London, 1931. 4 parts in one volume, modern cloth, original wrappers bound in. A fine copy. Trebizond 18-1 1983 $80

THORNE, EDWARD   Decorative Draperies & Upholstery. Grand Rapids, Mich.: Dean-Hicks Co., 1929. Folio. 74 color plates + numerous text illus. Karmiole 76-103 1983 $60

THORNE, JAMES   Handbook to the Environs of London. John Murray, 1876. First edition, 2 vols. Well bound in red cloth, gilt spine lettering, v.g. Jarndyce 31-301 1983 £35

THORNTON, E.   Illustrations of the History and Practices of the Thugs. London, 1837. Paper label on spine, slight wear. 8vo. Orig. cloth. With the Elphinstone Carberry Tower label. Good. Edwards 1044-706 1983 £130

THORNTON, E.   The History of the British Empire in
India. London, 1841-45. 2 vols., together 8 vols. Full cont. straight
grained morocco. Spine gilt in compartments. From the Marquis of
Tweeddale's Library, with his signature and bookplates. Fine copy
in an 'Indian' binding. 8vo. Good. Edwards 1044-705 1983 £550

THORNTON, E.   India, Its State and Prospects. London,
1835. Paper label on spine, some wear. 8vo, orig. cloth. Presentation copy "The Rt. Honle. Lord Ellenborough from the Author." Good.
Edwards 1044-703 1983 £85

THORNTON, E.   Leaves from an Afghan Scrapbook. London,
1910. Map, plates. 8vo. Orig. cloth. Good. Edwards 1044-704 1983
£25

THORNTON, JAMES   The "T & M" System of Ladies' Garment
Cutting and Practical Tailoring..." Thornton & Moulton, circa, 1915.
Fenning 62-364 1983 £16.50

THORNTON, JESSE QUINN   Oregon and California in 1848. N.Y.?
1849. 2 vols., 12 plates, color folding map. Original cloth.
Jenkins 151-336 1983 $475

THORNTON, JOHN W.   The Pulpit of the American
Revolution. Boston, 1860. First edition. Illus. Orig. cloth.
Library stamps on title page. Ginsberg 46-11 1983 $35

THORNTON. WILLIAM THOMAS   Over-Population and Its Remedy. Longman,
Brown, 1846. First edition. 32 pp ads. Orig. green cloth, spine.
Sl. darkened, v.g. Jarndyce 31-387 1983 £140

THORNTON, WILLIAM THOMAS   A Plea for Peasant Proprietors.
John Murray, 1848. First edition, half title, 2 pp ads. Orig.
purple-brown cloth, paper label, v.g. Jarndyce 31-205 1983 £34

THOROLD, ALGAR   The Life of Henry Labouchere. London:
Constable & Co., Ltd., 1913. First edition. Frontis. port. Orig.
cloth. Dust jacket. Front inner hinge starting. Fine. MacManus
279-3102 1983 $20

THOROLD, ALGAR   Six Masters of Disillusion. London,
Constable, 1909. Gilt stamped blue cloth, mostly unopened (some
fraying, corners bumped), else very good. Harold Acton's copy signed
and dated by him, 1921. Very good. Houle 22-890 1983 $45

THORP, JOSEPH   Early Days in the West Along the Missouri.
(Liberty, Mo., 1924). Orig. printed wrappers. Fine. Jenkins 152-467
1983 $75

THORP, JOSEPH   Eric Gill. London, Cape, 1929.
First edition. 4to, 38 plates. Gilt stamped black cloth. Very
good. Houle 22-406 1983 $65

THORP, N. HOWARD (JACK)   Pardner of the Wind. Caldwell, Idaho:
1945. First edition. Illus. Blue cloth. Some sun fading on cover,
dust jacket chipped. Bradley 66-616 1983 $67.50

THORP, RAYMOND W.   Bowie Knife. NM: Univ. of N. Mexico,
1948. 1st ed., illus, cloth, very good in chipped dw. King 46-686
1983 $25

THORPE, JAMES   English Illustration: The Nineties.
Faber, 1935. 1st edn. Frontis. & 122 b&w illus. Purple cloth,
t.e.g. (bkstrip sl. faded & soiled). A.L.S. from author dd. 1st
Sept. 1938 tipped in. fr. ep. V.g. copy. Hodgkins 27-575 1983
$45

THORPE, THOMAS BANGS   The Hive of "The Bee-Hunter"... N.Y.,
Appleton, 1854. 8vo. Frontis. & 8 plates. Orig. decorated cloth.
1st ed. Fine. O'Neal 50-54 1983 $200

THORY, C. A.   Monographie ou histoire naturelle du
genre Groseiller. Paris, 1829. 24 plain plates, 8vo, half morocco.
A scarce work. Some slight foxing and the binding trifle affected
by damp. Lacks the portrait. An uncut copy. Wheldon 160-2020 1983
£45

THOUGHTS on the Corn Laws. London: John Olliver, 1856. 3rd edition,
8vo, disbound. Pickering & Chatto 21-28 1983 $45

THRASHER, HALSEY   The Hunter and Trapper. New York,
(1868). 1st ed. 6 plates plus text illus. 12mo. Binding slightly
faded. Morrill 286-477 1983 $40

THRASHER, MARION   Long Life in California. Chicago,
(1915). Illus. Orig. cloth. First edition. Inscribed
presentation copy from Thrasher. Ginsberg 47-187 1983 $25

THE THRE Kynges of Coleyne. (London: Wynkyn de Worde, 1526).
Fourth extant edition. Black Letter. Small 4to. 18th century calf.
Lacking the title-page and last four leaves. Previous owned by
William Herbert, with his signature on fly-leaf and a bookplate
of a later member of the Herbert family. Slight stains but in good
condition. Traylen 94-207 1983 £2,300

THE THREE Americas Railway. St. Louis, 1881. 1st ed. By Hinton
Rowan Helper, et al. Small 8vo. Bottom third of backstrip torn and
part lacking, stain on back cover. Morrill 287-586 1983 $25

THREE Courses and a Dessert. Lon., 1845. 3rd edition. 51 illus. by
George Cruikshank. Spine frayed and chipped, cover worn, hinges
cracked, good. Quill & Brush 54-335 1983 $50

THREE Letters, the First from an Officer in His Majesties Army...
Oxford: by Leonard Lichfield, May 24, 1643. 4to. Modern
quarter morocco. Heath 48-192 1983 £45

THREE Memorials of the Citizens of the United States, Residents of
Leavenworth County, Kansas Territory, Praying the Immediate Admission
to Said Territory into the Union as a State. Wash., 1856. First
edition. Dbd. Ginsberg 46-390 1983 $25

THREE New Mexico Chronicles... Albuquer: Quivira Soc., 1942. Plate
and 2 folding maps. Orig. cloth-backed boards. Mostly unopened.
First English edition. Fine. Jenkins 153-436 1983 $150

THREEPLAND, MONCRIEFF   Letters respecting the performance at
the Theatre Royal, Edinburgh. Edinburgh: printed for G. Gray, by
W. Bell, 1800. 8vo, recent calf (amateurish), 1st edition. Tears in
a couple of blank margins, but a sound copy. Ximenes 64-542 1983
$125

3600 Bonnes Femmes Comiques. Paris: Dambuyant & Guignard, n.d. (ca.
1900). 4to. 16 colour plates, divided in 4, making many different
arrangements. Colour pictorial boards, light wear. Greer 40-146
1983 £60

THE THREE Trials of William Hone, For Publishing Three Parodies.
London, 1818. Boards, worn, spine badly chipped. With subscription
list. King 46-341 1983 $50

THRELFALL, T. R.   Long Live Love. London: Ward Lock,
1905. First edition. Orig. cloth. With a full-page presentation
inscription from the author on the flyleaf. Very good. MacManus 280-
5246 1983 $25

THUCYDIDES   Eight Bookes of the Peloponnesian Warre
Written by Thvcydides the sonne of Olorva. London, Hen: Seile,
1629. Folio, cont. calf rebacked, worn, signature of W. Stanely
Jevons, the Victorian economist on endpaper, bookplate. Ravenstree
95-131 1983 $750

THUCYDIDES   The Hystory Writtone by Thucidedes the
Athenyan of the Warre, which was Betwene the Peloponesians and the
Athenyans. London, 1550. Rare errata leaf. Contemporary calf,
rebacked. Folio, printed in black letters, woodcut border on title.
1st ed. in English. Fine copy. Jenkins 155-1215 1983 $3500

THUCYDIDES   The History Writtone by Thucidides
the Athenyan of the Warre... (London) Imprinted (by W. Tylle), 1550.
Folio, old calf sometime rebacked, worn, old age and dust soiling
and some waterstaining throughout, few minor holes touching a letter
here and there, bookplate of King's College Cambridge and cancelled
stamp on verso of title, but not a bad copy. First translation into
English. Ravenstree 95-130 1983 $1,600

THUCYDIDES   Tetarte. London, 1889. 8vo, cloth.
Salloch 385-781 1983 $20

THUDICHUM, J. L. W.   A Treatise on the Pathology of the
Urine... London, 1877. Second edition. 8vo. Cloth. Gurney JJ-
400 1983 £25

THURBER, JAMES   The Beast in Me and Other Animals. NY,
(1948). Minor cover stains, else very good in moderately chipped
and wearing, good dustwrapper. Quill & Brush 54-1366 1983 $40

THURBER, JAMES   The Beast in Me and Other Animals. NY,
(1948). First issue, bright, very good or better in lightly chipped
and frayed, slightly soiled, very good dustwrapper. Quill & Brush 54-
1367 1983 $30

THURBER, JAMES   The Beast in Me and Other Animals. N.Y.,
Harcourt, (1948). First edition, second state of binding color "light
lime green" (faded spot on top of spine). Dust jacket (small nicks)
else very good. Houle 22-891 1983 $25

THURBER, JAMES   The Beast in Me and Other Animals. L,
(1949). End pages very slightly foxed, very good in slightly frayed
and chipped, very good dustwrapper, owner's name. Quill & Brush 54-
1365 1983 $40

THURBER, JAMES   Thurber's Men, Women, and Dogs. N.Y.,
Harcourt, (1943). First edition. Dark blue cloth. Dust jacket (a
few small chips) else very good. Houle 22-894 1983 $35

THURBER, JAMES   The White Deer. N.Y., Harcourt, (1945).
First edition with "I" on verso of title page. Dust jacket (back a
bit darkened) else fine. Illus. in color and b/w by the author and
Don Freeman. Houle 22-893 1983 $30

THURLOE, JOHN   A Collection of State Papers of John
Thurloe. London, 1742. Portrait by G. Vertue. Embossed stamp on
blank portion and engraved headpieces. 7 vols., small folio, contemp.
calf, leather labels. Ex-library; worn; backstrips partly torn; 2
covers lacking and 4 covers loose; other hinges cracked. Morrill 290-
536 1983 $75

THURLOW, EDWARD   Ariadne. Wm. Bulmer for Messrs Longman,
1814. First edition, half title. Rebound in maroon moire-patterned
cloth, label. Jarndyce 30-858 1983 £10.50

THURMAN, WALLACE   The Blacker the Berry. N.Y.: Macaulay,
1929. First edition. Lacking the dust wrapper. Argosy 714-745
1983 $125

THURMOND, JOHN   An Exact Description of the Two Fam'd
Entertainments of Harlequin Doctor Faustus. London: printed for T.
Payne, (1724). 8vo, disbound in wrappers, extremely rare. Pickering
& Chatto 19-77 1983 $850

THURSTON, E.   Castes and Tribes of Southern India.
Madras, 1909. Numerous plates. 7 vols. Thick 8vo. Orig. cloth.
Good. Edwards 1044-707 1983 £200

THURSTON, E.   The Madras Presidency with Mysore, Coorg
and the Associated States. Cambridge, 1914. Maps, illus. 8vo. Orig.
cloth. Good. Edwards 1044-708 1983 £18

THURSTON, E. TEMPLE   The Passionate Crime. London: Chapman
& Hall, 1915. First edition. Orig. cloth. Presentation copy to Hugh
Walpole. MacManus 280-5247 1983 $22.50

THURSTON, E. TEMPLE   Poems 1918-1923. London, 1923. First
edition. Lower corners a little bruised. Author's signed autograph
presentation inscription to E. Marsh. Very nice. Rota 230-391 1983
£12

THURSTON, E. TEMPLE   Richard Furong. London: Chapman & Hall,
1913. First edition. Orig. cloth. Dust jacket (spine and covers
faded and worn at the margins). Slight offsetting to the endpapers.
Near-fine. MacManus 280-5248 1983 $25

THURSTON, LORRIN A.   A Hand-Book on the Annexation of
Hawaii. (St. Joseph, Mich., Morse, 1898). Orig. printed wraps.
First edition. Ginsberg 46-308 1983 $100

THURSTONE, WILLIAM   Statistics and Information Relative
to the Trade and Commerce of Buffalo for the Year Ending...1874.
Buffalo, 1875. Orig. printed wraps. First edition. Ginsberg 46-
544 1983 $35

THWAITES, REUBEN GOLD   Wisconsin in Three Centuries, 1634-1905.
N.Y.: Century Hist. Co., (1906). Illus. & maps, 4 vols., g.t., ex-
lib. Argosy 710-619 1983 $75

TIBULLUS   Tibulli et Propertii Opera. Glasguae,
Excudebant Robertus & Andreas Foulis, 1753. 8vo, cont. calf very
worn, covers nearly detached, some age-browning and foxing throughout.
Ravenstree 95-132 1983 $45

TICE, HENRY A.   Early Railroad Days in New Mexico, 1880.
Santa Fe: Stagecoach Press, 1965. Illus. Limited to 700 copies.
Jenkins 153-394 1983 $25

TICEHURST, C. B.   A History of the Birds of Suffolk.
1932. Map and 18 plates, 8vo, cloth, covers slightly affected by
damp. Wheldon 160-901 1983 £38

TICKNOR, GEORGE   Life, Letters, and Journals of George
Ticknor. Sampson Low, Marston, Searle & Rivington, 1876. Bickersteth
75-185 1983 £14

TICKNOR, GEORGE   Life of William Hickling Prescott.
Routledge, 1864. Front. port. Half title. Maroon calf, gilt
borders, spine faded. First English edition. Jarndyce 30-1107
1983 £16

TIEDEMANN, FRIEDRICH   Dissertatio inauguralis medica de cordis
polypis. Marburg: Krieger, 1804. 8vo. Wrappers. Kraus 164-228
1983 $120

TIESCHOWITZ, BERNARD VON   Das Chorgestuhl des Kilner Domes. Berlin, 1930. Large 4to, 96 plates. Cloth. Ars Libri SB 26-232 1983
$65

TIETJENS, EUNICE   Leaves in Windy Weather. New York,
(1929). 8vo. Cloth. Review copy with slip laid in. From library
of Alexander Laing, signed by same on front flyleaf. Cloth is
faded, else vg-fine. In Our Time 156-796 1983 $20

TIETZE, HANS   Albrecht Altdorfer. Leipzig: Insel,
1923. 127 illus. 4to. Boards, 1/4 cloth. From the library of
Jakob Rosenberg. Ars Libri 32-5 1983 $50

TIETZE, HANS   Kritisches Verzeichnis der Werke
Albrecht Durers. Augsburg/Basel/Leipzig: Benno Filser/Holbein
Verlag, 1928-1938. 2 vols. in 3. Prof. illus. throughout. Large
4to. Cloth. From the library of Jakob Rosenberg. Rare. Ars
Libri 32-189 1983 $875

TIETZE-CONRAT, E.   Osterreichische Barockplasti. Wien,
1920. 144pp. 97 plates. 4to. Boards (head of spine taped).
From the library of Jakob Rosenberg. Ars Libri SB 26-233 1983
$40

TILDEN, J.   Minnesota Algae, Vol. 1, The Myxophyceae
of North America and Adjacent Regions. Minneapolis, 1910. 20 double-
page plates, 8vo, cloth. Covers spotted, contents good. Wheldon
160-1907 1983 £17

TILGHMAN, ZOE A.   Marshall of the Last Frontier. Glendale,
1949. First edition. Illus. Red cloth. Spine trifle faded, else
very good. Houle 21-1166 1983 $75

TILGHMAN, ZOE A.   Marshall of the Last Frontier. Glendale,
CA: Arthur H. Clark Co., 1949. 9 leaves of plates plus folding map.
Red cloth. Karmiole 74-96 1983 $50

TILGHMAN, ZOE A.   Outlaw Days. Oklahoma City, 1926.
Wraps., fine. Reese 19-557 1983 $40

TILGHMAN, ZOE A.　　Outlaw Days: A True History of Early
Day Oklahoma Characters. Oklahoma City, 1926. Wrp. Illus. Scarce.
Jenkins 153-637　1983　$25

TILKE, MAX　　Le Costume en Orient. Berlin:
Ernst Wasmuth, (1922). Folio. 128 color plates, printed on leaf
rectos only. Yellow silk, gilt-stamped. Karmiole 72-37　1983　$185

TILLER, TERENCE　　Poems. London, 1941. First edition.
Dust wrapper. Fine. Rota 231-604　1983　£12

TILLOTSON, JOHN　　A Discourse Against Transubstantiation.
Printed for Brabazon Aylmer...and William Rogers, 1684. 4to, wrapper,
a very good copy. Fenning 61-451　1983　£18.50

TILLOTSON, JOHN　　A Sermon Preached at the First General
Meeting of the Gentlemen...who were Born within the County of York.
Printed for Brabazon Aylmer...and William Rogers, 1679. 4to.
Fenning 62-365　1983　£24.50

TILLOTSON, JOHN　　A Sermon Preached before the Queen, at
White-Hall, February the 27th, 1690. Printed for Brabazon Aylmer...
and William Rogers, 1691. 4to. Fenning 62-366　1983　£24.50

TILLOTSON, JOHN　　Stories of the Wars, 1574-1658...
Beeton, 1867. 1st edn. Frontis. & 7 col. plates & numerous wood
engrs. in text. Blue sand grain decor. cloth, a.e.g. (top rear cvr.
sl. marked, label fr. ep.), v.g. copy. Hodgkins 27-398　1983　£17.50

TILNEY, FREDERICK　　The Brain from Ape to Man. N.Y., 1928.
First edition. 557 illus., many in color. 2 vols. Thick 4to, cloth.
D.w. Argosy 713-540　1983　$250

TILNEY, FREDERICK　　Form and Functions of the Central System.
N.Y., 1923. Illus., 56 colored. 4to, buckram. Argosy 713-541　1983
$85

TILTON, CLINT CLAY　　The Centennial Book...Vermilion.
(Danville, 1926). Illus. Pictorial wrappers. Bradley 63-65　1983
$20

TILTON, ELEANOR　　Amiable Autocrat: A Biography of
Dr. Oliver Wendell Holmes. New York, 1947. First edition. 8vo.
Orig. binding. Dust wrapper. Fye H-3-789　1983　$20

TIMBERLAKE, HENRY　　The Memoirs of Lieut. Henry Timberlake.
London: Printed for the author, 1765. Folding map and plate. Orig.
(or contemporary) quarter calf and marbled boards, gilt, morocco
label. A fine, untrimmed and unpressed copy. Reese 18-82　1983
$4,000

TIMBREL, WILLIAM HALL　　Practical Observations on the Management
of Ruptures... Boston, 1809. 1st American ed. 2 engraved plates.
12mo., contemporary calf, leather label. Rubbed; hinges partly
cracked. Morrill 289-232　1983　$50

TIMELY advice, from the major part of the old souldiers in the army...
(London): printed in the year of our Lord 1659. First edition.
Small 4to. Disbound. Very scarce. Ximenes 63-107　1983　$107

TIMLIM, WILLIAM　　The Ship that Sailed to Mars. G.G. Harrap, n.d. 4to. Mounted decorated title with inscription. 48 mounted
colour plates & 47 mounted pp of text, little loose. Quarter white
vellum decorated gilt, grey boards. Good. Greer 40-223　1983　£325

TINDALL, WILLIAM YORK　　D.H. Lawrence and Susan His Cow. N.Y.,
Columbia, 1939. First edition. Dust jacket. Very good-fine. Houle
21-551　1983　$45

TINELLI, LOUIS　　An Address...Before an Assembly of
Silk Culturists. New York, 1840. Printed wraps. Inscribed by the
author. Felcone 22-224　1983　$30

TINGSEN, HERBERT　　Political Behaviour. Studies in Election
Statistics. London, P. S. King, 1937. 1st ed. in English, 8vo,
original gilt stamped black cloth, slightly rubbed. Pickering &
Chatto 21-125　1983　$85

TINKER, CHAUNCEY BREWSTER　　Painter and Poet. Cambridge, Mass.:
Harvard University Press, 1938. First edition. Orig. cloth. Dust
jacket (spine faded). Fine. MacManus 280-5250　1983　$35

TINKER, CHAUNCEY BREWSTER　　The Wedgewood Medallion of Samual Johnson. Cambridge, 1926. 4to, cloth-backed blind-stamped boards, gilt.
Illus. One of 385 copies. Perata 28-152　1983　$75

TINKLE, LON　　An American Original: The Life of J.
Frank Dobie. Boston: (1978). First edition. Illus. Dark green
cloth. 1/250 signed copies. Mint in slipcase. Print of a Tom Lea
drawing laid in. Bradley 66-538　1983　$200

TINTI, MARIO　　Ramano Romanelli. Firenze: Alinari,
1924. 35 plates. 4to. Boards, 1/4 cloth. Ars Libri 33-570　1983
$30

TIPHAIGNE DE LA ROCHE, CHARLES-FRANCOIS　　L'Empire des Zaziris sur
les Humains, ou La Zazirocratie. Pekin, 1761. 12mo, boards.
Rostenberg 88-76　1983　$315

TIRLONI, PIETRO　　Andrea Fantoni, scultore. Milano:
Silvana, 1959. 56 plates (partly in color). Small folio. Boards.
Ars Libri 33-134　1983　$85

TISSANDIER, GASTON　　A History and Handbook of Photography.
Sampson Low, etc., London, 1878. Second edition. 8vo, with a
Woodburytype frontis. and 20 plates (15 wood engravings and 5
examples of permanent processes); orig. cloth, rebacked with orig.
spine laid down. Quaritch NS 5-106　1983　$500

TISSOT, SAMUEL AUGUSTE　　An essay on the disorders of people
of fashion and a treatise on the diseases incident to literary and
sedentary persons. Edinburgh: printed by A. Donaldson, and sold
at his shop, 1772. 2 parts in one vol. 12mo. Cont. calf, spine
gilt. First edition of this translation. Bit worn, upper hinge
weak, lacks label. Some pencil markings. Ximenes 63-294　1983　$200

TISSOT, SAMUEL AUGUSTE　　A letter from the celebrated Dr. Tissot,
to Dr. Zimmerman... London: Kearsly, 1776. First edition in English.
8vo. Disbound. Wanting half-title. Ximenes 63-293　1983　$85

TISSOT, SIMON ANDRE　　Advice to the People in General, with
Regard to their Health. Printed for T. Becket and P.A. de Hondt,
1765. 8vo, cont. calf, spine rubbed, chipped at the top, slit
beginning at foot of joint of upper cover. First edition in English.
Bickersteth 75-264　1983　£70

TITCHENER, EDWARD B.　　An Outline of Psychology. NY:
Macmillan, 1916 (1897). Third edition. Gach 94-660　1983　$20

TITCHENER, EDWARD B.　　A Text-Book of Psychology. NY:
Macmillan, 1911 (1909). Spine tips and edges rubbed. Gach 94-659
1983　$25

TO Remember Gregg Anderson. Tributes by Members of The Columbiad
Club, The Rounce and Coffin Club, The Roxburghe & Zamorano Clubs.
N.p.: 1949. Sm 8vo, black cloth, gilt. Illustrated. Containing
a bibliography of Anderson's work. A fine copy. Perata 27-2
1983　$65

TO the Farmers of England. Foreign Corn. Remarks on the Cost Price
of Producing Wheat in Foreign Countries, and Matters therewith
connected. London: William Edward Painter, (1841). 1st ed., 8vo,
disbound. Pickering & Chatto 21-27　1983　$45

TO the People of the United States, by a Member of the Late Board.
Phila., 1807. Folded tables, full leather. First edition. Ginsberg
47-483　1983　$1,000

TO the People of Virginia! Richmond, 1859. Sewn as issued. On back
wrapper, "Printed by order of the State Central Committee." Jenkins
153-662　1983　$35

TOBIE, EDWARD P.　　Service of·the Cavalry in the Army
of the Potomac. Providence, 1882. Orig. printed wraps. First
edition. Ginsberg 46-743　1983　$30

TOD, JAMES   Annals and Antiquities of Rajas'than,
or the Central and Western States of India. London: Smith, Elder,
1829-32. 1st ed., large 4to, 2 vols., cont. half calf gilt, boards.
Presentation copy from the author to a close friend. Bookplates.
49 engraved plates, two folding tables, one engraved plan. Lacking
the folding map. Binding somewhat scuffed, but a very clean and
internally fine copy. Trebizond 18-147 1983 $300

TOD, JAMES   Annals and Antiquities of Rajast'han.
Madras, 1873. Second edition. Folding coloured map, repaired, 4 folding tables, 1 folding plate. 2 vols. Half morocco, marbled boards.
8vo. Good. Edwards 1044-713 1983 £75

TODD, HERBERT GEORGE   Armory and Lineages of Canada.
Yonkers, N.Y.: The Author, 1913. 24 1/2cm. Green cloth. Fine.
Scarce. McGahern 53-189 1983 $75

TODD, JAMES H.   St. Patrick, Apostle of Ireland.
Dublin: Hodges, Smith, 1864. First edition. Fenning 62-367 1983
£18.50

TODD, ROBERT BENTLEY   Clinical Lectures on Paralysis. Phila.,
1855. Orig. cloth. Argosy 713-542 1983 $85

TODD, ROBERT BENTLEY   Clinical Lectures on Paralysis,
Disease of the Brain, and Other Affections of the Nervous System.
Philadelphia, 1855. 1st American ed. 8vo. Binding partly faded.
Morrill 289-233 1983 $20

TODHUNTER, ISAAC   William Whewell, D.D. London: Mac-
millan, 1876. First edition. 2 vols. 8vo. Orig. brown cloth.
A bit rubbed and soiled, traces of library numbers on spines.
Ximenes 63-540 1983 $85

TOESCA, PIETRO   Masolino a Castiglione Olona.
Milano: Amilcare Pizzi, 1946. 32 color plates. Large 4to.
Flexible boards, 1/4 cloth. Light wear. Ars Libri 33-230 1983
$ 30

THE TOILET of Flora. London: J. Murray and W. Nicoll. 1779.
12mo, engraved frontis. A few preliminary leaves bound in
incorrect order; nevertheless complete. Later calf; extremities a
bit rubbed. Karmiole 71-92 1983 $175

THE TOKEN and Atlantic Souvenir. Boston: David Williams, 1842.
Plates. 1st ed. Orig. fullgreen embossed morocco, gilt, a.e.g.
First appearances by Longfellow, Lowell, et al. The binding is
signed in the embossing plate by Bradley (binder) and Morin
(Philadelphia designer). Very light rubbing, else a fine copy.
Jenkins 155-855 1983 $50

TOLBECQUE, J. B.   Quadrille de Contredanses. Paris,
Janet & Cotelle, n.d. (19th century). Oblong folio, engraved music.
Salloch 387-242 1983 $45

TOLBECQUE, J. B.   Quadrille de Contredanses sur les plus
Jolis Motifs de "Marie". Paris, n.d. Oblong folio, engraved music.
Orig. imprint of Meissonier whose rubberstamp is on the title, has
been pasted over by that of Hanry, Editeur de Musique, Rue Neuve des
Petits Champs. Salloch 387-243 1983 $45

TOLKIEN, JOHN RONALD REUEL   The Devil's Coach-Horses. London: Sidgwick & Lackson, Ltd., (1925). First separate edition. Orig. brown
wrappers, stitched. Fine. Bradley 66-340 1983 $185

TOLKIEN, JOHN RONALD REUEL   Farmer Giles of Ham. B, 1950. Illus.
by P. D. Baynes. Spine edges very slightly rubbed, else fine in
very good, bright dustwrapper with minor wear. Quill & Brush 54-1369
1983 $100

TOLKIEN, JOHN RONALD REUEL   The Hobbit. London, 1937. First
edition. Slightly bumped at head and foot of spine. The dustwrapper
has small pieces missing from two corners, some rubbing on the front
panel and spine, and two small pieces missing from the head and foot of
spine. First issue. Gekoski 2-195 1983 £850

TOLKIEN, JOHN RONALD REUEL   The Hobbit. London, 1972. 8vo.
Cloth, reprint. 7th impression. Signed by Tolkien on title page.
Small inscription on half-title page. Else fine copy in dj. In
Our Time 156-799 1983 $200

TOLKIEN, JOHN RONALD REUEL   Tree and Leaf. London, 1964. Advance
Proof, with publisher's stamp. Slightly fading green covers, laid
into a torn and soiled dustwrapper of the first edition. Fine.
Gekoski 2-196 1983 £100

TOLLEMACHE, MRS. W. A.   Spanish towns and Spanish pictures.
London: Hayes, 1870. First edition. 8vo. Orig. brown cloth.
Illus. with three mounted photographs of paintins. Map. Ximenes
63-639 1983 $85

TOLLER, ERNEST   Der Deutsche Hindemann. Potsdam, 1923.
8vo. Boards. Tipped in is the orig. program for the performance
as well as a newspaper account of the opening. This copy also
contains a holograph letter, written on postcard, by Toller to
Untermeyer. Note is dated Dec. 7th, 1922. Some light wear to
spine, else fine. In Our Time 156-801 1983 $400

TOLLER, ERNEST   Masse Mensch. Verlag/Potsdam, 1922.
8vo. Boards. Probably the 2nd ed., but with a new preface by
Toller. From library of Louis Untermyer. Laid into the vol. are
two postcards from Toller to Untermeyer. One card is dated Nov.
1922. The letter bears the prison control stamp. The other card
is from Jerusalem. In Our Time 156-800 1983 $450

TOLLER, ERNEST   Das Schwalbenbuch. Potsdam, (1924).
8vo. Boards. With errata slip laid in. Inscribed by Toller to
Jean and Louis Untermeyer and signed "gratitude Ernest Toller, 29th
of August, 1924". Some light tanning to spine, else fine. In Our
Time 156-802 1983 $300

TOLLER, ERNEST   Vormorgen. Potsdam, (1924). 8vo.
Boards. Inscribed by Toller to Louis Untermeyer and bears his
initials dated 1924. Some light spotting to boards, mainly a fine
copy. In Our Time 156-803 1983 $300

TOLLINGTON, R. R.   Alexandrine Teaching on the Universe.
London, 1932. 8vo, cloth. Salloch 385-194 1983 $20

TOLMAN, EDWARD CHACE   Drives Toward War. NY: D. Appleton-
Century, (1942). First edition. Publisher's blue cloth. Gach
94-661 1983 $25

TOLNAY, CHARLES DE   Hieronymus Bosch. Bale: Editions
Holbein, 1937. 128 plates. 4to. Cloth. From the library of
Jakob Rosenberg. Ars Libri 32-54 1983 $60

TOLNAY, CHARLES DE   Pierre Bruegel L'Ancien. Bruxelles:
Nouvelle Societe d'Editions, 1935. 2 vols. 117 plates. 4to.
Wrappers. Ars Libri 32-71 1983 $150

TOLSTOI, LEV NIKOLAEVICH (1828-1910)   Katia. New York, Gottsberger,
1887. First ed. in English, 12mo. Orig. cloth (defective). Fine.
MacManus 280-5252 1983 $200

TOLSTOI, LEV NIKOLAEVICH (1828-1910)   The Parables of a Prophet.
Review of Reviews Annual (W.T. Stead's Annual), 1906. First edition,
illus., folio, wrappers, lacking six loose plates, very nice. Rota
230-601 1983 £12

TOLSTOY, LEV NIKOLAEVICH (1828-1910)   Childhood, Boyhood, Youth.
New York: Thomas Crowell, (1886). Frontis. First edition in English.
Orig. mauve cloth, gilt. Very fine copy and scarce. Jenkins 155-1219
1983 $165

TOLSTOY, LEV NIKOLAEVICH (1828-1910)   Childhood. Boyhood, Youth.
New York, (1886). First english edition. Orig. tan cloth, gilt. Some
light smudging on spine, but very nice copy. Jenkins 155-1428 1983
$150

TOLSTOY, LEV NIKOLAEVICH (1828-1910)   The Novels and Other Works.
New York, 1913-17. 24 vols. 8vo. Blue cloth, gilt, t.e.g., others
uncut. Frontis. to each volume. Traylen 94-830 1983 £220

TOLSTOY, LEV NIKOLAEVICH (1828-1910)   The Complete Works. London,
1904-05. 24 vols. 8vo. Orig. maroon cloth, gilt, t.e.g., others
uncut. 72 plates. Traylen 94-829 1983 £240

TOMBLESON, WILLIAM   Eighty Picturesque Views of the Thames
and Medway Engraved on Steel by the First Artists. Ca. 1840. 80
plates only and two plates slightly frayed, spine relaid. 4to.
K Books 307-188 1983 £200

TOMES, JOHN   System of Dental Surgery. Phila., 1859. 272 illus. Thick 8vo, disbound, ex-lib. First American edition. Argosy 713-543 1983 $60

TOMKINS, THOMAS   Keyboard Music. London, Musica Britannica, 1955. 2 plates, music in modern notation. Folio, orig. flexible bds., (repaired). Salloch 387-244 1983 $75

TOMLINS, FREDERICK GUEST   The nature and state of the English drama. London: C. Mitchell, 1841. 16mo, later wrappers. First edition. Very good copy of a scarce little pamphlet. Ximenes 64-543 1983 $40

TOMLINS, FREDERICK GUEST   Remarks on the present state of the English drama. London: Hailes Lacy, 1851. 16mo, later wrappers. First edition. Very good copy. Ximenes 64-544 1983 $45

TOMLINSON, HENRY MAJOR   All Our Yesterdays. NY, 1930. Limited to 350 numbered and signed copies, many pages uncut, front hinge starting, spine label slightly darkened and chipped, else near fine in remnants of slipcase. Quill & Brush 54-1370 1983 $50

TOMLINSON, HENRY MAJOR   All Our Yesterdays. Lon., 1930. Limited to 1025 numbered and signed copies, t.e.g., page edges slightly foxed, spine soiled, else very good in soiled, very good slipcase. Quill & Brush 54-1371 1983 $50

TOMLINSON, HENRY MAJOR   All Our Yesterdays. London: William Heinemann Ltd., 1930. First edition. Frontis. port. Orig. cloth. One of 1025 copies signed by author. Inner hinge strained. Very good. MacManus 280-5254 1983 $40

TOMLINSON, HENRY MAJOR   All Our Yesterdays. London, 1930. Roy. 8vo. Buckram, gilt, t.e.g., others uncut, in a slip-case. Limited edition of 1,025 copies, numbered and signed by the author, with a drawing by Percy Smith. Traylen 94-831 1983 £20

TOMLINSON, HENRY MAJOR   Brown Owl. Garden City: Henry & Longwell, Publishers in Petto, 1928. First edition. Small 8vo. Orig. decorated boards with paper label, tissue jacket. Limited to 107 copies signed by author, the publishers and Christopher Morley. Fine. MacManus 280-5255 1983 $150

TOMLINSON, HENRY MAJOR   Gallions Reach. N.Y.: Harper & Brothers, 1927. First edition. Orig. cloth-backed boards. One of 350 copies signed by author. In a worn publisher's slipcase. MacManus 280-5257 1983 $40

TOMLINSON, HENRY MAJOR   Gallions Reach. London: William Heinemann Ltd., (1927). First edition. Orig. cloth. Dust jacket (a little foxed). Very good. MacManus 280-5258 1983 $20

TOMLINSON, HENRY MAJOR   Gifts of Fortune. London: William Heinemann Ltd., 1926. First edition. Orig. cloth. Dust jacket (soiled). Very good. MacManus 280-5259 1983 $20

TOMLINSON, HENRY MAJOR   Illusion: 1915. L, 1929. No. 172 of 520 signed and limited copies, edges bumped, otherwise very good. Quill & Brush 54-1372 1983 $35

TOMLINSON, HENRY MAJOR   Illusion: 1915. First edition. Orig. cloth-backed boards. Dust jacket (worn). One of 525 copies signed by author. Very good. MacManus 280-5261 1983 $25

TOMLINSON, HENRY MAJOR   London River. L, 1921. Flys offset else very good in chipped and aging dustwrapper. Quill & Brush 54-1373 1983 $35

TOMLINSON, HENRY MAJOR   Mars His Idiot. N.Y.: Harper & Brothers, 1935. First American edition. Orig. cloth. Dust jacket. Signed by author. Fine. MacManus 280-5263 1983 $20

TOMLINSON, HENRY MAJOR   Morning Light. London: Hodder & Stoughton, (1946). Advance Reading Copy of the first edition. Orig. printed wrappers. Top of spine a little chipped. A bit soiled. Very good. MacManus 280-5264 1983 $45

TOMLINSON, HENRY MAJOR   Old Junk. London: Andrew Melrose Ltd., 1918. First edition. Orig. cloth. Dust jacket (a trifle worn). Signed by Tomlinson on the half-title. Preserved in a blue half-morocco slipcase. Fine. MacManus 280-5265 1983 $175

TOMLINSON, HENRY MAJOR   Old Junk. London: Andrew Melrose Ltd., 1918. First edition. Orig. cloth. Dust jacket (chipped). In a half-morocco slipcase. Very good. MacManus 280-5266 1983 $100

TOMLINSON, HENRY MAJOR   The Sea and the Jungle. London: Duckworth & Co., (1912). First edition. Frontis. Orig. decorated cloth. Contents a trifle shaken. In a half-morocco slipcase. Bookplates of John C. Eckel and Katherine de Berkeley Parsons. Near-fine. MacManus 280-5269 1983 $350

TOMLINSON, HENRY MAJOR   The Sea and the Jungle. London: Duckworth & Co., (1912). First edition. Frontis. Orig. decorated cloth. Signed by author. In a green half-morocco slipcase. Very fine. MacManus 280-5268 1983 $275

TOMLINSON, HENRY MAJOR   The Sea and the Jungle. London, 1912. 8vo. Cloth. Bookplate on inside endboard, else vg-fine copy. In protective contemporary glassine wrapper which has some light wear. In Our Time 156-805 1983 $175

TOMLINSON, HENRY MAJOR   The Sea and The Jungle. L, (1912). Edges rubbed and slightly worn, else very good. Quill & Brush 54-1375 1983 $125

TOMLINSON, HENRY MAJOR   The Sea and The Jungle. L, (1912). Second issue with a 20 page catalog at rear, cover shows some wear and bumping but still good tight copy. Quill & Brush 54-1374 1983 $60

TOMLINSON, HENRY MAJOR   The Sea and the Jungle. London, 1930. First edition thus. Woodcuts by C. Leighton. One of 515 numbered copies, signed by author. Spine faded. Very nice. Rota 230-602 1983 £20

TOMLINSON, HENRY MAJOR   The Sea & The Jungle. London: Duckworth, 1930. First illus. trade edition. Woodcuts by C. Leighton. Orig. cloth-backed batik boards. Dust jacket (one short tear, partially faded). Fine. MacManus 280-5270 1983 $35

TOMLINSON, HENRY MAJOR   The Snows of Helicon. London: William Heinemann Ltd., (1933). First edition. Orig. brown buckram. Cellophane dust jacket (torn). Limited to 175 copies signed by author. Endpapers lightly foxed. Bottom of spine a trifle worn. Fine. MacManus 280-5272 1983 $65

TOMLINSON, HENRY MAJOR   South to Cadiz. N.Y.: Harper & Brothers Publishers, 1934. First American edition. Orig. cloth. Dust jacket. Fine. MacManus 280-5273 1983 $20

TOMLINSON, HENRY MAJOR   Thomas Hardy. NY, 1929. One of 761 numbered and signed copies. Litho. on stone of Hardy signed by Z. Gay. Top of spine slightly worn, else near fine. Quill & Brush 54-608 1983 $30

TOMLINSON, HENRY MAJOR   Under the Red Ensign. London: Williams & Norgate, Ltd., 1926. First edition. Orig. cloth. Presentation copy to author's brother, inscribed on the half-title: "This dip of the ensign from Hal to Phil, Christmas 1926." Endpapers browned. In a cloth slipcase. Fine. MacManus 280-5274 1983 $175

TOMLINSON, HENRY MAJOR   Under the Red Ensign. London: Williams & Norgate, Ltd., 1926. First edition. Orig. cloth. Dust jacket. Fine. MacManus 280-5275 1983 $35

TOMLINSON, HENRY MAJOR   Waiting for Daylight. London: Cassell, 1922. First edition. Orig. cloth. dust jacket. Fine. MacManus 280-5276 1983 $45

TOMLINSON, HENRY MAJOR   War Books. Cleveland, Ohio: The Rowfant Club, 1930. First edition. Orig. cloth-backed boards with paper label on spine. In publisher's slipcase. Limited to 215 copies printed by D.B. Updike at the Merrymount Press. Very fine. MacManus 280-5277 1983 $85

TOMLINSON, LAURENCE E.   Gutenberg and the Invention of Printing. (Washington, Judd & Detweiler, 1938). Illustrations and facsimiles. Tall 8vo, original buckram. Bookplate and former owner's inscrip.; very nice. Morrill 290-540 1983 $35

TOMLINSON, P. B.   Anatomy of the Monocotyledons, Vol. 7. 1981. 16 plates and 98 text-figures, 8vo, cloth. Wheldon 160-1576 1983 £51.50

TONE, WILLIAM T. W.   The Autobiography of Theobald Wolfe Tone, 1763-1798. T. Fisher Unwin, 1893. First edition thus, with 6 portraits and a folding plate of facs. 2 vols., roy. 8vo, orig. cloth, t.e.g., little foxing of flyleaves, but a very good copy. Fenning 61-453 1983 £85

TONNA, CHARLOTTE E.   Letters from Ireland, 1837. R.B. Seeley and W. Burnside, 1838. First edition, 8vo, orig. cloth, the spine neatly repaired, a very good copy. Fenning 60-411 1983 £48.50

TOOKE, WILLIAM   The Life of Catherine II Empress of Russia. Printed for T.N. Longman and O. Reese; and J. Debrett, 1799. 3 vols., 8vo, folding map and 2 engraved plates incorporating seven portraits, cont. calf. Bickersteth 77-82 1983 £46

TOOLE, JOHN KENNEDY   A Confederacy of Dunces. L.S.U. Press, 1980. 8vo. Cloth. Signed by Walker Percy on title page. Fine copy in dj. In Our Time 156-804 1983 $175

TOOR, FRANCES   Mexican Popular Arts. Mexico: Frances Toor Studios, 1939. Illus. by L. Alice Wilson. Prof. illus. Large 8vo. Cloth. Presentation copy, inscribed by the author. Ars Libri 34-500 1983 $37.50

TOOR, FRANCES   Las obras de Jose Guadalupe Posada, grabador mexicano. Mexico: Mexican Folkways, 1930. 208 plates with 406 illus. Folio. Cloth. Ars Libri 32-531 1983 $225

TOOR, FRANCES   Orozco's Frescoes in Guadalajara. Mexico: Frances Toor Studios, 1940. 44 plates, 1 map. Small 4to. Orig. wrappers. Ars Libri 32-499 1983 $50

TOOR, FRANCES   Three Worlds of Peru. New York: Crown, 1949. 73 plates. Large 8vo. Cloth. Dust jacket. Ars Libri 34-501 1983 $30

TOPFFER, R.   Les Amours de Mr. Vieux Bois. Paris, 1860. "Premiere edition." 92 plates. Oblong 4to. Faded red cloth pictorial. Greer 40-229 1983 £35

TOPFFER, R.   Le Docteur Festus. Paris: Garnier Freres, n.d. (ca.1860). Oblong 4to. Half-title, pictorial title & 87 plates. Faded red cloth pictorial, gilt. Greer 40-224 1983 £35

TOPFFER, R.   Histoire de M. Cryptograme. Paris, n.d. (ca.1860). Oblong 4to. Seventh edition. 64 plates. Faded red cloth pictorial, gilt. Greer 40-230 1983 £35

TOPFFER, R.   Histoire de Mr. Crepin. Paris, n.d. (ca.1860). Oblong 4to. 86 plates. Faded red cloth pictorial, gilt. Greer 40-227 1983 £35

TOPFFER, R.   Histoire de Mr. Jabot. Paris, n.d. (ca.1860). Oblong 4to. 52 plates. Faded red cloth, gilt. Greer 40-226 1983 £35

TOPFFER, R.   Histoire de Mr. Pensil. Paris: Garnier Freres, n.d. (ca.1860). Oblong 4to. 70 plates. Faded red cloth pictorial, gilt. Greer 40-228 1983 £35

TOPINARD, PAUL   De l'Ataxie Locomotrice... Paris, 1864. First edition. 8vo. Quarter-morocco. Signed presentation copy to Dr. Barthez. Binding rubbed. Gurney JJ-404 1983 £25

TOPONCE, ALEXANDER   Reminiscences of...Pioneer. (Ogden, Utah, 1923). Portraits and plates. Jenkins 153-639 1983 $150

TOPOR, TOM   Bloodstar. New York: Norton, (n.d.). Printed wraps. Uncorrected proofs of the first edition. Light offset from label, else very fine, with proof dust jacket inserted. Reese 20-1065 1983 $20

TOPSELL, E.   The History of Four-footed Beasts and Serpents. (1658). Facsimile reprint, New York, 1967. Numerous illus., 3 vols., folio, decorated boards. Wheldon 160-528 1983 £130

TORMO Y MONZO, ELIAS   Rodrigo de Osona, padre e hijo, y su escuela. Madrid, 1933. 90 plates. 4to. Cloth, 1/4 leather. Orig. wrappers bound in. Ars Libri 32-500 1983 $75

TORQUEMADA, JUAN DE   Primera (Segunda, Tercera) Parte De Los Veinte I Vn Libros Rituales I Monarchia Indiana. Madrid, 1723. Second edition, revised, corrected, and augmented by Gonzalez Barcia. 3 vols. Complete, 3 finely engraved allegorical frontis., folding engraved map of America. Woodcut initials and other ornamentation. Folio. Fully cont. limp vellum. Unusually fine. Jenkins 152-426 1983 $3,500

TORRENCE, RIDGELY   Poems. New York, 1941. 8vo. Cloth. Review copy with slip laid in as well as name of reviewer on fly. A vg-fine copy in dj. In Our Time 156-806 1983 $25

TORRENS, HENRY   Madame de Malguet. Longman, etc., 1848. First edition, 3 vols. Half titles, half green calf, marbled boards, spines gilt, maroon labels, v.g. Jarndyce 30-572 1983 £58

TORRES MARTIN, RAMON   Blas de Ledesma y el bodegon espagnol. Madrid: Privately Printed, 1974. 160 illus. (25 color plates). Small folio. Boards. Dust jacket. Edition limited to 2500 copies. Ars Libri 32-43 1983 $175

TORRIANO, PIERO   Carlo Carra. Milano: Garzanti, 1942. 51 plates (many in color). Folio. Cloth. Ars Libri 33-433 1983 $50

TORRICELLI, EVANGELISTA   Lezioni Accademiche. Florence: Jacopo Guiducci e Santi Franchi, 1715. Engraved portrait. First edition. 3 text woodcuts. Title vignette. Woodcut head- and tail-pieces, woodcut initials. Small folio. Orig. vellum. Backstrip torn. Kraus 164-96 1983 $1,500

TORRITI, PIERO   Pietro Tacca da Carrara. Genova: Sagep, 1975. 75 illus. (numerous color). Small folio. Cloth. Dust jacket. Ars Libri 33-351 1983 $75

TOSCANO, SALVADOR   Arte precolombino de Mexico y de la America Central. Mexico: Universidad Nacional Autonoma, 1944. Prof. illus. Folio. Cloth. Head of spine torn. Ars Libri 34-502 1983 $100

TOSQUINET, J.   Ichneumonides d'Afrique. Brussels, Mem. Soc. Ent. Belg., 1896. 8vo, wrappers (used). Wheldon 160-1177 1983 £18

THE TOTAL eclipse: a grand politico-astronomical phenomena... London: Dolby, n.d. (1820). First edition. 8vo. Disbound. 9 wood-engravings by Robert Cruikshank. Ximenes 63-518 1983 $50

TOULMIN, CAMILLA   Lays and Legends. Jeremiah How, 1845. 83 illus. Dark green morocco, gilt. First edition. Sl. rubbed, a.e.g. Jarndyce 30-859 1983 £12.50

TOULMIN, JOSHUA   Addressed to Young Men. Printed by C. Stower...for J. Johnson, 1803. First edition, including errata leaf, possibly wanting a half-title, large 12mo, slightly later half calf. Fenning 62-368 1983 £28.50

TOULOUSE-LAUTREC, HENRI DE   Catalogue of a Collection of Fine Lithographs and Drawings by...London, Oct. 6, 1966. Numerous illus., some in color. Tall 8vo, original boards, dust wrapper. Morrill 290-542 1983 $100

TOULOUSE-LAUTREC, HENRI DE   H. de Toulouse-Lautrec: One Hundred Ten Unpublished Drawings. Boston: Boston Book and Art, 1955. 110 plates. Large oblong 4to. Cloth. Boxed. Edition limited to 1500 copies, printed by Jacomet. Ars Libri 32-668 1983 $85

A TOUR to the Isle of Love. London: for Theophilus Thornton, 1788. First edition. 12mo. 19th-century half calf. Complete with half-title. Calf rubbed, text somewhat soiled in places. Ximenes 63-648 1983 $450

TOURETTE, GILLES DE LA   Leonard de Vinci. Paris: Albin Michel, 1932. 96 collotype plates. Square 4to. Cloth, 3/4 leather. Orig. wrappers bound in. Edition limited to 2000 numbered copies. Ars Libri 33-193 1983 $100

THE TOURIST in Wales. Ca. 1840. Engr. and printed titles, frontis. and 48 steel-engr. plates of views after Castineua, Partlett, etc. Roy. 8vo, minor foxing but a bright copy in the orig. gilt cloth. K Books 307-178 1983 £40

TOURNEUR, CYRIL   The Works. London: the Fanfrolico Press, (1929). 4to. Orig. green buckram, decorated gilt, t.e.g., others uncut, in a slipcase. Drawing by Percy Smith. Limited edition of 1,025 copies, numbered and signed by the author. Traylen 94-831 1983 £20

TOUSSAINT-SAMSON, MME. AD.   A Parisian in Brazil. Boston, 1891. 1st ed. in English. Illus. 12mo. Some light cover stains. Morrill 287-464 1983 $35

TOUT, OTIS B.   The First Thirty Years, 1901-1931. San Diego: Otis B. Tout, (1931). Fabricoid. Dawson 471-284 1983 $100

TOVEY, CHARLES   A Free Library for Bristol. London/ Bristol, 1855. 8vo. Orig. cloth. Heath 48-437 1983 £45

TOWER, CHARLEMAGNE   The Charlemagne Tower Collection of American Colonial Laws. (Phila.): Historical Soc. of Pennsylvania, 1890. Privately printed. 4to. Argoys 710-108 1983 $45

TOWER, W. L.   An Investigation of Evolution. Washington, 1906 30 plates (some coloured), royal 8vo, half leather, good ex-library copy. Wheldon 160-1178 1983 £15

TOWGOOD, MICHAIAH   The Dissenting Gentleman's Answer to the Reverend Mr. White's Three Letters. New York: James Parker, 1748. Disbound. Signature "Nath. Huntting June 23 1748." Felcone 22-241 1983 $35

TOWN Talk; or, Living Manners. London: For J. Johnson, 1811-1814. First ed., 5 vols., illus. with numerous folding colored plates by G. Cruikshank. Full red crushed mor., gilt by Riviere. Plates silked. Fine. MacManus 277-1231 1983 $1250

TOWNE, CHARLES HANSON   The Shop of Dreams. New York: D. Appleton-Century Co., 1939. First edition. 8vo. Cloth, dust jacket. Oak Knoll 48-66 1983 $30

TOWNE, R. M.   Plant lore of Shakespeare. Louisville, KY, 1975. Folio, three-quarter brown leather, gilt, g.e., in a slip case. Edition limited to 2,500 copies. A nice copy. Wheldon 160-107 1983 £120

TOWNLEY, EDWARD   A Practical Treatise on Humanity to Honey Bees. New York, 1843. First edition. Cloth. Foxed. Very good. Felcone 20-11 1983 $40

TOWNLEY, JAMES   High Life Below Stairs. Newbery and Carnon, 1768. Modern blue boards, v.g. Eighth edition. Jarndyce 31-64 1983 £16.50

TOWNS of New England and Old England, Ireland and Scotland. Boston: State Street Trust Co., 1920. Photographic illus., square 8vo, mod. buckram, ex library. Parts 1 & 2 bound together. Argosy 710-329 1983 $30

TOWNSEND, CHAUNCY HARE   Poems. Thomas Boys, 1821. First edition, green calf, blocked in blind and gilt, spine label, sl. chipped. Very good. Inscribed presentation copy from the author: 'Mrs. Taunton from her affectionate cousin. The Author, April 1821'. Also signed by Octavia Townsend 1898. Jarndyce 30-860 1983 £25

TOWNSEND, JOHN KIRK   Sport Excursions in the Rocky Mountains, including a Journey to the Columbia River, and a Visit to the Sand-wich Islands. London: Henry Colburn, 1840. 2 vols., cont. half calf with marbled boards. Frontis. Nice set. First English edition. Jenkins 151-337 1983 $300

TOWNSEND, JOHN KIRK   Sporting Excursions in the Rocky Mountains... London, 1840. Two vols. Orig. cloth, stamped in blind. Frontis. plates. Spines sunned, otherwise a fine, partially unopened set. Reese 19-558 1983 $450

TOWNSHEND, C. V. F.   My Campaign in Mesopotamia. London, (1920). Maps, plans, portrait. 8vo. Orig. cloth. Good. Edwards 1044-714 1983 £16

TOWNSHEND, CHARLES HERVEY   The Quinnipiack Indians and their Reservation. New Haven, (1900). Numerous plates and facs. Cloth. Felcone 22-242 1983 $25

TOWNSHEND, CHAUNCY HARE   Facts in Mesmerism, with Reasons for a Dispassionate Inquiry into It. 1844. Second edition. Half title, 2 pp. ads., orig. blue-green cloth. Fine. Jarndyce 31-388 1983 £60

TOWNSHEND, DOROTHEA   Life and Letters of Mr. Wndymion Porter. T. Fisher Unwin, 1897. First edition, with 5 plates, 8vo, orig. cloth, gilt, t.e.g., a very good copy. Fenning 60-412 1983 £10.50

TOWNSHEND, FREDERICK T.   Ten Thousand Miles of Travel, Sport, and Adventure... London, 1869. Illus. Orig. cloth. First edition. Ginsberg 47-887 1983 $175

TOWNSHEND, RICHARD B.   Last Memories of a Tenderfoot. London: (1926). First edition. Illus. Green cloth. Spine sun faded. Book-plate. Bradley 66-617 1983 $50

TOWNSHEND, RICHARD B.   Last Memories of a Tenderfoot. London: John Lane the Bodley Head Limited, 1926. Frontis. and plates. Fine. Jenkins 153-137 1983 $45

TOYNBEE, ARNOLD J.   Armenian Atrocities. The Murder of a Nation. Hodder & Stoughton, 1915. 1st ed., small 8vo, original printed wrappers, slightly dust-soiled. Pickering & Chatto 21-126 1983 $25

TOYNBEE, ARNOLD J.   The Belgian Deportations. London: T. Fisher Unwin, Ltd., (1916). First edition. Orig. wrappers. Dust-soiled. Very good. MacManus 280-5279 1983 $50

TOYNBEE, ARNOLD J.   The Destruction of Poland. London: T. Fisher Unwin, Ltd., n.d. (1916). First edition. Orig. wrappers (a bit torn and dust-soiled). Very good. MacManus 280-5280 1983 $50

TOYNBEE, ARNOLD J.   "The Murderous Tyranny of the Turks." London: Hodder & Stoughton, 1917. First edition. Orig. wrappers (dusty). Fine. MacManus 280-5281 1983 $50

TOYNBEE, ARNOLD J.   A Study of History. London, Oxford, 1934-71. First editions. 8vo and 4to. Illus. Dust jackets. Very good - fine. 12 vols. complete. Houle 22-899 1983 $350

TOYNBEE, ARNOLD J.   Turkey: A Past and a Future. N.Y.: George H. Doran Co., 1917. First American edition. Orig. wrappers (dust-soiled). Front wrapper somewhat chipped. Good. MacManus 280-5282 1983 $35

TOZZER, ALFRED M.   Animal Figures in the Maya Codices. Cambridge, 1910. 39 plates. 24 text illus. Small 4to. Wrappers. Ars Libri 34-505 1983 $35

TOZZER, ALFRED M.   A Preliminary Study of the Prehistoric Ruins of Nakum, Guatemala. Cambridge, 1913. 23 plates (3 folding). 54 text illus. Folio. Cloth. Ars Libri 34-504 1983 $75

TRACY, ALBERT   The Utah War. S.L.C., 1945. Illus. Orig. cloth. First edition. Ginsberg 46-762 1983 $25

TRACY, MILTON C.   The Colonizer: A Saga of Stephen F. Austin. El Paso, 1941. 1st ed. in dj. Illus., maps. Jenkins 153-557 1983 $25

TRADITIONER af Swenska Folk-Sansar. Stockholm 1814-1815. Four parts in one volume. 4 engraved titles, 72 pages engraved music. 4to, 1/2 calf, spine gilt, with label. Salloch 387-239 1983 $500

TRAHERNE, JOHN P.   The Habits of the Salmon. London 1889.
Gilt-pict. cloth, spine darkened, rubbed. King 46-688 1983 $22.50

TRAIL, WILLIAM   Elements of Algebra for the use of
Sutdents in Universities. Edinburgh: reprinted for C. Elliot...,
1779. 8vo. Cont. half calf, gilt. Very good copy. Heath 48-534
1983 £65

TRAIN, GEORGE FRANCIS   Championship of Woman. Leavenworth,
KS, 1867. Orig. pr. wraps. Light stain on front. Argosy 716-230
1983 $25

TRAIN, GEORGE FRANCIS   Young America in Wall-Street. N.Y.,
1857. Original cloth, 1st ed. Jenkins 151-338 1983 $65

TRANSACTIONS of the Perkinean Society... London: printed by A.
Topping, etc., 1804. 12mo. Orig. light blue printed wrappers.
Fine copy. Ximenes 63-295 1983 $125

TRANSFORMING Performers With Surprise Pictures. London: Dean & Son,
(ca. 1875). Octavo. 6 chromolithographed plates, each of which has
four flaps which, when turned back reveal a new picture, also in
color. Two pages torn and very neatly repaired. Near fine in orig.
pictorial boards, slightly chipped at top and bottom of spine.
Bromer 25-397 1983 $225

TRAQUAIR, R. H.   Les Poissons Wealdiens de Bernissart.
Brussels, Mus. Roy. Hist., 1911. 12 plates, 4to, half cloth.
Wheldon 160-1479 1983 £15

TRAQUAIR, RAMSAY   The Old Architecture of Quebec.
Toronto: Macmillan, 1947. 4to. 179 plates. Tired dust jacket.
A fine copy. McGahern 53-161 1983 $200

TRASENSTER, PAUL   Aux Etats-Unis. Liege, 1885. Printed
wraps. (a bit chipped at edges, rebacked with paper). First edition.
Felcone 22-245 1983 $35

TRASK, JOHN B.   Report on the Geology of Northern and
Southern California Embracing the Mineral and Agricultural Resources
of Those Sections; with Statistics of the Northern, Southern and
Middle Mines. (Sacramento), Allen, 1856. Dbd. First edition.
Ginsberg 47-189 1983 $50

TRASK, SPENCER   Bowling Green. NY, 1898. Many illus,
some photo. Pict. cloth, g.t., ex library. Argosy 710-385 1983
$30

TRATADO do jogo do voltarete, com as leis geraes do jogo. Lisbon:
Simao Thaddeo Ferreira, etc., 1794. Small 8vo. Cont. calf. A
bit worn. Ximenes 63-59 1983 $70

TRATTINNICK, L.   Fungi Austriaci. Vienna, 1830.
New ed., hand-coloured plates, 4to, original wrappers. Some very
foxing, but a good copy. Wheldon 160-108 1983 £450

TRAUBEL, HORACE L.   Camden's Compliment To Walt Whitman
May 31, 1889. Philadelphia, 1889. Portrait, cloth, t.e.g., extremities worn. First edition. King 46-355 1983 $65

TRAVASSOS VALDEZ, FRANCISCO   Six Years of a Traveller's Life in Western Africa. Hurst and Blackett, 1861. First edition, with 14 illus.
on 12 plates and a few other illus., including half-titles, 2 vols.,
8vo, orig. cloth, some light foxing of the preliminary leaves and with
some wear to the spines, but otherwise a very good copy in a fitted
cloth folding library case. With a presentation inscription by the
author, signed in full, dated November 30th, 1861. Fenning 60-415
1983 £195

TRAVEL and Exploration. 1909-11. Vols. 1 to 5 no. 2, 8vo, vols.
1-4 in cloth, rest in parts. Wheldon 160-447 1983 £20

TRAVEN, B.   The Death Ship. The Story of An
American Sailor. London: Chatto & Windus, 1934. First edition
in English. 8vo. Orig. cloth. Dust jacket. Dime-size spot
on front cover of jacket, otherwise a fine copy. Jaffe 1-376
1983 $875

TRAVEN, B.   The Death Ship, the Story of an American
Sailor. New York: Knopf, 1934. 1st American ed. Orig. black cloth,
gilt, dj. Very fine copy in very good dj (printed on soft fuzzy
paper that does not hold up well). Scarce. Jenkins 155-1221 1983
$200

TRAVEN, B.   The Death Ship. NY, 1934. Very good.
Quill & Brush 54-1376 1983 $50

TRAVEN, B.   Government. London: Chatto & Windus,
1935. First edition in English. 8vo. Orig. cloth. Dust jacket,
slightly torn at head of spine, spine faded beneath jacket, otherwise a fine copy. Jaffe 1-378 1983 $475

TRAVEN, B.   Der Marsch Ins Reich Der Caoba, Ein
Kriegsmarsch. Zurich, (ca. 1933). Very good in moderately
chipped dust wrapper. King 46-342 1983 $150

TRAVEN, B.   The Treasure of the Sierra Madre.
London: Chatto & Windus, 1934. First edition in English. 8vo.
Orig. cloth. Publisher's flyer on the author and his work laid
in. Fine copy. Jaffe 1-377 1983 $275

TRAVEN, B.   The Treasure of the Sierra Madre. New
York: Knopf, 1935. 1st American ed. Orig. black cloth, gilt, dj
with large chip from base of spine. Fine copy in creased dj.
Uncommon; rare with dj. Jenkins 155-1222 1983 $200

TRAVEN, B.   The Treasure of The Sierra Madre. NY,
1935. Very good in worn and chipped dustwrapper. Quill & Brush 54-
1377 1983 $200

TRAVERS, P. L.   Mary Poppins Opens the Door. NY:
(1943). First edition. Illus. About fine with slightly chipped
pictorial dust wrapper. Owner's signature and stamp. Bromer 25-
398 1983 $35

TRAVES, FREDERICK   The Cradle of the Deep. Smith, Elder,
1908. With 4 maps and 41 plates, roy. 8vo, orig. cloth, gilt, t.e.g.
A very good copy. Fenning 61-455 1983 £12.50

TRAYLOR, SAMUEL W.   Out of the Southwest. (Allentown, Pa.,
1936). Illus. Privately printed. Signed. Argosy 716-538 1983
$35

TRAZ, GEORGES DE   Tintoret. Paris: Albin Michel, 1929.
100 phototype plates. Stout 4to. Wrappers. Ars Libri 33-366 1983
$100

TREADWELL, EDWARD F.   The Cattle King, a Dramatized Biography.
New York, 1931. Frontis., plates, 1st ed. Nice copy. Jenkins 151-
340 1983 $55

TREADWELL, EDWARD F.   The Cattle King. New York, 1931. End
maps, illus. Clark 741-208 1983 $38.50

TREADWELL, EDWARD F.   The Cattle King. N.Y.: Macmillan, 1931.
Plates. Cloth. Dawson 471-285 1983 $25

THE TREASURES of the Deep. London, Nelson, 1876. Illus. Small 8vo.
Morrill 287-467 1983 $27.50

TREAT, LAWRENCE   D as in Dead. N.Y., Duell, (1941).
First edition. Dust jacket (tiny tears, nicks) else, very good.
Houle 22-902 1983 $35

TREDWELL, DANIEL M.   A Monograph on Privately Illustrated
Books. Flatbush, Long Island: Privately printed, 1892. Tall 8vo,
indices. Printed by the De Vinne Press. Blue cloth, upper right
hand corner bumped. Leather spine label. Karmiole 72-21 1983
$60

TREGELLAS, J. T.   Cornish Tales. Truro: James R. Nether-
ton, 1865. First edition. Gori. cloth. Edges and corners very
slightly worn. Offsetting to endpapers. A little light foxing. Very
good. MacManus 280-5286 1983 $185

TREGENNA, JAMES HAMLEY   The Autobiography of A Cornish Rector. London: Tinsley Brothers, 1872. First edition. 2 vols. Orig. bright blue cloth. Spines darkened and worn at the ends and edges. Former owner's signature. Good. MacManus 280-5287 1983 $165

TRELAWNEY, HARRIET JANE   Sister. London: Smith, Elder, & Co., 1879. First edition. 2 vols. Orig. decorated cloth. Spine ends slightly worn. Covers a trifle soiled. Former owner's signature on front free endpapers. Very good. MacManus 280-5288 1983 $135

TRELAWNY, EDWARD JOHN   Letters... Henry Frowde, 1910. First edition, tall 8vo, half title. Illus., orig. blue cloth, v.g. Jarndyce 30-1160 1983 £18

TRELAWNY, EDWARD JOHN   Recollections of the Last Days of Shelley and Byron. London: Edward Moxon, 1858. First edition. Illus. Rebound in 3/4 morocco & cloth. Very good. MacManus 280-4737 1983 $125

TRELAWNY, EDWARD JOHN   Records of Shelley, Byron and the Author. Pickering and Chatto, 1887. 4 pp. ads., half title, with two portraits, orig. blue cloth, paper label rubbed. Jarndyce 30-1159 1983 £15

TRELAWNY, EDWARD JOHN   Records of Shelley, Byron, and the Author. London: Basil Montagu Pickering, 1878. First edition. Frontis. ports. 2 vols. Rebound in 3/4 maroon morocco & cloth. Fine. MacManus 280-4738 1983 $125

TREMENHEERE, HUGH SEYMOUR   Notes on Public Subjects Made During a Tour in the United States and Canada. London: John Murray, 1852. Orig. cloth, gilt. Nice copy of a scarce book. Jenkins 153-642 1983 $250

TREMENHEERE, HUGH SEYMOUR   Notes on Public Subjects. London: John Murray, 1852. 20cm. Ads. Rear folding map. Orig. blind stamped green cloth expertly restored, but wanting the top third of the spine cap, with loss of title else very good copy. McGahern 53-163 1983 $75

TRENCK, FREDERIC   The Life of Baron. Providence: David Heaton, 1808. 18mo, orig. calf-backed boards, (worn, edges chipped, prelim. pp. wormholed). Argosy 716-299 1983 $40

TRENTSENSKY, M.   Exercises in Coloring - French Military. Vienna, (c.1860). 6 coloured lithograph plates with duplicate set of plates uncoloured. Oblong sm. folio. Orig. wrappers, slightly worn. Printed label. Good. Edwards 1042-490 1983 £60

TREVELYAN, G. E.   Appius and Virginia. London: Martin Secker, 1932. First edition. Orig. cloth. Dust jacket. Very fine. MacManus 280-5289 1983 $25

TREVELYAN, JANET PENROSE   The Life of Mrs. Humphrey Ward. London: Constable & Co., (1923). First edition. Orig. cloth. Two corners bumped. Very slightly foxed. Former owner's signature. Good. MacManus 280-5389 1983 $20

TREVELYAN, L. R.   A Year in Pashawur. London, 1880. Boards rubbed. 8vo. Orig. cloth. Good. Edwards 1044-717 1983 £45

TREVELYAN, R. C.   The Oresteia of Aeschylus. Liverpool: University Press of Liverpool, Ltd., Hodder & Stoughton, Ltd., London, (1922). First edition. Orig. holland-backed blue boards. Paper label on spine, tissue jacket. Spare label tipped in at the front. Fine. MacManus 280-5290 1983 $25

TREVITHICK, RICHARD   Life of Richard Trevithick, with an Account of His Inventions... E. and F. N. Spon, London, 1872. 2 vols. 8vo, with an engr. portrait by W. Holl and 17 lithographed plates, mostly folding. First edition. Orig. brown cloth, gilt. Good. Quaritch NS 5-107 1983 $200

TREVOR-BATTYE, AUBYN   Ice-Bound on Kolguev. 1895. 3 folding maps, 25 plates by Whymper, J.T. Nettleship, and the author, roy. 8vo. K Books 307-180 1983 £35

TREYSSAC DE VERGY, PIERRE HENRI   The Lovers: Or the Memoirs of Lady Sarah B. and the Countess P. Published by Mr. Treyssac de Vergy, Printed for the Editor, 1769. 8vo, later qtr. calf, cloth sides; half-title, two plates. Hill 165-133 1983 £185

TRIAL of Charles Pinney, Esq... Bristol: by Gutch & Martin..., 1833. 8vo. Half polished red calf, gilt. Fine copy. Heath 48-228 1983 £45

TRIAL of Mary Ann Burdock... Bristol: W.H. Somerston, (1835). 8vo. Stitched as issued. Little soiled. Heath 49-232 1983 £25

TRIAL of Thomas O. Selfridge, Attorney at Law. Boston, (1806). First edition. Contemp. boards, rebacked. This copy has the errata leaf but lacks the map. Severely foxed throughout. Contents page at end and last printed leaf repaired, with some loss of type in publisher's routine note stating this is a condensed version. Rare. Bradley 64-172 1983 $35

TRIALS; a Tale. G. & W. B. Whittaker. First edition, 3 vols. Half titles, half blue calf, sl. rubbed. Jarndyce 30-282 1983 £160

THE TRIALS of Samuel Goodere, Esq... London: for A. Millar..., 1741. Folio. Half green morocco. Heath 48-225 1983 £125

TRIANA, J.   Les Melastomacees. Linn. Trans., 1871. 7 plates, 4to, wrappers. Wheldon 160-1577 1983 £12

TRIANA, S. PEREZ   Down the Orinoco in a Canoe. London, 1902. First English edition. First with intro. by R. B. C. Graham. Nice. Rota 230-256 1983 £12

TRIBUNE Hand-Book of Minneapolis, with Map and Illustrations. Minneapolis, 1884. Large folding map. Wraps., good. Reese 19-368 1983 $125

TRIEM, EVE   Paradise of Doves. New York, 1946. 8vo. Cloth. 1 of 850 copies. Small erasure mark on front flyleaf, else fine in chipped dj. In Our Time 156-809 1983 $20

TRILL, HEW   Good King Wenceslas. Montreal, 1934. 8vo, parchment-backed decorated boards, paper label, d/w, decorated slipcase. Wood-cut frontis. One of 170 copies printed for Charles Corbett Ronalds by the Ronalds Company, Limited. Very good. Perata 28-172 1983 $65

TRILLER, DANIEL WILHELM   Dissertatio medica inauguralis de Tabici Ptarmici Abusu... Wittenberg: Ephraim Gottlob Eichsfeld, 1761. First edition. Decorative woodcut head- and tail-pieces and initial. Small 4to. Modern boards. Kraus 164-242 1983 $250

TRIMBLE, DAVID   Fellow Citizens. (Washington? 1822). Dsb. Very good. Reese 18-565 1983 $75

TRIP to Greece, Photographs by Jerome Hill. NY: E. Weyhe, 1936. Limited to 1000 copies, designed by Merle Armitage. Photos, cloth, very good. King 46-764 1983 $85

TRIPP, F. E.   British Mosses. 1874. 39 hand-coloured plates, 2 decorated title-pages, 2 vols., royal 8vo, original cloth. A very limited number of these volumes was issued. Wheldon 160-1908 1983 £80

TRISTRAM, HENRY BAKER   The Great Sahara: Wanderings south of the Atlas Mountains. London: John Murray, 1860. 8vo. 2 folding maps. 11 plates. 1/2 maroon morocco, rubbed. Adelson Africa-140 1983 $110

TRISTRAM, W. OUTRAM   Coaching Days and Coaching Ways. L, 1893. Very good. Quill & Brush 54-1360 1983 $50

TRITES, WILLIAM B.   The Gypsy. Nice, the Green Lane Press, circa, 1926. First edition, 8vo, orig. printed wrapper, inscribed by the author. Fenning 60-414 1983 £10.50

THE TRIUMPH of Beauty. London: Printed for C. Corbett...1740. Folio, disbound. First and only edition. Quaritch NS 7-132 1983 $325

TROBRIAND, PHILIPPE   Vie Militaire Dans le Dakota Notes et
Souvenirs 1867-1869. Paris: Librairie Ancienne Honore Champion, 1926.
Portrait. Jenkins 153-155 1983 $100

TROGUS POMPEIUS
Please turn to
JUSTINUS, MARCUS JUNIANUS

TROLLOPE, ANTHONY   Alice Dugdale. Daldy, Isbister, 1878.
First edition, 4to, illus. by G.G.K. Orig. pink printed wraps. sl.
chipped, v.g. Jarndyce 31-951 1983 £85

TROLLOPE, ANTHONY   The American Senator. London: Chapman
& Hall, 1877. First edition. 3 vols. Orig. decorated cloth. Spines
slightly faded and rubbed. Covers of volumes I & III a trifle rubbed
and soiled where library labels have been expertly removed. Slight
foxing to the preliminary pages and edges. Near-fine. MacManus 280-
5291 1983 $2,250

TROLLOPE, ANTHONY   The American Senator. London, Chapman
& Hall, 1877. 3 vols., orig. pinkish ochre cloth, worn faded and
shaken, W.H. Smith's subscription library label inside covers, some
smudging throughout; uncut. First binding of the first edition.
Ravenstree 96-271 1983 $425

TROLLOPE, ANTHONY   An Autobiography. Edinburgh: William
Blackwood & Sons, 1883. First edition. 2 vols. Orig. cloth. Spines
faded, all edges a little worn. Covers a little soiled. Very good,
tight set. MacManus 280-5292 1983 $200

TROLLOPE, ANTHONY   An Autobiography. Blackwood, 1883.
First edition. 2 vols., half titles, front. port. vol. I. 24 pp ads.
vol. II. Orig. smooth dark red cloth, spines faded, v.g. Jarndyce
30-256 1983 £56

TROLLOPE, ANTHONY   An Autobiography. Blackwood, 1883.
First edition. 2 vols., half titles, front. port. Vol. I. Ex-
library copy, library stamps. Rebound in maroon moire-patterned cloth,
label. Jarndyce 30-257 1983 £25

TROLLOPE, ANTHONY   An Autobiography. Edinburgh: William
Blackwood & Sons, 1883. Second edition. Photogravure frontis. port.
2 vols. Orig. cloth. Publisher's blind-stamped presentation copy.
Spines slightly faded. Extremities of spines a trifle rubbed. Very
good. MacManus 280-5293 1983 $40

TROLLOPE, ANTHONY   Ayala's Angel. London, Chapman & Hall,
1881. 3 vols., 8vo, bound in cont. dark red half morocco gilt,
hinges and spine ends rubbed, owner's stamp on endpapers. Ravenstree
96-272 1983 $425

TROLLOPE, ANTHONY   The Barsetshire Novels. London,
1906. 8 vols. 8vo. Cloth, gilt, t.e.g. Portrait. Traylen 94-
834 1983 £48

TROLLOPE, ANTHONY   The Belton Estate. Chapman & Hall,
1866. Vols. I & II. First edition; vol. III, 2nd edition. Half
brown morocco, worn, but sound. Jarndyce 30-241 1983 £85

TROLLOPE, ANTHONY   British Sports and Pastimes. London:
Virtue & Co., 1868. First edition. Orig. green cloth. With the
"Brackenburn" bookplate of Hugh Walpole. Head of spine nicked. Corners
a bit worn. Small stain on front cover. Good. MacManus 280-5294
1983 $350

TROLLOPE, ANTHONY   British Sports and Pastimes. London:
Virtue & Co., 1868. First edition, remainder or reissue binding.
Orig. green cloth. Orig. sheets and title-page with top-edge trimmed,
in the Daldy, Isbister & Co. binding. Extremities of spine a trifle
rubbed. Very good. MacManus 280-5295 1983 $185

TROLLOPE, ANTHONY   Can You Forgive Her? London, Chapman &
Hall, 1864. 2 vols., bound without half titles in 1 in cont. half
crimson morocco gilt a bit rubbed and worn. First edition.
Ravenstree 96-273 1983 $90

TROLLOPE, ANTHONY   Chronicles of Barsetshire. Chapman
and Hall, 1891-4. Collected edition, 8vo. Front. half titles, 2pp
ads. vol. V. Orig. dark-olive diagonal-grained cloth, blocked in
black on upper cover, spines gilt-lettered, v.g. Jarndyce 31-954
1983 £120

TROLLOPE, ANTHONY   The Chronicle of Barsetshire. Chapman &
Hall, 1889-93. 8 vols., fronts., half titles, ads. Orig. dark
olive-green cloth; blocked in black on upper cover, gilt spine
lettering, v.g. Jarndyce 30-259 1983 £58

TROLLOPE, ANTHONY   The Claverings. Smith, Elder, 1867.
2 vols., 16 illus. by M. Ellen Edwards. A little worn internally.
Ex-library copy. Sturdily bound in half calf, a little rubbed.
Jarndyce 30-244 1983 £38

TROLLOPE, ANTHONY   Doctor Thorne. London: Chapman & Hall,
1866. "Ninth edition." Orig. pictorial boards. Head and foot of
spine, and all edges, a bit worn. Bookplate and shelf number. Endpapers a little browned. Good. MacManus 280-5296 1983 $150

TROLLOPE, ANTHONY   Doctor Thorne. Chapman & Hall, 1866.
9th edition, inserted leaf of adverts. Orig. green cloth, v.g.
Jarndyce 30-240 1983 £18.50

TROLLOPE, ANTHONY   Dr. Wortle's School. Chapman and Hall,
1881. First edition in book form, 2 vols. 8vo, orig. cloth. Cancelled library labels on front endpapers, casing a little weak and
bindings a little rubbed at the corners. A very good copy in a folding
cloth library case. Fenning 60-416 1983 £195

TROLLOPE, ANTHONY   Dr. Wortle's School. London, Chapman &
Hall, 1881. 2 vols., 8vo, orig. cloth worn, slightly bubbled, the
"freak binding" with cover stamping reversed onto rear covers.
First edition. Ravenstree 96-274 1983 $195

TROLLOPE, ANTHONY   Framley Parsonage. New York, Harpers,
1861. 8vo, orig. cloth gilt, worn, spine snagged and torn, bit
shaken, name on endpaper. First American edition. Ravenstree 96-275
1983 $85

TROLLOPE, ANTHONY   Framley Parsonage. London: Smith,
Elder, 1878. New edition. 8vo. Orig. red cloth. Four wood-
engraved plates. Spine a trifle faded. Ximenes 63-163 1983
$35

TROLLOPE, ANTHONY   The Golden Lion of Granpere. London:
Tinsley Brothers, 1872. First edition, first binding. Orig. reddish
brown cloth. Covers slightly worn at edges, short tear at top of spine.
Inner hinges cracked. Free endpapers foxed. Former owner's signature
on flyleaf. Good. MacManus 280-5297 1983 $135

TROLLOPE, ANTHONY   Harry Heathcote of Gangoil. London:
Ward, Lock & Co., n.d. (1883). "Third edition." Orig. pictorial bds.
A yellowback. Corners, head and foot of spine worn. Covers a bit
soiled. Good. MacManus 280-5298 1983 $175

TROLLOPE, ANTHONY   He Knew He Was Right. London: Virtue &
Co., 1868-69. First edition, part-issue A. Illus. by M. Stone. Orig.
32 weekly parts, in pictorial wrappers (a bit soiled and frayed). In
a badly worn and faded cloth folding box. Very good. MacManus 280-
5299 1983 $1,500

TROLLOPE, ANTHONY   He Knew he was Right. London, Strahan,
1869. 2 vols., bound in 3/4 crimson morocco gilt, top edge gilt.
First edition. Ravenstree 96-276 1983 $145

TROLLOPE, ANTHONY   He Knew He Was Right. London: Strahan
& Co., 1869. First edition. 64 illus. by M. Stone. Orig. cloth.
2 vols. All edges rather worn. Covers soiled. Hinges cracking.
Bookplates. Shabby. MacManus 280-5300 1983 $75

TROLLOPE, ANTHONY   He Knew He Was Right. Strahan & Co.,
1869. 2 vols. bound as one. Illus. by Marcus Stone. Half calf, a
little rubbed. Internally v.g. except for taped repair to leading
blank. Jarndyce 30-245 1983 £30

TROLLOPE, ANTHONY   How the "Mastiffs" Went to Iceland.
London: Virtue & Co., 1878. First edition. Illus. by Mrs. H. Blackburn. 4to. Orig. decorated cloth. Presentation copy from Trollope,
inscribed: "Mrs. Carnegie, with the author's kind regards." With
the bookplate of Duff Cooper. All edges and corners rather worn.
Hinges cracked. Covers slightly soiled. Some light foxing. MacManus
280-5301 1983 $1,250

TROLLOPE, ANTHONY   Hunting Sketches. L, 1865. Rebound in
full leather without May ads, front hinge starting at title, spine
darkened and edges worn, very good, bookplate. Quill & Brush 54-1379
1983 $250

TROLLOPE, ANTHONY   John Caldigate. Chapman & Hall, 1879.
First edition, 3 vols. A good copy rebound in maroon moire-patterned
cloth, black labels, v.g. Jarndyce 31-952 1983 £58

TROLLOPE, ANTHONY   The Kellys and the O'Kellys. Chapman &
Hall, 1875. 8th edition, front. half blue calf, a little rubbed.
This copy with the armorial bookplate of 'Kelly of the Castle'.
Jarndyce 30-234 1983 £24

TROLLOPE, ANTHONY   Lady Anna. London: Chapman & Hall,
1874. "New edition." Full calf with gilt spine and marbled endpapers.
Inscribed on the first blank leaf to Miss Allen, dated Nov. 6, 1875.
Armorial bookplate. Binding a bit rubbed and soiled. Corners bumped.
Rear inner hinges cracking. Good. MacManus 280-5302 1983 $1,000

TROLLOPE, ANTHONY   Lady Anna. Chapman & Hall, 1874.
First edition, 2 vols. Sl. staining of title page vol. I, otherwise
a good clean copy rebound in maroon moire-patterned cloth, black
labels, v.g. Without half titles. Jarndyce 31-950 1983 £58

TROLLOPE, ANTHONY   The Last Chronicle of Barset. London:
Smith, Edler, 1866-67. First edition. 32 parts. Orig. pictorial
wrappers. Some soiling. Spines a bit soiled and worn. In a 3/4
morocco solander case. Very good. MacManus 280-5303 1983 $1,000

TROLLOPE, ANTHONY   The Last Chronicle of Barset. London:
Smith, Elder & Co., 1867. First edition. 2 vols. Decorated cloth.
All edges worn. Covers a bit soiled. Former owner's signature on the
front free endpaper of Vol. I. Very good, tight set. MacManus 280-
5304 1983 $350

TROLLOPE, ANTHONY   The last chronicle of Barset.
London: Smith, Elder, 1867. First edition. 2 vols. Large 8vo.
Orig. blue cloth. Spines a little rubbed and slightly worn at
the ends, corners rubbed. Ximenes 63-164 1983 $200

TROLLOPE, ANTHONY   The Last Chronicle of Barset. New
York: Harper, 1867. 1st American ed. Orig. blue-green cloth, gilt.
Small nick at base of spine and tiny corner torn from end paper, else
fine. Jenkins 155-1223 1983 $150

TROLLOPE, ANTHONY   The Last Chronicle of Barset. New
York, Harpers, 1867. 8vo, orig. cloth gilt, bit worn and spotted,
spine ends little frayed, name pencilled on flyleaf. First American
edition. Ravenstree 96-277 1983 $115

TROLLOPE, ANTHONY   Mr. Scarborough's Family. Chatto &
Windus, 1883. 3 vols., half titles, vol. 1 (March 1883). Leading
free end papers laid down. Orig. light blue cloth rubbed. Jarndyce
30-254 1983 £48

TROLLOPE, ANTHONY   Mr. Scarborough's Family. Chatto &
Windus, 1883. First edition. 3 vols. Half red roan, rubbed.
Jarndyce 30-255 1983 £45

TROLLOPE, ANTHONY   Nina Balakta. (1879). First edition,
2nd issue. 2 vols. in one, half titles to each vol; new title to
both vols. Orig. ochre-brown cloth, inner hinges a little weak.
Jarndyce 30-242 1983 £85

TROLLOPE, ANTHONY   The Noble Jilt. London: Constable & Co.
Ltd., 1923. First edition. Orig. cloth. Limited to 500 copies. Good.
MacManus 280-5305 1983 $100

TROLLOPE, ANTHONY   North America. London, 1862.
2 vols. Folding map. Cloth (worn). Third edition. Felcone 22-246
1983 $30

TROLLOPE, ANTHONY   An Old Man's Love. Blackwood, 1884.
First edition, 2 vols. Half maroon roan, rubbed. Jarndyce 30-258
1983 £45

TROLLOPE, ANTHONY   Orley Farm. London, 1862. 8vo.
Cloth. 2 vols. 1st ed. Some rebacking to spines, else a vg-fine
set. In Our Time 156-810 1983 $150

TROLLOPE, ANTHONY   Orley Farm. Chapman & Hall, 1862.
2 vols., illus. by J.E. Millais. Half titles. Half brown morocco,
rubbed on spines. Jarndyce 30-238 1983 £42

TROLLOPE, ANTHONY   Phineas Finn. New York, Harpers, 1868.
Tall 8vo, orig. cloth gilt, bookplate, trifle worn. First American
edition. Ravenstree 96-278 1983 $125

TROLLOPE, ANTHONY   Phineas Finn, the Irish Member. Virute
& Co., 1869. First English edition in book form, with 20 plates. 2
vols. 8vo, orig. green cloth, gilt. Fenning 60-417 1983 £165

TROLLOPE, ANTHONY   Phineas Finn, the Irish Member. London:
Virtue & Co., 1869. First edition. 20 illus. by J.E. Millais, R.A.
2 vols. Orig. decorated cloth. Edges and corners slightly worn.
Covers a little soiled and scratched. Very good. MacManus 280-5306
1983 $650

TROLLOPE, ANTHONY   Phineas Finn, The Irish Member. London:
Ward, Lock, & Co., n.d. "New edition." Orig. pictorial glazed yellow
boards. Spine somewhat worn. Light soiling. Good. MacManus 280-
5307 1983 $150

TROLLOPE, ANTHONY   The Prime Minister. Chapman & Hall,
1876. First edition. 4 vols., half calf, labels v.g. Jarndyce 30-250
1983 £120

TROLLOPE, ANTHONY   The Prime Minister. Chapman & Hall,
1877. Half title, front. 16 pp. ads. Orig. brown dec. cloth a little
rubbed. Second edition, with a new frontis. Jarndyce 30-251 1983 £20

TROLLOPE, ANTHONY   Rachel Ray. Chapman & Hall, 1863.
First edition, 2 vols., repair to one page vol. I. Ex-library copy,
in sturdy maroon cloth. Jarndyce 30-239 1983 £45

TROLLOPE, ANTHONY   Ralph the Heir. Hurst & Blackett,
1871. First edition, 3 vols. Well rebound in maroon moire-patterned
cloth, black labels, v.g. Jarndyce 31-949 1983 £56

TROLLOPE, ANTHONY   Ralph the Heir. London: Strahan, 1871.
1st ed. in 1 vol. Contemporary 3/4 crimson calf and marbled boards,
raised bands, gilt compartments, label, gilt. Fine copy. Jenkins
155-1224 1983 $75

TROLLOPE, ANTHONY   Ralph the Heir. 1871. Tall 8vo, illus.
by F. A. Fraser. Half black roan, rubbed. A good sound copy.
First one-volume edition. Jarndyce 30-246 1983 £46

TROLLOPE, ANTHONY   Ralph the Heir. 1871. Illus. by F.A.
Fraser. Half calf, spine heavily rubbed, green label. Jarndyce 30-
247 1983 £46

TROLLOPE, ANTHONY   Sir Harry Hotspur of Humblethwaite. NY,
1871. Very minor cover wear and rubbing. Quill & Brush 54-1380 1983
$200

TROLLOPE, ANTHONY   The Three Clerks. London: Richard
Bentley, 1858. First edition. 3 vols. Full gilt-stamped morocco
with gilt edges and marbled endpapers. Edges very slightly rubbed.
Bookplates and shelf numbers (of the Earl of Carysfort). Near-fine.
MacManus 280-5308 1983 $850

TROLLOPE, ANTHONY   The Three Clerks. New York: Harper
& Brothers, 1860. First U.S. edition. 8vo. Orig. cloth. With
the bookseller's label of I.T. Heald of Wilmington and a private
library stamp of Theo. Rogers of Delaware on the title page. Spine
extremities chipped, light foxing throughout. Oak Knoll 49-376
1983 $65

TROLLOPE, ANTHONY   The Three Clerks. Richard Bentley, 1867.
Repair to verso of front. Ex-library copy, a little worn internally;
sturdy half calf, a little rubbed. Jarndyce 30-236 1983 £12.50

TROLLOPE, ANTHONY   The warden. London: Longman, etc.,
1859. New edition. 8vo. Orig. pink cloth. Ximenes 63-165 1983
$45

TROLLOPE, ANTHONY   The Warden. Longmans, Green, 1866.
Half title, 2 pp ads, orig. pink cloth, v.g. Jarndyce 30-235 1983
£24

TROLLOPE, ANTHONY   The Way We Live Now. Lon., 1875. Two
vols., cover rubbed, hinges starting, some interior foxing and stains,
else good or better. Quill & Brush 54-1381 1983 $200

TROLLOPE, ANTHONY   The way we live now. London:
Chapman and Hall, 1875. First edition. 2 vols. 8vo. Orig. green
cloth. With 40 plates by Luke Fildes. Recased, rather rubbed and
dull. Lacks the half-title in Vol. 1. Ximenes 63-166 1983 $50

TROLLOPE, FRANCES   Charles Chesterfield. Henry Colburn,
1841. First edition. 3 vols. Frontis. & illus. by Phiz. 8 pp. ads.
vol. III. Orig. blue cloth bound in. Rebound in light blue cloth,
maroon leather labels, t.e.g. Very good. Jarndyce 31-957 1983 £62

TROLLOPE, FRANCES   Jessie Phillips. London: Henry Colburn,
1844. First one-volume edition. 3/4 morocco with marbled endpapers,
bound by Bayntun. Illus. by J. Leech. Covers and some page margins
slightly soiled. Very good. MacManus 280-5312 1983 $85

TROLLOPE, FRANCES   Mable's Progress. Chatto and Windus,
1884. New edition, 2pp, 32pp ads. Orig. brown dec. cloth, v.g.
Jarndyce 31-960 1983 £10.50

TROLLOPE, FRANCES   Paris and the Parisians in 1835. London:
Bentley, 1836. First edition. 2 vols. 8vo. Cont. half calf, spines
gilt. Vignette titles and 12 etched plates. Some imprints shaved.
Binding rubbed, ends of spines a trifle worn. Ximenes 63-640 1983
$75

TROLLOPE, FRANCES   The Refugee in America. London: Whitaker, Treacher & Co., 1832. First edition. 3 vols. Orig. boards with
paper labels on spines. Spines and labels worn and split. Former
owner's signature on front covers. Bookplates on endsheets. Fringes
firm. Good. MacManus 280-5314 1983 $650

TROLLOPE, FRANCES   Tremordyn Cliff. Richard Bentley, 1835.
First edition. 3 vols. Half titles, half dark green morocco, rubbed,
lacking one label. Jarndyce 31-958 1983 £48

TROLLOPE, FRANCES   Uncle Walter. Colburn & Co., 1852.
First edition. 3 vols. Half titles. Orig. boards, cloth spines,
but a subscription library copy which has blue paper affixed to boards,
partially removed. Lacking free end papers vol. III. Internally good.
Jarndyce 31-959 1983 £30

TROLLOPE, FRANCES   The widow married. London: Colburn,
1840. First edition. 3 vols. 8vo. Cont. half morocco. 21 plates
(several captions and outer margins shaved). Binding rubbed, spines
evenly faded. Ximenes 63-168 1983 $200

TROLLOPE, THOMAS ADOLPHUS   Leonora Casaloni. London: Chapman &
Hall, 1868. First edition. 2 vols. Orig. cloth. In a green pub.
(remainder?) cloth binding. Spine of volume one stained. A bit worn
along the edges and extremities. Very good. MacManus 280-5317 1983
$250

TROTMAN, EDWARD   Haec Epitome Undecim Librorum Relationum
...Edwardi Coke. London, 1640. 8vo. Title page dusty, some lightish
embrowning throughout, rebound in 1/2 brown morocco, spine double-gilt-
ruled & lettered, with black leather label, similarly gilt. Good copy.
1st & only ed. of 1st abridgment. Boswell 7-47 1983 $350

TROTSKII, LEV (1879-1940)   Moya Zhizn'. Berlin, 1930. 1st ed.,
2 vols., 8vo, edges slightly browned, original orange cloth, spines
a little faded. Exceedingly rare first edition, in Russian. Pickering
& Chatto 21-127 1983 $2,500

TROTSKII, LEV (1879-1940)   La Nouvelle Politique Economiqe Des
Soviets et la Revolution Mondiale. Paris, Librairie de l'Humanite,
1923. First ed. in French, 8vo, original orange printed wrappers.
Pickering & Chatto 21-129 1983 $200

TROTSKII, LEV (1879-1940)   Novaya Ekonomicheskaya Politika. Moscow,
1923. 1st ed., large 8vo, original printed covers, spotted, internally
clean. Pickering & Chatto 21-128 1983 $325

TROTTER, LIONEL J.   A Leader of Light Horse. Edinburgh,
1901. 2 maps, portrait. 2nd impression. K Books 307-181 1983 £26

TROTTER, R. G.   Canadian Federation. Its origins
and achievements. Toronto: Dent, 1924. 20 1/2cm. Folding map,
pen underlining else good to very good. McGahern 53-164 1983
$20

TROTTER, R. G.   Canadian History. A Syllabus and Guide
to Reading. Toronto: Macmillan, 1926. 22 1/2cm. Ex-lib. else
very good. McGahern 53-165 1983 $20

TROTTER, THOMAS   View of the Nervous Temperament. Troy,
NY: Wright, Goodenow & Stockwell, 1808. 12mo. Modern calf with
leather label. Slight foxing. Gach 95-503 1983 $275

TROTTER, W   The Collected Papers of Wilfred
Trotter. London, 1946. 8vo. Orig. binding. Fye H-3-574 1983
$30

TROTTER, W.   Instincts of the Herd in Peace and War.
NY: Macmillan, 1916. First edition. Spinal tips and front joint
worn. Review copy, stamp on titlepage. Gach 95-504 1983 $25

TROUETTE, E.   De l'introduction et de l'acclimation
des Quinquinas a l'Ile de la Reunion. Paris, 1879. 8vo, wrappers.
Wheldon 160-2188 1983 £12

TROUP, J. ROSE   With Stanley's Rear Column. London, 1890.
Second edition. Portrait frontis. 8vo. Orig. cloth. Folding map
and 13 plates. Very slightly worn. Good. Edwards 1042-492 1983 £45

TROUP, R. S.   The Silviculture of Indian Trees.
Oxford, 1921. First edition. Folding map, 4 folding tables. 89
coloured plates and numerous illus. 3 vols. 4to. Half morocco by
Paterson of Edinburgh. Good. Edwards 1044-720 1983 £65

TROUP, R. S.   The Silviculture of Indian Trees.
Oxford, 1921. Map, 490 illustrations (many coloured), 3 vols.,
imp. 8vo, new cloth. Trifle used internally. Wheldon 160-2109
1983 £65

TROW CO.   Specimen Book of Type, Borders,
Ornaments, Initials. N.P.: (Trow Co., 1905). Small 8vo.
Full pebbled cloth stamped in blind and gilt. A fine copy.
Oak Knoll 48-370 1983 $25

TROWBRIDGE, JOHN T.   Cudjo's Cave. Boston: Tilton, 1864.
Engraved title. 1st ed., 2nd state. Orig. green cloth, gilt. Small
nick to spine, else a bright copy. Jenkins 155-1225 1983 $60

A TRUE Description of All Trades. Published in Frankfort in the
Year 1568. With six of the illustrations (the printer, the bookbinder, the typefounder, the papermaker, the draughtsman and the
woodcutter) by Jobst Amman. Brooklyn: 1930. 12mo, parchment-
backed decorated bds. One of 400 copies printed in Linotype Granjon
on Kelmscott hand-made paper. Signed, presentation from George W.
Jones, the printer. Perata 28-10 1983 $75

A TRUE Relation of the Unjust, Cruel and Barbarous proceedings
against the English at Amboyna in the East Indies... London: by
Will Bentley for Will Hope..., 1651. 12mo. Engraved frontis.
cont. sheep. Couple of small tears, no loss. Heath 48-588 1983
£150

TRUEMAN, TIMOTHY   The New Jersey Almanack for ... 1779.
Trenton: Isaac Collins, (1778). Stitched. Two inch piece cut from
top of one leaf. Nice. Felcone 19-39 1983 $200

TRUMAN, BEN C.   Occidental Sketches. San Francisco:
San Francisco New Company, 1881. Ads. 1st ed. Orig. cloth. Some
wear. Presentation copy from the author. Jenkins 153-644 1983 $85

TRUMAN, NATHAN E.   Maine de Biran's Philosophy of Will.
Cornell Studies in Philosophy No. 5. NY: Macmillan, 1904. First
edition. Modern black cloth. Gach 94-234 1983 $40

TRUMBO, DALTON　　　　　　Johnny Got His Gun. Philadelphia,
Lippincott, 1939. First edition, fifth printing. Signed and
inscribed by the author, Beverly Hills, November 11, 1940. Fine.
Houle 22-904　1983　$150

TRUMBO, DALTON　　　　　　Johnny Got His Gun. Ph., (1939). Spine
lightly soiled, else very good or better. Quill & Brush 54-1382　1983
$30

TRUMBO, DALTON　　　　　　The Remarkable Mr. Andrew. Philadelphia:
Lippincott, (1941). Cloth. First edition. A fine copy in dust
jacket, which shows only slight rubbing at the extremities. Reese
20-1069　1983　$50

TRUMBO, DALTON　　　　　　Washington Jitters. N.Y., Knopf, 1936.
First edition. Dust jacket (a few small nicks) else very good.
Houle 22-905　1983　$75

TRUMBULL, BENJAMIN　　　　　A Plea, in Vindication of the
Connecticut Title to the Contested Lands, Lying West of the Province
of New-York... New Haven, 1774. Errata leaf. Later three-quarter
morocco, very good. Reese 18-107　1983　$300

TRUMBULL, GORDON　　　　　　Names and Portraits of Birds. NY (1888).
Illus, cloth, inner hinges cracked, spine frayed, back cover paint
stained. King 46-691　1983　$25

TRUMBULL, HENRY　　　　　　Life and Adventures of Robert, the
Hermit of Massachusetts, who has Lived 14 Years in a Case, Secluded
from Human Society... Providence, 1829. Color frontis., later
wraps., edges worn, good. Reese 18-644　1983　$135

TRUMBULL, HENRY　　　　　　Life and Adventures of Robert, the
Hermit of Massachusetts. Providence: H. Trumbull, 1829. 3/4
morocco (broken); library markings. First edition. Felcone 21-105
1983　$125

TRUMBULL, JOHN　　　　　　Life and Remarkable Adventures of Isreal
R. Potter. Providence: Printed by Henry Trumbull, 1824. First
edition. Frontis. With errata at foot of final page. Orig. half calf
and marbled boards. A rubbed copy with marginal tears in a few leaves.
Jenkins 152-767　1983　$350

TRUMBULL, JOHN　　　　　　Poetical Works. Hartford, 1820.
Port., extra engr. titles, 4 copperplates after Tisdale, 2 vols.,
8vo lea., worn, some foxing & pencil notes. 1st collected ed.,
with half-titles. Argosy 710-466　1983　$75

TRUMBULL, JOHN　　　　　　The Poetical Works of... Hartford:
Samuel Goodrich, 1820. Two vols. bound in one. Three quarter
pebbled morocco. Frontis. Engraved title, first edition. Illus.
Front hinge reinforced internally, else a very good copy. Reese
18-547　1983　$45

TRUSLER, JOHN　　　　　　A Description of the Road from London
to Bath and Bristol. London: by Shepperson & Co..., 1797. 8vo.
Slightly discoloured. Stitched as issued, uncut. Heath 48-574
1983　£65

TRUTH opposed to fiction. Or, an impartial and authentic review of
the life of the late Right Honourable the Earl of Barrymore...by a
personal observer. London: printed for C. and G. Kearsley, 1793.
8vo, wrappers, 1st edition. With a frontis. portrait. An uncut copy.
Scarce. Ximenes 64-546　1983　$225

THE TRYAL of Spencer Cowper, SQ. London, 1699. Folio. Half-calf.
Title soiled. Gurney JJ-405　1983　£120

TRYE, CHARLES BRANDON　　　　　Remarks on Morbid Retentions of Urine.
Glocester: Printed by R. Raikes, 1784. 8vo, 2 folding engraved
plates, library stamps on the plates, cont. calf, rebacked,
presentation inscription by the author on the front fly. First
edition. Bickersteth 77-325　1983　£48

TSCHUDY, JEAN J. C. R. BARON DE　　Essai sur la Greffe de l'Herbe
des Plantes et des Arbres. Metz: chez Antoine, 1819. First edition.
8vo. Boards. Folding engraved plate. Light waterstains. Heath
48-16　1983　£40

TSIMMERMAN, EDUARD R.　　　　　Puteschestvie Po Amerikie, 1869-1870.
Moscow: K.J. Goldatenkov, 1872. Contemp. green marbled boards. 3rd
ed. A great rarity. Jenkins 153-645　1983　$3500

TSUJI, K.　　　　　　Practical Poultry Husbandry. Toyohashi
City, 1980. 131 illus. and 133 graphs and tables, 8vo, cloth. Wheldon
160-903　1983　£47

TUBINO, FRANCISCO M.　　　　　Pablo de Cespedes. Madrid, 1868.
Chart. Map. Large 4to. New cloth. Presentation copy, inscribed
by the author. Ars Libri 32-86　1983　$100

TUCKER, BEVERLY　　　　　　The Partisan Leader. N.Y., 1861.
2 vols., small 8vo, orig. pr. wrs. Argosy 716-89　1983　$35

TUCKER, GEORGE　　　　　　A dissertation on Slavery: with a
Proposal for the Gradual Abolition of It, in the State of Virginia.
NY: reprinted, 1861. Pr. wrs. Argosy 710-27　1983　$25

TUCKER, HENRY ST. GEORGE　　　　Memorials of Indian Government. London,
1853. Straight-grain morocco, some wear. Rebacked with the Tucker
Arms stamped in gilt on boards. 8vo. Good. Edwards 1044-721　1983
£55

TUCKER, HENRY ST. GEORGE　　　　Reflections On The Present State Of
Great Britain. Edinburgh: Archibald Constable, and Longman, Hurst,
Rees, Orme, and Brown, London, 1813. 1st ed., 8vo, occasional
inked marginalia, cont. marbled boards, rebacked, rubbed, bookplate.
Rare. Pickering & Chatto 21-130　1983　$385

TUCKER, J. C.　　　　　　To the Golden Goal and Other Sketches.
San Francisco: William Doxey, 1895. Frontis. portrait. Illus. Orig.
pictorial cloth. Covers worn. Fairly nice. Jenkins 152-475　1983
$250

TUCKER, JOSIAH　　　　　　Four Tracts, on Political and Commercial
Subjects. Gloucester, England, 1776. Quarter-leather and boards,
hinge starting. Very good. Reese 18-117　1983　$135

TUCKER, JOSIAH　　　　　　A Series of Answers to Certain Popular
Objections, Against Separating from the Rebellious Colonies,
and Discarding them Entirely... Glocester: R. Raikes, 1776.
Uncut. Later wraps. First edition. Felcone 21-106　1983　$100

TUCKER, JOSIAH　　　　　　Tract V. The Respective Pleas
and Arguments of the Mother Country, and of the Colonies, Distinctly
set Forth... Glocester, Raikes, 1776. Second edition. Dbd.
Ginsberg 46-12　1983　$100

TUCKER, SARAH　　　　　　Abbeokuta; or Sunrise within the Tropics:
an Outline of the Origine and Progress of the Yoruba Mission. London:
James Nisbet, 1853. First edition, 12mo, cont. calf gilt, rebacked.
Folding map, six plates, two of them in color. Advertisement leaf.
A very good copy. Trebizond 18-165　1983　$200

TUCKER, SARAH　　　　　　Abbeokuta. London: James Nisbet &
Co., 1853. Third edition. 12mo. Folding map, plan, 6 plates (2
colored). Orig. blue cloth. Rubbed, spine ends worn. Adelson
Africa-141　1983　$100

TUCKER, SARAH　　　　　　South Indian Sketches. London, 1842.
2 parts bound in one. 3 maps, 1 folding, frontis., illus. Sm.8vo.
Half calf, label, gilt. With the bookplate of the Marquess of Tweeddale. Good. Edwards 1044-723　1983　£50

TUCKER, T. G.　　　　　　Life in the Roman World of Nero and St.
Paul. NY, 1917. 8vo, cloth. Salloch 385-260　1983　$35

TUCKER, W. R.　　　　　　A Short Account of the Outram Statue.
Calcutta, 1879. Plan, 3 plates of tipped-in photographs. 4to.
Pictorial cloth. Inscribed in pencil on title. Good. Edwards 1044-
722　1983　£35

TUCKERMAN, FREDERICK GODDARD　The Cricket. (N.p.): Cummington Press,
1950. Tall narrow quarto. First edition. One of 290 copies. About
fine. Reese 20-1070　1983　$60

TUCKERMAN, FREDERICK GODDARD The Sonnets of Frederick Goddard Tuckerman. New York, 1931. Edited with an intro. and notes by Witter Bynner. 8vo. Cloth, boards. Fine copy. In Our Time 156-811 1983 $35

TUCKERMAN, JOSEPH The Distinctive Character and Claims of Christianity: A Sermon Preached...in New-Bedford, Dec. 17, 1823. New Bedford, 1824. Dsb. Very good. Reese 18-582 1983 $25

TUCKEY, JAMES HINGSTON Narrative of an Expedition to Explore the River Zaire... London: John Murray, 1818. 4to, folding map, 13 plates (1 coloured). Half brown calf, marbled boards. Lightly rubbed, some browning to plates. Adelson Africa-142 1983 $350

TUCZEK, FRANZ Beitrage zur Pathologischen Anatomie und zur Pathologie der Dementia Paralytica. Berlin, 1884. 3 folding lithographic plates. Thin 8vo, cloth backed boards. First edition. Argosy 713-544 1983 $35

TUER, ANDREW W. Bartolozzi and His Works. London: Field & Tuer, 1881. 2 vols. in 4. 18 hinged tipped-in plates. Large 4to. Full leather. No. 32 of the Collector's Edition, limited to 50 copies, signed in the colophon by the author. Binding somewhat rubbed. Ars Libri 32-22 1983 $250

TUER, ANDREW W. History of the Horn Book. London: Leadenhall Press, 1896. 2 vols. 4to, with frontis., numerous illus., partly full-page, 7 horn-books in pocket flaps. Full gilt vellum. Bookplate of Joseph Y. Jeanes, Philadelphia, in each vol. First edition. Rostenberg 88-47 1983 $850

TUER, ANDREW W. Old London Street Cries... New York: Old London Street Company, 1887. First U.S. edition. 12mo. Orig. boards, paper cover label, cord-ties. Frontis. Spine missing. Other than the cover wear, a very good copy internally. Oak Knoll 48-363 1983 $25

TUER, ANDREW W. Stories from Old-Fashioned Children's Books. Leadenhall Press, 1899-1900. 33pp adverts. Dark blue cloth gilt, t.e.g. others uncut, eps. some foxing. Adorned with 250 cuts. Very good. Hodgkins 27-206 1983 £30

TUGWELL, GEORGE On the mountain: being the Welsh experiences of Abraham Black and Jonas White... London: Bentley, 1862. First edition. 8vo. Orig. violet-blue cloth. Bookplate removed. Ximenes 63-641 1983 $45

TUKE, DANIEL HACK (1827-1895) Illustrations of the Influence of the Mind Upon the Body. Philadelphia: Henry C. Lea, 1873 (1872). Modern blue cloth, leather lable, library stamp on title. Gach 95-505 1983 $60

TUKE, DANIEL HACK (1827-1895) Illustrations of the Influence of the mind upon the body... London: Churchill, 1884. Second edition, re-vised. 2 vols. 8vo. Orig. dark blue cloth. Frontis. in each vol. A little rubbed. Some light spotting. Ximenes 63-296 1983 $125

TUKE, DANIEL HACK (1827-1895) Illustrations of the Influence of the Mind upon the Body in Health and Disease. Phila., 1884. 8vo. Orig. cloth. Argosy 713-545 1983 $85

TUKE, DANIEL HACK (1827-1895) Insanity in Ancient and Modern Life. London, 1878. First edition. Sm. 8vo. Light cover stains. Lacks front endleaf. Morrill 289-237 1983 $32.50

TUKE, J. BATTY The Insanity of Over-Exertion of the Brain. Edinburgh: Oliver & Boyd, (1894). First edition. Folding color frontis. Gach 95-506 1983 $50

TUKE, JAMES A Visit to Connaught in the Autumn of 1847. Charles Gilpin; York: John L. Linney, 1848. 2nd edition. Sl. tear to title with no loss. Stabbed pamphlet as issued. Jarndyce 31-207 1983 £58

TULANE UNIVERSITY Tribes and Temples. New Orleans, 1926-1927. 2 vols. 7 folding plates and maps. 347 text illus. 4to. Cloth. Ars Libri 34-384 1983 $85

TULLY, RICHARD Narrative of a ten years' residence at Tripoli in Africa. London: Henry Colburn, 1817. Second edition. 4to. Folding map. 7 hand-colored plates. Modern 1/2 tan calf, marbled boards. Adelson Africa-143 1983 $450

TUMBLETY, FRANCIS A Few Passages in the Life of... Cincinnati: by the author, 1866. 12mo, orig. pr. pict. wraps. Argosy 716-243 1983 $50

TUNIS, W. E. Tunis's Topographical and Pictorial Guide to Niagara... Niagara Falls, (N.Y.): W.E. Tunis, 1856. 15 1/2cm. 4 folding plates and 2 folding maps, frontis. and 14 views, text illustrations. Orig. blind stamped brown cloth, gilt titles on the upper cover. A very good copy. Very scarce. McGahern 53-166 1983 $200

TUNNICLIFFE, WILLIAM A Topographical Survey of the Counties of Somerset, Gloucester, Worcester, Stafford, Chester, and Lancaster. Bath, printed and sold by R. Cruttwell, 1789. 2nd ed., 8vo, 6 large folding engraved maps, 56 engraved plates, full tree calf, gilt, black morocco label, marbled endpapers, one joint cracked, some maps trifle trimmed in margins and with two or three small tears in inner margins repaired, slight fraying and creasing to margins of one or two maps, 2 plates soiled. Deighton 3-287 1983 £185

TUPPER, CHARLES Recollections of Sixty Years in Canada. London, N.Y., Toronto, Melbourne: Cassell, 1914. 22 1/2cm. Wanting the front free fly, lib. stamp on the rear endpaper else fine. McGahern 53-191 1983 $35

TUPPER, FERDINAND BROCK The History of Guernsey and its Bailiwick. Guernsey, 1876. Second edition. 7 collotype plates, covers rather faded. K Books 301-181 1983 £45

TUPPER, MARTIN FARQUHAR A Modern Pyramid. London: Joseph Rickerby, 1839. First edition. Orig. cloth. Corners very slightly bumped. Bookseller's stamp on endpaper. Near-fine. MacManus 280-5318 1983 $125

TUPPER, MARTIN FARQUHAR Proverbial Philosophy. Joseph Rickerby, 1839. 3rd edition, half title, 4 pp ads. Orig. brown cloth, v.g. Jarndyce 30-863 1983 £10.50

TUPPER, MARTIN FARQUHAR Proverbial Philosophy. London: Hatchard, 1855. 21st edition. Small 8vo. Adv. leaf, uncut in original dark green cloth elegantly stamped in blind, spine slightly faded and with very short nick at head. A fine clean and crisp copy. Bookplates. Deighton 3-288 1983 £15

TUPPER, MARTIN FARQUHAR Proverbial Philosophy. Moxon, 1867. New edn. with 65 illus. by Gustave Dore, H.N. Humphries, Tenniel, Gilbert, Tupper, et al. (1st & 2nd series) Green decor. cloth gilt, bevelled boards, a.e.g. (eps. cracked at hinges corners sl. worn, occ. foxing, p.vii has sml. tear at fore-edge), autographed note from author tipped in, v.g. Hodgkins 27-335 1983 £30

TUPPER, MARTIN FARQUHAR Stephan Langton. London: Hurst & Black-ett, (1858). First edition. 2 vols. Full cont. calf with morocco labels on spines. Presentation copy, inscribed on a special inserted leaf in each volume to William John Evelyn, dated Dec. 2, 1858. Leather bookplates. Fine. MacManus 280-5319 1983 $175

TURBERVILLE, A. S. Johnson's England. Oxford: Clarendon Press, 1933. First edition. 2 vols. Orig. cloth. Dust jackets (spines faded). Rather worn publisher's box. Fine. MacManus 279-3000 1983 $75

THE TURF. Henry Colburn and Richard Bentley, 1831. First edition. Half titles, 4 pp ads. vol. II. Foxing to L and M vol. I. Uncut. Orig. boards, paper spines sl. chipped, paper labels. Jarndyce 30-283 1983 £72

TURGENEV, IVAN Pervoe Sobrianie 1840-1883. St. Peters-burg: Tip M. M. Stasiulibicha, 1884. Cont. half calf and boards. First edition. A very good copy, complete with the half-title. Reese 20-1071 1983 $100

TURGENEV, IVAN Smoke: Or the Life at Baden. London: Richard Bentley, 1868. First English edition. 2 vols. Frontis. Orig. cloth. Spine and covers a bit worn and faded. Front inner hinge of Vol. I slightly cracking. Former owner's signature. Good. MacManus 280-5321 1983 $225

TURGENEV, IVAN　　　　　　Torrents of Spring. A. Colish, 1976.
8vo, 8 full-page colour illus. and 12 black and white illus. by
Lajos Szalay. Qtr. green morocco lettered in gilt over marbled
paper boards, tiny natural flaw in spine, otherwise fine in slipcase. 1,600 numbered copies signed by Szalay. Deighton 3-289 1985
£36

TURGOT, ANNE ROBERT JACQUES　Oeuvres De Turgot. Paris: Guillaumin,
1844. 2nd ed., large 8vo, 2 vols., frontis. portrait to vol. I,
some light browning, original calf backed boards, joints neatly
repaired. Pickering & Chatto 21-131 1983 $300

TURNBULL, JOHN　　　　　　A voyage round the world... London:
A. Maxwell, 1813. Second edition. 4to. Half calf, spine gilt.
Half-title present. A fine copy. Ximenes 63-611 1983 $1,200

TURNER, FRANCIS　　　　　　Dies Academica. Cambridge: Reprinted
for private circulation only..., at the University Press, 1869. 4to.
Boards, cloth spine. Limited edition of 150 copies. Traylen 94-838
1983 £30

TURNER, FRANCIS　　　　　　Dies Academica. 1869. (1935?). 8vo,
boards with cloth spine. Ltd. to 150 numbered copies. Bickersteth
75-187 1983 £12

TURNER, FREDERICK JACKSON　Rueben Gold Thwaites, a Memorial Address.
Madison, 1914. Frontis. Cloth, near fine. Reese 19-559 1983 $75

TURNER, FREDERICK JACKSON　Reuben Gold Thwaites. Madison: State
Historical Society of Wisconsin, 1914. Frontis. portrait of Thwaites.
Also included is a bibliography of Thwaites' works. Jenkins 152-476
1983 $35

TURNER, FREDERICK JACKSON　The Significance of Sections in American
History. NY, (1932). Argosy 716-198 1983 $35

TURNER, FREDERICK JACKSON　The Significance of Sections in
American History. N.Y., (1932). Backstrip faded. Argosy 716-623
1983 $20

TURNER, FREDERICK JACKSON　The United States, 1830-1850. NY, (1935).
Port., maps. Argosy 716-199 1983 $35

TURNER, GEORGE　　　　　　Mary Stuart, Forgotten Forgeries. (1933).
8vo, portrait, orig. cloth, first edition. Bickersteth 77-177 1983
£15

TURNER, HATTON　　　　　　Astra Castra. London, 1865. Frontis.
33 plates, 5 portrait plates, illus. in text. 4to. Cont. brown
boards. Worn, rebacked in black leather. Red morocco label. Uncut.
Bookplate. Good. Edwards 1042-612 1983 £190

TURNER, HENRY SMITH　　　　The Original Journals of... Norman,
1966. Plates. 1st ed. in dj. Jenkins 153-647 1983 $20

TURNER, JAMES A.　　　　　To Learn To Sing... (Boston, 1752).
16mo., printed two up. 1st and only known ed. Orig. plain front
wrapper with 1760 owner's inscription, sewn. Near fine copy.
Jenkins 155-1226 1983 $850

TURNER, THOMAS　　　　　　Narrative of a Journey associated
with a Fly... London: for Private Distribution only, 1840. 8vo.
Half title. Orig. quarter roan, gilt. Engraved plates. Presentation
copy to Mrs. Raikes. Some light foxing and discolouring, light
wear to calf. Heath 48-575 1983 £75

TURNER, W.　　　　　　　　Report on the Human Crania. 1884-86.
10 plates, 2 parts, 4to, new wrappers. Wheldon 160-298 1983 £18

TURNER, W. J.　　　　　　Blow for Balloons, Being The First
Hemisphere of The History of Henry Airbubble. London: J.M. Dent &
Sons Ltd., (1935). First edition. 8vo. Orig. cloth. Dust jacket
designed by E. Bawden. Fine copy. Jaffe 1-379 1983 $65

TURNER, WILLIAM　　　　　The Names of Herbes a.d. 1548. London,
1881. 8vo. Orig. cloth. Gurney JJ-409 1983 £25

TURNEY, IDA VIRGINIA　　　Paul Bunyon Comes West. (Portland,
ca. 1920). Woodcut illus. & border designs. Sq. 8vo, pr. wrs.,
tied. Printed on uncut rag paper. Argosy 710-600 1983 $30

TURQUAN, J.　　　　　　　The Sisters of Napoleon. London, 1908.
Photogravure frontis. 8vo, orig. cloth. 33 plates, very slightly
faded. Some slight foxing throughout. Bookplate. Good. Edwards
1042-494 1983 £15

TURRECREMATA, JOANNES DE
Please turn to
TORQUEMADA, JUAN DE

TURRELL, CHARLES　　　　　Miniatures. London, 1912. Lg. 4to, full
English vellum, elaborate designes and lettering in gilt, a.e.g. One
of 100 copies signed by the artist. Fine. Perata 28-174 1983 $300

TURRILL, GARDNER S.　　　　A Tale of the Yellowstone. Turrill,
1901. Illus., about 100 views. Orig. pictorial cloth, front cover
soiled, rear cover stained. First edition. Ginsberg 47-1002 1983
$175

TUSSER, THOMAS　　　　　　Five hundred pointes of good husbandrie...
London: Henrie Denham, 1580. Woodcut border of title. Printer's
device at end. Small 4to. Calf. A fine copy. Kraus 164-243 1983
$2,200

TUTCHIN, JOHN　　　　　　The Western Martyrology... London:
for John Marshall, 1705. Fifth edition. 8vo. Engraved frontis.
Cont. calf, rebacked. Slight damage where corner of frontis. has
stuck to title. Heath 48-215 1983 £55

TUTHILL, FRANKLIN　　　　　The History of California. San Fran.:
H.H. Bancroft, 1866. First edition. Some fading and chipping to
spine. Jenkins 153-109 1983 $85

TUTT, J. W.　　　　　　　British Moths. 1902. 12 coloured plates,
cr. 8vo, prize calf, gilt (slightly rubbed). Ms. captions added to
some plates. Wheldon 160-1181 1983 £12

TUTTLE, CHARLES RICHARD　　General History of the State of Michigan.
Detroit, 1873. Original cloth. First edition. Jenkins 151-216
1983 $100

TUTTLE, CHARLES RICHARD　　General History of the State of
Michigan. Detroit, 1873. Illus., nicely rebound in green lea. back.
Cloth, bookplate, minor wear. King 46-197 1983 $35

TWAIN, MARK, PSEUD.
Please turn to
CLEMENS, SAMUEL LANGHORNE

TWAINIANA Notes from the Annotations of Walter Bliss. Hartford, Conn.:
1930. Edited with an introduction by Francis M. Edwards. 12mo, blue
cloth, gilt. One of 1000 copies. Fine. Perata 28-175 1983 $30

TWEDDELL, GEORGE MARKHAM　　Furness, Past and Present. Barrow-in-
Furness, 1870-80. 2 vols. in one, numerous illus. including coloured
and tinted lithographs, maps, text illus., thick 4to, gilt-edges,
half green morocco. K Books 307-182 1983 £125

TWEEDDALE, ARTHUR, MARQUIS OF　A List of the Birds Known to Inhabit
the Philippine Archipelago. Trans. Zoo. Soc., 1875. 4to, half morocco. Wheldon 160-907 1983 £20

TWEEDALE, VIOLET　　　　　The Veiled Woman. London: Herbert Jenkins, 1918. First edition. Orig. cloth. Presentation copy to Lady
Conan Doyle inscribed: "To Lady Conan Doyle in affectionate rememberance of February 23rd, 1923 from Violet Tweedale". Covers worn and
faded, contents slightly shaken. Good. MacManus 278-1641 1983 $125

TWELVE Jews. London: Rich & Cowan Limited, 1934. First edition.
8vo. Illus. Orig. cloth. Dust jacket. Spine of jacket slightly
darkened, upper edge worn, but a very good copy. Jaffe 1-15 1983
$85

20 FACTS About Redlands. Redlands, Ca., ca. 1910. Illus. Orig. wraps. First edition. Ginsberg 47-193 1983 $25

25 CHANSONS de la Vieille France. Stuttgart, n.d. Small 8vo, 1/2 cloth over pictorial boards. Illus. Salloch 387-258 1983 $25

TWICHELL, HORACE E.   History of Minisink Country. (Port Jervis, 1912). Illus., cloth with photo. front. Privately printed. Argosy 710-368 1983 $30

TWIGDEN, B. L.   Pisces Tropicani. Melbourne, 1979. Quarter calf, coloured plates, folio. Edition limited to 350 numbered and signed copies. Wheldon 160-109 1983 £125

TWITCHELL, RALPH E.   The History of the Military Occupation of the Territory of New Mexico from 1846-1851. 8vo, illus. Pict. plate on cover. Argosy 716-339 1983 $40

TWITCHELL, RALPH E.   The Military Occupation of New Mexico. Denver: Smith and Brooks, 1909. Illus. Orig. cloth with pictorial paper label on front cover. Some spotting. 1st ed. Fine. Jenkins 153-395 1983 $75

TWITCHELL, RALPH E.   Old Santa Fe... Santa Fe, 1925. Orig. pictorial cloth. Plates. 1st ed. A limited and numbered ed. Jenkins 153-396 1983 $125

221B Studies in Sherlock Holmes By Various Hands. NY, 1940. First edition. Cloth, ink name, spine slightly darkened, some light wear, else a very good copy. King 46-278 1983 $50

THE TWO Putnams, Israel and Rufus in the Havana Expedition 1762. Hartford: Conn. Histo. Soc., 1931. 8vo, 2 prts., cloth-backed boards, boxed. Argosy 710-127 1983 $35

TYLER, DANIEL   A Concise History of the Mormon Battalion in the Mexican War. 1846-1847. Orig. full presentation leather. First edition. Ginsberg 47-888 1983 $250

TYLER, DANIEL   A Concise History of the Mormon Battalion. N.p., 1881. Original full morocco, some wear to corners, fairly nice copy. Jenkins 151-341 1983 $225

TYLER, JOHN   Message from...Communicating...Copies of Correspondence with the Government of Mexico. Wash., 1842. Half morocco. First edition. Ginsberg 46-740 1983 $125

TYLER, JOHN   Message from... Communicating Copies of Correspondence with the Government of Mexico... Wash., 1844. Dbd. Ginsberg 47-194 1983 $25

TYLER, JOHN   Message from...Transmitting the Correspondence in Relation to the Proceedings and Conduct of the Choctaw Commission, Under the Treaty of Dancing Rabbit Creek. Wash., 1844. Cloth with leather label. First edition. Ginsberg 46-182 1983 $75

TYLER, JOHN   Message from the President of the United States. Wash., 1842. Folded tables. Dbd. First edition. Ginsberg 47-879 1983 $45

TYLER, JOSIAH   Livingstone Lost and Found, or Africa and its Explorers. Hartford, Conn.: Mutual Pub. Co., 1873. Tall thick 8vo, index. Orig. green gilt-stamped cloth. Karmiole 76-1 1983 $65

TYLER, LYON G.   The Cradle of the Republic. Richmond, Va., 1906. Second edition, with a frontis., 2 folding maps and nearly 100 other illus., 8vo, orig. cloth, gilt. Fenning 61-456 1983 £10

TYLER, MASON WHITING   Recollections of the Civil War. New York, 1912. First edition. Maps and illustrations. 8vo, unopened, dust wrapper, fine. Morrill 290-548 1983 $22.50

TYLER, MOSES COIT   The Literary History of the American Revolution, 1763-83. N.Y., 1941. 2 vols. Argosy 716-478 1983 $35

TYLER, PARKER   Chaplin. New York: Vanguard, (1948). Cloth. First edition. Illus, Pub.'s review copy, with slip laid in. Fine in dust jacket, with small mend at top edge of rear panel. Reese 20-1078 1983 $35

TYLER, PARKER   Florine Stettheimer. A life in art. New York: Farrar, Straus, 1963. 66 plates (10 color). 4to. Cloth. Dust jacket. Ars Libri 32-646 1983 $75

TYLER, PARKER   The Granite Butterfly. (N.p.): Bern Porter, 1945. Large quarto. Pictorial wraps. First edition. One of 494 numbered copies (of 502). There is some slight fraying of the overlap edges, and two small stains, otherwise an internally fine copy. This copy is signed by Tyler, and as well inscribed by him to Cleanth Brooks. Reese 20-1076 1983 $100

TYLER, PARKER   A Little Boy Lost. New York: Prospero Pamphlets, 1947. Pictorial wraps. First edition. One of 400 copies (of 420). Fine. Reese 20-1077 1983 $40

TYNAN, KATHERINE
Please turn to
HINKSON, KATHERINE TYNAN

TYNDALL, JOHN   Essays on the Floating-Matter of the Air in Relation to Putrefaction and Infection. Longmans, Green & Co., London, 1881. 8vo, with wood-engravings in text; orig. cloth, slightly faded. First edition. Quaritch NS 5-108 1983 $450

TYNDALL, JOHN   Faraday as a Discoverer. London: Longmans, 1868. 8vo. Orig. cloth. First edition. 2 portraits. Spine slightly warped, otherwise a fine copy. Zeitlin 264-144 1983 $110

TYNDALL, JOHN   Faraday as a Discoverer. London: Longmans, 1870. New edition. 8vo. Orig. cloth. 2 portraits. Dampstained. Zeitlin 264-145 1983 $40

TYNDALL, JOHN   Fragments of Science for Unscientific People. London: Longmans, Green, 1871. Ads. Publisher's purple cloth, spine faded, joints rubbed. Very good copy. First edition. Gach 95-507 1983 $75

A TYPICAL American; or Incidents in the Life of Dr. Swinburne of Albany... Albany, 1888. First edition. 8vo. Orig. binding. Fye H-3-968 1983 $25

TYRANNY triumphant! And liberty lost; the muses run mad; Apollo struck dumb; and all Covent-Garden confounded. London: printed for G. Lyon, 1743. 8vo, wrappers, first edition. Very scarce. Title a little dusty, else a very good copy. Ximenes 64-549 1983 $375

TYRRELL, F.   Waterways and Railways. London, 1874. Large folding map. Sm.8vo. Spine faded. Orig. cloth. Good. Edwards 1044-725 1983 £25

TYSON, LIEUTENANT   Le Poalaris: le Radeau de Glace, 1870-3. (Paris, 1875). Illus. with wood engravings, small folio, wrs. Argosy 710-11 1983 $35

TYTLER, ALEXANDER FRASER   Essay on the principles of translation. London: Cadell and Davies, 1797. Second edition, corrected and enlarged. 8vo. Cont. half calf. Spine gilt. Front hinge tender. Scarce. Ximenes 63-252 1983 $100

TYTLER, JAMES   A Treatise on the Plague and Yellow Fever. Salem: Joshua Cushing for B.B. Macanulty, 1799. Errata. Part of folding table lacking. Full calf. Front endsheet wanting. First edition. Felcone 22-147 1983 $85

TYTLER, SARAH, PSEUD.
Please turn to
KEDDIE, HENRIETTA

U

UBBELOHDE-DOERING, HEINRICH　Auf den Konigsstrassen der Inka. Berlin: Wasmuth, 1941. 304 plates. 4to. Cloth. Ars Libri 34-509　1983　$40

IICHARD, MARIO　My Uncle Barbassou. London: Vizetelly, 1888. Illus. with 40 etchings by P. Avril. Extra illus. with 18 pen & ink drawings by D. Garber. Fully crushed morocco, t.e.g. Fine. MacManus 280-5325　1983　$75

UDELL, JOHN　Incidents of Travel to California, Across the Great Plains. Jefferson, Ohio, 1856. Frontis. Later three-quarter leather and boards. Fine. Reese 19-560　1983　$850

UDELL, JOHN　Journal Kept During a Trip Across the Plains. Los Angeles, Novak, 1946. First edition thus. Half blue morocco. Illus. with eight plates. One of 35 deluxe copies, signed by the editor. Fine. Houle 21-1167　1983　$135

UEXKULL, J. VON (1864-1944)　Theoretical Biology. NY: Harcourt, 1926. First American edition. Dust jacket slightly worn. Gach 95-508　1983　$35

UKERS, WILLIAM H.　The Romance of Tea. NY: Knopf, 1936. With 58 illus. Green cloth; spine and extremities of front cover faded. Karmiole 73-105　1983　$40

ULLMAN, ALLAN　Sorry Wrong Number. N.Y., Random, 1948. First edition. Dust jacket (creases, slight rubbing) else very good. Advertising sheet for the film starring Barbara Stanwyck laid in loose. Houle 22-912　1983　$27.50

ULMANN, DORIS　A Book of Portraits of the Faculty of the Medical Department of the Johns Hopkins University Baltimore. Baltimore: Johns Hopkins Press, 1922. Folio. Clothbacked, paper covered boards, t.e.g., untrimmed. Printed at the shop of William E. Rudge, Mt. Vernon, N.Y. A very good copy. Very rare. Fye H-3-577　1983　$400

UNAMUNO, MIGUEL DE　The Tragic Sense of Life in Men and in Peoples. London: Macmillan, 1921. Cloth. First edition in English. Slight rubbing at head and toe of spine, else very good. Reese 20-1082 1983　$30

UNDER Canvas. New York, Atlantic Publishing and Engraving Co., 1876. 1st ed. Portrait and 2 plates. 8vo. Contributions by Stephen H. Tyng, Jr., William B. Mucklow, et al. Morrill 288-648　1983　$35

UNDERHILL, GEORGE F.　The Helterskelter Hounds. London: Chapman & Hall, Ltd., 1894. First edition. Illus. by L. Thackeray. Orig. pictorial boards. Bookplate on front endsheet. Covers rubbed. Good. MacManus 280-5326　1983　$50

UNDERHILL, GEORGE F.　Hunting and practical hints for hunting men. London: Bliss, Sands and Co., 1897. First edition. 8vo. Orig. yellow cloth. Fine copy. Ximenes 63-562　1983　$55

UNDERHILL, H. H.　Sailing Ship Rigs and Rigging. Glasgow, 1945. Imperial 8vo. Orig. cloth. Frontis., 48 full page plans, 31 text illus. Slightly worn. Good. Edwards 1042-173　1983　£12

UNDERHILL, JOHN　Gentleman, Soldier of Fortune. NY, 1934. 4to, cloth, paper label. Signed by the designer, B. Hutchinson. Mounted port. & plates. Argosy 716-103　1983　$35

UNDERHILL, RUTH　Pueblo Crafts. Washington: U.S. Department of the Interior, 1944. 98 illus. 4to. Boards, 3/4 cloth. Orig. wrappers bound in. Ars Libri 34-511　1983　$20

UNDERWOOD, MICHAEL　Traite des Maladies des Enfans. Paris, 1786. First French edition. 8vo, cont. mottled calf. Argosy 713-547　1983　$300

UNDSET, SIGRID　Men, Women, and Places. N.Y., Knopf, 1939. First American edition. Dust jacket (small nicks, faded), else very good. Houle 21-552　1983　$37.50

UNGEBAUR, IOHANNES ANDREAS　Dissertatio osteologica de dentitione secunda iuniorum. Leipzig: J.C. Langenheim, 1738. Woodcut initial and head-piece. 1 engraved plate. Small 4to. Cont. stenciled paper backstrip. Light foxing. Plate bound in upside-down. Kraus 164-61　1983　$240

UNGER, FREDERICK WILLIAM　With "Bobs" and Kruger. Philadelphia, 1901. 1st ed. Illus. 8vo, pictorial front cover, mint. Morrill 288-492　1983　$20

THE UNION Pacific Railway, Eastern Division.　Washington: Joseph L. Pearson, 1868. First edition. Large folding map. Printed wrappers, bound into boards and morocco with wrappers preserved. Bradley 66-640　1983　$150

THE UNITED States Army Sanitary Commission. A Succinct Narrative of Its Work and Purposes. New York, 1864. 1st ed. 8vo. Orig. wrappers. Morrill 189-201　1983　$25

THE UNITED States Biographical Dictionary and Portrait Gallery of Eminent and Self-Made Men. Chicago: American Biographical Pub. Co., 1877. Orig. full morocco, gilt with some shelf wear. A.e.g. Frontis. is J.T. Lewis. Nice copy. Jenkins 153-703　1983　$100

UNITED STATES. CONGRESS. HOUSE OF REPRESENTATIVES.　A Bill to Enable the People of Iowa to Form a Constitution and State Government, for the Admission of Such State into the Union. Washington, 1839. Laid in half morocco slipcase. Folio. Jenkins 152-170　1983　$750

UNITED STATES. CONGRESS. HOUSE OF REPRESENTATIVES.　A Bill to Reduce the Duties on Certain, Wines, and to Declare Free of Duty, Books Printed in Foreign Languages. Washington, 1818. Folio. Jenkins 152-175　1983　$150

UNITED STATES. CONGRESS. HOUSE OF REPRESENTATIVES.　Journal of the House of Representatives of the United States, at the First (second) Session of the Second Congress. Philadelphia, 1792-1793. Stitched as issued, fine. 2 vols. Each laid in a folio half morocco slipcase. Reese 18-173　1983　$450

UNITED STATES. CONGRESS. HOUSE OF REPRESENTATIVES.　Military Commission to Europe, in 1855 and 1856. Washington, 1861. Presentation from Alfred Avery Burnham. 21 plates. 4to. Nice. Morrill 287-288 1983　$87.50

UNITED STATES. CONGRESS. SENATE.　A Bill to Organize and Arm the Militia of Oregon. Washington, 1849. Folio. Laid in half morocco case. Jenkins 152-730　1983　$250

UNITED STATES. CONGRESS. SENATE.　Copies of All Reports of the Engineers and Other Persons Employed, to Make Explorations and Surveys...for a Railroad from the Mississippi River to the Pacific Ocean. (Washington), 1854. 2 large folding maps, disbound. Minor dampstains. Very good copy. Bradley 64-130　1983　$30

UNITED STATES. CONGRESS. SENATE.　In Senate of the United States...the Committee on the Memorial of the Legislative Council and House of Representatives of the Mississippi Territory... Washington, 1816. Good. Reese 18-500　1983　$50

UNITED STATES. CONGRESS. SENATE.　Journal of the Senate, 1st Session of the 2nd Congress. Phila.: John Fenno, 1791 (1792). 1st ed. Folio, orig. calf, tear in title with loss of few letters. Argosy 710-424　1983　$150

UNITED STATES. CONGRESS. SENATE.   Journal of the Senate of the United States of America, Being the First Session of the Second Congress. Philadelphia, 1791. Buckram, very good. Reese 18-174 1983 $225

UNITED STATES. CONGRESS. SENATE.   Report of the Expedition to the Black Hills, Under Command of Bvt. Maj. Gen. George A. Custer. Feb. 26, 1875. Clark 741-215 1983 $75

UNITED STATES. CONSTITUTION.   The Constitutions of the United States, According to the Latest Amendments. Philadelphia, 1791. Worn calf, internally good. Reese 18-173 1983 $500

UNITED STATES. CONSTITUTION.   The Declaration of Independence and Constitution of the United States of America. New York: R. Spalding, 1865. 8vo, orig. cloth, blocked in blind, lettered gilt on the upper cover, spine worn at head and foot, and small chip in centre of spine. Bickersteth 77-200 1983 £20

UNITED STATES. DEPARTMENT OF AGRICULTURE.   The Western Range Letter from the Secretary of Agriculture. Wash., 1936. Illus., numerous map and tables. Orig. green printed wraps. Ginsberg 46-164 1983 $100

UNITED STATES. DEPARTMENT OF AGRICULTURE.   The Western Range: Letter from the Secretary of Agriculture. Wash., 1936. Tables. Orig. wraps. Ginsberg 47-911 1983 $75

UNITED STATES. DEPARTMENT OF THE INTERIOR.   Annual Reports of the Department of the Interior for the Fiscal Year Ended June 30, 1898. Wash., HD5, 1898. Folding maps, charts, and illus. Orig. cloth. Jenkins 152-22 1983 $145

UNITED STATES. DEPARTMENT OF THE INTERIOR.   Five Civilized Tribes of Oklahoma. Wash., 1913. Illus. Orig. printed wraps., chipped. Ginsberg 46-591 1983 $50

UNITED STATES. DEPARTMENT OF THE INTERIOR.   Geology and Water Resources of the Eastern Portion of the Panhandle of Texas. Wash., 1906. Later cloth. Illus. Folding maps. Index. Jenkins 152-820 1983 $45

UNITED STATES. DEPARTMENT OF THE INTERIOR.   Indian Affairs in the Territories of Oregon and Washington. Wash., 1858. Dbd. Cloth box. First edition. Ginsberg 46-69 1983 $75

UNITED STATES. LAWS.   Acts Passed at a Congress of the United States of America. New York: Hodge, Allen and Campbell; also T. Floyd, 1789. Full cont. calf (spine label wanting, hinges glued). Felcone 21-107 1983 $300

UNITED STATES. LAWS.   Acts Passed at the Second Session of the Eighth Congress of the United States of America...1804. (Washington? 1805). Stitched in orig. plain wraps., unopened, very good. Reese 18-270 1983 $300

UNITED STATES. LAWS.   The Laws of the United States of America. Philadelphia, 1796. 8vo. 3 vols. Some spotting and embrowning throughout, newly and attractively bound in full, panelled calf, the spines with uniform black morocco labels, gilt-ruled, decorated and labelled. Boswell 7-148 1983 $500

UNITED STATES. LAWS.   Laws of the United States of America. Phila.: R. Folwell, 1796. 2 vols. (of 3). 8vo, cont. calf, (few chips in backstrip, some corners marginally stained). Argosy 716-237 1983 $75

UNITED STATES. LAWS.   Laws of the United States of America. Washington, 1805. 8vo, cont. lea., (some pp foxed). Vols. 7, 8, 9. Argosy 716-238 1983 $85

UNITED STATES. TREASURY DEPARTMENT.   Report of the Secretary of the Treasury... (Philadelphia), 1795. Ten tables on five folded sheets. Printed self-wrappers, sewn. A fine, untrimmed copy. Reese 18-201 1983 $150

UNITED STATES. TREASURY DEPARTMENT.   Report from the Secretary of the Treasury. Wash., 1838. Illus. 12 maps. Cloth with leather label. First edition. Ginsberg 47-486 1983 $50

UNITED STATES. TREASURY DEPARTMENT.   Report of the Secretary of the Treasury, On the State of the Finances for the Year Ending June 30, 1863. Washington: GPO, 1863. Bookplate, lacks f.e.p., minor cover spotting, worn. King 46-77 1983 $20

UNITED STATES. TREATIES.   Treaty Between the United States of America and the Klamath and Moadoc Tribes and Yahooskin Band of Snake Indians. (Washington, 1870). Small folio. Printed self wrappers. Bound into red cloth boards. Text little soiled, shows three horizontal folds, small breaks mended by tape. Bradley 66-560 1983 $200

UNITED STATES. WAR DEPARTMENT.   Letter from the Secretary of War, in Relation to the Construction of a Canal from Lake Erie to Lake Ontario. Wash., 1836. 3 very large folding maps. 4 folding elevation tables. Leather and boards, very good. Reese 19-403 1983 $200

UNITED STATES. WAR DEPARTMENT.   Letter from the Secretary of War...March 31, 1862. Richmond, 1862. Staples, boxed, first edition. Ginsberg 46-200 1983 $100

UNITED STATES. WAR DEPARTMENT.   Letter from...Transmitting... Correspondence Regarding the Apache Inidans. Wash., 1890. Later wrappers. Jenkins 153-732 1983 $55

UNITED STATES. WAR DEPARTMENT.   Letter from the Secretary of War... Transmitting...Reports Relative to the Treatment of Certain Apache Indians. Wash., 1890. Later wrappers. Jenkins 153-731 1983 $45

UNITED STATES. WAR DEPARTMENT.   Letter from the Secretary of War, Transmitting Statements of Expenditure and Application...for the Use of the Military Department... Washington, 1815. 2 folio leaves and folding table. Very good. Reese 18-480 1983 $40

UNITED STATES. WAR DEPARTMENT.   Report from the Secretary of War... in Relation to the Establishment of a Line of Military Posts from the Missouri to the Oregon or Columbia River. Wash., 1840. Folded. Jenkins 153-439 1983 $45

UNITED STATES. WAR DEPARTMENT.   Report from the Secretary of War...in Reference to the Construction of the Potomac Aqueduct. Wash., 1841. Dbd. First edition. Ginsberg 46-649 1983 $25

UNITED STATES. WAR DEPARTMENT.   Report of the Secretary of War... Information Respecting the Purchase of Camels for the Purposes of Military Transportation. Wash., 1857. Folding plate. Illustrated. Original cloth, fine copy. Jenkins 153-111 1983 $125

UNITED STATES. WAR DEPARTMENT.   Report of the Secretary of War (Henry D. Wallen), Communicating...the Report of Captain...of His Expedition, in 1859, from Dalles City to Great Salt Lake, and Back... (Wash., 1860). Illus., folded map. Half morocco. First edition. Ginsberg 47-912 1983 $125

UNITED STATES. WAR DEPARTMENT.   Report of the Secretary of War... Washington, 1871. Cloth, spine somewhat chipped, good. Reese 19-576 1983 $25

UNITED STATES. WAR DEPARTMENT.   Report of the Secretary of War... Relative to the Number and Situation of the Indians on the Frontiers of the United States. Wash., 1836. First edition. Dbd. Ginsberg 46-353 1983 $25

UNIVERSITY OF PENNSYLVANIA. DEPARTMENT OF ARCHAEOLOGY AND PALAEONTOLOGY.   Objects used in religious ceremonies and charms and implements for divination. Philadelphia, 1892. Wrappers. Presentation copy from the editor, Stewart Culin. Ars Libri 34-60 1983 $40

UNONIUS, GUSTAF   Minnen Fran en Sjuttonarig Vistelse I Nordvestra Amerika. Upsala, 1862. 3 vols. in 2. Half morocco, orig. printed wrappers bound in. Illus. Jenkins 153-651 1983 $250

UNTERMEYER, JEAN STARR   Private Collection. New York, 1965.
8vo. Cloth. Inscribed by author to her ex-husband Louis Untermeyer
dated Jan. 7, 1965. Clipping about poet's death pasted in by Louis
Untermeyer. Fine in lightly worn dj. In Our Time 156-826 1983
$150

UNTERMEYER, JEAN STARR   Steep Ascent. New York, 1927. 8vo.
Cloth. Inscribed by the poet to her husband Louis Untermeyer:
"To Louis-no ascent is too steep if I shall find him on the summit
Jean 1928." Some very light spotting to cloth, mainly a fine copy.
In Our Time 156-823 1983 $150

UNTERMEYER, JEAN STARR   Steep Ascent. New York, 1927. 8vo.
Cloth. Inscribed and dated Dec. 1928. In Our Time 156-824 1983
$50

UNTERMEYER, JEAN STARR   Winged Child. New York, 1936. 8vo.
Cloth. Inscribed by poet to her husband: "For Louis and December
twenty-sixth Jean Christmas 1936." Tipped into the rear is a two
and one-half page ALS from Jean to Louis. With envelope. Fine in
lightly worn dj. In Our Time 156-825 1983 $175

UNTERMEYER, LOUIS   "...and Other Poets". New York, 1916.
8vo. Cloth. A copy used by Untermeyer for a possible later ed.
Signed by Untermeyer on front fly and dated Feb. 1916. Untermeyer
has noted that there are corrections on pages 41, 51, 46, 42. With
holograph corrections by same. On endboard Untermeyer has pasted a
caricature of himself by William Rose Benet. Fine in dj. In Our
Time 156-829 1983 $150

UNTERMEYER, LOUIS   "...and Other Poets". New York, 1916.
8vo. Cloth. An author's copy of the book, signed by Untermeyer on
front flyleaf and with his bookplate. Fine in dj which has some light
wear. In Our Time 156-828 1983 $100

UNTERMEYER, LOUIS   First Love. Boston: Sherman, French &
Company, 1911. Cloth and boards. First edition. Pub.'s prospectus
laid in. Inscribed by the author at a later date. The spine is
slightly soiled, but a very good copy. Reese 20-1084 1983 $75

UNTERMEYER, LOUIS   Roast Leviathan. New York (1923). 8vo.
Cloth. Inscribed by Untermeyer to Alexander Laing. Spine faded, else
vg-fine. In Our Time 156-830 1983 $25

UNTERMEYER, LOUIS   The Younger Quire. NY: The Moods
Publishing Co., 1911. Of an edition of 100, 1/10 signed by Under-
meyer. Inscribed to William Braithwaite. Cream boards rubbed and
soiled. Bromer 25-121 1983 $200

UNWIN, WILLIAM J.   Education, the Work of the People.
Ward & Co., (1856). First edition, stabbed pamphlet as issued, v.g.
Jarndyce 31-158 1983 £16.50

UPDIKE, DANIEL BERKELEY   On the Dedications of American Churches.
Cambridge: Riverside Press, 1891. First edition. Tall 8vo. Orig.
paper front wrapper, spine and black wrapper missing. Except for
binding, a fine copy. Oak Knoll 48-375 1983 $55

UPDIKE, DANIEL BERKELEY   Printing Types, Their History Forms,
and Use. Cambridge: Harvard University Press, 1951. Second
printing of second, revised edition. 8vo. Cloth. Dust jackets.
Well illus. Some chipping and soiling of jackets. Oak Knoll 49-
385 1983 $75

UPDIKE, JOHN   Assorted Prose. New York, 1965. 8vo.
Cloth. One of a small number of copies issued with an extra leaf
tipped in and signed by Updike. Fine copy in dj. In Our Time
156-834 1983 $300

UPDIKE, JOHN   Bech: A Book. NY, 1970. Limited to
500 specially bound, numbered and signed copies, faint red "H" stamp
on red endpaper, else fine in fine dustwrapper in fine slipcase.
Quill & Brush 54-1417 1983 $100

UPDIKE, JOHN   Bech: A Book. NY, 1970. Limited to
500 specially bound, numbered and signed copies, crease on front end
paper, owner's name and address on half-title, very good, dustwrapper
and slipcase very good. Quill & Brush 54-1418 1983 $75

UPDIKE, JOHN   Bech: A Book. New York: Knopf, 1970.
1st ed., 1 of 500 numbered and signed copies. Orig. cloth, dj,
boxed. Mint copy. Jenkins 155-1228 1983 $75

UPDIKE, JOHN   The Coup. New York, 1978. 8vo. Wraps.
Uncorrected proof copy. Names of a few reviewers on front wrapper,
a fine copy. In Our Time 156-835 1983 $250

UPDIKE, JOHN   Ego and Art in Walt Whitman. New York:
Targ Editions, 1980. Cloth and patterned boards. First edition in
book form. One of 350 numbered copies, printed at the Bird & Bull
Press, and signed by the author. Mint as issued in plain dust jacket.
Reese 20-106 1983 $75

UPDIKE, JOHN   Midpoint and Other Poems. NY, 1969.
Limited to 500 specially bound, numbered and signed copies, mint in
mint dustwrapper in fine slipcase. Quill & Brush 54-1419 1983
$125

UPDIKE, JOHN   The Music School. New York, 1966.
8vo. Cloth. 1st ed., 1st issue with transposed lines on p. 46.
A copy for review with publicity photo of Updike tipped in and
publisher's slip laid in giving date and price of publication. Fine
copy in dj. In Our Time 156-833 1983 $200

UPDIKE, JOHN   People One Knows. CA, 1908. Limited to
100 numbered and signed deluxe copies, mint in mint slipcase. Quill &
Brush 54-1421 1983 $100

UPDIKE, JOHN   Problems, and Other Stories. New York:
Knopf, 1979. 1st ed., limited to 350 numbered and signed copies.
Orig. cloth, dj, boxed. Mint copy. Jenkins 155-1235 1983 $75

UPDIKE, JOHN   Problems and Other Stories. N.Y., 1979.
First edition. Limited to 350 numbered copies, signed by author.
Cloth. Dust wrapper and slipcase. Very good. King 45-272 1983 $75

UPDIKE, JOHN   The Same Door. NY, 1959. Signed, spine
and rear board slightly sunned, corners lightly bumped, else very good.
Quill & Brush 54-1422 1983 $90

UPHAM, CHARLES W.   Life Explorations and Public Services
of John Charles Fremont. Boston, 1856. Blue cloth, very good.
Reese 19-561 1983 $50

UPHAM, CHARLES W.   Salem Witchcraft. Boston, 1867.
2 vols., 2 frontis., folding map. 8vo, (vol. 1 backstrip 1/2 lacking,
few pp. loose, some unopened). Argosy 716-286 1983 $50

UPHAM, EDWARD   Rameses. For G.B. Whittaker, 1824.
First edition, 3 vols., half titles, orig. half calf, marbled
boards, very sl. defect in calf, bottom of spine vol. III. Calf
missing from corner on vol. I, otherwise fine. Jarndyce 30-576
1983 £75

UPHAM, EDWARD   Rameses. For G.B. Whittaker, John
Upham and Charles Upham, 1824. First edition. 3 vols. 8vo, three
half-titles, but lacks last leaves of vols. I and II, presumably
blank. Cont. half calf (worn). Occasional slight stains. Hannas
69-216 1983 £30

UPHAM, SAMUEL C.   Notes of a Voyage to California via
Cape Horn...with Scenes in El Dorado...1849-50. Phila., published by
the author, 1878. Illus. Orig. pictorial cloth, minor repairs to
spine. First edition. Ginsberg 46-758 1983 $150

UPHAM, THOMAS COGSWELL (1799-1872)   Outlines of Disordered Mental
Action. NY: Harper, 1840. 12mo. Contemporary printed cloth.
First edition. Gach 95-509 1983 $50

UPHAM, WARREN   The Geology of Central and Western
Minnesota. St. Paul, Pioneer Press, 1880. Orig. printed wraps.
Map. Author's separate with complimentary slip inserted. Ginsberg
46-484 1983 $50

UPHAM, WARREN   Minnesota in Three Centuries 1655-1903.
(NY), 1908. 4 vols., many illus., 8vo, blue buckram, ex library.
Argosy 710-319 1983 $60

URDANG, GEORGE   Pharmacy's Part in Society. Madison, 1946. 8vo. Limited edition. Orig. binding. Fye H-3-578 1983 $25

URDANG, GEORGE   Wessen und Bedeutung der Feschichte der Pharmazie. Berlin, 1927. 8vo, pr. wrs. Argosy 713-549 1983 $50

UREN, LESTER C.   A Textbook of Petroleum Production Engineering. New York, 1924. First edition. Illus. Jenkins 152-477 1983 $65

URQUHART, HUGH M.   Arthur Currie. Toronto, Vancouver: Dent, 1950. 23cm. Frontis. portrait and 5 illus. 7 maps. Spine faded else fine. McGahern 54-177 1983 $20

URSPRUNG, OTTO   Die Katholische Kirchenmusik. Potsdam, 1931. 13 plates (some tipped-in and color), numerous text illus. and musical samples. Folio, cloth with leather label (new binding). Salloch 387-404 1983 $65

URSPRUNG und Ordnungen der Bergwerge inn Konigreich Boheim... Leipzig: Lorenz Kober for Henning Gross, jr., 1616. Wide title border, engraved by Andreas Bretschneider III, and 13 text engravings. Woodcut armorial title vignettes, publisher's devices, and decorative initials. Some contemporary marginalia. Small folio. Half morocco. First 2 ff. torn and laid down, affecting small portions of title border, 3rd leaf frayed and remargined, two tears mended. From the library of Wilhelm Kreutz, with stamp. Kraus 164-164 1983 $650

THE USEFULNESS of the Edinburgh Theatre seriously considered. Edinburgh: 1757. 8vo, wrappers, 1st edition. An excellent copy, complete with half-title; outer edges uncut. Rare. Ximenes 64-550 1983 $400

USSHER, RICHARD J.   The Birds of Ireland. Gurney & Jackson, 1900. First edition, with 7 plates, 2 folding maps and 7 other illus. 8vo, orig. cloth, a small watercolour sketch mounted on the front endpaper, otherwise a very good copy. Fenning 62-371 1983 £45

UTAH. CONSTITUTION.   Constitution of the State of Utah. S.L.C., Deseret News Co., 1882. Orig. printed wraps. Ginsberg 46-760 1983 $250

UTAH'S Greatest Manhunt. The True Story of the Hunt for Lopez... (Salt Lake: Press of the F.W. Gardiner Co., 1913.) Orig. red pic. wrappers. Scarce. Jenkins 153-653 1983 $75

UTAH'S Greatest Manhunt. (Salt Lake: n.d.). First edition. Illus. Pictorial red wrappers. Very good. Bradley 66-682 1983 $37.50

UTLEY, HENRY M.   Michigan As a Province, Territory and State. Publishing Society of Michigan, 1906. 4 vols. Illus. Cloth. An unusually nice set. King 46-198 1983 $100

UTTLEY, ALISON   Little Grey Rabbit & the Weasels. Collins, 1947. Pictures by Margaret Tempest. 17 col. plates. Blue bds. with col. plate fr. cvr., insc. verso title page, corners sl. bruised, vg. Hodgkins 27-209 1983 £12.50

UTZINGER, RUDOLF   Indianer Kunst. Munchen: O.C. Recht, 1921. 43 plates. 4to. Boards. Ars Libri 34-512 1983 $35

UZANNE, OCTAVE   The French Bookbinders of the Eighteenth Century. Chicago: Caxton Club, 1904. First edition. One of 252 copies printed. Small folio. Plates. Orig. cloth-backed boards, label. Uncut. Printed on handmade paper by the Lakeside Press for the Caxton Club. Trifle dusty. Fine. Jenkins 152-786 1983 $200

UZANNE, OCTAVE   The Sunshade-The Glove-The Muff. London: 1883. Octavo. Illus. by Paul Avril. Deluxe edition. Rebound by Zaehnsdorf in full mustard morocco with blue and brown onlay, gilt design. Raised bands on spine. Orig. silk covers bound-in as the doublures surrounded by richly gilt dentelles. A.e.g. Spine slightly darkened, else fine. Preserved in fleece-lined cloth slip-case, lightly rubbed. Bromer 25-156 1983 $475

V

VACHON, MARIUS   Puvis de Chavannes. Paris: Braun/
Lahure, 1895. 15 photogravure plates with tissue guards. Folio.
Marbled boards, 3/4 leather. T.e.g. Uncut. Edges slightly rubbed.
Ars Libri 32-542 1983 $150

VAIL, ROBERT WILLIAM GLENROIE   Alive in Wonderland. N.Y.: New
York Public Library, 1928. First edition. Illus. Orig. printed
wrappers. Covers slightly faded; a trifle foxed throughout. Bookplate.
Near-fine. MacManus 278-1588 1983 $25

VAIL, ROBERT WILLIAM GLENROIE   The Voice of the Old Frontier.
Philadelphia: Univ. Of Penn. Press, 1949. Cloth. Dawson 470-296
1983 $20

VAILLANT, GEORGE C.   Excavations at Ticoman. New York,
1931. 40 plates. 6 maps. Small 4to. Wrappers. Ars Libri 34-
514 1983 $30

VAILLANT, GEORGE C.   Excavations at Zacatenco. New York,
1930. 54 plates. 4 maps. Small 4to. Wrappers (detached). Ars
Libri 34-515 1983 $30

VALCARCEL, LUIS E.   Indians of Peru. New York: Pantheon,
1950. Photographs by Pierre Verger. 87 plates. Small square 4to.
Cloth. Ars Libri 34-516 1983 $50

VALE, ROBERT B.   Wings, Fur & Shot. Harrisburg 1936.
First edition. Illus., cloth, ink name covers moderately rubbed. King
46-692 1983 $22.50

VALENTINE, MRS.   Shakespearian Tales in Verse. F. Warne,
n.d. 4to. Half-title. Colour frontis. Colour decorated title. 21
colour plates (3 double-page) & 76 text illus. Olive decorated cloth,
gilt. Very good. Greer 39-15 1983 £35

VALENTINER, WILHELM R.   Frans Hals Paintings in America.
Westport, Connecticut: Frederic Fairchild Sherman, 1936. 104
plates. 4to. Boards, 1/4 cloth. Limited edition of 200 copies.
With the 4pp. supplement loosely inserted. From the library of
Jakob Rosenberg. Ars Libri 32-301 1983 $150

VALENTINER, WILHELM R.   Georg Kolbe. Plastik und Zeichnung.
Munchen: Kurt Wolff, 1922. 61 plates. 3 text illus. Large 4to.
Boards, 1/4 cloth. Ars Libri 32-377 1983 $50

VALENTINER, WILHELM R.   Origins of Modern Sculpture. New York,
1946. 4to, 138 illus., cloth. Ars Libri SB 26-238 1983 $40

VALENTINER, WILHELM R.   Pieter De Hooch. Des Meisters Gemalde.
Stuttgart: Deutsche Verlags-Anstalt, 1929. 180 illus. 4to. Cloth.
Ars Libri 32-329 1983 $150

VALENTINER, WILHELM R.   Rembrandt Paintings in America. New
York: S.W. Frankel, 1931. 175 fine photogravure plates with titled
tissue guards. Folio. Cloth, 3/4 leather. Ars Libri 32-569 1983
$150

VALENTINER, WILHELM R.   Studies of Italian Renaissance Sculpture.
London, 1950. Large 4to, 247 illus., cloth. Ars Libri SB 26-239
1983 $85

VALENTYN, F.   Beschryvinge Van Het Eyland Ceylon.
(Dortrecht and Amsterdam, 1724-26). 2 folding maps, 2 plans, 1 folding.
11 plates, 4 folding, 8 half page illus. Folio. Very slight marginal
staining and worming. Modern paper-covered boards. 8vo. Good.
Edwards 1044-792 1983 £200

VALENTYN, F.   Beschryving Der Kust van Choromandel.
(Dortecht and Amsterdam, 1724-26). 2 folding maps, folding plan, 3
plates. Half page illus. slightly trimmed. Folio. PP.1-198, lightly
dampstained in early leaves affecting one map, some marginal worming.
Modern paper-covered boards. 8vo. Good. Edwards 1044-790 1983 £100

VALENTYN, F.   Levens Der Groote Mogols. (Dortrecht &
Amsterdam, 1724-26). Full page plan, 18 engr. plates, 19 engr. half-
page illus. Folio. Fine in modern paper-covered boards. Edwards
1044-791 1983 £265

VALERIUS MAXIMUS, GAIUS   Addition Indice Perbrevi, Cev ad Omneis
Historias Asylo Tvtissimo. Parisiis, Apud Simonem Colinaeum, 1531.
8vo, cont. calf, front joint cracked, back cover detached, somewhat
worn, bookplate, name on end-leaf, title soiled, light stain to
blank gutter, outer blank tips rounded (or evenly gnawed), few minor
spots. Ravenstree 95-137 1983 $87.50

VALLANCE, AYLMER   Art in England During the Elizabethan
and Stuart Periods. The Studio, 1908. With many full-page and
other illus., plates, etc. (10 in colour), small folio, orig. cloth,
gilt, t.e.g., very good. Fenning 61-457 1983 £12.50

VALLEMONT, PIERRE LE LORRAIN DE   Description de l'aimant, qui s'est
forme a la pointe du clocher neuf de N. Dame de Chartres... Paris:
chez Laurent d'Houry, etc., 1692. First edition. 12mo. Cont. stiff
wrappers. Some light browning, but a fine copy. Rare. Ximenes 63-
541 1983 $400

VALSALVA, ANTONIO MARIA   De Aure Humana Tractatus... Utrecht:
W. vande Water, 1707. 4to. Modern half-goat, uncut. 10 folding
plates. Insignificant worming in title. Fine copy. Gurney 90-116
1983 £200

VALSECCHI, MARCO   Cantatore. Milano: Luigi Maestri,
1968. 113 tipped-in color plates, 3 text illus. Large stout 4to.
Cloth. Ars Libri 33-425 1983 $85

VALSECCHI, MARCO   Carlo Fornara pittore. Milano:
Insegna del Pesce d'Oro, 1971. 205 plates (numerous color).
Large square 4to. Boards. Dust jacket. Edition limited to
200 numbered copies. Ars Libri 33-471 1983 $85

VALSECCHI, MARCO   Gli arazzi dei mesi del Bramantino.
Milano: Cassa di Risparmio delle Provincie Lombarde, 1968. 130
illus. mostly in color, partly folding. Small folio. Boards, 1/4
leather. Slipcase. Ars Libri 33-50 1983 $150

VALSECCHI, MARCO   Mario Tozzi. Milano: Insegna del
Pesce d'Oro, 1970. 113 plates (predominantly tipped-in color).
17 text illus. Small folio. Cloth. Edition limited to 1400
numbered copies. Ars Libri 33-602 1983 $85

VALSECCHI, MARCO   Tesori in Lombardia. Avori e
oreficerie. Milano, 1973. 167pp. Prof. illus., mostly in color.
Sm. folio. Cloth. D.j. Ars Libri SB 26-240 1983 $125

VAMBERY, ARMINIUS   Travels in Central Asia. NY: Harper
& Brothers, 1865. Illus. with 12 plates + a large folding map in
rear pocket. Brown cloth; lower outer corners water-stained.
Karmiole 71-93 1983 $65

VAN BERKEN, TINE   Katjesspel. Amsterdam: Becht, n.d.
Octavo. Heavy, coated paper with color and b&w illus. About fine
in pictorial stiff wrappers. Bromer 25-332 1983 $75

VANBRUGH, JOHN   Plays... London: for J. Rivington,
etc., 1776. 2 vols. 12mo. Cont. speckled calf, gilt spines with
crimson and black morocco labels, gilt. With engraved portrait by
T. Miller, general title-pages and separate title-page to each play.
Traylen 94-839 1983 £50

VANBRUGH, JOHN   A short vindication of the Relapse and
the Provok'd Wife, from immorality and prophaneness. London: printed
for H. Walwyn, 1698. 8vo, cont. panelled calf, spine gilt (spine
rubbed, short split in upper hinge). 1st edition. Early armorial
bookplate on the verso of the title. A fine copy, complete with
half-title. Ximenes 64-552 1983 $375

VANBRUGH, JOHN   The Complete Works of... Bloomsbury:
Nonesuch Press, 1927. Four octavo vols. Limited to 1300 copies. Very
fine set in cloth-backed boards, uniformly sunned at spines. Bromer
25-263 1983 $85

VAN BUREN, MARTIN   Calendar of the Papers of. Washington,
1910. First edition. Portrait. 4to, inner hinges cracked. Morrill
290-551 1983 $25

VAN BUREN, MARTIN   Capture of the Mexican Brig Urrea. Wash.,
1838. Dbd. First edition. Ginsberg 47-880 1983 $75

VAN BUREN, MARTIN   Message from...Communicating...Copies
of Correspondence Imputing Malpractices to the American Consul at
Havana, In Regard to Granting Papers to Vessels Engaged in the Slave-
Trade. Wash., 1841. Cloth. First edition. Ginsberg 46-694 1983
$50

VAN BUREN, MARTIN   Texas Invasion-Louisiana. Wash.,
1839. Dbd. First edition. Ginsberg 47-882 1983 $50

VANCE, ETHEL   Escape. Boston, Little Brown, 1939.
First edition. Dust jacket (rubbing and small nicks) else very good.
Houle 22-921 1983 $35

VANCE, LOUIS JOSEPH   The Bronze Bell. London: Grant Richards,
1909. First English edition. Orig. cloth. Very good. MacManus 280-
5332 1983 $35

VANCE, WILSON J.   Stone's River: The Turning-Point of the
Civil War. New York: Neale, 1914. First edition. Jenkins 152-714
1983 $25

VAN CLEEF, F. L.   Index Antiphonteus. Phil., 1895.
8vo, cloth. Salloch 385-425 1983 $30

VAN CLEVE, CHARLOTTE OUISCONSIN   "Three Score Years and Ten."
(Minneapolis), 1888. Frontis. Brown cloth, very fine. Reese 19-564
1983 $125

VAN DAAL, GEERT   Marbled Papers. Buren: Frits Knuf,
1980. Quarto. Limited to 50 copies signed by Van Daal. 20 large
tipped-in samples of marbled papers made by author. Mint in cloth-
covered boards with wide band of marbled paper folded around both
covers. Slip-case. Bromer 25-274 1983 $450

VANDERBILT, GERTRUDE LEFFERTS   The Social History of Flatbush, and
Manners and Customs of the Dutch Settlers in Kings County. New York,
1881. Map, small 8vo. Ex-library, ends of spine worn. Morrill
286-664 1983 $20

VANDERBILT, HAROLD S.   On the Winds Highway: Tanger, Rainbow
Racing. N.Y., Scribner, 1939. First edition. 4to, illus. with
halftones. Pictoria cloth, pub.'s slipcase (worn else, very good.
Houle 22-1187 1983 $45

VANDERBILT, HAROLD S.   On The Wind's Highway. N.Y., 1939.
First edition. Pictorial cloth. Covers slightly worn. Frayed
glassine dust wrapper. Very good. King 45-533 1983 $22.50

VANDERCOOK, JOHN W.   King Cane. N.Y., Harper 1939. First
edition. Illus. Cloth, very good. Houle 21-1086 1983 $20

VAN DER ZEE, JACOB   The British In Iowa. Iowa City, 1922.
Illus. Orig. cloth. First edition. Ginsberg 47-385 1983 $30

VAN Dongen. Paris: H. Floury, 1925. 118 plates (12 color facsimile
and tipped-in). Text illus. 4to. New cloth. Orig. wrappers bound
in. Ars Libri 32-168 1983 $125

VAN DOREN, CARL   James Branch Cabell. N.Y.: Lit. Gld.,
1932. Revised edition. 8vo. Cloth backed pictorial boards. Very
good to fine. Aleph-bet 8-46 1983 $20

VAN DOREN, CARL   Secret History of the American
Revolution. N.Y., Viking, 1941. First edition. Illus. with portraits,
maps, and facs. Red cloth, one of 590 copies, signed by the author.
Fine. Houle 21-1168 1983 $55

VAN DOREN, CARL   Swift. New York: Viking, 1930.
Frontis. 1st ed. Orig. cloth, gilt. Light fading but a little used
copy with author's presentation inscription in ink on front end
paper, and a later inscription, signed, below the first. Jenkins
155-1237 1983 $22.50

VAN DOREN, CARL   Three Worlds. N.Y., Harper & Brothers,
1936. First edition. Dust jacket (small nicks). Very good. Author's
autograph laid in loose. Houle 22-922 1983 $20

VAN DOREN, MARK   Prize Poems, 1913-1929. New York:
Boni, 1930. 1st ed. Orig. pictorial wrappers. Fine copy with work
of T.S. Eliot, Benet Cummings, Cowley, Frost, et al. Jenkins 155-
365 1983 $20

VAN DOREN, MARK   That Careless Clock. NY, (1947). Illus.
by Waldo Peirce. Signed by author and illus., edges very lightly
rubbed, bottom corners slightly bumped, else near fine in very lightly
chipped and soiled, very good dustwrapper. Quill & Brush 54-1427
1983 $35

VAN DYKE, HENRY   Builders. N.Y., Scribner, 1902.
Sm 8vo, gilt stamped green cloth, t.e.g., uncut. Presentation copy
from the author to Los Angeles pioneer attorney, Henry M. O'Melvenny,
May 27, 1903. Houle 21-891 1983 $30

VAN DYKE, JOHN C.   The New New York: a Commentary on the
Place & the People. NY, 1909. 1st ed. G.t. Illus. by Joseph
Pennell, some in color. Argosy 710-386 1983 $30

VAN DYKE, THEODORE STRONG   Southern California. NY: Fords,
Howard, & Hulbert, 1886. 20 cm. Orig. green cloth, gilt-lettered
spine, beveled edges; uncut. Very good; front inner hinge cracking,
a preliminary blank leaf stamped. First edition. Grunder 7-9 1983
$45

VANEL, CHARLES   The Royal Mistresses of France. London,
Henry Rhodes and John Harris, 1695. 8vo, 19th century polished calf,
spine defective, joints repaired; preserved in quarter morocco case.
First and only edition. Ravenstree 96-281 1983 $300

VAN GOGH, VINCENT   Letters of...to His Brother. 1872-
1886. London, Constable, 1927-1929. First edition, dust jackets
(some chips), else very good-fine. 3 vols. With 150 plates.
Houle 21-892 1983 $150

VAN HISE, C. R.   Pre-Cambrian Geology of North America.
Washington, U.S. Geo. Survey Bull. 360, 1909. 2 maps, 8vo, cloth.
Wheldon 160-1482 1983 £15

VAN LOON, H   The Arts. N.Y., Simon & Schuster, 1937.
First edition. Color and b/w illus. by the author. Pictorial
dust jacket (some rubbing and small nicks) else very good. Book mark
by author laid in loose. Houle 22-923 1983 $30

VAN LOON, H   The Story of Mankind. NY, (1922). Later
printing, with signed, dated, inscribed drawing from Van Loon, author's
picture tipped-in, edges sligtly rubbed, cover lightly soiled, else
very good, bookplate. Quill & Brush 54-1429 1983 $35

VAN MILLINGEN, ALEXANDER   Constantinople. London, 1906. 8vo,
pictorial cloth, t.e.g. First edition thus. Contains 63 color plates
by Goble. Very nice. Perata 27-46 1983 $75

VANNES, RENE   1252 Etiquettes de Luthiers. Paris,
1935. 8vo, printed wrs. Salloch 387-405 1983 $25

VAN NOSTRAND, JEANNE   San Fransicso, 1806-1906. SF: 1975.
In Contemporary Paintings, Drawings and Watercolors. Folio, cloth,
gilt, vignette on upper cover. Containing 53 plates. One of 500
copies. Limitation slip laid in. A fine copy. Perata 27-114
1983 $200

VAN OVEN, BERNARD   On the Decline of Life in Health &
Disease. London, 1853. 8vo, cloth, (rebacked). First edition.
Pub.'s catalogue bound in. Argosy 713-550 1983 $65

VAN RIJN, REMBRANDT   Rembrandt's Etchings. London:
Phaidon, 1952. 2 vols. 325 illus. 48 plates. Large 4to. Cloth.
Dust jacket. Boxed. Ars Libri 32-562 1983 $175

VAN RIJN, REMBRANDT   Seven Letters by Rembrandt. The Hague:
L.J.C. Boucher, 1961. 6 plates. illus. 4to. Cloth. Dust jacket.
From the library of Jakob Rosenberg. Ars Libri 32-556 1983 $85

VAN VECHTEN, CARL   Feathers. New York, 1930. 8vo.
Stiff wraps. 1 of 875 copies. Very good copy. In Our Time 156-838
1983 $20

VAN VECHTEN, CARL   Music After the Great War and Other
Studies. New York: Schirmer, 1915. Cloth, paper label. First
edition. A very good to fine copy, sans dust jacket. Reese 20-1085
1983 $50

VAN VECHTEN, CARL   Spider Boy. New York: Knopf, 1928. One
Large octavo. Cloth and pastepaper boards. First edition. One of
220 numbered copies, specially printed and bound, and signed by the
author. An unopened copy, in the orig. glassine, in slipcase (Bumped
at one edge). Reese 20-1086 1983 $100

VAN VECHTEN, CARL   Spider Boy. Lon., 1928. Cover and
page edges lightly stained, else very good in slightly chipped and
frayed, internally mended dustwrapper. Quill & Brush 54-1430 1983
$35

VAN VECHTEN, CARL   The Tattooed Countess. N.Y., Knopf,
1924. Tall 8vo, half pink cloth over patterned boards (spine a bit
faded), uncut. Slipcase. One of 150 copies signed by the author.
Very good. Houle 22-1221 1983 $165

VANVITELLI, LUIGI   Vita di Luigi Vanvitelli. Roma:
Banco di Roma, 1975. 10 color plates. 263 illus. Large 4to.
Cloth. Ars Libri 33-378 1983 $175

VAN VOORHIES, WILLIAM   Oration Before the Society of California
Pioneers, at Their Celebration of the Anniversary of the Admission
of the State of California into the Union. San F., 1853. Dbd.
First edition. Ginsberg 47-195 1983 $65

VANWINKLE, H. E.   Nine Years of Democratic Rule In
Mississippi. Jackson, MI, 1847. 1/2 calf, marbled boards. Lacks
f.e.p. Hinges cracked, covers very worn. King 46-208 1983 $150

VARENDONCK, J.   The Evolution of the Conscious Faculties.
London: George Allen & Unwin, (1923). First edition in English.
Gach 95-511 1983 $40

VARENIUS, BERNARD   Geographia Generalis, in qua Affectiones
Generales Telluris Explicantur... Joann. Hayes, Cambridge, 1681.
8vo, with 5 folding engraved plates; cont. sprinkled calf. Second
Newton edition. Quaritch NS 5-109 1983 $450

VARET, ALEXANDRE   The Hunns Complaint Against the
Fryars. Printed by E.H. for Robert Pawlett, 1676. First edition
in English, 8vo, unlettered sheep, old short repair to head of
spine. Fenning 62-372 1983 £120

VARIGNANA, FRANCA   Le collezioni d'arte della Cassa di
Risparmio in Bologna. Le incisioni. I: Giuseppe Maria Mitelli.
Bologna: Edizioni Alfa, 1978. 281 plates. 9 color. 560 catalogue
illus. 4to. Cloth. Ars Libri 33-252 1983 $120

VARIGNON, PIERRE   Traite du Mouvement, et de la Mesure
des eaux Coulantes et Jaillissantes. Pissot, Paris, 1725. 4to,
with 5 folding engraved plates; cont. mottled sheep, gilt spine,
a little rubbed. First edition. Quaritch NS 5-110 1983 $650

VARLO, CHARLES   A New System of Husbandry... Phila.,
1785. 2 vols. New half morocco, a fine set. Reese 19-566 1983 $675

VARNEY, ALMON C.   Our Homes and Their Adornments. Detroit,
1882. Numerous illus. of old houses. Cloth. Hinges broken. Covers
very worn. Rear endpapers with recipes. King 45-458 1983 $25

VARNEY, JOHN   Poems for a Prose Age. London: The
Unicorn Press, (1960). Cloth. First edition. Laid in is a two
page a.l.s. from Edith Sitwell to Varney, dated 1961. Also laid in is
a two page a.l.s. from Varney to Martin Secker. Note on the dust
jacket that the letter from E.S. is contained herein, and cont. review,
docketed in his hand, laid in. Very fine. Reese 20-1087 1983 $150

VARTHEMA, LUDOVICO DI   The travels of Ludovico di Varthema...
London: Hakluyt Soc., 1863. 8vo. 2 maps. Modern blue cloth.
Ex-library. Adelson Africa-230 1983 $50

VARTY-SMITH, AUGUSTA A.   Matthew Tindale. London: Richard Bentley & Co, 1891. First edition. 3 vols. Orig. blue cloth. Rear
inner hinge of first volume cracking. Minor wear at extremities of
spine. Very good. MacManus 280-5335 1983 $350

VARTY-SMITH, AUGUSTA A.   Matthew Tindale. London: Bentley, 1891.
First edition. 3 vols. Orig. cloth. Presentation copy to her sister,
signed on the (loose) flyleaf in vol. I. With a number of reviews of
book tipped in, one in the author's hand. Fine. MacManus 280-5334
1983 $250

VASON, GEORGE   An authentic Narrative of Four Years'
Residence at Tongataboo, one of the Friendly Islands, in the South
Sea. London: Longman, 1810. First (only) edition, 8vo, cont.
marbled boards, rebacked. Engraved frontis., engraved map. A very
good copy, complete with the errata leaf at end. Trebizond 18-167
1983 $500

VATTEL, EMERICH DE   The Law of Nations. London, 1793. 8vo.
Spotting, moreso to the preliminary and last leaves, bound in full
contemp. tree calf, quite worn, neatly rebacked, spine double-gilt
ruled, with orig. crimson morocco label, gilt lettered, preserved.
Else clean. Boswell 7-150 1983 $175

VAUGHAN, HENRY   Sacred Poems... London, Pickering, 1847.
First edition thus. Small 8vo, cont. full black morocco, a.e.g., a
little rubbed, else very good. Houle 22-379 1983 $475

VAUGHAN, THOMAS   The Works of... London: Theosophical
Pub. House, 1919. First edition. Gach 95-526 1983 $75

VAUX, ROBERTS   Letter on the Penitentiary System of
Pennsylvania. Philadelphia, 1827. Dsb., some foxing. Presentation
copy. Reese 18-616 1983 $100

THE VAUXHALL affray; or, the Macaronies defeated: being a compilation
of all the letters, squibs, etc., on both sides of that dispute.
London: sold by J. Williams, 1773. 8vo, cont. half calf (worn).
3rd edition. Folding frontis. caricature plate. Ximenes 64-553
1983 $300

VECHTEN, CARL VAN
Please turn to
VAN VECHTEN, CARL

VEGA, GARCILASO DE LA
Please turn to
GARCILASO DE LA VEGA

VEILLER, BAYARD   The Fun I've Had. N.Y., Reynal &
Hitchcock, 1941. First edition. Illus. Pictorial dust jacket (nicked,
lightly soiled). Presentation copy: signed and inscribed by the
author, "Dear...When I think of you spending money for this my heart
bleeds..." Very good. Houle 22-677 1983 $45

VELOSO, JOSE MARIANO DA CONCEICAO   Memoria sobre a Cultura do
Loureiro Cinamomo vulgo, Canelleira de Ceilao. (Lisbon:) Officina
de S. T. Ferreira, 1798. Only edition, 12mo, modern half calf
gilt, marbled boards. Fine folding plate. Half-title. A very
fine copy. Trebizond 18-181 1983 $375

VELPEAU, ALFRED A. L. M.   New Elements of Operative Surgery.
N.Y., 1847. First edition in English. 3 vols., thick 4to, sheep
(worn & foxed some dampstains). Lacks the atlas volume. Argosy
713-551 1983 $150

VENEGAS, MIGUEL   Histoire Naturelle Et Civile De La California. Paris: Durand, 1767. First French edition. 3 vols. Complete, fine folding engraved map of California. Full cont. mottled calf, spines gilt with raised bands and red leather labels. Fine. Jenkins 152-427 1983 $450

VENN, SUSANNA CARNEGIA   The Husband of One Wife. London: Hurst & Blackett, 1894. First edition. 3 vols. Orig. cloth. Spine a little faded. Slightly stained. Fine. MacManus 280-5336 1983 $300

VENNOR, HENRY G.   Our Birds of Prey... Montreal: Dawson Brothers, 1876. 4to. 30 photographic plates by Wm. Notman. Green cloth, black and gilt stamped titles and decorations. A fine copy. Rare. McGahern 54-195 1983 $350

VENTURE and Valour. London: W. & R. Chambers, 1900. With 8 page illus. by W. Boucher. Orig. pictorial cloth. First appearance in book form of Doyle's "The Surgeon of Gaster Fell." Fine. MacManus 278-1679 1983 $125

VENTURI, ADOLFO   Paolo Veronese. Milano: Ulrico Hoepli, 1928. 145 illus. Small 4to. Boards, 3/4 cloth. Orig. wrappers bound in. Ars Libri 33-385 1983 $65

VENTURI, LIONELLO   Cezanne. Son art, son oeuvre. Paris: Paul Rosenberg, 1936. 2 vols. 406 plates with 1634 illus. Large 4to. Orig. cloth. Ars Libri 32-92 1983 $2,500

VENTURI, LIONELLO   Georges Rouault. New York: E. Weyhe, 1940. 153 plates (3 tipped-in color). Large 4to. Wrappers. Worn. Ars Libri 32-592 1983 $75

VENTURI, LIONELLO   Il Perugino. Torino: Edizioni Radio Italiana, 1955. 13 color plates. Text illus. Large 4to. Boards. Dust jacket. Edition limited to 1000 numbered copies. Ars Libri 33-268 1983 $85

VENTURI, LIONELLO   Marc Chagall. New York: Pierre Matisse Editions, 1945. 64 collotype plates. 26 text illus. (2 tipped-in color). 4to. Boards. Edition limited to 1450 numbered copies. Ars Libri 32-103 1983 $100

VERBEEK, ALBERT   Die Niederrheinansichten Jan de Beyers. Essen: Fredebeul & Koenen, 1957. 180 illus. 4to. Cloth. Dust jacket. Ars Libri 32-37 1983 $100

VERCOE, A. GUY   English Warships. London, 1933. 8vo. Orig. cloth. 24 plates, 4 pages of ads. at end. Coloured printed illus. pasted onto upper cover. Ink signature on endpaper. Good. Edwards 1042-174 1983 £15

VERDOORN, F.   Plants and plant science in Latin America. Chronica Botanica, 1945. 38 plates and 45 text-figures, royal 8vo, cloth, good ex-library. Wheldon 160-1776 1983 £20

VEREY, JOSEPH   Martyrs to Fashion. London: Tinsley Brothers, 1868. First edition. 3 vols. Orig. cloth. W.H. Smith library blindstamping on front free endpaper of first volume. Former owner's signature on same leaf. With offsetting onto title-page. Later owner's ink stamp on endsheets. Covers a little rubbed and dust-soiled. Good. MacManus 280-5337 1983 $225

VERGA, GIOVANNI   Little Novels of Sicily. New York: Thomas Seltzer, 1925. First edition. 8vo. Orig. red cloth with paper label. Dust jacket. About fine copy. Jaffe 1-222 1983 $125

VERGA, GIOVANNI   Little Novels of Sicily. New York: Seltzer, 1925. 1st ed. Orig. brown cloth, paper label, dj. Very fine copy in a dj that is fine but for closed split in spine paper. Jenkins 155-776 1983 $65

VERGILIUS, POLYDORUS   An Abridgemet of the Notable Worke of Polidore Virgile... London: Richard Grafton, 1546. First English edition. Small 8vo. Modern brown morocco, red edges. Woodcut initials, small woodcut on verso of A8, title and a few leaves very slightly soiled. Traylen 94-840 1983 £600

VERGILIUS, POLYDORUS   An Abridgemente of the Notable worke of Polidore Virgile... London: John Tisdale, (ca. 1560). Small 8vo. Later calf, rebacked. Woodcut border title, repaired neatly at corner and laid down, few minor repairs. Heath 48-478 1983 £250

VERGILIUS MARO, PUBLIUS   Aeneis. Berlin, 1933. Bds. 8vo, cloth. Salloch 385-793 1983 $20

VERGILIUS MARO, PUBLIUS   Bucolica, Georgica, et AEneis. Birminghamiae, Johannis Baskerville, 1757. 4to, full crimson morocco gilt, a.e.g., by Riviere. Minor worming to blank inner edge of leaves X1 to 3C1, faint watermarking and some foxing. Ravenstree 95-141 1983 $450

VERGILIUS MARO, PUBLIUS   Publii Virgilii Maronis Bucolica, Georgica, et AEneis. In Aedibus Academicis Excudebant Robertus et Andreas Foulis, 1758. 8vo, later calf, gilt spine, hinges cracked, note on endpaper, foxing throughout, complete with the final leaf 2B8, with the short note in the middle of the page. Ravenstree 95-142 1983 $65

VERGILIUS MARO, PUBLIUS   Bucolica, Georgica et Aeneis. London: printed by T. Bensley for A. Dulau, 1800. 2 vols. 8vo. Cont. straight-grained blue morocco, two-line gilt borders on sides with inner gilt panels, gilt panelled spines, edges gilt. 14 engraved plates after Bartolozzi, Fittler, etc. Presentation inscription by E. Hawtrey, the headmaster at Eton College. Traylen 94-842 1983 £38

VERGILIUS MARO, PUBLIUS   Catalepton. Assen, 1949. 8vo, cloth. Salloch 385-794 1983 $30

VERGILIUS MARO, PUBLIUS   Eclogues & Georgics. London, 1898. 8vo, cloth. Salloch 385-795 1983 $35

VERGILIUS MARO, PUBLIUS   Virgilii Maronis Opera. Parisiis, Ex officina Roberti Stephani, 1532. Folio, old vellum (covers detached, covers wormed, some minor staining and spotting, end leaves a bit wormed, but no text affected, few early annotations and index separately printed by Estienne in 1529, with separate title. Ravenstree 95-138 1983 $265

VERGILIUS MARO, PUBLIUS   Opera. London, 1881-1884. 3 vols. 8vo, cloth. Salloch 385-789 1983 $110

VERGILIUS MARO, PUBLIUS   Opera. Lg, 1894/5. 4 vols. in 2. 8vo, cloth. Salloch 385-791 1983 $60

VERGILIUS MARO, PUBLIUS   Opera in tres Tomos divisa. 1680. 3 vols., stout 8vos, cont. calf, joints breaking, the Earl of Bridgewater copies with the Bridgewater Library bookplate. Brunet V, 1290 notes this is a "Bonne edition." Ravenstree 95-139 1983 $165

VERGILIUS MARO, PUBLIUS   Second Eclogue. Cambridge: (Golden Head Press), 1958. Octavo. 9 images by Raymond Lister combining text and illus. Printed in monochrome on one side of page only. Hand-colored by Lister. Limited to 36 copies signed by Lister. Extremely fine in quarter-leather and cloth-covered boards. Bromer 25-250 1983 $350

VERGILIUS MARO, PUBLIUS   The Works of Virgil. London, printed for Jacob Tonson, 1697. Folio, 19th century polished Russia gilt in the style of Hering, hinges cracked, corners worn, blank side of frontis. strengthened, with usual age-spotting throughout. Large, fine copy. Ravenstree 95-143 1983 $520

VERGILIUS MARO, PUBLIUS   The Works. London: for J. & F. Rivington, etc., 1772. 4 vols. 12mo. 18th century mottled calf, gilt decorated spines with crimson and blue morocco labels, gilt. 18 engraved plates after J. Collyer, half-titles. Traylen 94-841 1983 £70

VERHAEREN, EMILE   James Ensor. Bruxelles: G. Van Oest, 1908. 35 plates. 4to. Marbled boards, 3/4 leather. T.e.g. Orig. wrappers bound in. Cover designed by Ensor. Presentation copy, inscribed by Ensor to Sam Salz. Binding rubbed. Ars Libri 32-208 1983 $225

VERHEYEN, PHILIPPO   Corporis Humani Anatomiae Liber Primus. Bruzellis, 1710. Small 4to, boards (worn). Profusion of plates, some folding (a few mutilated or lacking); marginal annotations. Argosy 713-552 1983 $200

VERINI, GIOVAM BAPTISTA   Luminario, or the Third Chapter of the Liber Elementorum Litterarum on the Construction of Roman Capitals. Cambridge: Harvard College Library, 1947. First edition of this version. Large 4to. Cloth slipcase. Limited to 500 copies, of which this is one of the 300 printed on wove paper. Lightly worn slipcase. Fine copy. Oak Knoll 48-90 1983 $125

THE VERITABLE History of Mr. Bachelor butterfly. London: Vizetelly Brothers, 1845. Oblong 8vo. Cont. half morocco, leather label. 66 pp. of lithograph illus. Traylen 94-20 1983 £35

VERLAINE, PAUL   Dans les Limbes. Paris, 1894. Port. frontis. Later boards, orig. wraps. and backstrip neatly bound in. Wilmerding bookplate. A fine copy. First edition. Laid in are two love letters to Verlaine, one from Philomene "Esther" Boudin, the other from Eugenie Krantz. Also laid in are three cabinet photos of Verlaine by Otto of Paris. Felcone 21-108 1983 $750

VERLAINE, PAUL   Liturgies Intimes. Paris: Leon Vanier, 1893. Half morocco, orig. wrappers preserved. A very fine copy. Reese 20-1090 1983 $100

VERLOT, J. B.   Catalogue Raissone des Plantes Vascu-laires du Dauphine. Grenoble, 1872. 8vo, leather-backed boards. Wheldon 160-1777 1983 £18

VERNE, JULES   Abandoned. NY, 1876. Edges worn and green pic. cover slightly rubbed, good, bookplate. Quill & Brush 54-1431 1983 $50

VERNE, JULES   Adventures of Three Englishmen and Three Russians in South Africa. London, Sampson, Low, Marsten, 1896. New edition. Illus. Pictorial red cloth (slight soiling), very good. Houle 21-893 1983 $45

VERNE, JULES   At the North Pole. Ph. (1874). Spine edges rubbed and softened, rear cover frayed, interior clean, good. Quill & Brush 54-1432 1983 $50

VERNE, JULES   Meridiana. NY: Scribner, Armstrong & Co., 1874. First American edition. With 48 illus. Brown gilt-stamped cloth. Karmiole 75-114 1983 $65

VERNE, JULES   Michael Strogoff. N.Y., Scribner, (1927). First edition. 4to, with 12 color illus., including 9 full page; title page design; cover label and endpapers, all by Wyeth. Black cloth, large pictorial label, very good. Houle 21-972 1983 $85

VERNE, JULES   The Tour of the World in 80 Days. B, 1873. Cover soiled, edges rubbed and slightly worn, top and bottom of spine frayed, good. Quill & Brush 54-1433 1983 $40

VERNEDE, R. E.   The Fair Dominion. New York: James Pott & Co., 1911. 21cm. First edition. 12 colour plates from paintings by Cyrus Cuneo. Three colour decorated cloth. T.e.g. A fine copy. McGahern 53-168 1983 $20

VERNER, WILLOUGHBY   History & Campaigns of the Rifle Brigade. London, 1912-1919. 2 photogravure portrait frontis. 8 coloured plates of uniform, 5 photogravure and 11 other plates, 28 folding maps (24 coloured). 2 vols. 4to. Orig. green and black gilt decorated cloth. A.e.g. Very slightly worn and faded. Fine. Edwards 1042-550 1983 $180

VERNOIS, J. VON VERDY DU   With the Royal Headquarters. London, 1897. 8vo. Orig. cloth. Portrait frontis. Large folding map. 58 pp. publishers ads. Spine faded. Small library stamp. Good. Edwards 1042-499 1983 $20

VERNON, G.   Observations Respecting His Majesty's Ship Columbine. London, 1827. Sm. 8vo. Orig. cloth. Orig. wrappers, worn, within new boards. Paper label. Good. Edwards 1042-175 1983 £25

VERNON, JOSEPH   Along the Old Trail... Cimarron, Kan., (1910). Illus. Orig. pictorial stiff wrappers. Jenkins 153-656 1983 $75

VERRALL, G. H.   British Flies, Vol. 5. Stratiomyidae. 1909. 407 text-figures, royal 8vo, original cloth. Wheldon 160-1182 1983 $50

VERZEICHNIS des Musikalien-Verlags Von D Rahter. Leipzig, 1900-1910. 8vo, orig. cloth (binding worn). Salloch 387-359 1983 $35

VESEY, ARTHUR HENRY   A Cheque for Three Thousand. Bristol: J.W. Arrowsmith, 1905. Half title, 16pp ads. Orig. green cloth, lettered in gilt, lined in black with paper 'cheque' laid onto front cover, v.g. Jarndyce 31-963 1983 £10.50

VESEY-FITZGERALD, BRIAN   Game Fish of the World. London (1949). Illus, gilt-dec. cloth, very good in chipped and frayed d.w. King 46-693 1983 $25

VESLING, JOHANNES   The Anatomy of the Body of Man. London: Peter Cole, 1653. First English edition. Title and advertisement leaf pasted together. 24 engraved plates. Folio. Cont. calf. Worn rebacked, corners restored. From the library of Crawford W. Adams. Browning and soiling throughout. Some lower corners thumbed and chipped. Kraus 164-246 1983 $850

VESTAL, STANLEY   Bigfoot Wallace A Biography. Boston, 1942. Illus., 1st ed. in dust jacket. Scarce. Jenkins 151-343 1983 $65

VESTAL, STANLEY   Fandango. Ballads of the Old West. Boston, 1927. Original cloth backed boards. Fine copy of the 1st ed. in dust jacket. Quite scarce. Jenkins 151-344 1983 $75

VESTAL, STANLEY   The Missouri. New York, 1945. First edition in dust jacket. Illus. & maps. Jenkins 152-483 1983 $25

VESTAL, STANLEY   The Old Santa Fe Trail. Boston, 1939. Illus., 1st ed. in dust jacket. Fine copy. Scarce. Jenkins 151-345 1983 $50

VESTAL, STANLEY   Revolt on the Border. Boston, 1938. 1st ed. in dust jacket. Fine copy. Scarce. Jenkins 151-346 1983 $45

VESTAL, STANLEY   Short Grass Country. New York, 1941. 1st ed. in dj. Presentation from the author. Jenkins 153-657 1983 $40

VESTAL, STANLEY   Sitting Bull. Boston, Houghton Mifflin, 1932. First edition. Illus.; map. Dust jacket (a few nicks). Very good. Houle 22-1188 1983 $55

VESTAL, STANLEY   Sitting Bull Champion of the Sioux. Boston, 1932. Illus., 1st ed., some fading to the gold stamping on spine, else a fine copy. Jenkins 151-313 1983 $45

VESTAL, STANLEY   Warpath and Council Fire. New York, 1948. Illus. 1st ed. in dust jacket. Fine copy. Jenkins 151-347 1983 $35

VESTAL, STANLEY   Warpath The Story of the Fighting Sioux. Boston, 1934. Frontis and illus. 1st ed. Maps on endsheets. Some spotting to spine. Nice copy overall. Jenkins 151-348 1983 $50

VETH, J.   Albrecht Durers niederlandische Reise. Berlin/Utrecht: G. Grote/A. Oosthoek, 1918. 2 vols. 79 hinged collotype plates. Numerous text illus. Folio. Cloth. Uncut. Light foxing. Rare. Ars Libri 32-190 1983 $750

VIALE, VITTORIO   Gaudenzio Ferrari. Torino: ERI. Edizioni RAI. Radiotelevisione Italiana, 1969. 49 color plates. 100 illus. Folio. Dust jacket. Cloth. Slipcase. Ars Libri 33-138 1983 $100

VIALE FERRERO, MERCEDES   Filippo Juvarra. Scenografo e
architetto teatrale. Torinto: Fratelli Pozzo, 1970. 192 plates
(partly tipped-in color). Numerous reference illus. Large oblong
4to. Cloth. Dust jacket. Slipcase. Ars Libri 33-189 1983
$125

VIBART, E.   The Sepoy Mutiny. London, 1898. Folding
plan, portrait, 10 plates. Spine worn. 8vo. Orig. cloth. Good.
Edwards 1044-727 1983 £30

VICAIRE, GEORGES   Bibliographie Gastronomique. Lon.,
1954, second edition, near fine in slightly chipped and torn, very good
dustwrapper. Quill & Brush 54-1625 1983 $75

VICARS, JOHN   England Worthies. London, John Russell
Smith, 1845. First edition. With full page engraved portraits.
Full green morocco, spine stamped in gilt, covers ruled in gilt,
gilt inner dentelles, t.e.g., marbled endpapers (spine faded to a
rich brown, minor rubbing). Engraved bookplate of Hugh & Edward
Greenfield Doggett. One of four copies printed on India paper (so
inscribed and signed by the publisher, Sept. 26, 1845). Very good.
Houle 22-924 1983 $225

VICARS, THOMAS   Edom and Babylon against Jerusalem...
London: by E.P. for Henry Seyle, 1633. Sole edition. Small 8vo.
Cont. vellum, gilt lines, and central gilt device on each cover.
Damp.affecting the top of a few leaves, else good copy. Heath
48-561 1983 £125

VICKERS, A.   Phycologia Barbadensis. Paris, 1908.
93 coloured plates, 4to, original half cloth. Scarce. Edition
limited to 300 copies. Some very slight foxing. Wheldon 160-1909
1983 £100

VICTO, FRANCISCO   Decrizione d'un Apparecchio di
Macchine per Cavare... Bologna: Nell Instituto delle Scienze,
1788. First edition. Square 8vo. Uncut in orig. paper wrappers.
Engraved vignette on title, 2 folding engraved plates. Heath
48-535 1983 £75

VICTOR, BENJAMIN   The Widow of the Wood. London, printed
for C. Corbett, 1755. 8vo, orig. calf now badly worn, joints broken,
no half title or blank endleaves, name on title, title and end leaf
bit soiled and torn with minor hole in blank edge of title. First
edition. Ravenstree 96-282 1983 $265

VICTOR, BENJAMIN   The Widow of the Wood. For C. Corbet,
1755. First edition. 12mo, half-title, final advert. leaf for the
State-lottery. Cont. calf. Hannas 69-217 1983 £95

VICTOR, BENJAMIN   The Widow of the Wood. Printed for C.
Corbett, 1755. 12mo, cont. calf, worn at corners and head and foot
of spine. First edition. Bickersteth 77-83 1983 £85

VICTOR, FRANCIS FULLER   The River of the West. Hartford, 1870.
Calf and cloth, slightly rubbed, very good. Reese 19-569 1983 $135

VICTOR Hammer, Artist and Printer. Lexington: The Anvil Press,
1981. Small 4to. Cloth. Cardboard slipcase. One of 500 numbered
copies of a total edition of 550. Designed by Martino Mardersteig
in Dante type and printed at the Stamperia Valdonega in Verona.
Fine. Oak Knoll 49-213 1983 $75

THE VICTORIA Golden Almanack. London: Howlett, 1840. Entirely
printed in gold on deep blue paper. Elaborately decorated front cover
with center portrait of the Queen and Greek key borders on every page.
Lightly rubbed, else fine in self-wrappers. (3 1/2 x 2; 89x51mm).
Bromer 25-409 1983 $65

VIDAL, GORE   The City and the Pillar. N.Y., 1948.
First edition, d.w. Argosy 714-896 1983 $75

VIDAL, GORE   The City and The Pillar. NY, 1948.
Appears to be Wilma Dykeman's copy, cover dulled, else very good in
slightly worn and creased dustwrapper. Quill & Brush 54-1439 1983
$40

VIDAL, GORE   Creation. New York: Random House,
(1981). Cloth. First edition. One of 500 numbered copies, specially
bound, and signed by the author. Fine in slipcase. Reese 20-1092
1983 $35

VIDAL, GORE   In a Yellow Wood. NY, 1947. Edges
slightly rubbed, else very good or better in lightly frayed and slightly chipped dustwrapper. Quill & Brush 54-1437 1983 $75

VIDAL, GORE   The Season of Comfort. New York, 1949.
First edition. Fine, in a slightly faded dust wrapper. Argosy 714-
773 1983 $50

VIDAL, GORE   A Thirsty Evil. Zero Press, 1956.
8vo. Cloth. Signed by Vidal on half-title page. Fine copy in dj.
In Our Time 156-839 1983 $125

VIDAL, GORE   Williwaw. N.Y., Dutton, 1946. First
edition. Dust jacket (two short tears, some occasional light
rubbing) else very good. Houle 22-925 1983 $175

VIDAL, GORE   Williwaw. New York, 1946. First
edition. D.w. Very good copy. Argosy 714-774 1983 $100

VIDOUDEZ, PIERRE   L'Arche de Noe. Lucerne: Editions
Novos S. A., (1946). Oblong octavo. 7 colored full-page illus. by
Marcel Vidoudez. Slight rubbing to extremities, otherwise fine in
cloth-backed, color-printed board covers, staple-bound. Bromer 25-
319 1983 $30

VIEILLOT, L. J. P.   Histoire naturelle des oiseaux de
l'Amerique septentrionale. Paris, 1807 (-1809). 2 vols., roy. folio,
half morocco, coloured plates by Pretre. Some foxing, heavy on the
text at the beginning of vol. 1, and with occasional spotting.
Contemporary double-page map, coloured in outline, is bound in.
Wheldon 160-110 1983 £3,500

VIEILLOT, L. J. P.   Songbirds of the Torrid Zone. Kent,
Ohio, 1979. Imp. 4to, full leather, gilt, g.e., coloured plates.
A facsimile. Edition limited to 1,500 copies. Wheldon 160-111 1983
£145

VIELE, EGBERT L.   Sanitary & Topographical Map of the City
& Island of New York. NY, 1865. Very large, long map in 2 parts,
colored, with key to match. Argosy 716-385 1983 $1,500

VIELE, EGBERT L.   The Topography and Hydrology of New
York (City). New York, Robert Craighead, Printer, 1865. 1st ed.
Folding map on thin paper-few tears repaired with transparent tape.
8vo. Morrill 289-470 1983 $37.50

VIERORDT, OSWALD   Rhachitis und Osteomalacie. Wien, 1896.
Illus., wrs. Argosy 713-555 1983 $25

VIETH, FREDERICK HARRIS D.   Recollections of the Crimean Campaign
and the Expedition to Kinburn in 1855. Montreal: John Lovell, 1907.
22 1/2cm. 68 illus. Green cloth. Fine. McGahern 53-167 1983 $35

VIETOR, CASPAR   Disputatio de Crisibus Pior (-Posterior).
Strassburg: Johann Andrea, 1627. 2 parts in 1 vol. Marginalia in
first part. 4to. Modern boards. Blank corner of title torn off.
Tears in last leaf repaired partly obscuring one line. Kraus 164-247
1983 $240

VIEWS of Akron Ohio and Vicinity. Portland, Me.: L.H. Nelson Co.,
ca. 1900. Cover title. Original printed purple wrappers. Fine
copy. Illus. with photographs. Jenkins 151-258 1983 $35

VIEWS of Asbury Park and Ocean Grove. Portland: Nelson Co., (ca.
1905). Photos, no text. Oblong 8vo, pr. wrs., edges faded.
Argosy 710-333 1983 $40

VIEWS of Buffalo. Buffalo: Nelson Co., (ca. 1905). Photos, oblong
8vo, pr. wrs. Argosy 710-346 1983 $40

VIEWS of East London, South Africa. East London, South Africa:
Hebbes & Co., 1891. 24 leaves of photogravure plates, each with
tissue guard with printed description. Bound in cont. full calf,
rubbed. Gilt-stamped front cover. Karmiole 73-83b 1983 $50

VIGNAUD, HENRY   Histoire Critique de la Grande Entreprise de Christophe Colomb. Paris, 1911. 2 vols., pp. uncut, many unopened. Thick 8vo, pr. wrs. Argosy 710-135 1983 $40

VILBERT, CH.   Precis de Medecine Legale. Paris: J.-B. Billiere, 1890. Second edition, revised. Library bookplate and spine label. Unopened copy. Gach 95-513 1983 $27.50

VILLA, GUIDO   Contemporary Psychology. London: 1903. First edition. Spine tips rubbed. Gach 94-288 1983 $25

VILLARD, HENRY   The Early History of Transportation in Oregon. Eugene, 1944. 1st ed. Ptd. wrp. Jenkins 153-802 1983 $30

VILLEFOSSE, HERON DE   A Tribute to Precious Stones. (Paris): Cartier, 1947. Small folio, with an orig. color lithograph frontis. by Derain. This is one of 1472 copies. Folded sheets loose within printed wraps.; extremities lightly chipped. Karmiole 73-37 1983 $100

VILLIERS, ALAN J.   The Coral Sea. New York, 1949. First edition. 8vo. Orig. cloth. 3 text maps, (1 full page). Endpaper maps, 21 text illus., slightly worn and soiled. Good. Edwards 1042-176 1983 £15

VILLIERS, ALAN J.   Cruise of the Conrad. N.Y., 1937. First edition. Illus. 8vo, dust wrapper. Morrill 286-962 1983 $20

VILLIERS, ALAN J.   The Cutty Sark, Last of a Glorious Era. Hodder and Stoughton, 1953. Fenning 62-375 1983 £12

VILLIERS, ALAN J.   Last of the Wind Ships. New York, William Morrow (ca. 1934). 1st American ed. Photographs by author. 8vo., plates. Morrill 286-497 1983 $35

VILLIERS, ALAN J.   The Sea in Ships. George Routledge, 1932. First edition, with folding plan and 112 plates from photographs by the author, 4to, v.g. Slightly frayed dust wrapper. Fenning 62-376 1983 £14.50

VILLIERS, ALAN J.   Sons of Sinbad. New York, 1940. First edition. 8vo. Orig. cloth. Frontis. 15 plates, 2 full page maps, 1 text map and endpaper maps. Orig. dust jacket. Fine. Edwards 1042-177 1983 £40

VILLIERS, GEORGE, DUKE OF BUCKINGHAM
Please turn to
BUCKINGHAM, GEORGE VILLIERS, DUKE OF

VILLIERS, H. MONTAGU   Balls and theatres; or, the duty of reproving the works of darkness. A sermon. London: James Nisbet and Co., 1846. 12mo, wrappers, first edition. Rare. Ximenes 64-526 1983 $25

VILLON, FRANCOIS   The Ballads of Francois Villon. San Francisco: Windsor Press, 1927. With 2 hand-colored illus and dec. color initial. Text printed in red, blue and black. Edition limited to 200 numbered copies. Bound in full vellum, gilt-stamped cover; one tie lacking. In slipcase, repaired with tape. Karmiole 74-98 1983 $100

VILLON, FRANCOIS   Sundry Ballades. SF, 1922. Sm 4to, parchment-backed bds., leather label. Translated out of the Old Frence by John Payne. Cover, title-page and initials by Joseph Sinel. One of 210 copies. A fine copy Perata 27-56 1983 $135

VILMORIN, M. L.   Fruticetum Vilmorinianum. Paris, 1904. Text-figures, royal 8vo, cloth (trifle stained). Wheldon 160-2024 1983 £22

VIMERCATO, GIO BATTISTA   Dialogo Del Molto Rever... In Venegia Appresso Gabriel Giolito De' Ferrari MDLXV, (1565). 4to, three folding woodcut diagrams. In full new red morocco and new endpapers. Toned throughout. Some waterstaining in margins. Second edition. Good. Arkway 22-73 1983 $575

VINCENT, FRANK   Actual Africa, or, the coming continent. New York: D. Appleton, 1895. 8vo. Folding map. Plates. Orig. green cloth. Ex-lib. Adelson Africa-231 1983 $30

VINCENT, WILLIAM   The Commerce and Navigation of the Ancients in the Indian Ocean. London: T. Cadell & W. Davies, 1807. First collected edition, large 4to, 2 vols., cont. half calf gilt, marbled boards, 13 maps, 2 engraved frontispieces. Foxing of some maps, but a fine, tight copy. Trebizond 18-168 1983 $550

VINCENT, WILLIAM THOMAS   Warlike Woolwich: A History and Guide. Woolwich: A.W. & J.P. Jackson, London: Simpkin, Marshall, (1874). Front. & illus. Numerous illus. ads. Neat strengthening of inner hinges. Orig. pink cloth a little rubbed. Signed presentation copy from the author, Dec 30, '74. Jarndyce 31-304 1983 £36

VINCENT DE BEAUVAIS   Speculum Naturale. (Strassburg: Adolf Rusch, not after 1476). 2 vols. Editio princeps. Incl. first and last blanks. Initials supplied in red; rubricated. Large folio. Cont. blind-stamped pigskin over wooden boards, (wormed), by Paulus, the Heidelberg binder. Metal parts of two-clasps preserved on each vol. From the libraries of Georg Kloss, with his bookplate, and of Harrison D. Horblit. Very fine. Kraus 164-248 1983 $52,000

VINCENTIUS BELLOVACENSIS
Please turn to
VINCENT DE BEAUVAIS

VINER, GEORGE H.   A Descriptive Catalogue of the Bookplates Designed and Etched by George W. Eve. Kansas City: The American Bookplate Society, 1916. With 9 plates, tinted brown. Index. Edition ltd. to 250 copies on handmade paper. Bookplate removed. Boards. Karmiole 72-20 1983 $85

VINING, EDWARD P.   An Inglorious Columbus. New York: D. Appleton & Company, 1885. First edition. Frontis. map and 31 illus. Orig. green cloth. Library plate on front pastedown. Cover extremities worn (top of spine frayed), but very good and sound copy. Bradley 66-687 1983 $125

VIRCHOW, RUDOLF   Cellular Pathology. Phila., 1863. Orig. cloth, (backstrip repaired); ex-lib. Tall 8vo. 144 wood engrs. Argosy 713-556 1983 $125

VIRCHOW, RUDOLF   Cellular Pathology. Ann Arbor, 1940. Facsimile of 1860 edition. 8vo. Orig. binding. Fye H-3-582 1983 $30

VIRGIL
Please turn to
VERGILIUS MARO, PUBLIUS

VIRGIL, POLYDORE
Please turn to
VERGILIUS, POLYDORUS

VIRGINIA. LAWS.   Acts of the General Assembly of the State of Virginia, Passed in 1861-62. Richmond, Ritchie, 1862. Half calf. First edition. Ginsberg 46-765 1983 $250

VIRGINIA. LAWS.   Acts of the General Assembly of the State of Virginia, Passed at Called Session 1863. Richmond, 1863, 4. Linen-backed boards, bound in 1 vol. Argosy 710-552 1983 $175

VIRGINIA. LAWS.   The Code of Virginia: With the Declaration of Rights and Constitution of Virginia. Richmond, 1849. Calf, tall, thick 8vo, each page interleaved. Argosy 710-554 1983 $40

VISCHER, EDWARD   Drawings of the California Missions 1861-1878. With a Biography of the Artist. San Francisco, Book Club of Ca., 1982. 44 plates. Orig. cloth, d.j. Ltd. to 600 copies. Ginsberg 46-127 1983 $250

A VISIT to Texas: Being the Journal of a Traveller Through Those Parts Most Interesting to American Settlers. N.Y., 1838. Full calf. Library stamp on title-page. Upper right corner of one leaf in fac. Jenkins 153-626 1983 $150

THE VISITATION Sermon. Bristol: for W. Browne, 1788. Sole edition. 4to. Uncut, stitched as issued. Small ownership stamp. Dust soiled. Very rare. Heath 48-442 1983 £200

THE VISITING Day. For T. Lowndes, 1768. First edition. 2 vols. 12mo, half-title in vol. I. Five ad. pages in collation at end of vol. II. Cont. paper boards, sheep spines (worn), uncut. Hannas 69-218 1983 £250

VISSCHER, WILLIAM L.   A Thrilling and Truthful History of the Pony Express. Chicago, 1908. Illus. Orig. pictorial cloth. Many illus. Jenkins 153-441 1983 $30

VITALI, LAMBERTO   Disegni di Modigliani. Milano: Ulrico Hoepli, 1929. 31 plates. Small 8vo. Wrappers. Edition limited to 1100 numbered copies. Ars Libri 33-545 1983 $25

VITALI, LAMBERTO   Morandi. Catalogo generale. Milano: Electa, 1977. 2 vols. 1345 illus. hors texte. Large square 4to. Cloth. Dust jacket. Slipcase. Edition limited to 999 numbered copies. Ars Libri 33-553 1983 $200

VITALI, LAMBERTO   Quarantacinque disegni di Modigliani. Torino: Giulio Einaudi, 1959. 45 color facsimiles plates each under passepartout, loose in portfolio as issued. Large square folio. Cloth. No. 315 of a limited edition of 1000 copies. Ars Libri 33-546 1983 $375

VITALI, LAMBERTO   Quarantacinque disegni di Alberto Giacometti. Torino: Giulio Einaudi, 1963. 45 color facsimile plates each under passepartout, loose in portfolio as issued. Large Square folio. Cloth. No. 183 of a limited edition of 1250 copies. Ars Libri 32-257 1983 $275

VIZETELLY, HENRY   Extracts Principally from the English Classics. London: (the author), 1888. First edition. Orig. cloth-backed boards. 12 copies printed. Covers soiled. Endpapers browning. Good. MacManus 280-5341 1983 $350

VIZETELLY, HENRY   Facts about Champagne and Other Sparkling Wines. Ward, Lock, 1879. First edition, 40 plates and many other illus., 2 inserted slips, cr. 8vo, recent boards, very good copy. Fenning 61-459 1983 £35

VIZETELLY, HENRY   Four Months Among the Gold-Finders in Alta California... London: David Bogue, Fleet Street, 1849. Map. Orig. embossed red cloth with new spine. Some wear but fairly nice copy. Jenkins 153-663 1983 $150

VIZETELLY, HENRY   Four Months Among the Gold-Finders in Alta California. London, 1849. Map, half morocco. Second edition. Ginsberg 47-196 1983 $75

VIZETELLY, HENRY   The Story of the Diamond Necklace. Tinsley Brothers, 1867. 2nd edition, revised. 2 vols. Front. 3 pp ads. vol. I. Orig. maroon cloth, recased, v.g. Jarndyce 30-577 1983 £28

VOGE, WILHELM   Die deutschen Bildwerke und die der anderen cisalpinen Lander. Berlin, 1910. Zweite Auflage. (Konigliche Museen zu Berlin. Beschreibung der Bildwerke der christlichen Epochen. Vol. 4.) viii, 338pp., 36 hinged collotype plates. Lrg. 4to. Boards (slightly worn). Ars Libri SB 26-242 1983 $450

VOGE, WILHELM   Jorg Syrlin Der Altere und sein Bilwerke. Berlin: Deutscher Verein fur Kunstwissenschaft, 1950. 78 plates. 85 illus. Large 4to. Boards, 1/4 cloth. From the library of Jakob Rosenberg. Ars Libri 32-658 1983 $100

VOGEL, CLAUDE L.   The Capuchins in French Louisiana... Wash., 1928. 1st ed. Cloth, orig. printed wrappers bound in. Illus., maps. Very scarce. Jenkins 153-343 1983 $100

VOGEL, EL F. DE   Seedlings of Dicotyledons. The Hague, 1980. Watercolours and drawings, royal 8vo, cloth. Wheldon 160-1578 1983 £40

VOGEL, EMIL   Marco da Gagliano. Leipzig, 1889. 8vo, pamphlet binding. Salloch 387-406 1983 $24

VOLCK, ADELBERT J.   Confederate War Etchings. (Philadelphia, 1880's,). Index leaf, correctly issued without title page and 29 line etchings on India paper, each 8 by 10 1/4 inches, mounted on stiff larger sheets. In a cont. cloth portfolio. First edition. Reese 19-570 1983 $1,250

VOLKHOVSKY, FELIX   A China Cup. n.d. Illus. by Malischeff. Frontis. & 1 illus. Bkstrip discol'd & cvrs. marked, lower fr. corner of fr. free ep. eaten by silver-fish, 2 pp rear sl. crumpled, good. Hodgkins 27-45 1983 £10.50

VOLLGRAF, W.   Collection of Articles and Reprints. V.p., n.d. 8vo, cloth. Salloch 385-315 1983 $30

VOLNEY, CONSTANTIN FRANCOIS Travels through Syria and Egypt... London: G.G.J. & J. Robinson, 1787. First English edition. 2 vols. 8vo. 2 folding maps. 3 plates. Cont. 1/4 vellum. Marbled boards. Adelson Africa-144 1983 $200

VOLNEY, CONSTANTIN FRANCOIS Travels in Syria and Egypt. Perth, 1801. 2 folding maps, plan, 2 plates. 2 vols. 12mo. Mottled calf, labels, gilt. Some wear to corners and head and tail of spines. Good. Edwards 1044-729 1983 £110

VOLNEY, CONSTANTIN FRANCOIS A View of the Soil and Climate of the United States of America. Philadelphia, J. Conrad, 1804. First American ed. 8vo., Contemp. calf. gilt, mor. label (nicked). Plates, half title, front flyleaf detached but present. Trebizond 18-170 1983 $375

VOLTAIRE, FRANCOIS MARIE AROUET DE   The Age of Louis XIV. London: R. Dodsley, 1752. First English edition. 2 vols. 8vo. Illus. Later 3/4 brown morocco & cloth. Foxing, ink smudge on title-page of first volume. Very good. MacManus 280-1542 1983 $150

VOLTAIRE, FRANCOIS MARIE AROUET DE   The Age of Louis XV. Dublin: G. Faulkner, J. Exshaw, et al., 1770. First English edition. Extra-illus. 2 vols. Small 8vo. Full cranberry calf, gilt. Fine. MacManus 280-5343 1983 $225

VOLTAIRE, FRANCOIS MARIE AROUET DE   Le Brutus, de M. de Voltaire, avec un Discours sur la Tragedie. Paris: J. Fr. Josse, 1731. 1st ed., 8vo, modern calf antique, original morocco label, approbation leaf, advertisements. A fine copy of an uncommon title. Trebizond 18-126 1983 $300

VOLTAIRE, FRANCOIS MARIE AROUET DE   Candide. N.p. (Germany), 1759. 12mo, title page (with vignette) printed in red. Cont. mottled sheep (rubbed), gilt spine, red edges. A clean, unused copy. Hannas 69-220 1983 £130

VOLTAIRE, FRANCOIS MARIE AROUET DE   Candide. N.Y.: The Bennett Libraries, Inc., 1927. 10 etchings by C. Tice. Full decorated calf. Copy No. 1 of 250 copies printed from type cast by Joh. Enschede en Zonen from orig. Didot matrices on Pannekoek paper. Soiled. MacManus 280-5344 1983 $20

VOLTAIRE, FRANCOIS MARIE AROUET DE   Candide. N.Y., Random, 1928. 4to, illus. with drawings by Kent. Tan cloth (spine a bit sunned), else a fine copy. Pub.'s cloth slipcase. One of 1470 copies, signed by Kent. Houle 21-468 1983 $145

VOLTAIRE, FRANCOIS MARIE AROUET DE   Candide. New York, 1929. 4to. Cloth. Laid into the book is an issue of Wings which contains an article by Carl Van Doren on why the book was selected for the Literary Guild. A fine copy in lightly worn but intact dj. In Our Time 156-466 1983 $30

VOLTAIRE, FRANCOIS MARIE AROUET DE   Den Babyloniska Prinsessan. Stockholm, J.C. Holmberg, 1786. Small 8vo, disbound. Last few leaves water-stained. Hannas 69-219 1983 £50

VOLTAIRE, FRANCOIS MARIE AROUET DE   The History of Charles XII, King of Sweden. London 1807. Recent full lea., very good. King 46-771 1983 $25

VOLTAIRE, FRANCOIS MARIE AROUET DE   The History of the War of Seventeen Hundred and Forty One. London: J. Nourse, 1756. 1st ed. in English, 8vo, cont. calf gilt, morocco label. 2 parts in one volume. Half-title not called for. Advertisement leaf. Top of spine chipped but a fine copy. Trebizond 18-216 1983 $175

VOLTAIRE, FRANCOIS MARIE AROUET DE   L'Ingenu; Or, The Sincere Huron. Dublin: Printed for J. Milliken, 1768. 12mo, contemporary calf. First Dublin edition. Hill 165-135 1983 £50

A VOLUNTEER Haversack Containing Contributions of Certain Writers to the Queen's Rifle Volunteer Brigade. Edinburgh: Printed for the Brigade, 1902. Gilt parchment. Illus. First edition. Parchment trifle rubbed, else fine. Reese 20-34 1983 $35

VOM RAUMER, FREDERICK   Contributions to Modern History, from the British Museum and the State Paper Office. Charles Knight & Co., 1836. 8vo, portrait, cont. calf, spine gilt. Bickersteth 77-181 1983 £20

VON FALKE, JACOB   Art in the House. Boston, L. Prang and Company, 1879. 1st American ed. Illus. with chromo-lithographs, albertotypes and typographic etchings. 4to. Corners rubbed. Morrill 286-145 1983 $95

VON HOHENHEIM, PHILIP AUREOL THEOPHRAST BOMBAST   Badenfart Buchlin... Frnkfurt: Peter Schmidt, 1566. Second edition. Full-page woodcut. Title in red and black, decorated woodcut initials. 8vo. Modern boards. Tiny tear on fore-edge of title. Kraus 164-176 1983 $875

VON HOHENHEIM, PHILIP AUREOL THEOPHRAST BOMBAST   Ein schoner Tractat... Strassburg: Christian Muller, 1571. First edition. Woodcut printer's mark on last leaf. 8vo. Modern boards. Small wormhole in lower margin of 3 signatures, few pages with some under- lining in faded ink. Kraus 164-179 1983 $750

VON HOHENHEIM, PHILIP AUREOL THEOPHRAST BOMBAST   Funff Bucher vonn dem Langen leben. Strassburg: Bernhard Jobin, 1574. Title in red and black with woodcut border. Full-page woodcut portrait. 8vo. Modern boards. Early inscription on title of de Wahlberg. Kraus 164-180 1983 $850

VON HOHENHEIM, PHILIP AUREOL THEOPHRAST BOMBAST   Liber Vexationum. (Basle: S. Apiarius, 1567). First edition. 8vo. Modern boards. Very light stain at top of first few leaves. Rare. Kraus 164-178 1983 $950

VON HOHENHEIM, PHILIP AUREOL THEOPHRAST BOMBAST   Pharmacandi modus. Strassburg: Christian Muller, 1578. 2 blank ff. Woodcut printer's device on title and on last leaf. 8vo. Modern boards. Second edition. Kraus 164-181 1983 $530

VON HOHENHEIM, PHILIP AUREOL THEOPHRAST BOMBAST   Spittal Buch... Frankfurt am Main: Peter Schmid, 1566. Second edition. 1 blank. Title in black and red. 8vo. Modern boards. Kraus 164-177 1983 $950

VONNEGUT, KURT   Deadeye Dick. (New York): Delecorte, (1982). Cloth, a.e.g. First edition. One of 350 numbered copies, specially bound, and signed by the author. Mint as issued in cloth slipcase. Reese 20-1095 1983 $75

VONNEGUT, KURT   Jailbird. NY, (1979). One of 500 num- bered and signed copies, fine in fine slipcase. Quill & Brush 54- 1445 1983 $75

VONNEGUT, KURT   Slapstick. New York: Delacourte Press, (1976). 1st ed., 1 of 250 numbered and signed copies. Orig. cloth, boxed. Mint copy. Jenkins 155-1245 1983 $75

VON RHAU, HENRY   Tale of the Nineties. New York: Privately Printed, 1930. Roy. 8vo. Orig. illus. boards, cloth spine. 6 black and white plates by Frank Peers. Limited edition of 1,050 numbered copies. Traylen 94-844 1983 £12

VON STROHEIM, ERICH   Paprika. N.Y., Macaulay, (1935). First edition. Gilt stamped red cloth (spot on cover). Inscribed and signed to Sid Grauman Feb. 24, 1935. Houle 22-926 1983 $125

VON TROIL, UNO   Letters on Iceland. 1780. With engr. frontis. and folding engr. map, 8vo. Second edition corrected and improved. A little age browned and foxed but good in modern quarter morocco. K Books 307-187 1983 £110

VON WAGNER-JAUREGG, J.   Baron Constantine von Economo, His Life and Work. Burlington, 1937. First edition in English. 8vo. Orig. binding. Very scarce. Fye H-3-986 1983 $50

VON WITZLEBEN, H. D.   Herz-Und Kreislauferkrankungen in Thren Beziehungen Zum Nervensystem Und Zur Psyche. Leipzig: Georg Thieme, 1939. First edition. Ads. Inscribed to Adolf Meyer. Blue buckram preserving orig. wrappers. Library bookplate removed, stamp on rear paste-down. Gach 95-514 1983 $30

VOORN, HENK   Old Ream Wrappers; an Essay on Early Ream Wrappers of Antiquarian Interest. North Hills: Bird & Bull Press, 1969. Small 4to. Leather spine, marbled paper over boards. Gray paper folder containing two copper-plate prints of 19th century Dutch ream wrappers. One of 375 numbered copies. Scarce. Fine. Oak Knoll 39-44 1983 $325

VORONOFF, SERGE   Rejuvenation by Grafting. N.Y., (1925). 8vo, cloth. 38 illus. First edition in English. Argosy 713-557 1983 $75

VORSE, MARY HEATON   The Ninth Man. (NY): Press of the Woolly Whale. 1936. Small 4to, illus. throughout. Beige cloth, leather spine and cover labels. Karmiole 72-111 1983 $35

VOSS, G.   Der Hypnotismus. Halle: Carl Marhold, 1907. First edition. Modern cloth. M. J. Karpas' copy (unsigned), heavily underlined. Gach 95-227 1983 $30

VOYNICH, E. L.   The Gadfly. NY, 1897. Pic. cover slightly rubbed, fore-edges slightly stained, good, owner's name. Quill & Brush 54-1448 1983 $35

VRIES, A. B. DE   Jan Vermeer van Delft. London: B.T. Batsford, 1948. New edition. 73 plates. 4to. Cloth. Dust jacket. Ars Libri 32-687 1983 $44

VRIES, HUGO DE   Die Mutationstheorie. Von Veit, Leipzig, 1901-03. 2 vols., 8vo, with 12 chromolithographed plates; occasional slight foxing of text and 4 plates; a very good copy in orig. half cloth. First edition. Quaritch NS 5-31 1983 $650

VRIES, HUGO DE   Opera e Periodicis Collata. Utrecht, 1918-20. Portrait, 6 vols., 8vo, original cloth. Wheldon 160-1579 1983 £70

VROMAN, A. C.   The Genesis of the Story of Ramona. Los Angeles: Press of Kingsley-Barnes & Neuner, 1899. Unpaged. In tattered and repaired wrappers. Dawson 471-293 1983 $30

VROOMAN, JOHN J.   Forts and Firesides of the Mohawk Country, New York. Philadelphia, 1943. First edition. Autographed. Plates. 4to. Morrill 290-374 1983 $37.50

VULLIAMY, BENJAMIN LEWIS   Some considerations on the subject of public clocks... London: printed by B. McMillan, 1828. First edition. 4to. Cont. maroon straight-grained morocco, gilt, spine gilt. A fine copy. Very scarce. Ximenes 63-75 1983 $225

VULLO, SALVATRICE   Antonino Manno. Palermo: Michele Greco, 1938. Frontis. Small 4to. Wrappers. Ars Libri 33-216 1983 $37.50

VYSE, CHARLES   The New London Spelling-Book. Gainsborough: Henry Mozley, 1814. Half title, front. port. sheep. Very good. Jarndyce 31-666 1983 £38

W

WAAL, ANTON DE   Roma Sacra. Heidelberg, 1925. Profusely illus. 4to. Cloth. Salloch 385-392 1983 $40

WADDELL, HELEN   The Abbe Provost. London: Constable & Co. Ltd., (1933). First edition. Woodcut frontis. by H.W. Bray. Orig. vellum & cloth. Dust jacket. Limited to 750 copies signed by the author. Small bookplate. Fine. MacManus 280-5344a 1983 $40

WADDELL, HELEN   The Abbe Prevost. London, 1933. First Trade edition. One of 750 copies, signed by author. Dust wrapper. Fine. Rota 231-612 1983 £12

WADDELL, L. A.   Among the Himalayas. London, 1899. First edition. 4 maps, 1 folding. Numerous illus. Modern quarter calf. 8vo. Good. Edwards 1044-731 1983 £145

WADDINGTON, C. W.   Indian India. London, 1933. Folding map, 30 plates, folio. Buckram-backed cloth. 8vo. Good. Edwards 1044-732 1983 £30

WADSWORTH, BENJAMIN   The Saint's Prayer to Escape Temptations. Boston, 1715. Later antique calf, very good. Reese 19-38 1983 $400

WADSWORTH, CHARLES   War a Discipline. San F., 1864. Orig. printed wraps. First edition. Ginsberg 47-197 1983 $35

WAGEMANN, CLARA E.   Covered Bridges of New England. Rutland, Vt., 1931. Ed. limited to 500 signed copies. Full-page etchings by George T. Plowman. 8vo, orig. suede-covered boards. Morrill 287-485 1983 $35

WAGENER, G. R.   Beitrage zur Entwicklungs-Geschichte der Eingeweidewurmer. Haarlem, 1855. 37 plates (29 coloured), 4to, wrappers. Wheldon 160-1349 1983 £18

THE WAGGON of Life and other lyrics by Russian poets of the nineteeth century. Cambridge University Press for Cresset Press, 1947. Slim 8vo, parallel Russian and English texts, uncut in cream buckram gilt, covers slightly darkened, neat bookplate and signature. 1,500 numbered copies. Deighton 3-253 1983 £32

WAGNER, GLENDOLIN D,   Old Neutriment. Boston: Ruth Hill, Publisher, 1934. 1st ed. in dust jacket. Plates. Fine copy signed by the author. Jenkins 151-57 1983 $125

WAGNER, GLENDOLIN D.   Old Neutriment. Boston, Ruth Hill, 1934. Illus. Orig. cloth, first edition. Ginsberg 46-217 1983 $100

WAGNER, HENRY R.   Bullion to Books. Los Angeles, 1942. Cloth, fine. Reese 19-572 1983 $125

WAGNER, HENRY R.   California Voyages, 1529-1541. San Francisco, 1925. Orig. cloth, faded. First edition. Ginsberg 46-128 1983 $75

WAGNER, HENRY R.   The Plains & the Rockies. San F., 1982. Illus. Cloth. Fourth edition. Ginsberg 46-789 1983 $150

WAGNER, HENRY R.   The Plains & the Rockies. San Francisco: John Howell Books, 1982. Large 8vo, frontis. Index. Fine, as new. Karmiole 72-6 1983 $150

WAGNER, HENRY R.   The Spanish Southwest 1542-1794. Albuquerque: Quivira Society, 1937. 2 vols., plates. Boards, cloth spines. 1 of 401 numbered sets. Fine. Dawson 470-298 1983 $250

WAGNER, RICHARD   Der Fliegende Hollaender. Dresden, Meser, n.d. (1843). Orig. printed wrs. Small 8vo, slightly foxed. First edition. Salloch 387-248 1983 $90

WAGNER, RICHARD   The Flying Dutchman. (N.p.): The Corvinus Press, (1938). Quarto. Full gilt vellum. One of 130 copies, printed in red and black on Barcham Green Medway paper, with the English translation facing the German original. With a fine presentation inscription from the printer on the front blank. Fine in orig. linen and boards chemise, ribbon ties. Reese 20-279 1983 $200

WAGNER, RICHARD   The Flying Dutchman. Corvinus Press, (1938). 4to, German and English parallel texts printed in red and black throughout, full vellum gilt, t.e.g., others uncut, very fine. Deighton 3-85 1983 £95

WAGNER, RICHARD   Gesammelte Schriften und Dichtungen. Leipzig, 1897. 10 vols., bound in 5. Third edition, 8vo, 3/4 morocco with labels, gilt tooled, gilt edges. Fine set. Salloch 387-246 1983 $175

WAGNER, RICHARD   The Rhinegold & The Valkyrie. N.Y.: Doubleday; London: Hein., 1910. First American edition. Blue cloth. Gilt pictorial stamped. Light spine wear. 34 tipped in color plates with tissue guards and 14 black & whites. Pictorial endpapers. Very good to fine. Aleph-bet 8-213 1983 $130

WAGNER, RICHARD   Tannhaeuser und der Saengerkrieg auf Wartburg. Dresden, Meser, 1845. Small 8vo, orig. wrs. First edition. Salloch 387-249 1983 $75

WAGNER, RICHARD   Tannhaeuser und der Saengerkrieg auf Wartburg. Dresden, Meser, N.d. (ca. 1850). Small 8vo, wraps. Salloch 387-174 1983 $20

WAGNER, RICHARD   Tannhauser. N.Y., (ca.1930's). Black cloth. Unpaginated, untrimmed foredge. Frayed and holed dust wrapper. Every page decorated plus 8 full page plates by W. Pogany. King 45-421 1983 $25

WAGNER, RICHARD   Ueber Schauspieler und Saenger. Leipzig, 1872. First edition. 8vo, 3/4 cloth, orig. wrs., bound in. Salloch 387-247 1983 $150

WAHLENBERG, G.   Flora Upsaliensis. Upsala, 1820. 8vo, modern cloth, rare. Lacking map. Blank corner torn from the title-page, which bears a small library stamp, and a little foxing and soiling throughout. Wheldon 160-1780 1983 £40

WAIT, W. E.   Manual of the Birds of Ceylon. 1925. Map and 20 plain plates, 4to, cloth (trifle used). Wheldon 160-913 1983 £40

WAITE, ARTHUR EDWARD (1857-1942)   Azoth. London: The Theosophical Pub. Society, 1893. First edition. Covers a bit worn. Gach 95-515 1983 $125

WAITE, ARTHUR EDWARD (1857-1942)   A Book of Mystery and Vision. London: Philip Wellby, 1892. First edition. Publisher's gilt stamped cloth. Gach 95-516 1983 $65

WAITE, ARTHUR EDWARD (1857-1942)   The Hidden Church of the Holy Grail. London: Rebman, Ltd., 1909. First edition. Fair to good copy in publisher's red cloth (worn), front blank leaves lacking. Gach 95-517 1983 $50

WAITE, ARTHUR EDWARD (1857-1942)   The Life of Louis Claude de Saint-Martin. London: Philip Wellby, 1901. First edition. Cloth spine, boards. Gach 95-518 1983 $60

WAITE, ARTHUR EDWARD (1857-1942)   Lives of Alchemystical Philosophers. London: George Redway, 1888. Gach 95-519 1983 $125

WAITE, ARTHUR EDWARD (1857-1942)   The Pictorial Key to the Tarot.
London: William Rider & Son, 1922 (1910). Gach 95-520 1983 $35

WAITE, ARTHUR EDWARD (1857-1942)   The Quest of the Golden Stairs.
London: The Theosophical Pub. House, (1927). First edition. Cloth
spine, boards. Gach 95-521 1983 $75

WAITE, ARTHUR EDWARD (1857-1942)   The Real History of the Rosi-
crucians. London: George Redway, 1887. First edition. Tips
lightly worn. Gach 95-522 1983 $100

WAITE, ARTHUR EDWARD (1857-1942)   The Secret Tradition in Free-
masonry. NY: Rebman Co., 1911. First American edition. Two vols.
Publisher's gilt-stamped cloth. Gach 95-523 1983 $175

WAITE, ARTHUR EDWARD (1857-1942)   Strange House of Sleep. London:
Philip Sinclair Wellby, 1896. First edition. #132/250 copies.
Frontis photo. Parchment, top edge gilt. Gach 95-524 1983 $175

WAITE, ORIS F. R.   Vermont in the Great Rebellion, containing Historical and Biographical Sketches. Claremont, N.H., 1869. First
edition, illus. A nice copy. Scarce. Jenkins 151-342 1983 $45

WAKE, WILLIAM   A Discourse of the Holy Eucharist.
Printed for Richard Chiswell, 1687. First edition, 4to, wrapper,
without the imprimatur leaf, some very light soiling but a very good
copy. Fenning 61-462 1983 £14.50

WAKE, WILLIAM   An Exposition of the Doctrine of the
Church of England. Printed for Richard Chiswell, 1686. First
edition, 4to, wrapper, a very good copy. Fenning 61-463 1983 £14.50

WAKE, WILLIAM   The Missionarie's Arts Discovered.
Printed, and sold by Randal Taylor, 1688. First edition, wanting
imprimatur leaf or half-title, 4to, wrapper, a very good copy.
Fenning 61-464 1983 £18.50

WAKE, WILLIAM   A Second Defence of the Exposition of the
Doctrine of the Church of England. Printed for Richard Chiswell, 1687.
First edition. Includes imprimatur leaf. 4to, wrapper. Very good
copy. Fenning 61-466 1983 £12.50

WAKE, WILLIAM   Twenty Two Sermons Preached upon
Several Occasions... London: for R.S., 1737. 2 vols. 8vo.
Cont. polished calf, gilt. Traylen 94-845 1983 £24

WAKEFIELD, E. M.   Common British Fungi. 1981. Second
edition, completely revised by R. W. G. Dennis, 111 coloured plates
and 8 text-figures, 8vo, cloth. Edition limited to 1,500 copies.
Wheldon 160-1910 1983 £39.50

WAKEFIELD, EDWARD GIBBON   Facts relating to the punishment of
death in the metropolis. London: James Ridgway, 1831. First
edition. Small 8vo. Orig. grey boards, printed paper label.
A fine copy. Very uncommon. Ximenes 63-84 1983 $500

WAKEFIELD, GILBERT   Memoirs of the Life of Gilbert Wakefield. London: for J. Johnson and T. Bensley, 1804. New edition
with his latest corrections. 2 vols. Roy. 8vo. Cont. half blue
straight-grained morocco, gilt, gilt panelled spines, edges gilt.
Mezzotint portrait. Beckford's copy with a note on the fly-leaf,
"This copy of Wakefield's Memoirs with notes in both volumes in the
hand-writing of Mr. Beckford were sold by me at Fonthill Abbey Sept.
1823. H. Phillip." Traylen 94-846 1983 £270

WAKEFIELD, H. RUSSELL   The Clock Strikes Twelve. Sauk City:
Arkham House, 1946. First edition. Cloth. Fine in lightly worn
dust jacket. Bradley 66-147 1983 $22.50

WAKEFIELD, JOHN A.   Wakefield's History of the Black Hawk
War. Chicago, 1908. Frontis. Vellum and boards, very good. Reese
19-573 1983 $125

WAKEFIELD, PRISCILLA   An Introduction to Botany. Printed for
E. Newberry; Darton and Harvey; and Vernor and Hood, 1796. 12mo,
half title. 11 engraved plates, plate 4 with extra folding table,
orig. pink boards, rebacked. First edition. Bickersteth 75-265
1983 £40

WAKEFIELD, PRISCILLA   An Introduction to Botany. 1798.
12mo, 11 plates, plate 4 with extra folding table, orig. grey boards
and paper spine. Bickersteth 75-266 1983 £30

WAKELY, J. B.   Lost Chapters Recovered from the Early
History of American Methodism. New York, 1858. First edition. Illus.
Numerous woodcut and steel engraved plates. Cloth. Covers worn, fox-
ing. Good copy only. Felcone 20-104 1983 $25

WAKEMAN, FRANCIS   The Plough Press, 1967-1981. Fifteen
Years Printing in a Loughborough Garage. (Oxford): The Plough
Press, 1982. First edition. Tall 8vo. Half morocco over marbled
paper coverd boards. Limited to 120 numbered copies. Illus. in
the text and numerous specimens of printing tipped in. Oak Knoll
48-469 1983 $100

WAKEMAN, GEOFFREY   Victorian Colour Printing. (Loughborough), 1981. Lg. 4to, leather-backed marbled boards, gilt. One of
150 copies. Fine. Perata 28-214 1983 $250

WAKEMAN, JOEL   The Maine Law Triumphant.
Boston, 1859. Frontis, cloth, top of spine slightly chipped.
King 46-221 1983 $25

WAKOSKI, DIANE   Abalone. Los Angeles, Black Sparrow
Press, 1974. First edition. One of 26 lettered copies, signed by
the author. Plain white dust jacket (yellow line across rear cover)
else fine. Houle 22-929 1983 $75

WAKOSKI, DIANE   Black Dream for Billy the Kid. Black
Sparrow Press, 1970. 12mo. Boards. 1 of 26 copies lettered and
signed by poet. Fine in acetate jacket. In Our Time 156-849 1983
$100

WAKOSKI, DIANE   The Diamond Merchant. The Sans Souci
Press, Cambridge, Mass. (1968). 8vo. Cloth. Total ed. is 99 copies
signed by poet. Inscribed by Wakoski on front flyleaf. Letter from
the publisher laid in noting that this is the only copy which has an
experimental deckle label on front of dj. Fine. In Our Time 156-847
1983 $150

WAKOSKI, DIANE   The Lament of the Lady Bank Dick. Sans
Souci Press, Cambridge, Mass., 1969. 8vo. Cloth, boards. Total ed.
is 99 copies (numbered), of which this is 1 of 10 copies for presentation and signed by Wakoski and publisher. With an orig. drawing
by poet. Fine in glassine jacket. In Our Time 156-848 1983 $125

WAKOSKI, DIANE   Making a Sacher Torte. Mt. Horeb:
Perishable Press, 1981. Octavo. First edition. Illus. Limited to
225 copies. Mint in leather-backed paste-paper over boards. Bromer
25-279 1983 $225

WAKOSKI, DIANE   The Pumpkin Pie. Black Sparrow Press,
1972. 8vo. Wraps. Issued as a Christmas Greeting from the Press.
First (unpublished) issue of the book. 8 copies were run off with
"page 13" improperly placed at head of "page 16." Of the 8 copies,
publisher asked poet to sign 6. 1 of 6 signed copies. Fine. In
Our Time 156-850 1983 $150

WAKOSKI, DIANE   The Pumpkin Pie. Black Sparrow Press,
1972. 12mo. Boards. 1 of 26 copies lettered and signed by poet.
Fine in acetate jacket. In Our Time 156-851 1983 $100

WAKOSKI, DIANE   The Ring. Black Sparrow Press, 1977.
8vo. Cloth. 1 of 40 copies signed by poet with orig. ink drawing
by same. Fine in acetate jacket. In Our Time 156-853 1983 $125

WAKOSKI, DIANE   Smudging. Black Sparrow Press, 1972.
8vo. Cloth, boards. 1 of 30 copies signed by poet with holograph
poem by same. Fine in acetate jacket. In Our Time 156-852 1983
$100

WAKOSKI, DIANE   Trophies. Black Sparrow Press, 1979.
8vo. Cloth, boards. 1 of 50 copies signed by poet, with orig. water
color by same. Fine in acetate jacket. In Our Time 156-854 1983
$100

WAKSMAN, SELMAN A.   Microbial Antagonisms and Antibiotic
Substances. N.Y., 1945. Illus. First edition. Argosy 713-559
1983 $75

WALCOTT, MAC KENZIE E. D.   The Memorials of Westminster. F. & J. Rivington, 1851. A new edition. Front. & illus. Orig. purple cloth, faded. Very good. Jarndyce 31-305 1983 £24

WALDACK, CHARLES   Treatise on Photography. Cincinnati, 1865. 14 leaves of ads. for photographic material cloth, backstrip very chipped, internally good. Reese 19-426 1983 $600

WALDEGRAVE, a Novel. Henry Colburn, 1829. First edition. 3 vols. Half titles. Half calf, black labels. Jarndyce 31-415 1983 £60

WALDO, FRANCIS W.   Trial of Lieutenant Joel Abbot... Boston, 1822. First edition. Presentation from Abbot to William Sullivan, lawyer, writer, politician. 8vo, orig. boards. Ex-library, covers loose, lacks label. Morrill 287-487 1983 $35

WALDRON, GEORGE   The Complete Works in Verse and Prose. Printed for the Widow and Orphans. MDCCXXXI. Folio, large paper, plate of Manx coins. Title and some margins lightly foxed. Cont. calf, rebacked. First and only edition. Good. Quaritch NS 7-136 1983 $675

WALDSTEIN, CHARLES   The Argive Heraeum. Boston, 1902-5. First edition. Profusely illustrated. 2 vols., small folio, ex-library. Morrill 290-570 1983 $50

WALEY, ARTHUR   A Hundred and Seventy Chinese Poems. London, 1918. First edition. Corners just a little bruised. Very nice. Rota 230-612 1983 £35

WALEY, ARTHUR   The Temple and other poems. London, 1923. First edition. Spine just a little darkened. Nice. Rota 230-613 1983 £20

WALEY, ARTHUR   Three Ways of Thought in Ancient China. London, 1939. First edition. Covers a little soiled. Very nice. Rota 230-614 1983 £12.50

WALKER, A. EARL   A History of Neurological Surgery. Baltimore, 1951. First edition. 8vo. Orig. binding. Fye H-3-589 1983 $100

WALKER, ADAM   A Journal of Two Campaigns of the Fourth Regiment of U.S. Infantry, in the Michigan and Indiana Territories... Keene, N.H.: Printed at the Sentinel Press by the author, 1816. Orig. paper over wood boards, backed at an early date with paper, edges untrimmed, one marginal orig. paper flaw, otherwise a fine copy. The Littel copy. Boxed. Reese 18-508 1983 $1,250

WALKER, ADAM   A Philosophical Estimate of the Causes, Effects, and Cure, of Unwholsome Air in Large cities. (London): Robson, Johnson, and the author, 1777. 8vo, with folding plates fo diagrams. Boards. Rostenberg 88-87 1873 $385

WALKER, ADAM   A System of Familiar Philosophy. London: For the author, 1799. First edition. Large 4to, half-title lacking. Illus. with 47 engraved folding plates. Cont. calf, rebacked. Armorial bookplate. Karmiole 73-91 1983 $275

WALKER, ALEXANDER   Beauty: illustrated chiefly by an analysis and classification of beauty in woman. London: Wilson, 1836. First edition. Large 8vo. 19th-century half red morocco. Frontis. and 23 lithographed plates (on india paper, mounted). Ximenes 63-656 1983 $125

WALKER, ALEXANDER   Beauty. E. Wilson, 1836. 1st edn. Frontis. & 22 engr'd plates. Illus. with drawings by Henry Howard. Brown fine diaper grained blind stamped cloth, gilt decor. bkstrip, uncut (plates some foxing), v. nice copy. Hodgkins 27-337 1983 £35

WALKER, ALEXANDER   Beauty; illustrated chiefly by an Analysis and Classification of Beauty in Women... London, 1836. First edition. 8vo. Orig. cloth. 23 plates. One plate loose. Gurney JJ-416 1983 £25

WALKER, ALEXANDER   Intermarriage. New York, Langley, 1839. 1st American ed. 8 plates. Small 8vo. Morrill 289-240 1983 $22.50

WALKER, BETTINA   My Musical Experiences. Richard Bentley, 1890. First edition, with 2 plates, errata slip, 8vo, orig. cloth, gilt. A very good copy. Fenning 61-467 1983 £12.50

WALKER, DAVID H.   Pioneers of Prosperity. San Francisco, 1895. Ads. Orig. cloth. Fine. Jenkins 152-495 1983 $50

WALKER, FRANCIS A.   Hancock in the Rebellion. (N.Y., 1892). Orig. printed wrapper. Jenkins 152-651 1983 $45

WALKER, FRANCIS A.   Money. Macmillan, 1891. 1 p ads., index. Orig. brown cloth. Jarndyce 31-396 1983 £10.50

WALKER, FRANCIS A.   The World's Fair. Philadelphia, 1876. New York: A.S. Barnes, 1878. Orig. cloth. Jenkins 152-496 1983 $45

WALKER, FRANKLIN   A Literary History of Southern California. Berkeley, U. of Ca., 1950. Orig. cloth, dust jacket. First edition. Ginsberg 47-198 1983 $25

WALKER, GEORGE   Descriptive catalogue of a choice assemblage of original pictures... London, n.d. (1807). First edition. 8vo. Cont. half calf, rebacked. Interleaved. Ximenes 63-23 1093 $150

WALKER, GEORGE   The Vagabond. Dublin; Printed by D. Graisberry, for G. Burnet, P. Wogan (etc), 1800. 12mo, contemporary sheet, a little rubbed. Rather scarce. Hill 165-136 1983 £45

WALKER, HUGH   John B. Leicester Warren, Lord de Tabley. London: Chapman & Hall, 1903. First edition. Orig. wrappers (very slightly worn and soiled). Very good. MacManus 278-1479 1983 $45

WALKER, LEORY POPE   Speech of Gen. L.P. Walker on State and National Affairs... (Madison, 1878). 1st ed. Signed by author. Orig. printed wrappers, bound in later cloth, morocco label. Scarce. Jenkins 153-727 1983 $100

WALKER, MARY ALDEN   The Beginnings of Printing in the State of Indiana. Crawfordsville, R.E. Banta, 1934. First edition. Small folio. Morrill 290-200 1983 $75

WALKER, ORADIAH   Of Education. Oxon, at the Theater, Ann., 1773. 12mo, fine engraving on title of the University arms, with preliminary blank, and final errata leaf, nineteenth century speckled calf antique gilt, a little rubbed, a.e.g. Bickersteth 77-85 1983 £125

WALKER, OBADIAH   Some Instructions Concerning the Art of Oratory... Oxford, printed by L. Lichfield for the author and are to be sold by Jo. Crosley, 1682. 8vo, final blank leaf, orig. speckled calf, rubbed, slit at top of upper joint. Bickersteth 77-86 1983 £95

WALKER, R.   The Flora of Oxfordshire. Oxford, 1833. Folding table and 12 engraved plates, 8vo, original cloth, neatly repaired. Plates somewhat foxed. Wheldon 160-1633 1983 £45

WALKER, TIMOTHY   Annual Discourse, Delivered Before the Ohio Historical and Philosophical Society at Columbus, on the 23D of December, 1837. Cincinnati, 1838. Orig. front wrapper. First edition. Autograph presentation copy from "the author." Ginsberg 46-587 1983 $50

WALKER, WILLIAM   An Epitome of Astronomy, with the New Discoveries. Printed for the author, by C. Brightly; Bungay, 1802. 8vo, wrapper, recto of half-title a little dusty; a very good copy. Fenning 60-421 1983 £24.50

WALL, BERNHARDT   Following Abraham Lincoln 1809-1865. New York: The Wise-Parslow Company, (1943). Thick 4to. Cloth. Dust jacket. Dust jacket chipped and rubbed. Oak Knoll 49-390 1983 $30

WALL, BERNHARDT   Gen. Robert E. Lee. Sierra Madre, California, 1949. 36 leaves of engraved etchings on handmade paper. Limited to 100 signed and numbered copies. Stiff paper binding. Jenkins 152-498 1983 $250

WALL, BERNHARDT   Man's Best Friend. New York: Etched by Bernhardt Wall, 1920. Quarto. Orig. cloth and boards, etched paper label. First edition. One of 125 numbered copies, signed by Wall. Bookplate, else fine. Reese 20-1043 1983 $275

WALLACE, ALFRED RUSSEL (1823-1913)   Australasia. London, Edward Stanford, 1893. Vol. 1. Folding maps and illustrations. Small 8vo. Ex-library in library binding. Backstrip partly torn. Morrill 287-489 1983 $30

WALLACE, ALFRED RUSSEL (1823-1913)   Darwinism. London: Macmillan, 1889. Cloth. Portrait. Second edition, corrected. Inner hinges slightly tender, else about fine. Reese 20-1098 1983 $50

WALLACE, ALFRED RUSSEL (1823-1913)   Darwinism, an Exposition of the Theory of Natural Selection. 1890. Second ed. Portrait, map, illus., 8vo. Cloth. Wheldon 160-199 1983 £18

WALLACE, ALFRED RUSSEL (1823-1913)   The Malay Archipelago. London, 1869. First ed., 8 maps, 2 folding. 9 plates, 1 neatly repaired, illus. 2 vols. Half calf, labels, 8vo. Good. Edwards 1044-735 1983 £225

WALLACE, ALFRED RUSSEL (1823-1913)   The Malay Archipelago. Macmillan & Co., 1869. 2 vols. 8vo. Numerous text illus. Frontis. in each volume. 2 folding maps (one coloured), and 6 plates. Orig. green pictorial cloth gilt, gilt a little faded, small rectangular paper with library number at foot of each spine, 2 library stamps on each title, and 1 stamp on dedication page in first volume. Otherwise clean internally. First edition. Bickersteth 75-267 1983 £185

WALLACE, ALFRED RUSSEL (1823-1913)   The Malay Archipelago. London, 1869. First edition. 9 maps, 2 folding. 8 plates, numerous illus. 2 vols. Quarter red morocco. Tipped in is a 'P.S." from Wallace to an unknown correspondent. 8vo. Good. Edwards 1044-734 1983 £150

WALLACE, ALFRED RUSSEL (1823-1913)   The Malay Archipelago. London, 1869. 2 folding maps, 8 plates, maps and illus. in text. 2 vols. Front board of vol. 1 marked, some wear, good. ⅜vo. Edwards 1044-736 1983 £90

WALLACE, ALFRED RUSSEL (1823-1913)   The Malay Archipelago. New York, 1869. First American edition. Maps and illustrations. 8vo. Ex-library. Morrill 290-572 1983 $40

WALLACE, ALFRED RUSSEL (1823-1913)   The Malay Archipelago. Macmillan and Co., 1886. 2 folding maps, 7 plates, and other maps and illus. in text. Orig. cloth, stamps of the Royal Entomological Society of London on title and some other pages. Bickersteth 77-326 1983 £18

WALLACE, EDGAR   The Four Just Men. Lon., 1905. First issue with both folding frontis and competition solution sheet, cover soiled, interior foxed, hinges starting, good or better, book store embossed stamp, owner's name. Quill & Brush 54-1453 1983 $125

WALLACE, EDGAR   The Four Just Men. Lon., 1905. Covers soiled, interior foxed, hinges cracking, lacks frontis, has competition slip, good, bookplate. Quill & Brush 54-1454 1983 $75

WALLACE, EDGAR   The Four Just Men. London, 1905. First edition. 8vo. Orig. black printed orange cloth. Folding frontis. and competition slip at end. Traylen 94-847 1983 £25

WALLACE, EDGAR   Mr. Justice Maxell. London, Ward, Lack, (1927). First edition. Dust jacket (small chips) else very good. Houle 22-930 1983 $65

WALLACE, EDGAR   Writ in Barracks. London, 1900. First edition. 8vo, cloth; unopened. Fine. Argosy 714-778 1983 $65

WALLACE, HENRY   Uncle Henry's Letters to the Farm Boy. Des Moines, Iowa: Wallace Pub. Co., 1897. Orig. pictorial cloth. Frontis. Littel bookplate. 2nd ed. Presentation copy from author. Slipcased. Quite scarce. Very fine copy. Jenkins 153-665 1983 $55

WALLACE, HENRY   Uncle Henry's Own Story of His Life. Wallace, Iowa, 1917-1919. 3 vols. Orig. printed wrappers. Nice set. Jenkins 153-666 1983 $150

WALLACE, LEW   The Fair God. Bos., (1898). Illus. by Eric Pape. Two vols., edges slightly rubbed, spines darkened, else very good, owner's name. Quill & Brush 54-1455 1983 $40

WALLACE, LEW   The Prince of India. New York, 1893. First edition. 2 vols. Sm.8vo. Orig. cloth. Good. Edwards 1044-737 1983 £40

WALLACE, LEW   The Prince of India. N.Y., Harper & Bros., 1893. First edition, orig. blue cloth blocked in red, silver and gilt, v.g. Jarndyce 30-578 1983 £12.50

WALLACE, PHILIP   Colonial Ironwork in Old Philadelphia. NY, (1930). Photographic illus., measured drawings by Wm. Allen Dunn, small folio, 1/2 cloth. Argosy 710-408 1983 $50

WALLACE, R. G.   Memoirs of India. London, 1824. Half morocco by C. Lewis. Gilt, with square corner pieces, gilt edges. Manuscript note by Beckford on the front free endpaper. 8vo. Good. Edwards 1044-738 1983 £165

WALLACE, ROBERT (1858-1939)   Farming Industries of Cape Colony. 1896. 81 plates. 8vo. Cloth. Wheldon 160-2147 1983 £15

WALLACE, THOMAS   British Slavery. W.F. Ramsay; Ward & Co., 1850. Orig. brown cloth, 12mo, v.g. First edition. Jarndyce 31-398 1983 £46

WALLACE, W. S.   Pictorial History of the Great War. Canada in the Great War. Toronto: John A. Hertel Co., 1919. 4to. 25 1/2cm. Extensively illus (inc. 48 full-page colour maps). Bound in black fabrikoid, marbled edges. Very good to fine. McGahern 54-56 1983 $25

WALLACE, WILLIAM H.   Speeches of... Kansas City, ca. 1906. Orig. printed wrappers. Jenkins 153-281 1983 $75

WALLACE, WILLIAM VINCENT   Lurline. Grand Romantic Opers. NY, 1860. With composer's engraved portrait. Folio, new cloth. Salloch 387-254 1983 $200

WALLACE, WILLIAM VINCENT   Mein Fatherland. Dublin: Eddard's, circa 1830. First edition, folio, disbound. Fenning 62-378 1983 £35

WALLACK, LESTER   Memories of Fifty Years. New York: Charles Scribner's Sons, 1889. Front. port. & illus. Half title, facs. playbill. Orig. blue cloth, v.g. First edition. Jarndyce 30-1166 1983 £20

WALLER, EDMUND   Poems, etc. written upon several occasions... London: H. Herringman, 1668. Third edition. 8vo. Cont. calf. Trifle rubbed. Ximenes 63-384 1983 $300

WALLER, EDMUND   Poems, &c. written upon several Occasions... London: H. Herringham, 1682. Fourth edition, with several additions. 8vo. Cont. mottled calf, gilt. spine. 2 engraved portraits, title printed in red and black. Bound in at end of vol. are 26 pp. in ms. in a cont. hand entitle "Some Things written by Mr. Waller which are left out in this Impression." Traylen 94-848 1983 £130

WALLER, EDMUND   The Works of...in Prose and Verse. Printed for J. Tonson, 1730. With an engraved portrait and 3 plates, large 12mo, cont. calf, recently and neatly rebacked, very good copy. Second Fenton edition. Fenning 62-379 1983 £35

WALLER, JOHN ROWELL   Rambles and Musings. Darlington, Wm. Dresser, 1886. First edition, front. 4pp Press Opinions. Orig. red cloth, v.g. Jarndyce 31-870 1983 £10.50

WALLET, WILLIAM FEDERICK   The public life of W. F. Wallett, the Queen's jester. London: Bemrose and Sons, etc., 1870. 8vo, old half morocco (spine wear), 2nd edition. With a portrait; half-title present. Ximenes 64-563 1983 $75

WALLICH, NATHANIEL   Plantae Asiaticae Rariories. London, 1830-32. Map, 295 fine hand-coloured lithograph plates, bound from the orig. parts, with stab marks in margins. 3 vols. Cont. half green morocco, right angled leather corners, 'watered' calico boards. 8vo. The Plesch copy, with the half titles in vols. 1 & 3, and the plates in superb condition. Edwards 1044-739 1983 £12,000

WALLIN, GEORGIUS   De Prudentia in Cantionibus Ecclesiasticis Adhibenda. Wittenberg, 1723. 4to, wrs. First edition. Salloch 387-255 1983 $90

WALLIS, I. HENRY   The Cloud Kingdom. John Lane, n.d. (ca.1905). Frontis. Decorated title. 17 full-page & 60 text illus. Decorated endpapers. Green decorated cloth, gilt, spotted. Greer 40-194 1983 £38

WALLIS, I. HENRY   The Cloud Kingdom. John Lane, n.d. (ca.1905). Frontis. Decorated title. 17 full-page & 60 text illus. Decorated endpapers. Green decorated cloth gilt, rubbed. Greer 39-105 1983 £25

WALLIS, RUTH SAWTELL   Too Many Bones. N.Y., Dodd, Mead, 1943. First edition. Dust jacket (small hole in tear panel) else very good - fine. Houle 22-933 1983 $37.50

WALN, ROBERT   An Account of the Asylum for the Insane. Philadelphia: Benjamin & Thomas Kite, 1825. Disbound. Early library stamp. Felcone 22-150 1983 $35

WALPOLE, EDWARD H.   Mount Usher, 1868-1928. (Dublin: 1928). First edition, with 29 mounted plates, some coloured, 4to, orig. cloth-backed boards. Fenning 60-422 1983 £14.50

WALPOLE, HORACE   The Castle of Otranto. London, printed for Tho. Lownds, 1765. 8vo, deep green hard grain morocco gilt, a.e.g., only very minor wear. Only 500 copies were printed at first. First edition. Ravenstree 96-285 1983 $2,500

WALPOLE, HORACE   The Castle of Otranto. London, J. Dodsley, 1782. 8vo, cont. calf worn, joints breaking, rubbed, name on end-paper, above average copy complete with the half title. Ravenstree 96-286 1983 $142

WALPOLE, HORACE   A catalogue of the royal and noble authors of England... London: R. and J. Dodsley, etc., 1759. 2 vols. Second edition, corrected and enlarged. 8vo, cont. calf, gilt, spine gilt. Frontis. in vol. 1, and a plate of music. Calf rubbed, but sound. Ximenes 63-253 1983 $125

WALPOLE, HORACE   A Catalogue of the Royal and Noble Authors of England, Scotland and Ireland. London, 1806. 5 vols. Bound in morocco, e.g. Many fine engravings throughout the work. Some scuffing to the bindings and some foxing in text, otherwise a fine set. In Our Time 156-855 1983 $300

WALPOLE, HORACE   A Catalogue of the Royal and Noble Authors of England, Scotland, and Ireland. London, John Scott, 1806. 5 vols. 8vo. 150 engraved portraits. Full dark green straight-grained morocco, sides with several borders & panels in gold & blind, gilt-tooled backs, aeg. Enlarged ed. Fine. O'Neal 50-55 1983 $200

WALPOLE, HORACE   Journal of the Printing-Office at Strawberry Hi.. (London): Printed at the Chiswick Press for Constable and Co., ltd. 1923. 4to, edition ltd. to 650 copies on handmade paper. Prospectus laid-in. Two-tone boards. Fine in dust jacket. Karmiole 73-106 1983 $125

WALPOLE, HORACE   The Letters of Horace Walpole, Fourth Earl of Orford. London: Richard Bentley and Son, 1891. 9 vols. 8vo. Orig. blue cloth, gilt. Engraved frontis., vignette title-pages and numerous portraits. Slightly soiled. Traylen 94-849 1983 £25

WALPOLE, HORACE   A Selection of the Letters... N.Y. & London: Harper & Brothers, 1926. First edition. Fully illus. 2 vols. Orig. cloth-backed boards with paper labels on spines. Fine. MacManus 280-5347 1983 $45

WALPOLE, HUGH   Above the Dark Circus. Lon., 1932. Limited to 200 signed copies, edges very slightly worn, spine label very slightly foxed, else fine in slightly chipped and darkened, very good dustwrapper. Quill & Brush 54-1456 1983 $35

WALPOLE, HUGH   The Blind Man's House. London: Macmillan & Co., 1941. First edition. Orig. cloth. Dust jacket. Fine. MacManus 280-5350 1983 $20

WALPOLE, HUGH   The Cathedral. N.Y.: George H. Doran Co., 1922. Orig. cloth-backed boards. Publisher's box. First edition. One of 500 large paper copies signed by author. Very good. MacManus 5352 1983 $25

WALPOLE, HUGH   The Duchess of Wrexe. London: Martin Secker, 1914. First edition. Orig. cloth. Dust jacket. Mint. MacManus 280-5355 1983 $45

WALPOLE, HUGH   Fortitude, Being a True and Faithful Account. London: Martin Secker, (1913). First edition. Orig. cloth. Good. MacManus 280-5356 1983 $20

WALPOLE, HUGH   The Fortress, a Novel. London, 1932. Roy. 8vo. Orig. boards, linen spine, printed paper label, uncut edges. Limited edition of 310 large paper copies, signed by the author. Traylen 94-850 1983 £20

WALPOLE, HUGH   Hugh Walpole and the English Lake District. London: Macmillan & Co., 1933. First edition. Orig. wraps. Wrappers a bit soiled. Good. MacManus 280-5359 1983 $30

WALPOLE, HUGH   A Letter to a Modern Novelist. London: Hogarth Press, 1932. First edition. Orig. decorated wrappers. Fine. MacManus 280-5363 1983 $20

WALPOLE, HUGH   The Silver Thorn. London: Macmillan & Co., 1928. First edition. Orig. cloth. Dust jacket. Inscribed by author for Katherine Parsons, whose bookplate is on the front endpaper. In a cloth slipcase (rubbed). Near mint. MacManus 280-5368 1983 $40

WALPOLE, J. K.   Recollections and Historical Notices of Cambridge. Printed by Kemp and Fairfax, Lower George Street, 1847. 8vo, title in red and black, printed slip tipped in after the final page, orig. cloth with paper label. Bickersteth 75-188 1983 £120

WALSH, ANNIE   Scandinavian Relations with Ireland During the Viking Period. Dublin: Talbot, 1922. First edition, cr. 8vo, orig. cloth, a very good copy in dust wrapper. Fenning 61-468 1983 £12.50

WALSH, C.   Indian Village Crimes. London, 1929. Edges spotted. 8vo. Orig. cloth. Good. Edwards 1044-740 1983 £18

WALSH, E. H.   The Monk of Gethsemane Abbey. Brooklyn, 1893. 1st ed. Illus. Small 8vo. Inner hinges slightly cracked. Morrill 287-490 1983 $20

WALSH, J. FRANCIS   The Anatomy & Functions of the Muscles of the Hand & the Extensor Tendons of the Thumb. Phila., 1897. 8vo, cloth; 10 text illus. First edition. Presentation copy, signed on fly-leaf. Argosy 713-560 1983 $40

WALSH, JAMES   Makers of Modern Medicine. New York, 1915. 8vo. Orig. binding. Fye H-3-592 1983 $20

WALSH, PAUL   Gleanings from Irish Manuscripts, Chiefly of the Seventeenth Century. Dublin: Dollard, 1918. First edition, 8vo, orig. printed paper wrapper, very good copy. Fenning 61-470 1983 £12.50

WALSH, PAUL   Irish Men of Learning. Dublin: Three Candles, 1947. First collected edition, with 4 folding tables, 8vo, orig. cloth. Fenning 62-380 1983 £24.50

WALSH, RICHARD H.   Elementary Treatise on Metallic Currency. Dublin: James M'Glashan, 1853. First edition, 8vo, orig. cloth, the backstrip discoloured, otherwise a nice copy. Fenning 60-423 1983 £35

WALSH, RICHARD JOHN   Making of Buffalo Bill. Indianapolis,
Bobbs, (1928). First edition. Illus. Green cloth (minor rubbing),
very good. Houle 21-1169 1983 $45

WALSH, RICHARD JOHN   The Making of Buffalo Bill: a Study
in Heroics. Indianapolis, (1928). 1st ed., illus. Argosy 710-602
1983 $25

WALSH, RICHARD JOHN   The Making of Buffalo Bill. Indianapolis,
1958. First edition. Frontis. and illus. Mended dust jacket. Fine.
Jenkins 152-36 1983 $40

WALSH, ROBERT (1772-1852)   Narrative of a Journey from Constantinople
to England. Frederick Westley and A.H. Davis, 1828. First edition,
with 2 folding maps and 8 litho plates (1 folding), 8vo, orig. boards,
uncut, with printed paper label, just a little wear to the spine, but
still a nice copy in orig. state. Fenning 60-425 1983 £75

WALSH, THOMAS   Journal of the late campaign in Egypt.
London: T. Cadell & W. Davies, 1803. 4to. 50 plates and maps on
39 sheets, (6 hand-colored). Modern 1/2 brown morocco, marbled
boards, some foxing. Adelson Africa-145 1983 $350

WALSH, WILLIAM   Ode for the Thanksgiving Day.
London: for Jacob Tonson, 1706. First edition. Modern wrappers.
Title lightly dust soiled. Heath 48-452 1983 £125

WALTER, JOHANNES   Eine Kleine Sammlung Alter und Neuer
Geistreicher Lieder. Reading (Pa.), Johann Ritter, 1810. 18mo,
contemporary calf. Small gash on backstrip, title-page and last leaf
torn with no loss of text. Morrill 286-500 1983 $25

WALTER, WILLIAM P.   The Great Understander. Aurora (Ill.),
Walter, (1931). First edition. Frontis. Grey cloth stamped in
black and gilt. Very good - fine. Houle 22-1189 1983 $25

WALTERS, J. CUMMING   Phases of Dickens. Chapman & Hall, 1911.
Half title, front. port. Orig. dark green cloth. First edition.
Jarndyce 30-231 1983 £15

WALTERS, LORENZO   Tombstone's Yesterday. Tucson: Acme
Printing Co., 1928. Plates. Original cloth. First edition. Very
scarce. Jenkins 153-16 1983 $100

WALTHER, J.   Bau und Bildung der Erde. Leipzig, 1925.
23 plates and 217 text-figures, 8vo, cloth (slightly affected by
damp). Wheldon 160-1483 1983 £12

WALTON, EVANGELINE   Witch House. Sauk City: Arkham House,
1945. First edition. Cloth. Very fine in dust jacket. Bradley 66-
149 1983 $37.50

WALTON, IZAAK   The Complete Angler. London, 1766.
Second edition, 2 vols. in one, engraved frontis. (the first one
backed), 15 other engraved plates, 17 engravings of fishes in the
text, one engraved and several woodcut headpieces, 8vo, some leaves
browned. Cont. calf, rebacked. K Books 307-190 1983 £240

WALTON, IZAAK   The Complete Angler. London: John
Major, 1824. Two vols. bound in one, each with title-page. Second
edition. Karmiole 76-43 1983 $150

WALTON, IZAAK   The Complete Angler. London, Nathaniel
Cooke, 1854. Second edition. Illustrated. Small 8vo, full straight
grain morocco, all edges gilt, raised bands, fishing decorations in
gilt on spine. A few additional portraits and illustrations have
been bound in, including a fine colored double-page plate of Ilam
Hall. Attractive copy. Morrill 290-576 1983 $85

WALTON, IZAAK   The Complete Angler. J.C. Nimmo and
Bain, 1883. With 8 plates of etchings by Damman, each in two
states, and 74 woodcut text illus., each a mounted india proof,
8vo, orig. cloth, gilt, t.e.g., by Leighton, Son and Hodge. Fenning
62-381 1983 £65

WALTON, IZAAK   The Complete Angler. London, 1889.
With six orig. etchings, two portraits, and seventy-four wood
engravings. Modern quarter calf gilt. K Books 307-189 1983 £80

WALTON, IZAAK   Complete Angler. London, Major, 1823.
First edition by Major. Small 8vo, with 77 woodcuts and 14 copper
plates, full gilt stamped calf. Very good. Houle 21-904 1983 $150

WALTON, IZAAK   The Compleat Angler. London: the
Nonesuch Press, 1929. 9 illus. stencilled in colour by T.L. Poulton,
5 copper-engraved portraits by C. Sigrist, 2 seals in red. 8vo.
Full niger morocco, gilt, marbled endpapers, t.e.g., others uncut,
preserved in the orig. marbled slip-case. Limited edition of 1,600
numbered copies. Traylen 94-852 1983 £90

WALTON, IZAAK   The Compleat Angler...Illustrated by
Arthur Rackham. London: Harrap, (1931). Frontis., color plates.
1st trade ed. Orig. pictorial blue cloth, gilt, t.e.g., in dj, with
a few chips at edges, but very good. Fine copy. Jenkins 155-1048
1983 $150

WALTON, IZAAK   The Compleat Angler. Ph., (1931).
Illus. by Arthur Rackham. First American edition, 12 full color full-
page illus., corners slightly rubbed, else very good in slightly
chipped and soiled, very good dustwrapper with few tears. Quill &
Brush 54-1131 1983 $150

WALTON, IZAAK   The Compleat Angler...Illustrated by
Arthur Rackham. London: Harrap, (1931). Frontis., color plates.
1st trade ed. Orig. pictorial blue cloth, gilt, t.e.g., in dj. Dj
with a few chips at edges, but very good. Fine copy. Jenkins 153-830
1983 $150

WALTON, IZAAK   The Compleat Angler. Phila.: David McKay,
(1931). First American trade edition. Illus. by A. Rackham. Orig.
pictorial cloth. Dust jacket (rather chipped, with a few small tears).
Finely illustrated, including 12 full-page color plates. Fine. Mac-
Manus 280-4319 1983 $125

WALTON, IZAAK   The Compleat Angler. 1931. Illus. by
Arthur Rackham. First trade edition, 12 coloured plates, other illus.
and decorated end papers by Rackham, crown 4to, orig. cloth, t.e.g.
Good. K Books 307-188 1983 £75

WALTON, IZAAK   The Complete Angler. Phila.: McKay,
n.d. (1931). First American edition. 4to. Green cloth. Gilt
decorated. Torn pictorial dust wrapper. With pictorial endpapers.
12 full-page color plates, 25 black & whites. Fine. Aleph-bet 8-214
1983 $110

WALTON, J.   An Introduction to the Study of Fossil
Plants. 1940. 139 illus., royal 8vo, cloth. Wheldon 160-1484 1983
£15

WALTON, JAMES E.   Model Yachts and Model Yacht Sailing.
London, (ca.1890). Signet Library copy. 8vo. Orig. gilt-decorated
dark green cloth. Numerous engravings in text, 4-page publisher's
catalogue at beginning. Slightly soiled, endpapers browned. Good.
Edwards 1042-179 1983 £18

WALTON, JOSEPH S.   Conard Weiser and The Indian Policy of
Colonial Pennsylvania. Phila.: George W. Jacobs & Co., 1900. Frontis.
Illus. Orig. pictorial cloth. Slight wear to spine. T.e.g. Jenkins
152-499 1983 $85

WALWORTH, MANSFIELD T.   Warwick: Or the Lost Nationalities
of America. New York: Carleton, 1879. 1st ed. Orig. green cloth,
gilt. Fine copy. Jenkins 155-1248 1983 $22.50

WANDELL, SAMUEL   Aaron Burr, a Biography. NY, 1927.
64 illus. 2 vols. Argosy 716-445 1983 $22.50

THE WANDERER or Surprising Escape. Glasgow, 1752. First edition.
8vo. 19th Century cloth. Heath 48-180 1983 £90

WANDREI, DONALD   The Web of Easter Island. Sauk City:
Arkham House, 1948. First edition. Black cloth. Fine in near-fine
dj. Bradley 64-179 1983 $30

WANDREI, DONALD   The Web of Easter Island. Sauk City:
Arkham House, 1948. First edition. Black cloth. Very good in rubbed
dj. Bradley 64-180 1983 $20

WANDREI, DONALD   Poems for Midnight. Sauk City, 1964.
Illus. by Howard Wandrei. Review copy with slip laid-in, limited to
742 copies, fine in slightly sunned near fine dustwrapper. Quill &
Brush 54-1457 1983 $125

WAR horns, make room for the bucks with green bowes. London: for
F. Haris (sic), 1682. First edition. Small 4to. Calf. Title
slightly soiled. Ximenes 63-385 1983 $350

WARBASSE, JAMES P.   The Doctor and the Public. New York,
1935. First edition. 8vo. Orig. binding. Ex-library. Fye H-3-594
1983 $25

WARBURTON, GEORGE   Hochelaga; or, England in the New
World. London, 1846. First edition. 2 vols. 8vo. Cont. polished
calf, gilt, gilt panelled spines, morocco labels, gilt. Tinted
lithographe frontis. to vol. 1. Traylen 94-853 1983 £60

WARBURTON, R.   Eighteen Years in the Khyber. London,
1900. Folding map, portrait frontis., water-stained. Plates. 8vo.
Orig. cloth. Good. Edwards 1044-741 1983 £30

WARD, ARTEMUS, PSEUD.
Please turn to
BROWNE, CHARLES FARRAR (1834-1867)

WARD, CATHERINE G.   The Cottage on the Cliff, a Sea-Side
Story. George Virtue, 1823. First edition, front. & engraved
title, (foxed), illus. 2pp ads. Half black calf. Jarndyce 31-964
1983 £28

WARD, CHRISTOPHER   The Dutch & Swedes on the Delaware,
1609. First edition, colored frontis. Argosy 716-104 1983 $40

WARD, EDWARD   The Delights of the Bottle. London:
Printed for Sam. Briscoe...MDCCXX. 8vo, fine engraved frontis.
of Bacchus by James Sympson, quarter green morocco. First edition.
Quaritch NS 7-134 1983 $800

WARD, EDWARD   The Forgiving Husband, and Adulteress
Wife. London: Printed and sold by H. Hills...(1709). 8vo, modern
quarter morocco and cloth. Pirated edition. Quaritch NS 7-135
1983 $250

WARD, HARRY PARKER   Some American College Bookplates... Columbus, Ohio: The Champlin Press, 1915. First edition. 8vo. Decorated cloth. Hundreds of illus. bookplates including some that have
been tipped in. Limited to 500 numbered and signed copies. Very fine.
Oak Knoll 48-64 1983 $125

WARD, HARRY PARKER   Some American College Bookplates.
Columbus: Champlin Press, 1915. Profusely illus. with facs. bookplates + 12 orig. bookplates, tipped-in. Ltd. to 500 copies, signed
by the author. Gilt-stamped green cloth. Bookplate. Karmiole 71-
32 1983 $85

WARD, MRS. HUMPHREY
Please turn to
WARD, MARY AUGUSTA ARNOLD (1851-1920)

WARD, JAMES   Heredity and Memory. Being the Henry
Sidgwick Memorial Lecture Delivered at Newnham College, 9 Nov. 1912.
Cambridge: 1913. First edition. Rubbed. Gach 94-662 1983 $20

WARD, JAMES   Historic Ornament. Chapman and Hall,
1909. With 441 full-page and other illus., 8vo, orig. cloth,
a very good copy. Fenning 60-426 1983 £18.50

WARD, JAMES   Psychological Principles. Cambridge:
At the Univ. Press/NY: G.P. Putnam's Sons, 1919. First edition,
American issue in green cloth. Fine copy. Gach 94-663 1983 $40

WARD, JOHN   The Roman Era in Britain. London, 1911.
8vo, cloth. Salloch 385-262 1983 $24

WARD, LESLIE   Forty Years of 'Spy'. Chatto & Windus,
1915. First edition, half title, front. numerous illus. Orig.
green cloth, t.e.g., v.g. Jarndyce 30-1170 1983 £24

WARD, LESTER (1841-1913)   Dynamic Sociology. NY: D. Appleton
& Co., 1883, 1902. Two vols. Vol. I first edition. Vol. II second
edition. Ads. Few blemishes, but good sound set. Gach 95-528 1983
$40

WARD, LYND   Madman's Drum. NY, (1930). Edges
lightly rubbed, else bright, near fine copy in lightly chipped and
worn dustwrapper. Quill & Brush 54-1458 1983 $100

WARD, MARCUS   Sing a Song of Sixpence. Edinburgh:
W.P. Nimmo, n.d. (ca.1870). Oblong 8vo. 4 colour plates. 2pp of music.
Green pictorial wrappers. Greer 39-133 1983 £14

WARD, MARY AUGUSTA (ARNOLD) (1851-1920)   Amiel's Journey. London:
Macmillan & Co., 1885. First edition. 2 vols. Orig. cloth. Covers
rubbed. MacManus 280-5374 1983 $50

WARD, MARY AUGUSTA (ARNOLD) (1851-1920)   The Coryston Family. London: Macmillan & Co., 1913. First edition. Orig. decorated cloth.
Corners slightly worn. Covers soiled. With a bookseller's stamp on
front paste-down endpaper. Good. MacManus 280-5375 1983 $35

WARD, MARY AUGUSTA (ARNOLD) (1851-1920)   Fenwick's Career. London:
Smith, Elder, 1906. First edition. Orig. cloth. MacManus 280-5376
1983 $50

WARD, MARY AUGUSTA (ARNOLD) (1851-1920)   Helbeck of Bannisdale.
London: Smith, Elder, 1898. First edition. Orig. cloth. Near fine.
MacManus 280-5378 1983 $75

WARD, MARY AUGUSTA (ARNOLD) (1851-1920)   The History of David
Grieve. London: Smith, Elder & Co., 1892. First edition. 3 vols.
Orig. cloth. Spine of vol. II with a small puncture. Fine. MacManus
280-5379 1983 $300

WARD, MARY AUGUSTA ARNOLD (1851-1920)   The History of David Grieve.
Smith, Elder, 1892. First edition, 3 vols., half titles, endpapers
laid down vol. 2, Mudie's labels on leading boards. Orig. maroon
cloth little rubbed. Jarndyce 30-579 1983 £38

WARD, MARY AUGUSTA (ARNOLD) (1851-1920)   Marcella. London: Smith,
Elder, 1894. First edition. 3 vols. Orig. cloth. Spines uniformly
faded. Very good, tight set. MacManus 280-5381 1983 $250

WARD, MARY AUGUSTA (ARNOLD) (1851-1920)   The Marriage of William
Ashe. London: Smith, Elder, 1905. First edition. Orig. cloth.
Near-fine. MacManus 280-5382 1983 $50

WARD, MARY AUGUSTA (ARNOLD) (1851-1920)   Robert Elsmere. London:
Macmillan & Co., 1888. Early two-volume edition. Orig. cloth. Former
owner's bookplates on front endsheets. Name on half-titles. Very
good. MacManus 280-5384 1983 $35

WARD, MARY AUGUSTA (ARNOLD) (1851-1920)   Robert Elsmere. N.Y.:
John B. Alden, 1888. First American edition. Orig. cloth. Front
inner hinge cracking. Endsheet a bit chewed. Contents somewhat
shaken. Good. MacManus 280-5383 1983 $20

WARD, MARY AUGUSTA (ARNOLD) (1851-1920)   Sir George Tressady. Lon-
don: Smith, Elder & Co., 1896. Second edition. 2 vols. Orig. cloth.
Presentation copy, inscribed "To Lord Roberts, with the author's best
wishes. January 1897." Bookplate of Frederick Sleigh, Lord Roberts of
Kandahar. Edges slightly worn. Covers and endpapers slightly soiled.
Good. MacManus 280-5385 1983 $450

WARD, MARY AUGUSTA (ARNOLD) (1851-1920)   Sir George Tressady. London: Smith, Elder & Co., 1898. Second edition. 2 vols. Orig. light
green cloth. Presentation copy to Field Marshall Lord Roberts inscribed and dated January 1897. Spine and covers slightly worn. Bookplates of Lord Roberts. Nice set. MacManus 280-5386 1983 $450

WARD, MARY AUGUSTA (ARNOLD) (1851-1920)   The Story of Bessie Cost-
rell. London: Smith, Elder & Co., 1895. First edition. Orig. cloth.
Near-fine. MacManus 280-5387 1983 $50

WARD, MARY AUGUSTA (ARNOLD) (1851-1920)   Towards the Goal. London:
John Murray, 1917. First edition. Orig. cloth with paper labels.
Spine faded. Inscription on flyleaf. Very good. MacManus 280-5388
1983 $35

WARD, MARY AUGUSTA ARNOLD (1851-1920)   The Writings of Mrs. Humphrey Ward. London, 1911. Westmoreland edition, one of 250 copies signed by author. Inscribed by author to Beatrix C. Jones. Few labels have some light chipping, else fine. With recipient's bookplate. In Our Time 156-856 1983 $350

WARD, MATTHEW F.   A Full and Authentic Report of the Testimony on the Trial of Matt F. Ward...New York, 1854. First ed. 8vo, original wrapper. Lacks part of backstrip and all of back wrapper; front cover frayed; backstrip cracked. Morrill 290-577 1983 $20

WARD, MATTHEW W.   Trial of Matt. F. Ward, for the Murder of Prof. W. H. G. Butler, Before the Hardin Criminal Court, April Term 1854. Louisville, KY, 1854. 1st ed., original yellow printed wrappers. Jenkins 151-163 1983 $150

WARD, ROBERT PLUMER   De Clifford, or The Constant Man. London: Henry Colburn, 1841. First edition. 4 vols. Cloth-backed boards with paper spine labels. Edges and spine labels slightly worn. Covers a trifle soiled. Bookplates. Very good to near-fine. MacManus 280-5390 1983 $450

WARD, ROBERT PLUMER   De Clifford, or the Constant Man. London, 1841. 4 vols. Rebound in leather, a.e.g. A fine set. In Our Time 156-857 1983 $200

WARD, ROBERT PLUMER   De Vere. Henry Colburn, 1827. First edition, 4 vols. Grey boards, blue cloth spines. A fine set. Jarndyce 30-580 1983 £58

WARD, ROBERT PLUMER   De Vere. Henry Colburn, 1827. Henry Colburn, 1827. First edition, 4 vols. Large 12mo, lacks half-titles, and final ad. leaves in vol. IV. Cont. half calf, gilt spine (a little rubbed at head and tail). Occasional light stains. Hannas 69-225 1983 £45

WARD, ROBERT PLUMER   De Vere. Henry Colburn, June 1833. 3 vols., front. port. vol. I. Half green calf, black labels, v.g. Jarndyce 30-581 1983 £40

WARD, ROBERT PLUMER   Tremaine, or the Man of Refinement. London: Henry Colburn, 1825. First edition. 3 vols. 8vo. Orig. boards, uncut, paper labels. Engraved frontis. of Evelyn Hall. Joints a little defective. Traylen 94-854 1983 £95

WARD, ROBERT PLUMER   Tremaine, Or the Man of Refinement. Printed for Henry Colburn, 1825. 3 vols, 12mo, calf gilt, m.e.; no half-titles; frontispiece in vol. I (slightly foxed and offset); a fine copy; bookplates of Henry Drummond, Albury Park. 1st ed. Hill 165-137 1983 £85

WARD, ROBERT PLUMER   Tremaine, or the Man of Refinement. London: Henry Colburn, 1825. Second edition. Illus. 3 vols. Cont. 3/4 black morocco & marbled boards. Some foxing. Very good. MacManus 280-5391 1983 $125

WARD, ROBERT PLUMER   Tremaine. Henry Colburn, 1833. Front. vol. I. Half green calf, black labels, v.g. Jarndyce 30-583 1983 £20

WARD, THOMAS   Some Queries to the Protestants Concerning the English Reformation. Printed by Nathaniel Thompson, 1687. First edition, 4to, wrapper, a very good copy. Fenning 61-471 1983 £24.50

WARD, THOMAS HUMPHRY   The English Poets. London, 1889-95. 4 vols. 8vo. Full olive green crushed levant morocco, gilt, t.e.g. Traylen 94-855 1983 £60

WARD, THOMAS HUMPHRY   Men of the Reign. Routledge, 1885. First edition, orig. olive cloth, a little rubbed. Jarndyce 30-1167 1983 £12.50

WARDEN, CARL JOHN (1890-1961)   A Short Outline of Comparative Psychology. NY: Norton, (1927). 12mo. First edition. Fine in chipped dust jacket. Gach 95-529 1983 $40

WARDLAW, C. W.   Green havoc in the lands of the Caribbean. 1935. 8 plates, 8vo, cloth. Wheldon 160-2148 1983 £15

WARE, CHARLES E.   Home Seeker's Guide to Arkansas. (St. Louis), 1888. Orig. color pictorial wrappers bound in later cloth. Morocco label. Illus. Jenkins 152-15 1983 $175

WARE, EUGENE F.   The Indian War of 1864. Topeka, Kan., 1911. 1st ed. Illus., text maps. Clark 741-289 1983 $85

WARE, J. REDDING   Passing English of the Victorian Era. George Routledge, n.d. (c. 1900). Half title, orig. red cloth. Jarndyce 31-668 1983 £30

WARE, JAMES   The Antiquities and History of Ireland. Printed for A. and C. Churchill, 1705. First collected edition, complete with the 6 plates, 9 parts in 1 volume, thick folio, cont. calf, gilt, wanting the label and the upper joint cracked but the cords strong. A fine copy. Fenning 60-428 1983 £85

WARE, JOSEPH E.   The Emigrants' Guide to California. Princeton, 1932. Folding map. From the Library of LeRoy Hafen. Jenkins 153-670 1983 $25

WARE, N. A.   Notes on Political Economy. N.Y., 1844. Second edition. Orig. paper boards, cloth backed spine, with printed paper label. Signed by Joseph P. Huard, New Orleans, February 6, 1847. Bearing pencil marginal notations throughout. Library stamps. Slight foxing. Good. Jenkins 152-772 1983 $250

WARFEL, HARRY R.   Noah Webster, Schoolmaster to America. NY, 1936. Illus. Argosy 710-487 1983 $20

WARING, E. S.   A History of the Mahrattas. London, 1810. 2 plates, slightly spotted. 4to. Boards, rebacked. Good. Edwards 1044-742 1983 £150

WARING, EDWARD J.   Bibliotheca Therapeutica, or Bibliography of Therapeutics. London: New Sydenham Society, 1878/9. First edition. Argosy 713-568 1983 $100

WARING, GUY   My Pioneer Past. Boston: Bruce Humphries, 1936. Plates. Privately printed and hard to locate. Jenkins 153-671 1983 $60

WARING, THOMAS   A Treatise on Archery or the Art of Shooting with the English Bow... London, R. Hamm, 1847. Ninth edition. Small 8vo, frontis. illus. of three archers; full page plate with six diagrams. Cont. boards (rebacked). Very good. Houle 22-1008 1983 $150

WARMSTREY, THOMAS   A Convocation Speech, by...Against Images, Altars, Crosses, the New Canons, and the Oath, &c. Printed in the Yeare, 1641. First edition, 4to, wrapper. Fenning 60-429 1983 £24.50

WARNER, CHARLES DUDLEY   Mummies and Moslems. Hartford, Conn., 1876. Frontis. Decorated cloth. Minor cover wear. Nice. King 45-541 1983 $35

WARNER, ELLEN REBECCA   Herbert-Lodge. Richard Cruttwell, Bath. Wilkie & Robinson, 1808. First edition, 3 vols. 2 leaves loose vol. I. Half green calf. Jarndyce 30-584 1983 £170

WARNER, FRANK W.   Montana Territory History and Business Directory 1879. Helena, 1879. Illus., folded map. Orig. printed boards, leather spine. Ginsberg 49-588 1983 $750

WARNER, REX   Poems. London: Boriswood, (1937). First edition. 8vo. Orig. cloth. Dust jacket. Covers warping, otherwise a fine copy. Jaffe 1-380 1983 $150

WARNER, REX   Poems and Contradictions. (London): Lane, (1945). Cloth. Fine in dust jacket. Reese 20-1099 1983 $20

WARNER, REX   Views of Attica and its Surroundings. London, 1950. First English edition. Slight stain on upper cover. Chipped and rubbed, price-clipped dustwrapper. Very good. Jolliffe 26-572 1983 £16

WARNER, REX   The Wild Goose Chase. London: Boriswood, (1937). First edition. 8vo. Orig. cloth. Dust jacket. Lightly dampstained, otherwise a very good copy. Jaffe 1-381 1983 $45

WARNER, REX   The Wild Goose Chase. Boriswood, 1937. First edition. Initials on front endpaper. Nice. Rota 231-614 1983 £15

WARNER, RICHARD   Illustrations, Historical, Biographical and Miscellaneous of the Novels by the Author of Waverley... London: Longman, Hurst..., 1823. First edition. 12mo. Cont. straight grain morocco, gilt. Engraved frontis. Heath 48-448 1983 £35

WARNER, RICHARD   Literary Recollections. London: for Longman, Rees..., 1830. First edition. 2 vols. 8vo. Cont. half calf, full gilt spine. Half titles. Heath 48-449 1983 £40

WARNER, RICHARD   Miscellanies. Bath: by Richard Crutwell..., 1819. First edition. 2 vols. in 1. 12mo. Orig. cloth. Fine copy. Heath 48-450 1983 £70

WARNER, RICHARD   A Tour through Cornwall in the Autumn of 1808. Bath: by Richard Cruttwell..., 1809. First edition. 8vo. Uncut in orig. boards, respined. Sepia Aquatint plates. Heath 48-577 1983 £60

WARNER, SYLVIA TOWNSEND   Elinor Barley. The Cresset Press Ltd., 1930. First edition. Illus. in dry point by I.R. Hodgkins. 4to. Orig. vellum-backed marbled boards. One of 380 copies signed by the author. With the publisher's prospectus laid in. Vellum very slightly discolored in a few places. Extremities of boards a bit worn. Fine. MacManus 280-5392 1983 $75

WARNER, SYLVIA TOWNSEND   The Espalier. London, 1925. First edition. Spine a little faded and some light foxing. Nice. Rota 230-616 1983 £20

WARNER, SYLVIA TOWNSEND   Mr. Fortune's Maggot. London: Chatto & Windus, 1927. First edition. 8vo. Orig. cloth. Spine of dust jacket darkened, otherwise a fine copy. Jaffe 1-382 1983 $50

WARNER, SYLVIA TOWNSEND   Moral Ending and other stories. London, 1931. 4to. Buckram, t.e.g. Frontis. by William Kermode. Limited edition of 550 copies, this copy unnumbered. Traylen 94-856 1983 £18

WARNER, SYLVIA TOWNSEND   Opus 7. N.Y.: Viking Press, 1931. First American edition. Orig. cloth-backed boards. Dust jacket. Very fine. MacManus 280-5393 1983 $37.50

WARNER, SYLVIA TOWNSEND   Opus 7. London: Chatto & Windus, 1931. First edition. 8vo. Orig. decorated boards. Dust jacket. Very fine copy. Jaffe 1-383 1983 $25

WARNER, SYLVIA TOWNSEND   The Salutation. London: Chatto & Windus, 1932. First edition. 8vo. Orig. cloth. Dust jacket. Fine copy. Jaffe 1-384 1983 $40

WARNER, SYLVIA TOWNSEND   A Spirit Rises. London: Chatto & Windus, 1962. First edition. Orig. wrappers with paper label on front wrapper. Uncorrected proof copy, so marked on the front wrapper. Wrappers a bit faded and worn. Title of book written in pen on the spine. Good. MacManus 280-5395 1983 $60

WARNER, SYLVIA TOWNSEND   The True Heart. London, 1929. First English edition. Edges spotted. Dustwrapper browned and slightly stained at the spine. Fine. Jolliffe 26-574 1983 £45

WARREN, ARTHUR   The Charles Whittinghams Printers. New York: The Grolier Club, 1896. First and only edition. Tall 8vo. Orig. levant over boards, slipcase. Limited to 388 copies. Printed on hand-made paper. Fine in rubbed box. Oak Knoll 49-394 1983 $300

WARREN, EDWARD ROYAL   The Mammals of Colorado. NY, 1910. Illus and 3 folding maps. Modern buckram. Ex-library. Argosy 710-112 1983 $35

WARREN, ELIZA   Sixteen fancy-work designs for sofa and chair tidies... London: W.H. Collingridge, n.d. (1869). First edition. Oblong 8vo. Orig. pink glazed printed wrappers. Three folding plates. Numerous ads. Wrappers a bit worn. Very good copy. Scarce. Ximenes 63-88 1983 $125

WARREN, HERBERT L.   The Foundations of Classic Architecture. NY, 1919. Illus., 4to, cloth. Salloch 385-318 1983 $20

WARREN, JOHN (1753-1815)   An Eulogy on the Honourable Thomas Russell, Esq.,.... Boston, 1796. 1st ed. 8vo, orig. wrappers. Morrill 287-493 1983 $25

WARREN, JOHN C.   The Preservation of Health with Remarks on Constipation, Old Age, Use of Alcohol in the Preparation of Medicines. Boston, 1854. 1st ed. 16mo. All edges gilt. Morrill 289-244 1983 $22.50

WARREN, ROBERT PENN   All The King's Men. L, (1948). Flys slightly offset, fore-edges slightly foxed, else near fine in very good dustwrapper, slightly frayed at spine edges and one small chip. Quill & Brush 54-1462 1983 $90

WARREN, ROBERT PENN   At Heaven's Gate. New York, 1949. First paperback edition. Wrappers. With the ownership signature of Theodore Roethke. Upper cover slightly creased. Very good. Jolliffe 26-448 1983 £20

WARREN, ROBERT PENN   Incarnations, Poems 1966-1968. New York: Random House, (1968). 1st ed., 1 of 250 numbered and signed copies. Orig. cloth, dj, boxed. Mint copy. Jenkins 155-1250 1983 $85

WARREN, ROBERT PENN   Or Else: Poem/Poems. NY, (1974). Signed, near fine in near fine dustwrapper. Quill & Brush 54-1463 1983 $75

WARREN, ROBERT PENN   Selected Poems, New and Old, 1923-1966. New York: Random House, (1966). 1st ed., 1 of 250 numbered and signed copies. Orig. cloth, dj, boxed. Mint copy of a fine vol. Jenkins 155-1252 1983 $100

WARREN, ROBERT PENN   Selected Poems: New and Old, 1923-1966. NY: (1966). Limited to 250 copies signed by the poet. Mint with dust wrapper and slip-case. Bromer 25-123 1983 $100

WARREN, ROBERT PENN   Selected Poems 1923-1975. N.Y., (1976). First edition. Limited to 250 numbered and signed copies. Cloth. Slipcase. Very good. King 45-275 1983 $75

WARREN, ROBERT PENN   World Enough and Time. N.Y., (1950). Ltd. first edition. Argosy 714-780 1983 $25

WARREN, SAMUEL   Ten Thousand A-Year. Edinburgh and London, 1841. First English edition, with an engraved plates, ad. leaf, with the half-titles, 3 vols. 8vo, orig. plum cloth, a trifle shaken. Fenning 62-384 1983 £55

WARREN, SAMUEL   Ten Thousand a Year. Wm. Blackwood, 1841. First edition, 3 vols. Half calf, marbled boards. Raised bands, gilt. Labels, v.g. Jarndyce 30-585 1983 £45

WARREN, SAMUEL   Ten Thousand a Year. William Blackwood & Sons, Edinburgh & London, 1841. First Book Edition, 3 vols, lge. 12mo, half calf, marbled sides; with the half-titles. Hill 165-138 1983 £35

WARREN, SAMUEL   Titlebat Titmouse. N.Y., Funk & Wagnall, 1903. First edition, second printing. Illus. by Will Crawford. Dust jacket (small chips). Very good. Pictorial binding. Houle 21-908 1983 $75

WARREN MANUFACTURING COMPANY   Fifty Years of Papermaking... N.p.: Warren, 1923. 4to. Cloth. Illus. Oak Knoll 49-307 1983 $25

WARTON, JOSEPH   Odes on Various Subjects. London:
R. Dodsley, 1747. 2nd ed., 4to, disbound. A very good copy.
Trebizond 18-98 1983 $65

WARTON, THOMAS   The History of English Poetry. London,
1824. A new ed. revised with additional notes from Mr. Ritson. 4
vols. 8vo. Leather. Some light foxing, mainly a fine set. In Our
Time 156-860 1983 $150

WARTON, THOMAS   The Poetical Works... Oxford: at
the University Press for W. Hanwell and J. Parker, etc., 1802.
2 vols. Roy. 8vo. Cont. crimson morocco, two-line gilt and blind-
tooled panels, panelled spines blindtooled and gilt, inner gilt
dentelles, edges gilt. Large paper copy, with engraved portrait
after Reynolds. From the library of Lord Leigh of Stoneleigh,
with book-plate in each vol. Traylen 94-858 1983 £140

WARWICK, EDEN   The Poet's Pleasuance. Longmans, 1847.
1st edn. Many b&w illus. borders designed by Henry Noel Humphreys
engr'd on wood by W. Dickes & Henry Visetelly. Pub's red morocco
gilt, raised bands, bevelled boards, a.e.g., marbled eps. (1st 20 pp.
stained at sewn edge, some foxing mainly at prelims., leather presen.
plate & insc. 2nd ep.), v.g. Hodgkins 27-339 1983 £45

WASHBURN, MARGARET FLOY (1871-1939)   The Animal Mind. NY:
Macmillan, 1908. First edition. Publisher's brown cloth. Near
fine copy. Gach 95-530 1983 $40

WASHINGTON, BOOKER T.   An Autobiography, The Story of My Life
and Work. Naperville, Ill. (1901). Revised edition. Photos. Drawings by F. Beard. Blind-stamped cloth. Couple illus. loose. Covers
soiled. Extremities well worn. King 45-572 1983 $20

WASHINGTON, BOOKER T.   The Future of the American Negro. B,
1899. Ex-lib. with marks where packet and label were removed, good
or better copy. Quill & Brush 54-1466 1983 $150

WASHINGTON, GEORGE   Diaries, 1748-99. Boston, 1925. First
edition, Regents' ed. Frontispieces, 4 vols., g.t. Argosy 710-569
1983 $85

WASHINGTON, GEORGE   Letters & Recollections. London, 1906.
Plates. (Backstrip faded). Argosy 716-606 1983 $35

WASHINGTON, GEORGE   Writings, from the Original Manuscript
Sources, 1745-1799. Washington: G.P.O. (1931-44). 8vo, blue
cloth. Argosy 710-570 1983 $750

WASHINGTON, City and Capital...WPA...American Guide Series.
Washington, 1937. First edition. Maps and illustrations. Thick 8vo.
Morrill 290-588 1983 $30

WASHINGTON. LAWS.   An Act to Provide for the Assessment
and Collection of Taxes in the State of Washington, and Declaring
an Emergency. Olympia, 1891. Orig. printed wraps. First edition.
Ginsberg 47-951 1983 $50

WASHINGTON TERRITORY. LAWS. Session Laws of the Territory of Wash-
ington: And the Resolutions and Memorials of the Ninth Regular
Session of the Legislative Assembly...1861-2. Olympia, 1862.
First edition. Dbd. Ginsberg 47-947 1983 $75

WASHINGTON TERRITORY. LAWS. Statutes of the Territory of Washington,
Made and Passed...1864. Olympia, 1864. Dbd. First edition.
Ginsberg 47-953 1983 $75

WASMUND, CASPAR   Disputatio philosophica de coctionibus.
Herborn: Christopher Corvia, 1592. Woodcut vignette on title. 4to.
Boards. Kraus 164-249 1983 $125

WASON, RIGBY   A Letter to Lord Chief Justice Cockburn.
E. Truelove, 1868. 2nd edition, orig. red cloth, a little marked.
Jarndyce 31-220 1983 £14.50

WASSERMAN, JEANNE L.   Daumier Sculpture. A critical and
comparative study. Greenwich: New York Graphic Society, 1969.
Prof. illus. Large 4to. Cloth. Dust jacket. Ars Libri 32-144
1983 $40

WASSING, RENE S.   African Art. Its background and
traditions. New York: Abrams, 1968. Prof. illus. Large square
4to. Cloth. Slightly shaken. Ars Libri 34-773 1983 $125

WASSON, GEORGE S.   Sailing Days on the Penobscot. Salem,
Mass.: Marine Research Society, 1932. Tall 8vo, with 25 plates.
Karmiole 74-67 1983 $75

WASSON, ROBERT GORDON (b. 1898)   The Hall Carbine Affair. Danbury,
Conn., 1971. "Definitive Edition," privately printed. One of 276
numbered copies printed in Dante type on Tescia handmade paper. Designed by Giovanni Mardersteig and produced at his Stamperia Valdonega
in Verona. Facsimilies. Orig. blue cloth and morocco, gilt, t.e.g.
Mint in orig. slipcase and shipping carton. Bradley 65-149 1983 $200

WASSON, ROBERT GORDON (b. 1898)   The Hall Carbine Affair. Danbury,
Conn., 1971. "Definitive Edition," Facsimilies. Half blue morocco.
One of 250 copies designed by Giovanni Mardersteig and produced at his
Stamperia Valdonega in Verona, Italy. Mint in orig. slipcase and ship-
ping carton. Bradley 66-689 1983 $200

THE WATER of Life. London: Raphael Tuck, (ca. 1890). 5 full-page
chromolithographs. Front and rear covers chromolithographed. Bound
with pale blue cord with tassels. Owner's inscription dated Easter,
1890. Near mint. (4 1/8 x 3 1/2; 105x90mm). Bromer 25-478 1983 $30

WATERHOUSE, BENJAMIN   The Botanist. Boston, 1811. 8vo.
Rebound in cloth. Tiny chip at edge of title page (not affecting
any text) otherwise a fine copy. In Our Time 156-861 1983 $125

WATERHOUSE, BENJAMIN   The Botanist. Boston, 1811. 1st ed.
8vo, orig. boards, uncut. Lacks part of backstrip including paper
label, covers partly rubbed and dust-soiled. Morrill 287-496 1983
$100

WATERHOUSE, ELLIS   Gainsborough. London: Spring Books,
1966. 8 color plates. 292 illus. Large 4to. Cloth. Dust jacket.
Ars Libri 32-237 1983 $100

WATERHOUSE, SYLVESTER   The Resources of Missouri. St. Louis,
1867. Orig. printed wrappers. Good. Jenkins 152-710 1983 $25

WATERLOO, STANLEY   These Are My Jewels. Chicago:
Coolidge & Waterloo, 1902. 1st ed. Orig. cloth. Jenkins 155-1256
1983 $20

WATERMAN, T. T.   The Delineation of the Day-Signs in
Aztec Manuscripts. Berkeley: University of California Press, 1916.
38 illus. 4to. Wrappers. Worn. Ars Libri 34-528 1983 $30

WATERS, DAVID W.   The Art of Navigation in England. London,
1958. First edition. Roy. 8vo. Orig. cloth. Frontis., numerous
plates and maps, illus. in text. Orig. dust jacket. Fine. Edwards
1042-180 1983 £95

WATERS, EDMUND   The opera glass; exhibiting all the
curious proceedings of the King's Theatre. London: printed for C.
Chapple, 1808. 8vo, wrappers, 1st ed. A fine uncut copy. Rare.
Ximenes 64-564 1983 $225

WATERS, EDMUND   A statement of matters, relative to the
King's Theatre. London: published by J. Ebers; Hookham and Sons;
E. Lloyd; and J. Pentum, 1818. 8vo, wrappers. First edition. Rare.
Ximenes 64-565 1983 $175

WATERS, FRANK   The Colorado. New York, (1946). 1st
ed., 1st issue, with the Rinehart monogram. Maps and Fechin drawings.
Red cloth. Some cover soiling but a sound copy. Bradley 63-135 1983
$20

WATERS, FRANK   Masked Gods. Albuquerque: U. of New
Mexico Press, (1950). Cloth, first edition. Fine copy. In dust
jacket, which is a bit chipped at the top edge. Reese 19-583 1983
$50

WATERS, FRANK   Leon Gaspard. Flagstaff: Northland
Press, 1964. Limited edition of 500 copies specially bound and
signed by the author. Illus. by Gaspard with many in color.
Jenkins 151-359 1983 $150

WATERS, FRANK   Midas of the Rockies. New York: Covici, Friede Publishers, 1937. First edition. Frontis. Nice. Jenkins 152-59 1983 $40

WATERS, RUSSELL J.   El Estranjero: A Story of Southern California. Chicago, 1910. Orig. pictorial cloth. Illus. by Will E. Chapin. Bright copy. Jenkins 153-675 1983 $40

WATERS, S. D.   Clipper Ship to Motor Liner. N.Z. Shipping Co. Ltd., 1939. 8vo. Orig. cloth. Frontis. 7 plates. Good. Edwards 1042-181 1983 £12

WATERS, W. G.   Italian Sculptors. London, 1911. Small 4to, 78 illus. hors texte, cloth. Ars Libri SB 26-245 1983 $40

WATERS, WILSON   History of Chelmsford, Massachusetts. Lowell, 1917. 1st ed. Maps and illus. Thick 8vo, uncut and partly unopened, very nice. Morrill 287-265 1983 $75

WATHEN, JAMES   Journal of a Voyage, in 1811 and 1312. 1814. 4to, full panelled calf, spine relaid, a little thumbed, a few minor tears, inner hinges strengthened. 24 coloured aquatint plates. K Books 307-191 1983 £330

WATKIN, EDWARD WILLIAM   India. London: C.F. Roworth, 1889. Tall 8vo, frontis. This copy signed by Watkin. Orig. brown cloth; spine extremities chipped. Karmiole 74-60 1983 $45

WATKINS, JOHN   A biographical dictionary of the living authors of Great Britain and Ireland. London: Colburn, 1816. First edition. 8vo. Cont. diced calf. Front hinge tender. Very good copy. Ximenes 63-41 1983 $100

WATKINS, JOHN   Life, poetry, and letters of Ebenezer Elliott, the Corn-Lay Rhymer. London: John Mortimer, 1850. First edition. 8vo, orig. green cloth. Frontis., slightly rubbed. Very good copy. Ximenes 63-40 1983 $60

WATKINS, LURA W.   Cambridge Glass, 1818 to 1888. Boston, (1930). 1st ed. 8vo, illus, dust wrapper. Morrill 286-504 1983 $25

WATKINS, THOMAS   A Table of Redemption. London: J. Roberts, 1717. 1st ed., folio, uncut, stitched as issued. Pickering & Chatto 21-132 1983 $50

WATKINS, VERNON   The Lamp and the Veil. London, 1945. First edition. Inscription on flyleaf. Very nice. Rota 231-615 1983 £12.50

WATROUS, JOHN C.   Case of Judge John C. Watrous. Washington, 1860. Dsb., very good. Reese 19-585 1873 $40

WATSON, DOUGLAS S.   California in the Fifties. San Francisco: John Howell, 1936. Originally drawn on stone by Kuchel & Dresel and other early San Francisco lithographers. Unpaged. Large oblong format. Cloth. Dawson 471-298 1983 $200

WATSON, ELKANAH   History of the Rise, Progress, and Existing Condition of the Western Canals in the State of New-York, from September 1788, to...in 1819. Albany, 1820. Plates. 2 maps. Half morocco, slight stains, good. Reese 18-549 1983 $225

WATSON, FREDERICK   The Life of Sir Robert Jones. London, 1934. First edition. 8vo. Orig. binding. Inscribed by the author. Fye H-3-814 1983 $45

WATSON, FREDERICK   Robert Smith Surtees. London: George G. Harrap & Co., (1933). First edition. Illus. Orig. cloth. Dust jacket. Very good. MacManus 280-4961 1983 $20

WATSON, H. B. MARRIOTT   At the First Corner and Other Stories. London: John Lane, Vigo St., Boston: Roberts Bros., 1895. First edition. Orig. decorated cloth. Former owner's signature on front flyleaf. Spine faded. Covers a little worn. Good. MacManus 280-5397 1983 $35

WATSON, H. B. MARRIOTT   Captain Fortune. London: Methuen & Co., (1904). First edition. Mint. MacManus 280-5398 1983 $25

WATSON, H. B. MARRIOTT   Lady Faint-Heart. London: Chapman & Hall, 1890. First edition. 3 vols. Orig. cloth. Covers a little soiled. Fine. MacManus 280-5401 1983 $225

WATSON, H. B. MARRIOTT   The Privateers. London: Methuen, (1907). First edition. Orig. cloth. Fine. MacManus 280-5403 1983 $20

WATSON, H. B. MARRIOTT   Twisted Eglantine. London: Methuen, (1905). First edition. Illus. Orig. cloth. A bit worn and soiled. MacManus 280-5404 1983 $25

WATSON, HEWETT COTTRELL (1804-1881)   The New Botanist's Guide to the Localities of the Rarer Plants of Britain, Vol. 1. 1835. 8vo. Orig. cloth. Wheldon 160-1634 1983 £20

WATSON, JOHN   The Mercahant and Trader's Daily Companion. Dublin: Printed for Pat. Wogan and Rich. Cross, 1790. Unnumbered pages, tall narrow 12mo, some light signs of use, but a very good copy in recent boards. Sixth edition. Fenning 60-430 1983 £28.50

WATSON, JOHN BROADUS (1878-1958)   The Battle of Behavorism. NY: W. W. Norton & Co., (1929). First edition. Fine in dust jacket. Gach 95-476 1983 $60

WATSON, JOHN BROADUS (1878-1958)   Behavior. An Introduction to Comparative Psychology. NY: Holt, (1914). Second printing. Very good. Gach 94-664 1983 $25

WATSON, JOHN BROADUS (1878-1958)   Behaviorism. NY: The People's Institute Pub. Co., (1925). Correct first edition with the People's Institute imprint. Cloth rubbed. Gach 95-477 1983 $40

WATSON, JOHN BROADUS (1878-1958)   Behaviorism. NY: 1928. First trade edition with Norton imprint. Near fine. Gach 94-665 1983 $25

WATSON, JOHN BROADUS (1878-1958)   Behaviorism. NY: Norton, (1930). First printing of revised edition. Publisher's black cloth, rubbed. Fair to good copy. Gach 95-477a 1983 $25

WATSON, JOHN BROADUS (1878-1958)   Psychological Care of Infant and Child. NY: Norton, (1928). First edition. Spine tips rubbed. Gach 94-666 1983 $25

WATSON, JOHN BROADUS (1878-1958)   Psychology from the Standpoint of a Behaviorist. Phila: Lippincott, (1919). First edition. Gach 94-667 1983 $30

WATSON, JOHN BROADUS (1878-1958)   Psychology From the Standpoint of a Behaviorist. Philadelphia: J. B. Lippincott, (1924). Second ed. Publisher's russet cloth. Gach 95-478 1983 $25

WATSON, JOHN BROADUS (1878-1958)   The Ways of Behaviorism. NY: Norton, 1928. First edition. Short tear to spine label. Near fine. Gach 94-668 1983 $25

WATSON, JOHN F.   Annals of Philadelphia and Pennsylvania, in the Olden Time. Philadelphia, 1898. 3 vols. Plates. Cloth. A fine set. Felcone 22-192 $60

WATSON, RALPH   A Brief Explantory Statement. London, 1829. 8vo. Orig. cloth. Orig. paper backed boards. Slightly worn. Uncut. Some slight foxing. Presentation copy inscribed to T.P. Bart. Good. Edwards 1042-182 1983 £75

WATSON, RICHARD   Anecdotes of the Life of Richard Watson, Bishop of Landaff. Printed for T. Cadell and W. Davies, 1817. 4to, engraved portrait after Romney (lightly spotted in margins), neatly written pencil notes, very pale, in a cont. hand on several pages, the margins of two leaves folded in so that the notes were not trimmed off when the book was bound, early 19th century calf gilt, a little rubbed. First edition. Bickersteth 77-328 1983 £45

WATSON, RICHARD   An Apology for the Bible, in a Series of Letters Addressed to Thomas Paine. New Brunswick: Abraham Blauvelt, 1796. Full calf. Contains the list of subscribers' names and the leaf advertising Watson's Apology for Christianity. Very good. Felcone 19-55 1983 $50

WATSON, RICHARD   An Apology for the Bible, in a Series of Letters, Addressed to Thomas Paine. Lichfield, CT: T. Collier, 1797. 12mo, cont. calf. Karmiole 75-115 1983 $60

WATSON, ROBERT SPENCE   The History of English Rule and Policy in South Africa. Newcastle-upon-Tyne, J. Forster, 1879. Slip. Disbound. Jarndyce 31-113 1983 £28

WATSON, ROSAMUND MARRIOTT   After Sunset. London: John Lane, The Bodley Head, 1804(sic). First edition. Orig. cloth. Very good. MacManus 280-5405 1983 $25

WATSON, ROSAMUND MARIOTT   The Art of the House. George Bell, The Connoisseur Series, 1897. First collected edition, with 40 illus. and plates, 8vo, orig. cloth, gilt, t.e.g., a little light foxing but a very good copy. Fenning 61-472 1983 £14.50

WATSON, W.   Orchids, their culture and management. (1890). 52 plates (8 coloured), 117 text-figures, 13 parts in 12, 8vo, original wrappers. First edition, very rare in this state. Wrappers a trifle used, but a good set. Wheldon 160-2064 1983 £60

WATSON, WILLIAM (1858-1935)   The Collected Poems. London: John Lane, 1899. First edition. Thick large 8vo. Frontis. Orig. buckram. One of 120 large-paper copies, of which 90 were for sale. Presentation copy to G.F. Watts, dated January, 1899. Covers worn and darkened. Inner hinges cracked. MacManus 280-5406 1983 $85

WATSON, WILLIAM (1858-1935)   The Eloping Angels. London: Elkin Mathews & John Lane, 1983. First edition. Orig. cloth. Inner hinges a bit stained. Very good. MacManus 280-5407 1983 $20

WATSON, WILLIAM (1858-1935)   Epigrams of Art, Life and Nature. Liverpool: Gilbert G. Walmsley, 1884. First edition. Orig. cloth with printed paper label. Spine label darkened and slightly chipped. Spine slightly worn. Some offsetting to the endpapers. Former owner's signature. Very good. MacManus 280-5408 1983 $65

WATSON, WILLIAM (1858-1935)   Excursions in Criticism. London: Elkin Mathews & John Lane, 1893. First edition. Orig. cloth. Fine. MacManus 280-5409 1983 $25

WATSON, WILLIAM (1858-1935)   The Father of the Forest and Other Poems. Chicago: Stone & Kimball, 1895. First American edition. 12mo. Orig. cloth. Fine. MacManus 280-5410 1983 $35

WATSON, WILLIAM (1858-1935)   The Heralds of the Dawn. London: John Lane, The Bodley Head, 1912. First edition. Orig. cloth. Dust jacket (soiled and chipped). Edges very slightly worn. Rear free endpaper slightly browned. Very good. MacManus 280-5413 1983 $45

WATSON, WILLIAM (1858-1935)   The Hope of the World and Other Poems. London: John Lane, 1898. First edition. Orig. cloth. One of 125 large-paper copies. Spine darkened. Very good. MacManus 280-5416 1983 $45

WATSON, WILLIAM (1858-1935)   The Hope of the World and Other Poems. London: John Lane, 1898. First edition. Orig. cloth. Large paper copy limited to 125 copies, 75 of which are for sale. Spine darkened. Very good. MacManus 280-5415 1983 $35

WATSON, WILLIAM (1858-1935)   New Poems. Greenfield: John Lane, 1902. First edition. Orig. brown wrappers. Copy No. 1 of 50 copies on hand-made paper, printed to secure copyright. Very fine. MacManus 280-5420 1983 $100

WATSON, WILLIAM (1858-1935)   New Poems. London: John Lane, The Bodley Head, 1909. First edition. Orig. cloth. Endpapers foxed. Very good. MacManus 280-5419 1983 $20

WATSON, WILLIAM (1858-1935)   The Poems. N.Y.: John Lane Co., 1905. First American edition. 2 vols. Frontis. port. Orig. cloth. Fine. MacManus 280-5422 1983 $20

WATSON, WILLIAM (1858-1935)   The Prince's Quest and Other Poems. London: C. Kegan Paul & Co., 1880. First edition, first issue. Orig. decorated cloth. Binding worn and spotted. One inner hinge strained. Good. MacManus 280-5423 1983 $75

WATSON, WILLIAM (1858-1935)   The Prince's Quest and Other Poems. London: Elkin Mathews & John Lane, 1893. Second edition. Orig. cloth. With a new brief foreward by author. Good. MacManus 280-5424 1983 $20

WATSON, WILLIAM (1858-1935)   The Purple East. Chicago: Stone & Kimball, 1896. First American edition. Orig. boards. Signature & price on front flyleaf. Boards slightly torn & soiled. Good. MacManus 280-5425 1983 $25

WATSON, WILLIAM (1858-1935)   The Purple East. London: John Lane, 1896. First edition. Frontis. by G.F. Watts. Orig. purple wrappers. Very good. MacManus 280-5426 1983 $20

WATSON, WILLIAM (1858-1935)   Sable and Purple with other poems. N.Y.: John Lane Co., 1910. First American edition. Orig. purple cloth. Tissue jacket. Review copy. Publisher's slip laid in. Small piece nicked from outer hinge. Fine. MacManus 280-5429 1983 $25

WATSON, WILLIAM (1858-1935)   Selected Poems. London: Thornton Butterworth Ltd., (1928). First edition. Frontis. port. Orig. cloth. Dust jacket (chipped). Signed by author on the flyleaf. Very good. MacManus 280-5430 1983 $35

WATT, ALEXANDER   The Art of Paper-Making... New York: D. Van Nostrand Co., 1907. Third edition. 8vo. Modern cloth, paper spine label. Some pages professionally repaired. Oak Knoll 49-306 1983 $65

WATT, G.   The Pests and Blights on the Tea Plant. Calcutta, 1898. Half morocco, worn. 8vo. Good. Edwards 1044-744 1983 £20

WATT, ROBERT   Bibliotheca Britannica; or a General Index to British and Foreign Literature. Edinburgh, 1824. First edition. 4 vols. 4to. Cont. diced calf, gilt, gilt spines with crimson and green morocco labels, gilt. A little worn. Traylen 94-859 1983 £165

WATT, ROBERT   Bibliotheca Britannica. New York: Burt Franklin, n.d. 1 of the largest of the Franklin reprints, printed on 300-year paper. 4 vols., cloth. Reprint of the 1824 ed. Dawson 470-300 1983 $175

WATTERS, WILLIAM   A Short Account of the Christian Experience... Alexandria, Va.: S. Snowden, (1806?). Full calf. Very good. Felcone 20-182 1983 $25

WATTS, ALARIC A   Aurora. Henry S. King, 1875. First edition, orig. brown cloth, v.g. Jarndyce 30-866 1983 £10.50

WATTS, ALARIC A.   Poetical Sketches. Hurst, Robinson, 1824. Half title, engr. title and illus. Straight-grained morocco, v.g. 3rd edition. Jarndyce 30-865 1983 £14

WATTS, GEORGE C.   The Long Trail. (Oakland, 1949.) 1st ed. A very scarce privately printed work. Jenkins 153-676 1983 $40

WATTS, ISAAC (1674-1748)   Divine & Moral Songs... Van Voorst, 1848. 1st edn. thus. 30 wood engrs. by C.W. Cope engr'd by John Thompson. Crimson calf with gilt & blind tooled borders cvrs., gilt titling, a.e.g., cvrs. sl. & marks, contents foxed & thumbed, good copy. Hodgkins 27-211 1983 £15

WATTS, ISAAC (1674-1748)   Divine and Moral Songs for Children. S. Low, 1866. 1st edn. Numerous illus. by Wimperis, Kennedy, Allen, et al. Dark green sand grain cloth gilt (designed by Albert Warren), bevelled boards, a.e.g. (bookpl. fr. ep., corners sl. bruised), v.g. Hodgkins 27-340 1983 £16.50

WATTS, ISAAC (1674-1748)   The Doctrine of the Passions Explained and Improved. Elizabeth Town: Shepard Kollock for Robert Hodge & Co., 1795. Full calf. Front endsheet lacking. Very good. Felcone 19-56 1983 $45

WATTS, ISAAC (1674-1748)   Evangelical discourses on several subjects. London: J. Oswald, etc., 1747. First edition. 8vo. Cont. calf. Minor wear. Fine copy. Ximenes 63-591 1983 $125

WATTS, ISAAC (1674-1748)   A Guide to Prayer. Elizabeth Town: Shepard Kollock, 1797. Full calf (worn). Spine label wanting. Very good. Felcone 19-57 1983 $45

WATTS, ISAAC (1674-1748)   Hymns and Spiritual Songs. London, H.J. for John Lawrence, 1709. 12mo, 3/4 calf. Small repairs on title. Salloch 387-256 1983 $200

WATTS, ISAAC (1674-1748)   Psalms Carefully Suited to the Christian Worship in the United States. Elizabeth Town: Shepard Kollock, 1797. Full calf. Several signatures of Joseph Alling and two Alling family death dates. Kollock's name alone appears in each imprint. Very good. Felcone 19-59 1983 $60

WATTS, JOHN   Letter Book, Merchant and Councillor of New York, Jan. 1, 1762 - Dec. 22, 1765. NY; NY Hist. Soc., 1928. Argosy 710-387 1983 $30

WATTS-DUNTON, THEODORE   Aylwin. London: Hurst & Blackett, 1902. Illustrated edition. Frontis. port. Orig. decorated cloth. Presentation copy inscribed to W.E. Garrett-Fisher. Spine and covers slightly worn. Front inner hinge cracking, webbing intact. Bookplate. Very good. MacManus 280-5432 1983 $135

WAUGH, ALEC   Going Their Own Ways. N.Y., Farrar & Rinehart, (1939). First edition. Black cloth stamped in gilt (short tears at head of spine). Inscribed to Evelyn del Barrio, 1939. Good-very good. Houle 22-936 1983 $30

WAUGH, ALEC   Hot Countries. N.Y., Farrar, (1930). Frontis. and woodcuts by Lynd Ward. Signed by the author, 1930. Bookplate of actor Jean Hersholt. Very good. Houle 21-909 1983 $30

WAUGH, ALEC   Resentment. London: Grant Richards, 1918. Boards, paper label. First edition. Very slight foxing at top edge of a few leaves, otherwise a fine copy. Reese 20-1102 1983 $75

WAUGH, ARTHUR   Alfred Lord Tennyson: A Study of His Life and Work. Wm. Heinemann, 1893. 2nd edition, tall 8vo. Half title, front. 16 pp ads. Orig. maroon cloth. Jarndyce 30-1149 1983 £10.50

WAUGH, ARTHUR   A Hundred Years of Publishing. Chapman & Hall, 1930. First edition, with 41 plates & facs., 8vo, orig. cloth, a very good copy. Fenning 61-65 1983 £18.50

WAUGH, ARTHUR   Tradition and Change, Studies in Contemporary Literature. Chapman & Hall, 1919. First edition. Half title, orig. blue cloth, sl. rubbed. Jarndyce 31-1002 1983 £10.50

WAUGH, EDWIN   The Chimney Corner. Manchester: Abel Heywood, 1879. First edition, 4to, half title, front., orig. green cloth boards, rebacked with green morocco, matching orig. New e.p.s. Very good. Signed presentation copy from the author. Jarndyce 30-869 1983 £15

WAUGH, EVELYN   Basil Seal Rides Again, or the Rake's Progress. Boston: Little, Brown, (1963). 1st ed., 1 of 1,000 numbered and signed copies. Illus. by Kathleen Hale. Orig. blue linen, gilt, t.e.g., uncut. Mint copy. Jenkins 155-1258 1983 $200

WAUGH, EVELYN   Basil Seal Rides Again. Boston, Little, Brown, (1963). First American edition. Color frontis. by Kathleen Hale. Blue cloth, t.e.g., acetate jacket. One of 1,000 copies, signed by Waugh. Fine. Houle 21-911 1983 $175

WAUGH, EVELYN   Basil Seal Rides Again or the Rake's Progress. Boston: (1963). First American edition. Colored frontis. by Kathleen Hale. Limited to 1000 copies signed by Waugh. Near mint. Bromer 25-124 1983 $85

WAUGH, EVELYN   Black Mischief. London: Chapman and Hall, Ltd., (1932). First edition. 8vo. Frontis. Orig. marbled cloth. Dust jacket, very slightly darkened and dust-soiled, but a fine copy. Jaffe 1-389 1983 $450

WAUGH, EVELYN   Black Mischief. L, (1932). Minor interior foxing, spine slightly faded, edges starting to fray, otherwise good. Quill & Brush 54-1473 1983 $60

WAUGH, EVELYN   Black Mischief. NY, (1932). Cover faded with some soiling, front hinge starting, good. Quill & Brush 54-1468 1983 $30

WAUGH, EVELYN   Brideshead Revisited. B, 1945. Limited to 600 copies, cover slightly soiled and dulled. Quill & Brush 54-1474 1983 $150

WAUGH, EVELYN   Brideshead Revisited. Boston: Little, Brown, 1946. 1st trade ed. Orig. cloth, dj. Fine copy in dj with very little rubbing but a few small taped tears. Jenkins 155-1259 1983 $35

WAUGH, EVELYN   Edmund Campion. London: Longmans, Green and Co., (1935). First edition. Tall 8vo. Orig. cloth. Dust jacket, partially soiled and slightly torn. A fine copy. Jaffe 1-392 1983 $275

WAUGH, EVELYN   A Handful of Dust. London: Chapman and Hall Ltd., (1934). First edition. 8vo. Frontis. Orig. marbled cloth. Dust jacket. Orig. Book Society wraparound band. A very fine copy. Rare. Jaffe 1-390 1983 $1,250

WAUGH, EVELYN   The Holy Places. London: Queen Anne Press, 1953. Illus. with wood engravings by Reynolds Stone. Of an edition of 1000, 1/50 bound in full morocco and signed by author and artist. Slight rubbing to extremities, else very fine. Pictorial dust wrapper faintly chipped. Bromer 25-125 1983 $950

WAUGH, EVELYN   Labels. (London): Duckworth, 1930. First edition. Illus. Orig. cloth. Decorated endpapers. One of 110 copies signed by author, with a page of the orig. manuscript tipped-in. This copy contains the first page of the manuscript, which bears numerous corrections and revisions by Waugh. Foxing. Very fine. MacManus 280-5434 1983 $1,500

WAUGH, EVELYN   Labels. A Mediterranean Journal. (London): Duckworth, 1930. First edition. Tall 8vo. Frontis. Orig. cloth. Dust jacket. Spine bumped and lightly faded, otherwise a very good copy. Jaffe 1-387 1983 $225

WAUGH, EVELYN   Labels - a Mediterranean Journal. London, 1930. First edition. Black and white frontis. by the author. Spine faded. Covers very slightly marked. Very good. Jolliffe 26-579 1983 £65

WAUGH, EVELYN   The Loved One. (L, 1948). Illus. by Stuart Boyle. Edges very slightly rubbed, else near fine in slightly frayed, slightly rubbed, very good dustwrapper. Quill & Brush 54-1482 1983 $75

WAUGH, EVELYN   The Loved One. (London): Chapman & Hall, (1948). 1st ed. Orig. blue cloth, gilt. Fine copy without dj. Jenkins 155-1262 1983 $30

WAUGH, EVELYN   The Loved One. Boston: Little, Brown & Co., 1948. First American edition. Orig. cloth. Dust jacket (spine and covers faded and worn). Very good. MacManus 280-5436 1983 $25

WAUGH, EVELYN   Mr. Loveday's Little Outing And Other Sad Stories. London: Chapman & Hall, Ltd., (1936). First edition. 8vo. Frontis. Orig. marbled cloth. Dust jacket. Small tear in back panel of jacket, otherwise a very fine copy. Jaffe 1-393 1983 $750

WAUGH, EVELYN   Mr. Loveday's Little Outing. L, (1936). "Colonial Edition" stamped on copyright page, hinge tape and frontis added by publisher, some interior foxing, edges rubbed, else very good. Quill & Brush 54-1477 1983 $60

WAUGH, EVELYN   Ninety-Two Days. London: Duckworth, 1934. First edition. Map and 24 illus. Tall 8vo, orig. cloth. Dust jacket. A few slight nicks at edge of jacket, otherwise a very fine copy. Jaffe 1-391 1983 $1,000

WAUGH, EVELYN   Put Out More Flags. B, 1942. Cover and endpapers stained, else good in remnants of dustwrapper. Bookplate. Quill & Brush 54-1479 1983 $30

WAUGH, EVELYN   Remote People. London: Duckworth, (1931). First edition. Tall 8vo. Illus. Orig. cloth. Dust jacket, chipped. Top of spine slightly faded, otherwise a fine copy. Jaffe 1-388 1983 $250

WAUGH, EVELYN   Rossetti. His Life and Works. London: Duckworth, 1928. First edition. Tall 8vo. Illus. Orig. cloth. Fine copy. Jaffe 1-385 1983 $250

WAUGH, EVELYN   Scoop. Boston, 1938. 8vo. Cloth. 1st American ed. A fine copy in intact but browned and slightly scuffed dj. In Our Time 156-862 1983 $200

WAUGH, EVELYN   Scoop. B, 1938. Bookplate taped onto front pastedown, else very good in chipped and worn dustwrapper. Quill & Brush 54-1480 1983 $100

WAUGH, EVELYN   Unconditional Surrender. L, 1961. Fine in bright near fine, price clipped dustwrapper that is slightly stained on rear panel. Quill & Brush 54-1485 1983 $75

WAUGH, EVELYN   Vile Bodies. London: Chapman & Hall, Ltd, 1930. First edition. 8vo. Orig. marbled cloth. Fine copy. Jaffe 1-386 1983 $150

WAUGH, EVELYN   When the Going Was Good. Boston: Little, Brown & Co., 1947. First American edition. Color frontis port. Orig. cloth. Dust jacket (lightly worn). Good. MacManus 280-5438 1983 $65

WAUGH, EVELYN   Wine in Peace and War. London, (1947). First English edition. Decorations by Rex Whistler. Endpapers spotted as usual. Covers sprung. Tail of lower cover stained. Very good. Jolliffe 26-581 1983 £40

WAUGH, LORENZO   Autobiography of... Oakland: Pacific Press, 1883. Portrait and illus. Orig. cloth, gilt. The scarce orig. ed. Jenkins 153-677 1983 $100

WAUGH, LORENZO   Autobiography. Oakland, 1883. Illus. Orig. cloth. First edition. Ginsberg 47-199 1983 $35

WAY, HERBERT W. L.   Round the World for Gold. London: Sampson Low, Marston & Co., ltd. 1912. 46 leaves of plates, purple cloth. With illus. and maps. Karmiole 73-102 1983 $50

THE WAY of the Cross. Sussex: Douglas Pepler, 1918. Illus. with wood engravings by Eric Gill. Orig. printed wrappers. Spine slightly faded and worn. Near-fine. MacManus 278-2183 1983 $150

WAYLAND, FRANCIS   The Elements of Intellectual Philosophy. Boston: Phillips, Sampson & Co., 1855 (1854). 12mo. Publisher's cloth, lightly worn. Gach 94-669 1983 $25

WAYLAND, JOHN W.   The Political Opinions of Thomas Jefferson. N.Y., Neale, 1907. Orig. cloth. First edition. Ginsberg 46-377 1983 $35

WEADOCK, JACK   Dust of the Desert Plain. New York, 1936. First edition. Frontis. & illus. Some staining and browning to cloth. Signed by author. Fairly nice. Jenkins 152-505 1983 $35

WEATHERLY, F. E.   Told in the Twilight. N.Y.: Dutton, n.d., (ca.1880). 8vo. Cloth backed pictorial boards. Light edgewear. Victorian colorplate. Illus. by M.E. Edwards & J. Staples. Very good to fine. Aleph-bet 8-260 1983 $55

WEAVER, LAWRENCE   Memorials & Monuments. London, 1915. 1st ed. Illus. 8vo, orig. boards, buckram back. Morrill 287-498 1983 $30

WEAVER, THOMAS   Plantagenets tragicall story: or, the death of King Edward the Fourth... London: M.F. for Richard Tomlins, 1649. First edition. 8vo. Cont. calf. Engraved portrait. Calf worn. Ximenes 63-386 1983 $300

WEAVER, WARREN A.   Lithographs of N. Currier and Currier & Ives. NY: The Holport Publishing Co., (1925). Illus. with 15 plates. With two supplements to the text by Weaver, 1926, one bound-in, the other one laid in. Green cloth, sl. stained. Karmiole 72-114 1983 $35

WEAVER, WILLIAM D.   Catalogue of the Wheeler Gift of Books, Pamphlets and Periodicals... New York: American Institute of Elec. Engineers, 1909. 2 vols., cloth, scuffed and dull. Dawson 470-301 1983 $150

WEAVER, WILLIAM D.   Catalogue of the Wheeler Gift of Books... New York, American Institute of Electrical Engineers, 1909. Portraits, illus., & facs. 2 vols., 8vo. Morrill 288-514 1983 $100

WEBB, DANIEL   Remarks on the Beauties of Poetry. London: R. & J. Dodsley, 1762. 1st ed., 8vo, uncut copy in original wrappers, with half-title. Outer edges of wrappers and of half-title worn, else a very good copy. Trebizond 18-99 1983 $175

WEBB, JEAN FRANCIS   No Match for Murder. N.Y., MacMillian, 1942. First edition. Dust jacket (several short tears) else very good. Houle 22-939 1983 $25

WEBB, JOHN   The Government of Christ Considered and Applied. Boston: J. Draper for H. Procter and S. Eliot, 1738. Stitched. Signature "Thomas Wiswell His Book July ye 18 1738." Felcone 22-261 1983 $35

WEBB, MARIA   The Fells of Swart-moor Hall and Their Friends. A.W. Bennett, 1865. First edition, with 8 plates, 8vo, orig. cloth, by Westleys, with their ticket. Fenning 62-385 1983 £26.50

WEBB, MARIA   The Penns & Peningtons of the Seventeenth Century. F. Bowyer Kitto, 1867. First edition, 8vo, orig. cloth. Fenning 60-431 1983 £12.50

WEBB, MARION ST. JOHN   The Littlest One Again. G.G. Harrap, 1926. 4to. Colour frontis. Pictorial title. 3 colour plates & 22 text illus. Buff boards. Onlaid colour plate, light wear. Greer 40-220 1983 £15

WEBB, MARY   The Chinese Lion. London: Bertram Rota Ltd., 1937. First edition. 12mo. Orig. cloth-backed boards. One of 350 copies. Some light foxing. In the publisher's slipcase. Fine. MacManus 280-5443 1983 $35

WEBB, MARY   The Golden Arrow. London: Constable, 1916. First edition. Orig. cloth. Covers a bit worn. MacManus 280-5444 1983 $50

WEBB, MARY   Precious Bane. London: Jonathan Cape, 1924. First edition. Orig. cloth. With a bookplate by A. Rackham. Covers rather faded. Little foxing. In a half-morocco folding box. MacManus 280-5445 1983 $150

WEBB, MARY   Precious Bane. London, 1924. First edition. The first gathering has been somewhat clumsily re-inserted. Erasure from flyleaf. Inserted is a signed photograph of the author dressed up for the part of Madeline in "Nicholas Nickleby" in 1924, (damaged at edges, but subject is not affected). Very nice. Rota 231-617 1983 £50

WEBB, MARY   The Spring of Joy. London: J.M. Dent & Sons, 1917. First edition. Orig. cloth. With the bookplate of G.L. Lazarus, designed by A. Rackham. Covers slightly soiled. Edges a little worn. In a cloth box. Good. MacManus 280-5446 1983 $125

WEBB, MARY   The Spring of Joy. London, 1917. First
edition. Very nice. Rota 230-619 1983 £45

WEBB, RICHARD D.   The Life and Letters of Captain John
Brown. Smith, Elder (Dublin printed), 1861. First edition, with a
photo. frontis. portrait, small 8vo, orig. mauve cloth, by John
Mowat of Dublin, with his ticket, a little weakness in the inside
front joint but still a nice copy. Fenning 61-476 1983 £24.50

WEBB, SIDNEY   The Story of the Durham Miners.
Fabian Society and Labour Publishing Co., 1921. First edition, half
title, front. 2pp ads. Orig. blue card printed wraps. Jarndyce 31-
1003 1983 £12.50

WEBB, THOMAS SMITH   The Freemason's Monitor. Montpelier,
Vt., 1816. 12mo, contemporary calf, leather label. Morrill 287-499
1983 $30

WEBB, WALTER PRESCOTT   Divided We Stand. New York, 1937.
Maps. 1st ed. Spine faded. Presentation copy from Webb--quite
scarce. Jenkins 153-679 1983 $50

WEBB, WALTER PRESCOTT   The Great Plains. Boston: Ginn & Co.,
1931. First edition, first issue, with errors on p.10. Plates, maps,
text illus. Orig. blue pictorial cloth stamped in silver. Unusually
fine. Jenkins 152-506 1983 $150

WEBB, WALTER PRESCOTT   The Great Plains. (Boston, 1931).
First edition. Illus. & maps. Argosy 716-624 1983 $50

WEBB, WALTER PRESCOTT   The Texas Rangers: a Century of Frontier
Defense. Boston, 1935. 1st ed. Illus. by Lonnie Rees. Photos.
Argosy 710-531 1983 $40

WEBB, WILLIAM S.   An Archaelogical Survey of Wheeler on the
Tennessee River. Washington: 1939. Map frontis, large folding map,
122 plates, numerous text illus. Green wrappers. Very good. Bradley
66-445 1983 $20

WEBBER, CHARLES W.   The Gold Mines of the Gila. N.Y., 1849.
2 vols. bound in one. Half morocco. First edition. Ginsberg 47-966
1983 $375

WEBBER, SAMUEL   Logan, an Indian Tale. Cambridge:
Hilliard and Metcalf, 1821. Orig. gilt straight grain red morocco.
First edition. The spine and hinges have been crudely, but securely
repaired with library tape, but internally a fine copy. Reese 18-558
1983 $45

WEBER, A.   The History of Indian Literature. London,
1914. 8vo. Orig. cloth. Slight wear. Good. Edwards 1044-745 1983
£14

WEBER, CARL J.   A Thousand and one Fore-Edge Paintings.
Waterville, Maine: Colby College Press, 1949. First edition,
limited to 1000 copies. Tall 8vo. Cloth. Leather spine label,
dust jacket. 24 illus., some in color. Jacket worn, erasures from
endpaper. Oak Knoll 48-377 1983 $225

WEBER, ERNST HEINRICH   Wellenlehre auf Experimente gegrundet
oder uber die Wellen tropfbarer Flussigkeiten mit Anwendung auf die
Schallund Lichtwellen. Leipzig: G. Fleischer, 1825. 8vo. Old
boards. Errata leaf, with 18 folding plates. Fine copy. Gurney
90-118 1983 £350

WEBER, ERNST HEINRICH   Zusatze zur Lehre vom Baue und den
Verrichtungen der Geschlechtsorgane. Leipzig, 1846. 4to. Orig.
wrappers. Uncut, unopened. 9 lithograph plates. Offprint. Back
slightly torn. Gurney 90-119 1983 £30

WEBER, MAX   Cubist Poems. Elkin Mathews, 1914.
First edition. Exceptionally fine. Rota 231-618 1983 £30

WEBER, MAX   The Methodology of the Social Sciences.
Glencoe, Il.: The Free Press, (1949). First edition. Dust jacket.
Gach 95-479 1983 $20

WEBSTER, BENJAMIN   The series of dramatic entertainments
performed by royal command, before Her Majesty the Queen, His Royal
Highness Prince Albert, the Royal Family, and the Court at Windsor
Castle, 1848-9. London: published by Mr. Mitchell; Mr. McLean's;
and at the National Acting Drama Office; printed by W. S. Johnson,
n.d. (1849). 4to, original purple cloth, decorated in gilt (neatly
rebacked, original spine preserved). 1st edition. A color-printed
title-page and frontis. A very good copy. Ximenes 64-566 1983 $150

WEBSTER, CHARLES K.   Britain and the Independence of Latin
America, 1812-1830. 1938. First edition, roy. 8vo, 2 vols., orig.
cloth. Fenning 61-477 1983 £45

WEBSTER, DANIEL   Discourse, Del. at Plymouth, Dec. 22,
1820. Boston, 1821. 8vo, orig. pr. wraps. Argosy 716-105 1983
$125

WEBSTER, DANIEL   A Discourse in Commemoration of the
Lives and Services of John Adams and Thos. Jefferson, in Faneuil
Hall, Boston, Aug. 2. Boston, 1826. Pr. wraps. (front mended).
Argosy 716-447 1983 $30

WEBSTER, DANIEL   Speech of the Hon...on a Bill Making
Further Provision for Filling the Ranks of the Regular Army...
Alexandria, 1814. Dsb. Gocd. Reese 18-466 1983 $30

WEBSTER, DANIEL   Speech on the Subject of the Three
Millions Appropriation, Senate, Jan. 14. Wash., 1836. Tall 8vo,
uncut. (Unbound). First edition. "From the Author" written on
title. Argosy 716-448 1983 $35

WEBSTER, DANIEL   Speech, upon the Subject of Slavery.
Boston, 1850. Pr. wrs. Argosy 716-27 1983 $35

WEBSTER, DANIEL   The Works. Boston, 1851. First edition.
6 vols. 2 fine engraved ports. 2 views. Full calf, gilt spine,
leather labels, marbled edges. Signed by Webster. Subscriber's copy.
Argosy 716-449 1983 $375

WEBSTER, F. A. M.   The Hill of Riches. London: Hutchinson
& Co., n.d. First edition. Orig. cloth. Presentation copy to Doyle
inscribed: "To Sir Arthur Conan Doyle with all wishes and regards.
F.A.M. Webster Christmas 1923." Spine slightly faded and worn. Some
offsetting to the free endpapers. Very good. MacManus 278-1642 1983
$150

WEBSTER, JOHN   The Displaying of Supposed Witchcraft.
London, 1677. 1st ed. 4to, new boards, paper label. Professional
repair to blank portion of Imprimatur leaf, otherwise nice. Morrill
287-500 1983 $250

WEBSTER, JOHN   The Duchess of Malfi/The White Devil.
New York, (1930). 8vo. Cloth. Illus. by Henry Keen. A fine copy.
In Our Time 156-452 1983 $35

WEBSTER, JOHN WHITE   A Description of the Island of St.
Michael. Boston: R. P. & C. Williams, 1821. First (only) ed.,
8vo, modern half calf antique, marbled boards. Two large folding maps,
two engraved plates, folding table. Some foxing and offsetting of
plates, but a very good copy. Trebizond 18-128 1983 $265

WEBSTER, NOAH   The Elementary Spelling Book. New
Brunswick, 1836. Worn and fragile, good. Quill & Brush 54-1659
1983 $25

WEBSTER, NOAH   Elementary Spelling Book. NY, (1880).
Rev. ed., 12mo, orig. pr. bds., cloth-backed. Argosy 710-486 1983
$20

WEBSTER, NOAH   The Prompter. Boston: I. Thomas and
E.T. Andrews, 1793. Illus. Calf-backed wooden boards. Binding
worn and separating from text, endsheets lacking; internally a very
nice copy. Felcone 22-262 1983 $175

WEBSTER, NOAH   The Revolution in France. New York:
George Bunce, 1794. First edition. Signed and inscribed by Webster.
Half morocco. Jenkins 152-508 1983 $450

WEBSTER, NOAH   Rudiments of English Grammar. New Haven: Durrie & Peck, 1831. Orig. cloth and boards, stained, broken at hinge. Dawson 471-301 1983 $20

WEBSTER, NOAH   Webster Genealogy... Brooklyn, 1876. Ed. limited to 250 copies. 4to, orig. wrappers. Morrill 286-704 1983 $25

WECKERLIN, J. B.   Chansons de France pour les Petits Francais. Paris: Plon, 1927. Oblong 4to. Colour pictorial title & 48pp of colour pictorial decorations. Little loose. Red decorated cloth, gilt. Greer 40-87 1983 £22.50

WEDDERBURN, ALEXANDER   A song: or, a sermon. A new ballad. (Edinburgh): 29th January, 1757. Sm. 4to, two leaves, disbound, 1st edition. Very rare. Upper portion stained, but a sound copy. Ximenes 64-568 1983 $300

WEDDERBURN, JOHN   Quatuor Problematum quae Martinus Horky Contra Nuntium Sidereum de Quatuor Planetis Disputanda proposuit. Padua: Pietro Marienelli, 1610. First edition. 4to. Tan calf, gilt line borders, gilt back and dentelles, g.e. From the library of Piero Ginori Conti with his bookplate. Skillful restoration to outermost corners of title not affecting print. Kraus 164-97 1983 $14,000

WEDGWOOD, H. A.   The Bird Talisman. London, 1939. First edition. 8 colour plates and numerous drawings by Gwen Raverat. Fore-edge slightly soiled. A few pages slightly thumb-marked. Very good. Jolliffe 26-427 1983 £25

WEED, LEWIS H.   The Development of the Cerebro-Spinal Spaces in Pig and in Man. Washington, DC: Carnegie Inst., 1917. 4to. 27 plates. Library bookplate and spine label. Inscribed to Adolf Meyer. Gach 95-531 1983 $35

THE "WEEK-END" Calendar. London: Geoffrey Bles, 1932. First edition. 8vo. Orig. cloth. Dust jacket. Fine copy. Jaffe 1-10 1983 $150

WEEKS, FRED B.   Bibliograpn and Index of North American Geology, Paleontology, Petrology, and Mineralogy for 1903. Wash., 1904. Jenkins 152-509 1983 $50

WEEKS, GEORGE F.   California Copy. Washington, D.C.: Washington College Press, 1928. Illus. Orig. cloth in dj. 1st ed. Presentation copy from author. Jenkins 153-681 1983 $65

WEEKS, LEONIE BELLE   Leaves in the Sun. San Francisco, John Henry Nash, 1935. First edition. Half beige cloth over marbled boards (slight rubbing). One of 250 copies. Very good. Houle 22-1141 1983 $45

WEEKS, LYMAN HORACE   A History of Paper-Manufacturing in the United States, 1690-1916. New York: Lockwood Trade Journal Co., 1916. First edition. 8vo. Cloth. Over 150 illus. of papermills and papermakers. Scarce. Covers soiled. Oak Knoll 48-312 1983 $95

WEELER, EARL V.   Ballads of Eldorado. S.F., 1940. Half cloth over pictorial boards. One of 300 copies. Printed by Ward Ritchie. Very good. Houle 21-1178 1983 $90

WEGELIN, OSCAR   Early American Poetry. New York: Published by the Compiler, 1907. 1st ed., 1 of 150 numbered copies printed. Orig. boards, labels. Rebacked, but very good copy. Scarce. Jenkins 155-1359 1983 $60

WEHLE, HARRY B.   American Miniatures 1730-1850. GC, (1937). 173 portraits with description, cover slightly soiled, else very good, bookplate, owner's name. Quill & Brush 54-1633 1983 $35

WEHMER, CARL   Deutscher Buchdruck in Jahrhundert Guttenbergs. Leipzig, 1940. Large folio. 100 plates, some in red & black. Cloth-backed printed boards. Plates are fullpage facsimiles of specimen pages from German incunabula. Much of the incunabula is illus. with woodcuts. Fine. O'Neal 50-120 1983 $100

WEHNERT, E.   The Enchanted Toasting Fork. Tinsley Bros., 1869. Sm. 8vo. Title vignette & 70 illus. Blue decorated cloth, gilt. Greer 40-236 1983 £18.50

WEIBEL, JOHANN E.   Vierzig Jahre Missionar in Arkansas. Luzern, (Switzerland), 1927. 1st ed. Illus. Extremely scarce. Jenkins 153-734 1983 $100

WEIDMAN, JEROME   Letter of Credit. NY, 1940. Near fine in very good dustwrapper with slight wear to edges and one short tear. Quill & Brush 54-1488 1983 $25

WEIGALL, ARTHUR E. P.   Travels in the Upper Egyptian Deserts. Edinburgh: Blackwood, 1909. First edition, with 34 plates, 8vo, orig. cloth, t.e.g., a very good copy. Fenning 61-478 1983 £10.50

WEIGEL, C. E.   Observationes Chemicae et Mineralogicae. Gottingen, 1771. First edition. 4to. Boards. 1 plate. Title lightly dustsoiled. Gurney 90-120 1983 £60

WEIL, OSCAR   Oscar Weil, Letters and Papers. San Francisco: The Book Club of California, 1923. 4to, tipped-in photo by Dorothea Lange from a Painting. Text printed in red and black. Edition ltd. to 400 numbered copies, printed by the Grabhorn Press. Black cloth over boards; spine and cover labels. Karmiole 72-50 1983 $85

WEIR, JAMES   The Dawn of Reason, or Mental Traits in the Lower Animals. NY: The Macmillan Co., 1899. Ad leaf, publisher's green cloth. First edition. Gach 94-83 1983 $27.50

WEIR, R. W.   A History of the Scottish Borderers Militia. Dumfries, 1877. 8vo. Orig. cloth. Very slightly soiled. Good. Edwards 1042-565 1983 £25

WEISENBURG, THEODORE   Aphasia. NY: The Commonwealth Fund, 1935. First edition. Dusty ex-library copy with Leo Kanner's book-ticket. Gach 95-532 1983 $30

WEISMANN, AUGUST   Essays upon Heredity and Kindred Biological Problems. Oxford, 1889. 8vo, cloth. Binding worn, joints splitting. Wheldon 160-200 1983 £18

WEISMANN, AUGUST   Das Keimplasma. Jena, 1892. 24 text illus. Tall 8vo, orig. pr. wrs.; uncut & unopened. First edition. Argosy 713-563 1983 $175

WEISMILLER, EDWARD   The Faultless Shore and Other Poems. Boston, 1946. 8vo. Cloth. Review copy with slip laid in. Review of book pasted on inside endboard (under flap of jacket), else fine in dj. In Our Time 156-864 1983 $30

WEISS, E. R.   The Four Gospels... Leipzig: Printed by Poeschel & Trepte, 1932. 1st ed., 1 of 1500 numbered copies, signed by Weiss. Orig. vellum-backed tan boards, gilt, uncut, box. Fine copy in slightly rubbed box. Jenkins 155-1265 1983 $100

WEISSBERGER, JOSE A.   They Still Draw Pictures! NY 1938. Illus, wraps with silver title label, partially stained and rubbed. King 46-770 1983 $25

WEISSE, FRANK   The Art of Marbling. North Hills, PA: Bird & Bull Press, 1980. 4to, 14 leaves of specimens (tipped-in). 15 plates of photographic illus. Edition ltd. to 300 copies, printed on handmade paper. Fine copy in 1/4 oasis leather over marbled boards. Karmiole 76-83 1983 $350

WELBECK, ABBEY   Christening of the Marquis of Titchfield, May 22nd, 1893. (J. Linney, printer, Mansfield, 1893). With 12 actual photos., mounted on 11 plates, all but two measuring 6 by 8 inches approximately, the remaining two being 4 by 6 inches, titled, oblong 8vo, orig. stiff paper boards, gilt, a very good copy. Signed by both the Duke and the Duchess of Portland. Fenning 60-433 1983 £75

WELBY, T. EARLE   The Dinner Knell. London: Methuen & Co. Ltd., (1932). First edition. Orig. cloth. Dust jacket. Very fine. MacManus 280-5448 1983 $20

WELCH, EMILY SEDGWICK   A Biographical Sketch: John Sedwick, Major-General. (N.Y., Devinne Press), printed for private circulation, 1899. Orig. dec. cloth. First edition. One of 500 numbered copies. Ginsberg 46-681 1983 $50

WELCH, MOSES C.   An Excellent Spirit Forms the Character of a Good Ruler. Hartford: Hudson & Goodwin, 1812. Disbound. Very good. Felcone 20-30 1983 $20

WELCH, WILLIAM   Adaptation in Pathological Processes. Baltimore: Johns Hopkins Press, 1937. Uncut; ex-lib. Argosy 713-564 1983 $45

WELCH, WILLIAM   The Interdependence of Medicine with other Sciences of Nature. Baltimore, 1934. 8vo. Orig. binding. Limited edition of 225 copies. Backstrip age-darkened. Fye H-3-606 1983 $20

WELCH, WILLIAM   Papers and Addresses. Baltimore, 1920. 3 vols. 8vo. Orig. binding. First edition. Fye H-3-617 1983 $150

WELCH, WILLIAM   Papers and Addresses. Baltimore, 1920. First edition. 3 vols. 8vo. Orig. binding. Ex-library. Fye H-3-618 1983 $125

WELD, ISAAC   Travels through the States of North America... London: John Stockdale, 1799. First edition. Folding map (outlined in colour), 2 plans, 2 maps, and 11 full-page engraved views. Expertly rebound in full speckled calf, raised bands, red morocco labels, and blind stamped decorations on the boards. Some foxing else a fine copy. McGahern 53-170 1983 $1,100

WELLCOME, HENRY   Spanish Influence on the Progress of Medical Science. London: Wellcome Foundation, 1935. 8vo, cloth; ex-lib. Illus. Argosy 713-566 1983 $30

WELLES, SUMNER   Naboth's Vineyard, the Dominican Republic 1844-1924. NY, 1928. 2 vols., illus., thick 8vo, light spot on vol. 1 front. Argosy 710-617 1983 $100

WELLINGS, JAMES H.   Directory of the City of Detroit. Detroit, 1846. Leather spine, cloth. Ink names, some spine wear, foxed. King 46-201 1983 $125

WELLINGTON, ARTHUR WELLESLEY, DUKE OF   The Dispatches of... During His Various Campaigns in India, Denmark, Portugal, Spain, the Low Countries, and France. John Murray, 1852. In 8 vols., cont. half calf over marbled boards, gilt spines, with red and black labels, a little scratching of the sides and corner of 3 labels rubbed. Fenning 62-387 1983 £165

WELLMAN, JOHN   Opera Brevis. (N.p.): The Heron Press, 1977. Quarter morocco and marbled boards. First edition. One of only 20 numbered copies, printed by Daniel Keleher in Monotype Fournier and handset Bembo, on Czechoslovakian handmade paper, and signed by the author. Bound by E.G. Parrot, and illus. with block prints by Bruce Chandler, including a foldout frontis., initialed in margin. 250 copies were also issued in wraps., unsigned. Very fine in orig. glassine. Reese 20-513 1983 $125

WELLMAN, PAUL I.   Broncho Apache. N.Y., MacMillian, 1936. First edition. Dust jacket. Cloth slipcase. With a full page inscription: "To...who collects books and also friends...with the sincere friendship of Paul I. Wellman April 7, 1948." Houle 22-1196 1983 $175

WELLMAN, PAUL I.   The Chain. Garden City, Doubleday, 1949. First edition. Inscribed and signed by the author. Dust jacket. Fine. Houle 22-1197 1983 $85

WELLMAN, PAUL I.   Death in the Desert. N.Y., Macmillan, 1935. First edition. Illus. Dust jacket. Inscribed and signed by the author. Fine copy. Houle 21-1180 1983 $150

WELLMAN, PAUL I.   Jubal Troop. N.Y., Carrick & Evans, (1939). First edition. Illus. by F. Miller. Dust jacket. Inscribed and signed by the author. Very good. Houle 21-1181 1983 $95

WELLMAN, PAUL I.   Trampling Herd. N.Y., Carrick & Evans, (1939). First edition. Illus. by F. Miller. Inscribed and signed by the author. Very good. Houle 21-1182 1983 $95

WELLMANN, PAUL I.   The Trampling Herd. New York: Carrick & Evans, 1939. First edition. Illus. by Miller. Slightly worn dust jacket. Fine. Jenkins 152-510 1983 $85

WELLNHOFER, P.   Encyclopedia of Paleoherpetology. Stuttgart, 1981. Part 2, Gymnophiona, Caudata. 31 figures, royal 8vo, wrappers. Wheldon 160-1407 1983 £39

WELLS, CARLOLYN   Gilt Edges Guilt. Phila., (1938). First edition. D.w. Argosy 714-897 1983 $30

WELLS, CAROLYN   The Technique of the Mystery Story. Sp., (1913). Front hinge cracked, edges slightly worn, good or better. Quill & Brush 54-1490 1983 $50

WELLS, CHARLES KNOX POLK   Life and Adventures of Polk Wells. (Halls, Montana): G.A. Warnica, (1907). With 20 illus. Orig. red cloth; spine extremities fraying. Karmiole 74-103 1983 $65

WELLS, CHARLES KNOX POLK   Life and Adventures of Polk Wells, the Notorious Outlaw. (Halls, Mo., 1907). Corrected 1st ed. Ports., illus. Clark 741-402 1983 $52

WELLS, CHARLES W.   Frontier Life. Cincinnati, (1902). 12mo. Fine. Clark 741-256 1983 $67.50

WELLS, DAVID   Our Burden and Our Strength. Troy, 1864. First edition, orig. pr. wraps. Argosy 716-146 1983 $20

WELLS, EVELYN   Fremont Older. N.Y., Appleton-Century, 1936. First edition. Illus. Dust jacket. Very good-fine. Houle 21-1183 1983 $20

WELLS, GABRIEL   The Carter-Pollard Disclosures. Garden City: Doubleday, Doran & Co., 1934. First edition. 8vo. Paper wrappers. Postscript tipped in to the end. Oak Knoll 49-403 1983 $30

WELLS, GABRIEL   What Is Truth? London: Heinemann, 1924. 1st ed. Orig. boards, dj moderately rubbed. Presentation inscription at front from author to Arthur Swann, signed and dated in year of publication. Fine copy. Jenkins 155-1266 1983 $35

WELLS, GEORGE   The Tale of Charles Dickens. Rochester: The Journal Co., (1906). First edition. Frontispiece. Orig. white printed boards. Spine and covers slightly soiled. Spine cracking in several parts. Good. MacManus 278-1565 1983 $35

WELLS, GERARD   Naval Customs and Traditions. London, 1930. First edition. 8vo. Orig. cloth. Frontis. and 11 plates. Edges slightly foxed. Fine. Edwards 1042-183 1983 £18

WELLS, GERARD   Naval Customs and Traditions. Philip Allan, 1930. First edition, with 12 plates, 8vo, orig. cloth, very good copy. Fenning 60-436 1983 £14.50

WELLS, HENRY P.   Fly-Rods and Fly-Tackle. New York, 1901. Revised and enlarged ed. Illus. 8vo, very nice. Morrill 288-519 1983 $30

WELLS, HERBERT GEORGE   The Adventures of Tommy. London: Geo. G. Harrap & Co. Ltd., (1929). First edition. 4to. Facsimile of the orig. manuscript. Illus. in color by author. Orig. cloth-backed pictorial boards. Gilt dust jacket (chipped). Fine. MacManus 280-5449 1983 $125

WELLS, HERBERT GEORGE   The Adventures of Tommy. London, (1929). First edition. Color illus. by the author. Thin 4to, boards. Argosy 714-783 1983 $50

WELLS, HERBERT GEORGE   After Democracy. London: Watts & Co.,
(1932). First edition. Orig. cloth. Presentation copy to J.F.
Horrabin, inscribed: "Japhet. The real stuff. From H.G." Tipped in
is a letter from Horrabin to Wells, dated Oct. 20, 1932. Spine rather
sunned. Good. MacManus 280-5450 1983 $225

WELLS, HERBERT GEORGE   All Aboard For Ararat. NY, 1941. Flys
slightly darkened, very good in chipped, good dustwrapper worn along
edges, owner's name and address. Quill & Brush 54-1495 1983 $60

WELLS, HERBERT GEORGE   The Anatomy of Frustration. London:
The Cresset Press, 1936. First edition. Orig. cloth. Dust jacket
(spine and covers slightly worn and soiled). Edges a bit dusty.
Near-fine. MacManus 280-5451 1983 $65

WELLS, HERBERT GEORGE   Anticipations of the Reaction of
Mechanical and Scientific Progress upon Human Life and Thought.
NY: Harper & Brothers, 1902. First American edition. Ads. Boards;
paper spine label. Fine copy in a linen dust jacket, spotted on
spine and front cover; paper spine label. Karmiole 73-114 1983 $45

WELLS, HERBERT GEORGE   The Autocracy of Mr. Parham. London:
William Heinemann, (1930). First edition. Illus. Orig. red cloth.
Presentation copy to the illustrator. Spine and covers slightly worn
and faded. Good. MacManus 280-5452 1983 $125

WELLS, HERBERT GEORGE   Babes in the Darkling Wood. London:
Secker and Warburg, 1940. First edition. Orig. cloth. Presentation
copy to J.F. Horrabin. Edges slightly worn. Spine very slightly faded.
Good. MacManus 280-5454 1983 $150

WELLS, HERBERT GEORGE   The Brothers. London: Chatto & Windus,
1938. First edition. 8vo. Orig. cloth. Dust jacket, chipped.
Fine copy. Jaffe 1-396 1983 $35

WELLS, HERBERT GEORGE   The Brothers. London: Chatto & Windus,
1938. First edition. Orig. cloth. Dust jacket (slightly torn).
Very good. MacManus 280-5455 1983 $25

WELLS, HERBERT GEORGE   Brynhild. London: Methuen & Co. Ltd.,
1937. First edition. Orig. cloth. Dust jacket. Inscribed by author
on title-page "For Henry Hollowell, good wishes, H. G. Wells, Oct. 27,
37." Very fine. MacManus 280-5456 1983 $200

WELLS, HERBERT GEORGE   Brynhild. London: Methuen And Company,
Limited, 1937. First edition. 8vo. Orig. cloth. Dust jacket. Fine
copy. Jaffe 1-395 1983 $45

WELLS, HERRERT GEORGE   Certain Personal Matters. Lawrence &
Bullen, 1898. First edition, half title, 32pp ads. Orig. blue cloth
dulled. Jarndyce 31-965 1983 £12.50

WELLS, HERBERT GEORGE   Christina Alberta's Father. London:
Capte, (1925). 1st ed. Orig. red cloth, gilt. Spine cloth just
beginning to show signs of fading, but a fine copy inscribed by
Wells in ink on front end paper: "Mrs. R.D. Blumenfeld as ever from
H.G. Wells." Jenkins 155-1267 1983 $165

WELLS, HERBERT GEORGE   Christina Alberta's Father. London:
Jonathan Cape, 1925. First edition. Orig. cloth. Presentation copy
to J.F. Horrabin. Spine slightly sunned. Back cover slightly dampstained. Endpapers very lightly browned. MacManus 280-5457 1983
$125

WELLS, HERBERT GEORGE   Christina Albert's Father. London:
Cape, (1925). First edition. Orig. cloth. Dust jacket. Very fine.
MacManus 280-5458 1983 $85

WELLS, HERBERT GEORGE   Christina Alberta's Father. London,
1925. Presentation copy from the author, inscribed. Covers
slightly marked. Spine very slightly faded. Very good. Jolliffe
26-587 1983 £35

WELLS, HERBERT GEORGE   Common Sense of World Peace. London,
Hogarth Press, 1929. First edition. Dust jacket (few sm chips),
very good. Houle 21-913 1983 $80

WELLS, HERBERT GEORGE   The Country of the Blind. London, (1911).
First edition of this collection. Intro. by author. Spine a little
darkened. Bookplate. Very nice. Rota 230-625 1983 £17.50

WELLS, HERBERT GEORGE   The Croquet Player. London: Chatto &
Windus, 1936. First edition. Orig. cloth. Dust jacket (a bit faded
and chipped). Presentation copy inscribed to J.F. Horrabin. Base of
spine very slightly worn. Near-fine. MacManus 280-5459 1983 $150

WELLS, HERBERT GEORGE   The Croquet Player. London: Chatto
& Windus, 1936. First edition. 8vo. Orig. cloth. Dust jacket,
chipped at base of spine, otherwise a fine copy. Jaffe 1-394 1983
$35

WELLS, HERBERT GEORGE   The Croquet Player. N.Y., Viking, 1937.
First edition. Blue and red dust jacket designed by Martinot with
an unusual design. Fine copy. Houle 22-944 1983 $75

WELLS, HERBERT GEORGE   Crux Ansata. Penguin Books, (1943).
8vo, orig. orange and white stiff wrappers. First edition.
Bickersteth 75-190 1983 £12

WELLS, HERBERT GEORGE   The Dream. London: Jonathan Cape,
(1924). First edition. Orig. red cloth. Presentation copy to J.F.
Horrabin. Spine and covers faded, worn and spotted. Good. MacManus
280-5461 1983 $100

WELLS, HERBERT GEORGE   The Dream. NY, 1924. Endpapers offset,
edges bumped, very good or better in slightly chipped dustwrapper.
Quill & Brush 54-1492 1983 $35

WELLS, HERBERT GEORGE   First & Last Things. London: Constable
& Co., 1908. First edition. Orig. cloth. Half-morocco slipcase.
Very good. MacManus 280-5462 1983 $40

WELLS, HERBERT GEORGE   First and Last Things. London, 1908.
First edition. Argosy 714-784 1983 $25

WELLS, HERBERT GEORGE   The First Men in the Moon. London:
Newnes, 1901. Frontis., plates. 1st ed., later state of binding.
Orig. blue cloth, stamped in black. Near fine copy. Jenkins 155-
1270 1983 $125

WELLS, HERBERT GEORGE   The First Men in the Moon. London, 1901.
First edition, late binding. Lettered in black. Extremities rubbed.
Blind-stamp on flyleaf. Good. Rota 230-624 1983 £35

WELLS, HERBERT GEORGE   Floor Games. London, 1911. First
edition. 4to. Orig. dark blue cloth with mounted coloured illus.
on front cover. Frontis. and marginal drawings by J.R. Sinclair.
A mint copy. Traylen 94-861 1983 £48

WELLS, HERBERT GEORGE   The Food of the Gods. London:
MacMillan, 1904. 1st ed., 1st binding, earliest catalogue. Orig.
green cloth, gilt, t.e.g. From the library of R.D. Blumenfeld with
his pencil signature on front end paper, and publisher's embossed
presentation stamp on title. Two faint stains to cloth, and very
light rubbing at some edges, but very good association copy.
Jenkins 155-1271 1983 $125

WELLS, HERBERT GEORGE   The Food of the Gods and How it Came to
Earth. Macmillan and Co. ltd., 1904. 8vo, ad. leaf, 16 page pub.'s
catalogue, orig. cloth, blocked in blind. First edition. Bickersteth
75-200 1983 £34

WELLS, HERBERT GEORGE   God the Invisible King. London, 1917.
First English edition. Presentation copy from the author, inscribed.
Spine faded. Corners bumped. Upper cover slightly soiled. Very good.
Jolliffe 26-583 1983 £45

WELLS, HERBERT GEORGE   Guide to the New World. London: Victor
Gollancz, 1941. First edition. Orig. cloth. Presentation copy to
J.F. Horrabin, with a typewritten inscription tipped in on stationery
bearing Wells' address. Horrabin signed his name and the date 1941 at
the bottom of the tipped-in sheet. Spine rather faded. Some pencilling in margins. MacManus 280-5463 1983 $75

WELLS, HERBERT GEORGE   The History of Mr. Polly. London:
Thomas Nelson & Sons, (1910). First edition. Frontis. Orig. cloth.
Very good. MacManus 280-5464 1983 $35

WELLS, HERBERT GEORGE   The History of Mr. Polly. London, 1910.
First edition. Enamel on spine slightly chipped. Very nice. Rota
231-622 1983 £12.50

WELLS, HERBERT GEORGE   In the Days of the Comet. New York:
Century, 1906. 1st American ed. Orig. blue pictorial cloth. Fine.
Jenkins 155-1273 1983 $100

WELLS, HERBERT GEORGE   The Invisible Man. C. Arthur Pearson
ltd., 1897. 8vo, ad. leaf, orig. pictorial cloth. Covers slightly
soiled at the edges, but a good copy without ownership inscriptions.
First edition. Bickersteth 75-196 1983 £45

WELLS, HERBERT GEORGE   The Island of Dr. Moreau. London:
Heinemann, 1896. Frontis. 1st ed., early issue previously unrecorded. Orig. mustard cloth, stamped in black and rust. Light
spots on end papers, else a fine and rare copy. Jenkins 155-1274
1983 $250

WELLS, HERBERT GEORGE   The Island of Doctor Moreau. William
Heinemann, 1896. 8vo, preliminary blank leaf, frontis., final ad.
leaf, 32 pub.'s catalogue, orig. pictorial cloth. Ownership
inscription on front fly, otherwise a fine copy. First edition.
Bickersteth 75-194 1983 £25

WELLS, HERBERT GEORGE   Joan and Peter. L, (1918). Some slight
interior foxing, cover stained and a little limp, good plus. Quill &
Brush 54-1491 1983 $35

WELLS, HERBERT GEORGE   Kipps the Story of a Simple Soul.
Macmillan and Co. ltd., 1905. 8vo, blank leaf, pub.'s 8-page
catalogue dated 10.10.'05., orig. cloth blocked in blind. First
edition. Bickersteth 75-202 1983 £28

WELLS, HERBERT GEORGE   Love and Mr. Lewisham. Harper & Brother,
1900. 8vo, half title, 2 ad. leaves, orig. cloth. Paler rectangular
patch on the upper cover where a label has been removed. Small rubber
name stamp on inside back and front covers and in the margins of 11
pages of text, and larger oval stamp of a library at beginning or end
of chapters. First edition. Bickersteth 75-197 1983 £25

WELLS, HERBERT GEORGE   Man Who Could Work Miracles. London:
Cresset Press, 1936. First edition. Orig. cloth. Presentation copy
to J.F. Horrabin. Edges slightly worn and faded. Good. MacManus
280-5468 1983 $125

WELLS, HERBERT GEORGE   Mankind in the Making. Chapman and
Hall, 1903. 8vo, orig. cloth. Light spotting on the preliminary
pages. First edition. Bickersteth 75-198 1983 £30

WELLS, HERBERT GEORGE   Marriage. London, 1912. First edition.
8vo, cloth. Argosy 714-785 1983 $40

WELLS, HERBERT GEORGE   Marriage. Macmillan and Co. ltd., 1913.
8vo, 4 leaves of advertisements, orig. cloth. Inscribed by the author
on the title page. A fine copy inscribed by Wells. Bickersteth 75-
205 1983 £40

WELLS, HERBERT GEORGE   Meanwhile. Lon., 1927. Edges slightly
rubbed, rear board slightly creased, fore edge lightly stained, else
very good in soiled and chipped, mended dustwrapper. Quill & Brush
54-1449 1983 $40

WELLS, HERBERT GEORGE   Meanwhile. London: Ernest Benn, 1927.
First edition. Orig. cloth. Dust jacket (chipped and soiled). Mac-
Manus 280-5470 1983 $20

WELLS, HERBERT GEORGE   Men Like Gods. London: Cassell,
(1923). 1st ed. Orig. green cloth, gilt. Near fine copy inscribed
by Wells in ink on half-title: "Mrs. R.D.B. with good wishes for
R.D.B.'s recovery, H.G." Jenkins 155-1275 1983 $175

WELLS, HERBERT GEORGE   Men Like Gods. London, 1923. First
English edition. Presentation copy from the author, inscribed.
Spine faded. Corners bumped. Very good. Jolliffe 26-585 1983
£36

WELLS, HERBERT GEORGE   Men Like Gods. London, (1923). First
edition. 8vo, green cloth; backstrip faded. Argosy 714-786 1983
$20

WELLS, HERBERT GEORGE   The Misery of Boots. London: Fabian
Society, 1907. 1st ed. Orig. wrappers, uncut, label. Reprinted.
Very good. Jenkins 155-1287 1983 $20

WELLS, HERBERT GEORGE   Mr. Belloc Objects to "The Outline of
History." London: Watts, 1926. First edition. 12mo. Orig. boards.
Dust jacket. Half morocco slipcase. Mint. MacManus 280-5471 1983
$100

WELLS, HERBERT GEORGE   Mr. Belloc Objects to "The Outline of
History". Watts & Co., 1926. 8vo, 2 plates, orig. cloth in dust
wrapper. First edition. Bickersteth 75-206 1983 £15

WELLS, HERBERT GEORGE   Mr. Blettsworthy on Rampole Island.
London: Ernest Benn, 1928. First edition. Orig. cloth. Presentation
copy to J.F. Horrabin, inscribed. Spine a bit scratched. Covers very
slightly dampstained. Good. MacManus 280-5472 1983 $125

WELLS, HERBERT GEORGE   Mr. Blettsworthy on Rampole Island.
London: Ernest Benn, 1928. Cloth. First edition. Very slight traces
of foxing, otherwise a very fine copy in pictorial dust jacket. Reese
20-1111 1983 $50

WELLS, HERBERT GEORGE   Mr. Blettsworthy on Rampole Island.
Lon., 1928. Cover and page edges lightly stained, else very good in
slightly frayed and soiled, very good dustwrapper. Quill & Brush 54-
1450 1983 $40

WELLS, HERBERT GEORGE   Mr. Britling. London: Collins, n.d.
A reprint of "Mr. Britling Sees Its Through" (1916). Illus. by N.
Syers. With an ANS to J.F. Horrabin tipped in. Edges a bit worn.
Good. MacManus 280-5473 1983 $65

WELLS, HERBERT GEORGE   The New America: The New World. Lon.,
(1935). Very good in slightly soiled, very good dustwrapper. Quill
& Brush 54-1493 1983 $35

WELLS, HERBERT GEORGE   The New America. London, (1935).
First edition. 12mo, d.w. Stains on rear of dust wrapper. Argosy
714-787 1983 $30

WELLS, HERBERT GEORGE   New Worlds For Old. N.T.: The Macmillan
Co., 1908. First American edition. Orig. cloth. Newspaper photo.
of Wells pasted to front endsheet. Very good. MacManus 280-5475
1983 $75

WELLS, HERBERT GEORGE   The Open Conspiracy. London: Victor
Gollancz, 1928. First edition. Orig. cloth. Presentation copy
inscribed to J.F. Horrabin. Edges slightly worn. Little foxing.
One hinge cracked. MacManus 280-5477 1983 $150

WELLS, HERBERT GEORGE   The Outline of History. London: Cassell
& Co., 1920. "Revised and corrected edition." Illus. by J.F. Horrabin.
Orig. cloth. Presentation copy inscribed to J.F. Horrabin, dated Sept.
2, 1920. Laid in are a photograph of Wells and a postcard from an H.
H. Winslow to Horrabin. Clippins pasted to endpapers. Rebacked, with
portions of orig. spine retained. Edges a bit worn. MacManus 280-
5479 1983 $300

WELLS, HERBERT GEORGE   The Outline of History. London: George
Newnes Ltd., n.d. (1920). First edition. Illus. in 24 parts. 4to.
Orig. pictorial wrappers. A few backstrips slightly rubbed. Very good.
MacManus 280-5480 1983 $100

WELLS, HERBERT GEORGE   The Outlook for Homo Sapiens. London:
Secker & Warburg, (1942). First edition. Orig. cloth. Presentation
copy inscribed to J.F. Horrabin. Tipped in is a letter, 1 page, from
Wells to Horrabin, dated March 7, 1942. Edges and spine faded. Covers
a bit soiled. Good. MacManus 280-5481 1983 $250

WELLS, HERBERT GEORGE   The Passionate Friends, A Novel.
London: Macmillan, 1914. 1st ed., 4th issue. Orig. green cloth,
gilt. This issue consists of the sheets of the 1st ed. with a cancel
title dated 1914 and a slug on the verso falsely claiming this to be
a reprint. Fine copy with presentation inscription from Wells on
title: "From a passionate friend of...H.G. Wells." Jenkins 155-
1277 1983 $150

WELLS, HERBERT GEORGE   The Passionate Friends. London: Macmillan & Co., 1913. First edition. Orig. cloth. Bookplate. MacManus 280-5483 1983 $75

WELLS, HERBERT GEORGE   Russia in the Shadows. London: Hodder & Stoughton, (1920). First edition. Illus. Orig. cloth. Former owner's inscription on front flyleaf. Spine faded. Good. MacManus 280-5484 1983 $20

WELLS, HERBERT GEORGE   Russia in the Shadows. N.Y.: George H. Doran Co., (1921). First American edition. Illus. Orig. cloth. Presentation copy inscribed to J.F. Horrabin. Endpapers browned. Covers a bit soiled. MacManus 280-5485 1983 $125

WELLS, HERBERT GEORGE   The Salvaging of Civilization. London: Cassell, 1921. 1st ed. Orig. green cloth. Spine lettering slightly dulled. Presentation copy inscribed in ink by Wells: "Daisy with love of H.G." Fine copy. Jenkins 155-1278 1983 $150

WELLS, HERBERT GEORGE   The Salvaging of Civilization. London, 1921. First English edition. Presentation copy from the author, inscribed. Top edge faded. Very good. Jolliffe 26-584 1983 £30

WELLS, HERBERT GEORGE   The Science of Life. Garden City, N.Y.: Doubleday, Doran & Co., Inc., 1931. First edition. 4 vols. Large 8vo. Colored frontis. Illus. Orig. cloth with paper labels on spines. Limited to 750 signed by authors. Fine. MacManus 280-5486 1983 $200

WELLS, HERBERT GEORGE   The Sea Lady. New York: Appleton, 1902. Frontis., plates. 1st American ed. Orig. pictorial pale green cloth, gilt. Illus. by Lewis Baumer. Cover signed RR. Very good copy with little fading, and only traces of rubbing. Jenkins 155-1280 1983 $80

WELLS, HERBERT GEORGE   The Sea Lady. London: Methuen, 1902. 1st ed. Orig. red cloth, gilt. Very good copy. Jenkins 155-1281 1983 $50

WELLS, HERBERT GEORGE   Select Conversations with an Uncle. New York, 1895. 8vo. Cloth. 1st American ed. Some light spotting on spine, else a fine copy. In Our Time 156-867 1983 $300

WELLS, HERBERT GEORGE   A Short History of the World. London: Cassell & Co., 1922. First edition. Illus. Orig. cloth. Presentation copy inscribed to J.F. Horrabin. Spine rather badly worn at head and foot. Back cover dampstained. MacManus 280-5488 1983 $150

WELLS, HERBERT GEORGE   The Soul of the Bishop. NY, 1917. Slight wear to edges, good in dustwrapper with an inch missing from bottom of spine and front edge. Quill & Brush 54-1494 1983 $30

WELLS, HERBERT GEORGE   The Stolen Bacillus and Other Incidents. 1895. 8vo, pub.'s 32 page catalogue dated September 1895 at the end, title with ornamental design in gilt on both spine and upper cover. Bookplate inside the front cover, otherwise fine. Signed by H.G. Wells in ink in the middle of the blank leaf preceding the half title. First edition. Bickersteth 75-192 1983 £70

WELLS, HERBERT GEORGE   Tales of Space and Time. New York: Doubleday, 1899. 1st American ed., and possibly the true 1st ed. Orig. maroon cloth, gilt. Spine sunned, but a clean lightly used copy. Jenkins 155-1286 1983 $125

WELLS, HERBERT GEORGE   Tales of Space and Time. NY: 1899. First American(?) edition. Inside front hinge started and covers spotted. Bromer 25-126 1983 $75

WELLS, HERBERT GEORGE   The Time Machine. William Heinemann, 1895. 8vo, 32 page pub.'s catalogue, orig. pictorial cloth, a little soiled, contents fine. First edition. Bickersteth 75-191 1983 £65

WELLS, HERBERT GEORGE   The Time Machine. London, 1895. Second issue, with the edges cut. Spine a little darkened. Name on flyleaf. Nice. Rota 230-620 1983 $75

WELLS, HERBERT GEORGE   Tono-Bungay. London: Macmillan & Co., 1909. First edition, first issue. Orig. decorated cloth. Presentation copy inscribed to Clarence Rook. Spine and covers faded and slightly worn. A few small tears to the spine ends. Good. MacManus 280-5491 1983 $135

WELLS, HERBERT GEORGE   Tono-Bungay. London: Macmillan, 1909. Heavily gilt cloth. First edition, earliest state of the ads, dated '1.09.' Neat ink name, otherwise a fine copy. Reese 20-1110 1983 $75

WELLS, HERBERT GEORGE   Tono-Bungay. London: Macmillan & Co., 1909. First edition, second issue. Orig. cloth. Rear hinge cracking. Half morocco slipcase. MacManus 280-5492 1983 $50

WELLS, HERBERT GEORGE   Twelve Stories and a Dream. Macmillan and Co. ltd., 1903. 8vo, ads., 16 page pub.'s catalogue dated 20.9.03, orig. green cloth, blocked in blind. First edition. Bickersteth 75-199 1983 £38

WELLS, HERBERT GEORGE   The Undying Fire, A Contemporary Novel. London: Cassell, (1919). 1st ed., 2nd issue. Orig. green cloth, gilt. In this copy pp. 249-50 is a cancelled leaf with 249.11 reading "crescent." Fine copy with ink presentation inscription from Wells on half-title: "Mrs. R.D.B. Bless her! Love H.G." Jenkins 155-1288 1983 $165

WELLS, HERBERT GEORGE   The Undying Fire. London: Cassell & Co., Ltd., (1919). First edition. Orig. cloth. Presentation copy. Front hinge weak. Front outer hinge & bottom of spine a bit worn. MacManus 280-5493 1983 $75

WELLS, HERBERT GEORGE   The Undying Fire. London, n.d. First English edition. Presentation copy from the author, inscribed. Front free endpaper creased. Corners slightly bumped. Very good. Jolliffe 26-586 1983 £36

WELLS, HERBERT GEORGE   The Undying Fire, A Contemporary Novel. London: Cassell, (1919). 1st issue with pp. 249-50 uncancelled and reading "group" at 249.11. Orig. green cloth, gilt. Fine. Jenkins 155-1289 1983 $20

WELLS, HERBERT GEORGE   The War in the Air. New York: MacMillan, 1908. Frontis., plates. 1st American ed. Orig. pic. cloth. Ink presentation inscription by Wells on half-title: "E.V.L. from H.G.W." Light wear to spine cloth. Jenkins 155-1290 1983 $350

WELLS, HERBERT GEORGE   The War in the Air. London, 1908. First edition. Illus. 8vo, blue cloth; backstrip faded. Variant binding, with color reproduction of frontis. front cover. Argosy 714-789 1983 $150

WELLS, HERBERT GEORGE   The War in the Air and Particularly How Mr. Bert Smallways Fared While it Lasted. London: Bell, 1908. Cloth, pictorial onlay. Frontis. and plates. First edition, second state of the binding, without gilding on covers. Bookplate, edges a bit foxed, but a very good to fine copy with the hinges intact. Reese 20-1109 1983 $85

WELLS, HERBERT GEORGE   The War in the Air and Particularly How Mr. Bert Smallways fared while it lasted. 1908. 8vo, ad. leaf, 16 plates, orig. blue cloth, lettered gilt, the title repeated in gilt in a frame on the upper cover. First edition. Bickersteth 75-203 1983 £45

WELLS, HERBERT GEORGE   The War in the Air. London, 1908. First English edition. Illus. by A.C. Michael. Some internal foxing. Covers slightly rubbed. Very good. Jolliffe 26-582 1983 £45

WELLS, HERBERT GEORGE   The War in the Air. George Bell, 1908. First edition, second issue, with 16 plates, 8vo, orig. blue cloth, with design and lettering in blind on upper cover with frontis. printed in colours pasted on it, lettered in gilt on spine, the fore and lower edges uncut, binding little dull but sound. Fenning 62-388 1983 £25

WELLS, HERBERT GEORGE   The War of the Worlds. London, 1898. First edition. 8vo, gray cloth; front inner hinge starting. Argosy 714-788 1983 $200

WELLS, HERBERT GEORGE   The War of the Worlds. London, 1898.
First edition, late issue. Lacking ads. Spine darkened and a little
worn at hinges. Covers marked. Bookplate. Very good. Rota 230-622
1983 £40

WELLS, HERBERT GEORGE   When the Sleeper Wakes. London, 1899.
First edition. Spine faded. Bookplate. Blind-stamp on flyleaf.
Nice. Rota 230-623 1983 £25

WELLS, HERBERT GEORGE   The Wife of Sir Isaac Harman. London:
Macmillan & Co., 1914. First edition. Orig. decorated cloth. Presentation copy inscribed to A.T.S. Pages 63-84 slightly wrinkled in the
upper right-hand corner. Spine margins a trifle rubbed. Very good.
MacManus 280-5494 1983 $100

WELLS, HERBERT GEORGE   The Work, Wealth, and Happiness of Mankind. London: William Heinemann, (1932). First English edition.
Illus. Orig. cloth. J.F. Horrabin's copy, with a note in his hand.
Tipped in is a one-page ALS from Wells to "my dear Horry," dated Jan.
16, 1931. Edges rather worn. Spine faded and repaired. MacManus
280-5496 1983 $125

WELLS, HERBERT GEORGE   Works. N.Y., Scribner, 1924-1927.
Atlantic edition. Thick 8vo, frontis. portraits and facs. Tan
cloth over blue boards, paper labels, uncut and mostly unopened
(some foxing to labels). 28 vols., complete. One of 1050 numbered
copies, signed by the author. Houle 22-945 1983 $895

WELLS, HERBERT GEORGE   The World of William Clissold. London:
Ernest Benn, 1926. Vol. I of the first edition. Orig. cloth. Presentation copy inscribed to J.F. Horrabin. Spine a bit scratched. Some
foxing. MacManus 280-5497 1983 $125

WELLS, HERBERT GEORGE   The World of William Clissold. N.Y.:
George Doran Co., (1926). First American edition. 2 vols. Orig.
cloth. In a half morocco slipcase. Very good. MacManus 280-5498
1983 $50

WELLS, HERBERT GEORGE   The World of William Clissold. London:
Ernest Benn Ltd., 1926. First edition. 3 vols. Orig. cloth. Dust
jacket. Small bookplate. Very good. MacManus 280-5499 1983 $35

WELLS, HERBERT GEORGE   You Can't Be Too Careful. London:
Secker & Warburg, 1941. First edition. Orig. cloth. Presentation
copy inscribed to J.F. Horrabin. With a note from Wells to Horrabin
tipped in. Corners slightly bumped. Very good. MacManus 280-5500
1983 $225

WELLS, ROLLA   Episodes in My Life. St. Louis, 1933.
Illus. Orig. boards with leather spine boxed. First edition.
Inscribed presentation copy signed by the author. Ginsberg 47-967
1983 $100

WELLS, W. G. B.   Cooly Tamil. Colombo, 1927. 8vo.
Orig. cloth. Good. Edwards 1044-747 1983 £16

WELLS, WILLIAM V.   A Visit to the Quicksilver Mines of
New Almaden Belonging to the Quicksilver Mining Company. (N.Y., 1863).
Illus. Orig. printed wraps. First edition. Ginsberg 47-201 1983
$100

WELSH, HERBERT   Report of a Visit to the Navajo, Pueblo,
and Hualapais Indians of New Mexico and Arizona. Phila., 1885.
Orig. printed wraps. First edition. Ginsberg 47-969 1983 $125

WELSH, WILLIAM   Report and Supplementary Report of
a Visit to Spotted Tail's Tribe of Brule Sioux Indians. Phila., 1870.
Orig. printed wraps. First edition. Ginsberg 47-970 1983 $75

WELSH, WILLIAM   Report of a Visit to the Sioux and Ponka
Indians. Wash., 1872. Wraps., very good. Reese 19-587 1983 $125

WELSH, WILLIAM   Report of a Visit to the Sioux and
Ponca Indians on the Missouri River, Made by...to the Secretary of the
Interior. Wash., 1872. Orig. printed wraps. First edition. Ginsberg
47-972 1983 $60

WELSH, HERBERT   Reports of a Visit to the Great
Sioux Reserve Made in Behalf of the Indian Rights Association.
(Germantown, Pa., 1883). First edition. Dbd. Ginsberg 47-968
1983 $45

WELSTED, LEONARD   The Dissembled Wanton: or, my son get
money. London: printed for John Watts, 1727. 1st ed. 8vo, epilogue
and advertisements, modern red quarter morocco, spine lettered in
gilt. Pickering & Chatto 19-81 1983 $250

WELTY, EUDORA   Delta Wedding. NY, (1946). Very good
in worn dustwrapper. Quill & Brush 54-1496 1983 $60

WELTY, EUDORA   The Golden Apples. New York: Harcourt,
(1949). Cloth and boards. First edition. A fine copy in dust
jacket. Reese 20-1114 1983 $125

WELTY, EUDORA   The Golden Apples. NY, (1949). Edges
very lightly rubbed, else very good in slightly chipped and rubbed,
very good dustwrapper with darkened spine. Quill & Brush 54-1501
1983 $125

WELTY, EUDORA   The Golden Apples. NY,(1949). Cover
lightly stained, edge of cloth spine slightly rubbed, else very good
in slightly frayed and rubbed, internally reinforced, very good dustwrapper with slightly discolored spine. Quill & Brush 54-1500 1983
$75

WELTY, EUDORA   The Ponder Heart. NY, (1954). Advance
copy from pub., slip laid-in, edges very slightly rubbed, else near
fine in slightly soiled and rubbed, very good dustwrapper with slight
edge wear. Quill & Brush 54-1502 1983 $125

WELTY, EUDORA   Retreat. N.p., Palaemon Press, (1981).
First edition. Tall 8vo, one of 150 numbered copies, signed by the
author. Half cloth over patterned boards, uncut. Houle 22-946
1983 $80

WELTY, EUDORA   Three Papers on Fiction. Smith
College, Mass., 1962. 8vo. Wraps. A fine copy. In Our Time
156-866 1983 $100

WEMYSS, FRANCIS COURTNEY   Theatrical biography: or, the life of
an actor and manager. Glasgow: published by R. Griffin and Co.,
1848. 12mo, original green cloth (rather worn, old library labels on
front cover). 1st English edition. Ximenes 64-569 1983 $45

WENCKEBACH, K. F.   Die Arhythmie als Ausdruck bestimmter
Funktionsstorungen des Herzens. Leipzig: W. Englemann, 1903. First
edition. 8vo. Half-cloth. 7 folding plates, and figures in text.
Gurney 90-121 1983 £55

WENDELL, BARRETT   A Literary History of America. New
York: Scribner, 1900. 1st ed. Orig. cloth, gilt, t.e.g., uncut.
Nice copy. Jenkins 155-1292 1983 $20

WENDELL, LEHMAN   The Systematic Development of X-Ray
Plates & Films. St. Louis, 1919. First edition. 8vo, 4 plates,
33 illus. Argosy 713-568 1983 $45

WENTWORTH, E. N.   American Sheep Trails. Ames: Univ. of
Iowa Press, 1948. First edition. Illus., plates, portraits, maps.
Large 4to. Orig. tan pictorial cloth. Fine. Jenkins 152-511 1983
$75

WENTWORTH, FRANK L.   The Winsted Wildman and Other Tales.
Iowa City, Mercer Printing Co., 1929. First edition. 8vo. Morrill
290-72 1983 $20

WENTWORTH, JOHN   Early Chicago: A Lecture... Chicago,
1876. First edition. Portrait. Small 8vo, new cloth, all edges
gilt, fine. Morrill 290-197 1983 $27.50

WEPFER, JOHANN JACOB   Disputatio Medica De Chylificatione.
Basel: George Decker, 1644. 4to. Paper backstrip. Kraus 164-252
1983 $100

WEPFER, JOHANN JACOB   Peri Aneurysmatos. Basel: Georg
Decker, 1659. 4to. Paper backstrip. Kraus 164-251 1983 $180

WERFEL, FRANZ   Die Troerinnen des Euripides. Leipzig,
1916. 8vo, cloth. Salloch 385-60 1983 $25

WERICH, J. LORENZO   Pioneer Hunters of the Kankakee.
N.p., 1920. Illus. Orig. cloth. First edition. Ginsberg 46-342
1983 $35

WERNER, E.   A Heavy Reckoning. London: Richard
Bentley & Son, 1890. First edition. 3 vols. Orig. green cloth.
Front inner hinges repaired on volumes II & III. Spines and covers
slightly worn and a trifle spotted. Good. MacManus 280-5507 1983
$150

WERNER, E. T. C.   Chinese Weapons. Shanghai 1932.
Illus, cloth, some wear. King 46-695 1983 $50

WERNER, HERMAN   On the Western Frontier with the U. S.
Cavalry Fifty Years Ago. (N.p., 1934). Orig. printed wraps. Frontis.
Slight soiling to wraps., else fine. Reese 19-588 1983 $85

WERNER, J. R.   A visit to Stanley's Rear-Guard at
Major Barttelot's Camp... Edinburgh: Wm. Blackwood & Sons, 1889.
8vo. 47 adv. Folding map, 18 plates. Orig. green cloth. Rubbed.
Adelson Africa-152 1983 $80

WERTH, LEON   Bonnard. Paris: G. Cres, 1923.
70 plates. Text illus. 4to. Marbled boards, 3/4 morocco. Orig.
wrappers bound in. Ars Libri 32-48 1983 $60

WERTHEIMER, OTTO   Nicolaus Gerhaert. Berlin: Deutscher
Verein fur Kunstwissenschaft, 1929. 70 plates. 31 text illus. Large
4to. Cloth. Occasional foxing. Ars Libri 32-253 1983 $75

WESCOTT, GLENWAY   Apartment in Athens. NY, (1945). Signed,
very good or better in very good dustwrapper with few short tears.
Quill & Brush 54-1503 1983 $35

WESCOTT, GLENWAY   The Babe's Bed. P, 1930. No. 168 of
375 numbered and signed copies, third publication of Harrison of Paris
Press, cover lightly soiled, very good or better. Quill & Brush 54-
1504 1983 $125

WESCOTT, GLENWAY   A Calendar of Saints for Unbelievers.
(Paris): Harrison of Paris, 1932. Gilt cloth. First edition. Illus.
by Pavel Tchelitchew. One of 695 numbered copies, designed by
Monroe Wheeler. Bookplate neatly removed, a modicum of shelf rubbing
at edges; a very good copy, sans slipcase. Reese 20-490 1983 $100

WESCOTT, GLENWAY   Good-Bye Wisconsin. New York, 1928.
8vo. Cloth. Fine copy in dj which reinforced on front flap at top
with scotch tape. In Our Time 156-868 1983 $45

WESCOTT, GLENWAY   Like a Lover. Macon: for Monroe
Wheeler, Villefranche-sur-Mer, 1926. First edition. Presentation
copy, signed "Glenway." Ltd. to 200 copies. Argosy 714-791 1983
$200

WESENBERG-LUND, C.   Biologie der Susswasserinsekten.
Copenhagen 1943. 13 plates and 501 text-figures, royal 8vo, new
cloth. The scarce original issue. Wheldon 160-1185 1983 £50

WESLEY, CHARLES   The Protestant Association...June 1780.
Printed by J. Paramore: And sold at Mr Atlay's, 1781. 12mo, final
blank leaf, uncut, partly unopened, penultimate leaf and final blank
both torn and creased, but no loss of paper or text, modern calf,
lettered gilt on the upper cover and wrongly assigning authorship of
John Wesley. First edition. Bickersteth 77-88 1983 £165

WESLEY, JOHN   A Calm Address to Our American Colonies.
London: R. Hawes, 1775. First edition. Jenkins 152-512 1983 $300

WESLEY, JOHN   The Desideratum: or, Electricity made
Plain and Useful. Printed by R. Hawes, and sold at the Foundery in
Moorfields. Printed by R. Hawes, and sold at the Foundery in Moorfields; and at the Rev. Mr. Wesley's Preaching-Houses, in Town and
Country, 1778. 12mo, orig. wraps. bound in, methodist hymn in
ink in cont. hand on final page and lower wrapper, modern calf,
lettered in gilt on upper cover. Bickersteth 77-90 1983 £80

WESLEY, JOHN   Directions for Renewing our Covenant
with God. Printed by J. Paramore: And sold at the New Chapel, City
Road: and at the Rev. Mr. Wesley's Preaching-Houses in Town and
Country, 1781. 12mo, calf antique, lettered gilt. Bickersteth 77-91
1983 £48

WESLEY, JOHN   An Extract from the Christian-Pattern.
Published by John Wesley, printed in the year 1788. 16mo, cont.
calf, rebacked. Bickersteth 77-92 1983 £48

WESLEY, JOHN   A Sermon on the Death of the Rev. Mr.
George Whitefield. Printed by J. and W. Oliver, 1770. 8vo, 32
plates, modern calf, lettered in gilt on the upper cover. First
edition. Bickersteth 77-89 1983 £110

WESLEY, JOHN   Some Observations on Liberty... London:
Printed by R. Hawes, 1776. Half polished calf. 1st ed. Jenkins 153-
684 1983 $150

WEST, ANTHONY   John Piper. 1979. Med. 4to, double
portrait photographic frontis., 33 colour plates and 238 in black and
white, t.e.g., burgundy morocco, spine gilt, cloth boards slip-case.
Limited edition of 126 copies, containing, loosely tipped in, an
original lithograph by John Piper, signed in full in pencil.
Deighton 3-241 1983 £200

WEST, EARL IRVIN   The Search for an Ancient Order.
(Nashville, 1949 & Indianapolis, 1950). First edition. Illus. 2
vols., 8vo. Morrill 290-590 1983 $20

WEST, GILBERT   A Canto of the Fairy Queen. London:
Printed for G. Hawkins, at Milton's Head. MDCCXXXIX. Folio, partly
uncut, complete with initial ad. leaf, disbound. First edition.
Quaritch NS 7-138 1983 $200

WEST, HERBERT FAULKNER   Cunningham Graham: His Life & Work.
London, 1932. 8vo. Cloth. Presentation inscription by West to
Alexander Laing, dated 1933. Cloth has some spotting and fading,
otherwise a vg-fine copy. In Our Time 156-869 1983 $45

WEST, HERBERT FAULKNER   Don Roberto. Privately Printed. 8vo.
Boards. 1 of 100 copies signed by West. Inscribed to Alexander
Laing. In Our Time 156-871 1983 $35

WEST, HERBERT FAULKNER   The Mind on the Wing. New York, 1947.
First edition. Slightly frayed dust wrapper. Nice. Rota 231-623
1983 £12.50

WEST, HERBERT FAULKNER   Modern Book Collecting for the
Impecunious Amateur. Boston, 1936. 8vo. Cloth, boards. Inscribed
by author to Alexander Laing and dated 1936. Vg-fine copy. In Our
Time 156-870 1983 $45

WEST, JANE   A Gossip's Story. Longman & Rees, 1804.
5th edition, 2 vols. Half ttiles, tree calf, spines a little rubbed,
black labels. Jarndyce 30-587 1983 £24

WEST, JANE   The Refusal. Phila.: for M. Carey, by
A. Small, 1810. First American edition. Argosy 716-166 1983 $50

WEST, JANE   A Tale of the Times. Alexandria:
Printed by Cotton & Stewart, 1801. First American edition. 2 vols.
8vo. Full cont. calf with red morocco labels on spines. Free endpapers lacking at backs of both volumes. Minor wear. Very good.
MacManus 280-5508 1983 $125

WEST, JANE   A Tale of the Times. Longman & Reese,
1803. In three vols. 3rd edition, half titles vols. II & III. Tree
calf, spines rubbed, and large chip from head of spine vol. II, black
labels. Jarndyce 30-586 1983 £24

WEST, JULIUS   G. K. Chesterton. A Critical Study.
N.Y.: Dood, Mead & Co., 1916. First American edition. Frontis. port.
Orig. cloth. Dust jacket. Red half-morocco slipcase. Very fine.
MacManus 277-961 1983 $65

WEST, NATHANAEL   The Day of the Locust. N.Y., (1939).
First edition. 8vo, red cloth; extremes of backstrip faded; d.w.
Owner's name on flyleaf. Argosy 714-792 1983 $200

WEST, NATHANAEL   The Day of the Locust. New York: Random
House, (1939). First edition. Orig. red cloth, paper spine label.
Spine sunned. Lacking dust jacket. Fine. Jenkins 152-513 1983 $125

WEST, NATHANAEL   The Dream Life of Balso Snell. Paris & New York: Contact Editions, (1931). Orig. printed wraps. First edition. One of 500 numbered copies. Wraps. slightly browned at edges, slight fraying, internally fine. Reese 20-1116 1983 $550

WEST, REBECCA   Black Lamb and Grey Falcon. London, 1941. First edition. 2 vols. Cloth one spine of Vol. I just a little bubbled. Very nice. Rota 230-627 1983 £30

WEST, REBECCA   Black Lamb & Grey Falcon. London, 1942. First edition. Maps on endpapers. 32 plates. 2 vols. 8vo. Orig. cloth. Good. Edwards 1044-748 1983 £25

WEST, REBECCA   The Return of the Soldier. NY, 1918. Slightly worn, good plus. Quill & Brush 54-1506 1983 $35

WEST, RICHARD S.   Gideon Welles, Lincoln's Navy Department. Indianapolis, (1943). First edition, Connecticut edition, limited and signed by the author. Very good in slightly frayed and soiled dust wrappers. King 46-83 1983 $25

WEST, SAMUEL   Essays on Liberty and Necessity... New-bedford: Printed by John Spooner, 1795. Later 3/4 calf, chipped. Small tear in title, affecting two letters, otherwise a good, untrimmed copy. Reese 18-206 1983 $150

WEST, WILLIAM   Fifty Years Recollections of an Old Bookseller. (With): Three hundred and Fifty Years Retrospection of an Old Bookseller. Cork: Privately printed by the author, 1836. Second edition. 8vo. Modern half leather over cloth. 11 plates. Some light foxing, else a very good copy. Oak Knoll 48-379 1983 $150

WESTALL, WILLIAM   Roy of Roy's Court. London: Ward & Downey, 1892. First edition. 2 vols. Orig. cloth. Near-fine. MacManus 280-5514 1983 $125

WESTALL, WILLIAM   Sons of Belial. London: Chatto & Windus, 1895. First edition. 2 vols. Orig. embossed cloth. Library labels neatly removed from front covers. Covers slightly rubbed at edges. Very good. MacManus 280-5515 1983 $135

WESTCOTT, EDWARD NOYES   David Harum, A Story of American Life. New York: Appleton, 1898. 1st ed., 1st issue with perfect J at p. 40. Orig. yellow decorated cloth. Nice copy. Jenkins 155-1296 1983 $45

WESTCOTT, EDWARD NOYES   David Harum, A Story of American Life. New York: Appleton, 1898. 1st ed., 2nd issue with broken J at p. 40. Orig. yellow decorated cloth. Fine. Jenkins 155-1297 1983 $25

WESTCOTT, EDWARD NOYES   David Harum: a Story of American Life. NY, 1898. 1st ed. Argosy 710-164 1983 $25

WESTERGEN, A. M.   Echini. Echinoneus and Micropetalon. Cambridge, Mass., 1911. 31 plates (1 coloured), 4to, new cloth. Wheldon 160-1350 1983 £15

WESTERMAN, PERCY F.   A Watchdog of the North Sea. London, 1916. First English edition. Pictorial covers. Fine. Jolliffe 26-589 1983 £35

WESTERMEIER, CLIFFORD P.   Man, Beast, Dust: The Story of Rodeo. N.p.: Privately published, (1947). Plates. Cloth in dust wrapper. Signed by author. Dawson 471-302 1983 $30

WESTERN and Other Americana; Canadiana... New York: Parke-Bernet, 1941. Collection of Currier & Ives and other American lithographs. Cloth, top edge gilt, orig. wrappers bound in. Dawson 470-232 1983 $20

WESTERN TYPE FOUNDRY   Specimen Book of Type and Rule. Chicago: Western Type Foundry, June, 1917. Tall 8vo. Stiff paper covers. Bottom of spine bumped. Oak Knoll 48-371 1983 $25

WESTERNERS Brand Book 1944... Original Papers...March 1944 - March 1945. Chicago, (1946). Pict. cloth. Argosy 710-604 1983 $40

WESTERNERS Brand Book 1945-46, Papers Presented During the Second Years. Chicago, (1947). Pict. cloth. Argosy 710-605 1983 $40

WESTERNERS Brand Book, Los Angeles Corral, 1948. (Los Angeles, 1949). illus., 4to. Limited to 600 copies. Argosy 710-606 1983 $50

WESTGARTH, WILLIAM   Half a Century of Australasian Progress. Sampson Low, 1889. First edition, with 3 folding maps, 8vo, recent calf-backed marbled boards, gilt, with label. Fenning 61-479 1983 £55

WESTHEIM, PAUL   Oskar Kokoschka. Potsdam-Berlin: Gustav Kiepenheuer, 1918. 62 illus. 4to. Boards, 1/4 cloth. Dust jacket. Ars Libri 32-376 1983 $75

WESTHEIM, PAUL   Wilhelm Lehmbruck. Das Werk Lehmbrucks. Potsdam/Berlin: Gustav Kiepenheuer, n.d. 84 plates. 4to. Boards, 1/4 cloth. Slightly worn and shaken. Ars Libri 32-397 1983 $37.50

WESTMACOTT, CHARLES MOLLOY   Fitzalleyne of Berkeley. A romance of the present items. London: published by Sherwood and Co., 1825. 2 vols., 8vo, dark blue half morocco, spines gilt, t.e.g. First ed. Wood-engraved vignettes on titles; half-titles present. Ximenes 64-570 1983 $125

WESTWOOD, JOHN OBADIAH   An Introduction to the Modern Classification of Insects. London: Longman, Orme, Brown, Green, and Longmans, 1839-40. Two vols. 8vo, hand-colored frontis. plate. Numerous text figures. Orig. pub.'s green blind-stamped cloth. Quite shaken, spines faded, heavy wear. Internally very good. Partially unopened. Grunder 7-77 1983 $50

WESTWOOD, JOHN OBADIAH   Observations on the Uraniidae. Trans. Zoo. Soc. 1879. 4 plates (2 coloured), 4to, sewed. Wheldon 160-1186 1983 £15

WETHERELL, ELIZABETH   Queechy. London: James Nisbet & Co., 1852. 2 vols. Orig. blue cloth, slightly soiled. Karmiole 72-98 1983 $75

WETHERELL, ELIZABETH   Queechy. James Nisbet, 1852. First English edition. 2 vols. Orig. half calf, red labels, marbled boards, sl. brown discoloration on t.p. vol. I, otherwise good. Jarndyce 30-588 1983 £18.50

WETHEY, HAROLD E.   El Greco and His School. Princeton: Princeton University Press, 1962. 405 illus. hors texte. 4to. Cloth. Dust jacket. Ars Libri 32-285 1983 $225

WETHEY, HAROLD E.   Gil de Siloe and His School. Cambridge: Harvard University Press, 1936. 82 plates. Large 4to. Cloth. Ars Libri 32-636 1983 $150

WETMORE, ALPHONSO   Gazetter of Missouri. With an Appendix Containing Frontier Sketches, and Illustrations of Indian Character. St. Louis: Pub. by C. Keemle, 1837. Orig. cloth with paper label which is chipped. Some staining to text. Frontis. Large folding map. Overall a nice copy for this book. Jenkins 153-685 1983 $500

WETMORE, ALPHONSO   Gazetteer of the State of Missouri. St. Louis, 1837. Illus., frontis., large folded map. Orig. cloth. First edition. Ginsberg 47-974 1983 $500

WETMORE, HELEN CODY   Last of the Great Scouts. Chicago & Duluth, Duluth Press, (1899). Revised edition. Illus. with 16 plates, 2 by Frederick Remington; 10 by E.W. Deming; 1 by Rosa Bonheur; 3 halftones. Maroon cloth stamped in gilt and blind, t.e.g., uncut. Inscribed and signed by the author. Houle 21-1184 1983 $150

WETMORE, HELEN CODY   Last of the Great Scouts Life Story of Col. W.F. Cody. Duluth, 1899. Plates. Original pictorial embossed cloth. T.e.g. Fine copy. Jenkins 153-127 1983 $75

WEVER, ERNEST G.   Theory of Hearing. NY: John Wiley & Sons, (1949). First printing. Gach 94-765 1983 $25

WEWITZER, RALPH　　A brief dramatic chronology of actors, etc. on the London stage. London: printed for John Miller; sold by Mr. Asperne, and Mr. Chapple, 1817. 12mo, original grey boards, large printed paper side-labels, new edition. Ends of spine worn. Very good copy, in original condition, of a scarce title. Ximenes 64-571　1983　$100

WEYGANDT, WILHELM　　Atlas Und Grundriss Der Psychiatrie. Munich: J. F. Lehmann's Verlag, 1902. Ads. Thick 12mo. Publisher's embossed cloth. 24 color plates, 276 text illus., folding map. Gach 95-533　1983　$75

WEYLLAND, JOHN MATHIAS　　These Fifty Years. (1884). Front. & illus. 2 pp ads. Orig. light blue cloth, v.g. Jarndyce 31-306　1984 £16.50

WEYMAN, STANLEY　　The Abbess of Vlaye. London: Longmans, 1904. First edition. Orig. cloth. Covers a bit marked. Inscribed to Beatrice Hall, dated October 10, 1904. Good. MacManus 280-5518 1983　$75

WEYMAN, STANLEY　　Count Hannibal. London: Smith, Elder & Co., 1901. First edition. Orig. cloth. Edges very slightly worn. Bookseller's blind-stamp on front free endpaper. Very good to near-fine. MacManus 280-5533　1983　$35

WEYMAN, STANLEY　　A Gentleman of France. London: Longmans, Green, & Co., 1893. First edition. 3 vols. Orig. cloth. Bookplates on front endsheets. Prelims lightly foxed. Each volume in a half-morocco slipcase. Fine. MacManus 280-5522　1983　$350

WEYMAN, STANLEY　　A Gentleman of France. London: Longmans, Green & Co., 1893. First edition. 3 vols. Orig. cloth. Library labels faintly removed from two volumes. Spines a little dark. Very good, sound set. MacManus 280-5523　1983　$185

WEYMAN, STANLEY　　The Great House. London: John Murray, 1919. First edition. 8vo. Orig. cloth. Good. MacManus 280-5524 1983　$35

WEYMAN, STANLEY　　The House of the Wolf. London: Longmans, 1890. First edition. Orig. pictorial cloth. Extremities and edges of spine worn. Good, sound copy. MacManus 280-5525　1983　$65

WEYMAN, STANLEY　　In Kings' Byways. London: Smith Elder, 1902. First edition. Orig. cloth. MacManus 280-5526　1983　$40

WEYMAN, STANLEY　　The Long Night. London: Longmans, Green & Co., 1903. First edition. 8vo. Orig. cloth. Covers a bit soiled. MacManus 280-5527　1983　$20

WEYMAN, STANLEY　　My Lady Rotha. London: A.D. Innes, 1894. First edition. 8 illus. by J. Williamson. Orig. cloth. Half morocco slipcase. MacManus 280-5529　1983　$25

WEYMAN, STANLEY　　Ovington's Bank. London: John Murray, 1922. First edition. Frontis. by C.L. Cary. Orig. cloth. Faded. Good. MacManus 280-5531　1983　$20

WEYMAN, STANLEY　　The Red Cockade. N.Y., Longmans, Green, 1898. With 48 illus. Title page on a stub. Fine decorated light brown cloth stamped in gilt, black, and red with sword and buckler. Very good - fine. Houle 22-993　1983　$22.50

WEYMAN, STANLEY　　Shrewsbury. London: Longmans, Green & Co., 1898. First edition. Illus. Orig. decorated cloth. Spine and covers slightly worn and soiled. Good. MacManus 280-5534　1983　$35

WEYMAN, STANLEY　　The Story of Francis Cludde. London: Cassell & Co., 1891. First edition, first issue. Orig. decorated cloth. Hinges weak or cracking. Bookplate. Edges and corners a bit worn. Covers slightly soiled. Good. MacManus 280-5537　1983　$75

WEYMAN, STANLEY　　Under the Red Robe. London: Methuen & Co., 1894. First edition. Illus. by R. C. Woodville. 2 vols. Orig. red cloth. Inner hinges a bit strained, covers slightly soiled. Bookplates. In a rubbed half-morocco slipcase. Very good. MacManus 280-5538　1983　$350

WHARTON, EDITH　　The Decoration of Houses. N.Y., 1897. First edition. Woodcut title & 56 plates. Sq. tall 8vo, marbled boards, paper label, (corners rubbed). Argosy 714-797　1983　$125

WHARTON, EDITH　　Ethan Frome. N.Y., Scribner, 1911. First edition, first issue. Red cloth stamped in gilt, t.e.g., acetate wrapper. Bookplate of Lucy Smith Battson. Very good - fine. Houle 22-948　1983　$175

WHARTON, EDITH　　Ethan Frome. NY, 1911. First issue, t.e.g., bottom corners of pages dampstained, very good. Quill & Brush 54-1513　1983　$125

WHARTON, EDITH　　Fruit of the Tree. N.Y., Appleton, 1907. First edition. Three plates by Alonzo Kimball. Gilt stamped red cloth. Very good. Houle 21-924　1983　$60

WHARTON, EDITH　　The Gods Arrive. N.Y., Appleton, 1932. First edition. Dust jacket. Fine copy. Houle 22-949　1983 $85

WHARTON, EDITH　　The Gods Arrive. NY, 1932. Bright, fine copy in lightly chipped and frayed, very good dustwrapper. Quill & Brush 54-1515　1983　$45

WHARTON, EDITH　　Hudson River Bracketed. N.Y., Appleton, 1929. First edition. Blue cloth. Bookplate. Very good. Houle 21-926　1983　$22.50

WHARTON, EDITH　　A Motor-Flight through France. N.Y., Scribners, 1908. First edition. Green cloth stamped in blind and gilt, t.e.g, acetate wrapper. Illus. with 47 photographic plates. Very good. Houle 22-950　1983　$65

WHARTON, EDITH　　Reef. N.Y., Appleton, 1912. First edition, first printing, gilt stamped red cloth. Very good. Houle 21-928　1983　$55

WHARTON, EDITH　　Sanctuary. NY, 1903. Front hinge starting, edges rubbed, good. Quill & Brush 54-1514　1983　$30

WHARTON, FRANCIS　　A Monograph on Mental Unsoundness. Philadelphia, Kay & Brother, 1855. 1st ed. 8vo. Orig. boards, cloth back. Boards lightly dampstained, dust-soiled and rubbed; some light dampstains in text. Morrill 289-246　1983　$100

WHARTON, GRACE　　The Queens of Society. London, Hogg, (ca. 1870). Illus. by C.A. Doyle and the Dalziel Bros. Full tan calf by Tout, spines decorated in gilt, red leather spine labels, covers ruled in gilt, gilt inner dentelles, a.e.g., marbled endpapers (joints starting) else very good. 2 vols. Houle 22-951　1983　$85

WHARTON, HENRY　　The Enthusiasm of the Church of Rome Demonstrated in Some Observations Upon the Life of Ignatius Loyola. Printed for Ric. Chiswell, 1688. First edition, including half-title, 4to, wrapper. Fenning 61-481　1983　£24.50

WHARTON, JOHN　　The Virginia Wreath. Winchester, Va.: For the author, by J. Foster, 1814. Full calf (rear hinge cracked). Very good. Felcone 20-183　1983　$35

WHARTON, WILLIAM　　Birdy. New York (1979). 8vo. Cloth. Signed "William Wharton" on front flyleaf. A fine copy in dj. In Our Time 156-872　1983　$100

WHEAT, CARL I.　　Books of the California Gold Rush. San Francisco: Colt Press, (1949). 1 of 500 copies printed at the Grabhorn Press. Unpaginated. Cloth and boards, endpapers browned, otherwise fine. Dawson 470-305　1983　$150

WHEAT, CARL I.　　The Pioneer Press of California. Oakland, 1948. Three facsimiles mounted. Royal 8vo, cloth-backed boards. No. 15, edition limited to 450 copies. Clark 741-167　1983 $135

WHEAT, CARL I.　　Trailing the Forty-Niners through Death Valley. S.F., 1939. Illus. with photos and a folding map. Printed wraps. Signed by the author. Very good. Houle 21-1186　1983 $45

WHEATLEY, DENNIS   The Black Baroness. NY, 1932. Interior and cover foxed, else near very good in frayed and chipped dustwrapper. Quill & Brush 54-1516 1983 $30

WHEATLEY, DENNIS   Crime File Number 1. N.Y., Morrow, (1936). First edition. 4to, illus. with halftones, clues, etc. Stiff printed boards, stitched (as issued). Fine. A complete copy with the "clue" package at the end unopened. Houle 22-952 1983 $125

WHEATLEY, PHILLIS   Poems on Various Subjects. London: Printed for A. Bell, 1773. Portrait frontis. 1st ed. Orig. sheep, raised bands. Publisher's trade binding. In full leather folding case. Repair to head of title, else very good. Jenkins 155-1303 1983 $1,750

WHEELER, ALFRED   Celebration of the Seventy-Third Anniversary of the Declaration of Independence on Board the Barque "Hannah Sprague" at Sea, July 4, 1849. N.Y., 1849. Orig. printed wraps. First edition. Ginsberg 47-203 1983 $60

WHEELER, ALFRED   Celebration of the Seventy-Third Anniversary of the Declaration of Independence...New York, 1849. wrps. Scarce. Clark 741-168 1983 $50

WHEELER, ANDREW C.   The Iron Trail. NY, 1876. Sq. 12mo, orig. pict. wraps. This copy without Colorado mentioned in title. Argosy 716-453 1983 $50

WHEELER, ARTHUR O.   The Selkirk Range. Ottawa, 1905. With 95 plates and many other illus., 14 maps, charts, etc. Matching bookcase, 2 vols., roy. 8vo, orig. cloth, gilt. Fenning 61-483 1983 £85

WHEELER, BENJAMIN I.   Alexander the Great. London, 1900. Maps. 8vo, cloth. Salloch 385-263 1983 $28

WHEELER, DANIEL   Memoirs of the Life and Gospel Labours of the Late Daniel Wheeler, a Minister of the Society of Friends. Harvey & Darton, 1842. First edition, with folding map of the Friendly Society and Sandwich Islands. Errata leaf, 8vo, orig. cloth, neat repair to spine, a very good copy. Fenning 62-391 1983 $55

WHEELER, DAVID E.   A Discourse Delivered at the Request of the Order of United Americans. N.Y., 1851. Orig. printed wraps. First edition. Autograph presentation copy from Wheeler. Ginsberg 46-593 1983 $35

WHEELER, HOMER W.   Buffalo Days. Forty Years in the Old West... Indianapolis, 1925. Frontis and plates. Fine copy. Jenkins 153-686 1983 $35

WHEELER, HOMER W.   The Frontier Trail. Los Angeles, 1923. 1st ed. Plates (one by C.M. Russell). Distributor's stamp on title page, otherwise mint. Clark 741-257 1983 $58.50

WHEELER, POST   Russian Wonder Tales. Black, 1912. 1st Eng. edn. 12 illus. in colour by Bilibin. Black col. pictorial cloth, scarce, very nice copy. Hodgkins 27-212 1983 £30

WHEELER, W. M.   The Social Insects. 1928. 79 illus., 8vo, cloth. Wheldon 160-1187 1983 £18

WHEELOCK, JOHN HALL   Dear Men and Women. New York (1966). 8vo. Cloth. Inscribed to Louis Untermeyer. Contains one letter and two postcards from Wheelock to Untermeyer. Fine in dj. In Our Time 156-876 1983 $150

WHEELOCK, JOHN HALL   The Gardner and Other Poems. New York, 1961. 8vo. Cloth. Inscribed by Wheelock to Louis Untermeyer and one card (typed both sides). With envelopes. Fine in dj. In Our Time 156-875 1983 $100

WHEELOCK, JOHN HALL   Poems 1911-1936. New York, 1936. 8vo. Cloth. A presentation by Wheelock to Louis Untermeyer and dated August, 1936. Five lines of verse penned by Wheelock on front flyleaf. One page TLS from Wheelock to Untermeyer dated September 8, 1936. Fine in lightly rubbed dj. In Our Time 156-873 1983 $100

WHEELOCK, JOHN HALL   Poems Old and New. New York (1956). 8vo. Cloth. An early copy, inscribed by Wheelock to Louis Untermeyer and dated June, 1956. Contains 2 postcards and one holograph letter from Wheelock to Untermeyer. Fine in dj. In Our Time 156-874 1983 $150

WHEELWRIGHT, JOHN   Mirrors of Venus. Boston: Bruce Humphries, 1938. First edition. 8vo, cloth; backstrip faded. Argosy 714-800 1983 $20

WHEELRIGHT, JOHN   Forty Days. 1928. 8vo. Stapled wraps. 1st separate ed. Front cover of red wrappers dampstained, otherwise a very good copy. In Our Time 156-878 1983 $85

WHEN Grass Was King. Boulder: 1956. First edition. Illus. One of 1500 copies. Fine in dust jacket. Bradley 66-493 1983 $80

WHEWELL, WILLIAM   On the free motion of points... Cambridge: Deighton, etc., 1832. 8vo. Orig. green cloth, gilt. 4 folding plates. Some foxing. Ximenes 63-542 1983 $50

WHILT, JAMES W.   Rhymes of the Rockies. (Chicago, 1922). 2nd ed. Sq. 16mo. Signed. Argosy 710-40 1983 $25

WHINCOP, THOMAS   Scanderbeg: or, love and liberty. A tragedy. London: printed for W. Reeve, 1747. 8vo, cont. calf, gilt, spine gilt (bit rubbed, later label). 1st edition. With a frontis. and 5 plates. 8 page list of subscribers. Half-title present. Nice copy. Ximenes 64-572 1983 $175

WHIPPING rods, for trifling, scurrhill, scriblers. London: printed for M. Cooper, 1752. 8vo, disbound, 1st edition. A fine copy, with the outer margins uncut. Very rare. Ximenes 64-573 1983 $425

WHIPPLE, EDWIN PERCY   Charles Dickens, the Man and His Work. Boston & N.Y., Houghton Mifflin, 1912. Half titles, front. & engr. titles. Orig. green cloth, t.e.g. First edition. 2 vols. No. 304 of 550 copies. Jarndyce 30-233 1983 £24

WHIPPLE, GUY M.   Manual of Mental and Physical Tests. Baltimore: Warwick & York, 1914, 1915. Two vols. First printing of the greatly enlarged second edition. Photographs of early psychometric apparatus. Gach 94-674 1983 $50

WHIPPLE, HENRY B.   Address of...Bishop of Minnesota. Faribault: Alex. Johnston, 1862. Orig. salmon printed wrappers. Fine. Jenkins 152-256 1983 $125

WHIPPLE, MAURINE   This is the Place: Utah. New York, 1945. First edition. Colored frontis. Map and illus. Presentation copy from author. Jenkins 152-479 1983 $30

WHISTLER, LAURENCE   Armed October And Other Poems. London: Cobden-Sanderson, 1932. First edition. Illus. with 13 vignettes by Rex Whistler. 8vo. Orig. cloth-backed decorated boards. Dust jacket. Fine copy. Jaffe 1-397 1983 $125

WHISTLER, LAURENCE   Audible Silence. (London): Hart-Davis, 1961. First edition. Orig. boards. Dust jacket. Presentation copy inscribed to Siegfried Sasson, dated Sept. 1961. Laid in is an ALS from the author to Sassoon. Very fine. MacManus 280-5539 1983 $225

WHISTLER, LAURENCE   Emperor Heart. London, Heinemann, 1936. First edition. Dust jacket design, title page, and head pieces all by Rex Whistler. Dust jacket. Presentation copy from the author to Siegfried Sassoon, 1937. Top edge a bit foxed, else very good. Houle 21-934 1983 $350

WHISTLER, LAURENCE   The Emperor Heart. London: William Heinemann Ltd., 1936. First edition. 8 wood-cut vignettes by Rex Whislter. 8vo. Orig. decorated purple cloth. Dust jacket. Orig. King's Medal wraparound band. A fine copy. Jaffe 1-399 1983 $125

WHISTLER, LAURENCE   Four Walls. London: William Heinemann, Ltd., (1934). First edition. 8vo. Orig. cloth. Dust jacket. Fine copy. Jaffe 1-398 1983 $75

WHISTLER, LAURENCE   Four Walls. London: William Heinemann,
1934. First edition. 8vo. Orig. cloth, gilt, slight wear to top
of spine. Traylen 94-864 1983 £12

WHISTLER, LAURENCE   The Konigsmark Drawings. Richards Press,
1952. Large 4to. 10 mounted sepia plates, one mounted text illus.
Red cloth, gilt. Edition limited to 1000 copies, No. 180. Greer
40-240 1983 £35

WHISTLER, LAURENCE   Poems. London: Hart-Davis, 1956. First
edition. Orig. boards. Dust jacket (slightly worn). Presentation
copy inscribed to Siegfried Sassoon. Fine. MacManus 280-5540 1983
$150

WHISTLER, LAURENCE   Rex Whistler: His Life and Drawings.
London: Art & Tech., 1948. First edition. 8vo. Cloth. Worn dust
wrapper. Illus. Fine. Aleph-bet 8-262 1983 $25

WHISTLER, LAURENCE   The World's Room. London: William
Heinemann, 1949. First edition. Illus. by R. Whistler. Orig. cloth.
Dust jacket (slightly worn, with a small tear to the rear cover).
Presentation copy inscribed to Siegfried Sassoon, dated July 1949.
Loosely laid in is a fine ALS, 3 pages, North Devon, 12 July 1949.
Fine. MacManus 280-5541 1983 $385

WHITAKER, FESS   History of Corporal Fess Whitaker.
(Louisville), 1918. Portraits. Plates. Illus. Gilt cloth. First
four leaves creased slightly, otherwise a fine, bright copy. Reese 19-
599 1983 $125

WHITAKER, FESS   History of Corporal Fess Whitaker. Louisville, 1918. Illus. Orig. cloth. First edition. Ginsberg 46-818
1983 $35

WHITAKER, FESS   History of Corporal Fess Whitaker. Louisville, 1918). First edition. Illus. Green cloth. Fine. Bradley
66=696 1983 $85

WHITAKER, FESS   History of Corporal Fess Whitaker.
(Louisville, 1918). 1st ed. Illus. 8vo. Morrill 286-514 1983
$25

WHITAKER, J.   Scribblings of a hedgerow naturalist.
1904. 13 plates, 8vo, cloth. T. Parkin's copy with 2 letters from
the author inserted. Binding a little rubbed and some pages foxed.
Wheldon 160-451 1983 £20

WHITAKER, JOHN   Mary Queen of Scots Vindicated. 1787-
1788. 3 vols., 8vo, uncut, 19th century half morocco with marbled
end papers, rebacked, preserving the very rubbed 19th century spines.
First edition. Bickersteth 77-182 1983 £18

WHITAKER, THOMAS DUNHAM   A History of Richmondshire, in the North
Riding of the County of York; Together with those Parts of the Ever-
wicshire of Domesday... 1843. First edition, 2 vols., engr. frontis.
44 engr. plates, 27 double-page and other pedigrees, folio, half morocco, gilt. Handsome crisp set. K Books 307-194 1983 £200

WHITBY, BEATRICE   The Awakening of Mary Fenwick. Hurst
& Blackett, 1889. First edition, 3 vols., half titles, half maroon
roan, v.g. Jarndyce 30-589 1983 £34

WHITE, A. S.   A Bibliography of Regimental Histories.
London, 1965. First edition. Imperial 8vo. Bookplate. Orig. dust
jacket. Orig. cloth. Fine. Edwards 1042-511 1983 £60

WHITE, ANDREW D.   A Letter to William Howard Russell,
LLD. Syracuse, 1863. Orig. printed wraps. First American edition.
Ginsberg 46-819 1983 $50

WHITE, CHRISTOPHER   Rembrandt As an Etcher. London:
A. Zwemmer, 1969. 2 vols. 348 plates. Large 4to. Cloth. Ars
Libri 32-570 1983 $185

WHITE, DABNEY   East Texas: Its History and Its Markers.
N.Y., Lewis Pub. Co., 1940. 4 vols. Folio. Many illus. Jenkins
153-586 1983 $225

WHITE, EDMUND H.   Athelstan, a Tragedy. Wm. Strange, 1847.
2nd edition, subscribers' list. 4 pp ads. Orig. pink cloth, very
good. Jarndyce 30-871 1983 £10.50

WHITE, ELIJAH   Ten Years in Oregon. Ithaca, 1850.
Orig. cloth, backstrip faded. With 30 pages added of Fremont's extracts. Clark 741-373 1983 $60

WHITE, ELWYN BROOKS   The Trumpet of the Swan. N.Y., (1970).
First edition. 12mo, cloth, d.w. Presentation copy: "For-that
dreamer-who failed with me, to experience that 'day that will live in
tympani.' But thanks anyway." Fine. Argosy 714-805 1983 $200

WHITE, F. B. W.   The Flora of Perthshire. Edinburgh,
1898. Portrait and coloured map, 8vo, original cloth. Wheldon
160-1636 1983 £35

WHITE, G. F.   Views in India. London, 1830. Engraved
title, 28 plates, some spotting. Folio. Orig. decorative morocco,
spine faded. 8vo. Good. Edwards 1044-749 1983 £200

WHITE, GILBERT   The Natural History and Antiquities
of Selborne... London: by T. Bensley, 1789. First edition. 4to.
Cont. tree calf, gilt panels on sides, neatly rebacked with morocco
label, gilt. Folding engraved frontis. and 6 engraved plates, as
well as other illus., engraved and printed title-pages and errata
leaf. Traylen 94-865 1983 £750

WHITE, GILBERT   Natural History of Selbourne. London,
Lane, 1902. Illus. by Edmund H. Finely bound in 3/4 gilt stamped
brown morocco by Birdsall. The spine with a fine inlay in various
colored leathers of a woodpecker climbing a tree. Fine. Houle 22-
955 1983 $250

WHITE, GILBERT   The Natural History of Selborne. 1825.
New edition, 2 vols., with the coloured bird plate and 3 other
engravings, some slight foxing, half green morocco, faded. K Books
301-189 1983 £55

WHITE, HENRY C.   The Life and Art of Dwight William
Tryon. Boston, 1930. First edition. Illustrated. 4to, original
boards, cloth back. Corners slightly rubbed. Morrill 290-592 1983
$35

WHITE, HENRY KIRKE   The Poetical Works. London, 1867.
Cr. 8vo. Dark blue calf, two-line gilt borders with corner ornaments,
gilt panelled spine, morocco label, gilt. Portrait, vignette title-
page. Traylen 94-866 1983 £16

WHITE, JAMES   The Adventures of John of Gaunt, Duke
of Lancaster. Dublin: Printed for J. Jones, W. Jones, Grueber
and M'Allister, and R. White, 1790. 2 vols, 12mo, contemporary calf;
vol. II lacks labels, but with half-title. A very good copy.
Hill 165-139 1983 £135

WHITE, JAMES   A Compendium of the Veterinary Art.
London, ca. 1810. Thick 12mo. Half calf, title-page lacking. Some
dampstaining. 14 copperplates, some neatly hand-colored. Argosy 713-
570 1983 $100

WHITE, JAMES   A Compendium of the Verterinary Art.
London: Longmans, 1829. Illus. 3 vols. Old 3/4 calf. Uniformly
bound, consisting of the fifteenth edition of vol. one, fifth edition
of vol. two, seventh edition of vol. three. MacManus 280-5543 1983
$125

WHITE, JAMES   The Falstaff Letters. London: Chatto &
Windus, 1907. First edition. Orig. boards. Dust jacket (defective).
Association copy inscribed to Siegfried Sassoon from Edmund Blunden.
Two pencelled annotations by Blunden. Endpapers faded. Very good.
MacManus 277-470 1983 $135

WHITE, JOHN   The Adventures of Sir Frizzle Pumpkin.
Edinburgh: William Blackwood & Sons, etc., 1836. First edition.
Illus. by George Cruikshank. Full red morocco, gilt, by Sangorski &
Sutcliffe. Top of spine a trifle worn. Bookplate on front endsheet.
MacManus 277-1204 1983 $125

WHITE, JOHN   Planter's Plea, 1630. Rockport, Ma.,
1930. Cloth-backed boards, edges darkened. Argosy 710-110 1983
$30

WHITE, JOSIAH   Josiah White's History. N.p., n.d. Limited to 100 copies, cover slightly rubbed and soiled, else very good. Quill & Brush 54-1518 1983 $50

WHITE, NELSON C.   Abbott H. Thayer. (Hartford, Conn.): Connecticut Printers, Inc. 1951. 4to, color frontis. 67 plates (a number in color). Presentation copy, signed "Nelson & Aida", and a line note signed "N.C.W." Blue cloth. With an exhibition catalog on Thayer from the Lyman Allyn Museum laid in. Karmiole 72-12 1983 $100

WHITE, NELSON C.   The Life and Art of J. Frank Currier. Cambridge: The Riverside Press, 1936. 4to, 48 leaves of plates, each with tissue guard. And with 12 plates in text. This is a presentation copy, signed by White. Black cloth over boards. Karmiole 72-13 1983 $85

WHITE, NEWMAN IVEY   Shelley. N.Y.: Alfred A. Knopf, 1940. First edition. 2 vols. Orig. cloth. Dust jackets (slightly sunned at spines). In a rather worn publisher's box. Fine. MacManus 280-4740 1983 $40

WHITE, OWEN P.   The Autobiography of a Durable Sinner. New York: G.P. Putnam's Sons, 1942. First edition, first issue. Orig. cloth. Some wear to spine. Fairly nice. Jenkins 152-516 1983 $200

WHITE, OWEN P.   The Autobiography of a Durable Sinner. New York: 1942. First published edition. Black cloth. Pages 239-244 tipped-in with matter substituted under threat of a law suit. Fine in chipped dust jacket. Bradley 66-697 1983 $47.50

WHITE, OWEN P.   Out of the Desert. El Paso, Texas: McMath Co., 1923. Orig. cloth. Jenkins 152-517 1983 $150

WHITE, OWEN P.   Them Was the Days. New York: Minton, Balch & Co., 1925. First edition. Frontis. Illus. by Ross Santee. Fine. Jenkins 152-518 1983 $45

WHITE, OWEN P.   Trigger Fingers. New York: G.P. Putnam's Sons, 1926. Orig. cloth. This vol. has a presentation from Owen P. White to James DeShields. Very scarce. Jenkins 153-687 1983 $150

WHITE, PHILO   Philo White's Narrative of a Cruize in the Pacific to South America and California on the U. S. Sloop-of-War "Dale" 1841-1843. Denver: Old West Publishing Co., 1965. Frontis. and illus. A very fine copy of this first edition, limited to 1000 copies. Jenkins 151-371 1983 $75

WHITE, ROMA   Moonbeams & Brownies. Innes., 1894. Illus. by Leslie Brooke. Frontis. & 6 illus. & 5 text illus. Pink decor. cloth, t.e.g. others uncut, nice copy. Hodgkins 27-213 1983 £10.50

WHITE, STEPHEN   Apologia pro Hibernia adversus Cambri Calumnias. Dublinii: apud Johannem O'Daly, 1840. First edition, roy. 8vo, cont. half calf, a very good to nice copy. Fenning 60-438 1983 £85

WHITE, STEWART EDWARD   Arizona Nights. New York: McClure, 1907. First edition. Color plates by N.C. Wyeth. Orig. green cloth with colored pictorial label pasted on. Cloth slipcase. Fine. Jenkins 152-519 1983 $100

WHITE, STEWART EDWARD   Arizona Nights. New York, 1907. 1st ed. Full-page color plates of N.C. Wyeth paintings. Green cloth with Wyeth pictorial cover painting in color. Nolograph postcard from J. Frank Dobie laid in, along with a small clipped picture of White and a newspaper notice of his death. Very good copy. Scarce. Bradley 63-137 1983 $85

WHITE, STEWART EDWARD   A Collection of His Works. 24 vols. including his rare 1st book, in both wrappers (inscribed presentation copy, fine) and cloth (fine) and most other titles in fine condition. Jenkins 155-1305 1983 $325

WHITE, STEWART EDWARD   Old Califronia in Picture & Story. New York, 1937. First edition in dust jacket. Profusely illus. Fine. Jenkins 152-584 1983 $35

WHITE, T. H.   England Have My Bones. NY, 1936. Very good in frayed dustwrapper that is heavily chipped at top edge with no loss of lettering. Quill & Brush 54-1519 1983 $40

WHITE, WALTER   Eastern England, from the Thames to the Humber. London: Chapman and Hall, 1865. First edition. 2 vols. 8vo. Orig. green cloth. A trifle rubbed, one spine wrinkled. Ximenes 63-642 1983 $70

WHITE, WILLIAM   England's true wealth. London: Groombridge, 1849. First edition. 8vo. Cont. limp green moire cloth. Fine copy. Ximenes 63-4 1983 $75

WHITE, WILLIAM ALANSON (1870-1937)   The Meaning of Disease. Baltimore: Williams & Wilkins, 1926. First edition. Gach 95-535 1983 $27.50

WHITE, WILLIAM ALLEN   The Autobiography of William Allen White. New York, 1946. First edition, first printing (so stated), and first binding. Illustrated. Blue cloth. Scarce in this blue cloth binding. Fine copy in worn and repaired dj. Bradley 64-183 1983 $25

WHITE, WILLIAM CHARLES   Tomb Tile Pictures of Ancient China. Toronto: Royal Ontario Museum of Archaeology, 1939. 4to, illus. and maps (some full-page). Index. Dust jacket. Karmiole 75-41 1983 $125

WHITE, WILLIAM F.   A Picture of Pioneer Times in California. San Francisco: Hinton, 1881. First edition. Orig. gilt pictorial mauve cloth. Light wear. Fine. Jenkins 152-521 1983 $100

WHITE, WILLIAM F.   A Picture of Pioneer Times in California Illustrated with Anecdotes and Stories Taken from Real Life. San Francisco: Hinton, 1881. 8vo, orig. gilt and blind-stamped brown cloth. Binding faded and worn, hinges strengthened. 1st ed. Fair copy. Jenkins 153-688 1983 $75

WHITE, WILLIAM HALE   The Autobiography of Mark Rutherford. London: Trubner, 1881. First edition. Orig. boards. Paper label. Board covers darkened and worn. Good, tight copy. MacManus 280-4467 1983 $65

WHITE, WILLIAM HALE   Catherine Furze. London: Unwin, 1893, 1894. First edition, vol. I, Second edition, vol. II. 2 vols. Orig. cloth. Covers slightly worn. MacManus 280-4469 1983 $85

WHITE, WILLIAM HALE   Catherine Furze. London: Unwin, 1893. First edition. 2 vols. Orig. half green cloth. Spines defective. Good. MacManus 280-4468 1983 $65

WHITE, WILLIAM HALE   Mark Rutherford's Deliverance. London: Trubner & Co., 1885. First edition. Orig. boards with paper spine labels (worn and darkened). Holbrook Jackson's copy with his signature and finely designed bookplage loosely laid in. Spine ends and edges rather worn. Inner hinges weak. Good, clean. MacManus 280-4470 1983 $125

WHITE, WILLIAM HALE   Miriam's Schooling. London: Kegan, Paul, Trench, Trubner & Co., 1890. First edition. Frontis. Orig. blue cloth. Spines and covers slightly worn and a trifle soiled. Good, tight. MacManus 280-4471 1983 $85

WHITE Mountain and Winnepissiogee Lake Guide Book. Boston: Jordan & Wiley, 1846. 16mo, orig. cloth wraps., (last flyleaf torn). Argosy 716-330 1983 $30

WHITEAVES, J. F.   Catalogue of the Marine Invertebrata of Eastern Canada. Ottawa, 1901. Royal 8vo, half morocco, worn, marginal stain. Wheldon 160-1351 1983 £15

WHITEFIELD, EDWIN   Homes of Our Forefathers in Boston, Old England, and in Boston, New England, From Original Drawings. Boston (U.S.A.), 1889. 2 parts in one vol., with 64 tipped-in coloured plates, 4to, a fine copy in half morocco gilt, gilt top. K Books 307-195 1983 £70

WHITEFIELD, EDWIN   Homes of Our Forefathers in Boston, Old England, and Boston, New England. Boston, 1889. 1st ed. Colored illus. 8vo. Ex-library. Morrill 289-315 1983 $35

WHITEFIELD, GEORGE   A Continuation of the Reverend Mr. Whitefield's Journal, After His Arrival in Georgia... London, 1741. One
leaf. Half calf and boards, a good copy. Reese 18-55 1983 $200

WHITEFIELD, GEORGE   Letter from...to the Rev. John Wesley,
on Universal Redemption. Boston, 1814. Stitched, good. Reese 18-
467 1983 $20

WHITEHEAD, ALFRED N.   An Enquiry Concerning the Principles of
Natural Knowledge. Cambridge: At the University Press, 1925. Gilt
cloth. Very fine. Reese 20-1123 1983 $45

WHITEHEAD, CHARLES E.   The Camp-Fires of the Everglades.
Edinburgh 1891. Illus., gilt-pict. cloth, t.e.g., spine and corners
frayed, covers loose, spine sunned. King 46-698 1983 $65

WHITEHEAD, EMMA   Pierce Falcon, the Outcast. Richard Bentley, 1835. First edition. 3 vols. Half title, half red roan, rubbed
at heads of spines. Jarndyce 31-966 1983 £48

WHITEHEAD, JAMES   On the Transmission, from Parent to
Offspring... London, John Churchill, 1851. 8vo, orig. cloth, worn,
stained, ex-library stamp on title, few smudges, else very good copy
internally. First edition. Ravenstree 97-99 1983 $95

WHITEHEAD, JOHN   A Small Treatise. London, printed for
Robert Wilson, 1661. 4to, disbound, worn, age-browned, some minor
age stains. First edition. Ravenstree 97-174 1983 $71

WHITEHEAD, PAUL   Manners: a Satire. London: R. Dodsley,
1739. 1st ed., first state. Folio, modern boards, cloth spine.
Uncut copy, vignette title page, half-title. Some soiling throughout,
especially on half-title, but a good copy. Trebizond 18-100 1983
$95

WHITEHEAD, PAUL   A New Ballad on Lord D--n---l's
altering his Chapel... London: for M. Moore, 1746. First edition.
Folio. 19th Century quarter morocco. 3 small library stamps,
evidence of orig. fold, spine worn. Heath 48-453 1983 £140

WHITEHEAD, PAUL   Satires written by Mr. Whitehead. London,
1739. 8vo, half title, uncut in marbled wrappers. A fine copy.
Pickering & Chatto 19-83 1983 $250

WHITEHEAD, WILLIAM   The Danger of Writing Verse: an
Epistle. London: printed for R. Dodsley and sold by T. Cooper, 1741.
1st ed., folio, disbound in modern wrappers. Pickering & Chatto 19-
84 1983 $350

WHITEHEAD, WILLIAM   The danger of writing verse. London:
for R. Dodsley, etc., 1741. First edition. Folio. Disbound.
Ximenes 63-387 1983 $150

WHITEHEAD, WILLIAM   Variety. London: Printed for J.
Dodsley...MDCCLXXVI. 4to, new wraps. A fine copy. First edition.
Quaritch NS 7-139 1983 $100

WHITEHEAD, WILLIAM   Verses to the People of England. 1758.
London: R. & J. Dodsley, 1758. 1st ed., 4to, disbound. Some creasing
at center of leaves, but a good copy. Trebizond 18-101 1983 $75

WHITEHEAD, WILLIAM A.   Documents relating to the Colonial
History of the State of New Jersey, 1631-1737. Newark, 1880-82.
5 vols., scuffed. Argosy 710-342 1983 $40

WHITEHOUSE, FRANCIS CECIL   Plain Folks. A Story of the Canadian
Prairies. Ottawa: Graphic, 1926. 20cm. Yellow cloth. Very good to
fine. McGahern 53-172 1983 $20

WHITEHURST, JOHN   An Inquiry into the Original State and
Formation of the Earth. Printed for W. Bent, 1792. 4to, uncut, 7
folding engraved plates, orig. boards, rebacked. Bickersteth 77-329
1983 £110

WHITEING, RICHARD   The Island or an Adventure of a Person
of Quality. London: Longmans, 1888. First edition. Orig. cloth.
MacManus 280-4456 1983 $25

WHITEING, RICHARD   No. 5 John Street. London: Grant
Richards, 1899. First edition. Orig. cloth. Presentation copy
inscribed to A.P. Watt. Watt's bookplate on the front endsheet. Covers
faded. Inner hinges cracked. Front endpaper cracking at hinge. Some
foxing. Excellent association copy. Cheaply bound and found in poor
condition. MacManus 280-5547 1983 $50

WHITEING, RICHARD   No. 5 John Street. N.Y.: The Century
Co., 1899. First American edition. Orig. cloth. Fromer owner's ink
stamp on free endpaper. Good. MacManus 280-5548 1983 $20

WHITEWAY, R. S.   The Portuguese expedition to Abyssinia...
London: Hakluyt Soc., 1902. 8vo. Frontis. Folding map. Orig.
blue cloth. Spine darkened, rubbed, ex-lib. Adelson Africa-232
1983 $30

WHITFIELD, E.   The Log of the Yawl "Sea Bird"...
Reading, 1939. First edition. Wrappers. One of 75 copies. Wood
engravings by M.E. Mills. Covers slightly marked and faded at the
spine and edges. Very good. Jolliffe 26-206 1983 £30

WHITFIELD, HENRY   A Glorious Manifestation of the further
Progress of the Gospel Amongst the Indians in New-England. London,
1652, NY, 1865. Thin, small 4to, printed wrappers. Sabin's reprints
quarto series, one of 250 copies initialed by Savin. Argosy 710-111
1983 $35

WHITFORD, WILLIAM C.   Colorado Volunteers in the Civil War...
Denver, 1906. 1st ed. Illus. Maps. Orig. stiff wrappers.
Jenkins 153-689 1983 $65

WHITIN, ALBERT H.   The Queen's Reverie. The Obelisk Press,
Paris, 1932. Small 4to, 13 plates, orig. cloth gilt, spine faded,
upper cover with small bubbles in the cloth. Bickersteth 77-183 1983
£15

WHITING, JOHN   Persecution Exposed, in Some Memoirs
Relating to the Sufferings of John Whiting... 1791. Second edition.
Modern quarter calf. K Books 307-196 1983 £34

WHITING, LILIAN   The Brownings. Their Life and Art.
Boston: Little, Brown & Co., 1911. First edition. Illus. Orig.
cloth with pictorial labels. Very good. MacManus 277-738 1983 $20

WHITLEY, WILLIAM T.   Gilbert Stuart. Cambridge: Harvard
University Press, 1932. 7 plates. 4to. Cloth. Ars Libri 32-655
1983 $75

WHITLOCK, BRAND   Big Matt. New York, 1928. 8vo.
Cloth. A fine copy in new dj. In Our Time 156-882 1983 $35

WHITLOCKE, BULSTRODE   Memorials of the English Affairs...
London: For E. Curll, etc., 1709. First edition. Folio. Cont.
calf, gilt panels on sides with corner ornaments, gilt panelled
spine with heart decorations, morocco label, gilt. Traylen 94-867
1983 £95

WHITMAN, ALFRED   Charles Turner. London: George Bell
& Sons, 1907. First edition. Thick 4to. Cloth. T.e.g., others
uncut. Limited to 500 copies. With 32 full page plates. Spine
extremities worn, especially the top. Oak Knoll 48-487 1983 $50

WHITMAN, WALT   Autobiographia or The Story of a Life.
NY 1892. First edition. Frontis, cloth, couple corners bumped,
moderately rubbed cut still a nice copy. King 46-351 1983 $25

WHITMAN, WALT   The Book of Heavenly Death. Portland:
T.B. Mosher, 1907. Second edition. Port. Boards; uncut. One of
500 copies. Argosy 714-807 1983 $20

WHITMAN, WALT   Leaves of Grass. Brooklyn, 1855.
1st ed. of this facsimile ed. 1 of 250 copies with the binding
in facsimile of the orig. Orig. green cloth, gilt. Very fine.
Jenkins 155-1306 1983 $125

WHITMAN, WALT   Leaves of Grass. Boston: Thayer &
Eldridge, 1860-61. Third edition, first issue, with the Rand &
Avery imprint on copyright page, portrait on tinted ground, and gilt
butterfly on spine. Thick 12mo, blind-stamped brown cloth. Frontis.
dampstained; very shaken. Signed by Whitman beneath the portrait-
"Truly Yours, Walt Whitman." Argosy 714-810 1983 $25

WHITMAN, WALT   Leaves of Grass. B, (n.d.). Third edition, third issue, first pirated edition, hinges starting, spine
faded, good or better. Quill & Brush 54-1527 1983 $125

WHITMAN, WALT   Leaves of Grass. Camden, N.J., 1876.
Author's edition. 6th edition, signed "John Inman/from his friend/
the author" and again signed "Walt Whitman" under verse on title page.
Resewn and rebacked, very good. Quill & Brush 54-1528 1983 $750

WHITMAN, WALT   Leaves of Grass. Camden, 1876.
Two plates. Modern cloth, morocco label, by Gaebel. Prospectus
bound in. Signed by Whitman on the titlepage. A fine copy.
Felcone 21-110 1983 $375

WHITMAN, WALT   Leaves of Grass. Ph., 1882. First
Philadelphia edition, very good bright copy with slip tipped to front
end paper announcing "Whitman Prose Works" as ready. Quill & Brush
54-1526 1983 $200

WHITMAN, WALT   Leaves of Grass. Phila., 1882. 8vo,
orig. gilt dec. cloth. Printed from the plates of the 3rd edition.
Argosy 714-810 1983 $25

WHITMAN, WALT   Leaves of Grass. Philadelphia:
McKay, (1891). Death-bed ed., 1st paper back issue. Orig. printed
wrappers, label. From the library of Whitman's literary executor,
Thomas B. Harned, with his signature and bookplate, and his ink
notes on rear wrapper. A few corners turned down in text, with
Harned's marginal pencil notes. Nice copy. Jenkins 155-1307 1983
$150

WHITMAN, WALT   Leaves of Grass. Ph., 1892. Complete
1892 edition. Edges rubbed and slightly worn at corners, front hinge
starting at contents page, else very good. Quill & Brush 54-1525
1983 $250

WHITMAN, WALT   Manuscripts, Autograph Letters, First
Editions and Portraits of Walt Whitman. New York, Anderson Galleries,
1936. Facsimiles. 8vo, original stiff wrappers. Morrill 290-593
1983 $25

WHITMAN, WALT   Song Of The Broad-Axe. Philadelphia:
The Centaur Press, 1924. First edition thus. Illus. cut on wood
by Wharton H. Esherick. 4to. Orig. decorated boards. Dust jacket.
Limited to 400 copies. Presentation copy from the artist, inscribed.
Publisher's prospectus laid in. Fine copy. Jaffe 1-86 1983 $175

WHITMAN, WALT   Specimen Days and Collect. Phil.:
McKay, 1882-3. 1st ed., later issue. Orig. mustard cloth, gilt.
Near fine. Jenkins 155-1308 1983 $45

WHITMAN, WALT   Specimen Days & Collect. Philadelphia,
1882-83. First edition, first issue. Cloth, inner hinges cracked,
top of spine frayed, covers soiled. King 46-353 1983 $75

WHITMAN, WALT   Two Rivulets. Camden: Author's Eds.,
1876. 1st ed., privately printed and distributed by author. Orig.
3/4 white morocco. This copy inscribed from Thomas B. Harned, one
of Whitman's literary executors, to his son, and although it bears
the mounting sheet for photograpic frontispiece the photo has never
been inserted. Expertly rebacked, else fine. Jenkins 155-1309 1983
$200

WHITMAN, WALT   The Wound Dresser. Boston 1898.
First edition, first issue. Portrait, cloth, t.e.g., covers slightly
darkened else very good. King 46-354 1983 $75

WHITMER, DAIVD   An Address to All Believers in Christ.
Richmond, Mo.: David Whitmer, 1887. First edition. Printed wrappers. Numerous pencil markings in text. Wrappers chipped. Bradley
66-606 1983 $35

WHITMORE, WILLIAM H.   Catalogue of the American Portion of
the Library of the Rev. Thomas Prince... Boston: J.K. Wiggin &
Wm. Parsons Lunt, 1868. First edition. 8vo. Three-quarter
leather over cloth. Covers rubbed. Oak Knoll 48-471 1983 $55

WHITNEY, ASA   Memorial of...Praying a Grant of Public
Land to Enable Him to Construct a Railroad from Lake Michigan to
the Pacific Ocean. Wash., 1846. Folded map. First edition.
Ginsberg 46-622 1983 $60

WHITNEY, ASA   A Project for a Railroad to the
Pacific. New York, 1849. 2 folding maps. Disbound. Felcone 21-111
1983 $200

WHITNEY, ASA   Whitney's Railroad to the Pacific...
Location and Construction of,a National Railroad and Electric
Telegraph from the Mississippi Rover to the Pacific Ocean. Wash.,
1850. Illus. Folded map. Half morocco. Ginsberg 47-797 9183
$75

WHITNEY, HENRY C.   Life on the Circuit with Lincoln.
Boston, (1892). Illustrated with 67 plates, first edition. Jenkins
151-182 1983 $75

WHITNEY, JOEL P.   Silver Mining Regions of Colorado with
Some Account of the Different Processes Now Being Introduced for
Working the Gold Ores of that Territory. N.Y., 1865. Half morocco.
First edition. Ginsberg 46-194 1983 $300

WHITTAKER, THOMAS   Sights and Scenes in Oxford City and
University. London: Cassell & Co., n.d. First edition. Intro. by
G. Saintsbury. Orig. decorated cloth. Covers slightly worn and soiled.
Inner hinges repaired with cloth tape. Some light foxing. MacManus
280-5549 1983 $25

WHITTELSEY, CHAUNCEY   A Sermon Preach'd at New-Haven on the
Sabbath...Wherein is Considered the True Notion of a Faithful
Improvement of Our Talents... New London, Conn., 1744. Rebound.
Fine. Reese 18-58 1983 $100

WHITTEN, WILFRED   Nollekens and His Times. London:
John Lane The Bodley Head, 1917. 2 vols. 42 plates and 50 plates.
4to. Cloth. Frontis. loose in Vol. 1. Ars Libri 32-494 1983
$100

WHITTIER, JOHN GREENLEAF (1807-1892)   The Bay of Seven Island and
Other Poems. B, 1883. Tan dec. cover, very good or better. Quill &
Brush 54-1532 1983 $35

WHITTIER, JOHN GREENLEAF (1807-1892)   At Sundown. Cambridge, 1892.
8vo. Full vellum. Illus. fron designs by E. H. Garrett. Limited
edition. One of 250 numbered copies. Argosy 714-812 1983 $30

WHITTIER, JOHN GREENLEAF (1807-1892)   Maud Muller. Boston, 1867.
First edition. Thin 8vo. Blindstamped publishers mocorro. Illus.
by W. J. Hennessy. Fine. Argosy 714-813 1983 $35

WHITTIER, JOHN GREENLEAF (1807-1892)   Old Portraits and Modern
Sketches. Boston: Ticknor, Reed, 1850. First edition. 8vo. Orig.
brown bevelled cloth, spine gilt, ads. A very good copy. Trebizond
18-102 1983 $45

WHITTIER, JOHN GREENLEAF (1807-1892)   The Panorama. B, 1856. First
issue without ads, spine edges slightly chipped, cover slightly
stained, good. Quill & Brush 54-1534 1983 $40

WHITTIER, JOHN GREENLEAF (1807-1892)   The Pennsylvania Pilgrim. B,
1872. Edges of spine and corners worn, front hinge cracked, otherwise
good to very good. Quill & Brush 54-1535 1983 $30

WHITTIER, JOHN GREENLEAF (1807-1892)   The Pennsylvania Pilgrim. B,
1872. Ex-lib with usual markings to interior, spine edges rubbed,
otherwise very good. Quill & Brush 54-1536 1983 $30

WHITTIER, JOHN GREENLEAF (1807-1892)   Poems Written During the Progress of the Abolition Question in the United States, Between the Years
1830 and 1838. Boston: Knapps, 1837. Frontis., illus. First edition, first issue. Orig. green diamond-grain cloth, gilt. Front free
endpaper excised and faint stain to first three leaves, else a fine
unworn copy. Rare. Jenkins 155-1315 1983 $125

WHITTIER, JOHN GREENLEAF (1807-1892)   Poems Written During the Progress of the Abolition Question in the United States, Between the Years
1830 and 1838. Boston: Knapps, 1837. Frontis., illus. First edition, second issue. Orig. brown cloth. Foxing and a few light spots.
Jenkins 155-1316 1983 $75

WHITTIER, JOHN GREENLEAF (1807-1892)   Snow-Bound. B, 1866. First
edition second issue, page 52 not numbered, cover slightly rubbed,
corners and edges of spine fraying, otherwise very good, bookplate.
Quill & Brush 54-1531 1983 $60

WHITTIER, JOHN GREENLEAF (1807-1892)   Visions of Light. London: Collins Clear-Type Press, n.d. Full-color title-page illus. Fine in gilt-stamped alligator skin, slightly rubbed at extremities. (3 x 2 x 3/16; 75x55mm). Bromer 25-480 1983 $35

THE WHOLE Family, a Novel by Twelve Authors. New York & London: Harper, 1908. Frontis., plates. 1st ed., primary binding. Orig. blue cloth, decorated in gilt. Spine trifle dull, but attractive copy. Jenkins 155-712 1983 $125

WHY South Dakota Offers Better Opportunities and Possibilities to the Home Seeker and Home Builder than any Other State. Pierre, ca. 1898. Illus. Orig. pictorial wrappers. First edition. Ginsberg 47-299 1983 $75

WHYMPER, C.   Egyptian Birds. 1909. 51 coloured plates, text-figures, 8vo, original decorated cloth. Very scarce. Wheldon 160-924 1983 £40

WHYMPER, EDWARD   Scrambles Amongst the Alps. Cleveland, Ohio, ca 1880 (?). 2 works in one vol., numerous illus., blank upper margin of frontis. cut away, roy 8vo, slightly age-browned but good in the orig. decorated cloth, gilt edges. K Books 301-190 1983 £34

WHYMPER, EDWARD   Travels amongst the Great Andes of the Equator. 1892. 20 plates, 118 text-figures and 4 maps, 8vo, binder's cloth (label removed from inside of cover). Wheldon 160-453 1983 £25

WHYTE, CHRISTINA GOWANS   The Adventures of Merrywink. Hodder & Stoughton, n.d. (1906). 4to. Colour frontis. Title vignette. 4 colour plates (1 damaged). 16 full-page & 37 text illus. Little loose. Colour pictorial white cloth, rubbed. Presentation copy from Wheel-house, with a 4pp letter. Greer 39-136 1983 £85

WHYTE, SAMUEL   The theatre: a didactic essay. Dublin: printed by Zachariah Jackson, for John Jones, 1790. 8vo, disbound, 1st edition. Trimmed a trifle close at the top, touching a couple of headlines. Two leaves are present in cancelled and uncancelled state. With an errata leaf at the end. Rare. Ximenes 64-575 1983 $375

WHYTE-MELVILLE, GEORGE JOHN   Black but Comely. London: Chapman & Hall, 1879. First edition. 3 vols. Orig. cloth. Bindings a bit rubbed and shaken. MacManus 280-5550 1983 $40

WHYTE-MELVILLE, GEORGE JOHN   The Gladiators. London: Green, et al, 1863. First edition. 3 vols. Orig. red cloth. Presentation copy from the publisher with his small blindstamp on the title-page. Spines and covers slightly worn and faded. Very good. MacManus 280-5551 1983 $350

WHYTE-MELVILLE, GEORGE JOHN   Holmby House. London: Parker, 1860. Second edition. 2 vols. Orig. cloth. Two-tone frontis. in vol. one. Fine. MacManus 280-5552 1983 $25

WHYTE-MELVILLE, GEORGE JOHN   Katerfelto. London: Chapman & Hall, 1875. Orig. cloth. Illus. Extremities of spine slightly worn. MacManus 280-5554 1983 $25

WHYTE-MELVILLE, GEORGE JOHN   M. or N. London: Chapman & Hall, 1869. First edition. 2 vols. Orig. cloth. Spine of Vol. I faded. Near-fine. MacManus 280-5555 1983 $175

WHYTE-MELVILLE, GEORGE JOHN   Rosine. London: Chapman & Hall, 1877. First edition. Orig. cloth (a bit soiled and rubbed). Inner hinges cracked. Bookplate. Frontis. and other illus. by M. Kerns. MacManus 280-5556 1983 $25

WHYTE-MELVILLE, GEORGE JOHN   Roy's Wife. London: Chapman & Hall, 1878. First edition. 2 vols. Orig. decorated cloth. Front inner hinge of Vol. I cracked. Fine. MacManus 280-5557 1983 $250

WHYTE-MELVILLE, GEORGE JOHN   Sister Louise. London: Chapman & Hall, 1876. First edition. Orig. cloth (slightly rubbed; inner hinges cracked). Faint trace of library label removed from front cover. Frontis. and other illus. by M. Kerns. MacManus 280-5558 1983 $40

WHYTE-MELVILLE, GEORGE JOHN   Works. London, (ca. 1900). 12 vols. 8vo. Half green calf, gilt, sporting emblems on spines. Frontis. and other illus. Traylen 94-868 1983 £85

WICK, JEAN   Stories Editors Buy and Why. Boston (1921). 8vo. Cloth. Contributions by Edna Ferber, Booth Tarkington et al. Fine copy in scarce dj which has tiny hole on spine. In Our Time 156-884 1983 $35

WICKENDEN, JOSEPH F.   Seven Days in Attica in the Summer of 1852. Thomas Harrison, 1853. First edition, with the 2 maps and 23 plates and folding panoramas, from Sketches by the author. Linen-backed and loose as issued, with the text of pages, in the orig. printed paper wraps., all in the orig. roy. 8vo cloth library case, with the large litho labels on each bord, inner cloth folder in need of repair and the case a little worn at the corners, but otherwise a very good copy in orig. state. Fenning 62-392 1983 £145

WICKERSHAM, JAMES   A Bibliography of Alaskan Literature 1724-1924. Cordova, Ak: Cordova Daily Times Print, 1927. Cloth. Ex-library with stamps, a little used. Dawson 471-305 1983 $150

WICKSELL, KNUT   Forelasningar I Nationalekonomi. Stockholm, Fritzes, 1915. 2nd, revised edition, large 8vo, uncut in original printed wrappers. Pickering & Chatto 21-133 1983 $100

WICKSON, E. J.   California's Magazine. Vol., No. 1, 1915. Numerous illus., many in color. Ink inscrip-tion, covers dull and rubbed. King 46-30 1983 $25

WICKSTEED, JOSEPH H.   Blake's Innocence and Experience. London & Toronto: J.M. Dent & Sons Ltd., New York: E.P. Dutton & Co., 1928. First edition. Thick 8vo. Illus. with reproductions in color & black & white. Orig. cloth, dust jacket (a bit chipped). Fine. MacManus 277-435 1983 $125

WICKSTEED, JOSEPH H.   Blake's Innocence and Experience. Dent, 1928. First edition, thick sq. 8vo, 4 colour plates, green cloth gilt, fine in dustwrappers. Deighton 3-43 1983 £80

WICKSTEED, JOSEPH H.   William Blake's Jerusalem. New York: The Beechhurst Press, (1955). 8vo. Red leather. A fine copy. In Our Time 156-84 1983 $100

WICKSTEED, THOMAS   An Experimental Inquiry Concerning the Relative Power of, and Useful Effect Produced by, the Cornish and Boulton and Watt Pumping Engines, and Cylindrical Waggon-Head Boilers. John Weale, London, 1841. 4to, with 7 tables on 5 leaves, 2 folding, of which one is mounted on linen; 40 pp. ads.; presentation copy inscribed "Dr. Darwin from the Author" on free endpaper; orig. cloth, gilt, faded and worn. First edition. Quaritch NS 5-113 1983 $350

WIDDEMER, MARGARET   A Tree with a Bird in it. N.Y., (1922). 12mo, cloth; pict. label. Illus. by William Saphier. Argosy 714-593 1983 $25

WIDDESS, J. D. H.   An Account of the Schools of Surgery Royal College of Surgeons, Dublin 1789-1948. Baltimore, 1949. First edition. 8vo. Orig. binding. Fye H-3-623 1983 $30

WIDE-Awake Vocalist, or, Rail Splitters' Song Book...for the Repub-lican Campaign of 1860. N.Y.: E. A. Daggett, 1860. Original printed wrappers. A tattered copy, but complete and intact. Jenkins 151-184 1983 $150

WIEL, ALATHEA   The Navy of Venice. London, 1910. First edition. Thick 8vo. Orig. cloth. Frontis., 20 plates (1 fold-ing)., illus. Gilt, spine faded. Some slight foxing throughout. Good. Edwards 1042-186 1983 £40

WIENERS, JOHN   The Hotel Wentley Poems. (San Francisco: Auerhahn Press), 1958. Pictorial wraps. First edition. Inscribed by the author, with a 1 1/2 page a.l.s. from him laid in. Fine. Reese 20-1130 1983 $75

WIGFORSS, ERNST   Materialistisk Historieuppfattning Och Klasskamp. Malmo, Fram, 1908. 1st ed., 8vo, original printed red wrappers. Pickering & Chatto 21-134 1983 $60

WIGGIN, J. B.   The Wild Artist in Boston. Boston:
Wiggin, 1888. 1st ed. Orig. cloth, gilt. Very light use, and
signed by author on flyleaf. Jenkins 155-1320 1983 $30

WIGGIN, KATE DOUGLAS   Bluebeard. N.Y., 1914. First edition.
16mo, pict. blue cloth. Argosy 714-816 1983 $20

WIGGLESWORTH, MICHAEL   Meat out of the Eater. Boston, 1717.
Orig. calf, somewhat worn, over birch boards. Text lightly foxed
in places. Slight tear to last leaf, otherwise a fine copy.
Reese 18-39 1983 $5,000

WIGHT, FANNY   Nellie's Christmas Eve. NY: McLoughlin Bros., (ca. 1870's). Quarto. 6 full-page color illus. Fine in
slightly rubbed pictorial self-wrappers. Bromer 25-372 1983 $45

WIGHTWICK, GEORGE   Hints to young architects. London:
Lockwood, 1860. 8vo. Orig. green cloth. "Second issue", so
designated on the title-page. Numerous woodcut illus. in the text.
Pub's catalogue. Title-page foxed, otherwise a very fine copy.
Ximenes 63-24 1983 $125

WILBERFORCE, SAMUEL   Life of Wm. Wilberforce. John Murray,
1868. Half title, front. port. Orig. blue cloth. Jarndyce 30-178
1983 £10.50

WILBRAND, HERMANN   Die Hemianopischen Cesichtsfeld-Formen.
Weisbaden: J. F. Bergmann, 1890. First edition. Contemporary 1/2
leather, spine rubbed. Illus. with 24 text figures and 22 plates.
From Adolf Meyer's collection. Gach 95-538 1983 $45

WILBUR, RICHARD   A Bestiary. NY: Pantheon Books.
(1955). Folio. Profusely illus. with drawings by Calder, many
full-page. This is copy XIII, perhaps a special copy for author and
illustrator, signed by both Wilbur and Calder. (Total edition 825).
Printed at the Spiral Press. Karmiole 75-31 1983 $200

WILD, ROLAND   MacNab. The Last Laird. London:
Methuen, 1938. 21 1/2cm. First edition. Colour frontis. and 8
monotone plates. Wine cloth. Fine. Scarce. McGahern 54-178
1983 $45

WILD Bill McCanles Tragedy... Lincoln, 1927. Cloth. Illus. Fld.
map. Jenkins 153-382 1983 $25

WILD Flowers of America. New York, 1894. 288 coloured plates,
oblong 4to, cloth. Wheldon 160-1781 1983 £25

WILDE, OSCAR   Birthday of the Infanta. N.Y.,
Macmillan, 1929. Illus. by Pamela Bianco. Half cloth (spine faded);
pub.'s slipcase worn, else very good. One of 500 copies, signed
by Bianco. Houle 21-937 1983 $60

WILDE, OSCAR   The Complete Writings. New York, 1909.
10 vols. Thick 8vo. Half dark blue morocco, gilt, t.e.g., others
uncut. Frontis. to each vol. Traylen 94-870 1983 £195

WILDE, OSCAR   Fisherman and His Soul. (S.F.,
Grabhorn Press, 1939). 4to, title page, six headpieces, and six
initials by Mallette Dean. Half yellow cloth (a trifle faded),
else very good. One of 200 copies. Houle 21-382 1983 $95

WILDE, OSCAR   The Fisherman and His Soul. Portland:
Thos. Mosher, 1907. 24mo, parchment wraps.; uncut. One of 425
copies. Second edition. Argosy 714-818 1983 $20

WILDE, OSCAR   The Happy Prince and Other Tales. Stamford: Overbrook Press, 1936. Octavo. Illus. with 6 wood engravings.
Appears to be sample submitted by binder. Cloth-backed decorated
paper over boards. Inside rear hinge slightly cracked, pencilled note
on rear endpaper. Colophon page not printed in book. Two proofs of
colophon are laid-in. Fine in slip-case. Bromer 25-271 1983 $185

WILDE, OSCAR   The Happy Prince & Other Tales. Phila.:
Winst, (1940). 8vo. Dust wrapper. Full-page color illus. plus black
& whites by E. Shinn. Fine. Aleph-bet 8-264 1983 $20

WILDE, OSCAR   The Happy Prince and the Selfish Giant.
Trovillion Private Press, Herrin, Ill., 1945. 1 of 497 signed by
Violet and Hal Trovillion. With an inscription by the Trovillions
on front flyleaf. Illus. by W.J. Goodacre. Yellow boards. Fine.
Bradley 63-126 1983 $30

WILDE, OSCAR   Hellenism. Edinburgh: Tragara Press,
1909. 8vo. Cloth. 1st and only ed. Total ed. is 95 copies. Fine
copy. In Our Time 156-885 1983 $50

WILDE, OSCAR   The Importance of Being Earnest. N.Y.:
New York Public Library, 1956. 2 vols. 2nd vol. is facsimile. White,
gilt-decorated boards. Slipcase. Limited to 500 numbered copies.
Nice. King 45-278 1983 $250

WILDE, OSCAR   Impressions of America. Sunderland:
Keystone Press, 1906. Wraps. Soiled. Covers badly chipped, stained
and detached. Limited to 500 copies. As is. King 45-279 1983 $25

WILDE, OSCAR   Intentions... N.Y., Dodd, Mead, (n.d.,
1891). 8vo. Orig. rose cloth. Spine mod. soiled, top & bottom of
spine lightly chipped. 1st American ed. (English sheets with diff.
title and half-title). Only 600 copies issued, scarcer than English
ed. Very good. O'Neal 50-121 1983 $75

WILDE, OSCAR   The Picture of Dorian Gray. London/NY,
1891. Limited edition, one of 250 numbered and signed copies in gray
beveled boards with vellum spine. Top edge of spine whole with tear
which is reinforced internally. Bottom edge has half-inch chip missing,
minor cover stains, Chinese character stamp on front pastedown and half-
title, fore-edges slightly soiled, bookplate, very good. Quill & Brush
54-1537 1983 $2000

WILDE, OSCAR   The Picture of Dorian Gray. London, 1891.
Sq. 8vo, parchment backed gray boards, cover & spine with gilt
decorations after Charles Ricketts; t.e.g., other uncut; in 1/4
blue morocco slipcase. Ltd. large-paper edition. One of 250 copies,
signed by Wilde. Some wear to spine, but a good copy. Argosy
714-819 1983 $1,200

WILDE, OSCAR   The Plays of Oscar Wilde. New York,
Modern Library, (1932). First edition, small 8vo., dust jacket,
very good. Houle 22-958 1983 $30

WILDE, OSCAR   Poems. London, Methuen (1908). First
edition thus. Full purple morocco by Bayntun, the spine with gilt
stylized floral design, gilt inner dentelles top edge gilt,
marbled
endpapers, uncut. One of 1,000 on handmade paper. Fine copy.
Houle 21-938 1983 $350

WILDE, OSCAR   Salome. SF, 1927. 4to, cloth-backed
decorated bds., gilt. Frontis and marginal decorations from wood
blocks designed & cut by Valenti Angelo. Worn slipcase. Perata 27-
59 1983 $250

WILDE, OSCAR   The Sphinx. John Lane, 1920. Edition
limited to 1000 copies. Frontis. 13 text illus. & 11 plates in black
& blue. Lacks tissueguard. White cloth, ornate gilt & blue design.
Very nice. Greer 39-1 1983 £160

WILDE, OSCAR   The Works. London, 1908-22. First
collected edition. 15 vols. 8vo. White buckram, gilt, t.e.g.,
other edges uncut. Limited to 1,000 sets, finely printed on hand-
made paper. Traylen 94-869 1983 £420

WILDEMAN, E. DE   Icones selectae Horti Thenensis.
Brussels, 1899-1909. Vols. 1 to 6, 240 plates, 6 vols., royal 8vo, in
parts as issued. Scarce. Wheldon 160-2031 1983 £30

WILDEMAN, E. DE   Plantae novae vel minus cognitae ex
Herbario Horti Thenensis. Brussels, 1904-10. Vol. 1 and vol. 2 parts
1 to 3, 101 plates, 10 parts, royal 8vo, original wrappers. Scarce.
Wheldon 160-2032 1983 £20

WILDENSTEIN, GEORGES   Chardin. Biographie et catalogue
critiques. Paris: Les Beaux-Arts, 1933. 128 plates with 236
illus. Small stout folio. Cloth. Ars Libri 32-105 1983 $150

WILDENSTEIN, GEORGES   Ingres. London: Phaidon, 1956.
Second revised edition. 120 plates (8 tipped-in color). 200 reference
illus. Large 4to. Cloth. Dust jacket. Ars Libri 32-339 1983 $175

WILDENSTEIN, GEORGES   Lancret. Biographie et catalogue critiques. Paris: Les Beaux-Arts, 1924. 214 beautifully printed heliogravure plates. Sm. folio. Marbled boards, 1/4 leather. Orig.
wrappers bound in. Ex-library. Very slightly rubbed. Ars Libri
32-390 1983 $175

WILDENSTEIN, GEORGES   The Paintings of Fragonard. New York:
Phaidon, 1960. Complete edition. 350 illus. (16 color). Small
folio. Cloth. Dust jacket. Slipcase. Ars Libri 32-225 1983
$175

WILDENSTEIN, GEORGES   Le peintre Aved. Paris: Les Beaux-
Arts, 1922. 2 vols. Prof. illus. with heliogravure and tipped-in
plates hors texte. Figures. Small folio. Wrappers. Uncut.
Edition limited to 500 numbered copies. Ars Libri 32-13 1983 $275

WILDER, AMOS   Battle-Retrospect. New Haven: Yale,
1923. Printed wraps. over boards. First edition. Fine. Reese 20-
1131 1983 $45

WILDER, AMOS   The Healing of the Waters: Poems.
New York, 1943. 8vo. Cloth. Review copy with slip laid in.
Clipping about book on inside endboard, else fine in dj. In Our
Time 156-886 1983 $25

WILDER, DANIEL W.   The Annals of Kansas. Topeka: Geo. W.
Martin, 1875. Full calf, some scuffing. 1st ed. Jenkins 153-305
1983 $75

WILDER, DANIEL W.   The Annals of Kansas. Topeka, 1875.
Tables. Orig. cloth. First edition. Ginsberg 47-425 1983 $65

WILDER, DANIEL W.   The Annals of Kansas. Topeka: 1875.
First edition. New cloth. Nicely rebound. Bradley 66-573 1983
$55

WILDER, DAVID   The History of Leominster. Fitchburg,
1853. 1st ed. Small 8vo. Binding partly faded. Morrill 287-266
1983 $20

WILDER, LUCY   The Mayo Clinic. New York, 1938.
First edition. 8vo. Orig. binding. Fye H-3-625 1983 $20

WILDER, THORNTON   The Angel That Troubled the Waters and
Other Plays. New York: Coward-McCann, 1928. First edition. 1/775
signed by author. Frontis. photo. Blue boards. Former owner's name
in ink on flyleaf. Mint in plain blue dust jacket and slipcase.
Bradley 66-361 1983 $135

WILDER, THORNTON   The Angel That Troubled the Waters and
Other Plays. New York: Coward-McCann, 1928. First edition. 1/775
signed by author. Frontis. photo. Blue boards. Bookplate and
defective slipcase. Bradley 66-362 1983 $100

WILDER, THORNTON   The Angel That Troubled the Waters.
New York: Coward-McCann, 1928. 1st ed., 1 of 2,000 copies signed
by the publisher. Orig. cloth-backed boards, uncut. Fine copy.
Jenkins 155-1323 1983 $35

WILDER, THORNTON   Bridge of San Luis Rey. London,
Longmans, 1929. First illustrated edition. 16 tipped-in woodcuts by
Leighton. Dust jacket (a trifle soiled), very good-fine. Houle
21-559 1983 $125

WILDER, THORNTON   The Bridge of San Luis Rey. New York:
Boni, 1927. 1st ed. Orig. mauve cloth. Fine copy lacking dj.
Jenkins 155-1324 1983 $35

WILDER, THORNTON   Heaven's My Destination. London:
(1934). First English edition. Red cloth. Fine in worn dust
jacket. Bradley 66-364 1983 $35

WILDER, THORNTON   The Ides of March. N.Y., Harper,
(1948). First edition. Dust jacket. One of 750 copies, signed by
the author. Fine copy. Houle 22-962 1983 $85

WILDER, THORNTON   The Ides of March. New York: (1948).
First edition. Dark blue cloth. Small red ink price mark on back
paste-down, otherwise fine in dust jacket. Bradley 66-365 1983
$25

WILDER, THORNTON   The Long Christmas Dinner. New Haven:
Yale Univ. Press, 1931. 1st ed., 1 of 525 (no. 525) numbered and
signed copies. Orig. imitation parchment-backed patterned boards,
uncut. Fine copy. Jenkins 155-1325 1983 $85

WILDER, THORNTON   The Long Christmas Dinner and Other Plays
in One Act. NY, 1931. Cover slightly discolored, 1/4 inch nick on
front board, else very good in remnants of dustwrapper. Quill & Brush
54-1539 1983 $35

WILDER, THORNTON   The Skin of Our Teeth. NY, 1942. Small
stain to rear cover, else very good in lightly chipped and worn, good
dustwrapper, owner's name, bookplate. Quill & Brush 54-1540 1983
$40

WILDER, THORNTON   The Woman of Andros. London: 1930.
First English edition. Tipped-in frontis. drawing. Blue cloth.
1/260 signed. Corners slightly bumped, otherwise fine. Bradley 66-
366 1983 $125

THE WILDER Quarter-Century Book. Ithaca, 1893. 1st ed. Presentation
from Wilder. Illus. Large 8vo, uncut and partly unopened. Top of
spine chipped. Morrill 288-533 1983 $20

WILDFOWL Inquiry. Cambridge, 1941-39. 2 vols., 8vo, cloth.
Wheldon 160-925 1983 £13

WILDS, WILLIAM   Elementary and Practical Instructions on
the Art of Building Cottages and Houses for the Humbler Classes.
John Weale, 1835. First edition, with 6 plates and 26 other illus.,
8vo, some light spotting but a very good copy in recent boards.
Fenning 60-439 1983 £45

WILES, BERTHA HARRIS   The Fountains of Florentine Sculptors and
Their Followers from Donatello to Bernini. Cambridge, 1933. 220 illus.
hors texte. Frontis. Large 4to, cloth. Ars Libri SB 26-250 1983
$150

WILEY, SAMUEL T.   History of Monongalia County, West
Virginia. Kingwood, 1883. Plates. Cloth. First edition. Felcone
22-264 1983 $85

WILKES, CHARLES   Statement of...a Commander in the U.S.
Navy of the Survey of the Mouth of the Columbia River by the U.S.
Exploring Expedition. Wash., 1846. First edition. Ginsberg 47-762
1983 $25

WILKES, CHARLES   Western America. Phila., 1849. 8vo,
later calf-backed boards, (spine worn). 3 folding maps. Argosy 716-
625 1983 $300

WILKES, JOHN   Letters between the Duke of Grafton,
the Earls of Halifax, Egremont, Chatham, Temple and Talbot...
London, 1769. First edition. 12mo. Half title. Cont. calf.
Heath 48-458 1983 £100

WILKES, THOMAS   A General View of the Stage. London:
printed for J. Coote, and W. Whetstone, 1759. 8vo, cont. calf (spine
worn, hinges weak). First edition. A scarce title. With an engr.
vignette on the title-page. Ximenes 64-576 1983 300

WILKIE, F. B.   "Walks About Chicago". Chicago, 1869.
First edition. Rebacked folding frontis, cloth, ink name,
bookplate, spine ends and corners frayed. King 46-108 1983 $75

WILKINS, H. ST. CLAIR   Reconnoitring in Abyssinia. London,
1870. Folding map mounted on linen in pocket. 10 tinted lithograph
plates, 2 diagrams. Green quarter morocco, raised bands. 8vo. Good.
Edwards 1044-757 1983 £125

WILKINS, JOHN H.   Elements of Astronomy. Boston, 1831.
Stereotype edition. Illus. Calf spine. Marbled boards. Ink inscriptions. Hinges loose. Spine worn, text heavily foxed. King 45-647
1983 $30

WILKINS, W. A.   The Cleverdale Mystery. NY, 1882.
First edition. Pict. cloth, bookplate, minor wear. King 46-357
1983 $35

WILKINS, W. J.   Daily Life and Work in India. T.
Fisher Unwin, 1888. 59 illus. 30 pp ads. Orig. green cloth,
bevelled boards, blocked in black, lettered in gilt, t.e.g. Jarndyce
31-196 1983 £16

WILKINS, WILLIAM   Songs of Study. C. Kegan, Paul & Co.,
1881. First and only edition, name cut from blank portion of title,
8vo, orig. cloth, gilt, a fine copy. Fenning 61-489 1983 £35

WILKINS, WILLIAM GLYDE   First and Early American Editions of
the Works of Charles Dickens. New York, 1968. Grey cloth, v.g.
Jarndyce 31-623 1983 £10.50

WILKINSON, CHARLES   Epitome of the history of Malta and
Gozo. London: printed for William Miller, by W. Bulmer and Co.,
1804. First edition. 8vo. Cont. calf, spine gilt. Rubbed, front
hinge tender. Ximenes 63-644 1983 $85

WILKINSON, EDWARD   Wisdom, a Poem. New York: Isaac
Collins, 1797. Orig. plain wraps. A fine copy. Felcone 22-265
1983 $85

WILKINSON, JAMES   Memoirs of My Own Times. Philadelphia,
1816. 3 vols. and atlas. 8 maps and 11 plans. Orig. boards,
printed labels intact, preserved in folding cloth bases with leather
labels. Reese 18-510 1983 $1,500

WILKINSON, JAMES   Memoirs of My Own Times. Philadelphia:
Abraham Small, 1816. 3 vols. Facs. and tables (most folding).
Full calf. 19 maps and plans, some folding). Paper-covered boards,
calf spine label. Text vols. with light foxing. Atlas boards a bit
worn and creased, water stain on title leaf, maps and plans in perfect
state. Felcone 22-266 1983 $900

WILKINSON, NEVILLE R.   Yvette in Italy and Titania's Palace.
Humphrey Milford, 1923. With 20 plates, 4 in colour, and some other
illus. 4to, orig. cloth. Inscribed by the author "...architect-in-
chief & designer-in-ordinary to her residence..." Fenning 60-442 1983
£12.50

WILKINSON, NORMAN   The Dardanelles. London, 1915. First
edition. Roy. 8vo. Orig. decorated cloth gilt. Coloured frontis.,
29 coloured plates, and numerous illus. by author. 1 full-page map.
Spine slightly soiled. T.e.g. Others uncut. Good. Edwards 1042-
187 1983 £35

WILKINSON, TATE   Memoirs of His Own Life. York:
for the Author, by Wilson, Spence, and Mawman, 1790. First
edition. 4 vols. 12mo. Cont. tree calf, gilt spines with
crimson morocco labels, gilt. Traylen 94-872 1983 £295

WILKINSON, TATE   Memoirs of his own life. Dublin:
printed for P. Byrne, etc., 1791. 3 vols., 12mo, cont. diced calf,
gilt, spines gilt (spines a bit rubbed). First Irish edition.
Half-title present in the first volume. Nice copy of a very scarce
printing. Ximenes 64-577 1983 $350

WILKINSON, TATE   The Wandering Patentee. York:
printed for the Author, 1795. First edition. 4 vols. 12mo.
Half brown morocco, gilt, t.e.g., others uncut. 4 half-titles.
Traylen 94-873 1983 £335

WILKINSON, W.   A Compleat History of the Trials of
the Rebel Lords... London: for the Compiler, (1746?). First edition.
8vo. 19th Century cloth. Heath 48-181 1983 £60

WILKINSON, WILLIAM FRANCIS   The Rector in Search of a Curate.
J. Hatchard and Son, 1848. First edition. 12mo, original cloth,
a fine copy. Hill 165-140 1983 £48

WILKS, M.   Historical Sketches of the South of India.
London, 1810-1817. First edition. 2 folding coloured maps. 3 vols.
4to. Finely bound in full calf, boards ruled with a French fillet.
Gilt inner dentelles, gilt edges. Fine. Edwards 1044-751 1983 £550

WILL, P.   Practical Philosophy of Social Life.
Lansingburth (NY?): Penniman & Bliss, 1805. Comtemporary calf.
First American edition. Gach 95-537 1983 $75

WILL She Bear It? A Tale Of The Weald. London: Samuel Tinsley, 1872.
Orig. green decorated cloth. First edition. Spines and covers rather
worn and soiled. Inner hinges weak or cracked. Fair copy. MacManus
277-92 1983 $125

WILLARD, EMMA   Late American History. N.Y.: A.S.
Barnes & Co., 1856. Map in color. Portrait. Ads. Cloth, frontis.
offsetting. Dawson 471-91 1983 $50

WILLARD, EMMA   A Treatise on the Motive Powers Which
Produce Circulation of the Blood. New York, 1846. 1st ed. Text
illus. Small 8vo. Few cover stains. Morrill 289-248 1983 $45

WILLARD, JOSEPH   Topographical and Historical Sketches of
the Town of Lancaster. Worcester: Printed for the Proprietors, By
Charles Griffin, 1826. Tall untrimmed copy. Some soiling. Part of
front plain wrapper missing. Presentation copy. Jenkins 152-233 1983
$100

WILLARD, SIMON   The Columbian Union, Containing General
and Particular Explanations of Government and the Columbian Constitution... Albany: The author, 1815. Calf-backed boards, foxed, boards
rubbed. Signature "Apollos Kent/Salem/Ashtabula County/ Ohio".
Felcone 22-267 1983 $50

WILLARD, T. A.   Bride of the Rain God. Cleveland: The
Burrows Bros. Co., (1930). First edition. Frontispiece and 10
full-page plates. Green cloth. Dj is whole but is chipped and has a
few small tears. Fine in the pictorial silver dj printed in black.
Bradley 64-187 1983 $25

WILLARD, WARREN WYETH   Steeple Jim. Princeton, N.J., Princeton
Publishing House, 1929. 1st ed. 3 illus. 8vo. Morrill 288-536
1983 $20

WILLCOCKS, MARY   Caraboo. A Narrative of a Singular
Imposition... Bristol: by J.M. Gutch..., 1817. First edition.
8vo. 2 portraits, one folding. Half title. Wrappers. Heath
48-208 1983 £75

WILLERS, DIEDRICH   The Centennial Celebration of General
Sullivan's Campaign Against the Iroquois, in 1779. Waterloo, N.Y.:
Observer Steam Print, 1880. First edition. Illus. Orig. cloth.
Jenkins 152-522 1983 $50

WILLES, THOMAS   A Word in Season, for a Warning to
England. London, 1659. 1st ed. Frontispiece & attached leaf of
text. 12mo, contemporary calf, leather label. Rubbed, covers loose,
some repair to frontispiece and leaf of text. Morrill 287-515 1983
$25

WILLETT, EDWARD   Letters addressed to Mrs. Bellamy,
occasioned by her apology. London: printed and sold by J. Rozea;
sold also by G. Robinson, n.d. (1785). 8vo, modern marbled boards,
1st edition. A few faint dampstains, but a nice copy, complete
with half-title. Ximenes 64-579 1983 $250

WILLEY, A.   Convergence in Evolution. 1911. 8vo,
cloth. 12 text-figures. Wheldon 160-201 1983 £12

WILLEY, AUSTON   The History of the Antislavery Cause in
State and Nation. Portland, 1886. 1st ed. Illus, orig. pict. cloth,
ex-library. Argosy 710-28 1983 $35

WILLIAM HIGGINS AND SONS   The growth, treatment, and manufacture
of flax into linen. Salford: Jackson, n.d. (1851). 8vo. Orig.
yellow printed wrappers. Folding lithographed plate. Ximenes 63-
572 1983 $65

WILLIAM OF SWEDEN, PRINCE   Wild African Animals I Have Known. Boston, 1925. First American edition. 211 illus. from photographs by Oskar Olson. 4to. Morrill 290-595 1983 $25

WILLIAMS, A. LUKYN   Famines in India. London, 1876. 8vo. Orig. cloth. Worn. Good. Edwards 1044-752 1983 £14

WILLIAMS, ALFRED   Round About the Upper Thames. London, 1922. First edition. Author's autograph signature. From the library of Leonard Clark, with his autograph signature and bookplate. Good copy only. Rota 230-640 1983 £20

WILLIAMS, ALFRED   Villages of the White Horse. London, 1913. First edition. Covers marked and worn and foxing throughout. Author's autograph signature. Leonard Clark's copy, with his autograph signature and bookplate. Good. Rota 230-638 1983 £20

WILLIAMS, ALFRED   A Wiltshire Village. London, 1912. First edition. Covers marked and worn and some foxing throughout. Author's autograph signature. Leonard Clark's copy, with his autograph signature and bookplate. Good. Rota 230-637 1983 £20

WILLIAMS, ALFRED M.   Sam Houston and the War of Independence in Tax. Boston, 1895. Fld. map. A fine copy. Jenkins 151-134 1983 $60

WILLIAMS, AMOS   Scrap Book Amos Williams and Early Danville, Illinois. Danville: Recording & Statistical Corp., n.d. Stiff printed wrappers. Illus. Presentation copy from the Woodbury family. Fine. Jenkins 152-167 1983 $50

WILLIAMS, BASIL   Erskine Childers 1870-1922. Privately printed, 1926. First edition. Wrappers a little dust-marked. Very nice. Rota 231-116 1983 £21

WILLIAMS, BASIL   The Life of William Pitt, Earl of Chatham. London, 1913. 2 vols. 8vo. Half green crushed levant morocco, gilt, gilt panelled spines, t.e.g. 3 portraits and 3 coloured folding maps. Traylen 94-661 1983 £32

WILLIAMS, BEN AMES   Splendor. New York, (1927). 1st ed. 6-line inscription by author. 8vo, orig. boards, cloth back. Morrill 286-697 1983 $20

WILLIAMS, BEN AMES   The Strange Woman. Camb., 1941. Advance reading copy, paperwraps, cover slightly soiled and worn, else good or better. Quill & Brush 54-1542 1983 $35

WILLIAMS, BEN AMES   Time of Peace. B, 1942. Advance copy, printed paperwraps, very good. Quill & Brush 54-1543 1983 $50

WILLIAMS, BENJAMIN SAMUEL (1822-1890)   The Orchid Grower's Manual. (1894) 1973. 7th (last edition). 300 illus. Imp. 8vo. cloth. A facsimile reprint in an enlarged format. Wheldon 160-2065 1983 £39

WILLIAMS, CHARLES   The Descent of the Dove. London, 1939. First edition. Dust wrapper. Fine. Rota 231-629 1983 £15

WILLIAMS, CHARLES   The Region of the Summer Stars. London, 1944. First edition. Frayed dust wrapper. Fine. Rota 231-630 1983 £15

WILLIAMS, CHARLES   A Short Life of Shakespeare. Oxford, 1933. First edition. Very good. Rota 230-643 1983 £12

WILLIAMS, CHARLES   Witchcraft. London, 1941. First English edition. Slightly torn, strengthened dustwrapper. Fine. Jolliffe 26-597 1983 £25

WILLIAMS, CHARLES HANBURY   A dialogue between G--s E---e and B--b D---n. London: Taylor, 1741. First edition. Folio. Disbound. An uncut copy. Ximenes 63-388 1983 $250

WILLIAMS, CHAUNCEY PRATT   Lone Elk. Denver: John Van Male, 1935-36. 2 vols. Wrappers. Dawson 471-307 1983 $30

WILLIAMS, FREDERIC C.   Journalistic Jumbles or Trippings in Type. Field & Tuer, n.d. Oblong 8vo. Frontis. 15 text vignettes. Cream vellum, gilt. Printed on vellum thru'out. 14pp of ads. Greer 40-126 1983 £45

WILLIAMS, FREDERICK S.   Our Iron Roads. Ingram, Cooke, and Co., 1852. First edition, with a frontis. and additional engraved title-page, and with many full-page and other illus., final leaf blank but for imprint, 8vo, orig. red cloth, gilt. Fenning 60-444 1983 £38.50

WILLIAMS, GARDNER F.   The diamond mines of South Africa. New York: Macmillan, 1902. 8vo. Folding map. 30 plates (5 colored). Orig. cloth. Lightly rubbed. Adelson Africa-146 1983 $150

WILLIAMS, GEORGE C. F.   The Fine Library of Dr. George C. F. Williams Sold by His Order. NY, 1926. Cloth-backed boards, paper label. Argosy 710-467 1983 $35

WILLIAMS, H. N.   The Women Bonapartes. London, 1908. First edition. Portrait frontis. 34 plates. 2 vols. Gilt. Very slightly soiled. 8vo. Orig. cloth. Good. Edwards 1042-514 1983 £30

WILLIAMS, HELEN MARIA   A Residence in France. Elizabeth Town: Shepard Kollock for Cornelius Davis, 1798. Full calf. Nice. Felcone 19-60 1983 $50

WILLIAMS, IOLO A.   Points in 18th Century Verse. London: Constable & Co., 1934. First edition. 8vo. Parchment backed marbled boards. Limited to 500 copies. A few facsimile title pages. Fine. Oak Knoll 48-492 1983 $160

WILLIAMS, IOLO A.   Points in Eighteenth-Century Verse. London, 1934. 8vo. Orig. vellum backed marbled boards, uncut edges. 4 plates and 9 facsimiles. Limited edition of 500 copies. Traylen 94-874 1983 £70

WILLIAMS, J. J.   The Isthmus of Tehuanatepec: Being the Results of a Survey for a Railroad to Connect the Atlantic and the Pacific Oceans. New York, 1852. First edition. 14 tinted lithographic plates, large folding map, table, plan. Orig. brown cloth. Light foxing. With printed errata slip. Fine. Jenkins 152-523 1983 $700

WILLIAMS, J. WHITRIDGE   A Sketch of the History of Obstetrics in the United States up to 1860. N.p., ca. 1904. Tall 8vo, cloth; ex-lib. First separate edition. Argosy 713-571 1983 $35

WILLIAMS, JAMES   Seventy-Five Years on the Border. Kansas City, 9112. Illus. Orig. cloth. First edition. Ginsberg 47-552 1983 $45

WILLIAMS, JOHN   An Answer to the Address Presented to the Ministers of the Church of England. Printed for Ric. Chiswell, 1688. First edition, including imprimatur leaf, 4to, wrapper. Fenning 61-490 1983 £14.50

WILLIAMS, JOHN   A Discourse Concerning the Celebration of Divine Service, in an Unknown Tongue. Printed for Richard Chiswell, 1685. First edition, including leaf of ad. and errata, 4to, wrapper, a very good copy. Fenning 61-491 1983 £14.50

WILLIAMS, JOHN   The Papist Represented. Printed for Ric. Chiswell, 1687. First edition, 4to, wrapper. Fenning 61-492 1983 £18.50

WILLIAMS, JOHN   A Short Discourse Concerning the Churches Authority in Matters of Faith. Printed for Randal Taylor, 1687. First edition, 4to, wrapper, a very good copy. Fenning 61-495 1983 £16.50

WILLIAMS, JOHN (1761-1818)   The children of Thespis, a poem. London: printed for Kirby and Co., 1792. 12mo, 19th-cent. half maroon morocco, spine gilt (trifle rubbed). 13th edition; first collected edition. Lacks a half-title, signature torn from blank corner of title, else a very good copy. Ximenes 64-580 1983 $200

WILLIAMS, JOHN (1761-1818)   The eccentricities of John Edwin, comedian. London: printed for J. Strahan, n.d. (1791). 2 vols., 8vo, cont. half calf, spines gilt (spines rather rubbed). First ed. Half-titles present, and a leaf of ads at the end of Vol. II. Uncommon. Ximenes 64-581 1983 $300

WILLIAMS, JOHN (1761-1818)   The eccentricities of John Edwin, comedian. Dublin: printed by Zachariah Jackson, for P. Byrne, etc., 1791. 2 vols., 12mo, cont. calf, spines gilt, contrasting morocco labels (slight stains). First Irish edition. A fine set. Very scarce. Ximenes 64-582 1982 $225

WILLIAMS, JOHN (1761-1818)   The Life of the late Earl of Barrymore. London: printed for H. D. Symonds, 1793. maroon half calf, 1st edition. Bound in by a late owner are notes, portraits, and a large broadside showing the results of a parliamentary election in which Barrymore participated. With a frontis. portrait in sepia. Wanting a half-title; margins uncut. Ximenes 64-583 1983 $300

WILLIAMS, JOHN (1761-1818)   The pin-basket to the children of Thespis. London: printed for H. D. Symonds; and T. Bellamy, 1797. 12mo, original pink boards, light blue paper backstrip, printed paper label (some wear, but sound; a bit soiled). First edition. An uncut copy in original condition. Ximenes 64-584 1983 $225

WILLIAMS, JOHN (1761-1818)   Satires and biography. London: printed for Lackington and Allen; and H. D. Symonds, n.d. (1800). 8vo, cont. calf (rather worn). 1st edition. Ximenes 64-585 1983 $200

WILLIAMS, JOHN H.   A Brief History of the Rise and Progress of the Independent Order of Odd Fellows in the United States. Boston, 1845. Orig. printed wraps. First edition. Ginsberg 46-343 1983 $35

WILLIAMS, JOHN LEE   The Territory of Florida. New York: A.T. Goodrich, 1837. Frontis. 2 plates. Folding map lacking, orig. cloth. First edition. Scattered foxing. Felcone 22-66 1983 $150

WILLIAMS, JOHN S.   History of the Invasion and Capture of Washington and of the Events which Preceded and Followed. New York, 1857. Cloth, hinges cracking. Ex. lib. Reese 19-591 1983 $25

WILLIAMS, JOSEPH   An Essay on the Use of Narcotics and Other Remedial Agents Calculated to Produce Sleep in the Treatment of Insanity. London, 1845. 1st ed. Small 8vo. Few pencil marks in text. Morrill 289-249 1983 $25

WILLIAMS, M.   Modern India and the Indians. London, 1878. Second edition. 8vo. Orig. cloth. Good. Edwards 1044-755 1983 £18

WILLIAMS, MARY   The Dickens Concordance. Francis Griffiths, 1907. First edition, half title, 6 pp ads. Orig. green cloth, t.e.g. Jarndyce 31-624 1983 £10.50

WILLIAMS, MEADE C.   Early Mackinac. A Sketch, Historical & Descriptive. St. Louis, 1901. 3rd ed., rev. & enlarged. 12mo, red pr. wrs. Argosy 710-313 1983 $25

WILLIAMS, MICHAEL   Some London Theatres, Past and Present. Sampson Low, 1883. First edition, errata slip, 32 pp ads. Orig. brown cloth, v.g. Jarndyce 31-307 1983 £14.50

WILLIAMS, OSCAR   The Golden Darkness. New Haven: Yale, 1921. Printed wraps. over boards. First edition. Very slight chipping along top overlap edge of wrapper, else fine. Reese 20-1135 1983 $65

WILLIAMS, OSCAR   New Poems: 1940, An Anthology of British and American Verse. New York: 1941. First edition. Cloth. Fine in worn dust jacket. Bradley 66-367 1983 $27.50

WILLIAMS, OTHNIEL S.   The Early History of Clinton. Clinton, L.W. Payne, 1848. Orig. printed wraps. Ginsberg 46-545 1983 $125

WILLIAMS, PETER   Letters concerning Education. London: by Messrs Rivington..., 1785. First edition. 8vo. Orig. boards. One joint repaired. Very good copy. Heath 48-459 1983 £60

WILLIAMS, PETER   Letters concerning Education addressed to a Gentleman... London: Rivington..., 1785. First edition. 8vo. Orig. boards. Front cover detached. Heath 48-42 1983 £60

WILLIAMS, ROBERT FOLKESTONE   Shakespeare and His Friends. London: Colburn, 1838. First edition. 3 vols. 3/4 morocco, t.e.g. Bound without half-titles (as issued?). Very good. MacManus 280-5563 1983 $75

WILLIAMS, ROBERT FOLKESTONE   Shakespeare and His Friends. Henry Colburn, 1838. First edition. 3 vols. 4 pp. ads. vol. II. Orig. boards, cloth spines, paper labels (chipped). Inner hinges weak, otherwise good. Jarndyce 30-592 1983 £38

WILLIAMS, ROBERT FOLKESTONE   The Youth of Shakespeare. London: Colburn, 1839. First edition. 3 vols. Orig. cloth-backed boards. Paper labels. Ex-library set with the usual marks of acession and one outer hinge torn. Very good, tight copy. MacManus 280-5564 1983 $125

WILLIAMS, ROGER   A Key into the Language of America. Providence, 1827. Frontis. 8vo, disbound. Argosy 716-492 1983 $35

WILLIAMS, S. WELLS   Our Relations with the Chinese Empire. San Francisco, 1877. Orig. printed wraps. First edition. Ginsberg 46-131 1983 $75

WILLIAMS, SAMUEL   Sketches of the War Between the United States and the British Isles... Rutland, 1815. Two vols. bound in one. Orig. boards, untrimmed. One board detached, and a bit of age staining, otherwise very good. Reese 18-439 1983 $85

WILLIAMS, SIDNEY HERBERT   A Bibliography of the Writings of Lewis Carroll. London, 1924. 8vo, two-tone cloth; eight facs. title pages. One of 700 numbered copies. Duschnes 240-38 1983 $100

WILLIAMS, SIDNEY HERBERT   Bibliography of the Writings of Lewis Carroll. London, 1924. Facs. Title-pages. Tall 8vo; d.w. One of 700 numbered copies. Fine copy. Argosy 714-137 1983 $75

WILLIAMS, STEPHEN W.   American Medical Biography. Greenfield, Mass., 1845. 1st ed. Portraits. 8vo. Ex-library; rubbed; backstrip partly torn; cracks along front hinge. Morrill 289-250 1983 $35

WILLIAMS, TENNESSEE   Battle of Angles. Murray: Pharos Numbers 1 & 2, 1945. Orig. printed wraps. First edition. Slight crease at one corner of the front wrapper, and some slight sunning and use of the overlap edges, but essentially a fine copy. Reese 20-1136 1983 $300

WILLIAMS, TENNESSEE   It Happened the Day the Sun Rose. Los Angeles, 1981. First edition. Title page woodcut by Achilles Droungas. Black patterned cloth stamped in gilt, uncut. One of 300 numbered copies, signed by the author. Fine. Houle 22-966 1983 $80

WILLIAMS, TENNESSEE   Memoirs. N.Y., Doubleday, 1975. Illus. Gilt stamped green cloth. One of 400 copies, signed by Williams. Slipcase. Houle 22-967 1983 $165

WILLIAMS, TENNESSEE   Moise and the World of Reason. New York: (1975). First edition. Dark blue morocco. 1/350 signed. Very fine. Bradley 66-371 1983 $85

WILLIAMS, TENNESSEE   The Roman Spring of Mrs. Stone. (NY, 1950). Signed inscription from "this old thing" Tennessee Williams on front end paper, endpapers slightly offset, top of spine creased, very good in very good dustwrapper. Quill & Brush 54-1547 1983 $100

WILLIAMS, TENNESSEE   The Roman Spring of Mrs. Stone. (N.Y., 1950). First edition. Fine. Autographed by the author. Argosy 714-898 1983 $50

WILLIAMS, TENNESSEE   A Streetcar Named Desire. (New York): A New Directions Book, (1947). First edition. Tall 8vo, orig. pictorial boards. Dust jacket. Fine. Jaffe 1-400 1983 $350

WILLIAMS, TENNESSEE   Streetcar Named Desire. (N.Y., New Directions, 1947). First edition. Dust jacket (sm. nick), else a fine fresh copy. Houle 21-944 1983 $250

WILLIAMS, TENNESSEE   Tennessee William's Letters to Donald Wyndham 1940-1965. Verona, Sandy Campbell, 1976. First edition. Acetate jacket. Slipcase. One of 500 numbered copies on Favini paper. Printed under the supervision of Martino Mardersteig. Houle 22-969 1983 $125

WILLIAMS, WILLIAM   The Duty and Interest of a People, Among whom Religion has been Planted. Boston: S. Kneeland and T. Green, 1736. Cont. full calf. Felcone 22-57 1983 $125

WILLIAMS, WILLIAM   The Great Salvation Revealed and Offered in the Gospel Explained, and an Hearty Acceptance of It Urged. Boston: T. Crump for S. Gerrish and D. Henchman, 1717. Cont. calf (front hinge repaired). Endsheets wanting. Felcone 22-268 1983 $75

WILLIAMS, WILLIAM CARLOS   The Broken Span. Norfolk, Conn., (1941). First edition. Thin 8vo, pr. wrs.; darkened. Argosy 714-825 1983 $20

WILLIAMS, WILLIAM CARLOS   Build-Up. N.Y., Random (1952). First edition. Dust jacket. Fine copy. Houle 21-945 1983 $75

WILLIAMS, WILLIAM CARLOS   The Build-Up. New York: (1942). First edition, first printing. Boards and cloth. New Directions sticker over Random House imprint on title page. Fine in dust jacket with inner mend. Bradley 66-369 1983 $35

WILLIAMS, WILLIAM CARLOS   The Complete Collected Poems...1906-1938. Norfolk, (1938). First binding. Review copy, so stamped on front endpaper. Fine. Bromer 25-127 1983 $85

WILLIAMS, WILLIAM CARLOS   In the American Grain. New York: Albert & Charles Boni, 1925. Black cloth, first edition, bookplate, and a couple of small spots at edges, otherwise a very good copy. Reese 20-1039 1983 $35

WILLIAMS, WILLIAM CARLOS   Kora in Hell: Improvisations. Bos., 1920. Boards soiled and worn, edges of spine chipped, good, limited to 1000 copies. Quill & Brush 54-1551 1983 $100

WILLIAMS, WILLIAM CARLOS   Kora in Hell. Boston: The Four Seas Co., 1920. First edition. Frontis. Thin tall 8vo, pr. boards. The boards are darkened & rubbed, and the front flyleaf is lacking. Argosy 714-826 1983 $60

WILLIAMS, WILLIAM CARLOS   Kora in Hell. Boston, 1920. First edition. Extremities rubbed, label removed from foot of spine. Erasure from flyleaf. Good reading copy. Rota 230-644 1983 £25

WILLIAMS, WILLIAM CARLOS   A Note on the Turn of the View Toward Poetic Technique. Hanover, (1958). Printed wrapper. First separate edition. Light soil, else fine. Reese 20-1142 1983 $85

WILLIAMS, WILLIAM CARLOS   The Selected Letters... N.Y., McDowell, Obolensky, (1957). 8vo. Orig. cloth in orig. box with paper label. 1st ed. Some flaking of color on spine lettering area. i of 75 specially bound copies, numbered and signed by Williams. Extremely scarce, fine. O'Neal 50-56 1983 $275

WILLIAMS, WILLIAM CARLOS   The Selected Letters. NY, (1957). Signed, fine in dustwrapper with few tiny chips and tears. Quill & Brush 54-1555 1983 $135

WILLIAMS, WILLIAM CARLOS   Sour Grapes: A Book of Poems. B, 1921. Cover skinned, endpapers stamped, spine edges slightly worn, spine label chipped, pages poorly opened (one torn), good. Quill & Brush 54-1554 1983 $200

WILLIAMS, WILLIAM CARLOS   The Tempers. London: Elkin Mathews, 1913. Small 16mo, gilt boards. First edition. Bookplate of the "Library of the Andiron Club," some slight soiling, and the spine is a trifle rubbed. Reese 20-1138 1983 $350

WILLIAMS, WILLIAM CARLOS   The Wedge. (N.p.): The Cummington Press, 1944. Small octavo. Pastepaper boards. First edition. One of 380 copies on Dacian paper. There are very slight traces of rubbing at the extremity tips, otherwise a fine copy. Reese 20-1140 1983 $275

WILLIAMS, WILLIAM FRITH   An Historical and Statistical Account of the Bermudas, from their Discovery to the present Time. London: T. C. Newby, 1848. First (only) edition, 8vo, modern half morocco gilt, marbled boards. Folding colored map. Advertisement leaf, library blind-stamp on title, some foxing, but a very good copy. Trebizond 18-171 1983 $450

WILLIAM'S Tour with His Papa. J. Fairburn, nd (1845). 14 woodcuts. Pink pictorial wrappers. Bound in black calf backed marbled bds. with 3 blank leaves at front & 32 blank leaves at rear, blank pp. some foxing & fr. cvr. sl. dust soiled. Earl of Rosebery's copy with "Durdans" stamp on fr. cvr. & his bookpl. fr. ep. Scarce, nice copy. Hodgkins 27-217 1983 £45

WILLIAMSON, DAVID BRAINERD   Illustrated Life, Services, Martyrdom, and Funeral of Abraham Lincoln. Philadelphia, Peterson, (1865). Illustrated. 12mo. Small gash on back hinge at backstrip. Morrill 290-596 1983 $20

WILLIAMSON, GEORGE C.   Francesco Raibolini, Called Francia. London: George Bell & Sons, 1907. 42 plates. Small 4to. Cloth. Ars Libri 33-147 1983 $30

WILLIAMSON, GEORGE C.   George C. Pinwell & His Works. Bell, 1900. 1st edn. Limited to 350 copies. Frontis. & 51 illus. Apple green cloth, t.e.g. others uncut (bkstrip faded, corners bumped, bk-strip some soiling & titling sl. rubbed), scarce, v.g. Hodgkins 27-576 1983 £45

WILLIAMSON, GEORGE C.   John Russell, R.A. George Bell, 1894. First edition, with 52 plates and 38 other illus., and a double-page genealogical table, folio, orig. cloth gilt, t.e.g., very light discolouration of the binding but otherwise a nice copy. Fenning 61-379 1983 £125

WILLIAMSON, GEORGE C   Murray Marks and His Friends, A Tribute of Regard. Lond 1919. Illus., cloth, ink inscription, worn and very soiled copy. King 46-415 1983 $25

WILLIAMSON, HENRY   The Ackymals. N.p.: The Windsor Press, 1929. First edition. Orig. cloth-backed decorated boards. One of 225 copies signed by author. Foot of spine slightly worn. Endpapers very slightly browned. In a worn publisher's box. Very good. Mac-Manus 280-5565 1983 $125

WILLIAMSON, HENRY   The Gold Falcon or The Haggard of Love. London: Faber & Faber Limited, (1933). First edition. 8vo. Orig. cloth. Dust jacket. Fine copy. Jaffe 1-401 1983 $85

WILLIAMSON, HENRY   The Linhay on the Downs. London: Elkin Mathews, 1929. Small 4to. Orig. green dustwrapper. Limited edition of 530 copies, numbered and intialed by the author. Mint. Traylen 94-878 1983 £65

WILLIAMSON, HENRY   The Linhay on the Downs. London: Elkin Mathews & Marrot, 1929. First edition. Orig. boards. Dust jacket. One of 530 copies signed by author. Fine. MacManus 280-5567 1983 $65

WILLIAMSON, HENRY   Norfolk Life. London, 1943. First edition. 8vo. Cloth. Orig. dustwrapper. Traylen 94-880 1983 £18

WILLIAMSON, HENRY   The Pathway. London: Jonathan Cape, (1928). First edition. Orig. green cloth. Presentation copy inscribed to Wm. H. McCarthy, dated March 2, 1931. Spine and covers slightly faded and rubbed. A Few very small tears to the spine ends. Good. MacManus 280-5569 1983 $150

WILLIAMSON, HENRY   The Patriot's Progress... London, 1930. Roy. 8vo. Cloth. Orig. dustwrapper. Illus. by William Kermode. First edition. Traylen 94-881 1983 $30

WILLIAMSON, HENRY   The Phasian Bird. London, 1948. First edition. Orig. dustwrapper. Traylen 94-882 1983 £12.50

WILLIAMSON, HENRY   The Scanderoon. London, 1972. 8vo. Blue morocco, gilt, edges gilt, preserved in a slip-case. Limited edition of 250 numbered copies, signed by the author, with illus. by Ken Lilly. Traylen 94-886 1983 £42

WILLIAMSON, HENRY   The Star-Born. London: Faber & Faber, (1933). First edition. Orig. vellum. One of 70 copies printed on handmade paper and signed by H. Williamson. Spine faded. A bit stained. Very good. MacManus 280-5574 1983 $250

WILLIAMSON, HENRY   The Sun in the Sands. London, 1945. First edition. 8vo. Cloth. Orig. dustwrapper. Portrait. Traylen 93-888 1983 £16

WILLIAMSON, HENRY   Tarka the Otter. London, 1932. First illus. edition. Numerous full-page black and white by Charles Tunnicliffe. Chipped dustwrapper. Very good. Jolliffe 26-598 1983 £45

WILLIAMSON, HENRY   The Wet Flanders Plain. (London: The Beaumont Press, 1929). First edition. Cover & title-page decorated by R. Schwabe. Orig. vellum-backed boards. One of 80 copies signed by auther, illustrator and publisher. Fine. MacManus 280-5575 1983 $185

WILLIAMSON, HENRY   The Wet Flanders Plain. London: the Beaumont Press, 1929. Roy. 8vo. Boards, buckram spine. Coloured vignette on title-page by Randolph Schwabe. Limited edition of 320 numbered copies. Traylen 94-889 1983 £38

WILLIAMSON, HUGH ROSS   Gods & Mortals in Love. Country Life, 1935. 4to. Colour frontis. 8 colour plates. Blue grey cloth. Extra colour plate from a magazine loosely inserted. Greer 40-96 1983 £38

WILLIAMSOM, JOSEPH   A Bibliography of the State of Maine... Portland: Thurston Print, 1896. 2 vols., cloth, hinges weakening, outer leaves browned. Dawson 470-309 1983 $60

WILLIAMSON, K.   The Atlantic Islands, a study of the Faeroe life and scene. 1948. 8vo, cloth. Wheldon 160-454 1983 £18

WILLIAMSON, R. J. T.   History of the Old County Regiment of Lancashire Militia. London, 1888. 8vo. Orig. cloth. Photographic frontis. 3 photographic and 16 other plates. Spine slightly faded. Good. Edwards 1042-562 1983 £35

WILLIAMSON, ROBERT W.   Religion and Social Organization in Central Polynesia. Cambridge, 1937. First edition. Thick 8vo, dust jacket, very good. Houle 21-946 1983 $75

WILLIAMSON, T.   The East India Vade-Mecum. London, 1810. 2 vols. Half calf, slight wear. 8vo. With the bookplate of Robert Smyth, Lt. Col. of the Bengal Artillery. Good. Edwards 1044-756 1983 £95

WILLIAMSON, T   The European in India. London: Edward Orme, 1813. First edition. 4to. 20 hand-colored plates. Orig. full red morocco gilt, skillfully rebacked, a.e.g. 1 plate foxed. Adelson Africa-147 1983 $550

WILLINGHAM, CALDER   End As A Man. New York: Vanguard Press, Inc., (1947). First edition. 8vo. Orig. cloth. Dust jacket. Fine copy. Jaffe 1-402 1983 $100

WILLIS, B.   Index to the Stratography of North America. Washington, U. S. Geol. Survey, 1912. 19 figures, 5 folding tables and a coloured geological map, 4to, new cloth (map in picket at back). Wheldon 160-1487 1983 £20

WILLIS, FRANCIS   A Treatise on Mental Derangement. London, 1823. 1st ed. 8vo. Orig. boards, cloth back, paper label. Rubbed; lacks front endleaf. Morrill 289-251 1983 $37.50

WILLIS, J. C.   The Birth and Spread of Plants. Geneva, 1949. 8vo, cloth, trifle marked. A few pencil annotations. Wheldon 160-1582 1983 £20

WILLIS, J. C.   A Dictionary of the Flowering Plants and Ferns. Cambridge, (1931). Sixth edition, 8vo, cloth, faded. Wheldon 160-1581 1983 £12

WILLIS, NATHANIEL P.   American Scenery. London, Virtue, 1852. Illus. from drawings by W.H. Bartlett. 2 vols. 4to. 2 engraved titles, map, 117 steel engraved plates. Maroon cloth dec. in gold & blind, aeg. Corners bumped, light to mod. foxing to about half the plates (mostly in margins). Very good set. O'Neal 50-57 1983 $500

WILLIS, NATHANIEL P.   Canadian Scenery. London, Virtue, 1842. Illus. from drawings by W.H. Bartlett. 2 vols. 4to. Map, 2 engraved vignette titles, 117 steel-engraved plates. Cont. half green morocco & marbled boards. Without portrait of Bartlett. Mod. browning, mostly to margins, of about half the plates. Nice copy. O'Neal 50-58 1983 $850

WILLIS, NATHANIEL P   The Poems, Sacred, Passionate, and Humorous. NY, 1850. First edition. Frontis., extra engr. title. Orig. blind-stamped cloth, (backstrip lightly faded, faded). Argosy 716-422 1983 $50

WILLIS, THOMAS   Pathologiae Cerebri et Nervosi Generis Specimen. Londini, Typis S. Roycroft, Impensis Jo. Martyn, 1678. 12mo, cont. calf, worn, insect damaged, title stained, some smudges throughout, first several leaves and last 2 leaves strengthened and mended in outer blank edge. Ravenstree 97-100 1983 $250

WILLISON, JOHN   Reminiscences, Political and Personal. Toronto: M&S, 1919. 23cm. Frontis. and 8 portrait illus. Maroon cloth. Gilt titles. A fine copy in fine dust jacket. McGahern 54-180 1983 $20

WILLISON, JOHN   Sir George Parkin. A Biography. London: Macmillan, 1929. 22cm. Frontis. portrait and 3 plates. Blue cloth. Very good. McGahern 53-174 1983 $20

WILLISON, JOHN   Sir Wilfrid Laurier and the Liberal Party. Toronto: George N. Morang & Co., 1903. 24cm. 2 vols. Photogravure frontis. portrait, the limited edition of 100 copies, this being no. 11. Signed by the publisher. Full tan linen with paper labels. Extra labels tipped in. Very good. McGahern 54-181 1983 $85

WILLIUS, FREDERICK   A History of the Heart and Circulation. Philadelphia, 1948. First edition. 8vo. Orig. binding. Fye H-3-628 1983 $50

WILLKOMM, M.   Prodromus Florae Hispanicae. Stuttgart, 1870-80, 1893. 3 vols. and supplement, together 4 vols. in 2, 8vo, cloth. Rare original printing. Slight dampstaining at the beginning of vol. 1 but generally a good copy. Wheldon 160-1782 1983 £150

WILLMOTT, E.   The Genus Rosa. 1914. Illus. in black and white, 132 plates in colours. 2 vols., folio, half morocco, t.e.g. Some slight offsetting of a few plates on the text but generally a good copy. Wheldon 160-112 1983 £750

WILLOUGHBY, JOHN C.   East Africa and its big game. London: Longmans, Green, 1889. 8vo. Folding map. 18 plates. Orig. decorated cloth. Rubbed. Label removed from spine. Adelson Africa-148 1983 $160

WILLS, ALFRED   Wanderings among the High Alps. Richard Bentley, 1858. Small 8vo, a.e.g., 4 tinted litho plates, 4 wood-engraved plates, and maps in the text, orig. pictorial green cloth, prize label inside the front cover. Bickersteth 77-252 1983 £48

WILLSON, BECKLES   The Great Company. Toronto: The Copp, Clark Company, 1899. Illustrations. Original pictorial cloth. First edition. Fine copy. Jenkins 153-215 1983 $125

WILLSON, BECKLES   The Life and Letters of James Wolfe. London, 1909. First edition. Illustrations and plans. 8vo, ex-library, nice. Morrill 290-597 1983 $25

WILLSON, BECKLES   Lord Strathcona. The Story of his
Life. London: Methuen & Co., 1902. 22cm. 8 plates. Red cloth.
Very good. McGahern 53-173 1983 $20

WILLUGHBY, FRANCIS   De Historia Piscium. (London, 1686).
Facsimile Reprint, New York, 1978. 188 plates, 4to, art leather.
Wheldon 160-1012 1983 £47

WILLUGHBY, FRANCIS   Ornithologiae libri tres. 1676.
Folio, cont. calf (neatly repaired), engraved plates. Small tears
in 3 plates repaired without loss of surface and a little minor
browning and staining, but a large and generally clean copy of the
rare first edition, first issue with the title printed in red and
black. Wheldon 160-113 1983 £600

WILLUMSEN, J.-F.   La jeunesse du peintre El Greco.
Paris: G. Cres, 1927. 106 plates. Numerous text illus. Stout
4to. Wrappers. Edition limited to 1100 numbered copies. Ars
Libri 32-286 1983 $175

WILLYAMS, JANE LOUISA   Chillon. J. Hatchard, 1845. First
edition, 2 vols., half title and (36)pp ads. vol. II. Orig. blue
cloth, sl. mottled. Jarndyce 30-593 1983 £28

WILM, HUBERT   Die Gotische Holzfigur. Leipzig, 1923.
Large 4to, 196 plates, 312 illus. Cloth. Ars Libri SB 26-251 1983
$15-

WILM, HUBERT   Die Sammlung Georg Schuster. Munchen,
1937. 45, (3)pp., 50 plates with 95 illus. Frontis. Lrg. 4to.
Cloth. Ars Libri SB 26-252 1983 $100

WILMANUS, KARL   Zur Psychopathologie Des Landstreichers.
Leipzig: Johann A. Barth, 1906. First edition. Cloth spine, paper
label, boards. Gach 95-539 1983 $40

WILSON, ALEXANDER (1766-1813)   American Ornithology. (Philadelphia,
1823). Plate volume only. 76 hand colored engr. plates. New morocco
bonding. All plates in fine condition. Reese 19-592 1983 $14,500

WILSON, ALEXANDER (1766-1813)   American Ornithology. Edinburgh,
1831. Portrait and vignette titles. 4 vols. 12mo. Orig. cloth.
Wheldon 160-926 1983 £35

WILSON, ALEXANDER (1766-1813)   The Foresters. Newton, Pa.: S. Seigfried & J. Wilson, July 1818. Full calf (worn, covers detached).
First edition. Felcone 22-269 1983 $85

WILSON, ALEXANDER (1766-1813)   The Foresters. West Chester, Pa.:
Joseph Painter, 1838. Full calf (worn, covers detached). Felcone
22-270 1983 $35

WILSON, AMOS   The Sweets of Solitude! or Directions
to Mankind how they may be happy in a 'Miserable World!'. Boston:
John Wilkey, 1822. 2nd ed., 8vo, original printed wrappers, sewn as
issued, uncut copy, frontis. woodcut illus., repeated on back wrappers
(torn but complete). Margins of leaves soiled, but a very good copy
of a fragile work. Trebizond 18-217 1983 $85

WILSON, AUGUSTA JANE EVANS   Inez: A Tale of the Alamo. New York:
Harper & Bros., 1855. Orig. cloth, first edition, very slight
scattered foxing, and short snags in the crown and toe of the backstrip,
otherwise a fine copy. Reese 19-549 1983 $125

WILSON, C. B.   The Copepods of the Woods Hole Region,
Massachusetts. Washington, 1932. 41 plates (1 coloured), 8vo, 316
text-figures, new cloth. Wheldon 160-1352 1983 £30

WILSON, CAROL GREEN   California Yankee. Claremont, Saunders
Press, 1946. First edition. Illus. Dust jacket. One of 1,500
copies. Signed by the author. Very good. Houle 21-1188 1983 $22.50

WILSON, DANIEL   Prehistoric Man. Cambridge: Macmillan,
1862. First edition, with 2 coloured plates, 1 other plate and 69
text illus., including half-titles, 2 vols., 8vo, a very good copy
in cont. half calf, gilt spines, red & black labels. Fenning 61-496
1983 £45

WILSON, E. H.   Aristocrats of the Garden. 1937.
Wheldon 160-2033 1983 £12

WILSON, E. H.   A Monograph of Azalea. Cambridge,
Mass., (1921) 1942. 8vo, wrappers. The facsimile reissue which is
almost as rare as the original issue. Wheldon 160-2110 1983 £40

WILSON, EDMUND   A Book of Princeton Verse. Pr., 1916.
Edges slightly bumped, flys slightly offset, still near very good in
worn and frayed dustwrapper. Quill & Brush 54-1559 1983 $150

WILSON, EDMUND   A Book of Princeton Verse. Pr., 1916.
Edges slightly worn, else very good. Quill & Brush 54-1560 1983
$90

WILSON, EDMUND   The Boys in the Back Room. The Colt
Press, 1941. 8vo. Cloth, boards. Fine copy in lightly spotted dj
which is lightly nicked. In Our Time 156-890 1983 $200

WILSON, EDMUND   Memoirs of Hecate County. L, (n.d.).
Cover slightly stained, very good in soiled and slightly worn dustwrapper. Quill & Brush 54-1558 1983 $40

WILSON, EDMUND   A Prelude, Landscapes, Characters
and Conversations from the Earlier Years of My Life. NY (1967).
First edition, inscribed & signed by the author. Photos, cloth, a
bit soiled else good in worn dw. King 46-359 1983 $100

WILSON, EDMUND   This Room & This Gin & These Sandwiches.
New York: The New Republic, 1937. Pictorial wraps. First edition.
Slight adhesive offset from wrapper protector on endsheets, otherwise
a very fine copy. Reese 20-1151 1983 $225

WILSON, EDWARD LIVINGSTONE   Wilson's quarter century in photography. New York: Wilson, 1887. First edition. 4to. Orig.
green cloth. 386 text wood-engravings. Signature of W.F. Walker
on endpaper. Ximenes 63-575 1983 $125

WILSON, ERASMUS   On Diseases of the Skin. Phila., 1847.
20 colored litho. plates. 2 vols. 8vo, orig. embossed cloth; ex-lib.
Argosy 713-574 1983 $125

WILSON, FRAZER E.   The Peace of Mad Anthony. Cleveland:
The Arthur H. Clark Co., 1909. Plates. Jenkins 151-376 1983 $45

WILSON, GEORGE   Sanitary Defects in Villages and
Country Districts. J. & A. Churchill, 1876. First edition.
Jarndyce 31-350 1983 £12.50

WILSON, H. W.   Ironclads in Action. London, 1896.
Third edition. 8vo. Orig. blue decorated cloth. 2 vols. Frontis.,
44 plates, 30 maps (2 folding). Gilt. T.e.g. Slightly worn. Good.
Edwards 1042-189 1983 £100

WILSON, H. W.   With the Flag to Pretoria. London, 1900-
1902. 4 vols. Frontis. Numerous illus., many full page, 2 large
folding coloured maps. 4to, cont. binder's cloth. Spine faded. Very
slightly worn. Good. Edwards 1042-515 1983 £40

WILSON, HENRY   An Account of the Pelew Islands. MA,
(n.d.). Worn, chipped, fragile. Quill & Brush 54-1676 1983 $75

WILSON, HENRY   History of the Antislavery Measures of
the Thirty-Seventh and Thirty-Eighth United States Congresses. Boston,
1865. Spine a bit faded. Revised and enlarged over the 1864 orig.
Jenkins 152-525 1983 $65

WILSON, J. M.   Tales of the Borders, and of Scotland.
London, 1888. 12 vols. Cr. 8vo. Half polished calf, gilt, gilt
panelled spines with morocco labels, gilt, edges gilt. Traylen
94-890 1983 £105

WILSON, JAMES GRANT   Thackeray in the United States. London:
Smith, Elder & Co., 1904. First edition. 2 vols. Orig. cloth.
Spines slightly faded and soiled. Six Score illus. and a bibliography
by F.S. Dickson. Very good. MacManus 280-5142 1983 $35

WILSON, JAMES H.   Life of Charles A. Dana. NY, 1907.
Port., backstrip spotted. Argosy 710-388 1983 $75

WILSON, JOHN (1785-1854)   The Isle of Palms, and Other Poems.
Edinburgh: Longman, etc., 1812. First edition. Half title, 10 pp.
ads. Old boards, worn, rebacked red label. Jarndyce 30-873 1983
£22

WILSON, JOHN (1785-1854)   The Isle of Palms, and Other Poems.
Edinburgh: Longman; Merthyr: White...1837. Rebound in dull brown
cloth, leather label. First edition. Jarndyce 30-872 1983 £16.50

WILSON, JOHN (1785-1854)   The Recreations of Christopher North.
Edinburgh: William Blackwood & Sons, 1842. First edition. 3 vols.
Orig. green cloth. Gilt-decorated spines. Half-title bound in upside
down in Vol. III. Very fine. MacManus 280-5580 1983 $300

WILSON, JOHN (1785-1854)   The Trials of Margaret Lyndsay. Edinburgh: William Blackwood, 1823. First edition. Cont. full morocco
with leather spine label and marbled endpapers. Each leaf lightly
waterstained. Front cover a bit scratched. Very good. MacManus 280-
5581 1983 $85

WILSON, JOHN (1785-1854)   The Trials of Margaret Lindsay. Edinburgh: William Blackwood, and T. Cadell, 1823. First edition. 8vo,
half-title. Cont. half calf. Some stains. Hannas 69-226 1983 £30

WILSON, JOHN J.   The Rural Cyclopedia. Edinburgh:
A. Fullarton and Co. 1847-49. 4 vols., large 8vo, 69 engraved plates,
some fo them coloured, cont. half calf. Edges of binding slightly
rubbed, but a sound, well-bound set. Bickersteth 77-254 1983 £85

WILSON, MONA   The Life of William Blake. London:
the Nonesuch Press, 1927. 4to. Boards, parchment spine. 24 plates.
Limited edition of 1,480 numbered copies. Traylen 94-84 1983 £60

WILSON, NEIL   Treasure Express. N.Y., Macmillan.
First edition. Illus. Dust jacket. Very good. Inscribed and signed
by the author. Houle 21-1206 1983 $85

WILSON, NEILL C.   Silver Stampede. N.Y., Macmillan,
1937. First edition. Illus. Dust jacket (small nicks), else very
good. Signed and inscribed by the author. Houle 21-1190 1983 $60

WILSON, R. K.   Textbook of Automatic Pistols.
Plantersville, S. C. (1943). Illus, cloth, sm. hole in spine else
very good in chipped dw. King 46-703 1983 $45

WILSON, R. MC NAIR   Napoleon the Man. London, 1927.
First edition. 8 plates. 8vo. Half purple morocco, gilt, gilt
panelled spine with Napoleonic emblems, by Bayntun. Traylen
94-633 1983 £28

WILSON, R. MCNAIR   Napoleon: The Man. London, 1927.
First edition. Portrait frontis. Orig. cloth. 8vo. 7 plates. Ink
inscription on endpaper. Good. Edwards 1042-437 1983 £25

WILSON, ROBERT THOMAS   History of the British Expedition to
Egypt. London: T. Egerton, 1802. First edition. 4to, portrait, 3
folding military plans, 2 folding tables. Orig. tree calf, gilt,
rubbed, repair to tear on title. Adelson Africa-149 1983 $275

WILSON, ROBERT THOMAS   History of the British Expedition of
Egypt. London, 1802. Folding map. 2 folding plans. Portrait frontis.
4to. Half diced calf, some wear to hinges and corners. Good. Edwards
1044-758 1983 £50

WILSON, ROBERT THOMAS   History of the British Expedition to
Egypt. London, 1802. 4to, 2 folding tables, uncut in modern boards.
K Books 301-192 1983 £48

WILSON, ROMER   The Hill of Cloves. (London): William
Heinemann Ltd., 1929. First edition. Orig. cloth-backed decorated
boards. Limited to 775 copies signed by author. Near-fine. MacManus
280-5582 1983 $25

WILSON, RUFUS ROCKWELL   What Lincoln Read. Wash., Feb. 12,
1932. Narrow 8vo, cloth-backed boards, embossed with port. One of
250 numbered copies, signed. Argosy 710-266 1983 $30

WILSON, S. S.   A Narrative of the Greek Mission.
London, 1839. Coloured frontis. Vignette on title. 3 illus.
Binding worn and marked, spine faded. 8vo. Good. Edwards 1044-
759 1983 £85

WILSON, WOODROW   Chugach National Forest Alaska. Washington, 1919. Folio. Elephant folio map of the national forest with numerous inset maps. Jenkins 152-5 1983 $45

WILSON, WOODROW   A Collection of Approximately 150
Folio Printed Executive Orders and Proclamations Executed by Wilson,
Chiefly 1917-1918. Preserved in a cloth folding slipcase, fine.
Reese 19-438 1983 $1,000

WILSON, WOODROW   A History of the American People.
N.Y., 1902. 5 vols. Special issue of the first edition, printed
on large paper, limited to 350 numbered sets, autographed by the
future president. Jenkins 151-374 1983 $550

WILSON, WOODROW   History of the American People. N.Y.,
1903. Maps & illus. 5 vols. Cloth, g.t. Argosy 716-201 1983
$75

WILSON, WOODROW   State and Federal Governments of the
United States. D.C., 1889. Spine edges lightly chipped, corners
slightly worn, rear fly removed, else good, bookplate. Quill & Brush
54-1616 1983 $30

WILSON, WOODROW   Why the U.S. President Must Not Wear
a Uniform. Privately Printed. New York, 1918. 8vo. Wraps. With
a pen portrait of the President by Guido Bruno. Fine. In Our Time
156-893 1983 $25

WILSTACH, FRANK J.   Wild Bill Hickok, The Prince of
Pistoleers. New York, 1926. Illus. Dust jacket. Jenkins 153-697
1983 $20

WILSTACH, PAUL   Potomac Landings. New York, 1921.
Illus. and folding map. 1st ed. Light foxing. Scarce. Fairly
nice copy. Jenkins 153-698 1983 $50

WILTSEE, ERNEST A.   Gold Rush Steamers of the Pacific.
San Francisco: The Grabhorn Press, 1938. Illus. Few pencil marks.
Cloth, slightly soiled. Dawson 471-309 1983 $200

WILTSEE, ERNEST A.   The Pioneer Miner and the Pack Mule
Express. San Francisco, 1931. Plates, fldg. and other maps, facs.
Royal 8vo, illus. Clark 741-166 1983 $88.50

WILTSEE, ERNEST A.   The Truth About Fremont: An Inquiry.
San Francisco: John Henry Nash, 1936. 1st ed. in dj. Presentation
copy from author. Fine copy. Jenkins 153-699 1983 $100

WINCH, FRANK   Thrilling Lives of Buffalo Bill and
Pawnee Bill. (NY, 1911). Exceptionally nice in chipped, internally
reinforced orig. dustwrapper. Quill & Brush 54-1561 1983 $125

WINCH, FRANK   Thrilling Lives of Buffalo Bill, and
Pawnee Bill. (N.Y., 1911). 53 illus. D.w. Argosy 716-626 1983
$30

WINCHESTER, CLARENCE   Shipping Wonders of the World. London,
(1936-7). 4to. Orig. blue decorated cloth. 28 coloured plates,
numerous illus., maps, plans, etc. Some full page. Very slightly
worn, spines faded. Good. Edwards 1042-190 1983 £30

WINCHILSEA, ANNE FINCH, COUNTESS OF   The Tunbridge Prodigy.
London: printed and sold by J. Morphew, (1706). Single sheet folio,
small tear affecting two letters of text, a trifle browned, entirely
uncut in buckram folding case. An extremely rare edition.
Pickering & Chatto 19-85 1983 $2,000

WINDHAM, WILLIAM   An Account of the Glaciers or Ice Alps in Savoy. Printed for Peter Martel, 1744. First edition, with 2 folding engraved plates, 4to, calf-backed marbled boards, a very good copy. First and only eighteenth century edition. Fenning 61-497 1983 £265

WINDOM, WILLIAM   Northern Pacific Railroad. Speech of... Wash., 1869. Double columns. Dbd. First edition. Ginsberg 47-697 1983 $25

WINES, ENOCH C.   A Trip to Boston... Boston, 1838. 1st ed. 12mo, paper label. Some binding stains and foxing. Morrill 287-267 1983 $30

WINFIELD, CHARLES H.   The Block-House by Bull's Ferry. NY, 1904. Maps, ports., & illus. Uncut & unopened. One of 200 numbered copies. Argosy 710-468 1983 25

WING, CONWAY P.   A Historical and Genealogical Register of John Wing. NY: De Vinne Press, 1888. 2nd ed, engr., ports, large 4to, cloth, paper label. Argosy 710-179 1983 $85

WING, VINCENT   Astronomia Britannica. London: John Macock for George Sawbridge, 1669. First edition. With engraved portrait. Engraved title vignette. Folio. Cont. deerskin (some repairs). With ms. exlibris of James Hamilton, dated Nov. 22, 1669. Kraus 164-254 1983 $675

WING, VINCENT   An Ephemerides of the Coelestiall Motions for VII Years, Beginning Anno 1652, ending Anno 1658. London: Robert and William Leybourne, 1652. 4to. Cont. calf. Ms. exlibris of George Croxton dated 1652. Engraved armorial bookplate of George Kenyon of Peel. Kraus 164-255 1983 $675

WING, VINCENT   Geodaetes Practicus: or, the Art of Surveying. London: William Leybourne, 1664. First edition. 2 engraved plates, one of which is by Walter Hayes. Small 8vo. Cont. calf (some mends). Kraus 164-256 1983 $450

WINGERT, PAUL S.   An Outline Guide to the Art of the South Pacific. New York: Columbian University Press, 1947. 2 plates. Small 4to. Boards, 1/4 cloth. Ex-library. Ars Libri 34-861 1983 $35

WINGET, DAN   Anecdotes of Buffalo Bill That Have Never Appeared in Print. Chicago, 1927. Binding soiled. Clark 741-182 1983 $32.50

WINGFIELD, LEWIS   Barbara Philpot. Richard Bentley, 1885. First edition, 3 vols. Half title vol. I. Signs of library label removal from upper covers. Orig. brown cloth. A good set. Jarndyce 30-594 1983 £48

WINKLER, CLEMENS A.   Handbook of Technical Gas-Analysis. 1885. Fenning 62-394 1983 £18.50

WINKLER, ERNEST W.   Check List of Texas Imprints, 1846-1860. Austin, 1949. Orig. cloth, dust jacket. First edition. Ginsberg 47-884 1983 $20

WINKLER, FRIEDRICH   Durer. Des Meisters Gemalde, Kupferstiche und Holzschnitte. Stuttgart: Deutsche Verlags-Anstalt, (1928). 4to. Cloth. From the library of Jakob Rosenberg. Ars Libri 32-191 1983 $125

WINKLER, FRIEDRICH   Durer und die Illustrationen zum Narrenschiff. Berlin: Deutscher Verein fur Kunstwissenschaft, 1951. 88 plates. 15 text illus. 4to. Cloth. From the library of Jakob Rosenberg. Ars Libri 32-192 1983 $125

WINKLER, FRIEDRICH   Die Zeichnungen Hans Suss von Kulmbachs und Hans Leonhard Schaufeleins. Berlin: Deutscher Verein fur Kunstwissenschaft, 1942. 274 plates. Small folio. Boards, 1/4 cloth. Ars Libri 32-380 1983 $175

WINSCOM, JANE   Poems on Various Subjects. Bristol: Printed for the author. MDCCLXXXVI. 12mo, old cloth boards, a little worn, with leather lettering piece; frontis. portrait of the author. Second edition. Quaritch NS 7-141 1983 $250

WINSHIP, GEORGE PARKER   Cabot Bibliography... London: Henry Stevens, Son & Stiles, 1900. First edition. 8vo. Orig. gilt stamped red cloth, t.e.g., others uncut. First edition. Minor cover spotting, one corner bumped. Scarce. Oak Knoll 48-409 1983 $45

WINSHIP, GEORGE PARKER   William Caxton & His Work. Berkeley, Book Arts Club of the University of California, 1937. First edition. Blue cloth stamped in black (spine faded). One of 525 copies. Very good. Houle 22-971 1983 $30

WINSLOW, HUBBARD   Intellectual Philosophy: Analytical, Synthetical, and Practical. Boston: Brewer & Tileston, 1863 (1952). Eighth edition. Publisher's cloth. Fine copy. Gach 94-678 1983 $20

WINSOR, JUSTIN   Cartier to Frontenac. Boston, 1894. 1st ed. Illus. 8vo. Backstrip time-darkened, otherwise nice. Morrill 288-539 1983 $27.50

WINSOR, JUSTIN   Cartier to Frontenac. Boston, 1894. First edition. Illustrated. 8vo, leather label. Occasional cover stains; inner hinges very slightly cracked. Morrill 290-600 1983 $22.50

WINSOR, JUSTIN   The Mississippi Basin: The Struggle in America Between England and France, 1697-1763. Boston, (1895). Pict. cloth, t.e.g., illus. maps. Jenkins 151-377 1983 $45

WINSOR, JUSTIN   The Mississippi Basin. Boston, 1895. 1st ed. Illus. 8vo. Backstrip time-darkened, otherwise nice. Morrill 288-540 1983 $27.50

WINSOR, JUSTIN   The Westward Movement. Boston, 1897. 1st ed. Illus. 8vo. Backstrip time-darkened, otherwise nice. Morrill 288-541 1983 $27.50

WINSTON, W. R.   Four Years in Upper Burma. London, 1892. Folding map, plates. Cr.8vo. Some slight wear. Good. Edwards 1044-760 1983 £18

WINTER, GEORGE   Animal Magnetism History of... Bristol: by George Routh..., (1801). First edition. 8vo. Modern quarter calf. Very rare. Heath 48-539 1983 £150

WINTER, MILO   Illustrated Bible Story Book. Old Testament. Chicago: Rand Mc., (1923). First edition. Folio. Pictorial paste-on. Light wear to rear cover. Full-page & in-text color illus. Very good to fine. Aleph-bet 8-265 1983 $28

WINTER, MILO   Illustrated Bible Story Book. New Testament. Chicago: Rand., (1925). First edition. Folio, cloth. Pictorial paste-on. Frayed dust wrapper. Fine. Aleph-bet 8-266 1983 $30

WINTER, PETER VON   The Music of the Grand Mythologic Ballet. M. Kelly, w.m., 1804. Ballet composed by I. Degville. Folio, disbound. Fenning 62-395 1983 £21.50

WINTER, WILLIAM   The Wallet of Time, Containing Personal, Biographical, and Critical Reminiscence of the American Theatre. N.Y., Moffat, Yard, 1913. First edition. Each volume illus. with portraits of various actors on frontis. 32 halftone plates. Two vols. Uncut. Very good. Zane Grey's copy. Houle 22-971 1983 $30

WINTER From Home. NY, 1852. 12mo, orig. pr. wraps. Argosy 716-547 1983 $35

WINTERICH, JOHN T.   Books and The Man. New York: Greeberg Publisher, 1929. First edition. Tall 8vo. Cloth-backed boards, paper spine label, t.e.g. Limited to 210 numbered and signed copies printed on Utopian laid paper. Many illus. Fine copy. Oak Knoll 48-382 1983 $55

WINTERICH, JOHN T.   • Collector's Choice. N.Y., Greenberg, 1928. First edition. Dust jacket. Very good. Bookplate of Adrian Goldstone. Houle 21-152 1983 $30

WINTERICH, JOHN T.   Early American Books & Printing.
Boston: Riverside Press, (1935). 8vo, cloth, leather label,
slipcase, illus. One of 300 copies signed by the author. Duschnes
240-216 1983 $100

WINTERICH, JOHN T.   Three Lantern Slides. Urbana, U. Ill.,
1949. First edition. Half cloth. Very good. Houle 21-949 1983
$20

WINTERS, YVOR   Three Poems. (N.p.): The Cummington
Press, 1950. Marbled wraps. First edition. One of 300 copies.
Fine. Reese 20-1153 1983 $20

WINTHER, OSCAR OSBURN   Express and Stagecoach Days in
California... Stanford University Press, (1936). First edition.
Illus. Dust jacket. Fine. Houle 22-1200 1983 $45

WINTHROP, GRENVILLE LINDALL   A Catalogue of the Collection of Prints
from the Liber Studiorum of Joseph Mallard William Turner... Boston:
Privately Printed, 1916. 91 sepia-toned gravure illus. Large 4to.
Boards, 1/4 cloth. Printed by D.B. Updike at the Merrymount Press
on van Gelder. Ex-library. Somewhat worn. Ars Libri 32-681 1983
$75

WINTHROP, JOHN   History of New England, 1630-49. Boston,
1825-26. 2 vols., orig. boards, paper labels, (spines worn). Argosy
716-326 1983 $65

WINTHROP, THEODORE   The Canoe and the Saddle, or Klalam and
Klickatat. Tacoma: John H. Williams, 1913. Intro. and notes by J.H.
Williams. Plates. Cloth. Vellum spine. Dawson 471-310 1983 $50

WINTON, JOHN F.   The Engineer's Encyclopaedia. Phila.,
1893. New edition. Over 600 engravings in text and a series of
plates. 2 vols., 8vo. Morrill 290-601 1983 $35

WINTRINGHAM, TOM   Weapons and Tactics. London, 1943. First
edition. 6 plates, 15 illus. (1 full page). 8vo, orig. cloth. Very
slightly worn and soiled. Good. Edwards 1042-517 1983 £25

WINTZ, SOPHIA G.   Our Blue Jackets. London, 1894. Sm. 8vo.
Orig. blue pictorial cloth. Portrait frontis. 7 full page illus.
Good. Edwards 1042-191 1983 £15

WINZINGER, FRANZ   Albrecht Altdorfer. Zeichnungen.
Gesamtausgabe. Munchen: R. Piper, 1952. 171 illus. hors texte
(4 color plates). Large 4to. Cloth. Dust jacket. Ars Libri
32-8 1983 $150

WINZINGER, FRANZ   Albrecht Altdorfer. Die Gemalde.
Munchen: Hirmer Verlag, 1975. 258 illus. hors texte (48 color
plates). Large square 4to. Cloth. Dust jacket. Ars Libri 32-6
1983 $125

WINZINGER, FRANZ   Albrecht Altdorfer Graphik. Munchen:
R. Piper, 1963. 364 illus. hors texte. Large 4to. Cloth. Dust
jacket. Ars Libri 32-7 1983 $150

WINZINGER, FRANZ   Die Zeichnungen Martin Schongauers.
Berlin: Deutscher Verlag fur Kunstwissenschaft, 1962. 86 plates.
Large 4to. Cloth. Ars Libri 32-622 1983 $125

WIRT, WILLIAM   Sketches of the Life and Character of
Patrick Henry. Philadelphia, 1817. 8vo, contemporary calf, leather
label. 1st ed. Hinges partly cracked, rubbed, top of spine worn,
first and last several leaves dampstained. Morrill 289-579 1983
$25

WISCONSIN TERRITORY. LAWS. Laws of Wiskonsan Territory, Passed by
the Fourth Assembly. Madison, W.T., Syman, 1844. Orig. half sheep.
First edition. Ginsberg 46-830 1983 $175

WISE, HENRY A.   Los Gringos. N.Y.: Baker & Scribner,
1849. Cloth, foxed. Some signatures loosening. Dawson 471-311 1983
$50

WISE, JENNINGS C.   The Red Man in the New World Drama.
Washington, W.F. Roberts, (1931). First edition. Illustrated.
Large 8vo. Morrill 290-603 1983 $25

WISE, THOMAS J   A Conrad Library. London, Privately
printed, 1928. 4to, numerous facs. plates of title pages,
manuscripts, etc. Gilt stamped red cloth, bevelled edges, t.e.g.,
uncut. One of 180 copies on antique paper. With the bookplate of
Adrian Goldstone. Fine copy. Houle 22-125 1983 $325

WISE, THOMAS J.   Literary Anecdotes of the Nineteenth
Century. London: Hodder & Stroughton, 1895-96. 2 vols. 1st ed.
Orig. peach cloth, gilt, uncut. Very good set. Scarce. Jenkins
155-1429 1983 $175

WISEMAN, NICHOLAS   The Papal and royal supremacies
contrasted. London: Thomas Richardson and Son, n.d. (1850).
First edition. 8vo. Cont. calf, gilt, a.e.g. Six lectures of
Cardinal Newman bound in. Fine copy. Ximenes 63-592 1983 $25

WISEMAN, NICHOLAS   Two Letters on Some Parts of the
Controversy Concerning I. John v.7. Rome, Joseph Salviucci and Son,
1835. First collected edition, folding plate, 8vo., wrapper, ltd.
to a few copies. Fenning 61-498 1983 £28.50

WISEMAN, RICHARD   Severall Chirurgical Treatises.
London, 1676. Folio. First edition. Cont. brown morocco, gilt
panelled sides, slightly rubbed, neatly repaired, g.e. Gurney
90-124 1983 £1,050

WISHART, ALFRED W.   Short History of Monks and Monasteries.
Trenton, Brandt, 1900. First edition. Illus. Gilt stamped red cloth,
t.e.g. (two small holes in spine), else very good. Houle 21-953 1983
$27.50

WISLIZENUS, FREDERICK ADOLPHUS   A Journey to the Rocky Mountains in
the Year 1839. St. Louis: Missouri Historical Soc., 1912. Orig.
cloth and boards. Some wear. Folding map and frontis. Limited to
500 copies. The first is a very rare book. Jenkins 153-705 1983
$125

WISLIZENUS, FREDERICK ADOLPHUS   Memoir of a Tour to Northern Mexico
Conducted with Col. Doniphan's Expedition, in 1846 and 1847. Wash.,
1848. 3 maps. Some repairs. Later boards. A good copy. The W. J.
Holliday copy, with his bookplate. Reese 190597 1983 $325

WISSCHER, WILLIAM L.   Black Mammy. Cheyenne: Bristol & Knabe,
1886. Gilt pictorial cloth. Illus. Very good copy. Second edition.
Reese 19-606 1983 $125

WISSMANN, HERMANN VON   My second journey through Equatorial
Africa from the Congo to the Zambesi... London: Chatto & Windus,
1891. 8vo. Folding map. 32 plates. Orig. orange cloth. Rubbed.
Adelson Africa-150 1983 $120

WISTAR, ISAAC J.   Autobiography of... Phila., 1914.
2 vols. Illus., map, 2 plates. Orig. cloth with leather labels
on spines. First edition. One of 250 numbered sets published.
Ginsberg 47-978 1983 $275

WISTAR, ISAAC J.   The Autobiography of... Philadelphia:
1937. Illus. Cloth. Very fine copy. In dust jacket. Bradley 66-
701 1983 $32.50

WISTER, OWEN   A Collection of His Works. 19 vols.,
some with Remington illus., mostly fine condition, including a pres.
copy and a limited signed ed. Jenkins 155-1332 1983 $500

WISTER, OWEN   Journey in Search of Christmas. Toronto,
Musson (1910). First Canadian edition. Pictorial red cloth, t.e.g.,
uncut. Frontis. portrait, two plates; pictorial endpapers and
decorative borders by Remington. A fine copy. Houle 21-1133 1983
$65

WISTER, OWEN   A Journey in Search of Christmas. New
York: Harper & Brothers, 1904. T.e.g. Illus. by Frederic Remington.
Orig. pictorial cloth. 1st ed. with October, 1904 on copyright page.
Nice copy. Jenkins 153-464 1983 $45

WISTER, OWEN   Padre Ignacio. New York: Harper,
1911. Frontis. 1st ed. Orig. pictorial cloth, label on front
cover, dj. Very fine copy, scarce with dj. Jenkins 155-1335 1983
$45

WISTER, OWEN   The Virginia, a Horseman of the Plains.
New York: MacMillan, 1902. Frontis., plates. 1st ed. Orig. pic.
tan cloth, gilt. Light wear, but very good copy. Jenkins 155-1337a
1983 $100

WISZNIEWSKI, MICHEL, PRINCE DE   Sketches and characters, or the
natural history of the human intellect. London: Saunders and
Otley, 1853. First edition. 8vo. Orig. violet cloth. Presentation
copy, inscribed by the author to Miss Zephine Watts Russell. Rather
rubbed and dull, slight fraying of spine. Ximenes 63-300 1983 $65

WITHERING, W.   A Botanical Arrangement of all the
Vegetables Naturally Growing in Great Britain. Birmingham, 1776.
12 plates (1 folding), 2 vol., 8vo, contemporary calf. The rare
first edition. A few minor stains and light offsets and the joints of
the binding are beginning to crack, but a nice copy. Half-titles
and front fly-leaves lacking. Wheldon 160-1638 1983 £100

WITHERS, ALEXANDER SCOTT   Chronicles of Border Warfare, or a
History of the Settlement by the Whites, of North-Western Virginia.
Clarksburg, Va.: Joseph Israel, 1831. 1st ed., original calf, some
outer wear only. Ad leaf. Jenkins 151-379 1983 $300

WITHERS, ALEXANDER SCOTT   Chronicles of Border Warfare. Clarksburg, Va.: 1831. First edition, first issue, with ad leaf. Reason-
ably good condition. Folio on p. 83 printed upside down. Covers
rubbed, dampstaining throughout, several tiny holes on leaves 61-2
and 71-2 not obscuring type. Name stamp on front pastedown, top inch
of front free end paper torn off. Bradley 66-702 1983 $185

WITHERS, ALEXANDER SCOTT   Chronicles of Border Warfare. Cincinnati,
1895. Enlarged edition. Portrait, 8vo, ex-library. Morrill 290-567
1983 $47.50

WITHERS, PHILIP   Alfred, or a Narrative of the daring
and illegal measures to suppress a pamphlet... London: for the
Author, 1789. First edition. 8vo. Wrappers. Lightly foxed. Heath
48-204 1983 £65

WITHERSPOON, JOHN   A serious enquiry into the nature and
effects of the stage. Glasgow: printed by J. Bryce and D. Peterson,
1757. 8vo, wrappers, 1st edition. Scarce. Ximenes 64-588 1983
$300

WITHINGTON, MARY C.   A Catalogue of Manuscripts in the
Collection of Western Americana Founded by William Robertson Coe, Yale
University Library. New Haven, 1952. Cloth, fine. Reese 19-74
1983 $75

WITKOWSKI, GUSTAVE-JULES   Les Accouchements a la Cour. Paris,
(c. 1887). Large 8vo, pr. wrs. (foxed); uncut. Argosy 713-576 1983
$100

WITTELS, FRITZ   Sigmund Freud. His Personality, His
Teaching, and His School. London: George Allen & Unwin, (1924).
First edition in English. Gach 94-179 1983 $35

WITTING, FELIX   Lancelot Blondeel. Strassburg: J.E.
Ed. Heitz, 1917. 3 collotype plates. 4to. Wrappers. Ars Libri
32-45 1983 $35

WITTLIFF, WILLIAM D.   Vaquero: Genesis of the Texas Cowboy.
San Antonio, (1972). Oblong 12mo, printed paper over boards. Photos.
Very fine copy in dust jacket and slipcase. Reese 19-598 1983 $75

WITTMEYER, ALFRED V.   Registers of the Births, Marriages,
and Deaths of the "Eglise Francoise a la Nouvelle York," from 1688
to 1804. NY: Hugenot Society of America, 1886. Illus. Thick 8vo,
later buckram. Argosy 716-386 1983 $45

WITTY, Humorous and Merry Thoughts. Glasgow: David Bryce, (ca.
1900). Very fine in red leather, gilt-stamped. Bookplate of Arthur
A. Houghton. (1 1/16 x 3/4; 27x19mm). Bromer 25-482 1983 $240

WITTY, Humorous and Merry Thoughts. (ca. 1900). American issue with
NY, Frederick A. Stokes imprint. Very fine in wine leather, gilt-
stamped. (1 1/16 x 11/16; 27x20mm). Bromer 25-483 1983 $225

WODEHOUSE, PELHAM GRENVILLE   Cary on, Jeeves! NY, (1927). Cover
soiled and lightly stained, edges rubbed, endpapers lightly soiled,
else good or better. Bookplate. Quill & Brush 54-1562 1983 $50

WODEHOUSE, PELHAM GRENVILLE   The Crime Wave at Blandings. GC, 1937.
Small circular stain on rear board, front fly slightly skinned, else
very good in frayed and slightly chipped, wearing dustwrapper with
price clipped. Quill & Brush 54-1568 1983 $90

WODEHOUSE, PELHAM GRENVILLE   Full Moon. L, (n.d.). Bright, near fine
in slightly frayed, bright dustwrapper. Quill & Brush 54-1563 1983
$50

WODEHOUSE, PELHAM GRENVILLE   He Rather Enjoyed It. N.Y., Doran
(1925). First edition. Red cloth (faded on spine), good. Houle
21-955 1983 $35

WODEHOUSE, PELHAM GRENVILLE   Jeeves. NY, (1923). Corners and spine
edges slightly worn, front hinge starting, small stain to fore edge,
else good or better, gift inscription. Quill & Brush 54-1564 1983
$75

WODEHOUSE, PELHAM GRENVILLE   Leave it to Psmith. London, Jenkins,
1924 (1923). First edition, with eleven titles on verso of half title.
Pictorial green cloth. Good. Houle 21-957 1983 $45

WODEHOUSE, PELHAM GRENVILLE   Luck of the Bodkins. Boston, Little,
Brown, 1936. First American edition, reset and printed in USA.
Green cloth, spine a bit faded, else good-very good. Houle 21-
958 1983 $45

WODEHOUSE, PELHAM GRENVILLE   Meet Mr. Mulliner. London: Herbert
Jenkins Limited, (1927). First edition. Orig. cloth. Former owner's
inscription on front free endpaper. Fine. MacManus 280-5596 1983
$85

WODEHOUSE, PELHAM GRENVILLE   Mr. Mulliner Speaking. London:
Herbert Jenkins Limited, (1929). First edition. 8vo. Orig. cloth.
A bit rubbed, but a very good copy. Jaffe 1-403 1983 $75

WODEHOUSE, PELHAM GRENVILLE   Mr. Mulliner Speaking. N.Y. Doubleday,
1930. First American edition. Blue pictorial cloth (spine a bit
faded), else very good. Houle 21-959 1983 $27.50

WODEHOUSE, PELHAM GRENVILLE   Money for Nothing. N.Y., Doubleday,
1928. First American edition. Blue cloth blocked in orange. Some
stains. Good - very good. Houle 22-973 1983 $35

WODEHOUSE, PELHAM GRENVILLE   Sam in the Suburbs. NY, (1925). Corners
lightly worn, green cloth binding slightly pitted, else very good.
Quill & Brush 54-1565 1983 $75

WODEHOUSE, PELHAM GRENVILLE   Sam the Sudden. London: Methuen & Co.
Ltd., (1925). First edition, variant binding. Orig. yellow cloth.
Fine. MacManus 280-5601 1983 $75

WODEHOUSE, PELHAM GRENVILLE   Summer Moonshine. GC, 1937. Small
stain at bottom edge of front cover, else fine in dustwrapper with
very slightly sunned spine and minor wear to edges. Quill & Brush
54-1566 1983 $150

WODEHOUSE, PELHAM GRENVILLE   Thank You, Jeeves. B, 1934. Edges very
slightly worn, minor cover spotting, else very good. Quill & Brush
54-1567 1983 $30

WODEHOUSE, PELHAM GRENVILLE   Ukridge. London, Jenkins, 1924.
First edition. Pictorial green cloth. Edges lightly foxed, else very
good. Houle 21-962 1983 $85

WODEHOUSE, PELHAM GRENVILLE   Ukridge. London, Jenkins, 1924. First
edition, with list of 31 titles on verso of half-title page.
Pictorial green cloth stamped in dark green (edges slightly foxed,
small stain on p. 139) else very good. Houle 22-977 1983 $60

WODEHOUSE, PELHAM GRENVILLE   Uncle Fred in the Springtime. N.Y.,
Doubleday, 1939. First edition. Green cloth stamped in brown (a
bit soiled). Very good. Houle 22-978 1983 $45

WODEHOUSE, PELHAM GRENVILLE   William Tell Told Again. London,
Black, 1904. First edition. 16 color plates by Philip Dadd. Pictorial
cloth (backstrip reattached, contents shaken). Good. Inscribed
and signed by the author. Houle 21-963 1983 $275

WOELFL, JOSEPH   La Surprise de Diane. Printed & sold
for the author, by Lavenu & Mitchell, circa, 1806. Folio, disound.
Fenning 62-396 1983 £21.50

WOELMONT, ARNOLD DE   Souvenirs du Far-West. Paris, 1883.
Disbound; orig. front paper wrapper preserved. First edition.
Felcone 22-272 1983 $50

WOERMANN, KARL   Geschichte der Kunst aller Zeiten
und Volker. Leipzig: Bibliographisches Institut, 1924. 62
plates (8 color). 362 text illus. 4to. Boards. Ars Libri 34-82
1983 $50

WOERTERBUCH der Antike. Stuttgart, 1933. Map. 8vo, cloth. Salloch
385-92 1983 $22

WOLCOT, JOHN (1738-1819)   The Works of Peter Pindar. London, 1794-
1801. 8vo., calf, leather labels. 5 vols. Little foxing, mainly a
fine set. In Our Time 156-633 1983 $200

WOLF, A.   A History of Science, Technology and
Philosophy in the 16th and 17th centuries. London, 1950. New
edition. 8vo. Cloth. Plates. Gurney JJ-424 1983 £15

WOLF, F. A.   The Fungi. New York, 1947. 235 text
figures, portrait, 2 vols., 8vo, cloth. Wheldon 160-1911 1983 £18

WOLF, EDWIN   A Descriptive Catalogue of the John Frederick Lewis Collection of European Manuscripts... Phila., 1937. Presentation initialled by A. S. W. Rosenbach. 42 plates. Cloth. One of
1,000 copies. Very good. Dawson 470-310 1983 $50

WOLF, SIMON   The American Jew as Patriot, Soldier
and Citizen... Phila., 1895. First edition. Frontis, two-tone
cloth, covers rubbed. King 46-124 1983 $35

WOLFE, HUMBERT   The Craft of Verse: Oxford Poetry Essay.
NY, 1928. One of 395 numbered and signed copies, corners worn, else
very good or better. Quill & Brush 54-1570 1983 $75

WOLFE, HUMBERT   Cursory Rhymes. London: Ernest Benn
Limited, 1927. First edition. Illus. by A. Rutherston. Orig. cloth-
backed boards with paper label on spine. Dust jacket. Limited to
500 copies signed by author. Very good. MacManus 280-5606 1983 $25

WOLFE, HUMBERT   Dialogues and Monologues. Victor
Gollancz, 1928. First edition, 8vo, orig. cloth, with printed
paper label. Fine. Fenning 62-398 1983 £35

WOLFE, HUMBERT   Early Poems. Oxford: Basil Blackwell,
1930. First edition. Orig. cloth. Dust jacket (chipped, partially
faded). Very good. MacManus 280-5608 1983 $25

WOLFE, HUMBERT   New of the Devil. London: Ernest Benn
Ltd., 1926. First edition. Orig. cloth with paper label on spine.
Dust jacket. Limited to 265 copies signed by author. Very good.
MacManus 280-5611 1983 $30

WOLFE, HUMBERT   Notes on English Verse Satire. London:
The Hogarth Press, 1929. First edition. Orig. cloth. Dust jacket
(spine darkened). Very good. MacManus 280-5612 1983 $45

WOLFE, HUMBERT   Portrait of Heine. London: The Cresset
Press, 1930. First edition. Orig. limp green morocco. One of 500
copies on hand-made paper, signed by author. Extremities a little
rubbed. MacManus 280-5614 1983 $25

WOLFE, HUMBERT   Requiem. London: Ernest Benn Ltd., 1927.
First edition. Orig. cloth. Dust jacket (a bit soiled). Very good.
MacManus 280-5615 1983 $20

WOLFE, HUMBERT   Shylock Reasons with Mr. Chesterton.
Oxford: Basil Blackwell, 1920. First edition. Orig. cloth. Very
good. MacManus 280-5621 1983 $35

WOLFE, HUMBERT   The Uncelestial City. London: Victor
Gollancz Ltd., 1930. First edition. Orig. cloth. Dust jacket (some-
what soiled). Limited to 400 copies signed by author. Very good.
MacManus 280-5618 1983 $25

WOLFE, HUMBERT   The Uncelestial City. Victor Gollancz,
1930. First edition, 8vo, orig. cloth, with printed paper label.
Fine copy in d.w. Fenning 62-399 1983 £14.50

WOLFE, HUMBERT   The Unknown Goddess. London: Methuen
& Co., Ltd., (1925). First edition. Orig. cloth-backed boards with
paper label on spine. Dust jacket. Boards somewhat faded. Very good.
MacManus 280-5619 1983 $20

WOLFE, HUMBERT   A Winter Miscellany...(with) Orig.
Poems. by the Editor. Eyre and Spottiswoode, 1930. Decorated by
Frank Adams. Fenning 62-400 1983 £16.50

WOLFE, RICHARD J.   Jacob Bigelow's American Medical
Botany, 1817-1821. North Hills: Bird & Bull Press, 1979. Small
4to. Leather spine, decorated paper over boards. One of 300
numbered copies. This copy is additionally signed by Henry Morris.
Two plates, one hand-colored the other uncolored. Fine. Oak Knoll
39-40 1983 $350

WOLFE, THOMAS   From Death To Morning. New York:
Charles Scribner's Sons, 1935. First edition. 8vo. Orig. cloth.
Dust jacket, a little rubbed at head of spine, otherwise a fine
copy. Jaffe 1-405 1983 $85

WOLFE, THOMAS   From Death to Morning. N.Y., Scribner,
1935. First edition. Dust jacket (a few small chips). Bookplate.
Very good. Houle 22-979 1983 $75

WOLFE, THOMAS   Look Homeward, Angel. New York:
Charles Scribner's Sons, 1929. First edition, first issue. 8vo.
Orig. cloth. Dust jacket (defective). Very good copy. Jaffe
1-404 1983 $450

WOLFE, THOMAS   Look Homeward, Angel. NY, 1929. First
state, hinges starting, edges worn, internally reinforced tear top of
spine edge, good. Quill & Brush 54-1573 1983 $90

WOLFE, THOMAS   Look Homeward, Angel. NY, 1947. First
illus. edition. Illus. by D. Gorsline, fine in fine dustwrapper.
Quill & Brush 54-1572 1983 $75

WOLFE, THOMAS   Look Homeward, Angel. NY, 1947. First
illus. edition, endpapers slightly offset, spine stained, else very
good in frayed and torn dustwrapper. Quill & Brush 54-1574 1983 $45

WOLFE, THOMAS   Mannerhouse. NY, 1948. One of 500 numbered, specially bound and printed, with holograph letter, fine in
slightly sunner, near fine, price clipped dustwrapper in worn slipcase.
Quill & Brush 54-1575 1983 $150

WOLFE, THOMAS   Mannerhouse. New York: Harper &
Brothers, 1948. First edition. 8vo. Orig. cloth. Dust jacket.
Fine copy. Jaffe 1-407 1983 $45

WOLFE, THOMAS   Of the Time and the River. New York:
Charles Scribners, 1935. Cloth. First edition. Inscribed on the
front free endpaper: "For Bert Cross..." About fine in dust jacket,
in a half morocco folding case. Reese 20-1157 1983 $1,950

WOLFE, THOMAS   The story of a Novel. New York:
Charles Scribner's Sons, 1936. First edition. 8vo. Orig. cloth.
Dust jacket, a trifle nicked at head of spine, otherwise a fine
copy. Jaffe 1-406 1983 $85

WOLFE, THOMAS   The Story of a Novel. New York:
Scribner, 1936. 1st ed. Orig. cloth, dj. Pencil annotations by
Lyman Butterfield, editor... Fine copy in near fine dj. Jenkins
155-1339 1983 $65

WOLFE, THOMAS   The Web and the Rock. NY, 1939. Minor
cover stains, cover and spine design slightly rubbed, good or better
copy in internally reinforced, worn dustwrapper with price clipped.
Quill & Brush 54-1578 1983 $100

WOLFE, THOMAS   The Web and the Rock. London:
Heinemann, (1947). Cloth. First British edition, a very fine copy in
dust jacket. Reese 20-1158 1983 $45

WOLFE, THOMAS   You Can't Go Home Again. N.Y., Harper,
(1940). First edition, thick 8vo, blue cloth stamped in red and gilt.
Bookplate. Dust jacket (nicks and a bit rubbed). Very good. Houle
22-980 1983 $85

WOLFE, THOMAS   You Can't Go Home Again. N.Y., (1940).
8vo, cloth. First edition. Argosy 714-833 1983 $20

WOLFF, FRIEDRICH   Michael Pacher. Berlin: Franz Stoedt-
ner, 1909. 96 collotype plates with 143 illus. Folio. Portfolio.
Boards, 1/4 vellum. From the library of Victor Emmanuel III, King
of Italy. Ars Libri 32-502 1983 $200

WOLFF, JOSEPH   Narrative of a Mission to Bokhara, in
the Years 1843-1845. London: Published for the author, 1845. 1st
ed., 8vo, 2 vols., orig. cloth, spines gilt, engraved frontis., 7
engraved plates. Uncut copy with the half-titles, advertisements,
armorial bookplate. Three plates dampstained, others lightly foxed;
nevertheless a good copy. Uncommon. Trebizond 18-172 1983 $350

WOLFF, JOSEPH   Narrative of a Mission to Bokhara. London, 1846. Fifth edition. 8vo. Orig. cloth. Presentation copy to
"Miss Jessy Grant from Joseph Wolff", with quotations in English and
in Persian on the half-title. Good. Edwards 1044-761 1983 £85

WOLFF, MARITTA   Night Shift. NY, (1942). Printed paperwraps, proof copy, book cocked and cover soiled, else very good. Quill
& Brush 54-1581 1983 $50

WOLFF, WERNER   Island of Death. New York: J.J.
Augustin, 1948. 20 plates. Frontis., text figures. 4to. Cloth.
Ars Libri 34-862 1983 $30

WOLLASTON, T.   Catalogue of Coleopterous Insects
of the Canaries. British Museum, 1864. 8vo, cloth. Good ex-
library copy. Wheldon 160-1190 1983 £30

WOLLASTON, WILLIAM   The Religion of Nature Delineated.
London: by Samuel Palmer, 1726, 4to. Cont. panelled calf, gilt.
Engraved vignette on title-page and engraved head and tail-pieces.
Traylen 94-893 1983 £18

WOLLE, F.   Desmids of the United States and list
of American Pediastrums. Bethlehem, Pa., 1884. 53 coloured plates
of 1100 figures, royal 8vo, original cloth, rare. Wheldon 160-1912
1983 £80

WOLLSTONECRAFT, MARY (1759-1797)
Please turn to
GODWIN, MARY WOLLSTONECRAFT (1759-1797)

WOLLSTONECRAFT, MARY (1797-1851)
Please turn to
SHELLEY, MARY WOLLSTONECRAFT GODWIN

WOMACK, EMMETT   History and Business Methods of the
Department of the Interior. Wash., 1897. Printed wrappers. Jenkins
153-706 1983 $20

WOMOCK, LAURENCE   Sober Sadnes. Oxford: for W. Webb,
1643. Small 4to, 18-1/2 cm. Later red morocco-backed marbled
boards, worn at edges. Text with stains and browning. First
edition, second issue. Grunder 7-79 1983 $65

WOOD, ANNIE M.   Noman's Land. New Bedford, 1931. First
edition. Illustrated. 8vo. Morrill 290-303 1983 $20

WOOD, CASEY A.   Fundus Oculi of Birds. Chicago: Lakeside Press, 1917. Folio. 61 colored paintings & 145 text drawings
by Arthur W. Head. First edition. Argosy 713-577 1983 $175

WOOD, CASEY A.   An Introduction to the Literature of
Vertebrate Zoology. (Oxford, 1931). Reprint, Hildesheim, 1974.
Royal 8vo, cloth. Wheldon 160-285 1983 £39

WOOD, CHARLES ERSKINE SCOTT A Book of Indian Tales. N.Y.: Vanguard,
(1929). 12mo. Cloth. Dust wrapper. Lengthy inscription by Wood on
half-title. Very good to fine. Aleph-bet 8-267 1983 $40

WOOD, CHARLES ERSKINE SCOTT The Poet in the Desert. Portland, Oregon, 1915. 8vo. Cloth backed boards (somewhat discolored). Inscribed
on title page by Wood. Limited to 1000 copies printed at the press of
F.W. Baltes. Very good. Aleph-bet 8-268 1983 $40

WOOD, E.   The Shadow of Ashlydat. London: Bentley,
1863. First edition, regular binding. 3 vols. Orig. cloth. Covers
faded, soiled and worn. Inner hinges cracked. Sound copy. MacManus
280-5626 1983 $450

WOOD, E.   Verner's Pride. London: Bradbury &
Evans, 1863. First edition. 3 vols. Orig. green cloth. Corners of
rear flyleaves in vols. I-II slightly torn. Lacking rear flyleaf in
vol. III. Covers slightly rubbed. Very good. MacManus 280-5627
1983 $325

WOOD, ELLEN (PRICE) (1814-1887)   The Channings. London: Richard
Bentley, 1862. First edition. 3 vols. Orig. cloth. Spines a little
darkened and worn. Few signatures starting. Good. MacManus 280-5622
1983 $250

WOOD, ELLEN (PRICE) (1814-1887)   Edina. London: Richard Bentley &
Son, 1876. Orig. cloth. 3 vols. Presentation copy inscribed to
Mrs. Parker, dated 1876. Covers and spines slightly worn. Inner
hinges cracking. Some foxing to the preliminary pages. Very good.
MacManus 280-5623 1983 $350

WOOD, ELLEN (PRICE) (1814-1887)   Johnny Ludlow. London: R. Bentley & Son, 1885. First edition. 3 vols. Orig. cloth. Spines faded.
Upper edges slightly soiled, corners a bit worn. Former owner's signature on each half-title. A little light foxing. Very good. Mac-
Manus 280-5624 1983 $350

WOOD, ELLEN (PRICE) (1814-1887)   Oswald Gray. Edinburgh: Adam &
Charles Black, 1864. First edition. 3 vols. Orig. cloth. Front
cover of vol. I wormed. Inner hinges cracked, soiled and shaken.
MacManus 280-5625 1983 $250

WOOD, ELLEN (PRICE) (1814-1887)   Oswald Gray. Edinburgh: Adam &
Charles Black, 1864. First edition. 3 vols. Half titles, foxing to
prelims. Purple/brown wavy-grain cloth, boards blocked in blind,
spines lettered in gilt. Very good. Jarndyce 30-595 1983 £110

WOOD, EMMA CAROLINA   Rosewarn, A Novel. London: Chapman &
Hall, 1866. First edition. 3 vols. Illus. with orig. photographs of
drawings. Half-morocco with cloth borads and marbled endpapers.
Printed on albumen paper (drawings). Rear cover to vol. I detached.
Spines and covers rather worn at the edges. Bookplate. Internally
clean. Good. MacManus 280-5026 1983 $250

WOOD, G. B.   Dispensatory of the United States.
Phila., 1858. Thick large 8vo, orig. sheep, leather labels, (rubbed).
Argosy 713-578 1983 $45

WOOD, GEORGE   Introductory Lectures and Addresses
on Medical Subjects... Philadelphia, 1872. Second edition. 8vo.
Orig. binding. Inscribed by the author. Top of backstrip torn,
else fine. Fye H-3-635 1983 $50

WOOD, GEORGE   Peter Schlemihl in America. Phila., 1848.
First edition. Ads. Cloth. Binding quite worn, with front hinge
partially broken. Foxed. Felcone 20-44 1983 $35

WOOD, GEORGE   Peter Schlemihl in America. Phila.,
1848. First edition. Ads. Foxed. Argosy 716-167 1983 $35

WOOD, MRS. HENRY
Please turn to
WOOD, ELLEN PRICE (1814-1887)

WOOD, HENRY TRUEMAN   A History of the Royal Society of Arts.
London: John Murray, 1913. Thick 8vo, with 31 plates and some text
illus. Blue cloth. Karmiole 73-108 1983 $40

WOOD, J. E. R.   Detour. The Story of Oflag IVC.
London: The Falcon Press, 1946. 25cm. 64 plates (some in colour).
Cloth backed boards. Very good to fine. McGahern 54-183 1983
$25

WOOD, JOHN GEORGE   Common Objects of the Country.
Routledge, etc., 1859 (Shilling series). New edn. Frontis. & 11 b&w
illus., many text engrs. by W.S. Coleman. Yellow paper covered bds.
with pictorial fr. cvr. & bkstrip printed by Edmund Evans (top of
bkstrip worn, long contemp. insc. recto frontis.), v.g. copy.
Hodgkins 27-344 1983 £12

WOOD, JOHN MAXWELL   Smuggling in the Solway and Around the
Galloway Seaboard. Dumfries: J. Maxwell, (1908). First and
apparently only edition, with full-page and other illus., cr. 8vo,
orig. cloth, a very good copy. Illus. by John Copland. Fenning 61-
499 1983 £24.50

WOOD, NICHOLAS   A Practical Treatise on Rail-Roads and
Interior Communication in General. For Knight and Lacey, London,
1825. 8vo, with 6 folding engraved plates; offsetting on plates
and a large brown stain on plate VI but a crisp copy in orig. boards,
uncut, rebacked with orig. printed paper label preserved. First
edition. Quaritch NS 5-115 1983 $700

WOOD, R. D.   A Revision of the Characeae. 1964-65.
387 plates, 2 vols., royal 8vo, cloth. A clean secondhand copy.
Wheldon 160-1913 1983 £50

WOOD, RUSSELL E.   Records of the Lanarkshire Yeomanry.
Edinburgh, c.1910. Orig. cloth. Handcoloured engraved frontis. of
uniform by Skeoch Cumming. 5 photogravure plates and 13 illus. Imp.
8vo. T.e.g. Printed in a numbered limited edition of 100 copies for
private circulation. 3 ALS from author and numerous relevant newspaper
cuttings, etc. on endpapers. Fine. Edwards 1042-561 1983 £85

WOOD, SILAS   Sketch of the First Settlement of the
Several Towns on Long-Island. Brooklyn, 1828. 3rd ed. 100 copies
printed. 8vo, new cloth. Text partly water-stained. Morrill 287-
318 1983 $50

WOOD, STANLEY   Over the Range to the Golden Gate.
Chicago, 1891. Illus. Pictorial cloth. Spine darkened with
lettering faint. Felcone 22-273 1983 $30

WOOD, SUMNER GILBERT   Ulster Scots and Blandford Scouts.
West Medway, Author, 1928. First edition. Presentation copy.
Illustrated. 8vo. Portions of covers from fore-edge water-stained.
Morrill 290-304 1983 $20

WOOD, WILLIAM (1774-1857)   Index Entomologicus or a complete
illustrated catalogue...of the Lepidopterous Insects of Great
Britain. 1854. New and revised (last) edition, with supplement,
hand-coloured plates, royal 8vo, original half green morocco, gilt.
Very scarce. A little minor foxing. Wheldon 160-1192 1983 £125

WOOD, WILLIAM B.   Personal Recollections of the Stage...
Philadelphia, 1855. 1st ed. Portrait. Small 8vo. Binding partly
faded and lightly stained. Morrill 286-523 1983 $25

WOOD-JONES, F. W.   The Matrix of the Mind. 1929. 8vo,
cloth, 80 figures. Wheldon 160-203 1983 £15

WOODBRIDGE, WILLIAM C.   A System of Universal Geography.
Hartford, 1829. 3rd ed., illus, maps and engravings, thick 12mo,
lea.-backed boards, lea. label, ex-lib. Argosy 710-198 1983 $40

WOODBURY, AUGUSTUS   A Narrative of the Campaign of the
First Rhode Island Regiment... Providence, 1862. 1st ed. Map
and portrait. Small 8vo. Morrill 286-417 1983 $30

WOODBURY, C. J. H.   Bibliography of the Cotton Manufacture.
Waltham, Mass., 1909. 1st ed. Presentation copy. Frontispiece.
Tall 8vo, bookplate. Morrill 288-545 1983 $25

WOODBURY, JOSEPHINE CURTIS   Christian Science Voices. 1885-1897.
Boston: Press of Samuel Usher, 1897. Photogravure frontis.
Green gilt-stamped cloth; outer front hinge with a few small gouges.
Karmiole 73-27 1983 $75

WOODBURY, JOSEPHINE CURTIS   Echoes. NY: Putnam's, 1897.
Tall 8vo, illus. with 29 full-page plates by Pape and other text
decorations by Pape; dec. initial letters by Alice Pape. In orig.
silver and gilt-stamped beige cloth, sl. soiled. Front cover
with some erasure marks from someone who had tried to clean the
cloth binding. Karmiole 76-82 1983 $75

WOODBURY, LEVI   Condition of the State Banks. Wash.,
1841. Full calf. First edition. Ginsberg 46-49 1983 $100

WOODBURY, LEVI   Land Claims in Missouri- Arguments, etc.
Letter from...Transmitting a Communication from the Commissioner of
the General Land Office... Wash., 1836. Dbd. First edition.
Ginsberg 47-553 1983 $35

WOODFORD, JACK   Evangelical Cockroach. New York:
Louis Carrier & Co., 1929. Cloth. First edition. About fine in
lightly chipped, fragile foil pictorial dust jacket. Reese 20-1164
1983 $75

WOODFORDE, JAMES   The Diary of a Country Parson...
London: Oxford University Press, 1924-31. First edition.
27 plates and a folding map of Norfolk. 5 vols. Roy. 8vo. Lime
green morocco spines, marbled paper sides, vellum tips, gilt lettered
spines, t.e.g., by Douglas Cockerell. The orig. binder's bill is
loosely inserted. Traylen 94-894 1983 £225

WOODMAN, DAVID   Guide to Texas Emigrants. Boston: M.
Hawes, 1835. Orig. cloth, spine gilt, rare buffalo plate and folding
map, prepared by Woodman containing an inset made by Alexander
Thompson. 1st ed. of one of the rarest Texas books. Very fine copy.
Jenkins 153-587 1983 $5,500

WOODROFFE, JOSEPH F.   The Upper Reaches of the Amazon.
NY: Macmillan, 1914. Index. With twenty-one illus. and a map.
Red cloth. Bookplate. Karmiole 75-76 1983 $40

WOODROOFFE, ANNA   The History of Michael Kemp, the Happy
Farmer's Lad. Bath: Printed by Wood and Co, (etc), 1821. Second
edition, 12mo, contemporary boards, a little worn; new backstrip;
uncut. Hill 165-141 1983 £38

WOODRUFF, CHARLES S.   Legalized Prostitution. Boston, Bela
Marsh, 1862. 1st ed. 12mo. Presentation from publisher. Top of
spine frayed. Morrill 289-253 1983 $65

WOODS, ALVA   Valedictory Address. Tuscaloosa,
Slade, 1832. Dbd. First edition. Ginsberg 46-5 1983 $50

WOODS, GEORGE L.   Message of the Governor of Oregon,
to the Legislative Assembly. Salem, 1868. First edition. Dbd.
Ginsberg 46-613 1983 $100

WOODS, HARRIET F.   Historical Sketches of Brookline, Mass.
Boston, Author, 1874. 1st ed. With the signature and bookplate of
Edward Atkinson. 8vo. Rubbed and faded, tears on backstrip. Morrill
287-268 1983 $30

WOODS, JAMES   Recollections of Pioneer Work in
California by...A Pioneer Minister. San Francisco: Winterburn, 1878.
12mo, orig. green cloth. 1st ed. Very fine. Jenkins 153-707 1983
$45

WOODS, JULIAN EDMUND   Geological Observations in South Austral-
ia, Principally in the District South-East of Adelaide. London, 1862.
Map and wood-engraved illus., orig. gilt-lettered cloth. Bright.
K Books 307-109 1983 £120

WOODS, MARGARET L.   Esther Vanhomrigh. John Murray, 1891.
First edition, 3 vols. Half titles, library labels, orig. red cloth
a little dulled. Jarndyce 30-596 1983 £28

WOODS, MATTHEW   In Spite of Epilepsy. N.Y., 1913.
Ports. 8vo, cloth. Argosy 713-579 1983 $40

WOODWARD, ALICE B.   Banbury Cross & Other Nursery Rhymes.
J.M. Dent. 1895. Sm. slim 8vo. Frontis. Decorated title. 21 plates.
57 text illus. Pictorial endpapers. Yellow pictorial cloth, gilt.
Greer 40-244 1983 £28

WOODWARD, ALICE B.   The Pinafore Picture Book. London:
George Bell, 1908. 4to. Pictorial cloth, some foxing on preliminary
pages. Few spots scattered throughout. Color plates plus black &
whites by Woodward. Very good. Aleph-bet 8-269 1983 $20

WOODWARD, ARTHUR   Don Santiago Kirker. L.A., privately
printed, 1948. Orig. cloth. 200 copies printed. Ginsberg 47-683
1983 $35

WOODWARD, ARTHUR   Lances at San Pascual. San Francisco:
California Historical Society, 1948. Cloth. Special Publication 22.
Dawson 471-312 1983 $75

WOODWARD, ASHBEL   Life of General Nathaniel Lyon. Hartford,
1862. Map, 2 views, stamped stipple cloth, (backstrip top worn,
frontis. & t.p. foxed). Argosy 716-92 1983 $50

WOODWARD, EDWARD M.   Precis of information concerning
the Uganda Protectorate. London: His Majesty's Stationery Office,
1902. 8vo. 6 large folding maps in pocket. Orig. printed boards.
Adelson Africa-151 1983 $150

WOODWARD, GEORGE E.   Woodward's Country Homes. New York,
Woodward, 1865. 1st ed. Illus. and floor plans. 12mo. Corners
rubbed. Morrill 289-580 1983 $45

WOODWARD, HENRY   The beggar's pantomime; or, the contend-
ing columbines: a new comic interlude. London: printed for C.
Corbett; and W. Warner, 1736. 12mo, disbound, 2nd edition. Rare.
Ximenes 64-589 1983 $500

WOODWARD, HENRY   A letter from Henry Woodward, comedian,
the meanest of all characters. London: printed for M. Cooper, 1752.
8vo, half calf. 3rd edition. Title slight dusty, but a nice
copy. Ximenes 64-590 1983 $125

WOODWARD, J. J.   The Medical and Surgical History of
the War of Rebellion, 1861-65. Washington, 1870-88. Only
edition. Six vols. Orig. cloth. Recased with new endpapers, orig.
covers and backstrips laid down. Overall, a fine set. Fye-102
1983 $900

WOODWARD, JOHN   Remarks on the antient and present
state of London... London: printed for A. Bettesworth, etc.,
1723. Third edition. 8vo. Disbound. Slightly spotted. Ximenes
63-9 1983 $30

WOODWARD, JOHN   A Treatise on Heraldry, British and
Foreign, with English and French Glossaries. Edinburgh & London,
1892. 8vo. Leather, cloth. 2 vols. With 56 plates. Two page
ALS from John Woodward laid in. Some scuffing to binding, mainly
fine. In Our Time 156-894 1983 $150

WOODWARD, R. PITCHER   On a Donkey's Hurricane Deck. New York:
Blanchard, 1902. First edition. Frontis. portrait of author. Numer-
ous photoillus. from the trek. Orig. green pictorial cloth. Fine.
Jenkins 152-533 1983 $45

WOODWARD, SAMUEL PECKWORTH (1821-1865)   A Manual of the Mollusca.
(1880). 4th (last) edition. Map, 24 plates, text figures. Cr. 8vo.
Cloth. Wheldon 160-1239 1983 £25

WOODWORTH, ROBERT SESSIONS (1869-1962)   Dynamic Psychology. NY:
Columbia Univ. Press, 1918. First edition. Ads. Handsome copy in
publisher's crimson cloth. Gach 95-483 1983 $25

WOODWORTH, ROBERT SESSIONS (1869-1962)   Experimental Psychology.
NY: 1947 (1938). First edition, later printing. Gach 94-679 1983
$25

WOODWORTH, ROBERT SESSIONS (1869-1962)   Psychological Issues. NY:
Columbia Univ. Press, 1939. First edition. Leonard Carmichael's
copy. Gach 95-488 1983 $30

WOODWORTH, ROBERT SESSIONS (1869-1962)   The Puzzle of Color
Vocabularies. Orig. printed self-wrappers, unopened copy. Gach 95-
487 1983 $20

WOODYATT, N.   Under Ten Viceroys. London, 1922.
Plates. 8vo. Orig. cloth. Good. Edwards 1044-765 1983 £20

WOOLER, THOMAS J.   A political lecture on heads. London:
J. Johnston, 1820. First edition. 8vo. Disbound. Scarce. Ximenes
63-519 1983 $45

WOOLF, BELLA SIDNEY   Right Against Might. Cambridge, 1914.
Photographic illus., some on printed mounts. Thin 8vo, pict. boards.
First edition. Argosy 714-834 1983 $60

WOOLF, VIRGINIA   Annees. Paris: Editions Stock, 1938.
First edition in French. Orig. wrappers. Tissue guard. Fine. Mac-
Manus 280-5630 1983 $75

WOOLF, VIRGINIA   Between the Acts. N.Y.: Harcourt,
Brace & Co., (1941). First American edition. Orig. cloth. Dust
jacket. Review copy. Fine. MacManus 280-5632 1983 $75

WOOLF, VIRGINIA   Between The Acts. NY, (1941). Fine in
slightly chipped, near fine Vanessa Bell designed dustwrapper, discreet
owner's name and date. Quill & Brush 54-1586 1983 $50

WOOLF, VIRGINIA   Between the Acts. London: The Hogarth
Press, (1941). First edition. Orig. cloth. Dust jacket designed by
V. Bell. Former owner's signature on front flyleaf. Jacket dust-
soiled and worn at edges. Good. MacManus 280-5631 1983 $40

WOOLF, VIRGINIA   Between the Acts. New York, (1941).
First American edition. 8vo. Blue cloth, spine faded. Traylen
94-895 1983 £12

WOOLF, VIRGINIA   The Captain's Death and Other Essays.
London: The Hogarth Press, 1950. 8vo. Cloth. Some light fading
to lettering on spine, fine copy in dj. In Our Time 156-898 1983
$100

WOOLF, VIRGINIA   The Common Reader. London: The Hogarth
Press, 1925. First edition. Orig. cloth-backed decorated boards
designed by V. Bell. 1250 copies printed. Former owner's signature
on front endsheet. Spine slightly stained. Good. MacManus 280-5633
1983 $85

WOOLF, VIRGINIA   The Common Reader. London: The Hogarth
Press, 1932. First edition. Second Series. Orig. cloth. Dust jacket
(darkened & torn). With the publisher's prospectus (dusty) laid in.
Very good. MacManus 280-5634 1983 $125

WOOLF, VIRGINIA   The Common Reader. London: The Hogarth
Press, 1933-1935. Uniform edition. 2 vols. Orig. cloth. Dust
jackets (spines darkened, a bit worn). Inscriptions on flyleaves.
Very good. MacManus 280-5635 1983 $25

WOOLF, VIRGINIA   Flush. London: Hogarth Press, 1933.
Cloth. First edition. Illus. with four drawings by Vanessa Bell.
Binding slightly foxed, else a very good copy in slightly chipped
and soiled dust jacket. Reese 20-1169 1983 $75

WOOLF, VIRGINIA   A Haunted House and Other Stories. NY,
(1944). Flys slightly offset from laid-in Welty review, else bright
copy with slightly rubbed edges and some pencil underlinings in text
in lightly chipped dustwrapper, owner's inscription. Quill & Brush
54-1584 1983 $50

WOOLF, VIRGINIA   A Haunted House and Other Stories. NY,
(1944). Near fine in lightly chipped, very good dustwrapper that was
designed by Vanessa Bell. Quill & Brush 54-1583 1983 $50

WOOLF, VIRGINIA   The Hogarth Letters. London: Hogarth
Press, 1933. First edition. Thick 12mo, buff pictorial boards;
brown cloth spine; slightly rubbed. Argosy 714-845 1983 $250

WOOLF, VIRGINIA   Jacob's Room. New York, (1923).
First American edition. 8vo. Orig. yellow cloth, printed paper
label. Traylen 94-897 1983 £16

WOOLF, VIRGINIA   A Letter to a Young Poet. L, 1932.
Paperwraps, cover slightly soiled, very good, owner's name. Quill &
Brush 54-1585 1983 $75

WOOLF, VIRGINIA   A Letter to a Young Poet. London:
Hogarth Press, 1932. First edition. Printed wraps.; darkened.
Argosy 714-835 1983 $25

WOOLF, VIRGINIA   A Letter to a Young Poet. London:
The Hogarth Press, 1932. First English edition. Wrappers. Endpapers and edges slightly spotted. Very good. Jolliffe 26-612
1983 £12

WOOLF, VIRGINIA   Mrs. Dalloway. New York, (1925).
8vo. Orig. orange cloth boards, printed paper label. Spine faded.
Traylen 94-899 1983 £12

WOOLF, VIRGINIA   The Moment and Other Essays. London:
The Hogarth Press, 1947. Flexible cloth. First edition. Top edge
slightly dusty, otherwise fine in slightly used dust jacket.
Reese 20-1170 1983 $85

WOOLF, VIRGINIA   The Moment and Other Essays. London:
Hogarth Press, 1947. First edition. Orig. cloth. Dust jacket (soiled
and torn). Covers a bit warped and stained. MacManus 280-5639 1983
$40

WOOLF, VIRGINIA   The Moment and other essays. London,
1947. First edition. Slightly frayed dust wrapper. Fine. Rota
231-634 1983 £12

WOOLF, VIRGINIA   The Moment and Other Essays. NY, (1948).
Edges very slightly rubbed, else very good plus with some pencil underlining in text, Vanessa Bell dustwrapper with slightly faded spine,
owner's name. Quill & Brush 54-1591 1983 $40

WOOLF, VIRGINIA   The Moment and other Essays. New
York, 1948. First American edition. 8vo. Orig. cloth. Traylen
94-898 1983 £12

WOOLF, VIRGINIA   Monday or Tuesday. N.Y.: Harcourt,
Brace & Co., 1921. First American edition. Orig. cloth with paper
spine label. Spine and covers slightly wron. Very good. MacManus
280-5640 1983 $100

WOOLF, VIRGINIA   Monday or Tuesday. NY, 1921. Edges
slightly worn, endpapers slightly foxed, good or better. Quill &
Brush 54-1588 1983 $75

WOOLF, VIRGINIA   Monday or Tuesday. N.Y., 1921. First
American edition. Small 8vo, cloth backed boards. Spine label
chipped. Argosy 714-836 1983 $50

WOOLF, VIRGINIA   Night and Day. New York, (1920).
First American edition. 8vo. Orig. brown cloth. Traylen 94-900
1983 £18

WOOLF, VIRGINIA   Orlando. NY, 1928. Limited edition of
861 numbered and signed copies, many pages uncut, very minor cover
wear, bookplate. Quill & Brush 54-1589 1983 $500

WOOLF, VIRGINIA   Orlando. Hogarth Press, 1928.
First edition. Tall 8vo; orange cloth; corners bumped. Argosy
714-840 1983 $75

WOOLF, VIRGINIA   Roger Fry: A Biography. London:
The Hogarth Press, 1940. 8vo. Cloth. Orig. dj is chipped at top
of spine. Fine. In Our Time 156-897 1983 $100

WOOLF, VIRGINIA   Roger Fry. London: Hogarth Press, 1940.
First edition. Illus. 8vo, green cloth; faded. One page prospectus
for the book is enclosed. Argosy 714-841 1983 $60

WOOLF, VIRGINIA   A Room Of One's Own. London: The
Hogarth Press, 1929. First edition. Tall 8vo. Orig. cloth.
One of 492 copies signed by the author. Without dust jacket as
issued. Very fine copy. Jaffe 1-408 1983 $675

WOOLF, VIRGINIA   A Room Of One's Own. London: The
Hogarth Press, 1929. First edition. Orig. brown cloth. This copy
was inscribed for a student who was at Girton when author read the two
papers on which this essay is based. Edges very slightly worn. Endpapers lightly browned. Good. MacManus 280-5641 1983 $650

WOOLF, VIRGINIA   A Room of One's Own. New York, 1929.
First American edition. 8vo. Orig. blue cloth. With presentation
inscription on the fly-leaf, "Aunt Gertrude with a great deal of
love from Virginia, Christmas, 1929." Spine faded. Traylen 94-
902 1983 £35

WOOLF, VIRGINIA   Street Haunting. San Francisco:
The Westgate Press, 1930. 8vo. Leather, boards. Total ed. is
500 copies signed by Woolf. Name of owner on front fly, tiny nick
at top edge of spine, mainly a fine copy. In Our Time 156-896
1983 $400

WOOLF, VIRGINIA   Three Guineas. London: Hogarth Press,
1938. First edition. Orig. cloth. Dust jacket with design by V.
Bell (faded and torn). MacManus 280-5642 1983 $75

WOOLF, VIRGINIA   Three Guineas. New York, (1938).
First American edition. 5 plates. 8vo. Orig. pink cloth. Traylen
94-903 1983 $12

WOOLF, VIRGINIA   To the Lighthouse. N.Y., (1927).
First American edition. 8vo, light green cloth, slightly rubbed.
Owner's name on flyleaf. Argosy 714-842 1983 $125

WOOLF, VIRGINIA   To the Lighthouse. N.Y., Modern Library,
(1937). First edition thus, (so stated). Pictorial dust jacket
(slight rubbing, trifle nicked) else, very good. Houle 22-985 1983
$35

WOOLF, VIRGINIA   The Voyage Out. London, 1915. Bookplate of G.L. Lazarus. A little rubbed. Slightly used and reinforced
cream dustwrapper printed in blue, missing a small piece from the
lower corner of the front panel. This is a variant dustwrapper.
Very good. Gekoski 2-203 1983 £1,550

WOOLF, VIRGINIA   The Voyage Out. London, 1915. First
edition. 8vo, green cloth; slightly rubbed at edges; owner's bookplate. A good copy. Argosy 714-843 1983 $450

WOOLF, VIRGINIA   The Voyage Out. Duckworth, 1915.
First edition, 16 ads., 8vo, orig. green cloth. A very good copy in
a fitted fleece-lined folding cloth library case. Fenning 62-401
1983 £250

WOOLF, VIRGINIA   The Voyage Out. New York, (1920).
First American edition. 8vo. Orig. green cloth. Spine faded.
Traylen 94-905 1983 £18

WOOLF, VIRGINIA   The Waves. London: The Hogarth Press,
1931. First edition. Orig. cloth. Dust jacket (slightly chipped).
Some foxing. Very good. MacManus 280-5644 1983 $150

WOOLF, VIRGINIA   The Waves. N.Y.: Harcourt, Brace & Co.,
(1931). First American edition. Orig. cloth. Dust jacket (darkened).
Signature of former owner on flyleaf. Good. MacManus 280-5645 1983
$35

WOOLF, VIRGINIA   The Waves. London: The Hogarth Press,
1931. First edition. Orig. cloth. Very good. MacManus 280-5643
1983 $85

WOOLF, VIRGINIA   The Waves. N.Y., (1931). First
American edition. 8vo, blue cloth. Argosy 714-844 1983 $25

WOOLF, VIRGINIA   The Waves. New York, (1931). First
American edition. 8vo. Cloth. Spine faded. Traylen 94-906 1983
£15

WOOLF, VIRGINIA   A writer's diary. London: Hogarth
Press, 1953. First edition. Slight foxing to endpaper. Laid
in are Stephen Spender's 1p. holograph notes on the text, and the 2pp.
corrected typescript of his essay on Woolf. Very good. Gekoski
2-175 1983 £140

WOOLF, VIRGINIA   A Writer's Diary. London: The Hogarth
Press, 1953. 8vo. Cloth. A fine copy in dj which has a few minimal
tears. In Our Time 156-899 1983 $100

WOOLF, VIRGINIA   The Years. London: The Hogarth Press,
1937. First edition. Orig. cloth. Dust jacket (a bit faded and
foxed). Fine. MacManus 280-5648 1983 $350

WOOLF, VIRGINIA   The Years. New York, 1937. First
American edition. Dust wrapper severely faded at the portion covering
the spine. Very nice. Rota 230-648 1983 £30

WOOLF, VIRGINIA   The Years. New York, (1937). First
American edition. 8vo. Orig. blue cloth. Spine faded. Traylen
94-908 1983 £15

WOOLF, VIRGINIA   The Years. N.Y.: Harcourt, Brace &
Co., (1937). First American edition. Orig. cloth (spine faded, edges
rubbed). Cont. ownership inscription on free endpaper. Very good.
MacManus 280-5647 1983 $20

WOOLL, JOHN   Biographical Memoirs of the late
Revd. Joseph Warton... London: for T. Cadell, and W. Davies, 1806.
First edition. 4to. Half calf, neatly rebacked, gilt. Engraved
portrait after Reynolds. With author's presentation inscription
on fly-leaf. Traylen 94-857 1983 £30

WOOLLCOTT, ALEXANDER   His Life and His World. N.Y., (1945).
First edition. 8vo, cloth. Argosy 714-847 1983 $20

WOOLLEY, HELEN THOMPSON   An Experimental Study of Children. NY:
Macmillan, 1926. First edition. Ex-library copy. Gach 94-680 1983
$25

WOOLLEY, L. H.   California 1849-1913. Oakland: 1913.
First edition. Portrait frontis. Blue-gray wrappers. Fine copy,
covers lightly faded. Bradley 66-660 1983 $125

WOOLMAN, JOHN   The Journal of... B, 1871. Cover
slightly rubbed and top of spine slightly frayed, otherwise very good,
bookplate. Quill & Brush 54-1533 1983 $40

WOOLMAN, JOHN   The Journal and Essays. Philadelphia,
1922. Illus. 8vo. Morrill 287-528 1983 $22.50

WOOLMAN, JOHN   Serious Considerations on Various
Subjects of Importance. New York: Collins, Perkins and Co. for
Samuel Wood, 1805. Full calf. With five added titlepages. The
Samuel Wood line on the first title is on a slip pasted over the
address line of the Collins firm. Felcone 22-274 1983 $25

WOOLWARD, SAMUEL FRANCIS   The Beauties of Friendship. (Wichita,
Goldsmith, 1906). Tall narrow 8vo, unusual green suede leather
Craftsmen binding with a large green patinated brass oak leaf on
upper cover, with a large mother of pearl stone. Houle 21-114
1983 $85

WOOTTON, A. C.   Chronicles of Pharmacy. London, 1910.
8vo. 2 vols. Cloth. Gurney JJ-426 1983 £30

WORCESTER, NOAH   A Solemn Review of the Custom of War...
Hartford, 1815. Stitched, good. Reese 13-490 1983 $25

WORCESTER, SAMUEL   Calamity, Danger, and Hope... Salem,
1812. Stitched, good. Reese 18-404 1983 $20

WORCESTER, SAMUEL M.   California. Outlines of an Address Before the Naumkeag Mutual Trading and Mining Company...1849. (Salem,
Mass., 1849). Orig. printed wraps. First edition. Thomas W. Streeter's copy with his bookplate. Ginsberg 47-207 1983 $175

WORDSWORTH, WILLIAM   Gleanings of Verse. London: Printed
for Private Circulation Only, 1899. 4to. White buckram, gilt,
t.e.g., others uncut. With presentation inscription on the title-
page, "F.T. Dryden from her Cousin the Author, Nov. 1899." Traylen
94-910 1983 £12

WORDSWORTH, WILLIAM   Lyrical Ballads. London, Printed for
J & A Arch, 1798. 12mo. Errata & ads. Small dampstain in top margin
of last 30 leaves. Full olive green levant morocco gilt, gilt inner
dentelles, aeg by Aaehnsdorf. 1st ed., 2nd issue. 1st issue with
orig. Bristol titlepage-extremely rare. Very fine. O'Neal 50-60
1983 $2,000

WORDSWORTH, WILLIAM   Lyrical Ballads. London, Printed for
T.N. Longman and O. Rees, 1800. 2 vols. 12mo. Errata. Full olive
green levant morocco by Azehnsdorf, gilt, gilt inner dentelles, aeg.
2nd ed. of vol. 1; 1st ed., 1st issue of vol. 2. 500 copies printed.
Very fine. O'Neal 50-61 1983 $1500

WORDSWORTH, WILLIAM   Memorials of a Tour on the Continent,
1820. London: Printed for Longman, Hurst, Rees, Orme and Brown, 1822.
First edition. Orig. boards (dampstained). Spine worn with slightly
chipped spine label. Slight foxing. In a half-morocco slipcase.
Very good. MacManus 280-5655 1983 $200

WORDSWORTH, WILLIAM   Our English Lakes, Mountains & Water-
falls. Provost & Co., 1870. 4th edn. with mounted frontis. & 7
mounted photo illus. by Thomas Ogle. Blue pebble grain cloth gilt,
bevelled boards, a.e.g. (2" wear to top joint top & bottom of bkstrip,
lower corners bumped & sl. worn, insc. fr. ep.), contents fine.
Hodgkins 27-352 1983 £40

WORDSWORTH, WILLIAM   Poems. London, Longman, et al., 1807.
2 vols. 12mo. Errata. Light foxing. Full green levant morocco,
spines gilt, gilt inner dentelles, uncut edges, by Riviere. 1st ed.
With both half-titles, the errata leaf, and the ads. Fine. O'Neal
50-59 1983 $750

WORDSWORTH, WILLIAM   Poems. London: Longman, etc., 1815.
First collected edition. 2 vols. 8vo. Cont. calf. Spines gilt.
Frontis. in each vol. (some offsetting). Spines rubbed, a couple
of hinges tender. Ximenes 63-428 1983 $250

WORDSWORTH, WILLIAM   Poems for the Young. A. Strahan, 1863.
Sq. 8vo. First edition. Title vignette by Millais. Frontis. & 47
illus. engraved by D. Brothers. Light red ornately gilt cloth. 10pp
of ads. Greer 40-141 1983 £25

WORDSWORTH, WILLIAM   The poetical works. Paris: Galignani,
1828. Large 8vo. Orig. grey boards, printed paper label. Portrait.
Some wear. Ximenes 63-429 1983 $100

WORDSWORTH, WILLIAM   The Poetical Works... London, 1859.
Illus. Early ed. Contemporary full red morocco, fully gilt, a.e.g.
Very good. Jenkins 155-430 1983 $300

WORDSWORTH, WILLIAM   Yarrow Revisited. London: Printed for
Longman, Rees, Orme, Brown, Green & Longman, ... & Edward Moxon, 1836.
Second edition. 8vo. Orig. boards with paper label on spine. Bookplate. Cont. owner's signature on endsheet. Spine somewhat worn at
hinges. Label darkened & chipped. Good. MacManus 280-5656 1983 $50

THE WORK of Frank Lloyd Wright: The Life-Work of the American
Architect Frank Lloyd Wright. New York: Horizon Press, 1965.
Most prof. illus. Small square folio. Cloth. The posthumous
edition of the Wendingen Edition, retaining the orig. typographical
format and mis-en-page, the double-fold pages, and the specially
hinged binding designed by Wright. Very light wear. Ars Libri
32-712 1983 $175

WORKMAN, F. B.   Ice-Bound Heights of the Mustagh. London, 1908. First edition. 2 folding maps, 2 colour plates. 3 sepia
photograph plates, numerous other illus., many full page. New quarter
calf with raised bands, morocco label, gilt. 8vo. Good. Edwards
1044-767 1983 £165

WORLD'S Columbian Exposition Chicago. (Germany, ca. 1893). Narrow 12mo, spine top worn. Accordion-folded photographic views. Argosy 710-153 1983 $27.50

WORLIDGE, JOHN   Vinetum Britannicum: or, a Treatise of Cider... London: by J.C. for Tho. Dring and Tho. Burrel, 1676. First edition. 8vo. Frontis., and 2 plates. Licence leaf. Full modern old style panelled calf gilt. Frontis. trimmed close in one corner. Heath 48-18 1983 £350

WORSHAM, JOHN H.   One of Jackson's Foot Cavalry...During the War, 1861-1865. N.Y.: Neale, 1912. 1st ed., illus. An exquisite copy in original cloth. Included original four-page advance promotional for the book. Slipcased. Jenkins 151-237 1983 $300

WORSLEY, FRANCIS   Gazella. Saunders & Otley, 1839. First edition, half title. Orig. orange cloth, sl. rubbed. Jarndyce 30-764 1983 £24

WORSLEY, PHILIP STANHOPE   Poems and Translations. Blackwood, 1863. First edition, 1 p ads., half title. Tear from leading free end papers. Orig. blue cloth. Jarndyce 30-765 1983 £12.50

WORTHINGTON, E. B.   Science in Africa. 1938. 8vo, cloth, 5 maps and 8 plates. Wheldon 160-287 1983 £12

WORTHINGTON, G   A Bibliography of the Waverley Novels. London: Constable & Co., (1931). First edition. 8vo. Parchment-backed marbled boards. Limited to 500 copies. Slight soiling of parchment and rubbing along edges, else fine. Oak Knoll 48-476 1983 $150

WORTHINGTON, G   A Bibliography of the Waverly Novels. London, Constable, (1931). Tall 8vo, orig. quarter vellum, boards, spine a bit age-darkened, few pencil marks, uncut, one of only 500 copies. First and only edition. Ravenstree 96-211 1983 $125

WORTHINGTON, STELLA   Inland Waters of Africa. Macmillan, 1933. With a folding map, 4 other maps, 40 plates and some other illus. 8vo, orig. cloth, very slight discoloration of the boards. Fenning 62-402 1983 £18.50

WORTMAN, TUNIS   An Address, to the Republican Citizens of New York, on the Inauguration of Thomas Jefferson. New York: William Durell, 1801. Disbound. Very good. Felcone 20-71 1983 $20

WOTTON, HENRY   Reliquiae Wottonianae. London: Printed by Thomas Maxey, for R. Marriot, G. Bedel, & T. Garthwait, 1651. First edition. Illus. with engraved port. Full cont. calf. Cont. signature on flyleaf. Bookplate of Richard Prime on front endsheet. Outer hinges weak, top of spine worn. Good. MacManus 280-5661 1983 $250

WOTTON, HENRY   Reliquiae Wottonianae. 1651. First edition, 3 engraved portraits (lacking portrait of Wotton), small 12mo, cont. calf. K Books 301-196 1983 £40

WOTY, WILLIAM   The Shrubs of Parnassus. Printed for the author; and sold by J. Newbery, 1760. 12mo, orig. calf, slight wear at head and foot of the spine. There is a 17-page list of subscribers. First edition. Bickersteth 77-93 1983 £120

WOULFE, PATRICK   Sloinnte Gaedheal is Gall. Dublin: Gill, 1923. Cr. 8vo, orig. cloth, in worn dust wrapper. Fenning 62-403 1983 £24.50

WRAXHALL, NATHANIEL WILLIAM (1751-1831)   A Short Review of the Political State of Great Britain at the Commencement of the Year One Thousand Seven Hundred and Eighty-Seven. Printed for J. Debrett, 1787. Half-title and final blank leaf. 8vo. Wrapper. Fenning 61-500 1983 £85

THE WREATH & Other Pastorals. London: Marcus Ward, (ca. 1880). Oblong octavo. Illus. with 8 full-page and several small chomolithographs, many floral borders and other decorations printed in gold. Cloth-backed colored pictorial boards rubbed at corners, else fine. A.e.g. Bromer 25-405 1983 $60

WREN, CHRISTOPHER   Numismatum Antiquorum Sylloge Populis Graecis, Municipiis & Coloniis Romanis Cusorum, ex Cimeliarchio Editoris. Londini, apud Davidem Mortier, 1708. First edition, with 6 engraved plates, 4to, orig. stiff floral paper wraps. Fenning 60-448 1983 £35

WRIGHT, ANDREW   Court Hand Restored. London: Benjamin White, 1776. First edition. Small 4to. 19th century cloth, leather spine label. 20 engraved plates. One hing partially cracked else a very good copy. Oak Knoll 48-385 1983 $300

WRIGHT, ANDREW   Court Hand Restored. 1776. 20 plates, 4to, morocco. K Books 301-197 1983 £60

WRIGHT, ANDREW   Court-Hand Restored. Charles Trice Martin, 1879. 30 plates with accompanying letterpress. Cloth. 9th ed., corrected and enlarged. Worn and bumped, hinges repaired and tight. Dawson 470-312 1983 $40

WRIGHT, ARTHUR W.   Biographical Memoir of Benjamin Silliman. Washington: National Academy of Sciences, 1911. Authors separate. Orig. printed wrappers. Fine copy. Jenkins 153-513 1983 $25

WRIGHT, AUSTIN TAPPAN   Islandia. New York, Toronto: Farrar & Rinehart Inc., (1942). First edition, first issue. Large 8vo. Orig. cloth. Dust jacket. Aside from a single short tear to jacket, a very fine copy. Jaffe 1-409 1983 $275

WRIGHT, AUSTIN TAPPAN   Islandia. NY, (1942). Very slight soiling to cover and small tear on top of front end paper where price was erased, otherwise very good. Quill & Brush 54-1593 1983 $40

WRIGHT, CHARLES   A History of Lloyd's. London, 1928. Well illus. Index. Covers a bit dull with very minor wear. King 45-453 1983 $25

WRIGHT, FRANK LLOYD   An Autobiography. New York: Duell, Sloan & Pearce, 1943. 10 plates. Decorative section dividers (color) designed by Wright. Stout oblong 4to. Cloth. Ars Libri 32-710 1983 $75

WRIGHT, FRANK LLOYD   When Democracy Builds. Ch., (1945). Second printing, minor ink notation, else very good. Quill & Brush 54-1669 1983 $20

WRIGHT, HAROLD J. L.   The Etchings and Drypoints of Sir D.Y. Cameron. London: The Print Collector's Club, 1947. 18 plates. 4to. Cloth. Edition limited to 400 numbered copies. Ars Libri 32-77 1983 $50

WRIGHT, HENRY CLARKE (1797-1870)   Marriage and Parentage. Boston: Bela Marsh, 1854. 12mo. First edition. Orig. embossed mauve cloth. Gach 95-490 1983 $40

WRIGHT, JAMES A.   Historical Sketches of the Town of Moravia from 1791 to 1918. Auburn, N.Y.,: Cayuga County News, ca. 1918. Frontis. Portraits. Fine copy of the first edition in original cloth. Jenkins 151-250 1983 $45

WRIGHT, JOHN   The Flower Grower's Guide. London, ca 1880. 3 vols., with 46 coloured plates and several hundred text-illustrations, 4to, a little shaken but good in the orig. decorated cloth, gilt edges. K Books 301-198 1983 £120

WRIGHT, LOUISE W.   A Southern Girl in '61. New York, 1905. Cloth, fine. Reese 19-602 1983 $75

WRIGHT, MICHAEL   An Account of His Excellence Roger Earl of Castlemaine's Embassy, from...James the IId...to His Holiness Innocent XI. London: Snowden, 1688. Small folio, with engraved frontis., portrait of Mary of Modena, 16 plates & large folding plate. Calf. Bayfield Hall Library book-ticket. Illus. fete book. Plates by Flemish artist Westerhout. Rostenberg 88-55 1983 $775

WRIGHT, RICHARD   Black Boy. N.Y., (1945). First edition. D.w. Eslanda Goode Robeson's copy, with her autograph, and the notation "review copy". Argosy 714-848 1983 $60

WRIGHT, RICHARD　　　　　Black Boy. NY, (1945). Bright, fine copy in slightly rubbed, slightly frayed dustwrapper. Quill & Brush 54-1595　1983　$60

WRIGHT, RICHARD　　　　　Black Boy. (Paris): NRF/Gallimard, (1947). Orig. printed wraps. First French edition. One of only 100 numbered copies, printed on velin pur fil Nafuma-Navarre. A very fine copy. Reese 20-1171　1983　$60

WRIGHT, RICHARD　　　　　An Essay, on the Principles of Dissent... London, 1815. Later wraps., stitched. Good. Reese 18-491　1983　$35

WRIGHT, RICHARD　　　　　Native Son. New York: Harpers, 1940. 1st ed., 1st binding, 1st dj. Orig. dark blue cloth, stamped in red and white, in green and yellow dj. Fine copy in near fine dj, and scarce thus. Jenkins 155-1344　1983　$100

WRIGHT, RICHARD　　　　　Native Son. NY, 1940. Very good in very lightly chipped, slightly creased first issue dustwrapper. Quill & Brush 54-1598　1983　$90

WRIGHT, RICHARD　　　　　12 Million Black Voices. NY, 1941. Spine gutters very slightly darkened, else fine in frayed and chipped dustwrapper that is rubbed along edges. Quill & Brush 54-1594　1983　$75

WRIGHT, ROBERT　　　　　A Memoir of General James Oglethorpe. Chapman and Hall, 1867. First edition, with a map, 8vo, recent boards. Fenning 62-404　1983　£24.50

WRIGHT, ROBERT MARR (b. 1840)　　　Dodge City. (Wichita, 1913). First edition. Frontis. in color. Ullus. 12mo. Minor wear at lower front corners of cover. Nice copy. Most of the ed. was destroyed by the printer, hence its scarcity. Clark 741-223　1983　$195

WRIGHT, ROBERT MARR (b. 1840)　　　Dodge City, the Cowboy Capital. (Wichita, 1913). Cloth. Second issue, without the colored frontis. Very good. Reese 19-609　1983　$75

WRIGHT, ROBERT MARR (b. 1840)　　　Dodge City, The Cowboy Capital. (Wichita, 1913.) Plates. Orig. pictorial cloth, worn. Lacking frontis. Scarce. Jenkins 153-709　1983　$45

WRIGHT, THOMAS　　　　　Miscellanea Graphica. London, Chapman & Hall, 1857. 4to, illus. with 11 chromo plates, 33 lithos. Full diced tan calf, stamped in blind and gilt (moderate rubbing on spine, short cracks at joints). Marbled endpapers and edges, red leather label on spine. Foxing on some pages.　Good - very good. Houle 22-991　1983　$225

WRIGHT, THOMAS GIORDANI　　　Cholera in the Asylum. 1850. 8vo, 4 folding tables, and a plan, inscription on half title, orig. cloth, blocked in blind.　Spine a little faded, but a crisp copy. Bickersteth 77-330　1983　£90

WRIGHT, W. B.　　　　　The Quaternary Ice Age. (1936) 1937. Second edition, 23 plates and 155 text-figures, 8vo, cloth. Wheldon 160-1490　1983　£20

WRIGHT, WALTER P.　　　　Cassell's Popular Gardening. London, Cassell & Co., n.d. (ca. 1920s). Colored plates, illus. 2 vols. 4to. Morrill 286-556　1983　$22.50

WRIGHT, WILLIAM　　　　The Big Bonanza, an Authentic Account of the Discovery, History, and Working of the Comstock Lode in Nevada. NY, 1947. Illus. Argosy 710-325　1983　$35

WRIGHT, WILLIAM　　　　A History of the Comstock Mines. Virginia City, Nev., 1889. Orig. printed wraps. First edition. Ginsberg 47-668　1983　$75

WRIGHT, WILLIAM H.　　　　The Black Bear. New York, 1910. 1st ed. Illus. from photographs by author and J. B. Kerfoot. 8vo. Minor cover stains, otherwise nice. Morrill 286-557　1983　$20

WRIGHT, WILMER CAVE　　　　A Short History of Greek Literature. NY, 1907. 8vo, cloth.　Salloch 385-204　1983　$25

WRIGHTSON, RICHARD　　　　An Introductory Treatise on Sanscrit Hagiographa. Dublin: M'Glashan & Gill, 1859. First edition, cr. 8vo, orig. cloth-backed boards, with printed paper label. Fenning 62-405　1983　£18.50

WRISBERG, H. A.　　　　De Insitione Variolarum nonnulla momenta recensit et simul ad Sermonem Academicum de Physiologia Errores quosdam expurgante. Gottingen, 1765. First edition. 4to. Stitched as issued. 1 plate. Gurney 90-125　1983　£30

WRISBERG, H. A.　　　　De Respiratione Prima Nervo Phrenico et Calore Animali. Gottingen, 1763. First edition. 4to. Wrappers paper backed. Gurney 90-127　1983　£30

WRISBERG, H. A.　　　　Sylloge Commentationum Anatomicarum. Gottingen: J.C. Dieterich, 1786. First edition. 4to. Boards. Title slightly dust coloured. Gurney 90-128　1983　£70

WRONG, GEORGE M.　　　　A Canadian Manor and Its Seigneurs. Toronto: Macmillan, 1926. 23cm. 8 illus. and 2 maps. Limited to 900 copies. Green cloth. Spine slightly faded else very good. McGahern 53-177　1983　$25

WROTH, LAWRENCE C.　　　　The Colonial Printer. Portland, Maine: Southworth-Anthoensen Press, 1938. 8vo, green cloth, gilt, t.e.g. Illus throughout. Second edition, revised and enlarged. One of 1500 copies. Very fine copy in lightly rubbed slipcase. Perata 28-196　1983　$125

WROTH, LAWRENCE C.　　　　A History of Printing in Colonial Maryland 1686-1776. Baltimore: Typothetae, 1922. 3/4 morocco with morocco label. Light stain to title page. Limited to 500 copies. Illustrations. Handsome. Jenkins 153-47　1983　$175

WUESTENFELD, F.　　　　Geschichte der Arabischen Aerzte und Naturforscher. Gottingen, 1840. 8vo. Old wrappers, rebacked, uncut. First edition. 2 stamps on title, some foxing. Gurney JJ-428　1983　£60

WUNDT, MAX　　　　Platons Leben und Werk. 1914. 3/4 cl. 8vo. Salloch 385-695　1983　$24

WUNDT, WILHELM (1832-1920)　　　Einleitung in Due Philosophie. Leipzig: Verlag von Wilhelm Engelmann, 1901. First edition. Publisher's blue cloth. Gach 95-491　1983　$100

WUNDT, WILHELM (1832-1920)　　　Elemente Der Voelkerpsychologie. Leipzig: Alfred Kroener Verlang, 1912. Very fine in orig. blue linen, gilt. First edition. Gach 95-492　1983　$135

WUNDT, WILHELM (1832-1920)　　　Elements of Folk Psychology. London, 1916. First English edition. Cloth a little dirty, spine dull. Gach 95-493　1983　$85

WUNDT, WILHELM (1832-1920)　　　The Facts of Moral Life. London: Swan Sonnenschein & Co., 1897. First English edition. Publisher's vertically rubbed brown cloth. Near fine. Gach 95-494　1983　$50

WUNDT, WILHELM (1832-1920)　　　An Introduction to Psychology. NY: Macmillan, 1912. 12mo. Publisher's green cloth. First American edition. Near fine copy. Gach 95-495　1983　$50

WUNDT, WILHELM (1832-1920)　　　Lectures on Human and Animal Psychology. London: Swan Sonnenschein & Co., 1894. Some pencilling to first chapter, minor fraying to joints, else very good copy. Gach 95-496　1983　$75

WUNDT, WILHELM (1832-1920)　　　Outlines of Psychology. London/NY: 1907. Third revised English edition. Minor staining and pencil-lining. Gach 95-497　1983　$50

WUNDT, WILHELM (1832-1920)　　　The Principles of Morality. London: Swan Sonnenschein, 1901. First English edition. Gach 95-498　1983　$50

WUNSCH, JOSEF   Blasius Hofel. Geschichte seines Lebens und seiner Kunst und Verzeichnis seiner Werke. Wien: Gesellschaft fur Vervielfaltigende Kunst, 1910. 14 plates. Large 4to. Wrappers. Ars Libri 32-311 1983 $100

WYATT, MATTHEW DIGBY (1820-1827)   The history and manufacture of clocks... London, 1868. First edition, "privately printed." 16mo. Orig. limp salmon cloth. Spine a bit worn, upper hinge reinforced. Rare. Ximenes 63-76 1983 $60

WYATT, MATTHEW DIGBY (1820-1827)   Metal-Work and its Artistic Design. Printed in colours, and published by Day & Son, 1852. 48 chromo-litho plates, incl. the additional coloured title, folio, orig. calf-backed cloth, gilt, loose in case and a few margins lightly dusty. The missing plates are nos. 18 & 20. Fenning 61-501 1983 £45

WYATT, THOMAS   The Poetical Works. London, 1866. Cr. 8vo. Dark blue calf, two-line gilt borders with corner ornaments, gilt panelled spine, morocco label, gilt. Portrait, vignette title-page. Traylen 94-911 1983 £16

WYETH, JOHN ALLAN   Life of General Nathan Bedford Forrest. NY, 1899. First edition. T.e.g., lacks f.e.p., spine torn and heavily darkened. Back cover mildly stained. King 46-84 1983 $65

WYETH, NATHANIEL J.   The Correspondence and Journals of... Eugene, Ore.: University Press, 1899. Two folding maps, orig. printed wrappers, chipped. Spine repaired. Nice. Jenkins 152-536 1983 $75

WYLDE, KATHARINE   Mr. Bryant's Mistake. London: Richard Bentley & Son, 1890. First edition. Orig. cloth. 3 vols. Spine ends very slightly worn. Little light foxing. Near-fine. MacManus 280-2665 1983 $225

WYLDE, KATHARINE   The Princes Royal. London: Richard Bentley & Co., 1894. First edition. 3 vols. Orig. embossed cloth. Author's own copy, inscribed with her signatures in all volumes. The first with date of Oct. 16, 1894, with press cuttings pasted to front endpapers. Covers a little dull. Inner hinges tender. Very good. MacManus 277-1050 1983 $185

WYLIE, ANDREW   Opinion of...of the Supreme Court of the District of Columbia. Wash., 1866. Orig. printed wraps. First edition. Ginsberg 47-208 1983 $85

WYLIE, ELINOR   Angels and Earthly Creatures. New York, 1929. First edition. One of 200 numbered copies printed by the Plimpton Press on Swedish hand-made paper. Very good. Jolliffe 26-615 1983 £48

WYLIE, ELINOR   Incidental Numbers. London, 1912. Boards. First edition. A fine copy. In cloth slipcase. Reese 20-1172 1983 $4,000

WYLIE, ELINOR   Last Poems of... NY, 1943. Cover lightly stained, else very good in frayed and wearing, good dustwrapper, owner's name. Quill & Brush 54-1600 1983 $30

WYLIE, ELINOR   Trivial Breath. London and New York: 1928. First edition. 1/100 numbered copies signed by poet. Decorated cloth, printed paper spine label. Fine, most unopened. Bradley 66-388 1983 $125

WYLIE, PHILIP   Babes and Sucklings. NY, 1929. Very good in remnants of dustwrapper, bookplate. Quill & Brush 54-1601 1983 $30

WYLIE, PHILIP   Corpses at Indian Stones. NY, (1943). Edges slightly rubbed, else near fine in lightly chipped, very good dustwrapper. Quill & Brush 54-1602 1983 $30

WYLIE, PHILIP   The Other Horseman. NY, (1942). Very good with minor pencil notes in wearing, price clipped, good dustwrapper. Quill & Brush 54-1603 1983 $30

WYLLIE, ROBERT C.   Notes on the Shipping, Trade, Agriculture, Climate, Diseases, Religious Institutions... Honolulu, Oahu, S.I., 1845. Folio. Dbd. Ginsberg 46-309 1983 $75

WYLLY, H. C.   History of the Manchester Regiment. London, 1923-5. Frontis. (1 coloured), 10 coloured plates, 23 other plates, 6 folding coloured maps in pocket at end of vol. 2 (usually lacking), 5 maps and 2 text maps. 2 vols. Imp. 8vo. Spines slightly faded. Some very slight foxing. Good. Edwards 1042-545 1983 £125

WYLLY, H. C.   The Military Memoirs of Lieut.-General Sir Joseph Thackwell. London, 1908. Photogravure frontis., portrait. 1 plate, 8 coloured maps (4 folding), and 1 full-page map, some slight, mostly marginal, foxing. 8vo. Good. Edwards 1044-694 1983 £40

WYLLY, H. C.   The Military Memoirs of Lt. Gen. Sir Joseph Thackwell. London, 1908. 8vo, orig. cloth. Maps and plates. Good. Edwards 1044-766 1983 £20

WYLLYS, RUFUS KAY   The French in Sonora (1850-1854). Berkeley: University of California Press, 1932. Illus. Wrapper, frayed. Dawson 471-314 1983 $20

WYMAN, SETH   The Life and Adventures of Seth Wyman. Manchester, N.H., 1843. Cloth, somewhat stained, but overall very good. Reese 19-604 1983 $200

WYNNE, GEORGE R.   The O'Tooles of Glean Imaal. S.W. Partridge, (1868). First edition, with a frontis., cr. 8vo, orig. cloth, gilt. Fenning 61-502 1983 £35

WYNNE, JOHN HUDDLESTONE   Fables of Flowers, for the Female Sex. Printed for E. Newbery, and G. Riley, 1781. 12mo, 6 engraved plates, each with 5 vignettes illus. different flowers and plants, orig. sheep. No front fly, first plate, the frontis., laid down, lower margin trimmed, and detached, leather defective at top of spine. Bickersteth 77-94 1983 £55

WYNNE, JOHN HUDDLESTONE   The Prostitute, a Poem. London: for J. Wheble, 1771. First edition. 4to. Engraved vignette on title. Uncut copy in modern quarter calf. Title repaired at top and laid down, small holes repaired in first few leaves, some light dramping. Heath 48-461 1983 £75

WYNTER, ANDREW   Subtle brains and lissom fingers. London: Hardwicke, 1863. First edition. 8vo. Orig. purple cloth. A bit rubbed and faded. Ximenes 63-576 1983 $90

WYNTER, ANDREW   Subtle Brains and Lissom Fingers. Robert Hardwicke, 1869. 3rd edition, half title, 2 pp ads. Orig. green cloth. Jarndyce 31-402 1983 £10.50

X Y Z

X Marks the Spot. The Spot Publishing Co., 1930. Photos, large paper-wraps, cover slightly soiled and creased, four pages loose, very good or better. Quill & Brush 54-1670 1983 $40

XENOPHON   The Expedition of Cyrus into Persia. London: for D. Browne, etc., 1749. Second edition. 2 vols. 8vo. Cont. calf, gilt spines with morocco labels, gilt. Title-pages printed in red and black, folding map. Traylen 94-912 1983 £25

XENOPHON   The History of the Affairs of Greece. London, R.H., 1685. 8vo, cont. calf rebacked, inner hinges reinforced; large copy of the first edition of this translation. Ravenstree 95-144 1983 $83

XENOPHON   I Sette Libri de Xenophonte della Impresa de Ciro Minore Tradotti per M. Lodovico Domenichi. In Vinegia Appresso Gabriel Giolito de Ferrari, 1547. 8vo, orig. vellum, two small holes in blank portion of title, else fine. The first edition in Italian. Ravenstree 95-145 1983 $75

XIMENEZ DE LA TARSAL, EUGENIO   Discurso del Globo de Luz... Madrid, 1726. 4to. Middle Hill boards. From the library of Sir Thomas Phillipps, from Puttick & Simpson, 1868. Kraus 164-43 1983 $220

YAMAZAKI, AKIRA   Nippon Colours: The Japanese Art. (Kamakura: Getumei-Kai), 1959. Octavo. Limited to 300 copies. Some offsetting from thread samples on facing blank pages, else near mint. Bromer 25-231 1983 $350

YANKS: A. E. F. Verse. New York, 1919. 8vo, cloth. A fine copy in the uncommon dust jacket. Jacket is chipped and worn around top edges. In Our Time 156-469 1983 $35

YARD, ROBERT STERLING   The Publisher. Boston: Houghton Mifflin Co., 1913. First edition. Small 8vo. Cloth. Signed. Oak Knoll 49-410 1983 $20

YARRANTON, ANDREW   England's Improvement By Sea and Land. London: printed by R. Everingham for the author, 1677. 1st ed., small 4to, 7 folding engraved plates, repaired, narrow worm hole in 1 slightly affects the illustration, imprimatur leaf before the title-page, cont. calf, rebacked, corners worn. Bookplate. Pickering & Chatto 21-137 1983 $250

YARRELL, WILLIAM   A History of British Birds. London, 1856. 3 vols. 3rd ed., illustrated by 550 wood engravings. Bound in red morocco, a.e.g. Fine set. In Our Time 156-903 1983 $450

YARRELL, WILLIAM   A History of British Birds. 1843. 3 vols., imperial 8vo, half green levant morocco gilt. Only a few copies of imperial octavo issued. Wheldon 160-114 1983 £350

YARRELL, WILLIAM   A History of British Fishes. London, 1859. 2 vols. 3rd ed., illustrated by 522 wood engravings. Bound in full red morocco, a.e.g. Fine. In Our Time 156-904 1983 $350

YARRELL, WILLIAM   A History of British Birds. 1871-85. 4th edition, 564 wood engravings, 4 vols., 8vo, binder's cloth (not uniform). Wheldon 160-928 1983 £40

YARRELL, WILLIAM   A History of British Fishes. 1859. 522 woodcuts and a portrait, 2 vols., 8vo, original cloth (neatly repaired). Wheldon 160-1013 1983 £45

YATES, EDMUND   Black Sheep. London: Tinsley Brothers, 1867. First edition. 3 vols. Orig. cloth. Vol. I rebacked, with new endpapers supplied. Library labels removed from endsheets of Vols. II and III. Good. MacManus 280-5667 1983 $185

YATES, EDMUND   The Business of Pleasure. Chapman & Hall, 1865. First edition, 2 vols. Half titles, orig. green cloth, v.g. Jarndyce 30-598 1983 £75

YATES, EDMUND   Kissing the rod. London: Tinsley, 1866. First edition. 3 vols. 8vo. Orig. green cloth. Slightly rubbed, inner hinges of one volume cracked. Ximenes 63-169 1983 $300

YATES, GEORGE WORTHING   If a Body. N.Y., Morrow, 1941. First edition. Dust jacket (a bit rubbed, small nicks) else very good. Houle 22-999 1983 $25

YAZDANI, G.   The Early History of the Deccan. Oxford, 1960. Folding map, 65 plates. 11 parts in 2 vols. Roy.8vo. Orig. cloth. Good. Edwards 1044-769 1983 £45

THE YEARS at the Spring. London, 1920. First edition. 24 full-page illus., 12 in color, as well as many decorations by Harry Clarke. Fine. Jolliffe 26-96 1983 £75

YEARSLEY, MACLEOD   Doctors in Elizabethan Drama. London, 1933. Ex-lib. Argosy 713-582 1983 $75

YEATS, JOHN BUTLER   Passages from the Letters. Dundrum: Cuala Press, 1917. First edition. Thin 8vo, linen backed boards; paper label. One of 400 copies. Argosy 714-851 1983 $135

YEATS, WILLIAM BUTLER   Autobiographies. MacMillan, 1926. First collected edition, with 4 portraits and a coloured plate. 8vo, orig. cloth, inside joints neatly repaired. A very good copy. Fenning 61-503 1983 £35

YEATS, WILLIAM BUTLER   Autobiographies. NY: Macmillan, 1927. Illus. with a frontis. and four plates, including one mounted color plate. Edition limited to 250 numbered copies, signed by Yeats. Cloth spine over boards, with paper labels on spine and cover. Karmiole 71-97 1983 $250

YEATS, WILLIAM BUTLER   Autobiographies. N.Y., 1927. Ltd. edition. Illus. & some colored full-page plates, by Jack B. Yeats. Ltd. One of 250 copies, signed by the author. Argosy 714-852 1983 $75

YEATS, WILLIAM BUTLER   The Book of the Rhymers' Club. London: Elkin Mathews, 1892. Cloth, paper label. First edition. One of 450 copies, 350 for sale. Pub.'s complimentary copy, so inscribed on front free endsheet. Boards slightly darkened, slight fraying of headstrip and label, but a very good to near fine copy. Reese 20-1177 1983 $275

YEATS, WILLIAM BUTLER   The Collected Works in Verse and Prose. Stratford-on-Avon, 1908. Shakespeare Head Press edition, printed on hand-made paper. 8 vols. 8vo. Orig. half vellum, gilt, t.e.g., others uncut. Portraits. A mint set. Traylen 94-913 1983 £475

YEATS, WILLIAM BUTLER   The Cutting of an Agate. London, 1919. First English edition. Inscription. Spine darkened. Very good. Jolliffe 26-616 1983 £20

YEATS, WILLIAM BUTLER   The Cutting of an Agate. NY, 1912. Front fly removed, spine slightly stained, spine label rubbed and chipped, good. Quill & Brush 54-1609 1983 $30

YEATS, WILLIAM BUTLER   The Death of Synge. Dublin: The Cuala Press, 1928. First edition. Title-page vignette. Orig. holland-backed boards with paper label on spine (a trifle rubbed). Limited to 400 copies. Fine. MacManus 280-5669 1983 $150

YEATS, WILLIAM BUTLER   Deirdre. London: A.H. Bullen, 1907. First edition. Orig. cloth-backed boards. Edges rather worn. Book-plate. Good. MacManus 280-5670 1983 $65

YEATS, WILLIAM BUTLER   The Dome. London, Unicorn Press, 1897-1898. Illus. (some colored and tipped-in), by Pieranesi, Laurence Housman, William Nicholson, B. Shaw, et. al. Orig. boards, a bit rubbed. Good-very good. Houle 21-978 1983 $285

YEATS, WILLIAM BUTLER   Dramatis Personae. Dublin: The Cuala Press, 1935. First edition. Orig. cloth-backed boards with paper label on spine. Limited to 400 copies. Fine. MacManus 280-5671 1983 $150

YEATS, WILLIAM BUTLER   Early Poems and Stories. N.Y., MacMillian, 1925. First American edition. One of 250 numbered copies signed by the author. Green cloth over brown boards, paper labels, uncut and unopened. Very good. Houle 22-1000 1983 $300

YEATS, WILLIAM BUTLER   Early Poems and Stories. NY: Macmillan, 1925. 1st American edition. Edition ltd. to 250 numbered copies, signed by Yeats. Cloth spine over boards; paper label on spine and cover. Karmiole 71-98 1983 $250

YEATS, WILLIAM BUTLER   Early Poems and Stories. London: Macmillan & Co., 1925. First edition. Orig. blind-stamped cloth. Spine faded and a trifle soiled. Good. MacManus 280-5672 1983 $30

YEATS, WILLIAM BUTLER   Essays. N.Y., MacMillian, 1924. Ltd. edition. Green cloth over brown boards, paper labels, uncut and unopened. One of 250 numbered copies signed by the author. Very good. Houle 22-1001 1983 $325

YEATS, WILLIAM BUTLER   Essays. NY: Macmillan, 1924. Revised edition. Edition ltd. to 250 numbered copies, signed by Yeats. Cloth spine over boards; with paper label on spine and cover. Karmiole 71-99 1983 $250

YEATS, WILLIAM BUTLER   Essays. London, 1924. First edition. Cover design by C. Richetts. Spine a little faded. Very nice. Rota 231-635 1983 $20

YEATS, WILLIAM BUTLER   Estrangement. Dublin: Cuala Press, 1926. First edition. Orig. cloth-backed boards. Paper label on spine. Plain dust jacket. One of 300 copies. Fine. MacManus 280-5673 1983 $200

YEATS, WILLIAM BUTLER   Form: A Quarterly of the Arts. London & New York, 1916. First edition. Folio, wrappers slightly foxed and frayed at edges. Rebacked and preserved in a cloth portfolio, silk ties, lettered in gilt. Portfolio a little rubbed at corners and marked. Very nice. Rota 231-638 1983 £75

YEATS, WILLIAM BUTLER   Four Plays for Dancers. London, 1921. First English edition. 7 black and white illus., 4 full-page, by Edmund Dulac. Decorated covers by Sturge Moore. Endpapers browned. Last gathering slightly loose. Very good. Jolliffe 26-618 1983 £40

YEATS, WILLIAM BUTLER   Four Years. Dundrum: The Cuala Press, 1921. First edition. Orig. cloth-backed boards with paper label on spine. Limited to 400 copies. John Roland Abbey's bookplate on front free endpaper. Bookplate of C.G. Hamilton Dicker on endsheet. Faint discoloring to front cover. Fine. MacManus 280-5674 1983 $150

YEATS, WILLIAM BUTLER   A Full Moon in March. London: Macmillan, 1935. First edition. Dark green cloth. Fine in dust jacket. Bradley 66-389 1983 $175

YEATS, WILLIAM BUTLER   A Full Moon in March. London, 1935. 8vo. Cloth. Fine copy in dj. In Our Time 156-907 1983 $150

YEATS, WILLIAM BUTLER   A Full Moon In March. London: Macmillan And Co Ltd, 1935. First edition. 8vo. Orig. cloth. Dust jacket. Very fine copy. Jaffe 1-411 1983 $85

YEATS, WILLIAM BUTLER   The Herne's Egg. London: Macmillan & Co. Ltd., 1938. First edition. Orig. cloth. Dust jacket. 1600 copies printed. Very fine. MacManus 280-5675 1983 $100

YEATS, WILLIAM BUTLER   If I Were Four and Twenty. Cublin: The Cuala Press, 1940. Cloth and boards. First edition. One of 450 numbered copies. A very fine, unopened copy, in slightly frayed glassine jacket. Reese 20-1176 1983 $150

YEATS, WILLIAM BUTLER   The King's Threshold. N.Y.: Printed for Private Circulation, 1904. Large 8vo. Orig. blue-grey paper boards. Tissue jacket. In orig. publisher's box. One of 100 copies printed for John Quinn on cream-colored Italian paper. With a card inscribed by Yeats: "To Miss Dorothy Coates with kind regards W.B. Yeats, July, 1904," laid in. Near mint. MacManus 280-5687 1983 $1,250

YEATS, WILLIAM BUTLER   The Land of Heart's Desire. Chicago: Stone & Kimball, 1814 (i.e.1894). First American edition. Orig. grey boards. Paper label on spine. Limited to 450 copies. Small bookplate on front endsheet. Shelf number in white on spine. Covers soiled. MacManus 280-5676 1983 $60

YEATS, WILLIAM BUTLER   The Land of Heart's Desire. Portland, Maine, Thomas B. Mosher, 1903. First edition thus. Uncut and unbound. Loose as issued in pub.'s slipcase enclosed in a cloth box. One of only 10 numbered copies printed on fine pure vellum, signed by Mosher. With pub.'s device printed in red on title and colophon. Fine. Houle 22-1002 1983 $850

YEATS, WILLIAM BUTLER   The Land of Heart's Desire. SF, 1926. Foreword by James S. Johnson. SF, 1926. 12mo, bds., paper label. Illustrated. One of only 10 copies (of an edition of 750) bound in boards. A very nice copy. Perata 27-191 1983 $40

YEATS, WILLIAM BUTLER   Later Poems. N.Y., Macmillan, 1924. Half green cloth, paper labels, uncut and mostly unopened. One of 250 numbered copies, signed by Yeats. Very good. Houle 21-975 1983 $250

YEATS, WILLIAM BUTLER   Michael Robartes and the Dancer. Ir., 1920. Limited to 400 copies, some pages unopened, cover slightly rubbed and stained, edges slightly worn, minor interior soiling on top of page edges, near very good. Quill & Brush 54-1605 1983 $125

YEATS, WILLIAM BUTLER   New Poems. Dublin: Cuala Press, 1938. First edition, limited to 450 copies. Extremely fine in cloth-backed boards with chipped glassine. Bromer 25-129 1983 $130

YEATS, WILLIAM BUTLER   On the Boiler. Dublin: Cuala Press, (1939). Pictorial blue wrappers. First published edition. With the front cover illustration by Jack B. Yeats. Second printing. Blue wrappers have mostly faded to green, few chips at edges. Bradley 64-210 1983 $25

YEATS, WILLIAM BUTLER   A Packet for Ezra Pound. Dublin, 1929. First edition. Half cloth, paper label. One of 425 copies. Printed by the Cuala Press. Very good. Houle 21-979 1983 $200

YEATS, WILLIAM BUTLER   Per Amica Silentia Lunae. London, 1918. 8vo. Cloth. This copy bears the publisher's blind stamp for "presentation" on title page. Vg-fine. In Our Time 156-905 1983 $150

YEATS, WILLIAM BUTLER   Per Amica Silentia Lunae. Macmillan, 1918. First edition, with errata slip, 8vo, orig. cloth. Fenning 61-504 1983 £38.50

YEATS, WILLIAM BUTLER   Plays and Controversies. London: Macmillan & Co., 1923. First edition. Frontis. port. Orig. blind-stamped cloth. Spine faded. Extremities of spine rubbed. Good. MacManus 280-5677 1983 $30

YEATS, WILLIAM BUTLER   Plays and Controversies. N.Y., Macmillan, 1924. Frontis. portrait by John Singer Sargent; seven other plates. Half green cloth, paper labels, uncut and unopened. One of 250 numbered copies, signed by the author. Very good-fine. Houle 21-976 1983 $250

YEATS, WILLIAM BUTLER   Plays for an Irish Theatre. A.H. Bullen, 1911. First edition. 4 plates, 8vo, orig. cloth-backed boards, with paper label, a very good copy. With white end-papers. Fenning 61-505 1983 £55

YEATS, WILLIAM BUTLER   Plays in Prose and Verse. London, 1922. First edition. Cover design by C. Ricketts. Spine a little faded. Endpapers foxed. Blind presentation stamp on title-page. Very nice. Rota 230-652 1983 £20

YEATS, WILLIAM BUTLER   Plays in Prose and Verse. NY:
Macmillan, 1924. "New and revised edition." Edition ltd. to 250
numbered copies, signed by Yeats. CLoth over boards; paper
cover and spine labels. Karmiole 71-100 1983 $250

YEATS, WILLIAM BUTLER   Poems, 1899-1905. A. H. Bullen, 1906.
First edition. 8vo, orig. cloth, gilt. A very good copy. Fenning
61-595 1873 £38.50

YEATS, WILLIAM BUTLER   Responsibilities: Poems And A Play.
Churchtown, Dundram: The Cuala Press, 1914. First edition. 8vo.
Orig. cloth-backed boards. One of 400 copies printed. Fine copy.
Jaffe 1-410 1983 $175

YEATS, WILLIAM BUTLER   Reveries Over Childhood and Youth. NY,
1916. Frontis. backing torn, not affecting tipped in color plate,
otherwise very good. Quill & Brush 54-1606 1983 $35

YEATS, WILLIAM BUTLER   The Second Book of the Rhymers' Club.
London: Elkin Mathews, 1894. Gilt cloth. First edition. One of
500 copies for distribution in England. Slightest rubbing, else a
fine, unopened copy. Light ink name. Reese 20-1178 1983 $150

YEATS, WILLIAM BUTLER   Seven Poems and a Fragment. Dundram:
The Cuala Press, 1922. First edition. Orig. cloth-backed boards.
Limited to 500 copies. John Roland Abbey's copy, with his bookplate
on front endsheet. Fine. MacManus 280-5678 1983 $150

YEATS, WILLIAM BUTLER   The Shadowy Water. London: 1900.
First edition. Fine copy. T.e.g. Bromer 25-130 1983 $175

YEATS, WILLIAM BUTLER   Stories of Michael Robartes and His
Friends. Dublin: The Cuala Press, 1931. First edition. Orig. cloth-
backed boards with paper label on spine. Plain dust jacket (torn).
Limited to 450 copies. Very fine. MacManus 280-5679 1983 $125

YEATS, WILLIAM BUTLER   Stories of Red Hanrahan. Dundrum: The
Dun Emer Press, 1904. First edition. Orig. linen-backed boards.
Limited to 500 copies. Very fine. MacManus 280-5680 1983 $250

YEATS, WILLIAM BUTLER   Synge and the Ireland of His Time.
Dundrum: The Cuala Press, 1911. First edition. Orig. cloth-backed
boards. One of 350 copies. Spine and covers slightly foxed. Former
owner's signature. Very good. MacManus 280-5081 1983 $125

YEATS, WILLIAM BUTLER   The Tables of the Law. London: Elkin
Mathews, 1904. First published edition. Orig. blue paper wrappers.
Mint. MacManus 280-5681 1983 $150

YEATS, WILLIAM BUTLER   The Ten Principal Upanishads. New York,
1937. First American edition. Spine and edges of covers faded. Very
good. Rota 230-655 1983 £12

YEATS, WILLIAM BUTLER   The Trembling of the Veil. London:
T. Werner Laurie, Ltd., 1922. First edition. 1/1000 signed by
Yeats. Portrait frontis. Pale blue boards and cream parchment
spine, paper label. Fine copy, partly unopened. In dust jacket.
Bradley 66-390 1983 $325

YEATS, WILLIAM BUTLER   Two Plays For Dancers. (Dundrum): The
Cuala Press, 1919. First edition. Woodcut title-page. Orig. holland-
backed boards. Paper label on spine. Limited to 400 copies. Fine.
MacManus 280-5682 1983 $150

YEATS, WILLIAM BUTLER   Two Plays for Dancers. Churchtown:
Cuala Press, 1919. 8vo, boards with linen back. One of 400 copies
printed in red and black. First edition. Duschnes 240-217 1983
$75

YEATS, WILLIAM BUTLER   Vision. London: Macmillan & Co., Ltd.,
1937. First of this revised and enlarged edition. Illus. Orig.
cloth-backed decorated boards. Dust jacket. One of 1500 copies
printed. Very fine. MacManus 280-5683 1983 $275

YEATS, WILLIAM BUTLER   A Vision. London, 1937. New edition,
revised and enlarged. Dust wrapper. Fine. Rota 230-653 1983 £35

YEATS, WILLIAM BUTLER   Wheels & Butterflies: New Plays.
London, 1934. 8vo. Cloth. Fine copy in dj. In Our Time 156-
906 1983 $150

YEATS, WILLIAM BUTLER   Wheels and Butterflies. London: Macmillan & Co., Limited, 1934. First edition. Orig. cloth. Dust jacket.
Almost as new. MacManus 280-5684 1983 $100

YEATS, WILLIAM BUTLER   The Wild Swans at Coole, Other
Verses and a Play in Verse. Churchtown: The Cuala Press, 1917.
Holland-backed boards, paper label. First edition. One of 400
copies. A fine, unopened copy in glassine dust jacket. Reese 20-1175
1983 $60

YEATS, WILLIAM BUTLER   The Wild Swans at Coole. London, 1919.
First English edition. Inscription. Spine dull. Very good.
Jolliffe 26-617 1983 £20

YEATS, WILLIAM BUTLER   The Words Upon the Window Pane. Dublin:
Cuala Press, 1934. First edition. One of 350 copies. Cloth spine
a little soiled. Nice. Rota 231-636 1983 £55

THE YELLOW Book. Hartford, Edwin Valentine Mitchell, 1928. 8vo, 21
cm. Plates as called for. Orig. pictorial yellow cloth. As new in
fine dust wrapper. Grunder 7-80 1983 $65

THE YELLOW Book. Lon., (n.d.). Very good in soiled, internally
mended, worn dustwrapper. Quill & Brush 54-43 1983 $35

YERKES, ROBERT MEANS   The Dancing Mouse: A Study in Animal
Behavior. NY: Macmillan, 1907. Publisher's cloth, somewhat rubbed,
but a good copy. First edition. Gach 94-86 1983 $37.50

YERKES, ROBERT MEARNS   The Great Apes. New Haven, Yale Univ.
Press, 1929. First edition, 4to. Endpapers foxed. Illus. Very
good copy. Gach 95-502 1983 $125

YONGE, CHARLOTTE MARY   The Armourer's Prentices. London: Macmillan, 1884. First edition. 2 vols. Orig. cloth. Inner hinges
cracked. Very good. MacManus 280-5690 1983 $75

YONGE, CHARLOTTE MARY   Beechcroft at Rockstone. London: Macmillan & Co., 1888. First edition. 2 vols. Orig. cloth. Spines a
little rubbed. Several inner hinges cracked. Former owner's inscriptions on versos of front free endpapers. Very good. MacManus 280-
5691 1983 $165

YONGE, CHARLOTTE MARY   Beechcroft at Rockstone. Macmillan,
1888. First edition, 2 vols. Half titles, Martin's Circulating
Library labels on upper covers, orig. green cloth. Jarndyce 30-605
1983 £27

YONGE, CHARLOTTE MARY   The Caged Lion. London: Macmillan & Co.,
1870. First edition. Illus. Orig. cloth. Edges of covers rubbed.
Inner hinges cracked, shaken. Good. MacManus 280-5692 1983 $85

YONGE, CHARLOTTE MARY   The Chaplet of Pearls. London: Macmillan, 1868. First edition. 2 vols. Orig. cloth. Very good.
MacManus 280-5693 1983 $85

YONGE, CHARLOTTE MARY   The Chaplet of Pearls. Macmillan, 1868.
First edition. 2 vols. Half titles, 2 pp. ads. vol. I. Names cut
from corners of leading free end papers. Orig. green cloth, very
slightly rubbed. Jarndyce 30-603 1983 £38

YONGE, CHARLOTTE MARY   Countess Kate. London, 1948. First
edition. Numerous black and white drawings by Gwen Raverat. Torn
and chipped dustwrapper, by Raverat, faded at the spine and edges.
Very good. Jolliffe 26-428 1983 £16

YONGE, CHARLOTTE MARY   The Daisy Chain. John W. Parker, 1856.
First edition, one volume bound as two. Half green calf, spine
gilding, maroon labels, v.g. Jarndyce 30-599 1983 £42

YONGE, CHARLOTTE MARY   The Danvers Papers: An Invention. London: Macmillan & Co., 1867. First edition. Orig. cloth. Former
owner's signatures on half-title. Covers a little soiled. Good.
MacManus 280-5694 1983 $65

YONGE, CHARLOTTE MARY   The Danvers Papers. Macmillan, 1867.
First edition, half title. Orig. brown cloth, bevelled boards, a.e.g.
A little rubbed. Jarndyce 31-972 1983 £28

YONGE, CHARLOTTE MARY   The Dove in the Eagle's Nest. London:
Macmillan & Co., 1866. First edition. 2 vols. Orig. bright blue
cloth. Unusually fine. MacManus 280-5695 1983 $85

YONGE, CHARLOTTE MARY   The Dove in the Eagle's Nest. Macmillan,
1866. First edition, 2 vols. Half titles, orig. blue cloth, a little
rubbed at heads and tails of spines. Jarndyce 30-607 1983 £35

YONGE, CHARLOTTE MARY   Dynevor Terrace; or, The Clue of Life.
London: John W. Parker & Son, 1857. First edition. 2 vols, orig.
cloth. Spines a bit soiled. All edges and corners slightly worn.
Very good. MacManus 280-5696 1983 $150

YONGE, CHARLOTTE MARY   Dynevor Terrace. John W. Parker and
Son, 1857. First edition. 2 vols. 8vo, cont. half calf, (with
some slight insect damage). Lightly foxed at beginning and end.
Hannas 69-228 1983 £30

YONGE, CHARLOTTE MARY   Grisly Grisell or The Laidly Lady of
Whitburn. London: Macmillan & Co., 1893. First edition. 2 vols.
Orig. cloth. Presentation copy inscribed to Lucy Wilcox, dated May
1893. Spines and covers somewhat worn and soiled. Some discoloring
to the endpapers. Very good. MacManus 280-5697 1983 $250

YONGE, CHARLOTTE MARY   History of Christian Names. Parker,
Son & Bourn, 1863. First edition, 2 vols. Orig. maroon cloth,
spines dulled, a sl. worm at heads of spines, otherwise, v.g.
Jarndyce 31-971 1983 £70

YONGE, CHARLOTTE MARY   History of Christian Names. London:
Parker, Son, & Bourn, 1863. First edition. 2 vols. Orig. cloth.
Inscriptions and ink blotting on front endpapers. Spines a little
faded and rubbed. Very good. MacManus 280-5698 1983 $100

YONGE, CHARLOTTE MARY   Hope and Fears; or, Scenes from the Life
of a Spinster. London: John W. Parker, 1860. First edition. 2 vols.
Orig. cloth. Inner hinges weak. Near-fine. MacManus 280-5699 1983
$250

YONGE, CHARLOTTE MARY   Hopes and Fears. John W. Parker, 1860.
First edition, 2 vols. Half titles. Half dark green morocco.
Jarndyce 30-600 1983 £42

YONGE, CHARLOTTE MARY   Lady Hester, or, Ursula's Narrative.
Macmillan, 1874. First edition, half title. 56pp ads. Inner
hinges weakening. Orig. green cloth, a little rubbed. Jarndyce 31-
973 1983 £22

YONGE, CHARLOTTE MARY   The Lances of Lynwood. London: John
W. Parker & Son, 1855. First edition. Illus. by J.B. Inscription
on title-page. Very good. MacManus 280-5700 1983 $85

YONGE, CHARLOTTE MARY   Love and Life. London: Macmillan, 1880.
First edition. 2 vols. Orig. cloth. Front inner hinge in volume one
cracked. Extremities worn. Former owner's inscriptions in both vols.
Good. MacManus 280-5701 1983 $60

YONGE, CHARLOTTE MARY   Love and Life. Macmillan, 1880. First
edition, 2 vols. Half titles. Inner hinges a little loose, orig.
green cloth. Jarndyce 30-601 1983 £28

YONGE, CHARLOTTE MARY   Magnum Bonum. Macmillan, 1879. First
edition, 3 vols. Orig. green cloth, v.g. Jarndyce 30-602 1983
£56

YONGE, CHARLOTTE MARY   The Miz Maze. Macmillan, 1883. First
edition, half title. Orig. dark green cloth. Jarndyce 31-974 1983
£20

YONGE, CHARLOTTE MARY   My Young Alcides. A Faded Portrait.
London: Macmillan & Co., 1875. First edition. Orig. cloth.
Prize inscriptions on endpapers. Edges slightly worn. Very good.
MacManus 280-5702 1983 $150

YONGE, CHARLOTTE MARY   The Pilgrimage of the Ben Beriah.
Macmillan, 1897. First edition, half title, front. and 3 other illus.
16pp ads. A few marginal marks. Orig. maroon cloth. Jarndyce
31-975 1983 £18.50

YONGE, CHARLOTTE MARY   Pioneers and Founders or Recent Workers
in the Mission Field. (London): Macmillan & Co., (1871). First
edition. Engraved frontis. & title-page. Spine darkened. Good.
MacManus 280-5703 1983 $50

YONGE, CHARLOTTE MARY   The Population of an Old Pear Tree.
London: Macmillan & Co., 1870. First edition. Numerous illus. by
Backer. Orig. pictorial cloth. Edges and corners slightly worn.
Hinges cracking. Binder's ticket. Tiny stain on back cover. Very
good. MacManus 280-5704 1983 $60

YONGE, CHARLOTTE MARY   The Railroad Children. J. & C. Mozley,
1855. First edition, 12mo, orig. green printed wraps. sl. worn,
v.g. Jarndyce 31-970 1983 £28

YONGE, CHARLOTTE MARY   Recollections of Colonel De Gonneville.
London: Hurst & Blackett, 1875. First edition. 2 vols. 2 vols in
one. Orig. cloth. Front inner hinge cracking. Covers slightly
rubbed. Fine. MacManus 280-5705 1983 $100

YONGE, CHARLOTTE MARY   Stray Pearls. London: Macmillan, 1883.
First edition. 2 vols. Orig. cloth. Very good. MacManus 280-5706
1983 $65

YONGE, CHARLOTTE MARY   The Trial; or, More Links of the Daisy
Chain. London: Macmillan & Co., 1864. First edition. 2 vols. Orig.
cloth. Edges and corners slightly worn. Hinges cracking. Spines a
little darkened. Covers a bit soiled. Good. MacManus 280-5708
1983 $150

YONGE, CHARLOTTE MARY   The Two Sides of the Shield. London:
Macmillan & Co., 1885. First edition. 2 vols. Orig. cloth. Spines
a bit rubbed. Fine. MacManus 280-5709 1983 $165

YONGE, CHARLOTTE MARY   The Two Sides of the Shield. Macmillan,
1885. First edition, 2 vols. Half titles, 2 pp ads. vol. II. Orig.
green cloth, a little darkened, v.g. Jarndyce 30-604 1983 £48

YONGE, CHARLOTTE MARY   The Two Sides of the Shield. London:
Macmillan & Co., 1885. First one-volume edition. Orig. cloth. Ex-
tremities rubbed. Ownership inscription. Inner hinges cracking.
MacManus 280-5710 1983 $20

YONGE, CHARLOTTE MARY   Unknown to History. London: Macmillan
& Co., 1882. First edition. 2 vols. Orig. cloth. Cont. inscription
on front free endpapers. Inner hinges cracking. Spines a bit dull.
Very good. MacManus 280-5711 1983 $85

YORICK, PSEUD.
Please turn to
STERNE, LAURENCE

THE YOSEMITE Valley, and the Mammoth Trees and Geysers of California.
N.Y.: T. Nelson & Sons, n.d. (1870's?) 12 color plates. Decorated
cloth, a bit of wear. Dawson 471-315 1983 $65

YOUATT, WILLIAM   The Dog. London: Longman, Brown,
Green and Longmans, 1852. Pub.'s catalogue. Text profusely illus.
with woodcuts. Orig. cloth. Karmiole 72-100 1983 $75

YOUATT, WILLIAM   Sheep: Their Breeds, Management and
Diseases. London: Robert Baldwin, (n.d. ca. 1837). Tall 8vo,
illus. Orig. green cloth; spine sl. faded. Bookplate. Karmiole
73-110 1983 $60

YOUNG, ANDREW   The Bird-Cage. London, 1926. First
edition. Some foxing throughout. Several cont. newspaper reviews
mounted on rear endpaper. Author's autograph presentation inscription: "To Margaret from The Writer, Christmas 1926". Nice. Rota
231-639 1983 £40

YOUNG, ANDREW   Collected Poems. London, 1936. First
English edition. Very slightly rubbed dustwrapper. Fine. Jolliffe
26-620 1983 £30

YOUNG, ANDREW   Collected Poems. London, 1936. First
edition. Name on flyleaf. Author's autograph signature. Nice.
Rota 231-640 1983 £15

YOUNG, ARTHUR   The Farmer's Tour through the East of
England. 1771. 4 vols., 8vo, 29 engraved plates on 28 leaves, or
which 19 are folding, one folding table, orig. calf, volume 2
rebacked, preserving the orig. spine, upper joints cracked on the
other vols., but bindings firm. Waterstaining at foot of inner
joint at beginning of vol. 2. First edition. Bickersteth 75-100
1983 £140

YOUNG, ARTHUR   Letters concerning the present state
of the French nation. London: Nicoll, 1769. First edition. 8vo.
Cont. calf, spine gilt. Rubbed, front hinge tender. Ximenes 63-644
1983 $85

YOUNG, ARTHUR   Rural Economy, or Essays on the Practical
Parts of Husbandry. Burlington: Isaac Neale, 1792. Full calf (worn,
hinges breaking). Very good. Felcone 19-61 1983 $100

YOUNG, ARTHUR   A Six Months Tour through the North of
England. 1770. 4 vols., 8vo, 28 plates (of which 12 are folding),
6 printed tables, orig. calf, slight wear at head and foot of spines,
joints cracked, but bindings firm. Bickersteth 75-99 1983 £140

YOUNG, ARTHUR   Travels During the Years 1787, 1788,
& 1789. London - Bury St. Edmunds: Richardson, 1794. 2 vols. Large
4to, with 3 folding maps (one hand-colored). Orig. boards. 2nd
edition. Large fine set. Rostenberg 88-144 1983 $375

YOUNG, BRIGHAM   Governor's Message to the First General
Assembly of the State of Deseret. (SLC, 1862). Argosy 716-584 1983
$350

YOUNG, BRIGHAM   Governor's Message to the First
General Assembly of the State of Deseret. (SLC, 1897). Folio, orig.
color pict. wraps., tied. Argosy 716-583 1983 $75

YOUNG, BRIGHAM   The Resurrection. Salt Lake City,
1884. Pr. wraps. Argosy 716-586 1983 $40

YOUNG, C. B.   The Stalk-Eyed Crustacea of British
Guiana, West Indies and Bermuda. 1900. 7 coloured plates, 8vo, cloth
(foxed). Wheldon 160-1353 1983 £25

YOUNG, CALVIN M.   Little Turtle (Me-She-Kin-No-Quah) The
Great Chief of the Miami Indian Nation. Greenville, Ohio, 1917.
Frontis. and illus. 1st edition in original cloth. Jenkins 151-
208 1983 $50

YOUNG, CHARLES   Harald, First of the Vikings. G.G.
Harrap, 1911. Frontis. & 15 plates. Blue pictorial cloth. Rubbed.
Greer 39-72 1983 £14

YOUNG, DAVID   The Perusal. Elizabeth-Town: Peter Chatterton, 1819. Second edition. 16mo, cont. calf (lacks front cover).
Argosy 716-423 1983 $50

YOUNG, DAVID   The Wonderful History of the Morristown
Ghost. Newark, 1826. Orig. boards, front detached. Good. Reese
18-608 1983 $250

YOUNG, DAVID   The Wonderful History of the Morristown
Ghost. Newark: Benjamin Olds (J.C. Totten, pr.), 1826. Linen-backed
boards. Very good. Felcone 20-124 1983 $150

YOUNG, EDWARD   Busiris, King of Egypt. Dublin:
Printed by S. Powell, 1730. 12mo, wrapper, a very good copy.
Fenning 60-450 1983 £18.50

YOUNG, EDWARD   The Complaint. Dublin...for Peter Wilson,
1747. First complete one-volume edition of all nine parts. 12mo.
Later half calf, gilt spine. A very good copy. Fenning 61-507 1983
£85

YOUNG, EDWARD   Love of Fame, the Universal Passion.
In Seven Characteristical Satires. London: J. Tonson, 1730. 3rd
collected edition, 8vo, disbound. Despite light dampstaining of
initial leaves, a good copy. Trebizond 18-104 1983 $70

YOUNG, EDWARD   The Passions Personify'd. Printed for
J. Whiston and M. Lawrence, (1773). First edition, with an engraved
frontis. and 12 plates by Miller, 8vo, cont. calf. Fenning 62-408
1983 £65

YOUNG, EDWARD   The Poetical Works. London, 1858.
2 vols. Cr. 8vo. Dark blue calf, two-line borders with corner
ornaments, gilt panelled spines, morocco labels, gilt. Portrait,
vignette title-page. Traylen 94-914 1983 £30

YOUNG, EGERTON R.   Stories from Indian Wigwams and Northern
Campfires. New York, 1893. Frontis. Illus. Gilt-stamped pictorial
cloth, rubbed at edges. Very good. Reese 19-611 1983 $25

YOUNG, FILSON   Venus and Cupid. London, 1906. First
edition. One of 422 numbered copies, signed by author. 4to. Covers
a little rubbed and marked. Very good. Rota 230-657 1983 £15

YOUNG, FRANCIS BRETT   Deep Sea. London & Glasgow: Collins'
Clear-Type Press, n.d. (1914). First edition. Orig. embossed cloth.
Inscr. by Young to Hugh Walpole. With Walpole's Brackenburn book-
plate on the front endsheet. Spine a bit faded and rubbed. Very good.
MacManus 280-5716 1983 $85

YOUNG, FRANCIS BRETT   Jim Redlake. London: William Heinemann
Ltd., (1930). First edition. Orig. cloth. Dust jacket. Fine.
MacManus 280-5717 1983 $20

YOUNG, FRANCIS BRETT   Poems. 1916-1918. London: W. Collins
& Sons & Co., (1919). First edition. Orig. cloth-backed boards. Dust
jacket (covers and spine slightly faded and worn). Some offsetting to
the free endpapers. Slight foxing throughout. Bookplate and former
owner's signature in pencil. Very good. MacManus 280-5720 1983 $75

YOUNG, FRANCIS BRETT   Portrait of a Village. London, 1937.
First edition. Roy. 8vo. Buckram, gilt. Frontis. and 29 wood-
engravings by Joan Hassell. Traylen 94-915 1983 £10

YOUNG, FRANCIS BRETT   White Ladies. London: William Heinemann Ltd., (1935). First edition. Orig. 3/4 calf and boards. One
of 25 copies specially bound for presentation. Inscribed "For Nora &
St. John Ervine with love from Francis Brett Young." Spine and corners
a bit rubbed. Very good. MacManus 280-5722 1983 $150

YOUNG, GEORGE   A Geological Survey of the Yorkshire
Coast. Whitby, 1822. First edition, coloured folding map, coloured
folding plate of strata, frontis., 17 coloured lithograph plates, list
of subscribers, 4to, new old-style half calf. Scarce. K Books 307-200
1083 £160

YOUNG, GEORGE   Manitoba Memories. Toronto: William
Biggs, 1897. Illus., including a frontis. portrait of the author.
Fine copy. Karmiole 71-36 1983 $40

YOUNG, H. A.   The East India Company's Arsenals & Man-
ufactories. Oxford, 1937. Orig. cloth. 8vo. Good. Edwards 1044-
770 1983 £35

YOUNG, HUGH H.   Hugh Young - A Surgeon's Autobiography.
New York, 1940. First edition. 8vo. Orig. binding. Fye H-3-1004
1983 $25

YOUNG, HUGH H.   Young's Practice of Urology. Ph.,
(1926). 2 vols., 20 color plates, minor cover soiling, light interior
foxing, else near fine. Quill & Brush 54-1641 1983 $60

YOUNG, JAMES   Reminiscences of the Early History of
Galt and the Settlement of Dumfires... Toronto: Hunter, Rose & Co.,
1880. 18cm. Illus. fron wood-engravings, blind and gilt stamped blue
cloth. Wanting the rear free fly, otherwise fine. McGahern 54-185
1983 $185

YOUNG, JOHN   A Catalogue of the Manuscripts in the
Library of the Hunterian Museum in the University of Glasgow. Glasgow,
1908. First edition. 8vo. Orig. binding. Very fine copy. Fye
H-3-1082 1983 $80

YOUNG, JOHN   Selina, and Other Poems. Perth: Published by the author, 1878. First edition, half title, orig. green dec. cloth bevelled boards. T.e.g. Very good. Jarndyce 30-877 1983 £10.50

YOUNG, JOHN P.   Journalism in California. San Francisco, 1915. Illus. Orig. cloth. First edition. Autograph presentation copy from the author. Ginsberg 47-210 1983 $35

YOUNG, JOHN P.   Journalism in California, Pacific Coast & Exposition Biographies. San Francisco: Chronicle Pub. Co., (1915). Many ports., 8vo, buckram, ex-library. Argosy 710-43 1983 $25

YOUNG, JOHN R.   Memoirs of John R. Young, Utah Pioneer. Salt Lake City: The Deseret News, 1920. First edition. Portrait frontis, portraits of two of his wives. Cloth. Pencil marks throughout. S. H. Goodwin's copy, signed and dated by him at Zion, "9-6-27." Bradley 66-607 1983 $40

YOUNG, JULIAN CHARLES   A memoir of Charles Mayne Young, tragedian. London: Macmillan and Co., 1871. 2 vols., 8vo, cont. half calf, spines gilt (some rubbing). 1st edition. With a frontis. in each volume, and 3 other plates. Ximenes 64-591 1983 $60

YOUNG, LAMBTON J. H.   Sea-fishing as a sport. London: Groombridge, 1865. First edition. 8vo. Orig. blue cloth. With eight wood-engraved plates. Minor wear to binding. Very good copy. Ximenes 63-563 1983 $65

YOUNG, LEVI EDGAR   The First Hundred Years. Salt Lake City, 1930. Illus. Folio, wraps. Argosy 716-588 1983 $50

YOUNG, LEVI EDGAR   The Mormon Tabernacle with its World-Famed Organ & Choir. Salt Lake: Bur. Information, 1930. Inscribed. 12mo, pict. wraps. Illus. Argosy 716-589 1983 $20

YOUNG, MARY JULIA   A Summer at Brighton. A Modern Novel. Printed by D. N. Shury for J. F. Hughes, 1807. Third edition, 12mo, 5 vols, contemporary qtr. calf, marbled sides; four half-titles, advertisement leaf in vol. II. Hill 165-142 1983 £50

YOUNG, MARY JULIA   A Summer at Weymouth; Or, The Star of Fashion. Printed for J. F. Hughes, 1808. First edition. 3 vols, 12mo, new qtr. calf, old marbled sides, uncut; three half-titles, advertisement leaf in vol. III. Hill 165-143 1983 £95

YOUNG, N.   The Growth of Napoleon. London, 1910. First edition. Portrait frontis. 8vo. Orig. cloth. 16 plates, 3 maps, 2 folding tables. Very slightly worn and soiled. Some slight foxing throughout. Bookplate. Good. Edwards 1042-438 1983 £15

YOUNG, ROBERT W.   The Navaho Language. (Phoenix, 1943). Orig. cloth. First edition. Ginsberg 47-611 1983 $1,250

YOUNG, SAMUEL   Considerations on the Bank of the United States... Albany, 1832. Stitched. Title slightly soiled. Very good. Felcone 20-5 1983 $22.50

YOUNG, SAMUEL   Suggestions on the Best Mode of Promoting Civilization and Improvement. Albany: Hoffman & White, 1837. 8vo. Orig. printed pink wraps. Back cover & spine slightly damaged. Presentation inscription to Mr. Rantoul from Mrs. M. Coriche. Rostenberg 88-99 1983 $45

YOUNG, STANLEY P.   The Puma, Mysterious American Cat. Wash.: American Wildlife Inst., 1946. First edition. Argosy 716-310 1983 $35

YOUNG, STANLEY P.   The Wolf in North American History. Caldwell, Id.: Caxton Printers, 1946. 53 illus. D.w. Argosy 716-627 1983 $30

YOUNG, THOMAS   A Course of Lectures on Natural Philosophy and the Mechanical Arts. London, 1807. First edition. 4to. 2 vols. Old polished calf, gilt, arms of Edinburgh University on sides (prize binding). 58 plates (2 coloured). Copy awarded as the prize of physics at Edinburgh, each volume with the award in manuscript on a leaf before the title, signed by the professor of physics John Leslie. The recipient of the prize was David Milne. A.l.s. from Milne inserted. Fine. Gurney 90-129 1983 £875

YOUNG, THOMAS   A Course of Lectures in Natural Philosophy and the Mechanical Arts. London, 1845. Second edition. 8vo. 2 vols. Polished calf, gilt, arms of University College on sides. 2 tables and illus. in text. 43 double page plates (2 coloured). Fine copy. Gurney 90-130 1983 £150

THE YOUNG Clerk's Magazine. In the Savoy, 1740. Second edition. 12mo, rebound in panelled calf, label, v.g. Jarndyce 31-43 1983 £62

THE YOUNG Lady's Book of Botany. Robert Tyas, 1838. Coloured frontis., 11 coloured plates of 43 figures, sm. 8vo, original green morocco, gilt, worn. The spine has broken away and has been carelessly replaced. Scarce. Wheldon 160-1584 1983 £25

YOUNGHUSBAND, FRANCIS   Kashmir. London: Adam and Charles Black, 1909. Tall 8vo, 70 leaves of color plates, each with printed tissue guard. Folding color map at rear. Dec. gilt-stamped cloth. Bookplate. Karmiole 75-65 1983 $25

YOUNGHUSBAND, FRANCIS   Kashmir. London, 1911. Folding map. 70 coloured plates by Maj. E. Molyneux. Decorative cloth. 8vo. Good. Edwards 1044-772 1983 £40

YOUNGHUSBAND, G. J.   The Philippines... London, 1899. First edition. Folding map and 18 plates. Uncut. 8vo. Orig. cloth. Good. Edwards 1044-774 1983 £55

YOUNGHUSBAND, G. J.   The Relief of Chitral. London, 1895. Map, 2 folding plans, plates. 8vo. Orig. cloth. Good. Edwards 1044-775 1983 £60

YOUNGHUSBAND, G. J.   The Story of the Guides. London, 1908. 8vo. Orig. cloth. 16 plates. Good. Edwards 1044-773 1983 £36

YOUNGMAN, W. E.   Gleanings From Western Prairies. Cambridge: 1882. First edition. Blue decorated cloth with beveled edges. Fine copy. Bradley 66-637 1983 $60

YOURCENAR, MARGUERITE   The Alms of Alcippe. New York: Targ Editions, 1982. 1st ed., limited to 250 numbered and signed copies. Orig. linen-backed embossed boards. 1st ed. in English. Printed in Centaur types on Frankfurt paper. Mint, in glassine dj. Jenkins 155-1350 1983 $75

YULE, A. F.   A Memoir of Colonel Sir Henry Yule... London, 1903. 8vo. Orig. cloth. With a 3-page ALS from the author to A.J. Macdonald. With Macdonald's bookplate and inscribed on the half-title. Good. Edwards 1044-776 1983 £25

YULE, H.   A Narrative of the Mission sent by the Governor-General of India to the Court of Ava. London, 1858. Folding map in pocket at end. 3 coloured maps, plan, 20 tinted lithographs, 6 other plates. Numerous illus. Some occasional spotting. 4to. Half morocco, a few plates marginally stained. Presentation copy to "Harriette Helen White with the affectionate regards of the Author.H.Y." Good. Edwards 1044-777 1983 £220

YUTANG, LIN   The Importance of Living. NY (1937). Limited to 500 numbered copies, signed by the author. Lea. back, cloth, t.e.g., spine ends rubbed, a bit soiled. King 46-491 1983 $35

YUZON, AMADO M.   The Citizen's Poems. Printed in the Phillipines, (1960). 8vo. Decorative stiff wrappers. 2nd ed., enlarged, signed by poet. Blurbs on front cover. This copy bears a lengthy presentation inscription by poet to T.J. Eliot. In turn, Eliot has inscribed the book to Richard Church. A fine copy. In Our Time 156-245 1983 $200

ZACHARIAS, THOMAS   Joseph Emanuel Fischer Von Erlach. Wien/Munchen: Herold, 1960. 225 illus. hors texte. Large 4to. Cloth. Dust jacket. Ars Libri 32-222 1983 $85

ZAHN, LEOPOLD   Paul Klee. Leben/Werk/Geist. Potsdam: Gustav Kiepenheuer, 1920. 55 plates, text illus. 4to. Boards, 1/4 cloth. Ars Libri 32-368 1983 $150

ZAMBONI, SILLA   Ludovico Mazzolino. Milano: Silvana,
1968. 81 plates (16 tipped-in color). Catalogue illus. Large 4to.
Cloth. Dust jacket. Ars Libri 33-231 1983 $85

ZAMORANO CLUB   The Zamorano 80. Los Angeles: Zamorana
Club, 1945. Plates, cloth, used. In dust wrapper repaired internally
with tape. 1 of 500 numbered copies. Dawson 470-314 1983 $100

ZAMORANO CLUB   The Zamorano 80. Los Angeles, 1945.
8vo, cloth. Illus., folding frontis. One of 500 copies printed at
the Castle Press. Bookplate. A very nice copy in lightly worn d/w.
Perata 28-197 1983 $90

ZAMPETTI, PIETRO   Carlo Crivelli. Milano: Aldo Martello,
1961. 189 plates (24 tipped-in color). Large 4to. Cloth. Ars
Libri 33-126 1983 $125

ZAMPETTI, PIETRO   Giovanni Boccati. Firenze: Electa,
1971. 154 plates. Large square 4to. Cloth. Dust jacket. Ars
Libri 33-36 1983 $75

ZANER, C. P.   Gems of Flourishing. Columbus, OH.:
Zaner & Bloser, (1888). First edition. Oblong 8vo. Cloth spine,
printed boards. Ink inscription else a fine copy. Oak Knoll 48-
81 1983 $85

ZANGWILL, ISRAEL   Dreamers of the Ghetto. London: Heinemann, 1898. First edition. Orig. cloth. MacManus 280-5723 1983
$35

ZANGWILL, ISRAEL   The Mantle of Elijah. London: Heinemann,
1900. First edition. Orig. cloth. Bookplate. Good. MacManus 280-
5726 1983 $25

ZANGWILL, ISRAEL   Merely Mary Ann. N.Y.: The Macmillan
Co., 1904. Later edition. Illus. Orig. quarter-calf with cloth
boards. Presentation copy to Page Taylor. Spine and covers soiled
and worn. Former owner's signature. Good. MacManus 280-5727 1983
$45

ZANGWILL, ISRAEL   The Complete Works. London, 1925.
14 vols. 8vo. Half red morocco, gilt decorated spines, t.e.g.
Edition-de-Luxe limited to 1,000 numbered sets, signed by the author,
with a pen portrait of Zangwill and coloured frontis. to each
volume by Alfred A. Wolmark. Traylen 94-917 1983 £180

ZANZOTTO, ANDREA   Circhi & Cene. (Verona): Plain
wrapper Press. (1979). Folio. With two orig. full-page color
etchings. Edition ltd. to 150 numbered copies, printed on handmade
paper and signed by the author and the artist. Beige cloth; green
cloth slipcase. Karmiole 74-77 1983 $200

ZARA, LOUIS   Give Us This Day. Indianapolis, Bobbs-
Merrill, 1936. First edition. Dust jacket (slight rubbing, small
taped tears) else good. Signed and inscribed by the author May, 1936.
Houle 22-1005 1983 $45

ZATURENSKA, MARYA   Threshold and Hearth. New York, 1934.
8vo. Cloth. Fine in dj. In Our Time 156-911 1983 $35

ZBYSZEWSKI, K.   The Fight for Narvik. London, 1940.
Frontis map. Illus. on title. 11 plates. Numerous illus. by J.
Natanson. Imperial 8vo. Orig. cloth. Ink inscription on half-title
"To my great friends Mr and Mrs J.C. Anderson in remembrance of their
great kindness for me Jozef Natanson, Christmas 1940." Good. Edwards
1042-520 1983 £15

ZEHDER, HUGO   Wassily Kandinsky. Dresden: Rudolf
Kaemmerer, 1920. 11 plates (1 tipped-in color). 4to. Boards.
Backstrip defective. Light foxing. Ars Libri 32-356 1983 $75

ZEITSCHRIFT fur Ethnologie. Berlin, 1869-1982. Vols. 1-107 plus
index. Uniformly bound in new cloth. Ars Libri 34-83 1983 $9,250

ZEMSKY, JAMES L.   Oral Diseases. Brooklyn, 1930. First
edition. Tall 8vo, cloth (worn). Argosy 713-583 1983 $35

ZENARI, GIULIO CESARE   Antelo Dall'Oca Bianca. Verona:
Libreria Dante, 1948. 16 plates. Wrappers. Dust jacket. Ars
Libri 33-452 1983 $22.50

ZERBE, J. S.   Aeroplanes. New York, 1915. First
edition. Frontis. 92 illus. (3 full page). Orig. buff decorated
cloth. 8vo. Good. Edwards 1042-613 1983 £25

ZERVOS, CHRISTIAN   Dessins de Picasso. Paris: Editions
"Cahiers d'Art", 1949. 199 heliotype plates. Small folio. Boards.
Ars Libri 32-527 1983 $75

ZERVOS, CHRISTIAN   Georges Braque. Nouvelles sculptures
et plaques gravees. Paris: Albert Morance, n.d. 32 plates (8
color), loose as issued. Small folio. Wrappers. Dust jacket.
Ars Libri 32-65 1983 $75

ZERVOS, CHRISTIAN   Les oeuvres du Greco en Espagne. Paris:
Cahiers d'Art, 1939. Prof. illus. Folio. Boards. From the library
of Jakob Rosenberg. Head of spine taped. Ars Libri 32-287 1983
$125

ZERVOS, CHRISTIAN   Rousseau. Paris: Cahiers d'Art,
1927. 96 heliogype plates. Large 4to. No. 542 of 743 copies
on velin de Torpes, from the limited edition of 800 copies. Backstrip cracked. Ars Libri 32-594 1983 $85

ZIEBER, EUGENE   Heraldry in America. Phila., 1895.
950 illus., some color plates, 4to. Argosy 710-207 1983 $40

ZIEGLER, ADRIAN   Disputatio medica inauguralis de odontalgia... Utrecht: Franz Halm, 1697. Woodcut title-page vignette
and two initials. Small 4to. Boards. Kraus 164-62 1983 $250

ZILBOORG, GREGORY   A History of Medical Psychology. NY:
Norton, (1941), later printing. Cloth rubbed. Gach 94-294 1983 $20

ZIMMER, HENRY   Hindu Medicine. Baltimore, 1948.
First edition. 8vo. Orig. binding. Ex-library. Fye H-3-640
1983 $20

ZIMMERMAN, JAMES F.   Impressment of American Seamen. New
York, 1925. Orig. printed wraps., fine. Reese 19-612 1983 $30

ZIMMERMAN, JOHANN GEORG   Solitude Considered with Respect to Its
Influence on the Mind and Heart. Brooklyn, Alden Spooner, 1813.
12mo. Contemporary calf, leather label. Rubbed. Morrill 289-256
1983 $27.50

ZINNSER, HANS   Rats, Lice and History. London, 1935.
8vo. Cloth. Dust wrapper. Torn. Gurney JJ-430 1983 £12

ZION'S Bank: Or Bible Promises Secured to All Believers. Boston:
1857. Gilt-stamped midnight blue wrappers, rubbed at extremities.
(2 3/16 x 1 1/2; 55x37mm). Bromer 25-484 1983 $55

ZION'S Bank. Boston, Henry Hoyt, 1857. Orig. wrappers. Morrill
286-559 1983 $30

ZOLA, EMILE   The Attack on the Mill. London: William
Heinemann, 1892. First English edition. Orig. decorated cloth. A
bit worn and slightly foxed. Good. MacManus 280-5729 1983 $60

ZOLA, EMILE   The Downfall (La Debacle). London:
Chatto & Windus, 1892. First edition in English. Orig. cloth. Former
owner's booklabel on front free endpaper. Prelims slightly foxed.
Covers slightly rubbed. Very good. MacManus 280-5730 1983 $40

ZOLA, EMILE   Fruitfulness (Fecondite). London:
Chatto & Windus, 1900. First edition in English. Orig. cloth. Former
owner's inscription on front endsheet. Spine slightly faded. Very
good. MacManus 280-5732 1983 $40

ZOLA, EMILE   Germinal; or Master and Man. London:
Vizettelly, 1886. First English edition. Illus. Orig. pictorial
cloth. Bound in green pictorial diagonal fine-ribbed cloth without
final page of adverts. and with a later (April 1886) catalogue at
back. Spine and cover lettering dull. Very good. MacManus 280-
5731 1983 $20

ZOLA, EMILE   Jacques Damour. Boston: Copeland &
Day, 1895. 1st American ed. Orig. yellow printed cloth. Light
wear, but a very good copy. Jenkins 155-1351 1983 $60

ZOLA, EMILE   The Ladies' Paradise. London: Tinsley
Brothers, 1883. First edition in English. 3 vols. Orig. cloth.
Covers slightly soiled. A trifle stained. Rear hinges cracked. Very
good. MacManus 280-5733 1983 $250

ZOLA, EMILE   The Ladies Paradise. London: Tinsley
Bros., 1883. First English edition. 3 vols. bound in one. Orig.
publisher's cloth. In a publisher's remainder binding, incorporating
the orig. sheets of the three decker issue. Fine. MacManus 280-5734
1983 $125

ZOLA, EMILE   L'Assommior. London: Privately printed,
1928. Orig. boards. Dust jacket (worn). Limited to 1000 copies
signed by Symons. MacManus 280-5041 1983 $35

ZOLA, EMILE   Paris. London: Chatto & Windus, 1898.
First English edition. Orig. decorated cloth. MacManus 280-5735
1983 $30

ZOLA, EMILE   Piping Hot! London: Vizetelly & Co.,
1885. First English edition. Illus. Orig. decorated cloth. Contains
a 2-page publisher's advertisement for Moore's "A Mummer's Wife" as
well as a preface (14pp.) by him for "Piping Hot!" Spine and covers
slightly rubbed. Edges slightly foxed. Good. MacManus 279-3834
1983 $225

ZOLA, EMILE   The Soil. London: Vizetelly, 1888.
First English edition. Orig. cloth. Covers slightly worn. MacManus
280-5736 1983 $35

ZOLOTOV, YU   Antoine Watteau. Leningrad: Aurora,
1972. 20 color plates. Prof. illus. Folio. Cloth. Dust jacket.
Ars Libri 32-698 1983 $75

ZOOLOGICAL Records. Aves. 1947-66. 5 vols., 8vo and royal 8vo,
half cloth. Wheldon 160-929 1983 £100

ZOUCH, THOMAS   The crucifixion: a poetical essay.
Cambridge: printed by J. Bentham, etc., 1765. First edition.
4to. Disbound. Ximenes 63-389 1983 $50

ZUCKER, PAUL   Theater Und Lichtspiel-Hauser.
Berlin: Verlag Ernst Wasmuth, 1926. Folio. With 168 photographic
and architectural plates. Red cloth; some foxing. Karmiole 76-5
1983 $75

ZUCKERMAN, SOLLY, (b. 1904)   Functional Affinities of Man, Monkeys and
Apes. NY: Harcourt, Brace, 1933. First American edition. Illus.
with 12 plates. Fine in dust jacket. Gach 94-88 1983 $35

ZUKOFSKY, LOUIS   Little, A Fragment for Careenagers.
Black Sparrow Press, 1967. 8vo. Boards. 1 of 50 copies bound in
boards signed by author. Issued sans jacket. Fine. In Our Time
156-914 1983 $200

ZULCH, W. K.   Der historische Grunewald. Munchen:
F. Bruckmann, 1938. 224 illus. Large 4to. Cloth. Ars Libri 32-
297 1983 $175

ZUM Funfsigsten Jubilaum Evangelischen Zions-Gemeinde... (St. Joseph,
Missouri, 1908). Orig. printed wrappers. Illus. Jenkins 153-798
1983 $25

ZURBRUCKEN, MICHAEL   Dissertatio inauguralis medica de Odon-
talgia... Vienna: Georg Ludvig Schulz, 1763. Woodcut head-piece.
Small 4to. Cont. paper backstrip. With manuscript exlibris of
Dominici Michon. Title somewhat dustsoiled. Small tear in backstrip.
Kraus 164-63 1983 $180

ZUZZERI, GIO LUCA   D'una Antica Villa Scoperta sul
dosso del Tusculo. In Venezia, MDCCXLVI. Apresso Modesto Fenzo,
(1746). 4to, one fold. plate. Bound in full patterned paper
wrappers. Hinges rubbed. Lightly toned. Arkway 22-74 1983 $575

ZWEIG, ARNOLD   Aufzeichnungen Uber Eine Familie
Klopfer. Munchen (1911). First ed. No. 110 of Kleine Bibliothek
Langen. Paper label on boards, spine sunned, rubbed. King 46-369
1983 $25

ZWEIG, PAUL   Images & Footsteps, a Poem. (Verona,
1970). Tall quarto, paper covered boards with green leather
backstrip. With five etchings by Berta Moltke. One of 200 copies
printed by hand on handmade paper, each copy signed by the author
and artist. Slipcase. Duschnes 240-185 1983 $150

ZWEIG, STEFAN   The Invisible Collection. (New York:
Pynson Printers), 1926. First separate edition in English. Illus.
by J. Malay. Orig. decorated cloth-backed boards. Glassine jacket.
In a very slightly soiled publisher's box. Fine. MacManus 280-5738
1983 $35

ZWEIG, STEFAN   The Queen of Scots. (1935). 8vo, 8
plates, cloth. Bickersteth 77-185 1983 £12

ZWELFER, JOH.   Pharmacopieia Regia, seu Dispensatorium
Novum locupletatum et absolutum, annexa etiam Mantissa Spagyrica...
Nuremberg: B.J. Endter, 1693. 4to. Half-calf, new back and corners.
2 engravings and 1 woodcut. Some browning; tear in one leaf repaired;
slight marginal worming in a few leaves. Gurney 90-132 1983 £145

LIBRARY OF THE